Collins

Collins

Collins
Russian
Dictionary

Collins

Collins
Russian
Dictionary

HarperCollins Publishers
Westerhill Road
Bishopbriggs
Glasgow
G64 2QT
Great Britain

Second Edition 2000

Latest Reprint 2006

© HarperCollins Publishers 1994, 2000

ISBN-13 978-0-00-720891-3
ISBN-10 0-00-720891-X

www.collins.co.uk

A catalogue record for this book is available
from the British Library

HarperCollins Publishers,
10 East 53rd Street, New York, NY 10022

COLLINS RUSSIAN CONCISE DICTIONARY.
Second US Edition 2000

ISBN-13 978-0-06-095661-5
ISBN-10 0-06-095661-5

Library of Congress Cataloging-in-
Publication Data has been applied for

www.harpercollins.com

HarperCollins books may be purchased
for educational, business, or sales
promotional use. For information, please
write to: Special Markets Department,
HarperCollins Publishers, 10 East 53rd Street,
New York, NY 10022

Dictionary text typeset by Tradespools Ltd,
Frome, Somerset

Printed in Italy by Legoprint S.P.A.

Acknowledgements
We would like to thank those authors and
publishers who kindly gave permission for
copyright material to be used in the Collins
Word Web. We would also like to thank Times
Newspapers Ltd for providing valuable data.

АВТОРСКИЙ КОЛЛЕКТИВ/MAIN CONTRIBUTORS

Albina Ozieva • Olga Stott • Marina Hepburn • Katya Butler
Maria Marquise • Elena Cook • Irina Moore • Dr Lara Ryazanova
Dr Natasha Vasilyeva McGrath • Tanya Herries • Fatima Eloyeva
Daniel Brennan • Rose France • Rebecca Brown
Michael Cowan-Young • Sheila Bentley
Professor D. Ward

РЕДАКТОР СЕРИИ/SERIES EDITOR

Lorna Sinclair Knight

ЗАВЕДУЮЩИЙ РЕДАКЦИЕЙ/EDITORIAL MANAGEMENT

Jeremy Butterfield

ВЕДУЩИЙ РЕДАКТОР/EDITOR

Maree Airlie

РЕДАКТОРЫ/EDITORIAL STAFF

Judith Turtle • Andrew Knox • Isobel Gordon
Sandra Harper • Elspeth Anderson
Mary Steele • Merle Read

КОМПЬЮТЕРНОЕ ОБСЛУЖИВАНИЕ/COMPUTING

André Gautier • Colette Clenaghan

СОДЕРЖАНИЕ		CONTENTS	

ТОВАРНЫЕ ЗНАКИ ®

TRADEMARKS ®

ВВЕДЕНИЕ

INTRODUCTION

Мы рады, что Вы выбрали словарь, подготовленный издательством Коллинз. Мы надеемся, что он окажется Вам полезен, где бы Вы им ни пользовались – дома, на отдыхе или на работе.

В настоящем введении излагаются некоторые советы по эффективному использованию данного издания: его обширного словника и сведений, содержащихся в каждой словарной статье. Правильное и максимально полное использование приводимой информации поможет Вам не только читать и понимать современный английский, но также овладеть устной речью.

В начале словаря Коллинз помещён список условных сокращений, используемых в корпусе словаря. Далее следуют произносительные таблицы для русского и английского языков. Между двумя частями словаря помещён раздел, посвящённый русской грамматике. В конце англо-русской части даётся список английских неправильных глаголов а также таблицы русских неправильных форм. Некоторые словарные статьи отсылают читателя к данным таблицам для получения нужной грамматической информации. Числительные и фразы, обозначающие даты и время, находятся в самом конце словаря.

We are delighted that you have decided to use the Collins Russian Dictionary and hope that you will enjoy it and benefit from using it at home, on holiday or at work.

This introduction gives you a few tips on how to get the most out of your dictionary – not simply from its comprehensive wordlist but also from the information provided in each entry. This will help you to read and understand modern Russian, as well as communicate and express yourself in the language.

The Collins Russian Dictionary begins by listing the abbreviations used in the text, followed by a guide to Russian and English pronunciation. Between the two sides of the dictionary you will find a section on Russian grammar, and at the end of the English-Russian text are listed English irregular verbs, plus the tables of irregular Russian forms to which entries in the text are referred. Numbers and expressions using time and date are situated at the very back of the dictionary.

О Пользовании Словарём

Заглавные слова

Заглавными называются слова, начинающие словарную статью. Они напечатаны жирным шрифтом и расположены в строго алфавитном порядке. При многих из них приводятся словосочетания и сращения, частью которых выступает данное заглавное слово. Они напечатаны жирным шрифтом меньшего размера. Два заглавных слова в верхней части страницы указывают на первое и последнее слово, отрезка словника, представленного на данной странице.

Перевод

Перевод заглавных слов напечатан обычным шрифтом. Как правило, варианты перевода рассматриваемого слова разделяются запятой, если они синонимичны и взаимозаменяемы в значении, обозначенном пометой. Различные значения много-значного слова разделены точкой с запятой. Более подробно о пометах см. ниже.

Переводы для различных значений многозначных производных слов часто разделены только точкой с запятой и перед ними даётся одна помета типа (см прил). Это означает, что последовательное разделение значений рассматриваемого слова и их переводов даётся при слове, от которого данное производное слово образовано. Например, **annul/annulment**.

В некоторых случаях точный эквивалент перевода невозможен, например, когда английское слово обозначает явление или учреждение, не существующие в России, или же существующие в несколько иной форме. Если возможен приблизительный эквивалент перевода, то он обозначается знаком (≈). Если же культурный эквивалент в языке перевода отсутствует, то вместо него приводится толкование.

Пометы

Пометы, служат для разделения значений многозначного слова. Они приводятся на языке-источнике. Их цель – помочь читателю выбрать перевод, наиболее подходящий в том или ином контексте. Пометы являют собой либо синоним, либо слово, указывающее на характерную для данного значения слова лексическую сочетаемость. Пометы также обозначают переносные значения. Пометы напечат-аны курсивом и заключены в круглые скобки.

При многих заглавных словах даны необходимые стилистические пометы, обозначающие разговорное или просторечное использование этих слов. Эмоционально – стилистическая окраска перевода обычно совпадает с окраской переводимого слова. Нецензурные или грубые слова помечены восклицательным знаком (!).

Произношение

В англо-русской части словаря все заглавные слова снабжены фонетической транскрипцией, которая заключена в квадратные скобки. В тех случаях, где в роли заглавного слова выступает словосочетание, состоящее из двух или более слов, которые, в свою очередь, приводятся в словаре по отдельности, их произношение указывается только там, где они даны как одиночные слова в алфавитном порядке. Список фонетических знаков приводится на страницах xxix–xxx.

В русско-английской части словаря все русские слова снабжены знаком ударения, поскольку их произношение большей частью достаточно ясно, если указано место ударения. В тех словах, где возможно двоякое ударение, обычно указывается только одно, наиболее часто употребляющееся. Омографы (слова, имеющие одинаковое написание, но различное ударение и значение) приводятся как самостоятельные заглавные слова в том порядке, в котором в них проставлено ударение, например, первым даётся слово за́мок, затем - замо́к. Более подробную информацию о принципах русского произношения читатель может найти в разделе на страницах xxiv-xxviii.

Служебные слова

В словаре уделяется особое внимание тем русским и английским словам, которые обладают сложной грамматической или семантической структурой. Таковыми являются в первую очередь служебные слова, вспомогательные глаголы, местоимения, частицы итп. Они обозначены пометой KEYWORD.

Английские фразовые глаголы

Фразовыми глаголами называются устойчивые сочетания глагола с элементами **in**, **out**, **up** итп, типа **blow up**, **cut down** итп. Они приводятся в словарной статье базовых глаголов, таких как **blow**, **cut**, и сгруппированы в алфавитном порядке.

Аббревиатуры и собственные имена существительные

Аббревиатуры, сложносокращённые слова и собственные имена существительные включены в общий словник словаря в алфавитном порядке.

Употребление "Вы/ты" при переводе "You"

При переводе на русский язык английских фраз, содержащих местоимения "you/ your", даются две формы местоимения:одна в ед. числе, а другая во мн. числе --» "ты/твой", "Вы/Ваш". Если в состав фразы входит глагол в форме повелительного наклонения, то он также переводится двумя формами: 2-го лица ед. числа / 2-го лица мн. числа. В тех случаях, где эмоционально-стилистическая окраска фразы является явно неформальной, для местоимения даётся только форма "ты/твой", а для глаголов в повелительном наклонении форма 2-го лица ед. числа, например, "get lost!" переводится как "отстань!"

Употребление or/или, косой черты и скобок

В англо-русской части словаря между взаимозаменяемыми вариантами перевода, а также частями фразы на языке-источнике употребляется союз "*or*". В русско-английской части словаря ему соответствует союз "*или*". Косая черта (/) означает, что приведённые варианты перевода или фразы в языке-источнике не являются взаимозаменяемыми. В круглые скобки заключаются необязательные но возможные в данном выражении слова, как в переводе, так и во фразе на языке-источнике.

Употребление тильды (~)

Тильда в англо-русской части заменяет заглавное слово в словосочетаниях. Например, если в качестве заглавного выступает слово "**order**", то фраза "**out of order**" будет представлена следующим образом: **out of** ~. В русско-английской части тильда заменяет: 1) целое заглавное слово: например, в статье "**до́брый**" фраза "**до́брый день**" показана следующим образом: ~ **день**. 2) тильда заменяет часть заглавного слова, предшествующую вертикальной черте: например, в статье "**до́бр|ый**" фраза "**до́брое у́тро**" показана следующим образом: **~ое у́тро**.

Употребление звёздочки (*)

При переводе звёздочкой (*) отмечаются те существительные, в склонении которых наблюдаются те или иные отклонения от нормы. В русско-английской части даётся дополнительная информация относительно отклонений от правил склонения и спряжения.

USING THE DICTIONARY

Headwords

The **headword** is the word you look up in a dictionary. Headwords are listed in alphabetical order, and printed in bold type so that they stand out on the page. Each headword may contain other references such as **phrases** and **compounds**, which are in smaller bold type. The two headwords appearing at the top of each page indicate the first and last word dealt with on the page in question.

Translations

The translations of the headword are printed in ordinary roman type. As a rule, translations separated by a comma can be regarded as interchangeable for the meaning indicated. Translations separated by a semi-colon are not interchangeable, though the different meaning splits are generally marked by an indicator (see below). Where a semi-colon separates translations and the indicator refers to a different part of speech eg. (*see adj*), the translations mirror the splits shown at the other part of speech eg. **annul/annulment**.

It is not always possible to give an exact translation equivalent, for instance when the English word denotes an object or institution which does not exist or exists in a different form in Russia or in the Republics. If an approximate equivalent exists, it is given preceded by ≈. If there is no cultural equivalent, a *gloss* is given to explain the source item.

Indicators

An *indicator* is a piece of information in the source language about the usage of the headword to guide you to the most appropriate translation. Indicators give some idea of the contexts in which the headword might appear, or they provide synonyms for the headword. They are printed in italic type and shown in brackets.

Colloquial and informal language in the dictionary is marked at the headword. You should assume that the translations will match the source language in register, and rude or offensive translations are also marked with (!).

Pronunciation

On the English-Russian side of the dictionary you will find the phonetic spelling of the word in square brackets after the headword. Where the entry is composed of two or more unhyphenated words, each of which is given elsewhere in this dictionary, you will find the pronunication of each word in its alphabetical position. A list of the symbols used is given on pages xxix-xxx.

For Russian-English, stress is given on all Russian words as a guide to pronunciation. Where stress can be placed over either of two vowels, the most common or correct stress position is shown for the purpose of this dictionary. Words which are spelt in the same way, but have different stress positions are treated as separate entries, the order following the order of the stress eg. **зáмок** comes before **замóк**. The section on pages xxiv-xxviii explains Russian pronunciation in more detail.

Keywords

In this dictionary we have given special status to "key" Russian and English words. As these words can be grammatically complex and often have many different usages, they have been given special attention in the dictionary, and are labelled with KEYWORD.

Abbreviations and proper names

Abbreviations, acronyms and proper names have been included in the word list in alphabetical order.

"You" in phrases

In translations of English phrases containing "you/your" or the imperative, "Вы/Ваш" and the formal form is given, unless the phrase is very colloquial eg. "get lost!" where it would be more natural to give the familiar form of the imperative.

Use of or/или, oblique and brackets

The words "*or*" on the English-Russian side, and "*или*" on the Russian-English side are used between interchangeable parts of a translation or source phrase. The oblique (/) is used between non-interchangeable alternatives in the translation or source phrase. Round brackets are used to show optional parts of the translation or source phrase.

Use of the swung dash (~)

The swung dash (~) is used on the English-Russian side of the dictionary to stand for the headword in phrases eg. at "order" the phrase "**out of order**" is shown as "**out of ~**". On the Russian- English side of the dictionary the swung dash can either stand for the full headword eg. at "**добр|ый**" the phrase "**добрый день**" is shown as "~ **день**", or it can stand for the part of the word before the hairline eg. at "**добр|ый**" the phrase "**доброе утро**" appears as "~**ое утро**".

Use of the superior asterisk (*)

The asterisk (*) is used to mark translations which are in some way irregular in their declension. The Russian-English side of the dictionary contains further information on irregularities.

American variants

American spelling variants are generally shown at the British headword eg. **colour/color** and also as a separate entry if they are not alphabetically adjacent to the British form. Variant forms are generally shown as headwords in their own right eg. **trousers/pants**, unless the British and American forms are alphabetically adjacent, in which case the American form is only shown separately if phonetics are required eg. **jump leads/jumper cables**.

Russian reflexive verbs

Russian reflexive verbs eg. **мыться, краситься** are listed under the basic verb eg. **мыть, красить**.

STYLE AND LAYOUT OF THE DICTIONARY

RUSSIAN-ENGLISH

Inflectional and grammatical information

Inflectional information is shown in the dictionary in brackets immediately after the headword and before the part of speech eg. **стол (-á)** *м*.

Grammatical information is shown after the part of speech and refers to the whole entry eg. **завйд|овать (-ую**; *perf* **позавйдовать)** *несов неперех* (+*dat*).

Where grammatical information eg. *no perf* is given in the middle of the entry, it then governs all the following senses.

Use of hairline (|)

The hairline is used in headwords to show where the inflection adds on eg. **кнйг|а (-и)**. It is also used for swung dash relacement where the swung dash stands for the part of the word before the hairline in phrases.

Stress

Stress changes are shown where they occur, the last form given being indicative of the rest of the pattern eg. **игр|á (-ы́**; *nom pl* **-ы)**. In this example the stress is on the last syllable for the singular declension, moves to the first syllable for the plural and remains there for the rest of the plural declension.

Tables

Some headwords which have particularly irregular inflections are declined in full in tables at the back of the dictionary. Shown in these tables are a small group of nouns, verbs, all cardinal and collective numerals, and personal, interrogative and negative pronouns.

Nouns

In order to help you determine the declension and stress pattern of nouns, we have shown the genitive singular for all singular nouns, and the genitive plural for all plural nouns. This is given as the first piece of information after the headword and is not labelled eg. **стол (-á)**.

Where the noun has further irregularities in declension such as irregular plural forms, partitive genitive, locative singular in "у/ю" or change in stress throughout the declension these are shown at the headword and labelled eg. **я́блок|о (-а**; *nom pl* **-и)**.

Adjectives

As the declension of a large number of adjectives in the long form is governed by regular rules, we have not shown the long form endings for these adjectives.

Long form endings have been shown for adjectives which may cause problems in declension in the long form such as adjectives ending in **-ий**, where you might be unsure whether the adjective is "soft" or not, and adjectives ending in **-ин** and **-ов**.

Short form endings have been shown for all adjectives where they exist.

Numerals and pronouns

The genitive has been shown for all numerals and pronouns.

Verbs

Where to look:

The majority of verbs are dealt with in aspectual pairs, and we have chosen to show the translation of the verb at the base form of the pair.

Where the perfective is formed by adding a prefix to the imperfective, the imperfective is considered to be the base form and the translation is shown there. The corresponding perfective aspect can also be found in the dictionary in its alphabetical position, cross-referred to the imperfective aspect.

Where the aspect to be cross-referred is alphabetically adjacent to the aspect to which it will be referred, it is not shown separately unless there is some irregularity in its declension. With the pair **завинчивать/завинтить, завинчивать** is not shown separately.

Where the imperfective is formed by adding a suffix to the perfective, the perfective is considered to be the base form and the translation is shown there. The corresponding imperfective aspect can also be found in the dictionary in its alphabetical position, cross-referred to the perfective aspect.

Verbs which do not occur in aspectual pairs are dealt with at their individual headwords.

In phrases both aspects are shown if both work in the context.

To help you see how a verb conjugates, inflections are shown immediately after the verb headword for all verbs according to the following rules:

– for regular 1st conjugation verbs the 1st person singular only is shown eg. **работа|ть (-ю)**

– for 1st conjugation verbs which contain vowel/consonant mutation the 1st and 2nd person singular are shown eg. **жд|ать (-у, -ёшь)**
пи|сать (-шу́, -шешь)

– for regular 2nd conjugation verbs the 1st and 2nd person singular are shown eg. **говор|и́ть (-ю́, -и́шь)**

– for 2nd conjugation verbs which contain vowel/consonant mutation, insert "л", or where the stress changes throughout the declension the 1st and 2nd person singular are shown eg. **люб|и́ть (-лю́, -ишь)**

– for verbs where the verb form changes more than once throughout the conjugation, the 1st, 2nd person singular and 3rd person plural are shown. *umn* is inserted after the 2nd person singular to show that the pattern continues until the next form shown eg. **тол|о́чь (-ку́, -чёшь** *umn*, **-ку́т)**

– for verbs which are not used in the 1st person singular, the inflections are shown for their usual usage eg. **темне|ть** (*3sg* **-ет**) Where the restriction applies to one of the senses, the inflections are shown at the sense itself only if they are irregular.

The imperative mood is shown at the headword where it is irregularly formed.

The past tense is shown at the headword where it is irregularly formed or contains a change in stress.

Inflections given as separate entries

Irregular inflected forms are also shown at their alphabetical position and cross-referred to the base headword. In places an inflected form appears as a separate entry and is followed by *umn*, meaning that there are other inflected forms of the same headword which follow the same pattern eg. **отца́** *umn* means that the other inflections of **оте́ц** follow the same pattern by dropping a vowel in oblique cases.

Spelling rules

Russian has the following spelling rules which we have not taken as irregular when showing inflection information:

- after ж,ч,ш,щ,г,к and х, ы is replaced by и, я by a and ю by у.
- after ж,ч,ш,щ and ц, е replaces an unstressed о.
- the letter и is replaced by ы following a prefix ending in a consonant.

ENGLISH-RUSSIAN

Gender

The gender of Russian nouns given as translations is not shown for:

- masculine nouns which end in a hard consonant eg. труд, in -й eg. музе́й or in a hard or soft sibilant eg. нож, плащ
- feminine nouns which end in -a eg. страна́ or in -я eg. земля́
- neuter nouns which end in -o eg. окно́, in -е eg. мо́ре or in -ё eg. ружьё.

Nouns for which the gender is shown are:

- those ending in -ь which can be either masculine or feminine eg. дождь
- neuter nouns ending in -я
- masculine nouns ending in -a eg. па́па or -я eg. дя́дя

Nouns which have a common gender eg. сирота́ are labelled *m/f*.

Indeclinable nouns are labelled with gender followed by the abbreviation *ind* eg. кино́ *nt ind*.

Adjectives used as nouns are labelled with gender followed by the abbreviation *adj* eg. столо́вая *f adj*.

Where the feminine form of a masculine noun is also given as a translation, and the gender of the masculine noun is shown according to the guidelines given above, the gender of the feminine is shown as follows: учи́тель(ница) *m(f)*.

Plural noun translations are always labelled with the abbreviation *pl*, eg. кани́кулы *pl*, and the gender is shown if a singular form exists.

Noun translations are only marked with *sg* where a plural noun headword has a singular translation.

The label *no pl* is used for nouns which do not have a plural form and are only used in the singular eg. лу́ковица, unless the English is also not used in the plural.

Feminine forms

The following conventions are used in this dictionary to show feminine forms of masculine nouns.

- If the feminine ending adds on to the masculine form, the feminine ending is bracketed eg. учи́тель(ница).

- If the feminine ending substitutes part of the masculine form, the last common letter of the masculine and feminine form is shown before the feminine ending, preceded by a dash and enclosed in brackets eg. актёр(-три́са). Where an adjective is used as a noun and has a feminine form, the last common letter does not have to be given eg. безрабо́тный(- ая).

- If the feminine form is given in full, it is bracketed and separated from the masculine form by a character space eg. чех (че́шка).

Adjectives

Russian translations of adjectives are always given in the masculine, unless the adjective relates only to a feminine noun eg. бере́менная.

The masculine short form (or feminine if the adjective only applies to a feminine noun) is also given where it is appropriate.

Verbs

In translation of the headword, imperfective and perfective aspects are shown in full where they both apply eg. **to do** де́лать (сде́лать *perf*). If only one aspect is shown, it means that only one aspect works for this sense.

In infinitve phrases, if the two aspects apply they are shown and labelled eg. **to buy sth** покупа́ть (купи́ть *perf*) что-н.

Where the English phrase contains the construction "to do" standing for any verb, it has been replaced by +*infin*/+*impf infin*/+*perf infin* in the Russian translation, depending on which aspects of the Russian verb work in the given context.

Where the English phrase contains the past tense of a verb in the 1st person singular, the Russian translation gives only the masculine form eg. **I was glad** я был рад

Where both the present tense and the past tense of the verb "to be" are given in a phrase, eg. **he is/was** ..., it means that the Russian translation will govern the nominative case in either tense. If, however, only the present tense is shown, it can be assumed that the past tense of the Russian translation will govern the instrumental case.

Prepositions

Unless they are bracketed, prepositions and cases which follow verbs, adjectives etc are obligatory as part of the translation eg. **to inundate with** зава́ливать (завали́ть *perf*) +*instr*

Where they are separated by *or* they are interchangeable.

An oblique (/) is used to separate prepositions when the preposition depends on the following noun rather than on the preceding verb eg. идти в/на.

УСЛОВНЫЕ СОКРАЩЕНИЯ В АНГЛО-РУССКОЙ ЧАСТИ

сокращение	*abbr*	abbreviation
винительный падеж	*acc*	accusative
прилагательное	*adj*	adjective
администрация	*ADMIN*	administration
наречие	*adv*	adverb
сельское хозяйство	*AGR*	agriculture
анатомия	*ANAT*	anatomy
архитектура	*ARCHIT*	architecture
автомобильное дело	*AUT*	automobiles
вспомогательный глагол	*aux vb*	auxiliary verb
авиация	*AVIAT*	aviation
биология	*BIO*	biology
ботаника	*BOT*	botany
британский английский	*BRIT*	British English
химия	*CHEM*	chemistry
коммерция	*COMM*	commerce
компьютер	*COMPUT*	computing
союз	*conj*	conjunction
строительство	*CONSTR*	construction
сращение	*cpd*	compound
кулинария	*CULIN*	culinary
дательный падеж	*dat*	dative
склоняется	*decl*	declines
определённый артикль	*def art*	definite article
уменьшительное	*dimin*	diminutive
экономика	*ECON*	economics
электроника	*ELEC*	electricity
особенно	*esp*	especially
и тому подобное	*etc*	et cetera
междометие	*excl*	exclamation
женский род	*f*	feminine
в переносном значении	*fig*	figurative
родительный падеж	*gen*	genitive
география	*GEO*	geography
геометрия	*GEOM*	geometry
безличный	*impers*	impersonal
несовершенный вид	*impf*	imperfective verb
несклоняемое	*ind*	indeclinable
неопределённый артикль	*indef art*	indefinite article
разговорное	*inf*	informal
грубо	*infl*	offensive
инфинитив	*infin*	infinitive
творительный падеж	*instr*	instrumental
неизменяемое	*inv*	invariable
неправильный	*irreg*	irregular
лингвистика	*LING*	linguistics

Условные Сокращения в Англо-Русской Части

местный падеж	*loc*	locative
мужской род	*m*	masculine
субстантивированное прилагательное	*m/f/nt adj*	adjectival noun
математика	**MATH**	mathematics
медицина	**MED**	medicine
военный термин	**MIL**	military
музыка	**MUS**	music
имя существительное	*n*	noun
морской термин	**NAUT**	nautical
именительный падеж	*nom*	nominative
существительное во множественном числе	*npl*	plural noun
средний род	*nt*	neuter
числительное	*num*	numeral
себя	*o.s.*	oneself
разделительный	*part*	partitive
пренебрежительное	*pej*	pejorative
совершенный вид	*perf*	perfective verb
фотография	**PHOT**	photography
физика	**PHYS**	physics
физиология	**PHYSIOL**	physiology
множественное число	*pl*	plural
политика	**POL**	politics
страдательное причастие	*pp*	past participle
предлог	*prep*	preposition
местоимение	*pron*	pronoun
предложный падеж	*prp*	prepositional
психология	**PSYCH**	psychiatry
прошедшее время	*pt*	past tense
железнодорожный термин	**RAIL**	railways
религия	**REL**	religion
кто-нибудь	*sb*	somebody
просвещение	**SCOL**	school
единственное число	*sg*	singular
что-нибудь	*sth*	something
подлежащее	*subj*	subject
превосходная степень	*superl*	superlative
техника	**TECH**	technology
теле(связь)	**TEL**	telecommunications
театр	**THEAT**	theatre
телевидение	**TV**	television
типографский термин	**TYP**	printing

УСЛОВНЫЕ СОКРАЩЕНИЯ В АНГЛО-РУССКОЙ ЧАСТИ

американский английский	*US*	American English
обычно	*usu*	usually
глагол	*vb*	verb
непереходный глагол	*vi*	intransitive verb
глагольное слобосочетание	*vt fus*	inseparable verb
переходный глагол	*vt*	transitive verb
зоология	*ZOOL*	zoology
зарегистрированный товарный знак	®	registered trademark
вводит культурный эквивалент	≈	introduces a cultural equivalent

ABBREVIATIONS USED IN RUSSIAN-ENGLISH

aviation	**АВИА**	авиация
automobiles	**АВТ**	автомобильное дело
administration	**АДМИН**	администрация
anatomy	**АНАТ**	анатомия
architecture	**АРХИТ**	архитектура
impersonal	**безл**	безличный
biology	**БИО**	биология
botany	**БОТ**	ботаника
parenthesis	**вводн сл**	вводное слово
military	**ВОЕН**	военный термин
reflexive	**возв**	возвратный глагол
geography	**ГЕО**	география
geometry	**ГЕОМ**	геометрия
verb	**глаг**	глагол
offensive	**груб!**	грубо
singular	**ед**	единственное число
feminine	**ж**	женский род
zoology	**ЗООЛ**	зоология
history	**ИСТ**	история
et cetera	**итп**	и тому подобное
predicate	**как сказ**	как сказуемое
commercial	**КОММ**	коммерция
computing	**КОМП**	компьютер
somebody	**кто-н**	кто-нибудь
culinary	**КУЛИН**	кулинария
linguistics	**ЛИНГ**	лингвистика
masculine	**м**	мужской род
mathematics	**МАТ**	математика
medicine	**МЕД**	медицина
exclamation	**межд**	междометие
pronoun	**мест**	местоимение
plural	**мн**	множественное число
nautical	**МОР**	морской термин
music	**МУЗ**	музыка
adverb	**нареч**	наречие
invariable	**неизм**	неизменяемое
intransitive	**неперех**	непереходный глагол
indeclinable	**нескл**	несклоняемое
imperfective	**несов**	несовершенный вид
attributive	**опред**	определение
figurative	**перен**	в переносном значении
transitive	**перех**	переходный
subject	**подлеж**	подлежащее
politics	**ПОЛИТ**	политика
superlative	**превос**	превосходная степень
preposition	**предл**	предлог

ABBREVIATIONS USED IN RUSSIAN-ENGLISH

pejorative	**пренебр**	пренебрежительное
adjective	**прил**	имя прилагательное
possessive	**притяж**	притяжательный
school	**ПРОСВЕЩ**	просвещение
psychology	**ПСИХОЛ**	психология
informal	**разг**	разговорное
religion	**РЕЛ**	религия
see	**см**	смотри
collective	**собир**	собирательное
perfective	**сов**	совершенный вид
abbreviation	**сокр**	сокращение
neuter	**ср**	средний род
comparative	**сравн**	сравнительная степень
construction	**СТРОИТ**	строительство
noun	**сущ**	имя существительное
agriculture	**С.-Х.**	сельское хозяйство
television	**ТЕЛ**	телевидение
technology	**ТЕХ**	техника
printing	**ТИПОГ**	типографский термин
diminutive	**уменьш**	уменьшительное
physics	**ФИЗ**	физика
photography	**ФОТО**	фотография
chemistry	**ХИМ**	химия
particle	**част**	частица
somebody's	**чей-н**	чей-нибудь
numeral	**чис**	числительное
something	**что-н**	что-нибудь
economics	**ЭКОН**	экономика
eletricity	**ЭЛЕК**	электроника
law	**ЮР**	юридический термин
registered trademark	®	зарегистрированный товарный знак
introduces a cultural equivalent	≈	вводит культурный эквивалент

Vowels

1. Russian vowels are inherently short, whereas in English some vowels are inherently long (eg. **beat**) while others are inherently short (eg. **bit**). Russian stressed vowels, however, tend to be slightly longer than unstressed vowels. In unstressed positions all vowels are "reduced" ie. their individual characteristics are not as definite as those of their stressed counterparts.

2. In unstressed positions the letter **o** has the same value as the letter **a** eg. **города** [gərʌ'da]. Some loanwords and acronyms are exceptions eg. **páдио** ['raḍio], **госбáнк** [goz'bank].

3. In unstressed positions the letter **e** is pronounced like **bit** eg. **селó** [şi'lo]. The same is true of **я** before stressed syllables eg. **пятú** [pi'ţi], and of **a** when it follows **ч** or **щ** eg. **щадúть** [ʃɨi'ḍiţ]. After **ж, ц** and **ш** unstressed **e** is pronounced as [ɨ] eg. **женá** [ʒɨ'na].

4. All Russian diphthongs end in [j], which in diphthongs is pronounced as [i] (eg. **sheet**) with the tongue very close to the roof of the mouth.

N.B. The letter **ё**, always stressed, is not an independent letter of the alphabet, being used only in grammar books, dictionaries etc. to avoid ambiguity eg. **нéбо** and **нёбо**.

Consonants

1. The consonants **п, б, м, ф, в, т, д, н, с, з, л, р, к, г, x** have "soft" or "palatalised" consonants, which are indicated by a "softening" vowel letter **e, ё, и, ю, я** or the soft sign **ь** following the consonant letter: **те** [ţɛ], **нúва** ['ṇivə], **ся́ду** ['şadu], **мать** [maţ]. Consonants preceding a "soft" consonant may also be pronounced soft, usually if they are pronounced in the same place in the mouth (ie. are "homorganic") eg. **стих** [şţix], though this is not always the case eg. **свет** [şүɛt].

2. The "soft" consonants **п, б, м, ф, в, г** are pronounced like their "hard" counterparts with simultaneous [j] (as in **yet**).

3. In pronouncing "soft" **т, д, н** the tip of the tongue is drawn back slightly from the position for **т, д, н** and in these "soft" consonants, togther with "soft" **с, з**, the front of the tongue is arched up towards the [j] position.

4. "Soft" **л** is very different from **л**. The front of the tongue is raised to the [j] position, while the back of the tongue must not be raised at all, cf. **лот** [lot] and **лёт** [ḷot], **пóлка** ['polkə] and **пóлька** ['poḷkə].

5. In "soft" **к, г, x** the back of the tongue is raised somewhat further forward in the mouth than in **к, г, x** and a good portion of the middle of the tongue touches or approaches the roof of the mouth eg. **рукú** [ru'ḳi], **ногú** [nʌ'gi].

6. The consonants **т, д, н** eg. **ток** [tok], **дом** [dom], **нас** [nas] are pronounced with the tongue-tip slightly further forward in the mouth than in the English counterparts.

7. The consonants **п, т, к** eg. **пасть** [paşţ], **ток** [tok] and **кот** [kot] are pronounced without the slight puff of air which follows them in English before stressed vowels.

8. **л** eg. **лóдка** ['lotkə] is pronounced with the tongue-tip in the same position as in English [l], but the back of the tongue is raised as if one were pronouncing [u], while the middle of the

tongue is depressed. The result is an л which is even "darker" than that at the end of English **wall**.

9. There are pairs of voiced and voiceless consonants –

Voiced: **б, в, д, з, г** and their "soft" counterparts
Voiceless: **п, ф, т, с, к** and their "soft" counterparts

a) At the end of a word a voiced consonant is replaced by the corresponding voiceless consonant eg. **го́род** ['gorət] (cf. **го́рода** ['gorədə]).

b) When a voiced consonant occurs before a voiceless consonant in the same word or at the close juncture of two words it is replaced by the corresponding voiceless consonant eg. **городка́** [gərʌt'ka], **из того́** [is tʌ'vo] (cf. **из э́того** [ɪ'zɛtəvə]).

c) When a voiceless consonant occurs before one of the voiced members of the pairs (except **в** and its "soft" counterpart), the converse happens, and the voiceless consonant is replaced by a voiced consonant eg. **сдава́ть** [zd 'vatʲ] (cf. **сойти́** [šʌj'tʲi]), but **свой** [svoj], **свет** [şγɛt].

N.B. The spelling does not reflect these consonant changes except that the prefixes **воз-/вз-**, **из-**, **(с)низ-** and **раз-/роз-** change to **вос-/вс-**, **ис-**, **(с)нис-** and **рас-/рос-** respectively in the appropriate circumstances eg. **изойти́** [ɪzʌj'tʲi] to **исходи́ть** [isxʌ'dʲitʲ].

RUSSIAN PRONUNCIATION

Vowels and Diphthongs

Symbol	Russian Example	English Example/Explanation
[ɑ]	д**а**ть	pronounced like the beginning of diphthong in "eye"
[æ]	ч**а**сть	c**a**t
[ʌ]	д**а**вáл, **а**двокáт	c**u**p
[ə]	стýл**а**	**a**long
[ɪ]	ч**а**сы́, щ**а**ди́ть	b**i**t
[ɛ]	с**е**л	g**e**t
[e]	с**é**ли	pronounced like the beginning of diphthong in "eight"
[jɛ]	**е**л	**ye**t
[je]	**е**сть	only before "soft" consonants
[ɪ]	с**е**ло́	b**i**t
[ji]	**е**гó	**yi**p
[ɨ]	ж**е**нá	see note 3 under Vowels
[o]	дёсны, чёрный	**aw**e
[jo]	**ё**лка, мо**ё**	**yaw**n
[i]	**и**х, ни́ва	sh**ee**t
[ɪ]	**и**грá	b**i**t
[ɨ]	ж**и**ть	after "ж, ц, ш"
[j]	**й**од, мо**й**	**y**ield
[o]	к**о**т	**aw**e
[ʌ]	**но**гá, **о**ткрывáть	c**u**p
[ə]	к**о**лбасá, я́бл**о**к**о**	**a**long
[u]	**у**м	sh**oo**t
[ɨ]	с**ы**н	pronounced like "ee", but with the tongue arched further back in the mouth
[ɛ]	**э́**то	g**e**t
[e]	**э́**то	pronounced like the beginning of diphthong in "eight"
[ɨ]	съ**э**коно́мить	not after "soft" consonants
[u]	ут**ю**г	n**oo**n
[ju]	**ю**г, обо**ю**дный	**you**, **you**th
[a]	т**я́**жкий	pronounced like the beginning of diphthong in "eye"

xxvi

[ja]	я́сно	initially and after vowels
[æ]	ся́дь	c*a*t
[jæ]	я́сень	*ya*k
[ɪ]	пя́ти́	b*i*t
[jɪ]	язы́к, пояса́	*yi*p
[ə]	ды́ня	*a*long
[jə]	сча́стья	"y" + *a*long

Consonants

Symbol	Russian Example	English Example/Explanation
[b]	*б*анк	*b*ut
[b̦]	о*б*е́д	*see note 2 under Consonants*
[p]	зу*б*, ю́*б*ка	*p*ut
[p̦]	го́лу*бь*	*see note 2 under Consonants*
[v]	*в*от	*v*at
[ɣ]	*в*е́тка	*see note 2 under Consonants*
[f]	ле*в*	*f*at
[f̦]	бро*вь*	*see note 2 under Consonants*
[g]	*г*од	*g*ot
[g̦]	но*г*и́	*see note 5 under Consonants*
[k]	но*г*, но́*г*ти	*c*at
[d]	*д*ом	*d*og
[d̦]	*д*е́вушка	*see note 3 under Consonants*
[t]	са*д*	*t*op
[ț]	ло́ша*дь*	*see note 3 under Consonants*
[ʒ]	*ж*ена́	mea*s*ure
[ʃ]	ё*ж*, ло́*ж*ка	*sh*oot
[z]	*з*а́втра	do*z*e
[z̦]	га*з*е́та	*see note 3 under Consonants*
[s]	га*з*	ga*s*
[ș]	гря*зь*	at end of word or before voiceless consonant
[ʒ]	и*з*жо́га	mea*s*ure
[k]	*к*от	*c*ot
[k̦]	ру*к*и́	*see note 5 under Consonants*

[ʃ]	и<u>з</u> шёлка	<u>sh</u>oot
[ɪ]	и<u>з</u> чего́	<u>sh</u>eet
[l]	<u>л</u>о́дка	wa<u>ll</u>
[ļ]	<u>л</u>ес	*see note 4 under Consonants*
[m]	<u>м</u>ать	<u>m</u>at
[ɱ]	<u>м</u>ять	*see note 2 under Consonants*
[n]	<u>н</u>ас	<u>n</u>o
[ɳ]	<u>н</u>ет	*see note 3 under Consonants*
[p]	<u>п</u>асть	<u>p</u>ut
[p̡]	<u>п</u>еть	*see note 2 under Consonants*
[b]	ослё<u>н</u>	<u>b</u>ut
[r]	<u>р</u>от	pronounced like rolled Scots "r"
[ɾ]	<u>р</u>яд	*see note 2 under Consonants*
[s]	<u>с</u>ад	<u>s</u>at
[ş]	<u>с</u>ел	*see note 3 under Consonants*
[z]	<u>с</u>дава́ть	do<u>z</u>e
[ʐ]	<u>с</u>де́лать	before some voiced consonants
[ɪ]	<u>с</u>шить	<u>sh</u>oot
[ʒ]	<u>с</u>жать	mea<u>s</u>ure
[ɪ]	<u>с</u>чи́стить	<u>sh</u>eet
[t]	<u>т</u>ок	<u>t</u>op
[ḏ]	<u>т</u>е	*see note 3 under Consonants*
[d]	о<u>т</u>говори́ть	<u>d</u>og
[ṯ]	о<u>т</u>де́лать	before "soft" "д"
[f]	<u>ф</u>о́рма	<u>f</u>at
[f̡]	бу<u>ф</u>е́т	*see note 2 under Consonants*
[v]	а<u>ф</u>га́нец	<u>v</u>at
[x]	<u>х</u>од	pronounced like Scots "ch" in "loch"
[x̡]	<u>х</u>и́мик	*see note 5 under Consonants*
[ts]	<u>ц</u>ель	bi<u>ts</u>
[dz]	оте́<u>ц</u> <u>б</u>ы	a<u>dz</u>e
[tʃ]	<u>ч</u>а́сто	<u>ch</u>ip
[dʒ]	до<u>чь</u> <u>б</u>ы	<u>j</u>ig
[ʃ]	<u>ш</u>у́тка	<u>sh</u>oot
[ɕ]	<u>щ</u>ит	fre<u>sh sh</u>eets

АНГЛИЙСКОЕ ПРОИЗНОШЕНИЕ

Гласные и дифтонги

Знак	Английский Пример	Русское Соответствие/Описание
[ɑ:]	f*a*ther	м*а́*ма
[ʌ]	b*u*t, c*o*me	*а*льянс
[æ]	m*a*n, c*a*t	*э́*тот
[ə]	fath*e*r, *a*go	ра́н*а*, п*а*рохо́д
[ə:]	b*i*rd, h*ea*rd	ф*ё*дор
[ɛ]	g*e*t, b*e*d	ж*е*ст
[ɪ]	*i*t, b*i*g	к*и*т
[i:]	t*ea*, s*ea*	*и́*ва
[ɔ]	h*o*t, w*a*sh	х*о*д
[ɔ:]	s*a*w, *a*ll	*о́*чень
[u]	p*u*t, b*oo*k	б*у*к
[u:]	t*oo*, y*ou*	*у́*лица
[aɪ]	fl*y*, h*i*gh	л*а́й*
[au]	h*ow*, h*ou*se	*а́у*т
[ɛə]	th*ere*, b*ear*	произно́сится как сочета́ние зву́ков "э" и кра́ткого "а"
[eɪ]	d*ay*, ob*ey*	*эй*
[ɪə]	h*ere*, h*ear*	произно́сится как сочета́ние зву́ков "и" и кра́ткого "а"
[əu]	g*o*, n*o*te	*о́у*
[ɔɪ]	b*oy*, *oi*l	б*ой*
[uə]	p*oo*r, s*ure*	произно́сится как сочета́ние зву́ков "у" и кра́ткого "а"
[juə]	p*ure*	произно́ситься как сочета́ние зву́ков "ю" и кра́ткого "а"

Согласные

Знак	Английский Пример	Русское Соответствие/Описание
[b]	**b**ut	**б**ал
[d]	men**d**e**d**	аре́н**д**а
[g]	**g**o, **g**et, bi**g**	**г**ол, ми**г**
[dӡ]	**g**in, ju**dge**	**дж**и́нсы, и́ми**дж**
[ŋ]	si**ng**	произно́сится как ру́сский "н", но не ко́нчиком языка́, а за́дней ча́стью его́ спи́нки
[h]	**h**ouse, **h**e	**х**а́ос, **х**и́мия
[j]	**y**oung, **y**es	**й**од, **й**емен
[k]	**c**ome, mo**ck**	**к**а́мень, ро**к**
[r]	**r**ed, t**r**ead	**р**от, т**р**ава́
[s]	**s**and, ye**s**	**с**ад, ри**с**
[z]	ro**s**e, **z**ebra	ро́**з**а, **з**е́бра
[ʃ]	**sh**e, ma**ch**ine	**ш**и́на, ма**ш**и́на
[tʃ]	**ch**in, ri**ch**	**ч**ин, кули́**ч**
[v]	**v**alley	**в**альс
[w]	**w**ater, **wh**ich	**у**о́тергейт, **у**и́к-э́нд
[ӡ]	vi**s**ion	ва́**ж**ный
[θ]	**th**ink, my**th**	произно́сится как ру́сский "с", но ко́нчик языка́ нахо́дится ме́жду зуба́ми
[ð]	**th**is, **th**e	произно́сится как ру́сский "з", но ко́нчик языка́ нахо́дится ме́жду зуба́ми
[f]	**f**ace	**ф**акт
[l]	**l**ake, **l**ick	**л**ай, **л**ом
[m]	**m**ust	**м**ат
[n]	**n**ut	**н**ет
[p]	**p**at, **p**ond	**п**арохо́д
[t]	**t**ake, ha**t**	э́**т**от, не**т**
[x]	lo**ch**	**х**од

xxx

[ɑʒ]	**А,**	а
[be]	**Б,**	б
[ve]	**В,**	в
[ge]	**Г,**	г
[de]	**Д,**	д
[je]	**Е,**	е
[jɔ]	**Ё,**	ё
[ʒe]	**Ж,**	ж
[ze]	**З,**	з
[i]	**И,**	и
[i'kratkɔje]	**Й,**	й
[ka]	**К,**	к
[ɛl]	**Л,**	л
[ɛm]	**М,**	м
[ɛn]	**Н,**	н
[ɔ]	**О,**	о
[pe]	**П,**	п
[ɛr]	**Р,**	р
[ɛs]	**С,**	с
[te]	**Т,**	т
[u]	**У,**	у
[ɛf]	**Ф,**	ф
[xa]	**Х,**	х
[tse]	**Ц,**	ц
[tʃe]	**Ч,**	ч
[ʃa]	**Ш,**	ш
[ʃta]	**Щ,**	щ
['tyɔrd+ znak]	**Ъ,**	ъ
[+]	**Ы,**	ы
['makk+ znak]	**Ь,**	ь
[ɛ]	**Э,**	э
[ju]	**Ю,**	ю
[ja]	**Я,**	я

A, a [eɪ]
B, b [biː]
C, c [siː]
D, d [diː]
E, e [iː]
F, f [ɛf]
G, g [dʒiː]
H, h [eɪtʃ]
I, i [aɪ]
J, j [dʒeɪ]
K, k [keɪ]
L, l [ɛl]
M, m [ɛm]
N, n [ɛn]
O, o [əu]
P, p [piː]
Q, q [kjuː]
R, r [ɑː*]
S, s [ɛs]
T, t [tiː]
U, u [juː]
V, v [viː]
W, w ['dʌblju]
X, x [ɛks]
Y, y [waɪ]
Z, z [zɛd, (US) ziː]

~ A, a ~

A, a *сущ нескл (буква)* the 1st letter of the Russian alphabet; **от ~ до я** from A to Z.

a *союз* **1** *(выражает противопоставление)* but; **он согласи́лся, а я отказа́лся** he agreed, but I refused; **я чита́л, а он рисова́л** I was reading and he was drawing

2 *(выражает присоединение)* and; **снача́ла говори́л он, а пото́м мы** first he spoke, and then we did

3 *(перед перечислением)* namely; *(перед уточнением)* to be exact *или* precise; **пришли́ дво́е, а и́менно: Ивано́в и Петро́в** two people came, namely Ivanov and Petrov; **я до́лжен встать ра́но, а и́менно в 6 утра́** I have to get up early, at 6 am to be exact *или* precise

4 *(во фразах)*: **а (не) то** or (else); **спеши́, а (не) то опозда́ешь** hurry, or (else) you'll be !ate; **а и́менно** *(то есть)* that is; **а вот** but

♦ *част* **1** *(усиливает обращение)* hey; **Ма́ша, а Ма́ша!** hey, Masha!

2 *(обозначает отклик)*: **иди́ сюда́! — а, что тако́е!** come here! — yes? what is it?; **а как же** *(разг)* of course; **ты обе́дал? а как же** have you had lunch? of course

♦ *межд (выражает припоминание, догадку)* ah; *(выражает ужас, боль)* oh; **а ну** *(разг)* go on; **а ну, беги́ в дом!** go on, run along in!; **а ну́ его́!** *(разг)* stuff him!

А- *сокр*: **~72, ~76** *different grades of petrol.*

абажу́р (-а) *м* lampshade.

абба́т (-а) *м (в монастыре)* abbot.

абба́ти|са (-ы) *ж* abbess.

абба́тств|о (-а) *ср* abbey.

аббревиату́р|а (-ы) *ж* abbreviation.

Аберди́н (-а) *м* Aberdeen.

абза́ц (-а) *м* paragraph.

абитурие́нт (-а) *м entrant to university, college etc.*

абитурие́нт|ка (-ки; *gen pl* -ок) *ж см* **абитурие́нт.**

абонеме́нт (-а) *м* season ticket.

абонеме́нтный *прил (концерт, лекция)* for season-ticket holders.

абоне́нт (-а) *м* subscriber.

абориге́н (-а) *м* aborigine.

або́рт (-а) *м* abortion; **де́лать (сде́лать** *perf*) **~** to have an abortion.

абрази́в (-а) *м* abrasive.

абракада́бр|а (-ы) *ж* gobbledegook.

абрико́с (-а) *м (плод)* apricot; *(дерево)* apricot tree.

абсолю́тен *прил см* **абсолю́тный.**

абсолюти́зм (-а) *м* absolutism.

абсолю́тно *нареч* absolutely.

абсолю́т|ный (-ен, -на, -но) *прил* absolute; **~ная монопо́лия** absolute monopoly; **абсолю́тный слух** perfect pitch.

абсорби́р|овать (-ую) *(не)сов перех* to absorb.

абстраги́р|оваться (-уюсь) *(не)сов возв*: **~ (от** +*gen*) to detach o.s. (from).

абстра́кт|ный (-ен, -на, -но) *прил* abstract; **абстра́ктное (и́мя) существи́тельное** abstract noun.

абстра́кци|я (-и) *ж* abstraction.

абсу́рд (-а) *м* absurdity; **доводи́ть (довести́** *perf*) **что-н до ~а** to take sth to the point of absurdity.

абсу́рд|ный (-ен, -на, -но) *прил* absurd.

абсце́сс (-а) *м* abscess.

аванга́рд (-а) *м (также ВОЕН)* vanguard; *(ИСКУССТВО)* avant-garde; **в ~е** (+*gen*) in the vanguard (of).

авангарди́зм (-а) *м* the avant-garde.

ава́нс (-а) *м (КОММ)* advance; **~ в счёт платеже́й** advance against payments.

аванси́р|овать (-ую) *(не)сов перех*: **~ что-н кому́-н** to advance sb sth; *(КОММ)* to make sb an advance payment of sth.

ава́нсом *нареч* in advance.

авансце́н|а (-ы) *ж* proscenium.

авантю́р|а (-ы) *ж* adventurism; **втя́гивать (втяну́ть** *perf*) **кого́-н в ~у** to involve sb in a risky undertaking.

авантюри́ст (-а) *м* adventurist.

авантюри́ст|ка (-ки; *gen pl* -ок) *ж см* **авантюри́ст.**

авари́йный *прил (служба, машина)* emergency *опред*; *(дом, состояние техники)* unsafe; **авари́йный сигна́л** alarm signal.

ава́ри|я (-и) *ж* accident; *(повреждение:*

механизма, аппаратуры) breakdown; **терпéть (потерпéть** *perf*) **~ю** (*машина, самолёт итп*) to crash; **попáсть** (*perf*) **в ~ю** to have an accident.

áвгуст (-а) м August; *см также* **октя́брь.**

áвгустовск|ий (-ая, -ое, -ие) *прил* August *опред.*

áвиа *нескл* (*авиапочта*) air mail.

авиали́ни|я (-и) ж flight path.

авиано́с|ец (-ца) м aircraft carrier.

авиацио́нный *прил* aviation *опред.*

авиа́ци|я (-и) ж aviation; **гражда́нская ~** civil aviation.

ави́зо *ср нескл* (*КОММ*) advice note.

авитамино́з (-а) м vitamin deficiency, avitaminosis.

аво́сек *сущ см* **аво́ська.**

аво́сь *част* (*разг*) perhaps; **на ~** (*разг*) on the off chance; (: *наугад*) by guesswork; **надéяться** (*impf*) **на ~** to trust to luck.

аво́|ська (-ьки; *gen pl* **-ек**) ж (*разг*) (string) bag.

авра́л (-а) м (*МОР*) emergency task; (*перен: разг*) rush job.

австрали́ек *сущ см* **австрали́йка.**

австрали́|ец (-йца) м Australian.

австрали́йка (-йки; *gen pl* **-ек**) ж *см* **австрали́ец.**

австрали́йский (-ая, -ое, -ие) *прил* Australian.

австрали́йца *итп сущ см* **австрали́ец.**

Австра́ли|я (-и) ж Australia.

австри́ек *сущ см* **австри́йка.**

австри́|ец (-йца) м Austrian.

австри́йка (-йки; *gen pl* **-ек**) ж *см* **австри́ец.**

австри́йский (-ая, -ое, -ие) *прил* Austrian.

австри́йца *итп сущ см* **австри́ец.**

Áвстри|я (-и) ж Austria.

авт. *сокр* (= *автомоби́льный*) auto. (= *automobile*); = **автоно́мный, áвторский,** **áвтор.**

авто- *часть сложных слов* (*со значением автоматический*) indicating sth done automatically eg. *автопило́т*; (*со значением автомобильный*) indicating a connection with vehicles eg. *автозаво́д*; (*со значением свой, само-*) self- or auto-, indicating a connection with oneself eg. *автобиография.*

автоба́з|а (-ы) ж depot (*where a company's vehicles are kept and maintained*).

автобиографи́ческ|ий (-ая, -ое, -ие) *прил* autobiographical.

автобиогра́фи|я (-и) ж autobiography.

авто́бус (-а) м bus; (*на дальние расстояния*) coach (*BRIT*), bus (*US*).

авто́бусный *прил* (*см сущ*) bus *опред*; coach *опред* (*BRIT*).

автовокза́л (-а) м bus *или* coach (*BRIT*) station.

авто́граф (-а) м autograph.

автодоро́жный *прил* (*происшествие*) road *опред*; (*инспекция*) traffic *опред.*

автозаво́д (-а) м car (*BRIT*) *или* automobile (*US*) plant.

автозапра́вочн|ая (-ой; *decl like adj*) ж (*также:* **~ ста́нция**) filling station.

автока́р (-а) м fork-lift truck.

автола́в|ка (-ки; *gen pl* **-ок**) ж mobile shop.

автомагистра́л|ь (-и) ж motorway (*BRIT*), expressway (*US*).

автома́т (-а) м automatic machine; (*ВОЕН*) sub-machine-gun.

автоматиза́ци|я (-и) ж automation.

автоматизи́р|овать (-ую) (*не*)*сов перех* to automate.

автома́тик|а (-и) ж automatic equipment.

автомати́ческ|ий (-ая, -ое, -ие) *прил* automatic.

автомаши́н|а (-ы) ж (motor)car, automobile (*US*).

автомоби́л|ь (-я) м (motor)car, automobile (*US*); **легково́й ~** (passenger) car.

автоно́мен *прил см* **автоно́мный.**

автоно́ми|я (-и) ж autonomy.

автоно́м|ный (-ен, -на, -но) *прил* autonomous; (*ТЕХ*) independent; (*КОМП*) off-line, stand-alone.

автоотве́тчик (-а) м answering machine.

автопило́т (-а) м automatic pilot.

автопортре́т (-а) м self-portrait.

áвтор (-а) м author.

авторефера́т (-а) м abstract (*of dissertation*).

авториз|ова́ть (-у́ю) (*не*)*сов перех* to authorize.

авторита́р|ный (-ен, -на, -но) *прил* authoritarian.

авторите́т (-а) м authority; **по́льзоваться** (*impf*) **~ом** to enjoy authority; **завоёвывать** (**завоева́ть** *perf*) **~** to gain authority.

авторите́т|ный (-ен, -на, -но) *прил* authoritative.

áвторск|ий (-ая, -ое, -ие) *прил* author's; **áвторский ве́чер** (*поэта итп*) reading; (*композитора*) recital (*given by the composer*); **áвторское пра́во** copyright; **áвторское свиде́тельство** patent.

авторуч|ка (-ки; *gen pl* **-ек**) ж fountain pen.

автосто́п (-а) м (*способ путешествия*) hitchhiking.

автостра́д|а (-ы) ж motorway (*BRIT*), expressway (*US*).

автотра́нспорт (-а) м road transport.

авуа́р|ы (-ов) *мн* (*КОММ*) assets *мн.*

ага́ *межд* aha ♦ *част* (*разг: выражает согласие*) uh huh.

ага́т (-а) м agate.

аге́нт (-а) м agent.

аге́нтств|о (-а) *ср* agency; **телегра́фное ~** news agency; **аге́нтство печа́ти** press agency.

агенту́р|а (-ы) ж intelligence service ♦ *собир* agents *мн.*

агита́тор (-а) м (political) campaigner; (*на выборах*) canvasser.

агитацио́нный *прил* (political) promotional.

агита́ци|я (-и) ж campaigning.

агити́р|овать (-ую) *несов неперех:* **~ (за** +*acc*) to campaign (for).

аго́ни|я (-и) ж death throes *мн.*

агра́рный *прил* agrarian.
агрега́т (-а) *м* machine; (*узел*) unit (*of machine*).
агресси́вный (-ен, -на, -но) *прил* aggressive.
агре́сси|**я** (-и) *ж* aggression.
агроно́м (-а) *м* agronomist.
агрономи́ческ|**ий** (-ая, -ое, -ие) *прил* agronomic.
агроно́ми|**я** (-и) *ж* agronomy.
ад (-а) *м* hell.
ада́жио *ср нескл, нареч* adagio.
ада́мово *прил*: **А~ я́блоко** Adam's apple.
адапта́ци|**я** (-и) *ж* adaptation.
ада́птер (-а) *м* adaptor.
адапти́р|**овать** (-ую) (*не*)*сов перех* to adapt
► **адапти́роваться** (*не*)*сов возв* to adapt.
адвока́т (-а) *м* (*ЮР*) ≈ barrister (*BRIT*), ≈ attorney (*US*); (*консультант*) solicitor; **колле́гия ~ов** ≈ the Bar (*BRIT*).
адвокату́р|**а** (-ы) *ж собир* ≈ the Bar (*BRIT*).
АДД *м сокр* (= автореферат диссерта́ции на соиска́ние учёной сте́пени до́ктора нау́к) abstract of doctoral thesis.
Адди́с-Абе́б|**а** (-ы) *ж* Addis Ababa.
адеква́т|**ный** (-ен, -на, -но) *прил* adequate; (*совпадающий*) identical.
адено́ид|**ы** (-ов) *мн* (*МЕД*) adenoids *мн*.
адм. *сокр* (= администра́ция) admin (= *administration*).
административн|**ый** *прил* administrative; (*способности*) managerial, management *опред*; **в ~ом поря́дке** by authority; **~ тон** an official tone of voice.
администра́тор (-а) *м* administrator; (*в театре, гостинице, кино*) manager.
администра́ци|**я** (-и) *ж, собир* administration; (*гостиницы*) management.
администри́р|**овать** (-ую) *несов неперех* (+*instr*) to administrate.
адмира́л (-а) *м* admiral.
АДМП *ж сокр* = Агра́рно-демократи́ческая па́ртия.
а́дрес (-а; *nom pl* -**а́**) *м* address; **в ~** +*gen* (addressed) to; **Ва́ше обвине́ние не по ~у** (*разг*) you've got the wrong person; **по ~у кого́-н** concerning *или* about sb; **абсолю́тный/относи́тельный ~** (*КОМП*) absolute/relative address.
а́дресный *прил*: **~ стол** address bureau.
адрес|**ова́ть** (-у́ю) (*не*)*сов перех*: **~ что-н кому́-н** to address sth to sb; (*критику*) to direct sth at sb.
адриати́ческ|**ий** (-ая, -ое, -ие) *прил*: **А~ое мо́ре** the Adriatic (Sea).
а́дск|**ий** (-ая, -ое, -ие) *прил* (*РЕЛ*) infernal; (*разг: холод, условия*) diabolical; (: *терпение, выносливость*) fantastic; (*замысел*) cunning.
адъюта́нт (-а) *м* aide-de-camp.
аж *част, союз* (*разг*) even; **он ~ вскри́кнул от удивле́ния** he even cried out in surprise.

ажиота́ж (-а) *м* (*перен*) commotion; (*КОММ*) stockjobbing.
ажу́р (-а) *м keeping of books up to date*; **в ~е** (*разг*) in cracking order.
ажу́рный *прил* lace; **ажу́рная рабо́та** fine *или* delicate work.
АЗС *ж сокр* (= автозапра́вочная ста́нция) filling station.
аз|**ы́** (-о́в) *мн* (*перен*) basics *мн*; **начина́ть (нача́ть** *perf*) **с ~о́в** to start from scratch.
аза́ли|**я** (-и) *м* azalea.
аза́рт (-а) *м* ardour (*BRIT*), ardor (*US*); **с ~ом** with zest; **входи́ть (войти́** *perf*) **в ~** to get carried away.
аза́рт|**ный** (-ен, -на, -но) *прил* ardent; **аза́ртная игра́** game of chance.
а́збук|**а** (-и) *м* alphabet; (*буква́рь*) first reading book; (*перен: основны́е нача́ла*) rudiments *мн*; **но́тная ~** the system of musical notation; **а́збука Мо́рзе** Morse code.
а́збучный *прил* alphabetical; **а́збучная и́стина** truism.
Азербайджа́н (-а) *м* Azerbaijan.
азербайджа́н|**ец** (-ца) *м* Azerbaijani.
азербайджа́н|**ка** (-ки; *gen pl* -**ок**) *ж см* **азербайджа́нец**.
азербайджа́нск|**ий** (-ая, -ое, -ие) *прил* Azerbaijani.
азербайджа́нца *итп сущ см* **азербайджа́нец**.
азиа́т (-а) *м* Asian.
азиа́т|**ка** (-ки; *gen pl* -**ок**) *ж см* **азиа́т**.
азиа́тск|**ий** (-ая, -ое, -ие) *прил* Asian.
а́зимут (-а) *м* azimuth.
А́зи|**я** (-и) *ж* Asia.
азо́вск|**ий** (-ая, -ое, -ие) *прил*: **А~ое мо́ре** the Sea of Azov.
азо́рск|**ий** (-ая, -ое, -ие) *прил*: **А~ие острова́** the Azores.
азо́т (-а) *м* nitrogen.
азо́тный *прил* nitric.
а́ист (-а) *м* stork.
ай *межд* (*выражает боль*) ow, ouch; (*выражет испуг, страх*) oh; **~ да Мари́я!** good for Maria!
айв|**а́** (-ы́) *ж* (*плод*) quince; (*де́рево*) quince tree.
айда́ *межд* (*разг*) let's go; **~ купа́ться!** let's go for a swim!
а́йсберг (-а) *м* iceberg.
акад. *сокр* = **акаде́мик**.
акаде́мик (-а) *м* academician.
академи́ческ|**ий** (-ая, -ое, -ие) *прил* (*также перен*) academic; **академи́ческий теа́тр** *honorary title given to theatres*.
акаде́ми|**я** (-и) *ж* academy; **акаде́мия нау́к** the Academy of Sciences; **акаде́мия худо́жеств** the Academy of Arts.
а́ка|**ть** (-ю) *несов неперех to pronounce unstressed "o" as "a" in Russian*.

акáци|я (-и) ж acacia.
акваланг (-а) м aqualung.
аквамарúн (-а) м aquamarine.
аквамарúновый прил aquamarine.
акварéл|ь (-и) ж watercolours мн (BRIT),
watercolors мн (US); (картина) watercolo(u)r.
акварéльный прил watercolour опред (BRIT),
watercolor опред (US).
аквáриум (-а) м aquarium, fish tank.
акватóри|я (-и) ж: ~ пóрта area of water near
the port.
акведýк (-а) м aqueduct.
АКД м сокр (= авторефéрат диссертáции на
соискáние учёной стéпени кандидáта наýк)
abstract of dissertation for first level of
postgraduate degree.
акклиматизáци|я (-и) м acclimatization,
acclimation (US).
акклиматизúр|оваться (-уюсь) (не)сов возв
to acclimatize, acclimate (US).
аккомпанемéнт (-а) м (МУЗ, перен)
accompaniment.
аккомпанúр|овать (-ую) несов неперех (+dat;
МУЗ) to accompany.
аккóрд (-а) м chord; **брать (взять** perf) ~ to play
a chord; **заключúтельный** ~ (перен) climax.
аккордеóн (-а) м accordion.
аккóрдный прил: **~ая рабóта** piecework; **он на
~ой оплáте** he is on piecework.
аккредитúв (-а) м letter of credit.
аккредитúвный прил credit опред.
аккредитóванный прил: ~ **агéнт** accredited
agent.
аккредит|овáть (-ýю) (не)сов перех to accredit.
аккумулúр|овать (-ую) (не)сов перех (ТЕХ,
перен) to accumulate.
аккумуля́тор (-а) м accumulator.
аккурáтен прил см аккурáтный.
аккурáтно нареч (регулярно) regularly;
(старательно) carefully; (опрятно) neatly.
аккурáтность (-и) ж (см прил) regularity;
meticulousness; accuracy; neatness.
аккурáтный (-ен, -на, -но) прил (посещение)
regular; (работник) meticulous; (работа)
accurate; (костюм) neat.
акр (-а) м acre.
акрúл (-а) м acrylic.
акрúловый прил acrylic.
акробáт (-а) м acrobat.
акробáтик|а (-и) ж acrobatics.
акселерáт (-а) м early developer (physically).
акселерáтор (-а) м accelerator.
акселерáци|я (-и) ж early physical maturity.
аксессуáр (-а) м (одежды) accessory; см также
аксессуáры.
аксессуáр|ы (-ов) мн (перен: в живописи
итп) details мн; (: в теáтре) props мн
(= properties).
аксиóм|а (-ы) ж axiom.
акт (-а) м act; (торжественное собрание)
ceremony; **составлять (состáвить** perf) ~ to

draw up a formal document; **áкты
граждáнского состоя́ния** register (of births,
marriages, deaths).
актёр (-а) м actor.
актúв (-а) м activists мн (in organization);
(КОММ) assets мн; **запúсывать (записáть** perf)
что-н в ~ to count sth as an asset;
заморóженные ~ы (КОММ) frozen assets.
актúвен прил см актúвный.
активизúр|овать (-ую) (не)сов перех to
enliven.
актúвно нареч (участвовать) actively;
(работать) energetically.
актúвный (-ен, -на, -но) прил active; **актúвный
балáнс** balance of assets; **актúвный словáрь
или запáс слов** active vocabulary.
актрúс|а (-ы) ж actress.
актуáлен прил см актуáльный.
актуáльность (-и) ж topicality.
актуáльный (-ен, -ьна, -ьно) прил topical.
акýл|а (-ы) ж shark.
акупунктýр|а (-ы) ж acupuncture.
акýстик|а (-и) ж acoustics ед; (в зале, в студии)
acoustics мн.
акустúческ|ий (-ая, -ое, -ие) прил acoustic(al);
~ **соединúтель** (КОМП) acoustic coupler.
акушёр (-а) м obstetrician.
акушёрк|а (-и; gen pl -ок) ж midwife.
акушёрск|ий (-ая, -ое, -ие) прил obstetric(al).
акцéнт (-а) м accent; **дéлать (сдéлать** perf) ~ **на**
+prp (перен) to emphasize; **расставлять
(расстáвить** perf) **все ~ы** (перен) to draw
attention to the most important things.
акцентúр|овать (-ую) (не)сов перех (перен) to
accentuate.
акцéпт (-а) м (КОММ, ЮР) acceptance.
акцéптный прил (КОММ): ~ **банк** accepting
house.
акцепт|овáть (-ýю) (не)сов перех (КОММ) to
accept.
акцúз (-а) м (КОММ) excise (tax).
акцúзный прил (КОММ) excise опред.
акционéр (-а) м shareholder.
акционéрный прил joint-stock опред;
акционéрное óбщество joint-stock company;
акционéрный капитáл share capital.
акционéрск|ий (-ая, -ое, -ие) прил (права,
доля) shareholders'.
áкци|я (-и) ж (КОММ) share; (действие) action;
именнáя/обыкновéнная ~ registered/ordinary
share; **пакéт ~й** block of shares; **пóлностью
оплáченная** ~ fully-paid share; **~и без прáва
гóлоса** non-voting shares; **дипломатúческая** ~
diplomatic move.
албáн|ец (-ца) м Albanian.
Албáни|я (-и) ж Albania.
албáн|ка (-ки; gen pl -ок) ж см албáнец.
албáнск|ий (-ая, -ое, -ие) прил Albanian.
албáнца итп сущ см албáнец.
áлгебр|а (-ы) ж algebra.
алгорúтм (-а) м algorithm.

алеба́стр (-а) *м* alabaster.
алеба́стровый *прил* alabaster *опред*.
александри́т (-а) *м* (*ГЕО*) alexandrite.
Александри́|я (-и) *ж* Alexandria.
але́|ть (-ю) *несов неперех* (*флаг, мак*) to show scarlet; (*закат*) to glow scarlet; (*perf* **зале́ть**; *закат, небо*) to turn scarlet.
Алжи́р (-а) *м* Algeria.
алжи́р|ец (-ца) *м* Algerian.
алжи́р|ка (-ки; *gen pl* -ок) *ж см* **алжи́рец**.
алжи́рский (-ая, -ое, -ие) *прил* Algerian.
алжи́рца *итп сущ см* **алжи́рец**.
а́либи *ср нескл* alibi.
алиме́нтщик (-а) *м* (*разг: пренебр*) *man paying alimony or maintenance*.
алиме́нт|ы (-ов) *мн* alimony *ед*, maintenance *ед*.
алка́ш (-а́) *м* (*разг: пренебр*) alky.
алкоголи́зм (-а) *м* alcoholism.
алкого́лик (-а) *м* alcoholic.
алкоголи́ч|ка (-ки; *gen pl* -ек) *ж* (*разг*) *см* **алкого́лик**.
алкого́л|ь (-я) *м* alcohol.
Алла́х (-а) *м* Allah.
аллего́ри|я (-и) *ж* allegory.
алле́гро *ср нескл, нареч* allegro.
аллерге́н (-а) *м* allergen.
аллерги́ческ|ий (-ая, -ое, -ие) *прил* allergic.
аллерги́|я (-и) *ж* allergy.
алле́|я (-и) *ж* alley.
аллига́тор (-а) *м* alligator.
аллилу́йя *межд* hallelujah.
алло́ *межд* hello (*on answering phone*).
аллю́р (-а) *м* gait (*of horses*).
Алма-Ата́ (-ы́) *ж* Alma-Ata.
алма́з (-а) *м* diamond.
алма́зный *прил* diamond *опред*; (*инструмент*) diamond-tipped.
ало́э *ср нескл* aloe.
алта́р|ь (-я́) *м* (*в церкви*) chancel; (*жертвенник*) altar; **возлага́ть** (**возложи́ть** *perf*) **что-н на ~ чего́-н** to sacrifice on the altar of sth.
алфави́т (-а) *м* alphabet; **по ~у** in alphabetical order.
а́лчен *прил см* **а́лчный**.
а́лчност|ь (-и) *ж* greed.
а́лч|ный (-ен, -на, -но) *прил* greedy.
а́л|ый (-, -а, -о) *прил* scarlet.
алыч|а́ (-и́) *ж* cherry plum.
альбо́м (-а) *м* album; (*по искусству*) *book of art reproductions*.
альмана́х (-а) *м* anthology.
альпи́йский (-ая, -ое, -ие) *прил* alpine; (*в Альпах*) Alpine.
альпини́зм (-а) *м* mountaineering.
Альп|ы (-) *мн* the Alps.
альт (-а́) *м* (*голос*) alto; (*инструмент*) viola.
альтернати́в|а (-ы) *ж* alternative.
альтернати́вный *прил* alternative.

альтруи́зм (-а) *м* altruism.
алья́нс (-а) *м* alliance.
Аля́ск|а (-и) *ж* Alaska.
алюми́ниевый *прил* aluminium *опред* (*ВRIT*), aluminum *опред* (*US*).
алюми́ни|й (-я) *м* aluminium (*ВRIT*), aluminum (*US*).
аляпова́т|ый (-, -а, -о) *прил* gaudy.
амазо́н|ка (-ки; *gen pl* -ок) *ж* (*всадница*) horsewoman (*мн* horsewomen); (*платье*) riding habit.
амальга́м|а (-ы) *ж* (*хим, перен*) amalgam.
амба́р (-а) *м* barn.
амбицио́з|ный (-ен, -на, -но) *прил* (*человек*) arrogant; (*планы*) presumptuous.
амби́ци|я (-и) *ж* (*самолюбие*) pride, arrogance; (*обычно мн: притязания*) ambition; **ударя́ться** (**уда́риться** *perf*) **в ~ю** (*разг*) to go into a huff.
амбулато́ри|я (-и) *ж* doctor's surgery (*ВRIT*) *или* office (*US*).
амво́н (-а) *м* (*РЕЛ*) ≈ pulpit.
амёб|а (-ы) *ж* amoeba (*ВRIT*), ameba (*US*).
Аме́рик|а (-и) *ж* America.
америка́н|ец (-ца) *м* American.
американиза́ци|я (-и) *ж* Americanization.
американизи́р|овать (-ую) (*не*)*сов перех* to Americanize.
америка́н|ка (-ки; *gen pl* -ок) *ж см* **америка́нец**.
америка́нский (-ая, -ое, -ие) *прил* American.
америка́нца *итп сущ см* **америка́нец**.
амети́ст (-а) *м* amethyst.
аминокисл|ота́ (-оты́; *nom pl* -о́ты) *ж* amino acid.
ами́н|ь *част* (*РЕЛ*) amen.
аммиа́к (-а) *м* ammonia.
АМН *ж сокр* (= Акаде́мия медици́нских нау́к) Academy of Medical Sciences.
амнисти́р|овать (-ую) (*не*)*сов перех* to grant (an) amnesty to.
амни́сти|я (-и) *ж* amnesty; **попада́ть** (**попа́сть** *perf*) **под ~ю** to be granted (an) amnesty.
амора́лен *прил см* **амора́льный**.
амора́льност|ь (-и) *ж* (*см прил*) immorality; amorality.
амора́л|ьный (-ен, -ьна, -ьно) *прил* (*поступок*) immoral; (*человек*) amoral.
амортиза́тор (-а) *м* (*ТЕХ*) shock absorber.
амортизацио́нный *прил* (*ТЕХ*) shock-absorbing; (*ЭКОН*) depreciation *опред*; **амортизацио́нные отчисле́ния** (*ЭКОН*) depreciation deductions *мн*; **амортизацио́нный срок** (*ЭКОН*) period of depreciation.
амортиза́ци|я (-и) *ж* (*ТЕХ*) shock absorption; (*ЭКОН*) depreciation; (*КОММ*) amortization.
амо́рф|ный (-ен, -на, -но) *прил* amorphous.
ампе́р (-а) *м* amp (= *ampère*).
амплиту́д|а (-ы) *ж* amplitude.
амплуа́ *ср нескл* (*актёра*) speciality; **это не**

моё ~ (*разг*) that's not (in) my line.
áмпул|а (-ы) *ж* ampoule (*BRIT*), ampule (*US*).
ампутáци|я (-и) *ж* amputation.
ампути́р|овать (-ую) (*не*)*сов перех* to amputate.
АМТС *ж сокр* (= *автомати́ческая междугоро́дная телефо́нная связь*) ≈ STD (*BRIT*) (= *subscriber trunk dialling*).
амуни́ци|я (-и) *ж собир* ammunition.
Аму́р (-а) *м* Cupid; *см также* **аму́ры**.
аму́р|ы (-ов) *мн* (*разг: любовные дела*) intrigues *мн*, love affairs *мн*.
амфи́би|я (-и) *ж* amphibian.
амфитеа́тр (-а) *м* amphitheatre (*BRIT*), amphitheater (*US*).
АН *ж сокр* (= *Акаде́мия нау́к*) Academy of Sciences ♦ *м сокр* = *самолёт констру́кции О. К. Анто́нова*.
Ан *м сокр* = **АН**.
ана́лиз (-а) *м* analysis; **сдава́ть (сдать** *perf*) **кровь/мочу́ на ~** to give a blood/urine sample; **подверга́ть (подве́ргнуть** *perf*) **~у** to analyse (*BRIT*), analyze (*US*); **~ изде́ржек и при́были** (*КОММ*) cost-benefit analysis; **~ эффекти́вности рабо́ты** time and motion study; **ана́лиз кро́ви** blood test.
анализи́р|овать (-ую; *perf* **проанализи́ровать**) *несов перех* to analyse (*BRIT*), analyze (*US*).
анали́тик (-а) *м* (*специалист*) analyst; **он хоро́ший ~** (*склонный к анализу*) he has a very analytical mind.
ана́лог (-а) *м* analogue (*BRIT*), analog (*US*).
аналоги́ч|ный (-ен, -на, -но) *прил* analogous.
аналоги|я (-и) *ж* analogy; **по ~и** (**с** +*instr*) in a similar way (to); **проводи́ть (провести́** *perf*) **~ю ме́жду** +*instr* to draw an analogy between.
анало́|й (-я) *м* lectern.
ана́мнез (-а) *м* (*МЕД*) case history.
анана́с (-а) *м* pineapple.
анархи́зм (-а) *м* anarchism.
анархи́стск|ий (-ая, -ое, -ие) *прил* anarchist опред.
ана́рхи|я (-и) *ж* anarchy.
анато́ми|я (-и) *ж* anatomy.
ана́фем|а (-ы) *ж* anathema; **предава́ть (преда́ть** *perf*) **~е** to anathematize.
анахрони́зм (-а) *м* anachronism.
анахрони́ч|ный (-ен, -на, -но) *прил* anachronistic.
анга́р (-а) *м* hangar.
а́нгел (-а) *м* (*также разг*) angel.
а́нгельск|ий (-ая, -ое, -ие) *прил* angelic; **а́нгельское терпе́ние** the patience of a saint.
ангин|а (-ы) *ж* tonsillitis, quinsy.
англи́йск|ий (-ая, -ое, -ие) *прил* English; (*британский*) British; **~ язы́к** English; **англи́йская була́вка** safety pin; **англи́йский газо́н** lawn.
англика́нск|ий (-ая, -ое, -ие) *прил* Anglican; **англика́нская це́рковь** the Anglican church.

англича́н|ин (-ина; *nom pl* **-е**, *gen pl* **-**) *м* Englishman (*мн* Englishmen).
англича́н|ка (-ки; *gen pl* **-ок**) *ж* Englishwoman (*мн* Englishwomen).
А́нгли|я (-и) *ж* England.
Анго́л|а (-ы) *ж* Angola.
анго́л|ец (-ьца) *м* Angolan.
анго́л|ка (-ки; *gen pl* **-ок**) *ж см* **анго́лец**.
анго́льск|ий (-ая, -ое, -ие) *прил* Angolan.
анго́льца *итп сущ см* **анго́лец**.
анго́рск|ий (-ая, -ое, -ие) *прил* angora опред; **анго́рская шерсть** angora (wool).
А́нд|ы (-) *мн* the Andes.
анекдо́т (-а) *м* joke; **со мной случи́лся ~** (*разг*) something funny happened to me.
анекдоти́ч|ный (-ен, -на, -но) *прил* (*смешной и странный*) funny.
анеми́ч|ный (-ен, -на, -но) *прил* anaemic (*BRIT*), anemic (*US*).
анеми́|я (-и) *ж* anaemia (*BRIT*), anemia (*US*).
анестезио́лог (-а) *м* anaesthetist (*BRIT*), anesthesiologist (*US*).
анестези́р|овать (-ую) (*не*)*сов перех* to anaesthetize (*BRIT*), anesthetize (*US*).
анестези́|я (-и) *ж* anaesthesia (*BRIT*), anesthesia (*US*); **ме́стная/о́бщая ~** local/general ana(e)sthesia.
анили́н (-а) *м* aniline.
анили́новый *прил* aniline опред.
ани́совый *прил* aniseed опред; **ани́совая во́дка** aniseed vodka.
АНК *м сокр* (= *Африка́нский национа́льный конгре́сс*) ANC (= *African National Congress*).
Анкар|а (-ы) *ж* Ankara.
анке́т|а (-ы) *ж* (*опросный лист*) questionnaire; (*бланк для сведений*) form; (*сбор сведений*) survey; **проводи́ть (провести́** *perf*) **~у** to carry out a survey.
анке́тный *прил*: **~ые да́нные** personal details *мн*; **анке́тный лист** questionnaire.
анна́л|ы (-ов) *мн* annals *мн*; **в ~ах исто́рии** in the annals of history.
анне́кси|я (-и) *ж* annexation.
аннота́ци|я (-и) *ж* précis.
анноти́р|овать (-ую; *perf* **проанноти́ровать**) *несов перех* to summarize.
аннуите́т (-а) *м* (*КОММ*) annuity; **пожи́зненный ~** life annuity.
аннули́́́рование (-я) *ср* (*см глаг*) annulment; repeal; cancellation.
аннули́р|овать (-ую) (*не*)*сов перех* (*брак, договор*) to annul; (*закон*) to repeal; (*долг*) to cancel.
ано́д (-а) *м* anode.
анома́льный (-ен, -ьна, -ьно) *прил* anomalous.
ано́ним (-а) *м* anonymous author.
анони́мен *прил см* **анони́мный**.
анони́м|ка (-ки; *gen pl* **-ок**) *ж* (*разг: пренебр*) poison-pen letter.
анони́м|ный (-ен, -на, -но) *прил* anonymous.
анони́мок *сущ см* **анони́мка**.
ано́нс (-а) *м* announcement.

анорекси|я (-и) ж anorexia; **она страдает ~ей** she is anorexic.
ансамбл|ь (-я) м ensemble; (*танцоров*) troupe; (*эстрадный*) group.
АНТ м *сокр* = *самолёт конструкции А. Н Туполева*.
антагони́зм (-а) м antagonism.
Антаркти́д|а (-ы) ж Antarctica.
Анта́рктик|а (-и) ж Antarctica, the Antarctic.
антаркти́ческий (-ая, -ое, -ие) *прил* Antarctic.
Антве́рпен (-а) ж Antwerp.
анте́нн|а (-ы) ж aerial (*BRIT*), antenna (*US*); **~ косми́ческой свя́зи** satellite dish.
антибио́тик (-а) м antibiotic.
антивое́нный *прил* antiwar.
антидемократи́ческий (-ая, -ое, -ие) *прил* antidemocratic.
антиква́р (-а) м antiquary.
антиквариа́т (-а) м *собир* antiques *мн*.
антиква́р|ный *прил* antique *опред*; **антиква́рный магази́н** antique shop.
антило́п|а (-ы) ж antelope.
антинау́ч|ный (-ен, -на, -но) *прил* antiscientific.
антипати́ч|ный (-ен, -на, -но) *прил* unlikable.
антипа́ти|я (-и) ж antipathy.
антипо́д (-а) м antithesis.
антирелигио́зный *прил* antireligious.
антисанита́рен *прил* см **антисанита́рный**.
антисанитари́|я (-и) ж unhygienic *или* insanitary conditions *мн*.
антисанита́р|ный (-ен, -на, -но) *прил* unhygienic, insanitary.
антисеми́т (-а) м anti-Semite.
антисемити́зм (-а) м anti-Semitism.
антисеми́т|ка (-ки; *gen pl* -ок) ж см **антисеми́т**.
антисеми́ток *сущ* см **антисеми́тка**.
антисеми́тский (-ая, -ое, -ие) *прил* anti-Semitic.
антисе́птик (-а) м antiseptic.
антисепти́ческий (-ая, -ое, -ие) *прил* antiseptic.
антите́з|а (-ы) ж antithesis.
антите́л|о (-а; *nom pl* -á) *ср* (*обычно мн*) antibody.
антифаши́стский (-ая, -ое, -ие) *прил* antifascist.
антифри́з (-а) м antifreeze.
анти́христ (-а) м Antichrist.
антицикло́н (-а) м anticyclone.
анти́чность (-и) ж antiquity.
анти́чный *прил* classical; **анти́чный мир** the Ancient World.
антоло́ги|я (-и) ж anthology.
анто́ним (-а) м antonym.
анто́нов|ка (-ки; *gen pl* -ок) ж antonovka (*apple*).
антра́кт (-а) м interval.
антраци́т (-а) м anthracite.
антреко́т (-а) м entrecôte.
антрепренёр (-а) м impresario.

антресо́л|и (-ей) *мн* (*полуэтаж*) mezzanine *ед*; (*балкон*) gallery *ед*; (*под потолком*) cupboard *ед*.
антрополо́ги|я (-и) ж anthropology.
анфа́с *нареч* full face.
анфила́д|а (-ы) ж suite (*of rooms*).
анчо́ус (-а) м anchovy.
аншла́г (-а) м (*объявление*) sellout; (*заголовок*) banner headline; **проходи́ть** (**пройти́** *perf*) **с ~ом** to be a sellout.
аню́тины *прил*: **~ гла́зки** pansy *ед*.
АО ж *сокр* = *автоно́мная о́бласть* ♦ м *сокр* = *автоно́мный о́круг*.
А/О *ср сокр* (= *акционе́рное о́бщество*) joint-stock company.
ао́рт|а (-ы) ж aorta.
АП м *сокр* (= *Ассо́шиэйтед пресс*) AP (= *Associated Press*).
апартеи́д (-а) м apartheid.
апати́ч|ный (-ен, -на, -но) *прил* apathetic.
апа́ти|я (-и) ж apathy.
апелли́р|овать (-ую) (*не*)*сов неперех* (*ЮР*) to appeal; **~** (*impf/perf*) **к** +*dat* to appeal to.
апелляцио́нный *прил* (*ЮР*) appeal *опред*; **апелляцио́нный суд** court of appeal.
апелля́ци|я (-и) ж (*ЮР*) appeal; **~ к** +*dat* appeal to.
апельси́н (-а) м orange.
апельси́нный *прил* = **апельси́новый**.
апельси́новый *прил* orange.
аперити́в (-а) м aperitif.
АПК м *сокр* = *агра́рно-промы́шленный ко́мплекс*.
аплоди́р|овать (-ую) *несов неперех* (+*dat*) to applaud.
аплодисме́нт|ы (-ов) *мн* applause *ед*.
апло́мб (-а) м assurance; **с ~ом** with aplomb.
АПН *ср сокр* (= *аге́нтство печа́ти "Но́вости"*) "Novosti" Press Agency ♦ ж *сокр* (= *Акаде́мия педагоги́ческих нау́к*) Academy of Pedagogical Sciences.
апоге́|й (-я) м (*также перен*) apogee; **он в ~е сла́вы** he is at the height of his fame.
апока́липсис (-а) м (*РЕЛ*) (the Book of) Revelation, the Apocalypse.
аполити́ч|ный (-ен, -на, -но) *прил* apolitical.
апологе́т (-а) м apologist.
апо́стол (-а) м apostle; (*книга*) the Acts of the Apostles and the Epistles.
апо́стольский (-ая, -ое, -ие) *прил* apostolic.
апостро́ф (-а) м apostrophe.
апофео́з (-а) м (*восхваление*) apotheosis; (*ТЕАТР*) grand finale.
аппара́т (-а) м apparatus; (*ФИЗИОЛОГИЯ*) system; (*штат*) staff; **телефо́нный ~** telephone; **госуда́рственный ~** state apparatus.
аппара́т|ная (-ой; *decl like adj*) ж equipment room.
аппарату́р|а (-ы) ж *собир* apparatus, equipment;

(*приборы*) instruments мн.
аппара́тчик (-а) м operative; (*разг: работник аппара́та*) apparatchik.
аппе́ндикс (-а) м appendix.
аппендици́т (-а) м appendicitis.
аппети́т (-а) м appetite; (*обычно мн: перен: раза*) craving; **прия́тного ~а!** bon appétit!; **перебива́ть** (**переби́ть** *perf*) ~ to spoil one's appetite; **во́лчий** ~ a voracious appetite.
аппети́тный (-ен, -на, -но) прил appetizing.
апплика́ция (-и) ж appliqué.
апре́ль (-я) м April; *см также* **октя́брь**.
апроби́ровать (-ую) (*не)сов перех* to approve.
апте́ка (-и) ж dispensing chemist's (BRIT), pharmacy.
апте́карский (-ая, -ое, -ие) прил (*товары*) pharmaceutical.
апте́карь (-я) м chemist (BRIT), pharmacist.
апте́чка (-ки; *gen pl* -ек) ж medicine chest; (*первой помощи*) first-aid kit.
апте́чный прил chemist's.
апчхи межд: ~! atishoo!
ара́б (-а) м Arab.
арабе́ска (-ки; *gen pl* -ок) ж arabesque (ART).
ара́бка (-ки; *gen pl* -ок) ж см **ара́б**.
ара́бский (-ая, -ое, -ие) прил (*страны*) Arab; ~ язы́к Arabic; **ара́бские ци́фры** Arabic numerals.
арави́ек сущ см **арави́йка**
арави́ец (-йца) м Arabian.
арави́йка (-йки; *gen pl* -ек) ж см **арави́ец**.
арави́йский (-ая, -ое, -ие) прил Arabian опред.
арави́йца итп сущ см **арави́ец**.
Ара́вия (-и) ж Arabia.
ара́льский (-ая, -ое, -ие) прил: **А~ое мо́ре** Aral Sea.
аранжи́ровать (-ую) (*не)сов перех* to arrange.
аранжиро́вка (-ки; *gen pl* -ок) ж arrangement.
ара́хис (-а) м peanut.
ара́хисовый прил peanut опред.
АРБ ж сокр (= Ассоциа́ция росси́йских ба́нков) association of Russian banks.
арби́тр (-а) м (*в спорах*) arbitrator; (*в футболе*) referee; (*в бейсболе, теннисе*) umpire.
арбитра́ж (-а) м arbitration; (*орган*) arbitration service.
арбитра́жный прил arbitration опред.
арбу́з (-а) м watermelon.
Аргенти́на (-ы) ж Argentina.
аргенти́нец (-ца) м Argentinian.
аргенти́нка (-ки; *gen pl* -ок) ж см **аргенти́нец**.
аргенти́нский (-ая, -ое, -ие) прил Argentinian.
аргенти́нца итп сущ см **аргенти́нец**.
арго́н (-а) м argon.
аргуме́нт (-а) м (*также* МАТ) argument.
аргумента́ция (-и) ж argument.
аргументи́ровать (-ую) (*не)сов перех* to argue.
аре́на (-ы) ж (*в цирке*) ring; (*часть стадиона, перен*) arena.
аре́нда (-ы) ж (*наём*) lease; (*плата*) rent; **сдава́ть** (**сдать** *perf*) **в ~у** to lease.

аренда́тор (-а) м leaseholder.
аре́ндный прил lease опред; **на ~ых нача́лах** on a rental basis; **аре́ндная пла́та** rent; **аре́ндный подря́д** rental agreement, lease.
арендова́ть (-у́ю) (*не)сов перех* to lease.
аре́ст (-а) м (*преступника*) arrest; (*имущества*) sequestration; **брать** (**взять** *perf*) **кого́-н под** ~ to place sb under arrest; **налага́ть** (**наложи́ть** *perf*) ~ **на** +*acc* to sequester; **находи́ться** (*impf*) **под ~ом** to be under arrest.
аресто́ванная (-ой; *decl like adj*) ж см **аресто́ванный**.
аресто́ванный (-ого; *decl like adj*) м person held in custody.
аресто́вать (-у́ю; *impf* **аресто́вывать**) сов перех (*преступника*) to arrest; (*имущество*) to sequestrate.
аристокра́т (-а) м aristocrat.
аристократи́ческий (-ая, -ое, -ие) прил aristocratic.
аристокра́тия (-и) ж aristocracy.
а́рия (-и) ж aria.
АРКА м сокр (= Америка́но-Росси́йский комме́рческий алья́нс) American-Russian commercial alliance.
а́рка (-ки; *gen pl* -ок) ж arch.
арка́да (-ы) ж (АРХИТ) arcade.
арка́н (-а) м lasso.
арка́нить (-ю, -ишь; *perf* **заарка́нить**) несов перех to lasso.
А́рктика (-и) ж the Arctic.
аркти́ческий (-ая, -ое, -ие) прил Arctic.
арлеки́н (-а) м harlequin.
армату́ра (-ы) ж собир (СТРОИТ) steel framework; (*вспомога́тельные устро́йства*) fittings мн.
арме́йский (-ая, -ое, -ие) прил army опред.
Арме́ния (-и) ж Armenia.
а́рмия (-и) ж army; (*перен*): ~ +*gen* (*помо́щников, чита́телей*) army of.
армяни́н (-а; *nom pl* **армя́не**, *gen pl* **армя́н**) м Armenian.
армя́нка (-ки; *gen pl* -ок) ж см **армяни́н**.
армя́нский (-ая, -ое, -ие) прил Armenian опред; ~ язы́к Armenian.
а́рок сущ см **а́рка**.
арома́т (-а) м (*цветов*) fragrance; (*кофе итп*) aroma; (*перен: молодости*) spirit.
арома́тен прил см **арома́тный**.
ароматический (-ая, -ое, -ие) прил aromatic.
арома́тный (-ен, -на, -но) прил fragrant.
арсена́л (-а) м (*склад*) arsenal; (*завод*) munitions factory; **в ~е** (*перен*) at one's disposal.
арта́читься (-усь, -ишься) несов возв (*разг*) to be pig-headed.

артезиа́нск|ий (-ая, -ое, -ие) *прил* artesian.
арте́л|ь (-и) *ж worker's or peasant's cooperative.*
арте́льн|ый *прил* collective *опред*; **на ~ых нача́лах** on a collective basis.
артериа́льн|ый *прил*: **~ое давле́ние** blood pressure.
арте́ри|я (-и) *ж* (*также перен*) artery; **со́нная ~** carotid artery.
арти́кл|ь (-я) *м* (*линг*) article.
артиллери́йск|ий (-ая, -ое, -ие) *прил* artillery *опред.*
артиллери́ст (-а) *м* artilleryman (*мн* artillerymen), gunner (*ВРИТ*).
артилле́ри|я (-и) *ж* artillery.
арти́ст (-а) *м* artist(e); (*кино*) actor; **он ~ расска́зывать исто́рии** he's ace at telling stories.
артисти́ческ|ий (-ая, -ое, -ие) *прил* artistic; **~ая убо́рная** dressing room.
арти́ст|ка (-ки; *gen pl* -ок) *ж* (*см м*) artist(e); actress.
артишо́к (-а) *м* (globe) artichoke.
артри́т (-а) *м* arthritis.
а́рф|а (-ы) *ж* harp.
арфи́ст (-а) *м* harpist.
арфи́ст|ка (-ки; *gen pl* -ок) *ж см* **арфи́ст.**
арха́изм (-а) *м* archaism.
архаи́чн|ый (-ен, -на, -но) *прил* archaic.
арха́нгел (-а) *м* archangel.
Арха́нгельск (-а) *м* Archangel.
архео́лог (-а) *м* archaeologist (*ВРИТ*), archeologist.
археологи́ческ|ий (-ая, -ое, -ие) *прил* archaeological.
археоло́ги|я (-и) *ж* archaeology.
архи́в (-а) *м* (*учреждение, отдел*) archive; (*собрание рукописей итп*) archives *мн*; **сдава́ть (сдать** *perf*) **что-н в ~** (*перен*) to consign sth to history.
архива́риус (-а) *м* archivist.
архи́вный *прил* archival; **~ файл** (*КОМП*) archive file.
архиепи́скоп (-а) *м* archbishop.
архиере́|й (-я) *м general term for upper orders of the church.*
архимандри́т (-а) *м* archimandrite.
архипела́г (-а) *м* archipelago.
архите́ктор (-а) *м* architect.
архитекту́р|а (-ы) *ж* architecture.
архитекту́рный *прил* architectural.
арши́н (-а; *gen pl* - *или* -ов) *м* (*устаревший*) arshin (*unit of measurement equal to 0.71 m*); **ме́рить** (*impf*) **кого́-н на свой ~** (*перен*) to judge sb by one's own standards.
арши́нный *прил* (*разг*) *very big, tall, high or long.*
ас (-а) *м* (*лётчик*) ace; (*перен*) expert.
асбе́ст (-а) *м* asbestos.
АСЕА́Н *ж сокр* ASEAN (= *Association of South-*

East Asian Nations).
асепти́ческ|ий (-ая, -ое, -ие) *прил* aseptic.
асимметри́чн|ый (-ен, -на, -но) *прил* asymmetric(al).
асимме́три|я (-и) *ж* asymmetry.
аске́т (-а) *м* ascetic.
аскети́зм (-а) *м* asceticism.
аскети́ческ|ий (-ая, -ое, -ие) *прил* ascetic *опред.*
аскорби́нов|ый *прил*: **~ая кислота́** ascorbic acid.
аспе́кт (-а) *м* aspect; **в ~е** + *gen* in (the) light of.
аспира́нт (-а) *м* postgraduate (*doing a PhD*).
аспиранту́р|а (-ы) *ж* postgraduate studies *мн* (*leading to a PhD*).
аспири́н (-а) *м* aspirin.
ассамбле́|я (-и) *ж* assembly; **Генера́льная А~ Организа́ции Объединённых На́ций** General Assembly of the United Nations.
ассе́мблер (-а) *м* (*КОМП*) assembler.
ассениза́ци|я (-и) *ж* sewage disposal system.
ассигнова́ни|е (-я) *ср* allocation.
ассигн|ова́ть (-у́ю) (*не*)*сов перех* to allocate.
ассимили́р|овать (-ую) (*не*)*сов перех* to assimilate
▸ **ассимили́роваться** (*не*)*сов возв* to become assimilated.
ассимиля́ци|я (-и) *ж* assimilation.
ассисте́нт (-а) *м* assistant; (*в вузе*) assistant lecturer.
ассисти́р|овать (-ую) *несов неперех* (+*dat*) to assist.
ассорти́ *ср нескл* assortment.
ассортиме́нт (-а) *м* assortment.
ассоциати́вн|ый (-ен, -на, -но) *прил* based on association.
ассоциа́ци|я (-и) *ж* association.
ассоции́р|овать (-ую) (*не*)*сов перех*: **~ что-н с кем-н/чем-н** to associate sth with sb/sth
▸ **ассоции́роваться** (*не*)*сов возв*: **~ся с** +*instr* to be associated with.
АССР *ж сокр* (*ист*. = *автоно́мная сове́тская социалисти́ческая респу́блика*) ASSR (= *Autonomous Soviet Socialist Republic*).
астеро́ид (-а) *м* asteroid.
астигмати́зм (-а) *м* astigmatism.
а́стм|а (-ы) *ж* asthma.
астма́тик (-а) *м* asthmatic.
астмати́ческ|ий (-ая, -ое, -ие) *прил* asthmatic.
а́стр|а (-ы) *ж* aster.
астро́лог (-а) *м* astrologist.
астроло́ги|я (-и) *ж* astrology.
астрона́вт (-а) *м* astronaut.
астрона́втик|а (-и) *ж* astronautics.
астроно́м (-а) *м* astronomer.
астрономи́ческ|ий (-ая, -ое, -ие) *прил* (*также перен*) astronomic(al).
астроно́ми|я (-и) *ж* astronomy.

АСУ ж сокр (= автоматизированная система управления) automatic control system.

асфа́льт (-а) м asphalt.

асфальти́р|овать (-ую; perf **заасфальти́ровать**) (не)сов перех to asphalt.

асфикси́я (-и) ж asphyxia.

ата́к|а (-и) ж (также перен) attack; **идти́ (пойти́** perf**) в ~у** to launch an attack; **~ на кого́-н/что-н** an attack on sb/sth.

атак|ова́ть (-ую) (не)сов перех (также перен) to attack.

атама́н (-а) м ataman (Cossack leader); (перен: банды) leader.

атеи́зм (-а) м atheism.

атеи́ст (-а) м atheist.

атеи́ст|ка (-ки; gen pl -ок) ж см **атеи́ст**.

атеисти́ческий (-ая, -ое, -ие) прил atheist опред.

атеи́сток сущ см **атеи́стка**.

ателье́ ср нескл (художника, фотографа) studio; (мод) tailor's shop; **телевизио́нное ~** television repair shop; **ателье́ прока́та** rental shop.

атланти́ческий (-ая, -ое, -ие) прил: **А~ океа́н** Atlantic Ocean.

а́тлас (-а) м atlas.

атла́с (-а) м satin.

атла́сный прил satin; (шелковистый) satiny; **атла́сная ко́жа** (перен) skin like satin.

атле́т (-а) м athlete; (крепкий человек) muscleman.

атлети́зм (-а) м (телосложение) athletic build; (культуризм) body building.

атле́тик|а (-и) ж athletics; **лёгкая ~** track and field events; **тяжёлая ~** weightlifting.

атлети́ческий (-ая, -ое, -ие) прил athletic.

АТМ ж сокр (= автоматическая кассовая машина) ATM (= automated telling machine).

атмосфе́р|а (-ы) ж (также перен) atmosphere.

атмосфе́рный прил atmospheric.

а́том (-а) м atom.

а́томный прил atomic; **а́томный вес** atomic weight.

а́томщик (-а) м (разг) atomic scientist.

атрибу́т (-а) м attribute.

атрибути́вный прил (линг) attributive.

атрофи́рованный прил atrophied.

атрофи́р|оваться (3sg -уется, 3pl -уются) (не)сов возв to atrophy.

атрофи́|я (-и) ж atrophy.

АТС ж сокр (= автоматическая телефонная станция) automatic telephone exchange.

атташе́ м нескл attaché.

аттеста́т (-а) м certificate; **аттеста́т зре́лости** certificate attained for passing school-leaving examinations.

аттеста́ци|я (-и) ж certification; (отзыв) recommendation.

аттест|ова́ть (-ую) (не)сов перех (давать характеристику) to recommend; (оценивать знания) to give a mark.

аттракцио́н (-а) м (цирковой номер) attraction; (качели, карусель итп) amusement.

ау́ межд (cry for attention).

аудие́нци|я (-и) ж (приём) audience.

ауди́т (-а) м (комм) audit; **о́бщий ~** general audit.

аудито́ри|я (-и) ж (помещение) lecture hall ◆ собир (слушатели) audience.

аукцио́н (-а) м auction; **продава́ть (прода́ть** perf**) что-н с ~a** to sell sth by auction; **покупа́ть (купи́ть** perf**) что-н на ~e** to buy sth at an auction.

аукционе́р (-а) м person attending an auction.

аукциони́ст (-а) м auctioneer.

аул (-а) м aul (mountain village in the Caucasus and Middle Asia).

а́ут (-а) м (в теннисе) out; (в футболе): **мяч в а́уте** the ball is out of play; (в боксе): **~!** knockout!

аутенти́чный (-ен, -на, -но) прил authentic.

аутоге́нный прил: **~ая трениро́вка** autogenic training.

аутса́йдер (-а) м outsider.

афга́н|ец (-ца) м Afghan; (ветеран) Afghan war veteran.

Афганиста́н (-а) м Afghanistan.

афга́н|ка (-ки; gen pl -ок) ж см **афга́нец**.

афга́нца итп сущ см **афга́нец**.

афе́р|а (-ы) ж swindle.

афери́ст (-а) м swindler.

афери́ст|ка (-ки; gen pl -ок) ж см **афери́ст**.

Афи́н|ы (-) мн Athens.

афи́ш|а (-и) ж poster.

афиши́р|овать (-ую) (не)сов перех to parade.

афори́зм (-а) м aphorism.

А́фрик|а (-и) ж Africa.

африка́н|ец (-ца) м African.

африка́н|ка (-ки; gen pl -ок) ж см **африка́нец**.

африка́нский (-ая, -ое, -ие) прил African.

африка́нца итп сущ см **африка́нец**.

аффе́кт (-а) м fit of passion.

ах межд: **~!** oh!, ah!; **~ да!** (разг) ah yes!; **не ~** (разг) not up to much.

а́ха|ть (-ю; perf **а́хнуть**) несов неперех (разг) to express surprise, regret etc.

ахилле́сова прил: **~ пята́** Achilles' heel.

ахине́|я (-и) ж (разг) rubbish; **нести́** (impf) **~ю** to talk rubbish.

а́хн|уть (-у, -ешь) сов от **а́хать** ◆ неперех (разг: орудие итп) to bang ◆ перех (разг: сломать) to smash; (: выпить) to knock back; **он и ~ не успе́л, как они́ убежа́ли** (разг) before he could get a word out, they ran away.

АХО м сокр (= административно-хозяйственный отдел) department concerned with property and maintenance.

а́хти межд (разг): **не ~ как** not specially; **не ~ (како́й)** (разг) not specially good.

ацето́н (-а) м acetone.

Ашхаба́д (-а) м Ashkhabad.

аэро́бик|а (-и) ж aerobics.

аэро́бус (-а) м airbus.

аэровокзáл (-а) *м* air terminal (*BRIT*).
аэродинáмик|а (-и) *ж* aerodynamics.
аэродинами́ческ|ий (-ая, -ое, -ие) *прил*
  aerodynamic; **аэродинами́ческая трубá** wind
  tunnel.
аэродрóм (-а) *м* aerodrome.
аэрозóл|ь (-я) *м* aerosol.
аэрóн (-а) *м* air-sickness tablets *мн*.

аэроплáн (-а) *м* aeroplane (*BRIT*), airplane (*US*).
аэропóрт (-а; *loc sg* -ý) *м* airport.
аэростáт (-а) *м* aerostat.
аэрофотосъём|ка (-ки; *gen pl* -ок) *ж* aerial
  photography.
АЭС *ж сокр* (= *áтомная электростáнция*)
  atomic power station.
аятолл|á (-ы́) *м* ayatollah.

~ Б, б ~

Б, б *сущ нескл* (*буква*) the 2nd letter of the Russian alphabet.

б *част см* бы.

ба *межд* well, well!; ~! кого́ я ви́жу! gosh! look who it is!

ба́б|а (-ы) *ж* (*разг*) woman; (: *пренебр: мужчина*) old woman.

ба́б|а-яга́ (-ы, -и́) *ж* Baba Yaga (*old witch in Russian folk-tales*); (*разг*) old witch (*fig*).

ба́б|ий (-ья, -ье, -ьи) *прил* (*разг: пренебр*) womanish; **ба́бье ле́то** Indian summer; **ба́бьи разгово́ры** women's talk; **ба́бьи ска́зки** old wives' tales.

ба́б|ка (-ки; *gen pl* -ок) *ж* (*бабушка*) grandmother; (*разг: старуха*) old woman.

ба́боч|ка (-ки; *gen pl* -ек) *ж* butterfly; (*галстук*) bow tie.

ба́буш|ка (-ки; *gen pl* -ек) *ж* grandma, granny; (*разг: старуха*) old woman; ~ на́двое сказа́ла we shall see (what we shall see).

Бава́ри|я (-и) *ж* Bavaria.

бава́рск|ий (-ая, -ое, -ие) *прил* Bavarian.

бага́ж (-а́) *м* luggage (*BRIT*), baggage (*US*); **сдава́ть (сдать** *perf*) **ве́щи в** ~ to check in one's luggage (*BRIT*) *или* bags (*US*); **отправля́ть (отпра́вить** *perf*) **багажо́м** to send as unaccompanied baggage; **бага́ж зна́ний** knowledge.

бага́жник (-а) *м* (*в автомобиле*) boot (*BRIT*), trunk (*US*); (*на крыше автомобиля*) roof rack; (*на велосипеде*) carrier.

бага́жный *прил* luggage *опред* (*BRIT*), baggage *опред* (*US*).

бага́мск|ий (-ая, -ое, -ие) *прил*: **Б~ие острова́** Bahama Islands, Bahamas.

Багда́д (-а) *м* Baghdad.

багрове́|ть (-ю; *perf* **побагрове́ть**) *несов непрех* to turn crimson; (*no perf; цветы*) to show crimson.

багро́в|ый (-, -а, -о) *прил* crimson.

багря́н|ый (-, -а, -о) *прил* crimson.

бадминто́н (-а) *м* badminton.

бадминтони́ст (-а) *м* badminton player.

бадминтони́ст|ка (-ки; *gen pl* -ок) *ж см* **бадминтони́ст**.

ба́з|а (-ы) *ж* basis; (*ВОЕН, АРХИТ*) base; (*для туристов, спортсменов*) centre (*BRIT*), center (*US*); (*продовольствия, товаров*) warehouse; **на ~е** +*gen* on the basis of; **ба́за да́нных** database.

база́льт (-а) *м* basalt.

база́р (-а) *м* market; (*новогодний, книжный итп*) fair; (*перен: разг*) racket; **пти́чий** ~ bird colony.

база́рный *прил* market *опред*; **база́рная ба́ба** (*разг*) fishwife.

базили́к|а (-и) *ж* basilica.

бази́р|овать (-ую) *несов перех*: ~ **что-н на** +*prp* to base sth on

▶ **бази́роваться** *несов возв* to be based; ~**ся** (*impf*) **на** +*prp* (*на фактах итп*) to be based on.

ба́зис (-а) *м* basis.

байда́р|ка (-ки; *gen pl* -ок) *ж* canoe.

ба́й|ка (-и) *ж* flannelette.

Байка́л (-а) *м* Lake Baikal.

ба́йковый *прил* flannelette.

байт (-а; *gen pl* -) *м* byte.

бак (-а) *м* tank; (*МОР*) forecastle, fo'c'sle.

бакале́йн|ый *прил*: ~ **магази́н** grocer's shop (*BRIT*), grocery store (*US*); ~**ые това́ры** groceries.

бакале́|я (-и) *ж* (*в магазине*) grocery section; (*товары*) groceries *мн*.

ба́кен (-а) *м* buoy.

бакенба́рд|ы (-) *мн* sideburns *мн*.

баклажа́н (-а; *gen pl* -или -ов) *м* aubergine (*BRIT*), eggplant (*US*).

баклу́ши *мн*: **бить** ~ (*разг*) to idle away one's time.

бактериологи́ческ|ий (-ая, -ое, -ие) *прил* bacteriological; **бактериологи́ческая война́** germ *или* bacteriological warfare.

бактерици́дный *прил* bactericidal, germicidal.

бакте́ри|я (-и) *ж* bacterium (*мн* bacteria).

Баку́ *м нескл* Baku.

бал (-а; *loc sg* -у́, *nom pl* -ы́) *м* (*вечер*) ball.

балага́н (-а) *м* (*перен: разг*) farce.

балала́й|ка (-йки; *gen pl* -ек) *ж* balalaika.

бала́нс (-а) *м* (*также КОММ*) balance; (*ведомость*) balance sheet; **расчётный** ~ balance of claims and liabilities; **бухга́лтерский** ~ balance sheet; **платёжный/торго́вый** ~ balance of payments/trade.

баланси́р|овать (-ую) *несов непрех*: ~ (**на** +*prp*) to balance (on) ♦ (*perf* **сбаланси́ровать**) *перех* (*КОММ*) to balance; ~ (*impf*) **на гра́ни чего́-н** (*перен*) to be poised on the verge *или* brink of sth.

бала́нсовый *прил* balance *опред*; **бала́нсовый**

балахо́н (-а) м (*разг*) sack (*baggy garment*).
балда́ (-ы́) м/ж chump.
балери́н|а (-ы) ж ballerina.
бале́т (-а) м ballet.
балетме́йстер (-а) м ballet master.
ба́л|ка (-ки; *gen pl* -ок) ж (*железобетонная, деревянная*) beam; (*металлическая*) girder; (*овраг*) gully.
Балка́н|ы (-) мн the Balkans.
балко́н (-а) м (*АРХИТ*) balcony; (*ТЕАТР*) circle (*BRIT*), balcony (*US*).
балл (-а) м (*на экзамене*) mark; (*на соревновании*) point; **проходно́й ~** pass mark; **ве́тер си́лой в 5 ба́ллов** a force 5 wind.
балла́д|а (-ы) ж ballad.
балла́ст (-а) м ballast; (*перен*) dead weight.
балли́стик|а (-и) ж ballistics.
баллисти́ческ|ий (-ая, -ое, -ие) *прил* ballistic *опред*; **баллисти́ческая раке́та** ballistic missile.
балло́н (-а) м (*газовый*) cylinder; (*с жидкостью*) jar; (*с кислотой, щёлочью*) carboy; (*АВТ*) balloon tyre.
баллоти́р|овать (-ую) *несов перех* to vote for
▶ **баллоти́роваться** *несов возв*: **~ся в** +*acc* или **на пост** +*gen* to stand (*BRIT*) или run (*US*) for.
баллотиро́вочный *прил*: **~ бюллете́нь** ballot paper.
ба́л|овать (-ую; *perf* изба́ловать) *несов перех* to spoil
▶ **ба́ловаться** *несов возв* to fool around.
ба́лок *сущ см* **ба́лка**.
балти́йск|ий (-ая, -ое, -ие) *прил*: **Б~ое мо́ре** the Baltic (Sea).
бальза́м (-а) м balsam; (*перен*) balm.
бальзами́р|овать (-ую) (*не*)*сов перех* to embalm.
ба́льный *прил*: **~ое пла́тье** ball gown; **ба́льные та́нцы** ballroom dancing.
балюстра́д|а (-ы) ж balustrade.
БАМ (-а) м *сокр* (= Байка́ло-Аму́рская (железнодоро́жная) магистра́ль) Baikal-Amur Railway.
бамбу́к (-а) м bamboo.
ба́мпер (-а) м bumper.
БАН м *сокр* (= Библиоте́ка Акаде́мии нау́к) library of the Academy of Sciences.
бана́лен *прил см* **бана́льный**.
бана́льность (-и) ж banality, platitude.
бана́льный (-ен, -ьна, -ьно) *прил* banal, trite.
бана́н (-а) м banana.
Бангладе́ш (-а) м Bangladesh.
бангладе́шск|ий (-ая, -ое, -ие) *прил* Bangladeshi.
ба́нд|а (-ы) ж gang.
банда́ж (-а́) м support bandage.
бандеро́л|ь (-и) ж package; **я посла́л кни́гу ~ю**

I packaged the book and sent it.
банди́т (-а) м bandit.
банк (-а) м bank; **сберега́тельный ~** savings bank; **акционе́рный ~** joint-stock bank; **экспортно-и́мпортный ~** export-import bank.
ба́н|ка (-ки; *gen pl* -ок) ж (*стеклянная*) jar; (*жестяная*) tin (*BRIT*), can (*US*); (*обычно мн: МЕД*) cupping glass.
банке́т (-а) м banquet.
банки́р (-а) м banker.
банкно́т (-а; *gen pl* -) м banknote.
ба́нковск|ий (-ая, -ое, -ие) *прил* bank *опред*.
банкома́т (-а) м cash machine.
банкро́т (-а) м bankrupt; **объявля́ть** (**объяви́ть** *perf*) **кого́-н ~ом** to declare sb bankrupt.
банкро́тств|о (-а) *ср* bankruptcy.
ба́нный *прил* bath *опред*.
ба́нок *сущ см* **ба́нка**.
бант (-а) м bow.
ба́н|я (-и; *gen pl* -ь) ж bathhouse; (*разг: мытьё*) bath; **фи́нская ~** sauna; **ру́сская/туре́цкая ~** Russian/Turkish baths; **задава́ть** (**зада́ть** *perf*) **кому́-н ~ю** (*разг*) to give sb what for.
бапти́зм (-а) м baptism.
бапти́ст (-а) м Baptist.
бар (-а) м bar; (*gen pl* -; *ФИЗ*) bar.
бараба́н (-а) м drum.
бараба́н|ить (-ю, -ишь) *несов неперех* to drum.
бараба́нн|ый *прил*: **~ая перепо́нка** eardrum.
бара́к (-а) м barracks мн.
бара́н (-а) м sheep; **смотре́ть** (*impf*) **на кого́-н/что-н как ~ на но́вые воро́та** (*разг*) to gawk at sb/sth; **ста́до ~ов** (*также перен: пренебр*) flock of sheep.
бара́н|ий (-ья, -ье, -ьи) *прил* (*суп, котлета*) lamb; (*тулуп*) sheepskin.
бара́нин|а (-ы) ж mutton; (*молодая*) lamb.
бара́н|ка (-ки; *gen pl* -ок) ж small, hard bread ring; (*перен: разг*) wheel.
барахл|о́ (-а́) *ср собир* junk; (*разг: человек, вещь*) trash.
барахо́л|ка (-ки; *gen pl* -ок) ж flea market.
бара́хта|ться (-юсь) *несов возв* (*разг*) to flounder; (*играя*) to wallow.
бара́ш|ек (-ка) м (*разг*) lamb; (*шкура*) lambskin; *см также* **бара́шки**.
бара́ш|ки (-ов) мн (*облака*) fleecy clouds мн; (*волны*) white horses мн, whitecaps мн.
барбари́с (-а) м barberry.
бард (-а) м singer-songwriter.
барда́к (-а́) м (*груб!: беспорядок*) hell broke loose (!).
барелье́ф (-а) м bas-relief.
ба́ренцев (-а, -о, -ы) *прил*: **Б~о мо́ре** Barents Sea.
ба́рж|а (-и) ж barge.
ба́рин (-а; *nom pl* господа́, *gen pl* госпо́д) м (*ИСТ*) ≈ lord (*member of the landowning gentry*);

жить (impf) как ~ to live like a king.
баритóн (-а) м baritone.
бáрмен (-а) м barman (мн barmen), bartender (US).
барокáмер|а (-ы) ж pressure chamber.
барóкко ср нескл baroque.
барóметр (-а) м barometer.
баррéль (-я) м barrel (unit of measurement).
баррикáд|а (-ы) ж barricade; **быть** (impf) **по рáзные стóроны баррикáд** to be on opposite sides of the fence.
баррикадú́р|овать (-ую; perf **забаррикадúровать**) несов перех to barricade.
барс (-а) м snow leopard.
Барселóн|а (-ы) ж Barcelona.
бáрск|ий (-ая, -ое, -ие) прил (перен) lordly, haughty; **бáрская усáдьба** manor house.
барсýк (-á) м badger.
бáртер (-а) м barter; **по ~у** on a barter basis.
бáртерн|ый прил: ~**ая торгóвля** goods мн for barter; **на ~ой оснóве** on a barter basis.
бáрхат (-а) м velvet.
бáрхатный прил velvet; (перен: кожа, голос) velvety; **бáрхатный сезóн** warm autumn days by the sea.
барьéр (-а) м (в беге) hurdle; (на скачках) fence; (перен) barrier; **тарúфный ~** tariff barrier.
бас (-а; nom pl **-ы́**) м bass.
бáсен сущ см **бáсня**.
баскетбóл (-а) м basketball.
баскетболúст (-а) м basketball player.
баскетболúст|ка (-ки; gen pl **-ок**) ж см **баскетболúст**.
баснослóв|ный (-ен, -на, -но) прил fabulous.
бáс|ня (-ни; gen pl **-ен**) ж fable; (обычно мн: перен: разг) fairy story.
басóвый прил bass опред.
бассéйн (-а) м (swimming) pool; (реки, озера итп) basin; **каменноугóльный ~** coalfield.
баст|овáть (-ýю) несов неперех to be on strike.
батальóн (-а) м battalion.
батарé|йка (-йки; gen pl **-ек**) ж (ЭЛЕК) battery.
батарé|я (-и) ж (отопительная) radiator; (ВОЕН, ЭЛЕК) battery.
батúст (-а) м cambric, lawn.
батóн (-а) м (white) loaf (long or oval).
батрáк (-á) м farm hand.
батрá|чка (-ки; gen pl **-ек**) ж см **батрáк**.
баттерфля|й (-я) м butterfly (stroke).
бáтюш|ка (-ки; gen pl **-ек**) м (также РЕЛ) father; см также **бáтюшки**.
бáтюшки межд: ~ **(мой)!** good heavens!
бах межд bang.
бáх|нуть (-у, -ешь; impf **бáхать**) сов (не)перех to bang.
Бахрéйн (-а) м Bahrain.
бахром|á (-ы́) ж fringe.
бахч|á (-ú) ж melon or pumpkin patch.
бахчевы́е прил: ~ **культýры** melons or pumpkins.
бацúлл|а (-ы) ж bacillus (мн bacilli).

бáшен сущ см **бáшня**.
башк|á (-ú) ж (разг) head.
башмáк (-á) м (туфля) shoe; (ботинок) boot; **деревя́нный ~** clog; **быть** (impf) **под башмакóм у когó-н** to be under sb's thumb.
бáш|ня (-ни; gen pl **-ен**) ж tower; (ВОЕН) gun turret; (разг) tower block.
баю-бáй межд refrain (in lullaby).
баю́ка|ть (-ю) несов перех to lull to sleep.
бáюшки-баю́ межд см **баю-бáй**.
бая́н (-а) м bayan (kind of concertina).
БВЛ ж сокр (= Библиотéка всемúрной литератýры) series of books on world literature.
бдúтельн|ый (-ен, -ьна, -ьно) прил vigilant.
бег (-а) м running; (СПОРТ) race; ~ **на длúнные дистáнции** long-distance race; ~ **на корóткие дистáнции** sprint; см также **бегá**.
бег|á (-óв) мн the races мн; **быть** (impf) **в ~х** (разг) to be on the run или go.
бéга|ть (-ю) несов неперех to run; (челнок) to and fro; ~ (impf) **от** +gen (разг) to avoid; ~ (impf) **за кем-н** (разг) to chase или run after sb; **у негó глазá ~ли** he looked shifty.
бегемóт (-а) м hippopotamus.
бегú(те) несов см **бежáть**.
беглéц (-á) м fugitive.
бéгло нареч (читать, говорить) fluently; (просмотреть, ознакомиться) cursorily.
бéглый прил (каторжник, преступник) escaped; (крепостной) runaway опред; (речь, чтение) fluent; (обзор) cursory; **бéглые глáсные** fleeting vowels; **бéглый огóнь** (ВОЕН) rapid fire.
бегля́н|ка (-ки; gen pl **-ок**) ж см **беглéц**.
беговóй прил (лошадь) race опред; (лыжи) racing; ~**ая дорóжка** running track.
бегóм нареч quickly; (перен: разг) in a rush; **бежáть** (impf) ~ to race, fly.
бегóни|я (-и) ж begonia.
бéгств|о (-а) ср (из плена) escape; (из дома) flight; (с поля боя) rout; **обращáть** (**обратúть** perf) **в ~** to rout; **спасáться** (**спастúсь** perf) ~**м** to escape.
бегý итп несов см **бежáть**.
бегýн (-á) м runner.
бегýнь|я (-и) ж см **бегýн**.
бед|á (-ы́; nom pl **-ы**) ж tragedy; (личная) misfortune; **прóсто** ~**!** it's just awful!; **попадáть** (**попáсть** perf) **в ~ý** to get into trouble; **быть** (impf) **в ~é** to be in trouble; ~ **в том, что ...** the trouble is (that) ...; ~ (**мне**) **с ним** (разг) he's nothing but trouble (to me); **на ~ý** (разг) unfortunately; **не** ~**!** (разг) (it's) nothing!; **лихá** ~ **начáло** (разг) the first step is always the hardest.
бéден прил см **бéдный**.
бéдер сущ см **бедрó**.
бедн|éть (-ю; perf **обеднéть**) несов неперех to become poor.
бéдность| (-и) ж (также перен) poverty.

бе́д|ный (-ен, -на́, -но) *прил* poor.
бедня́г|а (-и) *м/ж* (*разг*) poor thing.
бедня́к (-а́) *м* poor man.
бе́дренный *прил* (*см сущ*) thigh *опред*; hip *опред*.
бедр|о́ (-а́; *nom pl* **бёдра**, *gen pl* **бёдер**) *ср* (*верхняя часть ноги*) thigh; (*таз*) hip.
бе́дственный (-, -на, -но) *прил* disastrous.
бе́дстви|е (-я) *ср* disaster.
бе́дств|овать (-ую) *несов неперех* to live in poverty.
бежа́ть (*см* **Table 20**) *несов неперех* to run; (*время*) to fly; (*облака*) to scud ♦ (*не*)*сов* (*из плена, из тюрьмы*) to escape.
бе́жевый *прил* beige.
бе́жен|ец (-ца) *м* refugee.
бе́жен|ка (-ки; *gen pl* -ок) *ж см* **бе́женец**.
бе́женца *итп сущ см* **бе́женец**.
бежи́шь *итп несов см* **бежа́ть**.
без *предл* (+*gen*) without; ~ **пяти́/десяти́ мину́т шесть** five to/ten to six; **не** ~ +*gen* (*труда, осложений*) not without; **и** ~ **того́** (*и так уже*) already; **не** ~ **того́** (*разг*) sort of; ~ **у́стали** tirelessly; ~ **тебя́ пробле́м хвата́ет** there are enough problems without you adding to them *.
безава́рийный *прил* accident-free.
безалабе́р|ный (-ен, -на, -но) *прил* (*разг*) sloppy.
безалкого́льный *прил* nonalcoholic, alcohol-free; **безалкого́льный напи́ток** soft drink.
безапелляцио́н|ный (-ен, -на, -но) *прил* (*тон, ответ*) peremptory; (*юр: решение*) final; **~ый пригово́р** *a sentence without the right of appeal*.
безбе́д|ный (-ен, -на, -но) *прил* comfortable.
безбиле́тник (-а) *м* (*разг: пассажир*) fare dodger.
безбиле́тниц|а (-ы) *ж см* **безбиле́тник**.
безбо́жен *прил см* **безбо́жный**.
безбо́жник (-а) *м* (*разг*) heathen.
безбо́жно *нареч* (*разг*) shamelessly.
безбо́ж|ный (-ен, -на, -но) *прил* (*разг*) shameless.
безболе́знен|ный (-, -на, -но) *прил* (*также перен*) painless.
безбоя́знен|ный (-, -на, -но) *прил* fearless.
безбра́чи|е (-я) *ср* celibacy.
безбре́ж|ный (-ен, -на, -но) *прил* (*также перен*) boundless.
безве́ст|ный (-ен, -на, -но) *прил* unknown.
безве́трен|ный (-, -на, -но) *прил* calm.
безвку́сен *прил см* **безвку́сный**.
безвку́сиц|а (-ы) *ж* bad taste.
безвку́с|ный (-ен, -на, -но) *прил* tasteless.
безвла́сти|е (-я) *ср* anarchy.
безво́д|ный (-ен, -на, -но) *прил* (*среда, почва*) arid.
безвозвра́т|ный (-ен, -на, -но) *прил* irretrievable; **безвозвра́тная ссу́да**

nonrepayable subsidy.
безвозме́здно *нареч* for free.
безвозме́здный *прил* free.
безво́л|ьный (-ен, -ьна, -ьно) *прил* weak-willed.
безвре́д|ный (-ен, -на, -но) *прил* harmless.
безвре́мен|ный (-ен, -на, -но) *прил* untimely.
безвы́ездно *нареч* continuously.
безвы́ход|ный (-ен, -на, -но) *прил* hopeless.
безгла́сный *прил* (*перен*) silent.
безголо́в|ый (-, -а, -о) *прил* (*перен: разг*) brainless.
безголо́с|ый (-, -а, -о) *прил*: ~ **пе́вец** singer with a weak voice.
безгра́мот|ный (-ен, -на, -но) *прил* illiterate; (*работник*) incompetent.
безграни́ч|ный (-ен, -на, -но) *прил* (*также перен*) boundless.
безгре́ш|ный (-ен, -на, -но) *прил* sinless.
безда́р|ный (-ен, -на, -но) *прил* (*писатель, музыкант*) talentless; (*произведение, роман*) mediocre.
бе́здар|ь (-и) *ж* (*разг*) nobody.
безде́йств|овать (-ую) *несов неперех* (*машина, предприятие*) to be out of action; (*человек*) to take no action.
безделу́ш|ка (-ки; *gen pl* -ек) *ж* (*разг*) trinket, knick-knack.
безде́ль|е (-я) *ср* idleness.
безде́льник (-а) *м* (*разг*) loafer.
безде́льниц|а (-ы) *ж см* **безде́льник**.
безде́льнича|ть (-ю) *несов неперех* (*разг*) to loaf *или* lounge about.
безде́нежный *прил* (*расчёт, перевод*) noncash; (*разг: человек*) hard up.
безде́т|ный (-ен, -на, -но) *прил* childless.
безде́ятел|ьный (-ен, -ьна, -ьно) *прил* inactive.
бе́здн|а (-ы) *ж* abyss; **у меня́ ~ дел** (*разг*) I've got heaps of things to do.
бездоказа́тел|ьный (-ен, -ьна, -ьно) *прил* unsubstantiated.
бездо́м|ный (-ен, -на, -но) *прил* (*человек*) homeless; (*собака*) stray *опред*.
бездо́н|ный (-ен, -на, -но) *прил* bottomless; **бездо́нная бо́чка** (*разг*) bottomless pit; (: *человек*) (old) soak.
безду́м|ный (-ен, -на, -но) *прил* thoughtless.
безду́ш|ный (-ен, -на, -но) *прил* (*человек*) heartless; (*игра актёра*) soulless.
безе́ *ср нескл* meringue.
безжа́лост|ный (-ен, -на, -но) *прил* ruthless.
безжи́знен|ный (-, -на, -но) *прил* lifeless; (*взгляд, лицо*) expressionless.
беззабо́т|ный (-ен, -на, -но) *прил* carefree.
беззако́нен *прил см* **беззако́нный**.
беззако́ни|е (-я) *ср* lawlessness; (*поступок*) unlawful act.

беззако́н|ный (-ен, -на, -но) *прил* unlawful.

беззасте́нчив|ый (-, -а, -о) *прил* shameless; ~ лгун barefaced liar.

беззащи́т|ный (-ен, -на, -но) *прил* defenceless (*BRIT*), defenseless (*US*).

беззву́ч|ный (-ен, -на, -но) *прил* inaudible.

беззло́б|ный (-ен, -на, -но) *прил* good-natured.

беззу́б|ый (-, -а, -о) *прил* toothless; (*перен*) feeble.

безли́к|ий (-ая, -ое, -ие; -, -а, -о) *прил* nondescript.

безли́чный *прил* (*линг*) impersonal.

безлю́д|ный (-ен, -на, -но) *прил* (*улица, место*) deserted, empty; **безлю́дная техноло́гия** automated technology; **безлю́дный фонд** *funds for employees not on regular staff.*

безме́р|ный (-ен, -на, -но) *прил* (*счастье, любовь*) boundless; (*требования*) unlimited.

безмо́зглый *прил* (*разг*) brainless.

безмо́лв|ный (-ен, -на, -но) *прил* (*также перен*) silent; ~**ное согла́сие** tacit agreement.

безмяте́ж|ный (-ен, -на, -но) *прил* tranquil.

безнадёж|ный (-ен, -на, -но) *прил* hopeless; ~ **больно́й** hopeless case (*MED*).

безнака́за|нный (-, -на, -но) *прил* unpunished.

безнали́чный *прил* noncash; **безнали́чный расчёт** clearing settlement.

безно́г|ий (-ая, -ое, -ие) *прил* one-legged; (*без двух ног*) legless.

безнра́вствен|ный (-, -на, -но) *прил* immoral.

безо *предл см* **без**.

безоби́д|ный (-ен, -на, -но) *прил* (*шутка, высказывание*) inoffensive, innocuous.

безо́блач|ный (-ен, -на, -но) *прил* cloudless; (*перен: жизнь, детство*) carefree; (: *счастье*) unclouded.

безобра́зен *прил см* **безобра́зный**.

безобра́зи|е (-я) *ср* (*физическое уродство*) ugliness; (*поступок*) outrage; ~**!** it's outrageous!, it's a disgrace!

безобра́зник (-а) *м* (*разг*) (little) horror.

безобра́зниц|а (-ы) *ж см* **безобра́зник**.

безобра́знича|ть (-ю; *perf* **набезобра́зничать**) *несов неперех* (*разг*) to carry on.

безобра́з|ный (-ен, -на, -но) *прил* ugly; (*поступок, действие*) outrageous, disgraceful.

безогово́роч|ный (-ен, -на, -но) *прил* unconditional.

безопа́сен *прил см* **безопа́сный**.

безопа́сность (-и) *ж* safety; (*международная*) security; **в** ~**и** out of danger; **Сове́т Б**~**и** Security Council; **те́хника** ~**и** health and safety; **безопа́сность движе́ния** road safety.

безопа́с|ный (-ен, -на, -но) *прил* safe.

безору́ж|ный (-ен, -на, -но) *прил* unarmed; (*перен: в споре*) defenceless (*BRIT*), defenseless (*US*).

безостано́вочно *нареч* incessantly.

безотве́т|ный (-ен, -на, -но) *прил* (*любовь*) unrequited; (*существо*) meek.

безотве́тственность (-и) *ж* irresponsibility.

безотве́тствен|ный (-, -на, -но) *прил* irresponsible.

безотка́з|ный (-ен, -на, -но) *прил* reliable.

безотлага́тел|ьный (-ен, -ьна, -ьно) *прил* urgent.

безотноси́тельно *нареч* ~ **к** +*dat* irrespective of.

безотра́д|ный (-ен, -на, -но) *прил* (*жизнь*) dreary; (*положение*) bleak.

безотхо́д|ный (-ен, -на, -но) *прил*: ~**ное произво́дство** *production process which recycles waste.*

безотчёт|ный (-ен, -на, -но) *прил* (*чувство*) irrational; (*поведение*) unaccountable.

безоши́боч|ный (-ен, -на, -но) *прил* (*решение, догадка*) correct; (*судья, ценитель*) infallible.

безрабо́тиц|а (-ы) *ж* unemployment.

безрабо́т|ная (-ой; *decl like adj*) *ж см* **безрабо́тный**.

безрабо́т|ный *прил* unemployed ♦ (-ого; *decl like adj*) *м* unemployed person; ~**ые** the unemployed.

безра́дост|ный (-ен, -на, -но) *прил* (*жизнь, детство*) cheerless, joyless; (*голос, взгляд*) dull.

безразде́л|ьный (-ен, -ьна, -ьно) *прил* (*господство, владение*) absolute; (*внимание*) undivided.

безразли́чен *прил см* **безразли́чный**.

безразли́чно *нареч* indifferently ♦ *как сказ*: **мне** ~ it doesn't matter to me, it makes no difference to me; ~, **придёт он и́ли нет** it makes no difference whether he comes or not; ~ **кто/что** no matter who/what.

безразли́ч|ный (-ен, -на, -но) *прил* indifferent.

безразме́р|ный *прил*: ~**ые носки́/чулки́** one-size socks/stockings.

безрассу́д|ный (-ен, -на, -но) *прил* (*поведение*) reckless; (*любовь*) impulsive.

безрезульта́т|ный (-ен, -на, -но) *прил* fruitless.

безро́пот|ный (-ен, -на, -но) *прил* uncomplaining.

безрука́в|ка (-ки; *gen pl* -ок) *ж* (*кофта*) sleeveless top; (*куртка*) sleeveless jacket.

безру́к|ий (-ая, -ое, -ие; -, -а, -о) *прил* one-armed; (*без двух рук*) with no arms; (*перен: разг*) ham-fisted.

безры́б|ье (-я) *ср*: **на** ~ **и рак ры́ба** something is better than nothing.

безубы́точ|ный (-ен, -на, -но) *прил*: ~**ное предприя́тие** *business which is not making a loss.*

безуда́р|ный (-ен, -на, -но) *прил* (*линг*) unstressed.

безукори́знен|ный (-, -на, -но) *прил* (*поведение, человек*) irreproachable; (*работа*) flawless.

безу́мен *прил см* **безу́мный**.

безу́м|ец (-ца) *м* madman (*мн* madmen).

безу́ми|е (-я) *ср* madness; **до** ~**я** madly.

безу́мно *нареч* (*любить*) madly; (*устать*) terribly.

безу́м|ный (**-ен, -на, -но**) *прил* (*план, намерение*) mad; (*счастье, ярость итп*) wild; **он зараба́тывает ~ные де́ньги** (*разг*) he earns crazy money; **~ная ро́скошь** unbelievable luxury.

безу́мца *итп сущ см* **безу́мец**.

безупре́ч|ный (**-ен, -на, -но**) *прил* (*поведение, человек*) irreproachable; (*работа*) flawless.

безусло́вен *прил см* **безусло́вный**.

безусло́вно *нареч* (*повиноваться, доверить*) unconditionally ♦ *част* (*несомненно*) without a doubt; **~, я бу́ду рад помо́чь Вам** naturally, I'll be happy to help you.

безусло́в|ный (**-ен, -на, -но**) *прил* (*повиновение, доверие*) unconditional; (*успех, превосходство*) indisputable.

безуспе́ш|ный (**-ен, -на, -но**) *прил* unsuccessful.

безуча́ст|ный (**-ен, -на, -но**) *прил* disinterested.

безъя́дерный *прил* nuclear-free.

безымя́н|ный (**-ен, -на, -но**) *прил* (*река, гора*) unnamed; (*герой, автор*) anonymous; **безымя́нный па́лец** ring finger.

безысхо́д|ный (**-ен, -на, -но**) *прил* hopeless.

бей(ся) *несов см* **би́ть(ся)**.

Бейру́т (**-а**) *м* Beirut.

бе́йте(сь) *несов см* **би́ть(ся)**.

беко́н (**-а**) *м* bacon.

БелА́З (**-а**) *м сокр* = **Белору́сский автомоби́льный заво́д**; (*автомоби́ль*) *vehicle manufactured at the Belorussian car factory*.

Беларус|ь (**-и**) *ж* Belarus.

Белгра́д (**-а**) *м* Belgrade.

беле́|ть (**-ю**; *perf* **побеле́ть**) *несов неперех* (*лицо*) to go *или* turn white; (*no perf; цветы*) to show white.

белиберд|а́ (**-ы́**) *ж* (*разг*) gobbledegook.

Бели́з (**-а**) *м* Belize.

бели́л|а (**-**) *мн* emulsion *ед*.

бел|и́ть (**-ю́, -ишь**; *perf* **побели́ть**) *несов перех* to whitewash.

бе́личий (**-ья, -ье, -ьи**) *прил* squirrel's; (*шуба*) squirrel (fur).

бе́л|ка (**-ки**; *gen pl* **-ок**) *ж* squirrel; **верте́ться** (*impf*) **как ~ в колесе́** to run round in circles.

белка́ *итп сущ см* **бело́к**.

белко́вый *прил* proteinous.

беллетри́стик|а (**-и**) *ж* fiction; (*лёгкое чтение*) light reading.

белови́к (**-а́**) *м* fair copy.

белогварде́|ец (**-йца**) *м* (*ИСТ*) White Guardsman (*мн* Guardsmen).

бело́к *сущ см* **бе́лка**.

бел|о́к (**-ка́**) *м* protein; (*яйца*) (egg) white; (*АНАТ*) white (of the eye).

белокро́ви|е (**-я**) *ср* (*МЕД*) leukaemia (*BRIT*), leukemia (*US*).

белоку́р|ый (**-, -а, -о**) *прил* (*человек*) fair(-haired); (*волосы*) fair.

белору́с (**-а**) *м* Belorussian.

белору́с|ка (**-ки**; *gen pl* **-ок**) *ж см* **белору́с**.

белору́сский (**-ая, -ое, -ие**) *прил* Belorussian.

белору́ч|ка (**-ки**; *gen pl* **-ек**) *м/ж* (*разг: пренебр*) shirker.

белосне́ж|ный (**-ен, -на, -но**) *прил* snow-white.

белу́г|а (**-и**) *ж* beluga (*sturgeon*).

белу́жий (**-ья, -ье, -ьи**) *прил* beluga *опред*.

Бе́лфаст (**-а**) *м* Belfast.

бе́л|ые (**-ых**; *decl like adj*) *мн* (*ШАХМАТЫ*) white *ед*.

бе́л|ый (**-, -а́, -о**) *прил* white; (*гриб*) сер ♦ (**-ого**; *decl like adj*) *м* (*человек*) white (person); **средь ~а дня** (*разг*) in broad daylight; **бе́лая воро́на** the odd one out; **бе́лая гва́рдия** (*ИСТ*) the White Guard; **бе́лая горя́чка** the DT's (= *delirium tremens*); **бе́лое духове́нство** secular clergy; **бе́лый медве́дь** polar bear; *см также* **бе́лые**.

бельги́ек *сущ см* **бельги́йка**.

бельги́|ец (**-йца**) *м* Belgian.

бельги́|йка (**-йки**; *gen pl* **-ек**) *ж см* **бельги́ец**.

бельги́йский (**-ая, -ое, -ие**) *прил* Belgian.

бельги́йца *итп сущ см* **бельги́ец**.

Бе́льги|я (**-и**) *ж* Belgium.

бель|ё (**-я́**) *ср собир* linen; (*стиранное*) washing; **ни́жнее ~** underwear; **посте́льное ~** bedclothes, bed linen.

бельэта́|ж (**-а**) *м* (*ТЕАТР*) dress circle; (*АРХИТ*) first floor, second floor (*US*).

беля́ш (**-а́**) *м* meat pie.

бемо́л|ь (**-я**) *м* (*МУЗ*) flat.

бенефи́с (**-а**) *м performance commemorating and featuring an actor.*

бензи́н (**-а**) *м* petrol (*BRIT*), gas (*US*).

бензи́новый *прил* petrol (*BRIT*), gas (*US*); **~ дви́гатель** petrol engine.

бензоба́к (**-а**) *м* petrol (*BRIT*) *или* gas (*US*) tank.

бензоколо́н|ка (**-ки**; *gen pl* **-ок**) *ж* petrol (*BRIT*) *или* gas (*US*) pump.

Бенилю́кс (**-а**) *м* Benelux.

бенуа́р (**-а**) *м* (*ТЕАТР*) boxes *мн*.

бе́рег (**-а**; *loc sg* **-у́**, *nom pl* **-а́**) *м* (*моря, озера*) shore; (*реки*) bank.

берёг(ся) *итп несов см* **бере́чь(ся)**.

берегов|о́й *прил* (*см сущ*) coastal; riverside; **берегова́я ли́ния** coastline; **берегова́я слу́жба** coastguard.

берегу́(сь) *итп несов см* **бере́чь(ся)**.

бе́режен *прил см* **бе́режный**.

бережёшь(ся) *итп несов см* **бере́чь(ся)**.

бережли́вость (**-и**) *ж* economy, thrift.

бережли́в|ый (**-, -а, -о**) *прил* economical, thrifty.

бе́режность (**-и**) *ж* care.

бе́реж|ный (**-ен, -на, -но**) *прил* (*заботливый*)

caring; (*осторожный*) careful.
берёз|а (-ы) *ж* birch (tree).
Берёз|ка (-ки; *gen pl* -ок) *ж* Beriozka (*hard-currency shop in the USSR*).
берёзовый *прил* birch.
Берёзок *сущ см* **Берёзка**.
берём *несов см* **брать**.
бере́мене|ть (-ю; *perf* **забере́менеть**) *сов неперех* to get pregnant.
бере́менн|ая (-ая) *прил* pregnant ♦ (-ой; *decl like adj*) *ж* pregnant woman.
бере́менность (-и) *ж* pregnancy.
бере́т (-а) *м* beret.
берёт *итп несов см* **брать**.
бере́чь (-егу́, -ежёшь *итп*, -егу́т; *pt* -ёг, -егла́, -егло́) *несов перех* (*документы*) to keep; (*деньги*) to be careful with; (*время*) to make good use of; (*здоровье, детей*) to look after, take care of; ~ (*impf*) **как зени́цу о́ка** to guard with one's life
► **бере́чься** (*perf* **побере́чься**) *несов возв* (+*gen*) to watch out for; **~еги́тесь просту́ды** take care you don't catch a cold; **~еги́тесь!** watch out!
бе́рингов (-а, -о, -ы) *прил*: **Б~ проли́в** Bering Strait.
Берли́н (-а) *м* Berlin.
берму́дск|ий (-ая, -ое, -ие) *прил*: **Б~ие острова́** Bermuda, the Bermudas.
Берн (-а) *м* Berne.
беру́(сь) *итп несов см* **брать(ся)**.
берцо́в|ый *прил*: **~ая кость** shinbone.
бес (-а) *м* demon, devil; (*перен*) devil.
бесе́д|а (-ы) *ж* conversation; (*не официальная*) chat; (*популярный доклад*) discussion.
бесе́д|ка (-ки; *gen pl* -ок) *ж* pavilion.
бесе́д|овать (-ую) *несов неперех*: ~ (**с** +*instr*) to talk (to); (*не официально*) to chat (to).
бесе́док *сущ см* **бесе́дка**.
бе|си́ть (-шу́, -сишь; *perf* **взбеси́ть**) *несов перех* to infuriate
► **беси́ться** *несов возв* (*разг*) to run wild; (*perf* **взбеси́ться**; *раздражаться*) to become furious; **с жи́ру ~ся** (*impf*) (*разг*) to become spoilt and fussy.
бескла́ссовый *прил* classless.
бескомпроми́сс|ный (-ен, -на, -но) *прил* uncompromising.
бесконе́чен *прил см* **бесконе́чный**.
бесконе́чно *нареч* (*очень долго*) endlessly; (*чрезвычайно*) infinitely.
бесконе́чность (-и) *ж* infinity; **до ~и** (*очень долго*) endlessly; (*очень сильно*) infinitely.
бесконе́ч|ный (-ен, -на, -но) *прил* (*пространство, дорога*) endless; (*время, удовольствие*) endless, infinite; (*число*) infinite; (*вечер, песня*) interminable; (*любовь, ненависть*) undying.
бесконтро́л|ьный (-ен, -ьна, -ьно) *прил* uncontrolled.
бескоры́стен *прил см* **бескоры́стный**.

бескоры́сти|е (-я) *ср* unselfishness.
бескоры́ст|ный (-ен, -на, -но) *прил* unselfish.
бескро́в|ный (-ен, -на, -но) *прил* bloodless.
беспардо́н|ный (-ен, -на, -но) *прил* shameless, brazen.
бесперебо́|йный (-ен, -йна, -йно) *прил* uninterrupted.
бесперспекти́в|ный (-ен, -на, -но) *прил* (*работа*) without prospects; (*отношения*) with no future.
беспе́чен *прил см* **беспе́чный**.
беспе́чность (-и) *ж* carefreeness.
беспе́ч|ный (-ен, -на, -но) *прил* carefree.
беспла́т|ный (-ен, -на, -но) *прил* free.
беспло́ден *прил см* **беспло́дный**.
беспло́ди|е (-я) *ср* (*женщины*) infertility; (*земли*) barrenness, infertility.
беспло́д|ный (-ен, -на, -но) *прил* (*женщина*) infertile; (*брак*) childless; (*почва*) barren, infertile; (*попытки, дискуссии*) fruitless.
бесповоро́т|ный (-ен, -на, -но) *прил* irrevocable.
бесподо́б|ный (-ен, -на, -но) *прил* (*разг*) fantastic.
беспоко́ен *прил см* **беспоко́йный**.
беспоко́|ить (-ю, -ишь) *несов перех* (*причинять боль*) to trouble; (*perf* **побеспоко́ить**; *мешать*) to disturb; (*perf* **обеспоко́ить**; *тревожить*) to bother, worry
► **беспоко́иться** *несов возв* (*утруждать себя*) to put o.s. out, trouble o.s.; (*тревожиться*): **~ся о** +*prp* или **за** +*acc* to worry about; **не ~йтесь, я сде́лаю всё сам** don't put yourself out, I'll do it myself.
беспоко́йный (-ен, -йна, -йно) *прил* (*человек*) anxious; (*взгляд*) uneasy, anxious; (*поездка*) uncomfortable; (*ребёнок*) fidgety, restless; (*море, сон, время*) troubled; **э́то о́чень ~йная рабо́та** it's a very stressful job.
беспоко́йств|о (-а) *ср* anxiety, unease; (*заботы, хлопоты*) trouble; **прости́те за ~!** sorry to trouble you!
бесполе́з|ный (-ен, -на, -но) *прил* useless.
беспо́мощен *прил см* **беспо́мощный**.
беспо́мощность (-и) *ж* (*см прил*) helplessness; weakness.
беспо́мощ|ный (-ен, -на, -но) *прил* helpless; (*перен*) weak.
беспоря́дк|и (-ов) *мн* disturbances *мн*.
беспоря́д|ок (-ка) *м* disorder; **в ~ке** (*комната, дела*) in a mess; *см также* **беспоря́дки**.
беспоря́доч|ный (-ен, -на, -но) *прил* (*груда бумаг*) disorderly, untidy; (*рассказ, записи*) confused.
беспоса́дочный *прил* nonstop.
беспо́чвен|ный (-, -на, -но) *прил* groundless.
беспо́шлинный *прил* duty-free.
беспоща́д|ный (-ен, -на, -но) *прил* (*наказание, удар*) merciless; (*критика, сатира*) ruthless; ~ **к** +*dat* ruthless *или* merciless towards.
беспра́вен *прил см* **беспра́вный**.

беспра́ви|е (-я) *ср* (*беззаконие*) lawlessness.
беспра́в|ный (-ен, -на, -но) *прил* without rights.
беспреде́л (-а) *м* lawlessness.
беспреде́л|ьный (-ен, -ьна, -ьно) *прил* (*пространство, море*) boundless; (*любовь, ненависть*) immeasurable.
беспрекосло́в|ный (-ен, -на, -но) *прил* unquestioning.
беспрепя́тственно *нареч* without difficulty.
беспрепя́тствен|ный (-, -на, -но) *прил* unimpeded.
беспрецеде́нт|ный (-ен, -на, -но) *прил* unprecedented.
беспри́быль|ный (-ен, -ьна, -ьно) *прил* unprofitable.
беспризо́рен *прил см* **беспризо́рный**.
беспризо́рник (-а) *м* (street) urchin.
беспризо́рниц|а (-ы) *ж см* **беспризо́рник**.
беспризо́р|ный (-ен, -на, -но) *прил* (*ребёнок*) homeless; (*дом, хозяйство*) neglected.
беспринци́п|ный (-ен, -на, -но) *прил* unscrupulous.
беспристра́ст|ный (-ен, -на, -но) *прил* unbias(s)ed.
беспричи́н|ный (-ен, -на, -но) *прил* irrational.
беспросве́т|ный (-ен, -на, -но) *прил* (*нужда*) desperate; (*грусть*) hopeless; (*ночь, мгла*) impenetrable.
беспроце́нтный *прил* interest-free.
Бессара́би|я (-и) *ж* Bessarabia.
бессвя́з|ный (-ен, -на, -но) *прил* disjointed.
бессерде́чен *прил см* **бессерде́чный**.
бессерде́чность (-и) *ж* heartlessness.
бессерде́ч|ный (-ен, -на, -но) *прил* heartless.
бесси́лен *прил см* **бесси́льный**.
бесси́ли|е (-я) *ср* (*больного, старика*) debility; (*чувства*) impotence.
бесси́ль|ный (-ен, -ьна, -ьно) *прил* (*больной, старик*) feeble, weak; (*гнев, ненависть*) impotent; **он/президе́нт ~ен измени́ть ситуа́цию)** he/the president is powerless (to change the situation).
бессме́ртен *прил см* **бессме́ртный**.
бессме́рти|е (-я) *ср* immortality.
бессме́рт|ный (-ен, -на, -но) *прил* immortal.
бессмы́сленность (-и) *ж* (*слов*) meaninglessness; (*поступка*) senselessness, pointlessness.
бессмы́слен|ный (-, -на, -но) *прил* (*слова*) meaningless; (*поступок*) senseless, pointless; (*взгляд, улыбка*) inane.
бессо́вест|ный (-ен, -на, -но) *прил* (*нечестный*) unscrupulous; (*наглый*) shameless.
бессодержа́тель|ный (-ен, -ьна, -ьно) *прил* (*слова*) empty; (*статья*) thin.
бессозна́тель|ный (-ен, -ьна, -ьно) *прил* (*страх, действия*) instinctive; **быть** (*impf*) **в**

~ьном состоя́нии to be unconscious.
бессо́нниц|а (-ы) *ж* insomnia.
бессо́нный *прил* (*ночь*) sleepless; (*страж, сиделка*) wakeful.
бесспо́рен *прил см* **бесспо́рный**.
бесспо́рно *нареч* indisputably ◆ *част* (*несомненно*) absolutely; **он, ~, умён** he is indisputably clever.
бесспо́р|ный (-ен, -на, -но) *прил* indisputable.
бессро́ч|ный (-ен, -на, -но) *прил* indefinite.
бесстра́ш|ный (-ен, -на, -но) *прил* fearless.
бессты́д|ный (-ен, -на, -но) *прил* shameless, brazen; (*ложь*) barefaced.
беста́кт|ный (-ен, -на, -но) *прил* tactless.
бе́сти|я (-и) *м/ж* (*разг*) rogue.
бестолко́в|ый (-, -а, -о) *прил* (*глупый*) stupid; (*невразумительный*) incoherent.
бестсе́ллер (-а) *м* best seller.
бесхи́трост|ный (-ен, -на, -но) *прил* simple.
бесхо́зный *прил* ownerless.
бесхозя́йствен|ный (-, -на, -но) *прил* (*руководитель*) inefficient; (*политика*) uneconomic; **~ная же́нщина** a bad housekeeper.
бесцве́т|ный (-ен, -на, -но) *прил* colourless (*BRIT*), colorless (*US*).
бесце́ль|ный (-ен, -ьна, -ьно) *прил* pointless, futile.
бесце́н|ный (-ен, -на, -но) *прил* (*коллекция, сокровища*) priceless; (*друг, жена*) invaluable.
бесце́нок *м*: **за ~** dirt cheap, for next to nothing.
бесцеремо́н|ный (-ен, -на, -но) *прил* unceremonious, familiar.
бесчелове́ч|ный (-ен, -на, -но) *прил* inhuman.
бесче́|стить (-щу, -стишь; *perf* **обесче́стить)** *несов перех* (*девушку*) to violate.
бесчи́слен|ный (-ен, -на, -но) *прил* numerous.
бесчу́вствен|ный (-, -на, -но) *прил* (*жестокий*) unfeeling; (*лишённый сознания*) senseless.
бето́н (-а; *part gen* **-у)** *м* concrete.
бетони́р|овать (-ую; *perf* **забетони́ровать)** *несов перех* to concrete.
бефстро́ганов *м нескл* boeuf *или* beef stroganoff.
бе́шенств|о (-а) *ср* (*перен*) rage; (*МЕД*) rabies; **приходи́ть (прийти́** *perf*) **в ~** to fly into a rage.
бе́шен|ый *прил* (*взгляд*) furious; (*характер, темперамент, ураган*) violent; (*МЕД*) rabid; (*разг: деньги, цены*) crazy; **э́то сто́ит ~ых де́нег** (*разг*) it costs a bomb.
бешу́(сь) *несов см* **беси́ть(ся)**.
биатло́н (-а) *м* biathlon.
биатлони́ст (-а) *м* biathlete.
биатлони́ст|ка (-ки; *gen pl* **-ок)** *ж см* **биатлони́ст**.
Би-би-си *ж сокр* (= *Брита́нская радиовеща́тельная корпора́ция*) BBC (=

British Broadcasting Corporation).

библе́йск|ий (-ая, -ое, -ие) *прил* biblical.

библиографи́ческ|ий (-ая, -ое, -ие) *прил* bibliographical; **библиографи́ческая ре́дкость** rare edition.

библиогра́фи|я (-и) *ж* bibliography.

библиоте́к|а (-и) *ж* library.

библиоте́кар|ь (-я) *м* librarian.

библиоте́чный *прил* library *опред*.

Би́бли|я (-и) *ж* the Bible.

бигуди́ *ср/мн нескл* curlers *мн*; **накру́чивать (накрути́ть** *perf*) **во́лосы на** ~ to put one's hair in curlers.

бидо́н (-а) *м* (*для молока*) churn; (*маленький*) can.

бижуте́ри|я (-и) *ж* costume jewellery.

би́знес (-а) *м* business; **де́лать (сде́лать** *perf*) ~ **на** +*prp* to make a living from.

бизнесме́н (-а) *м* businessman (*мн* businessmen).

бики́ни *ср нескл* bikini.

биле́т (-а) *м* ticket; (*члена организации*) (membership) card; **обра́тный** ~ return (*BRIT*) *или* roundtrip (*US*) ticket; **казначе́йский** ~ banknote; **входно́й** ~ ticket (*for standing room*).

биллио́н (-а) *м* billion (*one thousand million*).

билья́рд (-а) *м* (*игра*) billiards; (*стол*) billiard table.

бино́кл|ь (-я) *м* binoculars *мн*.

бинт (-а́) *м* bandage; **накла́дывать (наложи́ть** *perf*) ~ **ы на** +*acc* to put a bandage on.

бинт|ова́ть (-у́ю; *perf* **забинтова́ть**) *несов перех* to bandage.

био́граф (-а) *м* biographer.

биогра́фи|я (-и) *ж* biography.

био́лог (-а) *м* biologist.

биоло́ги|я (-и) *ж* biology.

би́рж|а (-и) *ж* (*КОММ*) exchange; **валю́тная** ~ exchange market; **це́нных бума́г** securities exchange; **това́рная** ~ commodity exchange; **фо́ндовая** ~ stock exchange *или* market; **игра́ть** (*impf*) **на** ~**е** to play the stock exchange.

биржеви́к (-а́) *м* stockbroker.

биржево́й *прил* (*сделка*) stock-exchange; **биржево́й бро́кер** stockbroker.

би́рк|а (-ки; *gen pl* -ок) *ж* tag.

Бирминге́м (-а) *м* Birmingham.

би́рок *сущ см* **би́рка**.

бирюз|а́ (-ы́) *ж* (*ГЕО*) turquoise.

бис *межд*: **Б**—! encore!; **исполня́ть (испо́лнить** *perf*) **что-н на** ~ to do sth as an encore.

би́сер (-а; *part gen* -у) *м собир* glass beads *мн*; **мета́ть** (*impf*) ~ **пе́ред сви́ньями** to cast pearls before swine.

бискви́т (-а) *м* sponge (cake).

бистро́ *ср нескл* bistro.

бит (-а) *м* (*КОМП*) bit.

би́тв|а (-ы) *ж* battle.

битко́м *нареч*: ~ (**наби́т**) (*разг*) chock-a-block, jam-packed.

би́тый *прил* broken; **би́тый час** (*разг*) a good hour.

бить (**бью, бьёшь;** *imper* **бей(те)**, *perf* **поби́ть**) *несов перех* (*также перен*) to beat; (*стёкла*) to break ♦ (*perf* **проби́ть**) *неперех* (*часы*) to strike; ~ (*impf*) **в** +*acc* (*в дверь*) to bang at; (*дождь, ветер*) to beat against; (*орудие*) to hit; ~ (*impf*) **на** +*acc* (*стремиться к*) to aim for; ~ (*impf*) **по столу́** to bang on the table; ~ (*impf*) **в бараба́н** to beat a drum; **свет бьёт мне в глаза́** the light is blinding me; ~ (*impf*) **по чьим-н недоста́ткам** to severely criticize sb's failings; ~ (*impf*) **по карма́ну** to hit one's pocket; **э́то бьёт по мои́м интере́сам** it conflicts with my interests; **его́ бьёт озно́б** he's got a fit of the shivers

▸ **би́ться** *несов возв* (*сердце, пульс*) to beat; (*стекло, фарфор*) to be breakable; (*сражаться*) to fight; **би́ться** (*impf*) **о** +*acc* to bang against; **би́ться** (*impf*) **над** +*instr* (*над зада́чей, над реше́нием*) to struggle with; **хоть голово́й об сте́ну бе́йся** you might as well bang your head against a brick wall.

бифште́кс (-а) *м* steak.

бич (-а́) *м* (*плеть*) whip; (*перен*) scourge.

Бишке́к (-а) *м* Bishkek.

б-ка *сокр* = **библиоте́ка**.

бла́г|а (-) *мн* rewards *мн*; **всех благ!** all the best!

бла́г|о (-а) *ср* benefit; **на** ~ +*gen* for the benefit of; *см также* **бла́га**.

благови́дн|ый (-ен, -на, -но) *прил* (*предлог*) plausible; (*стремления, поступки*) seemingly well-intentioned.

благодар|и́ть (-ю́, -и́шь; *perf* **поблагодари́ть**) *несов перех* to thank.

благода́рност|ь (-и) *ж* gratitude, thanks; **приноси́ть (принести́** *perf*) ~ **кому́-н** to express one's gratitude to sb.

благодаря́ *предл* (+*dat*) thanks to ♦ *союз*: ~ **тому́, что** owing to the fact that; **здоро́в, ~ тому́, что занима́юсь спо́ртом** I'm healthy thanks to *или* owing to the fact that I play sport.

благоде́тел|ь (-я) *м* benefactor.

благоде́тельниц|а (-ы) *ж* benefactress.

благ|о́й *прил*: ~**и́е наме́рения** good intentions *мн*; **крича́ть** (*impf*) ~**и́м ма́том** (*разг*) to shout at the top of one's voice.

благонадёжн|ый (-ен, -на, -но) *прил* trustworthy.

благополу́чи|е (-я) *ср* (*в семье, в отношениях*) wellbeing; (*материальная обеспеченность*) prosperity; **жела́ю Вам вся́кого** ~**я** I wish you all the very best.

благополу́чн|ый (-ен, -на, -но) *прил* successful.

благоприя́тн|ый (-ен, -на, -но) *прил* favourable (*BRIT*), favorable (*US*).

благоприя́тствовани|е (-я) *ср*: **усло́вия/поли́тика наибо́льшего** ~**я** the most favourable (*BRIT*) *или* favorable (*US*) conditions/policy.

благоразу́ми|е (-я) *ср* prudence.

благоразу́м|ный (-ен, -на, -но) *прил* prudent.
благоро́д|ный (-ен, -на, -но) *прил* noble; **он ~ного происхожде́ния** he is of noble birth; **благоро́дные га́зы** the noble gases; **благоро́дные мета́ллы** precious metals.
благоро́дств|о (-а) *ср* nobility.
благослов|и́ть (-лю́, -и́шь; *impf* **благословля́ть**) *сов перех* to bless; ~ *(perf)* **кого́-н (на что-н)** to give sb one's blessing (for sth).
благосостоя́ни|е (-я) *ср* wellbeing.
благотвори́тел|ь (-я) *м* philanthropist.
благотвори́тельниц|а (-ы) *ж см* **благотвори́тель.**
благотвори́тельност|ь (-и) *ж* charity.
благотвори́тельн|ый *прил* charitable; ~**ая организа́ция** charity (organization); ~ **конце́рт** charity concert.
благоустро́ен|ный (-, -на, -но) *прил* (*кварти́ра, дом*) *with all modern conveniences*; ~ **го́род** a city with every amenity; ~**ная ку́хня** a well-equipped kitchen.
блаже́н|ный (-, -на, -но) *прил* blissful; (*no short form*; *РЕЛ*) Blessed.
блаже́нств|о (-а) *ср* bliss; **быть** *(impf)* **на верху́ ~а** to be in seventh heaven.
бланк (-а) *м* form.
блат (-а) *м* (*разг*) connections *мн*; **по бла́ту** (*разг*) through (one's) connections.
блатно́й *прил* criminal.
бле́ден *прил см* **бле́дный.**
бледне́|ть (-ю; *perf* **побледне́ть**) *несов неперех* to (grow) pale; (*перен*): ~ **(пе́ред** +*instr*) to pale (beside).
бле́дност|ь (-и) *ж* (*см прил*) pallor, paleness; dullness.
бле́д|ный (-ен, -на́, -но) *прил* pale; (*перен*) dull.
бле́кн|уть (-у, -ешь; *perf* **поблёкнуть**) *несов неперех* to fade.
блеск (-а; *part gen* -у) *м* (*огней, мо́лнии*) brilliance, brightness; (*мета́лла*) shine; (*перен*) brilliance; **во всём бле́ске** in full splendour (*BRIT*) *или* splendor (*US*); **с бле́ском** brilliantly; **сдать** *(perf)* **экза́мен с бле́ском** to pass an exam with flying colours.
блесн|у́ть (-у́, -ёшь) *сов неперех* to flash; **у него́ ~у́ла мысль** a thought flashed through his mind; **~у́ла наде́жда** there was a ray of hope.
бле|сте́ть (-щу́, -сти́шь *или*, -щешь) *несов неперех* (*звёзды, мета́лл*) to shine; (*ка́мни, глаза́*) to sparkle; **она́ бле́щет красото́й** she is dazzling; **он бле́щет умо́м** he shines intellectually.
блестя́ще *нареч* brilliantly; **дела́ иду́т** ~ everything's going brilliantly.
блестя́щ|ий (-ая, -ее, -ие; -, -а, -е) *прил* (*звезда́*) bright; (*мета́лл*) shining; (*глаза́*) sparkling; (*перен*) brilliant.

блещу́ *итп несов см* **блесте́ть.**
бле́|ять (-ю) *несов неперех* to bleat.
ближа́йш|ий (-ая, -ее, -ие) *прил* (*го́род, дом*) the nearest; (*год*) the next; (*пла́ны*) immediate; (*друг*) closest; **в ~ем бу́дущем** in the near future; **при ~ем уча́стии** with the close cooperation of; **при ~ем рассмотре́нии** on closer inspection; **ближа́йший ро́дственник** next of kin.
бли́же *сравн прил от* **бли́зкий.**
бли́жн|ий (-яя, -ее, -ие) *прил* (*го́род, дере́вня*) neighbouring (*BRIT*), neighboring (*US*); **е́хать** (**пое́хать** *perf*) **~им путём** to take the shortest route; **Б~ Восто́к** Middle East.
бли́зк|ие (-их; *decl like adj*) *мн* (*ро́дственники*) relatives *мн*.
бли́зк|ий (-ая, -кое, -кие; -ок, -ка́, -ко) *прил* (*го́род*) nearby; (*коне́ц*) imminent; (*друг, отноше́ния*) close; ~ +*dat* (*интере́сы, те́ма*) similar *или* close to; ~ **по** +*dat* (*по содержа́нию, по це́ли*) similar *или* close to; **они́ близки́ во мне́ниях** they think alike; **бли́зкий ро́дственник** close relative.
бли́зко *нареч* near *или* close by ♦ *как сказ* not far off; ~ **от** +*gen* near, close to; **го́род** ~ the town isn't far off; ~ **узна́ть** *(perf)* **кого́-н** to get to know sb well; **принима́ть** (**приня́ть** *perf*) **что-н ~ к се́рдцу** to take sth to heart.
близне́ц (-а́) *м* (*обычно мн*) twin; **бра́тья/сёстры-близнецы́** twin brothers/ sisters; *см также* **Близнецы́.**
Близнец|ы́ (-о́в) *мн* (*созве́здие*) Gemini.
бли́зок *прил см* **бли́зкий.**
близору́к|ий (-ая, -ое, -ие; -, -а, -о) *прил* short-sighted (*BRIT*), nearsighted (*US*).
близору́кост|ь (-и) *ж* (*см прил*) short-sightedness, nearsightedness.
бли́зост|ь (-и) *ж* proximity; (*интере́сов, мне́ний*) closeness; (*бли́зкие отноше́ния*) intimacy.
блин (-а́) *м* pancake.
бли́нчик (-а) *м уменьш от* **блин.**
блок (-а) *м* (*ПОЛИТ*) bloc; (*ТЕХ*) unit.
блока́д|а (-ы) *ж* (*ВОЕН*) siege; (*ЭКОН*) blockade; **устана́вливать** (**установи́ть** *perf*)/**снима́ть** (**снять** *perf*) ~**у** to impose/lift a blockade.
блоки́р|овать (-ую) *(не)сов перех* to blockade; (*СПОРТ, КОМП*) to block.
блокно́т (-а) *м* notebook.
блонди́н (-а) *м*: **он – ~** he is blond.
блонди́н|ка (-ки; *gen pl* -ок) *ж* blonde.
блох|а́ (-и́; *nom pl* -и) *ж* flea.
блужда́|ть (-ю) *несов неперех* to wander *или* roam (around); (*перен: мы́сли*) to wander; (: *взгляд*) to rove.
блу́з|ка (-ки; *gen pl* -ок) *ж* blouse.
блю́д|о (-а) *ср* dish.
блю|сти́ (-ду́, -дёшь; *pt* -л, -ла́-ло́, *perf*

соблюсти́) *несов перех* (*интересы*) to guard; (*чистоту*) to maintain.

блядь (**-и**) *ж* (*груб!:* проститу́тка) whore (*!*) ♦ *м/ж* (*груб!:* же́нщина) bitch (*!*); (*: мужчина*) bastard (*!*)

бля́х|а (**-и**) *ж* (*на фо́рме*) badge; (*на ремне́*) buckle.

БМП *ж сокр* (= боева́я маши́на пехо́ты) *armoured car for infantry.*

БМР *м сокр* (= Банк междунаро́дных расчётов) BIS (= *Bank for International Settlements*).

боб (**-а́**) *м* bean; **на ~а́х оста́ться** (*perf*) to be left high and dry.

бобр (**-а́**) *м* beaver.

Бог (**-а**; *voc* **Бо́же**) *м* God; **ве́рить** (*impf*) **в Бо́га** to believe in God; **~ зна́ет** *или* **весть что** God knows what; **благослови́ Вас ~!** God bless you!; **не дай ~!** God forbid!; **ра́ди Бо́га!** for God's sake!; **сла́ва Бо́гу** (*к сча́стью*) thank God.

богате́|ть (**-ю**; *perf* **разбогате́ть**) *несов неперех* to become rich.

бога́тств|а (**-**) *мн* resources *мн*.

бога́тств|о (**-а**) *ср* wealth, riches *мн*; (*обстано́вки, оде́жды*) richness; *см также* **бога́тства**.

бога́т|ый (**-**, **-а**, **-о**) *прил* rich; **~ урожа́й** bumper harvest; **~** +*instr* (*ископа́емыми, собы́тиями*) rich in; **чем ~ы, тем и ра́ды** what's ours is yours.

богаты́р|ь (**-я́**) *м warrior hero of Russian folk epics*; (*перен*) Hercules.

бога́ч (**-а́**) *м* rich man (*мн* men).

бога́че *сравн прил от* **бога́тый**.

боге́м|а (**-ы**) *ж собир* bohemians *мн*; (*о́браз жи́зни*) bohemian lifestyle.

боги́н|я (**-и**) *ж* goddess.

богоро́диц|а (**-ы**) *ж* the Virgin Mary.

богосло́ви|е (**-я**) *ср* theology.

богослуже́ни|е (**-я**) *ср* service; **соверша́ть** (**соверши́ть** *perf*) **~** to take a service.

боготвор|и́ть (**-ю́**, **-и́шь**) *несов перех* to worship, idolize.

богоуго́дн|ый *прил*: **~ое заведе́ние** *charitable institution.*

богоху́льный *прил* blasphemous.

бод (**-а**) *м* (*КОМП*) baud.

бода́|ть (**-ю**; *perf* **забода́ть**) *несов перех* to butt.

бо́дрост|ь (**-и**) *ж* (*см прил*) energy, liveliness; cheerfulness.

бо́др|ый (**-**, **-а́**, **-о**) *прил* (*челове́к, похо́дка*) energetic, lively; (*настрое́ние, му́зыка*) cheerful.

боеви́к (**-а́**) *м* (*солда́т*) fighter; (*фильм*) action movie.

боево́й *прил* military; (*настрое́ние, дух*) fighting; **боевы́е иску́сства** martial arts *мн*.

боеголо́в|ка (**-ки**; *gen pl* **-ок**) *ж* warhead.

бо́ек *прил см* **бо́йкий**.

бо́ен *сущ см* **бо́йня**.

боеприпа́с|ы (**-ов**) *мн* ammunition *ед*.

бо|е́ц (**-йца́**) *м* (*солда́т*) soldier; (*уча́стник бо́я*) fighter.

Бо́же *сущ см* **Бог** ♦ *межд*: **~ (ты мой)!** good Lord *или* God!; **~!** кака́я красота́! God, it's beautiful!; **~ сохрани́** *или* **упаси́** *или* **избави** (*разг*) God forbid.

бо́жеск|ий (**-ая**, **-ое**, **-ие**) *прил* (*РЕЛ*) divine; (*разг: це́ны, усло́вия*) half-decent; **приводи́ть** (**привести́** *perf*) **кого́-н/что-н в ~ вид** to make sb/sth look decent.

боже́ствен|ный (**-ен**, **-на**, **-но**) *прил* divine.

бо́ж|ий (**-ья**, **-ье**, **-ьи**) *прил* God's; **ка́ждый ~ день** every single day; **бо́жий дар** God-given talent; **бо́жья коро́вка** ladybird.

бо|й (**-я**; *loc sg* **-ю́**, *nom pl* **-и́**, *gen pl* **-ёв**) *м* battle; (*боксёров, быко́в*) fight; (*бараба́нов*) beating; (*часо́в*) striking.

бо́йкий (**-йкая**, **-йкое**, **-йкие**; **-ек**, **-йка́**, **-йко**) *прил* (*распоряди́тель, продаве́ц*) smart; (*движе́ния*) brisk; (*речь, отве́т*) quick; (*no short form*; *ме́сто, база́р*) busy.

бойко́т (**-а**) *м* boycott.

бойкоти́р|овать (**-ую**) (*не*)*сов перех* to boycott.

бо́йлер (**-а**) *м* boiler.

бо́йн|я (**-и**; *gen pl* **-ен**) *ж* slaughterhouse, abattoir.

бойца́ *итп сущ см* **бое́ц**.

бо́йче *сравн прил от* **бо́йкий**.

бок (**-а**; *part gen* **-у**, *loc sg* **-у́**, *nom pl* **-а́**) *м* side; **под бо́ком** (*разг*) right nearby; **~ о́ ~** side by side.

бока́л (**-а**) *м* (*wine*)glass, goblet; **поднима́ть** (**подня́ть** *perf*) **~ за кого́-н/что-н** to raise one's glass to sb/sth.

бо́ком *нареч* (*вы́йти, пройти́*) sideways; **э́то ему́ ~ вы́шло** (*разг*) it was all screwed up for him.

бокс (**-а**) *м* (*СПОРТ*) boxing; (*МЕД*) cubicle.

боксёр (**-а**) *м* boxer.

болва́н (**-а**) *м* (*разг*) blockhead.

болга́р|ин (**-ина**; *nom pl* **-ы**, *gen pl* **-**) *м* Bulgarian.

Болга́ри|я (**-и**) *ж* Bulgaria.

болга́р|ка (**-ки**; *gen pl* **-ок**) *ж см* **болга́рин**.

болга́рск|ий (**-ая**, **-ое**, **-ие**) *прил* Bulgarian; **~ язы́к** Bulgarian.

бо́лее *нареч* more; **~ и́ли ме́нее** more or less; **~ того́** what's more; **тем ~** all the more so; **~ чем** more than.

боле́знен|ный (**-**, **-на**, **-но**) *прил* sickly; (*уко́л, перевя́зка*) painful; (*перен: подозри́тельность*) unhealthy; **у него́ ~ное самолю́бие** he's ultra-sensitive.

боле́зн|ь (**-и**) *ж* illness; (*зара́зная*) disease; **~и ро́ста** growing pains.

боле́льщик (**-а**) *м* fan.

боле́льщиц|а (**-ы**) *ж см* **боле́льщик**.

бо́лен *прил см* **больно́й**.

бол|е́ть (**-е́ю**) *несов неперех*: **~** (+*instr*) to be ill (with); (*3sg* **-и́т**, *3pl* **-я́т**; *подлеж: ру́ки итп*) to ache; **~** (*impf*) **за** +*acc* to be a fan of; **у меня́ душа́ ~и́т за них** (*перен*) I'm very worried about them.

болеутоля́ющ|ий (-ая, -ее, -ие) *прил*: ~ее сре́дство painkiller.

болон|ка (-ки; *gen pl* -ок) *ж* lapdog.

болоны|я (-и) *ж* (*ткань*) *lightweight waterproof material.*

боло́т|о (-а) *ср* marsh, bog; (*перен*) backwater.

болт (-а́) *м* bolt.

болта́|ть (-ю) *несов перех* (*разг*) to talk ♦ *неперех* (*разговаривать*) to chat; (: *много*) to chatter; (*без толку*) to drivel; (*лишнее*) to blab; ~ (*impf*) **по-англи́йски** to chatter away in English; ~ (*impf*) **нога́ми** to dangle one's legs

▶ **болта́|ться** *несов возв* (*разг*) to dangle; ~**ся** (*impf*) **без де́ла** to hang around with nothing to do.

болтовн|я́ (-и́) *ж* (*разг*) waffle.

болту́н (-а́) *м* chatterbox.

болту́ш|ка (-ки; *gen pl* -ек) *ж см* **болту́н.**

бол|ь (-и) *ж* pain, ache; **зубна́я** ~ toothache; **головна́я** ~ headache; ~ **в груди́/животе́** chest/abdominal pain.

больни́ц|а (-ы) *ж* hospital; **ложи́ться** (**лечь** *perf*) **в** ~**у** to go into hospital; **выпи́сываться** (**вы́писаться** *perf*) **из** ~**ы** to be discharged from hospital.

больни́чный *прил* hospital *опред*; **больни́чный лист** medical certificate.

бо́льно *нареч* (*удариться, упасть*) badly, painfully; (*обидеть*) deeply; ~**!** that hurts!; **мне** ~ I am in pain; **де́лать** (**сде́лать** *perf*) ~ **кому́-н** to hurt sb; **мне** ~ **поду́мать об э́том** it hurts me to think about it.

больн|о́й *прил* (*рука итп*) sore; (*воображе́ние*) unhealthy; (-**ен, -ьна́, -ьно**; *нездоро́в*) ill, sick ♦ (-**ьно́го**; *decl like adj*) *м* (*тот, кто боле́ет*) sick person; (*пациент*) patient; **у неё** ~ **вид** she doesn't look very well; **де́ти** ~**ьны́** the children are ill *или* sick; **больно́е се́рдце** a bad heart; **больно́й вопро́с** a sore point.

бо́льше *сравн прил от* **большо́й** ♦ *сравн нареч от* **мно́го** ♦ *нареч*: ~ +*gen* (*часа, килогра́мма итп*) more than; ~ **не бу́ду** (*разг*) I won't do it again; ~ **так не де́лай** don't do that again; ~ **того́** what's more; ~ **всего́** most of all; **ни** ~ **ни ме́ньше** (**чем** *или* **как**) no more, no less (than); **она́ здесь** ~ **не живёт** she doesn't live here any more.

большеви́к (-а́) *м* Bolshevik.

большинств|о́ (-а́) *ср* majority; **в** ~**е́** (**слу́чаев**) in most cases; **подавля́ющее** ~ an overwhelming majority.

больш|о́й *прил* (*дом, река, де́рево*) big, large; (*ра́дость*) great; (*де́ти*) grown-up; **бо́льшей ча́стью, по бо́льшей ча́сти** for the most part; **я не** ~ **люби́тель бале́та** I'm not a great ballet fan; **я не** ~ **знато́к э́того де́ла** I'm no expert in this matter; **больша́я бу́ква** capital letter; **большо́й па́лец** (*руки*) thumb; (*ноги́*) big toe.

боля́ч|ка (-ки; *gen pl* -ек) *ж* sore.

бо́мб|а (-ы) *ж* bomb.

бомб|и́ть (-лю́, -и́шь) *несов перех* to bomb.

бомбоубе́жищ|е (-а) *ср* bomb shelter.

бо́н|а (-ы) *ж* (*обычно мн*: *комм*) bond; (*временны́е де́ньги*) voucher.

бордо́вый *прил* dark red.

бордю́р (-а) *м* border; (*тротуа́ра*) kerb (*вял*), curb (*US*).

бор|е́ц (-ца́) *м* (*за свобо́ду итп*) fighter; (*спорт*) wrestler.

бормо|та́ть (-чу́, -чешь) *несов перех* to mutter.

бо́рн|ый *прил*: ~**ая кислота́** boric acid.

борови́к (-а́) *м сер.*

бор|ода́ (*acc sg* -оду, *gen sg* -оды́, *nom pl* -оды, *gen pl* -о́д, *dat pl* -ода́м) *ж* beard; **отпуска́ть** (**отпусти́ть** *perf*) **бо́роду** to grow a beard; с ~**одо́й** (*перен*: *разг*) ancient; **анекдо́т с** ~**одо́й** an old chestnut.

борода́в|ка (-ки; *gen pl* -ок) *ж* (*на па́льцах итп*) wart.

борозд|и́ть (-жу́, -ди́шь; *perf* **изборозди́ть**) *несов перех* to furrow; (*кора́бль*) to leave a wake.

бор|о́ться (-ю́сь, -ешься) *несов возв* (*спорт*) to wrestle; ~ (*impf*) (**с** +*instr*) to fight (with *или* against); ~ (*impf*) **с** +*instr или* **про́тив** +*gen* (*с конкуре́нтами*) to compete with *или* against; (*с предрассу́дками, с нарко́тиками*) to fight (against); ~ (*impf*) **за** +*acc* (*за мир*) to fight for.

борт (-а; *acc sg* **за́ борт** *или* **за бо́рт**, *instr sg* **за бо́ртом** *или* **за бо́ртом**, *loc sg* -у́, *nom pl* -а́) *м* side; **на** ~**у́** *или* ~ on board, aboard; **челове́к за** ~**о́м!** man overboard!; **остава́ться** (**оста́ться** *perf*) **за** ~**о́м** (*перен*) to be left behind.

бортпроводни́к (-а́) *м* steward (*on plane*).

бортпроводни́ц|а (-ы) *ж* air hostess, stewardess (*on plane*).

борца́ *итп сущ см* **боре́ц.**

борщ (-а́) *м* borsch (*beetroot-based soup*).

борьб|а́ (-ы́) *ж* fight; (*спорт*) wrestling.

босико́м *нареч* barefoot.

бос|о́й (-, -а́, -о) *прил* barefoot.

босоно́ж|ка (-и) *ж* (*обычно мн*) sandal; (: *закры́тым носо́м*) slingback.

босс (-а) *м* boss.

Босфо́р (-а) *м* Bosphorus.

бося́к (-а́) *м* tramp.

бося́ч|ка (-ки; *gen pl* -ек) *ж см* **бося́к.**

бота́ник|а (-и) *ж* botany.

боти́н|ок (-ка; *обычно мн*) ankle boot.

бо́цман (-а) *м* boatswain, bosun.

бо́ч|ка (-ки; *gen pl* -ек) *ж* (*сосуд*) barrel.

бо|я́ться (-ю́сь, -и́шься) *несов возв*: ~ (+*gen*) to be afraid (of); ~ (*impf*) +*infin* to be afraid of doing *или* to do; **я** ~**ю́сь ходи́ть** (*impf*) **но́чью** I'm afraid of being out *или* to be out at night; ~**ю́сь сказа́ть** I wouldn't like to say.

бра́во *межд* bravo.
брази́л|ец (**-ьца**) *м* Brazilian.
Брази́ли|я (**-и**) *ж* Brazil.
брази́льск|ий (**-ая, -ое, -ие**) *прил* Brazilian.
брази́льца *итп сущ см* **брази́лец**.
бразилья́н|ка (**-ки**; *gen pl* **-ок**) *ж см* **брази́лец**.
бразды́ *мн*: ~ **правле́ния** the reins of power *или* government.
брак (**-а**) *м* (*супружество*) marriage; (*продукция*) rejects *мн*; (*деффект*) flaw; **вступа́ть** (**вступи́ть** *perf*) **в** ~ to get married; **расторга́ть** (**расто́ргнуть** *perf*) ~ to dissolve a marriage.
брако́ванн|ый *прил* reject *опред*.
брак|ова́ть (**-у́ю**; *perf* **забракова́ть**) *несов перех* to reject.
браконье́р (**-а**) *м* poacher.
браконье́рств|о (**-а**) *ср* poaching.
бракосочета́ни|е (**-я**) *ср* marriage ceremony.
брасле́т (**-а**) *м* bracelet; (*кольцо из металла, кости итп*) bangle.
брасс (**-а**) *м* breaststroke.
брат (**-а**; *nom pl* **-ья**, *gen pl* **-ьев**) *м* brother; **сво́дный** ~ stepbrother; **двою́родный** ~ cousin.
Братисла́в|а (**-ы**) *ж* Bratislava.
бра́ти|я (**-и**) *ср* brotherhood.
бра́тск|ий (**-ая, -ое, -ие**) *прил* brotherly, fraternal; **бра́тская моги́ла** communal grave.
бра́тств|о (**-а**) *ср* (*содружество*) brotherhood.
бра|ть (**беру́, берёшь**; *pt* **-л, -ла́, -ло́**, *perf* **взять**) *несов перех* to take; (*билет*) to take; (*няню*) to take on; (*крепость, город*) to take, seize; (*высоту*) to conquer; (*барьер*) to clear; ~ (*impf*) **нало́г у кого́-н/за что-н** to tax sb/sth; ~ (**взять** *perf*) **что-н в расчёт** *или* **во внима́ние** to take sth into account *или* consideration
► **бра́ться** (*perf* **взя́ться**) *несов возв*: **бра́ться за** +*acc* (*дотронуться*) to touch; (*хватать рукой*) to take hold of; (*за чтение, за работу*) to get down to; (*за перо*) to take up; (*за книгу*) to begin; (*решение проблемы*) to take on, undertake; **отку́да у тебя́ вре́мя берётся?** where do you find the time?; **отку́да у него́ де́ньги беру́тся?** where does he get the money?; **бра́ться** (**взя́ться** *perf*) **за ум** to come to one's senses.
бра́тья *итп сущ см* **брат**.
бра́чный *прил* (*контракт*) marriage *опред*; (*союз*) conjugal.
бревн|о́ (**-а́**; *nom pl* **брёвна**, *gen pl* **брёвен**) *ср* log; (*СПОРТ*) the beam; (*перен*) oaf.
бред (**-а**; *loc sg* **-у́**) *м* delirium; (*перен*) nonsense; ~ **сумасше́дшего** the ravings of a madman.
бре́|дить (**-жу, -дишь**) *несов неперех* to be delirious; ~ (*impf*) **кем-н/чем-н** to be mad about sb/sth.
бредо́вый *прил* (*разг*) crazy.
бреду́ *итп несов см* **брести́**.
бре́жу *несов см* **бре́дить**.
бре́зга|ть (**-ю**) *несов* = **бре́зговать**.

брезгли́в|ый (**-, -а, -о**) *прил* (*человек*) fastidious; (*взгляд*) disgusted.
бре́зг|овать (**-ую**; *perf* **побре́зговать**) *несов неперех* (+*instr*) to be fastidious about.
брезе́нт (**-а**; *part gen* **-у**) *м* tarpaulin.
брёл *итп несов см* **брести́**.
бре́м|я (**-ени**; *как* **вре́мя**; *см* **Table 4**) *ср* burden.
бр|ести́ (**-еду́, -едёшь**; *pt* **-ёл, -ела́, -ело́**) *несов неперех* (*человек*) to trudge; (*лошадь*) to plod.
брета́нский (**-ая, -ое, -ие**) *прил* Breton.
Брета́н|ь (**-и**) *ж* Brittany.
брето́нский (**-ая, -ое, -ие**) *прил* = **брета́нский**.
Брето́н|ь (**-и**) *ж* = **Брета́нь**.
бре́ш|ь (**-и**) *ж* (*пролом*) breach.
бре́ю(сь) *итп несов см* **бри́ть(ся)**.
брига́д|а (**-ы**) *ж* (*ВОЕН*) brigade; (*в поезде*) crew; (*на производстве*) (work) team.
бригади́р (**-а**) *м* (*в поезде*) ≈ chief guard (*BRIT*), ≈ senior conductor (*US*); (*на производстве*) team leader.
бриз (**-а**) *м* sea breeze.
бриллиа́нт (**-а**) *м* (cut) diamond.
бриллиа́нтовый *прил* diamond *опред*.
брита́н|ец (**-ца**) *м* Briton; **~цы** the British.
Брита́ни|я (**-и**) *ж* Britain.
брита́н|ка (**-ки**; *gen pl* **-ок**) *ж см* **брита́нец**.
брита́нск|ий (**-ая, -ое, -ие**) *прил* British.
брита́нца *итп сущ см* **брита́нец**.
бри́тв|а (**-ы**) *ж* razor; **безопа́сная** ~ safety razor.
бр|ить (**-е́ю, -е́ешь**; *perf* **побри́ть**) *несов перех* (*человека*) to shave; (*бороду*) to shave off
► **бри́ться** (*perf* **побри́ться**) *несов возв* to shave.
бри́финг (**-а**) *м* briefing.
бро́в|ь (**-и**; *gen pl* **-е́й**) *ж* eyebrow; **попа́сть** (*perf*) **не в** ~, **а в глаз** to hit the nail on the head; **он и бро́вью не повёл** he didn't bat an eyelid.
бро|ди́ть (**-жу́, -дишь**) *несов неперех* to wander; (*perf* **вы́бродить**; *вино, пиво*) to ferment.
бродя́г|а (**-и**) *м/ж* tramp; (*любящий странствовать*) drifter.
броже́ни|е (**-я**) *ср* fermentation; (*перен*) ferment.
брожу́ *несов см* **броди́ть**.
бро́йлер (**-а**) *м* broiler.
бро́кер (**-а**) *м* broker; **биржево́й** ~ stockbroker.
бро́керск|ий (**-ая, -ое, -ие**) *прил* broker's.
бром (**-а**) *м* bromine.
бронемаши́н|а (**-ы**) *ж* armoured (*BRIT*) *или* armored (*US*) car.
бронетранспортёр (**-а**) *м* armoured (*BRIT*) *или* armored (*US*) personnel carrier.
бро́нз|а (**-ы**) *ж* bronze.
бро́нзовый *прил* bronze; **бро́нзовый век** the Bronze Age; **бро́нзовый призёр** bronze medallist (*BRIT*) *или* medalist (*US*).
брони́рова́ни|е (**-я**) *ср* reservation.
брони́р|овать (**-ую**; *perf* **заброни́ровать**) (*не*)*сов перех* to reserve.
бронх (**-а**; *обычно мн*) bronchial tube.
бронхи́т (**-а**) *м* bronchitis.
брон|ь (**-и**) *ж* (*разг*) reservation.

бро́н|я (-и) ж reservation.

брон|я́ (-и́) ж armour (*BRIT*) *или* armor (*US*) plating.

броса́|ть (-ю) *несов от* **бро́сить**

► **броса́ться** *несов от* **бро́ситься** ♦ *возв:* ~ся **снежка́ми/камня́ми** to throw snowballs/stones at each other; ~ся (*impf*) **деньга́ми** to throw one's money around; ~ся (*impf*) **друзья́ми** to abandon one's friends.

бро́с|ить (-шу, -сишь; *impf* **броса́ть**) *сов перех* (*камень, мяч итп*) to throw; (*якорь*) to drop, cast; (*сети*) to cast; (*семью, дру́га*) to abandon; (*войска, отряд*) to dispatch; (*спорт*) to give up; **броса́ть** (~ *perf*) **замеча́ние** to pass comment; **меня́** ~**сило в жар** I broke out in a (cold) sweat; **броса́ть** (~ *perf*) +*infin* to give up doing; ~**сьте!** stop it!

► **бро́ситься** (*impf* **броса́ться**) *сов возв:* ~ся на +*acc* (*на врага, на оби́дчика*) to throw o.s. at; **броса́ться** (~ся *perf*) **в дра́ку/ата́ку** to rush into the fray/to the attack; **броса́ться** (~ся *perf*) **кому́-н на по́мощь** to rush to sb's aid; ~ся (*perf*) **по ле́стнице вниз** to rush downstairs; ~ся (*perf*) **кому́-н в объя́тия** to fall into sb's arms; **кра́ска** ~**силась ему́ в лицо́** the colour rushed to his face.

бро́совый *прил* (*разг*) trashy; **бро́совая цена́** giveaway price; **бро́совый э́кспорт** (*комм*) dumping.

бро́ш|ка (-ки; *gen pl* -ек) ж brooch.

бро́шу(сь) *сов см* **бро́сить(ся)**.

брош|ь (-и) ж *см* **бро́шка**.

брошю́р|а (-ы) ж (*небольшая книжка*) pamphlet; (*рекламный буклет*) brochure.

брус (-а; *nom pl* -ья, *gen pl* -ьев) м beam; *см также* **бру́сья**.

бруска́ *итп сущ см* **брусо́к**.

брусни́к|а (-и) ж cowberry.

брусо́к (-ка́) м (*камень для точки*) whetstone; (*мыла*) bar.

бру́сь|я (-ев) мн parallel bars мн.

бру́тто *прил неизм* gross *опред*.

бры́з|гать (-жу, -жешь) *несов неперех* (*фонтан, грязь*) to splash; (~ **гаю**) (*опрыскивать*): ~ **на** +*acc* to splash.

бры́зг|и (-) мн splashes мн; (*мелкие*) spray *ед*; (*стекла, камня*) fragments мн, splinters мн.

бры́зжу *итп сущ см* **бры́згать**.

бры́нз|а (-ы) ж brynza (*sheep's milk cheese*).

брысь *межд* shoo.

брю́кв|а (-ы) ж swede.

брю́к|и (-) мн trousers мн, pants мн (*US*).

брюне́т (-а) м: **он** ~ he has dark hair.

брюне́т|ка (-ки; *gen pl* -ок) ж brunette.

Брюссе́л|ь (-я) м Brussels.

брю́х|о (-а) *ср* (*также разг*) belly; (*разг: толстое*) pot.

брюшно́й *прил* abdominal; **брюшно́й тиф**

typhoid fever.

БСЭ ж сокр = **Больша́я Сове́тская Энциклопе́дия**.

бубён *сущ см* **бу́бны**.

бу́блик (-а) м ≈ bagel.

бу́б|ны (-ён; *dat pl* -нам) мн (*карты*) diamonds мн.

буго́р (-ра́) м mound; (*на коже*) lump.

Будапе́шт (-а) м Budapest.

будди́зм (-а) м Buddhism.

будди́ст (-а) м Buddhist.

будди́ст|ка (-ки; *gen pl* -ок) ж *см* **будди́ст**.

бу́дем *несов см* **быть**.

бу́дет *несов см* **быть** ♦ *част* that's enough; **попла́кали и** ~ that's enough crying; ~ **тебе́!** that's enough from you!

бу́дешь *итп несов см* **быть**.

буди́льник (-а) м alarm clock; **заводи́ть** (**завести́** *perf*) ~ **на** +*acc* to set the alarm (clock) for.

бу|ди́ть (-жу́, -дишь; *perf* **разбуди́ть**) *несов перех* to wake (up), awaken; (*perf* **пробуди́ть**; *перен*) to awaken.

бу́д|ка (-ки; *gen pl* -ок) ж (*сторожа*) hut; (*для собаки*) kennel; **часова́я** ~ sentry box; **телефо́нная** ~ telephone booth *или* box.

бу́дн|и (-ей) мн working *или* week days мн; (*перен: обыденная жизнь*) routine *ед*.

бу́док *сущ см* **бу́дка**.

будора́жить (-у, -ишь) *несов от* **взбудора́жить**.

бу́дто *союз* (*якобы*) apparently; (*словно*): (**как**) ~ (**бы**) as if; **уверя́ет,** ~ **сам её ви́дел** he claims to have seen her himself; **он** ~ **бы до́лжен е́хать в Москву́** apparently he has to go to Moscow; **он улыба́лся,** ~ (**бы**) **был рад ви́деть нас** he smiled as if he were glad to see us.

бу́ду *итп несов см* **быть**.

бу́дущее (-его; *decl like adj*) *ср* the future; **в** ~**ем** in the future; **на** ~ for the future; **не де́лайте э́того в** ~**ем** don't do it in future.

бу́дущий (-ая, -ее, -ие) *прил* (*следующий*) next; (*предстоящий*) future; **бу́дущее вре́мя** future tense.

бу́дь(те) *несов см* **быть** ♦ *союз:* **будь то** to be it.

бу́ен *прил см* **бу́йный**.

бужени́н|а (-ы) ж cold cooked and seasoned pork.

бужу́ *несов см* **буди́ть**.

бу́|й (-я; *nom pl* -и́) м buoy.

бу́йвол (-а) м buffalo.

бу́йволиц|а (-ы) ж *см* **бу́йвол**.

бу́йный (-ен, -йна́, -йно) *прил* wild; (*обильный: растительность*) luxuriant, lush.

бук (-а) м beech.

бу́кв|а (-ы) ж letter; (*перен*): ~ +*gen* (*закона, документа*) the letter of; **прописна́я/строчна́я**

~ capital/small letter; ~ **в бу́кву** word for word.

буква́льно *нареч* literally.

буква́льный *прил* literal.

буква́рь (**-я́**) *м* first reading book.

буке́т (**-а**) *м* (*цвето́в, вина́*) bouquet; (*перен: разг: боле́зней, недоста́тков*) range.

букини́ст (**-а**) *м* *second-hand bookseller*.

букинисти́ческий (**-ая, -ое, -ие**) *прил*: ~ **магази́н** second-hand bookshop.

букле́т (**-а**) *м* booklet.

букси́р (**-а**) *м* tug; (*трос*) towrope; **тяну́ть** (*impf*) *или* **вести́** (*impf*) **на ~е** to give sb a tow.

була́вка (**-ки**; *gen pl* **-ок**) *ж* pin; **англи́йская ~** safety pin.

була́ный (**-ого**; *decl like adj*) *м* dun.

була́т (**-а**) *м* Damascus *или* damask steel.

бу́лка (**-ки**; *gen pl* **-ок**) *ж* roll; (*бе́лый хлеб*) loaf.

бу́лочка (**-ки**; *gen pl* **-ек**) *ж см* **бу́лка**.

бу́лочная (**-ой**; *decl like adj*) *ж* baker, baker's (shop).

булы́жник (**-а**) *м* cobblestone.

булы́жный *прил*: **~ая мостова́я** cobbled street.

бульва́р (**-а**) *м* boulevard.

бульва́рный *прил* boulevard *опред*; **~ рома́н** trashy novel; **бульва́рная пре́сса** gutter press.

бульдо́г (**-а**) *м* bulldog.

бульдо́зер (**-а**) *м* bulldozer.

бульо́н (**-а**; *part gen* **-у**) *м* stock.

бум (**-а**) *м* (*оживле́ние*) boom.

бума́га (**-и**) *ж* paper; **~ за по́дписью кого́-н** a document signed by sb; **це́нные ~и** securities; **ге́рбовая ~** headed paper; *см также* **бума́ги**.

бума́ги (**-**) *мн* papers *мн*.

бума́жка (**-ки**; *gen pl* **-ек**) *ж* piece of paper.

бума́жник (**-а**) *м* wallet, pocketbook (*US*).

бума́жный *прил* paper; (*бюрократи́ческий*) bureaucratic; **бума́жная волоки́та** red tape.

бумера́нг (**-а**) *м* boomerang.

бу́нгало *ср нескл* bungalow.

бу́нкер (**-а**) *м* bunker.

бунт (**-а**) *м* (*мяте́ж*) riot; (: *на корабле́*) mutiny.

бунтова́ть (**-у́ю**) *несов непер* (*см сущ*) to riot; to mutiny.

бура́вить (**-лю, -ишь**) *perf* **пробура́вить**) *несов перех* to drill.

бура́к (**-а́**) *м* beetroot.

бура́н (**-а**) *м* blizzard, snowstorm.

бу́ргер (**-а**) *м* burger.

бургоми́стр (**-а**) *м* ≈ mayor.

бурда́ (**-ы́**) *ж* (*разг*): **э́тот чай про́сто ~** the tea is just like dishwater.

бу́рен *прил см* **бу́рный**.

буре́ние (**-я**) *ср* boring, drilling.

буржуази́я (**-и**) *ж* bourgeoisie; **ме́лкая ~** petty bourgeoisie.

буржуа́зный *прил* bourgeois.

буржу́й (**-я**) *м* (*разг*) bourgeois.

бури́ть (**-ю́, -и́шь**; *perf* **пробури́ть**) *несов перех* to bore, drill.

бу́ркнуть (**-у, -ешь**) *сов перех* (*разг*) to grunt.

бурли́ть (**-ю́, -и́шь**) *несов непер* (*вода́*) to boil; (*руче́й*) to bubble; (*толпа́*) to seethe (*with*

---

excitement).

бу́рный (**-ен, -на́, -но**) *прил* (*пого́да, океа́н*) stormy, rough; (*р эка́*) turbulent; (*чу́вство, поры́в*) wild; (*спор*) heated; (*рост*) rapid.

бурови́к (**-а́**) *м* driller.

урово́й *прил* boring, drilling; **бурова́я вы́шка** derrick; **бурова́я сква́жина** bore(hole).

бурча́ть (**-у́, -и́шь**; *perf* **пробурча́ть**) *несов непер* (*разг: ворча́ть*) to mutter; **~ (пробурча́ть** *perf*) **себе́ под нос** to mutter *или* grumble to o.s.

бу́рый (**-, -а́, -о**) *прил* brown; **бу́рый у́голь** (*ГЕО*) brown coal, lignite.

бу́ря (**-и**) *ж* storm; (*перен*) burst; **~ в стака́не воды́** storm in a teacup.

буря́т (**-а**; *gen pl* **-**) *м* Buryat.

Буря́тия (**-и**) *ж* Buryatia.

буря́тка (**-ки**; *gen pl* **-ок**) *ж см* **буря́т**.

бу́сы (**-**) *мн* beads *мн*.

бутафо́рия (**-и**) *ж* (*ТЕА́ТР*) props *мн* (= properties;) (*перен*) sham.

бутербро́д (**-а**) *м* sandwich.

буто́н (**-а**) *м* bud.

бу́тса (**-ы**) *ж* (*обы́чно мн*) football boot.

буты́лка (**-ки**; *gen pl* **-ок**) *ж* bottle.

буты́лочный *прил* bottle *опред*; (*цвет*) bottle-green.

бу́фер (**-а**; *nom pl* **-а́**) *м* (*та́кже перен, КОМП*) buffer.

буфериза́ция (**-и**) *ж* (*КОМП*) buffering.

бу́ферный *прил* (*та́кже перен*) buffer *опред*.

буфе́т (**-а**) *м* (*для прода́жи заку́сок*) snack bar; (*шкаф*) sideboard.

буфе́тчик (**-а**) *м* assistant (*in snack bar*).

буфе́тчица (**-ы**) *ж см* **буфе́тчик**.

бух *межд*: **~!** bang!; (*разг: упа́л*) whoops!

буха́нка (**-ки**; *gen pl* **-ок**) *ж* loaf.

Бухаре́ст (**-а**) *м* Bucharest.

бу́хать (**-ю**) *несов от* **бу́хнуть**.

бухга́лтер (**-а**) *м* accountant, book-keeper; **~-реви́зор** auditor.

бухгалте́рия (**-и**) *ж* accountancy, book-keeping; (*отде́л*) accounts office.

бухга́лтерский (**-ая, -ое, -ие**) *прил* book-keeping *опред*, accountancy *опред*; **бухга́лтерские кни́ги** books; **бухга́лтерский учёт** book-keeping, accountancy.

бу́хнуть (**-у, -ешь**; *impf* **бу́хать**) *сов непер* (*дверь*) to bang; (*пу́шка*) to thunder ◆ *несов непер* to swell.

бу́хта (**-ы**) *ж* bay.

бу́хты-бара́хты *нареч*: **с ~** just like that; (*внеза́пно*) out of the blue.

бушева́ть (**-у́ю**) *несов непер* (*пожа́р, урага́н*) to rage.

Буэ́нос-А́йрес (**-а**) *м* Buenos Aires.

БЦЖ *ж сокр* BCG (= *Bacillus Calmette-Guérin*).

> **KEYWORD**

бы *часть* **1** (*выража́ет предположи́тельную возмо́жность*): **купи́л бы, е́сли бы бы́ли де́ньги** I would buy it if I had the money; **я бы**

давнó ужé купи́л э́ту кни́гу, éсли бы у меня́ бы́ли дéньги I would have bought this book long ago if I had had the money
2 (*выражает пожелание*): я бы хотéл поговори́ть с тобóй I would like to speak to you; я бы не хотéл об э́том говори́ть I would rather not talk about it; чáю бы I could do with some tea
3 (*выражает совет*): ты бы написáл ей you should write to her
4 (*выражает опасение*): не захвати́л бы нас дождь I hope we don't get caught in the rain; отдохну́ть/погуля́ть бы it would be nice to have a rest/walk; не опоздáть бы better not be late.

бывáло *част* expresses a repeated action in the past; ~ сиди́м и разговáриваем we used to *или* would sit and talk.

бывá|ть (-ю) *несов неперех* (*приходить, посещать*) to be; (*случаться, происходить*) to happen, take place; он ~ет у нас чáсто he often comes to see us; ~ют стрáнные слу́чаи strange things happen; как не ~ло (*разг*) as if it had never been; как ни в чём не ~ло (*разг*) as if nothing had happened; с кем не ~ет it happens to the best of us.

бы́вш|ий (-ая, -ее, -ие) *прил* former; (*жена, муж*) ex-, former.

бык (-á) *м* bull; (*рабочий*) ox; брать (взять *perf*) ~á за рогá to take the bull by the horns.

был *итп несов см* быть.

были́н|а (-ы) *ж* bylina (*Russian folk epic*).

бы́ло *част* expresses non-fulfilment of an intended action; он нáчал ~ говори́ть, но останови́лся he was about to say something, but stopped; мы нáчали ~ уходи́ть, но пошёл дождь we were about to leave, but it began to rain.

был|ь (-и) *ж* (*рассказ*) true story.

бы́стро *нареч* quickly.

быстрот|á (-ы́) *ж* speed; (*ума, рук*) quickness.

быстрохóд|ный (-ен, -на, -но) *прил* fast.

бы́стр|ый (-, á, -о) *прил* fast; (*лошадь*) swift, fast; (*проворный, беглый*) quick.

быт (-á; *loc sg* -ý) *м* life; (*повседневная жизнь*) everyday life; э́то вошлó в ~ this has become a part of our everyday life; слу́жба бы́та consumer services *мн*.

бытовóй *прил* everyday *опред*; **бытовáя жи́вопись** genre painting; **бытовóе обслу́живание населéния** consumer services *мн*; **бытовóе явлéние** everyday occurrence.

KEYWORD

быть (*см* **Table 21**) *несов* **1** (*omitted in present tense*) to be; кни́га на столé the book is on the table; зáвтра я бу́ду в шкóле I will be at school tomorrow; дом был на краю́ гóрода the house stood on the edge of the town; на ней краси́вое плáтье she is wearing a beautiful dress; вчерá был дождь it rained yesterday
2 (*часть составного сказ*) to be; я хочу́ быть учи́телем I want to be a teacher; я был рад ви́деть тебя́ I was happy to see you; так и быть! so be it!; как быть? what is to be done?; э́того не мóжет быть that's impossible; кто/какóй бы то ни был whoever/whatever it might be; бу́дьте добры́! excuse me, please!; бу́дьте добры́ – позови́те егó! would you be so good *или* kind as to call him?; бу́дьте здорóвы! take care!
3 (*образует будущее время*: +*impf vb*): вéчером я бу́ду писáть пи́сьма I'll be writing letters this evening; я бу́ду люби́ть тебя́ всегдá I'll love you forever.

бью(сь) *итп несов см* бить(ся).

Бэ́йсик (-а) *м* (*комп*) BASIC.

бюджéт (-а) *м* budget; дохóдный ~ income, revenue; расхóдный ~ expenditure.

бюджéтный *прил* budgetary.

бюллетéн|ь (-я) *м* bulletin; (*листок: для голосования*) ballot paper; (: *нетрудоспособности*) medical certificate; **быть** (*impf*) **на** ~е to be off sick (*from work*).

бюрó *ср нескл* office, agency; спрáвочное ~ inquiry office; бюрó (дóбрых) услу́г domestic help agency; бюрó нахóдок lost property office; бюрó по трудоустрóйству employment agency.

бюрокрáт (-а) *м* bureaucrat.

бюрократи́зм (-а) *м* bureaucracy.

бюрократи́ческий (-ая, -ое, -ие) *прил* bureaucratic.

бюрокрáти|я (-и) *ж* bureaucracy.

бюст (-а) *м* bust.

бюстгáльтер (-а) *м* bra (= *brassiere*).

бяз|ь (-и) *ж* calico.

~ *В, в* ~

В, в *сущ нескл* (*буква*) the 3rd letter of the Russian alphabet.

В *сокр* (= **вольт**) v. (= *volt*).

KEYWORD

в *предл* (+*acc*) **1** (*о месте направления*) in(to); **я положи́л кни́гу в портфе́ль** I put the book in(to) my briefcase; **я сел в маши́ну** I got in(to) the car

2 (*уехать, пойти*) to; **он уе́хал в Москву́** he went to Moscow; **идти́** (**пойти́** *perf*) **в учителя́** to become a teacher; **выбира́ть** (**вы́брать** *perf*) **кого́-н в комите́т** to elect sb to a committee

3 (*об изменении состояния*): **погружа́ться в рабо́ту** to be absorbed in one's work; **погружа́ться** (*impf*) **в разду́мье** to be deep in thought

4 (*об объекте физического действия*): **он постуча́л в дверь** he knocked on the door; **он посмотре́л мне в глаза́/в лицо́** he looked me in the eyes/face; **мать поцелова́ла меня́ в щёку** mother kissed me on the cheek

5 (*обозначает форму, вид*): **брю́ки в кле́тку** checked trousers; **лека́рство в табле́тках** medicine in tablet form; **разрыва́ть** (**разорва́ть** *perf*) **что-н в клочья́** to tear sth to shreds; **растира́ть** (**растере́ть** *perf*) **что-н в порошо́к** to grind sth to a powder

6 (*о размере, количестве*): **ве́сом в 3 то́нны** 3 tons *или* tonnes in weight; (: +*prp*): **дра́ма в трёх частя́х** a drama in three acts; **отря́д в де́сять челове́к** a detachment of ten men; **в пяти́ ме́трах от доро́ги** five metres (*BRIT*) *или* meters (*US*) from the road

7 (*о соотношении величин*): **в два ра́за бо́льше/дли́ннее/то́лще** twice as big/long/thick; **во мно́го раз лу́чше/умне́е** much better/cleverer; **во мно́го раз поле́знее/краси́вее** much more useful/beautiful

8 (*о времени совершения чего-н*): **он пришёл в понеде́льник** he came on Monday; **я ви́дел его́ в про́шлом году́** I saw him last year; **я встре́тил его́ в два часа́** I met him at two o'clock; **э́то случи́лось в ма́рте/в двадца́том ве́ке** it happened in March/in the twentieth century

9 (+*prp*; *о месте*) in; **ко́шка сиди́т в корзи́не** the cat is sitting in the basket; **я живу́ в дере́вне** I live in the country; **сын у́чится в шко́ле/университе́те** my son is at school/university; **в отдале́нии/сосе́дстве** in the distance/the neighbourhood

10 (*о чём-н облегающем, покрывающем*): **ру́ки в кра́ске/са́же** hands covered in paint/soot; **това́р в упако́вке** packaged goods; **не́бо в ту́чах** the sky is overcast

11 (*об одежде*) in; **мужчи́на в очка́х/в ша́пке** a man in *или* wearing glasses/a hat

12 (*о состоянии*): **быть в у́жасе/негодова́нии** to be terrified/indignant.

в. *сокр* (= **век**) c (= *century*); (= **восто́к**) E (= *East*); (= **восто́чный**) E (= *East*).

ва-ба́нк *нареч* (*также перен*): **идти́ ~** to stake everything.

ваго́н (**-а**) *м* (*пассажирский*) carriage (*BRIT*), coach (*BRIT*), car (*US*); (*товарный*) wagon (*BRIT*), truck (*BRIT*); **спа́льный ~** couchette car; **мя́гкий ~** ≈ sleeping car; **ваго́н-рестора́н** dining (*BRIT*) *или* club (*US*) car.

вагоне́т|ка (**-ки**; *gen pl* **-ок**) *ж* trolley (*RAIL*).

ваго́нный *прил* carriage *опред* (*BRIT*), car *опред* (*US*); **ваго́нный парк** train depot.

вагоноремо́нтный *прил* (*завод*) coach (*BRIT*) *или* car (*US*) reparation *опред*.

вагонострои́тельный *прил* (*завод*) coach (*BRIT*) *или* car (*US*) building *опред*.

ва́жен *прил см* **ва́жный**.

ва́жнича|ть (**-ю**) *несов неперех* to act in a self-important manner.

ва́жность (**-и**) *ж* importance; (*надменность*) self-importance; (**не**) **велика́ ~** what does it matter.

ва́ж|ный (**-ен, -на́, -но**) *прил* important; (*гордый*) pompous.

ВАЗ (**-а**) *м сокр* = **Во́лжский автомоби́льный заво́д**; (*автомобиль*) *vehicle manufactured at the Volga car factory*.

ва́з|а (**-ы**) *ж* vase.

вазели́н (**-а**; *part gen* **-у**) *м* Vaseline®.

вака́нси|я (**-и**) *ж* vacancy; **откры́лась ~ в бухгалте́рии** a vacancy has now arisen in accounts.

вака́нт|ный (**-ен, -на, -но**) *прил* vacant; **~ная до́лжность** vacancy.

ва́кс|а (**-ы**) *ж* black shoe polish.

ва́куум (**-а**) *м* (*также перен*) vacuum.

вакци́н|а (**-ы**) *ж* vaccine.

вакцини́р|овать (-ую) *(не)сов перех* to vaccinate.

вал (-а; *loc sg* -ý, *nom pl* -ы́) *м* (*насыпь*) bank; (: *крепости*) rampart; (*стержень*) shaft; (*волна*) breaker; (*ЭКОН*) gross product.

вале́жник (-а) *м собир* dead wood.

ва́лен|ок (-ка) *м* (*обычно мн*) felt boot.

валериа́н|а (-ы) *ж* valerian.

валериа́нк|а (-и) *ж* valerian drops *мн*.

валериа́нов|ый *прил*: ~ые ка́пли valerian drops.

валерья́н|а (-ы) *ж* = **валериа́на**.

вале́т (-а) *м* (*КАРТЫ*) jack.

валидо́л (-а) *м type of mild sedative.*

ва́лик (-а) *м* (*в механизме*) cylinder; (*для краски*) roller; (*подушка*) bolster.

вал|и́ть (-ю́, -ишь; *perf* **свали́ть** *или* **повали́ть**) *несов перех* (*заставить падать*) to knock over; (*рубить*) to fell; (*perf* **свали́ть**; *разг*: *бросать*) to dump ♦ *неперех* (*no perf*; *народ*) to flock; (*дым, пар*) to pour out; ~ (**свали́ть** *perf*) вину́ на +*acc* (*разг*) to point the finger at; **ва́лит снег** it's snowing heavily; **толпа́ ~и́ла на конце́рт** the crowd flocked to the concert

▶ **вали́ться** (*perf* **свали́ться** *или* **повали́ться**) *несов возв* (*падать*) to fall; (*разг*: *опускаться*) to flake out; **все бе́ды ва́лятся на него́** he attracts misfortune; **у него́ всё ва́лится из рук** everything he does fails; ~**ся** (*impf*) **с ног** (*разг*) to be dead on one's feet.

валово́й *прил* (*доход*) gross *опред*; **валово́й вну́тренний проду́кт** gross domestic product; **валово́й национа́льный проду́кт** gross national product; **валова́я при́быль** gross profit; ~ **объём прода́жи** gross sales *мн*.

ва́лом *нареч*: ~ **вали́ть** (*разг*: *народ*) to flock.

валто́рн|а (-ы) *ж* French horn.

валу́н (-а́) *м* boulder.

вальс (-а) *м* waltz.

вальцева́ть (-у́ю) *несов перех* to roll.

вальц|ы́ (-о́в) *мн* (*станок*) rolling press *ед*.

валю́т|а (-ы) *ж* currency ♦ *собир* foreign currency; **твёрдая** ~ hard currency.

валю́тно-фина́нсовый *прил* monetary.

валю́тный *прил* currency *опред*; ~ **контро́ль** exchange control; **валю́тный курс** rate of exchange; **валю́тный фонд** currency reserves *мн*.

валю́тчик (-а) *м* (*разг*) *person illegally dealing in foreign currency.*

валю́тчиц|а (-ы) *ж см* **валю́тчик**.

валя́|ть (-ю) *несов перех* (*катать*) to roll; (*perf* **сваля́ть**; *скатывать*) to shape

▶ **валя́ться** *несов возв* (*кататься*) to roll about; (*разг*: *человек, бумаги итп*) to lie about; (: *с гриппом итп*) to be laid up; **де́ньги на земле́** *или* **на доро́ге не ~ются** (*разг*) money doesn't grow on trees.

вам *итп мест см* **вы**.

вампи́р (-а) *м* vampire.

ВАН *м сокр* (= **Ве́стник Акаде́мии нау́к Росси́и**) Bulletin of the Russian Academy of Science.

вандали́зм (-а) *м* vandalism.

ванили́н (-а; *part gen* -у) *м* vanillin.

вани́л|ь (-и) *ж* vanilla.

ва́нн|а (-ы) *ж* bath; **принима́ть (приня́ть** *perf*) ~у to take *или* have a bath.

ва́нн|ая (-ой; *decl like adj*) *ж* bathroom.

ва́рвар (-а) *м* barbarian.

ва́рварск|ий (-ая, -ое, -ие) *прил* barbaric.

ва́рварств|о (-а) *ср* (*бескультурие*) barbarism; (*жестокость*) barbarity.

ва́реж|ка (-ки; *gen pl* -ек) *ж* (*обычно мн*) mitten.

варе́ник (-а) *м* (*обычно мн*) sweet dumpling (*with curd or fruit filling*).

варёный *прил* boiled.

варе́нь|е (-я) *ср* jam.

вариа́нт (-а) *м* version; (*возможность*) option; (*разновидность*) variant.

вариа́ци|я (-и) *ж* variation.

вар|и́ть (-ю́, -ишь; *perf* **свари́ть**) *несов перех* (*обед*) to cook; (*суп, кофе*) to make; (*картофель, мясо*) to boil; (*ТЕХ*) to weld; (*сталь*) to found; **у него́ голова́** *или* **котело́к ва́рит** (*разг*) he has a good head on his shoulders

▶ **вари́ться** (*perf* **свари́ться**) *несов возв* (*приготовляться*) to be cooking; ~**ся** (*impf*) **в со́бственном соку́** (*перен*) to live in a world of one's own; **до́лго/бы́стро** ~**ся** (*impf*) to cook slowly/quickly.

Варша́в|а (-ы) *ж* Warsaw.

варьете́ *ср нескл* variety show.

варьи́р|овать (-ую) *несов (не)перех* to vary.

вас *мест см* **вы**.

василёк (-ька́) *м* cornflower.

ВАТА *ж сокр* (= **Всеми́рная ассоциа́ция тури́стических аге́нтств**) IATA (= *International Association of Travel Agencies*).

ва́т|а (-ы) *ж* cotton wool (*BRIT*), (absorbent) cotton (*US*).

вата́г|а (-и) *ж* (*ребят*) gang.

ватерли́ни|я (-и) *ж* water line.

ватерпа́с (-а) *м* spirit level.

ватерполи́ст (-а) *м* water-polo player.

ватерпо́ло *ср нескл* water polo.

вати́н (-а) *м* padding.

ва́т|ка (-и) *ж* cotton wool ball.

ва́тман (-а) *м heavy paper for drawing etc.*

ва́тник (-а) *м* quilted jacket.

ва́тный *прил* cotton-wool (*BRIT*), absorbent cotton *опред* (*US*); **ва́тное одея́ло** quilt.

ватру́ш|ка (-ки; *gen pl* -ек) *ж* curd tart.

ватт (-а) *м* watt.

ва́учер (-а) *м* voucher.

ва́фельный *прил*: ~ **торт** waffle.

ва́фл|я (-ли; *gen pl* -ель) *ж* wafer.

ва́хт|а (-ы) ж watch; **стоя́ть** (impf) **на ~е** to keep watch.

ва́хтенный прил (служба) watch опред; **ва́хтенный журна́л** log(book).

вахтёр (-а) м caretaker, janitor.

Ваш мест см **ваш**.

ваш (-его; f -а, nt -е, pl -и; как наш; см Table 9) притяж мест your; **э́то ва́ше** this is yours; **наш дом бо́льше ва́шего** our house is bigger than yours; см также **ва́ши**.

ва́ш|и (-их; decl like adj) мн your nearest and dearest мн; **и на́шим и ~м** (разг: пренебр) all things to all people.

Вашингто́н (-а) м Washington.

вбежа́ть (как **бежа́ть**; см Table 20; impf **вбега́ть**) сов неперех: ~ **(в** +acc) to run in(to).

вберу́ итп сов см **вобра́ть**.

вбива́|ть (-ю) несов от **вбить**.

вбира́|ть (-ю) несов от **вобра́ть**.

вбить (вобью́, вобьёшь; impf **вбива́ть**) перех: ~ **(в** +acc) to drive или hammer in(to); **я не могу́ ~ э́то ей в го́лову** (разг) I can't seem to get it into her thick skull.

вблизи́ нареч nearby ◆ предл: ~ +gen или **от** +gen near (to).

вбок нареч sideways.

вбра́сыва|ть (-ю) несов от **вбро́сить**.

вброд нареч: **переходи́ть (перейти́** perf**) ~** to ford.

вбро́сить (-шу, -сишь; impf **вбра́сывать**) сов перех to throw in; **вбра́сывать (~** perf**) мяч** (СПОРТ) to take a throw-in.

ввал|и́ться (-ю́сь, -ишься; impf **вва́ливаться** сов возв (разг): ~ **(в** +acc) to burst in(to); (щёки, глаза́) to become sunken.

введе́ни|е (-я) ср introduction; (войск) sending in; (да́нных) input.

ввезти́ (-у́, -ёшь; pt ввёз, -ла́, -ло́, impf **ввози́ть**) сов перех (в дом итп) to take in; (в страну) to import.

вве́рг|нуть (-у, -ешь; impf **ввергать**) сов перех (перен): ~ **в** +acc to reduce to; **он вверга́ет меня́ в тоску́** he depresses me.

вверн|у́ть (-у́, -ёшь; impf **ввёртывать**) сов перех to screw in; (перен: разг: слово) to put in.

вверх нареч up ◆ предл: ~ **по** +dat up; ~ **по тече́нию** upstream; **всё в до́ме/в ко́мнате ~ дном** (разг) everything in the house/room is topsy-turvy; ~ **нога́ми** (разг) upside down.

вверху́ нареч up ◆ предл (+gen) at the top of.

вве|сти́ (-ду́, -дёшь; pt -ёл, -ела́, -ело́, impf **вводи́ть**) сов перех to take in; (машину в гара́ж) to put in; (иглу́: в ве́ну итп) to slip in; (лека́рство, раство́р) to inject; (в компью́тер) to enter; (устано́вить: зако́н, пошли́ны итп) to introduce; (сде́лать де́йствующим): ~ **что-н в** +acc to put sth into; **вводи́ть (~** perf**) кого́-н в заблужде́ние/искуше́ние** to mislead/tempt sb; **вводи́ть (~** perf**) кого́-н в расхо́ды** to cause sb expense; **вводи́ть (~** perf**) что-н в мо́ду** to bring sth into fashion; **вводи́ть (~** perf**) кого́-н в курс**

собы́тий to bring sb up-to-date with events.

ввиду́ предл (+gen) in view of ◆ союз: ~ **того́, что** in view of the fact that; ~ **плохо́й пого́ды рейс отло́жен** the flight has been delayed because of the bad weather.

ввин|ти́ть (-чу́, -ти́шь; impf **вви́нчивать**) сов перех to screw in.

ввод (-а) м bringing in; (да́нных) input, feeding in; (электри́ческий, телефо́нный) lead-in.

вво|ди́ть (-жу́, -дишь) несов от **ввести́**.

вво́дн|ый прил (статья) introductory; (устро́йство) lead-in опред; **вво́дное отве́рстие** input; **вво́дное сло́во** parenthesis.

ввожу́ несов см **ввози́ть**.

ввоз (-а) м (проце́сс) importation; (и́мпорт) imports мн; **беспо́шлинный ~** duty-free imports.

вво|зи́ть (-жу́, -зишь) несов от **ввезти́**.

ввозно́й прил imported; **ввозны́е по́шлины** import duty ед.

вво́лю нареч to one's heart's content.

ввосьмеро́м нареч in a group of eight; **они́ живу́т там ~** there are eight of them living there.

ВВП м сокр (= валово́й вну́тренний проду́кт) GDP (= gross domestic product).

ВВС мн сокр (= вое́нно-возду́шные си́лы) ≈ RAF (= Royal Air Force ед).

ВВФ м сокр (= Вое́нно-возду́шный флот) ≈ RAF (= Royal Air Force ед).

ввысь нареч upwards.

ввяза́ться (-жу́сь, -жешься; impf **ввя́зываться**) сов возв (разг) to get involved.

вгиба́|ть (-ю) несов от **вогну́ть**.

вглубь нареч (down) into the depths ◆ предл (+gen; вниз) into the depths of; (внутрь) into the heart of.

вгля|де́ться (-жу́сь, -ди́шься; impf **вгля́дываться**) сов возв: ~ **в** +acc to peer at.

вгоню́ итп сов см **вогна́ть**.

вгоня́|ть (-ю) несов от **вогна́ть**.

вда|ва́ться (-ю́сь) несов от **вда́ться**.

вдав|и́ть (-лю́, -ишь; impf **вда́вливать**) сов перех: ~ **(в** +acc) to press in(to).

вдадим итп сов см **вда́ться**.

вдалеке́ нареч in the distance; ~ **от** +gen a long way from.

вдали́ нареч = **вдалеке́**.

вдаль нареч into the distance.

вда́ться (как **дать**; см Table 14; impf **вдава́ться**) сов возв: ~ **в** +acc to jut out into; (перен: в рассужде́ния) to get caught up in; **вдава́ться** (impf) **в подро́бности** to go into details.

вдво́е нареч (сложи́ть) in two; ~ **сильне́е/умне́е** twice as strong/clever.

вдвоём нареч: **они́ живу́т/рабо́тают ~** the two of them live/work together.

вдвойне́ нареч (получи́ть, заплати́ть) double (the amount).

вде́ла|ть (-ю; impf **вде́лывать**) сов перех: ~ **в** +acc (вста́вить) to set into.

вде|ть (-ну, -нешь; *impf* **вдева́ть**) *сов перех* to put in; **вдева́ть** (~ *perf*) **ни́тку в иго́лку** to thread a needle.

ВДНХ *ж сокр* (= **Вы́ставка достиже́ний наро́дного хозя́йства СССР**) exhibition of economic achievements of the USSR.

вдоба́вок *нареч* (*разг*) in addition ♦ *предл*: ~ **к** +*dat* in addition to.

вдов|а́ (-ы́; *nom pl* -ы) *ж* widow.

вдове́ц (-ца́) *м* widower.

вдо́воль *нареч* to one's heart's content; **(в до́ме) всего́** ~ there is plenty of everything (in the house).

вдовца́ *итп сущ см* **вдове́ц**.

вдо́вый *прил* widowed.

вдого́нку *нареч* (*бежать*) behind ♦ *предл*: ~ **за** +*instr* after.

вдоль *нареч* (*сломаться, расколо́ться*) lengthways ♦ *предл* (+*gen*) along; ~ **и поперёк** here, there and everywhere; (*перен*) inside out.

вдох (-а) *м*: **де́лать** (**сде́лать** *perf*) ~ to breathe in.

вдохнове́ни|е (-я) *ср* inspiration.

вдохнове́н|ный (-ен, -на, -но) *прил* inspired.

вдохнов|и́ть (-лю́, -и́шь; *impf* **вдохновля́ть**) *сов перех* to inspire; ~ (*perf*) **кого́-н на что-н** to inspire sb to sth

▶ **вдохнови́ться** (*impf* **вдохновля́ться**) *сов возв* (+*instr*) to be inspired by.

вдохн|у́ть (-у́, -ёшь; *impf* **вдыха́ть**) *сов перех* (*воздух*) to breathe in; (*дым, лекарство*) to inhale; **вдыха́ть** (~ *perf*) **уве́ренность/ве́ру в кого́-н** to inspire confidence/faith in sb.

вдре́безги *нареч* to smithereens.

вдруг *нареч* suddenly; (*а если*) what if; ~ **он не придёт** what if he doesn't come.

вду́ма|ться (-юсь; *impf* **вду́мываться**) *сов возв*: ~ **в** +*acc* to think over.

вду́мчив|ый (-, -а, -о) *прил* contemplative.

вду́мыва|ться (-юсь) *несов от* **вду́маться**.

вдыха́ни|е (-я) *ср* inhalation.

вдыха́|ть (-ю) *несов от* **вдохну́ть**.

веб (-а) *м* the (World Wide) Web.

вегетариа́н|ец (-ца) *м* vegetarian.

вегетариа́н|ка (-ки; *gen pl* -ок) *ж см* **вегетариа́нец**.

вегетариа́нск|ий (-ая, -ое, -ие) *прил* vegetarian.

вегетариа́нца *сущ см* **вегетариа́нец**.

вегета́ци|я (-и) *ж* vegetation.

ве́да|ть (-ю) *несов перех* (*знать*) to know ♦ *непepex*: ~ +*instr* (*делами*) to be in charge of.

ведём *несов см* **вести́**.

ве́дени|е (-я) *ср* authority; **принима́ть** (**приня́ть** *perf*) **в своё** ~ to take charge of; **быть** (*impf*) **в** ~**и кого́-н** to be under sb's authority.

веде́ни|е (-я) *ср* (*урока, сле́дствия*) conducting; (*войны́*) waging; ~ **хозя́йства** housekeeping.

вёдер *сущ см* **ведро́**.

ведёт(ся) *итп несов см* **вести́(сь)**.

ве́домо *ср*: **с/без ве́дома кого́-н** (*согла́сие*) with/without sb's consent; (*уведомле́ние*) with/without sb's knowledge.

ве́домост|и (-ей) *мн* gazette *ед*.

ве́домост|ь (-и; *gen pl* -ей) *ж* register; **расчётная** *или* **платёжная** ~ payroll; *см также* **ве́домости**.

ве́домственный *прил* departmental; (*подхо́д*) narrow-minded.

ве́домств|о (-а) *ср* department.

ведр|о́ (-а́; *nom pl* **вёдра**, *gen pl* **вёдер**) *ср* bucket, pail; **(дождь) льёт, как из** ~**á** it's pouring *или* bucketing (with rain).

веду́(сь) *итп несов см* **вести́(сь)**.

веду́ща|я (-ей; *decl like adj*) *ж см* **веду́щий**.

веду́щ|ий (-ая, -ее, -ие) *прил* leading ♦ (-его; *decl like adj*) *м* presenter.

ведь *нареч* (*в вопросе*): ~ **ты хо́чешь пое́хать?** you do want to go, don't you?; (*в утвержде́нии*): ~ **она́ не спра́вится одна́!** she surely can't manage alone! ♦ *союз* (*указывает на причину*) seeing as; ~ **она́ ра́да?** she is glad, isn't she?; **пое́шь,** ~ **ты го́лоден** you should eat, seeing as you're hungry; ~ **я проси́л тебя́!** I asked YOU!

ведьм|а (-ы) *ж* (*также перен*) witch; **охо́та за** ~**ми** *или* **на ведьм** witch-hunt.

ве́ер (-а; *nom pl* -á) *м* fan.

ве́жливо *нареч* politely.

ве́жливост|ь (-и) *ж* politeness.

ве́жлив|ый (-, -а, -о) *прил* polite.

вёз *итп несов см* **везти́**.

везде́ *нареч* everywhere; ~ **и всю́ду** everywhere you go.

вездесу́щ|ий (-ая, -ее, -ие; -, -а, -е) *прил* (*Бог*) omnipresent; (*челове́к*) ubiquitous.

вездехо́д (-а) *м* ≈ Landrover®.

везе́ни|е (-я) *ср* luck.

вез|ти́ (-у́, -ёшь; *pt* **вёз, -ла́, -ло́**) *несов перех* to transport, take; (*дви́гать: за собо́й*) to pull; (: *перед собо́й*) to push ♦ (*perf* **повезти́**) *безл* (+*dat*; *разг*) to be lucky; **ему́** (**ча́сто**) ~**ёт** he is (often) lucky.

Везу́ви|й (-я) *м* Vesuvius.

везу́ч|ий (-ая, -ее, -ие; -, -а, -е) *прил* lucky.

вей(те) *несов см* **вить**.

век (-а; *loc sg* -ý, *nom pl* -á) *м* century; (*истори́ческий пери́од*) age; (*чья-н жизнь*) lifetime; **це́лый** ~ **тебя́ не ви́дел** I haven't seen you for ages; **на** ~**á** forever; **в ко́и-то ве́ки** (*разг*) for the first time in ages; **жить** (*impf*) **в** ~**áх** to live on forever; **во ве́ки** ~**о́в** forever.

ве́к|о (-а) *ср* eyelid.

веково́й *прил* (*тради́ция, де́рево*) ancient.

ве́ксел|ь (-я; *nom pl* -я́) *м* promissory note; **переводно́й** ~ bill of exchange; **казначе́йский**

~ treasury bill; **плати́ть (заплати́ть** *perf*) **по ~ю** to settle an account.

вёл(ся) *итп несов см* **вести́(сь)**.

вел|е́ть (-ю́, -и́шь) *(не)сов неперех* (+*dat*) to order; **он ~е́л мне прийти́, он ~е́л, что́бы я пришёл** he ordered me to come.

велика́н (-а) *м* giant.

вели́к|ий (-ая, -ое, -ие; -, -а́, -о́) *прил* great; (*no full form*; *велика́, одежда*) too big; **сапоги́ велики́** the boots are too big; **вели́кие держа́вы** the Great Powers.

Великобрита́ни|я (-и) *ж* Great Britain.

великоду́шный (-ен, -на, -но) *прил* magnanimous, big-hearted.

великоле́п|ный (-ен, -на, -но) *прил* (*роскошный*) magnificent, splendid; (*разг*) fantastic.

великому́ченик (-а) *м* holy martyr.

великоро́сс (-а) *м* (*ист: обычно мн*) Great Russian (*old name for a Russian*).

вели́чествен|ный (-, -на, -но) *прил* majestic.

вели́честв|о (-а) *ср*: **Ва́ше** *итп* ~ Your *итп* Majesty.

вели́чи|е (-я) *ср* grandeur.

величин|а́ (-ы́) *ж* size; (*МАТ*) quantity; (*КОМП: значение*) value.

вел|о́(сь) *несов см* **вести́(сь)**.

велого́н|ка (-ки; *gen pl* **-ок)** *ж* (*СПОРТ: обычно мн*) cycle race.

велодро́м (-а) *м* velodrome.

велосипе́д (-а) *м* bicycle; **го́ночный ~** racing bicycle, racer.

велосипеди́ст (-а) *м* cyclist.

велосипеди́ст|ка (-ки; *gen pl* **-ок)** *ж см* **велосипеди́ст**.

вельве́т (-а) *м* corduroy.

вельмо́ж|а (-и) *м* dignitary.

велю́р (-а) *м* velours.

Ве́н|а (-ы) *ж* Vienna.

ве́н|а (-ы) *ж* vein.

венге́р|ка (-ки; *gen pl* **-ок)** *ж см* **венгр**.

венге́рский (-ая, -ое, -ие) *прил* Hungarian; ~ **язы́к** Hungarian.

венгр (-а) *м* Hungarian.

Ве́нгри|я (-и) *ж* Hungary.

Вене́р|а (-ы) *ж* Venus.

венери́ческий (-ая, -ое, -ие) *прил*: ~**ая боле́знь** venereal disease.

венероло́ги|я (-и) *ж* venereology.

Венесуэ́л|а (-ы) *ж* Venezuela.

венесуэ́лец (-ьца) *м* Venezuelan.

венесуэ́л|ка (-ки; *gen pl* **-ок)** *ж см* **венесуэ́лец**.

венесуэ́льский (-ая, -ое, -ие) *прил* Venezuelan.

венесуэ́льца *итп сущ см* **венесуэ́лец**.

вен|е́ц (-ца́) *м* crown; (*АСТРОНОМИЯ*) corona; **идти́ (пойти́** *perf*) **под ~ с кем-н** to walk down the aisle with sb.

венециа́нский (-ая, -ое, -ие) *прил* Venetian.

Вене́ци|я (-и) *ж* Venice.

ве́нзел|ь (-я; *nom pl* **-я)** *м* monogram.

ве́ник (-а) *м* broom, besom.

венка́ *итп сущ см* **вено́к**.

вено́зный *прил* venous.

вен|о́к (-ка́) *м* wreath.

вентили́р|овать (-ую; *perf* **провентили́ровать)** *несов перех* (*помещение*) to ventilate.

ве́нтил|ь (-я) *м* valve.

вентиля́тор (-а) *м* (ventilator) fan.

вентиля́ци|я (-и) *ж* ventilation.

венца́ *итп сущ см* **вене́ц**.

венча́ни|е (-я) *ср* (*коронование*) coronation; (*бракосочетание*) church wedding.

венча́|ть (-ю; *perf* **обвенча́ть** *или* **повенча́ть)** *несов перех* (*соединять браком*) to marry; (*находиться наверху*) to crown; ~ (*impf*) **на ца́рство кого́-н** to crown sb

► **венча́ться** (*perf* **обвенча́ться**) *несов возв* to be married (*in church*).

ве́нчик (-а) *м* (*БОТ*) corolla.

венчу́рный *прил*: ~**ое предприя́тие** venture; ~ **капита́л** venture capital.

ве́р|а (-ы) *ж* faith; (*в бога*) belief; ~ **в кого́-н/что-н** faith in sb/sth; ~**ой и пра́вдой служи́ть** (*impf*) **кому́-н/чему́-н** to serve sb/sth faithfully; **на ~у принима́ть (приня́ть** *perf*) **что-н** to take sth on trust.

вера́нд|а (-ы) *ж* verandah.

ве́рб|а (-ы) *ж* pussy willow.

верба́льный *прил* verbal.

верблю́д (-а) *м* camel.

верблю́диц|а (-ы) *ж см* **верблю́д**.

ве́рб|ный *прил*: ~**ое воскресе́нье** ≈ Palm Sunday.

верб|ова́ть (-у́ю; *perf* **завербова́ть)** *несов перех* to recruit.

вербо́в|ка (-ки; *gen pl* **-ок)** *ж* recruitment.

верди́кт (-а) *м* verdict; **выноси́ть (вы́нести** *perf*) **обвини́тельный/оправда́тельный ~** to pronounce a verdict of guilty/not guilty.

верёв|ка (-ки; *gen pl* **-ок)** *ж* (*толстая*) rope; (*тонкая*) string; (*для белья*) line; **вить** (*impf*) ~**ки из кого́-н** to twist sb round one's little finger.

ве́рен *прил см* **ве́рный**.

верени́ц|а (-ы) *ж* (*предметов*) line; (*людей*) file; (*перен: мыслей итп*) series.

ве́реск (-а) *м* heather.

верет|ено́ (-ена́; *nom pl* **-ёна)** *ср* spindle.

верещ|а́ть (-у́, -и́шь) *несов неперех* (*женщина*) to chatter.

верзи́л|а (-ы) *м/ж* (*разг*) beanpole.

вери́г|а (-и) *ж* (*обычно мн*) chain (*worn for religious reasons*).

вери́тельный *прил*: ~**ая гра́мота** credentials *мн*.

ве́р|ить (-ю, -ишь; *perf* **пове́рить)** *несов неперех* (+*dat*) to believe; (*доверять*) to trust; ~ (**пове́рить** *perf*) **в кого́-н/что-н** to believe *или* have faith in sb/sth; ~ (*impf*) **(в Бо́га)** to believe (in God); ~ (**пове́рить** *perf*) **на́ сло́во кому́-н** to take sb at his *итп* word; **я не ~ю свои́м**

глаза́м/уша́м I don't believe my eyes/ears
▶ **ве́риться** *несов безл:* **не ~ится, что э́то пра́вда** it's hard to believe it's true.
вермише́л|ь (-и) *ж* vermicelli.
ве́рмут (-а) *м* vermouth.
верне́е *вводн сл* or rather; **~ всего́** most likely.
вернисаж (-а) *м* private view (*of art exhibition etc*).
ве́рно *нареч* (*преданно*) faithfully; (*правильно*) correctly ♦ *как сказ* that's right ♦ *вводн сл* probably; **она́, ~, больна́** she must be *или* is probably ill.
верноло́дданн|ая (-ой; *decl like adj*) *ж см* **верноподданный**.
верноподданн|ый (-ого; *decl like adj*) *м* loyal subject.
ве́рност|ь (-и) *ж* (*преданность*) faithfulness, loyalty; (*правильность*) correctness; **для ~и** just to make sure.
верну́|ть (-у́, -ёшь) *сов перех* to return, give back; (*долг*) to pay back; (*здоровье, надежду итп*) to restore; **~** (*perf*) **кого́-н к действи́тельности** to bring sb back (down) to earth; **~** (*perf*) **кого́-н про́шлому** to take sb back
▶ **верну́ться** *сов возв:* **~ся (к +dat)** to return (to).
ве́рн|ый (-ен, -на́, -но) *прил* (*преданный*) faithful; (*надёжный*) sure; (*правильный*) correct; (*no short form*; *неизбежный*) certain; **~ сло́ву** true to one's word; **она́ верна́ само́й себе́** she acts true to herself.
ве́рование (-я) *ср* (*обычно мн*) belief.
ве́р|овать (-ую) *несов неперех* to believe (in God).
вероисповеда́ние (-я) *ср* faith.
вероло́мный (-ен, -на, -но) *прил* (*друг*) treacherous; (*нападение*) deceitful.
вероотсту́пник (-а) *м* apostate.
веротерпи́мост|ь (-и) *ж* (*РЕЛ*) tolerance.
вероуче́ние (-я) *ср* teachings *мн*.
вероя́тен *прил см* **вероя́тный**.
вероя́тно *как сказ* it is likely *или* probable ♦ *вводн сл* probably.
вероя́тност|ь (-и) *ж* probability; **по всей ~и** in all probability.
вероя́т|ный (-ен, -на, -но) *прил* likely, probable; **~нее всего́** most likely *или* probably.
ве́рси|я (-и) *ж* version.
верст|а́ (-ы́; *nom pl* **вёрсты**) *ж* verst (*former Russian unit of measurement equal to 1.06 km*); **ви́дно за ~у́** it is visible from a long way away.
верста́к (-а́) *м* (*ТЕХ*) (work)bench.
верста́|ть (-ю; *perf* **сверста́ть**) *несов перех* to set.
вёрстк|а (-и) *ж* (page)proof.
ве́ртел (-а; *nom pl* -а́) *м* spit (*for roasting*).
верт|е́ть (-чу́, -ишь) *несов перех* (*руль*) to turn; **~** (*impf*) +*instr* (*зонтиком, тростью*) to twirl;

как ни ~ти́, а он прав (*разг*) no matter which way you look at it, he's right; **~** (*impf*) **в рука́х что-н** to fiddle with sth
▶ **верте́|ться** *несов возв* (*колесо*) to spin; (*человек*) to fidget; (: *хлопотать*) to be kept busy; **~ся** (*impf*) **в голове́** (*разг*: *мысль*) to go round and round in one's head; **его́ и́мя ве́ртится у меня́ на языке́** his name is on the tip of my tongue; **~ся** (*impf*) **под нога́ми** (*разг*) to get *или* be under one's feet.
вертика́л|ьный (-ен, -ьна, -ьно) *прил* vertical.
вертихво́ст|ка (-ки; *gen pl* -ок) *ж* flirt.
вертолёт (-а) *м* helicopter.
вертолётчик (-а) *м* helicopter pilot.
верту́шк|а (-ки; *gen pl* -ек) *ж* revolving object; (*разг*: *о человеке*) featherbrain; **дверь-~** revolving door.
ве́рующ|ая (-ей; *decl like adj*) *ж см* **ве́рующий**.
ве́рующ|ий (-его; *decl like adj*) *м* believer.
верф|ь (-и) *ж* shipyard; (*военная*) dockyard.
верх (-а; *loc sg* -у́, *nom pl* -и́) *м* (*дома, стола*) top; (*экипажа, коляски*) hood; (*шубы*) outer layer; (*обуви*) upper; **~ соверше́нства/глу́пости** the height of perfection/stupidity; **оде́рживать** (**оде́ржать** *perf*) *или* **брать** (**взять** *perf*) **~ над кем-н** to get the upper hand over sb; *см также* **верхи́**.
верх|и́ (-о́в) *мн*: **в ~а́х** at the top; **встре́ча/ перегово́ры в ~а́х** summit meeting/talks.
ве́рхн|ий (-яя, -ее, -ие) *прил* top; **ве́рхняя оде́жда** outer clothing *или* garments *мн*.
верхо́вный *прил* (*главный*) supreme; **Верхо́вный Сове́т** Supreme Soviet; **Верхо́вный Суд** High Court (*BRIT*), Supreme Court (*US*).
верхов|о́й *прил*: **~а́я езда́** riding, horseback riding (*US*); **~а́я ло́шадь** mount.
верхо́вь|е (-я) *ср* upper reaches *мн*.
верхола́з (-а) *м* steeplejack.
верхо́м *нареч* astride; **~ на ло́шади** on horseback.
верху́шк|а (-ки; *gen pl* -ек) *ж* (*дерева, насыпи*) top; (*перен*: *правящая*) elite.
верчу́(сь) *несов см* **верте́ть(ся)**.
верши́н|а (-ы) *ж* (*холма, дерева*) top; (*горы*) summit, peak; **на ~е сла́вы** at the height of his *итп* fame; **на ~е сча́стья** in seventh heaven.
верш|и́ть (-у́, -и́шь) *несов перех* (*суд*) to conduct ♦ *неперех*: **~** +*instr* (*судьбами*) to control.
вес (-а; *part gen* -у, *nom pl* -а́) *м* weight; (*перен*: *влияние*) authority; **ве́сом в 5 килогра́мм** weighing 5 kilogrammes; **закрепля́ть** (**закрепи́ть** *perf*) **что-н на ~у́** to suspend sth; **прибавля́ть** (**приба́вить** *perf*) **в ве́се** to put on weight; **бо́рец лёгкого/тяжёлого ве́са** light-/heavyweight wrestler; **цени́ться** (*impf*) *или* **быть** (*impf*) **на ~ зо́лота** to be worth one's weight in

gold.

ве́сел *прил см* **весёлый**.

ве́сел *сущ см* **весло́**.

веселе́ть (-ю; *perf* **повеселе́ть**) *несов неперех* to cheer up.

весели́ть (-ю́, -и́шь; *perf* **развесели́ть**) *несов перех* to amuse.

▸ **весели́ться** *несов возв* to have fun.

ве́село *нареч* (*сказать*) cheerfully ♦ *как сказ*: **здесь ~** it's fun here; **мне ~** I'm having fun.

весёлый (-ел, -ла́, -ло) *прил* cheerful.

весе́лье (-я) *ср* (*настроение*) cheerfulness; (*времяпровождение*) merriment.

весе́нний (-яя, -ее, -ие) *прил* spring *опред*.

ве́сить (-шу, -сишь) *несов неперех* to weigh.

ве́ский (-кая, -кое, -кие; -ок, -ка, -ко) *прил*: **~ аргуме́нт** an argument that carries a lot of weight.

весло́ (-а́; *nom pl* **вёсла**, *gen pl* **вёсел**) *ср* oar.

весна́ (-ы́; *nom pl* **вёсны**, *gen pl* **вёсен**) *ж* spring.

весно́й *нареч* in (the) spring.

весно́ю *нареч* = **весно́й**.

весну́шка (-ки; *gen pl* **-ек**) *ж* (*обычно мн*) freckle.

весово́й *прил* (*хлеб, конфеты итп*) *sold or bought by weight*; **весова́я катего́рия** (weight) category (*in boxing etc*).

ве́сок *прил см* **ве́ский**.

весо́мый (-, -а, -о) *прил* (*перен*) substantial.

вест (-а) *м* (*МОР*) west; (*ветер*) west wind.

ве́стерн (-а) *м* western.

вести́ (-ду́, -дёшь; *pt* **вёл**, **-ла́**, **-ло́**) *несов перех* to take; (*машину, поезд*) to drive; (*корабль*) to navigate; (*войско, отряд*) to lead; (*собрание, заседание*) to chair; (*работу, исследования*) to conduct; (*хозяйство*) to run; (*дневник, записи*) to keep ♦ (*perf* **привести́**) *неперех*: **~ к** +*dat* to lead to; **~** (*impf*) **себя́** to behave; **~** (*impf*) **речь о** +*prp* to talk about; **~** (*impf*) **нача́ло от** +*gen* to originate from

▸ **вести́сь** *несов возв* (*расследование*) to be carried out; (*переговоры*) to go on.

вестибю́ль (-я) *м* (*в гостинице*) lobby; (*в метро*) entrance hall.

ве́стник (-а) *м* messenger; (*перен*) herald; (*издание*) bulletin.

весть (-и) *ж* news; **пропада́ть** (**пропа́сть** *perf*) **без ~и** (*ВОЕН*) to go missing; **без ~и пропа́вший** (*ВОЕН*) missing feared dead; **Бог ~ кто/что** (*разг*) God knows who/what; **была́ не Бог ~ кака́я** (*разг*) the play wasn't up to much.

весы́ (-о́в) *мн* scales *мн*; (*созвездие*): **В~** Libra.

весь (*всего́*; *см* **Table 13**; *f* **вся**, *nt* **всё**, *pl* **все**) *мест* (*целый, полностью*) all; **~ день** all day; **я стара́лась изо всех сил** I tried with all my might; **он появи́лся ~ мо́крый/гря́зный** he appeared all wet/dirty; **при всём жела́нии я не смогу́ тебе́ помо́чь** with the best will in the world, I can't help you; **всего́ хоро́шего** *или* **до́брого!** all the best!; **без всего́** with nothing;

по всему́ (*по всем признакам*) by all the signs.

весьма́ *нареч* quite; **~ непло́хо** not bad.

ветвь (-и; *gen pl* **-е́й**) *ж* branch.

ве́тер (-ра) *м* wind; **каки́м ~ром его́ сюда́ занесло́?** (*разг*) what brought him here?; **у него́ ~ в голове́** (*разг*) he hasn't a serious thought in his head.

ветера́н (-а) *м* veteran.

ветерина́р (-а) *м* vet (*inf*) (= *veterinary surgeon,*) veterinarian (*US*).

ве́тка (-ки; *gen pl* **-ок**) *ж* branch; **железнодоро́жная ве́тка** branch line.

ве́то *ср нескл* veto; **накла́дывать** (**наложи́ть** *perf*) **~ на что-н** to veto sth.

ве́ток *сущ см* **ве́тка**.

ве́тра *сущ см* **ве́тер**.

ве́треный *прил* windy; (*девушка*) empty-headed.

ветро́вка (-и) *ж* windcheater.

ветрово́й *прил* wind *опред*; **ветрово́е стекло́** windscreen (*BRIT*), windshield (*US*).

ветря́нка (-ки) *ж* (*МЕД*) chickenpox.

ветряно́й *прил* (*двигатель*) wind-powered; **~áя ме́льница** windmill.

ве́тхий (-ая, -ое, -ие; -, -á, -о) *прил* (*старик*) decrepit; (*дом*) dilapidated; (*одежда*) shabby; **Ве́тхий Заве́т** the Old Testament.

ветхозаве́тный *прил* Old Testament *опред*; (*перен*) antediluvian.

ветчина́ (-ины́; *nom pl* **-и́ны**) *ж* ham.

ве́ха (-и) *ж* (*обычно мн*) landmark.

ве́че (-а) *ср* (*ИСТ*) *town assembly in medieval Russia.*

ве́чен *прил см* **ве́чный**.

ве́чер (-а; *nom pl* **-á**) *м* evening; (*праздник*) party; **на ~е** at a party.

вечере́ть (*3sg* **-ет**) *несов безл* to grow dark.

вечери́нка (-ки; *gen pl* **-ок**) *ж* party.

вече́рний (-яя, -ее, -ие) *прил* evening *опред*; **~ие ку́рсы** evening classes.

вече́рник (-а) *м* (*разг*) part-timer (*studying in the evening*).

ве́чером *нареч* in the evening.

ве́чно *нареч* eternally; (*разг: жаловаться*) perpetually.

вечнозелёный *прил* evergreen.

ве́чность (-и) *ж* eternity; **не ви́дел тебя́ це́лую ~** (*разг*) I haven't seen you for ages.

ве́чный (-ен, -на, -но) *прил* eternal, everlasting; (*бессрочный*) indefinite; (*no short form*; *разг: непрестанный*) perpetual; **ве́чная мерзлота́** permafrost; **ве́чные снега́** everlasting snows.

ве́шалка (-ки; *gen pl* **-ок**) *ж* (*планка*) rack; (*стойка*) hatstand; (*плечики*) coat hanger; (*гардероб*) cloakroom; (*петля*) loop.

ве́шать (-ю; *perf* **пове́сить**) *несов перех* to hang; (*perf* **све́шать**; *товар*) to weigh; **~** (**пове́сить** *perf*) **го́лову** to look downcast.

▸ **ве́шаться** (*perf* **пове́ситься**) *несов возв* to hang o.s.; **~ся** (*impf*) **на ше́ю кому́-н** (*разг: пренебр*) to throw o.s. at sb.

вéшу *несов см* **вéсить.**

вещá|ть (*3sg* -ет, *3pl* -ют) *несов неперех* to broadcast; ~ (*impf*) **на Москвý** to broadcast to Moscow.

вещéственный *прил* material; **вещéственное доказáтельство** material evidence.

вещество́ (-á) *ср* substance.

вéщ|ий (-ая, -ее, -ие) *прил* prophetic.

вещь (-и; *gen pl* -éй) *ж* thing; (*книга, фильм*) piece; **онá остáвила вéщи в машине** she left her things in the car; **называ́ть (назвáть** *perf*) **вéщи свои́ми имена́ми** to call a spade a spade.

вéяни|е (-я) *ср* breath; (*перен: в искусстве*) trend.

вé|ять (-ю, -ешь) *несов неперех* (*ветер*) to blow lightly; (*флаг, парус*) to flutter; **в во́здухе ~ет весно́й** spring is in the air.

вжи́|ться (-ву́сь, -вёшься; *pt* -лся, -лáсь, -ло́сь, *impf* **вжива́ться**) *сов возв*: ~ **в роль** to get into a role.

взад *нареч*: ~**вперёд** (*разг*) back and forth; **он не дви́гался ни ~ ни вперёд** he didn't budge (an inch).

взаи́мен *прил см* **взаи́мный.**

взаи́мность (-и) *ж* mutual feeling; **любо́вь без ~и** unrequited love; **отвеча́ть** (*impf*) **кому́-н ~ю** to reciprocate sb's feelings; **по́льзоваться** (*impf*) ~**ю** to be loved in return.

взаи́м|ный (-ен, -на, -но) *прил* mutual.

взаимовы́руч|ка (-ки; *gen pl* -ек) *ж* team spirit.

взаимоде́йстви|е (-я) *ср* (*связь*) interaction; (*поддержка*) cooperation.

взаимообусло́вленность (-и) *ж* interdependence.

взаимоотноше́ни|е (-я) *ср* (*обычно мн*) (inter) relationship.

взаимопо́мощь (-и) *ж* mutual assistance *или* aid.

взаимопонима́ни|е (-я) *ср* mutual understanding; **достига́ть (дости́гнуть** *или* **дости́чь** *perf*) ~**я** to come to *или* reach a mutual understanding.

взаимосвя́зь (-и) *ж* interconnection.

взаймы́ *нареч*: **дава́ть/брать де́ньги** ~ to lend/ borrow money.

взаме́н *нареч* in exchange ◆ *предл* (+*gen*; *вместо*) instead of; (*в обмен*) in exchange for; **он ничего́ не про́сит** ~ he doesn't want anything in return.

взаперти́ *нареч* under lock and key; **сиде́ть** (*impf*) ~ (*перен*) to stay indoors.

взахлёб *нареч* (*разг*) eagerly; ~ **хвали́ть** (*impf*) **что-н** to gush over sth.

взбодри́|ть (-ю) *несов от* **взбодри́ть.**

взба́лмошн|ый (-ен, -на, -но) *прил* (*разг*) hysterical.

взба́лтыва|ть (-ю) *несов перех от* **взболта́ть.**

взбе́й(те) *сов см* **взбить.**

взберу́сь *сов см* **взобра́ться.**

взбе|си́ть(ся) (-шу́(сь), -сишь(ся)) *сов от* **беси́ть(ся).**

взбива́|ть (-ю) *несов от* **взбить.**

взбира́|ться (-юсь) *несов от* **взобра́ться.**

взбить (**взобью́, взобьёшь**; *imper* **взбей(те)**) *сов перех* (*яйца*) to beat; (*сливки*) to whip; (*волосы*) to fluff up; (*подушки*) to plump up.

взбодри́|ть (-ю, -и́шь; *impf* **взба́дривать**) *сов перех* (*эмоционально*) to hearten, cheer; (*физически*) to invigorate.

взболта́|ть (-ю; *impf* **взба́лтывать**) *сов перех* to shake.

взбре|сти́ (-ду́, -дёшь; *pt* **взбрёл, -лá, -ло́**) *сов неперех*: ~ **нá гору** to slog up a hill; **ему́ ~ло́ в го́лову** +*infin* ... (*разг*) he took it into his head to ....

взбудора́ж|ить (-у, -ишь; *impf* **взбудора́живать** *или* **будора́жить**) *сов перех* to agitate.

взбунт|ова́ться (-у́ю(сь)) *сов возв* to rebel.

взбу́ч|ка (-ки; *gen pl* -ек) *ж* (*разг*) dressing-down.

взвал|и́ть (-ю́, -ишь; *impf* **взва́ливать**) *сов перех*: ~ **что-н на** +*acc* to haul sth up onto; **взва́ливать** (~ *perf*) **отве́тственность на кого́-н** (*перен: разг*) to burden sb with responsibility.

взведу́ *итп сов см* **взвести́.**

взвёл *сов см* **взвести́.**

взве́|сить (-шу, -сишь; *impf* **взве́шивать**) *сов перех* (*товар*) to weigh; (*перен: факты*) to weigh up, consider.

взве|сти́ (-ду́, -дёшь; *pt* **взвёл, -лá, -ло́**, *impf* **взводи́ть**) *сов перех*: **взводи́ть куро́к** to cock a gun.

взве́шен|ный (-, -на, -но) *прил* (*обдуманный*) considered; **во ~ном состоя́нии** (*перен: разг*) in suspense.

взве́шива|ть (-ю) *несов от* **взве́сить.**

взве́шу *сов см* **взве́сить.**

взвива́|ться (-юсь) *несов от* **взви́ться.**

взви́згн|уть (-у, -ешь; *impf* **взви́згивать**) *сов неперех* to let out a squeal.

взвин|ти́ть (-чу́, -ти́шь; *impf* **взви́нчивать**) *сов перех* (*разг: цены*) to jack up.

взви́нчен|ный (-, -на, -но) *прил* (*состояние*) agitated; **он взви́нчен** he is worked up.

взв|и́ться (-овью́сь, -овьёшься; *impf* **взвива́ться**) *сов возв* to shoot up; (*перен*) to fly off the handle.

взвод (-а) *м* platoon; **на взво́де** (*курок*) cocked; (*разг: человек*) on edge.

взво|ди́ть (-жу́, -ди́шь) *несов от* **взвести́.**

взволно́ван|ный (-, -на, -но) *прил* (*в тревоге*) agitated; (*радостный*) excited.

взволн|ова́ть(ся) (-у́ю(сь)) *сов от* **волнова́ть(ся).**

взв|ыть (-о́ю, -о́ешь) *сов неперех* (*животное,*

челове́к) to howl; (сире́на) to wail; ~ (perf) **от бо́ли** to howl in или with pain.

взгляд (-а) м glance; (выраже́ние) look; (перен: мне́ние) view; **с пе́рвого взгля́да, на пе́рвый** ~ at first sight или glance; **обме́ниваться (обменя́ться** perf) **взгля́дами** to exchange glances; **на мой/твой** ~ in my/your view; **остана́вливать (останови́ть** perf) ~ **на** +acc to rest one's gaze on.

взгляну́ть (-у́, -ешь; impf **взгля́дывать)** сов непе́рех: ~ **на** +acc to look at; (кра́тко) to glance at; (no impf; обрати́ть внима́ние) to look at.

взгромозди́ть (-жу́, -ди́шь; impf **взгроможда́ть)** сов перех: ~ **(на** +prp) to haul up (onto).

взгрустну́ться (3sg -ётся) сов безл (+dat; разг) to feel sad.

вздёрну́ть (-у, -ешь; impf **вздёргивать)** сов перех to jerk up; (ру́ку) to throw up; ~ (perf) **кого́-н на ви́селицу** (разг) to string sb up.

вздор (-а) (разг) rubbish; **нести́** (impf) или **моло́ть** (impf) ~ (разг) to talk rubbish.

вздо́рен прил см **вздо́рный**.

вздо́рить (-ю, -ишь; perf **повздо́рить)** несо́в непе́рех to squabble.

вздо́рн|ый (-ен, -на, -но) прил (неле́пый) absurd; (сварли́вый) crotchety.

вздорожа́|ть (-ю) сов от **дорожа́ть**.

вздох (-а) м (облегче́ния итп) sigh; (у́жаса) gasp.

вздохну́ть (-у́, -нёшь; сов непе́рех to sigh; (разг: отдохну́ть) to have a breather; **мне** ~ **не́когда** I'm rushed off my feet.

вздра́гива|ть (-ю) несо́в от **вздро́гнуть**.

вздремну́ть (-у́, -ёшь; сов непе́рех (разг) to have a nap или snooze.

вздро́гну|ть (-у, -ешь) сов непе́рех to shudder.

вздува́|ться (-юсь) несо́в от **вздуться**.

вздума|ть (-ю) сов непе́рех (разг): **он** ~**л заня́ться ру́сским языко́м** he took it into his head to learn Russian; **не** ~**йте лгать!** don't even think of lying!

вздуть (-ю, -ешь) сов перех (разг: це́ны) to inflate; **у него́ вздуло живо́т** his stomach became bloated

▶ **вздуться** (impf **вздува́ться)** сов возв (щека, живо́т) to swell up; (разг: це́ны) to shoot up.

вздыма́|ться (3sg -ется, 3pl -ются) несо́в возв (грудь) to heave; (во́лны) to rise.

вздыха́|ть (-ю) несо́в непе́рех to sigh; (тоскова́ть): ~ **о** +prp (о мо́лодости) to yearn for; ~ (impf) **по** +dat to pine for.

взима́ни|е (-я) ср collecting.

взима́|ть (-ю) несо́в перех to collect.

взла́мыва|ть (-ю) несо́в от **взлома́ть**.

взлеле́|ять (-ю) сов от **леле́ять**.

взлёт (-а) м (самолёта) takeoff; (перен: мы́сли) flight.

взле|те́ть (-чу́, -ти́шь; impf **взлета́ть)** сов непе́рех (пти́ца) to soar; (самолёт) to take off;

взлета́ть (~ perf) **на во́здух** to explode.

взлётно-поса́дочн|ый прил: **взлётно-поса́дочная полоса́** runway.

взлётн|ый прил: ~**ая полоса́** или **доро́жка** runway, airstrip.

взлечу́ сов см **взлете́ть**.

взлома́|ть (-ю; impf **взла́мывать)** сов перех to break open, force.

взло́мщик (-а) м burglar.

взлохма́|тить (-чу, -тишь) сов от **лохма́тить**.

взма́лива|ться (-юсь) несо́в от **взмоли́ться**.

взмахну́ть (-у́, -ёшь; impf **взма́хивать)** сов непе́рех (+instr; руко́й) to wave; (крыло́м) to flap.

взметну́ться (-у́сь, -ёшься) сов возв (пыль, и́скры) to fly up; (пла́мя, конь) to leap up.

взмоли́|ться (-ю́сь, -ишься; impf **взма́ливаться)** сов возв to beg.

взмо́рь|е (-я) ср seashore.

взму|ти́ть (-чу́, -ти́шь) сов от **мути́ть**.

взмы|ть (-ю, -ёшь; impf **взмыва́ть)** сов непе́рех to soar.

взнос (-а) м (страхово́й) payment; (в фонд) contribution; (чле́нский, вступи́тельный) fee; **ежеме́сячный** ~ monthly instalment.

взобра́|ться (взберу́сь, взберёшься; pt -лся, -ла́сь, -ло́сь, impf **взбира́ться)** сов возв: ~ **на** +acc to climb (up) onto; **взбира́ться** (~ perf) **на́ гору** to climb (up) a hill.

взобью́ итп сов см **взбить**.

взовью́сь итп сов см **взви́ться**.

взойти́ (как **идти́**; см Table 18; impf **всходи́ть** или **восходи́ть)** сов непе́рех (со́лнце, луна́) to rise; (семена́) to come up; (на го́ру, на престо́л) to ascend.

взор (-а) м glance; (выраже́ние) look.

взорва́|ть (-у́, -ёшь; pt -а́л, -ала́, -а́ло, impf **взрыва́ть)** сов перех (бо́мбу) to detonate; (дом, мост) to blow up

▶ **взорва́ться** (impf **взрыва́ться)** сов возв (грана́та, бо́мба) to explode; (мост, дом) to be blown up; (разг: не сдержа́ться) to blow up.

взошёл итп сов см **взойти́**.

взрасти́ть (-щу́, -сти́шь; impf **взра́щивать)** сов перех to cultivate, grow; (перен) to nurture.

взреве́ть (-у́, -ёшь) сов непе́рех to roar.

взро́сл|ая (-ой; decl like adj) ж см **взро́слый**.

взросле́|ть (-ю; perf **повзросле́ть)** несо́в непе́рех to grow up; (духо́вно) to mature.

взро́сл|ый прил (челове́к) grown-up опред; (фильм, биле́т, живо́тное) adult опред ♦ (-ого; decl like adj) м adult.

взрыв (-а) м explosion; (до́ма) blowing up; (+gen; возмуще́ния) outburst of; **разда́лся** ~ there was an explosion; ~ **сме́ха** a burst of laughter.

взрыва́|ть(ся) (-ю(сь)) несо́в от **взорва́ть(ся)**.

взрывно́й прил: ~**а́я волна́** blast.

взрывоопа́сн|ый (-ен, -на, -но) прил (та́кже перен) explosive.

взрывча́т|ка (-ки; gen pl -ок) ж explosive

(substance); **закла́дывать (заложи́ть** *perf)* **~ку** to plant an explosive.

взры́вчатый *прил* explosive.

взрыхл|и́ть (-ю, -и́шь) *сов от* **рыхли́ть ♦** *(impf* **взрыхля́ть)** *перех* to break up.

взъеро́ш|ить (-ю, -ишь) *сов от* **еро́шить**.

взыва́|ть (-ю; *perf* **воззва́ть)** *несов неперех:* **~ к кому́-н о** +*prp* to appeal to sb for; **~ (воззва́ть** *perf)* **к чьему́-н милосе́рдию/ра́зуму** to appeal to sb's sense of compassion/reason.

взыска́ни|е (-я) *ср (долга)* recovery; *(штрафа)* exaction; *(выговор)* reprimand; **накла́дывать (наложи́ть** *perf)* **~ на кого́-н** to reprimand sb.

взыска́тел|ьный (-ен, -ьна, -ьно) *прил (публика)* demanding; *(начальник)* exacting; *(критика)* severe.

взы́|ска́ть (-щу́, -щешь; *impf* **взы́скивать)** *сов перех (долга)* to recover; *(штраф)* to exact ♦ *неперех:* **~ с кого́-н** to call sb to account; **не ~щи́те!** I'm sorry!

взя́ти|е (-я) *ср (власти, территории)* seizure; *(города, крепости)* capture.

взя́т|ка (-ки; *gen pl* **-ок)** *ж (подкуп)* bribe; *(карты)* trick; **дава́ть (дать** *perf)* **кому́-н ~ку** to bribe sb; **брать** *(impf)* **~ку** to take a bribe.

взя́точник (-а) *м* bribe-taker.

взя́точниц|а (-ы) *ж см* **взя́точник**.

взя|ть (возьму́, возьмёшь; *pt* **-л, -ла́, -ло)** *сов от* **брать ♦** *перех (разг)* to nick; **возьму́ и или да и откажу́сь** *(разг)* I could refuse just like that; **~л да и пое́хал** *(разг)* he upped and left; **~ или возьми́те хотя́ бы тако́й приме́р** let's take this example; **с чего́ или отку́да ты ~л** *(разг: пренебр)* whatever gave you that idea?

▶ **взя́|ться** *сов от* **бра́ться ♦** *возв:* **отку́да ни возьми́сь, появи́лась Ма́ша** Masha appeared from out of the blue *или* as if from nowhere.

вибри́р|овать (-ую) *несов неперех* to vibrate.

вивисе́кци|я (-и) *ж* vivisection.

вид (-а; *part gen* **-у,** *loc sg* **-у́)** *м (внешность)* appearance; *(состояние: предмета)* form; *(панорама)* view; *(разновидность: растений, животных)* species; *(: спорта)* type; *(: искусства)* form; *(линг)* aspect; *(состояние):* **у него́ больно́й/серди́тый ~** he looks ill/angry; **в ви́де** +*gen* in the form of; **на ~у́** +*gen* in full view of; **под ви́дом** +*gen* in the guise of; **~ на о́зеро/го́ры/пло́щадь** a view of the lake/hills/square; **в ви́де шу́тки** as a joke; **име́ть** *(impf)* **в ~у́** to mean; *(учитывать)* to bear in mind; **скрыва́ться (скры́ться** *perf)***/исчеза́ть (исче́знуть** *perf)* **из ви́да** to hide/disappear from view; **де́лать (сде́лать** *perf)* **~** to pretend; **упуска́ть (упусти́ть** *perf)* **из ви́ду что-н** *(перен)* to lose sight of sth; **теря́ть (потеря́ть** *perf)* **кого́-н из ви́ду** to lose sight of sb; **вид на жи́тельство** residence permit; *см также* **ви́ды**.

вида́|ть (-ю; *perf* **повида́ть)** *несов перех* to see;

(испыта́ть) to know ♦ *вводн сл* obviously; **где э́то ви́дано!** *(разг)* whatever next!

▶ **вида́|ться** *(perf* **повида́ться)** *несов возв (разг)* to see each other.

ви́ден *прил см* **ви́дный**.

ви́дени|е (-я) *ср* vision.

виде́ни|е (-я) *ср (во сне)* vision; *(призрак)* apparition.

видеоза́пис|ь (-и) *ж* video (recording).

видеоигр|а́ (-ы́; *nom pl* **-ы)** *ж* video game.

видеока́мер|а (-ы) *ж* camcorder, videocamera.

видеокассе́т|а (-ы) *ж* video cassette.

видеомагнитофо́н (-а) *м* video (recorder).

видеоплёнк|а (-ки; *gen pl* **-ок)** *ж* (video) tape.

видеофи́льм (-а) *м* video (film).

ви́|деть (-жу, -дишь) *несов перех* to see ♦ *(perf* **уви́деть)** *перех* to see; *(испыта́ть)* to know; **рад Вас ~** it's good to see you; **~дите ли** you see; **(там) уви́дим** *(разг)* we'll see

▶ **ви́|деться** *несов от* **привиде́ться ♦** *(perf* **уви́деться)** *возв* to see each other; **вы́ход ~дится в эконо́мии сре́дств** economizing is viewed as the solution; **мы с ним ча́сто ~димся** we see a lot of each other.

ви́димо *вводн сл* it looks like; **он, ~, не придёт** it looks like he's not coming.

ви́димо-неви́димо *нареч (разг):* **наро́ду на пло́щади ~** there are masses of people in the square.

ви́димост|ь (-и) *ж* visibility; *(подобие)* outward appearance; **по всей ~и** seemingly; **для ~и** for the sake of appearances.

ви́дим|ый (-, -а, -о) *прил* visible; *(no short form; кажущийся)* superficial; **~ э́кспорт/и́мпорт** visible exports/imports *мн*.

видне́|ться (3sg -ется, 3pl -ются) *несов возв* to be visible.

ви́дно *как сказ (можно ви́деть)* one can see; *(можно поня́ть)* clearly ♦ *вводн сл* probably; **из окна́ ~ го́ры** you can see the hills from the window; **~, что он волну́ется** clearly he is worried; **~, он уста́л** he is probably tired; **тебе́ видне́е** you know best; **как ~** as it happens; **там ~ бу́дет** we'll see.

ви́дн|ый (-ен, -на́, -но, -ны́) *прил (заме́тный)* visible; *(no short form; изве́стный)* prominent; *(привлека́тельный):* **он ~ мужчи́на** he's a fine figure of a man; **~ен успе́х** success is in sight.

видоизмен|и́ть (-ю́, -и́шь; *impf* **видоизменя́ть)** *сов перех* to modify

▶ **видоизмени́|ться** *(impf* **видоизменя́ться)** *сов возв* to alter.

ви́д|ы (-ов) *мн* prospects *мн*; **име́ть** *(impf)* **~ на что-н** to have one's sights set on sth.

ви́жу(сь) *несов см* **ви́деть(ся)**.

ви́з|а (-ы) *ж* visa; *(дире́ктора, реда́ктора)* official stamp.

византи́йск|ий (-ая, -ое, -ие) *ж* Byzantine.

Византи́|я (-и) ж Byzantine Empire.
визг (-а) м (*собаки*) yelp; (*ребёнка, поросёнка*) squeal; (*человека*) shriek; (*металла, тормозов итп*) screech.
визж|а́ть (-у́, -и́шь) *несов неперех* (см *сущ*) to yelp; to squeal; to shriek; to screech.
визи́р|овать (-ую; *perf* завизи́ровать) *несов перех* (*документ*) to stamp; **ему́ ~ова́ли па́спорт** he was issued with a visa.
визи́т (-а) м visit; **прибыва́ть (прибы́ть** *perf*) **с ~ом** to arrive on an official visit; **де́лать (сде́лать** *perf*) **или наноси́ть (нанести́** *perf*) ~ **кому́-н** to visit sb.
визи́тн|ый *прил*: ~ая ка́рточка (business) card.
визуа́л|ьный (-ен, -ьна, -ьно) *прил* visual.
вика́ри|й (-я) м vicar.
виктори́н|а (-ы) ж quiz game.
ви́л|ка (-ки; *gen pl* -ок) ж fork; **ште́псельная ~** two-pin plug.
ви́лл|а (-ы) ж villa.
ви́лок *сущ см* ви́лка.
ви́л|ы (-) *мн* pitchfork *ед*; ~ами на воде́ пи́сано (*разг*) it's pie in the sky.
вильн|у́ть (-у́, -ёшь) *сов неперех*: ~ +*instr* (*хвостом*) to wag; (*бёдрами*) to wiggle; (*дорога, река итп*) to bend sharply.
Ви́льнюс (-а) м Vilnius.
виля́|ть (-ю) *несов неперех*: ~ +*instr* (*хвостом*) to wag; (*бёдрами*) to wiggle; (*дорога, река итп*) to wind (along); (*перен: разг: человек*) to be shifty.
вин|а́ (-ы́; *nom pl* -ы) м (*чувство*) guilt; (*ответственность*) blame; **возлага́ть (возложи́ть** *perf*) ~у́ **на** +*acc* to place the blame on; **ава́рия произошла́ по его́ ~е** the accident was his fault, he was to blame for the accident.
винегре́т (-а) м beetroot salad.
вини́тельный *прил*: ~ паде́ж accusative (case).
вини́|ть (-ю, -ишь) *несов перех*: ~ **кого́-н в** +*prp* to blame sb for; (*упрекать*): ~ **кого́-н за** +*acc* to accuse sb of.
вин|о́ (-а́; *nom pl* -а) *ср* wine.
винова́т|ый *прил* (*взгляд итп*) guilty; (-, -а, -о): ~ (**в** +*prp*) (*в проигрыше, неудаче*) responsible (for), to blame (for); ~! sorry!, excuse me!; **чу́вствовать** (*impf*) **себя́ ~ым** to feel guilty; **он винова́т пе́ред дру́гом** he has failed his friend; **он винова́т в том, что ...** it is his fault that ....
вино́вен *прил см* вино́вный.
вино́вн|ая (-ой; *decl like adj*) ж см вино́вный.
вино́вник (-а) м culprit; **он – ~ траге́дии** he is to blame for the tragedy.
вино́вниц|а (-ы) ж см вино́вник.
вино́вность (-и) ж guilt; **устана́вливать (установи́ть** *perf*) ~ to establish guilt.
вино́вн|ый (-ен, -на, -но) *прил* guilty ◆ (-ного; *decl like adj*) м guilty party; **признава́ть (призна́ть** *perf*) **себя́ ~ым** to plead guilty.
виногра́д (-а) м (*растение*) (grape)vine; (*ягоды*) grapes *мн*.
виногра́дник (-а) м vineyard.

виноде́ли|е (-я) *ср* wine-making.
винт (-а́) м screw; (*самолёта*) propeller.
ви́нтик (-а) м screw.
винто́в|ка (-ки; *gen pl* -ок) ж rifle.
виньéт|ка (-ки; *gen pl* -ок) ж vignette.
вио́л|а (-ы) ж (*МУЗ*) viol.
виолончели́ст (-а) м cellist.
виолончели́ст|ка (-ки; *gen pl* -ок) ж см виолончели́ст.
виолонче́л|ь (-и) ж cello.
ви́ра *межд*: ~! lift!
вира́ж (-а́) м (*поворот*) turn; (*СПОРТ*) bend.
виртуа́льный *прил* (*КОМП*) virtual.
виртуо́з (-а) м virtuoso.
виртуо́зн|ый (-ен, -на, -но) *прил* masterly; ~ное исполне́ние a virtuoso performance.
ви́рус (-а) м virus.
вис *сущ см несов см* ви́снуть.
ви́селиц|а (-ы) ж gallows *ед*.
висе́ть (-шу́, -сишь) *несов неперех* to hang; (*угрожать*): ~ **над** +*instr* to hang over; ~ (*impf*) **в во́здухе** (*перен*) to be up in the air; **у него́ на ше́е ~ся́т ро́дственники жены́** (*разг*) his wife's relatives are a burden to him; ~ (*impf*) **на телефо́не** (*разг*) to spend ages on the phone.
виска́ *сущ см* висо́к.
ви́ски *ср нескл* whisky (*BRIT*), whiskey (*US, IRELAND*).
виско́з|а (-ы) ж viscose.
Ви́сл|а (-ы) ж Vistula (*river*).
ви́с|нуть (-ну, -нешь; *pt* -, -ла, -ло, *perf* пови́снуть) *несов неперех* (*цветы*) to droop; (*волосы*) to hang limply; ~ (*impf*) **у кого́-н на ше́е** (*перен*) to cling to sb.
висо́к (-ка́) м (*АНАТ*) temple.
високо́сный *прил*: ~ год leap year.
вист (-а) м whist.
вися́ч|ий (-ая, -ее, -ие) *прил*: ~ мост suspension bridge; **закрепля́ть (закрепи́ть** *perf*) **что-н в ~ем положе́нии** to suspend sth.
витами́н (-а) м vitamin.
вита́|ть (-ю) *несов неперех* (*запах*) to hang in the air; ~ *perf* **над** +*instr* (*опасность, смерть*) to hang или hover over; ~ (*impf*) **в облака́х** (*перен*) to have one's head in the clouds.
витиева́т|ый (-, -а, -о) *прил* flowery.
витка́ *сущ см* вито́к.
вито́й *прил* twisted; (*лестница*) spiral.
вито́к (-ка́) м (*спирали*) twist; (*перен: этап*) stage.
витра́ж (-а́) м stained-glass window.
витри́н|а (-ы) ж (*в магазине*) shop window; (*в музее*) display case.
витри́нно-вы́ставочн|ый *прил*: ~ая рекла́ма display advertising.
ви|ть (вью, вьёшь; *pt* -л, -ла́, -ло, *imper* вей(те), *perf* свить) *несов перех* (*венок, верёвку*) to weave; (*гнездо*) to build
▶ **ви́ться** *несов возв* (*растения*) to trail; (*волосы*) to curl; (*флаг, лента*) to flutter; (*дым*) to spiral up.
вихо́р (-ра́) м forelock.

вихр|ь (-я) *м* whirlwind; (*перен: революции*) maelstrom; (: *развлечений*) whirl.

ви́це-председа́тел|ь (-я) *м* vice-chairman.

ви́це-президе́нт (-а) *м* vice president.

ВИЧ *м сокр* (= *ви́рус иммунодефици́та челове́ка*) HIV (= *human immunodeficiency virus*); **~-инфици́рованный** HIV-positive.

ви́шен *сущ см* **ви́шня**.

вишнёвый *прил* cherry.

ви́шн|я (-ни; *gen pl* -ен) *ж* (*дерево*) cherry (tree); (*плод*) cherry.

вишу́ *несов см* **висе́ть**.

вишь *част* (*разг*) (just) look (*used sarcastically*); ~ **(ты), како́й он сме́лый** look how brave he is, what a hero.

вка́лыва|ть (-ю) *несов от* **вколо́ть** ♦ *неперех* (*no perf*; *разг*) to slog.

вка́пыва|ть (-ю) *несов от* **вкопа́ть**.

вкати́|ть (-чу́, -тишь; *impf* **вка́тывать**) *сов перех* (*тачку, коля́ску*) to wheel in; (*бочку*) to roll in; (*перен: разг*): ~ **кому́-н пощёчину/вы́говор** to give sb a slap across the face/a dressing-down.

вклад (-а) *м* (*действие*) investment; (*в банке*) deposit; (*в науку, в литерату́ру*) contribution; **вноси́ть** (**внести́** *perf*) ~ **в** +*acc* to make a contribution to.

вкла́дчик (-а) *м* investor.

вкла́дчиц|а (-ы) *ж см* **вкла́дчик**.

вкла́дыва|ть (-ю) *несов от* **вложи́ть**.

вкла́дыш (-а) *м* (*в книге, в альбоме*) insert; (*в детали*) inlay.

включа́|ть (-ю) *несов от* **включи́ть** ♦ *перех*: ~ **(в себя́)** to include

► **включа́ться** *несов от* **включи́ться**.

включа́|я *предл* (+*acc*) including; **пришли́ все ~ дире́ктора** everybody came including the director.

включи́тельно *нареч* inclusive; **с 1-го по 5-ое ма́я ~** from (the) 1st to (the) 5th of May inclusive.

включ|и́ть (-у́, -и́шь; *impf* **включа́ть**) *сов перех* to turn *или* switch on; **включа́ть** (~ *perf*) **кого́-н в что-н** to include sb in sth

► **включи́ться** (*impf* **включа́ться**) *сов возв* to come on; (*присоедини́ться*): ~**ся в** +*acc* to join in.

вколо́|ть (-ю́, -ешь; *impf* **вка́лывать**) *сов перех* to stick in.

вконе́ц *нареч* completely and utterly.

вкопа́|ть (-ю; *impf* **вка́пывать**) *сов перех*: ~ **что-н в** +*acc* to sink sth into.

вкось *нареч* at an angle; **смотре́ть** (**посмотре́ть** *perf*) ~ **на кого́-н** to look at sb out of the corner of one's eye.

вкрад|у́сь *итп сов см* **вкра́сться**.

вкра́дчивый (-, -а, -о) *прил* ingratiating.

вкра́дыва|ться (-юсь) *несов от* **вкра́сться**.

вкрапле́ни|е (-я) *ср* (*обычно мн: в горных породах*) fragment; (*в тексте*) interspersion.

вкра́|сться (-ду́сь, -дёшься; *impf* **вкра́дываться**) *сов возв* to creep in; **вкра́дываться** (~ *perf*) **в дове́рие к кому́-н** to worm one's way into sb's confidence.

вкра́тце *нареч* briefly.

вкривь *нареч*: ~ **и вкось** (*разг*) squint.

вкругову́ю *нареч*: **ходи́ть** ~ to go the long way round.

вкру|ти́ть (-чу́, -тишь; *impf* **вкру́чивать**) *сов перех* to screw in.

вкруту́ю *нареч* hard-boiled; **вари́ть** (**свари́ть** *perf*) **яйцо́** ~ to hard-boil an egg.

вкру́чива|ть (-ю) *несов от* **вкрути́ть**.

вкручу́ *сов см* **вкрути́ть**.

вку́пе *нареч*: ~ **с** +*instr* together with.

вкус (-а; *part gen* -у) *м* taste; **про́бовать** (**попро́бовать** *perf*) **что-н на** ~ (*еду*) to taste sth; **на чей-н** ~, **в чьём-н вку́се** to sb's taste; **приходи́ться** (**прийти́сь** *perf*) **кому́-н по вку́су** to be to sb's taste *или* liking; **она́ оде́та со вку́сом** she is tastefully dressed; **входи́ть** (**войти́** *perf*) **во** ~ to start to enjoy o.s.; **о вку́сах не спо́рят** there is no accounting for taste.

вку́сен *прил см* **вку́сный**.

вку́сно *нареч* tastily ♦ *как сказ*: **о́чень** ~ it's delicious; **она́ ~ гото́вит** she is a good cook; **здесь ~ ко́рмят** the food here is very good.

вку́сный (-ен, -на́, -но) *прил* tasty; **обе́д был о́чень** ~ the lunch was delicious.

вла́г|а (-и) *ж* moisture.

влага́лищ|е (-а) *ср* vagina.

владе́л|ец (-ьца) *м* (*магазина, завода*) owner, proprietor; (*книги, картины*) owner.

владе́лиц|а (-ы) *ж см* **владе́лец**.

владе́льц|е *сущ см* **владе́лец**.

владе́ни|е (-я) *ср* estate; (*заводом*) ownership; (*обычно мн: брита́нские итп*) possession; **вступа́ть** (**вступи́ть** *perf*) **во** ~ **чем-н** to assume ownership *или* possession of sth.

владе́|ть (-ю) *несов неперех* (+*instr*; *обладать*) to own, possess; (*уметь пользоваться*): **хорошо́ ~ шпа́гой** to be a proficient *или* skilful swordsman; ~ **собо́й** to control o.s.; ~ (*impf*) **рука́ми/нога́ми** to have the use of one's arms/legs; **она́ в соверше́нстве ~ет англи́йским** she has a perfect command of English.

Владивосто́к (-а) *м* Vladivostok.

Владикавка́з (-а) *м* Vladikavkaz.

вла́жность (-и) *ж* humidity.

вла́ж|ный (-ен, -на́, -но) *прил* (*земля, воздух*) damp; (*глаза, кожа*) moist.

вла́ств|овать (-ую) *несов неперех*: ~ **над** +*instr* to rule; (*перен*) to hold sway over.

вла́стен *прил см* **вла́стный**.

вла́ст|и (-ей) *мн* authorities *мн*.

вла́ст|ный (-ен, -на, -но) *прил* (*человек*,

хара́ктер) imperious; **он не ～ен** +*infin* ... it's not within his power to ....

власт|ь (-и; *gen pl* -**ей**) *ж* (*полити́ческая*) power; (*роди́тельская*) authority; **быть** (*impf*) **у вла́сти** to be in power; **приходи́ть** (**прийти́** *perf*) **к вла́сти** to come to power; **теря́ть** (**потеря́ть** *perf*) **～ над собо́й** to lose one's self-control; *см та́кже* **вла́сти.**

вле́во *нареч* (to the) left; **～ от доро́ги** to the left of the road.

влез|ть (-у, -ешь; *pt* -, -ла, -ло, *impf* **влеза́ть**) *сов неперех*: **～ на** +*acc* (*на де́рево*) to climb (up); (*на кры́шу, на сту́л итп*) to climb onto; **влеза́ть** (**～** *perf*) **в** +*acc* (*забра́ться*) to climb into; (*разг: в трамва́й, в авто́бус итп*) to get on; (*пренебр: в разгово́р*) to butt in on; (: *в де́ло*) to meddle in; **ешь ско́лько вле́зет** (*разг*) eat as much as you want *или* like.

влей(те) *сов см* **влить.**

влёк *итп несов см* **влечь.**

влеку́ *итп несов см* **влечь.**

влет|е́ть (-чу́, -ти́шь; *impf* **влета́ть**) *сов неперех*: **～ в** +*acc* to fly into ♦ *безл* (+*dat*; *разг*) to be told off; **ему́ ～те́ло от учи́теля за опозда́ние** he was told off by his teacher for being late.

влече́ни|е (-я) *ср*: **～ (к** +*dat*) (*к челове́ку*) attraction (to); (*к иску́сству итп*) liking (for); (*к нау́ке, к поли́тике*) interest (in).

влечу́ *сов см* **влете́ть.**

вле|чь (-ку́, -чёшь *итп*, -ку́т; *pt* влёк, -кла́, -кло́, *perf* **повле́чь**) *несов перех*: **～ за собо́й** to lead to; (*no perf*): **его́ ～чёт нау́ка** he is drawn to science.

влива́ни|е (-я) *ср* injection.

влива́|ть (-ю) *несов от* **влить.**

вли́п|нуть (-ну, -нешь; *pt* -, -ла, -ло) *сов неперех* (*в мёд*) to get stuck; (*перен: разг*) to get into a mess.

вли|ть (волью́, вольёшь; *pt* -л, -ла́, -ло, *imper* **влей(те)**, *impf* **влива́ть**) *сов перех* to pour in; (*перен: сре́дства*) to inject
▶ **вли́ться** *сов возв*: **вли́ться в** +*acc* to flow into.

влия́ни|е (-я) *ср* influence; **ока́зывать** (**оказа́ть** *perf*) **～ на** +*acc* to influence, have an influence on; **под ～м** +*gen* under the influence of.

влия́тельный (-ен, -ьна, -ьно) *прил* influential.

влия́|ть (-ю) *несов неперех*: **～ на** +*acc* (*на люде́й, на собы́тия*) to influence; (*на органи́зм, на кли́мат*) to affect; **хорошо́/пло́хо ～** (*impf*) **на** +*acc* to have a good/bad influence on.

ВЛКСМ *м сокр* (*ист*: = **Всесою́зный Ле́нинский Коммунисти́ческий Сою́з Молодёжи**) Leninist Communist Youth League.

вложе́ни|е (-я) *ср* (*обы́чно мн: экон*) investment.

влож|и́ть (-у́, -ишь; *impf* **вкла́дывать**) *сов перех* (*сре́дства, де́ньги*) to invest; (*положи́ть внутрь*) to insert.

влюб|и́ться (-лю́сь, -ишься; *impf* **влюбля́ться**) *сов возв*: **～ в** +*acc* to fall in love

with; **влюбля́ться** (**～** *perf*) **в кого́-н с пе́рвого взгля́да** to fall in love with sb at first sight.

влюблён|ный (-, -а́, -о) *прил* in love; (*no short form; взгляд, глаза́*) loving ♦ (-**ного**) *м*: **～ные** lovers; **смотре́ть** (*impf*) **на кого́-н ～ными глаза́ми** to look lovingly at sb.

влюблю́сь *сов см* **влюби́ться.**

влюбля́|ться (-юсь) *несов от* **влюби́ться.**

вмен|и́ть (-ю́, -и́шь; *impf* **вменя́ть**) *несов перех*: **～ что-н кому́-н в вину́** to lay the blame for sth on sb; **вменя́ть** (**～** *perf*) **кому́-н в обя́занность** +*infin* to charge sb to do.

вменя́ем|ый (-, -а, -о) *прил* (*ЮР*) of sound mind.

вменя́|ть (-ю) *несов от* **вмени́ть.**

вме́сте *нареч* together; **～ с** +*instr* together with; **～ с тем** at the same time.

вмести́тельн|ый (-ен, -ьна, -ьно) *прил* (*помеще́ние, авто́бус*) spacious; **э́тот чемода́н о́чень ～** this suitcase holds a lot.

вме|сти́ть (-щу́, -сти́шь; *impf* **вмеща́ть**) *сов перех* (*подлеж: зал*) to hold; (: *гости́ница*) to accommodate; (*умести́ть*): **～ что-н/кого́-н в** +*acc* to fit sth/sb into
▶ **вмести́ться** (*impf* **вмеща́ться**) *несов возв* to fit in.

вме́сто *предл* (+*gen*; *взаме́н*) instead of; (*замеща́я*) in place *или* instead of ♦ *союз*: **～ того́ что́бы** instead of, rather than; **пошли́ в теа́тр ～ конце́рта** let's go to the theatre instead of the concert; **он рабо́тает ～ отца́** he's standing in for his father; **～ того́ что́бы критикова́ть, постара́йтесь поня́ть** try and understand instead of just criticizing.

вмеша́тельств|о (-а) *ср* (*в разгово́р, в спор*) interference; (*ВОЕН, ЭКОН*) intervention.

вмеша́|ть (-ю; *impf* **вме́шивать**) *сов перех* (*доба́вить*) to mix in; (*перен*): **～ кого́-н в** +*acc* to get sb mixed up in
▶ **вмеша́ться** (*impf* **вме́шиваться**) *сов возв* (*вто́ргнуться*) to interfere; (*присоедини́ться*: *в перегово́ры итп*) to intervene.

вмеща́|ть(ся) (-ю(сь)) *несов от* **вмести́ть(ся).**

вмещу́(сь) *сов см* **вмести́ть(ся).**

вмиг *нареч* instantly.

вмонти́р|овать (-ую) *сов перех*: **～ что-н в** +*acc* to fix sth to.

вмя́тин|а (-ы) *ж* dent.

внаём *нареч*: **отдава́ть ～** to let, rent out; „**сдаётся ～**" (*объявле́ние*) "to let (*BRIT*) *или* rent (*US*)".

внаймы́ *нареч* = **внаём.**

внакла́де *как сказ* (*разг*): **остава́ться ～** to come out worse off.

внача́ле *нареч* at first; **～ она́ испуга́лась** at first she was scared.

вне *предл* (+*gen*) outside; (*чьих-н обя́занностей*) outwith; (*сверх: пла́на*) over and above; **～ о́череди** out of turn; **он был ～ себя́** he was beside himself; **э́то ～ вся́кого сомне́ния** that is beyond any doubt.

внебра́чный *прил* (*отноше́ния*) extramarital;

(*ребёнок*) illegitimate.
внедорóжник (-а) *м* four-wheel drive.
внедрéние (-я) *ср* introduction.
внедр|и́ть (-ю́, -и́шь; *impf* **внедря́ть**) *сов перех*
(*ввести*) to introduce
▸ **внедри́ться** (*impf* **внедря́ться**) *сов возв*
(*методы*) to become established; (*идеи, традиции*) to take root.
внезáп|ный (-ен, -на, -но) *прил* sudden.
внеклáссный *прил* extracurricular.
внемáточ|ный *прил*: ~ная берéменность ectopic pregnancy.
внеочереднóй *прил* unscheduled; (*заседание*) extraordinary.
внес|ти́ (-у́, -ёшь; *pt* внёс, -слá, -слó, *impf* вноси́ть) *сов перех* (*вещи, мебель итп*) to carry *или* bring in; (*взнос, сумму*) to pay; (*законопроект*) to bring in; (*поправку, параграф*) to insert; (*раздор, путаницу*) to cause; вноси́ть (~ *perf*) предложéние/плáту to make a proposal/payment; он внёс оживлéние в вечери́нку he livened up the party; вноси́ть (~ *perf*) я́сность в дéло to shed light on the proceedings.
внешкóльный *прил* extracurricular.
внéшне *нареч* outwardly.
внешнеполити́ческ|ий (-ая, -ое, -ие) *прил* foreign-policy.
внешнеторгóв|ый *прил* (*связи, оборот*) foreign-trade.
внéшн|ий (-яя, -ее, -ие) *прил* (*стена*) exterior *орпед*; (*спокойствие*) outward; (*связи*) external; ~яя охрáна outer guard; ~ мир outside world; ~яя сторонá +*gen* the outside of; внéшний вид appearance; внéшняя поли́тика foreign policy; внéшняя торгóвля foreign trade.
внéшност|ь (-и) *ж* appearance; у неё прия́тная ~ she is good-looking.
внештáтный *прил* freelance.
Внешторгбáнк (-а) *м сокр* (= Банк для внéшней торгóвли) foreign trade bank.
вниз *нареч*; ~ (по +*dat*) down; ~ по течéнию downstream.
внизу́ *нареч* below; (*в здании*) downstairs ◆ *предл* (+*gen*): ~ страни́цы at the foot *или* bottom of the page; дорóга прохóдит ~ the road runs down below; ~ магази́н нахóдится there is a shop on the ground (*BRIT*) *или* first (*US*) floor.
вни́к|нуть (-ну, -нешь; *pt* -, -ла, -ло, *impf* вника́ть) *сов неперех*: ~ в +*acc* to understand.
внимáни|е (-я) *ср* attention; ~ю покупáтелей/пассажи́ров! attention all shoppers/passengers!; привлекáть (привлéчь *perf*) ~ к +*dat* to draw attention to; принимáть (приня́ть *perf*) во ~ что-н to take sth into account *или* consideration; окáзывать (оказáть *perf*) ~

кому́-н to pay attention to sb.
внимáтельност|ь (-и) *ж* (*в работе*) care; (*заботливость*) attentiveness.
внимáтел|ьный (-ен, -ьна, -ьно) *прил* (*сосредоточенный*) attentive; (*тщательный*) careful; (*заботливый*) ~ к +*dat* attentive to.
внимáть (-ю) *несов от* внять.
вничью́ *нареч* (*СПОРТ*): сыгрáть ~ to draw.
вновь *нареч* again.
вно|си́ть (-шу́, -сишь) *несов от* внести́.
ВНП *м сокр* (= валовóй национáльный продýкт) GNP (= *gross national product*).
внук (-а; *nom pl* -ки *или* -чáта) *м* grandson; *см также* внýки.
внýк|и (-ов) *мн* grandchildren *мн*.
внýтренне *нареч* inwardly.
внýтренн|ий (-яя, -ее, -ие) *прил* (*поверхность, стенка*) interior; (*побуждение, голос*) inner; (*политика, рынок*) domestic; (*рана, кровотечение*) internal; Министéрство внýтренних дел ≈ the Home Office (*BRIT*), ≈ the Department of the Interior (*US*); внýтренние óрганы internal organs *мн*.
внýтренност|и (-ей) *мн* (*АНАТ*) insides *мн*; (*КУЛИН*) offal *ед*.
внýтренност|ь (-и) *ж*: ~ (+*gen*) interior (of); *см также* внýтренности.
внутри́ *нареч* inside; (*в пределах, в рамках*) within ◆ *предл*: ~ +*gen* (*дома, ящика*) inside; (*организации*) within.
внутривéнный *прил* intravenous.
внутриполити́ческ|ий (-ая, -ое, -ие) *прил* (*кризис*) internal political *опред*; ~ая борьбá political infighting.
внутрь *нареч* inside ◆ *предл* (+*gen*) inside; принимáть (*impf*) лекáрство ~ to be taken internally.
внучáта *сущ см* внук.
внучáт(н)ый *прил*: ~ племя́нник great-nephew.
внýч|ка (-ки; *gen pl* -ек) *ж* granddaughter.
внушáть (-ю) *несов от* внуши́ть.
внуши́тельный (-ен, -ьна, -ьно) *прил* (*внешность*) imposing; (*сумма, успех*) impressive.
внуш|и́ть (-у́, -и́шь; *impf* внушáть) *сов перех* (*вызвать*) to inspire; внушáть (~ *perf*) что-н кому́-н to instil (*BRIT*) *или* instill (*US*) sth in sb.
вня́т|ный (-ен, -на, -но) *прил* (*отчётливый*) clear; (*вразумительный*) intelligible.
вня́|ть (*pt* -л, -лá, -ло, *impf* внимáть) *сов неперех* (+*dat*; *просьбам*) to heed.
В.О. *м сокр* = Васи́льевский óстров (Петербург).
ВО *м сокр* = воéнный óкруг.
во *предл см* в ◆ *част* (*разг*: *вот*) there; (: *выражает согласие*) that's it; (: *выражает оценку*) great.
вóбл|а (-ы) *ж* Caspian roach.

вобра́ть (вберу́, вберёшь; *pt* -л, -ла́, -ло, *impf* **вбира́ть**) *сов перех* (*воздух, во́ду*) to take in; **вбира́ть** (~ *perf*) **в себя́** to incorporate; **вбира́ть** (~ *perf*) **го́лову в пле́чи** to hunch one's shoulders.

вове́к(и) *нареч* (*навек*) forever; (*никогда*) never; ~ **его́ не прощу́** I will never forgive him.

вовле́чь (-еку́, -ечёшь *итп* -еку́т; *pt* -ёк, -екла́, -екло́, *impf* **вовлека́ть**) *сов перех*: ~ **кого́-н в** +*acc* (*в разговор, в спор*) to draw sb into; (*в рабо́ту*) to involve sb in.

во́время *нареч* on time.

во́все *нареч* (*разг*) completely; ~ **нет** not at all; **она́ на тебя́ ~ не се́рдится** she's not angry with you at all.

вовсю́ *нареч* (*разг*): **бежа́ть/гнать (маши́ну)** ~ to run/drive as fast as one can; **он стара́ется ~** he is giving it his all.

во-вторы́х *вводн сл* secondly, in the second place.

вогна́ть (вгоню́, вго́нишь; *pt* -л, -ла́, -ло, *impf* **вгоня́ть**) *сов перех*: ~ (**во что-н**) to drive in(to sth); **вгоня́ть** (~ *perf*) **кого́-н в отча́яние** to drive sb to despair; **вгоня́ть** (~ *perf*) **в кра́ску кого́-н** to make sb blush.

во́гнутый (-, -а, -о) *прил* concave.

вогну́ть (-у́, -ёшь; *impf* **вгиба́ть**) *сов перех* to bend *или* curve inwards.

вода́ (*acc sg* -у, *gen sg* -ы́, *nom pl* -ы) *ж* water; (*no pl*; *перен*: *в докладе*) padding; **что ты как ~ы в рот набра́л?** (*разг*) has the cat got your tongue?; **как в во́ду опу́щенный** (*разг*) down in the dumps; **похо́жи как две ка́пли ~ы** as like as two peas in a pod; **выходи́ть (вы́йти** *perf*) **сухи́м из ~ы** (*разг*) to get off scot-free; **выводи́ть (вы́вести** *perf*) **на чи́стую во́ду кого́-н** (*разг*) to force sb to come clean; *см также* **во́ды**.

водвори́ть (-ю́, -и́шь) *сов перех* (*посели́ть*) to settle; (*тишину́*) to establish

▸ **водвори́ться** *возв* (*тишина́*) to be established.

водеви́ль (-и) *ж* musical comedy.

води́тель (-я) *м* driver.

води́тельский (-ая, -ое, -ие) *прил*: ~**ие права́** driving licence (*BRIT*), driver's license (*US*).

води́ть (-жу́, -дишь) *несов перех* (*ребёнка, собаку*) to take; (*лошадь, войско*) to lead; (*маши́ну, поезд*) to drive; (*самолёт*) to fly; (*корабль*) to sail; ~ (*impf*) **дру́жбу/знако́мство с кем-н** to be friends/acquainted with sb; ~ (*impf*) **за́ нос кого́-н** to lead sb on

▸ **води́ться** *несов возв* (*рыба итп*) to be (found); ~**ся** (*impf*) **с** +*instr* (*разг*) to be pals with; **у него́ во́дятся де́ньги** (*разг*) he's got money; **как во́дится** (*разг*) as is usually the way.

во́дка (-и) *ж* vodka.

во́дный *прил* water *опред*; **во́дные лы́жи** water-skiing; **во́дное по́ло** water polo; **во́дные проце́дуры** hydrotherapy.

водоворо́т (-а) *м* whirlpool; (*перен*) whirlpool, maelstrom.

водоём (-а) *м* reservoir.

водоизмеще́ние (-я) *ср* displacement; **су́дно ~м в 10 ты́сяч тонн** a vessel of 10 thousand tons displacement.

водока́чка (-ки; *gen pl* -ек) *ж* (*TEX*) waterworks.

водола́з (-а) *м* (*челове́к*) diver.

Водоле́й (-я) *м* (*созве́здие*) Aquarius.

водолече́бница (-ы) *ж* hydrotherapy clinic.

водолюби́вый *прил* (*расте́ние*) water-loving.

водонапо́рный *прил*: ~**ая ба́шня** water tower.

водонепроница́емый *прил* waterproof.

водоотта́лкивающий (-ая, -ее, -ие) *прил* water-repellent.

водоочистно́й *прил* water-purifying.

водопа́д (-а) *м* waterfall.

водопо́й (-я) *м* (*для живо́тных*) (water) trough.

водопрово́д (-а) *м* water supply system; **у них в до́ме ~** their house has running water.

водопрово́дный *прил* (*труба́, кран*) water *опред*; (*систе́ма*) plumbing *опред*.

водопрово́дчик (-а) *м* plumber.

водоразде́л (-а) *м* (*также перен*) watershed.

водоро́д (-а) *м* hydrogen.

водоро́дный *прил* hydrogen *опред*; **водоро́дная бо́мба** hydrogen bomb.

во́доросль (-и) *ж* (*обы́чно мн*) algae *мн*; (*разг*: *в реке*) waterweed; (*в море*) seaweed.

водосбро́с (-а) *м* floodgate.

водосто́чный *прил*: ~**ая труба́** drainpipe; ~**ая кана́ва** gutter.

водохрани́лище (-а) *ср* reservoir.

водрузи́ть (-ужу́, -узи́шь; *impf* **водружа́ть**) *сов перех* to raise.

во́ды (-) *мн* (*госуда́рственные, нейтра́льные*) waters *мн*; (*минера́льные исто́чники*) spa *ед*.

водяни́стый *прил* watery.

водяно́й *прил* water *опред*; **водяно́й знак** watermark; **водяно́й пар** steam.

воева́ть (-ю́ю) *несов* (*страна́*) to be at war; (*челове́к*) to fight; ~ (*impf*) **с бюрокра́тами** *или* **про́тив бюрокра́тов** (*перен*) to wage war on *или* against bureaucracy.

воедино *нареч* together.

военача́льник (-а) *м* (*military*) commander.

военизи́ровать (-ую) (*не*)*сов перех* to militarize.

военкома́т (-а) *м сокр* (= *вое́нный комиссариа́т*) ministry for war.

вое́нно-возду́шный *прил*: **вое́нно-возду́шные си́лы** (the) air force.

вое́нно-морско́й *прил*: ~ **флот** (the) navy.

военнообя́занный (-ого; *decl like adj*) *м person eligible for compulsory military service.*

военнопле́нный (-ого; *decl like adj*) *м* prisoner of war.

вое́нно-полево́й *прил* (*го́спиталь*) field *опред*; **вое́нно-полево́й суд** court martial.

вое́нно-промы́шленный *прил*: ~ **ко́мплекс** military-industrial complex.

военнослу́жащий (-его; *decl like adj*) *м*

serviceman (*мн* servicemen).

вое́нн|ые (**-ых**; *decl like adj*) *мн собир* the military.

вое́нн|ый *прил* military; (*врач*) army *опред* ♦ (**-ого**; *decl like adj*) *м* serviceman (*мн* servicemen); **вое́нное положе́ние** martial law; **вое́нная промы́шленность** military-related industry; *см также* **вое́нные**.

вое́нщин|а (**-ы**) *ж собир* (*пренебр*) warmongers *мн*.

вожа́к (**-а́**) *м* leader.

вожа́т|ый (**-ого**; *decl like adj*) *м* (*в горах*) guide.

вожделе́ни|е (**-я**) *ср* (*к женщине*) lust; (*к власти, к пище*) craving.

вожде́ни|е (**-я**) *ср* (*машины, поезда*) driving; (*судна*) steering; (*яхты*) sailing; (*самолёта*) flying.

вожд|ь (**-я́**) *м* (*племени*) chief, chieftain; (*движения, партии*) leader.

вожж|а́ (**-и́**; *nom pl* **-и**, *gen pl* **-е́й**) *ж* (*обычно мн*) rein.

вожу́(сь) *несов см* **води́ть(ся)**, **вози́ть(ся)**.

ВОЗ *м сокр* (= *Всеми́рная организа́ция здравоохране́ния*) WHO (= *World Health Organization*).

воз (**-а**; *loc sg* **-у́**, *nom pl* **-ы́**) *м* loaded cart; (*перен: разг*) loads *мн*, heaps *мн*.

возбраня́|ться (*3sg* **-ется**, *3pl* **-ются**) *несов возв* (*запреща́ется*) to be prohibited.

возбуди́м|ый (**-**, **-а**, **-о**) *прил* excitable.

возбуди́тел|ь (**-я**) *м* (*МЕД*) pathogen.

возбуди́ть (**-ужу́**, **-у́дишь**; *impf* **возбужда́ть**) *сов перех* (*вызвать*) to arouse; (*взволновать*) to excite; **возбужда́ть** (**~** *perf*) **де́ло** *или* **проце́сс про́тив** +*gen* to bring a case *или* institute proceedings against; **возбужда́ть** (**~** *perf*) **иск** to begin legal proceedings; **возбужда́ть** (**~** *perf*) **хода́тайство о** +*prp* to submit a petition for; **возбужда́ть** (**~** *perf*) **не́нависть** to incite hatred

▶ **возбуди́ться** *сов возв* (*возникнуть*) to be aroused; (*взволноваться*) to become excited.

возбужда́ющий (**-ая**, **-ее**, **-ие**) *прил*: **~ее сре́дство** stimulant.

возбужде́ни|е (**-я**) *ср* (*волнение*) agitation; (: *радостное*) excitement.

возбуждённый *прил* (*см сущ*) agitated; excited.

возбужу́(сь) *сов см* **возбуди́ть(ся)**.

возведе́ни|е (**-я**) *ср* (*здания, стены итп*) elevation.

возвели́ч|ить (**-у**, **-ишь**; *impf* **возвели́чивать**) *сов перех* to extol.

возве|сти́ (**-ду́**, **-дёшь**; *pt* **возвёл**, **-ла́**, **-ло́**, *impf* **возводи́ть**) *сов перех* to erect; **возводи́ть** (**~** *perf*) **что-н в при́нцип** to adopt sth as a fundamental principle; **э́то бы́ло ~дено́ в зако́н** it was enshrined in law; **возводи́ть** (**~**

perf) **обвине́ние на кого́-н** to level an accusation against sb; **возводи́ть** (**~** *perf*) **клевету́ на кого́-н** to slander sb; **возводи́ть** (**~** *perf*) **что-н к** +*dat* to trace sth back to.

возве|сти́ть (**-щу́**, **-сти́шь**; *impf* **возвеща́ть**) *сов перех* to proclaim.

возво|ди́ть (**-жу́**, **-дишь**) *несов от* **возвести́**.

возвра́т (**-а**) *м* return; (*долга, займа*) repayment; **без ~а** irrevocably; **подлежа́щий ~у** returnable; **не подлежа́щий ~у** nonreturnable; **возвра́т нало́га** tax refund.

возвра|ти́ть (**-щу́**, **-ти́шь**; *impf* **возвраща́ть**) *сов перех* (*книгу, покупку*) to return; (*долг, ссуду*) to repay; (*свободу, здоровье, счастье*) to restore; **возвраща́ть** (**~** *perf*) **кого́-н к жи́зни** (*больного*) to bring sb back from the brink of death

▶ **возврати́ться** (*impf* **возвраща́ться**) *сов возв*: **~ся** (**к** +*dat*) to return *или* come back (to).

возвра́тный *прил* (*КОММ*) repayable; (*ЛИНГ*) reflexive.

возвраща́|ть(ся) (**-ю(сь)**) *несов от* **возврати́ть(ся)**.

возвраще́ни|е (**-я**) *ср* return.

возвращу́(сь) *сов см* **возврати́ть(ся)**.

возвы́|сить (**-шу**, **-сишь**; *impf* **возвыша́ть**) *сов перех* (*работника итп*) to elevate; **возвыша́ть** (**~** *perf*) **кого́-н в чьих-н глаза́х** to raise sb in sb's estimation

▶ **возвы́ситься** (*impf* **возвыша́ться**) *сов возв* to be elevated.

возвыша́|ться (**-юсь**) *несов возв* to tower.

возвыше́ни|е (**-я**) *ср* elevation.

возвы́шен|ный (**-**, **-на**, **-но**) *прил* (*перен: идея, цель*) lofty; (*натура, музыка*) sublime; (*берег*) high.

возвы́шу(сь) *сов см* **возвы́сить(ся)**.

возгла́в|ить (**-лю**, **-ишь**; *impf* **возглавля́ть**) *сов перех* to head.

во́зглас (**-а**) *м* exclamation.

возда|ва́ть (**-ю́**) *несов от* **возда́ть**.

возда́ть (*как* **дать**; *см* Table 14; *impf* **воздава́ть**) *сов перех*: **~ хвалу́** *или* **по́чести кому́-н** to eulogize sb, pay homage to sb; **воздава́ть** (**~** *perf*) **кому́-н по заслу́гам** (*в награду*) to reward sb for their services; (*в наказание*) to give sb what they deserve; **воздава́ть** (**~** *perf*) **до́лжное кому́-н** to give sb their due.

воздви́г *итп сов см* **воздви́гнуть**.

воздвига́|ть (**-ю**; *perf* **воздви́гнуть**) *несов перех* to erect.

воздви́г|нуть (**-ну**, **-нешь**; *pt* **-**, **-ла**, **-ло**) *несов от* **воздвига́ть**.

возде́йстви|е (**-я**) *ср* effect; (*идеологическое, педагогическое*) influence; **ока́зывать** (**оказа́ть** *perf*) **~ на** +*acc* to influence; **под ~м** +*gen* under the influence of.

возде́йств|овать (**-ую**) (*не*)*сов неперех*: **~ на**

+*асс* (*(по)влиять*) to have an effect on; (*оказать действие*) to influence.

возде́ла|ть (-ю; *impf* **возде́лывать**) *сов перех* (*обрабатывать*) to cultivate; (*растить*) to grow.

воздержа́вш|аяся (-ейся; *decl like adj*) *ж см* **воздержа́вшийся**.

воздержа́вш|ийся (-егося; *decl like adj*) *м* (*полит*) abstainer.

возде́ржан|ный (-, -на, -но) *прил* frugal; (*в напитках, еде*) abstemious; **он возде́ржан в оце́нках/в сужде́ниях** he is cautious in his evaluations/judgements.

возде|ржа́ться (-ржу́сь, -ржишься; *impf* **возде́рживаться**) *сов возв*: ~ **от** +*gen* (*от комментариев, от курения*) to refrain from; (*от голосования, от спиртного*) to abstain from; **~ержа́лось 10 челове́к** there were 10 abstentions.

во́здух (-а) *м* air; (*перен*) atmosphere; **на (откры́том) ~е** outside, outdoors; **в ~е но́сится опа́сность** there is danger in the air.

возду́шн|ый *прил* air *опред*; (*десант*) airborne; **посыла́ть (посла́ть** *perf*) **кому́-н ~ поцелу́й** to blow sb a kiss; **возду́шная трево́га** air-raid warning; **возду́шная я́ма** air pocket; **возду́шный флот** air force.

воззва́ни|е (-я) *ср* appeal.

воззва́ть (-ову́, -вёшь) *сов от* **взыва́ть**.

воззре́ни|е (-я) *ср* view.

воз|и́ть (-жу́, -зишь) *несов перех* to take; **нас ~зи́ли по Ло́ндону на авто́бусе** we were taken round London on a bus; **ка́ждый день она́ во́зит дете́й в шко́лу на маши́не** every day she takes *или* drives the children to school; ~ (*impf*) **во́ду на ком-н** (*разг*) to work sb into the ground

► **воз|и́ться** *несов возв* to potter about; (*дети*) to romp around *или* about; **~ся** (*impf*) **с** +*instr* (*разг*: *с работой итп*) to make heavy weather of; (*с детьми итп*) to spend a lot of time with.

возлага́|ть (-ю) *несов от* **возложи́ть**.

во́зле *нареч* nearby ♦ *предл* (+*gen*) near; **де́ти игра́ли ~** the children were playing nearby; **дом был ~ реки́** the house stood near the river.

возлож|и́ть (-у́, -ишь; *impf* **возлага́ть**) *сов перех* (*положить*) to lay, place; (*поручить*) to entrust; **возлага́ть (~** *perf*) **вину́ на кого́-н** to lay the blame on sb; **возлага́ть (~** *perf*) **отве́тственность на кого́-н** to hold sb responsible; **возлага́ть (~** *perf*) **наде́жды на кого́-н** to pin one's hopes on sb.

возлю́бленн|ая (-ой) *ж см* **возлю́бленный**.

возлю́бленн|ый (-ого; *decl like adj*) *м* beloved.

возме́зди|е (-я) *ср* retribution.

возме|сти́ть (-щу́, -сти́шь; *impf* **возмеща́ть**) *сов перех* (*ущерб, убытки*) to compensate for; (*затраты*) to refund, reimburse.

возмеще́ни|е (-я) *ср*: **~ убы́тков** compensation; **~ затра́т** reimbursement; **изде́ржки ~я** replacement cost; **сто́имость страхово́го ~я** (*комм*) replacement value.

возмещу́ *сов см* **возмести́ть**.

возмо́жен *прил см* **возмо́жный**.

возмо́жно *как сказ* it is possible ♦ *вводн сл* (*может быть*) possibly ♦ *нареч*: ~ **лу́чше/ быстре́е** as well/quickly as possible; ~ **ему́ помо́чь** it is possible to help him; ~, **он согласи́тся** he may possibly agree.

возмо́жност|и (-ей) *мн* (*творческие*) potential; **фина́нсовые** *или* **материа́льные ~** financial resources.

возмо́жност|ь (-и) *ж* opportunity; (*допустимость*) possibility; **по (ме́ре) ~и** as far as possible; **име́ть** (*impf*) ~ +*infin* to be able to do; **при пе́рвой ~и** at the first opportunity; *см также* **возмо́жности**.

возмо́жн|ый (-ен, -на, -но) *прил* possible.

возмужа́|ть (-ю) *сов от* **мужа́ть**.

возмути́тел|ьный (-ен, -ьна, -ьно) *прил* appalling.

возму|ти́ть (-щу́, -ти́шь; *impf* **возмуща́ть**) *сов перех* to appal (*BRIT*), appall (*US*)

► **возму|ти́ться** (*impf* **возмуща́ться**) *сов возв* to be appalled.

возмуще́ни|е (-я) *ср* indignation.

возмущённо *нареч* indignantly.

возмущённ|ый *прил* indignant.

возмущу́(сь) *сов см* **возмути́ть(ся)**.

вознагра|ди́ть (-жу́, -ди́шь; *impf* **вознагражда́ть**) *сов перех* to reward; (*комм*) to remunerate.

вознагражде́ни|е (-я) *ср* reward.

вознагражу́ *сов см* **вознагради́ть**.

возненави́|деть (-жу, -дишь) *сов перех* to come to hate.

Вознесе́ни|е (-я) *ср* Ascension Day.

вознес|ти́ (-у́, -ёшь; *pt* **вознёс, -ла́, -ло́**, *impf* **возноси́ть**) *сов перех* (*хвалить*) to exalt; **возноси́ть (~** *perf*) **чьи-н досто́инства** to extol (*BRIT*) *или* extoll (*US*) sb's virtues

► **вознес|ти́сь** (*impf* **возноси́ться**) *сов возв* to rise (up).

возни́к *итп сов см* **возни́кнуть**.

возника́|ть (-ю) *несов от* **возни́кнуть**.

возникнове́ни|е (-я) *ср* emergence.

возни́к|нуть (-ну, -нешь; *pt* **-, -ла, -ло**, *impf* **возника́ть**) *сов неперех* to arise.

возно|си́ть (-шу́, -сишь) *несов от* **вознести́**.

возн|я́ (-и́) *ж* (*при игре*) frolicking; (*перен*: *интриги*) intrigue; ~ **с** +*instr* (*хлопоты*) bother with; **мыши́ная ~** (*перен*) a lot of fuss about nothing.

возоблада́|ть (*3sg* -ет, *3pl* -ют) *сов неперех*: ~ **над** +*instr* to prevail over.

возобнов|и́ть (-лю́, -и́шь; *impf* **возобновля́ть**) *сов перех* (*начать снова*) to resume; **возобновля́ть (~** *perf*) **контра́кт** to renew a contract

► **возобнови́ться** (*impf* **возобновля́ться**) *сов возв* to resume.

возомн|и́ть (-ю́, -и́шь) *сов перех*: ~ **себя́ ге́нием/поэ́том** to consider o.s. a genius/poet.

возража́|ть (-ю) *несов от* **возрази́ть**.

возраже́ни|е (-я) *ср* objection; **предложе́ние встре́тило ~я** the proposal met with opposition.

возра|зи́ть (-жу́, -зи́шь; *impf* **возража́ть**) *сов непере*х: ~ (+*dat*) to object (to); **возража́ть** (~ *perf*) **на замеча́ние/обвине́ние** to object to a remark/an allegation.

во́зраст (-а) *м* age; **ребёнок в ~е десяти́ лет** a ten-year-old child; **он был уже́ в ~е** he was getting on in years; **вы́йти** *(perf)* **из ~а** to be over the age limit.

возр|асти́ (*3sg* -асте́т, *3pl* -асту́т, *pt* -о́с, -осла́, -осло́, *impf* **возраста́ть**) *сов непере*х to grow.

возрастно́й *прил* age *опред*.

возро|ди́ть (-жу́, -ди́шь; *impf* **возрожда́ть**) *сов перех* to revive.

▶ **возроди́ться** (*impf* **возрожда́ться**) *сов возв* to revive.

возрожде́ни|е (-я) *ср* (*хозяйства, традиции*) revival; (*нации, веры*) rebirth; (*территории, демократии*) regeneration; **В~** Renaissance.

возро́с *итп сов см* **возрасти́**.

возыме́|ть (-ю) *сов перех*: ~ **де́йствие** to take effect.

возьму́(сь) *итп сов см* **взя́ть(ся)**.

во́ин (-а) *м* warrior.

во́инск|ий (-ая, -ое, -ие) *прил* military; **во́инская пови́нность** conscription.

во́инствен|ный (-ен, -на, -но) *прил* (*племена*) warlike; (*вид, тон, намерения*) belligerent; (*воинствующий*) militant.

во́истину *нареч* in truth.

во́|й (-я) *м* howl.

войду́ *итп сов см* **войти́**.

во́йлок (-а) *м* felt.

войн|а́ (-ы́; *nom pl* -ы) *ж* war; **вести́** *(impf)* **~у́** to wage war; **идти́ (пойти́** *perf)* **на ~у́** to go to war.

во́йск|о (-а; *nom pl* -а́) *ср* (*обычно мн*) (the) forces *мн*.

войти́ (*как* **идти́**; *см* Table 18; *impf* **входи́ть**) *сов непере*х: ~ (**в** +*асс*) to enter, go in(to); (*включиться*) to become a member (of); (*уместиться*) to fit in(to); **в шкаф вхо́дит мно́го книг** the cupboard holds a lot of books; **э́та статья́ не вошла́ в сбо́рник** this article was not included in the collection; **входи́ть** (~ *perf*) **в спи́сок** to be added to the list; **входи́ть** (~ *perf*) **в систе́му** (*КОМП*) to log in.

вокали́ст (-а) *м* vocalist.

вока́льн|ый *прил* vocal; (*конкурс*) singing *опред*; **она́ у́чится на ~ом отделе́нии** she is studying singing.

вокза́л (-а) *м* station.

вокру́г *нареч* around, round ◆ *предл*: ~ +*gen* (*кругом*) around, round; (*по поводу*) about, over; ~ **го́рода** лес the town is surrounded by a forest; ~ **рефо́рмы бы́ло мно́го спо́ров** there was a lot of controversy surrounding *или* over the reforms; **ходи́ть** *(impf)* ~ **да о́коло** (*разг*) to beat about the bush.

вол (-а́) *м* ox (*мн* oxen), bullock.

вола́н (-а) *м* (*на одежде*) flounce; (*в бадминтоне*) shuttlecock.

Во́лг|а (-и) *ж* Volga.

Волгогра́д (-а) *м* Volgograd.

волды́р|ь (-я́) *м* blister.

волево́й *прил* (*человек, характер*) strong-willed; (*усилие, натура*) determined.

волейбо́л (-а) *м* volleyball.

волейболи́ст (-а) *м* volleyball player.

волейболи́ст|ка (-ки; *gen pl* -ок) *ж см* **волейболи́ст**.

во́лей-нево́лей *нареч* (*без желания*) like it or not; **ему́ ~ пришло́сь э́то сде́лать** he had no choice but to do it.

во́лен *прил см* **во́льный**.

во́лжск|ий (-ая, -ое, -ие) *прил* Volga *опред*, of the Volga.

волк (-а; *gen pl* -о́в) *м* wolf (*мн* wolves); **во́лком смотре́ть** *(impf)* **на кого́-н** to look daggers at sb.

волкода́в (-а) *м* wolfhound.

волн|а́ (-ы́; *nom pl* **во́лны**) *ж* (*также перен*) wave; **на коро́тких/сре́дних/дли́нных во́лнах** on short/medium/long wave.

волне́ни|е (-я) *ср* (*на море*) choppiness; (*человека: радостное*) excitement; (: *нервное*) agitation; (*обычно мн: в массах*) disturbance, unrest *ед*.

волни́ст|ый (-, -а, -о) *прил* (*волосы*) wavy.

волн|ова́ть (-у́ю; *perf* **взволнова́ть**) *несов перех* (*общество, человека*) to be concerned about ; (*море*) to agitate.

▶ **волнова́ться** (*perf* **взволнова́ться**) *несов возв* (*море*) to be rough *или* choppy; (*человек*) to worry.

волоки́т|а (-ы) *ж* red tape.

вол|окно́ (-окна́; *nom pl* -о́кна, *gen pl* -о́кон) *ср* fibre (*BRIT*), fiber (*US*).

волонтёр (-а) *м* volunteer.

во́лос (-а; *gen pl* **воло́с**, *dat pl* -а́м) *м* hair *только ед*; ~**ы рвать** *(impf)* **на себе́** (*перен*) to kick o.s.; **э́то притя́нуто за́ волосы** that's a bit far-fetched.

волоса́т|ый (-, -а, -о) *прил* (*грудь*) hairy.

волос|о́к (-ка́) *м* hair; (*лампочки*) filament; **быть** *(impf)* *или* **находи́ться** *(impf)* **на ~ или на волоске́ от** +*gen* to be within a hair's-breadth of; **висе́ть** *(impf)* *или* **держа́ться** *(impf)* **на ~ке́** to hang by a thread.

во́лост|ь (-и) *ж* volost (*administrative division*).

волосяно́й *прил* (*покров*) hair *опред*.

воло|чи́ть (-у́, -чишь) *несов перех* to drag; **едва́** *или* **еле но́ги** ~ *(impf)* to drag o.s. along.

волча́та *итп сущ см* **волчо́нок**.

во́лч|ий (-ья, -ье, -ьи) *прил* wolf *опред*; ~ **зако́н** the law of the jungle; ~ **аппети́т** voracious appetite.

волчи́ц|а (-ы) *ж* she-wolf.

волчо́нок (-о́нка; *nom pl* -**я́та**, *gen pl* -**я́т**) *м* wolf cub.

волше́бник (-а) *м* wizard.

волше́бница (-ы) *ж* (good *или* white) witch.

волше́бный *прил* magic *опред*; (*перен*: *чарующий*) magical.

волшебство́ (-а́) *ср* (*также перен*) magic.

волы́нка (-ки; *gen pl* -ок) *ж* bagpipes *мн*; (*разг*: *канитель*) palaver.

вольго́тный (-ен, -на, -но) *прил* free and easy.

вольёр (-а) *м* enclosure.

вольнича́ть (-ю) *несов неперех* (*разг*) to take liberties.

во́льно *нареч* freely; ~**!** (*ВОЕН*) at ease!; ~ **или** нево́льно willing or not.

вольноду́м|ец (-ца) *м* freethinker.

вольнолюби́в|ый (-, -а, -о) *прил* freedom-loving.

вольнонаёмный *прил* (*рабочий*, *труд*) casual.

во́льность (-и) *ж* (*нескромность*) licence (*BRIT*), license (*US*).

во́л|ьный (-ен, -ьна́, -ьно) *прил* (*свободный*) free; (*нескромный*) familiar ♦ *как сказ* (*no full form*): ~**ен** +*infin* he is free to do; **во́льная борьба́** freestyle wrestling; **во́льные упражне́ния** free floor routine; **во́льный перево́д** free translation.

вольт (-а; *gen pl* -) *м* volt.

вольтме́тр (-а) *м* voltmeter.

волью́ *итп сов см* **влить**.

во́л|я (-и) *ж* will; (*стремление*): ~ **к побе́де/достиже́нию чего́-н** the will to win/to achieve sth; **дава́ть** (**дать** *perf*) ~**ю слеза́м/языку́** to cry/speak without restraint; **дава́ть** (**дать** *perf*) ~**ю чу́вствам** to give free rein to one's feelings; **де́лать** (**сде́лать** *perf*) **что-н по свое́й** ~**е** to do sth of one's own volition *или* free will; **э́то не в мое́й** ~**е** it's not in *или* within my power.

вон *нареч* (*разг*: *прочь*) out; (: *там*) (over) there ♦ *част*: ~ **туда́ иди́те** you need to go THAT way; ~ **отсю́да**! get lost!; **вы́йди** ~! get out!; ~ **она́ идёт** look, there she is; ~ (**оно́**) **что** so that's it!

вон|зи́ть (-жу́, -зи́шь; *impf* **вонза́ть**) *сов перех*: ~ (**в** +*acc*) (*иголка*, *кинжал*) to stick in(to); (*зубы*, *когти*) to sink in(to)

▶ **вонзи́ться** (*impf* **вонза́ться**) *сов возв* (*иголка*, *кинжал*) to stick out; (*когти*, *зубы*) to sink in.

вон|ь (-и) *ж* (*разг*) pong.

воню́ч|ий (-ая, -ее, -ие; -, -а, -е) *прил* (*разг*) pongy.

воня́|ть (-ю) *несов неперех* (*разг*) to pong.

вообража́|ть (-ю) *несов от* **вообрази́ть** ♦ *неперех* (*разг*: *гордиться*) to think a lot of o.s.

вообра|зи́ть (-жу́, -зи́шь; *impf* **вообража́ть**) *сов перех* to imagine; **он** ~**зи́л, что все про́тив него́** he imagined that everyone was against him; **он** ~**зи́л себя́ ге́нием** he fancied himself as a genius; ~**зи́те**! (just) imagine!

вообще́ *нареч* **1** (*в общем*) on the whole; **она́ вообще́ до́брая** on the whole she is kind **2** (*при любых обстоятельствах*) absolutely; **ходи́ть в кино́ он вообще́ запрети́л нам** he absolutely forbade us to go to the cinema; **э́то нам вообще́ не подхо́дит** that does not suit us at all **3** (+*noun*; *не касаясь частностей*) in general; **мы говори́ли о поли́тике вообще́** we talked about politics in general; **вообще́ говоря́** generally speaking.

воодушев|и́ть (-лю́, -и́шь; *impf* **воодушевля́ть**) *сов перех* to inspire; ~ (*perf*) **кого́-н на то, что́бы** +*infin* to inspire sb to do

▶ **воодушеви́ться** *сов возв* (+*instr*) to be inspired by.

воодушевле́ни|е (-я) *ср* enthusiasm.

воодушевлю́ *сов см* **воодушеви́ть**.

воодушевля́|ть (-ю) *несов от* **воодушеви́ть**.

вооружа́|ть(ся) (-ю(сь)) *сов см* **вооружи́ть(ся)**.

вооруже́ни|е (-я) *ср* (*процесс*) arming; (*оружие*) arms *мн*; (*техника*) armament equipment; **брать** (**взять** *perf*) **на** ~ (*перен*) to make use of.

вооружённость (-и) *ж* (*оснащённость*) armed capability; **техни́ческая** ~ technical capability.

вооружённый *прил* armed; **вооружённые си́лы** (the) armed forces.

вооруж|и́ть (-у́, -и́шь; *impf* **вооружа́ть**) *сов перех* to arm; (*перен*) to equip

▶ **вооружи́ться** (*impf* **вооружа́ться**) *сов возв* (*человек*, *полиция*) to arm o.s.; (*население*) to take up arms; **вооружа́ться** (~**ся** *perf*) **терпе́нием** to arm o.s. with patience.

воо́чию *нареч* with one's own eyes.

во-пе́рвых *нареч* firstly, first of all.

воп|и́ть (-лю́, -и́шь) *несов неперех* (*разг*: *кричать*) to shriek; (*громко плакать*) to keen.

вопию́щий (-ая, -ее, -ие) *прил* (*ошибка*, *несправедливость*) glaring; (*безобразие*, *обман*) brazen ♦ (-его; *decl like adj*) *м*: **глас** ~**его в пусты́не** a voice in the wilderness.

вопло|ти́ть (-щу́, -ти́шь; *impf* **воплоща́ть**) *сов перех* to embody; **воплоща́ть** (~ *perf*) **в себе́** to be the embodiment of; **воплоща́ть** (~ *perf*) **в жизнь** to realize

▶ **воплоти́ться** (*impf* **воплоща́ться**) *сов возв*: ~**ся в** +*prp* to be embodied in; **воплоща́ться** (~**ся** *perf*) **в жизнь** to be realized.

воплоще́ни|е (-я) *ср* embodiment.

воплощу́ *сов см* **воплоти́ть**.

вопл|ь (-я) *м* scream.

воплю́ *несов см* **вопи́ть**.

вопреки́ *предл* (+*dat*; *ожиданию*, *прогнозу*) contrary to; (*желанию*, *приказу*) against.

вопро́с (-а) *м* question, issue; (*проблема*) question, issue; **задава́ть** (**зада́ть** *perf*) ~ to ask a question; **ста́вить** (**поста́вить** *perf*) **под** ~ to call into question; **быть** (*impf*) *или* **находи́ться**

(impf) под ~ом to be in question; поднима́ть (подня́ть *perf*) ~ to raise an issue; э́то ~ де́нег/вре́мени it's a question of money/time; ~ по поря́дку веде́ния *(ЮР)* point of order.

вопроси́тельный *прил (взгляд, интона́ция)* questioning; *(линг)* interrogative; вопроси́тельный знак question mark.

вопью́сь *итп сов см* впи́ться.

вор (-а; *gen pl* -о́в) *м* thief.

ворва́|ться (-у́сь, -ёшься; *pt* -а́лся, -ала́сь, -а́лось, *impf* врыва́ться) *сов возв* to burst in; *(звуки)* to flood in.

ворк|ова́ть (-у́ю) *несов непере (также перен)* to coo.

вороб|е́й (-ья́) *м* sparrow.

воро́ванный *прил* stolen.

вор|ова́ть (-у́ю) *несов пере* to steal.

воро́в|ка (-ки; *gen pl* -ок) *ж см* вор.

воровств|о́ (-а́) *ср* theft.

во́рон (-а) *м* raven.

воро́н|а (-ы) *ж* crow; *(перен: разг)* scatterbrain.

воро́н|ить (-ю, -ишь; *perf* проворо́нить) *сов пере (разг)* to miss.

воро́н|ка (-ки; *gen pl* -ок) *ж (для перелива́ния)* funnel; *(после взрыва)* crater.

вороно́й *прил* black ♦ (-о́го; *decl like adj*) *м* black horse.

воро́нок *сущ см* воро́нка.

во́рот (-а) *м* neck *(of clothes)*.

воро́т|а (-) *мн* gates *мн*; *(вход)* gateway *ед*; *(СПОРТ)* goal *ед*; э́то ни в каки́е ~ не ле́зет *(разг)* this is daft.

вороти́л|а (-ы) *м (разг)* big shot.

воротни́к (-а́) *м* collar.

во́рох (-а; *nom pl* -а́) *м* heap.

воро́ча|ть (-ю) *несов пере* to shift ♦ *непере (+instr; разг)* to have control of

▶ воро́чаться *несов возв* to toss and turn.

вороши́ть (-у́, -и́шь) *несов пере (листья, пепел)* to stir up; ~ се́но to toss hay; ~ *(impf)* про́шлое to stir up the past.

ворс (-а) *м (на тка́ни)* nap.

ворча́ни|е (-я) *ср (живо́тного)* growling; *(челове́ка)* grumbling.

ворч|а́ть (-у́, -и́шь) *несов непере (см сущ)* to growl; to grumble.

ворчли́в|ый (-, -а, -о) *прил* querulous.

ворчу́н (-а́) *м (разг)* whinger.

восемна́дцати *чис см* восемна́дцать.

восемна́дцат|ый (-ая, -ое, -ые) *чис* eighteenth; *см также* пя́тый.

восемна́дцат|ь (-и; *как* пять; *см* Table 27) *чис* eighteen; *см также* пять.

во́с|емь (-ьми́; *как* пять; *см* Table 27) *чис* eight; *см также* пять.

во́с|емьдесят (-ьми́десяти; *как* пятьдеся́т; *см* Table 29) *чис* eighty; *см также* пятьдеся́т.

восемьсо́т (-ьмисо́т; *как* пятьсо́т; *см* Table

34) *чис* eight hundred; *см также* сто.

воск (-а; *part gen* -у) *м* wax.

восклик|нуть (-у, -ешь; *impf* восклица́ть) *сов непере* to exclaim.

восклица́ни|е (-я) *ср* exclamation.

восклица́тельный *прил (интона́ция)* exclamatory; восклица́тельный знак exclamation mark *(BRIT)* или point *(US)*.

восклица́|ть (-ю) *несов от* воскли́кнуть.

восково́й *прил* wax; *(цвет)* waxen.

воскре́с *итп сов см* воскре́снуть.

воскреса́|ть (-ю) *несов от* воскре́снуть.

воскресе́ни|е (-я) *ср (РЕЛ)* resurrection; *(перен: обновле́ние)* regeneration; *(: иде́и, движе́ния)* revival.

воскресе́нь|е (-я) *ср* Sunday; в ~ on Sunday; по ~ям on Sundays; в сле́дующее/про́шлое ~ next/last Sunday; сего́дня ~ деся́тое ма́я today is Sunday (the) 10th (of) May.

воскре|си́ть (-шу́, -си́шь; *impf* воскреша́ть) *сов пере* to resurrect, raise from the dead; *(перен)* to revive.

воскре́с|нуть (-ну, -нешь; *pt* -, -ла, -ло, *impf* воскреса́ть) *сов непере* to be resurrected, rise from the dead; *(перен)* to be revived.

воскре́сный *прил* Sunday *опред*.

воскреша́|ть (-ю) *несов от* воскреси́ть.

воскреше́ни|е (-я) *ср* resurrection.

воскрешу́ *сов см* воскреси́ть.

воспале́ни|е (-я) *ср* inflammation; воспале́ние лёгких pneumonia.

воспал|и́ться (-ю́сь, -и́шься; *impf* воспаля́ться) *сов возв* to become inflamed.

воспе́|ть (-ою́, -оёшь; *impf* воспева́ть) *сов пере* to extol *(BRIT)*, extoll *(US)*.

воспита́ни|е (-я) *ср* upbringing; *(шко́льников, гра́ждан)* education; ~ че́стности instilling of honesty; брать (взять *perf*) на ~ to adopt.

воспи́танник (-а) *м (учи́теля, тре́нера)* pupil; *(вуза)* student; *(приёмный ребёнок)* adopted child.

воспи́танниц|а (-ы) *ж см* воспи́танник.

воспи́тан|ный (-, -на, -но) *прил* well-brought-up.

воспита́тел|ь (-я) *м* teacher; *(в ла́гере, в коло́нии)* instructor.

воспита́|ть (-ю; *impf* воспи́тывать) *сов пере (ребёнка)* to bring up; *(трудолю́бие, че́стность итп)* to foster, cultivate; воспи́тывать *(~ perf)* из кого́-н специали́ста/спортсме́на to make a specialist/sportsman of sb.

воспламен|и́ться (-ю́сь, -и́шься; *impf* воспламеня́ться) *сов возв* to ignite.

воспо́лн|ить (-ю, -ишь; *impf* восполня́ть) *сов пере (недоста́тки)* to make up или compensate for; *(пробелы)* to fill in.

воспо́льз|оваться (-уюсь) *сов от*

пóльзоваться.

воспоминáни|е (-я) *ср* memory, recollection; *см также* **воспоминáния**.

воспоминáния (-й) *мн* memoirs *мн*, reminiscences *мн*.

воспою́ *итп сов см* **воспéть**.

воспрепя́тств|овать (-ую) *сов от* **препя́тствовать**.

воспре|ти́ть (-щу́, -ти́шь; *impf* **воспреща́ть**) *сов перех* to forbid.

воспреща́|ться (*3sg* -ется, *3pl* -ются) *несов возв* to be forbidden; **посторóнним вход** ~**ется** no entry to unauthorized persons.

воспрещу́ *сов см* **воспрети́ть**.

восприи́мчив|ый (-, -а, -о) *прил* (*легко усваивающий*) receptive; (*подверженный*) susceptible.

воспри|ня́ть (-иму́, -и́мешь; *impf* **воспринимáть**) *сов перех* to perceive; (*идею, смысл*) to comprehend.

восприя́ти|е (-я) *ср* perception.

воспроизведéни|е (-я) *ср* (*звука, мелодии*) reproduction; (*событий, пейзажа*) re-creation.

воспроизв|ести́ (-еду́, -едёшь; *pt* -ёл, -лá, -лó, *impf* **воспроизводи́ть**) *сов перех* to restore; (*капитал*) to reproduce.

воспроизв|оди́ть (-ожу́, -óдишь) *несов от* **воспроизвести́**.

воспроти́в|иться (-люсь, -ишься) *сов от* **проти́виться**.

воспря́|нуть (-у, -ешь) *сов неперех*: ~ **дýхом** to take heart.

воссозда|вáть (-ю́) *несов от* **воссоздáть**.

воссозда́ть (*как* **дать**; *см* Table 14; *impf* **воссоздавáть**) *сов перех* (*образ, события*) to re-create.

восста|вáть (-ю́, -ёшь) *несов от* **восстáть**.

восстанá|вливать(ся) (-ю(сь)) *несов от* **восстанови́ть(ся)**.

восстáни|е (-я) *ср* uprising.

восстанови́тельн|ый *прил* (*работы*) restoration *опред*; ~ **перио́д** period of restoration.

восстан|ови́ть (-овлю́, -óвишь; *impf* **восстанá|вливать**) *сов перех* to restore; **восстанá|вливать** (~ *perf*) **когó-н в дóлжности** to reinstate sb; **восстанá|вливать** (~ *perf*) **когó-н в правáх** to restore sb's rights; **восстанá|вливать** (~ *perf*) **когó-н прóтив когó-н/чегó-н** to turn *или* set sb against sb/sth

▶ **восстанови́ться** (*impf* **восстанá|вливаться**) *сов возв* to be restored.

восстá|ть (-ну, -нешь; *impf* **восставáть**) *сов неперех*: ~ (**прóтив** +*gen*) to rise up (against); (*перен*) to take a stand (against).

востóк (-а) *м* east; **В**~ the East, the Orient; **éхать** (*impf*) **на** ~ to travel east; **лежáть** (*impf*)/ **находи́ться** (*impf*) **к** ~**у от** +*gen* to lie/be situated to the east of.

востóрг (-а) *м* rapture; **быть** (*impf*) **в** ~**е от** +*gen* to be enraptured by; **приходи́ть** (**прийти́** *perf*) **в**

~ **от** +*gen* to be thrilled by.

восторгá|ть (-ю) *несов перех* to delight, enrapture

▶ **восторгá|ться** *несов возв* (+*instr*) to be delighted *или* enraptured by.

восторженн|ый (-, -на, -но) *прил* (*зритель, поклонник итп*) ecstatic; (*слова, похвалá*) rapturous.

восторжеств|овáть (-ýю) *сов неперех*: ~ (**над** +*instr*) to triumph (over).

востóчн|ый *прил* eastern; ~ **вéтер** east wind.

вострéбовани|е (-я) *ср* (*багажá, грýза*) claim; **письмó до** ~**я** a letter sent poste restante (*BRIT*) *или* general delivery (*US*).

вострéб|овать (-ую) *сов перех* to claim.

вострó *нареч*: **держáть ýхо** ~ (*разг*) to keep an ear to the ground.

восхити́тельн|ый (-ен, -на, -но) *прил* (*мýзыка, стихи итп*) delightful; (*красáвица*) ravishing.

восхи|ти́ть (-щý, -ти́шь; *impf* **восхищáть**) *сов перех*: **меня́** ~**щáет он/егó хрáбость** I admire him/his courage

▶ **восхити́ться** (*impf* **восхищáться**) *сов возв* (+*instr*) to be delighted with.

восхищéни|е (-я) *ср* admiration; (*востóрг*) delight; **приходи́ть** (**прийти́** *perf*) **в** ~ **от** +*gen* to be enraptured *или* delighted by; **приводи́ть** (**привести́** *perf*) **в** ~ **когó-н** to delight sb.

восхищ|ý(сь) *сов см* **восхити́ть(ся)**.

восхóд (-а) *м*: ~ **сóлнца** sunrise; ~ **луны́** moonrise.

восх|оди́ть (-ожý, -óдишь) *несов от* **взойти́** ♦ *неперех*: ~ **к** +*dat* (*к периóду врéмени*) to date back to; (*к традиции*) to be based on.

восходя́щ|ий (-ая, -ее, -ие) *прил* rising.

восхожý *несов см* **восходи́ть**.

восьм|áя (-óй; *decl like adj*) *ж*: **однá** ~ one eighth.

восьмёр|ка (-ки; *gen pl* -ок) *ж* (*разг*: *цифрá*) eight; (*грýппа из восьми́*) group of eight; (*разг*: *автóбус, трамвáй итп*) (number) eight (*bus, tram etc*); **лóдка**~ eight (*ROWING*).

вóсьмер|о (-ы́х; *как* **чéтверо**; *см* Table 36a) *чис* eight; *см также* **двóе**.

восьми́ *чис см* **вóсемь**.

восьми́десяти *чис см* **вóсемьдесят**.

восьмидесятилéти|е (-я) *ср* (*срок*) eighty years *мн*; (*годовщи́на*) eightieth anniversary; (*день рождéния*) eightieth birthday.

восьмидесятилéтн|ий (-яя, -ее, -ие) *прил* (*перио́д*) eighty-year; (*стари́к*) eighty-year-old.

восьмидеся́т|ый (-ая, -ое, -ые) *чис* eightieth; *см также* **пятидеся́тый**.

восьмиднéвн|ый *прил* eight-day.

восьмиклáссни|к (-а) *м* pupil in eighth year at school (*usually 14 years old*).

восьмиклáссни|ца (-ы) *ж см* **восьмиклáссник**.

восьмикрáтн|ый *прил*: ~ **чемпиóн** eight-times champion; **в** ~**ом размéре** eightfold.

восьмилéти|е (-я) *ср* (*срок*) eight years; (*годовщи́на*) eighth anniversary.

восьмиле́тн|ий (-яя, -ее, -ие) *прил (период)* eight-year; *(ребёнок)* eight-year-old.
восьмиме́сячный *прил* eight-month; *(ребёнок)* eight-month-old.
восьминеде́льный *прил* eight-week; *(ребёнок)* eight-week-old.
восьмисо́т *чис см* **восемьсо́т**.
восьмисотле́тие (-я) *ср (срок)* eight hundred years *мн*; *(годовщина)* eight-hundredth anniversary, octocentenary.
восьмисотле́тн|ий (-яя, -ее, -ие) *прил (период)* eight hundred-year; *(дерево)* eight hundred-year-old.
восьмисо́т|ый (-ая, -ое, -ые) *чис* eight-hundredth.
восьмиуго́льник (-а) *м* octagon.
восьмичасово́й *прил (рабочий день)* eight-hour; *(поезд)* eight-o'clock.
восьм|о́й (-а́я, -о́е, -ы́е) *чис* eighth; *см также* **пя́тый**.

KEYWORD

вот *част* **1** *(при указании)*: **вот моя́ ма́ма** there is my mother; **вот мои́ де́ти** here are my children; **вот он идёт** here he comes
2 *(выражает указания)*: **вот в чём де́ло** this is what it's about; **вот где ну́жно иска́ть** this is where we need to look
3 *(при эмфатике)*: **вот посмотри́, како́е безобра́зие** just look at the mess; **вот ты и сде́лай э́то** YOU do this; **вот негодя́й!** what a rascal!
4 *(как часть сказ)*: **но́вая кни́га – вот моя́ цель** a new book – that's my goal; **вот-во́т** *(разг: вот и́менно)* you've got it; **он вот-во́т ля́жет спать** he is just about to go to bed; **вот ещё!** *(разг)* not likely!; **вот (оно́) как** *или* **что**! is that so *или* right?; **вот тебе́ (и) погуля́ли!** *(разг)* so much for the walk!; **вот тебе́ и на** *или* **те раз!** *(разг)* well I never!

воткн|у́ть (-у́, -ёшь; *impf* **втыка́ть**) *сов перех (иголку, нож)* to stick in; **втыка́ть** (~ *perf*) **кол в зе́млю** to drive a stake into the ground.
вотру́(сь) *итп сов см* **втере́ть(ся)**.
во́тум (-а) *м*: ~ **дове́рия/недове́рия** vote of confidence/no confidence.
вошёл *итп сов см* **войти́**.
вошь (**вши**; *instr sg* **во́шью**, *nom pl* **вши**) *ж* louse (*мн* lice).
вошью́ *итп сов см* **вшить**.
вощёный *прил* waxed.
во́ю *итп несов см* **выть**.
впада́|ть (-ю) *несов от* **впасть** ♦ *неперех*: ~ **в** +*acc* to flow into.
впа́дин|а (-ы) *ж (в земле)* gully; *(на дне моря)* trench; **глазна́я** ~ eye socket.
впа|сть (-ду́, -дёшь; *impf* **впада́ть**) *сов неперех (щёки, глаза)* to become sunken; **впада́ть** (~

perf) **в отча́яние** to fall into despair; **впада́ть** (~ *perf*) **в исте́рику** to go into hysterics; **впада́ть** (~ *perf*) **в па́нику** to get into a panic; **впада́ть** (~ *perf*) **в оши́бку** to err; **впада́ть** (~ *perf*) **в кра́йность** to go to extremes; **впада́ть** (~ *perf*) **в заблужде́ние** to be deluded.
впервы́е *нареч* for the first time.
вперёд *нареч (идти, смотреть итп)* (straight) ahead, forward; *(заплатить, требовать)* in advance.
впереди́ *нареч* in front; *(в будущем)* ahead ♦ *предл* (+*gen*) in front of; **у Вас вся жизнь** ~ you have your whole life in front of you.
вперемешку *нареч* higgledy-piggledy.
впечатле́ни|е (-я) *ср* impression; **находи́ться** *(impf)* **под** ~**м чего́-н** to be impressed by sth; **производи́ть (произвести́** *perf*) ~ **на** +*acc* to make an impression on; **тако́е** ~, **что** *или* **бу́дто** it looks as if.
впечатли́тельный (-ен, -ьна, -ьно) *прил* impressionable.
впечатля́|ть (-ю) *несов неперех* to be impressive.
впива́|ться (-юсь) *несов от* **впи́ться**.
впи|са́ть (-шу́, -шешь; *impf* **впи́сывать**) *сов перех* to insert, include
► **впи́са́ться** (*impf* **впи́сываться**) *сов возв (перен)* to fit in well.
впита́|ть (-ю; *impf* **впи́тывать**) *сов перех* to absorb; *(перен)* to absorb, take in
► **впита́ться** *сов возв* to be absorbed.
впи́ться (**вопью́сь, вопьёшься**; *impf* **впива́ться**) *сов возв*: ~ **в** +*acc (комар)* to bite; **впива́ться** (~ *perf*) **глаза́ми в** +*acc* to fix *или* fasten one's eyes on; **впива́ться** (~ *perf*) **когтя́ми/зуба́ми в** +*acc* to sink one's claws/teeth into.
впишу́(сь) *итп сов см* **вписа́ть(ся)**.
ВПК *сокр* (= **вое́нно-промы́шленный ко́мплекс**) ≈ military-industrial complex.
вплавь *нареч* by swimming.
вплотну́ю *нареч (близко)* close (by) ♦ *предл*: ~ **к** +*dat (близко: к городу)* right up close to; (: **к стене́**) right up against; **занима́ться (заня́ться** *perf*) **чем-н** *или* **бра́ться (взя́ться** *perf*) **за что-н** ~ to get down to sth in earnest.
вплоть *предл*: ~ **до** +*gen (вечера, зимы)* right up till; *(включая)* right up to; ~ **до того́, что ...** to the extent that ....
вполго́лоса *нареч (говорить, спросить)* in hushed tones; *(петь)* softly.
впо́ру *как сказ*: ~ +*infin* there is nothing for it but to do; **пла́тье/шля́па** ~ the dress/hat fits nicely.
впосле́дствии *нареч* subsequently.
впотьма́х *нареч* in the dark.
впп *ж сокр* (= **взлётно-поса́дочная полоса́**) landing strip.
впра́ве *как сказ*: ~ +*infin* to do rightly *или* justly;

The spelling rules for Russian are shown on page xvii.

он не ~ так поступа́ть he's got no right to behave like that.
впра́вить (-лю, -ишь; *impf* **вправля́ть)** *сов перех* to set.
впра́во *нареч* to the right; **~ от до́ма** to the right of the house.
впредь *нареч* in future ♦ *предл:* **~ до** +*gen* pending.
впритьк *нареч (разг)* right up close.
впро́голодь *нареч:* **жить ~** to live from hand to mouth.
впрок *нареч* for future use ♦ *как сказ:* **идти́ ~ кому́-н** to do sb good.
впроса́к *нареч:* **попа́сть(ся) ~** *(разг)* to get (o.s.) into a fix.
впро́чем *союз* however, though ♦ *вводн сл* but then again; **пого́да здесь хоро́шая, ~ не всегда́** the weather's good here, though not always; **~, я не уве́рен** but then again, I'm not sure.
впряг *итп сов см* **впрячь**.
впряга́ть (-ю) *несов от* **впрячь**.
впрягу́ *итп сов см* **впрячь**.
впрямь *част:* **и ~ (разг)** really; **он и ~ испуга́лся** he really got a fright.
впря́чь (-гу́, -жёшь *итп,* **-гут;** *pt* **-г, -гла́, -гло́,** *impf* **впряга́ть)** *сов перех* to harness.
впусти́ть (-щу́, -стишь; *impf* **впуска́ть)** *сов перех (в дом, в зал)* to admit, let in.
впу́тать (-ю) *сов от* **пу́тать** ♦ *(impf* **впу́тывать)** *перех (разг):* **~ кого́-н (в** +*acc)* to get sb mixed up (in)
▶ **впу́таться** *сов от* **пу́таться** ♦ *(impf* **впу́тываться)** *возв* to get involved.
впущу́ *сов см* **впусти́ть**.
впя́теро *нареч (больше, меньше)* five times; *(увеличить)* fivefold.
впятеро́м *нареч* in a group of five.
в-пя́тых *вводн сл* fifthly, in the fifth place.
враг (-а́) *м* enemy ♦ *собир (ВОЕН)* the enemy.
вражда́ (-ы́) *ж* enmity, hostility; **пита́ть (impf)** **~у́ к** +*dat* to harbour enmity towards.
вражде́бный (-ен, -на, -но) *прил (отношение, тон)* hostile; *(лагерь, сторона)* enemy *опред*.
враждова́ть (-у́ю) *несов неперех:* **~ (с** +*instr)* to be on hostile terms (with).
враз *нареч (разг)* at once.
вразбро́д *нареч* separately.
вразбро́с *нареч (разг)* scattered about.
вразва́лку *нареч (разг):* **ходи́ть ~** to waddle.
вразнобо́й *нареч (разг)* in a muddled way.
вразно́с *нареч:* **торгова́ть ~** to peddle.
вразре́з *нареч:* **~ с** +*instr* in contravention of.
вразуми́тельный (-ен, -ьна, -ьно) *прил* comprehensible.
вразуми́ть (-лю, -и́шь; *impf* **вразумля́ть)** *сов перех:* **~ кого́-н** to make sb understand.
враньё (-я́) *ср (разг)* lies *мн*.
врасплóх *нареч* unawares.
врассыпну́ю *нареч* in all directions.
врата́рь (-я́) *м* goalkeeper.

врать (-у́, -ёшь; *pt* **-ал, -ла́, -ло,** *perf* **наврать** *или* **соврать)** *несов неперех (разг: человек)* to fib; *(: часы)* to be wrong.
врач (-а́) *м* doctor.
враче́бный *прил* medical.
враща́ть (-ю) *несов перех (колесо)* to turn
▶ **враща́ться** *несов возв (колесо, планета)* to revolve, rotate; **~ся (impf) в полити́ческих круга́х** to move in political circles; **разгово́р ~лся вокру́г теа́тра** the conversation revolved around the theatre.
враще́ние (-я) *ср* revolution, rotation.
вред (-а́) *м (делу, здоровью)* damage; *(человеку)* harm, injury ♦ *предл:* **во ~** +*dat* to the detriment of; **его́ де́йствия бы́ли во ~ интере́сам фи́рмы** his actions were against the company's interests; **причиня́ть (причини́ть** *perf) или* **приноси́ть (принести́** *perf)* **~ кому́-н** to harm sb, do sb harm; **причиня́ть (причини́ть** *perf) или* **приноси́ть (принести́** *perf)* **~ чему́-н** to damage *или* cause damage to sth.
вре́ден *прил см* **вре́дный**.
вреди́тель (-я) *м (насекомое)* pest; *(человек)* saboteur.
вреди́ть (-жу́, -ди́шь; *perf* **навреди́ть)** *несов неперех (+dat)* to harm, hurt; *(здоровью)* to damage; *(врагу́)* to inflict damage on.
вре́дно *нареч:* **~ влия́ть на** +*acc* to have a harmful effect on ♦ *как сказ:* **кури́ть ~** smoking is bad for you; **ему́ ~ есть жи́рное** fatty foods are bad for him.
вре́дный (-ен, -на́, -но) *прил* harmful; *(no short form; разг)* nasty.
вре́зать (-жу, -жешь) *сов перех (замок)* to fit ♦ *неперех (разг: уда́рить):* **~ кому́-н** to bash sb.
врежу́ *несов см* **вреди́ть**.
вре́заться (-жусь, -жешься; *impf* **вреза́ться)** *сов возв:* **~ в** +*acc (пила, верёвка)* to cut into; *(ворва́ться)* to plough *(BRIT) или* plow *(US)* into; *(в се́рдце, в па́мять)* to engrave itself on.
времена́ (-ён; *dat pl* **-ена́м)** *мн (эпоха)* the time *ед;* **~ Петра́ Пе́рвого** the time of Peter the First.
времена́ми *нареч* at times.
вре́мени *итп сущ см* **вре́мя**.
вре́менный (-ен, -на, -но) *прил* temporary.
вре́мя (-ени; *см* **Table 4)** *ср* time; *(линг)* tense ♦ *предл:* **во ~** +*gen* during ♦ *союз:* **в то ~ как** *или* **когда́** while; **(a) в то же ~** (but) at the same time; **во вре́мя** during; **~ от вре́мени** from time to time; **в после́днее ~** recently; **в своё ~** *(когда́ необходи́мо)* in due course; **в своё ~ она́ была́ краса́вицей** she was a real beauty in her day; **на ~** for a while; **со ~енем** with *или* in time; **тем ~енем** meanwhile; **ско́лько ~ени?** what time is it?; **в 8 часо́в по моско́вскому ~ени** at 8 o'clock (by) Moscow time; **~ до́ступа (комп)** access time; **~ реализа́ции зака́за (комм)** lead time; **лу́чшее эфи́рное ~** prime time; **хорошо́ проводи́ть (провести́** *perf)* **~** to have a good time; **вре́мя го́да** season; *см также* **времена́**.

времяисчисле́ни|е (-я) *ср* calendar.
времяпрепровожде́ни|е (-я) *ср* way of spending time.
время́н|ка (-ки; *gen pl* -ок) *ж* (*печка*) makeshift stove; (*жилище*) makeshift hut (*next to new rural dwelling*).
вро́вень *нареч*: ~ **с** +*instr* level with.
вро́де *предл* (+*gen*) like ♦ *част* it looks as if; **он у меня́ ~ сове́тника** he's like an advisor to me; **он ~ уе́хал** it looks as if he's gone.
врождённый *прил* (*способности*) innate; (*уродство, болезнь*) congenital.
врозь *нареч* (*жить*) apart; (*работать, ехать*) separately ♦ *предл*: ~ **с** +*instr или* **от** +*gen* (*разг*) separate from.
вро́|ю *итп сов см* **врыть**.
вру́|ю *несов см* **врать**.
вруб|и́ть (-лю́, -ишь; *impf* **вруба́ть**) *сов перех* (*разг*: *включить*) to turn on.
врун (-а́) *м* (*разг*) fibber.
вру́нь|я (-и) *ж см* **врун**.
вруч|и́ть (-у́, -и́шь; *impf* **вруча́ть**) *сов перех*: ~ **что-н кому́-н** to hand sth (over) to sb; (*орден, пре́мию*) to present sb with sth.
вручну́ю *нареч* (*разг*) by hand.
врыва́|ться (-юсь) *несов от* **ворва́ться**.
вр|ыть (-о́ю, -о́ешь; *impf* **врыва́ть**) *сов перех* (*столб*) to sink into; (*дерево*) to plant firmly.
вряд *част*: ~ **ли** hardly; ~ **ли он согласи́тся** he's hardly likely to agree.
ВС *мн сокр* (= **Вооружённые Си́лы**) armed forces *мн*; (= **Верхо́вный Сове́т**) Supreme Soviet.
вса|ди́ть (-жу́, -дишь; *impf* **вса́живать**) *сов перех*: ~ **в** +*acc* (*нож, стрелу́*) to sink into; **вса́живать** (~ *perf*) **пу́лю в лоб кому́-н** (*разг*) to put a bullet in sb's head.
вса́дник (-а) *м* rider, horseman (*мн* horsemen).
вса́дниц|а (-ы) *ж* rider, horsewoman (*мн* horsewomen).
вса́жива|ть (-ю) *несов от* **всади́ть**.
всажу́ *сов см* **всади́ть**.
вса́сыва|ть (-ю) *несов от* **всоса́ть**.
все *мест см* **весь**.

KEYWORD

всё (**всего́**) *мест см* **весь**
♦ *ср* (*как сущ: без исключе́ния*) everything; **вот и всё**, **э́то всё** that's all; **ча́ще всего́** most often; **лу́чше всего́ написа́ть ей письмо́** it would be best to write to her; **меня́ э́то волну́ет ме́ньше всего́** that is the least of my worries; **мне всё равно́** it's all the same to me; **Вы хоти́те чай и́ли ко́фе? – всё равно́** do you want tea or coffee? – I don't mind; **я всё равно́ пойду́ туда́** I'll go there all the same
♦ *нареч* **1** (*разг*: *всё вре́мя*) all the time
2 (*разг*: *до сих пор*) still
3 (*то́лько*) all; **э́то всё он винова́т** it's all his fault

4 (*о нараста́нии при́знака*): **шум всё уси́ливается** the noise keeps getting louder
5 (*о постоя́нстве при́знака*): **всё так же** still the same; **всё там же** still there; **всё же** all the same; **всё ещё** still.

всевла́сти|е (-я) *ср* absolute power.
всевозмо́ж|ный (-ен, -на, -но) *прил* all sorts of.
всегда́ *нареч* always.
всего́ *мест см* **весь, всё** ♦ *нареч* in all ♦ *част* only; ~ **лишь** (*разг*) only; ~**-на́всего** (*разг*) all in all.
вселе́нн|ая (-ой; *decl like adj*) *ж* the whole world; **В~** universe.
всел|и́ть (-ю́, -и́шь; *impf* **вселя́ть**) *сов перех* (*жильцо́в*) to install; (*перен*) to instil (*BRIT*), instill (*US*)
▶ **всели́ться** (*impf* **вселя́ться**) *сов возв* (*жильцы́*) to move in; (*перен*) to be instilled.
всем *мест см* **весь, всё, все**.
всеме́рный *прил* (*по́мощь*) all possible.
всемеро́м *нареч* in a group of seven.
все́ми *мест см* **все**.
всеми́рный *прил* worldwide; (*конгре́сс*) world *опред*.
всемогу́щ|ий (-ая, -ее, -ие; -, -а, -е) *прил* omnipotent, all-powerful.
всему́ *мест см* **весь, всё**.
всенаро́ден *прил см* **всенаро́дный**.
всенаро́дно *нареч* publicly.
всенаро́д|ный (-ен, -на, -но) *прил* national.
всено́щн|ая (-ой; *decl like adj*) *ж* (*РЕЛ*) vespers.
всео́буч (-а) *м сокр* (= **всео́бщее обуче́ние**) general education.
всео́бщ|ий (-ая, -ее, -ие; -, -а, -е) *прил* universal; **всео́бщая забасто́вка/пе́репись** general strike/census.
всеобъе́млющ|ий (-ая, -ее, -ие; -, -а, -о) *прил* comprehensive.
всеору́жи|е (-я) *ср*: **во ~и зна́ний** armed with knowledge; **встреча́ть** (**встре́тить** *perf*) **врага́ во ~и** to be primed for battle.
всеросси́йск|ий (-ая, -ое, -ие) *прил* All-Russia.
всерьёз *нареч* in earnest; **ты э́то говори́шь ~?** are you serious?
всеси́ль|ный (-ен, -ьна, -ьно) *прил* all-powerful.
всесторо́н|ний (-няя, -нее, -ние; -ен, -ня, -не) *прил* comprehensive.
всё-таки *част* still, all the same ♦ *союз*: **а ~** all the same, nevertheless; **мо́жет, ~ пое́дем?** can we not still go?; **бы́ло ску́чно, и ~ я не ушёл** I was bored, but all the same I didn't leave.
всеуслы́шание *ср*: **во ~** publicly.
всех *мест см* **все**.
вселе́ло *нареч* completely.
всея́дный *прил* omnivorous.
вска́кива|ть (-ю) *несов от* **вскочи́ть**.
вска́пыва|ть (-ю) *несов от* **вскопа́ть**.

вскарáбка|**ться** (-юсь) *сов от* **карáбкаться**.
вскачь *нареч* at a gallop; **пускáть** (**пустúть** *perf*) **коня** ~ to break into a gallop.
вскúн|**уть** (-у, -ешь; *impf* **вскúдывать**) *сов перех* (*на плечи*) to shoulder; (*голову*) to jerk up; (*руки*) to throw up; **вскúдывать** (~ *perf*) **что-н на что-н** to throw sth on(to) sth; **вскúдывать** (~ *perf*) **глазá на когó-н** to glance up at sb.
вскип|**éть** (-лю́, -úшь; *impf* **кипéть**) *сов неперех* to boil; (*перен*) to flare up; ~ (*perf*) **от гнéва** to fly into a rage.
вскипя|**тúть(ся)** (-чý(сь), -тúшь(ся)) *сов от* **кипятúть(ся)**.
всклокóченный *прил* (*разг*) tousled.
всколыхн|**ýть** (-ý, -ёшь) *сов перех* (*подлеж: ветер*) to stir; (*перен: массы*) to stir up
▶ **всколыхнýться** *сов возв* (*перен*) to become stirred up.
вскользь *нареч* in passing.
вскопá|**ть** (-ю; *impf* **вскáпывать**) *сов перех* to dig (over).
вскóре *нареч* soon ♦ *предл*: ~ **пóсле** +*gen* soon *или* shortly after.
вскоч|**úть** (-ý, -ишь; *impf* **вскáкивать**) *сов неперех*: ~ **в/на** +*acc* (*на коня, в седлó*) to leap up onto; **вскáкивать** (~ *perf*) (**нá ноги**) to leap to one's feet.
вскрúкн|**уть** (-у, -ешь; *impf* **вскрúкивать**) *сов неперех* to cry out.
вскрóю(сь) *итп сов см* **вскрыть(ся)**.
вскруж|**úть** (-ý, -ишь) *сов перех*: ~ **гóлову комý-н** to turn sb's head (*fig*).
вскрывá|**ть** (-ю) *несов от* **вскрыть**.
вскрытие (-я) *ср* (*трупа*) postmortem (examination); (*сейфа итп*) opening.
вскр|**ыть** (-óю, -óешь; *impf* **вскрывáть**) *сов перех* (*открыть*) to open; (: *с силой*) to force open; (*выявить*) to reveal; (*нарыв*) to lance; (*труп*) to carry out a postmortem on
▶ **вскрыться** *сов возв* (*перен: выявиться*) to come to light, be revealed; **рекá ~ылась** the ice on the river cracked.
всласть *нареч* to one's heart's content.
вслед *нареч* (*бежáть*) behind ♦ *предл*: ~ (**за** +*instr*) after; ~ +*dat* (*другу, поезду*) after.
вслéдствие *предл* (+*gen*) as a result of, because of ♦ *союз*: ~ **тогó что** because; ~ **чегó** as a result of which.
вслепýю *нареч* blindly; **печáтать** (*impf*) **на машúнке** ~ to touch-type.
вслух *нареч* aloud; **сказáть** (*perf*) **что-н** ~ to say sth out loud.
вслýша|**ться** (-юсь; *impf* **вслýшиваться**) *сов возв*: ~ **в** +*acc* to listen carefully to.
ВСМ *м сокр* (= *Всемúрный Совéт Мúра*) World Peace Council.
всмотр|**éться** (-ю́сь, -ишься; *impf* **всмáтриваться**) *сов возв*: ~ **в** +*acc* to peer at.
всмятку *нареч*: **яйцó** ~ soft-boiled egg.
всóвыва|**ть** (-ю) *несов от* **всýнуть**.

всос|**áть** (-ý, -ёшь; *impf* **всáсывать**) *сов перех* (*втянуть*) to suck; (*впитать*) to absorb.
вспáрхива|**ть** (-ю) *несов от* **вспорхнýть**.
вспах|**áть** (-шý, -шешь) *сов от* **пахáть**.
вспéн|**иться** (-юсь, -ишься) *сов от* **пéниться**.
всплеск (-а) *м* (*волны*) splash.
всплесн|**ýть** (-ý, -ёшь; *impf* **всплёскивать**) *сов неперех* (*рыба, пловец*) to splash; ~ (*perf*) **рукáми** to throw up one's hands.
всплывá|**ть** (-ю) *несов от* **всплыть**.
всплывý *итп сов см* **всплыть**.
всплытие (-я) *ср* surfacing.
всплы|**ть** (-вý, -вёшь; *pt* -л, -лá, -ло, *impf* **всплывáть**) *сов неперех* to surface, come to the surface; (*перен*) to come to light; **всплывáть** (~ *perf*) **в пáмяти** to pop into one's head; **всплывáть** (~ *perf*) **в сознáнии** to appear before one.
всполош|**úть(ся)** (-ý(сь), -úшь(ся)) *сов от* **полошúть(ся)**.
вспóмн|**ить** (-ю, -ишь; *impf* **вспоминáть**) *сов перех* to remember ♦ *неперех*: ~ **о** +*prp* to remember about.
вспомогáтельный *прил* (*материал, литература*) supplementary; (*судно, отряд*) auxiliary; **вспомогáтельный глагóл** auxiliary verb.
вспорхн|**ýть** (-ý, -ёшь; *impf* **вспáрхивать**) *сов неперех* to fly off.
вспот|**éть** (-ю) *сов от* **потéть**.
вспрýсн|**уть** (-у, -ешь; *impf* **вспры́скивать**) *сов перех* to spray.
вспугн|**ýть** (-ý, -ёшь; *impf* **вспýгивать**) *сов перех* to scare away *или* off.
вспýхн|**уть** (-у, -ешь) *сов от* **пýхнуть** ♦ (*impf* **вспухáть**) *неперех* to swell up.
вспýч|**иться** (*3sg* -ится, *3pl* -атся) *несов от* **пýчиться**.
вспыл|**úть** (-ю́, -úшь) *сов неперех* to lose one's temper.
вспы́льчивость (-и) *ж* short-temperedness.
вспы́льчив|**ый** (-, -а, -о) *прил* short-tempered.
вспы́хн|**уть** (-у, -ешь; *impf* **вспы́хивать**) *сов неперех* (*солома, бумага*) to burst into flames; (*спичка, конфликт, страсть*) to flare up; (*покраснеть: человек*) to blush; **в окнé ~ул свет** the window lit up.
вспы́ш|**ка** (-ки; *gen pl* -ек) *ж* flash; (*энтузиазма*) burst; (*гнева*) outburst; (*болезни*) outbreak.
вспять *нареч* back.
ВСРФ *мн сокр* = *вооружённые сúлы россúйской федерáции*.
вста|**вáть** (-ю́; *imper* -**вáй(те)**) *несов от* **встать** ♦ *неперех*: **рабóтать/писáть не ~вáя** to work/write without a break.
встáв|**ить** (-лю, -ишь; *impf* **вставля́ть**) *сов перех* to insert, put in; **вставля́ть** (~ *perf*) **зýбы** to have a set of dentures *или* false teeth made; **вставля́ть** (~ *perf*) **кáмень в опрáву** to set a stone.
встáв|**ка** (-ки; *gen pl* -ок) *ж* insertion; (*в одежде*)

inset.

вста́влю *сов см* **вста́вить.**

вставля́ть (-ю) *несов от* **вста́вить.**

вставн|о́й *прил (рамы)* removable; ~**ы́е зу́бы** dentures, false teeth.

вста́вок *сущ см* **вста́вка.**

вста|ть (-ну, -нешь; *impf* **встава́ть**) *сов неперех (на ноги)* to stand up; *(с постели)* to get up; *(солнце)* to rise; *(трудности, вопрос)* to arise; *(no impf, разг: часы, мотор)* to stop; **пе́ред на́ми вста́ли но́вые тру́дности** we were faced with new difficulties.

встопо́рщ|ить(ся) (-ю(сь), -ишь(ся)) *сов от* **топо́рщить(ся).**

встрева́|ть (-ю) *несов неперех (разг: вмешиваться)* to stick one's oar in.

встрево́женн|ый (-, -а, -о) *прил* anxious.

встрево́ж|ить(ся) (-у(сь), -ишь(ся)) *несов от* **трево́жить(ся).**

встрепен|у́ться (-у́сь, -ёшься) *сов возв* to give a start.

встре́|тить (-чу, -тишь; *impf* **встреча́ть**) *сов перех* to meet; *(гостей, делегацию итп)* to meet, welcome; *(обнаружить: слово, цитату)* to come across; *(оппозицию, сопротивление)* to meet with, encounter; *(праздник итп)* to celebrate

▸ **встре́|титься** (*impf* **встреча́ться**) *сов возв:* ~**ся с** +*instr* to meet; *(перен: с сопротивлением итп)* to meet with, encounter; **мне** ~**тились друзья́/интере́сные фа́кты** I came across some friends/interesting facts.

встре́ч|а (-и) *ж* meeting; *(поединок)* match.

встреча́|ть (-ю) *несов от* **встре́тить**

▸ **встреча́|ться** *несов от* **встре́титься** ♦ *возв (регулярно видеться)* to meet; *(попадаться)* to be found.

встре́чн|ый *прил (машина, поезд итп)* oncoming; *(мера)* counter *опред* ♦ *(-ого; decl like adj)* м *someone coming from the opposite direction;* ~ **ве́тер** head wind; **пе́рвый** ~ *(разг)* anyone; **встре́чная ата́ка** counterattack; **встре́чный иск** counterclaim.

встре́чу(сь) *сов см* **встре́тить(ся).**

встря́с|ка (-ки; *gen pl* -ок) *ж (потрясение)* shock; *(системы)* upheaval.

встряхн|у́ть (-у́, -ёшь; *impf* **встря́хивать**) *сов перех* to shake (out); *(перен: общество)* to shake (up).

вступа́|ть(ся) (-ю(сь)) *несов от* **вступи́ть(ся).**

вступи́тельный *прил (речь, статья)* introductory; **вступи́тельный взнос** subscription fee; **вступи́тельный экза́мен** entrance exam.

вступ|и́ть (-лю́, -ишь; *impf* **вступа́ть**) *сов неперех:* ~ **в** +*acc* to enter; *(в партию, в общество)* to join; *(в спор, в переговоры)* to enter into; **вступа́ть** (~ *perf*) **на** +*acc* to mount;

вступа́ть (~ *perf*) **в бой** to join battle

▸ **вступи́ться** (*impf* **вступа́ться**) *сов возв:* ~**ся за** +*acc* to stand up for.

вступле́ни|е (-я) *ср (войск: в город)* entry; *(в партию)* joining; *(в стадию)* entering; *(в книге, в статье)* introduction; *(в бесе́де)* preamble.

вступлю́ *сов см* **вступи́ть.**

всу́н|уть (-у, -ешь; *impf* **всо́вывать**) *сов перех:* ~ **в** +*acc* to pour into ♦ *неперех:* ~ **кому́-н** *(разг: отчитать)* to give sb what for.

всухомя́тку *нареч:* **пита́ться** ~ to live off cold snacks; **есть** (*impf*) **хлеб** ~ to eat dry bread.

всучи́|ть (-у́, -ишь; *impf* **всу́чивать**) *сов перех (навязать)* to palm off.

всхлип (-а) *м* sob.

всхли́пыва|ть (-ю) *несов неперех* to sob.

всхо|ди́ть (-жу́, -дишь) *несов от* **взойти́.**

всхо́д|ы (-ов) *мн* shoots *мн*.

всхожу́ *сов см* **всходи́ть.**

всы́п|ать (-лю, -лешь; *impf* **всыпа́ть**) *сов перех:* ~ **в** +*acc* to pour into ♦ *неперех:* ~ **кому́-н** *(разг: отчитать)* to give sb what for.

всю *мест см* **вся.**

всю́ду *нареч* everywhere.

вс|я (-ей) *мест см* **весь.**

вся́к|ий (-ая, -ое, -ие) *мест (каждый)* every; *(разнообразный)* all kinds of; *(любой)* any ♦ *(-ого; decl like adj)* м *(любой)* anyone; *(каждый)* everyone; **здесь продаю́т** ~**ие това́ры** all kinds of goods are sold here; **у меня́ пропа́ло** ~**ое жела́ние помо́чь** I have lost all desire to help; **без** ~**ого сомне́ния/интере́са/жела́ния** without the slightest doubt/interest/desire; **безо** ~**ого** *или* ~**их согласи́ться** *(perf)*/**приня́ть** *(perf) (разг)* to agree/accept without a second thought.

вся́ко *нареч (разг)* all sorts of things.

вся́чески *нареч* in every possible way.

вся́ческ|ий (-ая, -ое, -ие) *мест (поддержка, сопротивление)* all possible; *(товары)* all kinds of.

вся́чин|а (-ы) *ж (разг):* **вся́кая** ~ all sorts of things.

Вт *сокр* (= *ватт*) W (= *watt*).

вта́йне *нареч* secretly, in secret.

вта́лкива|ть (-ю) *несов от* **втолкну́ть.**

вта́птыва|ть (-ю) *несов от* **втопта́ть.**

втащ|и́ть (-у́, -ишь; *impf* **вта́скивать**) *сов перех:* ~ **(в** +*acc*) to drag in(to).

втёк *итп сов см* **втечь.**

втека́|ть (3*sg* -ет, 3*pl* -ют) *несов неперех* to flow in(to).

втеку́т *сов см* **втечь.**

втере́|ть (вотру́, вотрёшь; *pt* втёр, втёрла, втёрло, *impf* **втира́ть**) *сов перех:* ~ **(в** +*acc*) to rub in(to)

▸ **втере́ться** (*impf* **втира́ться**) *сов возв* to be absorbed; *(разг: пренебр)* to worm one's way in; ~**ся** (*perf*) **в дове́рие кому́-н** to worm one's way into sb's confidence.

вте|чь (*3sg* -чёт, *3pl* -кут, *pt* втёк, -кла, -кло, *impf* **втекать**) *сов неперех*: ~ в +*acc* to flow into.

втира|ть(ся) (-ю(сь)) *несов от* **втереть(ся)**.

втисн|уть (-у, -ешь; *impf* **втискивать**) *сов перех*: ~ (в +*acc*) to cram in(to)

▶ **втиснуться** *сов возв* (*разг*) (*impf* **втискиваться**): ~ся (в +*acc*) (*человек*) to squeeze in(to).

втихомолку *нареч* (*разг*) on the quiet.

втолкн|уть (-у, -ёшь; *impf* **вталкивать**) *сов перех*: ~ (в +*acc*) to push in(to).

втолк|овать (-ую; *impf* **втолковывать**) *сов перех* (*разг*): ~ что-н кому-н to get sth through to sb.

втоп|тать (-чу, -чешь; *impf* **втаптывать**) *сов перех*: ~ (в +*acc*) to trample in(to); **втаптывать** (~ *perf*) кого-н в грязь (*перен*) to humiliate sb.

втор|ая (-ой; *decl like adj*) *ж*: **одна** ~ one half.

вто́рг|нуться (-усь, -ешься; *impf* **вторга́ться**) *сов возв*: ~ в +*acc* (*в страну*) to invade; (*вмешаться*) to interfere with *или* in.

втор|ить (-ю, -ишь) *несов неперех* (+*dat*; *петь*) to sing the second part to; (*разг*: поддакивать) to parrot.

вторичный *прил* (*повторный*) second; (*второстепенный*) secondary; **вторичное сырьё** recyclable materials.

вто́рник (-а) *м* Tuesday; **во** ~ on Tuesday; **по** ~**ам** on Tuesdays; **в сле́дующий/про́шлый** ~ next/last Tuesday; **сего́дня** ~, **деся́тое ма́я** today is Tuesday (the) 10th (of) May.

второго́дник (-а) *м pupil repeating a year at school*.

второго́дниц|а (-ы) *ж см* **второго́дник**.

втор|о́е (-о́го; *decl like adj*) *ср* main course; **на** ~ ~ **бифште́кс** the main course is steak.

второ́й (-а́я, -о́е, -ы́е) *прил* second; (*роль*) secondary; **быть** (*impf*) **на** ~**о́м пла́не** to stay in the background; **сейча́с** ~ **час** it's after one; **сейча́с полови́на** ~**о́го** it's half past one; **второ́е дыха́ние** second wind; **втора́я мо́лодость** second wind; **второ́й сорт** second class; *см также* **пя́тый**.

второкла́ссник (-а) *м pupil in second year at school (usually eight years old)*.

второкла́ссниц|а (-ы) *ж см* **второкла́ссник**.

второпя́х *нареч* in a hurry.

второсо́рт|ный (-ен, -на, -но) *прил* second-class; (*посредственный*) second-rate.

второстепе́н|ный (-ен, -на, -но) *прил* secondary.

в-тре́тьих *вводн сл* thirdly, in the third place.

втри́дорога *нареч* (*разг*): **плати́ть** ~ to pay a mint *или* bomb.

втро|е *нареч* (*больше, меньше*) three times; (*увеличить*) threefold.

втроём *нареч* in a group of three.

втройне́ *нареч* three times as much.

вту́л|ка (-ки; *gen pl* -ок) *ж* (*пробка*) plug; (*ТЕХ*) bush.

втыка́|ть (-ю) *несов от* **воткну́ть**.

втян|у́ть (-у́, -ешь; *impf* **втя́гивать**) *сов перех* (*втащить*) to pull in; (*вобрать*) to take in; **втя́гивать** (~ *perf*) кого-н в +*acc* (*перен: в дело*) to involve sb in; (: *в конфликт итп*) to draw sb into

▶ **втяну́ться** (*impf* **втя́гиваться**) *сов возв*: ~ся в +*acc* to get involved in; (*привыкнуть*) to settle into.

вуали́р|овать (-ую; *perf* **завуали́ровать**) *несов перех* to veil.

вуа́л|ь (-и) *ж* veil.

вуз (-а) *м сокр* (= **вы́сшее уче́бное заведе́ние**) institution of higher education.

ву́зовск|ий (-ая, -ое, -ие) *прил* university *опред*; ~**ая систе́ма** higher education system.

вулка́н (-а) *м* volcano; **де́йствующий/поту́хший** ~ active/extinct volcano.

вульга́рен *прил см* **вульга́рный**.

вульга́рност|ь (-и) *ж* vulgarity.

вульга́р|ный (-ен, -на, -но) *прил* (*человек, слова*) vulgar.

вундерки́нд (-а) *м* child prodigy.

вход (-а) *м* (*движение*) entry; (*место*) entrance; (*ТЕХ*) inlet; (*КОМП*) input.

вхо|ди́ть (-жу́, -дишь) *несов от* **войти́**.

входно́й *прил* (*дверь*) entrance *опред*; (*КОМП*) input *опред*; **входно́й биле́т** entrance ticket.

входя́щий (-ая, -ее, -ие) *прил* incoming.

вхожу́ *сов см* **входи́ть**.

вхолосту́ю *нареч*: **рабо́тать** ~ to idle.

вцеп|и́ться (-лю́сь, -ишься; *impf* **вцепля́ться**) *сов возв*: ~ в +*acc* to seize.

ВЦСПС *м сокр* (= **Всеросси́йский Центра́льный Сове́т профессиона́льных сою́зов**) *central trade-union council*.

ВЧ *ж сокр* (= **высо́кая частота́**) HF (= *high frequency*) ♦ *прил* (*высокочасто́тный*) HF = high-frequency).

вчера́ *нареч, м нескл* yesterday.

вчера́шн|ий (-яя, -ее, -ие) *прил* (*также перен*) yesterday's; **жить** (*impf*) ~**им днём** to live in the past.

вчерне́ *нареч* in rough.

вче́тверо *нареч* (*больше, меньше*) four times; (*увеличить*) fourfold.

вчетверо́м *нареч* in a group of four.

в-четвёртых *нареч* fourthly, in the fourth place.

вчита́|ться (-юсь; *impf* **вчи́тываться**) *сов возв*: ~ (в +*acc*) to get the gist (of).

вшей(те) *сов см* **вшить**.

вше́стеро *нареч* (*больше, меньше*) six times; (*увеличить*) sixfold.

вшестеро́м *нареч* in a group of six.

вши *итп сущ см* **вошь**.

вшива́|ть (-ю) *несов от* **вшить**.

вши́ве|ть (-ю; *perf* **завши́веть**) *несов неперех* to become lice-ridden.

вши́вый *прил* lice-ridden.

вши́рь *нареч* in breadth; **раздава́ться** (**разда́ться** *perf*) ~ to put on weight.

вшить (**вошью́, вошьёшь**; *imper* **вшей(те)**; *impf*

вшива́ть *сов перех* to sew in.

въеда́|ться (**-юсь**) *несов от* **въе́сться**.

въе́дешь *итп сов см* **въе́хать**.

въе́длив|ый (**-**, **-а**, **-о**) *прил* meticulous.

въе́ду *итп сов см* **въе́хать**.

въедя́тся *сов см* **въе́сться**.

въезд (**-а**) *м* (*движение*) entry; (*место*) entrance.

въездно́й *прил* entry *опред*.

въезжа́|ть (**-ю**) *несов от* **въе́хать**.

въе́сться (*3sg* **-стся**, *3pl* **-дя́тся**, *impf* **въеда́ться**) *сов возв*: ~ **в** +*acc* (*кислота*, *ржавчина*) to eat into; (*краска*, *грязь*) to become ingrained in.

въе́хать (*как* **е́хать**; *см* **Table 19**; *impf* **въезжа́ть**) *сов неперех* to enter; (*в новый дом*) to move in; (*наверх*: *на машине*) to drive up; (: *на коне*, *велосипеде*) to ride up.

вы- *префикс* (*in verbs*; *об исчерпанности действия*) indicating completion of action *eg*. **вы́яснить**, **вы́спаться**; (*о движении изнутри*) indicating movement outwards *eg*. **вы́бежать**.

Вы (**Вас**; *см* **Table 5b**) *мест* you; **быть** (*impf*) **на** ~ **с кем-н** to be on formal terms with sb.

вы (**вас**; *см* **Table 5b**) *мест* you (*plural*).

вы́бе|жать (*как* **бежа́ть**; *см* **Table 20**; *impf* **выбега́ть**) *сов неперех* to run out.

вы́бей(те) *сов см* **вы́бить**.

вы́бел|ить (**-ю**, **-ишь**) *сов от* **бели́ть**.

вы́беру(сь) *итп сов см* **вы́брать(ся)**.

вы́бива|ть(ся) (**-ю(сь)**) *несов от* **вы́бить(ся)**.

выбира́|ть (**-ю**) *несов от* **вы́брать** ♦ *перех*: ~ **слова́** to choose one's words.

▸ **выбира́ться** *несов от* **вы́браться**.

вы́б|ить (**-ью**, **-ьешь**; *imper* **вы́бей(те)**, *impf* **выбива́ть**) *сов перех* to knock out; (*противника*) to oust; (*ковер*) to beat; (*надпись*) to carve; (*разг*: *деньги*, *контракт*) to manage to get; **выбива́ть** (~ *perf*) **чек** (*кассир*) to ring up the total; **выбива́ть** (~ *perf*) **чек в ка́ссе** (*покупатель*) to get a ticket from the cashier (*to claim purchase*)

▸ **вы́биться** (*impf* **выбива́ться**) *сов возв*: ~**ся из** +*gen* (*освободиться*) to get out of; **выбива́ться** (~**ся** *perf*) **из сил** to wear o.s. out; **выбива́ться** (~**ся** *perf*) **из гра́фика** to fall behind schedule; ~**ся** (*perf*) **в лю́ди** to make one's way up in the world.

вы́боин|а (**-ы**) *ж* (*на дороге*) pothole; (*на металле*, *в стене*) dent.

вы́бор (**-а**) *м* choice; (*ассортимент*) choice, selection; **предлага́ть** (**предложи́ть** *perf*) **что-н на** ~ to offer a selection of sth; **по чьему́-н** ~**у** of sb's choice.

вы́бор|ка (**-ки**; *gen pl* **-ок**) *ж* (*обычно мн*: *из текста*) extract; (*статистическая*) sample.

вы́борный *прил* (*собрание*, *кампания*) election

опред; (*бюллетень*) ballot *опред*; (*должность*, *орган*) elective.

вы́борок *сущ см* **вы́борка**.

вы́бороч|ный (**-ен**, **-на**, **-но**) *прил* selective.

вы́борщик (**-а**) *м* (*полит*) ≈ elector (*US*), *elected representative taking part in elections on a higher level.*

вы́бор|ы (**-ов**) *мн* election *ед*.

вы́бра́сыва|ть(ся) (**-ю(сь)**) *несов от* **вы́бросить(ся)**.

вы́б|рать (**-еру**, **-ерешь**; *impf* **выбира́ть**) *сов перех* to choose; (*отобрать*) to pick; (*голосованием*) to elect

▸ **вы́браться** (*impf* **выбира́ться**) *сов возв* to manage to get out; (*разг*: *в театр*) to find time to go.

вы́бр|ить (**-ею**, **-еешь**; *impf* **выбрива́ть**) *сов перех* to shave.

вы́бро|дить (**-жу́**, **-дишь**) *сов от* **броди́ть**.

вы́брос (**-а**) *м* (*газа*, *радиации*) emission; (*отходов*) discharge; (*нефти*) spillage; (*десанта*) landing.

вы́бро|сить (**-шу**, **-сишь**; *impf* **выбра́сывать**) *сов перех* to throw out; (*разг*: *с работы*) to sack; (*отходы*) to discharge; (*газы*) to emit; (*десант*) to land; **выбра́сывать** (~ *perf*) **на ры́нок** to bring onto the market

▸ **вы́броситься** (*impf* **выбра́сываться**) *сов возв* (*из окна*) to throw o.s. out; **выбра́сываться** (~**ся** *perf*) **с балко́на** to throw o.s. off the balcony; **выбра́сываться** (~**ся** *perf*) **с парашю́том** to bale out.

вы́быть (*как* **быть**; *см* **Table 21**; *impf* **выбыва́ть**) *сов неперех*: ~ **из** +*gen* to leave.

вы́бью *итп сов см* **вы́бить**.

вы́вал|ить (**-ю**, **-ишь**; *impf* **выва́ливать**) *сов перех*: ~ (**из** +*gen*) to empty (out of)

▸ **вы́валиться** (*impf* **выва́ливаться**) *сов возв* (*выпасть*) to fall out; (*разг*: *толпа*) to pour out.

выведе́ни|е (**-я**) *ср* (*формулы*) deduction; (*цыплят*, *птенцов*) hatching; (*сорта*, *породы*) breeding; (*вредителей*) extermination.

вы́веду(сь) *итп сов см* **вы́вести(сь)**.

вы́вез|ти (**-у**, **-ешь**; *impf* **вывози́ть**) *сов перех* to take; (*товар*: *из страны*) to take out.

вы́вер|ить (**-ю**, **-ишь**; *impf* **выверя́ть**) *сов перех* to check; (*часы*) to set (*to the right time*).

вы́верн|уть (**-у**, **-ешь**; *impf* **вывёртывать** *или* **вывора́чивать**) *сов перех* (*винт*, *лампу*) to unscrew; (*пробку*) to pull out; (*карманы*, *рукава*) to turn inside out

▸ **вы́вернуться** (*impf* **вывёртываться** *или* **вывора́чиваться**) *сов возв* (*винт*, *лампа*) to come unscrewed; (*пробка*) to come out; (*человек*: *из беды*) to get out.

выверя́|ть (**-ю**) *несов от* **вы́верить**.

вы́ве|сить (**-шу**, **-сишь**; *impf* **выве́шивать**) *сов перех* (*флаг*, *лозунг*) to put up; (*бельё*) to hang out; (*объявление*) to post (up).

вы́вес|ка (-ки; *gen pl* -ок) *ж* sign; (*перен*) front; **под ~кой чего́-н** under the guise of sth.

вы́вес|ти (-ду, -дешь; *impf* **выводи́ть**) *сов перех* to take out; (*войска: из города*) to pull out; (: *на парад*) to bring out; (*формулу*) to deduce; (*заключение*) to draw; (*птенцов*) to hatch; (*сорт, породу*) to breed; (*вредителей*) to exterminate; (*КОМП*) to output; (*изобрази́ть*) to portray; (*исключить*): ~ **кого́-н из** +*gen* (*из партии, из комитета*) to expel sb from; (*из игры*) to take sb off; **выводи́ть** (~ *perf*) **кого́-н из шо́ка/из тра́нса** to bring sb out of a shock/trance; **выводи́ть** (~ *perf*) **кого́-н из терпе́ния** to exasperate sb; **выводи́ть** (~ *perf*) **кого́-н из равнове́сия** to disturb sb's equilibrium; **выводи́ть** (~ *perf*) **кого́-н в лю́ди** to help sb on in life; **выводи́ть** (~ *perf*) **кого́-н из себя́** to drive sb mad

▶ **вы́вестись** (*impf* **выводи́ться**) *сов возв* (*цыплята*) to hatch (out); (*исчезнуть*) to be eradicated.

вы́ветр|иться (*3sg* -ится, *3pl* -ятся, *impf* **выве́триваться**) *сов возв* (*запах, дым*) to disperse; (*берег, горные породы*) to weather.

выве́шива|ть (-ю) *несов от* **вы́весить**.

вы́вешу *сов см* **вы́весить**.

вы́вих (-а) *м* dislocation.

вы́вихн|уть (-у, -ешь; *impf* **выви́хивать**) *сов перех* to dislocate.

вы́вод (-а) *м* (*войск: из города*) withdrawal; (*формулы*) deduction; (*умозаключение*) conclusion; (*ЭЛЕК*) outlet; (*КОМП*) output; **приходи́ть (прийти́** *perf*) **к ~у** to come to a conclusion.

вы́води́ть(ся) (-вожу́(сь), -во́дишь(ся)) *несов от* **вы́вести(сь)**.

вы́вод|ок (-ка) *м* brood.

вывожу́(сь) *несов см* **выводи́ть(ся)**, **вывози́ть**.

вы́воз (-а) *м* removal; (*детей: на дачу*) taking out; (*товаров*) export.

вывози́ть (-вожу́, -во́зишь) *несов от* **вы́везти**.

вывозно́й *прил* export *опред*.

вывора́чива|ть(ся) (-ю(сь)) *несов от* **вы́вернуть(ся)**.

вы́гада|ть (-ю; *impf* **выга́дывать**) *сов перех* (*получить преимущество*) to gain; (*сэкономить*) to save.

вы́гиб (-а) *м* curve.

выгиба́|ть (-ю) *несов от* **вы́гнуть**.

вы́гла|дить (-жу, -дишь) *сов от* **гла́дить**.

вы́гля|деть (-жу, -дишь) *несов неперех* to look; **она́ хорошо́ ~дит сего́дня** she looks nice today; **он ~дит печа́льным** he looks sad.

выгля́дыва|ть (-ю) *несов от* **вы́глянуть**.

вы́гляжу *несов см* **вы́глядеть**.

вы́глян|уть (-у, -ешь; *impf* **выгля́дывать**) *сов неперех* to look out.

вы́гн|ать (-оню, -онишь; *impf* **выгоня́ть**) *сов*

перех to throw out; (*из страны*) to banish; (*разг: с работы*) to sack; (*стадо, табун*) to drive out.

вы́гн|уть (-у, -ешь; *impf* **выгиба́ть**) *сов перех* to bend; (*спину*) to arch.

выгова́рива|ть (-ю) *несов от* **вы́говорить**.

вы́говор (-а) *м* (*произношение*) accent; (*за провинность*) reprimand; **де́лать (сде́лать** *perf*) ~ **кому́-н за что́-н** to tell sb off for sth; **выноси́ть (вы́нести** *perf*) ~ **кому́-н** to issue sb with a reprimand.

вы́говор|ить (-ю, -ишь; *impf* **выгова́ривать**) *сов перех* (*произнести*) to pronounce; (*сказать*) to say

▶ **вы́говориться** *сов возв* (*разг*) to say what's on one's mind.

вы́год|а (-ы) *ж* advantage, benefit; (*прибыль*) profit; **кака́я ему́ от э́того ~?** what does he hope to gain from this?

вы́годно *нареч* (*продать*) at a profit ♦ *как сказ* it is profitable; **мне э́то ~** this is to my advantage; (*финансово*) this is profitable for me.

вы́годн|ый (-ен, -на, -но) *прил* (*сделка*) profitable; (*условия*) advantageous; (*впечатление*) favourable (*BRIT*), favorable (*US*); **выставля́ть (вы́ставить** *perf*) *или* **представля́ть (предста́вить** *perf*) **что-н в ~ном све́те** to show sth to (the) best advantage.

вы́гоню *итп сов см* **вы́гнать**.

выгоня́|ть (-ю) *несов от* **вы́гнать**.

вы́гор|еть (*3sg* -ит, *3pl* -ят, *impf* **выгора́ть**) *сов неперех* (*сгореть*) to burn down; (*высохнуть*) to be scorched; (*выцвести*) to fade; (*разг: удаваться*) to come off.

вы́горо|дить (-жу, -дишь; *impf* **выгора́живать**) *сов перех* (*разг*) to fence off.

выгравир|ова́ть (-ую) *несов от* **гравирова́ть**.

вы́гре|сти (-бу, -бешь; *pt* -б, -ла, -ло, *impf* **выгреба́ть**) *сов перех* to rake out.

вы́гру|зить (-жу, -зишь; *impf* **выгружа́ть**) *сов перех* to unload; (*КОМП*) to dump

▶ **вы́грузиться** (*impf* **выгружа́ться**) *сов возв* to unload; (*высадиться*) to disembark; (: *из поезда*) to get off.

выдава́|ть (-ю) *несов от* **вы́дать**

▶ **выдава́ться** *несов от* **вы́даться** ♦ *возв*: ~**ся чем-н** to stand out by virtue of sth.

вы́дав|ить (-лю, -ишь; *impf* **выда́вливать**) *сов перех* (*лимон*) to squeeze; (*ягоды*) to press; (*дверь*) to break down; **выда́вливать** (~ *perf*) **что-н из чего́-н** to squeeze sth out of sth.

вы́да|ть (*как дать; см Table 14; impf* **выдава́ть**) *сов перех* to give out; (*свидетельство, патент итп*) to issue; (*продукцию*) to produce; (*тайну, сообщников*) to give away; **выдава́ть** (~ *perf*) **кого́-н/что-н за** +*acc* to pass sb/sth off as; **выдава́ть** (~ *perf*) **де́вушку за́муж** to marry a girl off

▶ **вы́даться** (*impf* **выдава́ться**) *сов возв* (*берег*) to jut out; **сего́дня ~лся хоро́ший день** (*разг*) it's turned out fine today.

вы́дач|а (-и) ж (*справки*) issue; (*зарплаты*)
payment; (*продукции*) output; (*заложников*)
release.

вы́дашь(ся) *сов см* **вы́дать(ся)**.

выдаю́щийся (-аяся, -ееся, -иеся) *прил*
outstanding.

выдвига́|ть(ся) (-ю(сь)) *несов от*
вы́двинуть(ся).

выдвиже́ни|е (-я) *ср* (*кандидата*) nomination;
(*предложения*) proposal.

выдвижно́й *прил* sliding.

вы́двин|уть (-у, -ешь; *impf* **выдвига́ть**) *сов*
перех to pull out; (*предложение, гипотезу,*
человека) to put forward; (*обвинение*) to level
▶ **вы́двинуться** (*impf* **выдвига́ться**) *сов возв*
to slide out; (*работник*) to get ahead, advance;
выдвига́ться (*~ся perf*) **на руководя́щую**
рабо́ту to be promoted to a management
position.

вы́двор|ить (-ю, -ишь; *impf* **выдворя́ть**) *сов*
перех (*разг*) to kick out.

вы́дела|ть (-ю; *impf* **выде́лывать**) *сов перех* to
treat.

выделе́ни|е (-я) *ср* (*средств*) allocation;
(*физиология*) secretion; (*обычно мн: в*
гинекологии) discharge.

вы́дел|ить (-ю, -ишь; *impf* **выделя́ть**) *сов перех*
to assign, allocate; (*время*) to allot; (*отличить:*
ученика, цитату) to pick out; (*пот*) to secrete;
(*газы, вредные вещества*) to emit
▶ **вы́делиться** (*impf* **выделя́ться**) *сов возв* (*в*
отдельное предприятие) to split off; (*пот*) to
be secreted; (*газ, вредные вещества*) to be
emitted; **выделя́ться** (*~ся perf*) **чем-н** to stand
out by virtue of sth.

вы́делк|а (-и) ж treatment.

выде́лыва|ть (-ю) *несов от* **вы́делать** ◆ *перех*
(*разг: вытворять*) to get up to; **что э́то он там**
~ет? what is he up to?

выделя́|ть(ся) (-ю(сь)) *несов от*
вы́делить(ся).

выдёргива|ть (-ю) *несов от* **вы́дернуть**.

вы́держанный (-, -на, -но) *прил* (*человек*)
self-possessed; (*no short form; изложение,*
теория) consistent; (*вино, сыр*) mature;
(*древесина*) seasoned.

вы́держ|ать (-у, -ишь; *impf* **выде́рживать**) *сов*
перех (*давление, тяжесть*) to withstand;
(*боль*) to bear; (*экзамен, испытание*) to get
through; (*график, параметры*) to keep to;
(*вино, сыр*) to let mature; (*древесину*) to season
◆ *неперех*: **он не ~ал и рассмея́лся** he
couldn't contain his laughter; **кни́га ~ала мно́го**
изда́ний the book has been published in several
editions; **выде́рживать** (*~ perf*) **хара́ктер** to
hold one's ground.

вы́держек *сущ см* **вы́держка**.

выде́ржива|ть (-ю) *несов от* **вы́держать**.

вы́держк|а (-ки; *gen pl* -ек) ж (*самообладание*)
self-control; (*из текста*) excerpt; (*вина*)
maturing; (*древесины*) seasoning; (*ФОТО*)
exposure.

вы́дёргива|ть (-у, -ешь; *impf* **выдёргивать**) *сов*
перех to pull out.

вы́деру *итп сов см* **вы́драть**.

выдира́|ть (-ю) *несов от* **вы́драть**.

вы́долб|ить (-лю, -ишь) *сов от* **долби́ть**.

вы́дох (-а) *м* exhalation; **де́лать (сде́лать** *perf*)
~ to breathe out.

вы́дохн|уть (-у, -ешь; *impf* **выдыха́ть**) *сов*
перех to exhale, breathe out
▶ **вы́дохнуться** (*impf* **выдыха́ться**) *сов возв*
(*вино, духи*) to lose all smell; (*разг*) to be
washed out.

вы́др|а (-ы) ж otter.

вы́дра|ить (-ю, -ишь) *сов от* **дра́ить**.

вы́др|ать (-еру, -ерешь) *сов от* **драть** ◆ (*impf*
выдира́ть) *перех* (*разг: вырвать*) to tear out.

вы́дрессир|овать (-ую) *сов от*
дрессирова́ть.

вы́дуб|ить (-лю, -ишь) *несов от* **дуби́ть**.

выдува́|ть (-ю) *несов от* **вы́дуть**.

вы́думанный *прил* made-up.

вы́дума|ть (-ю; *impf* **выду́мывать**) *сов перех*
(*историю*) to make up, invent; (*игру*) to invent.

вы́думк|а (-ки; *gen pl* -ок) ж invention.

выду́мыва|ть (-ю) *несов от* **вы́думать**.

вы́ду|ть (-ю; *impf* **выдува́ть**) *сов перех* to blow
out; (*разг: водку итп*) to knock back; (*impf*
выдыва́ть *или* **ду́ть**; *тех*) to blow.

выдыха́ни|е (-я) *ср* exhalation.

выдыха́|ть(ся) (-ю(сь)) *несов от*
вы́дохнуть(ся).

выеда́|ть (-ю) *несов от* **вы́есть**.

вы́еду *итп сов см* **вы́ехать**.

вы́езд (-а) *м* (*отъезд*) departure; (*место*) way
out.

вы́езд|ить (-жу, -дишь; *impf* **выезжа́ть**) *сов*
перех (*лошадь*) to break in.

вы́ездк|а (-и) ж (*СПОРТ*) dressage.

вы́ездно́й *прил* (*виза, документ*) exit *опред*;
(*сессия суда*) in temporary premises;
(*спектакль*) travelling (*BRIT*), traveling (*US*); **~**
матч away match.

выезжа́|ть (-ю) *несов от* **вы́ехать**.

вы́езжу *сов см* **вы́ездить**.

вы́ем|ка (-ки; *gen pl* -ок) ж (*писем*) collection;
(*грунта*) excavation; (*углубление*) hollow.

вы́есть (*как есть; см* **Table 15**; *impf* **выеда́ть**)
сов перех (*съесть*) to eat; (*испортить*) to eat
through.

вы́е|хать (*как ехать; см* **Table 19**; *impf*
выезжа́ть) *сов неперех* (*уехать*) to leave;
(*машина, танк*) to drive out; (*всадник*) to ride
out; **выезжа́ть** (*~ perf*) **на ком-н/чём-н** (*перен:*
разг) to use sb/sth.

вы́жа|ть (-му, -мешь; *impf* **выжима́ть**) *сов перех* (*лимон*) to squeeze; (*ягоды*) to press; (*бельё*) to wring (out); **выжима́ть** (~ *perf*) **что-н из чего́-н** to squeeze sth out of sth; **выжима́ть** (~ *perf*) **что-н из кого́-н** (*перен*) to wring sth out of sb.

вы́жгу *итп сов см* **вы́жечь**.

вы́жда|ть (-у, -ешь; *impf* **выжида́ть**) *сов перех*: ~ **подходя́щий моме́нт** to pick one's moment.

вы́же|чь (-гу, -жешь *итп* -гут; *pt* -ег, -гла, -гло, *impf* **выжига́ть**) *сов перех* to burn; (*подлеж: солнце*) to scorch; **выжига́ть** (~ *perf*) **клеймо́** to brand; **выжига́ть** (*impf*) **по де́реву** to do pokerwork.

выжива́ни|е (-я) *ср* survival.

выжива́|ть (-ю) *несов от* **вы́жить**.

вы́живу *итп сов см* **вы́жить**.

выжига́|ть (-ю) *несов от* **вы́жечь**.

выжида́тельный (-ен, -ьна, -ьно) *прил* (*тактика, политика*) delaying; **занима́ть** (**заня́ть** *perf*) ~**ную пози́цию** to play a waiting game.

выжида́|ть (-ю) *несов от* **вы́ждать**.

выжима́|ть (-ю) *несов от* **вы́жать**.

вы́жи|ть (-ву, -вешь; *impf* **выжива́ть**) *сов непрех* to survive ♦ *перех* (*разг*) to drive out; ~ (*perf*) **из ума́** to become senile.

вы́жму *итп сов см* **вы́жать**.

вы́зва|ть (-ову, -овешь; *impf* **вызыва́ть**) *сов перех* to call; (*гнев, критику*) to provoke; (*восторг*) to arouse; (*пожар*) to cause; **вызыва́ть** (~ *perf*) **кого́-н на что-н** to challenge sb to sth; **вызыва́ть** (~ *perf*) **что-н к жи́зни** to give rise to sth; **вызыва́ть** (~ *perf*) **врача́ на́ дом** to call out a doctor

▶ **вы́зва|ться** (*impf* **вызыва́ться**) *сов возв*: ~**ся** +*infin* to volunteer to do.

вы́зво́л|ить (-ю, -ишь; *impf* **вызволя́ть**) *сов перех* (*разг*) to bale out.

вы́здоров|еть (-лю, -ишь; *impf* **выздора́вливать**) *сов непрех* to recover.

вы́зов (-а) *м* call; (*в суд, к директору*) summons; ~ +*dat* (*обществу, родителям итп*) challenge; **броса́ть** (**бро́сить** *perf*) ~ **кому́-н/чему́-н** to challenge sb/sth.

вы́зову(сь) *сов см* **вы́звать(ся)**.

вы́зубр|ить (-ю, -ишь) *сов от* **зубри́ть**.

вызыва́|ть(ся) (-ю(сь)) *несов от* **вы́звать(ся)**.

вызыва́ющий (-ая, -ее, -ие) *прил* provocative.

вы́игра|ть (-ю; *impf* **выи́грывать**) *сов перех* to win ♦ *непрех* (*получить выгоду*) to gain, benefit.

вы́игрыш (-а) *м* (*матча*) winning; (*крупный, де́нежный*) winnings *мн*; (*выгода*) advantage; ~ **пал на но́мер 10** number 10 wins.

вы́игрышн|ый (-ен, -на, -но) *прил* (*выгодный*) advantageous; ~ **вклад** ≈ premium bonds.

вы́йти (*как* **идти́**; *см* **Table 18**; *impf* **выходи́ть**) *сов непрех* to leave; (*из игры*) to drop out; (*сойти*) to get off; (*появиться*) to come out; (*случиться*) to ensue; (*КОМП*) to exit; (*иссякнуть*) to run out; (*оказаться*): ~ +*instr* to

come out; **выходи́ть** (~ *perf*) **из** +*gen* (*из затруднения*) to get out of; (*из употребления, из мо́ды*) to go out of; (*из крестья́н*) to be descended from; (*из гра́фика, из расписа́ния*) to fall behind; **выходи́ть** (~ *perf*) **на** +*acc* (*разг*) to get in with; **выходи́ть** (~ *perf*) **за́муж за** +*acc* to marry (*of woman*), get married to; **выходи́ть** (~ *perf*) **из больни́цы** to leave hospital; **выходи́ть** (~ *perf*) **из себя́** to lose one's temper; **выходи́ть** (~ *perf*) **из систе́мы** (*КОМП*) to log off; **из него́** ~**шел хоро́ший врач** he has turned out to be a good doctor; **из э́того ничего́ не** ~**шло** nothing came of it.

выка́пыва|ть (-ю) *несов от* **вы́колоть**.

выка́пыва|ть (-ю) *несов от* **вы́копать**.

выкара́бка|ться (-юсь; *impf* **выкара́бкиваться**) *сов возв*: ~ (**из** +*gen*) to clamber out (of); (*разг: из тру́дностей*) to get o.s. out (of); (: *из боле́зни*) to pull through.

выка́рмлива|ть (-ю) *несов от* **вы́кормить**.

вы́ка|тить (-чу, -тишь; *impf* **выка́тывать**) *сов перех* (*что-н кру́глое*) to roll out; (*что-н на колёсах*) to wheel out; **выка́тывать** (~ *perf*) **глаза́** (*разг*) to open one's eyes wide.

вы́кача|ть (-ю; *impf* **выка́чивать**) *сов перех* to pump out; (*перен: разг: деньги*) to squeeze *или* wring out.

вы́качу *сов см* **вы́катить**.

выка́шива|ть (-ю) *несов от* **вы́косить**.

выки́дыва|ть (-ю) *несов от* **вы́кинуть**.

вы́кидыш (-а) *м* miscarriage.

вы́ки|путь (-у, -ешь; *impf* **выки́дывать**) *сов перех* (*мусор*) to throw out; (*пропустить*) to omit; (*разг: товар*) to put on sale; **выки́дывать** (~ *perf*) **шту́ку** *или* **фо́кус** (*разг*) to play a trick.

вы́кип|еть (3*sg* -ит, 3*pl* -ят, *impf* **выкипа́ть**) *сов непрех* to boil away.

вы́кла́д|ка (-ки; *gen pl* -ок) *ж* (*облицовка*) facing; (*обычно мн: расчёты*) calculation.

выкла́дыва|ть(ся) (-ю(сь)) *несов от* **вы́ложить(ся)**.

выключа́тел|ь (-я) *м* switch.

вы́ключ|ить (-у, -ишь; *impf* **выключа́ть**) *сов перех* to turn off; (*исключить*) to expel

▶ **вы́ключ|иться** (*impf* **выключа́ться**) *сов возв* (*мотор, телеви́зор итп*) to go off; (*свет*) to go out; (*перен*) to switch off.

вы́клянч|ить (-у, -ишь) *сов от* **кля́нчить**.

вы́ко|вать (-ую; *impf* **выко́вывать**) *сов перех* (*металл*) to forge.

выкола́чива|ть (-ю) *несов от* **вы́колотить**.

вы́коло|тить (-чу, -тишь; *impf* **выкола́чивать**) *сов перех* (*ковёр*) to beat; (*налоги*) to wring out.

вы́коло|ть (-ю, -ешь; *impf* **выка́лывать**) *сов перех* to poke out.

вы́колочу *сов см* **вы́колотить**.

вы́копа|ть (-ю; *impf* **выка́пывать** *или* **копа́ть**) *сов перех* (*яму*) to dig; (*колодец*) to sink; (*овощи*) to dig up.

вы́корм|ить (-лю, -ишь; *impf* **выка́рмливать**) *сов перех* to rear.

вы́корч|евать (-ую; *impf* **выкорчёвывать** *или* **корчева́ть**) *сов перех* to uproot; (*перен*) to root out.

вы́ко|сить (-шу, -сишь; *impf* **выка́шивать**) *сов перех* to mow.

выкра́дыва|ть (-ю) *несов от* **вы́красть**.

выкра́ива|ть (-ю) *несов перех* to cut out.

вы́кра|сить(ся) (-шу(сь), -сишь(ся)) *сов от* **кра́сить(ся)**.

вы́кра|сть (-ду, -дешь; *impf* **выкра́дывать**) *сов перех* to steal.

вы́крик (-а) *м* shout.

вы́крикн|уть (-у, -ешь; *impf* **выкри́кивать**) *сов перех* to shout *или* cry out.

вы́кристаллиз|ова́ться (*3sg* -уется, *3pl* -уются) *сов от* **кристаллизова́ться**.

вы́кроек *сущ см* **вы́кройка**.

вы́кро|ить (-ю, -ишь) *сов от* **кро́ить** ◆ (*impf* **выкра́ивать**) *перех* (*перен*): ~ **вре́мя на** +*acc* to find time for; ~ (*perf*) **де́ньги на** +*acc* to scrape together money for.

вы́кройка (-йки; *gen pl* -ек) *ж* pattern.

выкрута́с|ы (-ов) *мн* (*разг: в танце*) fancy footwork *ед*; (*перен: в речи*) fancy turns *мн* of phrase; (: *в поведении*) foibles *мн*.

вы́кру|тить (-чу, -тишь; *impf* **выкру́чивать**) *сов перех* to unscrew; **выкру́чивать** (~ *perf*) **ру́ки кому́-н** (*также перен*) to twist sb's arm

▶ **вы́крутиться** *сов возв* to come unscrewed; (*перен*) to get o.s. out.

вы́куп (-а) *м* (*действие: заложника*) ransoming; (: *вещей*) redemption; (*плата*) ransom.

выкупа́|ть(ся) (-ю(сь)) *несов от* **купа́ть(ся)**.

вы́куп|ить (-лю, -ишь; *impf* **выкупа́ть**) *сов перех* (*заложника*) to ransom; (*вещи*) to redeem.

вы́кур|ить (-ю, -ишь; *impf* **выку́ривать**) *сов перех* (*трубку*) to smoke; (*зверя*) to smoke out.

выла́влива|ть (-ю) *несов от* **вы́ловить**.

вы́лаз|ка (-ки; *gen pl* -ок) *ж* (*ВОЕН*) sortie.

выла́мыва|ть (-ю) *несов от* **вы́ломать**.

вылеза́|ть (-ю) *несов от* **вы́лезти**.

вы́лез|ти (-у, -ешь; *pt* -, -ла, -ло, *impf* **вылеза́ть**) *сов неперех* (*волосы, шерсть*) to fall out; **вылеза́ть** (~ *perf*) (**из** +*gen*) to climb out (of); (*разг: из долгов*) to get o.s. out (of); (: *из болезней*) to pull through; (: *рубашка*) to hang out.

вы́леп|ить (-лю, -ишь) *сов от* **лепи́ть**.

вы́лет (-а) *м* departure.

вы́ле|теть (-чу, -тишь; *impf* **вылета́ть**) *сов неперех* to fly out; (*машина*) to hurtle out; **его́ и́мя ~тело у меня́ из головы́** his name has slipped my mind.

вы́леч|ить (-у, -ишь; *impf* **вылё́чивать** *или* **лечи́ть**) *сов перех* to cure

▶ **вы́лечиться** (*impf* **вылё́чиваться** *или* **лечи́ться**) *несов возв* to be cured.

вы́лечу *сов см* **вы́лететь**.

вылива́|ть(ся) (-ю(сь)) *несов от* **вы́лить(ся)**.

вы́ли|зать (-жу, -жешь; *impf* **выли́зывать**) *сов перех* (*тарелку*) to lick clean; (*разг: дом*) to spring-clean.

вы́л|ить (-ью, -ьешь; *impf* **вылива́ть**) *сов перех* to pour out; (*impf* **лить**; *деталь, статую*) to cast

▶ **вы́литься** (*impf* **вылива́ться**) *сов возв* (*также перен*) to pour out; **вылива́ться** (~ся *perf*) **в** +*acc* to turn into.

вы́лов|ить (-лю, -ишь; *impf* **выла́вливать**) *сов перех* to catch.

вы́лож|ить (-у, -ишь; *impf* **выкла́дывать**) *сов перех* to lay out; (*перен: правду*) to lay bare; **выкла́дывать** (~ *perf*) **что-н чем-н** (*кирпичом, плиткой*) to face sth with sth

▶ **вы́ложиться** (*impf* **выкла́дываться**) *сов возв* to apply o.s.

вы́лома|ть (-ю; *impf* **выла́мывать**) *сов перех* to break open.

вы́луп|иться (*3sg* -ится, *3pl* -ятся, *impf* **вылу́пливаться**) *сов возв* (*птенцы*) to hatch (out).

вы́лью(сь) *итп сов см* **вы́лить(ся)**.

вы́ма|зать (-жу, -жешь) *сов от* **ма́зать** ◆ (*impf* **выма́зывать**) *перех* (*покрыть*) to coat; (*разг: запачкать*) to smear

▶ **вы́мазаться** *сов от* **ма́заться**.

выма́лива|ть (-ю) *несов от* **вы́молить**.

выма́н|ить (-ю, -ишь; *impf* **выма́нивать**) *сов перех* (*зверя*) to lure out; **выма́нивать** (~ *perf*) **что-н у кого́-н** to cheat sb out of sth.

вы́мара|ть(ся) (-ю(сь)) *сов от* **мара́ть(ся)**.

выма́чива|ть (-ю) *несов от* **вы́мочить**.

вы́мени *итп сущ см* **вы́мя**.

вы́м|ереть (*3sg* -рет, *3pl* -рут, *impf* **вымира́ть**) *сов неперех* (*динозавры*) to die out, become extinct; (*город, селение*) to be dead.

вы́ме|сти (-ту, -тешь; *pt* -л, -ла, -ло, *impf* **вымета́ть**) *сов перех* to sweep out.

вы́ме|стить (-щу, -стишь; *impf* **вымеща́ть**) *сов перех*: ~ **что-н на ком-н** to take sth out on sb.

вымета́|ть (-ю) *несов от* **вы́мести**.

вы́мету *итп сов см* **вы́мести**.

вымеща́|ть (-ю) *несов от* **вы́местить**.

вы́мещу *сов см* **вы́местить**.

вымира́|ть (*3sg* -ет, *3pl* -ют) *несов от* **вы́мереть**.

вымога́тел|ь (-я) *м* extortionist.

вымога́тельств|о (-а) *ср* extortion.

вымога́|ть (-ю) *несов перех* to extort.

вы́мокн|уть (-ну, -нешь; *pt* -, -ла, -ло) *сов неперех* to get soaked through.

вы́молв|ить (-лю, -ишь) *сов перех* to utter.

вы́мол|ить (-ю, -ишь; *impf* **выма́ливать**) *перех* to successfully plead for.

вы́моч|ить (-у, -ишь; *impf* **выма́чивать**) *сов*

перех to soak.

вы́мощу *сов см* **вы́мостить**.

вы́мою *итп сов см* **вы́мыть**.

вы́мпел (-а) *м* (*на мачте корабля*) pennant; (*награда*) award (*in the form of a pennant*).

вы́мрет *итп сов см* **вы́мереть**.

вы́муштр|овать (-ую) *сов от* **муштрова́ть**.

вымыва́|ть (-ю) *несов от* **вы́мыть**.

вы́мыс|ел (-ла) *м* fantasy; (*ложь*) fabrication.

вы́м|ыть (-ою, -оешь; *impf* **мыть**) *сов перех* to wash; (*impf* **вымыва́ть**; *яму*) to hollow out; (*русло*) to channel out.

вы́мышлен|ный (-, -на, -но) *прил* fictitious.

вы́м|я (-ени; *как* **вре́мя**; *см* Table 4) *ср* udder.

вына́шива|ть (-ю) *несов от* **вы́носить**.

вы́нес|ти (-у, -ешь; *pt* -, -ла, -ло, *impf* **выноси́ть**) *сов перех* to carry *или* take out; (*приговор, вердикт*) to pass, pronounce; (*впечатления, знания*) to gain; (*боль, оскорбление*) to bear; **выноси́ть** (~ *perf*) **кому́-н благода́рность** to officially thank sb; **выноси́ть** (~ *perf*) **кому́-н вы́говор** to issue sb with a reprimand

▶ **вы́нестись** (*impf* **выноси́ться**) *сов возв* to fly *или* rush out.

вынима́|ть (-ю) *несов от* **вы́нуть**.

вы́нос (-а) *м* (*тела*) bearing out (*of coffin*); **продава́ть** (*impf*) **на** ~ to do take-aways.

выно|си́ть (-шу, -сишь; *impf* **вына́шивать**) *сов перех* (*перен*) to nurture; (*младенца*) to carry to term.

вын|оси́ть (-ошу́, -о́сишь) *несов от* **вы́нести** ♦ *перех*: **я его́ не ~ошу́** I can't bear *или* stand him

▶ **выноси́ться** *несов от* **вы́нестись**.

вынос́лив|ый (-, -а, -о) *прил* hardy.

вы́ношу *сов см* **вы́носить**.

выношу́(сь) *несов см* **выноси́ть(ся)**.

вы́ну|дить (-жу, -дишь; *impf* **вынужда́ть**) *сов перех*: ~ **кого́-н/что-н к чему́-н** to force sb/sth into sth; **вынужда́ть** (~ *perf*) **кого́-н/что-н** +*infin* to force sb/sth into doing.

вы́нужденный *прил* forced; **вы́нужденная поса́дка** emergency landing.

вы́нужу *сов см* **вы́нудить**.

вы́нут|ь (-у, -ешь; *impf* **вынима́ть**) *сов перех* to take out.

вы́нырн|уть (-у, -ешь; *impf* **выны́ривать**) *сов неперех* (*из воды*) to surface; (*разг: из-за угла*) to pop up.

вы́пад (-а) *м* (*враждебное действие*) attack; (*СПОРТ*) lunge (*in fencing*).

выпада́|ть (-ю) *несов от* **вы́пасть**.

выпаде́ни|е (-я) *ср* (*осадков*) fall; (*зубов, волос*) falling out.

вы́паду *итп сов см* **вы́пасть**.

вы́пал|ить (-ю, -ишь) *сов от* **пали́ть** ♦ (*impf* **выпа́ливать**) *перех* (*перен: разг*) to blurt out.

вы́пар|иться (*3sg* -ится, *3pl* -ятся, *impf* **выпа́риваться**) *сов возв* to evaporate.

вы́па|сть (-ду, -дешь; *impf* **выпада́ть**) *сов неперех* to fall out; (*осадки*) to fall; (+*dat*;

задание, задача итп) to fall to; **мне** ~**л слу́чай/сча́стье встре́тить его́** I chanced to/ had the luck to meet him.

вы́пачка|ть(ся) (-ю(сь)) *сов от* **па́чкать(ся)**.

вы́пей(те) *итп сов см* **вы́пить**.

выпека́|ть (-ю) *несов от* **вы́печь**.

вы́пеку *итп сов см* **вы́печь**.

вы́пер|еть (-ру, -решь; *pt* -ер, -ерла, -ерло, *impf* **выпира́ть**) *сов перех* (*разг*) to chuck out.

вы́пест|овать (-ую) *сов от* **пе́стовать**.

вы́печк|а (-и) *ж* baking.

вы́печн|о́й *прил*: ~**ы́е изде́лия** bakery products *мн*.

вы́пе|чь (-ку, -чешь *итп*, -кут; *impf* **выпека́ть**) *сов перех* to bake.

вы́пивк|а (-и) *ж* (*разг: попойка*) boozing ♦ *собир* (*спиртное*) booze.

выпира́|ть (-ю) *несов от* **вы́переть** ♦ *неперех* (*разг: выпячиваться*) to stick out.

выпи|са́ть (-шу, -шешь; *impf* **выпи́сывать**) *сов перех* (*цитату, данные*) to copy *или* write out; (*пропуск, счёт, рецепт*) to make out; (*газету, журнал*) to subscribe to; (*пациента*) to discharge; (*с местопроживания*) to change sb's residence permit

▶ **вы́писаться** (*impf* **выпи́сываться**) *несов возв* (*из больницы*) to be discharged; (*с местопроживания*) to change one's residence permit.

вы́пис|ка (-ки; *gen pl* -ок) *ж* (*действие*) copying *или* writing out; (*цитата*) extract; ~ **с ба́нковского счёта** bank statement.

выпи́сыва|ть(ся) (-ю(сь)) *несов от* **вы́писать(ся)**.

вы́п|ить (-ью, -ьешь; *imper* -ей(те)) *сов от* **пить**.

вы́пишу(сь) *итп сов см* **вы́писать(ся)**.

вы́плав|ить (-лю, -ишь; *impf* **выплавля́ть**) *сов перех* to smelt.

вы́плав|ка (-ки; *gen pl* -ок) *ж* (*действие*) smelting; (*продукция*) smelted metal.

вы́плавлю *сов см* **вы́плавить**.

выплавля́|ть (-ю) *несов от* **вы́плавить**.

вы́плавк|а *сущ см* **вы́плавка**.

вы́плат|а (-ы) *ж* payment.

вы́пла|тить (-чу, -тишь; *impf* **выпла́чивать**) *сов перех* to pay; (*долг*) to pay off.

вы́плёвыва|ть (-ю) *несов от* **вы́плюнуть**.

вы́плесн|уть (-у, -ешь; *impf* **выплёскивать**) *сов перех* to pour out.

вы́плы|ть (-ву, -вешь; *impf* **выплыва́ть**) *сов неперех* to swim out; (*всплыть*) to surface; (*перен*) to emerge, come to light.

вы́плюн|уть (-у, -ешь; *impf* **выплёвывать**) *сов перех* to spit out.

вы́полз|ти (-у, -ешь; *pt* -, -ла, -ло, *impf* **выполза́ть**) *сов неперех* to crawl out.

выполни́м|ый (-, -а, -о) *прил* practicable, feasible.

вы́полн|ить (-ю, -ишь; *impf* **выполня́ть**) *сов перех* (*задание, заказ*) to carry out; (*план, условие*) to fulfil (*BRIT*), fulfill (*US*); (*рисунок, условие*) to fulfil (*BRIT*), fulfill (*US*); (*рисунок,* *чертёж*) to execute; (*КОМП*) to run.

вы́полоска|ть (**-ю**) *сов от* полоска́ть.

вы́пол|оть (**-ю, -ешь**) *сов от* поло́ть.

вы́пор|оть (**-ю, -ешь**) *сов от* поро́ть.

вы́порхн|у́ть (**-у, -ешь**) *сов неперех* to dart out.

вы́потрош|и́ть (**-у, -ишь**) *сов от* потроши́ть.

вы́прав|ить (**-лю, -ишь;** *impf* **выправля́ть**) *сов перех* (*расспрямить*) to straighten (up); (*текст, чертёж*) to correct; (*положение, ситуацию*) to rectify, put right

► **вы́правиться** (*impf* **выправля́ться**) *несов возв* (*что-н кривое*) to straighten (out); (*положение, ситуация*) to be rectified.

вы́прав|ка (**-ки;** *gen pl* **-ок**) *ж* bearing.

вы́правлю(сь) *сов см* вы́править(ся).

выправля́|ть(ся) (**-ю(сь)**) *несов от* вы́править(ся).

вы́правок *сущ см* вы́правка.

выпра́шива|ть (**-ю**) *несов перех* to beg for.

вы́про|си́ть (**-шу, -сишь**) *сов перех*: **он ~си́л у отца́ маши́ну** he persuaded his father to give him the car.

вы́пру *итп сов см* вы́переть.

вы́прыгн|уть (**-у, -ешь;** *impf* **выпры́гивать**) *сов неперех* to jump out.

вы́прям|ить (**-лю, -ишь;** *impf* **выпрямля́ть**) *сов перех* to straighten (out)

► **вы́прямиться** (*impf* **выпрямля́ться**) *несов возв* to straighten (up).

выпрямля́|ть(ся) (**-ю(сь)**) *несов от* вы́прямить(ся).

вы́пуклый *прил* (*лоб, глаза итп*) bulging; (*стекло, линза*) convex; (*буква*) embossed.

вы́пуск (**-а**) *м* (*продукции*) output; (*газа, воздуха*) emission, release; (*книги*) instalment (*BRIT*), installment (*US*); (*денег, марок, акций*) issue; (*учащиеся*) school leavers *мн* (*BRIT*), graduates *мн* (*US*).

выпуска́|ть (**-ю**) *несов от* вы́пустить.

выпускни́к (**-а́**) *м* final-year student; (*окончивший вуз*) graduate.

выпускни́ц|а (**-ы**) *ж см* выпускни́к.

выпускн|о́й *прил* (*класс*) final-year; (*ТЕХ*): ~ **кла́пан** exhaust valve; ~**о́е отве́рстие** outlet; **выпускно́й ве́чер** graduation; **выпускно́й экза́мен** final exam, finals *мн*.

вы́пу|стить (**-щу, -стишь;** *impf* **выпуска́ть**) *сов перех* to let out; (*дым*) to exhale; (*заключённого, заложника*) to release; (*специалистов*) to turn out; (*продукцию*) to produce; (*книгу, газету итп*) to publish; (*заём, марки*) to issue; (*деньги*) to put into circulation; (*исключить: часть текста, параграф*) to omit; **выпуска́ть** (~ *perf*) (**из рук**) to let go of; **выпуска́ть** (~ *perf*) **в свет** (*книгу, журнал*) to publish; **выпуска́ть** (~ *perf*) **из рук возмо́жность/шанс** to miss an opportunity/a chance; **выпуска́ть** (~ *perf*) **кого́-н/что-н из**

вы́ду to let sb/sth out of sight.

вы́пута|ться (**-юсь;** *impf* **выпу́тываться**) *сов возв* (*также перен*) to extricate o.s.

выпу́тыва|ться (**-юсь**) *несов от* вы́путаться.

вы́пущу *сов см* вы́пустить.

вы́пью *итп сов см* вы́пить.

вы́пя|тить (**-чу, -тишь;** *impf* **выпя́чивать**) *сов перех* (*разг: грудь*) to stick out; **выпя́чивать** (~ *perf*) **губу́** to pout.

вы́работа|ть (**-ю;** *impf* **выраба́тывать**) *сов перех* to produce; (*план*) to work out; (*характер, стиль, привычку*) to develop.

вы́работ|ка (**-ки;** *gen pl* **-ок**) *ж* (*действие*) production; (*годовая, промышленная*) output, production; (*продукты*) yield.

выража́|ть(ся) (**-ю(сь)**) *несов от* вы́разить(ся).

выража́|ть (**-ю**) *несов от* вы́разить

► **выража́ться** *несов от* вы́разиться ♦ *возв* (*разг*) to swear.

выраже́ни|е (**-я**) *ср* expression.

вы́ражу(сь) *сов см* вы́разить(ся).

вырази́тельно *нареч* (*читать*) expressively.

вырази́тельный (**-ен, -ьна, -ьно**) *прил* expressive.

вы́ра|зить (**-жу, -зишь;** *impf* **выража́ть**) *сов перех* to express

► **вы́разиться** (*impf* **выража́ться**) *сов возв* (*чувство, состояние*) to manifest *или* express itself; (*человек*) to express o.s.

выраста́|ть (**-ю**) *несов от* вы́расти.

вы́ра|сти (**-асту, -астешь;** *pt* **-ос, -осла, -осли**) *сов от* расти́ ♦ (*impf* **выраста́ть**) *неперех* (*горы, башня*) to rise up; **выраста́ть** (~ *perf*) **в** +*acc* to become; **выраста́ть** (~ *perf*) **из оде́жды** to grow out of one's clothes.

вы́ра|стить (**-щу, -стишь;** *impf* **выра́щивать**) *сов перех* (*детей*) to raise; (*растение*) to grow; (*животных*) to rear.

выра́щива|ние (**-я**) *ср* (*растений*) cultivation; (*животных*) rearing.

выра́щива|ть (**-ю**) *несов от* вы́растить.

вы́ращу *сов см* вы́растить.

вы́рв|ать (**-у, -ешь;** *impf* **вырыва́ть**) *сов перех* to pull out; (*отнять*): ~ **что-н у кого́-н** to snatch sth from sb; (*перен*) to wring sth from sb ♦ (*impf* **рвать**) *безл* (*разг*): **её ~ало** she threw up; **ему́ ~али зуб** he had his tooth taken out

► **вы́рваться** (*impf* **вырыва́ться**) *сов возв* (*из объя́тий*) to free o.s.; (*из рук, из пут*) to break free, escape; (*из тюрьмы*) to make a break; (*перен: в театр, на концерт*) to manage to get away; (*пламя*) to shoot out; (*дым*) to pour out.

вы́режу *итп сов см* вы́резать.

вы́рез (**-а**) *м*: **пла́тье с больши́м ~ом** a low-cut dress.

вы́ре|зать (**-жу, -жешь;** *impf* **выреза́ть**) *сов перех* (*фотографию итп*) to cut out; (*опухоль,* *гнойник*) to remove; (*из дерева, из кости итп*) to carve; (*на камне, на металле итп*) to engrave; (*население, животных*) to slaughter.

вы́рез|ка (-ки; *gen pl* -ок) *ж* (*газетная*) cutting, clipping; (*мясная*) fillet.

вы́рис|оваться (*3sg* -уется, *3pl* -уются, *impf* **вырисо́вываться**) *сов возв* (*стать видным*) to stand out; (*стать явным*) to appear; (*перен: ситуация*) to emerge.

вы́ровня|ть (-ю) *сов от* **ровня́ть** ♦ (*impf* **выра́внивать**) *перех* to level

▸ **вы́ровняться** (*impf* **выра́внивать́ся**) *сов возв* (*отряд*) to form ranks; (*перен: характер*) to improve.

вы́род|иться (*3sg* -ится, *3pl* -ятся, *impf* **вырожда́ться**) *сов возв* (*также перен*) to degenerate.

вы́род|ок (-ка) *м* (*разг*) degenerate.

вырожда́|ться (-юсь) *несов от* **вы́родиться**.

вырожде́ни|е (-я) *ср* degeneration.

вы́рон|ить (-ю, -ишь) *сов перех* to drop.

вы́рос *итп сов см* **вы́расти**.

вы́рост (-а) *м*: **покупа́ть оде́жду на ~** (*разг*) *to buy clothes with room for growth*.

вы́рою *итп сов см* **вы́рыть**.

выруба́|ть (-ю) *несов от* **вы́рубить**.

вы́руб|ить (-лю, -ишь; *impf* **выруба́ть**) *сов перех* (*лес, деревья*) to cut down; (*яму, углубление*) to hew out; (*свет, сигнализацию*) to cut off.

выруга́|ть(ся) (-ю(сь)) *сов от* **руга́ть(ся)**.

выруч|ить (-у, -ишь; *impf* **выруча́ть**) *сов перех* to rescue, help out; (*деньги*) to make; **выруча́ть** (**~** *perf*) **кого́-н из беды́** to help sb out of trouble.

вы́руч|ка (-и) *ж* rescue; (*деньги*) takings *мн*; **приходи́ть** (**прийти́** *perf*) **на ~у кому́-н** to come to sb's rescue.

вырыва́|ть(ся) (-ю(сь)) *несов от* **вы́рвать(ся)**, **вы́рыть**.

вы́р|ыть (-ою, -оешь) *сов от* **рыть** ♦ (*impf* **вырыва́ть**) *перех* (*картофель, камень итп*) to dig up.

вы́са|дить (-жу, -дишь; *impf* **выса́живать**) *сов перех* (*растение*) to plant out; (*пассажира: дать выйти*) to drop off; (*: заставить выйти*) to throw out; (*войска, отряд*) to land; **~** (*perf*) **деса́нт** to make a landing

▸ **вы́садиться** (*impf* **выса́живаться**) *сов возв*: **~ся (из** +*gen*) to get off.

выса́сыва|ть (-ю) *несов от* **вы́сосать**.

высве́тлива|ть (-ю; *perf* **вы́светлить**) *несов перех* (*также комп*) to highlight.

высве́чивани|е (-я) *ср* (*комп*) highlighting.

высвобо|дить (-жу, -дишь; *impf* **высвобожда́ть**) *сов перех* (*ногу, руку*) to free; (*рабочую силу, средства*) to release; (*время*) to set aside.

вы́сек *итп сов см* **вы́сечь**.

высека́|ть (-ю) *несов от* **вы́сечь**.

вы́секу *итп сов см* **вы́сечь**.

вы́сел|ить (-ю, -ишь; *impf* **выселя́ть**) *сов перех* to evict.

вы́се|чь (-ку, -чешь *итп*, -кут; *pt* -к, -кла, -кло) *сов от* **сечь** ♦ (*impf* **высека́ть**) *перех* (*фигуру*) to carve, sculpt; (*надпись*) to engrave.

вы́си|деть (-жу, -дишь; *impf* **выси́живать**) *сов перех* to hatch; (*перен: лекцию*) to sit out.

вы́с|иться (*3sg* -ится, *3pl* -ятся) *несов возв* to tower.

выска́блива|ть (-ю) *несов от* **вы́скоблить**.

выска|за́ть (-жу, -жешь; *impf* **выска́зывать**) *сов перех* to express; **я ему́ всё ~зал** I told him exactly what I thought

▸ **вы́сказаться** (*impf* **выска́зываться**) *сов возв* to speak one's mind; **выска́зываться** (**~ся** *perf*) **про́тив** +*gen*/**за** +*acc* to speak out against/in favour of.

выска́зывани|е (-я) *ср* (*мнения*) expression; (*суждение*) statement.

выска́зыва|ть(ся) (-ю(сь)) *несов от* **вы́сказать(ся)**.

выска́кива|ть (-ю) *несов от* **вы́скочить**.

выска́льзыва|ть (-ю) *несов от* **вы́скользнуть**.

вы́скобл|ить (-ю, -ишь; *impf* **выска́бливать**) *сов перех* (*очистить*) to scrape; (*удалить скоблением*) to remove.

вы́скользн|уть (-у, -ешь; *impf* **выска́льзывать**) *сов неперех* (*также перен*) to slip out.

вы́скоч|ить (-у, -ишь; *impf* **выска́кивать**) *сов неперех* to jump out; **его́ и́мя ~ило у меня́ из головы́** (*разг*) his name has slipped my mind.

вы́скоч|ка (-ки; *gen pl* -ек) *м/ж* (*разг: пренебр*) upstart.

вы́|слать (-шлю, -шлешь; *impf* **высыла́ть**) *сов перех* (*посылку, деньги*) to send off; (*полит*) to exile; (*шпиона*) to deport.

вы́сле|дить (-жу, -дишь; *impf* **высле́живать**) *сов перех* to track down.

вы́слу|га (-и) *ж*: **за ~у лет** for long service.

вы́служ|ить (-у, -ишь; *impf* **выслу́живать**) *сов перех* (*пенсию, повышение*) to qualify for; (*орден, награду*) to earn

▸ **вы́служиться** *сов возв* to work one's way up.

вы́слуша|ть (-ю; *impf* **выслу́шивать**) *сов перех* to hear out.

вы́сме|ять (-ю; *impf* **высме́ивать**) *сов перех* to ridicule.

вы́сморка|ть (-ю) *сов от* **сморка́ть** ♦ *перех*: **~ нос** to blow one's nose

▸ **вы́сморкаться** *сов возв от* **сморка́ться**.

высо́выва|ть(ся) (-ю(сь)) *несов от* **вы́сунуть(ся)**.

высо́к|ий (-ая, -ое, -ие; -, -а́, -о́) *прил* high; (*человек*) tall; (*честь, ответственность*) great; (*гость*) distinguished; **быть** (*impf*) **~ого мне́ния о** +*prp* to have a high opinion of; **высо́кая вода́** high tide.

высоко́ *нареч* high (up) ♦ *как сказ* it's high (up), it's a long way up; **до верши́ны ~** it is a long way to the top.

высокого́рный *прил* alpine.

высокока́чественный *прил* high-quality.
высококвалифици́рованный *прил* (*учитель, юрист*) highly qualified; (*слесарь, токарь*) highly skilled.
высокоме́рен *прил см* **высокоме́рный**.
высокоме́ри|е (-я) *ср* haughtiness, arrogance.
высокоме́р|ный (-ен, -на, -но) *прил* haughty, arrogant.
высокоопла́чиваемый *прил* highly paid.
высокопа́р|ный (-ен, -на, -но) *прил* (*речь*) high-flown, pompous.
высокопоста́вленный *прил* high-ranking.
высокопроизводи́тель|ный (-ен, -ьна, -ьно) *прил* highly productive.
вы́сос|ать (-у, -ешь; *impf* **выса́сывать**) *сов перех* to suck out; (*насосом*) to pump out.
высот|а́ (-оты́; *nom pl* -о́ты) *ж* height; (*ГЕО*) altitude; (*звука*) pitch; (*давления, температуры*) level; **набира́ть (набра́ть** *perf*) ~**оту́** to climb, gain height; **на большо́й** ~**оте́** at a high altitude *или* great height; **быть** (*impf*) *или* **оказа́ться** (*perf*) **на** ~**оте́ (положе́ния)** to be equal to the occasion.
высо́т|ный *прил* (*полёт*) high-altitude; (*здание*) high-rise.
вы́сох|нуть (-ну, -нешь; *pt* -, -ла, -ло) *сов от* **со́хнуть** ♦ (*impf* **высыха́ть**) *непepex* (*бельё, дрова*) to dry out; (*лужа, река*) to dry up.
высо́честв|о (-а) *ср*: **Ва́ше** *итп* **В~** Your *итп* Highness.
вы́сп|аться (-люсь, -ишься; *impf* **высыпа́ться**) *сов возв* to sleep well.
вы́став|ить (-лю, -ишь; *impf* **выставля́ть**) *сов перех* (*поставить наружу*) to put out; (*грудь*) to stick out; (*кандидатуру*) to put forward; (*требования*) to lay down; (*картину*) to exhibit; (*товар*) to display; (*часовых, охрану*) to post; (*разг: выгнать*) to chuck out; **выставля́ть** (~ *perf*) **кого́-н в дурно́м све́те** to show sb in an unfavourable light
▶ **вы́ставиться** (*impf* **выставля́ться**) *сов возв* (*на выставке*) to exhibit.
вы́став|ка (-ки; *gen pl* -ок) *ж* exhibition, show; ~**-прода́жа книг** book fair.
выставлю(сь) *сов см* **вы́ставить(ся)**.
выставля́|ть(ся) (-ю(сь)) *несов от* **вы́ставить(ся)**.
вы́ставок *сущ см* **вы́ставка**.
выста́ива|ть (-ю) *несов от* **вы́стоять**.
вы́стега|ть (-ю) *сов от* **стега́ть**.
вы́ст|лать (-елю, -елешь; *impf* **выстила́ть**) *сов перех*: ~ **что-н чем-н** to line sth with sth.
вы́сто|ять (-ю, -ишь; *impf* **выста́ивать**) *сов непepex* (*долго простоять*) to stand; (*удержаться*) to remain standing; (*не сдаться*) to stand one's ground.
вы́страда|ть (-ю) *сов перех* to suffer; (*счастье, свободу*) *to achieve through much suffering.*

выстра́ива|ть(ся) (-ю(сь)) *несов* = **стро́ить(ся)**.
вы́стрел (-а) *м* shot; **разда́лся** ~ a shot rang out.
вы́стрел|ить (-ю, -ишь) *сов непepex* to fire; ~ (*perf*) **из ружья́/из пу́шки** to fire a gun/cannon.
вы́строга|ть (-ю) *сов от* **строга́ть**.
вы́стро|ить(ся) (-ю(сь), -ишь(ся)) *сов от* **стро́ить(ся)**.
вы́ступ (-а) *м* ledge.
выступа́|ть (-ю) *несов от* **вы́ступить** ♦ *непepex* (*берег*) to jut out; (*скулы*) to protrude.
вы́ступ|ить (-лю, -ишь; *impf* **выступа́ть**) *сов непepex* (*против закона, в защиту друга*) to come out; (*из толпы, из рядов*) to step out; (*оркестр, актёр*) to perform; (*пот, сыпь*) to break out; (*в поход, на поиски*) to set off *или* out; **выступа́ть** (~ *perf*) **с ре́чью** to make a speech.
выступле́ни|е (-я) *ср* (*МУЗ*) performance; (*в поход*) departure; (*в печати*) article; (*речь*) speech.
вы́ступлю *сов см* **вы́ступить**.
вы́сун|уть (-у, -ешь; *impf* **высо́вывать**) *сов перех* to stick out; **бежа́ть** (*impf*), ~**ув язы́к** (*перен: разг*) to run flat out
▶ **вы́сунуться** (*impf* **высо́вываться**) *сов возв* to lean out; (*рука, нога*) to stick out; (*перен: разг*): ~**ся с** +*instr* to come out with.
вы́суш|ить(ся) (-у(сь), -ишь(ся)) *сов от* **суши́ть(ся)**.
вы́счита|ть (-ю; *impf* **высчи́тывать**) *сов перех* to calculate.
вы́сш|ий (-ая, -ее, -ие) *прил* (*орган власти, начальство*) highest, supreme; **в** ~**ей сте́пени** extremely; **това́ры** ~**его со́рта** goods of the highest quality; **вы́сшая ме́ра наказа́ния** capital punishment; **вы́сшая шко́ла** higher education; **вы́сшее образова́ние** higher education; **вы́сшее уче́бное заведе́ние** higher education establishment.
высыла́|ть (-ю) *несов от* **вы́слать**.
вы́сыл|ка (-ки; *gen pl* -ок) *ж* (*посылки, денег*) sending; (*осуждённого*) exile; (*шпиона*) deportation.
вы́сып|ать (-лю, -лешь; *impf* **высыпа́ть**) *сов перех* to pour out ♦ *непepex* (*сыпь, прыщи*) to break out; (*разг: толпа, народ итп*) to pour out
▶ **вы́сыпаться** (*impf* **высыпа́ться**) *сов возв* to pour out.
высыха́|ть (-ю) *несов от* **вы́сохнуть**.
выс|ь (-и) *ж* height.
выта́лкива|ть (-ю) *несов от* **вы́толкнуть**.
выта́птыва|ть (-ю) *несов от* **вы́топтать**.
вытара́щ|ить(ся) (-у(сь), -ишь(ся)) *сов от* **тара́щить(ся)**.
выта́скива|ть (-ю) *несов см* **вы́тащить**.
вы́тащ|ить (-у, -ишь) *сов от* **тащи́ть** ♦ (*impf* **выта́скивать**) *перех* (*мебель*) to drag out.

вы́твер|дить (-жу, -дишь) *сов от* **тверди́ть**.
вытворя́|ть (-ю) *сов перех* (*разг*) to get up to.
вы́тек *итп сов см* **вы́течь**.
вытека́|ть (*3sg* -ет, *3pl* -ют) *несов от* **вы́течь** ♦ *непepex* (*вывод*) to follow; (*река*) to flow out.
вы́тер|еть (-ру, -решь; *pt* -ер, -ерла, -ерло, *impf* **вытира́ть**) *сов перех* (*грязь, лужу*) to wipe up; (*посуду*) to dry (up); (*руки, глаза*) to wipe; **вытира́ть** (~ *perf*) **пыль** to dust
▸ **вы́тер|еться** (*impf* **вытира́ться**) *сов возв* (*человек*) to dry o.s.
вы́терп|еть (-лю, -ишь) *сов перех* to bear, endure.
вы́тесн|ить (-ю, -ишь; *impf* **вытесня́ть**) *сов перех* (*удалить*) to oust; (*заменить собой*) to supplant.
вы́течь (*3sg* -чет, *3pl* -кут, *pt* -к, -кла, -кло, *impf* **вытека́ть**) *сов непepex* to flow out.
вытира́|ть(ся) (-ю(сь)) *несов от* **вы́тереть(ся)**.
вы́тк|ать (-у, -ешь) *сов перех* to weave.
вы́толкн|уть (-у, -ешь; *impf* **выта́лкивать**) *сов перех* to push out.
вы́топ|тать (-чу, -чешь; *impf* **выта́птывать**) *сов перех* to trample down.
вы́точ|ить (-у, -ишь) *сов от* **точи́ть**.
вы́трав|ить (-лю, -ишь; *impf* **вытра́вливать**) *сов перех* (*пятно*) to remove; (*крыс, тараканов*) to exterminate; (*рисунок*) to etch.
вытрезви́тел|ь (-я) *м* overnight police cell for drunks.
вы́тру(сь) *итп сов см* **вы́тереть(ся)**.
вы́тряс|ти (-у, -ешь; *pt* -, -ла, -ло) *сов от* **трясти́**.
вы́тряхн|уть (-у, -ешь; *impf* **вытря́хивать**) *сов перех* to shake out.
выть (во́ю, во́ешь) *несов непepex* (*зверь, ветер, вьюга*) to howl; (*сирена*) to wail; (*разг: плакать*) to howl, wail.
вытя́гива|ть(ся) (-ю(сь)) *несов от* **вы́тянуть(ся)**.
вы́тяжк|а (-ки; *gen pl* -ек) *ж* (*действие: дыма, вредных частиц*) extraction; (*экстракт*) extract.
вы́тян|уть (-у, -ешь; *impf* **вытя́гивать**) *сов перех* to pull out; (*дым, вредные вещества*) to extract; (*руки, ноги, ткань*) to stretch ♦ *непepex* (*разг: выдержать*) to last out; ~ (*perf*) (**всю**) **ду́шу из кого́-н** (*разг*) to wear sb out; **из него́ слова́ не ~ешь** (*разг*) you won't get a word out of him
▸ **вы́тян|уться** (*impf* **вытя́гиваться**) *сов возв* (*дым, газ*) to escape; (*одежда*) to stretch; (*на диване, вдоль берега*) to stretch out; (*разг: вырасти*) to shoot up; (*встать смирно*) to stand at attention; **у него́ ~улось лицо́** (*перен*) his face fell.
вы́у|дить (-жу, -дишь; *impf* **выу́живать**) *сов перех* (*рыбу*) to catch; (*перен: разг: сведения*) to wheedle out.
вы́тюж|ить (-у, -ишь) *сов от* **утю́жить**.

выучива|ть (-ю) *несов* to learn.
вы́уч|ить(ся) (-у(сь), -ишь(сь)) *сов от* **учи́ть(ся)**.
выха́жива|ть (-ю) *несов от* **вы́ходить**.
выхва́т|ить (-чу, -тишь; *impf* **выхва́тывать**) *сов перех* (*вырвать*) to snatch; (*пистолет*) to draw.
вы́хлопн|ой *прил* exhaust *опред*; **выхлопны́е га́зы** exhaust fumes.
вы́ход (-а) *м* (*войск*) withdrawal; (*из партии, из комиссии*) departure; (*из кризиса*) way out; (*на сцену*) appearance; (*в море*) sailing; (*книги*) publication; (*на экран*) showing; (*место, комп*) exit; **дава́ть** (**дать** *perf*) ~ **чему́-н** to give vent to sth.
вы́ход|ец (-ца) *м*: **он ~ из Росси́и** he is of Russian origin *или* is Russian by birth.
вы́ходит *вводн сл* (*разг*) it turns out.
вы́хо|дить (-жу, -дишь; *impf* **выха́живать**) *сов перех* (*больного*) to nurse (back to health).
выхо|ди́ть (-жу́, -ди́шь) *несов от* **вы́йти** ♦ *непepex*: ~ **на** +*acc* (*юг, север*) to face; **окно́ ~дит в парк** the window looks out onto the park; **дверь ~дит в коридо́р** the door opens onto the corridor.
выхо́дк|а (-и) *ж* prank.
выходн|о́й *прил* exit *опред*; (*платье, костюм*) best ♦ (-о́го; *decl like adj*) *м* (*также*: ~ **день**) day off (work); ~**о́е отве́рстие** outlet; **сего́дня** ~ (*разг*) today is a holiday; **я сего́дня** ~ (*разг*) I have a day off today; ~**ы́е** weekend *ед*; **выходна́я дверь** exit; **выходно́е посо́бие** redundancy payment; **выходны́е да́нные** imprint.
вы́ходца *итп сущ см* **вы́ходец**.
вы́хожу *сов см* **вы́ходить**.
выхожу́ *несов см* **выходи́ть**.
вы́цара́па|ть (-ю; *impf* **выцара́пывать**) *сов перех* to scratch out; (*перен: де́ньги, путёвку*) to wring out.
вы́цвес|ти (*3sg* -тет, *3pl* -тут, *impf* **выцвета́ть**) *сов непepex* to fade.
вы́черкн|уть (-у, -ешь; *impf* **вычёркивать**) *сов перех* to cross *или* score out.
вы́черпа|ть (-ю; *impf* **вычёрпывать**) *сов перех* (*извлечь*) to scoop out; (*опорожнить*) to drain; **вычёрпывать** (~ *perf*) **во́ду из ло́дки** to bail out a boat.
вы́чес|ть (-ту, -тешь; *impf* **вычита́ть**) *сов перех* (*мат*) to subtract; (*долг, налог*) to deduct.
вы́чет (-а) *м* deduction ♦ *предл*: **за** ~**ом** +*gen* minus; **до** ~**а нало́гов** pre-tax.
вычисле́ни|е (-я) *ср* calculation.
вычисли́тельный *прил* (*операция, функция*) computing; **вычисли́тельная маши́на** computer; **вычисли́тельная те́хника** computers *мн*; **вычисли́тельный центр** computer centre (*BRIT*) *или* center (*US*).
вы́числ|ить (-ю, -ишь; *impf* **вычисля́ть**) *сов перех* to calculate.
вы́чис|тить (-щу, -стишь) *сов от* **чи́стить**.

вычита́ни|е (-я) *ср* subtraction.

вычита́|ть (-ю; *impf* **вычи́тывать**) *сов перех* (*разг: узнать*) to find out (*by reading*).

вычита́|ть (-ю) *несов от* **вы́честь**.

вычи́тыва|ть (-ю) *несов от* **вы́читать**.

вычур|ный (-ен, -на, -но) *прил* elaborate.

вы́швырн|уть (-у, -ешь; *impf* **вышвы́ривать**) *сов перех* (*также перен: разг*) to chuck out.

вы́ше *сравн прил от* **высо́кий** ♦ *нареч* higher; (*в тексте*) above ♦ *предл* (+*gen*) above; **мы подняли́сь** ~ we went further up, we climbed higher; ~ **мы привели́ но́вые да́нные** we have cited new data above; **самолёт лете́л** ~ **облако́в** the plane was flying above the clouds; **э́то** ~ **моего́ понима́ния** it is beyond me *или* my comprehension.

вы́шек *сущ см* **вы́шка**.

вы́шел *сов см* **вы́йти**.

вышестоя́|щий (-ая, -ее, -ие) *прил* higher; **~ее лицо́** superior.

вы́шиб|ить (-у, -ешь; *pt* -, -ла, -ло, *impf* **вышиба́ть**) *сов перех* (*выбить*) to knock out; (*разг: прогнать*) to chuck out.

вышива́ни|е (-я) *ср* needlework.

вышива́|ть (-ю) *несов от* **вы́шить**.

вышив|ка (-ки; *gen pl* -ок) *ж* embroidery.

вышин|а́ (-ы́) *ж* (*высота*) height.

вы́ш|ить (-ью, -ьешь; *impf* **вышива́ть**) *сов перех* to embroider.

вы́ш|ка (-ки; *gen pl* -ек) *ж* (*высокое строение*) tower; (*разг: преступнику*) death penalty; (*спорт*) diving board; **бурова́я** *или* **нефтяна́я** ~ derrick; **прыжки́ в во́ду с** **~ки** high diving.

вы́школ|ить (-ю, -ишь) *сов перех* to train.

вы́шла *итп сов см* **вы́йти**.

вы́шлю *итп сов см* **вы́слать**.

вы́шью *итп сов см* **вы́шить**.

вы́щипа|ть (-ю; *impf* **выщи́пывать**) *сов перех* to pluck.

вы́яв|ить (-лю, -ишь; *impf* **выявля́ть**) *сов перех* (*талант*) to discover; (*недостатки*) to expose

▸ **вы́явиться** (*impf* **выявля́ться**) *сов возв* to come to light, be revealed.

вы́ясн|ить (-ю, -ишь; *impf* **выясня́ть**) *сов перех* (*обнаружить*) to find out; (*сделать ясным*) to clarify; **нам ну́жно** ~ **отноше́ния** we have to sort things out between us

▸ **вы́ясниться** (*impf* **выясня́ться**) *сов возв* to become clear.

Вьетна́м (-а) *м* Vietnam.

вьетна́м|ец (-ца) *м* Vietnamese.

вьетна́м|ка (-ки; *gen pl* -ок) *ж см* **вьетна́мец**.

вьетна́мск|ий (-ая, -ое, -ие) *прил* Vietnamese.

вьетна́мца *итп сущ см* **вьетна́мец**.

вью́г|а (-и) *ж* snowstorm, blizzard.

вью́чн|ый *прил*: **~ое живо́тное** beast of burden.

вяжу́ *сов см* **вяза́ть**.

вя́жущ|ий (-ая, -ее, -ие) *прил* (*вкус*) acerbic; (*материал, состав*) binding, cementing.

вяз *итп несов см* **вя́знуть** ♦ (-а) *м* elm.

вяза́ни|е (-я) *ср* (*снопов*) tying, binding; (*рукоделие*) knitting.

вя́заный *прил* knitted.

вя|за́ть (-жу́, -жешь; *perf* **связа́ть**) *несов перех* to tie up, bind; (*кофту, носки*) to knit ♦ *безл* (*no perf*): **э́то лека́рство вя́жет во рту** this medicine burns the inside of your mouth.

вя́з|кий (-кая, -кое, -кие; -ок, -ка́, -ко) *прил* (*тягучий*) viscous; (*топкий*) boggy.

вя́з|нуть (-ну, -нешь; *pt* -, -ла, -ло, *perf* **завя́знуть** *или* **увя́знуть**) *несов неперех*: ~ (**в** +*prp*) to get stuck (in).

вя́зок *прил см* **вя́зкий**.

вя́леный *прил* dried.

вя́л|ить (-ю, -ишь) *несов перех* to dry.

вя́ло *нареч* (*говорить*) dully.

вя́лост|ь (-и) *ж* sluggishness.

вя́л|ый (-, -а, -о) *прил* (*листья, цветы*) wilted, withered; (*человек, речь*) sluggish.

вя́|нуть (-ну, -нешь; *perf* **завя́нуть** *или* **увя́нуть**) *несов неперех* (*цветы*) to wilt, wither; (*перен: красота*) to fade; **его́ слу́шать – у́ши ~нут** (*разг*) it makes you sick to listen to him.

~ Г, г ~

Г, г *сущ нескл (буква)* the 4th letter of the Russian alphabet.

г *сокр (= грамм)* g, gm (= *gram*).

г. *сокр = год, город.*

га *м сокр (= гектáр)* ha (= *hectare*).

Гаáр|а (**-и**) *ж* The Hague.

габарит (**-а**) *м (обычно мн: ТЕХ)* dimension; *см также* **габариты.**

габариты (**-ов**) *мн (разг: человека)* size *ед.*

ГАБТ (**-а**) *м сокр (= Госудáрственный академический Большóй теáтр)* (State Academic) Bolshoi Theatre (*BRIT*) *или* Theater (*US*).

Гавáйи *м нескл* Hawaii.

Гавáн|а (**-ы**) *ж* Havana.

гáван|ь (**-и**) *ж* harbour (*BRIT*), harbor (*US*).

гáвка|ть (**-ю**) *несов неперех (разг: также* перен*)* to yap.

гагáр|а (**-ы**) *ж* diver (*BRIT*), loon (*US*).

гагáт (**-а**) *м (ГЕО)* jet.

гад (**-а**) *м (разг)* rat.

гадáл|ка (**-ки**; *gen pl* **-ок**) *ж* fortune-teller.

гадá|ть (**-ю**) *несов неперех (строить предположения)* to guess; (*perf* **погадáть**): ~ **комý-н** to tell sb's fortune; ~ (**погадáть** *perf*) **на кáртах** to read the cards; ~ (*impf*) **на кофéйной гýще** ≈ to read the tea leaves.

гáдин|а (**-ы**) *ж (разг)* rat.

гáдить (**-жу, -дишь**; *perf* **нагáдить**) *несов неперех (разг: животное)* to defecate; ~ (**нагáдить** *perf*) +*dat (разг)* to do the dirty on.

гáд|кий (**-кая, -кое, -кие; -ок, -кá, -ко**) *прил* loathsome.

гáдко *нареч (поступить)* terribly ♦ *как сказ:* **э́то** ~ — it's disgusting.

гáдост|ь (**-и**) *ж (поступка, слов)* nastiness; *(разг)* filth; **дéлать (сдéлать** *perf***)/говорить (сказáть** *perf***)** ~**и** to do/say nasty things; **э́то** ~ it's disgusting.

гадю́к|а (**-и**) *ж* viper.

гáек *сущ см* **гáйка.**

гáечный *прил:* ~ **ключ** spanner.

гáже *сравн прил от* **гáдкий** ♦ *сравн нареч от* **гáдко.**

гáжу *несов см* **гáдить.**

ГАЗ (**-а**) *м сокр (автомобиль)* vehicle manufactured at the Gorky car factory.

газ (**-а**; *part gen* **-у**) *м* gas; **готóвить (приготóвить** *perf***) на гáзе** to cook with gas; **давáть (дать** *perf***)** ~ *(разг)* to put one's foot down (*BRIT*), step on the gas (*US*); *см также* **гáзы.**

газéт|а (**-ы**) *ж* newspaper.

газéтный *прил* newspaper *опред.*

газéтчик (**-а**) *м (разг: сотрудник)* journalist; *(продавец)* newspaper vendor.

гáзик (**-а**) *м (разг)* car manufactured at the Gorky car plant.

газирóванн|ый *прил:* ~**ая водá** carbonated water.

газирóв|ка (**-ки**; *gen pl* **-ок**) *ж (разг)* soda.

газóвщи|к (**-á**) *м (разг)* gasman (*мн* gasmen).

гáзов|ый *прил* gas; **гáзовая кáмера** gas chamber.

газóн (**-а**) *м* lawn.

газопровóд (**-а**) *м* gas pipeline.

гáз|ы (**-ов**) *мн (МЕД)* wind *ед.*

ГАИ *ж сокр (= Госудáрственная автомобильная инспéкция)* state motor vehicle inspectorate.

Гаи́ти *м нескл* Haiti.

гаитя́н|ский (**-ая, -ое, -ие**) *прил* Haitian.

гаи́шник (**-а**) *м (разг)* ≈ traffic cop.

гáй|ка (**-йки**; *gen pl* **-ек**) *ж* nut; **закрýчивать (закрути́ть** *perf***)** ~**йки** *(разг)* to put the screws on.

гаймори́т (**-а**) *м* sinusitis.

галá *прил неизм* gala *опред.*

галáктик|а (**-и**) *ж* galaxy; **Нáша Г**~ the Galaxy.

галáнтен *прил см* **галáнтный.**

галантерé|я (**-и**) *ж* haberdashery (*BRIT*), notions store (*US*).

галáнтн|ый (**-ен, -на, -но**) *прил* gallant.

галерé|я (**-и**) *ж* gallery.

галéт|а (**-ы**) *ж sort of biscuit.*

галиматья́ (**-и́**) *ж (разг)* gobbledygook.

галифé *мн/ср нескл* riding breeches *мн* ♦ *прил неизм:* **брю́ки** ~ jodhpurs.

гáл|ка (**-ки**; *gen pl* **-ок**) *ж* jackdaw.

галлóн (**-а**) *м* gallon.

галлюцинáци|я (**-и**) *ж* hallucination.

гáлок *сущ см* **гáлка.**

галóп (**-а**) *м (бег лошади)* gallop; *(танец)* galop.

галóпом *нареч* at a gallop; **я прочитáл кни́гу** ~ *(разг)* I raced through the book.

гáлоч|ка (**-ки**; *gen pl* **-ек**) *ж (в тексте)* tick, check (*US*).

галóш|а (**-и**) *ж (обычно мн: обувь)* galosh; **сажáть (посади́ть** *perf***) когó-н в** ~**у** *(разг)* to put sb on the spot; **сади́ться (сесть** *perf*) **в ~у** (*разг*) to get into a jam.

гáлстук (**-a**) *м* tie, necktie (*US*); **завя́зывать (завяза́ть** *perf*) **~** to tie a tie.

гальваниза́ци|я (**-и**) *ж* galvanization.

гальванизи́р|овать (**-ую**) *(не)сов перех* to galvanize.

гáльк|а (**-и**) *ж, собир* pebble.

гам (**-a**) *м* uproar.

гамáк (**-á**) *м* hammock.

гамáш|а (**-и**) *ж* (*обычно мн*) gaiter.

Гáмбург (**-a**) *м* Hamburg.

гáмбургер (**-a**) *м* hamburger.

гáмм|а (**-ы**) *ж* (*муз*) scale; (*чувств, красок*) range.

гáмма-глобули́н (**-a**) *м* gamma globulin.

гáмма-излуче́ни|е (**-я**) *ср* gamma radiation.

Гáн|а (**-ы**) *ж* Ghana.

гангре́н|а (**-ы**) *ж* gangrene.

гáнгстер (**-a**) *м* gangster.

гандбóл (**-a**) *м* handball.

гандболи́ст (**-a**) *м* handball player.

гандболи́ст|ка (**-ки**; *gen pl* **-ок**) *ж см* гандболи́ст.

гантéл|ь (**-и**) *ж* dumbbell.

гарáж (**-á**) *м* garage.

гарáнт (**-a**) *м* guarantor.

гаранти́йный *прил* guarantee *опред*, warranty *опред*; **гаранти́йное письмó** letter of guarantee.

гаранти́р|овать (**-ую**) *(не)сов перех* to guarantee; **~** (*impf/perf*) **когó-н от** +*gen* to protect sb against.

гарáнти|я (**-и**) *ж* guarantee; **~ от убы́тков** guarantee against damage; **товáр с ~ей** item under guarantee; **бáнковская ~** bank's letter of guarantee; **авари́йная ~** warranty; **~ зáнятости** job security.

гардерóб (**-a**) *м* wardrobe; (*в общественном здании*) cloakroom.

гардерóбщик (**-a**) *м* cloakroom attendant.

гардерóбщиц|а (**-ы**) *ж см* гардерóбщик.

гарди́н|а (**-ы**) *ж* curtain.

гáрев|ый *прил*: **~ая дорóжка** cinder track.

гарéм (**-a**) *м* harem.

гармóник|а (**-и**) *ж* concertina; **губнáя ~** mouth organ.

гармони́р|овать (**-ую**) *несов неперех*: **~ с** +*instr* (*со средой*) to be in harmony with; (*одежда*) to go with.

гармони́ст (**-a**) *м* concertina player.

гармони́ч|ный (**-ен, -на, -но**) *прил* harmonious.

гармóни|я (**-и**) *ж* harmony.

гармóш|ка (**-ки**; *gen pl* **-ек**) *ж* (*разг*) ≈ squeeze-box; (*одежда*): **в ~ку** creased; **при удáре маши́на смя́лась в ~ку** the car concertinaed on impact.

гарнизóн (**-a**) *м* garrison.

гарни́р (**-a**) *м* side dish.

гарниту́р (**-a**) *м* (*одежды*) outfit; (*украшения*) set; (*мебели*) suite.

гарпу́н (**-á**) *м* harpoon.

гар|ь (**-и**) *ж* (*угля*) cinders *мн*; **пáхнет гáрью** there's a smell of burning.

гас *итп несов см* **гáснуть**.

гаси́ть (**-шу́, -сишь**; *perf* **погаси́ть**) *несов перех* (*лампу, свет*) to put out; (*пожар*) to extinguish, put out; (*скорость*) to reduce; (*звук*) to deaden; (*марку*) to frank; (*no perf*; *перен: инициативу*) to stifle, suppress; **~ (погаси́ть** *perf*) **задóлженность** to settle one's debts; **~ (погаси́ть** *perf*) **и́звесть** to slake lime.

гáс|нуть (**-ну, -нешь**; *pt* **- или -нул, -ла, -ло,** *perf* **погáснуть** *или* **угáснуть**) *несов неперех* (*огни*) to go out; (*звезды, чувства, надежда*) to fade.

гастри́т (**-a**) *м* gastritis.

гастрóл|и (**-ей**) *мн performances of a touring company*; **éздить/éхать (поéхать** *perf*) **на ~** to go on tour.

гастроли́р|овать (**-ую**) *несов неперех* to be on tour.

гастронóм (**-a**) *м* food store.

гастрономи́ческ|ий (**-ая, -ое, ие**) *прил*: **~ магази́н** = гастронóм.

гастронóми|я (**-и**) *ж* delicatessen.

ГАТТ *м сокр* (= Генерáльное соглаше́ние о тари́фах и торгóвле) GATT (= *General Agreement on Tariffs and Trade*).

гауптвáхт|а (**-ы**) *ж* (*воен*) guardroom (*as a place of detention*); **сажáть (посади́ть** *perf*) **когó-н на ~у** to confine sb to the guardroom.

гашён|ый *прил* (*марка*) franked; **~ая и́звесть** slaked lime.

гаши́ш (**-a**) *м* hashish.

гашу́ *несов см* **гаси́ть**.

ГБ *ж сокр* = госбезопáсность.

гвалт (**-a**) *м* (*разг*) row.

гвардéй|ец (**-йца**) *м* (*воен*) guardsman (*мн* guardsmen).

гвáрди|я (**-и**) *ж* (*воен*) Guards *мн*; **Крáсная/ Бéлая ~** (*ист*) the Red/White Guard.

Гватемáл|а (**-ы**) *ж* Guatemala.

Гвинé|я (**-и**) *ж* Guinea.

гвозди́к|а (**-и**) *ж* (*цветок*) carnation; (*пряность*) cloves *мн*.

гвозд|ь (**-я́**; *nom pl* **-и**, *gen pl* **-éй**) *м* nail; **~ прогрáммы** the highlight of the show; **и никаки́х ~éй!** (*разг*) and that's that!

гг *сокр* = гóды; (= господá) Messrs (= *messieurs*).

ГД *ж сокр* = Госудáрственная Дýма.

Гдáньск (**-a**) *м* Gdansk.

где *нареч* where; (*разг: где-нибудь*) somewhere, anywhere ♦ *союз* where; **~ Вы живёте?** where do you live?; **подýмайте, не забы́ли ли ~** try and think whether you left it anywhere *или* somewhere; **гóрод, ~ я жил** the town where I lived; **ты скóро бýдешь богáтым – ~ уж там!**

(*разг*) you'll soon be rich – hardly!

где́-либо *нареч* = **где́-нибудь**.

где́-нибудь *нареч* somewhere; (*в вопросе*) anywhere.

где́-то *нареч* somewhere.

ГДР *ж сокр* (*ИСТ*: = Герма́нская Демократи́ческая Респу́блика) GDR (= *German Democratic Republic*).

гегемони́зм (-а) *м* hegemony.

ге́йзер (-а) *м* geyser.

гейм (-а) *м* (*СПОРТ*) game.

гекта́р (-а) *м* hectare.

гел|ь (-я) *м* gel (*for hair*).

гемоглоби́н (-а) *м* haemoglobin (*BRIT*), hemoglobin (*US*).

геморро́|й (-я) *м* haemorrhoids *мн* (*BRIT*), hemorrhoids *мн* (*US*), piles *мн*.

гемофили́|я (-и) *ж* haemophilia (*BRIT*), hemophilia (*US*).

ген (-а) *м* gene.

ге́ндерный *прил* (*проблема*) gender *опред*.

генеалоги́ческ|ий (-ая, -ое, -ие) *прил*: ~**ое де́рево** genealogical chart; (*семьи*) family tree.

генеало́ги|я (-и) *ж* genealogy.

ге́незис (-а) *м* genesis.

генера́л (-а) *м* (*ВОЕН*) general.

генера́льн|ый *прил* general; (*главный*) main; ~**ая убо́рка** spring-clean; **генера́льная репети́ция** dress rehearsal; **генера́льное сраже́ние** decisive battle; **генера́льный штаб** chief headquarters.

генера́тор (-а) *м* generator.

гене́тик (-а) *м* geneticist.

гене́тик|а (-и) *ж* genetics.

генети́чески *нареч*: ~ **модифици́рованный** genetically modified.

генети́ческий (-ая, -ое, -ие) *прил* genetic.

гениа́льно *нареч* (*написанный*) superbly ♦ *как сказ* it's great.

генна́льн|ый (-ен, -ьна, -ьно) *прил* great.

ге́ни|й (-я) *м* genius.

ге́нный *прил* genetic; **ге́нная инжене́рия** genetic engineering.

геноци́д (-а) *м* genocide.

генсе́к (-а) *м сокр* = генера́льный секрета́рь; General Secretary (*of the Communist Party*).

Ге́ну|я (-и) *ж* Genoa.

гео́граф (-а) *м* geographer.

геогра́фи|я (-и) *ж* geography.

геоде́зи|я (-и) *ж* geodesy.

гео́лог (-а) *м* geologist.

геоло́ги|я (-и) *ж* geology.

геоме́три|я (-и) *ж* geometry.

геополи́тик|а (-и) *ж* geopolitics.

георги́н (-а) *м* dahlia.

георги́н|а (-ы) *ж* = георги́н.

гепа́рд (-а) *м* cheetah.

гепати́т (-а) *м* hepatitis.

гера́льдик|а (-и) *ж* heraldry.

гера́н|ь (-и) *ж* geranium.

герб (-а́) *м* coat of arms; **госуда́рственный** ~ national emblem.

герба́ри|й (-я) *м* herbarium.

гербици́д (-а) *м* herbicide.

ге́рбов|ый *прил* heraldic; (*с гербом*) bearing a coat of arms; **ге́рбовая бума́га** headed paper; **ге́рбовая ма́рка** official stamp (*relating to stamp duty*); **ге́рбовый сбор** stamp duty.

геркуле́с (-а) *м* (*человек*) Hercules; (*кулин*) porridge oats *мн*.

герма́н|ец (-ца) *м* (*обычно мн: ист*) Teuton.

Герма́ни|я (-и) *ж* Germany.

герма́нский (-ая, -ое, -ие) *прил* German.

герметизи́р|овать (-ую), *perf* **загермети- зи́ровать** *несов неперех* to make airtight.

герметти́чный (-ен, -на, -но) *прил* hermetic.

геро́изм (-а) *м* heroism.

геро́ин (-а) *м* heroin.

геро́и́н|я (-и) *ж* heroine.

герои́ческий (-ая, -ое, -ие) *прил* heroic; **герои́ческий э́пос** heroic epic.

геро́|й (-я) *м* hero.

герц (-а) *м* hertz.

ге́рцог (-а) *м* duke.

герцоги́н|я (-и) *ж* duchess.

геста́по *ср нескл* the Gestapo.

геста́пов|ец (-ца) *м* member of the Gestapo.

гетероге́нный *прил* heterogeneous.

гетр|а (-ы) *ж* (*обычно мн*) legwarmer.

ге́тто *ср нескл* ghetto.

г-жа *ж сокр* = **госпожа́**.

гжел|ь (-и) *ж type of ceramic made in Gzhel*.

гиаци́нт (-а) *м* hyacinth.

гиб *итп несов см* **ги́бнуть**.

ги́белен *прил см* **ги́бельный**.

ги́бел|ь (-и) *ж* (*человека*) death; (*армии*) destruction; (*самолета, надежды, ценностей*) loss; (*карьеры*) ruin; **они́ бы́ли обречены́ на** ~ they were doomed; **на краю́** ~**и** (*дело*) on the brink of disaster; (*человек*) on the verge of death.

ги́бельный (-ен, -ьна, -ьно) *прил* disastrous.

ги́бк|ий (-ая, -ое, -ие; -ок, -ка́, -ко) *прил* flexible; **ги́бкий диск** (*КОМП*) floppy disk; **ги́бкое произво́дство** (*ТЕХ*) flexible production methods.

ги́бкост|ь (-и) *ж* flexibility.

ги́б|нуть (-ну, -нешь; *pt* -, -ла, -ло, *perf* **поги́бнуть**) *несов неперех* to perish; (*растения*) to die; (*перен*) to come to nothing; ~ (**поги́бнуть** *perf*) **от** +*gen* to die of.

ги́бок *прил см* **ги́бкий**.

Гибралта́р (-а) *м* Gibraltar.

ги́бри́д (-а) *м* hybrid.

ги́бче *сравн прил от* **ги́бкий**.

гига́нт (-а) *м* giant; **пласти́нка-**~, **диск-**~ twelve-inch record.

гига́нтский (-ая, -ое, -ие) *прил* gigantic.

гигие́н|а (-ы) *ж* hygiene.

гигиени́ческ|ий (-ая, -ое, -ие) *прил* sanitary; **гигиени́ческий тампо́н** tampon.

гигиени́чный (-ен, -на, -но) *прил* hygienic.

гигроскопи́чный *прил* absorbent.

гид (-а) *м* guide.

гидравли́ческий (-ая, -ое, -ие) *прил*

hydraulic.

гидрокостюм (-а) *м* diving suit.

гидрометцентр (-а) *м сокр* =
  Гидрометеорологический центр.

гидростанци|я (-и) *ж см*
  гидроэлектростанция.

гидроэлектростанци|я (-и) *ж* hydroelectric
  power station.

гие́н|а (-ы) *ж* hyena.

ги́льди|я (-и) *ж* guild.

ги́льз|а (-ы) *ж* cartridge case.

гильоти́н|а (-ы) *ж* guillotine.

Гимала́|и (-ев) *мн* the Himalayas.

гимн (-а) *м* (*государственный*) anthem;
  (*хвалебная песня*) hymn.

гимнази́ст (-а) *м* ≈ grammar school student.

гимнази́ст|ка (-ки; *gen pl* -ок) *ж см* **гимнази́ст.**

гимна́зи|я (-и) *ж* ≈ grammar school.

гимна́ст (-а) *м* gymnast.

гимнастёр|ка (-ки; *gen pl* -ок) *ж* soldier's blouse.

гимна́стик|а (-и) *ж* exercises *мн*; (**спорти́вная**)
  ~ gymnastics *мн*; **худо́жественная** ~ modern
  rhythmic gymnastics; **де́лать (сде́лать** *perf*) ~**у**
  to do one's exercises.

гимна́ст|ка (-ки; *gen pl* -ок) *ж см* **гимна́ст.**

гинеко́лог (-а) *м* gynaecologist (*BRIT*),
  gynecologist (*US*).

гинеколо́ги|я (-и) *ж* gynaecology (*BRIT*),
  gynecology (*US*).

гипе́рбол|а (-ы) *ж* hyperbole.

гиперто́ник (-а) *м person suffering from high
  blood pressure.*

гипертони|я (-и) *ж* high blood pressure.

гипертрофи́рованный *прил* (*МЕД*)
  hypertrophied; (*перен*) excessive.

гипно́з (-а) *м* hypnosis.

гипнотизи́р|овать (-ую; *perf*
  загипнотизи́ровать) *несов перех* to hypnotize.

гипо́тез|а (-ы) *ж* hypothesis; **выдвига́ть
  (вы́двинуть** *perf*) ~**у** to put forward a
  hypothesis.

гипотети́ческ|ий (-ая, -ое, -ие) *прил*
  hypothetical.

гипото́ник (-а) *м person suffering from low
  blood pressure.*

гипотони|я (-и) *ж* low blood pressure.

гиппопота́м (-а) *м* hippopotamus.

гипс (-а) *м* (*ГЕО*) gypsum; (*ИСКУССТВО*) plaster of
  Paris; (*МЕД*) plaster; **накла́дывать (наложи́ть**
  perf) ~ **на** что-н to put sth in plaster.

гипю́р (-а) *м* (guipure) lace.

гирля́нд|а (-ы) *ж* garland.

ги́р|я (-и) *ж* (*весов*) weight; (*СПОРТ*) dumbbell.

гита́р|а (-ы) *ж* guitar.

гитари́ст (-а) *м* guitarist.

гитари́ст|ка (-ки; *gen pl* -ок) *ж см* **гитари́ст.**

ГК *м сокр* (= *Гражда́нский Ко́декс*) civil code.

гл. *сокр* (= *глава́*) ch. (= *chapter*).

глав|а́ (-ы́; *nom pl* -ы) *ж* (*делегации, семьи*) head;
  (*церкви*) dome; (*книги, статьи*) chapter; **во ~é
  с** +*instr* headed by; **во ~é** +*gen* at the head of; **во
  ~у́ угла́ ста́вить (поста́вить** *perf*) **что-н** to give
  top priority to sth.

глава́р|ь (-я́) *м* (*банды*) leader.

главе́нств|о (-а) *ср* leading role.

главе́нств|овать (-ую) *несов неперех*: ~ **над**
  +*instr* to hold sway over.

главк (-а) *м сокр* (= *гла́вный комите́т*) *chief
  administrative body within a ministry.*

гла́вное *вводн сл* the main thing; **он, ~, все
  отрица́ет** the main thing is, he denies
  everything.

главнокома́ндующ|ий (-его; *decl like adj*) *м*
  commander in chief.

гла́вн|ый *прил* main; (*старший по положению*)
  senior, head *опред*; ~**ым о́бразом** chiefly,
  mainly; **гла́вная кни́га** (*КОММ*) general ledger.

глаго́л (-а) *м* verb.

гла́ди|льный (-ен, -ьна, -ьно) *прил*: ~**ьная
  доска́** ironing board.

гладио́лус (-а) *м* gladiolus.

гла́|дить (-жу, -дишь; *perf* **погла́дить**) *несов
  перех* to iron; (*волосы*) to stroke; **они́ тебя́ не
  погла́дят по голо́вке за э́то** they won't be best
  pleased with you for this.

гла́дкий (-кая, -кое, -кие; -ок, -ка́, -ко) *прил*
  (*ровный*) smooth; (*одноцветный*) plain,
  unpatterned; (*плавный*) flowing; (*прямой*)
  straight.

гла́дко *нареч* (*ровно*) smoothly; (*причёсанный*)
  tightly; ~ **вы́бритый** clean-shaven.

гла́же *сравн прил от* **гла́дкий** ♦ *сравн нареч от*
  гла́дко.

гла́жу *несов см* **гла́дить.**

глаз (-а; *loc sg* -у́, *nom pl* -а́, *gen pl* -) *м* (*также
  перен*) eye; (*зрение*) eyesight; **в ~а́х** +*gen* in the
  eyes of; **на ~а́х у кого́-н** before sb's eyes; **с
  гла́зу на ~** tête à tête; **на ~** roughly; **она́ всегда́
  говори́т о нём за ~а́** (*разг*) she is always
  talking about him behind his back; **за ним
  ну́жен ~ да ~** you need to keep your eye on
  him; **куда́ ~а́ гляди́т идти́ (пойти́** *perf*) to
  go where one's fancy takes one; **де́лать
  (сде́лать** *perf*) **больши́е ~а́** to look amazed.

глаза́стый *прил* (*разг*) with big eyes; (*зоркий*)
  sharp-eyed.

Гла́зго *м нескл* Glasgow.

глазе́|ть (-ю) *несов неперех*: ~ **на** +*acc* to stare
  at.

глазир|ова́ть (-у́ю) (*не*)*сов перех* (*также* *ТЕХ*)
  to glaze; (*торт*) to ice, frost (*US*).

глазка́ *сущ см* **глазо́к.**

глазни́к (-а) *м* (*разг*) eye doctor.

глазни́ц|а (-ы) *ж* eyeball.

глазно́й *прил* eye *опред*.

глаз|о́к (-ка́) *м* peephole.

глазоме́р (-а) *м*: у него́ хоро́ший ~ he has a good eye.

глазу́нь|я (-и) *ж* fried egg.

глазу́р|ь (-и) *ж* (*на кера́мике итп*) glaze; (*на торте*) icing, frosting (*US*).

гла́нд|а (-ы) *ж* (*обычно мн*) tonsil.

глас|и́ть (*3sg* -и́т, *3pl* -я́т) *несов перех* to state; **зако́н/пра́вило** ~**и́т, что** ... the law/rule states that ...; **уста́в** ~**и́т, что** the regulations stipulate that.

гла́сность (-и) *ж* openness; (*ИСТ*) glasnost; **предава́ть** (**преда́ть** *perf*) ~**и** to make public.

гла́сный *прил* (*суд, процесс*) public; (*ЛИНГ*) voiced ♦ (*-ого*; *decl like adj*) *м* vowel.

глауко́м|а (-ы) *ж* glaucoma.

гли́н|а (-ы) *ж* clay.

глинтве́йн (-а; *part gen* -у) *м* mulled wine.

гли́няный *прил* clay.

глист (-а́) *м* (*обычно мн*) (intestinal) worm.

глицери́н (-а) *м* glycerin(e).

глици́ни|я (-и) *ж* wisteria.

глоба́л|ьный (-ен, -ьна, -ьно) *прил* (*перен*) thorough; (*no short form*; *климат, политика*) global.

гло́бус (-а) *м* globe.

глода́ть (-ю) *несов перех* to gnaw at.

глота́|ть (-ю; *perf* **проглоти́ть**) *несов перех* to swallow; (*разг: обед*) to scoff; (*перен: книгу*) to devour; ~ (**проглоти́ть** *perf*) **слёзы** to choke back one's tears.

гло́тк|а (-ки; *gen pl* -ок) *ж* gullet.

глот|о́к (-ка́) *м* gulp, swallow; (*воды, чая*) drop.

гло́х|нуть (-ну, -нешь; *pt* -, -ла, -ло, *perf* **огло́хнуть**) *несов неперех* to grow deaf; (*perf* **загло́хнуть**; *шум*) to die away; (*мотор*) to stall.

глу́бже *сравн прил от* **глубо́кий** ♦ *сравн нареч от* **глубоко́**.

глуб|ина́ (-ины́; *nom pl* -и́ны) *ж* depth; (*дно*) depths *мн*; (*леса*) heart; (*зала, сада*) middle; (*перен*): ~ +*gen* (*идеи итп*) profundity of; **на** ~**ине́ 10 ме́тров** at a depth of 10 metres (*BRIT*) *или* meters (*US*); **в** ~**ине́ души́** in one's heart of hearts; **до** ~**ины́ души́ тро́нут** deeply moved; **до** ~**ины́ души́ удивлён** astounded; **до** ~**ины́ души́ огорчён** cut to the quick.

глубо́к|ий (-ая, -ое, -ие; -, -а́, -о́) *прил* deep; (*провинция*) remote; (*мысль, интерес*) profound; (*зима, осень*) late; ~**ая ста́рость** ripe old age; ~**ая ночь** the dead of night; ~ **снег** deep snow; ~ **покло́н** deep bow; ~**ая та́йна** deep secret.

глубоко́ *нареч* deeply ♦ *как сказ*: **здесь** ~ it's deep here.

глубоково́д|ный (-ен, -на, -но) *прил* deep; (*no short form*; *исследования*) deep-sea.

глубокомы́слен|ный (-, -на, -но) *прил* (*речь, замечание*) profound; (*взгляд, вид*) thoughtful.

глубокоуважа́емый *прил* dear.

глуб|ь (-и) *ж* (*леса*) heart; (*океана*) depths *мн*.

глум|и́ться (-лю́сь, -и́шься) *несов возв*: ~ **над** +*instr* to mock.

глупе́|ть (-ю; *perf* **поглупе́ть**) *несов неперех* to grow stupid.

глуп|и́ть (-лю́, -и́шь; *perf* **сглупи́ть**) *несов неперех* to be silly *или* stupid.

глу́по *нареч* stupidly ♦ *как сказ* it's stupid *или* silly.

глу́пость (-и) *ж* stupidity, silliness; (*поступок*) stupid *или* silly thing; (*слова*) nonsense; **де́лать** (*impf*) ~**и** to do silly things; **написа́ть ей письмо́ бы́ло** ~**ю** it was foolish *или* stupid to write to her; **име́ть** (*impf*) ~ +*infin* to be foolish enough to do; ~**и! никуда́ не пойдёшь** nonsense! you're not going anywhere.

глу́п|ый (-, -а́, -о) *прил* stupid, silly.

глуха́р|ь (-я́) *м* (*ЗООЛ*) capercaillie.

глух|о́й (-, -а́, -о) *прил* deaf; (*волнение, недовольство*) suppressed, pent-up; (*звук*) muffled; (*no short form*; *пора*) dead; ~ **лес** dense forest; ~**а́я стена́** blank wall; **он глух к про́сьбам/жа́лобам** he is deaf to requests/complaints.

глухонем|о́й *прил* deaf-and-dumb ♦ (*-о́го*; *decl like adj*) *м* deaf-mute; **а́збука для** ~**ы́х** deaf-and-dumb alphabet.

глухот|а́ (-ы́) *ж* deafness.

глуши́тел|ь (-я) *м* (*ТЕХ*) silencer; (*АВТ*) silencer (*BRIT*), muffler (*US*); (*перен*) suppressor.

глуш|и́ть (-у́, -и́шь; *perf* **заглуши́ть**) *несов перех* (*звуки, шум итп*) to muffle; (*мотор*) to turn off; (*перен: инициативу*) to stifle, suppress; (*perf* **оглуши́ть**; *рыбу*) to stun; ~ (*impf*) **во́дку/вино́** to hit the vodka/wine.

глуш|ь (-и́; *instr sg* -ью, *loc sg* -и́) *ж* wilderness; (*леса*) deepest part; (*перен*) backwoods *мн*.

глы́б|а (-ы) *ж* (*ледяна́я*) block; **ка́менная** ~ boulder.

глюко́з|а (-ы) *ж* glucose.

гля|де́ть (-жу́, -ди́шь; *perf* **погляде́ть**) *несов неперех* to look; (*заботиться*): ~ **за** +*instr* to look after; (*оценивать*): ~ **на** +*acc* to look at; **на́ ночь гля́дя** (so) late at night; **на́ зиму гля́дя** just before winter; **я захоте́л есть, гля́дя на тебя́** seeing you eat has made me hungry; **того́ и** ~**ди́ дождь пойдёт** (*разг*) it looks like it could rain any minute; **того́ и** ~**ди́ де́ньги зако́нчатся** the money might run out at any time; **там погляди́м** (*разг*) we'll see

▸ **гляде́ться** *несов возв*: ~**ся в** +*acc* to look at o.s. in.

гля́н|ец (-ца) *м* lustre (*BRIT*), luster (*US*), sheen; **наводи́ть** (**навести́** *perf*) ~ **на что-н** (*перен*) to add the finishing touches to sth.

гля́нцевый *прил* glossy.

гм *межд* h'm.

гн|ать (**гоню́, го́нишь**; *pt* -л, -ла́, -ло) *несов перех* (*стадо*) to drive; (*зверя*) to chase; (*удалять: человека*) to throw out; (*лошадь*) to drive *или* urge on; (*машину*) to drive fast; (*водку итп*) to distil (*BRIT*), distill (*US*); (*разг: продукцию*) to churn out; ~ (*impf*) **от себя́** to drive off *или* away; ~ (*impf*) **кого́-н с** +*instr* to rush sb with; **гони́те де́ньги/еду́!** (*разг*) give us your money/some food!

▶ **гна́ться** *несов возв*: **гна́ться за** +*instr* (*преследовать*) to pursue; (*добиваться*) to strive after.

гнев (**-а**) *м* wrath; **быть** (*impf*) **в гне́ве** to be in a rage.

гне́ваться (**-юсь**) *несов возв* to be angry.

гне́вен *прил см* **гне́вный**.

гневи́ть (**-лю́, -и́шь**) *несов перех* to anger; **не ~й Бо́га!** ≈ you should count your blessings!

гне́вный (**-ен, -на́, -но**) *прил* wrathful.

гнедо́й *прил* (*масть лошади*) bay.

гнезди́ться (*3sg* **-и́тся**, *3pl* **-я́тся**) *несов возв* (*птицы*) to nest; (*мысль, чувство*) to take root.

гнездо́ (**-á**; *nom pl* **гнёзда**, *gen pl* **гнёзд**) *ср* (*у птиц*) nest; (*для патронов*) socket, pocket; (*для посуды*) compartment; (*линг*) word family; **вить** (**свить** *perf*) **~** to build a nest.

гнездо́вье (**-я**) *ср* nesting.

гнести́ (**-ту́, -тёшь**) *несов перех* to gnaw.

гнёт (**-а**) *м* (*бедности итп*) yoke; **под ~ом** under the yoke.

гнету́щий (**-ая, -ее, -ие**) *прил* depressing.

гни́да (**-ы**) *ж* nit; (*разг: пренебр*) louse.

гнило́й (**-, -á, -о**) *прил* (*продукты, ткань итп*) rotten; (*климат*) unhealthy; (*перен: настроения, теория*) decadent.

гниль (**-и**) *ж* rotten stuff.

гни́ть (**-ю́, -ёшь**; *perf* **сгни́ть**) *несов неперех* to rot.

гно́ить (**-ю́, -и́шь**; *perf* **сгнои́ть**) *несов перех* to let rot.

▶ **гно́иться** *несов возв* (*рана*) to discharge.

гной (**-я**) *м* pus.

гно́йник (**-á**) *м* boil.

гном (**-а**) *м* gnome.

гнуса́вить (**-лю, -ишь**) *несов неперех* to talk through one's nose.

гнуса́вый (**-, -а, -о**) *прил* (*голос, тон*) affected and nasal.

гну́сен *прил см* **гну́сный**.

гну́сность (**-и**) *ж* (*клеветы, поведения*) vileness; (*поступок*) vile thing.

гну́сный (**-ен, -на́, -но**) *прил* vile.

гну́ть (**-у, -ёшь**; *perf* **согну́ть**) *несов перех* to bend; **~** (*impf*) **свою́ ли́нию** (*разг*) to have things one's own way; **куда́** *или* **к чему́ он ~ёт?** (*разг*) what's he driving at?; **~** (*impf*) **спи́ну на кого́-н** to slave away for sb

▶ **гну́ться** *несов возв* (*ветка, полка*) to bend.

гнуша́ться (**-юсь**; *perf* **погнуша́ться**) *несов возв* (+*gen*) to abhor; **ниче́м не ~** (*impf*) to have no scruples whatsoever.

гобеле́н (**-а**) *м* tapestry.

гобо́й (**-я**) *м* oboe.

гове́ть (**-ю**) *несов неперех* to fast and attend church in preparation for confession and Communion.

говню́ (**-á**) *ср* (*груб!*) shit (*!*)

го́вор (**-а**) *м* (*линг*) dialect; (*звуки разговора*) voices *мн*.

говори́ть (**-ю́, -и́шь**; *perf* **сказа́ть**) *несов перех* to say; (*правду*) to tell ♦ *неперех* to speak, talk; (*обсуждать*): **~ о** +*prp* to discuss, talk about; (*общаться*): **~ с** +*instr* to talk to *или* with; **~йт** it's said, they say; **~** (*impf*) **по-ру́сски** to speak Russian; **что вы ~йте?** you don't say!, really?; **не ~я́ (уже́) о** +*prp* not to mention; **что и ~!** (*разг*) what else is there to say?; **что ни ~й!** (*разг*) say what you like!; **коро́че** *или* **коро́тко ~я́** in short; **стро́го ~я́** strictly speaking; **открове́нно ~я́** to be frank; **по пра́вде ~я́** to tell (you) the truth; **и́наче ~я́** in other words

▶ **говори́ться** *несов возв* (*произноситься*) to be said; **как ~и́тся** as they say.

говорли́вый (**-, -а, -о**) *прил* talkative.

говя́дина (**-ы**) *ж* beef.

го́гот (**-а**) *м* (*гусей*) honking; (*разг: пренебр*) guffaw.

гогота́ть (**-чу́, -чешь**; *perf* **прогогота́ть**) *несов неперех* (*гуси*) to honk; to guffaw.

год (**-а**; *part gen* **-у**, *loc sg* **-у́**, *nom pl* **-ы**, *gen pl* **-о́в/ лет**) *м* year; **прошло́ 3 го́да/5 лет** 3/5 years passed; **из го́да в ~** year in year out; **кру́глый ~** all year round; **с ~а́ми** with the years; **~ от го́да** from year to year; *см также* **го́ды**.

года́ми *нареч* for years.

го́ден *прил см* **го́дный**.

годи́ться (**-жу́сь, -ди́шься**) *несов возв* (+*dat*) to suit; **~** (*impf*) **в** +*nom pl* to be (well) suited to be; **~** (*impf*) **для** +*gen* to be suitable for; **куда́ э́то ~ди́тся?** (*разг*) what good is this?; **~** (*impf*) **в отцы́/в ма́тери кому́-н** to be old enough to be sb's father/mother; **~** (*impf*) **в сыновья́ кому́-н** to be young enough to be sb's son.

го́дность (**-и**) *ж* suitability; (*билета*) validity; **срок ~и** shelf life.

го́дный (**-ен, -на́, -но**) *прил*: **~ к** +*dat* или **для** +*gen* fit или suitable for; **биле́т ~ен до** ... the ticket is valid until ....

годовщи́на (**-ы**) *ж* anniversary; **~ со дня сме́рти кого́-н** the anniversary of sb's death.

го́ды (**-о́в**) *мн*: **де́тские/вое́нные ~** childhood/ war years; **он уже́ в года́х** he's getting on (in years) now; **пятидеся́тые ~** the Fifties *или* 1950s.

гожу́сь *несов см* **годи́ться**.

Гозна́к (**-а**) *м сокр* = *Гла́вное управле́ние производством госуда́рственных зна́ков, моне́т и орде́нов.*

гол (**-а**; *nom pl* **-ы**) *м* goal; **забива́ть** (**заби́ть** *perf*) **~** to score a goal.

голеносто́пный *прил*: **~ суста́в** ankle.

го́лень (**-и**) *ж* shin; (*у животного*) shank.

голки́пер (**-а**) *м* goalkeeper.

голла́нд|**ец** (-ца) м Dutchman (мн Dutchmen).
Голла́нди|**я** (-и) ж Holland.
голла́нд|**ка** (-ки; gen pl -ок) ж Dutchwoman (мн Dutchwomen).
голла́ндск|**ий** (-ая, -ое, -ие) прил Dutch; ~ **язы́к** Dutch; »**Г~ аукцио́н**" (комм) Dutch auction.
голла́ндца итп сущ см **голла́ндец**.
Голливу́д (-а) м Hollywood.
голов|**а́** (-овы́; acc sg -ову, dat sg -ове́, nom pl -овы, gen pl -о́в, dat pl -ова́м) ж head; **с ~овы́ до ног** from head to foot; **его́ и́мя вы́летало у меня́ из ~овы́** his name slipped my mind; **на ~ову вы́ше кого́-н** head and shoulders above sb; **де́лать (сде́лать** perf**) что-н на свою́/чью-н го́лову** (разг) to make matters worse for o.s./sb; **они́ де́йствовали че́рез мою́/его́ го́лову** they acted over my/his head.
голове́ш|**ка** (-ки; gen pl -ок) ж smouldering (BRIT) или smoldering (US) log.
голо́в|**ка** (-ки; gen pl -ок) ж (гвоздя) head; (чеснока) bulb; ~ **лу́ка** onion.
головно́й прил (платок итп) head опред; (отряд) front опред; (предприятие) main; **головно́й мозг** brain.
голо́вок сущ см **голо́вка**.
головокруже́ни|**е** (-я) ср giddiness.
головокружи́тельный прил (высота) dizzy; (карьера) breath-taking.
головоло́м|**ка** (-ки; gen pl -ок) ж (также перен) puzzle; **задава́ть (зада́ть** perf**) (кому́-н) ~ку** (перен) to pose a problem (to sb).
головомо́йк|**а** (-и) ж (разг) telling off.
головоре́з (-а) м (бандит) cutthroat.
го́лод (-а) м hunger; (длительное недоедание) starvation; (массовое бедствие) famine; (перен): **кни́жный/бума́жный ~** severe shortage of books/paper; **умира́ть (умере́ть** perf**) с ~у** или **от ~а** to die of hunger.
голода́ни|**е** (-я) ср starvation; (воздержание) fasting; **кислоро́дное ~** oxygen deficiency.
голода́|**ть** (-ю) несов неперех to starve; (воздерживаться от пищи) to fast.
гол|**о́дный** (-оден, -одна́, -одно) прил hungry; (год, время) hunger-stricken; (край) barren; **~о́дные бо́ли** hunger pangs; **~о́дная смерть** death from starvation.
голодо́в|**ка** (-ки; gen pl -ок) ж hunger strike; (разг) famine; **объявля́ть (объяви́ть** perf**) ~ку** to go on hunger strike.
гололё́д (-а) м (на дорогах) black ice.
гололе́диц|**а** (-ы) ж (на деревьях) ice; (на дорогах) black ice.
го́лос (-а; part gen -у, nom pl -а́) м voice; (в хоре) part; (крови) the call; (полит) vote; ~ **рассу́дка/со́вести** the voice of reason/conscience; **подава́ть (пода́ть** perf**) ~** to vote; **пра́во ~а** the right to vote; **в оди́н ~** with one voice; **во весь ~** at the top of one's voice; см также **голоса́**.
голос|**а́** (-о́в) мн foreign-controlled radio

stations broadcasting to the Soviet Union.
голоси́ст|**ый** (-, -а, -о) прил loud.
голосло́в|**ный** (-ен, -на, -но) прил unsubstantiated.
голосова́ни|**е** (-я) ср ballot, vote; **откры́тое/та́йное ~** open/secret ballot; **манда́тное** или **представи́тельское ~** card или block vote.
голос|**ова́ть** (-у́ю; perf **проголосова́ть**) несов неперех to vote; (разг) to hitch (a lift); ~ **(проголосова́ть** perf**) за** +acc/**про́тив** +gen to vote for/against.
голосов|**о́й** прил vocal; ~**ые свя́зки** vocal chords.
голубе́|**ть** (-ю) несов неперех to show blue; (perf **поголубе́ть**) to turn blue.
голубе́ц (-ца́) м (обычно мн) stuffed cabbage leaf.
голуби́|**ка** (-и) ж great bilberry.
голу́б|**ка** (-и) ж (обращение) pet.
голуб|**о́й** прил light blue ♦ (-о́го; decl like adj) м (разг: гомосексуали́ст) gay; **голуба́я мечта́** pipe dream; **голубо́й экра́н** small screen.
голу́буш|**ка** (-и) ж см **голу́бчик**.
голубца́ итп сущ см **голубе́ц**.
голу́бчик (-а) м (разг) (my) dear.
го́луб|**ь** (-я; gen pl -е́й) м pigeon; dove; ~ **ми́ра** dove of peace.
голубя́тн|**я** (-ни; gen pl -ен) ж pigeon loft; dovecot.
го́л|**ый** (-, -а́, -о) прил (человек) naked; (череп) bald; (дерево, стены) bare; (no short form; правда) naked; (цифры, факты) bare; ~**ыми рука́ми** with one's bare hands; **его́ ~ыми рука́ми не возьмёшь** (перен) he's a slippery character; **го́лый про́вод** bare wire.
голышо́м нареч starkers.
гол|**ь** (-и) ж собир rabble; ~ **на вы́думки хитра́** ≈ necessity is the mother of invention.
гольф (-а) м golf; (обычно мн: чулки) knee sock; см также **го́льфы**.
го́льф|**ы** (-ов) мн (брюки) plus-fours мн.
гомеопа́т (-а) м homoeopath (BRIT), homeopath (US).
гомеопати́ческ|**ий** (-ая, -ое, -ие) прил homoeopathic (BRIT), homeopathic (US); ~**ая до́за** (перен) tiny amount.
гомеопа́ти|**я** (-и) ж homoeopathy (BRIT), homeopathy (US).
гомери́ческ|**ий** (-ая, -ое, -ие) прил: ~ **смех** или **хо́хот** roar of laughter.
гомоге́нный прил homogenous.
го́мон (-а) м (толпы) hubbub; **пти́чий ~** chorus of birdsong; **поднима́ть (подня́ть** perf**) ~** to make a din.
гомосексуали́зм (-а) м homosexuality.
гомосексуали́ст (-а) м homosexual.
гонг (-а) м gong; **уда́рить** (perf) **в ~** to beat a gong.
гондо́л|**а** (-ы) ж gondola; (дирижабля) car (of airship).

Гондура́с (-a) м Honduras.

гоне́ни|е (-я) ср persecution; **подверга́ться (подве́ргнуться** perf) **~ям** to be persecuted; **~я на кого́-н/что́-н** persecution of sb/sth.

гоне́|ц (-ца́) м messenger.

го́н|ка (-ки; gen pl **-ок**) ж (разг: спешка) rush; (обычно мн: соревнования) racing; **го́нка вооруже́ний** arms race.

Гонко́нг (-a) м Hong Kong.

го́нок итп сущ см **го́нка**.

го́нор (-a) м arrogance.

гонора́р (-a) м fee; **а́вторский ~** royalty.

гоноре́|я (-и) ж gonorrhoea (BRIT), gonorrhea (US).

го́ночный прил racing опред; **го́ночный велосипе́д** racer.

гонт (-a) м (СТРОИТ) shingles мн.

гонца́ итп сущ см **гоне́ц**.

гонча́р (-а́) м potter.

го́нч|ая (-ей; decl like adj) ж hound.

го́нщик (-a) м (автомобиля) racing (BRIT) или race car (US) driver; (велосипеда) racing cyclist.

гоню́(сь) итп несов см **гнать(ся)**.

гоня́|ть (-ю, **-ешь**) несов перех (стадо) to drive; (птиц, поклонников) to chase off или away; (разг: курьера) to keep on the go; (: мяч) to knock about; (: ученика) to grill ◆ неперех to race; **~** (impf) **голубе́й** (СПОРТ) to race pigeons; (перен: разг) to loaf around; **~** (impf) **чай** (разг) to lounge around drinking tea

▶ **гоня́|ться** несов возв: **~ся за** +instr (преследовать) to chase (after); (перен) to pursue.

гоп-компа́ни|я (-и) ж (разг) rowdy bunch.

гор. сокр = **го́род, городско́й**.

гор|а́ (acc sg **-у**, gen sg **-ы́**, nom pl **-ы**, dat pl **-а́м**) ж mountain; (небольшая) hill; (перен: разг) heap; **идти́ (пойти́** perf) **в го́ру** to go uphill; (перен: разг: улучшаться) to be looking up; (: делать карьеру) to go up in the world; **идти́ (пойти́** perf) **под ~у** (также перен: разг) to go downhill; **у меня́ ~ с плеч свали́лась** (разг) that's a weight off my mind; **обеща́ть** (impf) **золоты́е го́ры** to promise the earth; **стоя́ть** (impf) **~о́й за кого́-н** (разг) to stand up for sb; **пир ~о́й** (разг) celebratory blowout; см также **го́ры**.

гора́зд (-a, -o) как сказ (разг): **~ на что́-н/**+infin very good at sth/at doing; **кто во что ~** (разг: пренебр) everyone doing his own thing.

гора́здо нареч much.

горб (-а́; loc sg **-у́**) м hump; **тащи́ть** (impf) **всё на ~у́** (перен: разг) to take everything upon o.s.; **испы́тывать (испыта́ть** perf) **что́-н на своём ~у́** (разг) to learn sth the hard way; **он зарабо́тал всё свои́м ~о́м** (разг) he earned everything through his own hard graft.

горба́т|ый (-, -а, -о) прил (человек)

hunchbacked; (нос) hooked; **~ого моги́ла испра́вит** he итп will never change, ≈ a leopard can't change his spots.

горби́н|ка (-ки; gen pl **-ок**) ж: **нос с ~кой** Roman nose.

го́рб|ить (-лю, -ишь; perf **сго́рбить**) несов перех: **~ спи́ну** to stoop.

▶ **го́рб|иться** (perf **сго́рбиться**) несов возв to stoop; (от старости) to develop a stoop.

горбоно́с|ый (-, -а, -о) прил hooknosed.

горбу́н (-а́) м hunchback.

горбу́нь|я (-и) ж см **горбу́н**.

горбу́ш|а (-и) ж (hunchback) salmon.

горбу́ш|ка (-ки; gen pl **-ек**) ж crust.

горде́ли́в|ый (-, -а, -о) прил proud.

горди́ться (-жу́сь, -ди́шься) несов возв (+instr) to be proud of.

го́рдост|ь (-и) ж pride; (+instr: победой, успехами) pride in; **он - ~ на́шей семьи́** he's the pride and joy of the family.

го́рд|ый (-, -а́, -о, -ы́) прил proud; (+instr: победой, успехами) proud of.

го́р|е (-я) ср (скорбь) grief, sorrow; (несчастье) misfortune; **хлебну́ть** (perf) **~я** (разг) to suffer one's share of misfortune; **помога́ть (помо́чь** perf) **~ю** to help out in times of trouble; **с ~я** with или from grief; **в ~** in (one's) grief; **как на ~** (разг) as ill luck would have it; **~ ты моё!** you'll be the death of me!; **ему́ и ~я ма́ло** (разг) he couldn't care less.

гор|ева́ть (-ю́ю) несов неперех to grieve; **~** (impf) **o** +prp to grieve for; **не ~ю́й!** cheer up!

го́рек прил см **го́рький**.

горе́л|ка (-ки; gen pl **-ок**) ж burner; **па́яльная ~** blowtorch.

горе́лый прил burnt.

горелье́ф (-a) м high relief.

горемы́|ка (-и) м/ж (разг) poor soul.

горе́стный (-ен, -на, -но) прил sorrowful.

го́рест|ь (-и) ж grief; (обычно мн: несчастье) trouble.

гор|е́ть (-ю́, -и́шь; perf **сгоре́ть**) несов неперех to burn; (по дрова, лес) to be on fire; (больной, лоб) to be burning hot; (рана) to smart; (глаза) to shine; (+instr: ненавистью, нетерпением) to burn with; **зака́т ~е́л** there was a blazing sunset; **~** (impf) **от стыда́/любопы́тства** to burn with shame/curiosity; **он ~и́т на рабо́те** he puts everything into his work; **план/спекта́кль ~и́т!** the plan/play is in danger of being a complete failure!; **~й всё си́ним огнём** или **пла́менем!** (разг) to hell with it!; **не ~и́т** (разг) there's no hurry; **у меня́ душа́ ~и́т** I'm bursting with enthusiasm.

го́р|ец (-ца) м mountain dweller.

го́речь (-и) ж bitter taste; (потери) bitterness.

горже́т|ка (-ки; gen pl **-ок**) ж boa.

горжу́сь несов см **горди́ться**.

горизо́нт (-а) м horizon; **появля́ться
(появи́ться** *perf*) **на чьём-н ~е** to come into
sb's life.
горизонта́лен *прил см* **горизонта́льный**.
горизонта́л|ь (-и) ж horizontal; (*на ка́рте*)
contour; (*на ша́хматной доске́*) rank.
горизонта́льный (-ен, -ьна, -ьно) *прил*
horizontal.
гори́лл|а (-ы) ж gorilla.
горисполко́м (-а) м *сокр* (*ИСТ* = *городско́й
исполни́тельный комите́т*) town *или* city
executive committee.
гори́стый *прил* mountainous.
го́р|ка (-ки; *gen pl* -ок) ж hill; (*склон*) slope;
(*шкаф*) cabinet; (*кучка*) small pile; (*АВИА*) steep
climb.
го́ркнуть (*3sg* -ет, *perf* **прого́ркнуть**) *несов
неперех* (*масло*) to go rancid.
горко́м (-а) м *сокр* (*ИСТ* = *городско́й комите́т*)
town *или* city committee.
горла́н|ить (-ю, -ишь) *несов неперех* (*разг*) to
bawl.
горла́стый (-, -а, -о) *прил* (*разг*) noisy.
го́рлиц|а (-ы) ж turtledove.
го́рл|о (-а) ср throat; (*у сосуда*) neck; **стать** (*perf*)
поперёк ~а кому́-н (*перен: разг*) to stick in
sb's throat; **во всё ~** (*разг*) at the top of one's
voice; **пристава́ть (приста́ть** *perf*) **к кому́-н с
ножо́м к ~у** (*разг: пренебр*) to pester the life
out of sb; **у меня́ рабо́ты по ~** (*разг*) I'm up to
my ears in work; **я сыт по ~** (*разг*) I'm stuffed;
(: *перен: обеща́ниями, упрёками*) I've had it up
to here.
го́рлышк|о (-ка; *nom pl* -ки, *gen pl* -ек) ср
(*бутылки, сосуда*) neck.
гормо́н (-а) м hormone.
гормона́льный *прил* hormonal.
горн (-а) м (*для переплавки*) furnace; (*для
обжига*) kiln; (*муз*) bugle.
горни́ст (-а) м bugler.
го́рничн|ая (-ой; *decl like adj*) ж chambermaid.
горно-бурово́й *прил* mining *опред*, mine-
excavation *опред*.
горнодобыва́ющ|ий (-ая, -ее, -ие) *прил*
mining *опред*.
горнозаво́дск|ий (-ая, -ое, -ие) *прил* mining
опред.
горноль́жный *прил* ski *опред*.
горнопромы́шленный *прил* =
горнозаво́дский.
горнопрохо́дческ|ий (-ая, -ое, -ие) *прил*: ~**ие
рабо́ты** tunnelling work *ед*.
горнорабо́ч|ий (-его; *decl like adj*) м miner.
горноспаса́тельный *прил* mountain-rescue
опред.
горноста́|й (-я) м stoat; (*мех*) ermine.
го́рный *прил* mountain *опред*; (*лыжи*) downhill
опред; (*страна*) mountainous; (*богатства*)
mineral *опред*; (*промышленность*) mining
опред; ~**ые поро́ды** rocks; ~ **хруста́ль** rock
crystal; **го́рная боле́знь** altitude sickness;

го́рный хребе́т mountain range.
горня́к (-а́) м (*рабочий*) miner; (*инженер*)
mining engineer.
го́род (-а; *nom pl* -а́) м (*большой*) city;
(*небольшой*) town; **е́хать (пое́хать** *perf*) **за́
го́род** to go out of town; **жить** (*impf*) **за́ го́родом**
to live out of town.
горо|ди́ть (-жу́, -ди́шь) *несов перех*: ~ **ерунду́**
или **вздор** *или* **чушь** (*разг: пренебр*) to talk
rubbish.
городо́к (-ка́) м small town; **спорти́вный ~**
sports complex; **вое́нный ~** military settlement;
университе́тский ~ (university) campus;
де́тский ~ playground.
городско́й *прил* urban; (*сад*) municipal; ~
жи́тель town dweller; (*большого города*) city
dweller.
горожа́н|ин (-ина; *nom pl* -е, *gen pl* -) м city
dweller.
горожа́н|ка (-ки; *gen pl* -ок) ж *см* **горожа́нин**.
горожу́ *несов см* **городи́ть**.
го́рок *сущ см* **го́рка**.
гороско́п (-а) м horoscope.
горо́х (-а; *part gen* -у) м собир peas мн; (*на
платье итп*) polka dots мн; **как об сте́ну ~** like
talking to a brick wall.
горо́ховый *прил* (*суп*) pea; **шут ~** (*разг:
пренебр*) buffoon.
горо́ш|ек (-ка) м собир peas мн; (*на платье
итп*) polka dots мн; **ткань в ~** spotted material;
зелёный ~ garden peas мн; **души́стый ~** sweet
pea.
горо́шин|а (-ы) ж pea.
горо́шка *итп сущ см* **горо́шек**.
горсове́т (-а) м *сокр* (= *городско́й сове́т*) ≈
town *или* city council.
го́рст|ка (-ки; *gen pl* -ок) ж (*также перен*)
handful.
горст|ь (-и; *gen pl* -е́й) ж (*руки*) cupped hand;
(*также перен*) handful.
горта́нный *прил* guttural.
горта́н|ь (-и) ж larynx.
горте́нзи|я (-и) ж hydrangea.
го́рца *итп сущ см* **го́рец**.
го́рче *сравн прил от* **го́рький** ♦ *сравн нареч от*
го́рько.
горч|и́ть (*3sg* -и́т, *3pl* -а́т) *несов неперех* to taste
bitter.
горчи́ц|а (-ы) ж mustard.
горчи́чник (-а) м mustard plaster.
горчи́чный *прил* mustard.
го́рше *сравн прил от* **го́рький** ♦ *сравн нареч от*
го́рько.
горш|о́к (-ка́) м pot; (*также: ночно́й ~*) chamber
pot; **цвето́чный ~** flowerpot.
го́р|ы (-; *dat pl* -а́м) мн mountains мн.
го́рький (-ькая, -ькое, -ькие; -ек, -ька́, -ько)
прил (*вкус, разочарова́ние*) bitter; (*обида,
событие*) painful; **го́рькая и́стина** the painful
truth; **го́рький пья́ница** (*разг*) a hopeless
drunkard; **го́рькие слёзы** bitter tears; **го́рький**

смех bitter laughter.

го́рько *нареч* (*пла́кать*) bitterly ♦ *как сказ:* **во рту** ~ I have a bitter taste in my mouth; **мне** ~, **что меня́ не понима́ют** I feel bitter that nobody understands me.

горю́ч|ее (-**его**; *decl like adj*) *ср* fuel.

горю́ч|ий (-**ая**, -**ее**, -**ие**) *прил* flammable; ~**ие слёзы** bitter tears.

горя́чек *сущ см* **горя́чка**.

горя́ч|ий (-**ая**, -**ее**, -**ие**; -, -**а́**, -**о́**) *прил* hot; (*перен: любо́вь*) passionate; (: *спор*) heated; (: *жела́ние*) burning; (: *челове́к*) hot-tempered; (*день итп*) hectic; ~ **хара́ктер** hot temper; **де́лать** (**сде́лать** *perf*) **что-н по** ~**им следа́м** to do sth without delay; **я попа́л ему́ под** ~**ую ру́ку** I caught him while he was in a bad mood; **горя́чая то́чка** trouble spot.

горя́ч|иться (-**у́сь**, -**и́шься**; *perf* **разгорячи́ться**) *несов возв* to get worked up.

горя́ч|ка (-**ки**; *gen pl* -**ек**) *ж* (*разг*) frenzy; **поро́ть** (*impf*) ~**ку** to rush.

горя́чность (-**и**) *ж* irascibility.

горячо́ *нареч* (*спо́рить, люби́ть*) passionately ♦ *как сказ* it's hot.

Госба́нк (-**а**) *м сокр* (= *госуда́рственный банк*) state bank.

госбезопа́сность (-**и**) *ж сокр* (*ИСТ:* = *госуда́рственная безопа́сность*) national security.

госбюдже́т (-**а**) *м сокр* (= *госуда́рственный бюдже́т*) state budget.

госдепарта́мент (-**а**) *м сокр* (= *госуда́рственный департа́мент*) State Department.

Госкомизда́т *м сокр* = Госуда́рственный комите́т Сове́та Мини́стров по дела́м изда́тельства полигра́фии и кни́жной торго́вли.

госкомите́т (-**а**) *м сокр* (= *госуда́рственный комите́т*) state committee.

госкреди́т (-**а**) *м сокр* (= *госуда́рственный креди́т*) state credit.

госпитализи́р|овать (-**ую**) (*не*)*сов перех* to hospitalize.

го́спиталь (-**я**) *м* army hospital.

Госпла́н *м сокр* (*ИСТ:* = Госуда́рственная пла́новая коми́ссия) state planning committee.

господа́ *итп сущ см* **господи́н**.

го́споди *межд:* Г~! good Lord!

госп|оди́н (-**оди́на**; *nom pl* -**ода́**, *gen pl* -**о́д**) *м* gentleman (*мн* gentlemen); (*хозя́ин*) master; (*при обраще́нии*) sir; (*при фами́лии, зва́нии*) Mr (= *Mister*).

госпо́дств|о (-**а**) *ср* supremacy; (*над страно́й*) dominion; (*иде́й*) predominance.

госпо́дств|овать (-**ую**) *несов непepex* to rule; (*мне́ние*) to prevail; ~ (*impf*) **на мо́ре** to rule the seas; ~ (*impf*) **над** +*instr* (*ме́стностью*) to tower

above, dominate.

госпо́дствующ|ий (-**ая**, -**ее**, -**ие**) *прил* (*па́ртия, класс*) ruling; (*взгля́ды*) prevailing; (*гора́, ба́шня итп*) imposing.

Госпо́дь (Го́спода; *voc* Го́споди) *м* (*та́кже:* ~ **Бог**) the Lord; **не дай Го́споди!** God forbid!; **сла́ва тебе́ Го́споди!** Glory be to God!; (*разг*) thank God!

госпож|а́ (-**и́**) *ж* lady; (*хозя́йка*) mistress; (*при обраще́нии, зва́нии*) Madam; (*при фами́лии:* замужняя) Mrs; (: *незамужняя*) Miss; (: *замужняя или незамужняя*) Ms.

Госстра́х (-**а**) *м сокр* (= Гла́вное управле́ние госуда́рственного страхова́ния Министе́рства фина́нсов Росси́и) department dealing with national insurance.

госстра́х (-**а**) *м сокр* (= *госуда́рственное страхова́ние*) ≈ national insurance.

ГОСТ (-**а**) *м сокр* (= *госуда́рственный общесою́зный станда́рт*) standard manufacturing specifications under the Soviet system.

гост (-**а**) *м сокр* = **ГОСТ**.

гостеприи́м|ный (-**ен**, -**на**, -**но**) *прил* hospitable.

гости́н|ая (-**ой**; *decl like adj*) *ж* living *или* sitting room, lounge (*BRIT*); (*ме́бель*) living-room suite.

гости́ница (-**ы**) *ж* hotel.

го|сти́ть (-**щу́**, -**сти́шь**) *несов непepex* to stay.

гост|ь (-**я**; *gen pl* -**е́й**) *м* guest; **идти́** (**пойти́** *perf*) **в го́сти к кому́-н** to go to see sb; **быть** (*impf*) **в** ~**я́х у кого́-н** to be at sb's house; **в** ~**я́х хорошо́, а до́ма лу́чше** there's no place like home.

го́ст|ья (-**ьи**; *gen pl* -**ий**) *ж см* **гость**.

госуда́рствен|ный *прил* state *опред*; ~ **язы́к** official language; ~ **строй** government system; **госуда́рственное пра́во** public law; **госуда́рственный экза́мен** Finals *мн*.

госэкза́мен (-**а**) *м сокр* (= *госуда́рственный экза́мен*) ≈ finals *мн*.

госуда́рств|о (-**а**) *ср* state.

госуда́рын|я (-**и**; *gen pl* -**ь**) *ж* sovereign; (*при обраще́нии*) Your Majesty; **ми́лостивая** ~ Madam.

госуда́р|ь (-**я**) *м* sovereign; (*при обраще́нии*) Your Majesty; **ми́лостивый** ~ Sir.

го́ти|ка (-**и**) *ж* Gothic.

готи́ческ|ий (-**ая**, -**ое**, -**ие**) *прил* Gothic.

готова́льн|я (-**ьни**; *gen pl* -**ен**) *ж* (*архите́ктора*) drawing instruments *мн*; (*шко́льника*) geometry set.

гото́в|ить (-**лю**, -**ишь**; *perf* **пригото́вить**) *несов перех* to get ready; (*уро́ки*) to prepare; (*обе́д*) to prepare, make; (*perf* **подгото́вить**; *специали́ста*) to train; (*ученика́*) to coach ♦ *непepex* to cook; **она́ хорошо́** ~**ит** she's a good cook

▸ **готóвиться** (*perf* **приготóвиться**) *несов возв*: ~**ся к** +*dat* (*к отъéзду*) to get ready for; ~**ся** (**подготóвиться** *perf*) **к** +*dat* (*к экзáмену*) to prepare for; ~**ятся большúе собы́тия/изменéния** great events/changes are in the offing.

готóвность (**-и**) *ж* readiness; ~ +*infin* readiness *или* willingness to do; **в боевóй** ~**и** ready for action.

готóво *как сказ* that's it.

готóв|ый (**-**, **-а**, **-о**) *прил* (*обéд*) ready; (*no short form*; *издéлие*) ready-made; ~ **к** +*dat*/+*infin* prepared for/to do; ~ **на переговóры** prepared *или* willing to negotiate; ~ **на всё** ready for anything; **онá живёт на всём** ~**ом** her every need is catered for; **готóвое плáтье** off-the-peg (*BRIT*) *или* off-the-rack (*US*) dress.

гофриróванный *прил* (*юбка*) pleated; (*жесть*) corrugated.

гофриров|áть (**-ýю**) *несов перех* (*см прил*) to pleat; to corrugate.

гощý *несов см* **гостúть**.

ГПТУ *ср сокр* (= **городскóе профессионáльно-технúческое учúлище**) ≈ CTC (= city technology college).

гр. *сокр* (= **грáдус**) d. (= *degree*); (= **гражданúн**) Mr (= *Mister*); (= **граждáнка**) Mrs; = **грýппа**.

граб (**-а**) *м* hornbeam.

грабёж (**-ежá**) *м* (*также перен*) robbery; (*дóма*) burglary; ~ **срéди бéла дня** (*разг*) daylight robbery.

грáбель *сущ см* **грáбли**.

грабúтел|ь (**-я**) *м* (*см сущ*) robber; burglar.

грабúтельск|ий (**-ая**, **-ое**, **-ие**) *прил* (*война*) predatory; (*цены*) extortionate; ~**ое нападéние** (*на дом*) burglary; (*на банк*) robbery; (*на странý*) pillage.

грáб|ить (**-лю**, **-ишь**; *perf* **ограбить**) *несов перех* (*также перен: человéка*) to rob; (*дом*) to burgle; (*гóрод*) to pillage.

грáб|ли (**-ель** *или* **-лей**) *мн* rake *ед*.

грáблю *несов см* **грáбить**.

гравёр (**-а**) *м* engraver.

грáв|ий (**-я**) *м* gravel.

гравиров|áть (**-ýю**; *perf* **вы́гравировать**) *несов перех* to engrave ◆ *неперех* to etch.

гравитáци|я (**-и**) *ж* gravitation.

гравю́р|а (**-ы**) *ж* (*оттиск*) engraving; (*офорт*) etching.

град (**-а**) *м* (*также перен*) hail; (*перен*): ~ +*gen* (*пуль*) hail of; (*упрёков*) stream of.

градáци|я (**-и**) *ж* gradation.

грáдин|а (**-ы**) *ж* hailstone.

градúрн|я (**-ни**; *gen pl* **-ен**) *ж* cooling tower.

грáдом *нареч* thick and fast; **катúться** (*impf*) ~ (*слёзы*) to stream down.

градострóител|ь (**-я**) *м* town (*BRIT*) *или* city (*US*) planner.

градострóительств|о (**-а**) *ср* town (*BRIT*) *или* city (*US*) planning.

грáдус (**-а**) *м* degree; **под** ~**ом** (*разг*) tiddly.

грáдусник (**-а**) *м* thermometer.

граждани́н (**-а**; *nom pl* **грáждане**, *gen pl* **грáждан**) *м* citizen.

граждáн|ка (**-ки**; *gen pl* **-ок**) *ж см* **граждани́н**.

граждáнск|ий (**-ая**, **-ое**, **-ие**) *прил* civil; (*долг*) civic; (*плáтье*) civilian; **граждáнская войнá** civil war; **граждáнская панихúда** civil funeral service; **граждáнский кóдекс** civil code.

граждáнств|о (**-а**) *ср* citizenship; **получáть** (**получúть** *perf*) ~ *или* **правá граждáнства** to be granted citizenship.

грамзáпис|ь (**-и**) *ж* recording; **ópера в** ~**и** recording of an opera.

грамм (**-а**; *gen pl* **-** *или* **-ов**) *м* gramme (*BRIT*), gram (*US*); **у негó (нет) ни грáмма сóвести** (*разг*) he doesn't have an ounce of conscience.

грамматик|а (**-и**) *ж* grammar.

граммати́ческ|ий (**-ая**, **-ое**, **-ие**) *прил* (*ошибка*) grammatical; (*упражнéние*) grammar *опред*.

грáмот|а (**-ы**) *ж* reading and writing; (*документ*) certificate; **для меня́ э́то китáйская** ~ (*разг*) it's Greek *или* double Dutch (*BRIT*) to me; **почётная** ~ certificate of merit.

грáмотн|ый (**-ен**, **-на**, **-но**) *прил* (*человéк*) literate; (*текст*) properly *или* correctly written; (*специалúст*, *план*) competent.

грампласти́н|ка (**-и**) *ж* gramophone (*BRIT*) *или* phonograph (*US*) record.

гранáт (**-а**) *м* (*плод*) pomegranate; (*дéрево*) pomegranate (tree); (*минерáл*) garnet.

гранáт|а (**-ы**) *ж* grenade.

гранáтов|ый *прил* (*сок*) pomegranate *опред*; (*браслéт*) garnet *опред*; (*цвет*) deep red.

гранатомёт (**-а**) *м* grenade launcher.

грандиóз|ный (**-ен**, **-на**, **-но**) *прил* (*сооружéние*) grand; (*масштáбы*, *плáны*) grandiose.

гранёный *прил* (*стакáн*) cut-glass *опред*; (*алмáз*) cut *опред*.

грани́т (**-а**) *м* granite.

грани́тный *прил* (*плитá*) granite.

гран|и́ть (**-ю́**, **-и́шь**) *несов перех* to cut.

грани́ц|а (**-ы**) *ж* (*госудáрства*) border; (*учáстка*) boundary; (*обычно мн: перен*) limit; **éхать** (**поéхать** *perf*) **за** ~**у** to go abroad; **жить** (*impf*) **за** ~**ей** to live abroad; **из-за** ~**ы** from abroad; **в** ~**х прилúчия/закóна** within the bounds of decency/the law; **егó поведéние перехóдит все** ~**ы!** he's gone too far!

грани́ч|ить (**-у**, **-ишь**) *несов неперех*: ~ **с** +*instr* to border on; (*перен*) to verge on.

грáн|ка (**-ки**; *gen pl* **-ок**) *ж* (*ТИПОГ*) proof.

грант (**-а**) *м* grant.

грáнул|а (**-ы**) *ж* granule.

гран|ь (**-и**) *ж* (*ГЕОМ*) face; (*алмáза*) facet; (*перен*) bounds *мн*; **переступáть** (**переступúть** *perf*) ~ to overstep the mark; **на грáни** +*gen* on the brink *или* verge of.

граф (**-а**) *м* count, earl (*BRIT*).

граф|á (**-ы́**) *ж* column.

грáфик (**-а**) *м* (*МАТ*) graph; (*план*) schedule,

timetable; (художник) graphic artist; **работать** (impf) по ~у to work to schedule; **поезд идёт по** ~у the train is running to time; ~ **расчёта точки „нулевой" прибыли** (комм) break-even chart.

графика (-и) ж graphic art; (буквы) script ◆ собир (рисунки) graphics мн.

графин (-а) м (для воды) water jug; (для вина) decanter; (: открытый) carafe.

графиня (-и) ж countess.

графит (-а) м (минерал) graphite; (грифель) (pencil) lead.

графить (-лю, -ишь; perf **разграфить**) несов перех to rule (lines).

графический (-ая, -ое, -ие) прил graphic.

графлю несов см **графить**.

графство (-а) ср county.

грациозный (-ен, -на, -но) прил graceful.

грация (-и) ж grace; (корсет) corset.

грач (-а) м rook.

грёб итп несов см **грести**.

гребёнка (-ки; gen pl -ок) ж (также ТЕХ) comb; **стричь** (impf) **всех под одну** ~ку to lump everyone together.

гребень (-ня) м comb; (волны, горы) crest.

гребец (-ца) м oarsman (мн oarsmen), rower.

гребешок (-ка) м comb; (также: морской ~) scallop.

гребля (-и) ж rowing.

гребной прил: ~ **спорт** rowing.

гребня итп сущ см **гребень**.

гребок (-ка) м stroke.

гребу итп несов см **грести**.

гребца итп сущ см **гребец**.

грёжу(сь) несов см **грёзить(ся)**.

грёза (-ы) ж (обычно мн) daydream.

грёзить (-жу, -зишь) несов неперех to (day)dream, fantasize

▶ **грёзиться** (perf **пригрёзиться**) несов возв: **ему** ~ится... he dreams of ....

грейдер (-а) м grader; (разг: дорога) dirt road.

грейпфрут (-а) м grapefruit.

грек (-а) м Greek (man) (мн men).

грелка (-ки; gen pl -ок) ж hot-water bottle; **электрическая** ~ electric blanket.

греметь (-лю, -ишь; perf **прогреметь**) несов неперех (поезд) to thunder by; (выстрелы) to thunder out; (гром) to rumble; (перен) to resound; ~ (**прогреметь** perf) +instr (ведром, кастрюлями) to clatter; (ключами) to jangle.

гремучий (-ая, -ее, -ие) прил: ~**ая змея** rattlesnake; ~ **газ** firedamp.

Гренада (-ы) ж Grenada.

гренадёр (-а; gen pl -или -ов) м (солдат) grenadier; **он настоящий** ~ (разг) he's a real hulk.

гренка итп сущ см **гренок**.

Гренландия (-и) ж Greenland.

гренландский (-ая, -ое, -ие) прил Greenlandic.

гренок (-ка; nom pl -ки) м (обычно мн) crouton.

грести (-бу, -бёшь; pt грёб, -бла, -бло) несов неперех to row; (веслом, руками) to paddle ◆ перех to rake.

греть (-ю) несов перех (подлеж: солнце, печь) to heat, warm; (: шуба) to keep warm; (воду) to heat (up); (руки) to warm; ~ (impf) **руки на чём-н** (разг) to line one's pockets with sth

▶ **греться** несов возв (человек) to warm o.s.; (вода) to warm или heat up.

грех (-а) м sin ◆ **как сказ**: ~ +infin (разг) it's a sin to do; **как на** ~ (разг) as ill luck would have it; **от** ~ **подальше** just to be on the safe side; **уйди от** ~**а подальше!** go away and stay out of trouble!; **с** ~**ом пополам** (разг) by a hair('s breadth).

греховный (-ен, -на, -но) прил sinful.

грехопадение (-я) ж the Fall.

Греция (-и) ж Greece.

грецкий (-ая, -ое, -ие) прил: ~ **орех** walnut.

гречанка (-ки; gen pl -ок) ж Greek (woman) (мн women).

греческий (-ая, -ое, -ие) прил Greek; (культура) (Ancient) Greek; ~ **язык** Greek.

гречиха (-и) ж buckwheat.

гречка (-и) ж buckwheat.

гречневый прил buckwheat.

грешен прил см **грешный**.

грешить (-у, -ишь; perf **согрешить**) несов неперех to sin; (perf **погрешить**; противоречить): ~ **против** +gen to sin against.

грешник (-а) м sinner.

грешница (-ы) ж см **грешник**.

грешный (-ен, -на, -но) прил sinful.

гриб (-а) м fungus (мн fungi); (съедобный) (edible) mushroom; **несъедобный** ~ toadstool.

грибка итп сущ см **грибок**.

грибник (-а) м mushroom picker.

грибница (-ы) ж mushroom spore.

грибной прил (суп) mushroom; ~**ое место** a good place for mushrooms; **грибной дождь** rain during sunshine.

грибок (-ка) м (на коже) fungal infection; (на дереве) fungus; (на хлебе итп) mould; (укрытие) mushroom-shaped shelter in a playground, on the beach etc.

грива (-ы) ж mane.

гривенник (-а) м (разг) ten-kopeck piece.

грим (-а) м stage make-up, greasepaint.

гримаса (-ы) ж grimace; **строить** (**состроить** perf) или **корчить** (**скорчить** perf) ~**ы** to make или pull faces.

гримасничать (-ю) несов неперех to make или pull faces.

гримёр (-а) м make-up artist.

гримёрная (-ой; decl like adj) ж dressing room.

гримировать (-ую; perf **загримировать**) несов перех: ~ **кого-н** to make sb up

▶ **гримирова́ться** (*perf* **загримирова́ться** *или* **нагримирова́ться**) *несов возв* to put on one's make-up.

грипп (-а) *м* flu.

гриппо́зн|ый *прил* flu *опред*; **у больно́го ~ое состоя́ние** the patient has influenza.

гриф (-а) *м* (ЗООЛ) vulture; (МИФОЛОГИЯ) griffin; (МУЗ) fingerboard; (*штемпель*) stamp.

гри́фель (-я) *м* (pencil)lead.

гроб (-а; *loc sg* -у́, *nom pl* -ы́) *м* coffin; **вогна́ть (вогна́ть** *perf*) **кого́-н в ~** (*разг*) to drive sb to their grave; **в ~у́ я э́то ви́дел!** (*разг*) I don't give a damn about it!

гро́б|ить (-лю, -ишь; *perf* **угро́бить**) *несов перех* (*разг*) to screw up.

гробни́ц|а (-ы) *ж* tomb.

гробов|о́й *прил*: **~ го́лос** sepulchral tones *мн*; **гробово́е молча́ние** deathly silence; **гробова́я тишина́** deathly hush.

грог (-а; *part gen* -у) *м* grog.

грожу́(сь) *несов см* **грози́ть(ся)**.

гр|оза́ (-озы́; *nom pl* -о́зы) *ж* thunderstorm; (*перен*): **~ +gen** (*садов, зверей*) threat to.

гроздь (-и; *gen pl* -е́й) *ж* (*винограда*) bunch; (*сирени*) cluster.

гро́зен *прил см* **гро́зный**.

гро|зи́ть (-жу́, -зи́шь) *несов неперех* (*no perf*; *опасности*) to loom; (+*instr*; *катастрофой*) to be threatened by; (*perf* **погрози́ть**): **~ кому́-н чем-н** to threaten sb with sth; **~ (пригрози́ть** *perf*) **кому́-н разво́дом** to threaten sb with divorce; **он пригрози́л нача́льнику уйти́** he threatened the boss that he would resign

▶ **грози́ться** (*perf* **пригрози́ться**) *несов возв* to threaten.

гро́зн|ый (-ен, -на́, -но) *прил* (*взгляд, письмо*) threatening; (*противник, оружие*) formidable; (*царь*) severe, harsh; (*учитель*) strict.

грозов|о́й *прил*: **~а́я ту́ча** storm cloud.

гром (-а; *gen pl* -о́в) *м* thunder; (*перен*) din; **пока́ ~ не гря́нет** (*разг*) until it's too late; **мета́ть** (*impf*) **гро́мы и мо́лнии** (*перен: разг*) to rant and rave.

грома́д|а (-ы) *ж* bulk.

грома́ден *прил см* **грома́дный**.

грома́дин|а (-ы) *ж* (*разг*) whopper, monster.

грома́дный *прил* enormous, huge.

гром|и́ть (-лю́, -и́шь) *несов перех* to destroy; (*перен: разг*) to slag (off).

гро́м|кий (-кая, -кое, -кие; -ок, -ка́, -ко) *прил* (*голос*) loud; (*no short form*; *скандал*) big; (*имя, дело*) famous; (*слова*) high-flown.

гро́мко *нареч* loudly.

громкоговори́тель (-я) *м* (loud)speaker.

громлю́ *несов см* **громи́ть**.

громов|о́й *прил* (*голос*) thunderous; **~ые раска́ты** thunderclaps *мн*.

громогла́с|ный (-ен, -на, -но) *прил* very loud; **~ное заявле́ние** public announcement.

громозди́ть (-жу́, -ди́шь; *perf* **нагромозди́ть**) *несов перех* to pile up

▶ **громозди́ться** (*perf* **нагромозди́ться**) *несов возв* (*скалы*) to loom; **~ся** (**взгромозди́ться** *perf*) **на +acc** (*разг*) to clamber up onto.

громо́зд|кий (-кая, -кое, -кие; -ок, -ка, -ко) *прил* cumbersome; (*перен*) clumsy.

громозжу́(сь) *несов см* **громозди́ть(ся)**.

гро́мок *прил см* **гро́мкий**.

громоотво́д (-а) *м* lightning conductor.

гро́мче *сравн прил от* **гро́мкий** ◆ *сравн нареч от* **гро́мко**.

громыха́|ть (-ю; *perf* **прогромыха́ть**) *несов неперех* (*разг: гром*) to rumble; (*колёса*) to rattle; ~ (**прогромыха́ть** *perf*) +*instr* (*кастрюлями, ведром*) to clatter.

гроссме́йстер (-а) *м* grandmaster.

грот (-а) *м* (*пещера*) grotto; (*парус*) mainsail.

гроте́ск (-а) *м* grotesque.

гро́хн|уть (-у, -ешь) *сов неперех* (*разг: выстрел*) to ring out; (: *рассмея́ться*) to go into stitches ◆ *перех* (*разг: вазу итп*) to smash; (: *мешок*) to bang down

▶ **гро́хнуться** (*impf* **гро́хаться**) *сов возв* (*разг*) to come crashing down.

гро́хот (-а) *м* racket.

грох|ота́ть (-очу́, -о́чешь; *perf* **прогрохота́ть**) *несов неперех* to rumble.

грош (-а́) *м* half-kopeck coin; **э́то сто́ит ~й** it costs next to nothing; **у меня́ нет ни ~á** (*разг*) I'm stony broke; **~á ло́маного не сто́ит** (*разг*) it's not worth a brass farthing (*BRIT*) *или* a plugged nickel (*US*).

гроше́вый *прил* (*разг: вещь*) dirt-cheap; (*сумма*) paltry; (*расчёты*) petty.

грубе́|ть (-ю; *perf* **огрубе́ть**) *несов неперех* (*человек*) to grow rude; (*душа*) to grow hard; (*perf* **загрубе́ть**; *кожа*) to become rough; (*perf* **погрубе́ть**; *черты*) to harden.

груб|и́ть (-лю́, -и́шь; *perf* **нагруби́ть**) *несов неперех* (+*dat*) to be rude to.

грубия́н (-а) *м* rude person (*мн* people).

грубия́н|ка (-ки; *gen pl* -ок) *ж см* **грубия́н**.

грублю́ *несов см* **груби́ть**.

гру́бо *нареч* (*отвеча́ть*) rudely; (*разгова́ривать*) crudely; (*обточи́ть, подсчита́ть*) roughly; **~ говоря́** roughly speaking.

гру́бость (-и) *ж* (*выраже́ние*) crudeness, coarseness; (*посту́пок*) rudeness.

гру́б|ый (-, -а́, -о) *прил* (*человек, поведе́ние*) rude; (*ткань, пища*) coarse; (*кожа, подсчёт*) rough; (*голос*) gruff; (*оши́бка, шу́тка*) crude; (*наруше́ние пра́вил*) gross.

гру́д|а (-ы) *ж* pile, heap.

груди́н|ка (-и) *ж* (*говя́дина*) brisket; (*копчёная свини́на*) bacon; **бара́нья ~** breast of lamb; **свина́я ~** pork fillet.

грудни́ц|а (-ы) *ж* mastitis.

грудн|о́й *прил* (*молоко*) breast *опред*; (*кашель*) chest *опред*; (*младе́нец*): **~ ребёнок** baby; **грудно́й го́лос** chest voice; **грудны́е же́лезы** mammary glands *мн*; **грудна́я кле́тка** thorax;

грудно́**е кормл**е́**ние** breast-feeding.

гру**дь** (-уди́; *instr sg* -у́дью, *nom pl* -у́ди) ж (*АНАТ*) chest; (: *женщины*) breasts мн; ~ руб**а́шки** shirt front; вста**ва́ть (встать** *perf*) ~у́**дью на защи́ту** ко**го́-н/чего́-н** to stake one's life in defence (*BRIT*) *или* defense (*US*) of sb/sth; **корми́ть** (*impf*) ~у́**дью** to breast-feed.

гружёный *прил* loaded.

гружу́(сь) *несов см* **грузи́ть(ся)**.

груз (-а) *м* (*тяжесть*) weight; (*товар*) cargo, freight.

груздь (-я) *м* milk agaric.

гру́зен *прил см* **гру́зный**.

грузи́ло (-а) *ср* sinker, weight.

грузи́н (-а) *м* Georgian.

грузи́нка (-ки; *gen pl* -ок) ж *см* **грузи́н**.

грузи́нский (-ая, -ое, -ие) *прил* Georgian.

гру́зи́ть (-ужу́, -у́зишь; *perf* **загрузи́ть** *или* **нагрузи́ть**) *несов перех* (*корабль итп*) to load (up); ~ (**погрузи́ть** *perf*) (**в/на** +*acc*) (*товар*) to load (onto)

▶ **грузи́ться** (*perf* **погрузи́ться**) *несов возв* (*люди*) to board; (*судно*) to take on cargo; (*машина*) to be loaded up.

Гру́зия (-и) ж Georgia.

гру́зный (-ен, -на́, -но) *прил* (*человек*) hefty; (*походка*) lumbering.

грузови́к (-а́) *м* lorry (*BRIT*), truck (*US*).

грузово́**й** *прил* (*судно*, *самолёт*) cargo *опред*; **грузова́я маши́на** goods vehicle; **грузово́е такси́** removal (*BRIT*) *или* moving (*US*) van.

грузооборо́т (-а) *м* turnover of goods.

грузоотправи́тель (-я) *м* consignor of goods.

грузоподъёмность (и) ж freight *или* cargo capacity.

грузополуча́тель (-я) *м* consignee.

гру́зчик (-а) *м* (*на складе*) warehouse porter; (*в магазине*) stockroom worker; (*в порту*) docker (*BRIT*), stevedore (*US*); (*на вокзале*) porter.

грунт (-а) *м* soil, earth; (*дно водоёма*) bottom; (*краска*) primer.

грунто**ва́ть** (-у́ю; *perf* **загрунтова́ть**) *несов перех* to prime.

грунто́вка (-и) ж undercoat.

грунтово́**й** *прил*: ~**а́я доро́га** dirt road; ~**а́я кра́ска** primer.

гру́ппа (-ы) ж group; **гру́ппа кро́ви** blood group.

группи́рова́ть (-у́ю; *perf* **сгруппирова́ть**) *несов перех* (*людей*) to group; (*отдел*) to establish, set up; (*данные, цифры*) to group, classified.

▶ **группирова́ться** (*perf* **сгруппирова́ться**) *несов возв* (*объединяться*) to form groups; (*классифицироваться*) to be grouped *или* classified.

группи́ровка (-ки; *gen pl* -ок) ж grouping; (*религиозная*) group.

группово́й *прил* group *опред*.

гру́стен *прил см* **гру́стный**.

гру́сти́ть (-щу́, -сти́шь) *несов неперех* to be melancholy, feel very sad; ~ (*impf*) **по** +*dat или* **о** +*prp* (*семье, дому*) to pine for.

гру́стно *нареч* sadly ◆ *как сказ* (+*dat*): **мне** ~ I feel sad.

гру́стный (-ен, -на́, -но) *прил* (*настроение*) sad, melancholy; (*no short form*; *конец*) sad.

грусть (-и) ж sadness, melancholy.

гру́ша (-и) ж (*плод*) pear; (*дерево*) pear (tree).

грущу́ *несов см* **грусти́ть**.

гры́жа (-и) ж hernia.

грыз *итп несов см* **грызть**.

грызня́ (-и) ж (*разг: собак итп*) scrap; (*перен: пренебр*) squabble.

гры́зть (-у́, -ёшь; *pt* -, -ла, -ло) *несов перех* (*печенье, яблоки*) to nibble (at); (*perf* **разгры́зть**; *кость*) to gnaw (on); (*орехи*) to nibble; (*перен: разг: человека*) to get at; ~ (*impf*) **но́гти** to bite one's nails; **меня́ гры́зло раска́яние/сомне́ние** I was consumed by remorse/doubt

▶ **гры́зться** *несов возв* (*собаки итп*) to fight; (*перен: разг*) to squabble.

грызу́н (-а́) *м* rodent.

гряда́ (-ы́; *nom pl* -ы) ж row (*of flowers, vegetables*); (*гор*) range; (*волн*) series; ~ **облако́в** bank of cloud.

грядёт *итп несов см* **грясти́**.

гря́дка (-ки; *gen pl* -ок) ж row.

гряду́щее (-его; *decl like adj*) *ср* the future.

гряду́щий (-ая, -ее, -ие) *прил* (*год*) coming; **на сон** ~ before going to bed.

грязелече́ние (-я) *ср* mud cure.

гря́зен *прил см* **гря́зный**.

гря́зи (-ей) ж mud cure; (*место*) mud baths мн.

грязни́ть (-ю́, -и́шь; *perf* **загрязни́ть**) *несов перех* (*платье*) to get dirty; (*пол*) to make dirty; (*перен: репутацию*) to tarnish ◆ (*perf* **нагрязни́ть**) *неперех* (*в доме*) to make a mess; (*на улице*) to drop litter

▶ **грязни́ться** (*perf* **загрязни́ться**) *несов возв* to become dirty.

грязну́ля (-и) *м/ж* (*разг*) pig; (: *ребёнок*) mucky kid.

гря́зный (-ен, -на́, -но) *прил* dirty; (*ребёнок, платье*) dirty, grubby; (*перен: анекдот, личность*) sordid; (*цвет*) murky; ~**ное де́ло** dirty business; ~**ная война́** dirty war.

гряз**ь** (-и; *loc sg* -и́) ж dirt; (*на дороге*) mud; (*перен*) filth; **облива́ть (обли́ть** *perf*) **кого́-н гря́зью, меша́ть (смеша́ть** *perf*) **кого́-н с гря́зью** (*перен*) to sling mud at sb; *см также* **гря́зи**.

гря́нуть (-у, -ешь) *сов перех* (*марш*) to strike up ◆ *неперех* (*выстрел*) to ring out; (*война*) to break out; ~ *(perf)* **пе́сню** to burst into song; ~**ул гром** there was a clap of thunder.

гря|сти́ *(3sg -дёт, 3pl -ду́т) несов непepex* to draw near.

гуа́ш|ь (-и) *ж* gouache.

губ|а́ (-ы́; *nom pl* **-ы,** *dat pl* **-а́м)** *ж* lip; (*обычно мн*: *тиски́*) jaw (*of pliers etc*); (*залив*) bay (*in North Russia*); **дуть (наду́ть** *perf*) **гу́бы** (*перен*: *разг*) to be in a huff; **у него́ ~ не ду́ра** (*разг*) he knows what's good for him.

губе́рни|я (-и) *ж* gubernia (*administrative region*).

губерна́тор (-а) *м* governor.

губе́рнск|ий (-ая, -ое, -ие) *прил* gubernia, regional.

губи́тел|ьный (-ен, -ьна, -ьно) *прил* (*климат*) unhealthy; (*влия́ние*) pernicious; (*после́дствия*) ruinous; (*привы́чка*) harmful; (*моро́з*): ~ **(для** +*gen*) disastrous (for).

губи́ть (-лю́, -ишь; *perf* **погуби́ть)** *несов перех* to kill; (*урожа́й, здоро́вье*) to ruin; **он её погу́бит** he'll be the ruin of her.

гу́б|ка (-ки; *gen pl* **-ок)** *ж* sponge.

гублю́ *несов см* **губи́ть.**

губн|о́й *прил*: ~**а́я пома́да** lipstick; ~**а́я гармо́шка** harmonica.

губо́к *сущ см* **гу́бка.**

ГУВД *сокр* (= *Гла́вное управле́ние вну́тренних дел*) ≈ police headquarters.

гуверна́нт|ка (-ки; *gen pl* **-ок)** *ж* governess.

гуверн|ёр (-а) *м* (*private*) tutor.

гугу́ *как сказ*: **она́ ни** ~ (*разг*) she doesn't say a word; **ни** ~! (*разг*) not a word!

гуде́ни|е (-я) *ср* (*жуко́в*) drone; (*проводо́в*) hum; (*ве́тра*) moan.

гу|де́ть (-жу́, -ди́шь) *несов неперех* (*шмель, провода́*) to hum; (*ве́тер*) to moan; (*толпа́*) to murmur; (*маши́на*) to hoot; (*разг: ноги́ итп*) to throb.

гуд|о́к (-ка́) *м* (*устро́йство: автомоби́ля*) horn; (: *парохо́да, заво́да*) siren; (*звук*) hoot.

гудро́н (-а) *м* tar.

гужу́ *несов см* **гуде́ть.**

гул (-а) *м* (*маши́н, голосо́в*) drone; (*мо́ре*) murmur.

гу́л|кий (-кая, -кое, -кие; -ок, -ка́, -ко) *прил* (*уда́р, шаги́*) resounding; (*свод*) echoing.

гу́лькин *прил*: **с ~ нос** (*разг*) next to nothing.

гуля́нь|е (-ья; *nom pl* **-ий)** *ср*: **наро́дное** ~ *outdoor merrymaking on a public holiday.*

гуля́|ть (-ю; *perf* **погуля́ть)** *несов неперех* (*прогу́ливаться*) to stroll; (*быть на у́лице*) to be out; (*на сва́дьбе*) to have a good time, enjoy

o.s.; **идти́ (пойти́** *perf*) ~ to go for a walk; **я сего́дня ~ю** (*разг*) I am taking the day off today.

гуля́ш (-а́) *м* goulash.

ГУМ (-а) *м сокр* (= *Госуда́рственный универса́льный магази́н*) *state department store.*

гуманита́р|ный *прил* (*по́мощь*) humanitarian; (*образова́ние, факульте́т*) arts *опред*; **гуманита́рные нау́ки** the humanities *или* arts.

гума́нност|ь (-и) *ж* humaneness, humanity.

гума́н|ный (-ен, -на, -но) *прил* humane.

гумн|о́ (-а́) *ср* (*сара́й*) barn; (*площа́дка*) threshing floor.

гурма́н (-а) *м* gourmet.

гурт (-а́) *м* (*коро́в*) herd.

гурто́м *нареч* (*разг: отпра́виться*) en masse; (: *прода́ть, купи́ть*) in bulk.

гурьб|а́ (-ы́) *ж* crowd; **ходи́ть** (*impf*) *или* **гуля́ть** (*impf*) ~**о́й** to go about in a gang.

гуса́к (-а́) *м* gander.

гу́сениц|а (-ы) *ж* caterpillar; (*тра́ктора*) caterpillar track.

гусёнок (-ёнка; *nom pl* **-я́та,** *gen pl* **-я́т)** *м* gosling.

гуси́|ный *прил* (*яйцо́*) goose; ~**ое ста́до** gaggle of geese; ~**ая ко́жа** goose flesh, goose pimples (*BRIT*) *или* bumps (*US*).

густе́|ть (3sg -ет, 3pl -ют, *perf* **погусте́ть)** *несов неперех* (*тума́н*) to grow *или* become denser; (*perf* **загусте́ть;** *ка́ша*) to thicken.

густ|о́й (-, -á, -о) *прил* (*лес, облака́*) dense; (*бро́ви*) bushy; (*суп, во́лосы*) thick; (*цвет, бас*) deep, rich.

густонаселённый *прил* densely-populated.

густот|а́ (-ы́) *ж* (*воло́с, ка́ши*) thickness; (*заросле́й, ды́ма*) density; (*го́лоса, цве́та*) richness, deepness.

гусы́н|я (-и) *ж* goose (*female*).

гус|ь (-я; *gen pl* **-е́й)** *м* goose; **как с гу́ся вода́** (*разг*) like water off a duck's back; **хоро́ш** ~! (*разг. пренебр*) a fine one!

гуся́та *итп сущ см* **гусёнок.**

гуся́тниц|а (-ы) *ж* casserole (*dish*).

гутали́н (-а) *м* shoe polish.

гу́щ|а (-и) *ж* (*ко́фейная*) grounds *мн*; (*пивна́я*) lees *мн*, dregs *мн*; (*су́па*) solids (*in soup etc*); (*ле́са*) thicket; **в ~е собы́тий/толпы́** in the thick of things/the crowd.

гу́ще *сравн прил от* **густо́й.**

Гц *сокр* (= *герц*) Hz (= *hertz*).

ГЭС *ж сокр* (= *гидроэлектроста́нция*) hydroelectric power station.

~ Д, д ~

Д, д сущ нескл (буква) the 5th letter of the Russian alphabet.

д. сокр = **дерéвня, дом**.

KEYWORD

да част **1** (выражает утверждение, согласие) yes

2 (не так ли): **ты придёшь, да?** you're coming, aren't you?; **ты меня любишь, да?** you love me, don't you?; **я получил письмó от мáмы – да?** I got a letter from my mum – really?

3 (при воспоминании, размышлении) oh, yes

4 (пусть: в лозунгах, призывах): **да – миру!** yes to peace!; **да здрáвствует демокрáтия!** long live democracy!; **вот это да!** (разг) cool!; **ну да!** (разг) sure!; (выражает недоверие) I'll bet!; **да ну!** (разг) no way!

♦ союз (и) and; (но, однако) but; **помогáет мáло, да и то неохóтно** he doesn't help much, and then only unwillingly; **у неё тóлько однó плáтье, да и то стáрое** she only has one dress and even that's old; **плáчет, да и тóлько** he does nothing but cry.

дáбы союз: ~ +infin in order to do; **он спрятал дéньги, ~ никтó не нашёл** he hid the money in order that it wouldn't be found.

давáй(те) несов см давáть ♦ част let's; ~ **пить чай** let's have some tea; ~ **помоги(те) мне!** come on, give me a hand!; **давáй-давáй!** (разг) come on!, get on with it!

давáть (-ю; imper **давáй(те)**) несов от **дать** ♦ перех (no perf; разг: продавáть) to sell; **вот (во) ~ёт!** (разг) that's incredible!; **в магазúне ~ют мясо** (разг) they sell meat in the shop

► **давáться** несов от **дáться** ♦ возв (иметь место) to take place.

давúть (-лю, -ишь) несов перех (подлеж: обувь) to pinch; (perf **задавúть**; калéчить) to crush, trample; (подлеж: машúна) to run over; (perf **раздавúть**; насекóмых) to squash; (подлеж: чувства) to oppress; ~ (impf) **на** +acc (налегáть тяжестью) to press или weigh down on; ~ (impf) **когó-н своúм авторитéтом** (разг) to intimidate sb; **воротнúк дáвит** the collar feels tight

► **давúться** несов возв (разг: в автóбусе, в

тесной комнате) to be crushed или squashed; ~**ся** (**подавúться** perf) +instr (кóстью, словáми) to choke on.

дáвка (-ки; gen pl -ок) ж crush.

давлéние (-я) ср (газа, жидкости, вóздуха) pressure; **кровянóе** ~ blood pressure; **атмосфéрное** ~ atmospheric pressure; **под** ~**м** +gen under the pressure of; **окáзывать** (**оказáть** perf) ~ **на** +acc to put pressure on.

давлю́(сь) несов см давúть(ся).

дáвний (-яя, -ее, -ие) прил: **в** ~**ие временá** a long time ago; **с** ~**их пор** for a long time; **это** ~ **слýчай** it happened a long time ago.

давнó нареч (случúться, встрéтиться) a long time ago; (ждать) for a long time; ~ **бы так!** about time too!

дáвность (-и) ж (ЮР: срок) prescription; (длительное существование): **дрýжба/ враждá имéет большýю** ~ the friendship/feud is of long standing; **за** ~**ю лет** due to the number of years which have elapsed.

давны́м-давнó нареч (разг) ages ago.

дáвок сущ см дáвка.

дадúм(ся) итп сов см дать(ся).

дáже част even; **так испугáлся,** ~ **вскрúкнул** I was so frightened, I even screamed; ~ **я согласúлся** even I agreed.

дáйджест (-а) м newspaper rubric.

дáй(те) сов см дать ♦ част (разг): ~ **я подýмаю** let me think.

дактилоскопúя (-и) ж fingerprinting.

дал итп сов см дать.

дáлее нареч further; **и так** ~ and so on; **не** ~ **как** или **чем вчерá** only yesterday.

далёкий (-ая, -ое, -ие; -, -á, -ó) прил (странá, звýки) distant, far-off; (прошлое, будущее) distant; (путь, путешéствие) long; **в** ~**ие гóды** in the distant past; **онú далекú друг от дрýга** they have nothing in common; ~ **от реáльности** far removed from reality; **онá – человéк** ~ **от наýки** she's far from being an expert when it comes to science.

далекó нареч (о расстоянии) far (away); (о врéмени) a long way off ♦ как сказ (распол-агáться) it's a long way away; **до гóрода ещё** ~ the town is still a long way off; **до лéта** ~

The spelling rules for Russian are shown on page xvii.

summer is a long way off; ~ **от** +*gen* far (away) from; ~ **за** +*acc* long after; **ему́** ~ **за 50** he's well over 50; ~ **не** far from, by no means; ~ **пойти́** (*perf*) (*перен*) to go far; **мне** ~ **до него́** I'm no match for him.

да́ло *итп см см* **дать**.

даль (**-и;** *loc sg* **-й**) *ж* faraway place; **это така́я** ~ (*разг*) it's such a long way (away).

дальне́йш|ий (**-ая, -ее, -ие**) *прил* further; **в** ~**ем** in the future.

да́льн|ий (**-яя, -ее, -ие**) *прил* distant; **Д~ Восто́к** the Far East; **раке́та** ~**его де́йствия** long-range missile; **по́езд/авто́бус** ~**его сле́дования** long-distance train/bus.

дальнобо́йный *прил* (*воен*) long-range.

дальнови́д|ный (**-ен, -на, -но**) *прил* far-sighted.

дальнозо́р|кий (**-кая, -кое, -кие; -ок, -ка, -ко**) *прил* long-sighted (*врит*), far-sighted (*US*); (*дальновидный*) far-sighted.

да́льше *сравн прил от* **далёкий ♦ сравн нареч от далеко́ ♦ нареч** next; **так пло́хо,** ~ **не́куда** (*разг*) things couldn't be any worse; **не** ~ **как** *или* **чем вчера́/у́тром** only yesterday/this morning.

дам(ся) *сов см* **дать(ся)**.

да́м|а (**-ы**) *ж* lady; (*карты*) queen.

Дама́ск (**-а**) *м* Damascus.

дама́сский (**-ая, -ое, -ие**) *прил*: ~**ая сталь** Damascus steel, damask.

да́мб|а (**-ы**) *ж* dam.

да́м|ка (**-ки;** *gen pl* **-ок**) *ж* king (*in draughts or checkers*).

да́мск|ий (**-ая, -ое, -ие**) *прил* ladylike; (*одежда, парикмахер*) ladies'.

Да́ни|я (**-и**) *ж* Denmark.

да́нность (**-и**) *ж* actuality.

да́нн|ые (**-ых;** *decl like adj*) *мн* (*сведения*) data *ед*, information *ед*; (*способности*) talent *ед*.

да́нный *прил* this, the given; **в** ~**ом слу́чае** in this case; **в** ~ **моме́нт** at present.

дань (**-и**) *ж* tribute; (*перен: моде, традиции*) concession; **отдава́ть** (**отда́ть** *perf*) ~ **кому́-н/чему́-н** to pay tribute to sb/sth.

дар (**-а;** *nom pl* **-ы́**) *м* (*также перен*) gift; **получа́ть** (**получи́ть** *perf*) **что-н в** ~ to be given sth as a present.

дари́ть (**-ю́, -ишь;** *perf* **подари́ть**) *несов перех* to give; ~ (*impf*) **что-н кому́-н** to give sb sth as a present.

дармово́й (**-а́я, -о́е, -ы́е**) *прил* (*разг*) free.

дармое́д (**-а**) *м* (*разг*) sponger.

дарова́ни|е (**-я**) *ср* gift.

дарови́тый (**-, -а, -о**) *прил* gifted.

да́ром *нареч* (*бесплатно*) free, for nothing; (*бесполезно*) in vain; **теря́ть** (**потеря́ть** *perf*) **вре́мя** ~ to waste time; **э́то ему́** ~ **не пройдёт** he'll pay for this; ~ **пропада́ть** (**пропа́сть** *perf*) to be wasted, go to waste.

да́рственн|ый *прил*: ~**ая на́дпись** dedication.

даст(ся) *сов см* **дать(ся)**.

да́т|а (**-ы**) *ж* date; **кру́глая** ~ *anniversary which is a multiple of ten years*; ~ **вступле́ния в си́лу** effective date.

да́тельный *прил*: ~ **паде́ж** dative case.

дати́р|овать (**-ую**) (*не*)*сов перех* to date.

да́тск|ий (**-ая, -ое, -ие**) *прил* Danish; ~ **язы́к** Danish.

датча́н|ин (**-ина;** *nom pl* **-е,** *gen pl* **-**) *м* Dane.

датча́н|ка (**-ки;** *gen pl* **-ок**) *ж см* **датча́нин**.

да́тчик (**-а**) *м* sensor.

дать (*см* **Table 14;** *impf* **дава́ть**) *сов* to give; (*разг: ударить*) to clout; (*устроить: концерт, спекта́кль*) to put on; (*позволить*): ~ **кому́-н** +*infin* to allow sb to do, let sb do; **дава́ть** (~ *perf*) **кому́-н что-н** to give sb sth, give sth to sb; **дава́ть** (~ *perf*) **себя́ знать** to make itself felt; **зима́ даёт себя́ знать** winter is making its presence felt; **ни** ~ **ни взять** (*разг*) no more, no less; **я тебе́ дам!** (*угроза*) I'll get you!; ~ (**дава́ть** *impf*) **кому́-н знать о чём-н** (*сообщить*) to let sb know about sth

▶ **да́ться** (*impf* **дава́ться**) *сов возв* (*разг*): **я не да́мся им в ру́ки** I won't let them catch me; **ей легко́ даю́тся языки́** languages come easily to her; **дала́сь тебе́ э́та те́ма!** (*разг*) you're obsessed with the subject!

да́ч|а (**-и**) *ж* (*дом*) dacha (*holiday cottage in the country*); (*корма*) portion; (*показаний, консультаций*) provision; **они́ всё ле́то живу́т на** ~**е** they are spending the whole of the summer at their dacha.

да́чник (**-а**) *м* person who spends time at his or her dacha.

да́чниц|а (**-ы**) *ж см* **да́чник**.

дашь(ся) *сов см* **дать(ся)**.

ДВ *сокр* (= *дли́нные во́лны*) LW= *long wave ед ♦ прил сокр* (= *длинноволно́вой*) LW (= *long-wave*).

дв|а (**-ух;** *см* **Table 23;** *f* **две,** *nt* **два**) *м чис* two ♦ *м нескл* (*ПРОСВЕЩ*) ≈ poor (*school mark*); **ей** ~ **го́да** she is two (years old); **они́ живу́т в до́ме но́мер** ~ they live at house number two; **о́коло** ~**ух** about two; **кни́га сто́ит** ~ **рубля́** the book costs two roubles; ~ **с полови́ной часа́** two and a half hours; ~**е с полови́ной мину́ты** two and a half minutes; **сейча́с** ~ **часа́** it's two o'clock; **я́блоки продаю́тся по** ~**е шту́ки** the apples are sold in twos; **дели́ть** (**раздели́ть** *perf*) **что-н на** ~ to divide sth into two; **в** ~**ух шага́х** (**от** +*gen*) within a stone's throw (of *или* from); **в** ~**ух слова́х** in a few words; **в** ~ **счёта** (*разг*) in a jiffy.

двадцати́ *чис см* **два́дцать**.

двадцатиле́ти|е (**-я**) *ср* (*срок*) twenty years; (*годовщина*) twentieth anniversary.

двадцатиле́тн|ий (**-яя, -ее, -ие**) *прил* (*период*) twenty-year; (*человек*) twenty-year-old.

двадцатипятиле́ти|е (**-я**) *ср* (*срок*) twenty-five years; (*годовщина*) twenty-fifth anniversary.

двадца́т|ый (**-ая, -ое, -ые**) *чис* twentieth; *см также* **пятидеся́тый**.

двáдцат|ь (-и; *как* **пять;** *см* **Table 27**) *чис* twenty; *см также* **пятьдесят.**

двáжды *нареч* twice; **он приходил сюдá** ~ he has come here twice; ~ **три – шесть** two times three is six; **я́сно как** ~ **два** (*разг*) as plain as day.

две *ж чис см* **два.**

двенáдцати *чис см* **двенáдцать.**

двенадцатиперстн|ый *прил*: ~**ая кишкá** duodenum.

двенадцатичасов|óй *прил* (*рабочий день*) twelve-hour; (*отправление*) twelve-o'clock.

двенáдцат|ый (-ая, -ое, -ые) *чис* twelfth; *см также* **пя́тый.**

двенáдцат|ь (-и; *как* **пять;** *см* **Table 27**) *чис* twelve; *см также* **пять.**

двéрц|а (-ы; *gen pl* -**ец**) *ж* door.

двер|ь (-и; *loc sg* -и, *gen pl* -**éй**) *ж* door; **при закры́тых** ~**я́х** behind closed doors; **стоя́ть** (*impf*) **в** ~**я́х** to stand in the doorway; **показáть** (*perf*) **на** ~ **комý-н** (*перен*) to show sb the door; **день откры́тых** ~**éй** open day.

двéсти (-**ухсóт;** *см* **Table 31**) *чис* two hundred; *см также* **сто.**

двигáтель (-я) *м* engine, motor; (*перен*) driving force; ~ **внýтреннего сгорáния** internal-combustion engine.

дви́г|ать (-аю; *perf* **дви́нуть**) *несов перех* to move; (*3sg* -**жет,** *3pl* -**жут;** *перен*) to further; (*no perf; механизм*) to drive; **им** ~**жет зáвисть/ любóвь** he is motivated by envy/love; ~ (**дви́нуть** *perf*) **пáльцами/рукóй** to move one's fingers/hand

▶ **дви́гаться** (*perf* **дви́нуться**) *несов возв* to move; (*отправляться*): ~**ся в/на** +*acc* to set off *или* start out for; ~**ся** (**дви́нуться** *perf*) **в путь** to set off on a journey; **дéло не** ~**гается** we are making no progress.

движéни|е (-я) *ср* movement; (*дорожное*) traffic; (*перен*) impulse; **приводи́ть** (**привести́** *perf*) **что-н в** ~ to set sth in motion; **прáвила дорóжного** *или* **у́личного** ~**я** ≈ the Highway Code; ~ **в защи́ту ми́ра** the peace movement.

дви́жимост|ь (-и) *ж* movables *мн.*

дви́жим|ый (-, -а, -о) *прил*: ~ +*instr* motivated by; **дви́жимое иму́щество** movables.

движ|óк (-кá) *м* (*ТЕХ*) *sliding part of a mechanism.*

дви́нуть(ся) (-у(сь), -ешь(ся)) *сов от* **дви́гать(ся).**

дво|é (-и́х; *см* **Table 36а**) *м чис* two; ~ **часóв/санéй** two watches/sledges; ~ **брюк/ нóжниц** two pairs of trousers/scissors; **их бы́ло** ~ there were two of them; **он не спал** ~ **сýток** he didn't sleep for forty-eight hours; **есть** (*impf*) **за двои́х** to eat enough for two; **на свои́х двои́х** (*разг*) on foot.

двоебóрь|е (-я) *ср* biathlon.

двоебрáчи|е (-я) *ср* bigamy.

двоевлáсти|е (-я) *ср* dual power, diarchy.

двóек *сущ см* **двóйка.**

двóен *сущ см* **двóйня.**

двоетóчи|е (-я) *ср* (*ЛИНГ*) colon.

двóечник (-а) *м* (*разг*) dimwit.

двóечниц|а (-ы) *ж см* **двóечник.**

двои́м *итп чис см* **двóе.**

двои́ться (*3sg* -**и́тся**) *несов возв*: **у негó в глазáх** ~**и́тся** he is seeing double.

двои́х *чис см* **двóе.**

двои́чный *прил* binary.

двóйк|а (-и; *gen pl* -**ек**) *ж* (*цифра, карта*) two; (*ПРОСВЕЩ*) ≈ D (*school mark*); (*разг: автóбус, трамвáй итп*) number) two (*bus, tram etc*).

двойн|óй (-áя, -óе, -ы́е) *прил* double; **двойнáя игрá** double-dealing.

двóйн|я (-и; *gen pl* -**ен**) *ж* twins *мн.*

двóйственн|ый (-, -на, -но) *прил* ambiguous.

двор (-á) *м* (*между домами*) courtyard, yard; (*при отдельном доме*) yard; (*крестьянское хозяйство*) homestead; (*королевский*) court; **монéтный** ~ mint; **при** ~**é** at court; **на** ~**é темнó** (*разг*) it's dark outside; **не ко** ~**ý оказáться** (*perf*) *или* **прийти́сь** (*perf*) (*разг*) to be like a fish out of water.

двор|éц (-цá) *м* palace; ~ **бракосочетáния** wedding palace (*venue for wedding ceremonies*), ≈ registry office (*BRIT*); **двор|éц спóрта** sports centre (*BRIT*) *или* center (*US*).

двóрник (-а) *м* (*работник*) road sweeper; (*АВТ*) windscreen (*BRIT*) *или* windshield (*US*) wiper.

дворня́г|а (-и) *ж* mongrel.

дворня́жк|а (-и; *gen pl* -**ек**) *ж* = **дворня́га.**

дворцá *сущ см* **дворéц.**

дворцóв|ый *прил* palace *опред.*

дворя́н|ин (-яни́на; *nom pl* -**я́не,** *gen pl* -**я́н**) *м* nobleman (*мн* noblemen).

дворя́нк|а (-и; *gen pl* -**ок**) *ж* noblewoman (*мн* noblewomen).

дворя́нств|о (-а) *ср* nobility.

двоюрóдн|ый *прил*: ~ **брат** (first) cousin (*male*); ~**ая сестрá** (first) cousin (*female*).

двоя́к|ий (-ая, -ое, -ие; -, -ка, -ко) *прил* dual.

двубóртный *прил* double-breasted.

двузнáчный *прил* (*число*) two-digit; (*слово, выражение*) ambiguous.

двукрáтн|ый *прил*: ~ **чемпиóн** two-times champion; **в** ~**ом размéре** twofold.

двули́чный (-ен, -на, -но) *прил* two-faced.

двум *итп чис см* **два.**

двумстáм *итп чис см* **двéсти.**

двунапрáвленный *прил* (*КОМП*) bidirectional.

двунóг|ий (-ая, -ое, -ие) *прил* two-legged.

двуслóжн|ый *прил* two-syllable.

двусмы́слен|ный (-, -на, -но) *прил* ambiguous; ~**ная шýтка** double entendre.

двуспáльн|ый *прил*: ~**ая кровáть** double bed;

двуспа́льная пала́тка two-person tent.

двуство́льн|ый *прил*: ~ое ружьё double-barrelled (*BRIT*) *или* double-barreled (*US*) shotgun.

двусторо́н|ний (-няя, -нее, -ние; -ен, -ня, -не) *прил (движение)* two-way; (*соглашение, переговоры*) bilateral; ~нее воспале́ние лёгких double pneumonia.

двух *чис см* два.

двухгоди́чный *прил* two-year.

двухдне́вный *прил* two-day.

двухкопе́ечный *прил*: ~ная моне́та two-kopeck coin.

двухле́ти|е (-я) *ср (срок)* two years; (*годовщина*) second anniversary.

двухле́тн|ий (-яя, -ее, -ие) *прил (период)* two-year; (*ребёнок*) two-year-old; (*БОТ*) biennial.

двухме́стный *прил (номер)* double; (*купе, каюта*) two-berth.

двухме́сячный *прил* two-month; (*ребёнок*) two-month-old; (*издание*) bimonthly.

двухнеде́льный *прил* two-week; (*ребёнок*) two-week-old; (*издание*) fortnightly.

двухпала́тный *прил (ПОЛИТ)* two-chamber.

двухсме́н|ка (-ки; *gen pl* -ок) *ж (разг) two shift working pattern.*

двухсо́т *чис см* две́сти.

двухсотле́ти|е (-я) *ср (срок)* two hundred years; (*годовщина*) bicentenary (*BRIT*), bicentennial (*US*).

двухсотле́тн|ий (-яя, -ее, -ие) *прил (период)* two-hundred-year; (*дерево*) two-hundred-year-old.

двухсо́т|ый (-ая, -ое, -ые) *чис* two hundredth.

двухста́х *чис см* две́сти.

двухто́мник (-а) *м* two-volume edition.

двухцве́тный *прил* two-coloured (*BRIT*), two-colored (*US*).

двухчасов|о́й (-а́я, -о́е, -ы́е) *прил (фильм)* two-hour; (*отправление*) two-o'clock.

двухэта́жный *прил* two-storey (*BRIT*), two-story (*US*).

двуш|ка (-ки; *gen pl* -ек) *ж (разг)* two-kopeck coin.

двуязы́ч|ный (-ен, -на, -но) *прил* bilingual.

дебарка́дер (-а) *м* landing stage.

дебати́р|овать (-ую) *несов перех* to debate.

деба́т|ы (-ов) *мн* debate *ед*.

де́бет (-а) *м* debit; заноси́ть (занести́ *perf*) что-н в ~ to debit sth.

дебетова́ни|е (-я) *ср*: прямо́е ~ direct debit.

дебет|ова́ть (-у́ю) *(не)сов перех* to debit.

дебето́вый *прил*: ~ оста́ток debit balance; дебето́вое авиз|о debit note.

дебил (-а) *м (разг: пренебр)* moron.

дебито́р (-а) *м* debtor.

де́бр|и (-ей) *мн (в лесу)* thicket *ед*; (*перен*): ~ +*gen (науки, техники)* maze of.

·дебю́т (-а) *м* debut; (*в шахматах*) opening.

дебюта́нт (-а) *м person making his debut.*

дебюта́нт|ка (-ки; *gen pl* -ок) *ж см* дебюта́нт.

де́в|а (-ы) *ж*: ста́рая ~ spinster; (*созвездие*): Д~ Virgo.

девальва́ци|я (-и) *ж* devaluation.

девальви́р|овать (-ую) *(не)сов перех* to devalue.

дева́|ть (-ю) *несов от* деть ♦ *сов перех (разг)* to put; мне не́куда ~ де́ньги/вре́мя I've got more money/time than I know what to do with

► дева́ться *несов от* де́ться ♦ *сов возв (разг)*: куда́ она́ ~лась? where has she got to?; куда́ ~ся it can't be helped.

де́вер|ь (-я) *м* brother-in-law (*wife's brother*).

деви́з (-а) *м* motto.

де́виц|а (-ы) *ж (ФОЛЬКЛОР)* maiden.

деви́ц|а (-ы) *ж (девушка)* girl.

деви́честв|о (-а) *ср (до замужества)* girlhood; в ~е Петро́ва née Petrova.

де́вич|ий (-ья, -ье, -ьи) *прил*: ~ья фами́лия maiden name.

де́в|ка (-ки; *gen pl* -ок) *ж (разг: девушка)* girl.

де́воч|ка (-ки; *gen pl* -ек) *ж (ребёнок)* little girl; (*разг: девушка*) girl.

де́вуш|ка (-ки; *gen pl* -ек) *ж* girl; (*разг: обращение*) miss.

девчо́н|ка (-ки; *gen pl* -ок) *ж (разг: девочка)* little girl, kid.

девяно́ст|о (-а; *как* сто; *см* Table 30) *чис* ninety; *см также* пятьдеся́т.

девяностоле́ти|е (-я) *ср (срок)* ninety years; (*годовщина*) ninetieth anniversary.

девяностоле́тн|ий (-яя, -ее, -ие) *прил (период)* ninety-year; (*человек*) ninety-year-old.

девяно́ст|ый (-ая, -ое, -ые) *чис* ninetieth; *см также* пятидеся́тый.

девя́т|ая (-ой; *decl like adj*) *ж*: одна́ ~ one ninth.

де́вятер|о (-ы́х; *как* че́тверо; *см* Table 36a) *чис* nine; (*ботинок, перчаток*) nine pairs; *см также* дво́е.

девяти́ *чис см* де́вять.

девятидне́вный *прил* nine-day.

девятикла́ссник (-а) *м pupil in ninth year at school (usually 15 years old).*

девятикла́ссни|ца (-ы) *ж см* девятикла́ссник.

девятикра́тный *прил*: ~ чемпио́н nine-times champion; в ~ом разме́ре ninefold.

девятиле́ти|е (-я) *ср (срок)* nine years; (*годовщина*) ninth anniversary.

девятиле́тн|ий (-яя, -ее, -ие) *прил (период)* nine-year; (*ребёнок*) nine-year-old.

девятиме́сячный *прил* nine-month; (*ребёнок*) nine-month-old.

девятинеде́льный *прил* nine-week; (*ребёнок*) nine-week-old.

девятисо́т *чис см* девятьсо́т.

девятисотле́ти|е (-я) *ср (срок)* nine hundred years *мн*; (*годовщина*) nine-hundredth anniversary.

девятисотле́тн|ий (-яя, -ее, -ие) *прил (период)* nine hundred-year; (*дерево*) nine hundred-year-old.

девятисо́т|ый (-ая, -ое, -ые) *чис* nine-

hundredth.
девятистáм *итп чис см* **девятьсóт**.
девятичасов|óй (-áя, -óе, -ы́е) *прил*
(*операция*) nine-hour; (*отправление*) nine
o'clock.
девя́т|ка (-ки; *gen pl* -ок) ж (*цифра, карта*) nine;
(*группа из девяти*) group of nine; (*разг:
автобус, трамвай итп*) (number) nine (*bus,
tram etc*).
девятнáдцати *чис см* **девятнáдцать**.
девятнáдцат|ый (-ая, -ое, -ые) *чис* nineteenth;
см также **пя́тый**.
девятнáдцат|ь (-и; *как* пять; *см* **Table 27**) *чис*
nineteen; *см также* **пять**.
девя́ток *сущ см* **девя́тка**.
девя́т|ый (-ая, -ое, -ые) *чис* ninth; *см также*
пя́тый.
де́вят|ь (-и; *как* пять; *см* **Table 27**) *чис* nine; *см*
также **пять**.
девятьсóт (-исóт; *как* пятьсóт; *см* **Table 34**)
чис nine hundred; *см также* **сто**.
девятью́ *чис см* **де́вять** ♦ *нареч* nine times; ~
пять – сóрок пять nine times five is forty-five.
девятьюстáми *чис см* **девятьсóт**.
дегенерати́в|ный (-ен, -на, -но) *прил*
degenerate.
дегенерáци|я (-и) ж degeneration.
дёг|оть (-тя) м tar.
дегради́р|овать (-ую) *(не)сов неперех* to
degenerate.
дёгтя *сущ см* **дёготь**.
дегусти́р|овать (-ую) *(не)сов перех* to taste,
sample.
дед (-а) м grandfather; (*разг*) old man; **Дед
Морóз** ≈ Father Christmas; *см также* **деды́**.
де́довск|ий (-ая, -ое, -ие) *прил* grandfather's;
(*перен*) old-fashioned.
дедовщи́н|а (-ы) ж *the abuse of new conscripts
by older soldiers*.
деду́кци|я (-и) ж deduction.
дед|ы́ (-óв) *мн* (*разг*) *final-year conscripts*.
деепричáсти|е (-я) *ср* gerund.
дееспосóб|ный (-ен, -на, -но) *прил* (*войска*)
functional; (*ЮР*) responsible.
дежу́р|ить (-ю, -ишь) *несов неперех* (в порядке
очереди) to be on duty; ~ (*impf*) **у чегó-н** to
guard sth; ~ (*impf*) **у постéли больнóго** to sit at
a patient's bedside.
дежу́рн|ая (-ой; *decl like adj*) ж *см* **дежу́рный**.
дежу́рн|ый *прил* (*пренебр: цитаты, остроты*)
hackneyed; ~ **врач/милиционéр** doctor/
(police) officer on duty ♦ (**-ого**; *decl like adj*) м
person on duty; (*по станции*) assistant station
master; **дежу́рный магази́н** late-night shop;
дежу́рное блю́до dish of the day.
дезерти́р (-а) м deserter.
дезерти́р|овать (-ую) *(не)сов неперех* to
desert.

дезинсéкци|я (-и) ж pest control (*of insects*).
дезинфéкци|я (-и) ж disinfection.
дезинфици́р|овать (-ую) *(не)сов перех* to
disinfect.
дезинформáци|я (-и) ж misinformation.
дезинформи́р|овать (-ую) *(не)сов перех* to
misinform.
дезодорáнт (-а) м antiperspirant.
дезорганизáци|я (-и) ж disorganization.
дезorganиз|овáть (-у́ю) *(не)сов перех* to
disorganize.
дезориенти́р|овать (-ую) *(не)сов перех* to
disorientate.
дéйственн|ый (-, -на, -но) *прил* effective.
дéйстви|е (-я) *ср* (*механизма, закона*)
functioning; (*романа итп*) action; (*часть
пьесы*) act; (*лекарства, предупреждения*)
effect; **вводи́ть (ввести́** *perf*) **в** ~ (*фабрику*) to
open; (*турбину*) to activate; (*закон*) to
introduce; **приводи́ть (привести́** *perf*) **в** ~ to
carry out, implement; **под** ~**м** +*gen* under the
influence of; *см также* **дéйствия**.
дéйствител|ен *прил см* **дéйстви́тельный**.
дéйстви́тельно *нареч, вводн сл* really; **онá** ~
краси́ва she is really beautiful; ~, **ужé порá
идти́** it really is time to go.
дéйстви́тельност|ь (-и) ж reality; **в** ~**и** in
reality.
дéйстви́тельн|ый *прил* (*факт, польза*) real,
actual; (-ен, -ьна, -ьно) *прил* (пропуск,
удостоверение) valid; **дéйстви́тельный залóг**
active voice; **дéйстви́тельная вóеннaя
слу́жба** active service (*BRIT*) *или* duty (*esp US*).
дéйстви|я (-й) *мн* (*поступки*) actions мн; (*ВОЕН*)
operations мн.
дéйств|овать (-ую) *несов неперех* (*человек*) to
act; (*механизмы, закон*) to operate, work; (*perf
подéйствовать; влиять*): ~ **на** +*acc*
(*лекарство, уговоры*) to have an effect on.
дéйствующ|ий (-ая, -ее, -ие) *прил*: ~**ие ли́ца**
(*персонажи*) characters мн; (*участники
событий*) protagonists мн; **дéйствующая
áрмия** standing army; **дéйствующий вулкáн**
active volcano.
декабри́ст (-а) м (*ИСТ*) Decembrist.
декáбр|ь (-я́) м December; *см также* **октя́брь**.
декáд|а (-ы) ж ten-day period; ~ **францу́зского
кинó** ten-day festival of French cinema.
декадéнт (-а) м decadent.
декадéнтск|ий (-ая, -ое, -ие) *прил* decadent.
декадéнтств|о (-а) *ср* decadence.
декáн (-а) м dean.
деканáт (-а) м faculty office.
деклами́р|овать (-ую; *perf
продеклами́ровать*) *несов перех* to recite.
декларáци|я (-и) ж declaration; **тамóженная** ~
customs declaration; ~ **судовóго гру́за** ship's
manifest.

деклари́р|овать (-ую) *(не)сов перех* to declare.
декласси́рованн|ый *прил*: ~ые элеме́нты
social outcasts.
декóдер (-а) *м (комп)* decoder.
декоди́р|овать (-ую) *(не)сов перех* to decode.
декольтé *ср нескл, прил неизм* décolleté.
декорати́вный *прил (растения)* ornamental;
  (искусство) decorative.
декорáци|я (-и) *ж (ТЕАТР)* set.
декрéт (-а) *м (постановление)* decree; *(разг:
  отпуск)* maternity leave; **издавáть (издáть**
  perf) ~ **о** +*prp* to issue a decree on; **уходи́ть**
  (уйти́ *perf)* **в** ~ *(разг)* to take maternity leave.
декрéтный *прил*: ~ óтпуск maternity leave.
дéланный *прил (смех)* false.
дéла|ть (-ю; *perf* сдéлать) *сов перех* to make;
  (упражнения, опыты, подлость итп) to do; ~
  (сдéлать *perf)* **урóки** to do one's homework; ~
  (сдéлать *perf)* **прыжóк** to jump; ~ **(сдéлать**
  perf) **из когó-н что-н** to make sth out of sb; ~
  (impf) **нéчего** ~ there is nothing to be done; **от**
  нéчего ~ for want of something better to do; **что**
  ~**?** what can be done?
► дéла|ться *(perf* сдéлаться) *несов возв*
  (происходить) to happen; ~ся **(сдéлаться** *perf)*
  +*instr* to become.
делегáт (-а) *м* delegate.
делегáт|ка (-ки; *gen pl* -ок) *ж см* делегáт.
делегáци|я (-и) *ж* delegation.
дéлен *прил см* дéльный.
делéни|е (-я) *ср* division; *(на линейке, в*
  термометре) point.
делéц (-ьцá) *м* dealer.
Дéли *м нескл* Delhi.
деликатéс (-а) *м* delicacy.
деликáтно *нареч* tactfully.
деликáтный *прил* delicate.
дел|и́ть (-ю́, -ишь; *perf* подели́ть *или*
  раздели́ть) *несов перех (также* МАТ) to divide;
  ~ **(раздели́ть** *perf)* **что-н на** +*acc* to divide sth
  by; ~ **(раздели́ть** *perf)* **что-н с** +*instr* to share sth
  with; ~ **(раздели́ть** *perf)* **рáдость/гóре (с**
  кем-н) to share one's joy/grief (with sb)
► дел|и́ться *(perf* раздели́ться) *несов возв*: ~ся
  (на +*acc) (отряд)* to divide *или* split up (into);
  ~ся *(impf)* **на** +*acc (книга, статья)* to be
  divided into; (МАТ) to be divisible by; ~ся
  (подели́ться *perf)* **чем-н с кем-н** to share sth
  with sb.
дéл|о (-а) *ср* matter; *(надобность, также* КОММ)
  business; *(положение)* situation; *(поступок)* act;
  (ЮР) case; *(АДМИН)* file; **э́то моё** ~ that's my
  business; **э́то не твоё** ~ it's none of your
  business; **я пришёл по** ~**у** I've come on
  business; **у меня́ к Вам** ~ I have something to
  discuss with you; **как делá?** how are things?; **в**
  чём ~? what's wrong?; ~ **в том, что** ... the thing
  is that ...; **не в э́том** ~ this isn't the issue; **на**
  (сáмом) ~е in (actual) fact; **на** ~е in practise;
  пéрвым ~**м** in the first case *или* instance; **за** ~
  fairly; **ме́жду** ~**м** in between times; **то и** ~ every

now and then.
делови́тост|ь (-и) *ж* businesslike manner.
делови́тый (-, -а, -о) *прил* businesslike.
делов|óй (-áя, -óе, -ы́е) *прил (встреча, круги)*
  business *опред*; *(человек)* efficient; *(вид, тон)*
  businesslike.
делопроизводи́тел|ь (-я) *м* clerk.
делопроизвóдств|о (-а) *ср* clerical work.
дéл|ьный (-ен, -ьна, -ьно) *прил (человек)*
  businesslike, efficient; *(совет, предложение)*
  practical.
дéльт|а (-ы) *ж* delta.
дельтаплáн (-а) *м* hang-glider.
дельфи́н (-а) *м* dolphin.
дельцá *итп сущ см* делéц.
деля́г|а (-и) *м (разг: пренебр)* wheeler-dealer.
демагóг (-а) *м* demagogue.
демагóги|я (-и) *ж* demagogy; **разводи́ть**
  (развести́ *perf)* ~**ю** *(разг)* to talk a lot of hot air.
демаркациóнн|ый *прил*: ~ая ли́ния
  demarcation line.
демилитаризáци|я (-и) *ж* demilitarization.
демисезóнн|ый *прил*: ~ое пальтó *coat for*
  spring and autumn wear.
демобилизáци|я (-и) *ж* demobilization.
демобилиз|овáться (-у́юсь) *(не)сов возв* to
  be demobilized.
демографи́ческ|ий (-ая, -ое, -ие) *прил*
  (исследование) population *опред*, demographic;
  демографи́ческий взрыв population
  explosion.
демогрáфи|я (-и) *ж* demography.
демокрáт (-а) *м* democrat.
демократи́зм (-а) *м* democracy.
демократи́ческ|ий (-ая, -ое, -ие) *прил*
  democratic.
демокрáти|я (-и) *ж* democracy.
дéмон (-а) *м* demon.
демонстрáнт (-а) *м* demonstrator.
демонстрáнт|ка (-ки; *gen pl* -ок) *ж см*
  демонстрáнт.
демонстрати́в|ный (-ен, -на, -но) *прил*
  (поведение, уход) theatrical.
демонстрáци|я (-и) *ж* demonstration; *(показ:*
  фильма) showing; *(: экспонатов)* show.
демонстри́р|овать (-ую) *(не)сов неперех*
  (ПОЛИТ) to demonstrate ♦ *несов перех* to show.
демонти́р|овать (-ую) *(не)сов перех* to
  dismantle.
деморализáци|я (-и) *ж* demoralization.
дéмпинг (-а) *м (КОММ)* dumping.
дéмпинговый *прил*: ~ые цéны artificially
  lowered prices.
денатурáт (-а) *м* meths.
денационализáци|я (-и) *ж* denationalization.
денационализи́р|овать (-ую) *(не)сов перех*
  to denationalize.
дендрáри|й (-я) *м* arboretum.
дéнег *сущ см* дéньги.
дéнежный *прил (реформа)* monetary; *(рынок)*
  money *опред*; *(разг)* well-off; **дéнежный знак**

banknote; **дéнежный штраф** fine.
деноминáци|я (-и) ж (ЭКОН) denomination.
дéну(сь) итп сов см **дéть(ся)**.
день (дня) м day; **Д~ Побéды** ≈ V-E Day,
Victory Day (*the anniversary of the USSR's
victory over Germany in World War 2*);
световóй ~ daylight; **~ ото дня** day by day;
изо дня в ~ day in, day out; **чéрез ~** every
other day; **со дня нá ~** (*постепенно*) from one
day to the next; (*скоро*) in the next few days; **на
другóй ~** the next day; **на днях** (*скоро*) in the
next few days; (*недавно*) the other day; **день
рождéния** birthday.
дéн|ьги (-ег; *dat pl* **-ьгáм**) *мн* money *ед*; **бросáть**
(*impf*) *или* **швырять** (*impf*) **~ на вéтер** to throw
money down the drain; **бумáжные ~** paper
money, banknotes; **налúчные ~** (ready) cash.
департáмент (-а) м department.
депéш|а (-и) ж dispatch.
депó *ср нескл* depot.
депозúт (-а) м deposit.
депозúтный *прил* deposit *опред*.
депозúтор (-а) м depositor.
депонéнт (-а) м = **депозúтор**.
депонúр|овать (-ую) (*не*)*сов перех* to deposit.
депортáци|я (-и) ж deportation.
депортúр|овать (-ую) (*не*)*сов перех* to deport.
депрéсси|я (-и) ж depression.
депутáт (-а) м deputy (POL).
депутáтск|ий (-ая, -ое, -ие) *прил* deputies'.
дéрга|ть (-ю) *несов перех* to tug *или* pull (at);
(*перен: разг*) to hassle ♦ *неперех* (+*instr*;
плечом, головой) to jerk
▶ **дéргаться** *несов возв* (*машина, лошадь*) to
jerk; (*лицо, губы*) to twitch; (*перен: разг*) to
(make a) fuss.
деревенé|ть (-ю; *perf* **одеревенéть**) *несов
неперех* to grow *или* go numb.
деревéнск|ий (-ая, -ое, -ие) *прил* (*дом,
житель*) country *опред*; (*тишина, пейзаж*)
rural; (*площадь, колодец*) village *опред*.
дерéв|ня (-ни; *gen pl* **-éнь**, *dat* **-ням**) ж (*селение*)
village; (*местность*) the country;
олимпúйская ~ Olympic Village.
дéр|ево (-ева; *nom pl* **-éвья**, *gen pl* **-éвьев**) *ср*
tree; (*древесина*) wood; **родослóвное ~** family
tree; **крáсное ~** mahogany.
деревообрабóт|ка (-ки; *gen pl* **-ок**) ж timber
processing.
дерéвья итп *сущ см* **дéрево**.
деревянный *прил* (*также перен*) wooden.
держáв|а (-ы) ж (*государство*) power;
(*эмблема*) orb; **велúкие ~ы** The Great (World)
Powers.
держáтел|ь (-я) м holder.
держáть (-ý, -ишь) *сов перех* to keep; (*в руках,
во рту, в зубах*) to hold; (*не отпускать*) to
keep hold of; (*поддерживать*) to hold up;

(*нанимать*) to take on; **~ речь** to make a
speech; **~** (*impf*) **экзáмен** to sit an exam; **~** (*impf*)
отвéт to be responsible; **~** (*impf*) **слóво** to keep
one's word; **~** (*impf*) **себя прóсто/
высокомéрно** to behave simply/haughtily; **~**
(*impf*) **себя в рукáх** to keep one's head
▶ **держáться** *несов возв* to stay; (*на колоннах,
на сваях*) to be supported; (*иметь осанку*) to
stand; (*вести себя*) to behave; **~ся** (*impf*) **+***gen*
(*берега, стены* итп) to keep to; (*перен*) to
adhere to; **~ся** (*impf*) **за** +*acc* (*за сумку, за
стену*) to hold onto; **~ся** (*impf*) **за гóлову** to
hold one's head.
дерз|úть (*2sg* **-úшь**, *3sg* **-úт**) *несов неперех* **~
комý-н** to be rude to sb.
дéрз|кий (-кая, -кое, -кие: -ок, -кá, -ко) *прил*
(*грубый*) impertinent; (*смелый*) audacious.
дéрзость (-и) ж (*см прил*) impertinence;
audacity; **говорúть** (**сказáть** *perf*) **~и** to be
impertinent; **имéть** (*impf*) **~** +*infin* to have the
cheek to do.
дериват (-а) м (ЛИНГ) derivative.
дерматúн (-а) м leatherette.
дерматолóги|я (-и) ж dermatology.
дёрн (-а) м turf.
дёрн|уть (-у, -ешь) *несов перех* to tug (at) ♦
неперех (+*instr*; плечом, головой) to jerk; **~уло
меня** *или* **чёрт ~ул меня сдéлать это** (*разг*) I
don't know what possessed me to do it
▶ **дёрнуться** *несов возв* (*машина*) to start with a
jerk; (*лошадь*) to shy; (*лицо, губы*) to twitch.
дерý(сь) *несов перех см* **дрáть(ся)**.
дерьм|ó (-á) *ср* (*груб'; также перен*) shit (*!*),
crap (*!*)
десáнт (-а) м landing troops *мн*; (*высадка войск*)
landing; **высáживать** (**высадить** *perf*) **~** to
make a landing.
десáнтник (-а) м (ВОЕН) paratrooper.
дéсен *сущ см* **деснá**.
десéрт (-а) м dessert.
дéскать *част*: **онá, ~, ничегó не знáет** she
claims she doesn't know anything.
десн|á (-ы́; *nom pl* **дёсны**, *gen pl* **дёсен**) ж (АНАТ)
gum.
деспотúческ|ий (-ая, -ое, -ие) *прил* despotic.
деся́т|ая (-ой; *decl like adj*) ж: **однá ~** one tenth.
деся́теро (-ы́х; *как* **чéтверо**; *см* **Table 36a**) *чис*
ten; (*дéсять пар*) ten pairs; *см также* **двóе**.
десяти *сущ см* **дéсять**.
десятибóр|ец (-ца) м decathlete.
десятибóрь|е (-я) *ср* decathlon.
десятиднéвный *прил* ten-day.
десятиклáссник (-а) м *pupil in tenth year at
school* (*usually 17 years old*).
десятиклáссни|ца (-ы) ж *см* **десятиклáссник**.
десятикопéечн|ый *прил*: **~ая монéта** ten-
kopeck coin.
десятикрáтн|ый *прил*: **~ чемпиóн** ten-times

champion; в ~ом разме́ре tenfold.

десятиле́ти|е (-я) ср (срок) decade; (годовщина) tenth anniversary.

десятиле́т|ка (-ки; gen pl -ок) ж (разг) ≈ secondary school (BRIT), ≈ high school (US).

десятиле́тний (-яя, -ее; период) прил ten-year; (ребёнок) ten-year-old.

десятиле́ток сущ см **десятиле́тка**.

десятиме́сячный прил ten-month; (ребёнок) ten-month-old.

десяти́н|а (-ы) ж old unit of measurement approximately equal to 2.7 acres.

десятинеде́льный прил ten-week; (ребёнок) ten-week-old.

десятирублёв|ка (-ки; gen pl -ок) ж (разг) ten-rouble note.

десятичасов|о́й (-а́я, -о́е, -ы́е) прил (операция) ten-hour; (отправление) ten o'clock опред.

десяти́чный прил decimal.

деся́т|ка (-ки; gen pl -ок) ж (цифра) ten; (группа из десяти) group of ten; (разг: денежный знак) tenner; (: автобус, трамвай итп) (number) ten (bus, tram etc).

деся́т|ки (-ов) мн: ~ люде́й/книг scores of people/books.

деся́т|ок (-ка) м ten; он не ро́бкого ~ка he's not afraid of anything; ему́ пошёл шесто́й ~ he has turned fifty; см также **деся́тки**.

деся́тый (-ая, -ое, -ые) прил tenth; см также **пя́тый**.

де́сять (-и; как пять; см Table 27) чис ten; см также **пять**.

дета́лен прил см **дета́льный**.

детализи́р|овать (-ую) (не)сов перех to work out in detail.

дета́л|ь (-и) ж detail; (механизма, прибора) component, part.

дета́льно нареч (обсудить) in detail.

дета́льный (-ен, -ьна, -ьно) прил detailed.

детвор|а́ (-ы́) ж собир little children мн.

детдо́м (-а; nom pl -а́) м сокр (= де́тский дом) children's home.

детдо́мов|ец (-ца) м child in care.

детдо́мов|ка (-ки; gen pl -ок) ж см **детдо́мовец**.

детдо́мовца сущ см **детдо́мовец**.

детекти́в (-а) м (следователь) detective; (фильм) detective film; (книга) detective novel.

детекти́вный прил detective опред.

дете́ктор (-а) м detector.

детёныш (-а) м cub.

де́т|и (-е́й; dat pl -ям, instr pl -ьми́, prp pl -ях, nom sg ребёнок) мн children мн.

дети́н|а (-ы) м (разг) hulk.

дети́ще (-а) ср creation.

де́тка (-и) ж (в обращении) sweetheart.

детона́тор (-а) м detonator.

детса́д (-а; nom pl -ы́) м сокр (= де́тский сад) kindergarten.

де́тск|ая (-ой; decl like adj) ж nursery.

де́тск|ий (-ая, -ое, -ие) прил (годы, болезнь) childhood; (книга, игра) children's; (рассуждение, затея) childish; **де́тская площа́дка** playground; **де́тский дом** children's home; **де́тский сад** kindergarten.

де́тств|о (-а) ср childhood; **впада́ть (впасть** perf**) в ~** to go senile.

де|ть (-ну, -нешь; impf **дева́ть**) сов перех (разг) to put; (время, деньги) to do with; **куда́ же я ~л э́ту кни́гу?** what on earth have I done with that book?; **э́того никуда́ не де́нешь** there's no arguing with that

▶ **де́ться** (impf **дева́ться**) сов возв (разг) to get to; **куда́ она́/кни́га де́лась?** where has she/the book got to?; **не́куда ~ва́ться** (impf) (разг) there's nothing else for it.

де-фа́кто нареч de facto.

дефе́кт (-а) м defect.

дефекти́в|ный (-ен, -на, -но) прил (умственно) mentally defective; (физически) physically handicapped.

дефе́ктный прил defective.

дефектоскопи́|я (-и) ж (ТЕХ) detection of flaws.

дефи́с (-а) м hyphen.

дефици́т (-а) м (ЭКОН) deficit; (нехватка): ~ +gen или в +prp shortage of; ~ **платёжного бала́нса** (ЭКОН) balance of payments deficit.

дефици́тный прил (предприятие, производство) unprofitable; (товар, сырьё) scarce, in short supply.

дефля́ци|я (-и) ж (ЭКОН) deflation.

деформа́ци|я (-и) ж deformation.

деформи́р|овать (-ую) (не)сов перех to deform

▶ **деформи́роваться** (не)сов возв to be deformed.

децентрализа́ци|я (-и) ж decentralization.

децентрализ|ова́ть (-у́ю) (не)сов перех to decentralize.

媒дециб́л (-а) м decibel.

дециме́тр (-а) м decimetre (BRIT), decimeter (US).

дешеве́|ть (3sg -ет, 3pl -ют, perf **подешеве́ть**) несов неперех to go down in price.

дешёв|ка (-ки; gen pl -ок) ж (перен: пренебр): **э́та карти́на ~** this picture is tacky; **купи́ть** (perf)**/прода́ть** (perf) **что-н по ~ке** to buy/sell sth dirt-cheap.

деше́вле сравн прил от **дешёвый** ◆ сравн нареч от **дёшево**.

дёшево нареч (купить) cheaply.

дешёвый (дёшев, дешева́, дёшево) прил (также разг) cheap.

дешифр|ова́ть (-у́ю) (не)сов перех to decipher.

де-ю́ре нареч de jure.

де́ятелен прил см **де́ятельный**.

де́ятел|ь (-я) м: **госуда́рственный ~** statesman; **полити́ческий ~** politician; **~ культу́ры** person involved in the arts.

де́ятельност|ь (-и) ж (научная, педагоги́ческая) work, activity; (сердца, мозга)

activity.
де́ятел|ьный (-ен, -ьна, -ьно) *прил* active,
energetic.
джаз (-а) *м* jazz.
джем (-а) *м* jam.
дже́мпер (-а) *м* jumper.
джентльме́н (-а) *м* gentleman (*мн* gentlemen).
джин (-а) *м* gin.
джи́нсов|ый *прил* denim; **джи́нсовая ткань**
denim.
джи́нс|ы (-ов) *мн* jeans *мн*.
джо́йстик (-а) *м* (*КОМП*) joystick.
джо́кер (-а) *м* (*КАРТЫ*) joker.
джу́нгл|и (-ей) *мн* jungle *ед*.
джут (-а) *м* jute.
дзюдо́ *ср нескл* judo.
дзюдои́ст (-а) *м* judoist.
диабе́т (-а) *м*: **са́харный** ~ diabetes.
диабе́тик (-а) *м* diabetic.
диа́гноз (-а) *м* diagnosis; **ста́вить (поста́вить**
perf) ~ to make a diagnosis.
диагности́р|овать (-ую) (*не*)*сов перех* (*МЕД*)
to diagnose; (*ТЕХ*) to check.
диагона́л|ь (-и) *ж* diagonal.
диагра́мм|а (-ы) *ж* diagram.
диакрити́ческ|ий (-ая, -ое, -ие) *прил*: ~ **знак**
diacritical mark.
диале́кт (-а) *м* dialect.
диале́ктик|а (-и) *ж* dialectics; (*событий,*
процесса) dialectic.
диало́г (-а) *м* dialogue.
диало́говый *прил* (*КОМП*) conversational.
диа́метр (-а) *м* diameter.
диапазо́н (-а) *м* range; (*частот*) waveband;
(*голоса, звука*) range, diapason.
диапозити́в (-а) *м* (*ФОТО*) slide.
диате́з (-а) *м* diathesis.
диафи́льм (-а) *м* (*ФОТО*) slide film.
диафра́гм|а (-ы) *ж* diaphragm.
дива́н (-а) *м* sofa.
дива́н-крова́т|ь (-и) *ж* sofa bed.
ди́вен *прил см* **ди́вный**
диверса́нт (-а) *м* saboteur.
диверсифика́ция (-и) *ж* diversification.
диве́рси|я (-и) *ж* sabotage; **соверша́ть**
(**соверши́ть** *perf*) ~**ю** to commit sabotage.
дивертисме́нт (-а) *м* divertissement.
дивиде́нд (-а) *м* dividend; **приноси́ть**
(**принести́** *perf*) ~**ы** to pay dividends.
дивизио́н (-а) *м* unit; (*военных кораблей*)
division.
дивизи|я (-и) *ж* division.
ди́в|ный (-ен, -на, -но) *прил* marvellous.
дидакти́ческ|ий (-ая, -ое, -ие) *прил* didactic.
дие́з (-а) *м* (*МУЗ*) sharp.
дие́т|а (-ы) *ж* diet; **быть** (*impf*) **на** ~**е** to be on a
diet; **соблюда́ть** (*impf*) ~**у** to keep to a diet.
диети́ческ|ий (-ая, -ое, -ие) *прил* dietetic.
диза́йн (-а) *м* design.

диза́йнер (-а) *м* designer.
ди́зел|ь (-я) *м* diesel engine.
дизентери́|я (-и) *ж* dysentery.
дика́р|ка (-ки; *gen pl* -ок) *ж* savage; (*перен*) *shy,*
unsociable woman or girl.
дика́р|ь (-я́) *м* savage; (*перен*) *shy, unsociable*
man or boy; (: *разг*) independent holidaymaker;
éхать (поéхать *perf*) **дикарём на юг/на мо́ре** to
go off on spec to the South/the seaside.
ди́к|ий (-ая, -ое, -ие) -, -á, -о) *прил* wild;
(*человек*) savage; (*ребёнок*) shy and unsociable;
(*голод, холод*) terrible.
дикобра́з (-а) *м* porcupine.
дико́вин|а (-ы) *ж* (*разг*) marvel; **э́то мне в** ~**у**
this is all too new.
дико́вин|ка (-ки; *gen pl* -ок) *ж* = **дико́вина**.
дикорасту́щ|ий (-ая, -ее, -ие) *прил* wild.
ди́кост|ь (-и) *ж* wildness; (*поступка, мысли*)
absurdity.
дикта́нт (-а) *м* dictation.
дикта́тор (-а) *м* dictator.
диктату́р|а (-ы) *ж* dictatorship.
дикт|ова́ть (-у́ю; *perf* **продиктова́ть**) *несов*
перех to dictate.
дикто́в|ка (-ки; *gen pl* -ок) *ж* dictation; **под чью-н**
~**ку** (*записывать*) from sb's dictation;
(*действовать*) at sb's bidding.
ди́ктор (-а) *м* announcer; (*читающий новости*)
newsreader.
диктофо́н (-а) *м* Dictaphone®.
ди́кци|я (-и) *ж* diction.
дилéмм|а (-ы) *ж* dilemma.
ди́лер (-а) *м*: ~ (**по** +*prp*) dealer (in).
дина́мик (-а) *м* (loud)speaker.
дина́мик|а (-и) *ж* (*физ*) dynamics; (*развития,*
процесса) dynamics *мн*.
динами́т (-а) *м* dynamite.
динами́|чный (-ен, -на, -но) *прил* dynamic.
дина́сти|я (-и) *ж* dynasty.
диноза́вр (-а) *м* dinosaur.
дио́д (-а) *м* diode.
диоптри́|я (-и) *ж* dioptre (*BRIT*), diopter (*US*).
дипко́рпус (-а) *м сокр* (= **дипломати́ческий**
ко́рпус) CD (= *Corps Diplomatique*).
дипло́м (-а) *м* (*ПРОСВЕЩ: свидетельство*)
degree certificate; (: *на конкурсе*) certificate,
diploma; (*научная работа*) dissertation (*for*
undergraduate degree); **защища́ть (защити́ть**
perf) ~ to have a viva (*for undergraduate*
degree).
диплома́нт (-а) *м* award winner.
диплома́т (-а) *м* diplomat; (*разг: портфель*)
briefcase.
дипломати́ческ|ий (-ая, -ое, -ие) *прил*
diplomatic.
дипломати́|я (-и) *ж* diplomacy.
дипломи́рованный *прил* qualified.
дир. *сокр* (= **дире́ктор**) dir. (= *director*).

директи́в|а (-ы) ж directive.

дире́ктор (-а; *nom pl* -á) м director; ~ **шко́лы** headmaster; ~-**распоряди́тель** managing director; **гла́вный исполни́тельный** ~ chief executive.

дире́кци|я (-и) ж (*завода, фабрики*) management; (*школы*) ≈ board (of governors); (*фирмы*) board (of directors).

дирижа́бл|ь (-я) м airship, dirigible.

дирижёр (-а) м (*муз*) conductor.

дирижёрск|ий (-ая, -ое, -ие) *прил*: ~**ая па́лочка** (conductor's) baton.

дирижи́р|овать (-ую) *несов неперех* (+*instr*) to conduct.

дисгармо́ни|я (-и) ж discord.

диск (-а) м (*также комп*) disk; (*спорт*) discus; (*муз*) record; **ги́бкий/жёсткий** ~ floppy/hard disk; ~ **с удво́енной пло́тностью** double-density floppy disk.

дисквалифици́р|овать (-ую) (*не*)*сов перех* (*врача, юриста*) to strike off; (*спортсмена*) to disqualify.

диске́т (-а) м diskette.

диске́т|а (-ы) ж = **диске́т**.

диск-жоке́й (-я) м disc jockey.

ди́ско *ср нескл* disco.

диско́нт (-а) м (*комм*) discount.

дискоте́к|а (-и) ж (*собрание пластинок*) record collection; (*танцы*) discotheque.

дискредити́р|овать (-ую) (*не*)*сов перех* to discredit.

дискримина́ци|я (-и) ж discrimination.

дискримини́р|овать (-ую) (*не*)*сов перех* to discriminate against.

дискуссио́нный *прил* (*спорный*) debat(e)able.

дискусси|я (-и) ж discussion.

дискути́р|овать (-ую) *несов перех* to discuss.

дислока́ци|я (-и) ж (*воен*) deployment; (*мед*) dislocation.

дислоци́р|овать (-ую) (*не*)*сов перех* (*воен*) to deploy.

диспансе́р (-а) м dispensary.

диспе́тчер (-а) м controller; **авиацио́нный** ~ air-traffic controller.

диспе́тчерск|ая (-ой; *decl like adj*) ж controller's office; (*авиа*) control tower.

диспе́тчерск|ий (-ая, -ое, -ие) *прил*: ~**ая слу́жба** control section; ~**ая вы́шка** control tower.

дисплей (-я) м (*комп*) display.

диспропо́рци|я (-и) ж disproportion.

ди́спут (-а) м debate.

диссерта́нт (-а) м (*post-graduate*) *student defending a PhD thesis*.

диссерта́ци|я (-и) ж ≈ PhD thesis; **защища́ть** (*impf*) ~**ю** to be examined on one's thesis; **защити́ть** (*perf*) ~**ю** to pass a viva.

диссиде́нт (-а) м dissident.

диссона́нс (-а) м (*муз*) dissonance; (*перен*) discord; **вноси́ть** (**внести́** *perf*) ~ **во что-н** (*перен*) to bring a note of discord into sth.

дистанцио́нн|ый *прил*: ~**ое управле́ние** remote control.

диста́нци|я (-и) ж distance; **сохраня́ть** (**сохрани́ть** *perf*) ~**ю** (*перен*) to keep one's distance; **он сошёл с** ~**и** (*спорт*) he didn't last the distance.

дистилли́р|овать (-ую) (*не*)*сов перех* to distil (*brit*), distill (*us*).

дистрибью́тор (-а) м distributor.

дистрофи́|я (-и) ж dystrophy.

дисципли́н|а (-ы) ж discipline.

дисциплини́рован|ный (-, -на, -но) *прил* disciplined.

дит|я́ (-и; *nom pl* **де́ти**) *ср* child; *см также* **де́ти**.

дифтери́т (-а) м diphtheria.

дифто́нг (-а) м diphthong.

дифференциа́льный *прил* (*экон*) differential *опред*.

дифференци́рованн|ый *прил*: ~**ая зарпла́та** differential.

дифференци́р|овать (-ую) (*не*)*сов перех* to differentiate.

дича́|ть (-ю; *perf* **одича́ть**) *несов неперех* to grow wild.

дич|ь (-и) ж *собир* game; (*разг*) rubbish.

диэле́ктрик (-а) м dielectric.

ДК *сокр* (= **Дворе́ц культу́ры, Дом культу́ры**) *centre for social and cultural activities*.

длин|а́ (-ы) ж length; **в** ~**у́** lengthways; ~**о́й 10 ме́тров** 10 metres (*brit*) *или* meters (*us*) long; ~ **тка́ни — 10 метро́в** the cloth is 10 metres long.

дли́нен *прил см* **дли́нный**.

длинноволно́в|о́й *прил* long-wave.

длинноволо́сый *прил* long-haired.

длинноно́г|ий (-ая, -ое, -ие) *прил* long-legged.

длиннору́к|ий (-ая, -ое, -ие) *прил* with long arms.

дли́нно *нареч* (*рассужда́ть*) at length ♦ *как сказ*: **пла́тье мне** ~ the dress is too long for me.

дли́нн|ый (-ен, -на́, -но) *прил* long; (*разг: челове́к*) tall; **у него́** ~ **язы́к** (*разг*) he's got a big mouth; **дли́нный рубль** (*разг*) easy money.

дли́тельност|ь (-и) ж length.

дли́тельный *прил* lengthy.

дли́ться (*3sg* -**ится**, *3pl* -**ятся**, *perf* **продли́ться**) *несов возв* (*урок, бесе́да*) to last.

KEYWORD

для *предл* (+*gen*) **1** for; **для о́бщего бла́га** for the general good; **ме́сто для по́дписи** space for a signature; **крем для лица́** face cream; **альбо́м для рисова́ния** sketch pad

2 (*в отношении кого-н/чего-н*): **для меня́ э́то име́ет большо́е значе́ние** this is very important to me; **для того́ что́бы** in order to; **для него́ э́то про́сто рабо́та** this is just work to him; **э́то поле́зно для здоро́вья** this is good for one's health; **для своего́ во́зраста он о́чень развито́й** he is very advanced for his age
---

дм *сокр* (= **дециме́тр**) dm= *decimetre* (*brit*) *или decimeter* (*us*).

дн|ева́ть (-ю́ю, -ю́ешь) *несов неперех*: ~ **и**

ночева́ть где́-нибудь (*разг*) to be somewhere day and night.

дневни́к (-á) м diary; (*ПРОСВЕЩ*) register; **вести́** (*impf*) ~ to keep a diary.

дневн|óй *прил* (*выработка, заработок*) daily; ~**áя фóрма обучéния** full-time education; ~ **свет** daylight; ~**óе врéмя** daytime; **дневнóй спектáкль** matinee.

днём *сущ см* **день** ♦ *нареч:* ~ in the daytime; (*после обéда*) in the afternoon; **егó ~ с огнём не найти́** he is absolutely nowhere to be found.

Днепр (-а) м Dnieper.

Днестр (-а) м Dniester.

дни *итп сущ см* **день**.

дни́ще (-а) *ср* bottom.

ДНК *ж сокр* (= *дезоксирибонуклеи́новая кислотá*) DNA (= *deoxyribonucleic acid*).

дн|о (-а) *ср* (*моря, реки*) bottom, bed; (*ямы, оврага*) bottom; (*nom pl* **дóнья**, *gen pl* **дóньев**; *бочки, ящика*) bottom; **идти́ (пойти́** *perf*) **ко ~у** to sink to the bottom; (*перен: предприятие*) to go under; (: *человек*) to sink.

дня *итп сущ см* **день**.

KEYWORD

до *предл* (+*gen*) **1** (*о предéле движéния*) as far as, to; **мы доéхали до реки́** we went as far as *или* to the river; **я проводи́л егó до стáнции** I saw him off at the station

2 (*о расстоя́нии*) to; **до гóрода 3 киломéтра** it is 3 kilometres (*BRIT*) *или* kilometers (*US*) to the town

3 (*о временнóм предéле*) till, until; **я отложи́л заседáние до утрá** I postponed the meeting till *или* until morning; **я рабóтаю с восьми́ до пяти́** I work from eight to five; **до свидáния!** goodbye!

4 (*перед*) before; **мы закóнчили до перерывá** we finished before the break

5 (*о предéле состоя́ния*): **мне бы́ло оби́дно до слёз** I was so hurt I cried; **он кричáл до хрипоты́** he shouted himself hoarse; **нáдо нагрéть вóду до кипéния** the water must be heated until it boils

6 (*полностью*): **я отдáл ей всё до копéйки** I gave her everything down to my last kopeck; **он вы́пил буты́лку до днá** he drank the bottle dry

7 (*направлéние дéйствия*): **ребёнок дотрóнулся до игрýшки** the child touched the toy; **мне до негó нет никакóго дéла** (*разг*) I have no truck with him

♦ *ср нескл* (*муз*) doh.

до- *префикс* (*in verbs*; *доведéние дéйствия до концá*) indicating completion of action eg. *добежáть*; (*о достижéнии какóго-нибудь результáта*) indicating achievement of a certain goal eg. *дозвони́ться*; (*in adverbs*;

доведéние кáчества до какóго-нибудь предéла) indicating attainment of a quality to a certain degree eg. *докраснá*; (*о дополни́тельном дéйствии*) indicating supplement to an action eg. *добáть*; (*in adjectives*; *бы́вший прéжде чегó-н*) pre-.

добáв|ить (-лю, -ишь; *impf* **добавля́ть**) *сов перех* to add.

добáв|ка (-ки; *gen pl* -ок) ж (*к обéду*) additional helping; (*пищевáя, бетóнная*) additive.

добавлéни|е (-я) *ср* addition; **дéлать (сдéлать** *perf*) ~**я к** +*dat* to make an addition to; **в** ~ **к** +*dat* in addition to.

добáвлю *сов см* **добáвить**.

добавля́|ть (-ю) *несов от* **добáвить**.

добáвок *сущ см* **добáвка**.

добáвочн|ый *прил* additional ♦ (-ого; *decl like adj*) м (*также:* ~ **телефóн**) extension number.

добе|жáть (*как* **бежáть**; *см* **Table 20**; *impf* **добегáть**) *сов неперех:* ~ **до** +*gen* to run to *или* as far as; (*звýки, вóлны*) to reach.

добелá *нареч:* **отмы́ть что-н** ~ to wash sth clean; **раскали́ть** (*perf*) **что-н** ~ to heat sth until it's white-hot.

доберýсь *итп сов см* **добрáться**.

добивá|ть(ся) (-ю(сь)) *несов от* **доби́ть(ся)**.

добирá|ться (-юсь) *несов от* **добрáться**.

доби́|ть (-ью, -ьёшь; *impf* **добивáть**) *сов перех* (*уби́ть*) to finish off; (*разби́ть*) to break

► **доби́ться** (*impf* **добивáться**) *сов возв* (+*gen*) to achieve; **добивáться** (~**ся** *perf*) **своегó** to get what one wants.

дóблестн|ый (-ен, -на, -но) *прил* valiant.

дóблест|ь (-и) ж valour (*BRIT*), valor (*US*).

добр|áться (-ерýсь, -ерёшься; *impf* **добирáться**) *сов возв:* ~ **до** +*gen* to get to, reach; (*решéния*) to reach; **добирáться** (~ *perf*) **до сýти (дéла)** to get to the heart of the matter; **я до тебя́** ~**ерýсь!** (*разг*) I'll get you!

добрé|ть (-ю; *perf* **подобрéть**) *несов неперех* to become kinder; (*perf* **раздобрéть**; *разг*) to fill out.

добр|ó (-á) *ср* good; (*разг: имýщество*) things *мн* ♦ *част* (*разг: лáдно*) fine; **желáть (пожелáть** *perf*) **комý-н** ~**á** to wish sb well; ~ **пожáловать (в Москвý)!** welcome (to Moscow)!; **давáть (дать** *perf*) **комý-н** ~ **на что-н** to give sb the go-ahead for sth; **получáть (получи́ть** *perf*) ~ **(на что-н)** to get the go-ahead (for sth).

добровóл|ец (-ьца) м volunteer; **идти́ (пойти́** *perf*) ~**ьцем** to volunteer.

добровóл|ьный (-ен, -ьна, -ьно) *прил* voluntary; **на** ~**ьных начáлах** on a voluntary basis.

добровóльца *итп сущ см* **добровóлец**.

добродéтел|ь (-и) ж virtue.

добродéтельный *прил* virtuous.

добродýш|ный (-ен, -на, -но) *прил* good-natured.

доброжелáтельност|ь (-и) *ж* benevolence.

доброжелáтельный *прил* benevolent.

доброкáчествен|ный (-, -на, -но) *прил* (*продукт, изделие*) quality *опред*; (*no short form*; *опухоль*) benign.

добропорядоч|ный (-ен, -на, -но) *прил* respectable.

добросердéч|ный (-ен, -на, -но) *прил* (*человек*) kind-hearted; (*слова*) kind.

добросóвест|ный (-ен, -на, -но) *прил* conscientious.

добрососéдств|о (-а) *ср* neighbourliness (*BRIT*), neighborliness (*US*).

добротá (-ы́) *ж* kindness.

добрóт|ный (-ен, -на, -но) *прил* good-quality.

дóбр|ый (-, -á, -о, -ы) *прил* kind; (*совет, имя*) good; (*милый: друг итп*) dear; бýдьте добры́! excuse me!; бýдьте добры́, позвони́те нам зáвтра! would you be so good as to phone us tomorrow?; всегó ~ого! all the best!; ~ого здорóвья! take care!; ~ день/вéчер! good afternoon/evening!; ~ое ýтро! good morning!; по ~ой вóле of one's own free will; чегó ~ого (*разг*) it's not impossible.

добýду *итп сов см* добы́ть.

добыва́|ть (-ю) *несов от* добы́ть.

добыва́|ющий (-ая, -ее, -ие) *прил*: ~ая промы́шленность *mining, gas and oil industries*.

добы́тчик (-а) *м* (*золота*) miner; (*нефти*) oil worker.

добы́ть (*как* быть; *см* Table 21; *impf* добыва́ть) *сов перех* (*денег, машину*) to get; (*нефть*) to extract; (*руду, золото*) to mine.

добы́ч|а (-и) *ж* (*процесс: нефти*) extraction; (: *руды*) mining, extraction; (*то, что добыто*) output; (: *на охоте, ловле*) catch.

добью́(сь) *итп сов см* добы́ть(ся).

доведý(сь) *итп сов см* довести́(сь).

довез|ти́ (-ý; *pt* довёз, -лá, -лó, *impf* довози́ть) *сов перех*: ~ когó-н до +*gen* to take sb to *или* as far as.

довёл(ся) *итп сов см* довести́(сь).

довéренност|ь (-и) *ж* power of attorney; дéйствовать (*impf*) по ~и to act by proxy.

довéренн|ый (-ого; *decl like adj*) *м* (*также*: ~ое лицó) proxy.

довéри|е (-я) *ср* confidence, trust; пóльзоваться (*impf*) чьим-н ~м to enjoy sb's confidence; входи́ть (войти́ *perf*) в чьё-н ~ to gain sb's confidence; выходи́ть (вы́йти *perf*) из чьегó-н ~я to lose sb's confidence.

довéрителен *прил см* довéрительный.

довéрител|ь (-я) *м person who empowers another to act on his or her behalf*.

довéрительный (-ен, -ьна, -ьно) *прил* trusting.

довéр|ить (-ю, -ишь; *impf* доверя́ть) *сов перех*: ~ что-н комý-н to entrust sb with sth

► довéриться (*impf* доверя́ться) *сов возв*: ~ся +*dat* to confide in; (*положиться*) to trust.

дóверху *нареч* (up) to the top; напóлненный ~ full to the brim.

довéрчивост|ь (-и) *ж* trustingness.

довéрчив|ый (-, -а, -о) *прил* trusting.

доверша́|ть (-ю) *несов от* доверши́ть.

доверше́ни|е (-я) *ср* completion; в ~ *или* к доверше́нию всегó on top of everything else.

доверш|и́ть (-ý, -и́шь; *impf* доверша́ть) *сов перех* to complete.

доверя́|ть (-ю) *несов от* довéрить ♦ *неперех*: ~ +*dat* to trust.

дове|сти́ (-дý, -дёшь; *pt* довёл, -лá, -лó, *impf* доводи́ть) *сов перех*: ~ когó-н/что-н до +*gen* to take sb/sth to *или* as far as; доводи́ть (~ *perf*) что-н до концá to see sth through to the end; доводи́ть (~ *perf*) когó-н до слёз to reduce sb to tears; доводи́ть (~ *perf*) когó-н до отчáяния to drive sb to despair; доводи́ть (~ *perf*) что-н до совершéнства to perfect sth; доводи́ть (~ *perf*) скóрость до предéла to reach the speed limit; доводи́ть (~ *perf*) что-н до свéдения когó-н to inform sb of sth

► довести́сь *сов безл*: мне не ~дётся вернýться тудá I won't get the opportunity *или* chance to go back there; передáйте привéт, éсли Вам ~дётся встрéтить её say hello if you happen to see her.

дóвод (-а) *м* argument; приводи́ть (привести́ *perf*) ~ to put forward an argument.

дово|ди́ть (-жý, -дишь) *несов от* довести́

► дово|ди́ться *несов от* довести́сь ♦ *возв*: он дово́дится ей брáтом/внýком (*разг*) he is her brother/grandson.

довоéнный *прил* prewar.

дово|жý(сь) *несов см* доводи́ть(ся).

дово|зи́ть (-жý, -зишь) *несов от* довезти́.

довóлен *прил см* довóльный.

довóльно *нареч* (*известный, сильный*) quite; (*улыбаться, сказать*) with satisfaction ♦ *как сказ* it's enough; ~ спóров *или* спóрить! that's enough arguing!

довóл|ьный (-ен, -ьна, -ьно) *прил* satisfied, contented; он ~ен рабóтой/жи́знью he's satisfied *или* happy with his work/life.

довóльств|оваться (-уюсь) *несов возв*: ~ +*instr* to be happy *или* content with; он ~уется мáлым *или* немнóгим it doesn't take much to make him happy.

довооруж|и́ть (-ý, -и́шь; *impf* довооружáть) *сов перех* (*окончательно*) to arm; (*дополнительно*) to provide with additional arms.

довы́бор|ы (-ов) *мн* ≈ by-election *ед*.

дог (-а) *м* (*ЗООЛ*) Great Dane.

догадá|ться (-юсь; *impf* догáдываться) *сов возв* to guess.

догáд|ка (-ки; *gen pl* -ок) *ж* guess; стро́ить (*impf*) ~ки о +*prp* to speculate about; теря́ться (*impf*) в ~x to be baffled *или* at a loss.

догáдлив|ый (-, -а, -о) *прил* quick-witted.
догáдок *сущ см* **догáдка**.
догáдыва|ться (-юсь) *несов от* **догадáться**.
дóгм|а (-ы) *ж* dogma.
догмáт (-а) *м* (*РЕЛ*) dogma.
догмати́ческ|ий (-ая, -ое, -ие) *прил* dogmatic.
догн|áть (-оню́, -óнишь; *impf* **догоня́ть**) *сов перех* to catch up with; ~ (*perf*) **когó-н/чтó-н до** +*gen* to drive sb/sth to.
догова́рива|ться (-юсь) *несов от* **договори́ться**.
договóр (-а) *м* (*ПОЛИТ*) treaty; (*КОММ*) agreement; ~ **о** +*prp*/**на** +*acc* agreement on *или* about; **заключáть (заключи́ть** *perf*)/ **расторгáть (расто́ргнуть** *perf*) ~ to sign/annul a treaty.
договорённост|ь (-и) *ж* agreement; **достигáть (дости́гнуть** *perf*) ~**и в чём-н** to reach an agreement on *или* about sth; **по** ~**и** by agreement.
договоренó *как сказ*: ~ **о** +*prp* ... there's been an agreement on ....
договор|и́ться (-ю́сь, -и́шься; *impf* **догова́риваться**) *сов возв*: ~ **с кем-н о чём-н** (*о встрече*) to arrange sth with sb; (*о цене*) to agree sth with sb; **мы** ~**и́лись до глу́постей/гру́бостей** we ended up talking nonsense/insulting each other; **мы** ~**и́лись встрéтиться** we agreed to meet.
договóрник (-а) *м* (*разг*) contract worker.
договóрн|ый *прил* (*цена*) agreed; (*обязательство*) contractual; **на** ~**ых начáлах** on a contractual basis.
догола́ *нареч*: **раздéться** ~ to strip bare; **постри́чься** (*perf*) ~ to have all one's hair cut off.
догоню́ *итп сов см* **догнáть**.
догоня́|ть (-ю) *несов от* **догнáть**.
догор|éть (-ю́, -и́шь; *impf* **догорáть**) *сов неперех* to burn out.
догру|зи́ть (-жу́, -зишь) *сов перех* to finish loading.
дод|áть (*как* **дать**; *см* **Table 14**; *impf* **додавáть**) *сов перех*: ~ **кому́-н 10 рублéй** to give sb an extra 10 roubles.
додéла|ть (-ю; *impf* **додéлывать**) *сов перех* to finish.
доду́ма|ться (-юсь; *impf* **доду́мываться**) *сов возв*: ~ **до** +*gen* to hit on; **как ты мог до такóго** ~? what on earth gave you that idea?
доедá|ть (-ю) *несов от* **доéсть**.
доéдешь *итп сов см* **доéхать**.
доеди́м *итп сов см* **доéсть**.
доéду *итп сов см* **доéхать**.
доезжáй(те) *сов см* **доéхать**.
доезжá|ть (-ю) *несов от* **доéхать**.
доéсть (*как* **есть**; *см* **Table 15**; *impf* **доедáть**) *сов перех* to finish off, eat up.

доéхать (*как* **éхать**; *см* **Table 19**; *impf* **доезжáть**) *сов неперех*: ~ **до** +*gen* to reach.
доéшь *сов см* **доéсть**.
дожд|áться (-у́сь, -ёшься; *pt* -áлся, -алáсь, -алóсь, *imper* -и́(те)сь) *сов неперех*: ~ **когó-н/чегó-н** to wait until sb/sth comes; ~ (*perf*) **пóезда** to wait until the train arrives; **он** ~**ётся вы́говора** (*разг*) he'll end up getting told off; **ты у меня** ~**ёшься!** (*разг*) just you wait!; **он ждёт не** ~**ётся** (*разг*) he can't wait.
дождли́в|ый (-, -а, -о) *прил* rainy.
дожд|ь (-я́) *м* rain; (*перен*) cascade; **гуля́ть** (*impf*) **в** ~ to go for a walk in the rain; ~ **идёт** it's raining; ~ **пошёл** it has started to rain; **попадáть (попáсть** *perf*) **под** ~ to get caught in the rain; ~ **льёт как из ведрá** it's bucketing (with rain).
дожива́|ть (-ю) *несов от* **дожи́ть** ♦ *неперех* (*жизнь, годы*) to live out.
дожидá|ться (-юсь) *несов возв* (+*gen*) to wait for.
дожи́|ть (-ву́, -вёшь; *impf* **дожива́ть**) *несов неперех*: ~ **до** +*gen* (*до старости*) to live to; (*до конца года*) to live until.
дóз|а (-ы) *ж* dose; ~ **облучéния** dose of radiation.
дозвáнива|ться (-юсь) *несов от* **дозвони́ться**.
дозвóленный *прил* permitted.
дозвон|и́ться (-ю́сь, -и́шься; *impf* **дозвáниваться**) *сов возв* to get through.
дози́метр (-а) *м* dosimeter (*BRIT*), dosimeter (*US*).
дози́р|овать (-ую) (*не)сов перех* to measure out.
дозóр (-а) *м* patrol; **быть** (*impf*) **в** ~**е** to be on patrol.
доигрá|ть (-ю; *impf* **доигрывать**) *сов перех* to finish (playing).
доигрывани|е (-я) *ср* (*СПОРТ*) playing to a finish.
доигрыва|ть (-ю) *несов от* **доигрáть**.
доистори́ческ|ий (-ая, -ое, -ие) *прил* prehistoric.
до|и́ть (-ю́, -ишь; *perf* **подои́ть**) *несов перех* to milk.
дóйн|ый *прил*: ~**ая корóва** dairy cow.
доймý *итп сов см* **доня́ть**.
дойти́ (*как* **идти́**; *см* **Table 18**; *impf* **доходи́ть**) *сов неперех*: ~ **до** +*gen* to reach; (*традиции, предания*) to be passed down to; (*слова, смысл*) to get through to; **доходи́ть** (~ *perf*) **до отчáяния/истощéния** to reach the point of desperation/exhaustion; **до моегó свéдения дошлó, что ...** it has been brought to my attention that ....
док (-а) *м* dock.
докажý *итп сов см* **доказáть**.

доказа́тельств|о (-а) *ср* (*правоты, дружбы*) proof, evidence; (*теории*) demonstration; **служи́ть** (**послужи́ть** *perf*) **~м** +*gen* to be evidence of.

доказа́ть (-жу́, -жешь; *impf* **дока́зывать**) *сов перех* (*правду, виновность*) to prove; (*теорему*) to demonstrate.

дока́нчива|ть (-ю) *несов от* **докончи́ть**.

дока́пыва|ть (-ю) *несов от* **докона́ть**.

дока́пыва|ться (-юсь) *несов от* **докопа́ться**.

докати́ться (-чу́сь, -тишься; *impf* **дока́тываться**) *сов возв* (*звуки, шум*) to reach; **дока́тываться** (**~** *perf*) **до** +*gen* (*мяч, волны*) to roll in to; **дока́тываться** (**~** *perf*) **до преступле́ния** to stoop to crime.

до́кер (-а) *м* docker.

докла́д (-а) *м* (*на съезде итп*) paper; (*директору итп*) report.

докладн|а́я (-о́й; *decl like adj*) *ж* (*также*: **~ запи́ска**) memo.

докла́дчик (-а) *м* speaker.

докла́дчиц|а (-ы) *ж см* **докла́дчик**.

докла́дыва|ть (-ю) *несов от* **доложи́ть**.

докона́ть (-ю; *impf* **дока́нивать**) *сов перех* (*разг*): **~ кого́-н** to do sb in.

доко́нч|ить (-у, -ишь; *impf* **дока́нчивать**) *сов перех* to finish off.

докопа́ться (-юсь; *impf* **дока́пываться**) *сов возв*: **~ до** +*gen* (*перен: разг: до фактов, истины*) to dig up; (*до клада, воды*) to dig down to.

до́ктор (-а; *nom pl* **-а́**) *м* doctor; **~ нау́к** Doctor of Sciences (*postdoctoral research degree in Russia*).

до́кторск|ий (-ая, -ое, -ие) *прил* (*МЕД*) doctor's; (*ПРОСВЕЩ*) postdoctoral.

доктри́н|а (-ы) *ж* doctrine.

докуме́нт (-а) *м* document.

докуча́|ть (-ю) *несов неперех*: **~ кому́-н чем-н** to pester sb with sth.

документа́льн|ый (-ен, -ьна, -ьно) *прил* documentary; **документа́льный фильм** documentary.

документа́ци|я (-и) *ж собир* documentation.

документи́р|овать (-ую) (*не*)*сов перех* to document.

долб|и́ть (-лю́, -и́шь; *perf* **продолби́ть**) *несов перех* to hollow out; (*no perf*; *разг: зубри́ть*) to learn by rote; **~** (*impf*) **в дверь** (*разг*) to hammer on the door.

долг (-а; *loc sg* **-у́**, *nom pl* **-и́**) *м* debt; **вне́шний/ госуда́рственный ~** (*ЭКОН*) foreign/national debt; **дава́ть** (**дать** *perf*)/**брать** (**взять** *perf*) **что-н в ~** to lend/borrow sth; **входи́ть** (**войти́** *perf*)/**залеза́ть** (**зале́зть** *perf*) **в ~й** to get/fall into debt; **быть** (*impf*) **в ~у́ пе́ред кем-н** *или* **у кого́-н** to be indebted to sb; **по до́лгу слу́жбы** in the course of duty; **пе́рвым до́лгом** (*разг*) first of all.

до́лг|ий (-гая, -гое, -гие; *-ог, -га́, -го*) *прил* long; **в ~ я́щик откла́дывать** (**отложи́ть** *perf*) **что-н**

to put sth off, postpone sth; **до́лгий гла́сный** long vowel.

до́лго *нареч* for a long time; **как ~ продли́тся фильм?** how long will the film last?

долгове́чн|ый (-ен, -на, -но) *прил* (*материал*) durable, long-lasting; (*дружба*) lasting.

долгов|о́й *прил*: **~а́я распи́ска** IOU; **~о́е обяза́тельство** promissory note.

долговре́менный *прил* prolonged.

долгожда́нный *прил* long-awaited.

долгожи́тел|ь (-я) *м* long-lived person.

долгожи́тельниц|а (-ы) *ж см* **долгожи́тель**.

долгоигра́ющ|ий (-ая, -ее, -ие) *прил*: **~ая пласти́нка** L.P. (= *long-playing record*).

долголе́тн|ий (-яя, -ее, -ие) *прил*: **~ее сотру́дничество** long-standing cooperation.

долгосро́чный *прил* long-term.

долгот|а́ (-ы́) *ж* length; (*ГЕО*) longitude.

до́лее *сравн прил от* **до́лгий** ♦ *сравн нареч от* **до́лго**.

до́лек *сущ см* **до́лька**.

доле|те́ть (-чу́, -ти́шь; *impf* **долета́ть**) *сов неперех*: **~ до** +*gen* to fly to, reach; (*звук, слухи*) to reach.

KEYWORD

до́лжен (-на́, -но́, -ны́) *часть сказуемого* (+*infin*) **1** (*обязан*): **я до́лжен уйти́** I must go; **я до́лжен бу́ду уйти́** I will have to go; **она́ должна́ была́ уйти́** she had to go

2 (*выража́ет предположе́ние*): **он до́лжен ско́ро прийти́** he should arrive soon

3 (+*dat*; *о до́лге*): **ты до́лжен мне 5 рубле́й** you owe me 5 roubles

4: **должно́ быть** (*вероя́тно*) probably; **кто́-то, должно́ быть сто́рож, закры́л дверь** somebody, probably the night watchman, closed the door; **должно́ быть, она́ о́чень уста́ла** she must have been very tired.

должни́к (-а́) *м* debtor.

должни́ц|а (-ы) *ж см* **должни́к**.

до́лжн|ое (-ого; *decl like adj*) *ср* due; **отдава́ть** (**отда́ть** *perf*) *или* **воздава́ть** (**возда́ть** *perf*) **~ кому́-н** to give sb his итп due.

должностн|о́й *прил* official; **~о́е преступле́ние** malfeasance; **должностно́е лицо́** official.

до́лжност|ь (-и; *gen pl* **-е́й**) *ж* (*пост*) post; (*обязанность*) duties *mn*; **вступи́ть** (**вступа́ть** *perf*) **в ~ кого́-н** to assume sb's post; **по ~и** ex officio.

до́лжн|ый *прил* (*уровень*) required; (*внимание*) sufficient.

доли́н|а (-ы) *ж* valley.

до́ллар (-а) *м* dollar.

до́лларов|ый *прил* dollar *опред*; **~ счёт** dollar account.

долож|и́ть (-у́, -ишь; *impf* **докла́дывать**) *сов перех* to report ♦ *неперех*: **~ о** +*prp* to give a report on; (*perf*) **о прихо́де кого́-н** to announce sb.

доло́й *нареч* away with; **~ апарте́йд!** down

with apartheid!

дол|ото́ (-ота́; *nom pl* -о́та) *ср* chisel; (*для бурения*) drill.

до́льше *сравн прил от* **до́лгий ♦** *сравн нареч от* **до́лго**.

до́ль|ка (-ки; *gen pl* -ек) *ж* (*апельсина*) segment.

до́л|я (-и; *gen pl* -е́й) *ж* share; (*пирога*) portion; (*судьба*) lot, fate; ~ **секу́нды/сантиме́тра** a fraction of a second/centimetre (*BRIT*) *или* centimeter (*US*); **входи́ть** (**войти́** *perf*) **в** ~**ю с кем-н** to go shares with sb; **выпада́ть** (**вы́пасть** *perf*) **на чью-н** ~**ю** to fall to sb's lot.

дом (-а; *nom pl* -а́) *м* house; (*многоэтажный*) block of flats (*BRIT*), apartment building (*US*); (*свое жильё*) home; (*семья*) household; ~ **Рома́новых** the house of Romanov; ~ **культу́ры** *centre for social and cultural activities*; **рабо́тать** (*impf*) **на** ~**у́** to work from home; **рабо́тать** (*impf*) **по до́му** to do the housework; **дом моде́лей** fashion house; **дом о́тдыха** ≈ holiday centre (*BRIT*) *или* center (*US*).

до́ма *нареч* at home; **быть** (*impf*) *или* **чу́вствовать** (*impf*) **себя́ как** ~ to feel at home; **его́ нет** ~ he's out *или* not at home; **сиде́ть** (*impf*) ~ to stay in *или* at home; **у него́ не все** ~ (*разг*) he's not all there.

дома́шн|ий (-яя, -ее, -ие) *прил* (*адрес, телефон*) home *опред*; (*еда*) home-made; (*животное*) domestic; ~**ие ту́фли** (carpet) slippers; ~**ее пла́тье** housecoat; **дома́шняя хозя́йка** housewife; **дома́шняя рабо́тница** domestic help (*BRIT*), maid (*US*); **дома́шнее зада́ние** homework.

до́менн|ый *прил* (*цех*) smelting *опред*; ~**ая печь** blast furnace.

доминика́нск|ий (-ая, -ое, -ие) *прил*: **Д**~**ая Респу́блика** Dominican Republic.

доминио́н (-а) *м* dominion.

домини́р|овать (-ую) *несов неперех* (*идея, мелодия*) to predominate; ~ (*impf*) **над** +*instr* to dominate.

домино́ *ср нескл* (*игра*) dominoes *ед*; (*фишка, костюм*) domino.

домко́м (-а) *м сокр* (= *домово́й комите́т*) ≈ residents' association.

домкра́т (-а) *м* (*TEX*) jack.

домовладе́л|ец (-ьца) *м* home owner.

домовладе́ни|е (-я) *ср* (*дом с участком*) *house with grounds attached*; (*владение домом*) home ownership.

домово́дств|о (-а) *ср* home economics.

домов|о́й (-о́го; *decl like adj*) *м* (*ФОЛЬКЛОР*) house spirit.

домо́вый *прил* (*ворота*) house *опред*; **домо́вая кни́га** property register.

домога́|ться (-юсь) *несов возв*: ~ +*gen* (*власти*) to strive for; ~ (*impf*) **чьей-н руки́** to court *или* woo sb.

домо́й *нареч* home; **мне пора́** ~ it's time for me to go home.

доморо́щенный *прил* (*разг: пренебр*) homespun.

домосе́д (-а) *м* stay-at-home.

домоуправле́ни|е (-я) *ср* ≈ housing department.

домофо́н (-а) *м* intercom.

домохозя́|йка (-йки; *gen pl* -ек) *ж* (= *дома́шняя хозя́йка*) housewife.

домоча́д|ец (-ца) *м* (*обычно мн*) member of the household.

домрабо́тни|ца (-ы) *ж* (= *дома́шняя рабо́тница*) domestic help (*BRIT*), maid (*US*).

домч|а́ться (-у́сь, -и́шься) *сов возв*: ~ (**до** +*gen*) to rush (to).

до́мысе|л (-ла) *м* conjecture.

донага́ *нареч*: **разде́ть кого́-н** ~ to strip sb naked.

дона́шива|ть (-ю) *несов от* **доноси́ть**.

доне́льзя *нареч* (*разг*) terribly.

донёс *итп сов см* **донести́**.

донесе́ни|е (-я) *ср* report.

донес|ти́ (-у́, -ёшь; *pt* **донёс**, -ла́, -ло́, *impf* **доноси́ть**) *сов перех* to carry ♦ *неперех*: ~ **на** +*acc* to inform on; ~ (*perf*) **o** +*prp* to report on
▶ **донести́сь** (*impf* **доноси́ться**) *сов возв*: ~**сь до** +*gen* to reach.

до́низу *нареч* to the bottom; **све́рху** ~ from top to bottom.

донима́|ть (-ю) *несов от* **доня́ть**.

до́нор (-а) *м* donor.

до́норск|ий (-ая, -ое, -ие) *прил* donor *опред*.

доно́с (-а) *м*: ~ (**на** +*acc*) denunciation (of); **де́лать** (**сде́лать** *perf*) ~ **на кого́-н** to inform on sb.

доно|си́ть (-шу́, -сишь) *несов от* **донести́ ♦** (*impf* **дона́шивать**) *сов перех* (*одежду*) to wear out; (*ребёнка*) to carry to term; **дона́шивать** (~ *perf*) **ве́щи за кем-н** to wear sb's hand-me-downs
▶ **доноси́ться** *несов от* **донести́сь**.

доно́счик (-а) *м* informer.

доно́счи|ца (-ы) *ж см* **доно́счик**.

доношу́(сь) *сов см* **доноси́ть(ся)**.

до́нья *итп сущ см* **дно**.

доня́|ть (-йму́, -ймёшь; *impf* **донима́ть**) *сов перех* (*разг*) to exasperate.

доп. *сокр* = **дополни́тельный**.

допе́й(те) *сов см* **допи́ть**.

допива́|ть (-ю) *несов от* **допи́ть**.

до́пинг (-а) *м* drugs *мн*.

допи|са́ть (-шу́, -шешь; *impf* **допи́сывать**) *сов перех* (*письмо*) to finish (writing); (*картину*) to finish (painting); (*написать дополнительно*) to add.

допи́|ть (**допью́, допьёшь**; *pt* -, -ла́, -ло, *imper* **допе́й(те)**, *impf* **допива́ть**) *сов перех* to drink up.

допишу́ *итп сов см* **дописа́ть**.

допла́т|а (-ы) *ж* additional payment; **~ за бага́ж** excess baggage (charge).

доплы́|ть (-ву́, -вёшь; *pt* **-л, -ла́, -ло,** *impf* **доплыва́ть)** *сов неперех:* **~ до** +*gen* **(на корабле́)** to sail to; **(вплавь)** to swim to.

допо́длинно *нареч:* **~ изве́стно** for certain.

допоздна́ *нареч (разг)* till late.

дополне́ни|е (-я) *ср* supplement; *(линг)* object; **в ~ (к** +*dat)* in addition (to); **прямо́е/ко́свенное ~** direct/indirect object.

дополни́тельно *нареч* in addition.

дополни́тельный *прил* additional.

дополн|ить (-ю, -ишь; *impf* **дополня́ть)** *сов перех* to supplement; **дополня́ть (~** *perf)* **кого́-н** to add to what sb has said; **дополня́ть** *(impf)* **друг дру́га** to complement one another.

допото́пный *прил (разг)* ancient.

допра́шива|ть (-ю) *несов от* **допроси́ть**.

допро́с (-а) *м* interrogation; **подверга́ть (подве́ргнуть** *perf)* **кого́-н ~у** to subject sb to an interrogation.

допро|си́ть (-шу́, -сишь; *impf* **допра́шивать)** *сов перех* to interrogate, question.

до́пуск (-а) *м (к зда́нию)* admittance; *(к докуме́нтам)* access; *(ТЕХ)* tolerance.

допуска́|ть (-ю; *perf* **допусти́ть)** *несов перех* to admit, allow in; *(предположи́ть)* to assume; **~ (допусти́ть** *perf)* **оши́бку (де́лать)** to make a mistake; *(позволя́ть)* to allow for a mistake; **~ (допусти́ть** *perf)* **кого́-н до уча́стия/ соревнова́ния** to allow sb to participate/ compete.

допу́стим *вводн сл* let us assume.

допусти́м|ый (-, -а, -о) *прил* permissible, acceptable; *(мысль)* feasible.

допу|сти́ть (-щу́, -стишь) *несов от* **допуска́ть**.

допуще́ни|е (-я) *ср (см глаг)* admittance; assumption.

допущу́ *сов см* **допусти́ть**.

допью́ *итп сов см* **допи́ть**.

дорабо́та|ть (-ю; *impf* **дораба́тывать)** *сов неперех:* **~ до** +*gen* to work until ◆ *перех* to finish.

дорас|ти́ (-у́, -ёшь; *pt* **доро́с, доросла́, доросло́,** *impf* **дораста́ть)** *сов неперех:* **~ до** +*gen (до потолка́)* to grow to; *(до како́го-н во́зраста)* to reach; **он доро́с до дире́ктора** he rose to become a director.

дорва́|ться (-у́сь, -ёшься; *pt* **-а́лся, -ала́сь, -ало́сь,** *impf* **дорыва́ться)** *сов неперех:* **~ до** +*gen (разг: до вла́сти)* to grab; *(: до еды́)* to fall (up)on.

дореволюцио́нный *прил* pre-revolutionary.

доро́г|а (-и) *ж* way; *(путь сообще́ния)* road; **по ~е** on the way; **мне с тобо́й** *или* **нам по ~е** we're going the same way; **сбива́ться (сби́ться** *perf)* **с ~и** *(также перен)* to lose one's way; **желе́зная ~** railway *(BRIT)*, railroad *(US)*.

до́рого *нареч (купи́ть, прода́ть)* at a high price

◆ *как сказ* it's expensive; **заплати́ть** *(perf)* **~ за что-н** *(перен)* to pay dearly for sth; **~ бы дал** *или* **заплати́л I** *итп* would give anything; **э́то ~ сто́ит** it's expensive.

дорогови́зн|а (-ы) *ж* high prices *мн*.

дорого́й *нареч* on the way.

доро́г|ой (-ог, -ога́, -ого) *прил (кни́га, дом)* expensive; *(цена́)* high; *(no short form; друг, мать)* dear; *(no full form;* воспомина́ния, *пода́рок)* cherished ◆ **(-ого́го;** *decl like adj)* dear, darling; **~ цено́й плати́ть (заплати́ть** *perf)* **за что-н** *(перен)* to pay dearly for sth.

дорож|а́ть (3sg **-ет,** *3pl* **-ют,** *perf* **вздорожа́ть** *или* **подорожа́ть)** *несов неперех* to rise *или* go up in price.

доро́же *сравн прил от* **дорого́й** ◆ *сравн нареч от* **до́рого**.

доро́жек *сущ см* **доро́жка**.

дорож|и́ть (-у́, -и́шь) *несов неперех:* **~** +*instr* to value.

доро́ж|ка (-ки; *gen pl* **-ек)** *ж* pathway; *(для пла́вания)* lane; *(для бе́га, на магнитофо́не)* track; *(ковёр)* runner; *(в аэропорту́)* runway.

доро́жный *прил (знак, строи́тельство)* road *опред; (костю́м, расхо́ды)* travelling *(BRIT)*, traveling *(US)*; *(су́мка)* travel; **доро́жный чек** traveller's cheque *(BRIT)*, traveler's check *(US)*.

доро́с *итп сов см* **дорасти́**.

дорыва́|ться (-юсь) *несов от* **дорва́ться**.

ДОС *ж сокр (= ди́сковая операцио́нная систе́ма)* DOS *(= disk operating system)*.

ДОСА́АФ *м сокр (= Доброво́льное о́бщество соде́йствия а́рмии, авиа́ции и фло́ту)*.

Доса́аф *м сокр* = **ДОСА́АФ**.

доса́д|а (-ы) *ж* annoyance; **с ~ы** out of annoyance; **~ берёт меня́** I am annoyed.

доса́дный (-ен, -на, -но) *прил* annoying.

доск|а́ (-и́; *nom pl* **-ки,** *gen pl* **-ок)** *ж* board; *(мра́морная)* slab; *(чугу́нная)* plate; **их нельзя́ ста́вить на одну́ до́ску** they're not in the same league; **доска́ объявле́ний** notice *(BRIT)* *или* bulletin *(US)* board.

доска|за́ть (-жу́, -жешь; *impf* **доска́зывать)** *сов перех* to finish (telling).

доскона́л|ьный (-ен, -ьна, -ьно) *прил* thorough.

дослед|ование (-я) *ср (ЮР)* further examination *или* inquiry.

досло́вно *нареч* verbatim, word for word.

досло́вный *прил* literal, word-for-word.

дослуж|и́ться (-усь, -ишься; *impf* **дослу́живаться)** *сов возв:* **~ до** +*gen* to rise to the rank of.

дослу́ша|ть (-ю; *impf* **дослу́шивать)** *сов перех* to listen to.

досма́трива|ть (-ю) *несов от* **досмотре́ть**.

досмо́тр (-а) *м:* **тамо́женный ~** customs examination.

досмотр|е́ть (-ю́, -ишь; *impf* **досма́тривать)** *сов перех* to watch the end of; *(бага́ж)* to check; **~ (perf) до** +*gen* to watch until.

досо́к *сущ см* **доска́**.

доспе́х|**и** (-ов) *мн* (*рыцаря*) armour *ед* (*BRIT*), armor *ед* (*US*); (*перен: разг*) gear *ед*.

досро́чно *нареч* early, ahead of time.

досро́чный *прил* early.

доста|**ва́ть(ся)** (-ю́(сь)) *несов от* **доста́ть(ся)**.

доста́в|**ить** (-лю, -ишь; *impf* **доставля́ть**) *сов перех* (*груз*) to deliver; (*пассажиров*) to carry, transport; (*удовольствие, возможность*) to give; (*трудности*) to cause.

доста́в|**ка** (-ки; *gen pl* -ок) *ж* delivery; **с ~кой на́ дом** ≈ recorded delivery (*BRIT*), ≈ certified mail (*US*).

доста́влю *сов см* **доста́вить**.

доставля́|ть (-ю) *несов от* **доста́вить**.

доста́вок *сущ см* **доста́вка**.

доста́ну(сь) *итп сов см* **доста́ть(ся)**.

доста́нь(те) *сов см* **доста́ть**.

доста́т|**ок** (-ка) *м*: **жить в ~ке** to be well provided for.

доста́точно *нареч*: ~ **хорошо́/подро́бно** good/detailed enough ♦ *как сказ* that's enough; ~ **де́нег/хле́ба** enough money/bread; ~ **шепта́ться/болта́ть!** that's enough whispering/chattering!; ~ **уви́деть, что́бы поня́ть** one only has to see to understand; ~ **сказа́ть, что** ... suffice it to say, that ....

доста́|ть (-ну, -нешь; *imper* **доста́нь(те)**, *impf* **достава́ть**) *сов перех* to take; (*раздобыть*) to get ♦ *неперех*: ~ **до** +*gen* to reach

▶ **доста́|ться** (*impf* **достава́ться**) *сов возв* (+*dat*; *при разделе*): **мне ~лся дом** I got the house; **мно́го забо́т ему́ ~лось** he was burdened down with a lot of worries; **мне ~лось** (*разг*) I got it in the neck.

дости́г *итп сов см* **дости́чь**.

достига́|ть (-ю) *несов от* **дости́гнуть**, **дости́чь**.

дости́гну *итп сов см* **дости́чь**.

дости́гн|**уть** (-у, -ешь) *сов см* **дости́чь**.

достиже́ни|**е** (-я) *ср* achievement; (*предела, возраста*) reaching.

достижи́м|**ый** (-, -а, -о) *прил* achievable, attainable.

дости́|**чь** (-гну, -гнешь; *pt* -г, -гла, -гло, *impf* **достига́ть**) *сов неперех* (+*gen*) to reach; (*результата, цели*) to achieve; (*положения*) to attain.

достове́р|**ный** (-ен, -на, -но) *прил* reliable; **из ~ных исто́чников** from reliable sources.

досто́ен *прил см* **досто́йный**.

досто́инств|**о** (-а) *ср* (*книги, плана*) merit; (*моральные качества*) virtue; (*уважение к себе*) dignity; (*КОММ*) value; **чу́вство со́бственного ~а** self-respect; **счита́ть** (**посчита́ть** *perf*) **что́-н ни́же своего́ ~а** to consider sth beneath one's dignity; **ба́нковский биле́т ~м в 100 рубле́й** a banknote to the value

of 100 roubles; **оце́нивать** (**оцени́ть** *perf*) **по ~у кого́-н/что́-н** to judge sb/sth on his/its merits.

досто́йно *нареч* with dignity.

досто́йный *прил* (*награда, кара*) fitting; (*челове́к*) worthy; (-ен, -йна, -йно; +*gen*): ~ **любви́/уваже́ния** worthy of love/respect.

достопримеча́тельност|**ь** (-и) *ж* sight; (*музея*) interesting exhibit; **осма́тривать** (**осмотре́ть** *perf*) ~**и** to go sightseeing.

достопримеча́тел|**ьный** (-ен, -ьна, -ьно) *прил* noteworthy.

достоя́ни|**е** (-я) *ср* property; **стать** (*perf*) *или* **сде́латься** (*perf*) ~**м наро́да** to become public property.

до́ступ (-а) *м* admittance; (*к документам итп*) access; **открыва́ть** (**откры́ть** *perf*) ~ **кому́-н куда́-нибудь** to give sb access to somewhere; **нет ~а во́здуха/кислоро́да** there is no way for air/oxygen to get in.

досту́п|**ный** (-ен, -на, -но) *прил* (*место*) accessible; (*цены*) affordable; (*объяснение, изложение*) comprehensible; (*челове́к*) approachable.

досу́г (-а) *м* leisure (time); **на ~е** in one's spare *или* free time.

до́суха *нареч*: **вы́тереть** ~ to dry.

до́сыта *нареч*: **их накорми́ли** ~ they were fed until they could eat no more.

досье́ *ср нескл* dossier, file; **заводи́ть** (**завести́** *perf*) ~ **на кого́-н** to open a file on sb.

досяга́емост|**ь** (-и) *ж*: **вне ~и** unattainable; **в преде́лах** ~**и** attainable.

досяга́ем|**ый** (-, -а, -о) *прил* (*зада́ча, цель*) attainable; (*место*) accessible.

дота́скива|**ть(ся)** (-ю(сь)) *несов от* **дотащи́ть(ся)**.

дота́ци|**я** (-и) *ж* subsidy.

дотащ|**и́ть** (-у́, -ишь; *impf* **дота́скивать**) *сов перех* to lug; **е́ле дота́скивать** (~ *perf*) **но́ги** to drag one's feet

▶ **дотащ**|**и́ться** (*impf* **дота́скиваться**) *сов возв* (*разг*): ~**ся до** +*gen* to drag o.s. to.

дотемна́ *нареч* until dark.

дотла́ *нареч*: **сгоре́ть** ~ to burn down (to the ground).

дото́ш|**ный** (-ен, -на, -но) *прил* (*разг*) meticulous.

дотро́н|**уться** (-усь, -ешься; *impf* **дотра́гиваться**) *сов возв*: ~ **до** +*gen* to touch.

дотя́н|**уть** (-у́, -ешь; *impf* **дотя́гивать**) *сов перех*: ~ **что-н до** +*gen* to extend sth as far as; **он ~у́л рабо́ту до ве́чера** he dragged the work out until the evening

▶ **дотя́н**|**уться** (*impf* **дотя́гиваться**) *сов возв*: ~**ся до** +*gen* to reach.

доучи́ться (-у́сь, -ишься; *impf* **доу́чиваться**) *сов возв* to complete one's education; ~ (*perf*) **до конца́ го́да/пя́того кла́сса** to study up until the end of the year/of fifth form.

дóхл|ый *прил* dead; (*разг: слабосильный*) wimpish.

дóх|нуть (-ну, -нешь; *pt* -, -ла, -ло, *perf* **подóхнуть**) *несов неперех* (*животное*) to die; (*разг: человек*) to snuff it.

дохн|ýть (-ý, -ёшь) *сов неперех* (*разг: человек*) to breathe; **мне ~ нéкогда** (*разг*) I don't get a moment's rest.

дохóд (-а) *м* (*предприятия*) income, revenue; (*человека*) income; **национáльный ~** the national income; **давáть** (**дать** *perf*) *или* **приносúть** (**принестú** *perf*) **~** to generate income; **извлекáть** (**извлéчь** *perf*) **~ из чегó-н** to make a profit from sth.

дохóд|ен *прил см* **дохóдный**.

дохóдить *несов от* **дойтú**.

дохóд|ный (-ен, -на, -но) *прил* profitable.

дохóдчив|ый (-, -а, -о) *прил* clear, easy to understand.

доцéнт (-а) *м* ≈ reader (*BRIT*), ≈ associate professor (*US*).

дóчек *сущ см* **дóчка**.

дóчери *итп сущ см* **дочь**.

дóчер|ний (-яя, -ее, -ее) *прил* daughter's; **~яя компáния/фúрма** subsidiary company/firm.

дóчерью *итп сущ см* **дочь**.

дóчиста *нареч* clean.

дочита|́ть (-ю; *impf* **дочúтывать**) *сов перех* to finish (reading); **~** (*perf*) **до +gen** to read until.

дóч|ка (-ки; *gen pl* -ек) *ж* daughter.

доч|ь (-ери; *см* **Table 2**) *ж* daughter.

дошёл *сов см* **дойтú**.

дошкóльник (-а) *м* preschool child.

дошкóльниц|а (-ы) *ж см* **дошкóльник**.

дошкóльный *прил* preschool.

дошлá *сов см* **дойтú**.

дощáтый *прил* made of boards.

доя́р|ка (-ки; *gen pl* -ок) *ж* milkmaid.

ДПР *ж сокр* = **Демократúческая пáртия Россúи**.

др. *сокр* = **другóй, другúе**.

драгоцéнность (-и) *ж* jewel; (*перен*) gem, treasure.

драгоцéнный *прил* (*камень, металл*) precious; (*время, сведения, мех*) valuable.

дражé *ср нескл* dragée.

дразн|úть (-ю́, -ишь) *несов перех* to tease; (*аппетит, воображение*) to stimulate.

дра|́ить (-ю, -ишь; *perf* **надрáить**) *несов перех* to scrub.

дра́к|а (-и) *ж* fight; (*битва*) battle; **лезть** (**полéзть** *perf*) *или* **ввя́зываться** (**ввязáться** *perf*) **в ~у** to get into a fight.

дракóн (-а) *м* dragon; (*ЗООЛ*) draco *или* flying lizard.

дракóновск|ий (-ая, -ое, -ие) *прил*: **~ие мéры** Draconian measures.

дра́м|а (-ы) *ж* drama; (*событие*) crisis; **переживáть** (**пережúть** *perf*) **тяжёлую ~у** to go through a crisis.

драматизúр|овать (-ую) (*не*)*сов перех* to dramatize.

драматúческ|ий (-ая, -ое, -ие) *прил* dramatic; (*актёр*) stage *опред*; **драматúческий кружóк** drama group; **драматúческий теáтр** theatre, theater (*US*).

драматýрг (-а) *м* playwright.

драматургú|я (-и) *ж* drama ♦ *собир* plays.

драмкружóк (-кá) *м сокр* (= **драматúческий кружóк**) drama group.

дрáный *прил* (*разг*) ragged.

драп (-а) *м* thick woollen cloth.

драпир|овать (-ую; *perf* **задрапировáть**) *несов перех*: **~ (чем-н)** to drape (with sth).

драпирóв|ка (-ки; *gen pl* -ок) *ж* drapery.

драть (**дерý, дерёшь**; *perf* **раздрáть**) *несов перех* (*бумагу, одéжду*) to tear *или* rip up; (*perf* **задрáть**; *подлеж: волк, лиса*) to tear to pieces; (*perf* **вы́драть**; *разг: побить*) to thrash; (*perf* **содрáть**; *кору, обои*) to strip; **~ (содрáть** *perf*) **шкýру с живóтного** to skin an animal; **~ (содрáть** *perf*) **дéньги с когó-н** (*разг*) to rip sb off; **он с меня́ шкýру сдерёт** (*разг*) he'll have my guts for garters; **~ (*impf*) гóрло** (*разг*) to bawl

▶ **дрáться** *несов возв*: **дрáться (с +instr)** to fight (with); (*perf* **подрáться**; *дети*) to fight.

дребедéн|ь (-и) *ж* (*разг*) rubbish.

дребезг (-а) *м*: **разбúться с ~ом** to shatter; **разбивáть** (**разбúть** *perf*) **в мéлкие ~и** to smash to smithereens.

дребезж|áть (*3sg* -úт, *3pl* -áт) *несов неперех* to jingle.

древесúн|а (-ы) *ж собир* wood.

древéсный *прил* wood; **древéсные порóды** species of tree; **древéсный ýголь** charcoal.

древк|о (-а) *ср* (*копья*) shaft; **~ флáга** flagpole.

дрéвн|ий (-яя, -ее, -ие) *прил* ancient; **дрéвняя истóрия** ancient history.

дрéвность (-и) *ж* antiquity.

дрезúн|а (-ы) *ж* trolley (*BRIT*), handcar (*US*).

дрейф (-а) *м* drift; **снимáться** (**сня́ться** *perf*) **с дрéйфа** to regain course; **лежáть** (*impf*) **в дрéйфе** to heave to.

дрейф|овáть (-ýю) *несов неперех* to drift.

дрель (-и) *ж* drill.

дрем|áть (-лю́, -лешь) *несов неперех* to doze; **враг не дрéмлет** (*перен*) the enemy never sleeps.

дремóт|а (-ы) *ж* drowsiness.

дремýч|ий (-ая, -ее, -ие; -, -а, -е) *прил* dense; (*перен: невежда*) absolute.

дренáж (-á) *м* (*почвы*) drainage; (*раны*) draining.

дрессир|овáть (-ýю; *perf* **вы́дрессировать**) *несов перех* to train.

дрóбен *прил см* **дрóбный**.

дроб|úть (-лю́, -úшь; *perf* **раздробúть**) *несов перех* (*камень, кость*) to crush; (*силы, отряд*) to divide.

дроблёный *прил* (*орехи*) crushed.

дрóб|ный (-ен, -на, -но) *прил* (*перечень,*

список) itemized; *(стук, шаг)* staccato; *(no short form*; *МАТ)* fractional.

дроб|ь (-и; *gen pl* **-éй**) *ж* fraction; *(дождя, шагов)* patter; *(барабана)* beat.

дров|á (-; *dat pl* **-áм**) *мн* firewood *ед*; **он наломáл ~!** *(перен: разг)* he made a hash of it!; **кто в лес, кто по ~** at sixes and sevens.

дро́гн|уть (-у, -ешь) *сов неперех (стёкла, руки, голос)* to shake, tremble; *(лицо)* to quiver; *(свет, огонь)* to flicker; *(человек)* to waver; **у меня́ рука́ не ~ет** +*infin* ... I won't hesitate to ....

дрожáни|е (-я) *ср (стёкол)* vibration; *(колён, голоса)* trembling; *(лица)* quivering; *(света, огня)* flickering.

дрожá|ть (-ý, -и́шь) *несов неперех (стёкла)* to vibrate; *(руки, голос)* to shake, tremble; *(лицо)* to quiver; *(свет, огонь)* to flicker; **~** *(impf)* **за** +*acc или* **над** +*instr (разг)* to fuss over; **~** *(impf)* **над (кáждой) копéйкой** to grudge every penny; **~** *(impf)* **пéред кем-н** to tremble before sb.

дро́жж|и (-éй) *мн* yeast *ед*.

дрожь (-и) *ж (от холода)* shiver; *(от страха)* shudder; **егó бросáет в ~** he is shuddering.

дрозд (-á) *м* thrush; **чёрный ~** blackbird.

дру|г (-га; *nom pl* **-зья́**, *gen pl* **-зéй**) *м* friend; *(разг: обращение)* mate; **~ дру́га** one another, each other; **~ дру́гу** *(говорить)* to one another *или* each other; **~ за дру́гом** one after another; **~ о дру́ге** *(говорить)* about one another *или* each other.

други́е (-их; *decl like adj*) *мн* others *мн*.

друг|о́й *прил (иной)* another; *(второй)* the other; *(не такой, как этот)* different ◆ *(-óго; decl like adj)* *м (кто-то иной)* another (person); *(второй)* the other (one); **~óе мнéние** different opinion; **в ~ раз** another time; **и тот и ~** both; **чтó-то ~óе** something else; **~и́ми словáми** in other words; **на ~ день** the next day; **э́то ~óе дéло** that's a different matter; *см также* **други́е**.

дру́жб|а (-ы) *ж* friendship.

дружелю́би|е (-я) *ср* friendliness.

дружелю́б|ный (-ен, -на, -но) *прил* friendly, amicable.

дру́жен *прил см* **дру́жный**.

дру́жески *нареч* in a friendly manner, amicably.

дру́жеск|ий (-ая, -ое, -ие) *прил* friendly.

дру́жествен|ный (-ен, -на, -но) *прил* friendly.

дружи́н|а (-ы) *ж (ИСТ, ВОЕН)* host.

дружи́|ть (-ý, -ишь) *несов неперех*: **~ с** +*instr* to be friends with

▶ **дружи́ться** *(perf* **подружи́ться)** *несов возв*: **~ся с** +*instr* to make friends with.

дружи́щ|е (-а) *м (разг)* mate.

дру́жн|ый (-ен, -нá, -но) *прил (семья, коллектив)* close-knit; *(аппплодисменты, смех)* general; *(усилия)* concerted.

друж|óк (-кá) *м (друг)* friend; *(разг: пренебр)* crony; *(обращение)* love.

друзья́ *итп сущ см* **друг**.

дры́га|ть (-ю) *несов неперех*: **~ нога́ми** to kick.

дры́хн|уть (-у, -ешь) *несов неперех (разг)* to kip, sleep.

дря́бл|ый (-, -á, -о) *прил (кожа)* sagging; *(человек, тело)* flabby.

дря́зг|и (-) *мн (разг)* squabbles *мн*.

дрянн|óй *прил (разг: товар, работа)* trashy; *(: характер)* rotten.

дрян|ь (-и) *ж (разг)* rubbish *(BRIT)*, trash *(US)*.

дряхлé|ть (-ю; *perf* **одряхлéть**) *несов неперех* to become infirm.

дря́хл|ый (-, -á, -о) *прил (человек)* infirm; *(здание)* dilapidated, decrepit.

ДСО *ср сокр* (= **доброво́льное спорти́вное о́бщество**) amateur sports association.

ДТП *сокр* (= **доро́жно-тра́нспортное происше́ствие**) RTA (= *road traffic accident*).

дуб (-а; *loc sg* **-ý**, *nom pl* **-ы́**) *м (БОТ)* oak (tree); *(древесина)* oak; *(перен: разг)* blockhead.

дуби́н|а (-ы) *ж* club ◆ *м/ж (разг)* blockhead.

дуби́н|ка (-ки; *gen pl* **-ок**) *ж* cudgel; **рези́новая ~** truncheon.

дуб|и́ть (-лю́, -ишь; *perf* **вы́дубить**) *несов перех* to tan.

дублён|ка (-ки; *gen pl* **-ок**) *ж* sheepskin coat.

дублёный *прил (мех)* tanned.

дублёр (-а) *м* backup; *(ТЕАТР)* understudy; *(КИНО)* double.

дубликáт (-а) *м* duplicate.

Ду́блин (-а) *м* Dublin.

дубли́р|овать (-ую) *несов перех (деятельность)* to duplicate; *(ТЕАТР)* to understudy; *(КИНО)* to dub; *(КОМП)* to back up.

дубл|ь (-я) *м (КИНО)* take.

дубо́вый *прил* oak; *(перен: стиль, язык)* ponderous.

дуг|á (-и́; *nom pl* **-и**) *ж (ГЕОМ)* arc.

дудé|ть (*2sg* **-и́шь**, *3sg* **-и́т**) *несов неперех* to play the pipe.

ду́д|ка (-ки; *gen pl* **-ок**) *ж (МУЗ)* pipe; **пляса́ть** *(impf)* **под чью-н ~ку** *(перен)* to dance to sb's tune.

ду́ж|ка (-ки; *gen pl* **-ек**) *ж (серёг)* hoop; *(ведра)* handle.

ду́л|о (-а) *ср (отверстие ствола)* muzzle; *(сам ствол)* barrel.

ду́м|а (-ы) *ж (размышление)* meditation, thought; **Д~** *(ПОЛИТ)* the Duma *(lower house of the Russian parliament)*; **Госуда́рственная Д~** the State Duma.

ду́ма|ть (-ю) *несов неперех*: **~ (о чём-н)** to think (about sth); **~** *(impf)* **над чем-н** to think sth over; **он ~ет маши́ну** he is thinking of buying a car; **я ~ю, что да/нет** I think/don't think so; **и не ~йте!** *(разг)* don't even think of it!

▶ **ду́маться** *(perf* **поду́маться)** *несов безл* (+*dat*) to seem; **мне ~ется, он прав** I think he's right.

Дуна́|**й** (**-я**) *м* Danube.
дунове́ни|**е** (**-я**) *ср* breath.
ду́н|**уть** (**-у, -ешь**) *сов непepex* to blow.
дупл|**о́** (**-а́;** *nom pl* **-ла,** *gen pl* **-ел**) *ср (дерева)*
hollow; *(зуба)* cavity.
ду́р|**а** (**-ы**) *ж (разг)* fool, idiot.
дура́к (**-а́**) *м (разг)* fool, idiot; **игра́ть** *(impf)* **в**
дурака́ to play "durak" *(Russian card game);* **он**
не ~ вы́пить/пое́сть *(разг)* he loves his drink/
food; **дурака́ валя́ть** *(impf) (разг: дура́читься)*
to clown about, play the fool; (: *безде́льничать)*
to lounge about; **остава́ться (оста́ться** *perf)* **в**
дурака́х *(перен: разг)* to be made a fool of.
дура́цк|**ий** (**-ая, -ое, -ие**) *прил (разг)* stupid,
idiotic.
дура́честв|**о** (**-а**) *ср* stupidity, idiocy.
дура́ч|**ить** (**-у, -ишь;** *perf* **одура́чить**) *несов*
перех (разг) to con
▶ **дура́читься** *несов возв (разг)* to play the fool.
дурачьё (**-я́**) *ср собир (разг)* bunch of idiots.
дурён *сущ см* **дурно́й**.
ду́р|**ень** (**-ня**) *м (разг)* dimwit, fool.
дуре́|**ть** (**-ю;** *perf* **одуре́ть**) *несов непepex (разг):*
~ от +*gen* to grow stupid from.
ду́р|**ий** (**-ья, -ье, -ьи**) *прил:* **~ья голова́** *или*
башка́ *(разг)* dope, fool.
дур|**и́ть** (**-ю́, -и́шь**) *несов непepex (разг:*
челове́к) to fool around; *(живо́тное)* to be
stubborn; **~ (задури́ть** *perf)* **го́лову кому́-н**
(разг) to mix sb up.
дурма́н (**-а**) *м* thorn apple, jimson weed (*US*);
(опьяняю́ще сре́дство) intoxicant; (: *перен)*
drug.
дурма́н|**ить** (**-ю, -ишь;** *perf* **одурма́нить**) *несов*
перех to intoxicate.
дурне́|**ть** (**-ю;** *perf* **подурне́ть**) *несов непepex* to
lose one's looks.
ду́рно *нареч (па́хнуть, вы́глядеть)* bad; *(вести́*
себя́) badly ♦ *как сказ:* **мне** ~ I don't feel well;
ему́ сде́лалось ~ he felt faint.
дур|**но́й** (**-ён, -на́, -но**) *прил* nasty; *(пита́ние)*
bad; **она́ ~на́ собо́й** she is very plain; **дурно́й**
при́знак bad omen.
дурнот|**а́** (**-ы́**) *ж* faintness.
ду́рня *итп сущ см* **ду́рень**.
ду́роч|**ка** (**-ки;** *gen pl* **-ек**) *ж (разг)* silly girl.
дуршла́г (**-а**) *м* colander.
дур|**ь** (**-и**) *ж (разг)* rubbish, nonsense; **вы́брось**
э́ту ~ из головы́! *(разг)* get that foolish idea
out of your head!; **ду́рью ма́яться** *(impf) или*
му́читься *(impf) (разг)* to muck around.
ду́тый *прил* hollow; *(перен)* exaggerated,
inflated.
ду́|**ть** (**-ю, -ешь**) *несов непepex* to blow ♦ *(perf*
вы́дуть) *перех* to blow; **здесь ду́ет** it's
draughty (*BRIT*) *или* drafty (*US*) in here.
дух (**-а;** *part gen* **-у**) *м* spirit; *(разг):* **перевести́** ~
to get one's breath back; **в ду́хе** +*gen* in the spirit
of; **па́дать** *(impf)* **ду́хом** to lose heart; **быть**
(impf) **в ду́хе/не в ду́хе** to be in high/low spirits;

сохраня́ть (сохрани́ть *perf)* **прису́тствие ду́ха**
to retain one's presence of mind; **у меня́ не**
хва́тит ду́ху на э́то *(разг)* I don't have the heart
to do this; **во весь** ~ *(разг)* at full *или* top
speed; **чтоб ду́ху твоего́ здесь не́ было!**
(разг) get out of my sight!
дух|**и́** (**-о́в**) *мн* perfume *ед*, scent *ед*.
духове́нств|**о** (**-а**) *ср собир* clergy;
(правосла́вное, католи́ческое) priesthood.
духо́вк|**а** (**-и**) *ж* oven.
духо́вник (**-а**) *м* confessor.
духо́вность (**-и**) *ж* spirituality.
духо́вный *прил (интере́сы, запро́сы)* spiritual;
(си́ла, мир, жизнь) inner; *(му́зыка)* sacred,
church *опред;* **духо́вная акаде́мия** seminary;
духо́вное зва́ние ecclesiastical rank; **духо́вное**
лицо́ ecclesiastic, cleric; **духо́вный сан** holy
orders *мн*.
духово́й *прил (муз)* wind *опред*.
духот|**а́** (**-ы́**) *ж* stuffiness; *(жара́)* closeness.
душ (**-а**) *м* shower; **принима́ть (приня́ть** *perf)* ~
to have *или* take a shower.
душ|**а́** (**-и́;** *nom pl* **-и**) *ж* soul; *(ист: крестья́нин)*
serf; **до́брая** ~ kind heart; **ни́зкая/по́длая** ~
mean/ignoble spirit; ~ **моя́** my dear; **рабо́тать**
(impf) **с ~о́й** to put one's heart into one's work; **в**
~**е́** at heart; **на ду́шу (населе́ния)** per head (of
the population); **он в ней ~й не ча́ет** she's the
apple of his eye; **быть** *(impf)* ~**о́й** +*gen*
(о́бщества, де́ла) to be the life and soul of; **не**
име́ть *(impf)* **гроша́ за ~о́й** to be without a
penny to one's name; **говори́ть** *(impf)/*
бесе́довать *(impf)* **по ~м** to have a heart-to-
heart talk/chat; **отводи́ть (отвести́** *perf)* **ду́шу** to
pour out one's heart; **как Бог на́ ~у поло́жит**
(разг) any old way; **у меня́ ~ в пя́тки ушла́**
(разг) I was scared to death; **от всей ~й** from
the bottom of one's heart; **в глубине́ ~й** in
one's heart of hearts.
Душанбе́ *м нескл* Dushanbe.
душевнобольн|**а́я** (**-о́й;** *decl like adj) ж см*
душевнобольно́й.
душевнобольн|**о́й** (**-о́го;** *decl like adj) м*
mentally-ill person.
душе́вн|**ый** *прил (си́лы, подъём)* inner;
(разгово́р) sincere, heartfelt; *(челове́к)* kindly;
~**ое потрясе́ние** shock.
душегре́йк|**а** (**-и;** *разг) ж* body warmer.
душегу́б (**-а**) *ж (разг)* butcher.
душегу́б|**ка** (**-ки;** *gen pl* **-ок**) *ж см* **душегу́б;**
(автомаши́на) mobile gas chamber.
ду́шен *сущ см* **ду́шный**.
душераздира́ющий (**-ая, -ее, -ие;** **-, -а, -е**)
прил (крик) bloodcurdling; *(плач)* heart-rending.
души́стый *прил (цвето́к)* fragrant; *(мы́ло)*
perfumed.
души́тель (**-я**) *м (перен)* suppressor.
душ|**и́ть** (**-у́, -ишь;** *perf* **задуши́ть** *или* **удуши́ть**)
несов перех to strangle; *(свобо́ду, прогре́сс)* to
stifle, suppress; *(perf* **надуши́ть;** *плато́к)* to
scent; **его́ ду́шит смех** he is choking with

laughter; ~ *(impf)* **в объятиях кого́-н** to smother sb in one's embrace.

душ́ица (-ы) *ж* marjoram.

д́ушно *как сказ* it's stuffy *или* close; **в ко́мнате** ~ the room is very stuffy; **мне ~, откро́йте окно́** I find it very stuffy *или* close, open the window.

д́уш|ный (-ен, -на́, -но) *прил* stuffy; *(жаркий)* sultry.

ду́эл|ь (-и) *ж* duel; **вызыва́ть (вы́звать** *perf)* **кого́-н на ~** to challenge sb to a duel.

ду́эт (-а) *м (произведение)* duet, duo; *(исполнители)* duo.

д́ыбом *нареч:* **встава́ть ~** *(волосы, шерсть)* to stand on end.

дыб́ы (-о́в) *мн:* **на ~ станови́ться** *(лошадь)* to rear up; *(перен: разг)* to kick up a fuss.

дым (-а; *part gen* **-у,** *loc sg* **-у́,** *nom pl* **-ы́)** *м* smoke; **поруга́ться** *(perf)* **в ~** to fall out completely.

дым́ить (-лю́, -ишь; *perf* **надыми́ть)** *несов неперех (печь, дрова)* to smoulder *(BRIT),* smolder *(US); (разг):* ~ *+instr* to puff on

▸ **дым́иться** *несов возв (труба)* to be smoking.

дым́ка (-и) *ж* haze.

д́ымно *как сказ;* **(здесь)** ~ it's smoky (in here).

д́ымный *прил (дрова, головешка)* smouldering *(BRIT),* smoldering *(US); (комната, помещение)* smoky, smoke-filled.

дымохо́д (-а) *м* flue.

д́ымчатый *прил (кот)* smoky; **ды́мчатые очки́** tinted glasses.

д́ын|я (-и) *ж* melon.

дыр́а́ (-ы́; *nom pl* **-ы)** *ж* hole; **в дыра́х** full of holes.

д́ыр|ка (-ки; *gen pl* **-ок)** *ж* hole.

дыроко́л (-а) *м* punch.

дыр́яв|ый (-, -а, -о) *прил (разг)* holey; **у него́ ~ая голова́** *(разг)* he has a head like a sieve.

дых́ани|е (-я) *ср* breathing, respiration; **~ весны́** a breath of spring; **с затае́нным ~м** with bated breath; **второ́е ~** second wind; **иску́сственное ~** artificial respiration.

дых́ательный *прил (упражнения)* breathing *опред; (процесс)* respiratory; **дыха́тельное го́рло** windpipe; **дыха́тельные пути́** respiratory tract *ед.*

дыш́ать (-у́, -ишь) *несов неперех* to breathe; ~ *(impf) +instr (ненавистью)* to exude; *(любовью)* to radiate

▸ **дыш́аться** *несов возв (+dat):* **мне здесь ле́гче ды́шится** I can breathe more easily here.

дья́вол (-а) *м* devil; **за каки́м ~ом я до́лжен идти́ туда́!** *(разг)* why the devil should I go there!; **како́го ~а ...!** what the devil ...!

дьяв́ольск|ий (-ая, -ое, -ие) *прил* diabolic(al); *(разг: холод)* devilish; **~ое терпе́ние** ≈ the patience of Job.

дья́кон (-а) *м* deacon.

дюж́ин|а (-ы) *ж* dozen; **чёртова ~** baker's dozen.

дюйм (-а) *м* inch.

дю́н|а (-ы; *gen pl* **-)** *ж (обычно мн)* dune.

дюралюм́ини|й (-я) *м* Duralumin®.

дюш́ес (-а) *м (БОТ)* Duchess pear.

дя́гил|ь (-я) *м* angelica.

дя́дь|ка (-ьки; *gen pl* **-ек)** *м* uncle; *(разг)* guy.

дя́д|я (-и) *м* uncle; *(разг)* man; *(: обращение)* mister.

дя́т|ел (-ла) *м* woodpecker.

~ E, e ~

Е, е *сущ нескл (буква)* the 6th letter of the Russian alphabet.

ЕАСТ *ж сокр (= Европейская ассоциация свободной торговли)* EFTA (= *European Free Trade Association*).

ЕБРР *м сокр (= Европейский банк реконструкции и развития)* EBRD (= *European Bank for Reconstruction and Development*).

евангелие (-я) *ср* the Gospels *мн*; *(одна из книг)* gospel.

евангелист (-а) *м* evangelist.

евангелический (-ая, -ое, -ие) *прил* evangelical.

евангельский (-ая, -ое, -ие) *прил*: ~ **текст** gospel.

евнух (-а) *м* eunuch.

Евразия (-и) *ж* Eurasia.

евреек *сущ см* **еврейка**.

еврей (-я) *м* Jew.

еврейка (-йки; *gen pl* -ек) *ж* Jewess.

еврейский (-ая, -ое, -ие) *прил (народ, обычаи)* Jewish; ~ **язык** Hebrew.

евроазиатский (-ая, -ое, -ие) *прил* Eurasian.

Евровидение (-я) *ср* Eurovision.

Европа (-ы) *ж* Europe.

европеец (-йца) *м* European.

европейка (-и) *ж см* **европеец**.

европейский (-ая, -ое, -ие) *прил* European; **европейский совет** Council of Europe; **европейский суд** European Court of Justice; **европейское сообщество** European Community.

европейца *итп сущ см* **европеец**.

ЕВС *ж сокр (= Европейская валютная система)* EMS (= *European Monetary System*).

ЕВФ *м сокр (= Европейский валютный фонд)* (= *European monetary fund*).

егерь (-я) *м (на охоте)* huntsman (*мн* huntsmen).

Египет (-та) *м* Egypt.

египетский (-ая, -ое, -ие) *прил* Egyptian.

Египта *итп сущ см* **Египет**.

египтянин (-ина; *nom pl* -е, *gen pl* -) *м* Egyptian.

египтянка (-ки; *gen pl* -ок) *ж см* **египтянин**.

его *мест см* **он, оно** ◆ *притяж мест (относительно мужчины итп)* his; *(относительно предмета итп)* its.

егожу *несов см* **егозить**.

егоза (-ы) *м/ж (разг)* fidget.

егозить (-жу, -зишь) *несов неперех (разг)* to fidget; ~ (*impf*) **перед** +*instr (перен)* to fawn on.

еда (-ы) *ж (пища)* food; *(процесс)*: **за ~ой, во время ~ы** at mealtimes; **мойте руки перед ~ой** wash your hands before eating.

KEYWORD

едва *нареч* 1 *(с трудом: нашёл, достал, доехал итп)* only just

2 *(только, немного)* barely, hardly; **больной едва дышит** the patient is barely *или* hardly breathing; **едва созревший плод** a barely ripe fruit

3 *(только что)* just; **ему едва исполнилось 20 лет** he has just turned 20

◆ *союз (как только)* as soon as; **едва он пришёл, начал работать** as soon as he arrived, he set to work; **едва ли** hardly; **уже поздно, едва ли он придёт** it's late, he's hardly likely to come now; **едва ли не** almost; **он едва ли не самый лучший ученик** he is almost the best pupil.

едем *итп сов см* **ехать**.

едим *несов см* **есть**.

единение (-я) *ср* unity.

единица (-ы) *ж (цифра)* one; *(изображение)* the figure 1; *(ПРОСВЕЩ)* ≈ very poor (*school mark*); *(измерения, часть целого)* unit; **денежная ~** monetary unit; **штатная ~** member of staff; *см также* **единицы**.

единицы (-) *мн* a few; **остались в живых ~** only a few people survived.

единичный (-ен, -на, -но) *прил (редкий: экземпляр)* single; *(случай)* isolated.

единоборство (-а) *ср* single combat; **вступать (вступить** *perf*) **в ~ с** +*instr* to enter into combat with.

единобрачие (-я) *ср* monogamy.

единовластен *прил см* **единовластный**.

единовластие (-я) *ср* autocracy.

единовластный (-ен, -на, -но) *прил* autocratic.

единовременный (-ен, -на, -но) *прил* one-off; **~ное пособие** one-off benefit payment.

единогласен *прил см* **единогласный**.

единогласие (-я) *ср* unanimity.

единогласно *нареч* unanimously; **принято ~** carried unanimously.

единоглá|сный (-ен, -на, -но) *прил* unanimous.
единодýши|е (-я) *ср* unanimity.
единодýшно *нареч* unanimously.
единодýшный *прил* unanimous.
единокрóвный *прил*: ~ **брат** half-brother (*with the same father*).
единолúчник (-а) *м* (*ист*) peasant smallholder; (*пренебр*) maverick.
единолúчный *прил* (*индивидуальный: власть, решение*) individual.
единомýсли|е (-я) *ср* like-mindedness.
единомýшленник (-а) *м* like-minded person; (*сообщник*) confederate.
единоначáли|е (-я) *ср* one-man rule.
единообрáз|ный (-ен, -на, -но) *прил* unified.
единорóг (-а) *м* unicorn.
единоутрóбный *прил*: ~ **брат** half-brother (*with the same mother*).
едúнственен *прил см* **едúнственный**.
едúнственно *част* (*только*) only ♦ *нареч*: ~ **прáвильный/возмóжный путь** the only correct/possible way; ~, **о чём я прошý** the only thing I ask.
едúнствен|ный (-ен, -на, -но) *прил* (the) only; ~ **в своём рóде** one of a kind; ~**ная надéжда** the only hope; **он** – ~ **ребёнок** he is an only child; **едúнственное числó** (*линг*) singular.
едúнств|о (-а) *ср* unity.
едúн|ый *прил* (*цельный*) united; (*общий*) common; (*только один*) one, single; ~**ое цéлое** a unified whole; **все до** ~**ого** to a man; **едúный** (**проездной**) **билéт** travel pass (*for use on all forms of transport*).
едúте *несов см* **есть**.
éд|кий (-кая, -кое, -кие; -ок, -кá, -ко) *прил* (*также перен*) caustic; (*запах, дым*) acrid.
éдкост|ь (-и) *ж* (*хим*) causticity; (*перен*) acerbity.
éдок *прил см* **éдкий**.
едóк (-á) *м*: **у негó в семьé пять едокóв** he has five mouths to feed.
éду *итп несов см* **éхать**.
едя́т *несов см* **есть**.
её *мест от* **онá** ♦ *притяж мест* (*относительно женщины итп*) her; (*относительно предмета итп*) its.
ёж (-á) *м* hedgehog; **морскóй** ~ sea urchin; **ежý поня́тно** (*разг*) it's as plain as the nose on your face.
ежевú|ка (-и) *ж* (*растение*) bramble; (*ягода*) blackberry; (*собир*) blackberries *мн*, brambles *мн*.
ежевúчный *прил* (*варенье, куст*) blackberry *опред*, bramble *опред*.
ежегóдник (-а) *м* annual (publication).
ежегóдно *нареч* annually.
ежегóдный *прил* annual *опред*.
ежеднéвен *прил см* **ежеднéвный**.

ежеднéвник (-а) *м* (*блокнот-дневник*) diary.
ежеднéвно *нареч* daily, every day.
ежеднéв|ный (-ен, -на, -но) *прил* daily; (*повседневный*) everyday.
ежемéсячник (-а) *м* (*периодическое издание*) monthly.
ежемéсячно *нареч* monthly.
ежемéсячный *прил* monthly *опред*.
ежеминýтен *прил см* **ежеминýтный**.
ежеминýтно *нареч* every minute; (*постоянно*) constantly.
ежеминýт|ный (-ен, -на, -но) *прил*: ~**ная провéрка** checks at one-minute intervals; (*очень частый*) constant.
еженедéльник (-а) *м* weekly.
еженедéльно *нареч* weekly.
еженедéльный *прил* weekly *опред*.
ежесекýнд|ный (-ен, -на, -но) *прил* occurring every second; (*чрезвычайно частый*) incessant.
ёжик (-а) *м* hedgehog; (*причёска*) crew cut; **стрúчься (постричься** *perf*) ~**ом** to have a crew cut.
ёж|иться (-усь, -ишься; *perf* **съёжиться**) *несов возв*: ~ **от** +*gen* (*от холода*) to huddle up from; (*от страха, от стыда*) to cringe with.
ёжовый *прил*: **держáть когó-н в ёжовых рукавúцах** to rule sb with a rod of iron.
ездá (-ы́) *ж* (*перемещение: на велосипеде, верхом*) riding; (: *на машине*) driving; (*мера: на машине*) drive; **в двадцатú минýтах** ~**ы́ от** +*gen* a twenty-minute drive from.
éз|дить (-жу, -дишь) *несов неперех* to go; ~ (*impf*) **на** +*prp* (*на лошади, на велосипеде*) to ride; (*на поезде, на автобусе итп*) to travel *или* go by; (*разг: эксплуатировать*) to make use of.
ездовóй *прил*: **ездовáя собáка** sled dog; **ездовáя лóшадь** draught horse.
ездóк (-á) *м* rider; **тудá я бóльше не** ~ I'm not going there again.
éзжу *несов см* **éздить**.
ей *мест см* **онá**.
ей-бóгу *межд* (*разг*) really, truly.
ЕКА *ср сокр* (= *Европéйское космúческое агéнство*) ESA (= *European Space Agency*).
Екатеринбýрг (-а) *м* Ekaterinburg.
ёка|ть (*3sg* -**ет**, *3pl* -**ют**, *perf* **ёкнуть**) *несов неперех* (*сердце*) to miss a beat.
ёкн|уть (*3sg* -**ет**, *3pl* -**ут**) *сов от* **ёкать**.
ел *итп несов см* **есть**.
éле *нареч* (*с трудом*) only just; (*едва*) barely, hardly.
éле-éле *нареч*: **он** ~ **спáсся** he had a narrow escape; **лóшадь** ~ **плетётся** the horse is on its last legs.
елéй|ный (-ен, -йна, -йно) *прил* (*перен: слащавый*) unctuous.
ёл|ка (-ки; *gen pl* -**ок**) *ж* fir (tree); (*бот*) spruce; (*праздник*) New Year party for children;

(рожде́ственская *или* новогодняя) ~ ≈ Christmas tree.

ело́в|ый *прил* fir; (*бот*) spruce.

ёлок *сущ см* **ёлка**.

ёлочн|ый *прил*: ~ые украше́ния *или* игру́шки Christmas-tree decorations *мн*.

ел|ь (-и) *ж* fir (tree); (*бот*) spruce.

е́льник (-а) *м* (*лес*) fir grove; (*плантация*) fir plantation; (*ветки*) fir branches *мн*.

ем *несов см* **есть**.

ёмк|ий (-кая, -кое, -кие; -ок, -ка, -ко) *прил* (*вместительный*) capacious; (*перен*: *содержательный*) meaningful.

ёмкост|ь (-и) *ж* (*вместимость*) capacity; (*вместилище*) container; **ме́ры** ~и units of volume.

ёмок *прил см* **ёмкий**.

ему́ *мест см* **он**, **оно́**.

ено́т (-а) *м* raccoon.

ено́товый *прил* raccoon.

епа́рхи|я (-и) *ж* diocese; (*в правосла́вной церкви*) eparchy.

епи́скоп (-а) *м* bishop.

ерала́ш (-а) *м* (*разг*: *беспорядок*) mess.

Ерева́н (-а) *м* Yerevan.

е́рес|ь (-и) *ж* heresy; (*перен*) nonsense.

ерети́к (-а́) *м* heretic.

ерети́ческ|ий (-ая, -ое, -ие) *прил* heretical.

ёрза|ть (-ю) *несов неперех* (*разг*: *беспокойно сиде́ть*) to fidget.

еро́ш|ить (-у, -ишь; *perf* взъеро́шить) *несов перех* (*волосы*: *разг*) to ruffle.

ерунд|а́ (-ы́) *ж* (*разг*: *чепуха*) rubbish, nonsense; э́то ~ (*пустяк*) it's a mere trifle, it's nothing.

ёрш (-а́) *м* (*рыба*) ruff(e); (*щётка*) brush.

ерш|и́ться (-у́сь, -и́шься) *несов возв* (*о волосах*) to stick up; (*разг*: *горячиться*) to fly off the handle.

ЕС *ср сокр* (= Европе́йское соо́бщество *или* сою́з) EC (= *European Community*) ♦ *м сокр* (= Европе́йский сове́т) Council of Europe.

есау́л (-а) *м* esaul (*rank equivalent to captain in Cossack army*).

KEYWORD

е́сли *союз* **1** (*в том случае когда*) if; **е́сли она́ придёт, дай ей э́то письмо́** if she comes, give her this letter; **е́сли ..., то ...** (*если*) if ..., then ...; **е́сли он опозда́ет, то иди́ оди́н** if he is late, (then) go alone

2 (*об усло́вном де́йствии*): **е́сли бы(, то/тогда́)** if; **е́сли бы я мог, (то) помо́г бы тебе́** if I could, I would help you

3 (*выража́ет си́льное жела́ние*): **(ах** *или* **о) е́сли бы** if only; **ах е́сли бы он позвони́л!** oh, if only he would phone (*брит*) *или* call (*us*)!

4 (*выража́ет противопоставле́ние*) if; **е́сли с ма́мой я ча́сто спо́рю, то с отцо́м мне легко́** if I argue with Mum, I get on all the better with Dad; **е́сли не ..., то ...** if not ..., then ...; **е́сли не ка́ждый день, то ча́сто** often, if not every day; **е́сли уж на то пошло́** if it comes to it; **е́сли**

хоти́те *или* **уго́дно** (*возмо́жно*) perhaps; **что е́сли...?** (*а вдруг*) what if...?

ест *несов см* **есть**.

есте́ственен *прил см* **есте́ственный**.

есте́ственно *нареч* naturally ♦ *вводн сл* (*коне́чно*) of course.

есте́ственност|ь (-и) *ж* (*норма́льность*) naturalness; (*непринуждённость*) spontaneity.

есте́ственн|ый (-ен, -на, -но) *прил* natural; ~ые нау́ки natural sciences; ~ая смерть death from natural causes.

естествозна́ни|е (-я) *ср* natural sciences *мн*.

естествоиспыта́тел|ь (-я) *м* (natural) scientist.

есть (*см* **Table 15**; *perf* пое́сть *или* съесть) *несов перех* (*пита́ться*) to eat; (*perf* съесть; *разруша́ть хими́чески*: *мета́лл*) to corrode; (*no perf*; *раздража́ть*) to sting, irritate; **мне хо́чется** ~ I'm hungry; ~ (*impf*) **кого́-н глаза́ми** (*разг*) to gaze at sb.

есть *несов* (*оди́н предме́т*) there is; (*мно́го предме́тов*) there are ♦ *межд*: ~! (*воен*) yes, sir!; ~ **мно́го возмо́жностей** there are many possibilities; **на столе́** ~ **я́блоки** there are apples on the table; **у меня́** ~ **друг** I have a friend.

ЕФР *м сокр* (= Европе́йский фонд разви́тия) EDF (= *European Development Fund*).

ефре́йтор (-а) *м* (*воен*) lance corporal.

е́хать (*см* **Table 19**) *несов неперех* to go; (*поезд, автомоби́ль*: *приближа́ться*) to come; (: *дви́гаться*) to go, travel; (*разг*: *скользи́ть*) to slide; ~ (*impf*) **на** +*prp* (*на ло́шади, на велосипе́де*) to ride; ~ (*impf*) +*instr или* **на** +*prp* (*на по́езде, на авто́бусе*) to travel *или* go by.

ехи́ден *прил см* **ехи́дный**.

ехи́дн|а (-ы) *ж* echidna, spiny anteater.

ехи́дничать (-ю; *perf* съехи́дничать) *несов неперех* (*разг*: *язви́ть*) to make spiteful remarks.

ехи́дный (-ен, -на, -но) *прил* malicious, spiteful.

ехи́дств|о (-а) *ср* (*язви́тельность*) spite.

ешь *несов см* **есть**.

KEYWORD

ещё *нареч* **1** (*дополни́тельно*) more; **хочу́ ещё ко́фе** I want more coffee; **купи́ ещё 3 кни́ги** buy 3 more books; **на́до ещё порабо́тать** we must do some more work

2 (*опя́ть*: *прие́ду, позвоню́ итп*) again; **позвоню́ ещё за́втра** I'll phone again tomorrow

3 (*до сих пор*) still; **ты ещё не зна́ешь, что случи́лось?** do you still not know what happened?; **нет ещё** not yet

4 (*уже́*): **он зако́нчил рабо́ту ещё вчера́** he had already finished the work the day before; **она́ уе́хала ещё три го́да наза́д** she left as long as three years ago; **ещё студе́нтом он сде́лал ва́жное откры́тие** while still a student he made an important discovery

5 (*о наличии возможности*) still; **ещё успéю на самолёт** I can still catch the plane
6 (+*comparative*; *лучше, красивее итп*) even; **в результáте он стал ещё богáче** as a result he became even richer
♦ *част* (*усиливает выразительность*): **ещё как рассердился/испугáлся** boy, did he get angry/frightened; **дай мне книгу! какýю ещё книгу!** give me the book! what book for goodness sake!; **всё ещё** still; **они всё ещё не помирились** they still haven't made up; **ещё бы!** (*разг*) you bet!; **вот ещё!** (*разг*) not likely!; **ещё чегó!** (*разг*) not likely!

ЕЭС *ср сокр* (= *Европéйское экономúческое сообщество*) EEC (= *European Econoтic Community*).
éю *мест см* **онá**.

~ Ж, ж ~

Ж, ж *сущ нескл (буква)* the 7th letter of the Russian alphabet.

ж *союз, част см* **же**.

жаб|а (-ы) *ж (ЗООЛ)* toad.

жабо́ *ср нескл* jabot.

жа́бр|а (-ы) *ж (ЗООЛ: обычно мн)* gill; **брать (взять** *perf***) за ~ы кого-н** *(разг)* to twist sb's arm.

жа́воронок|ок (-ка) *м (ЗООЛ)* lark.

жа́ден *прил см* **жа́дный**.

жа́дин|а (-ы) *м/ж (разг: пренебр)* meanie.

жа́дничать (-ю; *perf* **пожа́дничать**) *несов неперех (разг)* to be mingy.

жа́дност|ь (-и) *ж:* ~ **(к** +*dat***)** *(к вещам, к деньгам)* greed (for); *(к жизни)* lust (for); *(к развлечениям)* desire (for); ~ **к еде́** greedy; **с ~ю (есть)** greedily; *(слушать, смотреть)* avidly.

жа́д|ный (-ен, -на́, -но) *прил* greedy; *(на работу)* eager.

жа́жд|а (-ы) *ж* thirst; ~ **зна́ний** *(перен)* thirst for knowledge; ~ +*infin* eagerness to do; **утоля́ть (утоли́ть** *perf***)** ~**у** to quench one's thirst.

жа́жд|ать (-у, -ешь) *несов неперех:* ~ +*gen (перен: мира)* to long for; ~ *(impf)* +*infin (познавать)* to long to do.

жаке́т (-а) *м* (woman's) jacket.

жал(ся) *итп несов см* **жать(ся)**.

жале́|ть (-ю; *perf* **пожале́ть**) *несов перех* to feel sorry for; *(скупиться)* to grudge ◆ *неперех:* ~ **о** +*prp* to regret; **не ~я сил** sparing no effort; ~ **(пожале́ть** *perf***), что ...** to regret that ....

жа́л|ить (-ю, -ишь; *perf* **ужа́лить**) *несов перех (подлеж: оса)* to sting; *(: змея)* to bite.

жа́лкий (-кая, -кое, -кие; -ок, -ка, -ко) *прил (вид)* pitiful, pathetic; *(одежда)* shabby; *(трус)* abject.

жа́лко *как сказ* = **жаль**.

жа́л|о (-а) *ср (пчелы)* sting; *(змеи)* forked tongue.

жа́лоб|а (-ы) *ж* complaint; **подава́ть (пода́ть** *perf***)** ~**у на кого-н** to lodge a complaint against sb.

жа́лоб|ный (-ен, -на, -но) *прил (голос, песня)* plaintive; *(лицо)* sorrowful; **жа́лобная кни́га** complaints book *(in shop, post office etc)*.

жалова́нь|е (-я) *ср* salary.

жа́л|овать (-ую) *несов перех (разг):* **колле́ги его́ не ~уют** he is not very popular with his colleagues

▶ **жа́ловаться** (*perf* **пожа́ловаться**) *несов возв:* ~**ся на** +*acc* to complain about; *(разг:*

ябедничать) to tell on.

жа́лок *прил см* **жа́лкий**.

жа́лостен *прил см* **жа́лостный**.

жа́лостлив|ый (-, -а, -о) *прил* sympathetic.

жа́лост|ный (-ен, -на, -но) *прил* mournful; ~ **фильм** tear-jerker.

жа́лост|ь (-и) *ж:* ~ **к** +*dat* sympathy for; **кака́я** ~ what a shame; **де́лать (сде́лать** *perf***) что-н из** ~**и** to do sth out of pity.

KEYWORD

жаль *как сказ* **1** (+*acc*; *о сострадании*): **(мне) жаль дру́га** I am sorry for my friend

2 (+*acc или* +*gen*; *о сожалении, о досаде*): **(мне) жаль вре́мени/де́нег** I grudge the time/money

3 (+*infin*): **жаль уезжа́ть так бы́стро** it's a pity *или* shame to leave so soon; **жаль, что ты меня́ не понима́ешь** it's a pity *или* shame you don't understand me

◆ *вводн сл (к сожалению)* unfortunately; **хоте́л пое́хать в Ло́ндон, да, жаль, нет вре́мени** I wanted to go to London, but unfortunately I didn't have time.

жанр (-а) *м (лирический)* genre; *(перен)* style.

жар (-а; *part gen* -**у**, *loc sg* -**у́**) *м (тепло)* heat; *(перен)* fervour *(BRIT)*, fervor *(US)*; *(МЕД)* fever; **его́ бро́сило в** ~ *(перен)* he broke out in a sweat.

жар|а́ (-ы́) *ж* heat.

жарго́н (-а) *м* slang; *(профессиональный)* jargon.

жа́реный *прил (на сковороде)* fried; *(в духовке)* roast.

жа́р|ить (-ю, -ишь; *perf* **зажа́рить**) *несов перех (на сковороде)* to fry; *(в духовке)* to roast

▶ **жа́риться** (*perf* **зажа́риться**) *несов возв* to fry; ~**ся** *(impf)* **на со́лнце** *(разг)* to bask in the sun.

жа́рк|а (-и) *ж* frying.

жа́р|кий (-кая, -кое, -кие; -ок, -ка́, -ко) *прил* hot; *(перен)* heated; **жа́ркие стра́ны** tropical countries.

жа́рко *нареч (спорить)* heatedly; *(целовать)* passionately ◆ *как сказ* it's hot; **мне** ~ I'm hot; **ему́ ни хо́лодно ни** ~ *(разг)* it's all the same to him.

жарко́|е (-ого; *decl like adj*) *ср* meat *(fried)*.

жа́рок *прил см* **жа́ркий**.

жаропонижа́|ющий (-ая, -ее, -ие) *прил* febrifugal.

жаропро́ч|ный (-ен, -на, -но) *прил* (*материал*) heat-resistant; (*посуда*) ovenproof.
жар-пти́ц|а (-ы) *ж* Firebird.
жа́рче *сравн прил от* **жа́ркий.**
жасми́н (-а) *м* jasmine.
жа́тв|а (-ы) *ж* harvest.
жать (**жму, жмёшь**) *несов перех* (*руку*) to shake; (*лимон, сок*) to squeeze; (**жну, жнёшь;** *perf* **сжать;** to harvest; **сапоги́ мне жмут;** my boots are pinching (my feet); **э́то пла́тье жмёт в та́лии;** this dress is too tight at the waist;
► **жа́ться; жмусь, жмёшься**) ♦ *несов возв* (*от холода*) to huddle up; (*разг: колеба́ться*) to dither; (: *скупи́ться*) to be stingy.
жва́чк|а (-ки; *gen pl* **-ек**) *ж* cud; (*разг: жева́тельная рези́нка*) chewing gum.
жгу(сь) *итп несов см* **жечь(ся).**
жгут (-а́) *м* (*из соло́мы*) rope; (**МЕД**) tourniquet.
жгу́ч|ий (-ая, -ее, -ие; -, -а, -е) *прил* (*также перен*) burning; (*моро́з*) biting; **жгу́чий брюне́т** man with jet-black hair.
ж.д. *сокр* (= **желе́зная доро́га**) R., r. (= railway), RR (*US*) (= railroad).
ж/д *сокр* = **ж.д.**
ж.-д. *сокр* = **ж.д.**
жд|ать (-у, -ёшь; *pt* -ал, -ала́, -а́ло) *несов перех* (*also* +*gen*; *письмо́, дождя́, госте́й*) to expect; (*друга, по́езда*) to wait for; (*надея́ться: награ́ды, поща́ды*) to hope for; **что нас ~ёт?** what's in store for us?; **~а́ли, что он извини́тся** they hoped that he would apologize; **вре́мя не ~ёт** there's no time to lose; **я ~у не дожду́сь кани́кул** (*разг*) I can't wait for the holidays.

же *союз* **1** (*при противопоставле́нии*) but; **я не люблю́ матема́тику, литерату́ру же обожа́ю** I don't like mathematics, but I love literature
2 (*вво́дит дополни́тельные све́дения*) and; **успе́х зави́сит от нали́чия ресу́рсов, ресу́рсов же ма́ло** success depends on the presence of resources, and the resources are insufficient
♦ *част* **1** (*ведь*): **вы́пей ещё ча́ю, хо́чешь же!** have more tea, you want some, don't you?
2 (*и́менно*): **приду́ сейча́с же** I'll come right now; **когда́ же ты уйдёшь?** when will you go then?
3 (*выража́ет схо́дство*): **тако́й же** the same; **тако́й же дом** the same (kind of) house; **в э́том же году́** this very year; **те же лю́ди** the same (kind of) people.

жева́ть (-у́ю) *несов перех* to chew.
жёг(ся) *итп несов см* **жечь(ся).**
жезл (-а) *м* baton.
жела́нен *прил см* **жела́нный.**
жела́ни|е (-я) *ср* (*про́сьба*) request; **~ +**gen/+infin** desire for/to do; **горе́ть** (*impf*) **~м** +infin to be eager to do.
жела́нн|ый (-ен, -на, -но) *прил* (*гость, весть*) welcome.
жела́телен *прил см* **жела́тельный.**
жела́тельно *как сказ*: **~ +**infin** it is desirable to do; **~, что́бы Вы пришли́** it would be preferable if you could come.
жела́тельн|ый (-ен, -ьна, -ьно) *прил* desirable.
жела́|ть (-ю; *perf* **пожела́ть**) *несов неперех* (+*gen*) to desire; **~** (**пожела́ть** *perf*) +*infin* to wish *или* want to do; **~** (**пожела́ть** *perf*) **кому́-н сча́стья/всего́ хоро́шего** to wish sb happiness/all the best; **Ва́ша рабо́та оставля́ет ~ лу́чшего** your work leaves much to be desired.
жела́ющ|ий (-его; *decl like adj*) *м* (*обы́чно мн*): **~ие пое́хать/порабо́тать** those interested in going/working; **~ие есть?** is anybody interested?
желва́к (-а́) *м* (*разг*) lump.
желе́ *ср нескл* jelly.
желе́з|а (-ы́; *nom pl* **-ы, *gen pl* **-ёз, *dat pl* **-еза́м**) *ж* gland.
железнодоро́жник (-а) *м* rail(way) *или* railroad (*US*) worker.
железнодоро́жн|ый *прил* (*вокза́л*) railway *опред* (*BRIT*), railroad *опред* (*US*); (*тра́нспорт*) rail *опред*.
желе́зн|ый *прил* (*также перен*) iron; (: *ло́гика*) cast-iron; **~ые не́рвы** nerves of steel; **желе́зная доро́га** railway (*BRIT*), railroad (*US*).
желе́з|о (-а) *ср* iron.
железобето́н (-а) *м* reinforced concrete.
жёлоб (-а; *nom pl* -а́) *м* (*водосто́чный*) gutter.
желте́|ть (-ю; *perf* **пожелте́ть**) *несов неперех* to turn yellow; (*no perf*; *видне́ться*) to show yellow.
желт|о́к (-ка́) *м* yolk.
желторо́т|ый (-, -а, -о) *прил* yellow-beaked (*of young birds*); (*разг*: *пренебр*): **он ещё ~ юне́ц** he's still wet behind the ears.
желту́х|а (-и) *ж* jaundice.
жёлт|ый (-, -а́, -о) *прил* yellow; **жёлтая пре́сса** the gutter press.
желу́д|ок (-ка) *м* (**АНАТ**) stomach; **расстро́йство ~ка** stomach upset.
желу́дочный *прил* (*боль*) stomach *опред*; (*сок*) gastric.
жёлуд|ь (-я) *м* acorn.
жёлчн|ый *прил*: **~ пузы́рь** gall bladder; (-ен, -на, -но; *перен*) bilious.
жёлч|ь (-и) *ж* (*также перен*) bile.
жема́нн|ый (-ен, -на, -но) *прил* affected.
жёмчуг (-а; *nom pl* -а́) *м* pearls *мн*; **бу́сы из ~а** pearl necklace.
жемчу́жин|а (-ы) *ж* pearl; (*перен*) treasure.
жемчу́жный *прил* pearl; (*перен*: *зу́бы*) pearly.
жен|а́ (-ы́; *nom pl* **жёны, *gen pl* **жён**) *ж* wife.
жена́т|ый (-, -ы) *прил* married (*of man*); **он**

жена́т на +prp he is married to; **они́ ~ы** they are married.

Жене́в|а (-ы) ж Geneva.

жен|и́ть (-ю́, -ишь) (не)сов перех (сына, внука): **~ (на** +prp) to marry (off) (to); (perf **пожени́ть**; разг) to marry

▸ **жени́ться** (не)сов возв: **~ся на** +prp to marry (of man); (perf **пожени́ться**; разг) to get hitched.

жени́х (-а́) м (до свадьбы) fiancé; (на свадьбе) (bride)groom.

женонави́стник (-а) м misogynist, woman-hater.

женоподо́б|ный (-ен) прил effeminate.

же́нск|ий (-ая, -ое, -ие) прил (одежда, раздевалка) women's; (логика, органы) female; **же́нская консульта́ция** ≈ gynaecological and antenatal (BRIT) или gynecological and prenatal (US) clinic; **же́нский пол** the female sex; **же́нский род** feminine gender.

же́нственный прил feminine.

же́нщин|а (-ы) ж woman.

женьше́н|ь (-я) м ginseng.

жерд|ь (-и; gen pl **-е́й)** ж pole.

жеребёнок (-ёнка; nom pl **-я́та,** gen pl **-я́т)** м foal.

жеребе́ц (-ца́) м stallion.

жереб|и́ться (3sg **-и́тся,** 3pl **-я́тся,** perf **ожереби́ться)** несов возв to foal.

жеребца́ итп сущ см **жеребе́ц**.

жеребьёв|ка (-ки; gen pl **-ок)** ж casting или drawing of lots.

жеребя́та итп сущ см **жеребёнок**.

жерл|о́ (-а́; nom pl **-а)** ср (пушки, вулкана) mouth.

жёрнов (-а; nom pl **-а́)** м millstone.

же́ртв|а (-ы) ж victim; (РЕЛ) sacrifice; **приноси́ть (принести́** perf) **кого́-н/что-н в ~у кому́-н/чему́-н** to sacrifice sb/sth for sb/sth; **челове́ческие ~ы** casualties; **пасть** (perf) **~ой чего́-н** to fall victim to sth.

же́ртв|овать (-ую, perf **поже́ртвовать)** несов неперех (+instr) to sacrifice ◆ перех to donate.

жертвоприноше́ни|е (-я) ср (РЕЛ) sacrifice; **соверша́ть (соверши́ть** perf) **~** to offer up a sacrifice.

жест (-а) м gesture; **язы́к же́стов** sign language.

жестикули́р|овать (-ую) несов неперех to gesticulate.

жёст|кий (-кая, -кое, -кие; -ок, -ка́, -ко) прил (кровать, человек) hard; (мясо) tough; (волосы) coarse; (условия) strict; **жёсткий ваго́н** railway carriage with hard seats; **жёсткая вода́** hard water; **жёсткий диск** hard disk.

жесто́к|ий (-ая, -ое, -ие; -, -а́, -о) прил cruel; (перен) severe; **~ая необходи́мость** cruel necessity.

жесто́ко нареч (расправиться) cruelly.

жесто́кост|ь (-и) ж cruelty.

жёстче сравн прил от **жёсткий**.

жест|ь (-и) ж tin-plated sheet metal.

жестя́н|ка (-ки; gen pl **-ок)** ж tin box.

жето́н (-а) м tag; (в метро) token.

жечь (жгу, жжёшь итп, **жгут;** pt **жёг, жгла, жгло,** perf **сжечь)** несов перех to burn

▸ **жёчься** несов возв (утюг) to be very hot; (крапива) to sting; (perf **обжёчься;** разг) to burn o.s.

жже́ни|е (-я) ср burning sensation.

жжёшь(ся) итп несов см **жечь(ся)**.

живи́тел|ьный (-ен, -ьна, -ьно) прил (воздух) invigorating.

жи́во нареч (представить себе) vividly; (откликнуться) animatedly.

жив|о́й (-, -а́, -о) прил alive; (no short form; организм) living; (животное) live; (человек: энергичный) lively; (выразительный) vivid; **~ приме́р** a living example; **он ~ наде́ждой/ воспомина́ниями** he lives in hope/for his memories; **он ещё ~?** is he still alive?; **жив – здоро́в** (разг) alive and well; **в нём ещё ~á оби́да** the insult still rankles with him; **ни жив ни мёртв** (разг) petrified; **задева́ть (заде́ть** perf) **кого́-н за ~о́е** to cut sb to the quick; **остава́ться** (perf) **в ~ых** to survive; **жива́я и́згородь** hedge; **живо́й уголо́к** area in school where pets are kept for pupils to look after; **живо́й язы́к** living language; **живы́е цветы́** fresh flowers.

живопи́сен прил см **живопи́сный**.

живопи́с|ец (-ца) м painter.

живопи́с|ный (-ен, -на, -но) прил picturesque.

живопи́сца итп сущ см **живопи́сец**.

жи́вопис|ь (-и) ж (искусство) painting.

живо́т (-а́) м stomach, abdomen; (разг) belly, tummy.

животново́д (-а) м farmer specializing in animal husbandry.

животново́дств|о (-а) ср animal husbandry.

живо́тн|ое (-ого; decl like adj) ср (также перен) animal.

живо́тный прил animal опред; (перен) bestial.

живу́ итп несов см **жить**.

живу́ч|ий (-ая, -ее, -ие; -, -а, -е) прил hardy; (обычай, представление) enduring; (предрассудки) deep-rooted; **он ~ как ко́шка** he has nine lives.

живьём нареч alive.

жи́д|кий (-кая, -кое, -кие) прил liquid; (-ок, -ка́, -ко; молоко, суп) watery; (состояние, мускулы, голос) weak; (волосы) sparse, thin; **жи́дкое то́пливо** liquid fuel.

жи́дкост|ь (-и) ж liquid.

жи́док прил см **жи́дкий**.

жи́ж|а (-и) ж slurry.

жи́же сравн прил от **жи́дкий**.

жизнеде́ятельност|ь (-и) ж (организма, клетки) (vital) activity.

жи́знен|ный (-, -на, -но) прил (вопрос, интересы) vital; (необходимость) basic; **~ у́ровень** standard of living; **~ о́пыт** experience;

~ **путь** journey through life.
жизнера́достн|ый (**-ен, -на, -но**) *прил* cheerful.
жизнеспосо́бн|ый (**-ен, -на, -но**) *прил* (*также перен*) viable.
жизн|ь (**-и**) *ж* life; **о́браз жи́зни** way of life; **у́ровень жи́зни** standard of living; **как ~?** (*разг*) how's life?
жи́л|а (**-ы**) *ж* (*также ГЕО*) vein; (*сухожилие*) tendon, sinew; **золота́я ~** (*перен: разг*) gold mine.
жиле́т (**-а**) *м* waistcoat (*BRIT*), vest (*US*); **спаса́тельный ~** life jacket.
жил|е́ц (**-ьца́**) *м* (*квартиросъёмщик*) tenant; (*квартирант*) lodger; **он не ~** (*разг*) he's not long for this world.
жи́листый (**-, -а, -о**) *прил* (*мясо*) stringy; (*старик*) sinewy; (*рука*) veiny.
жили́щ|е (**-а**) *ср* (*дом*) dwelling.
жили́щный *прил* housing *опред*.
жи́л|ка (**-ки**; *gen pl* **-ок**) *ж* vein; (*перен: склонность*) streak.
жило́й *прил* (*дом, зда́ние*) residential; (*ко́мната, помеще́ние*) inhabited; **жила́я пло́щадь** accommodation.
жи́лок *сущ см* **жи́лка**.
жилпло́щад|ь (**-и**) *ж сокр* = **жила́я пло́щадь**.
жиль|ё (**-я́**) *ср* (*челове́ческое*) habitation; (*жилище*) accommodation (*BRIT*), lodgings *мн*.
жильца́ *итп сущ см* **жиле́ц**.
жи́молост|ь (**-и**) *ж* honeysuckle.
жир (**-а**; *part gen* **-у**, *loc sg* **-у́**, *nom pl* **-ы́**) *м* (*живо́тный*) fat; (*расти́тельный*) oil; **с жи́ру беси́ться** (*impf*) (*разг*) to become spoilt; **ры́бий ~** (*МЕД*) cod-liver oil.
жира́ф (**-а**) *м* giraffe.
жире́н *прил см* **жи́рный**.
жире́|ть (**-ю**; *perf* **разжире́ть** *или* **ожире́ть**) *несов непе́рех* to grow fat.
жи́р|ный (**-ен, -на́, -но**) *прил* (*пища*) fatty; (*челове́к*) fat; (*no short form*; *во́лосы*) greasy; (*черно́зём, и́звесть*) rich; **жи́рный шрифт** bold type.
жирови́к (**-а́**) *м* lipoma.
жирорасчёт (**-а**) *м* Giro.
жите́йск|ий (**-ая, -ое, -ие**) *прил* (*му́дрость*) worldly; (*пробле́мы*) everyday; **де́ло ~ое!** (*разг*) that's nothing unusual!
жи́тел|ь (**-я**) *м* resident; **городско́й ~** city dweller.
жи́тельниц|а (**-ы**) *ж см* **жи́тель**.
жи́тельств|о (**-а**) *ср* residence; **ме́сто постоя́нного ~a** permanent place of residence.
жи́тниц|а (**-ы**) *ж* (*перен*) breadbasket.
жи|ть (**-ву́, -вёшь**; *pt* **-л, -ла́, -ло**) *несов непе́рех* to live; (*также перен*): ~ **в** +*prp* to live in; ~ (*impf*) +*instr* (*детьми́, нау́кой*) to live for; ~ (*impf*) **на** +*acc*/**с** +*instr* to live on/with; ~ (*impf*) **на свои́ сре́дства** to support o.s.; **~л-был** there once

was, once upon a time there was
▶ **жи́ться** *несов возв* (*разг*): **ему́ ве́село/ тоскли́во ~вётся** he's having a good/miserable time; **как Вам ~вётся?** how's life?
жмот (**-а**) *м* (*разг*) skinflint.
жму(сь) *итп несов см* **жа́ть(ся)**.
жму́р|ить (**-ю, -ишь**; *perf* **зажму́рить**) *несов непе́рех*: ~ **глаза́** to screw up one's eyes
▶ **жму́риться** (*perf* **зажму́риться**) *несов возв* to squint; **~ся** (**зажму́риться** *perf*) **от све́та** to squint in the light.
жму́р|ки (**-ок**) *мн* blind man's buff *ед*; **игра́ть** (*impf*) **в ~** to play blind man's buff.
жне́ц (**-а́**) *м* reaper.
жни́ц|а (**-ы**) *ж см* **жнец**.
жну *итп несов см* **жать**.
жоке́й (**-я**) *м* jockey.
жонглёр (**-а**) *м* juggler.
жонгли́р|овать (**-ую**) *несов непе́рех*: ~ +*instr* to juggle (with).
жо́п|а (**-ы**) *ж* (*груб!*) arse (*BRIT*) (!), ass (*US*) (!)
жр|ать (**-у, -ёшь**; *pt* **-ал, -ала́, -а́ло**, *perf* **сожра́ть**) *несов перех* (*разг*) to scoff.
жре́би|й (**-я**) *м*: **броса́ть ~** to cast lots.
жре|ц (**-а́**) *м* (*РЕЛ*) (pagan) priest; (*перен*) devotee.
жри́ц|а (**-ы**) *ж* (*РЕЛ*) (pagan) priestess.
ЖСК *м сокр* (= *жили́щно-строи́тельный кооперати́в*) *housing cooperative*.
жу́желиц|а (**-ы**) *ж* ground beetle.
жужж|а́ть (**-у́, -и́шь**) *несов непе́рех* to buzz.
жук (**-а́**) *м* beetle.
жу́лик (**-а**) *м* swindler; (*в игре́*) cheat.
жу́льнича|ть (**-ю**; *perf* **сжу́льничать**) *несов непе́рех* (*разг*) to cheat.
жу́льничеств|о (**-а**) *ср* underhandedness; (*в игре́*) cheating.
жура́вл|ь (**-я́**) *м* crane.
жур|и́ть (**-ю́, -и́шь**) *несов перех* (*разг*) to chide.
журна́л (**-а**) *м* magazine; (*судово́й*) journal; (*кла́ссный*) register; (*КИНО*) short; ~ **протоко́лов** minute book.
журнали́ст (**-а**) *м* journalist.
журнали́ст|ка (**-ки**; *gen pl* **-ок**) *ж см* **журнали́ст**.
журнали́стик|а (**-и**) *ж* journalism.
журнали́стк|а *сущ см* **журнали́стка**.
журч|а́ть (**-у́, -и́шь**) *несов непе́рех* (*руче́й итп*) to babble, murmur.
жу́тк|ий (**-ая, -ое, -ие**; **-ок, -ка́, -ко**) *прил* terrible.
жу́тко *нареч* (*неприя́тный*) terribly ◆ *как сказ*: **здесь ~** it's terrifying here; **мне ~** I am terrified.
жу́ток *прил см* **жу́ткий**.
жут|ь (**-и**) *ж* (*разг*) terror ◆ *как сказ* it's terrible; **кака́я ~!** (*разг*) how terrible!
жу́хлый *прил* faded.
ЖЭК (**-а**) *м сокр* (= *жили́щно-эксплуатацио́нная конто́ра*) ≈ housing office.
жюри́ *ср нескл* panel of judges.

~ З, з ~

З, з *сущ нескл (буква)* the 8th letter of the Russian alphabet.

з. *сокр* (= **за́пад**) W (= *West*); (= **за́падный**) W (= *West*).

KEYWORD

за *предл* (+*acc*) **1** (*out* (*of*)) **вы́йти** (*perf*) **за дверь** to go out (of) the door

2 (*позади*) behind; **спря́таться** (*perf*) **за де́рево** to hide behind a tree

3 (*около: сесть, встать*) at; **сесть** (*perf*) **за стол** to sit down at the table

4 (*свыше какого-н предела*) over; **ему́ за со́рок** he is over forty; **моро́з за два́дцать гра́дусов** over twenty degrees of frost

5 (*при указании на расстояние, на время*): **за пять киломе́тров отсю́да** five kilometres (*BRIT*) *или* kilometers (*US*) from here; **за три часа́ до нача́ла спекта́кля** three hours before the beginning of the show; **за э́ти де́сять лет он постаре́л** he has aged over the last ten years

6 (*при указании объекта действия*): **держа́ться за** +*acc* to hold onto; **ухвати́ться** (*perf*) **за** +*acc* to take hold of; **взять** (*perf*) **кого́-н за́ руку** to take sb by the hand; **взя́ться** (*perf*) **за рабо́ту** to start work

7 (*об объекте чувств*) for; **ра́доваться** (*impf*) **за сы́на** to be happy for one's son; **отвеча́ть** (*impf*) **за успе́х предприя́тия** to be responsible for the success of an enterprise; **беспоко́иться** (*impf*) **за му́жа** to worry about one's husband

8 (*о цели*) for; **сража́ться** (*impf*) **за побе́ду** to fight for victory

9 (*в пользу*) for, in favour (*BRIT*) *или* favor (*US*) of; **голосова́ть** (*impf*) **за предложе́ние** to vote for *или* in favour (*BRIT*) *или* favor (*US*) of a proposal

10 (*по причине, в обмен*) for; **благодарю́ Вас за по́мощь** thank you for your help; **плати́ть** (**заплати́ть** *perf*) **за что-н** to pay for sth; **быть** (*impf*) **нака́занным за воровство́** to be punished for stealing; **я сде́лал э́то за де́ньги** I did it for money

11 (*вместо кого-н*) for; **рабо́тать** (*impf*) **за дру́га** to fill in for a friend

♦ *предл* (+*instr*) **1** (*по другую сторону*) on the other side of; **жить** (*impf*) **за реко́й** to live on the other side of the river

2 (*вне*) outside; **жить** (*impf*) **за́ городом** to live

outside the town; **за грани́цей** abroad

3 (*позади*) behind; **стоя́ть** (*impf*) **за две́рью** to stand behind the door; **я шёл за ним** I walked behind him; **бежа́ть** (*impf/perf*) **за престу́пником** to run after a criminal

4 (*около: стоять, сидеть*) at; **сиде́ть** (*impf*) **за столо́м** to sit at the table

5 (*о смене событий*) after; **год за го́дом** year after year; **за зимо́й идёт весна́** spring comes after winter

6 (*во время чего-н*) over; **поговори́ть** (*perf*) **за за́втраком** to talk over breakfast

7 (*о объекте внимания*): **смотре́ть** *или* **уха́живать за** +*instr* to look after; **моя́ сестра́ за́мужем за врачо́м** my sister is married to a doctor

8 (*с целью получить, достать что-н*) for; **я посла́л его́ за газе́той** I sent him out for a paper; **он пошёл за врачо́м** he went to fetch the doctor

9 (*по причине*) owing to; **за отсу́тствием доказа́тельств** in the absence of proof

♦ *как сказ* (*согласен*) in favour (*BRIT*) *или* favor (*US*); **кто за?** who is in favour (*BRIT*) *или* favor (*US*)?

♦ *ср нескл* pro; **взве́сить** (*perf*) **все за и про́тив** to weigh up all the pros and cons.

за- *префикс* (*in verbs; о начале действия*) indicating beginning of an action eg. **зааплоди́ровать**; (*о доведении действия до крайней степени*) indicating taking sth to an extreme degree eg. **завра́ться**; (*образует совершенный вид*) used in the formation of some perfective aspects eg. **заасфальти́ровать**; (*in nouns and adjectives; находящийся по ту сторону чего-н*) trans-.

заале́|ть (*3sg* -**ет**, *3pl* -**ют**) *сов неперех* to turn scarlet.

заарка́н|ить (-**ю**, -**ишь**; *impf* **заарка́нивать**) *сов неперех* to lasso.

заарта́ч|иться (-**усь**, -**ишься**) *сов возв* (*разг*) to become obstinate.

заасфальти́р|овать (-**ую**) *сов от* **асфальти́ровать**.

заба́в|а (-**ы**) *ж* amusement.

заба́вен *прил см* **заба́вный**.

забавля́|ть (-**ю**) *несов перех* to amuse

▶ **забавля́ться** *несов возв* to amuse o.s.

забáвно *нареч* (*рассказывать*) in an amusing way ◆ *как сказ* it's funny.

забáв|ный (-ен, -на, -но) *прил* amusing.

забаллоти́р|овать (-ую) *сов перех* to reject.

забальзами́р|овать (-ую) *сов от* **бальзами́ровать**.

забарахл|и́ть (*3sg* -и́т, *3pl* -я́т) *сов неперех* (*разг: мотор, компьютер итп*) to go on the blink.

забаррикади́р|овать (-ую) *сов от* **баррикади́ровать**.

забаст|овáть (-ýю) *сов неперех* to go on strike.

забастóв|ка (-ки; *gen pl* -ок) *ж* strike; **всеóбщая ~** general strike; **сидя́чая ~** sit-in.

забастóвочный *прил* strike *опред*.

забастóвщик (-а) *м* striker.

забастóвщиц|а (-ы) *ж см* **забастóвщик**.

забвéни|е (-я) *ср* (*забытьё*) oblivion; **предавáть** (**предáть** *perf*) **что-н ~ю** to consign sth to oblivion.

забéг (-а) *м* (*СПОРТ*) race; **предвари́тельный ~** preliminary heat; **~ на сто мéтров** the hundred metres.

забегáть (-ю) *сов неперех* (*люди*) to start running; (*глаза*) to roam about.

забежáть (*как* **бежáть**; *см* Table 20; *impf* **забегáть**) *сов неперех*: **~ (в** +*acc*) (*в дом, в деревню*) to run in(to); (*разг: в музéй*) to drop in(to); **забегáть (~** *perf*) **к знакóмым** (*разг*) to drop in on one's friends; **забегáть (~** *perf*) **со стороны́** (*разг*) to come up from the side; **забегáть (~** *perf*) **вперёд** to run ahead; (*перен*) to race ahead.

заберéмене|ть (-ю) *сов от* **берéменеть**.

заберý(сь) *итп сов см* **забрáть(ся)**.

забеспокó|иться (-юсь, -ишься) *сов возв* to start to worry.

забетони́р|овать (-ую) *сов от* **бетони́ровать**.

забивáть(ся) (-ю(сь)) *несов от* **заби́ть(ся)**.

забинт|овáть (-ýю; *impf* **бинтовáть** *или* **забинтóвывать**) *сов перех* to bandage.

забирáть(ся) (-ю(сь)) *несов от* **забрáть(ся)**.

заби́т|ый (-, -а, -о) *прил* cowed.

заби́|ть (-ью, -ьёшь) *сов неперех* (*часы*) to begin to strike; (*орудие, пушка*) to start firing; (*озноб, лихорадка*) to begin to spread; (*вода*) to begin to flow; (*фонтан*) to start up ◆ (*impf* **забивáть**) *перех* (*гвоздь, сваю*) to drive in; (*СПОРТ: гол*) to score; (: *мяч, шар*) to drive home; (*окно, дом*) to board up; (*наполнить: склад, холодильник*) to overfill; (*засори́ть: трубу, сток*) to clog (up); (*скот, зверя*) to slaughter; (*перен: человека*) to knock flat; **~** (*perf*) **в барабáн/кóлокол** to start drumming/ringing a bell; **забивáть (~** *perf*) **гóлову чем-н** to fill one's head with sth

▶ **заби́ться** *сов возв* (*сердце, пульс*) to start beating; (*impf* **забивáться**; *спря́таться*) to hide

(away); (*засори́ться: труба, сток*) to clog up; **~ся** (*perf*) **в судорогах** to have a fit; **~ся** (*perf*) **в истéрике** to have a fit of hysterics.

заби́я|ка (-и) *м/ж* (*разг*) bully.

заблаговрéменно *нареч* in good time.

заблагорассýд|иться (*3sg* -ится) *сов безл* (*взду́маться*): **поступáйте, как Вам ~ится** act as you see fit.

забле|стéть (-щý, -сти́шь) *сов неперех* (*река, слёзы*) to glisten; (*глаза*) to light up; (*металл*) to gleam.

заблýд|ший (-ая, -ее, -ие) *прил*: **~ человéк** person who has lost his or her way; **заблýдшая овцá** (*перен*) a lost sheep.

заблужд|áться (-áюсь) *несов возв* to be mistaken.

заблуждéни|е (-я) *ср* error, delusion; **вводи́ть (ввести́** *perf*) **когó-н в ~** to delude sb; **выводи́ть (вы́вести** *perf*) **когó-н из ~я** to open sb's eyes.

заблужýсь *сов см* **заблуди́ться**.

забодá|ть (*3sg* -ет, *3pl* -ют) *сов от* **бодáть**.

забóй (-я) *м* (*ГЕО*) (working) face; (*действие: скота*) slaughtering.

забóйщик (-а) *м* face worker.

заболевáемост|ь (-и) *ж* (*по стране*) incidence (*of illness*).

заболевáни|е (-я) *ср* illness.

заболé|ть (-ю; *impf* **заболевáть**) *сов неперех*: **~** +*instr* (*ветря́нкой, гри́ппом*) to fall ill with; (*разг: компьютерами, театром итп*) to get hooked on; (*нога, горло*) to begin to hurt.

заболóченн|ый (-, -а, -о) *прил* marshy, boggy.

забóр (-а) *м* fence.

забóт|а (-ы) *ж* (*беспокойство*) worry; (*уход*) concern; (*обычно мн: хлопоты*) trouble.

забóт|ить (-чу, -тишь) *несов перех* to worry, trouble

▶ **забóтиться** (*perf* **позабóтиться**) *несов возв*: **~ся о** +*prp* to take care of.

забóтлив|ый (-, -а, -о) *прил* (*человек*) caring, thoughtful.

забóчу(сь) *несов см* **забóтить(ся)**.

забрак|овáть (-ýю; *impf* **браковáть** *или* **забракóвывать**) *сов перех* to reject.

забрáл|о (-а) *ср* (*у шлема*) visor; (*ТЕХ*) screen.

забрáсыва|ть (-ю) *несов от* **забросáть**, **забрóсить**.

заб|рáть (-ерý, -ерёшь; *pt* -рáл, -ралá, -рáло, *impf* **забирáть**) *сов перех* to take; (*разг: захвати́ть*) to nick; (*перен: подлеж: страх, тоскá*) to grip; **забирáть (~** *perf*) **впрáво/влéво** to veer off to the right/left

▶ **забрáться** (*impf* **забирáться**) *сов возв* (*спря́таться*) to hide (o.s.) away; (*разг: уéхать*) to go off; **забирáться (~ся** *perf*) **в/на**

+*acc* (*в шкаф, в дом*) to get inside *или* into; (*на дерево*) to climb up; (*в скважину*) to go down; **забира́ться** (**~ся** *perf*) **под одея́ло** to crawl under the blanket; **забира́ться** (**~ся** *perf*) **внутрь/наве́рх** to get inside/to the top.

забреда́|ть (-ю) *несов от* **забрести́**.

забреду́ *итп сов см* **забрести́**.

забре́зж|ить (*3sg* -ит) *сов непepex* (*огонь*) to flicker; (*рассвет, утро*) to break.

забр|ести́ (-еду́, -едёшь; *pt* -ёл, -ела́, -ело́, *impf* **забреда́ть**) *сов непepex* (*разг: в лес*) to saunter off; (: *в гости*) to drop in.

заброни́р|овать (-ую) *сов от* **брони́ровать**.

заброса́|ть (-ю) *несов от* **забра́сывать** *сов перех*: **~ что-н чем-н** (*канаву, яму*) to fill with; (*камнями*) to pelt with; (*цветами*) to shower with; (*перен: фактами, вопросами*) to bombard with.

забро́|сить (-шу, -сишь; *impf* **забра́сывать**) *сов перех* (*мяч, камень*) to fling; (*десант*) to drop; (*шпиона*) to plant; (*разг: доставить*) to drop off; (*не заниматься*) to neglect.

забро́шен|ный (-, -а, -о) *прил* (*дом*) derelict; (*шахта*) disused; (*вид, сад, ребёнок*) neglected.

забро́шу *сов см* **забро́сить**.

забры́зга|ть (-ю; *impf* **забры́згивать**) *сов перех* to splash.

забу́ду(сь) *итп сов см* **забы́ть(ся)**.

забыва́|ть (-ю(сь)) *несов от* **забы́ть(ся)**.

забы́вчив|ый (-, -а, -о) *прил* forgetful.

забы́ть (*как быть; см* Table 21; *impf* **забыва́ть**) *сов перех* to forget; **~удь туда́/сюда́ доро́гу!** don't go there/come here any more!; **себя́ не забыва́ть** (**~** *perf*) to look out for o.s.

▶ **забы́ться** (*impf* **забыва́ться**) *сов возв* (*задремать*) to doze off; (*в мечтах*) to lose o.s.; (*сорваться*) to forget o.s.; (*события, факты*) to be forgotten.

забытьё (-я́) *ср* (*беспамятство*) oblivion; (*полусон*) drowsiness; (*задумчивость*) pensiveness; **впа́дать** (**впасть** *perf*) **в ~** to lose consciousness; (*уснуть*) to doze off.

забью́(сь) *итп сов см* **забить(ся)**.

зав (-а) *м сокр* (*разг*: = **заве́дующий**) boss.

зав. *сокр* = **заве́дующий**.

зава́л (-а) *м* obstruction; (*искусственный*) barrier; **у нас сейча́с ~ с рабо́той** we have a backlog of work.

завал|и́ть (-ю́, -а́лишь; *impf* **зава́ливать**) *сов перех* (*вход, дверь*) to block off; (*дом, стену*) to knock down; (*разг: экзамен, мероприятие*) to mess up; **зава́ливать** (**~** *perf*) (*дорогу*) *+instr*: (*снегом*) to cover with; (*яму: землёй*) to fill with; (*разг: магазины: товарами*) to cram with; (*перен: разг: поручениями*) to saddle with

▶ **завал|и́ться** (*impf* **зава́ливаться**) *сов возв* (*упасть*) to fall; (*стена, забор*) to collapse; (*разг: дело*) to go to the wall; (: *на экзамене*) to come a cropper; **зава́ливаться** (**~ся** *perf*) **в го́сти к кому́-н** (*разг*) to turn up on sb's doorstep; (**хоть**) **~али́сь!** (*разг: очень много*)

you can't move for them!

завал|я́ться (*3sg* -ется, *3pl* -ются) *сов возв* (*разг*) to be kicking about.

завар|и́ть (-арю́, -а́ришь; *impf* **зава́ривать**) *сов перех* (*чай, кофе*) to brew; (*TEX*) to weld; **зава́ривать** (**~** *perf*) **ка́шу** (*разг*) to stir up trouble

▶ **завари́ться** (*impf* **зава́риваться**) *сов возв* (*чай, кофе*) to brew; (*разг: дело, кутерьма*) to start.

зава́р|ка (-и) *ж* (*действие*: *чая, кофе*) brewing; (*разг: сухой чай*) char; (*заваренный чай*) brew.

заварн|о́й *прил* (*кулин*): **~о́е те́сто** choux pastry; **~ крем** custard filling.

заведе́ни|е (-я) *ср* (*учреждение*) establishment; **уче́бное ~** educational establishment.

заве́д|овать (-ую) *несов непepex* (*+instr*) to be in charge of.

заве́домый *прил* (*обманщик, лжец*) notorious; (*обман, ложь*) blatant.

заведу́(сь) *итп сов см* **завести́(сь)**.

заве́дующ|ая (-ей) *ж см* **заве́дующий**.

заве́дующ|ий (-его; *decl like adj*) *м* (*складом, редакцией*) manager; (*лабораторией, кафедрой*) head.

зав|езти́ (-езу́, -езёшь; *pt* -ёз, -езла́, -езло́, *impf* **завози́ть**) *сов перех* to drop off; (*увезти*) to take.

заверб|ова́ть (-у́ю) *сов от* **вербова́ть**.

заве́ни|е (-я) *ср* assurance.

заве́ренный *прил* (*копия, подпись*) authenticated, certified.

завери́тел|ь (-я) *м* (*документа, копии*) witness, attestant.

заве́р|ить (-ю, -ишь; *impf* **заверя́ть**) *сов перех* (*копию, подпись*) to witness; **заверя́ть** (**~** *perf*) **кого́-н в чём-н** to assure sb of sth.

заверн|у́ть (-у́, -ёшь; *impf* **завёртывать** *или* **завора́чивать**) *сов перех* (*рукав*) to roll up; (*кран*) to turn off; (*гайку*) to tighten up; (*налево, направо, за угол*) to turn; (*разг: в гости, к другу*) to drop by *или* round; **завёртывать** *или* **завора́чивать** (**~** *perf*) (**в** *+acc*) (*посылку, книгу, ребёнка*) to wrap (in)

▶ **заверну́ться** (*impf* **завёртываться** *или* **завора́чиваться**) *сов возв* (*рукав*) to roll up; **завёртываться** *или* **завора́чиваться** (**~ся** *perf*) **в** *+acc* (*в полотенце, в плед*) to wrap o.s. up in.

завер|те́ть (-ерчу́, -е́ртишь) *сов непepex* (*+instr*: *верёвкой*) to twirl; (*глазами*) to roll

▶ **заверте́ться** *сов возв* (*колесо, карусель*) to start turning; (*разг: захлопотаться*) to be run off one's feet.

завёртыва|ть(ся) (-ю(сь)) *несов см* **заверну́ть(ся)**.

заверчу́(сь) *сов см* **заверте́ть(ся)**.

заверша́|ть(ся) (-ю(сь)) *несов от* **заверши́ть(ся)**.

заверша́ющ|ий (-ая, -ее, -ие) *прил* final.

заверше́ни|е (-я) *ср* (*работы*) completion;

(разговора, лекции) conclusion; **в ~** *+gen* at the conclusion of.

заверш|и́ть (-у́, -и́шь; *impf* **завершать**) *сов перех* to complete; *(разговор)* to end

▶ **завершиться** *(impf* **завершаться**) *сов возв* to be completed; *(разговор)* to end.

заверя́|ть (-ю) *несов от* **заве́рить**.

заве́с|а (-ы) *ж (перен)* veil; **дымова́я ~** *(перен)* smoke screen.

заве́|сить (-шу, -сишь; *impf* **заве́шивать**) *сов перех (окно)* to curtain; *(картину, лампу)* to cover.

заве|сти́ (-еду́, -едёшь; *pt* **-ёл, -ела́, -ело́**, *impf* **заводи́ть**) *сов перех* to take; *(увести далеко)* to lead; *(приобрести)* to get; *(установить)* to introduce; *(переписку, разговор)* to initiate; *(часы)* to wind up; *(машину)* to start; *(разг: разозлить)*: **~ кого́-н** to wind sb up

▶ **завести́сь** *(impf* **заводи́ться**) *сов возв (появиться)* to appear; *(мотор, часы)* to start working; *(разг: разозлиться)* to get (all) wound up.

заве́т (-а) *м (наставление)* precept; *(РЕЛ)*: **Ве́тхий/Но́вый ~** the Old/New Testament.

заве́т|ный (-ен, -на, -но) *прил* treasured.

заве́ша|ть (-ю; *impf* **заве́шивать**) *сов перех* to hang; **заве́шивать** *(~ perf)* **сте́ны карти́нами** to hang pictures on the walls.

заве́шива|ть (-ю) *несов от* **заве́сить, заве́шать**.

заве́шу *сов см* **заве́сить**.

завеща́ни|е (-я) *ср (документ)* will; *(наставление)* precept.

завеща́|ть (-ю) *(не)сов перех*: **~ что-н кому́-н** *(наследство)* to bequeath sth to sb; **~** *(impf/perf)* **кому́-н** *+infin* to call upon sb to do.

завзя́тый *прил (разг: курильщик)* inveterate; **он ~ футболи́ст/охо́тник** he is a football/hunting fanatic.

завива́|ть(ся) (-ю(сь)) *несов от* **зави́ть(ся)**.

зави́вк|а (-и) *ж (волос)* curling; *(причёска)* curly hair.

зави́ден *прил см* **зави́дный**.

зави́дно *нареч*: **он ~ краси́в/умён** he has enviable good looks/intelligence ◆ *как сказ*: **~ как она́ говори́т по-англи́йски** her English is enviable; **ему́ ~** he feels envious.

зави́дный (-ен, -на, -но) *прил* enviable.

зави́д|овать (-ую; *perf* **позави́довать**) *несов неперех* to envy, be jealous of *(+dat)*.

завизжа́|ть (-у́, -и́шь) *сов неперех* to begin to yelp.

завизи́р|овать (-ую) *сов от* **визи́ровать**.

завин|ти́ть (-чу́, -ти́шь; *impf* **зави́нчивать**) *сов перех* to tighten (up).

завира́|ться (-юсь) *несов от* **завра́ться**.

зави́|сеть (-шу, -сишь) *сов неперех*: **~ от** *+gen* to depend on.

зави́симост|ь (-и) *ж (отношение)* correlation; **~ (от** *+gen)* dependence (on); **в ~и от** *+gen* depending on.

зави́сим|ый (-, -а, -о) *прил (человек, страна)* dependent; **~ от** *+gen (погоды, обстоятельств)* dependent on.

зави́стлив|ый (-, -а, -о) *прил* envious.

за́вист|ь (-и) *ж* envy, jealousy; **она́ вы́глядит на ~ хорошо́** *(разг)* it makes you sick how well she looks.

завитк|а́ *сущ см* **завито́к**.

завито́й *прил (волосы)* curly; *(девушка)* curly-haired; *(проволока, шнур)* coiled.

завито́к (-ка́) *м (локон)* curl; *(спирали)* twist; *(орнамента)* flourish, whorl.

зав|и́ть (-ью, -ьёшь; *pt* **-и́л, -ила́, -и́ло**, *impf* **завива́ть**) *сов перех (волосы, усы)* to curl; *(проволоку, шнур)* to twist

▶ **зави́ться** *(impf* **завива́ться**) *сов возв (волосы, усы)* to curl; *(проволока, шнур)* to get twisted; *(сделать завивку)* to curl one's hair.

завихре́ни|е (-я) *ср* whirl; *(перен)* peculiarity.

зави́шу *несов см* **зави́сеть**.

завладе́|ть (-ю; *impf* **завладева́ть**) *сов неперех* *(+instr; имуществом)* to take possession of; *(ВОЕН, вниманием)* to capture.

завл|е́чь (-еку́, -ечёшь *итп*, **-еку́т**; *pt* **-ёк, -екла́, -екло́**, *impf* **завлека́ть**) *сов перех (зверя, врага)* to lure; *(перен)* to captivate.

заво́д (-а) *м* factory; *(в часах, у игрушки)* clockwork; *(действие)* winding up; **ко́нный ~** stud farm.

заво́д|ить(ся) (-ожу́(сь), -о́дишь(ся)) *несов от* **завести́(сь)**.

заводно́й *прил (механизм, игрушка)* clockwork *опред; (ключ, ручка)* winding *опред; (разг: человек)* easily excitable.

заводско́й *прил* factory *опред*.

за́вод|ь (-и) *ж* backwater.

завоева́ни|е (-я) *ср (земель, страны)* conquest; *(обычно мн: достижения)* achievement.

завоева́тел|ь (-я) *м* conqueror.

завоева́тельн|ый *прил (политика)* aggressive; *(набеги)* offensive; **~ые во́йны** wars of conquest.

завое|ва́ть (-ю́ю; *impf* **завоёвывать**) *сов перех* to conquer; *(перен: доверие)* to win.

завожу́ *несов см* **заводи́ть, завози́ть**.

завожу́сь *несов см* **заводи́ться**.

заво́з (-а) *м* delivery.

заво|зи́ть (-ожу́, -о́зишь) *несов от* **завезти́**.

заволн|ова́ться (-у́юсь) *сов возв* to become agitated.

завора́чива|ть(ся) (-ю(сь)) *несов от* **заверну́ть(ся)**.

за́ворот (-а) *м*: **~ кишо́к** *(МЕД)* acute intestinal illness.

заворо́т (-а) *м (реки, дороги)* bend; *(движение)*

turn.

заворч|а́ть (-у́, -и́шь) *сов неперех* to start grumbling.

заво́ю *итп сов см* **завы́ть**.

завр|а́ться (-у́сь, -ёшься; *pt* -а́лся, -ала́сь, -а́лось, *impf* **завира́ться**) *сов возв* (*разг*) to get tied (up) in knots (*by lying*).

завсегда́та|й (-я) *м* (*разг*) regular.

за́втра *нареч, ср нескл* tomorrow; **до ~**! see you tomorrow!; **откла́дывать** (**отложи́ть** *perf*) **что-н на** *или* **до ~** to put sth off until tomorrow.

за́втрак (-а) *м* breakfast.

за́втрака|ть (-ю; *impf* **поза́втракать**) *несов неперех* to have breakfast.

за́втрашн|ий (-яя, -ее, -ие) *прил* tomorrow's; **за́втрашний день** tomorrow.

завуали́р|овать (-ую) *сов от* **вуали́ровать**.

за́вуч (-а) *м сокр* = **заве́дующий уче́бной ча́стью**; (*в школе, в училище*) ≈ deputy head.

завхо́з (-а) *м сокр* = **заве́дующий хозя́йством**; (*в школе, в институте*) bursar; (*на заводе*) *person in charge of supplies.*

завши́ве|ть (-ю) *сов от* **вши́веть**.

завыва́ни|е (-я) *ср* (*собак, метели*) howling; (*сирены*) wail; (*самолёта*) shriek.

завыва́|ть (-ю) *несов неперех* (*собака, метель*) to howl; (*сирена*) to wail; (*самолёт*) to shriek.

завы́|сить (-шу, -сишь; *impf* **завыша́ть**) *сов перех* (*нормы, цены*) to increase excessively; **~** (*perf*) **план** to set unreasonable targets.

зав|ы́ть (-о́ю, -о́ешь) *сов неперех* (*собака*) to begin to howl; (*сирена*) to start to wail.

завыша́|ть (-ю) *несов от* **завы́сить**.

завыше́ни|е (-я) *ср* excessive increase.

завы́шен|ный (-, -а, -о) *прил* excessively increased.

завы́шу *сов см* **завы́сить**.

завью́(сь) *итп сов см* **зави́ть(ся)**.

зав|яза́ть (-яжу́, -я́жешь; *impf* **завя́зывать**) ♦ (-я́жу, -я́жешь; *impf* **завя́зывать**) *сов перех* (*верёвку, ленту*) to tie; (*руку, посылку*) to bind; (*разговор*) to start (up); (*дружбу*) to form; (*отношение*) to establish; (*разг: пить, воровать*) to quit; **завя́зывать** (**~** *perf*) **глаза́ кому-н** to blindfold sb.

► **завяза́ться** (*impf* **завя́зываться**) *сов возв* (*шнурки, бант*) to be tied; (*разговор*) to start (up); (*дружба*) to form; (*отношения*) to become established; (*БОТ*) to set.

завя́з|ка (-ки; *gen pl* -ок) *ж* (*тесьма*) band; (*лента*) ribbon; (*разговора, событий*) beginning; (*боя*) onset; (*романа, рассказа*) opening.

завя́з|нуть (-у, -ешь; *impf* **завяза́ть** *или* **вя́знуть**) *сов неперех* (*в снегу, в грязи*) to get stuck; (*перен: разг*): **~ в** +*prp* (*в трудностях, в долгах*) to be up to one's neck in.

завя́зок *сущ см* **завя́зка**.

завя́зыва|ть(ся) (-ю(сь)) *несов от* **завяза́ть(ся)**.

завя́н|уть (-у, -ешь) *сов от* **вя́нуть**.

загада́|ть (-ю; *impf* **зага́дывать**) *сов перех* (*загадку*) to set; (*шараду*) to act out; (*число, слово*) to think of; (*желание*) to make ♦ *неперех* (*разг*) to guess.

зага́|дить (-жу, -дишь) *сов перех* (*разг*) to mess up.

зага́д|ка (-ки; *gen pl* -ок) *ж* riddle; (*перен*) puzzle, mystery.

зага́доч|ный (-ен, -на, -но) *прил* (*явление, событие*) puzzling, mysterious; (*выражение лица, слова*) enigmatic.

зага́дыва|ть (-ю) *несов от* **загада́ть**.

зага́жу *сов см* **зага́дить**.

загазо́ван|ный (-, -а, -о) *прил* (*атмосфера*) polluted.

зага́р (-а) *м* (sun)tan.

загво́зд|ка (-и) *ж* (*разг*) obstacle; **в э́том вся ~** (*разг*) that's the whole problem.

загерметизи́р|овать (-ую) *сов от* **герметизи́ровать**.

заги́б (-а) *м* (*на бумаге*) crease; (*перен: разг*) twist.

загиба́|ть(ся) (-ю(сь)) *несов от* **загну́ть(ся)**.

загипнотизи́р|овать (-ую) *сов от* **гипнотизи́ровать**.

загла́ви|е (-я) *ср* title.

загла́вн|ый *прил*: **~ая бу́ква** capital letter; **загла́вная роль** title role.

загла́|дить (-жу, -дишь; *impf* **загла́живать**) *сов перех* (*складки*) to iron; (*лист*) to fold; (*сгиб*) to make; (*перен: ошибки*) to put right; (: *обиду*) to make up for; **загла́живать** (**~** *perf*) **вину́** to make amends.

загло́х|нуть (-у, -ешь) *сов от* **гло́хнуть** ♦ *неперех* (*сад, тропинка*) to become overgrown; (*перен: разг: стройка, дело*) to die a death.

загло́хш|ий (-ая, -ее, -ие) *прил* overgrown.

заглуша́|ть (-ю; *perf* **заглуши́ть**) *несов перех* = **глуши́ть**.

заглуш|и́ть (-у́, -и́шь) *сов от* **глуши́ть**, **заглуша́ть**.

загляде́нь|е (-я) *ср* (*разг*) feast for the eyes.

загляде́|ться (-жу́сь, -ди́шься; *impf* **загля́дываться**) *сов возв* to gaze.

загля|ну́ть (-ну́, -нешь; *impf* **загля́дывать**) *сов неперех* (*в окно, в спальню*) to peep; (*в книгу, в словарь*) to glance; (*разг: к соседу, к друзьям*) to pop in; **загля́дывать** (**~** *perf*) **вперёд** to take a brief look ahead.

загна́ива|ться (-юсь) *несов от* **загнои́ться**.

заг|на́ть (-оню́, -о́нишь; *pt* -на́л, -нала́, -на́ло, *impf* **загоня́ть**) *сов перех* (*коров, детей*) to drive; (*разг: гвоздь, нож*) to ram in; (: *продать*) to flog (*BRIT*), sell; (*изнурить: лошадь*) to ride too hard; (: *рабочих*) to drive into the ground.

загн|и́ть (-ию́, -иёшь; *pt* -и́л, -ила́, -и́ло, *impf* **загнива́ть**) *сов неперех* to begin to rot.

загно|и́ться (-ю́сь, -и́шься; *impf* **загна́иваться**) *сов возв* (*рана*) to fester; (*глаз*) to become inflamed.

за́гнут|ый (-, -а, -о) *прил* bent.

загну́ть (-у́, -ёшь; *impf* **загиба́ть**) *сов перех* (*гвоздь*) to bend; (*край*) to fold; (*страницу*) to dog-ear; (*разг: сказать*) to spout; **загиба́ть** (~ *perf*) **рука́в вверх/вниз** to pull a sleeve up/down
▶ **загну́ться** (*impf* **загиба́ться**) *сов возв* (*гвоздь*) to bend; (*край*) to fold; (*страница*) to become dog-eared; (*воротник*) to twist; (*разг: умере́ть*) to kick the bucket.

загова́рива|ть (-ю) *несов от* **заговори́ть** ♦ *неперех:* **зу́бы ~ кому́-н** (*разг*) to steer sb off a subject
▶ **загова́риваться** *несов возв* (*говорить бессвязно*) to rave.

за́говень|е (-я) *ср* (*РЕЛ*) eve of fast, ≈ Shrove Tuesday.

за́говор (-а) *м* conspiracy; (*от боле́зни*) spell.

заговор|и́ть (-ю́, -и́шь) *сов неперех* (*начать говорить*) to begin to speak; (*по-английски, по-ру́сски*) to be able to speak; (*перен: совесть, гордость итп*) to stir ♦ (*impf* **загова́ривать**) *перех* (*болезнь, боль*) to magic away; **загова́ривать** (~ *perf*) **кого́-н** to wear sb out through constant talk; **в нём ~ла со́весть** his conscience stirred in him.

загово́рщик (-а) *м* conspirator.

загово́рщиц|а (-ы) *ж см* **загово́рщик**.

загол`ов|ок (-ка) *м* headline.

заго́н (-а) *м* (*скота́, ове́ц*) driving in; (*для скота́*) enclosure; (*для ове́ц*) pen; **быть** (*impf*) **в ~е** (*разг*) to be pushed to one side.

загоня́|ть (-ю) *несов от* **загна́ть**.

загора́жива|ть(ся) (-ю(сь)) *несов от* **загороди́ть(ся)**.

загора́|ть(ся) (-ю(сь)) *несов от* **загоре́ть(ся)**.

загоре́л|ый (-, -а, -о) *прил* tanned.

загор|е́ть (-ю́, -и́шь; *impf* **загора́ть**) *сов неперех* to go brown, get a tan
▶ **загоре́ться** (*impf* **загора́ться**) *сов возв* (*дрова, костёр*) to light; (*зда́ние итп*) to catch fire; (*ла́мпочка, глаза́*) to light up; **загора́ться** (~**ся** *perf*) **жела́нием** +*infin* to have a burning desire to do; **он ~е́лся э́той иде́ей** the idea fired his imagination.

за́город (-а) *м* (*разг*) the country.

загор|оди́ть (-ожу́, -о́дишь; *impf* **загора́живать**) *сов перех* (*у́лицу, вход*) to block off; (*свет*) to block out; **загора́живать** (~ *perf*) **кого́-н собо́й** to shield sb; **загора́живать** (~ *perf*) **кому́-н доро́гу** (*перен*) to stand on sb's way
▶ **загороди́ться** (*impf* **загора́живаться**) *сов возв:* ~**ся** (**от** +*gen*) (*от со́лнца, от уда́ра*) to shield o.s. (from).

загоро́д|ка (-ки; *gen pl* **-ок**) *ж* barrier; (*в ко́мнате*) partition.

за́городн|ый *прил* (*экску́рсия*) out-of-town; (*дом*) country *опред;* **~ая пое́здка** a trip out of

town *или* into the country.

загоро́док *сущ см* **загоро́дка**.

загорожу́(сь) *сов см* **загороди́ть(ся)**.

загота́влива|ть (-ю) *несов от* **загото́вить**.

загото́ви́тел|ь (-я) *м* person responsible for state procurements of timber, grain etc.

загото́ви́тельный *прил:* ~ **пункт** collection point; **загото́ви́тельная цена́** state procurement price.

загото́в|ить (-лю, -ишь; *impf* **загота́вливать** *или* **заготовля́ть**) *сов перех* (*се́но, корм итп*) to lay in; (*биле́ты, докуме́нты итп*) to prepare.

загото́в|ка (-ки; *gen pl* **-ок**) *ж* (*де́йствие: кормо́в, ле́са итп*) laying in; (*заку́пка госуда́рством*) procurement; (*полуфабрика́т*) component; (*: для ту́фель*) upper.

загото́влю *сов см* **загото́вить**.

заготовля́|ть (-ю) *несов от* **загото́вить**.

загото́вок *сущ см* **загото́вка**.

загради́тельн|ый *прил:* ~**ое сооруже́ние** barrier; **загради́тельный ого́нь** (*ВОЕН*) defensive fire; **загради́тельный патру́ль** roadblock.

загра|ди́ть (-жу́, -ди́шь; *impf* **загражда́ть**) *сов перех* to obstruct.

загражде́ни|е (-я) *ср* barrier.

заграж`у́ *сов см* **загради́ть**.

заграни́ц|а (-ы) *ж* (*разг*) foreign countries *мн.*

заграни́чный *прил* foreign; **заграни́чный па́спорт** passport (*issued specifically for travel abroad*).

За́греб (-а) *м* Zagreb.

загрёб *итп сов см* **загрести́**.

загреба́|ть (-ю) *несов от* **загрести́** ♦ *неперех* (*вёслами*) to row; (*рука́ми, ла́пами*) to paddle ♦ *перех:* ~ **де́ньги** (*разг*) to rake in the money.

загребу́ *итп сов см* **загрести́**.

загрем|е́ть (-лю́, -и́шь) *сов неперех* (*гром*) to crash out; (*го́лос*) to thunder; (*таре́лки итп*) to start to rattle.

загре|сти́ (-бу́, -бёшь; *pt* **-ёб**, **-ебла́**, **-ебло́**, *impf* **загреба́ть**) *сов перех* (*му́сор, ли́стья итп*) to rake up.

загри́в|ок (-ка) *м* (*у ло́шади*) withers *мн;* **взять** (*perf*) **кого́-н за** ~ (*разг*) to grab sb by the scruff of the neck.

загримир|ова́ть (-у́ю; *impf* **загримиро́вывать** *или* **гримирова́ть**) *сов перех* to make up
▶ **загримирова́ться** (*impf* **загримиро́вываться** *или* **гримирова́ться**) *сов возв* to make o.s. up.

загро́бный *прил:* ~ **мир** the next world; (*перен: го́лос*) gloomy; **загро́бная жизнь** the afterlife.

загромозд|и́ть (-жу́, -ди́шь; *impf* **загромо`жда́ть**) *сов перех* to clutter (up).

загрубе́л|ый (-, -а, -о) *прил* (*ко́жа, ру́ки*) calloused, rough; (*лицо́*) coarse; (*го́лос*) gruff; (*перен: челове́к, душа́*) hardened.

загрубе́ть (-ю) *сов от* **грубе́ть**.
загрузи́ть (-ужу́, -у́зишь) *сов от* **грузи́ть** ♦
(*impf* **загружа́ть**) *перех* (*машину, судно*) to load
up; (*КОМП*) to boot, load up; (*перен:
сотру́дников, ученико́в*) to load with work;
(: *день*) to fill up; (: *печь, до́мну*) to load.
загру́зк|**а** (-и) *ж* (*маши́ны, су́дна*) loading;
(*предприя́тия, станка́*) capacity.
загрунт|**ова́ть** (-у́ю) *impf* **загрунто́вывать** *или*
грунтова́ть) *сов перех* to prime.
загру|**сти́ть** (-щу́, -сти́шь) *сов неперех* to
become sad; ~ (*perf*) **по до́му** to start to feel
homesick.
загр|**ы́зть** (-ызу́, -ызёшь; *impf* **загрыза́ть**) *сов
перех* (*овцу́, петуха́*) to kill; (*no impf; перен:
разг: замучи́ть*) to nag to death; **её** ~**ы́зла
со́весть** she was tormented by her conscience.
загрязне́ни|**е** (-я) *ср* pollution; **загрязне́ние
окружа́ющей среды́** (environmental) pollution.
загрязнённый (-ён, -ена́, -ено́) *прил* polluted.
загрязн|**и́ть** (-ю́, -и́шь; *impf* **загрязня́ть**) *перех* (*во́здух, водоём*) to pollute;
загрязня́ть (~ *perf*) **что-н** (*сапоги́, пла́тье итп*)
to get sth dirty
▸ **загрязни́ться** *сов от* **грязни́ться** ♦ (*impf*
загрязня́ться) *возв* (*см перех*) to become
polluted; to get dirty.
ЗАГС (-а) *м сокр* (= за́пись а́ктов гражда́нского
состоя́ния) ≈ registry office.
загуб|**и́ть** (-лю́, -у́бишь) *сов от* **губи́ть** ♦
перех (*челове́ка*) to destroy; (*расте́ние*) to kill;
(*жизнь, ве́чер*) to ruin; (*разг: де́ньги, сре́дства*)
to waste.
загу|**де́ть** (-жу́, -ди́шь) *сов неперех* (*маши́на*) to
honk; (*гудо́к*) to sound.
загу́л (-а) *м* (*разг*) drinking session; **уда́риться**
(*perf*) **в** ~ to go on a bender.
загуля́|**ть** (-ю) *impf* **загу́ливать** *сов неперех*
(*разг: кути́ть*) to booze.
загусте́ть (*3sg* -е́т, *3pl* -е́ют) *сов от* **густе́ть**.
зад (-а; *part gen* -у, *loc sg* -у́, *nom pl* -ы́, *gen pl* -о́в)
м (*челове́ка*) behind, rear; (*живо́тного*) rump;
(*маши́ны, до́ма*) rear.
зада́брива|**ть** (-ю) *несов от* **задо́брить**.
зада|**ва́ть** (-ю́, -ёшь) *несов от* **зада́ть**
▸ **задава́ться** *несов от* **зада́ться** ♦ *возв* (*разг:
важничать*) to be cocky.
зада|**ви́ть** (-авлю́, -а́вишь) *сов от* **дави́ть** ♦
перех to crush; **её** ~**ави́ло де́ревом** she was
crushed under a tree; **его́** ~**ави́ла маши́на** he
was run over by a car.
зада́м(**ся**) *итп сов см* **зада́ть**(**ся**).
зада́ни|**е** (-я) *ср* (*поруче́ние*) task; (*упражне́ние*)
exercise; (*ВОЕН*) mission; **дома́шнее** ~
homework.
задар|**и́ть** (-рю́, -а́ришь; *impf* **зада́ривать**) *сов
перех*: ~ **кого́-н пода́рками** to shower sb with
presents.
зада́ром *нареч* (*разг: дёшево*) for next to
nothing; (: *зря*) for nothing.
зада́ст(**ся**) *сов см* **зада́ть**(**ся**).

зада́тк|**и** (-ов) *мн* (*о спосо́бностях*) ability *ед*.
зада́т|**ок** (-ка) *м* deposit; **дава́ть** (**дать** *perf*) ~ to
put down a deposit; *см та́кже* **зада́тки**.
зада́ть (*как* **дать**; *см* **Table 14**; *impf* **задава́ть**)
сов перех to set; **задава́ть** (~ *perf*) **кому́-н
вопро́с** to ask sb a question; **задава́ть** (~ *perf*)
пир (*разг*) to lay on a spread; **я тебе́** ~**а́м!**
(*разг*) just you wait!
▸ **зада́ться** (*impf* **задава́ться**) *сов возв*: ~**ся
це́лью** +*infin* (*сде́лать, написа́ть итп*) to set
o.s. the task of doing; ~**ся** (*perf*) **вопро́сом** to
ask o.s.
зада́ч|**а** (-и) *ж* task; (*МАТ*) problem; **ста́вить**
(**поста́вить** *perf*) **пе́ред собо́й** ~**у** to set o.s. a
task; **реша́ть** (**реши́ть** *perf*) ~**у** to solve a
problem.
зада́чник (-а) *м* book of problems.
зада́ш(**ся**) *сов см* **зада́ть**(**ся**).
задви́га|**ть** (-ю) *сов неперех* (+*instr*) to begin to
move
▸ **задви́гаться** *сов возв* to begin to move.
задвига́ть(**ся**) (-ю(сь)) *несов от*
задви́нуть(**ся**).
задви́жк|**а** (-и) *ж* bolt; **закрыва́ть** (**закры́ть** *perf*)
дверь на ~**у** to bolt the door.
задвижн|**о́й** *прил*: ~**а́я дверь** sliding door.
задви́н|**уть** (-у, -ешь; *impf* **задвига́ть**) *сов перех*
to push; (*я́щик, занаве́ски*) to close
▸ **задви́нуться** (*impf* **задвига́ться**) *сов возв* to
close.
задво́рк|**и** (-ок) *мн* backyard *ед*; **на** ~**ках
о́бщества** (*перен*) on the margins of society; **на**
~**ках исто́рии** (*перен*) in the footnotes of
history.
задева́|**ть** (-ю) *несов от* **заде́ть** ♦ *сов перех*
(*разг: положи́ть*) to put; **куда́ ты** ~**л мою́
су́мку?** where have you put my bag?
▸ **задева́ться** *сов возв* (*разг*) to go missing;
куда́ ~**лась моя́ ру́чка?** what's happened to my
pen?
заде́йств|**овать** (-ую) *сов перех*
(*обору́дование*) to render operational; (*полк,
диви́зию*) to mobilize ♦ *неперех* (*взя́ться за
де́ло*) to get busy.
заде́л (-а) *м* groundwork; **создава́ть** (**созда́ть**
perf) ~ **на бу́дущее** to create foundations for the
future.
заде́ла|**ть** (-ю; *impf* **заде́лывать**) *сов перех* to
seal up.
заде́ну *итп сов см* **заде́ть**.
задёрга|**ть** (-ю) *сов неперех* (+*instr*; *ного́й,
во́жжами*) to jerk ♦ *перех* (*разг: изму́чить*) to
wear out
▸ **задёргаться** *сов возв* (*те́ло, глаз, гу́бы*) to
twitch; (*нача́ть не́рвничать*) to become
twitchy; (*разг: изму́читься*) to reach the end of
one's tether.
задёргива|**ть** (-ю) *несов от* **задёрнуть**.
задеревене́|**ть** (-ю) *сов неперех* to go stiff.
задержа́ни|**е** (-я) *ср* (*ЮР*) detention.

заде|ржа́ть (**-ержу́, -е́ржишь;** *impf*
заде́рживать) *сов перех (самолёт, поезд итп)*
to delay, hold up; *(зарплату, уплату долгов)* to
withhold; *(преступника)* to detain;
(школьников) to keep back; **я не хочу́ Вас
~е́рживать** I don't want to hold you back;
заде́рживать (**~** *perf*) **дыха́ние** to hold one's
breath; **заде́рживать** (**~** *perf*) **взгляд на** +*prp* to
stare at; **заде́рживать** (**~** *perf*) **шаг** to slow up
▶ **задержа́ться** (*impf* **заде́рживаться**) *сов возв*
to be delayed *или* held up; *(у две́ри, перед
до́мом итп)* to pause; **заде́рживаться** (**~ся**
perf) **с отве́том/рабо́той** to be late in
answering/finishing the work.

заде́рж|ка (**-ки;** *gen pl* **-ек**) *ж* delay, hold-up; **без
~ек** without further delay.

задёрн|уть (**-у, -ешь;** *impf* **задёргивать**) *сов
перех (шторы)* to pull shut; **задёргивать** (**~**
perf) **окно́ занаве́ской/што́рой** to shut the
curtains/blind.

заперу́(сь) *итп сов см* **задра́ть(ся)**.

заде́|ть (**-ну, -нешь;** *impf* **задева́ть**) *сов перех:* **~**
(**за** +*acc*) *(стол итп)* to brush against; *(кость,
лёгкое)* to graze; *(перен: самолюбие, человека)*
to wound; **его́ тон меня́ ~л** I found his tone
offensive; **~** (*perf*) **кого́-н за живо́е** to cut sb to
the quick.

задира́ (**-ы**) *м/ж (разг)* troublemaker.

задира́|ть(ся) (**-ю(сь)**) *несов от* **задра́ть(ся)**.

задири́ст|ый (**-, -а, -о**) *прил* quarrelsome.

за́дн|ий (**-яя, -ее, -ие**) *прил* back *опред;*
помеча́ть (**поме́тить** *perf*) **~им число́м** to
backdate; **опла́чивать** (**оплати́ть** *perf*) **~им
число́м** to make a back payment; **она́ ~им
умо́м крепка́** she's simply being wise after the
event; **он был без ~их ног** *(разг)* he was dead
on his feet; **~яя мысль** ulterior motive; **~ие
но́ги** hind legs; **за́дний прохо́д** *(АНАТ)* rectum;
за́дний ход back entrance.

за́дник (**-а**) *м (боти́нка)* back; *(ТЕА́ТР)* backdrop.

за́дница (**-ы**) *ж (разг)* backside.

задо́бр|ить (**-ю, -ишь;** *impf* **зада́бривать**) *сов
перех* to soften up.

задо́лго *нареч:* **~ до** +*gen* long before.

задолжа́|ть (**-ю**) *сов перех* to owe.

задо́лж|енность (**-и**) *ж* debts *мн; (по рабо́те,в
учёбе)* work outstanding.

за́дом *нареч* backwards; **~ наперёд** back to
front; **повора́чиваться** (**поверну́ться** *perf*) **~ к
кому́-н** to turn one's back to sb; **стоя́ть** (*impf*) **~
к кому́-н** to stand with one's back to sb.

задо́р (**-а**) *м* enthusiasm.

задо́р|ный (**-ен, -на, -но**) *прил* lively.

задохн|у́ться (**-у́сь, -ёшься;** *impf* **задыха́ться**)
сов возв (в дыму́) to suffocate; *(от бе́га, при
ходьбе́)* to be out of breath; *(от зло́сти, от
сме́ха)* to choke.

задра́|ить (**-ю, -ишь;** *impf* **задра́ивать**) *сов
перех (МОР)* to batten down.

задрапиро|ва́ть (**-у́ю**) *сов от* **драпирова́ть**.

задра́|ть (**-еру́, -ерёшь;** *pt* **-ра́л, -рала́, -ра́ло,**
impf **драть** *или* **задира́ть**) *сов перех (пла́тье,
ю́бка)* to hitch *или* hike up; *(растерзать)* to
savage; **задира́ть** (**~** *perf*) **го́лову** to tip one's
head back; **задира́ть** (**~** *perf*) **нос** *(разг)* to be
stuck-up
▶ **задра́ться** (*impf* **задира́ться**) *сов возв (разг:
пла́тье, руба́шка)* to hitch itself up; *(рука́в)* to
ruck.

задре|ма́ть (**-емлю́, -е́млешь**) *сов неперех* to
doze off.

задрож|а́ть (**-у́, -и́шь**) *сов неперех (челове́к,
го́лос)* to begin to tremble; *(зда́ние, стекло́)* to
begin to shake.

задува́|ть (**-ю**) *несов от* **заду́ть**.

заду́ма|ть (**-ю;** *impf* **заду́мывать**) *сов перех
(по́весть, план)* to think up; *(ка́рту, число́)* to
think of; *(+infin: уехать итп)* to think of doing
▶ **заду́маться** (*impf* **заду́мываться**) *сов возв
(погрузиться в разду́мье)* to be deep in
thought; **заду́мываться** (**~ся** *perf*) **над** +*instr*/**о**
+*prp (над зада́чей, над жи́знью)* to ponder; **о
чём Вы ~лись?** what are you thinking about?;
он отве́тил, не заду́мываясь he answered
without hesitation; **она́ на мину́ту ~лась** she
reflected for a moment.

заду́мчив|ость (**-и**) *ж* pensiveness; **быть** (*impf*)
в глубо́кой ~и to be deep in thought.

заду́мчив|ый (**-, -а, -о**) *прил* pensive,
thoughtful.

заду́мыва|ть(ся) (**-ю(сь)**) *несов от*
заду́мать(ся).

заду́|ть (**-ю, -ешь;** *impf* **задува́ть**) *сов перех
(ого́нь, свечу́ итп)* to blow out ♦ *неперех
(ветер)* to get up; **ве́тром ~ло песо́к в
ко́мнату** the wind blew sand into the room.

задуше́в|ный (**-ен, -на, -но**) *прил (мы́сли,
та́йна, разгово́р)* intimate; *(пе́сня, расска́з)*
soulful; *(друг, челове́к)* genial.

задуш|и́ть (**-у́, -у́шишь**) *сов от* **души́ть**.

задым|и́ть (**-лю́, -и́шь**) *сов неперех* to begin to
smoulder *(BRIT)* *или* smolder *(US)*
▶ **задыми́ться** *сов возв* to begin to give off
smoke.

задыха́|ться (**-юсь**) *несов от* **задохну́ться**.

заеда́|ть (**-ю**) *несов от* **зае́сть**.

зае́дешь *итп сов см* **зае́хать**.

заеди́м *итп сов см* **зае́сть**.

зае́ду *итп сов см* **зае́хать**.

заедя́т *сов см* **зае́сть**.

зае́зд (**-а**) *м (СПОРТ)* race *(in horse-racing,
motor-racing)*; (: *отбо́рочный*) heat;
(тури́стов, отдыха́ющих) arrival; **с ~ом/без
зае́зда в Москву́** with/without a stopoff in
Moscow.

зае́з|дить (**-жу, -дишь**) *сов перех (перен: разг):*

~ **кого́-н** to drive sb too hard.
заезжа́|ть (**-ю**) *несов от* **зае́хать**.
зае́зжу *сов см* **зае́здить**.
зае́л *итп сов см* **зае́сть**.
заём *итп сов см* **зае́сть**.
заём (**за́йма**) *м* loan.
заёмщик (**-а**) *м* borrower.
зае́сть (*как* **есть**; *см* Table 15; *impf* **заеда́ть**) *сов перех* (*подлеж*: *комары*) to eat; (*разг*: *подлеж*: *жена, нача́льник, среда́*) to get to ♦ *безл* (*разг*: *ружьё*) to jam; **пласти́нку зае́ло** (*разг*) the record is stuck; **заеда́ть** (~ *perf*) **лека́рство/во́дку чем-н** to eat sth to take away the taste of the medicine/vodka.
зае́хать (*как* **е́хать**; *см* Table 19; *impf* **заезжа́ть**) *сов неперех*: ~ **за кем-н** to go to fetch sb; **заезжа́ть** (~ *perf*) **в** +*acc* (*в кана́ву, во двор*) to drive into; (*в Москву́, в магази́н итп*) to stop off at; ~ (*perf*) **к друзья́м** to stop off at friends; ~ (*perf*) **кому́-н в лицо́** (*разг*) to smash sb in the face.
зажа́р|ить (**-ю, -ишь**) *сов от* **жа́рить** ♦ (*impf* **зажа́ривать**) *перех* (*на сковоро́дке*) to fry; (*в духо́вке*) to roast
► **зажа́риться** *сов от* **жа́риться** ♦ (*impf* **зажа́риваться**) *возв* (*см перех*) to fry; to roast.
зажа́|ть (**-му́, -мёшь**; *impf* **зажима́ть**) *сов перех* to squeeze; (*рот, у́ши*) to cover; (*перен*: *инициати́ву, прое́кт*) to stifle, suppress; (*разг*: *де́ньги*) to pocket; **зажима́ть** (~ *perf*) **нос** to hold one's nose; **зажима́ть** (~ *perf*) **рот кому́-н** (*перен*) to silence sb.
зажгу́(сь) *итп сов см* **заже́чь(ся)**.
зажда́ться (**-у́сь, -ёшься**) *сов возв* (+*gen*; *разг*) to be sick of waiting for.
заже́|чь (**-гу́, -жёшь, -гут**; *pt* **-ёг, -гла, -гло**, *impf* **зажига́ть**) *сов перех* (*свечу́, спи́чку итп*) to light; (*свет*) to turn on; (*перен*: *аудито́рию*) to inflame; (: *интере́с, любо́вь*) to spark (off)
► **заже́чься** (*impf* **зажига́ться**) *сов возв* (*свеча́, спи́чка итп*) to light; (*свет*) to go on; (*перен*: *интере́с, любо́вь*) to be sparked off.
зажива́|ть (**-ю**) *несов от* **зажи́ть**.
заживу́ *итп сов от* **зажи́ть**.
зажига́лк|а (**-и**) *ж* (cigarette) lighter; (*разг*: *бо́мба*) firebomb.
зажига́ни|е (**-я**) *ср* (*действие*) lighting; (*АВТ*) ignition; **включа́ть** (**включи́ть** *perf*) ~ to turn on the ignition.
зажига́тельный (**-ен, -ьна, -ьно**) *прил* (*также перен*) inflammatory; (*снаря́д*) incendiary; **зажига́тельный шнур** fuse wire.
зажига́|ть(ся) (**-ю(сь)**) *несов от* **заже́чь(ся)**.
зажи́м (**-а**) *м* (*ТЕХ*) clamp; (*ЭЛЕК*) terminal; (*инициати́вы, кри́тики*) stifling, suppression.
зажима́|ть (**-ю**) *несов от* **зажа́ть**.
зажи́точ|ный (**-ен, -на, -но**) *прил* prosperous.
зажи́|ть (**-иву́, -ивёшь**; *pt* **-ил, -ила́, -ило**, *impf* **зажива́ть**) *сов неперех* (*ра́на*) to heal (up); (*no impf*; *нача́ть жить*) to start to live; ~ (*perf*) **по-но́вому** to change one's lifestyle.

зажму́ *итп сов см* **зажа́ть**.
зажму́р|ить (**-ю, -ишь**) *сов от* **жму́рить** ♦ (*impf* **зажму́ривать**) *перех*: ~ **глаза́** to screw up one's eyes
► **зажму́риться** *сов от* **жму́риться** ♦ (*impf* **зажму́риваться**) *возв* to screw up one's eyes.
зажужж|а́ть (**-у́, -и́шь**) *сов неперех* to start buzzing.
зазва́|ть (**-ову́, -овёшь**; *pt* **-ва́л, -вала́, -ва́ло**, *impf* **зазыва́ть**) *сов перех* (*разг*): ~ **кого́-н в го́сти** to invite sb over.
зазвене́|ть (**-ю, -ишь**) *сов неперех* to start ringing; **у меня́ ~ло в уша́х** my ears started ringing.
зазвон|и́ть (**-ю́, -и́шь**) *сов неперех* to start ringing.
зазвуч|а́ть (**3sg -и́т, 3pl -а́т**) *сов неперех* to be heard.
заздра́вный *прил* congratulatory.
зазелене́|ть (**3sg -ет**) *сов неперех* to turn green.
заземле́ни|е (**-я**) *ср* (*ЭЛЕК*: *де́йствие*) earthing (*BRIT*), grounding (*US*); (: *устро́йство*) earth (*BRIT*), ground (*US*).
заземл|и́ть (**-ю́, -и́шь**; *impf* **заземля́ть**) *сов перех* to earth (*BRIT*), ground (*US*).
зазна|ва́ться (**-аю́сь**) *несов от* **зазна́ться**.
зазна́йк|а (**-йки**; *gen pl* **-ек**) *м/ж* (*разг*) bighead.
зазна́|ться (**-юсь**; *impf* **зазнава́ться**) *сов возв* (*разг*) to think a lot of o.s.
зазову́ *итп сов см* **зазва́ть**.
зазо́р (**-а**) *м* gap.
зазре́ни|е (**-я**) *ср*: **без ~я со́вести** without a twinge of conscience.
зазу́брен|ный (**-, -а, -о**) *прил* serrated, jagged.
зазу́брива|ть (**-ю**) *несов от* **зазубри́ть**.
зазу́брин|а (**-ы**) *ж* serration.
зазубр|и́ть (**-ю́, -и́шь**; *impf* **зазу́бривать**) *сов перех* (*разг*): ~ **что-н** to learn sth parrot-fashion.
зазыва́|ть (**-ю**) *несов от* **зазва́ть**.
заигра́|ть (**-ю**) *сов* (*не*)*перех* (*музыка́нт, орке́стр*) to begin to play ♦ *неперех* (*му́зыка*) to begin ♦ (*impf* **заи́грывать**) *перех* (*пласти́нку, коло́ду карт*) to wear out
► **заигра́ться** (*impf* **заи́грываться**) *сов возв* to be absorbed in one's games.
заи́грыва|ть (**-ю**) *несов от* **заигра́ть** ♦ *неперех*: ~ **с** +*instr* (*разг*: *любезничать*) to flirt with; (: *заискивать*) to suck up to
► **заи́грываться** *несов от* **заигра́ться**.
зайк|а (**-и**) *м/ж* stutterer.
заика́ни|е (**-я**) *ср* (*действие*) stuttering; (*поро́к ре́чи*) stutter.
заика́|ться (**-юсь**) *несов возв* to have a stutter; (*разг*: *от испу́га, от волне́ния*) to stammer; (*perf* **заикну́ться**): ~ **о** +*prp* (*пое́здке, приглаше́нии*) to drop hints about.
заимода́в|ец (**-ьца**) moneylender; (*пренебр*) loan shark.
заимообра́зно *нареч* on loan.
заи́мствовани|е (**-я**) *ср* borrowing.
заи́мств|овать (**-ую**; *impf* **позаи́мствовать**)

(не)сов перех (слова, сюжет) to borrow; *(опыт)* to benefit from.

заиндеве́вш|ий (**-ая, -ое, -ие**) *прил* frost-covered.

зай|ндеве|ть (**-ю**) *сов от* **и́ндеветь.**

заинтересо́ван|ный (**-, -а, -о**) *прил* interested; **я заинтересо́ван в э́том де́ле** I have an interest in the matter; **заинтересо́ванная сторона́** interested party.

заинтерес|ова́ть (**-у́ю**; *impf* **заинтерес-о́вывать**) *сов перех* to interest

▸ **заинтересова́ться** (*impf* **заинтерес-о́вываться**) *сов возв* (**+instr**) to become interested in.

заинтриг|ова́ть (**-у́ю**; *impf* **заинтриго́вывать**) *сов перех* to intrigue.

Заи́р (**-а**) *м* Zaire.

заи́рск|ий (**-ая, -ое, -ие**) *прил* Zairean.

заи́скива|ть (**-ю**) *несов неперех*: ~ **пе́ред** +*instr* to ingratiate o.s. with.

заи́скивающ|ий (**-ая, -ее, -ие**) *прил* ingratiating.

зайду́ *итп сов см* **зайти́.**

за́йма *сущ см* **заём.**

за́ймов|ый *прил*: ~**ая опера́ция** loan transaction; ~ **проце́нт** interest *(on loan).*

займу́(сь) *итп сов см* **заня́ть(ся).**

зайти́ (*как* **идти́;** *см* **Table 18;** *impf* **заходи́ть)** *сов неперех (солнце, луна)* to go down; *(спор, разговор)* to start up; *(посетить)*: ~ **(в/на** +*acc*)**/к** +*dat)* to call in (at); *(попасть)*: ~ **в/на** +*acc* to stray into; **заходи́ть (**~ *perf)* **за кем-н** to go to fetch sb; **заходи́ть (**~ *perf)* **за хле́бом/молоко́м** to pop in for bread/milk; **заходи́ть (**~ *perf)* **на рабо́ту/к дру́гу** to call in at work/a friend's; **заходи́ть (**~ *perf)* **спра́ва/сле́ва** to come in from the right/left; **мы зашли́ в незнако́мую часть го́рода** we strayed into an unfamiliar part of town; **заходи́ть (**~ *perf)* **в тупи́к** *(перен)* to reach a dead end; **де́ло зашло́ сли́шком далеко́** things have gone too far.

за́йца *сущ см* **за́яц.**

зайча́та *итп сущ см* **зайчо́нок.**

за́йчик (**-а**) *м уменьш от* **за́яц;** *(разг: также:* **со́лнечный ~**) reflection of the sun.

зайчи́х|а (**-и**) *ж* doe, female hare.

зайчо́нок (**-о́нка;** *nom pl* **-а́та,** *gen pl* **-а́т**) *м* leveret.

закабал|и́ть (**-ю́, -и́шь;** *impf* **закабаля́ть**) *сов перех* to enslave.

закавка́зск|ий (**-ая, -ое, -ие**) *прил* Transcaucasian.

закады́чный *прил*: ~ **друг** bosom friend.

закажу́ *итп сов от* **заказа́ть.**

зака́з (**-а**) *м (действие:* платья, обеда *итп)* ordering; (: *телефонного разговора)* booking; (: *портрета)* commissioning; *(заказанный предмет)* order; **де́лать (сде́лать** *perf)* **что-н**

на ~ to make sth to order; **по** ~**у** *(также перен)* to order.

заказа́ть (**-ажу́, -а́жешь;** *impf* **зака́зывать**) *сов перех (см сущ)* to order; to book; to commission.

заказн|о́й *прил*: ~**о́е письмо́** registered letter.

зака́зчик (**-а**) *м* customer.

зака́зчица (**-ы**) *ж см* **зака́зчик.**

зака́зыва|ть (**-ю**) *несов от* **заказа́ть.**

закалё́нный (**-ён, -ена́, -ено́**) *прил (физически)* resistant; *(нравственно)* resilient.

зака́лива|ние (**-я**) *ср (ребёнка, организма)* toughening up.

зака́л|ивать (**-ю, -ишь;** *impf* **зака́ливать** *или* **закаля́ть**) *сов перех (сталь)* to harden, temper; *(ребёнка, организм)* to toughen up; *(волю, характер)* to toughen

▸ **закали́ться** (*impf* **зака́ливаться** *или* **закаля́ться**) *сов возв (сталь)* to be hardened *или* tempered; *(ребёнок, организм)* to build up one's resistance; *(воля, характер)* to toughen.

зака́лк|а (**-и**) *ж (см глаг)* hardening, tempering; toughening up; toughening; *(стойкость)* toughness.

зака́лыва|ть (**-ю**) *несов от* **заколо́ть.**

закаля́|ть(ся) (**-ю(сь)**) *несов от* **закали́ть(ся).**

закамуфли́р|овать (**-ую**) *сов от* **камуфли́ровать.**

зака́нчива|ть(ся) (**-ю(сь)**) *несов от* **зако́нчить(ся).**

закапа́|ть (**-ю**; *impf* **зака́пывать**) *сов перех* *(платье, тетрадь итп)* to splatter; *(лекарство, капли)* to apply ◆ *неперех (no impf)*: **дождь** ~**л** it started spitting (with rain).

зака́пыва|ть (**-ю**) *несов от* **зака́пать, закопа́ть**

▸ **зака́пываться** *несов от* **закопа́ться.**

зака́т (**-а**) *м*: ~ **(со́лнца)** sunset; *(перен: жизни, карьеры)* twilight; **на** ~**е дней** in the twilight of one's years.

закат|а́ть (**-ю**; *impf* **зака́тывать**) *сов перех* to roll up.

закат|и́ть (**-ачу́, -а́тишь;** *impf* **зака́тывать**) *сов перех* to roll; **зака́тывать (**~ *perf)* **сканда́л** *(разг)* to create a scandal; **зака́тывать (**~ *perf)* **исте́рику** *(разг)* to get hysterical; **зака́тывать (**~ *perf)* **глаза́** to roll one's eyes

▸ **закати́ться** (*impf* **зака́тываться**) *сов возв* to roll; *(солнце)* to set.

закача́|ться (**-юсь**) *сов возв* to begin to sway.

закачу́(сь) *сов см* **закати́ть(ся).**

зака́шля|ть (**-ю**) *сов неперех* to start coughing

▸ **зака́шляться** *сов возв* to have a coughing fit.

заква́|сить (**-шу, -сишь;** *impf* **заква́шивать**) *сов перех (капусту)* to pickle; *(молоко)* to sour

▸ **заква́ситься** (*impf* **заква́шиваться**) *сов возв* to be pickled; to be soured.

заква́ск|а (**-и**) *ж (для теста)* leaven; *(для кефира)* culture.

заква́шива|ть(ся) (-ю(сь)) *несов от* **заква́сить(ся).**

заква́шу(сь) *сов см* **заква́сить(ся).**

закида́|ть (-ю; *impf* **заки́дывать**) *сов перех* = **заброса́ть.**

заки́|нуть (-у, -ешь; *impf* **заки́дывать**) *сов перех* to throw; **судьба́ ~ула меня́ в Шотла́ндию** fate has brought me to Scotland; **заки́дывать (~** *perf*) **у́дочку** to cast a line; (*перен: разг*) to put out feelers.

закипе́ть (*3sg* -и́т, *3pl* -я́т, *impf* **закипа́ть**) *сов неперех* to start to boil; (*перен: работа*) to increase.

заки́с|нуть (-ну, -нешь; *pt* -, -ла, -ло, *impf* **закиса́ть**) *сов неперех* (*тесто, квас*) to turn sour; (*перен*) to stagnate.

за́кис|ь (-и) *ж* oxide.

закла́д (-а) *м*: **в ~е** in pawn; **би́ться** (*impf*) **об ~** (*разг*) to bet.

закла́дк|а (-и) *ж* (*сада, фунда́мента*) laying; (*в кни́ге*) bookmark.

закладна́|я (-ой; *decl like adj*) *ж* mortgage deed.

закла́дыва|ть (-ю) *несов от* **заложи́ть.**

закл|ева́ть (-юю, -юёшь; *impf* **заклёвывать**) *сов перех* to peek at; (*перен: разг*) to harass.

закле́|ить (-ю, -ишь; *impf* **закле́ивать**) *сов перех* to seal (up)

▶ **закле́иться** (*impf* **закле́иваться**) *сов возв* to seal.

закле́йм|и́ть (-лю́, -и́шь) *сов от* **клейми́ть.**

заклепа́|ть (-ю; *impf* **заклёпывать**) *сов перех* to rivet.

заклёпк|а (-и) *ж* (*стержень*) rivet.

заклёпыва|ть (-ю) *несов от* **заклепа́ть.**

заклина́ни|е (-я) *ср* (*маги́ческие слова*) incantation; (*перен: мольба́*) plea.

заклина́|ть (-ю) *несов перех* (*духов, змея́*) to charm; (*перен: умоля́ть*) to plead with.

закли́н|ить (-ю, -ишь; *impf* **закли́нивать**) *сов перех* (*дверь итп*) to jam; **руль ~ило** the wheel has jammed.

заключа́|ть (-ю) *несов от* **заключи́ть.**

заключа́|ться (*3sg* -ется, *3pl* -ются) *несов возв*: **~ в** +*prp* (*состоя́ть в*) to lie in; (*содержа́ться в*) to be contained in; (*зака́нчиваться*): **~** +*instr* to conclude with; **де́ло/пробле́ма ~ется в том, что ...** the point/problem is that ...; **на́ша цель ~ется в том, что́бы привле́чь инвести́ции в го́род** our aim is to attract investment into the city.

заключе́ни|е (-я) *ср* conclusion; (*в тюрьме́*) imprisonment, confinement; **в ~** in conclusion; **тюре́мное ~** imprisonment; **находи́ться** (*impf*) **в ~и** to be held in confinement.

заключённ|ая (-ой; *decl like adj*) *ж см* **заключённый.**

заключённ|ый (-ого; *decl like adj*) *м* prisoner.

заключи́тельный *прил* concluding, final.

заключ|и́ть (-у́, -и́шь; *impf* **заключа́ть**) *сов перех* (*соглаше́ние, догово́р, сде́лку*) to conclude, seal; **заключа́ть (~** *perf*) **в себе́** to comprise; **заключа́ть (~** *perf*) **контра́кт** to conclude a contract; **заключа́ть (~** *perf*) **кого́-н в тюрьму́** to put sb in prison; **заключа́ть (~** *perf*) **кого́-н под стра́жу** to take sb into custody; **заключа́ть (~** *perf*) **кого́-н в объя́тия** to embrace sb.

закля́тый *прил*: **~ враг** sworn enemy.

зак|ова́ть (-ую́; *impf* **зако́вывать**) *сов перех* to chain up; (*подлеж: лёд*) to cover.

закоди́р|овать (-ую) *сов от* **коди́ровать.**

закола́чива|ть (-ю) *несов от* **заколоти́ть.**

заколдо́ванн|ый (-, -а, -о) *прил* enchanted; **заколдо́ванный круг** vicious circle.

заколд|ова́ть (-у́ю; *impf* **заколдо́вывать**) *сов перех* to bewitch.

зако́лк|а (-и) *ж* (*для воло́с*) hairpin, hairclip.

заколо́|тить (-чу́, -отишь; *impf* **закола́чивать**) *сов перех* (*окна, дом*) to board up; (*я́щик*) to nail up.

заколо́ть (-олю́, -о́лешь) *сов от* **коло́ть** ♦ (*impf* **зака́лывать**) *перех* (*свинью́, инде́йку*) to slaughter; (*во́лосы*) to pin up; (*га́лстук, воротни́к*) to pin back; **у меня́ ~оло́ло в боку́** I've got a stitch.

заколочу́ *сов см* **заколоти́ть.**

закомпости́р|овать (-ую) *сов от* **компости́ровать.**

зако́н (-а) *м* law; **вне ~а** outside the law; **объявля́ть (объяви́ть** *perf*) **кого́-н вне ~а** to outlaw sb; **Зако́н Бо́жий** religious education.

зако́нен *прил см* **зако́нный.**

зако́нность (-и) *ж* (*докуме́нта, завеща́ния*) legality; (*в стране́*) law and order.

зако́нн|ый (-ен, -на, -но) *прил* legitimate, lawful; (*пра́во, приём*) legal; (*докуме́нт*) valid; **на ~ном основа́нии** on a legal basis; **~ным о́бразом** legally, lawfully; **зако́нный брак/муж** lawful wedlock/wedded husband.

законода́тел|ь (-я) *м* legislator; (*перен: вку́сов, мне́ний*) arbiter; **~ мод** trendsetter.

законода́тельниц|а (-ы) *ж см* **законода́тель.**

законода́тельный *прил* legislative.

законода́тельств|о (-а) *ср* legislation.

закономе́рн|ый (-ен, -на, -но) *прил* (*результа́т, явле́ние*) predictable; (*поня́тный*) legitimate.

законопа́|тить (-чу, -атишь; *impf* **законопа́чивать**) *сов перех* to patch up.

законоположе́ни|е (-я) *ср* statute.

законопрое́кт (-а) *м* (*полит*) bill.

законсерви́р|овать (-ую) *сов от* **консерви́ровать.**

законспекти́р|овать (-ую) *сов от* **конспекти́ровать.**

законтракт|ова́ть (-у́ю; *impf* **законтракто́вывать**) *сов перех* to sign a contract for.

зако́нчен|ный (-, -на, -но) *прил* (*мысль, расска́з*) complete; (*него́дяй, мерза́вец*) utter.

зако́нч|ить (-у, -ишь; *impf* **зака́нчивать**) *сов перех* to finish, end

▶ **зако́нчиться** (*impf* зака́нчиваться) *сов возв* to finish, end.

закопа́ть (-ю; *impf* зака́пывать) *сов перех* (*деньги, золото итп*) to bury; (*канаву, яму*) to fill in

▶ **закопа́ться** (*impf* зака́пываться) *сов возв* (*в землю итп*) to bury o.s.

закопти́ть (-чу́, -ти́шь) *сов от* копти́ть

▶ **закопти́ться** *сов возв* to be covered in smoke.

закопчённый *прил* (*чайник итп*) charred; (*потолок*) smoke-stained.

закопчу́(сь) *сов см* закопти́ть(ся).

закорене́лый *прил* (*традиции, предрассудки итп*) deep-rooted; (*дурак, кокетка итп*) incorrigible; ~ **престу́пник** hardened criminal.

закорене́ть (-ю) *сов неперех*: ~ **в** +*prp* (*мнении, предрассудках*) to be entrenched in.

зако́рки (-ок) *мн* (*разг*): **посади́ть кого́-н на** ~ to lift sb onto one's back; **нести́** (*impf*) **кого́-н на** ~**ках** to give sb a piggyback.

закорю́чка (-ки; *gen pl* -ек) *ж* squiggle.

закосне́ть (-ю) *сов от* косне́ть.

закостене́лый *прил* stiff.

закостене́ть (-ю) *сов от* костене́ть.

закоу́лок (-ка) *м* (*города*) back street *или* alley; (*дома, замка, двора*) nook; **обы́скивать** (**обыска́ть** *perf*) **все** ~**ки** to look in all the nooks and crannies.

закочене́лый *прил* numb.

закочене́ть (-ю) *сов неперех* to go numb.

закрадётся *итп сов см* закра́сться.

закра́дыва ться (*3sg* -ется, *3pl* -ются) *несов от* закра́сться.

закра́сить (-шу, -сишь; *impf* закра́шивать) *сов перех* to paint over.

закра́сться (*3sg* -адётся, *3pl* -аду́тся, *pt* -а́лся, -а́лась, -а́лось, *impf* закра́дываться) *сов возв* to creep in.

закра́шива ть (-ю) *несов от* закра́сить.

закра́шу *сов см* закра́сить.

закрепи́тел ь (-я) *м* (*ФОТО*) fixative.

закрепи́ть (-лю́, -и́шь; *impf* закрепля́ть) *сов перех* (*деталь, грунт*) to fasten; (*победу, позицию*) to consolidate; (*ФОТО*) to fix; **закрепля́ть** (~ *perf*) **что-н за кем-н** to secure sth for sb; **закрепля́ть** (~ *perf*) **кого́-н за кем-н** to assign sb to sb

▶ **закрепи́ться** (*impf* закрепля́ться) *сов возв* (*деталь, грунт*) to be fastened; (*победа, успехи*) to be consolidated; (*слово, привычка*) to become established; (*ВОЕН*): ~**ся на** +*acc* (*на высоте*) to consolidate one's position on.

закре́пка (-и) *ж* fastener.

закрепляю́(сь) *сов см* закрепи́ть(ся).

закрепля́ть(ся) (-ю(сь)) *несов от* закрепи́ть(ся).

закрепости́ть (-щу́, -сти́шь; *impf* закрепоща́ть) *сов перех* to enslave.

закрепоще́ни е (-я) *ср* enslavement.

закрепощу́ *сов см* закрепости́ть.

закрича́ть (-у́, -и́шь) *сов неперех* to start shouting.

закро́йщик (-а) *м* cutter (*DRESSMAKING*).

закро́йщиц а (-ы) *ж см* закро́йщик.

за́кром (-а; *nom pl* -а́) *м* (*в амба́ре*) grain store; *см также* закрома́.

закром а́ (-о́в) *мн* (*перен*) breadbasket *ед* (*esp US*), granary *ед*.

закро́ю(сь) *итп сов см* закры́ть(ся).

закругле́ни е (-я) *ср* curve.

закруглённ ый (-, -на, -но) *прил* curved, rounded.

закругл и́ть (-ю́, -и́шь; *impf* закругля́ть) *сов перех* (*край*) to round off; (*поверхность*) to make round

▶ **закругли́ться** (*impf* закругля́ться) *сов возв* to become rounded; (*перен: разг: закончить*) to round off.

закру жи́ть (-ужу́, -у́жишь) *сов перех*: ~ **кого́-н** (*начать кружить*) (to start) to spin sb round; (*довести до головокружения*) to make sb dizzy

▶ **закружи́ться** *сов возв* (*начать кружиться*) to start spinning; (*ослабеть*) to start to feel dizzy; (*перен: разг: захлопотаться*) to get o.s. into a tizzy; **у меня́** ~**жи́лась голова́** my head has started spinning.

закру ти́ть (-чу́, -у́тишь; *impf* закру́чивать) *сов перех* (*волосы, усы*) to twist; (*верёвку, ленту*) to wind; (*кран*) to turn off; (*гайку*) to screw in

▶ **закрути́ться** (*impf* закру́чиваться) *сов возв* (*верёвка, лента*) to wind up; (*перен: разг: захлопотаться*) to get o.s. into a flap.

закрыва́ть(ся) (-ю(сь)) *несов от* закры́ть(ся).

закры́ти е (-я) *ср* (*магазина итп*) closing (time); (*сезона, конкурса*) close.

закры́т ый (-, -а, -о) *прил* shut, closed; (*no short form*) террáса, машина) enclosed; (*стадион, бассейн*) indoor; (*собрание, заседание*) closed, private; (*перелом, рана*) internal; **в** ~**ом помеще́нии** indoors; **при** ~**ых дверя́х** behind closed doors; **вопро́с закры́т** the matter is closed; **закры́тое голосова́ние** secret vote *или* ballot; **закры́тое мо́ре** inland sea; **закры́тое пла́тье** dress with a high neck; **закры́тый ко́нкурс** closed competition.

закры́ть (-о́ю, -о́ешь; *impf* закрыва́ть) *сов перех* to close, shut; (*заслонить, накрыть*) to cover (up); (*проход, проезд, границу*) to close (off); (*воду, газ итп*) to shut off; **закрыва́ть** (~ *perf*) **кого́-н в ко́мнате** to shut sb in a room; **закрыва́ть** (~ *perf*) **счёт** to close an account; **закрыва́ть** (~ *perf*) **глаза́ на что-н** to close one's eyes to sth

▶ **закры́ться** (*impf* закрыва́ться) *сов возв* to close, shut; (*магазин, предприятие*) to close *или* shut down; (*накрыться*) to cover o.s. up; (*запереться: в доме итп*) to shut o.s. up; (*рана*) to close up.

закули́сн|ый *прил* backstage *опред*; (*перен: интриги, борьба*) behind-the-scenes; **~ая жизнь** off-stage life.

закупи́ть (-уплю́, -у́пишь; *impf* **закупа́ть**) *сов перех* (*купить оптом*) to buy up; (*запастись*) to stock up with.

заку́пк|а (-и) *ж* purchase.

закуплю́ *сов см* **закупи́ть**.

закупор|ить (-ю, -ишь; *impf* **заку́поривать**) *сов перех* (*бутылку*) to cork (up); (*бочку*) to seal up.

заку́порк|а (-и) *ж* (*см перех*) corking; sealing; (*МЕД: кишечника, сосудов*) blockage; **заку́порка вен** (*МЕД*) embolism.

заку́почн|ый *прил*: **~ая цена́** purchase price.

заку́пщик (-а) *м* buyer.

закур|и́ть (-ю́, -у́ришь; *impf* **заку́ривать**) *сов перех* to light (up) ◆ *неперех* to start smoking.

закуса́ть (-ю) *сов перех* (*разг*) to bite; **меня́ ~ли комары́** I've been bitten to death by mosquitoes.

закус|и́ть (-ушу́, -у́сишь; *impf* **заку́сывать**) *сов неперех* (*поесть*) to have a bite to eat ◆ *перех*: **~ во́дку/лека́рство** *итп* to have sth to eat with the vodka/medicine; **заку́сывать** (**~** *perf*) **губу́** to bite one's lip; **заку́сывать** (**~** *perf*) **удила́** (*перен*) to take the bit between one's teeth.

заку́ск|а (-и) *ж* snack; (*обычно мн: для водки*) zakuska (*мн* zakuski), nibbles *мн*; (*в начале обеда*) hors d'oeuvre; **на ~у** (*перен: разг*) for the finale.

заку́сочн|ая (-ой; *decl like adj*) *ж* snack bar.

заку́сыва|ть (-ю) *несов от* **закуси́ть**.

заку́та|ть (-ю) *сов от* **ку́тать** ◆ (*impf* **заку́тывать**) *перех* (*ребёнка*) to wrap up; (*ноги итп*) to cover

▶ **заку́таться** *сов от* **ку́таться** ◆ (*impf* **заку́тываться**) *возв* to wrap (o.s.) up.

закут|о́к (-ка́) *м* (*разг*) dark corner.

заку́тыва|ть(ся) (-ю(сь)) *несов от* **заку́тать(ся)**.

закушу́ *сов см* **закуси́ть**.

зал (-а) *м* hall; (*в музее, в библиотеке*) room; **зал ожида́ния** waiting room.

зала́|дить (-жу, -дишь) *сов (не)перех* (*разг*) to harp on (about); (*+infin*) to take to doing.

зала́мыва|ть (-ю) *несов от* **заломи́ть**.

залата́|ть (-ю) *сов от* **лата́ть**.

зала́я|ть (-ю) *сов неперех* to start barking, start to bark.

залёг *итп сов см* **зале́чь**.

залега́|ть (-ю) *несов от* **зале́чь**.

заледене́лый *прил* covered in ice; (*пальцы, руки*) icy.

заледене́|ть (-ю) *сов неперех* (*дорога*) to ice over; (*перен: пальцы, руки*) to freeze.

залежа́лый (-, -а, -о) *прил* (*разг*) old.

залежа́|ться (-у́сь, -и́шься; *impf* **залёживаться**) *сов возв*: **~ в магази́не/в**

посте́ли to lie in the shop/in bed for too long.

за́леж|ь (-и) *ж* (*угля, золота*) seam; (*с-х*) fallow land.

зале́з|ть (-у, -ешь; *impf* **залеза́ть**) *сов неперех*: **~ на** +*acc* (*на крышу*) to climb onto; (*на дерево, на лестницу*) to climb up; (*разг*): **~ в** +*acc* (*в квартиру, в магазин*) to break into; **залеза́ть** (**~** *perf*) **кому́-н в карма́н** to pick sb's pockets; **залеза́ть** (**~** *perf*) **в долги́** to get into debt.

зале|пи́ть (-еплю́, -е́пишь; *impf* **залепля́ть**) *сов перех* (*дыру, трещину*) to plaster up; (*подлеж: снег, грязь*) to plaster; **~** (*perf*) **кому́-н пощёчину** (*разг*) to give sb a slap round the face.

зале|те́ть (-чу́, -ти́шь; *impf* **залета́ть**) *сов неперех*: **~** (**в** +*acc*) to fly in(to); **залета́ть** (**~** *perf*) **за** +*acc* (*за море, за облака итп*) to fly over; **залета́ть** (**~** *perf*) **далеко́** to fly a long way; (*перен*) to go far; **самолёт ~те́л в Москву́ за горю́чим** the plane stopped off in Moscow for refuelling.

зале|чи́ть (-ечу́, -е́чишь; *impf* **зале́чивать**) *сов перех* (*язву, рану*) to heal; **~** (*perf*) **кого́-н** (*разг*) to make sb feel worse (*by excessive medication*)

▶ **залечи́ться** (*impf* **зале́чиваться**) *сов возв* to heal (up).

залечу́ *сов см* **залете́ть**.

заля́|гу (-гу, -жешь *итп*, -гут; *рt* -ёг, -егла́, -егло́, *impf* **залега́ть**) *сов неперех* (*в постель*) to lie down; (*в нору*) to retreat; (*укрыться*) to lie low; (*ГЕО: уголь, золото*) to be deposited; **залега́ть** (**~** *perf*) **в заса́де** to lie in wait.

зали́в (-а) *м* bay; (*длинный*) gulf.

залива́|ть(ся) (-ю(сь)) *несов от* **зали́ть(ся)**.

заливн|о́е (-о́го; *decl like adj*) *ср* (*кулин*) fish or meat in aspic.

заливно́й *прил* (*рыба, мясо*) jellied; **заливно́й луг** water meadow.

зал|и́ть (-ью́, -ьёшь; *рt* -и́л, -ила́, -и́ло, *impf* **залива́ть**) *сов перех* to flood; (*костёр, огонь*) to extinguish; **залива́ть** (**~** *perf*) **руба́шку пи́вом** to spill beer on one's shirt; **залива́ть** (**~** *perf*) **бензи́н в маши́ну** to fill a car with petrol; **залива́ть** (**~** *perf*) **доро́гу асфа́льтом** to cover a road with asphalt; **залива́ть** (**~** *perf*) **го́ре** to drown one's sorrows; **слёзы ~и́ли его́ лицо́** the tears poured down her face

▶ **зали́ться** (*impf* **залива́ться**) *сов возв* (*луг, пол*) to be flooded; (*вода*) to seep; **залива́ться** (**~ся** *perf*) **слеза́ми/сме́хом** to burst into tears/out laughing; **её лицо́ ~и́лось румя́нцем** the colour flooded into her cheeks.

зало́г (-а) *м* (*действие: вещей*) pawning; (: *квартиры*) mortgaging; (*заложенная вещь*) security; (*ЛИНГ: активный, пассивный*) voice; (*перен: знак*) token.

зал|ожи́ть (-ожу́, -о́жишь; *impf* **закла́дывать**) *сов перех* (*покрыть*) to clutter up; (*отметить*) to mark; (*отдать в залог: кольцо, шубу*) to pawn; (: *дом*) to mortgage; (*заполнить: трубу, дыру*) to block up; **закла́дывать** (**~** *perf*) **что-н**

за что-н to put sth behind sth; **закла́дывать (~ perf) го́род** to lay the foundations of a city; **у меня́ ~ожи́ло нос/го́рло** (*разг*) my nose/throat is all bunged up.

зало́жник (**-a**) *м* hostage.

зало́жница (**-ы**) *ж см* **зало́жник**.

зало́ми́ть (**-омлю́, -о́мишь**; *impf* **зала́мывать**) *сов перех* to tear off; **зала́мывать (~ perf) ру́ки** to throw up one's hands; **зала́мывать (~ perf) высо́кую це́ну** to ask too high a price.

залп (**-a**) *м* salvo (*мн* salvoes), volley.

за́лпом *нареч* (*разг: проглоти́ть, проговори́ть*) all in one go; **вы́стрелить** (*perf*) **~** to fire a volley *или* salvo of bullets.

залы́сина (**-ы**) *ж* bald patch.

залью́(сь) *итп сов см* **зали́ть(ся)**.

залюбо́ва́ться (**-у́юсь**) *сов возв* (+*instr*; *карти́ной, де́вушкой*) to be transfixed by.

заля́гу *итп сов см* **зале́чь**.

заля́жешь *итп сов см* **зале́чь**.

заля́па́ть (**-ю**; *impf* **заля́пывать**) *сов перех* (*разг*) to mess up.

зам (**-a**) *м сокр* (*разг*: = **замести́тель**) number two.

зам. *м сокр* (= **замести́тель**) dep. (= *deputy*).

зам- *префикс* deputy.

зама́зать (**-жу, -жешь**; *impf* **зама́зывать**) *сов перех* (*пятно́, рису́нок*) to paint over; (*о́кна, ще́ли*) to fill with putty; (*запа́чкать*) to smear

▶ **зама́заться** (*impf* **зама́зываться**) *сов возв*: **~ся** (+*instr*) to become smeared (with).

зама́зка (**-и**) *ж* putty.

зама́зыва́ть(ся) (**-ю(сь)**) *несов от* **зама́зать(ся)**.

зама́лчива́ть (**-ю**) *несов от* **замолча́ть**.

замани́ть (**-аню́, -а́нишь**; *impf* **зама́нивать**) *сов перех* to lure, entice.

зама́нчив̨ый (**-, -a, -o**) *прил* tempting.

замара́ть(ся) (**-ю(сь)**) *сов от* **мара́ть(ся)**.

замарин̨ова́ть (**-у́ю**) *сов от* **маринова́ть**.

замаскиро́ван̨ный (**-, -a, -o**) *прил* disguised; (*намёк, угро́за*) veiled.

замаскиро́ва́ть (**-у́ю**; *impf* **замаскиро́вывать** *или* **маскирова́ть**) *сов перех* to disguise; (*самолёт, танк*) to camouflage

▶ **замаскирова́ться** (*impf* **замаскиро́вываться** *или* **маскирова́ться**) *сов возв* to disguise o.s.; (*солда́ты*) to camouflage o.s.

зама́тыва́ть(ся) (**-ю(сь)**) *несов от* **замота́ть(ся)**.

зама́ха́ть (**-ашу́, -а́шешь**) *сов непрех* (+*instr*; *па́лкой, газе́той итп*) to brandish; **~** (*perf*) **руко́й** to start waving.

замахну́ться (**-у́сь, -ёшься**; *impf* **зама́хиваться**) *сов возв*: **~ на** +*acc* (*на соба́ку, на ребёнка*) to raise one's hand to; (*перен*) to set one's sights on; **он ~у́лся на бо́льшее** he has

set his sights on bigger and better things.

зама́чива́ть (**-ю**) *несов от* **замочи́ть**.

зама́шки (**-ек**) *мн* manners *мн*.

замби́йский (**-ая, -ое, -ие**) *прил* Zambian.

За́мби̨я (**-и**) *ж* Zambia.

замедле́ни̨е (**-я**) *ср* slowing down; **без ~я** without delay.

заме́дленный *прил* retarded; **~ ход** reduced speed.

заме́дл̨ить (**-ю, -ишь**; *impf* **замедля́ть**) *сов перех* to slow down; (*no impf*; *задержа́ться*): **~ с** +*instr* to be slow with; **не ~** (*perf*) +*infin* to be quick to do

▶ **заме́длиться** (*impf* **замедля́ться**) *сов возв* to slow down.

замёл *итп сов см* **замести́**.

заме́н̨а (**-ы**) *ж* replacement; (*СПОРТ*) substitution.

замени́м̨ый (**-, -a, -o**) *прил* replaceable.

замени́тел̨ь (**-я**) *м* (*суррога́т*) substitute.

замени́ть (**-еню́, -е́нишь**; *impf* **заменя́ть**) *сов перех* to replace; **она́ ~ени́ла им мать** she was like a mother to them.

заме́р̨еть (**-ру́, -рёшь**; *pt* **-ер, -ерла́, -ерло**, *impf* **замира́ть**) *сов непрех* (*челове́к, живо́тное*) to stop dead; (*перен: душа́, се́рдце*) to stand still; (: *рабо́та, страна́*) to come to a standstill; (*звук*) to die away; (*шум, стрельба́*) to die down; **~** (*perf*) **на ме́сте** to stop dead in one's tracks.

замерза́ни̨е (**-я**) *ср* freezing; **то́чка ~я** freezing point.

замёрз̨нуть (**-ну, -нешь**; *pt* **-, -ла, -ло**, *impf* **замерза́ть**) *сов непрех* to freeze; (*река́*) to freeze (up); (*окно́*) to ice up; **я совсе́м замёрз** I'm completely frozen.

заме́р̨ить (**-ю, -ишь**; *impf* **замеря́ть**) *сов перех* to measure.

за́мертво *нареч*: **упа́сть** *или* **ру́хнуть ~** to collapse in a heap.

замеря̨́ть (**-ю**) *несов от* **заме́рить**.

заме̨си́ть (**-ешу́, -е́сишь**; *impf* **заме́шивать**) *сов перех* (*бето́н, гли́ну*) to mix up; (*те́сто*) to knead.

замести́ (**-ету́, -етёшь**; *pt* **-ёл, -ела́, -ело́**, *impf* **замета́ть**) *сов перех* (*му́сор, ли́стья*) to sweep up; (*подлеж: мете́ль: доро́гу итп*) to cover; **замета́ть (~ perf) следы́** (*также перен*) to cover one's tracks.

замести́тел̨ь (**-я**) *м* replacement; (*до́лжность*) deputy; **~ дире́ктора/премье́р-мини́стра** deputy director/prime minister.

замести́тельница (**-ы**) *ж см* **замести́тель**.

заме̨сти́ть (**-щу́, -сти́шь**) *сов от* **замеща́ть**.

замета̨́ть (**-ю**) *несов от* **замести́**.

замета́ться (**-чу́сь, -чешься**) *сов возв* (*в крова́ти, в бреду́*) to start tossing and turning; (*в отча́янии*) to get into a state; **он ~та́лся по**

ко́мнате he began to rush about the room.

замётен *прил см* **замётный**.

замётить (-чу, -тишь; *impf* **замечать**) *сов перех* to notice; (*запомнить*) to take note of; (*сказать*) to remark.

замё́т|ка (-ки; *gen pl* -ок) *ж* (*на дереве итп*) mark, notch; (*в записной книжке итп*) note; (*в газете итп*) short piece *или* article; **брать** (**взять** *perf*) **что-н на ~ку** to make a (mental) note of sth; **он на ~ке у мили́ции** (*разг*) the police have got their eye on him.

замётно *нареч* noticeably ♦ *как сказ* (*видно*) it is obvious.

замётный (-ен, -на, -но) *прил* noticeable; (*личность, человек*) prominent.

заметý *итп сов см* **замести́**.

замеча́ни|е (-я) *ср* comment, remark; (*выговор*) reprimand.

замеча́телен *прил см* **замеча́тельный**.

замеча́тельно *нареч* (*красив, умён*) extremely; (*писать*) wonderfully, brilliantly ♦ *как сказ*: ~! that's brilliant *или* wonderful!

замеча́тельный (-ен, -ьна, -ьно) *прил* (*очень хороший*) wonderful, brilliant; (*необыкновенный*) remarkable; (*выдающийся*) outstanding.

замеча́ть (-ю) *несов от* **замётить**.

замечта́ться (-юсь) *сов возв* to start daydreaming.

замéчу *сов см* **замётить**.

замечу́сь *итп сов см* **замета́ться**.

замеша́тельств|о (-а) *ср* confusion; **приводи́ть** (**привести́** *perf*) **кого́-н в ~** to throw sb into confusion; **приходи́ть** (**прийти́** *perf*) **в ~** to become confused.

замеша́ть (-ю; *impf* **замёшивать**) *сов перех*: ~ **кого́-н во что-н** to get sb mixed up in sth

► **замеша́ться** (*impf* **замёшиваться**) *сов возв*: ~**ся в** +*acc* (*в историю, в преступление*) to get mixed up in; (*скрыться: в толпе*) to mingle with.

замёшива|ть (-ю) *несов от* **замеси́ть**, **замеша́ть**

► **замёшиваться** *несов от* **замеша́ться**.

► **замёшка|ть** (-ю) *сов от* **мёшкать**

► **замёшкаться** *сов возв* (*разг: с работой, с ответом*) to drag one's heels; (: *пробыть дольше*) to faff about.

замешу́ *сов см* **замеси́ть**.

замеща́|ть (-ю) *несов перех* (*начальника итп*) to stand in *или* deputize for; (*perf* **замести́ть**; *заменять: работника*) to replace; (: *игрока*) to substitute; (*вакантную должность*) to fill.

замеще́ни|е (-я) *ср* (*работника, директора*) replacement; (*игрока*) substitution; ~ **вака́нтной до́лжности** filling of a vacancy.

замещу́ *сов см* **замести́ть**.

замина́ть(ся) (-ю(сь)) *несов от* **замя́ть(ся)**.

замини́рова|ть (-ую) *сов от* **мини́ровать**.

зами́н|ка (-и) *ж* (*в работе*) hitch; (*в речи*) stumble.

замира́|ть (-ю) *несов от* **замерёть**.

замире́ни|е (-я) *ср* appeasement.

за́мка *сущ см* **за́мок**.

замка́ *сущ см* **замо́к**.

за́мкнут|ый (-, -а, -о) *прил* (*среда, жизнь*) cloistered; (*человек, характер*) reclusive; **за́мкнутая цепь** (*ЭЛЕК*) closed circuit; **за́мкнутый круг** vicious circle.

замкн|у́ть (-у́, -ёшь; *impf* **замыка́ть**) *сов перех* to close

► **замкну́ться** (*impf* **замыка́ться**) *сов возв* to close; (*перен: обособиться*) to shut o.s. off; **замыка́ться** (~**ся** *perf*) **в себе́** to withdraw into o.s.

замну́(сь) *итп сов см* **замя́ть(ся)**.

замоги́льный *прил*: ~ **го́лос** ghostly voice.

за́м|ок (-ка) *м* castle.

замо́|к (-ка́) *м* lock; (*также*: **вися́чий** ~) padlock; (*браслета, цепочки*) clasp; **на** ~**кé** locked; **под** ~**ко́м** under lock and key; **храни́ть** (*impf*) **что-н за семью́** ~**ка́ми** to keep sth very closely guarded.

замо́к|нуть (*3sg* -нет, *pt* -, -ла, -ло, *impf* **замока́ть**) *сов неперех* to get soaked.

замо́лв|ить (-лю, -ишь) *сов перех*: ~ **сло́во за кого́-н** (**пе́ред кем-н**) (*разг*) to put in a word for sb (with sb).

замо́лч|ать (-у́, -и́шь; *pt* -, -ла, -ло, *impf* **замолка́ть**) *сов неперех* (*человек*) to go quiet; (*перестать писать*): **он** ~**а́л ещё два го́да наза́д** I haven't heard from him for two years ♦ (*impf* **зама́лчивать**) *перех* (*разг: факты, происшествие*) to hush up; ~**й!** be quiet!, shut up!

замора́живани|е (-я) *ср* (*продуктов, овощей*) refrigeration; **замора́живание цен/зарабо́тной пла́ты** price/wage freeze.

замора́жива|ть (-ю) *несов от* **заморо́зить**.

замор|и́ть (-ю́, -и́шь) *сов от* **мори́ть**.

заморо́|зить (-жу, -зишь; *impf* **замора́живать**) *сов перех* (*продукты, овощи*) to freeze; (*десну, палец*) to freeze, numb; (*перен: строительство*) to put on hold; **замора́живать** (~ *perf*) **це́ны/зарпла́ту/счёт** to freeze prices/wages/an account.

за́морозк|и (-ов) *мн* frosts *мн*.

заморо́ч|ить (-у, -ишь) *сов от* **моро́чить**.

замо́рский (-ая, -ое, -ие) *прил* (*разг*) foreign.

замо́рыш (-а) *м* (*разг*) weed, wimp.

замост|и́ть (-щу́, -сти́шь) *сов от* **мости́ть**.

замо́тан|ный (-, -а, -о) *прил* (*разг*) knackered, whacked.

замота́|ть (-ю; *impf* **зама́тывать**) *сов перех* (*разг: утомить*) to knacker out; (*верёвку, канат*): ~ **что-н во что-н** to wind sth around sth

► **замота́ться** (*impf* **зама́тываться**) *сов возв* (*в платок, шарфом*) to bundle o.s. up; (*разг: утомиться*) to be knackered (out).

замощу́ *сов см* **замости́ть**.

зам|очи́ть (-очу́, -о́чишь; *impf* **зама́чивать**) *сов перех*: ~ **кого́-н/что-н** to get sb/sth wet; (*бельё, ко́жу*) to soak.

замру́ *итп сов см* **замере́ть**.

за́муж *нареч*: **выходи́ть** ~ (**за** +*acc*) to get married (to), marry; **выдава́ть** (**вы́дать** *perf*) **кого́-н** ~ (**за** +*acc*) to marry sb off (to).

за́мужем *нареч* married; **быть** (*impf*) ~ **за кем-н** to be married to sb.

заму́жеств|о (-а) *ср* marriage.

заму́жн|яя *прил* married ♦ (-**ей**; *decl like adj*) *ж* married woman (*мн* women).

замур|ова́ть (-у́ю; *impf* **замуро́вывать**) *сов перех* (*отверстие, окно*) to brick up; (*челове́ка, це́нности*) to brick in.

заму́т|ить(ся) (-чу́(сь), -ти́шь(ся)) *сов от* **мути́ть(ся)**.

заму́ч|ить (-у, -ишь) *сов от* **му́чить** ♦ *перех* (*заста́вить страда́ть*) to torment; (*утоми́ть*) to exhaust; (*до сме́рти*) to torture to death
▸ **заму́читься** *сов от* **му́читься** ♦ *возв* (*утоми́ться*) to exhaust o.s.

замучу́(сь) *сов см* **замути́ть(ся)**.

за́мш|а (-и) *ж* suede.

за́мшевый *прил* suede.

замше́лый *прил* mossy, moss-covered.

замыва́|ть (-ю) *несов от* **замы́ть**.

замыка́ни|е (-я) *ср* (*та́кже*: **коро́ткое** ~) short circuit.

замыка́|ть (-ю) *несов от* **замкну́ть** ♦ *перех* (*коло́нну, ше́ствие*) to bring up the rear of
▸ **замыка́ться** *несов от* **замкну́ться**.

за́мыс|ел (-ла) *м* (*челове́ка, прави́тельства*) scheme; (*карти́ны, произведе́ния*) idea.

замы́сл|ить (-ю, -ишь; *impf* **замышля́ть**) *сов перех* (*план, побе́г*) to think up; (+*infin*) to think about doing; **он** ~**ил купи́ть себе́ дом** he is thinking about buying a house.

замыслова́т|ый (-, -а, -о) *прил* intricate.

замы́|ть (-о́ю, -о́ешь; *impf* **замыва́ть**) *сов перех* to wash out.

замышля́|ть (-ю) *несов от* **замы́слить**.

замя́|ть (-ну́, -нёшь; *impf* **замина́ть**) *сов перех* (*разг*: *сде́лать незаме́тным*: *вопро́с*) to hush up; (: *приостанови́ть*: *разгово́р*) to put an end *или* a stop to
▸ **замя́ться** (*impf* **замина́ться**) *сов возв* to clam up; (*разг*: *замолча́ть*) to stop short.

за́навес (-а) *м* (*ТЕА́ТР*) curtain; **желе́зный** ~ (*ИСТ*) the Iron Curtain.

занаве́|сить (-шу, -сишь; *impf* **занаве́шивать**) *сов перех* to hang a curtain over.

занаве́с|ка (-ки; *gen pl* -ок) *ж* curtain.

занаве́шива|ть (-ю) *несов от* **занаве́сить**.

занаве́шу *сов см* **занаве́сить**.

зана́шива|ть (-ю) *несов от* **заноси́ть**.

зан|ести́ (-есу́, -есёшь; *pt* -ёс, -есла́, -есло́, *impf* **заноси́ть**) *сов перех* (*принести́*) to bring;

(*подня́ть*: *но́гу, ру́ку*) to lift; (*записа́ть*) to take down; (*доста́вить*): ~ **что-н кому́-н** to drop sth off to sb; (*отнести́*): ~ **за** +*acc* to take behind; **доро́гу ~есло́ сне́гом** the road is covered over with snow; **судьба́ ~есла́ меня́ сюда́ мно́го лет наза́д** fate brought me here many years ago.

зани́|зить (-жу, -зишь; *impf* **занижа́ть**) *сов перех* to lower; **занижа́ть** (**занизи́ть** *perf*) **отме́тки кому́-н** to undermark sb.

занима́тельный (-ен, -ьна, -ьно) *прил* engaging.

занима́|ть (-ю) *несов от* **заня́ть**
▸ **занима́ться** *несов возв*: ~**ся** (+*instr*) (*учи́ться*) to study; (*рабо́тать*) to work (in); (*на роя́ле итп*) to practise (*BRIT*), practice (*US*); ~**ся** (*impf*) **англи́йским (языко́м)** to study English; ~**ся** (*impf*) **спо́ртом/му́зыкой** to play sports/music; **чем ~ется Ваш оте́ц?** what does your father do (for a living)?; **он ~ется би́знесом/поли́тикой** he's a businessman/politician; **чем ты сейча́с ~ешься?** what are you doing at the moment?

за́ново *нареч* again.

заножу́ *сов см* **занози́ть**.

зано́з|а (-ы) *ж* splinter.

заноз|и́ть (-жу́, -зи́шь) *сов перех* to get a splinter in.

зано́с (-а) *м* (*обы́чно мн*) drift; **сне́жные ~ы** snowdrift.

зан|оси́ть (-ошу́, -о́сишь) *несов перех от* **занести́** ♦ (*impf* **зана́шивать**) *сов перех* (*пла́тье, пальто́ итп*) to wear out.

зано́счив|ый (-, -а, -о) *прил* arrogant.

заноч|ева́ть (-у́ю) *сов непере*х to spend the night.

заношу́ (*не*)*сов см* **заноси́ть**.

зану́д|а (-ы) *м/ж* bore.

зану́дный (-ен, -на, -но) *прил* tiresome, tedious.

зан|ы́ть (-о́ю, -о́ешь) *сов непере*х (*ребёнок*) to start whinging; (*се́рдце, зуб*) to begin to ache.

за́нят (-, -а́, -о) *прил* busy; **он был о́чень** ~ he was very busy; **телефо́н** ~ the phone *или* line is engaged.

заня́т|ие *прил см* **заня́тный**.

заня́т|ие (-я) *ср* occupation; (*обы́чно мн*: *в шко́ле, в институ́те*) lesson, class; (*времяпрепровожде́ние*) pastime, pursuit; **нача́ло шко́льных ~й** (*нача́ло уче́бного го́да*) the beginning of the school year; (*у́тром*) the beginning of the school day.

заня́т|ный (-ен, -на, -но) *прил* entertaining.

заня́т|ой *прил* busy; **он ~ ~ челове́к** he is a busy man.

за́нятост|ь (-и) *ж* (*ЭКО́Н*) employment; **по́лная** ~ full employment.

зан|я́ть (**займу́, займёшь**; *pt* -ял, -яла́, -яло, *impf* **занима́ть**) *сов перех* (*кварти́ру, го́род*) to occupy; (*до́лжность, пози́цию*) to take up;

(де́ньги) to borrow; (вре́мя) to take; (развле́чь) to occupy; ~ (perf) ме́сто кому́-н to keep a place for sb; все ~я́ли свои́ места́ everyone took their places; ~ (perf) пе́рвое/второ́е ме́сто to take first/second place; э́та рабо́та ~я́ла (у меня́) два часа́ the work took (me) two hours; э́то займёт всего́ одну́ мину́тку it will only take a minute

▶ **заня́ться** сов возв: ~ся +instr (языко́м, предме́том, спо́ртом) to take up; (би́знесом, поли́тикой) to go into; (помо́чь): ~ся с кем-н (чем-н) to assist sb with sth; ~ся (perf) собо́й/детьми́ to devote time to o.s./one's children; ~ся (perf) убо́ркой to do the cleaning; ему́ пора́ ~ся де́лом it's time that he did something serious with his life.

заобла́чный прил lofty.

заодно́ нареч (вме́сте) as one; (попу́тно) at the same time; де́йствовать (impf) ~ to act as one или with one accord; мы с ни́ми ~ we are in total accord.

заостри́ть (-ю́, -и́шь) impf заостря́ть) сов перех (копьё, каранда́ш) to sharpen; (перен: мысль, вопро́с) to define; заостря́ть (~ perf) внима́ние на чём-н to focus one's attention on sth

▶ **заостри́ться** (impf заостря́ться) сов возв (черты́ лица́) to become more pointed.

зао́чник (-а) м part-time student (studying by correspondence).

зао́чница (-ы) ж см зао́чник.

зао́чно нареч: учи́ться ~ to study part-time (by correspondence); обсужда́ть (impf) кого́-н ~ to discuss sb in his итп absence.

зао́чный прил part-time; зао́чное обуче́ние distance learning; зао́чный институ́т correspondence school.

за́пад (-а) м west; 3~ (полит) the West.

запада́ть (3sg -ет, 3pl -ют) несов от запа́сть.

западёт итп сов см запа́сть.

за́падник (-а) м westernizer.

западноевропе́йск|ий (-ая, -ое, -ие) прил West European.

за́падный прил western; (ве́тер) westerly.

западня́ (-и́) ж snare; (перен) trap.

запа́ива|ть (-ю) несов от запая́ть.

запако́ва|ть (-ю) сов от пакова́ть ♦ (impf запако́вывать) перех to wrap up.

запако́|стить (-щу, -стишь) сов от па́костить.

запа́л (-а) м (заря́да) fuse; (разг: пыл) fire (fig).

запа́льчив|ый (-, -а, -о) прил (челове́к, хара́ктер) quick-tempered; (отве́т, тон) impatient.

запанибра́та нареч (разг): обраща́ться ~ с кем-н to be overly familiar with sb.

запаник|ова́ть (-у́ю) сов непе́рех (разг) to panic.

запа́рк|а (-и) ж (разг) mad rush.

запа́рыва|ть (-ю) несов от запоро́ть.

запа́с (-а) м (проду́ктов, то́плива итп) store, supply; (руды́, поле́зных ископа́емых) deposit;

(перен: зна́ний) store; (на брю́ках, на пла́тье) hem; (воен) the reserves мн; у меня́ два часа́ в ~е I've got two hours to spare; оставля́ть (оста́вить perf) себе́ что-н про ~ to put sth by; золото́й ~ gold reserves мн; запа́с слов vocabulary.

запаса́|ть(ся) (-ю(сь)) несов от запасти́(сь).

запа́сливый (-, -а, -о) прил thrifty.

запа́сник (-а) м (в музе́е) storage room; (разг: воен) reserve.

запасн|о́й прил spare ♦ (-о́го; decl like adj) м (спорт: та́кже: ~ игро́к) substitute; (воен) reservist; запасно́й вы́ход emergency exit; запасно́й путь siding; запасно́й соста́в (воен) the reserves.

запа́сный прил = запасно́й.

запа́с|ти́ (-у́, -ёшь; pt -а́с, -асла́, -асло́, impf запаса́ть) сов перех (дрова́, то́пливо) to lay in

▶ **запасти́сь** (impf запаса́ться) сов возв: ~сь (+instr) (хле́бом, молоко́м) to stock up (on); запаса́ться (~сь perf) терпе́нием to arm o.s. with patience.

запа́|сть (3sg -дёт, 3pl -ду́т, pt -л, -ла, -ло, impf запада́ть) сов непе́рех (глаза́, щёки) to become sunken; (перен: фра́за, слова́) to be imprinted; его́ слова́ ~ли мне в па́мять his words remain imprinted on my memory.

запатент|ова́ть (-у́ю) сов от патентова́ть ♦ (impf запатенто́вывать) перех to patent.

за́пах (-а; part gen -у) м smell.

запа́х (-а) м (хала́та, пальто́) fold.

запа́хива|ть (-ю) несов от запахну́ть.

запа́х|нуть (-ну, -нешь; pt -, -ла, -ло) сов непе́рех: ~ (+instr) to start to smell (of).

запахну́ть (-у́, -ёшь; impf запа́хивать) сов перех to wrap round.

запа́чка|ть (-ю) сов от па́чкать ♦ перех to soil, dirty; (перен: со́весть, и́мя) to tarnish, sully

▶ **запа́чкаться** сов от па́чкаться ♦ возв to get dirty.

запая́|ть (-ю; impf запа́ивать) сов перех to solder.

запева́л|а (-ы) м/ж (муз) leader (of a song).

запева́|ть (-ю) несов непе́рех to lead off ♦ перех: ~ пе́сню to start up a song.

запе́й(те) сов см запи́ть.

запе́к|(ся) итп сов см запе́чь(ся).

запека́нк|а (-и) ж (карто́фельная итп) bake; (сла́дкая) baked pudding.

запека́|ть(ся) (-ю(сь)) несов от запе́чь(ся).

запеку́|(сь) итп сов см запе́чь(ся).

запелена́|ть (-ю) сов от пелена́ть.

запеленг|ова́ть (-у́ю) сов от пеленгова́ть.

зап|ере́ть (-ру́, -рёшь; pt -ер, -ерла́, -ерло, impf запира́ть) сов перех (дверь, шкаф, замо́к) to lock; (дом, челове́ка, де́ньги) to lock up

▶ **запере́ться** (impf запира́ться) сов возв (дверь, шкаф, замо́к) to lock; (челове́к) to lock o.s. up; (перен: не призна́ться) to clam up.

зап|е́ть (-ою́, -оёшь) сов перех: ~ пе́сню to start singing a song.

запеча́та|ть (-ю; *impf* **запеча́тывать**) *сов перех* to seal up.

запечатле́|ть (-ю; *impf* **запечатлева́ть**) *сов перех* (*на карти́не, в по́вести итп*) to capture; (*в па́мяти*) to impress

▶ **запечатле́ться** (*impf* **запечатлева́ться**) *сов возв*: ~**ся в па́мяти** to be imprinted on one's memory.

запеча́тыва|ть (-ю) *несов от* **запеча́тать**.

запе|чь (-еку́, -ечёшь итп, -еку́т; *pt* -ёк, -екла́, -екло́, *impf* **запека́ть**) *сов перех* to bake

▶ **запе́чься** (*impf* **запека́ться**) *сов возв* to bake; (*кровь*) to congeal; (*гу́бы, рот*) to become parched.

запива́|ть (-ю) *несов от* **запи́ть**.

запина́|ться (-юсь) *несов от* **запну́ться**.

запи́н|ка (-ки; *gen pl* -ок) *ж* hesitation; **без** ~**ки** smoothly.

запира́тельств|о (-а) *ср* obstinacy.

запира́|ть(ся) (-ю(сь)) *несов от* **запере́ть(ся)**.

запи|са́ть (-ишу́, -и́шешь; *impf* **запи́сывать**) *сов перех* (*а́дрес, и́мя итп*) to write down; (*конце́рт, пласти́нку*) to record; (*в кружо́к, на ку́рсы*) to enrol; **запи́сывать** (~ *perf*) **ле́кцию** to take notes (*in a lecture*); ~ (*perf*) **кого́-н (на приём) к врачу́** to make a doctor's appointment for sb

▶ **записа́ться** (*impf* **запи́сываться**) *сов возв* (*в кружо́к, на ку́рсы*) to enrol (o.s.); (*музыка́нт: на плёнку*) to make a recording; ~**ся** (*perf*) (**на приём) к врачу́** to make a doctor's appointment.

за́пис|и (-ей) *мн* (*ле́кции итп*) notes *мн*.

запи́ск|а (-и) *ж* note; (*служе́бная*) memo; *см та́кже* **запи́ски**.

запи́ск|и (-ок) *мн* (*коро́ткие за́писи*) jottings *мн*; (*ЛИТЕРАТУ́РА*) notes *мн*, sketches *мн*.

записн|о́й *прил*: ~**а́я кни́жка** notebook.

запи́сок *сущ см* **запи́ски**.

запи́сыва|ть(ся) (-ю(сь)) *несов от* **записа́ть(ся)**.

за́пис|ь (-и) *ж* (*собы́тий, КОМП*) record; (*в дневнике́*) entry; (*МУЗ*) recording; (*в кружо́к, на ку́рсы*) enrolment (*BRIT*), enrollment (*US*); (*на приём к врачу́*) registration; *см та́кже* **за́писи**.

запи́|ть (-ью, -ьёшь; *pt* -и́л, -ила́, -и́ло, *imper* -е́й(те), *impf* **запива́ть**) *сов перех* (*лека́рство, обе́д*): ~ **что-н (чем-н)** to wash sth down (with sth) ◆ (*pt* -и́л,-ила́,-и́ло) *неперех* (*нача́ть пить*) to take to drink.

запиха́|ть (-ю; *impf* **запи́хивать**) *сов перех*: ~ **что-н в** +*acc* (*разг*) to stuff sth into.

запихн|у́ть (-у́, -ёшь) *сов* = **запиха́ть**.

запишу́(сь) *итп сов см* **записа́ть(ся)**.

запла́ка|нный (-, -а, -о) *прил* tearful; (*глаза́*) puffy.

запла́|кать (-чу, -чешь) *сов непе́рех* to start crying *или* to cry.

заплани́р|овать (-ую) *сов перех* to plan.

запла́т|а (-ы) *ж* patch.

заплати́|ть (-ачу́, -а́тишь) *сов от* **плати́ть**.

запла́т|ка (-ки; *gen pl* -ок) *ж* = **запла́та**.

заплачу́ *итп сов см* **запла́кать**.

заплачу́ *сов см* **заплати́ть**.

заплёвыва|ть (-ю; *impf* **заплёвывать**) *сов перех* (*пол итп*) to spit on; (*челове́ка*) to spit at.

заплёл *итп сов см* **заплести́**.

заплесневе́лый *прил* mouldy (*BRIT*), moldy (*US*).

заплесневе|ть (*3sg* -ет, *3pl* -ют) *сов от* **пле́сневеть**.

запл|ести́ (-ету́, -етёшь; *pt* -ёл, -ела́, -ело́, *impf* **заплета́ть**) *сов перех* (*во́лосы, ко́су*) to plait.

заплета́|ться (*3sg* -ется, *3pl* -ются) *несов возв*: **у него́ но́ги** ~**ются** he keeps tripping over his feet; **у неё язы́к** ~**ется** she is muddling her words.

заплету́ *итп сов см* **заплести́**.

запломбир|ова́ть (-у́ю) *сов от* **пломбирова́ть**.

заплы́в (-а) *м* (*СПОРТ*) race (*in swimming*); (: *отбо́рочный*) heat.

заплы́|ть (-ву́, -вёшь; *impf* **заплыва́ть**) *сов непе́рех* (*челове́к*) to swim off; (*кора́бль*) to sail off; (*бревно́*) to float off; (*глаза́*) to become swollen.

запн|у́ться (-у́сь, -ёшься; *impf* **запина́ться**) *сов возв* to falter, stumble.

запове́дник (-а) *м* (*приро́дный*) nature reserve; **пти́чий** ~ bird reserve.

запове́дный *прил* (*лес, террито́рия*) protected.

за́поведь (-и) *ж* (*РЕЛ*) commandment; (*перен*) cardinal rule; **де́сять** ~**ей** the Ten Commandments.

заподо́зр|ить (-ю, -ишь) *сов перех* to suspect; ~ (*perf*) **кого́-н в** +*acc* to suspect sb of.

запо́ем *нареч*: **пить** ~ to drink heavily; **он чита́ет** ~ (*разг*) he's an avid reader.

запозда́лый *прил* (*по́мощь, трево́га итп*) belated; (*гость, весна́*) late.

запо́|й (-я) *м* binge.

заполз|ти́ (-у́, -ёшь; *impf* **заполза́ть**) *сов непе́рех* to crawl.

заполне́ни|е (-я) *ср* (*ба́ка, резервуа́ра*) filling; (*анке́ты, бла́нка*) completion.

запо́лн|ить (-ю, -ишь; *impf* **заполня́ть**) *сов перех* (*бак, ко́мнату*) to fill (up); (*анке́ту, бланк*) to fill in *или* out

▶ **запо́лниться** (*impf* **заполня́ться**) *сов возв* to fill up.

заполя́рный *прил* polar.

запомина́|ть (-ю) *несов от* **запо́мнить**

▶ **запомина́ться** *несов от* **запо́мниться**; **легко́/тру́дно** ~**ся** (*impf*) to be easy/difficult to remember.

запомина́ющий (-ая, -ее, -ие) *прил* (*КОМП*):

~ее устро́йство memory; ~ее устро́йство с произво́льной вы́боркой random access memory.

запо́мн|ить (-ю, -ишь; *impf* **запомина́ть**) *сов перех* to remember

▸ **запо́мниться** (*impf* **запомина́ться**) *сов возв*: мне ~ились его́ слова́ I remembered his words.

за́понк|а (-и) *ж* cuff link.

запо́р (-а) *м* (МЕД) constipation; (*замок*) lock; **быть** (*impf*) **на** ~**е** to be locked.

запор|о́ть (-орю́, -о́решь; *impf* **запа́рывать**) *сов перех* (*разг: испортить*) to botch up.

запороши́ть (*3sg* -**и́т**) *сов перех безл* to sprinkle; **доро́гу** ~**и́ло сне́гом** a sprinkling of snow covered the road.

запотева́|ть (-ю) *несов от* **запоте́ть**.

запоте́вш|ий (-ая, -ее, -ие) *прил* misty.

запоте́|ть (-ю; *impf* **запотева́ть**) *сов неперех* to steam up.

запою́ *итп сов см* **запе́ть**.

запра́в|ить (-лю, -ишь; *impf* **заправля́ть**) *сов перех* (*рубашку*) to tuck in; (*лампу*) to fill; (*салат*) to dress; **заправля́ть** (~ *perf*) **маши́ну** to fill up the engine

▸ **запра́виться** (*impf* **заправля́ться**) *сов возв* (*разг: горючим*) to tank up; (: *поесть*) to fuel up.

запра́в|ка (-ки; *gen pl* -**ок**) *ж* (*машины, самолёта итп*) refuelling; (*кулин*) dressing; (*разг: также*: ~**очная ста́нция**) filling station.

запра́влю(сь) *сов см* **запра́вить(ся)**.

заправля́|ть (-ю) *несов от* **запра́вить** ♦ *неперех*: ~ (+*instr*) (*разг: делами итп*) to be in charge (of)

▸ **заправля́ться** *несов от* **запра́виться**.

запра́вк|а *сущ см* **запра́вка**.

запра́вск|ий (-ая, -ое, -ие) *прил* true, real.

запра́шива|ть (-ю) *несов от* **запроси́ть**.

запре́т (-а) *м*: ~ (**на** +*acc*/+*infin*) ban (on/on doing); **быть** (*impf*) **под** ~**ом** to be banned.

запре́тен *прил см* **запре́тный**.

запре|ти́ть (-щу́, -ти́шь; *impf* **запреща́ть**) *сов перех* to ban.

запре́тн|ый (-ен, -на, -но) *прил* forbidden; ~**ная те́ма** taboo subject; **запре́тная зо́на** restricted area *или* zone; **запре́тный плод** forbidden fruit.

запреща́|ть (-ю) *несов от* **запрети́ть**

▸ **запреща́ться** *несов возв* to be forbidden *или* prohibited.

запреще́ни|е (-я) *ср* banning.

запрещённ|ый (-, -а, -о) *прил* banned; **запрещённый приём** (СПОРТ) foul; (*перен*) underhand tactic.

запрещу́ *сов см* **запрети́ть**.

запрограмми́р|овать (-ую) *сов от* **программи́ровать**.

запроекти́р|овать (-ую) *сов от* **проекти́ровать**.

запроки́н|уть (-у, -ешь; *impf* **запроки́дывать**) *сов перех*: ~ **го́лову** to throw one's head back

▸ **запроки́нуться** (*impf* **запроки́дываться**) *сов возв* to jerk backwards.

запропа|сти́ться (-щу́сь, -сти́шься) *сов неперех* (*разг*) to disappear.

запро́с (-а) *м* inquiry; (*обычно мн*: *требования*) need, requirement; (*стремления*) expectation.

запр|оси́ть (-ошу́, -о́сишь; *impf* **запра́шивать**) *сов перех* (*мнение, ответ итп*) to request; (*цену*) to ask.

за́просто *нареч* (*разг: без усилий*) easily; (*без церемоний*) without making a fuss; **он обы́чно захо́дит к нам** ~ he usually just drops in.

запротест|ова́ть (-у́ю) *сов неперех* to start protesting.

запротоколи́р|овать (-ую) *сов от* **протоколи́ровать**.

запрошу́ *сов см* **запроси́ть**.

запру́(сь) *итп сов см* **запере́ть(ся)**.

запру́д|а (-ы) *ж* (*плотина*) weir; (*водоём*) millpond.

запру|ди́ть (-ужу́, -у́дишь; *impf* **запру́живать** *или* **пруди́ть**) *сов перех* (*реку, ручей*) to dam; (*impf* **запру́живать**; *перен: площадь итп*) to pack.

запры́га|ть (-ю) *сов неперех* to start jumping.

запря́|чь (-гу́, -жёшь *итп*, -гу́т; *pt* -я́г, -ягла́, -ягло́, *impf* **запряга́ть**) *сов перех* (*лошадь*) to harness, hitch up; (*разг: нагрузить работой*) to weigh down.

запу́ган|ный (-, -на, -но) *прил* frightened, scared.

запуга́|ть (-ю; *impf* **запу́гивать**) *сов перех* to frighten, scare.

за́пуск (-а) *м* (*мотора, станка*) starting; (*ракеты, спутника*) launch.

запуска́|ть (-ю) *несов от* **запусти́ть**.

запусте́ни|е (-я) *ср* neglect.

запу|сти́ть (-щу́, -у́стишь; *impf* **запуска́ть**) *сов перех* (*бросить*) to hurl; (*мотор, станок*) to start (up); (*ракету, спутник*) to launch; (*хозяйство, работу, болезнь*) to neglect; (*разг: руку, когти*) to plunge; (: *впустить*) to let in ♦ *неперех*: ~ **чем-н в кого́-н** to hurl sth at sb; **запуска́ть** (~ *perf*) **что-н в произво́дство** to launch production of sth.

запу́тан|ный (-, -на, -но) *прил* (*нитки, волосы*) tangled, entangled; (*дело, вопрос*) confused; (*фраза*) muddled.

запу́та|ть (-ю) *сов от* **пу́тать** ♦ (*impf* **запу́тывать**) *перех* (*нитки, волосы*) to tangle; (*вопрос, человека*) to confuse

▸ **запу́таться** *сов от* **пу́таться** ♦ (*impf* **запу́тываться**) *возв* (*нитки, волосы*) to become tangled (up); (*человек: в верёвках*) to get tangled *или* caught up; (*дело, вопрос*) to become confused; (*разг: сбиться с толку*) to get o.s. in a tangle; (: *сбиться с пути*) to get lost; **запу́тываться** (~**ся** *perf*) **в долга́х** to become trapped in debt; **запу́тываться** (~**ся** *perf*) **в отве́те** to get muddled up.

запу́щен|ный (-, -на, -но) *прил* neglected.

запущу́ *сов см* **запусти́ть**.

запча́сть (-и) *ж сокр = запасна́я часть*; *(обычно мн)* spare (part).

запыла́ть (-ю) *сов неперех (костёр, камин)* to flare up; *(щёки, человек)* to flush.

запыли́ть(ся) (-ю́(сь), -и́шь(ся)) *сов от* **пыли́ть(ся)**.

запыха́ться (-юсь) *сов возв* to be out of breath.

запью́ *итп сов см* **запи́ть**.

запя́стье (-ья; *gen pl* -ий) *ср* wrist.

запят|а́я (-о́й; *decl like adj*) *ж* comma.

запятна́ть (-ю) *сов от* **пятна́ть**.

зарабо́та|ть (-ю; *impf* **зараба́тывать**) *сов перех* to earn ♦ *неперех (no impf; начать работать)* to start up

▸ **зарабо́таться** (*impf* **зараба́тываться**) *сов возв (разг)* to work o.s. into the ground.

за́работка *сущ см* **за́работок**.

за́работн|ый *прил*: ~ая пла́та pay, wages *мн*.

за́работ|ок (-ка) *м* earnings *мн*.

зара́внива|ть (-ю) *несов от* **заровня́ть**.

заража́|ть(ся) (-ю(сь)) *несов от* **зарази́ть(ся)**.

зараже́ни|е (-я) *ср (организма, крови итп)* infection; *(местности, водоёма итп)* contamination.

заражён|ный (-, -а, -о) *прил (см сущ)* infected; contaminated.

заражу́(сь) *сов см* **зарази́ть(ся)**.

зара́з|а (-ы) *ж* infection ♦ *м/ж (разг: мерзавец)* pain, pest.

зара́зен *прил см* **зара́зный**.

зарази́тел|ьный (-ен, -ьна, -ьно) *прил (перен)* infectious.

зара|зи́ть (-жу́, -зи́шь; *impf* **заража́ть**) *сов перех (человека: также перен)* to infect; *(воду, местность)* to contaminate

▸ **зарази́ться** (*impf* **заража́ться**) *сов возв (+instr; гриппом, корью итп)* to catch; *(перен: страхом, весельем)* to be infected by.

зара́зн|ый (-ен, -на, -но) *прил* infectious.

зара́нее *нареч* in advance.

зар|асти́ (-асту́, -астёшь; *pt* -о́с, -осла́, -осло́, *impf* **зараста́ть**) *сов неперех (зажить: рана, порез)* to close up; **зараста́ть** (*~ perf*) *(+instr)* *(травой итп)* to be overgrown (with); **он** ~о́с щети́ной he has let his beard grow.

зарв|а́ться (-у́сь, -ёшься; *impf* **зарыва́ться**) *сов неперех (разг)* to go too far; **зарыва́ться** (*~ perf*) **в тре́бованиях** to demand too much.

зарёван|ный (-, -а, -о) *прил (разг)* = **запла́канный**.

зарев|е́ть (-у́, -ёшь) *сов неперех (медведь, лев)* to start roaring; *(бык)* to start bellowing; *(разг: заплакать)* to start bawling.

за́рев|о (-а) *ср* glow.

зарегистри́рованный *прил* registered; ~ **торго́вый знак** registered trademark.

зарегистри́р|овать (-ую) *сов от* **регистри́ровать**.

заре́жу(сь) *итп сов см* **заре́зать(ся)**.

заре́з (-а) *м*: по ~, до ~у *(разг)* badly; **мне по ~ нужна́ твоя́ по́мощь** I badly need your help.

заре́|зать (-жу, -жешь) *сов от* **ре́зать** ♦ *перех (человека)* to knife; *(impf* **ре́зать**; *козу, поросёнка)* to slaughter; *(разг: книгу, проект)* to axe *(BRIT)*, ax *(US)*

▸ **заре́заться** *сов возв (разг)* to knife o.s.

зарека́|ться (-юсь) *несов от* **заре́чься**.

зарекоменд|ова́ть (-у́ю; *impf* **зарекомéнд-о́вывать**) *сов перех*: ~ **себя́** +*instr* to prove *или* show o.s. to be; **он хорошо́ себя́** ~ова́л he proved to be good.

заре́|чься (-ку́сь, -чёшься итп, -ку́тся; *pt* -ёкся, -екла́сь, -екло́сь, *impf* **зарека́ться**) *сов возв (+infin)* to swear *или* vow never to do; **она́** ~екла́сь ходи́ть туда́ she vowed never to go there.

заржа́ве|ть (*3sg* -ет) *сов от* **ржа́веть**.

заржа́влен|ный (-, -а, -о) *прил* rusty.

заржа́|ть (-у́, -ёшь) *сов неперех (лошадь)* to neigh; *(разг: человек)* to roar with laughter.

зарис|ова́ть (-у́ю; *impf* **зари́совывать**) *сов перех (дом, лодку)* to sketch; **они́** ~ова́ли всю сте́ну *(разг)* they drew all over the wall.

зарисо́вк|а (-ки; *gen pl* -ок) *ж (действие)* sketching; *(обычно мн: рисунок)* sketch.

зари́совыва|ть (-ю) *несов от* **зарисова́ть**.

зарни́ц|а (-ы) *ж* sheet lightning.

заровня́|ть (-ю; *impf* **зара́внивать**) *сов перех (поверхность)* to level; *(яму, канаву)* to fill up.

зароди́|ться (*3sg* -и́тся, *3pl* -я́тся, *impf* **зарожда́ться**) *сов возв (явление)* to emerge; *(перен: идея)* to be born; *(: чувство, сомнения)* to arise.

заро́дыш (-а) *м (БИО)* embryo; *(растения, также перен)* germ; **в** ~**е** *(перен)* in embryo; **подавля́ть (подави́ть** *perf***) что-н в** ~**е** to nip sth in the bud.

зарожда́|ться (*3sg* -ется, *3pl* -ются) *несов от* **зароди́ться**.

зарожде́ни|е (-я) *ср (жизни)* emergence; *(идеи, чувства)* conception.

заро́к (-а) *м* pledge, vow.

зaро́с *итп сов см* **зарасти́**.

за́росл|ь (-и) *ж (обычно мн)* thicket.

зарпла́т|а (-а) *ж* pay.

заруба́|ть (-ю) *несов от* **заруби́ть**.

зарубе́жный *прил* foreign.

зарубе́жь|е (-я) *ср* overseas; **стра́ны бли́жнего** ~**я** "near abroad" (*the republics of the former USSR*).

зар|уби́ть (-ублю́, -у́бишь; *impf* **заруба́ть**) *сов перех* to hack down; ~**уби́ себе́ на носу́** *или* **лбу** *(разг)* mark my words.

зару́бк|а (-и) *ж* notch.

зарублю́ *сов см* **заруби́ть**.

зарубц|ева́ться (*3sg* -у́ется, *3pl* -у́ются) *сов от* **рубцева́ться ♦** (*impf* **зарубцо́вываться**) *возв* to cicatrize.

заруман|иться (-юсь, -ишься; *impf* **заруманиваться**) *сов возв* (*лицо, щёки*) to colour (*BRIT*), color (*US*); (*пирог, мясо*) to brown.

заручи́ться (-у́сь, -и́шься; *impf* **заруча́ться**) *сов возв* (+*instr*; *помощью, согласием*) to secure.

зарыва́|ть (-ю) *несов от* **зары́ть**

▶ **зарыва́ться** *несов от* **зары́ться, зарва́ться.**

зарыда́|ть (-ю) *сов неперех* to begin to weep.

зар|ы́ть (-о́ю, -о́ешь; *impf* **зарыва́ть**) *сов перех* to bury; (*яму, канаву*) to fill

▶ **зары́ться** (*impf* **зарыва́ться**) *сов возв:* ~**ся в** +*acc* (*в зе́млю, в песо́к*) to bury o.s. in; **зарыва́ться** (~**ся** *perf*) **в рабо́ту/учёбу** to bury o.s. in one's work/books; **она́** ~**ылась голово́й в поду́шку** she buried her head in the pillow.

зар|я́ (-и́; *nom pl* зо́ри, *gen pl* зорь, *dat pl* зо́рям) *ж* (*у́тренняя, та́кже перен*) dawn; (*вече́рняя*) sundown; (*ВОЕН*) reveille; **ни свет ни** ~ at the crack of dawn; **от** ~**й до** ~**й** from dawn to dusk.

заря́д (-а) *м* (*ВОЕН, ЭЛЕК*) charge; (*перен: бо́дрости, эне́ргии*) charge, boost.

заря|ди́ть (-жу́, -ди́шь; *impf* **заряжа́ть**) *сов перех* (*пистоле́т, пу́шку, фотоаппара́т*) to load; (*батаре́йку, аккумуля́тор*) to charge; **он** ~**ди́л одно́ и то же** (*разг*) he keeps going on about it; **дождь** ~**ди́л** (*разг*) it started pouring

▶ **заряди́ться** (*impf* **заряжа́ться**) *сов возв* (*батаре́йка, аккумуля́тор*) to recharge; **заряжа́ться** (~**ся** *perf*) **эне́ргией** (*перен*) to recharge one's batteries.

заря́д|ка (-и) *ж* (*упражне́ния*) exercises *мн*.

заряжа́|ть(ся) (-ю(сь)) *несов от* **заряди́ть(ся).**

заряжу́(сь) *сов см* **заряди́ть(ся).**

заса́д|а (-ы) *ж* ambush; (*отря́д*) ambush party; **устра́ивать** (**устро́ить** *perf*) ~**у** to set up an ambush; **сиде́ть** (*impf*) **в** ~**е** to lie in ambush.

заса|ди́ть (-жу́, -а́дишь; *impf* **заса́живать**) *сов перех* (*гря́дку, клу́мбу*): ~ (+*instr*) to plant (with); (*разг: нож, топо́р*): ~ **в** +*acc* to sink into; ~ (*perf*) **кого́-н за решётку** (*разг*) to stick sb behind bars; **заса́живать** (~ *perf*) **кого́-н за рабо́ту** to set sb to work.

заса́ленный *прил* greasy.

заса́лива|ть (-ю) *несов от* **засоли́ть, заса́лить**

▶ **заса́ливаться** *несов от* **заса́литься.**

заса́л|ить (-ю, -ишь; *impf* **заса́ливать**) *сов перех* to soil

▶ **заса́литься** (*impf* **заса́ливаться**) *сов возв* to get greasy.

заса́сыва|ть (*3sg* -ет, *3pl* -ют) *несов от* **засоса́ть.**

заса́харенн|ый *прил:* ~**ые фру́кты** crystallized fruits *мн.*

заса́хар|ить (-ю, -ишь; *impf* **заса́харивать**) *сов перех* to crystallize

▶ **заса́хариться** (*impf* **заса́хариваться**) *сов*

возв (*мёд, варе́нье*) to crystallize.

засверка́|ть (-ю) *сов неперех* (*мо́лния, глаза́*) to flash.

засве|ти́ть (-чу́, -тишь; *impf* **засве́чивать**) *сов перех* (*ФОТО*) to expose

▶ **засвети́ться** (*impf* **засве́чиваться**) *сов возв* to be exposed.

за́светло *нареч* before nightfall *или* dark.

засве́чива|ть(ся) (-ю(сь)) *несов от* **засвети́ть(ся).**

засвечу́(сь) *сов см* **засвети́ть(ся).**

засвиде́тельств|овать (-ую) *сов перех* (*факт*) to testify to; (*докуме́нт, ко́пию*) to certify.

засева́|ть (-ю) *несов от* **засе́ять.**

заседа́ни|е (-я) *ср* (*собра́ние*) meeting; (*парла́мента, суда́*) session, sitting.

заседа́тель (-я) *м:* **прися́жный** ~ member of the jury.

заседа́|ть (-ю) *несов неперех* (*на совеща́нии*) to meet; (*в парла́менте, в суде́*) to sit; (*парла́мент, суд*) to be in session.

засе́ива|ть (-ю) *несов от* **засе́ять.**

засёк *итп сов см* **засе́чь.**

засека́|ть (-ю) *несов от* **засе́чь.**

засекре́|тить (-чу, -тишь; *impf* **засекре́чивать**) *сов перех* (*све́дения, докуме́нты*) to restrict access to.

засекре́ченный *прил* (*све́дения, докуме́нты*) classified; (*заво́д итп*) secret.

засекре́чива|ть (-ю) *несов от* **засекре́тить.**

засекре́чу *сов см* **засекре́тить.**

засеку́ *итп сов см* **засе́чь.**

засёл *итп сов см* **засе́сть.**

заселе́ни|е (-я) *ср* (*земе́ль*) settlement; (*дома́*) occupation.

заселённ|ый (-ён, -ена́, -ено́) *прил* (*о́бласть, райо́н*) settled; (*дом, кварти́ра*) occupied.

засел|и́ть (-ю́, -и́шь; *impf* **заселя́ть**) *сов перех* (*зе́мли*) to settle; (*дом*) to take up occupancy of.

засе́|сть (-я́ду, -я́дешь; *pt* -е́л, -е́ла, -е́ло) *сов неперех* (*надо́лго оста́ться: до́ма*) to ensconce o.s.; (*спря́таться*) to sit tight; (*застря́ть*) to lodge; ~ (*perf*) **за что-н/**+*infin* to get down to sth/down to doing.

засе́ч|ка (-ки; *gen pl* -ек) *ж* notch.

засе́|чь (-еку́, -ечёшь *итп*, -еку́т; *pt* -ёк, -екла́, -екло́, *impf* **засека́ть**) *сов перех* (*ме́сто*) to locate; (*разг: заме́тить*) to nail down; (*вы́пороть*) to flog; **засека́ть** (~ *perf*) **вре́мя** to record the time.

засе́|ять (-ю; *impf* **засева́ть** *или* **засе́ивать**) *сов перех* to sow.

засиде́ться (-жу́сь, -ди́шься; *impf* **заси́живаться**) *сов неперех* to stay for a long time; **мы вчера́** ~**де́лись в гостя́х** we stayed late at friends yesterday.

заси́ль|е (-я) *ср* dominance.

заси́я|ть (-ю) *сов неперех* to begin to shine.

заско́к (-а) *м* (*разг: в мы́слях*) peculiarity.

заскору́зл|ый (-, -а, -о) *прил* (*ко́жа, ру́ки*)

calloused.

заскочи́ть (-очу́, -о́чишь) *сов неперех (разг: в гости)* to drop in.

заскрежета́ть (-ещу́, -е́щешь) *сов неперех*: ~ зуба́ми to grind one's teeth.

заскуча́ть (-ю) *сов неперех* to get bored; ~ *(perf)* по кому́-н/чему́-н to start to miss sb/sth.

засла́ть (-шлю́, -шлёшь; *impf* засыла́ть) *сов перех* to send out.

засло́н (-а) *м* screen, shield.

заслони́ть (-ю́, -и́шь; *impf* заслоня́ть) *сов перех* to block out; *(от ве́тра, от пу́ли)* to shield, screen.

засло́нка (-ки; *gen pl* -ок) *ж (пе́чи)* vent; *(шлю́за)* gate.

заслоня́ть (-ю) *несов от* заслони́ть.

заслу́га (-и) *ж (обычно мн)* service; ~и пе́ред страно́й services to one's country; награди́ть *(perf)* кого́-н по ~м to fully reward sb; его́ наказа́ли по ~м he got what he deserved.

заслу́женный *прил* well-deserved, well-merited; *(врач, учёный итп)* renowned; **Заслу́женный арти́ст Росси́и/ма́стер спо́рта** title awarded by the state in honour of cultural/ sporting achievement.

заслу́живать (-ю) *несов от* заслужи́ть ♦ *перех (дове́рия, внима́ния итп)* to deserve.

заслужи́ть (-ужу́, -у́жишь; *impf* заслу́живать) *сов перех* to earn.

заслу́шать (-ю; *impf* заслу́шивать) *сов перех* to listen to

▶ **заслу́шаться** (*impf* заслу́шиваться) *сов возв*: ~ся (+*instr*) *(му́зыкой, расска́зом)* to be captivated (by).

засма́триваться (-юсь) *несов от* засмотре́ться.

засмея́ть (-ю́, -ёшь; *impf* засме́ивать) *сов перех* to taunt

▶ **засмея́ться** *сов возв* to start laughing.

засмотре́ться (-отрю́сь, -о́тришься; *impf* засма́триваться) *сов неперех*: ~ на +*acc* to be transfixed by.

засне́женный (-, -а, -о) *прил* snow-covered.

засну́ть (-у́, -ёшь; *impf* засыпа́ть) *сов неперех* to go to sleep, fall asleep.

засо́в (-а) *м* bolt.

засо́вывать (-ю) *несов от* засу́нуть.

засо́л (-а) *м (ры́бы)* salting.

засоли́ть (-олю́, -о́лишь; *impf* заса́ливать) *сов перех* to salt.

засоре́ние (-я) *ср (рек)* pollution; *(ра́ковины, туале́та)* blockage; **засоре́ние желу́дка** stomach upset.

засори́ть (-ю́, -и́шь; *impf* засоря́ть) *сов перех (ко́мнату, поля́ну)* to litter; *(ра́ковину, туале́т)* to block *или* clog up; *(перен: мы́сли, речь)* to contaminate; ~ *(perf)* глаза́ to get grit in one's eyes; ~ *(perf)* желу́док to get a stomach upset

▶ **засори́ться** (*impf* засоря́ться) *сов возв (ра́ковина, туале́т)* to become clogged up.

засоса́ть (-у́, -ёшь; *impf* заса́сывать) *сов перех* to suck in ♦ *неперех (no impf; подлеж: младе́нец)* to start feeding.

засо́хнуть (-у, -ешь) *сов от* со́хнуть ♦ *(impf* засыха́ть) *неперех (грязь)* to dry up; *(расте́ние)* to wither.

за́спанный (-, -на, -но) *прил* sleepy.

заспо́рить (-ю, -ишь) *сов неперех* to start arguing.

заста́ва (-ы) *ж (та́кже:* пограни́чная ~) frontier post; *(ВОЕН: отря́д)* party, detachment.

застава́ть (-ю́, -ёшь) *несов от* заста́ть.

заста́вить (-лю, -ишь; *impf* заставля́ть) *сов перех (заня́ть)* to clutter up; *(закры́ть)* to block off; **заставля́ть** (~ *perf)* кого́-н +*infin* to force sb to do, make sb do; **он ~ил меня́ помо́чь ему́** he made me help him.

заста́иваться (*3sg* -ется, *3pl* -ются) *несов от* застоя́ться.

заста́ну *итп сов см* заста́ть.

застаре́лый *прил* old.

заста́ть (-ну, -нешь; *impf* застава́ть) *сов перех* to catch, find; **я его́ не ~л до́ма** I didn't manage to catch him at home; **я ~л её за рабо́той** I found her at work.

застегну́ть (-у́, -ёшь; *impf* застёгивать) *сов перех* to do up

▶ **застегну́ться** (*impf* застёгиваться) *сов возв (челове́к: на пу́говицы)* to button o.s. up; *(: на мо́лнию)* to zip o.s. up; *(пу́говицы, мо́лния)* to do up.

застёжка (-ки; *gen pl* -ек) *ж* fastener.

застекли́ть (-ю́, -и́шь; *impf* застекля́ть) *сов перех* to glaze.

застели́ть (-ю́, -ишь; *impf* застила́ть) *сов перех (крова́ть)* to make up; *(стол, пол)* to cover.

застелю́ *итп сов см* застла́ть.

засте́нка *сущ см* засте́нок.

застенографи́ровать (-ую) *сов от* стенографи́ровать.

засте́нок (-ка; *nom pl* -ки) *м* torture chamber.

засте́нчивый (-, -а, -о) *прил* shy.

застесня́ться (-юсь) *сов возв (разг)* to go all shy.

засти́г *итп сов см* засти́чь.

застига́ть (-ю) *несов от* засти́гнуть, засти́чь.

засти́гну *итп сов см* засти́чь.

засти́гнуть (-ну, -нешь; *pt* -или -нул, -ла, -ло, *impf* застига́ть) *сов = засти́чь.

застила́ть (-ю) *несов от* застели́ть, застла́ть.

застира́ть (-ю; *impf* засти́рывать) *сов перех (бельё, оде́жду)* to overwash; *(пятно́)* to wash off *или* out.

засти́чь (-гну, -гнешь; *pt* -г, -гла, -гло, *impf* застига́ть) *сов перех* to catch.

застл|áть (-елю́, -éлешь; *impf* **застилáть**) *сов
перех* (*подлеж*: облака, туман) to cover;
(: слёзы, дым) to blur.

застó|й (-я) *м* (*в делах, в работе*) standstill; (*в
жизни, в мыслях*) stagnation.

застóйный *прил* (*также перен*) stagnant.

застóльн|ый *прил*: ~ые разговóры table talk;
~ая пéсня drinking song.

застон|áть (-онý, -óнешь) *сов неперех* to groan.

застопор|ить (-ю, -ишь) *сов от* **стóпорить**
▸ **застопóриться** *сов возв* (машина, станок)
to come to a halt; (дело, работа) to be held up.

застоя́|ться (3sg -и́тся, 3pl -я́ться, *impf*
застáиваться) *сов перех* (вода) to go stagnant.

застрáива|ть (-ю) *несов от* **застрóить**.

застрахóванн|ый (-, -а, -о) *прил* insured.

застрах|овáть (-ýю; *impf* **застрахóвывать**) *сов
перех*: ~ (от +gen) (*также перен*) to insure
(against)
▸ **застраховáться** (*impf* **застрахóвываться**)
сов возв: ~ся (от +gen) to insure o.s. (against).

застрáчива|ть (-ю) *несов от* **застрочи́ть**.

застрева́|ть (-ю) *несов от* **застря́ть**.

застрел|и́ть (-елю́, -éлишь; *impf*
застрéливать) *сов перех* to shoot
▸ **застрели́ться** (*impf* **застрéливаться**) *сов
возв* to shoot o.s.

застрóенный *прил* built-up.

застрó|ить (-ю, -ишь; *impf* **застрáивать**) *сов
перех* to build on, develop.

застрóйк|а (-и) *ж* development.

застроч|и́ть (-ý, -и́шь; *impf* **застрáчивать**) *сов
перех* (выточки, складки) to stitch ◆ *неперех*
(*по impf*; пулемёт) to spray bullets; (начать
писать) to start scribbling away.

застря́|ть (-ну, -нешь; *impf* **застревáть**) *сов
неперех* to get stuck.

застуд|и́ть (-ужý, -ýдишь; *impf* **застýживать**)
сов перех (*разг*): ~ гóрло/ýши to get a sore
throat/sore ears.

заступ|и́ться (-люсь, -ýпишься; *impf*
заступáться) *сов возв*: ~ за +acc to stand up
for.

застýпник (-а) *м* defender.

застýпниц|а (-ы) *ж см* **застýпник**.

застывá|ть (-ю) *несов от* **застыть**.

застывш|ий (-ая, -ее, -ие) *прил* (*также перен*)
frozen; (лава) solidified; (цемент, желе) set.

засты́|ть (-ну, -нешь; *impf* **застывáть**) *сов
неперех* to freeze; (лава) to solidify; (цемент)
to set; ~ (*perf*) на мéсте to freeze,
stop dead; ~ (*perf*) от стрáха to be paralysed
with fear.

засуе|ти́ться (-чýсь, -ти́шься) *сов возв* to start
bustling about.

засýн|уть (-у, -ешь; *impf* **засóвывать**) *сов
перех*: ~ что-н в +acc to thrust sth into.

зáсух|а (-и) *ж* drought.

засухоусто́йчив|ый (-, -а, -о) *прил* drought-
resistant.

засуч|и́ть (-учý, -ýчишь; *impf* **засýчивать**) *сов

перех* (штани́ну, рукав) to roll up; ~учи́в
рукавá (*перен*) in earnest.

засуш|и́ть (-ушý, -ýшишь; *impf* **засýшивать**)
сов перех to dry up.

засýшлив|ый (-, -а, -о) *прил* dry.

засчита́|ть (-ю; *impf* **засчи́тывать**) *сов перех* to
take into account; (гол, результат) to allow (to
stand).

засыла́|ть (-ю) *несов от* **засла́ть**.

засы́п|ать (-лю, -лешь; *impf* **засыпáть**) *сов
перех* (яму, канаву) to fill (up); (покрыть) to
cover; (*разг*: студéнта) to flunk; (муку, крупу
итп) to pour; **засыпáть** (~ *perf*) когó-н
вопрóсами/подáрками to bombard sb with
questions/gifts; егó ~ало пескóм he was buried
under the sand
▸ **засыпáться** (*impf* **засыпáться**) *сов возв*: ~ся
+instr (песком, землёй) to be covered with;
(*разг*: попáсться) to cock up; (: на экзáмене) to
flunk; **засыпáться** (~ся *perf*) в +acc/за +acc to
get into/behind.

засыпá|ть (-ю) *несов от* **заснýть**, **засы́пать**
▸ **засыпáться** *несов от* **засы́паться**.

засы́плю(сь) *итп сов см* **засы́пать(ся)**.

засóхн|уть (-у) *несов от* **засóхнуть**.

зася́ду *итп сов см* **засéсть**.

зата|и́ть (-ю́, -и́шь; *impf* **затáивать**) *сов перех*
(неприязнь, мечту) to harbour (*BRIT*), harbour
(*US*); **затáивать** (~ *perf*) оби́ду to harbour a
grudge; **затáивать** (~ *perf*) дыхáние to hold
one's breath
▸ **затаи́ться** *сов возв* to hide.

затáлкива|ть (-ю) *несов от* **затолкáть**,
затолкнýть.

затáплива|ть (-ю) *несов от* **затопи́ть**.

затáптыва|ть (-ю) *несов от* **затопи́ть**.

затáскан|ный (-, -на, -но) *прил* worn-out.

затаскá|ть (-ю; *impf* **затáскивать**) *сов перех*
(*разг*: одéжду, шýтку) to wear out; **затáскивать**
(~ *perf*) когó-н по магази́нам (*разг*) to drag sb
round the shops; ~ (*perf*) когó-н по судáм (*разг*)
to drag sb through the courts.

затáскива|ть (-ю) *несов от* **затаскáть**,
затащи́ть.

затáчива|ть (-ю) *несов от* **заточи́ть**.

затащ|и́ть (-ащý, -áщишь; *impf* **затáскивать**)
сов перех to drag; ~ (*perf*) когó-н в кинó (*разг*)
to drag sb off to the cinema.

затвердевá|ть (3sg -ет, 3pl -ют) *несов от*
затвердéть.

затвердéл|ый *прил* hardened.

затвердéни|е (-я) *ср* (*МЕД*) callus.

затвердé|ть (3sg -ет, 3pl -ют, *impf*
затвердевáть) *сов неперех* (земля́, цемéнт) to
harden; (жи́дкость) to solidify.

затверд|и́ть (-жý, -ди́шь) *сов от* **тверди́ть** ◆
(*impf* **затвéрживать**) *перех* to learn by rote.

затвóр (-а) *м* (плоти́ны) floodgate;
(фотоаппарáта) shutter; (винтóвки) breech.

затвóрник *м* (*РЕЛ*) hermit; (*перен*) hermit,
recluse.

затво́рниц|**а** (-ы) ж см **затво́рник**.
затева́|**ть** (-ю) несов от **зате́ять**.
зате́йливый (-, -а, -о) прил intricate.
зате́йник (-а) м entertainer.
затёк итп сов см **зате́чь**.
затека́|**ть** (-ю) несов от **зате́чь**.
затеку́т сов см **зате́чь**.
зате́м нареч (потом) then; (для того) for that reason; ~ **что́бы** in order to.
затемне́ни|**е** (-я) ср (перен: рассудка) obscuring; (ВОЕН) blackout.
затемнённый прил (очки, стекло) tinted.
затемн|**и́ть** (-ю́, -и́шь; impf **затемня́ть**) сов перех to darken; (перен: рассудок) to obscure; (город, окна) to black out.
за́темно нареч (разг: до рассвета) before light; (: когда стемнело) after dark.
затемня́|**ть** (-ю) несов от **затемни́ть**.
затен|**и́ть** (-ю́, -и́шь; impf **затеня́ть**) сов перех to shade; (комнату) to darken.
зате́пл|**иться** (3sg -ится, 3pl -ятся) сов неперех (огонёк) to begin to flicker; (надежда) to appear.
зат|**ере́ть** (-ру́, -рёшь; pt -ёр, -ёрла, -ёрло, impf **затира́ть**) сов перех (пятно, надпись) to rub out; (перен: разг: работника) to shackle; **её** ~**ёрли в толпе́** she got caught up in the crowd; **кора́бль** ~**ёрло льда́ми** the ship was icebound.
зате́рянный прил (человек) forgotten; (место, дом) forsaken.
затер|**я́ться** (-ю́сь) сов от **теря́ться** ♦ возв (разг) to go missing, disappear; (в дали, в толпе́) to disappear.
зат|**е́чь** (3sg -ечёт, 3pl -еку́т, pt -ёк, -екла́, -екло́, impf **затека́ть**) сов неперех (опухнуть) to swell up; (онеметь) to go numb; (вода) ~ **за** +acc/**в** +acc to seep behind/into.
затещу́сь итп сов см **затеса́ться**.
зате́|**я** (-и) ж (замысел) idea, scheme; (забава) escapade; **без** ~**й** without frills.
зате́|**ять** (-ю; impf **затева́ть**) сов перех (разговор, игру) to start (up); **он, ка́жется, что́-то затева́ет** (разг) he's got something up his sleeve.
затира́|**ть** (-ю) несов от **затере́ть**.
затих|**нуть** (-ну, -нешь; pt -, -ла, -ло, impf **затиха́ть**) сов неперех (люди, место) to quieten (BRIT) или quiet (US) down; (шум, ветер, буря) to die down.
зати́шь|**е** (-я) ср lull.
заткн|**у́ть** (-у́, -ёшь; impf **затыка́ть**) сов перех to stop up, plug; ~ (perf) **что-н за** +acc/**в** +acc to stuff sth behind/into; **затыка́ть** (~ perf) **кого́-н** или **рот кому́-н** (разг) to shut sb up; **затыка́ть** (~ perf) **кого́-н за по́яс** (перен: разг) to outdo sb
▶ **заткну́ться** (impf **затыка́ться**) сов возв (разг: замолчать) to shut up; ~**и́сь!** (разг: пренебр) shut it!
затмева́|**ть** (-ю) несов от **затми́ть**.

затме́ни|**е** (-я) ср (солнца, луны) eclipse; (разг: ума) blackout; **на меня́ нашло́** ~ my mind went blank.
затм|**и́ть** (-и́шь; impf **затмева́ть**) сов перех (также перен) to eclipse.
зато́ союз (также: **но** ~: однако) but then (again); (поэтому) but (to make up for it); **кварти́ра ма́ленькая, (но)** ~ **в хоро́шем райо́не** the flat is small, but then again it's in a nice district.
затова́ривани|**е** (-я) ср (КОММ: скопление товаров) stockpiling; (склада, магазина) overstocking.
затова́р|**ить** (-ю, -ишь; impf **затова́ривать**) сов перех (см сущ) to stockpile; to overstock.
затолка́|**ть** (-ю; impf **зата́лкивать**) сов перех (разг) to shove; (в автобусе, в толпе) to squash.
затолкн|**у́ть** (-у́, -ёшь; impf **зата́лкивать**) сов перех to shove.
зат|**ону́ть** (-ону́, -о́нешь) сов неперех to sink.
зат|**опи́ть** (-оплю́, -о́пишь; impf **зата́пливать**) сов перех (печь, камин) to light; (impf **затопля́ть**; остров, деревню) to flood; (судно) to sink.
затопт|**а́ть** (-опчу́, -о́пчешь; impf **зата́птывать**) сов перех (цветы, газон) to trample on; (огонь, следы) to stamp out; (убить) to trample to death.
зато́р (-а) м congestion; (на улице) traffic jam; (на реке) log jam.
затормоз|**и́ть(ся)** (-жу́, -зи́шь) сов от **тормози́ть(ся)**.
затор|**опи́ться** (-оплю́сь, -о́пишься) сов возв to hasten.
затоск|**ова́ть** (-у́ю) сов неперех to begin to feel melancholic; ~ (perf) **по** +dat to start to miss.
заточа́|**ть** (-ю) несов от **заточи́ть**.
заточе́ни|**е** (-я) ср incarceration.
заточ|**и́ть** (-очу́, -о́чишь; impf **зата́чивать**) сов перех to sharpen; (impf **заточа́ть**; в тюрьму́) to incarcerate.
затошн|**и́ть** (3sg -и́т) сов безл: **меня́** ~**и́ло** I began to feel sick.
затр|**ави́ть** (-авлю́, -а́вишь) сов от **трави́ть** ♦ (impf **затра́вливать**) перех (зайца, утку) to hunt; (перен: человека) to harass.
затра́гива|**ть** (-ю) несов от **затро́нуть**.
затрапе́зный (-ен, -на, -но) прил (разг) shabby.
затра́т|**а** (-ы) ж expenditure.
затра́т|**ить** (-чу, -тишь; impf **затра́чивать**) сов перех to expend.
затре́б|**овать** (-ую) сов перех to request.
затрепе|**та́ть** (-ещу́, -е́щешь) сов неперех to begin to tremble.
затреща́|**ть** (-у́, -и́шь) сов неперех (стул, дерево) to start to split.

затрещин|а (-ы) ж whack.
затрóн|уть (-у, -ешь; *impf* **затрáгивать)** *сов*
перех (*подлеж: пуля*) to graze; (*перен: вопрос,*
тему) to touch on; (: *душу, человека*) to affect;
затрáгивать (~ *perf*) **чьё-н самолюбие** to dent
sb's ego.
затрý *итп сов см* **затерéть.**
затруднéни|е (-я) *ср* difficulty.
затруднённый (-ён, -енá, -енó) *прил* laboured
(*BRIT*), labored (*US*).
затрудни́тельный (-ен, -ьна, -ьно) *прил*
difficult, awkward.
затрудни́|ть (-ю, -ишь; *impf* **затрудня́ть)** *сов*
перех: **~ что-н** to make sth difficult; **éсли Вас**
не ~и́т if it isn't too much trouble
▸ **затрудни́ться (***impf* **затрудня́ться)** *сов возв:*
~ся с +*instr*/+*infin* to have difficulty with/doing;
я ~я́юсь (Вам) сказáть that is difficult to say.
затряст|и́сь (-ясу́сь, -ясёшься; *pt* **-я́сся,**
-ясла́сь, -ясло́сь) *сов возв* (to start) to shake.
затума́н|ить (-ю, -ишь) *сов от* **тума́нить**
▸ **затума́ниться** *сов от* **тума́ниться** ◆ (*impf*
затума́ниваться) *возв* (*небо*) to cloud over;
(*глаза*) to mist over; (*перен: сознание*) to
become blurred.
затуп|и́ть (-уплю́, -у́пишь) *сов от* **тупи́ть** ◆
(*impf* **затупля́ть)** *перех* to blunt
▸ **затупи́ться** *сов от* **тупи́ться** ◆ (*impf*
затупля́ться) *возв* to become blunt.
зату́х|нуть (*3sg* **-нет,** *3pl* **-нут,** *pt* **-, -ла, -ло,** *impf*
затуха́ть) *сов неперех* (*огонь*) to die out;
(*сигнал*) to die away; (*колебания*) to die down.
затуш|ева́ть (-у́ю; *impf* **затушёвывать)** *сов*
перех to shade (in); (*перен: сгладить*) to brush
over.
затуш|и́ть (-ушу́, -у́шишь) *сов от* **туши́ть.**
за́тхл|ый (-, -а, -о) *прил* stale; (*запах*) musty.
затыка́|ть(ся) (-ю(сь)) *несов от* **заткну́ть(ся).**
заты́л|ок (-ка) *м* the back of the head.
заты́чк|а (-ки; *gen pl* **-ек)** ж (*разг*) stopper.
затю́ка|ть (-ю) *сов перех* (*разг*) to bug.
затя́гива|ть(ся) (-ю(сь)) *несов от*
затяну́ть(ся).
затя́ж|ка (-ки; *gen pl* **-ек)** ж (*промедление*) delay;
(*при курении*) drag, puff.
затяжн|о́й *прил* protracted, prolonged;
затяжны́е дожди́ long periods of rain;
затяжно́й прыжо́к delayed drop.
затя|ну́ть (-ну́, -нешь; *impf* **затя́гивать)** *сов*
перех (*шнурки, гайку*) to tighten; (*замедлить*)
to drag out; (*вовлечь*): **~ кого́-н в** +*acc* to drag
sb into; **онá** **-ну́ла тáлию по́ясом** she pulled
the belt tight around her waist; **нéбо ~яну́ло**
тýчами storm clouds gathered in the sky;
затя́гивать (~ *perf*) **пéсню** to strike up a song
▸ **затяну́ться (***impf* **затя́гиваться)** *сов возв*
(*петля, узел*) to tighten; (*рана*) to close up;
(*дело, переговоры итп*) to drag on; (*при*
курении) to inhale; **затя́гиваться (~ся** *perf*)
+*instr* (*поясом, корсетом*) to tighten.
зау́м|ный (-ен, -на, -но) *прил* unintelligible.

зауны́в|ный (-ен, -на, -но) *прил* mournful.
заупоко́й|ный *прил:* **~ая моли́тва** prayer for
the dead; **заупоко́йная слýжба** funeral service.
заупря́м|иться (-люсь, -ишься) *сов возв* to
become stubborn.
зауря́д|ный (-ен, -на, -но) *прил* unexceptional,
mediocre.
заусéн|ец (-ца; *nom pl* **-цы)** *м* (*на металле*) burr;
(*у ногтя*) hangnail.
заýтрен|я (-и) ж (*РЕЛ*) dawn mass, ≈ matins.
заýчен|ный (-, -на, -но) *прил* (*ответ, жест*)
(pre)rehearsed.
заучи́|ть (-учý, -ýчишь; *impf* **заýчивать)** *сов*
перех to memorize, learn
▸ **заучи́ться (***impf* **заýчиваться)** *сов возв* (*разг*)
to study too hard.
зафаршир|ова́ть (-ýю) *сов от* **фарширова́ть.**
зафикси́р|овать (-ую) *сов от* **фикси́ровать.**
зафрахт|ова́ть (-ýю; *impf* **зафрахто́вывать**
или фрахтова́ть) *сов перех* to charter.
захвал|и́ть (-ю́, -ишь; *impf* **захва́ливать)** *сов*
перех to overpraise.
захвáт (-а) *м* seizure, capture; (*СПОРТ*) hold;
(*ТЕХ*) clamp.
захв|ати́ть (-ачý, -а́тишь; *impf* **захвáтывать)**
сов перех to seize, capture; (*взять с собой*) to
take; (*подлеж: музыка, работа*) to captivate;
(*болезнь, пожар*) to catch (in time); **дух**
~а́тывает it takes your breath away; **у меня́**
дух ~а́тило от волнéния I was breathless with
excitement.
захва́тнически|й (-ая, -ое, -ие) *прил*
(*намерения, политика*) aggressive; **~ая войнá**
war of aggression.
захвáтчик (-а) *м* invader.
захвáтывающ|ий (-ая, -ее, -ие) *прил* (*книга,*
занятие) gripping, absorbing; (*вид*)
breathtaking.
захвáтыва|ть (-ю) *несов от* **захвати́ть.**
захвачý *итп сов см* **захвати́ть.**
захвора́|ть (-ю) *сов неперех* (*разг*) to be taken
ill.
захире́|ть (-ю) *сов от* **хире́ть.**
захлам|и́ть (-лю́, -и́шь; *impf* **захламля́ть)** *сов*
перех to clutter up.
захламлён|ный (-ён, -енá, -енó) *прил*
cluttered.
захламлю́ *сов см* **захлами́ть.**
захламля́|ть (-ю) *несов от* **захлами́ть.**
захлебн|ýться (-ýсь, -ёшься; *impf*
захлёбываться) *сов возв* to choke; (*перен:*
атака, наступление) to be stopped in its tracks;
(: *мотор*) to fail to start; **захлёбываться (~**
perf) **от смéха/слёз** to choke with laughter/on
one's tears; **захлёбываться (~** *perf*) **от**
счáстья/восто́рга to gasp in joy/elation.
захлестн|ýть (-ý, -ёшь; *impf* **захлёстывать)** *сов*
перех (*подлеж: волна*) to swallow; (*перен:*
подлеж: чувство) to overwhelm ◆ *неперех*
(*вода*) to wash over.
захло́па|ть (-ю) *сов неперех* (*двери*) to slam;

(*выстрелы*) to crash out; (*слушатели, зрители*): ~ **(в ладо́ши)** to start clapping.

захло́пн|уть (-у, -ешь; *impf* **захло́пывать**) *сов перех*: ~ **что-н** to slam sth shut

▶ **захло́пнуться** (*impf* **захло́пываться**) *сов возв* to slam shut.

захо́д (-а) *м* (*также*: ~ **со́лнца**) sundown; (*в порт*) call; (*попытка*) go; **с пе́рвого/второ́го** ~**а** at the first/second attempt; **с** ~**ом/без захо́да в** +*acc* stopping off/without stopping off at.

захо|ди́ть (-ожу́, -о́дишь) *несов от* **зайти́** ♦ *сов непepex* to start pacing.

захолу́сть|е (-я) *ср* provincial backwater.

захороне́ни|е (-я) *ср* (*действие*) burial; (*могила, могильник*) burial ground.

захор|они́ть (-оню́, -о́нишь) *сов перех* to bury.

захоте́ть (*как* **хоте́ть**; *см* **Table 16**) *сов (не)перех* to want

▶ **захоте́ться** *сов безл* (+*dat*): **мне** ~**оте́лось есть/пить** I started to feel hungry/thirsty.

захуда́лый *прил* wretched.

зацв|ести́ (*3sg* -ете́т, *3pl* -ету́т, *pt* -ёл, -ела́, -ело́, *impf* **зацвета́ть**) *сов непepex* (*цветы*) to blossom, bloom; (*разг*: *сыр, хлеб*) to go mouldy (*BRIT*) *или* moldy (*US*).

зацел|ова́ть (-у́ю) *сов перех*: ~ **кого́-н** to smother sb with kisses.

зацементи́р|овать (-ую) *сов от* **цементи́ровать**.

зацеп|и́ть (-еплю́, -е́пишь; *impf* **зацепля́ть**) *сов перех* (*поддеть*) to hook up; (*разг*: *случайно задеть*) to catch against

▶ **зацепи́ться** (*impf* **зацепля́ться**) *сов возв*: ~**ся за** +*acc* (*задеть за*) to catch *или* get caught on; (*ухватиться за*) to grab hold of; **я** ~**епи́лся рука́вом за гвоздь** I caught my sleeve on a nail.

заце́п|ка (-ки; *gen pl* -ок) *ж* (*перен*) pretext.

зацеплю́(сь) *сов см* **зацепи́ть(ся)**.

зацепля́|ть(ся) (-ю(сь)) *несов от* **зацепи́ть(ся)**.

зацикл|иться (-юсь, -ишься; *impf* **заци́кливаться**) *сов возв*: ~ **на** +*acc* (*разг*) to be crazy about.

зачар|ова́ть (-у́ю; *impf* **зачаро́вывать**) *сов перех* to enthral (*BRIT*), enthrall (*US*).

зача|сти́ть (-щу́, -сти́шь) *сов непepex* to come more often; **дождь** ~**сти́л** the rain got heavier.

зачасту́ю *нареч* often.

зача́ти|е (-я) *ср* conception.

зача́т|ок (-ка; *nom pl* -ки) *м* (*обычно мн*: *любви, идеи итп*) beginning, germ *только ед*; **в** ~**ке** (*перен*) in embryo.

зача́точный (-ен, -на, -но) *прил* (*также перен*) embryonic; **в** ~**ном состоя́нии** in an embryonic state.

зач|а́ть (-ну́, -нёшь; *pt* -а́л, -ала́, -а́ло, *impf* **зачина́ть**) *сов (не)перех* to conceive.

зача́х|нуть (-ну, -нешь; *pt* -, -ла, -ло) *сов от* **ча́хнуть**.

зачащу́ *сов см* **зачасти́ть**.

заче́м *нареч* why; ~ **он э́то сде́лал?** why did he do it?; **ей ста́ло поня́тно,** ~ **он э́то сде́лал** it became clear to her why he had done it.

заче́м-нибудь *нареч* for any reason.

заче́м-то *нареч* for some reason.

зачеркн|у́ть (-у́, -ёшь; *impf* **зачёркивать**) *сов перех* to cross out; (*перен*: *прошлое*) to blot out.

зачерпн|у́ть (-у́, -ёшь; *impf* **заче́рпывать**) *сов перех* to scoop up.

зачерстве́|ть (-ю) *сов от* **черстве́ть**.

зачеса́ть (-ешу́, -е́шешь; *impf* **зачёсывать**) *сов перех* to comb.

зач|е́сть (-ту́, -тёшь; *pt* -ёл, -ла́, -ло́, *impf* **зачи́тывать**) *сов перех* (*одобрить*) to pass; (*засчитать*: *диплом, опыт*) to take into account; **ему́** ~**ли отрабо́танные дни в счёт о́тпуска** he was given time off in lieu

▶ **заче́сться** (*impf* **зачи́тываться**) *сов возв* to be taken into account.

зачёсыва|ть (-ю) *несов от* **зачеса́ть**.

зачёт (-а) *м* (*ПРОСВЕЩ*) test; **сдава́ть** (*impf*)/ **сдать** (*perf*) ~ **по фи́зике** to sit (*BRIT*) *или* take/ pass a physics test.

зачётный *прил*: **зачётная рабо́та** assessed essay (*BRIT*), term paper (*US*); **зачётная кни́жка** assessment record book.

зачешу́ *итп сов см* **зачеса́ть**.

зачина́тел|ь (-я) *м* originator.

зачина́|ть (-ю) *несов от* **зача́ть**.

зачи́нщик (-а) *м* instigator.

зачи́сл|ить (-ю, -ишь; *impf* **зачисля́ть**) *сов перех* (*в институт*) to enrol; (*на работу*) to take on; (*на счёт*) to enter; **зачисля́ть** (~ *perf*) **расхо́ды** to keep a record of expenditure

▶ **зачи́слиться** (*impf* **зачисля́ться**) *сов возв* (*в институт*) to enrol; (*на работу*) to be taken on.

зачита́|ть (-ю; *impf* **зачи́тывать**) *сов перех* (*прочесть вслух*) to read out; ~ (*perf*) **у кого́-н кни́гу** to borrow a book from sb and not give it back

▶ **зачита́ться** (*impf* **зачи́тываться**) *сов возв*: ~**ся** +*instr* (*книгой*) to be engrossed in; **я** ~**лся до утра́** I read until morning.

зачи́тыва|ть(ся) (-ю(сь)) *несов от* **заче́сть(ся)**, **зачита́ть(ся)**.

зачну́ *итп сов см* **зача́ть**.

зачту́(сь) *итп сов см* **заче́сть(ся)**.

зашага́|ть (-ю) *сов непepex* to start walking.

зашата́|ться (-юсь) *сов возв* (*здание*) to start to shake; (*дерево, пьяница*) to begin to sway.

зашвырн|у́ть (-у́, -нёшь; *impf* **зашвы́ривать**) *сов перех* to hurl.

зашвыр|я́ть (-ю) *сов перех*: ~ **кого́-н чем-н** to pelt sb with sth.

зашевел|и́ть (-ю́, -и́шь) *сов неперех* (+*instr*) to move
▸ **зашевели́ться** *сов возв* to move.
зашёл *сов см* **зайти́**.
заш|и́ть (-ью́, -ьёшь; *impf* **зашива́ть**) *сов перех* (*дырку, носки*) to mend; (*шов, рану*) to stitch.
зашифр|ова́ть (-у́ю; *impf* **зашифро́вывать**) *сов перех* to encode, put into code.
зашла́ *итп сов см* **зайти́**.
зашлю́ *итп сов см* **засла́ть**.
зашнур|ова́ть (-у́ю; *impf* **зашнуро́вывать**) *сов перех* to lace up.
зашпакл|ева́ть (-ю́ю) *сов от* **шпаклева́ть**.
заштопа|ть (-ю; *impf* **што́пать**) *сов перех* to darn.
заштрих|ова́ть (-у́ю; *impf* **заштрихо́вывать**) *сов перех* to shade (in).
зашум|е́ть (-лю́, -и́шь) *сов неперех* (*люди, толпа*) to become noisy; **внизу́ ~е́ли голоса́** from downstairs came the sound of voices.
зашью́ *итп сов см* **заши́ть**.
защёлк|а (-и) *ж* (*на двери*) latch; (*на шкатулке, у замка*) catch.
защёлкн|у́ть (-у, -ешь; *impf* **защёлкивать**) *сов перех* to shut
▸ **защёлкнуться** (*impf* **защёлкиваться**) *сов возв* to click shut.
защем|и́ть (-лю́, -и́шь; *impf* **защемля́ть**) *сов перех* to clamp.
защи́т|а (-ы) *ж* (*также ЮР, СПОРТ*) defence (*BRIT*), defense (*US*); (*от комаров, пыли*) protection; (*диплома, диссертации*) viva (*open to the public*); **брать** (**взять** *perf*) **под ~у** to defend.
защит|и́ть (-щу́, -ти́шь; *impf* **защища́ть**) *сов перех* to defend; (*от солнца, от комаров итп*) to protect; **защища́ть** (**~** *perf*) **диссерта́цию** to defend one's thesis (*at public viva*)
▸ **защити́ться** (*impf* **защища́ться**) *сов возв* to defend o.s.; (*диссертант, студент*) to defend one's thesis.
защи́тник (-а) *м* (*также СПОРТ*) defender; (*ЮР*) defence counsel (*BRIT*), defense attorney (*US*); **ле́вый/пра́вый ~** (*футбол*) left/right back.
защи́тный *прил* protective; **защи́тный цвет** khaki.
защища́|ть (-ю) *несов от* **защити́ть** ♦ *перех* (*подсудимого, преступника*) to defend
▸ **защища́ться** *несов от* **защити́ться**.
защищу́(сь) *сов см* **защити́ть(ся)**.
за|яви́ть (-явлю́, -я́вишь; *impf* **заявля́ть**) *сов перех* (*претензию, протест*) to declare ♦ *неперех*: **~ о** +*prp* to announce; **заявля́ть** (**~** *perf*) **о свои́х права́х** (**на** +*acc*) to claim one's rights (to); **заявля́ть** (**~** *perf*) **на кого́-н в мили́цию** to report sb to the police
▸ **заяви́ться** (*impf* **заявля́ться**) *сов возв* (*разг*) to turn up.
зая́в|ка (-ки; *gen pl* -ок) *ж*: **~ (на** +*acc*) application (for); (*на билеты*) order (for); **~ на изобрете́ние** patent application; **присыла́йте**

ва́ши ~ки по а́дресу ... please apply to the following address ....
заявле́ни|е (-я) *ср* (*правительства*) statement; (*просьба*): **~ (о** +*prp*) application (for); **де́лать** (**сде́лать** *perf*) **~** to make a statement; **подава́ть** (**пода́ть** *perf*) **~ на рабо́ту/об о́тпуске** to apply for a job/leave.
заявлю́(сь) *сов см* **заяви́ть(ся)**.
заявля́|ть(ся) (-ю(сь)) *несов от* **заяви́ть(ся)**.
за́йдлый *прил* (*разг: курильщик*) inveterate; **он ~ футболи́ст/охо́тник** he is a football/hunting fanatic.
за́|яц (-йца) *м* (*ЗООЛ*) hare; (*разг: безбиле́тник*) fare dodger.
за́ячий (-ья, -ье, -ьи) *прил* (*мех, хвост*) hare's; **за́ячья губа́** harelip.
зва́ни|е (-я) *ср* (*воинское*) rank; (*учёное, почётное*) title; **присва́ивать** (**присво́ить** *perf*) **кому́ ~** to award sb a title.
зва́ный *прил*: **~ гость** welcome guest; **зва́ный обе́д** dinner party.
зв|ать (зову́, зовёшь; *pt* -ал, -ала́, -а́ло, *perf* **позва́ть**) *несов перех* to call; (*приглашать*) to ask; (*no perf*; +*instr*; *называть*): **~ кого́-н кем-н** to call sb sth; **как Вас зову́т?** what is your name?; **меня́/его́ зову́т Алекса́ндр** my/his name is Alexander; **~** (**позва́ть** *perf*) **кого́-н в го́сти/в кино́** to ask sb over/to the cinema
▸ **зва́ться** *несов возв* (+*instr*) to be called.
звезд|а́ (-ы́; *nom pl* **звёзды**) *ж* (*также перен*) star; **морска́я ~** starfish.
звёздный *прил* (*ночь, небо*) starry, starlit; **э́то был его́ ~ час** that was his finest hour; **звёздные во́йны** Star Wars; **Звёздный городо́к** Star City (*training centre for Russian cosmonauts*).
звёздо́ч|ка (-ки; *gen pl* -ек) *ж уменьш от* **звезда́**; (*типог*) asterisk.
звен|е́ть (-ю́, -и́шь) *несов неперех* (*звонок*) to ring; (*колокольчик*) to jingle; (*голос*) to chime; (*стаканы*) to clink; (*монеты*) to jangle.
звен|о́ (-а́; *nom pl* -ья, *gen pl* -ьев) *ср* (*цепи, также перен*) link; (*конструкции*) section; (*ВОЕН: самолётов*) flight; (*в школе*) group; (*на работе*) team.
звере́|ть (-ю; *perf* **озвере́ть**) *несов неперех* to go wild.
звери́н|ец (-ца) *м* menagerie.
звери́ный *прил* (*вой, тропа, шкура*) (wild) animal *опред*; (*перен: законы*) bestial; (: *страх, инстинкт*) animal *опред*.
зверово́дств|о (-а) *ср* breeding of animals for their fur.
зверо́лов (-а) *м* trapper.
зве́рск|ий (-ая, -ое, -ие) *прил* (*убийство, поступок*) brutal, savage; (*разг: жара, аппетит*) wicked; (: *скука*) severe.
зве́рств|о (-а) *ср* (*жестокость*) brutality; (*обычно мн: ужас*) atrocity.
зве́рств|овать (-ую) *несов неперех* to commit atrocities.

зверь (-я; gen pl -**е́й**) м beast, wild animal; (перен) beast, animal.

звон (-а) м clinking; (колокола) peal, chime.

звона́рь (-я́) м bell-ringer.

звон|и́ть (-ю́, -и́шь; perf **позвони́ть**) несов неперех to ring; (по телефо́ну): ~ **кому́** to ring или phone или call (US) sb; ~ (impf) **в звоно́к** to ring the bell.

зво́нк|а сущ см **звоно́к**.

зво́нкий (-о́нок, -онка́, -о́нко) прил (го́лос, песня) sonorous; (дно, свод) resonant; **зво́нкий согла́сный** (линг) voiced consonant.

звоно́к (-ка́; nom pl -**ки́**) м (на двери, на велосипе́де) bell; (звук) ring; (по телефо́ну) (telephone) call; **отсиде́ть** (perf) **от ~ка́ до ~ка́** ≈ to work from nine to five.

зво́нче сравн прил от **зво́нкий**.

звук (-а) м sound; **он не произнёс ни зву́ка** he didn't utter a sound; **без зву́ка** (сде́лать, согласи́ться) without much as a word.

звуков|о́й прил sound опред, audio; **звукова́я волна́** sound wave; **звукова́я доро́жка** track (on audio tape); **звукова́я аппарату́ра** hi-fi equipment.

звукоза́пис|ь (-и) ж sound recording; **сту́дия ~и** recording studio.

звукоизоля́ци|я (-и) ж soundproofing.

звуконепроница́ем|ый (-, -а, -о) прил soundproof.

звукоопера́тор (-а) м sound technician.

звукоподража́ни|е (-я) ср onomatopoeia.

звукоподража́тельн|ый прил: **~ое сло́во** onomatopoeic word.

звукопрово́дност|ь (-и) ж conductivity (of sound).

звукопроводя́щий (-яя, -ее, -ие) прил conductive (of sound).

звукорежиссёр (-а) м sound engineer.

звукоснима́тел|ь (-я) м pick-up.

звуча́ни|е (-я) ср sound; (перен: полити́ческое итп) resonance.

звуч|а́ть (3sg -и́т, 3pl -а́т) несов неперех (издава́ть зву́ки) to sound; (раздава́ться) to be heard; **~и́т убеди́тельно** it sounds convincing; **в её го́лосе ~а́ла оби́да** she sounded hurt.

зву́чный (-у́чен, -учна́, -у́чно) прил (смех, го́лос) deep, resounding; (инструме́нт) rich-sounding.

звя́кн|уть (-у, -ешь; impf **звя́кать**) сов неперех (звоно́к) to ring; (стака́н) to clink; (стекло́) to tinkle; (+instr; стака́нами) to clink; (ключа́ми) to jangle.

зги: ни ~ не ви́дно it's pitch-black.

з-д сокр = **заво́д**.

зда́ни|е (-я) ср building.

здесь нареч here; **есть ~ кто́-нибудь?** is (there) anyone here?; ~ **нет ничего́ смешно́го** there's nothing funny about it.

зде́шн|ий (-яя, -ее, -ие) прил (разг) local.

здоро́ва|ться (-юсь; perf **поздоро́ваться**) несов возв: ~ **с** +instr to say hello to; ~ (**поздоро́ваться** perf) **друг с дру́гом** to greet each other; ~ (**поздоро́ваться** perf) **за́ руку** to shake hands.

здо́рово нареч (разг: отли́чно) really well; (: о́чень си́льно) terribly ◆ как сказ (разг) it's great.

здоро́в|ый (-о́в, -о́ва, -о́во) прил healthy; (пита́ние) wholesome; (перен: иде́я) sound; (-о́в, -ова́, -ово́; разг: большо́й) hefty; **бу́дьте ~овы!** (при проща́нии) take care!; (при чиха́нии) bless you!

здоро́вь|е (-я) ср health; **как Ва́ше ~?** how are you keeping?; **за Ва́ше ~!** (to) your good health!; **на ~!** enjoy it!

здра́вниц|а (-ы) ж convalescent home.

здра́во нареч sensibly.

здравомы́слящ|ий (-ая, -ее, -ие) прил sensible.

здравоохране́ни|е (-я) ср health care; **систе́ма ~я** ≈ the Health Service (BRIT), ≈ Medicaid (US); **министе́рство ~я** ≈ Department of Health.

здравоохрани́тельный прил health-care.

здра́вств|овать (-ую) несов неперех to thrive; **~уйте** hello; **да ~ует...!** long live ...!

здра́в|ый (-, -а, -о) прил (поли́тика, мысль) sound.

зе́бр|а (-ы) ж zebra; (пешехо́дный перехо́д) zebra crossing (BRIT).

зев (-а) м pharynx.

зева́к|а (-и) м/ж (разг) idler.

зева́|ть (-ю) несов неперех to yawn; (разг: глазе́ть) to gawp; (perf **прозева́ть**; разг) to miss out; **не ~й!** (разг) keep your wits about you!

зевка итп сущ см **зево́к**.

зевн|у́ть (-у́, -ёшь) сов неперех to yawn.

зев|о́к (-ка́; nom pl -**ки́**) м yawn.

зево́т|а (-ы) ж yawning.

зелене́|ть (-ю; perf **позелене́ть**) несов неперех to go или turn green; **на горизо́нте ~л лес** the green of the forest could be seen on the horizon.

зелён|ый (зе́лен, зелена́, зе́лено) прил (также перен) green; „**3~ые"** (полит) the Greens; **дать** (perf) **чему́-н ~ую у́лицу** to give sth the green light; **зелёные насажде́ния** trees and shrubs; **зелёный лук** spring onion.

зе́лен|ь (-и) ж (цвет) green ◆ собир (расти́тельность) greenery; (о́вощи и тра́вы) greens мн.

земе́ль сущ см **земля́**.

земе́льн|ый прил land опред; ~ **наде́л** или **уча́сток** plot of land.

землевладе́л|ец (-ьца) м landowner.

землевладе́ни|е (-я) ср landownership.

земледе́л|ец (-ьца) м arable farmer.
земледе́ли|е (-я) ср *(возде́лывание земли)* arable farming.
земледе́льца сущ см **земледе́лец**.
земледе́льческ|ий (-ая, -ое, -ие) прил *(райо́н)* agricultural; *(маши́ны)* farming опред.
землеме́рный прил surveying опред.
землепо́льзовани|е (-я) ср land tenure.
землеро́йн|ый прил: **~ые рабо́ты** dredging; **~ая маши́на** dredger.
землетрясе́ни|е (-я) ср earthquake.
землечерпа́лк|а (-и) ж dredger.
земли́ст|ый (-, -а, -о) прил *(цвет лица́)* sallow; *(песо́к, торф)* earthy.
земл|я́ (-и́; acc sg **-лю,** nom pl **-ли,** gen pl **-е́ль)** ж land; *(плане́та)* earth; *(пове́рхность)* ground; *(по́чва)* earth, soil.
земля́к (-а́) м compatriot.
земля́н|е (-) мн earth dwellers мн.
земляни́к|а (-и) ж *(расте́ние)* wild strawberry; *(собир: я́годы)* wild strawberries мн.
земля́нк|а (-и; gen pl **-ок)** ж dugout *(shelter)*.
земляно́й прил *(вал, пол)* earthen; **~ые рабо́ты** excavations; **земляно́й червь** earthworm.
земля́чк|а (-и; gen pl **-ек)** ж см **земля́к**.
земново́дн|ые (-ых; decl like adj) мн amphibians мн.
земново́дный прил amphibious.
земно́й прил *(пове́рхность, кора́)* earth's; *(перен: бла́га, жела́ния)* earthly; **земно́й шар** the globe.
зени́т (-а) м *(также перен)* zenith.
зени́т|ка (-и; gen pl **-ок)** ж anti-aircraft gun.
зени́тный прил *(АСТРОНО́МИЯ)* zenithal; *(ВО́ЕН)* anti-aircraft.
зёрен сущ см **зерно́**.
зерка́лен прил см **зерка́льный**.
зе́рк|ало (-ала; nom pl **-ала́,** gen pl **-а́л,** dat pl **-ала́м)** ср mirror; *(перен: во́ды, зали́ва)* glassy surface.
зерка́л|ьный (-ен, -ьна, -ьно) прил *(произво́дство)* mirror опред; *(пове́рхность)* glassy; **его́ пье́са - э́то ~ьное отображе́ние действи́тельности** his play is a true reflection of real life; **~ шкаф** mirror wardrobe; **зерка́льный карп** mirror carp.
зерни́ст|ый (-, -а, -о) прил *(ма́сса, снег)* granular; *(пове́рхность)* grainy; **зерни́стая икра́** unpressed caviar.
зерно́ (зерна́; nom pl **зёрна,** gen pl **зёрен)** ср *(пшени́цы)* grain; *(ко́фе)* bean; *(ма́ка)* seed; *(по́роха)* granule ◆ собир *(семенно́е, на хлеб)* grain; **~ и́стины** a grain of truth; **жемчу́жное ~** pearl.
зернов́ой прил *(торго́вля, запа́с)* grain опред; **зернов́ые культу́ры** cereals мн.
зернов́|ые (-ых; decl like adj) мн cereals мн.
зерносуши́лк|а (-и) ж grain drier.
зерноубо́рочный прил harvesting опред; **~ комба́йн** combine harvester.

зернохрани́лищ|е (-а) ср granary.
зефи́р (-а) м ≈ marshmallow.
зигза́г (-а) м zigzag.
зи́жд|иться (3sg -ится, 3pl -утся) несов возв: **~ на** +prp to be based on.
ЗИЛ м сокр = Моско́вский автомоби́льный заво́д и́мени И.А. Лихачёва; *(автомоби́ль)* vehicle manufactured at the Moscow car factory.
зим|а́ (-ы́; acc sg **-у,** dat sg **-е́,** nom pl **-ы)** ж winter.
Зимба́бве ср нескл Zimbabwe.
зимбабви́йск|ий (-ая, -ое, -ие) прил Zimbabwean.
зи́мн|ий (-яя, -ее, -ие) прил *(день)* winter's; *(пого́да)* wintry; *(лес, оде́жда)* winter опред.
зим|ова́ть (-у́ю; perf **прозимова́ть)** несов непере́х *(челове́к)* to spend the winter; *(пти́цы)* to winter.
зимо́в|ка (-ки; gen pl **-ок)** ж wintering place; *(для птиц)* wintering ground; **остава́ться (оста́ться** perf) **на ~ку** to spend the winter.
зимо́вь|е (-я) ср *(для люде́й)* winter hut; *(звере́й, птиц)* wintering ground.
зимо́й нареч in the winter.
зия́ть (3sg -ет, 3pl -ют) несов непере́х to gape.
злак (-а) м grass; **зернов́ой ~** cereal.
зла́чн|ый прил: **~ое ме́сто** *(разг)* den of iniquity.
зле́йш|ий (-ая, -ее, -ие) превос прил: **~ враг** worst enemy.
зл|ить (-ю, -ишь; perf **разозли́ть)** несов пере́х to annoy
▶ **зли́ться** *(perf* **разозли́ться)** несов возв to get angry.
зло (зла; gen pl **зол)** ср evil; *(неприя́тность)* harm ◆ нареч *(посмотре́ть, сказа́ть)* spitefully; **со зла** out of spite; **причиня́ть (причини́ть** perf) **кому́-н ~** to cause sb harm; **меня́ ~ берёт** *(разг)* it makes me angry; **у меня́ на неё зла не хвата́ет** *(разг)* she annoys me no end; **из двух зол выбира́ть (вы́брать** perf) **ме́ньшее** to choose the lesser of two evils.
зло́б|а (-ы) ж malice; **статья́ на ~у дня** an article tackling the burning issue of the moment.
зло́бн|ый (-ен, -на, -но) прил *(хара́ктер, челове́к)* mean; *(улы́бка)* hateful, wicked; *(тон, го́лос)* nasty.
злободне́вн|ый (-ен, -на, -но) прил topical.
злоб́ствовать (-ую) несов непере́х to rage.
злове́щ|ий (-ая, -ее, -ие; -, -а, -е) прил *(улы́бка, вид, слу́хи)* sinister; *(тишина́)* ominous.
злово́нен прил см **злово́нный**.
злово́ни|е (-я) ср noxious odour *(BRIT)* или odor *(US)*.
злово́нн|ый (-ен, -на, -но) прил rank, fetid.
зловре́дн|ый (-ен, -на, -но) прил mean, horrid.
злоде́й (-я) м villain.
злоде́йк|а (-и) ж см **злоде́й**.
злоде́йск|ий (-ая, -ое, -ие) прил wicked.
злоде́йств|о (-а) ср act of evil.
злодея́ни|е (-я) ср evil deed, crime.
злой (зол, зла, зло) прил *(челове́к, жена́)* mean,

bad-tempered; (*собака*) vicious; (*глаза, лицо*)
mean; (*мысли*) evil; (*карикатура, замечание*)
scathing; (*перен: разг: мороз*) cruel; (: *перец,
горчица*) lethal; **я зол на тебя́** I'm angry with
you; **без зло́го у́мысла** no harm meant; **зла́я
судьба́** cruel fate; **злы́е языки́** malicious talk.
злока́чествен|ный (-, -на, -но) *прил* malignant.
злоключе́ни|е (-я) *ср* misadventure.
злонаме́рен|ный (-, -на, -но) *прил* ill-
intentioned.
злопа́мят|ный (-ен, -на, -но) *прил* (*человек*)
unforgiving.
злополу́ч|ный (-ен, -на, -но) *прил* (*охотник*)
ill-fated; (*день, час*) fateful.
злопыха́тел|ь (-я) *м* malevolent person (*мн
people*).
злопыха́|ть (-ю) *несов неперех* to rant.
злора́д|ный (-ен, -на, -но) *прил* gloating.
злора́дств|о (-а) *ср* malicious pleasure.
злора́дств|овать (-ую) *несов неперех* to gloat.
злосло́ви|е (-я) *ср* abuse, ridicule.
злосло́в|ить (-лю, -ишь) *несов неперех* to
indulge in ridicule.
зло́ст|ный (-ен, -на, -но) *прил* (*намерение*)
malicious; (*правонарушитель*) persistent.
злост|ь (-и) *ж* malice; **сказа́ть** (*perf*) **что-н со
зло́стью** to say sth angrily.
злосча́ст|ный (-ен, -на, -но) *прил* ill-fated.
злоумы́шленник (-а) *м* conspirator.
злоумы́шленный *прил* (*поступок*) malicious.
злоупотреб|и́ть (-лю́, -и́шь; *impf*
злоупотребля́ть) *сов неперех* (+*instr*) to abuse;
(*доверием*) to breach; (*сладким*) to indulge in.
злоупотребле́ни|е (-я) *ср* (+*instr*) abuse of;
(*обычно мн: незаконные действия*)
malpractise; ~ **дове́рием** breach of confidence.
злоупотреблю́ *сов см* **злоупотреби́ть**.
злоупотребля́|ть (-ю) *несов от*
злоупотреби́ть.
злю́к|а (-и) *м/ж* crosspatch.
змееви́к (-а́) *м* coil.
змеёныш (-а) *м* (*перен*) little sneak.
змеи́|ный *прил* (*кожа*) snake opred; (*нора,
питомник*) snake's; (*перен: улыбка, усмешка*)
venomous; ~ **яд** venom.
зме́|й (-я; *gen pl* -**ев**) *м* serpent; (*также:
возду́шный* ~) kite; **змей-горы́ныч** many-
headed dragon.
зме|я́ (-и́; *nom pl* -**éи**, *gen pl* -**éй**) *ж* (*также перен*)
snake; **змея́ подколо́дная** (*разг*) snake in the
grass.
знак (-а) *м* sign; (*МАТ, МУЗ, ТИПОГ*) symbol;
(*КОМП*) character; **в** ~ +*gen* as a sign of; **под
зна́ком** +*gen* in an atmosphere of; **знак
ра́венства** equals sign; **зна́ки препина́ния**
punctuation marks; **зна́ки разли́чия** (*ВОЕН*)
stripes; **зна́ки отли́чия** decorations; **зна́ки
зодиа́ка** signs of the Zodiac.

знако́м|ая (-ой; *decl like adj*) *ж см* **знако́мый**.
знако́м|ить (-лю, -ишь; *perf* **познако́мить**)
несов перех: ~ **кого́-н с** +*instr* to introduce sb to;
(*perf* **ознако́мить**; **с приказом, с документом**)
to acquaint sb with
▶ **знако́миться** (*perf* **познако́миться**) *несов
возв*: ~**ся с** +*instr* (*с человеком*) to meet; (*perf*
ознако́миться; **с приказом, с документом**) to
acquaint o.s. with.
знако́мств|о (-а) *ср* (*отношения*) acquaintance;
~**а** (*круг знакомых*) acquaintances; ~ **с** +*instr*
acquaintance with; **пе́рвое** ~ **с** +*instr* first
introduction to; **завя́зывать** (**завяза́ть** *perf*) ~ **с
кем-н** to make sb's acquaintance.
знако́м|ый (-, -а, -о) *прил*: ~ (**с** +*instr*) familiar
(with) ◆ (-**ого**; *decl like adj*) *м* acquaintance.
знамена́телен *прил см* **знамена́тельный**.
знамена́тел|ь (-я) *м* denominator; **приводи́ть
(привести́** *perf*) **к о́бщему** ~**ю** to reduce to a
common denominator.
знамена́тел|ьный (-ен, -ьна, -ьно) *прил*
momentous.
зна́мени *итп сущ см* **зна́мя**.
знаме́ни|е (-я) *ср* (*предзнаменование*) omen;
зна́мение вре́мени sign of the times.
знамени́тост|ь (-и) *ж* celebrity.
знамени́т|ый (-, -а, -о) *прил* famous.
знаме́н|овать (-у́ю) *несов перех* to mark.
знамено́с|ец (-ца) *м* standard-bearer.
зна́м|я (-ени; *как вре́мя; см* **Table 4**) *ср* banner;
(*перен: руководящая идея*) flag; **под** ~**енем**
+*gen* (*перен*) under the banner of.
зна́ни|е (-я) *ср* knowledge *только ед*; **со** ~**м
де́ла** knowledgeably.
зна́тный (-а́тен, -атна́, -а́тно) *прил* (*род,
человек*) noble; (*перен*) prominent.
знато́к (-а́) *м* (*литературы*) expert; (*вина*)
connoisseur.
зна|ть (-ти) *ж* nobility; ◆ (-ю) *несов перех* to
know; **она́ не зна́ет ме́ры** she doesn't know
when to stop; ~ (*impf*) **своё ме́сто** to know one's
place; **кто** (**его́**) **зна́ет?** (*разг*) who knows?; **так
и** ~**й** (*разг*) mark my words; ~ (*impf*) **це́ну** +*instr*
to appreciate; **дава́ть** (**дать** *perf*) ~ **себя́** ~ to make
itself known; **как** ~ maybe; **как зна́ешь** as you
wish; **он не** ~**л пораже́ний** he had never known
defeat; **он не зна́ет уста́лости** he never tires; **я
не зна́ю поко́я** I don't have a moment's peace
▶ **зна́ться** *несов возв*: **зна́ться с** +*instr* (*разг*) to
associate with.
значе́ни|е (-я) *ср* (*слова, взгляда*) meaning;
(*решения, победы*) importance; **э́то не име́ет**
~**я** it's not important; **придава́ть** (**прида́ть** *perf*)
осо́бое/большо́е ~ **чему́-н** to attach special/
great importance to sth.
зна́чимост|ь (-и) *ж* (*важность*) significance;
(*наличие смысла*) meaningfulness.
зна́чим|ый (-, -а, -о) *прил* important; ~**ая часть**

сло́ва unit of meaning.

зна́чит *вводн сл (разъ)* so ◆ *союз (следовательно)* that means; **~, ты не зна́ешь** so, you don't know then; **идёт снег, ~, сего́дня бу́дет хо́лодно** it's snowing, that means it's going to be cold today.

значи́тельный *(-ен, -ьна, -ьно) прил* significant; *(вид, взгляд)* meaningful; **в ~ьной сте́пени** to a significant degree.

зна́чить *(-у, -ишь) несов (не)перех* to mean; **что э́то ~ит?** what does it mean?; **э́то ничего́ не ~ит** it doesn't mean anything

▸ **зна́читься** *несов возв (состоять)* to appear; *(числиться):* **~ся больны́м** to be considered ill; **его́ и́мя ~ится в спи́ске** his name appears on the list.

значо́к *(-ка́) м* badge; *(пометка)* mark.

зна́ющий *(-ая, -ее, -ие; -, -а, -е) прил* competent.

зноби́ть *(3sg -и́т) несов безл:* **его́ ~и́т** he's shivery.

зно́ен *прил см* **зно́йный**.

зной *(-я) м* intense heat.

зно́йный *(-ен, -йна, -йно) прил (день, лето)* scorching; *(перен: взгляд)* intense; *(: чувство)* burning.

зоб *(-а; loc sg -у́, nom pl -ы́) м (у птицы)* crop; *(МЕД)* goitre *(BRIT)*, goiter *(US)*.

зов *(-а) м (о помощи, громкий)* call; **приходи́ть (прийти́ perf) по пе́рвому зо́ву** to come at the first call.

зову́ *итп несов см* **звать**.

зодиа́к *(-а) м* zodiac.

зо́дчество *(-а) ср* architecture.

зо́дчий *(-его; decl like adj) м* architect.

зол *сущ см* **зло** ◆ *прил см* **злой**.

зола́ *(-ы́) ж* cinders *мн*.

золо́вка *(-ки; gen pl -ок) ж* sister-in-law, husband's sister.

золоти́стый *(-, -а, -о) прил* golden.

золоти́ть *(-чу́, -ти́шь; perf* **позолоти́ть***) несов перех* to gild; **со́лнце позолоти́ло верху́шки дере́вьев** the sun cast a golden light over the tree tops.

золотни́к *(-а) м* slide valve.

зо́лото *(-а) ср* gold; *(золотые нити)* gold thread; **она́ про́сто ~** *(перен)* she's a real gem.

золотоиска́тель *(-я) м* gold-digger.

золото́й *прил* gold; *(рубль, локоны, лучи солнца итп)* golden; *(перен: человек, время)* wonderful; *(: работник)* priceless ◆ *(-о́го; decl like adj) м* gold coin; *(дорогой)* precious; **золота́я сва́дьба** golden wedding *или* anniversary; **золота́я середи́на** the golden mean; **золото́е дно** gold mine; **золото́е се́рдце** heart of gold; **золото́е пра́вило** golden rule; **золото́й век** golden age; **золото́й фонд** gold reserves.

золотоно́сный *(-ен, -на, -но) прил:* **~ райо́н** goldfield.

золотопромы́шленность *(-и) ж* gold-

mining.

золочёный *прил* gilt.

золочу́ *несов см* **золоти́ть**.

Зо́лушка *(-и) ж* Cinderella.

зо́на *(-ы) ж* zone; *(лесная)* area; *(для заключённых)* prison; **при́городная ~** suburb; **~ о́тдыха** holiday area; **~ обстре́ла** field of fire.

зона́льный *(-ен, -ьна, -ьно) прил (граница, деление)* zone *опред*; *(особенности, соревнование)* regional.

зонд *(-а) м (МЕД, ТЕХ)* probe.

зонди́ровать *(-ую; perf* **прозонди́ровать***) несов перех* to probe; **~ (прозонди́ровать perf) по́чву** *или* **обстано́вку** *(перен)* to test the water.

зонт *(-а́) м (от дождя)* umbrella; *(от солнца)* parasol; *(над дверью, над ветриной)* awning.

зо́нтик *(-а) м (от дождя)* umbrella; *(от солнца)* parasol.

зоо́лог *(-а) м* zoologist.

зоологи́ческий *(-ая, -ое, -ие) прил* zoological.

зооло́гия *(-и) ж* zoology.

зоомагази́н *(-а) м* pet shop.

зоопа́рк *(-а) м* zoo.

зоотехни́к *(-а) м* animal geneticist.

зо́ри *итп сущ см* **заря́**.

зо́ркий *(-кая, -кое, -кие; -ок, -ка, -ко) прил (человек)* sharp-eyed; *(глаза, ум)* sharp; *(перен: наблюдатель)* observant.

зрачо́к *(-ка́) м (АНАТ)* pupil.

зре́лище *(-а) ср (предмет обозрения)* sight, spectacle; *(представление)* show.

зре́лищный *прил:* **~ые предприя́тия** entertainment venues *мн*.

зре́лость *(-и) ж (плода, яблока)* ripeness; *(организма, человека)* maturity.

зре́лый *(-, -а, -о) прил (плод, зерно)* ripe.

зре́ние *(-я) ср* (eye)sight.

зреть *(-ю; perf* **созре́ть***) несов неперех* to mature; *(плод, яблоко)* to ripen; *(решение, мысль)* to develop; *(обида)* to grow.

зри́тель *(-я) м (в театре, в кино)* member of the audience; *(на стадионе)* spectator; *(наблюдатель)* onlooker.

зри́тельный *прил (память, восприятие)* visual; **зри́тельный зал** auditorium; **зри́тельный нерв** optic nerve.

зря *нареч (разг: без пользы)* for nothing, in vain; **~ тра́тить** *(impf)* **де́ньги/вре́мя** to waste money/time; **~ ты ему́ э́то сказа́л** you shouldn't have told him about it; **ты ~ купи́л э́ту кни́гу** there was no need to buy this book.

зря́чий *(-ая, -ее, -ие) прил* sighted.

зуб *(-а; nom pl -ы, gen pl -о́в) м (МН teeth); (nom pl -ья, gen pl -ьев; пилы, шестерни)* tooth *(МН teeth); (грабель, вилки)* prong; **у неё ~ на́ ~ не попада́ет** her teeth are chattering; **говори́ть** *(impf)* **сквозь зу́бы** *(разг)* to talk through one's teeth; **э́то мне не по ~а́м** *(перен)* it's too much for me; **он вооружён до ~о́в** he's armed to the teeth; **она́ на него́ ~ име́ет** (*разг*) she bears a grudge against him; **ни в ~ ного́й** (*разг*) he *итп* doesn't have a clue; **зуб му́дрости** wisdom tooth.

зуба́ст|ый (-, -а, -о) *прил* (*разг: щука, соба́ка*) with big sharp teeth; (*перен: разг*) sharp-tongued.

зуб|е́ц (-ца́; *nom pl* -цы́) *м* (*пилы, шестерни́*) tooth (*мн* teeth); (*гра́бель, ви́лки*) prong.

зуби́л|о (-а) *ср* chisel.

зубка́ *итп* сущ см **зубо́к**.

зубно́й *прил* dental; **зубна́я боль** toothache; **зубна́я па́ста** toothpaste; **зубна́я щётка** toothbrush; **зубно́й врач** dentist; **зубно́й проте́з** dentures.

зубовраче́бный *прил*: ~ **кабине́т** dental surgery (*BRIT*), dentist's office (*US*).

зубоска́л (-а) *м* (*разг*) scoffer.

зубоска́л|ить (-ю, -ишь) *несов неперех* (*разг*) to scoff.

зубочи́ст|ка (-ки; *gen pl* -ок) *ж* toothpick.

зубр (-а) *м* bison; (*перен: ретрогра́д*) die-hard; (*разг: о́пытный специали́ст*) boffin.

зубри́л|а (-ы) *м/ж* (*разг*) swot (*BRIT*), grind (*US*).

зубр|и́ть (-ю, -и́шь; *impf* **вы́зубрить**) *несов перех* (*разг*) to swot (*BRIT*), grind (*US*).

зубца́ *итп* сущ см **зубе́ц**.

зубча́т|ый *прил* (*стена́, ба́шня*) castellated; ~**ое колесо́** cog(wheel); ~**ая переда́ча** toothed gear; ~ **край** serrated edge.

зуд (-а) *м* (*та́кже перен*) itch.

зуд|е́ть (*3sg* -и́т, *3pl* -я́т) *несов неперех* (*разг: чеса́ться*) to itch; (-жу́, -ди́шь; *комар, пчела́*) to buzz; (*перен: нуди́ться*) to nag.

ЗУПВ *сокр* (= запомина́ющее устро́йство с произво́льной вы́боркой) RAM (= *random access memory*).

зы́б|кий (-кая, -кое, -кие; -ок, -ка, -ко) *прил* (*пове́рхность о́зера*) ripply; (*грунт, боло́то*) swampy; (*основа́ние*) shaky; (*перен: положе́ние*) unstable.

зыбу́ч|ий (-ая, -ее, -ие; -, -а, -е) *прил*: ~**ие пески́** quicksands *мн*.

зыбь (-и) *ж* ripple.

зы́чн|ый (-ен, -на, -но) *прил* (*го́лос*) booming; (*хо́хот*) thunderous.

зя́бко *как сказ* (*разг: хо́лодно*): **мне** ~ I feel chilly.

зя́блик (-а) *м* chaffinch.

зя́бн|уть (-у, -ешь; *perf* **озя́бнуть**) *несов неперех* to be cold.

зябь (-и) *ж field ploughed in autumn ready for sowing in the spring*.

зят|ь (-я) *м* (*муж до́чери*) son-in-law; (*муж сестры́*) brother-in-law, sister's husband; (*муж золо́вки*) brother-in-law (*husband's sister's husband*).

~ И, и ~

И, и *сущ нескл (буква)* the 9th letter of the Russian alphabet.

и *союз* **1** and; **я и мой друг** my friend and I; **и вот показался лес** and then a forest appeared

2 *(тоже)*: **и он пошёл в театр** he went to the theatre too; **и он не пришёл** he didn't come either

3 *(даже)* even; **и сам не рад** even he himself is not pleased

4 *(именно)*: **о том и речь!** that's just it!

5 *(во фразах)*: **ну и наглец же ты!** what a cheek you have!; **туда и сюда** here and there; **и ... и ...** both ... and ....

йбо *союз (так как)* for, because.

йва (-ы) *ж* willow.

иван-чай (-я) *м (no pl)* rosebay willowherb.

йвовый *прил* willow.

йволга (-ги; *gen pl* -г) *ж* oriole.

игла (-ы; *nom pl* -ы) *ж* needle; *(у ежа)* spine; *(проигрывателя)* needle, stylus.

иглодержатель (-я) *м (МЕД)* needleholder; *(проигрывателя)* cartridge.

иглоукалывание (-я) *ср* acupuncture.

игнорировать (-ую; *perf* игнорировать *или* проигнорировать) *несов перех* to ignore.

йго (-а) *ср* yoke.

иголка (-ки; *gen pl* -ок) *ж* = игла; **сидеть** *(impf)* **как на ~х** to be on tenterhooks.

игольный *прил*: **~ое ушко** eye of a needle.

игольчатый *прил (мех)* spiky; *(подшипник)* needle *опред*.

игорный *прил*: **~ дом** gaming club.

игра (-ы; *nom pl* -ы) *ж* game; *(на скрипке итп)* playing; *(актёра)* performance; **~ воображения** fantasy; **~ слов** play on words.

игральный *прил*: **~ые карты** playing cards *мн*.

играть (-ю) *несов неперех* to play ♦ *(perf* **сыграть)** *перех* to play; *(пьесу)* to perform; **~** *(сыграть perf)* **в** +*acc (СПОРТ)* to play; **~** *(impf)* **в прятки** to play hide-and-seek *(BRIT)* или hide-and-go-seek *(US)*; **~** *(impf)* **людьми/в демократию** *(перен)* to play with people/at democracy; **~** *(impf)* **на** +*prp (МУЗ)* to play; **~** *(сыграть perf)* **конём/королём** to play one's knight/king; **~** *(сыграть perf)* **на чьих-н слабостях** to play on sb's weaknesses; **~** *(impf)* **на чьих-н нервах** to irritate sb; **~** *(сыграть perf)*

свадьбу to celebrate a wedding; **вино ~ло в бокале** the wine sparkled in the glass.

играючи *нареч (разг: легко)* with one's eyes closed.

игривый (-, -а, -о) *прил* playful.

игристый *прил* sparkling.

игровой *прил*: **~ая комната** playroom; **~ые виды спорта** team sports; **игровой автомат** fruit machine.

игрок (-а) *м* player; *(в азартные игры)* gambler.

игротека (-и) *ж (собрание игр)* compendium *(BRIT)*; *(комната)* games room.

игрушек *сущ см* **игрушка**.

игрушечный *прил* toy *опред*; *(перен)* tiny.

игрушка (-ки; *gen pl* -ек) *ж* toy; *(перен)* puppet; **ёлочные ~ки** Christmas tree decorations.

идеал (-а) *м* ideal; **~ демократии** democratic ideal; **он – мой ~** he's someone I look up to.

идеален *прил см* **идеальный**.

идеализировать (-ую) *(не)сов перех* to idealize.

идеализм (-а) *м* idealism.

идеалист (-а) *м* idealist.

идеалистический (-ая, -ое, -ие) *прил* idealistic.

идеалистичный *прил* idealistic.

идеальный (-ен, -ьна, -ьно) *прил* ideal.

идейный (-ен, -йна, -йно) *прил (идеологический)* ideological; *(прогрессивный)* radical; **~йная основа романа** the main theme of the novel.

идём *несов см* **идти**.

идентифицировать (-ую) *(не)сов перех* to identify.

идентичный (-ен, -на, -но) *прил* identical.

идеолог (-а) *м* ideologist.

идеологический (-ая, -ое, -ие) *прил* ideological.

идеология (-и) *ж* ideology.

идёшь *итп несов см* **идти**.

идея (-и) *ж* idea; **по ~е** *(разг)* supposedly; **по ~е** +*gen* in accordance with; **подавать (подать** *perf)* **кому-н ~ю** to give sb an idea.

идиллический (-ая, -ое, -ие) *прил* idyllic.

идиллия (-и) *ж* idyll.

идиома (-ы) *ж* idiom.

идиот (-а) *м (также МЕД)* idiot.

идиотизм (-а) *м (МЕД)* mental retardation; *(разг: глупость)* idiocy.

идио́тск|ий (**-ая, -ое, -ие**) *прил* idiotic.

и́дол (**-а**) *м* idol.

идти́ (*см* **Table 18**) *несов неперех* to go; (*пешком*) to walk; (*дни, годы*) to go by; (*фильм, спектакль итп*) to be on; (*часы*) to work; (*товар*) to sell; (*подходить: одежда*): ~ **к** +*dat* to go with; ~ (**пойти́** *perf*) (**в/на** +*acc*) to go (to); ~ (**пойти́** *perf*) +*instr* (**конём, тузом** *итп*) to play; **я шёл 3 часа́** I walked for 3 hours; **иди́ сюда́!** come here!; **иду́!** (I'm) coming!; **идёт по́езд/авто́бус** the train/bus is coming; **по́езд идёт до Москвы́** the train goes as far as Moscow; **маши́на идёт со ско́ростью 100км в час** the car is going at 100km per hour; **идёт дождь/снег** it's raining/snowing; **идёт зима́** winter is coming; **идёт гроза́** there is a storm coming; **дела́ иду́т хорошо́/пло́хо** things are going well/badly; **сейча́с иду́т перегово́ры/экза́мены** the talks/exams are in progress; **что сейча́с идёт в кино́?** what's on at the cinema just now?; **спекта́кль идёт 2 часа́** the play goes on for 2 hours; **мои́ часы́ иду́т ме́дленно/бы́стро** my watch is slow/fast; **Вам идёт э́та шля́па** the hat suits you; **из трубы́ идёт дым** there is smoke coming from the chimney; **у меня́ идёт кровь из но́са** my nose is bleeding; **ему́ идёт пя́тый год** he was four on his last birthday; ~ (**пойти́** *perf*) **пешко́м** to walk, go on foot; ~ (**пойти́** *perf*) **на рабо́ту/в теа́тр** to go to work/the theatre; ~ (**пойти́** *perf*) **на э́кспорт/прода́жу** to be for export/sale; **э́ти я́блоки пойду́т на варе́нье** these apples will do for making jam; ~ (**пойти́** *perf*) **на у́быль** to decrease; ~ (**пойти́** *perf*) **на сниже́ние** to descend; ~ (**пойти́** *perf*) **на риск** to take a risk; ~ (**пойти́** *perf*) **на компроми́сс** to go for a compromise; ~ (**пойти́** *perf*) **на хи́трость/обма́н** to resort to cunning/deception; **идёт!** (*разг*) fine!

иезуи́т (**-а**) *м* Jesuit.

иена (**-ы**) *ж* yen.

иера́рхи|я (**-и**) *ж* hierarchy.

иеро́глиф (**-а**) *м* (*китайский, японский*) character; (*египетский*) hieroglyph (*мн* hieroglyphics).

Иерусали́м (**-а**) *м* Jerusalem.

ИЖ *м сокр* = **Иже́вский мотоцикле́тный заво́д**; (*мотоцикл*) *motorcycle manufactured at the Izhevsk motorcycle factory.*

иждиве́н|ец (**-ца**) *м* (*ребёнок, престарелые*) dependant; (*бездельник*) sponger.

иждиве́ни|е (**-я**) *ср* maintenance; **состоя́ть** (*impf*) **или быть** (*impf*) **на ~и у** +*gen* to be dependent on.

иждиве́нца *итп сущ см* **иждиве́нец**.

иждиве́нчеств|о (**-а**) *ср* dependence.

KEYWORD

из *предл* (+*gen*) **1** (*о направлении действия откуда-нибудь*) out of; **он вы́шел из ко́мнаты** he went out of the room; **она́ доста́ла из карма́на плато́к** she took a handkerchief out of her pocket
2 (*при обозначении происхождения, источника*) from; **све́дения из кни́ги** information from a book; **из достове́рных исто́чников** from reliable sources; **я из Москвы́** I am from Moscow
3 (*при выделении части из целого*) of; **вот оди́н из приме́ров** here is one of the examples
4 (*при обозначении компонентов целого*) made of; **э́тот стол сде́лан из сосны́** this table is made of pine; **ва́за из стекла́** a glass vase; **варе́нье из я́блок** apple jam; **блу́за из нейло́на** nylon blouse
5 (*при указании причины*) out of; **из осторо́жности/за́висти** out of wariness/envy; **из эконо́мии** in order to save money
6 (*во фразах*): **из го́да в год** year in, year out; **я бежа́л изо всех сил** I ran at top speed.

изба́ (**-ы́**; *nom pl* **-ы**) *ж* hut.

избави́тел|ь (**-я**) *м* saviour.

избави́тельни|ца (**-ы**) *ж см* **избави́тель**.

изба́в|ить (**-лю, -ишь**; *impf* **избавля́ть**) *сов перех*: ~ **кого́-н от** +*gen* (*от проблем, от забот*) to relieve sb of; (*от врагов*) to deliver sb from

▶ **изба́виться** (*impf* **избавля́ться**) *сов возв*: ~**ся от** +*gen* (*от проблем, от посетителей*) to get rid of; (*от страха, от предрассудков*) to get over.

избало́ван|ный (**-, -на, -но**) *прил* spoilt.

избал|ова́ть (**-у́ю**) *сов от* **ба́ловать**.

избал|ова́ться (**-у́юсь**; *impf* **избало́вываться**) *сов возв* (*разг*) to become spoilt.

избега́|ть (**-ю**) *сов перех* (*разг*) to run around.

избега́|ть (**-ю**) *несов от* **избежа́ть**, **избе́гнуть** ♦ *неперех*: ~ **чего́-н/** +*infin* to avoid sth/doing.

избе́г|нуть (**-ну, -нешь**; *pt* **-, -ла, -ло**, *impf* **избега́ть**) *сов неперех* = **избежа́ть**.

избегу́ *итп сов см* **избежа́ть**.

избежа́ни|е (**-я**) *ср*: **во ~** +*gen* (in order to) avoid.

избежа́ть (*как* **бежа́ть**; *см* **Table 20**; *impf* **избега́ть**) *сов неперех*: ~ +*gen* to avoid.

изберу́ *итп сов см* **избра́ть**.

избива́|ть (**-ю**) *несов от* **изби́ть**.

избие́ни|е (**-я**) *ср* beating; (*массовое убийство*) massacre.

избира́телен *прил см* **избира́тельный**.

избира́тел|ь (**-я**) *м* voter.

избира́тельни|ца (**-ы**) *ж см* **избира́тель**.

избира́тельный *прил* (*система*) electoral; (**-ен, -ьна, -ьно**; *эффект*) selective; **~ьная кампа́ния** election campaign; **избира́тельный**

уча́сток polling station; **избира́тельный бюллете́нь** ballot paper.

избира́ть (-ю) *несов от* **избра́ть** ♦ *перех* to elect.

изби́тый (-, -а, -о) *прил* clichéd, hackneyed.

изби́ть (-обью́, -обьёшь; *impf* **избива́ть**) *сов перех (человека)* to beat; *(обувь)* to wear out.

изборозди́ть (-жу́, -ди́шь) *сов от* **борозди́ть**.

избра́ние (-я) *ср* election.

избра́нник (-а) *м* chosen one; ~ **судьбы́** fate's darling; **наро́дные** ~**и** deputies.

избра́нница (-ы) *ж см* **избра́нник**.

и́збранные (-ых; *decl like adj*) *мн* select *или* chosen few *мн*.

и́збранный *прил (рассказы, стихи)* selected; *(люди, круг)* select; *см также* **и́збранные**.

избра́ть (-еру́, -ерёшь; *pt* -ра́л, -рала́, -ра́ло, *impf* **избира́ть**) *сов перех (профессию)* to choose; *(президента)* to elect; **избира́ть** (~ *perf*) **кого́-н в парла́мент** to elect sb to parliament.

избы́ток (-ка) *м (излишек)* surplus; *(обилие)* excess; **име́ть** *(impf)* **что-н в** ~**ке** to have plenty of sth; **э́того хва́тит с** ~**ком** it is more than enough; **она́ запла́кала от** ~**ка чувств** overwhelmed by emotion, she burst into tears.

избы́точный (-ен, -на, -но) *прил (вес, влага)* excess *опред*; *(информация)* abundant; ~**ное предложе́ние** *(экон)* excess supply.

изва́яние (-я) *ср* effigy.

изве́дать (-ю; *impf* **изве́дывать**) *сов перех* to come to know.

изведу́(сь) *итп сов см* **извести́(сь)**.

изве́дывать (-ю) *несов от* **изве́дать**.

и́зверг (-а) *м* monster *(fig)*.

изве́ргнуть (-у, -ешь; *impf* **изверга́ть**) *сов перех* to spew (out).

изверже́ние (-я) *ср* eruption.

изве́риться (-юсь, -ишься) *сов возв*: ~ **в** +*prp* to lose faith in.

изверну́ться (-у́сь, -ёшься; *impf* **извёртываться** *или* **изворо́чиваться**) *сов возв* to twist around; *(перен)* to pull through.

изве́стен *прил см* **изве́стный**.

извести́ (-еду́, -едёшь; *pt* -ёл, -ела́, -ело́, *impf* **изводи́ть**) *сов перех (разг: истратить)* to fritter away; *(: изму́чить)* to exasperate; *(истребить)* to exterminate.

▶ **извести́сь** *(impf* **изводи́ться**) *сов возв* to torment o.s.

изве́стие (-я) *ср* news; *см также* **изве́стия**.

извести́ть (-щу́, -сти́шь; *impf* **извеща́ть**) *сов перех*: ~ **кого́-н о** +*prp* to inform sb of.

изве́стия (-й) *мн (издание)* bulletin *ед*.

изве́стка (-и) *ж* slaked lime.

изве́стно *как сказ*: ~, **что** ... it is well known that ...; **мне э́то** ~ I know about it; **наско́лько мне** ~ as far as I know; **как** ~ as is well known.

изве́стность (-и) *ж* fame; **по́льзоваться** *(impf)* ~**ю** to be well known; **ста́вить (поста́вить** *perf)* **кого́-н в** ~ to inform sb.

изве́стный (-ен, -на, -но) *прил* famous, well-known; *(no short form; разг: лентяй, бабник)* notorious; *(условия)* certain; ~ +*instr* famous *или* well-known for; **он** ~**ен как тала́нтливый руководи́тель** he is known to be a talented leader; ~**ное де́ло!** *(разг)* that's no surprise!

известня́к (-а́) *м* limestone.

и́звесть (-и) *ж* lime.

изве́чный (-ен, -на, -но) *прил (проблема, спор)* perpetual.

извеща́ть (-ю) *несов от* **извести́ть**.

извеще́ние (-я) *ср* notification; *(комм)* advice note; **почто́вое** ~ signed receipt of delivery.

извещу́ *сов см* **извести́ть**.

извива́ться (-юсь) *несов возв (змея)* to slither; *(человек)* to writhe; *(дорога, река)* to wind.

изви́лина (-ы) *ж* bend; ~ **мо́зга** convolution.

изви́листый (-, -а, -о) *прил* winding, twisting.

извине́ние (-я) *ср* apology; *(оправдание)* excuse; **проси́ть (попроси́ть** *perf)* ~**я (у кого́-н)** to apologize (to sb).

извини́тельный *прил (тон, улыбка)* apologetic; *(-ен, -ьна, -ьно; ошибка, слабость)* excusable, forgivable.

извини́ть (-ю́, -и́шь; *impf* **извиня́ть**) *сов перех (простить)*: ~ **что-н (кому́-н)** to excuse (sb for) sth; ~**и́те!** excuse me!; ~**и́те, Вы не ска́жете где вокза́л?** excuse me, could you tell me where the station is?; **в э́том, ~и́те, я с Ва́ми не согла́сен** sorry, but I cannot agree with you on that

▶ **извини́ться** *(impf* **извиня́ться**) *сов возв*: ~**ся (за** +*acc)* to apologize (for); **он ~и́лся, что не позвони́л** he apologized for not phoning *(BRIT)* *или* calling *(US)*.

извиня́ющийся (-аяся, -ееся, -иеся) *прил* apologetic.

извлёк *итп сов см* **извле́чь**.

извлека́ть (-ю) *несов от* **извле́чь**.

извлеку́ *итп сов см* **извле́чь**.

извлече́ние (-я) *ср (золота, пользы итп)* extraction; *(из документа)* extract, excerpt.

извле́чь (-еку́, -ечёшь итп, -еку́т; *pt* -ёк, -екла́, -екло́, *impf* **извлека́ть**) *сов перех (занозу, осколок)* to remove, take out; *(золото)* to extract; *(перен: пользу, выгоду итп)* to derive; **извлека́ть** (~ *perf)* **уро́к** to learn a lesson; **извлека́ть** (~ *perf)* **ко́рень** *(мат)* to find the root.

извне́ *нареч* from outside.

изводи́ть(ся) (-ожу́(сь), -о́дишь(ся)) *несов от* **извести́(сь)**.

изво́зчик (-а) *м (кучер)* coachman *(мн* coachmen); *(экипаж)* cab *(coach)*.

изво́лить (-ю, -ишь) *несов неперех*: ~ +*infin* to condescend to do; ~**ьте не крича́ть** would you mind not shouting.

извора́чиваться (-юсь) *несов от* **изверну́ться**.

изворо́тливый (-, -а, -о) *прил (человек)* wily; *(ум, делец)* shrewd.

извра|ти́ть (-щу́, -ти́шь; *impf* **извраща́ть**) *сов перех* to distort.

извраще́ни|е (-я) *ср* distortion; **полово́е ~** sexual perversion.

извращён|ный (-, -на, -но) *прил* perverted.

извращу́ *сов см* **извратить**.

изга́|дить (-жу, -дишь) *сов перех* (*разг*) to mess up.

изги́б (-а) *м* bend.

изгиба́|ть(ся) (-ю(сь)) *несов от* **изогну́ть(ся)**.

изгла́|дить (-жу, -дишь; *impf* **изгла́живать**) *сов перех*: **~ что-н из па́мяти** to blot sth out of one's memory

▶ **изгла́диться** (*impf* **изгла́живаться**) *сов возв* to be blotted out.

изгна́ни|е (-я) *ср* (*ссылка*) exile; (*врага*) expulsion; (*злых духов*) exorcism.

изгна́нник (-а) *м* exile.

изгна́нниц|а (-ы) *ж см* **изгна́нник**.

изг|на́ть (-оню́, -о́нишь; *pt* -на́л, -нала́, -на́ло, *impf* **изгоня́ть**) *сов перех* to drive out; (*сослать*) to exile.

изго́|й (-я) *м* outcast.

изголо́вь|е (-я) *ср*: **у ~я** at the head of the bed.

изголода́|ться (-юсь) *сов возв* to be starving; (*перен*): **~ по** +*dat* (*по книгам*) to long *или* yearn for; **~** (*perf*) **по ла́ске** to crave affection.

изгоню́ *итп сов см* **изгнать**.

изгоня́|ть (-ю) *несов от* **изгнать**.

и́згород|ь (-и) *ж* fence; **живая ~** hedge.

изгото́в|ить (-лю, -ишь; *impf* **изготовля́ть**) *сов перех* to manufacture.

изготовле́ни|е (-я) *ср* manufacture.

изготовлю́ *сов см* **изгото́вить**.

изготовля́|ть (-ю) *несов от* **изгото́вить**.

изгры́з|ть (-у́, -ёшь; *pt* -, -ла, -ло) *сов перех* to gnaw (away) at.

изд. *сокр* (= **изда́ние**) ed. (= *edition*).

изда|ва́ть (-ю́, -ёшь) *несов от* **изда́ть**.

и́здавна *нареч* for a long time.

издади́м *итп сов см* **изда́ть**.

издалека́ *нареч* from a long way off *или* away; **начина́ть** (**нача́ть** *perf*) **разгово́р ~** (*перен*) to start a conversation in a roundabout way.

и́здали *нареч* = **издалека́**.

изда́м *итп сов см* **изда́ть**.

изда́ни|е (-я) *ср* (*действие*) publication; (*изданная вещь*) edition.

изда́ст *сов см* **изда́ть**.

изда́тел|ь (-я) *м* publisher.

изда́тельск|ий (-ая, -ое, -ие) *прил* publishing *опред*.

изда́тельств|о (-а) *ср* publisher, publishing house.

изда́|ть (*как* **дать**; *см* **Table 14**; *impf* **издава́ть**) *сов перех* (*книгу*) to publish; (*закон, постановление*) to issue; (*крик, стон*) to let out; (*запах*) to give off.

изд-во *сокр* (= **изда́тельство**) pub(l). (= *publisher*).

издева́тельск|ий (-ая, -ое, -ие) *прил* (*насмешливый*) mocking, scoffing; (*оскорбительный*) abusive.

издева́тельств|о (-а) *ср* mockery; (*наглое*) jibe; (*жестокое*) abuse.

издева́|ться (-юсь) *несов возв*: **~ над** +*instr* (*над подчинёнными*) to make a mockery of; (*над книгой*) to pour scorn on; (*над чьей-н одеждой*) to mock, ridicule.

издёв|ка (-ки; *gen pl* -ок) *ж* (*разг*) jibe.

изде́ли|е (-я) *ср* (*товар*) article; **ювели́рные ~я** jewellery (*BRIT*), jewelery (*US*); **стекля́нные ~я** glassware; **игру́шка куста́рного ~я** handmade toy.

издёрган|ный (-, -на, -но) *прил* (*разг*) edgy.

издёрга|ть (-ю) *сов перех* (*разг*) to put on edge.

▶ **издёргаться** *сов возв* (*разг*) to become edgy.

изд|ержа́ть (-ержу́, -е́ржишь; *impf* **изде́рживать**) *сов перех* (*деньги*) to use up; (*ресурсы*) to exhaust.

изде́рж|ки (-ек) *мн* (*производственные*) expenses *мн*; **суде́бные ~** legal costs; **э́то всё – ~ плохо́го воспита́ния** it's all the result of bad upbringing.

издеру́ *итп сов см* **изодра́ть**.

издыха́ни|е (-я) *ср*: **при после́днем ~и** on one's deathbed.

изж|и́ть (-ву́, -вёшь; *pt* -л, -ла́, -ло, *impf* **изжива́ть**) *сов перех* (*плохую привычку*) to overcome; (*преступность*) to eliminate; **изжива́ть** (**~** *perf*) **себя́** to outlive its usefulness.

изжо́г|а (-и) *ж* heartburn.

из-за *предл*: **~** +*gen* (*занавески*) from behind; (*угла*) from around; (*по вине*) because of; **встава́ть** (**встать** *perf*) **~ стола́** to get up from the table; **~ того́ что** because; **~ тебя́ мы пропусти́ли по́езд** we missed the train because of you.

иззя́б|нуть (-ну, -нешь; *pt* -, -ла, -ло) *сов непepex* (*разг*) to be frozen stiff.

излага́|ть (-ю) *несов от* **изложи́ть**.

изла́мыва|ть (-ю) *несов от* **изломать**.

излече́ни|е (-я) *ср* (*лечение*) treatment; (*выздоровление*) recovery; **быть** (*impf*) **на ~и** to undergo treatment.

изле́чива|ть (-ю) *несов от* **излечи́ть**

▶ **изле́чиваться** *несов от* **излечи́ться ♦ возв** (*болезнь*) to be curable.

излечи́м|ый (-, -а, -о) *прил* curable.

изл|ечи́ть (-ечу́, -е́чишь; *impf* **изле́чивать**) *сов перех*: **~ кого́-н (от** +*gen*) to cure sb (of)

▶ **излечи́ться** *сов возв*: **~ся от** +*gen* (*от болезни*) to recover from; (*от наркомании, от алкоголизма*) to be cured of.

изл|и́ть (**изолью́, изоль́ёшь**; *pt* -л, -ла́, -ло, *impf* **излива́ть**) *сов перех* (*перен: тоску*) to pour

out; **изливать** (~ *perf*) **душу** to pour one's heart
out; **изливать** (~ *perf*) **гнев** to vent one's anger
► **излиться** (*impf* **изливаться**) *сов возв* to pour
one's heart out; **изливаться** (*impf*) **в**
благодарностях to express one's great
appreciation.

излишек (-ка) *м* (*остаток*) remainder; ~ +*gen*
(*влаги, веса*) excess of.

излишество (-а) *ср* overindulgence.

излишка *итп сущ см* **излишек**.

излишний (-няя, -нее, -ние; -ен, -ня, -не) *прил*
unnecessary; **комментарии** ~**ни** there is
nothing to add.

излияние (-я) *ср* (*чувств*) gush; (*обычно мн*:
дружеские, любовные) outburst.

изловчиться (-усь, -ишься) *сов возв*
(*приспособиться*) to manage.

изложение (-я) *ср* presentation.

изложить (-ожу, -ожишь; *impf* **излагать**) *сов*
перех (*события*) to recount; (*просьбу, решение*
итп) to state.

изломанный (-, -на, -но) *прил* (*судьба, жизнь*)
ruined; (*характер*) unbalanced.

изломать (-ю; *impf* **изламывать**) *сов перех*
(*забор, игрушку*) to smash; (*перен: жизнь*) to
ruin; (: *характер*) to unbalance.

излучать (-ю) *несов перех* (*также перен*) to
radiate

► **излучаться** *несов возв* to radiate.

излучение (-я) *ср* radiation.

излучина (-ы) *ж* bend.

излюбленный *прил* favourite (*BRIT*), favorite
(*US*).

измазать(ся) (-жу(сь), -жешь(ся)) *сов от*
мазать(ся).

измарать(ся) (-ю(сь)) *сов от* **марать(ся)**.

изматывать(ся) (-ю(сь)) *несов от*
измотать(ся).

измельчать (-ю) *сов от* **мельчать**.

измельчить (-у, -ишь) *сов от* **мельчить**

► **измельчиться** *несов возв* to crumble.

измена (-ы) *ж* (*родине*) treason; (*другу*)
betrayal; **государственная** ~ high treason;
супружеская ~ adultery.

изменение (-я) *ср* change; (*поправка*)
alteration.

изменить (-еню, -енишь; *impf* **изменять**) *сов*
перех to change ♦ *неперех*: ~ +*dat* (*родине,*
другу) to betray; (*супругу*) to be unfaithful to;
(*память*) to fail; **силы ему** ~**енили** his strength
failed him

► **измениться** (*impf* **изменяться**) *сов возв* to
change.

изменник (-а) *м* (*родине*) traitor.

изменница (-ы) *ж см* **изменник**.

изменчивый (-, -а, -о) *прил* changeable.

изменяемый (-, -а, -о) *прил* (*линг*): ~**ое**
окончание variable ending.

изменять(ся) (-ю(сь)) *несов от* **изменить(ся)**.

измерение (-я) *ср* (*действие: площади*)
measurement; (*величина*) dimension.

измерительный *прил* measuring *опред*.

измерить (-ю, -ишь; *impf* **измерять**) *сов перех*
to measure; **измерять** (~ *perf*) **температуру**
кому-н to take sb's temperature; ~ (*perf*) **кого-н**
взглядом to look sb up and down.

измеряться (*3sg* -ется, *3pl* -ются) *несов возв*
(+*instr*): ~ **килограммами/метрами** to be
measured in kilogrammes/metres (*BRIT*) *или*
meters (*US*).

измождение (-я) *ср* exhaustion.

измождённый (-, -á, -ó) *прил* (*человек*) worn
out; (-, -на, -но; *вид, лицо*) haggard.

измокнуть (-ну, -нешь; *pt* -, -ла, -ло) *сов*
неперех to get soaked.

измор (-а) *м*: **взять кого-н/что-н** ~**ом** (*город*)
to wage a war of attrition against sb/sth; (*перен*:
разг) to wear down.

изморозь (-и) *ж* hoarfrost.

изморось (-и) *ж* drizzle.

измотать (-ю; *impf* **изматывать**) *сов перех* to
wear out

► **измотаться** (*impf* **изматываться**) *сов возв* to
be worn out.

измученный (-, -а, -о) *прил* (*человек*) worn
out; (-, -на, -но; *лицо*) haggard.

измучить (-у, -ишь) *сов от* **мучить**.

измываться (-юсь) *несов возв*: ~ **над** +*instr*
(*разг*) to taunt.

измышление (-я) *ср* fabrication.

измять(ся) (-омну(сь), -омнёшь(ся)) *сов от*
мять(ся).

изнанка (-и) *ж* (*одежды*) inside; (*ткани*) wrong
side; (*перен: жизни, событий*) dark side.

изнасиловать (-ую) *сов от* **насиловать**.

изначальный (-ен, -ьна, -ьно) *прил* initial.

изнашивать(ся) (-ю(сь)) *несов от*
износить(ся).

изнеженный (-, -а, -о) *прил* pampered.

изнежить (-у, -ишь) *сов перех* to pamper

► **изнежиться** *сов возв* to be pampered.

изнемог *итп сов см* **изнемочь**.

изнемогать (-ю) *несов от* **изнемочь**.

изнемогу *итп сов см* **изнемочь**.

изнеможение (-я) *ср* exhaustion; **до** ~**я** to the
point of exhaustion.

изнеможённый (-, -á, -ó) *прил* (*человек*) worn
out; (-, -на, -но; *вид, лицо*) haggard.

изнемочь (-гу, -жешь *итп*, -гут; *pt* -г, -гла, -гло,
impf **изнемогать**) *сов неперех* to be exhausted.

износ (-а) *м* (*механизмов*) wear; (*перен*:
организма) ageing; **работать** (*impf*) **на** ~
(*перен*) to work o.s. into the ground.

износить (-ошу, -осишь; *impf* **изнашивать**) *сов*
перех to wear out

► **износиться** (*impf* **изнашиваться**) *сов возв* to
wear out.

изношенный (-, -а, -о) *прил* worn-out.

изношу(сь) *сов см* **износить(ся)**.

изнурённый (-, -á, -ó) *прил* (*человек*)
exhausted; (-, -на, -но; *лицо, вид*) haggard.

изнурительный (-ен, -ьна, -ьно) *прил*

exhausting.

изнур|**и́ть** (**-ю́, -и́шь**; *impf* **изнуря́ть**) *сов перех* to exhaust.

изнутри́ *нареч* from inside.

изныва́|**ть** (**-ю**) *несов неперех* to languish.

и́зо *предл* = из.

изоби́ли|**е** (**-я**) *ср* abundance; **в ~и** in abundance.

изоби́л|**овать** (*3sg* **-ует**, *3pl* **-уют**) *несов неперех* (**+***instr*) to abound in.

изоби́ль|**ный** (**-ен, -ьна, -ьно**) *прил* abundant.

изоблича́|**ть** (**-ю**) *несов от* **изобличи́ть** ♦ *перех* (*обнаружить*): ~ **кого́-н в** +*prp* (*подлеж: одежда, акцент итп*) to give sb away as.

изоблич|**и́ть** (**-у́, -и́шь**; *impf* **изоблича́ть**) *сов перех* (*шпиона, взяточника итп*) to expose; **изоблича́ть** (~ *perf*) **кого́-н во лжи/в моше́нничестве** to expose sb's lies/deception.

изобража́|**ть(ся)** (**-ю(сь)**) *несов от* **изобрази́ть(ся)**.

изображе́ни|**е** (**-я**) *ср* image; (*действие: событий*) depiction, representation.

изображу́(сь) *сов см* **изобрази́ть(ся)**.

изобрази́тель|**ный** (**-ен, -ьна, -ьно**) *прил* descriptive; **изобрази́тельное иску́сство** fine art.

изобра|**зи́ть** (**-жу́, -зи́шь**; *impf* **изобража́ть**) *сов перех* (*на карти́не, в рома́не итп*) to depict, portray; (*подлеж: лицо*) to show; (*копировать*) to impersonate; **изобража́ть** (~ *perf*) **из себя́ наи́вного/знатока́** to make o.s. out to be naive/an expert

▶ **изобрази́ться** (*impf* **изобража́ться**) *сов возв* to show; **на его́ лице́ ~и́лся у́жас** a look of horror came over his face.

изобр|**ести́** (**-ету́, -ете́шь**; *pt* **-ёл, -ела́, -ело́**, *impf* **изобрета́ть**) *сов перех* to invent.

изобрета́тель (**-я**) *м* inventor.

изобрета́тельниц|**а** (**-ы**) *ж см* **изобрета́тель**.

изобрета́тельность (**-и**) *ж* inventiveness.

изобрета́тельств|**о** (**-а**) *ср* innovation.

изобрета́|**ть** (**-ю**) *несов от* **изобрести́**.

изобрете́ни|**е** (**-я**) *ср* invention.

изобью́ *итп сов см* **избить**.

изогн|**у́ть** (**-у́, -ёшь**; *impf* **изгиба́ть**) *сов перех* to bend

▶ **изогну́ться** (*impf* **изгиба́ться**) *сов возв* to bend.

изо|**дра́ть** (**-деру́, -дерёшь**; *pt* **-одра́л, -одрала́, -одра́ло**) *сов перех* (*разг*) to rip to shreds.

изо|**йти́** (*как* **идти́**; *см* Table 18; *impf* **исходи́ть**) *сов неперех* to cry one's eyes out; **она́ ~шла́ го́рем** she was completely grief-stricken.

изоли́рованный *прил* (*случай, явление итп*) isolated; (*комната, провод*) insulated.

изоли́р|**овать** (**-ую**) (*не*)*сов перех* (*больного, преступника*) to isolate; (*вход*) to cut off; (*ТЕХ,*

ЭЛЕК) to insulate

▶ **изоли́роваться** (*не*)*сов возв* (*человек*) to isolate o.s.

изолью́(сь) *итп сов см* **изли́ть(ся)**.

изоля́тор (**-а**) *м* (*ТЕХ, ЭЛЕК*) insulator; (*в больни́це*) isolation unit; (*в тюрьме́*) solitary confinement.

изоляцио́нн|**ый** *прил*: ~**ая ле́нта** insulating tape.

изоля́ци|**я** (**-и**) *ж* (*см глаг*) isolation; insulation; **жить** (*impf*) **в ~и** to live in isolation.

изомну́(сь) *итп сов см* **измя́ть(ся)**.

изопью́ *итп сов см* **испи́ть**.

изорв|**а́ть** (**-у́, -ёшь**; *pt* **-а́л, -ала́, -а́ло**) *сов перех* to rip up; ~ (*perf*) **в кло́чья** to tear to shreds.

изото́п (**-а**) *м* isotope.

изотрётся *итп сов см* **истере́ться**.

изошёл *итп сов см* **изойти́**.

изощрён|**ный** (**-, -на, -но**) *прил* sophisticated.

изощр|**и́ться** (**-ю́сь, -и́шься**; *impf* **изощря́ться**) *сов возв* (*отличиться*) to surpass o.s.; (*вкус, ум*) to become sophisticated.

изощря́|**ться** (**-ю́сь**) *несов от* **изощри́ться** ♦ *неперех*: ~ **в** +*prp* to excel in.

из-под *предл* (**+***gen*) from under(neath); (*около*) from outside; ~ **стола́ вы́ползла ко́шка** a cat crawled from under the table; **он прие́хал** ~ **Ки́ева** he comes from outside Kiev; **вы́йти (вы́йти** *perf*) ~ **чьего́-н влия́ния** to free o.s. from sb's influence; **бежа́ть** (*impf*) ~ **стра́жи** to escape from custody; **ба́нка** ~ **варе́нья** jam jar; **буты́лка** ~ **во́дки** vodka bottle.

изразе́|**ц** (**-ца́**) *м* tile.

изразцо́вый *прил* tiled.

Изра́ил|**ь** (**-я**) *м* Israel.

изра́ильск|**ий** (**-ая, -ое, -ие**) *прил* Israeli.

израильтя́н|**ин** (**-ина**; *nom pl* **-е**, *gen pl* **-**) *м* Israeli.

израильтя́н|**ка** (**-ки**; *gen pl* **-ок**) *ж см* **израильтя́нин**.

изра́н|**ить** (**-ю, -ишь**) *сов перех* to injure badly.

израсхо́д|**овать** (**-ую**) *сов от* **расхо́довать**.

и́зредка *нареч* now and then *или* again.

изре́|**зать** (**-жу, -жешь**; *impf* **изреза́ть**) *сов перех* to cut up; (*подлеж: дороги, каналы*) to crisscross.

изрёк *итп сов см* **изре́чь**.

изрека́|**ть** (**-ю**) *несов от* **изре́чь**.

изреку́ *итп сов см* **изре́чь**.

изрече́ни|**е** (**-я**) *ср* utterance.

изр|**е́чь** (**-еку́, -ече́шь** *итп*, **-еку́т**; *pt* **-ёк, -екла́, -екло́**, *impf* **изрека́ть**) *сов перех* to utter.

изреше|**ти́ть** (**-чу́, -ти́шь**) *сов перех*: ~ **кого́-н пу́лями** to pepper sb with bullets.

изру|**би́ть** (**-ублю́, -у́бишь**; *impf* **изруба́ть**) *сов перех* (*убить*) to hack to pieces.

изрыга́|**ть** (**-ю**) *несов перех* (*лаву*) to spew (out); (*перен: проклятия*) to let out a torrent of.

изры́т|ый (-, -а, -о) *прил* (*поверхность*) pitted; ~ о́спой pockmarked.

изры́ть (-о́ю, -о́ешь) *сов перех* to riddle.

изря́дн|ый (-ен, -на, -но) *прил* (*сумма, доход*) fair; (*разг: мошенник, пьяница итп*) real.

изуве́р (-а) *м* monster.

изуве́рск|ий (-ая, -ое, -ие) *прил* monstrous.

изуве́рств|о (-а) *ср* monstrosity.

изуве́чить (-у, -ишь; *impf* изуве́чивать) *сов перех* to maim

► **изуве́читься** (*impf* изуве́чиваться) *сов возв* to be maimed.

изукра́сить (-шу, -сишь; *impf* изукра́шивать) *сов перех* to adorn; (*разг: избить*) to beat black and blue.

изуми́тельный (-ен, -ьна, -ьно) *прил* marvellous (*BRIT*), marvelous (*US*), wonderful.

изуми́ть (-лю́, -и́шь; *impf* изумля́ть) *сов перех* to amaze, astound

► **изуми́ться** (*impf* изумля́ться) *сов возв* to be amazed.

изумле́ни|е (-я) *ср* amazement; **приходи́ть** (**прийти́** *perf*) **в** ~ to be amazed; **с** ~м (*слушать, рассматривать*) in amazement; **я с** ~м **обнару́жил, что** ... to my great amazement I discovered that ....

изумлю́(сь) *сов см* изуми́ть(ся).

изумля́ть(ся) (-ю(сь)) *несов от* изуми́ть(ся).

изумру́д (-а) *м* emerald.

изумру́дный *прил* (*кольцо итп*) emerald; (*цвет*) emerald-green.

изуро́довать (-ую) *сов от* уро́довать.

изуча́ть (-ю) *несов от* изучи́ть ♦ *перех* (*о процессе*) to study.

изуче́ни|е (-я) *ср* study.

изучи́ть (-учу́, -у́чишь; *impf* изуча́ть) *сов перех* (*язык, предмет*) to learn; (*понять*) to get to know; (*исследовать*) to study.

изъеда́ть (*3sg* -ет, *3pl* -ют) *несов от* изъе́сть.

изъе́ден|ный (-, -а, -о) *прил*: ~ мо́лью motheaten; ~ кислото́й eaten away by acid.

изъеди́м *итп сов см* изъе́сть.

изъе́здить (-жу, -дишь) *сов перех* to travel (round).

изъе́сть (*как* есть; *см* Table 15; *impf* изъеда́ть) *сов перех* (*мех, ткань*) to eat away; (*металл*) to corrode.

изъяви́тельн|ый *прил* (*линг*): ~ое наклоне́ние the indicative mood.

изъяви́ть (-явлю́, -я́вишь; *impf* изъявля́ть) *сов перех* to indicate.

изъя́н (-а) *м* flaw.

изъясни́ть (-ю́, -и́шь; *impf* изъясня́ть) *сов перех* to clarify.

изъя́ти|е (-я) *ср* (*см глаг*) withdrawal; removal.

изъя́ть (изыму́, изы́мешь; *impf* изыма́ть) *сов перех* (*из обращения, из продажи*) to withdraw; (*отобрать*) to remove.

изыска́ни|е (-я) *ср* investigation; (*геологические*) exploration.

изы́сканность (-и) *ж* refinement.

изы́скан|ный (-, -на, -но) *прил* refined.

изыска́тель (-я) *м* surveyor.

изыска́тельск|ий (-ая, -ое, -ие) *прил* exploratory.

изыска́ть (-ыщу́, -ы́щешь; *impf* изы́скивать) *сов перех* to find.

изы́скива|ть (-ю) *несов от* изыска́ть ♦ *перех* (*искать*) to seek out.

изыщу́ *итп сов см* изыска́ть.

изю́м (-а) *м собир* raisins *мн*.

изю́мин|а (-ы) *ж* raisin.

изю́минк|а (-ки; *gen pl* -ок) *ж уменьш от* изю́мина; (*перен*) highlight; **без** ~ки lacklustre.

изя́щен *прил см* изя́щный.

изя́щество (-а) *ср* elegance.

изя́щный (-ен, -на, -но) *прил* elegant.

ика́ть (-ю) *несов неперех* to hiccup.

икну́ть (-у́, -ёшь) *сов неперех* to hiccup.

ико́н|а (-ы) *ж* (*РЕЛ*) icon.

иконопи́с|ец (-ца) *м* icon painter.

и́конопись (-и) *ж* icon painting.

иконоста́с (-а) *м* iconostasis.

икот|а (-ы) *ж* hiccups *мн*.

икр|а́ (-ы́) *ж* (*рыбы*) roe; (*чёрная, красная*) caviar; (*кабачковая, баклажанная*) pâté; (*nom pl* -ы; *АНАТ*) calf (*мн* calves).

икри́н|ка (-ки; *gen pl* -ок) *ж* grain of caviar.

икс (-а) *м* (*МАТ*) X; **ми́стер И**~ Mr X.

ИЛ (-а) *м сокр* = самолёт констру́кции С.В. Илью́шина.

ил (-а) *м* silt.

и́ли *союз* or; **чай** ~ **ко́фе** tea or coffee; ~ ... ~ ... either ... or ...; ~ **ты не понима́ешь?** (*разг*) don't you understand or something?

и́лист|ый (-, -а, -о) *прил* silt *опред*.

иллюзиони́ст (-а) *м* conjurer.

иллю́зи|я (-и) *ж* (*также перен*) illusion.

иллюзо́р|ный (-ен, -на, -но) *прил* illusory.

иллюмина́тор (-а) *м* (*корабля*) porthole; (*самолёта*) window.

иллюмина́ци|я (-и) *ж* illuminations *мн*.

иллюстра́тор (-а) *м* illustrator.

иллюстра́ци|я (-и) *ж* illustration.

иллюстри́р|овать (-ую; *perf* иллюстри́ровать *или* проиллюстри́ровать) *несов перех* to illustrate.

ильм (-а) *м* elm.

им *мест см* он, оно́, они́.

им. *сокр* = и́мени.

имби́рь (-я́) *м* ginger.

и́мени *итп сущ см* и́мя.

име́ни|е (-я) *ср* estate.

имени́нник (-а) *м person who is celebrating his name day or birthday*.

имени́нниц|а (-ы) *ж см* имени́нник.

имени́н|ы (-) *мн* (*РЕЛ*) name day *ед*.

имени́тельн|ый *прил* (*линг*): ~ паде́ж the nominative case.

имени́т|ый (-, -а, -о) *прил* renowned.

и́менно *част* exactly, precisely ♦ *союз* (*перед перечислением*): **а** ~ namely; **э́то на́до сде́лать** ~ **сего́дня** it has to be done today; ~ **в**

э́том до́ме я роди́лся it was in this house that I was born; ~ **так я и поступи́л** that is exactly what I did; **вот** ~**!** exactly!, precisely!; **на собра́нии прису́тствовало 6 челове́к а** ~: **Ивано́в, Петро́в** .... there were 6 people present at the meeting, namely Ivanov, Petrov ....

имен|но́й *прил* (*оружие, часы*) personalized; (*акции, чек*) nontransferable; **именно́й про́пуск** pass (*issued in somebody's name*); **именно́й спи́сок** nominal roll.

имен|ова́ть (-у́ю; *perf* **наименова́ть**) *несов перех* to name.

им|е́ть (-ю) *несов перех* to have; ~ (*impf*) **ме́сто** (*совершаться*) to take place; ~ (*impf*) **де́ло с** +*instr* to deal with; **я не хочу́** ~ **с ним де́ло** I don't want anything to do with him; ~ (*impf*) **в виду́** to bear in mind; (*подразумевать*) to mean; **я** ~**ю зада́чу/цель** *или* **зада́чей/це́лью** +*infin* my task/aim is to do; ~ (*impf*) **что́-нибудь про́тив** +*gen* to have something against; **ничего́ не** ~ (*impf*) **про́тив** +*gen* to have nothing against to name.

▶ **им|е́ться** *несов возв* (*сведения, средства*) to be available; **у нас** ~**ются ну́жные сре́дства** we have the necessary resources available.

и́ми *мест см* **они́**.

и́мидж (-а) *м* image.

и́миджме́йкер (-а) *м* image-maker.

имита́ци|я (-и) *ж* imitation.

имити́р|овать (-ую; *perf* **сымити́ровать**) *несов перех* to imitate.

иммигра́нт (-а) *м* immigrant.

иммигра́нт|ка (-ки; *gen pl* -ок) *ж см* **иммигра́нт**.

иммиграцио́нный *прил* immigration.

иммигра́ци|я (-и) *ж* immigration ♦ *собир* immigrants *мн*.

иммигри́р|овать (-ую) (*не*)*сов непepex* to immigrate.

иммуните́т (-а) *м* (*МЕД. перен*): ~ (**к** +*dat*) immunity (to); **выраба́тывать** (**вы́работать** *perf*) ~ **к** +*dat* to develop an immunity to; **у меня́** ~ **к шу́му/кри́тике** I'm immune to noise/criticism; **дипломати́ческий** ~ diplomatic immunity.

имму́нн|ый *прил* (*МЕД*): ~**ая систе́ма** immune system.

иммуноло́ги|я (-и) *ж* immunology.

императи́в (-а) *м* (*также линг*) imperative.

импера́тор (-а) *м* emperor.

импера́торск|ий (-ая, -ое, -ие) *прил* imperial.

императри́ц|а (-ы) *ж* empress.

империали́зм (-а) *м* imperialism.

империали́ст (-а) *м* imperialist.

империалисти́ческ|ий (-ая, -ое, -ие) *прил* imperialistic.

импе́ри|я (-и) *ж* empire.

импе́рск|ий (-ая, -ое, -ие) *прил* imperial.

импи́чмент (-а) *м* (*полит*) impeachment.

импланта́т (-а) *м* (*МЕД*) implant.

имплантаци|я (-и) *ж* implantation.

имплант|и́ровать (-ую) (*не*)*сов перех* to implant.

импони́р|овать (-ую) *несов непepex* (+*dat*) to appeal to.

и́мпорт (-а) *м* (*ввоз*) importation ♦ *собир* (*товары*) imports *мн*; (*разг: о заграничных товарах*) foreign goods *мн*; **по́шлины/нало́г на** ~ import duty/tax; **и́мпорт капита́ла** capital investment from abroad.

импортёр (-а) *м* importer.

импорти́р|овать (-ую) (*не*)*сов перех* to import.

и́мпортный *прил* imported; **и́мпортная кво́та** import quota.

импоте́нт (-а) *м* impotent male.

импоте́нт|ный (-ен, -на, -но) *прил* impotent.

импоте́нци|я (-и) *ж* (*МЕД*) impotence.

импреса́рио *м нескл* (*музыканта*) agent; (*устроитель концертов итп*) impresario.

импрессиони́зм (-а) *м* impressionism.

импрессиони́ст (-а) *м* impressionist.

импрессионисти́ческ|ий (-ая, -ое, -ие) *прил* impressionist.

импровиза́тор (-а) *м* improviser.

импровиза́ци|я (-и) *ж* improvisation.

импровизи́р|овать (-ую; *perf* **импровизи́ровать** *или* **сымпровизи́ровать**) (*не*)*сов перех* to improvise.

и́мпульс (-а) *м* (*ФИЗ, БИО*) impulse; (*перен*): ~ (**к** +*dat*) (**к работе, к реформам** *итп*) impetus (for).

импульси́в|ный (-ен, -на, -но) *прил* impulsive.

иму́щественный *прил* property *опред*.

иму́ществ|о (-а) *ср* property; (*принадлежности*) belongings *мн*; **дви́жимое** ~ (*ЮР*) movables; **недви́жимое** ~ (*ЮР*) property.

иму́щий (-ая, -ее, -ие) *прил* (*классы*) propertied; **власть** ~**ие** the powers that be.

и́м|я (-ени; *как* **вре́мя**; *см* **Table 4**) *ср* (*также перен*) name; (*также: ли́чное* ~) first *или* Christian name; (*знаменитый человек*) famous name; **во** ~ +*gen* (*ради*) in the name of; **на** ~ +*gen* (*письму*) addressed to; **биле́ты оста́влены на Ва́ше** ~ the tickets have been left under your name; **от** ~**ени** +*gen* on behalf of; **моё** ~ — **Мари́я** my name is Maria; **Теа́тр** ~**ени Че́хова** the Chekhov Theatre; ~**енем зако́на** in the name of the law; **называ́ть** (*impf*) **ве́щи свои́ми имена́ми** to call a spade a spade; **и́мя прилага́тельное** adjective; **и́мя существи́тельное** noun.

инакомы́слящий (-его; *decl like adj*) *м* dissident.

ина́че *нареч* (*по-другому*) differently ♦ *союз* otherwise, or else; **вы́глядеть** (*impf*) ~ to look different; **так и́ли** ~ one way or another; **а как же** ~**?** how else?

инвали́д (-а) *м* disabled person (*мн* people).

инвалидн|ый *прил*: ~ая коляска wheelchair;
инвалидный дом home for the disabled.
инвалидность (-и) *ж* disability; пенсия по ~и
disablement benefit; получать (получить *perf*)
~ to be registered as disabled.
инвалют|а (-ы) *ж сокр* (= иностранная
валюта) foreign currency.
инвалютный *прил* (поступления, счёт)
foreign-currency.
инвентаризаци|я (-и) *ж* stocktaking.
инвентар|ь (-я) *м* (предметы) equipment;
(опись) inventory.
инверси|я (-и) *ж* (линг) inversion.
инвести́р|овать (-ую) (не)сов (не)перех (ЭКОН)
to invest.
инвестиционный *прил* investment опред;
инвестиционный банк investment bank.
инвестици|я (-и) *ж* (обычно мн) investment;
иностранные ~ foreign investment; доход от
~й investment income.
инвестор (-а) *м* investor.
ингаля́тор (-а) *м* (МЕД) inhaler.
ингаля́ци|я (-и) *ж* inhalation.
ингредиент (-а) *м* ingredient.
ингуш (-á) *м* Ingush.
Ингушети|я (-и) *ж* Ingushetia.
ингуш|ка (-ки; *gen pl* -ек) *ж см* ингуш.
йндеве|ть (-ю; *perf* заиндеветь) *несов неперех*
to become covered in frost.
индеек *сущ см* индейка.
инде́|ец (-йца) *м* Native American, North
American Indian.
индей|ка (-йки; *gen pl* -ек) *ж* turkey.
индеец *итп сущ см* индеец.
йндекс (-а) *м* (цен, книг) index (мн indexes);
(также: почтовый ~) post (BRIT) или zip (US)
code; фондовый ~ share index; йндекс
(розничных/потребительских) цен (retail/
consumer) price index.
индекса́ци|я (и) *ж* (ЭКОН) index-linking (BRIT),
indexing (US).
индекси́р|овать (-ую) *несов перех* (ЭКОН:
зарплату) to index, index-link (BRIT).
индиа́н|ка (-ки; *gen pl* -ок) *ж см* индиец, индеец.
индиви́д (-а) *м* individual.
индивидуа́лен *прил см* индивидуальный.
индивидуали́зм (-а) *м* individualism.
индивидуали́ст (-а) *м* individualist.
индивидуа́льность (-и) *ж* (совокупность
черт) individuality; (личность) individual.
индивидуа́льн|ый (-ен, -ьна, -ьно) *прил*
individual.
индиви́дуум (-а) *м* individual.
инди́го *ср нескл* indigo.
инди́|ец (-йца) *м* Indian.
инди́йск|ий (-ая, -ое, -ие) *прил* Indian;
Индийский океан the Indian Ocean.
индийца *итп сущ см* индиец.
Инди|я (-и) *ж* India.
индонези|ек *сущ см* индонезийка.
индонези|ец (-йца) *м* Indonesian.
индонези|йка (-йки; *gen pl* -ек) *ж см*

индонези|ец.
индонези́йск|ий (-ая, -ое, -ие) *прил*
Indonesian.
индонези́йца *итп сущ см* индонези́ец.
Индоне́зи|я (-и) *ж* Indonesia.
индосса́нт (-а) *м* (КОММ) endorser.
индосса́т (-а) *м* (КОММ) endorsee.
индуи́зм (-а) *м* Hinduism.
инду́кци|я (-и) *ж* (ФИЗ) induction.
инду́с (-а) *м* Hindu.
индустриализа́ци|я (-и) *ж* industrialization.
индустриализи́р|овать (-ую) (не)сов перех
to industrialize.
индустриа́льный *прил* industrial.
индустри́|я (-и) *ж* industry; ~ мо́ды/
кино́/тури́зма the fashion/film/tourist
industry.
индю́к (-á) *м* turkey cock.
индю́ш|ка (-ки; *gen pl* -ек) *ж* (разг) = инде́йка.
йне|й (-я) *м* hoarfrost.
ине́рт|ный (-ен, -на, -но) *прил* (ФИЗ, ХИМ) inert;
(перен) inactive.
ине́рци|я (-и) *ж* (ФИЗ, перен) inertia; дви́гаться
(*impf*) по ~и (ФИЗ) to move by inertia; де́лать
(*impf*) что-н по ~и to do sth out of habit; я по ~и
дал ему́ ста́рый телефо́н I gave him my old
telephone number automatically.
инжене́р (-а) *м* engineer; ~ по те́хнике
безопа́сности health and safety officer;
инжене́р-меха́ник/-констру́ктор/-строи́тель
mechanical/design/construction engineer.
инжене́рн|ый *прил*: ~ая нау́ка engineering
(*science*); ~ое де́ло engineering (*profession*).
инжи́р (-а) *м* (дерево) fig ♦ собир (плоды) figs
мн.
ИНИО́Н (-а) *м сокр* = Институ́т нау́чной
информа́ции по обще́ственным нау́кам.
инициализи́р|овать (-ую) (не)сов перех
(КОМП) to initialize.
инициа́л|ы (-ов) *мн* initials *мн*.
инициати́в|а (-ы) *ж* initiative; по со́бственной
~e on one's own initiative.
инициати́вн|ый (-ен, -на, -но) *прил*
enterprising; он о́чень ~ челове́к he has a lot of
initiative; **инициати́вная гру́ппа** action group.
инициа́тор (-а) *м* initiator.
инкасса́тор (-а) *м* security guard (*employed to
collect and deliver money*).
инкасси́р|овать (-ую) (не)сов перех (КОММ) to
encash.
инка́ссо *ср нескл* (КОММ) encashment.
инквизи́тор (-а) *м* (перен) inquisitor.
инквизи́ци|я (-и) *ж* (перен) inquisition.
инко́гнито *нареч, м/с нескл* incognito.
Инкомба́нк (-а) *м сокр* (= Иностра́нный
комме́рческий банк) foreign commercial bank.
инкримини́р|овать (-ую) (не)сов перех: ~
что-н кому́-н to accuse sb of sth.
инкруста́ци|я (-и) *ж* inlay.
инкрусти́р|овать (-ую) (не)сов перех to inlay.
инкуба́тор (-а) *м* incubator.

инкубацио́нный *прил*: ~ **пери́од** (*БИО, МЕД*) incubation period.

инкуба́ци|я (*-и*) *ж* incubation.

иногда́ *нареч* sometimes.

иногоро́дн|ий (*-яя, -ее, -ие*) *прил* from another town ♦ (*-его; decl like adj*) *м person from another town*.

инозе́мный *прил* foreign.

ин|о́й *прил* different ♦ *мест* (*некоторый*) some (people); ~ **раз** at times; ~**ыми слова́ми** in other words; **не что ~о́е, как ...**, **не кто ~**, **как ...** none other than ...; ~**ые счита́ют, что ...** some (people) think (that) ....

ино́к (*-а*) *м* monk (*in the Orthodox Church*).

инопланетя́н|ин (*-ина; nom pl -е, gen pl -*) *м* alien.

иноро́д|ный (*-ен, -на, -но*) *прил* alien; **иноро́дное те́ло** (*МЕД*) foreign body.

иносказа́ни|е (*-я*) *ср* allegory.

иносказа́тел|ьный (*-ен, -ьна, -ьно*) *прил* allegorical.

иностра́н|ец (*-ца*) *м* foreigner.

иностра́н|ка (*-ки; gen pl -ок*) *ж см* **иностра́нец**.

иностра́нн|ый *прил* foreign; **Министе́рство ~ых дел** Ministry of Foreign Affairs, ≈ Foreign Office (*BRIT*), ≈ State Department (*US*).

иностра́нок *сущ см* **иностра́нка**.

иностра́нца *итп сущ см* **иностра́нец**.

иноязы́чн|ый *прил* (*слово*) foreign; ~**ое населе́ние** foreign-language-speaking population.

инсинуа́ци|я (*-и*) *ж* insinuation.

инспекти́р|овать (*-ую; perf* **проинспекти́ровать**) *несов перех* to inspect.

инспе́ктор (*-а*) *м* inspector.

инспе́кци|я (*-и*) *ж* inspection; (*организация*) inspectorate.

инста́нци|я (*-и*) *ж* (*ПОЛИТ*) body, authority.

инсти́нкт (*-а*) *м* instinct.

инстинкти́в|ный (*-ен, -на, -но*) *прил* instinctive.

институ́т (*-а*) *м* institute; (*семьи, брака*) institution.

институ́тск|ий (*-ая, -ое, -ие*) *прил* institute *опред*.

инструкти́р|овать (*-ую; perf* **проинструкти́ровать**) (*не*)*сов перех* to instruct.

инстру́ктор (*-а*) *м* instructor; ~ **по пла́ванию/лы́жам** swimming/ski instructor.

инстру́кци|я (*-и*) *ж* instructions *мн*; (*также:* ~ **по эксплуата́ции**) instructions (for use).

инструме́нт (*-а*) *м* (*МУЗ, ТЕХ, перен*) instrument ♦ *собир* instruments *мн*.

инструмента́льный *прил* (*МУЗ*) instrumental; **инструмента́льная му́зыка** instrumental music; **инструмента́льный анса́мбль** instrumental ensemble; **инструмента́льный**

цех tool workshop.

инсули́н (*-а*) *м* insulin.

инсу́льт (*-а*) *м* (*МЕД*) stroke.

инсцени́р|овать (*-ую*) (*не*)*сов перех* (*перен: обморок, ограбление*) to stage; (*роман*) to adapt.

инсцениро́вк|а (*-и*) *ж* adaptation.

ин-т *сокр* = **институ́т**.

интегра́л (*-а*) *м* (*МАТ*) integral.

интегра́льн|ый *прил*: ~**ое исчисле́ние** integral calculus.

интегри́р|овать (*-ую*) (*не*)*сов перех* (*также МАТ*) to integrate.

интегра́ци|я (*-и*) *ж* (*также МАТ*) integration.

интелле́кт (*-а*) *м* intellect.

интеллектуа́л (*-а*) *м* intellectual.

интеллектуа́л|ьный (*-ен, -ьна, -ьно*) *прил* intellectual; **интеллектуа́льная со́бственность** intellectual property.

интеллиге́нт (*-а*) *м* member of the intelligentsia.

интеллиге́нт|ный (*-ен, -на, -но*) *прил* cultured and educated.

интеллиге́нци|я (*-и*) *ж собир* the intelligentsia; **техни́ческая/тво́рческая** ~ the science/arts community.

интенда́нт (*-а*) *м* (*ВОЕН*) quartermaster.

интенси́в|ный (*-ен, -на, -но*) *прил* intensive; (*окраска*) intense.

интенсифика́ци|я (*-и*) *ж* intensification.

интенсифици́р|овать (*-ую*) (*не*)*сов перех* to intensify.

интеракти́вный *прил* (*КОМП*) interactive.

интерва́л (*-а*) *м* interval; (*ТИПОГ*) spacing; **с** ~**ом в 10 мину́т** with a 10 minute interval.

интервье́нт (*-а*) *м* interventionist.

интерве́нци|я (*-и*) *ж* intervention.

интервью́ *ср нескл* interview; **брать** (**взять** *perf*)/**дава́ть** (**дать** *perf*) ~ to do/give an interview.

интервьюи́р|овать (*-ую; perf* **проинтервью́и́ровать**) (*не*)*сов перех* to interview.

интере́с (*-а*) *м*: ~ (**к** +*dat*) interest (in); **представля́ть** (**предста́вить** *perf*) ~ (**для** +*gen*) to be of interest (to); *см также* **интере́сы**.

интере́сен *прил см* **интере́сный**.

интере́сно *нареч*: **он о́чень** ~ **расска́зывает** he is very interesting to listen to ♦ *как сказ*: ~(, **что ...**) it's interesting (that ...); **мне э́то о́чень** ~ I find it very interesting; **э́то никому́ не** ~ that is of no interest to anyone; ~, **где он э́то нашёл** I wonder where he found that; ~ **знать, где он был** I'd be interested to know where he was; **как** ~! that's really interesting!; ~! (*разг: выражает недовольство, возражение*) so!; **она́** ~ **мы́слит** she has an interesting way of thinking.

интере́с|ный (**-ен, -на, -но**) *прил* interesting; (*вне́шность, же́нщина*) attractive.
интерес|ова́ть (**-у́ю**) *несов перех* to interest
▶ **интересова́ться** *несов возв* (**+instr**) to be interested in; (*осведомля́ться*) to inquire after; **он ~ова́лся, когда́ ты приезжа́ешь/где ты бу́дешь жить** he was asking when you would be arriving/where you would be living.
интере́с|ы (**-ов**) *мн* (*госуда́рства, фи́рмы итп*) interests *мн*; (*духо́вные*) concerns *мн*; **в ~ах +gen** in the interests of; **затра́гивать (затро́нуть** *perf*) *или* **задева́ть (заде́ть** *perf*) **чьи-н ~** to touch on sb's interests.
интерлю́ди|я (**-и**) *ж* (*МУЗ*) interlude.
интерме́ди|я (**-и**) *ж* (*ТЕАТР*) interlude.
интерн (**-а**) *м* (*МЕД*) ≈ houseman (*BRIT*) (*мн* housemen), ≈ intern (*US*).
интерна́т (**-а**) *м* boarding school.
Интернациона́л (**-а**) *м* (*ИСТ*) the International.
интернационализа́ци|я (**-и**) *ж* internationalization.
интернационали́зм (**-а**) *м* internationalism.
интернационали́ст (**-а**) *м* internationalist.
интернациона́льный *прил* international.
Интерне́т (**-а**) *м* Internet.
ИНТЕРПО́Л (**-а**) *м сокр* (= *Междунаро́дная организа́ция уголо́вной поли́ции*) Interpol (= *International Criminal Police Organization*).
интерпрета́тор (**-а**) *м* interpreter.
интерпрета́ци|я (**-и**) *ж* interpretation.
интерпрети́р|овать (**-ую**) (*не*)*сов перех* to interpret.
интерфе́йс (**-а**) *м* (*КОМП*) interface.
интерье́р (**-а**) *м* (*зда́ния*) interior.
инти́м|ный (**-ен, -на, -но**) *прил* intimate.
интоксика́ци|я (**-и**) *ж* intoxication.
интона́ци|я (**-и**) *ж* (*ЛИНГ, МУЗ*) intonation; (*недово́льная, трево́жная итп*) note.
интри́г|а (**-и**) *ж* (*полити́ческая*) intrigue; (*любо́вная*) affair; (*рома́на*) plot.
интрига́н (**-а**) *м* intriguer.
интрига́н|ка (**-ки**; *gen pl* **-ок**) *ж см* **интрига́н.**
интриг|ова́ть (**-у́ю**; *perf* **заинтригова́ть**) *несов перех* to intrigue ◆ *несов неперех* (*no perf*): **~ про́тив +gen** to intrigue against.
интрове́рт (**-а**) *м* introvert.
интуити́в|ный (**-ен, -на, -но**) *прил* intuitive.
интуи́ци|я (**-и**) *ж* intuition.
Интури́ст (**-а**) *м сокр* (= *Гла́вное управле́ние по иностра́нному тури́зму*) *Russian tourist agency dealing with foreign tourism.*
инфа́ркт (**-а**) *м* (*та́кже:* **~ миока́рда**) heart attack; **обши́рный ~ (миока́рда)** massive heart attack.
инфекцио́нный *прил* infectious; **инфекцио́нная больни́ца** hospital for infectious diseases.
инфе́кци|я (**-и**) *ж* infection.
инфинити́в (**-а**) *м* infinitive.
инфици́рован|ный (**-, -на, -но**) *прил* infected.
инфля́ци|я (**-и**) *ж* (*ЭКОН*) inflation.
инфляцио́нный *прил* inflationary.

информати́в|ный (**-ен, -на, -но**) *прил* informative.
информа́тик|а (**-и**) *ж* information technology.
информа́тор (**-а**) *м* informant.
информацио́нный *прил* information *опред*; **информацио́нная програ́мма** news programme (*BRIT*) *или* program (*US*).
информа́ци|я (**-и**) *ж* information.
информи́рованный *прил* well-informed.
информи́р|овать (**-ую**; *perf* **информи́ровать** *или* **проинформи́ровать**) *несов перех* to inform.
инфракра́сный *прил* infrared.
инфраструкту́р|а (**-ы**) *ж* infrastructure.
инциде́нт (**-а**) *м* incident.
инъе́кци|я (**-и**) *ж* injection.
иня́з (**-а**) *м сокр* = **институ́т иностра́нных языко́в; факульте́т иностра́нных языко́в.**
и.о. *сокр* (= *исполня́ющий обя́занности*) acting.
ио́н (**-а**) *м* ion.
иорда́н|ец (**-ца**) *м* Jordanian.
Иорда́ни|я (**-и**) *ж* Jordan.
иорда́н|ка (**-ки**; *gen pl* **-ок**) *ж см* **иорда́нец.**
иорда́нск|ий (**-ая, -ое, -ие**) *прил* Jordanian.
иорда́нца *итп сущ см* **иорда́нец.**
ипоста́с|ь (**-и**) *ж* (*РЕЛ*) hypostasis; **в ~и +gen** (*перен*) in the role of.
ипоте́к|а (**-и**) *ж* (*КОММ*) mortgage.
ипоте́чн|ый *прил* mortgage; **~ая ссу́да** mortgage; **~ банк** ≈ building society.
ипохо́ндрик (**-а**) *м* hypochondriac.
ипохо́ндри|я (**-и**) *ж* hypochondria.
ипподро́м (**-а**) *м* racecourse (*BRIT*), racetrack (*US*).
иприт (**-а**) *м* mustard gas.
Ира́к (**-а**) *м* Iraq.
ира́к|ец (**-ца**) *м* Iraqi.
ира́кск|ий (**-ая, -ое, -ие**) *прил* Iraqi.
ира́кца *итп сущ см* **ира́кец.**
Ира́н (**-а**) *м* Iran.
ира́н|ец (**-ца**) *м* Iranian.
ира́н|ка (**-ки**; *gen pl* **-ок**) *ж см* **ира́нец.**
ира́нск|ий (**-ая, -ое, -ие**) *прил* Iranian.
ира́нца *итп сущ см* **ира́нец.**
и́рис (**-а**) *м* (*БОТ*) iris; (*ни́тки*) thread (*for embroidery etc*).
ири́с (**-а**) *м* (*конфе́та*) toffee.
ири́с|ка (**-ки**; *gen pl* **-ок**) *ж* (*paзг*) toffee.
ирла́нд|ец (**-ца**) *м* Irishman (*мн* Irishmen).
Ирла́нди|я (**-и**) *ж* Ireland.
ирла́нд|ка (**-ки**; *gen pl* **-ок**) *ж* Irishwoman (*мн* Irishwomen).
ирла́ндск|ий (**-ая, -ое, -ие**) *прил* Irish.
ирла́ндца *итп сущ см* **ирла́ндец.**
ИРЛИ *м сокр* = **Институ́т ру́сской литерату́ры.**
иронизи́р|овать (**-ую**) *несов неперех*: **~ (над +instr**) to be ironic (about).
ирони́чн|ый (**-ен, -на, -но**) *прил* ironic.
иро́ни|я (**-и**) *ж* irony; **~ судьбы́** the irony of fate.
иррациона́л|ьный (**-ен, -ьна, -ьно**) *прил* irrational.

иррегуля́рн|ый *прил*: ~ые войска́ irregular forces *мн*, irregulars *мн*.

иррига́ци|я (-и) *ж* irrigation.

иск (-а) *м* lawsuit; встре́чный ~ counterclaim; де́нежный ~ damages; предъявля́ть (предъяви́ть *perf*) кому́-н ~ to take legal action against sb.

искажа́|ть(ся) (-ю(сь)) *несов от* искази́ть(ся).

искаже́ни|е (-я) *ср* (*фактов*) distortion; (*в тексте*) error.

иска|зи́ть (-жу́, -зи́шь; *impf* искажа́ть) *сов перех* (*факты, смысл*) to distort; (*лицо*) to contort; (*комп*) to corrupt; зло́ба ~зи́ла его́ лицо́ his face contorted with malice

► искази́ться (*impf* искажа́ться) *сов возв* (*изображение, смысл*) to be distorted; (*выражение лица, голос*) to contort.

искале́ч|ить (-у, -ишь) *сов от* кале́чить.

иска́ни|е (-я) *ср* (*обычно мн: творческие, научные*) quest.

иска́тел|ь (-я) *м* (*золота*) prospector; (*стремящийся к новому*) explorer; ~ приключе́ний adventure seeker.

иска́тельниц|а (-ы) *ж см* иска́тель.

иска́ть (ищу́, и́щешь) *несов перех* to look *или* search for.

исключа́|ть (-ю) *несов от* исключи́ть.

исключа́я *предл* (+*acc*) excluding; не ~ +*gen* including.

исключе́ни|е (-я) *ср* (*из списка, из очереди*) exclusion; (*из института*) expulsion; (*отклонение от нормы*) exception; ~ из пра́вила exception to the rule; за ~м +*gen* with the exception of; де́лать (сде́лать *perf*) что-н в ви́де ~я to make an exception of sth.

исключи́телен *прил см* исключи́тельный.

исключи́тельно *нареч* (*особенно*) exceptionally; (*толькс*) exclusively.

исключи́тельный (-ен, -ьна, -ьно) *прил* exceptional; (*no short form*; *право*) exclusive.

исключ|и́ть (-у́, -и́шь; *impf* исключа́ть) *сов перех* (*удалить: из списка*) to exclude; (: *из института*) to expel; (*ошибку, случайность*) to exclude the possibility of; э́то ~ено́ that is out of the question; компроми́сс ~ён a compromise is out of the question.

исковёрка|ть (-ю) *сов от* ковёркать.

исколе|си́ть (-шу́, -си́шь) *сов перех* (*разг*) to travel; он ~си́л весь мир he's been all over the world.

иско́мка|ть (-ю) *сов от* ко́мкать.

иско́м|ый *прил* (*МАТ*): ~ая величина́ unknown value ♦ (-ого; *decl like adj*) *ср* (*МАТ*) unknown.

иско́н|ный (-ен, -на, -но) *прил* (*население*) original; (*право*) intrinsic; ~ язы́к the vernacular.

ископа́ем|ое (-ого; *decl like adj*) *ср* fossil; (*также*: поле́зное ~: обычно мн) mineral.

ископа́емый *прил* (*животное, растение*) fossilized.

искорёж|ить (-у, -ишь) *сов от* корёжить.

искорен|и́ть (-ю́, -и́шь; *impf* искореня́ть) *сов перех* to eradicate.

и́скоса *нареч* (*взглянуть, смотреть*) sideways; смотре́ть (*impf*) ~ на кого́-н (*перен*) to look askance at sb.

и́скр|а (-ы) *ж* (*огня, также перен*) spark; (*снега, бриллианта*) glint, glistening; у меня́ ~ы из глаз посы́пались I began to see stars; зарони́ть (*perf*) в ком-н ~у наде́жды to give sb a glimmer of hope.

и́скренне *нареч* sincerely; ~ Ваш Yours sincerely.

и́скрен|ний (-няя, -нее, -ние; -ен, -на, -но *или* -не) *прил* sincere.

и́скренность (-и) *ж* sincerity.

искрив|и́ть (-лю́, -и́шь; *impf* искривля́ть) *сов перех* to bend.

искривле́ни|е (-я) *ср* bend; искривле́ние позвоно́чника (*МЕД*) curvature of the spine.

искривлю́ *сов см* искриви́ть.

искривля́|ть (-ю) *несов от* искриви́ть.

искри́ст|ый (-, -а, -о) *прил* glistening, sparkling.

искр|и́ться (-ю́сь, -и́шься) *несов возв* to glisten, sparkle.

искромёт|ный (-ен, -на, -но) *прил* (*перен: взгляд*) fiery; (: *остроумие*) sparkling.

искромса́|ть (-ю) *сов от* кромса́ть.

искрош|и́ть (-у́, -и́шь) *сов от* кроши́ть.

искупа́|ть(ся) (-ю(сь)) *сов от* купа́ть(ся).

иску|пи́ть (-плю́, -пишь; *impf* искупа́ть) *сов перех* (*перен: вину, проступок*) to atone for, expiate; (*возмещать, также РЕЛ*) to redeem.

искупле́ни|е (-я) *ср* (*вины, проступка*) atonement, expiation; (*РЕЛ*) redemption.

искуплю́ *сов см* искупи́ть.

искуса́|ть (-ю; *impf* иску́сывать) *сов перех* (*подлеж: комары*) to bite all over; (: *пчёлы*) to sting all over.

иску́сен *прил см* иску́сный.

искуси́тел|ь (-я) *м* tempter.

иску́сник (-а) *м* master.

искусниц|а (-ы) *ж см* иску́сник.

иску́с|ный (-ен, -на, -но) *прил* (*работник*) skilful (*BRIT*), skillful (*US*); (*работа*) fine.

иску́сственник (-а) *м* bottle-fed baby.

иску́сственниц|а (-ы) *ж см* иску́сственник.

иску́сствен|ный *прил* artificial; (*волокно, ткань, камин*) synthetic; (*мех*) fake; (-, -на, -но; притво́рный: смех*) faked; иску́сственное дыха́ние artificial respiration; иску́сственный интелле́кт artificial intelligence; иску́сственный спу́тник Земли́ artificial satellite.

иску́сств|о (-а) *ср* art; де́лать (*impf*) что-н из любви́ к ~у (*разг*) to do sth for its own sake.

искусствове́д (-а) *м* art historian.
искусствове́ние (-я) *ср* art history.
иску́сыва|ть (-ю) *несов от* искуса́ть.
искуша́|ть (-ю) *несов перех* to tempt; ~ *(impf)* **судьбу́** to tempt fate.
искуше́ние (-я) *ср* temptation; **поддава́ться (подда́ться** *perf*) ~**ю** to give in to temptation.
искушё́н|ный (-, -á, -ó) *прил (зритель, публика)* sophisticated; *(политик)* seasoned; *(же́нщина)* worldly; **он искушён в таки́х дела́х** he is well versed in such matters.
исла́м (-а) *м* Islam.
исла́мск|ий (-ая, -ое, -ие) *прил* Islamic.
исла́нд|ец (-ца) *м* Icelander.
Исла́нди|я (-и) *ж* Iceland.
исла́нд|ка (-ки; *gen pl* -ок) *ж см* исла́ндец.
исла́ндск|ий (-ая, -ое, -ие) *прил* Icelandic; ~ **язы́к** Icelandic.
исла́ндца *итп сущ см* исла́ндец.
испа́ко|стить (-щу, -стишь) *сов от* па́костить.
испа́н|ец (-ца) *м* Spaniard.
Испа́ни|я (-и) *ж* Spain.
испа́н|ка (-ки; *gen pl* -ок) *ж см* испа́нец.
испа́нск|ий (-ая, -ое, -ие) *прил* Spanish; ~ **язы́к** Spanish.
испа́нца *итп сущ см* испа́нец.
испаре́ние (-я) *ср (действие: воды)* evaporation; *(обычно мн: продукт)* vapour *(BRIT)*, vapor *(US)*.
испа́рин|а (-ы) *ж* perspiration.
испар|и́ть (-ю́, -и́шь; *impf* испаря́ть) *сов перех* to evaporate.
▸ **испари́ться** (*impf* испаря́ться) *сов возв (также перен)* to evaporate.
испа́чка|ть(ся) (-ю(сь)) *сов от* па́чкать(ся).
испеку́(сь) *итп сов см* испе́чь(ся).
испепел|и́ть (-ю́, -и́шь; *impf* испепеля́ть) *сов перех* to reduce to ashes; **испепеля́ть** (~ *perf*) **кого́-н взгля́дом** to give sb a withering look.
испе́|чь(ся) (-ку́(сь), -чёшь(ся) *итп*, -ку́т(ся)) *сов от* пе́чь(ся).
испещр|и́ть (-ю́, -и́шь; *impf* испещря́ть) *сов перех* to speckle.
испи|са́ть (-шу́, -шешь; *impf* испи́сывать) *сов перех (тетрадь, дневник)* to fill up; *(каранда́ш, ру́чку)* to wear out; *(бума́гу)* to use up.
▸ **исписа́ться** (*impf* испи́сываться) *несов возв (каранда́ш)* to wear out; *(ру́чка)* to run out; *(разг: писа́тель)* to lose one's touch.
испи́|ть (изопью́, изопьёшь; *pt* -л, -ла́, -ло) *сов неперех (+gen; перен: го́ря, разочарова́ний)* to suffer; *(воды́)* to sup.
испишу́(сь) *итп сов см* исписа́ть(ся).
испове́да́льн|я (-ьни; *gen pl* -ен) *ж (РЕЛ)* confessional.
испове́дание (-я) *ср* denomination.
испове́да|ть(ся) (-ю(сь)) *(не)сов* = испове́довать(ся).
испове́дник (-а) *м (РЕЛ)* confessor.
испове́д|овать (-ую) *несов перех (религию,*

мора́ль, иде́ю) to profess ◆ *(не)сов перех (РЕЛ)* ~ **кого́-н** to hear sb's confession
▸ **испове́доваться** *(не)сов возв:* ~**ся кому́-н** *или* **у кого́-н** to confess to sb.
и́споведь (-и) *ж (РЕЛ, перен)* confession.
и́сподволь *нареч* unbeknown to all.
исподло́бья *нареч:* **гляде́ть на кого́-н** ~ to look at sb with mistrust.
исподти́шка *нареч (разг: де́йствовать)* on the sly *или* quiet.
испоко́н *предл:* ~ **веко́в** from time immemorial.
исполи́н (-а) *м* giant.
исполи́нск|ий (-ая, -ое, -ие) *прил* gargantuan.
исполко́м (-а) *м сокр (= исполни́тельный комите́т)* executive committee.
исполне́ние (-я) *ср (прика́за, ука́за)* execution; *(обеща́ния, жела́ния)* fulfilment *(BRIT)*, fulfillment *(US)*; *(симфо́нии, ро́ли итп)* performance; **в** ~**и** +*gen* performed by; **приводи́ть (привести́** *perf*) **что-н в** ~ to carry sth out; **э́кспортное** ~ *(КОММ)* export version.
испо́лнен|ный (-, -а, -о) *прил (+gen)* full of, filled with.
исполни́м|ый (-, -а, -о) *прил (про́сьба, жела́ние)* realizable.
исполни́телен *прил см* исполни́тельный.
исполни́тел|ь (-я) *м (пье́сы, ро́ли)* performer; *(прика́за, поли́тики)* executive; **суде́бный** ~ bailiff.
исполни́тельниц|а (-ы) *ж см* исполни́тель.
исполни́тельный *прил (комите́т, власть)* executive; (-ен, -ьна, -ьно; *стара́тельный)* efficient; **исполни́тельный дире́ктор** executive director; **исполни́тельный лист** *(ЮР)* court order.
исполн|и́ть (-ю, -ишь; *impf* исполня́ть) *сов перех (прика́з)* to carry out; *(обеща́ние, долг, жела́ние)* to fulfil *(BRIT)*, fulfill *(US)*; *(та́нец, симфо́нию, роль итп)* to perform; ~ *(perf)* **кого́-н наде́ждой/ра́достью** *итп* to fill sb with hope/joy *итп*.
▸ **испо́лниться** (*impf* исполня́ться) *сов возв (жела́ние)* to be fulfilled; *(+instr; наде́ждой, ра́достью итп)* to be filled with; **ему́** ~**илось 10 лет** he is 10.
испо́льзование (-я) *ср* use.
испо́льз|овать (-ую) *(не)сов перех* to use.
испо́р|тить(ся) (-чу(сь), -тишь(ся)) *сов от* по́ртить(ся).
испо́рченный *прил (замо́к)* broken; *(настрое́ние)* bad; *(ребёнок)* spoilt; *(КОМП)* corrupt.
испра́вен *прил см* испра́вный.
исправи́м|ый (-, -а, -о) *прил* correctable.
исправи́тельный *прил (меры)* corrective; **исправи́тельные рабо́ты** *(ЮР)* corrective labour.
исправи́тельно-трудово́й *прил:* **исправи́тельно-трудова́я коло́ния** labour *(BRIT)* или labor *(US)* colony.
испра́в|ить (-лю, -ишь; *impf* исправля́ть) *сов*

перех *(повреждение, телефон)* to repair;
(ошибку) to correct; *(характер, дисциплину)* to
improve

▶ **испра́виться** *(impf* **исправля́ться)** *сов возв*
(характер, человек) to change (for the better).

исправле́ни|е (-я) *ср (повреждения)* repairing;
(: характера) reforming; *(текста,*
преступника) correction; **вноси́ть (внести́** *perf)*
~я в +*acc* to make corrections to.

испра́влю(сь) *сов см* **испра́вить(ся)**.

исправля́|ть(ся) (-ю(сь)) *несов от*
испра́вить(ся).

испра́вност|ь (-и) *ж:* **в (по́лной) ~и** in (full)
working order; **всё в ~и** everything's in order.

испра́в|ный (-ен, -на, -но) *прил (механизм)* in
good working order; *(работник)* diligent.

испражне́ни|е (-я) *ср* faeces *мн.*

испражня́|ться (-юсь) *несов возв* to defecate.

испро́б|овать (-ую) *сов от* **про́бовать**.

испу́г (-а; *part gen* **-у)** *м* fright; **в ~е, с ~у** in *или*
with fright.

испу́ган|ный (-, -а, -о) *прил (человек)*
frightened; *(-, -на, -но; вид, взгляд)* frightened.

испуга́|ть(ся) (-ю(сь)) *сов от* **пуга́ть(ся)**.

испу|сти́ть (-щу́, -́стишь; *impf* **испуска́ть)**
перех (крик, стон) to let out; *(свет)* to give off,
emit.

испыта́ни|е (-я) *ср (машины, прибора итп)*
testing; *(нового работника)* trial; *(обычно мн:*
экзамен) test; *(несчастье)* ordeal.

испы́тан|ный (-, -на, -но) *прил (приём)* tried
and tested; *(друг)* proven.

испыта́тел|ь (-я) *м* tester; **лётчик-испыта́тель**
test pilot.

испыта́тельный *прил:* **~ срок** trial period,
probation; **испыта́тельная тра́сса** test circuit;
испыта́тельный полёт test flight.

испыта́|ть (-ю; *impf* **испы́тывать)** *сов перех*
(механизм) to test; *(работника)* to try out;
(нужду, трудности, радость итп) to
experience.

испыту́ющий (-ая, -ее, -ие; -, -а, -е) *прил:* **~**
взгляд searching look.

испы́тыва|ть (-ю) *несов от* **испыта́ть**.

иссе́|чь (-еку́, -ечёшь *итп,* **-еку́т;** *pt* **-ёк, -екла́,**
-екло́) *сов перех (кнутом)* to flog.

исси́ня- *префикс:* **~чёрный** blue-black.

иссле́довани|е (-я) *ср (см глаг)* research;
examination; *(научный труд)* study;
занима́ться *(impf)* **~ями в о́бласти** +*gen* to
conduct research into.

иссле́довател|ь (-я) *м* researcher.

иссле́довательск|ий (-ая, -ое, -ие) *прил:* **~ая**
рабо́та research; **~ институ́т** research institute.

иссле́д|овать (-ую) *(не)сов перех* to research;
(больного) to examine.

иссо́х|нуть (-ну, -нешь; *pt* **-, -ла, -ло,** *impf*
иссыха́ть) *сов неперех (водоём)* to dry up;

(трава) to dry out; *(исхудать)* to wither away.

и́сстари *нареч* since days of old.

исстрада́|ться (-юсь) *сов возв* to suffer a great
deal.

исстреля́|ть (-ю; *impf* **исстре́ливать)** *сов перех*
(патроны) to use up.

исступле́ни|е (-я) *ср* frenzy; **приходи́ть**
(прийти́ *perf)* **в ~** to go into a frenzy.

исступлён|ный (-, -на, -но) *прил* frenzied.

иссыха́|ть (-ю) *несов от* **иссо́хнуть**.

иссяк|нуть (3sg -нет, 3pl -нут, *pt* **-, -ла, -ло,** *impf*
иссяка́ть) *сов неперех (источник, запасы)* to
run dry; *(перен: терпение, силы)* to run out.

иста́плива|ть (-ю) *несов от* **истопи́ть**.

иста́птыва|ть (-ю) *несов от* **истопта́ть**.

иста́скан|ный (-, -на, -но) *прил (разг: вид)*
bedraggled.

иста́ска|ть (-ю; *impf* **иста́скивать)** *сов перех*
(разг) to wear out

▶ **иста́ска|ться (impf иста́скиваться)** *сов возв*
(разг) to wear out.

исте́блишмент (-а) *м* the Establishment.

истёк *итп сов см* **исте́чь**.

истека́|ть (-ю) *несов от* **исте́чь**.

истеку́т *итп сов см* **исте́чь**.

истёкш|ий (-ая, -ее, -ие) *прил* past, previous.

истер|е́ться (3sg изотрётся, 3pl изотру́тся, *pt*
-ёрся, -ёрлась, -ёрлось, *impf* **истира́ться)** *сов*
возв (подошвы, канат) to wear down.

истёрзан|ный (-, -на, -но) *прил (душа, вид)*
tortured.

истерза́|ть (-ю) *сов от* **терза́ть**.

исте́рик (-а) *м* hysterical man *(мн* men).

исте́рик|а (-и) *ж* hysterics *мн;* **устра́ивать**
(устро́ить *perf) или* **зака́тывать (закати́ть** *perf)*
~у to become hysterical.

истери́чек *сущ см* **истери́чка**.

истери́чен *прил см* **истери́чный**.

истери́ческ|ий (-ая, -ое, -ие) *прил (больной,*
смех, плач) hysterical; **~ припа́док** a fit of
hysterics.

истери́ч|ка (-ка; *gen pl* **-ек)** *ж* hysterical woman
(мн women).

истери́ч|ный (-ен, -на, -но) *прил* hysterical.

истери́|я (-и) *ж (МЕД, перен)* hysteria.

исте́ц (-ца́) *м* plaintiff.

истече́ни|е (-я) *ср:* **по ~и** +*gen (года, месяца*
итп) after a period of; **по ~и э́того сро́ка** once
this period has elapsed; **за ~м сро́ка Ва́шего**
па́спорта due to expiry of your passport.

исте́|чь (3sg -ечёт, 3pl -еку́т, *pt* **-ёк, -екла́, -екло́,**
impf **истека́ть)** *сов неперех (срок)* to expire;
(время) to run out; **истека́ть (~** *perf)* **кро́вью** to
bleed.

и́стин|а (-ы) *ж* truth.

и́стинен *прил см* **и́стинный**.

и́стинност|ь (-и) *ж* truthfulness.

и́стин|ный (-ен, -на, -но) *прил* true.

истира́|ться (*3sg* -ется, *3pl* -ются) *несов от* истере́ться.

истле́|ть (-ю; *impf* истлева́ть) *сов неперех* (*сгнить*) to decompose; (*сгореть*) to turn to ash.

исто́к (-а) *м* (*обычно мн: реки*) source *только ед*; (: *перен*) source.

истолкова́ть (-у́ю; *impf* истолко́вывать) *сов перех* to interpret.

истоло́|чь (-ку́, -чёшь *итп*, -ку́т; *pt* -о́к, -кла́, -кло́) *сов от* толо́чь.

исто́м|а (-ы) *ж* languour.

истом|и́ть(ся) (-лю́(сь), -и́шь(ся)) *сов от* томи́ть(ся).

истоп|и́ть (-оплю́, -о́пишь; *impf* иста́пливать) *сов перех* to heat up.

истопта́ть (-опчу́, -о́пчешь; *impf* иста́птывать) *сов перех* to trample all over; (*разг: обувь*) to wear out.

исто́рик (-а) *м* historian.

истори́ческий (-ая, -ое, -ие) *прил* historical; (*важный: событие, решение итп*) historic.

исто́ри|я (-и) *ж* (*наука, предмет*) history; (*рассказ, происшествие*) story; **попада́ть** (**попа́сть** *perf*) **в ~ю** (*разг*) to get into a tricky situation; **со мной произошла́ стра́нная/заба́вная ~** a strange/funny thing happened to me; **ве́чная ~!** (*разг*) it's the same old story!; **исто́рия боле́зни** (*МЕД*) case history.

истоскова́|ться (-у́юсь) *сов возв*: ~ **по** +*dat* to yearn for.

источа́|ть (-ю) *несов перех* (*аромат, свет, тепло*) to emit; (*ненависть, доброту итп*) to exude.

исто́чник (-а) *м* (*водный*) source, spring.

исто́щ|ный (-ен, -на, -но) *прил* (*крик*) desperate.

истоща́|ть(ся) (-ю(сь)) *несов от* истощи́ть(ся).

истоще́ни|е (-я) *ср* (*организма*) depletion; (*средств, запасов*) exhaustion; ~ **не́рвной систе́мы** nervous exhaustion; **доводи́ть** (**довести́** *perf*) **себя́ до по́лного ~я** to run o.s. into the ground.

истощённый (-ён, -ена́, -ено́) *прил* (*человек*) malnourished; (-ён, -ённа, -ённо; *вид, лицо*) drained.

истощ|и́ть (-у́, -и́шь; *impf* истоща́ть) *сов перех* (*организм*) to run down; (*почву, ресурсы*) to deplete

► **истощи́ться** (*impf* истоща́ться) *сов возв* (*силы, организм, почва*) to become depleted; (*запасы, терпение*) to run out.

истра́|тить(ся) (-чу(сь), -тишь(ся)) *сов от* тра́тить(ся).

истреби́тель (-я) *м* (*ВОЕН: самолёт*) fighter (plane); (: *лётчик*) fighter pilot; (*тараканов, мышей итп*) exterminator.

истреби́тельный *прил* (*огонь*) destructive; ~**ая война́** war of destruction; ~**ая авиа́ция** fighter planes.

истреб|и́ть (-лю́, -и́шь; *impf* истребля́ть) *сов*

перех (*лес, посевы итп*) to destroy; (*крыс, тараканов*) to exterminate.

истребле́ни|е (-я) *ср* (*см глаг*) destruction; extermination.

истреблю́ *сов см* истреби́ть.

истребля́|ть (-ю) *несов от* истреби́ть.

истреп|а́ть(ся) (-лю́(сь), -лешь(ся)) *сов от* трепа́ть(ся).

истре́ска|ться (*3sg* -ется, *3pl* -ются, *impf* истре́скиваться) *сов возв* to crack.

истука́н (-а) *м* idol.

истца́ *итп сущ см* исте́ц.

и́стый *прил* genuine.

истяза́ни|е (-я) *ср* torture.

истяза́|ть (-ю) *несов перех* to torture.

исхлеста́ть (-ещу́, -е́щешь; *impf* исхлёстывать) *сов перех* to whip.

исхо́д (-а) *м* outcome; **у меня́ де́ньги/терпе́ние на ~е** my money/patience is running out; **на ~е дня** at the end of the day; **с лета́льным ~ом** resulting in death.

исхо|ди́ть (-жу́, -дишь) *несов от* изойти́ ◆ *сов перех* (*обойти*) to walk all over ◆ *несов неперех*: ~ **из** +*gen* (*сведения, слухи*) to emanate from; (*основываться: из данных*) to be derived from; ~**одя́ из/от** +*gen* on the basis of; **я ~ожу́ из того́, что...** I am working on the premise that ....

исхо́дный *прил* (*идея, данные*) primary; ~ **те́зис** premise; **исхо́дное положе́ние** (*СПОРТ*) starting position; **исхо́дный пункт** starting point.

исходя́щий (-ая, -ее, -ие) *прил* (*корреспонденция*) outgoing; **исходя́щий но́мер** (*АДМИН*) reference number.

исхожу́ (*не*)*сов см* исходи́ть.

исхуда́лый *прил* emaciated.

исхуда́|ть (-ю) *сов неперех* to become emaciated.

исцара́па|ть (-ю; *impf* исцара́пывать) *сов перех* to scratch all over.

исцеле́ни|е (-я) *ср* healing.

исцел|и́ть (-ю́, -и́шь; *impf* исцеля́ть) *сов перех* to heal.

► **исцели́ться** (*impf* исцеля́ться) *сов возв* to recover.

исча́ди|е (-я) *ср*: ~ **а́да** the devil incarnate.

исчеза́|ть (-ю) *несов от* исче́знуть.

исчезнове́ни|е (-я) *ср* disappearance.

исче́знуть (-ну, -нешь; *pt* -, -ла, -ло, *impf* исчеза́ть) *сов неперех* to disappear.

исчёрка|ть (-ю; *impf* исчёркивать) *сов перех* to scribble over.

исчерпа́|ть (-ю; *impf* исче́рпывать) *сов перех* to exhaust; **инциде́нт ~н** the matter is closed

► **исчерпа́ться** (*impf* исче́рпываться) *несов возв* (*запасы, терпение*) to be exhausted.

исче́рпыва|ться (*3sg* -ется, *3pl* -ются) *несов от* исчерпа́ться ◆ *возв* (*разрешаться*) to end; **э́тим де́ло не ~ется** the matter does not end here.

исчёрпывающ|ий (-ая, -ее, -ие; -, -а, -е) *прил* exhaustive.

исчислёни|е (-я) *ср* (*расходов, стоимости итп*) calculation; (*мат*) calculus.

исчисл|ить (-ю, -ишь; *impf* **исчислять**) *сов перех* to calculate.

исчисля|ться (*3pl* -ются) *несов возв* (+*instr*; *тысячами*) to amount to.

ита́к *союз* thus, hence; ~, **мо́жно заключи́ть, что** ... thus it can be concluded that ....

Ита́ли|я (-и) *ж* Italy.

италья́н|ец (-ца) *м* Italian.

италья́н|ка (-ки; *gen pl* -ок) *ж см* **италья́нец**.

италья́нск|ий (-ая, -ое, -ие) *прил* Italian; ~ **язы́к** Italian.

италья́нца *итп сущ см* **италья́нец**.

ИТА́Р *м сокр* (= *Информацио́нное телегра́фное аге́нтство Росси́и*) *Russian telegraph agency*.

и т.д. *сокр* (= **и так да́лее**) etc. (= *et cetera*).

ИТК *м сокр* (= *исправи́тельно-трудова́я коло́ния*) labour (*BRIT*) *или* labor (*US*) colony.

ито́г (-а) *м* (*работы, переговоров итп*) result; (*общая сумма*) total; **в** ~**е** (*при подсчёте*) in total; **в** (**коне́чном**) ~**е** in the end; **подводи́ть** (**подвести́** *perf*) ~**и** to sum up.

итого́ *нареч* in total, altogether; ~, **мы зарабо́тали 100 рубле́й** in total *или* altogether

we made 100 roubles.

ито́говый *прил* (*сумма, цифры*) total; (*результат*) final; **ито́говый отчёт** (*комм*) financial report.

и т.п. *сокр* (= **и тому́ подо́бное**) etc. (= *et cetera*).

иудаи́зм (-а) *м* Judaism.

их *мест см* **они́** ♦ *притяж мест* their; ~ **дом бо́льше на́шего** their house is bigger than ours; **чья э́та маши́на? –** ~ whose car is this? – it's theirs.

и́хн|ий (-яя, -ее, -ие) *притяж мест* (*разг*) = **их**.

иша́к (-а́) *м* (*зоол*) donkey; (*перен: работя́га*) dogsbody.

иша́ч|ить (-у, -ишь) *несов неперех* (*разг*) to slog away.

и́шиас (-а) *м* sciatica.

ишь *част* (*разг*): ~ **чего́ захоте́л!** you're asking a lot, aren't you?; ~ **какой он на́глый!** how cheeky can he get!

ище́йка (-йки; *gen pl* -ек) *ж* bloodhound; **полице́йская** ~ sniffer dog.

ищу́ *итп несов см* **иска́ть**.

ию́л|ь (-я) *м* July; *см также* **октя́брь**.

ию́льск|ий (-ая, -ое, -ие) *прил* July *опред*.

ию́н|ь (-я) *м* June; *см также* **октя́брь**.

ию́ньск|ий (-ая, -ое, -ие) *прил* June *опред*.

~ Й, й ~

Й, й *сущ нескл (буква)* the 10th letter of the Russian alphabet.

Йе́мен (-a) *м* Yemen.

йе́мен|ец (-ца) *м* Yemeni.

йе́мен|ка (-ки; *gen pl* -ок) *ж см* **йе́менец**.

йе́менск|ий (-ая, -ое, -ие) *прил* Yemeni.

йог (-и) *ж* yogi.

йо́г|а (-и) *ж* yoga; **занима́ться** *(impf)* ~**ой** to do yoga.

йо́гурт (-a) *м* yoghurt.

йод (-a) *м* iodine.

йо́дистый *прил* = **йо́дный**.

йо́дный *прил* iodine *опред*.

Йорк (-a) *м* York.

йо́т|а (-ы) *ж*: **ни на** ~**y** not one iota.

йота́ци|я (-и) *ж* vowel softening.

Йоха́ннесбург (-a) *м* Johannesburg.

~ К, к ~

К, к сущ нескл (буква) the 11th letter of the Russian alphabet.

к предл (+dat) **1** (обозначает направление) towards; **я пошёл к до́му/вокза́лу** I went towards the house/station; **звать (позва́ть** perf**) кого́-н к телефо́ну** to call sb to the phone; **мы пое́хали к друзья́м** we went to see friends; **поста́вь ле́стницу к стене́** put the ladder against the wall

2 (обозначает добавление, включение) to; **к уже́ существу́ющим пробле́мам приба́вились но́вые осложне́ния** new complications were added to the existing problems; **э́та ба́бочка отно́сится к о́чень ре́дкому ви́ду** this butterfly belongs to a very rare species

3 (обозначает отношение) of; **любо́вь к му́зыке/поря́дку** love of music/order; **он привы́к к хоро́шей еде́** he is used to good food; **к моему́ удивле́нию** to my surprise

4 (обозначает назначение) with; **Вы хоти́те пече́нья к ча́ю?** would you like biscuits (BRIT) или cookies (US) with your tea?; **припра́вы к мя́су** seasonings for meat.

к. сокр = **копе́йка**.

-ка част (разг) used to moderate imperative or indicate indecision; **иди́-ка сюда́** could you come here; **пойду́-ка я домо́й** I think I'll maybe be off home.

каба́к (-а́) м tavern; (разг) pub.

кабал|а́ (-ы́) ж (перен) slavery; **быть** (impf) **в ~е́ у кого́-н** to be at sb's mercy.

каба́льный прил: ~ **труд** slave labour (BRIT) или labor (US); **~ая зави́симость** slavery (fig).

каба́н (-а́) м boar; (дикий) wild boar.

кабаре́ ср нескл cabaret.

кабач|о́к (-ка́) м уменьш от **кабак**; (БОТ, КУЛИН) marrow (BRIT), squash (US).

ка́бел|ь (-я) м cable.

ка́бельный прил cable опред; **ка́бельное телеви́дение** cable television.

каби́н|а (-ы) ж (телефонная) booth; (грузовика) cab; (самолёта) cabin; (лифта) cage; (для голосования) voting booth; **пля́жная ~** beach hut.

кабине́т (-а) м (в доме) study; (на работе) office; (ПРОСВЕЩ) classroom; (врача) surgery (BRIT), office (US); (ПОЛИТ: также: ~ **мини́стров**) cabinet.

каблогра́мм|а (-ы) ж cablegram.

каблу́к (-а́) м heel; **быть** (impf) **под каблуко́м у кого́-н** (разг) to be under sb's thumb.

кабота́ж (-а) м coastal shipping.

Кабу́л (-а) м Kabul.

кавале́р (-а) м (в танце) partner; (поклонник) suitor; (награждённый орденом): ~ +gen knight of; **Гео́ргиевский** ~ knight of St George.

кавалери́йск|ий (-ая, -ое, -ие) прил cavalry опред.

кавалери́ст (-а) м cavalryman (мн cavalrymen).

кавале́ри|я (-и) ж cavalry.

кавалька́д|а (-ы) ж cavalcade.

каварда́к (-а́) м (разг) mess.

ка́верз|а (-ы) ж dirty trick; **подстро́ить** (perf) **кому́-н** ~**у** to play a dirty trick on sb.

ка́верзный (-ен, -на, -но) прил tricky.

Кавка́з (-а) м Caucasus.

кавка́зск|ий (-ая, -ое, -ие) прил Caucasian.

кавы́чки (-ек; dat pl -**кам**) мн inverted commas мн, quotation marks мн; **открыва́ть (откры́ть** perf**)/закрыва́ть (закры́ть** perf**)** ~ to open/close inverted commas; **в** ~**ках** (также перен) in inverted commas.

каго́р (-а) м red dessert wine.

каде́нци|я (-и) ж cadence.

каде́т (-а) м (ВОЕН) cadet; (ИСТ: = **конституцио́нный демокра́т**) Cadet (Constitutional Democrat).

каде́тск|ий (-ая, -ое, -ие) прил (форма) cadet's; **каде́тский ко́рпус** officer training corps.

кади́л|о (-а) ср (РЕЛ) censer.

ка|ди́ть (-жу́, -ди́шь) несов неперех (РЕЛ) to burn incense.

ка́д|ка (-ки; gen pl -**ок**) ж vat.

ка́дми|й (-я) м cadmium.

ка́док сущ см **кадка**.

ка́дочный прил (огурцы, капуста итп) preserved in vats.

кадр (-а) м (ФОТО, КИНО) shot; (разг: работник) worker; см также **кадры**.

ка́дров|ый *прил* (*офицер, войска*) regular *опред*; (*админ*): ~**ая поли́тика** staffing policy.

ка́др|ы (-ов) *мн* (*работники*) personnel *ед*, staff *ед*; (*воен*) regular army personnel *ед*; (*партийные*) cadres *мн*; **отде́л** ~**ов** personnel department.

кады́к (-а́) *м* Adam's apple.

кае́м *сущ см* **кайма́**.

кае́м|ка (-ки; *gen pl* -ок) *ж* = **кайма́**.

каждодне́вный *прил* daily.

ка́ждый *прил* each, every.

кажу́ *несов см* **кади́ть**.

кажу́сь *итп несов см* **каза́ться**.

каза́к (-а́; *nom pl* **каза́ки**) *м* Cossack.

каза́н (-а́) *м large round copper cooking vessel*.

Каза́н|ь (-и) *ж* Kazan.

каза́рм|а (-ы) *ж* barracks *мн*.

каза́рменный *прил*: ~ **поря́док** barracks regime; **каза́рменное положе́ние** confinement to barracks.

ка|за́ться (-жу́сь, -жешься; *perf* **показа́ться**) *несов возв* (+*instr*) to look; (**мне**) **ка́жется/каза́лось, что ...** it seems/seemed (to me) that ...; **он** ~**за́лся ста́рше свои́х лет** he looked older than his years.

каза́х (-а) *м* Kazakh.

каза́хск|ий (-ая, -ое, -ие) *прил* Kazakh.

Казахста́н (-а) *м* Kazakhstan.

каза́цк|ий (-ая, -ое, -ие) *прил* = **каза́чий**.

каза́чек *сущ см* **каза́чка**.

каза́честв|о (-а) *ср собир* the Cossacks *мн*.

каза́ч|ий (-ья, -ье, -ьи) *прил* Cossack.

каза́ч|ка (-ки; *gen pl* -ек) *ж см* **каза́к**.

каземат (-а) *м* cell.

казённый *прил* public; (*отношение, язык*) officious; **на** ~ **счёт** at public expense; **казённая кварти́ра** tied accommodation; **казённое иму́щество** government property.

казино́ *ср нескл* casino.

казн|а́ (-ы́) *ж* treasury.

казначе́|й (-я) *м* treasurer.

казн|и́ть (-ю́, -и́шь) *несов перех* to execute; (*перен*) to punish

▶ **казни́ться** *несов возв* (*разг*) to torture o.s.

казн|ь (-и) *ж* execution; **сме́ртная** ~ the death penalty; **приговори́ть** (*perf*) **кого́-н к сме́ртной ка́зни** to sentence sb to death.

Каи́р (-а) *м* Cairo.

кайм|а́ (-ймы́; *nom pl* -ймы́, *gen pl* -ём) *ж* hem.

кайф (-а) *м* (*разг*) high, kick.

кайф|ова́ть (-у́ю) *несов неперех* (*разг: на пляже, в отпуске итп*) to chill out; (: *от наркотиков, от вина*) to get high.

KEYWORD

как *местоимённое нареч* **1** (*вопросительное*) how; **как Вы себя́ чу́вствуете?** how do you feel?; **как дела́/де́ти?** how are things/the children?; **как тебя́ зову́т?** what's your name?

2 (*относительное*) **я сде́лал, как ты проси́ла** I did as you asked; **я не зна́ю, как э́то могло́ случи́ться** I don't know how that could have happened

3 (*насколько*): **как бы́стро/то́чно/давно́** how quickly/accurately/long ago

4 (*до какой сте́пени*): **как краси́во/по́дло!** how beautiful/mean!; **как жаль!** what a pity *или* shame!

5 (*выражает возмущение*) what; **как! он опя́ть напи́лся!** what! he's drunk again!

6 (*о внеза́пном де́йствии*): **она́ как закричи́т/запла́чет** she suddenly cried out/burst into tears

◆ *союз* **1** (*подобно*) as; **мя́гкий, как ва́та** as soft as cotton wool; **как мо́жно скоре́е/гро́мче** as soon/loud as possible; **он оде́т, как бродя́га** he is dressed like a tramp

2 (*в качестве*) as; **как консульта́нт он о́чень поле́зен** as a consultant he is very useful

3 (*о временны́х отношениях*: *о будущем, об одновременности*) when; (: *о прошлом*) since; **как зако́нчишь, позвони́ мне** phone (*BRIT*) call (*US*) me when you finish; **как вспо́мню об э́том, хо́чется пла́кать** when I remember it I feel like crying; **прошло́ два го́да, как она́ исче́зла** two years have passed since she disappeared:

4: **как бу́дто, как бы** as if; **он согласи́лся как бы не́хотя** he agreed as if unwillingly; **как же** of course; **как говоря́т** *или* **говори́тся** as it were; **как ни** however; **как ника́к** after all; **как раз во́время/то, что на́до** just in time/what we need; **э́то пла́тье/пальто́ мне как раз** this dress/coat is just my size; **как ..., так и ...** both ... and ...; **как то́лько** as soon as.

какаду́ *м нескл* cockatoo.

кака́о *ср нескл* cocoa.

ка́ка|ть (-ю; *perf* **пока́кать**) *несов неперех* (*разг*) to do a pooh.

ка́к-либо *нареч* = **ка́к-нибудь**.

ка́к-нибудь *нареч* (*так или ина́че*) somehow; (*когда-нибудь*) sometime; (*кое-как*) anyhow; **уговори́те его́** ~ try to convince him somehow; **зайди́** ~ pop in sometime; **ты всё де́лаешь** ~ you're doing everything just anyhow.

како́в (-а́, -о́, -ы́) *мест* what; ~ **нагле́ц!** what a cheek!; ~ **он собо́й?** what does he look like?

KEYWORD

как|о́й (-а́я, -о́е, -и́е) *мест* **1** (*вопросительное*) what; **како́й тебе́ нра́вится цвет?** what colour do you like?; **кака́я сего́дня пого́да?** what's the weather like today?; **в како́м году́ э́то бы́ло?** in what year was that?

2 (*относительное*) which; **скажи́, кака́я кни́га интере́снее** tell me which book is more interesting; **скажи́, в како́м го́роде нахо́дится Колизе́й** tell me in which city the Coliseum is

3 (*выражает оценку*) what; **како́й подле́ц!** what a rascal!; **кака́я неожи́данность!** what a surprise!

4 (*в риторических вопросах: совсем не*) what kind of; **како́й он дире́ктор?** what kind of

director is he?
5 (*разг: неопределённое*) any; **нет ли каки́х вопро́сов?** are there any questions?; **како́й ни на есть** any you like; **ни в каку́ю** not for anything; **каки́м о́бразом** in what way; **како́е там!** no way!

како́й-либо (-а́я, -о́е, -и́е) *мест* = **како́й-нибудь**.

како́й-нибудь (-а́я, -о́е, -и́е) *мест* (*тот или иной*) any; (*приблизительно*) some; **он и́щет ~ рабо́ты** he's looking for any kind of work; **~й-нибудь два-три ме́сяца** in some two or three months.

како́й-то (-а́я, -о́е, -и́е) *мест*: **Вам ~о́е-то письмо́** there's a letter for you; (*напоминающий*): **она́ ~а́я-то стра́нная сего́дня** she's acting a bit oddly today; **э́то не ко́мната, а свина́рник ~** it's more like a pigsty than a room.

какофони́ческий (-ая, -ое, -ие) *прил* cacophonous.

какофо́ни|я (-и) *ж* cacophony.

ка́к-то *мест* (*каким-то образом*) somehow; (*в некоторой степени*) somewhat; (*разг*): **~ (раз)** once; **мне бы́ло ~ не по себе́** I was feeling somewhat *или* a little out of sorts; **я ~ встре́тил его́ на у́лице** I bumped into him once in the street.

ка́ктус (-а) *м* cactus (*мн* cacti).

кал (-а) *м* excrement.

каламбу́р (-а) *м* pun.

каламбу́р|ить (-ю, -ишь; *perf* **скаламбу́рить**) *несов неперех* to pun, make puns.

калан|ча́ (-и́; *gen pl* -е́й) *ж* watchtower; (*разг: человеке*) beanpole.

кала́ч (-а́) *м* = cottage loaf; **его́ кала́чо́м не зама́нишь** nothing will persuade him.

кала́чиком *нареч*: **сверну́ться ~** to curl up in a ball.

калейдоско́п (-а) *м* (*также перен*) kaleidoscope.

ка́лек *сущ см* **ка́лька**.

кале́к|а (-и) *м/ж* cripple.

календа́рный *прил*: **~ ме́сяц/год** calendar month/year.

календа́р|ь (-я́) *м* calendar.

кале́ни|е (-я) *ср* incandescence; **довести́** (*perf*) **кого́-н до бе́лого ~я** to send sb into a blind rage.

кале́н|ый *прил* red-hot; **выжига́ть (вы́жечь** *perf*) **~ым желе́зом** to brand.

кале́ч|ить (-у, -ишь; *perf* **покале́чить** *или* **искале́чить**) *несов перех* to cripple.

кали́бр (-а) *м* (*воен, перен*) calibre (*BRIT*), caliber (*US*); (*TEX*) gauge.

калибр|ова́ть (-у́ю) (*не*)*сов перех* to calibrate.

калибро́вк|а (-и) *ж* calibration.

ка́ли|й (-я) *м* potassium.

кали́н|а (-ы) *ж* guelder-rose.

кали́т|ка (-ки; *gen pl* -ок) *ж* gate.

Калифо́рни|я (-и) *ж* California.

каллиграфи́ческий (-ая, -ое, -ие) *прил*: **~ по́черк** beautiful handwriting.

каллигра́фи|я (-и) *ж* calligraphy.

калмы́к (-а) *м* Kalmyk.

Калмы́ки|я (-и) *ж* Kalmykia.

калмы́ч|ка (-ки; *gen pl* -ек) *ж см* **калмы́к**.

калори́йност|ь (-и) *ж* (*пищи*) calorie content; (*физ*) calorific value.

кало́ри|я (-и) *ж* calorie.

ка́ль|ка (-ьки; *gen pl* -ек) *ж* (*бумага*) tracing paper; (*копия*) traced copy; (*линг*) calque.

кальки́р|овать (-ую; *perf* **скалькировать**) *несов перех* (*чертёж*) to trace.

калькуля́тор (-а) *м* calculator.

кальма́р (-а) *м* squid.

кальсо́н|ы (-) *мн* long johns *мн*.

ка́льци|й (-я) *м* calcium.

КамА́З (-а) *м сокр* = **Ка́мский автомоби́льный заво́д**; (*автомобиль*) *vehicle manufactured at the Kamskiy car factory.*

ка́мбал|а (-ы) *ж* flatfish.

Камбо́дж|а (-и) *ж* Cambodia.

камбоджи́йский (-ая, -ое, -ие) *прил* Cambodian.

ка́мбуз (-а) *м* galley.

каме́ли|я (-и) *ж* camelia.

камене́|ть (-ю) *несов от* **окамене́ть**.

камени́ст|ый (-, -а, -о) *прил* (*почва*) stony.

каменноуго́льный *прил* coal *опред*; **~ бассе́йн** coalfield.

ка́менн|ый *прил* stone; (*перен*) stony; **у неё ~ое се́рдце** she has a heart of stone; **ка́менный век** the Stone Age.

каменоло́м|ня (-ни; *gen pl* -ен) *ж* quarry.

каменотёс (-а) *м* stonemason.

ка́менщик (-а) *м* bricklayer; **во́льный ~** Freemason.

ка́м|ень (-ня; *gen pl* -не́й) *м* stone; **драгоце́нный ~** precious stone; **краеуго́льный ~** (*перен*) cornerstone; **~ в по́чках** kidney stone; **~ преткнове́ния** stumbling block; **у него́ ~ на се́рдце лежи́т** there's a weight lying heavy on his heart; **у меня́ ~ с души́ свали́лся** it was a great weight off my mind; **держа́ть** (*impf*) **~ за па́зухой** to bear a grudge.

ка́мер|а (-ы) *ж* (*тюремная*) cell; (*АВТ*) inner tube; (*также: телека́мера, кинока́мера*) camera; (*ТЕХ, АНАТ*) chamber; **снима́ть (снять** *perf*) **что-н скры́той ~ой** to film sth secretly; **ка́мера хране́ния** (*на вокзале*) left-luggage office (*BRIT*), checkroom (*US*); (*в музее*) cloakroom.

камерди́нер (-а) *м* (*ист*) valet.

ка́мерный *прил* (*обстановка*) cosy; **ка́мерная му́зыка** chamber music; **ка́мерный орке́стр** chamber orchestra.

камертон (-а) м tuning fork.
камешек (-ка; nom pl -ки, gen pl -ков) м stone.
камея (-и) ж cameo (in jewellery).
камзол (-а) м frock coat.
камин (-а) м fireplace.
камнепад (-а) м avalanche (of rocks, stones).
камня итп сущ см **камень**.
каморка (-и) ж (разг) cubbyhole.
кампания (-и) ж campaign.
кампучийский (-ая, -ое, -ие) прил Kampuchean.
Кампучия (-и) ж Kampuchea.
камуфлировать (-ую; perf закамуфлировать) несов перех to camouflage.
камуфляж (-а) м camouflage.
камфора (-ы) ж camphor.
камфорный прил: ~ое масло camphorated oil.
камыш (-а) м rushes мн.
канава (-ы) ж ditch; сточная ~ gutter.
Канада (-ы) ж Canada.
канадец (-ца) м Canadian.
канадка (-ки; gen pl -ок) ж см канадец.
канадский (-ая, -ое, -ие) прил Canadian.
канадца итп сущ см **канадец**.
канал (-а) м (также АНАТ) canal; (связь, тел. перен) channel; **я буду действовать по своим ~ам** I shall use the means available to me.
канализационный прил: ~ая труба sewer pipe; **канализационная сеть** the sewers.
канализация (-и) ж sewerage.
каналья (-ьи; gen pl -ий) м/ж rogue.
канарейка (-йки; gen pl -ек) ж canary.
канарский (-ая, -ое, -ие) прил: **К~ие острова** the Canary Islands, the Canaries.
канат (-а) м cable.
канатный прил: ~ая дорога cable car.
канатоходец (-ца) м tightrope walker.
канва (-ы) ж (в вышивании) sampler; (перен: рассказа) outline.
кандалы (-ов) мн shackles мн.
канделябр (-а) м candelabra (мн candelabra).
кандидат (-а) м candidate; (ПРОСВЕЩ): ~ наук ≈ Doctor.
кандидатский (-ая, -ое, -ие) прил candidate's; **кандидатская диссертация** ≈ doctoral thesis; **кандидатский экзамен** entrance exam for postgraduate study.
кандидатура (-ы) ж candidacy; **выставлять (выставить** perf) чью-н ~у to nominate sb.
каникулы (-) мн holidays мн (BRIT), vacation ед (US); **парламентские** ~ parliamentary recess.
каникулярный прил holiday опред (BRIT), vacation опред (US).
канистра (-ы) ж jerry can.
канителиться (-юсь, -ишься) несов возв (разг): ~ (с +instr) to waste one's time (over).
канитель (-и) ж (золотая итп) thread; (перен) bore, drag; **тянуть** (impf) ~ (перен: разг) to drag things out.
канифоль (-и) ж (ХИМ) resin; (МУЗ) rosin.
канкан (-а) м cancan.
каннибал (-а) м cannibal.

каннибализм (-а) м cannibalism.
каноист (-а) м canoeist.
канон (-а) м canon.
канонада (-ы) ж cannonade.
канонизация (-и) ж (также перен) canonization.
канонизировать (-ую) (не)сов перех (также перен) to canonize.
каноник (-а) м canon (REL).
канонический (-ая, -ое, -ие) прил (РЕЛ) canonical; (перен: правила, образец) definitive; ~ое право canon law.
каноэ ср нескл canoe.
кантата (-ы) ж cantata.
кантовать (-ую; perf окантовать) несов перех (окаймлять) to mount; (no perf; переворачивать) to tilt; „не ~!" "keep upright!"
канун (-а) м eve; в ~ +gen on the eve of; ~ Нового года New Year's Eve.
кануть (-у, -ешь) сов неперех (исчезнуть) to vanish; ~ (perf) в Лету или вечность to fade into obscurity; **он словно в воду ~ул** he vanished into thin air.
канцеляризм (-а) м official jargon.
канцелярия (-и) ж office.
канцелярский (-ая, -ое, -ие) прил office опред; ~ слог или язык officialese.
канцелярщина (-ы) ж (формализм) red tape.
канцлер (-а) м (глава государства) chancellor.
каньон (-а) м canyon.
канюк (-а) м buzzard.
канючить (-у, -ишь) несов неперех (разг) to whinge.
каолин (-а) м kaolin.
капать (-ю) несов неперех (вода) to drip ♦ (perf накапать) перех (микстуру) to pour out drop by drop; **дождь** ~ет it's spotting with rain.
капелек сущ см **капелька**.
капелла (-ы) ж (МУЗ) choir; (РЕЛ) chapel.
капеллан (-а) м chaplain.
капель сущ см **капля**.
капель (-и) ж thaw.
капелька (-ьки; gen pl -ек) ж droplet; ~ +gen (молока итп) a drop of; (счастья, правды) a grain of; **всё до последней** ~ьки every last little bit.
капельку нареч (разг) a tad или touch; **ну ещё** ~ a little bit more; **почитай хоть** ~ read for just a little while at least.
капельмейстер (-а) м bandmaster.
капельница (-ы) ж (МЕД) drip(-feed); **ставить (поставить** perf) кому-н ~у to put sb on a drip.
каперсы (-ов) мн (КУЛИН) capers мн.
капилляр (-а) м capillary.
капитал (-а) м (КОММ) capital; (перен: политический) power; **выпущенный акционерный** ~ (КОММ) issued capital.
капитален прил см **капитальный**.
капитализация (-и) ж capitalization.
капитализировать (-ую) (не)сов перех (КОММ) to capitalize.

капитали́зм (-а) *м* capitalism.
капитали́ст (-а) *м* capitalist.
капиталисти́ческий (-ая, -ое, -ие) *прил* capitalist.
капиталовложе́ни|я (-й) *мн* capital investment *ед*.
капита́л|ьный *прил* (ЭКОН, КОММ) capital *опред*; (-ен, -ьна, -ьно; сооруже́ние, труд) main; (вопрос, покупка) major; **капита́льная стена́** supporting wall; **капита́льное строи́тельство** major construction work; **капита́льные расхо́ды** capital expenditure; **капита́льный ремо́нт** major repairs; **капита́льные това́ры** capital goods.
капита́н (-а) *м* captain.
капита́нск|ий (-ая, -ое, -ие) *прил* captain's; **капита́нский мо́стик** (МОР) bridge.
капите́л|ь (-и) *ж* (АРХИТ) capital.
капитули́р|овать (-ую) (не)сов неперех to capitulate.
капитуля́ци|я (-и) *ж* capitulation.
капка́н (-а) *м* trap.
ка́пл|и (-ель) *мн* (МЕД) drops *мн*.
ка́пл|я (-и; *gen pl* -ель) *ж* (также перен) drop; **ни ~ли** not a bit; **вы́пить** (*perf*) **всё до ~ли** to drink every last drop; **подожди́те хоть ~лю** (разг) wait just one second; **они́ похо́жи как две ~ли воды́** they're like two peas in a pod; **~ в мо́ре** a drop in the ocean; *см также* **ка́пли**.
капо́т (-а) *м* (АВТ) bonnet (*BRIT*), hood (*US*); (халат) housecoat.
капра́л (-а) *м* corporal.
капремо́нт (-а) *м сокр* = **капита́льный ремо́нт**.
капри́з (-а) *ж* caprice, whim.
капри́зен *прил см* **капри́зный**.
капри́знича|ть (-ю; *perf* **покапри́зничать**) *несов неперех* to behave capriciously.
капри́з|ный (-ен, -на, -но) *прил* (человек, характер) capricious; (мода, погода итп) fickle.
капро́н (-а) *м* synthetic thread.
ка́псул|а (-ы) *ж* (МЕД, ТЕХ) capsule.
капу́ст|а (-ы) *ж* cabbage; **брюссе́льская ~** Brussels sprouts *мн*; **цветна́я ~** cauliflower.
капу́стник (-а) *м* amateur revue.
капу́стный *прил* cabbage.
капу́т *м нескл*: **магнитофо́ну ~** (разг) the tape recorder's kaput; **ему́ ~** he's finished.
капюшо́н (-а) *м* hood.
ка́р|а (-ы) *ж* retribution.
караби́н (-а) *м* (ВОЕН) carbine; (ТЕХ) karabiner.
кара́бка|ться (-юсь; *perf* **вскара́бкаться**) *несов возв*: **~ на** +*acc* (человек) to clamber up; (растение) to creep up.
карава́|й (-я) *м* cob (*loaf*).
карава́н (-а) *м* (судов) convoy; (верблюдов) caravan.
карава́н-сара́|й (-я) *м* caravanserai.

карака́тиц|а (-ы) *ж* (ЗООЛ) cuttlefish; (перен: разг) clodhopper.
кара́кулевый *прил* astrakhan.
кара́кул|и (-ей) *мн* (разг) scrawl *ед*.
кара́кул|ь (-я) *м* astrakhan; *см также* **кара́кули**.
караме́л|ь (-и) *ж собир* (леденцы) caramels *мн*; (жжёный сахар) caramel.
каранда́ш (-а́; *gen pl* -е́й) *м* pencil.
каранти́н (-а) *м* quarantine.
карапу́з (-а) *м* (разг) fatty.
кара́с|ь (-я́) *м* crucian (*type of carp*).
кара́т (-а) *м* carat (*BRIT*), karat (*US*).
кара́тельный *прил* punitive; **~ отря́д** death squad.
кара́|ть (-ю; *perf* **покара́ть**) *несов перех* to punish.
каратэ́ *ср нескл* karate.
карау́л (-а) *м* guard; **выставля́ть** (**вы́ставить** *perf*) **~** to post a guard; **стоя́ть** (*impf*) **в ~е** to stand guard; **~! help!**
карау́л|ить (-ю, -ишь) *несов перех* to guard; (разг: ожидать) to lie in wait for.
карбо́ван|ец (-ца) *м* karbovanets (*Ukrainian currency unit*).
карбо́ловый *прил*: **~ая кислота́** carbolic acid.
карбу́нкул (-а) *м* (ГЕО, МЕД) carbuncle.
карбюра́тор (-а) *м* carburettor (*BRIT*), carburetor (*US*).
карг|а́ (-и́) *ж* (разг) hag.
кардамо́н (-а; *no pl*) *м* cardamom.
кардина́л (-а) *м* (РЕЛ) cardinal.
кардина́льно *нареч* (изменить) drastically.
кардина́л|ьный (-ен, -ьна, -ьно) *прил* cardinal *опред*, of cardinal importance.
кардио́лог (-а) *м* cardiologist, heart specialist.
кардиологи́ческ|ий (-ая, -ое, -ие) *прил* (отделение) cardiac.
кардиоло́ги|я (-и) *ж* cardiology.
каре́ *ср нескл* (ВОЕН) square formation; (КАРТЫ) four of a kind.
каре́т|а (-ы) *ж* carriage.
каре́т|ка (-ки; *gen pl* -ок) *ж* carriage.
ка́р|ий (-яя, -ее, -ие) *прил* (глаза) hazel; (масть) chestnut.
карикату́р|а (-ы) *ж* caricature.
карикату́рен *прил см* **карикату́рный**.
карикатури́ст (-а) *м* caricaturist.
карикату́р|ный (-ен, -на, -но) *прил* caricatured.
карка́с (-а) *м* shell (*of a building*).
ка́рка|ть (-ю) *несов неперех* (ворона) to caw; (*perf* **нака́ркать**; перен: разг) to predict the worst.
ка́рлик (-а) *м* dwarf.
ка́рликовый *прил* (племена) pygmy *опред*; (растения) dwarf *опред*.
ка́рлиц|а (-ы) *ж см* **ка́рлик**.
карма́н (-а) *м* pocket; **набива́ть** (**наби́ть** *perf*) **~** (пренебр) to line one's pockets; **э́то мне не по ~у** I can't afford it; **нало́ги уда́рили по ~у** the

taxes have hit the population hard; **держи́ ~ ши́ре!** fat chance!; **он не поле́зет за сло́вом в ~** he's never short of something to say.

карма́нн|ый *прил:* ~ые **де́ньги/часы́** pocket money/watch; **карма́нный вор** pickpocket; **карма́нный нож** pocketknife; **карма́нные расхо́ды** petty expenses.

карма́ш|ек (-ка) *м уменьш от* **карма́н**; *(мешочек)* pouch.

карнава́л (-а) *м* carnival.

карнава́льный *прил* carnival *опред.*

карни́з (-а) *м (под крышей здания)* cornice; *(над дверью)* lintel.

карп (-а) *м* carp.

Карпа́т|ы (-) *мн* Carpathians, Carpathian Mountains.

карт (-а) *м* go-cart.

ка́рт|а (-ы) *ж (ГЕО)* map; *(также:* **игра́льная ~)** (playing) card; **ста́вить (поста́вить** *perf)* **на ~у что-н** *(перен)* to put sth at stake; *см также* **ка́рты.**

карта́в|ый (-, -а, -о) *прил:* **он ~** he can't pronounce the letter "r" properly.

карто́жник (-а) *м* card player.

карто́жница (-ы) *ж см* **карто́жник.**

карте́л|ь (-и) *ж (ЭКОН)* cartel.

карти́н|а (-ы) *ж (также кино, перен)* picture; *(ТЕАТР)* scene; *(обычно мн: прошлого, природы)* image.

карти́н|ка (-ки; *gen pl* **-ок)** *ж уменьш от* **карти́на;** *(иллюстрация)* picture *(in book etc)*; **кни́га с ~ми** picture book; **пря́мо как ~!** it's beautiful!

карти́нный *прил* picture *опред;* **(-ен, -на, -но;** *красивый)* picturesque.

карто́граф (-а) *м* cartographer.

картографи́р|овать (-ую) *(не)сов перех* to map.

картографи́ческий (-ая, -ое, -ие) *прил* cartographic.

картогра́фи|я (-и) *ж* cartography.

картон (-а) *м* cardboard.

карто́нный *прил* cardboard.

картоте́к|а (-и) *ж* card index.

картофелин|а (-ы) *ж* potato *(мн* potatoes).

карто́фел|ь (-я) *м (растение)* potato plant; *(плод)* potatoes *мн;* **~ в мунди́ре** baked *или* jacket potatoes.

карто́фельный *прил* potato; **карто́фельное пюре́** mashed potato.

ка́рто|чка (-ки; *gen pl* **-ек)** *ж* card; *(также:* **фотока́рточка)** photo; **хле́бная/визи́тная ~** ration/business card.

ка́рточн|ый *прил:* ~ая **игра́** card game; ~ая **систе́ма** rationing; ~ **долг** gambling debt; ~ **до́мик** *(также перен)* house of cards.

карто́шка (-и) *ж собир* potatoes *мн;* **нос ~ой** bulbous nose.

ка́ртридж (-а) *м* cartridge.

карту́з (-а́) *м* peaked cap.

ка́рт|ы (-) *мн* cards *мн;* **игра́ть** *(impf)* **в ~** to play

cards; **раскрыва́ть (раскры́ть** *perf)* **свой ~** *(перен)* to show one's hand.

карусе́л|ь (-и) *ж* merry-go-round *(BRIT)*, carousel *(US)*.

ка́рцер (-а) *м* isolation cell.

карье́р (-а) *м (ТЕХ)* quarry; *(галоп)* full gallop; **пуска́ться (пусти́ться** *perf)* **с ме́ста в ~** *(перен)* to rush straight in.

карье́р|а (-ы) *ж* career; **де́лать (сде́лать** *perf)* ~у to build a career for o.s.

карьери́зм (-а) *м* careerism.

карьери́ст (-а) *м* careerist.

карьери́стск|ий (-ая, -ое, -ие) *прил* careerist *опред.*

каса́ни|е (-я) *ср* contact.

каса́|ться (-юсь; *perf* **косну́ться)** *несов возв:* ~ +gen *(дотрагиваться)* to touch; *(затрагивать)* to touch on; **э́то тебя́ не ~ется** it doesn't concern you; **что ~ется Вас, то ...** as far as you are concerned ....

ка́ск|а (-ки; *gen pl* **-ок)** *ж* helmet.

каска́д (-а) *м* cascade; *(трюк)* stunt; *(перен)* flood.

каскадёр (-а) *м* stunt man *(мн* men).

ка́сок *сущ см* **ка́ска.**

каспи́йск|ий (-ая, -ое, -ие) *прил:* **К~ое мо́ре** Caspian Sea.

ка́сс|а (-ы) *ж (ТЕАТР, КИНО)* box office; *(железнодорожная)* ticket office; *(в магазине)* cash desk; *(аппарат)* cash register; *(ящик)* cash box; *(деньги)* cash; *(ТИПОГ)* case.

кассацио́нный *прил:* ~ **суд** court of appeal.

касса́ци|я (-и) *ж (ЮР)* cassation, annulment; **подава́ть (пода́ть** *perf)* **на ~ю** to lodge an appeal.

кассе́т|а (-ы) *ж (магнитофонная)* cassette; *(ФОТО)* cartridge.

касси́р (-а) *м* cashier.

ка́ст|а (-ы) *ж* caste.

кастеля́нш|а (-и) *ж* laundrywoman *(мн* laundrywomen).

касте́т (-а) *м* knuckle-duster.

касто́р|ка (-и) *ж (разг)* = **касто́ровое ма́сло.**

касто́ров|ый *прил:* ~ое **ма́сло** castor oil.

кастри́р|овать (-ую) *(не)сов перех* to castrate.

кастрю́л|я (-и) *ж* saucepan.

катава́си|я (-и) *ж (разг)* mayhem.

катакли́зм (-а) *м* cataclysm.

катако́мб|ы (-) *мн* catacombs *мн.*

катализа́тор (-а) *м* catalyst.

катало́г (-а) *м* catalogue *(BRIT)*, catalog *(US)*.

каталогизи́р|овать (-ую) *(не)сов перех (книги)* to catalogue *(BRIT)*, catalog *(US)*.

ката́ни|е (-я) *ср:* ~ **на маши́не** driving; ~ **на велосипе́де** cycling; ~ **на конька́х** skating; ~ **на ло́шади** horse *(BRIT) или* horseback *(US)* riding; ~ **на лы́жах** skiing.

катапу́льт|а (-ы) *ж (ТЕХ)* catapult.

катапульти́р|оваться (-уюсь) *(не)сов возв* to eject.

ката́р (-а) *м* catarrh.

катара́кт|а (-ы) *ж* (*МЕД*) cataract.

катастро́ф|а (-ы) *ж* (*авиационная, железнодорожная*) disaster; (*перен*) catastrophe.

катастрофи́ческий (-ая, -ое, -ие) *прил* catastrophic, disastrous.

ката́|ть (-ю) *несов перех* (*что-н круглое*) to roll; (*что-н на колёсах*) to wheel; ~ (*impf*) **кого́-н на маши́не** to take sb for a drive

▸ **ката́ться** *несов возв*: ~**ся на маши́не/велосипе́де** to go for a drive/cycle; ~**ся** (*impf*) **на конька́х/ло́шади** (*BRIT*) *или* **horseback** (*US*) riding; ~**ся** (*impf*) **от бо́ли** to roll about in pain; ~**ся** (*impf*) **со́ смеху** to fall about laughing; **как сыр в ма́сле** ~**ся** (*impf*) to be in clover.

катафа́лк (-а) *м* hearse.

категори́чен *прил см* **категори́чный**.

категори́ческий (-ая, -ое, -ие) *прил* categoric.

категори́ч|ный (-ен, -на, -но) *прил* categorical.

категори́|я (-и) *ж* category.

ка́тер (-а) *м* boat; **сторожево́й/торпе́дный** ~ patrol/torpedo boat.

катехи́зис (-а) *м* catechism.

кати́ть (-чу́, -тишь) *несов перех* (*что-н круглое*) to roll; (*что-н на колёсах*) to wheel ♦ *неперех* (*разг: в автомобиле*) to bomb along; ~ (*impf*) **бо́чки на кого́-н** (*перен*) to snipe at sb.

катка́ *сущ см* **като́к**.

като́д (-а) *м* cathode.

като́к (-ка́) *м* ice *или* skating rink; (*ТЕХ: также:* **асфа́льтовый** ~) steamroller.

като́лик (-а) *м* Catholic.

католици́зм (-а) *м* Catholicism.

католи́чка *сущ см* **католи́чка**.

католи́ческий (-ая, -ое, -ие) *прил* Catholic.

католи́чка (-ки; *gen pl* -ек) *ж см* **като́лик**.

ка́торг|а (-и) *ж* hard labour (*BRIT*) *или* labor (*US*).

каторжа́н|ин (-ина; *nom pl* -е, *gen pl* -) *м* convict (*in a labour camp*).

каторжа́нк|а (-и) *ж см* **каторжа́нин**.

ка́торжник (-а) *м см* **каторжа́нин**.

кату́шк|а (-ки; *gen pl* -ек) *ж* spool.

каучу́к (-а) *м* rubber.

каучу́ковый *прил* rubber.

КАФ *м сокр* CAF (= *cost and freight*).

кафе́ *ср нескл* café.

ка́федр|а (-ы) *ж* (*ПРОСВЕЩ*) department; (*РЕЛ*) pulpit; (*лекторская*) rostrum; **заве́дующий** ~**ой** chair; **он получи́л** ~**у** he obtained a chair.

кафедра́льный *прил*: ~ **собо́р** cathedral.

ка́фель (-я) *м собир* tiles *мн*.

ка́фельный *прил* tiled.

кафете́ри|й (-я) *м* cafeteria.

кафта́н (-а) *м* caftan.

кача́лк|а (-ки; *gen pl* -ок) *ж* rocking chair.

кача́ни|е (-я) *ср* (*на качелях*) swinging; (*на волнах*) rocking, roll.

кача́|ть (-ю) *несов перех* (*колыбель*) to rock; (*подбрасывать*) to throw into the air; (*нефть*) to pump; ~ (*impf*) **голово́й** to shake one's head; **кора́бль си́льно** ~**ло** the ship was rocking violently

▸ **кача́ться** *несов возв* to swing; (*на волнах*) to rock, roll; (*от устало́сти*) to sway.

каче́л|и (-ей) *мн* swing *ед*.

ка́чественно *нареч* (*другой*) essentially; (*делать, работать*) to a high standard.

ка́чествен|ный *прил* qualitative; (-, -на, -но; *товар, изделие*) high-quality; **ка́чественное прилага́тельное** qualitative adjective.

ка́честв|о (-а) *ср* quality ♦ *предл*: **в** ~**е** +*gen* as; **в** ~**е приме́ра** by way of example; **я рабо́таю в** ~**е меха́ника** I work as a mechanic.

ка́чк|а (-и) *ж*: **бортова́я** ~ rolling; **килева́я** ~ pitching.

качн|у́ть (-у́, -ёшь) *сов перех* to swing

▸ **качну́ться** *сов возв* to swing.

ка́ш|а (-и) *ж* ≈ porridge; **у него́ в голове́** ~ he's totally mixed up.

кашало́т (-а) *м* sperm whale.

ка́ш|ель (-ля) *м* cough.

кашеми́р (-а) *м* cashmere.

ка́шля *сущ см* **ка́шель**.

ка́шлян|уть (-у, -ешь) *сов неперех* to cough.

ка́шля|ть (-ю) *несов неперех* to cough.

Кашми́р (-а) *м* Kashmir.

кашне́ *ср нескл* narrow scarf, *usually worn under a coat*.

кашта́н (-а) *м* (*дерево*) chestnut (tree); (*плод*) chestnut; (: *несъедобный*) conker; **таска́ть** (*impf*) ~**ы из огня́** to do the dirty work; **ко́нский** ~ horse chestnut.

кашта́новый *прил* (*аллея, волосы*) chestnut.

каю́к (-а) *как сказ* (*разг*): **ему́** ~ he's finished.

каю́т|а (-ы) *ж* (*МОР*) cabin.

каю́т-компа́ни|я (-и) *ж naval officers' lounge*.

ка́|яться (-юсь; *perf* **пока́яться**) *несов возв*: ~ (**в чём-н пе́ред кем-н**) to confess (sth to sb); **я хочу́ тебе́ пока́яться в чём-то** I must tell you something; **до́лжен пока́яться, я никогда́ не люби́л её** I must confess, I never loved her.

кБт *сокр* (= **килоба́йт**) KB, kbyte (= *kilobyte*); = **килоби́т**.

КВ *мн сокр* (= **коро́ткие во́лны**) SW= *short wave ед*.

кв. *сокр* (= **квадра́тный**) sq. (= *square*); (= **кварти́ра**) Apt. (= *apartment*).

квадра́т (-а) *м* square; **возводи́ть** (**возвести́** *perf*) **что-н в** ~ to square sth.

квадра́т|ный (-ен, -на, -но) *прил* square; ~ **ко́рень** square root; **квадра́тные ско́бки** square brackets.

ква́канье (-я) *ср* croaking.

ква́кн|уть (*3sg* -ет, *3pl* -ут) *сов неперех* to croak.

квалификацио́нный *прил*: ~ **экза́мен**

professional exam.

квалифика́ци|я (-и) ж qualification; (*профессия*) profession.

квалифици́рованно *нареч* competently.

квалифици́рован|ный (-, -на, -но) *прил* (*работник*) qualified; (*труд*) skilled.

квалифици́р|овать (-ую) (*не*)*сов перех* (*спортсмена*) to rank; (*преступление, поведение*) to categorize.

квант (-а) м quantum.

ква́нтов|ый *прил*: ~ая меха́ника/фи́зика quantum mechanics/physics.

кварта́л (-а) м quarter.

кварта́льный *прил* (*отчёт, план*) quarterly.

кварте́т (-а) м quartet.

кварти́р|а (-ы) ж flat (*BRIT*), apartment (*US*); (*снимаемое жильё*) lodgings мн; жить (*impf*) на ~е to rent a flat *или* apartment; съезжа́ть (съе́хать *perf*) с ~ы to move out of lodgings.

кварти́ра́нт (-а) м lodger.

кварти́ра́нт|ка (-ки; *gen pl* **-ок)** ж см кварти́ра́нт.

квартир|ова́ть (-у́ю) *несов неперех* (*разг*: снимать жильё) to rent a flat (*BRIT*) *или* apartment (*US*).

квартиросъёмщик (-а) м leaseholder.

квартпла́т|а (-ы) ж *сокр* (= кварти́рная пла́та) rent (*for a flat*).

кварц (-а) м quartz.

ква́рцев|ый *прил* (*порода, руда*) quartz; ~ая ла́мпа quartz lamp.

квас (-а; *nom pl* **-ы)** м kvass (*mildly alcoholic drink made from fermented rye bread, yeast or berries*).

ква́|сить (-шу, -сишь; *perf* **заква́сить)** *несов перех* to pickle; (*молоко*) to sour.

ква́шен|ый *прил* (*молоко*) sour; ~ая капу́ста sauerkraut, pickled cabbage.

кваш|ня́ (-и́; *gen pl* **-ёй)** ж (*кадушка*) fermenting bucket (*for dough*); (*разг*: человек) clodhopper.

ква́шу *несов см* ква́сить.

Квебе́к (-а) м Quebec.

квинте́т (-а) м quintet.

квинтэссе́нци|я (-и) ж quintessence.

квита́нци|я (-и) ж receipt.

кви́ты *как сказ* (*разг*): мы ~ we're quits.

КВН м *сокр* (= клуб весёлых и находчивых) contest in which teams compete in various activities.

кво́рум (-а) м quorum.

кво́т|а (-ы) ж quota; и́мпортная ~ import quota.

кВт *сокр* (= килова́тт) kW (= *kilowatt*).

кг *сокр* (= килогра́мм) kg (= *kilogram(me)*).

КГБ м *сокр* (*ист*: = Комите́т госуда́рственной безопа́сности) KGB.

ке́гл|и (-ей) мн skittles мн; (*игра*) skittles *ед*.

кедр (-а) м cedar (tree).

ке́д|ы (-) мн pumps мн.

Кейпта́ун (-а) м Cape Town.

кейф (-а) м = кайф.

кейф|ова́ть (-у́ю) *несов* = кайфова́ть.

кекс (-а) м (fruit)cake.

келе́ен *прил см* келе́йный.

келе́йно *нареч* secretly.

келе́й|ный *прил* (*жизнь*) reclusive; (*тишина*) sublime; (-ен, -йна, -йно; *перен*: переговоры, совещания) secret.

Кёльн (-а) м Cologne.

кельт (-а) м Celt.

ке́льтск|ий (-ая, -ое, -ие) *прил* Celtic.

ке́ль|я (-ьи; *gen pl* **-ий)** ж (*монашеская*) cell.

кем *мест см* кто.

Ке́мбридж (-а) м Cambridge.

ке́мпинг (-а) м camping site, campsite.

кенгуру́ *ср нескл* kangaroo.

кени́йск|ий (-ая, -ое, -ие) *прил* Kenyan.

Ке́ни|я (-и) ж Kenya.

ке́пи *ср нескл* peaked cap.

ке́п|ка (-ки; *gen pl* **-ок)** ж cap.

кера́мик|а (-и) ж *собир* ceramics мн.

керами́ческ|ий (-ая, -ое, -ие) *прил* ceramic.

кероси́н (-а) м paraffin, kerosene (*US*).

кероси́н|ка (-ки; *gen pl* **-ок)** ж paraffin stove.

ке́сарев *прил*: ~о сече́ние Caesarean (*BRIT*) *или* Cesarean (*US*) section.

кессо́нн|ый *прил*: ~ая боле́знь decompression sickness, the bends мн.

ке́т|а (-ы) ж Keta salmon.

кефа́л|ь (-и) ж grey mullet.

кефи́р (-а) м kefir (*yoghurt drink*).

киберне́тик (-а) м specialist in cybernetics.

киберне́тик|а (-и) ж cybernetics.

кибернети́ческ|ий (-ая, -ое, -ие) *прил* cybernetic.

киби́т|ка (-и) ж carriage.

кива́|ть (-ю) *несов неперех* (+*dat*) to nod; ~ (*impf*) на кого́-н (*разг*) to pin the blame on sb.

кив|ка́ *сущ см* кивок.

кивн|у́ть (-у́, -ёшь) *сов неперех* to nod.

кив|о́к (-ка́) м nod.

кида́|ть (-ю) *несов от* ки́нуть

▸ **(-ся)** *несов от* ки́нуться ♦ *возв*: ~ся камня́ми to throw stones at each other; ~ся (*impf*) деньга́ми to throw money around.

Ки́ев (-а) м Kiev.

кизи́л (-а) м cornel.

кизи́ловый *прил* cornel *опред*.

ки|й (-я; *nom pl* **-и́,** *gen pl* **-ёв)** м (*СПОРТ*) cue.

кикимо́р|а (-ы) ж *female goblin in Russian mythology*; (*пренебр*: человек) fright.

килоба́йт (-а) м kilobyte.

килова́тт (-а) м kilowatt.

килогра́мм (-а) м kilogram(me).

килограммо́вый *прил* of one kilogram(me).

киломе́тр (-а) м kilometre (*BRIT*), kilometer (*US*).

километро́вый *прил* (*расстояние*) of one kilometre (*BRIT*) *или* kilometer (*US*); (*гонка*) one-kilometre.

кил|ь (-я) м keel.

кильва́тер (-а) м wake.

ки́льк|а (-и) ж sprat.

кимоно́ *ср нескл* kimono.

кинемато́граф (-а) м (*киноиндустрия*) cinematography; (*кинотеатр*) cinema.
кинематографи́ст (-а) м cinematographer.
кинематографи́ческий (-ая, -ое, -ие) *прил* cinematographic.
кинематогра́фия (-и) ж cinematography.
кине́тика (-и) ж kinetics.
кинети́ческий (-ая, -ое, -ие) *прил* kinetic.
кинжа́л (-а) м dagger.
кино́ *ср нескл* cinema; (*разг: фильм*) film, movie (*US*); **идти́ (пойти́** *perf*) **в ~** (*разг*) to go to the pictures (*BRIT*) *или* movies (*US*); **э́то про́сто ~** (*разг*) it's an absolute joke.
киноактёр (-а) м (film) actor.
киноактри́са (-ы) ж (film) actress.
киноарти́ст (-а) м = **киноактёр**.
киноарти́стка (-ки; *gen pl* -ок) ж = **киноактри́са**.
кинокарти́на (-ы) ж film.
кинооперáтор (-а) м cameraman.
кинорежиссёр (-а) м (film) director.
киносту́дия (-и) ж film studio.
киносъёмка (-и) ж filming, shooting.
кинотеа́тр (-а) м cinema.
кинофи́льм (-а) м film.
ки́нуть (-у, -ешь; *impf* **кида́ть**) *сов перех* (*дрова, камень*) to throw; (*взгляд*) to cast; (*друзей*) to desert; (*силы, ресурсы*) to channel; (*разг: обмануть*) to swindle
▶ **ки́нуться** (*impf* **кида́ться**) *сов возв*: **~ся на** +*acc* (*на врага*) to attack; (*на еду*) to fall upon; **кида́ться** (**~ся** *perf*) **кому́-н на ше́ю** to fall on sb; **кида́ться** (**~ся** *perf*) **к кому́-н** to throw o.s. at sb; **кида́ться** (**~ся** *perf*) **со скалы́** to throw o.s. off a cliff.
кио́ск (-а) м kiosk.
кио́т (-а) м icon case.
ки́па (-ы) ж bundle.
кипари́с (-а) м cypress.
кипари́совый *прил* cypress *опред*.
кипе́ние (-я) *ср* boiling; **температу́ра** *или* **то́чка ~я** boiling point.
кипе́ть (-лю́, -и́шь; *perf* **вскипе́ть**) *несов неперех* (*вода, чайник*) to boil; **рабо́та ~и́т** work is in full swing; **жизнь ~и́т** life is busy; **~** (**вскипе́ть** *perf*) **негодова́нием/зло́бой** to seethe with indignation/anger.
Кипр (-а) м Cyprus.
киприо́т (-а) м Cypriot.
киприо́тка (-ки; *gen pl* -ок) ж *см* **киприо́т**.
кипу́чий (-ая, -ее, -ие; -, -а, -о) *прил* bubbling; (*перен*) busy.
кипяти́льник (-а) м element (*for heating water*).
кипяти́ть (-чу́, -ти́шь; *perf* **вскипяти́ть**) *несов перех* to boil
▶ **кипяти́ться** *несов возв* (*овощи*) to boil; (*шприцы, бельё*) to be boiled; (*перен: разг: горячиться*) to get shirty.

кипято́к (-ка́) м boiling water.
кипячёный *прил* boiled.
кипячу́(сь) *несов см* **кипяти́ть(ся)**.
кирги́з (-а) м Kirghiz.
Кирги́зия (-и) ж Kirghizia.
кирги́зка (-ки; *gen pl* -ок) ж *см* **кирги́з**.
кирги́зский (-ая, -ое, -ие) *прил* Kirghiz.
кири́ллица (-ы) ж the Cyrillic alphabet.
кирка́ (-и́) ж pick(axe).
кирпи́ч (-а́) м (*СТРОИТ*) brick.
кирпи́чный *прил* brick; **кирпи́чный заво́д** brickworks.
кисе́йный *прил* muslin; **~ая ба́рышня** *prim young miss*.
ки́сел *прил см* **ки́слый**.
кисе́ль (-я́) м fruit jelly; **седьма́я вода́ на киселе́** distant relative.
кисе́т (-а) м tobacco pouch.
кисея́ (-и́) ж muslin.
кисли́нка (-и) ж sour taste.
кислоро́д (-а) м oxygen.
ки́сло-сла́дкий (-кая, -кое, -кие; -ок, -ка, -ко) *прил* (*хлеб*) sweet with a bitter aftertaste; (*ягоды*) bittersweet.
кислота́ (-оты́; *nom pl* -о́ты) ж acid.
кисло́тность (-и) ж acidity.
кисло́тный *прил* acid; **~ дождь** acid rain.
ки́слый (-ел, -ла́, -ло) *прил* (*также перен*) sour; **ки́слая капу́ста** sauerkraut; **ки́слое молоко́** soured milk.
ки́снуть (-ну, -нешь; *pt* -, -ла, -ло, *perf* **проки́снуть** *или* **ски́снуть**) *несов неперех* to go off; (*no perf*; *перен: разг*) to mope (about).
киста́ (-ы́) ж cyst.
ки́сточка (-ки; *gen pl* -ек) ж (paint)brush; (*винограда*) bunch; (*на берете, на скатерти итп*) tassel.
кисть (-и) ж (*АНАТ*) hand; (*гроздь: рябины*) cluster; (: *винограда*) bunch; (*на скатерти, на одежде итп*) tassel; (*художника, маляра*) (paint) brush; **он хорошо́ владе́ет ки́стью** he's a good painter; **полотно́ ки́сти Мати́сса** painting by Matisse.
кит (-а́) м whale.
кита́ец (-йца) м Chinese.
Кита́й (-я) м China.
кита́йский (-ая, -ое, -ие) *прил* Chinese; **~ язы́к** Chinese; **~ая гра́мота** double Dutch.
кита́йца *итп сущ см* **кита́ец**.
китая́нка (-ки; *gen pl* -ок) ж *см* **кита́ец**.
ки́тель (-я; *nom pl* -и, *gen pl* -ей) м *military jacket*.
китобо́йный *прил* whaling *опред*.
кито́вый *прил* whale *опред*.
кичи́ться (-у́сь, -и́шься) *несов возв*: **~** +*instr* to preen o.s. on.
кичли́вый (-, -а, -о) *прил* conceited.
кише́ть (*3sg* -и́т, *3pl* -а́т) *несов неперех* (*мошкара, черви*) to swarm; **~** (*impf*) +*instr* (*людьми, рыбой*) to teem with.

The spelling rules for Russian are shown on page xvii.

кише́чник (-а) *м* intestines *мн*.

кише́чный *прил* intestinal.

Кишинёв (-а) *м* Kishinev.

кишка́ (-ки́; *gen pl* -о́к, *dat pl* -ка́м) *ж* gut, intestine; **пряма́я** ~ rectum; **то́лстая** ~ large intestine.

кишла́к (-а́) *м village in Central Asia*.

кишми́ш (-а) *м собир* seedless grapes *мн*; (*изюм*) currants *мн*.

кишмя́ *нареч* (*разг*): ~ **кише́ть** to swarm.

кишо́к *сущ см* **кишка́**.

кл. *сокр* = **класс**.

клавеси́н (-а) *м* harpsichord.

клавиату́ра (-ы) *ж* keyboard; (**ма́лая**) ~ (*комп*) keypad.

кла́виша (-и) *ж* key; ~ **-возвра́т каре́тки"/вы́хода** (*комп*) return/escape key.

кла́вишный *прил*: ~ **инструме́нт** keyboard instrument.

клад (-а) *м* treasure.

кла́дбище (-а) *ср* cemetery; (*возле церкви*) graveyard.

кладби́щенский (-ая, -ое, -ие) *прил* (*см сущ*) cemetery *опред*; graveyard *опред*; ~ **сто́рож** sexton.

кла́дезь (-я) *м* (*перен*): ~ **зна́ний или прему́дрости** mine of information.

кла́дка (-и) *ж* (*действие*) laying; **кирпи́чная** ~ brickwork; **ка́менная** ~ masonry.

кладова́я (-о́й; *decl like adj*) *ж* store.

кладо́вка (-ки; *gen pl* -ок) *ж* (*разг*) cubby-hole.

кладовщи́к (-а́) *м* storeman (*мн* storemen).

кладовщи́ца (-ы) *ж* storewoman (*мн* storewomen).

кладу́ *итп несов см* **класть**.

кладь (-и) *ж* load; **ручна́я** ~ hand luggage.

кла́ксон (-а) *м* horn.

клан (-а) *м* clan.

кла́няться (-юсь; *perf* **поклони́ться**) *несов возв* to bow; (*свидетельствовать уважение*) to send one's regards; (*перен: униженно просить*) to beg.

кла́пан (-а) *м* valve.

кларне́т (-а) *м* clarinet.

кларнети́ст (-а) *м* clarinetist.

класс (-а) *м* class; (*комната*) classroom ♦ **как сказ** (*выражает восхищение*) it's great; **он вёл** ~ **фортепья́но в консервато́рии** he taught the piano at the conservatory; **специали́ст высо́кого кла́сса** highly-qualified specialist; **пока́зывать** (**показа́ть** *perf*) ~ (*разг*) to show one's class.

кла́ссен *прил см* **кла́ссный**.

кла́ссик (-а) *м* (*литерату́ры, му́зыки*) classic; (*учёный*) classical scholar.

кла́ссика (-и) *ж* classics *мн*.

классификацио́нный *прил* (*экзамен*) assessment *опред*; (*таблица*) classification *опред*.

классифика́ция (-и) *ж* classification.

классифици́ровать (-ую) (*не*)*сов перех* to classify.

классици́зм (-а) *м* classicism.

класси́ческий (-ая, -ое, -ие) *прил* (*пример, работа*) classic; (*музыка, литература*) classical; (*разг: жулик, политикан итп*) typical; ~**ая гимна́зия** *grammar school specializing in Latin and Ancient Greek*; ~**ое образова́ние** classical education.

кла́ссный *прил* (*сочинение, собрание*) class *опред*; (-ен, -на, -но; *разг: водитель, обед*) great; **кла́ссный руководи́тель** form teacher.

кла́ссовый *прил* class *опред*.

класть (-ду́, -дёшь; *рt* -л, -ла, -ло, *perf* **положи́ть**; *несов перех* to put; (*perf* **сложи́ть**; *фундамент*) to lay; ~ (**положи́ть** *perf*) **основа́ние** to lay down the foundations; ~ (**положи́ть** *perf*) **жизнь за кого́-н/что-н** to lay down one's life for sb/sth; ~ (**положи́ть** *perf*) **что-н на му́зыку** to put sth to music; ~ (*impf*) **я́йца** to lay eggs.

кла́цанье (-я) *ср* (*разг*) chattering.

кла́цать (-ю) *несов неперех* (*разг*) to chatter.

клёв (-а) *м* bite; **сего́дня хоро́ший** ~ the fish are biting today.

клева́ть (-ю́ю) *несов перех* (*подлеж: птица*) to peck ♦ *неперех* (*рыба*) to bite; ~ (*impf*) **но́сом** to nod; **у меня́ ~ю́ёт** I've got a bite

► **клева́ться** *несов возв* to peck.

кле́вер (-а) *м* clover.

клевета́ (-ы́) *ж* (*устная*) slander; (*письменная*) libel.

клевета́ть (-ещу́, -е́щешь; *perf* **наклевета́ть**) *несов неперех*: ~ **на** +*acc* (*см сущ*) to slander; to libel.

клеветни́к (-а́) *м* slanderer.

клеветни́ческий (-ая, -ое, -ие) *прил* (*см сущ*) slanderous; libellous.

клевещу́ *итп несов см* **клевета́ть**.

кле́ек *прил см* **кле́йкий**.

клеёнка (-ки; *gen pl* -ок) *ж* oilcloth.

клеёнчатый *прил* oilskin *опред*.

кле́ить (-ю, -ишь; *perf* **скле́ить**) *несов перех* to glue

► **кле́иться** *несов возв* to stick; (*перен: работа*) to come together; (: *разговор*) to go smoothly.

клей (-я) *м* glue.

кле́йкий (-йкая, -йкое, -йкие; -ек, -йка, -йко) *прил* sticky; **кле́йкая ле́нта** sticky tape.

клеймёный *прил* (*товар*) stamped; (*скот*) branded.

клейми́ть (-лю́, -и́шь; *perf* **заклейми́ть**) *несов перех* (*товар, груз*) to stamp; (*скот, преступника*) to brand; (*перен: человека, поведение*) to stigmatize; ~ (**заклейми́ть** *perf*) **кого́-н позо́ром** to hold sb up to shame; **его́ заклейми́ли преда́телем** he was branded a traitor.

клеймо́ (-а́; *nom pl* -а, *gen pl* -) *ср* stamp; (*на теле скота, осуждённого*) brand; ~ **позо́ра** stigma.

кле́йстер (-а; *part gen* -у) *м* paste.

клéмм|а (-ы) ж (ЭЛЕК) terminal.

клён (-а) м maple.

клено́вый прил maple.

клеп|а́ть (-а́ю; perf **склепа́ть**) несов перех to rivet; ♦ (-лю́, -лешь; perf **наклепа́ть**) неперех (разг): ~ **на** +acc to snitch on.

клептома́н (-а) м kleptomaniac.

клептома́ни|я (-и) ж kleptomania.

клептома́н|ка (-ки; gen pl -ок) ж см **клептома́н**.

клерк (-а) м clerk.

клéт|ка (-ки; gen pl -ок) ж (для птиц, животных) cage; (на ткани) check; (на бумаге) square; (БИО) cell; **бума́га в ~ку** squared paper; **ткань в ~ку** checked material; **грудна́я ~** chest; **ле́стничная ~** landing.

клéточный прил (БИО) cell опред.

клетча́т|ка (-и) ж (no pl; БОТ) cellulose; (АНАТ) cell tissue.

клéтчатый прил (ткань, шарф итп) chequered, checked.

клёц|ка (-ки; gen pl -ек) ж (обычно мн) dumpling.

клёш (-а) м flare ♦ прил неизм: **брю́ки ~** flares; **ю́бка ~** flared skirt.

клешн|я́ (-и́; gen pl -éй) ж claw, pincer.

клещ (-а́) м (ЗООЛ) tick.

клéщ|и (-éй) мн tongs мн.

клиéнт (-а) м client.

клиéнт|ка (-ки; gen pl -ок) ж см **клиéнт**.

клиенту́р|а (-ы) ж собир clientèle.

кли́зм|а (-ы) ж enema.

клик (-а) м (человека) cry; (птицы) call.

кли́к|а (-и) ж clique.

клику́ш|а (-и) ж hysterical woman (мн women) ♦ м/ж panicmonger.

кли́макс (-а) м (БИО) menopause.

климактери́ческ|ий (-ая, -ое, -ие) прил menopausal; **климактери́ческий пери́од** menopause.

кли́мат (-а) м (также перен) climate.

климати́ческ|ий (-ая, -ое, -ие) прил climatic.

клин (-а; nom pl -ья или -ы́, gen pl -ьев или -о́в) м wedge; (солдат, журавлей) V-formation; **борода́ кли́ном** goatee; **~ кли́ном вышиба́ть** (impf) to fight fire with fire.

кли́ник|а (-и) ж clinic.

клини́ческ|ий (-ая, -ое, -ие) прил clinical; **клини́ческая больни́ца** training hospital; **клини́ческая смерть** (МЕД) clinical death.

клин|о́к (-ка́) м blade.

кли́пс|ы (-ов) мн clip-on earrings мн.

клир (-а) м собир (РЕЛ) the clergy.

кли́рик (-а) м clergyman (мн clergymen).

кли́ринг (-а) м (КОММ) clearing.

кли́рос (-а) м choir (part of church).

клич (-а) м cry; **боево́й ~** battle cry.

кли́ч|ка (-ки; gen pl -ек) ж (собаки, кошки итп) name; (человека) nickname.

клише́ ср нескл (перен) cliché; (типог) plate.

клоа́к|а (-и) ж (перен: загрязнённое место)

cesspit; (: безнра́вственная среда́) cesspool.

клобу́к (-а́) м (РЕЛ) cowl.

кло|к (-ка́; nom pl -чья, gen pl -чьев) м (волос) tuft; (ваты) wad.

клокота́ни|е (-я) ср (воды) gurgling.

клоко|та́ть (-чу́, -о́чешь) несов неперех (вода, поток) to gurgle; (перен: негодовать) to seethe.

клон|и́ть (-ю́, -ишь) несов перех to bow, bend ♦ неперех: ~ **к** +dat to drive at; **его́ ~и́ло ко сну** he was drifting off (to sleep); **ло́дку кло́нит на́ бок** the boat is tilting; **к чему́ ты кло́нишь?** what are you getting или driving at?

▶ **клони́ться** несов возв (пригибаться) to bend; (близиться): **~ся к** +dat to approach; **день ~и́лся к ве́черу** evening was drawing near.

клоп (-а́) м bedbug.

кло́ун (-а) м clown.

кло́унск|ий (-ая, -ое, -ие) прил clown's; (перен) clownish.

клоч|о́к (-ка́) м уменьш от **клок**; (земли) plot; (бумаги) scrap.

кло́чья итп сущ см **клок**.

клуб (-а) м (общество, здание) club; (обычно мн: дыма, пыли) cloud.

клу́б|ень (-ня) м (картофеля) tuber.

клуб|и́ться (3sg -и́тся, 3pl -я́тся) несов возв to swirl.

клубка́ сущ см **клубо́к**.

клубни́к|а (-и) ж strawberry ♦ собир strawberries мн.

клубни́чный прил strawberry.

клуб|о́к (-ка́) м (ниток, шерсти) ball; (перен: противоречий) tangle, knot; **сверну́ться (perf) ~ко́м** to curl up in a ball.

клу́мб|а (-ы) ж flowerbed.

клу́ш|а (-и) ж (разг: пренебр) clumsy woman.

клык (-а́) м (человека) canine (tooth); (животного) fang.

клюв (-а) м beak.

клюк|а́ (-и́) ж walking stick.

клю́кв|а (-ы) ж cranberry ♦ собир cranberries мн; **развеси́стая ~** tall story.

клю́квенный прил: ~ **морс/кисе́ль** cranberry juice/jelly.

клю́|нуть (-у, -ешь) сов перех to peck.

ключ (-а́) м (также перен) key; (родник) spring; (МУЗ): **скрипи́чный/басо́вый ~** treble/bass clef; **га́ечный ~** spanner; ~ **от входно́й две́ри** front-door key; **бить** (impf) или **кипе́ть** (impf) ~**о́м** (вода) to jet, spout; **жизнь бьёт** или **кипи́т ~о́м** life is really buzzing; **в пре́жнем ~é** (перен) as before; **сдава́ть (сдать** perf) **что-н под ~** (здание) to offer sth ready for immediate entry; **ключ зажига́ния** ignition key.

ключево́й прил (позиция, проблемы итп) key опред; **ключева́я вода́** spring water.

ключи́ц|а (-ы) ж collarbone.

клюш|ка (-ки; gen pl -ек) ж (ХОККЕЙ) hockey stick; (ГОЛЬФ) club.

кля́кс|а (-ы) ж smudge.

кляну́(сь) итп несов см **кля́сть(ся)**.

кля́нч|ить (-у, -ишь; perf вы́клянчить) несов перех (разг): ~ что-н у кого́-н to pester sb for sth.

кляп (-а) м gag; **засу́нуть** (perf) **кому́-н** в рот to gag sb.

кля|сть (-ну́, -нёшь; pt -л, -ла́, -ло) несов перех to curse

▶ **кля́сться** (perf покля́сться) несов возв to swear; **кля́сться** (покля́сться perf) в ве́чной любви́ to swear eternal love; **кля́сться** (покля́сться perf) жи́знью/Бо́гу to swear on one's life/to God.

кля́тв|а (-ы) ж oath; **дава́ть** (дать perf)/ **сде́рживать** (сдержа́ть perf) ~у to take или swear/keep an oath; **наруша́ть** (нару́шить perf) ~у to break one's oath.

кля́узничать (-ы) ж backbiting.

кля́уза прил см **кля́узный**.

кля́узник (-а) м (пренебр) scandalmonger.

кля́узнич|ать (-ю; perf накля́узничать) несов непер: ~ (на +acc) to spread gossip (about).

кля́уз|ный (-ен, -на, -но) прил: ~ное письмо́ slanderous letter.

кля́ч|а (-и) ж (разг: пренебр: лошадь) old nag.

км. сокр (= киломе́тр) km (= kilometre (BRIT) или kilometer (US)).

км/ч сокр (= киломе́тров в час) km/h (= kilometres per hour).

КНДР ж сокр (= Коре́йская Наро́дно-Демократи́ческая Респу́блика) DPRK (= Democratic People's Republic of Korea).

кне́л|и (-ей) мн quenelles мн.

кни́г|а (-и) ж book; **ка́ссовая** ~ cash-book; **телефо́нная** ~ telephone book или directory; ~ **зака́зов** order book; ~ **учёта** day book; **кни́га жа́лоб и предложе́ний** suggestions book.

книголю́б (-а) м book-lover.

книгопеча́тани|е (-я) ср book printing.

кни́ж|ка (-ки; gen pl -ек) ж book; **записна́я** ~ notebook; **зачётная** ~ (ПРОСВЕЩ) register; **трудова́я** ~ employment record book; **че́ковая** ~ chequebook (BRIT), checkbook (US).

кни́жник (-а) м (знаток книг) bibliophile.

кни́жный прил (перен: знания, стиль) bookish; **кни́жный магази́н** bookshop; **кни́жный шкаф** bookcase; **кни́жный червь** bookworm.

кни́зу нареч downwards.

кно́п|ка (-ки; gen pl -ок) ж (звонка, лифта) button; (канцеля́рская) drawing pin (BRIT), thumbtack (US); (застёжка) press stud, popper (BRIT).

КНР ж сокр (= Кита́йская Наро́дная Респу́блика) PRC (= People's Republic of China).

кнут (-а́) м whip; **поли́тика** ~**а́ и пря́ника** the carrot and the stick policy.

княги́н|я (-и) ж princess (wife of a prince).

княж|ить (-у, -ишь) несов непер to reign.

княжн|а́ (-ны́; gen pl -о́н) ж princess (daughter of a prince).

княз|ь (-я; nom pl -ья́, gen pl -е́й) м prince (in Russia); **вели́кий** ~ (ИСТ) grand prince (son or brother of the tsar).

ко предл см **к.**

коагули́р|овать (3sg -ует, 3pl -уют) несов перех to coagulate.

коагуля́ци|я (-и) ж coagulation.

коа́л|а (-ы) ж koala (bear).

коалицио́нн|ый прил: ~ое прави́тельство coalition government; ~ **догово́р** coalition pact.

коали́ци|я (-и) ж coalition.

ко́бальт (-а) м cobalt.

кобе́л|ь (-я́) м dog (male).

ко́бр|а (-ы) ж cobra.

кобур|а́ (-ы́) ж holster.

кобы́л|а (-ы) ж mare; (перен: разг) strapping lass.

ко́ван|ый (-, -а, -о) прил (меч, решётка итп) forged; (обитый железом) metal-bound.

кова́рен прил см **кова́рный**.

кова́рность (-и) ж treachery.

кова́рный (-ен, -на, -но) прил devious.

кова́рств|о (-а) ср deviousness.

ков|а́ть (кую́, куёшь; imper куй(те), perf скова́ть) несов перех to forge; **куй желе́зо пока́ горячо́** strike while the iron's hot.

ковбо́|й (-я) м cowboy.

ковёр (-ра́) м carpet; **вызыва́ть** (вы́звать perf) **на** ~ кого́-н to call sb to account.

коверканье (-я) ср mangling.

коверка|ть (-ю; perf искове́ркать) несов перех (произноше́ние, слова) to mangle; (язык) to butcher; (душу) to twist; **коверка́ть** (искове́ркать perf) чью-н мысль/чьи-н слова́ to twist sb's ideas/words.

ко́вк|а (-и) ж forging.

ковр|а́ итп сущ см **ковёр**.

коври́г|а (-и) ж loaf (мн loaves).

коври́ж|ка (-ки; gen pl -ек) ж ≈ gingerbread.

ко́врик (-а) м rug; (дверно́й) mat; ~ **для мы́шки** mouse pad.

ковро́в|ый прил: ~ая доро́жка runner.

ковроде́ли|е (-я) ср carpet weaving.

ковче́г (-а) м: **Но́ев** ~ Noah's Ark.

ковш (-а́) м ladle; (экскава́тора) shovel.

ковы́л|ь (-я́) м (БОТ) feather grass.

ковыля́|ть (-ю) несов непер to hobble.

ковыря́|ть (-ю) несов перех to dig up; ~ (impf) **в зуба́х/носу́** to pick one's teeth/nose

▶ **ковыря́ться** несов возв (медлить) to faff about; ~**ся** (impf) (в +prp) (копаться: в земле́) to root или poke about (in).

когда́ нареч when; (иногда) sometimes; ~ **ты зако́нчишь?** when will you finish?; **мы не зна́ем,** ~ **э́то произошло́** we don't know when it happened; ~ **пью ко́фе,** ~ **чай** sometimes I drink coffee, sometimes tea.

когда́-либо нареч = **когда́-нибудь**.

когда́-нибудь нареч (в вопроси́тельных предложе́ниях) ever; (в утверди́тельных *предложениях*) some *или* one day; **Вы ~ там бы́ли?** have you ever been there?; **я ~ туда́ пое́ду** I'll go there some *или* one day.

когда́-то *нареч* once; **он был ~ бога́т** he was once a rich man; **~ ещё я туда́ пое́ду** just when will I have another chance to go there?

кого́ *мест от* **кто**.

когóрт|а (-ы) *ж* (*перен*) cohort.

ко́г|оть (-тя; *gen pl* -те́й) *м* (*кошки, льва итп*) claw; (*орла*) talon; **пока́зывать (показа́ть** *perf*) **~ти** (*перен*) to bare one's teeth.

код (-а) *м* code; **передава́ть (переда́ть** *perf*) **сообще́ние по ко́ду** to send a message in code; **~ си́мвола** (*КОМП*) character code.

кодеи́н (-а) *м* codeine.

ко́декс (-а) *м* code; **гражда́нский/уголо́вный ~** (*ЮР*) civil/criminal code.

коди́р|овать (-ую; *perf* **закоди́ровать**) *несов перех* to encode, code.

кодиро́вк|а (-и) *ж* coding.

кодиро́вщик (-а) *м* coder.

коди́рующий (-ая, -ее, -ие) *прил*: **~ее устро́йство** (*КОМП*) encoder.

кодифика́ци|я (-и) *ж* (*ЮР*) codification.

кодифици́р|овать (-ую) (*не)сов перех* (*ЮР*) to codify.

ко́дов|ый *прил*: **~ые зна́ки** code symbols *мн*; **ко́довое назва́ние** codename.

ко́е-где́ *нареч* here and there.

ко́ек *сущ см* **ко́йка**.

ко́е-ка́к *нареч* (*небрежно*) any old how; (*с трудом*) somehow.

ко́е-како́й (**ко́е-како́го**) *мест* some; **нам нужна́ ко́е-кака́я по́мощь** we need some sort of help.

ко́е-когда́ *нареч* now and then, now and again.

ко́е-кто́ (**ко́е-кого́**) *мест* (*некоторые*) some (people).

ко́е-куда́ *нареч* (*разг*) this place and that.

ко́е-что́ (**ко́е-чего́**) *мест* (*нечто*) something; (*немногое*) a little.

ко́ж|а (-и) *ж* skin; (*материал*) leather; (*апельсина, яблока*) peel; **гуси́ная ~** goose bumps *мн или* pimples *мн*; **~ да ко́сти** (*разг*) all skin and bone; **из ~и вон лезть** (*impf*) to sweat blood.

ко́жаный *прил* leather.

ко́же́венный *прил* leather; **ко́же́венный заво́д** tannery.

ко́жник (-а) *м* (*МЕД*) dermatologist.

ко́жн|ый *прил*: **~ые боле́зни** skin diseases; **ко́жный врач** dermatologist; **ко́жный покро́в** skin.

кожур|а́ (-ы́) *ж* (*апельсина*) peel; (*ореха*) skin.

коз|а́ (-ы́; *nom pl* -ы) *ж* (nanny) goat.

козёл *сущ см* **ко́злы**.

козёл (-ла́; *nom pl* -лы́) *м* (billy) goat; (*в гимнастике*) horse; (*разг: игра*) dominoes; **от него́ как от ~ла́ молока́** (*разг*) he's worse than

useless; **забива́ть** (*impf*) **~ла́** to play dominoes; **козёл отпуще́ния** scapegoat.

Козеро́г (-а) *м* (*созвездие*) Capricorn.

ко́з|ий (-ья, -ье, -ьи) *прил* goat опред; **~ье молоко́** goat's milk.

козла́ *итп сущ см* **козёл**.

козлёнок (-ёнка; *nom pl* -я́та, *gen pl* -я́т) *м* (*ЗООЛ*) kid.

козли́ный *прил* (*голос*) reedy; **~ая боро́дка** goatee.

ко́з|лы (-ел) *мн* (*сиденье*) coach box *ед*; (*опора*) trestle *ед*.

козля́та *итп сущ см* **козлёнок**.

ко́зн|и (-ей) *мн* intrigues *мн*; **стро́ить** (*impf*) **~** to scheme.

козырёк (-ька́) *м* (*картуза, фуражки*) peak; (*навес*) lintel; **брать (взять** *perf*) **под ~** to salute.

козырн|о́й *прил*: **~а́я ка́рта** trump.

козырн|у́ть (-у́, -ёшь) *сов от* **козыря́ть**.

ко́зыр|ь (-я) *м* (*КАРТЫ*) trump; (*перен*) trump card.

козырька́ *сущ см* **козырёк**.

козыря́|ть (-ю; *perf* **козырну́ть**) *несов неперех* (*разг: в картах*) to play a trump; (*хвастаться*): **~ +instr** to show off about; (*: отдавать честь*): **~ть +dat** to salute.

козя́в|ка (-ки; *gen pl* -ок) *ж* (*разг: букашка*) bug; (*: пренебр: человек*) small fry только *ед*.

ко́йк|а (-йки; *gen pl* -ек) *ж* (*на судне*) berth; (*в казарме*) bunk; (*в больнице, общежитии*) bed.

кок (-а) *м* (*повар*) ship's cook; (*вихор*) quiff.

кока́ин (-а) *м* cocaine.

кокаини́ст (-а) *м* cocaine addict.

кокаини́ст|ка (-ки; *gen pl* -ок) *ж см* **кокаини́ст**.

кока́рд|а (-ы) *ж* cockade.

коке́т|ка (-ки; *gen pl* -ок) *ж* flirt, coquette.

коке́тливость (-и) *ж* flirtatiousness.

коке́тлив|ый (-, -а, -о) *прил* (*девушка, взгляд, смех*) flirtatious; (*шапочка, платье итп*) pretty.

коке́тнича|ть (-ю) *несов неперех* to flirt.

коке́ток *сущ см* **коке́тка**.

коке́тств|о (-а) *ср* flirting.

коклю́ш (-а) *м* whooping cough.

КОКОМ *сокр* СОСОМ.

ко́кон (-а) *м* cocoon.

коко́с (-а) *м* coconut.

коко́сов|ый *прил*: **~ая па́льма** coconut palm; **коко́совое молоко́** coconut milk; **коко́совый оре́х** coconut.

кокс (-а) *м* coke.

кокс|ова́ть (-у́ю) *несов перех* (*ТЕХ*) to coke.

кокте́йл|ь (-я) *м* cocktail.

кол (-а́; *loc sg* -у́, *nom pl* -ья, *gen pl* -ьев) *м* stake; (*nom pl* -ы́; *разг*: ПРОСВЕЩ) ≈ E (*school mark*); **у меня́ нет ни ~а́ ни двора́** I don't have a thing to my name; (*ему́ итп*) **хоть ~ на голове́ чеши** it's like talking to a brick wall.

ко́лб|а (-ы) ж (хим) flask.
колбас|а́ (-ы́) ж sausage.
кол-во сокр (= коли́чество) amt (= amount).
колго́т|ки (-ок) мн tights мн (BRIT), panty hose мн (US).
колдо́бин|а (-ы) ж (на доро́ге) pothole.
колд|ова́ть (-у́ю) несов непер to practise (BRIT) или practice (US) witchcraft; (перен): ~ **над** +instr (над карти́ной, над у́жином итп) to conjure up.
колдовско́й прил magical; (перен) bewitching.
колдовств|о́ (-а́) ср sorcery, witchcraft.
колду́н (-а́) м wizard, sorcerer.
колду́н|ья (-ьи; gen pl -ий, dat pl -ьям) ж sorceress.
колеба́ни|е (-я) ср (физ) oscillation; (ма́ятника) swing; (по́чвы, зда́ния) vibration; (перен: цен, температу́ры) fluctuation; (: обы́чно мн: нереши́тельность) wavering, vacillation.
колеба́тельный прил (физ) oscillatory.
кол|еба́ть (-е́блю, -е́блешь) несов перех to rock, swing; (perf **поколеба́ть**; авторите́т) to shake.
▶ **колеба́ться** (perf **поколеба́ться**) несов возв (физ) to oscillate; (ли́стья, пла́мя итп) to flicker; (це́ны, пого́да) to fluctuate; (сомнева́ться) to waver, vacillate.
кол|е́блющийся (-я́яся, -е́еся, -ие́ся) прил (свет, те́ни) flickering; (челове́к) vacillating.
коленко́р (-а) м calico.
коленко́ровый прил calico.
коле́нн|ый прил: ~**ая ча́шка** kneecap.
коле́н|о (-а; nom pl -и, gen pl -ей) ср knee; (nom pl -а; трубы́) joint; (разг: муз) phrase; (поколе́ние) generation; **встава́ть (встать** perf**) на** ~**и** to kneel (down); **стоя́ть** (impf) **на** ~**ях** to be kneeling (down); **опуска́ться (опусти́ться** perf**) на** ~**и** to go down on one's knees; **сиде́ть** (impf) **у кого́-н на** ~**ях** to sit on sb's knee или lap; **поста́вить** (perf) **кого́-н на** ~**и** (перен) to bring sb to his итп knees; **ей мо́ре по** ~ everything washes straight over her.
коленопреклонённый прил kneeling.
коле́нчатый прил: ~ **вал** crankshaft.
ко́лер (-а) м colour (BRIT), color (US).
колёсик|о (-а) ср уменьш от **колесо́**; (часово́е) wheel.
коле|си́ть (-шу́, -си́шь) несов непер to get around; **я** ~**си́л по всему́ го́роду** I've been all over town.
колесни́ц|а (-ы) ж chariot.
колес|о́ (-а́; nom pl -ёса) ср wheel; **пя́тое** ~ (перен) fifth wheel (fig); **жизнь на** ~**ёсах** life on the road; **жить** (impf) **на** ~**ёсах** to live out of a suitcase.
коле́ц сущ см **кольцо́**.
колешу́ несов см **колеси́ть**.
коле|я́ (-и́) ж (на доро́ге) rut; (для поездо́в) track; (перен) routine; **выбива́ть (вы́бить** perf**) из** ~**й** to get out of a rut.

ко́лик|и (-) мн colic ед.
коли́чественный прил quantitative.
коли́честв|о (-а) ср quantity.
ко́лк|а (-и) ж (дров) chopping; (льда) breaking up.
ко́лкий (-кая, -кое, -кие; -ок, -ка́, -ко) прил (хво́я, трава́) prickly; (перен: шу́тка, замеча́ния) biting.
ко́лкост|ь (-и) ж (нрава, замеча́ний) abrasiveness; (насме́шка) biting remark.
коллаборациони́зм (-а) м collaborationism.
коллаборациони́ст (-а) м collaborator.
колла́ж (-а) м collage.
коллег|а (-и) м/ж colleague.
коллегиа́лен прил см **коллегиа́льный**.
коллегиа́льност|ь (-и) ж: **при́нцип** ~**и** collective responsibility.
коллегиа́льный (-ен, -ьна, -ьно) прил collective.
коллеги|я (-и) ж (полит) collegium (executive body in charge of government ministry); **адвока́тская** ~ ≈ the Bar; **редакцио́нная** ~ editorial board.
ко́лледж (-а) м college.
коллекти́в (-а) м collective; **а́вторский** ~ (team of) contributors.
коллекти́вен прил см **коллекти́вный**.
коллективиза́ци|я (-и) ж (ист) collectivization (creation of collective farms in the late 1920's and 1930's).
коллекти́вн|ый (-ен, -на, -но) прил collective.
коллекционе́р (-а) м collector.
коллекциони́ровани|е (-я) ср collecting.
коллекциони́р|овать (-ую) несов перех to collect.
коллекцио́нный прил collectable.
колле́кци|я (-и) ж collection.
ко́лли м нескл collie.
колли́зи|я (-и) ж clash.
колло́квиум (-а) м (просвещ) seminar; (совеща́ние специали́стов) colloquium.
коловоро́т (-а) м (водоворот) eddy; (тех) ice drill; (перен: столпотворе́ние) hurly-burly; ~ **собы́тий** the vortex of events.
коло́д|а (-ы) ж (бревно́) block; (карт) pack, deck; **че́рез пень** ~ half-heartedly.
коло́дезн|ый прил: ~**ая вода́** water from the well.
коло́дец (-ца) м well; (в ша́хте) shaft.
коло́д|ка (-ки; gen pl -ок) ж (обувна́я) shoetree; (орденская) strip.
коло́дца итп сущ см **коло́дец**.
ко́лок прил см **ко́лкий**.
ко́локол (-а; nom pl -а́) м bell; **звони́ть** (impf) **в** ~ to ring a bell.
колоко́л|ьня (-ьни; gen pl -ен) ж bell tower; **смотре́ть** (impf) **со свое́й** ~**ьни на что-н** to take a narrow view of sth.
колоко́льчик (-а) м bell; (бот) bluebell.

колониали́зм (-а) *м* colonialism.
колониа́льный *прил* colonial.
колониза́тор (-а) *м* colonizer.
колонизи́р|овать (-ую) *(не)сов перех* to colonize.
колонизова́ть (-у́ю) *(не)сов* = **колонизи́ровать**.
колони́ст (-а) *м* colonist.
колони́ст|ка (-ки; *gen pl* -ок) *ж см* **колони́ст**.
коло́ни|я (-и) *ж* colony;
　исправи́тельно-трудова́я ~ penal colony; **~ для малоле́тних престу́пников** *или* **несовершенноле́тних** young offenders' institution.
коло́н|ка (-ки; *gen pl* -ок) *ж* column; *(газовая)* geyser (*BRIT*), water heater; *(для воды, для бензина)* pump.
колонка́ *сущ см* **колоно́к**.
колонко́вый *прил* polecat *опред*.
коло́нн|а (-ы) *ж (АРХИТ)* column; *(ряд)*: **~ солда́т/демонстра́нтов** column of soldiers/ demonstrators.
колонна́д|а (-ы) *ж* colonnade.
коло́нок *сущ см* **коло́нка**.
колоно́к (-ка́) *м* polecat.
колорату́рн|ый *прил*: **~ое сопра́но** coloratura (*soprano*).
колори́т (-а) *м (перен: эпохи, страны итп)* colour (*BRIT*), color (*US*); *(искусство)* use of colour; **ме́стный ~** local colour.
колори́т|ный (-ен, -на, -но) *прил* colourful (*BRIT*), colorful (*US*).
ко́л|ос (-оса; *nom pl* -о́сья, *gen pl* -о́сьев) *м* ear (*of corn, wheat*).
коло́сс (-а) *м (также перен)* colossus; **~ на гли́няных нога́х** a giant with feet of clay.
колосса́льн|ый (-ен, -ьна, -ьно) *прил* colossal; **~ьно!** that's fantastic!
колоти́ть (-очу́, -о́тишь) *несов неперех (по столу, в дверь)* to thump ♦ *перех (разг: бить)* to whack; **меня́ ~о́тит (дрожь)** I'm shaking all over
▶ **колоти́ться** *несов возв (сердце)* to thump; **~ся** *(impf)* **в дверь** to thump on the door.
ко́лот|ый *прил*: **~ са́хар** lump sugar; **~ая ра́на** stab wound.
кол|о́ть (-ю́, -ешь; *perf* **расколо́ть**) *несов перех (дрова)* to chop (up); *(орехи)* to crack; *(perf* **заколо́ть**; *штыком итп)* to spear; *(perf* **уколо́ть**; *иголкой итп)* to prick; *(разг: делать укол)*: **~ кого́-н** to give sb an injection; **~** *(impf)* **кому́-н что́-н** *(разг)* to inject sb with sth; **у меня́ ко́лет в боку́** I've got a stitch; **пра́вда глаза́** the truth is hard to swallow
▶ **коло́ться** *несов возв (ёж, шиповник)* to be prickly; *(орех)* to crack; *(наркоман)* to be on drugs.
колочу́(сь) *несов см* **колоти́ть(ся)**.

колпа́к (-а́) *м (шутовской, поварской)* hat; *(лампы)* lampshade.
колпач|о́к (-ка́) *м уменьш от* **колпа́к**; *(контрацептив)* (Dutch) cap.
колумби́йск|ий (-ая, -ое, -ие) *прил* Columbian.
Колу́мби|я (-и) *ж* Columbia.
колупа́|ть (-ю) *несов перех (разг)* to scratch.
колхо́з (-а) *м* kolkhoz, collective farm.
колхо́зник (-а) *м* kolkhoznik, collective farmer.
колхо́зный *прил* kolkhoz *опред*, collective farm *опред*.
колча́н (-а) *м* quiver.
колчеда́н (-а) *м* pyrite.
колыбе́ль (-и) *ж (также перен)* cradle; **с ~и** *(перен)* from the cradle.
колыбе́льн|ая (-ой; *decl like adj*) *ж (также:* **~ пе́сня**) lullaby.
колыма́г|а (-и) *ж (разг: машина)* old banger.
колыха́ни|е (-я) *ср* rocking, swaying.
колых|а́ть (-ы́шу, -ы́шешь) *несов перех* to rock
▶ **колыха́ться** *несов возв (море, грудь)* to heave; *(трава, дерево)* to sway.
ко́лышек (-ка) *м уменьш от* **кол**; *(для палатки)* (tent) peg.
колы́шу(сь) *итп несов см* **колыха́ть(ся)**.
колье́ *ср нескл* necklace.
кольн|у́ть (-у́, -ёшь) *сов перех (иголкой)* to prick; *(перен: обидным намёком)* to sting; **у меня́ ~у́ло в спине́** a pain shot up my back.
кольра́би *ж нескл* kohlrabi.
кольт (-а) *м* automatic (revolver).
кольцева́ть (-у́ю) *несов перех* to ring.
кольцево́й *прил* round, circular; **кольцева́я доро́га** ring road; **кольцева́я ли́ния** circle line.
кольц|о́ (-ца́; *nom pl* -ьца, *gen pl* -е́ц) *ср* ring; *(в маршруте автобуса итп)* circle.
кольчу́г|а (-и) *ж (ИСТ)* chain-mail shirt.
ко́лья *сущ см* **кол**.
колю́чк|а *сущ см* **колю́чка**.
колю́ч|ий (-ая, -ее, -ие; -, -а, -е) *прил (куст, усы, мороз)* prickly; *(перен: насмешка, замечание, юмор)* barbed; **колю́чая про́волока** barbed wire.
колю́ч|ка (-ки; *gen pl* -ек) *ж (чертополоха, розы)* thorn; *(проволоки)* barb.
коля́дк|а (-ки; *gen pl* -ок) *ж* ≈ Christmas carol *(sung in rural Russia)*.
колядова́ть (-у́ю) *несов неперех* ≈ to go carol singing.
коля́док *сущ см* **коля́дка**.
коля́с|ка (-ки; *gen pl* -ок) *ж (экипаж)* carriage; *(детская)* pram (*BRIT*), baby carriage (*US*); *(инвалидная)* wheelchair.
ком *мест см* **кто** ♦ (-а; *nom pl* -ья, *gen pl* -ьев) *м* lump; **у меня́ ~ к го́рлу подкати́л** I felt a lump in my throat; **пе́рвый блин ко́мом ...** *(перен)* ≈ if at first you don't succeed ....
ко́м|а (-ы) *ж* coma.

кома́нд|**а** (-ы) ж command; (*судна*) crew; (*СПОРТ*) team; **пожа́рная** ~ fire brigade; ~ **президе́нта** presidential team; **быть** (*impf*) **под** ~**ой кого́-н** to be under sb.

команди́р (-а) м commander, commanding officer.

командиро́ванн|**ый** (-ого; *decl like adj*) м = **командиро́вочный**.

командиро́ва́ть (-у́ю) (*не*)*сов перех* to post; **его́** ~**ова́ли в Москву́** he has been posted to Moscow.

командиро́в|**ка** (-ки; *gen pl* -ок) ж (*коро́ткая*) business trip; (*дли́тельная*) secondment (*BRIT*), posting; **е́хать** (**пое́хать** *perf*) **в** ~**ку** to go away on business; **получа́ть** (**получи́ть** *perf*) ~**ку** to be seconded (*BRIT*) *или* posted.

командиро́вочн|**ые** (-ых; *decl like adj*) мн (*де́ньги*) subsistence allowance *ед*.

командиро́вочн|**ый** *прил*: ~**ое удостовере́ние** permit issued to employee travelling on official business ♦ (-ого; *decl like adj*) м person on business.

кома́ндн|**ый** *прил* command *опред*; (*до́лжность*) managerial; (*СПОРТ*): ~**ое состяза́ние** team event; ~**ые высо́ты** (*ВОЕН, перен*) key positions; **кома́ндный соста́в** (*ВОЕН*) command personnel.

кома́ндовани|**е** (-я) *ср*: ~ (+*instr*) (*судном, во́йском*) command (of) ♦ *собир* (*ВОЕН*) command.

кома́нд|**овать** (-ую; *perf* **скома́ндовать**) *несов непере́х* to give orders; (*no perf*; +*instr*; *а́рмией*) to command; (*му́жем*) to order around.

кома́ндующ|**ий** (-его; *decl like adj*) м commanding officer, commander.

кома́р (-а́) м mosquito (*мн* mosquitoes); ~ **но́са не подто́чит** you can't fault it.

комато́зный *прил* comatose.

комба́йн (-а) м (*С -X*) combine (harvester); **кухо́нный** ~ food processor.

комбайнёр (-а) м combine operator.

комбико́рм (-а) м *сокр* (= **комбини́рованный корм**) mixed fodder.

комбина́т (-а) м plant; **моло́чный/пищево́й** ~ dairy-/food-processing plant.

комбина́ци|**я** (-и) ж combination; (*разг: план*) scheme; (*ШАХМАТЫ*) position; (*же́нское бельё*) slip.

комбинезо́н (-а) м overalls *мн*; (*де́тский*) dungarees *мн*.

комбини́рованный *прил* (*ме́тод, подхо́д*) integrated.

комбини́р|**овать** (-ую; *perf* **скомбини́ровать**) *несов перех* (*блю́да*) to combine; (*оде́жду*) to match up ♦ *непере́х* (*разг*) to scheme.

комедиа́нт (-а) м (*также перен*) comedian.

комедиа́нт|**ка** (-ки; *gen pl* -ок) ж comedienne.

комеди́йный (-ен, -йна, -йно) *прил* comic; (*актёр*) comedy *опред*.

коме́ди|**я** (-и) ж comedy; (*перен: смешно́е собы́тие*) farce; **лома́ть** (*impf*) ~**ю** to play-act.

коменда́нт (-а) м (*общежи́тия, тюрьмы́*) warden; (*ВОЕН*) commandant.

коменда́нтск|**ий** (-ая, -ое, -ие) *прил*: ~ **час** curfew.

комендату́р|**а** (-ы) ж (*ВОЕН*) commandant's office.

коме́т|**а** (-ы) ж comet.

коми́зм (-а) м comedy; ~ **ситуа́ции** the funny side of the situation.

ко́мик (-а) м (*актёр*) comedian, comic; (*разг: смешно́й челове́к*) comedian. =

Коминте́рн (-а) м *сокр* (*ИСТ*: = **Коммунисти́ческий Интернациона́л**) Comintern.

комисса́р (-а) м (*ИСТ: также:* **Наро́дный К**~) People's Commissar; (*мили́ции ООН*) commissioner.

комиссионе́р (-а) м agent.

комиссио́н|**ка** (-ки; *gen pl* -ок) ж (*разг*) second-hand shop which sells goods on a commission basis.

комиссио́нн|**ые** (-ых; *decl like adj*) мн commission.

комиссио́нный *прил*: ~ **магази́н** = **комиссио́нка**.

комиссио́нок *сущ см* **комиссио́нка**.

коми́сси|**я** (-и) ж (*ПОЛИТ, КОММ*) commission; **брать** (**взять** *perf*) **что-н на** ~**ю** to take sth on commission; **постоя́нная** ~ standing committee.

комите́т (-а) м committee; **Комите́т Госуда́рственной Безопа́сности** (*ИСТ*) the KGB.

коми́чен *прил см* **коми́чный**.

коми́ческий (-ая, -ое, -ие) *прил* comic; ~ **актёр** comic actor.

коми́чный (-ен, -на, -но) *прил* comical.

комка́ *сущ см* **комо́к**.

ко́мка|**ть** (-ю; *perf* **ско́мкать**) *несов перех* (*письмо́, бельё итп*) to crumple; (*перен: ле́кцию итп*) to make a mess of.

коммента́ри|**й** (-я) м (*поясне́ние, репорта́ж*) commentary; **дава́ть** (**дать** *perf*) ~ **к чему́-н** to provide a commentary on sth; ~**и изли́шни** it speaks for itself.

коммента́тор (-а) м commentator.

комменти́р|**овать** (-ую) (*не*)*сов перех* (*текст*) to comment on; (*собы́тия, матч*) to commentate on.

коммерса́нт (-а) м businessman (*мн* businessmen).

комме́рческ|**ий** (-ая, -ое, -ие) *прил* commercial; **комме́рческий банк** commercial bank; **комме́рческий дире́ктор** sales and finance director; **комме́рческий магази́н** privately-run shop.

коммивояжёр (-а) м travelling (*BRIT*) *или* traveling (*US*) salesman (*мн* salesmen).

комму́н|**а** (-ы) ж commune.

коммуна́л|**ка** (-ки; *gen pl* -ек) ж (*разг*) communal flat (*BRIT*) *или* apartment (*US*).

коммунáльный *прил* communal;
коммунáльная квартúра communal flat (*BRIT*)
или apartment (*US*); **коммунáльные платежú**
bills; **коммунáльные услýги** utilities.
коммунáр (-а) *м* (*ИСТ*) member of a commune.
коммунúзм (-а) *м* communism.
коммуникáбель|ный (-ен, -ьна, -ьно) *прил*
sociable.
коммуникатúвный *прил* (*методы*)
communicative.
коммуникациóнн|ый *прил*: ~**ая лúния** line of
communication.
коммуникáци|я (-и) *ж* communication.
коммунúст (-а) *м* communist.
коммунистúческ|ий (-ая, -ое, -ие) *прил*
communist.
коммунúст|ка (-ки; *gen pl* -ок) *ж см* **коммунúст**.
коммутáтор (-а) *м* (*ТЕЛ*) switchboard; (*ЭЛЕК*)
commutator.
коммутациóнн|ый *прил*: ~**ая доскá**
switchboard.
коммутáци|я (-и) *ж*: ~ **пакéтов/сообщéний**
(*КОМП*) packet/message switching.
коммюникé *ср нескл* communiqué.
кóмнат|а (-ы) *ж* room; **кóмната мáтери и**
ребёнка *room for mothers with young children*.
кóмнатный *прил* indoor *опред*; **кóмнатная**
температýра room temperature; **кóмнатное**
растéние house plant.
комóд (-а) *м* chest of drawers.
ком|óк (-кá) *м уменьш от* **ком**; (*ваты*) wad; ~
бумáги crumpled-up piece of paper; **он** – ~
нéрвов he's a bag *или* bundle of nerves.
компáкт-дúск (-а) *м* compact disc.
компáкт|ный (-ен, -на, -но) *прил* compact;
(*изложение, доклад*) concise.
компанéйск|ий (-ая, -ое, -ие) *прил* (*разг*): **он** ~
пáрень he's good company.
компáни|я (-и) *ж* (*друзья*) group of friends;
(*КОММ*) company; **вы́пей со мной за** ~**ю** have a
drink, to keep me company; **он тебé не** ~ he's
not the right company for you.
компаньóн (-а) *м* companion; (*КОММ*) partner.
компаньóн|ка (-ки; *gen pl* -ок) *ж* (*старой дамы*)
companion.
компáрти|я (-и) *ж* Communist party.
кóмпас (-а) *м* compass.
компенсациóнный *прил* compensatory.
компенсáци|я (-и) *ж* compensation.
компенсúр|овать (-ую) (*не*)*сов перех* to
compensate.
компетéнтен *прил см* **компетéнтный**.
компетéнтност|ь (-и) *ж* competence.
компетéнт|ный (-ен, -на, -но) *прил* competent;
(*соответствующий*) appropriate.
компетéнци|я (-и) *ж* jurisdiction; **э́то не вхóдит**
в нáшу ~**ю** that is outside our jurisdiction.
компилúр|овать (-ую; *perf* **скомпилúровать**)

несов перех (*пренебр*) to cobble together.
компилятúв|ный (-ен, -на, -но) *прил*: ~ **труд**
compilation.
компилятор (-а) *м* hack (writer).
компиляци|я (-и) *ж* rehash.
кóмплекс (-а) *м* (*упражнений, мер, знаний итп*)
range; **спортúвный** ~ sports complex;
кóмплекс неполноцéнности inferiority
complex.
кóмплексный *прил* integrated; (*соединение,*
число) complex.
комплéкт (-а) *м* set.
комплектáци|я (-и) *ж* assembly; **отдéл** ~**и** (*в*
библиотеке) acquisitions (department).
комплект|овáть (-ýю; *perf* **укомплектовáть**)
несов перех to build up.
комплéкци|я (-и) *ж* build (*of person*).
комплимéнт (-а) *м* compliment; **дéлать**
(**сдéлать** *perf*) **комý-н** ~ to pay sb a compliment;
говорúть (*impf*) ~**ы** (**комý-н**) to pay (sb)
compliments.
композúтор (-а) *м* composer.
композициóнный *прил* compositional.
композúци|я (-и) *ж* composition.
компонéнт (-а) *м* component.
компон|овáть (-ýю; *perf* **скомпоновáть**) *несов*
перех to arrange, set out.
компонóвк|а (-и) *ж* (*материалов*) arranging.
компóст (-а) *м* compost.
компóстер (-а) *м* ticket punch.
компостúр|овать (-ую; *perf*
закомпостúровать) *сов перех* to punch *или*
clip (*ticket*).
компóстн|ый *прил*: ~**ая я́ма** compost pit.
компóт (-а) *м* compote.
компрéсс (-а) *м* (*МЕД*) compress.
компрéссор (-а) *м* (*ТЕХ*) compressor.
компрометúр|овать (-ую; *perf*
скомпрометúровать) *несов перех* to
compromise.
компрометúрующ|ий (-ая, -ое, -ие) *прил*
(*поступок, слова*) damaging.
компромúсс (-а) *м* (*соглашение*) compromise;
идтú (**пойтú** *perf*) **на** ~ to (make a) compromise;
приходúть (**прийтú** *perf*) **к** ~**у** to come to a
compromise.
компромúссный *прил* compromise *опред*.
компью́тер (-а) *м* computer.
компью́терный *прил* computer *опред*.
комсомóл (-а) *м* Komsomol (*communist youth*
organization).
комсомóл|ец (-ьца) *м* komsomol member.
комсомóл|ка (-ки; *gen pl* -ок) *ж см*
комсомóлец.
комсомóльск|ий (-ая, -ое, -ие) *прил* komsomol
опред.
комсомóльца *сущ см* **комсомóлец**.
комý *мест см* **кто**.

комфóрт (-а) м comfort.

комфортáбел|ьный (-ен, -ьна, -ьно) прил comfortable.

комьéв итп сущ см ком.

кон (-á; nom pl -ы, gen pl -óв) м (партия) round; (для ставки) kitty; (место: в городках) wicket.

конвéйер (-а) м conveyor (belt); **постáвить** (perf) что-н на ~ to mass-produce sth; (перен) to churn sth out.

конвéйерн|ый прил: ~ая лéнта conveyor belt.

конвéнци|я (-и) ж convention.

конвергéнци|я (-и) ж convergence.

конвéрси|я (-и) ж conversion.

конвéрт (-а) м (почтовый) envelope; (для младенца) baby nest.

конвертú|ровать (-ую) (не)сов перех to convert.

конвертúруемый прил convertible.

конвоúр (-а) м escort.

конвоú|ровать (-ую) несов перех to escort.

конвó|й (-я) м escort; **под ~ем** under escort.

конвóйн|ый прил escort опред ♦ (-ого; decl like adj) м escort.

конвýльси|я (-и) ж convulsion.

конгломерáт (-а) м conglomerate.

Кóнго ср нескл Congo (river and state).

конголéзск|ий (-ая, -ое, -ие) прил Congolese.

конгрéсс (-а) м (съезд) congress; (в США) Congress.

конгрессмéн (-а) м Congressman (мн Congressmen).

конденсáтор (-а) м condenser.

конденсáци|я (-и) ж condensation.

конденсú|роваться (3sg -уется, 3pl -уются) (не)сов возв to condense.

кондúтер (-а) м confectioner.

кондúтерск|ая (-ой; decl like adj) ж confectioner's.

кондúтерск|ий (-ая, -ое, -ие) прил confectionery опред: **кондúтерский магазúн** confectioner's.

кондиционéр (-а) м air conditioner.

кондициóнный прил (условия поставки) conditional; (продукт, овощи итп) up to standard.

кондúци|я (-и) ж standard; **я сейчáс не в ~и** (разг) I'm not in good shape at the moment; **доводúть** (довестú perf) что-н до ~и to bring sth up to scratch.

кондóвый прил diehard опред.

кондрáшк|а (-и) ж: **егó хватúла ~** (разг) he had a fit.

кондýктор (-а) м (автобуса) conductor; (поезда) guard.

коневóд (-а) м horse-breeder.

коневóдств|о (-а) ср horse-breeding.

конёк (-ькá) м уменьш от конь; (обычно мн: спорт) skate; (перен: любимая тема) hobbyhorse; **катáться** (impf) на ~ькáх to skate; **садúться** (impf) **на своегó ~ькá** to get on(to) one's hobbyhorse; **морскóй ~** sea horse; см

также **конькú**.

кон|éц (-цá) м end; **без ~цá** endlessly; **из концá в ~** from end to end; **и дéло с ~цóм** (разг) and that's the end of it; **в ~цé концóв** in the end; **билéт в одúн ~** single (BRIT) или one-way ticket; **мне ~** (разг) I'm done for; **сводúть** (impf) **~цы с ~цáми** to make ends meet; **на худóй ~** (разг) if the worst comes to the worst; **под ~** towards the end; **отдáть** (perf) **~цы** (разг) to kick the bucket.

конéчно вводн сл of course, certainly; **мне мóжно закурúть? – ~** may I smoke? – of course.

конéчность (-и) ж (обычно мн) limb.

конéчн|ый (-ен, -на, -но) прил (цель, итог) final; (станция, остановка) last; **в ~ом счёте** или **итóге** in the final analysis; **конéчный пóльзователь** (комп) end user.

конúн|а (-ы) ж horse meat.

конúческий (-ая, -ое, -ие) прил conical.

конкрéтен прил см конкрéтный.

конкретизú|ровать (-ую) (не)сов перех: что-н to make sth more concrete.

конкрéтно нареч (говорить) specifically.

конкрéтн|ый (-ен, -на, -но) прил (реальный) concrete; (факт) actual.

конкурéнт (-а) м competitor.

конкурéнтк|а (-и) ж см конкурéнт.

конкурéнтн|ый прил: ~ая борьбá competition.

конкурентоспосóбн|ый (-ен, -на, -но) прил competitive.

конкурéнци|я (-и) ж competition; **наш товáр вне ~и** our product is in a class of its own.

конкурú|ровать (-ую) несов неперех: ~ с +instr to compete with.

кóнкурс (-а) м competition; **проходúть** (пройтú perf) **вне ~а** to be admitted to university etc under special provisions; **проходúть** (пройтú perf) **по ~у** to attain the pass mark.

кóнкурсн|ый прил competition опред; ~ая **комúссия** (в университете) examining committee; (в состязании) judging panel; **кóнкурсный экзáмен** entrance examination.

кóнниц|а (-ы) ж cavalry.

конногвардéе|ц (-йца) м cavalryman (мн cavalrymen).

коннозавóдчик (-а) м stud-farm owner.

кóнный прил (двор, сбруя) horse опред; **кóнная áрмия** cavalry; **кóнный завóд** stud farm; **кóнная милúция** mounted police.

конопá|тить (-чу, -тишь; perf законопáтить) несов перех (сруб, лодку, пол итп) to patch up.

конопá|тый (-, -а, -о) прил (разг: веснушчатый) freckled.

конопá|чу несов см конопáтить.

конопл|я (-и) ж hemp.

конопля́ный прил hemp.

коносáмент (-а) м bill of lading.

консерватúвность (-и) ж conservatism.

консерватúвн|ый (-ен, -на, -но) прил conservative.

консерва́тор (-а) *м* conservative; (*полит*) Conservative.

консервато́ри|**я** (-и) *ж* (*муз*) conservatoire (*BRIT*), conservatory (*US*).

консерва́ци|**я** (-и) *ж* (*стройки*) suspension; (*продуктов, здания*) preservation.

консерви́ровани|**е** (-я) *ср* (*в жестяных банках*) canning; (*в стеклянных банках*) bottling.

консерви́рованный *прил* (*см сущ*) canned; bottled.

консерви́р|**овать** (-ую) (*не*)*сов перех* to preserve; (*в жестяных банках*) to can; (*в стеклянных банках*) to bottle; (*стройку*) to suspend.

консе́рвный *прил*: ~ **заво́д** canned-food factory; **консе́рвная ба́нка** can.

консе́рв|**ы** (-ов) *мн* canned food *ед*.

конси́лиум (-а) *м consultation between doctors about a patient*.

консисте́нци|**я** (-и) *ж* consistency.

ко́нск|**ий** (-ая, -ое, -ие) *прил* horse's.

консолида́ци|**я** (-и) *ж* consolidation.

консолиди́р|**овать** (-ую) (*не*)*сов перех* to consolidate.

консо́ль (-и) *ж* cantilever.

консо́рциум (-а) *м* consortium.

конспе́кт (-а) *м* notes *мн*.

конспекти́в|**ный** (-ен, -на, -но) *прил*: **в ~ной фо́рме** in note form.

конспекти́р|**овать** (-ую; *perf* **законспекти́ровать**) *несов перех* to take notes on.

конспирати́вный *прил* conspiratorial; **конспирати́вная кварти́ра** safe house.

конспира́тор (-а) *м* conspirator.

конспира́ци|**я** (-и) *ж* conspiracy.

констата́ци|**я** (-и) *ж*: ~ **фа́ктов** stating of the facts.

констати́р|**овать** (-ую) (*не*)*сов перех* to certify; (*факты*) to state.

конституцио́нный *прил* constitutional.

конститу́ци|**я** (-и) *ж* constitution.

констру́и́р|**овать** (-ую; *perf* **сконструи́ровать**) *несов перех* to construct.

констру́кти́вен *прил см* **констру́кти́вный**.

констру́кти́вность (-и) *ж* constructiveness.

констру́кти́в|**ный** (-ен, -на, -но; *замысл, идея*) constructive.

констру́ктор (-а) *м* designer; (*детская игра*) construction set; **инжене́р-~** mechanical engineer.

констру́кторск|**ий** (-ая, -ое, -ие) *прил*: ~**ое бюро́** design studio.

констру́кци|**я** (-и) *ж* construction.

ко́нсул (-а) *м* consul.

ко́нсульск|**ий** (-ая, -ое, -ие) *прил* consular.

ко́нсульств|**о** (-а) *ср* consulate.

консульта́нт (-а) *м* consultant.

консультацио́нный *прил* consultative.

консульта́ци|**я** (-и) *ж* (*у врача, у юриста*) consultation; (*учреждение*) consultancy; **же́нская ~** ≈ gynaecological and antenatal (*BRIT*) *или* gynecological and prenatal (*US*) clinic; **дава́ть (дать** *perf*) ~**ю кому́-н** to give professional advice to sb.

консульти́р|**овать** (-ую; *perf* **проконсульти́ровать**) *несов перех* to give professional advice to

▶ **консульти́роваться** (*impf* **проконсульти́роваться**) *несов возв*: ~**ся с кем-н** to consult sb.

конта́кт (-а) *м* contact.

конта́кт|**ный** (-ен, -на, -но) *прил* (*человек*) approachable; **конта́ктные ли́нзы** contact lenses; **конта́ктный телефо́н** contact number.

конте́йнер (-а) *м* container.

конте́кст (-а) *м* context; **в ~е** +*gen* in the context of.

континге́нт (-а) *м* contingent.

контине́нт (-а) *м* continent.

континента́льный *прил* continental.

конто́р|**а** (-ы) *ж* office.

конто́рск|**ий** (-ая, -ое, -ие) *прил* office *опред*; **конто́рская кни́га** account book.

ко́нтр|**а** (-ы) *ж* (*разг*): **быть в ~х с кем-н** to be at odds with sb.

контраба́нд|**а** (-ы) *ж* smuggling; (*товары*) contraband.

контрабанди́ст (-а) *м* smuggler.

контрабанди́стк|**а** (-ки; *gen pl* -**ок**) *ж см* **контрабанди́ст**.

контраба́ндный *прил* contraband.

контраба́с (-а) *м* double bass.

контрабаси́ст (-а) *м* double-bass player.

контрадмира́л (-а) *м* rear admiral.

контра́кт (-а) *м* contract; **фо́рвардный ~** (*КОММ*) forward contract.

контра́льто *ср нескл* contralto.

контрама́рк|**а** (-ки; *gen pl* -**ок**) *ж* ≈ complimentary ticket.

контрапу́нкт (-а) *м* counterpoint.

контра́ст (-а) *м* contrast.

контра́стен *прил см* **контра́стный**.

контрасти́р|**овать** (-ую) *несов неперех*: ~ **с** +*instr* to contrast with.

контра́ст|**ный** (-ен, -на, -но) *прил* contrasting.

контрата́к|**а** (-и) *ж* counterattack.

контрацепти́в (-а) *м* contraceptive.

контрацепти́вный *прил* contraceptive *опред*.

контрибу́ци|**я** (-и) *ж* reparations *мн*; **налага́ть (наложи́ть** *perf*) ~**ю** to exact reparations.

контрнаступле́ни|**е** (-я) *ср* counteroffensive.

контролёр (-а) *м* (*железнодорожный*) (ticket) inspector; (*театральный*) ≈ usher; (*сберкассы*) cashier.

контроли́р|овать (-ую) *несов перех* to control.
контро́л|ь (-я) *м* (*наблюде́ние*) monitoring; (*прове́рка*) testing, checking; (*в тра́нспорте*) ticket inspection; (*в магази́не*) checkout ◆ *собир* (*проверя́ющие*) inspectors *мн*; **па́спортный ~** passport control; **~ за це́нами** price control; **~ ка́чества** quality control.
контро́льн|ая (-ой; *decl like adj*) *ж* (*та́кже*: **~ рабо́та**) class test.
контро́льн|ый *прил*: **~ая коми́ссия** inspection team; **~ая рабо́та по** +*prp* class test in; **контро́льные ци́фры** control figures.
контрразве́д|ка (-и) *ж* counterespionage.
контрреволюционе́р (-а) *м* counter-revolutionary.
контрреволю́ци|я (-и) *ж* counter-revolution.
контрфо́рс (-а) *м* buttress.
конту́|зить (-жу, -зишь) *сов безл*: **его́ ~зило** he was contused.
конту́зи|я (-и) *ж* (*МЕД*) contusion.
ко́нтур (-а) *м* contour.
ко́нтурный *прил* contour *опред*; **ко́нтурная ка́рта** contour map.
конур|а́ (-ы́) *ж* (*соба́чья*) kennel; (*перен*: *ко́мната*) shoe box.
ко́нус (-а) *м* cone.
конусообра́з|ный (-ен, -на, -но) *прил* conical.
конферансье́ *ср нескл* compère.
конфере́нц-за́л (-а) *м* conference room.
конфере́нци|я (-и) *ж* conference.
конфе́т|а (-ы) *ж* sweet.
конфетти́ *ср нескл* confetti.
конфигура́ци|я (-и) *ж* configuration.
конфиденциа́льный (-ен, -ьна, -ьно) *прил* confidential.
конфиска́ци|я (-и) *ж* confiscation.
конфиск|ова́ть (-у́ю) (*не*)*сов перех* to confiscate.
конфли́кт (-а) *м* (*вое́нный*) conflict; (*в семье́, на рабо́те*) tension.
конфли́ктный *прил* (*ситуа́ция*) conflict *опред*.
конфликт|ова́ть (-у́ю) *несов непере́х*: **~ с** +*instr* (*разг*) to be at loggerheads with.
конфо́р|ка (-ки; *gen pl* -ок) *ж* ring (*on cooker*).
конфронта́ци|я (-и) *ж* confrontation.
конфу́жу(сь) *несов см* **конфу́зить(ся)**
конфу́з (-а) *м* embarrassment.
конфу́|зить (-жу, -зишь; *perf* **сконфу́зить**) *несов перех* to embarrass
▶ **конфу́зиться** (*perf* **сконфу́зиться**) *несов возв* to get embarrassed.
конц|а́ *итп сущ см* **коне́ц.**
концентра́т (-а) *м* (*о ко́рме*) concentrate; (*о руде́*) concentration.
концентрацио́нный *прил*: **~ ла́герь** concentration camp.
концентра́ци|я (-и) *ж* concentration.
концентри́рованный *прил* concentrated.
концентри́р|овать (-ую; *perf* **сконцентри́ровать**) *несов перех* to concentrate
▶ **концентри́роваться** (*perf* **сконцентри́роваться**) *несов возв* (*капита́л*) to

be concentrated; (*учени́к*) to concentrate.
концентри́ческ|ий (-ая, -ое, -ие) *прил* concentric.
конце́пци|я (-и) *ж* concept.
конце́рн (-а) *м* (*ЭКОН*) concern.
конце́рт (-а) *м* concert; **дава́ть (дать** *perf*) **~** to give a concert; **~ для фортепья́но с орке́стром** piano concerto.
концерти́р|овать (-ую) *несов непере́х* to give concerts.
концертме́йстер (-а) *м* (*МУЗ*) leader, concertmaster (*US*); (*аккомпаниа́тор*) accompanist.
конце́ртный *прил* concert *опред*.
конце́сси|я (-и) *ж* concession; **отдава́ть (отда́ть** *perf*) **что-н на ~ю** to grant sth as a concession.
концла́гер|ь (-я; *nom pl* -я́) *м сокр* concentration camp.
концо́в|ка (-ки; *gen pl* -ок) *ж* ending.
конча́|ть (-ю) *несов от* **ко́нчить**
▶ **конча́ться** *несов от* **ко́нчиться** ◆ *возв*: **~ся на** +*acc* to end in; **всё хорошо́, что хорошо́ ~ется** all's well that ends well.
конча́|я *предл* (+*instr*) to; **начина́я с кого́-н/чего́-н и ~ кем-н/чем-н** from sb/sth to sb/sth; **яви́лись все, ~ са́мыми да́льними ро́дственниками** everyone turned up, including the most distant relatives.
ко́нченый *прил*: **он ~ челове́к** he's a lost cause.
ко́нчик (-а) *м* tip.
кончи́н|а (-ы) *ж* end.
ко́нч|ить (-у, -ишь; *impf* **конча́ть**) *сов перех* (*жизнь, представле́ние, отноше́ния*) to end; (*университе́т, игру, кни́гу, рабо́ту*) to finish; **конча́ть (~** *perf*) +*instr* (*банди́том*) to end up as; (*пье́сой, слова́ми*) to finish with; **конча́ть (~** *perf*) **рабо́ту** *или* **рабо́тать** to finish work; **он пло́хо ~ил** he ended up in a bad way
▶ **ко́нчиться** (*impf* **конча́ться**) *сов возв* (*разгово́р, кни́га, игра́*) to end, finish; (*запа́сы, де́ньги*) to run out; (*пусты́ня, лес итп*) to end.
конъюнктиви́т (-а) *м* conjunctivitis.
конъюнкту́р|а (-ы) *ж* climate; **~ ры́нка** state of the market; **понижа́тельная ры́ночная ~** (*КОММ*) falling market; **пониже́ние/повыше́ние ~ы** downturn/upturn of the market; **он хорошо́ чу́вствует ~у** he is good at gauging the climate.
конъюнкту́рный *прил* (*соображе́ния*) tactical; **~ые це́ны** market prices *мн*.
конъюнкту́рщик (-а) *м* opportunist.
ко́н|ь (-я; *nom pl* -и, *gen pl* -е́й) *м* (*ло́шадь*) horse; (*ша́хматы*) knight; **быть** (*impf*) **на ~е́** to be on the ball.
конька́ *итп сущ см* **конёк.**
конь|ки́ (-о́в) *мн* skates *мн*; (*разг*: *вид спо́рта*) skating *ед*.
конькобе́ж|ец (-ца) *м* speed skater.
конькобе́жный *прил* speed-skating; **конькобе́жный спорт** speed skating.

конькобе́ж|ца итп сущ см конькобе́жец.
конья́к (-а́) м brandy, cognac.
ко́нюх (-а) м groom (at stable).
коню́ш|ня (-ни; gen pl -ен) ж stable.
кооперати́в (-а) м cooperative; (разг: кварти́ра) flat in housing cooperative; жили́щный ~ form of house or flat ownership.
кооперати́вный прил cooperative; ~ магази́н или ларёк co-op; ~ дом cooperative (form of house or flat ownership).
коопера́тор (-а) м member of a private enterprise.
коопера́ци|я (-и) ж cooperative enterprise; (труда́) co-operation; потреби́тельская ~ cooperative (society).
коопери́р|овать (-ую) (не)сов перех (труд. сре́дства) to organize through a cooperative.
кооптир|овать (-ую) (не)сов перех to coopt.
координа́т|а (-ы) ж (ГЕОМ: обычно мн) coordinate; (разг: местонахожде́ние) number (and address).
координа́ци|я (-и) ж (уси́лий) coordination.
координи́р|овать (-ую) (не)сов перех (де́йствия, уси́лия, движе́ния) to coordinate; ~ (impf/perf) произво́дство с тре́бованиями ры́нка to adjust production to meet the demands of the market.
коп. сокр = копе́йка.
копа́|ть (-ю) несов от вы́копать ♦ перех to dig; (выка́пывать) to dig up; ~ (impf) под +acc (разг) to cook up a scheme against
▶ копа́|ться несов возв (в огоро́де) to potter about; (в чужи́х веща́х) to snoop about; (разг: в душе́) to search; (: до́лго вози́ться) to dawdle.
копе́ек сущ см копе́йка.
копе́ечк|а (-и) ж: э́то тебе́ вста́нет в ~у it'll cost you a pretty penny.
копе́йк|а (-йки; gen pl -ек) ж kopeck; остава́ться (оста́ться perf) без ~йки to be left without a penny.
Копенга́ген (-а) м Copenhagen.
копи́л|ка (-ки; gen pl -ок) ж piggy bank.
копира́йт (-а) м copyright.
копира́йтный прил copyrighted.
копи́рк|а (-и) ж (разг) carbon paper; писа́ть (impf) под ~у to make a carbon copy of.
копирова́льно-мно́жительный прил copying опред.
копирова́льн|ый прил: ~ая маши́на photocopying machine, photocopier; копирова́льная бума́га carbon paper.
копи́р|овать (-ую; perf скопи́ровать) несов перех to copy.
коп|и́ть (-лю́, -ишь; perf накопи́ть или скопи́ть) несов перех to save; (перен: оби́ды) to harbour (BRIT), harbor (US)
▶ копи́ться (perf накопи́ться или скопи́ться) несов возв to accumulate.

ко́пи|я (-и) ж copy; (перен) spitting image; он ~ ~ своего́ отца́! he's the spitting image of his father; снима́ть (снять perf) ~ю с чего́-н to make a copy of sth.
коплю́(сь) несов см копи́ть(ся).
копн|а́ (-ы́; nom pl -ы) ж (се́на) stack; (воло́с) thatch.
копн|у́ть (-у́, -ёшь) несов перех to dig; (перен): е́сли ~ поглу́бже ... if you dig deeper ....
ко́пот|ь (-и) ж layer of soot.
копоши́ться (-у́сь, -и́шься) несов возв (мышь) to busy itself; (перен: подозре́ния) to stir; (вози́ться) to dawdle.
копт|е́ть (-чу́, -ти́шь) несов непepex to give off black smoke; (корпе́ть): ~ над +instr to pore over.
копт|и́ть (-чу́, -ти́шь) несов непepex (ла́мпа) to give off soot ♦ (perf закопти́ть) перех (мя́со. ры́бу) to smoke; ~ (impf) не́бо to fritter one's life away.
копу́ш|а (-и) м/ж (разг) slowcoach (BRIT), slowpoke (US).
копче́ни|е (-я) ср (ветчины) smoking; ры́ба горя́чего/холо́дного ~я fish smoked at a high/ low temperature; см также копче́нья.
копчёност|и (-ей) мн smoked food ед.
копчёный прил smoked.
копчён|ья (-ий) мн = копчёности.
ко́пчик (-а) м coccyx (мн coccyxes).
копы́т|о (-а) ср hoof (мн hooves).
коп|ьё (-ья́; nom pl -ья, gen pl -ий) ср spear; (СПОРТ) javelin; мета́ние ~ья javelin.
кор. сокр (= корреспонде́нт) corr. (= correspondent).
кор|а́ (-ы́) ж (де́рева) bark; (АНАТ) cortex; земна́я ~ the earth's crust; ~ головно́го мо́зга cerebral cortex.
корабе́льный прил ship's.
кораблестрое́ни|е (-я) ср shipbuilding.
кораблестрои́тел|ь (-я) м shipbuilder.
кораблестрои́тельный прил shipbuilding.
кора́бл|ь (-я́) м ship; сжига́ть (сжечь perf) свои́ корабли́ to burn one's boats.
кора́лл (-а) м coral.
кора́лловый прил (также цвет) coral; кора́лловый риф coral reef.
Кора́н (-а) м the Koran.
кордебале́т (-а) м corps de ballet.
кордо́н (-а) м cordon; за ~ом (разг) abroad.
коре́ец (-йца) м Korean.
корёж|ить (-у, -ишь; perf искорёжить или покорёжить) несов перех (разг) to twist; (no perf; перен): его́ поведе́ние меня́ ~ит his behaviour makes me cringe.
коре́йк|а (-и) ж smoked brisket of pork.
коре́йский (-ая, -ое, -ие) прил Korean.
корена́ст|ый (-, -а, -о) прил stocky.
корени́ться (3sg -и́тся, 3pl -я́тся) несов возв: ~

в +*prp* to be rooted in.
коренн|о́й *прил (население, традиции)* indigenous; *(вопрос, преобразования)* fundamental; **~ым о́бразом** fundamentally; **коренно́й зуб** molar.
ко́р|ень (**-ня**; *nom pl* **-ни**, *gen pl* **-не́й**) *м* root; **в ~не** fundamentally; **пресека́ть (пресе́чь** *perf***) что-н в ~не** to nip sth in the bud; **пуска́ть (пусти́ть** *perf***) ~ни** to put down roots; **подруба́ть (подруби́ть** *perf***) под ~** to uproot; **смотре́ть** (*impf*) **в ~ вопро́са/де́ла** to examine the root of the problem/matter.
коре́нь|я (**-ев**) *мн (БОТ)* roots *мн.*
ко́реш (**-а**) *м (разг)* mate, pal.
корешо́к (**-ка́**) *м уменьш от* **ко́рень**; *(чековой книжки)* counterfoil; *(переплёта)* spine.
коре́йца *итп сущ см* **коре́ец**.
Коре́|я (**-и**) *ж* Korea.
коре́я́н|ка (**-ки**; *gen pl* **-ок**) *ж см* **коре́ец**.
корж (**-а́**) *м* layer *(of a cake)*.
ко́ржик (**-а**) *м уменьш от* **корж**; *(пряник)* ≈ shortbread.
корзи́н|а (**-ы**) *ж* basket; **валю́тная ~** *(ЭКОН)* basket of currencies.
корзи́н|ка (**-ки**; *gen pl* **-ок**) *ж* (small) basket.
корзи́ноч|ка (**-ки**; *gen pl* **-ек**) *ж (КУЛИН)* tart.
корзи́нщик (**-а**) *м* basket weaver.
кориа́ндр (**-а**) *м* coriander.
коридо́р (**-а**) *м* corridor.
коридо́рн|ая (**-ой**; *decl like adj*) *ж* chambermaid.
коридо́рн|ый (**-ого**; *decl like adj*) *м* room attendant *(in hotel)*.
кор|и́ть (**-ю́, -и́шь**) *несов перех* to chastise.
корифе́|й (**-я**) *м* luminary.
кори́ц|а (**-ы**) *ж* cinnamon.
кори́чневый *прил* brown.
ко́р|ка (**-ки**; *gen pl* **-ок**) *ж уменьш от* **кора́**; *(апельсинная)* peel; *(на коже)* scab; **прочита́ть** *(perf)* **что-н от ~ки до ~ки** to read sth from cover to cover.
корм (**-а**; *nom pl* **-а́**) *м (для скота)* fodder, feed; *(диких животных)* food.
корм|а́ (**-ы́**) *ж* stern.
корм|ёжка (**-и**) *ж (разг: скота)* feeding; (: *еда*) grub.
корми́л|ец (**-ьца**) *м* breadwinner.
корми́л|ица (**-ы**) *ж* breadwinner; *(грудного ребёнка)* wet nurse.
корми́л|о (**-а**) *ср*: **стоя́ть** *или* **быть у ~а вла́сти** to be at the helm.
корми́льца *сущ см* **корми́лец**.
корм|и́ть (**-лю́, -ишь**) *несов перех* to feed; *(perf* **прокорми́ть**; *содержа́ть)* to feed, keep; *(perf* **накорми́ть**): **~ кого́-н (чем-н)** to feed sb (sth); **~** (*impf*) **гру́дью** to breast-feed; **его́ хле́бом не ~й, то́лько дай в футбо́л поигра́ть** he's never happier than when he's playing football
▸ **корм|и́ться** *(perf* **прокорми́ться**) *несов возв (животное)* to feed; (+*instr; человек*) to live on.
кормле́ни|е (**-я**) *ср* feeding.
кормлю́(сь) *несов см* **корми́ть(ся)**.

кормов|о́й *прил* (*С*-*Х*): **~ые сорта́** fodder crops; **кормова́я свёкла** beet; **кормово́е весло́** rudder.
корму́шк|а (**-и**) *ж (для скота)* trough; *(для птиц)* bird table; *(перен: разг)* slush fund.
корневи́щ|е (**-а**) *ср* rhizome.
корнепло́д (**-а**) *м* root vegetable.
корнепло́дн|ый *прил*: **~ое расте́ние** root plant.
корне́т (**-а**) *м* cornet.
ко́рня *итп сущ см* **ко́рень**.
ко́роб (**-а**) *м* rectangular basket; **с три ~а наговори́ть** *(perf)* to talk through one's hat; **с три ~а наобеща́ть** *(perf)* **кому́-н** to promise sb the earth.
коро́б|ить (**-лю, -ишь**; *perf* **покоро́бить**) *несов перех* to warp; **меня́ ~ит от его́ шу́ток** his jokes make me cringe
▸ **коро́б|иться** *(perf* **покоро́биться**) *несов возв* to warp.
коро́б|ка (**-ки**; *gen pl* **-ок**) *ж* box; *(остов дома)* frame; **коро́бка скоросте́й** gearbox.
коробка́ *сущ см* **коробо́к**.
коро́блю(сь) *несов см* **коро́бить(ся)**.
коро́бок *сущ см* **коро́бка**.
коробо́к (**-ка́**) *м*: **~ спи́чек** box of matches.
коро́боч|ка (**-ки**; *gen pl* **-ек**) *ж уменьш от* **коро́бка**; *(БОТ)* boll.
коро́в|а (**-ы**) *ж* cow; *(разг: пренебр)* silly cow; **до́йная ~** dairy cow.
коро́в|ий (**-ья, -ье, -ьи**) *прил*: **~ье молоко́** cow's milk.
коро́вник (**-а**) *м* cowshed.
коро́вниц|а (**-ы**) *ж* milkmaid.
ко́рок *сущ см* **ко́рка**.
короле́в|а (**-ы**) *ж (также ШАХМАТЫ, перен)* queen; **короле́ва красоты́** beauty queen.
короле́вский (**-ая, -ое, -ие**) *прил* royal.
короле́вств|о (**-а**) *ср* kingdom.
короле́|ёк (**-ька́**) *м (апельсин)* blood orange; *(хурма)* sharon fruit; *(ЗООЛ)* goldcrest.
коро́л|ь (**-я**) *м (также ШАХМАТЫ, КАРТЫ)* king.
королька́ *сущ см* **короле́к**.
коро́н|а (**-ы**) *ж* crown.
корона́рный *прил* coronary *опред.*
корона́ци|я (**-и**) *ж* coronation.
коро́нный *прил (разг)* best, favourite; **~ но́мер** party piece.
коронова́ни|е (**-я**) *ср* crowning.
корон|ова́ть (**-у́ю**) *(не)сов перех* to crown.
коро́ст|а (**-ы**) *ж* scab.
коросте́л|ь (**-я́**) *м* corncrake.
корота́|ть (**-ю**; *perf* **скорота́ть**) *несов перех (вечер, время итп)* to while away; *(свои дни, жизнь)* to live out.
коро́тк|ий (**-ая, -ое, -ие**; **ко́роток, коротка́, ко́ротко, ко́ротки**) *прил* short; *(отношения)* close; **у него́ ~ая па́мять** he has a short memory; **у него́ ру́ки коротки́** he's not up to it; **мы с ним на ~ой ноге́** we're on good terms; **коро́ткие во́лны** short wave; **коро́ткое**

замыка́ние short circuit.

ко́ротко *нареч* briefly; (*стри́чься*) short; (*узна́ть*) intimately ♦ *как сказ:* э́то пла́тье мне ~ this dress is too short for me.

коротково́лновый *прил* short-wave *опред.*

короткометра́жный *прил:* ~ фильм short (film).

коротконо́г|ий (-ая, -ое, -ие) *прил* short-legged.

ко́роток *прил см* **коро́ткий.**

короты́ш (-а́) *м* (*разг*) shorty.

коро́че *сравн прил от* **коро́ткий** ♦ *сравн нареч от* **ко́ротко;** ~ **говоря́** to put it briefly.

коро́чк|а (-и) *ж уменьш от* **ко́рка;** (*на пироге итп*) crust.

корп|е́ть (-лю́, -и́шь) *несов неперех:* ~ **над** +*instr* to slave away at.

корпорати́вный *прил* corporate.

корпора́ци|я (-и) *ж* corporation.

ко́рпус (-а; *nom pl* -ы) *м* body; (*самолёта*) fuselage; (*nom pl* -а́; *остов: су́дна, зда́ния*) frame; (*зда́ние*) block; (*ист: уче́бное заведе́ние*) academy; (*дипломати́ческий, офице́рский*) corps.

корре́ктен *прил см* **корре́ктный.**

корректи́в (-а) *м* (*попра́вка: обычно мн*) amendment; **вноси́ть** (**внести́** *perf*) ~ы **в план** to amend a plan.

корректи́р|овать (-ую; *perf* **скорректи́ровать**) *несов перех* (*оши́бку*) to correct; (*perf* **откорректи́ровать;** *ру́копись, статью́*) to proofread.

корректиро́в|ка (-ки; *gen pl* -ок) *ж* (*комп: обновле́ние*) update.

корре́кт|ный (-ен, -на, -но) *прил* correct.

корре́ктор (-а) *м* proofreader.

корректу́р|а (-ы) *ж* (*исправле́ние оши́бок*) proofreading; (*о́ттиск с набо́ра*) proofs *мн.*

корре́кци|я (-и) *ж* correction.

корреля́ци|я (-и) *ж* correlation.

корреспонде́нт (-а) *м* correspondent.

корреспонде́нт|ка (-ки; *gen pl* -ок) *ж см* **корреспонде́нт.**

корреспонде́нци|я (-и) *ж* correspondence.

корри́д|а (-ы) *ж* bullfight.

корроди́р|овать (*3sg* -ует, *3pl* -уют) (*не)сов неперех* to corrode.

коррози́йный *прил* corrosive.

корро́зи|я (-и) *ж* corrosion.

коррумпи́рован|ный (-, -а, -о) *прил* corrupt.

корру́пци|я (-и) *ж* corruption.

корса́ж (-а) *м* bodice.

корсе́т (-а) *м* corset.

корт (-а) *м* (tennis) court.

корте́ж (-а) *м* (*тра́урный*) cortege; (*сва́дебный*) procession.

ко́ртик (-а) *м* dagger, knife (*мн* knives).

ко́рточ|ки (-ек) *мн:* **присе́сть на** ~ to squat down; **сиде́ть** (*impf*) **на** ~ках to squat.

корч|ева́ть (-у́ю) *несов от* **вы́корчевать** ♦ *перех* to uproot.

ко́рч|ить (-у, -ишь; *perf* **ско́рчить**) *несов перех* to contort ♦ *безл:* его́ всего́ ~ило от бо́ли he was doubled up in pain; ~ (**ско́рчить** *perf*) ро́жу to pull a face; ~ (*impf*) из себя́ дурака́/свято́го (*разг*) to act the fool/saint

▶ **ко́рчиться** (*perf* **ско́рчиться**) *несов возв* (*от бо́ли, от сме́ха*) to writhe about.

ко́ршун (-а) *м* (*зоол*) kite.

коры́ст|ный (-ен, -на, -но) *прил* (*интере́с, цель*) mercenary; (*любо́вь*) selfish.

корыстолюби́в|ый (-, -а, -о) *прил* mercenary.

корыстолю́би|е (-я) *ср* greed.

коры́ст|ь (-и) *ж* (*вы́года*) gain; (*корыстолю́бие*) greed.

коры́т|о (-а) *ср* tub; **оста́ться** (*perf*) **у разби́того** ~а to end up with nothing.

кор|ь (-и) *ж* measles *мн.*

корю́ш|ка (-ки; *gen pl* -ек) *ж* smelt (*fish*).

коря́в|ый (-, -а, -о) *прил* (*де́рево, па́льцы*) gnarled; (*по́черк*) squiggly; (*перен: фра́зы, стиль*) clumsy.

коря́г|а (-и) *ж* dead branch (*мн* branches).

кос|а́ (-ы́; *acc sg* -у, *dat sg* -е́, *nom pl* -ы) *ж* (*во́лосы*) plait; (*ору́дие*) scythe; **заплета́ть** (*perf*) **ко́сы кому́-н** to plait sb's hair; **носи́ть** (*impf*) **ко́сы** to wear one's hair in plaits; **нашла́** ~ **на ка́мень** they are an equal match for each other.

коса́р|ь (-я́) *м* mower (*person*).

коса́т|ка (-и) *ж* killer whale.

ко́свенный *прил* indirect; (*дополне́ние, паде́ж*) oblique; **ко́свенная речь** indirect speech.

ко́сен *прил см* **ко́сный.**

коси́л|ка (-ки; *gen pl* -ок) *ж* mower (*machine*).

ко́синус (-а) *м* cosine.

ко|си́ть (-шу́, -сишь; *perf* **скоси́ть**) *несов перех* (*газо́н, се́но*) to mow; (*перен: подлеж: эпиде́мия, боле́знь*) to wipe out; (*рот, глаза́*) to twist; (*глаза́*) to slant; **у него́** ~сят глаза́ he has a slight squint; ~ (*impf*) **под** +*acc* (*разг*) to pretend to be

▶ **коси́ться** (*perf* **скоси́ться**) *несов возв* (*зда́ние*) to lean to one side; ~ся (*impf*) **на кого́-н** (*смотре́ть и́скоса*) to give sb a sidelong glance; (*перен*) to look askance at sb.

коси́ч|ка (-ки; *gen pl* -ек) *ж* pigtail.

косма́т|ый (-, -а, -о) *прил* shaggy.

косме́тик|а (-и) *ж* make-up ♦ *собир* cosmetics *мн.*

косме́тичек *сущ см* **косме́тичка.**

космети́ческ|ий (-ая, -ое, -ие) *прил* cosmetic; ~ **декори́рование** decorating; **космети́ческий кабине́т** beauty salon.

космети́ч|ка (-ки; *gen pl* -ек) *ж* (*челове́к*) beautician; (*су́мочка*) make-up bag.

космето́лог (-а) *м* (*та́кже:* врач-~) beautician.

космето́ло́ги|я (-и) *ж* cosmeticology.

косми́ческ|ий (-ая, -ое, -ие) *прил (полёт, ракета)* space *опред*; *(теория)* cosmic; **~ая ско́рость** *(перен)* terrific speed; **косми́ческий кора́бль** spaceship; **косми́ческое простра́нство** (outer) space.

космодро́м (-а) *м* spaceport.

космоло́ги|я (-и) *ж* cosmology.

космона́вт (-а) *м* cosmonaut; *(в США итп)* astronaut.

космона́втик|а (-и) *ж* space technology and exploration.

космополи́т (-а) *м* cosmopolitan.

космополити́зм (-а) *м* cosmopolitanism.

ко́смос (-а) *м* the cosmos.

ко́см|ы (-) *мн (разг)* tousled locks *мн*.

косне́|ть (-ю; *perf* **закосне́ть**) *несов неперех*: **~ (в +*prp*)** to stagnate (in).

ко́сность| (-и) *ж* intransigence.

косну́ться (-у́сь, -ёшься) *сов от* **каса́ться**.

ко́с|ный (-ен, -на, -но) *прил (ум, человек)* inflexible; *(среда, общество)* stagnant.

ко́со *нареч (расположить)* squint; **~ смотре́ть** *(impf)* **на +*acc* (перен)** to look askance at.

кособо́к|ий (-ая, -ое, -ие; -, -а, -о) *прил* lopsided.

косоворо́т|ка (-ки; *gen pl* -ок) *ж* traditional Russian shirt with a collar fastening at the side.

косогла́зи|е (-я) *ср* squint.

косогла́з|ый (-, -а, -о) *прил* cross-eyed.

косого́р (-а) *м* hillside.

кос|о́й (-а́, -о) *прил (глаза)* squinty; *(дождь, лучи)* slanting; **броса́ть** *(impf)* **~ы́е взгля́ды (на +*acc*)** to look askance (at); **у него́ ~а́я са́жень в плеча́х** *(разг)* he's built like an ox.

косола́п|ый (-, -а, -о) *прил (человек)* pigeon-toed.

костене́|ть (-ю; *perf* **закостене́ть**) *несов неперех* to go stiff.

костёр (-ра́) *м* campfire.

кости́ст|ый (-, -а, -о) *прил* bony.

костля́в|ый (-, -а, -о) *прил* bony.

ко́стный *прил (АНАТ):* **~ мозг** (bone) marrow.

ко́сточ|ка (-ки; *gen pl* -ек) *ж уменьш от* **кость**; *(абрикосовая, вишнёвая)* stone; *(винограда)* seed; *(лимона)* pip; **перемыва́ть** *(impf)* **~ кому́-н** *(разг)* to bitch about sb.

костра́ *сущ см* **костёр**.

косты́л|ь (-я́) *м (инвалида)* crutch (*мн* crutches); *(гвоздь)* spike.

кост|ь (-и; *prp sg* -и́, *gen pl* -е́й) *ж* bone; *(игральная)* dice (*мн* die); **лечь** *(perf)* **~ми́** *(погибнуть)* to lay down one's life; *(перен)* to do everything possible; **промока́ть** **(промо́кнуть** *perf*) **до ~éй** to get soaked to the skin.

костю́м (-а) *м* outfit; *(маскарадный, на сцене)* costume; *(пиджак и брюки/юбка)* suit; **брю́чный ~** trouser (*BRIT*) *или* pant (*US*) suit.

костюме́р (-а) *м* wardrobe assistant.

костюми́рованн|ый *прил:* **~ бал** costume ball.

костя́к (-а́) *м* skeleton; *(перен)* backbone.

костян|о́й *прил (нож, украшение)* bone; **~а́я му́ка** bone meal.

костя́ш|ка (-ки; *gen pl* -ек) *ж (пальцев)* knuckle; *(на счётах)* bead; *(домино)* domino.

косу́л|я (-и) *ж (ЗООЛ)* roe deer.

косы́н|ка (-ки; *gen pl* -ок) *ж* (triangular) scarf.

кося́к (-а́) *м (двери)* jamb; *(рыб)* school, shoal; *(птиц)* flock.

кот (-а́) *м* tomcat; **там хле́ба ~ напла́кал** *(разг)* there's hardly any bread left; **вся рабо́та пошла́ ко́ту под хвост** *(разг)* all the work has gone down the plughole; **~ в мешке́** a pig in a poke.

котёл (-ла́) *м (сосуд)* pot; *(паровой)* boiler; **о́бщий ~** kitty; **вари́ться** *(impf)* **в одно́м ~ле́** to live in each other's pockets.

котел|о́к (-ка́) *м уменьш от* **котёл**; *(походная кастрюля)* billycan; *(шляпа)* bowler (hat) (*BRIT*), derby (*US*).

коте́льн|ая (-ой; *decl like adj*) *ж* boilerhouse.

котёнок (-ёнка; *nom pl* -я́та, *gen pl* -я́т) *м* kitten.

ко́тик (-а) *м уменьш от* **кот**; *(тюлень)* fur seal; *(мех)* sealskin.

ко́тиковый *прил* sealskin.

коти́р|овать (-ую) *(не)сов перех (КОММ)* to quote

▸ **коти́роваться** *несов возв (КОММ):* **~ся (в +*acc*)** to be quoted (at); *(также перен)* to have a high value.

котиро́в|ка (-и) *ж (КОММ)* quotation.

коти́ться (*3sg* -и́тся, *perf* **окоти́ться**) *несов возв (кошка)* to have kittens; *(зайцы, кролики итп)* to give birth.

котла́ *сущ см* **котёл**.

котле́т|а (-ы) *ж* rissole; *(также: отбивна́я ~)* chop.

котлова́н (-а) *м* pit.

котлови́н|а (-ы) *ж (ГЕО)* basin.

кото́м|ка (-ки; *gen pl* -ок) *ж* knapsack; *(разг)* bag.

KEYWORD

кото́р|ый (-ая, -ое, -ые) *мест* **1** *(вопросительное)* which; **в кото́рый день он пришёл?** which day did he come?; **кото́рый час?** what time is it?

2 *(относительное: о предмете)* which; *(: о человеке)* who; **собы́тие, кото́рое нас потрясло́** an event which shook us; **ребёнок, у кото́рого моро́женое** the child who has the ice-cream; **челове́к, с кото́рым я говори́л** the person with whom I was speaking; **же́нщина, сы́на кото́рой я зна́ю** the woman whose son I know; **же́нщина, кото́рую я люблю́** the woman I love

3 *(не первый):* **кото́рый день/год мы не ви́делись** we haven't seen each other for many days/years.

котте́дж (-а) *м* cottage.

котя́та *итп сущ см* **котёнок**.

ко́фе *м нескл* coffee; **~ в зёрнах** coffee beans.

кофева́р|ка (-ки; *gen pl* -ок) *ж* percolator.

кофе́|ен *сущ см* **кофе́йня**.

кофеи́н (-а) *м* caffeine.

кофе́йник (-а) *м* coffeepot.

кофе́йн|ый *прил* coffee *мн*; **~ого цве́та** coffee-coloured; **кофе́йный серви́з** coffee service.
кофе́йня (-йни; *gen pl* -ен) *ж* coffee shop.
кофемо́л|ка (-ки; *gen pl* -ок) *ж* coffee grinder.
ко́фт|а (-ы) *ж* blouse; (*шерстяная*) cardigan.
коча́н (-á) *м*: **~ капу́сты** cabbage.
коче́в|а́ть (-у́ю) *несов неперех* (*также перен*) to lead a nomadic life; (*животные*) to roam.
коче́вник (-а) *м* nomad.
кочево́й *прил* nomadic.
коче́в|ье (-ья; *gen pl* -ий) *ср* nomad camp.
кочега́р (-а) *м* stoker.
кочега́р|ка (-ки; *gen pl* -ок) *ж* furnace room.
ко́чек *сущ см* **ко́чка.**
коченé|ть (-ю; *perf* **окоченéть**) *несов неперех* (*руки, труп*) to go stiff; (*человек*) to get stiff.
кочерг|á (-и́; *gen pl* -ёр) *ж* poker.
кочеры́ж|ка (-ки; *gen pl* -ек) *ж* heart (*of cabbage*).
ко́ч|ка (-ки; *gen pl* -ек) *ж* tussock.
коша́р|а (-ы) *ж* sheepfold.
коша́тник (-а) *м* cat-lover.
коша́тниц|а (-ы) *ж см* **коша́тник.**
коша́ч|ий (-ья, -ье, -ьи) *прил* (*также перен*) feline; (*мех, лапа*) cat's.
ко́шек *сущ см* **ко́шка.**
кошел|ёк (-ька́) *м* purse.
кошёл|ка (-ки; *gen pl* -ок) *ж* basket.
кошелька́ *сущ см* **кошелёк.**
ко́ш|ка (-ки; *gen pl* -ек) *ж* cat; (*скалолаза: обычно мн*) crampon; **~ки-мы́шки** (*игра*) tag; **игра́ть** (*impf*) **в ~ки-мы́шки с кем-н** (*перен*) to play cat and mouse with sb.
кошма́р (-а) *м* (*также перен*) nightmare.
кошма́р|ный (-ен, -на, -но) *прил* (*сон*) nightmarish; (*перен*) dreadful, nightmarish.
кошу́(сь) *несов см* **коси́ть(ся).**
кощé|й (-я) *м*: **~ бессме́ртный** *evil spirit in Russian fairytales.*
кощу́нствен|ный (-, -на, -но) *прил* blasphemous.
кощу́нств|о (-а) *ср* blasphemy.
кощу́нств|овать (-ую) *несов неперех* to blaspheme.
коэффициéнт (-а) *м* coefficient; **коэффициéнт поле́зного де́йствия** efficiency.
КПСС *ж сокр* (*ист*: = **Коммунисти́ческая па́ртия Сове́тского Сою́за**) CPSU (= *Communist Party of the Soviet Union*).
краб (-а) *м* crab.
кра́деный *прил* stolen.
краду́(сь) *итп несов см* **красть(ся).**
кра́дучись *нареч* stealthily.
краеве́д (-а) *м* local historian.
краеве́дение (-я) *ср* local studies *мн*.
краеве́дческий (-ая, -ое, -ие) *прил*: **~ музе́й** local-history museum.
краево́й *прил* regional.
краеуго́льный *прил* fundamental;

краеуго́льный ка́мень cornerstone.
кра́ж|а (-и) *ж* theft; **~ со взло́мом** burglary.
кра|й (-я; *loc sg* -ю́, *nom pl* -я́, *gen pl* -ёв) *м* edge; (*чашки, коробки*) rim; (*местность*) region; (*полит*) krai (*regional administrative unit*); **непоча́тый ~ рабо́ты** an endless amount of work; **на ~ све́та** to the ends of the earth; **на ~ю́ све́та** at the ends of the earth; **да́льние/тёплые ~я́** far-off/warm climes; **родно́й ~** native country; **находи́ться** (*impf*) **на ~ю́ ги́бели** to be on the verge of disaster; **кра́ем у́ха слу́шать** (*impf*) to half listen; **кра́ем у́ха слы́шать** (*impf*) to overhear; **хвати́ть** (*perf*) **че́рез ~** to go too far; **бить** (*impf*) **че́рез ~** to overflow.
кра́йне *нареч* extremely.
кра́йн|ий (-яя, -ее, -ие) *прил* extreme; (*дом*) end *опред*; (*пункт, маршрута*) last, final; **в ~ем слу́чае** as a last resort; **по ~ей ме́ре** at least; **кра́йний напада́ющий** winger; **Кра́йний Се́вер** the Arctic; **кра́йний срок** (final) deadline.
кра́йност|ь (-и) *ж* (*крайняя степень*) extremity; (*противоположное*) extreme; **броса́ться** (*impf*) **в ~и** to go from one extreme to the other; **твоё поведе́ние надое́ло мне до ~и** I find your behaviour tedious in the extreme.
кра́л|я (-и) *ж* (*разг: подруга*) chick; (: *красотка*) queen bee.
крамо́л|а (-ы) *ж* subversion; **говори́ть** (*impf*)/**писа́ть** (*impf*) **~y** to say/write subversive things.
крамо́льный *прил* subversive.
кран (-а) *м* tap, faucet (*US*); (*строит*) crane.
кранов|щи́к (-á) *м* crane operator.
кранов|щи́ц|а (-ы) *ж см* **крановщи́к.**
крапи́в|а (-ы) *ж* nettle.
крапи́вниц|а (-ы) *ж* (*мед*) nettle rash.
крапи́вный *прил*: **~ щи** nettle soup.
кра́пин|а (-ы) *ж* = **кра́пинка.**
кра́пин|ка (-ки; *gen pl* -ок) *ж* fleck, speck.
краплёный *прил* (*карты*) marked.
кра́пчатый (-, -а, -о) *прил* speckled.
крас|á (-ы́) *ж* beauty; (*перен*): **~ +gen** (*школы итп*) the pride of.
краса́в|ец (-ца) *м* handsome *или* good-looking man (*мн* men).
краса́виц|а (-ы) *ж* beautiful woman (*мн* women).
краса́в|ка (-и) *ж* deadly nightshade.
краса́вца *итп сущ см* **краса́вец.**
кра́сен *прил см* **кра́сный.**
краси́вост|ь (-и) *ж* superficial beauty.
краси́вый (-, -а, -о) *прил* beautiful; (*мужчина*) handsome; (*решение, фраза, слова*) fine.
краси́льный *прил* dye *опред*; **краси́льные вещества́** dyestuffs.
краси́тель (-я) *м* dye.
кра́|сить (-шу, -сишь; *perf* **покра́сить**) *несов перех* to paint; (*волосы*) to dye; (*perf* **накра́сить**; *щёки, губы итп*) to paint; (*no perf;*

перен: украшать) to adorn; **тако́е поведе́ние тебя́ не ~сит** such behaviour does not become you

▸ **кра́ситься** (*perf* **покра́ситься**) *несов возв* to be covered in paint; (*разг: пачкать*) to run; (*perf* **накра́ситься**) to wear make-up.

кра́ск|а (-**ки**; *gen pl* -**ок**) *ж* paint; (*обычно мн: не́жные, весе́нние итп*) colour (*BRIT*), color (*US*); (*стыда*) blush; **опи́сывать (описа́ть** *perf*) **что-н чёрными ~ми** to paint a gloomy picture of sth.

красне́|ть (-**ю**; *perf* **покрасне́ть**) *несов неперех* to turn red; (*от стыда*) to blush, flush; (*от гне́ва*) to go red; (*перен*): ~ **пе́ред кем-н за кого́-н** to be ashamed of sb in front of sb; ~ (*impf*) **до корне́й воло́с** to blush to the roots of one's hair.

красноарме́|ец (-**йца**) *м* (*ист*) Red-Army soldier.

краснобай (-**я**) *м* (*разг*) waffler.

красногварде́|ец (-**йца**) *м* (*ист*) Red Guardsman (*мн* Guardsmen).

краснодере́вщик (-**а**) *м* cabinet-maker.

красноречи́в|ый (-, -**а**, -**о**) *прил* (*оратор, письмо*) eloquent; (*взгляд, жест*) expressive; (*цифры, факты*) revealing.

красноре́чи|е (-**я**) *ср* eloquence.

краснот|а́ (-**ы**) *ж* (*лица*) redness; (*в го́рле*) inflammation.

краснощёк|ий (-**ая**, -**ое**, -**ие**) *прил* rosy-cheeked.

красну́х|а (-**и**) *ж* German measles.

кра́с|ный (-**ен**, -**на́**, -**но**) *прил* red; **проходи́ть** (*impf*) ~**ной ни́тью** *или* **ли́нией** to run through; **кра́сная а́рмия** Red Army; **кра́сная ры́ба** salmon; **кра́сная строка́** new paragraph; **кра́сное вино́** red wine; **кра́сное де́рево** mahogany; **кра́сный пе́рец** paprika.

красова́ться (-**у́юсь**) *несов возв* (*перед зе́ркалом, людьми*) to parade.

кра́сок *сущ см* **кра́ска**.

красот|а́ (-**оты́**; *nom pl* -**о́ты**) *ж* beauty; ~! wonderful!; *см также* **красо́ты**.

красо́тк|а (-**и**) *ж* pretty girl.

красо́т|ы (-) *мн* (*приро́ды*) beautiful scenery *ед*.

кра́соч|ный (-**ен**, -**на**, -**но**) *прил* (*язык, расцветка*) colourful (*BRIT*), colorful (*US*).

кра|сть (-**ду́**, -**дёшь**; *perf* **укра́сть**) *несов перех* to steal

▸ **кра́сться** *несов возв* (*человек*) to creep, steal.

кра́сящ|ий (-**ая**, -**ее**, -**ие**) *прил*: ~**ее вещество́** dye.

крат *нареч*: **во́ сто** ~ a hundred times.

кра́тер (-**а**) *м* crater.

кра́т|кий (-**кая**, -**кое**, -**кие**; -**ок**, -**ка́**, -**ко**) *прил* short; (*бесе́да*) brief, short; (*слова́рь, отчёт*) concise; ~**кое прилага́тельное** short-form adjective; **«и»** ~**кое** the 10th letter of the *Russian alphabet*

кратковре́мен|ный (-**ен**, -**на**, -**но**) *прил* short.

краткосро́ч|ный (-**ен**, -**на**, -**но**) *прил* (*о́тпуск,*

командиро́вка) short; (*заём, ссу́да*) short-term.

кра́ткост|ь (-**и**) *ж* brevity.

кра́тный *прил* divisible.

кра́ток *прил см* **кра́ткий**.

кра́тче *сравн прил см* **кра́ткий**.

крах (-**а**) *м* collapse; (*перен*) destruction.

крахма́л (-**а**) *м* starch.

крахма́л|ить (-**ю**, -**ишь**; *perf* **накрахма́лить**) *несов перех* to starch.

крахма́льный *прил* starched.

кра́ше *сравн прил от* **краси́вый**.

краше́ни|е (-**я**) *ср* dyeing.

краше́н|ый *прил* (*мех, ткань*) dyed; (*стол, дверь*) painted; ~**ая блонди́нка** (*разг*) peroxide blonde.

краш|у́(сь) *несов см* **кра́сить(ся)**.

краю́х|а (-**и**) *ж* (*разг: хле́ба*) doorstep.

креве́тк|а (-**и**) *ж* shrimp.

креди́т (-**а**) *м* credit; (*полити́ческий*) credibility; **в** ~ on credit; **превыша́ть (превы́сить** *perf*) ~ to overdraw; **брать (взять** *perf*) ~ **в ба́нке** to arrange an overdraft.

креди́тный *прил* credit *опред*; ~ **оста́ток на счёте** credit balance; **креди́тная ка́рточка** credit card; **креди́тный счёт** credit account.

кредит|ова́ть (-**у́ю**) (*не*)*сов перех* to grant credit to.

кредито́р (-**а**) *м* creditor; **незастрахо́ванный** ~ unsecured creditor.

кредито́рск|ий (-**ая**, -**ое**, -**ие**) *прил* creditor's.

кредитоспосо́бност|ь (-**и**) *ж* solvency.

кредитоспосо́бный *прил* solvent.

кре́до *ср нескл* credo.

кре́йсер (-**а**) *м* (*воен*) battleship, cruiser.

крейси́р|овать (-**ую**) *несов неперех* to sail (*along a specific route*); (*воен*) to patrol.

кре́кинг (-**а**) *м* (*нефти*) cracking.

крем (-**а**) *м* cream; **сапо́жный** ~ shoe polish.

кремато́ри|й (-**я**) *м* crematorium.

крема́ци|я (-**и**) *ж* cremation.

кре́м|ень (-**ня́**) *м* flint.

крем|и́ровать (-**ую**) (*не*)*сов перех* to cremate.

кремл|ь (-**я́**) *м* citadel; **К**~ the Kremlin.

кремнёвый *прил* flint.

кре́мни|й (-**я**) *м* silicon.

кремня́ *итп сущ см* **кре́мень**.

кре́мовый *прил* cream.

крен (-**а**) *м* (*судна*) list; (*самолёта*) bank; ~ **в сто́рону чего́-н** (*перен*) a move towards sth.

кре́ндел|ь (-**я**; *nom pl* -**я́**) *м* krendel (*sweet pastry*).

крен|и́ть (-**ю́**, -**и́шь**; *perf* **накрени́ть**) *несов перех* (*судно*) to list; (*самолёт*) to bank

▸ **крени́ться** (*perf* **накрени́ться**) *несов возв* (*судно*) to list; (*самолёт*) to bank.

креозо́т (-**а**) *м* creosote.

креп (-**а**) *м* crêpe.

крепдеши́н (-**а**) *м* crêpe de chine.

крепёжный *прил* reinforcing *опред*.

крепи́тельный *прил* (*тех*) reinforcing *опред*; ~**ое сре́дство** anti-diarrhoea tablets.

креп|и́ть (-**лю́**, -**и́шь**) *несов перех* to fix;

(*делать прочным*) to reinforce; **меня́ ~и́т** I'm constipated.

кре́п|кий (-кая, -кое, -кие; -ок, -ка́, -ко) *прил* strong; (*мороз, удар*) hard; **~ оре́шек** (*перен*) tough nut; **кре́пкие напи́тки** spirits.

кре́пко *нареч* strongly; (*спать, любить*) deeply; (*завязать*) tightly.

кре́пко-на́крепко *нареч* (*связать, закрыть*) as tightly as possible.

крепле́ни|е (-я) *ср* (*свай*) reinforcement; (*обычно мн: лыжные*) binding.

креплён|ый *прил*: **~ое вино́** fortified wine.

креплю́ *несов см* **крепи́ть**.

кре́п|нуть (-ну, -нешь; *pt* -, -ла, -ло, *perf* **окре́пнуть**) *несов неперех* to get stronger; (*уверенность*) to grow.

кре́пок *прил см* **кре́пкий**.

крепостни́к (-а́) *м* (*ИСТ*) serf owner.

крепостни́чество (-а) *ср* (*ИСТ*) serfdom.

крепостн|о́й *прил* (*ИСТ: отношения*) serf *опред*; (*башня, сооружение*) fortress *опред* ♦ (-о́го; *decl like adj*) *м* (*ИСТ: также:* **~ крестья́нин**) serf; **крепостно́е пра́во** (*ИСТ*) serfdom.

кре́пост|ь (-и) *ж* strength; (*ВОЕН*) fortress.

крепча́|ть (*3sg* -ет, *3pl* -ют) *несов неперех* (*мороз*) to harden; (*ветер*) to get stronger.

кре́пче *сравн прил от* **кре́пкий** ♦ *сравн нареч от* **кре́пко**.

крепы́ш (-а) *м* (*разг: ребёнок*) chubby chops.

кре́сл|о (-а; *gen pl* -ел) *ср* armchair; (*в театре*) seat.

кре́сло-крова́т|ь (-а, -и) *ж* ≈ sofa bed.

крест (-а́) *м* cross; **поста́вить** (*perf*) **~ на ком-н/чём-н** to give sb/sth up for lost.

крест|е́ц (-ца́) *м* sacrum.

крест|и́ (-) *мн* (*разг: КАРТЫ*) clubs *мн*.

крести́н|ы (-) *мн* christening *ед*, baptism *ед*.

крес|ти́ть (-щу́, -сти́шь; *perf* **окрести́ть**) *несов перех* to christen, baptize; **~ (перекрести́ть** *perf*) **кого́-н** to make the sign of the cross over sb; **~ (окрести́ть** *perf*) **кого́-н кем-н** to christen sb sth

▸ **крести́ться** (*не)сов возв* to be christened *или* baptized; (*perf* **перекрести́ться**; *крестить себя*) to cross o.s.

крест-на́крест *нареч* crosswise.

кре́стник (-а) *м* godson.

кре́стниц|а (-ы) *ж* goddaughter.

кре́стн|ый *прил*: **~ое зна́мение** sign of the cross; **~ ход** religious procession.

кре́стн|ый *прил*: **~ая мать** godmother; **~ оте́ц** godfather.

кресто́в|ый *прил*: **~ похо́д** crusade; **~ая да́ма/деся́тка** (*разг*) the queen/ten of clubs.

крестоно́с|ец (-ца) *м* crusader.

крестца́ *итп сущ см* **крестец**.

крестья́н|ин (-ина; *nom pl* -е, *gen pl* -) *м* peasant.

крестья́н|ка (-ки; *gen pl* -ок) *ж см* **крестья́нин**.

крестья́нск|ий (-ая, -ое, -ие) *прил* peasant *опред*.

крестья́нств|о (-а) *ср* peasantry.

крети́н (-а) *м* imbecile.

кре́чет (-а) *м* gerfalcon.

креще́ндо *нареч, ср нескл* crescendo.

креще́ни|е (-я) *ср* (*обряд*) christening, baptism; (*праздник*) ≈ the Epiphany; **он получи́л боево́е ~** (*перен*) he fought his first battle.

креще́нск|ий (-ая, -ое, -ие) *прил*: **~ пра́здник** the Epiphany; **~ие моро́зы** *coldest time of the year, traditionally following the Epiphany*.

крещу́(сь) (*не)сов см* **крести́ть(ся)**.

крив|а́я (-о́й; *decl like adj*) *ж* (*МАТ*) curve.

криве́|ть (-ю; *perf* **окриве́ть**) *несов неперех* to become cockeyed.

кривизна́ (-ы́) *ж* (*пола, потолка*) unevenness; (*линии, позвоночника*) curvature.

крив|и́ть (-лю́, -и́шь; *perf* **скриви́ть** *или* **покриви́ть**) *несов перех* to curve; (*лицо, губы*) to twist; **~ (покриви́ть** *perf*) **душо́й** to be insincere

▸ **криви́ться** (*perf* **скриви́ться**) *несов возв* (*забор, стена итп*) to lean; (*лицо, губы*) to twist; (*человек*) to slouch.

кривля́|ться (-юсь) *несов возв* (*гримасничать*) to squirm; (*манерничать*) to show off.

крив|о́й (-, -а́, -о) *прил* (*линия, палка, улыбка*) crooked; (*ноги*) bandy; (*разг: человек*) cockeyed; **~о́е зе́ркало** (*перен*) distorting mirror.

криволине́йный *прил* (*движение*) curvilinear.

кривоно́г|ий (-ая, -ое, -ие) *прил* bow-legged.

кривото́лк|и (-ов) *мн* gossip *ед*.

кри́зис (-а) *м* crisis; (*болезни*) critical point, crisis.

кри́зисный *прил* crisis *опред*.

крик (-а; *part gen* -у) *м* cry; (*человека*) shout, cry; (*птиц*) call, cry; **после́дний ~ мо́ды** (*разг*) the last word in fashion.

кри́кет (-а) *м* (*СПОРТ*) cricket.

крикли́в|ый (-, -а, -о) *прил* (*женщина, платье*) loud; (*голос*) yapping.

кри́кн|уть (-у, -ешь) *сов неперех* to shout.

крику́н (-а́) *м* (*разг*) bawler.

крику́н|ья (-ьи; *gen pl* -ий) *ж см* **крикун**.

кримина́л (-а) *м* (*разг*) criminal case; **я не ви́жу здесь ~а** I don't see anything criminal in it.

криминали́ст (-а) *м* specialist in crime detection.

криминали́стик|а (-и) *ж* crime detection.

кримина́льный *прил* (*случай*) criminal; (*история, хроника*) crime *опред*.

кримино́лог (-а) *м* criminologist.

криминоло́ги|я (-и) *ж* criminology.

кри́н|ка (-ки; *gen pl* -ок) *ж ceramic container for milk*.

криста́лен *прил см* **криста́льный**.

криста́лл (-а) *м* crystal.

кристаллиза́ция (-и) *ж* crystallization.

кристаллизова́ться (*3sg* -у́ется, *3pl* -у́ются, *perf* **вы́кристаллизоваться**) *(не)сов возв* to crystallize.

криста́льный (-ен, -ьна, -ьно) *прил* (*све́тлый*) crystal-clear; (*безупре́чный*) pure.

Крит (-а) *м* Crete.

крите́рий (-я) *м* criterion (*мн* criteria).

кри́тик (-а) *м* critic.

кри́тика (-и) *ж* criticism; **литерату́рная ~** literary criticism; **э́то не выде́рживает никако́й ~и** it doesn't stand up to criticism; **подверга́ть (подве́ргнуть** *perf*) **кого́-н/что-н ~е** to subject sb/sth to criticism.

критика́н (-а) *м* (*разг: пренебр*) nit-picker.

критикова́ть (-у́ю) *несов перех* to criticize.

критици́зм (-а) *м* criticism.

крити́чен *прил см* **крити́чный**.

крити́ческий (-ая, -ое, -ие) *прил* critical; **~ отде́л** review section; **~ая статья́** critique.

крити́чный (-ен, -на, -но) *прил* critical.

крича́ть (-у́, -и́шь) *несов неперех* (*птица*) to сгу; (*челове́к: от бо́ли, от гне́ва*) to cry (out); (: *говори́ть гро́мко*) to shout; **~** (*impf*) **на** +*acc* (*брани́ть*) to shout at.

крича́щий (-ая, -ое, -ие) *прил* (*перен: наря́ды*) loud; (: *рекла́ма*) eye-catching.

кров (-а) *м* shelter; **остава́ться (оста́ться** *perf*) **без кро́ва** to have no roof over one's head.

крова́вый *прил* (*ру́ки, оде́жда*) bloodied; (*нож*) bloodstained; (*ра́на, би́тва*) bloody; (*диктату́ра*) ruthless; **~ая ба́ня** blood bath; **~ бифште́кс** rare steak.

крова́тка (-ки; *gen pl* -ок) *ж* cot (*BRIT*), crib (*US*).

крова́ть (-и) *ж* bed.

кро́вель *сущ см* **кро́вля**.

кро́вельный *прил* roofing *опред*.

кро́вельщик (-а) *м* roofer.

кровено́сный *прил* blood *опред*.

кро́вля (-ли; *gen pl* -ель) *ж* roof; **жить** (*impf*) **под одно́й ~лей** to live under one roof.

кро́вный *прил* (*родство́*) blood *опред*; (*оби́да*) grave; **~ые интере́сы** vested interests; **~ враг** deadly enemy; **~ые де́ньги** blood money; **кро́вная месть** blood feud.

кровожа́ден *прил см* **кровожа́дный**.

кровожа́дность (-и) *ж* bloodthirstiness.

кровожа́дный (-ен, -на, -но) *прил* bloodthirsty.

кровоизлия́ние (-я) *ср* haemorrhage (*BRIT*), hemorrhage (*US*).

кровообраще́ние (-я) *ср* (*МЕД*) circulation.

кровооста́навливающий (-ая, -ее, -ие) *прил* (*сре́дства*) clotting *опред*.

кровопи́йца (-ы) *м/ж* bloodsucker.

кровоподтёк (-а) *м* blood blister.

кровопроли́тен *прил см* **кровопроли́тный**.

кровопроли́тие (-я) *ср* bloodshed.

кровопроли́тный (-ен, -на, -но) *прил* bloody.

кровопуска́ние (-я) *ср* (*та́кже МЕД*) blood-letting.

кровосмеше́ние (-я) *ср* incest.

кровотече́ние (-я) *ср* bleeding.

кровоточи́ть (*3sg* -и́т, *3pl* -а́т) *несов неперех* to bleed.

кровь (-и; *loc sg* -и́) *ж* blood; **го́лос кро́ви** call of the blood; **по́ртить** (*impf*) **~ кому́-н** (*разг*) to make sb's blood boil; **пролива́ть (проли́ть** *perf*) **(свою́) ~ за кого́-н/что-н** to sacrifice o.s. for sb/sth; **пролива́ть (проли́ть** *perf*) **чью-н ~** to spill sb's blood; **пить** (*impf*) **чью-н ~** to suck the lifeblood out of sb; **~ с молоко́м** *about a healthy, ruddy-faced person*; **плоть и ~ (чья)** (sb's) flesh and blood; **у меня́ се́рдце кро́вью облива́ется** my heart bleeds.

кровяно́й *прил* blood *опред*; **кровяна́я колбаса́** black pudding; **кровяно́е давле́ние** blood pressure.

крои́ть (-ю́, -и́шь) *несов перех* to cut out.

крокоди́л (-а) *м* crocodile.

крокоди́лов (-а, -о, -ы) *прил*: **~ы слёзы** crocodile tears *мн*.

крокоди́ловый *прил* crocodile *опред*.

кро́лик (-а) *м* rabbit; (*мех*) rabbit fur; **ша́пка из ~а** rabbit-fur hat.

кро́личий (-ья, -ье, -ьи) *прил* rabbit *опред*.

крольча́тник (-а) *м* rabbit hutch.

крольчи́ха (-и) *ж* doe (*rabbit*).

кро́ме *предл*: ~ +*gen* (*за исключе́нием*) except; (*сверх чего́-н*) as well as; ~ **того́** besides; ~ **него́ я никого́ не ви́дел** I haven't seen anyone except for *или* apart from him; ~ **соба́ки у них есть ещё и ко́шка** as well as a dog, they also have a cat; ~ **шу́ток** (*разг*) joking apart; **ему́ ничего́ оста́лось ~ как уйти́** (*разг*) he had no choice but to leave; ~ **как от тебя́, ни от кого́ не́ было пи́сем** I didn't get a letter from anyone except (for) you; ~ **того́, мне на́до идти́ на собра́ние** apart from that *или* besides I have to go to a meeting.

кроме́шный *прил*: **ад ~** hell on earth; **здесь тьма ~ая** it's pitch-black in here.

кро́мка (-и) *ж* (*тка́ни*) trim; (*льда, по́ля*) edge.

кромса́ть (-ю; *perf* **искромса́ть**) *несов перех* (*хлеб, материа́л*) to hack off; (*перен: ру́копись, пье́су*) to chop.

кро́на (-ы) *ж* (*де́рева*) crown; (*де́ньги*) krona.

кроншта́йн (-а) *м* (*балко́на*) support; (*ла́мпы, по́лки*) bracket.

кропа́ть (-ю; *perf* **на́кропать**) *несов перех* (*разг*) to scribble.

кропи́ть (-лю́, -и́шь; *perf* **окропи́ть**) *несов перех* (*РЕЛ*) to sprinkle (*with holy water*).

кропотли́вый (-, -а, -о) *прил* (*рабо́та*) painstaking; (*челове́к*) fastidious.

кросс (-а) *м* (*бег*) cross-country; (*го́нки*) cross-country race.

кроссво́рд (-а) *м* crossword.

кроссо́вка (-ки; *gen pl* -ок) *ж* (*обы́чно мн*) trainer.

крот (-а́) *м* mole.

кро́ткий (-кая, -кое, -кие; -ок, -ка́, -ко) *прил*

meek.

кротóвый *прил* moleskin.

крóток *прил см* **крóткий**.

крóтость (-и) *ж* meekness.

крóх|а (-и) *ж (обычно мн)* scrap ♦ *м/ж (ребёнок)* little one.

крохобóр (-а) *м* miser.

крохобóрств|о (-а) *ср (пренебр)* stinginess.

крóхотный (-ен, -на, -но) *прил* tiny.

крóшек *сущ см* **крóшка**.

крóшечный (-ек, -на, -но) *прил (разг)* teeny-weeny, tiny.

крош|ить (-ý, -ишь) *несов перех (хлеб)* to crumble; *(кулин)* to dice ♦ *неперех (сорить)* to drop crumbs

► **крошиться** *несов возв (хлеб, мел)* to crumble.

крóш|ка (-ки; *gen pl* -ек) *ж (кусочек)* crumb; *(малютка)* little one.

крóю(сь) *итп несов см* **крыть(ся)**.

круг (-а; *nom pl* -й) *м* circle; *(СПОРТ)* lap; *(сыра, хлеба)* round; *(loc sg* -ý; *перен: знакомых)* circle; *(: обязанностей, интересов, вопросов)* range; **у меня головá крýгом идёт** my head is spinning; **ходить** *(impf)* **по крýгу** to go round and round; **беговóй** ~ racing track; **поля́рный** ~ polar circle; *см также* **кругú**.

кругú (-óв) *мн (литературные, политические)* circles *мн*.

круглé|ть (-ю; *perf* **округлéть**) *несов неперех (полнеть)* to fill out; *(становиться круглым)* to become round.

круглогодúчный *прил* all-year-round.

круглолиц|ый (-, -а, -о) *прил* round-faced.

круглосýточный *прил (работа)* round-the-clock; *(детский сад)* twenty-four-hour.

крýгл|ый (-, -á, -о) *прил* round; *(no short form; идиот, дурак)* complete; total; *(цифра)* round; ~ **год** all year (round); ~**ые сýтки** twenty-four hours; ~**ая сýмма** hefty sum.

круговóй *прил* circular; **кругова́я порýка** mutual dependence; *(у преступников)* mutual cover-up.

круговорóт (-а) *м* cycle; *(событий)* turmoil.

кругозóр (-а) *м*: **он человéк широ́кого** ~**а** he is knowledgeable.

кругóм *нареч* around; *(разг: совершенно)* entirely; **идти (пойти** *perf)* ~ to make a detour; ~! about turn! *(BRIT)*; about face! *(US)*.

кругооборóт (-а) *м (КОММ)* turnover.

кругосвéтный *прил* round-the-world.

кружевни́ц|а (-ы) *ж* lace-maker.

кружевнóй *прил* lace.

кружевⷭ|о (-а; *nom pl* -á, *gen pl* -) *ср* lace.

крýжек *сущ см* **крýжка**.

круж|и́ть (-ý, -ишь) *несов перех* to spin ♦ *неперех (птица)* to circle; *(по лесу итп)* to go round in circles

► **кружи́ться** *несов возв (в хороводе)* to move

in a circle; *(в танце)* to spin (around); **у меня головá кру́жится** my head's spinning.

круж|ка (-ки; *gen pl* -ек) *ж (жестяная, глиняная)* mug; *(для пожертвований)* collection box.

кружкá *сущ см* **кружóк**.

кружкóвый *прил*: ~**ые заня́тия** extracurricular activities.

кружóк (-ка́) *м* circle; *(организация)* club.

круи́з (-а) *м* cruise.

круп (-а) *м (лошади)* crupper; *(МЕД)* croup.

круп|á (-ы́; *nom pl* -ы) *ж* grain.

крýпен *прил см* **крýпный**.

крупи́н|ка (-ки; *gen pl* -ок) *ж (разг)* grain.

крупи́ц|а (-ы) *ж (таланта, здравого смысла)* ounce; *(истины)* grain.

крупнé|ть (-ю; *perf* **покрупнéть**) *несов неперех* to grow larger.

крýпно *нареч (нарезать)* coarsely; **писа́ть (написа́ть** *perf)* ~ to write in big letters; ~ **поссóриться** *(perf)* **с кем-н** to have a big row with sb.

крупномасшта́бный *прил* large-scale.

крýпн|ый (-ен, -на́, -но) *прил (песок, соль)* coarse; *(размеры, ребёнок, фирма)* large; *(талант)* great; *(учёный, дело, фабрикант)* prominent; *(ссора, событие, успех)* major; **у меня бýдут** ~**ые неприя́тности** I'll be in serious trouble; ~ **разговóр** *(разг)* serious talk; **крýпный гóрод** major city; **крýпный план** close-up; **крýпный рога́тый скот** *(с -х)* cattle.

крупóзн|ый *прил*: ~**ое воспалéние лёгких** pneumonia with croup.

крутизн|á (-ы́) *ж* steepness.

кру|ти́ть (-чу́, -тишь) *несов перех (руль)* to turn; *(perf* **скрути́ть**; *руки)* to twist; *(верёвку)* to splice; *(папиросу)* to roll; ~ *(impf)* **кем-н** *(разг)* to manipulate sb; ~ *(impf)* **рома́н с кем-н** *(разг)* to have an affair with sb; **как ни** ~**ти́, нам придётся ..** *(разг)* we've no choice but to ...

► **крути́ться** *несов возв (вертеться)* to turn around; *(: колесо)* to spin; *(: дети)* to fidget; *(перен: хлопотать)* to be kept busy.

крýто *нареч (подниматься)* steeply; *(поворачивать)* sharply; ~ **обойди́ться (обойти́сь** *perf)* **с кем-н** to give sb a hard time.

крут|óй (-, -á, -о) *прил (берег, подъём)* steep; *(поворот, перемены)* sharp; *(нрав, меры)* harsh; *(no short form; тесто)* stiff; *(каша)* thick; ~ **кипятóк** fiercely boiling water; ~ **па́рень** *(разг)* cool guy; **крутóе яйцó** hard-boiled egg.

крýч|а (-и) *ж* steep slope.

крýче *сравн прил от* **крутóй** ♦ *сравн нареч от* **крýто**.

кручёный *прил (нитки)* twisted; **кручёный уда́р** *(в теннисе)* spin shot.

кручý(сь) *несов см* **крути́ть(ся)**.

крушéни|е (-я) *ср (поезда)* crash; *(перен: надежд, планов)* shattering; **терпéть**

(потерпе́ть *perf*) ~ (*кора́бль*) to be wrecked; (*по́езд*) to crash.

круши́н|а (-ы) ж buckthorn (*used as a laxative*).

круши́|ть (-у́, -и́шь) *несов перех* (*враго́в*) to crush; (*дере́вья, дома́*) to wreck.

крыжо́вник (-а) м (*куста́рник*) gooseberry (bush); (*я́года*) gooseberry.

крыла́т|ый *прил* (*насеко́мые*) winged; ~ые слова́ proverbial expressions; крыла́тая раке́та (*ВОЕН*) cruise missile.

крыл|о́ (-а́; *nom pl* -ья, *gen pl* -ьев) *ср* wing; (*ветряно́й ме́льницы*) sail; подреза́ть (подре́зать *perf*) кры́лья кому́-н (*перен*) to clip sb's wings; расправля́ть (распра́вить *perf*) кры́лья (*перен*) to spread one's wings.

крылы́шк|о (-а) *ср* wing; под ~м у кого́-н under sb's wing.

крыльц|о́ (-а́) *ср* porch.

Крым (-а) м Crimea.

кры́мск|ий (-ая, -ое, -ие) *прил* Crimean.

кры́н|ка (-ки; *gen pl* -ок) ж = кри́нка.

кры́с|а (-ы) ж rat.

крыси́ный *прил* (*нора́, хвост*) rat's; ~ яд rat poison.

кры́тый *прил* covered.

кры|ть (-о́ю, -о́ешь; *perf* покры́ть) *несов перех* to cover; (*ка́рту*) to trump; ~ (*impf*) ма́том (*раза*) to turn the air blue (*with bad language*)

► кры́ться *несов возв*: ~ы́ться в +*prp* (*причи́на*) to lie; в расчётах ~ы́лась оши́бка the calculations contained a mistake; причи́на э́того явле́ния ~о́ется в том, что ... the reason for this lies in the fact that ....

кры́ш|а (-и) ж roof.

кры́ш|ка (-ки; *gen pl* -ек) ж (*я́щика, ча́йника*) lid; тут ему́ и ~ (*разг*) that was the end of him.

крэк (-а) м crack (*drug*).

крю́к (-ка́; *nom pl* -чья, *gen pl* -чьев) м (*в стене́*) hook; (*разг: ли́шнее расстоя́ние*) detour.

крю́чить (*3sg* -ит, *perf* скрю́чить) *несов безл*: его́ ~ит от бо́ли he is bent double in pain

► крю́читься (*perf* скрю́читься) *несов возв* to be bent double.

крючка́ *итп сущ см* крючо́к.

крючкова́т|ый (-, -а, -о) *прил* hooked.

крючо́к (-ка́) м hook; ~ для вяза́ния crochet hook.

крю́чья *итп сущ см* крюк.

крюшо́н (-а) м (*КУЛИН*) punch.

кря́ду *нареч*: дождь шёл пять дней ~ it rained for five whole days.

кряж (-а) м (*го́рный*) ridge.

кря́жист|ый (-, -а, -о) *прил* (*та́кже перен*) stumpy.

кря́канье (-я) *ср* quacking.

кря́ка|ть (-ю) *несов от* кря́кнуть.

кря́кн|уть (-у, -ешь) *сов неперех* (*утка*) to quack; (*перен: челове́к*) to grunt.

кряхте́ть (-чу́, -ти́шь) *несов неперех* to groan.

ксероко́пи|я (-и) ж photocopy, Xerox®.

ксе́рокс (-а) м (*автома́т*) photocopier; (*ко́пия*) photocopy, Xerox®.

ксилофо́н (-а) м xylophone.

ксилогра́фи|я (-и) ж (*образе́ц рабо́ты*) woodcut; (*проце́сс*) wood engraving.

кста́ти *вводн сл* (*ме́жду про́чим*) incidentally, by the way; (*случа́йно*) by any chance ◆ *нареч* (*к ме́сту*) relevant; ~, ты слы́шал, что ...? by the way, did you hear that ...?; Вы, ~, не зна́ете, что случи́лось? you don't, by any chance, know what happened?; де́ньги пришли́сь как нельзя́ ~ the money came just at the right time.

KEYWORD

кто (кого́; *см* Table 6) *мест 1* (*вопроси́тельное, относи́тельное*) who; кто там? who is there?; на́до узна́ть, кто приходи́л we must find out who has come

2 (*разг: кто-нибудь*) anyone; е́сли кто позвони́т, позови́ меня́ if anyone phones, please call me

3: ма́ло ли кто many (people); ма́ло кто few (people); ма́ло кто пошёл в кино́ only a few of us went to the cinema; кто-кто, а он всегда́ пра́вду говори́т I don't know about anyone else, but he always tells the truth; кто из вас ... which of you ...; кто (его́) зна́ет! who knows!

кто́-либо (кого́-либо; *как* кто; *см* Table 6) *мест* = кто́-нибудь.

кто́-нибудь (кого́-нибудь; *как* кто; *см* Table 6) *мест* (*в вопроси́тельных предложе́ниях*) anybody, anyone; (*в утверди́тельных предложе́ниях*) somebody, someone; мне ~ звони́л? did anybody *или* anyone phone for me?; ~ до́лжен ему́ помо́чь somebody *или* someone should help him.

кто́-то (кого́-то; *как* кто; *см* Table 6) *мест* somebody, someone; ~ Вам звони́л somebody *или* someone phoned for you.

куб (-а) м (*ГЕОМ, МАТ*) cube; 3 в ку́бе 3 cubed.

куб. *сокр* (= куби́ческий) cu. (= *cubic*).

Ку́б|а (-ы) ж Cuba.

ку́барем *нареч* (*разг*) headfirst.

куби́зм (-а) м cubism.

ку́бик (-а) м (*игру́шка*) building brick *или* block.

куби́н|ец (-ца) м Cuban.

куби́н|ка (-ки; *gen pl* -ок) ж *см* куби́нец.

куби́нск|ий (-ая, -ое, -ие) *прил* Cuban.

куби́нца *итп сущ см* куби́нец.

куби́ст (-а) м cubist.

куби́ческ|ий (-ая, -ое, -ие) *прил* cubic; куби́ческий ко́рень cube root.

ку́б|ок (-ка) м goblet; (*СПОРТ*) cup.

кубоме́тр (-а) м cubic metre (*BRIT*) *или* meter (*US*).

ку́брик (-а) м crew's quarters *мн*.

кува́лд|а (-ы) ж sledgehammer.

Куве́йт (-а) м Kuwait.

кувши́н (-а) м jug (*BRIT*), pitcher (*US*).

кувши́н|ка (-ки; *gen pl* -ок) ж water lily.

кувырка́|ться (-юсь) *несов возв* to somersault.

кувыркн|у́ться (-у́сь, -ёшься) *сов возв* to turn a somersault.

кувырко́м *нареч* head over heels; **жизнь у меня́ пошла́** ~ my life has been turned on its head.

кувыро́к (-ка́) *м* somersault.

KEYWORD

куда́ *нареч* **1** (*вопросительное, относительное*) where; **куда́ ты положи́л мою́ ру́чку?** where did you put my pen?; **скажи́, куда́ ты идёшь** tell me where you are going **2** (*разг: для чего*) why; **куда́ мне сто́лько де́нег?** why would I want so much money? **3** (+*dat*; *разг: о невозмо́жности чего-н*): **куда́ мне с ни́ми состяза́ться?** how can I compare with them? **4** (+*comparative*; *разг: гора́здо*) much; **мой дом куда́ бо́льше** my house is much bigger.

куда́-либо *нареч* = **куда́-нибудь**.

куда́-нибудь *нареч* (*в вопроси́тельных предложе́ниях*) anywhere; (*в утверди́тельных предложе́ниях*) somewhere; **Вы** ~ **съе́здили ле́том?** did you go anywhere in the summer?; **дава́й** ~ **пойдём** let's go somewhere.

куда́-то *нареч* somewhere; **он** ~ **ушёл** he has gone off somewhere.

куда́хтанье (-я) *ср* clucking.

куда́хтать (-чу, -чешь) *несов непepex* to cluck.

куде́сник (-а) *м* sorcerer.

ку́дри (-ей) *мн* curls *мн*.

кудря́вый (-, -а, -о) *прил* (*во́лосы*) curly; (*челове́к*) curly-haired; (*де́рево*) bushy; (*перен: слог*) flowery.

кузне́ц (-а́) *м* blacksmith.

кузне́чик (-а) *м* grasshopper.

кузне́чный *прил* blacksmith's; **кузне́чные меха́** bellows *мн*.

ку́зница (-ы) *ж* smithy, forge.

ку́зов (-а; *nom pl* -а́) *м* (*АВТ*) back (*of a van, lorry etc*).

куй(те) *несов см* **кова́ть**.

кукаре́кать (-ю) *несов непepex* to crow.

кукареку́ *межд* (*крик петуха́*) cock-a-doodle-doo.

ку́киш (-а) *м* fig; **он показа́л мне** ~ (*перен: разг*) ≈ he told me to get lost.

ку́кла (-лы; *gen pl* -ол) *ж* (*также перен*) doll; (*в теа́тре*) puppet; **теа́тр** ~**ол** puppet theatre (*BRIT*) *или* theater (*US*).

кукова́ть (-у́ю) *несов непepex* to cuckoo; (*перен: разг*) to twiddle one's thumbs.

ку́кол *сущ см* **ку́кла**.

ку́колка (-ки; *gen pl* -ок) *ж* уменьш от **ку́кла**; (*ЗООЛ*) pupa (*мн* pupae).

ку́кольный *прил* (*игру́шечный*): ~ **до́мик** doll's house; **ку́кольный теа́тр** puppet theatre (*BRIT*) *или* theater (*US*).

ку́кситься (-шусь, -сишься) *несов возв* (*разг*) to sulk.

кукуру́за (-ы) *ж* (*БОТ*) maize; (*КУЛИН*) (sweet) corn.

кукуру́зный *прил* (*см сущ*) maize; corn.

куку́шка (-и) *ж* cuckoo.

ку́кушусь *несов см* **ку́кситься**.

кула́к (-а́) *м* fist; (*ИСТ*) kulak (*member of the land-owning peasant class, eradicated during collectivization*).

кула́чный *прил*: ~ **бой** fist fight.

кулебя́ка (-и) *ж* pie made with meat, fish or rice.

куль (-ька́) *м* paper bag.

кули́к (-а́) *м* (*ЗООЛ*) wader.

кулина́р (-а) *м* master chef.

кулина́рия (-и) *ж* (*приготовле́ние пи́щи*) cookery; (*магази́н*) ≈ delicatessen ♦ *собир* (*проду́кты*) cooked foods and groceries.

кулина́рный *прил* (*иску́сство*) culinary.

кули́са (-ы) *ж* (*обы́чно мн*: *ТЕАТР*) wing; **за** ~**ми** (*также перен*) backstage, behind the scenes.

кули́ч (-а́) *м* kulich (*Easter cake*).

кули́чки *нареч* (*разг*): **у чёрта на кули́чках** in the middle of nowhere; **к чёрту на** ~ to the back of beyond.

куло́н (-а) *м* (*украше́ние*) pendant; (*ФИЗ*) coulomb.

кулуа́рный *прил* (*встре́чи, сде́лки*) backstage.

кулуа́ры (-ов) *мн* (*ПОЛИТ*) lobby *ед*; **в** ~**ах бесе́ды иду́т** behind-the-scene talks are currently in progress.

куль (-я́) *м* sack.

кулька́ *итп сущ см* **кулёк**.

кульминацио́нный *прил* climactic.

кульмина́ция (-и) *ж* (*АСТРОНОМИЯ*) culmination; (*перен*) high point, climax.

культ (-а) *м* (*служе́ние божеству́*) cult; (*совоку́пность обря́дов: правосла́вный*) religion; (*перен: красоты́, де́нег*) cult worship; **служи́тели ку́льта** church officials; **культ ли́чности** personality cult.

культиви́рование (-я) *ср* cultivation.

культиви́ровать (-ую) *несов перех* to cultivate.

ку́льтовый *прил* religious.

культу́ра (-ы) *ж* (*также с.-х., БИО*) culture; (*разведе́ние: льна итп*) cultivation, culture; (*бы́та*) high quality; ~ **труда́** work ethic.

культу́рен *прил см* **культу́рный**.

культури́зм (-а) *м* body building.

культури́ст (-а) *м* body builder.

культу́рный (-ен, -на, -но) *прил* cultural; (*no short form*; *расте́ние*) cultivated.

кум (-а; *nom pl* -овья́, *gen pl* -ове́й) *м* godfather.

кума́ (-ы́) *ж* godmother.

кума́човый *прил* calico.

куми́р (-а) *м* (*также перен*) idol.

кумовство́ (-а) *ср* nepotism.

кумовья́ (-ёв) *мн от* **кум**.

кумы́с (-а) *м* fermented horse's milk.

куни́ца (-ы) *ж* marten.

купа́льник (-а) *м* swimming *или* bathing costume (*BRIT*), bathing suit (*US*).

купáльный *прил*: ~ костю́м swimming *или* bathing costume (*BRIT*), bathing suit (*US*); ~ сезóн swimming season.

купáны|е (-я) *ср* bathing; (*плáвание*) swimming.

купá|ть (-ю; *perf* **вы́купать** *или* **искупáть)** *несов перех* to bath

▸ **купáться** (*perf* **вы́купаться** *или* **искупáться)** *несов возв* to bathe; (*плáвать*) to swim; (*в вáнне*) to have a bath; ~**ся** (*impf*) **в зóлоте** to be rolling in money.

купé *ср нескл* compartment (*in railway carriage*).

купéйный *прил*: ~ **вагóн** Pullman (car).

купéл|ь (-и) *ж* (*РЕЛ*) font.

купéц (-цá) *м* merchant.

купéческий (-ая, -ое, -ие) *прил* (*сослóвие*) merchant *опред*; (*перен: нрáвы*) vulgar.

купéчеств|о (-а) *ср собир* the merchants *мн*.

купи́рованный *прил* = **купéйный.**

купи́ть (-лю́, -ишь; *impf* **покупáть)** *сов перех* to buy.

куплéт (-а) *м* couplet; *см также* **куплéты.**

куплéт|ы (-ов) *мн satirical song in couplet form.*

куплю́ *сов см* **купи́ть.**

ку́пл|я (-и) *ж* purchase; ~**продáжа** buying and selling.

ку́пол (-а; *nom pl* **-á)** *м* cupola.

купóн (-а) *м* (*цéнных бумáг*) ticket: (*денежный знак*) coupon (*перен*: *used as the Ukrainian currency*); **стричь** (*impf*) ~**ы** to make easy money; **подáрочный** ~ gift voucher.

купцá *итп сущ см* **купéц.**

ку́пчий (-ая, -ее, -ие) *прил* (*также*: ~**ая крéпость**: *ЮР*) deed of purchase.

купчи́х|а (-и) *ж см* **купéц.**

купю́р|а (-ы) *ж* (*сокращение*) cut; (*ЭКОН*) denomination; **статья́ печáтается без купю́р** the article is printed in full.

ку́р|а (-ы) *ж* (*разг*) chicken.

курагá (-и) *ж собир* dried apricots *мн.*

курá|житься (-усь, -ишься) *несов возв*: ~ **над кем-н** to bully sb.

курáнт|ы (-ов) *мн* chiming clock *ед.*

курáтор (-а) *м* supervisor.

кургáн (-а) *м* (*моги́льник*) (burial) mound.

ку́рев|о (-а) *ср* (*разг*) smokes *мн*, fags *мн.*

курéни|е (-я) *ср* smoking.

кури́л|ка (-ки; *gen pl* **-ок)** *ж* (*разг*) smoking room.

кури́льщик (-а) *м* smoker.

кури́льщиц|а (-ы) *ж см* **кури́льщик.**

кури́ный *прил* (*яйцó*) hen's; (*бульóн, пéрья*) chicken; **кури́ная слепотá** (*МЕД*) night blindness.

кури́тельный *прил*: ~ **табáк** rolling tobacco; **кури́тельная кóмната** smoking room.

кур|и́ть (-ю́, -ишь) *несов (не)перех* to smoke; "~ **запрещáется**", "**не** ~" "no smoking"; "**у нас не ку́рят**" "kindly refrain from smoking"

▸ **кури́ться** *несов возв* (*вулкáн*) to smoke; (*вершины гор*) to be shrouded in mist.

ку́риц|а (-ицы; *nom pl* **ку́ры)** *ж* hen, chicken; (*мя́со*) chicken; ~**ам на смех** (*разг*) it's a

complete joke; **дéнег у неё** ~**ы не клю́ют** (*разг*) she's absolutely loaded.

куркá *сущ см* **курóк.**

курнóс|ый (-, -а, -о) *прил* snub-nosed.

курóк (-кá) *м* hammer (*on gun*); **взводи́ть** (**взвести́** *perf*) ~ to cock a gun.

куроле́|сить (-шу, -сишь) *несов неперех* to play up.

куропáт|ка (-ки; *gen pl* **-ок)** *ж* grouse.

курóрт (-а) *м* (*holiday*) resort.

курóртный *прил* (*зóна, гóрод*) resort *опред*; **курóртный сезóн** the holiday season.

курс (-а) *м* course; (*ПОЛИТ*) policy; (*КОММ*) exchange rate; (*ПРОСВЕЩ*) year (*of university studies*); **брать** (**взять** *perf*) ~ **на** +*acc* to set a course for; **идти́** (*impf*) **по ку́рсу** to be on (the right) course; **переходи́ть** (**перейти́** *perf*) **на четвёртый** ~ to go into the fourth year (*of university*); **быть** (*impf*) **в ку́рсе дéла** to be up on what's going on; **входи́ть** (**войти́** *perf*) **в** ~ **чего́-н** to put o.s. in the picture about sth; **вводи́ть** (**ввести́** *perf*) **кого́-н в** ~ (**чего́-н**) to put sb in the picture (about sth).

курсáнт (-а) *м* (*ВОЕН*) cadet.

курси́в (-а) *м* italics *мн*; "~ **мой**" "the italics are mine".

курси́вный *прил*: ~ **шрифт** italic font.

курси́р|овать (-ую) *несов неперех*: ~ **мéжду** +*instr* ... **и** +*instr* ... (*самолёт, автóбус*) to shuttle between ... and ...; (*судно*) to sail between ... and ...

курсов|óй *прил*: ~**áя рабóта** project; ~**óе собрáние** student's year meeting; ~**áя рáзница** (*КОММ*) difference in exchange rates.

ку́рсор (-а) *м* cursor.

ку́рт|ка (-ки; *gen pl* **-ок)** *ж* jacket.

курчáв|ый (-, -а, -о) *прил* (*вóлосы*) curly; (*человéк, живóтное*) curly-haired.

ку́р|ы (-) *мн от* **ку́рица.**

курьёз (-а) *м* curious thing.

курьёзный (-ен, -на, -но) *прил* curious.

курьéр (-а) *м* messenger; (*дипломати́ческий*) courier.

курьéрский (-ая, -ое, -ие) *прил*: ~ **отдéл** dispatch department; **курьéрский пóезд** express train.

курятин|а (-ы) *ж* chicken (*meat*).

курятник (-а) *м* chicken coop.

кусá|ть (-ю) *несов перех* to bite; (*сáхар, конфéты*) to crunch

▸ **кусáться** *несов возв* (*живóтное*) to bite; (*растéние*) to sting; (*разг: цéны, налóги*) to hurt.

кусá|чки (-ек) *мн* wire cutters *мн.*

кускá *итп сущ см* **кусóк.**

кусковóй *прил*: ~ **сáхар** lump sugar.

кусóк (-кá) *м* piece; ~ **сáхара** sugar lump; ~ **мы́ла** bar of soap; ~ **хлéба** (*перен*) daily bread.

куст (-á) *м* (*БОТ*) bush; **прятаться** (**спрятаться** *perf*) **в** ~**ы́** (*перен*) to run for cover.

кустáрник (-а) *м* shrubbery ◆ *собир* bushes *мн.*

кустáрный *прил* handicraft *опред*; (*перен: методы, оборудование*) crude, primitive; ~ **труд** craftwork; **кустáрные издéлия** handicrafts.

кустáрь (-**я́**) *м* craftsman (*мн* craftsmen).

кустúстый (-, -**а**, -**о**) *прил* bushy.

кýта|ть (-**ю**; *perf* **закýтать**) *несов перех* (*плечи, ноги итп*) to cover up; (*ребёнка*) to bundle up

▸ **кýтаться** (*perf* **закýтаться**) *несов возв*: ~**ся в** +*acc* to wrap o.s. up in.

кутёж (-**á**) *м* drinking spree.

кутерьм|á (-**ы́**) *ж* (*разг*) mayhem, chaos.

кутú|ть (-**чý**, -**тишь**) *несов неперех* to go on a drinking spree.

кутýз|ка (-**ки**; *gen pl* -**ок**) *ж* (*разг*) the slammer, the clink (*BRIT*).

кухáр|ка (-**ки**; *gen pl* -**ок**) *ж* cook.

кýх|ня (-**ни**; *gen pl* -**онь**) *ж* (*помещение*) kitchen; (*еда*) cooking; **рýсская** ~ Russian cuisine.

кухóнный *прил* kitchen *опред*.

кýхонь *сущ см* **кýхня**.

кýц|ый (-, -**а**, -**о**) *прил* (*собака*) with no tail; (*перен: программа, права*) limited.

кýч|а (-**и**) *ж* (*песка, листьев*) pile, heap; (+*gen*; *разг: денег, проблем*) heaps *или* loads of; **валúть** (*impf*) **всё в однý** ~**у** to lump everything together.

кучев|óй *прил*: ~**ые облакá** cumulus (clouds *мн*).

кýчер (-**а**; *nom pl* -**á**) *м* coachman (*мн* coachmen).

кучý *несов см* **кутúть**.

куш (-**а**) *м* jackpot; **срывáть** (**сорвáть** *perf*) ~ to hit the jackpot.

кушáк (-**á**) *м* sash.

кýшанье (-**ья**; *gen pl* -**ий**) *ср* food.

кýша|ть (-**ю**; *perf* **покýшать** *или* **скýшать**) *несов перех* to eat; ~**йте, пожáлуйста** have something to eat.

кушéт|ка (-**ки**; *gen pl* -**ок**) *ж* couch.

кювéт (-**а**) *м* gutter.

~ Л, л ~

Л, л *сущ нескл (буква)* the 12th letter of the Russian alphabet.

л. *сокр* (= лист) f. (= *folio*).

лабири́нт (-а) *м* maze; *(перен)* labyrinth.

лабора́нт (-а) *м (в лаборатории)* lab technician; *(на кафедре)* secretary.

лабора́нт|ка (-ки; *gen pl* -ок) *ж см* **лабора́нт**.

лаборато́ри|я (-и) *ж* laboratory.

ла́в|а (-ы) *ж* lava; *(забой)* drift.

лава́нд|а (-ы) *ж* lavender.

лава́ш (-а) *м* lavash (*Caucasian flat bread*).

лави́н|а (-ы) *ж (также перен)* avalanche.

лави́р|овать (-ую; *perf* **слави́ровать**) *несов неперех (МОР)* to tack; *(перен)* to manoeuvre (*BRIT*), maneuver (*US*).

ла́в|ка (-ки; *gen pl* -ок) *ж (скамья)* bench; *(магазин)* shop.

ла́воч|ка (-ки; *gen pl* -ек) *ж уменьш от* **ла́вка**; *(перен: разг)* shady business.

ла́вочник (-а) *м* shopkeeper.

лавр (-а) *м* laurel; *см также* **ла́вры**.

ла́вр|а (-ы) *ж* monastery.

лавро́вый *прил* laurel; **лавро́вый лист** bay leaf.

ла́вр|ы (-ов) *мн (венок)* laurels *мн*; **пожина́ть** *(impf)* ~ to be crowned with laurels; **почи́ть** *(perf)* **на** ~**ах** to rest on one's laurels.

лавса́н (-а) *м* lavsan (*synthetic polyester fibre or fabric*).

ЛАГ *м сокр* (= Ли́га ара́бских госуда́рств) Arab League.

ла́герный *прил* camp *опред*.

ла́гер|ь (-я; *nom pl* -**я**) *м* camp; *(nom pl* -**и**; *перен)* camp.

лагу́н|а (-ы) *ж* lagoon.

лад (-а; *loc sg* -**у́**, *nom pl* -**ы́**) *м (разг: гармония)* harmony; *(МУЗ: обычно мн: деление на грифе)* fret; *(: клавиша)* key; *(: строй)* mode; **быть** *(impf)* **не в** ~**а́х с** +*instr* to be at odds with; **на свой** ~ in one's own way; **на все** ~**ы́** in all sorts of ways, every which way (*US*); **руга́ть** *(impf)* **кого́-н на все** ~**ы́** to call sb every name under the sun; **де́ло идёт на** ~ things are getting better.

ла́дан (-а) *м* incense; **дыша́ть** *(impf)* **на** ~ *(разг)* to be on one's last legs.

ла́ден *прил см* **ла́дный**.

ла́д|ить (-жу, -дишь; *perf* **пола́дить**) *несов неперех:* ~ **с** +*instr* to get on (well) with

► **ла́диться** *несов возв* to go well.

ла́дно *част (разг)* O.K., all right; **пойдём в кино́ –** ~ let's go to the cinema – O.K. *или* all right; ~ **тебе́!** *(разг: не стоит, не надо)* don't be silly!; ~ **тебе́ жа́ловаться/крича́ть** that's enough of your complaining/shouting; **да** ~! you don't say!

ла́д|ный (-ен, -на́, -но) *прил (разг: хорошо сложенный)* well-built; **у него́** ~**ная фигу́ра** he's a fine figure of a man.

ла́дожск|ий (-ая, -ое, -ие) *прил:* **Л**~**ое о́зеро** Lake Ladoga.

ладо́н|ь (-и) *ж (АНАТ)* palm; **отсю́да Москва́ видна́ как на** ~**и** from here you can see Moscow clearly.

ладо́ш|и (-) *мн:* **бить в** ~ to clap one's hands; **хло́пать** *(impf)* **в** ~ to clap.

ладья́ (-ьи́; *gen pl* -е́й) *ж (ШАХМАТЫ)* rook, castle.

ЛАЗ (-а) *м сокр* = Льво́вский авто́бусный заво́д; *(автобус)* bus manufactured at the Lvov bus factory.

лаз (-а) *м* gap.

лазаре́т (-а) *м (ВОЕН)* field hospital.

ла́за|ть (-ю) *несов* = **ла́зить**.

лазе́й|ка (-йки; *gen pl* -ек) *ж* gap; *(перен: в правилах)* loophole.

ла́зер (-а) *м* laser.

ла́зерный *прил* laser *опред*; **ла́зерный при́нтер** laser printer.

ла́з|ить (-жу, -зишь) *несов неперех* to climb; *(под стол, под кровать итп)* to crawl.

лазури́т (-а) *м* lapis lazuli.

лазу́рный *прил* azure, sky-blue.

лазу́р|ь (-и) *ж* azure.

ла|й (-я) *м* barking.

ла́йк|а (-и) *ж* husky; *(кожа)* kid.

ла́йковый *прил* kid *опред*.

ла́йнер (-а) *м* liner.

лак (-а) *м (для ногтей, для пола)* varnish; *(для волос)* lacquer; **покрыва́ть (покры́ть** *perf)* **что-н ла́ком** to varnish sth.

лака́|ть (-ю) *несов перех* to lap up.

лаке́|й (-я) *м (слуга)* footman *(мн* footmen); *(подхалим)* lackey.

лаки́рованный *прил (шкатулка)* lacquered; *(туфли)* patent-leather.

лакир|ова́ть (-у́ю; *perf* **отлакирова́ть**) *несов перех (изделие)* to lacquer; *(кожу)* to patent.

лакиро́в|ка (-и) *ж (изделия)* lacquer.

ла́кмусов|ый *прил*: ~**ая бума́га** litmus paper.
ла́ковый *прил* (*изделия*) lacquered; (*раствор, краски*) lacquer *опред*; **ла́ковая ко́жа** patent leather.
ла́ком|иться (-люсь, -ишься; *perf* **пола́комиться**) *несов неперех* (+*instr*) to feast on.
ла́ком|ка (-ки; *gen pl* -ок) *м/ж* (*любящий вкусное*) gourmet; **она́ настоя́щая ~** (*сладкоежка*) she has a sweet tooth.
ла́комлюсь *несов см* **ла́комиться**.
ла́комство *сущ см* **ла́комка**.
ла́комый *прил* delicious; **ла́комый кусо́к** titbit (*BRIT*), tidbit (*US*).
лакони́зм (-а) *м* succinctness.
лакони́чно *нареч* laconically, succinctly.
лакони́чный *прил* (*речь*) laconic, succinct; (*формы здания, рисунок*) spare, austere.
лакто́з|а (-ы) *ж* lactose.
ла́м|а (-ы) *ж* (*ЗООЛ*) llama ♦ *м* (*РЕЛ*) lama.
Ла-Ма́нш (-а) *м* the (English) Channel.
ла́мп|а (-ы) *ж* (*осветительная, керосиновая*) lamp; (*ТЕХ*) tube; **ла́мпа дневно́го све́та** fluorescent light.
лампа́д|а (-ы) *ж* icon lamp.
лампа́с (-а) *м* (*обычно мн*) stripe (*down trouser leg*).
ла́мпоч|ка (-ки; *gen pl* -ек) *ж* lamp; (*для освещения*) light bulb; **ему́ всё до ~ки** (*разг*) he couldn't care less.
ланге́т (-а) *м* fillet steak.
ландша́фт (-а) *м* landscape.
ла́ндыш (-а) *м* lily of the valley.
ланоли́н (-а) *м* lanolin.
ланце́т (-а) *м* (*МЕД*) lancet.
лан|ь (-и) *ж* fallow deer.
Лао́с (-а) *м* Laos.
лао́сск|ий (-ая, -ое, -ие) *прил* Laotian.
ла́п|а (-ы) *ж* (*зверя*) paw; (*птицы*) foot; (*сосны, ёлки*) bough; (*якоря*) fluke; **попада́ть** (**попа́сть** *perf*) **кому́-н в ~ы** (*разг*) to fall into sb's clutches; **дава́ть** (**дать** *perf*) **кому́ в ~у** (*разг*) to give sb a backhander; **ходи́ть** (*impf*) **на за́дних ~х пе́ред кем-н** (*перен: разг*) to dance attendance on sb.
ла́п|оть (-тя; *nom pl* -ти, *gen pl* -те́й) *м* (*обычно мн*) bast shoe.
ла́поч|ка (-ки; *gen pl* -ек) *м/ж* (*разг*) dear, darling.
ла́пт|а (-ы́) *ж* lapta (*traditional Russian ball game*).
ла́птя *итп сущ см* **ла́поть**.
ла́пуш|ка (-и) *ж* dear, darling.
лапш|а́ (-и́) *ж* noodles *мн*; (*суп*) noodle soup.
ларёк (-ька́) *м* stall.
ларе́ц (-ца́) *м* (*шкатулка*) casket.
ларинги́т (-а) *м* laryngitis.
ларинголо́ги|я (-и) *ж* laryngology.
ларца́ *итп сущ см* **ларе́ц**.

лар|ь (-я́) *м* bin.
ларька́ *итп сущ см* **ларёк**.
ла́с|ка (-ки) *ж* tenderness; (*gen pl* -ок; *ЗООЛ*) weasel.
ласка́тельный *прил*: ~ **суффикс** (*линг*) diminutive suffix (*denoting affection*).
ласка́ть (-ю) *несов перех* (*ребёнка, девушку*) to caress; (*собаку*) to pet; ~ (*impf*) **слух/взор** to be pleasing to the ear/eye
▶ **ласка́ться** (*perf* **приласка́ться**) *несов возв*: ~**ся к** +*dat* (*ребёнок*) to snuggle up to; (*кошка*) to rub up against; (*собака*) to fawn on.
ла́сков|ый (-, -а, -о) *прил* affectionate; (*перен: ветер, солнце итп*) gentle.
ла́сок *сущ см* **ла́ска**.
ласт (-а) *м* (*ЗООЛ, СПОРТ: обычно мн*) flipper.
ла́стик (-а) *м* (*разг*) rubber (*BRIT*), eraser.
ла́сточ|ка (-ки; *gen pl* -ек) *ж* swallow; **городска́я/берегова́я ~** house/sand martin.
лат (-а) *м* lat (*Latvian currency unit*).
лата́|ть (-ю; *perf* **залата́ть**) *несов перех* to patch.
латви́йск|ий (-ая, -ое, -ие) *прил* Latvian.
Ла́тви|я (-и) *ж* Latvia.
лати́нск|ий (-ая, -ое, -ие) *прил* Latin; ~ **язы́к** Latin.
ла́т|ка (-ки; *gen pl* -ок) *ж* (*разг*) patch.
лату́н|ь (-и) *ж* brass.
ла́т|ы (-) *мн* armour *ед* (*BRIT*), armor *ед* (*US*).
латы́н|ь (-и) *ж* Latin.
латы́ш (-а́) *м* Latvian.
латы́ш|ка (-ки; *gen pl* -ек) *ж см* **латы́ш**.
латы́шск|ий (-ая, -ое, -ие) *прил* Latvian; ~ **язы́к** Latvian.
лауреа́т (-а) *м* winner (*of an award*).
лафа́ *как сказ* (*разг*): **нам здесь ~** we've got it easy here.
ла́цкан (-а) *м* lapel.
лачу́г|а (-и) *ж* hovel.
ла́я|ть (-ю; *perf* **прола́ять**) *несов неперех* to bark.
лба *итп сущ см* **лоб**.
ЛГ *ж сокр* (= „Литерату́рная газе́та") "Literary Gazette".
лгать (лгу, лжёшь *итп*, лгут; *perf* **солга́ть** или **налга́ть**) *несов неперех* to lie.
лгун (-а́) *м* liar.
лгу́н|ья (-ьи; *gen pl* -ий) *ж см* **лгун**.
ЛДПР *ж сокр* = Либера́льно-демократи́ческая па́ртия Росси́и.
лебед|а́ (-ы́) *ж* (*БОТ*) orache.
лебедёнок (-ёнка; *nom pl* -я́та, *gen pl* -я́т) *м* cygnet.
лебеди́н|ый *прил* swan *опред*; (*перен: шея*) swanlike; (*: поступь*) graceful; ~**ая ста́я** flock of swans; **лебеди́ная пе́сня** swan song.
лебёд|ка (-ки; *gen pl* -ок) *ж* winch.
ле́бед|ь (-я; *gen pl* -е́й) *м* swan.
лебедя́та *итп сущ см* **лебедёнок**.
лебез|и́ть (-жу́, -зи́шь) *несов неперех*: ~ (**пе́ред**

+*instr*) (*разг*) to fawn (on).
лебя́ж|ий (-ья, -ье, -ьи) *прил:* ~ **пух** swan's-down.
лев (льва) *м* lion; (*созвездие*): **Л~** Leo.
левко́й (-я) *м* (*бот*) stock.
левосторо́нн|ий (-яя, -ее, -ие) *прил* on the left; **в Великобрита́нии** ~**ее движе́ние** in Britain they drive on the left.
левш|а́ (-и́; *gen pl* -е́й) *м/ж* left-handed person; **он/она́** ~ he/she is left-handed.
ле́в|ый *прил* left, left-hand; (*партия, взгляды*) left-wing; ~**ая рабо́та** (*разг*) moonlighting.
лёг *итп сов см* **лечь**.
лега́в|ый (-ого) *decl like adj м* type of gun dog.
лега́лен *прил см* **лега́льный**.
легализи́р|овать (-ую) (*не*)*сов перех* to legalize.
лега́льный (-ен, -ьна, -ьно) *прил* legal.
леге́нд|а (-ы) *ж* legend; (*перен*) fairy story.
легенда́рн|ый (-ен, -на, -но) *прил* legendary.
легио́н (-а) *м* legion.
леги́рованн|ый *прил:* ~**ая сталь** steel alloy.
лёг|кий (-кая, -кое, -кие; -ок, -ка́, -ко́) *прил* (*нетяжёлый*) light; (*нетрудный, несерьёзный*) easy; (*боль, насморк*) slight; (*фигура*) graceful; (*характер, человек*) easy-going; **у него́ сли́шком** ~**кое отноше́ние к жи́зни** he doesn't take life seriously enough; **у него́** ~**кая рука́** he brings good luck; **он нашёл рабо́ту с мое́й** ~**кой руки́** he found work thanks to me; **он** ~**ок на подъём** (*разг*) he doesn't take much persuading; ~**ок на поми́не!** (*разг*) talk of the devil!; **лёгкая атле́тика** athletics (*BRIT*), track-and-field (*US*); **лёгкая промы́шленность** light industry.
легко́ *нареч* easily; ~ **сказа́ть** (*разг*) easier said than done; **мне здесь** ~ I feel at ease here; **э́то** ~ it's easy.
легкоатле́т (-а) *м* athlete (*in track and field events*).
легкоатле́т|ка (-ки; *gen pl* -ок) *ж см* **легкоатле́т**.
легкове́рн|ый (-ен, -на, -но) *прил* gullible, credulous.
легкове́сн|ый (-ен, -на, -но) *прил* superficial.
легков|о́й *прил:* ~**а́я маши́на**, ~ **автомоби́ль** car, automobile (*US*).
легкову́ш|ка (-ки; *gen pl* -ек) *ж* (*разг*) motor (*BRIT*), auto (*US*).
лёгк|ое (-ого) *decl like adj ср* (*обычно мн*) lung.
легкомы́сленн|ый (-, -на, -но) *прил* (*человек*) frivolous; (*поступок*) thoughtless; (*отношение*) frivolous, flippant.
легкомы́сли|е (-я) *ср* (*человека*) frivolity; (*поступка*) thoughtlessness.
легкоплáв|кий (-кая, -кое, -кие; -ок, -ка, -ко) *прил* fusible.
лёгкост|ь (-и) *ж* (*походки, веса*) lightness; (*задания*) simplicity, easiness; (*характера*) easy-going nature; **у него́ мно́го друзе́й благодаря́** ~**и его́ хара́ктера** he has many friends thanks to his easy-going nature.

лёгок *прил см* **лёгкий**.
лёгочный *прил* pulmonary, lung *опред*; ~ **больно́й** patient with a pulmonary *или* lung condition.
ле́гче *сравн прил от* **лёгкий** ♦ *сравн нареч от* **легко́** ♦ *как сказ:* **больно́му сего́дня** ~ the patient is feeling better today.
лёд (льда; *loc sg* льду) *м* ice; ~ **тро́нулся** (*перен*) things are moving now.
леден|е́ть (-ю; *perf* **заледене́ть** *или* **оледене́ть**) *несов неперех* to freeze; (*человек, руки*) to be freezing; **он оледене́л от стра́ха** fear made his blood run cold.
ледене́ц (-ца́) *м* fruit drop.
леден|и́ть (3sg -и́т, 3pl -я́т) *несов перех* to freeze; **у́жас** ~**и́т (его́) кровь** terror makes his blood run cold.
леденца́ *итп сущ см* **ледене́ц**.
леденя́щ|ий (-ая, -ее, -ие) *прил* (*ветер, вода*) icy; (*перен: ужас, страх*) chilling.
ле́ди *ж нескл* lady.
ледни́к (-а́) *м* glacier.
леднико́вый *прил* glacial.
ледо́вый *прил* ice *опред*.
ледоко́л (-а) *м* icebreaker.
ледору́б (-а) *м* ice axe.
ледохо́д (-а) *м breaking up and drifting of ice on rivers in spring*.
ледяно́й *прил* (*глыба, покров*) ice *опред*; (*ветер, вода, взгляд*) icy.
ле́ек *сущ см* **ле́йка**.
лежа́к (-а́) *м* lounger.
лежа́лый *прил* (*хлеб*) stale; (*товар*) old.
леж|а́ть (-у́, -и́шь) *несов неперех* (*человек, животное*) to lie; (*предмет, вещи: на столе, на полке*) to be (lying); (: *в ящике, в шкафу итп*) to be; ~ (*impf*) **в больни́це** to be in hospital; **на нём** ~**а́т забо́ты о семье́** he is responsible for looking after his family; **(у меня́) душа́ не** ~**и́т к э́той рабо́те** my heart's not in this work; **(у меня́) душа́ не** ~**и́т к нему́** I don't feel very well disposed towards him.
лежа́ч|ий (-ая, -ее, -ие) *прил* lying; ~ **больно́й** bedridden patient; **рабо́та – не бей** ~**его** (*разг*) it's a cushy job.
ле́жбищ|е (-а) *ср* rookery (*of seals etc*).
лежебо́к|а (-и) *м/ж* (*разг*) couch potato.
лез *итп несов см* **лезть**.
ле́зви|е (-я) *ср* blade.
лез|ть (-у, -ешь; *pt* -, -ла, -ло) *несов неперех* (*выпадать: волосы, шерсть*) to fall out; (*проникать куда-н*): ~ **в** +*acc* to climb in(to); ~ (*impf*) **на** +*acc* to climb (up); ~ (*impf*) **в карма́н** (*разг*) to reach into one's pocket; ~ (*impf*) **в чужи́е дела́** (*разг*) to poke one's nose into other people's business; ~ (*impf*) **в разгово́р** (*разг*) to butt into a conversation; ~ (*impf*) **кому́-н на глаза́** (*разг*) to hang around sb.
лей *сущ см* **лить** ♦ (**ле́я**) *м* lay (*Moldavian currency unit*).
лейбори́ст (-а) *м* Labour party member.

лейбори́стск|ий (-ая, -ое, -ие) *прил* Labour.
ле́й|ка (-йки; *gen pl* -ек) *ж* watering can.
лейко́з (-а) *м* leukaemia (*BRIT*), leukemia (*US*).
лейкопла́стыр|ь (-я) *м* sticking plaster (*BRIT*), adhesive tape (*US*).
лейкоци́т (-а) *м* (*обычно мн*) leucocyte.
Ле́йпциг (-а) *м* Leipzig.
ле́йте *несов см* лить.
лейтена́нт (-а) *м* lieutenant.
лейтмоти́в (-а) *м* (*также перен*) leitmotif.
лека́л|о (-а) *ср* French curve.
лека́рственный *прил* medicinal;
лека́рственная фо́рма medicine.
лека́рств|о (-а) *ср* medicine; ~ **от** +*gen* medicine for; ~ **от ка́шля** cough medicine; **принима́ть** (**приня́ть** *perf*)/**прописа́ть** (**прописа́ть** *perf*) ~ to take/prescribe medicine.
ле́ксик|а (-и) *ж* vocabulary.
лексико́граф (-а) *м* lexicographer.
лексикографи́ческ|ий (-ая, -ое, -ие) *прил* lexicographical.
лексикогра́фи|я (-и) *ж* lexicography.
лексиколо́ги|я (-и) *ж* lexicology.
лексико́н (-а) *м* vocabulary.
ле́ктор (-а) *м* lecturer; (*в клубе*) speaker.
лекцио́нный *прил* lecture *опред*; ~ **курс** course of lectures.
ле́кци|я (-и) *ж* lecture.
леле́|ять (-ю; *perf* **взлеле́ять**) *несов перех* (*также перен*) to cherish.
ле́мех (-а) *м* ploughshare (*BRIT*), plowshare (*US*).
лему́р (-а) *м* lemur.
лён (льна) *м* (*БОТ*) flax; (*ткань*) linen.
лени́в|ый (-, -а, -о) *прил* lazy.
Ленингра́д (-а) *м* Leningrad.
ленини́зм (-а) *м* Leninism.
лени́ться (-ю́сь, -ишься; *perf* **полени́ться**) *несов возв* to be lazy; ~ (**полени́ться** *perf*) +*infin* to be too lazy to do.
ле́нт|а (-ы) *ж* (*в косе, на шляпе*) ribbon; (*изоляционная, магнитная*) tape; (*фильм*) film.
ле́нточный *прил*: ~ **червь** tapeworm; ~ **транспортёр** conveyor belt.
лентя́ек *сущ см* **лентя́йка**.
лентя́|й (-я) *м* lazybones.
лентя́й|ка (-йки; *gen pl* -ек) *ж см* **лентя́й**.
лентя́йнича|ть (-ю) *несов неперех* (*разг*) to lounge about.
лен|ь (-и) *ж* laziness ♦ *как сказ*: **ему́** ~ **учи́ться/рабо́тать** he can't be bothered studying/working; (**все**) **кому́ не** ~ (*разг*) anyone who feels like it.
леопа́рд (-а) *м* leopard.
лепест|о́к (-ка́) *м* petal.
ле́пет (-а) *м* babble; **де́тский** ~ (*перен*) drivel.
лепёш|ка (-ки; *gen pl* -ек) *ж* flat bread.
леп|и́ть (-лю́, -ишь; *perf* **вы́лепить**) *несов перех* (*из глины, из пластилина*) to model; (*perf* **слепи́ть**; *соты, гнёзда*) to build

► **лепи́|ться** *несов возв* (*на дере́вьях, на склонах*) to cling.
ле́п|ка (-и) *ж* modelling (*BRIT*), modeling (*US*).
лепл|ю́(сь) *несов см* **лепи́ть(ся)**.
лепно́й *прил* modelled (*BRIT*), modeled (*US*); (*потолок*) moulded (*BRIT*), molded (*US*).
ле́пт|а (-ы) *ж* contribution; **вноси́ть (внести́** *perf***) свою́** ~**у (во что-н)** to do one's bit (for sth); (*внести́ де́ньги*) to make a contribution (to sth).
лес (-а; *loc sg* -ý, *nom pl* -а́) *м* (*большо́й*) forest; (*небольшо́й*) wood ♦ *собир* (*материал*) timber (*BRIT*), lumber (*US*); **кто в** ~, **кто по дрова́** at sixes and sevens; *см также* **леса́**.
лес|а́ (-о́в) *мн* (*СТРОИТ*) scaffolding *ед*.
лесбия́н|ка (-ки; *gen pl* -ок) *ж* lesbian.
леси́ст|ый (-, -а, -о) *прил* wooded.
ле́ск|а (-и) *ж* fishing line.
лесни́к (-а́) *м* forester.
лесни́честв|о (-а) *ср* (*участок леса*) area of forest; (*учреждение*) = forestry commission.
лесни́ч|ий (-его; *decl like adj*) *м* forest ranger.
лесно́й *прил* (*см сущ*) forest *опред*; woodland *опред*.
лесово́дств|о (-а) *ср* forestry.
лесозагото́в|ка (-ки; *gen pl* -ок) *ж* (*обычно мн*) logging *ед*.
лесозащи́тн|ый *прил*: ~**ая зо́на** shelter belt (*of trees*).
лесоматериа́л (-а) *м* (*обычно мн*) timber *только ед* (*BRIT*), lumber *только ед* (*US*).
лесонасажде́ни|е (-я) *ср* (*искусственный лес*) plantation; (*разведение леса*) afforestation.
лесопа́рк (-а) *м* woodland park.
лесопи́л|ка (-и) *ж* (*разг*) sawmill.
лесопромы́шленност|ь (-и) *ж сокр* (= лесна́я промы́шленность) timber (*BRIT*) *или* lumber (*US*) industry.
лесопромы́шленный *прил* timber-industry *опред* (*BRIT*), lumber-industry *орпед* (*US*).
лесоразрабо́т|ки (-ок) *мн* timber (*BRIT*) *или* lumber (*US*) processing.
лесору́б (-а) *м* lumberjack.
лесосе́|ка (-и) *ж* felling area.
лесоспла́в (-а) *м* timber rafting.
лесосте́п|ь (-и) *ж* forest-steppe (*area in which forest and steppe are mixed*).
ле́стен *сущ см* **ле́стный**.
ле́стниц|а (-ы) *ж* (*лестничная клетка*) staircase; (*ступени*) stairs *мн*; (*переносная*) ladder; (*стремянка*) stepladder; **служе́бная** ~ career ladder.
ле́стничн|ый *прил*: ~**ая площа́дка** landing; ~ **пролёт** stairway; ~**ая кле́тка** stairwell.
ле́стн|ый (-ен, -на, -но) *прил* flattering.
лест|ь (-и) *ж* flattery.
лёт (-а) *м*: **на лету́** in flight; (*перен: понима́ть, усва́ивать*) very quickly; **он по́нял всё с** ~**у** (*разг*) he understood everything in a flash.

лета́ (лет) *мн см* **год**; (*возраст*): **ско́лько Вам лет?** how old are you?; **ему́ 16 лет** he is 16 (years old); **он в ~х** he is getting on; **он одни́х лет со мной** he is the same age as me.

лета́льный (-ен, -ьна, -ьно) *прил* fatal; **~ьная до́за** lethal dose.

летарги́ческий (-ая, -ое, -ие) *прил* lethargic.

лета́тельный *прил* flying *опред*.

лета́ть (-ю) *несов неперех* to fly.

лете́ть (-чу́, -ти́шь) *несов неперех* to fly; (*перен: мчаться*) to fly, rush; (*perf* **полете́ть**; *разг*): **~ +gen** (*со стула*) to fall off; (*с лестницы*) to fall down; **вре́мя ~ти́т** time flies; **все на́ши пла́ны полете́ли** (*разг*) all our plans were dashed.

ле́тний (-яя, -ее, -ие) *прил* summer *опред*.

лётный *прил*: **~ая пого́да** good weather for flying; **лётное по́ле** airfield; **лётная шко́ла** flying school.

ле́то (-а) *ср* summer; **ско́лько лет, ско́лько зим!** it's been ages!

летопи́сец (-ца) *м* chronicler.

ле́топись (-и) *ж* chronicle.

летосчисле́ние (-я) *ср* calendar.

лету́чек *сущ см* **лету́чка**.

лету́чий (-ая, -ее, -ие) *прил* (*газ, масло*) volatile; (*семена*) winged; (*песок*) shifting; (*перен: собрание, разговор*) brief; **лету́чая мышь** bat.

лету́чка (-ки; *gen pl* -ек) *ж* (*разг: собрание*) brief meeting; (: *листок*) leaflet.

лётчик (-а) *м* pilot; **~-испыта́тель** test pilot; **~-истреби́тель** fighter pilot.

лётчица (-ы) *ж см* **лётчик**.

ле́чащий (-ая, -ее, -ие) *прил*: **~ врач** ≈ consultant-in-charge (*BRIT*), ≈ attending physician (*US*).

лече́бница (-ы) *ж* clinic.

лече́бный *прил* (*учреждение*) medical; (*свойства, трава*) medicinal; (*ванна*) medicated; **у него́ бога́тая ~ая пра́ктика** he has extensive clinical experience; **~ая гимна́стика** therapeutic exercise; **лече́бное сре́дство** medication.

лече́ние (-я) *ср* (*раненных, детей*) treatment; (*от простуды, от туберкулёза итп*) cure.

лечи́ть (-у́, -ишь) *несов от* **вы́лечить** ♦ *перех* to treat; (*больного*): **~ кого́-н от +gen** to treat sb for

▶ **лечи́ться** *несов от* **вы́лечиться** ♦ *возв* to undergo treatment.

лечу́ *несов см* **лете́ть**.

лечь (**ля́гу, ля́жешь** *итп*, **ля́гут**; *pt* **лёг, легла́, легло́,** *imper* **ля́г(те),** *impf* **ложи́ться**) *сов неперех* (*на землю, на диван итп*) to lie down; (*пойти спать*) to go to bed; (*снег*) to fall; (*перен*): **~ на +acc** (*ответственность, заботы*) to fall on; **ложи́ться** (**~** *perf*) **в больни́цу** to be in hospital; **ложи́ться** (**~** *perf*) **в дрейф** to drift.

ле́ший (-его; *decl like adj*) *м* wood goblin.

лещ (-а́) *м* bream.

лженау́ка (-и) *ж* pseudoscience.

лжесвиде́тель (-я) *м* perjurer.

лжесвиде́тельница (-ы) *ж см* **лжесвиде́тель**.

лжесвиде́тельство (-а) *ср* perjury.

лжесвиде́тельствовать (-ую) *несов неперех* to commit perjury.

лжец (-а́) *м* liar.

лжи *итп сущ см* **ложь**.

лжи́вость (-и) *ж* falseness.

лжи́вый (-, -а, -о) *прил* (*человек*) deceitful; (*улыбка, заверения*) false.

ли *част* (*в вопросе*): **зна́ешь ~ ты, что** ... do you know that ...; (*в косвенном вопросе*): **спроси́, смо́жет ~ он нам помо́чь** ask if he can help us ♦ *союз*: **придёт ~, не придёт, не ва́жно** it's not important if he comes or not; **она́ краси́ва, не так ~?** she's beautiful, isn't she?; **они́ бы́ли пра́вы, не так ~?** they were right, weren't they?

лиа́на (-ы) *ж* (*БОТ: растение*) liana.

либера́л (-а) *м* Liberal; (*о терпимом человеке*) liberal.

либера́лен *прил см* **либера́льный**.

либерализа́ция (-и) *ж* liberalization.

либерали́зм (-а) *м* liberalism; (*с бездельниками, с подчинёнными итп*) tolerance.

либера́льничать (-ю) *несов неперех*: **~ с** +*instr* (*с подчинёнными*) to fraternize with; (*с бездельниками*) to connive at.

либера́льный (-ен, -ьна, -ьно) *прил* liberal; (*no short form; партия*) Liberal.

ли́бо *союз* (*или*) or; **~ я, ~ он** it's either me or him.

либретти́ст (-а) *м* librettist.

либре́тто *ср нескл* libretto.

Лива́н (-а) *м* (the) Lebanon.

лива́нский (-ая, -ое, -ие) *прил* Lebanese.

ли́вень (-ня) *м* (*дождь*) downpour; (*перен: огня, свинца*) shower.

ли́вер (-а) *м* offal.

ли́верный *прил*: **~ая колбаса́** *sausage made with offal*.

Ливерпу́ль (-я) *м* Liverpool.

ли́вневый *прил*: **~ дождь** downpour; **~ые во́ды** rainwater.

ли́вня *итп сущ см* **ли́вень**.

ливре́я (-и) *ж* livery.

ли́га (-и) *ж* (*ПОЛИТ, СПОРТ*) league.

лигату́ра (-ы) *ж* (*МЕД, ЛИНГ*) ligature.

ли́дер (-а) *м* leader.

ли́дерство (-а) *ср* leadership.

лиди́ровать (-ую) *несов неперех* to be in the lead, lead.

лиза́ть (-у́, -жешь) *несов перех* (*тарелку, мороженое*) to lick; (*подлеж: пламя, волны*) to lap.

ли́зинг (-а) *м* leasing.

лизну́ть (-у́, -ёшь) *сов перех* to lick.

лик (-а) *м* countenance.

ликбе́з (-а) *м сокр* (*ИСТ*: = **ликвида́ция**

безгра́мотности) campaign against illiteracy; (*перен: обучение элементарному*) basic teaching.

ликвида́тор (**-а**) *м* (*пожара, последствий аварии*) relief worker; (*КОММ*) liquidator.

ликвида́ци|я (**-и**) *ж* (*также экон*) liquidation; (*оружия*) destruction; **доброво́льная ~** (*ЭКОН*) voluntary liquidation.

ликвиди́р|овать (**-ую**) (*не*)*сов перех* (*оружие*) to destroy; (*фирму, дела*) to liquidate

▶ **ликвиди́роваться** (*не*)*сов возв* (*ЭКОН: фирма, трест итп*) to be liquidated.

ликви́дност|ь (**-и**) *ж* liquidity.

ликви́дн|ый *прил*: **~ые акти́вы** *или* **сре́дства** liquid assets.

ликви́д|ы (**-ов**) *мн* liquid assets *мн*.

ликёр (**-а**) *м* liqueur.

ликёро-во́дочный *прил*: **~ заво́д** distillery.

ликова́ни|е (**-я**) *ср* rejoicing.

лик|ова́ть (**-у́ю**) *несов неперех* to be elated.

лилипу́т (**-а**) *м* midget.

лилипу́т|ка (**-ки**; *gen pl* **-ок**) *ж см* **лилипу́т**.

ли́ли|я (**-и**) *ж* lily.

лило́вый *прил* purple.

лима́н (**-а**) *м* mud flats *мн*.

лими́т (**-а**) *м* (*на электроэнергию, на бензин*) quota; (*цен*) limit.

лимити́р|овать (**-ую**) (*не*)*сов перех* (*потребление, импорт*) to limit; (*цены*) to cap.

лими́тчик (**-а**) *м* (*разг*) *person who holds a temporary residence permit issued in connection with work*.

лимо́н (**-а**) *м* (*дерево*) lemon tree; (*плод*) lemon; **он как вы́жатый ~** he's completely washed out.

лимона́д (**-а**) *м* lemonade; (*разг: любой газированный напиток*) fizzy drink.

лимо́нный *прил* lemon; **лимо́нная кислота́** citric acid.

лимузи́н (**-а**) *м* limousine.

лимфати́ческ|ий (**-ая**, **-ое**, **-ие**) *прил* lymphatic.

лингафо́нный *прил*: **~ кабине́т** language laboratory.

лингви́ст (**-а**) *м* linguist.

лингви́стик|а (**-и**) *ж* linguistics.

лингвисти́ческ|ий (**-ая**, **-ое**, **-ие**) *прил* linguistic.

лине́й|ка (**-йки**; *gen pl* **-ек**) *ж* (*линия*) line; (*инструмент*) ruler; (*шеренга*) ≈ assembly; **тетра́дь в ~йку** lined notebook.

лине́йн|ый *прил* (*расположение, построение*) linear; **~ солда́т** soldier of the line; **~ые ме́ры** linear measures; **лине́йные войска́** regular forces; **лине́йный кре́йсер** battle cruiser.

ли́нз|а (**-ы**) *ж* lens.

ли́ни|я (**-и**) *ж* line; (*перен: партийная, профсоюзная*) policy, line; **по ~и** *+gen* in the line of; **вести́** (*impf*) *или* **проводи́ть** (*impf*) **~ю**

на *+acc* to pursue a policy of; **проводи́ть** (**провести́** *perf*) **~ю** to draw a line; **вести́** (*impf*) *или* **гнуть** (*impf*) **свою́ ~ю** (*разг*) to have one's own way; **железнодоро́жная ~** railway (*BRIT*) *или* **railroad** (*US*) track; **возду́шная ~** airway; **морска́я ~** sea route; **трамва́йная ~** tramway; **ли́ния фро́нта** (*ВОЕН*) front line; **ли́ния воро́т** goal line.

линко́р (**-а**) *м сокр* (= **лине́йный кора́бль**) destroyer.

лино́ванный *прил* lined, ruled.

лин|ова́ть (**-у́ю**; *perf* **разлинова́ть**) *несов перех* to rule.

лино́леум (**-а**) *м* linoleum.

линч|ева́ть (**-у́ю**) (*не*)*сов перех* to lynch.

линя́лый *прил* discoloured (*BRIT*), discolored (*US*).

лин|я́ть (*3sg* **-я́ет**, *3pl* **-я́ют**, *perf* **полиня́ть**) *несов неперех* to run (*colour*); (*perf* **облиня́ть**; *животное*) to moult (*BRIT*), molt (*US*).

Лио́н (**-а**) *м* Lyon.

ли́п|а (**-ы**) *ж* (*дерево*) lime (tree); (*разг: фальшивка*) fake.

ли́п|кий (**-кая**, **-кое**, **-кие**; **-ок**, **-ка́**, **-ко**) *прил* sticky.

ли́п|нуть (**-ну**, **-нешь**; *pt* **-**, **-ла**, **-ло**, *perf* **прили́пнуть**) *несов неперех* (*грязь, тесто*) to stick; (*перен: человек*) to cling.

ли́повый *прил* (*цвет, лист*) lime; (*из липы*) lime-blossom *опред*; (*разг: фальшивый*) forged.

ли́пок *прил см* **ли́пкий**.

липу́ч|ка (**-ки**; *gen pl* **-ек**) *ж* (*разг: липкая лента*) sticky tape; (: *застёжка*) Velcro® fastening.

ли́р|а (**-ы**) *ж* (*МУЗ*) lyre; (*денежная единица*) lira.

лири́зм (**-а**) *м* lyricism.

ли́рик (**-а**) *м* lyric poet.

ли́рик|а (**-и**) *ж* lyric poetry.

лири́чен *прил см* **лири́чный**.

лири́ческ|ий (**-ая**, **-ое**, **-ие**) *прил* lyrical.

лири́чн|ый (**-ен**, **-на**, **-но**) *прил* lyrical.

лис (**-а**) *м* (male) fox, dog fox.

лис|а́ (**-ы́**; *nom pl* **-ы**) *ж* fox; (*перен: хитрый человек*) sly fox.

лис|ёнок (**-ёнка**; *nom pl* **-я́та**, *gen pl* **-я́т**) *м* fox cub.

ли́с|ий (**-ья**, **-ье**, **-ьи**) *прил* (*след, нора*) fox's; (*шуба, воротник, горжетка*) fox-fur.

лиси́ц|а (**-ы**) *ж* vixen.

лиси́ч|ка (**-ки**; *gen pl* **-ек**) *ж уменьш от* **лиса́**; (*гриб*) chanterelle.

лист (**-а́**; *nom pl* **-ья**) *м* (*растения, дерева*) leaf; (*nom pl* **-ы́**; *бумаги, железа*) sheet; **исполни́тельный ~** writ of execution; **опро́сный ~** questionnaire.

лист|а́ть (**-ю**) *несов перех* (*страницы*) to turn; **~** (*impf*) **кни́гу** to leaf through a book.

листв|а́ (**-ы́**) *ж собир* foliage, leaves *мн*.

ли́ственниц|а (-ы) ж larch.
ли́ственный *прил* deciduous.
листка́ *итп сущ см* **листо́к.**
листо́в|ка (-ки; *gen pl* -ок) ж leaflet.
листово́й *прил* (сталь, железо) sheet *опред*; (табак) leaf *опред*.
листо́вок *сущ см* **листо́вка.**
лист|о́к (-ка́) м (бумаги) sheet; (бланк: контрольный, техосмотра) certificate; **листо́к нетрудоспосо́бности** disability certificate.
листопа́д (-а) м fall of leaves.
ли́стья *итп сущ см* **лист.**
лися́та *итп сущ см* **лисёнок.**
лит (-а) м lit (*Lithuanian currency unit*).
лита́вр|ы (-) *мн* kettledrum *ед*; **бить** (*impf*) **в ~** (*перен: торжествовать*) to sound the trumpets.
Литв|а́ (-ы́) ж Lithuania.
лите́йный *прил*: ~ **цех** foundry.
лите́йщик (-а) м foundry worker.
ли́тер|а (-ы) ж (*типог*) type.
литера́тор (-а) м literary man.
литерату́р|а (-ы) ж literature; (*также:* худо́жественная ~) fiction.
литерату́рный *прил* literary; **литерату́рный язы́к** literary language.
литературове́д (-а) м literary critic.
литературове́дени|е (-я) *ср* literary criticism.
литературове́дческ|ий (-ая, -ое, -ие) *прил* literary.
ли́терный *прил* (*с цифрой*) lettered; ~ **набо́р** typesetting.
ли́ти|й (-я) м lithium.
лито́в|ец (-ца) м Lithuanian.
лито́в|ка (-ки; *gen pl* -ок) ж *см* **лито́вец.**
лито́вск|ий (-ая, -ое, -ие) *прил* Lithuanian; ~ **язы́к** Lithuanian.
лито́вца *итп сущ см* **лито́вец.**
литографи́ческ|ий (-ая, -ое, -ие) *прил* lithographic.
литогра́фи|я (-и) ж (*искусство*) lithograph; (*типог*) lithography.
лито́й *прил* (*тех*) moulded (*BRIT*), molded (*US*), cast; **лито́е изде́лие** cast.
литр (-а) м litre (*BRIT*), liter (*US*).
ли́тровый *прил* (*бутылка, фляга итп*) (one-) litre (*BRIT*), (one-)liter (*US*).
литурги́|я (-и) ж liturgy.
лить (лью, льёшь; *рт* лил, лила́, ли́ло) *несов перех* (*воду*) to pour; (*слёзы*) to shed; (*тех: детали, изделия*) to cast, mould (*BRIT*), mold (*US*) ♦ *неперех* (*вода, дождь*) to pour; **дождь льёт как из ведра́** it's pouring (down)
▸ **ли́ться** *несов возв* (*вода*) to pour; (*перен: звуки*) to float; (: *свет*) to flood.
литьё (-я́) *ср* (*действие: деталей*) casting, moulding (*BRIT*), molding (*US*) ♦ *собир* (*литые изделия*) casts *мн*.
лиф (-а) м bodice.
лифт (-а) м lift.
лифтёр (-а) м lift operator.
лифтёрш|а (-и) ж *см* **лифтёр.**

ли́фчик (-а) м bra.
лиха́ч (-а́) м (*разг*) reckless driver.
лиха́честв|о (-а) *ср* (*при вождении*) reckless driving; (*в поведении*) recklessness.
лихв|а́ (-ы́) ж: **он отплати́л мне с ~о́й за мою́ доброту́** he more than repaid me for my kindness; **тебе́ вре́мени/де́нег хва́тит с ~о́й** you've got more than enough time/money.
ли́х|о (-а) *ср*: **не помина́й(те) ~м** (*разг*) remember me kindly.
лих|о́й (-, -а́, -о) *прил* (*наездник*) dashing; (*скакун*) swift; (*пора, враг*) evil; ~**а́ беда́ нача́ло** the first step is the hardest.
лихора́дить (*3sg* -ит) *несов безл*: **меня́ ~ит** I feel feverish; **эконо́мику ~ит** the economy is ailing.
лихора́д|ка (-и) ж (*мед, также перен*) fever; (: *на губа́х*) cold sore; **золота́я ~** gold fever.
лихора́дочн|ый (-ен, -на, -но) *прил* (*также перен*) feverish.
Лихтенште́йн (-а) м Liechtenstein.
лицев|о́й *прил* (*нерв*) facial; ~**а́я сторона́ мате́рии** the right side of the material; **лицево́й счёт** personal account.
лицезре́ть (-ю, -ишь) *несов перех* to behold.
лице́ист (-а) м lycée pupil, ≈ secondary school pupil.
лице́й (-я) м lycée, ≈ secondary school.
лицеме́р (-а) м hypocrite.
лицеме́рен *прил см* **лицеме́рный.**
лицеме́ри|е (-я) *ср* hypocrisy.
лицеме́р|ить (-ю, -ишь) *несов неперех* to be hypocritical *или* a hypocrite.
лицеме́рный (-ен, -на, -но) *прил* hypocritical.
лицензи́ровани|е (-я) *ср* licensing.
лице́нзи|я (-и) ж licence (*BRIT*), license (*US*).
лиц|о́ (-а́; *nom pl* -а) *ср* face; (*перен: индивидуа́льность*) image; (*ткани итп*) right side; (*линг*) person; **от ~а́** +*gen* in the name of, on behalf of; **пе́ред ~м** +*gen* in the face of; **э́та блу́за тебе́ к ~цу́** that blouse suits you; **тебе́ не к ~цу́ безде́льничать** shame on you for being so lazy; **знать** (*impf*) **кого́-н в ~** to know sb's face; **на ней ~ца́ нет** she looks dreadful; **они́ не уда́рили в грязь ~м** they didn't disgrace themselves; **стира́ть** (**стере́ть** *perf*) **с ~ца́ земли́** to wipe from *или* off the face of the earth; **пе́рвое/тре́тье ~** (*линг*) first/third person; **показа́ть** (*perf*) **това́р ~м** to show sth to advantage; ~**м к лицу́** face to face; **официа́льное ~** official; **физи́ческое ~** (*юр*) natural person, individual.
личи́н|а (-ы) ж mask; **под ~ой** +*gen* under the guise of.
личи́н|ка (-ки; *gen pl* -ок) ж maggot.
ли́чно *нареч* (*знать*) personally; (*встре́тить*) in person; ~ **я** ... (*разг*) as for me ...; ~ **мне всё равно́** (*разг*) personally, I don't care; **он всё проверя́ет ~** he checks everything personally *или* himself.
ли́чность (-и) ж (*выдаю́щаяся, зага́дочная*)

individual; (обычно мн: обидные замечания) personal remark; устана́вливать (установи́ть perf) чью-н ~ to establish sb's identity.

ли́чный прил (персональный) personal; (частный) private; ли́чная ссу́да (комм) personal loan; ли́чное де́ло personal records; ли́чный соста́в staff.

лиша́й (-я) м herpes.

лиша́йник (-а) м lichen.

лиша́ть (-ю) несов от лиши́ть.

лише́н (-а́, -о́, -ы́) как сказ: он ~ та́кта/чу́вства ю́мора he is devoid of tact/a sense of humour; э́то не лишено́ основа́ния/смы́сла this is not totally lacking in reason/sense.

лише́ни|е (-я) ср (прав, привилегий) deprivation; (большое, горькое) loss; (обычно мн: нужда) privation; ~ свобо́ды imprisonment; терпе́ть (impf) ~я to suffer privation; ~ пра́ва со́бственности (ЮР) foreclosure.

лиши́ть (-у́, -и́шь; impf лиша́ть) сов перех: ~ кого-н/что-н +gen (отнять: прав, привилегий) to deprive sb/sth of; (покоя, счастья) to rob sb/sth of; лиша́ть (~ perf) кого́-н насле́дства to disinherit sb; лиша́ть (~ perf) жи́зни кого́-н to take sb's life; лиша́ть (~ perf) кого́-н сло́ва to deny sb the right to speak.

ли́шний (-яя, -ее, -ие) прил (вес) extra; (деньги, билет) spare; (расходы, вещи) unnecessary; ~ раз once again или more; не ~ее или ~е +infin ... it would not be a bad idea to ...; сказа́ть (perf) ~ее to say the wrong thing; три килогра́мма с ~им over three kilogrammes; тре́тий ~ three's a crowd.

лишь част (только) only ♦ союз (как только) as soon as; ~ бы она́ согласи́лась! if only she would agree!; ему́ не ва́жно что де́лать, ~ бы не рабо́тать he doesn't care what he does, as long as he doesn't have to work; ему́ ~ бы уйти́ he just wants to leave.

лоб (лба; loc sg лбу) м forehead; сказа́ть (perf) кому́-н в ~ (перен) to tell sb straight; у него́ на лбу напи́сано, что он врёт (разг) it's written all over his face that he's lying.

ло́бби ср нескл lobby.

лобби́ст (-а) м lobbyist.

ло́бзик (-а) м fret saw.

лобово́й прил frontal; лобово́е стекло́ windscreen (BRIT), windshield (US).

лоботря́с (-а) м (разг) lazybones.

лов (-а) м catching.

лов|е́ц (-ца́) м catcher; ~ же́мчуга pearl diver.

лови́ть (-лю́, -ишь; perf пойма́ть) несов перех to catch; (случай, момент) to seize; ~ (impf) ры́бу to fish; ~ (impf) кого́-н на лжи to catch sb out; пойма́ть (perf) кого́-н на сло́ве to take sb at their word; ~ (пойма́ть perf) на себе́ чей-н

взгляд to catch sb's eye; ~ (пойма́ть perf) себя́ на мы́сли, что ... to catch o.s. thinking that ....

ловка́ч (-а́) м (разг) dodgy character.

ло́в|кий (-кая, -кое, -кие; -ок, -ка́, -ко) прил (человек) agile; (прыжок, движение) nimble; (удар) swift; (разг: торговец) sharp.

ло́вко нареч (прыгнуть) nimbly; (придумать) smartly; (придумано, сделано) smartly ♦ как сказ that's smart.

ловлю́ несов см лови́ть.

ло́вл|я (-и) ж (действие) catching; ры́бная ~ fishing.

ло́вок прил см ло́вкий.

лову́ш|ка (-ки; gen pl -ек) ж (также перен) trap.

ловца́ итп сущ см лове́ц.

логари́фм (-а) м logarithm.

логарифми́чес|кий (-ая, -ое, -ие) прил: ~ая лине́йка slide rule.

ло́гик|а (-и) ж logic.

логи́чески нареч логи́чный.

логи́чес|кий (-ая, -ое, -ие) прил logical.

логи́чный (-ен, -на, -но) прил logical.

ло́говище (-а) ср (также перен) den, lair.

ло́гов|о (-а) ср = ло́говище.

ло́джи|я (-и) ж recess balcony.

ло́д|ка (-ки; gen pl -ок) ж boat; подво́дная ~ submarine.

ло́доч|ка (-ки; gen pl -ек) ж уменьш от ло́дка; (обычно мн: открытые туфли) court shoe.

ло́дочный прил (вёсла) boat's; ло́дочная ста́нция boat-hire place.

лоды́ж|ка (-ки; gen pl -ек) ж ankle.

ло́дырнича|ть (-ю) несов неперех (разг) to idle.

ло́дыр|ь (-я) м (разг) idler.

ло́ж|а (-и) ж (в театре, в зале) box; (массонская) lodge; ло́жа пре́ссы press gallery.

ложби́н|а (-ы) ж dip (in the ground).

ло́ж|е (-а) ср bed.

ло́жек сущ см ло́жка.

ло́жен прил см ло́жный.

ложи́ться (-у́сь, -и́шься) несов от лечь.

ло́ж|ка (-ки; gen pl -ек) ж spoon.

ло́ж|ный (-ен, -на, -но) прил false; (вывод) wrong; представля́ть (предста́вить perf) что-н в ~ном све́те to show sth in a false light; ло́жные показа́ния false evidence; ло́жная трево́га false alarm.

ложь (лжи; instr sg ло́жью) ж lie.

лоз|а́ (-ы́; nom pl -ы) ж (ивы итп) cane; (винограда) vine.

ло́зунг (-а) м (призыв) slogan; (плакат) banner.

лока́лен прил см лока́льный.

локализа́ци|я (-и) ж localization.

локализова́ть (-ую) (не)сов перех to localize.

лока́ль|ный (-ен, -ьна, -ьно) прил local.

лока́тор (-а) м: опти́ческий ~ radar; звуково́й ~ sonar.

локомоти́в (-а) м locomotive.
ло́кон (-а) м singlet.
ло́к|оть (-тя; *gen pl* -те́й, *dat pl* -тя́м) м elbow; **куса́ть** *(impf)* ~**ти** *(разг)* to kick o.s.; **чу́вство** ~**тя** team spirit.
ло́ктя *итп сущ см* **ло́коть**.
лом (-а) м crowbar ♦ *собир (для переработки)* scrap; **металли́ческий** ~ scrap metal.
лома́н|ый *прил* broken; ~**ая ли́ния** zigzag.
лома́|ть (-ю; *perf* **слома́ть** *или* **разлома́ть**) *несов перех (разделять на куски)* to break; *(perf* **слома́ть** *или* **полома́ть**; *приводить в негодность)* to break; *(perf* **полома́ть**; *устои, традиции)* to challenge; *(планы)* to frustrate; ~ *(impf)* **го́лову над чем-то** to rack one's brains over sth; ~ *(impf)* **привы́чки** to force o.s. to change one's habits; **жизнь слома́ла его́** life dealt him a cruel blow
▸ **лома́ться** *(perf* **полома́ться** *или* **слома́ться)** *несов возв* to break; *(no perf; перен: обычаи, устои)* to be challenged; *(: человек)* to show off; *(: заставлять себя просить)* to be fussy.
ломба́рд (-а) м pawnshop; **закла́дывать (заложи́ть** *perf)* **что-н в** ~ to pawn sth.
ломба́рдный *прил* pawn *опред*.
лом|и́ть (-лю́, -ишь) *несов безл:* **у меня́ ло́мит ко́сти** my bones are aching; **наро́д ло́мит туда́** *(разг)* the people are flocking there
▸ **ломи́ться** *несов возв (ветви, деревья)* to groan; *(разг: идти насильно)* to pour in; **стол** ~**и́лся от еды́** *(перен)* the table groaned under the food.
ло́мк|а (-и) ж breaking; *(разг)* cold turkey.
ло́мк|ий (-ая, -ое, -ие; -ок, -ка́, -ко) *прил (хрупкий: стекло)* fragile; *(: лёд)* brittle.
ломлю́(сь) *несов см* **ломи́ть(ся)**.
ломов|о́й *прил:* ~**а́я ло́шадь** carthorse; *(перен: разг)* dogsbody.
ло́мок *прил см* **ло́мкий**.
ломо́т|а (-ы) ж ache.
лом|о́ть (-тя) м slice.
ло́мтик (-а) м = **ломо́ть**.
ломтя *итп сущ см* **ломо́ть**.
Ло́ндон (-а) м London.
ло́ндон|ец (-ца) м Londoner.
ло́ндон|ка (-ки; *gen pl* -ок) ж см **ло́ндонец**.
ло́ндонца *итп сущ см* **ло́ндонец**.
ло́н|о (-а) ср *(женщины)* bosom; *(перен):* **на** ~**е приро́ды** in the open air.
ло́пас|ть (-и; *gen pl* -е́й) ж *(также тех)* blade.
лопа́т|а (-ы) ж spade.
лопа́т|ка (-ки; *gen pl* -ок) ж *уменьш от* **лопа́та**; *(АНАТ)* shoulder blade; **класть (положи́ть** *perf)* **кого́-н на о́бе** ~**ки** *(перен)* to beat sb hands down.
лопа́|ть (-ю; *perf* **сло́пать**) *несов перех (разг)* to gobble (up).
лопа́|ться (-юсь) *сов от* **ло́пнуть**.
ло́пн|уть (-ну, -нешь; *perf* **ло́паться**) *сов неперех (разрываться: шар)* to burst; *(стекло)* to shatter; *(верёвка, струна)* to snap; *(разг:*

банк, предприятие)* to go bust; **у меня́ терпе́ние ~**уло** *(разг)* I've run out of patience.
лопу́х (-á) м burdock; *(перен: разг: простак)* simpleton.
ЛОР м *сокр (= оториноларинго́логия)* ORL *(= otorhinolaryngology)*, ENT *(= ear-nose-throat)*.
лорд (-а) м lord.
лорне́т (-а) м lorgnette.
Лос-А́нджелес (-а) м Los Angeles.
лоси́н|а (-ы) ж *(кожа лося)* elkskin; *(мясо лося)* elk (meat); *см также* **лоси́ны**.
лоси́н|ы (-) *мн* leggings *мн*.
лоси́х|а (-и) ж female elk *или* moose *(мн* moose).
лоск (-а) м *(глянец)* shine; *(перен: в доме)* spotlessness; *(: в одежде)* flair; **наводи́ть (навести́** *perf)* ~ **на что-н** to give sth a polish.
лоску́т (-á) м *(материи, кожи)* scrap.
лоску́тн|ый *прил:* ~**ое одея́ло** patchwork quilt.
лосн|и́ться (-ю́сь, -и́шься) *несов возв (от жира, от крема)* to shine.
лососёвый *прил* salmon.
лососи́н|а (-ы) ж salmon *(meat)*.
лосо́с|ь (-я) м salmon.
лос|ь (-я; *gen pl* -е́й) м elk, moose *(мн* moose).
лосьо́н (-а) м lotion.
лот (-а) м *(МОР)* lead line; *(комм: на аукционе, на торгах)* lot.
лотере́йный *прил* lottery *опред*.
лотере́|я (-и) ж lottery.
лотка́ *итп сущ см* **лото́к**.
лото́ *ср нескл* lotto.
лот|о́к (-ка́) м *(прилавок)* stall; *(ящик для торговли)* trader's tray; *(жёлоб)* trough.
ло́тос (-а) м lotus.
пото́чник (-а) м stallholder.
лохма́|тить (-чу, -тишь; *perf* **взлохма́тить**) *несов перех* to fluff up.
лохма́т|ый (-, -а, -о) *прил (животное)* shaggy; *(волосы)* straggly; *(человек)* dishevelled.
лохма́чу *сов см* **лохма́тить**.
лохмо́ть|я (-ев) *мн* rags *мн*.
ло́цман (-а) м pilot *(on ship)*.
лошади́ный *прил (седло, упряжь)* horse's; *(лицо)* equine; **лошади́ная си́ла** horsepower.
лоша́дник (-а) м *(разг: любитель лошадей)* horse-lover; *(торговец лошадьми)* horse-trader.
ло́шад|ь (-и; *gen pl* -е́й) ж horse.
лощёный *прил (бумага)* glossy; *(перен: человек, внешность)* polished.
лощи́н|а (-ы) ж dell.
лоя́льный (-ен, -ьна, -ьно) *прил* loyal *(to the state)*.
л.с. *сокр (= лошади́ная си́ла)* h.p. *(= horsepower)*.
ЛСД м *сокр* LSD *(= lysergic acid diethylamide)*.
Луа́р|а (-ы) ж the Loire.
луб|о́к (-ка́) м *(кора)* bast; *(повязка)* splint; **ру́сский** ~ *(ФОЛЬКЛОР)* lubok *(popular colour print)*.

лубрикáтор (-а) м lubricant.

луг (-а; *loc sg* -ý, *nom pl* -á) м meadow.

лужи́ть (-жý, -ди́шь) *несов перех* to tin.

лýж|**а** (-и) ж (*на улице, на доро́ге*) puddle; (*на полý, на столе́*) pool; **сади́ться (сесть** *perf*) **в** ~**у** (*перен: разг*) to get o.s. into a mess.

лужáй|**ка** (-йки; *gen pl* -ек) ж (*полянка*) glade; (*газо́н*) lawn.

лужёный *прил* (*самова́р, ча́йник итп*) tin-plated; **у него́** ~**ая гло́тка** (*перен: разг*) he has iron lungs.

лужý *несов см* **луди́ть**.

лýз|**а** (-ы) ж pocket (*on a billiard table*).

лук (-а) м *собир* onions мн ♦ м (*оружие*) bow; **зелёный** ~ spring onion (*BRIT*), scallion; **рéпчатый** ~ onion bulbs.

лукáв|**ить** (-лю, -ишь; *perf* **слукáвить**) *несов неперех* to be deceitful; **ты, кáжется,** ~**ишь** you're being a bit vague.

лукáв|**ый** (-, -а, -о) *прил* (*челове́к, посту́пок*) crafty; (*взгляд, улы́бка*) sly; (*де́вушка*) coquettish.

лýкови|**ца** (-ы) ж bulb; (*воло́са*) follicle.

лукóш|**ко** (-ка; *gen pl* -ек) *ср* basket.

лун|**á** (-ы́) ж moon; **ты что, с** ~**ы́ свали́лся?** where've you been all this time?

лунá-пáрк (-а) м funfair (*BRIT*), amusement park (*US*).

лунáтик (-а) м sleepwalker.

лýн|**ка** (-ки; *gen pl* -ок) ж hole.

лýнный *прил:* ~**ые фáзы** phases of the moon; **лýнный свет** moonlight.

лунóк *сущ см* **лýнка**.

лунохóд (-а) м lunar research module.

лунь (-я́) м harrier.

лýп|**а** (-ы) ж magnifying glass.

лупи́ть (-лю, -ишь; *perf* **облупи́ть**) *несов перех* (*яйцо́*) to shell; (*perf* **отлупи́ть**; *разг: бить*) to thrash; (*no perf*; *разг: сильно ударя́ть*) to hammer or

➤ **лупи́ться** (*perf* **облупи́ться**) *несов возв* (*шелуши́ться*) to peel (off).

луч (-á) м ray; (*проже́ктора, фонаря́*) beam; **рентгéновские** ~**и** X-ray; ~ **надéжды** a ray of hope; **лáзерный** ~ laser beam.

лучевóй *прил* (*физ: эне́ргия*) beamed; ~**áя кость** radius (*bone*); **лучевáя болéзнь** radiation sickness.

лучезáр|**ный** (-ен, -на, -но) *прил* (*бýдущее*) glorious; (*улы́бка*) radiant.

лучи́н|**а** (-ы) ж (*ще́пка*) splinter ♦ *собир* (*ще́пки*) kindling wood *собир*.

лучи́ст|**ый** (-, -а, -о) *прил* (*улы́бка, лицо́*) beaming; (*глаза́*) shining.

лýчник (-а) м archer.

лýчни|**ца** (-ы) ж см **лýчник**.

лýчше *сравн прил от* **хорóший** ♦ *сравн нареч от* **хорошó** ♦ *как сказ:* **больнóму** ~ the patient is feeling better ♦ *част:* ~ **не опрáвдывайся** don't try and justify yourself ♦ *вводн сл:* ~ (**всегó**) **éсли ты позвони́шь ве́чером** it would be better if you phone in the evening; **от э́того никомý не** ~ it doesn't do anyone any good; **нам** ~ **чем им** we're better off than them; **будь остóрожен и́ли,** ~, **вообщé не ходи́ тудá** take care, or better still, don't go there at all; ~ **возьми́ маши́ну** you'd better take the car; **как нельзя́** ~ couldn't be better; ~ **не спрáшивай** don't ask.

лýчш|**ий** (-ая, -ее, -ие) *прил* (*са́мый хорóший*) best; **э́то** ~**ая рабóта в клáссе** it's the best work in the class; **в** ~**ем слýчае нам удáстся закóнчить рабóту зáвтра** if we're lucky we'll finish the work tomorrow; **за неимéнием** ~**его** for want of something better; **э́то (всё) к** ~**ему** it's (all) for the best.

лущи́ть (-ý, -и́шь; *perf* **облущи́ть**) *несов перех* (*се́мечки, оре́хи*) to crack (open); (*горо́х*) to shell.

лы́ж|**а** (-и) ж (*обы́чно мн*) ski; см *также* **лы́жи**.

лы́ж|**и** (-) *мн* (*вид спóрта*) skiing; **вóдные** ~ (*сами лы́жи*) water-skis; (*вид спóрта*) water-skiing; **гóрные** ~ downhill skis; **ходи́ть** (*impf*) **на** ~**ах** to go cross-country skiing.

лы́жник (-а) м skier.

лы́жни|**ца** (-ы) ж см **лы́жник**.

лы́жный *прил* (*крепле́ния, мазь итп*) ski *опред*; (*соревнова́ния*) skiing *опред*; **лы́жный костю́м** ski suit; **лы́жные пáлки** ski poles.

лыжня́ (-и́) ж ski track.

лы́к|**о** (-а) *ср* (*ли́пы, и́вы*) bast; **он** ~**а не вя́жет** (*разг*) he's roaring drunk; **он не** ~**м шит** (*разг*) he's someone to be reckoned with.

лысé|**ть** (-ю; *perf* **облысéть** *или* **полысéть**) *несов неперех* to go bald.

лы́син|**а** (-ы) ж bald patch.

лы́с|**ый** (-, -á, -о) *прил* (*голова́, челове́к*) bald; (*гора́, холм*) bare.

ль *част* = **ли**.

львёнок (-ёнка; *nom pl* -я́та, *gen pl* -я́т) м lion cub.

льви́н|**ый** *прил* (*шкýра, гри́ва итп*) lion's; ~**ая стáя** pride of lions; ~**ая дóля** the lion's share; **льви́ный зев** (*БОТ*) snapdragon.

льви́|**ца** (-ы) ж lioness.

Львов (-а) м Lvov.

львя́та итп *сущ см* **львёнок**.

льгóт|**а** (-ы) ж (*инвали́дам, бере́менным итп*) benefit; (*обы́чно мн: предприя́тиям, экспортёрам*) special term; (*эли́те, ветерáнам*) privilege; **налóговые** ~**ы** tax relief.

льгóтный *прил* (*тари́ф*) concessionary; (*усло́вия*) privileged; (*заём*) special-rate; **льгóтный биле́т** concessionary ticket.

льда итп *сущ см* **лёд**.

льди́н|**а** (-ы) ж ice floe.

льди́н|ка (-ки; *gen pl* -ок) *ж* piece of ice.
льна *итп сущ см* **лён**.
льново́дств|о (-а) *ср* flax-growing.
льн|у́ть (-у́, -ёшь; *perf* **прильну́ть**) *несов неперех:* ~ **к** +*dat* (*к ма́тери*) to cling to; (*перен: к богача́м, к влия́тельным лю́дям*) to try to get in with.
льняно́|й *прил* (*полоте́нце, пла́тье*) linen; (*цвет*) flaxen; ~**ое полотно́** linen; **льняно́е ма́сло** linseed oil.
льсте́ц (-а́) *м* flatterer.
льсти́в|ый (-, -а, -о) *прил* (*челове́к*) smarmy; (*улы́бка*) unctuous; (*завере́ния, речь*) flattering.
льс|ти́ть (-щу́, -сти́шь; *perf* **польсти́ть**) *несов неперех* (+*dat*; *хвали́ть из коры́сти*) to flatter; (*доставля́ть удовлетворе́ние*) to gratify; ~ (*impf*) **себя́ наде́ждой** to live in hope.
лью(сь) *итп несов см* **лить(ся)**.
любвеоби́льн|ый (-ен, -ьна, -ьно) *прил* loving.
любви́ *итп сущ см* **любо́вь**.
любе́зен *прил см* **любе́зный**.
любе́знича|ть (-ю) *несов неперех:* ~ **с** +*instr* (*разг*) to pay compliments to.
любе́зность (-и) *ж* (*одолже́ние*) favour (*BRIT*), favor (*US*); (*комплиме́нт*) compliment; (*в поведе́нии*) courtesy; **ока́зывать** (**оказа́ть** *perf*) ~ **кому́-н** to do sb a favour; **не откажи́те в** ~**и?** would you do me a favour?
любе́зн|ый (-ен, -на, -но) *прил* polite; **бу́дьте** ~**ны!** excuse me, please!; **бу́дьте** ~**ны, принеси́те нам ко́фе?** could you be so kind as to bring us some coffee?
люби́м|ая (-ой; *decl like adj*) *ж* beloved.
люби́м|ец (-ца) *м* (*челове́к, живо́тное*) favourite (*BRIT*), favorite (*US*).
люби́мица (-ы) *ж см* **люби́мец**.
люби́мца *итп сущ см* **люби́мец**.
люби́мчик (-а) *м* (*разг*) pet; **быть** (*impf*) **в** ~**ах у кого́-н** to be sb's pet.
люби́м|ый (-, -а, -о) *прил* (*же́нщина, брат*) beloved; (*писа́тель, заня́тие итп*) favourite (*BRIT*), favorite (*US*) ♦ (*-ого; decl like adj*) *м* beloved.
люби́тел|ь (-я) *м* (*непрофессиона́л*) amateur; ~ **му́зыки/спо́рта** music-/sports-lover.
люби́тельница (-ы) *ж:* ~ **му́зыки/чте́ния** music-/book-lover.
люби́тельск|ий (-ая, -ое, -ие) *прил* (*спорт, теа́тр итп*) amateur; **люби́тельские права́** driving licence (*BRIT*) *или* driver's license (*US*).
люб|и́ть (-лю́, -ишь) *несов перех* (*ро́дину, мать, му́жа итп*) to love; (*му́зыку, спорт итп*) to like; **я** ~**лю́ его́ всем се́рдцем** I love him with all my heart; **цветы́ лю́бят тепло́** plants like the warmth; **я** ~**лю́, когда́ мне говоря́т комплиме́нты** I like it when people pay me compliments; **я** ~**лю́, когда́ лю́ди прихо́дят во́время** I like it when people come on time.
люб|ова́ться (-у́юсь; *perf* **полюбова́ться**) *несов возв* (+*instr*) to admire; **полюбу́йтесь на**

него́! take a look at him!
любо́вник (-а) *м* lover.
любо́вница (-ы) *ж см* **любо́вник**.
любо́вный *прил* (*дела́, похожде́ния*) lover's; (*пе́сня, письмо́*) love *опред*; (*отноше́ние, подхо́д*) loving.
любо́в|ь (-ви́) *ж* love; (*привя́занность*): ~ **к** +*dat* (*к ро́дине, к ма́тери итп*) love for; (*к чте́нию, к иску́сству итп*) love of; **занима́ться** (*impf*) ~**ю** to make love.
любозна́телен *прил см* **любозна́тельный**.
любозна́тельность (-и) *ж* inquisitiveness.
любозна́тельн|ый (-ен, -ьна, -ьно) *прил* inquisitive.
любо́й *мест* (*вся́кий*) any ♦ (*-ого; decl like adj*) *м* (*любо́й челове́к*) anyone; **в** ~**ое вре́мя** at any time; ~ **цено́й** at any price.
любопы́тен *прил см* **любопы́тный**.
любопы́тно *нареч* curiously ♦ *как сказ:* ~**!** that's interesting!; (*мне*) ~ **узна́ть** I'm intrigued *или* curious to know.
любопы́тн|ый (-ен, -на, -но) *прил* (*приме́р, кни́га итп*) interesting; (*челове́к, толпа́*) curious.
любопы́тств|о (-а) *ср* curiosity; **из** ~**а** out of curiosity.
любя́щий (-ая, -ее, -ие) *прил* loving.
люд (-а) *м собир* (*разг*) folk.
лю́ден *прил см* **лю́дный**.
лю́д|и (-е́й; *dat pl* -ям, *instr pl* -ьми́, *prp pl* -ях) *мн* people *мн*; (*солда́ты и офице́ры*) men *мн*; (*ка́дры*) staff *ед*; **выходи́ть** (**вы́йти** *perf*) **в** ~ to get on in life; **на** ~**ях** (*разг*) in public; **молоды́е** ~ young men; (*молодёжь*) young people; *см также* **челове́к**.
лю́дн|ый (-ен, -на, -но) *прил* (*у́лица итп*) busy; (*го́род*) lively; (*сбо́рище*) crowded.
людое́д (-а) *м* (*челове́к*) cannibal; (*живо́тное*) man-eater; (*в ска́зке*) ogre.
людое́дств|о (-а) *ср* cannibalism.
людско́й *прил* human; **род** ~ humankind.
люк (-а) *м* (*та́нка, самолёта*) hatch; (*на доро́ге*) manhole; (*на сце́не*) trap door.
люкс (-а) *м* (*о ваго́не*) first-class carriage; (*о каю́те*) first-class cabin ♦ *прил неизм* (*вы́сшего кла́сса*) first-class; **мы живём в лю́ксе** we've got a luxury suite.
Люксембу́рг (-а) *м* Luxemburg.
лю́л|ька (-ьки; *gen pl* -ек) *ж* (*также* СТРОИТ) cradle; (*мотоци́кла*) sidecar.
лю́мпен (-а) *м* member of the lumpen proletariat.
люпи́н (-а) *м* lupin.
лю́рекс (-а) *м* lurex.
лю́стр|а (-ы) *ж* chandelier.
лю́тен *сущ см* **лю́тня**.
лютера́н|ин (-ина; *nom pl* -е, *gen pl* -) *м* Lutheran.
лютера́н|ка (-ки; *gen pl* -ок) *ж см* **лютера́нин**.
лютера́нск|ий (-ая, -ое, -ие) *прил* Lutheran.
лю́тик (-а) *м* buttercup.
лю́т|ня (-ни; *gen pl* -ен) *ж* lute.
лю́т|ый (-, -а́, -о) *прил* (*враг, зверь*) fierce;

(*ненависть, горе*) intense; (*мороз*) severe.

люце́рн|а (-ы) *ж* lucerne.

ля *ср нескл* (*муз*) lah.

ляга́|ть (-ю) *несов перех* (*подлеж: лошадь, корова*) to kick.

▶ **ляга́ться** *несов возв* (*лошадь, корова*) to kick.

лягн|у́ть (-у́, -ёшь) *сов перех* to kick.

ляг(те) *сов см* **лечь**.

ля́гу *итп сов см* **лечь**.

лягуша́та *итп сущ см* **лягушо́нок**.

лягуша́тник (-а) *м* (*разг*) shallow end.

лягу́ш|ка (-ки; *gen pl* -ек) *ж* frog.

лягушо́н|ок (-онка; *nom pl* -а́та, *gen pl* -а́т) *м* young frog.

ля́жек *сущ см* **ля́жка**.

ля́жешь *итп сов см* **лечь**.

ля́ж|ка (-ки; *gen pl* -ек) *ж* thigh.

лязг (-а) *м* (*звук: цепей, оружия*) clanging; (: *зубов*) gnash; (: *подков*) clatter.

ля́зга|ть (-ю) *несов неперех* (*засов, цепь*) to clang; (+*instr*; *зубами*) to gnash; (*ключами*) to rattle.

ля́м|ка (-ки; *gen pl* -ок) *ж* strap; **тяну́ть** (*impf*) ~**ку** (*разг*) to toil away.

ля́па|ть (-ю) *несов от* **ля́пнуть** ◆ (*perf* **сля́пать**) *перех* (*разг: делать наспех*) to slap together ◆ (*perf* **наля́пать**) *перех* to make a mess of ◆ *неперех* to make a mess.

ля́пн|уть (-у, -ешь; *impf* **ля́пать**) *сов перех*: ~ **глу́пость** to make a blunder.

ля́псус (-а) *м* blunder.

~ M, м ~

М, м *сущ нескл* *(буква)* the 13th letter of the Russian alphabet.

М *сокр* = **метро**; (= *мегабайт*) MB (= *megabyte*).

м *сокр* (= *метр*) m= *metre* (BRIT) *или* meter (US); (= *минута*) m (= *minute*).

мавзолей (-я) *м* mausoleum.

маг (-а) *м* magician, wizard; *(разг)* tape recorder.

магазин (-а) *м* shop; *(ружья)* magazine.

МАГАТЭ *ср сокр* (= *Международное агентство по атомной энергии*) IAEA (= *International Atomic Energy Agency*).

магистр (-а) *м* *(учёная степень)* master's degree; ~ **гуманитарных наук** Master of Arts.

магистраль (-и) *ж* *(железнодорожная)* main line; *(дорожная)* arterial road; **водная** ~ main waterway.

магистральный *прил* main.

магический (-ая, -ое, -ие) *прил* *(перен)* magic *опред*.

магия (-и) *ж* magic.

магнат (-а) *м* magnate.

магнезия (-и) *ж* magnesia.

магнетизм (-а) *м* magnetism.

магний (-я) *м* magnesium.

магнит (-а) *м* magnet.

магнитный *прил* magnetic; ~ **диск** (КОМП) magnetic disk.

магнитола (-ы) *ж* radio cassette player.

магнитофон (-а) *м* tape recorder; *(кассетный)* tape *или* cassette recorder.

магнитофонный *прил*: ~**ая запись** tape recording; ~**ая кассета** (audio)cassette.

магнолия (-и) *ж* magnolia.

Мадагаскар (-а) *м* Madagascar.

мадам *ж нескл* madame.

мадемуазель (-и) *ж* mademoiselle.

мадонна (-ы) *ж* madonna.

Мадрид (-а) *м* Madrid.

маёк *сущ см* **майка**.

маета (-ы́) *ж* *(разг)* bother.

мажор (-а) *м* (МУЗ) major key.

мажоритарный *прил*: ~**ая система** (ПОЛИТ) system of majority rule.

мажорный *прил* (МУЗ) major; *(перен: настроение)* cheerful.

МАЗ *м сокр* = *Минский автомобильный завод*; *(автомобиль)* vehicle manufactured at the Minsk car factory.

мазать (-жу, -жешь; *perf* **намазать** *или* **помазать**) *несов перех* to spread; *(perf* **измазать**; *разг: пачкать)* to get dirty; (: *рисовать*) to daub ◆ *(perf* **промазать**) *неперех (разг)* to miss; ~ **(намазать** *perf)* **чем-н что-н** to spread sth with sth; ~ **(намазать** *perf)* **губы помадой** to put on lipstick

▶ **мазаться** *(perf* **намазаться**) *несов возв (разг: делать макияж)* to put on make-up; *(perf* **вымазаться** *или* **измазаться**; *разг: пачкаться)* to get dirty; ~**ся (намазаться** *perf)* **кремом/мазью** to apply cream/ointment.

мазка *сущ см* **мазок**.

мазня (-и́) *ж (разг: о рисовании)* daub; (: *о письме*) scribble.

мазок (-ка́) *м (кисти)* stroke; *(МЕД)* smear.

мазурка (-и) *ж* mazurka.

мазут (-а) *м* fuel oil.

мазь (-и) *ж (МЕД)* ointment; *(лыжная)* wax; *(колёсная)* grease; **дело на ~й** *(разг)* things are going smoothly.

майс (-а) *м* maize (BRIT), corn (US).

майсовый *прил* maize (BRIT), corn (US).

май (-я) *м* May; *см также* **октябрь**.

майка (-йки; *gen pl* -ек) *ж* vest (BRIT), sleeveless undershirt (US).

майолика (-и) *ж собир* majolica.

майонез (-а) *м* mayonnaise.

майор (-а) *м* (ВОЕН) major.

майский (-ая, -ое, -ие) *прил* May *опред*; **майский жук** May beetle, cockchafer.

мак (-а) *м* poppy; *(КУЛИН)* poppy seeds *мн*.

макака (-и) *ж* macaque.

макаронник (-а) *м* pasta bake.

макароны (-) *мн* pasta *ед*.

макаронный *прил (КУЛИН)* pasta *опред*; **макаронные изделия** pasta.

макать (-ю) *несов перех* to dip.

македонец (-ца) *м* Macedonian.

Македония (-и) *ж* Macedonia.

македонка (-ки; *gen pl* -ок) *ж см* **македонец**.

македонский (-ая, -ое, -ие) *прил* Macedonian.

македонца *сущ см* **македонец**.

макет (-а) *м (модель)* model; *(КОМП)* breadboard

макинтош (-а) *м* mackintosh.

маклер (-а) *м* (КОММ) broker.

макнуть (-у́, -ёшь) *сов перех (перо, кисть)* to dip.

маковка (-и) *ж* poppyhead; *(разг: купол церкви)* (onion) dome.

ма́ков|ый (-, -а, -о) *прил* poppy-seed *опред*; **с ~о зёрнышко** as small as a pinhead; **у него с утра́ во рту́ ~ой роси́нки не́ было** he hasn't had a bite to eat since morning.

макраме́ *ср нескл* macramé.

макре́л|ь (-и) *ж* mackerel.

макроэконо́мик|а (-и) *ж* macroeconomics *мн*.

ма́кси *ср нескл* maxi ◆ *прил неизм* maxi *опред*.

макс(им). *сокр* (= максима́льный) max. (= *maximum*).

максима́лен *прил см* **максима́льный**.

максимали́ст (-а) *м* maximalist.

максима́льн|ый (-ен, -ьна, -ьно) *прил* maximum *опред*.

ма́ксимум (-а) *м* maximum ◆ *нареч* at most, maximum.

макулату́р|а (-ы) *ж собир* wastepaper (*for recycling*); (*перен: пренебр*) pulp literature.

маку́шк|а (-ки; *gen pl* -ек) *ж* (*разг: дерева, горы*) top; (*головы*) crown; **у него́ у́шки на ~ке** he's keeping his ear to the ground.

Мала́ви *ср нескл* Malawi.

мала́г|а (-и) *ж* (*вино*) Malaga (wine).

мала́|ец (-йца) *м* Malay.

Мала́йзи|я (-и) *ж* Malaysia.

мала́йк|а (-йки; *gen pl* -ек) *ж см* **мала́ец**.

мала́йск|ий (-ая, -ое, -ие) *прил* Malaysian.

мала́йца *сущ см* **мала́ец**.

малахи́т (-а) *м* malachite.

малева́|ть (-юю, -юешь; *perf* **намалева́ть**) *несов перех* (*разг*) to daub.

мале́йш|ий (-ая, -ое, -ие) *прил* (*ошибка, промах*) the slightest; **не име́ть** (*impf*) **ни ~его представле́ния о чём-н** to not have the slightest idea about sth.

мал|ёк (-ька́) *м* young (fish), fry.

ма́леньк|ий (-ая, -ое, -ие) *прил* small, little; (*незначительный*) slight; (*малолетний*) little ◆ (-ого; *decl like adj*) *м* little one; **моё де́ло ~ое** (*разг*) it's none of my business; **ма́ленькая бу́ква** small letter.

Мали́ *ср нескл* Mali.

мали́н|а (-ы) *ж* (*кустарник*) raspberry cane *или* bush; (*ягода*) raspberries *мн*; **не жизнь, а ~!** (*разг*) it's a cushy life!

мали́нник (-а) *м собир* raspberry canes *мн*.

малино́вк|а (-и) *ж* robin (redbreast).

мали́новый *прил* (*варенье, куст*) raspberry; (*цвет*) crimson.

KEYWORD

ма́ло *чис* (+*gen*; *друзей, книг*) only a few; (*работы, денег*) not much; **нам да́ли ма́ло книг** they only gave us a few books; **я ви́дел ма́ло друзе́й** I only saw a few friends; **у меня́ ма́ло де́нег** I don't have much money; **ма́ло ра́дости** little joy

◆ *нареч* not much; **она́ ма́ло измени́лась** she hasn't changed much; **они́ ма́ло рабо́тают** they don't work much

◆ *как сказ*: **критикова́ть ма́ло, на́до помо́чь** it's not enough to criticize, you have to help; **мне э́того ма́ло** this is not enough for me; **ему́ всё ма́ло** it is impossible to satisfy him; **ма́ло ли что** so what?; **ма́ло ли кто/где/когда́** it doesn't matter who/where/when; **ма́ло того́** (and) what's more; **ма́ло того́, она́ ещё груби́ла** (and) what's more, she was rude; **ма́ло того́ что** not only; **ма́ло того́ что бы́ло хо́лодно, нам ещё не да́ли у́жин** not only was it cold, but they didn't give us any supper.

малова́ж|ный (-ен, -на, -но) *прил* of little importance.

малова́т *как сказ* (*разг: о размере*) on the small side.

малова́то *нареч* (*разг*) not quite enough.

малове́р (-а) *м* sceptic.

маловеро́я́т|ный (-ен, -на, -но) *прил* improbable.

малово́д|ье (-ья; *gen pl* -ий) *ср* low water level; (*недостаток воды*) drought.

маловы́год|ный (-ен, -на, -но) *прил* unprofitable.

малогабари́т|ный (-ен, -на, -но) *прил* small.

малогово́ря́щий (-ая, -ее, -ие) *прил* unimpressive.

малогра́мот|ный (-ен, -на, -но) *прил* semiliterate; (*руководитель*) incompetent.

малодосту́п|ный (-ен, -на, -но) *прил* (*место*) inaccessible.

малоду́шен *прил см* **малоду́шный**.

малоду́шнича|ть (-ю; *perf* **смалоду́шничать**) *несов неперех* (*разг*) to be yellow (*fig*).

малоду́ш|ный (-ен, -на, -но) *прил* cowardly.

малозаме́т|ный (-ен, -на, -но) *прил* (*пятно, окраска*) hardly noticeable; (*человек, событие*) insignificant.

малознако́м|ый (-, -а, -о) *прил* unfamiliar.

малокали́берный *прил* small-bore, small-calibre (*BRIT*), small-caliber (*US*).

малокро́ви|е (-я) *ср* (sickle-cell) anaemia (*BRIT*) *или* anemia (*US*).

малоле́тк|а (-и) *м/ж* (*разг*) kid.

малоле́т|ний (-яя, -ее, -ие) *прил* young.

малолитра́жк|а (-ки; *gen pl* -ек) *ж* (*разг*) small car (*with small cylinder capacity*).

малолитра́жный *прил*: **~ автомоби́ль** small car (*with small cylinder capacity*).

малолю́д|ный (-ен, -на, -но) *прил* (*улица*) unfrequented; (*район, село*) sparsely populated.

ма́ло-ма́льски *нареч* (*разг*) quite.

малома́льск|ий (-ая, -ое, -ие) *прил* (*разг*) the slightest.

малому́щный (-ен, -на, -но) *прил* weak.

малонаселён|ный *прил* sparsely populated.

малообеспе́ченный *прил* disadvantaged.

малообла́ч|ный (-ен, -на, -но) *прил* (*небо,*

погода) slightly cloudy.
малообразóванн|ый (-, -на, -но) *прил*
undereducated.
малоподвúжный (-ен, -на, -но) *прил* (*образ
жизни*) sedentary.
мáло-помáлу *нареч* (*разг*) little by little.
малорáзвит|ый (-, -а, -о) *прил* underdeveloped.
малорóслый *прил* undersized.
малосемéйн|ый (-ен, -йна, -йно) *прил* with a
small family.
малосúль|ный (-ен, -ьна, -ьно) *прил*
(*двигатель*) low-powered; (*лошадь*) weak.
малосóл|ьный (-ен, -ьна, -ьно) *прил* pickled
(*in weak brine*).
мáлост|ь (-и) *ж* (*разг*) trifle ◆ *нареч* (*разг*) a bit.
малотирáжный *прил* (*газета, журнал*) with a
low circulation; (*книга*) *published in a small
edition*.
малочúслен|ный (-, -на, -но) *прил* small;
(*поселения*) scarce.
мáл|ый (-, -á, -о) *прил* small, little; (*доход,
скорость*) low ◆ (-ого; *decl like adj*) *м* (*разг*)
chap; (*молодой человек*) lad ◆ *как сказ* (*no full
form*): **плáтье/пальтó мáло** the dress/coat is too
small; **довóльствоваться** (*impf*) **~ым** to have
modest needs; **с ~ых лет** from childhood; **у
негó семья́ мал малá мéньше** he has a very
large family of small children; **он мал да удáл**
(*разг*) he's a smart little guy; **без ~ого два часá**
(*разг*) just before two o'clock; **сáмое ~ое** at the
very least; **Мáлая Áзия** Asia Minor.
малы́ш (-á) *м* little boy.
малы́шк|а (-ки; *gen pl* -ек) *ж* little girl.
малышня́ (-й) *ж собир* (*разг*) little kids *мн*.
мáльв|а (-ы) *ж* mallow.
мальдúвск|ий (-ая, -ое, -ие) *прил*: **М~ие
островá** Maldives, Maldive Islands.
малькá *сущ см* **малёк**.
Мáльт|а (-ы) *ж* Malta.
мальтú|ец (-йца) *м* Maltese.
мальтú|йка (-йки; *gen pl* -ек) *ж см* **мальтúец**.
мальтúйск|ий (-ая, -ое, -ие) *прил* Maltese.
мальтúйца *сущ см* **мальтúец**.
мáльчик (-а) *м* boy.
мальчúшек *сущ см* **мальчúшка**.
мальчúшеск|ий (-ая, -ое, -ие) *прил* (*задор,
вид*) boyish; (*несерьёзный*) childish, puerile.
мальчúшеств|о (-а) *ср* childishness.
мальчúшк|а (-ки; *gen pl* -ек) *м* (*разг*) boy;
(*неопытный мужчина*) child.
мальчúшник (-а) *м* stag night *или* party (*BRIT*),
stag (*US*).
малю́сеньк|ий (-ая, -ое, -ие) *прил* (*разг*) tiny,
wee (*esp SCOTTISH*).
малю́тк|а (-ки; *gen pl* -ок) *м/ж* baby;
кнúжка/фотоаппарáт~ miniature book/
camera.
маля́вк|а (-ки; *gen pl* -ок) *ж* small fish ◆ *м/ж*
(*разг: пренебр*) shrimp.
маля́р (-á) *м* painter (and decorator).
малярúйный *прил* malarial.

маляри́|я (-и) *ж* malaria.
маля́рн|ый *прил* painter's; **~ая кисть**
paintbrush.
мáм|а (-ы) *ж* mummy (*BRIT*), mommy (*US*).
мамалы́г|а (-и) *ж* polenta, maize porridge.
мамáш|а (-и) *ж* (*разг: мать*) mummy (*BRIT*),
mommy (*US*); (: *обращение к пожилой
женщине*) missus.
мáменькин (-а, -о, -ы) *прил*: **~ сынóк** (*разг:
пренебр*) mummy's boy; **~а дóчка** (*разг*)
mummy's girl.
мáмонт (-а) *м* mammoth.
манáтк|и (-ок) *мн* (*разг*) stuff *ед*.
мáнго *ср нескл* mango.
мангýст|а (-ы) *ж* mongoose.
мандарúн (-а) *м* tangerine.
мандарúновый *прил* tangerine.
мандáт (-а) *м* mandate.
мандолúн|а (-ы) *ж* mandoline.
манёвр (-а) *м* (*также перен*) manoeuvre (*BRIT*),
maneuver (*US*); *см также* **манёвры**.
маневрúр|овать (-ую; *perf* **сманеврúровать**)
несов неперех (*войска, дипломат итп*) to
manoeuvre (*BRIT*), maneuver (*US*); (*перен*): **~
+instr** (*ресурсами, финансами*) to make full use
of.
манёвр|ы (-ов) *мн* manoeuvres *мн* (*BRIT*),
maneuvers *мн* (*US*); (*на железной дороге*)
shunting *ед*.
манé|ж (-а) *м* (*для верховой езды*) manège;
(*цирка*) ring; (*для младенцев*) playpen; (*также:
легкоатлетúческий ~*) indoor stadium (*мн
stadia*).
манекéн (-а) *м* (*портного*) dummy; (*в витрине*)
dummy, mannequin.
манекéнщик (-а) *м* model.
манекéнщиц|а (-ы) *ж см* **манекéнщик**.
манé|р (-а) *м* (*разг*): **такúм ~ом** like this ◆
предл: **на ~ +gen** like.
манéр|а (-ы) *ж* manner; (*художника, поэта*)
style; *см также* **манéры**.
манéрен *прил см* **манéрный**.
манéрнича|ть (-ю) *несов неперех* to put on airs.
манéрн|ый (-ен, -на, -но) *прил* affected.
манéр|ы (-) *мн* manners *мн*.
манжéт|а (-ы) *ж* cuff.
маниакáльный *прил* maniacal.
маникю́р (-а) *м* manicure.
маникю́рный *прил* manicure *опред*.
маникю́рш|а (-и) *ж* manicurist.
Манúл|а (-ы) *ж* Manila.
манипулúр|овать (-ую) *несов неперех* (+instr;
также перен) to manipulate.
манипуля́ци|я (-и) *ж* (*также перен*)
manipulation.
ман|úть (-ю́, -ишь; *perf* **поманúть**) *несов перех*
to beckon; (*no perf*; *перен: привлекать*) to
attract.
манифéст (-а) *м* manifesto.
манифестáци|я (-и) *ж* demonstration.
манúшк|а (-ки; *gen pl* -ек) *ж* (*часть рубашки*)
shirt front; (*нагрудник*) dicky.

мани|я (-и) ж mania.

ма́нк|а (-и) ж (разг) semolina.

ма́нн|а (-ы) ж manna; **ждать** (impf) **как ~ы небе́сной** to await impatiently.

ма́нный прил: **~ая ка́ша**, **~ая крупа́** semolina.

мано́метр (-а) м manometer.

манса́рд|а (-ы) ж garret.

ма́нти|я (-и) ж robe.

манто́ ср нескл (ladies') fur coat.

мануфакту́р|а (-ы) ж (ист: фабрика) (textile) mill.

Манче́стер (-а) м Manchester.

Маньчжу́ри|я (-и) ж Manchuria.

манья́к (-а) м maniac.

мара́зм (-а) м (МЕД) dementia; (перен: разг) idiocy; **ста́рческий ~** senility, senile dementia.

мара́л (-а) м Siberian deer.

мара́|ть (-ю; perf **вы́марать** или **измара́ть**) несов перех (разг: пачкать) to get dirty; (perf **замара́ть**; перен: разг) to drag through the dirt; (perf **намара́ть**; разг: рисовать, писать) to scribble; **~** (impf) **ру́ки** (перен: разг) to get one's hands dirty

► **мара́|ться** (perf **вы́мараться** или **измара́ться**) несов возв (разг: пачкаться) to get dirty; (perf **замара́ться**; разг: портить репутацию) to ruin one's reputation.

марафе́т (-а) м (разг): **навести́ ~** to tidy up; (: прихорашиваться) to smarten (o.s.) up.

марафо́н (-а) м marathon.

марафо́н|ец (-ца) м marathon runner.

ма́рган|ец (-ца) м manganese.

марганцо́вк|а (-и) ж (разг) potassium permanganate.

маргари́н (-а) м margarine.

маргари́т|ка (-и; gen pl -ок) ж daisy.

маргина́льный прил marginal.

ма́рж|а (-и) ж (КОММ) margin.

марина́д (-а) м (соус) marinade; (обычно мн: маринованные овощи) pickle.

марин|ова́ть (-у́ю; perf **замаринова́ть**) несов перех (грибы, овощи) to pickle; (мясо, рыбу) to marinate, marinade; (no perf; разг: дело) to put off.

марионе́т|ка (-ки; gen pl -ок) ж (также перен) puppet.

марионе́точный прил (также перен) puppet опред.

Мариу́пол|ь (-я) м Mariupol.

ма́р|ка (-ки; gen pl -ок) ж (почтовая) stamp; (торговая) trademark; (сорт) brand; (качество) grade; (модель) make; (денежная единица) mark; **держа́ть** (impf) **~ку** to keep up one's reputation; **держи́те ~ку шко́лы/фи́рмы** don't let your school/the firm down.

ма́ркетинг (-а) м marketing.

ма́ркий (-кая, -кое, -кие; -ок, -ка, -ко) прил: **э́то пальто́ о́чень ~кое** this coat shows the dirt easily.

марки́р|ова́ть (-у́ю) несов перех (продукцию) to trademark.

маркси́зм (-а) м Marxism.

маркси́ст (-а) м Marxist.

ма́рлевый прил gauze.

ма́рл|я (-и) ж gauze.

мармела́д (-а; part gen -у) м fruit jellies мн.

мароде́р (-а) м looter; (разг: спекулянт) profiteer.

мароде́рств|о (-а) ср looting.

ма́рок сущ см **ма́рка** ♦ прил см **ма́ркий**.

Маро́кко ср нескл Morocco.

ма́рочный прил (изделие) branded; (вино) vintage.

Марс (-а) м Mars.

Марсе́л|ь (-я) м Marseilles.

март (-а) м March; см также **октя́брь**.

марты́ш|ка (-и) ж marmoset ♦ м/ж (перен: разг) monkey.

марципа́н (-а) м marzipan.

марш (-а) м (также перен) march ♦ межд (ВОЕН): **~I** forward march!; **ле́стничный ~** flight of stairs; **~ домо́й!** (разг) off you go home!

ма́ршал (-а) м marshal.

марши́р|ова́ть (-у́ю; perf **промарширова́ть**) несов неперех to march.

маршру́т (-а) м route.

маршру́т|ка (-ки; gen pl -ок) ж (разг) fixed-route taxi.

маршру́тный прил: **~ое такси́** fixed-route taxi.

маршру́ток сущ см **маршру́тка**.

ма́сел сущ см **ма́сло**.

ма́с|ка (-ки; gen pl -ок) ж (также перен) mask; (косметическая) face pack.

маскара́д (-а) м masked ball; (перен) masquerade.

маскир|ова́ть (-у́ю; perf **замаскирова́ть**) несов перех (также перен) to camouflage

► **маскирова́ться** (perf **замаскирова́ться**) несов возв to camouflage o.s.

маскиро́вк|а (-и) ж (ВОЕН) camouflage; (перен) disguise.

маскиро́вочный прил camouflage опред.

ма́слениц|а (-ы) ж ≈ Shrovetide.

масле́н|ка (-ки; gen pl -ок) ж butter dish; (ТЕХ) oilcan.

масле́нок (-ёнка; nom pl -я́та, gen pl -я́т) м annulated или yellow boletus (edible mushroom).

ма́сленый прил (в масле) buttery; (запачканный маслом) oily; (перен: разг: льстивый) slick; (: сластолюбивый) voluptuous; **ма́сленая неде́ля** ≈ Shrovetide.

масли́н|а (-ы) ж (дерево) olive (tree); (плод) olive.

ма́сл|ить (-ю, -ишь; perf **нама́слить** или

пома́слить) *несов перех* to butter.
ма́сличный *прил* oil-yielding.
ма́сло (-ла; *nom pl* -ла́, *gen pl* -ел) *ср* (*сливочное*) butter; (*растительное, смазочное*) oil; (*искусство*) oils *мн*; **де́ло идёт как по ~лу** (*разг*) things are going smoothly; **подлива́ть** (**подли́ть** *perf*) ~ла **в ого́нь** to add fuel to the fire; ~ **ма́сляное** (*разг*) tautology.
маслобо́йня (-йни; *gen pl* -ен) *ж* creamery.
маслозаво́д (-а) *м* creamery.
масляни́стый (-, -а, -о) *прил* oily.
ма́сляный *прил* (*краска, фильтр*) oil *опред*; (*пятно*) oily.
масля́та *итп сущ см* **маслёнок**.
ма́сок *прил см* **ма́ска**.
масо́н (-а) *м* Freemason, Mason.
масо́нский (-ая, -ое, -ие) *прил* Masonic.
ма́сса (-ы) *ж* (*также физ*) mass; (*керамическая*) paste; (*древесная*) pulp; (*no pl; много*) loads *мн*; **де́нежная** ~ money supply; *см также* **ма́ссы**.
масса́ж (-а) *м* massage; ~ **се́рдца** cardiac massage.
массажи́ст (-а) *м* masseur.
массажи́стка (-ки; *gen pl* -ок) *ж* masseuse.
масси́в (-а) *м* (*водный*) expanse; (*земельный, лесной*) tract; (*КОМП*) array; **го́рный** ~ massif; **жило́й** *или* **жили́щный** ~ housing estate (*BRIT*) *или* project (*US*).
масси́вный (-ен, -на, -но) *прил* massive.
масси́рованный *прил* (*атака*) all-out.
масси́ровать (-ую) *несов перех* to massage.
массови́к (-а́) *м* organizer of group activities.
массо́вка (-ки; *gen pl* -ок) *ж* (*КИНО, ТЕАТР*: *массовая сцена*) crowd scene; (: *статисты*) extras *мн*; (*разг*) group outing.
ма́ссовый *прил* mass; (*поставка*) bulk *опред*; **това́ры** ~**ого спро́са** mass-market goods; **ма́ссовое произво́дство** (*ЭКОН*) mass production.
ма́ссы (-) *мн* (*народ*) the masses *мн*.
маста́к (-а́) *м* (*разг*): ~ **на** +*acc*/**в** +*prp* a dab hand at.
ма́стер (-а; *nom pl* -а́) *м* master; (*на производстве*) foreman (*мн* foremen); (*ремесленник*) craftsman (*мн* craftsmen); **часово́й** ~ watchmaker; ~ **на** +*acc* expert at; ~ **на все ру́ки** handyman (*мн* handymen); **ма́стер спо́рта** master sportsman (*title awarded to sportsmen*).
мастери́ть (-ю́, -и́шь; *perf* **смастери́ть**) *несов перех* to make (by hand).
мастеро́к (-а́) *м* trowel.
мастерска́я (-о́й; *decl like adj*) *ж* (*часовая, столярная*) workshop; (*художника, скульптора*) studio; (*на заводе*) shop.
мастерство́ (-а́) *ср* (*квалификация*) skill; (*ремесло*) trade.
масти́ка (-и) *ж* mastic; (*для натирания полов*) floor polish.
масти́т (-а) *м* mastitis.
масти́тый (-, -а, -о) *прил* eminent.

масть (-и; *gen pl* -е́й) *ж* (*лошади*) colour (*BRIT*), color (*US*); (*карты*) suit.
масшта́б (-а) *м* scale.
масшта́бный *прил* scale *опред*; (-ен, -на, -но; *произведение, стройка*) large-scale; **масшта́бная лине́йка** scale.
мат (-а) *м* (*ШАХМАТЫ*) checkmate; (*половик, также СПОРТ*) mat; (*ругательства*) bad language; **руга́ться** (*impf*) **ма́том** (*разг*) to use bad language.
матадо́р (-а) *м* matador.
матема́тик (-а) *м* mathematician.
матема́тика (-и) *ж* mathematics.
математи́ческий (-ая, -ое, -ие) *прил* mathematical; (*факультет*) mathematics *опред*.
ма́тери *итп сущ см* **мать**.
материа́л (-а) *м* material; (*обычно мн*: *служебные, следствия*) document.
материа́лен *прил см* **материа́льный**.
материали́зм (-а) *м* materialism.
материали́ст (-а) *м* materialist.
материа́льный (-ен, -ьна, -ьно) *прил* material *опред*; (*no short form; финансовый*) financial, material *опред*; ~ **уще́рб** material damage; **материа́льная по́мощь** financial assistance.
матери́к (-а́) *м* continent; (*суша*) mainland.
материко́вый *прил* mainland *опред*.
матери́нский (-ая, -ое, -ие) *прил* maternal; (*БИО, БОТ*) parent *опред*.
матери́нство (-а) *ср* maternity, motherhood; (*чувство*) motherliness.
матери́ться (-ю́сь, -и́шься) *несов возв* (*разг*) to swear.
мате́рия (-и) *ж* matter; (*разг*: *ткань*) cloth; **говори́ть** (*impf*) **о высо́ких** ~**х** to speak about elevated matters.
ма́терный *прил* (*разг*) obscene.
мате́рчатый *прил* cloth.
матёрый *прил* (*волк, медведь*) mature, full-grown; (*перен*: *преступник*) hardened.
ма́терь (-и) *ж*: **М~ Бо́жья** Mother of God.
ма́терью *итп сущ см* **мать**.
ма́тка (-ки; *gen pl* -ок) *ж* uterus, womb; (*ЗООЛ*: *также*: **пчели́ная** ~) queen bee.
ма́товый (-, -а, -о) *прил* (*без блеска*) mat(t); **ма́товое стекло́** frosted glass.
ма́ток *сущ см* **ма́тка**.
матра́с (-а) *м* mattress.
матра́ц (-а) *м* = **матра́с**.
матрёшка (-ки; *gen pl* -ек) *ж* Russian doll.
матриарха́т (-а) *м* (*ИСТ*) matriarchy.
ма́тричный *прил*: ~ **при́нтер** (*КОМП*) dot-matrix printer.
матро́с (-а) *м* sailor.
матро́ска (-и) *ж* sailor top *или* shirt.
матро́сский (-ая, -ое, -ие) *прил* sailor's.
ма́тушка (-ки; *gen pl* -ек) *ж* (*мать*) mother; (*РЕЛ*) priest's wife.
матч (-а) *м* (*СПОРТ*) match.
мать (-ери; *см* Table 1) *ж* mother; (*разг*: *как обращение*) missus; **в чём** ~ **родила́** (*разг*) in

one's birthday suit; **мать-одино́чка** single mother.

мать-и-ма́чех|а (-и) ж coltsfoot.

мафио́зи м нескл mafioso.

мафио́зный прил mafia опред.

ма́фи|я (-и) ж the Mafia; (перен) Mafia.

мах (-а; part gen -у) м (крыла) flap; (колеса) turn; (ногой) swing; (рукой) swing, stroke; **дать** (perf) **ма́ху** (разг: ошибиться) to boob.

маха́ть (-шу́, -шешь) несов неперех (+instr) to wave; (крыльями) to flap; ~ (impf) **кому́-н руко́й** to wave to sb.

махи́н|а (-ы) ж (разг) monster (fig).

махина́тор (-а) м machinator, schemer.

махина́ци|я (-и) ж machination, scheme.

махну́ть (-у́, -ёшь) сов неперех to give a wave; (разг: поехать) to go; (через забор) to jump; ~ (perf) **на кого́-н/что-н руко́й** to give sb/sth up as a bad job

▸ **махну́ться** сов возв (разг: +instr) to swap.

махо́рк|а (-и) ж ≈ shag, coarse tobacco.

махро́в|ый прил (халат) towelling; (цветок) double; (перен: отъявленный) out-and-out; **~ая ткань** terry towelling.

ма́чех|а (-и) ж stepmother.

ма́чт|а (-ы) ж mast.

машбюро́ ср нескл сокр (= машинопи́сное бюро́) typing pool.

маши́н|а (-ы) ж (также перен) machine; (автомоби́ль) car.

машина́лен прил см машина́льный.

машина́льно нареч mechanically.

машина́льный (-ен, -ьна, -ьно) прил mechanical.

машини́ст (-а) м (комбайна, экскаватора) driver, operator; ~ **локомоти́ва** engine driver (esp BRIT), engineer (US).

машини́ст|ка (-ки; gen pl -ок) ж typist.

маши́н|ка (-ки; gen pl -ок) ж machine; **пи́шущая ~ typewriter**.

маши́нный прил (производство, части, масло) machine опред; (счёт, обработка) mechanical; **маши́нное отделе́ние** engine room; **маши́нный код/язы́к** (КОМП) machine code/language.

маши́нок сущ см маши́нка.

машинопи́сный прил (текст) typewritten; **машинопи́сное бюро́** typing pool.

машинопи́с|ь (-и) ж (печатание) typing; (текст) typescript.

машинострое́ни|е (-я) ср mechanical engineering.

машу́ итп несов см маха́ть.

мая́к (-а́) м lighthouse.

ма́ятник (-а) м (часов) pendulum.

ма́|яться (-юсь; perf ума́яться) несов возв (разг: томиться) to suffer.

мая́ч|ить (-у, -ишь) несов неперех (разг: виднеться) to be visible; (: надоедливо

возника́ть) to hang around.

МБ м сокр (= Министе́рство безопа́сности) ministry for security.

МБР м сокр (= Министе́рство безопа́сности Росси́и) Russian Ministry for security; (= межконтинента́льная баллисти́ческая раке́та) ICBM (= intercontinental ballistic missile).

МБРР ср сокр (= Междунаро́дный банк реконстру́кции и разви́тия) IBRD (= International Bank for Reconstruction and Development).

МВД ср сокр (= Министе́рство вну́тренних дел) ≈ the Home Office (BRIT), ≈ the Department of the Interior (US).

МВК м сокр (= механи́зм валю́тных ку́рсов) ERM (= Exchange Rate Mechanism).

МВФ м сокр (= Междунаро́дный валю́тный фонд) IMF (= International Monetary Fund).

МВЭС ср сокр (= Министе́рство внешнеэкономи́ческих свя́зей) ministry for foreign economic links.

мг. сокр (= миллигра́мм) mg (= milligram(me)).

мгл|а (-ы) ж haze; (вечерняя) gloom.

мгнове́нен прил см мгнове́нный.

мгнове́ни|е (-я) ср moment; **в одно́ ~** right away.

мгнове́нный (-ен, -на, -но) прил (решение, реакция, фотография) instant; (смерть) instantaneous; (злость, раздражение) momentary; (вспышка) lightning опред.

МГУ м сокр (= Моско́вский госуда́рственный университе́т) Moscow State University.

МГц сокр (= мегаге́рц) MHz (= megahertz).

ме́бел|ь (-и) ж собир furniture; **мя́гкая ~** three-piece suite.

ме́бельный прил furniture опред.

ме́бельщик (-а) м furniture-maker.

мегаба́йт (-а) м megabyte.

мегава́тт (-а) м megawatt.

мегафо́н (-а) м megaphone.

меге́р|а (-ы) ж (разг) dragon.

мёд (-а; part gen -у, loc sg -ý, nom pl -ы́) м honey.

медали́ст (-а) м (человек) medallist (BRIT), medalist (US).

медали́ст|ка (-ки; gen pl -ок) ж medallist (BRIT), medalist (US).

меда́л|ь (-и) ж medal; **оборо́тная сторона́ ~и** (перен) the other side of the coin.

медальо́н (-а) м medallion.

медбра́т (-а) м сокр (= медици́нский брат) nurse (male).

медве́диц|а (-ы) ж she-bear; **Больша́я М~** the Great Bear.

медве́д|ь (-я) м (также перен) bear.

медвежа́та итп сущ см медвежо́нок.

медве́ж|ий (-ья, -ье, -ьи) прил bear опред; **медве́жья услу́га** ≈ more of a hindrance than a help.

медвежо́нок (-о́нка; *nom pl* -а́та, *gen pl* -а́т) *м* bear cub.

ме́дик (-а) *м* medic.

медикаме́нт (-а) *м* (*обычно мн*) medicine.

медици́на (-ы) *ж* medicine.

медици́нский (-ая, -ое, -ие) *прил* medical.

ме́ди|я (-и) *ж* media *мн*.

ме́дленно *нареч* slowly.

ме́дленный *прил* slow.

медли́тельный (-ен, -ьна, -ьно) *прил* slow.

ме́дл|ить (-ю, -ишь) *несов неперех* to delay; ~ (*impf*) **с реше́нием/отве́том** to be slow in deciding/answering.

ме́дный *прил* copper; (*МУЗ*) brass.

медо́вый *прил* honey *опред*; ~ **вкус/арома́т** taste/smell of honey; **медо́вый ме́сяц** honeymoon.

медпу́нкт (-а) *м сокр* (= медици́нский пункт) ≈ first-aid post.

медсестр|а́ (-ы́) *ж сокр* (= медици́нская сестра́) nurse.

меду́з|а (-ы) *ж* jellyfish.

медь (-и) *ж* copper ♦ *собир* coppers *мн*.

медя́к (-а́) *м* (*разг*) copper (*coin*).

меж|а́ (-и́; *nom pl* -и) *ж* boundary.

междоме́ти|е (-я) *ср* interjection.

KEYWORD

ме́жду *предл* (+*instr*) **1** between; **ме́жду дома́ми/города́ми** between the houses/towns; **ме́жду заседа́ниями/ле́кциями** between the meetings/lectures; **доро́га ме́жду Москво́й и Петербу́ргом** the road between Moscow and St. Petersburg

2: **они́ договори́лись ме́жду собо́й** they agreed among themselves; **ме́жду на́ми (говоря́)** between ourselves

3 (+*gen*; *в окружении*) amongst; **ме́жду домо́в росло́ большо́е де́рево** a big tree grew in amongst the houses

4: **ме́жду про́чим** (*попутно*) in passing; (*кстати*) by the way; **ме́жду про́чим, мы ви́дели Ма́шу** by the way, we saw Masha; **ме́жду тем** meanwhile; **ме́жду тем как** while.

междуве́домственный *прил* interdepartmental.

междугоро́дный *прил* intercity.

междунаро́дный *прил* international.

мезони́н (-а) *м* attic.

Ме́кк|а (-и) *ж* Mecca.

Ме́ксик|а (-и) *ж* Mexico.

мексика́н|ец (-ца) *м* Mexican.

мексика́н|ка (-ки; *gen pl* -ок) *ж см* мексика́нец.

мексика́нский (-ая, -ое, -ие) *прил* Mexican.

мексика́нца *сущ см* мексика́нец.

мел (-а; *part gen* -у, *loc sg* -у́) *м* chalk.

меланхо́лик (-а) *м* melancholic.

меланхоли́чный *прил* melancholic *опред*.

меле́|ть (*3sg* -ет, *3pl* -ют, *perf* обмеле́ть) *несов неперех* to become shallower.

мелиора́ци|я (-и) *ж* soil improvement.

мелка́ *сущ см* мело́к.

ме́лкий (-кая, -кое, -кие; -лок, -лка́, -лко) *прил* (*почерк*) small; (*песок, дождь*) fine; (*неглубокий*) shallow; (*малозначительный*) petty; (*no short form*; *собственник*) small; (*несущественный*) minor; ~**кие де́ньги** (*мелочь*) small change; **ме́лкая буржуази́я** petty bourgeoisie.

ме́лко *нареч* (*резать, дробить*) finely; (*писать*) small ♦ *как сказ* (*у берега итп*) it's shallow.

мелкобуржуа́зный (-ен, -на, -но) *прил* petty-bourgeois.

мелководный (-ен, -на, -но) *прил* shallow.

мелкокали́берный *прил* small-bore, small-calibre (*BRIT*), small-caliber (*US*).

мелоди́чный (-ен, -на, -но) *прил* melodious.

мело́ди|я (-и) *ж* tune, melody.

мелодра́м|а (-ы) *ж* (*также перен*) melodrama.

мело́к *прил см* ме́лкий.

мел|о́к (-ка́) *м* piece of chalk.

мелома́н (-а) *м* music-lover.

мелочи́|ться (-у́сь, -и́шься) *несов возв* (*разг*) to be petty.

ме́лочный (-ен, -на, -но) *прил* petty; (*человек*) small-minded, petty.

ме́лоч|ь (-и; *gen pl* -е́й) *ж* (*пустяк*) triviality; (*подробность*) detail ♦ *ж собир* little things *мн*; (*мелкие монеты*) small change; **"Ты́сяча мелоче́й"** *name of shops selling household goods*; **разме́ниваться** (*impf*) **по мелоча́м** to waste one's talents.

мель (-и; *loc sg* -и́) *ж* shallows *мн*, shoal; **сади́ться (сесть** *perf*) **на** ~ (*МОР*) to run aground; **быть** (*impf*) **на мели́** (*перен*: *разг*) to be (stony (*BRIT*) *или* stone (*US*)) broke.

Ме́льбурн (-а) *м* Melbourne.

мелька́|ть (-ю) *несов неперех* (*появиться и исчезнуть*) to flash past; (*мерцать*) to twinkle; ~ (*impf*) **в уме́** *или* **голове́** to flash through one's mind.

мелькн|у́ть (-у́, -ёшь) *сов неперех* to flash.

ме́льком *нареч* in passing.

ме́льник (-а) *м* miller.

ме́льниц|а (-ы) *ж* mill.

ме́льничный *прил* mill *опред*.

мельхио́р (-а) *м* nickel silver.

мельча́|ть (-ю; *perf* измельча́ть) *несов неперех* (*река, залив*) to get shallower; (*интересы, люди*) to become petty; (*хозяйство итп*) to become smaller.

ме́льче *сравн прил от* ме́лкий ♦ *сравн нареч от* ме́лко.

мельч|и́ть (-у́, -и́шь; *perf* измельчи́ть *или* размельчи́ть) *несов перех* (*ножом*) to cut up small; (*в ступке*) to crush.

мелю́ *итп несов см* моло́ть.

мелюзга́ (-и́) *ж собир* (*разг*: *пренебр*) small fry.

мембра́н|а (-ы) *ж* (*ТЕХ*) diaphragm.

мемора́ндум (-а) *м* memorandum.

мемориа́л (-а) м memorial.

мемориа́льный прил memorial опред.

мемуа́ры (-ов) мн memoirs мн.

ме́неджер (-а) м manager; **~ по ма́ркетингу** marketing manager.

ме́неджмент (-а) м management.

ме́нее сравн нареч от **ма́ло ♦** нареч less; **тем не ~** nevertheless; **~ всего́** least of all; **~ всего́ удо́бный** least convenient of all.

мензу́рка (-ки; gen pl -ок) ж measuring glass.

менинги́т (-а) м meningitis.

менструа́ция (-и) ж menstruation.

менто́л (-а) м menthol.

ме́ньше сравн прил от **ма́лый, ма́ленький ♦** сравн нареч от **ма́ло ♦** нареч less than; **~ всего́** least of all.

ме́ньший (-ая, -ее, -ие) сравн прил от **ма́лый, ма́ленький ♦** прил (младший) younger; **по ~ей ме́ре** at least; **са́мое ~ее** no less than.

меньшинство́ (-а́) ср собир minority; **национа́льное ~** ethnic minority.

меню́ ср нескл menu.

меня́ мест см я.

меня́ть (-ю; perf **поменя́ть**) несов перех to change; **~ (поменя́ть** perf) **что-н на** +acc to exchange sth for

▶ **меня́ться** (perf **поменя́ться**) несов возв to change; (жилплощадью) to swap; (perf **измени́ться**; погода, вкусы) to change; **~ся (поменя́ться** perf) **чем-н с кем-н** to exchange sth with sb.

ме́ра (-ы) ж measure; (предел) limit; **без ~ы** extremely; **сверх ~ы** excessively; **в по́лной ~е** fully; **по ~е** +gen with; **по ~е того́ как** as; **по ~е сил** as much as one can; **по ~е возмо́жности** as far as possible; **принима́ть (приня́ть** perf) **~ы по** +prp to take measures as regards; **вы́сшая ~ наказа́ния** capital punishment.

ме́рен прил см **ме́рный**.

мере́ть (3sg мрёт, 3pl мрут, pt мёр, -ла, -ло) несов неперех (разг: умирать) to snuff it.

мере́щиться (-усь, -ишься; perf **помере́щиться**) несов возв (+dat) to appear; **ему́ ~ился о́браз** he thought he saw a figure.

мёрз итп несов см **мёрзнуть**.

мерза́вец (-ца) м (разг) nasty piece of work.

мерза́вка (-ки; gen pl -ок) ж см **мерза́вец**.

мерза́вца сущ см **мерза́вца**.

ме́рзкий (-кая, -кое, -кие; -ок, -ка́, -ко) прил (слова, личность, поступок) disgusting; (погода, настроение) foul.

мерзлота́ (-ы́) ж: **ве́чная ~** permafrost.

мёрзлый прил (земля́) frozen; (овощи) frost-damaged.

мёрзнуть (-ну, -нешь; pt -, -ла, -ло, perf **замё рзнуть**) несов неперех to freeze.

ме́рзок прил см **ме́рзкий**.

ме́рзость (-и) ж disgusting thing; (поступка)

baseness; **кака́я ~!** how disgusting!

меридиа́н (-а) м meridian.

мери́ло (-а) ср criterion (мн criteria).

ме́рин (-а) м gelding.

ме́рить (-ю, -ишь; perf **сме́рить** или **изме́рить**) несов перех to measure; (perf **поме́рить**; примерять) to try on; **~ (сме́рить** perf) **взгля́дом кого́-н** (перен) to look sb up and down

▶ **ме́риться** (perf **поме́риться**) несов возв (+instr): **~ся зна́ниями/си́лами с кем-н** to measure one's knowledge/strengths against sb.

мерк итп несов см **ме́ркнуть**.

ме́рка (-ки; gen pl -ок) ж measurements мн; (перен: критерий) standard; (мерило) measure; **снима́ть (снять** perf) **~ку с кого́-н** to take sb's measurements.

ме́ркнуть (3sg -нет, 3pl -нут, pt -, -ла, -ло, perf **поме́ркнуть**) несов неперех (также перен) to fade.

Мерку́рий (-я) м Mercury.

ме́рный (-ен, -на, -но) прил (размеренный) measured; (no short form; ТЕХ) measuring.

мерок сущ см **ме́рка**.

мероприя́тие (-я) ср measure; **культу́рное ~** cultural event.

мертве́ть (-ю; perf **омертве́ть**) несов неперех (от холода) to go numb; (perf **помертве́ть**; от страха, от горя) to be numb.

мертве́ц (-а́) м dead person (мн people).

мёртвый (-, -а́, -о́) прил dead; (взгляд, улица) lifeless; **спать** (impf) **~ым сном** to sleep the sleep of the dead; **лежа́ть** (impf) **~ым гру́зом** to lie unused; **мёртвый сезо́н** dead season; **мёртвая хва́тка** mortal grip; **мёртвый язы́к** dead language.

мертвя́щий (-ая, -ое, -ие) прил (обстановка) lifeless.

мерца́ть (3sg -ет, 3pl -ют) несов неперех to glimmer, flicker; (звёзды) to twinkle.

ме́сиво (-а) ср mush; (на дороге) slush.

меси́ть (-шу́, -сишь; perf **смеси́ть**) несов перех (тесто, глину) to knead; **~** (impf) **грязь** (перен) to wade through the mud.

ме́сса (-ы) ж (РЕЛ) Mass.

места́ (-) мн provinces мн.

места́ми нареч in places.

мести́ (-ту́, -тёшь; pt мёл, -ла́, -ло́, perf **подмести́**) несов перех (пол, комнату итп) to sweep; (мусор, листья итп) to sweep up; (подлеж: метель) to whirl; **на дворе́ ~тёт** it's a blizzard outside.

месткóм (-а) м сокр (= **ме́стный комите́т**) local trade-union committee.

ме́стность (-и) ж (холмистая, ровная) terrain; (сельская, дачная) area, district.

ме́стный прил local **♦** (-ого; decl like adj) м local (inhabitant); **ме́стные вла́сти** local authorities

мн; **ме́стный нарко́з** (*МЕД*) local anaesthetic
(*BRIT*) *или* anesthetic (*US*).

ме́ст|**о** (-а; *nom pl* -á) *ср* place; (*для постройки*)
site; (*действия, происшествия*) scene;
(*работа*) job; (: *вакантное*) post; (*в театре,
поезде итп*) seat; (*багажа, груза*) item; (*в
книге, в пьесе*) part; **сла́бое ~** weak spot; **здесь
не ~ говори́ть о деньга́х** this is not the place to
talk about money; **реши́ть** (*perf*) **на ~е** to decide
on the spot; **~а себе́ не находи́ть** (*impf*) to
worry; **к ~y** to the point; **спа́льное ~** berth; **на
Ва́шем ~е я бы ...** in your place *или* if I were
you, I would ...; **ни с ~a!** don't move!; **у меня́
душа́ *или* се́рдце не на ~е** I'm worried; *см
также* **места́.**

местожи́тельств|**о** (-а) *ср* place of residence.
местоиме́ни|**е** (-я) *ср* pronoun.
местонахожде́ни|**е** (-я) *ср* location.
местопребыва́ни|**е** (-я) *ср* residence.
месторожде́ни|**е** (-я) *ср* (*скопление*) deposit;
(*угля, нефти, золота*) field.
мест|**ь** (-и) *ж* vengeance, revenge.
ме́сяц (-а; *nom pl* -ы) *м* month; (*часть луны*)
crescent moon; (*диск луны*) moon.
ме́сячн|**ые** (-ых; *decl like adj*) *мн* (*разг*)
(menstrual) period *ед.*
ме́сячный *прил* monthly.
мета́лл (-а) *м* metal.
металли́ческий (-ая, -ое, -ие) *прил* metal;
(*блеск, скрежет*) metallic.
металлоло́м (-а) *м* scrap metal.
металлу́рги|**я** (-и) *ж* metallurgy.
метаморфо́з|**а** (-ы) *ж* metamorphosis.
мета́тел|**ь** (-я) *м* thrower; **~ ди́ска** discus
thrower.
мета́|**ть** (-чу́, -чешь) *несов перех* (*гранату, диск
итп*) to throw; (*perf* **намета́ть**; *шов*) to tack,
baste; (*perf* **промета́ть** *или* **смета́ть**; *для
примерки*) to tack; **~** (*impf*) **жре́бий** to draw lots;
~ (смета́ть *perf*) **стог се́на** to stack hay; **~
(вы́метать** *perf*) **икру́** to spawn; **рвать** (*impf*) **и ~
(impf*) (*разг*) to storm and rage
▸ **мета́**|**ться** *несов возв* (*в постели, в бреду*) to
toss and turn; (*по комнате*) to rush about.
мета́фор|**а** (-ы) *ж* metaphor.
мётел *сущ см* **метла́.**
мете́л|**ь** (-и) *ж* snowstorm, blizzard.
метео́р (-а) *м* meteor.
метеори́т (-а) *м* meteorite.
метеоро́лог (-а) *м* meteorologist.
метеороло́ги|**я** (-и) *ж* meteorology.
метеосво́дк|**а** (-ки; *gen pl* -ок) *ж сокр* (=
метеорологи́ческая сво́дка) weather forecast
или report.
метеоста́нци|**я** (-и) *ж сокр* (=
метеорологи́ческая ста́нция) weather station.
ме́|**тить** (-чу, -тишь; *perf* **поме́тить**) *несов перех*
to mark ◆ *неперех*: **~** *в* +*acc* (*в противника, в
цель*) to aim at; **он ~тил в профессора́/
нача́льники** his ambition was to become a
professor/manager

▸ **ме́титься** (*perf* **наме́титься**) *несов возв*: **~ся
в** +*acc* to aim at.
ме́тк|**а** (-ки; *gen pl* -ок) *ж* mark.
ме́ткий (-кая, -кое, -кие; -ок, -ка́, -ко) *прил*
(*точный*) apt; (*перен*) accurate; **име́ть** (*impf*) **~
глаз** to have a good aim.
метл|**а́** (-ы́; *nom pl* **мётлы**, *gen pl* **мётел**) *ж* broom;
но́вая ~ (*разг*) new broom (*fig*).
метн|**у́ть** (-у́, -ёшь) *сов перех* (*диск, камень*) to
throw
▸ **метну́ться** *сов возв* (*разг: устремиться*) to
rush.
ме́тод (-а) *м* method.
мето́дик|**а** (-и) *ж* (*преподавания*) teaching
methodology; (*исследований, работы*) methods
мн.
методи́ческий (-ая, -ое, -ие) *прил* systematic.
ме́ток *прил см* **ме́ткий.**
метр (-а) *м* metre (*BRIT*), meter (*US*); (*линейка*)
measure.
метра́ж (-á) *м* (*квартиры, помещения*) (metric)
area; (*ткани*) length.
метрдоте́л|**ь** (-я) *м* head waiter.
метри́к|**а** (-и) *ж* birth certificate.
метри́ческий (-ая, -ое, -ие) *прил* metric; **~ая
систе́ма мер** metric system; **~ая то́нна** metric
ton.
метро́ *ср нескл* metro, tube (*BRIT*).
мет|**у́** *итп несов см* **мести́.**
мех (-а; *loc sg* -у́, *nom pl* -á) *м* fur; *см также* **меха́.**
мех|**а́** (-о́в) *мн* (*кузнечный, аккордеона*) bellows
мн.
механиза́тор (-а) *м* (*с.-х.*) machine operator.
механизи́р|**овать** (-ую) (*не)сов перех* to
mechanize.
механи́зм (-а) *м* mechanism; (*перен:
бюрократический*) machinery.
меха́ник (-а) *м* mechanic.
меха́ник|**а** (-и) *ж* mechanics.
механи́ческий (-ая, -ое, -ие) *прил* mechanical;
(*цех*) machine *опред.*
Ме́хико (*нескл*) *м* Mexico City.
мехово́й *прил* fur; **~ магази́н** furrier's.
меч (-á) *м* sword.
ме́ченый *прил* marked.
мече́т|**ь** (-и) *ж* mosque.
мечт|**а́** (-ы́; *gen pl* -а́ний) *ж* dream; **не о́тдых, а ~!**
(*разг*) it's a dream holiday!
мечта́ни|**е** (-я) *ср* (*обычно мн*) daydream;
преде́л ~й ultimate dream.
мечта́тельный *прил* dreamy.
мечта́тел|**ь** (-я) *м* dreamer.
мечта́тельниц|**а** (-ы) *ж см* **мечта́тель.**
мечта́|**ть** (-ю) *несов неперех*: **~** (**о** +*prp*) to
dream (of); **~** (*impf*) **стать врачо́м/учи́ться** to
dream of becoming a doctor/studying.
ме́чу(сь) *сов см* **ме́тить(ся).**
мечу́(сь) *итп несов см* **мета́ть(ся).**
мешани́н|**а** (-ы) *ж* (*разг*) jumble.
меша́|**ть** (-ю; *perf* **помеша́ть**) *несов перех* (*суп,
чай*) to stir; (*perf* **смеша́ть**; *напитки, краски*) to

mix ◆ *неперех* (+*dat*; *быть помехой*) to disturb,
bother; (*создавать затруднения*) to hinder; **не**
~**ло бы пое́сть** (*разг*) it wouldn't hurt to eat; ~
(**помеша́ть** *perf*) **кому́-н** +*infin*
(*препятствовать*) to make it difficult for sb to
do
▸ **меша́ться** *несов возв* (*разг: ребёнок, вещи*)
to be a pain; (*perf* **смеша́ться**; *путаться*) to get
mixed up; ~**ся** (*impf*) **в** +*acc* (*вмешиваться*) to
meddle *или* interfere in.
мешка́ *сущ см* **мешо́к**.
ме́шка|ть (-ю; *perf* **заме́шкать**) *несов неперех*
(*разг*) to dawdle; ~ (**заме́шкать** *perf*) **с отве́том/
отъе́здом** to be slow in answering/leaving.
мешкова́т|ый (-, -а, -о) *прил* (*пальто, платье*)
baggy; (*фигура*) clumsy.
мешкови́н|а (-ы) *ж* sacking.
мешо́к (-ка́) *м* sack; (*спальный, вещевой*) bag;
(*разг: человек*) lump; ~ +*gen* sack(ful) of;
де́нежный ~ moneybags; **у него́** ~**ки под
глаза́ми** he has bags under his eyes; **костю́м
сиди́т на нём** ~**ко́м** his suit hangs like a sack on
him.
мешо́ч|ек (-ка) *м*: **в** ~ (*яйцо*) soft-boiled.
мешу́ *несов см* **меси́ть**.
меща́н|и́н (-ани́на; *nom pl* -**а́не**, *gen pl* -**а́н**) *м*
petty bourgeois.
меща́н|ка (-ы) *ж см* **меща́ни́н**.
меща́нск|ий (-ая, -ое, -ие) *прил* (*взгляды*)
petty-bourgeois; (*вкусы*) philistine.
меща́нств|о (-а) *ср* petty-bourgeois mentality;
(*вкусы*) vulgarity; (*сословие*) petty bourgeoisie.
ми *ср нескл* (*муз*) mi.
МИГ (-а) *м сокр* = **самолёт констру́кции А.И.
Микоя́на и М.И. Гуре́вича**.
миг (-а) *м* moment.
мига́|ть (-ю) *несов неперех* to wink; (*перен*) to
twinkle.
мигну́|ть (-у́, -ёшь) *сов неперех* to wink.
ми́гом *нареч* (*разг*) as quick as a flash; **приду́** ~!
I'll be there in a jiffy!
мигра́ци|я (-и) *ж* migration.
мигре́н|ь (-и) *ж* migraine.
МИД (-а) *м сокр* (= **Министе́рство
иностра́нных дел**) ≈ the Foreign Office (*BRIT*), ≈
the State Department (*US*).
ми́ди *ср нескл* midi ◆ *прил неизм* midi *опред*.
ми́ди|я (-и) *ж* mussel.
ми́зер|ный (-ен, -на, -но) *прил* meagre (*BRIT*),
meager (*US*).
мизи́н|ец (-ца) *м* (*на руке*) little finger; (*на ноге*)
little toe.
микроавто́бус (-а) *м* minibus.
микро́б (-а) *м* microbe.
микробио́лог (-а) *м* microbiologist.
микробиоло́ги|я (-и) *ж* microbiology.
микрокли́мат (-а) *м* microclimate; (*перен*)

atmosphere.
микро́н (-а) *м* micron.
микроорган́изм (-а) *м* microorganism.
микропроце́ссор (-а) *м* microprocessor.
микрорайо́н (-а) *м* ≈ catchment area
(*administrative subdivision of urban region in
Russia*).
микроско́п (-а) *м* microscope.
микроскопи́ческ|ий (-ая, -ое, -ие) *прил*
(*также перен*) microscopic.
микросхе́м|а (-ы) *ж* (micro)chip.
микрофи́льм (-а) *м* microfilm.
микрофи́ш|а (-и) *ж* microfiche.
микрофо́н (-а) *м* microphone.
микрохирурги́|я (-и) *ж* microsurgery.
микроэконо́мик|а (-и) *ж* microeconomics *мн*.
ми́ксер (-а) *м* mixer.
миксту́р|а (-ы) *ж* mixture; ~ **от ка́шля** cough
mixture *или* linctus.
Мила́н (-а) *м* Milan.
ми́леньк|ий (-ая, -ое, -ие) *прил* (*хорошенький*)
pretty *или* sweet little; (: *любимый*) darling; **он
сде́лает э́то как** ~ he'll do it or else.
милитари́зм (-а) *м* militarism.
милитариз|ова́ть (-ую) (*не*)*сов перех* to
militarize.
милитари́ст (-а) *м* militarist.
милиционе́р (-а) *м* policeman (*in Russia*) (*мн*
policemen).
мили́ци|я (-и) *ж, собир* police (*in Russia*); (*разг:
участок*) police station.
миллиа́рд (-а) *м* billion.
миллиарде́р (-а) *м* billionaire.
миллигра́мм (-а) *м* milligram(me).
миллиме́тр (-а) *м* millimetre (*BRIT*), millimeter
(*US*).
миллиметро́вк|а (-и) *ж* (*разг*) graph paper.
миллио́н (-а) *м* million.
миллионе́р (-а) *м* millionaire.
миллио́нн|ый (-ая, -ое, -ые) *чис* (*посетитель,
автомобиль итп*) millionth; (*исчисляемый
миллионами*) million-strong; **у него́** ~**ое
состоя́ние** he is worth millions.
ми́ло *нареч* (*улыбнуться*) sweetly ◆ *как сказ*:
как ~! how sweet!
ми́л|овать (-ую; *perf* **поми́ловать**) *несов перех*
to have mercy on.
милови́д|ный (-ен, -на, -но) *прил* pleasing; **она́**
~**на** she has a pleasing appearance.
милосе́рден *прил см* **милосе́рдный**.
милосе́рди|е (-я) *ср* compassion; **сестра́** ~**я**
nurse.
милосе́рд|ный (-ен, -на, -но) *прил*
compassionate.
ми́лостын|я (-и) *ж* alms.
ми́лост|ь (-и) *ж* (*доброта*) kind-heartedness;
де́лать (**сде́лать** *perf*) **что-н из** ~**и** to do sth out
of the kindness of one's heart; ~**и про́сим!**

welcome!; **по твое́й ~и опозда́ли** thanks to you we are late; **скажи́те на ~** you don't say.

ми́лочк|а (-и) ж (разг: обраще́ние) dearest.

ми́л|ый (-, -á, -о) прил (симпати́чный) pleasant, nice; (дорого́й ♦ (-ого; decl like adj) м (возлю́бленный) darling.

ми́л|я (-и) ж mile; **морска́я ~** nautical mile.

мим (-а) м mime (artist).

ми́мик|а (-и) ж expression.

ми́мо нареч past ♦ предл (+gen) past.

мимо́з|а (-ы) ж (БОТ) mimosa.

мимолётн|ый (-ен, -на, -но) прил fleeting.

мимохо́дом нареч on the way; (перен: упомяну́ть) in passing.

мин. сокр (= мину́та) min. (= minute); (= минима́льный) min. (= minimum).

ми́н|а (-ы) ж (ВОЕН) mine; (выраже́ние лица́) expression.

минаре́т (-а) м minaret.

миндалеви́дный прил almond-shaped; **у него́ миндалеви́дные глаза́** he is almond-eyed.

минда́лин|а (-ы) ж (МЕД: обы́чно мн) tonsil.

минда́л|ь (-я́) м almond.

минда́льный прил almond.

минёр (-а) м (ВОЕН) person who lays mines.

минера́л (-а) м mineral.

минера́лк|а (-и) ж (разг) mineral water.

минера́льный прил mineral.

минздра́в (-а) м сокр (= министе́рство здравоохране́ния) Ministry of Health.

ми́ни ср нескл mini; **~ ю́бка** miniskirt; **~ пла́тье** minidress.

миниатю́р|а (-ы) ж (ИСКУССТВО) miniature; (ТЕА́ТР) short play; **в ~е** in miniature.

миниатю́р|ный (-ен, -на, -но) прил (статуэ́тка) miniature опред; (перен: же́нщина) dainty.

минима́льный (-ен, -ьна, -ьно) прил minimum опред.

ми́нимум (-а) м minimum ♦ нареч minimum; **прожи́точный ми́нимум** minimum living wage.

мини́р|овать (-ую; perf замини́ровать) (не)сов перех (ВОЕН) to mine.

минисериа́л (-а) м mini-series.

министе́рский (-ая, -ое, -ие) прил ministerial.

министе́рств|о (-а) ср ministry.

мини́стр (-а) м (ПОЛИТ) minister.

мин|ова́ть (-у́ю) (не)сов перех to pass; (no impf; +gen; избежа́ть) to escape, avoid ♦ непере́х to pass, be over.

мино́г|а (-и) ж lamprey.

миноиска́тель (-я) м mine detector.

миноме́т (-а) м mortar.

мино́нос|ец (-ца) м destroyer.

мино́р (-а) м minor key.

мино́рный прил (МУЗ) minor; (перен) subdued.

Минск (-а) м Minsk.

мину́вш|ее (-его; decl like adj) ср the past.

мину́вший (-ая, -ее, -ие) прил past.

ми́нус (-а) м (та́кже МАТ) minus; (перен: недоста́ток) drawback ♦ м нескл minus; **пять ~ два – три** five minus two equals three.

ми́нусовый прил (температу́ра) subzero.

мину́т|а (-ы) ж minute; (одну́) ~у! (про́сьба подожда́ть) just a minute!; **~ в мину́ту** to the minute; **он без пяти́ мину́т врач/юри́ст** (разг) he's a step away from qualifying as a doctor/lawyer; **она́ придёт с ~ы на ~у** she will be here any minute.

мину́тный прил (стре́лка) minute опред; (де́ло, разгово́р) brief; (по́рыв, увлече́ние) momentary.

ми́н|уть (3sg -ет, 3pl -ут) сов непере́х (+dat; испо́лниться): **ей ~уло 16 лет** she has turned 16.

мину́ть (-у́, -ёшь) сов (не)перех to pass.

мир (-а; nom pl -ы́) м world; (Вселе́нная) universe; (loc sg -ý; РЕЛ) (secular) world; (состоя́ние без войны́) peace; **~ те́сен** it's a small world; **он не от ми́ра сего́** he has his head in the clouds; **заключа́ть (заключи́ть perf) ~** to make peace; **чемпио́н ми́ра** world champion.

мира́ж (-á) м (та́кже перен) mirage.

ми́рен прил см ми́рный.

мир|и́ть (-ю́, -и́шь; perf помири́ть или примири́ть) несов перех to reconcile.

▶ **мири́ться** (perf помири́ться) несов возв: **~ся с** +instr to make up или be reconciled with; (perf примири́ться; с недоста́тками, с положе́нием) to come to terms with, reconcile o.s to.

ми́р|ный (-ен, -на, -но) прил peaceful; **ми́рное вре́мя** peacetime; **ми́рное населе́ние** civilian population; **ми́рные перегово́ры** peace talks или negotiations.

мировоззре́ни|е (-я) ср (писа́теля, о́бщества) philosophy of life.

мирово́й прил world опред; (перен: разг: хоро́ший) fantastic.

мирозда́ни|е (-я) ср universe.

миролюби́вый (-, -а, -о) прил peaceable.

миропонима́ни|е (-я) ср conception of the world.

миротво́р|ец (-ца) м peacemaker.

миротво́рческ|ий (-ая, -ое, -ие) прил peacemaking; **миротво́рческие войска́** peacekeeping force ед.

мирско́й прил (РЕЛ) worldly.

ми́с|ка (-ки; gen pl -ок) ж bowl.

мисс ж нескл Miss.

миссионе́р (-а) м missionary.

ми́ссис ж нескл Mrs.

Миссиси́пи ср нескл Mississippi.

ми́сси|я (-и) ж mission.

ми́стер (-а) м Mr.

ми́стик|а (-и) ж mysticism; (разг: о чём-н загадочном) mystery.

мистифика́ци|я (-и) ж hoax.

мисти́ческий (-ая, -ое, -ие) прил mystical.

ми́тинг (-а) м mass meeting, rally.

митинг|ова́ть (-у́ю) несов непере́х to hold a mass meeting или rally.

митрополи́т (-а) м (РЕЛ) metropolitan.

миф (-а) м (также перен) myth.
мифи́ческий (-ая, -ое, -ие) прил mythical.
мифоло́гия (-и) ж mythology.
мише́нь (-и) ж (также перен) target.
ми́шка (-и) м (раза) bear; (игрушка) teddy (bear).
мишура́ (-ы́) м tinsel.
МКК м сокр (= Междунаро́дный Кра́сный Крест) IRC (= International Red Cross).
мл. сокр (= мла́дший) Junr (= junior).
младе́нец (-ца) м infant, baby.
младе́нческий (-ая, -ое, -ие) прил: ~ие го́ды infancy.
младе́нчество (-а) ср infancy, babyhood.
мла́дше сравн прил от **молодо́й**.
мла́дший (-ая, -ее, -ие) прил younger; (самый младший) (the) youngest; (сотрудник, класс) junior; ~ лейтена́нт second lieutenant.
млекопита́ющее (-его) decl like adj ср mammal.
млеть (-ю) несов неперех: ~ (от +gen) (от счастья, от любви) to be overcome (with).
мле́чный прил milky; **М~ Путь** the Milky Way; **мле́чный сок** latex.
млн. сокр = миллио́н.
мм сокр (= миллиме́тр) mm= millimetre (BRIT) или millimeter (US).
мне мест см **я**.
мне́ние (-я) ср opinion.
мни́мый прил (кажущийся) imaginary; (ложный) fake.
мни́телен прил см **мни́тельный**.
мни́тельность (-и) ж suspiciousness.
мни́тельный (-ен, -ьна, -ьно) прил suspicious.
мно́гие прил many ♦ (-их; decl like adj) мн (много людей) many (people).

<hr>

KEYWORD

мно́го чис (+gen) a lot of; **они́ созда́ли нам мно́го пробле́м** they created a lot of problems for us; **мно́го книг тебе́ да́ли?** did they give you many или a lot of books?; **мно́го рабо́ты тебе́ да́ли?** did they give you much или a lot of work?
♦ нареч **1** (разговаривать, пить итп) a lot; **он мно́го рабо́тает** he works a lot
2 (+comparative; гора́здо) much
♦ как сказ: **у него́ мно́го враго́в** he has a lot of enemies; **у него́ мно́го друзе́й?** does he have many friends?; **по мно́гу** +gen many; **они́ приходи́ли по мно́гу раз** they came many times.

<hr>

многобо́рец (-ца) м competitor in multi-event competition.
многобо́рье (-я) ср multi-event competition.
многогра́нен прил см **многогра́нный**.
многогра́нник (-а) м polyhedron.
многогра́нный (-ен, -на, -но) прил (талант,

ка́мень, ли́чность) multifaceted; (фигура) polyhedral.
многоде́тный (-ен, -на, -но) прил with many children.
мно́гое (-ого; decl like adj) ср a great deal.
многожёнство (-а) ср polygamy.
многозна́чен прил см **многозна́чный**.
многозначи́тельный (-ен, -ьна, -ьно) прил significant.
многозна́чный (-ен, -на, -но) прил (число, номер) multi-digit; (слово, глагол) polysemantic.
многокра́тный (-ен, -на, -но) прил (визиты) repeated; (виза) multiple(-entry); ~ чемпио́н/ призёр many-times champion/prizewinner.
многоле́тний (-яя, -ее, -ие) прил (планы) long-term; (труд, усилия) of many years; (растения) perennial.
многолю́дный (-ен, -на, -но) прил (улица) crowded; (митинг) well-attended.
многонациона́льный (-ен, -ьна, -ьно) прил multinational.
многопо́льзовательский (-ая, -ое, -ие) прил (комп) multiaccess.
многообеща́ющий (-ая, -ее, -ие) прил promising.
многообра́зен прил см **многообра́зный**.
многообра́зие (-я) ср (жизни) variety; (растений, животных) diversity.
многообра́зный (-ен, -на, -но) прил diverse, varied.
многосеме́йный (-ен, -йна, -йно) прил with a large family.
многосло́вный (-ен, -на, -но) прил verbose, long-winded.
многосло́жный прил polysyllabic.
многосторо́нний (-няя, -нее, -ние) прил (ГЕОМ) polygonal; (переговоры, встреча) multilateral; (вопрос, личность) many-sided; (-ен, -яя, -не; интересы) diverse.
многотира́жка (-и) ж (раза) factory news sheet.
многотира́жный прил with a large circulation.
многото́чие (-я) ср (линг) ellipsis.
многоуважа́емый прил esteemed; (в письме) Dear.
многоуго́льник (-а) м polygon.
многочи́сленный (-, -на, -но) прил numerous.
многочле́н (-а) м (МАТ) multinomial.
многоэта́жный прил multistorey (BRIT), multistory (US).
мно́жественный прил: ~ое число́ (линг) plural (number).
мно́жество (-а) ср (МАТ) set; ~ +gen a great number of.
мно́жительный прил: ~ая те́хника photocopying equipment.
мно́жить (-у, -ишь; perf умно́жить) несов перех (увеличивать) to multiply; (perf помно́жить;

МАТ): ~ **(на** +*acc*) to multiply (by)
▶ **мно́житься** (*perf* **умно́житься**) *несов возв* to multiply.
мной *мест см* я.
мнс *м сокр* (= **мла́дший нау́чный сотру́дник**) junior researcher.
мну(**сь**) *итп несов см* **мя́ть(ся)**.
моби́лен *прил см* **моби́льный**.
мобилиза́ция (**-и**) *ж* mobilization.
мобилизова́ть (**-ую**) (**не**)*сов перех* to mobilize; ~ (*impf/perf*) **кого́-н на что-н** to mobilize sb for sth.
моби́льн|**ый** (**-ен, -ьна, -ьно**) *прил* (**войска, дом**) mobile; (**ум, руково́дство**) active.
мог *несов см* **мочь**.
моги́л|**а** (**-ы**) *ж* grave; **стоя́ть** (*impf*) **одно́й ного́й в ~е** (*разг*) to have one foot in the grave.
моги́льник (**-а**) *м* burial ground; (*для радиоактивных отходов*) dumping ground.
моги́льный *прил* (**плита́**) grave *опред*; (**холм, уча́сток**) burial *опред*.
моги́льщик (**-а**) *м* grave digger.
могла́ *итп несов см* **мочь**.
могу́ *итп несов см* **мочь**.
могу́ч|**ий** (**-ая, -ее, -ие; -, -а, -е**) *прил* mighty; (*талант, ум*) great.
могу́ществен|**ный** (**-, -на, -но**) *прил* mighty, powerful.
могу́ществ|**о** (**-а**) *ср* might, power.
мо́д|**а** (**-ы**) *ж* fashion; (*разг: манера поведения*) habit; **по ~е** fashionably; **быть** (*impf*) **в ~е** to be in fashion; **входи́ть** (**войти́** *perf*) **в ~у** to come into fashion; **выходи́ть** (**вы́йти** *perf*) **из ~ы** to go out of fashion; *см также* **мо́ды**.
модели́р|**овать** (**-ую**) (**не**)*сов перех* (**оде́жду**) to design; (*perf* **смодели́ровать**; *процесс, поведение*) to simulate.
моде́л|**ь** (**-и**) *ж* model.
модельер (**-а**) *м* fashion designer.
моде́льный *прил* (**о́бувь, оде́жда**) high-fashion.
моде́м (**-а**) *м* (*КОМП*) modem.
мо́ден *прил см* **мо́дный**.
модерниза́ци|**я** (**-и**) *ж* modernization.
моде́рн (**-а**) *м* (*ИСКУССТВО*) art nouveau.
модернизи́р|**овать** (**-ую**) (**не**)*сов перех* to modernize.
модифика́ци|**я** (**-и**) *ж* modification.
мо́дник (**-а**) *м* (*разг*) snappy dresser.
мо́дниц|**а** (**-ы**) *ж см* **мо́дник**.
мо́днича|**ть** (**-ю**) *несов неперех* (*разг*) to be a snappy dresser.
мо́дно *нареч* (*одева́ться, стри́чься*) fashionably ♦ *как сказ*: ~ **носи́ть ми́ни** miniskirts are in fashion.
мо́дн|**ый** (**-ен, -на, -но**) *прил* fashionable; (*no short form; журнал*) fashion *опред*.
мо́ды (**-**) *мн* fashions *мн*; **журна́л мод** fashion magazine.
моё (**-его́**) *притяж мест см* **мой**.
мо́жет *несов см* **мочь** ♦ *вводн сл* (*разг*) maybe, perhaps.

мо́жешь *итп несов см* **мочь**.
можжеве́льник (**-а**) *м* juniper.
мо́жно *как сказ* (*возможно*): ~ +*infin* it is possible to do; ~ **кури́ть** smoking is allowed *или* permitted; ~ (**войти́**)**?** may I (come in)?; **как ~** (*разг: выражает осуждение*) how could he *итп*; **как ~ лу́чше/быстре́е** as well/quickly as possible.
моза́ик|**а** (**-и**) *ж* (*узор*) mosaic; (*искусство*) mosaic work.
моза́ичный (**-ен, -на, -но**) *прил* mosaic.
Мозамби́к (**-а**) *м* Mozambique.
мозг (**-а**; *loc sg* **-у́**, *nom sg* **-и́**) *м* brain; (*перен: центр*) nerve centre (*BRIT*) *или* center (*US*); **спинно́й** ~ spinal cord; **ко́стный** ~ (bone) marrow; **до мо́зга косте́й** through and through; **шевели́ть** (**пошевели́ть** *perf*) **~а́ми** (*разг*) to use one's head; *см также* **мозги́**.
мозг|**и́** (**-о́в**) *мн* (*КУЛИН*) brains *мн*.
мозг|**ова́ть** (**-у́ю**) *несов неперех* (*разг*) to think.
мозгови́тый *прил* (*разг*) brainy.
мозгово́й *прил* cerebral; (*интеллектуальный*) intellectual; ~ **центр** nerve centre (*BRIT*) *или* center (*US*).
мозо́лист|**ый** (**-, -а, -о**) *прил* calloused.
мозо́л|**ить** (**-ю, -ишь**) *несов перех*: ~ **глаза́ кому́-н** (*разг*) to bug sb by one's very presence.
мозо́л|**ь** (**-и**) *ж* corn, callus.
мозо́льный *прил*: ~ **пла́стырь** corn plaster.
мой (**моего́**; *см Table 8*; *f* **моя́**, *nt* **моё**, *pl* **мои́**) *притяж мест* my; **по-мо́ему** my way; (*по моему́ мнению*) in my opinion.
мо́йк|**а** (**-и**) *ж* (*мытьё*) washing; (*раковина*) sink.
МОК (**-а**) *м сокр* (= **Междунаро́дный олимпи́йский комите́т**) IOC (= *International Olympic Committee*).
мо́к|**нуть** (**-ну, -нешь**; *pt* **-, -ла, -ло**) *несов неперех* to get wet; (*лежа́ть в воде́*) to be soaking.
мо́кро *как сказ* it's wet.
мокро́т|**а** (**-ы**) *ж* phlegm.
мокрот|**а́** (**-ы́**) *ж* (*разг*) dampness.
мо́крый (**-, -а, -о**) *прил* wet.
мол (**-а**; *loc sg* **-у́**) *м* breakwater, mole ♦ *част* (*разг*): **он, ~, ничего́ не зна́ет** he says he knows nothing.
молв|**а́** (**-ы́**) *ж* rumour (*BRIT*), rumor (*US*).
молда́вск|**ий** (**-ая, -ое, -ие**) *прил* Moldavian.
Молдо́в|**а** (**-ы**) *ж* Moldova.
молдова́н|**ин** (**-ина**; *nom pl* **-е**) *м* Moldavian.
молдова́н|**ка** (**-ки**; *gen pl* **-ок**) *ж см* **молдова́нин**.
моле́б|**ен** (**-на**) *м* (*РЕЛ*) service.
моле́кул|**а** (**-ы**) *ж* molecule.
молекуля́рный *прил* molecular.
моле́ни|**е** (**-я**) *ср* praying; (*мольба́*) entreaty.
моли́тв|**а** (**-ы**) *ж* prayer.
моли́твенник (**-а**) *м* prayer book.
мол|**и́ться** (**-ю́сь, -ишься**; *perf* **помоли́ться**) *несов возв*: ~ +*dat* to pray to; (*no perf; перен*): ~ **на** +*acc* to idolize.

моллю́ск (-а) м mollusc.
молниено́с|ный (-ен, -на, -но) прил lightning опред.
мо́лни|я (-и) ж lightning; (застёжка) zip (fastener) (BRIT), zipper (US); **телегра́мма-~** express telegram.
молодёжный прил (клуб, театр) youth опред; (мода, газета) for young people.
молодёж|ь (-и) ж собир young people мн.
молоде́|ть (-ю; perf **помолоде́ть**) несов неперех (выглядеть моложе) to look younger; (чувствовать себя моложе) to feel younger; (население) to become younger.
мо́лод|ец (-ца) м (ФОЛЬКЛОР) brave lad, fine young man.
молод|е́ц (-ца́) м strong fellow; ~! (разг) well done!; **она́/он** ~! (разг) she/he has done well!; **держа́ться** (impf) ~цо́м to put up a good show.
молоде́цк|ий (-ая, -ое, -ие) прил (вид) dashing; (поступок) valiant.
моло|ди́ть (-жу́, -ди́шь) несов перех: ~ кого́-н to make sb look younger
▶ **молоди́ться** несов возв to try to look younger.
молодня́к (-а́) м собир (ЗООЛ) young (of animals); (БОТ) saplings мн.
молодожён (-а) м (обычно мн) newlywed.
молодо́й (**мо́лод, молода́, мо́лодо**) прил young; (картофель, листва) new; (задор, отвага) youthful; (no short form; вино, пиво) young; (сыр) unripe.
мо́лодост|ь (-и) ж youth; **он не пе́рвой ~и** he's getting on in years.
молодца́ итп сущ см **мо́лодец**.
молодца́ итп сущ см **молоде́ц**.
молодцева́тый прил sprightly.
молодчик (-а) м thug.
моложа́в|ый (-, -а, -о) прил (человек) young-looking; (вид, лицо) youthful.
моло́же сравн прил от **молодо́й**.
моложу́(сь) несов см **молоди́ть(ся)**.
молоко́ (-а́) ср milk.
молокосо́с (-а) м (разг: пренебр) greenhorn.
мо́лот (-а) м hammer.
молоти́л|ка (-ки; gen pl -ок) ж threshing machine.
моло|ти́ть (-очу́, -о́тишь) несов перех (пшеницу) to thresh; (разг: колотить) to hammer.
молот|о́к (-ка́) м hammer; **продава́ть (прода́ть** perf**) что-н с ~ка́** to sell sth by auction, auction sth.
мо́лотый прил (кофе, перец) ground.
моло́|ть (**мелю́, ме́лешь**; perf **смоло́ть** или **помоло́ть**) несов перех (зерно, кофе) to grind; ~ (impf) **вздор** или **чепуху́** (разг) to talk rubbish.
молочко́ (-а́) ср (жидкий крем) lotion.

моло́чник (-а) м (посуда) milk jug; (разносчик молока) milkman (мн milkmen).
моло́чниц|а (-ы) ж milklady.
моло́чный прил (продукты, скот) dairy опред; (каша, коктейль) milk опред; (поросёнок, телёнок) sucking; (железа) mammary; (хим) lactic; **моло́чная ку́хня** place where baby food is prepared; **моло́чная сестра́** foster sister; **моло́чный брат** foster brother; **моло́чный зуб** milk tooth.
молочу́ несов см **молоти́ть**.
мо́лча нареч (кивнуть, уйти) silently; (согласиться) tacitly.
молчали́в|ый (-, -а, -о) прил silent; (no short form; согласие, одобрение) tacit; ~ **мужчи́на** a man of few words.
молча́ни|е (-я) ср (безмолвие) silence; ~ – **знак согла́сия** silence can be taken to mean approval.
молч|а́ть (-у́, -и́шь) несов неперех to be silent; ~ (impf) **о** +prp to keep silent или quiet about.
мол|ь (-и) ж moth.
мольб|а́ (-ы́) ж entreaty.
мольбе́рт (-а) м easel.
моме́нт (-а) м moment; (в фильме) episode; (доклада, исследования) point; **теку́щий** ~ the current situation.
момента́лен прил см **момента́льный**.
момента́льно нареч instantly.
момента́л|ьный (-ен, -ьна, -ьно) прил instant.
мона́рх (-а) м monarch.
мона́рхи|я (-и) ж monarchy.
монасты́р|ь (-я́) м (мужской) monastery; (женский) convent.
мона́х (-а) м monk.
мона́хин|я (-и; gen pl -ь) ж nun.
мона́шеск|ий (-ая, -ое, -ие) прил (также перен) monastic.
мона́шеств|о (-а) ср monastic life.
Монбла́н (-а) м Mont Blanc.
монго́л (-а) м Mongol, Mongolian.
монго́л|ка (-ки; gen pl -ок) ж см **монго́л**.
монго́льск|ий (-ая, -ое, -ие) прил Mongolian.
Монго́ли|я (-и) ж Mongolia.
моне́т|а (-ы) ж coin; **плати́ть (отплати́ть** perf**) кому́-н той же ~ой** (отомсти́ть) to pay sb back in kind; **принима́ть (приня́ть** perf**) что-н за чи́стую ~у** to take sth at face value.
монетари́ст (-а) м monetarist.
монета́рный прил monetary.
моне́тный прил: ~ **двор** mint.
монито́р (-а) м monitor.
моногра́мм|а (-ы) ж monogram.
моногра́фи|я (-и) ж monograph.
моноли́т (-а) м monolith.
моноли́т|ный (-ен, -на, -но) прил (глыба, колонна) monolithic; (перен) united.
моноло́г (-а) м monologue.
монополиза́ци|я (-и) ж monopolization.
монополизи́р|овать (-ую) (не)сов перех to

monopolize.

монополи́ст (**-а**) *м* monopolist.

монопо́ли|я (**-и**) *ж* monopoly.

монопо́льный *прил* monopoly *опред*.

моното́н|ный (**-ен, -на, -но**) *прил* (*также перен*) monotonous.

монохро́мный *прил* (*комп*) monochrome.

Монреа́л|ь (**-я**) *м* Montreal.

монта́ж (**-а́**) *ж* (*сооружения*) erection; (*оборудования*) mounting, assembly; (*кадров, фильма*) editing.

монта́жник (**-а**) *м* (*на стройке*) rigger; (*на фабрике*) fitter.

монта́жни|ца (**-ы**) *ж* см **монта́жник**.

монтёр (**-а**) *м* fitter; (*электромонтёр*) electrician.

монти́р|овать (**-ую**; *perf* **смонти́ровать**) *несов перех* (*оборудование, схему*) to assemble; (*фильм, передачу*) to edit.

монуме́нт (**-а**) *м* monument.

монумента́льный (**-ен, -ьна, -ьно**) *прил* monumental.

мопе́д (**-а**) *м* moped (*with movable pedals*).

мор (**-а**) *м* pestilence, plague.

мора́лен *прил* см **мора́льный**.

морализи́р|овать (**-ую**) *несов неперех* to moralize.

мора́л|ь (**-и**) *ж* (*этика поведения*) morals *мн*, ethics *мн*; (*басни, сказки*) moral; (*разг: нравоучение*) moralizing.

мора́льный (**-ен, -ьна, -ьно**) *прил* moral; (*no short form; кодекс, нормы*) moral, ethical; **мора́льный изно́с, мора́льное устарева́ние** obsolescence.

морато́ри|й (**-я**) *м* moratorium.

морг (**-а**) *м* morgue.

морга́|ть (**-ю**) *несов неперех* to blink; (*подмигивать*): ~ (+*dat*) to wink (at).

моргн|у́ть (**-у́, -ёшь**) *сов неперех* to blink; (*подмигнуть*): ~ (+*dat*) to wink (at); **не ~у́в гла́зом** (*разг*) without batting an eyelid.

мо́рд|а (**-ы**) *ж* (*животного*) muzzle; (*разг: лицо*) mug.

мордви́н (**-а**) *м* Mordvin.

мордви́н|ка (**-ки**; *gen pl* **-ок**) *ж* см **мордви́н**.

Мо́рдви|я (**-и**) *ж* Mordvia.

мо́р|е (**-я**; *nom pl* **-я́**, *gen pl* **-е́й**) *ср* (*также перен*) sea; **откры́тое** ~ open sea; **ему́** ~ **по коле́но** (*разг*) he's afraid of nothing.

морепла́вани|е (**-я**) *ср* (*плавание*) seafaring; (*вождение судов*) navigation.

морепла́ватель (**-я**) *м* seafarer.

морехо́д|ка (**-и**) *ж* (*разг*) naval college.

морехо́дный *прил* (*училище, испытания*) naval; (*инструменты*) navigational.

морж (**-а́**) *м* walrus; (*перен*) *wintertime open-air bather*.

моржи́х|а (**-и**) *ж* см **морж**.

моржо́вый *прил* walrus *опред*.

мори́л|ка (**-и**) *ж* (*разг: краска*) stain; (*от насекомых*) insecticide.

мор|и́ть (**-ю́, -и́шь**; *perf* **помори́ть**) *несов перех* (*насекомых*) to exterminate; (*дерево*) to stain; (*дуб*) to fume; (*perf* **размори́ть**; *подлеж: сон, жара*) to exhaust, drain; ~ (**замори́ть** *perf*) **го́лодом кого́-н** to starve sb; ~ (**умори́ть** *perf*) **шу́тками кого́-н** (*разг*) to have sb in stitches with one's jokes.

морко́в|ка (**-ки**; *gen pl* **-ок**) *ж* (*разг: одна штука*) carrot; (*морковь*) carrots *мн*.

морко́вный *прил* carrot *опред*.

морко́в|ь (**-и**) *ж* carrots *мн*.

моро́жени|ца (**-ы**) *ж* (*аппарат*) ice-cream maker; (*кафе*) ice-cream parlour (*BRIT*) *или* parlor (*US*).

моро́жен|ое (**-ого**; *decl like adj*) *ср* ice cream.

моро́женый *прил* frozen; (*испорченный морозом*) frost-damaged.

моро́жу *несов* см **моро́зить**.

моро́з (**-а**) *м* frost; **у нас стоя́т** ~**ы** we're having a spell of freezing (cold) weather; **Дед М~** ≈ Father Christmas.

моро́зен *прил* см **моро́зный**.

морози́льник (**-а**) *м* freezer.

морози́льный *прил* freezing; **морози́льная ка́мера** deepfreeze.

моро́|зить (**-жу, -зишь**) *несов перех* to freeze ♦ *безл*; **на у́лице** ~**зит** it's freezing outside.

моро́зный (**-ен, -на, -но**) *прил* frosty.

морозосто́й|кий (**-йкая, -йкое, -йкие; -ек, -йка, -йко**) *прил* frost-resistant.

морос|и́ть (*3sg* **-и́т**, *3pl* **-я́т**) *несов неперех* to drizzle.

моро́ч|ить (**-у, -ишь**; *perf* **заморо́чить**) *несов перех* (*разг*) to fool; ~ (**заморо́чить** *perf*) **го́лову кому́-н** (*разг*) to pull sb's leg.

моро́шк|а (**-и**) *ж* cloudberry.

морс (**-а**; *part gen* **-у**) *м* (fruit) drink.

морск|о́й (**-а́я, -о́е, -и́е**) *прил* sea *опред*; (*БИО, ВОЕН*) marine; (*курорт, лечебница*) seaside *опред*; ~**о́е страхова́ние** marine insurance; ~**о́е пра́во** maritime law; **морска́я боле́знь** seasickness; **морско́й волк** sea dog; **морска́я сви́нка** guinea pig.

мо́рфи|й (**-я**) *м* morphine, morphia.

морфоло́ги|я (**-и**) *ж* morphology.

морщи́н|а (**-ы**) *ж* (*на лице*) wrinkle; (*на ткани*) crease.

морщи́нист|ый (**-, -а, -о**) *прил* (*лицо*) wrinkled.

мо́рщ|ить (**-у, -ишь**; *perf* **намо́рщить**) *несов перех* (*брови*) to knit; (*perf* **смо́рщить**; *нос, лоб*) to wrinkle; (*лицо*) to screw up

▶ **мо́рщиться** (*perf* **намо́рщиться**) *несов возв* to screw up one's face; (*одежда, ткань*) to crease; ~**ся** (**смо́рщиться** *perf*) **от** +*gen* (*от старости, от солнца*) to become wrinkled from; (*от боли*) to wince in.

морщ|и́ть (*3sg* **-и́т**, *3pl* **-а́т**) *несов неперех* (*разг*) to be wrinkled.

моря́к (**-а́**) *м* sailor.

Москва́ (**-ы́**) *ж* Moscow.

москви́ч (**-а́**) *м* Muscovite.

москви́ч|ка (-ки; *gen pl* -ек) *ж см* **москви́ч**.
мост (-а́; *loc sg* -ý) *м* bridge; (*телевизио́нный, косми́ческий*) link; (*АВТ*) axle.
мо́стик (-а) *м* bridge; **капита́нский** ~ bridge (*NAUT*).
мости́ть (-щу́, -сти́шь; *perf* **вы́мостить**) *несов перех* (*пло́щадь, у́лицу*) to pave; (*perf* **намости́ть**; *пол*) to lay.
мост|ки́ (-о́в) *мн* (*через лу́жу*) duckboard *ед*; (*у реки́, у пруда́*) wooden platform *ед*.
мостов|а́я (-о́й; *decl like adj*) *ж* road.
МОТ *ж сокр* (= междунаро́дная организа́ция труда́) ILO (= *International Labour Organization*).
мота́|ть (-ю; *perf* **намота́ть**) *несов перех* (*ни́тки*) to wind ♦ (*perf* **умота́ть**) *непарех* (*разг: уехать*) to go off; (*perf* **помота́ть**): ~ +*instr* (*голово́й*) to shake; ~**й отсю́да!** get lost!; ~ (*impf*) **кому́-н не́рвы** (*разг*) to get on sb's nerves
▶ **мота́|ться** *несов возв* to swing; (*разг: хлопотать*) to rush about.
моте́л|ь (-я) *м* motel.
моти́в (-а) *м* (*преступления*) motive; (*для развода*) grounds *мн*; (*мелодия*) motif.
мотиви́р|овать (-ую) (*не)сов перех* to justify.
мотка́ *сущ см* **мото́к**.
мотого́н|ка (-ки; *gen pl* -ок) *ж* (*обычно мн*) motorcycle race.
мотого́нщик (-а) *м* motorcycle racer.
мот|о́к (-ка́) *м* skein.
мото́р (-а) *м* motor; (*автомобиля, лодки*) engine.
мотори́ст (-а) *м* motor mechanic.
мото́рный *прил* motor *опред*; **мото́рная ло́дка** motorboat.
моторо́ллер (-а) *м* (motor) scooter.
мотоци́кл (-а) *м* motorcycle.
моты́г|а (-и) *ж* hoe.
мотыл|ёк (-ька́) *м* moth.
м|ох (мха; *loc sg* мху, *nom pl* мхи) *м* moss.
мохе́р (-а) *м* mohair.
мохе́ровый *прил* mohair.
мохна́тый (-, -а, -о) *прил* (*животное*) shaggy; (*ель, сосна*) bushy; (*no short form*; *плед, шапка*) fluffy.
махови́к (-а́) *м* (*БОТ*) variegated boletus.
моцио́н (-а) *м* (*прогулка*) constitutional.
моч|а́ (-и́) *ж* urine.
моча́л|ка (-ки; *gen pl* -ок) *ж* sponge.
мочево́й *прил*: ~ **пузы́рь** bladder.
мочего́нный *прил* diuretic.
мо́чек *сущ см* **мо́чка**.
мочёный *прил* (*яблоко, брусника*) preserved (*in sugar solution*).
мочи́ть (-ý, -ишь; *perf* **намочи́ть**) *несов перех* (*ноги, волосы, одежду*) to wet; (*perf* **замочи́ть**; *бельё*) to soak; (*яблоки*) to preserve
▶ **мочи́ться** (*perf* **помочи́ться**) *несов возв* to urinate.

мо́чк|а (-ки; *gen pl* -ек) *ж* ear lobe.
мо́чь (-гу́, -жешь *итп*, -гут; *pt* -г, -гла́, -гло́, *perf* **смочь**) *несов непарех*: ~ +*infin* to be able to do ♦ (-чи) *ж*: **йзо всей мо́чи** with all one's might; **я** ~**гу́ игра́ть на гита́ре/говори́ть по-англи́йски** I can play the guitar/talk English; **он мо́жет прийти́** he can come *или* is able to come; **она́ не** ~**гла́ купи́ть дом** she couldn't buy *или* wasn't able to buy the house; **я сде́лаю всё, что** ~**гу́** I will do all I can; **за́втра мо́жешь не приходи́ть** you don't have to come tomorrow; **он мо́жет оби́деться** he may well be offended; **не** ~**гу́ поня́ть э́того** I can't understand this; **мо́жешь бо́льше не извиня́ться** don't bother apologising any more; **мо́жет быть** maybe; **не мо́жет быть!** (*выражение сомнения*) it's impossible!
мо́шек *сущ см* **мо́шка**.
моше́нник (-а) *м* swindler, crook.
моше́нничаа|ть (-ю; *perf* **смоше́нничать**) *несов непарех* to swindle.
моше́ннический (-ая, -ое, -ие) *прил* devious.
моше́нничеств|о (-а) *ср* deviousness.
мо́шк|а (-ки; *gen pl* -ек) *ж* midge.
мошкар|а́ (-ы́) *ж собир* midges *мн*.
мо́щен *прил см* **мо́щный**.
мощёный *прил* paved.
мо́щност|и (-ей) *мн* facilities *мн*.
мо́щность (-и) *ж* power; (*воздействие*) force; **неиспо́льзуемая произво́дственная** ~ idle capacity; *см также* **мо́щности**.
мо́щный (-ен, -на́, -но) *прил* (*взрыв, выступле́ние*) powerful; (*организм, дуб*) mighty; (*рост, подъём*) vigorous; (*массивный*) massive; (*no short form*; *двигатель, агрегат*) powerful.
мощ|у́ *несов см* **мости́ть**.
мощь (-и) *ж* power, might.
мо́ю(сь) *итп несов см* **мы́ть(ся)**.
мо|я́ (-е́й) *притяж мест см* **мой**.
м.п. *сокр* = **ме́сто печа́ти**.
МП *м сокр* (= маши́нный перево́д) MT (= *machine translation*).
мрак (-а) *м* (*темнота*) darkness; (*перен*) gloom.
мракобе́с (-а) *м* obscurantist.
мра́мор (-а) *м* marble.
мра́морный *прил* (*также перен*) marble; (*узор, линолеум*) marbled; **Мра́морное мо́ре** Sea of Marmara.
мра́чен *прил см* **мра́чный**.
мрачне́|ть (-ю; *perf* **помрачне́ть**) *несов непарех* (*небо, горизонт*) to grow dark; (*взгляд, лицо*) to darken.
мра́чный (-ен, -на́, -но) *прил* (*небо, мысли, взгляд*) gloomy; (*времена, годы, период*) dark.
мсти́тел|ь (-я) *м* avenger.
мсти́тельниц|а (-ы) *ж см* **мсти́тель**.

мсти́тельный (-ен, -ьна, -ьно) прил vindictive.
мстить (мщу, мстишь; perf **отомсти́ть**) несов
неперех: ~ кому́-н to take revenge on sb.
МТП ж сокр (= междунаро́дная торго́вая
пала́та) ICC (= International Chamber of
Commerce).
МТС ж сокр (= междугоро́дная телефо́нная
ста́нция) ≈ intercity telephone exchange.
мудрёный (-ён, -ена́, -ено́) прил (непоня́тный)
strange; (сло́жный) tricky, complicated; **не**
~ено́, что ... it's no wonder that ....
мудре́ц (-а́) м wise man (мн men).
мудри́ть (-ю, -и́шь; perf **намудри́ть**) несов
неперех to try to be clever.
му́дрость (-и) ж wisdom; **зуб** ~и wisdom
tooth.
му́дрый (-, -á, -о) прил wise.
муж (-а; nom pl -ья́, gen pl -éй) м husband; (nom pl
-и́): госуда́рственный ~ elder statesman (мн
statesmen); **учёный** ~ man of science.
мужа́ть (-ю; perf **возмужа́ть**) несов неперех to
mature
▶ **мужа́ться** несов возв to take heart, have
courage.
мужеподо́бный (-ен, -на, -но) прил masculine.
му́жественный (-, -на, -но) прил (лицо́,
нату́ра) strong; (посту́пок, шаг) courageous.
му́жество (-а) ср courage.
мужи́к (-á) м (разг: мужчи́на) man (мн men);
(крестья́нин) muzhik.
мужикова́тый прил boorish.
мужско́й (-а́я, -о́е, -и́е) прил (боти́нки,
туале́т, парикма́хер) men's; (хара́ктер,
рукопожа́тие) masculine; (о́рганы, кле́тка)
male; **мужско́й пол** male sex; **мужско́й род**
masculine gender.
мужчи́на (-ы) м man (мн men).
мужья́ сущ см **муж**.
му́за (-ы) ж muse.
музе́й (-я) м museum.
музе́йный прил museum опред.
му́зыка (-и) ж (та́кже перен) music.
музыка́льный (-ен, -ьна, -ьно) прил musical;
музыка́льная шко́ла music school.
музыка́нт (-а) м musician.
му́ка (-и) ж torment.
мука́ (-и́) ж flour; (гру́бого помо́ла) meal;
ко́стная ~ bone meal; **карто́фельная** ~
(крахма́л) potato starch.
мул (-а) м mule.
мулла́ (-ы́) м mullah.
му́льтик (-а) м (разг) cartoon.
мультиплика́тор (-а) м animator.
мультипликацио́нный прил: ~ **фильм**
cartoon.
мультиплика́ция (-и) ж cartoon.
мультфи́льм (-а) м сокр (=
мультипликацио́нный фильм) cartoon,
animation film.
му́мия (-и) ж mummy.
мунди́р (-а) м uniform; **карто́фель в** ~е jacket
potatoes.

мундшту́к (-á) м cigarette holder; (муз)
mouthpiece.
муниципалите́т (-а) м municipality, city
council.
муниципа́льный прил municipal.
МУР (-а) м сокр (= Моско́вский уголо́вный
ро́зыск) Moscow Criminal Investigation
Department.
мура́ (-ы́) ж (разг) rubbish.
мураве́й (-ья́) м ant.
мураве́йник (-а) м ant hill.
муравьи́ итп сущ см **мураве́й**.
мура́шки (-ек) мн: у меня́ ~ по спине́ бе́гают
shivers are running down my spine;
покрыва́ться (**покры́ться** perf) ~ками to come
out in goose pimples (BRIT) или goose bumps
(US).
мурлы́кать (-чу, -чешь) несов неперех to purr
◆ (perf **промурлы́кать**) перех to hum.
муска́т (-а) м (оре́х) nutmeg; (сорт виногра́да)
muscat; (сорт вина́) muscat(el).
му́скул (-а) м muscle.
мускулату́ра (-ы) ж собир musculature.
мускули́стый (-, -а, -о) прил muscular.
му́сор (-а) м rubbish (BRIT), garbage (US).
му́сорить (-ю, -ишь; perf **наму́сорить**) несов
неперех to make a mess.
му́сорный прил rubbish опред (BRIT), garbage
опред (US); **му́сорное ведро́** dustbin.
мусоропрово́д (-а) м refuse или garbage (US)
chute.
мусс (-а) м (кули́н) mousse.
мусульма́нин (-а) м Muslim.
мусульма́нка (-ки; gen pl -ок) ж см
мусульма́нин.
мусульма́нский (-ая, -ое, -ие) прил Muslim.
мусульма́нство (-а) ср Islam.
му́тен прил см **му́тный**.
мути́ть (-чу́, -ти́шь; perf **взмути́ть** или
замути́ть) несов перех (жи́дкость) to muddy;
(perf **помути́ть**; перен: рассу́док) to cloud; (по
perf; разг: наро́д, толпу́) to work up ◆ несов
безл (разг): меня́ му́тит I feel sick
▶ **мути́ться** (perf **замути́ться**) несов возв (вода́,
раство́р) to become cloudy; (perf **помути́ться**;
перен: рассу́док) to become clouded ◆ безл
(разг): у меня́ в глаза́х или в голове́
помути́лось I felt giddy.
мутне́ть (3sg -ет, 3pl -ют, perf **помутне́ть**) несов
неперех (жи́дкость) to become cloudy; (взор,
глаза́) to grow dull; **он так уста́л, что у него́
созна́ние** ~ет he is so tired, he can't think
straight.
му́тный (-ен, -на́, -но) прил (жи́дкость) cloudy;
(стекло́, взор, глаза́) dull; (взор, глаза́) glazed;
(перен: голова́, рассу́док) confused.
муть (-и) ж sediment; (разг: фильм, кни́га итп)
rubbish; (перен: на душе́) ache.
му́фта (-ы) ж (ТЕХ) sleeve; (же́нская оде́жда)
muff.
му́ха (-и) ж fly; **де́лать** (**сде́лать** perf) **из** ~и

слона́ ≈ to make a mountain out of a molehill;
под ~ой (разг) legless.

мухомо́р (-а) м (БОТ) fly agaric.

муче́ни|е (-я) ср torment, torture.

му́ченик (-а) м martyr.

му́ченица (-ы) ж см му́ченик.

мучи́телен прил см мучи́тельный.

мучи́тел|ь (-я) м tormentor.

мучи́тельница (-ы) ж см мучи́тель.

мучи́тельный (-ен, -ьна, -ьно) прил agonizing.

му́чить (-у, -ишь; perf заму́чить или изму́чить) несов перех to torment

▸ **му́читься** (perf заму́читься) несов возв: ~ся +instr (сомнениями, угрызениями совести) to be tormented by; ~ся (заму́читься perf) от +gen (от боли, от приступов) to suffer from; ~ся (заму́читься perf) с +instr (разг) to have a lot of hassle with; ~ся (impf) над +instr to agonize over.

мучн|о́е (-о́го; decl like adj) ср starchy foods мн.

му́шк|а (-и; gen pl -ек) ж (для прицела) sight; (на лице) beauty spot; **брать (взять** perf) кого́-н/что-н на ~ку (прицелиться) to take aim at sb/sth; (перен) to keep a close eye on sb/sth.

муштр|ова́ть (-у́ю; perf вы́муштровать) несов перех (солдат) to drill.

мха итп сущ см мох.

МХАТ (-а) м сокр (= Моско́вский Худо́жественный академи́ческий теа́тр) Moscow Arts Theatre (BRIT) или Theater (US).

мч|ать (-у, -ишь) несов неперех (поезд, автомобиль) to speed along; (лошадь) to race along ◆ перех to rush

▸ **мча́ться** несов возв (поезд, автомобиль) to speed along; (лошадь) to race along; (перен: годы, время) to fly past.

мще́ни|е (-я) ср revenge, vengeance.

мщу несов см мстить.

мы (нас; см Table 5b) мест we; ~ с тобо́й/жено́й you/my wife and I; кто зако́нчил рабо́ту? – ~ who finished the job? – we did; кто винова́т? – ~ who is to blame? – we are.

мы́л|ить (-ю, -ишь; perf намы́лить) несов перех to soap

▸ **мы́литься** (perf намы́литься) несов возв to soap o.s.; (мыло, шампунь) to lather.

мы́л|о (-а) ср soap; он весь в ~е (перен: разг: в поту) he's in a lather.

мы́льниц|а (-ы) ж soap dish.

мы́льный прил soap опред.

мыс (-а; loc sg -у́, nom pl -ы) м cape, promontory.

мы́сленно нареч mentally.

мы́сленный прил mental.

мысли́тел|ь (-я) м thinker.

мысли́тельный прил (процесс) thought опред; (способности, уровень) intellectual.

мы́сл|ить (-ю, -ишь) несов неперех to think, reason ◆ перех to imagine; я не ~ю жи́зни без

рабо́ты I can't imagine life without work.

мысл|ь (-и) ж thought; (идея) idea: за́дняя ~ ulterior motive; о́браз мы́слей way of thinking; собира́ться (собра́ться perf) с мы́слями to collect one's thoughts; э́то ~! that's a thought!

мы́слящий (-ая, -ее, -ие) прил thinking опред.

мыть (мо́ю, мо́ешь; perf вы́мыть или помы́ть) несов перех to wash; рука́ ру́ку мо́ет partners in crime will always cover for each other

▸ **мы́ться** (perf вы́мыться или помы́ться) несов возв to wash o.s.

мыч|а́ть (-у́, -и́шь; perf промыча́ть) несов неперех (корова) to moo; (бык) to bellow; (разг: человек) to mumble.

мы́шек сущ см мы́шка.

мышело́в|ка (-ки; gen pl -ок) ж mousetrap.

мы́шечный прил muscular.

мыши́н|ый прил (цвет) grey (BRIT), gray (US); ~ая нора́ mouse hole; мыши́ная возня́ (перен) intrigue.

мы́шк|а (-и; gen pl -ек) ж уменьш от мышь; под ~кой under one's arm.

мышле́ни|е (-я) ср thought, thinking.

мы́шц|а (-ы) ж muscle.

мыш|ь (-и) ж (ЗООЛ, КОМП) mouse.

мышья́к (-а́; part gen -у́) м arsenic.

мэр (-а) м mayor.

мэ́ри|я (-и) ж city hall.

мя́гк|ий (-ая, -ое, -ие; -ок, -ка́, -ко) прил soft; (движения, похо́дка) smooth; (хара́ктер, челове́к) mild, gentle; (пригово́р, вы́говор, наказа́ние) lenient; (кли́мат, зима́, пого́да) mild; **мя́гкий ваго́н** railway carriage with soft seats; **мя́гкий знак** soft sign (Russian letter).

мя́гко нареч gently; (отруга́ть) mildly; ~ выража́ясь to put it mildly.

мягкосерде́чный (-ен, -на, -но) прил kind-hearted.

мя́гок прил см мя́гкий.

мя́гче сравн прил от мя́гкий ◆ сравн нареч от мя́гко.

мя́киш (-а) м crumb.

мя́кот|ь (-и) ж flesh; (мясо без косте́й) meat off the bone.

мя́мл|ить (-ю, -ишь; perf промя́млить) несов перех (разг) to mumble.

мяси́стый (-, -а, -о) прил meaty; (пле́чи, лицо́, плод) fleshy.

мясни́к (-а́) м butcher.

мясно́й прил (из мя́са) meat; (коро́ва, скот) beef; (отде́л, магази́н) butcher's; ~ы́е консе́рвы tinned meat.

мя́с|о (-а) ср meat; (разг: говя́дина) beef.

мясору́б|ка (-ки; gen pl -ок) ж mincer (BRIT), grinder (US).

мя́т|а (-ы) ж mint.

мятеж́ (-а́) м revolt.

мяте́жный прил rebellious; (душа́, хара́ктер)

restless.
МЯ́ТНЫЙ *прил* mint.
МЯ́ТЫЙ *прил* (*одежда*) creased; (*бумага*)
crumpled.
МЯТЬ (**мну, мнёшь**; *perf* **размя́ть**) *несов перех*
(*глину*) to knead; (*кожу*) to work; (*perf* **измя́ть**
или **смять**; *одежду*) to crease; (*бумагу*) to
rumple; (*волосы*) to ruffle

▶ **МЯ́ТЬСЯ** *несов возв* (*разг: человек*) to shillyshally; (*perf* **измя́ться** *или* **помя́ться** *или*
смя́ться; *одежда*) to get creased; (*бумага*) to
get rumpled.
МЯУ́КА|**ТЬ** (-**ю**; *perf* **промяу́кать**) *несов неперех*
to miaow, mew.
МЯЧ (-**á**) *м* ball; **ручно́й** ~ (*СПОРТ*) handball;
футбо́льный ~ football.

~ H, н ~

Н, н *сущ нескл* (*буква*) the 14th letter of the Russian alphabet.

KEYWORD

на *предл* (+*acc*) **1** (*направление на поверхность*) on; **положи таре́лку на стол** put the plate on the table; **я пове́сил карти́ну на сте́ну** I hung the picture on the wall; **на́до накле́ить ма́рку на конве́рт** you need to stick the stamp on the envelope

2 (*направление в какое-н место*) to; **на Юг/Украи́ну** to the South/Ukraine; **е́здить** (*impf*) **на мо́ре/рабо́ту/конфере́нции** to go to the seaside/to work/to a conference; **сесть** (*perf*) **на по́езд** to get on(to) the train

3 (*об объекте воздействия*): **обрати́ внима́ние на э́того челове́ка** pay attention to this man; **нажми́ на педа́ль/кно́пку** press the pedal/button; **я люблю́ смотре́ть на дете́й/на звёзды** I love watching the children/the stars

4 (*о времени, сроке*) for; **назнача́ть** (**назна́чить** *perf*) **на за́втра/на 5 часо́в** to arrange sth for tomorrow/for 5 o'clock; **он уе́хал на час/ме́сяц** he has gone away for an hour/a month

5 (*о цели, о назначении*) for; **де́ньги на кни́ги** money for books; **ткань на пла́тье** material for a dress; **на написа́ние докла́да ушло́ мно́го вре́мени** much time was spent writing the report; **прове́рка на сообрази́тельность** intelligence test

6 (*о мере*) into; **дели́ть** (*impf*) **что-н на ча́сти/пара́графы** to divide sth into parts/paragraphs

7 (*при сравнении*): **я получа́ю на сто рубле́й ме́ньше** I get one hundred roubles less

8 (*об изменении состояния*) into; **на́до перевести́ текст на англи́йский** the text must be translated into English; **мы перешли́ на ру́сский язы́к** we switched (in)to Russian; **я обменя́л маши́ну на я́хту** I exchanged the car for a yacht ♦ *предл* (+*prp*) **1** (*нахождение на поверхности*) on; **кни́га на по́лке** the book is on the shelf; **я сижу́ на дива́не** I am sitting on the sofa; **на де́вочке ша́пка/шу́ба** the girl has a hat/fur coat on

2 (*о пребывании где-н*) in; **на Украи́не/Кавка́зе** in the Ukraine/Caucasus; **на у́лице** in the street;

быть (*impf*) **на рабо́те/заседа́нии** to be at work/at a meeting

3 (*о времени осуществления чего-н*): **встре́тимся на сле́дующей неде́ле** let's meet next week; **на пе́рвых пора́х** at first; **на ходу́** (*сказать, бросить итп*) in passing; (*поймать*) without stopping

4 (*об объекте воздействия*) on; **сосредото́читься** (*perf*)**/останови́ться** (*perf*) **на чём-н** to concentrate/dwell on sth; **сойти́** (*perf*) **с ума́ на чём-н** to go mad about sth

5 (*о средстве осуществления чего-н*): **е́здить на по́езде/велосипе́де** to travel by train/bicycle; **игра́ть** (*impf*) **на роя́ле/скри́пке** to play the piano/violin; **ката́ться** (*impf*) **на лы́жах/конька́х** to go skiing/skating; **говори́ть** (*impf*) **на ру́сском/англи́йском языке́** to speak (in) English/Russian

6 (*о составной части предмета*): **раство́р на йо́де** iodine solution; **ка́ша на воде́** porridge made with water

7 (*раза: о большом количестве чего-н*): **оши́бка на оши́бке** mistake upon mistake.

на (**на́те**) *част* (*разг*) here (you are).

наб. *сокр* = **набережная**.

наба́вить (-лю, -ишь; *impf* **набавля́ть**) *сов перех* to increase.

набалда́шник (-а) *м* knob (*of walking stick*).

наба́лтывать (-ю) *несов от* **наболта́ть**.

наба́т (-а) *м* alarm bell; **бить** (*impf*) **в ~** (*перен*) to sound the alarm.

набе́г (-а) *м* raid.

набега́ть (-ю) *сов перех* (*километра итп*) to run; **~** (*perf*) **инфа́ркт** (*разг*) to give o.s. a heart attack (*by running*).

набега́ть (-ю) *несов от* **набежа́ть**.

набега́ться (-юсь) *сов возв* to wear o.s. out running.

набегу́ *итп сов см* **набежа́ть**.

набе́дренный *прил*: **~ая повя́зка** loincloth.

набежа́ть (*как* **бежа́ть**; *см* Table 20; *impf* **набега́ть**) *сов непepex* (*разг: тучи*) to gather; (: *толпа, букашки*) to come running; (: *вода*) to well up; (*проценты, выходные итп*) to mount up; (*наскочить*): **~ на** +*acc* to run into; (*волны: на берег*) to lap against.

набезобра́знича|ть (-ю) *сов от* **безобра́зничать**.

набекре́нь *нареч* (*шапка*) tilted to one side; **у него́ мозги́ ~** (*разг*) he's not with it.

на́бело *нареч*: **переписа́ть что-н ~** to write sth out in neat.

на́бережн|ая (-ой, *decl like adj*) ж embankment.

наберу́(сь) *итп сов см* **набра́ть(ся)**.

набива́|ть(ся) (-ю(сь)) *несов от* **наби́ть(ся)**.

наби́вк|а (-и) ж stuffing.

набивно́й *прил* (*матрас, подушка*) stuffed; (*ткань*) printed.

набира́|ть(ся) (-ю(сь)) *несов от* **набра́ть(ся)**.

наби́|ть (-ью, -ьёшь; *impf* **набива́ть**) *сов перех* (*прикрепить гвоздями*) to nail; (*полотно, ситец*) to print; (*разг: тарелок, чашек*) to smash; (: *настрелять*) to bag; **набива́ть** (~ *perf*) (+*instr*) (*матрас, чемодан итп*) to stuff (with); **~** (*perf*) **ши́шку/синя́к** (*разг*) to get a bump/bruise; **~** (*perf*) **оско́мину** (*перен*) to reach saturation point; **~** (*perf*) **ру́ку** (**на** +*prp*) (*разг*) to get the knack (of); **набива́ть** (~ *perf*) **це́ну** (*разг*) to talk up the price

▶ **наби́ться** (*impf* **набива́ться**) *сов возв* (*разг*): **~ся в** +*acc* (*в комнату, в автобус*) to pack; **она́ всё вре́мя ~ива́ется к нам в го́сти** she's always inviting herself round.

наблюда́телен *прил см* **наблюда́тельный**.

наблюда́тел|ь (-я) м observer.

наблюда́тельн|ый (-ен, -ьна, -ьно) *прил* (*человек*) observant; **~ пункт** observation point.

наблюда́|ть *несов перех* to observe; (*пациента*) to treat ♦ *неперех*: **~ за** +*instr* to monitor; (*за порядком, за детьми*) to watch over

▶ **наблюда́ться** *несов возв* (*случаться*) to be; **~ся** (*impf*) **у** +*gen* (*лечиться*) to be treated by; **в стране́ ~ется рост престу́пности** there has been an increase in crime across the country.

набо́жный (-ен, -на, -но) *прил* devout.

набо́йк|а (-йки; *gen pl* -ек) ж (*ткани, узора*) printing; (*ткань*) printed fabric; (*на каблуке*) heel.

на́бок *нареч* to one side.

наболева́|ть (*3sg* -ет) *несов от* **наболе́ть**.

наболе́вш|ий (-ая, -ее, -ие) *прил* (*перен: проблема, тема*) sensitive; **~ вопро́с** sore point.

наболе́|ть (*3sg* -ет, *impf* **наболева́ть**) *сов неперех* to become sore; (*проблема*) to become acute; **у неё ~ло на душе́** she has suffered a great deal.

наболта́|ть (-ю; *impf* **наба́лтывать**) *сов перех* (*разг*): **~ глу́постей** to talk a lot of rubbish ♦ *неперех*: **~ кому́-н про кого́-н** to tell sb stories about sb.

набо́р (-а; *совокупность*) set; (*студентов*) selection; (*армии, штата*) recruitment; (*типог*) typesetting; **~ слов** gibberish.

набо́рный *прил* (*типог*): **~ цех** typesetter's; **набо́рный стано́к** galley.

набо́рщик (-а) м (*типог*) typesetter.

набо́рщиц|а (-ы) ж см **набо́рщик**.

набра́сыва|ть (-ю) *несов от* **наброса́ть**, **набро́сить**

▶ **набра́сываться** *несов от* **набро́ситься**.

наб|ра́ть (-еру́, -ерёшь; *pt* -ра́л, -рала́, -ра́ло, *impf* **набира́ть**) *сов (не)перех* (+*acc или* +*gen*: *грибов, цветов*) to pick; (*воды*) to fetch; (*работы, студентов, работников*) to take on; (*армию, труппу*) to assemble; (*скорость, высоту, баллы*) to gain; (*код, номер телефона*) to dial; (*статью, текст*) to typeset; **набира́ть** (~ *perf*) **о́пыт** to gain experience

▶ **набра́ться** (*impf* **набира́ться**) *сов возв* (+*gen*: *много народу*) to gather; (*сумма денег*) to accumulate; (*разг: напиться*) to get sloshed; **~ся** (*perf*) +*gen* (*предрассу́дков итп*) to acquire; **набира́ться** (**~ся** *perf*) **сил** to build up one's strength; **набира́ться** (**~ся** *perf*) **хра́брости** to muster up courage; **набира́ться** (**~ся** *perf*) **терпе́ния** to arm o.s. with patience.

набр|ести́ (-еду́, -едёшь; *pt* -ёл, -ела́, -ело́, *impf* **набреда́ть**) *сов неперех* (*разг*): **~ на** +*acc* (*перен*) to come across; **~** (*perf*) **на мысль** (*перен*) to hit upon an idea.

наброса́|ть (-ю; *impf* **набра́сывать**) *сов перех* (*план, текст*) to sketch out ♦ (*не)перех* (+*acc или* +*gen*: *вещей, окурков*) to throw about.

набро́|сить (-шу, -сишь; *impf* **набра́сывать**) *сов перех* (*пальто, платок*) to throw on; (*покрывало*) to throw over

▶ **набро́ситься** (*impf* **набра́сываться**) *сов возв*: **~ся на** +*acc* (*на добы́чу, на же́ртву*) to fall upon; (*разг: на еду, на рабо́ту*) to get stuck into; **~ся** (*perf*) **на кого́-н** (*разг: с упрёками*) to lay into sb.

набро́с|ок (-ка) м (*плана*) sketch; (*статьи, письма*) draft.

набро́шу(сь) *сов см* **набро́сить(ся)**.

набры́зга|ть (-ю) *сов (не)перех*: **~** +*acc или* +*gen или* +*instr* to splash.

набу́х|нуть (*3sg* -нет, *3pl* -нут, *pt* -, -ла, -ло, *impf* **набуха́ть**) *сов неперех* to swell up.

набью́(сь) *итп сов см* **наби́ть(ся)**.

нава́г|а (-и) ж (*зоол*) type of cod.

наважде́ни|е (-я) *ср* apparition.

нава|ли́ть (-лю́, -лишь; *impf* **нава́ливать**) *сов (не)перех* (+*acc или* +*gen*: *му́сору, кирпиче́й итп*) to pile up ♦ *неперех* (*no impf*: *толпа*) to flock; **нава́ливать** (**~** *perf*) (**на** +*acc*) to pile on(to); **нава́ливать** (**~** *perf*) **на кого́-н рабо́ту/обя́занности** to load sb with work/responsibilities; **в э́том году́ ~али́ло мно́го сне́гу** there was a lot of snow this year

▶ **навали́ться** (*impf* **нава́ливаться**) *сов возв*: **~ся на** +*acc* (*на дверь итп*) to lean into; (*насыпаться: земля*) to pile up on; (*разг: набро́ситься: на еду*) to get stuck into; **на меня́ ~али́лось мно́го рабо́ты** (*разг*) I'm swamped with work.

навалом *нареч*: грузить ~ to pile up ♦ *как сказ*: ~ +*gen* (*разг*: *фруктов, денег итп*) there's loads of.

навар (-а) *м* (*бульон*) broth; (*жир*) fat; (*разг*: *прибыль*) take-in.

наваривать (-ю) *несов от* **наварить**.

наваристый (-, -а, -о) *прил* rich.

нава|рить (-арю, -аришь; *impf* **наваривать**) *сов перех* (*ТЕХ*: *стали*) to weld; (: *кусок металла*) to weld on ♦ (*не*)*перех* (+*acc или* +*gen*; *супа, варенья*) to make a lot of.

наве|вать (-ю) *несов от* **навеять**.

наведа|ться (-юсь; *impf* **наведываться**) *сов возв* (*разг*): ~ **к** +*dat* to call in on.

наведени|е (-я) *ср* (*порядка*) establishment; (*справок*) making; (*орудия*) aiming.

наведу *итп сов см* **навести**.

наведыва|ться (-юсь) *несов от* **наведаться**.

навезти (-езу, -езёшь; *pt* -ёз, -езла, -езло, *impf* **навозить**) *сов перех* to bring a lot of.

навек *нареч* (*навсегда*) for good, forever.

навеки *нареч* = **навек**.

навёл *итп сов см* **навести**.

наверно *вводн сл* probably ♦ *нареч* (*точно*) for sure.

наверное *нареч* = **наверно**.

наверн|уть (-у, -ёшь; *impf* **навёртывать**) *сов перех*: ~ (**на** +*acc*) (*навинтить*) to screw on(to); (*намотать*) to wrap (around)

▶ **навернуться** (*impf* **навёртываться**) *сов возв* (*слёзы*) to well up.

наверняка *вводн сл* (*конечно*) certainly ♦ *нареч* (*несомненно*) definitely, for sure; **он действует** ~ he doesn't take any chances.

наверста|ть (-ю; *impf* **навёрстывать**) *сов перех* (*типог*) to typeset; **навёрстывать** (~ *perf*) **упущенное** *или* **потерянное время** to make up for lost time.

навер|теть (-ерчу, -ертишь; *impf* **навёртывать**) *сов перех*: ~ (**на** +*acc*) to twist (around).

навёртыва|ть (-ю) *несов от* **навернуть**, **навертеть**

▶ **навёртываться** *несов от* **навернуться**.

наверх *нареч* up; (*на верхний этаж*) upstairs; (*на поверхность*) to the top; **посмотреть** (*perf*) ~ to look up; **обращаться (обратиться** *perf*) ~ (*перен*: *разг*) to go to the top.

наверху *нареч* (*также перен*) at the top; (*в верхнем этаже*) upstairs; (*на поверхности*) on (the) top ♦ *предл* (+*gen*) at the top of.

наверчу *сов см* **навертеть**.

навес (-а) *м* (*над прилавком, у подъезда*) canopy; (*скалы, берега*) overhang.

навеселе *нареч* (*разг*): **быть** ~ to be merry *или* tipsy.

наве|сить (-шу, -сишь; *impf* **навешивать**) *сов перех* (*дверь, замок*) to hang; (*разг*: *картин,*

плакатов) to hang up; (*СПОРТ*) to lob.

наве|сти (-еду, -едёшь; *pt* ёл, -ела, -ело, *impf* **наводить**) *сов перех* (*вызвать*: *ужас, грусть итп*) to cause; (*бинокль, объектив*) to focus; (*орудие*) to aim; (*мост*) to lay; (*лак, краску*) to apply; (*разг*: *гостей, приятелей, друзей*) to bring; (*порядок*) to establish; **наводить** (~ *perf*) **кого-н на** +*acc* (*на место, на след*) to lead sb to; **наводить** (~ *perf*) **справки** to make inquiries; **наводить** (~ *perf*) **чистоту** to clean up; **наводить** (~ *perf*) **красоту** (*разг*) to tart o.s. up; **эта музыка** ~**одит на меня тоску** this music makes me sad; **наводить** (~ *perf*) **кого-н на мысль** to give sb an idea; **его рассказ** ~**ёл меня на размышления** his story started me thinking.

наве|стить (-щу, -стишь; *impf* **навещать**) *сов перех* to visit.

навечно *нареч* for evermore.

навеша|ть (-ю; *impf* **навешивать**) *сов* (*не*)*перех* (+*acc или* +*gen*; *белья, картин, украшения*) to hang up; (*муки, печений*) to weigh out.

навешива|ть (-ю) *несов от* **навесить**, **навешать**.

навешу *сов см* **навесить**.

навеща|ть (-ю) *несов от* **навестить**.

навещу *сов см* **навестить**.

наве|ять (-ю, -ешь; *impf* **навевать**) *сов перех* (*перен*: *тоску итп*) to evoke.

навзничь *нареч* on one's back.

навзрыд *нареч*: **плакать** ~ to sob loudly.

навигатор (-а) *м* navigator.

навигаци|я (-и) *ж* navigation.

навин|тить (-чу, -тишь; *impf* **навинчивать**) *сов перех* (*гайку, пробку*) to screw in; (*крышку*) to screw on.

нави|снуть (-ну, -нешь; *pt* -, -ла, -ло, *impf* **нависать**) *сов неперех*: ~ **на** +*acc* (*волосы*: *на лоб*) to hang down over; **нависать** (~ *perf*) **на** +*prp* (*сосульки*: *на ветках*) to hang from; **нависать** (~ *perf*) **над** +*instr* (*скалы*) to overhang; (*тучи, опасность*) to loom over.

нависш|ий (-ая, -ее, -ие) *прил* (*берег, скала*) overhanging.

навл|ечь (-еку, -ечёшь *итп*, -екут; *pt* -ёк, -екла, -екло, *impf* **навлекать**) *сов перех* (*подозрения, несчастье*) to attract; **навлекать** (~ *perf*) **на кого-н беду** to bring sb bad luck; **навлекать** (~ *perf*) **на себя чей-н гнев** to incur sb's wrath.

навод|ить (-ожу, -одишь) *несов от* **навести**.

наводк|а (-и) *ж* (*объектива*) focusing; (*оружия*) aiming.

наводнени|е (-я) *ср* flood; (*рынков товаром*) flooding.

наводн|ить (-ю, -ишь; *impf* **наводнять**) *сов перех*: ~ **что-н** +*instr* (*товарами, продуктами*) to flood sth with.

наводчик (-а) *м* (*сообщник*) *informant who tips*

thieves off.

наводя́щий (-ая, -ее, -ие) *прил:* ~ **вопро́с**
pointer, hint.

наво́жу *несов см* **навози́ть.**

навожу́ *несов см* **наводи́ть, навози́ть.**

наво́з (-а) *м* manure.

наво́зить (-жу, -зишь; *perf* **унаво́зить**) *несов*
перех to fertilize.

навози́ть (-ожу́, -о́зишь) *несов от* **навезти́.**

наво́лоч|ка (-ки; *gen pl* -ек) *ж* pillowcase.

навостри́ть (-ю́, -и́шь) *сов перех* (*разг*): ~ **у́ши**
to prick up one's ears; ~ (*perf*) **лы́жи** (*разг*) to be
ready to shoot off.

наврá|ть (-у́, -ёшь; *pt* -а́л, -ала́, -а́ло) *сов от*
врать.

навре|ди́ть (-жу́, -ди́шь) *сов от* **вреди́ть.**

навсегда́ *нареч* forever; **раз и** ~ once and for
all.

навстре́чу *предл* (+*dat*) towards ◆ *нареч:*
бежа́ть ~ **к кому́-н** to run towards sb; **она́**
вы́шла ~ **гостя́м** she came out to meet the
guests; **идти́ (пойти́** *perf*) ~ **кому́-н** (*перен*) to
give sb a hand.

на́выворот *нареч* (*разг: наизна́нку*) inside out;
(*перен: наоборот*) the wrong way round.

на́вык (-а) *м* skill.

навы́кат(е) *нареч:* **глаза́** ~ bulging eyes.

навы́лет *нареч* right through; **его́ ра́нило**
пулёй ~ the bullet went right through him.

навы́нос *нареч* to take away (*BRIT*), to go (*US*);
мы не продаём ~ we don't do takeaways (*BRIT*)
или takeouts (*US*).

навы́пуск *нареч* outside, over; **он но́сит**
руба́шку ~ he wears his shirt outside his
trousers.

навы́тяжку *нареч:* **стоя́ть** ~ to stand to
attention.

навью́ч|ить (-у, -ишь; *impf* **навью́чивать**) *сов*
перех to load.

навя|за́ть (-жу́, -жешь; *impf* **навя́зывать**) *сов*
перех: ~ (**на** +*acc*) (*на шею, на удочку*) to tie
on(to); **навя́зывать** (~ *perf*) +*gen* (*связать*) to
knit a lot of; (*снопов, веников*) to tie a lot of;
(*венков*) to weave a lot of; **навя́зывать** (~ *perf*)
что-н кому́-н (*перен*) to impose sth on sb

▶ **навяза́ться** (*impf* **навя́зываться**) *сов возв*
(*разг*): ~**ся кому́-н в друзья́** to impose o.s. on
sb; ~**ся** (*perf*) **в го́сти** to invite o.s. round.

навя́зчив|ый (-, -а, -о) *прил* (*мысль*) persistent;
(*человек*) bothersome; **она́ ужа́сно** ~**ая** she's a
real pest.

навя́зыва|ть(ся) (-ю(сь)) *несов от*
навяза́ть(ся).

нагада́|ть (-ю; *impf* **нага́дывать**) *сов перех*
(*разг*) to predict.

нага́|дить (-жу, -дишь) *сов от* **га́дить.**

нага́дыва|ть (-ю) *несов от* **нагада́ть.**

нага́жу *сов см* **нага́дить.**

нага́й|ка (-йки; *gen pl* -ек) *ж* whip.

нага́н (-а) *м* revolver.

нага́р (-а) *м* snuff (*of candle*).

нагиба́|ть(ся) (-ю(сь)) *несов от* **нагну́ть(ся).**

нагишо́м *нареч* (*разг*) stark-naked.

нагла́|дить (-жу, -дишь; *impf* **нагла́живать**) *сов*
перех to iron.

нагле́|ть (-ю; *perf* **обнагле́ть**) *несов неперех* to
get impudent.

нагле́ц (-а́) *м* impudent upstart.

на́гло *нареч* impudently.

на́глост|ь (-и) *ж* impudence, impertinence.

наглота́|ться (-юсь) *сов возв* (+*gen*) to swallow.

на́глухо *нареч* tight, securely; **застёгиваться**
(**застегну́ться** *perf*) ~ to do one's coat right up.

на́гл|ый (-, -á, -о) *прил* insolent, impudent; ~**ая**
ложь brazen lie.

нагляде́н *прил см* **нагля́дный.**

нагля|де́ться (-жу́сь, -ди́шься) *сов возв:* ~ **на**
+*acc* to tire of looking at; **дай мне на тебя́** ~ let
me take a good look at you.

нагля́дн|ый (-ен, -на, -но) *прил* (*пример,*
случай) clear; (*no short form; метод обуче́ния*)
visual; **нагля́дные посо́бия** visual aids.

нагляжу́сь *сов см* **нагляде́ться.**

нагна́|ть (-оню́, -о́нишь; *pt* -на́л, -нала́, -на́ло,
impf **нагоня́ть**) *сов перех* (*беглеца́*) to catch up
with; (*упу́щенное, про́йденное*) to make up for;
(*подлеж: ветер: грозу́, тучи*) to blow; (*спирта,*
самого́на) to distil (*BRIT*), distill (*US*); **нагоня́ть**
(~ *perf*) **страх на кого́-н** to strike fear into sb;
нагоня́ть (~ *perf*) **тоску́ на кого́-н** to fill sb with
sadness.

нагне|сти́ (-ту́, -тёшь; *impf* **нагнета́ть**) *сов перех*
to pump.

нагнета́|ть (-ю) *несов от* **нагнести́** ◆ *перех*
(*перен: напряже́ние*) to heighten.

нагное́ни|е (-я) *ср* festering.

нагно|и́ться (*3sg* -и́тся, *3pl* -я́тся) *сов возв* to
fester.

нагну́|ть (-у́, -ёшь; *impf* **нагиба́ть**) *сов перех*
(*ветку, человека*) to pull down; (*шею, голову*)
to bend

▶ **нагну́ться** (*impf* **нагиба́ться**) *сов возв* to bend
down.

нагова́рива|ть(ся) (-ю(сь)) *несов от*
наговори́ть(ся).

нагово́р (-а) *м* (*разг: клевета́*) slander;
(*колдовско́й*) spell.

наговор|и́ть (-ю́, -и́шь; *impf* **нагова́ривать**) *сов*
перех (*текст: на плёнку*) to record ◆ *неперех*
(*разг: наклеветать*): ~ **на** +*acc* to slander; ~
(*perf*) **чепухи́** to talk a lot of nonsense; ~ (*perf*)
кому́-н комплиме́нтов to shower sb with
compliments

▶ **наговори́ться** (*impf* **нагова́риваться**) *сов*
возв to talk one's fill.

наго́|й (-, -á, -о) *прил* (*человек*) naked, nude;
(*руки, ноги, лес*) bare.

на́голо *нареч:* **остри́чься** ~ to shave one's
head; **обри́ть** (*perf*) **кого́-н** ~ to shave sb's head.

наголо́ *нареч:* **ша́шки** ~ drawn swords.

на́голову *нареч:* **разби́ть** *или* **разгроми́ть** ~ to
rout.

нагоню *итп сов см* **нагнать**.

нагоня́й (-я) *м* (*разг*): получи́ть ~ (от кого́-н) to get a ticking off (from sb).

нагоня́ть (-ю) *несов от* **нагна́ть**.

нагоре́ть (3sg -и́т, *impf* **нагора́ть**) *сов безл* (+gen; израсхо́доваться) to be used up.

наго́рный *прил* (па́стбище, расти́тельность) alpine, mountain *опред*; (гори́стый) hilly.

нагор|оди́ть (-ожу́, -о́дишь; *impf* **(не)переть** +acc или +gen; разг: постро́ек) to put up; он ~оди́л еру́нды (*разг*) he came out with a load of nonsense.

наго́рь|е (-я) *ср* plateau.

нагот|а́ (-ы́) *ж* nudity, nakedness.

нагота́вливать (-ю) *несов от* **наготовить**.

нагото́ве *нареч* at the ready.

нагото́в|ить (-лю, -ишь; *impf* **нагота́вливать**) *сов перех* (запасти́) to stock up with; (свари́ть) to cook.

награ́б|ить (-лю, -ишь) *сов перех* to plunder.

награ́д|а (-ы) *ж* reward; (за уче́бу, за рабо́ту) prize; (ВОЕН) decoration; дать (perf) что-н кому́-н в ~у to give sb sth as a reward.

награ|ди́ть (-жу́, -ди́шь; *impf* **награжда́ть**) *сов перех*: ~ кого́-н чем-н (орденом) to award sb sth, award sth to sb; (перен: спосо́бностями) to endow sb with sth; (: поцелу́ем, улы́бкой) to reward sb with sth.

награжде́ни|е (-я) *ср* awards ceremony.

награжу́ *сов см* **награди́ть**.

награба́|ть (-ю) *несов от* **нагрести́**.

нагребу́ *итп сов см* **нагрести́**.

нагрева́ни|е (-я) *ср* heating.

нагрева́тельный *прил*: ~ прибо́р heating appliance.

нагрева́|ть(ся) (-ю(сь)) *несов от* **нагре́ть(ся)**.

нагрест|и́ (-бу́, -бёшь; *pt* -ёб, -ебла́, -ебло́, *impf* **нагреба́ть**) *сов перех* to rake together.

нагре́|ть (-ю; *impf* **нагрева́ть**) *сов перех* to heat, warm; ~ (perf) ру́ки (на +prp) (перен) to line one's pockets (with)

▸ **нагре́ться** (*impf* **нагрева́ться**) *сов возв* to warm up.

нагримиров|а́ться (-у́юсь) *сов от* **гримирова́ться**.

нагроможда́|ть (-ю) *несов от* **громозди́ть**.

нагроможде́ни|е (-я) *ср* (предме́тов) pile; (фа́ктов) mound.

нагромозд|и́ть (-жу́, -ди́шь) *сов от* **громозди́ть**.

нагруб|и́ть (-лю, -и́шь) *сов от* **груби́ть**.

нагру́дник (-а) *м* bib; (ры́царский) breastplate.

нагру́дный *прил*: ~ карма́н breast pocket.

нагру|зи́ть (-жу́, -у́зишь) *сов от* **грузи́ть** ♦ (*impf* **нагружа́ть**) *перех* to load up; **нагружа́ть** (~ perf) кого́-н рабо́той to load sb with work.

нагру́зк|а (-и) *ж* (де́йствие) loading; (груз, та́кже ЭЛЕК, ТЕХ) load; (за́нятость) workload;

(обще́ственная) responsibilities *мн*.

нагрязн|и́ть (-ю́, -и́шь) *сов от* **грязни́ть**.

нагря́н|уть (-у, -ешь) *сов непере* (го́сти, поли́ция) to descend on; (хо́лода) to set in; ~ула беда́ tragedy struck.

нагуля́|ть (-ю; *impf* **нагу́ливать**) *сов перех* (разг): ~ аппети́т to work up an appetite; **нагу́ливать** (~ perf) румя́нец to get some colour in one's cheeks

▸ **нагуля́ться** *сов возв* to have a good walk.

над *предл* (+instr) above; рабо́тать (*impf*) ~ прое́ктом to work on a project; ду́мать (*impf*) ~ зада́чей to think about a problem; смея́ться (*impf*) ~ ребёнком to laugh at a child; сиде́ть (*impf*) ~ кни́гой to sit over a book.

над- *префикс* (*in verbs*; об увеличе́нии чего́-н) indicating an increase in sth eg. надстро́ить; (о непо́лном де́йствии) indicating an incomplete action eg. надкуси́ть; (*in nouns and adjectives*; пове́рх чего́-н) indicating position above sth eg. надзе́мный.

нада|ва́ть (-ю́, -ёшь) *сов перех* (разг): ~ кому́-н чего́-н (пода́рков, сове́тов, обеща́ний) to give sb lots of sth ♦ непере: ~ кому́-н (разг) to thrash sb.

нада|ви́ть (-авлю́, -а́вишь; *impf* **нада́вливать**) *сов (не)перех* (+acc или +gen; со́ку) to squeeze; (разг: тарака́нов *итп*) to squash ♦ непере: ~ на +acc (на дверь *итп*) to lean against; (на кно́пку) to press.

нада́ива|ть (-ю) *несов от* **надои́ть**.

надар|и́ть (-ю́, -ишь; *impf* **нада́ривать**) *сов перех* (разг): ~ кому́-н пода́рков to give sb lots of presents.

надба́в|ить (-лю, -ишь; *impf* **надбавля́ть**) *сов перех* (разг) = **наба́вить**.

надба́вк|а (-и) *ж* (к зарпла́те) rise; (к пе́нсии) supplement; (к цене́) surcharge; **надба́вка за вре́дность** danger money (*BRIT*), hazard pay (*US*).

надба́влю *сов см* **надба́вить**.

надбавля́|ть (-ю) *несов от* **надба́вить**.

надви́н|уть (-у, -ешь; *impf* **надвига́ть**) *сов перех*: ~ что-н (на +acc) to pull sth down (over)

▸ **надви́нуться** (*impf* **надвига́ться**) *сов возв* (гроза́, опа́сность, ста́рость) to approach; **надвига́ться** (~ся perf) (на +acc) (на лоб, на у́ши) to slide down (over).

надво́дный *прил* above water; (кора́бль) surface *опред*.

надво́е *нареч* in(to) two.

надво́рн|ый *прил*: ~ые постро́йки outbuildings *мн*.

надвяз|а́ть (-яжу́, -я́жешь; *impf* **надвя́зывать**) *сов перех* (сви́тер, рука́в) to lengthen (*knitted garment*); (верёвку, ни́тку) to tie on.

надгро́би|е (-я) *ср* gravestone, tombstone.

надгро́бный *прил* (речь) at the graveside;

(*надпись*) gravestone *опред*; **надгробный камень** headstone; **надгробный памятник** memorial.

надёванный *прил* (*разг*) worn.

надевать (-ю) *несов от* **надеть**.

надежда (-ы) *ж* hope; **в ~е на** +*acc* in the hope of; **питать** (*impf*) **~у на что-н** to hope for sth; **подавать** (*impf*) **~ы** to show promise.

надёжен *прил см* **надёжный**.

надёжно *нареч* securely.

надёжность (-и) *ж* reliability.

надёжный (-ен, -на, -но) *прил* reliable; (*дверь, механизм*) secure; (*средство, путь*) safe.

наделать (-ю) *сов* (*не*)*перех* (+*acc или* +*gen*; *ошибок, салатов*) to make lots of; (*неприятностей, вреда*) to cause a lot of; **не ~й глупостей** don't do anything stupid; **что ты ~л?** what have you done?

наделить (-ю, -ишь; *impf* **наделять**) *сов перех*: **~ кого-н чем-н** (*землёй, участком*) to grant sb sth; (*перен: талантом, умом*) to endow sb with sth.

надену *итп сов см* **надеть**.

надёргать (-ю; *impf* **надёргивать**) *сов* (*не*)*перех* (+*acc или* +*gen*; *перьев, сорняков*) to pull out; (*разг: цитат, примеров*) to choose carefully.

надёрнуть (-у, -ешь; *impf* **надёргивать**) *сов перех* to pull over.

надеть (-ну, -нешь; *impf* **надевать**) *сов перех* to put on.

надеяться (-юсь) *несов возв*: **~** +*infin* (*отдохнуть, успеть итп*) to hope to do; (*perf* **понадеяться**): **~ на** +*acc* (*на друга, на семью*) to rely on; (*на улучшение*) to hope for; **я надеюсь, что ...** I hope that ....

надземный *прил* (*сооружение*) overground; (*часть растения*) above ground.

надзиратель (-я) *м* guard.

надзор (-а) *м* control.

надираться (-юсь) *несов от* **надраться**.

надкусить (-ушу, -усишь; *impf* **надкусывать**) *сов перех* to take a bite of.

надламывать(ся) (-ю(сь)) *несов от* **надломить(ся)**.

надлежащий (-ая, -ее, -ие) *прил* appropriate, suitable; **~им образом** in the appropriate manner.

надлежит (*pt* -**ало**) *несов безл*: **ему ~ явиться в 9 часов** he is required to make an appearance at 9 o'clock.

надлом (-а) *м* (*на ветке*) crack; (*угнетение*) breakdown.

надломить (-омлю, -омишь; *impf* **надламывать**) *сов перех* (*также перен*) to break; (*здоровье, психику*) to damage

▶ **надломиться** (*impf* **надламываться**) *сов возв* to break; (*перен: здоровье*) to suffer; (: *человек*) to damage one's health.

надменный (-ен, -на, -но) *прил* haughty.

надо *как сказ* **1** (*о долженствовании*): **надо ему помочь** it is necessary to help him; **надо, чтобы он пришёл вовремя** he must come on time; **надо всегда говорить правду** one must always speak the truth; **мне/ему надо закончить работу** I/he must finish the job; **помочь тебе? – не надо!** can I help you? – there's no need!; **не надо!** (*не делай этого*) don't!

2 (*о потребности*): **надо много лет** it takes many years; **на варенье надо много сахара** you need a lot of sugar to make jam; **им надо 5 рублей** they need 5 roubles; **мне надо спать** I need to sleep; **что тебе надо?** what do you want?; **так ему/ей и надо** (*разг*) it serves him/her right; **надо же!** (*разг*) of all things!; **надо думать** (*вероятно*) probably; (*конечно*) of course; **что надо** (*разг*) excellent; **фильм что надо!** it's an excellent film!

надо *предл см* **над**.

надобность (-и) *ж* necessity.

надоедать (-ю) *несов от* **надоесть**.

надоедим *итп сов см* **надоесть**.

надоедливый (-, -а, -о) *прил* tedious, tiresome.

надоесть (*как есть; см* Table 15; *impf* **надоедать**) *сов неперех*: **~ кому-н** (+*instr*) (*разговорами, упрёками*) to bore sb (with); **мне ~ло ждать** I'm tired of waiting; **он мне ~л** I've had enough of him; **перестань мне надоедать!** stop bothering me!

надоить (-ю, -ишь; *impf* **надаивать**) *сов* (*не*)*перех* (+*acc или* +*gen*; *молока*) to get.

надолго *нареч* for a long time; **Вы здесь ~?** are you here for long?

надомник (-а) *м* homeworker.

надомница (-ы) *ж см* **надомник**.

надорвать (-у, -ёшь; *impf* **надрывать**) *сов перех* (*лист, материю*) to make a tear in; (*пакет*) to start to tear open; (*перен: голос*) to strain; (: *силы, здоровье*) to tax

▶ **надорваться** (*impf* **надрываться**) *сов возв* (*конверт, воротник*) to tear slightly; (*перенапрячься*) to do o.s. an injury; (*перен*) to overexhaust o.s.

надоумить (-лю, -ишь) *сов перех*: **~ кого-н** +*infin* (*разг*) to advise sb to do; **это он меня ~ил** he was the one who gave me the idea.

надписать (-ишу, -ишешь; *impf* **надписывать**) *сов перех* (*книгу, фотографию*) to inscribe; (*посылку, конверт*) to address; **надписывать** (**~** *perf*) **адрес на** +*acc* to address.

надпись (-и) *ж* inscription.

надпишу *итп сов см* **надписать**.

надрать (-ю, -ишь) *сов от* **драть**.

надраться (-ерусь, -ерёшься; *impf* **надираться**) *сов возв* (*разг*) to get sozzled.

надрежу *итп сов см* **надрезать**.

надрез (-а) *м* cut.

надрезать (-ежу, -ежешь; *impf* **надрезать**) *сов перех* to cut into.

надруга́тельств|о (-а) *ср*: ~ (над +*instr*) (*над памятью, над честью*) violation (of); (*над человеком*) abuse (of).

надруга́|ться (-юсь) (*не*)*сов возв*: ~ **над** +*instr* to abuse.

надры́в (-а) *м* (*надорванное место*) tear, rip; (*перен: физический*) strain; (: *в пении итп*) hysterical streak; **с ~ом в го́лосе** with a trembling voice.

надрыва́|ть (-ю) *несов от* **надорва́ть**
▶ **надрыва́|ться** *несов от* **надорва́ться** ◆ *возв* (*кричать*) to scream away; (*разг*): ~**ся** (**над** +*instr*) to break one's back (over) (*fig*); **у меня́ се́рдце** *или* **душа́** ~**ется** my heart bleeds.

надры́в|ный (-ен, -на, -но) *прил* hysterical.

надсмо́трщик (-а) *м* (*тюремный*) warden; (*на плантации*) overseer.

надсмо́трщиц|а (-ы) *ж см* **надсмо́трщик**.

надста́в|ить (-лю, -ишь; *impf* **надставля́ть**) *сов перех* to lengthen (*by adding extra material*).

надстра́ива|ть (-ю) *несов от* **надстро́ить**.

надстро́ек *сущ см* **надстро́йка**.

надстро́|ить (-ю, -ишь; *impf* **надстра́ивать**) *сов перех* (*стену, дом*) to build onto; (*этаж*) to add.

надстро́|йка (-йки; *gen pl* -ек) *ж* (*здания*) additional floor; (*ФИЛОСОФИЯ*) superstructure.

надува́тельств|о (-а) *ср* (*разг*) con.

надува́|ть(ся) (-ю(сь)) *несов от* **наду́ть(ся)**.

надувно́й *прил* inflatable.

наду́манный *прил* contrived.

наду́ма|ть (-ю; *impf* **наду́мывать**) *сов неперех* (+*infin*; *разг*) to take it into one's head to do.

наду́т|ый (-, -а, -о) *прил* (*почки, вена*) swollen; (*разг: высокомерный*) puffed-up; (: *обиженный*) sulky.

наду́|ть (-ю, -ешь; *impf* **надува́ть**) *сов перех* (*мяч, колесо*) to inflate, blow up; (*разг: обмануть*) to con ◆ *безл* (+*gen*; *пыли, холоду итп*) to blow; (*в ухо, в шею итп*) to catch a chill; **мне** ~**ло в грудь** I've caught a chill (on my chest).

▶ **наду́|ться** (*impf* **надува́ться**) *сов возв* (*матрас, мяч*) to inflate; (*парус*) to billow; (*почка, вена, река*) to swell; (*перен: от важности*) to swell up; (: *разг: обидеться*) to sulk; ~ (*perf*) **гу́бы** (*разг*) to go into a sulk.

надым|и́ть (-лю́, -и́шь) *сов от* **дыми́ть**.

надыша́|ть (-у́, -ишь) *сов неперех* (*в комнате, в купе*) to get warm (*from body heat*); ~ (*perf*) **на** +*acc* (*на стекло, на очки*) to breathe on

▶ **надыша́|ться** *сов возв* (+*instr*; *дымом, газом*) to breathe in; ~**ся** (*perf*) **во́здухом** to get plenty of fresh air; **пе́ред сме́ртью не нады́шишься** it's too late to do anything about it now.

наеда́|ться (-юсь) *несов от* **нае́сться**.

нае́дешь *итп сов см* **нае́хать**.

наеди́мся *сов см* **нае́сться**.

наедине́ *нареч*: ~ (**с** +*instr*) alone (with); **они́**

оста́лись ~ they were left on their own; **я до́лжен оста́ться** ~ **с собо́й** I need time to be by myself.

наеди́те(сь) *сов см* **нае́сть(ся)**.

нае́ду *сов см* **нае́хать**.

наедя́тся *сов см* **нае́сться**.

нае́зд (-а) *м* (*визит*) visit.

нае́здить (-зжу, -здишь; *impf* **наезжа́ть**) *сов перех* (*сто километров*) to clock up; (*дорогу*) to break in

▶ **нае́здиться** *сов возв* to travel a lot; **я** ~**здился в командиро́вки** I'm tired of going away on business.

нае́здник (-а) *м* rider.

нае́здниц|а (-ы) *ж см* **нае́здник**.

наезжа́|ть (-ю) *несов от* **нае́здить**, **нае́хать** ◆ *неперех*: ~ (**в го́сти**) **к кому́-н** to pay sb visits.

нае́зженный *прил* well-used.

нае́зжу(сь) *сов см* **нае́здить(ся)**.

нае́лся *итп сов см* **нае́сться**.

нае́мся *сов см* **нае́сться**.

нае́м (-йма) *м* hiring; (*квартиры*) renting.

наёмник (-а) *м* (*ВОЕН, также перен*) mercenary; (*наёмный работник*) casual worker.

наёмный *прил* (*труд, работник*) hired; (*помещение*) rented, leased; (*земля*) leased; ~ **уби́йца** hitman.

нае́сться (*как* **есть**; *см* Table 15; *impf* **наеда́ться**) *сов возв* (+*gen*; *сладкого, овощей*) to eat a lot of; (+*instr*; *супом*) to fill o.s. up on; **я нае́лся** I'm full.

нае́хать (*как* **е́хать**; *см* Table 19; *impf* **наезжа́ть**) *сов неперех* (*разг: туристы, гости*) to arrive in droves; **наезжа́ть** (~ *perf*) **на** +*acc* to drive into; (*угрожать*) to harass.

нае́шься *сов см* **нае́сться**.

нажа́л|оваться (-уюсь) *сов возв* (*разг*): ~ (**кому́-н на** +*acc*) to complain (to sb about).

нажа́р|ить (-ю, -ишь; *impf* **нажа́ривать**) *сов перех* to fry.

нажа́|ть (-му́, -мёшь; *impf* **нажима́ть**) *сов* (*не*)*перех* (+*acc или* +*gen*; *соку*) to squeeze; (*снопов, хлеба*) to reap ◆ *неперех* (*перен*): ~ **на** +*acc* (*на работников, на руководство*) to put pressure on; (*разг: на работу, на учёбу*) to get moving with; **нажима́ть** (~ *perf*) **на** +*acc* (*на кнопку*) to press; (*на рычаг*) to press (down).

нажгу́ *итп сов см* **нажёчь**.

нажда́к (-а) *м* emery.

нажда́чный *прил*: ~**ая бума́га** emery paper.

нажёчь (-гу́, -жёшь *итп*, -гу́т; *pt* -ёг, -гла́, -гло́, *impf* **нажига́ть**) *сов* (*не*)*перех* (+*acc или* +*gen*; *дров, угля, керосина*) to burn a lot of; (*разг: лицо, спину итп*) to burn.

нажи́ва|ть(ся) (-ю(сь)) *несов от* **нажи́ть(ся)**.

нажив|и́ть (-лю́, -и́шь; *impf* **наживля́ть**) *сов перех* to bait.

нажи́вк|**а** (**-и**) ж bait.

наживлю́ сов см **наживи́ть**.

наживля́|**ть** (**-ю**) несов от **наживи́ть**.

наживн|**о́й** прил: **де́ньги – де́ло** ~**о́е** money will start to roll in given time.

наживу́(**сь**) итп сов см **нажи́ть**.

нажига́|**ть** (**-ю**) несов от **нажѐчь**.

нажи́м (**-а**) м (также перен) pressure; **сде́лать** (perf) **что-н под** ~**ом** to do sth under pressure.

нажима́|**ть** (**-ю**) несов от **нажа́ть**.

нажира́ться (**-юсь**) несов от **нажра́ться**.

нажи́|**ть** (**-ву́**, **-вёшь**; impf **нажива́ть**) сов перех (состояние, миллионы) to acquire; ~ (perf) (себе́) **враго́в** to make enemies; ~ (perf) (себе́) **неприя́тность** to get o.s. into trouble; **наживёшь себе́ радикули́т** you'll end up with backache

▶ **нажи́ться** (impf **нажива́ться**) сов возв: ~**ся** (**на** +prp) (**на войне́, на спекуля́ции**) to gain (from).

нажму́ итп сов см **нажа́ть**.

нажра́ться (**-у́сь**, **-ёшься**; impf **нажира́ться**) сов возв (животное) to eat its fill; (разг: человек) to stuff o.s.; (: напиться) to get plastered.

наза́втра нареч (разг) next day.

наза́д нареч back; (нагну́ться, кати́ться итп) backwards; (тому́) ~ ago; **де́сять лет/неде́лю** (**тому́**) ~ ten years/one week ago.

назва́нива|**ть** (**-ю**) несов неперех (разг) to keep ringing.

назва́ни|**е** (**-я**) ср name; (отдельное издание) title; **под** ~**м** +gen named, called; **э́то не велосипе́д, а одно́** ~ you can hardly call it a proper bicycle; **торго́вое** ~ trade name.

назва́|**ть** (**-ову́**, **-овёшь**; pt **-ва́л**, **-вала́**, **-ва́ло**, impf **называ́ть**) сов перех to call; (ребёнка, собаку) to name, call; (назначить: кандидатов, день, цену) to set; **называ́ть** (~ perf) **ве́щи свои́ми имена́ми** to call a spade a spade

▶ **назва́ться** (impf **называ́ться**) сов возв (+instr; представиться) to call o.s.

назе́мный прил surface опред; **назе́мные войска́** ground troops.

на́земь нареч (упасть, бросить) to the ground.

назида́ни|**е** (**-я**) ср edification.

назида́тельный (**-ен**, **-ьна**, **-ьно**) прил edifying.

назло́ нареч out of spite; ~ **кому́-н** to spite sb; **как** ~ to make things worse.

назнача́|**ть** (**-ю**) несов от **назна́чить**.

назначе́ни|**е** (**-я**) ср (времени, цены итп) setting; (на работу) appointment; (лекарства) prescription; (функция) function; **пункт** или **ме́сто** ~ destination.

назна́ч|**ить** (**-у**, **-ишь**; impf **назнача́ть**) сов перех (начальником) to appoint; (время, цену) to set; (встречу) to arrange; (лекарство, курс лечения) to prescribe; **он** ~**ил ей свида́ние** he asked her to meet him.

назову́(**сь**) итп сов см **назва́ть**(**ся**).

назо́йлив|**ый** (**-**, **-а**, **-о**) прил (человек) tiresome; (вопрос, мысль) persistent.

назре́|**ть** (3sg **-ет**, 3pl **-ют**, impf **назрева́ть**) сов неперех to come to a head; (перен: вопрос, разговор) to become unavoidable.

назубо́к нареч (разг): **вы́учить/зна́ть** ~ to learn/know off by heart.

называ́емый прил: **так** ~ so-called.

называ́|**ть** (**-ю**) несов от **назва́ть**

▶ **называ́ться** несов от **назва́ться** ♦ возв (носить название) to be called; **как** ~**ется э́то ме́сто?** what is this place called?; **ситуа́ция, что** ~**ется, крити́ческая** the situation is what you might call critical.

наибо́лее нареч: ~ **интере́сный/краси́вый** the most interesting/beautiful.

наибо́льш|**ий** (**-ая**, **-ее**, **-ие**) прил the greatest.

наи́вн|**ый** (**-ен**, **-на**, **-но**) прил naive.

наивы́сш|**ий** (**-ая**, **-ее**, **-ие**) прил the highest.

наигра́нный прил artificial, false.

наигра́|**ть** (**-ю**; impf **наи́грывать**) сов перех (мелодию) to play; (для записи) to record

▶ **наигра́ться** сов возв to play for a long time.

наи́грыва|**ть** (**-ю**) несов от **наигра́ть** ♦ неперех: ~ **на** +prp (**на фле́йте**) to play quietly on.

на́игрыш (**-а**) м tune.

наизна́нку нареч inside out.

наизу́сть нареч: **знать/вы́учить** ~ to know/learn by heart.

наилу́чш|**ий** (**-ая**, **-ее**, **-ие**) прил the best.

наиме́нее нареч: ~ **уда́чный/спосо́бный** the least successful/capable.

наименова́ни|**е** (**-я**) ср name; (проекта, книги) title, name.

наимен|**ова́ть** (**-у́ю**) сов от **именова́ть**.

наиме́ньш|**ий** (**-ая**, **-ее**, **-ие**) прил (длина, высота итп) the smallest; (усилие) the least.

наискосо́к нареч (разг: разрезать) crosswise; (: идти) diagonally.

на́искось нареч diagonally.

наиху́дш|**ий** (**-ая**, **-ее**, **-ие**) прил the worst.

найдёныш (**-а**) м foundling.

найду́(**сь**) итп сов см **найти́**(**сь**).

на́йма итп сущ см **наём**.

наймит (**-а**) м hireling.

найму́(**сь**) итп сов см **наня́ть**(**ся**).

найти́ (**-йду́**, **-йдёшь**; pt **-шёл**, **-шла́**, **-шло́**, impf **находи́ть**) сов перех to find ♦ неперех (толпа, гости, тучи) to gather; (натолкнуться): ~ **на** +acc to stumble into; **на него́** ~**шла тоска́** he was overcome with sadness; **на меня́** ~**шёл смех** I couldn't help laughing; ~**шёл чем горди́ться!** (разг) is that all you've got to be proud of?; **находи́ть** (~ perf) **о́бщий язы́к** to find a common language; ~ (perf) **себя́** to find o.s.

▶ **найти́сь** (impf **находи́ться**) сов возв (ключи, ребёнок итп) to turn up; (добровольцы, желающие) to come forward; (не растеря́ться) to come up with an answer.

накажу́ *итп сов см* **наказа́ть**.

нака́з (-а) *м* (*полит*) mandate (*to govern*); (*наставление*) wish.

наказа́ние (-я) *ср* punishment; (*перен: разг*) pain, hassle.

наказа́ть (-ажу́, -а́жешь; *impf* **нака́зывать**) *сов перех* (*за проступок итп*) to punish; (*приказать*) to order.

нака́л (-а) *м* (*борьбы́*) heat.

накали́ть (-ю́, -и́шь; *impf* **нака́ливать** *или* **накаля́ть**) *сов перех* to heat up; (*перен: обстано́вку*) to hot up

► **накали́ться** (*impf* **нака́ливаться** *или* **накаля́ться**) *сов возв* to heat; (*перен: обстано́вка*) to become heated; (: *стра́сти*) to become inflamed; **~ся** (*perf*) **докрасна́/добела́** to become red-/white-hot.

нака́лывать(ся) (-ю(сь)) *несов от* **наколо́ть(ся)**.

накаля́ть(ся) (-ю(сь)) *несов от* **накали́ть(ся)**.

накану́не *нареч* the day before, the previous day ♦ *предл* (+*gen*) on the eve of.

нака́пать (-ю) *сов от* **ка́пать**.

нака́пливать(ся) (-ю(сь)) *несов от* **накопи́ть(ся)**.

нака́пывать (-ю) *несов от* **накопа́ть**.

нака́ркать (-ю) *сов от* **ка́ркать** ♦ *перех* (*разг*): **~ кому́-н беду́** to bring sb bad luck.

наката́ть (-ю; *impf* **нака́тывать**) *сов перех* to roll; (*доро́гу, колею́*) to flatten out; (*разг: написа́ть*) to rattle off

► **наката́ться** *сов возв* (*на конька́х*) to have a good time skating; (*на лы́жах*) to have a good time skiing.

накати́ть (-ачу́, -а́тишь; *impf* **нака́тывать**) *сов неперех* (*разг: толпа́, го́сти*) to surge forward; (*тоска́*) to be overwhelming ♦ *перех*: **~ что-н на** +*acc* to roll sth onto; **нака́тывать** (**~** *perf*) (**на** +*acc*) (*волна́*) to roll up (onto)

► **накати́ться** (*impf* **нака́тываться**) *сов возв*: **~ся на** +*acc* (*волна́, лави́на*) to roll up onto.

нака́тывать (-ю) *несов от* **наката́ть, накати́ть**

► **нака́тываться** *несов от* **накати́ться**.

нака́чать (-ю; *impf* **нака́чивать**) *сов (не)перех* (+*acc или* +*gen*; *во́ды, во́здуха*) to pump; (*ка́меру, ши́ну*) to pump up.

накида́ть (-ю; *impf* **наки́дывать**) *сов перех* to throw.

наки́дка (-ки; *gen pl* -ок) *ж* (*оде́жда*) wrap; (*покрыва́ло*) bedspread, thrower.

наки́дывать (-ю) *несов от* **накида́ть, наки́нуть**

► **наки́дываться** *несов от* **наки́нуться**.

наки́нуть (-у, -ешь; *impf* **наки́дывать**) *сов перех* (*плато́к*) to throw on; (*разг: наба́вить*) to add on

► **наки́нуться** (*impf* **наки́дываться**) *сов возв*: **~ся на** +*acc* (*на челове́ка*) to hurl o.s. at; (*разг:*

на еду́, на кни́гу) to get stuck into; **наки́дываться** (**~ся** *perf*) **на кого́-н с вопро́сами/жа́лобами** (*разг*) to bombard sb with questions/complaints.

накипе́ть (*3sg* -и́т, *impf* **накипа́ть**) *сов неперех* (*на́кипь, пе́на*) to form ♦ *безл* (*перен: зло́ба, оби́да*) to build up.

на́кипь (-и) *ж* (*на бульо́не*) scum; (*в ча́йнике*) fur (*BRIT*), scale (*US*).

накла́дка (-ки; *gen pl* -ок) *ж* (*шиньо́н*) hairpiece; (*разг: недоразуме́ние*) mix-up.

накладна́я (-о́й; *decl like adj*) *ж* (*КОММ*) bill of lading (*BRIT*), waybill (*US*); **грузова́я ~** consignment note.

накладно́й *прил* (*во́лосы, бо́рода*) false; (*карма́н*) sewn-on; **накладно́е зо́лото** rolled gold; **накладны́е расхо́ды** (*ЭКОН*) overheads *мн* (*BRIT*), overhead (*US*).

накла́док *сущ см* **накла́дка**.

накла́дывать (-ю) *несов от* **наложи́ть**.

наклевета́ть (-ещу́, -е́щешь) *сов от* **клевета́ть**.

наклёвываться (*3sg* -ется, *3pl* -ются) *несов от* **наклюну́ться**.

накле́ек *сущ см* **накле́йка**.

накле́ить (-ю, -ишь; *impf* **накле́ивать**) *сов перех* (*афи́шу, ма́рку итп*) to stick on; (*фона́риков, украше́ний итп*) to make (*with glue and paper*).

накле́йка (-йка; *gen pl* -ек) *ж* label.

наклепа́ть (-ю) *сов от* **клепа́ть** ♦ (*impf* **наклёпывать**) *перех* to rivet on.

наклёпка (-и) *ж* stud.

наклёпывать (-ю) *несов от* **наклепа́ть**.

накли́кать (-чу, -чешь; *impf* **наклика́ть**) *сов перех*: **~ кому́-н несча́стье** to bring misfortune on sb.

накло́н (-а) *м* incline, slope; (*головы́*) tilt; (*по́черка*) slope.

наклоне́ние (-я) *ср* (*ЛИНГ*) mood.

наклони́ть (-оню́, -о́нишь; *impf* **наклоня́ть**) *сов перех* to tilt

► **наклони́ться** (*impf* **наклоня́ться**) *сов возв* to bend down.

накло́нность (-и) *ж*: **~ к** +*dat* (*к му́зыке итп*) aptitude for; (*к меланхо́лии итп*) tendency toward; **дурны́е/хоро́шие накло́нности** bad/good habits.

накло́нный *прил* slanting.

наклоня́ть(ся) (-ю(сь)) *несов от* **наклони́ть(ся)**.

наклюну́ться (*3sg* -ется, *3pl* -утся, *impf* **наклёвываться**) *сов возв* (*цыплёнок*) to peck its way out of the shell; (*перен: по́чки, росто́к*) to form; (: *вы́годное де́ло*) to turn up.

наклязни́чать (-ю) *сов от* **клязни́чать**.

накова́льня (-ьни; *gen pl* -ен) *ж* anvil.

нако́жный *прил* skin *опред*.

наколе́нник (-а) *м* (*СПОРТ*) kneepad.
нако́лк|**а** (-и) *ж* (*разг: татуировка*) tattoo.
наколо́ть (-олю́, -о́лешь; *impf* нака́лывать) *сов перех* (*руку, палец*) to prick; (*татуировку*) to apply; (*прикрепить*): ~ (**на** +*acc*) (*на шляпу, на дверь*) to pin on(to) ♦ (*не*)*перех* (+*acc или* +*gen*; *дров*) to chop; (*сахару*) to break up
► **наколо́ться** (*impf* нака́лываться) *сов возв*: ~**ся** (**на** +*acc*) to prick o.s. (on).
наконе́ц *нареч* at last, finally ♦ *вводн сл* after all; ~**-то!** at long last!; **он ~ по́нял** he finally understood; **ты мог бы, ~,** позвони́ть if nothing else, you could have phoned; **ну, иди́ же ~!** come on, it really is time for you to go!
наконе́чник (-а) *м* tip, end.
накопа́ть (-ю; *impf* нака́пывать) *сов перех* to dig up.
накопи́тельств|**о** (-а) *ср* acquisitiveness.
накопи́ть (-лю́, -ишь) *сов от* копи́ть ♦ (*impf* нака́пливать) (*силы, информацию*) to store up; (*средства*) to accumulate
► **накопи́ться** *сов от* копи́ться ♦ (*impf* нака́пливаться) *возв* (*силы, толпа*) to build up; (*средства*) to accumulate; (*раздражение*) to mount.
накопле́ни|**е** (-я) *ср* (*действие*) accumulation; ~ **да́нных** (*КОМП*) data storage; *см также* накопле́ния.
накопле́ни|**я** (-й) *мн* (*сбережения*) savings *мн*.
накоплю́(сь) *сов см* накопи́ть(ся).
накопти́ть (-чу́, -ти́шь) *сов от* копти́ть ♦ *перех* (*рыбы, колбасы*) to smoke.
накорми́ть (-лю́, -ишь) *сов от* корми́ть.
накра́пыва|**ть** (*3sg* -ет) *несов неперех* to drizzle.
накра́сить (-шу, -сишь) *сов от* кра́сить ♦ (*impf* накра́шивать) *перех* to paint
► **накра́ситься** *сов от* кра́ситься ♦ (*impf* накра́шиваться) *возв* to put on make-up.
накрахма́л|**ить** (-ю, -ишь) *сов от* крахма́лить.
накра́шива|**ть(ся)** (-ю(сь)) *несов от* накра́сить(ся).
накра́шу(сь) *сов см* накра́сить(ся).
накрени́ть(ся) (-ю́(сь), -и́шь(ся)) *сов от* крени́ть(ся).
на́крепко *нареч* (*запереть, забить*) tight; (*также*: **кре́пко-~**: *запретить, наказать*) strictly; **запо́мни ~** be sure to remember.
на́крест *нареч* (*также*: **крест-~**) crosswise.
накрича́ть (-у́, -и́шь) *сов неперех*: ~ **на** +*acc* (*на ребёнка, на подчинённого*) to shout at
► **накрича́ться** *сов возв* (*разг*) to shout a lot; **ну что, ~а́лся?** are you through shouting?
накропа́ть (-ю) *сов от* кропа́ть.
накроши́ть (-у́, -и́шь) *сов от* кроши́ть.
накро́ю(сь) *итп сов см* накры́ть(ся).
накрути́ть (-учу́, -у́тишь; *impf* накру́чивать) *сов перех* (*верёвок, пряжи*) to twist; (*разг: ерунды, небылиц*) to spin; **накру́чивать** (~ *perf*) (**на** +*acc*) (*гайку: на болт*) to screw on(to);

(*канат: на столб*) to wind (round)
► **накрути́ться** (*impf* накру́чиваться) *сов возв* (*разг: завить*) to put one's hair in rollers; **накру́чиваться** (~**ся** *perf*) (**на** +*acc* to wind around.
накры́ть (-о́ю, -о́ешь; *impf* накрыва́ть) *сов перех* to cover; (*разг: преступника, вора*) to nail, nab; **накрыва́ть** (~ *perf*) (**на**) **стол** to lay the table
► **накры́ться** (*impf* накрыва́ться) *сов возв* (*разг: мероприятие, прогулка*) to fall through; **накрыва́ться** (~**ся** *perf*) (+*instr*) (*пледом, одеялом*) to cover o.s. up (with).
накупи́ть (-лю́, -ишь; *impf* накупа́ть) *сов перех* to buy lots of.
наку́ренный *прил* (*помещение, вагон*) smoke-filled; (*воздух*) smoky.
накури́ть (-урю́, -у́ришь; *impf* наку́ривать) *сов неперех*: ~ **в ко́мнате** to fill a room with smoke
► **накури́ться** (*impf* наку́риваться) *сов возв* to smoke too much.
налага́ть (-ю) *несов от* наложи́ть.
нала́дить (-жу, -дишь; *impf* нала́живать) *сов перех* (*мотор, станок*) to repair, fix; (*сотрудничество*) to initiate; (*хозяйство*) to sort out; (*порядок*) to establish; (*разг: гитару, рояль*) to tune
► **нала́диться** (*impf* нала́живаться) *сов возв* (*работа*) to go well; (*отношения, здоровье*) to improve.
нала́мыва|**ть** (-ю) *несов от* налома́ть.
налга́ть (-гу́, -жёшь) *сов от* лгать.
нале́во *нареч* (*повернуть, посмотреть*) (to the) left; (*разг: продать, сбыть*) on the side.
налёг *итп сов см* нале́чь.
налега́ть (-ю) *несов от* нале́чь.
налегке́ *нареч* (*ехать*) without luggage; (*в лёгкой одежде*) lightly-clad; **путеше́ствовать** (*impf*) ~ to travel light.
нале́зть (-у, -ешь; *impf* налеза́ть) *сов неперех* (*разг: насекомые, дети*) to accumulate; (*надеться*) to fit; (*шапка*): ~ **на** +*acc* (*на глаза*) to slide over.
налепи́ть (-лю́, -ишь) *сов от* лепи́ть ♦ (*не*)*перех* (+*acc или* +*gen*; *фигурок, птиц*) to model.
налёт (-а) *м* (*птиц, авиации*) flying in, approach; (*на врага, на город*) raid; (*на банк, на кварти́ру*) robbery; (*пыли, плесени*) thin layer; (*МЕД*) spot, patch; **с ~а(-у)** (*на полном ходу́*) at full pelt; (*перен: сразу*) in a flash.
налете́ть (-чу́, -ти́шь; *impf* налета́ть) *сов неперех*: ~ **на** +*acc* (*натолкнуться*) to fly against; (*перен: разг: на приятеля, на столб*) to run into; (*напасть*) to swoop down on; (*перен: разг: с бранью, с упрёками*) to lay into; (*буря, ветер*) to spring up; (*саранча, стая*) to fly in; (*пыль, листва*) to drift in.
налётчик (-а) *м* burglar.
налечу́ *сов см* налете́ть.
нале́чь (-я́гу, -я́жешь *итп*, -я́гут; *pt* -ёг, -егла́, -егло́, *impf* налега́ть) *сов неперех*: ~ **на** +*acc*

(*на стол*) to lean on; (*плечом: на дверь*) to press against; (*перен: на рабо́тников*) to exert pressure on; (: *на учёбу, на рабо́ту*) to apply o.s. to; (*роса, снег*) to settle on; **налега́ть** (~ *perf*) **на вёсла** to ply one's oars.

налива́ть(ся) (-ю(сь)) *несов от* **нали́ть(ся)**.

нали́в|ка (-ки; *gen pl* -ок) *ж* fruit liquor.

наливн|о́й *прил*: ~о́е су́дно tanker; (*я́блоко, хле́ба*) ripe.

нали́вок *сущ см* **нали́вка**

налип|ну́ть (*3sg* -ет, *3pl* -ут, *impf* **налипа́ть**) *сов непере*: ~ **на** +*acc* to stick to.

налит|о́й *прил* (*ко́лос, я́блоко*) ripe; (*му́скулы, щёки итп*) fleshy.

нал|и́ть (-ью́, -ье́шь; *impf* **налива́ть**) *сов перех* to pour (out); **налива́ть** (~ *perf*) **стака́н вина́** to pour a glass of wine

▶ **нали́ться** (*impf* **налива́ться**) *сов возв* (*нате́чь во что-н*): ~**ся в** +*acc* to pour into; (*напо́лниться*): ~**ся** +*instr* to fill with; (*рожь, плоды́*) to ripen; (*перен: зло́бой*) to brim over; ~**ся** (*perf*) **кро́вью** to turn red.

налицо́ *как сказ*: **фа́кты** ~ the facts are obvious; **доказа́тельство** ~ there is proof; **свиде́тели** ~ there are witnesses on hand.

нали́чи|е (-я) *ср* presence.

нали́чник (-а) *м* casing, jambs and lintel (*of door or window*).

нали́чност|ь (-и) *ж* cash.

нали́чн|ые (-ых; *decl like adj*) *мн* cash *ед*; **платёж** ~**ыми при доста́вке гру́за** cash on delivery.

нали́чн|ый *прил*: ~**ые де́ньги** cash; ~ **расчёт** cash payment; ~ **счёт** cash account.

наловч|и́ться (-у́сь, -и́шься) *сов возв* (*разг*: +*infin*) to get the hang of doing.

нало́г (-а) *м* (*экон*) tax; **подохо́дный** ~ income tax; **поиму́щественный** ~ property tax; ~ **на ввоз** +*gen* import duty on; ~ **на при́быль** profits tax; ~ **на предме́ты ро́скоши** luxury tax; ~ **на перево́д капита́ла** capital transfer tax; **ко́свенный** ~ hidden tax.

нало́говик (-а) *м* taxman.

нало́говый *прил* tax *опред*.

налогоплате́льщик (-а) *м* taxpayer.

налогоплате́льщиц|а (-ы) *ж см* **налогоплате́льщик**

нало́женн|ый *прил*: ~**ым платежо́м** cash on delivery.

нал|ожи́ть (-ожу́, -о́жишь; *impf* **накла́дывать**) *сов перех* to put *или* place on; (*мед*: **ши́ну**) to fasten; (: *компре́сс, бинт*) to apply; (*лак, позоло́ту*) to apply; (*печа́ть*) to affix; (*резолю́цию*) to append; (*ка́шу итп*) to dish up; (*дров: в пе́чку*) to put on; (*impf* **налага́ть**; *штраф*) to impose; (*запре́т*) to place.

налома́|ть (-ю; *impf* **нала́мывать**) *сов перех* (+*gen*) to break; ~ (*perf*) **дров** (*разг*) to do

something stupid.

налью́(сь) *итп сов см* **нали́ть(ся)**.

налюб|ова́ться (-у́юсь) *сов возв* to gaze one's fill; **не могу́** ~ **са́дом** I am lost in admiration for the garden.

наля́гу *итп сов см* **нале́чь**.

наля́па|ть (-ю) *сов от* **ля́пать**.

нам *мест см* **мы**.

нама́жу(сь) *итп сов см* **нама́зать(ся)**.

нама́з (-а) *м* (*РЕЛ*) (*Mohammedan*) prayer.

нама́з|ать(ся) (-жу(сь), -жешь(ся)) *сов от* **ма́зать(ся)**.

намалева́ть (-ю) *сов от* **малева́ть**.

нама́лыва|ть (-ю) *несов от* **намоло́ть**.

намара́|ть (-ю) *сов от* **мара́ть**.

нама́сл|ить (-ю, -ишь) *сов от* **ма́слить**.

нама́тыва|ть(ся) (-ю(сь)) *несов от* **намота́ть(ся)**.

намёк (-а) *м* (*также перен*) hint.

намека́|ть (-ю; *perf* **намекну́ть**) *несов непере*: ~ **на** +*acc* to hint at.

намелю́ *итп сов см* **намоло́ть**.

намен|я́ть (-ю) *сов* (*не*)*перех* (+*acc или* +*gen*; *де́нег, ма́рок, значко́в*) to get *или* obtain by exchange.

намерева́|ться (-юсь) *несов возв*: ~ +*infin* to intend to do.

наме́рен (-а, -о) *как сказ*: **он** ~ **уе́хать** he intends to leave.

наме́рени|е (-я) *ср* intention.

наме́ренн|ый (-, -на, -но) *прил* intentional, deliberate.

на́мертво *нареч* (*разг*) tightly, fast.

намётанн|ый *прил*: ~ **глаз** trained eye; **у него́ глаз намётан** he has a good eye.

намета́|ть (-ю) *сов от* **мета́ть**.

наме́т|ить (-чу, -тишь) *сов от* **ме́тить** ◆ (*impf* **намеча́ть**) *перех* to plan; (*план*) to project; (*ко́нтуры*) to outline

▶ **наме́титься** *сов от* **ме́титься** ◆ (*impf* **намеча́ться**) *возв* (*маршру́т*) to take shape; (*разногла́сия, усы́*) to begin to show.

намёт|ка (-и) *ж* (*ю́бки, пла́тья*) tacking (*BRIT*), basting; (*ни́тка*) tacking (*BRIT*) *или* basting thread; (*пла́на*) rough draft; (*маршру́та*) preliminary outline.

намеча́|ть(ся) (-ю(сь)) *несов от* **наме́тить(ся)**.

наме́чу(сь) *сов см* **наме́тить(ся)**.

на́ми *мест см* **мы**.

намина́|ть (-ю) *несов от* **намя́ть**.

намно́го *нареч* much, far; ~ **ху́же/интере́снее** much worse/more interesting.

намну́ *итп сов см* **намя́ть**.

намо́кн|уть (-у, -ешь; *impf* **намока́ть**) *сов непере*х to get wet.

намол|о́ть (-ю́, -е́шь; *impf* **нама́лывать**) *сов перех* to grind, mill.

намо́рдник (-а) *м* muzzle.

намо́рщить(ся) (-у(сь), -ишь(ся)) *сов от* **мо́рщить(ся)**.
намости́ть (-щу́, -сти́шь) *сов от* **мости́ть**.
намота́ть (-ю) *сов от* **мота́ть** ♦ (*impf* **нама́тывать**) *перех* to wind.
▸ **намота́ться** (*impf* **нама́тываться**) *сов возв* (*нитка на шпу́льку*) to be wound; (*разг: устать*) to run o.s. ragged.
намо́чить (-очу́, -о́чишь) *сов от* **мочи́ть**.
намощу́ *сов см* **намости́ть**.
намо́ю *итп сов см* **намы́ть**.
намудри́ть (-ю́, -и́шь) *сов от* **мудри́ть**.
намусо́рить (-ю, -ишь) *сов от* **му́сорить**.
наму́читься (-усь, -ишься) *сов возв* (*разг*) to wear o.s. out.
намы́лива|ть (-ю; *perf* **намы́лить**) *несов перех* = **мы́лить**.
намы́л|ить(ся) (-ю(сь), -ишь(ся)) *сов от* **мы́лить(ся)**.
нам|ы́ть (-о́ю, -о́ешь) *сов перех* to wash; (*плотину*) to deposit; (*золотину*) to pan out.
нам|я́ть (-ну́, -нёшь; *impf* **намина́ть**) *сов* (*не)перех* (+*acc или* +*gen; льна, кож, глины*) to mash; (*траву, солому*) to trample.
нан|ести́ (-есу́, -есёшь; *pt* -ёс, -есла́, -есло́, *impf* **наноси́ть**) *сов* (*не)перех* (+*acc или* +*gen; подарков, продуктов*) to bring; (*снегу, песку*) to heap, pile up ♦ *перех* (*лак, мазь, краску*) to apply; (*узор, рисунок, резьбу*) to draw; (*на карту, на схему*) to plot; (*удар*) to deliver; (*урон*) to inflict; **наноси́ть** (~ *perf*) **кому́-н оскорбле́ние** to insult; **наноси́ть** (~ *perf*) **кому́-н пораже́ние** to defeat sb; ~ (*perf*) **кому́-н визи́т** to pay sb a visit.
нани́зыва|ть (-ю) *несов перех* (*жемчуг, бусинки*) to string, thread; (*перен: слова, фразы*) to string.
нанима́тел|ь (-я) *м* tenant; (*рабочей силы*) employer.
нанима́тельниц|а (-ы) *ж см* **нанима́тель**.
нанима́ть(ся) (-ю(сь)) *несов от* **наня́ть(ся)**.
нано́с (-а) *м* (*речной*) alluvium; (*ледниковый, снежный*) drift.
нан|оси́ть (-ошу́, -о́сишь) *сов от* **нанести́** ♦ *перех* (*воды, песку, камней*) to bring.
нано́сный *прил* (*ил*) alluvial; (*перен: увлечения*) alien.
на|ня́ть (-йму́, -ймёшь; *pt* -нял, -няла́, -няло, *impf* **нанима́ть**) *сов перех* (*работника*) to hire; (*лодку, машину*) to hire, rent
▸ **наня́ться** (*impf* **нанима́ться**) *сов возв* to get a job; **нанима́ться** (~ся *perf*) **секретарём/ реда́ктором** to get a job as a secretary/editor.
наоборо́т *нареч* (*прочитать слово*) backwards; (*поступать, делать*) the wrong way (round) ♦ *вводн сл, част* (*при противопоставлении*) on the contrary.
наобу́м *нареч* (*разг: делать, отвечать*) without thinking; (*стрелять*) at random.
на́отмашь *нареч* with a bold swipe.
наотре́з *нареч* flatly, point-blank.

напада́|ть (-ю) *несов от* **напа́сть**.
напада́ющ|ий (-его; *decl like adj*) *м* (*СПОРТ*) forward.
нападе́ни|е (-я) *ср* attack; (*СПОРТ*) forwards *мн*.
напа́дк|и (-ок) *мн* attacks *мн*.
нападу́ *итп сов см* **напа́сть**.
напа́ко|стить (-щу, -стишь) *сов от* **па́костить**.
напа́лм (-а) *м* napalm.
напа́рник (-а) *м* fellow worker.
напа́рниц|а (-ы) *ж см* **напа́рник**.
напа́рыва|ться (-юсь) *несов от* **напоро́ться**.
напа|сти́сь (-у́сь, -ёшься) *сов возв: на тебя́ са́хара не ~ёшься* you haven't got in enough sugar.
напа́сть (-а́сти) *ж* (*разг: беда*) calamity; ♦ (-аду́, -адёшь; *pt* -а́л, -а́ла, -а́ло, *impf* **напада́ть**) *сов неперех*: ~ **на** +*acc* to attack; (*на золоту́ю жи́лу*) to come across, stumble (up)on; (*перен: на иде́ю*) to have; (*тоска, грусть, страх*) to grip, seize.
напе́в (-а) *м* tune, melody.
напева́|ть (-ю) *несов от* **напе́ть** ♦ *перех* (*песенку*) to hum.
напе́вный (-ен, -на, -но) *прил* melodious.
напёк *итп сов см* **напе́чь**.
напека́|ть (-ю) *несов от* **напе́чь**.
напеку́ *итп сов см* **напе́чь**.
наперебо́й *нареч* vying with each other.
наперевес *нареч*: **держа́ть ружьё** ~ to hold one's gun at the ready.
наперегонки́ *нареч* (*разг*) racing each other.
наперёд *нареч* (*знать, угада́ть*) in advance; **за́дом** ~ back to front.
наперекор *нареч* (*говорить, поступать, идти*) defiantly ♦ *предл* (+*dat; судьбе, врагу, здравому смыслу*) in defiance of.
напереро́з *нареч* (*бежать, идти, плыть итп*) in order to intercept.
нап|ере́ть (-ру́, -рёшь; *pt* -ёр, -ёрла, -ёрло, *impf* **напира́ть**) *сов неперех*: ~ **на** +*acc* (*разг: на дверь*) to push against.
наперечёт *нареч* (*знать, помнить*) without exception.
напёрст|ок (-ка) *м* thimble.
наперчи́ть (-у́, -и́шь) *сов от* **перчи́ть**.
нап|е́ть (-ою́, -оёшь; *impf* **напева́ть**) *сов перех* (*мотив, песню, мелодию*) to sing; **напева́ть** (~ *perf*) **пласти́нку** to make a recording of one's singing.
напеча́тать(ся) (-ю(сь)) *сов от* **печа́тать(ся)**.
нап|е́чь (-еку́, -ечёшь *итп*, -еку́т; *pt* -ёк, -екла́, -екло́, *impf* **напека́ть**) *сов перех* (*блинов, пирогов*) to bake ♦ *безл* (*разг: голову, плечи*) to burn.
напива́|ться (-юсь) *несов от* **напи́ться**.
напи́льник (-а) *м* file.
напира́|ть (-ю) *несов от* **напере́ть** ♦ *неперех*: ~ **на** +*acc* (*теснить*) to push against; (*перен*) to stress.
написа́ни|е (-я) *ср* writing; (*буквы*) spelling.
напи|са́ть (-шу́, -шешь) *сов от* **писа́ть**.

напи́т|ок (-ка) м drink.

напи́ться (-ьюсь, -ьёшься; *impf* **напива́ться**) сов возв (воды, сока, чаю) to have a drink; (квасом, лимонадом) to quench one's thirst; (разг: опьянеть) to get drunk.

напиха́ть (-ю; *impf* **напи́хивать**) сов перех (разг): **~ в** +acc to stuff into.

напи́чка|ть (-ю) сов от **пи́чкать**.

напишу́ итп сов см **написа́ть**.

наплака́ть сов перех: **кот напла́кал** (разг) very little; **у нас де́нег – кот напла́кал** we have very little money

▶ **напла́|каться ♦** (-чусь, -чешься) сов возв (ребёнок) to cry one's eyes out; **напла́чешься ты с ней** (перен) you'll have nothing but problems with her.

наплева́тельск|ий (-ая, -ое, -ие) прил (разг: отношение) harum-scarum.

наплева́ть (-юю) сов от **плева́ть ♦** неперех to spit; **~!** (разг) to hell with it!

наплы́|в (-а) м (перен: туристов) influx; (: заявлений, чувств) flood.

наплы́|ть (-ву́, -вёшь; *impf* **наплыва́ть**) сов неперех: **~ на** +acc (на мель, на камень) to run against; (облако, туча) to drift over или in front of; (тина, водоросли) to be washed up; (перен: воспоминания) to come flooding back.

напова́л нареч outright.

наподо́бие предл (+gen) like, resembling.

напо́|йть (-ою́, -о́ишь) сов от **пои́ть**.

напока́з нареч for show.

наполз|ти́ (-у́, -ёшь; *impf* **наполза́ть**) сов неперех: **~ на** +acc (на преграду) to crawl onto; (туча) to creep up; (муравьи) to crawl in.

напо́лн|ить (-ю, -ишь; *impf* **наполня́ть**) сов перех: **~** +instr to fill with

▶ **напо́лниться** (*impf* **наполня́ться**) сов возв: **~ся** +instr to fill with.

наполови́ну нареч (уменьшить, увеличить) by half; (наполнить, налить) half.

напо́льн|ый прил floor орпед; **~ые часы́** grandfather clock.

напомина́ни|е (-я) ср reminder.

напомина́|ть (-ю) несов см **напо́мнить ♦** перех (иметь сходство) to resemble; **он ~ет мне моего́ отца́** he resembles my father.

напо́мн|ить (-ю, -ишь; *impf* **напомина́ть**) сов перех: **~** +acc или **о** +prp to remind of.

напо́р (-а) м (воды, воздуха) pressure; (ветра) force; (войск) onslaught; (разг: настойчивость) push, go.

напо́рист|ый (-, -а, -о) прил forceful.

напор|о́ть (-ю, -ешь) сов от **поро́ть ♦** перех (разг: руку, ногу) to cut

▶ **напоро́ться** (*impf* **напа́рываться**) сов возв: **~ся на** +acc (разг: на гвоздь, на сучок) to cut o.s. on; (: на беду, на скандал) to run up against.

напо́р|тить (-чу, -тишь) сов (не)перех (+acc или

+gen; бумаги, материала) to spoil **♦** неперех (+dat; разг: делу) to wreck; (: другу) to harm.

напосле́док нареч (разг) in the end, finally.

напою́ итп сов см **напе́ть**.

напра́в|ить (-лю, -ишь; *impf* **направля́ть**) сов перех (взгляд, внимание, разговор) to direct; (в госпиталь, к врачу) to refer; (на завод) to assign; (телеграмму, послание) to send; **направля́ть (~** perf) **свой путь куда́-нибудь** to make one's way somewhere

▶ **напра́виться** (*impf* **направля́ться**) сов возв: **~ся в** +acc/**к** +dat (в город, к острову) to make for.

направле́ни|е (-я) ср direction; (специалистов) sending; (деятельности, также воен) line; (политики) orientation; (течения) school; (документ: в больницу) referral; (: на работу, на учёбу) directive; **по ~ю к** +dat towards.

напра́вленност|ь (-и) ж focus.

направлю́(сь) итп сов см **напра́вить(ся)**.

направля́|ть(ся) (-ю(сь)) несов от **напра́вить(ся)**.

напра́во нареч (идти, повернуть) (to the) right; (от дороги, от дома) to the right.

напра́сен прил см **напра́сный**.

напра́сно нареч in vain.

напра́сн|ый (-ен, -на, -но) прил (труд, усилия) vain; (тревога, страх) unfounded.

напра́шива|ться (-юсь) несов от **напроси́ться**.

наприме́р вводн сл for example или instance.

напрока́знича|ть (-ю) сов от **прока́зничать**.

напрока́т нареч: **взять ~** to hire; **отдава́ть** (**отда́ть** perf) **~** to hire out.

напролёт нареч without a break.

напроло́м нареч at nothing.

напроро́ч|ить (-у, -ишь) сов от **проро́чить**.

напро|си́ться (-шу́сь, -óсишься; *impf* **напра́шиваться**) сов возв (разг: в гости, на должность) to force o.s.; **напра́шиваться (~** perf) **на** +acc (на комплимент, на оскорбле́ние) to invite.

напро́тив нареч opposite **♦** вводн сл on the contrary **♦** предл (+gen) opposite.

на́прочь нареч (разг) completely.

напрошу́сь сов см **напроси́ться**.

напря́г(ся) итп сов см **напря́чь(ся)**.

напряга́|ть(ся) (-ю(сь)) несов от **напря́чь(ся)**.

напрягу́(сь) итп сов см **напря́чь(ся)**.

напряже́ни|е (-я) ср tension; (внимания, с ресурсами) strain; (физ: механическое) strain, stress; (: электрическое) voltage.

напряжённ|ый (-, -на, -но) прил tense; (отношения, голос, встреча) strained.

напрями́к нареч (идти, ехать) straight; (перен: сказать) straight out.

напря́|чь (-гу́, -жёшь итп, -гу́т; *pt* -г, -гла́,

-ягло́, *impf* напряга́ть) *сов перех* to strain
► напря́чься (*impf* напряга́ться) *сов возв* (мускулы, леска) to become tense; (внутренне) to strain o.s.
напуга́ть(ся) (-ю(сь)) *сов от* пуга́ть(ся).
напу́др|ить(ся) (-ю(сь), -ишь(ся)) *сов от* пу́дрить(ся).
напуска́ть(ся) (-ю(сь)) *несов от* напусти́ть(ся).
напускно́й *прил* (грубость) affected; (спокойствие) feigned.
напу|сти́ть (-щу́, -у́стишь; *impf* напуска́ть) *сов перех*: ~ +gen (дыму, воды) to fill with; (разг): ~ на +acc to put on; (разг: собак) to set on; напуска́ть (~ *perf*) на себя́ что-н to assume sth
► напусти́ться (*impf* напуска́ться) *сов возв* (разг): ~ся на +acc to attack.
напу́та|ть (-ю; *impf* напу́тывать) *сов (не)перех* (+acc или +gen; ниток, пряжи) to tangle; напу́тывать (~ *perf*) в +prp (в делах итп) to make a mess of.
напу́тственн|ый *прил* (речь) farewell опред; ~ое сло́во parting words мн.
напу́тстви|е (-я) *ср* parting words мн или wishes мн, farewell speech.
напу́тыва|ть (-ю) *несов от* напу́тать.
напущу́(сь) *сов см* напусти́ть(ся).
напы́ж|иться (-усь, -ишься) *сов от* пы́житься.
напыл|и́ть (-ю́, -и́шь) *сов от* пыли́ть.
напы́щен|ный (-, -на, -но) *прил* (вид, человек) pompous; (речь, рассказ) high-flown, bombastic.
напью́сь итп *сов см* напи́ться.
наравне́ *нареч*: ~ с +instr on an equal footing with; (по одной линии) on a level with.
нара́д|оваться (-уюсь) *сов возв*: ~ на +acc to fully enjoy.
нараспа́шку *нареч* (разг: одежда) unbuttoned; душа́ ~ у неё she is very open.
нараспе́в *нареч* drawlingly.
нарас|ти́ (3sg -тёт, 3pl -ту́т, *impf* нараста́ть) *сов неперех* (много грибов, трава) to spring up; (долги, проценты) to accumulate; (волнение, сопротивление) to grow; нараста́ть (~ *perf*) на +prp (мох) to grow on; (плесень) to form on; (водоросли) to build up on.
нара|сти́ть (-щу́, -сти́шь; *impf* нара́щивать) *сов перех* (мускулы) to develop; (канат, трубу) to lengthen.
нарасхва́т *нареч* (продаваться, покупаться) like hot cakes; таки́е специали́сты сейча́с ~ such specialists are in great demand nowadays.
нара́щива|ть (-ю) *несов от* нарасти́ть ♦ *перех* (темпы, объём итп) to increase.
наращу́ *сов см* нарасти́ть.
нарв|а́ть (-у́, -ёшь; *impf* нарыва́ть) *сов (не)перех* (+acc или +gen; травы, цветов, земляники) to pick; (бумаги) to tear
► нарва́ться (*impf* нарыва́ться) *сов возв* (разг): ~ся на +acc (на хулигана, грубияна) to run up against; (на оскорбление) to have to take

или swallow; нарыва́ться (~ся *perf*) на неприя́тность to run into some trouble.
наре́|зать (-жу, -жешь; *impf* нареза́ть) *сов (не)перех* (+acc или +gen; колбасы, хлеба, сыр) to slice, cut; (веток, цветов) to cut; (земли, участки) to allot (тех) to thread.
наре́зк|а (-и) *ж* (винта) thread.
нарека́ни|е (-я) *ср* reprimand, censure.
наре́чи|е (-я) *ср* (линг: говоры) dialect; (: часть речи) adverb.
нарза́н (-а) *м* Narzan (*kind of mineral water*).
нарис|ова́ть (-у́ю) *сов от* рисова́ть.
нарица́тельн|ый *прил*: и́мя ~ое (линг) common noun; ~ая сто́имость (экон) nominal cost.
наркоби́знес (-а) *м* drug dealing.
наркоделе́ц (-ьца́) *м* drug dealer.
нарко́з (-а) *м* (мед) narcosis, anaesthesia (*BRIT*), anesthesia (*US*).
наркокурье́р (-а) *м* drug trafficker.
нарко́лог (-а) *м* (мед) expert in narcotics.
наркологи́ческ|ий (-ая, -ое, -ие) *прил*: ~ диспансе́р drug-abuse clinic.
наркома́н (-а) *м* drug addict или abuser.
наркома́ни|я (-и) *ж* drug addiction или abuse.
наркома́н|ка (-ки; *gen pl* -ок) *ж см* наркома́н.
нарко́тик (-а) *м* narcotic, drug.
наро́д (-а; *part gen* -у) *м* people мн, nation; ру́сский ~ the Russian people; мно́го ~у many people.
наро́ден *прил см* наро́дный.
наро́дность (-и) *ж* nation; (литературы) national character.
наро́дн|ый (-ен, -на, -но) *прил* national; (фронт) popular; (искусство) folk опред; ~ поэ́т national poet или bard; ~ худо́жник/арти́ст *artist/actor who has received an official honour from the state*.
народонаселе́ни|е (-я) *ср* population.
нарожа́ть (-ю) *сов перех* (разг) to give birth to.
наро́ст (-а) *м* (наслоение) covering; (утолщение: на дереве) outgrowth; (: на суставах) growth.
наро́чи́т|ый (-, -а, -о) *прил* deliberate, intentional.
наро́чно *нареч* (опоздать, отвернуться) purposely, on purpose; (разг: сказать, заплакать) for fun; как ~ (разг) to make things worse; ~ не приду́маешь! (разг) this is quite something!
наро́чн|ый (-ого; *decl like adj*) *м* courier.
на́рт|а (-ы) *ж* sledge (*BRIT*) или sled (*US*) (*drawn by reindeer or dogs*).
наруб|и́ть (-лю́, -ишь; *impf* наруба́ть) *сов (не)перех* (+acc или +gen; дров, капусты) to chop.
нару́жен *прил см* нару́жный.
нару́жность (-и) *ж* exterior; (строения, города) outward appearance.
нару́жн|ый (-ен, -на, -но) *прил* (дверь, стена) exterior; (лекарство) for external application; (спокойствие, сдержанность) outward.

нару́жу *нареч* out.

наруме́н|ить(ся) (-ю(сь), -ишь(ся)) *сов от* **румя́нить(ся).**

нару́чник (-а) *м* (*обычно мн*) handcuff.

нару́чн|ый *прил*: ~ые часы́ wristwatch.

наруша́|ть(ся) (-ю(сь)) *несов от* **нару́шить(ся).**

наруши́тел|ь (-я) *м* (*закона*) transgressor, infringer; (*границы*) trespasser; (*ЮР: порядка*) offender; ~ **дисципли́ны** troublemaker.

наруши́тельни|ца (-ы) *ж см* **наруши́тель.**

нару́ш|ить (-у, -ишь; *impf* **наруша́ть**) *сов перех* (*покой, тишину*) to break, disturb; (*связь*) to break; (*правила, договор*) to break, violate; (*дисциплину*) to breach; **наруша́ть** (~ *perf*) **грани́цу** to illegally cross a border

► **нару́шиться** (*impf* **наруша́ться**) *сов возв* to be broken *или* disturbed.

нарци́сс (-а) *м* daffodil, narcissus.

на́р|ы (-) *мн* plank bed *ед*.

нары́в (-а) *м* (*МЕД*) abscess, boil.

нарыва́|ть (-ю) *несов от* **нарва́ть** ♦ *наперех* (*рана*) to fester; **у меня́ па́лец** ~ет I have a boil on my finger

► **нарыва́ться** *несов от* **нарва́ться.**

наря́д (-а) *м* (*одежда*) outfit; (*красивая одежда*) attire; (*распоряжение*) directive; (*КОММ*) order; (*ВОЕН: подразделение*) division; (: *задание*) assignment.

наря́ден *прил см* **наря́дный.**

наря́|дить (-жу́, -дишь; *impf* **наряжа́ть**) *сов перех* (*невесту итп*) to dress; (*в караул, на кухню итп*) to assign; **наряжа́ть** (~ *perf*) **ёлку** = to decorate (*BRIT*) *или* trim (*US*) the Christmas tree; **наряжа́ть** (~ *perf*) **кого́-н** +*instr*/**в** +*acc* to dress sb as/in

► **наряди́ться** (*impf* **наряжа́ться**) *сов возв*: ~ся (**в** +*acc*) to dress o.s. (in).

наря́дный (-ен, -на, -но) *прил* (*человек*) well-dressed; (*комната, улица*) well-decorated; (*шляпа, платье*) fancy.

наряду́ *нареч*: ~ **с** +*instr* at the same time as; (*наравне*) on an equal footing with.

наряжа́|ть(ся) (-ю(сь)) *несов от* **наряди́ть(ся).**

наряжу́(сь) *сов см* **наряди́ть(ся).**

нас *мест см* **мы.**

НАСА *ср сокр* NASA (= *National Aeronautics and Space Administration*).

наса́|дить (-жу́, -а́дишь; *impf* **наса́живать**) *сов перех* (*надеть*) to put.

наса́д|ка (-ки; *gen pl* -ок) *ж* (*для рыбы*) bait; (*ТЕХ*) nozzle.

насажде́ни|е (-я) *ср* (*БОТ*) plantation.

наса́живал|ть (-ю) *несов от* **насади́ть.**

насажу́ *сов см* **насади́ть.**

насви́стыва|ть (-ю) *несов перех*: ~ **мело́дию** to whistle a tune under one's breath.

наседа́|ть (-ю) *несов от* **насе́сть** ♦ *неперех*

(*разг: толпа*) to press forward.

насе́д|ка (-ки; *gen pl* -ок) *ж* broody hen.

насеко́м|ое (-ого; *decl like adj*) *ср* insect.

населе́ни|е (-я) *ср* population.

населённый *прил* (*район, область*) populated, inhabited; (*квартира*) inhabited; ~ **пункт** locality.

насел|и́ть (-ю́, -и́шь; *impf* **населя́ть**) *сов перех* (*край*) to settle; (*дом*) to move into.

населя́|ть (-ю) *несов от* **насели́ть** ♦ *перех* (*лес, страну*) to inhabit.

насе́ст (-а) *м* (*для кур итп*) roost.

насе́|сть (-я́ду, -я́дешь; *impf* **наседа́ть**) *сов неперех* (*пыль, копоть*) to settle; **наседа́ть** (~ *perf*) **на** +*acc* (*перен: разг: с просьбами, в вопросами*) to pester; (*на противника*) to fall upon.

наси́женн|ый *прил*: ~ое **ме́сто** (*разг*) familiar surroundings *мн*.

наси́ли|е (-я) *ср* (*физическое*) violence; (*над личностью*) suppression.

наси́л|овать (-ую; *perf* **изнаси́ловать**) *несов перех* (*женщину, девушку*) to rape; (*no perf; личность*) to suppress.

наси́лу *нареч* (*разг: успеть, догнать*) only just.

наси́льник (-а) *м person who commits an act of violence*; (*над женщиной*) rapist.

наси́льно *нареч* forcibly; ~ **заста́вить** (*perf*) **кого́-н** +*infin* to force sb to do.

наси́льственный *прил* (*меры*) violent; **наси́льственная смерть** violent death.

наска́кива|ть (-ю) *несов от* **наскочи́ть.**

наскво́зь *нареч* through; **ви́деть** (*impf*) ~ **кого́-н** to see (right) through sb.

наско́к (-а) *м* (*разг*) slagging; **с** ~**а** (*разг*) impromptu.

наско́лько *нареч* so much.

на́скоро *нареч* (*разг*) on the double.

наско|чи́ть (-очу́, -о́чишь; *impf* **наска́кивать**) *сов неперех*: ~ **на** +*acc* to run into; (*перен: разг: на обидчика, на оппонента*) to attack; (: *на неприятность*) to get into.

наскре|сти́ (-бу́, -бёшь; *pt* -ёб, -ебла́, -ебло́, *impf* **наскреба́ть**) *сов перех* (*крошек, муки*) to collect; (*перен: мелочи, денег*) to scrape together.

наску́ч|ить (-у, -ишь) *сов неперех*: ~ **кому́-н** to bore sb.

насла|ди́ться (-жу́сь, -ди́шься; *impf* **наслажда́ться**) *сов возв*: ~ +*instr* to enjoy.

наслажде́ни|е (-я) *ср* enjoyment.

наслажу́сь *сов см* **наслади́ться.**

насла́ива|ться (*3sg* -ется, *3pl* -ются) *несов см* **наслои́ться.**

насле́ди|е (-я) *ср* (*культурное*) heritage; (*идеологическое*) legacy.

насле|ди́ть (-жу́, -ди́шь) *сов от* **следи́ть.**

насле́дник (-а) м (*престо́ла, состоя́ния*) heir; (*перен: прее́мник*) inheritor.

насле́дница (-ы) ж (*см* м) heiress; inheritor.

насле́дный *прил*: ~ **принц** prince next in line (to the throne).

насле́дование (-я) *ср* inheritance; (*престо́ла*) succession.

насле́д|овать (-ую) (*не*)*сов перех* to inherit; (*престо́л*) to succeed.

насле́дственный *прил* inherited; (*черты́, боле́знь*) hereditary.

насле́дств|о (-а) *ср* (*иму́щество*) inheritance; (*культу́рное*) heritage; (*идеологи́ческое*) legacy; **получа́ть** (**получи́ть** *perf*) **что-н в** ~ to inherit sth.

наслежу́ *сов см* **насле́дить**.

наслое́ни|е (-я) *ср* (*ГЕО*) stratification.

насло|и́ться (*3sg* -и́тся, *3pl* -я́тся, *impf* **насла́иваться**) *сов возв*: ~ **на** +*acc* to settle on; (*перен*) to add to.

наслу́ша|ться (-юсь) *сов возв*: ~ +*gen* to hear a lot of; (*вдо́воль послу́шать*) to hear enough of.

наслы́шан *как сказ*: **я** ~ **об э́том/о нём** I have heard a lot about it/him.

наслы́ш|аться (-усь, -ишься) *сов возв* (*разг*): ~ **о** +*prp* to hear a lot about.

насма́рку *нареч* (*разг*): **идти́** ~ to be wasted.

на́смерть *нареч* (*сража́ться*) to the death; (*разби́ться, ра́нить*) fatally; (*перен: разг: перепуга́ться*) to death; (: *поруга́ться*) strongly.

насмеха́|ться (-юсь) *несов возв*: ~ **над** +*instr* to mock.

насме́шек *сущ см* **насме́шка**.

насмеш|и́ть (-у́, -и́шь) *сов от* **смеши́ть**.

насме́ш|ка (-ки; *gen pl* -ек) ж (*оби́дная шу́тка*) jibe; **сказа́ть** (*perf*) **что-н в** ~**ку** to say sth mockingly.

насме́шливый (-, -а, -о) *прил* mocking.

насме|я́ться (-ю́сь) *сов возв*: ~ **над** +*instr* to offend.

на́сморк (-а) м runny nose.

насмотр|е́ться (-ю́сь, -о́тришься) *сов возв*: ~ (**на** +*acc*) to see enough (of); (+*gen*; *чуде́с, люде́й*) to see a lot of.

насовсе́м *нареч* (*разг*) for good.

насол|и́ть (-ю́, -ишь) *сов перех* to preserve (*in brine*) ♦ *неперех* (+*dat*; *перен: разг: сде́лать неприя́тность*) to be nasty to.

насор|и́ть (-ю́, -и́шь) *сов от* **сори́ть**.

насо́с (-а) м pump.

на́спех *нареч* hurriedly.

наста|ва́ть (*3sg* -ёт, *3pl* -ю́т) *несов от* **наста́ть**.

настави́тельный (-ен, -ьна, -ьно) *прил* (*тон*) preaching.

наста́в|ить (-лю, -ишь) *сов неперех* (+*gen*; *поста́вить*) to put; (*синяко́в, ши́шек*) to cause ♦ (*impf* **наставля́ть**) *перех* (*пла́тье, рука́в*) to lengthen; (*револьве́р, ружьё*) to aim; **наставля́ть** (~ *perf*) **кого-н на путь и́стинный** to set sb on the right path.

наставле́ни|е (-я) *ср* (*поуче́ние*) lecture; (*руково́дство*) instructions *мн*.

наста́влю *сов см* **наста́вить**.

наставл|я́ть (-ю) *несов от* **наста́вить** ♦ *перех* (*ученико́в*) to teach.

наста́вник (-а) м mentor.

наста́ива|ть(ся) (-ю(сь)) *несов от* **настоя́ть(ся)**.

наста́|ть (*3sg* -нет, *3pl* -нут, *impf* **настава́ть**) *сов неперех* (*ле́то*) to begin; (*молча́ние, ночь*) to fall; (*день отъе́зда*) to come.

на́стежь *нареч* (*откры́ть*) wide; (*окно́, дверь итп*) wide open; **распахну́ть** (*perf*) ~ to fling wide open.

насте́л|ить (-ю́, -и́лишь) *сов от* **стели́ть**.

насте́нный *прил* wall *опред*.

настига́|ть (-ю) *несов от* **насти́чь**.

насти́гн|уть (-у, -ешь; *impf* **настига́ть**) *сов перех* = **насти́чь**.

насти́л (-а) м (*из се́на*) bedding; (*деревя́нный*) boarding.

насти́|чь (-гну, -гнешь; *pt* -г, -гла, -гло, *impf* **настига́ть**) *сов перех* to catch up with.

насто́ек *сущ см* **насто́йка**.

насто́й (-я) м infusion.

насто́й|ка (-йки; *gen pl* -ек) ж (*экстра́кт*) tincture; (*алкого́ль*) liqueur.

насто́йчивый (-, -а, -о) *прил* (*челове́к, хара́ктер*) persistent; (*про́сьба, взгляд итп*) insistent.

насто́лько *нареч* so.

насто́льн|ый *прил* (*ла́мпа, часы́*) table *опред*; (*календа́рь*) desk *опред*; ~**ая кни́га** (*перен*) bible; **насто́льный те́ннис** table tennis.

настора́жива|ть(ся) (-ю(сь)) *несов от* **насторожи́ть(ся)**.

насторо́же *нареч* on the alert ♦ *как сказ*: **он всегда́** ~ he is always on the alert.

насторо́женно *нареч* intently.

насторо́жен|ный (-, -на, -но) *прил* alert.

насторожённ|ый (-, -на, -но) *прил* = **насторо́женный**.

насторож|и́ть (-у́, -и́шь; *impf* **настора́живать**) *сов перех* to alert

▸ **насторожи́ться** (*impf* **настора́живаться**) *сов возв* to become more alert.

настоя́ни|е (-я) *ср*: **по** ~**ю кого-н** on sb's insistence.

настоя́тельный (-ен, -ьна, -ьно) *прил* (*про́сьба*) persistent; (*зада́ча*) urgent.

насто|я́ть (-ю́, -и́шь; *impf* **наста́ивать**) *сов неперех*: ~ **на** +*prp* to insist on ♦ *перех* (*рома́шку*) to infuse; **наста́ивать** (~ *perf*) **на своём** to insist on having one's own way

▸ **настоя́ться** (*impf* **наста́иваться**) *сов возв* (*чай, рома́шка*) to infuse.

настоя́щее (-его; *decl like adj*) *ср* the present.

настоя́щий (-ая, -ее, -ие) *прил* real; (*моме́нт, вре́мя*) present; (*да́нный: статья́*) this; **по-**~**ему** (*как на́до*) properly; (*пре́данный*) really; **настоя́щее вре́мя** (*линг*) the present tense.

настрада́|ться (-юсь) *сов возв* to suffer a lot.

настра́ива|ть(ся) (-ю(сь)) *несов от* **настро́ить(ся)**.

на́строго *нареч* (*разг*) strictly.

настрое́ни|е (-я) *ср* mood; (*антивоенное*) feeling; **не в ~и** in a bad mood; **обще́ственное ~** the mood in society.

настро́ить (-ю, -ишь; *impf* **настра́ивать**) *сов* (*не)перех* (+*acc или* +*gen*; *домов, мостов, больниц*) to build ♦ *перех* (*гитару, пианино итп*) to tune; (*приёмник*) to tune in; (*механизм*) to adjust; **настра́ивать** (~ *perf*) **кого́-н на** +*acc* to put sb in the right frame of mind for; **настра́ивать** (~ *perf*) **кого́-н про́тив** +*gen* to incite sb against

► **настро́иться** (*impf* **настра́иваться**) *сов возв* (*приёмник*) to be tuned in; (*дружелюбно, враждебно*) to be disposed; **~ся** (*perf*) +*infin* to be disposed to do.

настро́й (-я) *м* mood.

настро́йщик (-а) *м*: **~ роя́ля** piano tuner.

наступа́тельный (-ен, -ьна, -ьно) *прил* (*бой, действие*) offensive.

наступа́|ть (-ю) *несов от* **наступи́ть** ♦ *неперех* (*воен*) to go on the offensive.

наступи́ть (-уплю́, -у́пишь; *impf* **наступа́ть**) *сов неперех*: **~ на** +*acc* (*на камень, на ногу итп*) to step on; (*ночь, тишина*) to fall; (*утро, лето*) to begin; (*день отъезда*) to come.

наступле́ни|е (-я) *ср* (*воен*) offensive; (*весны, старости*) beginning; (*темноты*) fall; **с ~м зимы́** at the beginning of winter; **с ~м темноты́** at nightfall.

наступлю́ *сов см* **наступи́ть**.

настурци|я (-и) *ж* nasturtium.

насты́рн|ый (-ен, -на, -но) *прил* (*разг*) persistent.

на́сухо *нареч*: **вы́тереть что-н ~** to dry sth thoroughly.

насу́щн|ый (-ен, -на, -но) *прил* vital.

насчёт *предл* (+*gen*) regarding.

насчита́|ть (-ю; *impf* **насчи́тывать**) *сов перех* to count.

насчи́тыва|ть (-ю) *несов от* **насчита́ть** ♦ *неперех* to have; **дере́вня ~ет ты́сячу жи́телей** the village has a thousand inhabitants

► **насчи́тываться** *несов возв безл* to have.

насыпа́|ть (-лю, -лешь; *impf* **насыпа́ть**) *сов перех* to pour; (*набросать*) to strew.

на́сып|ь (-и) *ж* embankment.

насы́тить (-щу, -тишь; *impf* **насыща́ть**) *сов перех* (*голодного, ребёнка*) to satiate; (*запахом, водой, радостью*) to fill; (*раствор, рынок*) to saturate

► **насы́титься** (*impf* **насыща́ться**) *сов возв*

(*наесться*) to eat one's fill; (*земля*) to be saturated.

насы́щенный *прил* (*хим*) saturated; (*перен: жизнь*) rich.

насы́щу(сь) *сов см* **насы́тить(ся)**.

насяду *итп сов см* **насе́сть**.

ната́лкива|ть(ся) (-ю(сь)) *несов от* **натолкну́ть(ся)**.

натаска́|ть (-ю; *impf* **ната́скивать**) *сов (не)перех* (+*acc или* +*gen*; *дров, сучьев итп*) to bring; (*разг: перен: цитат, отрывков*) to fish out; (: *студента, ученика*) to coach (*for examination*).

натащ|и́ть (-у́, -ишь) *сов (не)перех* (+*acc или* +*gen*; *разг: камней, сучьев, грязи*) to bring in.

натвор|и́ть (-ю́, -и́шь) *сов (не)перех* (+*acc или* +*gen*; *разг*) to get up to.

натер|е́ть (-ру́, -рёшь; *pt* -ёр, -ёрла, -ёрло, *impf* **натира́ть**) *сов перех* (*ботинки, полы*) to polish; (*руку, шею итп*) to chafe; (*морковь, сыр итп*) to grate; **натира́ть** (~ *perf*) **что-н чем-н** (*руки итп: мазью, кремом*) to rub sth with sth; **натира́ть** (~ *perf*) **себе́ мозо́ли** to get a callus

► **натере́ться** (*impf* **натира́ться**) *сов возв*: **~ся** (+*instr*) (*мазью, кремом*) to rub o.s. (with).

натерп|е́ться (-лю́сь, -ишься) *сов возв*: **~** +*gen* (*разг: горя, беды*) to experience a lot of.

натира́|ть(ся) (-ю(сь)) *несов от* **натере́ть(ся)**.

на́тиск (-а) *м* pressure.

наткн|у́ться (-у́сь, -ёшься; *impf* **натыка́ться**) *сов возв*: **~у́ться на** +*acc* (*разг: на пень, на преграду*) to bump into; (*перен: на непонимание, на сопротивление*) to come up against.

НА́ТО *ср сокр* NATO (= *North Atlantic Treaty Organization*).

натолкн|у́ть (-у́, -ёшь; *impf* **ната́лкивать**) *сов перех*: **~ кого́-н на** +*acc* (*разг: на иде́ю*) to lead sb to; **ната́лкивать** (~ *perf*) **кого́-н на мысль** to put a thought into sb's head

► **натолкну́ться** (*impf* **ната́лкиваться**) *сов возв*: **~ся на** +*acc* (*также перен*) to bump into.

натоп|и́ть (-лю́, -ишь) *сов перех* (*избу, печь*) to heat; (*жир, воск*) to melt.

натопта́|ть (-чу́, -чешь) *сов перех* (*разг*) to make dirty footmarks across.

нато|чи́ть (-чу́, -чишь) *сов от* **точи́ть**.

натоща́к *нареч* on an empty stomach.

натрав|и́ть (-лю́, -ишь; *impf* **натравля́ть**) *сов перех*: **~ кого́-н на** +*acc* to set sb on; (*перен*) to incite sb against.

натрениро́ванн|ый (-, -а, -о) *прил* trained.

натрениров|а́ть(ся) (-у́ю(сь)) *сов от* **трениров́ать(ся)**.

на́три|й (-я) *м* sodium.

на́трое *нареч* in(to) three.

натру́(сь) *итп сов см* **натере́ть(ся)**.

натру|ди́ться (-жу́сь, -у́дишься) *сов возв* (*разг*) to work hard.

нату́г|а (-и) ж (разг) effort.

на́туго нареч (разг) tightly.

нату́ж|иться (-усь, -ишься; impf **нату́живаться**) сов возв (разг) to strain.

нату́р|а (-ы) ж (характер) nature; (натурщик) model (ART); **увиде́ть** (perf) **что-н/кого́-н ~е** to see sth/sb in real life; **рисова́ть** (impf) **с ~ы** to paint from nature; **~ой, в ~е** (ЭКОН) in kind.

натура́лен прил см **натура́льный**.

натурализа́ци|я (-и) ж naturalization.

натурали́зм (-а) м naturalism.

натурали́ст (-а) м naturalist.

натура́льный (-ен, -ьна, -ьно) прил natural; (мех, кожа, слёзы) real; (обмен, доходы, налог) in kind; **~ьная величина́** life-sized.

нату́рщик (-а) м model (ART).

нату́рщиц|а (-ы) ж см **нату́рщик**.

натыка́|ться (-юсь) несов от **наткну́ться**.

натюрмо́рт (-а) м still life.

натя́гива|ть (-ю(сь)) несов от **натяну́ть(ся)**.

натя́ж|ка (-ки; gen pl -ек) ж (в аргументах) distortion; **с ~кой** at a pinch.

натя́нут|ый (-, -а, -о) прил strained.

натян|у́ть (-у́, -ешь; impf **натя́гивать**) сов перех (струны, вожжи, холст) to pull tight; (разг: сапоги, перчатки) to pull on; (: одеяло) to pull over; **он ~у́л ему́ пятёрку** (разг) he stretched his mark to an A

▸ **натяну́ться** (impf **натя́гиваться**) сов возв to tighten.

науга́д нареч (идти, взять) at random; **отвеча́ть** (impf) **~** to guess.

нау́к|а (-и) ж science; (разг: урок) lesson; **есте́ственные ~и** science; **гуманита́рные ~и** arts.

наутёк нареч (разг: пуститься, броситься) at full tilt.

нау́тро нареч next morning.

нау́чен прил см **нау́чный**.

нау́ч|ить(ся) (-учу́(сь), -у́чишь(ся)) сов от **учи́ть(ся)**.

нау́чно-популя́рный прил (программа) science опред; (литература) scientific.

нау́чно-техни́ческ|ий (-ая, -ое, -ие) прил scientific.

нау́чный (-ен, -на, -но) прил scientific; **нау́чная фанта́стика** science fiction.

нау́шник (-а) м (обычно мн: на шапке) earflap; **магнитофо́нные ~и** headphones.

нафтали́н (-а; part gen -у) м naphthalene.

наха́л (-а) м (разг) cheeky beggar.

наха́лен прил см **наха́льный**.

наха́лк|а (-и) ж см **наха́л**.

наха́л|ьный (-ен, -ьна, -ьно) прил cheeky.

наха́льств|о (-а) ср cheek.

нахам|и́ть (-лю́, -и́шь) сов от **хами́ть**.

нахвата́|ть (-ю) сов неперех (+gen; разг: товаров, знаний) to pick up

▸ **нахвата́ться** сов возв (+gen; разг: знаний, привычек) to pick up; (: воды) to gulp.

нахле́бник (-а) м (разг) sponger.

нахлобу́ч|ить (-у, -ишь; impf **нахлобу́чивать**) сов перех (разг) to pull down.

нахлын|у́ть (3sg -ет, 3pl -ут) сов неперех (поток) to surge; (перен: толпа) to surge forward; (: мысли) to surge up; **~ули воспомина́ния** memories came flooding back.

нахму́р|ить(ся) (-ю(сь), -ишь(ся)) несов от **хму́рить(ся)**.

нах|оди́ть (-ожу́, -о́дишь) несов от **найти́**

▸ **находи́ться** несов от **найти́сь** ♦ возв (дом, город) to be situated; (человек) to be.

нахо́д|ка (-ки; gen pl -ок) ж (потерянного) discovery; (приём: писателя, актёра) innovation; **он ~ для нас** he is a real find for us; **Бюро́ ~ок** lost property office (BRIT), lost and found (US).

нахо́дчив|ый (-, -а, -о) прил (человек) resourceful; (ответ) apt.

нахожде́ни|е (-я) ср (преступника) whereabouts.

нахо́жен|ный (-, -а, -о) прил (тропа) well-trodden.

нахожу́(сь) несов см **находи́ть(ся)**.

нахохота́ться (-очу́сь, -о́чешься) сов возв to have a good laugh.

нахра́пист|ый (-, -а, -о) прил (разг: продавец, посетитель) pushy.

нахра́пом нареч (разг): **де́йствовать ~** to be pushy.

нахулига́н|ить (-ю, -ишь) сов от **хулига́нить**.

нацара́па|ть (-ю) сов от **цара́пать**.

нацед|и́ть (-ежу́, -е́дишь; impf **нацеживать**) сов перех to strain.

наце́лен|ный (-, -а, -о) прил: **~ на** +acc (на победу) aiming for.

наце́л|ить (-ю, -ишь) сов от **це́лить** ♦ (impf **наце́ливать**) перех: **~ кого́-н на** +acc to push sb towards

▸ **наце́литься** сов от **це́литься**.

наце́н|ка (-ки; gen pl -ок) ж (на товар) surcharge; (ресторанная) cover charge.

нацеп|и́ть (-лю́, -ишь; impf **нацепля́ть**) сов перех (повесить) to hang on; (разг: украшения) to doll o.s. up in.

наци́зм (-а) м Nazism.

национализа́ци|я (-и) ж nationalization.

национализи́р|овать (-ую) (не)сов перех to nationalize.

национали́зм (-а) м nationalism.

национали́ст (-а) м nationalist.

национали́ст|ка (-ки; gen pl -ок) ж см **национали́ст**.

национали́стск|ий (-ая, -ое, -ие) прил (политика, лозунг) nationalistic.

национа́льность (-и) ж (нация) nation; (принадлежность к нации) nationality.

национа́льный прил national; **национа́льный о́круг** administrative division of minor nationalities.

наци́ст (-а) м Nazi.

наци́стск|ий (-ая, -ое, -ие) *прил* Nazi.
на́ци|я (-и) *ж* nation; **Организа́ция Объединённых Н~й** United Nations Organization.
нацме́н (-а) *м сокр = представи́тель национа́льного меньшинства́*.
нач. *сокр = нача́льник*.
нача|ди́ть (-жу́, -ди́шь) *сов от* чади́ть.
нача́л|а (-) *мн (методы)* basis *ед*; *(принципы)* fundamentals *мн*; **на коллекти́вных/ комме́рческих ~х** on a collective/commercial basis.
нача́л|о (-а) *ср* beginning, start; *(основа: организующее, сдерживающее)* foundation; *(: волевое, поэтическое)* nature; **быть** *(impf)* **под ~м кого́-н** или **у кого́-н** to be under sb; **брать** *(impf)* **~** to start; **вести́** *(impf)* **своё ~ от** +*gen* to have its origins in; **положи́ть** *(perf)* или **дать** *(perf)* **~ чему́-н** to make a start on sth; *см также* нача́ла.
нача́льник (-а) *м (цеха)* floor manager; *(управления)* head; *(экспедиции)* leader.
нача́льническ|ий (-ая, -ое, -ие) *прил (тон)* authoritative.
нача́льный *прил (период, этап)* initial; *(глава книги)* first; *(первоначальный: сведения, уроки)* very first; **нача́льная шко́ла** *(ПРОСВЕЩ)* primary *(BRIT)* или elementary *(US)* school; **нача́льное образова́ние** *(ПРОСВЕЩ)* primary *(BRIT)* или elementary *(US)* education; **нача́льные кла́ссы** *(ПРОСВЕЩ)* the first three classes of primary school.
нача́льственный *прил* superior.
нача́льств|о (-а) *ср (власть)* authority ◆ *собир (руководители)* management; **под ~м кого́-н** *(служить, находиться)* under sb.
нача́льствующий (-ая, -ее, -ие) *прил* managing *опред*.
нача́тк|и (-ов) *мн* fundamentals *мн*.
нача́|ть (-ну́, -нёшь; *pt* -ал, -ала́, -ало, *impf* начина́ть) *сов перех* to begin, start; *(начать использовать)* to start; **начина́ть** (~ *perf*) +*infin* to start doing.
▸ **нача́ться** *(impf* начина́ться) *сов возв* to begin, start.
начеку́ *нареч:* **быть ~** to be on one's guard.
начерка́|ть (-ю) *сов от* черка́ть ◆ *перех (разг: линии, штрихи итп)* to draw *(randomly)*; *(записку)* to scribble.
начерн|и́ть (-ю́, -и́шь) *сов от* черни́ть.
на́черно *нареч (написать, подготовить)* roughly.
начерта́ни|е (-я) *ср (букв)* outline.
нач|ерти́ть (-ерчу́, -е́ртишь) *сов от* черти́ть.
начёс (-а) *м (на шерсти, на ткани)* nap; *(вид причёски)* bouffant.
начёт (-а) *м (денежное взыскание)* penalty.
начина́ни|е (-я) *ср* initiative.

начина́тел|ь (-я) *м* initiator.
начина́|ть(ся) (-ю(сь)) *несов от* нача́ть(ся).
начина́ющ|ая (-ей; *decl like adj*) *ж см* начина́ющий.
начина́ющ|ий (-ая, -ее, -ие) *прил (писатель, учитель)* novice *опред* ◆ (-его; *decl like adj*) *м* beginner.
начина́я *предл* (+*instr*) including; **~ с** +*gen* from; **~ от** +*gen* или **с** +*gen (включая)** including.
начин|и́ть (-ю́, -и́шь; *impf* начиня́ть) *сов перех (пирога)* to fill.
начи́н|ка (-ки; *gen pl* -ок) *ж* filling.
начиня́|ть (-ю) *несов от* начини́ть.
начисле́ни|е (-я) *ср (действие)* addition; *(начисленная сумма)* surcharge.
начи́сл|ить (-ю, -ишь; *impf* начисля́ть) *сов перех (проценты)* to add on.
начи́|стить (-щу, -стишь; *impf* начища́ть) *сов перех (туфли)* to clean ◆ *неперех* (+*gen*; *картошки)* to peel.
на́чисто *нареч (набело)* cleanly; *(разг: совершенно)* absolutely.
начистоту́ *нареч (разг)* straight.
начи́та|нный (-, -на, -но) *прил* well-read.
начита́|ть (-ю; *impf* начи́тывать) *сов перех* to read.
▸ **начита́ться** *сов возв* (+*gen*) to read a lot of.
начи́тыва|ть (-ю) *несов от* начита́ть.
начиха́|ть (-ю) *сов неперех (перен: разг):* **ему́ ~ на сове́ты** he doesn't give a toss about taking people's advice.
начища́|ть (-ю) *несов от* начи́стить.
начи́щу *сов см* начи́стить.
начме́д (-а) *м сокр* SG (= *Surgeon General*).
начну́(сь) *итп сов см* нача́ть(ся).
наш (-его; *см* Table 9; *f* -а, *nt* -е, *pl* -и) *притяж мест* our; **~ го́род о́чень ста́рый** our city is very old; **чей э́то дом? – ~** whose is this house? – ours; **чьи э́то кни́ги? – на́ши** whose are these books? – ours; **по-на́шему** our way; *(по нашему мнению)* in our opinion; **на́ша взяла́!** *(разг)* we won!; *см также* на́ши.
нашаты́рный *прил:* **~ спирт** *(МЕД)* liquid ammonia.
нашаты́р|ь (-я́) *м (хим)* ammonium chloride; *(разг: нашаты́рный спирт)* liquid ammonia.
на́ше (-его) *притяж мест см* наш.
наше́стви|е (-я) *ср* invasion.
на́ш|и (-их) *притяж мест см* наш; ◆ *decl like adj мн (о членах семьи)* relatives *мн*; *(о соотечественниках)* compatriots *мн*; **и ~м и ва́шим** *(разг)* all things to all people; **~ вы́играли** we won.
нашива́|ть (-ю) *несов от* наши́ть.
наши́в|ка (-ки; *gen pl* -ок) *ж (на погонах)* stripe *(showing rank)*.
на́шим *притяж мест см* наш, на́ше, на́ши.
на́шими *притяж мест см* на́ши.

нашинк|ова́ть (-у́ю) *сов от* **шинкова́ть**.
наш|и́ть (-ью́, -ьёшь; *impf* **нашива́ть**) *сов перех* (*тесьму́, эмбле́му*) to sew on ♦ *неперех* (*no perf*): ~ +*gen* (*наря́дов*) to sew.
на́ших *притяж мест см* **наш**.
нашлёп|ать (-ю) *сов перех* (*разг*) to smack.
нашпиг|ова́ть (-у́ю) *сов от* **шпигова́ть**.
нашум|е́ть (-лю́, -и́шь) *сов неперех* to make a lot of noise; (*фильм, кни́га*) to cause a stir.
нашью́ *итп сов см* **наши́ть**.
нащу́п|ать (-ю; *impf* **нащу́пывать**) *сов перех* (*также перен*) to find.
наэлектриз|ова́ть (-у́ю) *сов от* **электризова́ть**.
ная́беднича|ть (-ю) *сов от* **я́бедничать**.
наяву́ *нареч* in reality; **как ~** distinctly.
НДС *м сокр* (= *нало́г на доба́вленную сто́имость*) VAT (= *value-added tax*).
не *част* not; ~ **я написа́л э́то письмо́** I didn't write this letter; **я ~ рабо́таю** I don't work; ~ **пла́чьте/опозда́йте** don't cry/be late; ~ **могу́ ~ согласи́ться/не возрази́ть** I can't help agreeing/objecting; ~ **мне на́до помо́чь, а ему́** I am not the one who needs help, he is; **слу́шаю ~ без удово́льствия/удивле́ния** I listen not without pleasure/surprise; ~ **до** +*gen* no time for; **мне ~ до тебя́** I have no time for you; ~ **без того́** (*разг: в положи́тельных отве́тах*) that's about it; ~ **то** (*разг: в проти́вном слу́чае*) or else; **откро́й дверь, ~ то я её слома́ю** open the door or else I'll break it down.
неадеква́т|ный (-ен, -на, -но) *прил* inadequate.
неаккура́т|ный (-ен, -на, -но) *прил* (*челове́к*) untidy; (*подсчёт*) inaccurate; (*рабо́та*) sloppy.
неактуа́л|ьный (-ен, -ьна, -ьно) *прил* irrelevant.
неаполита́нск|ий (-ая, -ое, -ие) *прил* Neapolitan.
Неа́пол|ь (-я) *м* Naples.
небезопа́с|ный (-ен, -на, -но) *прил* somewhat dangerous.
небезоснова́тельный (-ен, -ьна, -ьно) *прил* not unreasonable.
небезызве́ст|ный (-ен, -на, -но) *прил* (*фа́кты*) reasonably well-known; (*спле́тник, интрига́н*) notorious.
небезынтере́с|ный (-ен, -на, -но) *прил* reasonably interesting.
небеса́ *итп сущ см* **не́бо**.
небе́сный *прил* (*небосво́д, сфе́ра*) celestial; (*перен*) heavenly; **небе́сные тела́** heavenly bodies; **небе́сные си́лы** (*РЕЛ*) the heavenly host; **небе́сный цвет** sky blue.
небесполе́з|ный (-ен, -на, -но) *прил* reasonably useful.
неблагови́д|ный (-ен, -на, -но) *прил* unseemly.
неблагода́рен *прил см* **неблагода́рный**.
неблагода́рность (-и) *ж* ingratitude.
неблагода́р|ный (-ен, -на, -но) *прил* (*челове́к*) ungrateful; (*заня́тие, рабо́та*) thankless.
неблагозву́ч|ный (-ен, -на, -но) *прил*

dissonant.
неблагополу́ч|ный (-ен, -на, -но) *прил* unsuccessful.
не́б|о (-а; *nom pl* **небеса́**, *gen pl* **небе́с**) *ср* sky; (*РЕЛ*) Heaven; **на седьмо́м ~е** in seventh heaven; **под откры́тым ~м** out in the open; **с ~а свали́ться** (*perf*) (*разг: неожи́данно появи́ться*) to appear out of nowhere; **я был ме́жду ~м и землёй** I didn't know whether I was coming or going; **превозноси́ть** (*impf*) **кого́-н до небе́с** to praise sb to the skies.
нёб|о (-а) *ср* (*АНАТ*) palate.
небога́т|ый (-, -а, -о) *прил* (*страна́*) not wealthy; (*вы́бор, уло́в*) fairly poor; **он челове́к ~** he has a modest income.
небольш|о́й *прил* small; (*расстоя́ние, промежу́ток вре́мени*) short; (*до́лжность, зва́ние*) minor; (*по́льза, авторите́т*) limited; **на ~ глубине́/высоте́** not very deep/high; **ей три́дцать (лет) с ~им** she is a little over thirty.
небосво́д (-а) *м* the heavens *мн*.
небоскрё́б (-а) *м* skyscraper.
небо́сь *вводн сл* (*разг*) I dare say.
небре́жен *прил см* **небре́жный**.
небре́жность (-и) *ж* (*в рабо́те, подсчётов*) carelessness; (*роди́телей, рабо́тников*) negligence; (*то́на, в обраще́нии*) offhandedness.
небре́ж|ный (-ен, -на, -но) *прил* (*челове́к, рабо́та, подсчёт*) careless; (*причёска, по́черк*) untidy; (*тон, отноше́ние*) offhand(ed).
небыва́л|ый (-, -а, -о) *прил* (*чу́вство, ощуще́ние*) unknown; (*слу́чай*) unprecedented.
небыли́ц|а (-ы) *ж* tall story.
небыти́|е (-я́) *ср* nonexistence.
Нев|а́ (-ы́) *ж* the Neva.
нева́жен *прил см* **нева́жный**.
нева́жно *нареч* (*рабо́тать, де́лать что-н*) not very well ♦ *как сказ* it's not important; **я чу́вствую себя́ ~** I'm not feeling too good; **он ~ у́чится в шко́ле** he isn't doing very well at school.
нева́ж|ный (-ен, -на, -но) *прил* unimportant; (*не о́чень хоро́ший*) poor; **обе́д был нева́жный** dinner wasn't great; **у неё ~ое здоро́вье** her health isn't very good.
невдалеке́ *нареч* (*слы́шаться, ви́деться*) not far off; ~ **от** +*gen* not far from.
невдомёк *как сказ* (+*dat*): **ей ~, что ...** (*разг*) she doesn't realize that ....
неве́дени|е (-я) *ср* ignorance; **сде́лать** (*perf*)/**сказа́ть** (*perf*) **что-н по ~ю** to do/say sth out of ignorance; **он пребыва́ет в по́лном ~и** he doesn't know anything (about it).
неве́домо *нареч*: ~ **кто/что/как** *итп* (*разг*) God knows who/what/how *итп*.
неве́дом|ый (-, -а, -о) *прил* unknown.
неве́ж|а (-и) *м/ж* boor.
неве́жд|а (-ы) *м/ж* ignoramus.
неве́жественный (-, -на, -но) *прил* ignorant.
неве́жеств|о (-а) *ср* ignorance.

невѐжлив|ый (-, -а, -о) *прил* impolite.
невезѐни|е (-я) *ср* (*разг*) bad luck.
невели́к|ий (-ая, -ое, -ие; -, -а́, -о́) *прил* (*по размеру*) small; (*по длине*) short; (*убытки, ущерб*) minor; **он ро́стом невели́к** he's not very tall; **невелика́ беда́!** (*разг*) it's no big deal!
невѐрен *прил см* **невѐрный**.
невѐри|е (-я) *ср* lack of faith.
невѐрно *нареч* incorrectly ◆ *как сказ:* (ѐто) ~ that's not right.
невѐрност|ь (-и) *ж* (*рассуждений, понятия*) incorrectness; (*друга, союзника*) disloyalty; (*жены, мужа*) infidelity.
невѐр|ный (-ен, -на, -но) *прил* (*см сущ*) incorrect; disloyal; unfaithful; (*шаги, движения*) unsteady; (*голос, звук*) faltering; (*нота*) false.
невероя́тен *прил см* **невероя́тный**.
невероя́тно *нареч* incredibly ◆ *как сказ* it's incredible.
невероя́тност|ь (-и) *ж* (*сообщения, результатов*) improbability; **до ~и** incredibly.
невероя́т|ный (-ен, -на, -но) *прил* (*неправдоподобный*) improbable; (*чрезвычайный*) incredible.
невѐрующ|ий (-ая, -ее, -ие) *прил* (*РЕЛ*) faithless ◆ (-его; *decl like adj*) *м* unbeliever.
невес|ёлый (-ѐсел, -есела́, -ѐсело) *прил* gloomy.
невесо́мост|ь (-и) *ж* (*ФИЗ*) weightlessness.
невесо́м|ый (-, -а, -о) *прил* weightless; (*перен: преимущество, превосходство*) negligible.
невѐст|а (-ы) *ж* (*после помолвки*) fiancée; (*на свадьбе*) bride.
невѐст|ка (-ки; *gen pl* -ок) *ж* (*жена сына*) daughter-in-law; (*жена брата*) sister-in-law.
невѐсть *нареч:* ~ **кто/что/куда́** *итп* (*разг*) goodness knows who/what/where *итп*.
невзго́д|а (-ы) *ж* (*обычно мн*) adversity.
невзира́|я *предл:* ~ **на** +*acc* in spite of.
невзл|юби́ть (-юблю́, -ю́бишь) *сов перех* to take a dislike to.
невзнача́й *нареч* (*разг*) by accident.
невзра́ч|ный (-ен, -на, -но) *прил* ordinary-looking.
невзыска́тел|ьный (-ен, -ьна, -ьно) *прил* undemanding.
нѐвидал|ь (-и) *ж* (*разг*) oddity; ~ **кака́я!** now there's a surprise!
невѝдан|ный (-, -на, -но) *прил* unprecedented.
невидѝм|ка (-ки; *gen pl* -ок) *м/ж* (*человек*) invisible being ◆ *ж* (*шпилька*) hairpin.
невидѝм|ый (-, -а, -о) *прил* invisible.
невидя́щий (-ая, -ее, -ие) *прил* unseeing.
невѝнен *прил см* **невѝнный**.
невѝнност|ь (-и) *ж* innocence.
невѝн|ный (-ен, -на, -но) *прил* innocent.
невино́вен *прил см* **невино́вный**.

невино́вност|ь (-и) *ж* innocence.
невино́в|ный (-ен, -на, -но) *прил* innocent.
невку́сен *прил см* **невку́сный**.
невку́сно *нареч:* **она́ ~ гото́вит** she is a bad cook; **здесь ~ ко́рмят** the food here is not very nice.
невку́с|ный (-ен, -на́, -но) *прил* (*суп, салат, пища*) tasteless.
невменя́емост|ь (-и) *ж* derangement; **в состоя́нии ~и** (*ЮР*) non compos mentis.
невменя́ем|ый (-, -а, -о) *прил* deranged.
невмеша́тельств|о (-а) *ср* non interference; (*ЭКОН*) laissez faire.
невнима́ни|е (-я) *ср* (*невнимательность*) lack of attention; (*равнодушие*) lack of concern.
невнима́телен *прил см* **невнима́тельный**.
невнима́тельност|ь (-и) *ж* (*см прил*) inattention; lack of consideration; carelessness.
невнима́тел|ьный (-ен, -ьна, -ьно) *прил* (*ученик, слушатель*) inattentive; (*незаботливый: сын, дочь*) inconsiderate; (: *отношение, обращение*) careless.
невня́т|ный (-ен, -на, -но) *прил* muffled.
нѐвод (-а) *м* fishing net.
невозвра́тен *прил см* **невозвра́тный**.
невозврати́м|ый (-, -а, -о) *прил* irretrievable.
невозвра́т|ный (-ен, на, -но) *прил* = **невозврати́мый**.
невозвраще́н|ец (-ца) *м* defector.
невозвраще́н|ка (-ки; *gen pl* -ок) *ж см* **невозвраще́нец**.
невозвраще́нц|а *итп сущ см* **невозвраще́нец**.
невоздержан|ный (-, -на, -но) *прил* highly strung (*BRIT*), high-strung (*US*).
невозмо́жен *прил см* **невозмо́жный**.
невозмо́жно *как сказ:* ~ +*infin* (*сделать, найти итп*) it is impossible to do ◆ *нареч* (*большой, трудный*) impossibly; (ѐто) ~ that's impossible.
невозмо́жност|ь (-и) *ж:* **до ~и** exceedingly.
невозмо́ж|ный (-ен, -на, -но) *прил* impossible; (*боль, жара*) unbearable; (*тон, поведение, вид*) insufferable.
невозмути́м|ый (-, -а, -о) *прил* (*человек*) unflappable; (*тон, ответ*) unruffled; (*тишина, спокойствие*) undisturbed.
нево́лен *прил см* **нево́льный**.
нево́л|ить (-ю, -ишь) *несов перех* (*разг*): ~ **кого́-н** +*infin* (*согласиться, отказаться итп*) to force sb to do.
нево́льник (-а) *м* slave.
нево́льниц|а (-ы) *ж см* **нево́льник**.
нево́ль|ный (-ен, -ьна, -ьно) *прил* (*ложь, вина*) unintentional; (*движение, улыбка, свидетель*) involuntary.
нево́л|я (-и) *ж* captivity; **в ~е** in captivity.
невообрази́м|ый (-, -а, -о) *прил* unimaginable.
невооружён|ный *прил* unarmed; **~ым гла́зом**

(без опти́ческих прибо́ров) with the naked eye; э́то ви́дно ~ым гла́зом *(перен)* it's plain for all to see.

невоспи́танный (-, -на, -но) *прил* ill-bred.

невоспри́мчив|ый (-, -а, -о) *прил:* ~ (к +*dat*) *(к зна́ниям)* unreceptive (to); *(к боле́зням)* immune (to).

невостре́бованный *прил* unclaimed.

невпопа́д *нареч (разг)* out of turn.

невразуми́тельный (-ен, -ьна, -ьно) *прил* unintelligible.

невралги́ческий (-ая, -ое, -ие) *прил* neuralgic.

невралги́|я (-и) *ж* neuralgia.

невра́стеник (-а) *м* neurotic.

неврастени́чный (-ен, -на, -но) *прил* neurotic.

неврастени́|я (-и) *ж (МЕД)* nervous tension.

невреди́м|ый (-, -а, -о) *прил (ло́дка, маши́на)* undamaged; *(челове́к)* unharmed.

невро́з (-а) *м* neurosis *(мн* neuroses).

невропато́лог (-а) *м* neurologist.

невтерпёж *как сказ (+dat)*: ей ~ пойти́/узна́ть she can't wait to go/find out; ему́ всё ~ he is always in a hurry.

невы́годный (-ен, -на, -но) *прил* unprofitable; *(усло́вия, ситуа́ция, впечатле́ние)* unfavourable *(BRIT)*, unfavorable *(US)*; *(вне́шность)* unattractive.

невы́держан|ный (-, -на, -но) *прил (челове́к, поведе́ние)* uncontrolled; *(стиль)* erratic.

невыноси́м|ый (-, -а, -о) *прил* unbearable, intolerable.

невыполне́ни|е (-я) *ср (обяза́тельства, пла́на)* failure to carry out; *(обеща́ния)* failure to keep.

невыполни́м|ый (-, -а, -о) *прил* not feasible.

невырази́м|ый (-, -а, -о) *прил* inexpressible.

невырази́тельный (-ен, -ьна, -ьно) *прил (лицо́, глаза́)* expressionless; *(расска́з, исполне́ние)* bland.

невысо́кий (-ая, -ое, -ие; -, -á, -о) *прил* low; *(челове́к)* short.

не́г|а (-и) *ж* bliss.

негати́в (-а) *м (ФОТО)* negative.

негати́вный (-ен, -на, -но) *прил* negative.

негашёный *прил*: **негашёная ма́рка** unused stamp; **негашёная и́звесть** quicklime.

не́где *как сказ (+infin)* there is nowhere to do; мне ~ жить I don't have anywhere to live; здесь ~ купи́ть еды́ there is nowhere to buy food around here.

неги́б|кий (-ая, -ое, -ие; -ок, -ка́, -ко) *прил (также перен)* inflexible.

негла́сный (-ен, -на, -но) *прил* secret.

неглубо́кий (-ая, -ое, -ие; -, -á, -о) *прил (я́ма, река́)* shallow; *(зна́ния, челове́к, чу́вство)* superficial; *(сон)* light.

неглу́п|ый (-, -á, -о) *прил* fairly clever; **он о́чень неглу́п** he's by no means stupid.

него́ *мест от* он, оно́.

него́ден *прил см* него́дный.

него́дность (-и) *ж* worthlessness; **приходи́ть**

(прийти́ *perf*) **в** ~ *(обору́дование)* to become defunct; *(оде́жда)* to be worn out.

него́дный (-ен, -на, -но) *прил (непригодный)* unusable; *(скве́рный)* good-for-nothing.

негодова́ни|е (-я) *ср* indignation.

негодова́ть (-ую) *несов неперех* to be indignant.

негоду́ющий (-ая, -ее, -ие) *прил* indignant.

негодя́|й (-я) *м* scoundrel.

негр (-а) *м* black man *(мн* men).

негра́мот|ный (-ен, -на, -но) *прил (челове́к, учени́к)* illiterate; *(содержа́щий оши́бки: речь)* ungrammatical; *(специали́ст, рабо́та)* incompetent.

негритёнок (-ёнка; *nom pl* -я́та, *gen pl* -я́т) *м* black child *(мн* children).

негритя́н|ка (-ки; *gen pl* -ок) *ж* black woman *(мн* women).

негритя́нский (-ая, -ое, -ие) *прил* black.

негритя́та *итп сущ см* негритёнок.

негро́м|кий (-кая, -кое, -кие; -ок, -ка́, -ко) *прил* quiet.

не́гры (-ов) *мн* black people *мн*.

неда́вн|ий (-яя, -ее, -ие) *прил* recent; до ~его вре́мени until recently.

неда́вно *нареч* recently.

недалёкий (-ая, -ое, -ие; -, -á, -ó) *прил (ме́сто)* nearby; *(расстоя́ние, путь)* short; *(неда́вний)* near; (-, -а, -о; *перен: челове́к, ум)* limited; **в** ~ом бу́дущем in the near future; **она́ недалека́ от и́стины** she is not far from the truth.

недалеко́ *нареч (жить, находи́ться)* nearby; *(идти́, е́хать)* not far ◆ *как сказ*: ~ (до +*gen*) it isn't far (to); ~ от +*gen* not far from; до утра́ ~ it will soon be morning.

недальнови́д|ный (-ен, -на, -но) *прил* short-sighted.

неда́ром *нареч (не напра́сно)* not in vain; *(не без це́ли)* for a reason; я ~ сто́лько учи́лся all of that studying has paid off; я ~ прие́хал сего́дня I do have a reason for coming today.

недви́жимость (-и) *ж* property.

недви́жимый *прил*: **недви́жимое иму́щество = недви́жимость**.

недвижи́м|ый (-, -а, -о) *прил (неподви́жный)* motionless; *(не спосо́бный дви́гаться: больно́й)* immobile.

недвусмы́слен|ный (-, -на, -но) *прил* unambiguous.

недееспосо́б|ный (-ен, -на, -но) *прил (ЮР: челове́к)* incapacitated; *(: организа́ция, структу́ра)* impotent, ineffective.

недействи́тельный (-ен, -ьна, -ьно) *прил* invalid.

неделика́т|ный (-ен, -на, -но) *прил (челове́к)* tactless; *(замеча́ние, вопро́с)* indelicate, tactless.

недели́м|ый (-, -а, -о) *прил* indivisible; **недели́мое число́** prime number.

неде́льный *прил (срок, о́тпуск)* one-week; *(запа́с, за́работок итп)* a или one week's.

неде́л|я (-и) *ж* week; **че́рез ~ю** in a week; **на про́шлой/э́той/сле́дующей ~е** last/this/next week.

недобо́р (-а) *м* shortage.

недоброжела́тел|ьный (-ен, -ьна, -ьно) *прил* hostile.

недоброка́чествен|ный (-, -на, -но) *прил* poor-quality.

недобросо́вест|ный (-ен, -на, -но) *прил* (*небрежный*) unconscientious; (*нечестный*) unscrupulous.

недо́бр|ый (-, -á, -о) *прил* unkind; (*чувства, намерения*) ill; (*время, сон, предчувствие*) bad; **~ые ве́сти** ill tidings.

недова́р|ить (-ю́, -áришь; *impf* **недова́ривать**) *сов перех* to undercook.

недове́ри|е (-я) *ср* mistrust, distrust; **относи́ться (отнести́сь** *perf*) **к кому́-н/чему́-н с ~м** to be mistrustful *или* distrustful of sb/sth.

недове́рчивость (-и) *ж* mistrust, distrust.

недове́рчив|ый (-, -а, -о) *прил* mistrustful, distrustful.

недове́с (-а) *м* shortfall (*in weight*).

недове́|сить (-шу, -сишь; *impf* **недове́шивать**) *сов перех*: **~ кому́-н чего́-н** to give sb too little of sth.

недово́л|ьный (-ен, -ьна, -ьно) *прил* discontented, dissatisfied; **она́ всем ~ьна** she is never satisfied.

недово́льстви|е (-а) *ср*: **~** (+*instr*) dissatisfaction (with).

недога́длив|ый (-, -а, -о) *прил* inscrutable.

недогля́|де́ть (-жу́, -ди́шь) *сов перех* (*ошибки, опечатки*) to overlook ♦ *неперех*: **~ за** +*acc* to fail to keep an eye on.

недоговор|и́ть (-ю́, -и́шь; *impf* **недогова́ривать**) *сов перех* to leave unsaid; **он что́-то недогова́ривает** there is something that he's not saying.

недоде́лан|ный (-, -на, -но) *прил* unfinished.

недоде́л|ка (-ки; *gen pl* -ок) *ж* loose end.

недоеда́|ть *несов неперех* to eat badly; **они́ постоя́нно ~ют** they never eat enough.

недозре́лый *прил* unripe.

недойм|ка (-ки; *gen pl* -ок) *ж* arrears *мн*.

недока́зан|ный (-, -на, -но) *прил* unproven.

недо́лг|ий (-ая, -ое, -ие; -ог, -á, -го) *прил* short.

недо́лго *нареч* for a short time, not for long ♦ *как сказ* (*разг*): **мне ~ э́то сде́лать** it won't take me long (to do); **~ по́сле** +*gen* not long after; **я там бу́ду ~** I won't be there for long; **ему́ оста́лось ~ (жить)** he hasn't got long (to live).

недолгове́ч|ный (-ен, -на, -но) *прил* short-lived.

недо́лог *прил см* **недо́лгий**.

недолю́блива|ть (-ю) *несов перех* to dislike.

недомога́ни|е (-я) *ср* queasiness; **чу́вствовать** (*impf*) **~** to feel queasy.

недомога́|ть (-ю) *несов неперех* to feel unwell.

недомо́лв|ка (-ки; *gen pl* -ок) *ж* indirect reference; **говори́ть** (*impf*) **о чём-н ~ми** to refer to sth indirectly.

недомы́сли|е (-я) *ср*: **по ~ю** without thinking.

недоно́шен|ный (-, -а, -о) *прил*: **~ ребёнок** premature baby.

недооцен|и́ть (-ю́, -éнишь; *impf* **недооце́нивать**) *сов перех* to underestimate.

недооце́н|ка (-и) *ж* underestimation.

недопусти́м|ый (-, -а, -о) *прил* not permissible.

недорабо́т|ка (-и) *ж* = **недоде́лка**.

недора́звит|ый (-, -а, -о) *прил* underdeveloped; (*разг*) dumb.

недоразуме́ни|е (-я) *ср* misunderstanding.

недо́рого *нареч* cheaply.

недорог|о́й (-, -á, -о) *прил* inexpensive.

недоса́лива|ть (-ю) *несов см* **недосоли́ть**.

недосмо́тр (-а) *м* oversight; **по ~у** through lack of attention.

недосм|отре́ть (-отрю́, -о́тришь) *сов неперех* = **недогляде́ть**.

недосол|и́ть (-ю́, -о́лишь; *impf* **недоса́ливать**) *сов перех*: **ты ~и́л суп** you haven't put enough salt in the soup.

недосп|а́ть (-лю́, -и́шь; *impf* **недосыпа́ть**) *сов неперех* to not get enough sleep.

недоста|ва́ть (*3sg* -ёт) *несов безл* (+*gen*; *не хватать*) to lack; (*быть нужным*) to need; **ей ~ёт терпе́ния** she lacks patience; **нам о́чень тебя́ ~ва́ло** we really needed you; **э́того ещё ~ва́ло!** as if that were not enough!

недоста́т|ок (-ка; *nom pl* -ки) *м* shortage, lack; (*в характере, в работе*) shortcoming.

недоста́точен *прил см* **недоста́точный**.

недоста́точно *нареч* insufficiently ♦ *как сказ* (+*gen*): **у нас ~ еды́/де́нег** we don't have enough food/money; **я ~ зна́ю об э́том** I don't know enough about it; **~ критикова́ть, на́до помо́чь** it's not enough to criticize, you need to help.

недоста́точность (-и) *ж* inadequacy; **серде́чная ~** heart failure.

недоста́точ|ный (-ен, -на, -но) *прил* insufficient.

недоста́ч|а (-и) *ж* (*разг: материалов, оборудования*) lack; (*денег: при проверке*) shortfall; **у нас в ка́ссе ~ де́нег** the till is short.

недостаю́щий (-ая, -ое, -ие) *прил* missing.

недостижи́м|ый (-, -а, -о) *прил* (*высота, уровень*) unreachable; (*мечта, идеал*) unattainable.

недостове́р|ный (-ен, -на, -но) *прил* unreliable.

недосто́й|ный (-ен, -йна, -йно) *прил*: **~** (+*gen*) unworthy (of).

недоступ|ный (-ен, -на, -но) *прил* (*также перен*) inaccessible; (*цена*) unaffordable; (*человек*) unapproachable; **это ~но моему пониманию** it is beyond my understanding.

недосуг *как сказ*: **ему ~** (+*infin* ...) (*разг*) he can never find the time (to ...).

недосчита́|ться (-юсь; *impf* **недосчи́тываться**) *сов возв* (+*gen*) to be short; **я ~лся пяти до́лларов** I'm five dollars short; **мы ~лись двух челове́к** we are missing two people.

недосыпа́|ть (-ю) *несов от* **недоспа́ть**.

недосяга́ем|ый (-, -а, -о) *прил* unattainable.

недотро́г|а (-и) *м/ж* (*разг*): **он тако́й ~** he's very touchy.

недоумева́|ть (-ю) *несов неперех* to be perplexed *или* bewildered.

недоумева́ющий (-ая, -ее, -ие) *прил* perplexed, bewildered.

недоуме́ни|е (-я) *ср* perplexity, bewilderment.

недоуме́нный *прил* perplexed, bewildered.

недоу́ч|ка (-ки; *gen pl* -ек) *м/ж* (*разг*): **он/она́ ~** he/she is badly educated.

недочёт (-а) *м* (*в подсчётах*) shortfall; (*обычно мн: в работе*) deficiency.

не́др|а (-) *мн* depths *мн*; **в ~х земли́** in the bowels of the earth; **в ~х души́** in the depths of one's soul; **в ~х о́бщества** at the heart of society.

недремлющий (-ая, -ее, -ие) *прил* vigilant.

не́друг (-а) *м* foe.

недружелюб|ный (-ен, -на, -но) *прил* unfriendly.

недуг (-а) *м* ailment.

недурно *нареч* not badly.

недур|ной (-ён, -на́, -но) *прил* not bad; **он ~ён собо́й** he's not bad-looking.

неё *мест см* **она́**.

неесте́ствен|ный (-, -на, -но) *прил* unnatural.

нежда́н|ный (-ен, -на, -но) *прил* unexpected.

нежела́ни|е (-я) *ср* unwillingness.

нежела́тель|ный (-ен, -ьна, -ьно) *прил* undesirable.

не́жен *прил см* **не́жный**.

нежена́т|ый *прил* unmarried.

не́жен|ка (-ки; *gen pl* -ок) *м/ж* (*разг*) softy.

неживо́й *прил* dead; (*природа, мир*) inorganic; (*перен: взгляд, голос*) lifeless.

нежизнеспосо́б|ный (-ен, -на, -но) *прил* (*организм, растение*) incapable of surviving; (*перен: теория*) impractical.

нежило́й *прил* nonresidential.

не́ж|иться (-усь, -ишься) *несов возв* to laze about; ~ (*impf*) **на со́лнце** to bask in the sun.

не́жнича|ть (-ю) *несов неперех* (*разг*): **~ с** +*instr* to make a fuss of.

не́жност|ь (-и) *ж* tenderness; **шепта́ть** (*impf*) **~и кому́-н на́ ухо** to whisper sweet nothings in sb's ear.

не́жно *нареч* gently.

не́ж|ный (-ен, -на́, -но) *прил* tender, gentle;

(*кожа, пух*) soft; (*запах*) subtle; (*сложение, здоровье*) fragile.

незабве́н|ный (-ен, -на, -но) *прил* beloved.

незабу́д|ка (-ки; *gen pl* -ок) *ж* forget-me-not.

незабыва́ем|ый (-, -а, -о) *прил* unforgettable.

незави́д|ный (-ен, -на, -но) *прил* unenviable.

незави́симо *нареч* independently; **~ от** +*gen* (*условий, времени*) regardless of.

незави́симост|ь (-и) *ж* independence.

незави́сим|ый (-, -а, -о) *прил* independent.

незави́сящий (-ая, -ее, -ие) *прил*: **по ~им от нас обстоя́тельствам** due to circumstances beyond our control.

незада́ч|а (-и) *ж* (*разг*) pain.

незада́члив|ый (-, -а, -о) *прил* (*разг*) unlucky.

незадо́лго *нареч*: **~ до** +*gen* *или* **пе́ред** +*instr* shortly before.

незаинтересо́ван|ный (-, -на, -но) *прил* (*ученик, слушатели итп*) indifferent; (*лицо, сторона*) disinterested.

незако́нност|ь (-и) *ж* illegality.

незако́н|ный (-ен, -на, -но) *прил* illegal; (*ребёнок*) illegitimate.

незако́нчен|ный (-, -на, -но) *прил* unfinished, incomplete.

незамедли́тель|ный (-ен, -ьна, -ьно) *прил* immediate.

незамени́м|ый (-, -а, -о) *прил* irreplaceable.

незаме́тен *прил см* **незаме́тный**.

незаме́тно *нареч* (*изменяться*) imperceptibly ♦ *как сказ* it isn't noticeable; **он ~ подошёл/ушёл** he approached/left unnoticed; **~, что ты всю ночь не спал** you may not have slept all night, but it doesn't show.

незаме́т|ный (-ен, -на, -но) *прил* not noticeable; (*перемены, изменения*) imperceptible; (*перен: человек, внешность*) unremarkable.

незаме́чен|ный (-, -на, -но) *прил* unnoticed.

незаму́жняя *прил* unmarried.

незамыслова́т|ый (-, -а, -о) *прил* uncomplicated.

неза́нят|ый *прил* (*дом, помещение*) unoccupied; (*человек, работник*) not occupied; (*вечер, утро*) free; **~ая часть населе́ния** the non-working population.

незапа́мятный *прил*: **с ~ых времён** from time immemorial; **в ~ые времена́** in the days of yore.

незара́з|ный (-ен, -на, -но) *прил* noncontagious.

незаслу́жен|ный (-, -на, -но) *прил* undeserved.

незауря́д|ный (-ен, -на, -но) *прил* exceptional.

не́зачем *как сказ* (*разг*): **~ ходи́ть/э́то де́лать** there's no reason to go/do it.

незва́н|ый *прил* uninvited.

нездоро́в|иться (*3sg* -ится) *несов безл*: **мне ~ится** I feel unwell, I don't feel well.

нездоро́в|ый (-, -а, -о) *прил* unhealthy; **он нездоро́в** he isn't well; **у него́ ~ цвет лица́** his face is an unhealthy colour; **у неё ~ вид** she doesn't look well.

неземно́й *прил* (*тело, объект итп*) alien;

(*силы, красота*) unearthly.
незнако́мец (-ца) *м* stranger.
незнако́м|ка (-ки; *gen pl* -ок) *ж см* **незнако́мец**.
незнако́мца *итп сущ см* **незнако́мец**.
незнако́м|ый (-, -а, -о) *прил* unfamiliar; **я незнако́м с ним** I am not acquainted with him; **я незнако́м с э́тими фа́ктами** I am not familiar with these facts.
незна́ни|е (-я) *ср* ignorance.
незнача́щий (-ая, -ее, -ие) *прил* meaningless.
незначи́тельный (-ен, -ьна, -ьно) *прил* (*небольшой*) insignificant; (*несущественный*) trivial.
незре́л|ый (-, -а, -о) *прил* (*яблоко итп*) unripe; (*человек, книга*) immature; (*мысль*) half-formed.
незри́м|ый (-, -а, -о) *прил* anonymous; (*бой*) hidden.
незы́блем|ый (-, -а, -о) *прил* unshakable.
неизбе́жен *прил см* **неизбе́жный**.
неизбе́жно *как сказ:* **э́то ~** it's inevitable.
неизбе́жный (-ен, -на, -но) *прил* inescapable, inevitable.
неизве́дан|ный (-, -на, -но) *прил* (*путь, пространство*) unexplored; (*счастье, чувство*) new.
неизве́стен *прил см* **неизве́стный**.
неизве́стно *как сказ* it's not known; **никому́ ~** nobody knows; **~ кто/что/почему́** Heaven (only) knows who/what/why.
неизве́стн|ое (-ого; *decl like adj*) *ср* (*МАТ*) unknown.
неизве́стност|ь (-и) *ж* uncertainty; (*незаметное существование*) obscurity.
неизве́стн|ый (-ен, -на, -но) *прил* unknown ♦ (-ного; *decl like adj*) *м* stranger.
неизглади́м|ый (-, -а, -о) *прил* indelible.
неизлечи́м|ый (-, -а, -о) *прил* (*болезнь*) incurable; (*больной*) terminally ill.
неизме́н|ный (-ен, -на, -но) *прил* (*постоянный*) unchanging; (*верный*) steadfast.
неизменя́ем|ый (-, -а, -о) *прил* invariable.
неизмери́мо *нареч* immeasurably.
неизмери́м|ый (-, -а, -о) *прил* immeasurable.
неизу́ченный *прил* (*вопрос, проблема*) unexplored.
неиме́ни|е (-я) *ср:* **за ~м** +*gen* for want of; **за ~м лу́чшего** for want of something better.
неимове́рный (-ен, -на, -но) *прил* extreme.
неиму́щий (-ая, -ее, -ие) *прил* deprived.
неинтере́с|ный (-ен, -на, -но) *прил* boring, uninteresting; (*некрасивый*) plain.
неискорени́м|ый (-, -а, -о) *прил* deep-rooted.
неи́скрен|ний (-няя, -нее, -ние; -ен, -на, -но или не) *прил* insincere.
неискушённый *прил* unsophisticated.
неисполне́ни|е (-я) *ср* failure to carry out.
неисполни́м|ый (-, -а, -о) *прил* unrealizable.

неиспо́льзованный *прил* unused.
неиспо́рченный *прил* (*человек*) innocent.
неиспра́вен *прил см* **неиспра́вный**.
неисправи́м|ый (-, -а, -о) *прил* (*ошибка*) irreversible; (*пьяница*) incorrigible.
неиспра́вност|ь (-и) *ж* (*механизма, станка*) fault.
неиспра́в|ный (-ен, -на, -но) *прил* (*механизм, станок*) faulty; (*плательщик, поставщик*) unreliable.
неиспы́танный *прил* (*самолёт, машина*) untested; (*чувство, счастье*) unexperienced.
неиссле́дованный *прил* (*вопрос, район*) unexplored.
неиссяка́ем|ый (-, -а, -о) *прил* inexhaustible.
нейстовств|о (-а) *ср* (*исступление*) frenzy; (*жестокость*) atrocity; **приходи́ть (прийти́** *perf*) **в ~** to go into a frenzy.
нейстовств|овать (-ую) *несов неперех* to be in a frenzy; (*перен: буря, метель*) to rage; (: *каратели*) to commit atrocities.
нейстов|ый (-, -а, -о) *прил* (*ужас, радость*) intense; (*крики*) frenzied; (*аплодисменты, буря*) wild; (*грохот*) crashing.
неистощи́м|ый (-, -а, -о) *прил* inexhaustible.
неисчерпа́ем|ый (-, -а, -о) *прил* inexhaustible.
неисчисли́м|ый (-, -а, -о) *прил* (*силы*) countless; (*неприятности*) innumerable.
ней *мест см* **она́**.
нейло́н (-а) *м* nylon.
нейло́новый *прил* nylon *опред*.
нейрохиру́рг (-а) *м* neurosurgeon.
нейрохирурги́|я (-и) *ж* neurosurgery.
нейтра́лен *прил см* **нейтра́льный**.
нейтрализа́ци|я (-и) *ж* neutrality.
нейтрализ|ова́ть (-у́ю) (*не*)*сов перех* to neutralize.
нейтралите́т (-а) *м* neutrality.
нейтра́л|ьный (-ен, -ьна, -ьно) *прил* neutral.
нейтро́н (-а) *м* neutron.
неказ́ист|ый (-, -а, -о) *прил* unsightly.
нека́чественно *нареч:* **~ сде́ланный** badly made.
нека́чествен|ный (-ен, -на, -но) *прил* poor-quality.
неквалифици́рован|ный (-, -на, -но) *прил* (*работник*) unqualified, unskilled; (*работа*) unskilled.
не́кем *мест см* **не́кого**.
не́к|ий (-ого; *f* -ая, *nt* -ое, *pl* -ие) *мест* a certain; (*момент, время*) some.
не́когда *как сказ* (*читать, гуля́ть*) there is no time; **ей ~** she is busy; **ей ~** +*infin* ... she has no time to ....
не́к|ого (*как кто; см* **Table 6**) *мест:* **~ спроси́ть/позва́ть** there is nobody to ask/call.
некомпете́нт|ный (-ен, -на, -но) *прил* (*человек*) incompetent; (*суждение*)

inappropriate.

не́кому *мест см* **не́кого**.

не́котор|ые (-ых) *мест* (*отде́льные*) several.

не́котор|ый (-ого; *f* -ая, *nt* -ое, *pl* -ые) *мест* some; **с ~ых пор** for some time; **в ~ой сте́пени** to a certain degree; **в ~ом ро́де** somewhat; **~ым о́бразом** somehow; *см также* **не́которые**.

некраси́в|ый (-, -а, -о) *прил* (*челове́к, лицо́*) unattractive, ugly; (*посту́пок, поведе́ние*) ugly.

некроло́г (-а) *м* obituary.

некста́ти *нареч* (*сказа́ть, яви́ться итп*) at the wrong time ♦ *как сказ*: **э́то ~** this is untimely.

некта́р (-а) *м* nectar.

не́кто *мест* a certain person (*мн* certain people).

не́куда *как сказ* (*идти́, пое́хать*) there is nowhere; **да́льше** *или* **ху́же/лу́чше ~** (*разг*) it can't get any worse/better.

некульту́р|ный (-ен, -на, -но) *прил* (*расте́ние*) uncultivated; (*челове́к, поведе́ние*) uncivilized.

некуря́щ|ий (-его; *decl like adj*) *м* non-smoker; ♦ (-ая, -ее, -ие) *прил*: **~ мужчи́на, некуря́щая же́нщина** non-smoker.

нела́дно *как сказ* (*в семье́, на душе́*) there's unease.

нела́д|ы (-ов) *мн* (*разг: в семье́, в коллекти́ве*) tension *ед*; (: *с учёбой, с рабо́той*) problems *мн*.

нелега́л|ьный (-ен, -ьна, -ьно) *прил* (*газе́та, въезд*) illegal.

нелегити́м|ный (-ен, -на, -но) *прил* illegitimate.

неле́г|кий (-кая, -кое, -кие; -ок, -ка́, -ко́) *прил* (*но́ша, груз*) heavy; (*зада́ние, рабо́та*) difficult.

нелегко́ *как сказ* it's not easy; **мне нелегко́ согласи́ться на э́то** it's not easy for me to agree to this.

неле́пост|ь (-и) *ж* stupidity; **говори́ть** (*impf*)/ **де́лать** (*impf*) **~и** to say/do stupid things.

неле́п|ый (-, -а, -о) *прил* stupid.

нелёст|ный (-ен, -на, -но) *прил* (*выска́зывание, характери́стика*) unflattering.

нелётный *прил*: **~ая пого́да** poor weather for flying; **~ое вре́мя** not a good time to fly.

нело́в|кий (-кая, -кое, -кие; -ок, -ка́, -ко) *прил* awkward; **нело́вкое положе́ние** awkward situation.

нело́вко *нареч* awkwardly ♦ *как сказ* (*говори́ть, проси́ть*) it's awkward; **мне ~ (перед ней)** I feel awkward (with her).

нело́вкост|ь (-и) *ж* awkwardness; **чу́вствовать** (*почу́вствовать* *perf*) **~** to feel awkward.

нело́вок *прил см* **нело́вкий**.

нелоги́чный (-ен, -на, -но) *прил* (*до́вод, доказа́тельство*) illogical.

нельзя́ *как сказ* (*невозмо́жно*) it is impossible; (*не разреша́ется*) it is forbidden; **~ ли?** would it be possible?; **~ сказа́ть, что она́ умна́** she can hardly be described as clever; **как ~ лу́чше** as well as could be expected.

нелюби́м|ый (-, -а, -о) *прил* unloved.

нелюди́м|ый (-, -а, -о) *прил* (*челове́к, сосе́д*)

unsociable.

нём *мест см* **он, оно́**.

нема́ло *нареч* (+*gen*; *де́нег*) a good deal of; (*иде́й, люде́й, книг*) a good few.

немалова́ж|ный (-ен, -на, -но) *прил* significant.

нема́л|ый *прил* (*дохо́д*) reasonable; (*труд*) much; (*успе́х*) considerable; (*чин, до́лжность*) important; **~ые де́ньги** a sizeable sum of money.

неме́длен|ен *прил см* **неме́дленный**.

неме́дленно *нареч* immediately.

неме́длен|ный (-ен, -на, -но) *прил* immediate.

немеркну́щий (-ая, -ее, -ие) *прил* (*также перен*) unfading.

немета́лл (-а) *м* (*хим*) nonmetal.

неме́|ть (-ю; *perf* **онеме́ть**) *несов неперех* (*от у́жаса, от восто́рга*) to be struck dumb; (*нога́, руки́*) to go numb.

не́мец (-ца) *м* German.

неме́ц|кий (-ая, -ое, -ие) *прил* German; **~ язы́к** German.

немило́ст|ь (-и) *ж* disfavour; **впада́ть (впасть** *perf*) **в ~** to fall out of favour (*BRIT*) *или* favor (*US*).

неминуе́м|ый (-, -а, -о) *прил* (*беда́, собы́тия*) unavoidable.

не́м|ка (-ки; *gen pl* -ок) *ж см* **не́мец**.

немно́г|ие (-их; *decl like adj*) *мн* few.

немно́г|ий (-ая, -ое, -ие) *прил* (*ча́сти, сло́ва, лю́ди*) a few; **~им ху́же/лу́чше/бо́льше/ ме́ньше** a little worse/better/more/less; **за ~им исключе́нием** with few exceptions.

немно́го *нареч* (*отдохну́ть, ста́рше*) a little, a bit; (*друзе́й, слов*) a few.

немно́г|ое (-ого; *decl like adj*) *ср* (*мо́жно сказа́ть уви́деть*) little.

немногосло́в|ный (-ен, -на, -но) *прил* (*о́тзыв, изложе́ние*) brief; (*челове́к*) laconic.

немногочи́слен|ный (-, -на, -но) *прил* (*оши́бки*) few; **на дипломати́ческом приёме бы́ло ~ное о́бщество** there weren't many (people present) at the diplomatic reception.

немно́жко *нареч* (*разг*) = **немно́го**.

немну́щийся (-аяся, -ееся, -иеся) *прил* (*брю́ки, мате́рия, ю́бка*) crease-resistant.

немо́|й (-, -а́, -о) *прил* (*челове́к*) dumb; (*перен: ночь, лес, глубина́*) silent; (: *вопро́с, упре́к*) implied ♦ (-о́го; *decl like adj*) *м* mute; **нема́я сце́на** situation in which somebody freezes in surprise, shock etc; **немо́й фильм** silent film.

немолодо́й (-о́лод, -олода́, -о́лодо) *прил* old.

немота́ (-ы́) *ж* (*ребёнка, мужчи́ны*) dumbness.

не́мощ|ный (-ен, -на, -но) *прил* (*стари́к, челове́к*) sick, ailing.

нему́ *мест от* **он, оно́**.

немудрён|ый (-, -а, -о) *прил* (*разг*) simple.

не́мца *итп сущ см* **не́мец**.

немы́слим|ый (-, -а, -о) *прил* unthinkable.

ненави́|деть (-жу, -дишь) *несов перех* to hate.

ненави́ст|ный (-ен, -на, -но) *прил* (*челове́к, рабо́та*) hateful.

нéнавист|ь (-и) *ж* hatred.

ненагля́дный *прил* (*разг*) beloved.

ненадёж|ный (-ен, -на, -но) *прил* (*человек, сведения*) unreliable; (*механизм*) unsafe.

ненадобност|ь (-и) *ж*: **вы́бросить что-н за ~ю** to throw sth out *или* away because it is not needed.

ненадóлго *нареч* for a short while.

ненападéни|е (-я) *ср* nonaggression.

ненарóком *нареч* (*разг: случайно*) without meaning to.

ненáст|ный (-ен, -на, -но) *прил* (*день, осень*) wet and dismal.

ненастоя́щий (-ая, -ее, -ие) *прил* (*мех, золото*) artificial; (*дружба, любовь*) contrived.

ненáсть|е (-я) *ср* awful weather.

ненасы́т|ный (-ен, -на, -но) *прил* (*также перен*) insatiable.

ненатурáл|ьный (-ен, -ьна, -ьно) *прил* (*мех, свет*) artificial; (*смех*) forced; (*поведение*) affected.

ненормáлен *прил см* **ненормáльный**.

ненормáльност|ь (-и) *ж* abnormality.

ненормáл|ьный (-ен, -ьна, -ьно) *прил* abnormal; (*разг: сумасшедший*) mad ◆ (-ьного; *decl like adj*) *м* (*разг*) crackpot.

ненýж|ный (-ен, -нá, -но) *прил* (*осторожность*) unnecessary; (*человек*) dispensable; (*инструмент*) inessential.

необдýманно *нареч* (*поступить*) rashly.

необдýман|ный (-, -на, -но) *прил* ill-considered.

необеспéченный *прил* poor.

необитáем|ый (-, -а, -о) *прил* (*место*) uninhabited; **~ óстров** desert island.

необозри́м|ый (-, -а, -о) *прил* (*просторы, дали*) vast.

необоснóван|ный (-, -на, -но) *прил* unfounded.

необрабóтанный *прил* (*земля*) uncultivated; (*деталь*) unfinished; (*металл, дерево*) untreated.

необразóван|ный (-, -на, -но) *прил* uneducated.

необýздан|ный (-, -на, -но) *прил* (*страсть*) unbridled; (*человек, характер*) ungovernable.

необходи́мо *как сказ* it is necessary; **мне ~ с Вáми поговори́ть** I really need to talk to you.

необходи́мост|ь (-и) *ж* (*увидеть, сделать*) need, necessity; **~ в** +*prp* need for; **по мéре ~и** as (far as is) necessary; **по ~и** out of necessity; **предмéты пéрвой ~и** bare essentials.

необходи́м|ый (-, -а, -о) *прил* necessary.

необщи́тел|ьный (-ен, -ьна, -ьно) *прил* unsociable.

необъекти́в|ный (-ен, -на, -но) *прил* (*отношение, критика*) not objective, bias(s)ed.

необъясни́м|ый (-, -а, -о) *прил* inexplicable.

необъя́т|ный (-ен, -на, -но) *прил* (*просторы, дали, познания*) vast.

необыкновéн|ный (-ен, -на, -но) *прил* exceptional.

необычáй|ный (-ен, -йна, -йно) *прил* = **необыкновéнный**.

необы́ч|ный (-ен, -на, -но) *прил* (*человек, явление*) unusual.

необязáтел|ьный (-ен, -ьна, -ьно) *прил* (*предмет, лекция*) optional; (*факты*) nonessential; (*человек*) unreliable.

неограни́чен|ный (-, -на, -но) *прил* unlimited; **неограни́ченная монáрхия** absolute monarchy.

неодинáков|ый (-, -а, -о) *прил* (*размер*) different.

неоднокрáтен *прил см* **неоднокрáтный**.

неоднокрáтно *нареч* (*говорить*) repeatedly; (*повторять*) time after time.

неоднокрáт|ный (-ен, -на, -но) *прил* repeated.

неоднорóд|ный (-ен, -на, -но) *прил* (*масса*) heterogeneous; (*тесто*) mixed; (*явления*) dissimilar.

неодобрéни|е (-я) *ср* disapproval.

неодобри́тел|ьный (-ен, -ьна, -ьно) *прил* disapproving.

неодоли́м|ый (-, -а, -о) *прил* (*упорство, страх*) insurmountable; (*сила*) invincible.

неодушевлённый *прил* inanimate.

неожи́данно *нареч* unexpectedly.

неожи́данност|ь (-и) *ж* (*атаки*) unexpectedness; (*приятная, большая*) surprise; **вздрáгивать** (**вздрóгнуть** *perf*) **от ~и** to start in surprise.

неожи́дан|ный (-, -на, -но) *прил* unexpected.

неокончáтел|ьный (-ен, -ьна, -ьно) *прил* (*вариант, решение*) not final.

неокóнченный *прил* unfinished.

неоли́т (-а) *м* Neolithic.

неологи́зм (-а) *м* neologism.

неóн (-а) *м* (*хим*) neon.

неонаци́зм (-а) *м* Neo-Nazism.

неóновый *прил* neon *опред*.

неопáсен *прил см* **неопáсный**.

неопáсно *нареч* safely ◆ *как сказ* it's safe, it's not dangerous.

неопáс|ный (-ен, -на, -но) *прил* (*путешествие, место*) safe; (*противник, заболевание*) harmless.

неописýем|ый (-, -а, -о) *прил* indescribable.

неоплáт|ный (-ен, -на, -но) *прил*: **~ долг** debt that cannot be repaid; **я твой ~ должни́к** I'm greatly indebted to you.

неоплáченный *прил* unpaid.

неопóзнан|ный (-, -на, -но) *прил* unidentified.

неоправдан|ный *прил* (*вывод, обвинение*) unjustified; (*траты, потери*) unwarranted.

неопределённост|ь (-и) *ж* uncertainty.

неопределён|ный (-, -на, -но) *прил (время, срок)* indefinite; *(путь)* undecided; *(ответ, выражение, жест)* vague; *(звук)* indistinct.

неопровержи́м|ый (-, -а, -о) *прил* irrefutable.

неопря́т|ный (-ен, -на, -но) *прил* untidy.

неопублико́ванный *прил* unpublished.

нео́пытен *прил см* **нео́пытный.**

нео́пытност|ь (-и) *ж* inexperience.

нео́пыт|ный (-ен, -на, -но) *прил* inexperienced.

неорганизо́ванный *прил* disorganized; *(массы)* unorganized.

неоргани́ческий (-ая, -ое, -ие) *прил* inorganic.

неосведомлённый *прил* ill-informed.

неосла́б|ный (-ен, -на, -но) *прил (надзор)* constant; *(контроль)* unrelenting.

неосмотри́тель|ный (-ен, -ьна, -ьно) *прил (человек)* careless; *(поступок)* imprudent.

неоспори́м|ый (-, -а, -о) *прил (преимущество)* unquestionable; *(доказательство)* incontrovertible.

неосторо́жен *прил см* **неосторо́жный.**

неосторо́жност|ь (-и) *ж* carelessness.

неосторо́ж|ный (-ен, -на, -но) *прил (поступок)* careless; *(поведение, высказывание)* imprudent.

неосуществи́м|ый (-, -а, -о) *прил* unrealizable, unattainable.

неотврати́м|ый (-, -а, -о) *прил* inevitable.

неотдели́м|ый (-, -а, -о) *прил:* ~ **(от** +*gen)* inseparable (from).

неотёсан|ный (-, -а, -о) *прил* unpolished; *(перен: разг)* crude.

нео́ткуда *как сказ:* мне *итп* де́нег взять ~ I *итп* can't get money from anywhere.

неотло́жен *прил см* **неотло́жный.**

неотло́жк|а (-и) *ж (разг: учреждение)* ambulance service; *(: машина)* emergency medical care.

неотло́ж|ный (-ен, -на, -но) *прил* urgent; **неотло́жная медици́нская по́мощь** emergency medical service.

неотрази́м|ый (-, -а, -о) *прил (атака, красота)* irresistible; *(перен: довод)* compelling; *(удар, впечатление)* powerful.

неотсту́п|ный (-ен, -на, -но) *прил (мечта, мысль)* constant; *(преследование)* relentless.

неотъе́млем|ый (-, -а, -о) *прил (право)* inalienable; *(часть)* integral.

неофаши́зм (-а) *м* Neo-fascism.

неофаши́ст (-а) *м* Neo-fascist.

неофаши́стский (-ая, -ое, -ие) *прил* Neo-fascist.

неофициа́ль|ный (-ен, -ьна, -ьно) *прил* unofficial.

неохо́т|а (-ы) *ж (разг: нежелание)* reluctance ♦ *как сказ:* мне ~ спо́рить I don't feel like arguing.

неохо́тно *нареч* reluctantly.

неохо́тный *прил* reluctant.

неоцени́м|ый (-, -а, -о) *прил* invaluable.

неощути́м|ый (-, -а, -о) *прил (незаметный)* imperceptible.

Непа́л (-а) *м* Nepal.

непа́льский (-ая, -ое, -ие) *прил* Nepalese.

непа́рный *прил (перчатки, ботинки)* odd.

непереводи́м|ый (-, -а, -о) *прил* untranslatable.

непередава́ем|ый (-, -а, -о) *прил (страх, впечатление)* inexpressible.

непереходный *прил:* ~ **глаго́л** *(линг)* intransitive verb.

непеча́тный *прил (разг)* unprintable.

непи́саный *прил* unwritten.

неплатёж (-ежа́) *м* nonpayment.

неплатёжеспосо́б|ный (-ен, -на, -но) *прил (человек)* unable to pay; *(предприятие)* insolvent.

неплате́льщик (-а) *м (налогов, алиментов)* defaulter.

неплате́льщиц|а (-ы) *ж см* **неплате́льщик.**

неплодоро́д|ный (-ен, -на, -но) *прил* infertile, barren.

непло́тно *нареч* not tightly *или* firmly.

непло́хо *нареч* not badly, quite well ♦ *как сказ* it's not bad.

непл|охо́й (-óх, -оха́, -óхо) *прил* not bad, quite good.

непобеди́м|ый (-, -а, -о) *прил* invincible.

неповинове́ни|е (-я) *ср* disobedience, insubordination.

неповоро́тлив|ый (-, -а, -о) *прил (неуклюжий)* clumsy; *(медлительный)* slow.

неповтори́м|ый (-, -а, -о) *прил* unique.

непого́д|а (-ы) *ж* bad weather.

непогреши́м|ый (-, -а, -о) *прил* infallible.

неподалёку *нареч (разг)* not far off ♦ *предл:* ~ **от** +*gen* not far from.

неподви́жен *прил см* **неподви́жный.**

неподви́жно *нареч* without moving.

неподви́ж|ный (-ен, -на, -но) *прил (больной, рука, туман)* motionless; *(взгляд)* fixed; *(лицо)* rigid; *(медлительный)* slow.

неподда́ющ|ийся (-аяся, -ееся, -иеся) *прил (разг: перевоспитанию, лечению)* resistant, unresponsive.

неподде́ль|ный (-ен, -ьна, -ьно) *прил (также перен)* genuine.

неподку́п|ный (-ен, -на, -но) *прил (человек, ревизор)* incorruptible; *(совесть, принципы)* honourable *(BRIT)*, honorable *(US)*.

неподража́ем|ый (-, -а, -о) *прил* inimitable.

неподходя́щ|ий (-ая, -ее, -ие) *прил (место)* unsuitable; *(время)* inappropriate.

неподчине́ни|е (-я) *ср (закону, властям)* insubordination.

неподъём|ный (-ен, -на, -но) *прил (разг)* very heavy.

непозволи́тель|ный (-ен, -ьна, -ьно) *прил* inadmissible.

непоколеби́м|ый (-, -а, -о) *прил* unshakable.

непоко́р|ный (-ен, -на, -но) *прил (конь, слуга)* recalcitrant; *(характер, нрав)* rebellious.

непокры́т|ый *прил:* с ~**ой голово́й**

bareheaded.

неполад|ки (-ок) *мн* fault *ед*, defect *ед*; (*разг: в семье*) quarrel *ед*.

неполноправный (-ен, -на, -но) *прил* not possessing full rights.

неполнот|а (-ы) *ж* incompleteness.

неполноценность (-и) *ж* lack; **комплекс ~и** inferiority complex.

неполноцен|ный (-ен, -на, -но) *прил* insufficient.

непол|ный (-он, -на́, -но) *прил* (*чашка, мешок*) not full; (*список, перечень, данные*) incomplete.

непомер|ный (-ен, -на, -но) *прил* excessive.

непонима|ние (-я) *ср* (*задачи, происходящее*) incomprehension; (*равнодушие*) indifference.

непонятен *прил см* **непонятный**.

непонятлив|ый (-, -а, -о) *прил* (*ученик, студент*) slow on the uptake, dull.

непонятно *нареч* incomprehensibly ♦ *как сказ* it is incomprehensible; **мне ~, что происходит** I cannot understand what is going on.

непонят|ный (-ен, -на, -но) *прил* incomprehensible.

непоправим|ый (-, -а, -о) *прил* (*ошибка*) irreparable; (*шаг, несчастье*) irreversible.

непороч|ный (-ен, -на, -но) *прил* pure, chaste.

непоряд|ок (-ка; *nom pl* -ки) *м* disorder.

непоряд|очный (-ен, -на, -но) *прил* (*человек, поведение*) dishonourable (*BRIT*), dishonorable (*US*).

непосед|а (-ы) *м/ж* (*разг*) fidget.

непоседлив|ый (-, -а, -о) *прил* restless.

непосил|ьный (-ен, -ьна, -ьно) *прил* (*труд, задача*) beyond one's strength.

непоследовательность (-и) *ж* inconsistency.

непоследовател|ьный (-ен, -ьна, -ьно) *прил* inconsistent.

непослуша|ние (-я) *ср* (*детей, подчинённых*) disobedience.

непослуш|ный (-ен, -на, -но) *прил* (*ребёнок, собака*) disobedient; (*перен: волосы, кудри*) unmanageable.

непосредственность (-и) *ж* spontaneity.

непосредствен|ный *прил* (*начальник*) immediate; (*результат, свидетель, участник*) direct; (-ен, -на, -но; *натура, тон*) spontaneous.

непостижим|ый (-, -а, -о) *прил* (*загадка, сила*) incomprehensible; **уму~о** it's incomprehensible.

непостоя́нный (-ен, -на, -но) *прил* changeable.

непостоянств|о (-а) *ж* inconstancy, changeability.

непотреб|ный (-ен, -на, -но) *прил* (*разг*) indecent.

непохо́ж|ий (-ая, -ее, -ие; -, -а, -е) *прил* dissimilar.

непоча́т|ый (-, -а, -о) *прил* (*бутылка, пачка*) unopened; (*чашка кофе*) full, untouched; (*перен: силы*) unused; (: *запас, энергии*)

untapped; **непоча́тый край** no end, a great deal.

непочте́ни|е (-я) *ср* disrespect.

непочти́тельно *нареч* disrespectfully.

непра́в (-а́, -о, -ы) *как сказ*: **ты ~** you are wrong.

непра́вд|а (-ы) *ж* lie, untruth ♦ *как сказ* it's not true; **э́то ~!** it's *или* this is a lie!

неправдоподо́б|ный (-ен, -на, -но) *прил* (*история, рассказ*) improbable, implausible.

непра́вилен *прил см* **непра́вильный**.

непра́вильно *нареч* (*решить*) incorrectly, wrongly ♦ *как сказ*: **э́то ~** it's wrong; **~ ду́мать, что ...** it's wrong to think that ...; **~ понима́ть** (**поня́ть** *perf*) to misunderstand; **~ написа́ть** (*perf*) to misspell.

непра́виль|ный (-ен, -ьна, -ьно) *прил* (*решение, произношение, идея*) wrong; (*черты лица, форма*) irregular; **непра́вильная дробь** (*МАТ*) improper fraction.

неправоме́р|ный (-ен, -на, -но) *прил* unjustifiable.

неправомо́ч|ный (-ен, -на, -но) *прил* (*неправомо́чная организа́ция*) *organization without legal authority*.

непревзойдё́н|ный (-, -на, -но) *прил* (*рекорд, мастерство*) unsurpassed; (*тупость, жестокость*) unprecedented.

непредви́денный *прил* unforeseen.

непреднаме́рен|ный (-, -на, -но) *прил* unpremeditated.

непредсказу́ем|ый (-, -а, -о) *прил* unpredictable.

непредубеждё́нный *прил* unbias(s)ed.

непредусмо́тренный *прил* unforeseen, unanticipated.

непредусмотри́тел|ьный (-ен, -ьна, -ьно) *прил* short-sighted.

непрекло́н|ный (-ен, -на, -но) *прил* (*человек*) unbending; (*противник*) uncompromising; (*воля*) unshakable; (*характер*) strong, firm; (*решения*) firm.

непрекраща́|ющийся (-яся, -ееся, -иеся) *прил* (*дождь*) persistent; (*ссора*) endless; (*стрельба*) continuous.

непрело́ж|ный (-ен, -на, -но) *прил* (*правило, закон*) immutable; **непрело́жная и́стина** unquestionable truth.

непреме́нен *прил см* **непреме́нный**.

непреме́нно *нареч* (*обязательно*) by all means.

непреме́н|ный (-ен, -на, -но) *прил* (*условие*) necessary; (*следствие*) unavoidable; (*деталь, черта*) indispensable.

непреодолим|ый (-, -а, -о) *прил* (*препятствие*) insurmountable; (*желание, смущение*) overwhelming.

непререка́ем|ый (-, -а, -о) *прил* (*авторитет*) unquestionable; (*интонация*) peremptory.

непреры́вен *прил см* **непреры́вный**.

The spelling rules for Russian are shown on page xvii.

непреры́вно *нареч* (*спрашивать, меняться*) uninterruptedly, continuously.

непреры́в|ный (-ен, -на, -но) *прил* uninterrupted, continuous.

неприве́тлив|ый (-, -а, -о) *прил* (*человек, тон*) unfriendly; (*перен: лес, место*) bleak.

непривлека́тел|ьный (-ен, -ьна, -ьно) *прил* unattractive.

непривы́чен *прил см* **непривы́чный**.

непривы́чк|а (-и) *ж*: с ~и к физи́ческому труду́ он бы́стро уста́л (*разг*) not being used to physical work, he got tired quickly.

непривы́чно *как сказ*: мне ~ +infin I'm not used to doing.

непривы́ч|ный (-ен, -на, -но) *прил* (*мысль*) unusual; (*обстановка*) not the usual; (*человек*) unaccustomed.

непригля́д|ный (-ен, -на, -но) *прил* (*вид, внешность*) unsightly, unattractive; (*поступок, поведение*) unseemly.

неприго́д|ный (-ен, -на, -но) *прил* unsuitable.

неприе́млем|ый (-, -а, -о) *прил* unacceptable.

непри́знанный *прил* (*писатель, художник*) unrecognized, unacknowledged.

неприка́ян|ный (-, -а, -о) *прил* (*разг*) restless and drifting.

неприкоснове́нность (-и) *ж* inviolability; дипломати́ческая ~ diplomatic immunity.

неприкоснове́н|ный (-ен, -на, -но) *прил* (*фонд*) reserve *опред*; (*ценность*) inviolable; (*лицо, личность*) protected by law; **неприкоснове́нный запа́с** emergency ration.

неприкра́шенный *прил* (*действительность*) plain, unvarnished; (*вид*) plain.

неприкры́т|ый (-, -а, -о) *прил* (*дверь*) open; (*отряд, батальон*) open, exposed; (*перен: правда*) plain; (: *ложь*) barefaced, blatant; (: *грубость*) undisguised.

неприли́чен *прил см* **неприли́чный**.

неприли́чи|е (-я) *ср*: до ~я extremely.

неприли́чно *нареч* indecently, improperly.

неприли́ч|ный (-ен, -на, -но) *прил* (*вид, анекдот, рисунок*) indecent; (*платье*) outrageous.

непримет|ный (-ен, -на, -но) *прил* (*незаметный*) imperceptible; (*непримечательный*) unremarkable.

непримири́м|ый (-, -а, -о) *прил* (*спорщики, противоречия*) irreconcilable; (*характер*) uncompromising.

непринуждённость (-и) *ж* (*беседы*) informality; (*движений*) freeness, casualness.

непринуждён|ный (-, -на, -но) *прил* informal, relaxed.

неприсоедине́ни|е (-я) *ср* (*полит*) nonalignment.

непристо́ен *прил см* **непристо́йный**.

непристо́йность (-и) *ж* obscenity.

непристо́й|ный (-ен, -йна, -йно) *прил* obscene.

непристу́п|ный (-ен, -на, -но) *прил* (*крепость*) impregnable; (*высота*) inaccessible; (*человек*) unapproachable; (*характер, вид*) unfriendly.

непритво́р|ный (-ен, -на, -но) *прил* unfeigned.

непритяза́тел|ьный (-ен, -ьна, -ьно) *прил* (*читатель, зритель, вкус*) undiscriminating; (*острота, стихи*) unsubtle.

неприхотли́в|ый (-, -а, -о) *прил* (*человек, студент*) unpretentious; (*вкус, требования*) modest; (*растение, цветок*) undemanding; (*простой: пища*) frugal; (: *рисунок*) simple.

неприя́знен|ный (-ен, -на, -но) *прил* hostile.

неприя́зн|ь (-и) *ж* hostility.

неприя́тел|ь (-я) *м собир* the enemy.

неприя́тен *прил см* **неприя́тный**.

неприя́ти|е (-я) *ср* rejection.

неприя́тно *как сказ*: ~ +infin (*думать, слушать*) it's unpleasant *или* disagreeable to do; мне ~ говори́ть об э́том I don't enjoy talking about it.

неприя́т|ный (-ен, -на, -но) *прил* unpleasant, disagreeable.

непробива́ем|ый (-, -а, -о) *прил* (*броня, борт*) impregnable; (*перен: спокойствие*) imperturbable; (: *разг: дурак*) utter.

непробу́д|ный (-ен, -на, -но) *прил* (*пьяница*) inveterate; ~ сон deep sleep; ~ное пья́нство drunken stupor.

непроводни́к (-а́) *м* (*физ*) nonconductor, dielectric.

непрогля́д|ный (-ен, -на, -но) *прил* (*ночь*) pitch-dark; (*тьма*) impenetrable.

непродолжи́тел|ьный (-ен, -ьна, -ьно) *прил* short.

непродукти́в|ный (-ен, -на, -но) *прил* unproductive.

непроду́манный *прил* ill-considered.

непрое́зж|ий (-ая, -ее, -ие) *прил* impassable.

непрозра́ч|ный (-ен, -на, -но) *прил* opaque.

непроизводи́тел|ьный (-ен, -ьна, -ьно) *прил* (*труд*) unproductive; (*расходы*) wasteful.

непроизво́л|ьный (-ен, -ьна, -ьно) *прил* involuntary.

непрола́з|ный (-ен, -на, -но) *прил* (*разг*) impassable.

непромока́ем|ый (-, -а, -о) *прил* (*куртка, сапоги*) waterproof.

непроница́ем|ый (-, -а, -о) *прил* (*мрак, туман*) impenetrable; (*перен: вид, лицо*) inscrutable; ~ для +gen impervious to.

непропорциона́л|ьный (-ен, -ьна, -ьно) *прил* disproportionate.

непрости́тел|ьный (-ен, -ьна, -ьно) *прил* unforgivable, inexcusable.

непроходи́мость (-и) *ж* (*мед*) blockage.

непроходи́м|ый (-, -а, -о) *прил* (*чаща, болото*) impassable; (*no short form; перен: разг: дурак*) utter.

непро́ч|ный (-ен, -на́, -но) *прил* (*дом*) unstable; (*материал*) flimsy; (*перен: чувства*) questionable; (: *привязанность*) precarious.

непро́шеный *прил (разг)* uninvited.

непрямо́й *прил (путь)* indirect; *(ответ)* evasive.

Непту́н (**-а**) *м* Neptune.

непью́щий (**-ая, -ее, -ие**) *прил (человек)* teetotal.

неработоспосо́бный (**-ен, -на, -но**) *прил* unable to work.

нерабо́чий (**-ая, -ее, -ие**) *прил:* ~**ее вре́мя** time off; ~**ая обстано́вка** atmosphere which is not conducive to work.

нера́вен *прил см* **нера́вный**.

нера́венство (**-а**) *ср* inequality; **знак** ~**а** *(МАТ)* inequality sign.

неравноду́шный (**-ен, -на, -но**) *прил:* ~ **(к** +*dat)* not indifferent (to); **он к ней** ~**ен** he finds her attractive.

неравноме́рный (**-ен, -на, -но**) *прил (развитие, глубина)* uneven; *(движения)* irregular.

неравнопра́вен *прил см* **неравнопра́вный**.

неравнопра́вие (**-я**) *ср* inequality (of rights).

неравнопра́вный (**-ен, -на, -но**) *прил* unequal.

нера́вный (**-ен, -на́, -но**) *прил* unequal.

неради́вый (**-, -а, -о**) *прил* careless, negligent.

неразбери́ха (**-и**) *ж (разг)* muddle.

неразбо́рчивый (**-, -а, -о**) *прил (буквы, почерк)* illegible; *(читатель, вкус)* undiscriminating; ~ **в сре́дствах** unscrupulous.

неразви́то́й (**-, -а, -о**) *прил* undeveloped.

неразга́данный *прил* unsolved.

неразгово́рчивый (**-, -а, -о**) *прил* taciturn.

неразде́льный (**-ен, -ьна, -ьно**) *прил* inseparable, indivisible.

неразличи́мый (**-, -а, -о**) *прил (схожий)* indistinguishable; *(издали, в темноте)* indiscernible.

неразлу́чный (**-ен, -на, -но**) *прил* inseparable.

неразрешённый *прил (запрещённый)* prohibited; *(оставшийся неясным)* unsolved.

неразреши́мый (**-, -а, -о**) *прил* insoluble.

неразрывный (**-, -а, -о**) *прил* indissoluble.

неразу́мный (**-ен, -на, -но**) *прил (поведение, поступок)* foolish; *(разг: малыш, ребёнок)* silly.

нераспростране́ние (**-я**) *ср* nonproliferation; ~ **я́дерного ору́жия** nonproliferation of nuclear weapons.

нерассуди́тельный (**-ен, -ьна, -ьно**) *прил* lacking (in) common sense.

нерасторжи́мый (**-, -а, -о**) *прил* indissoluble.

нерастаро́пный (**-ен, -на, -но**) *прил* slow, sluggish.

нерасчётливый (**-, -а, -о**) *прил* wasteful.

нерв (**-а**) *м (АНАТ)* nerve; **больны́е не́рвы** nervous disorder; **он всем де́йствует на не́рвы** he gets on everyone's nerves; **переста́нь трепа́ть мне не́рвы!** *(разг)* stop getting on my nerves!

нерви́ровать (**-ую**) *несов перех* to make nervous.

не́рвничать (**-ю**) *несов неперех* to fret.

не́рвно *нареч* nervously.

нервнобольно́й (**-о́го**; *decl like adj)* *м person suffering from a nervous disorder*.

не́рвный *прил* nervous; *(работа, занятие)* nerve-racking; *(окончания, клетки)* nerve *опред*; **не́рвная систе́ма** the nervous system.

нерво́зен *прил см* **нерво́зный**.

нерво́зность (**-и**) *ж* nervousness.

нерво́зный (**-ен, -на, -но**) *прил (человек)* nervous, highly *(ВRIТ)* или high *(US)* strung; *(тон, характер)* nervous; *(обстановка)* nerve-racking.

нервотрёпка (**-и**) *ж (разг)* hassle.

нереа́лен *прил см* **нереа́льный**.

нереа́льность (**-и**) *ж (событий, обстановки)* unreality; *(неосуществимость)* impracticality.

нереа́льный (**-ен, -ьна, -ьно**) *прил (мир, события)* unreal; *(неосуществимый)* impractical.

нерегуля́рный (**-ен, -на, -но**) *прил* irregular.

нере́дко *нареч (часто)* not infrequently, quite often.

нерента́белен *прил см* **нерента́бельный**.

нерента́бельность (**-и**) *ж* unprofitability.

нерента́бельный (**-ен, -на, -но**) *прил* unprofitable.

нере́ст (**-а**) *м* spawning.

нереши́мость (**-и**) *ж* indecision.

нереши́телен *прил см* **нереши́тельный**.

нереши́тельно *нареч* indecisively.

нереши́тельность (**-и**) *ж* indecision, indecisiveness; **быть** *(impf)* **в** ~**и** to be undecided.

нереши́тельный (**-ен, -ьна, -ьно**) *прил* indecisive.

нержаве́йка (**-йки**; *gen pl* **-ек**) *ж (разг)* stainless steel.

нержаве́ющий (**-ая, -ее, -ие**) *прил (крыша, бочка)* rustproof; **нержаве́ющая сталь** stainless steel.

неро́вно *нареч (порезать)* unevenly.

неро́вный *прил (поверхность, край)* uneven; *(местность)* rough, rugged; *(линия)* crooked; *(пульс)* irregular; *(характер, поведение)* unbalanced.

не́рпа (**-ы**) *ж (ЗООЛ)* seal.

неруши́мый *прил (союз)* indestructible.

неря́ха (**-и**) *м/ж (разг)* scruff.

неря́шливый (**-, -а, -о-**) *прил (человек, одежда)* scruffy; *(работа)* careless.

несамостоя́тельный (**-ен, -ьна, -ьно**) *прил* dependent; **Ва́ша рабо́та** ~**ьна** this is not all your own work.

несбы́точный (**-ен, -на, -но**) *прил* unrealizable;

~ные ме́чты pipe dreams.

несваре́ни|е (-я) *ср:* ~ желу́дка indigestion.

несве́дущий (-ая, -ее, -ие; -, -а, -е, -и) *прил* ignorant.

несве́ж|ий (-ая, -ее, -ие; -, -á, -о) *прил* (*рубашка*) dirty; **óвощи ~ие** the vegetables are not very fresh; **у тебя́** ~ **вид** you look weary.

несвоевре́мен|ный (-ен, -на, -но) *прил* untimely.

несвя́зный *прил* disjointed.

несгиба́емый *прил* staunch.

несгово́рчив|ый (-, -а, -о) *прил* pig-headed.

несгора́емый *прил* fireproof.

несде́ржанность (-и) *ж* fieriness.

несде́ржан|ный (-, -на, -но) *прил* (*характер, человек*) fiery; (*тон, поведение*) passionate.

несдоброва́ть *как сказ:* **ему́** ~ (*разг*) he's in trouble.

несе́ни|е (-я) *ср* (*охраны, службы*) carrying out; (*наказания*) taking.

несери́йный *прил* (*изделие*) custom-made.

несерьёз|ный (-ен, -на, -но) *прил* (*человек*) frivolous; (*предложение*) flippant; (*болезнь*) mild; ~**ная ра́на** flesh wound.

несимметри́ч|ный (-ен, -на, -но) *прил* asymmetrical.

несказа́н|ный (-ен, -на, -но) *прил* inexpressive.

нескла́д|ный (-ен, -на, -но) *прил* (*рассказ, жизнь*) disjointed; (*человек, фигура*) ungainly.

несклоня́емый *прил* (*линг*) indeclinable.

не́скольк|о (-их) *чис* (+*gen*) a few ♦ *нареч* (*немного: обидеться*) somewhat; **в ~их слова́х** in a few words, briefly.

несконча́емый (-, -а, -о) *прил* unending.

нескро́м|ный (-ен, -на, -но) *прил* (*человек, поведение*) immodest; (*вопрос*) indelicate; (*жест, предложение*) brazen.

нескрыва́емый (-, -а, -о) *прил* undisguised.

несло́ж|ный (-ен, -нá, -но) *прил* simple.

неслы́хан|ный (-, -на, -но) *прил* unheard of.

неслы́шно *нареч* (*сказать, проехать*) quietly ♦ *как сказ:* **мне** ~ I can't hear.

неслы́ш|ный (-ен, -на, -но) *прил* inaudible.

несме́т|ный (-ен, -на, -но) *прил* infinite.

несмолка́емый (-, -а, -о) *прил* unceasing.

несмотря́ *предл:* ~ **на** +*acc* (*трудности, усталость*) in spite of, despite; ~ **на то что ...** in spite of *или* despite the fact that ...; ~ **ни на что** no matter what.

несмыва́емый *прил* (*пятно*) indelible; (*позор*) ineradicable.

несмышлённый *прил* (*ребёнок*) innocent.

несно́с|ный (-ен, -на, -но) *прил* (*человек, поведение итп*) insufferable; (*жара, холод*) unbearable.

несоблюде́ни|е (-я) *ср* nonobservance.

несоверше́нен *прил см* **несоверше́нный**.

несовершеннолéт|ний (-его; *decl like adj*) *м* minor; ♦ (-яя, -ее, -ие) *прил:* ~ **ребёнок** minor.

несовершеннолéт|няя (-ей; *decl like adj*) *ж см* **несовершеннолéтний**.

несоверше́н|ный (-ен, -на, -но) *прил* flawed; **несоверше́нный вид** (*линг*) imperfective (aspect).

несоверше́нств|о (-а) *ср* (*общества, системы*) imperfect nature.

несовмести́мость (-и) *ж* incompatibility; **несовмести́мость тка́ней** (*мед*) antagonism.

несовмести́м|ый (-, -а, -о) *прил* incompatible.

несогла́си|е (-я) *ср* (*отказ*) refusal; (*в семье*) disagreement.

несогласо́ванность (-и) *ж* lack of coordination.

несогласо́ван|ный (-, -на, -но) *прил* (*действия*) uncoordinated.

несозна́телен *прил см* **несозна́тельный**.

несозна́тельность (-и) *ж* irresponsibility.

несозна́тель|ный (-ен, -ьна, -ьно) *прил* irresponsible.

несоизмери́м|ый (-, -а, -о) *прил* (*понятия*) disproportionate.

несокруши́м|ый (-, -а, -о) *прил* indestructible.

несомне́нен *прил см* **несомне́нный**.

несомне́нно *нареч* (*правильный, хороший итп*) indisputably ♦ *вводн сл* without a doubt ♦ *как сказ:* **э́то** ~ this is indisputable; ~, **что он придёт** there is no doubt that he will come.

несомне́нность (-и) *ж* indisputability.

несомне́н|ный (-ен, -на, -но) *прил* (*факт, успех*) indisputable.

несообра́зен *прил см* **несообра́зный**.

несообрази́тель|ный (-ен, -ьна, -ьно) *прил* (*человек*) slow, thick.

несообра́зность (-и) *ж* (*поведения*) foolishness; **говори́ть** (*impf*)/**де́лать** (*impf*) ~**и** to say/do foolish things.

несообра́з|ный (-ен, -на, -но) *прил* (*поведение*) foolish; ~ **с** +*instr* (*с возможностями, с обстоятельствами*) out of line with.

несоотве́тстви|е (-я) *ср:* ~ +*dat* (*правилам, закону*) nonconformity with; (*возможностям, обстоятельствам*) discrepancy with.

несоразме́р|ный (-ен, -на, -но) *прил* unbalanced.

несостоя́телен *прил см* **несостоя́тельный**.

несостоя́тельность (-и) *ж* (*довода*) lack of substantiation; (*комм*) insolvency; **обнару́живать** (**обнару́жить** *perf*) **свою́** ~ to prove to be worthless.

несостоя́тель|ный (-ен, -на, -но) *прил* (*довод*) unsubstantiated; (*комм: компания, должник*) insolvent; (*руководитель*) incompetent.

неспе́ш|ный (-ен, -на, -но) *прил* unhurried.

несподру́чно *как сказ* (*разг*) it is inconvenient; **мне** ~ **де́лать э́то** it's inconvenient for me to do this.

несподру́чный *прил* (*разг*) inconvenient.

неспоко́ен *прил см* **неспоко́йный**.

неспоко́йно *как сказ* (*в доме, в стране*) there's unease; **у меня́ на душе́** ~ I feel uneasy.

неспоко́й|ный (-ен, -йна, -йно) *прил* (*сон*

uneasy; (*жизнь*) troubled.

неспосо́бен *прил см* **неспосо́бный**.

неспосо́бност|ь (**-и**) *ж* inability; ~ **на** +*acc* (*на жертвы, на уступки итп*) inability to make.

неспосо́б|ный (**-ен, -на, -но**) *прил*: ~ **к** +*dat* incapable of; ~ **к языка́м/матема́тике** incapable of learning languages/doing maths; ~ **на** +*acc* (*на жертвы, на уступки*) incapable of making.

несправедли́во *нареч* unfairly, unjustly ♦ *как сказ*: э́то ~ this is unfair *или* unjust.

несправедли́вост|ь (**-и**) *ж* injustice.

несправедли́в|ый (**-, -а, -о**) *прил* (*человек, суд, упрёк*) unfair, unjust; (*сообщение*) unfounded.

неспроста́ *нареч* (*разг*) for a reason.

неспряга́емый *прил* (*линг*) inconjugable.

несрабо́танност|ь (**-и**) *ж* lack of harmony at work.

несравне́нен *прил см* **несравне́нный**.

несравне́нно *нареч* (*лучшее, красивее итп*) incomparably.

несравне́н|ный (**-ен, -на, -но**) *прил* incomparable.

несрави́мый (**-, -а, -о**) *прил* incomparable.

нестанда́рт|ный (**-ен, -на, -но**) *прил* (*подход*) original; (*товар*) substandard.

нестерпи́мый (**-, -а, -о**) *прил* intolerable.

нест|и́ (**-у́, -ёшь;** *pt* **нёс, -ла́, -ло́**) *несов перех* to carry; (*влечь: хаос, разруху, неприятности*) to bring; (*разг: чепуху, вздор*) to spout; (*perf* **понести́**; *службу, охрану*) to carry out; (*perf* **снести́**; *яйцо*) to lay ♦ *безл*: ~**ёт бензи́ном/во́дкой** there's a smell of petrol (*BRIT*) *или* gas (*US*)/of vodka; **с мо́ря** ~**ёт прохла́дой** coolness wafted in from the sea; ~ **(понести́** *perf***) наказа́ние** to take punishment; ~ **(понести́** *perf***) поте́ри** to suffer losses; ~ **(понести́** *perf***) уще́рб** to be damaged; **куда́ тебя́** ~**ёт?** (*разг*) where on earth are you going?; **кого́ э́то** ~**ёт?** (*разг*) who on earth is that?

нест|и́сь *несов возв* (*человек, машина*) to race; (*перен: сплетни, слухи*) to spread; (: *музыка*) to carry; (*perf* **снести́сь**; *курица*) to lay eggs.

несто́ящий (**-ая, -ее, -ие**) *прил* (*человек*) worthless; (*дело*) valueless.

нестро́йный (**-ен, -йна, -йно**) *прил* shapeless; (*ряды*) ragged.

несудохо́дный *прил* not navigable.

несура́зен *прил см* **несура́зный**.

несура́зност|ь (**-и**) *ж* silliness; **говори́ть** (*impf*)/**де́лать** (*impf*) ~**и** to say/do silly things.

несура́з|ный (**-ен, -на, -но**) *прил* silly; (*характер*) idiotic.

несуще́ственный *прил* inconsequential.

несхо́д|ный (**-ен, -на, -но**) *прил* dissimilar.

несча́стен *прил см* **несча́стный**.

несчастли́вый (**несчастли́в, несча́стлива,** **несча́стливо**) *прил* (*человек*) unhappy; (*попытка*) unfortunate.

несча́ст|ный (**-ен, -на, -но**) *прил* (*человек, лицо*) unhappy; (*день*) sad; (*no short form; разг: жалкий*) wretched; **у него́ о́чень** ~ **вид** he looks very unhappy; **несча́стная любо́вь** unrequited love; **несча́стный слу́чай** accident.

несча́сть|е (**-я**) *ср* (*беда*) misfortune; **к** ~**ю** unfortunately.

несчётный *прил* incalculable.

несъедо́б|ный (**-ен, -на, -но**) *прил* inedible.

KEYWORD

нет *част* **1** (*при отрицании, несогласии*) no; **ты согла́сен? – нет** do you agree? – no; **нет, э́то не то** no, that's not right; **тебе́ не нра́вится мой суп? – нет, нра́вится** don't you like my soup? – yes, I do

2 (*для привлечения внимания*): **нет, ты то́лько посмотри́ на него́!** would you just look at him!

3 (*выражает недоверие*): **нет, ты действи́тельно не се́рдишься?** so you are really not angry?

♦ *как сказ* (+*gen*; *не имеется: об одном предмете*) there is no; (: *о нескольких предметах*) there are no; **нет вре́мени** there is no time; **нет биле́тов** *или* **биле́тов нет** there are no tickets; **у меня́ нет де́нег** I have no money; **его́ нет в го́роде** he is not in town

♦ *союз*: **1**: (**так) нет (же)** (*разг: однако*) but; **я помога́л ему́ три дня, (так) нет (же) ему́ всё ма́ло** I helped him for three days, but it still wasn't enough; **своди́ть (свести́** *perf***) что-н на нет** to bring sth to nothing; **сойти́** (*perf*) **на нет** to come to nothing

2 (*во фразах*): **нет – так нет** it can't be helped; **нет-нет да и зайдёт/ска́жет** every now and then he called in/said; **чего́ то́лько нет?** what don't they have?; **нет чтобы извини́ться/** **сказа́ть пра́вду** (*разг*) instead of saying sorry/ telling the truth.

нетакти́чен *прил см* **нетакти́чный**.

нетакти́чност|ь (**-и**) *ж* tactlessness.

нетакти́чный (**-ен, -на, -но**) *прил* tactless.

нетвёрдый *прил* (*походка*) unsteady; (*решение*) shaky.

нетерпели́во *нареч* impatiently.

нетерпели́вый (**-, -а, -о**) *прил* impatient.

нетерпе́ни|е (**-я**) *ср* impatience; **с** ~**м ждать** (*impf*)/**слу́шать** (*impf*) to wait/listen impatiently.

нетерпи́мост|ь (**-и**) *ж* intolerance.

нетерпи́мый (**-, -а, -о**) *прил* (*недопустимый*) intolerant; (*непримиримый*): ~ **к** +*dat* (*ко лжи*) intolerant of.

неторопли́во *нареч* unhurriedly.

нетороплив|ый (**-, -а, -о**) *прил* unhurried.

нето́чност|ь (**-и**) *ж* (*данных, описания*) inexactness; (*в работе, в описании*) inexactitude.

неточ|ный (-ен, -но, -на) *прил* inexact.

нетребовательный (-ен, -ьна, -ьно) *прил* (*начальник*) undemanding; (*вкус, публика*) unsophisticated; (*человек*) unassuming.

нетрёзвый *прил* drunk; **в нетрёзвом состоянии** drunk.

нетронут|ый (-, -а, -о) *прил* (*снег*) virgin; (*обед*) untouched.

нетруден *прил см* **нетрудный**.

нетрудно *как сказ*: **это ~** it's easy *или* not difficult; **~ понять** it's easy *или* not difficult to understand.

нетруд|ный (-ен, -но, -на) *прил* easy.

нетрудовой *прил*: **~ доход** unearned income.

нетрудоспособен *прил см* **нетрудоспособный**.

нетрудоспособность (-и) *ж* disability; **пособие по ~и** disability living allowance.

нетрудоспособ|ный (-ен, -на, -но) *прил unable to work through disability.*

нётто *прил неизм* (*о весе*) net *опред*; **вес ~** net weight; **~активы** (*комм*) net assets.

неубеди́тел|ьный (-ен, -ьна, -ьно) *прил* unconvincing.

неубранный *прил* (*урожай*) ungathered; (*поля*) unharvested; (*постель*) unmade; (*комната*) untidy.

неуваже́ни|е (-я) *ср* disrespect.

неуве́ренно *нареч* uncertainly.

неуве́ренный *прил* (*человек*) unsure; (*тон*) uncertain; **~ в себе́** unsure of o.s.

неувяда́ем|ый (-, -а, -о) *прил* (*талант, слава*) enduring; (*красота*) unfading.

неувя́з|ка (-ки; *gen pl* -ок) *ж* (*разг: в описании, в аргументации*) discrepancy; (*недоразумение*) misunderstanding.

неугаси́м|ый (-, -а, -о) *прил* inextinguishable.

неугомо́нный (-ен, -на, -но) *прил* unruly.

неуда́ч|а (-и) *ж* (*в делах*) failure; **терпе́ть** (**потерпе́ть** *perf*) **~у** to meet with failure.

неуда́чен *прил см* **неуда́чный**.

неуда́члив|ый (-, -а, -о) *прил* (*человек*) unlucky.

неуда́чно *нареч* unsuccessfully; **её жизнь сложи́лась ~** her life was a failure.

неуда́|чный (-ен, -на, -но) *прил* (*попытка*) unsuccessful; (*фильм, стихи*) bad.

неудержи́м|ый (-, -а, -о) *прил* (*поток, бег*) uncontrollable; (*слёзы, радость*) unrestrained.

неудиви́тельно *как сказ* it's not surprising.

неудо́бен *прил см* **неудо́бный**.

неудо́бно *нареч* (*расположенный, сидеть*) uncomfortably ◆ *как сказ* it's uncomfortable; (*неприлично*) **мне ~** I am uncomfortable; **~ задава́ть лю́дям таки́е вопро́сы** it's awkward to ask people such questions; (*мне*) **~ сказа́ть ему́ об э́том** I feel uncomfortable telling him that.

неудо́б|ный (-ен, -на, -но) *прил* uncomfortable.

неудобовари́м|ый (-, -а, -о) *прил* (*также*

перен) indigestible.

неудо́бств|о (-а) *ср* (*неловкость*) discomfort; (*в поезде итп*) lack of comfort.

неудовлетворённость (-и) *ж*: **~ +instr** (*работой, жизнью*) dissatisfaction with.

неудовлетворённый *прил* (*любопытство*) unsatisfied; (*читатель, зритель*) dissatisfied.

неудовлетвори́телен *прил см* **неудовлетвори́тельный**.

неудовлетвори́тельно *нареч* (*сделать*) unsatisfactorily ◆ *ср нескл* (*ПРОСВЕЩ*) ≈ D (*school mark*).

неудовлетвори́тельный (-ен, -ьна, -ьно) *прил* unsatisfactory.

неудово́льстви|е (-я) *ср* dissatisfaction.

неуём|ный (-ен, -на, -но) *прил* (*энергия*) irrepressible; (*тоска*) unrestrained.

неуже́ли *част* really; **~ она́ так ду́мает?** does she really think that?

неужи́вчив|ый (-, -а, -о) *прил* unaccommodating.

неузнава́емость (-и) *ж*: **до ~и** beyond (all) recognition.

неузнава́ем|ый (-, -а, -о) *прил* unrecognizable.

неукло́нно *нареч* steadily.

неукло́н|ный (-ен, -на, -но) *прил* steady.

неуклю́ж|ий (-ая, -ее, -ие; -, -а, -е) *прил* clumsy.

неукосни́телен *прил см* **неукосни́тельный**.

неукосни́тельно *нареч* strictly.

неукосни́тел|ьный (-ен, -ьна, -ьно) *прил* strict.

неукроти́м|ый (-, -а, -о) *прил* (*гнев*) unrestrained; (*энергия*) irrepressible.

неулови́м|ый (-, -а, -о) *прил* imperceptible; (*человек*) elusive.

неуме́лый *прил* inept.

неуме́ни|е (-я) *ср* incapability.

неуме́рен|ный (-, -на, -но) *прил* (*восторг*) boundless; (*потребности*) unlimited.

неуме́ст|ный (-ен, -на, -но) *прил* inappropriate; **шу́тка была́ соверше́нно ~на** the joke was completely out of place.

неу́мный *прил* (*политика*) unintelligent.

неумоли́м|ый (-, -а, -о) *прил* (*мститель*) relentless; (*закон*) stringent.

неумо́л|чный (-ен, -на, -но) *прил* unremitting.

неумы́шленный *прил* (*поступок*) unintentional; (*убийство*) unpremeditated.

неупла́т|а (-ы) *ж* nonpayment.

неупоря́доченный *прил* disorderly.

неупотреби́тельный (-ен, -ьна, -ьно) *прил*: **э́то сло́во сейча́с ~ьно** this word is not in use any more.

неуправля́ем|ый (-, -а, -о) *прил* (*недисциплинированный*) unruly.

неуравнове́шенность (-и) *ж* irascibility.

неуравнове́шен|ный (-, -на, -но) *прил* unbalanced.

неурожа́|й (-я) *м* poor harvest.

неурожа́йный *прил*: **~ год** year with a poor harvest.

неуро́чный *прил* (*время, час*) unearthly.

неуря́диц|а (-ы) ж (разг: обычно мн: в семье, на работе) squabble.

неуспева́емост|ь (-и) ж poor performance.

неуспева́ющий (-ая, -ее, -ие) прил (ученик) poor.

неуста́нен прил см неуста́нный.

неуста́нно нареч indefatigably.

неуста́н|ный (-ен, -на, -но) прил indefatigable.

неусто́йка (-йки; gen pl -ек) ж (КОММ) penalty; (разг: неудача) flop.

неусто́йчивост|ь (-и) ж (цен) instability.

неусто́йчив|ый (-, -а, -о) прил (стул, цены) unstable; (погода) unsettled.

неустрани́м|ый (-, -а, -о) прил insurmountable.

неустраши́м|ый (-, -а, -о) прил fearless.

неустро́ен|ный (-, -на, -но) прил (жизнь, быт) uncomfortable.

неусы́п|ный (-ен, -на, -но) прил vigilant.

неуте́шен прил см неуте́шный.

неутеши́тел|ьный (-ен, -ьна, -ьно) прил upsetting.

неуте́ш|ный (-ен, -на, -но) прил inconsolable.

неутоли́м|ый (-, -а, -о) прил (жажда) unquenchable; (голод, также перен) insatiable.

неутоми́м|ый (-, -а, -о) прил untiring.

неу́ч (-а) м (разг) dunce.

неучти́вост|ь (-и) ж lack of civility; **говори́ть** (impf) **~и** to be uncivil.

неучти́в|ый (-, -а, -о) прил uncivil.

неую́тно нареч (сидеть) uncomfortably ♦ как сказ it's uncomfortable; **мне ~ с чужи́ми людьми́** I don't feel at ease with strangers.

неуязви́м|ый (-, -а, -о) прил (противник, позиция) impregnable; (аргумент) unassailable.

неформа́л (-а) м (разг) member of a nonconformist organization.

неформа́льный прил (отношение) relaxed; (организация) nonconformist.

нефри́т (-а) м (МЕД) nephritis; (ГЕО) jade.

нефтедобыва́ющий (-ая, -ее, -ие) прил (промышленность) oil опред.

нефтедобы́ч|а (-и) ж drilling for oil.

нефтедо́ллар|ы (-ов) мн petrodollars мн.

нефтено́сный прил: **~ пласт** oilfield.

нефтеперерабо́тк|а (-и) ж oil-processing plant.

нефтепрово́д (-а) м oil pipeline.

нефтепроду́кт (-а) м (обычно мн) oil product.

нефтехрани́лищ|е (-а) ср oil storage tank.

нефт|ь (-и) ж oil, petroleum.

нефтя́ник (-а) м worker in the oil industry.

нефтян|о́й прил: **~а́я платфо́рма** oil rig; **нефтяна́я вы́шка** (oil) derrick.

нехва́тк|а (-и) ж: **~ +gen** (разг) shortage of.

нехи́трый прил (простой) simple.

нехо́жен|ый (-, -а, -о) прил little-used.

нехоро́ший (-ая, -ее, -ие) прил bad.

нехорошо́ нареч (поступить) badly ♦ как сказ

it's bad; **мне ~** I'm not well; **~ на душе́** I feel uneasy; **он нехоро́ш собо́й** he isn't good-looking.

не́хотя нареч unwillingly.

нецензу́р|ный (-ен, -на, -но) прил unprintable; **~ное сло́во** swearword.

неча́янно нареч unintentionally.

неча́ян|ный (-на, -но) прил (неумышленный) unintentional; (неожиданный) chance опред.

не́чего как сказ: **~ рассказа́ть** there is nothing to tell; (разг: не следует) there's no need to do; **не́ для чего стара́ться** there is nothing to try for; **не́ к чему придра́ться** there is nothing to find fault with; **мне не́ с чем идти́** I have nothing to take; **не́ о чем говори́ть** there is nothing to talk about; **не́чему серди́ться** there is nothing to be angry about; **не́ за что!** (в ответ на благодарность) not at all!, you're welcome! (US); **~ (и) говори́ть** (разг: конечно) no buts about it; **~ сказа́ть!** (разг) would you credit it!; **от ~ де́лать** (разг) for want of something better to do; **де́лать ~** there's nothing else to be done.

нечелове́ческ|ий (-ая, -ое, -ие) прил inhuman; (колоссальный: усилия) superhuman.

нечёсаный прил unkempt.

нече́стен прил см нече́стный.

нече́стно нареч dishonestly ♦ как сказ: **э́то ~** this is dishonest.

нече́стност|ь (-и) ж dishonesty.

нече́ст|ный (-ен, -на, -но) прил dishonest.

нечётный прил (число) odd.

нечи́сто как сказ: **в ко́мнате ~** the room is untidy; **здесь что́-то ~** (разг) there's something fishy here.

нечистопло́т|ный (-ен, -на, -но) прил (неопрятный) untidy; (неразборчивый) unscrupulous.

нечисто́т|ы (-) мн sewage ед; (отбросы) waste ед.

нечи́ст|ый (-, -а, -о) прил (одежда, комната) dirty; (произношение) indistinct; (приёмы, игра) unscrupulous; **у него́ ~ая со́весть** he has a guilty conscience; **он нечи́ст на́ руку** (нечестен) he is dishonest; (ворует) he is light-fingered; **нечи́стая си́ла** evil spirit.

нечи́ст|ь (-и) ж собир (нечистая сила) evil spirit; (перен: преступная, нацистская) scum.

нечленоразде́л|ьный (-ен, -ьна, -ьно) прил inarticulate.

не́что мест something.

нечувстви́телен прил см нечувстви́тельный.

нечувстви́тельност|ь (-и) ж insensitivity.

нечувстви́тел|ьный (-ен, -ьна, -ьно) прил insensitive.

нечу́тк|ий (-ая, -ое, -ие) прил (человек) unsympathetic.

нешу́точ|ный (-ен, -на, -но) прил (серьёзный)

serious; (*значительный*) large; это ~ное дело
it's no laughing matter.

нещаден *прил см* **нещадный**.

нещадно *нареч* unmercifully.

нещадный (-ен, -на, -но) *прил* (*критика,
наказание*) merciless; (*перен: жара*) relentless.

неэкономичен *прил см* **неэкономичный**.

неэкономичность (-и) *ж* (*методов,
технологии*) inefficiency.

неэкономичный (-ен, -на, -но) *прил*
(*технология, отрасль*) inefficient; (*мотор*)
uneconomical.

неэтичный *прил* (*поведение*) unethical.

неэффективный (-ен, -на, -но) *прил*
ineffective.

неявка (-ки; *gen pl* -ок) *ж* (*на работу*) absence;
(*на суд*) failure to appear; за ~кой, по ~ке by
default.

неясен *прил см* **неясный**.

неясно *нареч*: он ~ объяснил положение he
didn't explain the situation clearly ♦ *как сказ* it's
not clear; мне ~, почему он отказался I'm not
clear *или* it's not clear to me why he refused.

неясность (-и) *ж* vagueness; (*в тексте*)
ambiguity.

неясный (-ен, -на, -но) *прил* (*очертания, звук*)
indistinct; (*мысль, вопрос*) vague.

НЗ *м сокр* = **неприкосновенный запас**.

KEYWORD

ни *част* **1** (*усиливает отрицание*) not a; ни
один not one, not a single; она не произнесла
ни слова she didn't say a word; она ни разу не
пришла she didn't come once; у меня не
осталось ни рубля I don't have a single rouble
left:

2: кто/что/как ни who/what/however; сколько
ни however much; что ни говори, а ей
приходится трудно whatever you say, it is hard
for her; как ни старайся, не убедишь его
however hard you try, you will not convince
him; куда ни посмотри, везде бедность
wherever you look, there is poverty
  ♦ *союз* (*in negative sentences; при перечислении*):
ни ..., ни ... neither ... nor ...; ни денег, ни еды у
неё нет she has neither money nor food; ни за
что no way; ни за какие деньги not for any
money; ни-ни! (*разг*) no way!

нива (-ы) *ж* field (*of crops*).

нивелировать (-ую) (*не*)*сов перех* (*перен*) to
even out.

нигде *нареч* nowhere; его ~ не было he was
nowhere to be found; ~ нет моей книги I can't
find my book anywhere, my book is nowhere to
be found; ~ не мог поесть I couldn't find
anywhere to get something to eat.

нигерийский (-ая, -ое, -ие) *ж* Nigerian.

Нигерия (-и) *ж* Nigeria.

нигилизм (-а) *м* nihilism.

нигилист (-а) *м* nihilist.

нидерландский (-ая, -ое, -ие) *прил* Dutch.

Нидерланды (-ов) *мн* the Netherlands.

ниже *сравн прил от* **низкий** ♦ *сравн нареч от*
низко ♦ *нареч* (*далее*) later on ♦ *предл* (+*gen*)
below; ~ речь пойдёт о +*prp* ... later (on) we
will deal with ...; он выступил ~ своих
возможностей he performed below his
capabilities.

нижеизложенный *прил*: ~ые данные/
аргументы the facts/arguments given below.

нижеподписавшийся (-аяся, -ееся, -иеся)
прил undersigned.

нижесказанное (-ого; *decl like adj*) *ср* what has
been said below.

нижестоящий (-ая, -ее, -ие) *прил* lower.

нижеуказанный *прил* undermentioned.

нижеупомянутый *прил см* **нижеуказанный**.

нижний (-яя, -ее, -ие) *прил* (*ступенька, ящик*)
bottom; (*течение реки*) lower reaches *мн*;
(*регистр*) low; ~ этаж ground (*BRIT*) *или* first
(*US*) floor; Н~ Новгород Nizhni Novgorod;
нижнее бельё underwear; **нижняя юбка**
underskirt.

низ (-а; *loc sg* -у, *nom pl* -ы) *м* (*стола, ящика итп*)
bottom; (*дома*) ground (*BRIT*) *или* first (*US*) floor;
по ~у along the bottom; *см также* **низы**.

низвергнуть (-у, -ешь; *impf* **низвергать**) *сов
перех* to overthrow

▶ **низвергнуться** *сов возв* to hurtle down.

низина (-ы) *ж* low-lying land.

низкий (-кая, -кое, -кие; -ок, -ка, -ко) *прил* low;
(*no short form*; *происхождение*) lowly; этот стол
мне ~ок this table is too low for me; ~ лоб
narrow forehead; ~кое место (*низменность*)
low-lying area; ~ поклон low bow; (*перен*)
forelock tugging.

низко *нареч* low.

низкооплачиваемый *прил* low-paid.

низкопоклонник (-а) *м* sycophant.

низкопоклонство (-а) *ср* sycophancy.

низкопробный (-ен, -на, -но) *прил* (*золото,
серебро*) low-grade; (*книга, газета*) trashy;
(*делец*) amoral.

низкорослый *прил* (*человек*) small; (*дерево,
кустарник*) stunted.

низкосортный (-ен, -на, -но) *прил* low-quality.

низкокачественный *прил* low-quality.

низложить (-ожу, -ожишь; *impf* **низлагать**) *сов
перех* to depose.

низменность (-и) *ж* (*ГЕО*) low-lying area;
(*интересов*) baseness.

низменный *прил* (*местность, болота*) low-
lying; (-, -на, -но; *интересы, мысли*) base;
(*инстинкты*) basic.

низовой *прил* (*организация*) grass-roots;
низовые работники the grass roots.

низовье (-ья; *gen pl* -ьев) *ср* lower reaches *мн*.

низок *прил см* **низкий**.

низом *нареч* along the bottom.

низость (-и) *ж* baseness; говорить (*impf*) ~и to
say base things; делать (*impf*) ~и to behave
basely.

ни́зш|ий (-ая, -ее, -ие) *сравн прил от* **ни́зкий**; (*звание*) junior; **~ие чины́** the lowest ranks.

ни́з|ы (-о́в) *мн* (*низший классы*) lowest classes *мн*; (*широкие массы*) masses *мн*; **он вы́шел из ~о́в** he came from the lowest classes of society; **опира́ться** (*impf*) **на ~** to rely for support on the masses.

ника́к *нареч* (*никаким образом*) no way; **~ не могу́ запо́мнить э́то сло́во** I can't remember this word at all; **дверь ~ не открыва́лась** the door just wouldn't open; **ему́ ~ не удава́лось её встре́тить** there's no way he could have managed to meet her; **~ нельзя́** +*infin* ... one can't do ....

никак|о́й (-а́я, -о́е, -и́е) *мест*: **~и́е де́ньги не помогли́** no amount of money would have helped; (*разг*): **~ он не врач** he's not a doctor at all; (: *плохой*): **писа́тель он ~** he can't be called a writer; **ни у како́го челове́ка не бу́дет сомне́ния** nobody will have any doubt about it; **ни к како́му де́лу он не спосо́бен** he is not capable of anything; **он не соглаша́лся ни с каки́м аргуме́нтном** he didn't agree with any of the arguments; **нет ~о́го сомне́ния** there is absolutely no doubt (at all); **у меня́ нет ~о́го сомне́ния** I have absolutely no doubts; **и ~и́х!** and that's that!

никара́гуа *ж нескл* Nicaragua.

никарагуа́нск|ий (-ая, -ое, -ие) *прил* Nicaraguan.

никелир|ова́ть (-у́ю; *perf* **отникелирова́ть**) *несов перех* to nickel.

никелиро́вк|а (-и) *ж* (*действие*) nickelling (*BRIT*), nickeling (*US*); (*покрытие*) nickel plate.

ни́кел|ь (-я) *м* (*хим*) nickel.

ни́кн|уть (-у, -ешь) *несов от* **пони́кнуть** ♦ *неперех* (*трава, цветы*) to droop.

никогда́ *нареч* never; **как ~** as never before.

нико́го *мест см* **никто́**.

нико́й *нареч*: **нико́им о́бразом** not at all; **ни в ко́ем слу́чае** under no circumstances.

ни|кто́ (-кого́; *как* кто; *см* **Table 6**) *мест* nobody ♦ *м*: **она́ мне ~** (*разг*: *не родственник*) she's not a relative of mine; (*не друг*) she's nothing to me; **ни у кого́ нет сомне́ний** nobody has any doubts; **ни к кому́ не подходи́л** I didn't approach anyone; **ни с кем не говори́л** I didn't speak to anyone; **ни о ком не зна́ю** I don't know anything about anyone.

никуда́ *местоимённое нареч* nowhere ♦ *как сказ* (*разг*): **обслу́живание здесь – ~** the service here is terrible; **я ~ не пое́ду** I'm not going anywhere; **~ я не пое́ду** I'm going nowhere; **э́то ~ не годи́тся** that just won't do.

никуды́шн|ый (-ен, -на, -но) *прил* (*разг*) good-for-nothing.

никче́мн|ый (-ен, -на, -но) *прил* no good for anything.

Нил (-а) *м* the Nile.

НИИ *м сокр* (= **нау́чно-иссле́довательский институ́т**) scientific research institute.

нимб (-а) *м* nimbus.

ниотку́да *местоимённое нареч* from nowhere; **~ нет по́мощи** I get no help from anywhere.

нипочём *как сказ*: **бе́дность ему́ ~** (*разг*) being poor doesn't bother him; **ему́ всё ~** (*разг*) nothing hassles him.

ни́ппел|ь (-я) *м* (*ТЕХ*) nipple.

ниско́лько *местоимённое нареч* not at all; (*не лучше, не полезнее*) no; (*не рад, не удивлён*) at all; **ты рад? – ~** are you pleased? – not at all *или* in the slightest.

ниспада́|ть (*3sg* -ет, *3pl* -ют) *несов неперех* to fall.

ниспрове́рг|нуть (-ну, -нешь; *pt* -, -ла, -ло, *impf* **ниспроверга́ть**) *сов перех* to overthrow.

нисходя́щ|ий (-ая, -ее, -ие) *прил* (*линия*) descending; (*интонация*) falling.

нитеви́дн|ый (-ен, -на, -но) *прил* long and thin.

ни́т|ка (-ки; *gen pl* -ок) *ж* (*обычно мн*: *для шитья*) thread *ед*; (*для вязания*) yarn; **~ жёмчуга** string of pearls; **~ газопрово́да** gas pipeline; **промо́кнуть** (*perf*) **до ~ки** to get soaked right through; **вдева́ть** (**вдеть** *perf*) **~ку в иго́лку** to thread a needle.

нитра́т (-а) *м* nitrate.

нит|ь (-и) *ж* thread; (*для вязания*) yarn; (+*gen*; *повествования, воспоминаний*) thread of; **ни́ти за́говора** strands of a plot; **ни́ти дру́жбы** threads of friendship.

них *мест см* **они́**.

ниц *м*: **па́дать ~** to prostrate o.s.

Ни́цц|а (-ы) *ж* Nice.

ничего́ *мест см* **ничто́** ♦ *нареч* fairly well; (**э́то**) **~, что** ... it's all right that ...; **извини́те, я Вас побеспоко́ю – ~!** sorry to disturb you – it's all right!; **как живёшь? – ~** how are you? – all right; **~ себе́** (*сносно*) fairly well; **~ себе́!** (*выражает удивление*) well, I never!

ниче́|й (-ьего́; *f* -ья́, *nt* -ьё, *pl* -ьи́; *как* чей; *см* **Table 7**) *мест* nobody's; **он не слу́шает ~ьих сове́тов** he doesn't follow anybody's advice; **ни к чьему́ сове́ту не прислу́шивается** he doesn't listen to anybody's advice; **ни с чьим мне́нием не счита́ется** he doesn't consider anyone's views; **ни о чьём благополу́чии не беспоко́ится** he doesn't worry about anyone's wellbeing.

ниче́йн|ый *прил* (*полоса, зона*) no man's; **~ая земля́** no-man's-land; **~ результа́т, ниче́йная па́рти|я** draw.

ничко́м *нареч* face down.

нич|то́ (-его́; *как* что; *см* **Table 6**) *мест, ср* nothing; **ни для чего́ не приго́дный** not suitable for anything; **ни с чем не согла́сен** I don't agree with anything; **ни о чём не прошу́** I don't ask for anything; ~ **мне не интере́сно** nothing interests me; ~**его́ с ним не случи́тся** nothing will happen to him; ~**его́ подо́бного не ви́дел** I've never seen anything like it; ~**его́ подо́бного!** (*разг: совсем не так*) nothing like it!; **всего́ ~его́** (*разг*) next to nothing; **ни за что!** (*ни в коем случае*) no way!; **ни за что не соглаша́йся** whatever you do, don't agree; **ни за что ни про что** for nothing; **я здесь ни при чём** it has nothing to do with me; ~**его́ не поде́лаешь** there's nothing to be done.

ничто́жен *прил см* **ничто́жный**.

ничто́жеств|о (-а) *ср* nonentity.

ничто́жный (-ен, -на, -но) *прил* paltry.

ничу́ть *местоименное нареч* (*нисколько*) not at all; (*не лучше, не больше*) no; (*не испугался, не огорчился*) at all; ~ **не быва́ло** not at all.

ничь|я́ (-éй) *ж* (*СПОРТ*) draw; **сыгра́ть** (*perf*) **в** ~**ю́** to draw (*BRIT*), tie (*US*).

ни́ш|а (-и) *ж* niche.

нища́|ть (-ю; *perf* **обнища́ть**) *несов неперех* to become impoverished.

ни́щ|ая (-ей; *decl like adj*) *ж* beggar.

ни́щенк|а (-ки; *gen pl* -ок) *ж =* **ни́щая**.

ни́щенск|ий (-ая, -ое, -ие) *прил* (*ничтожный*) beggarly; ~**ая жизнь** life of begging.

нищет|а́ (-ы́) *ж* poverty.

ни́щ|ий (-ая, -ее, -ие) *прил* poverty-stricken ◆ (-его; *decl like adj*) *м* beggar.

НЛО *м сокр* (*= неопознанный лета́ющий объе́кт*) UFO (*= unidentified flying object*).

но *союз* but ◆ *ср нескл* (*препятствие*) setback ◆ *межд* gee up; **я предложи́л ему́ по́мощь, ~ он отказа́лся** I offered to help him, but he refused; ~ **вдруг** then suddenly; ~ **то́лько** only; ~**но, осторо́жнее!** now then, be more careful!

нова́тор (-а) *м* innovator.

нова́торств|о (-а) *ср* innovation.

нова́ци|я (-и) *ж* innovation.

новелл|а (-ы) *ж* novella.

новелли́ст (-а) *м* writer of novellas.

новелли́стк|а (-ки; *gen pl* -ок) *ж см* **новелли́ст**.

но́веньк|ая (-ой; *decl like adj*) *ж* newcomer; (*в классе*) new pupil.

но́веньк|ий (-ая, -ое, -ие) *прил* (*разг*) new ◆ (-ого; *decl like adj*) *м* newcomer; (*в классе*) new pupil; **что** ~**ого?** what's new?

новизн|а́ (-ы́) *ж* (*идей, подхода*) novelty.

нови́н|ка (-ки; *gen pl* -ок) *ж* new product; ~ **мо́ды** new fashion item; **кни́жная** ~ new book; **мне это в** ~**ку** it's new to me.

новичо́к (-ка́) *м* newcomer; (*в классе*) new pupil; **я ~ в** +*prp* I am a newcomer to.

но́во *как сказ*: **здесь мне всё** ~ it's all new to me here.

новобра́н|ец (-ца) *м* new recruit.

новобра́чн|ая (-ой; *decl like adj*) *ж см* **новобра́чный**.

новобра́чн|ый (-ого; *decl like adj*) *м* newlywed.

нововведе́ни|е (-я) *ср* innovation.

нового́дн|ий (-яя, -ее, -ие) *прил* New Year

опред; **нового́дняя ёлка** ≈ Christmas tree.

новозела́ндск|ий (-ая, -ое, -ие) *прил* New Zealand *опред*.

новоиспечённый *прил* (*разг*) new.

новока́ин (-а) *м* (*МЕД*) Novocaine ®.

новолу́ни|е (-я) *ср* new moon.

новорождённ|ая (-ой; *decl like adj*) *ж* newborn girl.

новорождённ|ый *прил* newborn ◆ (-ого; *decl like adj*) *м* newborn boy.

новосёл (-а) *м* (*дома*) new owner.

новосе́лье (-ья; *gen pl* -ий) *ср* house-warming.

Новосиби́рск (-а) *м* Novosibirsk.

новостро́йк|а (-йки; *gen pl* -ек) *ж* (*строительство*) construction of new buildings; (*новое здание*) new building; **больни́ца-**~ newly-built hospital.

но́вост|ь (-и; *gen pl* -е́й) *ж* (*известие*) news; (*медицины, техники*) innovation.

новоявленный *прил* (*разг*) new.

но́вшеств|о (-а) *ср* (*в жизни, в обществе*) novelty; (*техническое*) innovation.

но́в|ый (-, -á, -о) *прил* new; **но́вая исто́рия** modern history; **Но́вый Заве́т** the New Testament; **Но́вая Зела́ндия** New Zealand; **Но́вая Земля́** Novaya Zemlya.

новь (-и) *ж* new era.

ног|а́ (-и́; *acc sg* -у, *nom pl* -и, *gen pl* -, *dat pl* -а́м) *ж* (*ступня*) foot; (*выше ступни*) leg; **переступа́ть** (*impf*) *или* **перемина́ться** (*impf*) **с** ~**и́ на** ~**у** to shift from one foot to the other; **идти́** (*impf*) **в но́гу со вре́менем** (*перен*) to move with the times; **он бежа́л со всех ног** he ran as fast as his legs would carry him; **сби́ться** (*perf*) **с ног** to be run off one's feet; **поста́вить** (*perf*) **кого́-н на** ~**и** (*перен: больного*) to get sb back on his *итп* feet; (*детей*) to make sb stand on his *итп* own two feet; **с ног на́ голову перевора́чивать** (*перевернуть* perf) *или* **ста́вить** (*поста́вить* perf) **что-н** to turn *или* put sth on its head; **éле но́ги унести́** (*perf*) to escape by the skin of one's teeth; ~**й моей там не бу́дет** (*разг*) I won't step foot there again; **в** ~**х** (*постели*) at the foot of the bed; **вверх** ~**ми** upside down; **в до́ме всё вверх** ~**ми** the house is completely topsy turvy; **жить** (*impf*) **на широ́кую но́гу** to live lavishly; **на коро́ткой** *или* **дру́жеской** ~**é с** +*instr* on friendly terms with.

ноготк|и́ (-о́в) *мн* marigold.

но́гот|ь (-тя; *gen pl* -те́й) *м* nail; **до ко́нчиков ногте́й** (*перен: совершенно*) from top to toe.

нож (-а́) *м* knife; **быть** (*impf*) **с кем-н на** ~**а́х** (*враждовать*) to be at daggers drawn with sb; **твои́ посту́пки мне** – ~ **о́стрый** (*перен: разг*) your behaviour gives me a lot of grief.

ножево́й *прил* (*рана*) knife *опред*.

но́жек *сущ см* **но́жка**.

но́жен *сущ см* **но́жны**.

но́жик (-а) *м*: **перочи́нный** ~ penknife; **складно́й** ~ flick knife (*BRIT*), switchblade (*US*)

но́ж|ка (-ки; *gen pl* -ек) *ж уменьш от* нога́; (*стула, стола итп*) leg; (*циркуля*) arm; **подставля́ть (подста́вить** *perf*) ~ку кому́-н (*также перен*) to trip sb up.

но́жниц|ы (-) *мн* (*инструмент*) scissors *мн*, pair *ед* of scissors (*мн* pairs of scissors); (*расхождение*) disproportion.

ножно́й *прил* foot *опред*.

но́ж|ны (-ен) *мн* (*для кинжала*) sheath *ед*; (*для шпаги, сабли итп*) scabbard *ед*.

ножо́в|ка (-ки; *gen pl* -ок) *ж* hacksaw.

ноздрева́т|ый (-, -а, -о) *прил* (*сыр*) holey.

ноздр|я́ (-и́; *nom pl* -и, *gen pl* -е́й) *ж* (*обычно мн*) nostril.

нока́ут (-а) *м* knockout.

нокаути́р|овать (-ую) (*не)сов перех* to knock out.

нокда́ун (-а) *м* knockdown.

нол|ь (-я́) *м* (*МАТ*) zero, nought; (*при исчислении температуры*) zero; (*перен: человек*) nothing; ~ це́лых пять деся́тых, 0.5 zero *или* nought point five, 0.5; **встре́титься** (*perf*) в де́сять ~ноль to meet at exactly ten o'clock.

номенклату́р|а (-ы) *ж* (*товаров, услуг*) list ♦ *собир* (*номенклатурные работники*) nomenklatura.

номенклату́рный *прил* (*единица*) listed; **номенклату́рный рабо́тник** nomenklatura.

но́мер (-а; *nom pl* -а́) *м* number; (*журнала, газеты*) issue; (*перчаток*) size; (*в гостинице*) room; (*концерта*) number, turn; **но́мер маши́ны** registration (number).

номерка́ *сущ см* **номеро́к**.

номерно́й *прил* (*завод*) *identified only by a number*; **номерно́й знак (автомоби́ля)** (car) number (*BRIT*) *или* license (*US*) plate; **номерно́й счёт (в ба́нке)** numbered account.

номер|о́к (-ка́) *ж* (*для пальто*) ≈ ticket.

номина́л (-а) *м* (*КОММ*) face value.

номина́льный (-ен, -ьна, -ьно) *прил* (*зарплата*) nominal; ~ьная цена́ face value.

но́нсенс (-а) *м* nonsense.

нор|а́ (-ы́; *nom pl* -ы) *ж* (*зайца*) burrow; (*лисы*) den; (*барсука*) set; (*перен*) hole.

Норве́ги|я (-и) *ж* Norway.

норве́ж|ец (-ца) *м* Norwegian.

норве́ж|ка (-ки; *gen pl* -ек) *ж см* **норве́жец**.

норве́жск|ий (-ая, -ое, -ие) *прил* Norwegian; ~ язы́к Norwegian.

норве́жца *итп сущ см* **норве́жец**.

но́р|ка (-ки; *gen pl* -ок) *ж* mink.

но́рковый *прил* mink *опред*.

но́рм|а (-ы) *ж* standard; (*выработки, прибыли*) rate; ~ **поведе́ния** behavioural norm; **войти́** (*perf*) *или* **прийти́** (*perf*) **в** ~**у** (*в обычное состояние*) to return to normal; **он сего́дня в** ~**е** (*разг*) he's fine today.

норма́лен *прил см* **норма́льный**.

нормализа́ци|я (-и) *ж* normalization.

нормализ|ова́ть (-у́ю) (*не)сов перех* (*обстановку, отношения*) to normalize

► **нормализова́ться** (*не)сов возв* to stabilize.

норма́льно *нареч* normally ♦ *как сказ*: э́то вполне́ ~ this is quite normal; **как дела́? –** ~ how are things? – not bad; **у нас всё** ~ everything's fine with us.

норма́льность (-и) *ж* normality.

норма́льный (-ен, -ьна, -ьно) *прил* normal; (*психически*) of sound mind.

Норма́нди|я (-и) *ж* Normandy.

норма́тив (-а) *м* norm.

нормати́вный *прил* normative.

норми́ровани|е (-я) *ср* (*цен*) standardization; (*мяса*) rationing.

норми́р|овать (-ую) (*не)сов перех* to standardize.

норов|и́ть (-лю́, -и́шь) *несов неперех* (*разг*): ~ +*infin* to take pains to do.

но́рок *сущ см* **но́рка**.

нос (-а; *part gen* -у, *loc sg* -у́, *nom pl* -ы́) *м* nose; (*корабля*) bow; (*птицы*) beak, bill; (*ботинка*) toe; **из-под но́са у** +*gen* from under the nose of; **отъе́зд/экза́мен на** ~**у́** (*разг*) the departure/ exam is imminent; **под но́сом** (*разг: близко*) under one's (very) nose; **с но́сом оста́ться** (*perf*) (*разг*) to be left with nothing; **води́ть** (*impf*) **кого́-н за** ~ to lead sb by the nose; **он не ви́дит да́льше со́бственного но́са** (*разг*) he can't see further than his own nose; **сова́ть** (*impf*) ~ **в** +*acc* (*разг*) to poke *или* stick one's nose into.

носа́т|ый (-, -а, -о) *прил* with a big nose.

но́сик (-а) *м* (*человека*) small nose; (*чайника*) spout.

носи́л|ки (-ок) *мн* (*для раненых*) stretcher.

носи́льщик (-а) *м* porter.

носи́тел|ь (-я) *м* (*идей, прогресса*) bearer; (*инфекции*) carrier; (*данных, информации*) transmitter; **носи́тель языка́** native speaker.

носи́тельниц|а (-ы) *ж* (*идей, прогресса*) bearer.

но|си́ть (-шу́, -сишь) *несов перех* (*вещи, камни*) to carry; (*платье, очки*) to wear; (*усы, бороду, причёску*) to sport; (*фамилию мужа*) to use; (*отличаться: подлеж: предложение, спор,*) to be characterized by; **на́ши отноше́ния но́сят делово́й хара́ктер** our relations are of a business nature; ~ (*impf*) **на рука́х** to carry; (*перен: любить*) to adore

► **носи́ться** *несов возв* (*человек*) to rush; (*слухи*) to spread; (*одежда*) to wear; (*разг: увлекаться*): ~**ся с** +*instr* (*с идеей*) to be preoccupied with; (*с человеком*) to make a fuss of; ~**ся** (*impf*) **в во́здухе** (*настроения*) to be in the air; (*идея*) to be widespread.

но́ск|а (-и) *ж* (*одежды, обуви*) wearing; **удо́бный в** ~**е** comfortable (to wear).

носка́ *итп сущ см* носо́к.

но́ский (-кая, -кое, -кие; -ок, -ка́, -ко) *прил* (туфли, ткань) hard-wearing.

носово́й *прил* (звук) nasal; **~а́я часть** bow; **носово́й плато́к** handkerchief.

но́сок *прил см* но́ский.

носо́к (-ка́; *gen pl* -о́к) *м* (обычно *мн:* чулок) sock; (*gen pl* -ко́в; ботинка, чулка, ноги) toe; **встава́ть** (**встать** *perf*) **на ~ки** to stand on tiptoe.

носоро́г (-а) *м* rhinoceros, rhino (*inf*).

ностальги́ческий (-ая, -ое, -ие) *прил* nostalgic.

ностальги́я (-и) *ж* (по дому) homesickness, nostalgia; (по утраченному) nostalgia.

но́та (-ы) *ж* note; *см также* но́ты.

нотариа́льный *прил* (услуги) notarial; **нотариа́льная конто́ра** notarial office.

нота́риус (-а) *м* notary (public).

нота́ция (-и) *ж* (выговор) lecture.

но́тный *прил:* **~ое письмо́** musical notation.

но́ты (-) *мн* (муз) sheet music; **как по ~ам** (перен) smoothly.

но́у-ха́у *ср нескл* know-how.

ночева́ть (-у́ю; *perf* **переночева́ть**) *несов неперех* to spend the night.

ночёвка (-ки; *gen pl* -ок) *ж:* **останови́ться на ~ку** to spend the night; **они́ прие́хали с ~кой** they came and stayed the night.

ночле́г (-а) *м* (место) somewhere to spend the night; **останови́ться** (*perf*) **на ~** to spend the night.

ночле́жный *прил:* **~ дом** hostel.

ночни́к (-а́) *м* night-light.

ночно́й *прил* (час, холод) night *опред*; **ночна́я руба́шка** nightshirt; **ночна́я сме́на** night shift.

ночь (-и; *loc sg* -и́, *nom pl* -и, *gen pl* -е́й) *ж* night; **с утра́ до ~и** from dawn to dusk; **на ~** before bed; **споко́йной но́чи!** good night!

но́чью *нареч* at night; **и днём и ~** day and night.

но́ша (-и) *ж* burden.

ноше́ние (-я) *ср* (действие) wearing; **~ ору́жия** (ЮР) carrying of offensive weapons.

но́шеный *прил* (одежда, туфли) second-hand.

ношу́(сь) *несов см* носи́ть(ся).

но́ю *итп несов см* ныть.

ноя́брь (-я́) *м* November; *см также* октя́брь.

ноя́брьский (-ая, -ое, -ие) *прил* November *опред*.

нрав (-а) *м* (человека) temperament; **э́то мне по нра́ву** this is to my liking; *см также* нра́вы.

нра́виться (-люсь, -ишься; *perf* **понра́виться**) *несов возв* (+*dat*): **мне ~ится э́тот фильм** I like this film; **мне ~ится чита́ть/гуля́ть** I like to read/go for a walk.

нравоуче́ние (-я) *ср* lecture on morals; (в басне) moral; **чита́ть** (*impf*) **кому́-н ~я** to give sb a lecture on morals.

нравоучи́тельный (-ен, -ьна, -ьно) *прил* (рассказ, история) with a moral; (тон) moralizing.

нра́вственность (-и) *ж* morals *мн*.

нра́вственный (-, -на, -но) *прил* moral.

нра́вы (-ов) *мн* (обычаи) customs *мн*.

н.с. *сокр* (= но́вого сти́ля) NS (New Style).

НТР *ж сокр* = нау́чно-техни́ческая револю́ция.

KEYWORD

ну *межд* **1** (выражает побуждение) come on; **ну, начина́й!** come on, get started!

2 (выражает восхищение) what; **ну и си́ла!** what strength!

3 (выражает иронию) well (well); **ну и у́мник же ты!** well (well), what a clever fellow you are!

♦ *част* **1** (неужели): (**да**) **ну?!** not really?!; **я женю́сь – да ну?!** I'm getting married – not really?!

2 (усиливает выразительность): **ну коне́чно!** why of course!; **ну, я тебе́ покажу́!** why, I'll show you!

3 (допустим): **ты говори́шь по-англи́йски? – ну, говорю́** do you speak English? – what if I do

4 (во фразах); **ну и ну!** (разг) well well!; **ну-ка!** (разг) come on!; **ну тебя́/его́!** (разг) to hell with you/him!

нувори́ш (-а) *м* nouveau riche.

нуга́ (-и́) *ж* nougat.

ну́ден *прил см* ну́дный.

нуди́ст (-а) *м* nudist.

нуди́стка (-и) *ж см* нуди́ст.

ну́дно *нареч* tediously.

ну́дный (-ен, -на́, -но) *прил* tedious.

нужда́ (-ы́; *nom pl* -ы) *ж* (no pl; бедность) poverty; (потребность): **~ (в** +*prp*) need (for); **ну́жды населе́ния** the needs of the population; **в э́том нет ~ы** there is no need for it.

нужда́ться (-юсь) *несов возв* (бедствовать) to be needy; **~** (*impf*) **в** +*prp* to need, be in need of.

ну́жен *прил см* ну́жный.

ну́жно *как сказ* (необходимо): **~ им помо́чь** или **~, что́бы им помогли́** it is necessary to help them; **~ хоро́шего специали́ста** a good specialist is needed; **мне ~ идти́** I have to go, I must go; **мне ~ 10 рубле́й** I need 10 roubles; **о́чень ~!** (разг) my foot!

ну́жный (-ен, -на́, -но, -ны) *прил* necessary.

нулево́й *прил:* **~а́я температу́ра** temperature of zero; **~а́я отме́тка** (mark of) zero; **~ результа́т** no result.

нуль (-я́) *м* (мат) zero, nought; (при исчислении температуры) zero; (перен: человек) nothing; **начина́ть** (**нача́ть** *perf*) **с ~я́** to start from scratch; **своди́ться** (**свести́сь** *perf*) **к ~ю́** to come to nothing.

нумера́ция (-и) *ж* numbering.

нумерова́ть (-у́ю; *perf* **пронумерова́ть**) *несов перех* to number.

нумизма́т (-а) *м* numismatist.

нумизма́тика (-и) *ж* numismatics.

ну́трия (-и) *ж* (зоол) coypu.

нутро́ (-а́) *ср* (разг: интуиция) instincts *мн*; **э́то**

мне не по ~ý I'm not too keen on this.

НФ *м сокр* (= *национáльный фронт*) NF (=
National Front;) (= *нау́чная фантáстика*)
sci-fi, SF (= *science fiction*).

НФС *сокр* (= *Национáльная федерáция спорт*)
national federation of sport.

НХЛ *ж сокр* (= *Национáльная хоккéйная ли́га*)
NHL (= *National Hockey League*).

НЧ *сокр* (= *ни́зкая частотá*) LF (= *low
frequency*) ◆ *прил* (*низкочастóтный*) LF (=
low-frequency).

ны́не *нареч* today.

ны́нешн|ий (**-яя, -ее, -ие**) *прил* (*события,
правительство*) the present; (*молодёжь*)
today's; ~**ее лéто** this summer.

ны́нче *нареч* (*разг: сегóдня*) today; (: *теперь*)
nowadays.

нырну́ть (**-ý, -ёшь**) *сов неперех* (*также перен*)
to dive.

ныря́льщик (**-а**) *м* diver.

ныря́льщиц|а (**-ы**) *ж см* **ныря́льщик**.

ныря́|ть (**-ю**) *несов неперех* (*также перен*) to
dive.

ныть (**нóю, нóешь**) *несов неперех* (*рана, зуб*) to
ache; (*жáловаться*) to moan.

Нью-Йóрк (**-а**) *м* New York.

н.э. *сокр* (= *нáшей э́ры*) AD (= *anno Domini*).

НЭП *м сокр* (*ИСТ:* = *нóвая экономи́ческая
поли́тика*) NEP (= *New Economic Policy*).

нюáнс (**-а**) *м* nuance.

Ню́рнберг (**-а**) *м* Nuremberg.

нюх (**-а**) *м* (*собáки*) nose; (*перен: разг*): ~ **на**
+*acc* nose for.

ню́ха|ть (**-ю**; *perf* **поню́хать**) *несов перех*
(*цветы́, вóздух*) to smell; (*спирт*) to sniff; ~
(*impf*) **табáк** to take snuff.

ня́нек *сущ см* **ня́нька**.

ня́неч|ка (**-ки**; *gen pl* **-ек**) *ж* (*разг*) = **ня́ня**.

ня́нч|ить (**-у, -ишь**) *несов перех* to mind

▶ **ня́нчиться** *несов возв:* ~**ся с** +*instr* (*с
младéнцем*) to mind; (*разг: с лентя́ем, с
му́жем*) to fuss over.

ня́нь|ка (**-ьки**; *gen pl* **-ек**) *ж* (*разг: ребёнка*)
nanny.

ня́н|я (**-и**; *gen pl* **-ь**) *ж* nanny; (*рабóтающая на
дому́*) child minder; (*в больни́це*) auxiliary
nurse; (*в детском саду́*) cleaner; **приходя́щая**
~ babysitter.

~ O, o ~

O, o сущ нескл *(буква)* the 15th letter of the Russian alphabet.

o предл *(+prp)* about; *(+acc; опереться, удариться)* against; *(споткнуться)* over ♦ межд oh; **кни́га ~ Росси́и** a book on *или* about Russia; **мы́сли ~ до́ме** thoughts of home; **во́лны бью́тся ~ ска́лы** the waves are beating against the cliffs; **~ да/нет!** oh yes/no!; **~, е́сли бы ты знал!** oh, if only you knew!

o. сокр *(= **о́стров**)* I *(= island)*; *(= **о́зеро**)* L *(= lake)*.

o- префикс *(in verbs; сделать каким-нибудь) indicating change of state eg.* округли́ть; *(снабдить чем-н) indicating suppy of sth eg.* озагла́вить; *(распространить действие на всю поверхность) indicating covering of a surface with sth eg.* охвати́ть; *(распространить действие на многих) indicating action involving many people eg.* одари́ть.

оа́зис (-а) *м (также перен)* oasis.

ОАЕ *ж сокр (= Организа́ция африка́нского еди́нства)* OAU *(= Organization of African Unity)*.

ОАПЕ́К *ж сокр (= Организа́ция ара́бских стран-экспортёров не́фти)* OAPEC *(= Organization of Arab Petroleum-Exporting Countries)*.

об предл = **о**.

об- префикс см **о-**.

об|а́ (-о́их; *см* **Table 26**; *f* **обе**, *nt* **о́ба**) *м чис* both; **смотре́ть** *(impf)* **в ~** *(разг: быть осторожным)* to watch out; *(: быть внимательным)* to keep one's eyes peeled.

обалде́ть (-ю; *impf* **обалдева́ть**) *сов неперех (разг)* to go crazy.

обанкро́|титься (-чусь, -тишься) *сов возв* to go bankrupt; *(перен: идея, политика)* to prove (to be) bankrupt.

обая́ние (-я) *ср* charm.

обая́тельный (-ен, -ьна, -ьно) *прил* charming.

обва́л (-а) *м (в шахте, в штольне)* rock fall; *(снежный)* avalanche; *(здания, этажа, рубля)* collapse.

обва́лива|ть (-ю) *несов от* **обваля́ть**.

обвал|и́ться (3sg -ится, 3pl -ятся, *impf* **обва́ливаться**) *сов возв* to collapse; *(потолок, крыша)* to cave in, collapse.

обваля́|ть (-ю; *impf* **обва́ливать**) *сов перех: ~*

кого́-н/что-н в *+prp* to roll sb/sth in.

обвар|и́ть (-ю́, -ришь; *impf* **обва́ривать**) *сов перех* to pour boiling water over; *(кулин)* to blanch; *(обжечь)* to scald

► **обвари́ться** (*impf* **обва́риваться**) *сов возв (обжечься)* to scald o.s.

обведу́ *итп сов см* **обвести́**.

обвенча́|ть (-ю; *impf* **венча́ть**) *сов перех* to marry

► **обвенча́ться** (*impf* **венча́ться**) *сов возв* to get married, marry.

обв|ести́ (-еду́, -едёшь; *pt* -ёл, -ела́, -ело́, *impf* **обводи́ть**) *сов перех (букву, чертёж)* to go over *(drawing, outline etc)*; *(окаймить: заголовок, рисунок)* to edge; *(футболиста)* to pass *(while keeping possession of the ball/puck etc)*; **обводи́ть** (*~ perf*) **вокру́г** *+gen (стола, дома)* to lead *или* take round; **обводи́ть** (*~ perf*) **что-н/кого́-н глаза́ми** to run one's eye over sth/sb; **~** (*perf*) **кого́-н вокру́г па́льца** *(разг)* to twist sb round one's little finger.

обве́тренный *прил* weather-beaten.

обве́тр|иться (-юсь, -ишься; *impf* **обве́триваться**) *сов возв* to become weather-beaten.

обветша́лый *прил* dilapidated.

обвива́|ть(ся) (-ю(сь)) *несов от* **обви́ть(ся)**.

обвине́ние (-я) *ср: ~* **(в** *+prp)* accusation (of); *(ЮР)* charge (of) ♦ *ссбир (обвиняющая сторона)* the prosecution; **свиде́тели ~я** witnesses for the prosecution.

обвини́тел|ь (-я) *м* accuser; *(ЮР)* prosecutor.

обвини́тельный *прил (речь, выступление)* accusatory; **~ пригово́р** *(ЮР)* verdict of guilty; **~ акт** *(ЮР)* indictment.

обвин|и́ть (-ю́, -и́шь; *impf* **обвиня́ть**) *сов перех: ~* **кого́-н** **(в** *+prp)* to accuse sb (of); *(ЮР)* to charge sb (with).

обвиня́ем|ая (-ой; *decl like adj) ж см* **обвиня́емый**.

обвиня́ем|ый (-ого; *decl like adj) м* the accused *или* defendant.

обвиня́|ть (-ю) *несов от* **обвини́ть** ♦ *перех (ЮР)* to prosecute.

обвиса́|ть (3sg -ет, 3pl -ют, *perf* **обви́снуть**) *несов неперех* to droop.

обви́слый *прил (разг: кожа)* sagging; *(: усы)* drooping; *(: тело)* flabby.

обви́с|нуть (3sg -нет, 3pl -нут, *pt* -, -ла, -ло) *сов от* **обвиса́ть**.

обви́ть (-овью́, -овьёшь; *impf* обвива́ть) *сов перех (подлеж: плющ, вьюн)* to twine around; обвива́ть (~ *perf*) кого́-н/что-н чем-н to wind sth round sb/sth; обвива́ть (~ *perf*) чью-н ше́ю рука́ми to wrap one's arms around sb's neck
► обви́ться (*impf* обвива́ться) *сов возв:* ~ся вокру́г +gen to twine around.

обв|оди́ть (-ожу́, -о́дишь) *несов от* обвести́.

обводн|и́ть (-ю́, -и́шь; *impf* обводня́ть) *сов перех* to irrigate.

обво́дный *прил:* ~ кана́л canal encircling a town.

обводня́|ть (-ю) *несов от* обводни́ть.

обвожу́ *несов см* обводи́ть.

обвора́жива|ть (-ю) *несов от* обворожи́ть.

обвор|ова́ть (-у́ю; *impf* обворо́вывать) *сов перех (разг: квартиру)* to do over; (: сосе́да) to rob.

обворожи́тел|ьный (-ен, -ьна, -ьно) *прил* captivating.

обворож|и́ть (-у́, -и́шь; *impf* обвора́живать) *сов перех* to captivate.

обвяз|а́ть (-яжу́, -я́жешь; *impf* обвя́зывать) *сов перех:* ~ кого́-н/что-н чем-н (верёвкой, платком) to tie sth round sb/sth; ~ (*perf*) что-н спи́цами/крючко́м to knit/crochet a border on sth
► обвяза́ться (*impf* обвя́зываться) *сов возв:* ~ся чем-н to tie sth round o.s.

обгл|ода́ть (-ожу́, -о́жешь; *impf* обгла́дывать) *сов перех* to pick clean.

обговор|и́ть (-ю́, -и́шь; *impf* обгова́ривать) *сов перех (разг)* to discuss.

обго́н (-а) *м* overtaking.

обгоню́ *итп сов см* обогна́ть.

обгоня́|ть (-ю) *несов от* обогна́ть.

обгора́|ть (-ю) *несов от* обгоре́ть.

обгоре́лый *прил (дом, дерево)* burnt; (*разг: спина, плечи)* sunburnt.

обгор|е́ть (-ю́, -и́шь; *impf* обгора́ть) *сов неперех (дом)* to be burnt; (*разг: на пожаре)* to get burnt; (: на со́лнце) to get sunburnt.

обгрыз|ть (-у́, -ёшь; *impf* обгрыза́ть) *сов перех (яблоко, кость)* to gnaw; обгрыза́ть (~ *perf*) но́гти to bite one's nails right down.

обдел|и́ть (-елю́, -е́лишь; *impf* обделя́ть) *сов перех:* он ~ели́л её деньга́ми he didn't give her the money; приро́да ~ели́ла его́ умо́м/си́лой he is not blessed with intelligence/strength; всем да́ли пода́рки, а его́ ~ели́ли everybody got a present but he was left out.

обдеру́ *итп сов см* ободра́ть.

обдира́|ть (-ю) *несов от* ободра́ть.

обду́ман|ный (-, -на, -но) *прил* considered.

обду́ма|ть (-ю; *impf* обду́мывать) *сов перех* to consider, think over.

обдур|и́ть (-ю́, -и́шь; *impf* обдуря́ть) *сов перех:* ~ кого́-н (разг: обмануть) to pull the wool over

sb's eyes; (: смошеннича́ть) to rip sb off.

о́б|е (-е́их) *ж чис см* о́ба.

обега́|ть (-ю; *impf* обега́ть) *сов перех (разг)* to rush round.

обега́|ть (-ю) *несов от* обе́гать, обежа́ть.

обегу́ *итп сов см* обежа́ть.

обе́д (-а) *м* lunch, dinner; (*время)* lunch *или* dinner time; (*разг: перерыв)* lunch break; за ~ом at lunch *или* dinner; по́сле ~а after lunch *или* dinner; (*после 12 часов дня)* in the afternoon; закры́т на ~ closed for lunch.

обе́да|ть (-ю; *perf* пообе́дать) *несов неперех* to have lunch *или* dinner; (*разг: уходить на перерыв)* to take a lunch break.

обе́ден *сущ см* обе́дня.

обе́денный *прил (стол, сервиз)* dinner *опред*; (*часы, время)* lunch *опред*, dinner *опред*.

обедне́вший (-ая, -ее, -ие) *прил* impoverished.

обедне́|ть (-ю) *сов от* бедне́ть.

обе́д|ня (-ни; *gen pl* -ен) *ж (РЕЛ)* Mass; идти́ (пойти́ *perf*) к ~не to go to Mass; служи́ть (*impf*) ~ню to hear Mass.

обежа́ть (*как* бежа́ть; *см* **Table 20**; *impf* обега́ть) *сов перех (разг: магазины)* to rush round ♦ *неперех:* ~ вокру́г +gen to run round.

обезбо́ливани|е (-я) *ж* anaesthetization (*BRIT*), anesthetization (*US*).

обезбо́лива|ть (-ю) *несов от* обезбо́лить.

обезбо́ливающ|ее (-его; *decl like adj*) *ср (разг)* painkiller.

обезбо́ливающ|ий (-ая, -ее, -ие) *прил* anaesthetic *опред (BRIT)*, anesthetic *опред (US)*.

обезбо́л|ить (-ю, -ишь; *impf* обезбо́ливать) *сов перех* to anaesthetize (*BRIT*), anesthetize (*US*); обезбо́ливать (~ *perf*) кому́-н ро́ды to give sb an anaesthetic (*BRIT*) *или* anesthetic (*US*) during childbirth.

обезво́|дить (-жу, -дишь; *impf* обезво́живать) *сов перех (землю)* to drain; (*организм)* to dehydrate.

обезво́жу *сов см* обезво́дить.

обезвре́|дить (-жу, -дишь; *impf* обезвре́живать) *сов перех (бомбу)* to defuse; (*воду)* to purify; (*преступника)* to make powerless.

обезгла́в|ить (-лю, -ишь; *impf* обезгла́вливать) *сов перех* to behead; (*перен: восстание)* to leave without a leader.

обездо́лен|ный (-, -на, -но) *прил* deprived.

обездо́л|ить (-ю, -ишь) *сов перех* to deprive.

обезжи́ренный *прил* fat-free.

обезжи́р|ить (-ю, -ишь; *impf* обезжи́ривать) *сов перех (молоко, творог)* to skim; (*шерсть)* to remove fat from.

обезли́ч|ить (-у, -ишь; *impf* обезли́чивать) *сов перех* to depersonalize; (*работу, руководство)* to remove individual responsibility from.

обезобра́|зить (-жу, -зишь; *impf*

обезобрá|живать) *сов перех* to disfigure.
обезопá|сить (-шу, -сишь) *сов перех* (*себя, друга*) to protect
▶ **обезопáситься** *сов возв* to protect o.s.
обезорý|жить (-у, -ишь; *impf* **обезорýживать)** *сов перех* (*также перен*) to disarm.
обезýме|ть (-ю) *сов неперех:* ~ **от** +*gen* (*страха, горя итп*) to go out of one's mind with.
обезья́н|а (-ы) *ж* (*с хвостом*) monkey; (*без хвоста*) ape; (*перен: разг*) copycat.
обезья́н|ий (-ья, -ье, -ьи) *прил* (*хвост*) monkey's; (*повадки*) apelike.
обезья́нича|ть (-ю; *impf* **собезья́нничать)** *несов неперех* (*разг*) to be a copycat.
обéих *чис см* **обé.**
обéй(те) *сов см* **обúть.**
обелúск (-а) *м* obelisk.
обел|úть (-ю́, -úшь; *impf* **обеля́ть)** *сов перех* to whitewash.
оберегá|ть (-ю) *несов перех* (*человека*) to protect; (*имущество*) to guard.
оберн|ýть (-ý, -ёшь; *impf* **обёртывать** *или* **оборáчивать)** *сов перех* (*книгу, посылку*) to wrap (up); (*impf* **оборáчивать;** *капитал*) to turn over; **обёртывать** *или* **оборáчивать** (~ *perf*) **что-н вокрýг** +*gen* (*талии, головы*) to wrap sth round; **оборáчивать** (~ *perf*) **дéло в свою́ пóльзу** (*перен*) to turn things to one's own advantage
▶ **обернýться** (*impf* **оборáчиваться**) *сов возв* (*повернуться назад*) to turn (round); (*капитал, деньги*) to be recovered; **оборáчиваться** (~*ся perf*) +*instr* (*неприятностями, сюрпризом*) to turn out to be; (*лебедем, волком*) to turn into.
обёрт|ка (-ки; *gen pl* **-ок)** *ж* (*книжная, конфетная*) wrapper; (*на посылке*) wrapping.
обёрточн|ый *прил:* ~**ая бумáга** wrapping paper.
оберý(сь) *итп сов см* **обобрáть(ся).**
обескрóв|ить (-лю, -ишь) *сов перех* (*перен*) to sap the strength of.
обескурáженный (-, -на, -но) *прил* baffled.
обескурá|жить (-у, -ишь; *impf* **обескурáживать)** *сов перех* (*озадачить*) to baffle.
обеспéчени|е (-я) *ср* (*мира, безопасности, договора*) guarantee; ~ +*instr* (*сырьём, продуктами*) provision of; **материáльное** ~ financial security.
обеспéченност|ь (-и) *ж* (*material*) comfort; (*школ, завода итп*) provision; **финáнсовая** ~ financial security.
обеспéчен|ный (-, -на, -но) *прил* well-off, well-to-do.
обеспéч|ить (-у, -ишь; *impf* **обеспéчивать)** *сов перех* (*семью*) to provide for; (*мир, успех*) to guarantee, ensure; **обеспéчивать** (~ *perf*) **когó-н/чтó-н чем-н** to provide sb/sth with sth, provide *или* supply sth for sb/sth.

обеспокó|ить (-ю, -ишь) *сов от* **беспокóить.**
обессú́ле|ть (-ю; *impf* **обессúлевать)** *сов неперех* to become *или* grow weak.
обессú́л|ить (-ю, -ишь; *impf* **обессúливать)** *сов перех* to weaken.
обесслáв|ить (-лю, -ишь) *сов перех* to besmirch.
обессмéр|тить (-чу, -тишь) *сов перех* to immortalize.
обесточ|ить (-у, -ишь; *impf* **обесточивать)** *сов перех* (*ТЕХ*) to cut off the power to.
обесцвé|тить (-чу, -тишь; *impf* **обесцвéчивать)** *несов перех* to bleach; (*перен: рассказ*) to tone down
▶ **обесцвéтиться** (*impf* **обесцвéчиваться**) *сов возв* to be bleached; (*ткань: от времени*) to fade; (*перен: рассказ*) to become flat.
обесцéнивани|е (-я) *ср* (*валюты*) depreciation; (: *намеренное*) devaluation.
обесцéн|ить (-ю, -ишь; *impf* **обесцéнивать)** *сов перех* (*также перен*) to devalue
▶ **обесцéниться** (*impf* **обесцéниваться**) *сов возв* to be devalued; (*вещь*) to depreciate.
обесчé|стить (-щу, -стишь) *сов от* **бесчéстить.**
обéт (-а) *м* vow.
обетóванн|ый *прил:* ~**ая земля́** the Promised Land.
обещáни|е (-я) *ср* promise.
обещá|ть (-ю; *perf* **обещáть** *или* **пообещáть)** *несов (не)перех* to promise.
обжáловани|е (-я) *ср* appeal.
обжáл|овать (-ую) *сов перех* to appeal against.
обжáр|ить (-ю, -ишь; *impf* **обжáривать)** *сов перех* to brown.
обж|éчь (-гý, -ожжёшь *итп*, **-огýт;** *pt* **-жёг, -огла́, -огло́)** *сов от* **жечь** ♦ (*impf* **обжигáть**) *перех* to burn; (*кирпич итп*) to fire; (*дерево итп*) to scorch; (*подлеж: крапива*) to sting
▶ **обжéчься** *сов от* **жéчься** ♦ (*impf* **обжигáться**) *возв* to burn o.s.; (*перен: потерпеть неудачу*) to get one's fingers burnt.
обжирá|ться (-юсь) *несов от* **обожрáться.**
обжитóй *прил* (*дом*) lived-in.
обжóр|а (-ы) *м/ж* (*разг*) pig, greedy guts.
обжóрств|о (-а) *ср* (*разг*) greediness.
обжýл|ить (-ю, -ишь; *impf* **обжýливать)** *сов перех* (*разг*) to con.
обзаве|стúсь (-дýсь, -дёшься; *impf* **обзаводúться)** *сов возв* (+*instr; разг*) to get o.s.
обзвон|úть (-ю́, -úшь; *impf* **обзвáнивать)** *сов перех* (*разг*) to phone round.
обзовý *итп сов см* **обозвáть.**
обзóр (-а) *м* view; (*статьи, новостей*) review.
обзóрн|ый *прил* general; ~**ая статья́** review.
обзывá|ть (-ю) *несов от* **обозвáть**
▶ **обзывáться** *несов возв* (*разг*) to call people names.
обивá|ть (-ю) *несов от* **обúть**
обúв|ка (-и) *ж* upholstery.
обú|да (-ы) *ж* (*несправедливость*) insult;

(*горечь*) grievance; **кака́я ~!** what a pity!; **наноси́ть (нанести́** *perf*) **~у кому́-н** to hurt *или* offend sb; **не дава́ть (дать** *perf*) **кого́-н в ~у** (*разг*) to stand *или* stick up for sb; **быть** (*impf*) **в ~е на кого́-н** to be in a huff with sb.

оби́ден *прил см* **оби́дный**.

оби́деть (-жу, -дишь; *impf* **обижа́ть**) *сов перех* to hurt, offend; **он ~жен умо́м/красото́й** (*разг*) he's not too smart/good-looking

▸ **оби́деться** (*impf* **обижа́ться**) *сов возв*: **~ся (на** +*acc*) to be hurt *или* offended (by).

оби́дно *как сказ* (*см прил*) it's offensive; it's annoying; **мне ~ слы́шать э́то** it hurts me to hear this; **~, что мы не встре́тились** it's annoying that we didn't meet.

оби́дный (-ен, -на, -но) *прил* (*оскорби́тельный*) offensive; (*разг: досадный*) annoying.

оби́дчив|ый (-, -а, -о) *прил* touchy.

обижа́ть(ся) (-ю(сь)) *несов от* **оби́деть(ся)**.

оби́жен|ный (-, -на, -но) *прил* aggrieved.

обижу́(сь) *сов см* **оби́деть(ся)**.

оби́лен *прил см* **оби́льный**.

оби́ли|е (-я) *ср* abundance.

оби́л|ьный (-ен, -ьна, -ьно) *прил* abundant; (+*instr*: *рыбой, талантами*) rich in; **~ьная еда́** food in abundance.

обиня́к (-а́) *м*: **без обиняко́в** plainly.

обира́ть (-ю) *несов от* **обобра́ть**.

обита́ем|ый (-, -а, -о) *прил* inhabited.

обита́тел|ь (-я) *м* inhabitant.

обита́|ть (-ю) *несов неперех* to live.

оби́|ть (-обью, -обьёшь; *imper* **обе́й(те)**, *impf* **обива́ть**) *сов перех*: **~** (+*instr*) to cover (with); **обива́ть** (**~** *perf*) **поро́ги у кого́-н** to camp on sb's doorstep.

обихо́д (-а) *м*: **быть в ~е** to be in use; **входи́ть (войти́** *perf*) **в ~** to come into use; **выходи́ть (вы́йти** *perf*) **из ~а** to go out of use.

обихо́д|ный (-ен, -на, -но) *прил* everyday.

обката́|ть (-ю; *impf* **обка́тывать**) *сов перех* (*поверхность, дорогу*) to flatten (out); (*машину*) to run in; (*станок итп*) to test (out).

обка́тк|а (-и) *ж* (*дороги*) flattening; (*машины, станка*) testing.

обка́тыва|ть (-ю) *несов от* **обката́ть**.

обкла́дыва|ть(ся) (-ю(сь)) *несов от* **обложи́ть(ся)**.

обкле́|ить (-ю, -ишь; *impf* **обкле́ивать**) *сов перех* (*плакатами, бумагой*) to cover; (*обоями*) to (wall)paper.

обко́м (-а) *м сокр* = **областно́й комите́т**; (*профсоюза, партии*) ≈ regional committee.

обкраду́ *итп сов см* **обокра́сть**.

обкра́дыва|ть (-ю) *несов от* **обокра́сть**.

обку́р|ить (-урю́, -у́ришь; *impf* **обку́ривать**) *сов перех* (*разг: комнату*) to fill with smoke; **ты меня́ совсе́м ~урил** your smoke is suffocating me.

обкуса́|ть (-ю; *impf* **обку́сывать**) *сов перех* to nibble; **обку́сывать (~** *perf*) **но́гти** to bite one's nails.

обл. *сокр* = **о́бласть**.

обла́в|а (-ы) *ж* (*на преступников*) roundup; **устро́ить** (*perf*) **~у на** +*acc* (*на зверя*) to close in on.

облага́|ть (-ю) *несов от* **обложи́ть**.

облагоде́тельств|овать (-ую) *сов перех*: **~ кого́-н** to do sb a great favour (*BRIT*) *или* favor (*US*).

облада́тел|ь (-я) *м* possessor.

облада́|ть (-ю) *несов неперех* (+*instr*) to possess; (*женщиной*) to have; **~** (*impf*) **здоро́вьем** to enjoy good health; **~** (*impf*) **красото́й** to be beautiful.

обла́|зить (-жу, -зишь) *сов перех* (*разг*) to go round.

обла́ива|ть (-ю) *несов от* **обла́ять**.

о́блак|о (-а; *nom pl* -а́, *gen pl* -о́в) *ср* (*также перен*) cloud; **вита́ть** (*impf*) **в облака́х** to have one's head in the clouds.

обла́мыва|ть(ся) (-ю(сь)) *несов от* **обломи́ть(ся)**.

обласка́|ть (-ю) *сов перех* to be kind to.

областно́й *прил* (*центр, театр*) ≈ regional, oblast *опред*; (*выражение, слово*) regional.

о́бласт|ь (-и; *gen pl* -е́й) *ж* region; (*АДМИН*) ≈ region, oblast; (*науки, искусства*) field; **в ~и** +*gen* (*в сфере*) in the field of.

облача́|ть *прил см* **обла́чный**.

о́блачност|ь (-и) *ж* cloud.

о́блач|ный (-ен, -на, -но) *прил* cloudy.

обла́|ять (-ю; *impf* **обла́ивать**) *сов перех* to bark at; (*перен: разг*) to swear at.

облёг *итп сов см* **обле́чь**.

облега́|ть (-ю) *несов от* **обле́чь** ♦ *перех* to fit.

облега́ющий (-ая, -ее, -ие) *прил* close-fitting.

облегча́|ть (-ю) *несов от* **облегчи́ть**.

облегче́ни|е (-я) *ср* (*условий труда, жизни*) improvement; (*успокоение*) relief.

облегчённо *нареч* with relief.

облегчённый *прил* (*ткань, инструмент*) light; (*труд, экзамен*) easier; (*ответ, улыбка*) relieved.

облегч|и́ть (-у́, -и́шь; *impf* **облегча́ть**) *сов перех* (*вес*) to lighten; (*экзамен, жизнь*) to make easier; (*боль, страдание*) to relieve; **облегча́ть** (**~** *perf*) **ду́шу** to ease one's mind.

обледене́лый *прил* (*ступени, горка*) icy; (*борода*) frozen.

обледене́|ть (-ю) *сов неперех* (*см прил*) to become icy; to freeze.

облеза́|ть (-ю) *несов от* **обле́зть**.

обле́злый *прил* (*разг: собака, птица*) mangy; (*вид, внешность*) scruffy; (*стены*) peeling.

обле́з|ть (-у, -ешь; *impf* **облеза́ть**) *сов неперех* *(разг)* to grow mangy; *(краска, обои)* to peel (off); *(стены)* to peel.

облёк *итп сов см* **облечь**.

облека́ть (-ю) *несов от* **облечь**.

облеку́ *сов см* **облечь**.

обл|ени́ться (-еню́сь, -е́нишься) *сов возв* to grow lazy.

обле|пи́ть (-еплю́, -е́пишь); *impf* **облепля́ть)** *сов перех (подлеж: грязь, глина)* to stick to; *(перен: подлеж: люди, мухи)* to surround; *(разг: покрыть)*: ~ **что-н чем-н** to plaster sth with sth.

обле|те́ть (-чу́, -ти́шь); *impf* **облета́ть)** *сов перех* to fly round; *(новость)* to spread ♦ *неперех (листья)* to fall off.

обле́|чь (-ку́, -чёшь *итп,* **-ку́т;** *pt* **-ёк, -екла́, -екло́,** *impf* **облека́ть)** *сов перех*: ~ **кого-н/что-н чем-н** *(властью, доверием)* to vest sb/sth with sth; *(тайной)* to shroud sb/sth in sth; *(impf* **облега́ть,** *3sg* **-я́жет,** *3pl* **-я́гут,** *pt* **-ёг, -егла́, -егло́)** to envelop; **облека́ть (~** *perf)* **что-н в** +*acc* to express sth in.

облива́|ть (-ю) *несов от* **обли́ть**

▶ **облива́ться** *несов от* **обли́ться** ♦ *возв*: ~**ся слеза́ми** to be in floods of tears; **у меня́ се́рдце кро́вью ~ется** my heart bleeds.

облига́ци|я (-и) *ж (комм)* debenture (bond); **премиа́льные ~и** premium bond; **прави́тельственные ~и** government stock.

обл|иза́ть (-ижу́, -и́жешь); *impf* **обли́зывать)** *сов перех (губы, ложку)* to lick; **пиро́г – па́льчики ~и́жешь** *(разг)* the pie is scrumptious

▶ **облиза́ться** *(impf* **обли́зываться)** *сов возв (человек)* to lick one's lips; *(собака, кошка)* to lick itself.

о́блик (-а) *м (внешний вид)* appearance; *(характер, также перен)* character.

облиня́|ть (-ю) *сов от* **линя́ть**.

об|ли́ть (-олью́, -ольёшь); *impf* **облива́ть)** *сов перех*: ~ **кого-н/что-н чем-н** *(намеренно)* to pour sth over sb/sth; *(случайно)* to spill sth over sb/sth; **облива́ть (~** *perf)* **кого-н гря́зью** *(перен)* to throw mud at sb; **облива́ть (~** *perf)* **кого-н презре́нием** to pour scorn on sb; **облива́ть (~** *perf)* **что-н слеза́ми** to shed tears over sth

▶ **обли́ться** *(impf* **облива́ться)** *сов возв*: ~**ся** +*instr (водой)* to sluice o.s. with; *(соком)* to spill over o.s.; **облива́ться (~ся** *perf)* **по́том** to be bathed in sweat.

облицева́|ть (-ю́); *impf* **облицо́вывать)** *сов перех*: ~ **что-н чем-н** to face sth with sth.

облицо́вк|а (-и) *ж* facing.

облицо́вывать (-ю) *несов от* **облицева́ть**.

облича́|ть (-ю) *несов от* **обличи́ть**.

обличи́тельный (-ен, -ьна, -ьно) *прил* damning.

обличи́|ть (-у́, -и́шь); *impf* **облича́ть)** *сов перех* to expose.

обло́жек *сущ см* **обло́жка**.

обложе́ни|е (-я) *ср (действие: налогом итп)* imposition; *(сбор)* levy.

обл|ожи́ть (-ожу́, -о́жишь); *impf* **облага́ть)** *сов перех*: ~ **нало́гом** to tax; *(impf* **обкла́дывать)** to surround; *(печь)* to face; *(подлеж: тучи, облака)* to cover; *(разг: обругать)* to swear at; **го́рло ~ожи́ло** my throat is furred

▶ **обложи́ться** *(impf* **обкла́дываться)** *сов возв*: ~**ся** +*instr* to surround o.s. with.

обло́жк|а (-и; *gen pl* **-ек)** *ж (книги, тетради)* cover; *(для паспорта итп)* holder.

облок|оти́ться (-очу́сь, -о́тишься; *impf* **облока́чиваться)** *сов возв*: ~ **на** +*acc* to lean on *(with elbows)*.

облома́|ть (-ю; *impf* **обла́мывать)** *сов перех (ветки, ногти итп)* to break off; *(перен: разг)*: ~ **кого-н** to talk sb round

▶ **облома́ться** *(impf* **обла́мываться)** *сов возв (ветка, ногти итп)* to break off.

обло́м|ок (-ка) *м* fragment.

облуп|и́ть (-лю́, -и́шь) *сов от* **лупи́ть** ♦ *(impf* **облу́пливать)** *перех* to peel

▶ **облупи́ться** *сов от* **лупи́ться** ♦ *(impf* **облу́пливаться)** *возв (разг)* to peel.

облу́пленный *прил (разг)* peeling; **знать** *(impf,* **кого-н как ~ого** *(разг)* to know sb inside out.

облу́пливать(ся) (-ю(сь)) *несов от* **облупи́ть(ся)**.

облуплю́(сь) *сов см* **облупи́ть(ся)**.

облуча́|ть(ся) (-ю(сь)) *несов от* **облучи́ть(ся)**.

облуче́ни|е (-я) *ср* irradiation.

облуч|и́ть (-у́, -и́шь); *impf* **облуча́ть)** *сов перех* to irradiate

▶ **облучи́ться** *(impf* **облуча́ться)** *сов возв* to be irradiated.

облущ|и́ть (-у́, -и́шь) *сов от* **лущи́ть**.

облыс|е́ть (-ю) *сов от* **лысе́ть**.

облюб|ова́ть (-у́ю); *impf* **облюбо́вывать)** *сов перех* to choose.

обля́жет *итп сов см* **облечь**.

обма́|зать (-жу, -жешь); *impf* **обма́зывать)** *сов перех*: ~ **кого-н/что-н чем-н** to coat sb/sth with sth; *(разг: испачкать)* to get sb/sth covered in sth.

обмакну́|ть (-у́, -ёшь); *impf* **обма́кивать)** *сов перех*: ~ **что-н в** +*acc* to dip sth into.

обма́н (-а) *м* deception; ~ **зре́ния** optical illusion.

обма́нный *прил* fraudulent; **обма́нным путём** fraudulently.

обм|ану́ть (-ану́, -а́нешь); *impf* **обма́нывать)** *сов перех* to deceive; *(поступить нечестно)* to cheat; *(не выполнить обещание)* to fail

▶ **обману́ться** *(impf* **обма́нываться)** *сов возв*: ~**ся в** +*prp* to be disappointed in.

обма́нчивый (-, -а, -о) *прил* deceptive.

обма́нщик (-а) *м* cheat.

обма́нщица (-ы) *ж см* **обма́нщик**.

обма́тыва|ть(ся) (-ю(сь)) *несов от* **обмону́ть(ся)**.

обма́тыва|ть(ся) (-ю(сь)) *несов от* **обмота́ть(ся)**.

обмахну́ть (-у́, -ёшь; *impf* **обма́хивать**) *сов перех* (*пыль*) to brush off; (*стол*) to wipe down; **обма́хивать** (~ *perf*) **лицо́ ве́ером** to fan one's face *или* o.s.

► **обмахну́ться** (*impf* **обма́хиваться**) *сов возв*: ~**ся ве́ером** to fan o.s.

обмеле́|ть (-ю) *сов от* **меле́ть**.

обме́н (-а) *м* (*также* экон) exchange; (*документов*) renewal; (*также*: ~ **веще́ств**: био) metabolism; (*также*: ~ **жилпло́щадью**) exchange (*of flats etc*); **в** ~ **на** +*acc* in exchange for.

обменя́|ть (-ю; *impf* **обме́нивать**) *сов перех* (*вещи, билеты*) to change

► **обменя́|ться** (*impf* **обме́ниваться**) *сов возв*: ~**ся** +*instr* to exchange.

обме́р|ить (-ю, -ишь; *impf* **обме́ривать**) *сов перех* (*участок итп*) to measure.

обме|сти́ (-ту́, -тёшь; *impf* **обмета́ть**) *сов перех* (*песок, паутину*) to brush away.

обм|ета́ть (-ечу́, -е́тишь; *impf* **обмётывать**) *перех* to oversew ♦ *безл* (*разг*): **гу́бы** ~**ета́ло** my lips are chapped.

обмету́ *итп сов см* **обмести́**.

обмётыва|ть (-ю) *несов от* **обмета́ть**.

обмечу́ *сов см* **обмета́ть**.

обмола́чива|ть (-ю) *несов от* **обмолоти́ть**.

обмо́лв|иться (-люсь, -ишься) *сов возв* (*разг*: *сказать невзначай*) to slip in; (: *оговориться*) to slip up; **сло́вом не** ~ (*perf*) (*разг*) to keep mum.

обмоло́т (-а) *м* (*действие*) threshing; (*количество*) yield (*from threshing*).

обмол|оти́ть (-очу́, -о́тишь; *impf* **обмола́чивать**) *сов перех* to thresh.

обморо́|зить (-жу, -зишь; *impf* **обмора́живать**) *сов перех*: ~ **но́гу/ру́ку** to get frostbite in one's foot/hand

► **обморо́|зиться** (*impf* **обмора́живаться**) *сов возв* to suffer from frostbite.

о́бморок (-а) *м* faint; **па́дать** (**упа́сть** *perf*) **в** ~ to faint.

обмота́|ть (-ю; *impf* **обма́тывать**) *сов перех*: ~ **кого́-н/что́-н чем-н** to wrap sth round sb/sth; (*обвить*): ~ **что́-н вокру́г** +*gen* (*пальца, столба*) to wind sth round

► **обмота́|ться** (*impf* **обма́тываться**) *сов возв*: ~**ся вокру́г** +*gen* to be wound round; **обма́тываться** (~**ся** *perf*) +*instr* (*разг*: *шарфом, одеялом*) to wrap o.s. in.

обмо́тк|а (-и) *ж* (ЭЛЕК) winding.

обмо́ю *итп сов см* **обмы́ть**.

обмундирова́ни|е (-я) *ср* (ВОЕН: *действие*) fitting out; (*комплект одежды*) uniform.

обмундир|ова́ть (-у́ю; *impf* **обмундиро́вывать**) *сов перех* to fit out.

обм|ы́ть (-о́ю, -о́ешь; *impf* **обмыва́ть**) *сов перех* (*рану*) to bathe; (*разг*: *событие, премию*)

to celebrate (*by drinking*).

обнагле́|ть (-ю) *сов от* **нагле́ть**.

обнадёж|ить (-у, -ишь; *impf* **обнадёживать**) *сов перех* to reassure; (*обещать*) to assure.

обнажа́|ть(ся) (-ю(сь)) *несов от* **обнажи́ть(ся)**.

обнажённый (-ён, -ена́, -ено́) *прил* bare; (*корни*) exposed.

обнаж|и́ть (-у́, -и́шь; *impf* **обнажа́ть**) *сов перех* to expose; (*руки, ноги*) to bare; (*ветки*) to strip bare; (*шпагу, меч*) to draw

► **обнаж|и́ться** (*impf* **обнажа́ться**) *сов возв* to be exposed; (*человек*) to strip; (*рука, нога итп*) to be bared; (*лес, дерево*) to become bare.

обнаро́довани|е (-я) *ср* (*см глаг*) publication; promulgation.

обнаро́д|овать (-ую) *сов перех* (*факты, статью́*) to make public; (*закон, указ*) to promulgate.

обнаруж|ить (-у, -ишь; *impf* **обнару́живать**) *сов перех* (*найти*) to find; (*проявить*) to show; (*раскрыть*) to reveal

► **обнаруж|иться** (*impf* **обнару́живаться**) *сов возв* (*найтись*) to be found; (*проявиться*) to show; (*стать явным*) to become evident.

обна́шива|ться (-юсь) *несов от* **обноси́ться**.

обн|ести́ (-есу́, -есёшь; *pt* -ёс, -есла́, -есло́, *impf* **обноси́ть**) *сов перех*: ~ **что́-н/кого́-н вокру́г** +*gen* to carry sth/sb round; (*огородить*): ~ **что́-н чем-н** to surround sth with sth; **обноси́ть** (~ *perf*) **кого́-н чем-н** (*вином*) to serve sb with sth.

обнима́|ть(ся) (-ю(сь)) *несов от* **обня́ть(ся)**.

обни́мк|а: **в** ~**у** (*разг*) with their arms around each other.

обниму́(сь) *итп сов см* **обня́ть(ся)**.

обнища́|ть (-ю) *сов от* **нища́ть**.

обнов|и́ть (-лю́, -и́шь; *impf* **обновля́ть**) *сов перех* (*оборудование, гардеро́б*) to replenish; (*репертуа́р, зна́ния*) to refresh; (*па́мятник, дом*) to renovate; (*жизнь, иску́сство*) to revitalize; (*разг*: *пла́тье*) to christen

► **обнов|и́ться** (*impf* **обновля́ться**) *сов возв* (*оборудование, гардеро́б*) to be replenished; (*репертуа́р*) to be refreshed; (*органи́зм, приро́да*) to be regenerated; (*жизнь, иску́сство*) to be revitalized.

обновле́ни|е (-я) *ср* (*см возв*) replenishment; refreshment; regeneration; revitalization.

обновлю́(сь) *сов см* **обнови́ть(ся)**.

обновля́|ть(ся) (-ю(сь)) *несов от* **обнови́ть(ся)**.

обн|оси́ть (-ошу́, -о́сишь) *несов от* **обнести́**.

обн|оси́ться (-ошу́сь, -о́сишься; *impf* **обна́шиваться**) *сов возв* (*разг*: *старик, ребёнок*) to wear out one's clothes; (: *одежда*) to become worn to bits.

обно́ск|и (-ов) *мн* old clothes *мн*.

обношу́(сь) несов см обноси́ть(ся).

обню́ха|ть (-ю; impf **обню́хивать**) сов перех to sniff.

обня́ть (-иму́, -и́мешь; pt -я́л, -яла́, -я́ло, impf **обнима́ть**) сов перех to embrace
▸ **обня́ться** (impf **обнима́ться**) сов возв to embrace (each other).

обо предл см о.

об|обра́ть (-еру́, -ерёшь; impf **обира́ть**) сов перех (сморо́дину, чере́шню) to pick; (разг: прохо́жего, клие́нта) to fleece
▸ **обобра́ться** сов возв: забо́т не ~ерёшься (разг) no end of worries.

обобща́|ть (-ю) несов от **обобщи́ть**.

обобще́ни|е (-я) ср generalization.

обобщён|ный (-, -а, -но) прил general.

обобществ|и́ть (-лю́, -и́шь; impf **обобществля́ть**) сов перех (произво́дство, хозя́йство) to socialize; (зе́млю, труд) to collectivize.

обобществле́ни|е (-я) ср socialization.

обобществлю́ сов см **обобществи́ть**.

обобществля́|ть (-ю) несов от **обобществи́ть**.

обобщ|и́ть (-у́, -и́шь; impf **обобща́ть**) сов перех (результа́ты, фа́кты) to generalize from; (статью́, выступле́ние) to summarize.

обобью́ итп сов см **обви́ть**.

обовью́(сь) итп сов см **обви́ть(ся)**.

обогати́ть (-щу́, -ти́шь; impf **обогаща́ть**) сов перех to enrich; (ру́ду) to concentrate
▸ **обогати́ться** (impf **обогаща́ться**) сов возв (челове́к, страна́) to be enriched; (по́чва, ру́да) to be concentrated.

об|огна́ть (-гоню́, -го́нишь; impf **обгоня́ть**) сов перех to overtake; (перен) to outstrip.

обогн|у́ть (-у́, -ёшь; impf **огиба́ть**) сов перех (стол, дом) to go round.

обогре́в (-а) м heating.

обогре́|ть (-ю; impf **обогрева́ть**) сов перех (помеще́ние) to heat; (замёрзших) to warm; (перен: приласка́ть) to be kind to
▸ **обогре́ться** (impf **обогрева́ться**) сов возв (согре́ться: челове́к) to warm o.s.; (помеще́ние) to heat up; (душа́) to be warmed.

о́б|од (-ода; nom pl -о́дья, gen pl -о́дьев) м rim; (раке́тки) frame.

ободо́к (-ка́) м уменьш от **о́бод**; (на рису́нке, пла́тье) border.

обо́дран|ный (-, -а, -о) прил (стена́) stripped; (дом, оде́жда) shabby; (ру́ки) scratched; (коле́ни) skinned.

об|одра́ть (-деру́, -дерёшь; impf **обдира́ть**) сов перех (кору́, шку́ру) to strip; (ру́ки) to scratch; (коле́ни) to skin; (перен: разг: покупа́теля, клие́нта) to fleece.

ободре́ни|е (-я) ср encouragement.

ободри́тельный (-ен, -ьна, -ьно) прил encouraging.

ободр|и́ть (-ю́, -и́шь; impf **ободря́ть**) сов перех to encourage.

обожа́|ть (-ю) несов перех to adore; ~ (impf) что-н/+infin (разг) to adore sth/doing.

обожгу́(сь) итп сов см **обже́чь(ся)**.

обожеств|и́ть (-лю́, -и́шь; impf **обожествля́ть**) сов перех to worship.

обожествле́ни|е (-я) ср worship.

обожествлю́ сов см **обожестви́ть**.

обожествля́|ть (-ю) несов от **обожестви́ть**.

обожжёшь(ся) итп сов см **обже́чь(ся)**.

обож|ра́ться (-у́сь, -ёшься; pt -а́лся, -ала́сь, -ало́сь, impf **обжира́ться**) сов возв (разг) to stuff o.s.

обо́з (-а) м convoy.

об|озва́ть (-зову́, -зовёшь; impf **обзыва́ть**) сов перех: ~ кого́-н кем-н (разг) to call sb sth.

обозли́ть(ся) (-ю́(сь), -и́шь(ся)) сов от **злить(ся)**.

обознача́|ть (-ю) несов от **обозна́чить** ♦ перех (о зна́ках) to signify
▸ **обознача́ться** несов от **обозна́читься**.

обозначе́ни|е (-я) ср (грани́цы, направле́ния) marking; (на ка́рте, в те́ксте итп) symbol.

обозна́ч|ить (-у, -ишь; impf **обознача́ть**) сов перех (грани́цу, направле́ние) to mark; (no impf): ~ что-н (нос, черты́ лица́) to make sth stand out
▸ **обозна́читься** (impf **обознача́ться**) сов возв to appear; (станови́ться ощути́мым) to become noticeable.

обозрева́тел|ь (-я) м (собы́тий) observer; (на ра́дио и телеви́дении) editor;
междунаро́дный/полити́ческий ~ international/political editor.

обозре́ни|е (-я) ср review; (представле́ние) revue.

обозри́м|ый (-, -а, -о) прил (простра́нство) visible; (собы́тия) observable; ~ое бу́дущее the foreseeable future.

обо́|и (-ев) мн wallpaper ед.

обо́их чис см **о́ба**.

обойду́ итп сов см **обойти́(ся)**.

обо́йм|а (-ы) ж (ВОЕН) (cartridge) clip; (ТЕХ) ring, hoop; (перен: вопро́сов, аргуме́нтов) round.

обойти́ (как идти́; см Table 18; impf **обходи́ть**) сов перех to go round; (пройти́ стороно́й: лу́жу, кана́ву) to skirt, go round; (перен: вопро́с, те́му) to skirt; (: зако́н, ука́з) to get round; (обогна́ть) to pass; (перен: обману́ть) to take in; обходи́ть (~ perf) что-н молча́нием to ignore
▸ **обойти́сь** (impf **обходи́ться**) сов возв (ула́диться) to turn out; (сто́ить): ~сь в +acc to cost; обходи́ться (~сь perf) с кем-н/чем-н to treat sb/sth; обходи́ться (~сь perf) +instr (разг) to get by with; обходи́ться (~сь perf) без +gen (разг) to get by without; (без сканда́ла) to be settled without.

об|окра́сть (-краду́, -крадёшь; impf

обкра́дывать) сов перех to rob.
оболга́ть (-гу́, -жёшь; pt -га́л, -гала́, -га́ло) сов
перех (разг: человека) to slander.
оболо́ч|ка (-ки; gen pl -ек) ж (плода) pericarp;
(зерна) testa, (seed) coat; (Земли) crust; (перен:
человека) shell; (: вопроса) surface;
(аэростата) hull; сли́зистая ~ mucous
membrane.
обо́лтус (-а) м (разг) waster.
обольсти́ть (-щу́, -сти́шь; impf обольща́ть)
сов перех (соблазнить) to seduce; (увлечь) to
captivate.
обольща́ться (-юсь) несов возв to be under a
delusion.
обольщу́ сов см обольсти́ть.
обольют(ся) итп сов см обли́ть(ся).
обомле́ть (-ю) сов неперех (разг) to freeze.
обоня́ние (-я) ср sense of smell.
обопру́сь итп сов см опере́ться.
обора́чиваемость (-и) ж (КОММ) turnover.
обора́чива|ть(ся) (-ю(сь)) несов от
оберну́ть(ся).
оборва́н|ец (-ца) м (разг) scruff.
обо́рван|ный (-, -а, -о) прил (разг: одежда)
tattered; (: рассказ, мысли) fragmented.
оборва́нца итп сущ см оборва́нец.
оборв|а́ть (-у́, -ёшь; pt -а́л, -ала́, -а́ло, impf
обрыва́ть) сов перех (верёвку, нитку) to
break, snap; (ягоды, цветы) to pick; (перен:
разговор, дружбу) to break off; (: разг:
говорящего) to cut short
▶ оборва́ться (impf обрыва́ться) сов возв
(верёвка, нитка) to break, snap; (со скалы) to
fall; (перен: жизнь, разговор, дружба) to be cut
short suddenly.
обо́р|ка (-ки; gen pl -ок) ж frill.
оборо́н|а (-ы) ж defence (BRIT), defense (US);
(линия сооружений) defences мн (BRIT),
defenses мн (US); занима́ть (заня́ть perf) ~у to
take up a defensive position; держа́ть (impf) ~у
to hold the defence.
оборо́нный прил (промышленность) defence
опред (BRIT), defense опред (US).
обороноспосо́бность (-и) ж defence (BRIT)
или defense (US) capacity.
обороня́ть (-ю) несов перех to defend
▶ обороня́ться несов возв (защищаться) to
defend o.s.
оборо́т (-а) м (полный круг) revolution; (КОММ)
turnover; (обратная сторона) back; (перен:
поворот событий) turn; (судов, вагонов)
turnaround; (словесное выражение) turn of
phrase; в ~е in use; входи́ть (войти́ perf) в ~ to
come into use; пуска́ть (пусти́ть perf) в ~
(деньги) to put into circulation; (средства,
сбережения) to invest; брать (взять perf)
кого́-н в ~ (разг) to take sb in hand.
оборо́тлив|ый (-, -а, -о) прил resourceful.

оборо́тный прил (КОММ) working опред.
обору́дование (-я) ср (действие: завода)
equipping; (предметы) equipment; (КОМП)
hardware.
обору́д|овать (-ую) (не)сов перех to equip.
обоснова́ни|е (-я) ср (действие: теории)
substantiation; (довод) basis.
обосно́ван|ный (-, -на, -но) прил substantiated;
~ изно́с (КОММ) fair wear and tear.
обосн|ова́ть (-у́ю; impf обосно́вывать) сов
перех (теорию, вывод) to substantiate
▶ обоснова́ться (impf обосно́вываться) сов
возв (расположиться) to be (situated); (разг:
прочно устроиться) to settle.
обосо́б|ить (-лю, -ишь; impf обособля́ть) сов
перех to set apart; (предложение) to detach
▶ обосо́биться (impf обособля́ться) сов возв
(от коллектива, от семьи) to alienate o.s.
обосо́блен|ный (-, -на, -но) прил (дом, также
линг) detached; (комната) separate; (жизнь)
solitary.
обосо́блю(сь) сов см обосо́бить(ся).
обособля́|ть(ся) (-ю(сь)) несов от
обосо́бить(ся).
обостре́ни|е (-я) ср (см глаг) sharpening;
intensification; aggravation; straining.
обостр|и́ть (-ю́, -и́шь; impf обостря́ть) сов
перех to sharpen; (желания, конфликт) to
intensify; (боль, какое-нибудь чувство) to
aggravate; (отношения) to strain
▶ обостри́ться (impf обостря́ться) сов возв to
sharpen; (желание, разногласия) to intensify;
(боль, какое-нибудь чувство) to become more
acute; (отношения) to become strained.
оботру́(сь) итп сов см обтере́ть(ся).
обо́чин|а (-ы) ж verge.
обошёл(ся) итп сов см обойти́(сь).
обошью́ итп сов см обши́ть.
обою́д|ный (-ен, -на, -но) прил mutual.
обрабо́та|ть (-ю; impf обраба́тывать) сов
перех (камень) to cut; (кожу) to cure; (деталь:
на станке) to turn; (статью, песню) to polish
up; (землю, поле) to till; (перен: разг:
человека) to work on.
обрабо́т|ка (-ки; gen pl -ок) ж (см глаг) cutting;
curing; turning; polishing up; tilling; (перен:
человека) influencing; ~ да́нных (КОМП)
computing; пла́та за ~ку (КОММ) handling
charge.
обра́д|овать(ся) (-ую(сь)) сов от
ра́довать(ся).
о́браз (-а) м image; (человека, зверя)
appearance; (ЛИТЕРАТУРА) figure; (жизни,
мыслей) way; (икона) icon; каки́м ~ом? in
what way?; таки́м ~ом in this way;
(следовательно) consequently; гла́вным ~ом
mainly; ра́вным ~ом similarly; не́которым
~ом to some extent.

óбразен прил см **óбразный**.

образе́ц (-ца́) м (ткани, изделий, оружия) sample; (скромности, мужества, также TEX) model.

óбраз|ный (-ен, -на, -но) прил vivid; **óбразное выраже́ние** (линг) figure of speech.

образова́ни|е (-я) ср formation; (получение знаний) education.

образо́ван|ный (-, -на, -но) прил educated.

образ|ова́ть (-у́ю), impf **образова́ть** или **образо́вывать** сов перех to form

▶ **образова́ться** (impf **образова́ться** или **образо́вываться**) сов возв (трещина, опухоль) to form; (группа, комиссия) to be formed; (разг: уладиться) to turn out all right.

образу́м|ить (-лю, -ишь) сов перех: ~ кого́-н to make sb see sense

▶ **образу́миться** сов возв (стать благоразумным) to come to one's senses.

образца́ итп сущ см **образе́ц**.

образцо́в|ый (-, -а, -о) прил exemplary.

образ|ти́ (-у́, -ёшь; pt **обро́с**, **обросла́**, **обросло́**, impf **обраста́ть**) сов неперех: ~ +instr (травой, деревьями) to become overgrown with; (разг: волосами, грязью) to be covered in; (: хозяйством, барахлом) to surround o.s. with.

обрати́м|ый (-, -а, -о) прил reversible.

обрати́ть (-щу́, -ти́шь; impf **обраща́ть**) сов перех (взгляд, мысли) to turn; **обраща́ть** (~ perf) кого́-н/что-н в +acc to turn sb/sth into; **обраща́ть** (~ perf) внима́ние на +acc to pay attention to; **обраща́ть** (~ perf) кого́-н в бе́гство to force sb to take flight; **обраща́ть** (~ perf) кого́-н в свою́ ве́ру to convert sb to one's own faith

▶ **обрати́ться** (impf **обраща́ться**) сов возв (подлеж: взгляд) to turn; (с вопросом) to inquire; (превратиться): ~ся в +acc to turn into; **обраща́ться** (~ся perf) к +dat (к врачу итп) to consult; (к зрителям) to address; **обраща́ться** (~ся perf) в суд to go to court; **обраща́ться** (~ся perf) в бе́гство to take flight.

обра́тно нареч back; **туда́ и** ~ there and back; **биле́т туда́ и** ~ return ticket (BRIT), round-trip ticket (US).

обра́тн|ое (-ого; decl like adj) ср the opposite; **убежда́ть** (**убеди́ть** perf) кого́-н в ~ом to convince sb of the opposite.

обра́тн|ый прил (порядок, движение, мысль) reverse; (дорога, путь) return опред; **на** ~ом пути́ on the way back; **в** ~ую сто́рону in the opposite direction; the other way; **обра́тная сторона́** reverse (side); **обра́тный а́дрес** return address; **обра́тный биле́т** return (BRIT) или round-trip (US) ticket.

обраща́|ть (-ю) несов от **обрати́ть**

▶ **обраща́ться** несов от **обрати́ться** ♦ возв (деньги, товар) to circulate; ~ся (impf) с +instr (применять) to use; (уметь справля́ться с) to handle; (с человеком) to treat.

обраще́ни|е (-я) ср address; (экон) circulation;

~ к +dat (к народу итп) address to; ~ с +instr (прибором, с огнём) handling of; (с животными, с больным) treatment of; **находи́ться** (impf) в ~и to be in circulation.

обращу́(сь) сов см **обрати́ть(ся)**.

обре́жу итп сов см **обре́зать**.

обре́з (-а) м (книги, альбома) edge; (оружие) sawn-off (BRIT) или sawed-off (US) shotgun; **вре́мени/де́нег в** ~ (разг) there's just enough time/money.

обре́зать (-жу, -жешь; impf **обреза́ть**) сов перех to trim; (разг: прервать) to cut short; (РЕЛ) to circumcise.

обре́з|ок (-ка) м scrap.

обрёк итп сов см **обре́чь**.

обрека́|ть (-ю) несов от **обре́чь**.

обреку́ итп сов см **обре́чь**.

обремени́тельный (-ен, -ьна, -ьно) прил onerous.

обремен|и́ть (-ю́, -и́шь; impf **обременя́ть**) сов перех: ~ кого́-н чем-н to load sb down with sth.

обр|ести́ (-ету́, -ете́шь; pt -ёл, -ела́, -ело́, impf **обрета́ть**) сов перех to find.

обречённ|ый (-ён, -ена́, -ено́) прил doomed.

обре́|чь (-ку́, -чёшь итп, -ку́т; pt -ёк, -екла́, -екло́, impf **обрека́ть**) сов перех: ~ кого́-н на что-н to condemn sb to sth.

обрис|ова́ть (-у́ю; impf **обрисо́вывать**) сов перех (перен) to describe.

обр|они́ть (-оню́, -о́нишь) сов перех to drop; (замечание, фразу) to let drop.

обро́с итп сов см **обрасти́**.

обруб|и́ть (-лю́, -у́бишь; impf **обруба́ть**) сов перех to lop off.

обру́б|ок (-ка) м (пень, хвоста) stump; (дерева) chunk.

обруга́|ть (-ю) сов перех (выбранить) to curse; (обозвать) to swear at; (разг: раскритиковать) to pan, slate (BRIT).

о́бруч (-а) м hoop; (для волос) (Alice) band.

обруча́льн|ый прил: ~ое кольцо́ wedding ring.

обруча́|ть(ся) (-ю(сь)) несов от **обручи́ть(ся)**.

обруче́ни|е (-я) ср betrothal.

обруч|и́ть (-у́, -и́шь; impf **обруча́ть**) сов перех to betroth

▶ **обручи́ться** (impf **обруча́ться**) сов возв to get betrothed.

обру́ш|ить (-у, -ишь; impf **обру́шивать**) сов перех (стену, крышу) to bring down; **обру́шивать** (~ perf) что-н на +acc to bring sth down onto; ~ (perf) **обвине́ния/угро́зы на кого́-н** to bombard sb with accusations/threats

▶ **обру́шиться** (impf **обру́шиваться**) сов возв (крыша, здание) to collapse; **обру́шиваться** (~ся perf) на +acc (на голову) to crash down onto; (на врага) to fall upon; (на человека: с упрёками) to come down on; **на него́** ~илась беда́ he was struck down by misfortune.

обры́в (-а) м (ГЕО) precipice; (на линии) break.

обрыва́|ть(ся) (-ю(сь)) несов от

оборва́ть(ся).

обры́вист|ый (-, -а, -о) *прил (склон, берег)* steep; *(мысли, фразы)* fragmentary.

обры́в|ок (-ка) *м (верёвки)* piece; *(бумаги)* scrap; *(обычно мн: мыслей, воспоминаний)* fragment; *(: разговора)* snatch.

обры́воч|ный (-ен, -на, -но) *прил* fragmentary.

обры́зга|ть (-ю; *impf* обры́згивать) *сов перех*: ~ кого́-н/что́-н +*instr (водой)* to splash sb/sth with; *(грязью, краской)* to splatter sb/sth with

► обры́згаться *(impf* обры́згиваться) *сов возв*: ~ся +*instr (см перех)* to get splashed with; to get splattered with.

обря́д (-а) *м* ritual.

обря́довый *прил (песни)* ceremonial; *(действия)* ritual.

обса́сыва|ть (-ю) *несов от* обсоса́ть.

обсервато́ри|я (-и) *ж* observatory.

обсле́довани|е (-я) *ср (см глаг)* inspection; examination.

обсле́д|овать (-ую) *(не)сов перех* to inspect; *(больного)* to examine.

обслу́живани|е (-я) *ср* service; медици́нское ~ health care; сфе́ра ~я service industry.

обслу́жива|ть (-ю) *несов от* обслужи́ть ♦ *перех (подлеж: магазин)* to supply; *(: поликлиника)* to see to.

обслу́живающий (-ая, -ее, -ие) *прил*: ~ персона́л ancilliary staff.

обслу́ж|и́ть (-у́жу, -у́жишь; *impf* обслу́живать) *сов перех (покупателей)* to serve; *(клиентов)* to attend to; *(подлеж: поликлиника, магазин)* to see to; *(станки)* to operate.

обсос|а́ть (-у́, -ёшь; *impf* обса́сывать) *сов перех* to suck.

обста́в|ить (-лю, -ишь; *impf* обставля́ть) *сов перех (квартиру, кабинет)* to furnish; обставля́ть *(~ perf)* стол сту́льями to put chairs around the table.

обстано́в|ка (-ки; *gen pl* -ок) *ж (квартиры, кабинета)* furnishings *мн*; *(в мире, в семье)* situation; междунаро́дная ~ the international situation.

обстоя́тельно *нареч* in detail.

обстоя́тель|ный (-ен, -ьна, -ьно) *прил* detailed; *(разг: человек)* solid.

обстоя́тельств|о (-а) *ср* circumstance; *(линг)* adverbial modifier; ни при каки́х ~ах under no circumstances; стече́ние обстоя́тельств coincidence; смотря́ по ~ам depending on the circumstances; *(как ответ на вопрос)* it depends.

обсто|я́ть (*3sg* -и́т, *3pl* -я́т) *несов неперех (дела, работа, учёба)* to be; как ~я́т дела́? how are things going?; всё ~и́т хорошо́ everything is going well.

обстра́гива|ть (-ю) *несов от* обострога́ть.

обстре́л (-а) *м* fire; артиллери́йский ~ artillery fire.

обстреля́|ть (-ю; *impf* обстре́ливать) *сов перех* to fire at.

обстри́|чь (-гу́, -жёшь *итп*, -гу́т) *сов от* стричь.

обстрога́|ть (-ю; *impf* обстра́гивать) *сов перех* to plane.

обстру́кци|я (-и) *ж* obstruction.

обступ|и́ть (*3sg* -у́пит, *3pl* -у́пят, *impf* обступа́ть) *сов перех* to surround.

обсуд|и́ть (-у́жу, -у́дишь; *impf* обсужда́ть) *сов перех* to discuss.

обсужде́ни|е (-я) *ср* discussion; предложи́ть *(предлага́ть impf)* что-н на ~ to bring sth up for discussion.

обсужу́ *сов см* обсуди́ть.

обсчита́|ть (-ю; *impf* обсчи́тывать) *сов перех* to overcharge; *(результат, параметры)* to calculate

► обсчита́ться *(impf* обсчи́тываться) *сов возв (разг)* to miscalculate.

обсы́п|ать (-лю, -лешь; *impf* обсыпа́ть) *сов перех*: ~ что-н чем-н to sprinkle sth with sth

► обсы́паться *(impf* обсыпа́ться) *сов возв*: ~ся +*instr* to get covered in.

обта́чива|ть (-ю) *несов от* обточи́ть.

обтека́ем|ый (-, -а, -о) *прил (поверхность, форма)* streamlined; *(разг: ответ, объяснение)* ambiguous.

обтере́|ть (-тру́, -трёшь; *impf* обтира́ть) *сов перех* to wipe

► обтере́ться *(impf* обтира́ться) *сов возв* to sponge o.s. down.

обтеса́|ть (-ешу́, -е́шешь; *impf* обтёсывать) *сов перех (бревно)* to trim; *(разг: манеры, человека)* to bring up to scratch.

обтира́|ть(ся) (-ю(сь)) *несов от* обтере́ть(ся).

обточ|и́ть (-очу́, -о́чишь; *impf* обта́чивать) *сов перех (на станке)* to turn; *(на точильном камне)* to sharpen.

обто́ч|ка (-и) *ж (см глаг)* turning; sharpening.

обтрёпан|ный (-, -на, -но) *прил* shabby.

обтреп|а́ть (-лю́, -лешь) *сов перех* to wear out

► обтрепа́ться *сов возв (износиться)* to wear out.

обтя́гива|ть (-ю) *несов от* обтяну́ть.

обтя́жк|а (-и) *ж*: в ~у skintight.

обтяну́|ть (-яну́, -я́нешь; *impf* обтя́гивать) *сов перех (кресло, диван)* to cover; *(фигуру)* to fit tightly.

обува́|ть(ся) (-ю(сь)) *несов от* обу́ть(ся).

обувно́й *прил* shoe *опред*.

о́бувь (-и) *ж* footwear.

обу́гл|иться (*3sg* -ится, *3pl* -ятся, *impf* обу́гливаться) *сов возв* to become charred.

обужива|ть (-ю) *несов от* обу́зить.

обужу́ *сов см* обу́зить.

обу́з|а (-ы) *ж* burden; быть *(impf)* ~ой для

кого́-н (*разг*) to be a burden to sb.

обу́зить (-жу, -зишь; *impf* **обу́живать**) *сов перех* to make too tight.

обусло́в|ить (-лю, -ишь; *impf* **обусла́вливать**) *сов перех* (*явиться причиной*) to lead to; **обусла́вливать** (~ *perf*) **что-н чем-н** to make sth conditional on sth.

обу́т|ый (-, -а, -о) *прил*: ~ **в ту́фли/сапоги́** wearing shoes/boots; (*no full form*; *обеспеченный обувью*) provided with shoes or boots.

обу́|ть (-ю; *impf* **обува́ть**) *сов перех* (*туфли, сапоги*) to put on; (*разг*: *снабдить обувью*) to provide with shoes or boots; (*ребёнка*) to put shoes on

▶ **обу́ться** (*impf* **обува́ться**) *сов возв* to put on one's shoes or boots; (*разг*: *обеспечить себя обувью*) to provide o.s. with shoes or boots.

о́бух (-а) *м* (*топора*) blunt end; **как ~ом по голове́** like a bolt from the blue.

обуча́|ть(ся) (-ю(сь)) *несов от* **обучи́ть(ся)**.

обуче́ни|е (-я) *ср*: ~ +*dat* (*преподавание*) teaching of, instruction in; (*изучение*) education in.

обу|чи́ть (-учу́, -у́чишь; *impf* **обуча́ть**) *сов перех*: ~ **кого́-н чему́-н**/+*infin* to teach sb sth/to do

▶ **обучи́ться** (*impf* **обуча́ться**) *сов возв*: ~**ся чему́-н**/+*infin* to learn sth/to do.

обуя́|ть (3sg -ет, 3pl -ют) *сов перех* to overcome.

обхам|и́ть (-лю, -и́шь) *сов перех* (*разг*) to be rude to.

обхва́т (-а) *м* circumference (*measured by putting arms around object*); **в ~е** in circumference.

обхва|ти́ть (-чу́, -а́тишь; *impf* **обхва́тывать**) *сов перех*: ~ **что-н** (**рука́ми**) to put one's arms round sth.

обхо́д (-а) *м* (*путь*) way round; (*в больнице, на предприятии*) round; (*ВОЕН*) turning movement; **в ~** +*gen* (*озера, закона*) bypassing; **идти́** (*impf*) **в ~ чего́-н** to go round sth; (*закона, правил*) to evade this.

обходи́тельный (-ен, -ьна, -ьно) *прил* courteous.

обх|оди́ть(ся) (-ожу́(сь), -о́дишь(ся)) *несов от* **обойти́(сь)**.

обходно́й *прил* (*путь*) detour *опред*; (*маневр, движение*) turning; **обходно́й лист** *a certificate which must be signed on leaving job to prove that all property has been returned*.

обхожде́ни|е (-я) *ср* manners *мн*.

обхожу́(сь) *несов см* **обходи́ть(ся)**.

обхох|ота́ться (-очу́сь, -о́чешься) *сов возв* (*разг*) to kill o.s. laughing.

обчи́|стить (-щу, -стишь) *сов от* **чи́стить**.

обша́р|ить (-ю, -ишь; *impf* **обша́ривать**) *сов перех* (*разг*) to ransack.

обшива́|ть (-ю) *несов от* **обши́ть**.

обши́в|ка (-ки; *gen pl* -ок) *ж* (*платья, пальто*) trim; (*корабля*) plating; (*дома*) cladding.

обши́р|ный (-ен, -на, -но) *прил* extensive;

(*комната*) spacious.

обши́т|ый (-, -а, -о) *прил*: ~ +*instr* (*бахромой, мехом*) trimmed with; (*досками*) faced with; (*металлом*) plated with.

об|ши́ть (-ошью, -ошьёшь; *impf* **обшива́ть**) *сов перех* (*разг*: *семью итп*) to make clothes for; **обшива́ть** (~ *perf*) (+*instr*) (*мехом, бахромой*) to trim (with); (*деревом*) to face (with); (*металлом*) to plate *или* cover (with).

обшла́г (-ага́; *nom pl* -ага́) *м* cuff.

обща́|ться (-юсь) *несов возв*: ~ **с** +*instr* (*с друзьями, с родственниками*) to spend time with; (*с политиками, с преступниками итп*) to associate with; **я бо́льше с ним не ~юсь** I don't see him any more.

общевойсково́й *прил* military.

общегородско́й *прил* town *опред*, city *опред*.

общегосуда́рственный *прил* state *опред*.

общедосту́пный *прил* (*средства, способ*) available to everyone; (*цены*) affordable; (*изложение, лекция*) accessible.

о́бщ|ее (-его; *decl like adj*) *ср* similarity; **в ~ем** (*разг*) on the whole; **в ~ем и це́лом** by and large; **у них мно́го/нет ничего́ ~его** they have a lot/nothing in common.

общежи́ти|е (-я) *ср* (*рабочее*) hostel; (*студенческое*) hall of residence (*BRIT*), dormitory *или* hall (*US*); (*сосуществование*) communal living.

общеизве́ст|ный (-ен, -на, -но) *прил* well-known.

общенаро́дный *прил* national *опред*.

общенациона́льный *прил* national *опред*.

обще́ни|е (-я) *ср* (*деловые, дружеские*) relations *мн*; (*с природой, с друзьями*) communication.

общеобразова́тельный *прил* comprehensive.

общепи́т (-а) *м сокр* (= *обще́ственное пита́ние*) public catering.

общепри́знанный *прил* universally recognized.

общепри́нят|ый *прил* generally accepted; **в ~ом смы́сле сло́ва** in the accepted sense of the word.

общераспространённый *прил* widespread.

обще́ственност|ь (-и) *ж собир* community.

обще́ственный *прил* social; (*признание, собственность, жизнь*) public; (*организация*) civic; **обще́ственное мне́ние** public opinion; **обще́ственные нау́ки** social sciences.

о́бществ|о (-а) *ср* society; (*компания*) company; **в ~е** +*gen* in the company of.

обществове́дени|е (-я) *ср* social science.

общеупотреби́тельный (ен, -ьна, -ьно) *прил* commonly-used.

общечелове́ческ|ий (-ая, -ое, -ие) *прил* universal.

о́бщ|ий (-ая, -ее, -ие) *прил* general; (*труд*) communal; (*дом, книги*) shared; (*друзья*) mutual; (*интересы, увлечения, ненависть*) common; (*стоимость, количество*) total; (-, -á,

-ó; *картина, описание*) general; ~ими уси́лиями together; в ~ей сло́жности altogether; на ~их основа́ниях on equal terms; в ~их черта́х in general terms; находи́ть (найти́ *perf*) ~ язы́к to find a common language; ~ие слова́ waffle; óбщее образова́ние general education.

общи́н|а (-ы) *ж* community.

общипа́ть (-иплю́, -и́плешь; *impf* **общи́пывать**) *сов перех* to pluck.

общи́телен *прил см* **общи́тельный**.

общи́тельность (-и) *ж* sociability.

общи́тельный (-ен, -ьна, -ьно) *прил* sociable.

óбщность (-и) *ж* (*взгля́дов, це́лей*) similarity; (*истори́ческая, социа́льная: community*).

объеда́|ть(ся) (-ю(сь)) *несов от* **объе́сть(ся)**.

объе́дешь *итп сов см* **объе́хать**.

объеди́м(ся) *сов см* **объе́сть(ся)**.

объедине́ни|е (-я) *ср* (*сил, уси́лий, тала́нтов*) concentration; (*литера́торов, произво́дственное*) association; (*ВОЕН*) unit.

объединённый *прил* (*заседа́ние, собра́ние*) joint; (*уси́лия, ресу́рсы*) joint, united; **О~ые Ара́бские Эмира́ты** United Arab Emirates.

объедини́ть (-ю́, -и́шь; *impf* **объединя́ть**) *сов перех* to join, unite; (*ресу́рсы*) to pool; (*компа́нии*) to amalgamate

▸ **объедини́ться** (*impf* **объединя́ться**) *сов возв* (*лю́ди*) to unite; (*компа́нии*) to amalgamate.

объеди́те(сь) *сов см* **объе́сть(ся)**.

объе́дк|и (-ов) *мн* (*разг*) leftovers *мн*.

объе́ду *итп сов см* **объе́хать**.

объедя́т(ся) *сов см* **объе́сть(ся)**.

объе́зд (-а) *м* detour; (*с це́лью осмо́тра*) tour; **éхать (поéхать** *perf*) **в** ~ to make a detour.

объе́зд|ить (-жу, -дишь; *impf* **объезжа́ть**) *сов перех* (*ме́сто*) to travel round; (*ло́шадь*) to break in; (*друзе́й*) to visit.

объезжа́|ть (-ю) *несов от* **объе́здить, объе́хать**.

объе́зжу *сов см* **объе́здить**.

объе́кт (-а) *м* (*изуче́ния, наблюде́ния*) subject; (*СТРОИТ, ВОЕН*) site.

объекти́в (-а) *м* lens.

объекти́вен *прил см* **объекти́вный**.

объекти́вность (-и) *ж* objectivity.

объекти́вный (-ен, -на, -но) *прил* objective.

объе́л(ся) *итп сов см* **объе́сть(ся)**.

объе́м(ся) *сов см* **объе́сть(ся)**.

объём (-а) *м* (*ГЕОМ*) volume; (*ведра́, ча́шки*) capacity; (*рабо́ты, зна́ний*) amount.

объёмен *прил см* **объёмный**.

объёмист|ый (-, -а, -о) *прил* bulky.

объём|ный (-ен, -на, -но) *прил* (*ГЕОМ*) volumetric; (*изображе́ние, кино́*) three-dimensional; (*кни́га, па́пка*) bulky.

объе́сть (*как* **есть**; *см* **Table 15**; *impf* **объеда́ть**) *сов перех* (*кость, я́блоко*) to nibble

(at); ~ (*perf*) **кого́-н** (*разг*) to eat sb out of house and home

▸ **объе́сться** (*impf* **объеда́ться**) *сов возв* to overeat.

объе́хать (*как* **éхать**; *см* **Table 19**; *impf* **объезжа́ть**) *сов перех* (*ка́мень, я́му*) to go *или* drive round; (*с це́лью осмо́тра*) to travel round; (*друзе́й, стра́ны*) to visit.

объе́шь(ся) *сов см* **объе́сть(ся)**.

объяви́ть (-явлю́, -я́вишь; *impf* **объявля́ть**) *сов перех* to announce; (*войну́*) to declare ♦ *неперех*: ~ **о** +*prp* (*о реше́нии, о случи́вшемся*) to announce; (*объявля́ть* [~ *perf*) **собра́ние закры́тым/кого́-н победи́телем** to declare the meeting closed/sb the winner

▸ **объяви́ться** (*impf* **объявля́ться**) *сов возв* (*разг*) to turn up.

объявле́ни|е (-я) *ср* announcement; (*войны́*) declaration; (*рекла́мное сообще́ние*) advertisement; (*извеще́ние*) notice.

объявлю́(сь) *сов см* **объяви́ть(ся)**.

объявля́|ть(ся) (-ю(сь)) *несов от* **объяви́ть(ся)**.

объясне́ни|е (-я) *ср* explanation; ~ **в любви́** declaration of love.

объясни́м|ый (-, -а, -о) *прил* explicable.

объясни́ть (-ю́, -и́шь; *impf* **объясня́ть**) *сов перех* to explain

▸ **объясни́ться** (*impf* **объясня́ться**) *сов возв*: ~**ся** (**с** +*instr*) to clear things up (with); **всё ~и́лось** everything became clear; **объясня́ться** (~**ся** *perf*) (**кому́-н**) **в любви́** to declare one's love (to sb).

объясня́|ться (-юсь) *несов от* **объясни́ться** ♦ *возв* (*же́стами, на англи́йском языке́*) to communicate; ~ (*impf*) +*instr* (*тру́дностями, уста́лостью*) to be explained by.

объя́ти|е (-я) *ср* embrace; **встреча́ть (встре́тить** *perf*) **кого́-н с распростёртыми** ~ями to welcome sb with open arms.

обыва́тель| (-я) *м* (*пренебр*) philistine; (*ист*) resident.

обыва́тельск|ий (-ая, -ое, -ие) *прил* philistine.

обыгра́|ть (-ю; *impf* **обы́грывать**) *сов перех* (*кома́нду, сопе́рника*) to beat; (*разг: оши́бку, огово́рку*) to turn to one's advantage.

обы́денный (-, -на, -но) *прил* mundane.

обыкнове́ни|е (-я) *ср* habit; **име́ть** (*impf*) ~ +*infin* to be in the habit of doing; **по ~ю** as usual; **про́тив ~я** against the norm; **по своему́ ~ю** as is his *итп* wont.

обыкнове́нно *нареч* usually.

обыкнове́н|ный (-ен, -на, -но) *прил* (*зауря́дный: челове́к, явле́ние*) ordinary; (*ча́стый*) common.

óбыск (-а) *м* search; **производи́ть** (**произвести́** *perf*) ~ to carry out a search.

обы́ска́ть (-ыщу́, -ы́щешь; *impf* **обы́скивать**)

сов перех to search.

обы́ча|й (**-я**) *м* custom.

обы́чен *прил см* **обы́чный**.

обы́чно *нареч* usually.

обы́чн|ый (**-ен, -на, -но**) *прил* usual; (*зауря́дный*) ordinary.

обыщу́ *итп сов см* **обыска́ть**.

обяжу́(сь) *итп сов см* **обяза́ть(ся)**.

обя́занност|и (**-ей**) *мн* (*дире́ктора итп*) duties *мн*, responsibilities *мн*; **исполня́ть** (*impf*) ~ +*gen* to act as; **он исполня́ет** ~ **дире́ктора** he is the acting director.

обя́занност|ь (**-и**) *ж* duty; *см также* **обя́занности**.

обя́зан|ный (**-, -а, -о**) *прил*: ~ +*infin* (*помо́чь, сде́лать итп*) obliged to do; ~ +*dat* obliged *или* indebted to; **я Вам о́чень обя́зан** I am greatly obliged to you.

обяза́телен *прил см* **обяза́тельный**.

обяза́тельно *нареч* definitely, without fail; **не** ~ not necessarily.

обяза́тельн|ый (**-ен, -ьна, -ьно**) *прил* (*пра́вило, усло́вие*) binding; (*исполне́ние, обуче́ние*) compulsory, obligatory; (*челове́к, рабо́тник*) reliable; **в** ~**ьном поря́дке** as a compulsory measure.

обяза́тельств|о (**-а**) *ср* commitment, obligation; (*обычно мн: КОММ*) liability; **долгово́е** ~ (*КОММ*) promissory note; **брать** (**взять** *perf*) **на себя́** ~ to take on some commitment.

обяза́|ть (**-жу́, -жешь**; *impf* **обя́зывать**) *сов перех*: ~ **кого́-н** +*infin* to oblige sb to do; **Вы меня́** ~**жите, е́сли сде́лаете э́то** I would be very much obliged if you would do this; **он** ~**за́л меня́ свое́й добротой** I am obliged to him for his kindness

▸ **обяза́ться** (*impf* **обя́зываться**) *сов возв* to pledge.

обя́зыва|ть (**-ю**) *несов от* **обяза́ть** ♦ *перех* (*подлеж: пра́вила, зако́н, фа́кты*) to oblige; **положе́ние** ~**ет** his *итп* position demands it

▸ **обя́зываться** *несов от* **обяза́ться**.

ова́л (**-а**) *м* oval; **у неё краси́вый** ~ **лица́** her face is a lovely shape.

ова́льный (**-ен, -ьна, -ьно**) *прил* oval.

ова́ци|я (**-и**) *ж* ovation.

ОВД *м сокр* = **отде́л вну́тренних дел**.

овдове́|ть (**-ю**) *сов неперех* (*же́нщина*) to become a widow, be widowed; (*мужчи́на*) to become a widower, be widowed.

Ове́н (**-на́**) *м* (*созве́здие*) Aries.

ове́с (**-са́**) *м собир* oats *мн*.

ове́ц *сущ см* **овца́**.

ове́ч|ий (**-ья, -ье, -ьи**) *прил* (*шерсть, сыр*) sheep's; (*молоко́*) ewe's.

ОВИ́Р *м сокр* = **Отде́л виз и регистра́ции иностра́нных гра́ждан**.

овладе́|ть (**-ю, -ешь**; *impf* **овладева́ть**) *сов неперех*: ~ +*instr* (*го́родом, высото́й*) to capture, seize; (*перен: разгово́ром*) to take

control of; (: *внима́нием*) to capture; (: *языко́м, профе́ссией*) to master; **им** ~**ла ра́дость** he was overcome with joy.

Овна́ *сущ см* **Ове́н**.

о́вод (**-а**) *м* gadfly.

о́вощ (**-а**) *м* vegetable; *см также* **о́вощи**.

о́вощ|и (**-ей**) *мн* vegetables *мн*.

овощно́й *прил* (*суп, блю́до*) vegetable *опред*; **овощно́й магази́н** greengrocer's (*BRIT*), fruit and vegetable shop.

овра́г (**-а**) *м* ravine.

овса́ *итп сущ см* **овёс**.

овся́нк|а (**-и**) *ж собир* (*разг: крупа́*) oats *мн*; (*ка́ша*) porridge (*BRIT*), oatmeal (*US*).

овся́ный *прил* oat *опред*.

овуля́ци|я (**-и**) *ж* ovulation.

овц|а́ (**-ы́**; *nom pl* **-ы**, *gen pl* **-е́ц**) *ж* sheep (*мн* sheep); (*са́мка*) ewe.

овцево́дство (**-а**) *ср* sheep-farming.

ОВЧ *сокр* (= о́чень высо́кая частота́) VHF (= *very high frequency*).

овча́р|ка (**-ки**; *gen pl* **-ок**) *ж* sheepdog.

овча́рн|я (**-и**) *ж* sheepfold.

овчи́н|а (**-ы**) *ж* sheepskin.

ога́р|ок (**-ка**) *м* candle end.

огиба́|ть (**-ю**) *несов от* **обогну́ть**.

оглавле́ни|е (**-я**) *ср* (table of) contents.

огла|си́ть (**-шу́, -си́шь**; *impf* **оглаша́ть**) *сов перех* (*реше́ние, прое́кт*) to announce; (*прика́з, зако́н*) to proclaim; (*телегра́мму*) to read out; ~ (*perf*) **что-н чем-н** to fill sth with sth

▸ **огласи́ться** (*impf* **оглаша́ться**) *сов возв*: ~**ся** +*instr* to resound with.

огла́с|ка (**-и**) *ж* publicity; **предава́ть** (**преда́ть** *perf*) **что-н** ~**е** to make sth public.

оглаша́|ть(ся) (**-ю(сь)**) *несов от* **огласи́ть(ся)**.

оглашу́(сь) *сов см* **огласи́ть(ся)**.

оглоб|ля (**-ли**; *gen pl* **-ель**) *ж* shaft (*on cart*).

оглох|ну́ть (**-у, -нешь**) *сов от* **гло́хнуть**.

оглуша́|ть (**-ю**) *несов от* **оглуши́ть**.

оглуши́тельн|ый (**-ен, -ьна, -ьно**) *прил* deafening.

оглу|ши́ть (**-шу́, -ши́шь**; *impf* **оглуша́ть**) *сов перех*: ~ **кого́-н чем-н** (*зву́ками, кри́ками*) to deafen sb with sth; (*уда́ром*) to stun sb with sth.

огля|де́ть (**-жу́, -ди́шь**; *impf* **огля́дывать**) *сов перех* to look round

▸ **огляде́ться** (*impf* **огля́дываться**) *сов возв* to look around.

огля́д|ка (**-и**) *ж*: **с** ~**ой** with caution; **де́лать** (**сде́лать** *perf*) **что-н без** ~**и** to do sth resolutely; **он бежа́л без** ~**и** (*разг*) he ran as fast as his legs would carry him.

огля́дыва|ть (**-ю**) *несов от* **огляде́ть**

▸ **огля́дываться** *несов от* **огляде́ться**, **огляну́ться**.

огляжу́(сь) *сов см* **огляде́ть(ся)**.

огля|ну́ться (**-ну́сь, -нешься**; *impf* **огля́дываться**) *сов возв* to look back; (**я**) **не успе́л** ~, **как ...** before I knew it ....

огнево́й *прил* (*хара́ктер, взгляд*) fiery; **огнева́**

заве́са (*ВОЕН*) curtain of fire; **огнева́я пози́ция** firing position; **огнева́я то́чка** (*ВОЕН*) emplacement.

огнеды́шащ|ий (-ая, -ее, -ие) *прил* (*дракон*) fire-breathing; (*вулкан*) erupting.

огнемёт (-а) *м* flame-thrower.

о́гненный *прил* (*цвет, глаза, хара́ктер*) fiery; (*поцелуй*) passionate; ~ **столб** burst of flames.

огнеопа́с|ный (-ен, -на, -но) *прил* (in)flammable.

огнесто́йкий (-йкая, -йкое, -йкие; -ек, -йка, -йко) *прил* fireproof.

огнестре́льный *прил*: ~**ое ору́жие** firearms *мн*; **огнестре́льная ра́на** bullet wound.

огнетуши́тель (-я) *м* fire-extinguisher.

огнеупо́р|ный (-ен, -на, -но) *прил* (*материа́л*) fire-proof; **огнеупо́рная гли́на** fire clay; **огнеупо́рный кирпи́ч** firebrick.

огня́ *итп сущ см* **ого́нь**.

ого́ *межд*: ~! well!; ~, **каки́м ты стал взро́слым!** my, how you've grown!

оговор|и́ть (-ю́, -и́шь; *impf* **огова́ривать**) *сов перех* to slander; (*усло́вия, срок*) to agree (on); (*подлеж: пра́вила*) to stipulate

▸ **оговори́ться** (*impf* **огова́риваться**) *сов возв*: **я ~и́лся** it was a slip of the tongue.

оговор|ка (-ки; *gen pl* -ок) *ж* (*обмо́лвка*) slip of the tongue; (*усло́вие*) proviso; **я могу́ сказа́ть без** ~**ок, что** ... I can say without reservation that ....

оголённый (-ён, -ена́, -ено́) *прил* bare.

огол|и́ть (-ю́, -и́шь; *impf* **оголя́ть**) *сов перех* to bare, expose; (*дере́вья, про́вод, зе́млю*) to strip; (*меч, кинжа́л*) to draw; (*фронт, уча́сток*) to expose

▸ **оголи́ться** (*impf* **оголя́ться**) *сов возв* (*ше́я, плечо́ итп*) to become uncovered; (*дере́вья, земля́*) to become bare; (*про́вод*) to be exposed; (*фронт, уча́сток*) to become exposed.

оголте́лый (-, -а, -о) *прил* mad.

оголя́|ть(ся) (-ю(сь)) *несов перех от* **оголи́ть(ся)**.

огон|ёк (-ька́) *м уменьш от* **ого́нь**; (*блеск глаз*) twinkle; **рабо́тать** (*impf*) **с** ~**ько́м** to work enthusiastically *или* with enthusiasm; **заходи́ть** (**зайти́** *perf*) **на** ~ to drop in.

ог|о́нь (-ня́) *м* fire; (*фонаре́й, в окне́*) light; (*перен: любви́, негодова́ния*) flame; **разводи́ть** (**развести́** *perf*) ~ to light a fire; **зажига́ть** (**заже́чь** *perf*) ~ to turn on the light; **открыва́ть** (**откры́ть** *perf*) ~ to open fire; **в** ~**не́ сраже́ния** in the heat of battle; **боя́ться** (*impf*) **чего́-н/кого́-н как** ~**ня́** to be terrified by sb/sth; **игра́ть** (*impf*) **с** ~**нём** (*перен*) to play with fire; **ме́жду двух** ~**не́й** between two fires.

огонь́ка *итп сущ см* **огонёк**.

огора́жива|ть (-ю) *несов от* **огороди́ть**.

огоро́д (-а) *м* vegetable *или* kitchen garden.

огор|оди́ть (-ожу́, -о́дишь; *impf* **огора́живать**) *сов перех*: ~ **что-н (чем-н)** to fence sth in (with sth).

огоро́ш|ить (-у, -ишь; *impf* **огоро́шивать**) *сов перех* (*разг*) to astound.

огорча́|ть(ся) (-ю(сь)) *несов от* **огорчи́ть(ся)**.

огорче́ни|е (-я) *ср* distress; **к моему́** ~**ю** to my dismay.

огорчённый (-ён, -ена́, -ено́) *прил* distressed; **у него́ был** ~ **вид** he looked upset.

огорчи́тельный (-ен, -ьна, -ьно) *прил* distressing.

огорч|и́ть (-у́, -и́шь; *impf* **огорча́ть**) *сов перех* to distress

▸ **огорчи́ться** (*impf* **огорча́ться**) *сов возв* to be upset *или* distressed.

огра́б|ить (-лю, -ишь) *сов от* **гра́бить**.

ограбле́ни|е (-я) *ср* robbery.

огра́блю *сов см* **огра́бить**.

огра́д|а (-ы) *ж* (*стена́*) wall; (*забо́р*) fence; (*решётка*) railings *мн*.

ограл|и́ть (-жу́, -ди́шь; *impf* **огражда́ть**) *сов перех* (*перен*) to defend, protect.

огражде́ни|е (-я) *ср* barrier.

огражу́ *сов см* **огради́ть**.

огран|и́ть (-ю́, -и́шь; *impf* **ограни́вать**) *сов перех* to cut.

ограниче́ни|е (-я) *ср* restriction, limitation; (*пра́вило*) restriction.

ограни́чен|ный (-, -на, -но) *прил* limited; (*челове́к*) narrow-minded.

ограни́чива|ть(ся) (-ю(сь)) *несов от* **ограни́чить(ся)**.

ограничи́тел|ьный (-ен, -ьна, -ьно) *прил*: ~**ьные ме́ры** restrictive measures *мн*.

ограни́ч|ить (-у, -ишь; *impf* **ограни́чивать**) *сов перех* to limit, restrict

▸ **ограни́читься** (*impf* **ограни́чиваться**) *сов возв*: ~**ся** +*instr* (*удовлетвори́ться*) to content o.s with; (*свести́сь*) to become limited to.

огре́|ть (-ю) *сов перех* (*разг*) to whack.

огро́м|ный (-ен, -на, -но) *прил* enormous.

огрубе́лый *прил* (*ру́ки, ко́жа*) coarse; (*се́рдце, душа́*) hardened.

огрубе́|ть (-ю) *сов от* **грубе́ть**.

огрыза́|ться (-юсь) *несов возв* to snap.

огрызну́|ться (-у́сь, -ёшься) *сов возв* to snap.

огры́з|ок (-ка) *м* (*огурца́, я́блока*) half-eaten bit; (*карандаша́, ла́стика*) stub; (*бума́жки*) scrap.

огу́льный (-ен, -ьна, -ьно) *прил* unfounded.

огур|е́ц (-ца́) *м* cucumber; (*марино́ванный*) gherkin.

о́д|а (-ы) *ж* ode.

одалжива|ть (-ю) *несов от* **одолжи́ть**.

одарённый (-, -на, -но) *прил* gifted.

одар|и́ть (-ю́, -и́шь; *impf* **ода́ривать** *или* **одаря́ть**) *сов перех*: ~ **кого́-н чем-н** to give sb sth; **приро́да** ~**и́ла её красото́й** she is blessed with good looks.

одева́ть (-ю) *несов от* **оде́ть**

▶ **одева́ться** *несов от* **оде́ться** ◆ *возв* (носить одежду) to dress.

оде́жд|а (-ы) *ж* clothes *мн.*

одеколо́н (-а) *м* eau de Cologne.

одел|и́ть (-ю́, -и́шь; *impf* **оделя́ть**) *сов перех*: ~ кого́-н чем-н to give sth out to sb.

одену(сь) *итп сов см* **оде́ть(ся)**.

одёргива|ть (-ю) *несов от* **одёрнуть**.

одеревене́лый *прил* (руки, пальцы) numb; (человек) paralysed (BRIT), paralyzed (US).

одеревене́|ть (-ю) *сов от* **деревене́ть**.

одерж|а́ть (-ержу́, -е́ржишь; *impf* **оде́рживать**) *сов перех*: ~ побе́ду to be victorious; **оде́рживать** (~ *perf*) **верх на соревнова́нии/в спо́ре** to win a competition/argument.

одержи́м|ый (-, -а, -о) *прил*: ~ +*instr* (эмоциями) possessed by; (мыслью) obsessed by.

одёрн|уть (-у, -ешь; *impf* **одёргивать**) *сов перех* (одежду) to straighten; (разг: человека) to check.

Оде́сс|а (-ы) *ж* Odessa.

оде́т|ый (-, -а, -о) *прил* dressed; (разг: обеспеченный одеждой) clothed; (покрытый): ~ +*instr* (снегом итп) covered with.

оде́|ть (-ну, -нешь; *impf* **одева́ть**) *сов перех* to dress; (разг: снабдить одеждой) to clothe; (перен: снегом итп) to cover

▶ **оде́ться** (*impf* **одева́ться**) *сов возв* to get dressed; (также разг: тепло, легко, приобретать одежду) to dress; (покрываться): ~ся +*instr* to be covered with.

одея́л|о (-а) *ср* (шерстяное) blanket; (стёганое) quilt; (пуховое) eiderdown.

KEYWORD

оди́н (-ного; *см* Table 22; *f* **одна́**, *nt* **одно́**, *pl* **одни́**) *м чис* one; **одна́ кни́га** one book; **одни́ брю́ки** one pair of trousers; **ей оди́н год** she is one (year old); **они́ живу́т в до́ме но́мер оди́н** they live at number one; **кни́га сто́ит оди́н рубль** the book costs one rouble; **я́блоки продаю́тся по одно́й шту́ке** the apples are sold singly

◆ *прил* alone; (единственный, единый) one; (одинаковый, тот же самый) the same; **он идёт в кино́ оди́н** he goes to the cinema alone; **есть то́лько оди́н вы́ход** there is only one way out; **у них одни́ взгля́ды** they hold similar views; **я оди́н** (без супруги) I am single

◆ *мест 1* (какой-то): **оди́н мой знако́мый** a friend; **одни́ неприя́тности** nothing but problems

2 (во фразах): **оди́н из** +*gen pl* one of; **оди́н и то́т же** the same one; **одно́ и то́ же** the same thing; **оди́н раз** once; **оди́н на оди́н** one to one; **все до одного́** all to a man; **ни оди́н** not one; **оди́н за други́м** one after the other; **одно́ по одному́** one by one; **одно́ к одному́** (разг) one thing after another; **оди́н к одному́** one as good as another;

одно́ из двух one of two things; **одно́ вре́мя** for some time; **в оди́н го́лос** with one voice; **оди́н-еди́нственный** only one; **оди́н-одинёшенек** (разг) all alone.

одина́ково *нареч* in the same way.

одина́ков|ый (-, -а, -о) *прил* similar.

одина́рный *прил* single.

одиннадцатичасово́й *прил* eleven-hour; (отправление) eleven-o'clock.

оди́ннадцат|ый (-ая, -ое, -ые) *чис* eleventh; *см также* **пя́тый**.

оди́ннадцать (-и; *как* пять; *см* Table 27) *чис* eleven; *см также* **пять**.

оди́нок|ий (-ая, -ое, -ие; -, -а, -о) *прил* (дом, дерево) solitary; (жизнь, человек) lonely; (без семьи: женщина, мужчина) single.

одино́чек *сущ см* **одино́чка**.

одино́честв|о (-а) *ср* loneliness.

одино́ч|ка (-ки; *gen pl* -ек) *ж* (человек): **жить ~кой** to live alone; **байда́рка-~** one-man canoe; **в ~ку** on one's own; **сиде́ть** (*impf*) **в ~ке** (разг) to be in solitary confinement.

одино́чн|ый *прил* (стук, выстрел) single, lone; (прохожие, дома) solitary; ~ **полёт** solo flight; ~**ое заключе́ние** solitary confinement; **одино́чное ката́ние (на конька́х)** (СПОРТ) singles figure skating.

одио́зн|ый (-ен, -на, -но) *прил* odious.

одича́лый *прил* wild.

одича́|ть (-ю) *сов от* **дича́ть**.

одн|а́ (-о́й) *ж чис см* **оди́н**.

однажды *нареч* once.

однако *союз*, *вводн сл* however; **его́ повы́сили – ~!** he's been promoted – no, really!; ~ **же** even so.

одн|и́ (-х) *мн чис см* **оди́н**.

одн|о́ (-ого́) *ср чис см* **оди́н**.

одноа́ктный *прил* one-act, in one act.

однобо́ртный *прил* single-breasted.

одновре́ме́нно *нареч*: ~ (с +*instr*) at the same time (as).

одновре́ме́нный *прил* simultaneous.

одного́ *итп чис см* **оди́н, одно́**.

одного́д|ок (-ка) *м* (разг): **он мой** ~ he was born in the same year as me.

однодне́вн|ый *прил* (зарплата, работа) one day's; ~**ая пое́здка** day trip.

однозву́чн|ый (-ен, -на, -но) *прил* monotonous.

однозна́чн|ый (-ен, -на, -но) *прил* (тождественный) synonymous; (с одним значением: слово) monosemantic; (: выражение, ответ) unambiguous; (МАТ) single-figure; **однозна́чное число́** single-digit number.

одноиме́нный *прил* of the same name.

однокла́ссник (-а) *м* classmate.

однокла́ссниц|а (-ы) *ж см* **однокла́ссник**.

одноклёточный *прил* single-cell.

однcol|е́йный *прил* single-lane.

однокра́тный *прил* single.

однолётн|ий (-яя, -ее, -ие) *прил* annual.

одноме́стный прил (купе, номер) single; (каюта) single-berth.

однообра́зие (-я) ср monotony.

однообра́зный прил monotonous.

одноло́лый прил unisexual.

однора́зовый прил disposable; ~ про́пуск temporary pass (valid only once).

однор́одный (-ен, -на, -но) прил (явления, понятия) similar; (жидкость, масса) homogenous.

односло́жный (-ен, -на, -но) прил (также перен) monosyllabic.

односторо́нний (-няя, -нее, -ние) прил (ткань) one-sided; (разоружение) unilateral; (движение, связь) one-way; (-ен, -ня, -не; перен: воспитание, развитие) narrow; (: мышление) parochial; у него́ ~ парали́ч he is paralysed (BRIT) или paralyzed (US) down one side.

одноти́пный (-ен, -на, -но) прил of the same type или kind.

однотомный прил one-volume.

однофами́лец (-ьца) м namesake (with same surname).

однофами́лица (-ы) ж см однофами́лец.

однофами́льца итп сущ см однофами́лец.

одноцве́тный (-ен, -на, -но) прил plain.

одночле́н (-а) м monomial.

одноэта́жный прил single-storey (BRIT), single-story (US), one-storey (BRIT), one-story (US).

одобре́ние (-я) ср approval.

одобри́телен прил см одобри́тельный.

одобри́тельно нареч favourably.

одобри́тельный (-ен, -ьна, -ьно) прил (отзыв, реакция) favourable (BRIT), favorable (US); (восклицание, взгляд) of approval; (статья) positive.

одо́брить (-ю, -ишь; impf одобря́ть) сов перех to approve.

одоле́ть (-ю; impf одолева́ть) сов перех (врага) to overpower; (смущение, неприязнь) to overcome; (разг: книгу, задачу) to get through; (: подлеж: жара, комары) to bug; (науку) to master; его́ ~ла грусть/лень he was overwhelmed by sadness/a feeling of laziness.

одолже́ние (-я) ср favour (BRIT), favor (US); сде́лайте ~ would you do me a favour?; (ответ) be my guest.

одолжи́ть (-у, -йшь; impf ода́лживать) сов перех: ~ что-н кому́-н to lend sth to sb; ода́лживать (~ perf) что-н у кого́-н (разг) to borrow sth from sb.

одряхле́ть (-ю) сов от дряхле́ть.

одува́нчик (-а) м dandelion.

оду́маться (-юсь, impf оду́мываться) сов возв to think again.

одура́чить (-у, -ишь) сов от дура́чить.

одуре́лый прил (разг) befuddled.

одуре́ть (-ю) сов от дуре́ть.

одурма́нить (-ю, -ишь) сов от дурма́нить.

о́дурь (-и) ж: напи́ться до ~и (разг) to drink o.s. silly; набе́гаться (perf) до ~и (разг) to run until one is ready to drop; я насмотре́лся детекти́вов до ~и (разг) I've watched thrillers until I'm sick of them.

одутлова́тый (-, -а, -о) прил puffed up, puffy.

одухотворённый (-, -на, -но) прил (вид, лицо) spiritual; (речь) inspired.

одухотвори́ть (-ю, -йшь; impf одухотворя́ть) сов перех to inspire.

одышка (-и) ж: у него́ ~ he is short of breath; страда́ть (impf) ~ой to be short-winded.

ОЕЭС ж сокр (= Организа́ция европе́йского экономи́ческого сотру́дничества) OEEC (= Organization for European Economic Cooperation).

ожереби́ться (3sg -ится, 3pl -ятся) сов от жереби́ться.

ожере́лье (-я) ср necklace.

ожесточа́ть(ся) (-ю(сь)) несов от ожесточи́ть(ся).

ожесточе́ние (-я) ср bitterness; с ~м furiously.

ожесточённый (-, -на, -но) прил (человек) hardened, embittered; (спор, сражение) fierce.

ожесточи́ть (-у́, -йшь; impf ожесточа́ть) сов перех (человека) to harden, embitter

▶ **ожесточи́ться** (impf ожесточа́ться) сов возв to become hardened или embittered.

ожива́ть (-ю) несов от ожи́ть.

оживи́ть (-лю́, -йшь; impf оживля́ть) сов перех to revive; (глаза, лицо) to light up; (улицу, доли́ну) to bring to life; (торговлю, работу) to revitalize

▶ **оживи́ться** (impf оживля́ться) сов возв to liven up; (лицо) to brighten; (улица, школа) to come to life.

оживле́ние (-я) ср (на улице, в доме) bustle; (организма, растения) revival.

оживлённый (-, -на, -но) прил (беседа, спор) animated; (улица, место, деятельность) lively; (торговля) brisk; (-, -а́, -о́; человек) lively.

оживлю́(сь) сов см оживи́ть(ся).

оживля́ть(ся) (-ю(сь)) несов от оживи́ть(ся).

оживу́ итп сов см ожи́ть.

ожида́ние (-я) ср anticipation; (обычно мн: надежды) expectation; в ~и чего́-н in anticipation of sth; обма́нывать (обману́ть perf) чьи-н ~я to fail to come up to sb's expectations.

ожида́ть (-ю) несов перех (ждать) to expect; (+gen; надеяться) to expect; его́ ~ет блестя́щая карье́ра he has a brilliant career ahead of him; э́того мо́жно бы́ло ~ that was to be expected

▶ **ожида́ться** несов возв to be expected.

ожире́ни|е (-я) *ср* obesity.

ожире́ть (-ю) *сов от* жире́ть.

ожи́ть (-иву́, -ивёшь; *impf* ожива́ть) *сов неперех* to come to life; (*перен: чувства, человек*) to revive.

ожо́г (-а) *м* burn.

озабо́тить (-чу, -тишь) *сов перех* to worry, trouble.

озабо́чен|ный (-, -на, -но) *прил* worried.

озабо́чу *сов см* озабо́тить.

озагла́в|ить (-лю, -ишь; *impf* озагла́вливать) *сов перех* to entitle.

озада́чен|ный (-, -на, -но) *прил* puzzled.

озада́ч|ить (-у, -ишь; *impf* озада́чивать) *сов перех* to puzzle, perplex.

озар|и́ть (-ю́, -и́шь; *impf* озаря́ть) *сов перех* (*подлеж: солнце, улыбка*) to light up; (*: идея, догадка*) to dawn on

▶ **озари́ться** (*impf* озаря́ться) *сов возв*: ~ся +*instr* (*также перен*) to be lit up by.

озвере́ть (-ю) *сов от* звере́ть ♦ *неперех* to become violent.

озву́ч|ить (-у, -ишь; *impf* озву́чивать) *сов перех*: ~ фильм to record the soundtrack for a film.

оздорови́тельн|ый *прил*: ~ые мероприя́тия health-improving measures; оздорови́тельный ко́мплекс ≈ health farm.

оздоров|и́ть (-лю́, -и́шь; *impf* оздоровля́ть) *сов перех* (*перен: коллектив, обстановку*) to clean up; оздоровля́ть (~ *perf*) органи́зм to improve one's health; ~ (*perf*) ме́стность to improve the ecology of an area.

озелен|и́ть (-ю́, -и́шь; *impf* озеленя́ть) *несов перех* to green.

о́зер|о (-ера; *nom pl* -ёра) *ср* lake.

ози́м|ые (-ых; *decl like adj*) *мн* winter crops *мн*.

ози́м|ый *прил*: ~ая пшени́ца/рожь winter wheat/rye; *см также* ози́мые.

озира́|ться (-юсь) *несов возв*: ~ (по сторона́м) to glance about *или* around.

озло́б|ить (-лю, -ишь; *impf* озлобля́ть) *сов перех* to anger

▶ **озло́биться** (*impf* озлобля́ться) *сов возв* to become angry.

озлобле́ни|е (-я) *ср* anger.

озло́блен|ный (-, -на, -но) *прил* angry.

озлоблю́(сь) *сов см* озло́бить(ся).

озлобля́|ть(ся) (-ю(сь)) *несов от* озло́бить(ся).

ознако́м|ить (-лю, -ишь) *сов от* знако́мить ♦ (*impf* ознакомля́ть) *перех*: ~ кого́-н с +*instr* to familiarize sb with

▶ **ознако́миться** *сов от* знако́миться ♦ (*impf* ознакомля́ться) *возв*: ~ся с +*instr* to familiarize o.s. with.

ознамена́ни|е (-я) *ср*: в ~ +*gen* (*в память*) in commemoration of.

ознамен|ова́ть (-у́ю; *impf* ознамено́вывать) *сов перех* to commemorate, mark; его́ побе́да ~ова́ла э́тот год his victory made this a

memorable year

▶ **ознаменова́ться** (*impf* ознамено́вываться) *сов возв* (+*instr*) to be remembered for.

означа́|ть (-ю) *несов перех* to mean.

озно́б (-а) *м* shivering.

ОЗО *ср сокр* (= отделе́ние зао́чного обуче́ния) *extra-mural department*.

озо́н (-а) *м* ozone.

озо́новый *прил*: ~ слой ozone layer; озо́новая дыра́ hole in the ozone layer.

озорни́к (-а́) *м* (*разг*) scallywag.

озорно́й *прил* mischievous.

озорств|о́ (-а́) *ср* mischief.

озя́бн|уть (-у, -ешь) *сов от* зя́бнуть.

ой *межд*: ~! (*выражает испуг*) argh!; (*выражает удивление, восхищение*) oh!; (*выражает боль*) ouch!, ow!; им жило́сь ~ как тру́дно their life was ever so difficult.

ОК *м сокр* (= отде́л ка́дров) personnel department.

ока|за́ть (-ажу́, -а́жешь; *impf* ока́зывать) *сов перех*: ~ по́мощь/соде́йствие кому́-н to provide help/assistance for sb; ока́зывать (~ *perf*) влия́ние на +*acc* to exercise influence over *или* on; ока́зывать (~ *perf*) давле́ние на +*acc* to put pressure on *или* upon; ока́зывать (~ *perf*) внима́ние кому́-н to pay attention to sb; ока́зывать (~ *perf*) предпочте́ние кому́-н to give preference to sb; ока́зывать (~ *perf*) сопротивле́ние (кому́-н) to offer resistance (to sb); ока́зывать (~ *perf*) услу́гу кому́-н to do sb a service

▶ **оказа́ться** (*impf* ока́зываться) *сов возв* (*найтись: на столе итп*) to appear; (*очутиться: на острове итп*) to find o.s.; ока́зываться (~ся *perf*) +*instr* (*вором, шпионом*) to turn out to be; ~а́зывается, она́ была́ права́ it turns out that she was right; у него́ не ~аза́лось де́нег it turned out that he didn't have any money.

ока́зи|я (-и) *ж* opportunity; посыла́ть (посла́ть *perf*) что-н с ~ей to send sth with somebody.

ока́зыва|ть(ся) (-ю(сь)) *несов от* оказа́ть(ся).

окайм|и́ть (-лю́, -и́шь; *impf* окаймля́ть) *сов перех* (*рисунок*) to frame; (*платок*) to border.

окамени́ва|ть (-ю) *сов от* камене́ть.

окамене́лый *прил* (*дерево, растение*) fossilized; (*хлеб, сыр*) rock-hard; (*перен: человек, взгляд, лицо*) motionless.

окамене́ть (-ю; *impf* окаменева́ть *или* камене́ть) *сов неперех* (*дерево, растение*) to fossilize; (*хлеб, сыр*) to go stale; (*перен: лицо, взгляд*) to freeze; (*: душа, сердце*) to turn to stone; ~ (*perf*) от стра́ха to turn rigid with fear; ~ (*perf*) от го́ря to be numb with grief.

окант|ова́ть (-у́ю; *impf* оканто́вывать) *сов перех* (*картину, фотогра́фию*) to frame; (*воротник, платок*) to border.

ока́нчива|ть (-ю) *несов от* око́нчить

▶ **ока́нчиваться** *несов от* око́нчиться ♦ *возв*: ~ся на гла́сную/согла́сную to end in a vowel/

consonant; **эта у́лица ~ется тупико́м** this (street) is a dead end.

ока́пыва|ть(ся) (-ю(сь)) несов от **окопа́ть(ся)**.

ок|ати́ть (-ачу́, -а́тишь; impf **ока́чивать**) сов перех: **~ кого́-н/что-н чем-н** to pour sth over sb/sth.

океа́н (-а) м (также перен) ocean.

Океа́ни|я (-и) ж Oceania.

океаноло́ги|я (-и) ж oceanography.

оки́н|уть (-у, -ешь; impf **оки́дывать**) сов перех: **~ кого́-н/что-н взгля́дом** to glance over at sb/sth.

о́кис|ел (-ла) м oxide.

окисле́ни|е (-я) ср oxidation.

окисл|и́ть (3sg -и́т, 3pl -я́т, impf **окисля́ть**) сов перех to oxidize

▸ **окисли́ться** (impf **окисля́ться**) сов возв to oxidize.

о́кис|ь (-и) ж oxide.

оккупа́нт (-а) м (захватчик) occupier.

оккупацио́нный прил occupation опред.

оккупа́ци|я (-и) ж occupation.

оккупи́р|овать (-ую) (не)сов перех to occupy.

окла́д (-а) м (зарплата) salary; (на иконе) overlay.

оклеве|та́ть (-щу́, -щешь) сов перех to slander.

окле́|ить (-ю, -ишь; impf **окле́ивать**) сов перех: **~ что-н чем-н** to cover sth with sth; **окле́ивать** (**~** perf) **сте́ны обо́ями** to paper the walls.

оклик|ну́ть (-у, -ешь; impf **оклика́ть**) сов перех to call out to.

ок|но́ (-на́; nom pl -на, gen pl -он) ср window; (подоконник) windowsill; (разг: между уроками) gap.

око́в|ы (-) мн (также перен) fetters мн.

окола́чива|ться (-юсь) несов возв (разг) to hang about.

околд|ова́ть (-у́ю; impf **околдо́вывать**) сов перех (также перен) to bewitch.

околева́|ть (-ю) несов от **околе́ть**.

околе́сиц|а (-ы) ж (разг) claptrap, tripe; **нести́** (impf) **~у** to talk tripe.

околе́|ть (-ю; impf **околева́ть**) сов неперех (животное) to die.

о́коло нареч nearby ♦ предл (+gen; рядом с) near; (приблизительно) about.

околозе́мн|ый прил around the earth; **~ая орби́та** the earth's orbit.

око́льн|ый прил roundabout опред; (перен: метод) devious; **мы пошли́ ~ым путём** we took a roundabout route.

окольцева́ть (-у́ю) сов от **кольцева́ть**.

о́кон сущ см **окно́**.

оконе́чность (-и) ж tip.

око́нн|ый прил: **~ая ра́ма** window frame; **~ое стекло́** windowpane.

оконча́ни|е (-я) ср end; (линг) ending.

оконча́телен прил см **оконча́тельный**.

оконча́тельно нареч (решить, ответить) definitely; (разбить, победить, влюбиться) completely; (отредактировать, проверить) finally.

оконча́тельн|ый (-ен, -ьна, -ьно) прил (вывод, редакция, ответ) final; (победа, свержение) complete.

око́нч|ить (-у, -ишь; impf **ока́нчивать**) сов перех to finish; (вуз) to graduate from

▸ **око́нчиться** (impf **ока́нчиваться**) сов возв to finish; **~ся** (perf) +instr (скандалом, свадьбой) to result in.

око́п (-а) м trench.

окоп|а́ть (-ю; impf **ока́пывать**) сов перех: **~ расте́ние** to loosen the soil around a plant

▸ **окопа́ться** (impf **ока́пываться**) сов возв (ВОЕН) to dig (o.s.) in; (разг: в библиотеке, в кабинете) to bury o.s.

о́корок (-а; nom pl -а́) м gammon.

окосе́|ть (-ю) сов неперех (разг: косить) to squint; (: ослепнуть) to lose an eye; (: опьянеть) to get drunk.

окостенева́|ть (-ю) несов от **окостене́ть**.

окостене́л|ый прил ossified; (руки, ноги) stiff; (ум, жизнь) fossilized.

окостене́|ть (-ю; impf **окостенева́ть**) сов неперех to ossify; (руки, ноги) to stiffen; (ум) to fossilize.

око́т (-а) м (кошки) birth of kittens; (овцы) lambing.

окот|и́ться (3sg -и́тся, 3pl -я́тся) сов от **коти́ться**.

окочене́лый прил stiff with cold.

окочене́|ть (-ю) сов от **коченеть**.

окра́ин|а (-ы) ж (поля, леса) edge; (города) outskirts мн; (страны) remote parts мн.

окра́|сить (-шу, -сишь; impf **окра́шивать**) сов перех (ткань, волосы) to dye; (рассказ, жизнь) to colour (BRIT), color (US)

▸ **окра́ситься** (impf **окра́шиваться**) сов возв: **~ся в чёрный/кра́сный цвет** to come out black/red; **облака́ ~сились в ро́зовый цвет** the clouds were tinged with pink.

окра́ск|а (-ки; gen pl -ок) ж (ткани, волос) dyeing; (животного, выражения) colouring (BRIT), coloring (US); **принима́ть (приня́ть** perf) **совсе́м другу́ю ~ку** (перен) to take on a different complexion.

окра́шива|ть(ся) (-ю(сь)) несов от **окра́сить(ся)**.

окра́шу(сь) сов см **окра́сить(ся)**.

окре́пн|уть (-у, -ешь) сов см **кре́пнуть**.

окр|ести́ть (-ещу́, -е́стишь) сов от **крести́ть** ♦ сов перех: **~ кого́-н/что-н чем-н** (разг) to nickname sb/sth sth

▸ **окрести́ться** сов от **крести́ться**.

окре́стность (-и) ж (города, деревни) environs

мн; в ~и +*gen* in the vicinity of.

окре́стный *прил* (*города́, дере́вни*) neighbouring (*BRIT*), neighboring (*US*); **~ое населе́ние** the population of the surrounding area.

окрещу́(сь) *сов см* **окрести́ть(ся)**.

окриве́ть (-ю) *сов от* **криве́ть**.

о́крик (-а) *м* shout.

окри́кнуть (-у, -ешь; *impf* **окри́кивать**) *сов перех*: ~ **кого́-н** to shout to sb.

окрова́влен|ный (-, -а, -о) *прил* bloodstained.

окропи́|ть (-лю́, -и́шь) *сов от* **кропи́ть**.

окро́шк|а (-и) *ж* okroshka (*cold kvass soup with vegetables and cooked meat*).

о́круг (-а) *м* (*административный, военный*) district; (*избирательный*) ward; (*национальный*) territory; (*города*) area.

окру́г|а (-и) *ж* (*разг*) neighbourhood (*BRIT*), neighborhood (*US*).

округле́ть (-ю) *сов от* **круглеть**.

округл|и́ть (-ю́, -и́шь; *impf* **округля́ть**) *сов перех* (*форму, заготовку*) to round off; (*цифру, результат*) to round up *или* down; (*разг*: *сумму, капитал*) to increase; **округля́ть** (~ *perf*) **глаза́** от удивле́ния, от стра́ха to open one's eyes wide

► **округли́ться** (*impf* **округля́ться**) *сов возв* (*фигура, лицо*) to fill out; (*перен: разг*: *капитал, сумма*) to increase; **у неё ~и́лись глаза́** her eyes widened.

окру́глый *прил* rounded; (*лицо*) round.

округля́|ть(ся) (-ю(сь)) *несов от* **округли́ть(ся)**.

окружа́|ть (-ю) *несов от* **окружи́ть ♦** *перех* to surround.

окружа́ющее (-его; *decl like adj*) *ср* environment.

окружа́ющие (-их; *decl like adj*) *мн* (*также:* ~ **лю́ди**) the people around one; **ничего́ нельзя́ скрыть от ~их** you can't hide anything from (other) people.

окружа́ющий (-ая, -ее, -ие) *прил* surrounding; **окружа́ющая среда́** environment.

окруже́ни|е (-я) *ср* (*среда*) environment; (*компания*) company; (*ВОЕН*) encirclement; **в ~и** +*gen* (*в сопровождение*) in the company of; (*среди*) surrounded by.

окруж|и́ть (-у́, -и́шь; *impf* **окружа́ть**) *сов перех* to surround; **окружа́ть** (~ *perf*) **что-н** +*instr* to surround sth by; **окружа́ть** (~ *perf*) **кого́-н** +*instr* to surround sb with.

окружно́й *прил* (*центр, конференция*) regional; **окружна́я доро́га** bypass; **окружна́я избира́тельная коми́ссия** constituency electoral committee.

окру́жность (-и) *ж* circle; **на три киломе́тра в ~и** three kilometres (*BRIT*) *или* kilometers (*US*) in circumference.

О́ксфорд (-а) *м* Oxford.

окта́в|а (-ы) *ж* octave.

октя́бр|ь (-я́) *м* October; **прие́ду пе́рвого октября́** I shall arrive on the first of October; **в про́шлом/бу́дущем октябре́** last/next October; **в конце́/нача́ле/середи́не октября́** at the end of/beginning of/in the middle of October.

октя́брьск|ий (-ая, -ое, -ие) *прил* October *опред*.

окули́ст (-а) *м* ophthalmologist.

окун|у́ть (-у́, -ёшь; *impf* **окуна́ть**) *сов перех* to dip

► **окуну́ться** (*impf* **окуна́ться**) *сов возв* to plunge.

о́кун|ь (-я) *м* (*ЗООЛ*) perch.

окупа́емость (-и) *ж* viability.

окуп|и́ть (-лю́, -у́пишь; *impf* **окупа́ть**) *сов перех* (*расходы*) to cover; (*поездку, проект*) to cover the cost of

► **окупи́ться** (*impf* **окупа́ться**) *сов возв* to pay for itself; (*перен: усилия, работа*) to be rewarded.

окур|о́к (-ка; *nom pl* -ки) *м* stub, butt.

окута|ть (-ю; *impf* **оку́тывать**) *сов перех* (*подлеж: туман, дым*) to envelop; **оку́тывать** (~ *perf*) **что-н/кого́-н в чем-н** to wrap sth/sb (up) in sth

► **оку́таться** (*impf* **оку́тываться**) *сов возв*: ~**ся** +*instr* to wrap up in; (*перен: земля итп*) to be enveloped in.

оку́чи|ть (-у, -ишь; *impf* **оку́чивать**) *сов перех* to earth up.

ола́дь|я (-ьи; *gen pl* -ий) *ж* ≈ drop scone, ≈ (Scotch) pancake.

оледене́ни|е (-я) *ср* freezing.

оледене́ть (-ю) *сов от* **леденеть**.

оленёнок (-ёнка; *nom pl* -я́та, *gen pl* -я́т) *м* fawn.

оле́н|ий (-ья, -ье, -ьи) *прил* deer's; ~**ьи рога́** antlers.

оле́нин|а (-ы) *ж* venison.

оле́н|ь (-я) *м* deer (*мн* deer).

оленя́та *итп сущ см* **оленёнок**.

оли́вк|а (-и) *ж* olive.

оли́вковый *прил* olive *опред*; (*цвет*) olive-green.

олимпиа́д|а (-ы) *ж* (*СПОРТ*) the Olympics *мн*; (*по физике итп*) Olympiad; **Бе́лая/Ле́тняя О~** the Winter/Summer Olympics.

олимпи́йск|ий (-ая, -ое, -ие) *прил* Olympic *опред*; ~**ое споко́йствие** superhuman calm; **олимпи́йские и́гры** the Olympic Games.

оли́ф|а (-ы) *ж* drying oil.

олицетвор|и́ть (-ю́, -и́шь; *impf* **олицетворя́ть**) *сов перех* to personify.

о́лов|о (-а) *ср* (*ХИМ*) tin.

оловя́нный *прил* tin.

о́лух (-а) *м* (*разг*) oaf.

О́льстер (-а) *м* Ulster.

ольх|а́ (-и́) *ж* alder.

ом (-а) *м* ohm.

Ома́н (-а) *м* Oman.

ома́р (-а) *м* lobster.

оме́г|а (-и) *ж* omega.

омерзе́ни|е (-я) *ср* disgust.

омерзи́тел|ьный (**-ен, -ьна, -ьно**) *прил* disgusting.

омертве́лый *прил* dead.

омертве́|ть (**-ю**) *сов от* **мертве́ть**.

омле́т (**-а**) *м* omelette.

омоло|ди́ть (**-жу́, -ди́шь;** *impf* **омола́живать**) *сов перех* to rejuvenate

▶ **омолоди́ться** (*impf* **омола́живаться**) *сов возв* to be rejuvenated.

ОМО́Н *м сокр* (= *отря́д мили́ции осо́бого назначе́ния*) special police force.

омо́ним (**-а**) *м* homonym.

омоно́в|ец (**-ца**) *м member of* **ОМО́Н**.

омо́ю *итп сов см* **омы́ть**.

омрач|и́ть (**-у́, -и́шь;** *impf* **омрача́ть**) *сов перех* (*настрое́ние, ра́дость, лицо́*) to cloud; (*пра́здник, встре́чу*) to cast a cloud over

▶ **омрачи́ться** (*impf* **омрача́ться**) *сов возв* (*взгляд, лицо́, настрое́ние*) to darken.

ому́т (**-а**) *м* (*водоворо́т*) whirlpool.

омыва́|ть (**-ю**) *несов от* **омы́ть** ◆ *перех* (*подлеж: мо́ре, океа́н*) to wash.

омы́|ть (**-о́ю, -о́ешь;** *impf* **омыва́ть**) *сов перех* to wash.

он (**его́;** *см* **Table 5a**) *мест* (*челове́к*) he; (*живо́тное, предме́т*) it.

она́ (**её;** *см* **Table 5a**) *мест* (*челове́к*) she; (*живо́тное, предме́т*) it.

онани́зм (**-а**) *м* masturbation.

онда́тр|а (**-ы**) *ж* musquash, muskrat.

онеме́лый *прил* numb.

онеме́|ть (**-ю**) *сов от* **неме́ть**.

они́ (**их;** *см* **Table 5b**) *мест* they.

онко́лог (**-а**) *м* oncologist.

онкологи́ческ|ий (**-ая, -ое, -ие**) *прил* oncological; **~ая кли́ника** cancer clinic.

онла́йновый *прил* on-line.

оно́ (**его́;** *см* **Table 5a**) *мест* it; **~ и ви́дно!** (*разг*) sure! (*used ironically*); **я хоте́л помо́чь Вам – ~ и ви́дно** I was only trying to help you – sure you were; **вот ~ что** *или* **как!** (*разг*) so that's what it is!

ОНЧ *сокр* (= *о́чень ни́зкая частота́*) VLF (= *very low frequency*).

ООН *ж сокр* (= *Организа́ция Объединённых На́ций*) UNO (= *United Nations Organization*).

ООП *ж сокр* (= *Организа́ция освобожде́ния Палести́ны*) PLO (= *Palestine Liberation Organization*).

опада́|ть (*3sg* **-ет,** *3pl* **-ют**) *несов от* **опа́сть**.

опаду́т *итп сов см* **опа́сть**.

опа́здыва|ть (**-ю**) *несов от* **опозда́ть**.

опа́л (**-а**) *м* opal.

опа́л|а (**-ы**) *ж* (*перен*) disfavour (*BRIT*), disfavor (*US*); **быть** (*impf*) **в ~е** (**у** *+gen*) to be out of favour (with).

опал|и́ть (**-ю́, -и́шь;** *impf* **опа́ливать** *или* **опаля́ть**) *сов перех* (*во́лосы, кры́лья, де́рево*

итп) to singe; (*ко́жу, лицо́*) to burn; (*impf* **опа́ливать**; *ку́рицу, у́тку*) to singe.

опа́р|а (**-ы**) *ж* leaven.

опаса́|ться (**-юсь**) *несов возв*: **~ +gen** (*неприя́теля, реце́нзента*) to be afraid of; (*сквозня́ка, просту́ды*) to avoid; **~** (*impf*) **за** *+acc* to be worried about.

опа́сен *прил см* **опа́сный**.

опасе́ни|е (**-я**) *ср* apprehension.

опа́ск|а (**-и**) *ж*: **с ~ой** cautiously; **без ~и** fearlessly.

опа́сно *нареч* dangerously ◆ *как сказ* it's dangerous; **э́то ~ для жи́зни** it's life-threatening.

опа́сност|ь (**-и**) *ж* danger; **в ~и** in danger; **с ~ю для жи́зни** endangering one's life.

опа́с|ный (**-ен, -на, -но**) *прил* dangerous.

опа́|сть (*3sg* **-дёт,** *3pl* **-ду́т,** *impf* **опада́ть**) *сов непере́х* (*цветы́, ли́стья*) to fall; (*о́пухоль, ши́шка*) to go down; (*разг: щёки, бока́*) to get thinner.

ОПЕ́К *м/ж сокр* (= *Организа́ция стран-экспортёров не́фти*) OPEC (= *Organization of Petroleum-Exporting Countries*).

опе́к|а (**-и**) *ж* (*попечи́тельство: госуда́рства*) guardianship; (*: ма́тери, отца́*) custody; (*забо́та*) care ◆ *собир* guardians *мн*; **брать** (**взять** *perf*) **кого́-н под ~у** to take sb into one's care; **она́ рабо́тает под мое́й ~ой** she works under my supervision.

опека́|ть (**-ю**) *несов перех* to take care of; (*сироту́*) to be guardian to.

опеку́н (**-а́**) *м* (*сироты́*) guardian; (*насле́дника, насле́дства*) trustee.

опеку́нш|а (**-и**) *ж* (*сироты́*) guardian.

опёнок (**-ёнка;** *nom pl* **-я́та,** *gen pl* **-я́т**) *м* (*БОТ*) honey agaric.

о́пер|а (**-ы**) *ж* opera.

операти́вен *прил см* **операти́вный**.

операти́вност|ь (**-и**) *ж* efficiency.

операти́в|ный (**-ен, -на, -но**) *прил* (*рабо́та, гру́ппа, штаб*) executive *опред*; (*ме́ры, де́йствия, руково́дство*) efficient; (*хирурги́ческий*) surgical; **операти́вное вмеша́тельство** surgical intervention.

опера́тор (**-а**) *м* operator.

операцио́нн|ая (**-ой;** *decl like adj*) *ж* (*МЕД*) operating theatre (*BRIT*) *или* room (*US*).

операцио́нный *прил* (*инструме́нты, отделе́ние*) surgical; **операцио́нный стол** operating table.

опера́ци|я (**-и**) *ж* operation.

опере|ди́ть (**-жу́, -ди́шь;** *impf* **опережа́ть**) *сов перех* (*в бе́ге, в учёбе, в разви́тии*) to outstrip; **~** (*perf*) **кого́-н** (*в разгово́ре*) to beat sb to it.

опере́ни|е (**-я**) *ср* (*ЗООЛ*) plumage; (*АВИА*): **хвостово́е ~** tail.

опере́тт|а (**-ы**) *ж* operetta.

опере́ться (обопру́сь, обопрёшься; *pt*
   опёрся, оперла́сь, оперло́сь, *impf* опира́ться)
   сов непepex: ~ **на** +*acc* (*дерево, трость*) to
   lean on; (*перен: на товарища, на коллектив*)
   to rely on; (*перен: на факты, на теорию*) to be
   supported *или* backed up by.
опери́р|овать (-ую) *perf* опери́ровать *или*
   проопери́ровать) *несов перех* (*больного*) to
   operate on ◆ *непepex* (*no perf*; ВОЕН) to operate;
   ~ (*impf*) +*instr* (*акциями, ценными бумагами*) to
   deal in; (*перен: цифрами, фактами*) to use.
опери́ться (*3sg* -и́тся, *3pl* -я́тся, *impf*
   опери́ться) *сов возв* to become fully fledged.
о́перный *прил* (*ария, партитура*) operatic;
   (*певец*) opera *опред*; ~ **теа́тр** opera house.
оперя́ться (*3sg* -ется, *3pl* -ются) *несов от*
   опери́ться.
опеча́л|иться (-юсь) *сов от* печа́литься.
опеча́та|ть (-ю; *impf* опеча́тывать) *сов перех* to
   seal.
опеча́т|ка (-ки; *gen pl* -ок) *ж* misprint; **спи́сок**
   ~**ок** errata.
опеча́тыва|ть (-ю) *несов от* опеча́тать.
опеш|ить (-у, -ишь) *сов непepex* (*разг*) to be
   taken aback.
опи́л|ки (-ок) *мн* (*древесные*) sawdust *ед*;
   (*металлические*) filings *мн*.
опира́|ться (-юсь) *несов от* опере́ться.
описа́ни|е (-я) *ср* description.
описа́тел|ьный (-ен, -ьна, -ьно) *прил*
   descriptive.
опис|а́ть (-ишу́, -и́шешь; *impf* опи́сывать) *сов*
   перех to describe; (*составить перечень*) to
   make a list *или* an inventory of; (*наложить*
   арест) to distrain.
опис|а́ться (-ю́сь) *сов возв* (*разг*) to wet o.s.
опи́сыва|ть (-ю) *несов от* описа́ть.
о́пис|ь (-и) *ж* (*список*) list, inventory; (*арест*)
   distraint.
о́пиум (-а) *м* opium.
опишу́ *итп сов см* описа́ть.
опла́|кать (-чу, -чешь; *impf* опла́кивать) *сов*
   перех to mourn.
опла́т|а (-ы) *ж* payment.
опла|ти́ть (-чу́, -́тишь; *impf* опла́чивать) *сов*
   перех (*работу, труд*) to pay for; (*счёт*) to pay.
опла́чу *итп сов см* оплати́ть.
опла́чива|ть (-ю) *несов от* оплати́ть.
оплачу́ *сов см* оплати́ть.
оплеу́х|а (-и) *ж* (*разг*) clout; (*перен:*
   оскорбление) slap in the face.
оплодотворе́ни|е (-я) *ср* fertilization.
оплодотвор|и́ть (-ю́, -и́шь; *impf*
   оплодотворя́ть) *сов перех* to fertilize.
опломбир|ова́ть (-у́ю) *сов от* пломбирова́ть.
опло́т (-а) *м* stronghold, bastion.
оплоша́|ть (-ю) *сов непepex* (*разг*) to boob.
опло́шност|ь (-и) *ж* mistake; **допуска́ть**
   (**допусти́ть** *perf*) ~ to make a mistake.
опове|сти́ть (-щу́, -сти́шь; *impf* оповеща́ть)
   сов перех to notify.
оповеще́ни|е (-я) *ср* notification.

оповещу́ *сов см* оповести́ть.
опога́н|ить (-ю) *сов от* пога́нить.
опозда́вш|ий (-его; *decl like adj*) *м* latecomer.
опозда́ни|е (-я) *ср* lateness; (*поезда, самолёта*)
   late arrival; **приходи́ть** (**прийти́** *perf*) **с ~м/без**
   опозда́ния to arrive late/on time.
опозда́|ть (-ю; *impf* опа́здывать) *сов непepex*:
   опа́здывать (**в/на** +*acc*) (*в школу, на работу*
   итп) to be late (for); **опа́здывать** (~ *perf*) **с**
   чем-н to be late with sth; ~ (*perf*) **на**
   по́езд/самолёт to miss the train/plane.
опознава́тельный *прил* (*знак*) identifying;
   (*огни*) distinguishing.
опознава́|ть (-ю́) *несов от* опозна́ть.
опозна́ни|е (-я) *ср* identification.
опозна́|ть (-ю; *impf* опознава́ть) *сов перех* to
   identify.
опозо́р|ить(ся) (-ю(сь)) *сов от* позо́рить(ся).
опола́скива|ть (-ю) *несов от* ополосну́ть.
о́пол|зень (-зня) *м* landslide.
ополосн|у́ть (-у́, -ёшь; *impf* опола́скивать) *сов*
   перех (*посуду*) to rinse; (*лицо, руки*) to wash.
ополоу́ме|ть (-ю) *сов непepex* (*разг*) to go
   wild.
ополча́|ться (-юсь) *несов от* ополчи́ться.
ополче́н|ец (-ца) *м* member of the home guard.
ополче́ни|е (-я) *ср* home guard.
ополче́нца *итп сущ см* ополче́нец.
ополч|и́ться (-у́сь, -и́шься; *impf* ополча́ться)
   сов возв: ~ **на** +*acc или* **про́тив** +*gen* (*человека*)
   to turn against; (*теорию, недостатки*) to
   attack.
опо́мн|иться (-юсь, -ишься) *сов возв* (*прийти*
   в сознание) to come round; (*одуматься*) to
   come to one's senses; ~**ись, что ты де́лаешь!**
   think what you're doing!
опо́р (-а) *м*: **во весь ~** at top speed.
опо́р|а (-ы) *ж* (*также перен*) support; (*строит*)
   pile; **то́чка** ~**ы** fulcrum; **опо́ра**
   электропереда́ч (*обычно мн*) electricity pylon.
опо́рный *прил* supporting *опред*; **опо́рный**
   прыжо́к vault; **опо́рный пункт** base; (*воен*)
   strongpoint.
опорожн|и́ть (-ю́, -и́шь; *impf* опорожня́ть) *сов*
   перех to drain, empty.
опоро́с (-а) *м* farrowing.
опоро́ч|ить (-у, -ишь) *сов от* поро́чить.
опохмел|и́ться (-ю́сь, -и́шься; *impf*
   опохмеля́ться) *сов возв* (*разг*) to take the hair
   of the dog (*to cure a hangover*).
опо́шл|ить (-ю, -ишь; *impf* опошля́ть) *сов*
   перех (*мысль, человека, имя*) to debase,
   demean; (*слово, песню*) to vulgarize.
опоэтизи́р|овать (-ую) *сов от*
   поэтизи́ровать.
оппозицио́нный (-ен, -на, -но) *прил* (*партия*
   блок) opposition; ~**ные настрое́ния** mood of
   opposition.
оппози́ци|я (-и) *ж* opposition; **быть** (*impf*) **в ~и**
   (*полит*) to be in opposition; **быть** (*impf*) **в ~и к**
   +*dat* to oppose.

оппонéнт (-а) *м* external examiner (*for doctoral thesis*); (*в спóре*) opponent.

опрáв|а (-ы) *ж* frame.

оправдáни|е (-я) *ср* justification; (*ЮР*) acquittal; (*извинéние*) excuse; **говорúть (сказáть** *perf*) **что-н в своё ~** to say sth in one's defence (*BRIT*) *или* defense (*US*).

оправдáн|ный (-, -на, -но) *прил* justified.

оправдá|ть (-ю; *impf* **опрáвдывать**) *сов перех* to justify; (*ЮР*) to acquit, find not guilty

▸ **оправдáться** (*impf* **опрáвдываться**) *сов возв* to justify o.s.; (*надéжды, опасéния, расхóды*) to be justified.

опрáв|ить (-лю, -ишь; *impf* **оправлять**) *сов перех* (*плáтье, постéль*) to straighten; (*драгоцéнный кáмень, зéркало*) to mount; (*лúнзы*) to frame

▸ **опрáвиться** (*impf* **оправляться**) *сов возв*: **~ся от** +*gen* to recover from.

опрáшива|ть (-ю) *несов от* **опросúть**.

определéни|е (-я) *ср* determination; (*понятия, значéния*) definition; (*линг*) attribute; (*ЮР*) ruling.

определён|ный (-ен, -на, -но) *прил* (*устанóвленный*) definite; (*нéкоторый*) certain; (*явный: успéх, спосóбности*) unqualified; **при ~ных обстоятельствах** under certain circumstances.

определ|úть (-ю́, -úшь; *impf* **определять**) *сов перех* to determine; (*явлéние, понятие*) to define

▸ **определúться** (*impf* **определяться**) *сов возв* (*болéзнь*) to be diagnosed; (*задáчи*) to become clear; (*разг: харáктер*) to take shape; (*пилóт*) to get one's bearings.

опрéлост|ь (-и) *ж* rash; (*у младéнца*) nappy (*BRIT*) *или* diaper (*US*) rash.

опресн|úть (-ю́, -úшь; *impf* **опреснять**) *сов перех* to desalinate.

оприхóд|овать (-ую) *сов от* **прихóдовать**.

опрóб|овать (-ую) (*не*)*сов перех* to test.

опровéрг|нуть (-у, -ешь; *impf* **опровергáть**) *сов перех* to refute.

опровержéни|е (-я) *ср* refutation.

опрокú|нуть (-у, -ешь; *impf* **опрокúдывать**) *сов перех* (*стакáн, стул*) to knock over; (*лóдку*) to capsize, overturn; (*прохóжего, ребёнка*) to knock down *или* over; (*перен: войскá, наступлéние*) to repel; (: *взгляды, представлéния*) to demolish

▸ **опрокúнуться** (*impf* **опрокúдываться**) *сов возв* (*стакáн, стул, человéк*) to fall over; (*лóдка*) to capsize.

опромéтчив|ый (-, -а, -о) *прил* precipitate, hasty.

óпрометью *нареч* headlong.

опрóс (-а) *м* (*свидéтелей*) questioning; (*населéния*) survey; **опрóс обществéнного**

мнéния opinion poll.

опрос|úть (-ошу́, -óсишь; *impf* **опрáшивать**) *сов перех* (*свидéтелей*) to question; (*населéние*) to survey.

опрóсный *прил*: **~ лист** questionnaire.

опротест|овáть (-у́ю; *impf* **опротестóвывать**) *сов перех* (*ЮР*) to appeal against; (*вéксель*) to protest.

опротúве|ть (-ю) *сов неперех*: **мне э́то ~ло** I am sick of it.

опрошу́ *сов см* **опросúть**.

опры́ска|ть (-ю; *impf* **опры́скивать**) *сов перех* to spray.

опры́скиватель (-я) *м* sprayer; (*садóвый*) sprinkler.

опры́скива|ть (-ю) *несов от* **опры́скать**.

опрятный (-ен, -на, -но) *прил* neat, tidy.

óптик|а (-и) *ж* (*раздéл фúзики*) optics ◆ *собир* optical instruments *мн*.

оптимáльный (-ен, -ьна, -ьно) *прил* optimum.

оптимúзм (-а) *м* optimism.

оптимúст (-а) *м* optimist.

оптимистú|чный (-ен, -на, -но) *прил* optimistic.

оптúческ|ий (-ая, -ое, -ие) *прил* optical.

оптовúк (-á) *м* wholesaler.

оптóв|ый *прил* wholesale; **~ые закýпки** (*КОММ*) bulk buying.

óптом *нареч*: **купúть/продáть ~** to buy/sell wholesale.

опубликовáни|е (-я) *ср* (*статьú, кнúги*) publication; (*закóна*) promulgation.

опублик|овáть (-у́ю; *impf* **опубликóвывать** *или* **публиковáть**) *сов перех* (*статью́, кнúгу*) to publish; (*закóн*) to promulgate.

опускáть(ся) (-ю(сь)) *несов от* **опустúть(ся)**.

опустéлый *прил* (*дом, сад*) empty; (*улица*) deserted.

опустé|ть (*3sg* -ет, *3pl* -ют) *сов от* **пустéть**.

опу|стúть (-щý, -стишь; *impf* **опускáть**) *сов перех* to lower; (*гóлову*) to bow; (*ворóтник*) to turn down; (*слóво, пáраграф*) to miss out; **опускáть** (~ *perf*) **в** +*acc* (*в стакáн, в ящик*) to drop *или* put in(to); (*человéка: в яму*) to lower into; **опускáть** (~ *perf*) **рýки** (*перен*) to give up

▸ **опустúться** (*impf* **опускáться**) *сов возв* (*человéк: на дивáн, на зéмлю*) to sit (down); (*сóлнце*) to sink; (*мост, шлагбáум*) to be lowered; (*перен: человéк*) to let o.s. go.

опустошá|ть (-ю) *несов от* **опустошúть**.

опустошён|ный (-, -а, -о) *прил* (*человéк, душá*) empty.

опустошú|тельный (-ен, -ьна, -ьно) *прил* devastating.

опустош|úть (-ý, -úшь; *impf* **опустошáть**) *сов перех* (*странý, пóле*) to devastate; (*разг: бутылку, ящик*) to empty; (*перен: жизнь, человéка*) to ruin.

опу́та|ть (-ю; *impf* опу́тывать) *сов перех* (*подлеж: ветки, плющ*) to entangle; **опу́тывать** (~ *perf*) **чем-н** (*верёвками, интригами*) to enmesh in sth.

опу́хн|уть (-у, -ешь) *сов от* пу́хнуть ♦ (*impf* опуха́ть) *неперех* to swell (up).

о́пухол|ь (-и) *ж* (*на руке, на ноге*) swelling; (*внутренняя*) tumour (*BRIT*), tumor (*US*).

опу́хший (-ая, -ее, -ие) *прил* swollen.

опу́шк|а (-и) *ж* (*леса*) edge; (*шапки, воротника*) trim(ming).

опуще́ни|е (-я) *ср* (*деталей, слов*) omission; (*желудка, матки*) prolapse.

опущу́(сь) *сов см* опусти́ть(ся).

опыле́ни|е (-я) *ср* pollination.

опыл|и́ть (-ю́, -и́шь; *impf* опыля́ть) *сов перех* to pollinate; (*от вредителей*) to spray (*with insecticide*).

о́пыт (-а) *м* (*знания*) experience; (*эксперимент*) experiment; (*попытка*) attempt; **на со́бственном ~е** from (one's own) experience.

о́пыт|ный (-ен, -на, -но) *прил* (*врач, рабочий*) experienced; (*лаборатория, отдел*) experimental; (*экземпляр*) sample *опред*; (*полёт*) test *опред*; ~ **экземпля́р** (test) sample; **дока́зывать (доказа́ть** *perf*) **что-н ~ным путём** to prove sth by experiment; **~ный образе́ц** sample.

опьяне́ни|е (-я) *ср* intoxication.

опьяне́|ть (-ю) *сов от* пьяне́ть.

опьян|и́ть (-ю́, -и́шь; *impf* опьяня́ть *или* пьяни́ть) *сов перех* (*также перен*) to intoxicate.

опя́та *итп сущ см* опёнок.

опя́ть *нареч* again; ~ **же** (*разг*) yet again; ~ **два́дцать пять!** (*разг*) not again!

ора́в|а (-ы) *ж* (*разг*) gang.

орангута́н(г) (-а) *м* orang-utan.

ора́нжевый *прил* orange.

оранжере́йный *прил* hothouse *опред*.

оранжере́|я (-и) *ж* hothouse.

ора́тор (-а) *м* orator; (*выступающий*) speaker.

орато́ри|я (-и) *ж* oratorio.

ора́торский (-ая, -ое, -ие) *прил* oratorical.

ор|а́ть (-у́, -ёшь) *несов неперех* (*разг*) to yell; (: *ребёнок*) to bawl, howl; ~ (*impf*) **во всё го́рло** (*разг*) to yell at the top of one's voice.

орби́т|а (-ы) *ж* orbit.

орбита́льный *прил* orbital.

о́рган (-а) *м* (*также* АНАТ) organ; (*здравоохранения*) body; (*орудие*): ~ +*gen* (*пропаганды*) vehicle for; **ме́стные ~ы вла́сти** local authorities (*BRIT*) *или* government (*US*); **половы́е ~ы** genitals; *см также* о́рганы.

орга́н (-а) *м* (*МУЗ*) organ.

организа́тор (-а) *м* organizer.

организа́торский (-ая, -ое, -ие) *прил* organizational.

организацио́нный *прил* organizational.

организа́ци|я (-и) *ж* organization; (*устройство*) system; **Организа́ция**

Объединённых На́ций United Nations Organization.

органи́зм (-а) *м* organism.

организо́ван|ный (-, -на, -но) *прил* organized; **организо́ванная престу́пность** organized crime.

организ|ова́ть (-у́ю) (*не*)*сов перех* (*создать*) to organize

▶ **организ|ова́ться** (*не*)*сов возв* to be organized; (*в отряд, в ансамбль*) to organize o.s.; (*разг: жизнь*) to sort o.s. out.

органи́ст (-а) *м* organist.

органи́ческ|ий (-ая, -ое, -ие) *прил* organic; (*перен: неприязнь, отвраще́ние*) natural; ~ **поро́к се́рдца** heart defect.

о́рган|ы (-ов) *мн* (*разг*) the Ministry of Internal Affairs and the KGB.

о́рги|я (-и) *ж* orgy.

оргкомите́т (-а) *м сокр* (= организацио́нный комите́т) organizational committee.

орграбо́т|а (-ы) *ж сокр* (= организацио́нная рабо́та) organizational work.

оргте́хник|а (-и) *ж* office automation equipment.

орд|а́ (-ы́; *nom pl* **о́рды**) *ж* horde.

о́рден (-а; *nom pl* -а́) *м* order; (*nom pl* -ы; *рыцарский, масо́нский*) order.

орденоно́сный *прил* (*батальон, теа́тр*) order-bearing.

орденоно́сца *итп сущ см* орденоно́сец.

о́рдер (-а) *м* (*на аре́ст, на о́быск*) warrant; (*на кварти́ру*) authorization.

ордина́р|ный (-ен, -на, -но) *прил* ordinary.

ордина́тор (-а) *м* (*МЕД*) ≈ registrar (*BRIT*), ≈ resident (*US*).

ординату́р|а (-ы) *ж two-year period in which junior doctor specializes in particular field*.

ор|ёл (орла́; *nom pl* **о́рлы**) *м* eagle; (*перен: человек*) hero; ~ **или ре́шка?** (*разг*) heads or tails?

Оренбу́рг (-а) *м* Orenburg.

орео́л (-а) *м* halo; (*перен: славы, таинственности*) aura.

оре́х (-а) *м* nut; (*древесина*) walnut; **мне доста́лось на ~и** (*разг*) I got it in the neck.

оре́ховый *прил* nut; (*ме́бель*) walnut.

оре́шник (-а) *м* (*кустарник*) hazel; (*собир: заросль*) hazel grove.

ОРЗ *ср сокр* (= о́строе респирато́рное заболева́ние) ARD (= *acute respiratory disease*).

оригина́л (-а) *м* original; (*разг: чудак*) eccentric.

оригина́л|ьный (-ен, -ьна, -ьно) *прил* original.

ориента́ци|я (-и) *ж* orientation; **име́ть** (*impf*) **хоро́шую ~ю в чём-н** to have a good grasp of sth.

ориенти́р (-а) *м* landmark.

ориенти́р|овать (-ую) (*не*)*сов перех* to orient, orientate; (*перен*): ~ **кого-н на** +*acc* to orient *или* orientate sb towards

▶ **ориенти́р|оваться** (*perf* **ориенти́роваться**

или **сориенти́роваться**) *несов возв* to find *или* get one's bearings; (*перен: в ситуации*) to find one's feet; (*разбираться*) to be versed; **~ся** (*impf/perf*) **на** +*acc* (*перен*) to be oriented *или* orientated towards; (*на маяк, на солнце*) to find one's bearings by.

ориентиро́воч|ный (-ен, -на, -но) *прил* provisional; ~ **пункт** landmark.

орке́стр (-а) *м* orchestra.

оркестра́нт (-а) *м* member of an orchestra.

оркестро́в|ка (-ки; *gen pl* -ок) *ж* orchestration.

оркне́йск|ий (-ая, -ое, -ие) *прил*: **О~ие острова́** Orkney Islands, Orkneys.

орла́ *итп сущ см* **орёл**.

орли́ный *прил* (*клюв, гнездо*) eagle's; ~ **взгляд** proud look.

орна́мент (-а) *м* (decorative) pattern.

орнито́лог (-а) *м* ornithologist.

орнитоло́ги|я (-и) *ж* ornithology.

оробе́|ть (-ю) *сов от* **робе́ть**.

ороси́тельный *прил* irrigation *опред*.

оро|си́ть (-шу́, -си́шь; *impf* **ороша́ть**) *сов перех* to irrigate; (*подлеж: дождь*) to water.

ороше́ни|е (-я) *ср* irrigation.

орошу́ *сов см* **ороси́ть**.

ортодокса́л|ьный (-ен, -ьна, -ьно) *прил* orthodox.

ортопе́д (-а) *м* orthopaedic (*BRIT*) *или* orthopedic (*US*) surgeon.

ортопеди́ческ|ий (-ая, -ое, -ие) *прил* orthopaedic (*BRIT*), orthopedic (*US*).

ору́ди|е (-я) *ср* (*также перен*) tool; (*ВОЕН*) gun (*used of artillery*).

ору́д|овать (-ую) *несов неперех* (+*instr*; *разг*: *вёслами, лопатой*) to work away with; (: *вор, браконьер*) to be at work.

оруже́йный *прил*: ~ **заво́д** arsenal; ~ **ма́стер** armourer (*BRIT*), armorer (*US*); **Оруже́йная пала́та** The Armoury Palace.

ору́жи|е (-я) *ж* (*также перен*) weapon; (*собир*) arms *мн*.

орфографи́ческ|ий (-ая, -ое, -ие) *прил* orthographical.

орфогра́фи|я (-и) *ж* (*правописание*) spelling; (*правила*) orthography.

орхиде́|я (-и) *ж* orchid.

ос|а́ (-ы́; *nom pl* **о́сы**) *ж* wasp.

оса́д|а (-ы) *ж* siege; **снима́ть** (**снять** *perf*) ~**у** to lift a siege.

оса|ди́ть (-жу́, -ди́шь; *impf* **осажда́ть**) *сов перех* to besiege; (*хим*) to precipitate; (*impf* **оса́живать**; *коня, лошадь*) to rein in; **осажда́ть** (~ *perf*) **кого́-н чем-н** (*перен*) to besiege sb with sth; ~ (*perf*) **кого́-н** (*разг*) to put sb in his *итп* place.

оса́дка *сущ см* **оса́док**.

оса́д|ки (-ов) *мн* precipitation *ед*.

оса́дный *прил*: ~**ое положе́ние** state of siege.

оса́д|ок (-ка) *м* sediment; **у меня́ оста́лся неприя́тный** ~ **от э́той встре́чи** the meeting left me with an unpleasant aftertaste.

оса́дочный *прил* sedimentary.

осажда́|ть (-ю) *несов от* **осади́ть**.

▶ **осажда́ться** *несов возв* to precipitate.

оса́жива|ть (-ю) *несов от* **осади́ть**.

осажу́ *сов см* **осади́ть**.

оса́нист|ый (-, -а, -о) *прил* imposing.

оса́н|ка (-и) *ж* posture.

осатанева́|ть (-ю) *несов от* **осатане́ть**.

осатане́лый *прил* (*разг*) frenzied; (: *человек*) furious.

осатане́|ть (-ю; *impf* **осатанева́ть**) *сов неперех* (*разг*) to go wild; (: *надоедать*): ~ **кому́-н** to drive sb mad.

ОСВ *сокр* = **ограниче́ние стратеги́ческих наступа́тельных вооруже́ний**: **перегово́ры/догово́р** ~ SALT (= *Strategic Arms Limitation Talks/Treaty*).

осва́ива|ть(ся) (-ю(сь)) *несов от* **осво́ить(ся)**.

осведоми́тел|ь (-я) *м* informer.

осведоми́тельниц|а (-ы) *ж см* **осведоми́тель**.

осведом|и́ть (-лю́, -и́шь; *impf* **осведомля́ть**) *сов перех* to inform

▶ **осве́домиться** (*impf* **осведомля́ться**) *сов возв*: ~**ся о** +*prp* to inquire about; **осведомля́ться** (~**ся** *perf*) **о чьём-н здоро́вье** to inquire after sb's health.

осведомлён|ный (-, -на, -но) *прил* knowledgeable.

осведомлю́(сь) *сов см* **осве́домить(ся)**.

осведомля́|ть(ся) (-ю(сь)) *несов от* **осве́домить(ся)**.

освеж|и́ть (-у́, -и́шь; *impf* **освежа́ть**) *сов перех* (*воздух*) to freshen; (*комнату, платье*) to freshen up; (*краски*) to liven up; (*воспоминания, знания*) to refresh; **о́тдых** ~**и́л меня́** I feel refreshed after my rest

▶ **освежи́ться** (*impf* **освежа́ться**) *сов возв* (*воздух*) to freshen; (*человек: под душем итп*) to freshen up; (*краски*) to brighten up; (*воспоминания, знания*) to be refreshed.

освети́тел|ь (-я) *м* (*ТЕАТР*) lighting technician.

освети́тельный *прил*: ~ **прибо́р** light; **освети́тельная раке́та** flare.

осве|ти́ть (-щу́, -ти́шь; *impf* **освеща́ть**) *сов перех* (*также перен*) to light up; (*вопрос, проблему, дело*) to highlight

▶ **освети́ться** (*impf* **освеща́ться**) *сов возв* (*также перен*) to be lit up; (*лицо*) to light up.

освеще́ни|е (-я) *ср* lighting; (*вопроса, проблемы, дела*) coverage.

освещу́(сь) *сов см* **освети́ть(ся)**.

освист|а́ть (-ищу́, -и́щешь; *impf* **освистывать**) *сов перех* to boo.

освободи́тел|ь (-я) *м* liberator.

освободи́тельниц|а (-ы) *ж см*
освободи́тель.

освободи́тельный *прил* liberation *опред*;
~ая война́ war of liberation.

освобо|ди́ть (-жу́, -ди́шь; *impf* освобожда́ть)
сов перех to release; (*из капкана*) to free;
(*город, деревню*) to liberate; (*полку, комнату*)
to clear; (*дом, кварти́ру*) to vacate; (*время,
день*) to leave free; ~ (*perf*) кого́-н от
хлопо́т/наказа́ния to spare sb the trouble/from
punishment; ~ (*perf*) кого́-н от эксплуата́ции to
liberate sb from exploitation; ~ (*perf*) кого́-н от
до́лжности to dismiss sb

▸ освободи́ться (*impf* освобожда́ться) *сов
возв* (*из тюрьмы́*) to be released; (*из капкана*:
зверь) to free itself; (: *челове́к*) to free o.s.;
(*кварти́ра, дом*) to be vacated; (*место, полка*)
to be cleared; ~ся (*perf*) от наказа́ния to escape
punishment; ~ся (*perf*) от рабо́ты to finish
work.

освобожде́ни|е (-я) *ср* release, freeing;
(*города, деревни*) liberation; ~ от до́лжности
dismissal; ~ от нало́гов tax exemption.

освобожу́(сь) *сов см* освободи́ть(ся).

ОСВО́Д *м сокр* = Всеросси́йское о́бщество
спасе́ния на во́дах.

освое́ни|е (-я) *ср* (*см глаг*) mastering;
cultivation.

осво́|ить (-ю, -ишь; *impf* осва́ивать) *сов перех*
(*те́хнику, язы́к*) to master; (*зе́мли, пусты́ню*) to
cultivate

▸ осво́иться (*impf* осва́иваться) *сов возв* (*на
но́вой рабо́те*) to find one's feet.

освя|ти́ть (-щу́, -ти́шь; *impf* освяща́ть *или*
святи́ть) *сов перех* (*РЕЛ*) to bless.

оседа́|ть (-ю) *несов от* осе́сть.

оседла́|ть (-ю) *сов от* седла́ть ♦ (*impf*
осёдлывать) *несов перех* (*разг*: *стул, бревно́*)
to straddle; (: *ро́дственников, знако́мых*) to take
advantage of.

осе́длый *прил* settled.

осека́|ться (-юсь) *несов от* осе́чься.

осёкся *итп сов см* осе́чься.

осеку́сь *итп сов см* осе́чься.

осёл (-ла́) *м* donkey; (*перен*: *разг*) ass.

осе|ни́ть (*3sg* -и́т, *3pl* -я́т, *impf* осеня́ть) *сов
перех* (*подлеж*: *мысль*) to strike; меня́ ~и́ло,
что ... it struck me that ...; осеня́ть (~ *perf*)
кресто́м to bless.

осе́нний (-яя, -ее, -ие) *прил* autumn *опред*, fall
опред (*US*); (*похо́жий на о́сень*: *пого́да, день*)
autumnal, fall.

о́сен|ь (-и) *ж* autumn, fall (*US*).

о́сенью *нареч* in autumn, in the fall (*US*).

осеня́|ть (-ю) *несов от* осени́ть.

осе́|сть (-я́ду, -я́дешь; *impf* оседа́ть) *сов
непере́х* (*пол, дом*) to subside; (*пыль, осадок*) to
settle; они́ ~ли в го́роде they settled in the
city.

осети́н (-а; *gen pl* -) *м* Ossetian.

осети́н|ка (-ки; *gen pl* -ок) *ж см* осети́н.

Осе́ти|я (-и) *ж*: Се́верная/Ю́жная ~ North/
South Ossetia.

осётр (-етра́) *м* sturgeon (*ZOOL*).

осетри́н|а (-ы) *ж* sturgeon (*CULIN*).

осе́ч|ка (-ки; *gen pl* -ек) *ж* (*перен*: *раза*) cockup
(*BRIT*), mess (*US*); дава́ть (дать *perf*) ~ку to
misfire.

осе́|чься (-ку́сь, -чёшься *итп*, -ку́тся; *pt*
ёкся, -е́клась, -е́клось, *impf* осека́ться) *сов
непере́х* to stop short.

оси́л|ить (-ю, -ишь; *impf* оси́ливать) *сов перех*
(*проти́вника*) to overpower; (*разг*: *кни́гу*) to get
through; (: *фи́зику, упражне́ние*) to get to grips
with.

оси́н|а (-ы) *ж* aspen.

оси́новый *прил* aspen *опред*.

оси́ный *прил*: ~ое гнездо́ wasp's nest; (*перен*)
hornet's nest.

осипну́ть (-у, -ешь) *сов от* си́пнуть.

осироте́вш|ий (-ая, -ее, -ие) *прил* (*ребёнок*)
orphaned; (*перен*: *дом, сад*) abandoned.

осироте́лый *прил* = осироте́вший.

осироте́|ть (-ю) *сов от* сироте́ть.

оска́л|ить (-ю, -ишь; *impf* оска́ливать *или*
ска́лить) *сов перех*: ~ зу́бы (*также перен*) to
bare one's teeth.

▸ оска́литься (*impf* оска́ливаться *или*
ска́литься) *сов возв* (*также перен*) to bare
one's teeth; (*перен*: *осла́биться*) to smirk.

осканда́л|иться (-юсь, -ишься) *сов возв*
(*разг*) to show o.s. up.

оскверн|и́ть (-ю́, -и́шь; *impf* оскверня́ть) *сов
перех* to defile; (*чу́вства, иде́и*) to debase.

оскла́б|иться (-люсь, -ишься) *сов непере́х* to
grin.

оско́л|ок (-ка) *м* (*стекла́, ча́шки*) piece; (:
ме́лкий) sliver; (*бо́мбы, снаря́да*) shrapnel
только ед; (*перен*: *про́шлого*) fragment.

оско́лочный *прил* (*ра́на, бо́мба*) shrapnel
опред.

оско́мин|а (-ы) *ж* acidic taste; наби́ть (*perf*)
кому́-н ~у (*перен*) to bore sb stupid.

оскоп|и́ть (-лю́, -и́шь; *impf* оскопля́ть) *сов
перех* to castrate.

оскорби́тель|ный (-ен, -ьна, -ьно) *прил*
offensive.

оскорб|и́ть (-лю́, -и́шь; *impf* оскорбля́ть) *сов
перех* to insult, offend; оскорбля́ть (~ *perf*)
кого́-н в лу́чших чу́вствах to offend sb's finer
feelings; оскорбля́ть (~ *perf*) слух to offend the
ear

▸ оскорби́ться (*impf* оскорбля́ться) *сов возв*
to be offended, take offence *или* offense (*US*).

оскорбле́ни|е (-я) *ср* insult.

оскорбл|ю́(сь) *сов см* оскорби́ть(ся).

оскорбля́|ть(ся) (-ю(сь)) *несов от*
оскорби́ть(ся).

оскуде́|ть (-ю; *impf* оскудева́ть *или* скуде́ть)
сов непере́х (*страна́*) to become impoverished;
(*запа́сы итп*) to become depleted.

осла́ *итп сущ см* осёл.

осла́бе́ть (-ю; *impf* ослабева́ть *или* слабе́ть) *сов неперех* to weaken; (*давление, ветер*) to drop; (*внимание*) to wander; (*дождь*) to slacken *или* ease off; (*шум*) to die down; (*ремень*) to loosen; (*дисциплина*) to slacken.

осла́б|ить (-лю, -ишь; *impf* ослабля́ть) *сов перех* to weaken; (*внимание*) to let wander; (*ремень*) to loosen; (*дисциплина*) to relax.

ослабле́ни|е (-я) *ср* weakening; (*давления, шума*) reduction; (*внимания*) slackening; (*дисциплины*) decline; за́втра ожида́ется ~ ве́тра/дождя́ the wind/rain should ease off by tomorrow.

осла́блю *сов см* осла́бить.

ослабля́|ть (-ю) *несов от* осла́бить.

осла́бн|уть (-у, -ешь) *сов от* сла́бнуть.

осла́в|ить (-лю, -ишь) *сов перех* (*разг*) to smear
▶ осла́виться *сов возв* (*разг*) to get o.s. a bad name.

осл|ёнок (-ёнка; *nom pl* -я́та, *gen pl* -я́т) *м* foal (*of donkey*).

ослепи́тельный (-ен, -ьна, -ьно) *прил* dazzling.

ослеп|и́ть (-лю́, -и́шь; *impf* ослепля́ть) *сов перех* (*также перен*) to blind; (*подлеж: солнце, красота*) to dazzle.

ослепле́ни|е (-я) *ср* (*перен*) blindness.

ослеплю́ *сов см* ослепи́ть.

ослепля́|ть (-ю) *несов от* ослепи́ть.

ослеп|нуть (-ну, -нешь; *pt* -, -ла, -ло) *сов от* сле́пнуть ◆ *неперех* (*перен*): ~ от не́нависти/любви́ to be blinded by hatred/love.

осли́н|ый *прил* donkey's; ~ое упря́мство pigheadedness.

осли́ц|а (-ы) *ж* female donkey.

О́сло *м нескл* Oslo.

осложне́ни|е (-я) *ср* complication.

осложн|и́ть (-ю́, -и́шь; *impf* осложня́ть) *сов перех* to complicate
▶ осложни́ться (*impf* осложня́ться) *сов возв* to become complicated; (*болезнь*) to develop complications.

ослы́ш|аться (-усь, -ишься) *сов возв* to mishear.

осля́та *итп сущ см* ослёнок.

осма́трива|ть(ся) (-ю(сь)) *несов от* осмотре́ть(ся).

осме́ива|ть (-ю) *несов от* осме́ять.

осмеле́|ть (-ю) *несов от* смеле́ть.

осме́л|иться (-юсь, -ишься) *сов возв* to dare.

осме́|ять (-ю; *impf* осме́ивать) *сов перех* (*поведение, человека*) to mock; (*теорию*) to ridicule.

осмо́тр (-а) *м* inspection; (*больного*) examination; (*выставки, музея*) visit.

осм|отре́ть (-отрю́, -о́тришь; *impf* осма́тривать) *сов перех* (*см сущ*) to inspect; to examine; to visit

▶ осмотре́ться (*impf* осма́триваться) *сов возв* (*по сторонам*) to look around; (*перен: на но́вом ме́сте*) to settle in.

осмотри́тельность (-и) *ж* circumspection.

осмотри́тельный *прил* prudent, cautious.

осмысле́ни|е (-я) *ср* comprehension.

осмы́слен|ный (-, -на, -но) *прил* (*взгляд*) intelligent; (*поступок, поведение*) premeditated.

осмы́сл|ить (-ю, -ишь; *impf* осмы́сливать *или* осмысля́ть) *сов перех* to comprehend.

осна|сти́ть (-щу́, -сти́шь; *impf* оснаща́ть) *сов перех* (*предприятие, лабораторию*) to equip; (*судно*) to rig.

оснаще́ни|е (-я) *ср* (*предприятия, лаборатории, армии*) equipment; (*судна*) rigging.

оснащённость (-и) *ж* equipping.

оснащу́ *сов см* оснасти́ть.

осно́в|а (-ы) *ж* (*сооружения*) foundation; (*общества, развития*) basis; (*ткани, материи*) warp; (*линг*) stem; на ~е +*gen* on the basis of; класть (положи́ть *perf*) в ~у чего́-н to use as a basis for sth; быть (*impf*) *или* лежа́ть (*impf*) в ~е чего́-н to be the basis of sth; *см также* осно́вы.

основа́ни|е (-я) *ср* (*также мат, хим*) base; (*города, общества*) founding; (*теории, науки*) basis; (*опоздания, поступка*) grounds мн; (*здания*) foundation; без вся́ких ~й without any reason; до ~я completely; на ~и +*gen* on the grounds of; на како́м ~и? on what grounds?; на о́бщем ~и on an equal basis; с по́лным ~м with good reason.

основа́телен *прил см* основа́тельный.

основа́тел|ь (-я) *м* founder.

основа́тельниц|а (-ы) *ж см* основа́тель.

основа́тельный (-ен, -ьна, -ьно) *прил* (*причины, довод*) good; (*сооружение, человек*) solid; (*разг: вес, сумма*) fair; (*проверка, осмотр*) thorough.

основа́|ть (*pt* -л, -ла, -ло, *impf* осно́вывать) *сов перех* to found; осно́вывать (~ *perf*) что-н на +*prp* to base sth on sth upon
▶ основа́ться (*impf* осно́вываться) *сов возв* (*общество, компания*) to be founded; (*разг: в Москве́, на но́вом ме́сте*) to settle down.

основн|о́й *прил* (*цель, зада́ча*) main; (*закон, при́нцип*) fundamental, basic; в ~о́м on the whole.

основополо́жник (-а) *м* founder.

осно́выва|ть (-ю) *несов от* основа́ть
▶ осно́вываться *несов от* основа́ться ◆ *возв*: ~ся на +*prp* to be based on.

осно́в|ы (-) *мн* (*физики итп*) basics мн, rudiments мн.

осо́б|а (-ы) *ж* individual.

осо́бенен *прил см* осо́бенный.

особенно *нареч* particularly; (*смотреть, вести себя*) in an unusual way; (*приятно, хорошо*) especially, particularly; **не ~** (*разг*) not particularly.

особенность (-и) *ж* (*не обыкновенность*) uniqueness; (*свойство*) peculiarity; **в ~и** in particular.

особенн|ый (-ен, -на, -но) *прил* special; **ничего ~ного** (*разг*) nothing special.

особняк (-á) *м* mansion.

особняком *нареч* by oneself.

особ|ый *прил* (*вид, случай*) special, particular; (*вход, помещение*) separate; **у него ~ое мнение на этот счёт** he has his own opinion about this.

особь (-и) *ж* individual.

осовремен|ить (-ю, -ишь; *impf* **осовременивать**) *сов перех* to update.

осознава́ть (-ю, -ёшь) *несов от* **осозна́ть**.

осознанный *прил* (*риск, поступок*) calculated; (*необходимость*) acknowledged.

осозна́ть (-ю; *impf* **осознава́ть**) *сов перех* to realize.

осо́ка (-и) *ж* sedge.

осолове́ть (-ю) *сов от* **солове́ть**.

осп|а (-ы) *ж* smallpox; (*разг: шрам*) pockmarks *мн*.

оспа́рива|ть (-ю) *несов от* **оспо́рить** ♦ *перех* (*первенство*) to contend *или* compete for.

оспин|а (-ы) *ж* pockmark.

оспо́р|ить (-ю, -ишь; *impf* **оспа́ривать**) *сов перех* (*мнение, решение*) to question.

осрам|и́ть(ся) (-лю́(сь), -и́шь(ся)) *сов от* **срами́ть(ся)**.

остава́ться (-ю́сь, -ёшься) *несов от* **оста́ться** ♦ *возв*: **счастли́во ~**! good luck!, all the best!

оста́в|ить (-лю, -ишь; *impf* **оставля́ть**) *сов перех* to leave; (*сохранить*) to keep; (*задержать: после уроков*) to keep in; (*работу, занятие, разговор*) to stop; (*перен: мысли, мечты, надежды*) to give up; **~ь!** stop it!; **оставля́ть** (~ *perf*) **кого́-н позади́** (*перен*) to leave sb standing; **оставля́ть** (~ *perf*) **кого́-н/что́-н в поко́е** to leave sb/sth in peace *или* alone; **оставля́ть** (~ *perf*) **кого́-н на второ́й год** (*ПРОСВЕЩ*) to make sb repeat a year; **оставля́ть** (~ *perf*) **кого́-н в дурака́х** to make a fool of sb; **мы ~или госте́й ночева́ть** we asked our guests to stay overnight; **созна́ние ~ило его́** he lost consciousness.

остально́|е (-го; *decl like adj*) *ср* the rest; **в ~ом** in other respects.

остально́|й *прил* (*часть*) the remaining; **~ые де́ньги/де́ти** the rest of the money/children; **~ое вре́мя** the rest of the time.

остальны́|е (-ых; *decl like adj*) *мн* the others; **все ~** all the others; (*вещи*) all the rest.

остана́влива|ть(ся) (-ю(сь)) *несов от* **останови́ть(ся)**.

оста́нк|и (-ов) *мн* remains *мн*.

останов|и́ть (-овлю́, -о́вишь; *impf*

остана́влива|ть (-ю) *сов перех* to stop; **остана́вливать** (~ *perf*) **взгляд/внима́ние на чём-н** to let one's gaze/attention rest on sth; **остана́вливать** (~ *perf*) **свой вы́бор на** +*acc* to choose

▶ **останов|и́ться** (*impf* **остана́вливаться**) *сов возв* to stop; (*в гости́нице, у друзе́й*) to stay; **~ся** (*perf*) **на** +*prp* (*на вопро́се, на описа́нии*) to dwell on; (*на реше́нии, на заключе́нии*) to come to; (*взгляд*) to rest on; **не остана́вливаться (~ся** *perf*) **ни пе́ред чем** to stop at nothing.

остано́вк|а (-и) *ж* (*мотора, часов, эксперимента*) stopping; (*в речи, в работе*) pause; (*автобусная, поезда, в пути*) stop; **за кем/чем ~?** (*разг*) who/what is holding us up?

остановлю́(сь) *сов см* **останови́ть(ся)**.

оста́нусь *итп сов см* **оста́ться**.

оста́т|ок (-ка) *м* (*пищи, дня*) the remainder, the rest; (*материи*) remnant; (*МАТ*) remainder; **~ки** (*дома, стены*) remains *мн*; (*еды*) leftovers *мн*; (*красоты, чувства*) traces *мн*; **всё без ~ка** absolutely everything.

оста́|ться (-нусь, -нешься; *impf* **остава́ться**) *сов неперех* to stay; (*сохрани́ться: дом, чувство*) to remain; (*оказа́ться*) to be left; (*разг: проигра́ть*) to lose; **остава́ться** (~ *perf*) **сиде́ть/стоя́ть** to remain sitting/standing; **мне ~лось дочита́ть 2 страни́цы** I have 2 pages left to read; **остава́ться** (~ *perf*) **на второ́й год** (*ПРОСВЕЩ*) to repeat a year; **остава́ться** (~ *perf*) **при своём мне́нии** to stick to one's opinion; **остава́ться** (~ *perf*) **ни с чем** to end up with nothing; **остава́ться** (~ *perf*) **ни при чём** to be left out; **остава́ться** (~ *perf*) **в живы́х** to survive; **не остаётся ничего́ друго́го как ...** there is nothing for it but ....

остеклене́|ть (-ю) *сов от* **стеклене́ть**.

остепен|и́ться (-ю́сь, -и́шься; *impf* **остепеня́ться**) *сов неперех* to settle down.

остервене́лый *прил* frenzied, furious.

остервене́|ть (-ю) *сов от* **стервене́ть**.

остерега́|ть (-ю; *perf* **остере́чь**) *несов перех* to warn

▶ **остерега́ться** (*perf* **остере́чься**) *несов возв*: **~ся** +*gen* to be wary of; **~йтесь просту́ды!** mind you don't catch cold!

осто́в (-а) *м* (*здания, корабля*) frame; (*зверя*) skeleton; (*словаря, романа*) framework.

остолбене́|ть (-ю) *сов от* **столбене́ть**.

остоло́п (-а) *м* (*разг*) dimwit.

осторо́жен *прил см* **осторо́жный**.

осторо́жно *нареч* (*взять, подня́ть*) carefully; (*ходи́ть, выступа́ть, говори́ть*) cautiously; **~!** look out!

осторо́жность (-и) *ж* (*обраще́ния, ухо́да*) care; (*посту́пка, поведе́ния*) caution; **забыва́ть (забы́ть** *perf*) **о вся́кой ~и** to throw caution to the winds.

осторо́жн|ый (-ен, -на, -но) *прил* careful; (*осмотри́тельный*) cautious.

осточерте́|ть (-ю; *impf* **осточертева́ть**) *сов*

неперех (+dat; разг) to bore rigid.
остёр прил см **острый**.
остригу(сь) сов см **остричь(ся)**.
остри|ё (-я́) ср (пера, иглы, шпиля) point; (ножа, меча, бритвы) edge; (критики, сатиры) cutting edge.
остри́ть (-ю́, -и́шь) несов перех (нож, меч) to sharpen ♦ (perf **состри́ть**) неперех (шутить) to make witty remarks.
остри́|чь(ся) (-гу́(сь), -жёшь(ся) итп, -гу́т(ся)) сов от **стри́чь(ся)**.
о́стров (-а; nom pl -á) м (также перен) island.
остров|о́к (-ка́) м island; **острово́к безопа́сности** traffic island.
остроконе́ч|ный (-ен, -на, -но) прил pointed.
остроно́с|ый (-, -а, -о) прил (человек) sharp-nosed; (туфли) pointed.
острослов|ить (-лю, -ишь) несов неперех to be witty.
остросовреме́н|ный (-ен, -на, -но) прил (пьеса) extremely topical.
остросюже́т|ный (-ен, -на, -но) прил (фильм, пьеса) gripping; ~ **фильм**, ~ **рома́н** thriller.
остро́т|а (-ы) ж witticism.
острот|а́ (-ы́) ж (ножа) sharpness; (зрения, слуха) sharpness, keenness; (шутки, слова) wit; (запаха, вкуса) pungency; (пищи) spiciness; (желания, радости) poignancy; (положения, ситуации) acuteness; (игры) tension.
остроуго́л|ьный (-ен, -ьна, -ьно) прил acute-angled.
остроу́мен прил см **остроу́мный**.
остроу́ми|е (-я) ср wit; (рассказа) wittiness.
остроу́м|ный (-ен, -на, -но) прил witty.
о́стр|ый (-р или -ёр, -рá, -ро́ или -ро) прил (нож, память, вкус) sharp; (борода, нос, носок) pointed; (зрение, слух) keen; (шутка, слово) witty; (запах) pungent; (блюдо, еда) spicy; (сыр) strong; (желание) burning; (боль) acute; (ситуация) critical; (игра) tense; (no short form; аппендицит, воспаление лёгких) acute; **о́стрый у́гол** acute angle; **о́стрый язы́к** sharp tongue.
остря́к (-á) м (разг) wit.
остря́ч|ка (-ки; gen pl -ек) ж (разг) см **остря́к**.
осту|ди́ть (-жу́, -у́дишь; impf **остужа́ть** или **студи́ть**) сов перех (молоко, чай, суп) to cool; (перен: желания) to curb; (: чувства) to restrain.
оступи́ться (-уплю́сь, -у́пишься; impf **оступа́ться**) сов возв to trip, stumble; (разг: совершить ошибку) to trip up.
осты́|ть (-ну, -нешь; impf **остыва́ть**) сов неперех (также перен) to cool down; (чувства, желание) to cool; (суп) to get cold; **остыва́ть** (~ perf) **к** +dat (перен) to lose interest in.
осу|ди́ть (-жу́, -у́дишь; impf **осужда́ть**) сов перех to condemn; (приговорить) to convict.

осужде́ни|е (-я) ср (см глаг) condemnation; conviction.
осуждён|ная (-ой; decl like adj) ж см **осуждённый**.
осуждённ|ый (-ого; decl like adj) м convict.
осужу́ сов см **осуди́ть**.
осу́нуться (-усь, -ешься) сов возв to look drawn.
осуша́|ть (-ю) несов от **осуши́ть**.
осуше́ни|е (-я) ср drainage.
осуши́тельный прил drainage опред.
осу|ши́ть (-шу́, -у́шишь; impf **осуша́ть**) сов перех to drain.
осуществи́м|ый (-, -а, -о) прил (мечты, желания) realizable.
осуществле́ни|е (-я) ср (мечты, идеи, намерения) realization; (плана, реорганизации) implementation.
осуществ|и́ть (-лю́, -и́шь; impf **осуществля́ть**) сов перех (мечту, намерение) to realize; (идею) to put into practice; (план, реорганизацию) to implement
▸ **осуществи́ться** (impf **осуществля́ться**) сов возв (мечты) to come true; (идея) to materialize; (надежды) to be fulfilled.
осчастли́в|ить (-лю, -ишь) сов перех to make happy.
осыпа́|ть (-лю, -лешь; impf **осыпа́ть**) сов перех (кучу песка, землю) to knock down; **осыпа́ть** (~ perf) **кого́-н/что-н чем-н** to scatter sth over sb/sth; (перен: подарками, поцелуями) to shower sb/sth with sth; (оскорблениями) to heap sth on sb/sth
▸ **осыпа́ться** (impf **осыпа́ться**) сов возв (земля, насыпь, песок) to subside; (штукатурка, потолок) to crumble; (листья, цветы) to fall.
ос|ь (-и; loc sg -и́) ж (колеса, механизма) axle; (ГЕОМ) axis (мн axes); (перен: событий, происходящего) centre (BRIT), center (US), hub.
осьмино́г (-а) м octopus (мн octopuses).
ося́ду итп сов см **осе́сть**.
осяза́ем|ый (-, -а, -о) прил (перен: результат) tangible.
осяза́ни|е (-я) ср touch.
осяза́тельный прил (нервные окончания, органы) tactile; (перен: результат, разница, успех) tangible.

┌──────────┐
│ **KEYWORD** │
└──────────┘

от предл (+gen) **1** from; **он отошёл от стола́** he moved away from the table; **недалеко́ от меня́** not far from me; **он узна́л об э́том от дру́га** he found out about it from a friend; **у него́ есть сын от пе́рвого бра́ка** he has a son from his first marriage; **от ча́са до двух** from one (o'clock) to two (o'clock); **он ушёл от семьи́** he left his family
2 (указывает на причину): **бума́га размо́кла**

от дождя the paper got wet with rain; **от злости** with anger; **от радости** for или in joy; **от удивления** in surprise; **от разочарования/ страха** out of disappointment/fear

3 (*о подлежащем устранении*): **отмой лицо от грязи** wash the dirt off your face

4 (*указывает на что-н, против чего направлено действие*) for; **лекарство от кашля** medicine for a cough, cough medicine

5 (*о части целого*): **ручка/ключ от двери** door handle/key; **я потерял пуговицу от пальто** I lost the button off my coat

6 (*при противопоставлении*) from; **они не могут отличить добро от зла** they can't tell right from wrong

7 (*в датах*): **письмо от первого февраля** a letter of или dated the first of February

8 (*о временной последовательности*): **год от года** from year to year; **время от времени** from time to time.

от- *префикс* (*in verbs*; *прекращение действия*) indicating cessation of action eg. **отзвучать**; (*удаление от чего-н*) indictaing removal from sth eg. **открепить**; (*об уклонении от чего-н*) indicating avoidance of sth eg. **отшутиться**.

отаплива|ть (**-ю**) *несов перех* to heat
► **отапливаться** *несов возв* to be heated.

отар|а (**-ы**) *ж* flock (*of sheep*).

отбав|ить (**-лю, -ишь**; *impf* **отбавлять**) *сов перех* (*сахар, порцию*) to take away; (*молоко, воду*) to pour off; **хоть отбавляй** (*разг*) more than enough.

отбараба́н|ить (**-ю, -ишь**; *impf* **отбарабанивать**) *сов перех* (*мелодию*) to tap out; (*разг: ответ, вопрос*) to rattle off.

отбежа́ть (*как* **бежать**; *см* Table 20; *impf* **отбегать**) *сов неперех* to run off.

отбеливатель (**-я**) *м* bleach.

отбел|ить (**-елю, -елишь**; *impf* **отбеливать**) *сов перех* to bleach.

отберу́ *итп сов см* **отобрать**.

отбива́ть(ся) (**-ю**) *несов от* **отбить(ся)**.

отбивн|а́я (**-ой**; *decl like adj*) *ж* tenderized steak; (*также*: **~ котлета**) chop.

отбира́ть (**-ю**) *несов от* **отобрать**.

от|би́ть (**-обью, -обьёшь**; *impf* **отбивать**) *сов перех* (*отколоть*) to break off; (*мяч, удар*) to parry; (*атаку, нападение*) to repulse; (*город, пленных*) to recapture; (*разг: жениха, невесту*) to pinch; (*такт, мелодию*) to beat out; (*мясо*) to tenderize; **запах ~би́л у меня желание есть** the smell put me off my food; **я ~би́л себе ноги** my feet are sore
► **отби́ться** (*impf* **отбиваться**) *сов возв* (*отколоться*) to break off; (**~ся** (*perf*) **от** +*gen*) (*от нападающих, от собак*) to defend o.s. (against); (*от компании, от стада*) to fall behind; **~ся** (*perf*) **от рук** to get out of hand.

отблагодар|и́ть (**-ю́, -и́шь**) *сов перех* to show one's gratitude to.

о́тблеск (**-а**) *м* reflection.

отбо́|й (**-я**) *м* (ВОЕН: *ко сну*) the last post; (: *после воздушной тревоги*) all-clear (signal); (: *к отступлению*) retreat; **у неё ~ю нет от поклонников** (*разг*) she has an endless stream of admirers.

отбо́йный *прил*: **~ молоток** pickaxe (*BRIT*), pickax (*US*).

отбо́р (**-а**) *м* selection.

отбо́рн|ый *прил* (*картофель, семена*) selected; (*ругань, выражения*) well-chosen; **~ые войска** crack troops.

отбо́рочн|ый *прил* (*СПОРТ*) qualifying; **~ая комиссия** selection committee.

отбро́|сить (**-шу, -сишь**; *impf* **отбрасывать**) *сов перех* to throw aside; (*противника, войска*) to repel; (*перен: сомнения, тревоги итп*) to cast aside; (*тень, свет*) to cast.

отбро́с|ы (**-ов**) *мн* (*производства*) waste *ед*; (*пищевые*) scraps *мн*.

отбро́шу *сов см* **отбро́сить**.

отб|ы́ть (*как* **быть**; *см* Table 21; *impf* **отбывать**) *сов неперех*: **~ (из** +*gen*/**в** +*acc*) to depart (from/ for) ♦ (*pt* **-ы́л, -ыла́, -ы́ло**) *перех*: **~ наказание** to serve a sentence.

отва́г|а (**-и**) *ж* bravery.

отва́|дить (**-жу, -дишь**; *impf* **отва́живать**) *сов перех* (*разг*): **~ кого-н от чего-н** (*от вредных привычек*) to wean sb off sth; (*от дома*) to drive sb away from sth.

отва́жен *прил см* **отва́жный**.

отва́жива|ть (**-ю**) *несов от* **отва́дить**.

отва́ж|иться (**-усь, -ишься**; *impf* **отва́живаться**) *сов возв*: **~** +*infin* (*пойти, сказать итп*) to find the courage to do; **~** (*perf*) **на** +*acc* to venture on.

отва́жн|ый (**-ен, -на, -но**) *прил* brave.

отва́жу *сов см* **отва́дить**.

отва́жусь *сов см* **отва́житься**.

отва́л (**-а**) *м* (*породы, земли*) heap; **наесться** (*perf*) **до ~а** (*разг*) to eat one's fill; **накормить** (*perf*) **кого-н до ~а** to stuff sb with food.

отвал|и́ть (**-ю́, -алишь**; *impf* **отва́ливать**) *сов перех* (*камень, бревно*) to push aside; (*разг: кучу денег*) to fork out
► **отвали́ться** (*impf* **отва́ливаться**) *сов возв* (*обои, штукатурка*) to fall off; (*разг: откинуться назад*) to slump.

отва́р (**-а**; *part gen* **-у**) *м* (*из трав*) decoction; **мясно́й ~** meat broth.

отва́р|ить (**-ю́, -аришь**; *impf* **отва́ривать**) *сов перех* to boil
► **отвари́ться** (*impf* **отва́риваться**) *сов возв* to boil.

отварно́й *прил* boiled.

отведу́ *итп сов см* **отвести́**.

отв|езти́ (**-езу́, -езёшь**; *pt* **-ёз, -езла́, -езло́**; *impf* **отвозить**) *сов перех* (*увезти*) to take away; **отвози́ть** (**~** *perf*) **кого-н/что-н в го́род/на да́чу** to take sb/sth off to town/the dacha.

отве́ргн|уть (**-у, -ешь**; *impf* **отверга́ть**) *сов*

перех (*решение, помощь*) to reject; (*жениха*) to
spurn.

отвердéть (*3sg* -**ет**, *3pl* -**ют**, *impf* **отвердевáть**)
сов непepex to harden.

отвéрженн|ая (-**ой**; *decl like adj*) *ж см*
отвéрженный.

отвéрженн|ый *прил* outcast *опред* ♦ (-**ого**; *decl
like adj*) *м* outcast.

отвернýть (-**ý**, -**ёшь**; *impf* **отвёртывать**) *сов
перех* (*гайку, пробку*) to unscrew; (*кран*) to be
turned on; (*пола, рукав*) to turn back; (*impf*
отворáчивать: *лицо, голову*) to turn aside;
(*разг: отломать: ручку*) to twist off

▶ **отвернýться** (*impf* **отвёртываться**) *сов возв*
(*гайка, пробка*) to come unscrewed; (*кран*) to be
turned on; (*поля, рукав*) to be turned back; (*impf*
отворáчиваться: *человек*) to turn away; ~**ся**
(*perf*) **от когó-н** to ostracize sb.

отвéрсти|е (-**я**) *ср* opening.

отвёрт|ка (-**ки**; *gen pl* -**ок**) *ж* screwdriver.

отвёртывать(ся) (-**ю(сь)**) *несов от*
отвернýть(ся).

отвéс (-**а**) *м* (*груз*) plumb; ~ **скалы́** cliff face.

отвéсен *прил см* **отвéсный**.

отвé|сить (-**шу**, -**сишь**; *impf* **отвéшивать**) *сов
перех* to weigh out; ~ (*perf*) **комý-н пощёчину**
(*разг*) to give sb a slap in the face.

отвéс|ный (-**ен**, -**на**, -**но**) *прил* (*склон, берег,
стена*) vertical.

отве|стú (-**дý**, -**дёшь**; *pt* -**ёл**, -**елá**, -**елó**, *impf*
отводúть) *сов перех* (*человека: домой, к
врачу*) to take (off); (: *от окна*) to lead away;
(*войска, полк*) to relocate, move; (*воду, реку*) to
divert; (*ветки*) to push aside; (*глаза, взгляд*) to
avert, turn away; (*перен: беду, удар*) to avert;
(*заявление, кандидатуру*) to reject; (*участок,
сад*) to allot; (*средства*) to allocate; **отводúть**
(~ *perf*) **когó-н в стóрону** to take *или* lead sb
aside; **отводúть** (~ *perf*) **врéмя на что-н** (*себе*)
to set aside time for sth; (*другим*) to allocate
time for sth; **отводúть** (~ *perf*) **дýшу** to
unburden one's soul.

отвéт (-**а**) *м* (*на вопрос*) answer; (*реакция*)
response; (*на письмо, на приглашение*) reply; **в**
~ (**на** +*acc*) in response (to); **быть** (*impf*) **в** ~**е за**
+*acc* to be answerable for; **призывáть**
(**призвáть** *perf*) **к** ~**у** to call to account.

отвéтв|иться (*3sg* -**ится**, *3pl* -**ятся**, *impf*
отвéтвля́ться) *сов возв* to branch.

ответвлéни|е (-**я**) *ср* (*дерева, дороги*) branch;
(*перен: движения, религии*) branch, offshoot.

отвéтвля́|ться (*3sg* -**ется**, *3pl* -**ются**) *несов от*
отвéтвиться.

отвé|тить (-**чу**, -**тишь**; *impf* **отвечáть**) *сов
непepex* ~ (**на** +*acc*) to answer, reply (to); (**на
увольнение, на грубость**) to retaliate (against);
~ (*perf*) **за** +*acc* (*за преступление, за поступок*)
to answer for; **отвечáть** (~ *perf*) **любóвью на**

(**чью-н**) **любóвь** to return sb's love.

отвéтственность (-**и**) *ж* (*задания, заказа*)
importance; (*за поступки, за действия*)
responsibility; **нестú** (**понестú** *perf*) ~ **за** +*acc* to
be responsible for; **привлекáть** (**привлéчь** *perf*)
когó-н к ~**и** to call sb to account.

отвéтственн|ый (-, -**на**, -**но**) *прил* responsible;
(*работа, поручение, момент*) important;
отвéтственный квартиросъёмщик
responsible tenant; **отвéтственный рабóтник**
executive.

отвéтчик (-**а**) *м* (*ЮР*) defendant.

отвéтчиц|а (-**ы**) *ж см* **отвéтчик**.

отвечá|ть (-**ю**) *несов от* **отвéтить** ♦ *непepex*: ~
+*dat* (*требованиям*) to meet; (*описанию*) to
answer; (*интересам итп*) to suit; ~ (*impf*) **за
когó-н/что-н** to be responsible for sb/sth.

отвéчу *сов см* **отвéтить**.

отвéшива|ть (-**ю**) *несов от* **отвéсить**.

отвéшу *сов см* **отвéсить**.

отвúлива|ть (-**ю**; *perf* **отвильнýть**) *несов
непepex*: ~ **от** +*gen* (*разг: от работы итп*) to
dodge.

отвин|тúть (-**чý**, -**тúшь**; *impf* **отвúнчивать**) *сов
перех* to unscrew.

▶ **отвинтúться** (*impf* **отвúнчиваться**) *сов возв*
to come unscrewed.

отвисá|ть (*3sg* -**ет**, *3pl* -**ют**) *несов от*
отвúснуть.

отвúслый *прил* (*щёки*) sagging; (*уши*) droopy.

отвú|снуть (*3sg* -**ет**, *3pl* -**ут**, *impf* **отвисáть**) *сов
непepex* to sag.

отвлёк(ся) *сов см* **отвлéчь(ся)**.

отвлекá|ть(ся) (-**ю(сь)**) *несов от* **отвлéчь(ся)**.

отвлекý(сь) *итп сов см* **отвлéчь(ся)**.

отвлечéни|е (-**я**) *ср* (*внимания, интереса*)
distraction; (*абстракция*) abstraction.

отвлечённ|ый (-, -**на**, -**но**) *прил* abstract.

отвл|éчь (-**екý**, -**ечёшь**, -**екýт**; *pt* -**ёк**, -**еклá**,
-**еклó**, *impf* **отвлекáть**) *сов перех*: ~ (**от** +*gen*)
(*противника*) to divert (from); (*от дел*) to
distract (from); **отвлекáть** (~ *perf*) **чью-н
внимáние** to distract sb's attention

▶ **отвлéчься** (*impf* **отвлекáться**) *сов возв*: ~**ся**
(**от** +*gen*) to be distracted (from); (*от темы*) to
digress (from); (*абстрагироваться*) to abstract
o.s. (from).

отвóд (-**а**) *м* (*воды, газа*) diversion; (*войск*)
relocation; (*кандидатуры, судьи*) rejection; **для**
~**а глаз** (*разг*) as a distraction.

отводú|ть (-**ожý**, -**óдишь**) *несов от* **отвестú**.

отводнóй *прил* drainage *опред*.

отво|евáть (-**юю**; *impf* **отвоёвывать**) *сов перех*
(*также перен*) to win back ♦ *непepex* (*разг:
кончить воевать*) to finish fighting.

▶ **отвоевáться** *сов возв* (*разг: солдат, полк*) to
finish fighting.

отвожý *несов см* **отводúть**.

отво́зи́ть (-ожу́, -о́зишь) *несов от* **отвезти́**.

отвора́чива|ть(ся) (-ю(сь)) *несов от* **отверну́ть(ся)**.

отвор|и́ть (-ю́, -и́шь; *impf* **отворя́ть**) *сов перех* to open.

отвра́тен *прил см* **отвра́тный**.

отврати́телен *прил см* **орврати́тельный**.

отврати́тельно *нареч* (*пахнуть*) disgusting; (*поступить*) abominably ♦ *как сказ* it's disgusting.

отврати́тельный (-ен, -ьна, -ьно) *прил* disgusting.

отвра|ти́ть (-щу́, -ти́шь; *impf* **отвраща́ть**) *сов перех* to avert.

отвра́тный (-ен, -на, -но) *прил* (*разг*) revolting.

отвраща́|ть (-ю) *несов от* **отврати́ть**.

отвраще́ни|е (-я) *ср* disgust, repulsion.

отвращу́ *сов см* **отврати́ть**.

отвы́к|нуть (-ну, -нешь; *pt* -, -ла, -ло, *impf* **отвыка́ть**) *сов неперех*: ~ **от** (*от наркотиков*) to give up; (*от людей, от дома, от работы*) to become unaccustomed to; **отвыка́ть** (~ *perf*) **от куре́ния** to give up smoking; **он отвы́к от до́ма/рабо́ты** he is not used to living at home/working any more.

отвя|за́ть (-жу́, -жешь; *impf* **отвя́зывать**) *сов перех* (*верёвку*) to untie; (*собаку, коня*) to untie, untether

▸ **отвяза́ться** (*impf* **отвя́зываться**) *сов возв* (*верёвка*) to come undone; (*собака, конь*) to break loose; (*разг*): ~**ся от** +*gen* (*от человека*) to leave in peace; (*отделаться*) to get rid of; ~**жи́сь (от меня́)!** (*разг*) get lost!

отгада́|ть (-ю; *impf* **отга́дывать**) *сов перех* to guess.

отга́д|ка (-ки; *gen pl* -ок) *ж* answer (*to riddle*).

отга́дыва|ть (-ю) *несов от* **отгада́ть**.

отгиба́|ть(ся) (-ю(сь)) *несов от* **отогну́ть(ся)**.

отглаго́льный *прил* verbal.

отгла́|дить (-жу, -дишь; *impf* **отгла́живать**) *сов перех* to iron

▸ **отгла́диться** (*impf* **отгла́живаться**) *сов возв* to be ironed.

отговор|и́ть (-ю́, -и́шь; *impf* **отгова́ривать**) *сов перех*: ~ **кого́-н от чего́-н**/+*infin* to dissuade sb from sth/from doing

▸ **отговори́ться** (*impf* **отгова́риваться**) *сов возв* (+*instr*; *разг: незнанием, болезнью*) to plead; ~ (~ *perf*) **незна́нием** to plead ignorance; **он** ~**и́лся боле́знью** he gave the excuse that he was ill.

отгово́р|ка (-ки; *gen pl* -ок) *ж* excuse.

отголо́с|ок (-ка; *nom pl* -ки) *м* (*также перен*) echo.

отгоню́ *сов см* **отогна́ть**.

отгоня́|ть (-ю) *несов от* **отогна́ть**.

отгор|оди́ть (-ожу́, -о́дишь; *impf* **отгора́живать**) *сов перех* (*дом, участок*) to fence off; (*часть комнаты*) to partition off; (*от жизни*) to isolate; (*от забот*) to shelter

▸ **отгороди́ться** (*impf* **отгора́живаться**) *сов*

возв (*забором*) to fence o.s. off; (*ширмой*) to screen o.s. off; (*от жизни, от забот*) to cut o.s. off.

отгрёб *итп сов см* **отгрести́**.

отгреба́|ть (-ю) *несов от* **отгрести́**.

отгребу́ *итп сов см* **отгрести́**.

отгрем|е́ть (*3sg* -и́т, *3pl* -я́т) *сов неперех* (*гром, аплодисменты*) to stop; **его́ сла́ва** ~**е́ла** he is no longer famous; **бой** ~**е́л** the battle is over.

отгр|ести́ (-ебу́, -ебёшь; *pt* -ёб, -ебла́, -ебло́, *impf* **отгреба́ть**) *сов перех* (*листья, снег*) to rake away ♦ *неперех* (*от берега*) to row away.

отгру|зи́ть (-ужу́, -у́зишь; *impf* **отгружа́ть**) *сов перех* (*отправить*) to ship.

отгру́з|ка (-и) *ж* shipment.

отгры́з|ть (-у́, -ёшь; *pt* -, -ла, -ло, *impf* **отгрыза́ть**) *сов перех* to bite off.

отгу́л (-а) *м* day off.

отгуля́|ть (-ю; *impf* **отгу́ливать**) *сов перех* (*разз: отпуск, праздники*) to finish (*one's holidays etc*); (: *за дежурство, за сверхурочные*) to have time off; **мы** ~**ли о́тпуск** our holidays are over.

отда|ва́ть (-ю́, -ёшь) *несов от* **отда́ть** ♦ *неперех*: ~ +*instr* (*разг: пахнуть*) to reek of

▸ **отдава́ться** *несов от* **отда́ться**.

отда|ви́ть (-авлю́, -а́вишь; *impf* **отда́вливать**) *сов перех* to crush.

отдади́м(ся) *итп сов см* **отда́ть(ся)**.

отда́й(ся) *сов см* **отда́ть(ся)**.

отда́йте(сь) *сов см* **отда́ть(ся)**.

отдале́ни|е (-и) *ср* distance; **в** ~**и, на** ~**и** in the distance; **в** ~**и от** +*gen* some way away from.

отдал|и́ть (-ю́, -и́шь; *impf* **отдаля́ть**) *сов перех* (*смерть, разлуку*) to postpone; (*сына, друзей*) to alienate

▸ **отдали́ться** (*impf* **отдаля́ться**) *сов возв*: ~**ся от** +*gen* (*от берега, от города*) to move away from; (*от темы, от дел*) to digress from; (*от друзей, от семьи*) to become alienated from.

отда́|ть (*как* **дать**; *см* **Table 14**, *impf* **отдава́ть**) *сов перех* (*возвратить*) to return; (*дать*) to give; (*сдать: город, крепость*) to surrender; (*ребёнка: в школу, в детский сад*) to send; (*разз: заплатить*) to pay; (*подлеж: ружьё*) to kick; (: *боль*) to spread; **он** ~**л жизнь нау́ке** he devoted his life to science; **отдава́ть** (~ *perf*) **ту́фли в ремо́нт** to put one's shoes in for repair; **отдава́ть** (~ *perf*) **что-н за бесце́нок** to give sth away; **отдава́ть** (~ *perf*) **дочь за́муж** to give one's daughter away (*in marriage*); **отдава́ть** (~ *perf*) (**кому́-н) распоряже́ние/прика́з** to give (sb) instructions/an order; **отдава́ть** (~ *perf*) **кому́-н/чему́-н предпочте́ние** to give preference to sb/sth; **отдава́ть** (~ *perf*) **кого́-н под суд** to prosecute sb; **отдава́ть** (~ *perf*) **кому́-н честь** to salute sb; **отдава́ть** (~ *perf*) **себе́ отчёт** to realize; **отдава́ть** (~ *perf*) **до́лжное** *или* **справедли́вость кому́-н** to give

sb his *итп* due; **отдава́ть** (~ *perf*) кому́-н
после́дний долг to pay one's last respects to sb;
отдава́ть (~ *perf*) **концы́** (*разг: умере́ть*) to
kick the bucket

▸ **отда́ться** (*impf* **отдава́ться**) *сов возв* (*голос,
эхо*) to resound, reverberate; **отдава́ться** (~*ся*
perf) +*dat* to give o.s. up *или* surrender to;
(*воспомина́ниям*) to lose o.s. in; (*иску́сству*) to
devote o.s. to; (*любо́внику*) to give o.s. to; **боль
отдава́лась в спине́** the pain spread to his
back.

отда́ч|а (-и) *ж* (*при вы́стреле*) recoil; (*СПОРТ*)
return; **рабо́тать** (*impf*) **с по́лной ~ей** to put a
lot into one's work.

отда́шь(ся) *сов см* **отда́ть(ся)**.

отде́л (-а) *м* (*учрежде́ния, универма́га*)
department; (*кни́ги, газе́ты*) section; (*исто́рии,
нау́ки*) branch; **отде́л здравоохране́ния** health
department; **отде́л ка́дров** personnel
department; **отде́л отпра́вки** dispatch
department.

отде́лать (-ю; *impf* **отде́лывать**) *сов перех*
(*кварти́ру*) to do up; (*разг: поколоти́ть*) to do
over; **отде́лывать** (~ *perf*) **что-н чем-н**
(*пальто́: ме́хом*) to trim sth with sth; (*ко́мнату:
де́ревом*) to do sth out with sth

▸ **отде́латься** (*impf* **отде́лываться**) *сов возв*:
~ся от +*gen* (*разг: от рабо́ты, от дел*) to get
away from; (: *от челове́ка*) to get rid of; **~ся**
(*perf*) +*instr* (*разг: лёгким уши́бом*) to get away
with; **легко́ ~ся** (*perf*) to get off lightly; **он ~лся
обеща́ниями** he did no more than make a few
promises; **он ~лся испу́гом** more than anything
he got a fright.

отделе́ни|е (-я) *ср* (*де́йствие: от семьи́ итп*)
separation; (*пена́ла, стола́*) section; (*су́мки*)
compartment; (*уче́бного заведе́ния, больни́цы*)
department; (*ба́нка*) branch; (*конце́рта*) part;
(*ВОЕН*) section; **отделе́ние свя́зи** post office;
отделе́ние мили́ции police station.

отдели́ть (-елю́, -е́лишь; *impf* **отделя́ть**) *сов
перех*: **~** (**от** +*gen*) to separate (from); (*уча́сток,
часть ко́мнаты*) to separate *или* divide off (from)

▸ **отдели́ться** (*impf* **отделя́ться**) *сов возв*: **~ся**
(**от** +*gen*) to separate (from); **~ся** (*perf*) **от
роди́телей** to alienate o.s. from one's parents.

отде́л|ка (-ки; *gen pl* -ок) *ж* decoration; (*в
кварти́ре*) decor; (*на пла́тье*) trimmings *мн*.

отде́лочный *прил* (*материа́лы, тесьма́,
пу́говицы*) decorative; **отде́лочные рабо́ты**
decorating.

отде́лывать(ся) (-ю(сь)) *несов от*
отде́лать(ся).

отде́льно *нареч* separately.

отде́льность (-и) *ж*: **в ~и** separately.

отде́льный *прил* separate; (*едини́чный:
приме́ры, возраже́ния*) isolated.

отделя́ть(ся) (-ю(сь)) *несов от* **отдели́ть(ся)**.

отдёрнуть (-у, -ешь; *impf* **отдёргивать**) *сов
перех* to pull back.

отдеру́(сь) *итп сов см* **отодра́ть(ся)**.

отдира́ть (-ю) *несов от* **отодра́ть**.

отдохну́ть (-у́, -ёшь; *impf* **отдыха́ть**) *сов
непере́х* to (have a) rest; (*на мо́ре*) to have a
holiday; **я хорошо́ ~у́л** I had a good rest.

отдува́ться (-юсь) *несов непере́х* (*разг*) to
pant; (: *за оши́бки, за други́х*) to carry the can.

отду́шин|а (-ы) *ж* vent; (*пере́н*) escape.

о́тдых (-а) *м* rest; (*о́тпуск*) holiday; **на ~е** (*в
о́тпуске*) on holiday; **он на заслу́женном ~е**
(*на пе́нсии*) he is having a well-earned rest; **дом
~а** a holiday centre; **без ~а** without a moment's
rest.

отдыха́ть (-ю) *несов от* **отдохну́ть**.

отдыха́ющ|ая (-ей; *decl like adj*) *ж см*
отдыха́ющий.

отдыха́ющ|ий (-его; *decl like adj*) *м*
holidaymaker (*BRIT*).

отды́ша́ться (-ышу́сь, -ы́шишься) *сов возв* to
get one's breath back.

отёк (-а) *м* swelling; **отёк лёгких** (*МЕД*)
emphysema.

отёк *итп сов см* **отёчь**.

отека́ть (-ю) *несов от* **отёчь**.

отеку́ *итп сов см* **отёчь**.

отёл (-а) *м* calving.

оте́ли́ться (*3sg* -е́лится, *3pl* -е́лятся) *сов от*
тели́ться.

оте́л|ь (-я) *м* hotel.

оте́ц (-ца́) *м* (*также РЕЛ, пере́н*) father.

оте́ческий (-ая, -ое, -ие) *прил* fatherly, paternal.

оте́чественн|ый *прил* (*не иностра́нный:
промы́шленность*) domestic; **това́р ~ого
произво́дства** home-produced goods; **Вели́кая
О~ая Война́** Great Patriotic War (*World War
II*); **Оте́чественная Война́** patriotic war (*fought
in defence of one's country*).

оте́честв|о (-а) *ср* fatherland.

отёчный *прил* swollen.

отёчь (-еку́, -ечёшь *итп*, -еку́т; *pt* отёк, -екла́,
-екло́, *impf* **отека́ть**) *сов непере́х* to swell up.

отжа́ть (-ожму́, -ожмёшь; *impf* **отжима́ть**) *сов
перех* (*рука́ми*) to wring out; (*в стира́льной
маши́не*) to spin dry.

отзвене́ть (*3sg* -и́т, *3pl* -я́т) *сов непере́х* to stop
ringing.

отзвони́ть (-ю́, -и́шь) *сов перех* (*подле́ж:
ко́локол*) to ring out; **часы́ ~и́ли по́лночь** the
clock struck midnight.

о́тзвук (-а) *м* (*также пере́н*) echo.

отзвуча́ть (*3sg* -и́т, *3pl* -а́т) *сов непере́х* to come
to an end (*of music, speeches etc*).

отзову́(сь) *итп сов см* **отозва́ть(ся)**.

о́тзыв (-а) *м* (*мне́ние*) impression; (*реце́нзия*)
review; (*пере́н: в душе́*) echo; (*ВОЕН*) reply (*to a
password*).

отзы́в (-а) *м (представителя, посла)* recall.
отзыва́ть(ся) (-ю(сь)) *несов от* отозва́ть(ся).
отзы́вчив|ый (-, -а, -о) *прил* ready to help.
оти́т (-а) *м (МЕД)* otitis *(ear infection)*.
ОТК *м сокр = отдёл техни́ческого контро́ля.*
откажу́(сь) *итп сов см* отказа́ть(ся).
отка́з (-а) *м* refusal; *(на заявле́ние, от реше́ния)* rejection; *(меха́низма)* failure; **закру́чивать (закрути́ть** *perf)* **до ~а** to turn full on; **рабо́тать** *(impf)* **без ~а** to operate smoothly; **набива́ть (наби́ть** *perf)* **до ~а** to cram.
отка|за́ть (-ажу́, -а́жешь; *impf* **отка́зывать)** *сов непере́х*: ~ **кому́-н в чём-н** to refuse sb sth; *(лиши́ть кого́-н чего́-н)* to deny sb sth; *(мото́р, не́рвы)* to fail; **ему́ не ~а́жешь в тала́нте** you can't deny that he's talented
▶ **отка|за́ться** *(impf* **отка́зываться)** *сов возв*: ~**ся (от** +*gen)* to refuse; **отка́зываться (~ся** *perf)* **от свои́х слов** to retract one's words; **отка́зываться (~ся** *perf)* **от мы́сли** to give up on an idea; **не ~ажу́сь** I wouldn't say no.
отка́лыва|ть(ся) (-ю(сь)) *несов от* отколо́ть(ся).
отка́плива|ть (-ю) *несов от* откопа́ть.
отка́рмлива|ть (-ю) *несов от* откорми́ть.
отка|ти́ть (-ачу́, -а́тишь; *impf* **отка́тывать)** *сов перех (что-н кру́глое)* to roll away; *(что-н на колёсах)* to wheel away ♦ *непере́х (разг: бы́стро отъе́хать)* to speed off
▶ **откати́ться** *(impf* **отка́тываться)** *сов возв* to roll away.
отка́ча|ть (-ю; *impf* **отка́чивать)** *сов перех (жи́дкость, газ)* to pump (out); *(привести́ в чу́вство)* to resuscitate.
откачу́(сь) *сов см* откати́ть(ся).
отка́шлива|ться (-юсь) *несов от* отка́шляться.
отка́шля|нуть (-у, -ешь; *impf* **отка́шливать)** *сов перех* to cough up.
отка́шля|ться (-юсь; *impf* **отка́шливаться)** *сов возв* to clear one's throat. ♦
откидно́й *прил* foldaway.
отки́|нуть (-у, -ешь; *impf* **отки́дывать)** *сов перех* to throw; *(перен: трево́ги, сомне́ния)* to cast aside; *(верх, сиде́ние)* to open; *(ру́ку)* to throw back; *(во́лосы, го́лову)* to toss back; *(в дуршла́г: макаро́ны, рис)* to tip out; *(разг: войска́, проти́вника)* to push back
▶ **отки́|нуться** *(impf* **отки́дываться)** *сов возв*: ~**ся на** +*acc* to lean back against; **отки́дываться (~ся** *perf)* **наза́д** to lean backwards.
откла́дыва|ть (-ю) *несов от* отложи́ть.
откле́|ить (-ю, -ишь; *impf* **откле́ивать)** *сов перех* to peel off
▶ **откле́|иться** *(impf* **откле́иваться)** *сов возв* to come off.
о́тклик (-а) *м* response; *(перен)* echo; *(обы́чно мн: в печа́ти)* comment.
откли́к|нуться (-усь, -ешься; *impf* **откли́каться)** *сов возв*: ~ **(на** +*acc)* to answer;

(на собы́тия, на про́сьбу) to respond (to).
отклоне́ни|е (-я) *ср* deflection; *(перен: про́сьбы)* rejection; *(от ку́рса)* deviation; *(МЕД)* abnormality; ~ **от те́мы** digression.
отклон|и́ть (-оню́, -о́нишь; *impf* **отклоня́ть)** *сов перех (стре́лку)* to deflect; *(перен: предложе́ние, про́сьбу)* to reject
▶ **отклони́ться** *(impf* **отклоня́ться)** *сов возв (стре́лка)* to deflect; *(перен: в сто́рону, от уда́ра)* to dodge; *(от ку́рса, на се́вер)* to be deflected; **отклоня́ться (~ся** *perf)* **от те́мы** to digress.
отключ|и́ть (-у́, -и́шь; *impf* **отключа́ть)** *сов перех* to switch off; *(телефо́н)* to cut off
▶ **отключ|и́ться** *(impf* **отключа́ться)** *сов возв (та́кже перен)* to switch off.
отковыр|я́ть (-ю; *impf* **отковы́ривать)** *сов перех* to pick off.
откозыр|я́ть (-ю) *сов от* козыря́ть.
отколот|и́ть (-очу́, -о́тишь) *сов перех (разг)*: ~ **кого́-н** to give sb a thrashing.
откол|о́ть (-олю́, -о́лешь; *impf* **отка́лывать)** *сов перех (кусо́к)* to break off; *(бант, була́вку)* to unpin; ~ *(perf)* **но́мер** *(разг)* to pull a fast one
▶ **отколо́ться** *(impf* **отка́лываться)** *сов возв (та́кже перен)* to break off; *(бант, була́вка)* to come unpinned.
отколо́чу *сов см* отколоти́ть.
откомандиров|а́ть (-у́ю; *impf* **откомандиро́вывать)** *сов перех* to post, second.
откопа́|ть (-ю; *impf* **отка́пывать)** *сов перех* to dig up; *(перен: кни́гу, све́дения)* to unearth.
откорм|и́ть (-ормлю́, -о́рмишь; *impf* **отка́рмливать)** *сов перех* to fatten (up).
откорректи́р|овать (-ую) *сов от* корректи́ровать.
отко́с (-а) *м (горы́, бе́рега)* slope; *(желе́зной доро́ги)* embankment; **пуска́ть (пусти́ть** *perf)* **по́езд под** ~ to derail a train.
открепи́ть (-лю́, -и́шь; *impf* **открепля́ть)** *сов перех (значо́к, вы́веску)* to unfasten; *(снять с учёта)* to take off the register
▶ **открепи́ться** *(impf* **открепля́ться)** *сов возв (вы́веска)* to come unfastened; *(сня́ться с учёта)* to sign o.s. off the register.
открове́нен *прил см* открове́нный.
открове́ни|е (-я) *ср* revelation.
открове́нича|ть (-ю) *несов непере́х*: ~ **(с** +*instr)* to bare one's soul (to).
открове́нно *нареч* frankly; ~ **говоря́** frankly speaking.
открове́нност|ь (-и) *ж* frankness.
открове́н|ный (-ен, -на, -но) *прил* frank; *(ха́мство, обма́н)* blatant; *(разг: пла́тье, туале́т)* revealing.
откро́ю(сь) *итп сов см* откры́ть(ся).
открут|и́ть (-учу́, -у́тишь; *impf* **откру́чивать)** *сов перех* to unscrew.
открыва́л|ка (-ки; *gen pl* -ок) *ж (для консе́рвов)* tin-opener; *(для буты́лок)* bottle-opener.

открыва́ть(ся) (-ю(сь)) *несов от* **откры́ть(ся)**.

откры́ти|е (-я) *ср* (*также перен*) discovery; (*сезона, выставки, клуба*) opening.

откры́т|ка (-ки; *gen pl* -ок) *ж* postcard.

откры́т|ый (-, -а, -о) *прил* open; (*голова, шея*) bare; (*лицо, взгляд, человек*) frank; **в ~ую** openly; **на ~ом во́здухе** outside, outdoors; **музей под ~ым не́бом** open-air museum; **~ая маши́на** open-top car; **~ое пла́тье** low-cut dress; **откры́тая ра́на** open wound; **откры́тое голосова́ние/письмо́** open vote/letter; **откры́тый вопро́с** open question.

откры́ть (-о́ю, -о́ешь; *impf* **открыва́ть**) *сов перех* to open; (*лицо итп*) to uncover; (*намерения, правду итп*) to reveal; (*воду, кран*) to turn on; (*возможность, путь, позицию*) to open up; (*явление, закон*) to discover; **открыва́ть** (**~** *perf*) **торго́влю чем-н** to start selling sth; **открыва́ть** (**~** *perf*) **Аме́рику** (*перен*) to reinvent the wheel; **открыва́ть** (**~** *perf*) **счёт** (*КОММ*) to open an account; (*СПОРТ*) to open the scoring; **открыва́ть** (**~** *perf*) **ого́нь** to open fire

▶ **откры́ться** (*impf* **открыва́ться**) *сов возв* to open; (*возможность, путь, позиция*) to open up; (*тайна*) to be revealed; (*пейзаж, река*) to open out; **~ кому́-н** to open up to sb; **у него́ глаза́ ~ы́лись** (*перен*) he has begun to see things clearly.

отку́да *нареч* where from ◆ *союз* whence, from where; **Вы ~ ?** where are you from?; **~ ты приа́хали?** where have you come from?; **~ ты э́то зна́ешь?** how do you know about that?; **он не мог поня́ть, ~ слы́шался звук** he couldn't work out where the sound was coming from; **~ сле́дует...** hence ...; **~ ни возьми́сь** out of nowhere; **~ я зна́ю?** (*разг*) how do I know?

отку́да-нибудь *нареч* from somewhere (or other).

отку́да-то *нареч* from somewhere.

отку́п|иться (-лю́сь, -ишься; *impf* **откупа́ться**) *сов возв*: **~ от** +*gen* to buy one's way out of.

отку́пор|ить (-ю, -ишь; *impf* **отку́поривать**) *сов перех* to unseal.

отку́с|и́ть (-ушу́, -у́сишь; *impf* **отку́сывать**) *сов перех* (*зубами*) to bite off; (*кусачками*) to snip off.

отл. *сокр* (= **отли́чно**) ≈ O (*US*) (= *outstanding*), ≈ A (*BRIT*).

отлага́тельств|о (-а) *ср* delay.

отла́д|ка (-и) *ж* (*КОМП*) debugging.

отлакиров|а́ть (-у́ю) *сов от* **лакирова́ть**.

отла́мыва|ть(ся) (-ю) *несов от* **отлома́ть(ся)**, **отломи́ть(ся)**.

отлеж|а́ть (-у́, -и́шь) *сов перех*: **я ~а́л но́гу/ру́ку** my leg/arm has gone dead

▶ **отлежа́ться** (*impf* **отлёживаться**) *сов возв*

(*разг*) to rest up.

отлеп|и́ть (-еплю́, -е́пишь; *impf* **отлепля́ть**) *сов перех* to peel off

▶ **отлепи́ться** (*impf* **отлепля́ться**) *сов возв* to peel off.

отлёт (-а) *м* (*птиц*) flight; (*самолёта*) departure; **на ~е** (*жить*) on the outskirts; (*держать*) in one's outstretched hand.

отле|те́ть (-чу́, -ти́шь; *impf* **отлета́ть**) *сов неперех* to fly off; (*мяч*) to fly back; (*человек: от удара*) to be sent flying back.

отл|е́чь (*3sg* -я́жет, *3pl* -я́гут, *pt* -ёг, -егла́, -егло́) *сов безл*: **у меня́ ~егло́ от се́рдца** a weight has been lifted from my mind.

отли́в (-а) *м* (*в море*) ebb; (*оттенок*) sheen.

отлива́|ть (-ю) *несов от* **отли́ть** ◆ *неперех* (+*instr*; *серебром, лиловым*) to be tinted with.

отли́в|ка (-и) *ж* (*деталей, форм*) casting.

отл|и́ть (-олью́, -олье́шь; *pt* -ил, -ила́, -и́ло, *impf* **отлива́ть**) *сов перех* (*воду, вино*) to pour off; (*ТЕХ: деталь, форму*) to cast; **у него́ кровь ~ила́ от лица́** the blood drained from his face.

отлича́|ть (-ю) *несов от* **отличи́ть** ◆ *перех* (*подлеж: красота, новизна*) to be a feature of

▶ **отлича́ться** *несов от* **отличи́ться** ◆ *возв* (*не походить*): **~ся** (**от** +*gen*) to be different (from); **~ся** (*impf*) +*instr* (*оригинальностью, красотой итп*) to be distinguished by; **она́ ~ется умо́м** she has a distinguished mind.

отли́чен *прил см* **отли́чный**.

отли́чи|е (-я) *ср* distinction; **зна́ки ~я** decorations; **дипло́м с ~м** ≈ first-class degree with distinction; **в ~ от** +*gen* unlike.

отличи́тельный *прил* distinguishing.

отлич|и́ть (-у́, -и́шь; *impf* **отлича́ть**) *сов перех*: **~ кого́-н/что-н от** +*gen* to tell sb/sth from; (*наградить*) to honour (*BRIT*), honor (*US*); **отлича́ть** (**~** *perf*) **плохо́е от хоро́шего** to tell the difference between good and bad; **я не могу́ ~ их** (*друг от дру́га*) I can't tell them apart

▶ **отличи́ться** (*impf* **отлича́ться**) *сов возв* to distinguish o.s.; (*разг: сделать что-н необычное*) to outdo o.s.

отли́чник (-а) *м* 'A'grade pupil.

отли́чниц|а (-ы) *ж см* **отли́чник**.

отли́чно *нареч* extremely well ◆ *как сказ* it's great ◆ *ср нескл* (*ПРОСВЕЩ*) ≈ excellent *или* outstanding (*school mark*); **он ~ зна́ет, что он винова́т** he knows perfectly well that he's wrong; **здесь ~** it's great here; **учи́ться** (*impf*) **на ~** to get top marks; **~!** (that's) excellent!

отли́ч|ный (-ен, -на, -но) *прил* excellent; (*иной*): **~ от** +*gen* distinct from.

отло́г|ий (-ая, -ое, -ие; -, -а, -о) *прил* sloping.

отложе́ни|е (-я) *ср* (*ГЕО, МЕД*) deposit.

отлож|и́ть (-ожу́, -о́жишь; *impf* **откла́дывать**) *сов перех* to put aside; (*отсрочить*) to postpone; (*яйцо*) to lay.

отложнóй *прил (воротник, манжеты)* turndown.

отломá|ть (-ю; *impf* **отлáмывать**) *сов перех* to break off

▸ **отломáться** (*impf* **отлáмываться**) *сов возв* to break off.

отл|омúть (-омлю́, -óмишь; *impf* **отлáмывать**) *сов перех* to break off

▸ **отломúться** (*impf* **отлáмываться**) *сов возв* to break off.

отл|упúть (-уплю́, -у́пишь) *сов от* **лупúть**.

отлуч|úть (-у́, -úшь; *impf* **отлучáть**) *сов перех*: ~ когó-н от +gen (от дома, от семьи) to take sb from; **отлучáть** (~ *perf*) когó-н от цéркви to excommunicate sb

▸ **отлучúться** (*impf* **отлучáться**) *сов возв*: я дóлжен ~ся на полчасá I'll have to go out for half an hour.

отлы́|нивать (-ю) *несов неперех*: ~ от +gen to try to get out of.

отмáлчива|ться (-юсь) *несов от* **отмолчáться**.

отмáтыва|ть (-ю) *несов от* **отмотáть**.

отмахну́ться (-у́сь, -ёшься; *impf* **отмáхиваться**) *сов возв*: ~ от +gen (от мухи) to brush away; (от человека, от предложения) to brush *или* wave aside.

отмáчива|ть (-ю) *несов от* **отмочúть**.

отмеж|евáть (-у́юсь; *impf* **отмежёвываться**) *сов возв*: ~ от +gen (перен) to distance o.s. from.

óтмель (-и) *ж*: песчáная ~ sandbank.

отмéн|а (-ы) *ж* (*см глаг*) repeal; reversal; abolition; cancellation.

отмен|úть (-ю́, -éнишь; *impf* **отменя́ть**) *сов перех* (закон) to repeal; (решение, приговор) to reverse; (налог) to abolish; (лекцию) to cancel.

от|мерéть (3sg -омрёт, 3pl -омру́т, pt -мер, -мерлá, -мерло, *impf* **отмирáть**) *сов неперех* (ткань, ветка) to die; (перен: обычаи, привычки) to die (out).

отмёрз|нуть (3sg -нет, 3pl -нут, pt -, -ла, -ло, *impf* **отмерзáть**) *сов неперех* (ветки, побеги) to freeze; (разг: руки, ноги) to be frozen.

отмéр|ить (-ю, -ишь; *impf* **отмеря́ть**) *сов перех* to measure out.

отм|естú (-ету́, -етёшь; pt -ёл, -елá, -елó, *impf* **отметáть**) *сов перех* (мусор, снег) to sweep away; (перен: доводы, возражения) to sweep aside.

отмéстк|а (-и) *ж*: в ~у за +acc in revenge for.

отметá|ть (-ю) *несов от* **отместú**.

отмéтин|а (-ы) *ж* mark.

отмé|тить (-чу, -тишь; *impf* **отмечáть**) *сов перех* (на карте, в книге) to mark; (затраты, расходы) to record; (присутствующих, отсутствующих) to take a note of; (достоинства, недостатки, успехи) to recognise; (юбилей, день рождения) to celebrate; **ну́жно** ~, **что** ... it should be noted that ...

▸ **отмé|титься** (*impf* **отмечáться**) *сов возв* to register.

отмéт|ка (-ки; gen pl -ок) *ж* mark; (в документе, в паспорте) note.

отмету́ *itn сов см* **отместú**.

отмечá|ть (-ю) *несов от* **отмéтить**

▸ **отмечá|ться** *несов от* **отмéтиться** ♦ *возв* (успехи, талант) to be apparent.

отмéчу(сь) *сов см* **отмéтить(ся)**.

отмирá|ть (3sg -ет, 3pl -ют) *несов от* **отмерéть**.

отмóк|нуть (3sg -нет, 3pl -нут, pt -, -ла, -ло, *impf* **отмокáть**) *сов неперех* to get damp; (бельё) to soak; (отклеиться) to come off (*as a result of soaking*).

отмолчá|ться (-у́сь, -úшься; *impf* **отмáлчиваться**) *сов неперех* to keep silent.

отморó|зить (-жу, -зишь; *impf* **отморáживать**) *сов перех*: ~ ру́ки/нóги to get frostbite in one's hands/feet.

отмотá|ть (-ю; *impf* **отмáтывать**) *сов перех* to unwind.

отм|очúть (-очу́, -óчишь; *impf* **отмáчивать**) *сов перех* (наклейку, бинт) to soak off; (разг: глупость) to come out with.

отмóю(сь) *itn сов см* **отмы́ть(ся)**.

отму́ч|иться (-усь, -ишься) *сов возв*: он наконéц ~ился his suffering has finally come to an end.

отмы́|ть (-óю, -óешь; *impf* **отмывáть**) *сов перех*: ~ что-н to get sth clean; (грязь, пятно) to wash out

▸ **отмы́|ться** (*impf* **отмывáться**) *сов возв* (см перех) to wash; to wash out; **у меня́ ру́ки не** ~вáются I can't get my hands clean.

отмы́чк|а (-и) *ж* skeleton key.

отнéкива|ться (-юсь) *несов неперех* (разг: отказываться) to keep saying no; (не признаваться) to refuse to own up.

отн|естú (-есу́, -есёшь; pt -ёс, -еслá, -еслó, *impf* **относúть**) *сов перех* to take (off); (подлеж: течение, ветер) to carry off; (причислить к): ~ что-н к +dat (к периоду, к году) to date sth back to; (к разряду, к категории) to classify sth as; **относúть** (~ *perf*) что-н за или на счёт +gen to put sth down to, attribute sth to

▸ **отнестú|сь** (*impf* **относúться**) *сов возв*: ~сь к +dat (к человеку) to treat; (к преуведомлению, к событию) to take; **как он** ~ёсся **к Вáшему предложéнию?** what did he think of your suggestion?

отникелир|овáть (-у́ю) *сов от* **никелировáть**.

отнимá|ть(ся) (-ю(сь)) *несов от* **отня́ть(ся)**.

отниму́(сь) *itn сов см* **отня́ть(ся)**.

относúтелен *прил см* **относúтельный**.

относúтельно *нареч* relatively ♦ *предл* (+gen; в отношении) regarding, with regard to.

относúтельный (-ен, -ьна, -ьно) *прил* relative; **относúтельное местоимéние/ прилагáтельное** (линг) relative pronoun/ adjective.

отн|осúть (-ошу́, -óсишь) *несов от* **отнестú**

▶ **ОТНОСИ́ТЬСЯ** *несов от* **отнести́сь** ♦ *возв:* ~**ся к** +*dat* to relate to; (*к кла́ссу, к катего́рии*) to belong to; (*к го́ду, к эпо́хе*) to date from; **он к ней хорошо́** ~**о́сится** he likes her; **как ты** ~**о́сишься к нему́?** what do you think about him?; **э́то к нам не** ~**о́сится** it has nothing to do with us.

ОТНОШЕ́НИ|е (-я) *ср:* ~ **к** +*dat* attitude (to); (*связь*) relation (to); (*МАТ*) ratio; (*докуме́нт*) letter; **в** ~**и** +*gen* with regard to; **по** ~**ю к** +*dat* towards; **в э́том** ~**и** in this respect *или* regard; **в не́котором** ~**и** in certain respects *или* regards; **во всех** ~**ях** in all respects *или* regards; (*impf*) ~ **к** +*dat* to be connected with; **не име́ть** (*impf*) ~**я к** +*dat* to have nothing to do with; *см та́кже* **отноше́ния**.

ОТНОШЕ́НИЯ (-й) *мн* (*полити́ческие, семе́йные итп*) relations *мн*.

ОТНОШУ́(СЬ) *сов см* **относи́ть(ся)**.

ОТНЫ́НЕ *нареч* henceforth.

ОТНЮ́ДЬ *нареч:* ~ **не** by no means, far from; ~ **нет** absolutely not.

ОТНЯ́ТЬ (-иму́, -и́мешь; *pt* -я́л, -яла́, -я́ло, *impf* **отнима́ть**) *сов перех* to take away; (*си́лы, вре́мя*) to take up; (*но́гу, ру́ку*) to take off; **отнима́ть** (~ *perf*) **от груди́** to wean; **э́того у него́ не** ~**и́мешь** (*перен*) you can't take that away from him

▶ **ОТНЯ́ТЬСЯ** (*impf* **отнима́ться**) *сов возв:* **у него́** ~**яли́сь но́ги/ру́ки** he has lost the use of his legs/arms; **у меня́ язы́к** ~**я́лся** (*перен: разг*) I was left speechless.

ОТО *предл см* **от**.

ОТОБРАЖА́|ТЬ (-ю) *несов от* **отобрази́ть**.

ОТОБРАЖЕ́НИ|е (-я) *ср* representation.

ОТОБРАЗ|И́ТЬ (-жу́, -зи́шь; *impf* **отобража́ть**) *сов перех* to represent.

ОТ|ОБРА́ТЬ (-беру́, -берёшь; *pt* -обра́л, -обрала́, -обра́ло, *impf* **отбира́ть**) *сов перех* (*отня́ть*) to take away; (*вы́брать*) to select.

ОТОБЬЮ́(СЬ) *итп сов см* **отби́ть(ся)**.

ОТОВСЮ́ДУ *нареч* from all around.

ОТ|ОГНА́ТЬ (-гоню́, -го́нишь; *impf* **отгоня́ть**) *сов перех* to chase away; (*перен: мы́сли, сомне́ния*) to drive out.

ОТОГН|У́ТЬ (-у́, -ёшь; *impf* **отгиба́ть**) *сов перех* (*мета́лл*) to bend back; (*ска́терть, страни́цу*) to fold back

▶ **ОТОГНУ́ТЬСЯ** (*impf* **отгиба́ться**) *сов возв* to bend back.

ОТОГРЕ́|ТЬ (-ю; *impf* **отогрева́ть**) *сов перех* to warm

▶ **ОТОГРЕ́|ТЬСЯ** (*impf* **отогрева́ться**) *сов возв* to get warm.

ОТОДВИ́Н|УТЬ (-у, -ешь; *impf* **отодвига́ть**) *сов перех* (*шкаф*) to move; (*щеко́лду, засо́в*) to slide back; (*срок, экза́мен*) to put back

▶ **ОТОДВИ́НУТЬСЯ** (*impf* **отодвига́ться**) *сов возв*

(*челове́к*) to move; (*срок, экза́мен*) to be put back.

ОТ|ОДРА́ТЬ (-деру́, -дерёшь; *impf* **отдира́ть**) *сов перех* (*разг: оторва́ть*) to rip off; (: *вы́сечь*) to thrash

▶ **ОТОДРА́ТЬСЯ** *сов возв* (*разг*) to come off.

ОТОЖДЕСТВ|И́ТЬ (-лю́, -и́шь; *impf* **отождествля́ть**) *сов перех* to equate.

ОТОЖДЕСТВЛЕ́НИ|е (-я) *ср* equating.

ОТОЖДЕСТВЛЮ́ *сов см* **отождестви́ть**.

ОТОЖДЕСТВЛЯ́|ТЬ (-ю) *несов от* **отождестви́ть**.

ОТОЖМУ́ *итп сов см* **отжа́ть**.

ОТ|ОЗВА́ТЬ (-зову́, -зовёшь; *impf* **отзыва́ть**) *перех* to call back; (*посла́, представи́теля, докуме́нты*) to recall; **отзыва́ть** (~ *perf*) **кого́-н в сто́рону** to take sb aside; **отзыва́ть** (~ *perf*) **иск** (*ЮР*) to drop a case

▶ **ОТОЗВА́ТЬСЯ** (*impf* **отзыва́ться**) *сов возв:* ~**ся** (**на** +*acc*) to respond (to); **хорошо́/пло́хо** ~**ся** (*perf*) **о** +*prp* to speak well/badly of; ~**ся** (*perf*) **о** +*prp* (*о кни́ге*) to voice one's opinion about.

ОТ|ОЙТИ́ (*как* **идти́;** *см* **Table 18;** *impf* **отходи́ть**) *сов неперех:* ~ **от** +*gen* to move away from; (*перен: от друзе́й, от взгля́дов*) to distance o.s. from; (*от пи́сьма, от оригина́ла*) to depart from; (*по́езд, авто́бус*) to leave; (*войска́, полк*) to withdraw; (*обо́и, кра́ска*) to come off; (*пятно́, грязь*) to come out; (*отлучи́ться*) to go off; (*отта́ять*) to thaw; (*переста́ть серди́ться*) to calm down; **я** ~**йду́ на 5 мину́т** I'll be back in 5 minutes.

ОТОЛЬЮ́ *итп сов см* **отли́ть**.

ОТОЛАРИНГО́ЛОГ (-а) *м* ear, nose and throat specialist.

ОТОМРЁТ *итп сов см* **отмере́ть**.

ОТОМ|СТИ́ТЬ (-щу́, -сти́шь) *сов от* **мстить**.

ОТОПИ́ТЕЛЬНЫЙ *прил* (*прибо́р*) heating *опред;* ~ **сезо́н** the cold season.

ОТОПЛЕ́НИ|е (-я) *ср* heating.

ОТОПРУ́(СЬ) *итп сов см* **отпере́ть(ся)**.

ОТОПЬЮ́ *итп сов см* **отпи́ть**.

ОТО́РВАН|НЫЙ (-, -а, -о) *прил:* ~ **от** +*gen* (*от жи́зни, от друзе́й*) cut off from; (*воротни́к, пу́говица*) torn-off.

ОТОРВ|А́ТЬ (-у́, -ёшь; *impf* **отрыва́ть**) *сов перех:* ~ (**от** +*gen*) to tear away (from); (*воротни́к, пу́говицу*) to tear off; **ему́** ~**а́ло но́гу** his leg was blown off; **отрыва́ть** (~ *perf*) **что-н от себя́** to sacrifice sth

▶ **ОТОРВА́ТЬСЯ** (*impf* **отрыва́ться**) *сов возв:* ~**ся** (**от** +*gen*) (*от рабо́ты*) to tear o.s. away (from); (*от отря́да, от бегуно́в, от пресле́дователей*) to break away (from); (*от семьи́, от друзе́й, от жи́зни*) to lose touch (with); (*воротни́к, штани́на*) to tear; (*пу́говица*) to come off; **отрыва́ться** (~**ся** *perf*) **от земли́** to take off.

ОТОРОПЕ́ЛЫЙ *прил* (*разг*) dumbstruck.

оторопе́ть (-ю) *сов неперех* (*разг*) to be dumbstruck.

ото|сла́ть (-шлю́, -шлёшь; *impf* **отсыла́ть**) *сов перех*: ~ **кого́-н к** +*dat* to refer sb to; (*письмо, посылку*) to send (off); (*человека, машину*) to send back.

отоспа́ться (-лю́сь, -и́шься; *impf* **отсыпа́ться**) *сов перех* (*разг*) to have a good sleep.

оботру́ *итп сов см* **оттере́ть.**

от|очи́ть (-очу́, -о́чишь) *сов перех* to sharpen.

отошёл *итп сов см* **отойти́.**

отошлю́ *итп сов см* **отосла́ть.**

отоща́|ть (-ю) *сов от* **тоща́ть.**

отпада́ет *итп сов см* **отпа́сть.**

отпада́|ть (-ю) *несов от* **отпа́сть.**

отпа́ива|ть (-ю) *несов от* **отпая́ть, отпои́ть.**

отпа́рива|ть (-ю) *несов от* **отпа́рить.**

отпари́р|овать (-ую) *сов от* **пари́ровать.**

отпа́р|ить (-ю, -ишь; *impf* **отпа́ривать**) *сов перех* (*брюки, юбку*) to steam press.

отпа́ры|ва|ть(ся) (-ю(сь)) *несов от* **отпоро́ть(ся).**

отпа́|сть (3sg -дёт, 3pl -ду́т, *impf* **отпада́ть**) *сов неперех* (*обои, штукату́рка*) to come off; (*жела́ние, необходи́мость*) to pass; **у меня́ ~ла охо́та идти́ туда́** I don't feel like going there any more.

отпая́|ть (-ю; *impf* **отпа́ивать**) *сов перех* to melt off.

отпева́ни|е (-я) *ср* funeral service.

отпева́|ть (-ю) *несов от* **отпе́ть.**

от|пере́ть (-опру́, -опрёшь; *pt* -пер, -перла́, -перло, *impf* **отпира́ть**) *сов перех* to unlock

▶ **отпере́ться** (*impf* **отпира́ться**) *сов возв* (*дверь, ворота, шкаф*) to open.

отпе́тый *прил* (*разг*) out-and-out.

отпе́|ть (-о́ю, -о́ешь; *impf* **отпева́ть**) *сов перех* (*РЕЛ*) to read a service for.

отпеча́та|ть (-ю; *impf* **отпеча́тывать**) *сов перех* (*также ФОТО*) to print; (*на компьютере*) to finish typing; (*следы*) to leave; (*помеще́ние*) to open up

▶ **отпеча́таться** (*impf* **отпеча́тываться**) *сов возв* (*на земле, на песке*) to leave a print; (*перен: в памяти, в сознании*) to imprint itself.

отпеча́т|ок (-ка) *м* (*также перен*) imprint; **отпеча́тки па́льцев** fingerprints.

отпеча́тыва|ть(ся) (-ю(сь)) *несов от* **отпеча́тать(ся).**

отпива́|ть (-ю) *несов от* **отпи́ть.**

отп|или́ть (-илю́, -и́лишь; *impf* **отпи́ливать**) *сов перех* to saw off.

отпира́тельств|о (-а) *ср* denial.

отпира́|ть (-ю) *несов от* **отпере́ть**

▶ **отпира́ться** *несов от* **отпере́ться** ♦ *возв*: ~**ся (от** +*gen*) (*от слов итп*) to deny.

отпи|са́ться (-шу́сь, -шешься; *impf* **отпи́сываться**) *сов неперех* (*разг*) to send a formal reply.

отпи́с|ка (-ки; *gen pl* -ок) *ж* formal reply.

отпи́сыва|ться (-юсь) *несов от* **отписа́ться.**

от|пи́ть (-опью́, -опьёшь; *impf* **отпива́ть**) *сов*

перех (*полстакана итп*) to drink; ~ (*perf*) **глото́к** to take a sip.

отпихн|у́ть (-у́, -ёшь; *impf* **отпи́хивать**) *сов перех* (*разг*) to shove

▶ **отпихну́ться** (*impf* **отпи́хиваться**) *сов возв* (*разг*): ~**ся (от** +*gen*) (*от берега*) to push off (from).

отпишу́сь *итп сов см* **отписа́ться.**

отпла́т|а (-ы) *ж* repayment (*fig*); **в ~у за** +*acc* in repayment *или* as a reward for.

отпл|ати́ть (-ачу́, -а́тишь; *impf* **отпла́чивать**) *сов неперех* (+*dat*; *наградить*) to repay; (*отомстить*) to pay back.

отплыва́|ть (-ю) *несов от* **отплы́ть.**

отплыву́ *итп сов см* **отплы́ть.**

отплы́ти|е (-я) *ср* (*отправление*) departure.

отпл|ы́ть (-ву́, -вёшь; *impf* **отплыва́ть**) *сов неперех* (*человек*) to swim off; (*корабль*) to set sail.

о́тповед|ь (-и) *ж* rebuke.

отп|ои́ть (-ю́, -и́шь; *impf* **отпа́ивать**) *сов перех*: ~ **кого́-н чем-н** (*разг*) to give sb sth (to drink).

отполз|ти́ (-у́, -ёшь; *impf* **отполза́ть**) *сов неперех* to crawl away.

отполир|ова́ть (-у́ю) *сов от* **полирова́ть.**

отпо́р (-а) *м*: **дать** ~ +*dat* (*врагу*) to repel, repulse; (*идее*) to rebuff; **получа́ть** (**получи́ть** *perf*) **реши́тельный** ~ to be rebuffed.

отп|оро́ть (-орю́, -о́решь; *impf* **отпа́рывать**) *сов перех* (*рукав, пу́говицу*) to unstitch

▶ **отпоро́ться** (*impf* **отпа́рываться**) *сов возв* (*рукав*) to come unstitched; (*пуговица*) to come off.

отпою́ *итп сов см* **отпои́ть.**

отправи́тел|ь (-я) *м* sender.

отпра́в|ить (-лю, -ишь; *impf* **отправля́ть**) *сов перех* to send; **отправля́ть** (~ *perf*) **кого́-н на тот свет** to do away with sb

▶ **отпра́виться** (*impf* **отправля́ться**) *сов возв* (*человек*) to set off; (*поезд, теплоход*) to depart.

отпра́в|ка (-ки; *gen pl* -ок) *ж* (*письма, посы́лки*) posting; (*груза*) dispatch; (*поезда, теплохода*) departure.

отправле́ни|е (-я) *ср* (*письма, посы́лки*) dispatch; (*поезда, теплохода*) departure; (*обя́занностей, правосу́дия*) administration; (*заказно́е, почто́вое*) item; **отправле́ния органи́зма** bodily function.

отправлю́(сь) *сов см* **отпра́вить(ся).**

отправля́|ть (-ю) *несов от* **отпра́вить** ♦ *перех* (*обя́занности*) to exercise; (*правосу́дие*) to adminster

▶ **отправля́ться** *несов от* **отпра́виться.**

отправн|о́й *прил*: ~ **пункт** point of departure; ~**а́я цена́** (*КОММ*) reserve price (*BRIT*), upset price (*US*); **отправна́я то́чка** (*перен*) starting point.

отпра́здн|овать (-ую) *сов от* **пра́здновать.**

отпра́шива|ться (-юсь) *несов от* **отпроси́ться.**

отпресс|овать (-у́ю) *сов от* **прессовать**.
отпр|оси́ться (-ошу́сь, -о́сишься) *impf* **отпрашиваться**) *сов возв* to ask to be let off; **он ~оси́лся домо́й** he asked to be allowed to go home.
отпры́гн|уть (-у, -ешь; *impf* **отпры́гивать**) *сов неперех* to jump.
о́тпрыск (-а) *м* shoot; (*перен*) offspring.
отпря́г *итп сов см* **отпря́чь**.
отпряга́|ть (-ю) *несов от* **отпря́чь**.
отпря́гу *итп сов см* **отпря́чь**.
отпря́н|уть (-у, -ешь) *сов неперех* to recoil.
отпря́|чь (-гу́, -жёшь *итп*, -гу́т; *pt* -г, -гла́, -гло́, *impf* **отпряга́ть**) *сов перех* to unharness.
отпугн|у́ть (-у́, -ёшь; *impf* **отпу́гивать**) *сов перех* to scare off.
о́тпуск (-а) *м* leave, holiday (*BRIT*), vacation (*US*); (*ВОЕН*) leave; (*товаров*) sale; **ежего́дный ~** annual leave; **быть** (*impf*) **в ~** to be on holiday; **идти́ (пойти́** *perf*) **в ~** to go on holiday; **брать (взять** *perf*) **~** to take leave.
отпуска́|ть (-ю) *несов от* **отпусти́ть**.
отпускни́|к (-а́) *м* holiday-maker; (*ВОЕН*) soldier on leave.
отпускни́ц|а (-ы) *ж* (*разг*) *см* **отпускни́к**.
отпускны́|е (-х; *decl like adj*) *мн* (*также:* **~ де́ньги**) holiday pay *ед*.
отпусти́|ть (-ущу́, -у́стишь; *impf* **отпуска́ть**) *сов перех* to let out; (*из рук*) to let go of; (*товар, продукты*) to sell; (*деньги, средства*) to release; (*бороду, волосы*) to grow ◆ *безл* (*разг: боль*) to ease off; **отпуска́ть** (~ *perf*) **кому́-н грехи́** (*РЕЛ*) to absolve sb of his sins; **отпуска́ть** (~ *perf*) **комплиме́нт** (*разг*) to compliment sb; **отпуска́ть** (~ *perf*) **шу́тку** (*разг*) to crack a joke.
отраба́тыва|ть (-ю) *несов от* **отрабо́тать**.
отрабо́танный *прил* (*порода*) worked out; (*газ*) waste *опред*.
отрабо́та|ть (-ю; *impf* **отраба́тывать**) *сов перех* (*долги*) to work off; (*какое-то время*) to work; (*освоить*) to work on, polish ◆ *неперех* (*кончить работать*) to finish work.
отра́в|а (-ы) *ж* poison.
отрави́тель (-я) *м* poisoner.
отрави́тельниц|а (-ы) *ж см* **отрави́тель**.
отр|ави́ть (-авлю́, -а́вишь; *impf* **отравля́ть**) *сов перех* to poison; (*перен: удовольствие, праздник итп*) to spoil.
▶ **отрави́ться** *сов от* **трави́ться** ◆ (*impf* **отравля́ться**) *возв* to poison o.s.; (*едой*) to get food-poisoning; (*газом итп*) to be poisoned.
отравле́ни|е (-я) *ср* poisoning.
отравлю́(сь) *сов см* **отрави́ть(ся)**.
отравля́|ть(ся) (-ю(сь)) *несов от* **отрави́ть(ся)**.
отравля́ющий (-ая, -ее, -ие) *прил* poisonous, toxic.
отра́д|а (-ы) *ж* joy.

отра́дный (-ен, -на, -но) *прил* satisfying.
отража́тель (-я) *м* reflector.
отража́|ть(ся) (-ю(сь)) *несов от* **отрази́ть(ся)**.
отраже́ни|е (-я) *ср* (*см глаг*) reflection; deflection.
отра|зи́ть (-жу́, -зи́шь; *impf* **отража́ть**) *сов перех* (*также перен*) to reflect; (*нападение, удар*) to deflect
▶ **отрази́ться** (*impf* **отража́ться**) *сов возв* (*также перен*) to be reflected; **отража́ться** (~**ся** *perf*) **на** +*prp* (*на здоровье, на успехах итп*) to have an effect on.
отрапорт|ова́ть (-у́ю) *сов от* **рапортова́ть**.
отраслево́й *прил related to a particular branch of industry*.
о́трасл|ь (-и) *ж* branch (*of research, industry*).
отр|асти́ (*3sg* -астёт, *3pl* -асту́т, *pt* -о́с, -осла́, -осло́, *impf* **отраста́ть**) *сов неперех* to grow.
отра|сти́ть (-щу́, -сти́шь; *impf* **отра́щивать**) *сов перех* to grow.
отреаги́р|овать (-ую) *сов от* **реаги́ровать**.
отре́бь|е (-я) *ср собир* (*пренебр*) scum.
отрегули́р|овать (-ую) *сов от* **регули́ровать**.
отредакти́р|овать (-ую) *сов от* **редакти́ровать**.
отре́жу *итп сов см* **отре́зать**.
отре́з (-а) *м* piece of fabric; **ли́ния ~а** dotted line.
отре́|зать (-жу, -жешь; *impf* **отреза́ть**) *сов перех* to cut off ◆ *несов перех* (*разг: резко ответить*) to cut short.
отрезве́|ть (-ю) *сов от* **трезве́ть**.
отрезв|и́ть (-лю́, -и́шь; *impf* **отрезвля́ть**) *сов перех* (*также перен*) to sober up.
отре́зк|а *итп сущ см* **отре́зок**.
отрезно́й *прил* (*талон*) tear-off; (*рукав*) detachable.
отре́з|ок (-ка) *м* (*ткани*) piece; (*пути*) section; (*времени*) period; (*ГЕОМ*) segment.
отрека́|ться (-юсь) *несов от* **отре́чься**.
отрекоменд|ова́ть (-у́ю) *сов от* **рекомендова́ть**.
отрёкся *итп сов см* **отре́чься**.
отреку́сь *итп сов от* **отре́чься**.
отремонти́р|овать (-ую) *сов от* **ремонти́ровать**.
отрепети́р|овать (-ую) *сов от* **репети́ровать**.
отреставри́р|овать (-ую) *сов от* **реставри́ровать**.
отрецензи́р|овать (-ую) *сов от* **рецензи́ровать**.
отрече́ни|е (-я) *ср*: **~ от** +*gen* renunciation of; **отрече́ние от престо́ла** abdication.
отре́|чься (-ку́сь, -чёшься *итп*, -ку́тся; *pt* -ёкся, -екла́сь, -екло́сь, *impf* **отрека́ться**) *сов возв*: **~ от** +*gen* to renounce; **отрека́ться** (~ *perf*) **от престо́ла** to abdicate.
отреша́|ться (-юсь) *несов от* **отреши́ться**.

отрешён|ный (-, -а, -о) *прил* resolute.

отреш|и́ться (-у́сь, -и́шься; *impf* **отреша́ться**) *сов возв*: ~ **от** +*gen* to reject.

отрица́ни|е (-я) *ср* denial; (*линг*) negation.

отрица́тельный (-ен, -ьна, -ьно) *прил* (*также МАТ, ЭЛЕК*) negative.

отрица́|ть (-ю) *несов перех* to deny; (*литературу, моду итп*) to reject.

отро́г (-а) *м* (*ГЕО*) spur.

о́троду *нареч*: ~ **не** +*pt* (*разг*) never; **я** ~ **тако́го не ви́дел** I've never ever seen anything like it.

отро́дь|е (-я) *ср* (*разг: пренебр*) scum.

отро́с *итп сов см* **отрасти́**.

отро́сток (-ка) *м* (*побег*) shoot; (*ответвление*) branch; ~ **слепо́й кишки́** appendix.

о́трочеств|о (-а) *ср* adolescence.

отро́ю *итп сов см* **отры́ть**.

отруба́|ть (-ю) *несов от* **отруби́ть**.

о́труб|и (-ей) *мн* bran *ед*.

отруб|и́ть (-у́блю́, -у́бишь; *impf* **отруба́ть**) *сов перех* (*ветку, голову*) to chop off ♦ *неперех* (*разг: резко ответить*) to cut short.

отруга́|ть (-ю) *сов от* **руга́ть**.

отры́в (-а) *м*: ~ **от** (*отряда, семьи*) separation from; **ли́ния** ~**а** perforated line; **учи́ться** (*impf*) **без** ~**а от произво́дства** to study without giving up work; **быть** (*impf*) **в** ~**е от** +*gen* to be cut off from.

отрыва́|ть (-ю) *несов от* **оторва́ть**, **отры́ть**.

▸ **отрыва́ться** *несов от* **оторва́ться**.

отры́вист|ый (-, -а, -о) *прил* (*смех*) spasmodic; (*сигнал*) interrupted; (*речь, замечания*) disjointed.

отры́вк|а *итп сущ см* **отры́вок**.

отрывно́й *прил* (*блокнот, талоны*) tear-off.

отры́в|ок (-ка) *м* excerpt.

отры́воч|ный (-ен, -на, -но) *прил* fragmented, disjointed.

отрыгн|у́ть (-у́, -ёшь; *impf* **отры́гивать**) *сов* (*не)перех* to burp (*inf*).

отры́жк|а (-и) *ж* burp (*inf*).

отры́|ть (-о́ю, -о́ешь; *impf* **отрыва́ть**) *сов перех* (*также перен*) to dig up.

отря́д (-а) *м* party, group; (*ВОЕН*) detachment; (*ЗООЛ*) order; **поиско́вый** ~ search party.

отряхн|у́ть (-у́, -ёшь; *impf* **отря́хивать**) *сов перех* (*снег, пыль*) to shake off; (*пальто, сапоги*) to shake down

▸ **отряхну́ться** (*impf* **отря́хиваться**) *сов возв* to shake o.s. down.

отса|ди́ть (-жу́, -дишь; *impf* **отса́живать**) *сов перех* (*ученика, болтуна*) to move; (*растение, цветок*) to add new soil to.

отса́жива|ться (-юсь) *несов от* **отсе́сть**.

отсажу́ *сов см* **отсади́ть**.

отсалют|ова́ть (-у́ю) *сов от* **салютова́ть**.

отса́сыва|ть (-ю) *несов от* **отсоса́ть**.

о́тсвет (-а) *м* reflection.

отсве́чива|ть (*3sg* -ет, *3pl* -ют) *несов неперех* to reflect the light.

отсебя́тин|а (-ы) *ж* (*разг: пренебр*): **нести́** ~**у**

to say whatever comes into one's head; **занима́ться** (*impf*) ~**ой** to do whatever comes into one's head.

отсе́в (-а) *м* (*действие: шелухи*) separation; (*то, что отсеяно*) siftings *мн*; (*кандидатов*) elimination; (*студентов*) expulsion.

отсе́ива|ть(ся) (-ю(сь)) *несов от* **отсе́ять(ся)**.

отсе́к (-а) *м* (*судна, помещения*) compartment; (*ракеты*) module.

отсёк *итп сов см* **отсе́чь**.

отсека́|ть (-ю) *несов от* **отсе́чь**.

отсеку́ *итп сов см* **отсе́чь**.

отс|е́сть (-я́ду, -я́дешь; *impf* **отса́живаться**) *сов неперех*: ~ (**от** +*gen*) to move away (from); ~ (*impf*) **пода́льше** to sit further away.

отсе́|чь (-еку́, -ечёшь итп, -ку́т; *pt* -ёк, -екла́, -екло́, *impf* **отсека́ть**) *сов перех* to cut off.

отсе́|ять (-ю; *impf* **отсе́ивать**) *сов перех* (*семена, шелуху*) to sift out; (*перен: кандидатов*) to eliminate; (*: учеников*) to expel

▸ **отсе́яться** (*impf* **отсе́иваться**) *сов возв* (*см перех*) to be separated; to be eliminated; to drop out.

отси|де́ть (-жу́, -ди́шь; *impf* **отси́живать**) *сов неперех* (*просидеть*) to wait; (*лекцию*) to sit through; (*разг: в тюрьме*) to do time ♦ *перех*: **я** ~**де́л но́гу** my leg has gone dead; **я** ~**де́л там два часа́** I sat (and waited) there for two hours

▸ **отсиде́ться** (*impf* **отси́живаться**) *сов возв* (*разг*) to sit tight.

отска́блива|ть (-ю) *несов от* **отскобли́ть**.

отска́кива|ть (-ю) *несов от* **отскочи́ть**.

отскобл|и́ть (-ю́, -и́шь; *impf* **отска́бливать**) *сов перех* to scrub off.

отск|очи́ть (-очу́, -о́чишь; *impf* **отска́кивать**) *сов неперех*: ~ **от** +*gen* to bounce off; (*человек*) to jump off; (*в сторону, назад*) to jump; (*разг: пуговица, кнопка*) to come off; **отска́кивать** (~ *perf*) **в сто́рону/наза́д** to jump to the side/back.

отскре|сти́ (-бу́, -бёшь; *impf* **отскреба́ть**) *сов перех* to scratch off.

отсло|и́ть (-ю́, -и́шь; *impf* **отсла́ивать**) *сов перех* to strip away.

отслу|жи́ть (-жу́, -у́жишь) *сов неперех* (*какое-то время*) to serve ♦ *перех* (*военную службу*) to serve out; (*панихиду, молебен*) to conduct.

отсн|я́ть (-иму́, -и́мешь; *сов перех* (*плёнку*) to finish off, use up; (*фильм, серию*) to finish shooting.

отсове́т|овать (-ую) *сов неперех*: ~ **кому́-н** +*infin* (*делать, ездить итп*) to advise sb not to do *или* against doing.

отсоедин|и́ть (-ю́, -и́шь; *impf* **отсоединя́ть**) *сов перех* to disconnect.

отсо́с (-а) *м* (*действие*) suction; (*устройство*) suction pump.

отсос|а́ть (-у́, -ёшь; *impf* **отса́сывать**) *сов перех* to draw off.

отсо́хн|уть (-у, -ешь; *impf* **отсыха́ть**) *сов*

неперех to wither.

отсро́ч|ить (-у, -ишь; *impf* **отсро́чивать**) *сов перех* to defer.

отсро́чк|а (-и) *ж* deferral.

отстава́ни|е (-я) *ср* (*в работе, в учёбе*) falling behind; (*в развитии*) retardation.

отстав|а́ть (-ю́, -ёшь) *несов от* **отста́ть**.

отста́в|ить (-лю, -ишь; *impf* **отставля́ть**) *сов перех* to move aside; ~! (*ВОЕН*) as you were!

отста́в|ка (-ки; *gen pl* -ок) *ж* (*ВОЕН*) retirement; (*с государственной службы*) resignation; **подава́ть** (**пода́ть** *perf*) **в ~ку** to offer one's resignation; **уходи́ть** (**уйти́** *perf*) **в ~ку** to resign one's commission; **офице́р в ~ке** retired officer; ~ **прави́тельства/кабине́та** resignation of the government/cabinet.

отставля́ю *сов см* **отста́вить**.

отставля́ть (-ю) *несов от* **отста́вить**.

отста́вок *сущ см* **отста́вка**.

отста́ива|ть(ся) (-ю) *несов от* **отстоя́ть(ся)**.

отста́лост|ь (-и) *ж* backwardness.

отста́лый *прил* backward.

отста́|ть (-ну, -нешь; *impf* **отстава́ть**) *сов неперех*: ~ (**от** +*gen*) (*от группы, от друзей*) to fall behind; (*от поезда, от автобуса*) to be left behind; (*перен: в учёбе, в работе, в развитии*) to fall behind; (*обои, пластырь*) to come off; (*часы*) to be slow; ~**нь от меня́!** stop pestering me!; **часы́ отстаю́т на 5 мину́т** the clock is 5 minutes slow; **отстава́ть** (~ *perf*) **от вре́мени** (*перен*) to be behind the times; **отстава́ть** (~ *perf*) **от жи́зни** to be out of touch.

отстега́|ть (-ю) *сов от* **стега́ть**.

отстегн|у́ть (-у́, -ёшь; *impf* **отстёгивать**) *сов перех* (*крючок*) to unfasten; (*капюшон, рукава*) to detach

▶ **отстегну́ться** (*impf* **отстёгиваться**) *сов возв* (*крючок*) to come unfastened.

отстира́|ть (-ю; *impf* **отсти́рывать**) *сов перех* (*пятно, грязь*) to wash out; (*рубашку, юбку*) to wash clean

▶ **отстира́ться** (*impf* **отсти́рываться**) *сов возв* (*см перех*) to wash out; to wash clean.

отсто́|й (-я) *м* sediment.

отсто́йник (-а) *м* (*ТЕХ*) settling tank.

отсто|я́ть (-ю́, -и́шь; *impf* **отста́ивать**) *сов перех* (*город, своё мнение*) to defend; (*воду, раствор*) to allow to stand; (*службу, концерт*) to stand through; (*два часа итп*) to wait; **мы ~я́ли всю слу́жбу** we stood through the whole service; **я ~я́л два часа́ в о́череди** I stood (and waited) for two hours in the queue ♦ *несов неперех* (*no perf*): ~ **от** +*gen* to be situated away from; **их дом ~и́т на 3 киломе́тра от го́рода** their house is situated 3 kilometres from the town

▶ **отстоя́ться** (*impf* **отста́иваться**) *сов возв* to settle.

отстра́ива|ть (-ю) *несов от* **отстро́ить**.

отстран|и́ть (-ю́, -и́шь; *impf* **отстраня́ть**) *сов перех* (*уволить*): ~ **от** +*gen* (*от должности*) to relieve of; (*отодвинуть*) to push away

▶ **отстрани́ться** (*impf* **отстраня́ться**) *сов возв*: ~**ся от** +*gen* (*от должности*) to relinquish; (*отодвинуться*) to draw back.

отстреля́ться (-юсь; *impf* **отстре́ливаться**) *сов возв*: ~ **от** +*gen* to drive back (*with gunfire*); (*разг: кончить дела*) to do one's bit.

отстри́|чь (-гу́, -ижёшь *итп*, -игу́т; *impf* **отстрига́ть**) *сов перех* to cut off.

отстро́|ить (-ю, -ишь; *impf* **отстра́ивать**) *сов перех* to finish building.

о́тступ (-а) *м* (*в начале строки*) indentation.

отступ|и́ть (-уплю́, -у́пишь; *impf* **отступа́ть**) *сов неперех* to step back; (*ВОЕН*) to retreat; (*перен: перед трудностями, перед опасностью*) to give up; (*морозы, холода*) to abate; **отступа́ть** (~ *perf*) **наза́д** to step back; **он ~упи́л на 2 ша́га** he took 2 steps back; **отступа́ть** (~ *perf*) **от свои́х взгля́дов** to retreat from one's beliefs; **отступа́ть** (~ *perf*) **от те́мы** to digress

▶ **отступи́ться** (*impf* **отступа́ться**) *сов возв*: ~**ся от** +*gen* (*от взглядов, от требований итп*) to abandon.

отступле́ни|е (-я) *ср* (*также ВОЕН*) retreat; (*от темы*) digression.

отступлю́(сь) *сов см* **отступи́ть(ся)**.

отсту́пник (-а) *м* apostate.

отсту́пниц|а (-ы) *ж см* **отсту́пник**.

отсту́пничеств|о (-а) *ср* apostasy.

отступя́ *нареч* away, off; **немно́го от** +*gen* away from.

отсу́тстви|е (-я) *ср* (*человека*) absence; (*денег, вкуса*) lack; **в ~** +*gen* in the absence of.

отсу́тств|овать (-ую) *несов неперех* (*в классе итп*) to be absent; (*желание, аппетит*) to be lacking.

отсу́тствующ|ий (-ая, -ее, -ие) *прил* (*взгляд, вид*) absent ♦ (-его: *decl like adj*) *м* absentee.

отсчёт (-а) *м* (*шагов, минут*) calculation; ~ **вре́мени** time-keeping.

отсчита́|ть (-ю; *impf* **отсчи́тывать**) *сов перех* (*шаги, минуты*) to count; (*деньги*) to count out.

отсыла́|ть (-ю) *несов от* **отосла́ть**.

отсы́лк|а (-и) *ж* cross-reference.

отсы́п|ать (-лю, -лешь; *impf* **отсыпа́ть**) *сов перех* (+*gen*) to pour off; **отсыпа́ть** (~ *perf*) **кому́-н чего́-н** to give sb sth.

отсыпа́ться (-юсь; *несов от* **отоспа́ться**.

отсы́плю *сов см* **отсы́пать**.

отсыре́|ть (-ю; *impf* **отсырева́ть**) *сов неперех* to get damp.

отсыха́|ть (*3sg* -ет, *3pl* -ют) *несов от* **отсо́хнуть**.

отсю́да *нареч* from here; ~ **мо́жно заключи́ть, что ...** from this we can conclude that ....

отся́ду *итп сов см* **отсе́сть.**

Отта́в|**а** (**-ы**) *ж* Ottawa.

отта́ива|**ть** (**-ю**) *несов от* **отта́ять.**

отта́лкива|**ть(ся)** (**-ю(сь)**) *несов от* **оттолкну́ть(ся).**

отта́лкивающий (**-ая, -ее, -ие**) *прил* repellent.

отт|**ащи́ть** (**-ащу́, -а́щишь;** *impf* **отта́скивать**) *сов перех*: ~ (**от** +*gen*) (**от огня́, от окна́**) to drag away (from); (*в сторону, назад*) to drag.

отта́|**ять** (**-ю;** *impf* **отта́ивать**) *сов непepex* (*земля́*) to thaw; (*мясо, рыба*) to thaw out; (*перен: человек*) to soften ◆ *перех* (*разморо́зить*) to defrost.

оттен|**и́ть** (**-ю́, -и́шь;** *impf* **оттеня́ть**) *сов перех* (*рисунок, контур*) to shade in; (*перен: главное, подробности*) to highlight.

отте́н|**ок** (**-ка**) *м* (*также перен*) shade.

оттеня́|**ть** (**-ю**) *несов от* **оттени́ть.**

о́ттепель (**-и**) *ж* thaw; (*полит*) the Thaw (*the period of political liberalization*).

отт|**ере́ть** (**-ру́, -рёшь;** *pt* **-тёр, -тёрла, -тёрло,** *impf* **оттира́ть**) *сов перех* (*грязь, пятно́*) to rub out; (*щёки, ру́ки*) to rub.

оттесн|**и́ть** (**-ю́, -и́шь;** *impf* **оттесня́ть**) *сов перех* to drive back.

оттира́|**ть** (**-ю**) *несов от* **оттере́ть.**

о́ттиск (**-а**) *м* (*ступни, ладо́ни*) impression; (*рисунка, гравюры*) print; (*также*: **корректу́рный** ~) proof; (*статьи́*) offprint.

оттого́ *нареч* that is why; ~ **что** because.

оттолкн|**у́ть** (**-у́, -ёшь;** *impf* **отта́лкивать**) *сов перех* to push away; (*перен: друзе́й*) to shun

▶ **оттолкну́ться** (*impf* **отта́лкиваться**) *сов возв*: ~**ся от** +*gen* (*от бе́рега*) to push o.s. away *или* back from; (*перен: от како́го-н положе́ния, от да́нных*) to take as one's starting point.

оттопы́ренный *прил* (*карма́ны*) bulging; (*губа́*) pouting; (*у́ши*) protruding.

оттопы́р|**иться** (*3sg* **-ится,** *3pl* **-ятся,** *impf* **оттопы́риваться**) *сов возв* to stick out; (*карма́н*) to bulge.

отто́рг|**нуть** (**-у, -ешь;** *impf* **оттерга́ть**) *сов перех* (*МЕД: о́рган, ткань*) to reject; (*зе́мли, иму́щество*) to seize.

отторже́ни|**е** (**-я**) *ср* (*см глаг*) rejection; seizure.

отту́да *нареч* from there.

оття́гива|**ть** (**-ю**) *несов от* **оттяну́ть.**

отт|**я́жка** (**-ки;** *gen pl* **-ок**) *ж* delay.

отт|**яну́ть** (**-яну́, -я́нешь;** *impf* **оття́гивать**) *сов перех* to pull back; (*разг: челове́ка*) to pull away; (*карма́н*) to stretch; (*разг: выполне́ние, реше́ние*) to delay; **оття́гивать** (~ *impf*) **вре́мя** to play for time.

отупе́лый *прил* glazed, dazed.

отупе́ни|**е** (**-я**) *ср* stupor.

отупе́|**ть** (**-ю**) *сов от* **тупе́ть.**

отутю́ж|**ить** (**-у, -ишь**) *сов от* **утюжить.**

отуч|**и́ть** (**-учу́, -у́чишь;** *impf* **отуча́ть**) *сов перех*: ~ **от** +*gen* (*от куре́ния, от буты́лки*) to wean sb off; (+*infin*: *ворова́ть, врать*) to teach sb not to do

▶ **отучи́ться** (*impf* **отуча́ться**) *сов возв* (+*infin*) to get out of the habit of doing; **отуча́ться** (~**ся** *perf*) **от плохи́х привы́чек** to get out of bad habits.

отфильтр|**ова́ть** (**-у́ю;** *impf* **отфильтро́вывать**) *сов перех* to filter off.

отфутбо́л|**ить** (**-ю, -ишь;** *impf* **отфутбо́ливать**) *сов перех* (*разг*): ~ **кого́-н** to send sb packing.

отха́ркивающий (**-ая, -ее, -ие**) *прил* (*МЕД*): ~**ее сре́дство** expectorant.

отхв|**ати́ть** (**-ачу́, -а́тишь;** *impf* **охва́тывать**) *сов перех* (*разг: отруби́ть*) to cut off; (*: доста́ть*) to get.

отхлебн|**у́ть** (**-у́, -ёшь;** *impf* **отхлёбывать**) *сов перех* (*разг*) to take a swig of.

отхлеста́|**ть** (**-ю;** *impf* **отхлёстывать**) *сов перех* (*разг*): ~ **кого́-н** to give sb a hiding.

отхлы́н|**уть** (*3sg* **-ет,** *3pl* **-ут**) *сов непepex* (*во́лны*) to roll back; (*кровь от лица́*) to drain; (*перен: толпа́*) to draw back.

отхо́д (**-а**) *м* departure; (*ВОЕН*) withdrawal; ~ **от тради́ций/действи́тельности** departure from tradition/reality; *см также* **отхо́ды.**

отхо|**ди́ть** (**-ожу́, -о́дишь**) *несов от* **отойти́.**

отхо́дн|**ая** (**-ой;** *decl like adj*) *ж* (*РЕЛ*) prayer for the dying.

отхо́дчив|**ый** (**-, -а, -о**) *прил*: **он** ~ he doesn't stay angry for long.

отхо́ды (**-ов**) *мн* (*промы́шленности итп*) waste *мн*.

отхожу́ *несов см* **отходи́ть.**

отца́ *итп сущ см* **оте́ц.**

отцве|**сти́** (**-ту́, -тёшь;** *impf* **отцвета́ть**) *сов непepex* to finish blossoming.

отце|**ди́ть** (**-жу́, -дишь;** *impf* **отце́живать**) *сов перех* to strain off.

отцеп|**и́ть** (**-еплю́, -е́пишь;** *impf* **отцепля́ть**) *сов перех* (*ваго́н, парово́з*) to uncouple; (*колю́чку*) to unsnag

▶ **отцепи́ться** (*impf* **отцепля́ться**) *сов возв* (*ваго́н, парово́з*) to come uncoupled; ~**епи́сь от меня́!** (*разг*) leave me alone!

отцо́вский (**-ая, -ое, -ие**) *прил* father's; (*перен*) paternal, fatherly.

отцо́вств|**о** (**-а**) *ср* fatherhood.

отча́ива|**ться** (**-юсь**) *несов от* **отча́яться.**

отча́л|**ить** (**-ю, -ишь;** *impf* **отча́ливать**) *сов непepex* to set sail.

отча́сти *нареч* partially.

отча́яни|**е** (**-я**) *ср* despair.

отча́янно *нареч* (*пыта́ться*) desperately; (*крича́ть*) in despair; (*спо́рить*) terribly.

отча́янн|**ый** (**-, -на, -но**) *прил* desperate; (*сме́лый*) daring; (*разг: врун, болту́н итп*) terrible.

отча́|**яться** (**-юсь;** *impf* **отча́иваться**) *сов возв*: ~ (+*infin*) to despair (of doing).

отчего́ *нареч* (*почему*) why ◆ *союз* (*всле́дствие чего́*) which is why; ~ **же?** (*разг*) what for?

отчего́-либо *нареч* = **отчего́-нибудь.**

отчего́-нибудь *нареч* for any reason.

отчего́-то *нареч* for some reason.

отчека́н|ить (-ю, -ишь; *impf* **отчека́нивать**) *сов перех* (*монету*) to mint; (*изделие*) to emboss; (*перен: слово*) to pronounce distinctly; **отчека́нивать** (~ *perf*) **отве́т** to answer distinctly.

о́тчеств|о (-а) *ср* patronymic.

отчёт (-а) *м* account; **фина́нсовый** ~ financial report; **годово́й** ~ annual report; **отдава́ть** (**отда́ть** *perf*) **себе́** ~ **в чём-н** to realize sth.

отчётлив|ый (-, -а, -о) *прил* (*звук, отпеча́ток*) distinct; (*объясне́ние, повествова́ние*) clear.

отчётность (-и) *ж* accountability ◆ *собир* (*фина́нсовая, администрати́вная*) records *мн*.

отчётный *прил* (*собра́ние*) review *опред*; (*год*) current; ~ **докла́д** report; **отчётный пери́од** accounting period.

отчи́зн|а (-ы) *ж* mother country.

о́тчий (-ая, -ее, -ие) *прил* (*ла́ска, сове́т*) fatherly; ~ **дом** one's father's house.

о́тчим (-а) *м* stepfather.

отчисле́ни|е (-я) *ср* (*рабо́тника*) dismissal; (*студе́нта*) expulsion; (*обычно мн: на строи́тельство*) allocation *ед*; (: *де́нежные: удержа́ние*) deduction; (: *выделе́ние*) assignment.

отчи́сл|ить (-ю, -ишь; *impf* **отчисля́ть**) *сов перех* (*рабо́тника*) to dismiss; (*студе́нта*) to expel; (*де́ньги: удержа́ть*) to deduct; (: *вы́делить*) to assign

▶ **отчи́слиться** (*impf* **отчисля́ться**) *сов возв*: ~**ся** (**из** +*gen*) to leave.

отчи́|стить (-щу, -стишь; *impf* **отчища́ть**) *сов перех* (*грязь*) to clean off; (*пятно́*) to remove; (*пальто́, ту́фли*) to clean

▶ **отчи́ститься** (*impf* **отчища́ться**) *сов возв* (*грязь*) to come off; (*пятно́*) to come out; (*пальто́, ту́фли*) to come clean.

отчита́|ть (-ю; *impf* **отчи́тывать**) *сов перех* (*ребёнка*) to tell off

▶ **отчита́ться** (*impf* **отчи́тываться**) *сов возв* to report; **отчи́тываться** (~**ся** *perf*) **пе́ред** +*instr*/**о** +*prp* to report to/on.

отчища́|ть(ся) (-ю(сь)) *несов от* **отчи́стить(ся)**.

отчи́щу(сь) *сов см* **отчи́стить(ся)**.

отчуд|и́ть (-и́шь) *сов перех* (*разг*): **он сего́дня тако́е** ~**и́л!** he did something really weird today!

отчужда́|ть (-ю) *несов перех* (*также ЮР*) to alienate.

отчужде́ни|е (-я) *ср* (*прекраще́ние отноше́ний*) estrangement; (*ЮР*) alienation.

отчуждённость (-и) *ж* alienation.

отчуждённ|ый (-, -на, -но) *прил* (*взгляд, вид*) indifferent.

отшатн|у́ться (-у́сь, -ёшься; *impf* **отша́тываться**) *сов возв* (*от уда́ра*) to recoil;

(*наза́д, в сто́рону*) to move; **отша́тываться** (~ *perf*) **от** +*gen* (*разг: от друзе́й итп*) to ditch.

отшвырн|у́ть (-у́, -ёшь; *impf* **отшвы́ривать**) *сов перех* (*разг: предме́т*) to toss away; (: *челове́ка*) to shove aside.

отше́льник (-а) *м* (*также перен*) hermit.

отше́льниц|а (-ы) *ж см* **отше́льник**.

отши́б (-а) *м*: **на** ~**е** (*разг: жить*) alone, on one's tod (*BRIT*); (*стоя́ть: дом итп*) on its own.

отшиб|и́ть (-у́, -ёшь; *impf* **отшиба́ть**) *сов перех* (*разг: ру́ку, но́гу*) to hurt; **у меня́ па́мять отши́бло** (*разг*) my memory's gone.

отшлёпа|ть (-ю; *impf* **отшлёпывать**) *сов перех* (*разг*): ~ **кого́-н** (*ребёнка*) to give sb a walloping.

отшлиф|ова́ть (-у́ю; *impf* **отшлифо́вывать**) *сов перех* (*дета́ль, пове́рхность*) to grind; (*расска́з, пье́су*) to put the finishing touches to.

отштамп|ова́ть (-у́ю) *сов от* **штампова́ть**.

отштукату́р|ить (-ю, -ишь) *сов от* **штукату́рить**.

отшу|ти́ться (-чу́сь, -́тишься; *impf* **отшу́чиваться**) *сов возв* to reply with a joke.

отщеп|и́ть (-лю́, -ишь; *impf* **отщепля́ть**) *сов перех* (*кусо́чек де́рева итп*) to chip off

▶ **отщепи́ться** (*impf* **отщепля́ться**) *сов возв* (*кусо́чек де́рева итп*) to split off.

отъеда́|ться (-юсь) *несов от* **отъе́сться**.

отъе́дешь *итп сов см* **отъе́хать**.

отъеди́мся *итп сов см* **отъе́сться**.

отъе́ду *итп сов см* **отъе́хать**.

отъедя́тся *сов см* **отъе́сться**.

отъе́зд (-а) *м* departure; **быть** (*impf*) **в** ~**е** to be away.

отъезжа́|ть (-ю) *несов от* **отъе́хать**.

отъе́сться (*как* есть; *см* Table 15; *impf* **отъеда́ться**) *сов возв* (*по́сле го́лода*) to eat one's fill; (*потолсте́ть*) to grow fat.

отъе́хать (*как* е́хать; *см* Table 19; *impf* **отъезжа́ть**) *сов неперех* to travel; **отъезжа́ть** (~ *perf*) **от** +*gen* to move away from.

отъе́шься *сов см* **отъе́сться**.

отъя́вленный *прил* (*моше́нник итп*) absolute.

отыгра́|ть (-ю; *impf* **оты́грывать**) *сов перех* to win back

▶ **отыгра́ться** (*impf* **оты́грываться**) *сов возв* (*в ка́рты, в ша́хматы*) to win again; (*перен*) to get one's own back.

отыска́|ть (-щу́, -́щешь; *impf* **оты́скивать**) *сов перех* to hunt out; (*КОМП*) to retrieve

▶ **отыска́ться** (*impf* **оты́скиваться**) *сов возв* to turn up.

отяго|ти́ть (-щу́, -ти́шь; *impf* **отягоща́ть**) *сов перех*: ~ **кого́-н чем-н** to burden sb with sth.

отягча́ющий (-ая, -ее, -ие) *прил*: ~**ие обстоя́тельства** (*ЮР*) aggravating circumstances.

отягч|и́ть (-у́, -и́шь; *impf* **отягча́ть**) *сов перех* (вину, положение) to aggravate.

отяжеле́|ть (-ю) *сов от* **тяжеле́ть**.

о́фис (-а) *м* office.

офице́р (-а) *м* (ВОЕН) officer; (разг: ШАХМАТЫ) bishop.

офице́рск|ий (-ая, -ое, -ие) *прил* (звание, форма) officer's; (комната, столовая) officers'.

офице́рств|о (-а) *ср собир* officers *мн*.

официа́льный (-ен, -ьна, -ьно) *прил* official; **официа́льное лицо́** official.

официа́нт (-а) *м* waiter.

официа́нт|ка (-ки; *gen pl* -ок) *ж* waitress.

официо́зный (-ен, -на, -но) *прил*: ~**ная газе́та** *newspaper which supports the government*.

оформи́тел|ь (-я) *м*: ~ **интерье́ра/спекта́кля** interior/set designer; ~ **витри́ны** window-dresser.

оформи́тельниц|а (-ы) *ж см* **оформи́тель**.

офо́рм|ить (-лю, -ишь; *impf* **оформля́ть**) *сов перех* (книгу) to design the layout of; (витрину) to dress; (спектакль) to design the sets for; (документы, договор) to draw up; **оформля́ть** (~ *perf*) **кого́-н на рабо́ту** (+*instr*) to take sb on (as)

▸ **офо́рмиться** (*impf* **оформля́ться**) *сов возв* (мнение, взгляды) to form; **оформля́ться** (~*ся perf*) **на рабо́ту** (+*instr*) to be taken on (as).

оформле́ни|е (-я) *ср* design; (документов, договора) drawing up; (на работу) taking on; **музыка́льное** ~ music.

оформлю́(сь) *сов см* **офо́рмить(ся)**.

оформля́|ть(ся) (-ю(сь)) *несов от* **офо́рмить(ся)**.

офо́рт (-а) *м* etching.

офсе́т (-а) *м* offset (process).

офтальмо́лог (-а) *м* ophthalmologist.

ох *межд* oh.

оха́ива|ть (-ю) *несов от* **оха́ять**.

охаме́|ть (-ю) *сов от* **хаме́ть**.

оха́п|ка (-ки; *gen pl* -ок) *ж* armful; **схвати́ть** (*perf*) **что-н в** ~**ку** to grab sth in one's arms.

охарактеризова́ть (-у́ю) *сов от* **характеризова́ть**.

о́ха|ть (-ю) *несов неперех* (от боли) to groan; (от сожаления, печали) to sigh.

оха́|ять (-ю; *impf* **оха́ивать**) *сов перех* (разг) to slate (BRIT), to slag (off).

охвати́ть (-ачу́, -а́тишь; *impf* **охва́тывать**) *сов перех* (подлеж: пламя, чувства, темнота) to engulf; (подписчиков, население) to cover; (ВОЕН) to envelop; **охва́тывать** (~ *perf*) **что-н чем-н** (руками, лентой) to put sth round sth; **охва́тывать** (~ *perf*) **взгля́дом** to take in; **охва́тывать** (~ *perf*) **умо́м** to grasp.

охладе́|ть (-ю; *impf* **охладева́ть**) *сов неперех* (отношения) to cool; **охладева́ть** (~ *perf*) **к** +*dat* (к мужу, к невесте) to grow cool towards; (к футболу, к сладкому) to go off.

охла|ди́ть (-жу́, -ди́шь; *impf* **охлажда́ть**) *сов перех* (воду, чувства) to cool; (забияку) to cool

down

▸ **охлади́ться** (*impf* **охлажда́ться**) *сов возв* (печка, вода) to cool down; (человек: водой) to cool off.

охлажде́ни|е (-я) *ср* (также перен) cooling.

охлажу́(сь) *сов см* **охлади́ть(ся)**.

охламо́н (-а) *м* (разг: пренебр) loafer.

охмур|и́ть (-ю́, -и́шь; *impf* **охмуря́ть**) *сов перех* (разг) to lead on.

о́хн|уть (-у, -ешь) *сов неперех* to gasp.

охо́т|а (-ы) *ж* hunt; (желание): ~ **к чему́-н**/+*infin* desire for sth/to do; ~ **на лис** fox hunting (*to kill*); ~ **за лисо́й** fox hunting (*to catch*); **ходи́ть/идти́** (**пойти́** *perf*) **на** ~**у** to go hunting; ~ **за престу́пником/уби́йцей** the hunt for a criminal/murderer; **мне** ~ **посмотре́ть э́ту переда́чу** (разг) I fancy watching that programme; **что Вам за** ~ **спо́рить с ней?** (разг) what do you get out of arguing with her?; ~ **тебе́ спо́рить!** (разг) do you really have to argue?

охо́т|иться (-чусь, -тишься) *несов возв*: ~ **на** +*acc* to hunt (*to kill*); ~ (*impf*) **за** +*instr* to hunt (*to catch*); (перен: разг) to hunt for.

охо́тник (-а) *м* hunter; ~ +*infin* volunteer to do; **быть** (*impf*) **больши́м** ~**ом до** +*gen* (разг: до женщин, сладкого) to be crazy about.

охо́тничий (-ья, -ье, -ьи) *прил* hunting *опред*.

охо́тно *нареч* gladly.

охо́чусь *несов см* **охо́титься**.

о́хр|а (-ы) *ж* ochre, ocher (*US*).

охра́н|а (-ы) *ж* (защита: помещения, президента) security; (группа людей: президента) bodyguard; (: помещения) guard; (здоровья, растений, животных) protection; **под** ~**ой зако́на** protected by law; **охра́на поря́дка** maintenance of law and order; **охра́на приро́ды** nature conservation; **охра́на труда́** health and safety regulations *мн*.

охране́ни|е (-я) *ср* (также ВОЕН) protection.

охра́нник (-а) *м* guard.

охра́нниц|а (-ы) *ж см* **охра́нник**.

охра́нный *прил* (зона, территория) guarded; ~**ая ро́та** security company.

охран|я́ть (-ю) *несов перех* (помещение, президента) to guard; (здоровье) to look after; (природу) to protect.

охри́плый *прил* (разг: голос, крик) hoarse.

охри́пн|уть (-у, -ешь) *сов от* **хри́пнуть**.

охри́пший (-ая, -ее, -ие) *прил* hoarse.

охроме́|ть (-ю) *сов неперех* to go lame.

оцара́па|ть(ся) (-ю(сь)) *сов от* **цара́пать(ся)**.

оцен|и́ть (-ю́, -е́нишь; *impf* **оце́нивать**) *сов перех* (определить цену) to value; (определить уровень) to assess; (признать достоинства) to appreciate; **оце́нивать** (~ *perf*) **что-н по досто́инству** to appreciate the true value of sth.

оце́н|ка (-ки; *gen pl* -ок) *ж* (вещи) valuation; (работника, поступка) assessment; (отметка) mark.

оце́нщик (-а) м valuer.

оцепене́лый прил (взгляд, человек) stunned; оцепене́лое состоя́ние stupor.

оцепене́ни|е (-я) ср numbness; (био) dormancy.

оцепене́|ть (-ю) сов от цепене́ть.

оцеп|и́ть (-еплю́, -е́пишь; impf оцепля́ть) сов перех to cordon off.

оцепле́ни|е (-я) ср (действие) cordoning off; (группа) cordon.

оцеплю́ сов см оцепи́ть.

оцепля́|ть (-ю) несов от оцепи́ть.

оцинк|ова́ть (-у́ю; impf оцинко́вывать) сов перех (тех) to galvanize.

оча́г (-а́) м hearth; (перен: заболевания) source; (: культуры) heart; ~ войны́ flash point; дома́шний ~ hearth and home.

очарова́ни|е (-я) ср charm.

очарова́тельный (-ен, -ьна, -ьно) прил charming.

очар|ова́ть (-у́ю; impf очаро́вывать) сов перех to charm.

очеви́ден прил см очеви́дный.

очеви́д|ец (-ца) м eyewitness.

очеви́дно нареч, част obviously ♦ как сказ: ~, что он винова́т it's obvious that he is guilty ♦ вводн сл: ~, он не придёт apparently he's not coming; э́то соверше́нно ~! it is perfectly obvious!; он винова́т? – ~! is he guilty? – obviously!

очеви́дный (-ен, -но, -на) прил (факт, истина) plain; (желание, намерение) obvious.

очеви́дца итп сущ см очеви́дец.

о́чень нареч (+adv, +adj) very; (+vb) very much; ~ удо́бный/удо́бно very comfortable/comfortably; мы ~ хоти́м, что́бы она́ пришла́ we would very much like her to come.

очередно́й прил next; (ближайший: задача) immediate; (: номер газеты) latest; (следующий по порядку: собрание, отпуск) regular; (повторяющийся: ссора, глупость) usual.

о́черед|ь (-и) ж (порядок) order; (место в порядке) turn; (группа людей) queue (BRIT), line (US); (тоннеля, завода итп) section; в пе́рвую ~ in the first instance; в поря́дке ~и when one's turn comes; в свою́ ~ in turn; ~ за ни́ми it is their turn; по ~и in turn; стоя́ть (impf) на ~и на +acc (на квартиру итп) to be on the waiting list for; пулемётная ~ (ВОЕН) burst of automatic rifle fire; на ~и стои́т вопро́с/зада́ча this is the next question/task.

о́черк (-а) м (литературный) essay; (газетный) sketch.

очерн|и́ть (-ю́, -и́шь) сов от черни́ть.

очерств|е́ть (-е́ю) сов от черстве́ть.

очерта́ни|е (-я) ср (обычно мн) outline ед.

оч|ерти́ть (-ерчу́, -е́ртишь; impf оче́рчивать) сов перех to outline.

оче́чник (-а) м spectacle case.

оч|ини́ть (-иню́, -и́нишь; impf очиня́ть) сов перех to sharpen.

очисти́тельный прил purifying, purification опред.

очи́|стить (-щу, -стишь; impf очища́ть) сов перех to clean; (газ, во́ду) to purify; (со́весть, го́род, кварти́ру) to clear; (ду́шу) to cleanse; (разг: обокра́сть: дом итп) to clean out; (impf очища́ть или чи́стить; я́блоко, карто́шку) to peel; (ры́бу) to clean

► очи́ститься (impf очища́ться) сов возв (газ, во́да) to be purified; (перен: со́весть) to be cleared; (: душа́) to be cleansed; не́бо ~стилось от туч the sky cleared.

очи́стк|а (-и) ж purification; для ~и со́вести to ease one's conscience; см также очи́стки.

очи́стк|и (-ов) мн peelings мн.

очистн|о́й прил: ~ые сооруже́ния purification plant ед.

очища́|ть(ся) (-ю(сь)) несов от очи́стить(ся).

очи́щенный прил (хим) purified; (я́блоко, карто́шка) peeled; (ры́ба) cleaned.

очищу́(сь) сов см очи́стить(ся).

очк|и́ (-о́в) мн (для чте́ния) glasses мн, spectacles мн; (для пла́вания) goggles мн; со́лнечные ~ sunglasses; защи́тные ~ safety specs.

очк|о́ (-а́) ср (СПОРТ) point; (КАРТЫ) pip; дать (perf) сто ~в вперёд to be miles better.

очковтира́тель (-я) м deceiver.

очковтира́тельств|о (-а) ср deception.

очко́в|ый прил: ~ая змея́ cobra.

очну́|ться (-у́сь, -ёшься) сов возв (по́сле сна) to wake up; (по́сле обморока) to come to; (по́сле испуга) to steady o.s.

о́чный прил (обучение, институт итп) with direct contact between students and teachers; о́чная ста́вка (ЮР) confrontation.

очуме́|ть (-ю) сов неперех (разг) to go off one's head.

очу|ти́ться (2sg -ти́шься, 3sg -ти́тся) сов возв to find o.s.

ошара́ш|ить (-у, -ишь; impf ошара́шивать) сов перех (разг: вопросом, поведением) to dumbfound.

оше́йник (-а) м collar.

ошеломи́тельный (-ен, -ьна, -ьно) прил stunning.

ошелом|и́ть (-лю́, -и́шь; impf ошеломля́ть) сов перех to stun.

ошеломля́ющий (-ая, -ее, -ие; -, -а, -е) прил = ошеломи́тельный.

ош|иби́ться (-ибу́сь, -ибёшься; pt -и́бся, -и́блась, -и́блось, impf ошиба́ться) сов возв to make a mistake; ошиба́ться (~ perf) в ком-н to misjudge sb.

оши́бк|а (-и; gen pl -ок) ж mistake, error; (КОМП)

bug; **по ~ке** by mistake.

оши́боч|ный (-ен, -на, -но) *прил (мнение, представление)* mistaken, erroneous; *(суждение, вывод)* wrong.

ошива́|ться (-юсь) *несов возв (разг: пренебр)* to hang about.

ошпа́р|ить (-ю, -ишь; *impf* **ошпа́ривать**) *сов перех (разг: ногу, палец, помидор)* to scald

► **ошпа́риться** (*impf* **ошпа́риваться**) *сов возв (разг)* to scald o.s.

оштрафова́ть (-у́ю) *сов от* **штрафова́ть**.

оштукату́р|ить (-ю, -ишь) *сов от* **штукату́рить**.

ощен|и́ться (*3sg* -и́тся, *3pl* -я́тся) *сов от* **щени́ться**.

ощети́нива|ться (*3sg* -ется, *3pl* -ются) *несов =* **щети́ниться**.

ощети́н|иться (*3sg* -ится, *3pl* -ятся) *сов от* **щети́ниться**.

ощипа́|ть (-иплю́, -и́плешь) *сов от* **щипа́ть**.

ощи́пыва|ть (-ю) *несов перех =* **щипа́ть**.

ощу́па|ть (-ю; *impf* **ощу́пывать**) *сов перех (стол)* to feel for; *(лицо)* to feel.

о́щуп|ь (-и) *ж:* **на ~** by touch; **пробира́ться** (*impf*) **на ~** to grope one's way through.

о́щупью *нареч* by touch; *(перен)* blindly; **пробира́ться** (*impf*) ~ to grope one's way through.

ощути́м|ый (-, -а, -о) *прил (потепление, запах)* noticeable; *(успех, расходы)* appreciable.

ощути́тельный (-ен, -ьна, -ьно) *прил =* **ощути́мый**.

ощу|ти́ть (-щу́, -ти́шь; *impf* **ощуща́ть**) *сов перех (запах)* to notice; *(радость, желание, боль)* to feel.

ощуща́|ть (-ю) *несов от* **ощути́ть**.

ощуще́ни|е (-я) *ср (прикосновения, запаха)* sense; *(радости, боли)* feeling.

ОЭСР *ж сокр* (= Организа́ция экономи́ческого сотру́дничества и разви́тия) OECD (= *Organization for Economic Cooperation and Development*).

оягн|и́ться (*3sg* -и́тся, *3pl* -я́тся) *сов от* **ягни́ться**.

~ П, п ~

П, п *сущ нескл (буква)* the 16th letter of the Russian alphabet.

п. *сокр* (= **пара́граф**) par. (= *paragraph*); = **посёлок**.

па *ср нескл* (dance) step.

п.а. *сокр* (= **почто́вый а́дрес**) postal address.

павиа́н (-а) *м* baboon.

павильо́н (-а) *м* pavilion; *(кино)* studio.

павли́н (-а) *м* peacock.

па́водок (-ка) *м* flood.

па́губный (-ен, -на, -но) *прил (последствия)* ruinous; *(влияние, привычка)* pernicious.

па́даль (-и) *ж собир* carrion.

па́дать (-ю; *perf* **упа́сть** *или* **пасть**) *несов неперех* to fall; *(настроение)* to sink; *(дисциплина, нравы)* to decline; *(умирать: животное)* to die; *(no perf; снег)* to fall; ~ **(упа́сть** *perf***) на** +*acc (пожиться: тень)* to fall on; ~ **(пасть** *perf***) на** +*acc (подозрение)* to fall on; *(ответственность)* to fall to *или* on; ~ **(упа́сть** *perf***) ду́хом** to lose heart; **у неё упа́ло настрое́ние** her spirits sank; ~ **(упа́сть** *perf***) в чьих-н глаза́х** to fall in sb's estimation; ~ **(упа́сть** *perf***) в о́бморок** to faint.

паде́ж (-а́) *м (линг)* case.

паде́жный *прил (линг)* case *опред*.

Па-де-Кале́ *м нескл* Pas de Calais.

паде́ние (-я) *ср (также перен)* fall; *(нравов, дисциплины)* decline.

па́дкий (-кая, -кое, -кие; -ок, -ка, -ко) *прил:* ~ **на** +*acc* greedy for.

паду́ *итп сов см* **пасть**.

па́дчерица (-ы) *ж* stepdaughter.

па́дший (-ая, -ее, -ие) *прил* fallen.

паево́й *прил (экон)* share *опред;* **на** ~**ых нача́лах** on a shareholder basis.

паёк (-йка́) *м* ration; **сухо́й** ~ dry ration.

паж (-а́) *м* page(boy).

ПАЗ *м сокр* = **Па́вловский авто́бусный заво́д;** *(автобус) vehicle manufactured at the Pavlovsk car factory.*

паз (-а; *loc sg* -у́, *nom pl* -ы́) *м (ТЕХ)* groove.

па́зуха (-и) *ж* bosom; **держа́ть** *(impf)* **ка́мень за** ~**ой на кого́-н** to bear a grudge against sb, bear sb a grudge; **жить** *(impf)* **как у Христа́ за** ~**ой** *(разг)* to be without a care in the world.

пай (-я; *nom pl* -й) *м (ЭКОН)* share; **на** ~**я́х** jointly.

пайка́ *итп сущ см* **паёк**.

па́йщик (-а) *м* shareholder.

пакга́уз (-а) *м* warehouse.

паке́т (-а) *м (бумажный свёрток, комп)* package; *(мешок)* (paper *или* plastic) bag; *(конверт)* official envelope *(containing important or secret documents)*; *(КОММ):* **(контро́льный)** ~ **а́кций** (controlling) shareholding; ~ **програ́мм** *(КОМП)* software package; ~ **прикладны́х програ́мм** *(КОМП)* applications package.

паке́тный *прил:* ~**ая обрабо́тка** *(КОМП)* batch processing.

Пакиста́н (-а) *м* Pakistan.

пакиста́нец (-ца) *м* Pakistani.

пакиста́нка (-ки; *gen pl* -ок) *ж см* **пакиста́нец**.

пакиста́нский (-ая, -ое, -ие) *прил* Pakistani.

пакиста́нца *сущ см* **пакиста́нец**.

пакова́ть (-ую; *perf* **запакова́ть** *или* **упакова́ть**) *несов перех* to pack.

па́костен *прил см* **па́костный**.

па́костить (-щу, -стишь; *perf* **запа́костить**) *несов перех (разг)* to soil, dirty ◆ *(perf* **напа́костить**) *неперех:* ~ **(кому́-н)** to play a dirty trick (on sb).

па́костный (-ен, -на, -но) *прил (разг)* vile, nasty.

па́кощу *несов см* **па́костить**.

пакт (-а) *м* pact.

ПАЛ *сокр* PAL (= *phase alternation line*).

пала́с (-а) *м double-sided woven rug.*

пала́та (-ы) *ж (в больнице)* ward; *(полит)* chamber, house; **ве́рхняя/ни́жняя** ~ *(полит)* Upper/Lower Chamber; ~ **о́бщин/ло́рдов** House of Commons/Lords; **Кни́жная** ~ Book Chamber *(Bibliographical centre in Moscow)*; **Торго́вая** ~ Chamber of Commerce.

пала́тка (-ки; *gen pl* -ок) *ж (туристическая)* tent; *(ларёк)* stall.

пала́ч (-а́) *м* executioner.

Палести́на (-ы) *ж* Palestine.

палести́нский (-ая, -ое, -ие) *прил* Palestinian.

па́лец (-ьца) *м (руки)* finger; *(ноги)* toe; **безымя́нный** ~ fourth *или* ring finger; **большо́й** ~ *(руки)* thumb; *(ноги)* big toe;

сре́дний ~ middle finger; указа́тельный ~ index finger; знать *(impf)* что-н как свои́ пять ~ьцев to know sth like the back of one's hand; он ~ о ~ не уда́рил, он па́льцем не шевельну́л he didn't lift a finger; смотре́ть *(impf)* сквозь ~ьцы на что-н to shut one's eyes to sth.

палиса́дник (-а) *м* (small) front garden (*BRIT*) *или* yard (*US*).

пали́тр|а (-ы) *ж (также перен)* palette.

пали́|ть (-ю́, -и́шь; *perf* опали́ть) *несов перех (волосы)* to singe; (*perf* спали́ть; *подлеж: солнце)* to scorch; (*perf* вы́палить; *разг: стреля́ть)* to fire.

па́л|ка (-ки; *gen pl* -ок) *ж* stick; лы́жные ~ки ski poles; де́лать [сде́лать *perf*] что-н из-под ~ки *(разг)* to be bludgeoned into doing sth; э́то ~ о двух конца́х it cuts both ways; ~ки в колёса вставля́ть *(impf)* кому́-н to put a spoke in sb's wheel.

пало́мник (-а) *м* pilgrim.

пало́мничеств|о (-а) *ср* pilgrimage.

па́лоч|ка (-ки; *gen pl* -ек) *ж уменьш от* па́лка; *(мед)* bacillus *(мн* bacilli); дирижёрская ~ (conductor's) baton; волше́бная ~ magic wand.

па́лочн|ый *прил*: ~ая дисципли́на *(перен)* heavy-handed discipline.

па́луб|а (-ы) *ж (мор)* deck.

па́льм|а (-ы) *ж* palm (tree).

пальто́ *ср нескл* overcoat.

па́льца *итп сущ см* па́лец.

памфле́т (-а) *м* lampoon.

па́мятен *прил см* па́мятный.

па́мят|ка (-ки; *gen pl* -ок) *ж (туриста, отдыха́ющих)* guidelines *мн*; *(на работе)* memorandum *(мн* memoranda).

па́мятник (-а) *м* monument; *(на моги́ле)* tombstone; *(археологи́ческий)* relic; ~и старины́ ancient monuments; па́мятники пи́сьменности ancient manuscripts.

па́мятн|ый (-ен, -на, -но) *прил (незабыва́емый)* memorable; *(no short form; сде́ланный в па́мять)* commemorative.

па́мяток *сущ см* па́мятка.

па́мят|ь (-и) *ж (также комп)* memory; *(воспомина́ние)* memories *мн*; в чью-н ~, в ~ о ком-н in memory of sb; на ~ *(чита́ть стихи́)* from memory; *(подари́ть, взять)* as a memento; быть *(impf)* без ~и to be unconscious; он лю́бит её без ~и *(разг)* he is crazy about her; она́ без ~и от э́того актёра *(разг)* she's mad about that actor.

Пана́м|а (-ы) *ж* Panama.

пана́м|а (-ы) *ж* Panama (hat).

пана́мский (-ая, -ое, -ие) *прил*: П~ кана́л Panamanian Canal.

панаце́|я (-и) *ж* panacea.

па́нд|а (-ы) *ж* panda.

пандеми́|я (-и) *ж* pandemia.

пане́л|ь (-и) *ж (тротуа́р)* pavement (*BRIT*), sidewalk (*US*); *(строит)* panel; *(тех)* control panel.

панибра́тств|о (-а) *ср* familiarity.

па́ник|а (-и) *ж* panic.

паник|ова́ть (-у́ю) *несов неперех (разг)* to panic.

панихи́д|а (-ы) *ж (рел)* funeral service; гражда́нская ~ civil funeral.

пани́ческ|ий (-ая, -ое, -ие) *прил (состоя́ние, бе́гство итп)* panic-stricken; *(слу́хи)* alarming.

панно́ *ср нескл* decorative panel.

панора́м|а (-ы) *ж* panorama.

пансио́н (-а) *м (школа)* boarding school; *(по́лное содержа́ние)* (full) board and lodging.

пансиона́т (-а) *м* boarding house.

пантео́н (-а) *м* pantheon.

панте́р|а (-ы) *ж* panther.

пантоми́м|а (-ы) *ж* mime.

па́нцир|ь (-я) *м (черепа́хи)* shell; *(ры́царя)* coat of armour (*BRIT*) *или* armor (*US*).

па́п|а (-ы) *м* dad; *(также:* Ри́мский ~) the Pope.

папа́х|а (-и) *ж* papakha *(tall fur cap)*.

папа́ш|а (-и) *м (разг: па́па)* old man; (*: как обраще́ние)* grandad.

па́перт|ь (-и) *ж* church porch.

папиро́с|а (-ы) *ж type of cheap Russian cigarette with cardboard filter*.

папиро́сн|ый *прил*: ~ая бума́га *(для куре́ния)* cigarette paper; *(то́нкая бума́га)* tissue paper.

папи́рус (-а) *м* papyrus.

па́п|ка (-ки; *gen pl* -ок) *ж* folder (*BRIT*), file (*US*).

па́поротник (-а) *м* fern.

папье́-маше́ *ср нескл* papier-mâché.

пар (-а; *loc sg* -у́, *nom pl* -ы́) *м* steam; (*с -х*) fallow land; на всех ~а́х *(перен)* full steam ahead; *см также* па́ры.

па́р|а (-ы) *ж (ту́фель итп)* pair; *(супру́жеская)* couple; *(просвещ)* ≈ poor *(school mark)*; ~ слов/мину́т *(разг)* a couple of words/minutes; рабо́тать *(impf)*/игра́ть *(impf)* в ~е с кем-н to work/play with sb; э́то ~ пустяко́в *(разг)* it's child's play; они́ два сапога́ ~ *(разг)* they are as bad as each other.

Парагва́|й (-я) *м* Paraguay.

пара́граф (-а) *м* paragraph.

пара́д (-а) *м* parade; в по́лном *или* при всём ~е *(разг)* dressed up to the nines.

пара́дн|ая (-ой; *decl like adj)* ж = пара́дное.

пара́дн|ое (-ого; *decl like adj)* ср entrance.

пара́дн|ый *прил (обе́д)* formal; *(стол)* festive; *(вид)* smart (*BRIT*), stylish (*US*); *(вход, ле́стница)* front *опред*, main; пара́дный костю́м/пара́дная фо́рма full dress.

парадо́кс (-а) *м* paradox.

парадокса́льн|ый (-ен, -ьна, -ьно) *прил* paradoxical.

парази́т (-а) *м* parasite.

парализ|ова́ть (-у́ю) *(не)сов перех (также перен)* to paralyze; у́жас ~ова́л его́ he was paralyzed with fear.

парали́ч (-а́) *м* paralysis.

паралле́лен *прил см* паралле́льный.

параллéл|ь (-и) *ж (также перен)* parallel.
параллéльный (-ен, -ьна, -ьно) *прил* parallel.
парамéдик (-а) *м* paramedic.
парáметр (-а) *м (также перен)* parameter; *(комп)* default option.
паранджá (-й) *ж* yashmak.
паранóй|я (-и) *ж* paranoia.
парапéт (-а) *м* parapet.
парапсихолóги|я (-и) *ж* parapsychology.
парафи́н (-а) *м* paraffin (wax).
парафи́новый *прил* paraffin *опред*.
парашю́т (-а) *м* parachute.
парашюти́ст (-а) *м* parachutist.
парашюти́ст|ка (-ки; *gen pl* -ок) *ж см* парашюти́ст.
пáр|ень (-ня; *gen pl* -нéй) *м (разг: юноша)* lad, boy; (: *мужчина*) chap *или* fellow (*BRIT*), guy (*US*); **он свой ~** (*разг*) he's an easy-going guy.
пари́ *ср нескл* bet; **держáть** (*impf*) **~, что ...** to bet that ...; **заключáть (заключи́ть** *perf*) **~ с кем-н (на что-н)** to make a bet with sb (about sth).
Пари́ж (-а) *м* Paris.
парижá|нин (-нина; *nom pl* -е, *gen pl* -) *м* Parisian.
парижá|нка (-ки; *gen pl* -ок) *ж* Parisienne.
пари́жский (-ая, -ое, -ие) *прил* Parisian.
пари́к (-á) *м* wig.
парикмáхер (-а) *м* hairdresser.
парикмáхерск|ая (-ой; *decl like adj*) *ж* hairdresser's (*BRIT*), beauty salon (*US*).
пари́л|ка (-ки; *gen pl* -ок) *ж* steam room (*in sauna*).
пари́р|овать (-ую; *perf* **пари́ровать** *или* **отпари́ровать**) *несов перех (также перен)* to parry.
паритéт (-а) *м* parity.
пá|рить (-ю, -ишь) *несов перех (овощи)* to steam
► **пá|риться** *несов возв (овощи)* to be steamed; (*в бане*) to have a sauna; (*разг: в тёплой одежде*) to sweat.
пар|и́ть (-ю́, -и́шь) *несов неперех* to glide; **~** (*impf*) **в облакáх** (*перен*) to have one's head in the clouds.
парк (-а) *м* park; (*трамвáйный*) depot; **вагóнный ~** rolling stock; **автомоби́льный ~** fleet of cars.
паркéт (-а) *м* parquet.
парк|овáть (-у́ю) *несов перех* to park.
парлáмент (-а) *м* parliament.
парламентáри|й (-я) *м* parliamentarian.
парламéнтск|ий (-ая, -ое, -ие) *прил* parliamentary.
парни́к (-á) *м (из стеклá)* greenhouse; (*из полиэтилéна*) (poly)tunnel.
парникóв|ый *прил (растéние)* hothouse *опред*; **~ое хозя́йство** glasshouse nursery; **парникóвый эффéкт** greenhouse effect.
парнóй *прил* fresh.
пáрн|ый *прил*: **~ боти́нок/носóк** one of a pair of boots/socks; **~ое катáнье (на конькáх)** pairs' ice-skating; **где ~ боти́нок?** where is the other boot?
пáрня *итп сущ см* **пáрень**.
паровóз (-а) *м* steam engine *или* locomotive.
паровóй *прил* steam *опред*.
пароди́р|овать (-ую) *(не)сов перех* to parody.
парóди|я (-и) *ж (также перен)*: **~ (на** +*acc*) parody (of).
парóл|ь (-я) *м* password.
парóм (-а) *м* ferry.
парохóд (-а) *м* steamer, steamship.
парохóдств|о (-а) *ср* shipping; (*учреждéния*) ≈ port and navigation authority; (*фи́рма*) shipping company.
пáрт|а (-ы) *ж* desk.
партбилéт (-а) *м сокр* (= **парти́йный билéт**) (Party) membership card (*of the Communist Party*).
партéр (-а) *м* the stalls *мн*.
партизáн (-а; *gen pl* -) *м* partisan, guerrilla.
парти́йный *прил (съезд)* party *опред* ♦ (-ого; *decl like adj*) *м* Party member.
партиту́р|а (-ы) *ж* score.
пáрти|я (-и) *ж (полит)* party; (: *в СССР*) the (Communist) Party; (*муз*) part; (*грýза*) consignment; (*издéлий: в произвóдстве*) batch, lot; (*грýппа*): **пóисковая ~** search party; (*спорт*): **~ в шáхматы/волейбóл** a game of chess/volleyball.
парткóм (-а) *м сокр* (= **парти́йный комитéт**) (Communist) Party committee.
партнёр (-а) *м* partner.
партнёрств|о (-а) *ср (экóн)* partnership.
парторганизáци|я (-и) *ж сокр* (= **парти́йная организáция**) (Communist) Party organization.
пáрус (-а; *nom pl* -á) *м* sail; **на всех парусáх** (*перен*) at full speed.
паруси́н|а (-ы) *ж* canvas.
паруси́новый *прил* canvas *опред*.
пáрусник (-а) *м* sailing vessel.
парфюмéри|я (-и) *ж собир* perfume and cosmetic goods.
парч|á (-й) *ж* brocade.
парши́в|ый (-, -а, -о) *прил (разг)* lousy, rotten.
пар|ы́ (-óв) *мн* vapour *ед* (*BRIT*), vapor *ед* (*US*).
пас (-а) *м (спорт)* pass.
пас(ся *итп несов см* **пасти́(сь)**.
пáсек|а (-и) *ж* apiary.
пáсечник (-а) *м* bee keeper.
пáсквил|ь (-я) *м* send-up (*inf*).
паскýдный (-ен, -на, -но) *прил (разг)* nasty.
пáсмурен *прил см* **пáсмурный**.
пáсмурно *как сказ*: **сегóдня ~** it is overcast today.
пáсмурный (-ен, -на, -но) *прил* overcast, dull; (*перен*) gloomy.
пас|овáть (-у́ю) *несов перех (мяч)* to pass ♦

(*perf* спасова́ть) *неперех:* ~ пе́ред +*instr* to give in to.

па́спорт (-а; *nom pl* -á) м passport; (*автомобиля, станка*) registration document; загра́ничный ~ passport (*for foreign travel*).

пасса́ж (-а) м arcade; (*муз*) passage.

пассажи́р (-а) м passenger.

пассажи́р|ка (-ки; *gen pl* -ок) ж *см* пассажи́р.

пассажи́рский (-ая, -ое, -ие) *прил* passenger *опред*.

пасси́в (-а) м (*комм*) liabilities мн; (*линг*) passive (voice).

пасси́в|ный (-ен, -на, -но) *прил* (*также линг*) passive; (*no short form; комм*): ~ бала́нс unfavourable (*BRIT*) *или* unfavorable (*US*) balance; ~ партнёр (*комм*) silent partner.

па́ст|а (-ы) ж (*томатная*) purée; (*в ручке*) ink; зубна́я ~ toothpaste.

па́стбище (-а) *ср* pasture.

пасте́л|ь (-и) ж pastel.

пасте́льный *прил* pastel *опред*.

пастеризо́ванный *прил* pasteurized.

пастериз|ова́ть (-у́ю) (*не*)*сов перех* to pasteurize.

пастерна́к (-а) м parsnip.

пас|ти́ (-у́, -ёшь; *pt* -, -ла́, -ло́) *несов перех* (*скот*) to graze

► пасти́сь *несов возв* to graze.

пастил|а́ (-илы́; *nom pl* -и́лы) ж ≈ marshmallow.

па́стор (-а) м minister, pastor.

пасту́х (-а́) м (*коров*) herdsman (*мн* herdsmen); (*овец*) shepherd.

па́стыр|ь (-я) м pastor.

па|сть (-ду́, -дёшь; *pt* -л, -ла, -ло) *сов от* па́дать

♦ *неперех* (*no impf; крепость, правительство*) to fall ♦ (-сти) (*зверя*) mouth.

па́сх|а (-и) ж (*в иудаизме*) Passover; (*в христианстве*) ≈ Easter; (*кушанье*) paskha (*sweet dish made with cream cheese at Easter*).

па́сын|ок (-ка) м stepson.

пат (-а) м (*в шахматах*) stalemate.

пате́нт (-а) м (*на изобретение*) patent; (*торговый*) licence (*BRIT*), license (*US*).

пате́нтный *прил* patent *опред*; пате́нтное бюро́/пра́во patent office/rights.

патент|ова́ть (-у́ю; *perf* запатентова́ть) *несов перех* to patent.

патети́ческий (-ая, -ое, -ие) *прил* (*страстный*) passionate, emotional.

па́ток|а (-и) ж treacle.

патологи́ческий (-ая, -ое, -ие) *прил* (*также перен*) pathological.

патоло́ги|я (-и) ж pathology.

патриа́рх (-а) м patriarch.

патриарха́льный *прил* patriarchal.

патриа́рхи|я (-и) ж patriarchate.

патрио́т (-а) м patriot.

патриоти́зм (-а) м patriotism.

патрио́т|ка (-ки; *gen pl* -ок) ж *см* патрио́т.

патро́н (-а) м (*воен*) cartridge; (*дрели*) chuck; (*лампы*) socket; (*покровитель*) patron.

патрона́ж (́-а) м (*мед*) home visiting by a district nurse for newborn babies or the chronically ill.

патрона́жный *прил:* ~ая сестра́ (*мед*) ≈ district (*BRIT*) *или* visiting (*US*) nurse.

па́трубок (-ка) м branch pipe.

патрули́р|овать (-ую) *несов* (*не*)*перех* to patrol.

патру́л|ь (-я) м patrol.

па́уз|а (-ы) ж (*также муз*) pause.

пау́к (-á) м spider.

паути́н|а (-ы) ж spider's web, spiderweb (*US*); (*в помещении*) cobweb; (*перен*) web.

па́фос (-а) м zeal, fervour (*BRIT*), fervor (*US*).

пах (-а; *loc sg* -у́) м groin.

пах *итп несов см* па́хнуть.

па́хар|ь (-я) м ploughman (*BRIT*), plowman (*US*) (*мн* ploughmen *или* plowmen).

пах|а́ть (-шу́, -шешь; *perf* вспаха́ть) *несов перех* to plough (*BRIT*), plow (*US*).

па́х|нуть (-ну, -нешь; *pt* -, -ла, -ло) *несов неперех:* ~ (+*instr*) to smell (of); (*разг*): ~ +*instr* (*скандалом*) to smack of; от неё ~нет духа́ми she smells of perfume.

пахн|у́ть (*3sg* -ёт, *3pl* -у́т) *сов неперех* (+*instr*): ~у́ло ро́зами the scent of roses wafted by.

па́хот|а (-ы) ж ploughing (*BRIT*), plowing (*US*).

паху́чий (-ая, -ее, -ие; -, -а, -е) *прил* strong-smelling.

паца́н (-á) м (*разг*) boy, lad.

пацие́нт (-а) м patient.

пацие́нт|ка (-ки; *gen pl* -ок) ж *см* пацие́нт.

пацифи́ст (-а) м pacifist.

па́ч|ка (-ки; *gen pl* -ек) ж (*бумаг, денег итп*) bundle; (*чая, сигарет итп*) packet; (*балерины*) tutu.

па́чка|ть (-ю; *perf* запа́чкать *или* испа́чкать) *несов перех:* ~ что-н to get sth dirty; (*perf* запа́чкать; *перен: репутацию*) to sully, tarnish

► па́чкаться (*perf* запа́чкаться *или* испа́чкаться) *несов возв* to get dirty.

па́шн|я (-ни; *gen pl* -ен) ж ploughed (*BRIT*) *или* plowed (*US*) field.

паште́т (-а) м pâté.

пашу́ *итп несов см* паха́ть.

па́юс|ный *прил:* ~ая икра́ pressed caviar(e).

пая́льник (-а) м soldering iron.

пая́снича|ть (-ю) *несов неперех* (*разг*) to play the fool.

пая́|ть (-ю) *несов перех* to solder.

пая́ц (-а) м clown.

ПВО ж *сокр* (= противовозду́шная оборо́на) anti-aircraft defence (*BRIT*) *или* defense (*US*) system.

ПДВ м *сокр* (= преде́льно допусти́мый вы́брос) maximum permitted discharge.

певе́ц (-ца́) м singer.

певи́ц|а (-ы) ж *см* певе́ц.

певц|а́ *итп сущ см* певе́ц.

пе́вчий (-ая, -ее, -ие) *прил:* ~ая пти́ца songbird

♦ (-его; *decl like adj*) м chorister.

пе́гий (-ая, -ое, -ие) *прил* piebald *опред*.

педаго́г (-а) м (учитель) teacher.
педаго́гик|а (-и) ж education science.
педагоги́ческий (-ая, -ое, -ие) прил
(коллектив) teaching опред; ~ **институ́т**
teacher-training (BRIT) или teachers' (US)
college; **у неё ~ тала́нт** she has a talent for
teaching; **у него́ ~ое образова́ние** he trained as
a teacher.
педа́л|ь (-и) ж pedal.
педа́нт (-а) м pedant.
педиа́тр (-а) м paediatrician (BRIT), pediatrician
(US).
педиатри́|я (-и) ж paediatrics (BRIT), pediatrics
(US).
педикю́р (-а) м pedicure.
пединститу́т (-а) м сокр (= педагоги́ческий
институ́т) teacher-training college.
педсове́т (-а) м сокр (= педагоги́ческий сове́т)
staff meeting.
педучи́лище (-а) ср сокр (= педагоги́ческое
учи́лище) teacher-training college (for nursery
and primary level).
пей несов см пить.
пейза́ж (-а) м (также ИСКУССТВО) landscape;
морско́й ~ (ИСКУССТВО) seascape.
пейзажи́ст (-а) м landscape painter.
пе́йте несов см пить.
пёк(ся) итп несов см печь(ся).
пека́р|ня (-ни; gen pl -ен) ж bakery.
пе́кар|ь (-я) м baker.
Пеки́н (-а) м Beijing, Peking.
пе́кл|о (-а) ср (зной) scorching heat; (перен: ад)
hell.
пеку́(сь) итп несов см печь(ся).
пелен|а́ (-ы́) ж (тумана, облаков) veil, shroud; **у
него́ сло́вно ~ с глаз упа́ла** the scales fell from
his eyes.
пелена́|ть (-ю; perf запелена́ть) несов перех to
swaddle.
пеленг|ова́ть (-у́ю; perf запеленгова́ть) несов
перех (ТЕХ) to take the bearings of.
пелён|ка (-ки; gen pl -ок) ж swaddling clothes мн;
с ~ок (перен) from a very early age.
пелика́н (-а) м pelican.
пельме́н|ь (-я; nom pl -и) м (обычно мн) ≈ ravioli
только ед.
пе́мз|а (-ы) ж pumice (stone).
пе́н|а (-ы) ж (мыльная) suds мн; (морская) foam;
(бульонная) froth; **говори́ть** (impf) **с ~ой у рта́**
to foam at the mouth.
пена́л (-а) м pencil case.
пена́льти ср нескл penalty.
Пенджа́б (-а) м Punjab.
пенджа́бский (-ая, -ое, -ие) прил Punjabi.
пе́ней сущ см пе́ня.
пе́н|и (-ей) мн = пе́ня.
пе́ни|е (-я) ср singing.
пе́нистый прил frothy.

пе́н|иться (3sg -ится, 3pl -ятся, perf
вспе́ниться) несов возв to foam, froth.
пеницилли́н (-а) м penicillin.
пе́н|ка (-и) ж (на молоке) skin; **снима́ть** (impf) **~и**
(перен) to cream off the best for o.s.
пе́нни ср нескл penny.
пенопла́ст (-а) м foam plastic.
пенс (-а) м pence мн.
пенсионе́р (-а) м pensioner.
пенсионе́р|ка (-ки; gen pl -ок) ж см пенсионе́р.
пенсио́нный прил (фонд) pension опред;
пенсио́нный во́зраст pension age.
пе́нси|я (-и) ж pension; **~ по инвали́дности** ≈
invalidity benefit; **выходи́ть (вы́йти** perf) **на
~ю** to retire.
пенсне́ ср нескл pince-nez.
пень (пня) м (tree) stump; (разг: пренебр: о
челове́ке) dolt, blockhead.
пенька́ (-и́) ж hemp (fibre).
пеньюа́р (-а) м negligee.
пе́н|я (-и; gen pl -ей) ж fine.
пен|я́ть (-ю) несов неперех: **~ на себя́** (разг) to
blame или reproach o.s.; **пусть он ~ет на себя́**
he has only himself to blame.
пе́пел (-ла) м ash; (хлопья) ashes мн.
пепели́ще (-а) ср site of a fire.
пе́пельниц|а (-ы) ж ashtray.
пе́пла итп сущ см пе́пел.
пер. сокр = переу́лок.
пёр итп несов см переть.
перве́йш|ий (-ая, -ее, -ие) прил primary.
пе́рвен|ец (-ца) м first-born.
пе́рвенств|о (-а) ср (положение) first place;
(соревнование) championship.
пе́рвенств|овать (-ую) несов неперех to take
first place, come first.
пе́рвенца итп сущ см пе́рвенец.
перви́чный прил (самый ранний) initial опред,
primary; (низовой) grass root.
первобы́т|ный прил primeval; (-ен, -на, -но;
перен: методы) primitive.
пе́рв|ое (-ого; decl like adj) ср first course.
первозда́нный прил primordial.
первоисто́чник (-а) м primary source.
первокла́ссник (-а) м pupil in first year at
school (usually seven years old).
первокла́ссниц|а (-ы) ж см первокла́ссник.
первокла́ссный прил: **~ые инвести́ции**
(КОММ) blue-chip investment.
пе́рво-на́перво нареч (разг) first of all.
первонача́льный (-ен, -ьна, -ьно) прил
(исходный) original, initial опред.
первообра́з (-а) м prototype.
первооткрыва́тел|ь (-я) м discoverer.
первоочередно́й прил (неотложный)
immediate.
первоочерёдный прил = первоочередно́й.
первопрохо́д|ец (-ца) м (поселенец) pioneer;
(исследователь) explorer.

перворазря́дный *прил* first-class, top-class.
первосо́рт|ный (-ен, -на, -но) *прил* top-quality, top-grade, first-rate.
первостепе́н|ный (-ен, -на, -но) *прил* (*задача, значение*) paramount.
первоцве́т (-а) *м* primrose.
пе́рв|ый (-ая, -ое, -ые) *чис* first; (*по времени*) first, earliest; ~ эта́ж ground (*BRIT*) *или* first (*US*) floor; ~ое вре́мя at first; в ~ую о́чередь in the first place *или* instance; ~ час дня/но́чи after midday/midnight; из ~ых рук first-hand; он ~ учени́к he is top of the class; ~ым де́лом *или* до́лгом first of all; това́р ~ого со́рта top grade product (*on a scale of 1-3*); пе́рвая по́мощь first aid; *см также* пя́тый.
перга́мент (-а) *м* parchment.
пере- *префикс* (*in verbs*; *о направлении де́йствия че́рез что-н*) indicating movement over or across sth eg. переходи́ть; (*о направлении де́йствия из одного́ ме́ста в другое*) indicating movement from one place to another eg. передви́нуть; (*разделе́ние что-н на две ча́сти*) indicating division of sth into two parts eg. перепили́ть; (*изменение направленности де́йствия*) indicating redirection of sth eg. передове́рить; (*повторе́ние де́йствия*) indicating repetition of sth eg. переде́лать; (*обозначает превосхо́дство в чём-н*) indicating superiority in sth eg. переспо́рить; (*чрезме́рность де́йствия*) indicating excessive action eg. перепи́ть; (*прекраще́ние де́йствия по́сле длительного проявления*) indicating cessation of action after certain length of time eg. переволнова́ться; (*распростране́ние де́йствия на мно́го лиц или предме́тов*) indicating action involving of many people or objects eg. перечита́ть; (*обозначает взаи́мность де́йствия*) indicating reciprocal nature of action eg. перепи́сываться; (*in nouns*; *обозначает промежу́точность*) indicating intermediate stage of sth eg. переми́рие.
переадрес|ова́ть (-у́ю; *impf* переадресо́вывать) *сов перех* to readdress.
перебази́р|овать (-ую) *сов перех* to relocate.
перебо́рщива|ть (-ю) *несов от* переборщи́ть.
перебежа́ть (*как* бежа́ть; *см* Table 20) *сов неперех*: ~ (че́рез +*acc*) to run across; **перебега́ть** (~ *perf*) к +*dat* (*разг*: *к проти́внику итп*) to go over to.
перебе́й(те) *сов см* переби́ть.
переберу́(сь) *итп сов см* перебра́ть(ся).
переб|еси́ться (-е́шусь, -е́сишься) *сов возв* to run riot; (*разг*) to sow one's wild oats.
перебива́|ть(ся) (-ю(сь)) *несов от* переби́ть(ся).
перебира́|ть (-ю) *несов от* перебра́ть ♦ *перех*: ~ кла́виши to run one's fingers over the keys
► **перебира́ться** *несов от* перебра́ться.
переб|и́ть (-ью́, -ьёшь; *impf* перебива́ть) *сов*

перех to interrupt; (*убить*) to kill; (*разбить*) to break; (*оби́ть*) to reupholster; **перебива́ть** (~ *perf*) аппети́т to spoil *или* ruin one's appetite; **перебива́ть** (~ *perf*) мысль to interrupt one's train of thought; **перебива́ть** (~ *perf*) за́пах чего́-н to conceal the smell of sth
► **переби́ться** (*impf* перебива́ться) *сов возв* to make ends meet, get by; (*no impf*; *обойти́сь*): ~ся (без +*gen*) (*разг*) to do without; они́ с трудо́м ~йли́сь до зарпла́ты they managed to get by till payday; он ~ье́тся! he'll survive *или* manage!
перебо́|й (-я) *м* (*сердца*) irregularity; (*двигателя*) misfire; (*задержка*) interruption, break.
переболе́|ть (-ю) *сов неперех*: ~ +*instr* to recover from; (*дети, люди*: *корью, гриппом*) to come down with; у него́ душа́ ~ла he is over the heartache.
перебо́р (-а) *м* (*муз*) strumming; (*излишнее*): э́то уже́ ~ that's too much.
переб|оро́ть (-орю́, -о́решь) *сов перех* to overcome.
переборщ|и́ть (-у́, -и́шь; *impf* перебо́рщивать) *сов неперех*: ~ в +*prp* (*разг*) to go over the top with.
перебра́сыва|ть(ся) (-ю(сь)) *несов от* перебро́сить(ся).
переб|ра́ть (-еру́, -ерёшь; *impf* перебира́ть) *сов перех* (*пересмотре́ть*: *бума́ги*) to sort out; (: *крупу, я́годы*) to sort; (*мысленно воспроизвести́*) to go over *или* through (in one's mind); (*взять сли́шком мно́го*) to take too much; (*вы́пить ли́шнее*) to drink too much; (*стру́ны*) to pluck (*BRIT*), pick (*US*)
► **перебра́ться** (*impf* перебира́ться) *сов возв* (*разг*: *че́рез реку́*) to manage to get across; (*на но́вую кварти́ру*) to move.
перебро́|сить (-шу, -сишь; *impf* перебра́сывать) *сов перех* (*мяч, мешо́к*) to throw over; (*войска́*) to transfer, move
► **перебро́ситься** (*impf* перебра́сываться) *сов возв* (*войска́*) to be transferred; **перебра́сываться** (~ся *perf*) +*instr* (*мячо́м*) to throw (to each other); (*слова́ми*) to exchange (with one another).
перебыва́|ть (-ю) *сов неперех* (*у мно́гих люде́й*) to call on; (*во мно́гих места́х*): он везде́ ~л he has been all over the world.
перебью́(сь) *итп сов см* переби́ть(ся).
перева́л (-а) *м* (*в гора́х*) pass.
перева|ли́ть (-лю́, -́лишь; *impf* перева́ливать) *сов неперех*: ~ (че́рез +*acc*) to cross; **перева́ливать** (~ *perf*) за +*acc* (*разг*) to top.
перева́лочный *прил*: ~ пункт/ла́герь transit area/camp.
перева́р|ивать (-аю, -а́ришь; *impf* перева́ривать) *сов перех* to overcook (*by boiling*); (*пищу, информа́цию*) to digest
► **перевари́ться** (*impf* перева́риваться) *сов*

возв to be overdone *или* overcooked; (*пища*) to be digested.

переведу́(сь) *итп сов см* **перевести́(сь)**.

перев|езти́ (-езу́, -езёшь; *pt* -ёз, -езла́, -езло́, *impf* **перевози́ть**) *сов перех* (*переместить*) to take *или* transport across; (*доставить*) to transport, take.

переверну́ть (-у́, -ёшь; *impf* **перевёртывать** *или* **перевора́чивать**) *сов перех* to turn over; (*изменить*) to change (completely); (*по impf*; *комнату*) to turn upside down

► **переверну́ться** (*impf* **перевёртываться** *или* **перевора́чиваться**) *сов возв* (*человек*) to turn over; (*лодка, машина*) to overturn.

переве́с (-а) *м* (*преимущество*) advantage.

переве́|сить (-шу, -сишь; *impf* **переве́шивать**) *сов перех* (*товар*) to reweigh; (*подлеж: аргумент*) to outweigh.

перев|ести́ (-еду́, -едёшь; *pt* -ёл, -ела́, -ело́, *impf* **переводи́ть**) *сов перех* (*помочь перейти*) to take across; (*часы*) to reset; (*учреждение, сотрудника*) to transfer, move; (*текст*) to translate; (*: устно*) to interpret; (*переслать: деньги*) to send, transfer; (*доллары, метры итп*) to convert; (*разг: израсходовать*) to waste; **переводи́ть** (~ *perf*) **разгово́р** to change the subject; **переводи́ть** (~ *perf*) **текст с ру́сского языка́ на англи́йский** to translate a text from Russian into English; **переводи́ть** (~ *perf*) **дух** *или* **дыха́ние** to take a (deep) breath

► **перевести́сь** (*impf* **переводи́ться**) *сов возв* to move; (*разг: исчезнуть*) to die out.

переве́шива|ть (-ю) *несов от* **переве́сить**.

переве́шу *сов см* **переве́сить**.

перевида́|ть (-ю) *сов перех* to see.

перевира́|ть (-ю) *несов от* **перевра́ть**.

перево́д (-а) *м* (*на другую должность*) transfer; (*стрелки часов*) resetting; (*текст*) translation; (*деньги*) remittance; ~ **строки́** (*комп*) line feed; **креди́тный** ~ (*комм*) credit transfer, bank giro.

перев|оди́ть(ся) (-ожу́(сь), -о́дишь(ся)) *несов от* **перевести́(сь)**.

перево́дный *прил* in translation.

перево́дчик (-а) *м* translator; (*устный*) interpreter.

перево́дчиц|а (-ы) *ж см* **перево́дчик**.

перевожу́ *несов см* **перевози́ть**.

перевожу́(сь) *несов см* **переводи́ть(ся)**.

перево́з (-а) *м* (*груза*) transportation.

перев|ози́ть (-ожу́, -о́зишь) *несов от* **перевезти́**.

перево́з|ка (-ки; *gen pl* -ок) *ж* transportation, conveyance.

переволн|ова́ться (-у́юсь) *сов возв* to be worried sick.

перевооруж|и́ть (-у́, -и́шь; *impf* **перевооружа́ть**) *сов перех* (*армию*) to rearm; (*промышленность*) to re-equip.

перевопло|ти́ться (-щу́сь, -ти́шься; *impf* **перевоплоща́ться**) *сов возв* (*актёр*) to be transformed.

перевора́чива|ть(ся) (-ю(сь)) *несов от* **переверну́ть(ся)**.

переворо́т (-а) *м* (*полит*) coup (d'état); (*в судьбе*) upheaval.

перевоспита́|ть (-ю; *impf* **перевоспи́тывать**) *сов перех* to re-educate.

перевр"а́ть (-у́, -ёшь; *impf* **перевира́ть**) *сов перех* (*разг: содержание*) to muddle.

перевы́бор|ы (-ов) *мн* election *ед* (*occurring at regular intervals*).

перевы́полн|ить (-ю, -ишь; *impf* **перевыполня́ть**) *сов перех* (*задание, план*) to overfulfil; (*норму*) to exceed.

перевя|за́ть (-жу́, -жешь; *impf* **перевя́зывать**) *сов перех* (*руку, раненого*) to bandage; (*рану*) to dress, bandage; (*коробку*) to tie up; (*чулки, свитер*) to reknit.

перевя́з|ка (-ки; *gen pl* -ок) *ж* (*раны, раненых*) bandaging.

перевя́зочный *прил*: ~ **материа́л** bandage.

перевя́зыва|ть (-ю) *несов от* **перевяза́ть**.

перевя́з|ь (-и) *ж* shoulder-belt; (*для руки*) sling.

перега́р (-а) *м* smell *or* taste of (*stale*) alcohol; **от него́ несёт** ~**ом** he reeks of alcohol.

переги́б (-а) *м* (*страницы, ткани*) fold; (*перен: крайность*) excesses *мн*.

перегиба́|ть (-ю) *несов от* **перегну́ть**.

перегл|яну́ться (-яну́сь, -я́нешься; *impf* **перегля́дываться**) *сов возв*: ~ (**с** +*instr*) to exchange glances (with).

перег|на́ть (-оню́, -о́нишь; *pt* -на́л, -нала́, -на́ло, *impf* **перегоня́ть**) *сов перех* (*переместить: скот, машину*) to drive; (*обогнать: бегуна, конкурента*) to overtake; (*нефть*) to refine; (*спирт*) to distil (*BRIT*), distill (*US*).

перегно́|й (-я) *м* humus.

перегн|у́ть (-у́, -ёшь; *impf* **перегиба́ть**) *сов перех* (*бумагу*) to fold (over) ♦ *неперех* (*с критикой*) to go too far; **перегиба́ть** (~ *perf*) **па́лку** (*перен*) to go too far.

перегова́рива|ться (-юсь) *несов возв*: ~ (**с** +*instr*) to exchange remarks (with).

переговор|и́ть (-ю́, -и́шь) *сов неперех*: ~ **с** +*instr* (*обсудить*) to have a talk with ♦ *перех* (*разг*) to outtalk.

перегово́рный *прил*: ~ **пункт** telephone office (*for long-distance calls*).

перегово́р|ы (-ов) *мн* negotiations *мн*, talks *мн*; (*по телефону*) call *ед*; **зака́зывать** (**заказа́ть** *perf*) ~ **с** +*instr* to book a call to.

перего́н (-а) *м* (*на железной дороге*) stage (*between two railway stations*).

перего́н|ка (-ки; *gen pl* -ок) *ж* (*нефти*) refining; (*спирта*) distillation.

перегоню́ *итп сов см* **перегна́ть**.

перегоня́|**ть** (-ю) *несов от* **перегна́ть**.
перегора́живать (-ю) *несов от*
   перегороди́ть.
перегоре́ть (*3sg* -и́т, *3pl* -я́т, *impf* **перегора́ть**)
   сов неперех (лампочка) to fuse; (двигатель) to
   burn out.
перегоро|**ди́ть** (-жу́, -ди́шь; *impf*
   перегора́живать) *сов перех* (комнату) to
   partition (off); (дорогу) to block.
перегоро́д|**ка** (-ки; *gen pl* -ок) *ж* partition.
перегорожу́ *сов см* **перегороди́ть**.
перегре́|**ть** (-ю; *impf* **перегрева́ть**) *сов перех* to
   overheat
► **перегре́ться** (*impf* **перегрева́ться**) *сов возв*
   to overheat; **он ~лся на со́лнце** he got a touch
   of sunstroke.
перегру|**зи́ть** (-жу́, -у́зишь; *impf* **перегружа́ть**)
   сов перех to overload.
перегру́з|**ка** (-ки; *gen pl* -ок) *ж* overload; (обычно
   мн: нервные) strain.
перегры́з|**ть** (-у́, -ёшь; *impf* **перегрыза́ть**) *сов
   перех* to gnaw through
► **перегры́зться** (*impf* **перегрыза́ться**) *сов
   возв* to fight.

KEYWORD

пе́ред *предл* (+*instr*) **1** (о положении, в
   присутствии): in front of); **пе́ред до́мом/**
   зе́ркалом in front of the house/mirror; **он**
   робе́л пе́ред де́вушками he was shy in front of
   girls; **моли́ться** (*impf*) **пе́ред ико́ной** to pray
   before an icon
   2 (раньше чего-н: ужином, войной, концом
   итп) before; **я говори́л с ним пе́ред уро́ком** I
   spoke to him before the lesson
   3 (об объекте воздействия): **устоя́ть пе́ред**
   тру́дностями to stand one's ground in the face
   of difficulties; **извини́ться** (**извини́ться** *perf*)
   пе́ред кем-н to apologize to sb; **я винова́т**
   пе́ред тобо́й I am guilty in your eyes;
   отчи́тываться (**отчита́ться** *perf*) **пе́ред** +*instr*
   to report to
   4 (по сравнению) compared to; **пе́ред ним ты**
   челове́к ничто́жный compared to him, you are
   a nonentity
   5 (как союз): **пе́ред тем как** before; **пе́ред тем**
   как уйти́/зако́нчить before leaving/finishing.

перёд (переда) *м* front.
переда|**ва́ть(ся)** (-ю́(сь); *imper* **передава́й(те)**)
   несов от **переда́ть(ся)**.
передам(ся) *итп сов см* **переда́ть(ся)**.
переда́тчик (-а) *м* (*ТЕХ*) transmitter.
переда́ть (*как дать; см* **Table 14**; *impf*
   передава́ть) *сов перех*: ~ **что-н (кому́-н)**
   (письмо, подарок) to pass *или* hand sth (over)
   (to sb); (известие, любовь, интерес) to pass sth
   on (to sb); (идеи, эмоции) to convey sth *или* get
   sth across (to sb); ~**йте ему́ (мой) приве́т** give
   him my regards; ~**йте ей, что я не приду́** tell
   her I am not coming; **передава́ть** (~ *perf*) **что-н**
   по телеви́дению/ра́дио to televise/broadcast

sth; **передава́ть** (~ *perf*) **де́ло в суд** to take a
   case to court
► **переда́ться** (*impf* **передава́ться**) *сов возв*
   (+*dat*; эмоция): **его́ страх ~лся други́м** his fear
   communicated itself to the others; **ему́ ~лся**
   тала́нт отца́ he has inherited his father's talent.
переда́ч|**а** (-и) *ж* (известия) passing on;
   (концерта, новостей) transmission; (*ТЕЛ*,
   РАДИО: интересная) programme (*BRIT*),
   program (*US*); (больному, заключённому)
   parcel; **програ́мма переда́ч** television and
   radio guide.
переда́шь(ся) *сов см* **переда́ть(ся)**.
передвига́ть (-ю) *несов от* **передви́нуть**.
► **передвига́ться** *несов от* **передви́нуться** ◆
   возв (на машине, на танке *итп*) to move.
передвиже́ни|**е** (-я) *ср* (предмета, войск)
   movement; (срока) alteration, change; **сре́дства**
   ~**я** means of transport.
передвижно́й *прил* (выставка, цирк) travelling
   (*BRIT*), traveling (*US*); (лаборатория,
   библиотека) mobile.
передви́н|**уть** (-у, -ешь; *impf* **передвига́ть**) *сов
   перех* to move
► **передви́нуться** (*impf* **передвига́ться**) *сов
   возв* to move.
переде́ла|**ть** (-ю; *impf* **переде́лывать**) *сов
   перех* (работу) to redo; (характер) to change;
   (рассказ) to rewrite; ~ (*perf*) **все дела́** to get
   everything done.
переде́л|**ка** (-ки; *gen pl* -ок) *ж* (одежды)
   alteration; (характера) change; **попада́ть**
   (**попа́сть** *perf*) **в** ~**ку** (разг) to get into a fix;
   побыва́ть (*perf*) **в** ~**х** (разг) to be in a fix.
переде́лывать (-ю) *несов от* **переде́лать**.
передёргивать (-ю) *несов от* **передёрнуть**.
передержа́ть (-ержу́, -е́ржишь; *impf*
   переде́рживать) *сов перех*: **он ~ержа́л мя́со в**
   духо́вке he left the meat in the oven for too
   long.
передёрн|**уть** (-у, -ешь; *impf* **передёргивать**)
   сов перех (разг: факты, цифры) to massage ◆
   безл (+*acc*): **его́ ~уло от хо́лода** he convulsed
   from the cold; **его́ ~уло от отвраще́ния** he
   shuddered in disgust.
пере́дний (-яя, -ее, -ие) *прил* front; **П ~яя Áзия**
   the Middle East; ~ **план** (*КОМП*) foreground;
   пере́дний край (*ВОЕН, перен*) front line.
пере́дник (-а) *м* apron.
пере́дняя (-ей; *decl like adj*) *ж* (entrance) hall.
пе́редо *предл*: ~ **мно́й** in front of me.
передово́й|**я** (-о́й; *decl like adj*) *ж* (также: ~
   статья́) editorial; (также: ~ **пози́ция**: *ВОЕН*)
   vanguard.
передово́й *прил* (отряд) advance, forward;
   (машина) front *опред*; (технология) advanced;
   (писатель, взгляды) progressive.
передохну́ть (-у́, -ёшь; *сов неперех* (разг) to
   take a breather (*BRIT*) *или* break (*US*).
передра|**зни́ть** (-азню́, -а́знишь; *impf*
   передра́знивать) *сов перех* to mimic.

переду́ма|ть (-ю; *impf* **переду́мывать**) *сов неперех* to change one's mind.

переды́ш|ка (-ки; *gen pl* -ек) *ж* rest; *(перерыв)* (short) break.

пере́еду *итп сов см* **пере́ехать**.

пере́езд (-а) *м (в новый дом)* move; *(на железной дороге)* level crossing.

пере́е|хать (*как* **е́хать;** *см* **Table 19;** *impf* **переезжа́ть**) *сов неперех (переселиться)* to move; **переезжа́ть** (~ *perf*) *(че́рез +acc)* to cross.

пережгу́ *итп сов см* **переже́чь**.

пережда́|ть (-у́, -ёшь; *impf* **пережида́ть**) *сов перех:* ~ **дождь** to wait for the rain to pass.

переже́|чь (-гу́, -жёшь *итп,* -гу́т; *pt* -ёг, -гла́, -гло́, *impf* **пережига́ть**) *сов перех (зерна кофе)* to burn; *(глину)* to overfire.

пережива́ни|е (-я) *ср (обычно мн)* feeling.

пережива́|ть (-ю) *несов от* **пережи́ть ♦** *неперех:* ~ **(за** +acc) *(разг)* to worry (about).

переживу́ *итп сов см* **пережи́ть**.

пережига́|ть (-ю) *несов от* **пережечь**.

пережида́|ть (-ю) *несов от* **пережда́ть**.

пережи́т|ок (-ка) *м* relic.

пережи́|ть (-ву́, -вёшь; *impf* **пережива́ть**) *сов перех (прожить дольше)* to outlive; *(выжить)* to survive; *(испытать)* to experience; *(вытерпеть)* to suffer.

перезаря|ди́ть (-жу́, -ди́шь; *impf* **перезаряжа́ть**) *сов перех (аккумулятор)* to recharge; *(ружьё)* to reload.

перезвон|и́ть (-ю́, -и́шь; *impf* **перезва́нивать**) *сов неперех* to phone (*BRIT*) *или* call (*US*) back.

перезим|ова́ть (-у́ю) *сов от* **зимова́ть**.

перезре́|ть (-ю; *impf* **перезрева́ть**) *сов неперех* to become overripe.

переигра́|ть (-ю; *impf* **переи́грывать**) *сов перех (играть снова)* to replay **♦** *неперех (разг)* to overact; **э́то де́ло на́до** ~ *(разг)* this will have to be looked at again.

переизбра́|ть (-еру́, -ерёшь; *pt* -ра́л, -рала́, -ра́ло, *impf* **переизбира́ть**) *сов перех* to re-elect.

переиздава́|ть (-ю; *imper* **переизда́й(те)**) *несов от* **переизда́ть**.

переизда́м *итп сов см* **переизда́ть**.

переизда́ни|е (-я) *ср (действие)* republication; *(исправленное, дополненное)* new edition.

переизда́|ть (*как* **дать;** *см* **Table 14;** *impf* **переиздава́ть**) *сов перех* to republish.

переимен|ова́ть (-у́ю; *impf* **переимено́вывать**) *сов перех* to rename.

перейду́ *итп сов см* **перейти́**.

перейму́ *итп сов см* **переня́ть**.

перейти́ (*как* **идти́;** *см* **Table 18;** *impf* **переходи́ть**) *сов перех (че́рез +acc)* to cross **♦** *неперех:* ~ **в/на** +acc *(поменять место)* to go to; *(на другую работу)* to move to;

переходи́ть (~ *perf*) **к** +dat *(к сыну итп)* to pass to; *(к делу, к обсуждению)* to turn to; **переходи́ть** (~ *perf*) **в ата́ку** to launch an attack; **переходи́ть** (~ *perf*) **на** +acc to switch to; **переходи́ть** (~ *perf*) **грани́цу** to cross the frontier *или* border; *(перен)* to overstep the bounds *или* mark; **переходи́ть** (~ *perf*) **из рук в ру́ки** to change hands; **переходи́ть** (~ *perf*) **на гру́бости** to resort to bad language; **дру́жба** ~ **шла́ в любо́вь** friendship turned *или* developed into love.

перека́пыва|ть (-ю) *несов от* **перекопа́ть**.

перека́рмлива|ть (-ю) *несов от* **перекорми́ть**.

перека|ти́ть (-чу́, -а́тишь; *impf* **перека́тывать**) *сов перех (что-н круглое)* to roll; *(что-н на колёсах)* to wheel.

перека́шива|ть(ся) (-ю(сь)) *несов от* **перекоси́ть(ся)**.

переквалифици́р|оваться (-уюсь) *сов возв* to retrain.

перекидно́й *прил:* ~ **мост** gangplank; ~ **календа́рь** desk calendar.

переки́|нуть (-у, -ешь; *impf* **переки́дывать**) *сов перех* to throw over

▶ **переки́нуться** (*impf* **переки́дываться**) *сов возв:* ~+*instr (мячом)* to throw to each other.

перекла́дин|а (-ы) *ж* crossbeam; *(СПОРТ)* (horizontal *или* high) bar.

перекладны́|е (-ых; *decl like adj*) *мн* stagecoach *ед.*

перекла́дыва|ть (-ю) *несов от* **переложи́ть**.

переклика́|ться (-юсь) *несов возв (люди, животные)* to call to each other; ~ (*impf*) **(с** +*instr*) *(перен: образы, идеи)* to have something in common (with).

перекли́ч|ка (-ки; *gen pl* -ек) *ж* roll call.

переключа́тел|ь (-я) *м* switch.

переключа́|ть(ся) (-ю(сь)) *несов от* **переключи́ть(ся)**.

переключе́ни|е (-я) *ср* switching; *(скорости)* changing (*BRIT*), shifting (*US*).

переключ|и́ть (-у́, -и́шь; *impf* **переключа́ть**) *сов перех* to switch; **переключа́ть** (~ *perf*) **ско́рость** to change (*BRIT*) *или* shift (*US*) gear; **переключа́ть** (~ *perf*) **разгово́р** to change the subject

▶ **переключи́ться** (*impf* **переключа́ться**) *сов возв:* ~**ся (на** +acc) *(внимание)* to shift (to).

переко|ва́ть (-у́ю; *impf* **переко́вывать**) *сов перех (коня)* to reshoe; *(изделие, деталь)* to reforge.

перекопа́|ть (-ю; *impf* **перека́пывать**) *сов перех (огород)* to dig up; *(разг: чемодан, шкаф)* to rummage through.

перекорм|и́ть (-лю́, -ишь; *impf* **перека́рмливать**) *сов перех* to overfeed.

переко|си́ть (-шу́, -си́шь; *impf* **перека́шивать**)

сов перех (*рисуя*) to draw crooked; (*вырезая*) to cut crooked;

▶ **перекоси́ться** (*impf* **перека́шиваться**) сов возв (*деталь, рисунок*) to come out crooked; (*лицо, тело*) to become distorted.

перекочёва́ть (-*у́ю*; *impf* **перекочёвывать**) сов неперех (*стадо, табор*) to move on.

перекошу́(сь) сов см **перекоси́ть(ся)**.

перекра́ива|ть (-ю) несов от **перекро́ить**.

перекре|сти́ть (-*щу́*, -*е́стишь*) сов от **крести́ть**

▶ **перекрести́ться** сов от **крести́ться ♦** (*impf* **перекре́щиваться**) возв (*также перен*) to cross.

перекрёстка сущ см **перекрёсток**.

перекрёстный прил intersecting; **перекрёстный допро́с** cross-examination; **перекрёстный ого́нь** crossfire.

перекрёст|ок (-*ка*) м crossroads.

перекре́щива|ться (-*юсь*) несов от **перекрести́ться**.

перекрещу́(сь) сов см **перекрести́ть(ся)**.

перекрича́|ть (-*у́*, -*и́шь*; *impf* **перекри́кивать**) сов перех (*в споре*) to shout down; (*шум, музыку*) to shout above.

перекро́|ить (-*ю́*, -*и́шь*; *impf* **перекра́ивать**) сов перех (*платье*) to cut differently; (*карту*) to redraw.

перекро́ю итп сов см **перекры́ть**.

перекру|ти́ть (-*чу́*, -*у́тишь*; *impf* **перекру́чивать**) сов перех (*гайку, кран*) to overtighten

▶ **перекрути́ться** (*impf* **перекру́чиваться**) сов возв to get tangled up.

перекрыва́|ть (-ю) несов от **перекры́ть**.

перекры́ти|е (-*я*) ср ceiling; (*реки*) damming.

перекры́|ть (-*о́ю*, -*о́ешь*; *impf* **перекрыва́ть**) сов перех (*покрыть заново*) to re-cover; (*реку*) to dam; (*дорогу, улицу*) to close off; (*воду, газ*) to cut off; (*разг: план*) to exceed.

перекуп|и́ть (-*уплю́*, -*у́пишь*; *impf* **перекупа́ть**) сов перех (-ю) to buy.

перекупщик (-*а*) м dealer.

перекур (-*а*) м (*разг: перерыв*) cigarette break.

перекур|и́ть (-*ю́*, -*у́ришь*; *impf* **перекуривать**) сов перех (*разг*) to break for a cigarette; (: *сделать перерыв*) to take a break.

переку|си́ть (-*шу́*, -*у́сишь*; *impf* **переку́сывать**) сов перех to bite through ♦ неперех (*разг*) to have a snack.

перела́влива|ть (-ю) несов от **переловить**.

перелага́|ть (-ю) несов от **переложи́ть**.

перела́мыва|ть (-ю) несов от **переломи́ть**.

переле́з|ть (-*у*, -*ешь*; *pt* -, -*ла*, -*ло*, *impf* **перелеза́ть**) сов (*не*)*перех*: ~ (**через** +*acc*) (*забор, канаву*) to climb (over); **перелеза́ть** (~ *perf*) **в/на** +*acc* to get *или* climb into.

переле́с|ок (-*ка*) м (*небольшой лес*) copse, coppice; (*редкий лес*) sparsely wooded area.

перелёт (-*а*) м flight; (*птиц*) migration.

перелете́|ть (-*чу́*, -*ти́шь*; *impf* **перелета́ть**) сов

(*не*)*перех*: ~ (**через** +*acc*) to fly over.

перелётный прил (*птицы*) migratory.

перелечу́ сов см **перелете́ть**.

перели́в (-*а*) м (*красок, звуков*) (subtle) gradation; (*голоса*) modulation.

перелива́ни|е (-*я*) ср: ~ **кро́ви** blood transfusion.

перелива́|ть (-ю) несов от **перели́ть ♦** неперех (*блестеть*): ~ +*instr* to shimmer with; ~ (*impf*) **все́ми цвета́ми ра́дуги** to be iridescent.

перелиста́|ть (-ю; *impf* **перели́стывать**) сов перех (*просмотреть*) to leaf through; (*быстро перебрать*) to flick through.

перел|и́ть (-*ью́*, -*ьёшь*; *impf* **перелива́ть**) сов перех to pour (*from one container to another*); **перелива́ть** (~ *perf*) **кровь кому́-н** to give sb a blood transfusion.

перел|ови́ть (-*овлю́*, -*о́вишь*; *impf* **перела́вливать**) сов перех to catch.

переложе́ни|е (-*я*) ср (*пьесы, повести*) adaptation; (*музыкального произведения*) arrangement.

перел|ожи́ть (-*ожу́*, -*о́жишь*; *impf* **перекла́дывать**) сов перех to move, shift; (*impf* **перекла́дывать** или **перелага́ть**; *повесть, пьесу*) to adapt; **перекла́дывать** (~ *perf*) **что-н на кого-н** (*ответственность, работу итп*) to pass sth onto sb; ~ (*perf*) **со́ли в суп** to put too much salt in the soup.

перело́м (-*а*) м (*МЕД*) fracture; (*перен*) turning point.

перелома́|ть (-ю) сов перех to break.

перел|оми́ть (-*омлю́*, -*о́мишь*; *impf* **перела́мывать**) сов перех (*палку*) to break in two; (*перен: ход событий*) to change dramatically.

перело́мный прил critical.

перелью́ итп сов см **перели́ть**.

перема́|зать (-*жу*, -*жешь*; *impf* **перема́зывать**) сов перех to cover.

перема́лыва|ть (-ю) несов от **перемоло́ть**.

перем|ани́ть (-*аню́*, -*а́нишь*; *impf* **перема́нивать**) сов перех (*разг*) to entice.

перема́тыва|ть (-ю) несов от **перемота́ть**.

перемежа́|ть (-ю) сов неперех: ~ **что-н с чем-н** to alternate sth with sth

▶ **перемежа́ться** несов возв: ~**ся с** +*instr* to alternate with.

перемелю́ итп сов см **перемоло́ть**.

переме́н|а (-*ы*) ж change; (*в школе*) break (*BRIT*), recess (*US*).

перем|ени́ть (-*еню́*, -*е́нишь*) сов перех to change

▶ **перемени́ться** сов возв (*жизнь, погода*) to change; **он** ~**ени́лся в лице́** (*от волнения итп*) his expression changed.

переме́нный прил (*погода*) changeable; (*успех, ветер*) variable; **переме́нный ток** alternating current.

переме́р|ить (-ю, -ишь; *impf* **переме́ривать**)

сов перех (измерить снова) to remeasure; *(примерить)* to try on.

переме|стить (-щу́, -сти́шь; *impf* **перемеща́ть**) *сов перех (предмет)* to move, shift; *(людей)* to transfer
▶ **перемести́ться** (*impf* **перемеща́ться**) *сов возв* to move.

переметн|у́ть (-у́, -ёшь) *сов (не)перех*: ~ **(че́рез** +*acc*) to throw over
▶ **переметну́ться** *сов возв (на сторону противника итп)* to go over; **~ся** *(perf)* **че́рез** +*acc* to leap over.

перемеша́|ть (-ю; *impf* **переме́шивать**) *сов перех (кашу)* to stir; *(угли, дрова)* to poke; *(вещи, бумаги)* to mix up
▶ **перемеша́ться** (*impf* **переме́шиваться**) *сов возв* to get mixed up.

перемеща́|ть(ся) (-ю(сь)) *несов от* **перемести́ть(ся)**.

перемеще́ни|е (-я) *ср* reshuffle (*in government, of jobs*); *(передвижение)* transfer.

перемещённ|ый *прил*: ~**ое лицо́** *(обычно мн)* displaced person (*мн* people).

перемещу́(сь) *сов см* **перемести́ть(ся)**.

перемигн|у́ться (-у́сь, -ёшься; *impf* **перемигиваться**) *сов возв (разг)* to wink at each other; **он ~у́лся с де́вушкой** he winked at the girl and she winked back.

переминá|ться (-юсь) *несов возв*: ~ **с ноги́ на́ ногу** to shift from one foot to the other.

переми́ри|е (-я) *ср* truce.

перемнóж|ить (-у, -ишь; *impf* **перемножа́ть**) *сов перех (числа)* to multiply.

перемóлв|иться (-люсь, -ишься) *сов возв*: ~ **(слóвом) с кем-н** *(разг)* to pass the time of day with sb.

перемо|ло́ть (-елю́, -е́лешь; *impf* **перема́лывать**) *сов перех* to grind.

перемотá|ть (-ю; *impf* **перема́тывать**) *сов перех (нитку, шерсть)* to wind; *(магнитофонную плёнку)* to rewind.

перемы́|ть (-о́ю, -о́ешь; *impf* **перемыва́ть**) *сов перех* to wash; *(вымыть заново)* to wash again, rewash; **перемыва́ть** *(~ perf)* **ко́сточки кому́-н** *(разг)* to gossip about sb.

перемы́|чка (-ки; *gen pl* -ек) *ж (соединение)* crosspiece; *(перекрытие: окна, двери)* lintel.

перенапряг *итп сов см* **перенапря́чь**.

перенапряга́|ть (-ю) *несов от* **перенапря́чь**.

перенапрягу́ *итп сов см* **перенапря́чь**.

перенапряже́ни|е (-я) *ср (физическое, умственное)* overexertion.

перенапря|чь (-гу́, -жёшь *итп*, -гу́т; *pt* -г, -гла́, -гло́, *impf* **перенапряга́ть**) *сов перех* to overstrain, overexert.

перенаселён|ный (-, -а́, -о́) *прил* overpopulated.

перенасы́|тить (-щу, -тишь; *impf*

перенасыща́ть) *сов перех* to oversaturate; **он ~тил свою́ речь цита́тами** his speech was riddled with quotations.

перен|ести́ (-есу́, -есёшь; *pt* -ёс, -есла́, -есло́, *impf* **переноси́ть**) *сов перех*: ~ **что-н че́рез** +*acc* to carry sth over *или* across; *(поменять место)* to move; *(встречу, заседание)* to reschedule; *(болезнь)* to suffer from; *(несчастье, голод, холод итп)* to endure; **переноси́ть** (~ *perf*) **слóво на другу́ю строку́** to carry a word over to the next line
▶ **перенести́сь** (*impf* **переноси́ться**) *сов возв (также перен)* to be transported.

перенима́|ть (-ю) *несов от* **переня́ть**.

перенóс (-а) *м (вещей, предметов)* transfer; *(заседания)* rescheduling; *(линг)* hyphen.

перено|си́ть (-ошу́, -о́сишь) *несов от* **перенести́** ◆ *перех*: **не ~ антибио́тиков/самолёта** to react badly to antibiotics/flying; **он хорошо́ ~ёс доро́гу** he coped well with the journey; **она́ не ~о́сит его́** she can't stand him
▶ **переноси́ться** *несов от* **перенести́сь**.

перено́сиц|а (-ы) *ж* bridge of the nose.

переносно́й *прил* portable.

перено́сн|ый *прил (значение)* figurative.

перено́счик (-а) *м (МЕД)* carrier.

переноч|ева́ть (-у́ю) *сов от* **ночева́ть**.

переношу́(сь) *сов см* **переноси́ть(ся)**.

пере|ня́ть (-йму́, -ймёшь; *pt* -ня́л, -няла́, -ня́ло, *impf* **перенима́ть**) *сов перех (опыт, идеи)* to assimilate; *(обычаи, привычки)* to adopt.

переобору́д|овать (-ую) *сов перех* to re-equip.

переобу́|ть (-ю, -ешь; *impf* **переобува́ть**) *сов перех (туфли)* to change (out of); **переобува́ть** *(~ perf)* **кого́-н** to change sb's shoes.

переоде́|ть (-ну, -нешь; *impf* **переодева́ть**) *сов перех (одежду)* to change (out of); **переодева́ть** *(~ perf)* **кого́-н** to change sb's clothes
▶ **переоде́ться** (*impf* **переодева́ться**) *сов возв* to change, get changed.

переосмы́сл|ить (-ю, -ишь; *impf* **переосмы́сливать**) *сов перех (осмыслить заново)* to reassess.

переоце|ни́ть (-ню́, -нишь; *impf* **переоце́нивать**) *сов перех (дать новую цену)* to re-evaluate, revalue; *(оценить слишком высоко)* to overestimate.

переоце́н|ка (-ки; *gen pl* -ок) *ж (см глаг)* re-evaluation, revaluation; overestimation; ~ **це́нностей** *(перен)* reappraisal *или* reassessment of values.

перепа́д (-а) *м*: ~ +*gen* drop in.

перепада́|ть (*3sg* -ет, *3pl* -ют) *несов от* **перепа́сть**.

перепадёт *итп сов см* **перепа́сть**.

перепа́л|ка (-ки; *gen pl* -ок) *ж (разг)* row.

перепа́|сть (*3sg* -**дёт**, *3pl* -**ду́т**, *impf* **перепада́ть**) *сов неперех* (+*dat*; *доста́ться*) to come one's way; **мне ~ла ко́е-кака́я ме́бель** some furniture has come my way.

перепа́чка|ть (-**ю**) *сов перех* (*разг*) to get filthy.

перепева́|ть (-**ю**) *несов перех* (*перен*) to rehash.

пе́репел (-**а**; *nom pl* -**á**) *м* quail.

перепёл|ка (-**ки**; *gen pl* -**ок**) *ж см* **пе́репел**.

перепеча́та|ть (-**ю**) *сов перех* (*статью*) to reprint; (*ру́копись*) to type.

перепил|и́ть (-**илю́**, -**и́лишь**; *impf* **перепи́ливать**) *сов перех* (*мно́го дров*) to saw; (*до́ску*) to saw in two.

перепи|са́ть (-**ишу́**, -**и́шешь**; *impf* **перепи́сывать**) *сов перех* (*написа́ть за́ново*) to rewrite; (*скопи́ровать*) to copy; (*сде́лать спи́сок*) to list, make a list of; (*КОМП*) to overwrite.

перепи́с|ка (-**ки**; *gen pl* -**ок**) *ж* (*см глаг*) rewriting; copying; listing; (*делова́я*) correspondence ♦ *собир* (*пи́сьма*) letters *мн*; **быть** (*impf*) **в ~ке с** +*instr* to be in correspondence with.

перепи́сыва|ть (-**ю**) *несов от* **переписа́ть**

▶ **перепи́сываться** *несов возв*: **~ся** (**с** +*instr*) to correspond (with).

пе́репис|ь (-**и**) *ж* (*населе́ния*) census; (*иму́щества*) inventory.

перепишу́ *итп сов см* **переписа́ть**.

перепла|ти́ть (-**чу́**, -**тишь**; *impf* **перепла́чивать**) *сов неперех* to pay too much.

переплес|ти́ (-**ту́**, -**тёшь**; *pt* -**ёл**, -**ела́**, -**ело́**, *impf* **переплета́ть**) *сов перех* (*кни́гу*, *диссерта́цию*) to bind; (*верёвки*, *па́льцы*) to interlace

▶ **переплести́сь** (*impf* **переплета́ться**) *сов возв* to intertwine; (*перен: собы́тия*) to become interwoven.

переплёт (-**а**) *м* (*обло́жка*) binding; **попада́ть** (**попа́сть** *perf*) **в ~** (*перен: разг*) to get into a fix; **отдава́ть** (**отда́ть** *perf*) **кни́гу/диссерта́цию в ~** to have a book/thesis bound; **око́нный ~** window sash.

переплета́|ть(ся) (-**ю(сь)**) *несов от* **переплести́(сь)**.

переплётн|ая (-**ой**; *decl like adj*) *ж* (book) bindery.

переплету́(сь) *итп сов см* **переплести́(сь)**.

переплы́|ть (-**ву́**, -**вёшь**; *pt* -**л**, -**ла́**, -**ло**, *impf* **переплыва́ть**) *сов (не)перех*: **~ (че́рез** +*acc*) (*вплавь*) to swim (across); (*на ло́дке*, *на корабле́*) to sail (across).

переплю́|нуть (-**у**, -**ешь**) *сов перех* (*перен: разг*) to go one up on.

переподгото́в|ка (-**ки**; *gen pl* -**ок**) *ж* retraining.

переполз|ти́ (-**у́**, -**ёшь**; *pt* -**, -ла́**, -**ло́**, *impf* **переполза́ть**) *сов (не)перех* to crawl; **переполза́ть** (**~** *perf*) (**че́рез** +*acc*) (*доро́гу*, *по́ле итп*) to crawl across.

перепо́лн|ить (-**ю**, -**ишь**; *impf* **переполня́ть**) *сов перех* (*сосу́д*, *конте́йнер*) to overfill;

(*ваго́н*, *авто́бус итп*) to overcrowd; **моё се́рдце ~ено любо́вью** my heart is overflowing with love

▶ **перепо́лниться** (*impf* **переполня́ться**) *сов возв* (*сосу́д*) to be overfilled; (*душа́*, *се́рдце*) to overflow.

переполо́х (-**а**) *м* hullabaloo.

переполош|и́ть (-**у́**, -**и́шь**) *сов перех* (*разг*) to alarm

▶ **переполоши́ться** *сов возв* (*разг*) to become alarmed.

перепо́н|ка (-**ки**; *gen pl* -**ок**) *ж* membrane; **бараба́нная ~** eardrum.

перепра́в|а (-**ы**) *ж* crossing.

перепра́в|ить (-**лю**, -**ишь**; *impf* **переправля́ть**) *сов перех* (*че́рез ре́ку*, *грани́цу*) to take across; (*посы́лку*, *письмо́*) to forward; (*оши́бку*, *фра́зу*) to correct

▶ **перепра́виться** (*impf* **переправля́ться**) *сов возв* (*че́рез ре́ку*, *го́ры итп*) to cross.

перепро́б|овать (-**ую**) *сов перех* (*еду́*) to taste; (*спо́собы*) to try (out).

перепрода|ва́ть (-**ю́**; *imper* **перепродава́й(те)**) *несов от* **перепрода́ть**.

перепрода́ть (*как* **дать**; *см* **Table 14**; *impf* **перепродава́ть**) *сов перех* to resell.

перепроизво́дств|о (-**а**) *ср* overproduction.

перепры́г|нуть (-**у**, -**ешь**; *impf* **перепры́гивать**) *сов (не)перех*: **~ (че́рез** +*acc*) to jump (over).

перепу́г (-**а**) *м* (*разг*): **с ~у** in fright.

перепуга́|ть (-**ю**) *сов перех*: **~ кого́-н** to scare the life out of sb.

перепу́та|ть (-**ю**; *impf* **перепу́тывать** *или* **пу́тать**) *сов перех* (*ни́тки*, *провода́*) to tangle (up); (*фа́кты*) to confuse; (*имена́*, *адреса́*) to mix up

▶ **перепу́таться** (*impf* **перепу́тываться** *или* **пу́таться**) *сов возв* (*ни́тки*, *провода́*) to get tangled up; (*перен: мы́сли*, *воспомина́ния*) to get confused.

перепу́ть|е (-**я**) *ср* crossroads; **на ~** (*перен*) at a crossroads.

перерабо́та|ть (-**ю**; *impf* **перераба́тывать**) *сов перех* (*сырьё*, *нефть*) to process; (*иде́и*, *статью́*, *тео́рию*) to rework ♦ *неперех* (*переутоми́ться*) to be overworked.

перераспредел|и́ть (-**ю́**, -**и́шь**; *impf* **перераспределя́ть**) *сов перех* to redistribute.

перера|сти́ (-**сту́**, -**стёшь**; *pt* -**о́с**, -**осла́**, -**осло́**, *impf* **перераста́ть**) *сов перех* (*та́кже перен*) to outgrow; **перераста́ть** (**~** *perf*) **в** +*acc* (*преврати́ться*) to escalate into.

перерасхо́д (-**а**) *м* (*эне́ргии*, *де́нег*) overexpenditure; (*КОММ*) overdraft.

перерасхо́д|овать (-**ую**) *сов перех*: **~ эне́ргию/де́ньги** to expend too much energy/money.

перерасчёт (-**а**) *м* (*счёт за́ново*) recalculation; (*КОММ: в други́е едини́цы*) conversion.

перере́|зать (-**жу**, -**жешь**; *impf* **перереза́ть**) *сов перех* (*про́вод*) to cut in two; (*перен:*

преградить) to cut off.
перерис|ова́ть (-у́ю; *impf* **перерисо́вывать**) *сов перех* to copy.
переро|ди́ться (-жу́сь, -ди́шься; *impf* **перерожда́ться**) *сов возв* (*природа, общество*) to be regenerated; (*человек*) to be transformed.
перерожде́ни|е (-я) *ср* (*см глаг*) regeneration; transformation.
перерожу́сь *сов см* **перероди́ться**.
переро́с *итп сов см* **перерасти́**.
переро́ю *итп сов см* **перерыть**.
переруга́|ться (-юсь) *сов возв* to quarrel.
переры́в (-а) *м* break; **обе́денный** ~ lunch break; **де́лать** (**сде́лать** *perf*) ~ to take a break.
перер|ы́ть (-о́ю, -о́ешь) *сов перех* (*перекопать*) to dig up; (*разг: вещи, книги*) to rummage through.
перес|ади́ть (-ажу́, -а́дишь; *impf* **переса́живать**) *сов перех* to move; (*на другой поезд, самолёт итп*) to transfer; (*дерево, цветок, сердце*) to transplant; (*кость, кожу*) to graft; **переса́живать** (~ *perf*) **кого́-н на друго́е ме́сто** to move sb to another seat.
переса́д|ка (-ки; *gen pl* -ок) *ж* (*растения*) transplantation; (*на другой итп*) change; (*МЕД: сердца*) transplant; (*: кожи*) graft; **де́лать** (**сде́лать** *perf*) ~**ку в Москве́** to change in Moscow.
переса́жива|ть (-ю) *несов от* **пересади́ть**.
переса́жива|ться (-юсь) *несов от* **пересе́сть**.
пересажу́ *сов см* **пересади́ть**.
переса́лива|ть (-ю) *несов от* **пересоли́ть**.
передава|ть (-ю; *imper* **пересдава́й(те)**) *несов перех* to resit.
пересда́ть (*как* **дать**; *см* **Table 14**) *сов перех* (*экзамен, зачёт*) to pass (*after resit*).
пересе́к(ся) *итп сов см* **пересе́чь(ся)**.
пересека́|ть(ся) (-ю(сь)) *несов от* **пересе́чь(ся)**.
пересеку́(сь) *итп сов см* **пересе́чь(ся)**.
переселе́н|ец (-ца) *м* (*на новую территорию*) settler; (*временно переселяемый*) *person having to move to temporary accommodation.*
переселе́н|ка (-ки; *gen pl* -ок) *ж см* **переселе́нец**.
переселе́нца *итп сущ см* **переселе́нец**.
пересел|и́ть (-ю́, -и́шь; *impf* **переселя́ть**) *сов перех* (*на новые земли*) to settle; (*в новую квартиру*) to move
▸ **пересели́ться** (*impf* **переселя́ться**) *сов возв* (*в другую страну*) to emigrate; (*в новый дом*) to move
пересе́|сть (-я́ду, -я́дешь; *impf* **переса́живаться**) *сов неперех* (*на другое место*) to move; **переса́живаться** (~ *perf*) **на друго́е ме́сто** to move to another seat; **переса́живаться** (~ *perf*) **на друго́й по́езд/**

самолёт to change trains/planes.
пересече́ни|е (-я) *ср* (*действие*) crossing; (*место*) intersection.
пересе́ченный *прил* (*ГЕО: местность итп*) broken.
пересе́|чь (-ку́, -чёшь *итп*, -ку́т; *pt* -ёк, -екла́, -екло́, *impf* **пересека́ть**) *сов перех* to cross
▸ **пересе́чься** (*impf* **пересека́ться**) *сов возв* to intersect; (*интересы*) to cross.
пересил|ить (-ю, -ишь; *impf* **переси́ливать**) *сов перех* (*человека*) to overpower; (*чувство*) to overcome.
перескажу́ *итп сов см* **пересказа́ть**.
переска́з (-а) *м* (*содержания фильма*) retelling; (*изложение*) exposition.
переск|аза́ть (-ажу́, -а́жешь; *impf* **переска́зывать**) *сов перех* to tell.
переск|очи́ть (-очу́, -о́чишь; *impf* **переска́кивать**) *сов* (*не*)*перех:* ~ (**че́рез** +*acc*) to jump (over); (*перен*): ~ **на** +*acc* (*на другую тему*) to jump to.
пересла|сти́ть (-щу́, -сти́шь; *impf* **пересла́щивать**) *сов перех:* ~ **что-н** to put too much sugar in sth.
пере|сла́ть (-шлю́, -шлёшь; *impf* **пересыла́ть**) *сов перех* (*отослать*) to send; (*по другому адресу*) to forward.
пересла́щива|ть (-ю) *несов от* **пересласти́ть**.
переслащу́ *сов см* **пересласти́ть**.
пересма́трива|ть (-ю) *несов от* **пересмотре́ть**.
пересме́ива|ться (-юсь) *несов возв* to smile at each other.
пересме́н|а (-ы) *ж* (*на заводе, на вахте*) change of shift.
пересме́шник (-а) *м* mockingbird.
пересм|отре́ть (-отрю́, -о́тришь; *impf* **пересма́тривать**) *сов перех* (*книги, вещи*) to look through; (*решение, вопрос, позицию*) to reconsider.
пересн|я́ть (-иму́, -и́мешь; *pt* -я́л, -яла́, -я́ло, *impf* **переснима́ть**) *сов перех* (*документ*) to make a copy of; (*сцену в фильме*) to reshoot; (*фотографию*) to take again.
пересол|и́ть (-олю́, -о́лишь; *impf* **переса́ливать**) *сов перех:* ~ **что-н** to put too much salt in sth.
пересо́х|нуть (*3sg* -нет, *3pl* -нут, *pt* -, -ла, -ло, *impf* **пересыха́ть**) *сов неперех* (*почва, бельё*) to dry out; (*река, ручей*) to dry up.
пересп|а́ть (-лю́, -и́шь; *impf* **пересыпа́ть**) *сов неперех* (*спать слишком долго*) to oversleep; ~ (*perf*) **с кем-н** (*раз*) to sleep with sb.
переспе́лый *прил* overripe.
переспе́|ть (*3sg* -ет, *3pl* -ют) *сов неперех* to become overripe.
пересплю́ *сов см* **переспа́ть**.

переспо́р|ить (-ю, -ишь) *сов перех:* ~ **кого́-н** to defeat sb in an argument.

переспро|си́ть (-ошу́, -о́сишь; *impf* **переспра́шивать**) *сов перех* to ask again.

перессо́р|иться (-юсь, -ишься) *сов возв:* ~ (с +*instr*) to quarrel *или* fall out (with).

переста|ва́ть (-ю́; *imper* **перестава́й(те)**) *несов от* **переста́ть**.

переста́в|ить (-лю, -ишь; *impf* **переставля́ть**) *сов перех* to move; (*изменить порядок*) to rearrange.

переста́ну *итп сов см* **переста́ть**.

перестара́|ться (-юсь) *сов возв* to overdo it.

переста́|ть (-ну, -нешь; *impf* **перестава́ть**) *сов неперех* to stop; **перестава́ть** (~ *perf*) +*infin* to stop doing; **~ньте!** stop it!

перестира́|ть (-ю; *impf* **перести́рывать**) *сов перех* (*все вещи*) to wash; (*постирать заново*) to wash again, rewash.

перестоя́|ть (*3sg* -и́т, *3pl* -я́т) *сов неперех* (*квас, суп*) to stand too long; (*молоко*) to go off.

перестрада́|ть (-ю) *сов (не)перех* to suffer.

перестра́ива|ть(ся) (-ю(сь)) *несов от* **перестро́ить(ся)**.

перестрах|ова́ться (-у́юсь; *impf* **перестрахо́вываться**) *сов возв* (*комм*) to reinsure; (*перен*) to play safe.

перестрахо́в|ка (-ки; *gen pl* -ок) *ж* (*см глаг*) reinsurance; playing safe.

перестрахо́выва|ться (-юсь) *несов от* **перестрахова́ться**.

перестре́л|ка (-ки; *gen pl* -ок) *ж* exchange of fire.

перестро́ек *сущ см* **перестро́йка**.

перестро́ечный *прил* (*процессы, явления*) perestroika *опред*.

перестро́|ить (-ю, -ишь; *impf* **перестра́ивать**) *сов перех* (*дом, мост*) to rebuild, reconstruct; (*программу, экономику*) to reorganize; (*ряды, колонны*) to re-form; (*музыкальный инструмент*) to retune

► **перестро́иться** (*impf* **перестра́иваться**) *сов возв* (*человек*) to reorganize o.s.; (*фабрика, коллектив*) to restructure; (*солдаты, шеренги*) to re-form.

перестро́|йка (-йки; *gen pl* -ек) *ж* (*дома*) rebuilding, reconstruction; (*расписания, экономики*) reorganization; (*муз*) retuning; (*ист*) perestroika.

переступ|и́ть (-уплю́, -у́пишь; *impf* **переступа́ть**) *сов (не)перех* (*перен*) to overstep; **переступа́ть** (~ *perf*) (**че́рез** +*acc*) (*порог, предмет*) to step over.

пересу́д|ы (-ов) *мн* (*разг*) gossip *ед*.

пересчёт (-а) *м* count; (*повторный*) re-count; **ско́лько э́то в** ~**е на рубли́?** how much is it when converted into roubles?

пересчита́|ть (-ю; *impf* **пересчи́тывать**) *сов перех* to count; (*повторно*) to re-count, count again; (*в других единицах*) to convert.

пересыла́|ть (-ю) *несов от* **пересла́ть**.

пересы́л|ка (-ки; *gen pl* -ок) *ж* sending;

(*тюрьма*) transit prison (*where prisoners stay temporarily*).

пересы́п|ать (-лю, -лешь; *impf* **пересыпа́ть**) *сов перех* (*насыпать*) to pour; (*перен: речь, рассказ*) to intersperse.

пересыпа́|ть (-ю) *несов от* **переспа́ть**.

пересы́плю *итп сов см* **пересы́пать**.

пересыха́|ть (*3sg* -ет, *3pl* -ют) *несов от* **пересо́хнуть**.

переся́ду *итп сов см* **пересе́сть**.

перета́скива|ть (-ю) *несов от* **перетащи́ть**.

перетас|ова́ть (-у́ю; *impf* **перетасо́вывать**) *сов перех* (*карты*) to shuffle; (*перен: министров*) to reshuffle.

перета|щи́ть (-щу́, -щишь; *impf* **перета́скивать**) *сов перех* (*мешок*) to drag over.

перетру|ди́ться (-ужу́сь, -у́дишься; *impf* **перетружда́ться**) *сов возв* (*разг*) to be burnt out.

перетру́|сить (-шу, -сишь) *сов неперех* (*разг*) to be scared out of one's wits.

перетряс|ти́ (-у́, -ёшь; *pt* -, -ла́, -ло́) *сов перех* to shake out.

пере́|ть (пру, прёшь; *pt* пёр, пёрла, пёрло) *несов неперех* (*разг: идти*) to trudge; (*ломиться*) to barge through; (*perf* **спере́ть**; *красть*) to pinch

► **пере́|ться** *несов возв* (*разг: идти*) to trudge.

перетя|ну́ть (-ну́, -нешь; *impf* **перетя́гивать**) *сов перех* (*передвинуть*) to pull, tow; (*быть более тяжёлым*) to outweigh; (*стянуть*): ~ **что-н чем-н** to tie sth tightly round sth.

переубе|ди́ть (-жу́, -ди́шь; *impf* **переубежда́ть**) *сов перех:* ~ **кого́-н** to make sb change his mind.

переу́л|ок (-ка) *м* lane, alley.

переустро́йств|о (-а) *ср* reconstruction.

переутом|и́ться (-лю́сь, -и́шься; *impf* **переутомля́ться**) *сов возв* to tire o.s. out.

переутомле́ни|е (-я) *ср* exhaustion.

переутомлю́сь *сов см* **переутоми́ться**.

переутомля́|ться (-юсь) *несов от* **переутоми́ться**.

переучёт (-а) *м* stocktaking.

переуч|и́ть (-учу́, -у́чишь; *impf* **переу́чивать**) *сов перех* to retrain

► **переучи́ться** (*impf* **переу́чиваться**) *сов возв* to undergo retraining.

переформати́р|овать (-ую) *(не)сов перех* (*комп*) to reformat.

перефрази́р|овать (-ую) *(не)сов перех* to paraphrase.

перехва|ти́ть (-чу́, -а́тишь; *impf* **перехва́тывать**) *сов перех* (*захватить на пути*) to intercept; (*разг: переборщить*) to go too far; (*обязать*): ~ **что-н чем-н** to tie sth round sth; **у него́** ~**ти́ло дыха́ние** he caught his breath; **перехва́тывать** (~ *perf*) **бутербро́д** (*разг*) to grab a sandwich; **перехва́тывать** (~ *perf*) **чей-н взгляд** (*перен*) to catch sb's eye.

перехитрить (-ю, -ишь) *сов перех* to outwit.

переход (-а) *м* crossing; (*к другой системе*) transition; (*в здании, между зданиями*) passage.

переходить (-ожу, -одишь) *несов от* перейти.

переходный *прил* (*промежуточный*) transitional; **переходный глагол** transitive verb.

переходящий (-ая, -ее, -ие) *прил*: ~ кубок (*СПОРТ*) challenge cup.

перехожу *несов см* переходить.

перец (-ца) *м* pepper; (*зёрнышко*) peppercorn; жгучий ~ chilli pepper; болгарский ~ capsicum.

перечень (-ня) *м* list; ~ служебных обязанностей job specification.

перечеркнуть (-у, -ёшь; *impf* перечёркивать) *сов перех* to cross out; (*перен: надежды*) to shatter.

перечертить (-ерчу, -ертишь; *impf* перечёрчивать) *сов перех* (*начертить снова*) to draw again; (*скопировать*) to copy.

перечесть (-ту, -тёшь; *pt* -ёл, -ла, -ло) *сов перех* (*пересчитать*) to re-count, count again; (*перечитать*) to reread, read again.

перечисление (-я) *ср* transfer; платить (заплатить *perf*) по ~ю to pay by transfer.

перечислить (-ю, -ишь; *impf* перечислять) *сов перех* (*упомянуть*) to list; (*КОММ*) to transfer.

перечитать (-ю; *impf* перечитывать) *сов перех* to read; (*читать заново*) to reread, read again.

перечня *итп сущ см* перечень.

перечту *итп гл см* перечесть.

перешагнуть (-у, -ёшь; *impf* перешагивать) *сов* (*не*)*перех*: ~ (через +*acc*) to step over.

перешеек (-йка) *м* isthmus.

перешёл *итп сов см* перейти.

перешёптываться (-юсь) *несов возв* to whisper to each other.

перешить (-ью, -ьёшь; *impf* перешивать) *сов перех* (*платье, костюм*) to alter; (*пуговицу, крючок*) to move (*by sewing on somewhere else*).

перешлю *сов см* переслать.

перещеголять (-ю) *сов перех* (*разг*) to outshine.

переэкзаменовка (-ки; *gen pl* -ок) *ж* resit.

перила (-) *мн* railing *ед*; (*лестницы*) banisters *мн*.

периметр (-а) *м* perimeter.

перина (-ы) *ж* feather bed.

период (-а) *м* period; первый/второй ~ игры (*СПОРТ*) first/second half (of the game).

периодика (-и) *ж собир* periodicals *мн*.

периодически *нареч* periodically.

периодический (-ая, -ое, -ие) *прил* periodical

опред; **периодическая печать** the periodical press.

периодичность (-и) *ж* regularity.

перипетия (-и) *ж* (*обычно мн*) upheaval.

перитонит (-а) *м* peritonitis.

периферийный *прил* peripheral.

периферия (-и) *ж* the provinces *мн* ◆ *собир* (*КОМП*) peripherals *мн*, peripheral devices *мн*.

перифразировать (-ую) (*не*)*сов перех* to paraphrase.

перл (-а) *м* (*также перен*) pearl.

перламутр (-а) *м* mother-of-pearl.

перламутровый *прил* mother-of-pearl *опред*; (*цвет*) pearly.

перловка (-ки; *gen pl* -ок) *ж* (*разг*) pearl barley.

перловый *прил* (*суп, каша*) barley *опред*; ~ая крупа pearl barley.

перлюстрировать (-ую) *сов перех* to censor.

перманент (-а) *м* perm (= *permanent wave*).

перманентный (-ен, -на, -но) *прил* permanent.

пернатый (-ого; *decl like adj*) *м* (*обычно мн*) bird.

пёрнуть (-у, -ешь) *сов неперех* (*груб!*) to fart (!)

перо (-á; *nom pl* -ья, *gen pl* -ьев) *ср* (*птицы*) feather; (*для письма: гусиное*) quill; (: *стальное, золотое*) nib.

перочинный *прил*: ~ нож penknife (*мн* penknives).

перпендикулярный (-ен, -на, -но) *прил* perpendicular.

перрон (-а) *м* platform (*RAIL*).

перс (-а) *м* Persian.

персидский (-ая, -ое, -ие) *прил* Persian; Персидский залив Persian Gulf.

персик (-а) *м* (*дерево*) peach tree; (*плод*) peach.

Персия (-и) *ж* Persia.

персиянка (-ки; *gen pl* -ок) *ж см* перс.

персона (-ы) *ж* person; собственной ~ой in person.

персонаж (-а) *м* character.

персонал (-а) *м* (*АДМИН*) personnel, staff.

персональный *прил* personal; персональная выставка one-man exhibition; персональный компьютер PC (= *personal computer*).

перспектива (-ы) *ж* (*ГЕОМ*) perspective; (*вид*) view; ~ы (*планы*) prospects *мн*; в ~е (*в будущем*) in store.

перспективный *прил* (*изображение*) in perspective; (*планирование*) long-term; (*многообещающий*) promising; ~ план plan of future developments.

перстень (-ня) *м* ring.

Перу *ж нескл* Peru.

перуанский (-ая, -ое, -ие) *прил* Peruvian.

перфокарта (-ы) *ж сокр* (= *перфорационная карта*) punched *или* punch (*BRIT*) card.

перфолента (-ы) *ж сокр* (= *перфорационная лента*) punched tape.

пе́рхот|ь (**-и**) *ж собир* dandruff.
пе́рца *итп сущ см* **пе́рец**.
перча́т|ка (**-ки**; *gen pl* **-ок**) *ж* glove; (*боксёра*) (boxing) glove; **пе́рвая ~** (*СПОРТ*) champion boxer.
пе́рч|ить (**-у, -ишь**; *perf* **наперчи́ть** *или* **поперчи́ть**) *сов перех* to pepper.
перши́ть (*3sg* **-и́т**) *несов безл* (*разг*): **у меня́ ~и́т в го́рле** I've got a frog in my throat.
пе́рья *итп сущ см* **перо́**.
пёс (**пса**) *м* dog.
пе́сен *сущ см* **пе́сня**.
пе́сенник (**-а**) *м* songbook; (*композитор*) songwriter.
пес|е́ц (**-ца́**) *м* arctic fox.
песка́ *итп сущ см* **песо́к**.
песка́р|ь (**-я́**) *м* gudgeon.
песк|и́ (**-о́в**) *мн* sands *мн*.
песн|ь (**-и**; *gen pl* **-ей**) *ж* (*в поэме*) canto.
пе́сн|я (**-и**; *gen pl* **-ен**) *ж* song; **ста́рая ~** (*разг*) the same old story.
пес|о́к (**-ка́**; *part gen* **-ку́**) *м* sand; **са́харный ~** granulated sugar; *см также* **пески́**.
песо́чниц|а (**-ы**) *ж* sandpit (*BRIT*), sandbox (*US*).
песо́чный *прил* (*цвет*) sandy; (*тесто, печенье*) short; **песо́чные часы́** hourglass.
пессими́ст (**-а**) *м* pessimist.
пессимисти́ч|ный (**-ен, -на, -но**) *прил* pessimistic.
пестици́д (**-а**) *м* pesticide.
пе́ст|овать (**-ую**; *perf* **вы́пестовать**) *несов перех* (*перен*) to nurture.
пестр|е́ть (*3sg* **-е́т**, *3pl* **-ю́т**) *несов неперех* (*виднеться*) to be colourful (*BRIT*) *или* colorful (*US*); (*3pl* **-я́т**; *мелькать*) to make a colo(u)rful display; **в саду́/на лугу́ ~ю́т цветы́** the garden/meadow is bright with flowers.
пестр|и́ть (*3sg* **-и́т**, *3pl* **-я́т**) *несов неперех*: **~** +*instr* to be full of.
пёстр|ый (**-, -а́, -о**) *прил* (*ткань, ковёр*) multi-coloured (*BRIT*), multi-colored (*US*); (*перен: разнородный*) mixed.
песца́ *итп сущ см* **пес|е́ц**.
песча́ник (**-а**) *м* sandstone.
песча́ный *прил* (*берег, дно реки*) sandy; **песча́ная бу́ря** sandstorm.
пе́тель *сущ см* **пе́тля**.
Петербу́рг *сущ* = **Санкт-Петербу́рг**.
пети́ци|я (**-и**) *ж* petition.
петли́ц|а (**-ы**) *ж* (*петля*) buttonhole; (*нашивка*) tab (*on uniform*).
пе́тл|я (**-и**; *gen pl* **-ель**) *ж* loop; (*в вязании*) stitch; (*двери, крышки*) hinge; (*в одежде: для пуговицы*) buttonhole; (: *для крючка*) eye.
петля́|ть (**-ю**) *несов неперех* to meander.
петру́шк|а (**-и**) *ж* parsley.
пету́нь|я (**-и**) *ж* petunia.
пету́х (**-а́**) *м* cock, rooster (*US*).
петуши́ный *прил* (*пение*) cocks'; **~ бой** cockfight; **~ го́лос** a squeaky voice.
пе|ть (**пою́, поёшь**; *pt* **-л, -ла, -ло**, *imper* **пой(те)**, *perf* **спеть**) *несов перех* to sing.

пехо́т|а (**-ы**) *ж* infantry.
пехоти́н|ец (**-ца**) *м* infantryman (*мн* infantrymen).
пехо́тный *прил* infantry *опред*.
печа́лен *прил см* **печа́льный**.
печа́л|иться (**-юсь, -ишься**; *perf* **опеча́литься**) *несов возв* to be sad.
печа́л|ь (**-и**) *ж* (*грусть*) sadness, sorrow; **не́ было ~и!** (*разг*) what a nuisance!
печа́льно *нареч* (*петь, вы́глядеть*) sadly ♦ **как сказ** it's sad; **~, что мы не встре́тились** it's sad that we didn't meet; **~ изве́стный** notorious.
печа́льный (**-ен, -ьна, -ьно**) *прил* sad; (*ошибка, судьба, память*) unhappy; **~ьная изве́стность** *или* **сла́ва** ill repute.
печа́та|ть (**-ю**; *perf* **напеча́тать**) *несов перех* (*также ФОТО*) to print; (*публиковать*) to publish; (*на пишущей машинке*) to type
▸ **печа́таться** (*perf* **напеча́таться**) *несов возв* to have one's work published.
печа́тающ|ий (**-ая, -ее, -ие**) *прил*: **~ая голо́вка** (*КОМП*) printhead; **~ее колесо́** (*КОМП*) printwheel.
печа́т|ка (**-ки**; *gen pl* **-ок**) *ж* signet.
печа́тник (**-а**) *м* (*работник*) printer.
печа́тный *прил* (*станок*) printing *опред*; (*цех*) print *опред*; (*интервью итп*) published; **писа́ть (написа́ть** *perf*) **~ыми бу́квами** to print; **печа́тные бу́квы** block letters; **печа́тный лист** (*единица измерения*) printer's sheet.
печа́ток *сущ см* **печа́тка**.
печа́т|ь (**-и**) *ж* stamp, seal; (*на дверях, на сейфе*) seal; (*издательское дело*) printing; (*след: страданий*) mark ♦ *собир* (*пресса*) press; **выходи́ть (вы́йти** *perf*) **из ~и** to come out, be published.
пе́чек *сущ см* **пе́чка**.
печён|ка (**-ки**; *gen pl* **-ок**) *ж* liver; **в ~х сиде́ть** (*impf*) **у кого́-н** (*разг*) to get on sb's nerves.
печёный *прил* baked.
пе́чен|ь (**-и**) *ж* (*АНАТ*) liver.
пече́нь|е (**-я**) *ср* biscuit (*BRIT*), cookie (*US*).
пе́ч|ка (**-ки**; *gen pl* **-ек**) *ж* stove.
пе|чь (**-чи**; *loc sg* **-чи́**, *gen pl* **-е́й**) *ж* stove; (*ТЕХ*) furnace; (: *обжиговая*) kiln; ♦ (**-ку́, -чёшь** *итп*, **-ку́т**; *pt* **пёк, -кла́, -кло́**, *perf* **испе́чь**) *несов перех* to bake; **микроволно́вая ~** microwave oven
▸ **пе́чься** (*perf* **испе́чься**) *несов возв* to bake; (*заботиться*): **пе́чься о** +*prp* to look after (*BRIT*), take care of (*US*).
пе́шек *сущ см* **пе́шка**.
пешехо́д (**-а**) *м* pedestrian.
пешехо́дный *прил* pedestrian *опред*; (*совершаемый пешком*) on foot; **пешехо́дный мост** footbridge.
пе́ш|ий (**-ая, -ее, -ие**) *прил* (*солдат*) foot *опред*; (*движение*) pedestrian *опред*; (*совершаемый пешком*) on foot; **~им хо́дом** on foot.
пе́ш|ка (**-ки**; *gen pl* **-ек**) *ж* (*также перен*) pawn.
пешко́м *нареч* on foot.

пеще́р|а (-ы) ж cave.
пеще́рный прил (живопись) cave опред; пеще́рный челове́к caveman (мн cavemen).
ПЗУ ср сокр (= постоянное запоминающее устройство) ROM (= read-only memory).
пиала́ (-ы́) ж handleless cup used in Central Asia.
пиани́но ср нескл (upright) piano.
пиани́ст (-а) м pianist.
пиани́ст|ка (-ки; gen pl -ок) ж см пиани́ст.
пивн|а́я (-о́й; decl like adj) ж ≈ bar, ≈ pub (BRIT).
пивно́й прил (бар, бочка) beer опред; (дрожжи) brewer's.
пи́в|о (-а) ср beer.
пига́лица (-ы) ж (перен: пренебр) pipsqueak.
пигме́й (-я) м pygmy.
пигме́нт (-а) м pigment.
пигмента́ци|я (-и) ж pigmentation.
пиджа́к (-а́) м jacket.
пижа́м|а (-ы) ж pyjamas мн.
пи́жм|а (-ы) ж (трава) feverfew; (дерево) wild rowan.
пижо́н (-а) м (разг: пренебр) pose(u)r.
пик (-а) м (также перен) peak ♦ прил неизм (часы, период, время) peak опред; часы́ ~ (в работе транспорта) rush hour; (электростанции, телефона итп) peak period.
пи́к|а (-и) ж (рыцаря) lance; (солдата) pike; в ~у кому́-н to get at sb.
пика́нт|ный (-ен, -на, -но) прил (вкус) piquant; (случай, слухи) spicy; (женщина, внешность) alluring.
пике́т (-а) м picket.
пикети́р|овать (-ую) несов перех to picket.
пи́к|и (-) мн (в картах) spades мн.
пики́р|овать (-ую) (не)сов неперех (АВИА) to dive.
пикиро́вщик (-а) м (АВИА) dive-bomber.
пикни́к (-а́) м picnic.
пи́кн|уть (-у, -ешь) сов неперех (разг: животное) to let out a squeak; (: птица) to let out a squawk; он при ней не смел и ~ he wouldn't dare speak out in her presence.
пи́ковый прил (наивысший) peak опред; (в картах) of spades; ~ое положе́ние (разг) mess.
пи́ксел|ь (-я) м (КОМП) pixel.
пил итп несов см пить.
пил|а́ (-ы́; nom pl -ы) ж saw.
пилигри́м (-а) м pilgrim.
пилика́|ть (-ю) несов неперех (разг): ~ на +prp (на скрипке) to scrape away on.
пил|и́ть (-ю́, -ишь) несов перех to saw; (перен: разг) to nag.
пи́л|ка (-ки; gen pl -ок) ж nail file.
пиломатериа́л|ы (-ов) мн sawn timber ед.
пило́т (-а) м pilot; (СПОРТ) driver.
пилоти́р|овать (-ую) несов перех to pilot.

пило́т|ка (-ки; gen pl -ок) ж cloth cap worn as part of uniform.
пилю́л|я (-и) ж pill; проглоти́ть (perf) ~ю (перен) to swallow a bitter pill.
пиля́стр|а (-ы) ж pilaster.
пина́|ть (-ю) несов перех to kick.
пингви́н (-а) м penguin.
пинг-по́нг (-а) м table tennis, ping-pong.
пине́т|ка (-ки; gen pl -ок) ж (обычно мн) bootee.
пин|о́к (-ка́) м kick.
пинце́т (-а) м (МЕД) tweezers мн; (ТЕХ) pincers мн.
пио́н (-а) м peony.
пионе́р (-а) м pioneer; (в СССР) member of Communist Youth organisation.
пипе́т|ка (-ки; gen pl -ок) ж pipette.
пир (-а; loc sg -у́, nom pl -ы́) м feast.
пирами́д|а (-ы) ж pyramid.
пира́т (-а) м pirate.
пира́тский (-ая, -ое, -ие) прил pirate опред.
Пирене́|и (-ев) мн Pyrenees.
пир|ова́ть (-у́ю) несов неперех to feast.
пиро́г (-а́) м pie.
пирожка́ итп сущ см пирожо́к.
пирожко́в|ая (-ой; decl like adj) ж (тип закусочной) snack-bar.
пиро́жн|ое (-ого; decl like adj) ср cake, sweet pastry.
пирож|о́к (-ка́) м (с мясом) pasty, pie; (с вареньем) turnover, tart.
пирс (-а) м pier.
пируэ́т (-а) м pirouette.
пи́ршеств|о (-а) ср feast.
писа́|ка (-и) м/ж (разг: пренебр) scribbler.
писа́ни|е (-я) ср (действие) writing; Свяще́нное П~ Holy Scripture.
писани́н|а (-ы) ж (разг: пренебр) scribblings мн.
пи́саный прил (разг): она́ ~ая краса́вица she is a picture of beauty ♦ (-ого; decl like adj) м: говори́ть как по ~ому to speak fluently.
пи́сар|ь (-я) м clerk.
писа́тел|ь (-я) м writer.
писа́тельница (-ы) ж см писа́тель.
пис|а́ть (-шу́, -шешь; perf написа́ть) несов перех to write; (картину, пейзаж) to paint ♦ неперех (no perf; ребёнок, ученик) to be able to write; (ручка) to write; он написа́л, как дое́хал/где устро́ился he wrote to say he had arrived safely/where he was staying; ~ши пропа́ло (разг) it is as good as lost
▶ писа́ться несов возв (слово) to be spelt или spelled; как пи́шется э́то сло́во? how do you spell this word?; мне сего́дня не пи́шется I don't feel like writing today.
пи́сем сущ см письмо́.
пис|е́ц (-ца́) м (ИСТ) scribe.
писк (-а) м (ребёнка) squeak; (птицы) cheep.
писклявый прил (голос) squeaky.
пискля́вый прил = писклявый.

пи́скн|уть (-у, -ешь) *сов непepex* (*ребёнок, животное*) to give a squeak; (*птица*) to give a cheep.

пистоле́т (-а) *м* pistol.

писто́н (-а) *м* (*в патроне*) percussion cap.

писца́ *итп сущ см* **писе́ц**.

писчебума́жный *прил*: ~ **магази́н** stationer's.

пи́счий (-ая, -ее, -ие) *прил* writing *опред*.

пи́сьменно *нареч* in writing.

пи́сьменность (-и) *ж* written language; (*памятники*) literary texts *мн*.

пи́сьменн|ый *прил* (*просьба, экзамен*) written; (*стол, прибор*) writing; **в ~ой фо́рме** in writing.

пись|мо́ (-ьма́; *nom pl* -ьма, *gen pl* -ем) *ср* letter; (*no pl; иероглифическое, алфавитное*) script; (*искусство: манера*) style.

пита́ни|е (-я) *ср* (*больного, ребёнка*) feeding; (*ТЕХ*) supply; (*вегетарианское, плохое*) diet; **обще́ственное** ~ public catering.

пита́тел|ьный *прил* (*соли, вещества*) nutritious; (*крем, лосьон итп*) nourishing; (*клапан, станция, насос*) supply *опред*; (-ен, -ьна, -ьно; *каша, бульон*) filling; **пита́тельная среда́** (*БИО: перен*) breeding ground.

пита́|ть (-ю) *несов перех* (*кормить*) to feed; (*снабжать*) to supply; (*перен: испытывать*) to feel

► **пита́ться** *несов возв*: ~**ся** +*instr* (*человек, растение*) to live on; (*животное*) to feed on; (*ТЕХ*) to run on.

пито́м|ец (-ца) *м* (*воспитанник*) pupil.

пито́мник (-а) *м* (*БОТ*) nursery.

пито́н (-а) *м* python.

пи|ть (пью, пьёшь; *pt* -л, -ла́, -ло, *imper* **пе́й(те)**, *perf* **вы́пить**) *несов перех* to drink ◆ *непepex*: ~ **за кого́-н/что-н** to drink to sb/sth; **как ~ дать** (*разг*) for sure.

питьев|о́й *прил*: ~**а́я вода́** drinking water.

пиха́|ть (-ю) *несов перех* (*разг: толкать*) to shove; (*разг: засовывать*) to cram

► **пиха́ться** *несов возв* to push and shove (each other).

пихн|у́ть (-у́, -ёшь) *сов перех* to give a shove; (*сунуть*) to push.

пи́хт|а (-ы) *ж* fir (tree).

пи́цц|а (-ы) *ж* pizza.

пиццери|я (-и) *ж* pizzeria.

пи́чка|ть (-ю; *perf* **напи́чкать**) *несов перех* (*разг*): ~ **кого́-н чем-н** (*конфетами итп*) to stuff sb with sth; (*лекарствами*) to pour sth down sb's neck.

пишу́(сь) *итп несов см* **писа́ть(ся)**.

пи́шущ|ий (-ая, -ее, -ие) *прил*: ~**ая маши́нка** typewriter.

пи́щ|а (-и) *ж* food; ~ **для размышле́ний** *или* **ума́** food for thought; ~ **для воображе́ния** fuel to the imagination.

пища́|ть (-у́, -и́шь) *несов непepex* (*птицы*) to cheep; (*животные*) to squeak; (*ребёнок*) to cry.

пищебло́к (-а) *м* kitchen (*for catering*).

пищеваре́ни|е (-я) *ср* digestion.

пищев|о́й *прил* food *опред*; (*соль*) edible; **пищева́я со́да** baking soda.

пия́в|ка (-ки; *gen pl* -ок) *ж* leech.

ПК *м сокр* (= персона́льный компью́тер) PC (= *personal computer*).

пл. *сокр* (= пло́щадь) Sq. (= *Square*).

плав (-а) *м*: **на** ~**у́** afloat.

пла́вани|е (-я) *ср* swimming; (*на судне*) sailing; (*рейс*) voyage; **занима́ться** (*impf*) ~**м** to train as a swimmer.

пла́вательный *прил* swimming *опред* **пла́вательный бассе́йн** swimming pool.

пла́ва|ть (-ю) *несов непepex* (*человек, животное*) to swim; (*корабль*) to sail; (*лист, облако*) to float; (*перен: на экзамене итп*) to be out of one's depth; (*служить на судне*) ~ +*instr* to work (at sea) as.

пла́вен *прил см* **пла́вный**.

пла́в|ить (-лю, -ишь; *perf* **распла́вить**) *несов перех* to smelt

► **пла́виться** (*perf* **распла́виться**) *несов возв* to smelt; (*стекло, пластмасса*) to melt.

пла́в|ка (-ки; *gen pl* -ок) *ж* (*действие*) smelting; (*продукт*) smelted metal.

пла́в|ки (-ок) *мн* swimming trunks *мн*.

пла́влени|е (-я) *ср*: **температу́ра** *или* **то́чка** ~ melting point.

пла́вленый *прил*: ~ **сыр** processed cheese.

пла́влю(сь) *несов см* **пла́вить(ся)**.

плавни́к (-а́) *м* (*у рыб*) fin; (*у водных животных*) flipper.

пла́в|ный (-ен, -на, -но) *прил* smooth.

пла́вок *сущ см* **пла́вка, пла́вки**.

плаву́ч|ий (-ая, -ее, -ие) *прил* floating; **плаву́чая ба́за** (*в рыболовстве*) *floating unit for storing and processing fish*.

плагиа́т (-а) *м* plagiarism.

плагиа́тор (-а) *м* plagiarist.

пла́зм|а (-ы) *ж* plasma.

плака́т (-а) *м* poster.

пла́|кать (-чу, -чешь) *несов непepex* to cry, weep; ~ (*impf*) **от** +*gen* (*от боли итп*) to cry from; (*от радости*) to cry with; (*от горя*) to cry in; ~**кал мой выходно́й** (*разг*) so much for my day off; ~**кали мои де́ньги** (*разг*) that's my money up the spout; **па́лка по нему́** ~**чет** (*разг*) he's asking for a beating

► **пла́каться** *несов возв* (*разг*): ~**ся (на** +*acc*) (*на судьбу, на участь*) to moan (about).

плакир|ова́ть (-у́ю) (*не*)*сов перех* (*ТЕХ*) to plate.

пла́кс|а (-ы) *м/ж* crybaby.

плаку́ч|ий (-ая, -ее, -ие) *прил*: ~**ая и́ва** weeping willow.

пла́мени *итп сущ см* **пла́мя**.

пла́менный *прил* (*цвета пламени*) flame-coloured (*BRIT*), flame-colored (*US*); (*горячий*) burning; (*перен: страстный*) ardent.

пла́м|я (-ени; *как* **вре́мя**; *см* **Table 4**) *ср* flame.

план (-а) *м* plan; (*чертёж*) plan, map; **кру́пный**

~ (КИНО, ФОТО) close-up; **пла́ны на бу́дущее** future plans; **пере́дний** ~ foreground; **за́дний** ~ background; **на пе́рвом пла́не у неё учёба** her priority is studying; **в теорети́ческом пла́не** in theory; **отходи́ть (отойти́** perf**)** или **отступа́ть (отступи́ть** perf**) на второ́й** ~ to become less important.

планёр (-а) м glider.

планери́зм (-а) м gliding.

плане́т|**а** (-ы) ж planet.

планета́ри|**й** (-я) м planetarium.

плани́ровани|**е** (-я) ср planning; ~ **семьй** family planning.

плани́р|**овать** (-ую) несов перех to plan ◆ неперех (perf **заплани́ровать; намерева́ться**) to plan; (АВИА) to glide.

планир|**ова́ть** (-у́ю; perf **распланирова́ть**) несов перех to lay out.

плани́ровк|**а** (-и) ж (участка, квартиры) layout.

плани́ро́вщик (-а) м planner.

пла́н|**ка** (-ки; gen pl -ок) ж (деревянная) strip of wood; (металлическая) strip of metal.

планкто́н (-а) м plankton.

планови́к (-а́) м planner.

пла́новый прил (задание, продукция) planned; (отдел, комиссия) planning.

пла́нок сущ см **пла́нка**.

планоме́рный (-ен, -на, -но) прил systematic.

планта́ци|**я** (-и) ж plantation.

планше́т (-а) м mapcase.

пласт (-а́) м (также перен) stratum (мн strata).

пла́стик (-а) м = **пластма́сса**.

пла́стик|**а** (-и) ж (скульптура) the plastic arts мн; (гармония) grace; (балетная) eurhythmics; (МЕД) plastic surgery.

пластили́н (-а) м plasticine.

пласти́н|**а** (-ы) ж (ГЕО) plate.

пласти́н|**ка** (-ки; gen pl -ок) ж (уменьш от **пласти́на**; (МУЗ) record; **долгоигра́ющая** ~ album, L.P. (= long-playing record).

пласти́чен прил см **пласти́чный**.

пласти́ческ|**ий** (-ая, -ое, -ие) прил plastic опред; **пласти́ческая ма́сса** plastic; **пласти́ческая опера́ция** (МЕД) plastic surgery.

пласти́чный (-ен, -на, -но) прил (жесты, движения) graceful; (материалы, вещества) plastic опред.

пластма́сс|**а** (-ы) ж сокр (= **пласти́ческая ма́сса**) plastic.

пласту́нск|**ий** (-ая, -ое, -ие) прил: **ползти́ по**—**и** to crawl on one's belly.

пла́стыр|**ь** (-я) м (МЕД) plaster.

пла́т|**а** (-ы) ж (за труд, за услуги) pay, salary; (за квартиру) payment; (за проезд) fee; (перен: награда, кара) reward; **за́работная** ~ wages мн.

плата́н (-а) м plane (tree).

плат|**ёж** (-ежа́) м payment; **нало́женным** ~**ежо́м** cash on delivery.

платёжеспосо́бен прил см **платёжеспосо́бный**.

платёжеспосо́бност|**ь** (-и) ж solvency.

платёжеспосо́б|**ный** (-ен, -на, -но) прил (КОММ) solvent.

платёж|**ный** прил (КОММ): ~ **бланк** payslip; ~**ая ве́домость** payroll; ~**ое поруче́ние** или **тре́бование** payment order.

пла́тин|**а** (-ы) ж platinum.

пла|**ти́ть** (-чу́, -тишь; perf **заплати́ть** или **уплати́ть**) несов перех to pay ◆ неперех (перен): ~ **чем-н за что-н** to repay sth with sth; ~ (**заплати́ть** или **уплати́ть** perf**) нали́чными/нату́рой** to pay in cash/in kind

▸ **плати́ться** (perf **поплати́ться**) несов возв: ~**ся чем-н за что-н** to pay for sth with sth.

платка́ итп сущ см **плато́к**.

пла́тный прил (вход, стоянка) chargeable; (школа) fee-paying; (больница) private.

плато́ ср нескл plateau.

плато́к (-ка́) м (головной) headscarf (мн headscarves); (наплечный) shawl; (также: носово́й ~) handkerchief.

платфо́рм|**а** (-ы) ж platform; (маленькая станция) halt; (открытый вагон) open goods truck; (основание) foundation.

пла́ть|**е** (-я; gen pl -ев) ср dress ◆ собир (одежда) clothing, clothes мн.

плафо́н (-а) м decorated ceiling; (абажур) shade (for ceiling light).

пла́ха|**а** (-и) ж (ИСТ) (executioner's) block.

плац (-а; loc sg -у́) м (ВОЕН) parade ground.

плацда́рм (-а) м (ВОЕН) bridgehead.

плаце́нт|**а** (-ы) ж placenta.

плацка́ртный прил: ~ **ваго́н** railway car with open berths instead of compartments.

плач (-а) м crying.

плаче́вный (-ен, -на, -но) прил (бедственный) lamentable; (жалкий) pitiful.

пла́чу(сь) итп несов см **пла́кать(ся)**.

плачу́(сь) несов см **плати́ть(ся)**.

плашмя́ нареч flat.

плащ (-а́) м cloak; (пальто) raincoat.

плащани́ц|**а** (-ы) ж (РЕЛ) the shroud of Christ.

плащ-пала́т|**ка** (-ки; gen pl -ок) ж (ВОЕН) waterproof cape.

плебе́й (-я) м plebeian.

плебе́йск|**ий** (-ая, -ое, -ие) прил plebeian опред.

плев|**а́ть** (-ю́ю) несов неперех to spit; (perf **наплева́ть**; перен): ~ **на** +acc (разг: на правила, на мнение других) to not give a damn about; ~ (impf) **в потоло́к** (разг) to loaf (about)

▸ **плева́ться** несов возв to spit.

плев|**о́к** (-ка́) м spit, spittle.

плеври́т (-а) м pleurisy.

плёвый прил: (**э́то**) ~**ое де́ло** (разг) it's a piece of cake.

плед (-а) м (tartan) rug.

пле́йер (-а) м Walkman®.

плёл *итп несов см* **плести́**.

пле́мени *итп сущ см* **пле́мя**.

племенно́й *прил* (*язык, территория*) tribal; (*с.-х.: скот*) purebred; (*хозяйство, животноводство*) (pure-strain) stockbreeding *опред*; **племенно́й бык** pedigree bull; **племенна́я ло́шадь** thoroughbred (horse).

пле́м|я (-ени; *как вре́мя; см* **Table 4**) *ср* (*также перен*) tribe; **молодо́е ~** the younger generation.

племя́нник (-а) м nephew.

племя́нниц|а (-ы) ж niece.

плен (-а; *loc sg* -у́) м captivity; **брать (взять** *perf*) **кого́-н в ~** to take sb prisoner; **попада́ть (попа́сть** *perf*) **в ~** to be taken prisoner.

плена́рный *прил* plenary.

плени́тельный (-ен, -ьна, -ьно) *прил* captivating, charming.

плени́ть (-ю́, -и́шь; *impf* **пленя́ть**) *сов перех* (*очаро́вывать*) to captivate, charm.

плёнк|а (-и; *gen pl* -ок) ж (*также* ФОТО); (*кожица*) film, membrane; (*магнитофонная*) tape; **запи́сывать (записа́ть** *perf*) **что-н на ~ку** to record sth (on tape).

пле́нн|ая (-ой; *decl like adj*) ж см **пле́нный**.

пле́нник (-а) м (*пле́нный*) prisoner, captive.

пле́нниц|а (-ы) ж см **пле́нник**.

пле́нный *прил* captive *опред* ♦ (-ого; *decl like adj*) м prisoner, captive.

плёнок *сущ см* **плёнка**.

пле́нум (-а) м plenum.

пленя́ть (-ю) *несов от* **плени́ть**.

пле́сень (-и) ж mould (BRIT), mold (US).

плеск (-а) м splash.

плеска́ть (-щу́, -щешь) *несов неперех* to splash; (*слегка́*) to lap

▶ **плеска́ться** *несов возв* to splash; (*во́лны: слегка́*) to lap.

пле́сневе|ть (3sg -ет, 3pl -ют, perf **запле́сневеть**) *несов неперех* to go mouldy (BRIT) *или* moldy (US).

плести́ (-ету́, -етёшь; *pt* -ёл, -ела́, -ело́, perf **сплести́**) *несов перех* (*се́ти*) to weave; (*вено́к, во́лосы*) to plait; (*глу́пости*) to spout; **~** (*impf*) **интри́ги** *или* **ко́зни** to weave a web of intrigue; **~** (*impf*) **небыли́цы** (*разг*) to spin yarns

▶ **плести́сь** *несов возв* (*разг: челове́к: ме́дленно идти́*) to trudge, plod.

плетёный *прил* (*корзи́на, ме́бель*) wicker; (*санда́лии*) woven.

плете́нь (-ня́) м wattle fence.

плётк|а (-и; *gen pl* -ок) ж whip.

плетня́ *итп сущ см* **плете́нь**.

плёток *сущ см* **плётка**.

плету́(сь) *итп несов см* **плести́(сь)**.

плеть (-и; *gen pl* -е́й) ж whip.

пле́чик|и (-ов) *мн* (*ве́шалка*) coat hangers *мн*; (*подкла́дки*) shoulder pads *мн*.

плечи́ст|ый (-, -а, -о) *прил* broad-shouldered.

плеч|о́ (-а́; *nom pl* -и) *ср* shoulder; **~м к ~у́** shoulder to shoulder; **э́то мне не по ~у́** I am not up to it; **за ~а́ми у него́ 5 лет учёбы** he has 5 years of study behind him *или* under his belt; **с чужо́го ~а́** (*оде́жда*) second-hand; **выноси́ть (вы́нести** *perf*) **что-н на свои́х ~а́х** to carry sth on one's shoulders.

плеши́в|ый (-, -а, -о) *прил* bald.

плешь (-и) ж bald patch.

плёщет(ся) *итп несов см* **плеска́ть(ся)**.

плещу́сь *итп несов см* **плеска́ться**.

плея́д|а (-ы) ж (*учёных, музыка́нтов итп*) galaxy.

Пли́мут (-а) м Plymouth.

пли́нтус (-а) м skirting board (BRIT), baseboard (US).

плиссе́ *ср нескл* pleats *мн* ♦ *прил неизм*: **ю́бка/пла́тье ~** pleated skirt/dress.

плит|а́ (-ы́; *nom pl* -ы) ж (*ка́менная*) slab; (*металли́ческая*) plate; (*печь*) cooker, stove.

пли́тк|а (-и; *gen pl* -ок) ж (*керами́ческая, ка́фельная*) tile; (*шокола́да*) bar; (*электри́ческая*) hot plate; (*га́зовая*) camping stove.

плов (-а) м pilaff.

плов|е́ц (-ца́) м swimmer.

пловчи́х|а (-и) ж см **плове́ц**.

плод (-а́) м (БОТ) fruit; (БИО) foetus (BRIT), fetus (US); **~** +*gen* (*перен*) fruits of.

плоди́ться (3sg -и́тся, 3pl -я́тся, perf **расплоди́ться**) *несов возв* (*также перен*) to multiply.

плодови́т|ый (-, -а, -о) *прил* fertile; (*перен*) prolific.

плодово́дств|о (-а) *ср* fruit-growing.

плодоро́д|ный (-ен, -на, -но) *прил* fertile.

плодотво́р|ный (-ен, -на, -но) *прил* fruitful.

пло́мб|а (-ы) ж (*в зу́бе*) filling; (*на дверя́х, на се́йфе*) seal.

пломби́р (-а) м rich creamy ice-cream.

пломбиро́ва|ть (-ю; perf **запломбирова́ть**) *несов перех* (*зуб*) to fill; (perf **опломбирова́ть**; *дверь, сейф*) to seal.

пло́ский (-кая, -кое, -кие; -ок, -ка́, -ко) *прил* flat; (*перен: неоригина́льный*) feeble.

плоскогу́бц|ы (-ев) *мн* pliers *мн*.

пло́скост|ь (-и; *gen pl* -е́й) ж (*также перен*) plane.

пло́сок *прил см* **пло́ский**.

плот (-а́; *loc sg* -у́) м raft.

пло́тен *прил см* **пло́тный**.

плоти́н|а (-ы) ж dam.

пло́тник (-а) м carpenter.

пло́тно *нареч* (*закры́ть дверь*) tightly; (*пообе́дать*) well.

пло́тность (-и) ж density.

пло́т|ный (-ен, -на́, -но) *прил* (*дым, тума́н*) dense, thick; (*населе́ние, толпа́, лес*) dense; (*бума́га, ко́жа*) thick; (*те́ло, челове́к*) thick-set; (*за́втрак, обе́д*) substantial.

плотоя́д|ный (-ен, -на, -но) *прил* carnivorous; (перен) lustful.

пло́тск|ий (-ая, -ое, -ие) *прил* (желания) carnal.

пло́ттер (-а) м (КОМП) plotter.

плоть (-и) ж flesh; ~ и кровь flesh and blood; а́нгел/дья́вол во ~й angel/devil incarnate.

пло́хо *нареч* (учиться, работать) badly ♦ *как сказ* it's bad ♦ *ср нескл* (ПРОСВЕЩ) ≈ poor (*school mark*); без друзе́й ~ it's bad not to have friends; мне ~ I feel bad; в го́роде ~ с хле́бом there's a shortage of bread in the town; у меня́ ~ с деньга́ми I am short of money.

плох|о́й (-а́я, -о́е, -и́е; -, -а́, -о) *прил* bad; мать ста́ла ~а́ mother is in a bad way.

площа́д|ка (-ки; *gen pl* -ок) ж (де́тская) playground; (спорти́вная) ground; (строи́тельная) site; (часть вагона) corridor; ле́стничная ~ landing; поса́дочная ~ landing pad.

пло́щадь (-и; *gen pl* -е́й) ж (ме́сто) square; (пространство, также МАТ) area; (разг: также: жила́я ~) living space.

пло́ще *сравн прил от* **пло́ский**.

плуг (-а; *nom pl* -и́) м plough (*BRIT*), plow (*US*).

плут (-а́) м (моше́нник) cheat; (хитре́ц) rogue.

плута́|ть (-ю) *несов неперех* (разг) to wander.

плут|ова́ть (-у́ю; *perf* **сплутова́ть**) *несов неперех* to cheat.

Плуто́н (-а) м Pluto.

плуто́ний (-я) м plutonium.

плы|ть (-ву́, -вёшь; *pt* -л, -ла́, -ло) *несов неперех* (человек, животное) to swim; (судно) to sail; (лист, облако) to float.

плюга́вый (-, -а, -о) *прил* (разг: пренебр) wimpish.

плю́|нуть (-у, -ешь) *сов неперех* to spit; ~ (*perf*) на что-н (разг) to stop bothering about sth; плю́нь! (разг) forget it!; э́то мне раз ~ (разг) it's a doddle (for me).

плюрали́зм (-а) м pluralism.

плюралисти́ческ|ий (-ая, -ое, -ие) *прил* pluralist(ic).

плюс м нескл, союз plus ♦ (-а) м (разг: преиму́щество) plus (мн plusses); два ~ два – четы́ре two plus two is four; ~~ми́нус 2см plus or minus или give or take 2cm.

плюхн|уться (-усь, -ешься; *impf* плю́хаться) *сов возв* (человек) to flop down.

плюш (-а) м plush.

плю́ш|ка (-ки; *gen pl* -ек) ж bun.

плющ (-а́) м ivy.

плю́щ|ить (-у, -ишь; *perf* сплю́щить) *несов перех* to flatten.

пляж (-а) м beach.

пля|са́ть (-шу́, -шешь; *perf* сплясать) *несов перех* to dance.

пля́с|ка (-ки; *gen pl* -ок) ж dance.

пля́шу *итп несов см* **пляса́ть**.

пневмати́ческ|ий (-ая, -ое, -ие) *прил* pneumatic.

пневмони́|я (-и) ж pneumonia.

Пномпе́нь (-я) м Pnomh Penh.

пн|у́ть (-у, -ёшь) *сов перех* (разг) to boot.

пня *итп сущ см* **пень**.

ПО *ср сокр* = произво́дственное объедине́ние.

─ **KEYWORD** ─

по *предл* (+*dat*) **1** (о ме́сте де́йствия, вдоль) along; де́вочка идёт по у́лице the little girl is walking along the street; по берега́м расту́т кусты́ bushes grow along the banks; ло́дка плывёт по реке́ the boat is sailing on the river; спуска́ться (спусти́ться *perf*) по ле́стнице to go down the stairs

2 (при глаго́лах движе́ния) round; ходи́ть (*impf*) по ко́мнате/са́ду to walk round the room/ garden; путеше́ствовать (*impf*) по стране́ to travel round the country; плыть (*impf*) по тече́нию to go downstream; (перен) to swim with the tide; идти́ (*impf*) по ве́тру to sail with the wind

3 (об объе́кте возде́йствия) on; уда́рить (*impf*) кого́-н по плечу́/лицу́ to hit on the shoulder/ face; уда́рить (*impf*) по врагу́/по контрабанди́стам to deal a blow to the enemy/to the smugglers

4 (в соотве́тствии с): де́йствовать по зако́ну/пра́вилам to act in accordance with the law/the rules; по расписа́нию/пла́ну according to schedule/plan; он ушёл по со́бственному жела́нию he left voluntarily; получа́ть (получи́ть *perf*) де́ньги по счёту to receive payment of a bill

5 (об основа́нии): суди́ть по вне́шности to judge by appearances; жени́ться (*impf/perf*) по любви́ to marry for love

6 (всле́дствие): по отсу́тствовать (*impf*) по боле́зни to be absent due to illness; по невнима́тельности due to carelessness; по необходи́мости out of necessity

7 (посре́дством): говори́ть по телефо́ну to speak on the phone; отправля́ть (отпра́вить *perf*) что-н по по́чте to send sth by post; передава́ть (переда́ть *perf*) что-н по ра́дио/по телеви́дению to broadcast sth on radio/television

8 (с це́лью, для): рабо́та по повыше́нию эффекти́вности work towards increased efficiency; о́рганы по борьбе́ с престу́пностью organizations in the fight against crime; опера́ция по захва́ту моста́ an operation to seize the bridge; я позва́л тебя́ по де́лу I called you on you business

9 (о како́й-н характери́стике объе́кта) in; по интере́сам/до́лжности in interests/position; по профе́ссии by profession; дед по ма́тери maternal grandfather; това́рищ по шко́ле

---

school friend

10 (*о сфере деятельности*) in; **заня́тия по литерату́ре** studies in literature; **иссле́дование по хи́мии** research in chemistry

11 (*о мере времени*): **по вечера́м/утра́м** in the evenings/mornings; **по воскресе́ньям/пя́тницам** on Sundays/Fridays; **я рабо́таю по це́лым дням** I work all day long; **рабо́та рассчи́тана по мину́там** the work is planned by the minute

12 (*о единичности предметов*): **ма́ма дала́ всем по я́блоку** Mum gave them each an apple; **мы купи́ли по одно́й кни́ге** we bought a book each

♦ *предл* (+*acc*) **1** (*вплоть до*) up to; **стоя́ть** (*impf*) **по по́яс в воде́** to stand up to the waist in water; **по настоя́щее вре́мя** up to the present time; **с пе́рвой по пя́тую главу́** from the first to (*BRIT*) *или* through (*US*) the fifth chapter; **я за́нят по го́рло** (*разг: перен*) I am up to my eyes in work; **он до уши в неё влюблён** he is head over heels in love with her

2 (*при обозначении цены*): **по два/три рубля́ за шту́ку** two/three roubles each

3 (*при обозначении количества*): **по два/три челове́ка** in twos/threes

♦ *предл* (+*prp*; *после*) on; **по оконча́нии рабо́ты** on finishing work; **по прие́зде** on arrival

по- *префикс* (*in verbs*; *о начале действия*) *indicating the beginning of an action eg.* **побежа́ть**; (*об ограниченном действии*) *indicating limitation of an action eg.* **поговори́ть**; (*о прерывистом действии*) *indicating action carried out at intervals eg.* **погля́дывать**; (*о действии, совершаем многими*) *indicating action undertaken by many people eg.* **повскака́ть**; (*in adjectives and adverbs*; *о неинтенсивном качестве*) *indicating non-intensive quality of sth eg.* **помя́гче**; (*подобно чем-н*) *indicating comparison with sth eg.* **по-но́вому**.

п/о *сокр* = **почто́вое отделе́ние**; **произво́дственное объедине́ние**.

по-англи́йски *нареч* in English; **как ~ э́то сло́во?** what is this word in English?

побагрове́|ть (**-ю**) *сов от* **багрове́ть**.

поба́ива|ться (**-юсь**) *несов возв*: ~ +*gen* to be a bit frightened of.

поба́лива|ть (*3sg* **-ет**, *3pl* **-ют**) *несов неперех* (*разг: иногда*) to ache now and again; (: *слегка*) to hurt a bit.

побе́г (**-а**) *м* (*из тюрьмы́*) escape; (*БОТ*) shoot, sprout.

побегу́ *итп сов см* **побежа́ть**.

побегу́шк|и *мн* (*разг*): **быть на ~ах у кого́-н** to run errands for sb; (*перен*) to be at sb's beck and call.

побе́д|а (**-ы**) *ж* victory; **оде́рживать** (**одержа́ть** *perf*) ~**у над кем-н/чем-н** to win a victory over

sb/sth.

победи́тел|ь (**-я**) *м* (*в войне*) victor; (*в состяза́нии*) winner.

победи́тельница (**-ы**) *ж см* **победи́тель**.

победи́|ть (*2sg* **-и́шь**, *3sg* **-и́т**, *impf* **побежда́ть**) *сов перех* to defeat ♦ *неперех* to win.

побе́дный *прил* victorious, triumphant; (*марш, салют*) victory *опред*.

победоно́с|ный (**-ен, -на, -но**) *прил* (*армия, атака*) victorious; (*перен: вид, слова*) triumphant.

побежа́ть (*как* **бежа́ть**; *см* **Table 20**) *сов неперех* (*человек, животное*) to start running; (*дни, годы*) to start to fly by; (*ручьи, слёзы*) to begin to flow.

побежда́|ть (**-ю**) *несов от* **победи́ть**.

побежи́шь *итп сов см* **побежа́ть**.

побеле́|ть (**-ю**) *сов от* **беле́ть**.

побел|и́ть (**-ю́, -ишь**) *сов от* **бели́ть**.

побе́лк|а (**-и**) *ж* whitewash; (*действие*) whitewashing.

побере́г(ся) *итп сов см* **побере́чь(ся)**.

поберегу́(сь) *итп сов см* **побере́чь(ся)**.

побере́жь|е (**-я**) *ср* coast.

побере́|чь (**-гу́, -жёшь** *итп*, **-гу́т**; *pt* **-ёг, -егла́, -егло́**) *сов перех* (*де́ньги, вре́мя*) to save; (*здоро́вье, мать*) to take care of, look after

▸ **побере́чься** *сов возв* to take care of o.s.

побесе́д|овать (**-ую**) *сов неперех* to have a chat.

побеспоко́|ить (**-ю, -ишь**) *сов перех* to disturb, bother; **позво́льте Вас ~** may I trouble you?; ~ (*perf*) **кого́-н прие́здом** to inconvenience sb by one's arrival

▸ **побеспоко́иться** *сов возв* (*прояви́ть забо́ту*) to concern o.s.

поб|и́ть (**-ью́, -ьёшь**) *сов от* **бить** ♦ *перех* (*повреди́ть*) to destroy; (*перебить*) to kill; (*разби́ть*) to break; (*impf* **побива́ть**; *СПОРТ*) to beat; **побива́ть** (~ *perf*) **реко́рд** to break a record.

поблагодар|и́ть (**-ю́, -и́шь**) *сов от* **благодари́ть**.

побла́жк|а (**-ки**; *gen pl* **-ек**) *ж* (*разг*) indulgence.

побледне́|ть (**-ю**) *сов от* **бледне́ть**.

поблёк|нуть (**-ну, -нешь**; *pt* **-, -ла, -ло**) *сов от* **блёкнуть**.

побли́зости *нареч* nearby ♦ *предл*: ~ **от** +*gen* near (to), close to.

побо́|и (**-ев**) *мн* beating *ед*.

побо́рник (**-а**) *м* champion (*of cause*).

побо́рница (**-ы**) *ж см* **побо́рник**.

побор|о́ть (**-орю́, -о́решь**) *сов перех* (*также перен*) to overcome.

побо́р|ы (**-ов**) *мн* (*ист*) taxes *мн*, levies *мн*.

побо́чный (**-ен, -на, -но**) *прил* (*продукт, реакция*) secondary; ~ **эффе́кт** side effect.

побо́|яться (**-ю́сь, -и́шься**) *сов от* **боя́ться** ♦ *возв*: **побо́йся Бо́га!** (*разг*) have a heart!

побрати́м (**-а**) *м*: **города́-~ы** twin towns *или* cities.

побреду́ *итп сов см* **побрести́**.

побре́зга|ть (-ю) *сов от* **бре́згать**.

побре́зг|овать (-ую) *сов от* **бре́зговать**.

побре|сти́ (-еду́, -едёшь; *pt* -ёл, -ела́, -ело́) *сов непepex* to trudge.

побри́ть(ся) (-е́ю(сь), -е́ешь(ся)) *сов от* **бри́ть(ся)**.

поброса́|ть (-ю) *сов перех* (*вещи*) to throw about.

побря́ку|шка (-ки; *gen pl* -ек) *ж* (*обычно мн*) trinket.

побуди́ть (-ужу́, -у́дишь; *impf* **побужда́ть**) *сов перех*: ~ кого́-н к чему́-н/+*infin* to prompt sb (in)to sth/to do.

побу́ду *итп сов см* **побы́ть**.

побужда́|ть (-ю) *несов от* **побуди́ть**.

побужде́ни|е (-я) *ср* (*действие*) prompting; (*стремление*) motive.

побужу́ *сов см* **побуди́ть**.

побыва́|ть (-ю) *сов непepex*: ~ в Африке/у роди́телей to visit Africa/one's parents.

побы́ть (*как* быть; *см* **Table 21**) *сов непepex* to stay.

побью́ *итп сов см* **поби́ть**.

пова́|диться (-жусь, -дишься) *сов непepex*: ~ +*infin* to get into the way of doing.

пова́д|ка (-ки; *gen pl* -ок) *ж* (*разг*) way.

пова́жусь *сов см* **пова́диться**.

пова́лен *прил см* **пова́льный**.

повал|и́ть (-ю́, -а́лишь) *сов от* **вали́ть** ◆ *непepex* (*снег, град*) to begin to fall; (*толпа*) to come pouring in

▶ **повали́ться** *сов от* **вали́ться**.

пова́льный (-ен, -ьна, -ьно) *прил* mass.

по́вар (-а; *nom pl* -а́) *м* cook.

пова́ренный *прил*: ~ая кни́га cookery (*BRIT*) *или* cook (*US*) book; ~ая соль table salt.

повари́х|а (-и) *ж см* **по́вар**.

пове́да|ть (-ю) *сов* (*не*)*перех*: ~ что-н *или* о чём-н кому́-н to tell sb sth.

поведе́ни|е (-я) *ср* behaviour (*BRIT*), behavior (*US*).

поведу́(сь) *итп сов см* **повести́(сь)**.

повез|ти́ (-у́, -ёшь; *pt* -ёз, -езла́, -езло́) *сов от* **везти́** ◆ *перех* to take.

повели́тельный (-ен, -ьна, -ьно) *прил* imperious; **повели́тельное наклоне́ние** (*линг*) imperative mood.

повенча́|ть (-ю) *сов от* **венча́ть**.

поверг|ну́ть (-у, -ешь; *impf* **поверга́ть**) *сов перех* (*перен: врага*) to conquer; **поверга́ть** (~ *perf*) кого́-н в +*acc* (*в отчаяние, в уныние итп*) to plunge sb into.

пове́ренный (-ого; *decl like adj*) *м*: ~ в дела́х chargé d'affaires; **прися́жный** ~ (*ист*) barrister (*in tsarist Russia*).

пове́р|ить (-ю, -ишь) *сов от* **ве́рить** ◆ (*impf* **поверя́ть**) *перех*: ~ что-н кому́-н to confide sth to sb.

▶ **пове́риться** *сов от* **ве́риться**.

пове́р|ка (-и) *ж* (*перекличка*) rollcall; **на** ~у in fact.

поверн|у́ть (-у́, -ёшь; *impf* **повора́чивать**) *сов* (*не*)*перех* to turn

▶ **поверну́ться** (*impf* **повора́чиваться**) *сов возе* to turn; **де́ло** ~у́лось к лу́чшему/ ху́дшему things took a turn for the better/worse; **у меня́ язы́к не** ~ётся сказа́ть э́то (*разг*) I wouldn't have the guts to say that; ~ся не́где there isn't even room to turn round.

пове́рх *предл* (+*gen*) over.

пове́рхност|ный *прил* surface *опред*; (-ен, -на, -но; *перен*) superficial.

пове́рхност|ь (-и) *ж* surface; **лежа́ть** (*impf*) **на** ~и to be perfectly obvious.

пове́р|ье (-ья; *gen pl* -ий) *ср* (popular) belief.

поверя́|ть (-ю) *несов от* **пове́рить**.

повесел|е́ть (-ю) *сов от* **весеге́ть**.

пове́|сить(ся) (-шу(сь), -сишь(ся)) *сов от* **ве́шать(ся)**.

повествова́ни|е (-я) *ср* narrative.

повеств|ова́ть (-у́ю) *несов непepex*: ~ о +*prp* (*роман итп*) to tell (the story) of.

пов|ести́ (-еду́, -едёшь; *pt* -ёл, -ла́, -ло́) *сов перех* (*начать вести: человека*) to take; (: *войска*) to lead; (*машину, поезд*) to drive; (*войну, следствие итп*) to begin ◆ (*impf* **поводи́ть**) *непepex*: ~ +*instr* (*бровью*) to raise; (*плечом*) to shrug; (*perf*) **себя́ наха́льно** to start to behave impudently; **он и бро́вью не** ~ёл (*разг*) he didn't bat an eyelid

▶ **повести́сь** *сов возе* (*войти в обыкновение*) to become the custom; ~сь (*perf*) с кем-н to become friends with sb.

пове́ст|ка (-ки; *gen pl* -ок) *ж* summons (*мн* summonses); (*также*: ~ дня) agenda.

по́вест|ь (-и) *ж* story.

пове́три|е (-я) *ср* tendency.

пове́шени|е (-я) *ср* hanging; **сме́ртная казнь че́рез** ~ sentence of death by hanging.

пове́шу(сь) *сов см* **пове́сить(ся)**.

пове́|ять (3*sg* -ет, 3*pl* -ют) *сов безл* (+*instr*): ~яло прохла́дой/све́жестью there was a breath of cool/fresh air; ~яло свобо́дой/ сча́стьем there was a feeling of freedom/ happiness in the air.

повздо́р|ить (-ю, -ишь) *сов от* **вздо́рить**.

повзросл|е́ть (-ю) *сов от* **взросле́ть**.

повида́|ть(ся) (-ю(сь)) *сов от* **вида́ть(ся)**.

по-ви́димому *ввод сл* apparently.

повидл|о (-а) *ср* jam (*BRIT*), jelly (*US*).

пови́нн|ая (-ой; *decl like adj*) *ж* confession; **яви́ться** (*perf*) *или* **прийти́** (*perf*) **с** ~ой to give o.s. up.

пови́нност|ь (-и) *ж* duty; **во́инская** ~ conscription.

пови́н|ный (-ен, -на, -но) *прил* guilty.
повин|ова́ться (-у́юсь) *сов возв* (+*dat*) to obey.
повинове́ни|е (-я) *ср* obedience.
пови́с|нуть (-ну, -нешь; *pt* -, -ла, -ло, *impf* **повиса́ть**) *сов неперех* to hang; (*тучи*) to hang motionless; (*птица, вертолёт*) to hover.
повл|е́чь (-еку́, -ечёшь *итп*, -еку́т; *pt* -ёк, -екла́, -екло́) *сов от* **влечь**.
по́вод (-ода; *loc sg* -оду́, *nom pl* -о́дья, *gen pl* -ьев) *м* (*лошади*) rein; (*nom pl* -оды; *причина*) reason ♦ *предл*: **по ~у** +*gen* regarding, concerning; **дава́ть** (**дать** *perf*) **кому́-н ~ для чего́-н** to give sb cause for sth; **идти́** (*impf*) *или* **быть** (*impf*) **на поводу́ у кого́-н** to be under sb's thumb.
пово|ди́ть (-ожу́, -о́дишь) *несов от* **повести́** ♦ *перех* (*водить недолго*) to walk.
повод|о́к (-ка́) *м* lead, leash.
пово́дья *итп сущ см* **по́вод**.
повожу́ *сов см* **поводи́ть**.
пово́з|ка (-ки; *gen pl* -ок) *ж* cart.
поволо́к|а (-и) *ж* shroud, haze.
повора́чива|ть (-ю) *несов от* **поверну́ть**.
▶ **повора́чиваться** *несов от* **поверну́ться** ♦ *возв* (*разг: быстро действовать*) to get a move on.
поворо́т (-а) *м* (*действие*) turning; (*место*) bend, turn; (*перен*) turning point.
поворо́тлив|ый (-, -а, -о) *прил* (*человек*) agile, nimble.
поворо́тный *прил* (*ТЕХ*) revolving; **~ пункт** *или* **моме́нт** (*перен*) turning point; **~ день** crucial day; **поворо́тный круг** turntable.
повре|ди́ть (-жу́, -ди́шь) *сов от* **вреди́ть** ♦ (*impf* **поврежда́ть**) *перех* (*поранить*) to injure; (*поломать*) to damage.
поврежде́ни|е (-я) *ср* (*см глаг*) injury; damage.
поврежу́ *сов см* **повреди́ть**.
повремен|и́ть (-ю́, -и́шь) *сов неперех*: **~ с чем-н** to delay sth a little; **~** (*perf*) **с отве́том** to wait a little before answering.
повреме́нный *прил*: **повреме́нная опла́та** payment by the hour.
повседне́вен *прил см* **повседне́вный**.
повседне́вность (-и) *ж* everyday routine.
повседне́в|ный (-ен, -на, -но) *прил* everyday; (*занятия, встречи*) daily.
повсеме́ст|ный (-ен, -на, -но) *прил* widespread.
повск|ака́ть (*3sg* -а́чет, *3pl* -а́чут) *сов неперех* (*разг*) to jump up.
повстреча́|ть (-ю) *сов перех* (*разг*) to bump into
▶ **повстреча́ться** *сов возв* (*разг*): **~ся с кем-н** to bump into sb.
повсю́ду *нареч* everywhere.
по-вся́кому *нареч* in different ways.
повто́рен *прил см* **повто́рный**.
повторе́ни|е (-я) *ср* repetition.
повтор|и́ть (-ю́, -и́шь; *impf* **повторя́ть**) *сов перех* to repeat

▶ **повтори́ться** (*impf* **повторя́ться**) *сов возв* (*ситуация*) to repeat itself; (*болезнь*) to recur.
повто́р|ный (-ен, -на, -но) *прил* repeated.
повторя́|ть(ся) (-ю(сь)) *несов от* **повтори́ть(ся)**.
повы́|сить (-шу, -сишь; *impf* **повыша́ть**) *сов перех* to increase; (*интерес*) to heighten; (*качество, культуру*) to improve; (*работника*) to promote; **повыша́ть** (**~** *perf*) **кого́-н в обще́ственном мне́нии** to raise sb in the opinion of the public; **повыша́ть** (**~** *perf*) **го́лос** to raise one's voice
▶ **повы́ситься** (*impf* **повыша́ться**) *сов возв* to increase; (*интерес*) to heighten; (*качество, культура*) to improve.
повы́шенный *прил* (*спрос*) increased; (*интерес, чувствительность*) heightened; (*качество*) improved; **повы́шенное давле́ние** high blood pressure.
повы́шу(сь) *сов см* **повы́сить(ся)**.
повя|за́ть (-жу́, -жешь; *impf* **повя́зывать**) *сов перех* to tie.
повя́з|ка (-ки; *gen pl* -ок) *ж* bandage; (*стерильная*) dressing; **ги́псовая ~** plaster.
повя́зыва|ть (-ю) *несов от* **повяза́ть**.
погада́|ть (-ю) *сов от* **гада́ть**.
пога́н|ить (-ю, -ишь; *perf* **опога́нить**) *несов перех* (*разг*) to mess up.
пога́н|ка (-ки; *gen pl* -ок) *ж* toadstool.
пога́ный *прил* (*разг: отвратительный*) lousy; **~ гриб** toadstool.
пога́с *итп сов см* **пога́снуть**.
пога|си́ть (-ашу́, -а́сишь) *сов от* **гаси́ть** ♦ (*impf* **погаша́ть**) *перех* (*задолженность, вексель*,) to pay (off).
пога́с|нуть (-ну, -нешь; *pt* -, -ла, -ло) *сов от* **га́снуть**.
погаша́|ть (-ю) *несов от* **погаси́ть**.
погаше́ни|е (-я) *ср*: **срок ~я** (*КОММ*) maturity date.
погашу́ *сов см* **погаси́ть**.
поги́б *итп сов см* **поги́бнуть**.
погиба́|ть (-ю) *несов от* **поги́бнуть**.
поги́бель (-и) *ж*: **согну́ться в три ~и** (*разг*) to bend double.
поги́б|нуть (-ну, -нешь; *pt* -, -ла, -ло) *сов от* **ги́бнуть**.
поги́бш|ий (-его; *decl like adj*) *м* dead person; **~ие** the dead.
погла́|дить (-жу, -дишь) *сов от* **гла́дить**.
погло|ти́ть (-щу́, -о́тишь; *impf* **поглоща́ть**) *сов перех* to absorb; (*средства, время*) to take up; (: *усилия*) to demand.
поглоще́ни|е (-я) *ср*: **попы́тка ~я** (*КОММ*) takeover bid.
поглощу́ *сов см* **поглоти́ть**.
поглупе́|ть (-ю) *сов от* **глупе́ть**.
погля|де́ть (-жу́, -ди́шь) *сов от* **гляде́ть**.
погля́дыва|ть (-ю) *несов неперех* (*разг*) to have *или* take a squint.
погляжу́ *сов см* **погляде́ть**.

погна́ть (-оню́, -о́нишь) *сов перех* (*стадо, ло́шадь*) to drive; (*маши́ну, по́езд*) to drive fast
погна́ться *сов возв*: ~ся за кем-н/чем-н (*также перен*) to set off in pursuit of sb/sth.

погова́рива|ть (-ю) *несов неперех*: ~ о +*prp* to talk about; ~ют, что ... they say that ....

погово́р|ка (-ки; *gen pl* -ок) ж saying.

пого́д|а (-ы) ж weather; э́то не де́лает ~у it doesn't make a lot of difference.

погоди́ть (-жу́, -ди́шь) *сов неперех*: ~ с +*instr* (*разг: подожда́ть*) to take one's time with; немно́го ~дя́ after a while; ~ди́! (*угро́за*) just you wait!

пого́дный *прил* weather *опред*.

пого́жий (-ая, -ее, -ие; -, -а, -е) *прил* fine.

погожу́ *сов см* погоди́ть.

поголо́вный *прил* (*всео́бщий*) general.

поголо́вь|е (-я) *ср* (*скота́, лошаде́й*) total number.

поголубе́|ть (-ю) *сов от* голубе́ть.

пого́н (-а) *м* (*обы́чно мн*) (shoulder) stripe.

пого́нщик (-а) *м* (cattle) driver.

погоню́(сь) *итп см* погна́ть(ся).

пого́н|я (-и) ж: ~ за +*instr* (*также перен*) pursuit of ♦ *собир* (*пресле́дователи*) pursuers *мн*; в ~е за +*instr* in pursuit of.

погоня́ть (-ю) *несов перех* (*ло́шадь, скот*) to drive; (*перен: разг*): ~ кого́-н to hurry sb up.

погоре́ть (-ю́, -и́шь; *impf* погора́ть) *сов неперех* to lose everything (*in a fire*); **погора́ть** (~ *perf*) на взя́тках/кра́же (*разг*) to be caught taking bribes/stealing.

погорячи́ться (-у́сь, -и́шься) *сов возв* to get worked up.

погранзаста́в|а (-ы) ж сокр (= пограни́чная заста́ва) frontier post.

пограни́чник (-а) *м* frontier *или* border guard.

пограни́чный *прил* (*го́род, райо́н*) frontier *опред*, border *опред*; (*конфли́кт, знак*) border *опред*.

по́греб (-а; *nom pl* -á) *м* cellar; ви́нный ~ wine cellar.

погреба́льный *прил* funeral *опред*.

погребе́ни|е (-я) *ср* (*по́хороны*) burial, interment; (*моги́ла*) grave.

погрему́ш|ка (-ки; *gen pl* -ек) ж rattle.

погре́|ть (-ю; *impf* погрева́ть) *сов перех* to warm up
погре́ться *сов возв* to warm up.

погреши́ть (-у́, -и́шь) *сов от* греши́ть.

погре́шность (-и) ж error, mistake.

погрози́ть (-жу́, -зи́шь) *сов от* грози́ть.

погро́м (-а) *м* pogrom; (*разг: беспоря́док*) chaos.

погрубе́ть (-ю) *сов от* грубе́ть.

погру|зи́ть (-ужу́, -у́зишь) *сов перех от* грузи́ть ♦ *перех*: (-ужу́, -у́зишь; *impf*

погружа́ть; ~ что-н в +*acc*) to immerse sth in
► **погрузи́ться** *сов от* грузи́ться ♦ (*impf* **погружа́ться**) *возв* (*челове́к*) to immerse o.s.; (*предме́т*) to sink; **погружа́ться** (~ся *perf*) в +*acc* (*в сон, в апа́тию*) to sink into; **погружа́ться** (~ся *perf*) в размышле́ния to be deep in thought.

погру́з|ка (-ки; *gen pl* -ок) ж loading.

погру́зочный *прил* (*маши́на*) loading *опред*; ~ые рабо́ты loading.

погры́з|ться (-у́сь, -ёшься) *несов от* грызться.

погря́зн|уть (-у, -ешь; *impf* погряза́ть) *сов неперех*: ~ в +*prp* (*в грязи́*) to get stuck in; (*в долга́х, во лжи*) to sink into; (*в развра́те*) to wallow in.

погуби́ть (-ублю́, -у́бишь) *сов от* губи́ть.

погуля́ть (-ю) *сов от* гуля́ть.

погусте́ть (-ю) *сов от* густе́ть.

KEYWORD

под *предл* (+*acc*) **1** (*в направле́нии ни́же*) under; я положи́л су́мку под стол I put the bag under the table; идти́ (*impf*) по́д гору to go downhill
2 (*подде́рживая сни́зу*) by; брать (взять *perf*) кого́-н по́д руку to take sb by the arm
3 (*ука́зывает на положе́ние, состоя́ние*) under; под контро́ль/наблюде́ние under control/ observation; отдава́ть (отда́ть *perf*) кого́-н под суд to prosecute sb; попада́ть (попа́сть *perf*) под дождь to be caught in the rain
4 (*бли́зко к*): под у́тро/ве́чер towards morning/ evening; под пра́здники coming up to the holidays; под ста́рость approaching old age
5 (*ука́зывает на фу́нкцию*) as; мы приспосо́били помеще́ние под магази́н we fitted out the premises as a shop
6 (*в ви́де чего́-н*): ва́за под хруста́ль an imitation crystal vase; сте́ны под мра́мор marble-effect walls
7 (*в обме́н на*) on; брать (взять *perf*) что-н под зало́г/че́стное сло́во to take sth on security/ trust
8 (*в сопровожде́нии*): под роя́ль/скри́пку to the piano/violin; мне э́то не под си́лу that is beyond my powers
♦ *предл* (+*instr*) **1** (*ни́же чего́-н: о расположе́нии*) under; чемода́н под столо́м the suitcase is under the table
2 (*о́коло*) near; под Петербу́ргом near St. Petersburg; под бо́ком у кого́-н very near to sb; под но́сом у кого́-н under sb's nose; под руко́й to hand, at hand
3 (*об усло́виях существова́ния объе́кта*) under; быть (*impf*) под наблюде́нием/аре́стом to be under observation/arrest; под назва́нием, под и́менем under the name of
4 (*всле́дствие*) under; под влия́нием/ тя́жестью чего́-н under the influence/weight of

sth; **понима́ть** (*impf*)/**подразумева́ть** (*impf*) **под чем-н** to understand/imply by sth.

под- *префикс* (*in verbs*; *о движении снизу вверх*) *indicating movement upwards eg.* подбро́сить; (*о действии, совершающемся внизу*) *indicating movement below sth eg.* подби́ть; (*приближение*) *indicating movement towards eg.* подбежа́ть; (*добавление*) *indicating addition to sth eg.* подли́ть; (*ослабленная степень действия*) *indicating non-intensive quality of sth eg.* подкра́сить; (*тайное действие*) *indicating undercover nature of sth eg.* подслу́шать; (*in adjectives*; *расположенный ниже какой-нибудь поверхности*) *under–*; (*находящийся в ведении*) *indicating supervision of sth eg.* поднадзо́рный; (*in nouns*; *часть чего-н*) *sub–*; (*ниже по званию*) *indicating lower position or rank eg.* подмастерье.

подава́ть(ся) (-ю(сь)) *несов от* пода́ть(ся).

подави́ть (-авлю́, -а́вишь; *impf* подавля́ть) *сов перех* to suppress; **подавля́ть** (~ *perf*) **кого-н чем-н** to intimidate sb with sth
▸ **подави́ться** *сов от* дави́ться.

подавле́ние (-я) *ср* (*восстания*) suppression.

пода́вленность (-и) *ж* depression.

пода́вленный *прил* (*настроение, состояние, человек*) depressed; (*смех, стон*) suppressed.

подавлю́(сь) *сов см* подави́ть(ся).

подавля́ть (-ю) *несов от* подави́ть.

подавля́ющий (-ая, -ее, -ие) *прил* overwhelming.

пода́вно *нареч*: **он бога́т, а она́ и ~** (*разг*) he is rich and she is even more so; **е́сли я не могу́ э́то сде́лать, то ты и ~** (*разг*) if I can't do this, then you certainly can't.

пода́м(ся) *итп сов см* пода́ть(ся).

подари́ть (-арю́, -а́ришь) *сов от* дари́ть.

пода́рок (-ка) *м* gift, present.

пода́рочный *прил* (*магазин итп*) gift *опред*.

пода́ст(ся) *сов см* пода́ть(ся).

податливый (-, -а, -о) *прил* pliable; (*тело*) supple.

по́дать (-и) *ж* (*ИСТ*) tax.

пода́ть (*как* дать; *см* **Table 14**; *impf* подава́ть) *сов перех* to give; (*еду*) to serve up; (*поезд, такси итп*) to bring; (*заявление, жалобу итп*) to submit; (*СПОРТ: в теннисе*) to serve; (*: в футболе*) to pass; **подава́ть** (~ *perf*) **что-н кому́-н** to give sth to sb, give sb sth; (*еду*) to serve sb up with sth; **подава́ть** (~ *perf*) **го́лос за** +*acc* to cast a vote for; **подава́ть** (~ *perf*) **иде́ю** to put forward an idea; **подава́ть** (~ *perf*) **ре́плику** to make a comment; **подава́ть** (~ *perf*) **в отста́вку** to hand in *или* submit one's resignation; **подава́ть** (~ *perf*) **на кого́-н в суд** to take sb to court; **подава́ть** (~ *perf*) **кому́-н ру́ку** (*при встрече*) to give sb one's hand; (*в трудной ситуации*) to give sb a hand; **подава́ть** (~ *perf*) **кому́-н пальто́** to help sb into

their coat
▸ **пода́ться** (*impf* подава́ться) *сов возв* (*сдвинуться*) to give way; (*разг: уехать*) to make tracks.

пода́ча (-и) *ж* (*действие: заявления, прошения*) submission; (*: обеда*) serving up; (*СПОРТ: в теннисе*) serve; (*: в футболе*) pass.

пода́чка (-ки; *gen pl* -ек) *ж* (*собаке*) scraps *мн*; (*человеку*) hand-out.

пода́шь(ся) *сов см* пода́ть(ся).

подая́ние (-я) *ср* alms *мн*.

подба́вить (-лю, -ишь; *impf* подавля́ть) *сов перех* to add.

подба́дривать (-ю) *несов от* подбодри́ть.

подбежа́ть (*как* бежа́ть; *см* **Table 20**; *impf* подбега́ть) *сов неперех* to run up.

подберёзовик (-а) *м* (*БОТ*) shaggy boletus.

подберу́(сь) *итп сов см* подобра́ть(ся).

подбива́ть (-ю) *несов от* подби́ть.

подбира́ть(ся) (-ю(сь)) *несов от* подобра́ть(ся).

подби́ть (-обью́, -обьёшь; *impf* подбива́ть) *сов перех* (*птицу, самолёт*) to shoot down; (*глаз, крыло*) to injure; **подбива́ть** (~ *perf*) **каблуки́ на** +*prp* to reheel.

подбодри́ть (-ю́, -и́шь; *impf* подба́дривать) *сов перех* to cheer up.

подбо́р (-а) *м* selection; (*собрание*) collection; **как на ~** – *all alike and all the very best*.

подбо́рка (-и) *ж* (*журнальная*) collection of articles on one general theme.

подборо́док (-ка) *м* chin.

подбро́сить (-шу, -сишь; *impf* подбра́сывать) *сов перех* (*мяч, шар, камень итп*) to toss; (+*acc или* +*gen*; *добавить*) to put; (*тайно подложить: анониму*) to leave; (*: ворованный товар, наркотик*) to plant; (*разг: подвезти*) to give a lift.

подва́л (-а) *м* cellar; (*для жилья*) basement.

подва́льный *прил* (*помещение*) basement *опред*; **подва́льный эта́ж** basement.

подведе́ние (-я) *ср* (*линии электропередачи*) connecting; **подведе́ние ито́гов** summing-up.

подведу́ *итп сов см* подвести́.

подвезти́ (-езу́, -езёшь; *pt* -ёз, -езла́, -езло́, *impf* подвози́ть) *сов перех* (*машину, товар*) to take up; (*человека*) to give a lift.

подве́ргнуть (-ну, -нешь; *pt* -, -ла, -ло, *impf* подверга́ть) *сов перех*: ~ **кого́-н/что-н чему́-н** to subject sb/sth to sth; **подверга́ть** (~ *perf*) **кого́-н ри́ску/опа́сности** to put sb at risk/in danger
▸ **подве́ргнуться** (*impf* подверга́ться) *сов возв*: **~ся** +*dat* to be subjected to.

подве́рженный (-, -а, -о) *прил*: ~ +*dat* (*дурному влиянию*) subject to; (*простуде*) susceptible to.

подверну́ть (-у́, -ёшь; *impf* подвора́чивать) *сов перех* (*сделать короче*) to turn up; **подвора́чивать** (~ *perf*) **но́гу** to turn *или* twist one's ankle

▶ **подверну́ться** (*impf* **подвора́чиваться**) *сов возв* (*разг: попа́сться*) to turn up; **мне ~ýлась пóд руку интере́сная кни́га** I came across an interesting book; **у меня́ нога́ ~ýлась** I've twisted my ankle.

подве́|сить (-шу, -сишь; *impf* **подве́шивать**) *сов перех* to hang up.

подве́с|ка (-ки; *gen pl* -ок) *ж* pendant.

подвесно́й *прил* (*в вися́чем положе́нии*) hanging *опред*; **подвесно́й мост** suspension bridge.

подве́сок *сущ см* **подве́ска**.

подве|сти́ (-еду́, -едёшь; *pt* -ёл, -ела́, -ело́, *impf* **подводи́ть**) *сов перех:* ~ **к** +*dat* (*челове́ка*) to bring up to; (*маши́ну*) to drive up to; (*по́езд*) to bring into; (*кора́бль*) to sail up to; (*электри́чество*) to bring to; (*доро́гу*) to link to; (*разочарова́ть*) to let down; **подводи́ть** (~ *perf*) **глаза́/гу́бы** to put eyeliner/lipstick on; **подводи́ть** (~ *perf*) **ито́ги** to sum up.

подве́шива|ть (-ю) *несов от* **подве́сить**.

подве́шу *сов см* **подве́сить**.

по́двиг (-а) *м* exploit.

подвига́|ть(ся) (-ю(сь)) *несов от* **подви́нуть(ся)**.

подви́жен *прил см* **подви́жный**.

подви́жник (-а) *м* devotee.

подвижно́й *прил:* ~ **соста́в** (*на желе́зной доро́ге*) rolling stock.

подви́ж|ный (-ен, -на, -но) *прил* (*челове́к, живо́тное*) agile; (*no short form*; *войска́, конта́кт*) mobile.

подви́н|уть (-у, -ешь; *impf* **подвига́ть**) *сов перех* (*передви́нуть: челове́ка, предме́т*) to move; (*перен: рабо́ту, де́ло*) to push ahead with

▶ **подви́нуться** (*impf* **подвига́ться**) *сов возв* (*челове́к*) to move.

подвла́ст|ный (-ен, -на, -но) *прил:* ~ +*dat* (*зако́ну*) subject to; (*президе́нту*) under the control of.

подво́д|а (-ы) *ж* cart.

подво́|ди́ть (-ожу́, -óдишь) *несов от* **подвести́**.

подво́дник (-а) *м* (*моря́к*) submariner; (*водола́з*) diver.

подво́дный *прил* (*расте́ние, рабо́ты*) underwater *опред*; **подво́дная ло́дка** submarine; **подво́дное тече́ние** undercurrent.

подвожу́ *сов см* **подводи́ть**.

подво́|зи́ть (-ожу́, -óзишь) *несов от* **подвезти́**.

подвора́чива|ть (-ю) *несов от* **подверну́ть**.

подворо́т|ня (-ни; *gen pl* -ен) *ж* passage(way).

подво́х (-а) *м* (*разг: лову́шка*) catch.

подвя|за́ть (-жу́, -жешь; *impf* **подвя́зывать**) *сов перех* to tie.

подгиба́|ть(ся) (-ю(сь)) *несов от* **подогну́ть(ся)**.

подгля|де́ть (-жу́, -ди́шь; *impf* **подгля́дывать**) сов перех to peep through.

подговор|и́ть (-ю́, -и́шь; *impf* **подгова́ривать**) *сов перех:* ~ **кого́-н на что-н**/+*infin* to put sb up to sth/to doing.

подгоню́ *итп сов см* **подогна́ть**.

подгоня́|ть (-ю) *несов от* **подогна́ть**.

подгор|е́ть (*3sg* -и́т, *3pl* -я́т, *impf* **подгора́ть**) *сов неперех* (*мя́со, пиро́г*) to burn slightly.

подгота́влива|ть(ся) (-ю(сь)) *несов от* **подгото́вить(ся)**.

подготови́тельный *прил* (*предвари́тельный*) preparatory; **подготови́тельный класс** (*в нача́льной шко́ле*) reception.

подгото́в|ить (-лю, -ишь; *impf* **подгота́вливать**) *сов перех* to prepare

▶ **подгото́виться** (*impf* **подгота́вливаться**) *сов возв* to prepare (o.s.).

подгото́в|ка (-и) *ж* (*к экза́мену, к отъе́зду*) preparation; (*запа́с зна́ний, уме́ний*) training.

подготовлю́ (сь) *сов см* **подгото́вить(ся)**.

подгу́зник (-а) *м* nappy (*BRIT*), diaper (*US*).

поддава́|ться (-ю́сь) *несов от* **подда́ться** ◆ *возв:* **не ~ сравне́нию/описа́нию** to be beyond comparison/words.

поддади́мся *итп сов см* **подда́ться**.

подда́кива|ть (-ю) *несов неперех:* ~ +*dat* (*разг*) to agree with.

поддадѝмся *сов см* **подда́ться**.

по́дданн|ая (-ой; *decl like adj*) *ж см* **по́дданный**.

по́дданн|ый (-ого; *decl like adj*) *м* subject, citizen.

по́дданств|о (-а) *ср* nationality, citizenship.

подда́ться (*как* **дать**; *см* **Table 14**; *impf* **поддава́ться**) *сов возв* (*дверь итп*) to give way; **поддава́ться** (~ *perf*) +*dat* (*па́нике*) to give way to; (*влия́нию, собла́зну*) to give in to; **поддава́ться** (~ *perf*) +*dat или на* +*acc* (*на про́сьбы*) to give in to.

поддева́|ть (-ю) *несов от* **подде́ть**.

подде́ла|ть (-ю; *impf* **подде́лывать**) *сов перех* to forge

▶ **подде́латься** (*impf* **подде́лываться**) *сов возв:* ~**ся под** +*acc* to imitate.

подде́л|ка (-ки; *gen pl* -ок) *ж* forgery.

подде́лыва|ть(ся) (-ю(сь)) *несов от* **подде́лать(ся)**.

подде́льный *прил* (*докуме́нт*) forged; (*ра́дость, гостеприи́мство*) feigned.

подде́ну *итп сов см* **подде́ть**.

поддержа́ть (-ержу́, -е́ржишь; *impf* **подде́рживать**) *сов перех* (*па́дающего*) to hold on to; (*выступле́ние, предложе́ние итп*) to second; (*бесе́ду*) to keep up.

подде́ржива|ть (-ю) *несов от* **поддержа́ть** ◆ *перех* to support; (*перепи́ску*) to keep up; (*поря́док, отноше́ния*) to maintain.

подде́ржк|а (-и) *ж* support.

поддеть (-ну, -нешь; *impf* **поддевать**) *сов перех* (*приподнять*) to prise (*BRIT*) *или* prize (*US*) off; (*перен: разг*) to gibe at; **поддевать** (~ *perf*) **свитер под куртку** to put on a sweater under(neath) one's jacket; **поддевать** (~ *perf*) **крючком** to hook.

поддон (-а) *м* (*для грузов*) pallet; (*для жидкости*) tray.

поддувало (-а) *ср* damper.

подевать(ся) (-ю(сь)) *сов от* **девать(ся)**.

подействовать (-ую) *сов от* **действовать**.

поделать (-ю) *сов перех* (*разг*) to do; **ничего не ~ешь, ничего нельзя ~** (*разг*) it can't be helped.

поделить(ся) (-елю(сь), -елишь(ся)) *сов от* **делить(ся)**.

поделка (-ки; *gen pl* -ок) *ж* any kind of handmade craft.

поделом *нареч*: ~ **ему** it serves him right.

подёргиваться (-юсь) *несов от* **подёрнуться** ♦ *возв* (*лицо*) to twitch.

подержанный *прил* (*одежда, мебель итп*) second-hand.

подёрнуться (*3sg* -ется, *3pl* -утся, *impf* **подёргиваться**) *сов возв*: ~ +*instr* (*покрыться*) to be covered with; **у него волосы ~улись сединой** he had a lot of grey hair.

подерусь *итп см* **подраться**.

подешеветь (-ю) *сов от* **дешеветь**.

поджаристый (-, -а, -о) *прил* (*мясо*) well-done; (*картошка, пирожок*) crisp.

поджарый (-, -а, -о) *прил* lean.

поджать (-ожму, -ожмёшь; *impf* **поджимать**) *сов перех* (*губы*) to purse; (*живот*) to pull in; **поджимать** (~ *perf*) **ноги под себя** to tuck one's legs under o.s.; **поджимать** (~ *perf*) **колени** to pull one's knees up.

поджелудочный *прил*: ~ая железа pancreas.

поджечь (-огу, -ожёшь итп, -огут; *impf* **поджигать**) *сов перех* to set fire to.

поджигатель (-я) *м* arsonist.

поджигать (-ю) *несов от* **поджечь**.

поджидать (-ю) *несов перех* to wait for.

поджимать (-ю) *несов от* **поджать** ♦ *перех* (*разг*): **нас~ют сроки** we are working to a tight deadline.

поджог (-а) *м* arson.

подзаголовок (-ка) *м* subheading.

подзатыльник (-а) *м* (*разг*) clip round the ear.

подзащитная (-ой; *decl like adj*) *ж* (*ЮР*) *см* **подзащитный**.

подзащитный (-ого; *decl like adj*) *м* (*ЮР*) client.

подземелье (-ья; *gen pl* -ий) *ср* (*комната*) vault; (*проход*) underground passage; (*ряд помещений*) catacombs *мн*.

подземный *прил* underground.

подзову *итп сов см* **подозвать**.

подзорный *прил*: ~ая труба telescope.

подзывать (-ю) *несов от* **подозвать**.

поди *сов* (*разг*) go ♦ *вводн сл* (*наверное*) probably.

подирать (*3sg* -ет) *несов безл*: **у меня мороз по коже ~ет от этого** (*разг*) it makes my skin crawl *или* my flesh creep.

подкалывать (-ю) *несов от* **подколоть**.

подкапываться (-юсь) *несов от* **подкопаться**.

подкараулить (-ю, -ишь; *impf* **подкарауливать**) *сов перех* (*разг*) to lie in wait for.

подкармливать (-ю) *несов от* **подкормить**.

подкатить (-ачу, -атишь; *impf* **подкатывать**) *сов перех* (*что-н круглое*) to roll; (*что-н на колёсах*) to wheel ♦ *неперех* (*машина, экипаж*) to race up.

подкачать (-ю) *сов* (*не)перех* (*разг*) to fail.

подкачу *сов см* **подкатить**.

подкашивать(ся) (-ю(сь)) *несов от* **подкосить(ся)**.

подкидывать (-ю) *несов от* **подкинуть**.

подкидыш (-а) *м* abandoned baby.

подкинуть (-у, -ешь; *impf* **подкидывать**) *сов перех* (*кинуть вверх*) to toss; (+*acc или* +*gen*; *добавить*) to put; (*тайно подложить: анонимку*) to leave; (: *ворованный товар, наркотик*) to plant; **подкидывать** (~ *perf*) **кому-н денег** (*разг*) to give sb a sub; **подкидывать** (~ *perf*) **кого-н** (*разг*) to give sb a lift.

подкладка (-ки; *gen pl* -ок) *ж* lining.

подкладывать (-ю) *несов от* **подложить**.

подклеить (-ю, -ишь; *impf* **подклеивать**) *сов перех* to stick on.

подключить (-у, -ишь; *impf* **подключать**) *сов перех* (*телефон*) to connect; (*лампу*) to plug in; (*специалистов*) to involve; **подключать** (~ *perf*) **к системе/центральной сети** (*КОМП*) to network, hook up to the main network

▶ **подключиться** (*impf* **подключаться**) *сов возв* to get involved.

подкова (-ы) *ж* (*лошади итп*) shoe.

подковать (-ую) *сов от* **ковать** ♦ (*impf* **подковывать**) *перех* (*лошадь итп*) to shoe.

подколоть (-олю, -олешь; *impf* **подкалывать**) *сов перех* (*скрепить*) to pin up; (*разг: уязвить*) to taunt; **подкалывать** (~ *perf*) **документ к делу** to file a document.

подкоп (-а) *м* (*ход*) secret underground passage.

подкопаться (-юсь; *impf* **подкапываться**) *сов возв*: ~ **под** +*acc* (*под здание*) to tunnel under; (*разг: под начальника итп*) to undermine.

подкормить (-ормлю, -ормишь; *impf* **подкармливать**) *сов перех* (*животных*) to fatten up; (*ребёнка, больного*) to feed up.

подкосить (-ошу, -осишь; *impf* **подкашивать**) *сов перех* (*подлеж: удар, пуля*) to fell; (*несчастье*) to devastate; (*усталость*) to overcome

▶ **подкоситься** (*impf* **подкашиваться**) *сов возв*: **у него ноги/колени ~осились** his legs/knees gave way.

подкрасться (-дусь, -дёшься; *impf*

подкра́дываться) *сов возв* to sneak *или* steal up.

подкреп|и́ть (-лю́, -и́шь; *impf* **подкрепля́ть**) *сов перех* (сте́ну, кры́шу) to support; (мы́сли, утвержде́ние) to support, back up

подкрепи́ться (*impf* **подкрепля́ться**) *несов возв* to fortify o.s.

подкрепле́ни|е (-я) *ср* (ВОЕН) reinforcement.

подкреплю́(сь) *сов см* **подкрепи́ть(ся)**.

подкрепля́|ть(ся) (-ю(сь)) *несов от* **подкрепи́ть(ся)**.

по́дкуп (-а) *м* bribery.

подкуп|и́ть (-уплю́, -у́пишь; *impf* **подкупа́ть**) *сов перех* to bribe; (*перен*: добро́той) to win over.

подла́мыва|ться (*3sg* -ется, *3pl* -ются) *несов от* **подломи́ться**.

по́дле *нареч* (ря́дом) nearby ◆ *предл* (+*gen*) beside, next to.

подлеж|а́ть (*3sg* -и́т, *3pl* -а́т) *несов неперех*: ~ +*dat* (прове́рке, обложе́нию нало́гом) to be subject to; **пригово́р не ~и́т обжа́лованию** (ЮР) the sentence is not open to appeal; **э́то не ~и́т сомне́нию** there can be no doubt about that.

подлежа́щ|ее (-его; *decl like adj*) *ср* (ЛИНГ) subject.

подле|те́ть (-чу́, -ти́шь; *impf* **подлета́ть**) *сов неперех* (самолёт) to fly in; (пти́ца) to fly up; (*разг*: челове́к) to race up.

подле́ц (-а́) *м* scoundrel.

подле́ч|ить (-ечу́, -е́чишь; *impf* **подле́чивать**) *сов перех* to treat

▸ **подлечи́ться** (*impf* **подле́чиваться**) *сов возв* to undergo a short course of treatment.

подлечу́ *сов см* **подлете́ть**.

подлива́|ть (-ю) *несов от* **подли́ть**.

подли́в|ка (-ки; *gen pl* -ок) *ж* (КУЛИН) sauce.

подли́з|а (-ы) *ж* crawler.

подли́зыва|ться (-юсь; *perf* **подлиза́ться**) *несов возв*: ~ к +*dat* (*разг*) to crawl to.

по́длинен *прил см* **по́длинный**.

по́длинник (-а) *м* original.

по́длинн|ый (-ен, -на, -но) *прил* original; (докуме́нт) authentic; (*no short form*; геро́й, друг) true.

подл|и́ть (-олью́, -ольёшь; *pt* -и́л, -ила́, -и́ло, *impf* **подлива́ть**) *сов перех* to add; **подлива́ть** (~ *perf*) **вина́ в стака́н** to top up a glass with wine; **подлива́ть** (~ *perf*) **ма́сла в ого́нь** to add fuel to the fire *или* flames.

по́дло *нареч* (поступи́ть) meanly ◆ *как сказ* it's mean.

подло́г (-а) *м* forgery.

подло́жен *прил см* **подло́жный**.

подлож|и́ть (-ожу́, -о́жишь; *impf* **подкла́дывать**) *сов перех* (анони́мку) to leave; (воро́ванный това́р) to plant; (+*acc или* +*gen*;

добави́ть) to put; (дров, са́хара) to add; **подкла́дывать** (~ *perf*) **что-н под что-н** to put sth under sth.

подло́жн|ый (-ен, -на, -но) *прил* forged.

подлоко́тник (-а) *м* arm(rest).

подл|оми́ться (*3sg* -о́мится, *3pl* -о́мятся, *impf* **подла́мываться**) *сов возв*: ~ **под тя́жестью чего́-н** to give way under the weight of sth.

по́длост|ь (-и) *ж* (ка́чество) baseness; **кака́я ~!** what a base thing to do!

по́дл|ый (-, -а́, -о) *прил* base.

подмасте́р|ье (-я) *м* apprentice.

подма́чива|ть (-ю) *несов от* **подмочи́ть**.

подм|ени́ть (-еню́, -е́нишь; *impf* **подме́нивать**) *сов перех* (замени́ть) to substitute; **подме́нивать** (~ *perf*) **кого́-н** (*разг*) to stand in for sb.

подм|ести́ (-ету́, -етёшь; *pt* -ёл, -ела́, -ело́) *сов от* **мести́** ◆ (*impf* **подмета́ть**) *перех* (пол) to sweep; (му́сор) to sweep up.

подме́|тить (-чу, -тишь; *impf* **подмеча́ть**) *сов перех* to notice.

подмёт|ка (-и) *ж* (подо́шва) sole; **он в ~и ей не годи́тся** (*разг*) he's not worth her little finger.

подмету́ *итп сов см* **подмести́**.

подмеча́|ть (-ю) *несов от* **подме́тить**.

подмечу́ *сов см* **подме́тить**.

подмигн|у́ть (-у́, -ёшь; *impf* **подми́гивать**) *сов неперех*: ~ **кому́-н** to wink at sb.

подмина́|ть (-ю) *несов от* **подмя́ть**.

подмо́г|а (-и) *ж* (*разг*) help.

подмо́стк|и (-ов) *мн* (ТЕАТР) stage *ед*.

подм|очи́ть (-очу́, -о́чишь; *impf* **подма́чивать**) *сов перех* to dampen, moisten; (*разг*: репута́цию) to blacken.

подмо́ю *итп сов см* **подмы́ть**.

подмыва́|ть (-ю) *несов от* **подмы́ть** ◆ *безл* (*разг*): **его́ ~ло** +*infin* ... he felt an urge to ....

подм|ы́ть (-о́ю, -о́ешь; *impf* **подмыва́ть**) *сов перех* (ребёнка, больно́го) to wash; (бе́рег, мост) to undermine.

подмы́ш|ка (-ки; *gen pl* -ек) *ж* armpit.

подм|я́ть (-омну́, -омнёшь; *impf* **подмина́ть**) *сов перех* to crush.

поднево́льн|ый (-ен, -ьна, -ьно) *прил* (челове́к) subordinate; (труд) forced.

подне|сти́ (-су́, -сёшь; *impf* **подноси́ть**) *сов перех*: ~ **к** +*dat* to bring up to; (подари́ть): ~ **что-н кому́-н** to present sth to sb.

поднима́|ть(ся) (-ю(сь)) *несов от* **подня́ть(ся)**.

подниму́(сь) *итп сов см* **подня́ть(ся)**.

подновля́|ть (-лю́, -и́шь; *impf* **подновля́ть**) *сов перех* (зда́ние) to refurbish; (кра́ску) to touch up.

подного́тн|ая (-ой; *decl like adj*) *ж*: (вся) ~ the true nature.

подно́жек *сущ см* **подно́жка**.

подно́жи|е (-я) *ср* (*горы, памятника*) foot.

подно́жка (-ки; *gen pl* -ек) *ж* (*трамвая, автобуса итп*) step; **дать** (*perf*) *или* **поста́вить** (*perf*) **~ку кому́-н** to trip sb up.

подно́жный *прил*: **быть на ~ом корму́** (*с.-х.*) to be out at pasture.

подно́с (-а) *м* tray.

подн|оси́ть (-ошу́, -о́сишь) *несов от* поднести́.

подн|я́ть (-иму́, -и́мешь; *impf* поднима́ть) *сов перех* to raise; (*что-н лёгкое*) to pick up; (*что-н тяжёлое*) to lift (up); (*флаг*) to hoist; (*спящего человека*) to rouse; (*панику, восстание*) to start; (*экономику, дисциплину*) to improve; (*архивные материалы, документацию итп*) to unearth; **поднима́ть** (**~** *perf*) **крик** *или* **шум** to make a fuss; **поднима́ть** (**~** *perf*) **чьё-н настрое́ние** *или* **чей-н дух** to raise sb's spirits; **поднима́ть** (**~** *perf*) **кого́-н на́ смех** to make a laughing stock of sb

▶ **подня́ться** (*impf* поднима́ться) *сов возв* to rise; (*на другой этаж, на сцену*) to go up; (*с постели, со стула*) to get up; (*паника, метель, драка*) to break out; (**~ся** *perf*) **на́ го́ру** to climb a hill; **~я́лся крик** there was an uproar; **~я́лся ве́тер** the wind got up.

подо *предл см* под.

подоба́|ть (*3sg* -ет, *3pl* -ют) *несов неперех*: **~** **+dat** to befit; **Вам не ~ет отка́зываться** it does not befit you to refuse.

подоба́ющий (-ая, -ее, -ие) *прил* appropriate.

подо́бен *прил см* подо́бный.

подо́бно *предл*: **~ +dat** like, similar to ◆ *союз*: **~ тому́ как** in the same way as, just as.

подо́бный (-ен, -на, -но) *прил*: **~ +dat** (*сходный с*) like, similar to; **~ные лю́ди – ре́дкость** there are very few people like this *или* of this type; **и тому́ ~ное** et cetera, and so on; **ничего́ ~ного** (*разг*) nothing of the sort.

подобостра́стный (-ен, -на, -но) *прил* obsequious, servile.

подо|бра́ть (-беру́, -берёшь; *impf* подбира́ть) *сов перех* to pick up; (*приподнять вверх*) to gather (up); (*выбрать подходящее*) to select, pick

▶ **подобра́ться** (*impf* подбира́ться) *сов возв* (*коллектив*) to get together; (*библиотека, коллекция*) to be built up; (*подкрасться*) to steal up.

подобре́|ть (-ю) *сов от* добре́ть.

подобру́-поздоро́ву *нареч* (*разг*): **убира́йся ~!** get out while the going's good!

подобью́ *итп сов см* подби́ть.

подогна́ть (-гоню́, -го́нишь; *impf* подгоня́ть) *сов перех*: **~ к +dat** (*стадо, машину*) to drive up to; (*лодку*) to take in to; **подгоня́ть** (**~** *perf*) **под +acc** to fit.

подогн|у́ть (-у́, -ёшь; *impf* подгиба́ть) *сов перех* (*рукава, штанину*) to turn up

▶ **подогну́ться** (*impf* подгиба́ться) *сов возв* to curl under; **у него́ но́ги/коле́ни ~у́лись** his

legs/knees gave way.

подогре́|ть (-ю; *impf* подогрева́ть) *сов перех* to warm up; (*перен: любопытство*) to heighten.

пододви́н|уть (-у, -ешь; *impf* пододвига́ть) *сов перех* to move closer.

пододея́льник (-а) *м* ≈ duvet cover.

подожд|а́ть (-у́, -ёшь; *pt* -а́л, -ала́, -а́ло) *сов перех* to wait for; **~** (*perf*) **с чем-н** to put sth off; **~** (*perf*) **+infin** to put off doing; **~йте!** wait a minute!; **~йте, мо́жет всё не так пло́хо** wait a bit, maybe it won't be all that bad; **~йте, я ведь знал Ва́шего отца́** wait a minute, I think I knew your father.

подожгу́ *итп сов см* поджёчь.

подожму́ *итп сов см* поджа́ть.

подо|зва́ть (-зову́, -зовёшь; *pt* -озва́л, -озвала́, -озва́ло, *impf* подзыва́ть) *сов перех* to call over.

подозрева́|ть (-ю) *несов перех* to suspect; **~** (*impf*) **кого́-н в чём-н** to suspect sb of sth; **~** (*impf*) **(о чём-н)** to have an idea (about sth).

подозре́ни|е (-я) *ср* suspicion; **~ на +acc** (*предположение*) suspicion of; **быть** (*impf*) **под ~м** *или* **на ~и** to be under suspicion; **он был заде́ржан/аресто́ван по ~ю в уби́йстве** he was held/arrested on suspicion of murder.

подозри́тельный (-ен, -ьна, -ьно) *прил* suspicious.

подо|йти́ (-ю́, -ишь) *сов от* дойти́.

подой|ти́ (*как* идти́; *см* **Table 18**; *impf* подходи́ть) *сов неперех*: **~ к +dat** (*также перен*) to approach; (*соответствовать*): **~ти к +dat** (*юбка*) to go (well) with; **подходи́ть** (**~** *perf*) **на до́лжность** to be suited to a position; **э́то мне подхо́дит** this suits me; **подходи́ть** (**~** *perf*) **к концу́** to come to an end.

подоко́нник (-а) *м* windowsill.

подо́л (-а) *м* hem.

подо́лгу *нареч* for a long time.

подолью́ *итп сов см* подли́ть.

подомну́ *итп сов см* подмя́ть.

подо́н|ок (-ка) *м* scum.

подопе́чный (-ого; *decl like adj*) *м* ward ◆ *прил*: **~ ребёнок** ward; **~ная террито́рия** (*под опекой ООН*) trust territory, trusteeship.

подоплёк|а (-и) *ж* underlying reason.

подопру́ *итп сов см* подпере́ть.

подо́пытный *прил*: **~ое живо́тное** animal used in experiments; **~ кро́лик** (*перен*) guinea pig.

подорв|а́ть (-у́, -ёшь; *pt* -а́л, -ала́, -а́ло, *impf* подрыва́ть) *сов перех* to blow up; (*перен: авторитет, доверие*) to undermine; (: *здоровье*) to destroy

▶ **подорва́ться** (*impf* подрыва́ться) *сов возв* to be blown up; (*перен: авторитет*) to be undermined; (: *здоровье*) to be destroyed.

подорожа́|ть (-ю) *сов от* дорожа́ть.

подоро́жник (-а) *м* plantain.

подо|сла́ть (-шлю́, -шлёшь; *impf* подсыла́ть) *сов перех* to send (*secretly*).

подоспе́|ть (-ю; *impf* **подоспева́ть**) *сов неперех* to arrive in time.

подотру́ *итп сов см* **подтере́ть**.

подотчёт|ный (-ен, -на, -но) *прил* accountable; (*организация, работник итп*) accountable; **счёт ~ных сумм** expense account; **подотчётные де́ньги** expenses.

подо́хн|уть (-у, -ешь) *сов от* **до́хнуть**.

подохо́дный *прил*: ~ **нало́г** income tax.

подо́шв|а (-ы) *ж* (*обуви*) sole.

подошёл *итп сов см* **подойти́**.

подошлю́ *итп сов см* **подосла́ть**.

подошью́ *итп сов см* **подши́ть**.

подпа́|сть (-ду́, -дёшь) *сов неперех*: ~ **под** +*acc* to fall under.

подпева́|ть (-ю; *perf* **подпе́ть**) *несов неперех* (+*dat*) to join in with; (*перен: разг: пренебр*) to echo.

под|пере́ть (-опру́, -опрёшь; *pt* -пёр, -пёрла, -пёрло, *impf* **подпира́ть**) *сов перех*: ~ **что-н чем-н** to prop up; **подпира́ть** (~ *perf*) **щёку кулако́м** to rest one's head in one's hands.

подп|е́ть (-ою́, -оёшь) *сов от* **подпева́ть**.

подпира́|ть (-ю) *несов от* **подпере́ть**.

подписа́ни|е (-я) *ср* signing.

подп|иса́ть (-ишу́, -и́шешь; *impf* **подпи́сывать**) *сов перех* to sign

подписа́ться (*impf* **подпи́сываться**) *сов возв*: ~**ся под** +*instr* to sign; **подпи́сываться** (~**ся** *perf*) **на** +*acc* (*на газету, на журнал*) to subscribe to.

подпи́с|ка (-ки; *gen pl* -ок) *ж* subscription; (*о невыезде, о неразглашении*) signed statement.

подписно́й *прил* subscription *опред*; ~ **акционе́рный капита́л** (*КОММ*) subscribed capital; **подписно́й лист** list of subscribers.

подпи́сок *сущ см* **подпи́ска**.

подпи́счик (-а) *м* subscriber.

подпи́сыва|ть(ся) (-ю(сь)) *несов от* **подписа́ть(ся)**.

по́дпис|ь (-и) *ж* (*фамилия*) signature; (*под картиной*) title, caption; (*под стихами*) title.

подпишу́(сь) *итп сов см* **подписа́ть(ся)**.

подплы́|ть (-ву́, -вёшь; *pt* -л, -ла́, -ло, *impf* **подплыва́ть**) *сов неперех* (*лодка*) to sail (up); (*пловец, рыба*) to swim (up).

подполко́вник (-а) *м* lieutenant colonel.

подпо́ль|е (-я) *ср* (*подвал*) cellar; (*конспирация*) underground activities *мн*; **уходи́ть** (**уйти́** *perf*) **в** ~ to go underground.

подпо́льный *прил* underground *опред*.

подпо́р|ка (-ки; *gen pl* -ок) *ж* prop, support.

подпою́ *итп сов см* **подпе́ть**.

подпоя́|сать (-шу, -шешь; *impf* **подпоя́сывать**) *сов перех* to belt.

подпра́в|ить (-лю, -ишь; *impf* **подправля́ть**) *сов перех* to make minor corrections to.

подпрогра́мм|а (-ы) *ж* (*КОМП*) subroutine.

подпру́г|а (-и) *ж* girth.

подпры́гн|уть (-у, -ешь; *impf* **подпры́гивать**) *сов неперех* to jump.

подпуска́|ть (-ю) *несов от* **подпусти́ть** ♦ *перех*: ~ **к** +*dat* to allow access to.

подп|усти́ть (-ущу́, -у́стишь; *impf* **подпуска́ть**) *сов перех* (*человека, зверя*) to allow to approach.

подрабо́та|ть (-ю; *impf* **подраба́тывать**) *сов перех* (*статью*) to polish up ♦ (*не*)*перех* (+*acc или* +*gen*) to earn extra.

подра́внива|ть (-ю) *несов от* **подровня́ть**.

подра́гива|ть (-ю) *сов неперех* to tremble; (*ресницы*) to flutter.

подража́ни|е (-я) *ср* imitation.

подража́|ть (-ю) *несов неперех* (+*dat*) to imitate.

подразделе́ни|е (-я) *ср* (*воинское*) subunit; (*производственное*) subdivision.

подраздел|и́ть (-ю́, -и́шь; *impf* **подразделя́ть**) *сов перех* to subdivide.

подразделя́|ться (*3sg* -ется, *3pl* -ются) *несов возв* to be subdivided.

подразумева́|ть (-ю) *несов перех* to mean

▸ **подразумева́ться** *несов возв* to be implied.

подра́мник (-а) *м* stretcher.

подраст|и́ (-у́, -ёшь; *pt* -о́с, -осла́, -осло́, *impf* **подраста́ть**) *сов неперех* to grow (a little).

под|ра́ться (-еру́сь, -ерёшься) *сов от* **дра́ться**.

подре́з|ать (-жу, -жешь; *impf* **подреза́ть**) *сов перех* (*платье*) to shorten; (*волосы*) to cut; ~ (*perf*) **кры́лья кому́-н** (*перен*) to clip sb's wings.

подро́бен *прил см* **подро́бный**.

подро́бност|ь (-и) *ж* detail; **вдава́ться** (*impf*) **в** ~**и** to go into detail.

подро́б|ный (-ен, -на, -но) *прил* detailed.

подровня́|ть (-ю; *impf* **подра́внивать**) *сов перех* to trim.

подро́с *итп сов см* **подрасти́**.

подро́стка *сущ см* **подро́сток**.

подростко́вый *прил* (*одежда итп*) teenage *опред*; (*проблемы*) adolescent *опред*; **подростко́вый во́зраст** teens *мн*.

подро́ст|ок (-ка) *м* teenager, adolescent.

подру́г|а (-и) *ж* (girl)friend; **подру́га жи́зни** wife.

по-друго́му *нареч* (*иначе*) differently.

подруж|и́ть (-у́, -у́жишь) *сов от* **дружи́ть**

▸ **подружи́ться** *сов от* **дружи́ться** ♦ *возв*: ~**ся с** +*instr* to make friends with; **они́ бы́стро** ~**ужи́лись** they quickly became friends.

подрул|и́ть (-ю́, -и́шь; *impf* **подру́ливать**) *сов неперех* (*самолёт*) to taxi; (*автомобиль*) to drive (up).

подрумя́н|иться (-юсь, -ишься) *сов от* **румя́ниться** ♦ (*impf* **подрумя́ниваться**) *возв* (*женщина*) to put on blusher; (*пирожки,* бу́лочки) to brown.

подру́чн|ый *прил*: ~ **материа́л/инструме́нт** the material/instrument to hand ♦ **(-ого**; *decl like adj*) *м* assistant.

подрыва́|ть(ся) (-ю(сь)) *несов от* **подорва́ть(ся)**.

подрывно́й *прил* subversive.

подря́д *нареч* in succession ♦ **(-а)** *м (рабо́чий догово́р)* contract; **рабо́тали 5 дней** ~ they worked 5 days in a row *или* in succession; **все/всё** ~ everyone/everything without exception.

подря́дный *прил* contract *опред*.

подря́дчик (-а) *м* contractor.

подряхле́|ть (-ю) *сов от* **дряхле́ть**.

подса|ди́ть (-ажу́, -а́дишь; *impf* **подса́живать)** *сов перех (на коня́)* to help to mount; *(на высо́кий стул)* to help up; *(посади́ть ря́дом)* to place nearby.

подса́жива|ться (-юсь) *несов от* **подсе́сть**.

подсажу́ *сов см* **подсади́ть**.

подсве́чник (-а) *м* candlestick.

подсе́к *итп сов см* **подсе́чь**.

подсека́|ть (-ю) *несов от* **подсе́чь**.

подсеку́ *итп сов см* **подсе́чь**.

подсе́|сть (-я́ду, -я́дешь; *impf* **подса́живаться)** *сов неперех*: ~ **к** +*dat* to sit down beside.

подсе́|чь (-ку́, -чёшь *итп*, **-ку́т;** *pt* **-ёк, -екла́, -екло́,** *impf* **подсека́ть)** *сов перех* to cut down; *(перен: подлеж: несча́стье, боле́знь)* to lay low.

подсини́|ть (-ю, -ишь) *сов от* **сини́ть**.

подск|аза́ть (-ажу́, -а́жешь; *impf* **подска́зывать)** *сов перех (перен: иде́ю, реше́ние)* to suggest; *(разг: а́дрес, телефо́н)* to tell; **подска́зывать** *(~ perf)* **что-н кому́-н** to prompt sb with sth; **не ~а́жите, где у́лица Пу́шкина?** can you please tell me where Pushkin Street is?

подска́з|ка (-ки; *gen pl* **-ок)** *ж* prompt; **де́йствовать** *(impf)* **по чьей-н ~ке** *(перен)* to do as sb says.

подска́зыва|ть (-ю) *несов от* **подсказа́ть**.

подск|очи́ть (-очу́, -о́чишь; *impf* **подска́кивать)** *сов неперех (та́кже перен)* to jump; *(подбежа́ть)* to run up; **подска́кивать** *(~ perf)* **от испу́га/неожи́данности** to start (in fright/surprise*)*.

подсла|сти́ть (-щу́, -сти́шь; *impf* **подсла́щивать)** *сов перех* to sweeten.

подсле́дственн|ая (-ой; *decl like adj*) *ж см* **подсле́дственный**.

подсле́дственн|ый (-ого; *decl like adj*) *м* the accused, the defendant; **~ые** the accused.

подслу́ша|ть (-ю; *impf* **подслу́шивать)** *сов перех* to eavesdrop on.

подсма́трива|ть (-ю) *несов от* **подсмотре́ть**.

подсме́|иваться (-юсь) *сов возв*: ~ **над** +*instr* to poke gentle fun at.

подсм|отре́ть (-отрю́, -о́тришь; *impf* **подсма́тривать)** *сов перех (уви́деть)* to spy

on; ~ *(perf)*, **что ...** to notice that ...; **я ~отре́л, как он брал конфе́ты** I saw him take the sweets.

подсне́жник (-а) *м* snowdrop.

подсо́бный *прил (помеще́ние, хозя́йство)* subsidiary; **подсо́бный рабо́чий** auxiliary.

подсо́выва|ть (-ю) *несов от* **подсу́нуть**.

подсозна́ни|е (-я) *ср* the subconscious.

подсозна́тельный (-ен, -ьна, -ьно) *прил* subconscious.

подсо́лнечник (-а) *м* sunflower.

подсо́лнечн|ый *прил*: **~ое ма́сло** sunflower oil.

подсо́лнух (-а) *м (разг)* sunflower.

подсо́х|нуть (-ну, -нешь; *pt* **-, -ла, -ло,** *impf* **подсыха́ть)** *сов неперех* to dry out a little.

подспо́р|ье (-я) *ср* help.

подспу́дный (-ен, -на, -но) *прил* hidden.

подста́в|ить (-лю, -ишь; *impf* **подставля́ть)** *сов перех*: ~ **под** +*acc* to put under; **подставля́ть** *(~ perf)* **кого́-н под уда́р** *(перен)* to lay sb open to attack.

подста́в|ка (-ки; *gen pl* **-ок)** *ж* stand.

подста́влю *сов см* **подста́вить**.

подставля́|ть (-ю) *несов от* **подста́вить**.

подставно́й *прил (ло́жный)* false.

подста́вок *сущ см* **подста́вка**.

подстака́нник (-а) *м* glassholder.

подста́нци|я (-и) *ж* substation.

подстегн|у́ть (-у́, -ёшь; *impf* **подстёгивать)** *сов перех* to urge on; *(перен: разг)*: ~ **кого́-н** to get sb moving.

подст|ели́ть (-елю́, -е́лишь; *impf* **подстила́ть)** *сов перех (плед, простыню́)* to spread out.

подстерега́|ть (-ю) *несов от* **подстере́чь** ♦ *перех (ожида́ть)* to await.

подстере́|чь (-гу́, -жёшь *итп*, **-гу́т;** *impf* **подстерега́ть)** *сов перех* to lie in wait for.

подсти|ли́ть (-лю́, -лишь) *сов от* **подстели́ть**.

подсти́л|ка (-ки; *gen pl* **-ок)** *ж* covering.

подстра́ива|ть (-ю) *несов от* **подстро́ить**.

подстрах|ова́ть (-у́ю; *impf* **подстрахо́вывать)** *сов перех (гимна́ста)* to be on hand for; *(в риско́ванном де́ле)* to insure.

подстрека́тель (-я) *м* instigator.

подстрека́|ть (-ю) *несов перех*: ~ **кого́-н к** +*da[...]* to drive sb to.

подстр|ели́ть (-елю́, -е́лишь; *impf* **подстре́ливать)** *сов перех* to wing.

подстри́|чь (-гу́, -жёшь *итп*, **-гу́т;** *pt* **-г, -ла, -ло,** *impf* **подстрига́ть)** *сов перех* to trim; *(для укора́чивания)* to cut

▶ **подстри́чься** *(impf* **подстрига́ться)** *сов воз[...]* to have one's hair cut.

подстро́|ить (-ю, -ишь; *impf* **подстра́ивать)** *со[...] перех* to fix.

подстро́чн|ый *прил*: **~ое примеча́ние** footnote; **~ перево́д** word-for-word translation

по́дступ (-а) *м (обы́чно мн)* approach.

подступ|и́ть (-уплю́, -у́пишь; *impf* **подступа́ть)** *сов неперех (слёзы)* to well up; *(рыда́ния)* to rise; **подступа́ть** (~ *perf*) **к** +*dat* to approach

▶ **подступи́ться** (*impf* **подступа́ться**) *сов возв*: ~**ся к** +*dat* to approach.

подсу́ден *прил см* **подсу́дный**.

подсуди́м|ая (-**ой**; *decl like adj*) *ж см* **подсуди́мый**.

подсуди́мый (-**ого**; *decl like adj*) *м* (ЮР) the accused, the defendant; ~**ые** the accused.

подсу́дный (-**ен, -на, -но**) *прил* (ЮР) sub judice; ~**ное де́ло** (*подлежащий суду*) *case due to come before court*; (*преступление*) crime.

подсу́нуть (-**у, -ешь**; *impf* **подсо́вывать**) *сов перех* to shove; (*разг: что-н ненужное, плохое*) to get rid of.

подсуши́ть (-**ушу́, -у́шишь**; *impf* **подсу́шивать**) *сов перех* to dry slightly.

подсчёт (-**а**) *м* counting; (*обычно мн: итог*) calculation.

подсчита́ть (-**ю**; *impf* **подсчи́тывать**) *сов перех* to count (up).

подсыла́ть (-**ю**) *несов см* **подосла́ть**.

подсыха́ть (-**ю**) *несов от* **подсо́хнуть**.

подся́ду *итп сов см* **подсе́сть**.

подталкива́ть (-**ю**) *несов от* **подтолкну́ть**.

подтасова́ть (-**у́ю**; *impf* **подтасо́вывать**) *сов перех* to juggle (with).

подта́чивать (-**ю**) *несов от* **подточи́ть**.

подтверди́ть (-**жу́, -ди́шь**; *impf* **подтвержда́ть**) *сов перех* to confirm; (*фактами, цифрами*) to back up

▶ **подтверди́ться** (*impf* **подтвержда́ться**) *сов возв* to be confirmed.

подтвержде́ние (-**я**) *ср* confirmation.

подтвержу́(сь) *сов см* **подтверди́ть(ся)**.

подтёк (-**а**) *м* bruise.

подте́кст (-**а**) *м* hidden meaning.

подтере́ть (-**отру́, -отрёшь**; *impf* **подтира́ть**) *сов перех* to mop up.

подтолкну́ть (-**у́, -ёшь**; *impf* **подта́лкивать**) *сов перех* to nudge; (*перен*) to urge on.

подточи́ть (-**очу́, -о́чишь**; *impf* **подта́чивать**) *сов перех* to sharpen (a little); (*перен: силы*) to weaken; (: *здоровье*) to destroy.

подтя́гива|ть(ся) (-**ю(сь)**) *несов от* **подтяну́ть(ся)**.

подтя́ж|ка (-**ки**; *gen pl* -**ек**) *ж* (*обычно мн*) braces *мн* (BRIT), suspenders *мн* (US).

подтя́нутый (-, -**а, -о**) *прил* smart.

подтяну́ть (-**яну́, -я́нешь**; *impf* **подтя́гивать**) *сов перех* (*тяжёлый предмет*) to haul up; (*гайку, болт*) to tighten; (*войска*) to bring up

▶ **подтяну́ться** (*impf* **подтя́гиваться**) *сов возв* (*на брусьях, на перекладине*) to pull o.s. up; (*войска*) to move up; (*перен*) to get one's act together.

поду́ма|ть (-**ю**) *сов от* **ду́мать** ♦ *неперех*: ~ (о +*prp*) to think (about); ~ (*perf*) **над** +*instr или* **о** +*prp* to think about; ~, **что...** to think that ...; **он**

и не ~л извини́ться he didn't even think of apologizing *или* to apologize; ~**ешь купи́л но́вую маши́ну** so what if he's bought a new car!; ~ **то́лько!** (*разг*) just think!; **кто бы мог** ~! who would have thought it!; **и не ~ю!** (*разг*) I won't hear of it!

▶ **поду́маться** *сов от* **ду́маться**.

поду́мыва|ть (-**ю**) *несов неперех* (*разг*): ~ **о** +*prp*/*infin* to think about/of doing.

подурне́ть (-**ю**) *сов от* **дурне́ть**.

поду́ть (-**ю**) *сов неперех* to blow; (*ветер*) to begin to blow.

подучи́ть (-**учу́, -у́чишь**; *impf* **поду́чивать**) *сов перех* (*разг: выучить*) to learn; (*научить*) to teach.

поду́шек *сущ см* **поду́шка**.

подуши́ть (-**ушу́, -у́шишь**) *сов перех* to spray lightly with perfume.

поду́ш|ка (-**ки**; *gen pl* -**ек**) *ж* (*для сидения*) cushion; (*под голову*) pillow.

поду́шный *прил*: ~ **нало́г** poll tax.

подхали́м (-**а**) *м* toady.

подхали́м|ка (-**ки**; *gen pl* -**ок**) *ж см* **подхали́м**.

подхва́т (-**а**) *м*: **быть на** ~**е** (*разг*) to be at hand.

подхвати́ть (-**ачу́, -а́тишь**; *impf* **подхва́тывать**) *сов перех* (*падающее*) to catch; (*подлеж: течение, толпа*) to carry away; (*слова, идею, болезнь*) to pick up; (*песню, мелодию*) to join in.

подхлестну́ть (-**у́, -ёшь**; *impf* **подхлёстывать**) *сов перех* to whip on.

подхо́д (-**а**) *м* approach; **экза́мены на** ~**е** the exams are approaching.

подходи́ть (-**ожу́, -о́дишь**) *несов от* **подойти́**.

подходя́щий (-**ая, -ее, -ие**) *прил* (*дом*) suitable; (*момент, случай*) appropriate.

подхожу́ *несов см* **подходи́ть**.

подцепи́ть (-**еплю́, -е́пишь**) *сов перех* to attach; (*разг: болезнь, девушку, жениха*) to pick up.

подча́с *нареч* at times.

подчеркну́ть (-**у́, -ёшь**; *impf* **подчёркивать**) *сов перех* (*слова в тексте*) to underline; (*в речи*) to emphasize.

подчине́ние (-**я**) *ср* obedience.

подчинённый *прил* subordinate *опред* ♦ (-**ого**; *decl like adj*) *м* subordinate.

подчини́ть (-**ю́, -и́шь**; *impf* **подчиня́ть**) *сов перех* (*народ, страну*) to subjugate; **подчиня́ть** (~ *perf*) **что-н кому́-н** to place sth under the control of sb

▶ **подчини́ться** (*impf* **подчиня́ться**) *сов возв* (+*dat*) to obey.

подчи́стить (-**щу, -стишь**; *impf* **подчища́ть**) *сов перех* (*пол итп*) to clean; (*написанное*) to erase.

подше́й(те) *сов см* **подши́ть**.

подше́фный *прил*: ~ **де́тский дом** children's

home under patronage.

подшива́ть (-ю) *несов от* **подши́ть**.

подши́в|ка (-ки; *gen pl* -ок) *ж* (*газет, докуме́нтов*) bundle.

подши́пник (-а) *м* (*TEX*) bearing.

подши́ть (-ошью́, -ошьёшь; *imper* -ше́й(те), *impf* **подшива́ть**) *сов перех* (*рука́в*) to hem; (*подо́л*) to take up; (*докуме́нт*) to file; (*па́чку газе́т*) to bundle up.

подшути́ть (-учу́, -у́тишь; *impf* **подшу́чивать**) *сов неперех*: ~ **над** +*instr* to make fun of.

подъ- *преф см* **под-**.

подъе́ду *итп сов см* **подъе́хать**.

подъе́зд (-а) *м* (*к го́роду, к до́му*) approach; (*в зда́нии*) entrance.

подъезжа́й(те) *сов см* **подъе́хать**.

подъезжа́ть (-ю) *несов от* **подъе́хать**.

подъём (-а) *м* (*гру́за*) lifting; (*фла́га*) raising; (*на го́ру*) ascent; (*промы́шленный, культу́рный итп*) revival; (*в ре́чи, в де́йствиях*) enthusiasm; (*сигна́л: к пробужде́нию*) reveille.

подъёмник (-а) *м* lift (*BRIT*), elevator (*US*).

подъёмны|е (-ых; *decl like adj*) *мн* (*та́кже:* ~ **де́ньги**) relocation costs *мн*.

подъёмный *прил* lifting *опред*; **подъёмный кран** crane.

подъе́хать (*как* **е́хать**; *см* Table 19; *impf* **подъезжа́ть**) *сов неперех* (*на автомоби́ле*) to drive up; (*на коне́*) to ride up; (*разг*) to call in.

подыгра́ть (-ю; *impf* **подыгрывать**) *сов неперех* (+*dat*; *разг*) to accompany.

поды|ска́ть (-щу́, -щешь; *impf* **подыскивать**) *сов перех* to find.

подыто́ж|ить (-у, -ишь) *сов перех* (*расхо́ды, дохо́ды*) to add up; (*сде́ланное, ска́занное*) to sum up.

подыха́ть (-ю) *несов неперех* (*живо́тные*) to be dying; (*разг*): ~ **от** ‹ *gen* (*от го́лода, от ску́ки итп*) to be dying of.

подыша́ть (-шу́, -шешь) *сов неперех* to breathe.

подыщу́ *итп сов см* **подыска́ть**.

поеда́|ть (-ю) *несов от* **пое́сть**.

пое́дешь *итп сов см* **пое́хать**.

поеди́м *итп сов см* **пое́сть**.

поеди́н|ок (-ка) *м* duel.

поеди́те *сов см* **пое́сть**.

пое́ду *итп сов см* **пое́хать**.

поедя́т *сов см* **пое́сть**.

поёжиться (-усь, -ишься; *impf* **поёживаться**) *сов возв* to shiver slightly.

по́езд (-а; *nom pl* -а́) *м* train; **ско́рый** ~ express train; ~ **да́льнего сле́дования** long-distance train; **е́хать** (*impf*) ~**ом** *или* **на** ~**е** to travel by train; **е́хать** (*impf*) **в** ~ **в метро́** to travel by tube (*BRIT*) *или* subway (*US*).

пое́зд|ка (-ки; *gen pl* -ок) *ж* trip.

поезжа́й(те) *сов см* **пое́хать**.

пое́сть (*как* **есть**; *см* Table 15) *сов от* **есть** ♦ (*impf* **поеда́ть**) *перех*: ~ **чего́-н** to eat a little bit of sth; (*съесть всё*) to eat sth up; (*подлеж:*

моль) to eat sth away.

пое́хать (*как* **е́хать**; *см* Table 19) *сов неперех* (*автомоби́ль, по́езд итп*) to set off.

поёшь *сов см* **пое́сть**.

пожа́дничать (-ю) *сов от* **жа́дничать**.

пожале́|ть (-ю) *сов от* **жале́ть**.

пожа́л|овать (-ую) *сов от* **жа́ловать** ♦ *неперех*: ~ **к** +*dat* (*посети́ть*) to visit; **добро́** ~ welcome.

пожа́луй *вводн сл* (*возмо́жно*) perhaps; (*выража́ет предпочте́ние*) likely; **он**, ~, **не придёт** he may not come; **я**, ~, **пойду́** I'd better go.

пожа́луйста *част* please; (*в отве́т на благода́рность*) don't mention it, you're welcome; ~, **помоги́те мне** please help me; **скажи́те** ~! I you don't say!; **зако́нчил шко́лу и**, ~, **жени́лся** he left school and then, would you believe it, he got married.

пожа́р (-а) *м* fire; (+*gen*; *перен: войны́, револю́ции*) the fire.

пожа́рищ|е (-а) *ср* site of fire.

пожа́рник (-а) *м* (*разг*) fireman (*мн* firemen).

пожа́рный (-ого; *decl like adj*) *м* fireman (*мн* firemen) ♦ *прил*: ~**ая кома́нда** fire brigade (*BRIT*) *или* department (*US*); ~**ая маши́на** fire engine; **на вся́кий** ~ (**слу́чай**) (*разг*) in case of emergency.

пожа́ти|е (-я) *ср*: ~ (**руки́**) handshake.

пожа́ть (-му́, -мёшь; *impf* **пожима́ть**) *сов перех* to squeeze; **он** ~**а́л мне ру́ку** he shook my hand; **пожима́ть** (~ *perf*) **плеча́ми** to shrug one's shoulders.

пожела́ни|е (-я) *ср* wish; **прими́те мои́ наилу́чшие** ~**я** please accept my best wishes.

пожела́|ть (-ю) *сов от* **жела́ть**.

пожелте́|ть (-ю) *сов от* **желте́ть**.

пожен|и́ть (-ю́, -о́нишь) *сов от* **жени́ть** ♦ *перех* (*разг*) to marry

▸ **пожени́ться** *сов от* **жени́ться** ♦ *возв* to marry, get married.

поже́ртвовани|е (-я) *ср* donation.

поже́ртв|овать (-ую) *несов от* **же́ртвовать**.

пожива́|ть (-ю) *несов неперех* (*разг*): **как ты** ~**ешь?** how are you?

пожив|и́ться (-лю́сь, -и́шься) *сов возв* (+*instr*; *разг*) to live off.

поживу́ *итп сов см* **пожи́ть**.

пожи́зненный *прил* lifelong, life *опред*; **пожи́зненное заключе́ние** life imprisonment.

пожило́й *прил* elderly.

пожима́|ть (-ю) *несов от* **пожа́ть**.

пожира́|ть (-ю) *несов от* **пожра́ть** ♦ *перех* (*кни́ги*) to devour; **любопы́тство/честолю́бие** ~**ло его́** he was devoured by curiosity/ambition; ~ (*impf*) **кого́-н глаза́ми** to devour sb with one's eyes.

пожи́тк|и (-ов) *мн* (*разг*) belongings *мн*.

пожи́ть (-иву́, -ивёшь; *pt* -и́л, -ила́, -и́ло) *сов неперех* (*пробы́ть где-нибудь*) to stay for a while; ~**ивём – уви́дим** we shall see.

пожму *итп сов см* **пожать**.

пожр|ать (-у, -ёшь; *impf* **пожирать**) *сов перех* (*подлеж: животное*) to devour; (*no impf; разг: подлеж: человек*) to gobble up.

поз|а (-ы) *ж* posture; (*перен: поведение*) pose.

позабо|титься (-чусь, -тишься) *сов от* **заботиться**.

позави|довать (-ую) *сов от* **завидовать**.

позавтрака|ть (-ю) *несов от* **завтракать**.

позавчера *нареч* the day before yesterday.

позади *нареч* (*сзади*) behind; (*в прошлом*) in the past ♦ *предл* (+*gen*) behind.

позаймств|овать (-ую) *сов от* **заимствовать**.

позапрошл|ый *прил* before last; ~**ая неделя** the week before last.

позарез *нареч* (*разг*) terribly.

позв|ать (-ову, -овёшь) *сов от* **звать**.

позволе́ни|е (-я) *ср* permission; **с Вашего** ~**я** with your permission.

позвол|ить (-ю, -ишь; *impf* **позволять**) *сов неперех* (*погода, обстоятельства*) to permit ♦ *перех*: ~ **что-н кому-н** to allow sb sth; **позволять** (~ *perf*) **кому-н** +*infin* to allow sb to do; ~**ьте!** excuse me!; ~**ьте мне представить моего коллегу** allow me to introduce my colleague; ~**ьте пройти** excuse me please; **позволять** (*impf*) **себе что-н** to afford sth.

позвон|ить (-ю, -ишь) *сов от* **звонить**.

позвон|ок (-ка) *м* vertebra (*мн* vertebrae).

позвоночник (-а) *м* spine, spinal column.

позднее *сравн нареч от* **поздно** ♦ *нареч* later ♦ *предл* (+*gen*) after; (**не**) ~ +*gen* (no) later than.

поздн|ий (-яя, -ее, -ие) *прил* late; **самое** ~**ее** (*разг*) at the latest.

поздно *нареч* late ♦ **как сказ** it's late.

поздоро́ва|ться (-юсь) *сов от* **здороваться**.

поздоро́в|иться (*3sg* -ится) *сов возв*: **ему не** ~**ится** (*разг*) he's in trouble.

поздравительный *прил* greetings *опред*.

поздрав|ить (-лю, -ишь; *impf* **поздравлять**) *сов перех*: ~ **кого-н с** +*instr* to congratulate sb on; **поздравлять** (~ *perf*) **кого-н с днём рождения** to wish sb a happy birthday.

поздравле́ни|е (-я) *ср* congratulation; (*с днём рождения*) greeting.

поздравлю *сов см* **поздравить**.

поздравля|ть (-ю) *несов от* **поздравить**.

позелене́|ть (-ю) *сов от* **зеленеть**.

позже *нареч* = **позднее**.

пози́р|овать (-ую) *сов неперех* (+*dat*) to pose for.

позити́в (-а) *м* (*ФОТО*) positive.

позити́в|ный (-ен, -на, -но) *прил* positive.

пози́ци|я (-и) *ж* position; (*контракта, проекта*) item.

познава́тельный (-ен, -ьна, -ьно) *прил* educational.

познава́|ть (-ю) *несов от* **познать**

▶ **познава́ться** *несов возв* to become known.

познако́м|ить(ся) (-лю(сь), -ишь(ся)) *сов от* **знакомить(ся)**.

позна́ни|е (-я) *ср* familiarization; (*приобретение знаний*) cognition; *см также* **познания**.

позна́ни|я (-й) *мн* knowledge *ед*.

позна́|ть (-ю; *impf* **познавать**) *сов перех* (*любовь, бедность итп*) to experience.

позову́ *итп сов см* **позвать**.

позоло́т|а (-ы) *ж* gilding, gilt.

позолот|ить (-чу, -ти́шь) *сов от* **золотить**.

позо́р (-а) *м* disgrace; **выставлять** (**выставить** *perf*) **кого-н на** ~ to bring disgrace on sb.

позо́рен *прил см* **позорный**.

позо́р|ить (-ю, -ишь; *perf* **опозорить**) *несов перех* to disgrace

▶ **позо́риться** (*perf* **опозориться**) *несов возв* to disgrace o.s.

позо́р|ный (-ен, -на, -но) *прил* disgraceful.

позывн|ые (-ых; *decl like adj*) *мн* call sign *ед*.

поимённый *прил*: ~ **список** list of names.

пои́м|ка (-ки; *gen pl* -ок) *ж* capture.

по-ино́му *нареч* differently.

поинтерес|ова́ться (-у́юсь) *сов возв* (+*instr*) to take an interest in.

по́иск (-а) *м* (*научный, творческий итп*) quest; (*КОМП*) search; «~ **и заме́на**» "search and replace"; *см также* **поиски**.

поиск|а́ть (-ищу́, -и́щешь) *сов перех* to have a look for.

по́иск|и (-ов) *мн*: ~ (+*gen*) search *ед* (for); **в** ~**ах** +*gen* in search of.

пои́стине *нареч* truly.

по|и́ть (-ю́, -и́шь; *imper* **пои́(те)**, *perf* **напои́ть**) *несов перех*: ~ **кого-н чем-н** to give sb sth to drink; **его́ напои́ли во́дкой** he was plied with vodka.

поищу́ *итп сов см* **поиска́ть**.

пойду́ *итп сов см* **пойти́**.

по́йм|а (-ы) *ж* flood plain.

пойма́|ть (-ю) *сов перех* to catch.

пойму́ *итп сов см* **поня́ть**.

по́йнтер (-а) *м* pointer (*dog*).

по́й|(те) *несов см* **петь**.

пойти́ (*как* **идти́**; *см* **Table 18**) *сов неперех* to set off; (*по пути реформ*) to start off; (*о механизмах, к цели*) to start working; (*дождь, снег*) to begin to fall; (*дым, пар*) to begin to rise; (*кровь*) to start flowing; (*фильм итп*) to start showing; (*подойти*): ~ +*dat или* **к** +*dat* (*шляпа, поведение*) to suit; ~ (*perf*) **в кого́-н** (*в мать, в деда итп*) to look like sb; **е́сли на то пошло́** if it comes to that; **так не пойдёт** that won't work.

KEYWORD

пока́ *нареч* **1** (*некоторое время*) for a while; **я пока́ подожду́** I'll wait for a while
2 (*тем временем*) in the meantime; **я ушёл, а**

она́ пока́ остава́лась в до́ме I left, and in the meantime she stayed at home
♦ *союз* **1** (*в то время как*) while; **пока́ он чита́л, я вы́шел на балко́н** while he was reading, I went out onto the balcony **2** (*до того времени как*): **пока́ не** until; **ребёнок бу́дет крича́ть, пока́ не полу́чит конфе́ту** the child will go on shouting until he gets a sweet; **пока́!** so long!; **пока́ что** for the moment.

покажу́(сь) *итп сов см* **показа́ть(ся)**.

пока́з (-а) *м* (*фильма*) showing; (*опыта*) demonstration; (*изменений, тенденций итп*) portrayal, depiction.

показа́ние (-я) *ср* (*ЮР: обычно мн*) evidence *ед*; (*на счётчике итп*) reading.

показа́телен *прил см* **показа́тельный**.

показа́тель (-я) *м* indicator; (*МАТ, ЭКОН*) index (*мн* indices).

показа́тельный (-ен, -ьна, -ьно) *прил* (*явление, пример итп*) revealing; (*no short form*): **~ьное выступле́ние гимна́стов** gymnastics display; **~ о́пыт** demonstration (*of an experiment*).

показа́ть (-жу́, -жешь; *impf* **пока́зывать**) *сов перех* to show; (*подлеж: часы, счётчик итп*) to say; (*на суде*) to testify; **пока́зывать что-н/кого́-н кому́-н** to show sth/sb to sb; **пока́зывать** (~ *perf*) **на что-н/кого́-н** to point to sth/sb; **пока́зывать** (~ *perf*) **приме́р** to set an example; **пока́зывать** (~ *perf*) **себя́** to prove o.s.; **он ~за́л себя́ не в лу́чшем све́те** he didn't show himself in a very good light; **я тебе́ ~жу́!** (*разг*) I'll show you!

► **показа́ться** *сов от* **каза́ться** ♦ (*impf* **пока́зываться**) *возв* to appear; **~ся** (*perf*) **врачу́** to see a doctor.

показно́й *прил* (*энтузиазм, радость итп*) affected; (*роскошь*) ostentatious.

пока́зывать(ся) (-ю(сь)) *несов от* **показа́ть(ся)**.

пока́кать (-ю) *сов от* **ка́кать**.

покале́чить (-у, -ишь) *сов от* **кале́чить**.

пока́лывать (*3sg* -ет) *несов неперех*: **у меня́ ~ет се́рдце/желу́док** I keep getting stabbing pains in my chest/stomach.

пока́мест *нареч* (*разг*) in the meantime ♦ *союз* (*разг*) while.

покапри́зничать (-ю) *сов от* **капри́зничать**.

покара́ть (-ю) *сов от* **кара́ть**.

поката́ть (-ю) *сов перех*: **~ кого́-н на маши́не** to take sb for a drive; **~** (*perf*) **ребёнка на саня́х** to take a child sledging

► **поката́ться** *сов возв* to go for a ride.

покати́ть (-ачу́, -а́тишь) *сов перех* (*что-н кру́глое*) to roll; (*что-н на колёсах*) to wheel ♦ *неперех* (*машина*) to shoot off

► **покати́ться** *сов возв* to start rolling, start to roll; **~ся** (*perf*) **со́ смеху** (*разг*) to burst out laughing.

пока́тываться (-юсь) *несов возв*: **~ со́ смеху** (*разг*) to roll about with laughter *или* laughing.

пока́тый (-, -а, -о) *прил* sloping.

покача́ть (-ю) *сов перех* to rock; **~** (*perf*) **голово́й** to shake one's head

► **покача́ться** *сов возв* (*на каче́лях*) to swing.

пока́чивать (-юсь) *несов возв* to rock.

покачу́(сь) *сов см* **покати́ть(ся)**.

пока́яние (-я) *ср* repentance.

пока́яться (-юсь) *несов от* **ка́яться**.

по́кер (-а) *м* poker (*CARDS*).

поки́нуть (-у, -ешь; *impf* **покида́ть**) *сов перех* to abandon.

поклада́ть (-ю) *несов перех*: **не ~я рук** tirelessly.

покла́дистый (-, -а, -о) *прил* flexible.

покло́н (-а) *м* (*жест*) bow; (*приветствие*) greeting; **посыла́ть** (**посла́ть** *perf* *или* **передава́ть** (**переда́ть** *perf*) **кому́-н ~** to send sb one's regards.

поклони́ться (-оню́сь, -о́нишься) *сов от* **кла́няться** ♦ (*impf* **поклоня́ться**) *возв*: **~** (+*dat*) (*святым места́м*) to pay homage (at).

покло́нник (-а) *м* admirer.

поклоня́ться (-юсь) *несов от* **поклони́ться** ♦ *возв* (+*dat*) to worship.

покля́сться (-ну́сь, -нёшься) *сов от* **кля́сться**.

поко́иться (-юсь, -ишься) *несов возв* (*быть похоро́ненным*) to be at rest; (*осно́вываться*): **~ на** +*prp* to rest on.

поко́й (-я) *м* peace; **оставля́ть** (**оста́вить** *perf*) **кого́-н в ~е** to leave sb in peace; **он не даёт мне ~я** he doesn't give me any peace.

поко́йная (-ой; *decl like adj*) *ж см* **поко́йный**.

поко́йник (-а) *м* the deceased.

поко́йница (-ы) *ж см* **поко́йник**.

поко́йный *прил* the late ♦ (-ого; *decl like adj*) *м* the deceased.

поколеба́ть (-ю) *сов от* **колеба́ть**

► **поколеба́ться** *сов от* **колеба́ться** ♦ *возв* to waver.

поколе́ние (-я) *ср* generation.

поко́нчить (-у, -ишь) *сов неперех*: **~ с** +*instr* (*с дела́ми, с ремо́нтом итп*) to be finished with; (*с бе́дностью, с пробле́мой*) to put an end to; **~** (*perf*) **с собо́й** to kill o.s, commit suicide.

покорёжить (-у, -ишь) *несов от* **корёжить**.

поко́рен *прил см* **поко́рный**.

покори́тель (-я) *м* conqueror.

покори́ть (-ю́, -и́шь; *impf* **покоря́ть**) *сов перех* (*страну, наро́д*) to conquer; (*подлеж: же́нщина, стихи́*) to conquer the heart of; **~** (*perf*) **чьё-н се́рдце** to win sb's heart

► **покори́ться** (*impf* **покоря́ться**) *сов возв*: **~ся** (+*dat*) to submit (to).

покорми́ть (-ормлю́, -о́рмишь) *сов от* **корми́ть**.

поко́рный (-ен, -на, -но) *прил* submissive.

покоро́бить(ся) (-лю(сь), -ишь(ся)) *сов от* **коро́бить(ся)**.

покоря́|ть(ся) (-ю(сь)) *несов от* покори́ть(ся).

поко́с (-а) *м* (*трав*) mowing; (*время покоса*) haymaking.

поко|си́ть(ся) (-шу́(сь), -сишь(ся)) *сов от* коси́ть(ся).

покра́|сить(ся) (-шу(сь), -сишь(ся)) *сов от* кра́сить(ся).

покрасне́|ть (-ю) *сов от* красне́ть.

покрасова́ться (-у́юсь) *сов от* красова́ться.

покра́шу(сь) *сов см* покра́сить(ся).

покриви́|ть(ся) (-лю́(сь), -и́шь(ся)) *несов от* криви́ть(ся).

покри́кива|ть (-ю) *несов неперех* (*разг*): ~ (на +*acc*) to yell (at).

покро́в (-а) *м* (*верхний слой*) layer; (*РЕЛ*) shroud; сне́жный ~ a blanket of snow; под ~ом но́чи under cover of darkness.

покрови́тель (-я) *м* protector.

покрови́тельниц|а (-ы) *ж см* покрови́тель.

покрови́тельствен|ный (-ен, -на, -но) *прил* patronizing.

покрови́тельств|о (-а) *ср* protection.

покро́|й (-я) *ср* cut (*of clothing*).

покро́ю(сь) *итп сов см* покры́ть(ся).

покрупне́|ть (-ю) *сов от* крупне́ть.

покрыва́л|о (-а) *ср* bedspread.

покрыва́|ть(ся) (-ю(сь)) *несов от* покры́ть(ся).

покры́ти|е (-я) *ср* covering; ~ дивиде́нда (*КОММ*) dividend cover.

покр|ы́ть (-о́ю, -о́ешь) *сов от* крыть ♦ (*impf* покрыва́ть) *перех* (*звуки, шум*) to cover up; (*расходы, убытки, расстояние*) to cover; покрыва́ть (~ *perf*) (что-н/кого́-н чем-н) to cover (sth/sb with sth)

▸ покры́ться (*impf* покрыва́ться) *сов возв* (+*instr*; *одеялом*) to cover o.s. with; (*румянцем, снегом итп*) to be covered in.

покры́шк|а (-ки; *gen pl* -ек) *ж* (*ABT*) tyre (*BRIT*), tire (*US*).

покупа́тель (-я) *м* (*в магазине*) customer; (*товара, дома итп*) buyer, purchaser.

покупа́тельниц|а (-ы) *ж см* покупа́тель.

покупа́тельн|ый *прил*: ~ая спосо́бность purchasing power.

покупа́тельск|ий (-ая, -ое, -ие) *прил* (*спрос, интересы*) consumer *опред*.

покупа́|ть (-ю) *несов от* купи́ть.

поку́п|ка (-ки; *gen pl* -ок) *ж* purchase; де́лать (сде́лать *perf*) ~ки to go shopping.

покупно́й *прил* (*торт*) bought.

поку́почн|ый *прил*: ~ая цена́ purchase price.

поку́ша|ть (-ю) *сов от* ку́шать ♦ (*не)перех*: ~ чего́-н to have sth to eat.

покуша́|ться (-юсь) *несов возв*: ~ на +*acc* to attempt to take.

покуше́ни|е (-я) *ср*: ~ (на +*acc*) (*на свободу, на права*) infringement (of); (*на жизнь*) attempt

(on); соверша́ть (соверши́ть *perf*) ~ на кого́-н to make an attempt on sb's life.

пол (-а; *loc sg* -у́, *nom pl* -ы́) *м* floor; (*nom pl* -ы́, *gen pl* -о́в, *dat pl* -а́м) sex, gender.

пол|а́ (-ы́; *nom pl* -ы) *ж* (*обычно мн*: пальто́, пиджака́ итп) side; продава́ть (прода́ть *perf*) из-под ~ы́ to sell under the counter.

полага́|ть (-ю) *несов неперех* (*думать*) to suppose; на́до ~ supposedly; ~ (*impf*) нача́ло чему́-н to make a start on sth; ~ (*impf*) коне́ц чему́-н to put an end to sth.

полага́|ться (-юсь) *несов от* положи́ться ♦ *возв* (*быть должным*) to be expected; ~ется приходи́ть во́ время one is expected to be punctual.

пола́|дить (-жу, -дишь) *сов от* ла́дить.

пола́ком|иться (-люсь, -ишься) *сов от* ла́комиться.

полбеды́ *ж нескл*: э́то ещё ~ (*разг*) it could be worse.

пол|ве́ка (-уве́ка) *м* half a century.

пол|го́да (-уго́да) *м* half a year.

по́лдень (полу́дня *или* по́лдня) *м* midday, noon; 2 часа́ по́сле полу́дня 2 p.m.

по́лдник (-а) *м* (afternoon) tea.

по́лдня *сущ см* по́лдень.

полдоро́|ги (-) *ж*: на ~е halfway; остана́вливаться (останови́ться *perf*) на ~е (*также перен*) to stop halfway.

по́л|е (-я; *nom pl* -я́, *gen pl* -е́й) *ср* field; ~ де́ятельности sphere of activity; ~ зре́ния field of vision; *см также* поля́.

полево́дств|о (-а) *ср* crop cultivation.

полев|о́й *прил* field *опред*; ~ы́е рабо́ты work in the fields; полево́й госпита́ль field hospital.

полёг *итп сов см* поле́чь.

полежа́|ть (-у́, -и́шь) *сов неперех* (*человек*) to have a lie down; (*книга на полке, продукты в ящике итп*) to lie.

полеза́й(те) *сов см* лезть.

поле́з|ный (-ен, -на, -но) *прил* useful; (*пища*) healthy; чем могу́ быть ~ен? how can I be of help?; ~ная нагру́зка (*КОММ*) payload; поле́зные ископа́емые minerals; поле́зная жила́я пло́щадь living space.

поле́з|ть (-у, -ешь) *сов неперех* (*начать лезть*) to start climbing, start to climb; (*в дра́ку, в спор*) to get involved.

поле́мик|а (-и) *ж* polemic.

полеми́ческ|ий (-ая, -ое, -ие) *прил* polemical.

полен|и́ться (-ю́сь, -ишься) *сов от* лени́ться.

поле́н|о (-а; *nom pl* -ья, *gen pl* -ьев) *ср* log.

полёт (-а) *м* flight; ~ фанта́зии *или* мы́сли flight of fancy.

полете́|ть (-чу́, -ти́шь) *сов от* лете́ть ♦ *неперех* (*птица, самолёт*) to fly off; (*годы, дни*) to start to fly by; (*слухи, новости*) to start to fly.

поле́|чь (-гу, -жешь *итп*, -гут; *pt* -ёг, -егла́, -егло́) *сов неперех* (*травы*) to be flattened; (*перен: погибнуть*) to fall, perish.

по́лза|ть (-ю) *несов неперех* to crawl; ~ (*impf*) **в нога́х у кого́-н** to come crawling to sb.

ползко́м *нареч*: **продвига́ться** ~ to crawl along on one's stomach.

ползти́ (-у́, -ёшь; *pt* -, -ла́, -ло́) *несов неперех* to crawl; (*разг: медленно двигаться*) to crawl (along).

ползунки́ (-о́в) *мн* (*одежда*) rompers *мн*.

ползу́чий (-ая, -ее, -ие) *прил* (*животные*) crawling *опред*; (*растения*) creeping *опред*.

полива́|ть (-ю) *несов от* **поли́ть**.

поливитами́н|ы (-ов) *мн* multivitamins *мн*.

полига́ми|я (-и) *ж* polygamy.

полиго́н (-а) *м* (*для учений*) shooting range; (*для испытания оружия*) test(ing) site.

полиграфи́ст (-а) *м* printer.

полиграфи́|я (-и) *ж* printing.

поликли́ник|а (-и) *ж* clinic.

полиня́|ть (*3sg* -ет, *3pl* -ют) *сов от* **линя́ть**.

полиомиели́т (-а) *м* polio(myelitis).

полир|ова́ть (-у́ю; *perf* **отполирова́ть**) *несов перех* to polish.

по́лис (-а) *м*: **страхово́й** ~ insurance policy.

полисеми́|я (-и) *ж* polysemy.

политбюро́ *ср нескл* the Politburo.

политехнику́м (-а) *м* technical college.

политехни́ческ|ий (-ая, -ое, -ие) *прил*: ~ **институ́т** polytechnic.

поли́тик (-а) *м* politician.

поли́тик|а (-и) *ж* (*курс*) policy; (*события, наука*) politics.

политика́н (-а) *м* (*пренебр*) politico.

полити́ческ|ий (-ая, -ое, -ие) *прил* political; **полити́ческая эконо́мия** political economy; **полити́ческий обозрева́тель** political observer.

полито́лог (-а) *м* political scientist.

поли́|ть (-ью, -ьешь; *pt* -и́л, -ила́, -и́ло, *impf* **полива́ть**) *сов неперех* (*дождь*) to start pouring, start to pour ♦ *перех*: **~ что-н чем-н** to pour sth on sth; **полива́ть** (~ *perf*) **цветы́** to water the flowers

▸ **поли́ться** *сов возв* to pour out.

политэконо́ми|я (-и) *ж сокр* (= *полити́ческая эконо́мия*) Pol. Econ. (= *political economy*).

полице́йск|ий (-ая, -ое, -ие) *прил* police *опред* ♦ (-ого; *decl like adj*) *м* policeman (*мн* policemen); **полице́йский уча́сток** police station.

поли́ци|я (-и) *ж* the police; **вызыва́ть (вы́звать** (*perf*)) ~**ю** to call the police.

поли́чн|ое (-ого; *decl like adj*) *ср*: **пойма́ть кого́-н с** ~**ым** to catch sb at the scene of a crime; (*перен*) to catch sb red-handed *или* in the act.

полиэтиле́н (-а) *м* polythene.

полиэтиле́нов|ый *прил* polythene *опред*.

полк (-а́; *loc sg* -у́) *м* regiment.

по́л|ка (-ки; *gen pl* -ок) *ж* shelf; (*в поезде: для*

багажа) luggage rack; (: *для лежания*) berth.

полко́вник (-а) *м* colonel.

полково́д|ец (-ца) *м* commander.

пол-ли́тра (полули́тра) *м* half a litre (*BRIT*) *или* liter (*US*).

полне́|ть (-ю; *perf* **пополне́ть**) *несов неперех* to put on weight.

по́лно *как сказ* that's enough; ~ **серди́ться/ расстра́иваться** stop getting so angry/upset.

полно́ *как сказ* (+*gen*; *разг*): **в до́ме** ~ **книг** the house is stacked full of books; **наро́ду** ~ there are a lot of people.

полнове́сн|ый (-ен, -на, -но) *прил* (*аргумент, статья*) weighty; (*описание*) full-bodied.

полновла́стн|ый (-ен, -на, -но) *прил* fully empowered.

полново́дн|ый (-ен, -на, -но) *прил* deep.

полнокро́вн|ый (-ен, -на, -но) *прил* (*жизнь*) full-blooded.

полнолу́ни|е (-я) *ср* full moon.

полнометра́жный *прил*: ~ **фильм** full-length film.

полномо́чен *прил см* **полномо́чный**.

полномо́чи|е (-я) *ср* authority; (*обычно мн: право*) power; **облека́ть (обле́чь** (*perf*)) **кого́-н** ~**ями** +*infin* to authorize sb to do; **слага́ть (сложи́ть** (*perf*)) **с себя́** ~**я** to relinquish one's authority; **э́то не вхо́дит в мои́** ~**я** it is not within my jurisdiction.

полномо́чн|ый (-ен, -на, -но) *прил* fully authorized.

полнопра́вн|ый (-ен, -на, -но) *прил* (*гражданин*) fully-fledged; (*наследник*) rightful **он** ~ **владе́лец** he has full ownership rights.

по́лностью *нареч* fully, completely.

полнот|а́ (-ы́) *ж* (*целостность*) completeness; (*тучность*) stoutness; **облада́ть** (*impf*) **всей** ~**о́й вла́сти/прав** to enjoy full power/rights; **опи́сывать (описа́ть** *perf*) **что-н во всей** ~**е́** to describe sth in its entirety; **от** ~**ы́ чувств** *или* **души́** overcome by emotion.

полноце́нн|ый (-ен, -на, -но) *прил* (*отдых, пища*) proper; (*работа, исследование*) valuable; (*деньги, валюта*) valued.

по́лночь (-уночи) *ж* midnight.

по́лн|ый (-он, -на́, -но́ *или* -но) *прил* full; (*no short form; победа, власть, счастье итп*) complete, total; (*толстый*) stout; ~ +*gen или* +*instr* full of; (*тревоги, любви итп*) filled with; **ведро́,** ~**ное воды́** a bucket, full of water; **ко́мната была́ полна́ людьми́** the room was full of people; **она́ была́ полна́ трево́ги** she was filled with anxiety; ~**ным хо́дом** at full speed; **в** ~**ную си́лу** at full strength; **по́лным-полно́** (+*gen*) (*разг*) loads and loads (of); **по́лное собра́ние сочине́ний** complete works.

по́ло *ср нескл*: (**во́дное**) ~ (water) polo.

полови́к (-а́) *м* mat.

полови́н|а (-ы) *ж* half; **на** ~**е доро́ги** halfway; **сейча́с** ~ **пе́рвого/второ́го** it's (now) half past twelve/one; **приходи́те в ~е двена́дцатого** come at half past eleven; **встре́ча назна́чена на ~у деся́того** the meeting has been set for half past nine.

полови́нчат|ый (-, -а, -о) *прил (меры, решение)* half-baked.

поло́вник (-а) *м* ladle.

полово́дь|е (-я) *ср* high water.

полово́й *прил (тряпка, мастика)* floor *опред*; *(БИО)* sexual; **полова́я жизнь** sex life; **полова́я зре́лость** puberty; **половой о́рган** reproductive organ; **половы́е о́рганы** genitals.

поло́г|ий (-ая, -ое, -ие; -, -а, -о) *прил (склон)* gentle; *(гора, берег)* gently sloping.

положе́ни|е (-я) *ср* situation; *(географическое)* location, position; *(тела, головы итп)* position; *(социальное, семейное итп)* status; *(правила)* regulations *мн*; *(обычно мн: тезис)* point; **быть** *(impf)* **на высоте́ ~я** to be on top of the situation; **входи́ть (войти́** *perf)* **в чьё-н ~** to put o.s. in sb's position; **выходи́ть (вы́йти** *perf)* **из тру́дного/неприя́тного ~я** to get o.s. out of a difficult/unpleasant situation; **она́ в ~и** *(разг)* she's expecting; **положе́ние дел** the state of affairs.

положенный *прил* due.

положи́тельный (-ен, -ьна, -ьно) *прил* positive.

пол|ожи́ть (-ожу́, -о́жишь) *сов от* **класть** ◆ *(не)перех*: **~о́жим, ты прав/э́то так** let us assume that you're right/this is the case; **~ожа́ ру́ку на́ сердце** *(перен)* with hand on heart

положи́ться *(impf* **полага́ться**) *сов возв*: **~ся на** +*acc* to count on.

пол|оз (-оза; *nom pl* -о́зья) *м (обычно мн)* runner *(on sledge)*.

поло́к *сущ см* **по́лка**.

полома́ть(ся) (-ю(сь)) *сов от* **лома́ть(ся)**.

поло́м|ка (-ки; *gen pl* -ок) *ж (действие)* breakdown; *(повреждённое место)* damage.

поло́н *прил см* **по́лный**.

полос|а́ (-ы́; *nom pl* **по́лосы**, *gen pl* **поло́с**, *dat pl* **по́лосам**) *ж (ткани, металла итп)* stripe; *(на ткани, на рисунке итп)* stripe; *(тумана, леса итп)* belt; *(неудач, плохой погоды)* spell; *(в газете)* column.

полоса́тый (-, -а, -о) *прил* striped, stripy.

поло́с|ка (-ки; *gen pl* -ок) *ж (ткани, бумаги, металла)* (thin) strip; *(на одежде, на ткани)* (thin) stripe; **в ~ку** striped.

пол|оска́ть (-ощу́, -о́щешь; *perf* **прополоска́ть**) *несов перех (бельё, посуду)* to rinse; *(рот)* to rinse out; **~ (прополоска́ть** *perf)* **го́рло** to gargle.

поло́сок *сущ см* **поло́ска**.

по́лост|ь (-и; *gen pl* -е́й) *ж (АНАТ)* cavity.

полотен *сущ см* **полотно́**.

полоте́н|це (-ца; *gen pl* -ец) *ср* towel.

поло́тнищ|е (-а) *ср*: ~ **фла́га** flag.

полотн|о́ (-отна́; *nom pl* -о́тна, *gen pl* -о́тен) *ср* *(ткань)* sheet; *(картина)* canvas; **бле́дный как ~** white as a sheet.

пол|о́ть (-ю́, -ешь; *perf* **прополо́ть**) *несов перех* to weed.

полоу́мный *прил (разг: идея, речь)* crackpot *опред*.

полощу́ *итп несов см* **полоска́ть**.

полпре́д (-а) *м (= полномо́чный представи́тель)* plenipotentiary.

полпути́ *м нескл* half *(of journey)*; **на ~** halfway; *(перен: остановиться, бросить дело итп)* halfway through; **верну́ться** *(perf)* **с ~** to turn back halfway.

полсло́ва (- *или* **полусло́ва**) *ср* half of the word; **мо́жно Вас на ~?** could I have a quick word?; **прерыва́ть (прерва́ть** *perf)* **кого́-н на пол(у)сло́ве** to cut sb short; **понима́ть (поня́ть** *perf)* **с пол(у)сло́ва** to understand in an instant.

полти́нник (-а) *м (сумма)* 50 kopecks; *(монета)* 50-kopeck piece.

пол|тора́ (-у́тора; *f* **полторы́**) *м/ср чис* one and a half; **ей ~ го́да** she is one and a half; **ей о́коло ~у́тора лет** she is about one and a half; **кни́га сто́ит ~ рубля́/полторы́ ма́рки** the book costs one and a half roubles/one and a half marks.

полтора́ста (-у́тораста) *чис* one hundred and fifty.

полуботи́н|ок (-ка) *м (обычно мн)* ankle *или* desert boot.

полуве́ка *сущ см* **полве́ка**.

полуго́да *сущ см* **полго́да**.

полуго́ди|е (-я) *ср (ПРОСВЕЩ)* semester; *(ЭКОН)* half *(of the year)*.

полугоди́чный *прил* six-month.

полугодово́й *прил* six-monthly, half-yearly.

полу́дня *сущ см* **по́лдень**.

полузащи́т|а (-ы) *ж* midfield.

полузащи́тник (-а) *м* midfielder.

полукру́г (-а) *м* semicircle.

полукру́глый *прил* semicircular.

полуме́р|а (-ы) *ж* half-measure *(fig)*.

полуме́сяц (-а) *м* half-moon.

полумра́к (-а) *м* semidarkness.

полу́ночи *сущ см* **по́лночь**.

полуо́стров (-а) *м* peninsular.

полупальто́ *ср нескл* jacket, short coat.

полупроводни́к (-а́) *м (ЭЛЕК)* semiconductor.

полусапо́ж|ек (-ка; *gen pl* -ек) *м (обычно мн)* half-boot.

полусло́ва *сущ см* **полсло́ва**.

полуто́н (-а) *м (МУЗ)* semitone, half step *(US)*.

полу́тора *чис см* **полтора́**.

полуфабрика́т (-а) *м (КУЛИН) any products such as frozen foods and cake mixes which require partial preparation*; *(ТЕХ)* semifinished article.

полуфина́л (-а) *м* semifinal.
получа́са *сущ см* полчаса́.
получа́тель (-я) *м* recipient.
получа́ть(ся) (-ю(сь)) *несов от* получи́ть(ся).
получа́чек *сущ см* получа́чка.
получе́ни|е (-я) *ср* receipt; (*урожая, результата*) obtaining.
получи́ть (-учу́, -у́чишь; *impf* получа́ть) *сов перех* to receive, get; (*урожай, результат, насморк, удовольствие*) to get; (*известность, распространение, применение итп*) to gain ♦ *неперех* (*разг: быть наказанным*) to get it in the neck
▶ **получи́ться** (*impf* получа́ться) *сов возв* to turn out; (*удаться*) to work; (*фотография*) to come out; **из него́ ~у́чится хоро́ший учи́тель** he'll make a good teacher; **пиро́г хорошо́ ~учи́лся** the pie turned out well; **у меня́ э́то не ~уча́ется** I can't do it; **из э́того ничего́ не ~у́чится** it won't come to anything.
полу́ч|ка (-ки; *gen pl* -ек) *ж* (*разг*) pay.
полуша́ри|е (-я) *ср* hemisphere.
полушу́б|ок (-ка) *м* (*из овчины*) sheepskin jacket; (*из меха*) short fur coat.
полцены́ *ж нескл* (*разг*): **за ~** for next to nothing.
полчаса́ (-уча́са) *м* half an hour; **ка́ждые ~** every half hour; **прошло́** *или* **прошли́ ~** half an hour went by.
по́лчищ|е (-а) *ср* (*обычно мн: врагов*) horde; (: *насекомых, крыс*) swarm.
по́л|ый (-, -а, -о) *прил* hollow.
полы́нь (-и) *ж* wormwood.
полысе́|ть (-ю) *сов от* лысе́ть.
полыха́|ть (-ю) *несов неперех* to blaze.
по́льз|а (-ы) *ж* benefit; **в ~у** +*gen* in favour (*BRIT*) *или* favor (*US*) of; **идти́ (пойти́** *perf*) **на ~у кому́-н** to be of benefit to sb.
по́льзовани|е (-я) *ср*: **~** (+*instr*) use (of).
по́льзовател|ь (-я) *м* (*также КОМП*) user.
по́льзоваться (-уюсь; *perf* воспо́льзоваться) *несов возв* (+*instr*) to use; (*no perf*; *авторитетом, успехом итп*) to enjoy.
по́ль|ка (-ьки; *gen pl* -ек) *ж см* поля́к; (*танец*) polka.
по́льск|ий (-ая, -ое, -ие) *прил* Polish; **~ язы́к** Polish.
польсти́ть (-щу́, -сти́шь) *сов от* льстить.
По́льш|а (-и) *ж* Poland.
польщён|ный (-, -á, -ó) *прил*: **~** (+*instr*) flattered (by).
польщу́ *сов см* польсти́ть.
полью́(сь) *итп сов см* поли́ть(ся).
пол|юби́ть (-юблю́, -ю́бишь) *сов перех* (*человека*) to come to love; **~** (*perf*) **что-н**/+*infin* to develop a love for sth/doing.
полюб|ова́ться (-у́юсь) *сов от* любова́ться ♦ *возв* (*разг*): **~у́йтесь на него́/э́то!** take a look at him/that!
по́люс (-а; *nom pl* -á) *м* (*ГЕО, ЭЛЕК*) pole.
пол|я́ (-е́й) *мн* (*шляпы*) brim *ед*; (*на странице*)

margin *ед*.
поля́гу *итп сов см* поле́чь.
поля́к (-а) *м* Pole.
поля́н|а (-ы) *ж* glade.
поля́рный *прил* (*ГЕО*) polar *опред*; (*интересы, точки зрения итп*) diametrically opposed; **поля́рная звезда́** the Pole Star; **поля́рная ночь** Arctic night; **поля́рный день** Arctic day.
пома́д|а (-ы) *ж* (*также:* **губна́я ~**) lipstick.
пома́|зать (-жу, -жешь) *сов от* ма́зать.
помале́ньку *нареч* (*разг*) bit by bit; **живём ~** we're getting by.
пома́лкива|ть (-ю) *несов неперех* (*разг*) to keep quiet.
пом|ани́ть (-аню́, -а́нишь) *несов от* мани́ть.
пома́р|ка (-ки; *gen pl* -ок) *ж* crossing out (*мн* crossings out).
пома́сл|ить (-ю, -ишь) *сов от* ма́слить.
помаха́ть (-ашу́, -а́шешь) *сов неперех* (+*instr*) to wave.
помедл|ить (-ю, -ишь) *сов неперех*: **~ с** +*instr*/+*infin* to linger over sth/over doing.
помелю́ *итп сов см* помоло́ть.
поменя́|ть(ся) (-ю(сь)) *сов от* меня́ть(ся).
помере́щиться (*3sg* -ится, *3pl* -атся) *сов от* мере́щиться.
помер|ить(ся) (-ю(сь), -ишь(ся)) *сов от* ме́рить(ся).
померкнуть (-у, -ешь) *сов от* ме́ркнуть.
помертве́|ть (-ю) *сов от* мертве́ть.
помести́ть (-ещу́, -ести́шь; *impf* помеща́ть) *сов перех* to put; (*поставить*) to place, put; (*поселить*) to put up; (*устроить*) to settle
▶ **помести́ться** (*impf* помеща́ться) *сов возв* (*уместиться*) to fit.
поме́сть|е (-ья; *gen pl* -ий) *ср* estate.
помёт (-а) *м* dung.
помёт|а (-ы) *ж* (*в словаре*) explanatory note.
поме́|тить (-чу, -тишь) *сов от* ме́тить ♦ (*impf* помеча́ть) *перех* to note.
поме́т|ка (-ки; *gen pl* -ок) *ж* note.
поме́х|а (-и) *ж* hindrance; (*связь: обычно мн*) interference *ед*.
помеча́|ть (-ю) *несов от* поме́тить.
помечу́ *сов см* поме́тить.
помеша́н|ный (-, -а, -о) *прил* mad; (*разг*): **~ на** +*prp* crazy about.
помеша́тельств|о (-а) *ср* madness.
помеша́|ть (-ю) *сов от* меша́ть
▶ **помеша́ться** *сов возв* to go mad; (*разг*): **~ся на** +*prp* to become crazy about.
помеща́|ть (-ю) *несов от* помести́ть
▶ **помеща́ться** *несов от* помести́ться ♦ *возв* (*находиться*) to be situated.
помеще́ни|е (-я) *ср* room; (*под офис*) premises *мн*; **жило́е ~** living space.
поме́щик (-а) *м* landowner.
поме́щиц|а (-ы) *ж см* поме́щик.
помещу́(сь) *сов см* помести́ть(ся).
помидо́р (-а) *м* tomato (*мн* tomatoes).
поми́ловани|е (-я) *ср* (*преступника*) pardon.

поми́ловать (-ую) *сов от* ми́ловать ◆ *неперех:* ~у́йте! *(разг)* you can't be serious!

поми́мо *предл (+gen)* besides; *(без участия)* bypassing; ~ де́нег нам нужна́ маши́на besides money we need a car; ~ того́/всего́ про́чего apart from that/everything else.

поми́н (-а) *м:* э́того и в ~е нет it's nowhere to be found; его́ у нас и в ~е не́ было we haven't seen hide nor hair of him; лёгок на ~е *(разг)* speak of the devil.

помина́льный *прил (РЕЛ)* funeral *опред.*

помина́ть (-ю) *несов от* помяну́ть ◆ *неперех:* ~й как зва́ли *(разг)* just like that.

поми́нки (-ок) *мн* wake *ед;* справля́ть (спра́вить *perf)* ~ по кому́-н to give a wake for sb.

помину́тный (-ен, -на, -но) *прил* at intervals of one minute; *(очень частый)* constant; *(оплата)* by the minute.

помири́ть(ся) (-ю́(сь), -и́шь(ся)) *сов от* мири́ть(ся).

по́мнить (-ю, -ишь) *несов (не)перех:* ~ *(о +prp)* про *+acc)* to remember; я ~ю Ва́шу про́сьбу *или* о Ва́шей про́сьбе I remember your request; я ~ю, что Вы проси́ли об э́том I remember that you asked about that

▸ **по́мниться** *несов возв* to be remembered; мне ~ится на́ша встре́ча I remember our meeting; ~ится, мы об э́том говори́ли I remember that we spoke about that.

помножа́ть (-ю) *несов перех* = мно́жить.

помно́жить (-у, -ишь) *сов от* мно́жить.

помню́(сь) *итп сов см* помя́ть(ся).

помо́г *итп сов см* помо́чь.

помога́ть (-ю) *несов от* помо́чь.

помогу́ *итп сов см* помо́чь.

помо́ек *сущ см* помо́йка.

по-мо́ему *нареч* my way ◆ *вводн сл* in my opinion.

помо́жешь *итп сов см* помо́чь.

помо́и (-ев) *мн* dishwater; *(отходы)* slops *мн.*

помо́йка (-йки; *gen pl* -ек) *ж (помойная яма)* cesspit; *(для мусора)* rubbish *(BRIT) или* garbage *(US)* heap.

помо́л (-а) *м:* мука́/ко́фе ме́лкого/кру́пного ~а a fine-/coarse-ground flour/coffee.

помо́лвить (-лю, -ишь) *сов перех:* они́ ~лены they are engaged; она́ ~лена с ним she is engaged to him.

помоли́ться (-олю́сь, -о́лишься) *сов от* моли́ться.

помолоде́ть (-ю) *сов от* молоде́ть.

помоло́ть (-елю́, -е́лешь) *несов от* моло́ть.

помолча́ть (-у́, -и́шь) *сов неперех* to pause.

помори́ть (-ю́, -и́шь) *сов от* мори́ть.

помо́рщиться (-усь, -ишься) *сов возв* to screw up one's face.

помо́ст (-а) *м (для обозрения)* platform; *(для выступлений)* rostrum; *(для казни)* scaffold.

помота́ть (-ю) *сов от* мота́ть.

помо́читься (-очу́сь, -о́чишься) *сов от* мочи́ться.

помо́чь (-огу́, -о́жешь *итп,* -о́гут; *pt* -о́г, -огла́, -огло́, *impf* помога́ть) *сов неперех (+dat)* to help; *(в работе)* to help, assist; *(другой стране)* to aid.

помо́щник (-а) *м* helper; *(должностное лицо)* assistant; ~ капита́на mate.

помо́щница (-ы) *ж* helper.

по́мощь (-и) *ж* help, assistance; с ~ю, при по́мощи with; *(позва́ть perf)* на ~ to call for help; ока́зывать (оказа́ть *perf)* кому́-н ~ to help *или* assist sb; проси́ть (попроси́ть *perf)* о ~и to ask for help.

помо́ю(сь) *итп сов см* помы́ть(ся).

помпо́н (-а) *м* pompom.

помрачне́ть (-ю) *сов от* мрачне́ть.

помути́ть(ся) *(3sg* -и́т(ся), *3pl* -я́т(ся)) *сов от* мути́ть(ся).

помутне́ть (-ю) *сов от* мутне́ть.

помучи́ть (-у, -ишь) *сов перех* to torment

▸ **помучи́ться** *сов возв* to suffer.

по́мысел (-ла) *м* intention.

помы́слить (-ю, -ишь; *impf* помышля́ть) *сов неперех:* ~ о чём-н to have sth in mind.

помы́ть(ся) (-о́ю(сь), -о́ешь(ся)) *сов от* мы́ть(ся).

помышля́ть (-ю) *несов от* помы́слить.

помяну́ть (-яну́, -я́нешь; *impf* помина́ть) *сов перех (упомянуть)* to mention; *(устроить поминки)* to give a wake for; ~яни́те моё сло́во mark my words.

помя́тый (-, -а, -о) *прил (разг: одежда, внешность)* rumpled; *(бок машины)* dented.

помя́ть(ся) (-ну́(сь), -нёшь(ся)) *сов от* мя́ть(ся).

понаде́яться (-юсь) *сов от* наде́яться.

понадо́биться (-люсь, -ишься) *сов возв* to be needed *или* required.

понаслы́шке *нареч:* знать ~ о ком-н/чём-н to hear a rumour *(BRIT) или* rumor *(US)* about sb/sth.

по-настоя́щему *нареч* properly.

понача́лу *нареч (разг)* at first.

по-на́шему *нареч* our way ◆ *вводн сл* in our opinion.

понево́ле *нареч* against one's will.

понеде́льник (-а) *м* Monday; *см также* вто́рник.

понемно́гу *нареч* a little; *(постепенно)* little by little; как пожива́ете? – ~ how's life? – not too bad.

понести́ (-есу́, -есёшь; *pt* -ёс, -есла́, -есло́) *сов от* нести́ ◆ *перех (начать нести)* to take

▸ **понести́сь** *сов возв (человек)* to tear off; *(лошадь)* to charge off; *(машина)* to speed off.

пóни *м нескл* pony.

понижá|ть(ся) (-ю(сь)) *несов от* **понúзить(ся)**.

понижéни|е (-я) *ср* reduction; (*в должности*) demotion.

понú|зить (-жу, -зишь; *impf* **понижáть**) *сов перех* to reduce; (*в должности*) to demote; (*голос*) to lower

▸ **понúзиться** (*impf* **понижáться**) *сов возв* to be reduced.

пóнизу *нареч* (*близко к земле*) low.

понú|кнуть (-у, -ешь) *сов от* **нúкнуть**.

понимáни|е (-я) *ср* (*способность ума*) understanding; (*толкование*) interpretation; **относúться (отнестúсь** *perf*) **к чему-н с ~м** to be understanding about sth; **это вы́ше моегó ~я** this is beyond me.

понимá|ть (-ю) *несов от* **понять** ♦ *перех* to understand ♦ *неперех*: **~ в +prp** to know about; **~ете** you see; **вот это я ~ю!** (*разг*) that's great!

пономáр|ь (-я́) *м* (*РЕЛ*) ≈ acolyte.

понóс (-а) *м* diarrhoea (*BRIT*), diarrhea (*US*).

понос|úть (-ошý, -óсишь) *сов перех* to carry for a while; (*одежду*) to wear ♦ *несов перех* (*ругать*) to curse.

понóшен|ный (-, -на, -но) *прил* (*одежда*) worn.

ношý (*не*)*сов см* **носúть**.

понрáв|иться (-люсь, -ишься) *сов от* **нрáвиться**.

понт (-а) *м* (*разг*) pretence.

понтóн (-а) *м* pontoon bridge.

понукá|ть (-ю) *несов перех* to urge on.

понýр|ить (-ю, -ишь) *сов перех*: **~ гóлову** to hang one's head.

понýрый *прил* downcast.

пóнчик (-а) *м* doughnut (*BRIT*), donut (*US*).

поны́не *нареч* to this day.

понюха|ть (-ю) *сов от* **нюхать**.

понятен *прил см* **понятный**.

поняти|е (-я) *ср* (*времени, пространства итп*) conception; (*о политике, о литературе*) idea; **~я не имéю** (*разг*) I've no idea.

понятлив|ый (-, -а, -о) *прил* quick.

понятно *нареч* intelligibly ♦ *как сказ*: **мне ~** I understand; **~! I** see!

понятн|ый (-ен, -на, -но) *прил* intelligible; (*ясный*) clear; (*оправданный*) understandable.

понятóй (-óго; *decl like adj*) *м* (*ЮР*) witness (*during official search*).

по|нять (-ймý, -ймёшь; *pt* -нял, -нялá, -няло, *impf* **понимáть**) *сов перех* to understand; **давáть (дать** *perf*) **~ кому-н** to give sb to understand.

пообéда|ть (-ю) *сов от* **обéдать**.

пообещá|ть (-ю) *сов от* **обещáть**.

поóдаль *нареч* a little way away ♦ *предл*: **~ от +gen** a little way from.

поодинóчке *нареч* one at a time.

поочерёдный *прил* (*дежурство, обслуживание*) alternating.

поощрéни|е (-я) *ср* (*действие*) encouragement; (*то, чем поощряют*) incentive.

поощрúтельн|ый *прил*: **~ая плáта** (*КОММ*) incentive bonus.

поощр|úть (-ю, -úшь; *impf* **поощрять**) *сов перех* to encourage.

поп (-á) *м* (*разг*) priest.

пóп|а (-ы) *ж* (*разг*) bottom, bum.

попадáни|е (-я) *ср* hit.

попадá|ть(ся) (-ю(сь)) *несов от* **попáсть(ся)**.

попадý(сь) *итп сов см* **попáсть(ся)**.

попáрно *нареч* in pairs.

попá|сть (-дý, -дёшь; *impf* **попадáть**) *сов неперех*: **~ в +acc** (*в цель*) to hit; (*в ворота*) to end up in; (*в чужой город*) to find o.s. in; (*в беду*) to land in; **мы́ло ~ло в глазá** the soap got in my eyes; **он ~л мячóм в корзúну** he put the ball in the basket; **~** (*perf*) **в университéт/на кýрсы** to get into university/onto a course; **попадáть (~** *perf*) **в авáрию** to have an accident; **~** (*perf*) **в плен** to be taken prisoner; **попадáть (~** *perf*) **под дождь** to be caught in the rain; **емý ~ло** (*разг*) he got a hiding; **(Вы) не тудá ~ли** you've got the wrong number; **где ~ло** (*разг*) anywhere; **как ~ло** (*разг*) anyhow; **что ~ло** (*разг*) anything

▸ **попáсться** (*impf* **попадáться**) *сов возв* (*быть пойманным*) to be caught; **~ся** (*perf*) **на взя́тках/воровствé** to be caught taking bribes/stealing; **мне ~лась интерéсная кнúга** I came across an interesting book; **попадáться (~ся** *perf*) **кому-н на глазá** to catch sb's eye.

попéй(те) *сов см* **попúть**.

поперёк *нареч* crossways ♦ *предл* (+*gen*) across.

попеременно *нареч* in turns.

поперéчный *прил* horizontal.

поперхн|ýться (-ýсь, -ёшься) *сов возв* to choke.

попéрч|ить (-у, -ишь) *сов от* **перчúть**.

попечéни|е (-я) *ср* (*о детях*) care; (*о делах, о доме*) charge; **оставля́ть (остáвить** *perf*) **когó-н/что-н на чьё-н ~** to leave sb/sth in sb's care.

попечúтел|ь (-я) *м* guardian; (*КОММ*) trustee.

попирá|ть (-ю) *несов от* **попрáть**.

попис|áть (-ишý, -úшешь) *сов* (*не*)*перех* to write; **ничегó не ~úшешь** (*разг*) there's nothing you can do.

поп|úть (-ью́, -ьёшь; *pt* -úл, -илá, -úло, *imper* -éй(те)) *сов перех* to have a drink of.

попишý *итп сов см* **пописáть**.

пóпкорн (-а) *м* popcorn.

поплав|óк (-кá) *м* (*на удочке*) float.

поппл|атúться (-ачýсь, -áтишься) *сов от* **платúться**.

поплúн (-а) *м* poplin.

поплы́|ть (-вý, -вёшь; *pt* -л, -лá, -ло) *сов неперех* (*человек, животное*) to start swimming; (*судно*) to set sail.

пополáм *нареч* in half; **~ с +instr** mixed with.

пополнéни|е (-я) *ср* (*запасов*) replenishment; (*коллекции*) expansion; (*то, чем пополняется*) reinforcement.

пополнé|ть (-ю) *сов от* **полнéть.**

пополн|и́ть (-ю, -и́шь; *impf* **пополня́ть**) *сов перех*: ~ что-н +*instr* (*запасы*) to replenish sth with; (*коллекцию*) to expand sth with; (*коллектив*) to reinforce sth with; (*образование*) to supplement sth with

▶ **попо́лниться** (*impf* **пополня́ться**) *сов возв* (*запасы*) to be replenished; (*коллекция*) to be expanded.

поправи́м|ый (-, -а, -о) *прил* (*дело, ошибка*) rectifiable.

попра́в|ить (-лю, -ишь; *impf* **поправля́ть**) *сов перех* to correct; (*галстук, платье итп*) to straighten; (*причёску*) to tidy; (*здоровье, дела*) to improve

▶ **попра́виться** (*impf* **поправля́ться**) *сов возв* to improve; (*пополнеть*) to put on weight.

попра́в|ка (-ки; *gen pl* -ок) *ж* (*в решение, в закон*) amendment; **вноси́ть** (**внести́** *perf*) ~**ку в зако́н** to make an amendment to a law; **дéло идёт на** ~**ку** things are looking up.

поправлю́(сь) *сов см* **попра́вить(ся).**

поправля́|ть(ся) (-ю(сь)) *несов от* **попра́вить(ся).**

попра́вок *сущ см* **попра́вка.**

попра́|ть (*pt* -л, -ла, -ло, *impf* **попира́ть**) *сов перех* (*права*) to disregard; (*гордость*) to offend; (*закон*) to flout.

по-прéжнему *нареч* as before.

попрека́|ть (-ю) *несов перех* to reproach.

попрекн|у́ть (-у́, -ёшь) *сов перех* to reproach.

поприве́тств|овать (-ую) *сов от* **приве́тствовать.**

по́прищ|е (-а) *ср* (*науки итп*) field.

попро́б|овать (-ую) *сов от* **про́бовать** ♦ *неперех*: ~**уйте!** (*раза*) just you try!

попро|си́ть(ся) (-ошу́(сь), -о́сишь(ся)) *сов от* **проси́ть(ся).**

по́просту *част* simply; **он** ~ **уста́л** he's just *или* simply tired.

попрошу́(сь) *сов см* **попроси́ть(ся).**

попроща́|ться (-юсь) *сов возв*: ~ **с** +*instr* to say goodbye to.

попуга́|й (-я) *м* parrot.

популя́рен *прил см* **популя́рный.**

популяризи́р|овать (-ую) (*не*)*сов перех* to popularize.

популяриз|ова́ть (-у́ю) (*не*)*сов* = **популяризи́ровать.**

популя́рност|ь (-и) *ж* popularity.

популя́рн|ый (-ен, -на, -но) *прил* popular; (*изложение*) accessible.

популя́ци|я (-и) *ж* population (*of plants or animals*).

попурри́ *ср нескл* (*муз*) medley.

попусти́тельств|овать (-ую) *несов неперех* (+*dat*) to tolerate.

по́пусту *нареч* (*разг*) in vain.

попу́тн|ый *прил* (*замечание, исправление*) accompanying; (*машина*) passing; (*ветер*) favourable (*BRIT*), favorable (*US*); (: *мор*) fair.

попу́тчик (-а) *м* travelling (*BRIT*) *или* traveling (*US*) companion.

попыта́|ть (-ю) *сов перех*: ~ **сча́стья** to try one's luck

▶ **попыта́ться** *сов от* **пыта́ться.**

попы́т|ка (-ки; *gen pl* -ок) *ж* attempt; ~ **к бéгству** attempted escape; **со второ́й/с трéтьей** ~**ки** on *или* at the second/third attempt.

попью́ *итп сов см* **попи́ть.**

попя́|титься (-чусь, -тишься) *сов возв* to take a few steps backward.

попя́тн|ый *прил*: **идти́** *или* **пойти́ на** ~ *или* **на** ~**ую** to go back on one's word.

попя́чусь *сов см* **попя́титься.**

по́р|а (-ы) *ж* pore.

пор|а́ (-ы́; *acc sg* -у, *dat sg* -é, *nom pl* -ы) *ж* time ♦ **как сказ** it's time; **до каки́х** ~**р?** until when?; **до** ~**ры́ до врéмени** for the time being; **до сих пор** (*раньше*) up till now; (*всё ещё*) still; **до тех пор** until then; **до тех пор, пока́** until; **на пéрвых** ~**х** at first; **с каки́х пор?** since when?; (**мне**) ~ it's time (for me) to go; (**мне**) ~ **спать/рабо́тать** it's time (for me) to go to bed/ to work.

порабо|ти́ть (-щу́, -ти́шь; *impf* **порабоща́ть**) *сов перех* to enslave.

порабощéни|е (-я) *ср* enslavement.

порабощу́ *сов см* **порабо́тить.**

поравня́|ться (-юсь) *сов возв*: ~ **с** +*instr* (*человек*) to draw level with; (*машина*) to come alongside.

пора́д|овать(ся) (-ую(сь)) *сов от* **ра́довать(ся).**

поража́|ть(ся) (-ю(сь)) *несов от* **порази́ть(ся).**

поражéни|е (-я) *ср* (*цели*) hitting; (*мед: лёгких*) damage; (*в войне, в состяза́нии итп*) defeat; **наноси́ть** (**нанести́** *perf*) **кому́-н** ~ to defeat sb; **терпéть** (**потерпéть** *perf*) ~ to be defeated.

поражу́(сь) *сов см* **порази́ть(ся).**

порази́тельн|ый (-ен, -ьна, -ьно) *прил* (*красота, талант*) striking; (*жестокость*) astonishing.

пора|зи́ть (-жу́, -зи́шь; *impf* **поража́ть**) *сов перех* (*цель*) to hit; (*подлеж: болезнь*) to affect; (*изумить*) to astonish

▶ **порази́ться** (*impf* **поража́ться**) *сов возв* to be astonished.

поран|и́ть (-ю, -ишь) *сов перех* to hurt.

пор|асти́ (*3sg* -асте́т, *3pl* -асту́т, *pt* -о́с, -осла́, -осло́, *impf* **пораста́ть**) *сов неперех*: ~ +*instr* to become overgrown with.

порв|а́ть (-у́, -ёшь) *сов от* **рвать** ♦ *перех* to tear ♦ (*impf* **порыва́ть**) *неперех*: ~ **с** +*instr* (*с женой, с друзьями*) to break up with; **порыва́ть** (~ *perf*) **что-н с кем-н** to break off sth with sb

▶ **порва́ться** *сов от* **рва́ться** ♦ *возв* (*нить*) to break; (*пла́тье*) to tear.

пореде́ть (*3sg* -**ет**, *3pl* -**ют**) *несов от* **реде́ть**.

поре́жу(сь) *итп сов см* **поре́зать(ся)**.

поре́з (-**а**) *м* cut.

поре́зать (-**жу**, -**жешь**) *сов перех* to cut.

▶ **поре́заться** *сов возв* to cut o.s.

▶ **поре́й** (-**я**) *м* leek.

порекомендова́ть (-**ую**) *сов от* **рекомендова́ть**.

по́ристый (-, -**а**, -**о**) *прил* porous.

порица́ние (-**я**) *ср* reprimand.

порица́ть (-**ю**) *несов перех* to reprimand.

порнографи́ческий (-**ая**, -**ое**, -**ие**) *прил* pornographic.

порногра́фия (-**и**) *ж* pornography.

по́ровну *нареч* equally.

поро́г (-**а**) *м* (*та́кже перен*) threshold; (*на реке́*) rapids *мн*; **переступа́ть** (**переступи́ть** *perf*) ~ to cross the threshold; **я его́ на ~ не пущу́** he won't darken my door again.

поро́да (-**ы**) *ж* (*живо́тных*) breed; (*древе́сная*) species; (*го́рная*) rock; (*перен: люде́й*) type.

поро́дистый (-, -**а**, -**о**) *прил* pedigree *опред*; (*лицо́*) aristocratic.

породи́ть (-**жу́**, -**ди́шь**; *impf* **порожда́ть**) *сов перех* (*стать причи́ной*) to give rise to.

породни́ться (-**юсь**, -**и́шься**) *сов от* **родни́ться**.

порожда́ть (-**ю**) *несов от* **породи́ть**.

поро́жний (-**яя**, -**ее**, -**ие**) *прил* empty; **перелива́ть** (*impf*) **из пусто́го в ~ее** to rabbit on.

порожня́к (-**а́**) *м* empty vehicle.

порожняко́м *нареч* without a load.

порожу́ *сов см* **породи́ть**.

порозове́ть (-**ю**) *сов от* **розове́ть**.

поро́й *нареч* from time to time.

поро́к (-**а**) *м* vice; **поро́к се́рдца** heart disease.

пороло́н (-**а**) *м* foam rubber.

поро́с *итп сов см* **порасти́**.

поросёнок (-**ёнка**; *nom pl* -**я́та**, *gen pl* -**я́т**) *м* piglet.

по́росль (-**и**) *ж* (*побе́ги*) shoots *мн*; (*перен*) generation.

порося́та *итп сущ см* **поросёнок**.

поро́ть (-**ю́**, -**ешь**; *perf* **распоро́ть**) *несов перех* (*швы*) to unpick; (*perf* **вы́пороть**; *бить*) to belt; ~ (**напоро́ть** *perf*) **чушь** *или* **ерунду́** *или* **чепуху́** to talk nonsense; ~ (*impf*) **горя́чку** (*разг*) to get a move on.

по́рох (-**а**; *part gen* -**у**) *м* gunpowder.

поро́чен *прил см* **поро́чный**.

поро́чить (-**у**, -**ишь**; *perf* **опоро́чить**) *несов перех* to bring shame on; (*черни́ть: челове́ка*) to defame; (: *рабо́ту*) to bring into disrepute.

поро́чный (-**ен**, -**на**, -**но**) *прил* (*безнра́вственный*) depraved; (*непра́вильный*) flawed.

порошо́к (-**ка́**) *м* powder.

поро́ю *нареч* = **поро́й**.

порт (-**а**; *loc sg* -**у́**, *nom pl* -**ы**, *gen pl* -**о́в**) *м* port; **возду́шный ~** airport.

порта́л (-**а**) *м* (*архит*) portal.

порта́тивный *прил* portable.

портве́йн (-**а**) *м* port (*wine*).

по́ртить (-**чу**, -**тишь**; *perf* **испо́ртить**) *несов перех* (*механи́зм, здоро́вье, карье́ру*) to damage; (*настрое́ние, пра́здник, ребёнка*) to spoil; ~ (*impf*) **себе́ не́рвы** to worry

▶ **по́ртиться** (*perf* **испо́ртиться**) *сов возв* (*механи́зм*) to be damaged; (*здоро́вье, пого́да*) to deteriorate; (*настрое́ние*) to be spoiled; (*молоко́*) to go off; (*мя́со, о́вощи*) to go bad.

портни́ха (-**и**) *ж* dressmaker.

портно́й (-**о́го**; *decl like adj*) *м* tailor.

портно́вый *прил* от **портно́й**.

портре́т (-**а**) *м* portrait.

портсига́р (-**а**) *м* cigarette case.

Портсму́т (-**а**) *м* Portsmouth.

Португа́лия (-**и**) *ж* Portugal.

португа́льский (-**ая**, -**ое**, -**ие**) *прил* Portuguese; ~ **язы́к** Portuguese.

портфе́ль (-**я**) *м* briefcase; (*полит, комм*) portfolio; ~ **це́нных бума́г** (*комм*) investment portfolio.

портье́ *м нескл* (*в гости́нице*) porter.

портье́ра (-**ы**) *ж* curtain.

портя́нка (-**ки**; *gen pl* -**ок**) *ж* (*обы́чно мн*) puttee.

поруга́ние (-**я**) *ср* desecration.

поруга́ть (-**ю**) *сов перех* (*разг*) to scold

▶ **поруга́ться** *сов от* **руга́ться** ♦ *возв* (*разг*): ~**ся** (**с** +*instr*) to fall out (with).

пору́ка (-**и**) *ж*: **брать кого́-н на ~у** to take sb on probation; (*юр*) to stand bail for sb; **кругова́я ~** mutual dependence; (*у престу́пников*) mutual cover-up; **отпуска́ть** (**отпусти́ть** *perf*) **кого́-н на ~у** to release sb on bail.

по-ру́сски *нареч* (*разгова́ривать, написа́ть*) in Russian; **говори́ть** (*impf*)/**понима́ть** (*impf*) ~ to speak/understand Russian; **как ~ „book"?** what is the Russian for "book"?

поруча́ть (-**ю**) *несов от* **поручи́ть**.

поруче́ние (-**я**) *ср* (*зада́ние*) errand; (: *ва́жное*) mission; **по ~ю** +*gen* on behalf of.

по́ручень (-**ня**) *м* handrail.

пору́чик (-**а**) *м* (*ист*) first lieutenant.

поручи́тель (-**я**) *м* (*комм*) guarantor.

поручи́тельство (-**а**) *ср* guarantee.

поручи́ть (-**учу́**, -**у́чишь**; *impf* **поруча́ть**) *сов неперех*: ~ **кому́-н что-н** to entrust sb with sth; **поруча́ть** (~ *perf*) **кому́-н** +*infin* to instruct sb to do; **поруча́ть** (~ *perf*) **кому́-н кого́-н/что-н** (*отда́ть на попече́ние*) to leave sb/sth in sb's care.

поручи́ться (-**учу́сь**, -**у́чишься**) *сов от* **руча́ться**.

по́ручня *итп сущ см* **по́ручень**.

порха́ть (-**ю**) *несов перех* (*ба́бочка*) to flutter about; (*пти́ца*) to flit about.

по́рция (-**и**) *ж* portion; **принеси́те нам две ~и**

жа́реной говя́дины bring us two steaks.
по́рч|а (-и) ж damage.
по́рчу(сь) *сов см* **по́ртить(ся)**.
по́рш|ень (-ня) м (*в дви́гателе*) piston; (*в насо́се*) plunger.
поры́в (-а) м (*ве́тра*) gust; (*него́дования, восто́рга итп*) surge.
порыва́|ть (-ю) *несов от* **порва́ть**
▶ **порыва́ться** *несов возв*: ~**ся** +*infin* (*стреми́ться*) to strive to do.
поры́вист|ый (-, -а, -о) *прил* (*ве́тер*) gusty; (*движе́ния*) jerky; (*хара́ктер, челове́к*) impetuous.
поря́дка *итп сущ см* **поря́док**.
поря́дковый *прил* (*но́мер*) ordinal; **поря́дковое числи́тельное** ordinal number.
поря́дком *нареч* (*разг*) pretty; **я ~ уста́л** I'm pretty tired.
поря́д|ок (-ка) м order; (*пра́вила*) procedure; **в ~ке** +*gen* (*в ка́честве*) as; ~**ка** +*gen* about; **в рабо́чем ~ке** in the course of the proceedings; **э́то в ~ке веще́й** (*э́то норма́льно*) that's nothing out of the ordinary; **в ~ке** in order; **всё в ~ке** everything's OK; **поря́док дня** agenda; **поря́док слов** (*линг*) word order.
поря́дочно *нареч* decently; (*уста́л*) pretty; (*хорошо́*) quite well.
поря́доч|ный (-ен, -на, -но) *прил* (*че́стный*) decent; (*значи́тельный*) fair.
пос. *сокр* = **посёлок**.
посади́|ть (-ажу́, -а́дишь) *сов от* **сажа́ть**.
поса́д|ка (-ки; *gen pl* **-ок)** ж (*овоще́й, дере́вьев*) planting; (*пассажи́ров*) boarding; (*самолёта итп*) landing; **произво́дится ~ на самолёт ...** the flight ... is boarding.
поса́дочный *прил* (*трап, тало́н*) boarding *опред*; (*площа́дка, огни́*) landing *опред*.
посажу́ *сов см* **посади́ть**.
посва́та|ть(ся) (-ю(сь)) *сов от* **сва́таться**.
посвеже́|ть (-ю) *сов от* **свеже́ть**.
посве|ти́ть (-чу́, -тишь) *сов от* **свети́ть**.
посветле́|ть (-ю) *сов от* **светле́ть**.
посвечу́ *сов см* **посвети́ть**.
по-сво́ему *нареч* his *итп* way.
посвя|ти́ть (-щу́, -ти́шь; *impf* **посвяща́ть)** *сов перех*: ~ **что-н** +*dat* to devote sth to; (*кни́гу, стихи́*) to dedicate sth to; **посвяща́ть {~ perf**) **кого́-н в** +*acc* (*в та́йну*) to let sb into.
посвяща́|ть (-ю) *несов от* **посвяти́ть**.
посвяще́ни|е (-я) *ср* (*в кни́ге*) dedication.
посвящу́ *сов см* **посвяти́ть**.
посе́в (-а) м sowing; *см также* **посе́вы**.
посевн|о́й *прил*: ~**ы́е рабо́ты** sowing; **посевны́е пло́щади** (*с.-х.*) area sown with crops.
посе́в|ы (-ов) *мн* crops *мн*.
поседе́|ть (-ю) *сов от* **седе́ть**.
поселе́н|ец (-ца) м settler; (*вы́сланный*)

deportee.
поселе́ни|е (-я) *ср* (*селе́ние*) settlement; (*как наказа́ние*) deportation.
поселе́нца *итп сущ см* **поселе́нец**.
посе|ли́ть(ся) (-елю́(сь), -е́лишь(ся)) *сов от* **сели́ть(ся)**.
посёл|ок (-ка) м village; **да́чный ~** village made up of dachas.
посел|я́ть(ся) (-ю(сь)) *несов* = **сели́ть(ся)**.
посеребр|и́ть (-ю́, -и́шь) *сов от* **серебри́ть**.
посереди́не *нареч* in the middle ◆ *предл* (+*gen*) in the middle of.
посере́|ть (-ю) *сов от* **сере́ть**.
посети́тель (-я) м visitor.
посети́тельни|ца (-ы) ж *см* **посети́тель**.
посе|ти́ть (-щу́, -ти́шь; *impf* **посеща́ть)** *сов перех* to visit.
посе́това|ть (-ую) *сов от* **се́товать**.
посеща́емост|ь (-и) ж attendance.
посеща́|ть (-ю) *несов от* **посети́ть**.
посеще́ни|е (-я) *ср* visit.
посещу́ *сов см* **посети́ть**.
посе́|ять (-ю) *сов от* **се́ять** ◆ *перех* (*разг: потеря́ть*) to lose.
посиде́|ть (-жу́, -ди́шь) *сов неперех* to sit for a while.
поси́л|ьный (-ен, -ьна, -ьно) *прил* feasible.
посине́|ть (-ю) *сов от* **сине́ть**.
посин|и́ть (-ю́, -и́шь) *сов от* **сини́ть**.
поска|ка́ть (-чу́, -чешь) *сов от* **скака́ть**.
посканда́л|ить (-ю, -ишь) *сов от* **сканда́лить**.
поскачу́ *итп сов см* **поскака́ть**.
поскольз|ну́ться (-у́сь, -ёшься) *сов возв* to slip.
поско́льку *союз* as.
поскуп|и́ться (-лю́сь, -и́шься) *сов от* **скупи́ться**.
посла́ *итп сущ см* **посо́л**.
послабле́ни|е (-я) *ср* leniency.
посла́н|ец (-ца) м envoy.
посла́ни|е (-я) *ср* (*официа́льное*) dispatch; (*дру́жеское, любо́вное*) message.
посла́нни|к (-а) м (*дипломати́ческий*) diplomat.
посла́нца *итп сущ см* **посла́нец**.
по|сла́ть (-шлю́, -шлёшь; *impf* **посыла́ть)** *сов перех* to send; **посыла́ть {~ perf**) **кого́-н к чёрту** (*разг*) to tell sb to go to hell.
по́сле *нареч* (*пото́м*) afterwards ◆ *предл* (+*gen*) after ◆ *союз*: ~ **того́ как** after.
послевое́нный *прил* postwar.
после́д (-а) м placenta.
после́дн|ее (-его; *decl like adj*) *ср* the last; **до ~его** to the utmost.
после́дн|ий (-яя, -ее, -ие) *прил* last; (*но́вости, мо́да*) latest; (*разг*): ~ **негодя́й** utter rascal; **за или в ~ее вре́мя** recently; **руга́ться** (*impf*) ~**ими слова́ми** to use foul language.
после́дователь (-я) м follower.

после́довательност|**ь** (-и) *ж* sequence;
  (*политики*) consistency.
после́довательный *прил* (*этапы, движения*)
  consecutive; (*вывод, ход мысли*) consistent.
после́дова|**ть** (-ую) *сов от* **сле́довать**.
после́дстви|**е** (-я) *ср* consequence.
после́дующ|**ий** (-ая, -ее, -ие) *прил* subsequent.
послеза́втра *нареч* the day after tomorrow.
послеродово́й *прил* postnatal.
послесло́ви|**е** (-я) *ср* (*в книге*) epilogue.
посло́виц|**а** (-ы) *ж* proverb, saying; **войти** (*perf*)
  в ~у to become proverbial.
послу́ж|**и́ть** (-ужу́, -у́жишь) *сов от* **служи́ть**.
послужно́й *прил:* ~ **спи́сок** (*военного*) service
  record; (*работника*) work record.
послуша́ни|**е** (-я) *ср* (*покорность*) obedience.
послу́ша|**ть** (-ю) *сов от* **слу́шать** ◆ *перех:* ~
  что-н to listen to sth for a while; **~йте!** listen!
► **послу́шаться** *сов от* **слу́шаться**.
послу́шиш *прил см* **послу́шный**.
послу́шник (-а) *м* (*РЕЛ*) novice.
послу́шниц|**а** (-ы) *ж см* **послу́шник**.
послу́ш|**ный** (-ен, -на, -но) *прил* (*ребёнок,
  ученик*) obedient; (*механизм*) user-friendly.
послы́ш|**аться** (*3sg* -ется, *3pl* -атся) *сов от*
  слы́шаться.
послюня́в|**ить** (-лю, -ишь) *сов от* **слюня́вить**.
посма́трива|**ть** (-ю) *несов неперех* to glance
  occasionally.
посме́ива|**ться** (-юсь) *несов возв* (*смеяться*)
  to chuckle; ~ (*impf*) (**над** +*instr*) (*насмехаться*)
  to laugh at.
посме́нный *прил* shift *опред*.
посме́ртный *прил* posthumous.
посме́|**ть** (-ю) *сов от* **сметь**.
посме́шищ|**е** (-а) *ср* laughing stock;
  выставля́ть (*impf*) **кого́-н на** ~ to make a
  laughing stock of sb.
посме|**я́ться** (-ю́сь, -ёшься) *сов от* **смея́ться**.
посм|**отре́ть** (-отрю́, -о́тришь) *сов от*
  смотре́ть ◆ *неперех:* ~**о́трим** (*разг*) we'll see;
  там ~о́трим (*разг*) we'll see later
► **посмотре́ться** *сов от* **смотре́ться**.
посо́би|**е** (-я) *ср* (*помощь*) benefit; (*ПРОСВЕЩ:
  учебное*) handout; (: *наглядное*) visual aids *мн*;
  посо́бие по безрабо́тице unemployment
  benefit; **посо́бие по инвали́дности** disability
  living allowance.
посо́бник (-а) *м* accomplice.
посове́това|**ть(ся)** (-ую(сь)) *сов от*
  сове́товать(ся).
посоде́йств|**овать** (-ую) *сов от*
  соде́йствовать.
посо́л (-ла́) *м* ambassador; (-о́ла; *засол*) salting.
посо́л|**ить** (-ю́, -о́лишь) *сов от* **соли́ть**.
посо́льств|**о** (-а) *ср* embassy.
поспе́|**ть** (-ю) *сов от* **спеть** ◆ (*impf* **поспева́ть**)
  неперех (*успеть*) to make it.
поспе́шен *прил см* **поспе́шный**.
поспеш|**и́ть** (-у́, -и́шь) *сов от* **спеши́ть**.
поспе́ш|**ный** (-ен, -на, -но) *прил* rushed.

поспо́р|**ить** (-ю, -ишь) *сов от* **спо́рить** ◆
  неперех to argue.
поспосо́бств|**овать** (-ую) *сов от*
  спосо́бствовать.
посрам|**и́ть** (-лю́, -и́шь; *impf* **посрамля́ть**) *сов*
  перех to disgrace.
посреди́ *нареч* in the middle ◆ *предл* (+*gen*) in
  the middle of; ~ **толпы́** in the midst of the
  crowd.
посреди́не *нареч* in the middle ◆ *предл* (+*gen*)
  in the middle of.
посре́дник (-а) *м* intermediary; (*при
  конфли́кте*) mediator; **торго́вый** ~ middleman
  (*мн* middlemen).
посре́дническ|**ий** (-ая, -ое, -ие) *прил* (*КОММ*)
  intermediary *опред*.
посре́дничеств|**о** (-а) *ср* mediation.
посре́дственно *нареч* (*учиться, писать,
  сочинять*) averagely ◆ *ср нескл* (*ПРОСВЕЩ*) ≈
  satisfactory (*school mark*).
посре́дствен|**ный** (-, -на, -но) *прил* mediocre.
посре́дств|**о** (-а) *ср:* **при** ~**е** *или* **че́рез** ~ +*gen*
  by means of.
посре́дством *предл* (+*gen*) by means of.
поссо́р|**ить(ся)** (-ю(сь), -ишь(ся)) *сов от*
  ссо́рить(ся).
пост (-á; *loc sg* -у́) *м* (*люди*) guard; (*место*)
  lookout post; (*должность*) position, post; (*РЕЛ*)
  fast; ~ **автоинспе́кции** (*traffic*) police
  checkpoint.
поста́в|**ить** (-лю, -ишь) *сов от* **ста́вить** ◆ (*impf*
  поставля́ть) *перех* (*товар*) to supply.
поста́в|**ка** (-ки; *gen pl* -ок) *ж* (*снабжение*) supply.
поста́влю *сов см* **поста́вить**.
поставля́|**ть** (-ю) *несов от* **поста́вить**.
поста́вок *сущ см* **поста́вка**.
поставщ|**и́к** (-á) *м* supplier; **судово́й** ~ ship
  chandler.
постаме́нт (-а) *м* pedestal.
постан|**ови́ть** (-овлю́, -о́вишь; *impf*
  постановля́ть) *сов неперех:* ~ +*infin* to resolve
  to do.
постано́в|**ка** (-ки; *gen pl* -ок) *ж* (*памятника*)
  erection; (*учебного процесса*) organization;
  (*ТЕАТР*) production; **у неё хоро́шая** ~ **головы́**
  she holds her head well; ~ **вопро́са/пробле́мы**
  the formulation of the question/problem.
постановле́ни|**е** (-я) *ср* (*решение*) resolution;
  (*распоряжение*) decree.
постановлю́ *сов см* **постанови́ть**.
постановля́|**ть** (-ю) *несов от* **постанови́ть**.
постано́вок *сущ см* **постано́вка**.
постано́вщик (-а) *м* producer.
постара́|**ться** (-юсь) *сов от* **стара́ться**.
постаре́|**ть** (-ю) *сов от* **старе́ть**.
пост|**ели́ть(ся)** (-елю́(сь), -е́лишь(ся)) *сов от*
  стели́ть(ся).
посте́л|**ь** (-и) *ж* bed.
посте́льный *прил:* ~**ое бельё** bedclothes *мн*;
  он на ~ом режи́ме he is confined to bed.
постелю́ *итп сов см* **постла́ть**.

постепенно *нареч* gradually.
постепенный (-ен, -на, -но) *прил* gradual.
постесняться (-юсь) *сов от* стесняться.
постиг *итп сов см* постичь.
постигать (-ю) *несов от* постичь.
постигну *итп сов см* постичь.
постигнуть (-ну, -нешь; *pt* -, -ла, -ло) *сов* = постичь.
постилать (-ю) *несов* = стелить.
постирать (-ю) *сов от* стирать.
поститься (-щусь, -стишься) *несов возв* (РЕЛ) to fast.
постичь (-гну, -гнешь; *pt* -г, -гла, -гло, *impf* постигать) *сов перех* (*смысл, значение*) to grasp; (*подлеж: несчастье*) to befall; **я не могу ~, как он мог это сделать** I can't comprehend how he could do something like that; **его ~гло разочарование** he was disappointed.
постлать (-елю, -елешь) *сов от* стлать.
постный *прил* (*суп, обед*) vegetarian; (*мясо*) lean; (*разг: хмурый*) cheesed off; **постное масло** vegetable oil.
постовой *прил* (*служба, будка*) sentry *опред* ♦ (-ого; *decl like adj*) *м* militiaman on duty.
постольку *союз*: **~ ... поскольку** in so far as ....
посторониться (-онюсь, -онишься) *сов от* сторониться.
посторонний (-яя, -ее, -ие) *прил* (*чужой*) strange; (*помощь, влияние*) outside; (*вопрос*) irrelevant ♦ (-его; *decl like adj*) *м* stranger, outsider; **~им вход воспрещён** authorized entry only.
постоянный (-ен, -на, -но) *прил* (*работа, адрес*) permanent; (*шум, разговоры*) constant; (*вкус, взгляды*) consistent; **постоянная армия** regular army; **постоянный ток** direct current.
постоять (-ю, -ишь) *сов от* стоять ♦ *неперех* (*стоять недолго*) to stand for a while; **постойте!** (*подождите*) hang on!; **он за ценой не ~ит** (*разг*) money is no object to him.
пострадать (-ю) *сов от* страдать.
постричь(ся) *сов от* постричь(ся).
постригу(сь) *итп сов см* постричь(ся).
пострижение (-я) *ср* (*мужчины*) taking the habit; (*женщины*) taking the veil.
постричь (-гу, -жёшь *итп*, -гут; *pt* -г, -гла, -гло) *сов перех*: **~ кого-н** to cut sb's hair; **~** (*perf*) **кого-н в монастырь** to initiate sb into a monastery.
► постричься *сов возв* to have a haircut; **~ся** (*perf*) **в монастырь** to be initiated into a monastery.
построек *сущ см* постройка.
построение (-я) *ср* (*предложения, фразы*) construction.
построить(ся) (-ю(сь), -ишь(ся)) *сов от* строить(ся).
постройка (-йки; *gen pl* -ек) *ж* construction.

поступательный *прил* (*движение*) forward *опред*; **~ое развитие** progress.
поступить (-уплю, -упишь; *impf* поступать) *сов неперех* (*благородно, разумно*) to act; (*товар, известия*) to come in; (*жалоба: в суд*) to be received; **поступать** (**~** *perf*) **в** +*acc* (*в университет*) to enter; **поступать** (**~** *perf*) **на** +*acc* (*на работу, на курсы*) to start
► поступиться (*impf* поступаться) *сов возв*: **~ся** +*instr* to give up.
поступка *сущ см* поступок.
поступление (-я) *ср* (*действие: в университет*) entrance; (: *на работу*) starting; (: *жалобы: в суд*) receipt; (*то, что поступило: бюджетное*) revenue; (: *в библиотеке*) acquisition.
поступлю(сь) *сов см* поступить(ся).
поступок (-ка) *м* (*благородный, подлый*) deed.
поступь (-и) *ж* (*походка*) gait.
постучать(ся) (-у(сь), -ишь(ся)) *сов от* стучать(ся).
постыден *прил см* постыдный.
постыдиться (-жусь, -дишься) *сов от* стыдиться.
постыдный (-ен, -на, -но) *прил* shameful.
постыжусь *сов см* постыдиться.
посуда (-ы) *ж собир* crockery; **кухонная ~** kitchenware; **стеклянная ~** glassware; **мыть** (**помыть** *perf*) **~у** to wash *или* do (*BRIT*) the dishes.
посудить (-жу, -дишь) *сов*: **~дите сами** judge for yourself.
посулить (-ю, -ишь) *сов от* сулить.
посчастливиться (*3sg* -ится) *сов безл*: **мне ~илось** +*infin* ... I was lucky enough to ....
посчитать(ся) (-ю(сь)) *сов от* считать(ся).
посылать (-ю) *несов от* послать.
посылка (-ки; *gen pl* -ок) *ж* (*действие: книг, денег*) sending; (*отправление*) parcel; (*основание*) premise.
посыльный (-ого; *decl like adj*) *м* messenger.
посыпать (-лю, -лешь) *сов перех* to sprinkle.
посягательство (-а) *ср*: **~ на что-н** infringement on *или* of sth; **~ на чью-н жизнь** an attempt on sb's life.
посягнуть (-у, -ёшь; *impf* посягать) *сов неперех*: **~ на** +*acc* to infringe; **посягать** (**~** *perf*) **на чью-н жизнь** to make an attempt on sb's life.
пот (-а; *part gen* -у, *loc sg* -у, *nom pl* -ы) *м* sweat; **в поте лица** hard; **потом и кровью добывать** (**добыть** *perf*) **что-н** to sweat blood to get sth; **работать** (*impf*) **в поте лица** to sweat blood.
потайной *прил* secret *опред*.
потакать (-ю) *несов неперех*: **~** +*dat* (*агрессии*) to turn a blind eye to; (*агрессору*) to ignore.
потаскуха (-и) *ж* (*разг: пренебр*) hussy.
потасовка (-ки; *gen pl* -ок) *ж* (*разг*) punch-up.

по-твоему *нареч* your way ♦ *вводн сл* in your opinion.

потворств|овать (-ую) *несов неперех*: ~ +*dat* (*агрессии*) to turn a blind eye to; (*агрессору*) to ignore.

потёк *птп сов см* **потёчь**.

потекут *сов см* **потёчь**.

потём|ки (-ок) *мн* darkness *ед*.

потемне|ть (-ю) *сов от* **темнеть**.

потёмок *сущ см* **потёмки**.

потенциал (-а) *м* potential.

потенциал|ьный (-ен, -ьна, -ьно) *прил* potential.

потепление (-я) *ср* warmer spell.

потепле|ть (*3sg* -ет, *3pl* -ют) *сов от* **теплеть**.

потер|еть (-ру, -рёшь; *pt* -ёр, -ёрла, -ёрло) *сов перех* (*ушиб*) to rub; (*морковь*) to grate

► **потереться** *сов от* **тереться**.

потерпевш|ая (-ей; *decl like adj*) *ж см* **потерпевший**.

потерпевш|ий (-его; *decl like adj*) *м* (*ЮР*) victim ♦ *прил*: (-ая, -ее, -ие) ~ая сторона injured party.

потерп|еть (-ерплю, -ерпишь) *сов от* **терпеть**.

потёртый *прил* (*одежда*) worn.

потер|я (-и) *ж* loss; **нести** (**понести** *perf*) ~и (*в войне*) to suffer losses.

потерянно *нареч* (*смотреть*) lost.

потерян|ный (-, -на, -но) *прил* (*растерянный: вид итп*) lost.

потеря|ть(ся) (-ю(сь)) *сов от* **терять(ся)**.

потесн|ить (-ю, -ишь) *сов от* **теснить** ♦ *перех*: ~ кого-н to make sb squeeze up

► **потесниться** *сов возв* to squeeze up.

поте|ть (-ю; *impf* **вспотеть**) *несов неперех* to sweat.

пот|ечь (*3sg* -ечёт, *3pl* -екут, *pt* -ёк, -екла, -екло) *сов неперех* (*вода*) to start flowing; (*дни, жизнь*) to begin.

потеш|ить(ся) (-ю(сь)) *сов от* **тешить(ся)**.

потихоньку *нареч* (*разг: медленно*) at a snail's pace; (: *тайно*) on the sly.

потни|ца (-ы) *ж* (*МЕД*) heat rash.

потный *прил* sweaty.

потогон|ный *прил* (*перен*): ~ая система slave labour (*BRIT*) или labor (*US*).

пото|к (-а) *м* (*также ПРОСВЕЩ*) stream; **положительный/отрицательный** ~ **наличности** (*КОММ*) positive/negative cash flow.

потол|ок (-ка) *м* (*также перен*) ceiling; **брать** (**взять** *perf*) что-н с ~ка (*разг*) to pluck sth out of thin air.

потолсте|ть (-ю) *сов от* **толстеть**.

потом *нареч* (*после: пойдем, закончим итп*) later ♦ *союз* (*после*) then; (*разг: кроме того*) anyhow; **на** ~ (*разг*) for later.

потом|ки (-ов) *мн* descendants *мн*.

потомственный *прил* (*имение, деньги*) inherited; **он** - ~ **музыкант** he is descended from a family of musicians.

потомств|о (-а) *ср собир* descendants *мн*; (*дети*) offspring *мн*.

потому *нареч*: ~ (**и**) that's why; **я не приду**, ~ **что устал** I'm not coming because I'm tired; **потому что** because.

потон|уть (-ону, -онешь) *сов от* **тонуть**.

потоп (-а) *м* flood.

потоп|ить (-оплю, -опишь) *сов от* **топить**.

потоп|тать (-чу, -чешь) *сов от* **топтать**.

потораплива|ть (-ю) *несов перех*: ~ кого-н to hurry sb up

► **потораплиываться** *несов возв* to hurry.

потороп|ить(ся) (-лю(сь), -ишь(ся)) *сов от* **торопить(ся)**.

поточный *прил* (*производство*) mass *опред*; **поточная линия** production line.

потрав|ить (-лю, -ишь) *сов от* **травить**.

потра|тить(ся) (-чу(сь), -тишь(ся)) *сов от* **тратить(ся)**.

потребитель (-я) *м* consumer.

потребительск|ий (-ая, -ое, -ие) *прил* (*спрос, товар*) consumer *опред*: **потребительская кооперация** cooperative (society).

потреб|ить (-лю, -ишь) *сов от* **потреблять**.

потребление (-я) *ср* (*действие*) consumption; **товары широкого** ~я consumer goods.

потреблю *сов см* **потребить**.

потребля|ть (-ю; *perf* **потребить**) *несов перех* to consume.

потребность (-и) *ж* (*надобность*) requirement, demand; (*желание*) need.

потреб|овать(ся) (-ую(сь)) *сов от* **требовать(ся)**.

Потребсоюз (-а) *м сокр* = *Союз потребительских кооперации*.

потревож|ить(ся) (-у(сь), -ишь(ся)) *сов от* **тревожить(ся)**.

потрёпан|ный (-, -на, -но) *прил* (*книга, одежда*) tattered, tatty; (*вид, лицо*) worn.

потреп|ать(ся) (-лю(сь), -лешь(ся)) *сов от* **трепать(ся)**.

потреска|ться (*3sg* -ется, *3pl* -ются) *сов от* **трескаться**.

потрох|а (-ов) *мн* (*птицы*) giblets *мн*.

потрош|ить (-у, -ишь; *perf* **выпотрошить**) *несов перех* (*курицу, рыбу*) to gut.

потру|(сь) *итп см* **потереть(ся)**.

потруд|иться (-жусь, -дишься) *сов возв* to work; ~ (*perf*) +*infin* to take the trouble to do; ~**дитесь передать это письмо** if you could be so kind as to pass on this letter.

потряса|ть (-ю) *несов от* **потрясти**.

потрясающ|ий (-ая, -ее, -ие) *прил* (*музыка, стихи*) fantastic; (*красота*) stunning.

потрясение (-я) *ср* breakdown.

потряс|ти (-у, -ёшь; *pt* -, -ла, -ло) *сов перех* to shake; (*impf* **потрясать**; *взволновать*) to stun ♦ *неперех*: ~ +*instr* to shake.

потуг|а (-и) *ж* (*обычно мн*) contraction; (*перен: пренебр: усилия*) pathetic attempt.

потуп|ить (-лю, -ишь; *impf* **потуплять**) *сов*

перех (*голову, глаза*) to lower
► **поту́питься** *сов возв* to lower one's eyes.
потускне́|ть (-ю) *сов от* тускне́ть.
потусторо́нн|ий (-яя, -ее, -ие) *прил* (*РЕЛ*) on the other side.
поту́хн|уть (*3sg* -ет, *3pl* -ут, *impf* потуха́ть) *сов неперех* (*лампа, свет*) to go out; (*жизнь, веселье*) to end.
поту́ш|ить (-у́шу, -у́шишь) *сов от* туши́ть.
потяга́|ться (-юсь) *сов от* тяга́ться.
потя́гива|ть (-ю) *несов перех* (*верёвку*) to pull; (*вино, чай*) to sip
► **потя́гиваться** *несов от* потяну́ться.
потяжеле́|ть (-ю) *сов от* тяжеле́ть.
потя́н|уть (-я́ну, -я́нешь) *сов от* тяну́ть
► **потяну́ться** *сов возв* to start to drag; (*impf* **потя́гиваться**; *в постели, в кресле*) to stretch out.
поу́жина|ть (-ю) *сов от* у́жинать.
поумне́|ть (-ю) *сов от* умне́ть.
поуча́|ть (-ю) *несов перех* to teach.
поуче́ни|е (-я) *ср* preaching.
поучи́тел|ьный (-ен, -ьна, -ьно) *прил* (*пример, история*) instructive; (*тон, голос*) didactic; **его́ приме́р был для нас ~ен** we learnt from his example.
поха́б|ный (-ен, -на, -но) *прил* (*непристойный*) dirty.
поха́жива|ть (-ю) *несов неперех* (*в парке итп*) to stroll.
похвал|а́ (-ы́) *ж* praise; **отзыва́ться** (**отозва́ться** *perf*) **с ~о́й о ком-н** to praise sb.
похва́лен *прил см* похва́льный.
похва|ли́ть(ся) (-алю́(сь), -а́лишь(ся)) *сов от* хвали́ть(ся).
похва́л|ьный (-ен, -ьна, -ьно) *прил* praiseworthy; (*отзыв*) complimentary; **~ьное сло́во** word of praise; **похва́льная гра́мота** certificate of merit.
похва́ста|ть(ся) (-ю(сь)) *сов от* хва́стать(ся).
похити́тел|ь (-я) *м* (*см глаг*) thief; abductor; kidnapper.
похити́тельни|ца (-ы) *ж см* похити́тель.
похи́|тить (-щу, -тишь; *impf* похища́ть) *сов перех* (*предмет*) to steal; (*человека*) to abduct; (: *для выкупа*) to kidnap.
похище́ни|е (-я) *ср* (*см глаг*) theft; abduction; kidnap(ping).
похи́щу *сов см* похи́тить.
похло́па|ть (-ю) *сов перех* to pat ♦ *неперех* (*человек: в ладоши*) to clap; (*птица*) to flap.
похлоп|ота́ть (-очу́, -о́чешь) *сов от* хлопота́ть.
похме́лье (-я) *ср* hangover.
похо́д (-а) *м* (*военный*) campaign; (*туристический*) hike (*walking and camping expedition*).
похода́тайств|овать (-ую) *сов от*

хода́тайствовать.
похо|ди́ть (-жу́, -́дишь) *несов неперех*: **~ на кого́-н/что-н** to resemble sb/sth ♦ *сов неперех* to walk.
похо́д|ка (-и) *ж* gait.
похожде́ни|е (-я) *ср* (*обычно мн*) adventure.
похо́ж|ий (-ая, -ее, -ие) *прил*: **~** (**на** +*acc или* **с** +*instr*) similar (to); **он похо́ж на бра́та, они́ с бра́том ~и** he looks like his brother; **они́ ~и** they look alike; **~е на то, что ...** it looks as if ...; **э́то на него́ не ~е** it's not like him.
похож|у́ (*не*)*сов см* походи́ть.
похолода́ни|е (-я) *ср* cold spell.
похолода́|ть (*3sg* -ет) *сов от* холода́ть.
похолоде́|ть (-ю) *сов от* холоде́ть.
похор|они́ть (-оню́, -о́нишь) *сов от* хорони́ть.
похоро́нный *прил* funeral *опред*; **похоро́нное бюро́** undertaker's.
по́хор|оны (-о́н; *dat pl* -она́м) *мн* funeral *ед*.
похороше́|ть (-ю) *сов от* хороше́ть.
по́хот|ь (-и) *ж* lust.
похуде́|ть (-ю) *сов от* худе́ть.
поцара́па|ть (-ю) *сов от* цара́пать.
поцел|ова́ть(ся) (-у́ю(сь)) *сов от* целова́ть(ся).
поцелу́|й (-я) *м* kiss.
поцеремо́н|иться (-юсь) *сов от* церемо́ниться.
почасови́к (-а́) *м* part-time worker (*paid by the hour*).
почасов|о́й *прил* (*оплата*) hourly; **~а́я рабо́та** hourly-paid work.
поча́т|ок (-ка) *м* (*кукурузы*) cob.
по́чв|а (-ы) *ж* soil; (*перен*) basis; **на ~е** +*gen* owing to; **он потеря́л ~у под нога́ми** he lost his confidence.
по́чек *сущ см* по́чка.
почём *нареч* (*разг*) how much; **~ я́блоки?** how much are the apples?
почему́ *нареч* why; (**и**) **вот ~** and that is why.
почему́-либо *нареч* for some reason.
почему́-нибудь *нареч* = почему́-либо.
почему́-то *нареч* for some reason.
по́черк (-а) *м* handwriting; (*перен: художника, грабителя*) hallmark.
почерне́|ть (-ю) *сов от* черне́ть.
почерпн|у́ть (-у́, -ёшь) *сов перех* (*сведения*) to obtain; (*идею*) to draw.
почерстве́|ть (-ю) *сов от* черстве́ть.
поче|са́ть(ся) (-шу́(сь), -шешь(ся)) *сов от* чеса́ть(ся).
по́чест|ь (-и) *ж* (*обычно мн*) homage *ед*; **воздава́ть** (**возда́ть** *perf*) **~и кому́-н** to pay homage to sb.
поче́|сть (-ту́, -тёшь; *pt* -ёл, -ла́, -ло́, *impf* **почита́ть**) *сов неперех*: **~ за долг/честь** +*infin* to consider it one's duty/an honour (*BRIT*) *или* honor (*US*) to do.

почёт (-а) *м* honour (*BRIT*), honor (*US*).

почётный *прил* (*гость*) honoured (*BRIT*), honored (*US*); (*член академии*) honorary; (*обязанность*) honourable (*BRIT*), honorable (*US*); **почётный карау́л** guard of honour (*BRIT*) *или* honor (*US*).

по́чечный *прил* kidney *опред*, renal; (*камни*) kidney *опред*.

почешу́(сь) *итп сов см* **почеса́ть(ся)**.

почи́н (-а) *м* initiative.

почини́ть (-ию́, -инишь) *сов от* **чини́ть**.

почи́н|ка (-ки; *gen pl* -ок) *ж* (*обуви, телевизора*) repair.

почи́стить (-щу, -стишь) *сов от* **чи́стить**.

почита́тель (-я) *м* admirer.

почита́тельница (-ы) *ж см* **почита́тель**.

почита́|ть (-ю) *несов от* **поче́сть** ♦ *перех* (*поклоняться*) to admire ♦ *сов перех* to read.

почи́щу *сов см* **почи́стить**.

по́ч|ка (-ки; *gen pl* -ек; *БОТ*) bud; (*АНАТ*) kidney; **~ки** (*КУЛИН*) kidneys.

по́чт|а (-ы) *ж* (*учреждение*) post office; (*корреспонденция*) mail, post; **отправля́ть** (**отпра́вить** *perf*) **что-н ~ой** *или* **по ~е** to send sth by post.

почтальо́н (-а) *м* postman (*BRIT*) (*мн* postmen), mailman (*US*) (*мн* mailmen).

почта́мт (-а) *м* main post office.

почте́ние (-я) *ср* esteem.

почте́нный *прил* venerable; **~ые го́ды** advanced years.

почти́ *нареч* almost, nearly; **~ что** (*разг*) almost.

почти́тельный (-ен, -ьна, -ьно) *прил* respectful; **на ~ьном расстоя́нии** at a respectful distance.

почти́ть (*как* чтить; *см* **Table 17**) (-у́, -йшь) *сов перех* (*память*) to pay homage to; **~** (*perf*) **кого́-н свои́м прису́тствием** to honour (*BRIT*) *или* honor (*US*) sb with one's presence.

почто́вый *прил* (*служба, связь*) postal; (*марка*) postage *опред*; **почто́вая откры́тка** postcard; **почто́вая бума́га** writing paper; **почто́вый и́ндекс** postcode (*BRIT*), zip code (*US*); **почто́вый перево́д** (*деньги*) postal order; **почто́вый я́щик** postbox.

почту́ *итп сов см* **поче́сть**.

почу́вствовать (-ую) *сов от* **чу́вствовать**.

почу́диться (*3sg* -ится, *3pl* -ятся) *сов от* **чу́диться**.

почу́ять (-ю) *сов от* **чу́ять**.

пошатну́ть (-у́, -ёшь) *сов перех* (*веру*) to shake; (*здоровье*) to affect

▸ **пошатну́ться** *сов возв* to sway; (*авторитет*) to be undermined; (*здоровье*) to suffer.

поша́тыва|ться (-юсь) *несов возв* (*человек*) to sway slightly.

пошеве́лива|ться (-юсь) *несов возв* to stir; (*разг: поторапливаться*) to get a move on.

пошевели́ть(ся) (-ю́(сь), -и́шь(ся)) *сов от* **шевели́ть(ся)**.

пошевельн|у́ться (-у́сь, -ёшься) *сов возв* to stir.

пошёл *сов см* **пойти́**.

пошелохну́ться (-у́сь, -ёшься) *сов =* **шелохну́ться**.

пошиб (-а) *м* (*разг: пренебр*): **они́ лю́ди одного́ ~а** they are cut from the same cloth; **ни́зкий** *или* **невысо́кий ~** second-rate.

поши́в (-а) *м* (*действие*) sewing; **индивидуа́льный ~** tailoring.

пошла́ *итп сов см* **пойти́**.

пошли́н|а (-ы) *ж* duty; **суде́бная ~** legal costs *или* expenses; **облага́ть** (**обложи́ть** *perf*) **что-н ~ой** to impose a duty on sth.

по́шлинный *прил* customs *опред*.

пошло́ *сов см* **пойти́**.

по́шлость (-и) *ж* vulgarity; **говори́ть** (*impf*) **~и** to make trite and vulgar comments.

по́шл|ый (-, -á, -о) *прил* (*человек, поступок*) vulgar; (*анекдот*) corny; (*картинка*) kitsch; (*речи*) trite and vulgar.

пошлю́ *итп сов см* **посла́ть**.

пошля́к (-á) *м* (*разг*) vulgar person.

пошут|и́ть (-чу́, -у́тишь) *сов от* **шути́ть**.

пощад|а (-ы) *ж* mercy.

пощади́ть (-жу́, -ди́шь) *сов от* **щади́ть**.

пощекота́ть (-очу́, -о́чешь) *сов от* **щекота́ть**.

пощёчин|а (-ы) *ж* slap in the face.

пощу́па|ть (-ю) *сов от* **щу́пать**.

пощу́сь *несов см* **пости́ться**.

поэ́зи|я (-и) *ж* (*также перен*) poetry.

поэ́м|а (-ы) *ж* poem.

поэ́т (-а) *м* poet.

поэте́сс|а (-ы) *ж см* **поэ́т**.

поэтизи́р|овать (-ую; *perf* **опоэтизи́ровать**) *несов перех* to wax poetic about.

поэти́ческий (-ая, -ое, -ие) *прил* poetic.

поэ́тому *нареч* therefore.

пою́ *итп несов см* **петь**, **пои́ть**.

поя|ви́ться (-влю́сь, -вишься; *impf* **появля́ться**) *сов возв* to appear; **у него́ ~ви́лись иде́и/сомне́ния** he has had an idea/ begun to have doubts; **появля́ться** (**~ perf**) **на свет** to come into the world.

появле́ние (-я) *ср* appearance.

появлю́сь *сов см* **появи́ться**.

появля́|ться (-юсь) *несов от* **появи́ться**.

по́яс (-а; *nom pl* -á) *м* (*ремень*) belt; (*талия*) waist; (*ГЕО*) zone; **спаса́тельный ~** life belt; **тари́фный ~** (*ЭКОН*) tariff zone.

поясне́ние (-я) *ср* explanation.

поясни́ть (-ю́, -йшь; *impf* **поясня́ть**) *сов перех* to explain.

поясни́ц|а (-ы) *ж* small of the back.

поясня́|ть (-ю) *несов от* **поясни́ть**.

ППГ *м сокр* (= *полево́й подви́жный го́спиталь*) field hospital. ≈ **MASH** (*US*) (= *mobile army surgical hospital*).

пр. *сокр* = **прое́зд**, **проспе́кт**, **про́чее**, **про́чие**.

прабáб|ка (-ки; *gen pl* -ок) *ж* great-grandmother.

прабáбуш|ка (-ки; *gen pl* -ек) *ж* = **прабáбка**.

прав|а́ (-) *мн (также:* **води́тельские** ~) driving licence (*BRIT*), driver's license (*US*); **права́ челове́ка** human rights.

пра́вд|а (-ы) *ж* truth ♦ *нареч* really ♦ *вводн сл* true; **он** ~ **измени́лся** he really has changed; **он,** ~, **сам созна́лся** true, he did confess; **ты винова́т в э́том** – ~ you are to blame, it's true; ~**у** *или* **по** ~**е говоря́** *или* **сказа́ть** to tell the truth; **он уже́ уе́хал, не** ~ **ли?** he's already gone, hasn't he?; **хоро́шая пого́да, не** ~ **ли?** the weather's good, isn't it?

правди́в|ый (-, -а, -о) *прил* truthful.

правдоподо́б|ный (-ен, -на, -но) *прил* plausible.

пра́веден *прил см* **пра́ведный**.

пра́ведник (-а) *ж* (*РЕЛ*) righteous man (*мн* men).

пра́вед|ный (-ен, -на, -но) *прил* (*человек*) righteous; (*суд*) just.

пра́вилен *прил см* **пра́вильный**.

пра́вил|о (-а) *ср* rule; **э́то не в мои́х** ~**ах** that's not my way; **как** ~ as a rule; **по всем** ~**ам** by the rules; **пра́вила доро́жного движе́ния** rules of the road, ≈ Highway Code.

пра́вильно *нареч* correctly ♦ *как сказ* that's correct.

пра́вил|ьный (-ен, -ьна, -ьно) *прил* (*написание, произношение*) correct; (*вывод, ответ*) right; (*совет, суждение*) sound.

прави́тель (-я) *м* ruler.

прави́тельственный *прил* government *опред*.

прави́тельств|о (-а) *ср* government.

пра́в|ить (-лю, -ишь) *несов перех* (*исправлять*) to correct ♦ *неперех:* ~ +*instr* (*страной*) to rule, govern; (*машиной*) to drive.

пра́в|ка (-ки; *gen pl* -ок) *ж* proofreading.

правле́ни|е (-я) *ср* government; (*орган*) board.

пра́влю *несов см* **пра́вить**.

пра́внук (-а) *м* great-grandson.

пра́в|о (-а; *nom pl* -а́) *ср* (*нормы, наука*) law; (*свобода*) right ♦ *вводн сл* (*разг*) really; **име́ть** (*impf*) ~ **на что-н/**+*infin* to have the right *или* be entitled to sth/to do; **быть** (*impf*) **в** ~**е** +*infin* to be entitled *или* have the right to do; **на права́х** +*gen* as; **по** ~**у** (*законно*) by rights; (*с полным основа́нием*) rightly; **на ра́вных права́х с** +*instr* on equal terms with; *см также* **права́**.

правове́д (-а) *м* jurisprudent.

правове́дени|е (-я) *ср* jurisprudence.

правове́р|ный (-ен, -на, -но) *прил* orthodox.

правов|о́й *прил* (*нормы*) legal; **правово́е госуда́рство** lawful state.

правозащи́тник (-а) *м* human rights activist.

правозащи́тни|ца (-ы) *ж см* **правозащи́тник**.

пра́вок *сущ см* **пра́вка**.

правоме́р|ный (-ен, -на, -но) *прил* (*вопрос*) valid; (*сомнения*) justifiable; (*действие, поступок*) lawful.

правомо́ч|ный (-ен, -на, -но) *прил* (*орган*)

competent; (*лицо*) authorized.

правонаруше́ни|е (-я) *ср* offence.

правонаруши́тель (-я) *м* offender.

правоохрани́тельный *прил* (*орган*) law-enforcement.

правописа́ни|е (-я) *ср* spelling.

правопоря́д|ок (-ка) *м* law and order.

правосла́ви|е (-я) *ср* orthodoxy.

правосла́вн|ая (-ой; *decl like adj*) *ж см* **правосла́вный**.

правосла́вн|ый *прил* (*церковь, обряд*) orthodox ♦ (-ого; *decl like adj*) *м member of the Orthodox Church*.

правоспосо́б|ный (-ен, -на, -но) *прил* (*ЮР*) capable.

правосу́ди|е (-я) *ср* justice.

правот|а́ (-ы́) *ж* correctness; **я не сомнева́юсь в Ва́шей** ~**е́** I don't doubt that you are right.

пра́в|ый *прил* right; (*ПОЛИТ*) right-wing; (-, -а́, -о; *справедливый*) just; (*невиновный*) innocent; (*no full form*): **он прав** he is right; ~ **суд** fair trial.

пра́вящий (-ая, -ее, -ие) *прил* ruling *опред*.

Пра́г|а (-и) *ж* Prague.

прагмати́зм (-а) *м* pragmatism.

прагма́тик (-а) *м* pragmatist.

пра́дед (-а) *м* great-grandfather.

прадеду́ш|ка (-ки; *gen pl* -ек) *м* = **пра́дед**.

пра́зднеств|о (-а) *ср* festival.

пра́здник (-а) *м* (*по случаю какого-н события*) public holiday; (*религиозный*) festival; (*нерабочий день*) holiday; (*радость, торжество*) celebration; **с** ~**ом!** best wishes!

пра́здни́ч|ный (-ен, -на, -но) *прил* (*салют, обед*) celebratory; (*одежда, настроение*) festive; ~ **день, пра́здничная да́та** holiday.

пра́здн|овать (-ую) *несов перех* to celebrate.

пра́зд|ный (-ен, -на, -но) *прил* idle; ~**ная жизнь** life of idleness.

пра́ктик (-а) *м* (*о каком-н специалисте*) expert; (*практичный человек*) practical person (*мн* people); **он хоро́ший** ~, **но плохо́й теоре́тик** he's technically very good, but not so good at the theory.

пра́ктик|а (-и) *ж* practice; (*часть учёбы*) practical experience *или* work; **на** ~**е** in practice.

практика́нт (-а) *м* trainee (*on a placement*).

практика́нт|ка (-ки; *gen pl* -ок) *ж см* **практика́нт**.

практик|ова́ть (-у́ю) *несов перех* to practise (*BRIT*), practice (*US*)

▶ **практикова́ться** *несов возв* (*методы, приёмы*) to be used; (*обучаться*): ~**ся в чем-н** to practise sth.

практи́чен *прил см* **практи́чный**.

практи́чески *нареч* (*на практике*) in practice; (*по сути дела*) practically.

практи́ческ|ий (-ая, -ое, -ие) *прил* practical.

практи́ч|ный (-ен, -на, -но) *прил* practical.

пра́порщик (-а) *м* (*ВОЕН*) ≈ warrant officer.

прах (-а) *м* (*умершего*) ashes *мн*; **пойти́** (*perf*) **пра́хом** (*усилия, работа*) to be wasted.

пра́чек *сущ см* **пра́чка**.

пра́чечн|ая (-ой; *decl like adj*) *ж* laundry.

пра́ч|ка (-ки; *gen pl* -ек) *ж* laundress.

преа́мбул|а (-ы) *ж* preamble.

пребыва́ни|е (-я) *ср* (*в каком-н месте*) stay; ~ **у вла́сти** term of office.

пребыва́|ть (-ю) *несов неперех* (*находиться*) to be.

превали́р|овать (-ую) *несов неперех*: ~ (**над** +*instr*) to prevail (over).

превенти́вный *прил* preventive; ~ **уда́р** preemptive strike.

превзойти́ (*как* **идти́**; *см* **Table 18**; *impf* **превосходи́ть**) *сов перех* (*соперника, врага*) to beat; (*прежние результаты, ожидания*) to surpass; (*доходы, скорость*) to exceed; ~ (*perf*) **самого́ себя́** to surpass o.s.

превозмо́чь (-огу́, -о́жешь *etc* *impf*, -о́гут; *pt* -о́г, -огла́, -огло́, *impf* **превозмога́ть**) *сов перех* to overcome.

превозне|сти́ (-су́, -се́шь; *pt* -ёс, -есла́, -есло́) *сов перех* to extol.

превосхо́ден *прил см* **превосхо́дный**.

превосхо|ди́ть (-жу́, -дишь) *несов от* **превзойти́**.

превосхо́дно *нареч* excellently ♦ *как сказ* it's excellent.

превосхо́дный (-ен, -на, -но) *прил* superb; **превосхо́дная сте́пень** superlative degree.

превосхо́дств|о (-а) *ср* superiority.

превосхожу́ *несов см* **превосходи́ть**.

превра́тен *прил см* **превра́тный**.

превра|ти́ть (-щу́, -ти́шь; *impf* **превраща́ть**) *сов перех*: ~ **что-н в** +*acc* to turn sth into; **превраща́ть** (~ *perf*) **кого́-н в** +*acc* to turn *или* transform sb into

► **превра|ти́ться** (*impf* **превраща́ться**) *сов возв* to turn.

превра́тный (-ен, -на, -но) *прил* wrong.

превраща́|ть(ся) (-ю(сь)) *несов от* **превра́ти́ть(ся)**.

превраще́ни|е (-я) *ср* transformation.

превращу́(сь) *сов см* **превра́ти́ть(ся)**.

превы́|сить (-шу, -сишь; *impf* **превыша́ть**) *сов перех* to exceed; (*рекорд*) to break.

прегра́д|а (-ы) *ж* barrier.

прегра|ди́ть (-жу́, -ди́шь; *impf* **прегражда́ть**) *сов перех*: ~ **кому́-н доро́гу/вход** to block *или* bar sb's way/entrance.

предава́|ть(ся) (-ю(сь)) *несов от* **преда́ть(ся)**.

преда́м(ся) *etc сов см* **преда́ть(ся)**.

преда́ни|е (-я) *ср* legend.

пре́дан|ный (-, -на, -но) *прил* devoted; **он пре́дан де́лу/жене́** he is devoted to the cause/his wife.

преда́ст(ся) *сов см* **преда́ть(ся)**.

преда́тел|ь (-я) *м* traitor.

преда́тельниц|а (-ы) *ж см* **преда́тель**.

преда́тельск|ий (-ая, -ое, -ие) *прил* treacherous.

преда́тельств|о (-а) *ср* treachery.

преда́ть (*как* **дать**; *см* **Table 14**; *impf* **предава́ть**) *сов перех* to betray; **предава́ть** (~ *perf*) **что-н гла́сности** to make sth public; **предава́ть** (~ *perf*) **кого́-н суду́** to prosecute sb; **предава́ть** (~ *perf*) **забве́нию** to consign to oblivion

► **преда́ться** (*impf* **предава́ться**) *сов возв*: ~ +*dat* (*мечтам итп*) to give o.s. up to.

предвари́тельный (-ен, -ьна, -ьно) *прил* preliminary; (*продажа билетов*) advance *опред*; ~ **счёт-факту́ра** (*комм*) pro-forma invoice; **предвари́тельное заключе́ние** (*юр*) remand.

предвар|и́ть (-ю́, -и́шь; *impf* **предваря́ть**) *сов перех* (*события*) to anticipate.

предве́сти|е (-я) *ср* indication.

предвеща́|ть (-ю) *несов перех* (*будущее, успех*) to foretell; (*изменения, кризис*) to portend; (*плохую погоду*) to herald.

предвзя́тый (-, -а, -о) *прил* prejudiced.

предви́дени|е (-я) *ср* foresight; (*предположения*) prediction.

предви́|деть (-жу, -дишь) *сов перех* to foresee, predict

► **предви́деться** *сов неперех* to be expected.

предвкуша́|ть (-ю) *несов перех* to look forward to, anticipate.

предвкуше́ни|е (-я) *ср* anticipation.

предводи́тел|ь (-я) *м* leader.

предвосхи́|тить (-щу́, -ти́шь; *impf* **предвосхища́ть**) *сов перех* to anticipate.

предвы́борн|ый *прил* (*собрание*) pre-election *опред*; ~**ая кампа́ния** election campaign.

предго́рный *прил*: ~ **райо́н** foothills *мн*.

преддве́ри|е (-я) *ср*: **в** ~**и чего́-н** on the threshold of sth.

преде́л (-а) *м* (*обычно мн*: *города, страны*) boundary; (*перен*: *приличия*) bound; (: *терпения*) limit; (*изнеможения*) peak; (*совершенства, подлости*) height; (*мечтаний, желаний*) pinnacle; **на** ~**е** at breaking point; **дойти́** (*perf*) **до** ~**а** to reach the limit; **в** ~**ах** +*gen* (*закона, года*) within; (*приличия*) within the bounds of; **за** ~**ами** +*gen* (*страны, города*) outside.

преде́льный (-ен, -ьна, -ьно) *прил* maximum; (*восторг, важность*) utmost; **преде́льный срок** deadline.

предзнаменова́ни|е (-я) *ср* omen.

предика́т (-а) *м* (*линг*) predicate.

предисло́ви|е (-я) *ср* foreword, preface.

преде́дка *сущ см* **пре́док**.

пре́дк|и (-ов) *мн* ancestors *мн*.

предлага́|ть (-ю) *несов от* **предложи́ть**.

предло́г (-а) *м* pretext; (*линг*) preposition; **под** ~**ом** +*gen* on the pretext of; **под** ~**ом того́ что**, **под тем** ~**ом что** on the pretext that.

предложе́ни|е (-я) *ср* (*конкретное, умное*) proposal, suggestion; (*замужества*) proposal;

(*комм*) offer; (*экон*) supply; (*линг*) sentence; **де́лать (сде́лать** *perf*) **~ кому́-н** (*девушке*) to propose to sb; (*комм*) to make sb an offer; **вноси́ть (внести́** *perf*) **~** (*на собра́нии, на съе́зде*) to propose a motion.

предл|ожи́ть (**-ожу́, -о́жишь**; *impf* **предлага́ть**) *сов перех* to offer; (*план, кандидату́ру*) to propose ♦ *неперех* to suggest, propose; (*попроси́ть*) to ask; (*потре́бовать*) to ask; **предлага́ть (~** *perf*) **что-н кому́-н** to offer sth to sb, offer sb sth; **он ~ожи́л нам пойти́ туда́** he suggested that we went there.

предло́жный *прил* (*линг*) prepositional; **предло́жный паде́ж** prepositional case.

предме́сть|е (**-я**) *ср* suburb.

предме́т (**-а**) *м* object; (*обсужде́ния, изуче́ния*) subject; **на ~ +***gen* concerning; **предме́ты дома́шнего обихо́да** household goods; **предме́ты пе́рвой необходи́мости** necessities.

предназнача́|ть (**-ю**) *несов от* **предназна́чить** ▶ **предназнача́ться** *несов возв* (+*dat*) to be destined for.

предназначе́ни|е (**-я**) *ср* role.

предназна́ч|ить (**-у, -ишь**; *impf* **предназнача́ть**) *сов перех*: **~ что-н/кого́-н** +*dat* to intend sth/sb for.

преднаме́рен|ный (**-, -на, -но**) *прил* (*преступле́ние*) premeditated; (*обма́н итп*) deliberate.

пре́д|ок (**-ка**) *м* ancestor; *см также* **пре́дки**.

предопредел|и́ть (**-ю́, -и́шь**; *impf* **предопределя́ть**) *сов перех* (*определи́ть*) to predetermine; (*обусло́вить*) to bring about.

предоста́в|ить (**-лю, -ишь**) *сов перех*: **~ что-н кому́-н** to give sb sth ♦ *неперех*: **~ кому́-н** +*infin* (*выбира́ть, реша́ть*) to let sb do; **предоставля́ть (~** *perf*) **кого́-н самому́ себе́** to leave sb to his own devices; **предоставля́ть (~** *perf*) **кому́-н сло́во** to call upon sb to speak.

предостерёг *итп сов см* **предостере́чь.**

предостерега́|ть (**-ю**) *несов от* **предостере́чь.**

предостерегу́ *итп сов см* **предостере́чь.**

предостереже́ни|е (**-я**) *ср* warning.

предостер|е́чь (**-егу́, -ежёшь** *итп*, **-егу́т**; *pt* **-ёг, -егла́, -егло́,** *impf* **предостерега́ть**) *сов перех*: **~ кого́-н (от** +*gen*) to warn sb (about).

предосторо́жност|ь (**-и**) *ж* caution; **ме́ры ~и** precautionary measures, precautions.

предосуди́тел|ьный (**-ен, -ьна, -ьно**) *прил* reprehensible.

предотвра|ти́ть (**-щу́, -ти́шь**; *impf* **предотвраща́ть**) *сов перех* (*войну́, кри́зис*) to avert; (*боле́знь, ава́рии*) to prevent.

предотвраще́ни|е (**-я**) *ср* (*см глаг*) averting; prevention.

предотвращу́ *сов см* **предотврати́ть.**

предохрани́тел|ь (**-я**) *м* safety device; (*электри́ческий*) fuse (*BRIT*), fuze (*US*); (*руже́йный*) safety catch; (*замка́*) snib.

предохрани́тельный *прил* (*TEX*) safety опред.

предохран|и́ть (**-ю́, -и́шь**; *impf* **предохраня́ть**) *сов перех* to protect.

предписа́ни|е (**-я**) *ср* (*распоряже́ние*) instruction; (*: президе́нта, поли́ции*) order; (*: врача́*) prescription.

предпи|са́ть (**-шу́, -шешь**; *impf* **предпи́сывать**) *сов перех*: **~ что-н кому́-н** (*назна́чить*) to prescribe sth for sb ♦ *неперех*: **~ кому́-н** +*infin* to order sb to do.

предполага́|ть (**-ю**) *несов от* **предположи́ть** ♦ *перех* to demand ♦ *неперех*: **~** +*infin* (*намерева́ться*) to intend to do

▶ **предполага́ться** *несов неперех* (*намеча́ться*) to be planned.

предположе́ни|е (**-я**) *ср* (*дога́дка*) supposition; (*наме́рение*) intention.

предположи́тел|ьный (**-ен, -ьна, -ьно**) *прил* (*результа́т, вопро́с*) hypothetical; (*срок, дохо́д*) anticipated.

предпол|ожи́ть (**-ожу́, -о́жишь**; *impf* **предполага́ть**) *сов перех* (*допусти́ть возмо́жность*) to allow for; **~ожи́м** (*возмо́жно*) suppose; **~ожи́м, он опозда́ет** suppose he is late.

предпо|сла́ть (**-шлю́, -шлёшь**; *impf* **предпосыла́ть**) *сов перех*: **~ что-н чему́-н** to preface sth with sth.

предпосле́дн|ий (**-яя, -ее, -ие**) *прил* (*но́мер журна́ла*) penultimate; (*в о́череди*) last but one.

предпосыла́|ть (**-ю**) *несов от* **предпосла́ть.**

предпосы́л|ка (**-ки**; *gen pl* **-ок**) *ж* (*усло́вие*) precondition, prerequisite; (*исхо́дное положе́ние*) premise.

предпоч|е́сть (**-ту́, -тёшь**; *pt* **-ёл, -ла́, -ло́,** *impf* **предпочита́ть**) *сов перех*: **~ что-н/кого́-н** +*dat* to prefer sth/sb to ♦ *неперех*: **~** +*infin* to prefer to do.

предпочте́ни|е (**-я**) *ср* preference; **ока́зывать (оказа́ть** *perf*) *или* **отдава́ть (отда́ть** *perf*) **~ кому́-н/чему́-н** to show a preference for sb/sth.

предпочти́тел|ьный (**-ен, -ьна, -ьно**) *прил* preferable.

предпочту́ *итп сов см* **предпоче́сть.**

предпошлю́ *итп сов см* **предпосла́ть.**

предприи́мчив|ый (**-, -а, -о**) *прил* enterprising.

предприму́ *итп сов см* **предприня́ть.**

предпринима́тел|ь (**-я**) *м* entrepreneur, businessman (*мн* businessmen).

предпринима́тельск|ий (**-ая, -ое, -ие**) *прил* enterprise опред, business опред.

предпринима́тельств|о (**-а**) *ср* enterprise.

предприн|я́ть (**-иму́, -и́мешь**; *pt* **-и́нял, -иняла́,-и́няло,** *impf* **предпринима́ть**) *сов перех* to

undertake; (*атаку, наступление итп*) to
launch; (*меры*) to take.
предприятие (-я) *ср* enterprise, business.
предрасположение (-я) *ср* predisposition.
предрасположенность (-и) *ж* =
  предрасположение.
предрассудок (-ка) *м* prejudice.
предрекать (-ю) *несов перех* (*успех*) to
  foretell; (*плохую погоду*) to herald.
предрешить (-у, -ишь; *impf* **предрешать**) *сов*
  перех to predetermine.
председатель (-я) *м* chairman (*мн* chairmen).
председательство (-а) *ср* chairmanship; **под**
  ~**м** +*gen* under the chairmanship of.
председательствовать (-ую) *несов неперех*
  (*на заседании*) to be in the chair; (*работать*
  председателем) to be chairman; ~ (*impf*) **на**
  собрании to chair a meeting.
предскажу *итп сов см* **предсказать**.
предсказание (-я) *ср* (*действие*) predicting;
  (*то, что предсказано*) prediction.
предсказать (-ажу, -ажешь; *impf*
  предсказывать) *сов перех* to predict; (*чью-н*
  судьбу) to foretell.
предсмертный *прил* (*агония*) death *опред*;
  (*вздох*) dying; (*воля*) last.
представать (-ю) *несов от* **предстать**.
представитель (-я) *м* representative; (*разряда*
  животных итп) specimen.
представительница (-ы) *ж* representative.
представительный *прил* representative;
  (*видный*) imposing.
представительство (-а) *ср* (*учреждение*)
  representatives *мн*; (*наличие представителей*)
  representation; **торговое** ~ trade mission;
  дипломатическое ~ diplomatic corps.
представить (-лю, -ишь; *impf* **представлять**)
  сов перех to present; **представлять** (~ *perf*)
  кого-н кому-н (*познакомить*) to introduce sb to
  sb; **представить** (**представить** *perf*) **кого-н к**
  +*dat* (*к награде, к премии итп*) to recommend
  sb for, put sb forward for; **представлять** (~
  perf) **интерес** to be of interest; **представлять**
  (~ *perf*) **себе** to imagine; ~**ьте** (**себе**)**!** (just)
  imagine!
▸ **представиться** (*impf* **представляться**)
  несов возв (*при знакомстве*) to introduce o.s.;
  (*появиться: возможность*) to present itself;
  представляться (~**ся** *perf*) **кому-н** (*вид*) to
  appear before sb; (*интересная картина*) to
  meet sb's eyes; **ему** ~**илась будущая встреча**
  he pictured the future meeting; **ей** ~**илась**
  возможность поехать в Лондон an
  opportunity arose for her to go to London;
  представляться (~**ся** *perf*) **больным/спящим**
  to pretend to be ill/asleep.
представление (-я) *ср* presentation;
  (*документ*) statement; (*ТЕАТР*) performance;
  (*знание*) idea; (*ПСИХОЛ*) representation; **не**
  иметь (*impf*) (**никакого**) ~**я о** +*prp* to have no
  idea about.

представлю(сь) *сов см* **представить(ся)**.
представлять (-ю) *несов от* **представить** ◆
  перех (*действовать от имени*) to represent; ~
  (*impf*) **собой** *или* **из себя** (*являться*) to be; ~
  (*impf*) **себе что-н** (*понимать*) to understand sth;
  (*осознавать*) to appreciate sth; **он ничего из**
  себя не ~**ет** he doesn't amount to much
▸ **представляться** *несов от* **представиться**
  ◆ *возв*: **мне** ~**ется, (что) он прав** I think he's
  right; ~**ется, что ...** it appears that ....
предстать (-ну, -нешь; *impf* **представать**) *сов*
  неперех: ~ **перед** +*instr* (*появиться*) to appear
  before; (*проявиться: человек*) to show o.s.;
  (: *характер*) to show itself.
предстоять (*3sg* -**ит**, *3pl* -**ят**) *несов неперех* to
  lie ahead; **нам** ~**ит много работы** there is a lot
  of work ahead of us.
предстоящий (-ая, -ее, -ие) *прил* (*сезон*)
  coming; (*трудности*) impending; (*работа,*
  встреча) forthcoming.
предубеждение (-я) *ср* prejudice.
предугадать (-ю; *impf* **предугадывать**) *сов*
  перех to anticipate.
предупредительный (-ен, -ьна, -ьно) *прил*
  (*предохраняющий*) preventive; (*любезный*)
  solicitous, attentive.
предупредить (-жу, -дишь; *impf*
  предупреждать) *сов перех* to warn;
  (*предотвратить*) to prevent; (*опередить*) to
  anticipate; **предупреждать** (~ *perf*) **кого-н о**
  +*prp* to warn sb about.
предупреждение (-я) *ср* warning; (*аварии,*
  заболевания) prevention; (*извещение*) notice.
предупрежу *сов см* **предупредить**.
предусмотреть (-отрю, -отришь; *impf*
  предусматривать) *сов перех* (*учесть*) to
  foresee; (*принять меры*) to make provision for;
  (*подлеж: программа, закон*) to provide for.
предусмотрительный (-ен, -ьна, -ьно) *прил*
  prudent.
предчувствие (-я) *ср* premonition.
предчувствовать (-ую) *несов перех* to have a
  premonition of.
предшественник (-а) *м* predecessor.
предшествующий (-ая, -ее, -ие) *прил*
  previous; (*событие*) foregoing.
предъявитель (-я) *м* bearer.
предъявительница (-ы) *ж см*
  предъявитель.
предъявить (-явлю, -явишь; *impf*
  предъявлять) *сов перех* (*паспорт, билет*
  итп) to show; (*доказательства*) to produce;
  (*требования, претензии*) to make; (*иск*) to
  bring; **предъявлять** (~ *perf*) **права на что-н** to
  lay claim to sth.
предъявление (-я) *ср* (*паспорта, билета*
  итп) showing; (*претензий*) making; (*иска*)
  bringing; **по** ~**ю** (*КОММ*) at sight.
предъявлю *сов см* **предъявить**.
предъявлять (-ю) *несов от* **предъявить**.
предыдущий (-ая, -ее, -ие) *прил* previous.

предыстóри|**я** (-и) ж background.
преéмник (-а) м successor.
преéмниц|**а** (-ы) ж см **преéмник**.
преéмственность (-и) ж (*власти, традиций*) continuity.
преéмственный *прил* successive.
прéжде *нареч* (*в прошлом*) formerly; (*сначала*) first ◆ *предл* (+*gen*); ~ **всегó** first of all; ~ **чем** before; ~ **онá никогдá об э́том не дýмала** she never used to think about it.
преждеврéмен|**ный** (-ен, -на, -но) *прил* premature.
прéжн|**ий** (-яя, -ее, -ие) *прил* former.
презентáция (-и) ж presentation.
презервати́в (-а) м condom.
президéнт (-а) м president.
прези́диум (-а) м presidium.
презирá|**ть** (-ю) *несов перех* to hold in contempt.
презрéни|**е** (-я) *ср* (*ко лжи, к предателю*) contempt; (*к опасности*) disregard; (*к богатству итп*) scorn.
презри́тельный (-ен, -ьна, -ьно) *прил* contemptuous.
преиму́щественно *нареч* chiefly.
преиму́ществ|**о** (-а) *ср* advantage; (*ЮР*) privilege; **по** ~**у** (*главным образом*) chiefly; **имéть** (*impf*) ~ **пéред** +*instr* to have an advantage over.
преиспóлн|**иться** (-юсь; *impf* **преисполня́ться**) *сов возв*: ~ +*instr* to be filled with.
прейскурáнт (-а) м price list.
преклонéни|**е** (-я) *ср*: ~ (**пéред** +*instr*) admiration (for).
преклóнный *прил*: ~ **вóзраст** old age.
преклоня́|**ться** (-юсь) *несов возв*: ~ **пéред** +*instr* to admire.
прекрáсен *прил см* **прекрáсный**.
прекрáсн|**ое** (-ого; *decl like adj*) *ср* beauty.
прекрáс|**ный** (-ен, -на, -но) *прил* (*красивый: женщина, природа*) beautiful; (: *город, вид, день*) fine, beautiful; (*отличный*) excellent; **в оди́н** ~ **день** (*однажды*) one fine day.
прекрати́|**ть** (-щу́, -ти́шь; *impf* **прекращáть**) *сов перех* to stop; (*подачу энергии*) to cut off ◆ *неперех*: ~ +*infin* to stop doing; **прекращáть** (~ *perf*) **отношéния с кем-н** to break off relations with sb
▸ **прекрати́ться** (*impf* **прекращáться**) *сов возв* (*дождь, занятия*) to stop; (*отношения, знакомство*) to end.
прекращéни|**е** (-я) *ср* (*работы*) stopping; (*поставок*) cutting off; (*отношений*) breaking off.
прекращу́(сь) *сов см* **прекрати́ть(ся)**.
прелéстный (-ен, -на, -но) *прил* charming.
прéлест|**ь** (-и) ж charm; **какáя** ~! how

charming!
преломи́|**ться** (*3sg* -**óмится**, *3pl* -**óмятся**, *impf* **преломля́ться**) *сов возв* (*ФИЗ*) to be refracted; (*перен*) to take on a different cast.
прéлый *прил* rotten.
прельсти́ть (-щу́, -сти́шь; *impf* **прельщáть**) *сов перех* to attract; (*увлечь*): ~ **когó-н чем-н** to entice sb with sth
▸ **прельсти́ться** (*impf* **прельщáться**) *сов возв*: ~**ся** +*instr* (*возможностями*) to be attracted by; (*богатством*) to be enticed by.
прелю́ди|**я** (-и) ж prelude.
премиáльн|**ые** (-ых; *decl like adj*) мн bonus *ед*.
премиáльный *прил* bonus *опред*; см *также* **премиáльные**.
премир|**овáть** (-у́ю) (*не*)*сов перех* (*работника*) to give a bonus to; (*победителя*) to award a prize to.
прéми|**я** (-и) ж (*работнику*) bonus; (*победителю*) prize; (*КОММ*) premium.
прему́дрост|**ь** (-и) ж (*разг: обычно мн*) ins мн and outs мн.
премьéр (-а) м (*также:* ~-**мини́стр**) prime minister, premier.
премьéр|**а** (-ы) ж première.
премьéр-мини́стр (-а) м prime minister, premier.
пренебрёг *итп сов см* **пренебрéчь**.
пренебрегá|**ть** (-ю) *несов от* **пренебрéчь**.
пренебрегý *итп сов см* **пренебрéчь**.
пренебрежéни|**е** (-я) *ср* (*законами итп*) disregard; (: *обязанностями*) neglect; (*высокомерие*) contempt.
пренебрежёшь *итп сов см* **пренебрéчь**.
пренебрежи́тельный (-ен, -ьна, -ьно) *прил* contemptuous.
пренебрéчь (-егý, -ежёшь *итп*, -гýт; *pt* -ёг, -еглá, -еглó, *impf* **пренебрегáть**) *сов неперех*: ~ +*instr* (*опасностью, последствиями*) to disregard; (*модной одеждой, правилами*) to scorn; (*советом, просьбой*) to ignore.
прéни|**я** (-й) мн debate *ед*.
преобладá|**ть** (*3sg* -**ет**, *3pl* -**ют**) *несов неперех*: ~ (**над** +*instr*) to predominate (over).
преобрази́ть (-жý, -зи́шь; *impf* **преображáть**) *сов перех* to transform
▸ **преобрази́ться** (*impf* **преображáться**) *сов возв* to be transformed.
преобразовáни|**е** (-я) *ср* (*общества, жизни*) transformation; (*тока, энергии*) conversion; (*революционное, социальное*) reform.
преобразовáтел|**ь** (-я) м (*тока, радиосигналов*) transformer; (*общества*) reformer.
преобраз|**овáть** (-у́ю; *impf* **преобразóвывать**) *сов перех* to reorganize; **преобразóвывать** (~ *perf*) **что-н в** +*acc* (*превратить*) to convert sth into.

преодоле́ть (-ю; *impf* **преодолева́ть**) *сов*
перех to overcome; (*прегра́ду*) to break down;
(*тру́дный перехо́д итп*) to get through.
препара́т (-а) *м* (*МЕД, ХИМ*) preparation.
препина́ни|**е** (-я) *ср*: **зна́ки ~а** punctuation
marks *мн*.
препира́ться (-юсь) *несов возв*: ~ **(с** +*instr*) to
squabble *или* bicker (with).
преподава́ни|**е** (-я) *ср* teaching.
преподава́тел|**ь** (-я) *м* (*шко́лы, ку́рсов*)
teacher; (*ву́за*) lecturer.
преподава́тельни|**ца** (-ы) *ж см*
преподава́тель.
препода|**ва́ть** (-ю́, -ёшь) *несов перех* to teach.
препода́ть (*как* **дать**; *см* **Table 14**) *сов перех* to
teach; ~ (*perf*) **кому́-н уро́к терпе́ния** to teach sb
patience.
препод|**нести́** (-есу́, -есёшь; *pt* -ёс, -есла́,
-есло́, *impf* **преподноси́ть**) *сов перех*: ~ **что-н**
кому́-н to present sb with sth; (*но́вость,*
сюрпри́з) to give sb sth.
преподо́би|**е** (-я) *ср* (*РЕЛ*): **Ва́ше/Его́ ~** Your/
His Eminence.
преподо́бный *прил* (*РЕЛ*) venerable.
препя́тстви|**е** (-я) *ср* obstacle.
препя́тств|**овать** (-ую; *perf*
воспрепя́тствовать) *несов непере* (+*dat*) to
impede.
прерв|**а́ть** (-у́, -ёшь; *impf* **прерыва́ть**) *сов перех*
(*разгово́р, рабо́ту итп*) to cut short;
(*отноше́ния, знако́мство*) to break off;
(*говоря́щего*) to interrupt; (*КОМП*) to abort
▸ **прерва́ться** (*impf* **прерыва́ться**) *сов возв*
(*разгово́р, игра́*) to be cut short; (*отноше́ния,*
знако́мство) to be broken off.
препере|**ка́ться** (-юсь) *несов возв* to squabble *или*
bicker.
прерогати́в|**а** (-ы) *ж* prerogative.
прерыва́ть(ся) (-ю(сь)) *несов от*
прерва́ть(ся).
прерыви́ст|**ый** (-, -а, -о) *прил* (*звоно́к*)
intermittent; (*ли́ния*) broken.
пресе́к *итп сов см* **пресе́чь**.
пресека́ть (-ю) *несов от* **пресе́чь**.
пресеку́ *итп сов см* **пресе́чь**.
пре́сен *прил см* **пре́сный**.
пресече́ни|**е** (-я) *ср* suppression; **ме́ра ~я** (*ЮР*)
injunction.
пресе́чь (-еку́, -ечёшь *итп*, -еку́т; *pt* -ёк, -екла́,
-екло́, *impf* **пресека́ть**) *сов перех* to suppress.
пресле́довани|**е** (-я) *ср* pursuit; (*инакомы́слия*)
persecution.
пресле́д|**овать** (-ую) *несов перех* to pursue;
(*перен: же́нщину*) to chase; (*подлеж: мы́сли,*
чу́вства) to haunt; (*правозащи́тника*) to
persecute.
пресловут́ый *прил* notorious.
пресмыка́ться (-юсь) *несов возв* (*пренебр*): ~
пе́ред +*instr* (*унижа́ться*) to crawl to.
пресмыка́ющееся (-егося; *nom pl* -иеся) *ср*
reptile.

пресново́дный *прил* freshwater.
пре́сный (-ен, -на, -но) *прил* (*вода́*) fresh;
(*пи́ща*) bland; (*перен: шу́тка*) feeble;
(: *исто́рия, разгово́ры итп*) tedious.
пресс (-а) *м* (*ТЕХ*) press.
пре́сс|**а** (-ы) *ж собир* the press;
общенациона́льная ~ national press.
пресс-конфере́нци|**я** (-и) *ж* press conference.
пресс|**ова́ть** (-у́ю; *perf* **спрессова́ть**) *несов*
перех (*дета́ли*) to press; (*порошо́к, газ*) to
compress.
пресс-центр (-а) *м* press office.
престаре́лый *прил* aged; **дом (для) ~ых** old
people's home.
прести́ж (-а) *м* prestige.
прести́жный (-ен, -на, -но) *прил* prestigious.
престо́л (-а) *м* (*трон*) throne; **вступа́ть**
(вступи́ть *perf*) *или* **восходи́ть (взойти́** *perf*) **на**
~ to ascend the throne; **сверга́ть (све́ргнуть**
perf) **кого́-н с ~а** to dethrone sb.
престу́пен *прил см* **престу́пный**.
преступ|**и́ть** (-лю́, -у́пишь; *impf* **преступа́ть**)
сов перех to breach.
преступле́ни|**е** (-я) *ср* crime.
преступлю́ *сов см* **преступи́ть**.
престу́пник (-а) *м* criminal.
престу́пни|**ца** (-ы) *ж см* **престу́пник**.
престу́пност|**ь** (-и) *ж* criminal nature;
(*коли́чество*) crime; **организо́ванная ~**
organized crime.
престу́пный (-ен, -на, -но) *прил* criminal.
пресы́|**титься** (-щусь, -тишься; *impf*
пресыща́ться) *сов возв* (+*instr*) to satiate o.s.
with.
претвор|**и́ть** (-ю́, -и́шь; *impf* **претворя́ть**) *сов*
перех: ~ **что-н в жизнь** *или* **в де́ло** *или* **в**
действи́тельность (*пла́ны, за́мыслы*) to put
sth into practice; (*мечту́*) to realize sth.
претенде́нт (-а) *м* (**на престо́л** claimant; (**на**
до́лжность) candidate; (**на ру́ку же́нщины**)
suitor; (*СПОРТ*) contender; (*ША́ХМАТЫ*)
challenger.
претенд|**ова́ть** (-у́ю) *несов непере*: ~ **на** +*acc*
(*стреми́ться*) to aspire to: (*заявля́ть права́*) to
lay claim to.
прете́нзи|**я** (-и) *ж* (*обы́чно мн: на насле́дство,*
на престо́л) claim *ед*; (: **на ум, на красоту́ итп**)
pretension; (*жа́лоба*) complaint; **быть** (*impf*) **в**
~**и на** +*acc* to bear a grudge against.
претенцио́зный (-ен, -на, -но) *прил*
pretentious.
претерп|**е́ть** (-лю́, -, -ёпишь; *impf*
претерпева́ть) *сов перех* (*измене́ния*) to
undergo; (*невзго́ды*) to suffer.
прети́ть (*3sg* -и́т, *3pl* -я́т) *несов безл* (+*dat*): **ему́**
~**и́т жа́дность** greed disgusts *или* sickens him.
преткнове́ни|**е** (-я) *ср*: **ка́мень ~я** stumbling
block.
Прето́ри|**я** (-и) *ж* Pretoria.
пре|**ть** (-ю; *perf* **сопре́ть**) *несов непере*
(*ли́стья*) to rot; (*пи́ща*) to stew.

преувеличе́ни|е (-я) *ср* exaggeration.
преувели́ч|ить (-у, -ишь; *impf*
преувели́чивать) *сов перех* to exaggerate.
преуме́ньш|ить (-у, -ишь; *impf*
преуменьша́ть) *сов перех* (*недооценивать*) to
underestimate; (*показать в меньших размерах*)
to understate.
преуспева́|ть (-ю) *несов от* **преуспе́ть** ♦
неперех (*бизнесмен, писатель*) to be
successful.
преуспе́|ть (-ю; *impf* **преуспева́ть**) *сов неперех*
to be successful.
префе́кт (-а) *м* head of administrative area of
Moscow.
преходя́щ|ий (-ая, -ее, -ие: -, -а, -е, -и) *прил*
(*временный*) transient.
прецеде́нт (-а) *м* precedent.

KEYWORD

при *предл* (+*prp*) **1** (*возле*) by, near; **при
доро́ге/до́ме** by *или* near the road/house;
сраже́ние при Ватерло́о the battle of Waterloo
2 (*указывает на прикреплённость*) at; **при
институ́те есть столо́вая** there is a canteen at
the institute; **я бу́ду при гостя́х** I will be with
the guests
3 (*в присутствии*) in front of; **при мне он не
хо́чет говори́ть** he doesn't want to speak in
front of me; **при свиде́телях** in front of *или* in
the presence of witnesses; **он всегда́ чита́ет
при све́те ла́мпы** he always reads by the light
of a lamp
4 (*о времени*) under; **при коммуни́стах/
консерва́торах** under the communists/
Conservatives; **при короле́ве Викто́рии** in the
time of Queen Victoria
5 (*о наличии чего-н у кого-н*) on; **он всегда́ при
деньга́х** he always ˈhas money on him; **я
оставлю́ э́то при себе́** I'll keep it on me; **при
жела́нии мо́жно всё измени́ть** if you wish
everything can be changed; **при слу́чае
передай ему́ приве́т** if the occasion arises, give
him my regards ; **он при сме́рти** he is close to
death; **я здесь ни при чём** it has nothing to do
with me.

при- *префикс* (*in verbs*; *о доведении движения до
конечной цели*) indicating achievement of final
goal eg. **прибежа́ть**; (*добавление*) indicating
addition eg. **пристро́ить**; (*скрепление*)
indicating fastening onto sth eg. **привинти́ть**;
(*сближение*) indicating approach of sth eg.
придви́нуться; (*о слабой мере действия*)
indicating slight action eg. **приоткры́ть**; (*о
сопутствующем действии*) indicating
accompanying action eg. **припева́ть**; (*in nouns
and adjectives*; *примыкающий*) indicating
adjoining position eg. **примо́рский**.
приба́в|ить (-лю, -ишь; *impf* **прибавля́ть**) *сов*

перех to add; (*увеличить*) to increase;
прибавля́ть (~ *perf*) **в ве́се** to put on weight
► **приба́виться** (*impf* **прибавля́ться**) *сов возв*
(*проблемы, работа итп*) to mount up ♦ *безл*
(*воды в реке*) to rise; (*народу в толпе*) to grow.
прибавле́ни|е (-я) *ср* addition; (*к зарплате,
воды в реке*) rise; ~ **семе́йства** new addition to
the family.
приба́влю(сь) *сов см* **приба́вить(ся)**.
прибавля́|ть (-ю) *несов от* **приба́вить**.
прибавля́|ть (-ю) *несов от* **приба́вить**.
прибау́тк|а (-ки; *gen pl* -ок) *ж* catch phrase.
прибега́|ть (-ю) *несов от* **прибе́гнуть**,
прибежа́ть.
прибе́гн|уть (-у, -ешь; *impf* **прибега́ть**) *сов*
неперех: ~ **к** +*dat* to resort to.
прибегу́ *итп сов см* **прибежа́ть**.
прибедня́|ться (-юсь) *несов возв* (*разг*) to
pretend to be poor; (*преуменьшать свои
возможности*) to show false modesty.
прибежа́ть (*как* **бежа́ть**; *см* **Table 20**) *сов*
неперех to come running.
прибе́жищ|е (-а) *ср* refuge.
прибе́й(те) *сов см* **прибить**.
приберу́ *итп сов см* **прибра́ть**.
прибива́|ть(ся) (-ю(сь)) *несов от*
прибить(ся).
прибира́|ть (-ю) *несов от* **прибра́ть**.
прибьй|ть (-ью, -ьёшь; *imper* -е́й(те), *impf*
прибива́ть) *сов перех* (*прикрепить гвоздями*)
to nail; (*подлеж*: *вода, волна итп*) to wash up
► **прибиться** (*impf* **прибива́ться**) *сов возв*
(*лодка к берегу*) to be washed up.
приближа́|ть(ся) (-ю(сь)) *несов от*
прибли́зить(ся).
приближе́ни|е (-я) *ср* (*дня, события*) approach.
прибли́жу(сь) *сов см* **прибли́зить(ся)**.
приблизи́тельный (-ен, -ьна, -ьно) *прил*
approximate.
прибли́|зить (-жу, -зишь; *impf* **приближа́ть**)
сов перех (*придвинуть*) to move nearer;
(*ускорить*) to bring nearer
► **прибли́зиться** (*impf* **приближа́ться**) *сов
возв* (*человек к окну, машина к дому*) to
approach; (*развязка, победа итп*) to draw near.
прибо́й (-я) *м* breakers *мн*.
прибо́р (-а) *м* (*измерительный*) device;
(*оптический*) instrument; (*нагревательный*)
appliance; (*бритвенный, чернильный*) set.
прибра́|ть (-еру́, -ерёшь; *impf* **прибира́ть**) *сов
перех* to clear up; **прибира́ть** (~ *perf*) что-н к
рука́м to lay one's hands on sth; **прибира́ть** (~
perf) **кого́-н к рука́м** to take sb in hand.
прибре́жный *прил* (*у берега моря*) coastal; (*у
берега реки*) riverside *опред*.
прибу́ду *итп сов см* **прибы́ть**.
прибыва́|ть (-ю) *несов от* **прибы́ть**.
при́быль (-и) *ж* profit; **нереализо́ванная** ~
(*комм*) paper profit.

при́быль|ный (-ен, -ьна, -ьно) *прил* profitable.

прибы́ти|е (-я) *ср* arrival.

прибы́ть (*как* быть; *см* Table 21; *impf* **прибыва́ть**) *сов неперех* to arrive; (*вода в реке*) to rise.

прибью́(сь) *итп сов см* **прибить(ся)**.

привал (-а) *м* (*в пути*) stop; (*место остановки*) stopping place.

прив|али́ть (-алю́, -а́лишь; *impf* **прива́ливать**) *сов перех* (*придвинуть что-н тяжёлое*) to heave ♦ *неперех* (*перен: разг*) to turn up.

приватиза́ци|я (-и) *ж* (*ЭКОН*) privatization.

приватизи́р|овать (-ую) (*не*)*сов перех* to privatize.

приведе́ни|е (-я) *ср* (*чего-н в порядок*) bringing; (*примеров*) introduction; ~ **к прися́ге** swearing in; ~ **пригово́ра в исполне́ние** (*ЮР*) carrying out of a sentence; ~ **в движе́ние** setting in motion.

приведу́ *итп сов см* **привести́**.

прив|езти́ (-езу́, -езёшь; *pt* -ёз, -езла́, -езло́, *impf* **привози́ть**) *сов перех* to bring.

привере́длив|ый (-, -а, -о) *прил* fussy.

приве́ржен|ец (-ца) *м* (*идеи, традиции*) adherent.

приве́ржен|ный (-, -а, -о) *прил*: ~ (**к** +*dat*) dedicated (to).

приве́рженца *итп сущ см* **приве́рженец**.

прив|ести́ (-еду́, -едёшь; *pt* -ёл,-ела́,-ело́, *impf* **приводи́ть**) *сов перех* (*ребёнка: домой*) to bring; (*подлеж: дорога: к дому*) to take; (*пример*) to give; (*чьи-н слова*) to quote; ~ (*perf*) **в у́жас** to horrify; ~ (*perf*) **в отча́яние** to bring to the point of despair; ~ (*perf*) **в восто́рг** to delight; ~ (*perf*) **в изумле́ние** to astonish; ~ (*perf*) **в исполне́ние** to put into effect; ~ (*perf*) **в гото́вность** to make ready; ~ (*perf*) **в поря́док** to put in order; ~ (*perf*) **в движе́ние** to set in motion.

приве́т (-а) *м* greetings *мн*, regards *мн*; (*разг: при встрече*) hi; (: *при расставании*) bye; **посыла́ть** (**посла́ть** *perf*) *или* **передава́ть** (**переда́ть** *perf*) **кому́-н** ~ to send one's regards to sb; ~! **рад тебя́ ви́деть** hi! it's nice to see you.

приве́тлив|ый (-, -а, -о) *прил* friendly.

приве́тстви|е (-я) *ср* (*при встрече*) greeting; (*съезду, делега́ции*) welcome.

приве́тств|овать (-ую) *perf* **поприве́тствовать**) *несов перех* (*также перен*) to welcome.

привива́|ть(ся) (-ю(сь)) *несов от* **приви́ть(ся)**.

приви́в|ка (-ки; *gen pl* -ок) *ж* (*МЕД*) vaccination.

привиде́ни|е (-я) *ср* ghost.

приви́д|еться (*3sg* -ится, *3pl* -ятся, *impf* **ви́деться**) *сов безл* (+*dat*) to appear to; **мне** ~**елся стра́шный сон** I had a terrifying dream.

привилегиро́ванный *прил* privileged.

привиле́ги|я (-и) *ж* privilege.

привин|ти́ть (-чу́, -ти́шь; *impf* **приви́нчивать**)

сов перех to screw on.

приви́ть (-ью́, -ьёшь; *impf* **привива́ть**) *сов перех* (*растение*) to graft; (*МЕД*): ~ **кому́-н что-н** to inoculate *или* vaccinate sb against sth; (*перен*) to cultivate sth in sb

▸ **приви́ться** (*impf* **привива́ться**) *сов возв* (*приви́вка, черено́к*) to take; (*новшество*) to catch on.

при́вкус (-а) *м* flavour (*BRIT*), flavor (*US*).

привлёк *итп сов см* **привле́чь**.

привлека́тельный (-ен, -ьна, -ьно) *прил* attractive.

привлека́|ть (-ю) *несов от* **привле́чь**.

привлеку́ *итп сов см* **привле́чь**.

привлече́ни|е (-я) *ср* (*покупа́телей, внима́ния*) attraction; (*ресу́рсов*) use; ~ **к суду́** taking to court; ~ **к отве́тственности** calling to account.

привл|е́чь (-еку́, -ечёшь *итп*, -еку́т; *pt* -ёк, -екла́, -екло́, *impf* **привлека́ть**) *сов перех* to attract; **привлека́ть** (~ *perf*) **кого́-н к** +*dat* (*к рабо́те, к уча́стию*) to coax sb into; (*к суду́*) to take sb to; **привлека́ть** (~ *perf*) **кого́-н к разгово́ру** to draw sb into a conversation; **привлека́ть** (~ *perf*) **кого́-н к отве́тственности** to call sb to account.

привн|ести́ (-есу́, -есёшь; *pt* -ёс, -есла́, -есло́, *impf* **привноси́ть**) *сов перех*: ~ **что-н в** +*acc* to inject sth into.

привн|оси́ть (-ошу́, -о́сишь) *несов от* **привнести́**.

приво́д (-а) *м* (*электри́ческий*) drive; (*ручно́й*) gear.

приво́д (-а) *м* (*ЮР*) arrest.

прив|оди́ть (-ожу́, -о́дишь) *несов от* **привести́**.

привожу́ *несов см* **привози́ть**.

приво́з (-а) *м* (*това́ров, сырья́*) supply.

прив|ози́ть (-ожу́, -о́зишь) *несов от* **привезти́**.

привозно́й *прил* imported.

приво́лен *прил см* **приво́льный**.

приво́ль|е (-я) *ср* (*степно́е, полево́е*) expanse.

приво́ль|ный (-ен, -ьна, -ьно) *прил* (*луга́, поля́ итп*) expansive; (*жизнь*) free and easy.

привра́тник (-а) *м* doorman (*мн* doormen).

привста|ва́ть (-ю́) *несов от* **привста́ть**.

привста́ть (-ну, -нешь; *impf* **привстава́ть**) *сов неперех* to half rise.

привы́к|нуть (-ну, -нешь; *pt* -, -ла, -ло, *impf* **привыка́ть**) *сов неперех*: ~ +*infin* (*гуля́ть, тра́тить де́ньги*) to get into the habit of doing; **привыка́ть** (~ *perf*) **к** +*dat* (*к но́вым друзья́м, к шко́ле*) to get used to; **он** ~, **что́бы ему́ все помога́ли** he is used to everyone helping him.

привы́чек *сущ см* **привы́чка**.

привы́чен *прил см* **привы́чный**.

привы́ч|ка (-ки; *gen pl* -ек) *ж* habit; **по** ~**ке** out of habit.

привы́ч|ный (-ен, -на, -но) *прил* (*рабо́та, зву́ки*) familiar.

привью́(сь) *итп сов см* **приви́ть(ся)**.

привяжу́(сь) *итп сов см* **привяза́ть(ся)**.

привя́занность (-и) ж attachment.
привяза́ть (-яжу́, -я́жешь; *impf* **привя́зывать**) *сов перех*: ~ что-н/кого́-н к +*dat* to tie sth/sb to; **привя́зывать** (~ *perf*) к себе́ +*acc* (*вызвать любовь*) to endear o.s. to

▸ **привяза́ться** (*impf* **привя́зываться**) *сов возв*: ~ся к +*dat* (*ремнём к сиде́нью*) to fasten o.s. to; (*полюбить*) to become attached to; (*разг: надоеда́ть*) to pester.
при́вязь (-и) ж tie.
пригиба́ть(ся) (-ю(сь)) *несов от* **пригну́ть(ся)**.
пригла́дить (-жу, -дишь; *impf* **пригла́живать**) *сов перех* (*складки на платье*) to smooth out; (*волосы*) to smooth back.
пригласи́тельный *прил*: ~ биле́т invitation.
пригласи́ть (-шу́, -си́шь; *impf* **приглаша́ть**) *сов перех* to invite; (*врача́*) to call; **приглаша́ть** (~ *perf*) кого́-н в го́сти to invite sb; **приглаша́ть** (~ *perf*) кого́-н на та́нец to ask sb to dance.
приглаше́ни|е (-я) *ср* invitation; (*КОМП*) prompt.
приглашу́ *сов см* **пригласи́ть**.
приглуш|и́ть (-у́, -и́шь; *impf* **приглуша́ть**) *сов перех* (*звуки*) to deaden; (*радио*) to turn down; (*краски*) to tone down; (*то́на*) to soften; (*перен: боль, тоску́*) to lessen.
пригля|де́ться (-жу́, -ди́шь; *impf* **пригля́дывать**) *сов неперех*: ~ за +*instr* to look after ◆ *перех* to search out, find

▸ **пригляде́ться** (*impf* **пригля́дываться**) *сов возв*: ~ся (к +*dat*) (*к карти́не, к незнако́мцу*) to look closely (at).
пригля|ну́ться (-яну́сь, -я́нешься) *сов возв*: ~ кому́-н to attract sb.
приг|на́ть (-оню́, -о́нишь; *impf* **пригоня́ть**) *сов перех* to drive; (*костю́м*) to adjust, alter.
пригну́ть (-у́, -ёшь; *impf* **пригиба́ть**) *сов перех* (*ве́тку, кусты́*) to bend

▸ **пригну́ться** (*impf* **пригиба́ться**) *сов возв* (*нагну́ться: челове́к*) to bend down; (*ветки, кусты́*) to bend.
пригова́рива|ть (-ю) *несов от* **приговори́ть** ◆ *неперех* (*сопровождать словами*) to talk at the same time (*as doing sth*).
пригово́р (-а) *м* (*ЮР*) sentence; (*перен*) condemnation; **выноси́ть** (**вы́нести** *perf*) ~ to pass sentence.
приговор|и́ть (-ю́, -и́шь; *impf* **пригова́ривать**) *сов перех*: ~ кого́-н к +*dat* to sentence sb to.
приго́ден *прил см* **приго́дный**.
пригод|и́ться (-жу́сь, -ди́шься; *impf* **пригожда́ться**) *сов возв* (+*dat*) to be useful to.
приго́д|ный (-ен, -на, -но) *прил* suitable.
пригожда́|ться (-юсь) *несов от* **пригоди́ться**.
пригожу́сь *сов см* **пригоди́ться**.
пригоню́ *итп сов см* **пригна́ть**.
пригоня́|ть (-ю) *несов от* **пригна́ть**.

пригора́|ть (*3sg* -ет, *3pl* -ют) *несов от* **пригоре́ть**.
пригоре́лый *прил* burnt.
пригор|е́ть (*3sg* -и́т, *3pl* -я́т, *impf* **пригора́ть**) *сов неперех* to burn.
приго́рка *сущ см* **приго́рок**.
при́город (-а) *м* suburb.
при́городный *прил* (*посёлок, жи́тель*) suburban; (*поезд, авто́бус*) local.
пригор|ок (-ка) *м* hillock.
при́горшн|я (-ни; *gen pl* -ен) *ж* handful.
пригото́в|ить (-лю, -ишь) *сов от* **гото́вить** ◆ (*impf* **пригота́вливать** *или* **приготовля́ть**) *перех* to prepare; (*постель*) to make; (*ванну*) to run

▸ **пригото́виться** *сов от* **гото́виться** ◆ *возв*: ~ся (к +*dat*) (*к путеше́ствию*) to get ready (for); (*к уро́ку*) to prepare (o.s.) (for).
приготовле́ни|е (-я) *ср* preparation.
пригото́влю(сь) *сов см* **пригото́вить(ся)**.
приготовля́|ть (-ю) *несов от* **пригото́вить**.
пригрева́|ть (-ю) *несов от* **пригре́ть**.
пригре́|зиться (-жусь, -зишься) *сов от* **гре́зиться**.
пригре́|ть (-ю; *impf* **пригрева́ть**) *сов перех* (*подлеж: со́лнце: зе́млю*) to warm; (*перен: сироту́*) to take in.
пригро|зи́ть(ся) (-жу́(сь), -зи́шь(ся)) *сов от* **грози́ть(ся)**.
пригу́б|ить (-лю, -ишь; *impf* **пригу́бливать**) *сов перех* to take a sip of.
прида|ва́ть (-ю́, -ёшь) *несов от* **прида́ть**.
придав|и́ть (-авлю́, -а́вишь; *impf* **прида́вливать**) *сов перех* to press, to squash.
придаю́ *итп сов см* **прида́ть**.
прида́н|ое (-ого; *decl like adj*) *ср* (*неве́сты*) dowry; (*новорождённого*) layette.
прида́ст *сов см* **прида́ть**.
прида́т|ок (-ка) *м* (*также перен*) appendage.
прида́точный *прил*: **прида́точное предложе́ние** (*линг*) subordinate clause.
прида́ть (*как* **дать**; *см* **Table 14**; *impf* **придава́ть**) *сов неперех*: ~ чего́-н кому́-н (*уве́ренности*) to instil sth in sb; **придава́ть** (~ *perf*) что-н чему́-н (*вид, фо́рму*) to give sth to sth; (*ва́жности*) to attach sth to sth; **придава́ть** (~ *perf*) бо́дрости кому́-н to hearten sb; **придава́ть** (~ *perf*) сил кому́-н to strengthen sb.
прида́ч|а (-и) *ж*: в ~у in addition.
прида́шь *сов см* **прида́ть**.
придви́н|уть (-у, -ешь; *impf* **придвига́ть**) *сов перех*: ~ (к +*dat*) to move over *или* up (to).
придво́рн|ый *прил* court *опред* ◆ -ого; *decl like adj*) *м* courtier.
приде́ла|ть (-ю; *impf* **приде́лывать**) *сов перех*: ~ что-н к +*dat* to attach *или* fix sth to.
придерж|а́ть (-ержу́, -е́ржишь; *impf* **приде́рживать**) *сов перех* (*дверь*) to hold

(steady): (*лошадь*) to restrain.

придéрживаться (-юсь) *несов возв* (+*gen*: *каких-н взглядов*) to hold; (*за перила*): ~ **за** +*acc* to hold onto.

придерýсь *итп сов см* **придрáться**

придирáться (-ю) *несов от* **придрáться**.

придúрка (-ки: *gen pl* -ок) *ж* quibble.

придúрчивый (-, -а, -о) *прил* (*человек*) fussy; (*замечание, взгляд*) critical.

придрáться (-ерýсь, -ерёшься; *impf* **придирáться**) *сов возв*: ~ **к** +*dat* to find fault with.

придý(сь) *итп сов см* **прийти(сь)**.

придýмать (-ю; *impf* **придýмывать**) *сов перех* (*отговорку, причину*) to think of *или* up; (*новый прибор*) to devise; (*песню, стихотворение*) to make up: **он** ~**л, как спасти положéние** he thought of how to save the situation.

придýриваться (-юсь) *несов возв* (*разг*) to pretend to be ignorant.

придýсь *итп сов см* **прийтúсь**.

придыхáние (-я) *ср* (*линг*) aspiration.

приедáться (-юсь) *несов от* **приéсться**.

приедúмся *итп сов см* **приéсться**.

приéду *итп сов см* **приéхать**.

приедúтся *сов см* **приéсться**.

приéзд (-а) *м* arrival.

приезжáть (-ю) *несов от* **приéхать**

приéзжий (-ая, -ее, -ие) *прил* visiting.

приём (-а) *м* reception; (*у врача*) surgery (*BRIT*), office (*US*); (*борьбы, гимнастический*) technique; (*наказания, воздействия*) means: **за одúн** ~ in one go: **в два/в три** ~**а** in two/three attempts; **устрáивать** (**устрóить** *perf*) ~ to organize a reception; (**записáться** (**записáться** *perf*) **на** ~ **к** +*dat* to make an appointment to see.

приёмка (-и) *ж* (*товаров*) receipt.

приёмная (-ой; *decl like adj*) *ж* (*также:* ~ **кóмната**) reception.

приёмник (-а) *м* (*радиоприёмник*) radio; (*связь*) receiver.

приёмный *прил* (*часы*) reception *опред*; (*день*) visiting *опред*; (*экзамены*) entrance *опред*; (*комиссия*) selection *опред*; (*родители, дети*) adoptive: **приёмный покóй** *room where newly-arrived patients register and are given inital checkup before going to the ward.*

приéмся *сов см* **приéсться**.

приéсться (*как* **есть**; *см* **Table 15**; *impf* **приедáться**) *сов возв*: ~ **комý-н** (*разг*) to bore sb stiff.

приéхать (*как* **éхать**; *см* **Table 19**; *impf* **приезжáть**) *сов неперех* to arrive *или* come (*by transport*).

приéшься *сов см* **приéсться**.

прижáть (-мý, -мёшь; *impf* **прижимáть**) *сов перех* (*разг: притеснить*) to put the screws on; **прижимáть** (~ *perf*) **что-н/когó-н к** +*dat* to press sth/sb to *или* against

▸ **прижáться** (*impf* **прижимáться**) *сов возв*:

~**ся к** +*dat* to press o.s. against; (*ребёнок к груди*) to snuggle up to.

прижéчь (-гý, -жёшь *итп*, -гýт; *impf* **прижигáть**) *сов перех* to cauterize.

приживáться (-юсь) *несов от* **прижúться**

приживýсь *итп сов см* **прижúться**

прижигáть (-ю) *несов от* **прижéчь**.

прижúзненный *прил*: ~**ая слáва** fame during one's lifetime: **он вúдел мнóго** ~**ых издáний своúх поэм** many books of his poems were published during his lifetime.

прижимáть(ся) (-ю(сь)) *несов от* **прижáть(ся)**.

прижúмистый (-, -а, -о) *прил* (*разг*) tightfisted.

прижúться (-вýсь, -вёшься; *pt* -лся, -лáсь, -лось, *impf* **приживáться**) *сов возв* (*человек*) to settle in, get o.s. settled; (*животные*) to adapt, become acclimatized (*BRIT*) *или* acclimated (*US*): (*растения*) to take rest.

прижмý(сь) *сов см* **прижáть(ся)**.

приз (-а; *nom pl* -**ы**) *м* prize.

призадýматься (-юсь; *impf* **призадýмываться**) *сов возв*: ~ **над** +*instr или* **о** +*prp* to reflect upon.

призвáние (-я) *ср* (*к искусству, к науке итп*) vocation; (*предназначение*) calling: ~ **теáтра** — **воспúтывать** the purpose of the theatre is to educate.

призвáть (-овý, -овёшь; *pt* -вáл, -валá, -вáло, *impf* **призывáть**) *сов перех* (*на борьбу, к защите страны*) to call, summon: **призывáть** (~ *perf*) **к мúру/разоружéнию** to call for peace/disarmament; **призывáть** (~ *perf*) **когó-н к спокóйствию/повиновéнию** to appeal to sb to be calm/obedient; **призывáть** (~ *perf*) **когó-н к порáдку** to call sb to order; **призывáть** (~ *perf*) **в áрмию** to call up (to join the army).

приземúстый (-, -а, -о) *прил* (*человек*) squat.

приземлúть (-ю, -úшь; *impf* **приземлáть**) *сов перех* to land

▸ **приземлúться** (*impf* **приземлáться**) *сов возв* to land

призёр (-а) *м* prizewinner.

прúзма (-ы) *ж* prism: **сквозь** *или* **чéрез** ~**у** +*gen* (*перен*) in the light of.

признавáть(ся) (-ю(сь), -ёшь(ся)) *несов от* **признáть(ся)**.

прúзнак (-а) *м* (*кризиса, успеха*) sign; (*отравления*) symptom: **без** ~**ов жúзни** not showing any sign of life.

признáние (-я) *ср* (*государства, писателя*) recognition; (*своего бессилия, чьих-н достижений*) acknowledgment, recognition; (*в любви*) declaration; (*в преступлении*) confession.

прúзнанный (-, -а, -о) *прил* recognized.

признáтелен *прил см* **признáтельный**.

признáтельность (-и) *ж* gratitude.

признáтельный (-ен, -ьна, -ьно) *прил* grateful.

признáть (-ю; *impf* **признавáть**) *сов перех*

(*правительство, чьи-н права*) to recognize;
(*положительно оценить: книгу, фильм*) to
acclaim; (*счесть*) ~ **что-н/кого-н** +*instr* to
recognize sth/sb as

▶ **призна́|ться** (*impf* **признава́ться**) *сов возв*:
~**ся кому́-н в чём-н** (*в преступлении*) to
confess sth to sb; **признава́ться** (~**ся** *perf*)
кому́-н в любви́ to make a declaration of love to
sb; ~**ся** *или* **признаю́сь, я Вас не понима́ю** I
have to admit that I don't understand you.

призов|о́й *прил* (*деньги*) prize *опред*; ~**а́я
меда́ль** prizewinner's medal; ~**о́е ме́сто** medal
position.

призову́ *итп сов см* **призва́ть**.

призо́р (-а) *м*: **без** ~**а** (*разг*) unattended.

при́зрак (-а) *м* ghost.

при́зрач|ный (-ен, -на, -но) *прил* (*успех,
надежды*) illusory; (*опасность*) imagined.

при́зыв (-а) *м* (*к восстанию, к защите*) call: (: *в
армию*) conscription; (*лозунг*) slogan ◆ *собир*
call-up.

призыва́|ть (-ю) *несов от* **призва́ть**.

призывни́к (-а́) *м* conscript.

призывн|о́й *прил* (*возраст*) call-up *опред*;
(*пункт*) recruiting *опред*.

призы́вный *прил* summoning *опред*.

при́иск (-а) *м* mine.

прийти́ (*как* **идти́**; *см* **Table 18**; *impf*
приходи́ть) *сов неперех* (*идя, достичь*) to
come (*on foot*); (*письмо, телеграмма*) to arrive;
(*весна, час свободы*) to come; (*достигнуть*): ~
к +*dat* (*к власти, к выводу*) to come to; (*к
демократии*) to achieve; **приходи́ть** (~ *perf*) **в
у́жас/недоуме́ние** to be horrified/bewildered;
приходи́ть (~ *perf*) **в восто́рг** to go into
raptures; **приходи́ть** (~ *perf*) **в него́дность** to
become worthless; **приходи́ть** (~ *perf*) **в упа́док**
to go into decline; **приходи́ть** (~ *perf*) **в
запу́щенность** to fall into neglect; **приходи́ть**
(~ *perf*) **кому́-н в го́лову** *или* **на ум** to occur to
sb; **приходи́ть** (~ *perf*) **в себя́** (*после обморока*)
to come to *или* round; (*успокоиться*) to come to
one's senses

▶ **прийти́сь** (*impf* **приходи́ться**) *сов возв*: ~**сь
на** +*acc* to fall on; (*попасть*): ~**сь по** +*dat* to
land on; (*подойти*): ~**сь по** +*dat*/**к** +*dat* (*одежда,
ключ*) to fit; (*вещь: по вкусу*) to suit ◆ **безл**
(+*infin*; *уступить, пойти на компромисс итп*) to
have to do; (**нам**) **придётся согласи́ться**
we'll have to agree; **нам пришло́сь тяжело́** we
had a hard time; **как придётся** anyhow; **где
придётся** anywhere; **что придётся** anything.

прикажу́ *итп сов см* **приказа́ть**.

прика́з (-а) *м* order; **отдава́ть** (**отда́ть** *perf*) ~ to
give an order.

приказа́ни|е (-я) *ср* = **прика́з**.

приказа́|ть (-ажу́, -а́жешь; *impf* **прика́зывать**)
сов неперех: ~ **кому́-н** +*infin* to order sb to do;

как ~**а́жете** as you like.

приказн|о́й *прил* (*тон, жест*) commanding; **в
приказно́м поря́дке** in the form of an order.

прика́зчик (-а) *м* (*в магазине*) sales assistant
(*BRIT*) *или* clerk (*US*); (*в помещичьем
хозяйстве*) *manager of estate or farm*.

прика́зыва|ть (-ю) *несов от* **приказа́ть**.

прика́лыва|ть (-ю) *несов от* **приколо́ть**.

прика́нчива|ть (-ю) *несов от* **прико́нчить**.

прикарма́н|ить (-ю, -ишь; *impf*
прикарма́нивать) *сов перех* (*разг*) to pocket.

прика́рмлива|ть (-ю) *несов перех* (*младенца*)
to supplement the diet of.

прикаса́ни|е (-я) *ср* (*рук*) touch.

прикаса́|ться (-юсь) *несов от* **прикосну́ться**.

прика́т|ить (-ачу́, -а́тишь; *impf* **прика́тывать**)
сов перех to roll up ◆ *неперех* (*разг: приехать*)
to show up.

прики́|нуть (-у, -ешь; *impf* **прики́дывать**) *сов
неперех* (*разг: посчитать*) to work out
(roughly)

▶ **прики́нуться** (*impf* **прики́дываться**) *сов возв*
(+*instr*; *разг*) to pretend to be.

прикла́д (-а) *м* (*ружья, автомата*) butt (*of gun
etc*).

прикладн|о́й *прил* applied; **прикладна́я
програ́мма** (*КОМП*) application program;
прикладно́е иску́сство applied art.

прикла́дыва|ть(ся) (-ю(сь)) *несов от*
приложи́ть(ся).

прикле́|ить (-ю, -ишь; *impf* **прикле́ивать**) *сов
перех* to glue, stick

▶ **прикле́иться** (*impf* **прикле́иваться**) *сов возв*
to stick.

приключа́|ться (*3sg* -ется, *3pl* -ются) *несов от*
приключи́ться.

приключе́ни|е (-я) *ср* adventure.

приключе́нческ|ий (-ая, -ое, -ие) *прил*
adventure *опред*.

приключи́|ться (*3sg* -и́тся, *3pl* -а́тся, *impf*
приключа́ться) *сов возв* (*разг: произойти*) to
happen.

прико́выва|ть (-ю; *impf* **прико́вывать**) *сов перех*
(*перен: внимание, взгляд*) to fix; **прико́вывать**
(~ *perf*) **кого́-н к** +*dat* to chain sb to; (*перен*) to
confine sth to.

прико́л (-а) *м*: **стоя́ть на** ~**е** to be moored.

прикол|о́ть (-олю́, -о́лешь; *impf* **прика́лывать**)
сов перех to fasten, fix.

прикоманди́рова́|ть (-у́ю; *impf*
прикомандиро́вывать) *сов перех* to second.

прико́нч|ить (-у, -ишь; *impf* **прика́нчивать**) *сов
перех* (*умертвить*) to finish off.

прикорн|у́ть (-у́, -ёшь) *сов неперех* (*разг*) to
curl up.

прикосну́|ться (-у́сь, -ёшься; *impf*
прикаса́ться) *сов возв*: ~ **к** +*dat* to touch
lightly.

прикреп|и́ть (-лю́, -и́шь; *impf* **прикрепля́ть**) *сов перех:* ~ **что-н к** +*dat* (*деталь, бант*) to fix sth to; **прикрепля́ть** (~ *perf*) **кого́-н/что-н к** +*dat* (*советника к предприятию, институт к заводу*) to attach sb/sth to.

прикри́кн|уть (-у, -ешь; *impf* **прикри́кивать**) *сов неперех:* ~ **на** +*acc* to shout *или* yell at.

прикро́ю(сь) *итп сов см* **прикры́ть(ся)**.

прикрыва́|ть(ся) (-ю) *несов от* **прикры́ть(ся)**.

прикры́ти|е (-я) *ср* (*махина́ций*) cover-up; (*ты́ла, ВОЕН*) cover; **под** ~**м** +*gen* under the guise of.

прикр|ы́ть (-о́ю, -о́ешь; *impf* **прикрыва́ть**) *сов перех* to cover; (*закры́ть*) to close (over); (*разг: ликвиди́ровать*) to wind up; (*скрыва́ть*) to cover up

▸ **прикры́ться** (*impf* **прикрыва́ться**) *сов возв* (+*instr; одея́лом, плащо́м*) to cover o.s. with; (*отгово́рками, рито́рикой*) to hide behind; (*разг: ликвиди́роваться*) to close down.

прикур|и́ть (-урю́, -у́ришь; *impf* **прику́ривать**) *сов неперех* to get a light (*from lit cigarette*).

прикус|и́ть (-ушу́, -у́сишь; *impf* **прику́сывать**) *сов перех* (*губу, язы́к*) to bite.

прила́в|ок (-ка) *м* (*в магази́не*) counter; (*на ры́нке*) stall.

прилага́тельн|ое (-ого; *decl like adj*) *ср* (*ЛИНГ: также:* **и́мя** ~) adjective.

прилага́|ть (-ю) *несов от* **приложи́ть**.

прила́|дить (-жу, -дишь; *impf* **прила́живать**) *сов перех:* ~ **что-н к** +*dat* to fit sth on to.

приласка́|ть(ся) (-ю(сь)) *сов от* **ласка́ть(ся)**.

прилёг *итп сов см* **приле́чь**.

прилега́|ть (*3sg* -ет, *3pl* -ют) *несов неперех:* ~ **к** +*dat* (*каса́ться*) to fit tightly; (*находи́ться ря́дом*) to adjoin.

прилежа́ни|е (-я) *ср* diligence.

приле́ж|ный (-ен, -на, -но) *прил* diligent.

прилеп|и́ть (-еплю́, -е́пишь; *impf* **прилепля́ть**) *сов перех* to stick.

прилет|е́ть (-чу́, -ти́шь; *impf* **прилета́ть**) *сов неперех* to arrive (*by air*), fly in.

прил|е́чь (-я́гу, -я́жешь итп, -я́гут; *pt* -ёг, -егла́, -егло́) *сов неперех* to lie down for a while.

прили́в (-а) *м* (*в мо́ре, в океа́не*) tide; (*де́нег, тури́стов*) flood; (*негодова́ния, эне́ргии*) surge.

прилива́|ть (-ю) *несов от* **прили́ть**.

прилижу́ *итп сов см* **прилиза́ть**.

прили́занный *прил* (*разг: во́лосы*) slicked-down; (*вид*) fastidious; (*челове́к*) pernickety (*BRIT*), persnickety (*US*).

прили|за́ть (-жу́, -жешь; *impf* **прили́зывать**) *сов перех* (*разг: во́лосы*) to slick down.

прили́п|нуть (-ну, -нешь; *pt* -, -ла, -ло, *impf* **прилипа́ть** *или* **ли́пнуть**) *сов неперех:* ~ **к** +*dat* to stick to; (*разг: к де́вушке, к незнако́мцу*) to cling to.

прил|и́ть (*3sg* -ьёт, *3pl* -ью́т, *pt* -и́л, -ила́, -и́ло, *impf* **прилива́ть**) *сов неперех* (*вода́ в мо́ре*) to flow; (*кровь*) to rush.

прили́чен *прил см* **прили́чный**.

прили́чи|е (-я) *ср* decency; (*обычно мн*) manners *мн*.

прили́ч|ный (-ен, -на, -но) *прил* (*присто́йный: челове́к*) decent; (: *мане́ры*) proper; (*доста́точно хоро́ший, большо́й*) fair, decent.

приложе́ни|е (-я) *ср* (*си́лы, эне́ргии*) application; (*к журна́лу*) supplement; (*к документа́ции*) addendum (*мн* addenda).

прил|ожи́ть (-ожу́, -о́жишь; *impf* **прилага́ть**) *сов перех* (*присоедини́ть*) to affix; (*си́лу, зна́ния итп*) to apply; (*impf* **прикла́дывать**): ~ **что-н к** +*dat* (*ру́ку ко лбу*) to put sth to; (*тру́бку к уху*) to hold sth to; **прилага́ть** (~ *perf*) **ру́ку к** +*dat* to put one's hand to; **ума́ не** ~**ожу́** (*разг*) I don't have a clue

▸ **приложи́ться** (*impf* **прикла́дываться**) *сов возв:* ~**ся у́хом/губа́ми к** +*dat* to press one's ear/lips against; **остально́е** ~**о́жится** the rest is a matter of course.

прильёт *итп сов см* **прили́ть**.

прильн|у́ть (-у́, -ёшь) *сов от* **льнуть** ♦ *неперех* (*прини́кнуть*): ~ **к** +*dat* (*к чьей-н груди́*) to cling to; (*к две́ри, к окну́*) to press o.s. against.

приля́гу *итп сов см* **приле́чь**.

при́м|а (-ы) *ж* (*МУЗ: веду́щий го́лос*) lead; (*разг: о балери́не*) prima ballerina.

при́м|а-балери́н|а (-ы, -ы) *ж* prima ballerina.

прим|ани́ть (-аню́, -а́нишь) *сов перех* (*разг*) to lure.

прима́н|ка (-ки; *gen pl* -ок) *ж* bait.

примелька́|ться (-юсь) *сов возв* to become familiar.

примене́ни|е (-я) *ср* (*ору́жия*) use; (*маши́н, лека́рств*) application; (*мер, ме́тода*) adoption; **в** ~**и к** +*dat* in application to.

примени́м|ый (-, -а, -о) *прил* applicable.

примени́тельно *предл:* ~ **к** +*dat* in conformity with.

прим|ени́ть (-еню́, -е́нишь; *impf* **применя́ть**) *сов перех* (*ме́ры*) to implement; (*си́лу*) to use; **применя́ть** (~ *perf*) **что-н** (**к** +*dat*) (*ме́тод, тео́рию*) to apply sth (to); **применя́ть** (~ *perf*) **са́нкции к** +*dat* to impose sanctions on.

применя́|ться (*3sg* -ется, *3pl* -ются) *несов неперех* (*испо́льзоваться*) to be used.

приме́р (-а) *м* example; **к** ~**у** for example; **не в** ~ +*dat* unlike; **по** ~**у** +*gen* (*схо́дно с*) after the example of; **ста́вить** (**поста́вить** *perf*) **кого́-н/что-н в** ~ to hold sb/sth up as an example; **брать** (**взять** *perf*) ~ **с** +*gen* to follow the example of.

приме́рен *прил см* **приме́рный**.

примёрз|нуть (-ну, -нешь; *pt* -, -ла, -ло, *impf* **примерза́ть**) *сов неперех:* ~ (**к** +*dat*) to freeze (to).

приме́р|ить (-ю, -ишь; *impf* **примеря́ть**) *сов перех* to try on.

приме́р|ка (-ки; *gen pl* -ок) *ж* trying on.

приме́рно *нареч* (*образцо́во*) in an exemplary fashion; (*приблизи́тельно*) approximately.

приме́р|ный (-ен, -на, -но) *прил* (*образцовый*) exemplary; (*приблизительный*) approximate.

приме́рок *сущ см* **приме́рка**.

примеря́|ть (-ю) *несов от* **приме́рить**.

при́месь (-и) *ж* dash.

приме́т|а (-ы) *ж* (*признак*) sign; (*суеверная*) omen; **она́ у него́ на ~е** he has his eye on her.

примета́|ть (-ю; *impf* **примётывать**) *сов перех* to stitch on, tack on (*BRIT*).

приме́тен *прил см* **приме́тный**.

приме́|тить (-чу, -тишь; *impf* **примеча́ть**) *сов перех* (*разг*) to notice.

приме́т|ный (-ен, -на, -но) *прил* (*заметный*: *человек*) conspicuous; (: *событие*) prominent.

примётыва|ть (-ю) *несов от* **примета́ть**.

примеча́ни|е (-я) *ср* note, comment.

примеча́тель|ный (-ен, -ьна, -ьно) *прил* (*событие, внешность*) remarkable; (*изменение*) notable.

примеча́|ть (-ю) *несов от* **приме́тить**.

примечу́ *сов см* **приме́тить**.

примеша́|ть (-ю; *impf* **приме́шивать**) *сов перех* (*перен*) to bring; **приме́шивать** (~ *perf*) (в +*acc*) to add (to), mix in(to).

примина́|ть (-ю) *несов от* **примя́ть**.

примире́ни|е (-я) *ср* reconciliation.

примир|и́ть (-ю́, -и́шь; *impf* **примиря́ть** *или* **мири́ть**) *сов перех*: ~ **кого́-н с кем-н** to reconcile sb with sb; **примиря́ть** (~ *perf*) **кого́-н с чем-н** to help sb come to terms with sth

▶ **примири́ться** (*impf* **примиря́ться**) *сов возв*: ~**ся с** +*instr* (*с врагом, с мужем*) to be reconciled with; (*с действительностью*) to reconcile o.s. with.

примити́в|ный (-ен, -на, -но) *прил* primitive.

примкн|у́ть (-у́, -ёшь; *impf* **примыка́ть**) *сов неперех*: ~ **к** +*dat* (*к партии*) to join; (*к большинству*) to side with.

примну́ *итп сов см* **примя́ть**.

примо́лкн|уть (-у, -ешь) *сов неперех* (*разг*: *умолкнуть*) to shush.

примо́рск|ий (-ая, -ое, -ие) *прил* seaside *опред*.

примо́рь|е (-я) *ср* seaside.

примо|сти́ться (-щу́сь, -сти́шься) *сов возв* (*разг*) to perch o.s.

примо́ч|ка (-ки; *gen pl* -ек) *ж* (*процедура*) bathing; (*лекарство*) lotion.

примощу́сь *сов см* **примости́ться**.

приму́(сь) *итп сов см* **приня́ть(ся)**.

при́мул|а (-ы) *ж* (*БОТ*) primrose.

при́мус (-а) *м* Primus (stove) ®.

примч|а́ться (-у́сь, -и́шься) *несов возв* to come tearing up.

примыка́|ть (-ю) *несов от* **примкну́ть** ♦ *неперех* (*прилегать*): ~ **к** +*dat* to adjoin.

примя́|ть (-ну́, -нёшь; *impf* **примина́ть**) *сов перех* (*траву*) to trample on.

принадлеж|а́ть (-у́, -и́шь) *несов неперех*: ~

+*dat* to belong to; (*заслуга*) to go to; (*роль*) to be played by; ~ (*impf*) **к** +*dat* (*входить в состав*) to belong to, be a member of.

принадле́жность (-и) *ж* characteristic; (*обычно мн*: *охотничьи, рыболовные*) tackle; (*письменные*) accessories *мн*; (*вхождение в состав*): ~ **к** +*dat* membership of.

принево́л|ить (-ю, -ишь) *сов от* **нево́лить**.

прин|ести́ (-есу́, -есёшь; *pt* -ёс, -есла́, -есло́, *impf* **приноси́ть**) *сов перех* (*стул, ребёнка, удачу итп*) to bring; (*подлеж: животные*) to bear; (: *растения*) to yield; (*доход, прибыль итп*) to bring in; (*извинения, благодарность итп*) to express; (*присягу*) to take; **приноси́ть** (~ *perf*) **по́льзу** to be of use; **приноси́ть** (~ *perf*) **вред** to harm; **приноси́ть** (~ *perf*) **что-н в же́ртву** to sacrifice sth.

прини́|зить (-жу, -зишь; *impf* **принижа́ть**) *сов перех* (*унизить*) to humiliate; (*умалить*) to belittle.

прини́к|нуть (-ну, -нешь; *pt* -, -ла, -ло, *impf* **приника́ть**) *сов неперех*: ~ **к** +*dat* (*к земле*) to press o.s. to; (*к подушке итп*) to nestle up against; (*к другу*) to snuggle up to; (*к двери, к окну*) to press o.s. against.

принима́|ть(ся) (-ю(сь)) *несов от* **приня́ть(ся)**.

приноров|и́ться (-лю́сь, -и́шься; *impf* **принора́вливаться**) *сов возв*: ~ **к** +*dat* (*к обстоятельствам*) to adapt o.s. to; (*к машине*) to get used to; (+*infin*) to get used to doing.

прино|си́ть (-шу́, -сишь) *несов от* **принести́**.

при́нтер (-а) *м* (*КОМП*) printer.

принуди́тель|ный (-ен, -ьна, -ьно) *прил* (*труд, лечение итп*) forced; (*меры*) compulsory.

прину́|дить (-жу, -дишь; *impf* **принужда́ть**) *сов перех*: ~ **кого́-н/что-н к** +*dat*/+*infin* to force sb/sth into/to do.

принужде́ни|е (-я) *ср* compulsion; **по ~ю** under compulsion.

принуждё|нный (-ён, -на, -но) *прил* forced.

прину́жу *сов см* **прину́дить**.

принц (-а) *м* prince.

принце́сс|а (-ы) *ж* princess.

при́нцип (-а) *м* principle; **в ~е** (*в основном*) in principle; **из ~а** on principle; **по ~у** +*gen* on the principle of.

принципиа́ль|ный (-ен, -ьна, -ьно) *прил* (*человек, политика*) of principle; (*согласие, договорённость*) in principle.

при́нят|ый (-, -а, -о) *прил* accepted.

при|ня́ть (-му́, -мешь; *pt* -ня́л, -няла́, -няло́, *impf* **принима́ть**) *сов перех* to take; (*подарок, критику, условия*) to accept; (*какой-н пост*) to take up; (*гостей, делегацию, телеграмму*) to receive; (*закон, резолюцию, поправку*) to pass;

(*отношение, вид*) to take on; (*христианство итп*) to adopt; **принима́ть** (~ *perf*) **в/на** +*acc* (*в университет, на работу*) to accept for; **принима́ть** (~ *perf*) **что-н/кого́-н за** +*acc* to mistake sth/sb for; (*счесть*) to take sth/sb as; **принима́ть** (~ *perf*) **ро́ды** to deliver a baby

▶ **приня́ться** (*impf* **принима́ться**) *сов возв* (*растение*) to take root; (+*infin*; *приступить*) to get down to doing; **принима́ться за** +*acc* (*приступить*) to get down to; (*за лентяев, за преступников*) to take in hand; (*за десерт, за вино*) to start *или* get started on.

приободри́ть (-ю́, -йшь; *impf* **приободря́ть**) *сов перех* to cheer up

▶ **приободри́ться** (*impf* **приободря́ться**) *несов возв* to cheer up.

приобре́сти (-ету́, -ете́шь; *pt* -ёл, -ела́, -ело́, *impf* **приобрета́ть**) *сов перех* to acquire; (*друзей, врагов*) to make; (*опыт*) to gain.

приобрете́ние (-я) *ср* acquisition; (*комм*) procurement.

приобрету́ *итп сов см* **приобрести́**.

приобщи́ть (-у́, -йшь; *impf* **приобща́ть**) *сов перех* (*приложить*; *познакомить*): ~ **кого́-н/что-н к** +*dat* to introduce sb/sth to; **приобща́ть** (~ *perf*) **к де́лу** to file

▶ **приобщи́ться** (*impf* **приобща́ться**) *сов возв*: ~ **к** +*dat* to become involved in.

приоде́ть (-ну, -нешь) *сов перех* (*разг*) to dress up.

приорите́т (-а) *м* priority.

приорите́тный (-ен, -на, -но) *прил* main.

приостанови́ть (-овлю́, -о́вишь; *impf* **приостана́вливать**) *сов перех* to suspend.

приоткры́ть (-о́ю, -о́ешь; *impf* **приоткрыва́ть**) *сов перех* (*дверь*) to open slightly; (*глаза*) to half open.

припада́ть (-ю) *несов от* **припа́сть**.

припа́док (-ка) *м* (*сердечный*) attack; (*гнева*) fit; (*веселья*) outburst; **истери́ческий** ~ fit of hysterics.

припаду́ *итп сов см* **припа́сть**.

припа́ивать (-ю) *несов от* **припая́ть**.

припа́рка (-ки; *gen pl* -ок) *ж* (*мед*) poultice.

припасти́ (-асу́, -асёшь; *pt* -а́с, -асла́, -асло́, *impf* **припаса́ть**) *сов перех* (*еду*) to store up; (*деньги*) to save up.

припа́сть (-аду́, -адёшь; *impf* **припада́ть**) *сов неперех*: ~ **к** +*dat* to throw o.s. at.

припасу́ *итп сов см* **припасти́**.

припа́сы (-ов) *мн* (*еды, денежные*) supplies; (*воен: боевые, ружейные*) ammunition.

припая́ть (-ю; *impf* **припа́ивать**) *сов перех* (*приделать паянием*) to solder on.

припе́в (-а) *м* (*песни*) chorus, refrain.

припева́ючи *нареч* (*разг*): **жить** ~ to live the life of Riley.

припека́ть (*3sg* -ет) *несов неперех* (*солнце*) to be burning hot.

припере́ть (-ру́, -рёшь; *pt* -ёр, -ёрла, -ёрло, *impf* **припира́ть**) *сов перех* (*разг*): ~ **к** +*dat*

(*прижать*) to shove against; **припира́ть** (~ *perf*) **к сте́нке** (*перен: разг*) to put in a tight spot.

приписа́ть (-ишу́, -и́шешь; *impf* **припи́сывать**) *сов перех* (*написать в дополнение*) to add; (*прикрепить*): ~ **кого́-н/что-н к** +*dat* to attach sb/sth to; (*счесть следствием*): ~ **что-н чему́-н** to put sth down to sth; (*счесть принадлежащим*): ~ **что-н кому́-н** to attribute sth to sb.

припи́ска (-ки; *gen pl* -ок) *ж* (*в письме*) postscript; (: *в документе*) addition; (*обычно мн: ложные данные: в отчёте, в докладе*) tampering with facts and figures.

припи́сывать (-ю) *несов от* **приписа́ть**.

припишу́ *итп сов см* **приписа́ть**.

приплести́ (-ету́, -етёшь; *pt* -ёл, -ела́, -ело́, *impf* **приплета́ть**) *сов перех* (*вплетая, присоединить*) to plait in; (*перен: разг: имя*) to drag in; (: *событие, факт*) to drag up

▶ **приплести́сь** *сов возв* (*разг*) to drag o.s. along.

приплю́снутый (-, -а, -о) *прил* (*нос*) flat.

припля́сывать (-ю) *несов неперех* to skip.

приподнима́ть(ся) (-ю(сь)) *несов от* **приподня́ть(ся)**.

приподниму́(сь) *итп сов см* **приподня́ть(ся)**.

приподня́тый (-, -а, -о) *прил* (*оживлённый*) cheerful; (*торжественный*) elevated.

приподня́ть (-иму́, -и́мешь; *impf* **приподнима́ть**) *сов перех* (*чемодан*) to lift slightly; (*занавес*) to raise slightly

▶ **приподня́ться** (*impf* **приподнима́ться**) *сов возв* to raise o.s. a little.

припо́мнить (-ю, -ишь; *impf* **припомина́ть**) *сов перех* to remember; **припомина́ть** (~ *perf*) **что-н кому́-н** to make sb remember sth.

припра́ва (-ы) *ж* seasoning.

припру́ *итп сов см* **припере́ть**.

припря́тать (-чу, -чешь; *impf* **припря́тывать**) *сов перех* (*разг*) to stash (away).

припугну́ть (-у́, -ёшь; *impf* **припу́гивать**) *сов перех* (*разг*) to put the wind up.

при́пуск (-а) *м* allowance.

припусти́ть (-ущу́, -у́стишь; *impf* **припуска́ть**) *сов неперех* (*разг: побежать*) to speed up.

припу́хлый *прил* slightly swollen.

припущу́ *сов см* **припусти́ть**.

приравня́ть (-ю; *impf* **прира́внивать**) *сов перех*: ~ **кого́-н/что-н к** +*dat* to equate sb/sth with.

прирасти́ (-асту́, -астёшь; *pt* -о́с, -осла́, -осло́, *impf* **прираста́ть**) *сов неперех* (*прижиться*) to take; (*увеличиться*) to increase; (*перен*): ~ **к** +*dat* to become rooted to.

приро́да (-ы) *ж* nature; (*места вне города*) countryside; **от** ~**ы**, **по** ~**е** by nature; **живая** ~ natural world.

приро́дный *прил* natural; (*врождённый*) innate; **приро́дные бога́тства** natural resources; **приро́дный газ** natural gas.

природове́дение (-я) *ср* natural history.

природоохра́н|а (-ы) ж nature conservation.

природоохра́нный прил conservation опред.

прирождённый прил (чувство, грация) inborn; (учитель, художник) born.

приро́с итп сов см **прирасти́**.

приро́ст (-а) м (населения) growth; (доходов, урожая) increase.

приручи́|ть (-у́, -и́шь; impf **прируча́ть**) сов перех (животное) to tame; (перен: человека) to bring to heel.

приса́жива|ться (-юсь) несов от **присе́сть**.

приса́сыва|ться (-юсь) несов от **присоса́ться**.

присво́|ить (-ю, -ишь; impf **присва́ивать**) сов перех to appropriate; (дать): ~ **что-н кому́-н** to confer sth on sb.

приседа́ни|е (-я) ср squatting (physical exercise).

приседа́|ть (-ю) несов от **присе́сть**.

присе́ст (-а) м (разг): **в** или **за оди́н** ~ at one sitting или a single sitting.

прис|е́сть (-я́ду, -я́дешь; impf **приседа́ть**) сов непepex to squat; (impf **приса́живаться**) to sit down (for a short while).

приск|ака́ть (-ачу́, -а́чешь; impf **приска́кивать**) сов непepex (лошадь, всадник) to gallop up, come galloping up; (разг: быстро прийти/приехать) to come tearing up.

приско́рбен прил см **приско́рбный**.

приско́рби|е (-я) ср: **к мо́ему глубо́кому** ~**ю** to my deepest regret; **с глубо́ким** ~**м** with deepest regret.

приско́рб|ный (-ен, -на, -но) прил regrettable.

при|сла́ть (-шлю́, -шлёшь; impf **присыла́ть**) сов перех to send.

прислон|и́ть (-ю́, -и́шь; impf **прислоня́ть**) сов перех: ~ **что-н к** +dat to lean sth against

▶ **прислони́ться** (impf **прислоня́ться**) сов возв: ~**ся к** + dat to lean against.

прислу́г|а (-и) ж собир servants мн.

прислу́жива|ть (-ю) несов непepex (+dat; официанту) to wait on

▶ **прислу́живаться** несов возв to ingratiate o.s., grovel.

прислу́ша|ться (-юсь; impf **прислу́шиваться**) сов возв: ~ **к** +dat (к звуку) to listen to; (к совету) to take heed of.

присма́трива|ть (-ю) несов от **присмотре́ть**
◆ перех to look for

▶ **присма́триваться** несов от **присмотре́ться**.

присмире́|ть (-ю) сов непepex to quieten (BRIT) или quiet (US) down, calm down.

присмир|и́ть (-ю́, -и́шь; impf **присмиря́ть**) сов перех to quieten (BRIT), quiet (US).

присмо́тр (-а) м care.

присм|отре́ть (-отрю́, -о́тришь) сов перех (разг) to find ◆ (impf **присма́тривать**) непepex:

~ **за** +instr to look after

▶ **присмотре́ться** (impf **присма́триваться**) сов возв: ~**ся (к** +dat) to take a good look (at).

присни́|ться (3sg -и́тся, 3pl -я́тся) сов от **сни́ться**.

присовокуп|и́ть (-лю́, -и́шь; impf **присовокупля́ть**) сов перех (к делу) to file; (к сказанному) to add.

присоедине́ни|е (-я) ср (см глаг) attachment; connection; annexation; (к протесту итп) joining; (к чьему-л мнению) supporting.

присоедин|и́ть (-ю́, -и́шь; impf **присоединя́ть**) сов перех: ~ **что-н к** +dat to attach sth to; (провод) to connect sth to; (территорию) to annex sth to

▶ **присоедини́ться** (impf **присоединя́ться**) сов возв: ~**ся к** +dat (к экскурсии, к протесту итп) to join; (к чьему-н мнению) to support.

присос|а́ться (-у́сь, -ёшься; impf **приса́сываться**) сов возв to attach itself by suction.

приспе́шник (-а) м (пренебр) accomplice.

приспосо́б|ить (-лю, -ишь; impf **приспоса́бливать** или **приспособля́ть**) сов перех to adapt

▶ **приспосо́биться** (impf **приспоса́бливаться** или **приспособля́ться**) сов возв (к условиям, к климату) to adapt (o.s.); (делать что-н) to get used to.

приспосо́блен прил см **приспосо́бленный**.

приспособле́ни|е (-я) ср (к условиям итп) adaptation; (устройство, механизм итп) appliance.

приспосо́блен|ный (-, -а, -о) прил: ~ **к** +dat (пригодный) fit for, well-suited to.

приспосо́блю(сь) сов см **приспосо́бить(ся)**.

приспособля́|ть(ся) (-ю(сь)) несов от **приспосо́бить(ся)**.

пристава́ни|е (-я) ср pestering.

приста|ва́ть (-ю́, -ёшь) несов от **приста́ть**.

приста́в|ить (-лю, -ишь; impf **приставля́ть**) сов перех: ~ **что-н к** +dat to put sth against; (пистолет: к груди) to put sth to; **приставля́ть** (~ perf) **кого́-н к** +dat to assign sb to look after.

приста́в|ка (-ки; gen pl -ок) ж fitting; (линг) prefix.

приста́влю сов см **приста́вить**.

приставля́|ть (-ю) несов от **приста́вить**.

приста́вок сущ см **приста́вка**.

при́стальный (-ен, -ьна, -ьно) прил (взгляд, внимание) fixed; (интерес, наблюдение) determined, resolute.

приста́нищ|е (-а) ср refuge.

приста́ну итп сов см **приста́ть**.

при́стан|ь (-и) ж pier.

приста́|ть (-ну, -нешь; impf **пристава́ть**) сов непepex: ~ **к** +dat (прилипнуть) to stick to; (присоединиться) to join; (разг: с вопросами) to pester; (причалить) to put into; **ему́ не** ~**ло**

так поступа́ть (*разг*) he shouldn't behave like that.

пристегну́ть (-у́, -ёшь; *impf* **пристёгивать**) *сов перех* to fasten

▸ **пристегну́ться** (*impf* **пристёгиваться**) *сов возв* (в самолёте, в автомобиле) to fasten one's seat belt.

присто́йный (-ен, -йна, -йно) *прил* (приличный) decent.

пристра́ива|ть(ся) (-ю(сь)) *несов от* **пристро́ить(ся)**.

пристра́стен *прил см* **пристра́стный**.

пристра́сти|е (-я) *ср* (склонность) passion; (предубеждение) bias.

пристра|сти́ться (-щу́сь, -сти́шься) *сов возв*: ~ к +*dat* to develop a liking for.

пристра́ст|ный (-ен, -на, -но) *прил* bias(s)ed.

пристращу́сь *сов см* **пристрасти́ться**.

пристре|ли́ть (-елю́, -е́лишь; *impf* **пристре́ливать**) *сов перех* (животное) to put down; (разг: человека) to shoot.

пристро́ек *сущ см* **пристро́йка**.

пристро́|ить (-ю, -ишь; *impf* **пристра́ивать**) *сов перех* (комнату) to build onto; (разг: устроить) to fix up

▸ **пристро́иться** (*impf* **пристра́иваться**) *сов возв* (на диване, в углу) to settle o.s.; (разг: на работу, на службу) to get fixed up.

пристро́йк|а (-йки; *gen pl* -ек) *ж* extension.

при́ступ (-а) *м* (атака) attack; (смеха, гнева) fit; (кашля) bout; (припадок): **серде́чный** ~ heart attack; ~ **удущья** asthma attack.

приступ|и́ть (-уплю́, -у́пишь; *impf* **приступа́ть**) *сов неперех*: ~ к +*dat* (начать) to get down to.

пристыди́ть (-жу́, -ди́шь) *сов от* **стыди́ть**.

присуди́ть (-жу́, -у́дишь; *impf* **присужда́ть**) *сов перех*: ~ что-н кому-н (приз, алименты итп) to award sth to sb; (учёную степень) to confer sth on sb; (приговорить): ~ кого́-н к +*dat* to sentence sb to.

прису́тственный *прил* (день, часы) working опред.

прису́тстви|е (-я) *ср* presence; **в** ~и +*gen* in the presence of; ~ **ду́ха** presence of mind.

прису́тств|овать (-ую) *несов неперех* to be present.

прису́тствующи|е (-их; *decl like adj*) *мн* those present.

прису́щ|ий (-ая, -ее, -ие; -, -а, -о) *прил*: ~ +*dat* characteristic of.

присыла́|ть (-ю) *несов от* **присла́ть**.

присы́лк|а (-ки; *gen pl* -ок) *ж* (письма) sending.

присы́п|ка (-ки; *gen pl* -ок) *ж* powder.

прися́г|а (-и) *ж* oath; **под** ~**ой** under oath.

присяга́|ть (-ю; *perf* **присягну́ть**) *несов неперех* (+*dat*) to swear an oath to.

прися́ду *итп сов см* **присе́сть**.

прися́жн|ый (-ого; *decl like adj*) *м* (ЮР: *также:* ~ **заседа́тель**) juror; **суд** ~**ых** jury.

притаи́|ться (-ю́сь, -и́шься; *impf* **притаи́ваться**) *сов возв* to hide.

притащи́ть (-ащу́, -а́щишь; *impf* **прита́скивать**) *сов перех* (что-н тяжёлое или громоздкое) to drag; (заставить пойти) to drag along.

притво́рен *прил см* **притво́рный**.

притво|ри́ть (-орю́, -о́ришь; *impf* **притворя́ть**) *сов перех* to shut (not fully).

притвори́ться (-ю́сь, -и́шься; *impf* **притворя́ться**) *сов возв* (+*instr*) to pretend to be.

притво́рный (-ен, -на, -но) *прил* feigned.

притво́рств|о (-а) *ср* pretence.

притворю́(сь) *сов см* **притвори́ть(ся)**.

притворя́|ть(ся) (-ю(сь)) *несов от* **притвори́ть(ся)**.

притесне́ни|е (-я) *ср* (людей) oppression; (обычно мн: гонения) persecution.

притесни́тель (-я) *м* oppressor.

притесн|и́ть (-ю́, -и́шь; *impf* **притесня́ть**) *сов перех* to oppress.

прити́х|нуть (-ну, -нешь; *pt* -, -ла, -ло, *impf* **притиха́ть**) *сов неперех* to grow quiet.

приткну́ть (-у́, -ёшь; *impf* **притыка́ть**) *сов перех* to stick.

прито́к (-а) *м* (река) tributary; ~ +*gen* (сил, энергии, средств) supply of; (населения) influx of.

прито́м *союз* and what's more.

прито́н (-а) *м* den.

прито́рный (-ен, -на, -но) *прил* (вкус, торт итп) sickly sweet; (перен: улыбка, выражение лица) unctuous.

притро́н|уться (-усь, -ешься; *impf* **притро́гиваться**) *сов возв*: ~ к +*dat* to touch.

приту|пи́ться (*3sg* -у́пится, *3pl* -у́пятся, *impf* **притупля́ться**) *сов возв* (нож, бритва, топор) to go blunt; (перен: внимание итп) to diminish; (: чувства) to fade; (: слух) to fail.

при́тч|а (-и) *ж* parable.

притыка́|ть (-ю) *несов от* **приткну́ть**.

притяга́тел|ьный (-ен, -ьна, -ьно) *прил* attractive.

притя́гива|ть (-ю) *несов от* **притяну́ть**.

притяжа́тельный *прил* (линг) possessive.

притяза́ни|е (-я) *ср*: ~ **на** +*acc* (на наследство, на территорию) claim to; (на остроумие, на красоту итп) pretensions *мн* of.

притя|ну́ть (-яну́, -я́нешь; *impf* **притя́гивать**) *сов перех* (подтащить) to drag up; (привлечь) to attract; **притя́гивать** (~ *perf*) **факт за́ уши** to come up with a far-fetched fact.

приукра́|сить (-шу, -сишь; *impf* **приукра́шивать**) *сов перех* (события, чьи-н достоинства) to exaggerate.

приумно́ж|ить (-у, -ишь; *impf* **приумножа́ть**) *сов перех* to increase.

приуны́|ть (-о́ю, -о́ешь) *сов неперех* to get depressed.

приуро́ч|ить (-у, -ишь; *impf* **приуро́чивать**) *сов перех*: ~ что-н к +*dat* to time sth to coincide with.

приуса́дебный *прил:* ~ **уча́сток** allotment.
приу|чи́ть (-учу́, -у́чишь; *impf* **приуча́ть**) *сов перех:* ~ **кого́-н к** +*dat*/+*infin* to train sb for/to do
▸ **~ся к** +*dat*/+*infin* to train for/to do.
▸ **приучи́ться** (*impf* **приуча́ться**) *сов возв:*
прифронтово́й *прил* front(line) *опред.*
прихвастн|у́ть (-у́, -ёшь) *сов неперех (разг)* to blow one's own trumpet a bit.
прихва|ти́ть (-ачу́, -а́тишь; *impf* **прихва́тывать**) *сов перех (разг: схвати́ть)* to grab; (: **взять с собо́й**) to take ♦ *безл (о бо́ли)* to grip.
прихлеба́тел|ь (-я) *м (разг: пренебр)* sponger.
прихло́пн|уть (-у, -ешь; *impf* **прихло́пывать**) *сов перех (кры́шку)* to slam shut; *(разг: насеко́мое)* to swat.
прихлын|у́ть (*3sg* -ет, *3pl* -ут) *сов перех (волна́, толпа́)* to surge; *(перен: воспомина́ния)* to come flooding back.
прихо́д (-а) *м (по́езда, го́стя, весны́)* arrival; *(комм)* receipts *мн*; *(рел)* parish; ~ **и расхо́д** *(комм)* credit and debit.
прихо|ди́ть (-ожу́, -о́дишь) *несов от* **прийти́**
▸ **приходи́ться** *несов от* **прийти́сь** ♦ *возв:* **~ся кому́-н дя́дей/ро́дственником** to be sb's uncle/relative; **раз на раз не ~о́дится** no two times are ever the same.
прихо́дн|ый *прил (комм):* ~**ая кни́га** receipt book.
прихо́д|овать (-ую; *perf* **оприхо́довать**) *несов перех (комм: су́мму)* to enter (*in receipt book*).
прихо́дск|ий (-ая, -ое, ие) *прил (рел)* parish *опред.*
приходя́щий (-ая, -ее, -ие) *прил* nonresident; *(медсестра́)* visiting *опред;* ~**ая ня́ня** babysitter; ~ **больно́й** outpatient.
прихожа́н|ин (-ина; *nom pl* -е) *м (рел)* parishioner.
прихожа́н|ка (-ки; *gen pl* -ок) *ж (рел) см* **прихожа́нин.**
прихо́ж|ая (-ей; *decl like adj*) *ж* entrance hall.
прихожу́(сь) *несов см* **приходи́ть(ся).**
прихора́шива|ться (-юсь) *несов возв (разг)* to smarten o.s. up.
прихотли́в|ый (-, -а, -о) *прил (челове́к)* capricious, whimsical; *(вкус)* quirky; *(узо́р)* intricate.
при́хот|ь (-и) *ж* whim.
прихра́мыва|ть (-ю) *сов неперех* to limp slightly.
прице́л (-а) *м (ру́жья, пу́шки)* sight(s); *(прице́ливание)* aiming; **брать (взять** *perf)* **кого́-н/что-н на** ~ to aim at sb/sth; *(перен)* to keep a close watch on sb/sth.
прице́л|иться (-юсь, -ишься; *impf* **прице́ливаться**) *сов возв* to take aim.
прицени́ться (-еню́сь, -е́нишься; *impf* **прице́ниваться**) *сов возв:* ~ **к** +*dat* to enquire about the price of.

прице́п (-а) *м* trailer.
прицеп|и́ть (-еплю́, -е́пишь; *impf* **прицепля́ть**) *сов перех (ваго́н)* to couple
▸ **прицепи́ться** (*impf* **прицепля́ться**) *сов возв (перен: разг: приста́ть)* to be a pain in the neck; **прицепля́ться (~ся** *perf)* **к** +*dat* to stick to; *(перен: разг: к челове́ку)* to nag; (: **к слова́м**) to find fault with.
прича́л (-а) *м* mooring; *(пассажи́рский)* quay; *(грузово́й, ремо́нтный)* dock.
прича́л|ить (-ю, -ишь; *impf* **прича́ливать**) *сов (не)перех* to moor.
причасте́н *прил см* **прича́стный.**
прича́сти|е (-я) *ср (линг)* participle; *(рел)* communion.
причасти́ть (-щу́, -сти́шь; *impf* **причаща́ть**) *перех (рел)* to give communion to
▸ **причасти́ться** (*impf* **причаща́ться**) *сов возв (рел)* to receive communion.
прича́стн|ый *прил (линг)* participial; *(-ен, -на, -но; свя́занный):* ~ **к** +*dat* connected with.
причаща́|ть(ся) (-ю(сь)) *несов от* **причасти́ть(ся).**
причаще́ни|е (-я) *ср (рел)* Eucharist.
причащу́(сь) *сов см* **причасти́ть(ся).**
причём *союз* moreover.
причеса́ть (-ешу́, -е́шешь; *impf* **причёсывать**) *сов перех (во́лосы)* to comb, brush; **причёсывать (~** *perf)* **кого́-н** to comb *или* brush sb's hair; **причёсывать (~** *perf)* **го́лову** to comb one's hair
▸ **причеса́ться** (*impf* **причёсываться**) *сов возв* to comb *или* brush one's hair.
причёс|ка (-ки; *gen pl* -ок) *ж* hairstyle.
причёсыва|ть(ся) (-ь(сь)) *несов от* **причеса́ть(ся).**
причешу́(сь) *итп сов см* **причеса́ть(ся).**
причи́н|а (-ы) *ж* cause, reason; **по ~е** +*gen* on account of.
причин|и́ть (-ю́, -и́шь; *impf* **причиня́ть**) *сов перех* to cause.
причи́сл|ить (-ю, -ишь; *impf* **причисля́ть**) *сов перех:* ~ **кого́-н/что-н к** +*dat (отнести́ к)* to number sb/sth among.
причита́ни|е (-я) *ср* lamentation; *(похоро́нные)* keening; **сва́дебные ~я** old Russian wedding ritual where women wail and lament the bride.
причита́|ть (-ю) *несов неперех (на похорона́х)* to wail
▸ **причита́ться** *несов возв:* **мне ~ется 10 рубле́й** I am owed 10 roubles; **с Вас ~ется 10 рубле́й** you owe 10 roubles.
причу́д|а (-ы) *ж* whim.
причу́дли|вый (-, -а, -о) *прил (узо́р)* intricate.
пришварт|ова́ть (-ую) *сов от* **швартова́ть.**
прише́й(те) *сов см* **приши́ть.**
пришёл(ся) *сов см* **прийти́(сь).**
пришёл|ец (-ьца) *м* stranger.

прише́стви|е (-я) *ср* (*РЕЛ*) advent.
приши́бленный *прил* crestfallen.
приши́|ть (-ью, -ьёшь; *imper* **-е́й(те)**, *impf* **пришива́ть**) *сов перех* to sew on; (*перен: разг*): ~ кому́-н что́-н to pin sth on sb.
пришла́ *итп сов см* **прийти́**.
при́шлый *прил* (*человек*) strange; (*кошка*) stray.
пришлю́ *итп сов см* **присла́ть**.
пришпо́р|ить (-ю, -ишь; *impf* **пришпо́ривать**) *сов перех* to spur.
пришью́ *итп сов см* **приши́ть**.
прищем|и́ть (-лю́, -йшь; *impf* **прищемля́ть**) *сов перех* to catch.
прище́п|ка (-ки; *gen pl* -ок) *ж* clothes peg (*BRIT*), clothespin (*US*).
прищу́р|ить (-ю, -ишь; *impf* **прищу́ривать**) *сов перех* (*глаза*) to screw up
► **прищу́риться** (*impf* **прищу́риваться**) *сов возв* to screw up one's eyes.
прию́т (-а) *м* shelter; (*для сирот*) orphanage.
приют|и́ть (-чу́, -ти́шь) *сов перех* to shelter
► **приюти́ться** *сов возв* to take shelter.
прия́тел|ь (-я) *м* friend.
прия́тельница (-ы) *ж см* **прия́тель**.
прия́тен *прил см* **прия́тный**.
прия́тно *нареч* (*удивлён, поражён*) pleasantly ♦ *как сказ* it is nice *или* pleasant; **мне ~ э́то слы́шать** I'm glad to hear that; **о́чень ~** (*при знакомстве*) pleased to meet you.
прия́тный (-ен, -на, -но) *прил* (*встреча, пое́здка*) pleasant, enjoyable; (*разговор, вкус*) pleasant; (*человек, лицо, улыбка*) nice, pleasant.
ПРО *ж сокр* (= *противораке́тная оборо́на*) antimissile defence (*BRIT*) *или* defense (*US*) system.
про *предл* (+*acc*) about.
про- *префикс* (*in verbs*; *о действии, направленном сквозь что-н*) *indicating action through sth eg.* **прострели́ть**; (*о действии, распространяющемся на весь предмет*) *indicating action involving whole object eg.* **прогре́ть**; (*о движении мимо чего-н*) *indicating movement past sth eg.* **прохать**; (*об исчерпанности действия*) *indicating completion of action eg.* **пронумерова́ть**; (*о звучании, осуществляемом в один приём*) *indicating single occurence of sound eg.* **протруби́ть**; (*о длительном действии*) *indicating prolonged action eg.* **проработа́ть**; (*in nouns and adjectives*; *сторонник чего-н*) pro-.
проанализи́р|овать (-ую) *сов от* **анализи́ровать**.
проанноти́р|овать (-ую) *сов от* **аннота́ровать**.
про́б|а (-ы) *ж* (*испытание*) test; (*образец*) sample; (*драгоценного металла*) standard (*of precious metals*); (*клеймо*) hallmark.
пробе́г (-а) *м* (*СПОРТ: автомобильный, марафонский*) race; (*: лыжный*) run; (*АВТ*)

mileage.
пробе́га|ть (-ю) *сов неперех* to run around.
пробе|жа́ть (*как бежа́ть*; *см* **Table 20**; *impf* **пробега́ть**) *сов перех* (*бегло прочитать*) to skim; (*5 километров*) to cover ♦ *неперех* (*время, годы*) to pass; (*миновать бегом*): ~ **ми́мо** +*gen* to run past; (*появиться и исчезнуть*): ~ **по** +*dat* (*шум, дрожь*) to run through; (*по земле*) to run along; **пробега́ть** (~ *perf*) **че́рез** +*acc* to run through
► **пробежа́ться** *сов возв* to run.
пробе́ж|ка (-ки; *gen pl* -ек) *ж* run.
пробе́л (-а) *м* (*также перен*) gap.
пробер|у́(сь) *итп сов см* **пробра́ть(ся)**.
пробива́|ть(ся) (-ю(сь)) *несов от* **проби́ть(ся)**.
пробивно́й *прил* (*сила снаряда*) penetrating; (*перен: разг: человек*) pushy.
пробира́|ть(ся) (-ю(сь)) *несов от* **пробра́ть(ся)**.
проби́р|ка (-ки; *gen pl* -ок) *ж* test-tube.
проб|и́ть (-ью, -ьёшь) *сов от* **бить** ♦ (*impf* **пробива́ть**) *перех* (*дыру, отверстие*) to knock; (*крышу, стену*) to make a hole in; (*разг: с трудом добиться*) to force through; **пробива́ть** (~ *perf*) **себе́ доро́гу** (*перен*) to carve one's way
► **проби́ться** (*impf* **пробива́ться**) *сов возв* (*прорваться*) to fight one's way through; (*растения, ростки*) to push through *или* up; (*разг: прожить с трудом*) to struggle through.
про́б|ка (-ки; *gen pl* -ок) *ж* (*no pl*; *древесной коры*) cork; (*для закупоривания*) cork, stopper; (*перен: транспортная*) jam; (*ЭЛЕК*) fuse.
пробле́м|а (-ы) *ж* problem.
проблема́тик|а (-и) *ж собир* problems *мн*.
проблемати́чен *прил см* **проблемати́чный**.
проблемати́ческий (-ая, -ое, -ие) *прил* problematic(al).
проблемати́чный (-ен, -на, -но) *прил* = **проблемати́ческий**.
про́блеск (-а) *м* (*блеск*) ray; (*таланта, понимания*) hint; ~ **наде́жды** ray of hope.
про́бный *прил* (*образец, экземпляр*) trial *опред*; (*полёт*) test *опред*; ~ **ка́мень** (*перен*) touchstone.
про́б|овать (-ую; *perf* **попро́бовать**) *несов перех* (*мотор*) to test; (*пирог, вино*) to taste; (+*infin*; *пытаться*) to try to do.
прободе́ни|е (-я) *ср* (*МЕД*) perforation.
пробо́ин|а (-ы) *ж* hole.
пробо́к *сущ см* **про́бка**.
проболта́|ться (-юсь) *сов возв* (*разг: проговориться*) to blab; (: *пробездельничать*) to loaf about.
пробо́р (-а) *м* parting (*of hair*).
пробра́|ть (-еру́, -ерёшь; *impf* **пробира́ть**) *сов перех* (*разг: страх*) to strike; (*дрожь*) to come over; (*мороз*) to chill
► **пробра́ться** (*impf* **пробира́ться**) *сов возв* (*с трудом пройти*) to fight one's way through;

(тихо пройти) to steal past *или* through.

пробу́дешь *итп сов см* **пробы́ть**.

пробуди́ть (-ужу́, -у́дишь; *impf* **пробужда́ть** *или* **буди́ть**) *сов перех (массы, людей)* to rouse, stir; *(перен: желания, чувства)* to arouse

▸ **пробуди́ться** *(impf* **пробужда́ться**) *сов возв (проснуться)* to awake, wake up; *(перен: появиться)* to appear.

пробу́ду *итп сов см* **пробы́ть**.

пробу́дь(те) *сов см* **пробы́ть**.

пробужда́ть(ся) (-ю(сь)) *несов от* **пробуди́ть(ся)**.

пробужде́ни|е (-я) *ср (ото сна)* waking up; *(сознания, чувств)* awakening.

пробужу́(сь) *сов см* **пробуди́ть(ся)**.

пробура́в|ить (-лю, -ишь) *сов от* **бура́вить**.

пробур|и́ть (-ю́, -и́шь) *сов от* **бури́ть**.

пробурча́|ть (-у́, -и́шь) *сов от* **бурча́ть**.

пробы́ть (*как быть*; *см* Table 21) *сов неперех (прожить)* to stay, remain; *(провести)* to go; **он пробы́л 10 лет учи́телем** he was a teacher for 10 years.

пробью́(сь) *итп сов см* **проби́ть(ся)**.

прова́л (-а) *м (в почве, в стене)* hole; *(перен: неудача)* flop; *(: памяти)* failure.

провал|и́ть (-алю́, -а́лишь; *impf* **прова́ливать**) *сов перех (крышу, пол)* to cause to collapse; *(разг: перен: дело, затею)* to make a mess of; *(: студента)* to fail

▸ **провали́ться** *(impf* **прова́ливаться**) *сов возв (упасть)* to fall; *(рухнуть)* to collapse; *(разг: перен: студент, попытка)* to fail; *(: исчезнуть)* to vanish; **как сквозь зе́млю ~али́лся** he disappeared into thin air.

прова|ри́ть (-рю́, -́ришь; *impf* **прова́ривать**) *сов перех* to boil *(for a long time)*.

прове́да|ть (-ю; *impf* **прове́дывать**) *сов перех (навестить)* to call on; *(разг: узнать)* to find out.

проведе́ни|е (-я) *ср (урока)* taking; *(репетиции, конкурса)* holding; *(границы)* drawing; *(линии передачи)* installation; *(машины)* piloting.

проведу́ *итп сов см* **провести́**.

прове́дыва|ть (-ю) *несов от* **прове́дать**.

пров|езти́ (-езу́, -езёшь; *pt* -ёз, -езла́, -езло́, *impf* **провози́ть**) *сов перех (везя, доставить)*: ~ **по** +*dat*/**ми́мо** +*gen*/**че́рез** +*acc* to take along/past/across; *(контрабанду, наркотики)* to smuggle.

провентили́р|овать (-ую) *сов от* **вентили́ровать**.

прове́р|ить (-ю, -ишь; *impf* **проверя́ть**) *сов перех* to check; *(выполнение правил)* to monitor; *(знание ученика, двигатель)* to test

▸ **прове́риться** *(impf* **проверя́ться**) *сов возв (у врача)* to get a check-up.

прове́р|ка (-ки; *gen pl* -ок) *ж (см глаг)* check;

monitoring; test.

провер|ну́ть (-у́, -ёшь; *impf* **провора́чивать**) *сов перех (кран, винт)* to crank; *(перен: разг: дело, обмен кварти́ры)* to rush through.

прове́рок *прил см* **прове́рка**.

проверя́ющий (-его; *decl like adj*) *м* examiner.

проверя́|ть(ся) (-ю(сь)) *несов от* **прове́рить(ся)**.

пров|ести́ (-еду́, -едёшь; *pt* -ёл, -ела́, -ело́, *impf* **проводи́ть**) *сов перех (черту, границу)* to draw; *(дорогу, ход итп)* to build; *(линию передачи)* to install; *(план, реформу)* to implement; *(урок, репетицию)* to hold; *(операцию)* to carry out; *(детство, день)* to spend; *(обмануть)* to trick; **проводи́ть** (~ *perf)* **ми́мо** +*gen*/**че́рез** +*acc (людей, экскурсантов)* to take past/across; **проводи́ть** (~ *perf)* **что-н в жизнь** to put sth into effect.

прове́тр|ить (-ю, -ишь; *impf* **прове́тривать**) *сов перех* to air

▸ **прове́триться** *(impf* **прове́триваться**) *сов возв (комната, оде́жда)* to have an airing; *(человек: на свежем воздухе)* to take a breath of fresh air; *(перен: разг)* to have a change of scene.

прове́|ять (-ю) *сов от* **ве́ять**.

провиа́нт (-а) *м* provisions *мн*.

прови́де́ни|е (-я) *ср* foresight.

провиде́ни|е (-я) *ср (РЕЛ)* Providence.

провин|и́ться (-ю́сь, -и́шься) *сов возв*: ~ (**в** +*prp*) to be guilty (of).

прови́нность (-и) *ж* fault.

провинциа́л (-а) *м* provincial.

провинциа́л|ка (-ки; *gen pl* -ок) *ж см* **провинциа́л**.

провинциа́льный *прил* provincial.

прови́нци|я (-и) *ж* province; *(отдалённая местность)* provinces *мн*.

про́вод (-а; *nom pl* -а́) *м* cable.

проводи́мость (-и) *ж* conductivity.

провод|и́ть (-ожу́, -о́дишь) *несов от* **провести́**
♦ *(impf* **провожа́ть)** *сов перех* to see off; *(сына: в армию)* to send off; **провожа́ть** (~ *perf)* **глаза́ми/взгля́дом кого́-н** to follow sb with one's eyes/gaze.

прово́д|ка (-ки; *gen pl* -ок) *ж (ЭЛЕК)* wiring.

проводни́к (-а́) *м (в горах)* guide; *(в поезде)* steward *(BRIT)* *или* porter *(US)*; *(ЭЛЕК)* conductor; *(перен: идей, политики итп)* vehicle.

проводни́ц|а (-ы) *ж (в поезде)* stewardess *(BRIT)* *или* porter *(US)*.

прово́док *сущ см* **прово́дка**.

про́вод|ы (-ов) *мн (прощания)* send-off *ед*.

провожа́тый (-ого; *decl like adj*) *м* escort.

провожа́|ть (-ю) *несов от* **проводи́ть**.

провожу́ *(не)сов см* **проводи́ть**.

провожу́(сь) *несов см* **провози́ть(ся)**.

провóз (-а) *м* (*багажа*) transport; (*незаконный*) smuggling.

провозгла|сить (-шý, -сишь; *impf* **провозглашáть**) *сов перех* to proclaim; **провозглашáть** (~ *perf*) **когó-н/чтó-н** +*instr* to hail sb/sth as.

провозглашéни|е (-я) *ср* proclamation.

провозглашý *сов см* **провозгласить**.

пров|озить (-ожý, -óзишь) *несов от* **провезти**

▸ **провозиться** *сов возв* (*разг*) to muck around *или* about; **~ся** (*perf*) **с кем-н/чем-н** to spend time with sb/on sth.

провокáтор (-а) *м* agent provocateur.

провокациóнный *прил* provocative.

провокáци|я (-и) *ж* provocation; **поддавáться** (**поддáться** *perf*) **на ~ю** to give in to provocation.

прóволок|а (-и) *ж* wire.

проволóч|ка (-ки; *gen pl* -ек) *ж* (*разг*) hold-up.

провора́чива|ть (-ю) *несов от* **провернýть**.

провóр|ный (-ен, -на, -но) *прил* agile.

провор|овáться (-ýюсь; *impf* **проворóвываться**) *сов возв* (*разг*) to be caught stealing.

проворó|нить (-ю, -ишь) *сов от* **воронить**.

проворч|áть (-ý, -ишь) *сов неперех* (*человек*) to grumble ♦ *перех* to mutter.

провоци́р|овать (-ую; *perf* **спровоци́ровать**) *несов перех* to provoke; **~** (**спровоци́ровать** *perf*) **когó-н/чтó-н на чтó-н** to provoke sb/sth into sth.

провя́л|ить (-ю, -ишь) *сов от* **вялить**.

прогадá|ть (-ю; *impf* **прогáдывать**) *сов неперех* (*разг*) to miscalculate.

проги́б (-а) *м* (*пола, балки*) sagging; (*место*) sag.

прогибá|ть(ся) (-ю(сь)) *несов от* **прогнýть(ся)**.

проглоти́ть (-очý, -óтишь; *impf* **проглáтывать** *или* **глотáть**) *сов перех* (*также перен*) to swallow; (*перен: разг: книгу*) to devour; **язык ~óтишь, так вкýсно** (*разг*) it's so tasty it makes your mouth water.

прогляде́ть (-жý, -дишь) *сов перех* (*ошибку, изменения*) to overlook.

прогля́|нуть (*3sg* -янет, *3pl* -я́нут) *сов неперех* (*солнце*) to peek out; **на егó лицé ~я́нула улы́бка** there was a hint of a smile on his face.

прог|нáть (-оню́, -óнишь; *pt* -нáл, -налá, -нáло, *impf* **прогоня́ть**) *сов перех* (*заставить двигаться*) to drive; (*заставить уйти*) to turn out; (*уволить*) to dismiss; (*избавиться*) to drive away.

прогнева́|ть (-лю, -йшь) *сов от* **гневить**.

прогни́|ть (*3sg* -ёт, *3pl* -ю́т, *impf* **прогнивáть**) *сов неперех* to rot through.

прогнóз (-а) *м* forecast.

прогнози́р|овать (-ую) (*не*)*сов перех* to forecast.

прогнýть (-ý, -ёшь; *impf* **прогибáть**) *сов перех*: **~ чтó-н** to cause sth to sag

▸ **прогнýться** (*impf* **прогибáться**) *сов возв* to sag.

проговор|и́ть (-ю́, -и́шь; *impf* **проговáривать**) *сов перех* (*произнести*) to utter ♦ *неперех* (*по impf*; *разговаривать*) to chat

▸ **проговори́ться** (*impf* **проговáриваться**) *сов возв* to let out a secret; **~ся** (*perf*) **о чём-н** to reveal sth.

прогого|тáть (-чý, -чешь) *сов от* **гоготáть**.

проголос|овáть (-ýю) *сов от* **голосовáть**.

прогоню́ *итп сов см* **прогнáть**.

прогоня́|ть (-ю) *несов от* **прогнáть**.

прогор|éть (-ю́, -и́шь; *impf* **прогорáть**) *сов неперех* (*дрова*) to burn through; (*перен: разг: дело*) to go bust.

прогóрклый *прил* (*масло*) rancid.

прогóркн|уть (*3sg* -ет, *3pl* -ут) *сов от* **гóркнуть**.

прогрáмм|а (-ы) *ж* programme (*BRIT*), program (*US*); (*ПОЛИТ*) manifesto; (*также*: **вещáтельная ~**) channel; (*ПРОСВЕЩ*) curriculum; (*КОМП*) program.

программи́рование (-я) *ср* (*КОМП*) programming.

программи́р|овать (-ую; *perf* **запрограмми́ровать**) *несов перех* (*КОМП*) to program.

программи́ст (-а) *м* (*КОМП*) programmer.

прогрáмм|ка (-ки; *gen pl* -ок) *ж* (*разг*: *в театре*) programme (*BRIT*), program (*US*).

прогрáммный *прил* programmed (*BRIT*), programed (*US*); (*экзамен, зачёт*) set; (*КОМП*) programming (*BRIT*), programing (*US*); **прогрáммное обеспéчение** (*КОМП*) software; **прогрáммное управлéние** (*КОМП*) programmed (*BRIT*) *или* programed (*US*) control.

прогревá|ть(ся) (-ю(сь)) *сов от* **прогрéть(ся)**.

прогремé|ть (-лю́, -йшь) *сов от* **гремéть**.

прогрéсс (-а) *м* progress.

прогресси́вный *прил* (*писатель, идеи*) progressive.

прогресси́р|овать (-ую) *несов неперех* to progress.

прогрé|ть (-ю; *impf* **прогревáть**) *сов перех* to warm up

▸ **прогрéться** (*impf* **прогревáться**) *сов возв* to warm up.

прогромыхá|ть (-ю) *сов от* **громыхáть**.

прогрохо|тáть (-чý, -чешь) *сов от* **грохотáть**.

прогры́з|ть (-ý, -ёшь; *pt* -, -ла, -ло, *impf* **прогрызáть**) *сов перех* to gnaw through.

прогудé|ть (-жý, -дишь) *сов от* **гудéть**.

прогýл (-а) *м* (*на работе*) absence; (*в школе*) truancy.

прогýлива|ть (-ю) *несов от* **прогуля́ть** ♦ *перех* (*разг: собаку*) to take

▸ **прогýливаться** *несов от* **прогуля́ться**.

прогýл|ка (-ки; *gen pl* -ок) *ж* walk; (*недалекая поездка*) trip.

прогýльщик (-а) *м* (*работник*) absentee; (*ученик*) truant.

прогýльщиц|а (-ы) *ж см* **прогýльщик**.

прогуля́ть (-ю; *impf* **прогу́ливать**) *сов перех* (*работу*) to be absent from; (*уроки*) to miss ♦ *неперех* (*no impf*) to walk

▸ **прогуля́ться** (*impf* **прогу́ливаться**) *сов возв* to go for a walk.

продава́ть(ся) (-ю́(сь)) *несов от* **прода́ть(ся)**.

продаве́ц (-ца́) *м* seller; (*в магазине*) (shop-)assistant.

прода́вить (-авлю́, -а́вишь; *impf* **прода́вливать**) *сов перех* (*стекло*) to go through; **прода́вливать** (~ *perf*) **сиде́нье сту́ла** to make the seat of a chair sag.

продавца́ *итп сущ см* **продаве́ц**.

продавщи́ца (-ы) *ж см* **продаве́ц**.

продади́м(ся) *итп сов см* **прода́ть(ся)**.

прода́жа (-и) *ж* (*дома, товара*) sale; (*торговля*) trade; **быть** (*impf*) **в ~е, поступа́ть** (**поступи́ть** *perf*) **в ~у** to be on sale.

прода́жный *прил* (*цена*) sale *опред*; (*вещь*) for sale; (-ен, -на, -но; *человек, пресса*) corrupt.

продалбли́вать (-ю) *несов от* **продолби́ть**.

прода́ть (*как дать; см* **Table 14**; *impf* **продава́ть**) *сов перех* to sell; (*перен: друга*) to betray

▸ **прода́ться** (*impf* **продава́ться**) *сов возв* (*врагам*) to sell out.

продвига́ть(ся) (-ю(сь)) *несов от* **продви́нуть(ся)**.

продвиже́ние (-я) *ср* (*по территории*) advance; (*по службе*) promotion.

продви́нуть (-у, -ешь; *impf* **продвига́ть**) *сов перех* to move; (*перен: работника*) to promote

▸ **продви́нуться** (*impf* **продвига́ться**) *сов возв* to move; (*войска*) to advance; (*перен: работник*) to be promoted; (: *работа, строительство*) to progress.

продева́ть (-ю) *несов от* **проде́ть**.

продезинфици́ровать (-ую) *сов от* **дезинфици́ровать**.

продеклами́ровать (-ую) *сов от* **деклами́ровать**.

проде́лать (-ю; *impf* **проде́лывать**) *сов перех* (*отверстие*) to make; (*работу*) to do.

проде́лка (-ки; *gen pl* -ок) *ж* trick.

проде́лывать (-ю) *несов от* **проде́лать**.

продемонстри́ровать (-ую) *сов от* **демонстри́ровать**.

проде́ну *итп сов см* **проде́ть**.

продержа́ть (-ержу́, -е́ржишь) *сов перех* (*держать*) to hold; (: *библиоте́чную кни́гу, человека*) to keep

▸ **продержа́ться** *сов возв* (*держаться*) to hold out.

продеру́сь *итп сов см* **продра́ться**.

проде́ть (-ну, -нешь; *impf* **продева́ть**) *сов перех* to thread; **продева́ть** (~ *perf*) **ни́тку в иго́лку** to thread a needle.

продикто́вать (-у́ю) *сов от* **диктова́ть**.

продира́ться (-ю́сь) *несов от* **продра́ться**.

продлева́ть (-ю) *несов от* **продли́ть**.

продле́ние (-я) *ср* (*см глаг*) extension; prolongation.

продлённый *прил*: ~ **день** (*ПРОСВЕЩ*) extended school day (*for children whose parents work late*).

продли́ть (-ю́, -и́шь; *impf* **продлева́ть**) *сов перех* (*командиро́вку, о́тпуск*) to extend; (*жизнь*) to prolong.

продли́ться (*3sg* -и́тся, *3pl* -я́тся) *сов от* **дли́ться**.

продма́г (-а) *м* (= **продово́льственный магази́н**) grocer's (shop) (*BRIT*), grocery (*US*).

продово́льственный *прил* food *опред*; **продово́льственный магази́н** grocer's (shop) (*BRIT*), grocery (*US*).

продово́льствие (-я) *ср* provisions *мн*.

продолби́ть (-лю́, -и́шь) *сов от* **долби́ть**.

продолгова́тый (-, -а, -о) *прил* elongated.

продолжа́тель (-я) *м* successor.

продолжа́ть (-ю; *perf* **продо́лжить**) *несов перех* to continue, carry on; ~ (**продо́лжить** *perf*) +*impf infin* to continue *или* carry on doing

▸ **продолжа́ться** (*perf* **продо́лжиться**) *несов возв* to continue, carry on.

продолже́ние (-я) *ср* (*борьбы, лекции*) continuation; (*романа, рассказа*) sequel; **в ~** +*gen* for the duration of.

продолжи́телен *прил см* **продолжи́тельный**.

продолжи́тельность (-и) *ж* duration; **сре́дняя ~ жи́зни** life expectancy; **продолжи́тельность жи́зни** lifespan.

продолжи́тельный (-ен, -ьна, -ьно) *прил* (*болезнь, разговор*) prolonged; (*урок*) extended.

продо́лжить(ся) (-у(сь), -ишь(ся)) *сов от* **продолжа́ть(ся)**.

продо́льный *прил* longitudinal.

продра́ться (-еру́сь, -ерёшься; *impf* **продира́ться**) *сов возв*: ~ **сквозь** +*acc* to fight one's way through.

продро́гнуть (-у, -ешь) *сов неперех* to be frozen to the bone.

продува́ть (-ю) *несов от* **проду́ть** ♦ *перех*: **сквозня́к** ~**л ко́мнату** the draught blew through the room.

проду́кт (-а) *м* product; *см та́кже* **проду́кты**.

продукти́вен *прил см* **продукти́вный**.

продукти́вность (-и) *ж* productivity; (*КОМП*) throughput.

продукти́вный (-ен, -на, -но) *прил* productive.

проду́ктовый *прил* food *опред*.

проду́кты (-ов) *мн* (*также*:~ **пита́ния**) foodstuffs *мн*.

проду́кция (-и) *ж* produce.

проду́манный (-, -на, -но) *прил* well thought-out.

проду́мать (-ю; *impf* **проду́мывать**) *сов перех*

(*действия, выступление*) to think out; (*ответ*) to consider ◆ *непереx* to think.

продýть (-ю, -ешь; *impf* **продувáть**) *сов переx* (*трубу*) to blow through; (*разг: проиграть*) to lose ◆ *безл* (+*acc*): **меня ~ло** I've caught a chill.

продырявить (-лю, -ишь) *сов переx* to make a hole in.

продюсер (-а) *м* producer.

проедá|ть (-ю) *несов от* **проéсть**.

проéдешь *итп сов см* **проéхать**.

проедúм *итп сов см* **проéсть**.

проéду(сь) *итп сов см* **проéхать(ся)**.

проедят *итп сов см* **проéсть**.

проéзд (-а) *м* (*в транспорте*) journey; (*место*) passage.

проездной *прил* (*документ*) travel *опред*; **проездной билéт** travel card.

проéздом *нареч* en route.

проезжáй(те) *сов см* **проéхать**.

проезжá|ть (-ю) *несов от* **проéхать**.

проéзжий (-ая, -ее, -ие) *прил* (*человек*) passing ◆ (-его; *decl like adj*) *м* traveller (*BRIT*), traveler (*US*); ~**ая часть** (**улицы**) road.

проéкт (-а) *м* (*дома, памятника итп*) design; (*закона, договора*) draft; (*замысел*) project.

проектú|ровать (-ую; *perf* **спроектúровать**) *несов переx* (*дом*) to design; (*perf* **запроектúровать**) *наметить*) to plan.

проектúровщик (-а) *м* designer.

проéктор (-а) *м* (*оптика*) projector.

проéкци|я (-и) *ж* (*также геом*) projection.

проéм (-а) *м* (*дверной, оконный*) aperture.

проéсть (*как* **есть**; *см* **Table 15**; *impf* **проедáть**) *сов переx* to eat through; (*разг: деньги*) to blow on food.

проéхать (*как* **éхать**; *см* **Table 19**) *сов переx* (*миновать*) to pass; (*остановку, поворот итп*) to miss ◆ (*impf* **проезжáть**) *непереx*: ~ **мúмо** +*gen*/**по** +*dat*/**чéрез** +*acc* *итп* to drive past/along/across *итп*

▶ **проéхаться** *сов возв* (*на велосипеде, на санках*) to go for a ride; (*на машине*) to go for a drive.

проéшь *сов см* **проéсть**.

прожá|рить (-ю, -ишь; *impf* **прожáривать**) *сов переx* to fry

▶ **прожáриться** (*impf* **прожáриваться**) *возв* to be well-fried.

прожгý *итп сов см* **прожéчь**.

прождá|ть (-ý, -ёшь) *сов переx* to wait a long time for.

прожёг *итп сов см* **прожéчь**.

прожéктор (-а) *м* floodlight.

прожéчь (-гý, -жёшь *итп*, -гýт; *pt* -ёг, -глá, -гло, *impf* **прожигáть**) *сов переx* (*огнём, кислотой*) to burn a hole in.

проживáни|е (-я) *ср* (*в гостинице*) stay.

проживá|ть (-ю) *несов от* **прожúть** ◆ *непереx* to live.

проживý *итп сов см* **прожúть**.

прожигá|ть (-ю) *несов от* **прожéчь** ◆ *переx*: ~

жизнь (*перен*) to live life in the fast lane.

прожúл|ка (-ки; *gen pl* -ок) *ж* vein; (*дерева*) grain.

прожúти|е (-я) *ср*: **на** ~ to live on.

прожúточный *прил*: ~ **мúнимум** minimum living wage.

прожú|ть (-вý, -вёшь) *сов непереx* (*пробыть живым*) to live; (*жить*) to spend ◆ *переx* (*деньги, состояние*) to squander.

прожóрливый (-, -а, -о) *прил* voracious.

прóз|а (-ы) *ж* prose; (*повседневность*) routine.

прозáик (-а) *м* prosaist.

прозаúческ|ий (-ая, -ое, -ие) *прил* (*произведение*) prose *опред*; (*жизнь*) prosaic.

прозвáни|е (-я) *ср* nickname.

прозвá|ть (-ову, -овёшь; *impf* **прозывáть**) *сов переx* to nickname.

прозвенé|ть (*3sg* -úт, *3pl* -ят) *сов от* **звенéть**.

прóзвищ|е (-а) *ср* nickname.

прозвучá|ть (*3sg* -úт, *3pl* -áт) *сов непереx* (*стать слышным*) to resound; (*проявиться*) to come through.

прозевá|ть (-ю) *сов от* **зевáть**.

прозимó|вать (-ую) *сов от* **зимовáть**.

прозовý *итп сов см* **прозвáть**.

прозондú|ровать (-ую) *сов от* **зондúровать**.

прозорлúвый (-, -а, -о) *прил* (*человек, ум*) perceptive; (*политика*) farsighted.

прозрá|чный (-ен, -на, -но) *прил* (*стекло, намерение*) transparent; (*воздух, вода*) clear; (*ткань, одежда*) see-through.

прозрé|ть (-ю; *impf* **прозревáть**) *сов непереx* to gain one's sight; (*перен*) to see the light.

прозывá|ть (-ю) *несов от* **прозвáть**.

прозябá|ть (-ю) *несов непереx* (*человек*) to vegetate.

проигнорú|ровать (-ую) *сов от* **игнорúровать**.

проигрá|ть (-ю; *impf* **проúгрывать**) *сов переx* to lose; (*играть*) to play ◆ *непереx* (*по impf*; *играть*) to play.

проúгрыватель (-я) *м* record player.

проúгрывать (-ю) *несов от* **проигрáть**.

проúгрыш (-а) *м* loss.

произведéни|е (-я) *ср* (*литературы, искусства*) work; (*мат*) product.

произвест|ú (-éду, -éдешь; *pt* -ёл, -елá, -елó, *impf* **производúть**) *сов переx* (*обыск, операцию*) to carry out; (*впечатление, суматоху*) to create: **производúть** (~ *perf*) **посáдку** to land; **производúть** (~ *perf*) **когó-н в офицéры/в генерáлы** to confer the rank of an officer/a general on sb.

производú|тель *прил см* **производúтельный**.

производú|тель (-я) *м* producer.

производúтельность (-и) *ж* productivity.

производú|тельный (-ен, -ьна, -ьно) *прил* (*продуктивный*) productive; **производúтельные сúлы** (*экон*) labour (*BRIT*) *или* labor (*US*) force.

произв|оди́ть (-ожу́, -о́дишь) *несов от* **произвести́** ♦ *перех (изготовля́ть)* to produce.

произво́дный *прил* derivative *опред*; **произво́дное сло́во** derivative.

произво́дственный *прил (процесс, план)* production *опред*; ~ **несча́стный слу́чай** occupational accident; **произво́дственные отноше́ния** industrial relations.

произво́дств|о (-а) *ср (товаров)* production, manufacture; *(о́трасль)* industry; *(заво́д, фа́брика)* factory; *(о́пыта)* carrying out; **сельскохозя́йственное** ~ agricultural yield; *(о́трасль)* agriculture; **промы́шленное** ~ industrial output; *(о́трасль)* industry.

произвожу́ *несов см* **производи́ть**.

произво́л (-а) *м (самовла́стие)* arbitrary rule; **оставля́ть (оста́вить** *perf)* **или броса́ть (бро́сить** *perf)* **кого́-н на** ~ **судьбы́** to leave sb in the hands of fate.

произво́л|ьный (-ен, -ьна, -ьно) *прил (свобо́дный)* free; *(no short form; СПОРТ)* freestyle *опред*; *(неоснова́тельный)* arbitrary.

произн|ести́ (-есу́, -есёшь; *pt* -ёс, -есла́, -есло́, *impf* **произноси́ть**) *сов перех (вы́говорить)* to pronounce; *(сказа́ть)* to say; **произноси́ть** (~ *perf)* **речь/тост** to make a speech/toast.

произн|оси́ть (-ошу́, -о́сишь) *несов см* **произнести́**.

произноше́ни|е (-я) *ср* pronunciation.

произношу́ *несов см* **произноси́ть**.

произойти́ (*как* **идти́**; *см* **Table 18**; *impf* **происходи́ть**) *сов непе́рех (случи́ться)* to occur; **происходи́ть** (~ *perf)* **из** +*gen* to come from.

проиллюстри́р|овать (-ую) *сов от* **иллюстри́ровать**.

проинспекти́р|овать (-ую) *сов от* **инспекти́ровать**.

проинструкти́р|овать (-ую) *сов от* **инструкти́ровать**.

проинтервью́и́р|овать (-ую) *сов от* **интервью́и́ровать**.

проинформи́р|овать (-ую) *сов от* **информи́ровать**.

про́иск|и (-ов) *мн* machinations *мн*.

проистека́|ть (*3sg* -ет, *3pl* -ют) *несов непе́рех*: ~ **из/от** +*gen* to result from.

происх|оди́ть (-ожу́, -о́дишь) *несов от* **произойти́** ♦ *непе́рех*: ~ **от/из** +*gen* to come from.

происхожде́ни|е (-я) *ср* origin; **по** ~**ю** by birth.

происхожу́ *несов см* **происходи́ть**.

происше́стви|е (-я) *ср* event; **доро́жное** ~ road accident.

пройдёшь(ся) *итп сов см* **пройти́(сь)**.

пройдо́х|а (-и) *м/ж (разг)* cad.

пройду́(сь) *итп сов см* **пройти́(сь)**.

пройму́ *итп сов см* **проня́ть**.

пройти́ (*как* **идти́**; *см* **Table 18**; *impf* **проходи́ть**) *сов непе́рех* to pass; *(расстоя́ние)* to cover; *(слух, весть итп)* to spread; *(доро́га, кана́л итп)* to stretch; *(дождь, снег)* to fall; *(состоя́ться: опера́ция, перегово́ры итп)* to go ♦ *перех (заверши́ть: пра́ктику, слу́жбу итп)* to complete; *(изучи́ть: те́му итп)* to do; **проходи́ть** (~ *perf)* **в** +*acc (в институ́т итп)* to get in

▶ **пройти́сь** (*impf* **проха́живаться**) *сов возв (по ко́мнате)* to pace; *(по па́рку)* to stroll; ~**сь** (*perf)* **на чей-н счёт** *или* **по чьему́-н а́дресу** *(разг)* to give sb a bad name.

прок (-а; *gen part* -у) *м (разг)* use.

прока́з|а (-ы) *ж* mischief; *(МЕД)* leprosy.

прока́зник (-а) *м* mischief-maker.

прока́знича|ть (-ю; *perf* **напрока́зничать**) *несов непе́рех* to get up to mischief.

прока́лыва|ть (-ю) *несов от* **проколо́ть**.

прока́пчива|ть (-ю) *несов от* **прокопти́ть**.

прока́плыва|ть (-ю) *несов от* **прокопти́ть**.

прока́т (-а) *м (телеви́зора, пала́тки итп)* hire; *(мета́лл)* rolled iron; **брать (взять** *perf)* **что-н на** ~ to hire sth; **выпуска́ть (вы́пустить** *perf)* **фильм в** ~ to release a film.

прока|ти́ть (-ачу́, -а́тишь; *impf* **прока́тывать**) *сов перех (разг: раскритикова́ть)* to pick holes in; *(: обману́ть)* to cheat ♦ *непе́рех (разг)* to whizz past; **прока́тывать** (~ *perf)* **кого́-н (на маши́не итп)** to take sb for a ride

▶ **прокати́ться** (*impf* **прока́тываться**) *сов возв (та́кже перен: гром)* to roll; *(на маши́не)* to go for a spin; *(перен: вы́стрел)* to ring out.

прока́тк|а (-и) *ж (ТЕХ)* rolling.

прока́тный *прил (произво́дство, цех)* rolling; *(пункт, пла́та)* hire.

прока́тчик (-а) *м (в цеху́)* worker (*in steel rolling mill*).

прока́тыва|ть(ся) (-ю(сь)) *несов от* **прокати́ть(ся)**.

прокачу́(сь) *сов см* **прокати́ть(ся)**.

прокипя|ти́ть (-чу́, -ти́шь) *сов перех* to boil.

проки́с|нуть (*3sg* -нет, *3pl* -нут, *pt* -, -ла, -ло) *сов от* **ки́снуть** ♦ *(impf* **прокиса́ть**) *непе́рех* to go off.

прокла́дк|а (-ки; *gen pl* -ок) *ж (де́йствие: труб)* laying out; *(: ли́ний переда́чи)* laying; *(защи́тная)* padding.

прокла́дыва|ть (-ю) *несов от* **проложи́ть**.

проклина́|ть (-ю) *несов от* **прокля́сть** ♦ *перех* to curse.

прокл|я́сть (-яну́, -янёшь; *pt* -ял, -яла́, -яло, *impf* **проклина́ть**) *сов перех* to curse.

прокля́ти|е (-я) *ср* curse.

прокля́тый *прил* damned; **рабо́тать** *(impf)* **как про́клятый** *(разг)* to work like a dog.

прокол (-a) м (*действие: шины*) puncturing; (: *нарыва*) lancing; (: *ушей*) piercing; (*отверстие: в шине*) puncture; (*в ушах*) hole; (*раза: неудача*) flop.

прок|олоть (-олю, -олешь; *impf* **прокалывать**) *сов перех* (*шину*) to puncture; (*уши*) to pierce; (*нарыв*) to lance.

прокомментировать (-ую) *сов от* **комментировать**.

прокомпостировать (-ую) *сов от* **компостировать**.

проконсультировать(ся) (-ую(сь)) *сов от* **консультировать(ся)**.

прокопать (-ю; *impf* **прокапывать**) *сов перех* (*канаву, ход*) to dig out.

прокоп|тить (-чу, -тишь) *сов от* **коптить** ♦ (*impf* **прокапчивать**) *перех* (*копотью*) to cover with soot; (*дымом*) to fill with smoke.

прокорм (-a) м feeding.

прок|ормить(ся) (-ормлю(сь), -ормишь(ся)) *сов от* **кормить(ся)**.

прокр|асться (-адусь, -адёшься; *impf* **прокрадываться**) *сов возв*: ~ в +*acc*/мимо +*gen*/через +*acc* итп to creep (*BRIT*) или sneak (*US*) in(to)/past/through итп.

прокрич|ать (-у, -ишь) *сов перех* (*выкрикнуть*) to shout out ♦ *неперех* (*ребёнок*) to сгу.

прокр|утить (-учу, -утишь; *impf* **прокручивать**) *сов перех* (*провернуть*) to turn; (*мясо*) to mince; (*КОМП*) to scroll; (*разг: фильм*) to roll; (: *пластинку, видеоплёнку*) to play; (: *деньги*) to invest illegally.

прокручивани|е (-я) *ср* (*см глаг*) turning; mincing; rolling; playing.

прокручива|ть (-ю) *несов от* **прокрутить**.

прокручу *сов см* **прокрутить**.

прокуратур|а (-ы) ж (*ЮР*) public prosecution office ♦ *собир* procurators мн.

прок|урить (-урю, -уришь; *impf* **прокуривать**) *сов перех* to fill with smoke.

прокурор (-a) м (*района, города*) procurator; (*на суде*) counsel for the prosecution; **Генеральный** ~ (*ЮР*) general procurator, attorney general (*US*).

прокурорск|ий (-ая, -ое, -ие) *прил*: ~ надзор (*ЮР*) procurator's powers мн.

прок|усить (-ушу, -усишь; *impf* **прокусывать**) *сов перех* to bite through.

пролага|ть (-ю) *несов от* **проложить**.

проламыва|ть (-ю) *несов от* **проломить**.

пролаять (-ю) *сов от* **лаять**.

пролега|ть (*3sg* -ет, *3pl* -ют) *несов от* **пролечь**.

пролеж|ать (-у, -ишь) *сов неперех* to lie.

пролезть (-у, -ешь; *impf* **пролезать**) *сов неперех* to get through; (*перен: разг: в руководство*) to worm one's way in.

пролёт (-a) м span; ~ лестницы a flight of stairs.

пролетариа́т (-a) м proletariat.

пролетарск|ий (-ая, -ое, -ие) *прил* proletarian.

проле|теть (-чу, -тишь; *impf* **пролетать**) *сов неперех* to fly; (*человек, поезд*) to fly past; (*лето, отпуск*) to fly by.

прол|ечь (*3sg* -яжет, *3pl* -ягут, *impf* **пролегать**) *сов неперех* (*дорога, тропинка*) to stretch.

пролив (-a) м strait(s) (*мн*).

пролива́|ть(ся) (-ю(сь)) *несов от* **пролить(ся)**.

проливной *прил*: ~ дождь pouring rain.

прол|ить (-ью, -ьёшь; *pt* -ил, -ила, -ило, *impf* **проливать**) *сов перех* to spill; **проливать** (~ *perf*) чью-н кровь to spill sb's blood

► **пролиться** (*impf* **проливаться**) *сов возв* to spill.

пролог (-a) м prologue (*BRIT*), prolog (*US*).

прол|ожить (-ожу, -ожишь; *impf* **прокладывать**) *сов перех* (*протянуть*) to lay; **прокладывать** (~ *perf*) что-н чем-н to interlay sth with sth; ~ (*perf*) дорогу или путь кому-н/чему-н to pave the way for sb/sth.

пролом (-a) м (*льда*) cracking; (*место*) crack.

пролома́|ть (-ю; *impf* **проламывать**) *сов перех* to break through.

прол|омить (-омлю, -омишь; *impf* **проламывать**) *сов перех* (*лёд*) to break; (*череп*) to fracture; **проламывать** (~ *perf*) дыру в чём-н to make a hole in sth.

пролью(сь) итп *сов см* **пролить(ся)**.

проляжет итп *сов см* **пролечь**.

прома́|зать (-жу, -жешь) *сов от* **мазать**.

промаршир|овать (-ую) *сов неперех* to march past.

промасл|ить (-ю, -ишь; *impf* **промасливать**) *сов перех* (*растительным маслом*) to oil; (*сливочным маслом*) to grease.

проматыва|ть (-ю) *несов от* **промотать**.

промах (-a) м miss; (*перен*) blunder; **давать** (**дать** *perf*) ~ to miss the target; (*перен*) to make a blunder.

промахн|уться (-усь, -ёшься; *impf* **промахиватся**) *сов возв* to miss; (*перен: разг*) to blunder.

промачива|ть (-ю) *несов от* **промочить**.

промашк|а (-ки; *gen pl* -ек) ж stroke of bad luck; (*упущение*) blunder.

промедлени|е (-я) *ср* delay.

промедл|ить (-ю, -ишь) *сов неперех*: ~ с +*instr* to delay.

промежут|ок (-ка) м (*пространство*) gap; (*перерыв*) break.

промежуточный *прил* (*участок, период*) intervening; (*стадия, положение*) intermediate.

промелькн|уть (-у, -ёшь) *сов неперех* to flash past; ~ (*perf*) в +*prp* (*в голове, в памяти*) to flash through.

променя́|ть (-ю; *impf* **променивать**) *сов перех*: ~ кого-н/что-н на +*acc* to prefer sb/sth to.

промёрзн|уть (-у, -ешь; *impf* **промерзать**) *сов неперех* (*комната, дом*) to be chilled through; (*человек*) to freeze.

промета́|ть (-ю) *сов от* **метать**.

промо́зглый *прил* cold and wet.
промока́тельн|ый *прил*: ~ая бума́га blotting paper.
промока́|ть (-ю) *несов от* промо́кнуть ♦ *неперех* to let water through.
промока́ш|ка (-ки; *gen pl* -ек) *ж* (*разг*) blotting paper.
промо́кн|уть (-у, -ешь; *impf* промока́ть) *сов неперех* (*одежда, ноги*) to get soaked.
промокн|у́ть (-у́, -ёшь; *impf* промока́ть) *сов перех* to blot.
промо́лв|ить (-лю, -ишь) *сов перех* to utter.
промолч|а́ть (-у́, -и́шь) *сов неперех* to say nothing.
промота́|ть (-ю; *impf* прома́тывать) *сов перех* (*разг*) to blow.
промо|чи́ть (-чу́, -́чишь; *impf* прома́чивать) *сов перех* to get wet.
промо́|ю *итп сов см* промы́ть.
промтова́рный *прил*: ~ магази́н shop selling *manufactured goods*.
промтова́р|ы (-ов) *мн* (= промы́шленные това́ры) manufactured goods *мн*.
промурлы́ка|ть (-ю) *сов от* мурлы́кать.
промч|а́ться (-у́сь, -и́шься) *сов возв* (*год, лето, жизнь*) to fly by; ~ (*perf*) ми́мо +*gen*/ че́рез +*acc* (*поезд, человек*) to fly past/through.
промыва́ни|е (-я) *ср* (*желудка*) pumping; (*глаза, раны*) bathing.
промыва́|ть (-ю) *несов от* промы́ть.
про́мыс|ел (-ла) *м* (*ремесло*) trade; охо́тничий ~ hunting; пушно́й ~ trapping; ры́бный ~ fishing; *см также* про́мыслы.
промысло́вый *прил* trading; (*рыба, зверь*) marketable.
про́мысл|ы (-ов) *мн* (*нефтяные*) fields *мн*; (*горные, соляные*) mines *мн*.
пром|ы́ть (-о́ю, -о́ешь; *impf* промыва́ть) *сов перех* (*желудок*) to pump; (*рану, глаз*) to bathe; (*золотой песок*) to pan out.
промыч|а́ть (-у́, -и́шь) *сов от* мыча́ть.
промы́шленник (-а) *м* industrialist.
промы́шленност|ь (-и) *ж* industry; лёгкая/тяжёлая ~ light/heavy industry.
промы́шленный *прил* industrial.
промышля́|ть (-ю) *несов неперех*: ~ охо́той to hunt; ~ (*impf*) ры́бой to fish; ~ (*impf*) перево́дами (*разг*) to earn a living from translation.
промя́мл|ить (-ю, -ишь) *сов от* мя́млить.
промя́ука|ть (-ю) *сов от* мя́укать.
пронаблюда́|ть (-ю) *сов от* наблюда́ть.
прон|ести́ (-есу́, -есёшь; *pt* -ёс, -есла́, -есло́, *impf* проноси́ть) *сов перех* to carry; (*тайком*) to sneak in; (*сохранить*) to preserve ♦ *безл* (*перен*) to blow over
▶ **пронести́сь** (*impf* проноси́ться) *сов возв* (*машина, пуля, бегун*) to shoot by; (*лето, годы*

итп) to fly by; (*буря, тайфун итп*) to whirl past.
пронжу́ *сов см* пронзи́ть.
пронза́|ть (-ю) *несов от* пронзи́ть.
пронзи́тельн|ый (-ен, -ьна, -ьно) *прил* piercing; (*свет, цвет*) glaring.
прон|зи́ть (-жу́, -зи́шь; *impf* пронза́ть) *сов перех* (*также перен*) to pierce.
прон|иза́ть (-ижу́, -и́жешь; *impf* прони́зывать) *сов перех* to penetrate (into).
прони́к(ся) *итп сов см* прони́кнуть(ся).
проника́|ть(ся) (-ю(сь)) *несов от* прони́кнуть(ся).
проникнове́нный (-ен, -на, -но) *прил* (*слова*) heartfelt; (*голос*) emotional.
прони́кнут|ый (-, -а, -о) *прил* (+*instr*) full of.
прони́кн|уть (-у, -ешь; *pt* -, -ла, -ло, *impf* проника́ть) *сов перех*: ~ в +*acc* to penetrate (into); (*залезть*) to break into; (*распространиться*) to spread into; (*понять*) to understand
▶ **прони́кнуться** (*impf* проника́ться) *сов возв* (+*instr*) to be filled with.
пронима́|ть (-ю) *несов от* проня́ть.
проница́тельн|ый (-ен, -ьна, -ьно) *прил* (*человек, ум*) shrewd; (*взгляд*) penetrating.
проница́|ть (-ю) *несов неперех*: ~ в +*acc* (*свет*) to penetrate (into).
прон|оси́ть(ся) (-ошу́(сь), -о́сишь(ся)) *несов от* пронести́(сь).
пронумер|ова́ть (-у́ю) *сов от* нумерова́ть.
проны́р|а (-ы) *ж* (*разг*) dodgy character.
проны́рлив|ый (-, -а, -о) *прил* (*разг*) dodgy.
прон|я́ть (-йму́, -ймёшь; *impf* пронима́ть) *сов перех* (*разг*: *подлеж*: холод) to seize; (: *музыка*) to move.
проо́браз (-а) *м* (*образец*) model; (*прототип*) prototype.
прооперир|ова́ть (-ую) *сов от* опери́ровать.
пропага́нд|а (-ы) *ж* propaganda; (*спорта*) promotion.
пропаганди́р|овать (-ую) *несов перех* (*политическое учение*) to spread propaganda about; (*знаний, спорт*) to promote.
пропаганди́ст (-а) *м* propagandist.
пропаганди́стск|ий (-ая, -ое, -ие) *прил* (*шумиха, кампания*) propagandist *опред*.
пропада́|ть (-ю) *несов от* пропа́сть ♦ *неперех* (*разг*) to stay for a long time; он вечера́ми ~ет на рабо́те he spends all his evenings at work.
про́падом *нареч*: пропади́ ~ (*разг*) to hell with it.
пропаду́ *итп сов см* пропа́сть.
пропа́ж|а (-и) *ж* (*денег, документов*) loss; (*то, что пропало*) lost object.
пропа́лыва|ть (-ю) *несов от* прополо́ть.
про́паст|ь (-и) *ж* precipice; (*перен*: *во взглядах*) abyss; (*no pl*; *разг*) masses *мн*.

проп|а́сть (-аду́, -адёшь; *impf* **пропада́ть**) *сов непepex* to disappear; *(деньги, письмо)* to go missing; *(аппетит, голос, слух)* to go; *(усилия, билет в театр)* to be wasted: *(погибнуть)* to die; **пропада́ть** (~ *perf*) **без вести** *(человек)* to go missing.

проп|аха́ть (-ашу́, -а́шешь; *impf* **пропа́хивать**) *сов перех* to plough (*BRIT*), plow (*US*).

пропа́х|нуть (-ну, -нешь; *pt* -, -ла, -ло) *сов непepex* (+*instr*) to become filled with the smell of.

пропашу́ *итп сов см* **пропаха́ть**.

пропа́щий (-ая, -ее, -ие) *прил* (*разг: безнадёжный*) hopeless; *(долго не приходивший)* long-lost: **э́ти де́ньги ~ие** *(разг)* that money is lost for good.

пропе́й(те) *сов см* **пропи́ть**.

пропёк(ся) *итп сов см* **пропе́чь(ся)**.

пропека́|ть(ся) (-ю(сь)) *несов от* **пропе́чь(ся)**.

пропеку́(сь) *итп сов см* **пропе́чь(ся)**.

проп|е́ть (-ою́, -оёшь) *сов от* **петь** ♦ *перех* (*петь*) to sing.

проп|е́чь (-еку́, -ечёшь *итп*, -еку́т; *pt* -ёк, -екла́, -екло́, *impf* **пропека́ть**) *сов перех* to bake
▸ **пропе́чься** (*impf* **пропека́ться**) *сов возв* to be well-baked.

пропива́|ть (-ю) *несов от* **пропи́ть**.

проп|или́ть (-илю́, -и́лишь; *impf* **пропи́ливать**) *сов перех* to saw through.

проп|иса́ть (-ишу́, -и́шешь; *impf* **пропи́сывать**) *сов перех* (*человека*) to register; *(лекарство)* to prescribe; *(статью, письмо)* to write
▸ **прописа́ться** *сов возв* to register.

пропи́ск|а (-и) *ж* (*в городе, в доме*) registration.

прописн|о́й *прил* (*общеизвестный*) commonplace; **~а́я и́стина** truism; **прописна́я бу́ква** capital letter.

пропи́сыва|ть (-ю) *несов от* **прописа́ть**.

про́пис|ь (-и) *ж* (*ПРОСВЕЩ*) writing samples *мн*.

про́писью *нареч* in full; **писа́ть** (**написа́ть** *perf*) **су́мму ~** to write out a sum *или* amount in words.

пропита́ни|е (-я) *ср* food.

пропита́|ть (-ю; *impf* **пропи́тывать**) *сов перех* (*смочить*) to soak; *(насытить: бумагу)* to saturate; *(: комнату, воздух)* to fill
▸ **пропита́ться** (*impf* **пропи́тываться**) *сов возв*: **~ся чем-н** *(водой)* to be soaked in sth; *(запахом: воздух)* to be filled with sth; *(: одежда)* to be saturated with sth.

пропи́тк|а (-и; *gen pl* -ок) *ж* (*ткани, дерева*) soaking; *(водонепроницаемая)* impregnation; *(ромовая)* flavouring.

пропи́тыва|ть(ся) (-ю(сь)) *несов от* **пропита́ть(ся)**.

проп|и́ть (-ью́, -ьёшь; *pt* -и́л, -ила́, -и́ло, *imper* **пропе́й(те)**, *impf* **пропива́ть**) *сов перех* (*деньги, состояние*) to squander on drink; *(талант, карьеру)* to ruin (*through drinking*); *(no impf, пить)* to drink.

пропихн|у́ть (-у́, -ёшь) *сов перех* (*разг: в дверь итп*) to shove; *(: в университет итп*) to push.

пропишу́(сь) *итп сов см* **прописа́ть(ся)**.

пропла́ва|ть (-ю) *сов непepex* (*человека*) to swim; *(судно)* to sail.

пропла́|кать (-чу, -чешь) *сов непepex* to cry; **~** (*perf*) **все глаза́** to cry one's eyes out.

проплута́|ть (-ю) *сов непepex* to wander.

пропл|ы́ть (-ыву́, -ывёшь; *impf* **проплыва́ть**) *сов непepex* (*человек*) to swim; *(: миновать)* to swim past; *(судно)* to sail; *(: миновать)* to sail past; *(перен: птица, облака)* to sail by *или* past; *(: воспоминания, мысли итп*) to flash past.

пропове́дник (-а) *м* (*РЕЛ*) preacher; *(перен: убеждений, теории)* advocate.

пропове́дниц|а (-ы) *ж см* **пропове́дник**.

пропове́д|овать (-ую) *несов перех* (*РЕЛ*) to preach; *(идею)* to advocate.

про́повед|ь (-и) *ж* (*РЕЛ*) preaching; *(идей)* endorsement; *(речь)* sermon.

пропо́йц|а (-ы) *м* (*разг*) soak.

прополя́скива|ть (-ю) *несов от* **прополоска́ть**.

прополз|ти́ (-у́, -ёшь; *pt* -, -ла́, -ло́) *сов непepex*: **~ по** +*dat*/**в** +*acc итп* (*насекомое, человек*) to crawl along/in(to) *итп*; *(змея)* to slither along/in (to) *итп*.

пропо́лис (-а) *м* propolis.

пропо́лк|а (-и; *gen pl* -ок) *ж* weeding.

прополоска́|ть (-ю; *impf* **прополя́скивать** *или* **полоска́ть**) *сов перех* to rinse (out); **прополя́скивать** *или* **полоска́ть** (~ *perf*) **го́рло** to gargle.

проп|оло́ть (-олю́, -о́лешь; *impf* **пропя́лывать** *или* **поло́ть**) *сов перех* (*грядку итп*) to weed.

пропорциона́лен *прил см* **пропорциона́льный**.

пропорциона́льность (-и) *ж* proportion.

пропорциона́льный (-ен, -ьна, -ьно) *прил* (*фигура, тело*) well-proportioned; *(развитие, распределение)* proportional; **пропорциона́льное представи́тельство** proportional representation.

пропо́рци|я (-и) *ж* proportion.

пропоте́|ть (-ю; *impf* **пропотева́ть**) *сов непepex* to sweat profusely; *(пропитаться потом)* to be soaked with sweat.

пропою́ *итп сов см* **пропе́ть**.

про́пуск (-а) *м* (*действие: в зал, через границу итп*) admission; *(: в школе)* non-attendance; *(в тексте, в изложении)* gap; *(неявка: на работу, в школу)* absence; *(nom pl* -а́; *документ)* pass.

пропуска́|ть (-ю) *несов от* **пропусти́ть** ♦ *перех* (*чернила, свет итп*) to let through; *(воду, холод)* to let in.

проп|усти́ть (-ущу́, -у́стишь; *impf* **пропуска́ть**) *сов перех* to miss; *(дать дорогу, обслужить)* to admit; *(разрешить)* to allow; *(заставить пройти)* to put through; *(выпустить)* to miss out; **пропуска́ть** (~ *perf*) **кого́-н че́рез грани́цу** to let sb across the border; **пропуска́ть** (~ *perf*) кого-н вперёд to let sb go ahead.

пропылесо́с|ить (-ю, -ишь) *сов от* **пылесо́сить**.

пропыл|и́ться (-ю́сь, -и́шься) *сов возв* to be full of dust.

пропью́ *итп сов см* **пропи́ть**.

прора́б (-а) *м* (= производи́тель рабо́т) foreman (*мн* foremen).

прорабо́та|ть (-ю; *impf* **прораба́тывать**) *сов непереx* to work ♦ *переx* (учебник, статью, урок) to study in detail; (*разг*: критиковать) to rip into.

прор|асти́ (*3sg* -асте́т, *3pl* -асту́т, *pt* -о́с, -осла́, -осло́, *impf* **прораста́ть**) *сов непереx* (семена) to germinate; (трава) to sprout.

про́рв|а (-ы) *ж* (*разг*: очень много) heaps *мн*, masses *мн*; (: о человеке) pig.

прорв|а́ть (-у́, -ёшь; *pt* -а́л, -ала́, -а́ло, *impf* **прорыва́ть**) *сов переx* (одежду, сумку) to tear; (плотину) to burst; (оборону, фронт) to break through ♦ *безл* (+*acc*; *перен*) to explode; наконе́ц его́ ~а́ло (*перен*) he finally exploded

► **прорва́ться** (*impf* **прорыва́ться**) *сов возв* (карман, сумка) to tear; (плотина, шарик) to burst; (гнев, раздражение) to erupt; (горе) to break out; **прорыва́ться** (~ся *perf*) **в** +*acc* to burst in(to).

прореаги́р|овать (-ую) *сов от* **реаги́ровать**.

проре|ди́ть (-жу́, -ди́шь; *impf* **проре́живать**) *сов* (грядки, всходы) to thin out.

проре́|зать (-жу, -жешь) *сов от* **ре́зать** ♦ (*impf* **проре́зывать**) *переx* to cut through; (резать: мясо, рыбу итп) to cut; (: овощи, фрукты итп) to chop

► **проре́заться** *сов от* **ре́заться** ♦ (*impf* **проре́зываться**) *возв* (появиться: зубы) to come through; (: листья) to come out.

прорези́н|ить (-ю, -ишь; *impf* **прорези́нивать**) *сов переx* to cover with rubber.

прорезн|о́й *прил*: ~ карма́н slit pocket; ~а́я петля́ buttonhole.

проре́зыва|ть(ся) (-ю(сь)) *несов от* **проре́зать(ся)**.

про́рез|ь (-и) *ж* (на ткани) slit; (на прицеле орудия) aperture.

проре́ктор (-а) *м* vice-principal.

прорепети́р|овать (-ую) *сов от* **репети́ровать**.

прорефери́р|овать (-ую) *сов от* **рефери́ровать**.

проре́х|а (-и) *ж* (дыра) tear; (*разг*: недостаток) shortcoming.

прорецензи́р|овать (-ую) *сов от* **рецензи́ровать**.

проржа́ве|ть (*3sg* -ет, *3pl* -ют) *сов непереx* to rust through.

прорица́ни|е (-я) *ср* prophecy.

прорица́тел|ь (-я) *м* prophet.

прорица́тельниц|а (-ы) *ж см* **прорица́тель**.

прорица́|ть (-ю) *несов переx* to prophesy.

проро́к (-а) *м* (*РЕЛ, перен*) prophet.

прор|они́ть (-оню́, -о́нишь) *сов переx* (сказать) to utter.

проро́с *итп сов см* **прорасти́**.

проро́ческ|ий (-ая, -ое, -ие) *прил* (сон, слова, дар) prophetic.

проро́честв|о (-а) *ср* prophecy.

проро́ч|ить (-у, -ишь; *perf* **напроро́чить**) *несов переx* to predict.

проро́ю *итп сов см* **проры́ть**.

прор|уби́ть (-ублю́, -у́бишь; *impf* **проруба́ть**) *сов переx* (стену, лёд, гору) to make a hole in; **проруба́ть** (~ *perf*) **про́секу в лесу́** to make a clearing in a forest.

про́руб|ь (-и) *ж* ice-hole.

проры́в (-а) *м* (фронта) break-through; (плотины) bursting; (прорванное место) breach.

прорыва́|ть(ся) (-ю(сь)) *несов от* **прорва́ть(ся)**.

прор|ы́ть (-о́ю, -о́ешь; *impf* **прорыва́ть**) *сов переx* (прокопать) to dig.

прос|ади́ть (-ажу́, -а́дишь; *impf* **проса́живать**) *сов переx* (*разг*: истратить) to blow.

проса́лива|ть (-ю) *несов от* **просоли́ть**.

проса́чива|ться (*3sg* -ется, *3pl* -ются) *несов от* **просочи́ться**.

просверл|и́ть (-ю́, -и́шь; *impf* **просверливать** или **сверли́ть**) *сов переx* (отверстие) to bore, drill.

просве́т (-а) *м* (в тучах, в облаках) break; (в заборе, в занавесе) crack; (*перен*: в тяжёлой ситуации) light at the end of the tunnel.

просвети́тел|ь (-я) *м* person who *enlightens others about progressive ideas*.

просвети́тельниц|а (-ы) *ж см* **просвети́тель**.

просвети́тельный *прил* enlightening.

просве|ти́ть (-щу́, -ти́шь; *impf* **просвеща́ть**) *сов переx* to enlighten; (-чу́, -ти́шь; *impf* **просве́чивать**; лёгкие) to x-ray

► **просве|ти́ться** ♦ (-щу́сь, -ти́шься; *impf* **просвеща́ться**) *сов возв* to enlighten o.s.

просветле́ни|е (-я) *ср* (ясность) lucidity.

просветлённый *прил* lucid.

просветле́|ть (-ю) *сов от* **светле́ть**.

просве́чива|ть (-ю) *несов от* **просвети́ть** ♦ *непереx* (солнце) to shine through; (небо) to be visible through; (ткань) to let light through.

просвечу́ *сов см* **просвети́ть**.

просвеща́|ть(ся) (-ю(сь)) *несов от* **просвети́ть(ся)**.

просвеще́ни|е (-я) *ср* education; **Министе́рство** ~**я** ≈ Department of Education.

просвещённый (-, -на, -но) *прил* educated.

просвещу́(сь) *сов см* **просвети́ть(ся)**.

просвир|а́ (-ы́) *ж* (*РЕЛ*) communion bread, Host.

просви|сте́ть (-щу́, -сти́шь) *сов от* **свисте́ть** ♦

(*impf* **просви́стывать**) *перех* (*мотив, песню*) to whistle (through) ♦ *неперех* (*пуля, снаряд*) to whistle past.

про́седь (-и) *ж* grey (*BRIT*) *или* gray (*US*) streak.

просе́ивани|е (-я) *ср* (*муки, песка*) sifting.

просе́ива|ть (-ю) *несов от* **просе́ять**.

про́се|ка (-и) *ж* (*в лесу*) clearing.

просёл|ок (-ка) *м* dirt-track.

просёлочн|ый *прил*: ~*ая доро́га* dirt-track.

просе́я|ть (-ю; *impf* **просе́ивать**) *сов перех* (*муку, песок*) to sift.

просигнализи́р|овать (-ую) *сов от* **сигнализи́ровать**.

просигна́л|ить (-ю, -ишь) *сов от* **сигна́лить**.

просиде́|ть (-жу́, -ди́шь; *impf* **проси́живать**) *сов неперех* (*сидеть*) to sit; (*пробыть*) to stay.

проси́тельный *прил* pleading.

про|си́ть (-шу́, -сишь; *perf* **попроси́ть**) *несов перех* to ask; (*приглашать*) to invite; **~шу́ Вас!** if you please!; ~ **попроси́ть** *perf*) **кого́-н о чём-н**/+*infin* to ask sb for sth/to do; ~ (**попроси́ть** *perf*) **кого́-н за кого́-н** to ask sb a favour (*BRIT*) *или* favor (*US*) on behalf of sb

▶ **проси́ться** (*perf* **попроси́ться**) *несов возв* (*просить разрешения*) to ask permission; **сло́во так и** ~**ся** (*impf*) **с языка́** to have a word on the tip of one's tongue; **её лицо́ про́сится на карти́ну** her face was crying out to be painted.

просия́|ть (-ю) *сов неперех* (*солнце*) to begin to shine; (*радуга*) to appear; (*перен: человек*) to beam; (: *лицо*) to light up.

проска|ка́ть (-чу́, -чешь) *сов неперех* (*человек*) to hop; ~ (*perf*) **че́рез/сквозь** +*acc* (*лошадь*) to gallop across/through; (*олень, заяц*) to bound across *или* by/through.

проска́кива|ть (-ю) *несов от* **проскочи́ть**.

проска́льзыва|ть (-ю) *несов от* **проскользну́ть**.

проскачу́ *итп сов см* **проскака́ть**.

проскво|зи́ть (*3sg* -зи́т, *3pl* -зя́т) *сов безл* (+*acc*): **меня́** ~**зи́ло** I caught a chill.

просклоня́|ть (-ю) *сов от* **склоня́ть**.

проскользн|у́ть (-у́, -ёшь; *impf* **проска́льзывать**) *сов неперех* (*монета*) to slide in; (*человек*) to slip in; (*перен: сомнение, страх*) to creep in.

проско|чи́ть (-чу́, -о́чишь; *impf* **проска́кивать**) *сов неперех* (*проскользнуть*) to slide in; (*пройти, проехать*): ~ **в** +*acc*/**ми́мо** +*gen* *итп* to race in(to)/past *итп*; (*проникнуть*): ~ **в/че́рез** +*acc* to break in(to)/through.

проскуча́|ть (-ю) *сов неперех* to be bored.

просла́б|ить (*3sg* -ит, *3pl* -ят) *сов от* **сла́бить**.

просла́в|ить (-лю, -ишь; *impf* **прославля́ть**) *сов перех* (*сделать известным*) to make famous; (*impf* **прославля́ть** *или* **сла́вить**; *восхвалять*) to glorify

▶ **просла́виться** (*impf* **прославля́ться**) *сов возв* (*актёр, писатель*) to become famous; (*перен: разг: преступник*) to become notorious.

просла́вленный *прил* renowned.

просла́влю(сь) *сов см* **просла́вить(ся)**.

прославля́|ть(ся) (-ю(сь)) *несов от* **просла́вить(ся)**.

просле|ди́ть (-жу́, -ди́шь; *impf* **просле́живать**) *сов перех* (*следить глазами*) to follow; (*исследовать*) to trace ♦ *неперех*: ~ **за** +*instr* to follow; (*за выполнением приказа, за чьим-н поведением*) to monitor.

просле́д|овать (-ую) *сов неперех*: ~ (**ми́мо** +*gen*/**сквозь** +*acc*) to pass slowly (by/through).

просле́жива|ть (-ю) *несов от* **проследи́ть**.

прослежу́ *сов см* **проследи́ть**.

просле|зи́ться (-жу́сь, -зи́шься) *сов возв* to cry.

просло́|йка (-йки; *gen pl* -ек) *ж* (*слой*) layer; (*в горной породе*) stratum (*мн* strata).

прослу|жи́ть (-жу́, -у́жишь) *сов неперех* to serve; (*туфли, пальто итп*) to last.

прослу́ша|ть (-ю; *impf* **прослу́шивать**) *сов перех* to listen to; (*курс, лекции*) to attend; (*ответ, объяснение итп*) to miss; (*no impf*; *радио, музыку*) to listen to.

прослу́шива|ть (-ю) *несов от* **прослу́шать** ♦ *перех*: **их кварти́ру** ~**ют** their flat (*BRIT*) *или* apartment (*US*) is bugged.

просл|ы́ть (-ыву́, -ывёшь) *сов неперех* (+*instr*) to acquire a reputation as.

прослы́ша|ть (-у, -ишь) *сов неперех* (*разг*): ~ **о** +*prp* to hear about.

просма́лива|ть (-ю) *несов от* **просмоли́ть**.

просма́трива|ть (-ю) *несов от* **просмотре́ть**

▶ **просма́триваться** *несов возв* to be visible.

просмол|и́ть (-ю́, -и́шь; *impf* **просма́ливать**) *сов перех* to coat with tar.

просмо́тр (-а) *м* (*фильма, спектакля*) viewing; (*документов*) inspection; (*ошибка*) blunder.

просм|отре́ть (-отрю́, -о́тришь; *impf* **просма́тривать**) *сов перех* (*ознакомиться: читая*) to look through; (: *смотря*) to view; (*пропустить*) to overlook.

просн|у́ться (-у́сь, -ёшься; *impf* **просыпа́ться**) *сов возв* to wake up; (*перен: любовь, страх итп*) to be awakened.

про́с|о (-а) *ср* millet.

просо́выва|ть(ся) (-ю(сь)) *несов от* **просу́нуть(ся)**.

просо́дия (-и) *ж* prosody.

просол|и́ть (-ю́, -о́лишь; *impf* **проса́ливать**) *сов перех* to salt.

просо́х|нуть (-ну, -нешь; *pt* -, -ла, -ло, *impf* **просыха́ть**) *сов неперех* to dry out.

просоч|и́ться (*3sg* -и́тся, *3pl* -а́тся, *impf* **проса́чиваться**) *сов возв* (*также перен*) to filter through.

просп|а́ть (-лю, -и́шь; *pt* -а́л, -ала́, -а́ло) *сов неперех* (*спать*) to sleep; (*impf* **просыпа́ть**; *встать поздно*) to oversleep ♦ *перех* (*разг*: *остановку*) to sleep through.

проспе́кт (-а) *м* avenue; (*план*) draft; (*издание*) brochure.

просплю́ *сов см* **проспа́ть**.

проспо́р|ить (-ю, -ишь; *impf* проспо́ривать) *сов перех* to lose in a bet ♦ *неперех* (*no impf*; спо́рить) to argue.

проспряга́|ть (-ю) *сов от* спряга́ть.

просро́чек *сущ см* просро́чка.

просро́ч|ить (-у, -ишь; *impf* просро́чивать) *сов перех* (платёж) to be late with; (паспорт, биле́т) to let expire.

просро́ч|ка (-ки; *gen pl* -ек) *ж* (платежа́) expiry of time limit; (па́спорта, биле́та) expiry.

проста́в|ить (-лю, -ишь; *impf* проставля́ть) *сов перех* to fill in.

проста́ива|ть (-ю) *несов от* простоя́ть.

проста́к (-а́) *м* simpleton.

простега́|ть (-ю) *сов от* стега́ть.

простен|ок (-ка) *м* section of wall between windows or doors.

прост|ере́ть(ся) (*pt* -ёр(ся), -ёрла(сь), -ёрло(сь)) *сов от* простира́ть(ся).

просте́цк|ий (-ая, -ое, -ие) *прил* (*разг*) informal.

простира́|ть (-ю; *perf* простере́ть) *несов перех* (пла́ны, за́мыслы) to raise; (протя́гивать): ~ ру́ки to hold out one's hands ♦ (*impf* прости́рывать) *сов перех* (стира́ть тща́тельно) to wash thoroughly ♦ *неперех* (стира́ть) to wash

▸ простира́|ться (*perf* простере́ться) *несов возв* to extend.

простирн|у́ть (-у́, -ёшь) *сов перех* (*разг*): ~ что-н to give sth a quick wash.

прости́рыва|ть (-ю) *несов от* простира́ть.

прости́тел|ьный (-ен, -ьна, -ьно) *прил* excusable, forgivable.

проститу́т|ка (-ки; *gen pl* -ок) *ж* prostitute.

проститу́ци|я (-и) *ж* prostitution.

прост|и́ть (прощу́, прости́шь; *impf* проща́ть) *сов перех* (врага́, оши́бку итп) to forgive; проща́ть (~ *perf*) что-н кому́-н to excuse или forgive sb (for) sth; проща́ть (~ *perf*) долг кому́-н to cancel sb's debt; прости́те меня́, я был о́чень груб forgive me, I was very rude; прости́те, как пройти́ на ста́нцию? excuse me, how do I get to the station?; нет (уж) прости́те, я не согла́сен I'm sorry, but I cannot agree

▸ прост|и́ться (*impf* проща́ться) *сов возв*: ~ся с +*instr* to say goodbye to; (поки́нуть) to leave.

про́сто *нареч* (де́лать) easily; (интерпрети́ровать) simply ♦ *част* just; я зашёл ~ повида́ться I just popped in to see you; всё э́то ~ недоразуме́ние all this is simply a misunderstanding; ~ (так) for no particular reason; ~на́просто (*разг*) just.

простова́т|ый (-, -а, -о) *прил* simple-minded.

простоволо́с|ый (-, *разг*) bareheaded.

простоду́шен *прил см* простоду́шный.

простоду́ши|е (-я) *ср* ingenuousness.

простоду́ш|ный (-ен, -на, -но) *прил* ingenuous.

прост|о́й (-, -а́, -о) *прил* simple;

(незамыслова́тый, гру́бый) plain; (не тру́дный) easy, simple; (прямо́й и нецеремо́нный) unaffected; (*no short form*; обыкнове́нный) ordinary ♦ (-о́я) *м* downtime, idle time; (рабо́чих) stoppage; маши́на на ~о́е the machine is standing idle; пла́та за ~ су́дна demurrage; ~ым гла́зом with the naked eye; про́ще ~о́го (*разг*) as easy as pie; просто́е письмо́ ordinary letter; просто́й каранда́ш lead pencil; просты́е чулки́ cotton stockings.

простоква́ш|а (-и) *ж* soured milk (*type of yoghurt*).

простонаро́дный *прил* of the common people.

просто|на́ть (-ону́, -о́нешь) *сов* (*не*)*перех* to groan.

просто́р (-а) *м* expanse; (свобо́да) scope.

просто́рен *прил см* просто́рный.

просторе́чи|е (-я) *ср* common speech; э́то ~ it's a colloquial expression.

просторе́чный *прил* common.

просто́р|ный (-ен, -на, -но) *прил* roomy.

простосерде́ч|ный (-ен, -на, -но) *прил* open-hearted.

простот|а́ (-ы́) *ж* simplicity; (зада́чи) easiness, simplicity; (оде́жды, рису́нка) plainness; (хара́ктера) unaffectedness; по ~е́ душе́вной или серде́чной in all innocence.

простофи́л|я (-и) *м/ж* dimwit.

просто|я́ть (-ю́, -и́шь; *impf* проста́ивать) *сов неперех* to stand; (безде́йствуя) to stand idle; (*no impf*; просуществова́ть) to stand.

простра́н|ный (-ен, -на, -но) *прил* (подро́бный) verbose.

простра́нственный *прил* spatial.

простра́нств|о (-а) *ср* (*также* АСТРОНОМИЯ) space; (террито́рия) expanse.

прострел (-а) *м* backache.

простре́лива|ть (-ю) *несов от* прострели́ть ♦ *перех* (обстре́ливать) to cover (*with artillery fire*).

прострел|и́ть (-елю́, -е́лишь; *impf* простре́ливать) *сов перех* to shoot through.

простроч|и́ть (-очу́, -о́чишь) *сов от* строчи́ть.

просту́д|а (-ы) *ж* (МЕД) cold.

просту|ди́ть (-жу́, -у́дишь; *impf* простужа́ть) *сов перех*: ~ кого́-н to give a cold to sb; простужа́ть (~ *perf*) у́ши/го́рло to get a cold in one's ears/throat

▸ просту|ди́ться (*impf* простужа́ться) *сов возв* to catch a cold.

просту́дный *прил* cold-related.

просту́ж|енный (-, -а, -о) *прил*: ребёнок просту́жен the child has got a cold; у Вас ~ го́лос you sound as if you've got a cold.

простужу́(сь) *сов см* простуди́ть(ся).

просту|пи́ть (*3sg* -у́пит, *3pl* -у́пят, *impf*

проступа́ть) *сов непepex* (*пот, пятна*) to come through; (*очертания*) to appear.

просту́п|ок (-ка) *м* misconduct; (*ЮР*) misdemeanour (*BRIT*), misdemeanor (*US*).

простыва́ть (-ю) *несов от* **просты́ть**.

просты́ну *итп сов см* **просты́ть**.

простын|я́ (-й; *nom pl* **про́стыни**, *gen pl* **просты́нь**, *dat pl* **-я́м**) *ж* sheet.

просты́ть (-ну, -нешь; *impf* **простыва́ть**) *сов непepex* (*разг*) to catch a cold; **его́ и след ~л** (*разг*) he disappeared without a trace.

просу́н|уть (-у, -ешь; *impf* **просо́вывать**) *сов перех*: **~ сквозь/в** +*acc итп* to push through/in (to) *итп*

▶ **просу́нуться** (*impf* **просо́вываться**) *сов возв* (*разг*): **в дверь/в окно́ ~улась голова́** a head came round the door/appeared at the window.

просуши́ть (-ушу́, -у́шишь; *impf* **просу́шивать**) *сов перех* to dry.

просуществова́ть (-у́ю) *сов непepex* to exist.

просфор|а́ (-ы́) *ж* (*РЕЛ*) communion bread, Host.

просчёт (-а) *м* (*счёт*) counting; (*ошибка: в подсчёте*) error; (*: в действиях*) miscalculation.

просчита́ть (-ю; *impf* **просчи́тывать**) *сов перех* (*считать*) to count; (*ошибиться*) to miscount

▶ **просчита́ться** (*impf* **просчи́тываться**) *сов возв* (*при счёте*) to miscount; (*в планах, в предположениях*) to miscalculate; **мы ~лись на сто рубле́й** we are out by one hundred roubles.

просы́п|ать (-лю, -лешь; *impf* **просыпа́ть**) *сов перех* to spill

▶ **просы́паться** (*impf* **просыпа́ться**) *сов возв* to spill.

просыпа́ть (-ю) *несов от* **проспа́ть**, **просы́пать**

▶ **просыпа́ться** *несов от* **просну́ться**, **просы́паться**.

просы́плю(сь) *итп сов см* **просы́пать(ся)**.

просыха́ть (-ю) *сов от* **просо́хнуть**.

про́сьб|а (-ы) *ж* request; **выполня́ть (вы́полнить** *perf*) **~у** to fulfil a request; **обраща́ться (обрати́ться** *perf*) **к кому́-н с ~ой** to make a request to sb.

прота́лин|а (-ы) *ж* bare patch (*where snow has melted*).

прота́лкивать(ся) (-ю(сь)) *несов от* **протолкну́ть(ся)**.

прота́пливать (-ю) *несов от* **протопи́ть**.

прота́птывать (-ю) *несов от* **протопта́ть**.

протара́нить (-ю, -ишь) *сов от* **тара́нить**.

протаска́ть (-ю) *сов перех* (*разг: сумку*) to carry round; (*: платье*) to wear.

прота́скивать (-ю) *несов от* **протащи́ть**.

прота́чивать (-ю) *несов от* **проточи́ть**.

протащи́ть (-ащу́, -а́щишь; *impf* **прота́скивать**) *сов перех* (*разг: перен: силой устроить*) to wangle; (*: критиковать*) to pan; **прота́скивать** (**~** *perf*) **что-н по** +*dat*/**сквозь** +*acc* to drag sth along/through.

протеже́ *м/ж нескл* protégé(e).

проте́з (-а) *м* artificial *или* prosthetic limb; **зубно́й ~** denture.

протеи́н (-а) *м* protein.

протеи́новый *прил* protein *опред*.

протёк *сов см* **проте́чь**.

протека́ни|е (-я) *ср* (*болезни, явлений*) progression; (*в крыше*) leakage.

протека́ть (*3sg* -ет, *3pl* -ю́т) *несов от* **проте́чь** ♦ *непepex* (*вода*) to flow, run; (*болезнь, явление*) to progress.

протеку́т *итп сов см* **проте́чь**.

протекциони́зм (-а) *м* (*ЭКОН*) protectionism.

протекци|я (-и) *ж* patronage; **ока́зывать (оказа́ть** *perf*) **~ю кому́-н** to use one's influence on behalf of sb.

протелеграфи́р|овать (-ую) *сов от* **телеграфи́ровать**.

протер|е́ть (-ру́, -рёшь; *pt* -ёр, -ёрла, -ёрло, *impf* **протира́ть**) *сов перех* (*сделать дыру*) to wear a hole in; (*очистить*) to wipe; **протира́ть** (**~** *perf*) **что-н че́рез си́то** to rub sth through a sieve; **~** (*perf*) **глаза́** to rub one's eyes

▶ **протере́ться** (*impf* **протира́ться**) *сов возв* (*одежда итп*) to wear through.

протёртый *прил* mashed.

протест (-а) *м* protest; (*ЮР*) objection.

протеста́нт (-а) *м* Protestant.

протеста́нтск|ий (-ая, -ое, -ие) *прил* Protestant *опред*.

протест|ова́ть (-у́ю) *несов непepex*: **~ (про́тив** +*gen*) to protest (against) ♦ (*perf* **опротестова́ть**) *перех* (*вексель, решение суда*) to object to.

протесту́ющий (-его; *decl like adj*) *м* (*обычно мн*) protestor.

проте́чек *сущ см* **проте́чка**.

протечёт *итп сов см* **проте́чь**.

проте́ч|ка (-ки; *gen pl* -ек) *ж* leak.

проте́чь (*3sg* -ечёт, *3pl* -еку́т, *pt* -ёк, -екла́, -екло́, *impf* **протека́ть**) *сов непepex* (*вода*) to seep; (*крыша*) to leak; (*время, юность итп*) to pass by.

про́тив *предл* (+*gen*) against; (*прямо перед*) opposite ♦ *как сказ*: **я ~ да́нного предложе́ния** I am against the motion; **кто ~?** who is against?; **~ до́ма магази́н** opposite the house (there) is a shop; **~ и́мени/наименова́ния** against a name/ designation; **~ ве́тра/тече́ния/со́лнца** against the wind/current/sun; **~ пра́вил/во́ли роди́телей** against the rules/one's parents wishes; **~ ожида́ния** contrary to expectation; **~ конкуре́нтов/врага́** against the competition/ enemy; **лека́рство ~ ка́шля/головно́й бо́ли** medicine for a cough/headache.

проти́вен *прил см* **проти́вный**.

про́тив|ень (-ня) *м* baking tray.

проти́в|иться (-люсь, -ишься; *perf* **воспроти́виться**) *несов возв* (+*dat*) to oppose.

проти́вник (-а) *м* opponent ♦ *собир* (*ВОЕН*) the enemy.

проти́вниц|**а** (-ы) ж opponent.

проти́вно *нареч* offensively ♦ *как сказ безл* it's disgusting; **мне ~ ви́деть э́то** it disgusts me to see this.

проти́вн|**ое** (-ого; *decl like adj*) *ср* the opposite.

проти́вный *прил (точка зрения, мнение)* opposite *опред*, contrary *опред*; (**-ен, -на, -но;** *человек, работа*) disgusting, revolting; **~** +*dat* (*закону, разуму*) contrary to; **в ~ном слу́чае** otherwise; **проти́вная сторона́** the opposing side.

про́тивня *итп сущ см* **про́тивень.**

противоа́томный *прил (защита)* anti-nuclear; **~ое укры́тие** nuclear shelter.

противобо́рств|**о** (-а) *ср* struggle.

противобо́рств|**овать** (-ую) *несов неперех* (+*dat*) to fight.

противове́с (-а) *м (тех, перен)* counterbalance; **в ~ обще́ственному мне́нию** contrary to public opinion.

противовозду́шный *прил* anti-aircraft.

противога́з (-а) *м* gas mask.

противоде́йстви|**е** (-я) *ср* opposition; **встреча́ть (встре́тить** *perf*) **~ чему́-н** to meet with opposition over sth.

противоде́йств|**овать** (-ую) *несов неперех* (+*dat*) to oppose.

противоесте́ственный (**-, -на, -но**) *прил* unnatural.

противозако́нный (**-ен, -на, -но**) *прил* unlawful.

противозача́точный *прил* contraceptive *опред*; **противозача́точное сре́дство** contraceptive.

противопожа́рный *прил (меры)* fire-prevention; (*техника*) fire-fighting.

противопоказа́ни|**е** (-я) *ср* contraindication.

противопока́зан|**ный** (**-, -а, -о**) *прил:* **ему́ ~о есть жи́рное** he's been advised not to eat fatty things.

противополо́жен *прил см* **противополо́жный.**

противополо́жность (-и) ж *(мнений, политики)* contrast; *(противоположное явление)* opposite; **в ~** +*dat* in contrast to.

противополо́жный (**-ен, -на, -но**) *прил* (*берег, сторона итп*) opposite; (*мнение, политика итп*) opposing.

противопоста́в|**ить** (**-лю, -ишь;** *impf* **противопоставля́ть**) *сов перех:* **~ кого́-н/что-н** +*dat* to contrast sb/sth with; (*направить против*) to oppose sb/sth with.

противопоставле́ни|**е** (-я) *ср (мнений, взгля́дов)* contrasting; *(силы)* opposing.

противопоста́вл|**ю** *сов см* **противопоста́вить.**

противопоставля́|**ть** (-ю) *несов от* **противопоста́вить.**

противоречи́вость (-и) ж paradox.

противоречи́вый (**-, -а, -о**) *прил* paradoxical.

противоре́чи|**е** (-я) *ср* contradiction; (*классовое, полити́ческие*) conflict; (*возражение*) defiance (of); **быть** (*impf*) **в ~и с** +*instr* to be in conflict with.

противоре́ч|**ить** (**-у, -ишь**) *несов неперех:* **~** +*dat* (*человеку*) to contradict; (*логике, закону итп*) to defy; **их показа́ния ~ат друг дру́гу** their evidence is contradictory.

противосто|**я́ть** (**-ю, -и́шь**) *несов неперех:* **~** +*dat* (*ветру, буре*) to withstand; (*угово́рам, давле́нию*) to resist; **~** (*impf*) **друг дру́гу** to confront each other.

противоя́ди|**е** (-я) *ср (также перен)* antidote.

протира́|**ть(ся)** (**-ю(сь)**) *несов от* **протере́ть(ся).**

проти́сн|**уть** (**-у, -ешь;** *impf* **проти́скивать**) *сов перех* to squeeze through

▶ **проти́снуться** (*impf* **проти́скиваться**) *сов возв:* **~ся в** +*acc*/**сквозь** +*acc* to squeeze in(to)/through; **~ся** (*impf*) **вперёд** to push forward.

проткн|**у́ть** (**-у́, -ёшь;** *impf* **протыка́ть**) *сов перех* to pierce.

протодья́кон (-а) *м* archdeacon.

протоиере́й (-я) *м* high priest.

прото́к (-а) *м (рука́в реки)* tributary; (*соединя́ющая река*) channel; (*мед*) duct.

протоко́л (-а) *м (собрания)* minutes *мн*; (*допро́са*) transcript; (*соглашение*) protocol; **Дипломати́ческий ~** Diplomatic Protocol; **вести́** (*impf*) **~ собра́ния** to take the minutes of a meeting; **составля́ть (соста́вить** *perf*) **~ о́быска** to record the details of a search; **журна́л ~ов** minute book.

протоколи́р|**овать** (-ую; *perf* **запротоколи́ровать**) *несов перех (собрание, заседа́ние*) to minute; (*осмотр, обыск*) to record.

протоко́льный *прил (стиль)* condensed; **протоко́льная за́пись** record of proceedings; **~ журна́л** minutes book.

протолкн|**у́ть** (**-у́, -ёшь;** *impf* **прота́лкивать**) *сов перех (также перен)* to push through

▶ **протолкну́ться** (*impf* **прота́лкиваться**) *сов возв* to push one's way through.

прото́п|**ить** (**-оплю́, -о́пишь;** *impf* **прота́пливать**) *сов перех (комнату, дом*) to warm through; (*печь*) to stoke up.

протоп|**та́ть** (**-опчу́, -о́пчешь;** *impf* **прота́птывать**) *сов перех (тропинку, доро́жку)* to beat.

проторг|**ова́ть** (**-у́ю;** *impf* **проторго́вывать**) *сов перех (потеря́ть)* to make a loss of; (*no impf; торгова́ть: това́ры*) to sell; (*жизнь*) to fritter away.

проторённый *прил (дорога, путь)* well-trodden.

проторить (-ю, -ишь; *impf* **проторять**) *сов перех* to beat.

прототип (-а) *м person upon which a character of a novel, play etc is based.*

проточить (-очу, -очишь; *impf* **протачивать**) *сов перех* (*прогрызть отверстие*) to nibble through; (*ТЕХ*) to bore.

проточный *прил* (*вода*) running; **~ое озеро** lake with rivers flowing out of it; **~ая труба** pipe.

протралить (-ю, -ишь) *сов от* **тралить**.

протрезве́ть (-ю) *сов неперех* = **протрезвиться**.

протрезвить (-лю, -йшь; *impf* **протрезвлять**) *сов перех*: **~ кого-н** to sober sb up

▶ **протрезвиться** (*impf* **протрезвляться**) *сов возв* to sober up.

протру(сь) *итп сов см* **протереть(ся)**.

протрубить (-лю, -ишь) *сов от* **трубить**.

протухнуть (*3sg* -ет, *3pl* -ут, *impf* **протухать** *или* **тухнуть**) *сов неперех* to go bad *или* off.

протыкать (-ю) *несов от* **проткнуть**.

протягивать(ся) (-ю(сь)) *несов от* **протянуть(ся)**.

протяжен *прил см* **протяжный**.

протяжение (-я) *ср*: **на ~и двух недель/месяцев** over a period of two weeks/months; **на всём ~и пути** the whole way; **на ~и всего нашего визита** for the whole duration of our visit.

протяжённость (-и) *ж* length.

протяжённый (-, -на, -но) *прил* prolonged.

протяжный (-ен, -на, -но) *прил* (*песня, крик итп*) long drawn-out.

протянуть (-яну, -янешь; *impf* **протягивать**) *сов перех* (*верёвку*) to stretch; (*линию передачи*) to extend; (*руки, ноги*) to stretch (out); (*предмет*) to hold out; (*слово, ответ итп*) to say slowly; (*разг: критиковать*) to pan ◆ *неперех* (*разг: прожить*) to last; **~ (*perf*) ноги** (*разг*) to turn up one's toes; **протягивать (~ *perf*) руку помощи** to lend a (helping) hand

▶ **протянуться** (*impf* **протягиваться**) *сов возв* (*дорога*) to stretch; (*линия передачи*) to extend; (*рука*) to stretch out.

проулюк (-ка) *м* (*разг*) lane.

проучить (-учу, -учишь; *impf* **проучивать**) *сов перех* (*разг: наказать*) to teach a lesson; (*no impf*; *учить*) to study

▶ **проучиться** *сов возв* to study.

проф. *сокр* (= **профессор**) Prof. (= *Professor*).

профан (-а) *м* ignoramus.

профанация (-и) *ж* (*непочтительное отношение*) profanity; (*обман*) sham.

профашист (-а) *м* fascist sympathizer.

профашистский (-ая, -ое, -ие) *прил* fascist *опред*.

профбюро *ср нескл сокр* (= **профсоюзное бюро**) trade-union office.

профессионал (-а) *м* professional.

профессионализм (-а) *м* professionalism.

профессиональный *прил* professional *опред*; (*болезнь, привычка, обучение*) occupational; **профессиональный союз** trade (*BRIT*) *или* labor (*US*) union.

профессия (-и) *ж* profession; **по ~ он инженер** he is an engineer by profession; **получать (получить *perf*) *или* приобретать (приобрести *perf*) ~ю** to get professional qualifications.

профессор (-а; *nom pl* -á) *м* professor.

профессура (-ы) *ж* professorship ◆ *собир* professors *мн*.

профилактика (-и) *ж* prevention.

профилактический (-ая, -ое, -ие) *прил* (*меры*) prevent(at)ive; (*прививка*) prophylactic *опред*; **~ое средство** prophylactic.

профиль (-я) *м* profile; (*предмета, дороги*) cross section; (*учебного заведения*) type; (*работника*) field.

профильтровать (-ую) *сов от* **фильтровать**.

профком (-а) *м сокр* (= **профсоюзный комитет**) trade-union committee.

профорг (-а) *м сокр* (= **профсоюзный организатор**) trade-union boss.

проформа (-ы) *ж* formality.

профсоюз (-а) *м сокр* (= **профессиональный союз**) trade (*BRIT*) *или* labor (*US*) union.

профсоюзный *прил* trade-union.

прохаживаться *несов от* **пройтись**.

прохватить (*3sg* -áтит, *3pl* -áтят, *impf* **прохватывать**) *сов перех* (*подлеж: холод, мороз итп*) to chill to the bone.

прохвост (-а) *м* (*разг*) crook.

прохлада (-ы) *ж* cool.

прохладительный *прил*: **~ напиток** cool soft drink.

прохладно *нареч* (*встретить*) coolly ◆ *как сказ* it's cool.

прохладный *прил* (*также перен*) cool.

прохладца (-ы) *ж*: **с ~ей** coolly.

прохлаждаться (-юсь) *несов возв* (*разг: бездельничать*) to doss about.

прохлопать (-ю; *impf* **прохлопывать**) *сов перех* (*разг*) to miss.

проход (-а) *м* passage; **задний ~** (*АНАТ*) back passage, anus; **~а нет от кого-н/чего-н** you can't get away from sb/sth; **не давать** (*impf*) **~а кому-н** to pester sb.

проходимец (-ца) *м* swindler.

проходимость (-и) *ж* (*местности*) passability; (*АВТ*) off-road capability; (*МЕД*) permeability.

проходимый (-, -а, -о) *прил* passable.

проходить (-ожу, -одишь) *несов от* **пройти** ◆ *сов неперех* (*ходить*) to walk.

проходка (-ки; *gen pl* -ок) *ж* sinking of shafts.

проходная (-ой; *decl like adj*) *ж* checkpoint (*at entrance to factory etc*).

проходной *прил*: **~ая комната** hall;

прохо́дно́й балл pass mark.
прохо́док *сущ см* прохо́дка.
прохо́дчик (-а) *м person who sinks shafts.*
прохо́ж|ая (-ей; *decl like adj*) *ж см* прохо́жий.
прохожде́ни|е (-я) *ср* (*по доро́ге*) passage; (*испыта́ний*) passing; (*слу́жбы*) term.
прохо́ж|ий (-его; *decl like adj*) *м* passer-by.
прохожу́ (*не*)*сов см* проходи́ть.
проху́ди́ться (*3sg* -и́тся, *3pl* -я́тся) *сов непе́рех* (*разг*) to wear thin.
процвета́ть (-ю) *несов непе́рех* (*фи́рма, бизнесме́н*) to prosper; (*теа́тр, нау́ка*) to flourish; (*разг: челове́к, семья́*) to thrive.
процеди́ть (-ежу́, -е́дишь; *impf* проце́живать) *сов пе́рех* (*бульо́н, сок*) to strain; (*no impf*; *произнести́*): ~ (**сквозь зу́бы**) to say through one's teeth.
процеду́р|а (-ы) *ж* procedure; (*МЕД: обычно мн*) course of treatment.
процеду́рн|ый *прил* procedural; (*МЕД*): ~**ая сестра́** nurse; ~ **кабине́т** treatment room.
проце́жива|ть (-ю) *несов от* процеди́ть.
процежу́ *сов см* процеди́ть.
проце́нт (-а) *м* percentage; **в разме́ре 5 ~ов годовы́х** at a yearly rate of 5 percent; **на все сто ~ов** (*доверя́ть, подде́рживать*) one hundred percent; *см также* проце́нты.
проце́нтный *прил* (*вы́раженный в проце́нтах*) percentage *опред*; **проце́нтная ста́вка** interest rate.
проце́нт|ы (-ов) *мн* (*КОММ*) interest *ед*; (: *вознагражде́ние*) commission; **просты́е/сло́жные/наро́сшие** ~ simple/compound/accrued interest.
проце́сс (-а) *м* process; (*ЮР: поря́док разбира́тельства*) proceedings *мн*; (: *также*: **суде́бный** ~) trial; **воспали́тельный** ~ inflammation; **в ~е** +*gen* in the course of; **возбужда́ть** (**возбуди́ть** *perf*) ~ to institute proceedings.
проце́сси|я (-и) *ж* procession.
проце́ссор (-а) *м* word processor.
процессуа́льный *прил* (*ЮР*) procedural; **процессуа́льный ко́декс** procedural code.
процити́р|овать (-ую) *сов от* цити́ровать.
прочёл *сов см* проче́сть.
про́чен *прил см* про́чный.
про́черк (-а) *м* line.
прочерти́ть (-ерчу́, -е́ртишь; *impf* проче́рчивать) *сов пе́рех*: ~ **ли́нию** to draw a line.
прочеса́ть (-ешу́, -е́шешь; *impf* прочёсывать) *сов пе́рех* (*также перен*) to comb.
проче́сть (-ту́, -тёшь; *pt* -ёл, -ла́, -ло́) *сов от* чита́ть.
прочёсыва|ть (-ю) *несов от* прочеса́ть.
прочешу́ *итп сов см* прочеса́ть.
про́ч|ий (-ая, -ее, -ие) *прил* other; **поми́мо**

всего́ ~его on top of everything else; **и про́чее** and so on.
прочи́|стить (-щу, -стишь; *impf* прочища́ть) *сов пе́рех* to clean out; (*нос*) to clear.
прочита́|ть (-ю) *сов от* чита́ть.
про́ч|ить (-у, -ишь) *несов пе́рех*: ~ **что-н кому́-н** to predict sth for sb; **его́ роди́тели ~или его́ во врачи́** his parents intended him to be a doctor.
прочища́|ть (-ю) *несов от* прочи́стить.
прочи́щу *сов см* прочи́стить.
прочла́ *итп сов см* проче́сть.
про́чно *нареч* (*закрепи́ть*) firmly; (*заучи́ть*) well.
про́чност|ь (-и) *ж* (*материа́ла итп*) durability; (*отноше́ний, семьи́*) stability; **запа́с ~и** reliability.
про́ч|ный (-ен, -на́, -но) *прил* (*материа́л итп*) durable; (*постро́йка*) solid, stable; (*зна́ния*) sound; (*отноше́ние, семья́*) stable; (*мир, сча́стье*) lasting.
прочте́ни|е (-я) *ср* reading.
прочту́ *итп сов см* проче́сть.
прочу́вствованный *прил* heartfelt.
прочу́вств|овать (-ую) *сов пе́рех* to feel deeply; ~ (*perf*) **роль** to get inside a role.
прочь *нареч* (*в сто́рону*) away; **ру́ки ~!** hands off!; ~ **с доро́ги!** get out of the way!; **он не ~ вы́пить** he won't say no to a drink.
прошвырну́ться (-у́сь, -ёшься) *сов возв* (*разг*) to stretch one's legs.
проше́дш|ий (-ая, -ее, -ие) *прил* (*про́шлый*) past; **проше́дшее вре́мя** past tense.
проше́й(те) *сов см* проши́ть.
прошёл(ся) *сов см* пройти́(сь).
проше́ни|е (-я) *ср* plea; (*пи́сьменное ходата́йство*) petition; **подава́ть** (**пода́ть** *perf*) ~ **в** +*acc* to present a petition to.
прош|епта́ть (-епчу́, -е́пчешь) *сов пе́рех* to whisper.
проше́стви|е (-я) *ср*: **по ~и го́да/ме́сяца** after a year's/month's lapse.
прошиб|и́ть (-у́, -ёшь; *pt* -, -ла, -ло, *impf* прошиба́ть) *сов пе́рех* (*разг: дверь, окно́ итп*) to smash through; **пот проши́б его́** he broke out in a sweat; **дрожь ~ла её** a shiver went down her spine.
прош|и́ть (-ью, -ьёшь; *imper* -е́й(те), *impf* прошива́ть) *сов пе́рех* (*приши́ть*) to sew a seam on; (*перен: пу́лями сте́ны*) to pepper.
прошла́ *итп сов см* пройти́.
прошлого́дн|ий (-яя, -ее, -ие) *прил* last year's; ~**ие собы́тия** the events of last year.
про́шло|е (-го; *decl like adj*) *ср* the past; **отходи́ть** (**отойти́** *perf*) **в** ~ to become a thing of the past.
про́шл|ый *прил* last; (*пре́жний*) past; **в** ~ **раз** last time; **на** ~**ой неде́ле** last week; **в** ~**ом году́/ме́сяце** last year/month; **де́ло** ~**ое** it's in

the past.

прошмыгну́ть (-у́, -ёшь; *impf* **прошмы́гивать**) *сов неперех*: ~ ми́мо +*gen*/сквозь +*acc итп* (*разг*) to dart past/through *итп*.

проштампова́ть (-у́ю) *сов от* **штампова́ть**.

проштра́фиться (-люсь, -ишься) *сов возв* (*разг*) to lapse.

проштуди́ровать (-ую) *сов от* **штуди́ровать**.

прошу́(сь) *несов см* **проси́ть(ся)**.

прошью́ *итп сов см* **проши́ть**.

проща́йте *част* goodbye, farewell.

проща́льный *прил* parting *опред*; (*вечер, визит*) farewell *опред*.

проща́ни|е (-я) *ср* (*действие*) parting; **на** ~ on parting.

проща́|ть(ся) (-ю(сь)) *несов от* **прости́ть(ся)**.

про́ще *сравн нареч от* **про́сто** ♦ *сравн прил от* **просто́й**.

проще́ни|е (-я) *ср* (*ребёнка, друга итп*) forgiveness; (*преступника*) pardon; **проси́ть** (**попроси́ть** *perf*) ~я to say sorry; **прошу́** ~я! (I'm) sorry!

прощу́(сь) *сов см* **прости́ть(ся)**.

прощу́па|ть (-ю; *impf* **прощу́пывать**) *сов перех* to feel for; (*перен*) to check out; **прощу́пывать** (~ *perf*) по́чву to see how the land lies.

проэкзамен|ова́ть (-у́ю) *сов от* **экзаменова́ть**.

проявит́ель (-я) *м* (*ФОТО*) developer.

про|яви́ть (-явлю́, -я́вишь; *impf* **проявля́ть**) *сов перех* to display; (*ФОТО*) to develop; **проявля́ть** (~ *perf*) себя́ пло́хо/хорошо́ to show o.s. in a bad/good light

▶ **прояви́ться** (*impf* **проявля́ться**) *сов возв* (*талант, потенциал итп*) to reveal itself; (*решительность, смелость итп*) to show itself; (*ФОТО*) to be developed.

проявле́ни|е (-я) *ср* display; (*обычно мн: жизни*) manifestation.

проявлю́(сь) *сов см* **прояви́ть(ся)**.

проявля́|ть(ся) (-ю(сь)) *несов от* **прояви́ть(ся)**.

проясне́ни|е (-я) *ср* (*погоды*) brightening *или* clearing up; (*ситуации*) clarification; **у меня́ наступи́ло** ~ **созна́ния** *или* **ума́** my mind cleared.

прояснить (-ю́, -и́шь; *impf* **проясня́ть**) *сов перех* (*обстановку*) to clarify; (*мысли*) to sort out; **проясня́ть** (~ *perf*) чьё-н созна́ние to bring sb round

▶ **проясни́ться** (*impf* **проясня́ться**) *сов возв* (*погода, небо*) to brighten *или* clear up; (*обстановка*) to be clarified; (*мысли*) to be sorted out; **у него́** ~и́лось **созна́ние** his mind cleared.

пру(сь) *итп несов см* **пере́ть(ся)**.

пруд (-а́; *loc sg* -у́) *м* (*естественный*) pool, pond; (*искусственный*) pond.

пру|ди́ть (-жу́, -у́дишь; *perf* **запруди́ть**) *несов перех* to dam; **де́нег у него́ хоть** ~**у́д пруди́** (*разг*) he is rolling in cash.

пружи́н|а (-ы) *ж* (*ТЕХ*) spring; (*перен: движущая сила*) mainspring.

пружи́нист|ый (-, -а, -о) *прил* springy; **у него́** ~ **шаг** he has a spring in his step.

пружу́ *сов см* **пруди́ть**.

прут (-а́; *nom pl* -ья) *м* (*БОТ*) twig; (*ТЕХ*) rod.

прыга́л|ка (-ки; *gen pl* -ок) *ж* skipping-rope (*BRIT*), skip rope (*US*).

прыга́|ть (-ю) *несов неперех* to jump; (*мяч*) to bounce.

пры́гн|уть (-у, -ешь) *сов неперех* to jump; (*мяч*) to bounce.

прыгу́н (-а́) *м* (*СПОРТ*) jumper; ~ **в длину́** long jumper; ~ **в высоту́** high jumper.

прыгу́нь|я (-и; *gen pl* -ий) *ж см* **прыгу́н**.

прыж|о́к (-ка́) *м* (*через лужу, с парашютом*) jump; (*в воду*) dive; ~**ки́ в высоту́/длину́** high/long jump; ~**ки́ с шесто́м** pole vault; **опо́рный** ~ (*СПОРТ*) vault.

пры́сн|уть (-у, -ешь; *impf* **пры́скать**) *сов неперех* (*кровь*) to spurt; (+*instr*; *водой*) to sprinkle with; (*духами*) to spray with; **пры́скать** (~ *perf*) **со́ смеху** (*разг*) to go into a fit of giggles.

пры́т|кий (-кая, -кое, -кие; -ок, -ка́, -ко) *прил* (*разг: подвижный*) bouncy.

прыть (-и) *ж* (*разг: быстрота*) bounce; **во всю** ~ (*разг*) at full tilt.

прыщ (-а́) *м* spot.

прыща́в|ый (-, -а, -о) *прил* spotty.

пряди́льный *прил* spinning *опред*.

пряди́льщик (-а) *м* spinner.

пряди́льщиц|а (-ы) *ж см* **пряди́льщик**.

пряду́ *итп несов см* **прясть**.

пря́д|ь (-и) *ж* lock (*of hair*).

пря́ж|а (-и) *ж* yarn.

пря́ж|ка (-ки; *gen pl* -ек) *ж* (*на ремне*) buckle; (*на юбке*) clasp.

пря́л|ка (-ки; *gen pl* -ок) *ж* spinning wheel.

пряма́|я (-о́й; *decl like adj*) *ж* straight line; **по** ~**о́й** in a straight line.

прямико́м *нареч*: **он прошёл** ~ **че́рез сад** (*разг*) he went straight across the garden.

пря́мо *нареч* (*в прямом направлении*) straight ahead; (*ровно*) upright; (*непосредственно*) straight; (*откровенно*) directly ♦ *част* (*действительно*) really; **приступа́ть** (**приступи́ть** *perf*) ~ **к де́лу** to get straight down to business; **у меня́** ~ **сил нет!** I really haven't (got) the strength!; **помоги́те ему́ – (ну)** ~! (*разг*) help him? no way!

прямоду́ш|ный (-ен, -на, -но) *прил* (*человек*) forthright; (*ответ*) candid.

прям|о́й (-, -а́, -о) *прил* straight; (*путь, слова, человек*) direct; (*ответ, политика*) open; (*вызов, ответ*) obvious; (*no short form*; *сообщение, рейс, обязанность итп*) direct; (*выгода, смысл, польза итп*) real; (*значение слова*) literal; ~**ые изде́ржки** direct cost; **пряма́я кишка́** rectum; **пряма́я**

трансля́ция live broadcast; **прямо́е дополне́ние** direct object; **прямо́е попада́ние** direct hit; **прямо́й до́ступ** (комп) direct access; **прямо́й репорта́ж** live coverage; **прямо́й у́гол** right angle; **прямы́е вы́боры/нало́ги** direct elections/taxes.

прямолине́й|ный (-ен, -йна, -йно) прил (движение) along a straight line; (перен) blunt.

пря́мо-таки нареч (разг) really.

прямоуго́льник (-а) м rectangle.

прямоуго́льный прил rectangular.

пря́|ник (-а) м ≈ gingerbread.

пря́ность (-и) ж spice.

пря́н|ый (-, -а, -о) прил spicy.

пря|сть (-ду́, -дёшь; perf **спрясть**) несов перех to spin.

пря́|тать (-чу, -чешь; perf **спря́тать**) несов перех to hide; он ~тал глаза́ от меня́ he didn't look me straight in the eye

▸ пря́таться (perf **спря́таться**) несов возв to hide; (человек: от холода, ветра) to shelter; (солнце) to hide; ~ся (**спря́таться** perf) за чужу́ю спи́ну to redirect responsibility.

пря́т|ки (-ок; dat pl -кам) мн hide-and-seek ед; игра́ть (impf) в ~ с кем-н to play hide-and-seek with sb; (перен) to avoid sb.

пря́чу(сь) итп несов см пря́тать(ся).

пса итп сущ см пёс.

псал|о́м (-ма́) м psalm.

псало́мщик (-а) м sexton.

псалты́р|ь (-и) ж Psalter.

пса́рн|я (-и) ж kennels мн (for hunting dogs).

псевдони́м (-а) м pseudonym.

псих (-а) м (разг) psycho.

психиа́тр (-а) м psychiatrist.

психиатри́ческ|ий (-ая, -ое, -ие) прил psychiatric.

психиатри́|я (-и) ж psychiatry.

пси́хик|а (-и) ж psyche.

психи́ческ|ий (-ая, -ое, -ие) прил (заболевание, отклонение итп) mental.

психоана́лиз (-а) м psychoanalysis.

псих|ова́ть (-у́ю) несов неперех (разг) to freak out.

психо́з (-а) м (мед) psychosis; (странность в психике) neurosis.

психо́лог (-а) м psychologist.

психологи́ческ|ий (-ая, -ое, -ие) прил psychological.

психоло́ги|я (-и) ж psychology.

психопа́т (-а) м psychopath.

психопати́|я (-и) ж psychopathy.

психотерапе́вт (-а) м psychotherapist.

психотерапи́|я (-и) ж psychotherapy.

ПСС м сокр = по́лное собра́ние сочине́ний.

пта́х|а (-и) ж (разг) bird.

пта́ш|ка (-ки; gen pl -ек) ж bird.

птен|е́ц (-ца́) м chick.

пти́ц|а (-ы) ж bird ◆ собир: (дома́шняя) ~ poultry; ва́жная ~ (разг) big shot.

птицево́д (-а) м poulterer, poultry farmer.

птицево́дств|о (-а) ср poultry farming.

птицево́дческ|ий (-ая, -ое, -ие) прил: ~ая фе́рма poultry farm.

птицефа́брик|а (-и) ж poultry farm.

пти́чек сущ см пти́чка.

пти́ч|ий (-ья, -ье, -ьи) прил (корм, клетка) bird опред; вид с высоты́ ~ьего полёта bird's eye view; я сам здесь на ~ьих права́х I don't have any rights here myself; пти́чий база́р bird colony.

пти́ч|ка (-ки; gen pl -ек) ж уменьш от пти́ца; (разг: в тексте) tick (BRIT), check (US).

пти́чник (-а) м ≈ hen house.

ПТУ ср сокр (= профессиона́льно-техни́ческое учи́лище) ≈ tech (= technical college).

пуа́нт (-а) м (БАЛЕТ) ballet shoe.

пу́блик|а (-и) ж собир audience; широ́кая ~ the public; игра́ть (impf) на ~у to show off; на ~у in company.

публика́ци|я (-и) ж publication.

публик|ова́ть (-у́ю; perf **опубликова́ть**) несов перех to publish.

публици́ст (-а) м writer of sociopolitical literature.

публици́стик|а (-и) ж собир sociopolitical journalism.

публицисти́ческ|ий (-ая, -ое, -ие) прил sociopolitical.

публи́ч|ный (-ен, -на, -но) прил public; публи́чный дом brothel; публи́чные торги́, публи́чная прода́жа (public) auction, public sale.

пу́гал|о (-а) ср scarecrow; (перен: некрасивый человек) fright.

пуга́|ть (-ю; perf **испуга́ть** или **напуга́ть**) несов перех to frighten, scare

▸ пуга́ться (perf **испуга́ться** или **напуга́ться**) несов возв to be frightened или scared.

пугли́в|ый (-, -а, -о) прил timid.

пу́говиц|а (-ы) ж button; застёгивать (застегну́ть perf) ~у to fasten a button.

пуд (-а; nom pl -ы́) м pood (Russian measure of weight equivalent to 16 kilogrammes).

пу́дел|ь (-я) м poodle.

пу́динг (-а) м ≈ pudding.

пудо́в|ый прил: ~ая ги́ря a pood weight.

пу́др|а (-ы) ж powder; са́харная ~ icing sugar.

пу́дрениц|а (-ы) ж powder compact.

пу́др|ить (-ю, -ишь; perf **напу́дрить**) несов перех to powder; ~ (impf) мозги́ кому́-н (разг) to pull the wool over sb's eyes

▸ пу́дриться (perf **напу́дриться**) несов возв to powder one's face.

пуза́т|ый (-, -а, -о) прил (разг: человек) tubby; (перен: чайник, комод) rounded.

The spelling rules for Russian are shown on page xvii.

пу́з|о (-а) ср (разг: живот) belly; (брюхо) paunch.
пузыр|ёк (-ька́) м (уменьш) от пузы́рь; (для лекарства, чернил) vial.
пузыр|и́ться (3sg -и́тся, 3pl -я́тся) несов возв (жидкость) to bubble; (краска) to blister; (разг: одежда) to blow up.
пузы́р|ь (-я́) м (мыльный) bubble; (на коже) blister; (с водой) water bottle; жёлчный ~ gall bladder; мочево́й ~ (urinary) bladder.
пузырька́ итп сущ см пузырёк.
пук (-а; nom pl -и́) м bundle.
пу́ка|ть (-ю; perf пу́кнуть) несов неперех to fart.
пулево́й прил bullet опред.
пулемёт (-а) м machine gun.
пулемётчик (-а) м machine gunner.
пуленепробива́емый прил bullet-proof.
пуло́вер (-а) м pullover.
пульвериза́тор (-а) м atomizer.
пульс (-а) м (МЕД, перен) pulse.
пульси́р|овать (3sg -ует, 3pl -уют) несов неперех (артерии) to pulsate; (кровь) to pulse; (нарыв) to throb.
пульт (-а) м panel; (музыканта) stand; пульт управле́ния control panel.
пу́л|я (-и) ж bullet; ~ей вы́лететь (perf) (из +gen) (перен: разг) to shoot out (from).
пу́м|а (-ы) ж puma.
пункт (-а) м point; (документа) clause; (медицинский) centre (BRIT), center (US); (наблюдательный, командный) post; населённый ~ inhabited area.
пункти́р (-а) м dotted line.
пунктуа́льный (-ен, -ьна, -ьно) прил (человек) punctual.
пунктуа́ци|я (-и) ж punctuation.
пу́нкци|я (-и) ж (МЕД) lumber puncture.
пунцо́вый прил scarlet опред.
пунш (-а) м (кулин) punch.
пуп (-а́) м (разг) belly button; ~ земли́ (разг) the bee's knees.
пупка́ сущ см пупо́к.
пупови́н|а (-ы) ж umbilical cord.
пуп|о́к (-ка́) м (АНАТ) navel.
пупы́рыш|ек (-ка) м (разг: на коже) pimple.
пург|а́ (-и́) ж snowstorm.
пурге́н (-а) м phenol phthalene (used as laxative).
пурита́н|ин (-ина; nom pl -е, gen pl -) м puritan.
пурита́н|ка (-ки; gen pl -ок) ж см пурита́нин.
пурита́нский (-ая, -ое, -ие) прил puritanical.
пу́рпур (-а) м wine, Burgundy.
пурпу́рный прил wine опред, Burgundy опред.
пуск (-а) м (завода итп) starting up; ~ в эксплуата́цию commission.
пуска́й част, союз (разг) = пусть.
пуска́|ть(ся) (-ю(сь)) несов от пусти́ть(ся).
пусково́й прил (период) initial опред; (механизм, установка) starting опред; (платформа) launching опред.
пусте́|ть (3sg -ет, 3pl -ют, perf опусте́ть) несов

неперех to become empty.
пусти́|ть (-щу́, -стишь; impf пуска́ть) сов перех (руку, человека) to let go of; (лошадь, санки итп) to send off; (завод, станок, электростанцию) to start; (в вагон, в зал) to let in; (пар, дым) to give off; (камень, снаряд) to throw; (сплетни) to spread; (корни) to put out; пуска́ть (~ perf) что-н на +acc/под +acc (использовать) to use sth as/for; пуска́ть (~ perf) кого́-н куда́-нибудь to let sb go somewhere; пуска́ть (~ perf) това́р в прода́жу to put goods onto the market; пуска́ть (~ perf) пузыри́ to blow bubbles; пуска́ть (~ perf) слю́ни to dribble; пуска́ть (~ perf) во́ду/газ to turn on the water/gas
► пусти́|ться (impf пуска́ться) сов возв: ~ся в +acc (в объяснения) to go into; пуска́ться (~ся perf) в подро́бности to go into detail; пуска́ться (~ся perf) в пляс или пляса́ть to start dancing; пуска́ться (~ся perf) в путь to set off.
пу́сто нареч empty ♦ как сказ (ничего нет) there's nothing there; (никого нет) there's no-one there; в го́роде/холоди́льнике ~ the town/fridge is empty.
пуст|ова́ть (3sg -у́ет, 3pl -у́ют) несов неперех to be empty.
пуст|о́й (-, -а́, -о, -ы́) прил empty; (взгляд) vacant; (предлог, причина, затея) trifling; он ~ о́е ме́сто he's a real nobody; с ~ы́ми рука́ми empty-handed.
пустосло́ви|е (-я) ср idle talk.
пуст|ота́ (-оты́; nom pl -о́ты) ж emptiness; (полое место) cavity.
пу́стошь (-и) ж wasteland.
пусты́нный прил desert опред; (-ен, -на, -но; безлюдный) deserted.
пусты́н|я (-и; gen pl -ь) ж desert; (безлюдное место) wilderness.
пусты́рник (-а) м motherwort.
пусты́рь (-я́) м wasteland.
пусты́ш|ка (-ки; gen pl -ек) ж (разг: соска) dummy (BRIT), pacifier (US); (перен: о человеке) airhead.

KEYWORD

пусть част (+3sg/pl) 1 (выражает приказ, угрозу): пусть он придёт у́тром let him come in the morning; пусть она́ то́лько попро́бует отказа́ться let her just try to refuse
2 (выражает согласие): пусть бу́дет так so be it; пусть по-тво́ему have it your way
3 (всё равно) OK, all right; она́ вини́т меня́, пусть! OK или all right, so she blames me!
♦ союз (допустим) even if; пусть он плохо́й дире́ктор, зато́ хоро́ший челове́к even if he is a bad director, he is a good person; на́до оправда́ть все, пусть да́же небольши́е, затра́ты all expenses, even small ones, must be justified.

пустя́к (-а́) м trifle; (неценный предмет) trinket

♦ *как сказ:* э́то ~ it's nothing; **говори́ть** (*impf*) **пустяки́** to talk nonsense; **Вы огорчены́ ? – пустяки́!** are you upset? – it's nothing!

пустяко́вый *прил* (*разг: повод, жалоба*) trivial; э́то пустяко́вая рабо́та it's a piece of cake.

пустя́чный *прил* = **пустяко́вый**.

пу́та|ница (-ы) *ж* (*в мыслях, в делах*) muddle; (*дорог, дверей*) maze.

пу́таный (-, -а, -о) *прил* (*объяснение, рассказ*) muddled.

пу́та|ть (-ю; *perf* **запу́тать** *или* **спу́тать**) *несов перех* (*нитки, волосы*) to tangle (up); (*разг: сбить с толку*) to bamboozle; (*perf* **спу́тать** *или* **перепу́тать**: *бумаги, факты итп*) to mix up; (*perf* **впу́тать**; *разг*): ~ кого́-н в +*acc* to get sb mixed up in: я его́ с кем-то ~ю I'm confusing him with somebody else; **он всегда́ ~л на́ши имена́** he always got our names mixed up

▸ **пу́таться** (*perf* **запу́таться** *или* **спу́таться**) *несов возв* to get tangled (up); (*в рассказе, в объяснении*) to get mixed up; (*perf* **спу́таться**; *общаться*): ~ся с +*instr* (*с мошенниками, с хулиганами итп*) to get mixed up with.

путёв|ка (-ки; *gen pl* -ок) *ж* holiday voucher (*given by employer*); (*водителя*) manifest (*of cargo drivers*).

путеводи́тель (-я) *м* guidebook.

путево́д|ный *прил* (*перен: идея, теория*) guiding; ~ая нить guiding light.

путево́й *прил* (*пост. сигнал*) railway *опред*; (*записки, дневник*) travel *опред*; **путево́й лист** (*водителя*) = **путёвка**.

путёвок *сущ см* **путёвка**.

путёвый *прил* (*разг*) = **пу́тный**.

путе́й *сущ см* **путь**.

путём *сущ см* **путь** ♦ *предл* (+*gen*) by means of.

путеше́ственник (-а) *м* traveller (*BRIT*), traveler (*US*).

путеше́стви|е (-я) *ср* journey, trip; (*морской*) voyage.

путеше́ств|овать (-ую) *несов неперех* to travel.

пут|и́ *сущ см* **путь** ♦ (-е́й) *мн:* **дыха́тельные** ~ respiratory tract.

пу́тник (-а) *м* traveller (*BRIT*), traveler (*US*).

пу́тный *прил* (*человек*) decent; (*план, предложение*) practical.

путч (-а) *м* (*полит*) putsch.

пу́т|ы (-) *мн* (*также перен*) fetters *мн*.

пут|ь (-и́; *см* **Table 3**) *м* (*также перен*) way; (*платформа*) platform; (*рельсы*) track; (*путешествие*) journey; **запасно́й** ~ siding; **во́дные** ~**и** waterways; **возду́шные** ~**и** air lanes; **нам с Ва́ми не по** ~**й** we're not going the same way; (*перен*) we don't see eye to eye; **счастли́вого** ~**й!** have a good trip!; **быть** (*impf*)

на ~**й** к +*dat* to be on the road *или* way to; **провожа́ть** (**проводи́ть** *perf*) **кого́-н в после́дний** ~ to lay sb to rest; **пути́ сообще́ния** transport network *ед*; *см также* **пути́**.

пуф (-а) *м* pouffe.

пух (-а; *loc sg* -ý) *м* (*у животных*) fluff; (*у птиц, у человека*) down; **в** ~ **и прах** (*разг*) totally and utterly; **ни пу́ха ни пера́!** good luck!

пух *итп несов см* **пу́хнуть**.

пу́хлый (-, -á, -о) *прил* (*щёки, человек*) chubby; (*губы*) full; (*портфель, папка*) bulging.

пу́х|нуть (-ну, -нешь; *pt* -, -ла, -ло, *perf* **вспу́хнуть** *или* **опу́хнуть**) *несов неперех* to swell (up); **у меня́ голова́** ~**нет** (*разг*) my head's buzzing.

пухо́вый *прил* (*подушка*) feather *опред*; (*платок*) angora *опред*; ~ая ку́ртка padded jacket.

пучегла́зый *прил* (*разг*) goggle-eyed, pop-eyed.

пучи́н|а (-ы) *ж* the deep.

пу́ч|ить (-у, -ишь; *perf* **вы́пучить**) *несов перех:* ~ глаза́ to goggle; **он вы́пучил глаза́** his eyes popped out of his head; **меня́** ~**ит** I have flatulence

▸ **пу́читься** (*perf* **вспу́читься**) *несов возв* to swell (up).

пучо́к (-ка́) *м* bunch; (*света*) beam.

пу́шек *сущ см* **пу́шка**.

пуши́н|ка (-ки; *gen pl* -ок) *ж* piece of fluff; (*снега*) flake.

пуши́стый (-, -а, -о) *прил* (*мех, ковёр итп*) fluffy; (*волосы*) fuzzy; (*ткань*) fleecy; (*кот*) furry; (*цыплёнок*) downy.

пу́ш|ка (-ки; *gen pl* -ек) *ж* (*на танке*) artillery gun; (*ист*) cannon.

пушни́н|а (-ы) *ж собир* furs *мн*.

пушно́й *прил* furry; ~ **това́р** furs *мн*.

пушо́к (-ка́) *м уменьш от* **пух**; (*над губой*) fluff.

пу́щ|а (-и) *ж* dense forest.

пу́щий (-ая, -ее, -ие) *прил:* **для** ~**ей ва́жности** (*разг*) for more importance.

пущу́(сь) *сов см* **пусти́ть(ся)**.

пфе́ннинг (-а) *м* pfennig.

Пхенья́н (-а) *м* Pyongyang.

пчел|а́ (-ы́; *nom pl* **пчёлы**) *ж* bee.

пчели́ный *прил* (*мёд*) bee's; ~ **воск** beeswax; ~ **рой** swarm of bees.

пчелово́д (-а) *м* bee-keeper.

пчелово́дств|о (-а) *ср* bee-keeping.

пшени́ц|а (-ы) *ж* wheat.

пшени́чный *прил* wheat *опред*.

пшён|ка (-ки) *ж* (*разг*) millet porridge.

пшённый *прил:* ~ая ка́ша millet porridge.

пшен|о́ (-а́) *ср* millet.

пы́ж|иться (-усь, -ишься; *perf* **напы́житься**) *несов возв* (*разг: напрягаться*) to puff and pant; (*держаться важно*) to puff up.

пыл (-а; *loc sg* -ý) *м* (*перен*) ardour (*BRIT*), ardor (*US*); **в** ~ý **спóра/сражéния** in the heat of the argument/battle.

пылáть (-ю) *несов неперех* (*костёр*) to blaze; (*перен: лицо*) to burn; (+*instr*; *перен: любовью, гнéвом итп*) to burn with.

пýлен *прил см* **пýльный**.

пылесóс (-а) *м* vacuum cleaner, Hoover®.

пылесóсить (-ишь; *perf* **пропылесóсить**) *сов перех* to vacuum, hoover®.

пылúнка (-ки; *gen pl* -ок) *ж* speck of dust.

пылúть (-ю, -ишь; *perf* **напылúть**) *несов неперех* to raise dust

► **пылúться** (*perf* **запылúться**) *несов возв* to get dusty.

пылкий (-кая, -кое, -кие; -ок, -ка́, -ко) *прил* passionate.

пыль (-и; *loc sg* -и́) *ж* dust; **вытирáть** (**вытереть** *perf*) ~ to dust; **пускáть** (**пустú́ть** *perf*) ~ **в глазá** **комý**-н to give sb the wrong idea.

пыльный (-ен, -ьна́, -ьно) *прил* dusty.

пыльца́ (-ы́) *ж* pollen.

пырнýть (-ý, -ёшь) *сов перех* (*разг*) to stab; ~ (*perf*) **ножóм** to knife.

пытáть (-ю) *несов перех* to torture; ~ (*impf*) **когó**-н **о чём**-н to grill sb about sth

► **пытáться** (*perf* **попытáться**) *несов возв*: ~**ся** +*infin* to try to do.

пытка (-ки; *gen pl* -ок) *ж* torment.

пытлúвый (-, -а, -о) *прил* inquisitive.

пыток *сущ см* **пытка**.

пыхать (-шу, -шешь) *несов неперех*: ~ +*instr* to give off; ~ (*impf*) **злóбой/зáвистью** to burn with anger/envy; **онá** ~**шет здорóвьем** she's bursting with health.

пыхтéть (-чý, -тúшь) *несов неперех* (*тяжело дышáть*) to pant; (*самовáр*) to steam; (*паровóз*) to chug; ~ (*impf*) **над чем**-н (*разг*) to sweat over sth.

пышек *сущ см* **пышка**.

пышен *прил см* **пышный**.

пышка (-ки; *gen pl* -ек) *ж* doughnut (*BRIT*), donut (*US*).

пышноволóсый (-, -а, -о) *прил* fuzzy-haired.

пышногрýдый (-, -а, -о) *прил* busty.

пышность (-и) *ж* (*волос*) luxuriance; (*хвостá итп*) bushiness; (*обстанóвки, приёма итп*) splendour (*BRIT*), splendor (*US*); **придавáть** (**придáть** *perf*) ~ **волосáм** to give body to one's hair.

пышный (-ен, -на́, -но) *прил* (*волосы, хвост, усы итп*) bushy; (*полный*) voluptuous; (*роскóшный*) splendid.

пышу *итп несов см* **пыхать**.

пьедестáл (-а) *м* (*основáние*) pedestal; (*для победúтелей*) winners' rostrum.

пьéса (-ы) *ж* (*ЛИТЕРАТУРА*) play; (*МУЗ*) piece.

пью *итп несов см* **пить**.

пьющий (-его; *decl like adj*) *м* heavy drinker.

пьянéть (-ю; *perf* **опьянéть**) *несов неперех* to get drunk; (*перен*) to become intoxicated.

пьянúть (-ю, -úшь; *perf* **опьянúть**) *несов перех* to get drunk; (*перен: подлеж: воздух, счáстье итп*) to intoxicate.

пьянúца (-ы) *м/ж* drunkard.

пьянка (-ки; *gen pl* -ок) *ж* (*разг*) booze-up.

пьянство (-а) *ср* heavy drinking; **борьбá с** ~**м** anti-drinking campaign.

пьянствовать (-ую) *несов неперех* to drink heavily.

пьянчýга (-и) *м/ж* (*разг*) (old) soak.

пьяный (-, -á, -о) *прил* (*человéк*) drunk; (*крики, песни итп*) drunken ♦ (-ого; *decl like adj*) *м* drunk; **под** ~**ую рýку** (*разг*) in a drunken rage.

пэр (-а) *м* peer.

пюпитр (-а) *м* lectern.

пюрé *ср нескл* (*фруктóвое*) purée; **картóфельное** ~ mashed potato.

п/я *сокр* (= **почтóвый ящик**) POB (= *Post Office Box*).

пядь (-и) *ж* (*мéра*) span; (*небольшóе прострáнство*) stretch; **семú пядéй во лбу** extraordinarily intelligent.

пя́лец *сущ см* **пя́льцы**.

пя́литься (-юсь, -ишься) *несов возв* (*разг*) to gawk.

пя́льцы (-ец; *dat pl* -ьцам) *мн* tambour *ед*.

пята́ (-ы́) *ж*: **до пят** (*очень длинный*) to the ground; **с головы до пят** from head to toe; **ходúть** (*impf*) *или* **гнáться** (*impf*) **за кем**-н **по** ~**м** to follow hot on sb's heels.

пятáк (-á) *м* (*разг*) five-kopeck piece.

пятачóк (-ка́) *м* five-kopeck piece; (*небольшáя плóщадка*) spot; (*небольшóе прострáнство*) stretch; (*свинú*) snout.

пя́тая (-ой; *decl like adj*) *ж*: **однá** ~ one fifth.

пя́тен *сущ см* **пятнó**.

пятёрка (-ки; *gen pl* -ок) *ж* (*цифра, кáрта*) five; (*разг: денéжный знак*) fiver; (*ПРОСВЕЩ*) ≈ A (*school mark*); (*грýппа из пятú*) group of five; (*разг: автóбус, трамвáй итп*) (number) five (*bus, tram итп*).

пятерня́ (-ú) *ж* (*разг*) paw.

пя́теро (-ы́х; *как* **чéтверо**; *см* **Table 36b**) *чис* five; *см также* **дво́е**.

пятёрок *сущ см* **пятёрка**.

пятú *чис см* **пять**.

пятибóрье (-я) *ср* pentathlon.

пятидесятú *чис см* **пятьдеся́т**.

пятидесятилéтие (-я) *ср* fifty years *мн*; (*годовщúна*) fiftieth anniversary.

пятидесятилéтний (-яя, -ее, -ие) *прил* (*перúод*) fifty-year; (*человéк*) fifty-year-old.

пятидеся́тый (-ая, -ое, -ые) *чис* fiftieth; **я читáю** ~**ую странúцу** I am on page fifty; **я живý в** ~**ой квартúре** I live in flat fifty; **я приéхал в Петербýрг в** ~**ом годý** I came to Petersburg in nineteen fifty; ~**ые гóды** the Fifties; **в** ~**ых годáх** in the Fifties.

пятиднéвка (-ки; *gen pl* -ок) *ж* (*разг*) five-day week.

пятиднéвный *прил* five-day.

пятикла́ссник (-а) *м pupil in fifth year at school (usually eleven years old)*.

пятикла́ссниц|**а** (-ы) *ж см* **пятикла́ссник**.

пятикопе́ечный *прил* five-kopeck.

пятикра́тн|**ый** *прил*: ~ **чемпио́н** five-times champion; **в ~ом разме́ре** fivefold.

пятиле́ти|**е** (-я) *ср* (*срок*) five years; (*юбилей*) fifth anniversary.

пятиле́т|**ка** (-ки; *gen pl* -ок) *ж* (*ИСТ, ЭКОН*) five-year plan.

пятиле́тн|**ий** (-яя, -ее, -ие) *прил* (*промежуток*) five-year; (*ребёнок*) five-year-old.

пятиле́ток *сущ см* **пятиле́тка**.

пятиме́сячный *прил* five-month; (*ребёнок*) five-month-old.

пятимину́т|**ка** (-ки; *gen pl* -ок) *ж* (*разг*) short meeting (*at work*).

пятинеде́льный *прил* five-week; (*ребёнок*) five-week-old.

пятисо́т *чис см* **пятьсо́т**.

пятисотле́ти|**е** (-я) *ср* (*срок*) five hundred years; (*годовщина*) quincentenary.

пятисотле́тн|**ий** (-яя, -ее, -ие) *прил* (*период*) five-hundred-year; (*дерево*) five hundred-year-old.

пятисо́т|**ый** (-ая, -ое, -ые) *чис* five-hundredth.

пя́т|**иться** (-чусь, -тишься; *perf* **попя́титься**) *несов возв* to move backwards; **он попя́тился от меня́** he backed away from me.

пятиуго́льник (-а) *м* pentagon.

пятичасово́й *прил* (*рабочий день*) five-hour; (*поезд*) five-o'clock.

пятиэта́ж|**ка** (-ки; *gen pl* -ек) *ж* (*разг*) five-storey block of flats (*BRIT*), five-story apartment block (*US*).

пятиэта́жный *прил* five-storey.

пя́т|**ка** (-ки; *gen pl* -ок) *ж* heel; **наступа́ть** (*impf*) **кому́-н на ~ки** (*перен*) to tread on sb's toes.

пятна́дцатый (-ая, -ое, -ые) *чис* fifteenth; *см также* **пя́тый**.

пятна́дцать (-и; *как* **пять**; *см* **Table 27**) *чис см также* **пять**.

пятна́|**ть** (-ю; *perf* **запятна́ть**) *несов перех* to tarnish.

пятни́ст|**ый** (-, -а, -о) *прил* spotted.

пя́тниц|**а** (-ы) *ж* Friday; **в ~у** on Friday; **по ~м** on Fridays; **в сле́дующую/про́шлую ~у** next/

last Friday; **сего́дняя ~, деся́тое ма́я** today is Friday (the) tenth (of) May.

пятн|**о́** (-á; *nom pl* **пя́тна**, *gen pl* -**ен**) *ср* (*также перен*) stain; (*выделяющееся по цвету*) spot.

пя́ток *сущ см* **пя́тка**.

пят|**о́к** (-ка́) *м* (*разг*) five (*when buying eggs etc*).

пя́т|**ый** (-ая, -ое, -ые) *чис* fifth; **сего́дня ~ое ию́ля** today is the fifth of July *или* July the fifth; **прие́ду ~ого ию́ля** I will arrive on the fifth of July; **встре́ча отло́жена до ~ого ию́ля** the meeting was postponed until the fifth of July; **сего́дня уже́ ~ое** (*число́*) today is already the fifth; **сейча́с де́сять мину́т ~ого** it is ten minutes past four; **я прие́хал в Петербу́рг в ты́сяча девятьсо́т пятьдеся́т ~ом году́** I came to Petersburg in nineteen fifty five; **ле́кция бу́дет в ~ой аудито́рии** the lecture will take place in room five; **я зако́нчил ~ым** I finished fifth; **я был ~ым ребёнком в семье́** I was child number five in the family; **~ое – деся́тое** (*разг*) this and that; **переска́кивать** (*impf*) **с ~ого на деся́тое** (*разг*) to skip from one subject to another.

пять (-и́; *см* **Table 27**) *чис* five; (*ПРОСВЕЩ*) ≈ A (*school mark*); **ей ~ лет** she is five years old; **они́ живу́т в до́ме но́мер ~** they live at number five; **о́коло ~и́** about five; **кни́га сто́ит ~ рубле́й** the book costs five roubles; **~ с полови́ной часо́в** five and a half hours; **сейча́с ~ часо́в** it is five o'clock; **я́блоки продаю́тся по ~ штук** the apples are sold in fives; **дели́ть** (**раздели́ть** *perf*) **что-н на ~** to divide sth into five.

пятьдеся́т (-и́десяти; *см* **Table 29**) *чис* fifty; **здесь о́коло ~и́десяти челове́к** there are about fifty people here; **на сле́дующей неде́ле ему́ испо́лнится ~ (лет)** he will be fifty next week; **ему́ о́коло ~и́десят (лет)** he is about fifty (years old); **маши́на е́дет со ско́ростью ~ киломе́тров в час** the car is going at fifty kilometres (*BRIT*) *или* kilometers (*US*) per hour.

пятьсо́т (-исо́т; *см* **Table 34**) *чис* five hundred; *см также* **сто**.

пя́тью *нареч* five times; **~ два – де́сять** five times two is ten.

пятью́ *чис см* **пять**.

пя́чусь *несов см* **пя́титься**.

~ *P, р* ~

Р, р *сущ нескл* (*буква*) the 17th letter of the Russian alphabet.

р. *сокр* (= **река́**) R., r. (= *river*); (= **роди́лся**) b. (= *born*); (= **рубль**) R., r. (= *rouble*).

раб (**-á**) *м* (*также перен*) slave; ~ **любви́/мо́ды** *итп* a slave to love/fashion *итп*.

раб|á (**-ы́**; *no pl*) *ж см* **раб**.

рабовладе́л|ец (**-ьца**) *м* slave owner.

рабовладе́льческ|ий (**-ая, -ое, -ие**) *прил* slave-owning.

раболе́п|ный (**-ен, -на, -но**) *прил* servile.

раболе́пств|овать (**-ую**) *несов неперех*: ~ (**пе́ред** +*instr*) to crawl (to).

рабо́т|а (**-ы**) *ж* (*труд, произведе́ние*) work; (*исто́чник заработка*) work, job; (*функциони́рование*) working; **поступа́ть** (**поступи́ть** *perf*) **на** ~**у** to start a job; **постоя́нная/вре́менная/случа́йная** ~ permanent/temporary/casual work *или* employment; **сде́льная** ~ piecework; **сме́нная** ~ shiftwork.

рабо́та|ть (**-ю**) *несов неперех* to work; (*магази́н, библиоте́ка итп*) to be open; ~ (*impf*) **на кого́-н/что-н** to work for sb/sth; ~ (*impf*) **над чем-н** to work on sth; **кем Вы** ~**ете?** what do you do for a living?; **я** ~**ю инжене́ром** I'm an engineer

▸ **рабо́таться** *несов возв* (+*dat*): **сего́дня мне не** ~**ется** I can't get down to work today; **в библиоте́ке хорошо́** ~**ется** the library is a good place to work.

рабо́тник (**-а**) *м* worker; (*учрежде́ния*) employee; **руководя́щие** ~**и** management; **нау́чный** ~ researcher.

рабо́тниц|а (**-ы**) *ж* (female) worker.

работода́тел|ь (**-я**) *м* employer.

работоспосо́бност|ь (**-и**) *ж* (*челове́ка*) ability to work hard; (*маши́ны*) efficiency.

работоспосо́бный *прил* (*челове́к*) able to work hard; (*населе́ние*) working *опред*.

работя́г|а (**-и**) *м/ж* (*разг*) workhorse (*fig*).

работя́щ|ий (**-ая, -ее, -ие**) *прил* (*разг*) hard-working.

рабо́ч|ая (**-ей**; *decl like adj*) *ж см* **рабо́чий**.

рабо́ч|ий (**-ая, -ее, -ие**) *прил* (*движе́ние, посёлок, столо́вая итп*) worker's *опред*; (*челове́к, оде́жда, часть механи́зма, чертёж*) working *опред* ♦ (**-его**; *decl like adj*) *м* worker; **в** ~**ее вре́мя** during working hours; **у нас нехва́тка**

~**их рук** we are undermanned; **в** ~**ем поря́дке** in the course of the proceedings; **рабо́чая ло́шадь** workhorse; **рабо́чая си́ла** workforce; **рабо́чая ста́нция** (*комп*) work station; **рабо́чее ме́сто** (*помеще́ние*) workplace; (*пост*) position; **рабо́чие ру́ки** workers; **рабо́чий визи́т** working visit; **рабо́чий день** working day (*BRIT*), workday (*US*); **рабо́чий класс** the working class.

ра́бск|ий (**-ая, -ое, -ие**) *прил* (*существова́ние, усло́вия*) slave-like; (*послуша́ние, подража́ние*) slavish; ~ **труд** slave labour (*BRIT*) *или* labor (*US*).

ра́бств|о (**-а**) *ср* slavery.

рабфа́к (**-а**) *м* (*ист*: = **рабо́чий факульте́т**) ≈ working man's college.

рабы́н|я (**-и**) *ж* slave.

равви́н (**-а**) *м* rabbi.

ра́вен *прил см* **ра́вный**.

ра́венств|о (**-а**) *ср* equality; (*чисел*) equal value; **знак** ~**а** (*МАТ*) equals sign; **ста́вить** (**поста́вить** *perf*) **знак** ~**а ме́жду чем-н и чем-н** to equate sth with sth.

равни́н|а (**-ы**) *ж* plain.

равно́ *нареч* equally ♦ *союз*: ~ (**как**) **и** as well as ♦ *как сказ*: **э́то всё** ~ it doesn't make any difference; **мне всё** ~ it's all the same to me; **я всё** ~ **приду́** I'll come just the same; **два плюс пять** ~ **семи́** two plus five equals seven.

равнове́си|е (**-я**) *ср* (*также перен*) equilibrium; **теря́ть** (**потеря́ть** *perf*) ~ to lose one's balance; ~ **сил** balance of power.

равноде́нстви|е (**-я**) *ср* equinox.

равноду́шен *прил см* **равноду́шный**.

равноду́ши|е (**-я**) *ср*: ~ (**к** +*dat*) indifference (to).

равноду́шно *нареч* indifferently.

равноду́ш|ный (**-ен, -на, -но**) *прил*: ~ (**к** +*dat*) indifferent (to).

равноме́р|ный (**-ен, -на, -но**) *прил* even.

равнопра́вен *прил см* **равнопра́вный**.

равнопра́ви|е (**-я**) *ср* equal rights *мн*.

равнопра́в|ный (**-ен, -на, -но**) *прил* equal.

равноси́л|ьный (**-ен, -ьна, -ьно**) *прил*: ~ +*dat* equivalent *или* equal to.

равноце́н|ный (**-ен, -на, -но**) *прил* of equal value *или* worth.

ра́в|ный (**-ен, -на́, -но**) *прил* equal; ~**ным о́бразом** equally; **на** ~**ных** (*разг*) on an equal footing.

равня́|ть (-ю; *perf* **сравня́ть**) *несов перех*: ~ **(с** +*instr*) (*де́лать ра́вным*) to make equal (with); (*одина́ково оце́нивать*): ~ **кого́-н/что-н с** +*instr* to treat sb/sth the same as

▶ **равня́ться** (*perf* **сравня́ться**) *несов возв*: ~**ся по** +*dat* to draw level with; (*счита́ть себя́ ра́вным*): ~**ся с** +*instr* to compare o.s. with; (*быть равноси́льным*): ~**ся** +*dat* to be equal to; (*сле́довать приме́ру*): ~**ся на** +*acc* to emulate; **два плюс два ~ется четырём** two plus two equals four.

рагу́ *ср нескл* ragout.

рад (-а, -о, -ы) *как сказ*: ~ **(**+*dat*) glad (of); ~ +*infin* glad *или* pleased to do; ~ **познако́миться с Ва́ми** pleased to meet you; **я** ~ **за него́** I'm pleased *или* happy for him; **я всегда́** ~ **помо́чь** I'm always glad to be of help; **я уже́ и не ра́да, что согласи́лась** I'm already regretting that I agreed.

ра́ди *предл*: ~ **(**+*gen*) for the sake of; **чего́** ~? (*разг*) what for?; **шу́тки** ~ (*разг*) for a joke; ~ **Бо́га!** (*разг*) for God's sake!

радиа́льный *прил* radial.

радиа́тор (-а) *м* radiator.

радиа́ци|я (-и) *ж* radiation.

ра́ди|й (-я) *м* radium.

радика́л (-а) *м* (ПОЛИТ, МАТ) radical.

радика́льный (-ен, -ьна, -ьно) *прил* radical.

радикули́т (-а) *м* lower back pain.

ра́дио *ср нескл* radio; **по** ~ on the radio; **слу́шать** (*impf*) ~ to listen to the radio.

радиоакти́вность (-и) *ж* radioactivity.

радиоакти́вный *прил* radioactive.

радиовеща́ни|е (-я) *ср* (radio) broadcasting.

радиолока́тор (-а) *м* radar (*device*).

радиолока́ци|я (-и) *ж* radar (*system*).

радиолюби́тел|ь (-я) *м* radio ham.

радиопереда́ч|а (-и) *ж* radio programme (BRIT) *или* program (US).

радиоприёмник (-а) *м* radio (set).

радиосвя́з|ь (-и) *ж* radiocommunication.

радиослу́шател|ь (-я) *м* (radio) listener.

радиослу́шательни|ца (-ы) *ж см* **радиослу́шатель**.

радиоста́нци|я (-и) *ж* radio station.

радиотелефо́н (-а) *м* radiotelephone.

радиоте́хник|а (-и) *ж* radio engineering.

радиоу́з|ел (-ла́) *м* public-address facilities *мн*.

радиоэлектро́ник|а (-и) *ж* radio electronics.

ради́ст (-а) *м* radio operator.

ради́ст|ка (-ки; *gen pl* -ок) *ж см* **ради́ст**.

ра́диус (-а) *м* radius; (*перен: влия́ния, де́йствия*) range.

ра́д|овать (-ую; *perf* **обра́довать**) *несов перех*: ~ **кого́-н** to make sb happy, please sb; ~ (*impf*) **глаз/слух** to be a joy to behold/hear

▶ **ра́доваться** *несов возв* (*перен: душа́,*

се́рдце*) to rejoice; (*perf* **обра́доваться**; +*dat*: *со́лнцу, успе́хам*) to take pleasure in; **я обра́довалась ему́** *или* **встре́че с ним** I was overjoyed to see him.

ра́достен *прил см* **ра́достный**.

ра́достно *нареч* joyfully; **они́ меня́** ~ **встре́тили** they gave me a very warm welcome.

ра́достн|ый (-ен, -на, -но) *прил* joyful; (*день, но́вость*) joyous.

ра́дос|ть (-ти) *ж* joy; **от** ~**ти** (*пла́кать, смея́ться*) with joy; **пры́гать** (*impf*) **от** ~**ти** to jump for joy; **с** ~**ю** gladly; **на** ~**тях я его́ прости́л** (*разг*) I was so happy, I forgave him.

ра́дуг|а (-и) *ж* rainbow.

ра́дужн|ый (-ен, -на, -но) *прил* (*перен: настрое́ние, наде́жды*) bright; ~**ые цвета́** rainbow colours; **ра́дужная оболо́чка** (АНАТ) iris.

раду́шен *прил см* **раду́шный**.

раду́ши|е (-я) *ср* warmth.

раду́шн|ый (-ен, -на, -но) *прил* warm.

раз (-а; *nom pl* -ы́, *gen pl* -) *м* time ◆ *нескл* (*оди́н*) one ◆ *нареч* (*разг*: *одна́жды*) once ◆ *союз* (*разг*: *е́сли*) if; **в два/три/четы́ре ра́за бо́льше/ме́ньше** two/three/four times bigger/smaller; **в пять/шесть/семь** *итп* ~ **бо́льше/ме́ньше** five/six/seven *итп* times bigger/smaller; **не** ~ more than once; **в пе́рвый** ~ (*впервы́е*) for the first time; (*в пе́рвом слу́чае*) on the first occasion; **в тот/про́шлый/сле́дующий** ~ that/last/next time; **на э́тот** ~ this time; **ещё** ~ (once) again; ~ **и навсегда́** once and for all; **ни ра́зу** not once; (**оди́н**) ~ **в день** once a day; **вот тебе́ и** ~**!** (*разг*) that's a turn up for the books!; **в са́мый** ~ (*разг: о разме́ре*) just right; (: *о вре́мени*) at just the right time: ~**... то ...** (*разг*) if ... then ...; ~ **на** ~ **не прихо́дится** you can't win all the time; ~ **пришёл – сади́сь** now that you're here, have a seat.

раз- *префикс* (*in verbs*; *о разделе́нии на ча́сти eg.* **развяза́ть**; (*о распределе́нии по места́м, по пове́рхности*) *indicating positioning of sth somewhere eg.* **разложи́ть**; (*об интенси́вном де́йствии*) *indicating intensive action eg.* **разбушева́ться**; (*о направле́нии движе́ния в ра́зные сто́роны*) *indicating movement in different directions eg.* **разбежа́ться**; (*о прекраще́нии де́йствия*) *indicating cessation of action eg.* **разлюби́ть**; (*in adjectives*; *разг: о вы́сшей сте́пени ка́чества*) *indicating a great degree of a certain quality eg.* **развесёлый**.

разба́в|ить (-лю, -ишь; *impf* **разбавля́ть**) *сов перех* to dilute.

разбаза́р|ить (-ю, -ишь; *impf* **разбаза́ривать**) *сов перех* to squander.

разба́лива|ться (-юсь) *несов от* **разболе́ться**.

разба́лтыва|ть(ся) (-ю(сь)) *несов от* **разболта́ть(ся)**.

разбе́г (-а) *м* (*машины*) acceleration; (*атлета*) run-up; **прыжо́к с** ~**а** *или* ~**у** running jump.

разбежа́ться (*как* **бежа́ть**; *см* **Table 20**; *impf* **разбега́ться**) *сов возв* to run off, scatter; (*перед прыжком*) to take a run-up; (*перен: мысли*) to wander; **у меня́ глаза́ разбега́ются** (*разг*) I'm spoilt for choice.

разбе́й(те) *сов см* **разби́ть**.

разберу́(сь) *сов см* **разобра́ть(ся)**.

разбива́|ть(ся) (-ю(сь)) *несов от* **разби́ть(ся)**.

разби́в|ка (-ки; *gen pl* -ок) *ж* (*данных, людей*) arranging; (*сада, парка*) layout.

разбира́тельств|о (-а) *ср* (*ЮР*) examination.

разбира́|ть (-ю) *несов от* **разобра́ть** ♦ *перех* (*разг: сотрудника, нарушителя*) to take to task

▸ **разбира́ться** *несов от* **разобра́ться** ♦ *возв* (*разг: понимать*): ~**ся в** +*prp* to understand.

разби́тн|ый *прил* carefree.

разб|и́ть (-обью, -обьёшь; *imper* -бе́й(те), *impf* **разбива́ть**) *сов перех* (*стекло, тарелку, голову*) to break; (*машину*) to smash up; (*врага, армию*) to crush; (*на участки, на части*) to break up; (*аллею, клумбу*) to lay; (*счастье, мечты́*) to ruin; **разбива́ть** (~ *perf*) **ла́герь** to set up camp

▸ **разби́ться** (*impf* **разбива́ться**) *сов возв* to break, smash; (*при падении, в аварии*) to be badly hurt; (*на группы, на участки*) to break up.

разбогате́|ть (-ю) *сов от* **богате́ть**.

разбо́|й (-я) *м* robbery.

разбо́йник (-а) *м* robber; (*разг: шалун*) troublemaker.

разбо́йниц|а (-ы) *ж см* **разбо́йник**.

разбо́йнича|ть (-ю) *несов неперех* to thieve; (*разг: шалить*) to get up to mischief.

разбо́йн|ый *прил*: ~**ое нападе́ние** (*ЮР*) armed assault.

разболе́|ться (-юсь; *impf* **разба́ливаться**) *сов возв* (*разг: человек*) to be taken ill; (: *рука, живот итп*) to hurt badly; **у меня́ голова́** ~**лась** I've got a splitting headache.

разбо́лтан|ный (-, -на, -но) *прил* (*разг*) slack; ~**ная похо́дка** swagger.

разболта́|ть (-ю; *impf* **разба́лтывать**) *сов перех* (*порошок, смесь итп*) to mix in; (*замок, гайку*) to weaken; (*разг: секрет, новость*) to blab; ~ (*perf*) **дисципли́ну** (*разг*) to let discipline slip; ~ (*perf*) **ребёнка** (*разг*) to lose control over a child

▸ **разболта́ться** (*impf* **разба́лтываться**) *сов возв* (*порошок, мука*) to mix in; (*дверь, запор*) to come loose; (*дисциплина, поведение*) to slacken off; (*no impf; болтать*) to babble on.

разбомб|и́ть (-лю́, -и́шь) *сов перех* to bomb.

разбо́р (-а) *м* (*статьи, вопроса итп*) analysis; (*ЮР*) examination; (*линг*) parsing; **без** ~**а** without exception.

разбо́р|ка (-и) *ж* (*обычно мн*) infighting.

разбо́рный *прил* collapsible.

разбо́рчивость (-и) *ж* (*требовательность*) discernment; (*почерка*) legibility.

разбо́рчив|ый (-, -а, -о) *прил* (*человек, вкус*) discerning; (*почерк*) legible.

разбра́сыва|ть (-ю) *несов от* **разбро́са́ть**

▸ **разбра́сываться** *несов возв* (*разг*) to try to do too much (at once); (+*instr*; *друзьями, поклонниками итп*) to underrate.

разбр|ести́сь (-еду́сь, -едёшься; *pt* -ёлся, -ела́сь, -ело́сь, *impf* **разбреда́ться**) *сов возв* to wander off (*in different directions*).

разброса́|ть (-ю; *impf* **разбра́сывать**) *сов перех* to scatter.

разбуд|и́ть (-ужу́, -у́дишь) *сов от* **буди́ть**.

разбу́х|нуть (-ну, -нешь; *pt* -, -ла, -ло, *impf* **разбуха́ть**) *сов неперех* to swell; (*папка, чемодан итп*) to bulge; (*лицо, рука итп*) to swell up.

разбуш|ева́ться (-у́юсь) *сов возв* (*море*) to rage; (*разг*) to rant.

разва́л (-а) *м* (*в кварти́ре, в дела́х*) chaos; (*экономики*) ruin; (*системы*) break-up; **у нас до́ма по́лный** ~ our home is in a state of chaos.

разва́лива|ть(ся) (-ю(сь)) *несов от* **развали́ть(ся)**.

разва́лин|а (-ы) *ж* (*обычно мн*) ruins *мн*; (*перен: человек*) wreck.

разв|али́ть (-алю́, -а́лишь; *impf* **разва́ливать**) *сов перех* (*стену, дом*) to knock down; (*дело, хозяйство*) to ruin

▸ **развали́ться** (*impf* **разва́ливаться**) *сов возв* to collapse; **он** ~**али́лся в кре́сле** he sat slumped in the armchair.

разва́р|иться (3sg -ится, 3pl -ятся, *impf* **разва́риваться**) *сов возв* to be overcooked; **бы́стро** ~**а́риваться** (*impf*) to cook quickly.

ра́зве *част* really; ~ **он согласи́лся/не знал?** did he really agree/not know?; ~ **то́лько** *или* **что** except that.

развева́|ться (3sg -ется, 3pl -ются) *несов возв* (*флаг*) to flutter; (*волосы*) to flow.

разве́да|ть (-ю; *impf* **разве́дывать**) *сов перех* (*ГЕО*) to prospect; (*ВОЕН*) to reconnoitre (*BRIT*), reconnoiter (*US*); ~ (*perf*)(**о** +*prp*) to find out (about).

разведе́ни|е (-я) *ср* (*животных*) breeding; (*растений*) cultivation; (*костра*) building; (*клея, краски*) dilution; ~ **пчёл** beekeeping.

разведён|ный (-, -а́, -ы́) *прил* (*в разводе*) divorced; (*no short form; раствор, водка*) diluted.

разве́д|ка (-ки; *gen pl* -ок) *ж* (*ГЕО*) prospecting; (*полит*) intelligence; (*ВОЕН*) reconnaissance.

разведу́(сь) *итп сов см* **развести́(сь)**.

разве́дчик (-а) *м* (*ГЕО*) prospector; (*полит*) intelligence agent; (*ВОЕН*) scout; (*самолёт*) reconnaissance plane.

разве́дчиц|а (-ы) *ж* (*ВОЕН*) scout.

разве́дыва|ть (-ю) *несов от* **разве́дать**.

разв|езти́ (-езу́, -езёшь; *pt* -ёз, -езла́, -езло́, *impf* **развози́ть**) *сов перех* to deliver ♦ *безл*: **меня́** ~**езло́ от жары́/во́дки** the heat/vodka knocked me out; **доро́гу** ~**езло́** the road has become impassable.

развéива|ть(ся) (-ю(сь)) *несов от*
разве́ять(ся).

развéй(те) *сов см* разви́ть.

развенча́|ть (-ю; *impf* развéнчивать) *сов перех*
to discredit.

развёрнут|ый (-, -а, -о) *прил* detailed;
(*строительство*) extensive.

развернý|ть (-ý, -ёшь; *impf* развёртывать *или*
развора́чивать) *сов перех* (*бумагу, карту*) to
unfold; (*ковёр*) to unroll; (*парус, флаг*) to
unfurl; (*проект, торговлю итп*) to launch;
(*выставку, лагерь*) to set up; (*свои силы,
талант*) to develop fully; (*корабль, машину,
самолёт*) to turn around; (*батальон, полк итп*)
to deploy; ~ (*perf*) пле́чи to pull one's shoulders
back

▶ разверну́ться (*impf* развёртываться *или*
развора́чиваться) *сов возв* (*борьба, кампания,
работа*) to get under way; (*талант, человек*)
to develop fully; (*автомобиль, судно*) to turn
around; (*батальон*) to be deployed; (*вид,
зрелище*) to open up.

развесел|и́ть (-ю́, -и́шь) *сов от* весели́ть.

развеси́ст|ый (-, -а, -о) *прил* spreading *опред.*

разве́|сить (-шу, -сишь; *impf* развéшивать) *сов
перех* (*ветви*) to spread; (*картины, вещи*) to
hang; (*бельё*) to hang up *или* out; ~ (*perf*) у́ши
(*разг*) to listen wide-eyed.

развесно́й *прил* sold by weight.

разв|ести́ (-еду́, -едёшь; *pt* -ёл, -ела́, -ело́, *impf*
разводи́ть) *сов перех* to take; (*разъединить*)
to divorce; (*порошок*) to dissolve; (*сок, краску*)
to dilute; (*животных*) to breed; (*цветы, сад*) to
grow; (*мост*) to raise; разводи́ть (~ *perf*) дете́й
по дома́м to take the children home; разводи́ть
(~ *perf*) ого́нь to get a fire going; разводи́ть (~
perf) рука́ми ≈ to shrug one's shoulders;
разводи́ть (~ *perf*) пусту́ю болтовню́ (*разг*) to
talk hot air

▶ развести́сь (*impf* разводи́ться) *сов возв*
(*животные*) to breed; разводи́ться (~сь *perf*)
(*с +instr*) to divorce, get divorced (from).

разветв|и́ть (-лю́, -и́шь; *impf* разветвля́ть) *сов
перех* to expand

▶ разветви́ться (*impf* разветвля́ться) *сов возв*
(*дерево, река, дорога*) to branch; (*компания,
учреждение*) to branch out.

разветвле́ни|е (-я) *ср* (*действие: дорог, кроны
деревьев*) branching; (: *компании*) expansion;
(*место: железной дороги, канала*) fork.

разветвлённый (-ён, -ена́, -ено́) *прил*
extensive.

разветвлю́(сь) *сов см* разветви́ть(ся).

разветвля́|ть(ся) (-ю(сь)) *несов от*
разветви́ть(ся).

разве́ша|ть (-ю; *impf* развéшивать) *сов перех*
(*картины, фотографии*) to hang; (*бельё*) to
hang up *или* out.

развéшива|ть (-ю) *несов от* разве́сить,
разве́шать.

разве́шу *сов см* разве́сить.

разве́|ять (-ю; *impf* развéивать) *сов перех*
(*облака, туман*) to disperse; (*подозрения,
сомнения, грусть*) to dispel; развéивать (~
perf) миф to shatter a myth

▶ разве́яться (*impf* развéиваться) *сов возв*
(*облака*) to disperse; (*туман*) to lift; (*тоска,
сомнения, мрачные мысли*) to be dispelled;
(*человек*) to relax.

развива́|ть(ся) (-ю(сь)) *несов от* разви́ть(ся).

развива́ющ|ийся (-аяся, -оеся, -иеся) *прил*:
~аяся страна́ developing country.

разви́л|ка (-ки; *gen pl* -ок) *ж* fork (*in road*).

разви́ти|е (-я) *ср* development; высо́кое/
ни́зкое ~ a high/low level of development.

ра́звит|о́й (-, -а, -о) *прил* developed; (*духовно
зрелый*) mature.

разв|и́ть (-овью́, -овьёшь; *pt* -и́л, -ила́,
-и́ло, *imper* -ве́й(те), *impf* развива́ть) *сов
перех* to develop; (*наступление,
деятельность*) to step up; (*верёвку, плётку*) to
unwind; (*волосы*) to straighten; развива́ть (~
perf) ско́рость to gather speed; развива́ть (~
perf) ребёнка to help a child to develop

▶ разви́ться (*impf* развива́ться) *сов возв* to
develop; (*скорость*) to build up; (*верёвка, коса,
плётка*) to come unwound; (*волосы*) to become
straighter.

развлёк(ся) *итп сов см* развле́чь(ся).

развлека́тел|ьный (-ен, -ьна, -ьно) *прил*
entertaining.

развлека́|ть(ся) (-ю(сь)) *несов от*
развле́чь(ся).

развлеку́(сь) *итп сов см* развле́чь(ся).

развлече́ни|е (-я) *ср* (*гостей, публики*)
entertaining; (*спектакль итп*) entertainment.

развл|е́чь (-еку́, -ечёшь *итп*, -еку́т; *pt* -ёк,
-екла́, -екло́, *impf* развлека́ть) *сов перех* to
entertain

▶ развле́чься (*impf* развлека́ться) *сов возв* to
have fun.

разво́д (-а) *м* (*расторжение брака*) divorce;
(*моста*) opening; они́ в ~е they are divorced;
подава́ть (пода́ть *perf*) на ~ to apply for a
divorce.

разво|ди́ть(ся) (-ожу́(сь), -о́дишь(ся)) *несов
от* развести́(сь).

разводно́й *прил*: ~ ключ monkey wrench;
разводно́й мост drawbridge.

разво́д|ы (-ов) *мн* (*узор*) design *ед*; (*подтёки,
пятна*) stains *мн*.

развожу́(сь) *несов см* разводи́ть(ся).

разв|ози́ть (-ожу́, -о́зишь) *несов от* развезти́.

разволн|ова́ть (-у́ю) *сов перех* to alarm

▶ разволнова́ться *сов возв* to be alarmed.

развора́чива|ть(ся) (-ю(сь)) *несов от*

разверну́ть(ся).

разворова́ть (-у́ю; *impf* **разворо́вывать**) *сов перех* to loot.

разворо́т (-а) *м* (*машины*) U-turn; (*в книге*) double page.

разворо́тить (-чу́, -тишь) *сов перех* (*дорогу*) to dig up.

разврат (-а) *м* promiscuity; (*духовный*) depravity.

разврат\|ен *прил см* **развра́тный**.

разврати́ть (-щу́, -ти́шь; *impf* **развраща́ть**) *сов перех* to pervert; (*деньгами*) to corrupt.

▶ **разврати́ться** (*impf* **развраща́ться**) *сов возв* (*см перех*) to become promiscuous; to become corrupted.

развра́тник (-а) *м* promiscuous man (*мн* men).

развра́тниц\|а (-ы) *ж* promiscuous woman (*мн* women).

развра́тнича\|ть (-ю) *несов неперех* to lead a life of promiscuity.

развра́т\|ный (-ен, -на, -но) *прил* promiscuous.

развраща́\|ть(ся) (-ю(сь)) *несов от* **разврати́ть(ся)**.

развращу́(сь) *несов см* **разврати́ть(ся)**.

развяза́ть (-жу́, -жешь; *impf* **развя́зывать**) *сов перех* (*узел, шнурки, мешок*) to untie: (*перен: инициативу*) to unshackle; (: *войну, реакцию*) to unleash; **развя́зывать** (*~ perf*) **кому́-н ру́ки** (*перен*) to free sb's hands; **развя́зывать** (*~ perf*) **кому́-н язы́к** to loosen sb's tongue

▶ **развяза́ться** (*impf* **развя́зываться**) *сов возв* (*шнурки, бант итп*) to come untied: **~ся с** +*instr* (*разг: с людьми, с экзаменами*) to be through with; (: *с долгами*) to get rid of.

развя́з\|ка (-ки; *gen pl* -ок) *ж* (*конец*) ending; (*АВТ*) junction.

развя́з\|ный (-ен, -на, -но) *прил* overly familiar.

развя́зок *сущ см* **развя́зка**.

развя́зыва\|ть(ся) (-ю(сь)) *несов от* **развяза́ть(ся)**.

разгада́\|ть (-ю; *impf* **разга́дывать**) *сов перех* (*кроссворд, загадку*) to solve; (*замыслы, тайну*) to guess; (*сны*) to decipher; (*человека*) to fathom out.

разга́д\|ка (-ки; *gen pl* -ок) *ж* (*снов, мыслей*) deciphering; (*тайны*) key; (*феномена*) explanation; (*решение загадки*) solution.

разга́дыва\|ть (-ю) *несов от* **разгада́ть**.

разга́р (-а) *м*: **в ~е** +*gen* (*сезона*) at the height of; (*боя*) in the heart of; **кани́кулы в (по́лном) ~е** the holidays are in full swing.

разгиба́\|ть(ся) (-ю(сь)) *несов от* **разогну́ть(ся)**.

разгильдя́\|й (-я) *м* (*разг*) layabout.

разгла́\|дить (-жу, -дишь; *impf* **разгла́живать**) *сов перех* to smooth out.

разгла\|си́ть (-шу́, -си́шь; *impf* **разглаша́ть**) *сов перех* to divulge, disclose.

разгля\|де́ть (-жу́, -ди́шь; *impf* **разгля́дывать**) *сов перех* (*рассмотреть*) to scrutinize; (*no impf*:

поня́ть) to discern.

разгне́ван\|ный (-, -а, -о) *прил*: **~** (+*instr*) angry (with).

разгова́рива\|ть (-ю) *несов неперех*: **~** (*с* +*instr*) to talk (to); **она́ бо́льше со мной не ~ет** she doesn't talk to me any more.

разгово́р (-а) *м* conversation; **э́то друго́й ~!** (*разг*) that's another matter!; **без ~ов** without a word; *см также* **разгово́ры**.

разгово́рник (-а) *м* phrase book.

разгово́рный *прил* colloquial.

разгово́рчив\|ый (-, -а, -о) *прил* talkative.

разгово́р\|ы (-ов) *мн* (*толки*) gossip *ед*.

разго́н (-а) *м* (*демонстрации*) breaking up; (*самолёта, автомобиля*) acceleration; **устра́ивать** (**устро́ить** *perf*) **кому́-н ~** (*разг*) to give sb a roasting.

разгоня́\|ть(ся) (-ю(сь)) *несов от* **разогна́ть(ся)**.

разгоре́ться (*3sg* -и́тся, *3sg* -я́тся, *impf* **разгора́ться**) *сов возв* (*костёр, спор*) to flare up; (*закат*) to be ablaze; (*щёки, уши*) to burn; (*перен: страсти, любопытство*) to become inflamed.

разгорячён\|ный (-, -а́, -о́) *прил*: **~** (+*instr*) (*человек*) inflamed (by); (-, на́, -но́; *лицо*) excited.

разгорячи́\|ться (-у́сь, -и́шься) *сов от* **горячи́ться ♦** *возв* (*от волнения, от работы*) to get het up; (*от бега*) to be hot.

разграни́ч\|ить (-у, -ишь; *impf* **разграни́чивать**) *сов перех* (*район, земли*) to demarcate; (*обязанности, понятия*) to delimit.

разграфи́\|ть (-лю́, -и́шь) *сов от* **графи́ть**.

разгре\|сти́ (-бу́, -бёшь; *pt* -ёб, -ебла́, -ебло́, *impf* **разгреба́ть**) *сов перех* to sweep aside.

разгро́м (-а) *м* rout; (*разг: беспорядок*) mayhem, havoc; (*статьи*) savaging.

разгроми́\|ть (-лю́, -ишь) *сов перех* (*врага, сопротивление*) to crush; (*город, страну*) to destroy; (*политику, статью, соперника*) to savage.

разгро́мный *прил* (*речь, критика*) savage.

разгру\|зи́ть (-ужу́, -у́зишь; *impf* **разгружа́ть**) *сов перех* to unload; (*программу*) to ease; **разгружа́ть** (*~ perf*) **кого́-н** to lighten sb's load.

разгру́з\|ка (-ки; *gen pl* -ок) *ж* (*вагонов, баржи*) unloading; (*перен: человека*) unburdening; (: *программы, плана*) easing up.

разгру́зочн\|ый *прил*: **~ые рабо́ты** unloading; **разгру́зочный день** day during dieting programme on which diet is relaxed.

разгрыз\|ть (-у, -ёшь) *сов от* **грызть ♦** (*impf* **разгрыза́ть**) *перех* (*редиску, кость*) to gnaw at; (*орех*) to crack open.

разгу́л (-а) *м* revelry; (+*gen*; *реакции, национализма*) outburst of.

разгу́лива\|ть (-ю) *несов неперех* to have a wander

▶ **разгу́ливаться** *несов от* **разгуля́ться**.

разгуля́\|ться (-юсь; *impf* **разгу́ливаться**) *сов*

возв (дать себе волю) to let o.s. go; *(перен: ветер, море)* to get up; (: *погода, день*) to clear up.

раздава́|ть(ся) (-ю́(сь), -ёшь(ся)) *несов от* разда́ть(ся).

раздави́ть (-авлю́, -а́вишь) *сов от* дави́ть ♦ (*impf* разда́вливать) *перех* to squash.

разда́м(ся) *итп сов см* разда́ть(ся).

разда́точный *прил*: ~ пункт distribution centre (*BRIT*) *или* center (*US*).

разда́ть (*как* дать; *см* Table 14; *impf* раздава́ть) *сов перех* to give out, distribute

▸ **разда́ться** (*impf* раздава́ться) *сов возв (голос, шум итп)* to be heard; *(толпа)* to make way; *(обувь, сапоги)* to stretch; **раздава́ться** (~ся *perf*) **в бёдрах** *(разг)* to put weight on around the hips.

разда́ч|а (-и) *ж* distribution.

разда́шь(ся) *сов см* разда́ть(ся).

раздва́ива|ться (-юсь) *несов от* раздво́иться.

раздвига́|ть(ся) (-ю) *несов от* раздви́нуть(ся).

раздвижно́й *прил*: ~ за́навес curtain (*THEAT*); ~ стол extending table.

раздви́н|уть (-у, -ешь; *impf* раздвига́ть) *сов перех* to move apart; *(шторы)* to open; *(толпу)* to part; *(перен: рамки наблюдения, исследования)* to broaden

▸ **раздви́нуться** (*impf* раздвига́ться) *сов возв (шторы)* to open; *(толпа)* to part; *(перен: мир, возможности)* to open up.

раздво́ени|е (-я) *ср*: ~ ли́чности split personality.

раздво́|иться (-ю́сь, -и́шься; *impf* раздва́иваться) *сов возв (дорога, река)* to divide into two; *(перен: мнение)* to be divided.

раздева́л|ка (-ки; *gen pl* -ок) *ж* changing room.

раздева́|ть(ся) (-ю(сь)) *несов от* разде́ть(ся).

разде́л (-а) *м (действие: имущества)* division; *(часть, область)* section.

разде́ла|ть (-ю; *impf* разде́лывать) *сов перех (мясо, рыбу)* to dress; *(грядки)* to prepare; *(мебель)*: ~ что-н под дуб/мра́мор to give sth an oak/a marble finish

▸ **разде́латься** (*impf* разде́лываться) *сов возв (разг)*: ~ся с +*instr* (с делами, с долгами) to settle; *(с соперником, с хулиганом)* to take care of.

разделе́ни|е (-я) *ср* division; ~ труда́ division of labour (*BRIT*) *или* labor (*US*).

раздели́ть (-елю́, -е́лишь) *сов от* дели́ть ♦ (*impf* разделя́ть) *перех (мнение, взгляды, энтузиазм)* to share

▸ **раздели́ться** *сов от* дели́ться ♦ (*impf* разделя́ться) *возв (мнения, общество)* to become divided.

разде́лыва|ть(ся) (-ю(сь)) *несов от* разде́лать(ся).

разделя́|ть(ся) (-ю(сь)) *несов от* раздели́ть(ся).

раздеру́ *итп сов см* разодра́ть.

разде́|ть (-ну, -нешь; *impf* раздева́ть) *сов перех* to undress; *(разг: ограбить)*: ~ кого́-н to strip sb bare

▸ **разде́ться** (*impf* раздева́ться) *сов возв* to get undressed.

раздира́|ть (-ю) *несов от* разодра́ть ♦ *перех (душу, человека, общество)* to tear apart.

раздобре́|ть (-ю) *сов от* добре́ть.

раздоб|ы́ть (*как* быть; *см* Table 21; *impf* раздобыва́ть) *сов перех (разг)* to get hold of, lay one's hands on.

раздо́лен *прил см* раздо́льный.

раздо́ль|е (-я) *ср* expanse; *(перен)* freedom; мне здесь ~ I feel free here.

раздо́л|ьный (-ен, -ьна, -ьно) *прил* vast; *(перен)* free.

раздо́р (-а) *м (обычно мн)* strife *ед.*

раздоса́д|овать (-ую) *сов перех* to upset.

раздража́|ть(ся) (-ю(сь)) *несов от* раздражи́ть(ся).

раздраже́ни|е (-я) *ср* irritation.

раздражённо *нареч (сказать)* irritably.

раздражённый (-ён, -ена́, -ено́) *прил (человек, голос)* irritated; (-ён, -енна́, -енно́; *тон*) irritable; у меня́ не́рвы ~ены́ до преде́ла my nerves are on edge.

раздражи́тел|ьный (-ен, -ьна, -ьно) *прил* irritable.

раздраж|и́ть (-у́, -и́шь; *impf* раздража́ть) *сов перех (также МЕД)* to irritate; *(нервы)* to agitate; *(аппетит)* to stimulate

▸ **раздражи́ться** (*impf* раздража́ться) *сов возв (кожа, глаза)* to become irritated; *(человек)*: ~ся (+*instr*) to be irritated (by).

раздроб|и́ть (-лю́, -и́шь) *сов от* дроби́ть ♦ (*impf* раздробля́ть) *перех* to shatter.

раздро́блен|ный (-, -а, -о) *прил* fragmented.

раздроблю́ *сов см* раздроби́ть.

раздробля́|ть (-ю) *несов от* раздроби́ть.

раздува́|ть(ся) (-ю(сь)) *несов от* разду́ть(ся).

разду́ма|ть (-ю; *impf* разду́мывать) *сов неперех*: ~ +*infin* (пойти, жениться итп) to decide not to do, decide against doing.

разду́мыва|ть (-ю) *несов от* разду́мать ♦ *неперех*: ~ (о +*prp*) *(долго думать)* to contemplate.

разду́м|ье (-я; *gen pl* -ий) *ср* contemplation; *(обычно мн)* thought; впа́дать (впасть *perf*) в ~ to sink deep into thought; по́сле до́лгих ~ий on *или* after lengthy consideration.

разду́|ть (-ую; *impf* раздува́ть) *сов перех (огонь, костёр)* to fan; *(пузырь)* to blow; *(разг: дело, скандал)* to blow up; (: *штаты*) to overstaff; раздува́ть (~ *perf*) но́здри to flare

The spelling rules for Russian are shown on page xvii.

one's nostrils; **у неё ~у́ло щёку/но́гу** her cheek/leg has swollen up

► **разду́ться** (*impf* **раздува́ться**) *сов возв* (*парус*) to swell; (*щека, губа, также перен*) to swell up; (*карманы, портфель*) to bulge.

разева́ть (-ю) *несов от* **рази́нуть**.

разжа́лоб|ить (-лю, -ишь) *сов перех*: ~ **кого́-н** to evoke sympathy in sb.

разжа́л|овать (-ую) *сов перех* to demote; ~ (*perf*) **кого́-н в рядовы́е** to reduce sb to the ranks.

разжа́ть (-ожму́, -ожмёшь; *impf* **разжима́ть**) *сов перех* (*пальцы, губы*) to relax; (*пружину*) to uncoil

► **разжа́ться** (*impf* **разжима́ться**) *сов возв* (*см перех*) to relax; to uncoil.

разже́ва́ть (-ую; *impf* **разжёвывать**) *сов перех* to chew; (*перен: разг: мысль*) to spell out in simple terms.

разже́чь (-огу́, -ожжёшь *итп*, -огу́т; *pt* -жёг, -огла́, -огло́, *impf* **разжига́ть**) *сов перех* (*также перен*) to kindle; (*войну, ненависть*) to incite.

разживу́сь *итп сов см* **разжи́ться**.

разжига́|ть (-ю) *несов от* **разже́чь**.

разжима́|ть(ся) (-ю(сь)) *несов от* **разжа́ть(ся)**.

разжире́|ть (-ю) *сов от* **жире́ть**.

разжи́ться (-иву́сь, -ивёшься; *pt* -и́лся, -ила́сь, -ило́сь) *сов возв* (*разг: жить в достатке*) to do well for o.s.; ~ (*perf*) +*instr* (*деньгами*) to rake in.

раздадо́р|ить (-ю, -ишь; *impf* **раздадо́ривать**) *сов перех* to excite.

рази́н|уть (-у, -ешь; *impf* **разева́ть**) *сов перех* (*разг*): ~ **рот** to gape; **слу́шать** (*impf*) ~**ув рот** to listen open-mouthed.

рази́н|я (-и) *м/ж* (*разг*) scatterbrain.

рази́тел|ьный (-ен, -ьна, -ьно) *прил* striking.

рази́ть (-жу́, -зи́шь) *сов перех* to strike; (*перен: пороки*) to strike out ♦ *безл* (+*instr*; *разг*): **от неё ~зи́т духа́ми/чесноко́м** she reeks of perfume/garlic.

разлага́|ть(ся) (-ю(сь)) *несов от* **разложи́ть(ся)**.

разла́д (-а) *м* (*в делах, в работе*) disorder; (*с женой*) discord.

разла́мыва|ть (-ю) *несов от* **разлома́ть, разломи́ть**

► **разла́мываться** *несов от* **разлома́ться, разломи́ться** ♦ *возв* (*разг*): **у меня́ ~ется спина́/голова́** my back/head is killing me.

разлёгся *итп сов см* **разле́чься**.

разле|те́ться (-чу́сь, -ти́шься; *impf* **разлета́ться**) *сов возв* (*птицы, перья*) to fly off (*in different directions*); (*перен: выросшие дети*) to fly the nest; (*разг: стекло, ваза итп*) to shatter; (: *новости*) to get around; (: *поезд*) to speed up.

разле́чься (-я́гусь, -я́жешься *итп*, -я́гутся; *pt* -ёгся, -егла́сь, -егло́сь) *сов возв* (*разг*) to

stretch out.

разли́в (-а) *м* flooding; (*место, залитое водой*) flood plain; (*вина, воды*) bottling; (*металла*) casting.

разлива́|ть (-ю) *несов от* **разли́ть**

► **разлива́ться** *несов от* **разли́ться** ♦ *возв* (*соловьи*) to sing; (*перен*): ~**ся соловьём** to wax lyrical.

разливн|о́й *прил*: ~**о́е пи́во** beer on tap.

разлин|ова́ть (-у́ю; *impf* **разлино́вывать**) *сов перех* to rule (*page*).

разли́ть (-олью́, -олье́шь; *pt* -ли́л, -лила́, -ли́ло, *impf* **разлива́ть**) *сов перех* to pour out; (*по бутылкам*) to bottle; (*пролить*) to spill; **их водо́й не ~олье́шь** they are never apart

► **разли́ться** (*impf* **разлива́ться**) *сов возв* (*пролиться*) to spill; (*река*) to overflow; **румя́нец ~пи́лся по его́ щека́м** the colour flooded into his cheeks; **по её лицу́ ~лила́сь улы́бка** a smile spread across her face.

различа́|ть (-ю) *несов от* **различи́ть**

► **различа́ться** *несов возв*: ~**ся по** +*dat* to differ in.

разли́чен *прил см* **разли́чный**.

разли́чи|е (-я) *ср* difference; **без ~я** indiscriminately.

различи́ть (-у́, -и́шь; *impf* **различа́ть**) *сов перех* (*увидеть, услышать*) to make out; (*отличить*): ~ (*по* +*dat*) to distinguish (by); **я их не ~а́ю** I can't tell them apart.

разли́ч|ный (-ен, -на, -но) *прил* different.

разложе́ни|е (-я) *ср* (*хим, био*) decomposition; (*общества, армии итп*) disintegration; (*мат*) expansion (*of equation*).

разл|ожи́ть (-ожу́, -о́жишь; *impf* **раскла́дывать**) *сов перех* (*расположить*) to place, arrange; (*еду по тарелкам*) to dish out, serve; (*карту, диван, стол*) to open out; (*impf* **разлага́ть**; *хим, био*) to decompose; (*мат*) to expand; (*перен: армию*) to demoralize; **раскла́дывать** (~ *perf*) **костёр** to build a fire

► **разложи́ться** (*impf* **раскла́дываться**) *сов возв* (*разг: разместить свои вещи*) to spread; (*impf* **разлага́ться**; *хим, био*) to decompose; (*мат*) to expand; (*перен: армия, общество*) to fall apart.

разлома́|ть (-ю) *сов от* **лома́ть** ♦ (*impf* **разла́мывать**) *перех* to break up

► **разлома́ться** (*impf* **разла́мываться**) *сов возв* to break up; (*постройка*) to fall to pieces.

разл|оми́ть (-омлю́, -о́мишь; *impf* **разла́мывать**) *сов перех* (*на части: хлеб итп*) to break up

► **разломи́ться** (*impf* **разла́мываться**) *сов возв* to break up.

разлу́к|а (-и) *ж* separation; **жить** (*impf*) **в ~е с кем-н** to live apart from sb.

разлуч|и́ть (-у́, -и́шь; *impf* **разлуча́ть**) *сов перех*: ~ **кого́-н с** +*instr* to separate sb from

► **разлучи́ться** (*impf* **разлуча́ться**) *сов возв*: ~**ся** (*с* +*instr*) to be separated (from).

разлюб|и́ть (-юблю́, -ю́бишь) *сов перех*: ~ +*infin* (*читать, гулять итп*) to lose one's enthusiasm for doing; **он меня́ ~юби́л** he doesn't love me any more.

разля́гусь *итп сов см* разле́чься.

разма́|зать (-жу, -жешь; *impf* разма́зывать) *сов перех* to smear

▶ разма́заться (*impf* разма́зываться) *сов возв* to be smeared.

размазн|я́ (-и́) *м/ж* ditherer.

разма́зыва|ть(ся) (-ю) *несов от* разма́зать(ся).

размáлыва|ть (-ю) *несов от* размоло́ть.

разма́рива|ть (*3sg* -ет, *3pl* -ют) *несов от* размори́ть

▶ разма́риваться *несов от* размори́ться.

разма́тыва|ть (-ю) *несов от* размота́ть.

разма́х (-а) *м* (*рук, крыльев*) span; (*маятника, колокола*) swing; (*перен: деятельности*) scope; (: *проекта*) scale; **уда́рить** (*perf*) **кого́-н с ~у** to take a swing at sb; **он челове́к с ~ом** he thinks on a large scale.

разма́хива|ть (-ю) *несов от* размахну́ть ◆ *неперех*: ~ +*instr* (*руками, флажком*) to wave; (*шашкой*) to brandish

▶ разма́хиваться *несов от* размахну́ться.

размахн|у́ть (-у́, -ёшь; *impf* разма́хивать) *сов перех* (*руки, крыльа*) to spread ◆ *неперех*: ~ +*instr* (*кнутом, топором*) to swing

▶ размахну́ться (*impf* разма́хиваться) *сов возв* to swing one's arm back; (*перен: разг: со свадьбой, в делах итп*) to go to town.

разма́шист|ый (-, -а, -о) *прил* sweeping.

размельч|и́ть (-у́, -и́шь) *сов от* мельчи́ть.

размелю́ *итп сов см* размоло́ть.

разме́н (-а) *м* (*денег, пленных*) exchange; ~ кварти́ры flat swap (*in which one large flat is exchanged for two smaller ones*).

разме́нива|ть(ся) (-ю(сь)) *несов от* разменя́ть(ся).

разме́нн|ый *прил*: ~ автома́т change machine; ~ая моне́та (small) change.

разменя́|ть (-ю; *impf* разме́нивать) *сов перех* (*деньги*) to change; (*квартиру*) to exchange; (*перен: талант*) to waste; ~ (*perf*) со́весть to sell out (*fig*)

▶ разменя́ться (*impf* разме́ниваться) *сов возв* (*перен: разг: обменять жилплощадь*) to do a flat swap (*of one large flat for two smaller ones*); **разме́ниваться** (*impf*) **по мелоча́м** или **пустяка́м** (*разг*) to waste o.s.

разме́р (-а) *м* size; (*обычно мн: строительства: масштабы*) dimension; (*линг*) metre (*BRIT*), meter (*US*); **како́й у тебя́ ~?** what size do you take?

разме́рен|ный (-, -на, -но) *прил* (*звон, шаги*) measured; (*жизнь*) well-regulated.

разме|сти́ть (-щу́, -сти́шь; *impf* размеща́ть) *сов*

перех (*найти́ место для*) to place; (*расположить*) to arrange

▶ размести́ться (*impf* размеща́ться) *сов возв* to accommodate o.s.; **го́сти ~сти́лись за столо́м** the guests took their seats at the table.

разме|та́ть (-чу́, -чешь) *сов перех* (*листву, пепел итп*) to scatter; (*руки*) to fling open

▶ размета́ться *сов возв* (*волосы*) to fly everywhere; (*человек: во сне*) to sprawl out.

разме́тить (-чу, -тишь; *impf* размеча́ть) *сов перех* to mark out.

размечта́|ться (-юсь) *сов возв* to start dreaming.

разме́чу *сов см* разме́тить.

размечу́(сь) *итп сов см* размета́ть(ся).

размеша́|ть (-ю; *impf* разме́шивать) *сов перех* to stir.

размеща́|ть(ся) (-ю(сь)) *несов от* размести́ть(ся).

размеще́ни|е (-я) *ср* (*вещей*) placing; (*расположение*) arrangement; (*людей: по комнатам*) accommodation.

размещу́(сь) *сов см* размести́ть(ся).

размина́|ть(ся) (-ю(сь)) *несов от* размя́ть(ся).

размини́р|овать (-ую) (*не*)*сов перех*: ~ по́ле to clear a field of mines.

разми́н|ка (-ки; *gen pl* -ок) *ж* (*ног, мускулов*) loosening up; (*спортсмена*) warm-up.

размин|у́ться (-у́сь, -ёшься) *сов возв* (*не встретиться*) to miss each other; (*дать пройти*) to pass; **мы с ним ~у́лись** (**на 5 мину́т**) we missed each other (by 5 minutes).

размножа́|ть (-ю) *несов от* размно́жить

▶ размножа́ться *несов от* размно́житься ◆ *возв* (*био*) to reproduce.

размноже́ни|е (-я) *ср* (*также био*) reproduction.

размно́ж|ить (-у, -ишь; *impf* размножа́ть) *сов перех* to make (multiple) copies of

▶ размно́житься (*perf* размножа́ться) *сов возв* (*био*) to reproduce.

размо́ет *итп сов см* размы́ть.

размозж|и́ть (-у́, -и́шь) *сов перех* to smash.

размо́к|нуть (-ну, -нешь; *pt* -, -ла, -ло, *impf* размока́ть) *сов неперех* (*хлеб, картон*) to go soggy; (*почва*) to become sodden.

размо́лв|ка (-ки; *gen pl* -ок) *ж* squabble.

размо|ло́ть (-елю́, -е́лешь; *impf* размáлывать) *сов перех* to grind.

размора́жива|ть(ся) (-ю(сь)) *несов от* разморо́зить(ся).

размор|и́ть (*3sg* -и́т, *3pl* -я́т, *impf* разма́ривать) *сов перех* (*сон, усталость*) to come over; **меня́ ~и́ло от жары́/све́жего во́здуха** the heat/fresh air has made me drowsy

▶ размори́ться (*impf* разма́риваться) *сов возв* to become drowsy.

разморо́|зить (-жу, -зишь; *impf*

размора́живать) *сов перех* to defrost
▶ разморо́зиться (*impf* размора́живаться)
сов возв to defrost.
размота́|ть (-ю; *impf* разма́тывать) *сов перех*
to unwind.
размыва́|ть (*3sg* -ет, *3pl* -ют) *несов от*
размы́ть.
размыка́|ть(ся) (-ю) *несов от* разомкну́ть(ся).
размы́тый (-, -а, -о) *прил* blurred.
размы́|ть (*3sg* -о́ет, *3sg* -о́ют, *impf* размыва́ть)
сов перех to wash away.
размышле́ни|е (-я) *ср* reflection.
размышля́|ть (-ю) *несов неперех*: ~ (o +*prp*) to
think (about), reflect (on).
размягч|и́ть (у́, -и́шь; *impf* размягча́ть) *сов
перех* (воск, кожу, душу) to soften; (*перен*:
человека) to soften up.
размя́к|нуть (-ну, -нешь; *pt* -, -ла, -ло, *impf*
размяка́ть) *сов неперех* (глина, почва) to
soften; (*перен*: от спиртного, от духоты) to
(become) mellow; (: от похвалы) to soften up.
размя́ть (-омну́, -омнёшь) *сов от* мять ◆ (*impf*
размина́ть) *перех* to loosen up
▶ размя́ться (*impf* размина́ться) *сов возв* to
warm up.
разнаря́д|ка (-ки; *gen pl* -ок) *м* directive.
разна́шивать(ся) (-ю) *несов от*
разноси́ть(ся).
разн|ести́ (-есу́, -есёшь; *pt* -ёс, -есла́, -есло́,
impf разноси́ть) *сов перех* (письма, посылки) to
deliver; (еду) to serve (up); (тарелки, чашки) to
put out; (тучи, обрывки бумаги) to disperse;
(заразу, слухи) to spread; (разг: разбить) to
smash up; (: раскритиковать) to slam, pan ◆
безл (разг: опухнуть) to puff up; (: пополнеть)
to get fat; разноси́ть (~ *perf*) что-н в кло́чья to
smash sth to pieces
▶ разнести́сь (*impf* разноси́ться) *сов возв*
(весть, слух, запах) to spread; (звон, гудок,
крик) to resound.
разнима́|ть (-ю) *несов от* разня́ть.
разниму́ *итп сов см* разня́ть.
ра́зниц|а (-ы) *ж* difference; кака́я ~? what
difference does it make?; ~ в ве́се/в во́зрасте
weight/age difference; без ~ы (разг) it makes
no difference.
разнобо́|й (-я) *м* (в работе, в действиях) lack
of coordination; (в правилах) contradictions *мн*.
разнове́с (-а) *м* weights *мн* (*for set of scales*).
разнови́дность| (-и) *ж* (био) variety; (людей)
type, kind.
разногла́си|е (-я) *ср* disagreement.
разнообра́жу *сов см* разнообра́зить.
разнообра́зен *прил см* разнообра́зный.
разнообра́зи|е (-я) *ср* variety; для ~я for a
change.
разнообра́|зить (-жу, -зишь) *несов перех* to
vary.
разнообра́зный (-ен, -на, -но) *прил* (вкусы,
звуки, мнения) various; ~ные лю́ди different
sorts of people; ~ная пу́блика a diverse

audience.
разнорабо́ч|ий (-его; *decl like adj*) *м* labourer
(*BRIT*), laborer (*US*).
разноречи́в|ый (-, -а, -о) *прил* conflicting.
разноро́д|ный (-ен, -на, -но) *прил* (состав)
heterogeneous; (вещества, предметы) of
various sorts; (впечатления) varied.
разно́с (-а) *м* delivery; (разг: выговор)
pounding.
разн|оси́ть (-ошу́, -о́сишь) *несов от* разнести́
◆ (*impf* разна́шивать) *сов перех* (туфли,
сапоги) to break in
▶ разноси́ться *несов от* разнести́сь ◆ (*impf*
разна́шиваться) *сов возв* to wear loose.
разносторо́н|ний (-няя, -нее, -ие; -ен, -ня,
-не) *прил* (деятельность) wide-ranging;
(соглашение, договор) multilateral; (ум,
личность) multifaceted; он ~ челове́к he has a
wide range of interests; ~ее образова́ние a
broad education.
ра́зност|ь (-и) *ж* (также МАТ) difference.
разно́счик (-а) *м* (товара) delivery man (*мн*
men); (телеграмм) bearer; (инфекции) carrier.
разноцве́тный *прил* multicoloured (*BRIT*),
multicolored (*US*).
разночи́н|ец (-ца) *м* (ИСТ) raznochinets
(*educated person of nonaristocratic descent in
19th century Russia*).
разношёрстный *прил* (перен) motley.
разношу́(сь) (не)сов *см* разноси́ть(ся).
разноязы́чный *прил* speaking different
languages.
разну́здан|ный (-, -на, -но) *прил* (человек,
поведение) unruly.
ра́зный *прил* different.
разн|я́ть (-иму́, -и́мешь; *pt* -я́л, -яла́, -яло́, *impf*
разнима́ть) *сов перех* (руки, зубы) to unclench;
(драчунов, боксёров) to separate, pull apart.
разоблач|и́ть (-у́, -и́шь; *impf* разоблача́ть) *сов
перех* to expose.
разо|бра́ть (-беру́, -берёшь; *impf* разбира́ть)
сов перех (разг: раскупить, взять) to snatch
up; (привести в порядок) to sort out;
(подвергнуть анализу) to analyse (*BRIT*),
analyze (*US*); (распознать: вкус, подпись итп)
to make out; разбира́ть (~ *perf*) (на ча́сти)
(часы, механизм итп) to take apart; его́
~бира́ет смех (разг) he can hardly control his
laughter
▶ разобра́ться (*impf* разбира́ться) *сов возв*:
~ся в +*prp* (в вопросе, в деле) to form an
understanding of.
разобщён|ный (-, -на, -но) *прил* isolated.
ра́зовый *прил*: ~ биле́т single (*BRIT*) или one-
way ticket.
разовью́(сь) *итп сов см* разви́ть(ся).
раз|огна́ть (-гоню́, -го́нишь; *pt* -огна́л, -огнала́,
-огна́ло, *impf* разгоня́ть) *сов перех* (толпу,
демонстрацию) to break up; (разг:
организацию) to purge; (: бездельников,
тунеядцев) to come down on; (тучи, туман) to

disperse; *(перен: сон, тоску, мысли)* to drive away; *(машину, самолёт)* to increase the speed of

▶ **разогна́ться** *(impf* **разгоня́ться)** *сов возв* to build up speed.

разогну́ть (-у́, -ёшь; *impf* **разгиба́ть)** *сов перех (спину)* to straighten up; *(проволоку, скрепку)* to straighten out

▶ **разогну́ться** *(impf* **разгиба́ться)** *сов возв* to straighten up.

разогре́ть (-ю; *impf* **разогрева́ть)** *сов перех (чайник, суп)* to heat

▶ **разогре́ться** *(impf* **разогрева́ться)** *сов возв (суп)* to heat up; *(человек, двигатель)* to warm up.

разоде́тый (-, -а, -о) *прил* overdressed.

разоде́ться (-нусь, -нешься) *сов возв (разг)* to get dressed up.

разодра́ть (-деру́, -дерёшь; *impf* **раздира́ть)** *сов перех* to tear up.

разожгу́ *итп сов см* **разже́чь.**

разожму́(сь) *итп сов см* **разжа́ть(ся).**

разозли́ть (-ю́, -и́шь) *сов от* **злить** ♦ *перех* to anger

▶ **разозли́ться** *сов от* **зли́ться** ♦ *возв* to get angry.

разойти́сь (*как* **идти́; см Table 18;** *impf* **расходи́ться)** *сов возв (гости)* to leave; *(облака, туман, толпа)* to disperse; *(запасы, деньги)* to run out; *(тираж)* to sell out; *(не встретиться)* to miss each other; *(дать дорогу)* to pass each other; *(супруги)* to split up; *(прекратить дружбу)* to part company; *(шов, крепления)* to come apart; *(перен: мнения, взгляды)* to diverge; *(: разг: дать волю себе)* to get going; **на э́той доро́ге не** ~ the road is too narrow for passing.

разолью́(сь) *итп сов см* **разли́ть(ся).**

ра́зом *нареч (разг: все вместе)* all at once; *(: в один приём)* all in one go.

разомкну́ть (-у́, -ёшь; *impf* **размыка́ть)** *сов перех (цепь, крепление)* to unfasten; *(пальцы)* to uncurl; ~ *(perf)* **ру́ки** to let go (of each other's hands)

▶ **разомкну́ться** *(impf* **размыка́ться)** *сов возв (цепь, крепление)* to come unfastened; *(пальцы)* to open.

разомну́(сь) *итп сов см* **размя́ть(ся).**

разопью́ *итп сов см* **распи́ть.**

разорва́ть (-у́, -ёшь; *pt* -а́л, -ала́, -а́ло) *сов от* **рвать** ♦ *(impf* **разрыва́ть)** *перех (письмо, бумагу)* to tear *или* rip up; *(конверт, обёртку)* to tear *или* rip open; *(одежду)* to tear, rip; *(перен: знакомство, связь)* to break off; *(: договор, контракт)* to break ♦ *безл (ногу, руку)* to be blown off; *(танк, стену)* to be blown up

▶ **разорва́ться** *сов от* **рва́ться** ♦ *(impf* **разрыва́ться)** *возв (одежда)* to tear, rip;

(верёвка, цепь) to break; *(связь, знакомство)* to be severed; *(снаряд, ракета)* to explode.

разоре́ние (-я) *ср (см глаг)* plundering; impoverishment; ruin.

разори́тельный (-ен, -ьна, -ьно) *прил* ruinous.

разори́ть (-ю́, -и́шь; *impf* **разоря́ть)** *сов перех (деревню, гнездо)* to plunder; *(семью, население)* to impoverish; *(: компа́нию, страну́)* to ruin

▶ **разори́ться** *(impf* **разоря́ться)** *сов возв* to go to rack and ruin; *(человек)* to become impoverished; *(: разг)* ~**ся на** +*acc (потратить деньги)* to splash out on.

разоружа́ть(ся) (-ю(сь)) *несов от* **разоружи́ть(ся).**

разоруже́ние (-я) *ср (противника, пленных)* disarming; *(политический процесс)* disarmament.

разоружи́ть (-у́, -и́шь; *impf* **разоружа́ть)** *сов перех (также перен)* to disarm

▶ **разоружи́ться** *(impf* **разоружа́ться)** *сов возв* to disarm.

разоря́ть(ся) (-ю(сь)) *несов от* **разори́ть(ся).**

разосла́ть (-шлю́, -шлёшь; *impf* **рассыла́ть)** *сов перех* to send out.

разостла́ть (**расстелю́, рассте́лешь)** *несов* = **расстели́ть.**

разотру́(сь) *итп сов см* **растере́ть(ся).**

разочарова́ние (-я) *ср* disappointment; *(потеря веры)*: ~ **в** +*prp (в друге, в идеалах)* disenchantment with.

разочаро́ван|ный (-, -на, -но) *прил* disappointed; (-, -а, -о): ~ **в** +*prp* disenchanted with.

разочарова́ть (-у́ю; *impf* **разочаро́вывать)** *сов перех* to disappoint

▶ **разочарова́ться** *(impf* **разочаро́вываться)** *сов возв*: ~**ся в** +*prp* to become disenchanted with.

разошёлся *итп сов см* **разойти́сь.**

разошлю́ *итп сов см* **разосла́ть.**

разошью́ *итп сов см* **расши́ть.**

разрабо́тать (-ю; *impf* **разраба́тывать)** *сов перех (план, технологию, теорию)* to develop; *(месторождение)* to exploit.

разрабо́т|ка (-ки) *ж (см глаг)* development; exploitation; *(gen pl* -ок: *обычно мн: научные)* groundwork *ед; см также* **разрабо́тки.**

разрабо́тки (-ок) *мн (ГЕО)*: **га́зовые** ~ gas fields *мн*; **нефтяны́е** ~ oilfields *мн*; **методи́ческие** ~ guidelines *мн*.

разра́внивать (-ю) *несов от* **разровня́ть.**

разрази́ться (-жу́сь, -зи́шься; *impf* **разража́ться)** *сов возв (гроза, катастрофа)* to break out; ~ *(perf)* **аплодисме́нтами/сме́хом** to break into applause/laughter.

разрасти́сь (*3sg* -а́стётся, *3pl* -асту́тся, *pt* -о́сся, -осла́сь, -осло́сь, *impf* **разраста́ться)**

сов возв (*лес, растение*) to spread; (*город, движение*) to grow.

разреве́|ться (-у́сь, -ёшься) сов возв (*разг*) to start bawling.

разрежённый (-, -а́, -о́) *прил* rarified.

разре́жу сов см **разреза́ть**.

разре́з (-а) *м* (*на юбке*) slit; (*ГЕОМ*) section; **в ~е** +*gen* in the context of; **~ глаз** the shape of one's eyes.

разре́|зать (-жу, -жешь) сов от **ре́зать**.

разреза́|ть (-ю) *несов перех* to cut up.

разреклами́р|овать (-ую) сов перех to publicize.

разреша́|ть (-ю) *несов от* **разреши́ть**

▸ **разреша́ться** *несов от* **разреши́ться** ♦ *неперех* (*допускаться*) to be allowed *или* permitted; **здесь не ~ется кури́ть** smoking is not permitted here.

разреше́ни|е (-я) *ср* (*действие*) authorization; (*позволение, право*) permission, authorization; (*документ*) permit; (*решение*) resolution; **с Ва́шего ~я** with your permission.

разреш|и́ть (-у́, -и́шь; *impf* **разреша́ть**) сов перех (*решить*) to resolve; (*позволить*): **~ кому́-н** +*infin* to allow *или* permit sb to do; **~и́те** +*infin* ... may I ...; **~?** may I come in?; **~и́те пройти́** let me through; **разреша́ть** (**~** *perf*) **фильм/кни́гу** to pass a film for screening/book for publication

▸ **разреши́ться** (*impf* **разреша́ться**) сов возв to be resolved.

разрис|ова́ть (-у́ю; *impf* **разрисо́вывать**) сов перех (*карандашо́м*) to draw all over; (*краской*) to paint all over.

разровн|я́ть (-ю) сов от **ровня́ть** ♦ (*impf* **разра́внивать**) *перех* to level.

разро́знен|ный (-, -на, -но) *прил* (*действия, силы*) uncoordinated; (*коллекция, сервиз*) made up of odd parts; (*тома*) odd.

разро́сся *итп* сов см **разрасти́сь**.

разруб|и́ть (-лю́, -у́бишь; *impf* **разруба́ть**) сов перех to chop in two; **разруба́ть** (**~** *perf*) **на куски́** to chop up.

разрумя́н|ить(ся) (-ю(сь)) сов от **румя́нить(ся)**.

разру́х|а (-и) *ж* ruin; **в стране́ ~** the country is in ruins.

разруша́|ть(ся) (-ю(сь)) *несов от* **разру́шить(ся)**.

разруши́тельный (-ен, -ьна, -ьно) *прил* destructive.

разру́ш|ить (-у, -ишь; *impf* **разруша́ть**) сов перех to destroy; (*планы, жизнь*) to ruin

▸ **разру́шиться** (*impf* **разруша́ться**) сов возв (*см перех*) to be destroyed; to be ruined.

разры́в (-а) *м* (*дипломати́ческих отноше́ний, связе́й*) severance; (*провода, цепи*) breaking; (*разорванная часть*) tear; (*снаряда, гранаты*) explosion; (*несоответствие, промежуток времени*) gap; **с ~ом в 10 лет** with a gap of 10 years; **разры́в се́рдца** (*МЕД*) heart attack.

разрыва́|ть(ся) (-ю(сь)) *несов от* **разорва́ть(ся)**.

разрыхл|и́ть (-ю, -и́шь) сов от **рыхли́ть**.

разря́д (-а) *м* (*люде́й, расте́ний*) class; (*спортивный*) grade; (*профессиональный*) status; (*физ*) discharge.

разря|ди́ть (-жу́, -ди́шь; *impf* **разряжа́ть**) сов перех (*оружие*) to discharge; **разряжа́ть** (**~** *perf*) **обстано́вку** to diffuse the situation

▸ **разряди́ться** (*impf* **разряжа́ться**) сов возв (*перен*) to become less tense.

разря́д|ка (-ки; *gen pl* -ок) *ж* release, outlet; (*в те́ксте*) spacing; **~ (междунаро́дной) напряжённости** détente.

разряжа́|ть(ся) (-ю(сь)) *несов от* **разряди́ть(ся)**.

разряжу́(сь) сов см **разряди́ть(ся)**.

разубе|ди́ть (-жу́, -ди́шь; *impf* **разубежда́ть**) сов перех: **~ кого́-н** (**в** +*prp*) to dissuade sb (from).

разува́|ть(ся) (-ю(сь)) *несов от* **разу́ть(ся)**.

разуве́р|ить (-юсь, -ишься; *impf* **разуверя́ться**) сов возв: **~ в** +*prp* to lose faith in.

разузна́|ть (-ю; *impf* **разузнава́ть**) сов перех (*раз*) to find out.

разукра́|сить (-шу, -сишь; *impf* **разукра́шивать**) сов перех to decorate.

ра́зум (-а) *м* reason.

разу́мен *прил см* **разу́мный**.

разуме́|ться (3sg -ется) сов возв: **под э́тим ~ется, что** ... by this is meant that ...; (*само́ собо́й*) **~ется** that goes without saying; **он, ~ется, не знал об э́том** it goes without saying that he knew nothing about it.

разу́мный (-ен, -на, -но) *прил* intelligent; (*поступок, решение, довод*) reasonable.

разу́т|ый (-, -а, -о) *прил* (*без обуви*) barefoot; (*разг: нуждающийся в обуви*) shoeless.

разу́|ть (-ю; *impf* **разува́ть**) сов перех: **~ кого́-н** to take sb's shoes off

▸ **разу́ться** (*impf* **разува́ться**) сов возв to take one's shoes off.

разуч|и́ть (-у́, -у́чишь; *impf* **разу́чивать**) сов перех to learn

▸ **разучи́ться** (*impf* **разу́чиваться**) сов возв: **~ся** +*infin* to forget how to do.

разъеда́|ть (3sg -ет, 3pl -ют) *несов от* **разъе́сть** ♦ *перех* (*перен: душу*) to eat away at

▸ **разъеда́ться** *несов от* **разъе́сться**.

разъе́дешься *итп* сов см **разъе́хаться**.

разъеди́м(ся) сов см **разъе́сть(ся)**.

разъедин|и́ть (-ю́, -и́шь; *impf* **разъединя́ть**) сов перех (*провода, телефон*) to disconnect; (*друзей, любимых*) to separate.

разъеди́те(сь) сов см **разъе́сть(ся)**.

разъе́дься *итп* сов см **разъе́хаться**.

разъедя́т(ся) сов см **разъе́сть(ся)**.

разъе́зд (-а) *м* (*гостей*) departure; (*для поездо́в*) siding (*BRIT*), sidetrack (*US*); см также разъе́зды.

разъе́зд|ы (-ов) *мн (поездки)* travel *ед*; **он всё вре́мя в ~ах** he does a lot of travelling.

разъезжа́|ть (-ю) *несов неперех (по делам, по городам)* to travel around; *(катаъться: на тройке, на автомобиле)* to ride about; ~ *(impf)* **по гостя́м** to go around visiting friends

▶ **разъезжа́ться** *несов от* **разъе́хаться**.

разъе́сть (*как* **есть**; *см* Table 15; *impf* **разъеда́ть**) *сов перех* to corrode

▶ **разъе́сться** *(impf* **разъеда́ться***) сов возв (разг)* to get fat.

разъе́|хаться (*как* **е́хать**; *см* Table 19; *impf* **разъезжа́ться***) сов возв* to leave; *(разг: лыжи, ноги на льду)* to slide apart; **она́ ~халась с му́жем/ма́терью** she doesn't live with her husband/mother any more; **мы с ни́ми ~хались в темноте́** we missed each other in the darkness; **маши́ны не могли́ ~** the cars couldn't get past each other.

разъе́шь(ся) *сов см* **разъе́сть(ся)**.

разъярённый *прил (зверь, человек, лицо)* furious; *(перен: река, стихия)* raging.

разъяр|и́ть (-ю́, -и́шь; *impf* **разъяря́ть***) сов перех (толпу, человека)* to infuriate, enrage; *(зверя)* to provoke

▶ **разъяри́ться** *(impf* **разъяря́ться***) сов возв* to become infuriated.

разъясне́ни|е (-я) *ср* clarification.

разъясн|и́ть (-ю́, -и́шь; *impf* **разъясня́ть***) сов перех* to clarify

▶ **разъясни́ться** *(impf* **разъясня́ться***) сов возв* to be clarified.

разыгра́|ть (-ю; *impf* **разы́грывать***) сов перех (МУЗ, СПОРТ)* to play; *(сцену)* to act out; *(в лотерею, по жребию)* to raffle; *(разг: подшути́ть)* to play a joke *или* trick on

▶ **разыгра́ться** *(impf* **разы́грываться***) сов возв (увлечься игрой)* to get carried away with one's game; *(начать лучше играть)* to get going; *(перед концертом)* to warm up; *(перен: буря)* to rage; *(: драма, сражение)* to unfold; **у меня́ ~лась мигре́нь** I had a nasty migraine; **по́сле прогу́лки у него́ ~лся аппети́т** the walk gave him a big appetite.

разыск|а́ть (-ищу́, -и́щешь; *impf* **разы́скивать***) сов перех* to find

▶ **разыска́ться** *(impf* **разы́скиваться***) сов возв* to turn up.

РАИС *ср сокр (= Росси́йское аге́нтство интеллектуа́льной со́бственности)* copyright protection agency.

рай (-я; *loc sg* -ю́) *м (также перен)* paradise.

райко́м (-а) *м сокр (ИСТ: = райо́нный комите́т)* district committee *(of Communist Party or Komsomol)*.

райо́н (-а) *м* region; *(ПОЛИТ)* district.

райо́нный *прил* district *опред*.

ра́йск|ий (-ая, -ое, -ие) *прил (также перен)* heavenly.

райце́нтр (-а) *м сокр (= райо́нный центр)* main town *(of district)*.

рак (-а) *м (ЗООЛ: речной)* crayfish (*мн* crayfish); *(: морской)* crab; *(МЕД)* cancer; *(созвездие)*: **Р~** Cancer.

раке́т|а (-ы) *ж (также КОСМОС)* rocket; *(ВОЕН)* missile; *(судно)* hydrofoil.

раке́т|ка (-ки; *gen pl* -ок) *ж (СПОРТ)* racket; **пе́рвая ~** *(перен)* the top player.

раке́тный *прил (также КОСМОС)* rocket *опред*; *(ВОЕН)* missile *опред*; **раке́тное ору́жие** *(ВОЕН)* missiles *мн*.

раке́ток *сущ см* **раке́тка**.

ра́ковин|а (-ы) *ж (ЗООЛ)* shell; *(для умыва́ния)* sink; **ушна́я ~** aural cavity.

ра́ковый *прил (ЗООЛ, КУЛИН)* crab *опред*; *(МЕД)* cancer *опред*; **ра́ковая о́пухоль** malignant tumour.

ра́лли *ср нескл (СПОРТ)* rally.

ра́м|а (-ы) *ж* frame; *(АВТ)* chassis; **двойны́е ~ы** double glazing.

рамаза́н (-а) *м* Ramadan.

ра́м|ка (-ки; *gen pl* -ок) *ж (для фотографии, для картины)* frame; *(текста, рисунка)* border; *см также* **ра́мки**.

ра́м|ки (-ок) *мн: ~* +*gen (рассказа, разговора, обязанностей)* framework *ед* of; *(закона, устава)* limits *мн* of; **в ~ках** +*gen (закона, прили́чия)* within the bounds of; *(дискуссии, переговоров)* within the framework of; **за ~ками** +*gen* beyond the bounds of; **держа́ть** *(impf)* **себя́ в ~ках** to control o.s.

ра́мп|а (-ы) *ж (ТЕАТР)* **огни́ ~ы** footlights *мн*.

РАН *м сокр (= Росси́йская акаде́мия нау́к)* Russian Academy of Sciences.

ра́н|а (-ы) *ж (также перен)* wound.

Рангу́н (-а) *м* Rangoon.

ра́нен|ая (-ой; *decl like adj*) *ж см* **ра́неный**.

ране́ни|е (-я) *ср* injury.

ра́нен|ый *прил* injured; *(ВОЕН)* wounded ♦ (-ого; *decl like adj*) *м* injured person (*мн* people); *(ВОЕН)* wounded person (*мн* people).

ра́н|ец (-ца) *м (школьный)* satchel; *(солдатский, походный)* backpack.

рани́м|ый (-, -а, -о) *прил* vulnerable.

ра́н|ить (-ю, -ишь) *(не)сов перех (также перен)* to wound; ~ *(impf/perf)* **кого́-н в ру́ку/но́гу** to wound sb in the arm/leg; ~ *(impf/perf)* **кому́-н ду́шу** to wound sb *(fig)*.

ра́нн|ий (-яя, -ее, -ие) *прил* early.

ра́но *нареч* early ♦ *как сказ* it's early; **ещё ~** *(о раннем времени)* it's still early; ~ **де́лать** *(impf)* **вы́воды** it's too early to draw conclusions; **он жени́лся/у́мер** ~ he married/died young; ~ **и́ли по́здно** sooner or later.

ра́нца *итп сущ см* **ра́нец**.

рань (-и) ж (*разг*) early morning.

ра́ньше *сравн нареч от* **ра́но** ♦ *нареч* (*прежде*) before; (*сначала*) earlier ♦ *предл:* ~ +*gen* before; ~ **он жил в го́роде** he used to live in the city; ~ **поду́май, пото́м отвеча́й** think before you answer; ~ **вре́мени** (*радоваться итп*) too soon; ~ **ве́чера мы не зако́нчим** we won't finish before the evening; **он зако́нчил ~ всех** he finished before everybody else.

РАО *сокр* (= *Росси́йское акционе́рное о́бщество*) joint-stock company.

рапи́р|**а** (-ы) ж foil (*for fencing*).

ра́порт (-а) м report; **подава́ть** (**пода́ть** *perf*) ~ to submit a report.

рапорт|**ова́ть** (-у́ю) *perf* **отрапортова́ть**) (*не*)*сов неперех:* ~ (**кому́-н о** +*prp*) to report back (to sb on).

рас- *префикс см* **раз-**.

ра́с|**а** (-ы) ж race.

раси́зм (-а) м racism.

раси́ст (-а) м racist.

раси́ст|**ка** (-ки; *gen pl* -**ок**) ж *см* **раси́ст**.

раси́стск|**ий** (-ая, -ое, -ие) *прил* racist *опред*.

раска́ива|**ться** (-юсь) *несов от* **раска́яться**.

раскалённый *прил* burning hot.

раскал|**и́ть** (-ю́, -и́шь; *impf* **раскаля́ть**) *сов перех* to bring to a high temperature

▶ **раскали́ться** (*impf* **раскаля́ться**) *сов возв* to get very hot.

раска́лыва|**ть** (-ю) *несов от* **расколо́ть**

▶ **раска́лываться** *несов от* **расколо́ться** ♦ *возв:* **у меня́ ~ется голова́** I have a splitting headache.

раскал|**я́ть**(**ся**) (-ю́(**сь**)) *несов от* **раскали́ть**(**ся**).

раска́пыва|**ть** (-ю) *несов от* **раскопа́ть**.

раска́рмлива|**ть** (-ю) *несов от* **раскорми́ть**.

раска́т (-а) м (*обычно мн: грома, смеха*) peal.

раска́та|**ть** (-ю; *impf* **раска́тывать**) *сов перех* (*ковёр, рулон*) to unroll; (*тесто*) to roll out; (*дорогу, горку*) to flatten (out); (*брёвна, шары*) to send rolling (*in different directions*).

раска́тистый (-, -а, -о) *прил* booming.

раска́тыва|**ть** (-ю) *несов от* **раската́ть**.

раскача́|**ть** (-ю; *impf* **раска́чивать**) *сов перех* to swing; (*качели, ребёнка*) to push

▶ **раскача́ться** (*impf* **раска́чиваться**) *сов возв* (*лодка*) to rock; (*качели*) to swing; (*разг: медлить: человек*) to dither.

раска́яни|**е** (-я) *ср* repentance.

раска́|**яться** (-юсь; *impf* **раска́иваться**) *сов возв:* ~ (**в** +*prp*) to repent (of).

расквита́|**ться** (-юсь) *сов возв* (*разг*): ~ **с** +*instr* (*с кредиторами*) to settle up with; (*перен: с врагом, с обидчиком*) to settle a score with.

раскида́|**ть** (-ю; *impf* **раски́дывать**) *сов перех* to throw around, scatter; **жизнь ~ла их по всему́ све́ту** life has scattered them across the globe.

раски́дист|**ый** (-, -а, -о) *прил* spreading.

раски́дыва|**ть** (-ю) *несов от* **раскида́ть**, **раски́нуть**.

раски́н|**уть** (-у, -ешь; *impf* **раски́дывать**) *сов перех* (*руки*) to throw open; (*ковёр, сети*) to spread out; (*лагерь*) to set up; (*палатку, шатёр*) to pitch; ~ (*perf*) **что-н умо́м** *или* **мозга́ми** (*разг*) to think sth over

▶ **раски́нуться** (*impf* **раски́дываться**) *сов возв* to stretch out.

раскла́дк|**а** (-и) ж (*действие*) arranging; (*соотношение: сил, средств*) balance.

раскладно́й *прил* folding *опред*.

расклаау́шк|**а** (-ки; *gen pl* -**ек**) ж (*разг*) camp bed (*BRIT*), cot (*US*).

раскла́дыва|**ть**(**ся**) (-ю(**сь**)) *несов от* **разложи́ть**(**ся**).

раскла́ня|**ться** (-юсь; *impf* **раскла́ниваться**) *сов возв* (*актёр, выступающий*) to take a bow; (*при встрече, при расставании*) to bow.

раскле́и|**ть** (-ю, -ишь; *impf* **раскле́ивать**) *сов перех* (*конверт*) to unglue; (*плакаты, афиши, рекламы*) to paste up

▶ **раскле́иться** (*impf* **раскле́иваться**) *сов возв* to come unstuck; (*перен: разг: свадьба, дело*) to fall through; **я совсе́м ~ился** (*разг*) I feel (like) a complete wreck.

раско́ван|**ный** (-, -на, -но) *прил* relaxed.

раско́л (-а) м (*организации, движения*) split; (*РЕЛ*) schism.

раск|**оло́ть** (-олю́, -о́лешь; *impf* **раска́лывать**) *сов перех* (*дрова, страну, движение*) to split; (*лёд, орех*) to crack

▶ **расколо́ться** (*impf* **раска́лываться**) *сов возв* (*полено, орех*) to split open; (*перен: движение, организация*) to be split.

раскопа́|**ть** (-ю; *impf* **раска́пывать**) *сов перех* (*также перен*) to dig up.

раско́п|**ка** (-ки; *gen pl* -**ок**) ж (*действие*) excavation; *см также* **раско́пки**.

раско́п|**ки** (-ок) мн (*работы*) excavations *мн*; (*место*) (archaeological) dig *ед*.

раскорм|**и́ть** (-ормлю́, -о́рмишь; *impf* **раска́рмливать**) *сов перех* to overfeed.

раско́сый *прил* (*глаза*) slanting.

раскоше́л|**иться** (-юсь, -ишься; *impf* **раскоше́ливаться**) *сов возв* (*разг*): ~ (**на** +*acc*) to fork out (for).

раскра́ива|**ть** (-ю) *несов от* **раскрои́ть**.

раскра́|**сить** (-шу, -сишь; *impf* **раскра́шивать**) *сов перех* (*рисунок, картинку*) to colour (*BRIT*), color (*US*); (*вазу, поделку*) to paint.

раскра́ск|**а** (-и) ж (*см глаг*) colouring (*BRIT*), coloring (*US*); painting; (*цветовая гамма*) colours *мн* (*BRIT*), colors *мн* (*US*).

раскрасне́|**ться** (-юсь) *сов возв* to go red.

раскра́шива|**ть** (-ю) *несов от* **раскра́сить**.

раскра́шу *сов см* **раскра́сить**.

раскритик|**ова́ть** (-у́ю) *сов перех* to criticize severely.

раскро|**и́ть** (-ю́, -и́шь; *impf* **раскра́ивать**) *сов перех* to cut.

раскру|**ти́ть** (-учу́, -у́тишь; *impf* **раскру́чивать**) *сов перех (что-н сплетённое)* to untwist; *(что-н закрученное)* to unscrew; *(интригу, тайну)* to unravel; *(идею, политика)* to promote.

раскру́тк|**а** (**-и**) *ж (разг)* promotion.

раскры́ть (**-о́ю, -о́ешь**; *impf* **раскрыва́ть**) *сов перех* to open; *(перен)* to discover; **раскрыва́ть** (**~ *perf*) свои́ ка́рты** *(перен)* to show one's hand

▶ **раскры́ться** (*impf* **раскрыва́ться**) *сов возв* to open; *(перен: характер, дарование)* to be revealed; **~ся** *(perf)* **пе́ред кем-н** to open up to sb.

раск|упи́ть (**-уплю́, -у́пишь**; *impf* **раскупа́ть**) *сов перех* to buy up.

раск|уси́ть (**-ушу́, -у́сишь**) *сов перех (разг: понять)* to suss out; *(impf* **раску́сывать**; *яблоко, конфету)* to bite into.

ра́совый *прил* racial.

распа́д (**-а**) *м* break-up, collapse; *(хим)* decomposition.

распада́|ться (*3sg* **-ется**, *3pl* **-ются**) *несов от* **распа́сться** ♦ *возв (состоять из частей)*: **~ на** *+acc* to be divided into.

распадётся *итп сов см* **распа́сться**.

распа́рыва|ть (**-ю**; *perf* **распоро́ть**) *несов перех* = **поро́ть**.

распа́|сться (*3sg* **-дётся**, *3pl* **-ду́тся**, *impf* **распада́ться**) *сов возв* to break up; *(вещество, молекула)* to decompose; **распада́ться** (**~ *perf*) на ча́сти** to fall apart.

распа|ха́ть (**-шу́, -а́шешь**; *impf* **распа́хивать**) *сов перех* to plough (*BRIT*) *или* plow (*US*) up.

распахн|у́ть (**-у́, -ёшь**; *impf* **распа́хивать**) *сов перех* to throw open; **~** *(perf)* **ду́шу** to bare one's soul

▶ **распахну́ться** (*impf* **распа́хиваться**) *сов возв (дверь, шуба)* to fly open; *(поля, равнина)* to open out.

распашо́н|ка (**-ки**; *gen pl* **-ок**) *ж cotton baby top.*

распашу́ *итп сов см* **распаха́ть**.

распева́|ть (**-ю**) *несов неперех (разг)* to sing loudly ♦ *перех (разг)*: **~ пе́сню** to sing away.

распелена́|ть (**-ю**; *impf* **распелёнывать**) *сов перех* to unwrap.

распеча́та|ть (**-ю**; *impf* **распеча́тывать**) *сов перех (письмо, пакет)* to open; *(помещение)* to unseal; *(размножить)* to print off; *(КОМП)* to print out.

распеча́т|ка (**-ки**; *gen pl* **-ок**) *ж (доклада)* printout; *(КОМП)* hard copy.

распеча́тыва|ть (**-ю**) *несов от* **распеча́тать**.

распива́|ть (**-ю**) *несов от* **распи́ть**.

расп|или́ть (**-илю́, -и́лишь**; *impf* **распи́ливать**) *сов перех* to saw up.

распина́|ть (**-ю**) *несов от* **распя́ть**

▶ **распина́ться** *несов возв (разг)*: **~ся пе́ред** *+instr* to go out of one's way for.

расписа́ни|е (**-я**) *ср* timetable.

распи|са́ть (**-шу́, -шешь**; *impf* **распи́сывать**) *сов перех (дела, мероприятия, расходы итп)* to arrange; *(день, месяц)* to fill up; *(стены, шкатулку, вазу)* to paint; *(перен: разг: будущее, приключения)* to paint a rosy picture of; *(разг: жениха и невесту)* to marry (*in registry office*)

▶ **расписа́ться** (*impf* **распи́сываться**) *сов возв (поставить подпись)* to sign one's name; *(перен)*: **~ся в** *+prp (в невежестве, в бессилии)* to acknowledge; *(разг)*: **~ся (с** *+instr)* *(зарегистрировать брак)* to get married (to) *(in registry office)*; **распи́сываться** (**~ся** *perf*) **в получе́нии чего́-н** to sign for sth.

распи́с|ка (**-ки**; *gen pl* **-ок**) *ж (о получении денег)* receipt; *(гарантия)* warrant; **принима́ть** (**приня́ть** *perf*) **что-н под ~ку** to sign for sth.

расписно́й *прил* painted.

распи́сок *сущ см* **распи́ска**.

распи́сыва|ть(ся) (**-ю(сь)**) *несов от* **расписа́ть(ся)**.

расп|и́ть (**разопью́, разопьёшь**; *pt* **-и́л, -ила́, -и́ло**, *impf* **распива́ть**) *сов перех (разг)* to get through.

распиха́|ть (**-ю**; *impf* **распи́хивать**) *сов перех (разг: толпу, очередь)* to push through; *(: вещи, бумаги)* to stuff into.

распишу́(сь) *итп сов см* **расписа́ть(ся)**.

распла́в|ить (**-лю, -ишь**) *сов от* **пла́вить** ♦ *(impf* **расплавля́ть**) *перех* to melt

▶ **распла́виться** *сов от* **пла́виться** ♦ *(impf* **расплавля́ться**) *возв* to melt.

распла́ка|ться (**-чусь, -чешься**) *сов возв* to burst into tears.

распласта́|ть (**-ю**; *impf* **распла́стывать**) *сов перех (крылья, руки)* to spread

▶ **распласта́ться** (*impf* **распла́стываться**) *сов возв* to sprawl out.

распла́т|а (**-ы**) *ж* payment; *(перен)* retribution; **час ~ы** *(перен)* the day of reckoning.

распла|ти́ться (**-чу́сь, -а́тишься**; *impf* **распла́чиваться**) *сов возв*: **~ (с** *+instr)* *(с продавцом, с кредитором)* to pay; *(перен: с предателем, с негодяем)* to get even (with); **распла́чиваться** (**~ *perf*) за оши́бку/ преступле́ние** to pay for a mistake/crime.

распла́чусь *итп сов см* **распла́каться**.

распла́та — *see above*

расплёл(ся) *итп сов см* **расплести́(сь)**.

распл|еска́ть (**-ещу́, -е́щешь**; *impf* **расплёскивать**) *сов перех* to spill

▶ **расплеска́ться** (*impf* **расплёскиваться**) *сов возв* to spill.

распл|ести́ (**-ету́, -етёшь**; *pt* **-ёл, -ела́, -ело́**, *impf* **расплета́ть**) *сов перех (плётку)* to untwist; *(косу)* to unplait

▶ **расплести́сь** (*impf* **расплета́ться**) *сов возв* to come untwisted; *(коса)* to come out.

расплещу́(сь) *сов см* **расплеска́ть(ся)**.

расплоди́ться (*3sg* -и́тся, *3pl* -я́тся) *сов от* плоди́ться.

расплыва́ться (-ю́сь) *несов от* расплы́ться.

расплыву́сь *итп сов см* расплы́ться.

расплы́вчатый (-, -а, -о) *прил* (*рисунок, очертания*) blurred; (*перен: мысли, ответ, намёк*) vague.

расплы́ться (-ву́сь, -вёшься; *pt* -лся, -ла́сь, -ло́сь, *impf* расплыва́ться) *сов возв* (*утки итп*) to swim off; (*чернила, краски*) to run; (*нефть, дым*) to diffuse; (*облака*) to disperse; (*перен: фигуры, силуэт*) to be blurred; (*раза: расползтись*) to spread; (*: широко улыбнуться*) to beam; **он ~лся́ *или* его́ лицо́ ~ло́сь в улы́бке** a smile spread across his face.

расплющить (-у, -ишь; *impf* расплющивать) *сов перех* to crush.

распну́ *итп сов см* распя́ть.

распого́диться (*3sg* -ится) *сов возв* to clear up (*weather*).

распозна́ть (-ю; *impf* распознава́ть) *сов перех* to identify.

располага́ть (-ю) *несов от* расположи́ть ♦ *неперех*: ~ +*instr* (*данными, временем итп*) to have at one's disposal, have available; **Вы мо́жете мной ~** I am entirely at your disposal

располага́ться *несов от* расположи́ться ♦ *возв* (*находиться*) to be situated *или* located.

располага́ющий (-ая, -ее, -ие) *прил* welcoming.

расползти́сь (*3sg* -ётся, *3pl* -у́тся, *impf* располза́ться) *сов возв* to crawl off; (*туман, плющ*) to spread; (*пятно, строчки*) to smudge; (*разг: ткань, одежда*) to become threadbare.

расположе́ние (-я) *ср* (*действие: предметов*) arranging; (*место: отряда, лагеря*) location; (*комнат*) layout; (*мебели*) arrangement; (*симпатия*) disposition; ~ **ду́ха** mood; **я испы́тываю к нему́** ~ I am well-disposed towards him; **у меня́ нет сейча́с ~я е́хать туда́** I'm not in the mood for going there right now.

расположен|ный (-, -а, -о) *прил*: ~ **к** +*dat* (*к человеку*) well-disposed towards; (*к инфекции, к простуде*) susceptible to; ~ +*infin* (*читать, работать, играть*) in the mood for doing; **я не расположен э́то сейча́с обсужда́ть** I am not in the mood to discuss it right now.

расположи́ть (-ожу́, -о́жишь; *impf* располага́ть) *сов перех* (*мебель, вещи итп*) to arrange; (*отряд*) to station; (*лагерь*) to set up; **располага́ть** (~ *perf*) **кого́-н к себе́** to win sb over

► **расположи́ться** (*impf* располага́ться) *сов возв* (*человек: в кресле, под деревом итп*) to settle down; (*отряд*) to position itself.

распоро́ть (-орю́, -о́решь) *сов от* поро́ть.

распоряди́тель (-я) *м* (*КОММ*) manager; (*церемониала, вечера*) organizer.

распоряди́тельный *прил* (*хозяйка, начальник*) efficient; **распоряди́тельный дире́ктор** managing director;

распоряди́тельный комите́т management committee.

распоряди́ться (-жу́сь, -ди́шься; *impf* распоряжа́ться) *сов возв* to give out instructions; (+*infin*; *сделать что-н*) to order to do; (+*instr*; *деньгами, ресурсами*) to manage; **он ~ди́лся, что́бы все яви́лись к шести́** he instructed everyone to be there by six (o'clock).

распоря́д|ок (-ка) *м* routine; **пра́вила вну́треннего ~ка** regulations *мн*.

распоряжа́ться (-юсь) *несов от* распоряди́ться ♦ *возв*: ~ (+*instr*) to be in charge (of).

распоряже́ни|е (-я) *ср* (*управление*) management; (*приказ*) instructions *мн*; (*указ*) enactment; **ба́нковское** ~ banker's order; **в** ~ +*gen* at sb's/sth's disposal; **предоставля́ть (предоста́вить** *perf*) **что-н в чьё-н** ~ to place sth at sb's disposal; **я в Ва́шем ~и** I am at your disposal.

распоряжу́сь *сов см* распоряди́ться.

распоя́са|ться (-юсь; *impf* распоя́сываться) *сов возв* (*перен: разг*) to get cocky.

распра́в|а (-ы) *ж* reprisals *мн*.

распра́в|ить (-лю, -ишь; *impf* расправля́ть) *сов перех* (*складки, смятую бумагу*) to straighten out; (*грудь, плечи*) to straighten (up); (*крылья*) to spread

► **распра́виться** (*impf* расправля́ться) *сов возв* (*см перех*) to be straightened out; to straighten up; to unfurl; (*парус*) to unfurl; (*наказать*): ~**ся с** +*instr* (*с демонстрантами, с забастовщиками*) to take reprisals against; (*перен: разг*): **с дела́ми, с обе́дом итп** to be finished with.

распределе́ни|е (-я) *ср* distribution; (*после института*) work placement.

распредел|и́ть (-ю́, -и́шь; *impf* распределя́ть) *сов перех* (*обязанности, доходы*) to distribute; (*книги по по́лкам*) to arrange; (*учеников по кла́ссам*) to divide up; (*раза*): ~ **кого́-н (выпускника́)** to give sb a work placement

► **распредели́ться** (*impf* распределя́ться) *сов возв* (*раза: выпускники*) to get work placements; **распределя́ться** (~**ся** *perf*) (*по* +*dat*) (*по гру́ппам, по брига́дам*) to divide up (into).

распродава́ть (-ю́, -ёшь) *несов от* распрода́ть.

распродаю́т *итп сов см* распрода́ть.

распрода́ж|а (-и) *ж* sale.

распрода́ть (*как* дать; *см* Table 14; *impf* распродава́ть) *сов перех* (*вещи, имущество, товар*) to sell off; (*билеты*) to sell out of.

распростёртый *прил* (*руки*) outstretched; (*тело*) prostrate; **встреча́ть (встре́тить** *perf*) **кого́-н с распростёртыми объя́тиями** to welcome sb with open arms.

распрости́ться (-щу́сь, -сти́шься) *сов возв*: ~ **с** +*instr* to say *или* bid farewell to.

распростране́ни|е (-я) *ср* (*информации,*

опыта, знаний) dissemination; *(инфекции)* spreading; *(ядерного оружия)* proliferation; *(приказа, правила)* extension.

распространён|ный (-, -на, -но) *прил* widespread.

распростран|и́ть (-ю́, -и́шь; *impf* **распространя́ть**) *сов перех (информацию, знания)* to disseminate; *(опыт)* to share; *(сплетни, инфекцию)* to spread; *(правило, приказ)* to apply; *(владения)* to widen; *(газеты)* to distribute; *(запах)* to emit

▸ **распространи́ться** (*impf* **распространя́ться**) *сов возв* to spread; *(разг: подробно говорить)* to go into detail; ~**ся** *(perf)* **на** +*acc* to extend to; **э́тот прика́з ~я́ется на всех** this order applies to everybody.

распроща́|ться (-юсь) *сов возв* = **распрости́ться.**

распрощу́сь *сов см* **распрости́ться.**

ра́спр|я (-и; *gen pl* -ей) *ж (обычно мн)* feud.

распря́г *futp сов см* **распря́чь.**

распряга́|ть (-ю) *несов от* **распря́чь.**

распрягу́ *сов см* **распря́чь.**

распряжёшь *futp сов см* **распря́чь.**

распрям|и́ть (-лю́, -и́шь; *impf* **распрямля́ть**) *сов перех (проволоку, крючок)* to straighten (out); *(спину, грудь, плечи)* to straighten (up).

распря́|чь (-гу́, -жёшь *итп*, -гу́т; *pt* -г, -гла́, -гло́, *impf* **распряга́ть**) *сов перех* to unharness.

распуга́|ть (-ю; *impf* **распу́гивать**) *сов перех* to scare away *или* off.

распусти́ть (-ущу́, -у́стишь; *impf* **распуска́ть**) *сов перех (армию)* to disband; *(студентов, школьников)* to dismiss; *(шнурки, корсет, ремень)* to loosen; *(волосы, косу)* to let down; *(шов, вязанье)* to unpick; *(перен)*: ~ **кого́-н** *(ребёнка итп)* to let sb run wild; **распуска́ть** *(~ perf)* **парла́мент** to dissolve parliament; **распуска́ть** *(~ perf)* **слу́хи** to spread rumours

▸ **распусти́ться** (*impf* **распуска́ться**) *сов возв (цветы, почки)* to open out; *(шнуровка, завязки)* to come undone; *(дети, люди)* to get out of hand.

распу́та|ть (-ю; *impf* **распу́тывать**) *сов перех (узел, нитки)* to untangle; *(перен: дело, преступление, загадку)* to unravel; *(лошадь)* to unfetter

▸ **распу́таться** (*impf* **распу́тываться**) *сов возв (см перех)* to come untangled; to unravel itself.

распу́тиц|а (-ы) *ж period during autumn and spring when the roads become impassable.*

распу́тник (-а) *м* libertine.

распу́тниц|а (-ы) *ж см* **распу́тник.**

распу́тн|ый (-ен, -на, -но) *прил* depraved.

распу́тыва|ть(ся) (-ю(сь)) *несов от* **распу́тать(ся).**

распу́ть|е (-ья; *nom pl* -ий) *ср* crossroads; **быть** *(impf)* **на** ~ *(перен)* to be at a crossroads.

распу́хн|уть (-у, -ешь; *impf* **распуха́ть**) *сов неперех (лицо, нога итп)* to swell up; *(бумажник, папка)* to bulge.

распу́щен|ный (-, -на, -но) *прил* unruly; *(безнравственный)* dissolute.

распущу́(сь) *сов см* **распусти́ть(ся).**

распыли́тел|ь (-я) *м* spray.

распыл|и́ть (-ю́, -и́шь; *impf* **распыля́ть**) *сов перех* to spray.

распя́ти|е (-я) *ср* crucifixion.

распя́|ть (-ну́, -нёшь; *impf* **распина́ть**) *сов перех* to crucify.

расса́д|а (-ы) *ж собир (бот)* seedlings *мн.*

рассад|и́ть (-ажу́, -а́дишь; *impf* **расса́живать**) *сов перех (гостей, публику)* to seat; *(болтуно́в)* to seat apart; *(цветы)* to thin out.

расса́дник (-а) *м (перен)* hotbed.

расса́жива|ть (-ю) *несов от* **рассади́ть**

▸ **расса́живаться** *несов от* **рассе́сться.**

рассажу́ *сов см* **рассади́ть.**

расса́сыва|ться (*3sg* -ется, *3pl* -ются) *несов от* **рассоса́ться.**

рассве|сти́ (*3sg* -тёт, *pt* -ло́, *impf* **рассвета́ть**) *сов безл*: ~**та́ет** dawn is breaking; **уже́** ~**ло́** it's already light.

рассве́т (-а) *м* daybreak.

рассвета́|ть (*3sg* -ет) *несов от* **рассвести́.**

рассветёт *сов см* **рассвести́.**

рассвирепе́|ть (-ю) *сов от* **свирепе́ть.**

расседла́|ть (-ю; *impf* **рассёдлывать**) *сов перех* to unsaddle.

рассе́ива|ть(ся) (-ю(сь)) *несов от* **рассе́ять(ся).**

рассе́к *итп сов см* **рассе́чь.**

рассека́|ть (-ю) *несов от* **рассе́чь.**

рассеку́ *итп сов см* **рассе́чь.**

рассе́лин|а (-ы) *ж* fissure.

рассел|и́ть (-ю́, -и́шь; *impf* **рассели́ть**) *сов перех (по комнатам, по квартирам)* to accommodate, put up; **рассели́ть** *(~ perf)* **коммуна́льную кварти́ру** *to move the occupants of a communal flat into self-contained accommodation.*

рассе́лся *итп сов см* **рассе́сться.**

расселя́|ть (-ю) *несов от* **рассели́ть.**

рассерд|и́ть(ся) (-ержу́(сь), -е́рдишь(ся)) *сов от* **серди́ть(ся).**

рассе́сться (-я́дусь, -я́дешься; *pt* -е́лся, -е́лась, -е́лось) *сов возв (по столам, в зале)* to take one's seat; *(разг: развалиться: на дива́не, в кре́сле)* to slump.

рассе́чь (-еку́, -ечёшь *итп*, -еку́т; *pt* -ёк, -екла́, -екло́, *impf* **рассека́ть**) *сов перех (тушу, кана́т)* to cut in two; *(губу, лоб)* to cut; **рассека́ть** *(~ perf)* **во́лны** to cut through the water.

рассе́ян|ный (-, -на, -но) *прил (человек)* absent-minded; *(свет)* diffuse.

рассе́ять (-ю; *impf* рассе́ивать) *сов перех* (*семена, людей*) to scatter; (*свет*) to diffuse; (*перен: сомнения, подозрения*) to dispel; (*горе, тоску*) to alleviate

▶ рассе́яться (*impf* рассе́иваться) *сов возв* (*люди, семена*) to be scattered; (*тучи, туман, дым*) to disperse; (*сомнения, печаль*) to be dispelled; (*развлечься*) to find a distraction.

расскажу́ *итп сов см* рассказа́ть.

расска́з (-а) *м* story; (*свидетеля*) account.

рассказа́ть (-ажу́, -а́жешь; *impf* расска́зывать) *сов перех* to tell.

расска́зчик (-а) *м* storyteller; (*автор*) narrator.

расска́зчица (-ы) *ж см* расска́зчик.

расска́зыва|ть (-ю) *несов от* рассказа́ть.

рассла́б|ить (-лю, -ишь; *impf* расслабля́ть) *сов перех* (*мышцы, ноги, руки*) to relax; (*ремень, галстук*) to loosen; (*подлеж: болезнь, работа*) to weaken

▶ рассла́биться (*impf* расслабля́ться) *сов возв* to relax.

рассла́бленный (-, -на, -но) *прил* relaxed.

рассла́бл|ить(ся) (-ю(сь)) *несов от* рассла́бить(ся).

рассла́ива|ться (*3sg* -ется, *3pl* -ются) *несов от* расслои́ться.

рассле́довани|е (-я) *ср* investigation.

рассле́дова|ть (-ю) (*не*)*сов перех* to investigate.

расслои́ться (*3sg* -и́тся, *3pl* -я́тся, *impf* рассла́иваться) *сов возв* (*горная порода, общество*) to stratify; (*пирог, фанера*) to split.

рассл́ыш|ать (-у, -ишь) *сов перех* to hear; извини́те, я не ~ал I'm sorry, I didn't catch what you said.

рассма́трива|ть (-ю) *несов от* рассмотре́ть ♦ *перех:* ~ что-н как to regard sth as.

рассмеши́ть (-у́, -и́шь) *сов от* смеши́ть.

рассме|я́ться (-ю́сь, -ёшься) *сов возв* to start laughing.

рассмотре́ни|е (-я) *ср* examination.

рассм|отре́ть (-отрю́, -о́тришь; *impf* рассма́тривать) *сов перех* to examine; (*различить: в темноте, вдали*) to discern.

рассо́ва|ть (-ю́; *impf* рассо́вывать) *сов перех* (*разг*) ~ что-н в +*acc или* по +*dat* to stuff sth into.

рассо́л (-а; *part gen* -у) *м* brine.

рассо́льник (-а; *part gen* -у) *м* soup made with meat and pickled cucumbers.

рассоса́ться (*3sg* -ётся, *3pl* -у́тся, *impf* расса́сываться) *сов возв* (*опухоль*) to go down; (*перен: очередь, пробка*) to ease off; (*: толпа*) to thin out.

расспра́шива|ть (-ю) *несов от* расспроси́ть.

расспро́с (-а) *м* (*действие: свидетелей*) questioning; (*обычно мн: вопросы*) question.

расспро|си́ть (-ошу́, -о́сишь; *impf* расспра́шивать) *сов перех:* ~ (о +*prp*) to question (about).

рассро́ч|ка (-ки; *gen pl* -ек) *ж* installment, instalment (*US*); в ~ку (*купить, продать*) on hire purchase (*BRIT*), on the installment plan (*US*); выпла́чивать (вы́платить *perf*) в ~ку to pay in install(l)ments.

расстава́ни|е (-я) *ср* parting.

расста|ва́ться (-ю́сь, -ёшься) *сов от* расста́ться.

расста́в|ить (-лю, -ишь; *impf* расставля́ть) *сов перех* (*книги, мебель итп*) to arrange; (*шахматы*) to set up *или* out; (*знаки препинания, ударения*) to add; (*ножки циркуля*) to open; (*пальцы*) to splay; (*разг: расширить: платье, воротник*) to let out; **расставля́ть** (~ *perf*) **но́ги** to open one's legs.

расстано́в|ка (-ки; *gen pl* -ок) *ж* (*мебели, книг*) arrangement; ~ **сил** distribution of power; **чита́ть** (*impf*)/**говори́ть** (*impf*) с ~**кой** to read/ speak slowly and clearly.

расста́|ться (-нусь, -нешься; *impf* расстава́ться) *сов возв:* ~ с +*instr* to part with; (*с любимым делом*) to abandon; (*перен: с мечтой, с детством*) to say goodbye to.

расстегн|у́ть (-у́, -ёшь; *impf* расстёгивать) *сов перех* to undo

▶ расстегну́ться (*impf* расстёгиваться) *сов возв* (*человек*) to unbutton o.s.; (*рубашка, молния, пуговица*) to come undone.

расстел|и́ть (-ю́, -е́лешь; *impf* расстила́ть) *сов перех* to spread out.

расстила́|ться (*3sg* -ется, *3pl* -ются) *несов возв* (*равнина, степь*) to extend; (*туман*) to spread.

расстоя́ни|е (-я) *ср* distance; **держа́ть** (*impf*) **кого́-н на** ~**и** (*перен*) to keep sb at arm's length; **держа́ться** (*impf*) **на** ~**и** to keep one's distance.

расстра́ива|ть(ся) (-ю(сь)) *несов от* расстро́ить(ся).

расстре́л (-а) *м:* ~ +*gen* shooting *или* firing at; (*казнь*) execution (*by firing squad*); **пригова́ривать** (**приговори́ть** *perf*) **кого́-н к** ~**у** to sentence sb to be shot.

расстреля́|ть (-ю; *impf* расстре́ливать) *сов перех* (*демонстрацию*) to open fire on; (*казнить*) to shoot; (*патроны, снаряды*) to use up.

расстро́енный (-, -а, -о) *прил* (*здоровье, нервы*) weak; (*человек, вид*) upset; (*рояль, скрипка*) out of tune.

расстро́|ить (-ю, -ишь; *impf* расстра́ивать) *сов перех* (*планы, дела, свадьбу*) to disrupt; (*нервы*) to unsettle; (*человека, желудок*) to upset; (*здоровье*) to compromise; (*ряды противника*) to throw into confusion *или* disarray; (*муз*) to put out of tune

▶ расстро́иться (*impf* расстра́иваться) *сов возв* (*поездка, планы*) to fall through; (*дела, бизнес*) to fall apart; (*человек*) to get upset; (*колонна, ряды*) to fall into disarray; (*нервы*) to weaken; (*здоровье*) to become poorly; (*муз*) to go out of tune.

расстро́йств|о (-а) *ср* (*в делах, в хозяйстве*)

disorder; (*в рядах противника*) confusion, disarray; (*огорчение*) upset; (*речи, нервной* - *системы*) dysfunction; ~ **желу́дка** stomach upset; **приходи́ть (прийти́** *perf*) **в** ~ (*дела, хозяйство*) to be thrown into confusion; (*человек*) to become upset.

расступи́ться (*3sg* -**у́пится**, *impf* **расступа́ться**) *сов возв* (*толпа*) to make way; (*перен: тайга, волны, земля*) to part.

расстык|ова́ться (-**у́юсь**; *impf* **расстыко́вываться**) *сов возв* (*космос*) to undock.

расстыко́в|ка (-**ки**) *ж* undocking.

расстыко́выва|ться (-**юсь**) *несов от* **расстыкова́ться**.

рассуди́тельный (-**ен**, -**ьна**, -**ьно**) *прил* judicious.

рассу|ди́ть (-**жу́**, -**у́дишь**) *сов перех* (*спор*) to settle; (*люде́й*) to settle a dispute between ♦ *неперех*: **она́ ~уди́ла пра́вильно** she made the correct decision.

рассу́д|ок (-**ка**) *м* reason; **быть** (*impf*) **в своём** ~**ке** to be in possession of one's facilities.

рассужда́|ть (-**ю**) *несов неперех* to reason; ~ (*impf*) **о** +*prp* to debate.

рассужде́ни|е (-**я**) *ср* (*умозаключение: логическое итп*) judg(e)ment; (*обычно мн: о морали*) reasoning *ед*; **без** ~**й** without arguing.

рассужу́ *сов см* **рассуди́ть**.

рассчита́|ть (-**ю**; *impf* **рассчи́тывать**) *сов перех* (*стоимость, траекторию, политику*) to calculate; (*работника*) to lay off; **словарь рассчи́тан на студе́нтов** the dictionary is designed for students

▸ **рассчита́|ться** (*impf* **рассчи́тываться**) *сов возв* (*уволиться*) to hand in one's notice; (*воен: в строю*) to call out one's number; **рассчи́тываться** (~**ся** *perf*) (**с** +*instr*) (*с продавцом, в гостинице*) to settle up (with); (*перен: с врагом итп*) to settle a score (with).

рассчи́тыва|ть (-**ю**) *несов от* **рассчита́ть** ♦ *неперех*: ~ **на** +*acc* (*надеяться: на удачу, на друга*) to count *или* rely on; ~ (*impf*) +*infin* to count on doing

▸ **рассчи́тываться** *несов от* **рассчита́ться**.

рассыла́|ть (-**ю**) *несов от* **разосла́ть**.

рассы́п|ать (-**лю**, -**лешь**; *impf* **рассыпа́ть**) *сов перех* to spill; (*распределить*): ~ **по** +*dat* to pour into

▸ **рассы́паться** (*impf* **рассыпа́ться**) *сов возв* (*сахар, песок, бусы*) to spill; (*стена, холм*) to crumble; (*волосы*) to fall loose; (*толпа, стая*) to scatter; **он ~ался в благода́рностях** he was effusive in his thanks.

рассыпно́й *прил* sold loose.

рассы́пчат|ый (-, -**а**, -**о**) *прил* (*каша, рис*) fluffy; (*печенье, пирог*) crumbly.

рассяду́сь *итп сов см* **рассе́сться**.

раста́лкива|ть (-**ю**) *несов от* **растолка́ть**.

растамо́ж|ить (-**у**, -**ишь**) (*не*)*сов перех* to obtain customs clearance for.

раста́плива|ть (-**ю**) *несов от* **растопи́ть**.

раста́птыва|ть (-**ю**) *несов от* **растопта́ть**.

растаска́|ть (-**ю**; *impf* **раста́скивать**) *сов перех* (*разг: по комнатам*) to drag; (: *разворовать*) to filch.

раст|ащи́ть (-**ащу́**, -**а́щишь**) *сов* = **растаска́ть** ♦ *перех* (*разг: мальчишек*) to drag apart.

раста́|ять (-**ю**) *сов от* **та́ять**.

раство́р (-**а**) *м* (*хим*) solution; (*циркуля*) span, spread; (*строительный*) mortar; **цеме́нтный** ~ cement.

раствори́м|ый (-, -**а**, -**о**) *прил* soluble; **раствори́мый ко́фе** instant coffee.

раствори́тел|ь (-**я**) *м* solvent.

раствор|и́ть (-**ю́**, -**и́шь**; *impf* **растворя́ть**) *сов перех* (*окно, дверь*) to open; (*порошок, сахар*) to dissolve

▸ **раствори́ться** (*impf* **растворя́ться**) *сов возв* (*см перех*) to open; to dissolve; (*перен*): ~ **в** +*prp* (*в темноте, в тумане*) to vanish into.

растека́|ться (*3sg* -**ется**, *3pl* -**ются**) *несов от* **расте́чься**.

растёкся *итп сов см* **расте́чься**.

растеку́тся *итп сов см* **расте́чься**.

расте́ни|е (-**я**) *ср* plant.

растенниево́дств|о (-**а**) *ср* horticulture.

раст|ере́ть (**разотру́**, **разотрёшь**; *pt* -**ёр**, -**ёрла**, -**ёрло**, *impf* **растира́ть**) *сов перех* (*рану, тело*) to massage; **растира́ть** (~ *perf*) (**в порошо́к**) to grind (into a powder); **растира́ть** (~ *perf*) **кре́мом/ма́зью** to rub cream/ointment into; **растира́ть** (~ *perf*) **но́гу** to get blisters

▸ **растере́ться** (*impf* **растира́ться**) *сов возв*: ~**ся** (+*instr*) (*полотенцем, мочалкой*) to rub o.s. down (with).

растерза́|ть (-**ю**) *сов от* **терза́ть**.

растеря́нность (-**и**) *ж* confusion; **она́ стоя́ла в** ~**и** she stood there looking confused.

растеря́н|ный (-, -**а**, -**о**) *прил* confused.

растеря́|ться (-**юсь**) *сов возв* (*человек*) to be confused; (*письма*) to go missing.

расте́|чься (*3sg* -**чётся**, *3pl* -**ку́тся**, *pt* -**кся**, -**кла́сь**, -**кло́сь**, *impf* **растека́ться**) *сов возв* (*ручьи, вода*) to spill; (*чернила, краска*) to run.

раст|и́ (-**у́**, -**ёшь**; *pt* **рос**, **росла́**, **росло́**, *perf* **вы́расти**) *несов неперех* to grow; (*проводить детство*) to grow up; **он вы́рос за грани́цей** he grew up abroad; ~ (**вы́расти** *perf*) **в чьих-н глаза́х** to grow in sb's estimation.

растира́|ть(ся) (-**ю(сь)**) *несов от* **растере́ть(ся)**.

расти́тельность (-**и**) *ж собир* vegetation.

расти́тельн|ый *прил* (*бот*) plant *опред*; **расти́тельное ма́сло** vegetable oil; **расти́тельный мир** the plant kingdom;

расти́тельный покро́в vegetation.

ра|сти́ть (-щу́, -сти́шь; *perf* вы́растить) *несов перех* (*детей*) to raise; (*цветы*) to grow; (*животных*) to rear; (*перен: кадры*) to nurture; (: *талант, дарование*) to cultivate.

растолка́|ть (-ю; *impf* раста́лкивать) *сов перех* (*толпу, людей*) to push away; (*разг: разбудить*) to shake.

растолк|ова́ть (-у́ю; *impf* растолко́вывать) *сов перех:* ~ что-н (кому́-н) to clarify sth (for sb).

растол|о́чь (-ку́, -чёшь *итп*, -ку́т; *pt* -о́к, -кла́, -кло́) *сов от* толо́чь.

растолсте́|ть (-ю) *сов непepex* to put on weight.

раст|опи́ть (-оплю́, -о́пишь; *impf* раста́пливать) *сов перех* (*печку*) to light; (*воск, жир, лёд*) to melt

▸ растопи́ться *сов от* топи́ться.

раст|опта́ть (-опчу́, -о́пчешь; *impf* раста́птывать) *сов перех* (*также перен*) to trample on.

растопы́р|ить (-ю, -ишь; *impf* растопы́ривать) *сов перех* to spread.

растор́г|нуть (-ну, -нешь; *pt* -, -ла, -ло, *impf* расторга́ть) *сов перех* to annul.

растормош|и́ть (-у́, -и́шь) *сов перех* (*разг*) to shake.

растор́оп|ный (-ен, -на, -но) *прил* quick, efficient.

расточи́тельный (-ен, -ьна, -ьно) *прил* extravagant.

расточи́тельств|о (-а) *ср* extravagance.

растр|а́вить (-авлю́, -а́вишь; *impf* растравля́ть) *сов перех* (*перен*): ~ кому́-н ду́шу to torment sb.

растранжи́р|ить (-ю, -ишь) *сов от* транжи́рить.

растра́т|а (-ы) *ж* (*времени, сил, денег*) waste; (*хищение*) embezzlement; (*растраченная сумма*) loss.

растра́|тить (-чу, -тишь; *impf* растра́чивать) *сов перех* to waste; (*расхитить*) to embezzle.

растрево́ж|ить (-у, -ишь) *сов перех* to alarm; ~ (*perf*) кому́-н ду́шу to stir sb's emotions

▸ растрево́житься *сов возв* to become alarmed.

растрёпан|ный (-, -на, -но) *прил* (*вид, внешность*) bedraggled; (*волосы*) tousled; (*тетрадь, книга*) tatty; быть (*impf*) в ~ных чу́вствах (*разг*) to be all confused.

растреп|а́ть (-еплю́, -е́плешь) *сов перех* (*волосы*) to mess up; (*тетрадь, книгу*) to tatter; (*разг: разболтать*) to blab

▸ растрепа́ться *сов возв* (*разг: волосы*) to get messed up; (: *тетрадь, книга*) to become tattered.

растро́ган|ный (-, -на, -но) *прил* (*человек*) moved, touched; (*голос*) full of emotion.

растро́га|ть (-ю) *сов перех:* ~ кого́-н (+*instr*) (*письмом, вниманием*) to touch *или* move sb (by)

▸ растро́гаться *сов возв* to be touched *или* moved; ~ся (*perf*) до слёз to be moved to tears.

растру́б|ить (-лю́, -и́шь) *сов от* труби́ть.

растя́гива|ть(ся) (-ю(сь)) *несов от* растяну́ть(ся).

растяже́ни|е (-я) *ср* (*МЕД*) strain.

растяжи́м|ый (-, -а, -о) *прил:* ~ое поня́тие a loose concept.

растя́ну|тый (-, -а, -о) *прил* lengthy.

растя|ну́ть (-ну́, -нешь; *impf* растя́гивать) *сов перех* to stretch; (*скатерть*) to spread out; (*связки, сухожилие*) to strain; (*ногу, руку*) to sprain; (*доклад, рассказ*) to drag out; (*удовольствие*) to prolong; (*средства*) to stretch out

▸ растяну́ться (*impf* растя́гиваться) *сов возв* to stretch; (*человек, обоз*) to stretch out; (*связки, сухожилие*) to be strained; (*собрание, работа*) to drag on.

растя́п|а (-ы) *м/ж* (*разг*) bungler.

расфас|ова́ть (-у́ю) *сов от* фасова́ть.

расформир|ова́ть (-у́ю; *impf* расформиро́вывать) *сов перех* to disband.

расха́жива|ть (-ю) *несов непepex* to saunter.

расхвал|и́ть (-алю́, -а́лишь; *impf* расхва́ливать) *сов перех* to enthuse about.

расхвата́|ть (-ю; *impf* расхва́тывать) *сов перех* (*разг*) to snatch up.

расхити́тел|ь (-я) *м* embezzler.

расхи́|тить (-щу, -тишь; *impf* расхища́ть) *сов перех* to embezzle.

расхище́ни|е (-я) *ср* embezzlement.

расхля́бан|ный (-, -на, -но) *прил* (*жест, движение*) irreverent; (*человек, поведение*) lax.

расхо́д (-а) *м* (*энергии, воды*) consumption; (*обычно мн: затраты*) expense; (: *комм: в бухгалтерской книге*) expenditure; ~ы произво́дства production costs; вводи́ть (ввести́ *perf*) кого́-н в ~ to leave sb out of pocket.

расх|оди́ться (-ожу́сь, -о́дишься) *несов от* разойти́сь.

расхо́дный *прил:* ~ о́рдер (*комм*) expenses form.

расхо́д|овать (-ую; *perf* израсхо́довать) *несов перех* (*деньги*) to spend; (*материалы, энергию*) to expend; (*потреблять: бензин*) to consume.

расхожде́ни|е (-я) *ср* (*между словом и делом*) discrepancy; (*во взглядах*) divergence.

расхо́ж|ий (-ая, -ее, -ие) *прил* (*мнение*) widely accepted.

расхожу́сь *несов см* расходи́ться.

расхоте́ть (*как* хоте́ть; *см* Table 16) *сов непepex:* ~ +*infin* (*спать, гулять итп*) to no longer want to do; я расхоте́л есть I don't feel hungry any more

▸ расхоте́ться *сов безл:* (мне) расхоте́лось спать I don't feel sleepy any more.

расхохота́ться (-очу́сь, -о́чешься) *сов возв* to burst out laughing.

расхочу́(сь) *итп сов см* **расхоте́ть(ся)**.
расцара́па|ть (-ю) *сов перех* to scratch.
расцве|сти́ (-ту́, -тёшь; *pt* -ёл, -ела́, -ело́, *impf* **расцвета́ть**) *сов непepex (также перен)* to blossom; *(от радости)* to light up.
расцве́т (-a) *м (перен: науки, таланта)* blossoming; **он в ~e сил** he is in the prime of life.
расцвета́|ть (-ю) *несов от* **расцвести́**.
расцве́т|ка (-ки; *gen pl* -ок) *ж* colour *(BRIT)* или color *(US)* scheme.
расцвету́ *итп сов см* **расцвести́**.
расцел|ова́ть (-у́ю) *сов перех* to kiss
▸ **расцелова́ться** *сов возв* to kiss each other.
расце́нива|ться (*3sg* -ется, *3pl* -ются) *несов возв:* ~ **как** to be regarded as.
расце|ни́ть (-ню́, -е́нишь; *impf* **расце́нивать**) *сов перех* to judge; **расце́нивать** (~ *perf*) **что-н как** to regard sth as.
расце́н|ка (-ки; *gen pl* -ок) *ж (оплата работы)* rate; *(цена)* tariff.
расцеп|и́ть (-лю́, -е́пишь; *impf* **расцепля́ть**) *сов перех (состав)* to uncouple; *(дерущихся, пальцы)* to pull apart.
расч|ерти́ть (-ерчу́, -е́ртишь; *impf* **расче́рчивать**) *сов перех* to rule, line.
расч|еса́ть (-ешу́, -е́шешь; *impf* **расчёсывать**) *сов перех (волосы, гриву)* to comb; *(шерсть, лён)* to card; *(руку, царапину)* to scratch; **расчёсывать** (~ *perf*) **кого-н** to comb sb's hair.
расчёс|ка (-ки; *gen pl* -ок) *ж* comb.
расчёсыва|ть (-ю) *несов от* **расчеса́ть**.
расчёт (-a) *м (налога, стоимости итп)* calculation; *(оплата)* payment; *(предложение)* calculation; *(выгода)* advantage; *(бережливость)* economy; *(увольнение)* dismissal; *(ВОЕН, МОР)* crew; **из ~a** +*gen* on the basis of; **из ~a 5 проце́нтов годовы́х** at 5 percent per annum; **он ведёт дела́ с ~ом** he runs his business economically; **де́йствовать** (*impf*) **по ~y** to act in a calculated way; **исходи́ть** (*impf*) **из ~a, что ...** to act on the assumption that ...; **брать** (**взять** *perf*) или **принима́ть** (**приня́ть** *perf*) **что-н в ~** to take sth into account; **по мои́м ~ам мы зако́нчим к ве́черу** by my reckoning we will finish by evening; **я с Ва́ми в ~e** we are all even; **брать** (**взять** *perf*) ~ to hand in one's notice.
расчётлив|ый (-, -а, -о) *прил (экономный)* thrifty; *(руководитель, игрок)* calculating; *(движения)* deliberate.
расчётн|ый *прил (ТЕХ: скорость итп)* estimated; **расчётный день** payday; **расчётный счёт** debit account.
расчешу́ *итп сов см* **расчеса́ть**.
расчи́|стить (-щу, -стишь) *impf* **расчища́ть**) *сов перех* to clear
▸ **расчи́ститься** (*impf* **расчища́ться**) *сов возв*

to clear.
расчлен|и́ть (-ю́, -и́шь) *сов от* **расчленя́ть**, **члени́ть**.
расчленя́|ть (-ю) *несов от* **расчлени́ть**.
расчу́вств|оваться (-уюсь) *сов возв (разг)* to be overcome with emotion.
расшата́|ть (-ю; *impf* **расша́тывать**) *сов перех (стол, стул)* to make wobbly; *(здоровье)* to damage; **он ~л себе́ не́рвы** he's become a nervous wreck
▸ **расшата́ться** (*impf* **расша́тываться**) *сов возв (забор, столб)* to become wobbly; *(перен: нервы)* to give out; *(здоровье)* to be damaged.
расшвыр|я́ть (-ю) *сов перех (разг)* to hurl around; (: *перен: деньги*) to fritter away.
расшевел|и́ть (-ю́, -и́шь) *сов перех (разг):* ~ **кого-н** to give sb a shake; *(перен: слушателей)* to liven sb up
▸ **расшевели́ться** *сов возв* to stir; *(перен: начальство, игроки)* to get moving.
расшиб|и́ть (-у́, -ёшь; *impf* **расшиба́ть**) *сов перех (разг)* to smash
▸ **расшиби́ться** (*impf* **расшиба́ться**) *сов возв (о дверь, при падении)* to hurt o.s.; *(разг: для друга, для семьи)* to put o.s. out.
расшива́|ть (-ю) *несов от* **расши́ть**.
расшире́ни|е (-я) *ср* widening; *(связей, производства)* expansion; *(знаний)* broadening.
расши́рен|ный (-, -на, -но) *прил (проход)* widened; *(комитет, заседание)* expanded; *(зрачки, сосуды)* dilated.
расши́р|ить (-ю, -ишь; *impf* **расширя́ть**) *сов перех* to widen; *(производство)* to expand; **расширя́ть** (~ *perf*) **кругозо́р** to broaden one's horizons
▸ **расши́риться** (*impf* **расширя́ться**) *сов возв* to widen; *(завод, контакты, знания)* to expand; *(зрачки)* to dilate.
расши́тый *прил* embroidered.
ра|сши́ть (-зошью́, -зошьёшь; *impf* **расшива́ть**) *сов перех (вышить)* to embroider.
расшифр|ова́ть (-у́ю; *impf* **расшифро́вывать**) *сов перех (текст, шифровку)* to decode, decipher; *(перен: тайну, смысл слов)* to decipher.
расшнур|ова́ть (-у́ю; *impf* **расшнуро́вывать**) *сов перех* to unlace.
расшум|е́ться (-лю́сь, -и́шься) *сов возв (разг)* to make a racket; (: *начать спорить*) to kick up a fuss.
расще́др|иться (-юсь, -ишься; *impf* **расще́дриваться**) *сов возв (разг)* to become generous.
расще́лин|а (-ы) *ж (скалы, горы)* crevice; *(в дереве, в камне)* cleft.
расщеп|и́ть (-лю́, -и́шь; *impf* **расщепля́ть**) *сов перех (также ФИЗ)* to split; *(ХИМ)* to decompose
▸ **расщепи́ться** (*impf* **расщепля́ться**) *сов возв*

to splinter; (ФИЗ) to split; (ХИМ) to decompose.

расщепле́ни|е (-я) *ср* splintering; (ФИЗ) fission; (ХИМ) decomposition.

расщеплю́(сь) *сов см* **расщепи́ть(ся)**.

расщепля́|ть(ся) (-ю) *несов от* **расщепи́ть(ся)**.

ратифика́ци|я (-и) *ж* ratification.

ратифици́р|овать (-ую) *(не)сов перех* to ratify.

ра́унд (-а) *м* (СПОРТ) round; (ПОЛИТ): ~ **перегово́ров** round of talks.

ра́фик (-а) *м* (разг) minibus.

рафина́д (-а) *м* sugar cubes *мн*.

рафини́рованный *прил* refined.

рахи́т (-а) *м* (МЕД) rickets.

рацио́н (-а) *м* ration.

рациона́лен *прил см* **рациона́льный**.

рационализа́тор (-а) *м* innovator.

рационализа́ци|я (-и) *ж* rationalization.

рационализи́р|овать (-ую) *(не)сов перех* to rationalize.

рационали́ст (-а) *м* rationalist.

рациона́льный (-ен, -ьна, -ьно) *прил* (поступок) rational; (использование ресурсов, организация) effective; **~ьное пита́ние** well-balanced diet.

ра́ци|я (-и) *ж* walkie-talkie.

рацпредложе́ни|е (-я) *ср сокр* (= рационализа́торское предложе́ние) innovation proposal.

рачи́тельный (-ен, -ьна, -ьно) *прил* thrifty.

рвану́ть (-у, -ёшь) *сов перех* to pull at; (разг) to explode ♦ *неперех* (разг: лошадь, бегун) to shoot off; ~ *(perf)* **кого́-н за пиджа́к/за́ руку** to tug at sb's jacket/arm; ~ *(perf)* **пе́сню** (разг) to break into song

▸ **рвану́ться** *сов возв* to tear off.

рва́ный *прил* torn; (ботинки) ripped; (рана) lacerated.

рв|ать (-у, -ёшь; *perf* **порва́ть** *или* **разорва́ть)** *несов перех* (письмо, одежду, книгу) to tear, rip; (перен: отношения, дружбу) to break off; *(perf* **вы́рвать;** предмет из рук) to snatch; *(no perf;* подлеж: ветер: одежды, занавес) to tear at; *(perf* **сорва́ть;** цветы, траву) to pick; (ветки) to break off ♦ *(perf* **вы́рвать)** безл: **его́** *итп* **~а́ло всю ночь** he was vomiting *или* being sick all night; ~ *(разорва́ть perf)* **кого́-н/что-н на ча́сти** to tear sb/sth to bits; **меня́ ~ут на ча́сти** (перен) I'm in demand from all sides; ~ **(порва́ть** *perf)* **с про́шлым** to break with the past; ~ **(вы́рвать** *perf)* **кому́-н зуб** (разг) to pull sb's tooth out; ~ *(impf)* **и мета́ть** *(impf)* (разг) to rant and rave

▸ **рва́ться** *(perf* **порва́ться** *или* **разорва́ться)** *несов возв* (бумага, одежда) to rip; (перен: отношения, связи) to be severed; *(perf* **разорва́ться;** снаряд) to explode; **~а́ться** *(impf)* **к приключе́ниям/вла́сти** to be hungry for adventure/power; **~а́ться** *(impf)* **в дра́ку** to be spoiling for a fight; **у меня́ се́рдце** *или* **душа́ ~ётся на ча́сти** my heart is being torn in two.

рвач (-а́) *м* (разг: пренебр) taker.

рве́ни|е (-я) *ср* (в учёбе, в работе) enthusiasm; (патриотический, религиозный) zeal; ~ **+**infin desire to do.

рво́т|а (-ы) *ж* vomiting.

рво́тный *прил*: **~ое (сре́дство)** emetic.

ре *ср нескл* (МУЗ) re.

реабилита́ци|я (-и) *ж* rehabilitation.

реабилити́р|овать (-ую) *(не)сов перех* to rehabilitate.

реаги́р|овать (-ую) *несов неперех*: ~ **(на +**acc) (на свет, на раздражение) to react (to); *(perf* **отреаги́ровать** *или* **прореаги́ровать;** на критику, на слова) to react *или* respond (to).

реакти́в (-а) *м* (ХИМ) reagent.

реакти́вный *прил* (ХИМ) reactive; (ТЕХ) jet-propelled; **реакти́вный дви́гатель** jet engine; **реакти́вный самолёт** jet (plane).

реа́ктор (-а) *м* reactor.

реакционе́р (-а) *м* reactionary.

реакцио́нный *прил* reactionary.

реа́кци|я (-и) *ж* reaction.

реа́лен *прил см* **реа́льный**.

реализа́ци|я (-и) *ж* (см глаг) implementation; realization.

реали́зм (-а) *м* realism.

реализ|ова́ть (-у́ю) *(не)сов перех* (реформы, проект, предложение) to implement; (товар, ценные бумаги) to realize.

реали́ст (-а) *м* realist.

реалисти́чен *прил см* **реалисти́чный**.

реалисти́ческий (-ая, -ое, -ие) *прил* realistic; (искусство) realist *опред*.

реалисти́чный (-ен, -на, -но) *прил* realistic.

реа́льност|ь (-и) *ж* reality; (политики, плана, задачи) practicability, feasibility; **~и на́шего вре́мени** modern-day realities.

реа́льный (-ен, -ьна, -ьно) *прил* (не воображаемый) real; (осуществимый, практический) realistic; **в ~ьном вре́мени** (КОМП) real-time; **реа́льная за́работная пла́та** (ЭКОН) real wage.

реанима́ци|я (-и) *ж* resuscitation; **отделе́ние ~и** intensive care unit.

ребён|ок (-ка; *nom pl* **де́ти** *или* **ребя́та)** *м* child (*мн* children); (грудной) baby; **дом ~ка** children's home.

ребр|о́ (-а́; *nom pl* **рёбра,** *gen pl* **рёбер)** *ср* (АНАТ) rib; (монеты, стола, кубика *итп*) edge; **ста́вить (поста́вить** *perf)* **вопро́с ~м** to put a question bluntly.

ре́бус (-а) *м* rebus; (перен) riddle.

ребя́т|а (-) *мн от* **ребёнок;** (разг: парни) guys *мн*.

ребя́ческий (-ая, -ое, -ие) *прил* (душа, сознание) child's *опред*; (перен: поведение, суждение) childish.

рёв (-а) *м* roar; (разг: громкий плач) howling.

ревальва́ци|я (-и) *ж* (ЭКОН) revaluation.

рева́нш (-а) *м* revenge; (игра) revenge match; **взять** *(perf)* ~ to take revenge.

реваншйзм (-а) *м* revanchism.

реве́нь (-я́) *м* rhubarb.

реве́ть (-у́, -ёшь) *несов неперех* to roar; (*разг: плакать*) to howl.

ревизио́нный *прил:* ~**ая коми́ссия** audit commission.

реви́зия (-и) *ж* (*комм*) audit; (*взглядов, учения*) revision.

ревизова́ть (-у́ю) *(не)сов перех* (*предприятие*) to inspect; (*бухгалтерские книги*) to audit.

ревизо́р (-а) *м* (*комм*) auditor.

ревмати́зм (-а) *м* rheumatism.

ревмати́ческий (-ая, -ое, -ие) *прил* rheumatoid.

ревмато́лог (-а) *м* rheumatologist.

ревни́вый (-, -а, -о) *прил* jealous.

ревнова́ть (-у́ю) *несов неперех:* ~ (*кого-н*) to be jealous (of sb); **он** ~**у́ет меня́ к своему́ бра́ту** he is jealous of my relationship with his brother.

ре́вностный (-ен, -на, -но) *прил* ardent, zealous.

ре́вность (-и) *ж* jealousy.

револьве́р (-а) *м* revolver.

революционе́р (-а) *м* revolutionary.

революционе́рка (-ки; *gen pl* -ок) *ж см* **революционе́р**.

революцио́нный *прил* revolutionary.

револю́ция (-и) *ж* revolution.

реви́ю *ср нескл* revue.

рега́лия (-и) *ж* (*обычно мн*) regalia *ед*.

рега́та (-ы) *ж* regatta.

ре́гби *ср нескл* rugby.

регби́ст (-а) *м* rugby player.

регио́н (-а) *м* region.

региона́льный *прил* regional.

реги́стр (-а) *м* (*муз, комп, мор*) register; (*на пишущей машинке*): **ве́рхний/ни́жний** ~ upper/lower case.

регистра́тор (-а) *м* (*в поликлинике*) receptionist; (*в загсе*) registrar.

регистрату́ра (-ы) *ж* (*в поликлинике*) reception; (*на предприятии*) records department.

регистра́ция (-и) *ж* registration.

регистри́ровать (-ую; *perf* **регистри́ровать** *или* **зарегистри́ровать**) *несов перех* to register

► **регистри́роваться** (*не)сов возв* to register; (*оформлять брак*) to get married (*at a registry office*).

регла́мент (-а) *м* (*порядок заседаний*) order of business; (*время для выступления*) speaking time.

регла́н *прил неизм* raglan ◆ (-а) *м*: **(пальто́-)/(пла́тье-)**~ raglan coat/dress.

регули́ровать (-ую) *несов перех* to regulate; (*perf* **урегули́ровать**; *отношения*) to

normalize; (*perf* **отрегули́ровать**; *мотор, громкость*) to adjust.

регулиро́вщик (-а) *м* traffic policeman (*мн* policemen).

регуля́рен *прил см* **регуля́рный**.

регуля́рно *нареч* regularly.

регуля́рность (-и) *ж* regularity.

регуля́рный (-ен, -на, -но) *прил* regular; **регуля́рные войска́** regular army *ед*.

редакти́ровать (-ую; *perf* **отредакти́ровать**) *несов перех* to edit.

реда́ктор (-а) *м* (*также комп*) editor.

редакцио́нный *прил* (*поправки*): ~**ая колле́гия** editorial board; **редакцио́нная статья́** editorial.

реда́кция (-и) *ж* (*действие: текста, статьи*) editing; (*вариант произведения*) edition; (*формулировка: статьи закона*) wording; (*учреждение*) editorial offices *мн*; (*на радио*) desk; (*на телевидении*) division; **под** ~**ей** +*gen* edited by *n*.

реде́ть (*3sg* -ет, *3pl* -ют, *perf* **поре́деть**) *несов неперех* to thin out.

реди́с (-а) *м* radish.

реди́ска (-и) *ж* (*разг*) (red) radish ◆ *собир* radishes *мн*.

ре́дкий (-кая, -кое, -кие; -ок, -ка́, -ко) *прил* rare; (*выстрелы, письма, гость*) occasional; (*волосы*) thin; (*зубы*) gappy; (*лес*) sparse; (*ткань, материал*) loose-weave.

ре́дко *нареч* rarely, seldom; (*расти*) sparsely.

редколле́гия (-и) *ж сокр* = **редакцио́нная колле́гия**.

ре́дкость (-и) *ж* rarity; **на** ~ unusually; **он на** ~ **до́брый челове́к** he is a person of uncommon kindness; **таки́е приме́ры не** ~ such examples are not uncommon.

ре́док *прил см* **ре́дкий**.

ре́дька (-и) *ж* (white) radish ◆ *собир* radishes *мн*.

режи́м (-а) *ж* (*питания, также полит*) regime; (*больничный, тюремный итп*) routine; (*условия работы*) conditions *мн*; (*комп*) mode; ~ **безопа́сности** security system; **рабо́чий** ~ **дви́гателя** the operating conditions of the engine.

режиссёр (-а) *м* director (*of film, play etc*); **режиссёр-постано́вщик** (stage) director.

режиссу́ра (-ы) *ж* (*профессия*) directing; (*фильма, спектакля*) direction.

ре́зать (-жу, -жешь; *perf* **разре́зать**) *несов перех* (*хлеб*) to slice, cut up; (*металл, кожу*) to cut; (*разг: нарыв, живот*) to cut open; (*perf* **заре́зать**; *разг: гуся, свинью*) to slaughter; (*перен: разг: диссертацию*) to flunk; (*perf* **сре́зать**; *студента*) to fail; (*no perf: ложки, фигурки итп*) to carve; (*причинять боль: подлеж: воротник*) to dig into; (: *дым, ветер*)

to sting; (*наносить изображения*): ~ **+***dat*
(*по де́реву, по ка́мню*) to carve; (*по стеклу́*) to
cut; (*по мета́ллу*) to engrave; **ре́зать** (*impf*)
слух или **у́хо** to grate
▶ **ре́заться** (*perf* **проре́заться**) *несов возв*
(*зубы, рога́*) to come through; (*no perf; разг*):
~**ся в** +*acc* (*в ка́рты итп*) to play.
резв|и́ться (-**лю́сь, -и́шься**) *несов возв* to
frolic, frisk about.
ре́зво *нареч* (*бежа́ть*) energetically.
ре́зв|ый (-, **-а́, -о**) *прил* (*ребёнок*) playful;
(*быстрый в беге́: конь, заяц*) frisky.
резе́рв (-**а**) *м* (*СПОРТ*) reserve team; (*обычно мн:
материа́льные итп*) reserve; **ка́ссовый** ~
(*КОММ*) cash reserves.
резе́рвн|ый *прил* reserve *опред*; (*КОМП*) backup
опред; ~**ые войска́** (army) reserves;
резе́рвная валю́та reserve currency;
резе́рвный капита́л capital reserve;
резе́рвный фонд reserve fund.
резервуа́р (-**а**) *м* reservoir (*tank*).
резе́ц (-**ца́**) *м* (*инструмент*) cutting tool; (*АНАТ*)
incisor.
резиде́нт (-**а**) *м* spy.
резиде́нци|я (-**и**) *ж* residence.
рези́н|а (-**ы**) *ж* rubber; **тяну́ть** (*impf*) ~**у** (*разг*) to
drag things out.
рези́н|ка (-**ки**; *gen pl* -**ок**) *ж* (*ла́стик*) rubber
(*BRIT*), eraser (*esp US*); (*тесёмка*) elastic;
(*жва́чка*) chewing gum.
рези́новый *прил* rubber *опред*.
рези́нок *сущ см* **рези́нка**.
ре́з|кий (-**кая, -кое, -кие; -ок, -ка́, -ко**) *прил*
sharp; (*свет, звук, го́лос*) harsh; (*запах*)
pungent; (*стиль, мане́ра*) abrupt.
ре́зко *нареч* sharply; (*встать, вы́сказать*)
abruptly.
ре́зкост|ь (-**и**) *ж* (*поведе́ния, мане́ры*)
abruptness; (*ФОТО*) focus; **говори́ть (сказа́ть**
perf) **кому́-н** ~**и** to be rude to sb.
резно́й *прил* carved.
резн|я́ (-**и́**) *ж* slaughter.
ре́зок *прил см* **ре́зкий**.
резолю́ци|я (-**и**) *ж* (*съе́зда, заседа́ния*)
resolution; (*распоряже́ние*) directive.
резона́нс (-**а**) *м* (*ФИЗ*) resonance; (*перен*)
response.
резо́н|ный (-**ен, -на, -но**) *прил* reasonable.
результа́т (-**а**) *м* result; **в** ~**е** as a result; (*в
ито́ге*) in the end.
результати́вн|ый (-**ен, -на, -но**) *прил* (*де́ло,
встре́ча*) productive; (*спортсме́н*) successful.
ре́зче *сравн прил от* **ре́зкий** ◆ *сравн нареч от*
ре́зко.
ре́зус (-**а**) *м* (*также:* ~**-фа́ктор**) rhesus factor.
резца́ *итп сущ см* **резе́ц**.
резь| (-**и**) *ж* sharp pain.
резьб|а́ (-**ы́**) *ж* carving; (*винта́, шуру́па*) thread;
~ **по де́реву/ка́мню** carving in wood/stone.
резюме́ *ср нескл* resumé, summary.
резюми́р|овать (-**ую**) (*не*)*сов перех* to

summarize.
рейд (-**а**) *м* raid; (*МОР*) anchorage.
ре́й|ка (-**йки**; *gen pl* -**ек**) *ж* batten;
(*измери́тельная*) measuring rod.
Ре́йкьявик (-**а**) *м* Reykjavik.
Рейн (-**а**) *м* (the) Rhine.
рейнве́йн (-**а**) *м* hock (*wine*).
рейс (-**а**) *м* (*самолёта*) flight; (*авто́буса*) run;
(*парахо́да*) sailing.
ре́йсовый *прил* regular.
ре́йтинг (-**а**) *м* popularity rating.
рейту́з|ы (-) *мн* thermal pants.
рек|а́ (-**и́**; *acc sg* -**у**, *dat sg* -**е́**, *nom pl* -**и**) *ж* (*также
перен*) river.
ре́квием (-**а**) *м* requiem.
реквизи́р|овать (-**ую**) (*не*)*сов перех* to
requisition.
реквизи́т (-**а**) *м* (*ТЕАТР, КИНО*) props *мн*;
(*обычно мн: в докуме́нте*) stipulation.
рекла́м|а (-**ы**) *ж* (*де́йствие: торго́вая*)
advertising; (*сре́дство*) advert (*BRIT*),
advertisement; (*театра́льная*) publicity;
де́лать (сде́лать *perf*) **себе́** ~**у** to draw attention
to o.s.
реклами́р|овать (-**ую**) (*не*)*сов перех* to
advertise.
рекла́мный *прил* (*отде́л, коло́нка*) advertising
опред; (*статья́, фильм, спра́вочник*) publicity
опред; **рекла́мный ро́лик** advertisement;
(*фильма*) trailer.
рекоменда́тельн|ый *прил*: ~**ое письмо́** letter
of recommendation.
рекоменда́ци|я (-**и**) *ж* recommendation.
рекомендова́ть (-**у́ю**; *perf* **рекомендова́ть**
или **порекомендова́ть**) *несов перех* to
recommend; ~ (**порекомендова́ть** *perf*) **кого́-н
кому́-н/на рабо́ту** to recommend sb to sb/for a
job; ~ (**порекомендова́ть** *perf*) **кому́-н** +*infin* to
recommend sb to do.
реконструи́р|овать (-**ую**) (*не*)*сов перех*
(*промы́шленность*) to rebuild; (*па́мятник,
зда́ние*) to reconstruct.
реконстру́кци|я (-**и**) *ж* reconstruction.
реко́рд (-**а**) *м* record; **устана́вливать
(установи́ть** *perf*)**/поби́ть** (*perf*) ~ to set/break a
record.
реко́рдный *прил* record(-breaking) *опред*.
рекордсме́н (-**а**) *м* recordholder.
рекордсме́н|ка (-**ки**; *gen pl* -**ок**) *ж см*
рекордсме́н.
ре́ктор (-**а**) *м* ≈ principal.
ректора́т (-**а**) *м* principal's office.
религио́зн|ый (-**ен, -на, -но**) *прил* religious.
рели́ги|я (-**и**) *ж* religion.
рели́кви|я (-**и**) *ж* relic; (*семе́йная*) heirloom.
релье́ф (-**а**) *м* (*ГЕО, ИСКУ́ССТВО*) relief.
рельс (-**а**) *м* (*обычно мн*) rail; **на ре́льсы** +*gen*
(*перен*) towards.
ре́льсовый *прил*: ~ **путь** railway (*BRIT*) *или*
railroad (*US*) track.
рема́рк|а (-**и**) *ж* (*ТЕАТР*) stage directions *мн*;

(*замечание*) remark.

ремéнь (-ня́) м (*брюк, платья, также* TEX) belt; (*сумки*) strap; **привязны́е ~ни́** seat belt; **приводно́й ~** drive-belt.

ремёсел *сущ см* **ремесло́**.

ремéсленник (-а) м artisan, craftsman (*мн* craftsmen).

ремéсленный *прил* (*труд, мастерская*) artisan's, craftsman's; (*изделие*) handcrafted; (*перен: не творческий*) mechanical.

ремесл|о́ (-а́; *nom pl* **ремёсла**, *gen pl* **ремёсел**) *ср* trade; (*перен: нетворческая работа*) hack work.

ремеш|о́к (-ка́) м strap.

ремня́ *итп сущ см* **ремéнь**.

ремо́нт (-а) м repair; (*здания*) refurbishment; (: *мелкий*) redecoration; **на ~е** under repair; **теку́щий ~** maintenance; **сдава́ть (сдать** *perf*) **что-н в ~** to put sth in for repair; **у нас до́ма сейча́с идёт ~** our house is being redecorated.

ремонти́р|овать (-ую; *perf* **отремонти́ровать** *или* **отремонти́ровать**) *несов перех* to repair; (*квартиру, здание*) to do up.

ремо́нтн|ый *прил*: **~ые рабо́ты** repairs *мн*; **~ая мастерска́я** repair workshop.

рéнт|а (-ы) ж rent; **земéльная ~** ground rent.

рента́бельн|ый (-ен, -ьна, -ьно) *прил* profitable.

рентгéн (-а) м (*МЕД*) X-ray; (*ФИЗ*) roentgen; **дéлать (сдéлать** *perf*) **кому́-н ~** to X-ray sb.

рентгéновск|ий (-ая, -ое, -ие) *прил*: **кабинéт/аппара́т** X-ray room/machine; **~ сни́мок** X-ray; **~ие лучи́** X-rays.

рентгено́лог (-а) м radiologist.

реорганиза́ци|я (-и) ж reorganization.

реорганиз|ова́ть (-у́ю) (*не*)*сов перех* to reorganize.

рéп|а (-ы) ж (*no pl*) swede (*BRIT*), rutabaga (*US*).

репатриа́нт (-а) м repatriate.

репатриа́ци|я (-и) ж repatriation.

репатрии́р|овать (-ую) (*не*)*сов перех* to repatriate.

репéй (-я́) м (*разг*) = **репéйник**.

репéйник (-а) м (*БОТ*) burdock.

репертуа́р (-а) м repertoire.

репети́р|овать (-ую; *perf* **отрепети́ровать** *или* **прорепети́ровать**) *несов* (*не*)*перех* (*диалог, спектакль*) to rehearse.

репети́тор (-а) м (*преподаватель*) coach, private tutor.

репети́ци|я (-и) ж rehearsal.

рéплик|а (-и) ж (*слушателей*) remark; (*ТЕАТР*) line; (*ЮР*) objection.

репорта́ж (-а) м (*статья, передача*) report.

репортёр (-а) м reporter.

репрéсси|я (-и) ж (*обычно мн*) repression.

репроду́ктор (-а) м loudspeaker.

репроду́кци|я (-и) ж reproduction (*of painting etc*).

репти́ли|я (-и) ж reptile.

репута́ци|я (-и) ж reputation.

рéпчатый *прил*: **~ лук** onions *мн*.

репья́ *итп сущ см* **репéй**.

ресни́ц|а (-ы) ж (*обычно мн*) eyelash.

респекта́бельный (-ен, -ьна, -ьно) *прил* respectable.

респондéнт (-а) м respondent.

респу́блик|а (-и) ж republic.

республика́нск|ий (-ая, -ое, -ие) *прил* republican.

рессо́р|а (-ы) ж spring.

реставра́тор (-а) м restorer.

реставра́ци|я (-и) ж restoration.

реставри́р|овать (-ую; *perf* **реставри́ровать** *или* **отреставри́ровать**) *несов перех* to restore.

рестора́н (-а) м restaurant.

ресу́рс (-а) м (*обычно мн*) resource; **приро́дные ~ы** natural resources.

рéтро *прил неизм* (*мода, мебель*) retro.

ретрогра́д (-а) м reactionary.

ретроспекти́в|а (-ы) ж retrospective.

рефера́т (-а) м synopsis (*мн* synopses).

референдум (-а) м referendum (*мн* referenda).

референт (-а) м (*директора, министра*) aide.

рефери *м нескл* referee.

рефери́р|овать (-ую; *perf* **рефери́ровать** *или* **прорефери́ровать**) (*не*)*сов* to summarize.

рефлéкс (-а) м reflex.

рефлéктор (-а) м reflector.

рефо́рм|а (-ы) ж reform.

реформа́тор (-а) м reformer.

рефрижера́тор (-а) м (*судно*) refrigerator ship; (*грузовик*) refrigerated lorry (*BRIT*) *или* truck (*US*).

рехн|у́ться (-у́сь, -ёшься) *сов возв* (*разг*) to crack (up), flip; **~** (*perf*) **на чём-н** to be nuts about sth.

рецензи́р|овать (-ую; *perf* **прорецензи́ровать**) *несов перех* to review.

рецéнзи|я (-и) ж: **~** (**на** +*acc*) review (of).

рецéпт (-а) м (*МЕД*) prescription; (*КУЛИН, перен*) recipe.

рециди́в (-а) м (*преступления*) repetition; (*болезни*) recurrence.

рецидиви́ст (-а) м recidivist, habitual offender.

речев|о́й *прил* speech *опред*; **~ дефéкт** speech defect; **~ые на́выки** speaking skills.

рéчк|а (-ки; *gen pl* -ек) ж stream; (*разг*) river.

речни́к (-а) м river-transport worker.

речн|о́й *прил* river *опред*; **~а́я ры́ба** freshwater fish; **речно́й трамва́й** river bus.

речь (-и) ж speech; (*стиль: разговорная итп*) language; (*русская, французская*) spoken language; **русская ~** spoken Russian; **часть рéчи** part of speech; **прямая/ко́свенная ~**

direct/indirect speech; **ýстная/пи́сьменная ~** spoken/written language; **дар ре́чи** the gift of speech; **теря́ть (потеря́ть** *perf***) дар ре́чи** to be left speechless; **произноси́ть** (*impf*) **ýмные/пусты́е ре́чи** to make clever/empty pronouncements; **~ идёт о** +*prp* ... we are talking about ...; **о чём идёт ~?** what are you talking about?; **~ идёт о том, как/где/кто** *итп* ... the matter in question is how/where/who *итп* ...; **заводи́ть (завести́** *perf***) ~ о** +*prp* to raise the matter of; **об э́том не мо́жет быть и ре́чи** there can be absolutely no question of this; **об э́том ре́чи не́ было** nothing was said about this; **о чём ~!** (*разг*) sure!, of course!

реша́|ть(ся) (-ю(сь)) *несов от* реши́ть(ся).

реша́ющий (-ая, -ее, -ие) *прил* decisive; (*слово, матч*) deciding *опред*; **реша́ющий го́лос** casting vote.

реше́ние (-я) *ср* (*суда, собрания итп*) decision; (*ответ к задаче*) solution; (*действие: вопроса, дела*) solution, solving; (*: судьбы*) deciding.

реше́т|ка (-ки; *gen pl* -ок) *ж* (*садовая*) trellis; (*оконная*) grille; (*в камине*) grate; (*в духовке*) oven rack; **за ~кой** (*разг*) behind bars.

решет|о́ (-á) *ср* sieve.

решёток *сущ см* решётка.

решётчат|ый *прил* lattice *опред*, trellis *опред*; **~ое окно́** lattice window.

реши́мост|ь (-и) *ж* resolve.

реши́телен *прил см* реши́тельный.

реши́тельно *нареч* (*заявить, отказать*) resolutely; (*действовать*) with resolve, decisively; **я ~ не понима́ю, о чём Вы говори́те** I've got absolutely no idea what you are talking about.

реши́тельн|ый (-ен, -ьна, -ьно) *прил* (*человек, взгляд*) resolute; (*меры*) drastic; (*решающий*) decisive.

реши́|ть (-ý, -ишь; *impf* реша́ть) *сов перех* to decide; (*задачу, вопрос*) to solve; **реша́ть (~** *perf***) +*infin*** to decide to do

▶ **реши́ться** (*impf* реша́ться) *сов возв* (*вопрос, судьба*) to be decided; **реша́ться (~ся** *perf***) на** +*acc*/+*infin* to make up one's mind on/to do.

ре́ш|ка (-и) *ж* (*на монете*) tails *мн*; **орёл или ~?** heads or tails?

реэ́кспорт (-а) *м* re-export.

реэкспорти́р|овать (-ую) (*не*)*сов перех* re-export.

ре|я́ть (3sg -ет, 3sg -ют) *сов непер* (*птица*) to soar; (*флаг*) to fly.

ржа́ве|ть (3sg -ет, 3pl -ют, *perf* заржа́веть) *несов непер* to rust, go rusty.

ржа́вчин|а (-ы) *ж* rust.

ржа́в|ый *прил* rusty; (*вода*) brown; (*листва*) rust-coloured (*BRIT*) *или* -colored (*US*); **~ое пятно́** rust mark.

ржано́й *прил* rye *опред*.

ржать (-у, -ёшь) *несов непер* to neigh; (*разг: смеяться*) to roar with laughter.

ржи *итп сущ см* рожь.

РЖУ *ср сокр* = *районное жили́щное управле́ние*.

РИА *ср сокр* (= *Росси́йское информацио́нное аге́нтство*) Russian News Agency.

Ривье́р|а (-ы) *ж* the Riviera.

Ри́г|а (-и) *ж* Riga.

ри́з|а (-ы) *ж* (*одежда*) vestments *мн*; (*на иконе*) overlay.

рикоше́т (-а) *м* ricochet, rebound; **отска́кивать (отскочи́ть** *perf***) ~ом** to ricochet, rebound.

Рим (-а) *м* Rome.

ри́мский (-ая, -ое, -ие) *прил* Roman; **Па́па Р~** the Pope; **ри́мские ци́фры** Roman numerals.

ри́мско-католи́ческ|ий (-ая, -ое, -ие) *прил* Roman Catholic.

ринг (-а) *м* (boxing) ring.

ри́н|уться (-усь, -ешься) *сов возв* to charge; **~** (*perf*) **в рабо́ту** to throw o.s. into one's work.

Рио-де-Жане́йро *м нескл* Rio de Janeiro.

рис. *сокр* (= **рису́нок**) diag. (= *diagram*).

рис (-а) *м* rice.

риск (-а) *м* (*no pl*) risk; **на свой страх и ~** at one's own risk.

рискн|у́ть (-ý, -ёшь) *сов от* рискова́ть.

риско́ван|ный (-, -на, -но) *прил* risky; (*перен: разговор, шутка*) risqué.

риск|ова́ть (-у́ю; *perf* рискну́ть) *несов непер* to take risks; (*рискну́ть* *perf*) (*жизнью, здоровьем*) to risk; **~** (*impf*) **+*infin*** to risk doing; **Вы (си́льно) ~у́ете** you are taking a (big) risk.

ри́слинг (-а) *м* Riesling.

рисова́ни|е (-я) *ср* (*карандашом*) drawing; (*красками*) painting.

рис|ова́ть (-у́ю; *perf* нарисова́ть) *несов перех* (*карандашом*) to draw; (*красками*) to paint; (*перен: описывать*) to depict, portray; (*: подлеж: воображение, сознание*) to evoke a picture of

▶ **рисова́ться** *несов возв* (*виднеться*) to be seen; (*перен: в воображении*) to be conjured up; (*манерничать*) to show off.

ри́совый *прил* rice *опред*.

рису́н|ок (-ка) *м* drawing; (*на ткани, на обоях*) pattern; (*картины*) sketch; **акваре́льный ~** watercolour (*BRIT*), watercolor (*US*).

ритм (-а) *м* (*сердца, стиха*) rhythm; (*перен: жизни, работы*) pace.

ритми́чен *прил см* ритми́чный.

ритми́ческий (-ая, -ое, -ие) *прил* rhythmic(al); **ритми́ческая гимна́стика** aerobics.

ритми́чн|ый (-ен, -на, -но) *прил* (*музыка, стук*) rhythmic(al); (*работа, процесс*) smooth-running.

рито́рик|а (-и) *ж* rhetoric.

ритуа́л (-а) *м* ritual.

риф (-а) *м* reef.

рифлёный *прил* (*подошва*) grooved; **рифлёное желе́зо** corrugated iron.

ри́фм|а (-ы) *ж* rhyme.

рифм|ова́ть (-у́ю; *perf* срифмова́ть) *несов перех* (*строчки, слова*) to make rhyme

▶ **рифмова́ться** *несов возв* to rhyme.

РКП(б) *ж сокр (ист)* = Росси́йская Коммунисти́ческая па́ртия (большевико́в).

р-н *сокр* = райо́н.

РНК *ж сокр* (= рибонуклеи́новая кислота́) RNA (= *ribonucleic acid*).

робе́|ть (-ю; *perf* оробе́ть) *несов неперех* to go shy.

ро́б|кий (-кая, -кое, -кие; -ок, -ка́, -ко) *прил* shy.

ро́бот (-а) *м* robot.

робототе́хник|а (-и) *ж* robotics.

ро|в (-ва; *loc sg* -ву́) *м* ditch.

ро́вен *прил см* ро́вный.

рове́сник (-а) *м*: он мой ~ he is the same age as me.

рове́сниц|а (-ы) *ж*: она́ моя́ ~ she is the same age as me.

ро́вно *нареч* (*писа́ть*) evenly; (*черти́ть*) straight; (*дыша́ть*) regularly; (*че́рез год*) exactly; ~ в два часа́ at two o'clock sharp; я ~ ничего́ не по́нял I didn't understand a thing.

ро́в|ный (-ен, -на́, -но) *прил* even; (*степь*) flat; (*пробо́р, ли́ния*) straight; (*дыха́ние, пульс*) regular; (*перен: хара́ктер, челове́к*) stable; ~ счёт round number; ~ным счётом ничего́ (*разг*) absolutely nothing.

ровня́|ть (-ю; *perf* сровня́ть или вы́ровнять) *несов перех* (*строй, шере́нгу*) to straighten (up); (*perf* разровня́ть или сровня́ть; *доро́жку, площа́дку*) to level; сровня́ть (*perf*) с землёй to raze to the ground.

ро|г (-а; *nom pl* -а́) *м* (*та́кже муз*) horn; (*полуме́сяца*) cusp; оле́ний ~ antler; ~ изоби́лия horn of plenty; у чёрта на ~а́х (*разг*) in the middle of nowhere; взять (*perf*) быка́ за ~а́ (*разг*) to take the bull by the horns.

рога́лик (-а) *м* crescent-shaped roll.

рога́т|ка (-ки; *gen pl* -ок) *ж* (*для мета́ния ка́мешков*) catapult; (*на доро́ге*) roadblock: ста́вить (*impf*) ~ки кому́-н to create obstacles for sb.

рога́т|ый (-, -а, -о) *прил* horned; кру́пный ~ скот cattle.

рогови́ц|а (-ы) *ж* cornea.

рогово́й *прил* horn *опред*; рогова́я оболо́чка cornea.

рого́ж|а (-и) *ж* (*ткань*) sacking.

ро|д (-а; *part gen* -у, *loc sg* -у́, *nom pl* -ы́) *м* clan; (*ряд поколе́ний*) family; (*происхожде́ние*) stock; (*расте́ний, живо́тных*) genus (*мн* genera); (*де́ятельности, войск*) type; (*линг*) gender; (*одно́ поколе́ние*) generation; он ро́дом из По́льши he comes from Poland; он ро́дом из дворя́н he is of noble stock; своего́ ро́да a kind of; в не́котором ро́де to some extent; что-то в э́том или тако́м ро́де something like that; вся́кого или ра́зного ро́да all kinds of; вести́ *perf* свой ~ от кого́-н to be descended from sb;

э́то у нас в ~у́ it runs in the family; из ро́да в ~ from generation to generation; ему́ два́дцать лет от ~у (*разг*) he is twenty years old; он от ~у ничего́ тако́го не слы́шал he had never heard anything like this in his life.

род. *сокр* (= роди́лся) b. (= *born*).

роддо́м (-а) *м сокр* (= роди́льный дом) maternity hospital.

роди́льный *прил*: ~ дом maternity hospital.

роди́мый *прил* (*разг: край, земля́*) native; ~ дом family home; роди́мое пятно́ birthmark.

ро́дин|а (-ы) *ж* (*оте́чество*) homeland; (*ме́сто рожде́ния, появле́ния*) birthplace.

ро́дин|ка (-ки; *gen pl* -ок) *ж* birthmark.

роди́тел|и (-ей) *мн* parents *мн*.

роди́тельный *прил*: ~ паде́ж genitive case.

роди́тельский (-ая, -ое, -ие) *прил* (*обя́занности, права́, дом*) parental; (*де́ньги*) parents'; роди́тельское собра́ние parents' meeting.

ро|ди́ть (-жу́, -ди́шь; *pt perf* -ди́л, -дила́, -ди́ло, *pt impf* -ди́л, -ди́ла, -ди́ло, *impf* рожа́ть или рожда́ть) *сов перех* to give birth to; (*подлеж*: земля́, я́блоня) to bear a crop or

▶ **роди́ться** (*impf* рожда́ться) *сов возв* to be born ◆ (*perf* уроди́ться) *несов* (*пшени́ца, я́блоки*) to give a good yield; у них ~дила́сь дочь they had a daughter; ~ся (*perf*) в руба́шке (*разг*) to always land on one's feet.

родни́|к (-а́) *м* spring (*water*).

родни́ть (3sg -и́т, 3pl -я́т) *несов перех*: ~ кого́-н (с +*instr*) to bring sb closer (to)

▶ **родни́ться** ◆ (-ю́сь, -и́шься; *perf* породни́ться) *несов возв*: ~ся (с +*instr*) to become related (to).

родно́й *прил* (*брат, мать итп*) natural *опред*; (*го́род, страна́*) native; (*в обраще́нии*) dear; родно́й язы́к mother tongue; *см та́кже* родны́е.

родны́|е (-х; *decl like adj*) *мн* relations *мн*, relatives *мн*.

родн|я́ (-и́) *ж собир* (*ро́дственники*) relations *мн*, relatives *мн* ◆ *ж/м* (*разг*: ро́дственник) relative.

родови́т|ый (-, -а, -о) *прил* of noble birth.

родово́й *прил* (*ист*: строй, быт) tribal; (*поня́тие, при́знак*) generic; (*линг*) gender *опред*; (*име́ние*) family *опред*; (*мед*: су́дороги, тра́вма) birth *опред*.

родовспоможе́ни|е (-я) *ср* midwifery.

родонача́льник (-а) *м* (*семьи́, дина́стии*) forefather; (*перен*: уче́ния) founder; (: *тео́рии*) originator.

родосло́ви|е (-я) *ср* genealogy.

родосло́вн|ая (-ой; *decl like adj*) *ж* (*семьи́*) ancestry; (*соба́ки*) pedigree.

родосло́вный *прил*: ~ое де́рево family tree.

ро́дственник (-а) *м* relation, relative.

ро́дственниц|а (-ы) *ж см* ро́дственник.

ро́дствен|ный (-, -на, -но) *прил* family *опред*; (*языки, науки*) related; **ро́дственные свя́зи** family ties.

родство́ (-а́) *ср* relationship; (*душ, идей итп*) affinity.

ро́д|ы (-ов) *мн* labour *ед* (*BRIT*), labor *ед* (*US*); **умере́ть** (*perf*) **от ~ов** to die in childbirth; **принима́ть** (**приня́ть** *perf*) **~** to deliver a baby.

ро́ж|а (-и) *ж* (*разг: лицо*) face; (*неприятное лицо*) mug; (*МЕД*) erysipelas (*skin complaint*); **стро́ить** (*impf*) **~и** (*разг*) to make faces.

рожа́|ть (-ю) *несов от* **роди́ть**.

рожда́емость (-и) *ж* birth rate.

рожда́|ть(ся) (-ю(сь)) *несов от* **роди́ть(ся)**.

рожде́ни|е (-я) *ср* birth; **день ~я** birthday.

рожде́ственский (-ая, -ое, -ие) *прил* Christmas *опред*.

Рождество́ (-а́) *ср* (*РЕЛ*) Nativity; (*праздник*) Christmas; **с ~м!** Happy *или* Merry Christmas!

роже́ниц|а (-ы) *ж* (*рожающая женщина*) woman in labour; (*только что родившая*) woman who has given birth.

рожка́ *итп сущ см* **рожо́к**.

рожна́ *итп сущ см* **рожо́н**.

рожо́к (-ка́) *м* (*МУЗ*) horn; (*рогалик*) crescent-shaped roll; (*для надевания обуви*) shoehorn; (*макароны*) macaroni.

рожо́н (-на́) *м* (*разг*): **лезть на ~** to ask for trouble; **како́го ~на́ тебе́ на́до?** (*разг*) what the hell do you want?

рожу́(сь) (*не*)*сов см* **роди́ть(ся)**.

рожь (ржи) *ж* rye.

ро́з|а (-ы) *ж* (*растение*) rose(bush); (*цветок*) rose.

роза́ри|й (-я) *м* rose garden.

ро́з|га (-ги; *gen pl* -ог) *ж* birch (*for punishment*).

розе́т|ка (-ки; *gen pl* -ок) *ж* power point; (*блюдечко*) jam (*BRIT*) *или* jelly (*US*) dish; (*украшение*) rosette.

ро́зниц|а (-ы) *ж* retail goods *мн*; **продава́ть** (*impf*) **в ~у** to retail.

ро́зничный *прил* retail; (**рекомендо́ванная**) **ро́зничная цена́** (recommended) retail price.

розн|ь (-и) *ж*: **студе́нт студе́нту ~** there are students and students.

розове́|ть (-ю; *perf* **порозове́ть**) *несов неперех* to turn *или* go pink; **у него́ на лбу ~л шрам** he had a pink scar on his forehead.

ро́зовый *прил* rose *опред*; (*цвет*) pink; (*ребёнок, мечты*) rosy; **ви́деть** (*impf*) **кого́-н/что-н в ро́зовом све́те** to see sb/sth through rose-coloured spectacles (*BRIT*) *или* rose-colored glasses (*US*).

ро́зог *сущ см* **ро́зга**.

ро́зыгрыш (-а) *м* draw; (*шутка*) prank.

ро́зыск (-а) *м* search; **уголо́вный ~** Criminal Investigation Department (*BRIT*), Federal Bureau of Investigation (*US*).

ро́|иться (*3sg* -и́тся, *3pl* -я́тся) *несов возв* to swarm; (*перен: мысли*) to flood.

ро́|й (-я; *nom pl* -й) *м* (*пчёл, комаров*) swarm; (*снежинок, искр*) flurry; (*пыли*) cloud; (*перен: воспоминаний*) flood.

рок (-а) *м* (*злая судьба*) fate; (*рок-музыка*) rock ♦ *прил неизм* (*танец, стиль*) rock *опред*.

ро́кер (-а) *м* (*разг*) rocker.

рок-му́зык|а (-и) *ж* rock music.

рок-н-ро́лл (-а) *м* rock and roll.

роково́й *прил* fatal.

ро́кот (-а) *м* rumble.

рокот|а́ть (*3sg* -о́чет, *3pl* -о́чут) *несов неперех* to rumble.

рокфо́р (-а) *м* Roquefort.

ро́лик (-а) *м* (*вращающийся валик*) roller; (*на ножке*) caster; (*ЭЛЕК*) cleat; (*фотоплёнки, бумаги*) roll; (*обычно мн: разг: коньки на колесиках*) roller skate; **~ новосте́й** newsreel; **рекла́мный ~** advertisement; (*фильма*) trailer; *см также* **ро́лики**.

ро́лик|и (-ов) *мн* roller skates *мн*.

ро́ликов|ый *прил* (*ТЕХ*) roller *опред*; **~ые коньки́** roller skates.

рол|ь (-и; *gen pl* -е́й, *dat pl* -я́м) *ж* role; (*текст*) part; **в ро́ли** +*gen* as; **игра́ть** (*impf*) **~** to play a part; **входи́ть** (**войти́** *perf*) **в ~** to get into the part.

ром (-а) *м* rum.

рома́н (-а) *м* (*исторический, биографический*) novel; (*любовная связь*) affair.

романи́ст (-а) *м* (*писатель*) novelist; (*учёный*) Romance language philologist.

рома́нс (-а) *м* (*МУЗ*) romance.

рома́нский (-ая, -ое, -ие) *прил* Romance *опред*; (*архитектура*) Romanesque.

романти́зм (-а) *м* (*художественное течение*) Romanticism; (*умонастроение*) romantic mood.

рома́нтик (-а) *м* (*мечтатель*) romantic; (*писатель, композитор итп*) romanticist.

рома́нтик|а (-и) *ж* romance.

рома́ш|ка (-ки; *gen pl* -ек) *ж* camomile.

ромб (-а) *м* rhombus.

ро́мовый *прил* rum *опред*; **ро́мовая ба́ба** rum baba.

ромште́кс (-а) *м* rump steak.

РОНО́ *м сокр* (= *районный отдел народного образова́ния*) ≈ district education department.

рон|я́ть (-ю; *perf* **урони́ть**) *несов перех* to drop; (*перен: честь, авторитет*) to lose (*no perf*; *листву, перья*) to shed; **~** (*impf*) **слёзы** to shed tears; **~** (*impf*) **себя́ в чьих-н глаза́х** to lose face with sb; **~** (*impf*) **слова́** to make haughty remarks.

ро́пот (-а) *м* rumble.

рос *итп несов см* **расти́**.

рос|а́ (-ы́; *nom pl* -ы) *ж* dew.

роси́н|ка (-ки; *gen pl* -ок) *ж* dewdrop.

роско́ш|ный (-ен, -на, -но) *прил* (*наряд, дом*) luxurious; (*еда*) sumptuous; (*разг: волосы, растительность*) luxuriant; (: *день, погода*) splendid; **~ная жизнь** a life of luxury.

ро́скош|ь (-и) *ж* luxury; (*излишества*)

extravagance; *(приро́ды)* luxuriance; **предме́ты**
~и luxury items; **жить** *(impf)* **в ~и** to live in
luxury.

ро́слый *прил* tall.

ро́спис|ь (-и) *ж (де́йствие: собо́ра, ку́пола)*
painting; *(узо́р: на шкату́лке)* design; (: *на*
сте́нах) mural; *(расхо́дов, иму́щества)* list;
(по́дпись) signature.

ро́спуск (-а) *м (а́рмии)* disbandment;
(парла́мента) dissolution.

росси́йский (-ая, -ое, -ие) *прил* Russian;
Росси́йская Федера́ция the Russian
Federation.

Росси́|я (-и) *ж* Russia.

россия́н|ин (-ина; *nom pl* **-е,** *gen pl* **-)** *м* Russian.

россия́н|ка (-ки; *gen pl* **-ок)** *ж см* **россия́нин.**

ро́ссказн|и (-ей) *мн (разг)* old wives' tale.

ро́ссып|и (-ей) *мн (алма́зов, золоты́е итп)*
deposit *ед.*

ро́ссып|ь (-и) *ж (грибо́в)* scattering; *см также*
ро́ссыпи.

рост (-а) *м* growth; *(перен: мастерства́,*
производи́тельности) increase; *(разме́р:*
челове́ка) height; *(nom pl* **-á;** *дли́на: пальто́,*
пла́тья) length; **встава́ть (встать** *perf)* **во весь**
~ *(челове́к)* to stand up straight; *(пробле́ма,*
зада́ча) to become fully apparent.

ро́стбиф (-а) *м* roast beef.

ростка́ *итп сущ см* **росто́к.**

ростовщи́к (-á) *м* moneylender.

ростовщи́|ца (-ы) *ж см* **ростовщи́к.**

росто́к (-ká) *м (БОТ)* shoot; *(перен):* **~ки́** +*gen*
(демокра́тии, но́вого) beginnings *мн* of.

ро́счерк (-а) *м* stroke; **реша́ть (реши́ть** *perf)*
что-н одни́м ~ом пера́ to decide sth with one
stroke of the pen.

рот (рта; *loc sg* **рту)** *м* mouth; **говори́ть** *(impf)* **не**
закрыва́я рта *(разг)* to talk nonstop; **смотре́ть**
(impf) **в ~ кому́-н** *(перен)* to hang on sb's every
word; **она́ в ~ не берёт ры́бы** *(разг)* she
doesn't touch fish.

ро́т|а (-ы) *ж (ВОЕН)* company.

ротапри́нт (-а) *м* offset duplicator.

ротозе́|й (-я) *м (разг: безде́льник)* loafer;
(рази́ня) scatterbrain.

ро́тор (-а) *м* rotor.

Ро́ттердам (-а) *м* Rotterdam.

ро́щ|а (-и) *ж* grove.

роя́л|ь (-я) *м* grand piano.

р-р *сокр (=* **раство́р)** sol. *(= solution).*

р/с *сокр =* **расчётный счёт.**

РСО *ж сокр (=* **раке́та сре́дней да́льности)**
MRBM *(= medium-range ballistic missile).*

РСУ *ср сокр =* **ремо́нтно-строи́тельное**
управле́ние.

РСФСР *ж сокр (ист: =* **Росси́йская Сове́тская**
Федерати́вная Социалисти́ческая
Респу́блика) RSFSR *(= Russian Soviet Federal*

Socialist Republic).

рта *итп сущ см* **рот.**

рту́тный *прил* mercury *опред;* **~ сто́лбик**
mercury column.

рту́т|ь (-и) *ж* mercury.

руб. *сокр (=* **рубль)** R., r., rouble.

руба́н|ок (-ка) *м* plane *(tool).*

руба́х|а (-и) *ж (разг)* shirt; **~-па́рень** *(разг)*
straightforward chap *(BRIT) или* guy *(US).*

руба́ш|ка (-ки; *gen pl* **-ек)** *ж (мужска́я)* shirt;
(игра́льной ка́рты) back; **ни́жняя ~** *(же́нская)*
slip; **ночна́я ~** nightshirt; **смири́тельная ~**
(перен) straitjacket.

рубе́ж (-á) *м (госуда́рства)* border; (: *во́дный,*
лесно́й) boundary; *(ВОЕН)* line; **он живёт за**
рубежо́м he lives abroad; **он уе́хал за ~** he
went abroad; **на рубеже́ эпо́х** between the two
eras.

рубе́ц (-ца́) *м (от ран, по́сле опера́ции)* scar;
(кули́н) tripe.

руби́льник (-а) *м* knife switch.

руби́н (-а) *м* ruby.

руби́новый *прил* ruby *опред.*

руби́ть (-лю́, -ишь; *perf* **срубить)** *сов перех*
(де́рево) to fell; *(perf* **отруби́ть)** *(ве́тку)* to chop off; *(no perf:*
мя́со, капу́сту) to chop (up); *(го́лову)* to hack
off; *(да́чу, избу́)* to erect; **он ~ит сплеча́**
(перен) he doesn't mince his words.

ру́б|ка (-и) *ж (де́йствие: дере́вьев)* felling;
(избы́) erection; *(мя́са)* chopping; *(на су́дне, на*
радиоста́нции) cabin.

рублёвый *прил (моне́та, банкно́та)* rouble
опред; (пече́нье, конфе́ты) for one rouble;
(разг: това́р, пода́рок) cheap.

ру́блен|ый *прил (мя́со, о́вощи)* chopped;
(амба́р, изба́) made from logs; **~ые котле́ты**
rissoles.

руб|ль (-я́) *м* rouble; **переводно́й ~** convertible
rouble.

рублю́ *сов см* **руби́ть.**

ру́брик|а (-и) *ж (разде́л)* column; *(заголо́вок)*
heading.

рубца́ *итп сущ см* **рубе́ц.**

рубцева́ться (3sg -у́ется, *3pl* **-у́ются,** *perf*
зарубцева́ться) *несов возв* to form a scar.

ру́бчат|ый (-, -а, -о) *прил* ribbed.

ру́бчик (-а) *м* rib.

руга́н|ь (-и) *ж* bad language.

руга́тельн|ый *прил:* **~ое сло́во** swearword;
пье́са получи́ла мно́го ~ых о́тзывов the play
got a lot of bad reviews.

руга́тельств|о (-а) *ср* swearword.

руга́|ть (-ю; *perf* **вы́ругать** *или* **отруга́ть)** *несов*
перех (му́жа, ученика́) to scold; *(perf* **обруга́ть;**
пье́су, статью́) to take to pieces

▶ **руга́|ться** *несов возв (брани́ться):* **~ся с** +*instr*
to scold; *(perf* **вы́ругаться)** to swear; *(perf*
поруга́ться):* **~ся с +*instr (с му́жем, с родны́ми)*

to fall out with.

ругну́ться (-у́сь, -ёшься) *сов возв (разг)* to swear *(once)*.

руда́ (-ы́; *nom pl* -ы) *ж* ore.

рудни́к (-а́) *м* mine.

рудннко́вый *прил (предприятие)* ore-mining.

рудни́чный *прил* = **рудннко́вый**.

руже́йный *прил* rifle *опред*.

ружьё (-ья́; *nom pl* -ья, *gen pl* -ей) *ср* rifle.

руи́на (-ы) *ж (обычно мн)* ruin.

рука́ (-и́; *acc sg* -у, *nom pl* -и, *gen pl* -, *dat pl* -а́м) *ж* hand; *(верхняя конечность)* arm; *(разг: в верхах, в руководстве)* contact; **из пе́рвых рук** first hand; **в э́том чу́вствуется ~ ма́стера** one can tell this is the work of clever hands; **у неё на ~х тро́е дете́й** she has three children on her hands; **под руко́й, под ~ми** to hand, handy; **она́ шла с ним под ~у** she walked arm in arm with him; **проси́ть** *(impf)* **чьей-н ~и** to ask for sb's hand (in marriage); **подня́ть** *(perf)* **ру́ку на кого́-н** to raise one's hand to sb; **его́/э́то с ~ми оторву́т** *(разг)* he/it will be snapped up; **у меня́ все́ ру́ки не дохо́дят до э́того** I haven't got round to (doing) it; **отсю́да до го́рода ~о́й пода́ть** it's a stone's throw from here to the town; **у меня́ ру́ки че́шутся** +*infin* ... *(разг)* I'm itching to ...; **э́то ему́ на́ ~у** that's what suits him; **брать [взять** *perf*] **себя́ в ру́ки** to get a grip of o.s.; **ему́ всё схо́дит с рук** *(разг)* he gets away with everything; **э́то де́ло рук ма́фии** this is the work of the Mafia; **у него́ золоты́е ру́ки** he's very good with his hands; **дела́ иду́т из рук вон пло́хо** things have hit rock bottom; **прибира́ть [прибра́ть** *perf*] **что-н к ~м** to get one's hands on sth.

рука́в (-а́) *м (одежды)* sleeve; *(реки)* branch; *(пожарный, напорный)* hose; *(зерновой)* chute.

рукави́ца (-ы) *ж (обычно мн)* mitten.

руководи́тель (-я) *м* leader; *(кафедры, предприятия)* head.

руководи́тельница (-ы) *ж см* **руководи́тель**.

руково|ди́ть (-ожу́, -оди́шь) *несов неперех*: ~ +*instr (наступлением, действиями)* to lead; *(учреждением, цехом, лаборато́рией)* to be in charge of; *(страной)* to govern; *(аспира́нтами)* to supervise; **им ~оди́ла жа́дность** he was governed by greed.

руково́дств|о (-а) *м (походом, мероприятием)* leadership; *(заводом, институтом)* management; *(лаборато́рией)* supervision; *(к де́йствию, в поведе́нии)* guidelines *мн*; *(по рукоде́лию, по фотогра́фии)* handbook, manual; *(по эксплуата́ции, по ухо́ду)* instructions *мн* ♦ *собир (партии, страны)* leadership *(leaders)*; **под ~м** +*gen* under the leadership of.

руково́дств|оваться (-уюсь) *несов возв*: ~ +*instr* to follow; *(здра́вым смы́слом)* to be guided by.

руководя́щий (-ая, -ее, -ие) *прил (работник, кадры)* managerial; *(орган)* governing *опред*;

~**ие указа́ния** instructions.

руковожу́ *несов см* **руководи́ть**.

рукоде́ли|е (-я) *ср* needlework.

рукоде́льница (-ы) *ж* needlewoman.

рукомо́йник (-а) *м* washstand.

рукопа́шный *прил*: **они́ пошли́ в ~ бой** they went off to fight with their bare hands.

рукопи́сный *прил (текст)* handwritten; *(отдел библиоте́ки)* manuscript *опред*.

ру́копис|ь (-и) *ж* manuscript.

рукоплеска́ть (-ещу́, -е́щешь) *несов неперех*: ~ +*dat* to applaud.

рукопожа́ти|е (-я) *ср* handshake.

рукоприкла́дств|о (-а) *ср* beating.

рукоя́т|ка (-ки; *gen pl* -ок) *ж (кинжала, молотка)* handle; *(пульта управления)* crank.

рулев|о́й (-о́го; *decl like adj*) *м (МОР)* helmsman *(мн* helmsmen); *(перен: ведущий вперёд)* leader ♦ *прил*: ~**о́е колесо́** steering wheel; ~**о́е управле́ние** steering.

руле́т (-а) *м (картофельный)* croquette; *(с ма́ком, с джемом)* ≈ swiss roll; *(окорок без кости)* boned ham; **мясно́й** ~ meat loaf.

руле́т|ка (-ки; *gen pl* -ок) *ж (для измере́ния)* tape measure; *(в игорных дома́х)* roulette.

рул|и́ть (-ю́, -и́шь) *несов перех* to steer.

руло́н (-а) *м* roll.

рул|ь (-я́) *м* steering wheel; **стоя́ть** *(impf)* **у ~я́** *(перен)* to be at the helm.

румы́н (-а) *м* Romanian.

Румы́ни|я (-и) *ж* Romania.

румы́н|ка (-ки; *gen pl* -ок) *ж см* **румы́н**.

румы́нский (-ая, -ое, -ие) *прил* Romanian; ~ **язы́к** Romanian.

румя́н|а (-) *мн* blusher *ед*.

румя́н|ец (-ца) *м* glow.

румя́н|ить (-ю, -ишь; *perf* **нарумя́нить**) *несов перех (щёки, лицо́)* to put blusher on; *(perf* **разрумя́нить**): **моро́з** ~**ит ли́ца** the frost makes faces glow

▸ **румя́ниться** *(perf* **разрумя́ниться**) *несов возв* to flush; *(perf* **нарумя́ниться**; *женщина)* to put on blusher; *(perf* **подрумя́ниться**; *пирог)* to brown.

румя́нца *итп сущ см* **румя́нец**.

румя́ный (-, -а, -о) *прил* rosy; *(пирог)* browned.

РУОП *сокр (= Региона́льное управле́ние по борьбе́ с организо́ванной престу́пностью)* department fighting against organized crime.

ру́пор (-а) *м* loudspeaker; ~ +*gen (о газе́те, о журна́ле)* mouthpiece of.

руса́л|ка (-ки; *gen pl* -ок) *ж* mermaid.

руса́лоч|ий (-ья, -ье, -ьи) *прил* mermaid's.

ру́сел *сущ см* **ру́сло**.

руси́ст (-а) *м* Russianist.

руси́стик|а (-и) *ж* Russian studies.

руси́ст|ка (-ки; *gen pl* -ок) *ж см* **руси́ст**.

русифика́ци|я (-и) *ж* Russification.

русифици́р|овать (-ую) *(не)сов перех* to Russify

▸ **русифици́роваться** *(не)сов возв* to be

Russified.

ру́сло (-ла; *gen pl* -ел) *ср* bed (*of river, stream etc*); (*перен*: *путь развития чего-н*) course; **жизнь вошла́ в обы́чное ~** life has taken its usual course.

ру́сск|**ая** (-ой; *decl like adj*) *ж см* **ру́сский**.

ру́сск|**ий** (-ая, -ое, -ие) *прил* Russian ♦ (-ого; *decl like adj*) *м* Russian; **~ язы́к** Russian.

ру́с|**ый** *прил* (*волосы, борода*) light brown; (*человек*) with light brown hair.

Русь (-и) *ж* Russia.

рути́н|**а** (-ы) *ж* rut (*fig*).

рути́нный *прил* stale.

ру́хлядь (-и) *ж собир* (*разг*) junk.

ру́хн|**уть** (-у, -ешь) *сов* (*дерево, человек итп*) to crash down; (*дом, мост*) to collapse; (*перен*: *счастье, надежда*) to be shattered.

руча́тельств|**о** (-а) *ср* guarantee.

руча́|**ться** (-юсь; *perf* **поручи́ться**) *несов возв*: **~ за** +*acc* to guarantee; **я голово́й ~юсь, что мы успе́ем** (*разг*) I'll bet my life that we'll do it.

руче́й (-ья́) *м* stream; **~ слёз** floods of tears.

ру́чк|**а** (-ки; *gen pl* -ек) *ж уменьш от* **рука́**; (*двери, чемодана итп*) handle; (*кресла, дивана*) arm; (*для письма*) pen; **ша́риковая ~** ballpoint (pen).

ручн|**о́й** *прил* hand *опред*; (*животное, человек*) tame; **~а́я прода́жа** sale without a prescription; **ручна́я кладь, ручно́й бага́ж** hand luggage; **ручны́е часы́** (wrist)watch.

ручья́ *сущ см* **руче́й**.

ру́ш|**ить** (-у, -ишь; *perf* **обру́шить**) *несов перех* (*дома, деревья*) to pull down; (*no perf; разг*: *счастье, семью*) to wreck.

▶ **ру́шиться** *несов возв* (*дом, строение*) to collapse; (*перен*: *семья, планы*) to be wrecked.

РФ *ж сокр* (= **Росси́йская Федера́ция**) the Russian Federation.

ры́б|**а** (-ы) *м* fish; **ни ~ ни мя́со** neither here nor there; **чу́вствовать** (*impf*) **себя́ как ~ в воде́** to feel at home; *см также* **Ры́бы**.

рыба́к (-а́) *м* fisherman (*мн* fishermen).

рыба́лк|**а** (-ки; *gen pl* -ок) *ж* fishing.

рыба́цкий (-ая, -ое, -ие) *прил* fishing *опред*.

рыба́чек *сущ см* **рыба́чка**.

рыба́чий (-ья, -ье, -ьи) *прил* = **рыба́цкий**.

рыба́ч|**ить** (-у, -ишь) *несов неперех* to fish.

рыба́чк|**а** (-ки; *gen pl* -ек) *ж* fisherwoman (*мн* fisherwomen); (*разг*: *жена рыбака*) fisherman's wife (*мн* wives).

ры́би|**й** (-ья, -ье, -ьи) *прил* (*чешуя, хвост, клей*) fish *опред*; (*плавник*) fish's; **ры́бий жир** cod-liver oil.

рыбнадзо́р (-а) *м* fishing patrol.

ры́бный *прил* (*магазин*) fish *опред*; (*промышленность, хозяйство*) fishing *опред*; (*река, озеро*) full of fish; **ры́бные консе́рвы** tinned (*BRIT*) *или* canned fish; **~ день** *day when*

only fish is served in a canteen or restaurant.

рыболо́в (-а) *м* fisherman (*мн* fishermen), angler.

рыболо́вный *прил* fishing *опред*.

Ры́б|**ы** (-) *мн* (*созвездие*) Pisces.

рыв|**о́к** (-ка́) *м* (*человека, машины*) jerk; (*перен*: *в работе*) push; (: *бегуна*) dash.

рыга́|**ть** (-ю) *несов неперех* (*разг*) to belch, burp.

рыда́ни|**е** (-я) *ср* sobbing.

рыда́|**ть** (-ю) *несов неперех* to sob.

рыжеволо́с|**ый** (-, -а, -о) *прил* red-haired.

ры́ж|**ий** (-ая, -ее, -ие; -, -á, -е) *прил* (*усы, волосы, животное*) red *опред*; (*человек*) red-haired.

ры́ка|**ть** (-ю) *несов неперех* to roar.

ры́лец *сущ см* **ры́льце**.

ры́л|**о** (-а) *ср* (*свиное*) snout; (*разг*: *лицо*) mug.

ры́льце (-ьца; *gen pl* -ец) *ср* (*БОТ*) stigma (*мн* stigmata).

ры́н|**ок** (-ка) *м* market; **~ труда́** labour (*BRIT*) *или* labor (*US*) market; **~ки сбы́та** markets.

ры́ночный *прил* (*КОММ*) market *опред*; (*яйца, овощи*) from the market; **ры́ночная цена́** market price; **ры́ночная сто́имость** market value.

рыса́к (-а́) *м* trotter (*horse*).

ры́сий (-ья, -ье, -ьи) *прил* lynx *опред*.

ры́|**скать** (-щу, -щешь) *несов неперех* to roam, rove; **~** (*impf*) **глаза́ми** (*перен*) to let one's eyes roam.

рысц|**а́** (-ы́) *ж* jog trot.

рысь (-и) *ж* lynx; (*бег лошади*) trot.

ры́твин|**а** (-ы) *ж* pothole.

ры́ть (ро́ю, ро́ешь; *perf* **вы́рыть**) *несов перех* (*окопы, канал*) to dig; (*картошку итп*) to dig up

▶ **ры́ться** *несов возв* (*в земле, в песке*) to dig; (*в карманах, в шкафу*) to rummage; (*перен*: *в бумагах, в книгах*) to dig about; **ры́ться** (*impf*) **в па́мяти** to delve into one's memory.

рыхл|**и́ть** (-ю́, -и́шь; *perf* **взрыхли́ть** *или* **разрыхли́ть**) *несов перех* to loosen.

ры́хл|**ый** (-, -а, -о) *прил* (*снег, земля*) loose; (*кирпич, камень*) crumbly; (*перен*: *статья, план*) rough; (: *разг*: *тело, человек*) podgy (*BRIT*), pudgy (*US*).

ры́царский (-ая, -ое, -ие) *прил* (*доспехи, честь, долг*) knight's; (*турнир*) jousting *опред*; (*поступок, поведение*) chivalrous, knightly; **ры́царский рома́н** tale of chivalry.

ры́цар|**ь** (-я) *м* knight; **он настоя́щий ~** he's very chivalrous.

рыча́г (-а́) *м* (*ТЕХ*: *управления, скорости*) lever; (*телефона*) cradle; (*перен*: *воздействия, реформ*) linchpin.

рыч|**а́ть** (-у́, -и́шь) *несов неперех* to growl; (*разг*): **~ на** +*acc* (*на подчинённых, на учеников итп*) to snarl at.

ры́щу *итп несов см* **ры́скать**.

рья́н|**ый** (-, -а, -о) *прил* zealous.

рэ́кет (-а) *м* racket.

рэкети́р (-а) *м* racketeer.

рюкза́к (-а́) *м* rucksack.

рю́м|ка (-ки; *gen pl* -ок) *ж* (*сосуд*) ≈ liqueur glass; (*водки, коньяка итп*) shot.

рю́мочн|ая (-ой; *decl like adj*) *ж small bar selling alcohol and sandwiches*.

рю́ш|ка (-ки; *gen pl* -ек) *ж* frill.

ряби́н|а (-ы) *ж* (*дерево*) rowan, mountain ash ♦ *собир* (*ягоды*) rowan berry; (*разг: на коже*) pockmark; (*тёмное пятно*) speck.

ряби́новый *прил* (*куст*) rowan *опред*, mountain ash *опред*; (*настойка, варенье*) rowan-berry.

ряби́ть (*3sg* -и́т) *несов перех* (*воду*) to ripple; **у меня́ ~и́т в глаза́х** I'm seeing stars.

рябо́й (-, -а́, -о) *прил* (*лицо, тело*) pockmarked; (*курица, скворец*) speckled; (*гладь озера*) rippling; **Ку́рочка-ря́ба** speckled hen (*in fairytales*).

ря́бчик (-а) *м* hazelhen.

ряб|ь (-и) *ж* (*на воде*) ripple; (*в глазах*) stars *мн*.

ря́вка|ть (-ю) *несов неперех* (*разг*): ~ (**на** +*acc*) to bark (at).

ряд (-а; *loc sg* -у́, *nom pl* -ы́) *м* row; (*бойцов*) line; (*явлений, событий*) sequence; (*обычно мн: торговые, овощной*) stalls *мн*; (*prp sg* -е): ~ +*gen* (*вопросов, причин*) a number of; **из ря́да вон выходя́щий** extraordinary; *см также* **ряды́**.

рядов|о́й *прил* (*случай, жизнь, работник итп*) ordinary; (*член партии, боец*) rank-and-file ♦ (-о́го; *decl like adj*) *м* (*ВОЕН*) private.

ря́дом *нареч* close (by), near(by); **они́ сиде́ли ~** they sat side by side; ~ **с** +*instr* next to; **э́то совсе́м ~** it's really near.

ряд|ы́ (-о́в) *мн* (*состав: армии, партии*) ranks *мн*.

ря́женк|а (-и) *ж type of yoghurt*.

Ряза́н|ь (-и) *ж* Ryazan.

ря́с|а (-ы) *ж* cassock.

~ C, c ~

C, с *сущ нескл (буква)* the 18th letter of the Russian alphabet.

с *сокр* (= **се́вер**) N (= North;) (= **секу́нда**) s (= second).

с *предл* (+*gen*) **1** *(указывает на объект, от которого что-н отделяется)* off; **лист упа́л с де́рева** a leaf fell off the tree; **ма́льчик пры́гнул с кры́ши** the boy jumped off the roof; **письмо́ с ро́дины/Украи́ны** a letter from home/the Ukraine; **с ле́кции/рабо́ты/ свида́ния** from a lecture/work/a meeting **2** *(следуя чему-н)* from; **эски́з с нату́ры** a sketch from nature; **перево́д с ру́сского** a translation from Russian; **ко́пия с докуме́нта** a copy of a document **3** *(об источнике)* from; **де́ньги с зака́зчика** money from a customer; **с ребёнка спрос ма́ленький** one can't demand much from a child; **с меня́/него́ доста́точно** I've/he's had enough **4** *(начиная с)* since; **жду тебя́ с утра́** I've been waiting for you since morning; **с января́ по май** from January to May; **с утра́ до ве́чера** from morning till evening **5** *(на основании чего-н)* with; **зако́н введён с одобре́ния парла́мента** the law was brought in with the approval of parliament **6** *(по причине)*: **с го́лоду/хо́лода/го́ря** of hunger/cold/grief; **с испу́га/доса́ды** with fright/ anger; **со зла** out of spite; **я уста́л с доро́ги** I was tired from the journey

◆ *предл* (+*acc*; *приблизительно*) about; **с киломе́тр/то́нну** about a kilometre (*BRIT*) *или* kilometer (*US*)/ton *или* tonne

◆ *предл* (+*instr*) **1** *(совместно)* with; **я иду́ гуля́ть с дру́гом** I am going for a walk with a friend; **он познако́мился с де́вушкой** he has met a girl; **мы с ним о́чень ра́зные** he and I are very different **2** *(о наличии чего-н в чём-н)*: **пиро́г с мя́сом** a meat pie; **хлеб с ма́слом** bread and butter; **дикта́нт с оши́бками** a dictation containing mistakes; **челове́к с ю́мором** a man with a sense of humour (*BRIT*) *или* humor (*US*)

3 *(при указании на образ действия)* with; **слу́шать** *(impf)* **с удивле́нием** to listen with *или* in surprise; **ждать** *(impf)* **с нетерпе́нием** to wait impatiently *или* with impatience; **ждём с нетерпе́нием встре́чи с Ва́ми** we look forward to meeting you; **одева́ться** *(impf)* **со вку́сом** to dress with (good) taste; **он ел с жа́дностью** he ate greedily **4** *(при посредстве)*: **с курье́ром** by courier; **я уе́хал с пе́рвым по́ездом** I left on the first train **5** *(при наступлении чего-н)*: **с во́зрастом** with age; **мы вы́ехали с рассве́том** we left at dawn; **с отъе́здом госте́й нам ста́ло ску́чно** when the guests left we got bored **6** *(об объекте воздействия)* with; **поко́нчить** *(perf)* **с несправедли́востью** to do away with injustice; **поспеши́ть** *(perf)* **с вы́водами** to draw hasty conclusions; **случа́ться (случи́ться** *perf)* **с** +*instr* to happen to; **что с тобо́й?** what's the matter with you?

с. *сокр* = **село́**; (= **страни́ца**) p. (= *page*).

СА *ж сокр (ИСТ)* = *Сове́тская А́рмия*.

са́бля (*-ли*; *gen pl* **-ель**) *ж* sabre (*BRIT*), saber (*US*).

сабо́ *м/ср нескл (обычно мн)* clog.

сабота́ж (*-а*) *м* sabotage.

саботи́ровать (*-ую*) *(не)сов перех* to sabotage.

са́ван (*-а*) *м* shroud.

сава́нна (*-ы*) *ж* savannah.

са́га (*-и*) *ж* saga.

сагити́ровать (*-ую*) *сов от* **агити́ровать**.

са́го *ср нескл* sago.

сад (*-а*; *loc sg* **-у́**, *nom pl* **-ы́**) *м* garden; *(фруктовый)* orchard; *(также: де́тский ~)* nursery (school) (*BRIT*), kindergarten (*US*).

сади́зм (*-а*) *м* sadism.

са́дик (*-а*) *м уменьш от* **сад**; *(разг: детский сад)* nursery (*BRIT*), kindergarten (*US*).

сади́ст (*-а*) *м* sadist.

сади́ться (*-жу́сь, -ди́шься*) *несов от* **сесть**.

садо́вник (*-а*) *м* (professional) gardener.

садово́д (*-а*) *м (любитель)* gardener; *(специалист)* horticulturalist.

садово́дство (*-а*) *ср (хобби)* gardening; *(наука)* horticulture.

садо́в|ый *прил* garden *опред*; голова́ твоя́ ~ая (*разг*) you've got a head like a sieve.

са́ек *сущ см* са́йка.

са́жа (-и) *ж* soot.

сажа́ть (-ю; *perf* посади́ть) *несов перех* (*человека: на стол, в кресло*) to seat; (: *в поезд, в автобус*) to put; (*растения, дерево*) to plant; (*раза: заключить*) to lock up; (*самолёт*) to land; ~ (посади́ть *perf*) кого́-н в по́езд/на самолёт to put sb on a train/plane; ~ (посади́ть *perf*) кого́-н за рабо́ту to sit sb down to work; ~ (посади́ть *perf*) кого́-н в тюрьму́/под аре́ст to put sb in prison/under arrest.

са́жен|ец (-ца) *м* (*дерева*) sapling; (*растения*) seedling.

сажу́сь *несов см* сади́ться.

саза́н (-а) *м* carp.

са́йк|а (-и; *gen pl* -ек) *ж* (bread) roll.

сайт (-а) *м* (*КОМП*) web site.

саквоя́ж (-а) *м* travelling (*BRIT*) *или* traveling (*US*) bag.

сакрамента́л|ьный (-ен, -ьна, -ьно) *прил* (*РЕЛ*) sacramental; (*перен*) sacred.

саксофо́н (-а) *м* saxophone.

сала́з|ки (-ок) *мн* (*сани*) toboggan *ед*.

сала́к|а (-и) *ж* Baltic herring.

сала́т (-а) *м* (*БОТ*) lettuce; (*КУЛИН*) salad.

сала́тни|ца (-ы) *ж* salad bowl.

сала́тный *прил* salad *опред*; (*цвет*) pale green.

са́л|о (-а) *ср* (*животного*) fat; (*КУЛИН*) lard.

сало́н (-а) *м* salon; (*автобуса, самолёта итп*) passenger section; (*в гостинице*) lounge; (*на корабле*) saloon; худо́жественный ~ art salon.

салфе́т|ка (-ки; *gen pl* -ок) *ж* (*столовая*) napkin, serviette (*BRIT*); (*маленькая скатерть*) doily.

Сальвадо́р (-а) *м* El Salvador.

сальди́р|овать (-ую) *несов перех* (*КОММ*) to balance.

са́льдо *ср нескл* (*КОММ*) balance; ~ с перено́са balance brought forward.

са́льный *прил* greasy; (*шутка, слова*) dirty.

са́льто *ср нескл* somersault.

салю́т (-а) *м* salute.

салют|ова́ть (-у́ю) (*не*)*сов неперех* (+*dat*) to salute.

саля́ми *ж нескл* salami.

сам (-ого́; *f* сама́, *nt* само́, *pl* са́ми) *мест* (*я*) myself; (*ты*) yourself; (*он*) himself; (*как таковой*) itself; он ~ предложи́л э́то he himself suggested it; я ~ могу́ прове́рить I can check it myself; ты (и) ~ зна́ешь you know yourself; ~а его́ принципиа́льность важна́ his integrity itself is important; ~ по себе́ (*в отдельности*) per se, by itself; ~ собо́й (*непроизвольно*) of its own accord, by itself; фа́кты говоря́т ~и за себя́ the facts speak for themselves.

сам|а́ (-о́й) *мест* (*я*) myself; (*ты*) yourself; (*она*) herself; *см также* сам.

Сама́р|а (-ы) *ж* Samara.

самби́ст (-а) *м* sambo wrestler.

са́мбо *ср нескл* sambo (wrestling).

сам|е́ц (-ца́) *м* male (*ZOOL*).

са́м|и (-и́х) *мест* (*мы*) ourselves; (*они*) themselves; *см также* сам.

са́м|ка (-ки; *gen pl* -ок) *ж* female (*ZOOL*).

са́ммит (-а) *м* (*ПОЛИТ*) summit.

сам|о́ (-ого́) *мест* itself; ~ собо́й (разуме́ется) it goes without saying; *см также* сам.

самоана́лиз (-а) *м* self-analysis.

самобичева́ни|е (-я) *ср* (*перен*) self-reproach.

самобы́тен *прил см* самобы́тный.

самобы́тность (-и) *ж* originality.

самобы́т|ный (-ен, -на, -но) *прил* original.

самова́р (-а) *м* samovar.

самовлюблённый *прил* (*человек*) vain.

самово́ли|е (-я) *ср* wilfulness (*BRIT*), willfulness (*US*).

самово́л|ьный (-ен, -ьна, -ьно) *прил* (*человек*) self-willed; (*уход*) unauthorized.

самого́н (-а) *м* home-made vodka.

самоде́л|ка (-ки; *gen pl* -ок) *ж* home-made thing.

самоде́льный *прил* home-made.

самодержа́ви|е (-я) *ср* autocracy.

самодержа́вный *прил* autocratic.

самоде́ятельность (-и) *ж* initiative, self-motivation; (*также: худо́жественная ~*) amateur art and performance.

самоде́ятельный *прил* (*по личному почину*) self-motivated; (*не профессиональный*) amateur.

самодисципли́н|а (-ы) *ж* self-discipline.

самодовле́ющ|ий (-ая, -ее, -ие) *прил* self-sufficient.

самодово́л|ьный (-ен, -ьна, -ьно) *прил* self-satisfied.

самоду́р (-а) *м* tyrant (*fig*).

самозабве́нен *прил см* самозабве́нный.

самозабве́ни|е (-я) *ср* selflessness.

самозабве́н|ный (-ен, -на, -но) *прил* selfless.

самозва́н|ец (-ца) *м* impostor.

самозва́н|ка (-ки; *gen pl* -ок) *ж см* самозва́нец.

самозва́нный *прил* self-appointed.

самозва́н|ца *итп сущ см* самозва́нец.

са́мок *сущ см* са́мка.

самока́т (-а) *м* scooter (*child's*).

самоконтро́л|ь (-я) *м* self-control.

самокри́ти|ка (-и) *ж* self-criticism.

самокрити́ч|ный (-ен, -на, -но) *прил* self-critical.

самолёт (-а) *м* (aero)plane (*BRIT*), (air)plane (*US*).

самолётострое́ни|е (-я) *ср* aircraft manufacturing.

самолюби́в|ый (-, -а, -о) *прил* self-enamoured.

самолю́би|е (-я) *ср* self-esteem.

самомне́ни|е (-я) *ср* self-importance.

самонаде́ян|ный (-, -на, -но) *прил* self-important.

самооблада́ни|е (-я) *ср* self-possession.

самообма́н (-а) *м* self-deception.

самооборо́н|а (-ы) *ж* self-defence (*BRIT*), self-

defense (*US*).
самообразова́ни|**е** (-я) *ср* self-education.
самообслу́живани|**е** (-я) *ср* self-service.
самоокупа́емост|**ь** (-и) *ж* (ЭКОН) self-sufficiency.
самоопределе́ни|**е** (-я) *ср* self-determination.
самоопредел|**и́ться** (-ю́сь, -и́шься; *impf* **самоопределя́ться**) *сов возв* (*человек*) to determine one's position; (*нация*) to make its position clear.
самоотве́ржен|**ный** (-, -на, -но) *прил* self-sacrificing.
самоотво́д (-а) *м* withdrawal.
самоотрече́ни|**е** (-я) *ср* self-denial.
самооце́н|**ка** (-ки; *gen pl* -ок) *ж* self-appraisal.
самоочеви́д|**ный** (-ен, -на, -но) *прил* self-evident.
самопа́л (-а) *м* (*разг: кустарная вещь*) cheap fake.
самопоже́ртвовани|**е** (-я) *ср* self-sacrifice.
самопрове́р|**ка** (-ки; *gen pl* -ок) *ж* (КОМП) self-test.
самопроизво́льный (-ен, -ьна, -ьно) *прил* spontaneous.
саморекла́м|**а** (-ы) *ж* self-advertisement.
саморо́д|**ок** (-ка) *м* (*золотой*) nugget; (*перен: талант*) natural.
самосва́л (-а) *м* dump truck.
самосоверше́нствовани|**е** (-я) *ср* self-improvement.
самосозна́ни|**е** (-я) *ср* self-awareness.
самосохране́ни|**е** (-я) *ср* self-preservation.
самостоя́телен *прил см* **самостоя́тельный**.
самостоя́тельно *нареч* (*независимо*) independently; (*без помощи других*) on one's own.
самостоя́тел|**ьный** (-ен, -ьна, -ьно) *прил* independent.
самосу́д (-а) *м* mob law.
самотёк (-а) *м* (*перен*) chaos; **пуска́ть (пусти́ть** *perf*) **де́ло на** ~ to let things slide.
самоуби́йств|**о** (-а) *ср* suicide; **поко́нчить** (*perf*) **жизнь** ~**м** to commit suicide.
самоуби́йц|**а** (-ы) *м/ж* suicide (victim).
самоуваже́ни|**е** (-я) *ср* self-respect.
самоуве́рен|**ный** (-, -на, -но) *прил* self-confident, self-assured.
самоуниже́ни|**е** (-я) *ср* self-abasement, self-degradation.
самоунижче́ни|**е** (-я) *ср* self-humiliation.
самоуправле́ни|**е** (-я) *ср* self-administration.
самоупра́вств|**о** (-а) *ср* (*произвол*) arbitrariness.
самоуспокое́ни|**е** (-я) *ср* complacency.
самоустран|**и́ться** (-ю́сь, -и́шься) *сов возв*: ~ **от** +*gen* to evade, dodge.
самоутвержде́ни|**е** (-я) *ср* self-assertion.
самоу́чек *сущ см* **самоу́чка**.

самоучи́тел|**ь** (-я) *м* teach-yourself book.
самоу́ч|**ка** (-ки; *gen pl* -ек) *м/ж*: **он/она́** ~ he/she is self-taught.
самофинанси́ровани|**е** (-я) *ср* self-financing.
самохо́дный *прил* self-propelled.
самоцве́т (-а) *м* gem.
самоцве́тный *прил*: ~ **ка́мень** gemstone.
самоце́л|**ь** (-и) *ж* an end in itself.
самочу́встви|**е** (-я) *ср*: **как Ва́ше** ~? how are you feeling?
самца́ *итп сущ см* **саме́ц**.
са́м|**ый** (-ая, -ое, -ые) *мест* (+*noun*) the very; (+*adj*; *вкусный, красивый итп*) the most; **на** ~ **верх** to the very top; **в** ~**ом низу́** at the very bottom; **в** ~**ом нача́ле/конце́** right at the beginning/end; ~ **большо́й/ма́ленький/лу́чший/ху́дший** the biggest/smallest/best/worst; **тот же** ~ the same; **э́то тот** ~ **челове́к, о кото́ром мы говори́ли** this is the (same) person that we were talking about; ~**ое вре́мя уйти́/~ая пора́ уйти́/нача́ть** it is high time to go/start; **в** ~ **раз** (*разг: вовремя*) at just the right time; **э́ти ту́фли мне в** ~ **раз** (*разг*) these shoes are a perfect fit; ~**ая ма́лость** the tiniest little bit; **в** ~**ом де́ле** really; **на** ~**ом де́ле** in actual fact.
сан (-а) *м* (*звание*) rank; **духо́вный** ~ holy orders *мн*.
санато́ри|**й** (-я) *м* sanatorium (*BRIT*), sanitarium (*US*) (*мн* sanatoriums *или* sanatoria).
санда́ли|**я** (-и) *ж* (*обычно мн*) sandal.
са́н|**и** (-е́й) *мн* sledge *ед* (*BRIT*), sled *ед* (*US*); (*спортивные*) toboggan *ед*.
санита́р (-а) *м* (МЕД) orderly.
санитари́|**я** (-и) *ж* sanitation.
санита́р|**ка** (-ки; *gen pl* -ок) *ж* auxiliary.
санита́рный *прил* sanitary; **санита́рная те́хника** = **санте́хника**;; **санита́рное состоя́ние** sanitation; **санита́рный день** cleaning day; **санита́рный инспе́ктор** environmental health officer.
санита́рок *сущ см* **санита́рка**.
са́н|**ки** (-ок) *мн* sledge *ед* (*BRIT*), sled *ед* (*US*).
Санкт-Петербу́рг (-а) *м* St. Petersburg.
санкт-петербу́ргск|**ий** (-ая, -ое, -ие) *прил* St. Petersburg *опред*.
санкциони́ровани|**е** (-я) *ср* sanctioning.
санкциони́р|**овать** (-ую) (*не*)*сов перех* to sanction.
са́нкци|**я** (-и) *ж* (*разрешение*) sanction; (*мера*): **экономи́ческие/полити́ческие** ~ economic/political sanctions; ~ **на о́быск** search warrant; **с** ~**и** +*gen* with the sanction of; **дава́ть (дать** *perf*) ~**ю на** +*acc* to sanction.
са́нок *сущ см* **са́нки**.
са́ночник (-а) *м* (СПОРТ) tobogganist.
санте́хник (-а) *м сокр* (= санита́рный те́хник) plumber.
санте́хник|**а** (-и) *ж сокр* (= санита́рная

техника) *collective term for plumbing equipment and bathroom accessories.*

сантиме́тр (-а) *м* centimetre (*BRIT*), centimeter (*US*); (*линейка*) tape measure.

Сантья́го *м нескл* Santiago.

сану́зел (-ла) *м сокр* (= *санита́рный у́зел*) bathroom facilities *мн.*

Сан-Франци́ско *м нескл* San Francisco.

санча́сть (-и) *ж сокр* = *санита́рная часть*; (*BOEH*) medical unit.

сапёр (-а) *м* field engineer, sapper.

сапо́г (-а́; *nom pl* -и́, *gen pl* -) *м* boot.

сапо́жник (-а) *м* shoemaker; (*разг: пренебр*) bungler.

сапфи́р (-а) *м* sapphire.

сапфи́ровый *прил* sapphire *опред.*

Сара́ево (-а) *ср* Sarajevo.

сара́й (-я) *м* (*для дров, скотины*) shed; (*для сена*) barn.

саранча́ (-и́) *ж собир* locusts *мн.*

сарафа́н (-а) *м* (*платье*) pinafore (dress) (*BRIT*), jumper (*US*).

сарде́лька (-ьки; *gen pl* -ек) *ж* sausage.

сарди́на (-ы) *ж* sardine.

са́ржа (-и) *ж* serge.

сарка́зм (-а) *м* sarcasm.

саркасти́ческий (-ая, -ое, -ие) *прил* sarcastic.

саркофа́г (-а) *м* sarcophagus (*мн* sarcophaguses *или* sarcophagi).

сары́ч (-а́) *м* buzzard.

сатана́ (-ы́) *м* Satan.

сателли́т (-а) *м* (*также ПОЛИТ*) satellite.

сати́н (-а) *м* sateen.

сати́новый *прил* sateen *опред.*

сати́ра (-ы) *ж* satire.

сати́рик (-а) *м* satirist.

сатири́ческий (-ая, -ое, -ие) *прил* satirical.

Сату́рн (-а) *м* Saturn.

сау́довский (-ая, -ое, -ие) *прил*: **С~ая Ара́вия** Saudi Arabia.

са́уна (-ы) *ж* sauna.

Сахали́н (-а) *м* Sakhalin.

са́хар (-а; *part gen* -у) *м* sugar; **рабо́та у меня́ не ~** (*разг*) my work is no picnic; **хара́ктер у неё не ~** (*разг*) she's not all sweetness and light.

Саха́ра (-ы) *ж* Sahara.

сахари́н (-а) *м* saccharin.

са́харница (-ы) *ж* sugar bowl.

са́харный *прил* sugary; (*перен: белый*) white; (: *слащавый*) sugary; **са́харная ва́та** candy floss; **са́харная кость** marrowbone; **са́харная свёкла** sugar beet; **са́харный диабе́т** diabetes; **са́харный песо́к** granulated sugar; **са́харный тростни́к** sugar cane.

сахаро́за (-ы) *ж* sucrose.

сачо́к (-ка́) *м* (*для ловли рыб*) landing net; (*для бабочек*) butterfly net.

СБ *ж сокр* (= *слу́жба бы́та*) service industries *мн.*

сб. *сокр* (= *сбо́рник*) coll. (= *collection*).

сба́вить (-лю, -ишь; *impf* **сбавля́ть**) *сов перех* to reduce.

сба́грить (-ю, -ишь) *сов перех* (*разг*) to get rid *или* shot of.

сбаланси́рованный *прил* balanced.

сбаланси́ровать (-ую) *сов от* **баланси́ровать**.

сба́лтывать (-ю) *несов от* **сболта́ть**.

сбе́гать (-ю) *сов неперех* (*разг*): **~ в магази́н/за молоко́м** to run to the shop/for milk.

сбежа́ть (*как* **бежа́ть**; *см* **Table 20**; *impf* **сбега́ть**) *сов неперех* (*убежать*) to run away; **сбега́ть** (*~ perf*) *с +gen* (*с горы итп*) to run down; **сбега́ть** (*~ perf*) **с ле́стницы** to run downstairs; **сбега́ть** (*~ perf*) **из тюрьмы́** to escape from prison; **улы́бка ~жа́ла с его́ лица́** the smile vanished from his face

▶ **сбежа́ться** (*impf* **сбега́ться**) *сов возв* to come running.

сбей(те) *сов см* **сбить**.

сберёг *итп сов см* **сбере́чь**.

сберега́тельный *прил*: **~ банк** savings bank; **сберега́тельная ка́сса** = **сберка́сса;; сберега́тельная кни́жка** = **сберкни́жка**.

сберега́ть (-ю) *несов от* **сбере́чь**.

сберегу́ *итп сов см* **сбере́чь**.

сбереже́ние (-я) *ср* (*действие*) saving; **~я** savings *мн.*

сбере́чь (-егу́, -ежёшь *итп*, -егу́т; *pt* -ёг, -егла́, -егло́, *impf* **сберега́ть**) *сов перех* (*имущество*) to protect; (*здоровье, любовь, отношение*) to preserve; (*деньги*) to save (up).

сберка́сса (-ы) *ж сокр* (= *сберега́тельная ка́сса*) savings bank.

сберкни́жка (-ки; *gen pl* -ек) *ж сокр* (= *сберега́тельная кни́жка*) savings book.

сбива́ть(ся) (-ю(сь)) *несов от* **сбить(ся)**.

сби́вчивый (-, -а, -о) *прил* confused.

сбить (**собью, собьёшь**; *imper* **сбей(те)**, *impf* **сбива́ть**) *сов перех* to knock down; (*птицу, самолёт*) to shoot down; (*каблуки, туфли*) to wear down; (*цену, температуру*) to bring down; (*ящик из досок*) to knock together; (*сливки, яйца*) to beat; **сбива́ть** (*~ perf*) **кого́-н с пути́** (*перен*) to lead sb astray; **сбива́ть** (*~ perf*) **кого́-н с то́лку** to mislead sb

▶ **сби́ться** (*impf* **сбива́ться**) *сов возв* (*шапка, повязка итп*) to slip; (*каблуки, копыта*) to wear down; (*собраться вместе*) to flock together; (*сливки, крем, яйца*) to stiffen; **сбива́ться** (**сби́ться** *perf*) **с пути́** (*также перен*) to lose one's way; **сбива́ться** (**сби́ться** *perf*) **со счёта** to lose count; **сбива́ться** (**сби́ться** *perf*) **с ног** to be run off one's feet.

сближа́ть(ся) (-ю(сь)) *несов от* **сбли́зить(ся)**.

сближе́ние (-я) *ср* (*между государствами*) rapprochement; (*между людьми*) closeness.

сбли́зить (-жу, -зишь; *impf* **сближа́ть**) *сов перех* to bring closer together

▶ **сбли́зиться** (*impf* **сближа́ться**) *сов возв*: **~ся** (*друг с дру́гом*) to approach (one another); (*люди, государства*) to become closer.

СБО м сокр = спра́вочно-библиографи́ческий отде́л.

сбо́|й (-я) м (перебой) failure; (в работе людей) disruption.

сбо́ку нареч at the side ♦ предл: ~ от +gen at the side of, beside.

сболта́ть (-ю; impf сба́лтывать) сов перех to shake (up).

сболтну́ть (-у́, -ёшь) сов перех (разг): ~ ли́шнее/глу́пость to say too much/something stupid.

сбор (-а) м (урожая, данных) gathering; (налогов, взносов) collection; (валовой, годовой) yield; (плата: страховой, аукционный итп) fee; (выручка: от концерта, спектакля) takings мн, receipts мн; (собрание) assembly, gathering; (обычно мн: армейского запаса, спортсменов) training ед; ~ фру́ктов fruit-picking; тамо́женный/ге́рбовый ~ customs/stamp duty; ~ информа́ции (комп) data capture; порто́вые сбо́ры harbour dues; все в сбо́ре everyone is present; см также сбо́ры.

сбо́рищ|е (-а) ср (разг: пренебр) gang; (: собрание) mob.

сбо́р|ка (-ки; gen pl -ок) ж (изделия) assembly; (обычно мн: на юбке) gather.

сбо́рн|ая (-ой; decl like adj) ж (также: ~ кома́нда) national team.

сбо́рник (-а) м collection (of stories, articles).

сбо́рный прил: ~ пункт assembly point; сбо́рная ме́бель kit furniture; сбо́рная моде́ль model kit.

сбо́рок сущ см сбо́рка.

сбо́рочный прил assembly опред; ~ конве́йер assembly line.

сбо́рщик (-а) м (данных, урожая) gatherer; (машин) assembler; сбо́рщик нало́гов tax collector.

сбо́р|ы (-ов) мн (приготовления) preparations мн.

сбра́сыва|ть(ся) (-ю(сь)) несов от сбро́сить(ся).

сбр|ить (-е́ю, -е́ешь; impf сбрива́ть) сов перех to shave off.

сброд (-а) м (разг: пренебр) rabble.

сброс (-а) м (отходов) discharge; (воды) overflow.

сбро́|сить (-шу, -сишь; impf сбра́сывать) сов перех (бросить вниз) to throw down; (спустить) to let down; (свергнуть) to overthrow; (пальто итп) to throw off; (скорость, давление) to reduce; (карту) to throw away; (комп) to reset

▸ **сбро́ситься** (impf сбра́сываться) сов возв (разг: сложиться) to chip in; сбра́сываться (~ся perf) с +gen to throw o.s. from.

сбру́|я (-и) ж harness.

СБСЕ ср сокр (= Совеща́ние по безопа́сности и сотру́дничеству в Евро́пе) CSCE (= Conference on Security and Cooperation in Europe).

сбу́ду(сь) итп сов см сбыть(ся).

сбыва́ть(ся) (-ю(сь)) несов от сбыть(ся).

сбыт (-а) м sale; ры́нок сбы́та market; отде́л сбы́та sales department.

сбытово́й прил retail опред.

сбыть (как быть; см Table 21; impf сбыва́ть) сов перех (товар) to sell; (разг: избавиться) to get rid of; ~ (perf) кого́-н/что-н с рук to get sb/sth off one's hands

▸ **сбы́ться** (impf сбыва́ться) сов возв (надежды, предсказания) to come true.

СВ сокр (= сре́дние во́лны) MW = medium wave ед ♦ прил (средневолново́й) MW (= medium-wave).

св. сокр (= свято́й) St (= Saint).

сва́деб сущ см сва́дьба.

сва́дебный прил: ~ пода́рок wedding present; сва́дебное пла́тье wedding dress.

сва́дь|ба (-ьбы; gen pl -еб) ж wedding; игра́ть (сыгра́ть perf) ~ьбу to celebrate a wedding.

свал|и́ть (-алю́, -а́лишь) сов от вали́ть ♦ (impf сва́ливать) перех to throw down; (разг: свергнуть) to topple; меня́ ~али́ла уста́лость (разг) I feel whacked; её ~али́л грипп (разг) she's come down with the flu

▸ **свали́ться** сов от вали́ться ♦ (impf сва́ливаться) возв (разг: появиться) to turn up; (: заболеть и слечь) to collapse; вся рабо́та ~али́лась на него́ he was landed with all (of) the work.

сва́л|ка (-ки; gen pl -ок) ж (действие) dumping; (место) rubbish dump.

сваля́|ть (-ю) сов от валя́ть

▸ **сваля́ться** сов возв (волосы, шерсть) to become matted.

СВАПО ж сокр SWAPO (= South-West Africa People's Organization).

свар|и́ть (-арю́, -а́ришь) сов от вари́ть ♦ (impf сва́ривать) перех (шов) to weld

▸ **свари́ться** сов от вари́ться.

свар|ка (-и) ж welding.

сварли́вый (-, -а, -о) прил quarrelsome.

сва́рочный прил welding опред.

сва́рщик (-а) м welder.

сва́стик|а (-и) ж swastika.

сват (-а) м (сватающий) matchmaker; (родственник) the father of one's son-in-law or daughter-in-law.

сва́та|ть (-ю; perf посва́тать или сосва́тать) несов перех: ~ кого́-н (за +acc) (предлагать в супруги) to try to marry sb off (to); (no perf; перен): ~ кого́-н (кому́-н) to fix sb up (with sb)

▸ **сва́таться** (perf посва́таться) несов возв: ~ся к +dat или за +acc to court.

сва́ть|я (-и) ж mother of one's son-in-law or daughter-in-law.

сва́х|а (-и) ж matchmaker.

сва́|я (-и) ж (СТРОИТ) pile.

сведени|е (-я) ср (обычно мн: известия, данные) information ед; доводи́ть (довести́ perf) что-н до ~я кого́-н to bring sth to sb's attention; принима́ть (приня́ть perf) что-н к ~ю to take sth into consideration; к Ва́шему ~ю for your information; см также све́дения.

сведе́ни|е (-я) ср (пятен, грязи) removal; (в таблицу, в график итп) arrangement; ~ к +dat reduction to.

сведе́ни|я (-й) мн (знания) knowledge ед.

сведу́(сь) итп сов см свести́(сь).

све́дущ|ий (-ая, -ее, -ие; -, -а, -е) прил: ~ (в +prp) knowledgeable (about).

свежезаморо́женный прил fresh-frozen.

свежеиспечённый прил freshly-baked.

све́жест|ь (-и) ж (продуктов итп) freshness; (воздуха, воды) cleanliness; (погоды) briskness; э́ти о́вощи не пе́рвой ~и these vegetables aren't very fresh.

свеже́|ть (-ю; perf посвеже́ть) несов неперех (ветер) to turn brisk; (воздух) to clear; (человек) to look fresher.

све́ж|ий (-ая, -ее, -ие; -, -а́, -о́, -и) прил fresh; (воздух, вода) clean; (ветер) brisk; (журнал) recent; к ве́черу ста́ло свежо́ it grew chilly towards evening; обду́мывать (обду́мать perf) что-н на ~ую го́лову to come back to sth with a clear head.

све́зти (-зу́, -зе́шь; pt -ёз, -езла́, -езло́, impf свози́ть) сов перех: ~ (с +gen) (спусти́ть) to drive down; (собра́ть) to bring; (разг: отвезти́: на дачу) to take.

свёкл|а (-ы) ж beetroot.

свеко́льный прил beetroot опред; (цвет) beetroot(-coloured (BRIT) или colored (US)).

свёк|ор (-ра) м father-in-law, husband's father.

свекро́в|ь (-и) ж mother-in-law, husband's mother.

свёл(ся) итп сов см свести́(сь).

све́рг|нуть (-у, -ешь; impf сверга́ть) сов перех to overthrow.

сверже́ни|е (-я) ср overthrow.

све́р|ить (-ю, -ишь; impf сверя́ть) сов перех: ~ (с +instr) to check (against).

▶ све́риться (impf сверя́ться) сов возв: ~ся с +instr to check in.

сверка́|ть (-ю) несов неперех (звезда, глаза) to twinkle; (огни) to flicker; ~ (impf) умо́м/красото́й to sparkle with intelligence/ beauty.

сверк|ну́ть (-у́, -ёшь) сов неперех to flash; у меня́ ~у́ла мысль a thought flashed through my mind.

сверли́льный прил (ТЕХ): ~ стано́к drill; ~ая голо́вка drillstock.

сверл|и́ть (-ю́, -и́шь; perf просверли́ть) несов перех to drill, bore; (no perf; подлеж: сомнения

итп) to gnaw away at.

сверл|о́ (-ерла́; nom pl свёрла) ср drill.

сверн|у́ть (-у́, -ёшь; impf свёртывать или свора́чивать) сов перех (ската́ть: карту, ковёр итп) to roll up; (: сигаре́ту) to roll; (сократи́ть) to cut, reduce; (вре́менно прекрати́ть) to hold up ♦ (impf свора́чивать) непере́х (поверну́ть) to turn; ~ (perf) себе́ ше́ю to break one's neck; ~ (perf) кому́-н ше́ю (перен) to wring sb's neck; свора́чивать (~ perf) напра́во/нале́во to turn right/left

▶ сверну́ться (impf свёртываться или свора́чиваться) сов возв (карта, ковёр итп) to roll up; (человек, животное) to curl up; (молоко́) to curdle; (кровь) to clot.

сверста́|ть (-ю) сов от верста́ть.

све́рстник (-а) м peer; мы с ней ~и she and I are the same age.

све́рстниц|а (-ы) ж см све́рстник.

свёрт|ок (-ка) м package.

свёрты|ва(ть)(ся) (-ю(сь)) несов от сверну́ть(ся).

сверх предл (+gen; нормы) over and above; э́то ~ мои́х возмо́жностей it is out of my reach; ~ ожида́ния beyond all expectation; ~ обыкнове́ния unusually; ~ того́ moreover; ~ всего́ on top of everything else.

сверхзвуково́й прил supersonic.

сверхпла́новый прил over and above the plan.

сверхприбыл|ь (-и) ж surplus profit.

сверхсро́чн|ый прил: ~ая вое́нная слу́жба extended military service.

све́рху нареч (о направлении) from the top; (в верхней части) on the surface; прика́зы ~ orders from above; смотре́ть (impf) ~ вниз на кого́-н to look down on sb.

сверхуро́чно нареч: рабо́тать ~ to work overtime.

сверхуро́чн|ые (-ых; decl like adj) мн (плата) overtime pay ед.

сверхуро́чн|ый прил: ~ая рабо́та overtime; рабо́тать (impf) в ~ые часы́ to work on after hours.

сверхчелове́ческ|ий (-ая, -ое, -ие) прил superhuman.

сверхъесте́ственный прил (РЕЛ) supernatural; (перен: усилие, терпение итп) superhuman.

сверч|о́к (-ка́) м (ЗООЛ) cricket.

сверша́|ть(ся) (-ю(сь)) несов от сверши́ть(ся).

сверше́ни|е (-я) ср (надежд) fulfilment (BRIT), fulfilment (US); (дел, подвига итп) accomplishment; (кары) exacting.

сверш|и́ть (-у́, -и́шь; impf сверша́ть) сов перех to accomplish

▶ сверши́ться (impf сверша́ться) сов возв (событие) to take place; (надежды, замыслы) to be fulfilled.

сверя́|ть(ся) (-ю(сь)) несов от све́рить(ся).

све́|сить (-шу, -сишь; impf све́шивать) сов

перех to lower

► **свéситься** (*impf* **свéшиваться**) *сов возв*: **~ся из** +*gen*/**чéрез** +*acc* to hang from/over; (*ветви, дерéвья*) to overhang.

свести́ (**-едý, -едёшь**; *pt* **-ёл, -елá, -елó**, *impf* **своди́ть**) *сов перех*: **~ с** +*gen* to lead down; (*напрáвить в другýю стóрону*) to lead off; (*пятнó, грязь*) to shift; (*познакóмить*) to introduce; (*собрáть*) to arrange; **своди́ть** (**~** *perf*) **к ми́нимуму** to minimize; **своди́ть** (**~** *perf*) **когó-н с умá** to drive sb mad; **у меня́ ~елó нóгу** I've got cramp in my leg; **своди́ть** (**~** *perf*) **брóви** to knit one's brows; **своди́ть** (**~** *perf*) **рýки** to clasp one's hands (together)

► **свести́сь** (*impf* **своди́ться**) *сов возв*: **~сь к** +*dat* to be reduced to; **своди́ться** (**~сь** *perf*) **к нулю́** to come to nothing.

свет (**-а**; *loc sg* **-ý**) *м* light; (*Земля́*) the world; (*аристокрáтия*) (high) society; **при свéте лунý/свечи́** by moonlight/candlelight; **в свéте** +*gen* (*нóвой поли́тики, послéдних собы́тий*) in the light of; **в мрáчном/оптими́стическом свéте** in a gloomy/optimistic light; **ни ~ ни заря́** at the crack of dawn; **чуть ~** at daybreak; **выводи́ть** (**вы́вести** *perf*) **в ~** (*кни́га*) to be published; **выпускáть** (**вы́пустить** *perf*) **в ~** (*кни́гу*) to publish; **включáть** (**включи́ть** *perf*)/**выключáть** (**вы́ключить** *perf*) to switch *или* turn the light on/off; **проливáть** (**проли́ть** *perf*) **~ на что-н** to shed *или* throw light on sth; **тот ~** (*РЕЛ*) the next world; **ни за что на свéте не сдéлал бы э́то** (*разг*) I wouldn't do it for the world; **ругáть** (*impf*) *или* **брани́ть** (*impf*) **когó-н на чём ~ стои́т** (*разг*) to give sb hell.

светáть (*3sg* **-ет**) *несов безл* to get *или* grow light; **лéтом рáно ~ет** it gets light early in summer.

свéтел *прил см* **свéтлый**.

свети́л|**о** (**-а**) *ср*: **небéсное ~** heavenly body; (*перен: наýки итп*) leading light.

свети́льник (**-а**) *м* lamp.

свети́ть (**-ечý, -éтишь**) *несов неперех* to shine; (*perf* **посвети́ть**): **~ комý-н** (*фонарём итп*) to light the way for sb

► **свети́ться** *несов возв* (*также перен*) to shine; **её глазá ~éтились любóвью** her eyes shone with love; **он ~éтился от рáдости** he was radiant with joy.

светлéть (**-ю**; *perf* **посветлéть** *или* **просветлéть**) *несов неперех* (*также перен*) to lighten; (*ткань, вóлосы*) to go lighter; (*no perf*: *виднéться*) to shine light; **за óкнами ~ет** it's getting light outside.

светлó *как сказ*: **на ýлице ~** it's light outside.

свéтл|**ый** (**-ел, -лá, -ло**) *прил* bright; (*кóмната*) light, bright; (*вóлосы, глазá, крáски*) light; (*ум, мы́сли*) lucid; **~ло-крáсный/-зелёный** light-red/-green; **у негó ~лая головá** he is very

bright.

светов|**óй** *прил* light *опред*; **световóй день** time of the day during which it's light.

светопреставлéни|**е** (**-я**) *ср* doomsday.

светофóр (**-а**) *м* traffic light.

светочувстви́тельный *прил* light-sensitive.

свéтск|**ий** (**-ая, -ое, -ие**) *прил* (*круг, манéры*) refined; (*не духóвный*) secular; **~ое óбщество** high society; **~ человéк** man of the world.

свечá (**-и́**; *nom pl* **-и**, *gen pl* **-éй**) *ж* candle; (*МЕД*) suppository; (*ТЕХ*) spark(ing) plug; (*СПОРТ*) lob.

свéчк|**а** (**-ки**; *gen pl* **-ек**) *ж* candle.

свечý(**сь**) *сов см* **свети́ть(ся)**.

свéша|**ть** (**-ю**) *сов от* **вéшать**.

свéшива|**ть(ся)** (**-ю(сь)**) *несов от* **свéсить(ся)**.

свéшу(**сь**) *сов см* **свéсить(ся)**.

свивá|**ть** (**-ю**; *perf* **свить**) *несов перех* to weave

► **свивá́ться** *несов от* **сви́ться**.

свидá́ни|**е** (**-я**) *ср* rendezvous; (*делово́е*) appointment; (*с заключённым, с больны́м*) visit; (*влюблённых*) date; **до ~я** goodbye; **до скóрого ~я** see you soon; **назначáть** (**назнáчить** *perf*) **комý-н ~** to arrange to meet sb; (*о влюблённых*) to make a date with sb.

свидéтель (**-я**) *м* witness.

свидéтельниц|**а** (**-ы**) *ж см* **свидéтель**.

свидéтельск|**ий** (**-ая, -ое, -ие**) *прил* witness's.

свидéтельств|**о** (**-а**) *ср* evidence; (*докумéнт*) certificate; **свидéтельство о рождéнии/брáке** birth/marriage certificate.

свидéтельств|**овать** (**-ую**) *несов неперех*: **~ о** +*prp* (*свидéтель*) to give evidence about; (*ци́фры, собы́тия*) to testify to ♦ (*perf* **засвидéтельствовать**) *перех* (*пóдпись*) to certify.

свинáрник (**-а**) *м* (*также перен*) pigsty.

свинéц (**-цá**) *м* lead (*metal*).

свини́н|**а** (**-ы**) *ж* pork.

сви́нк|**а** (**-и**) *ж* (*МЕД*) mumps; **морскáя ~** guinea pig.

свиновóдств|**о** (**-а**) *ср* pig farming.

свин|**óй** *прил* (*сáло, корм*) pig *опред*; (*из свини́ны*) pork *опред*; **свинáя кóжа** pigskin.

сви́нск|**ий** (**-ая, -ое, -ие**) *прил* (*разг*) filthy.

сви́нств|**о** (**-а**) *ср* (*разг*) filth.

свинти́ть (**-чý, -ти́шь**; *impf* **сви́нчивать**) *сов перех* (*соедини́ть*) to screw together.

свинцá *итп сущ см* **свинéц**.

свинцóв|**ый** *прил* lead *опред*; (*цвет*) leaden.

сви́нчива|**ть** (**-ю**) *несов от* **свинти́ть**.

свинчý *сов см* **свинти́ть**.

свинь|**я́** (**-и́**; *nom pl* **-ьи**, *gen pl* **-éй**) *ж* pig; (*разг*: *пренебр*) pig, swine; **подклáдывать** *perf* **~ью комý-н** (*разг*) to do the dirty on sb.

свирéль (**-и**) *ж* (*МУЗ*) reed pipe.

свирепéть (**-ю**; *perf* **рассвирепéть**) *несов неперех* to turn savage.

свире́пств|овать (-ую) *несов неперех* to rage.
свире́п|ый (-, -а, -о) *прил* fierce, ferocious.
свиса́ть (*3sg* -ет, *3pl* -ют) *несов неперех* to hang.
свист (-а) *м* whistle; (*ветра*) whistling.
сви|сте́ть (-щу́, -сти́шь; *perf* **просвисте́ть**) *несов неперех* to whistle.
свистка́ *сущ см* **свисто́к**.
сви́стн|уть (-у, -ешь) *сов неперех* to give a whistle ♦ *перех* (*разг: украсть*) to nick (*BRIT*), pinch.
свист|о́к (-ка́) *м* whistle.
сви́т|а (-ы) *ж* retinue.
сви́тер (-а) *м* sweater.
свить (совью, совьёшь) *сов от* **вить**, **свива́ть**
▶ **сви́ться** (*impf* **свива́ться**) *сов возв* (*растения*) to intertwine.
свихн|у́ться (-у́сь, -ёшься) *сов возв* (*разг: помешаться*) to go round the bend *или* twist; ~ (*perf*) **на чём-н** (*на футболе, на кино*) to be mad *или* crazy about sth.
свищ (-а́) *м* (*МЕД*) fistula.
свищу́ *несов от* **свисте́ть**.
свобо́д|а (-ы) *ж* freedom; **лише́ние ~ы** imprisonment; **лиша́ть** (**лиши́ть** *perf*) **кого́-н ~ы** to imprison sb; **выпуска́ть** (**вы́пустить** *perf*) **кого́-н на ~у** to set sb free; **свобо́да ли́чности/печа́ти** freedom of the individual/press; **свобо́да сло́ва** freedom of speech.
свобо́ден *прил см* **свобо́дный**.
свобо́дно *нареч* (*передвигаться*) freely; (*говорить*) fluently; (*облегать*) loosely ♦ *как сказ*: **мне здесь ~** I feel free here; **в до́ме ~** there's a lot of room in the house; **здесь ~?** is this place free?; **он ~ говори́т по-ру́сски** he speaks Russian fluently.
свобо́дн|ый (-ен, -на, -но) *прил* free; (*незанятый: место, номер*) vacant; (: *комната*) spare; (*одежда*) loose-fitting; (*помещение*) spacious; (*движение, речь*) fluent; (*дыхание*) unrestricted; ~ **от** +*gen* (*от недостатков итп*) free from *или* of; **вход ~** free admission; **телефо́н ~ен** the telephone is free; **Вы ~ны, мо́жете идти́** you are free to go; **у меня́ сейча́с нет ~ных де́нег** I don't have any money to spare; **свобо́дный перево́д** free translation; **свобо́дный стиль** (*в плавании*) free style; **свобо́дный уда́р** (*в футболе*) free kick.
свободолюби́в|ый (-, -а, -о) *прил* freedom-loving.
свободомы́сли|е (-я) *ср* free thinking.
свод (-а) *м* (*пятен, грязи*) removal; (*частей в целое, данных в таблицу*) arrangement; (*правил итп*) set; (*летописей*) collection; (*здания, тоннеля*) vaulting; ~ **пра́вил** (*профессиональный*) code of practice; **свод зако́нов** legal code.
сво|ди́ть (-ожу́, -о́дишь) *несов от* **свести́** ♦ *сов перех* (*отвести*) to take
▶ **своди́ться** *несов от* **свести́сь**.

сво́д|ка (-ки; *gen pl* -ок) *ж*: ~ **пого́ды/новосте́й** weather/news summary; **операти́вная ~** (*ВОЕН*) situation report.
сво́дный *прил* (*таблица, график*) summary *опред*; **сво́дный брат** stepbrother; **сво́дная сестра́** stepsister.
сво́док *прил см* **сво́дка**.
сво́дчатый *прил* vaulted.
своё (-его́) *мест см* **свой**.
своево́л|ьный (-ен, -ьна, -ьно) *прил* self-willed.
своевре́мен|ный (-ен, -на, -но) *прил* timely.
своём *итп мест см* **свой**, **своё**.
своенра́в|ный (-ен, -на, -но) *прил* wilful (*BRIT*), willful (*US*).
своеобра́зен *прил см* **своеобра́зный**.
своеобра́зи|е (-я) *ср* distinctiveness.
своеобра́з|ный (-ен, -на, -но) *прил* (*оригинальный*) original; (*no short form*; *своего рода*) peculiar.
свожу́(сь) (*не*)*сов см* **своди́ть(ся)**.
св|ози́ть (-ожу́, -о́зишь) *несов от* **свезти́** ♦ *сов перех* to take; **он ~ози́л нас в кино́** he took us to the cinema.

KEYWORD

свой (-его́; *f* **своя́**, *nt* **своё**, *pl* **свои́**; *как мой; см* **Table 8**) *мест* **1** (*я*) my; (*ты*) your; (*он*) his; (*она*) her; (*оно*) its; (*мы*) our; (*вы*) your; (*они*) their; **я люблю́ свою́ рабо́ту** I love my work; **мы собра́ли свои́ ве́щи** we collected our things; **де́лать** (**сде́лать** *perf*) **что-н свои́ми рука́ми** to make sth oneself; **жить** (*impf*) **свои́м трудо́м** to live by one's own hard work; **крича́ть** (*impf*) **не свои́м го́лосом** to shout wildly; **называ́ть** (*impf*) **ве́щи свои́ми имена́ми** to call a spade a spade
2 (*собственный*) one's own; **у неё свой компью́тер** she has her own computer; **у меня́ своя́ маши́на** I have my own car
3 (*своеобразный*) its; **э́тот план име́ет свои́ недоста́тки** this plan has its shortcomings
4 (*близкий*): **свой челове́к** one of us; **он сам не свой по́сле случи́вшегося** he is not himself after what happened

---

сво́йск|ий (-ая, -ое, -ие) *прил* (*разг*) easy-going, laid-back.
сво́йствен|ный (-, -на, -но) *прил* (+*dat*) characteristic of; **ему́ ~но серди́ться** he has a tendency to get angry.
сво́йств|о (-а) *ср* (*человека*) characteristic; (*предмета*) property.
сво́лоч|ь (-и; *gen pl* -е́й) *ж* (*груб!*) bastard (*!*).
сво́р|а (-ы) *ж* (*собак*) (*волков*) pack; (*перен: хулига́нов, моше́нников*) pack, gang.
свора́чива|ть (-ю) *несов от* **сверну́ть**, **свороти́ть**
▶ **свора́чиваться** *несов от* **сверну́ться**.
своро|ти́ть (-чу́, -тишь; *impf* **свора́чивать**) *сов неперех* (*разг: сдвинуть*) (: *сверну́ть*) to turn.
своя́ (-е́й) *мест см* **свой**.

свояк (-á) *м* brother-in-law (*wife's sister's husband*).

своя́ченица (-ы) *ж* sister-in-law (*wife's sister*).

СВЧ *сокр* (= **сверхвысо́кая частота́**) SHF, shf (= *superhigh frequency*) ♦ *прил сокр* (**сверхвысокочасто́тный**) SHF, shf (= *superhigh frequency*).

СВЧ-печь (-и) *ж* microwave.

свы́кн|уться (-усь, -ешься; *impf* **свыка́ться**) *сов возв*: ~ **с** +*instr* to get *или* become used to.

свысока́ *нареч* condescendingly; **смотре́ть** (*impf*) **на кого́-н** ~ to look down on sb.

свы́ше *предл*: ~ +*gen* (**вы́ше**) beyond; (**бо́льше**) over, more than; **э́то** ~ **мои́х сил** it's beyond me.

свяжу́(сь) *итп сов см* **связа́ть(ся)**.

свя́зан|ный (-, -а, -о) *прил*: ~ (**с** +*instr*) connected (to *или* with); (**име́ющий свя́зи**): ~ **с** +*instr* (**с деловы́ми круга́ми, с худо́жниками** *итп*) associated with; (-, -на, -но; *несвобо́дный: движе́ния, речь*) restricted; **э́то** ~**о со значи́тельными расхо́дами** it involves considerable expense; **он был не́сколько лет свя́зан с э́той фи́рмой** he was involved with the company for several years.

связа́|ть (-жу́, -жешь) *сов от* **вяза́ть** ♦ (*impf* **свя́зывать**) *перех* (*верёвку итп*) to tie; (*вещи, челове́ка*) to tie up; (*перен: де́йствия, инициати́ву*) to bind; (*установи́ть сообще́ние, зави́симость*): ~ **что-н с** +*instr* to connect *или* link sth to; **с чем Вы э́то свя́зываете?** to what do you attribute this?; **я могу́ Вас с ним** ~ I can put you in touch with him; **он** ~**за́л свою́ жизнь с нау́кой** he devoted his life to science; **он двух слов** ~ **не мо́жет** (*перен*) he can't string two words together; **свя́зывать** (~ *perf*) **кого́-н по рука́м и нога́м** (*перен*) to bind sb hand and foot

▶ **связа́ться** (*impf* **свя́зываться**) *сов возв*: ~**ся с** +*instr* to contact; (*разг: с вора́ми итп*) to get mixed up with; (: **с невы́годным де́лом**) to get o.s. caught up in; **свя́зываться** (~**ся** *perf*) **с кем-н по телефо́ну** to get in touch with sb by phone.

свя́з|и (-ей) *мн* (*знако́мства*) connections *мн*; ~ **с обще́ственностью** public relations; **отде́л по** ~**ям с обще́ственностью** public relations department.

связи́ст (-а) *м* (*ВОЕН*) signalman (*мн* signalmen).

свя́з|ка (-ки; *gen pl* -**ок**) *ж* bunch; (*бума́г, дров*) bundle; (*АНАТ*) ligament; (*ЛИНГ*) copula.

связн|о́й (-о́го; *decl like adj*) *м* messenger.

свя́зный *прил* coherent.

свя́зок *сущ см* **свя́зка**.

свя́зующий (-ая, -ее, -ие) *прил* connecting.

свя́зывани|е (-я) *ср* tying.

свя́зыва|ть(ся) (-ю(сь)) *несов от* **связа́ть(ся)**.

связ|ь (-и) *ж* tie; (*причи́нная*) connection, link; (*почто́вая итп*) communications *мн*; (*та́кже:*

любо́вная ~) relationship; **в** ~**й с** +*instr* (*всле́дствие*) due to; (*по по́воду*) in connection with; **в э́той** ~**й** in this regard; **Министе́рство Свя́зи** Ministry of Communications; *см та́кже* **свя́зи**.

свят|а́я (-о́й; *decl like adj*) *ж см* **свято́й**.

святи́лищ|е (-а) *ср* (*РЕЛ*) sanctuary.

свя|ти́ть (-щу́, -ти́шь; *perf* **освяти́ть**) *несов перех* (*РЕЛ*) to sanctify.

свя́тк|и (-ок) *мн* ≈ Christmas(tide) *ед*.

свят|о́й *прил* holy; (-, -а, -о; *де́ло, обя́занность, и́стина*) sacred ♦ (-о́го; *decl like adj*) *м* (*РЕЛ*) saint; ~**а́я святы́х** the holy of holies; ~ **оте́ц** father (*used to address a priest*); **он/она́** ~ **челове́к** he/she is a real saint.

свя́ток *сущ см* **свя́тки**.

свя́тост|ь (-и) *ж* holiness; (*де́ла, чу́вства*) sanctity.

святота́тств|о (-а) *ср* sacrilege.

святы́н|я (-и) *ж* (*ме́сто*) sacred place; (*предме́т*) sacred object.

свяще́нник (-а) *м* priest.

священноде́йстви|е (-я) *ср* religious ceremony.

священноде́йств|овать (-ую) *несов неперех* to conduct a religious ceremony.

священнослужи́тел|ь (-я) *м* clergyman (*мн* clergymen).

свяще́нный *прил* holy, sacred; (*долг, обя́занность*) sacred; **Свяще́нное Писа́ние** Holy Scripture.

свяще́нств|о (-а) *ср собир* the priesthood.

свящу́ *несов см* **святи́ть**.

с.г. *сокр* = **сего́ го́да**.

сгиб (-а) *м* bend.

сгиба́|ть (-ю; *perf* **согну́ть**) *несов перех* to bend

▶ **сгиба́ться** (*perf* **согну́ться**) *несов возв* to bend down.

сги́н|уть (-у, -ешь) *сов неперех* (*разг*) to vanish.

сгла́|дить (-жу, -дишь; *impf* **сгла́живать**) *сов перех* to smooth out; (*перен: противоре́чия, остроту́ го́ря*) to smooth over; **сгла́живать** (~ *perf*) **углы́** (*перен*) to iron out difficulties

▶ **сгла́диться** (*impf* **сгла́живаться**) *сов возв* to be smoothed out.

сгла́|зить (-жу, -зишь) *сов перех* (*РЕЛ*) to put the evil eye on; (*разг*) to jinx.

сглуп|и́ть (-лю́, -и́шь) *сов от* **глупи́ть**.

сгнива́|ть (*3sg* -ет, *3pl* -ют) *несов неперех* to rot.

сгни|ть (-ю́, -ёшь) *сов от* **гнить**.

сгно|и́ть (-ю́, -и́шь) *сов от* **гнои́ть**.

сгова́рива|ться (-юсь) *несов от* **сговори́ться**.

сго́вор (-а) *м* agreement.

сговор|и́ться (-ю́сь, -и́шься; *impf* **сгова́риваться**) *сов возв*: ~ **с** +*instr* (*о встре́че, о сде́лке*) to come to an arrangement with; (*в диску́ссии, в бесе́де*) to reach an agreement with.

сговóрчив|ый (-, -а, -о) *прил* cooperative.
сгоню *итп сов см* **согнáть**.
сгоня́|ть (-ю) *несов от* **согнáть** ♦ *сов неперех* (*разг:* сбегать) to run ♦ *перех* (*послать*) to send.
сгорáни|е (-я) *ср* (*ТЕХ*) combustion.
сгорá|ть (-ю) *несов от* **сгорéть** ♦ *неперех:* ~ **от любопы́тства/нетерпéния** to be burning with curiosity/impatience.
сгóрб|ить(ся) (-лю(сь), -ишь(ся)) *сов от* **гóрбить(ся)**.
сгорéть (-ю, -ишь; *impf* **сгорáть** *или* **горéть**) *сов неперех* to burn; (*impf* **сгорáть**; *ЭЛЕК*) to fuse; (*на солнце*) to get burnt; (*перен: на рабóте*) to burn o.s. out.
сгоряча́ *нареч* in the heat of the moment.
сготóв|ить (-лю, -ишь) *сов от* **готóвить**.
сгре|стú (-бу́, -бёшь; *pt* -ёб, -ебла́, -ебло́, *impf* **сгребáть** *сов перех* (*собрать*) to rake up; (*скинуть*) ~ **с** +*gen* to shovel off.
сгруди́ться (*3sg* -и́тся, *1pl* -и́мся) *сов неперех* (*разг*) to crowd together.
сгру|зúть (-ужу́, -у́зишь; *impf* **сгружáть** *сов перех:* ~ (**с** +*gen*) to unload (from).
сгруппирова́ть(ся) (-у́ю(сь)) *сов от* **группировáть(ся)**.
сгуби́ть (-ублю́, -у́бишь) *сов от* **губи́ть**.
сгу|стúть (-щу́, -сти́шь; *impf* **сгущáть** *сов перех* to thicken; **сгущáть** (~ *perf*) **крáски** (*перен*) to paint an exaggerated picture
▸ **сгустúться** (*impf* **сгущáться**) *сов возв* to thicken.
сгу́ст|ок (-ка) *м* blob.
сгущá|ть(ся) (-ю(сь)) *несов от* **сгусти́ть(ся)**.
сгущённый *прил:* ~**ое молокó** condensed milk.
сгущу́(сь) *сов см* **сгусти́ть(ся)**.
с.-д. *сокр* = **социáл-демократи́ческий**.
сдава́|ть (-ю́, -ёшь; *imper* -**вáй(те)**) *несов от* **сдать** ♦ *перех:* ~ **экзáмен** to sit an exam
▸ **сдавáться** *несов от* **сдáться** ♦ *возв* (*отдаваться внаём*) to be leased out ♦ *безл* (+*dat; разг*): ~**ётся мне, что** ... I reckon that ...; „~**ётся внаём**" "to let".
сда|ви́ть (-авлю́, -а́вишь) *impf* **сдáвливать** *сов перех* to squeeze.
сда́влен|ный (-, -на, -но) *прил* (*голос, плач*) choked.
сда́влива|ть (-ю) *несов от* **сдави́ть**.
сдавлю́ *сов см* **сдави́ть**.
сда́м(ся) *итп сов см* **сдáть(ся)**.
сда́тчик (-а) *м* supplier.
сдать (*как* **дать**; *см* Table 14; *impf* **сдавáть** *сов перех* (*пальто, багáж, рабóту*) to hand in; (*сырьё, продýкцию*) to supply; (*дежýрство, рабóчее мéсто итп*) to hand over; (*дом, кóмнату итп*) to rent out; (*гóрод, пози́цию*) to surrender; (*сдáчу*) to give (back); (*no impf; экзáмен, зачёт итп*) to pass ♦ *неперех* (*ослабеть*) to give out; **сдать** (*perf*) **делá** to step down; **сдавáть** (**сдать** *perf*) **орýжие** to lay down one's arms; **он сдал мне 5 рублéй** he gave me 5

roubles change
▸ **сдать** (*impf* **сдавáться**) *сов возв* to give up; (*солдáт, гóрод*) to surrender; **сдавáться** (~**ся** *perf*) **на** +*acc* (*на уговóры итп*) to give in to; **на что мне сдали́сь э́ти дéньги?** (*разг*) what use is this money to me?; **сдавáться** (~**ся** *perf*) **в плен комý-н** to give o.s. up to sb.
сда́ч|а (-и) *ж* (*сырья́*) supply; (*экзáмена*) passing; (*дежýрства*) handing over; (*дóма*) letting; (*гóрода врагý*) surrender; (*изли́шек дéнег*) change; (*КАРТЫ*) deal; **дава́ть** (**дать** *perf*) **комý-н** ~**у** (*в магази́не*) to give sb his *итп* change; **дать** (*perf*) **комý-н** ~ (*разг*) to match sb blow for blow; ~ **с 10 рублéй** change from 10 roubles.
сда́шь(ся) *сов см* **сдáть(ся)**.
сдвиг (-а) *м* (*в рабóте, в учёбе*) progress; (*в сознáнии*) change; **у негó** ~ (*разг*) he's not all there.
сдви́н|уть (-у, -ешь; *impf* **сдвигáть** *сов перех* (*переместить*) to move; (*сблизить*) to move together; (*застáвить тронýться*) to shift
▸ **сдви́нуться** (*impf* **сдвигáться**) *сов возв:* ~**ся** (**с мéста**) to move; (*смести́ться*) to shift.
сдéла|ть(ся) (-ю(сь)) *сов от* **дéлать(ся)**.
сдéл|ка (-ки; *gen pl* -ок) *ж* deal; **заключа́ть** (**заключи́ть** *perf*) ~**ку** (**с** +*instr*) to do a deal (with); **пойти́** (*perf*) **на** ~**ку с сóвестью** to do a deal with the devil.
сдéльн|ый *прил:* ~**ая рабóта** piecework.
сдéльщик (-а) *м* pieceworker.
сдéльщиц|а (-ы) *ж см* **сдéльщик**.
сдёргива|ть (-ю) *несов от* **сдёрнуть**.
сдéржанно *нареч* (*сказáть, плáкать итп*) with restraint; (*отнести́сь, приня́ть*) with reserve.
сдéржан|ный (-, -на, -но) *прил* (*человéк*) reserved; (*чýвства*) contained.
сд|ержáть (-ержу́, -éржишь; *impf* **сдéрживать** *сов перех* to contain, hold back; **сдéрживать** (~ *perf*) **себя́** to contain o.s.; **сдéрживать** (~ *perf*) **слóво/обещáние** to keep one's word/promise; **сдéрживать** (~ *perf*) **кля́тву** to honour an oath
▸ **сдержáться** (*impf* **сдéрживаться**) *сов возв* to restrain o.s.
сдёрн|уть (-у, -ешь; *impf* **сдёргивать** *сов перех* to pull off.
сдерý *итп сов см* **содрáть**.
сдирá|ть (-ю; *perf* **содрáть** *несов перех* (*кóжуру, кóру*) to peel off.
сдóб|а (-ы) *ж* (*добáвки*) shortening ♦ *собир* (*бýлки*) buns *мн*.
сдóбный *прил* rich.
сдóхн|уть (-у, -ешь) *сов от* **дóхнуть**.
сдр|ужи́ть (-ужу́, -у́жишь) *сов перех* to bring together
▸ **сдружи́ться** *сов возв* to become friends.
сдубли́р|овать (-ую) *сов от* **дубли́ровать**.
сдувá|ть (-ю) *несов см* **сдуть**.
сдýру *нареч* (*разг*) stupidly.
сду|ть (-ю; *impf* **сдувáть** *сов перех* to blow away; (*разг: списáть*) to copy.
сдыхá|ть (-ю) *несов неперех* (*разг: человéк*) to

snuff it.

сё (**сего́**) *мест* this; **то да ~** (*разг*) this and that; **ни то ни ~** (*разг*) neither one thing nor the other.

сеа́нс (**-а**) *м* (*кино*) show; (*психотерапии итп*) session.

СЕА́ТО *ср сокр* (= Организа́ция догово́ра Юго-Восто́чной А́зии) SEATO (= *Southeast Asia Treaty Organization*).

себе́ *мест см* **себя́** ♦ *част* (*разг*): **так ~** so-so; **ничего́ ~**! wow!; **иди́ ~, не вме́шивайся**! just stay out of it!

себесто́имост|**ь** (**-и**) *ж* cost price.

KEYWORD

себя́ *мест* (*я*) myself; (*ты*) yourself; (*он*) himself; (*она́*) herself; (*оно́*) itself; (*мы*) ourselves; (*вы*) yourselves; (*они́*) themselves; **он тре́бователен к себе́** he asks a lot of himself; **она́ вини́т себя́** she blames herself; **представля́ть** (**предста́вить** *perf*) **что-н себе́** to imagine sth; **испы́тывать** (**испыта́ть** *perf*) **что-н на себе́** (*лекарство*) to test sth on o.s.; (*тру́дности*) to experience sth; **к себе́** (*домой*) home; (*в свою́ ко́мнату*) to one's room; **"к себе́"** (*на двери*) "pull"; **"от себя́"** (*на двери*) "push"; **по себе́** (*по своим вкусам*) to one's taste; **убира́ть** (**убра́ть** *perf*) **по́сле себя́** to tidy up after o.s.; **приходи́ть** (**прийти́** *perf*) **в себя́** to come to one's senses; **говори́ть** (*impf*)/**чита́ть** (*impf*) **про себя́** to talk/read to o.s.; **она́ себе́ на уме́** (*разг*) she is secretive; **он у себя́** (*в своём до́ме*) he is at home; (*в своём кабине́те*) he is in the office.

себялюби́в|**ый** (**-, -а, -о**) *прил* egotistical.

себялюби́е (**-я**) *ср* self-love.

сев (**-а**) *м* sowing.

Севасто́пол|**ь** (**-я**) *м* Sevastopol.

се́вер (**-а**) *м* north; **С~** (*Аркти́ка*) the Arctic North.

се́верн|**ый** *прил* north *опред*; (*ветер, направле́ние*) northerly; (*климат, полуша́рие*) northern; **С~ Кавка́з** the Northern Caucasus; **С~ая Коре́я** North Korea; **С~ Ледови́тый океа́н** Arctic Ocean; **се́верное сия́ние** the northern lights *мн*; **Се́верный по́люс** the North Pole.

се́веро-восто́к (**-а**) *м* northeast.

се́веро-за́пад (**-а**) *м* northwest.

северя́н|**ин** (**-ина**; *nom pl* **-е**, *gen pl* **-**) *м* northerner.

северя́н|**ка** (**-ки**; *gen pl* **-ок**) *ж см* **северя́нин**.

севрю́г|**а** (**-и**) *ж* sturgeon.

сегме́нт (**-а**) *м* segment.

сего́ *мест см* **сей, сия́**.

сего́дня *нареч, сущ нескл* today; **~ у́тром/ днём/ве́чером** this morning/afternoon/ evening; **встре́ча назна́чена на ~** this meeting has been set for today; **на ~ у нас ма́ло ресу́рсов** we currently have very few resources; **не ~за́втра** any day now.

сего́дняшн|**ий** (**-яя, -ее, -ие**) *прил* today's; **~ день** today; **на ~ день** at present; **жить** (*impf*) **~им днём** to live for the present.

сегрега́ци|**я** (**-и**) *ж* segregation.

сёдел *сущ см* **седло́**.

седе́|ть (**-ю**; *perf* **поседе́ть**) *несов неперех* to go grey (*BRIT*) или gray (*US*).

седин|**а́** (**-ины́**; *nom pl* **-и́ны**) *ж* grey (*BRIT*) или gray (*US*) hair.

седла́|ть (**-ю**; *perf* **оседла́ть**) *несов перех* to saddle.

седл|**о́** (**-а́**; *nom pl* **сёдла**, *gen pl* **сёдел**) *ср* saddle; **вы́шибить** (*perf*) или **вы́бить** (*perf*) **кого́-н из ~á** (*перен*) to knock sb out of his *итп* stride.

седовла́с|**ый** (**-, -а, -о**) *прил* grey-haired (*BRIT*), gray-haired (*US*).

седоволо́с|**ый** (**-, -а, -о**) *прил* = **седовла́сый**.

седо́|**й** (**-, -á, -о**) *прил* (*волосы*) grey (*BRIT*), gray (*US*); (*человек*) grey-haired (*BRIT*), gray-haired (*US*); **~áя старина́** ancient times.

седо́к (**-á**) *м* (*вса́дник*) rider; (*пассажир*) passenger.

седьм|**о́й** (**-áя, -óе, -ы́е**) *чис* seventh; **сейча́с ~ час** it's after six; **быть** (*impf*) **на ~óм не́бе** to be in seventh heaven; *см также* **пя́тый**.

сезо́н (**-а**) *м* season; **~ дожде́й** the rainy season.

сезо́нник (**-а**) *м* seasonal worker.

сезо́нный *прил* seasonal; **сезо́нный биле́т** season ticket.

сей (**сего́**; *см* Table 12) *мест* this; **сию́ мину́ту** *или* **секу́нду**! this minute!; **на ~ раз** on this occasion; **по ~ день** to this day; **5-го ма́я сего́ го́да** on the 5th (of) May this year; **от сих до сих** (*разг*) from here to here.

сейсми́ческ|**ий** (**-ая, -ое, -ие**) *прил* (*колеба́ния, волны*) seismic; (*станция, прибор*) seismological.

сейсмо́лог (**-а**) *м* seismologist.

сейф (**-а**) *м* (*ящик*) safe; (*помещение*) vault.

сейча́с *нареч* (*теперь*) now; (*скоро*) now; (*разг: недавно*) (only) just; **он ~ рабо́тает** he's working just now; **~ приду́** I'm just on my way; **~ же**! right now!

сёк *итп сов см* **сечь**.

СЕКА́М *м сокр* (= систе́ма цветно́го телеви́дения) SECAM (= *séquentiel couleur à mémoire*).

сека́тор (**-а**) *м* secateurs *мн*.

секре́т (**-а**) *м* secret; **по ~у** in secret; **под ~ом** confidentially; **держа́ть** (*impf*) **что-н в ~е** to keep sth a secret.

секретариа́т (**-а**) *м* secretariat.

секрета́рш|**а** (**-и**) *ж* (*разг*) secretary (*female*).

секрета́р|**ь** (**-я́**) *м* secretary; **генера́льный ~** secretary-general; **секрета́рь-машини́стка**

secretary.

секре́тен *прил см* **секре́тный**.

секрете́р (-а) *м* bureau (*BRIT*), secretaire.

секре́тнича|ть (-ю) *несов неперех* (*скрытничать*) to be secretive; (*разговаривать по секрету*) to talk secretively.

секре́тный (-ен, -на, -но) *прил* secret.

секс (-а) *м* sex.

сексопи́льность (-и) *ж* sex appeal.

сексопи́льный *прил* sexy.

сексуа́льный *прил* sexual; (-ен, -ьна, -ьно; *эроти́чный*) sexy; **сексуа́льная жизнь** sex life; **сексуа́льное образова́ние** sex education; **сексуа́льное домога́тельство** *или* **пресле́дование** sexual harassment.

се́кт|а (-ы) *ж* sect.

секта́нт (-а) *м* sect member.

секта́нт|ка (-ки; *gen pl* -ок) *ж см* **секта́нт**.

секта́нтск|ий (-ая, -ое, -ие) *прил* sectarian.

се́ктор (-а) *м* (*также экон, геом*) sector; (*здания*) section; (*учреждения*) department.

се́кторный *прил*: **се́кторная диагра́мма** pie chart.

секу́ *итп сов см* **сечь**.

секу́нд|а (-ы) *ж* second; **(одну́) ~у!** just one *или* a second!

секунда́нт (-а) *м* second (*of boxer, duellist*).

секу́ндн|ый *прил* (*пауза, заминка*) second's; **~ая стре́лка** second hand (*on clock*).

секундоме́р (-а) *м* stopwatch.

секцио́нный *прил* divided into sections.

се́кци|я (-и) *ж* section.

сел *итп сов см* **сесть**.

селёд|ка (-ки; *gen pl* -ок) *ж* herring.

селезён|ка (-и) *ж* spleen.

се́лез|ень (-ня) *м* drake.

селе́ктор (-а) *м* (*тел*) intercom.

селекционе́р (-а) *м* breeder.

селе́кци|я (-и) *ж* (*био*) selective breeding.

селе́ни|е (-я) *ср* village.

сел|и́ть (-ю́, -ишь; *perf* **посели́ть**) *несов перех* (*в местности*) to settle; (*в доме*) to house
► **сели́ться** (*perf* **посели́ться**) *несов возв* to settle.

сел|о́ (-а́; *nom pl* сёла) *ср* (*селение*) village; (*no pl*; *местность*) the country; **ни к ~у́ ни к го́роду** (*разг*) inappropriately.

сел|ь (-я) *м* mountain torrent.

сельдере́|й (-я) *м* celery.

сельд|ь (-и; *gen pl* -е́й) *ж* herring.

сельпо́ *ср нескл* (= **се́льское потреби́тельское о́бщество**) village shop.

се́льск|ий (-ая, -ое, -ие) *прил* (*см сущ*) village *опред*; country *опред*, rural; **се́льское хозя́йство** agriculture.

сельскохозя́йственный *прил* agricultural.

сельча́н|ин (-ина; *nom pl* -е, *gen pl* -) *м* villager.

сельча́н|ка (-ки; *gen pl* -ок) *ж см* **сельча́нин**.

сём *мест см* **сей**, **сиё**.

сема́нтик|а (-и) *ж* semantics.

семанти́ческ|ий (-ая, -ое, -ие) *прил* semantic.

семафо́р (-а) *м* semaphore.

сёмг|а (-и) *ж* salmon.

семе́йный *прил* family *опред*; **~ челове́к** family man.

семе́йственность (-и) *ж* nepotism.

семе́йств|о (-а) *ср* family.

се́мени *итп сущ см* **се́мя**.

семен|и́ть (-ю́, -и́шь) *несов неперех* to mince.

семенно́й *прил* (*для посева*) seed; (*био*) sperm.

семёр|ка (-ки; *gen pl* -ок) *ж* (*цифра, карта*) seven; (*группа из семи*) group of seven; (*разг*: *автобус, трамвай итп*) (number) seven (*bus, tram etc*).

се́мер|о (-ы́х; *как* **че́тверо**; *см* **Table 36b**) *чис* seven; *см также* **дво́е**.

семёрок *сущ см* **семёрка**.

семе́стр (-а) *м* term (*BRIT*), semester (*US*).

се́мечк|и (-ек) *мн* (*бот*) sunflower seeds *мн*.

се́мечк|о (-ка; *gen pl* -ек) *ср* seed; *см также* **се́мечки**.

семи́ *чис см* **семь**.

семи́десяти *чис см* **се́мьдесят**.

семидесятиле́ти|е (-я) *ср* (*промежуток*) seventy years; (*годовщина*) seventieth anniversary.

семидесятиле́тн|ий (-яя, -ее, -ие) *прил* seventy-year; (*человек*) seventy-year-old.

семидеся́т|ый (-ая, -ое, -ые) *чис* seventieth; *см также* **пятидеся́тый**.

семидне́вный *прил* seven-day.

семикла́ссник (-а) *м* pupil in seventh year at school (*usually 13 years old*).

семикла́ссниц|а (-ы) *ж см* **семикла́ссник**.

семикра́тн|ый *прил*: **~ чемпио́н** seven-times champion; **в ~ом разме́ре** sevenfold.

семиле́ти|е (-я) *ср* (*срок*) seven years; (*годовщина*) seventh anniversary.

семиле́тн|ий (-яя, -ее, -ие) *прил* seven-year; (*ребёнок*) seven-year-old.

семиме́сячный *прил* seven-month; (*ребёнок*) seven-month-old.

семина́р (-а) *м* seminar.

семинари́ст (-а) *м* seminarist.

семина́ри|я (-и) *ж* seminary.

семинеде́льный *прил* seven-week; (*ребёнок*) seven-week-old.

семисо́т *чис см* **семьсо́т**.

семисотле́ти|е (-я) *ср* (*срок*) seven hundred years *мн*; (*годовщина*) seven hundredth anniversary.

семисотле́тн|ий (-яя, -ее, -ие) *прил* (*период*) seven-hundred-year; (*дерево*) seven-hundred-year-old.

семисо́т|ый (-ая, -ое, -ые) *чис* seven hundredth.

семиуго́льник (-а) *м* heptagon.

семичасово́й *прил* (*рабочий день*) seven-hour; (*поезд*) seven o'clock.

семна́дцати *чис см* **семна́дцать**.

семна́дцат|ый (-ая, -ое, -ые) *чис* seventeenth; *см также* **пя́тый**.

семна́дцат|ь (-и; *как* **пять**; *см* **Table 27**) *чис* seventeen; *см также* **пять**.

сему́ *мест см* сей, сие́.

семь (-и; *как* пять; *см* Table 27) *чис* seven; *см также* пять.

се́м|ьдесят (-идесяти; *как* пятьдесят; *см* Table 29) *чис* seventy; *см также* пятьдесят.

семь|со́т (-исо́т; *как* пятьсо́т; *см* Table 34) *чис* seven hundred; *см также* сто.

се́мью *нареч:* ~ пять *итп* seven times five *итп*.

семью *чис см* семь.

семь|я́ (-и; *nom pl* -и) *ж* family.

семьяни́н (-a) *м* family man.

се́м|я (-ени; *как* вре́мя; *см* Table 4) *ср* (БОТ. *также перен*) seed; (*no pl*; БИО) semen.

Се́н|а (-ы) *ж* Seine.

сена́т (-a) *м* senate.

сена́тор (-a) *м* senator.

Сенега́л (-a) *м* Senegal.

се́н|и (-е́й) *мн* hall *ед*.

сенн|о́й *прил*: ~а́я лихора́дка hay fever.

се́н|о (-a) *м* hay.

сенова́л (-a) *м* hayloft.

сеноко́с (-a) *м* (*косьба*) haymaking; (*место*) hayfield.

сенсацио́нный *прил* sensational.

сенса́ци|я (-и) *ж* sensation.

сенте́нци|я (-и) *ж* maxim.

сентимента́л|ьный (-ен, -ьна, -ьно) *прил* sentimental.

сентя́бр|ь (-я́) *м* September; *см также* октя́брь.

сентя́брьск|ий (-ая, -ое, -ие) *прил* September *опред*.

сен|ь (-и; *prp sg* -и́) *ж* canopy; под се́нью +*gen* under the protection of.

сепарати́зм (-a) *м* separatism.

сепара́тный *прил* separate.

се́псис (-a) *м* septicaemia (BRIT), septicemia (US).

септи́ческ|ий (-ая, -ое, -ие) *прил* septic.

се́р|а (-ы) *ж* sulphur (BRIT), sulfur (US); (*в ушах*) earwax.

серб (-a) *м* Serb.

Се́рби|я (-и) *ж* Serbia.

се́рб|ка (-ки; *gen pl* -ок) *ж см* серб.

се́рбск|ий (-ая, -ое, -ие) *прил* Serbian.

серва́нт (-a) *м* buffet unit.

серви́з (-a) *м*: столо́вый/ча́йный ~ dinner/tea service.

сервир|ова́ть (-у́ю) (*не*)*сов перех*: ~ стол to set *или* lay the table.

се́рвис (-a) *м* service (*in shop, restaurant etc*).

серде́ц *итп сущ см* се́рдце.

серде́чен *прил см* серде́чный.

серде́чник (-a) *м* (ТЕХ) core; (*разг*): он ~ he's got a bad heart.

серде́чни|ца (-ы) *ж* (*разг*) *см* серде́чник.

серде́чн|ый *прил* heart *опред*, cardiac; (*любовный*) loving; (*волнения, обида*) deep-felt; (-ен, -на, -но; *человек*) warm-hearted; (*приём, разговор*) cordial; ~ная тоска́

heartache; серде́чная боле́знь heart disease; серде́чный при́ступ acute angina.

серди́т|ый (-, -а, -о) *прил* angry.

серди́ть (-жу́, -дишь; *perf* рассерди́ть) *несов перех* to anger, make angry

▶ серди́ться (*perf* рассерди́ться) *несов возв*: ~ся (на кого́-н/что-н) to be angry (with sb/ about sth).

сердобо́л|ьный (-ен, -ьна, -ьно) *прил* soft-hearted.

сердоли́к (-a) *м* carnelian.

се́рдц|е (-a; *nom pl* -а́, *gen pl* -е́ц, *dat pl* -а́м) *ср* (*также перен*) heart; в сердца́х in a fit of temper; в глубине́ ~ца in one's heart of hearts; от всего́ ~ца from the bottom of one's heart; принима́ть (приня́ть *perf*) что-н бли́зко к ~цу to take sth to heart; он мне по́ сердцу he's a man after my own heart; у него́ ~ не лежи́т к э́той рабо́те his heart isn't in the work.

сердцебие́ни|е (-я) *ср* (*нормальное*) heartbeat; (*учащённое*) palpitations *мн*.

сердцеви́н|а (-ы) *ж* (*стебля, плода*) core; (*перен: событий*) heart.

серебри́ст|ый (-, -а, -о) *прил* silver(-coloured (BRIT) *или* -colored (US)); (*перен: голос, смех*) silvery.

серебр|и́ть (-ю́, -и́шь; *perf* посеребри́ть) *несов перех* (*покрыть серебром*) to silver-plate; (*перен*) to turn silver.

серебр|о́ (-á) *ср, собир* silver.

сере́бряник (-a) *м* silversmith.

сере́бряный *прил* silver; сере́бряная сва́дьба silver wedding (anniversary).

серёг *сущ см* серьга́.

середи́н|а (-ы) *ж* middle; в ~е +*gen* in the middle of.

середи́нный *прил* middle-of-the-road.

серёд|ка (-и) *ж* (*разг*) middle.

серёж|ка (-ки; *gen pl* -ек) *ж уменьш от* серьга́; (БОТ) catkin.

серена́д|а (-ы) *ж* serenade.

сере́|ть (-ю; *perf* посере́ть) *несов неперех* to turn grey (BRIT) *или* gray (US); (*no perf*; *цветы*) to show grey.

сержа́нт (-a) *м* sergeant.

сержу́(сь) *несов см* серди́ть(ся).

сери́йн|ый *прил*: ~ое произво́дство serial production; сери́йный но́мер serial number.

се́ри|я (-и) *ж* series *ед*; (*кинофильма*) part.

се́рн|а (-ы) *ж* chamois.

се́рн|ый *прил*: ~ая кислота́ sulphuric (BRIT) *или* sulfuric (US) acid.

серп (-á) *м* sickle; лу́нный ~ crescent moon.

серпанти́н (-a) *м* (*бумажная лента*) streamer; (*дорога*) sharply winding road (*in the mountains*).

сертифика́т (-a) *м* certificate; (*товара*) guarantee (certificate).

се́р|ый *прил* grey (*BRIT*), gray (*US*); (-, -á, -о; *перен: погода, жизнь*) grey, drab; (*разг: малообразованный*) dim; **се́рый хлеб** brown bread.

сер|ьга́ (-ьги́; *nom pl* -ьги, *gen pl* -ёг, *dat pl* -ьга́м) *ж* earring.

серьёзен *прил см* **серьёзный.**

серьёзно *нареч, вводн сл* seriously; ~, **ты согла́сен?** do you really agree?

серьёзность (-и) *ж* seriousness.

серьёз|ный (-ен, -на, -но) *прил* serious.

се́сси|я (-и) *ж* (*суда, парламента*) session; (*также: экзаменацио́нная* ~) examinations *мн.*

сестр|а́ (-ы́; *nom pl* **сёстры**, *gen pl* **сестёр**) *ж* sister; (*также: медици́нская* ~) nurse.

сесть (**ся́ду, ся́дешь**; *pt* **сел, се́ла, се́ло**, *impf* **сади́ться**) *сов неперех* to sit down; (*птица, самолёт*) to land; (*солнце, луна*) to go down; (*одежда*) to shrink; (*батаре́йка, аккумуля́тор*) to run down; **сади́ться** (~ *perf*) **в по́езд/на самолёт** to get on a train/plane; **сади́ться** (~ *perf*) **за руль** to get behind the wheel; **сади́ться** (~ *perf*) **за рабо́ту** to sit down to work; **сади́ться** (~ *perf*) **в тюрьму́** to go to prison; **сади́ться** (~ *perf*) **под аре́ст** to be placed under arrest; **сади́ться** (~ *perf*) **за стол** to sit down at the table.

сет (-а) *м* (*ТЕННИС итп*) set.

се́т|ка (-ки; *gen pl* -ок) *ж* net; (*разг: сумка*) string bag; **тари́фная** ~ scale of charges.

се́тован|ие (-я) *ср* (*обычно мн*) complaint.

се́т|овать (-ую; *perf* **посе́товать**) *несов неперех:* ~ **на** +*acc* to complain about.

се́ток *сущ см* **се́тка.**

се́т|ь (-и; *prp sg* -и́, *gen pl* -е́й) *ж* (*для ловли рыб итп*) net; (*система, также КОМП*) network; **расставля́ть** (**расста́вить** *perf*) **кому́-н се́ти** to set a trap for sb; **Сеть** the Net, Internet.

Сеу́л (-а) *м* Seoul.

сече́ни|е (-я) *ср* (*поперечное, продольное итп*) section; **ке́сарево** ~ Caesarean (*BRIT*) *или* Cesarean (*US*) (section).

се́чк|а (-и) *ж* (*крупа*) chaff.

сечь (**секу́, сечёшь** итп, **секу́т**; *pt* **сёк, секла́, секло́**) *несов перех* (*рубить*) to cut up; (*perf* **вы́сечь**; *розгами итп*) to lash, flog.

се́ял|ка (-ки; *gen pl* -ок) *ж* seed drill.

се́|ять (-ю; *perf* **посе́ять**) *несов перех* (*также перен*) to sow ◆ *неперех* (*no perf*): ~**ет дождь** it's drizzling; ~ (**посе́ять** *perf*) **зна́ния/зло** to sow the seeds of knowledge/evil.

СЖ *м сокр* (= *Сою́з журнали́стов*) ≈ NUJ (= *National Union of Journalists*).

сжа́л|иться (-юсь, ишься) *сов возв:* ~ (**над** +*instr*) to have *или* take pity (on).

сжа́ти|е (-я) *ср* (*воздуха, газа*) compression; (*в груди, в горле*) constriction; (*сердца*) contraction.

сжа́т|ый (-, -а, -о) *прил* (*воздух, газ*) compressed; (*краткий*) condensed; **в** ~**ые сро́ки** in a short space of time.

сжать (**сожну́, сожнёшь**) *сов от* **жать** ◆ (**сожму́, сожмёшь**; *impf* **сжима́ть**) *перех* to squeeze; (*воздух, газ*) to compress; (*текст, статью́*) to condense; (*срок*) to reduce; **сжима́ть** (~ *perf*) **зу́бы** to grit one's teeth; **сжима́ть** (~ *perf*) **гу́бы** to purse one's lips

▶ **сжа́ться** (*impf* **сжима́ться**) *сов возв* (*пружина, гу́бка, воздух*) to contract; (*человек: от боли, испуга*) to tense up; (*перен: сердце*) to seize up.

сжечь (**сожгу́, сожжёшь**; *итп*, **сожгу́т**; *pt* **сжёг, сожгла́, сожгло́**, *impf* **сжига́ть** *или* **жечь**) *сов перех* to burn; (*impf* **сжига́ть**; *перен: подлеж: страсть, жела́ние*) to consume; (: *со́лнце*) to scorch; **его́ сжига́ла за́висть** he was consumed with envy; ~ (*perf*) **свои́ корабли́** *или* **за собо́й мосты́** to burn one's boats *или* bridges.

сжива́ть(ся) (-ю(сь)) *несов от* **сжи́ть(ся).**

сживу́(сь) *итп сов см* **сжи́ть(ся).**

сжига́|ть (-ю) *несов от* **сжечь.**

сжима́|ть(ся) (-ю(сь)) *несов от* **сжа́ть(ся).**

сжи́|ть (-ву́, -вёшь; *pt* -л, -лá, -ло, *impf* **сжива́ть**) *сов перех:* ~ **кого́-н со све́та** *или* **све́ту** to drive sb to his *итп* grave.

сжи́|ться (-ву́сь, -вёшься; *pt* -лся, -лáсь, -лось, *impf* **сжива́ться**) *сов возв:* ~ **с** +*instr* to become close to; (*привы́кнуть*) to grow used to; ~ (*perf*) **с ро́лью** to get inside a role.

сжу́льнича|ть (-ю) *сов от* **жу́льничать.**

сза́ди *нареч* (*подойти*) from behind; (*находи́ться*) behind ◆ *предл* (+*gen*) behind.

сзыва́|ть (-ю) *несов от* **созва́ть.**

си *ср нескл* (*МУЗ*) te.

сиби́рск|ий (-ая, -ое, -ие) *прил* Siberian.

Сиби́р|ь (-и) *ж* Siberia.

сибиря́к (-á) *м* Siberian.

сибиря́ч|ка (-ки; *gen pl* -ек) *ж см* **сибиря́к.**

си́в|ый *прил* (*масть ло́шади*) grey (*BRIT*), gray (*US*).

сига́р|а (-ы) *ж* cigar.

сигаре́т|а (-ы) *ж* cigarette.

сигна́л (-а) *м* signal; (*ABT*) horn.

сигнализа́тор (-а) *м* signalling device.

сигнализа́ци|я (-и) *ж* (*де́йствие*) signalling; (*система*) signalling system; (*в кварти́ре*) burglar alarm; **пожа́рная/автомоби́льная** ~ fire/car alarm.

сигнализи́р|овать (-ую) *perf* **сигнализи́ровать** *или* **просигнализи́ровать**) *несов неперех:* ~ (**о** +*prp*) to signal.

сигна́л|ить (-ю, -ишь; *perf* **просигна́лить**) *несов неперех* (*флажка́ми, фа́рами*) to signal; (*ABT*) to honk.

сигна́льный *прил* signal *опред*; **сигна́льный экземпля́р** proof copy; **сигна́льная бу́дка** signal box; **сигна́льные огни́** (*ABT*) indicators.

СИД *м сокр* (= *светоизлуча́ющий дио́д*) LED (= *light-emitting diode*).

сиде́л|ка (-ки; *gen pl* -ок) *ж* (sick) nurse.

сиде́ни|е (-я) *ср* sitting.

сиде́нь|е (-я) *ср* seat.

сид|е́ть (-жу́, -ди́шь) *несов неперех* to sit; (*не*

работать, отдыхать) to sit around; *(одежда)* to fit; ~ *(impf)* **дома** to stay at home; ~ *(impf)* **в тюрьме** to be in prison; ~ *(impf)* **с ребёнком** to look after a child; ~ *(impf)* **без денег/дела** to have no money/nothing to do; **он ~дел за книгой/работой** he was sitting reading a book/doing his work; ~ *(impf)* **на телефоне** *(разг)* to spend ages on the phone

▸ **сиде́ться** *безл:* **ему не ~дится на месте/дома** he can't keep still/bear sitting at home.

Сидне́й (-я) *м* Sydney.

сидя *нареч:* **работать/есть** ~ to work/eat sitting down.

сидя́чий (-ая, -ее, -ие) *прил (положение)* sitting *опред; (образ жизни)* sedentary; **сидя́чая забастовка** sit-down strike; **сидя́чие места** *(разг)* seats *мн.*

сие́ *мест см* сей.

сижу́ *несов см* сидеть.

СИЗО *сокр = следственный изолятор.*

си́зый (-, -á, -о) *прил* blue-grey *(ВRIT)*, blue-gray *(US).*

сим *мест см* сей.

си́л|а (-ы) *ж* strength; *(тока, ветра, закона)* force; *(воли, слова)* power; *(обычно мн: душевные, творческие)* energy; **в ~у того, что ...** owing to the fact that ...; **изо всей ~ы** *или* **всех сил** as hard as one can; **от ~ы** *(разг)* at (the) most; **это задание ему по ~м** *или* **под силу** he is capable of (doing) this task; **я не в ~х** **это сделать** I'm not able to do that; **он всё делает через ~у** it's an effort for him to do anything; **он ест через ~у** he's forcing himself to eat; **вступа́ть (вступи́ть** *perf)* **или входи́ть (войти́** *perf)* **в ~у** to come into *или* take effect; **теря́ть (потеря́ть** *perf)* **или утра́чивать (утра́тить** *perf)* **~у** to cease to be effective; **всё остаётся в ~е** everything will stay as it is; **применя́ть (примени́ть** *perf)* **~у** to use force; *см также* **силы.**

сила́ч (-á) *м* strong man *(мн* men).

силён *прил см* сильный.

си́л|иться (-юсь, -ишься) *несов возв:* ~ +*infin* to make an effort to do.

силово́й *прил* power *опред*; **силова́я борьба́** wrestling; **силово́й приём** throw *(in martial arts).*

си́лой *нареч* by force.

си́лос (-а) *м* silage.

силуэ́т (-а) *м (контур)* silhouette; *(одежды)* outline.

си́л|ы (-) *мн* forces *мн*; **~ами кого-н** with the help of; **свои́ми ~ами** by o.s.; **производи́тельные** ~ production force; **си́лы быстрого реаги́рования** quick-deployment forces.

си́льно *нареч* strongly; *(ударить)* hard;

(хотеть, понравиться итп) very much.

сильноде́йствующий (-ая, -ее, -ие) *прил (лекарство, яд)* powerful.

си́льный (-ён, -ьна́, -ьно) *прил* strong; *(мороз)* hard; *(впечатление, желание)* powerful; *(шум)* loud; *(дождь)* heavy.

сим *мест см* сей, сиё, сий.

си́мвол (-а) *м* symbol; *(КОМП)* character.

символизи́р|овать (-ую) *несов перех* to symbolize.

символи́зм (-а) *м (ИСКУССТВО)* symbolism.

симво́лик|а (-и) *ж (символическое значение)* symbolism ♦ *собир (военная, морская итп)* symbols *мн.*

символи́ческий (-ая, -ое, -ие) *прил* symbolic.

си́ми *мест см* сий.

симметри́ческий (-ая, -ое, -ие) *прил* symmetrical.

симметри́чный *прил* = **симметри́ческий.**

симме́три|я (-и) *ж* symmetry.

симпатизи́р|овать (-ую) *несов неперех:* ~ **кому-н** to like *или* be fond of sb.

симпати́чный (-ен, -на, -но) *прил* nice, pleasant.

симпа́ти|я (-и) *ж* liking, fondness.

симпо́зиум (-а) *м* symposium.

симпто́м (-а) *м* symptom.

симптомати́чный (-ен, -на, -но) *прил* symptomatic.

симули́р|овать (-ую) *(не)сов перех (нападение)* to simulate; *(болезнь)* to fake.

симфони́ческий (-ая, -ое, -ие) *прил* symphonic; **симфони́ческий орке́стр** symphony orchestra.

симфо́ни|я (-и) *ж (МУЗ)* symphony.

синаго́г|а (-и) *ж* synagogue.

Сингапу́р (-а) *м* Singapore.

синдика́т (-а) *м (ЭКОН)* syndicate.

синдро́м (-а) *м (МЕД)* syndrome.

синев|а́ (-ы́) *ж (синий цвет)* blue; *(моря, неба)* blueness.

сине́|ть (-ю; *perf* **посине́ть)** *несов неперех* to turn blue; *(no perf; виднеться)* to show blue.

си́н|ий (-яя, -ее, -ие) *прил* blue; **си́ний чулок** bluestocking.

син|и́ть (-ю, -и́шь; *perf* **посини́ть)** *несов перех (красить)* to paint blue.

сини́ц|а (-ы) *ж* tit.

синкрети́зм (-а) *м* syncretism.

сино́д (-а) *м* synod.

сино́ним (-а) *м* synonym.

синоними́ческий (-ая, -ое, -ие) *прил* synonymous.

синоними́|я (-и) *ж* synonimity.

сино́птик (-а) *м* weather forecaster.

си́нтаксис (-а) *м* syntax.

синтакси́ческий (-ая, -ое, -ие) *прил* syntactic; **~ая оши́бка** *(КОМП)* syntax error.

си́нтез (-а) *м* (*также хим*) synthesis (*мн* syntheses).

синтези́р|овать (-ую) (*не*)*сов перех* (*также хим*) to synthesize.

синте́тик|а (-и) *ж собир* (*материалы*) synthetic material; (*изделия*) synthetics *мн*.

синтети́ческий (-ая, -ое, -ие) *прил* (*материал*) synthetic.

синхро́нный *прил* (*движение*) synchronous; (*перевод*) simultaneous; **~ое пла́вание** synchronized swimming.

синь (-и) *ж* = **синева́**.

си́нька (-и) *ж* blue.

синя́к (-а́) *м* bruise.

сиони́зм (-а) *м* Zionism.

сиони́ст (-а) *м* Zionist.

сипе́ть (-лю́, -и́шь) *несов неперех* to croak.

си́плый (-, -а́, -о) *прил* hoarse.

сиплю́ *несов см* **сипе́ть**.

си́пн|уть (-у, -ешь; *perf* **оси́пнуть**) *несов неперех* to grow hoarse.

сире́н|а (-ы) *ж* (*гудок*) siren.

сире́невый *прил* lilac.

сире́н|ь (-и) *ж* (*кустарник*) lilac bush ♦ *собир* (*цветы*) lilac.

сири́ек *сущ см* **сири́йка**.

сири́ец (-йца) *м* Syrian.

сири́йка (-йки; *gen pl* -ек) *ж см* **сири́ец**.

сири́йский (-ая, -ое, -ие) *прил* Syrian.

сири́йца *итп сущ см* **сири́ец**.

Си́ри|я (-и) *ж* Syria.

сиро́п (-а) *м* syrup.

сирот|а́ (-оты́; *nom pl* -о́ты) *м/ж* orphan.

сироте́|ть (-ю; *perf* **осироте́ть**) *несов неперех* to be orphaned.

сиротли́вый (-, -а, -о) *прил* sad and lonely.

систе́м|а (-ы) *ж* system; (*конструкция*) make; **приводи́ть** (**привести́** *perf*) **в ~у** to put into order.

систематизи́р|овать (-ую) (*не*)*сов перех* to order.

системати́ческий (-ая, -ое, -ие) *прил* following a defined system; (*регулярный*) regular.

системати́чный *прил* = **системати́ческий**.

систе́мный *прил* relating to or based on a system; **систе́мный ана́лиз** systems analysis; **систе́мный диск** (*КОМП*) system disk.

си́т|ец (-ца) *м* cotton.

си́течк|о (-ка; *gen pl* -ек) *ср уменьш от* **си́то**; (*для чая*) (tea) strainer.

си́т|о (-а) *ср* sieve.

ситро́ *ср нескл* soft drink.

ситуа́ци|я (-и) *ж* situation.

си́тца *итп сущ см* **си́тец**.

си́тцевый *прил* (*ткань*) cotton.

СИФ *м сокр* c.i.f. (= *cost, insurance, freight*).

сифилис (-а) *м* syphilis.

сифо́н (-а) *м* siphon.

сих *мест см* **сий**.

сицилиа́нский (-ая, -ое, -ие) *прил* Sicilian.

Сици́ли|я (-и) *ж* Sicily.

сию́ *мест см* **сия́**.

сиюмину́тный (-ен, -на, -но) *прил* immediate.

сия́ *мест см* **сей**.

сия́ни|е (-я) *ср* (*солнца, луны, глаз*) shining; (*лица*) radiance; (*славы, успеха*) dazzle; **се́верное ~** the Northern lights *мн*.

сия́|ть (-ю) *несов неперех* (*солнце, звезда*) to shine; (*огонь*) to glow; **~** (*impf*) **от сча́стья** to beam with happiness; **ко́мната ~ла чистото́й** the room was spotlessly clean; **же́нщина ~ла красото́й** the woman was dazzlingly beautiful.

сия́ющий (-ая, -ее, -ие) *прил* (*глаза*) shining; (*лицо, улыбка*) beaming; (*человек*) radiant.

СК *м сокр* (= *Сою́з компози́торов*) ≈ MU (= *Musicians' Union*).

скажу́(сь) *итп сов см* **сказа́ть(ся)**.

сказа́ни|е (-я) *ср* legend.

сказа́ть (-ажу́, -а́жешь) *сов от* **говори́ть** ♦ *перех*; **~а́жем** (*разг*) let's say; **~ажи́те!** (*разг*) I say!; **как ~** (*разг*) how shall I put it; **кста́ти ~** by the way; **не́чего ~** (*разг: действительно*) indeed; **~ажи́те пожа́луйста** could you please tell me; **~ажи́те пожа́луйста!** well I never!; **так ~** so to speak

► **сказа́ться** (*impf* **ска́зываться**) *сов возв* (*способности, опыт итп*) to show; (*отразиться*): **~ся на** +*prp* to take its toll on; **ска́зываться** (**~ся** *perf*) +*instr* (*родственником, журналистом*) to pose as; **ска́зываться** (**~ся** *perf*) **больны́м** to pretend to be ill (*BRIT*) *или* sick (*US*).

ска́з|ка (-ки; *gen pl* -ок) *ж* fairy tale *или* story.

ска́зочен *прил см* **ска́зочный**.

ска́зочник (-а) *м* story teller.

ска́зочниц|а (-ы) *ж см* **ска́зочник**.

ска́зоч|ный *прил* fairy-tale; (-ен, -на, -но; *перен: необычайный*) fantastic.

сказу́емо|е (-ого; *decl like adj*) *ср* (*линг*) predicate.

ска́зыва|ться (-юсь) *несов от* **сказа́ться**.

скак *м*: **на (всём) ~у́** at top speed.

скака́л|ка (-ки; *gen pl* -ок) *ж* skipping rope.

скак|а́ть (-ачу́, -а́чешь) *несов неперех* (*человек*) to skip; (*животное*) to hop; (*мяч*) to bounce; (*разг: температура, цены итп*) to rise and fall; (*лошадь, всадник*) to gallop.

скакн|у́ть (-у́, -ёшь) *сов неперех* to leap.

скаков|о́й *прил*: **~а́я ло́шадь** racehorse; **скаковы́е соревнова́ния** race meeting.

скаку́н (-а́) *м* racehorse.

скал|а́ (-алы́; *nom pl* -а́лы) *ж* cliff.

скаламбу́р|ить (-ю, -ишь) *сов от* **каламбу́рить**.

скали́стый *прил* rocky; **С~ые го́ры** the Rocky Mountains *или* Rockies.

ска́л|ить (-ю, -ишь; *perf* **оска́лить**) *несов перех*: **~ зу́бы** to bare one's teeth

► **ска́литься** (*perf* **оска́литься**) *несов возв* to bare one's teeth.

ска́л|ка (-ки; *gen pl* -ок) *ж* (*кулин*) rolling-pin.

скалола́з (-а) *м* rock-climber.

скалола́зани|е (-я) *ср* rock-climbing.
ска́лыва|ть (-ю) *несов от* сколо́ть.
скальки́р|овать (-ую) *сов от* кальки́ровать.
ска́льпель (-я) *м* scalpel.
скаме́йка (-йки; *gen pl* -ек) *ж* bench.
скам|ья́ (-ьи́; *gen pl* -е́й) *ж* (*для сидения*) bench;
~ **подсуди́мых** (*ЮР*) the dock; **сесть** (*perf*) **на**
~**ью́ подсуди́мых** to stand trial; **со**
шко́льной/студе́нческой ~**ьи́** from one's
school/student days.
сканда́л (-а) *м* (*политический*) scandal; (*ссора*)
quarrel.
сканда́лен *прил см* сканда́льный.
скандализи́р|овать (-ую) (*не*)*сов перех* to
scandalize.
скандали́ст (-а) *м* troublemaker.
скандали́ст|ка (-ки; *gen pl* -ок) *ж см*
скандали́ст.
сканда́л|ить (-ю, -ишь; *perf* наскандали́ть)
несов неперех to quarrel.
сканда́льный (-ен, -ьна, -ьно) *прил* (*история*,
поступок) scandalous; (*no short form; человек*)
quarrelsome.
скандир|овать (-ую) (*не*)*сов перех* (*подлеж*:
толпа итп) to chant.
ска́нер (-а) *м* scanner.
ска́плива|ть(ся) (-ю(сь)) *несов от*
скопи́ть(ся).
скарб (-а) *м собир* (*разг*: *вещи*) stuff.
ска́редный (-ен, -на, -но) *прил* (*разг*) mingy.
скарлати́н|а (-ы) *ж* scarlet fever.
скармлива|ть (-ю) *несов от* скорми́ть.
скат (-а) *м* slope; (*АВТ*: *колесо*) wheel; (*ось*) axle.
ска|та́ть (-ю) *сов от* ката́ть ♦ (*impf* ска́тывать)
перех to roll up.
ска́терть (-и; *gen pl* -е́й) *ж* tablecloth; ~**ю**
доро́га (*разг*) good riddance.
ск|ати́ть (-ачу́, -а́тишь; *impf* ска́тывать) *сов*
перех to roll down.
► **скати́ться** (*impf* ска́тываться) *сов возв*
(*слеза*) to roll down; (*перен*): ~**ся к** +*dat*/**на**
+*acc* to slide towards/into; ~**ся** (*perf*) **на**
лы́жах/на саня́х to ski/sledge down.
ска́тыва|ть (-ю) *несов от* ската́ть, скати́ть
► **ска́тываться** *несов от* скати́ться.
скафа́ндр (-а) *м* (*водолаза*) diving suit;
(*космонавта*) spacesuit.
ска́чек *итп сущ см* ска́чки.
ска́чк|а (-и) *ж* galloping.
скачка́ *итп сущ см* скачо́к.
ска́чк|и (-ек) *мн* the races *мн*.
скач|о́к (-ка́) *м* leap.
скачу́(сь) *сов возв см* скати́ть(ся).
скачу́ *итп несов см* скака́ть.
ска́шива|ть (-ю) *несов от* скоси́ть.
СКВ *ж сокр* (= *свободно конвертируемая*
валюта) convertible currency.
сква́жин|а (-ы) *ж* (*нефтяная, газовая*) well;

замо́чная ~ keyhole; **бурова́я** ~ borehole.
сквер (-а) *м small public garden.*
скве́рен *прил см* скве́рный.
скверносло́ви|е (-я) *ср* foul language.
скверносло́в|ить (-лю, -ишь) *несов неперех*
to use foul language.
скве́рный (-ен, -на́, -но) *прил* foul; (*история*,
поступок) nasty.
сквита́|ться (-юсь) *сов возв*: ~ (**с** +*instr*)
(*отомстить*) to get even (with);
(*рассчитаться*) to pay in full.
сквоз|и́ть (*3sg* -и́т, *3pl* -я́т) *несов неперех*
(*чувство*) to show ♦ *безл*: **здесь** ~**и́т** it's
draughty here.
сквозн|о́й *прил* (*поезд*) through *опред*; **он**
получи́л ~**у́ю ра́ну** the bullet has gone right
through him; ~ **ве́тер** crosswinds *мн*.
сквозня́к (-а́) *м* (*в комнате*) draught (*BRIT*),
draft (*US*).
сквозь *предл* (+*acc*) through; **я слы́шал что́-то**
~ **сон** I heard something in my sleep.
скворе́|ц (-ца́) *м* starling.
скворе́чник (-а) *м* nesting box.
скворца́ *итп сущ см* скворе́ц.
скеле́т (-а) *м* (*также перен*) skeleton.
ске́псис (-а) *м* scepticism.
ске́птик (-а) *м* sceptic.
скептици́зм (-а) *м* scepticism.
скепти́ческ|ий (-ая, -ое, -ие) *прил* sceptical.
ски́д|ка (-ки; *gen pl* -ок) *ж* (*с цены*) discount,
reduction; (**сде́лать** perf) ~**ку на что́-н**
to make an allowance for sth; **со** ~**кой на что́-н**
taking sth into account; **нало́говая** ~ tax
allowance.
ски́|нуть (-ну, -нешь; *impf* ски́дывать) *сов перех*
(*сбросить*) to throw down; (: *одежду, одеяло*)
to throw off; (*разг*: *с цены*) to knock off
► **ски́нуться** *сов возв* (*разг*) to have a whip-
round.
ски́петр (-а) *м* sceptre (*BRIT*), scepter (*US*).
скирд|а́ (-ы́) *ж* stack; *pt* -, -ла, -ло) *сов от*
ки́снуть ♦ (*impf* скиса́ть) *неперех* to turn sour;
(*перен*: *разг*) to lose interest.
скита́л|ец (-ьца) *м* wanderer.
скита́ни|е (-я) *ср* wandering.
скита́|ться (-юсь) *несов возв* to wander.
склад (-а) *м* (*помещение*: *товарный*) store;
(*жизни*) way; (*оружия итп*) cache; ~ **ума́**
mentality; ~ **боеприпа́сов** ammunition dump.
скла́ден *прил см* скла́дный.
склади́р|овать (-ую) (*не*)*сов перех* to store.
скла́д|ка (-ки; *gen pl* -ок) *ж* (*на одежде*) pleat; (*на*
лице) furrow; (*на ткани*) crease; **ю́бка в** ~**ку**
или **со** ~**ми** pleated skirt.
складно́й *прил* folding.
скла́дный (-ен, -на, -но) *прил* (*статный*) well-
built; (*связный*) coherent.

скла́док *сущ см* **скла́дка.**

складско́й *прил* storage *опред.*

скла́дчин|а (-ы) *ж* (*сбор*) pool; **купи́ть** (*perf*) **что-н в ~у** to pool together to buy sth.

скла́дыван|е (-я) *ср* (*действие: предметов*) stacking; (*чисел*) addition.

скла́дыва|ть(ся) (-ю(сь)) *несов от* **сложи́ть(ся).**

скле́|ить (-ю, -ишь) *сов от* **кле́ить ◆** (*impf* **скле́ивать**) *перех* to glue together.

склеп (-а) *м* crypt.

склепа́|ть (-ю) *сов от* **клепа́ть.**

склеро́з (-а) *м* (*сосудов, лёгких*) sclerosis; **~ мо́зга** senility.

склеро́зный *прил* sclerotic.

склеро́тик (-а) *м* sclerotic.

склероти́ческ|ий (-ая, -ое, -ие) *прил* = **склеро́зный.**

скло́к|а (-и) *ж* squabble.

склон (-а) *м* slope; **на скло́не лет** *или* **жи́зни** *или* **дней** in one's later life.

скло́нен *прил см* **скло́нный.**

склоне́ни|е (-я) *ср* (*линг*) declension.

скло|ни́ть (-ню́, -ни́шь; *impf* **склоня́ть**) *сов перех* (*опустить*) to lower; **склоня́ть** (**~** *perf*) **кого́-н к побе́гу/на преступле́ние** to talk sb into escaping/committing a crime; **я ~они́л её на свою́ сто́рону** I talked her over to my side

► **склони́ться** (*impf* **склоня́ться**) *сов возв* (*нагнуться*) to bend; (*перен*): **~ся к** +*dat* to come round to

скло́нност|ь (-и) *ж*: **~ к** +*dat* (*к музыке, к математике*) aptitude for; (*к меланхолии, к полноте*) tendency to.

скло́н|ный (-ен, -на́, -но) *прил*: **~ к** +*dat* (*к простудам*) prone *или* susceptible to; **~** +*infin* (*согласиться, помириться*) inclined to do; **он ~ен к фи́зике** he has an aptitude for physics.

склоня́емый *прил* declinable.

склоня́|ть (-ю) *несов от* **склони́ть ◆** (*perf* **просклоня́ть**) *перех* (*линг*) to decline; **~** (*impf*) **кого́-н** to talk about sb a lot

► **склоня́ться** *несов от* **склони́ться ◆** *возв* (*линг*) to decline.

скло́чен *прил см* **скло́чный.**

скло́чник (-а) *м* (*разг*) quarrelsome man (*мн* men).

скло́чниц|а (-ы) *ж* (*разг*) quarrelsome woman (*мн* women).

скло́чн|ый (-ен, -на, -но) *прил* quarrelsome.

скля́н|ка (-ки; *gen pl* -ок) *ж* (*разг: сосуд*) bottle.

ско́б|а (-о́бы; *nom pl* -о́бы) *ж* (*для опоры, для держа́ния*) clamp; (*для крепления*) staple.

ско́б|ка (-ки; *gen pl* -ок) *ж уменьш от* **скоба́;** (*обычно мн: знак*) bracket, parentheses *мн*; **кру́глые/квадра́тные ~ки** round/square brackets; **брать** (**взять** *perf*) **сло́во в ~ки** to put a word in brackets *или* parentheses.

скобл|и́ть (-ю́, -и́шь) *несов перех* to scrape.

ско́бок *сущ см* **ско́бка.**

ско́ван|ный (-, -на, -но) *прил* (*человек,*

скова́ть (-ую́) *сов от* **кова́ть ◆** (*impf* **ско́вывать**) *перех* (*соединить*) to weld together; **страх ~ова́л его́** he was paralysed with fear; **лёд ~ова́л ре́ку** the river froze over.

сковород|а́ (-ы́; *nom pl* **ско́вороды**) *ж* frying-pan (*BRIT*), skillet (*US*).

сковоро́д|ка (-ки; *gen pl* -ок) *ж* = **сковорода́.**

ско́выва|ть (-ю) *несов от* **скова́ть.**

скол|оти́ть (-очу́, -о́тишь; *impf* **скола́чивать**) *сов перех* to hammer together; (*разг: банду, капитал*) to get together.

скол|о́ть (-олю́, -о́лешь; *impf* **ска́лывать**) *сов перех* (*снять*) to chop off; (*соединить*) to pin together.

сколочу́ *сов см* **сколоти́ть.**

сколь *нареч* (*как*) how; (*возможно*) as much as; **~ ... сто́ль** (*же*) ... as much ... as ....

скольз|и́ть (-жу́, -зи́шь) *несов неперех* to glide; (*теряя устойчивость*) to slide.

ско́льз|кий (-кая, -кое, -кие; -ок, -ка, -ко) *прил* slippery; (*ситуация, тема*) tricky; (*вопрос*) sensitive.

скольз|ну́ть (-у́, -ёшь) *сов неперех* to glide; (*быстро пройти*) to slip.

ско́льзок *прил см* **ско́льзкий.**

скользя́щ|ий (-ая, -ее, -ие) *прил* (*шаг*) gliding; (*непостоянный*) flexible.

KEYWORD

ско́льк|о (-их) *местоимённое нареч* **1** (+*gen*; *книг, часо́в, дней итп*) how many; (*сахара, сил, работы итп*) how much; **ско́лько люде́й пришло́?** how many people came?; **ско́лько де́нег тебе́ на́до?** how much money do you need?; **ско́лько э́то сто́ит?** how much is it?; **ско́лько тебе́ лет?** how old are you?

2 (*относительное*) as much; **бери́, ско́лько хо́чешь** take as much as you want; **ско́лько уго́дно** as much as you like

◆ *нареч* **1** (*насколько*) as far as; **ско́лько по́мню, он всегда́ был агресси́вный** as far as I remember, he was always aggressive

2 (*много*): **ско́лько люде́й!** what a lot of people!; **ско́лько вре́мени он отня́л у нас!** what a long time he has kept us!; **не сто́лько ... ско́лько ...** not so much ... as ....

скома́нд|овать (-ую) *сов от* **кома́ндовать.**

скомбини́р|овать (-ую) *сов от* **комбини́ровать.**

ско́мка|ть (-ю) *сов от* **ко́мкать.**

скоморо́х (-а) *м* (*комедиант*) mummer; (*перен*) buffoon.

скомпили́р|овать (-ую) *сов от* **компили́ровать.**

скомплект|ова́ть (-у́ю) *сов от* **комплектова́ть.**

скомпон|ова́ть (-у́ю) *сов от* **компонова́ть.**

скомпромети́р|овать (-ую) *сов от* **компромети́ровать.**

сконструи́р|овать (-ую) *сов от*

конструи́ровать.

сконфу́зить(ся) (-жу(сь), -зишь(ся)) *сов от* конфу́зить(ся).

сконцентри́ровать(ся) (-ую(сь)) *сов от* концентри́ровать(ся).

сконча́ни|е (-я) *ср:* до ~я ве́ка to the end of time.

сконча́|ться (-юсь) *сов возв* to pass away.

скоордини́ровать (-ую) *сов от* координи́ровать.

скопидо́м (-а) *м* miser.

скопи́р|овать (-ую) *сов от* копи́ровать.

скопи́ть(ся) (-лю(сь), -ишь(ся)) *сов от* копи́ть(ся).

ско́пищ|е (-а) *ср* horde.

скопле́ни|е (-я) *ср (людей, предметов)* mass.

скоплю́(сь) *сов см* скопи́ть(ся).

ско́пом *нареч (разг)* in a crowd.

ско́р|ая (-ой; *decl like adj) ж (разг: также:* ~ по́мощь) ambulance.

скорбен *прил см* ско́рбный.

скорб|е́ть (-лю́, -и́шь) *несов неперех:* ~ о +*prp* to grieve for.

ско́рб|ный (-ен, -на, -но) *прил* sorrowful; в ~ную мину́ту at a time of sorrow.

скорб|ь (-и; *gen pl* -е́й) *ж* grief.

скоре́е *сравн прил от* ско́рый ♦ *сравн нареч от* ско́ро ♦ *част* rather; ~...чем *или* нежели (*в большей степени*) more likely ... than; (*лучше, охотнее*) rather ... than; ~ всего́ они́ до́ма it's most likely they'll be (at) home; ~ всего́ он сего́дня не придёт he is most unlikely to come today; ~ бы он верну́лся I wish he would come back soon.

скорлупа́ (-упы́; *nom pl* -у́пы) *ж* shell; яи́чная ~ eggshell; оре́ховая ~ nutshell.

скорм|и́ть (-лю́, -ишь; *impf* ска́рмливать) *сов перех:* ~ что-н кому́-н to feed sth to sb.

скорня́ж|ный *прил:* ~ая мастерска́я furrier's workshop; ~ое де́ло furriery.

скорня́к (-а́) *м* furrier.

ско́ро *нареч* soon ♦ *как сказ* it's soon; ~ зима́ it will soon be winter; я ~ верну́сь I will be back soon.

скорова́р|ка (-ки; *gen pl* -ок) *ж* pressure cooker.

скороговор|ка (-ки; *gen pl* -ок) *ж* tongue-twister; (*быстрая речь*) gabble.

скоро́м|ный *прил:* ~ая пи́ща *food forbidden on fasting days.*

скоропали́тел|ьный (-ен, -ьна, -ьно) *прил* hasty.

скоропо́ртящийся (-аяся, -ееся, -иеся) *прил* (*кулин*) perishable.

скоропости́ж|ный (-ен, -на, -но) *прил:* ~ная смерть sudden death.

скороспе́лый *прил (бот)* early.

скоростно́й *прил (поезд)* high-speed; (*строительство*) speedy.

ско́рост|ь (-и; *gen pl* -е́й) *ж* speed; (*физ*) velocity; со ~ю 5 киломе́тров в час at (a speed of) 5 kilometres (*BRIT*) *или* kilometers (*US*) per hour; на (большо́й) ~и at (great) speed; ~ переда́чи (в ба́йдах) (*комп*) baud rate.

скоросшива́тел|ь (-я) *м* (loose-leaf) binder.

скорота́|ть (-ю) *сов от* корота́ть.

скороте́ч|ный (-ен, -на, -но) *прил* short-lived.

скорпио́н (-а) *м* scorpion; (*созвездие*) С~ Scorpio.

скорректи́р|овать (-ую) *сов от* корректи́ровать.

ско́рч|ить(ся) (-у(сь), -ишь(ся)) *сов от* ко́рчить(ся).

ско́р|ый (-, -а́, -о) *прил (езда, движение)* fast; (*разлука, визит*) impending; до ~ого свида́ния see you soon; в ~ом вре́мени shortly; пригото́вить (*perf*) что-н на ~ую ру́ку to rustle sth up; ско́рая по́мощь (*учреждение*) ambulance service; (*автомашина*) ambulance; ско́рый по́езд express (train).

скос (-а) *м (скошенная сторона)* slant; (*склон*) slope.

скос|и́ть (-ошу́, -о́сишь) *сов от* коси́ть ♦ (*impf* ска́шивать) *перех (траву)* to mow; (*пшеницу*) to reap; (*крышу*) to set on a slant; ска́шивать *или* коси́ть (~ *perf*) глаза́ to squint

▸ **скоси́ться** *сов от* коси́ться.

скот (-а́) *м собир* livestock; (*перен: разг*) animal; моло́чный/мясно́й ~ dairy/beef cattle.

скоти́н|а (-ы) *ж собир* livestock ♦ *ж (разг: человек)* swine.

ско́тник (-а) *м* herdsman (*мн* herdsmen).

ско́тниц|а (-ы) *ж* dairy maid.

ско́тный *прил:* ~ двор cattle-yard.

скотово́дств|о (-а) *ср* livestock farming.

ско́тск|ий (-ая, -ое, -ие) *прил (подлый)* beastly; (*грязный*) bestial.

скошу́ *сов см* скоси́ть.

скра́дыва|ть (*3sg* -ет, *3pl* -ют) *несов перех (звуки)* to keep out; (*полноту, морщины*) to conceal.

скра́|сить (-шу, -сишь; *impf* скра́шивать) *сов перех* to ease.

скреб(ся) *итп несов см* скрести́(сь).

скреб|о́к (-ка́) *м* scraper.

скребу́(сь) *итп несов см* скрести́(сь).

скре́жет (-а) *м (металла)* grating; (*колёс*) screech.

скреже|та́ть (-щу́, -щешь) *несов неперех (что-н металлическое)* to grate; ~ (*impf*) зуба́ми to grate one's teeth.

скреп|и́ть (-лю́, -и́шь; *impf* скрепля́ть) *сов перех (соединить)* to fasten together; (*перен: дружбу*) to strengthen; (*удостоверить*) to endorse; ~я́ се́рдце reluctantly.

скре́п|ка (-ки; *gen pl* -ок) *ж* paperclip.

скреплю́ *сов см* скрепи́ть.

скрепля́ть (-ю) *несов от* скрепи́ть.

скре́пок *сущ см* скре́пка.

скрести́ (-бу́, -бёшь; *pt* -ёб, -ебла́, -ебло́) *несов непер* (*мышь, кошка*) to scratch ♦ *перех* (*сковоро́дку*) to scour; (*дерево*) to sand; ~ебёт на душе́ *или* на се́рдце he *итп* has a nagging feeling inside

► скрести́сь *несов возв* (*мышь*) to scratch about; соба́ка ~ебётся в дверь the dog is scratching at the door.

скрести́ть (-щу́, -сти́шь; *impf* скре́щивать) *сов перех* to cross

► скрести́ться (*impf* скре́щиваться) *сов возв* to cross; (*перен: интере́сы, устремле́ния*) to clash.

скреще́ние (-я) *ср* crossing; (*интересов*) clash; ~ доро́г crossroads.

скре́щивание (-я) *ср* cross-breeding.

скре́щивать(ся) (-ю(сь)) *несов от* скрести́ть(ся).

скрещу́(сь) *сов см* скрести́ть(ся).

скриви́ть(ся) (-лю́(сь), -и́шь(ся)) *сов от* криви́ть(ся).

скрип (-а) *м* (*две́ри, по́ла*) creak; (*мета́лла*) grate; (*сне́га*) crunch; со скри́пом (*перен: разг*) with a struggle.

скрипа́ч (-а́) *м* violinist.

скрипа́чка (-ки; *gen pl* -ек) *ж см* скрипа́ч.

скрипе́ть (-лю́, -и́шь) *несов непер* to creak; (*перен: разг*) to struggle along.

скри́пка (-ки; *gen pl* -ок) *ж* violin; (*в наро́дной му́зыке*) fiddle; пе́рвая ~ (*в орке́стре*) first violin; (*в де́ле*) first fiddle.

скриплю́ *несов см* скрипе́ть.

скри́пок *сущ см* скри́пка.

скрипу́чий (-ая, -ее, -ие) *прил* (*дверь, пол*) creaky; (*го́лос*) croaky.

скро́йть (-ю́, -и́шь) *сов от* крои́ть.

скро́мен *прил см* скро́мный.

скро́мник (-а) *м* (*разг*) modest lad (*BRIT*) *или* guy (*US*).

скро́мница (-ы) *ж* (*разг*) modest girl.

скро́мность (-и) *ж* modesty; (*оде́жды итп*) plainness.

скро́мный (-ен, -на́, -но) *прил* modest; (*слу́жащий, до́лжность*) humble.

скро́ю(сь) *итп сов см* скры́ть(ся).

скрупулёзный (-ен, -на, -но) *прил* scrupulous.

скрути́ть (-учу́, -у́тишь) *сов от* крути́ть ♦ (*impf* скру́чивать) *перех* (*провода́, во́лосы*) to twist together; (*разг: аресто́ванного*) to tie up; (: *подлеж: боле́знь, го́ре*) to take a grip

► скрути́ться *сов возв* to twist together.

скрыва́ть (-ю) *несов от* скрыть

► скрыва́ться *несов от* скры́ться ♦ *возв* (*от поли́ции, от власте́й*) to hide; (*раздраже́ние в го́лосе*) to lurk; ~ся (*impf*) под чужи́м и́менем to hide behind another name.

скры́тный (-ен, -на, -но) *прил* secretive; (*возмо́жности*) potent.

скры́тый *прил* (*смысл, возмо́жности итп*)

hidden; (*не́нависть, оппози́ция*) secret; скры́тая ка́мера *или* съёмка hidden camera.

скрыть (-о́ю, -о́ешь; *impf* скрыва́ть) *сов перех* (*спря́тать*) to hide; (*фа́кты*) to conceal

► скры́ться (*impf* скрыва́ться) *сов возв* (*от дождя́, от пого́ни*) to take cover; (*со́лнце, луна́*) to disappear; от него́ ничего́ не ~о́ется nothing escapes him.

скрю́чить (-у, -ишь) *сов от* крю́чить ♦ (*impf* скрю́чивать) *перех* to bend

► скрю́читься *сов от* крю́читься ♦ (*impf* скрю́чиваться) *возв* to be stooped.

скря́га (-и) *м/ж* (*разг*) skinflint.

ску́ден *прил см* ску́дный.

скуде́ть (-ю; *perf* оскуде́ть) *несов непер* to run thin.

ску́дный (-ен, -на́, -но) *прил* (*запа́сы, сре́дства*) meagre (*BRIT*), meager (*US*); (*язы́к, све́дения*) limited; (*расти́тельность*) sparse; ~ +instr (*собы́тиями, витами́нами*) lacking in.

ску́ка (-и) *ж* boredom; там ужа́сная ~ it's dreadfully boring there.

скула́ (-улы́; *nom pl* -у́лы) *ж* (*обы́чно мн*) cheekbone.

скула́стый (-, -а, -о) *прил*: ~ое лицо́ a face with prominent cheekbones.

скули́ть (-ю́, -и́шь) *несов непер* to whine.

ску́льптор (-а) *м* sculptor.

скульпту́ра (-ы) *ж* sculpture.

ску́мбрия (-и) *ж* mackerel.

скупа́ть (-ю) *несов от* скупи́ть ♦ *перех* (*для перепрода́жи*) to buy up; (*кра́деного*) to buy.

скупи́ть (-уплю́, -у́пишь; *impf* скупа́ть) *сов перех* to buy up.

скупи́ться (-лю́сь, -и́шься; *perf* поскупи́ться) *несов возв*: ~ на +acc to skimp on; он не ~и́тся на обеща́ния/комплиме́нты he's generous with his promises/compliments.

ску́пка (-и) *ж* (*де́йствие*) buying up; (*магази́н*) second-hand shop.

скуплю́ *сов см* скупи́ть.

скупо́й (-, -а́, -о) *прил* mean; (*свет*) dim; (*речь*) terse; (*расти́тельность*) sparse; он скуп на де́ньги/похвалу́ he's sparing with money/ praise.

ску́почный *прил*: ~ магази́н second-hand shop; ~ пункт collection point.

ску́пщик (-а) *м* buyer.

скуфья́ (-и́; *gen pl* -е́й) *ж* tall hat worn by Orthodox priests.

скуча́ть (-ю) *несов непер* to be bored; (*тоскова́ть*): ~ по +dat *или* о +prp to miss.

ску́чен *прил см* ску́чный.

ску́чно *нареч* (*жить, расска́зывать итп*) boringly ♦ *как сказ*: здесь ~ it's boring here; мы о́чень ~ живём we lead a boring life; как ~! oh, how boring!; на уро́ке бы́ло ~ the lesson was boring; мне ~ I'm bored.

ску́чный (-ен, -на́, -но) *прил* (*челове́к, жизнь итп*) boring, dreary; (*испы́тывающий ску́ку: челове́к, го́лос итп*) bored.

скуша|ть (-ю) *сов от* **кушать**.

слабе|ть (-ю; *perf* **ослабеть**) *несов неперех* (*человек*) to grow weak; (*здоровье, интерес итп*) to weaken; (*мороз*) to ease off; (*ветер*) to drop; (*дисциплина*) to slacken.

слабительн|ое (-ого; *decl like adj*) *ср* laxative.

слабительный *прил* laxative.

слаб|ить (*3sg* -ит) *несов перех*: ~ **кого-н** to give sb diarrhoea (BRIT) *или* diarrhea (US); **его́ ~ит** he has diarrhoea.

слаб|нуть (-ну, -нешь; *perf* **ослабнуть**) *несов* = **слабеть**.

слабо *нареч* (*вскрикнуть*) weakly; (*нажать*) lightly; (*знать*) badly.

слабово́л|ьный (-ен, -ьна, -ьно) *прил* weak-willed.

слабост|ь (-и) *ж* weakness; (*голоса*) feebleness; (*дисциплины*) slackness; (*пристрастие*): ~ **к** +*dat* weakness for.

слабоу́мный *прил* feeble-minded.

слабохара́ктерный (-ен, -на, -но) *прил* weak.

слаб|ый (-, -á, -о) *прил* weak; (*ветер*) light; (*голос*) feeble; (*знания, доказательство итп*) poor; (*резинка, дисциплина итп*) slack; **слабая сторона́, слабое ме́сто** weak spot.

слав|а (-ы) *ж* (*героя*) glory; (*писателя, актёра итп*) fame; (*дурная, хорошая*) repute; (*разг: слухи*) rumour (BRIT), rumor (US); **во ~у** +*gen* to the greater glory of; **на ~у** splendidly; ~ **Бо́гу!** thank God!

славен *прил см* **славный**.

слави́р|овать (-ую) *сов от* **лави́ровать**.

сла́в|ить (-лю, -ишь) *несов от* **просла́вить** ♦ *перех* (*героев*) to glorify.

▶ **сла́виться** *несов возв*: ~**ся** +*instr* to be renowned for.

сла́вный (-ен, -ná, -но) *прил* (*человек, отдых*) pleasant; (*подвиг, имя*) famous.

славосло́в|ить (-лю, -ишь) *несов перех* to extol.

славяни́н (-яни́на; *nom pl* -я́не, *gen pl* -я́н) *м* Slav.

славя́н|ка (-ки; *gen pl* -ок) *ж см* **славяни́н**.

славя́нск|ий (-ая, -ое, -ие) *прил* Slavonic.

слага́ем|ое (-ого; *decl like adj*) *ср* (MAT) item; (*успеха*) component.

слага́|ть (-ю) *несов от* **сложи́ть**.

сла́|дить (-жу, -дишь; *impf* **сла́живать**) *сов неперех*: ~ **с** +*instr* (*с машиной, с лошадью*) to handle; (*с ребёнком*) to cope with.

сла́дк|ий (-ая, -ое, -кие; -ок, -ка́, -ко) *прил* sweet; (*жизнь*) pleasant.

сла́дко *нареч* (*пахнуть*) sweetly; (*спать*) deeply; (*улыбаться*) sweetly; ♦ *как сказ безл*: **во рту́ ~** I am left with a sweet taste in my mouth; **мне здесь не ~** (*разг*) I can't stand it here.

сла́дк|ое (-ого; *decl like adj*) *ср* sweet things *мн*; (*разг: десерт*) afters (BRIT), dessert (US); **что**

сего́дня на ~? what's for afters today?

сладкое́ж|ка (-ки; *gen pl* -ек) *м/ж* (*разг*) = **сласте́на**.

сла́док *прил см* **сла́дкий**.

сла́достен *прил см* **сла́достный**.

сла́дост|и (-ей) *мн* sweet things *мн*.

сла́достный (-ен, -на, -но) *прил* sweet.

сладостра́стный (-ен, -на, -но) *прил* sensual.

сла́дост|ь (-и) *ж* (*см прил*) sweetness; pleasantness; *см также* **сла́дости**.

сла́жен|ный (-, -на, -но) *прил* orderly.

сла́жива|ть (-ю) *несов от* **сла́дить**.

сла́жу *сов от* **сла́дить**.

сла́з|ить (-жу, -зишь) *сов неперех* to climb.

слайд (-а) *м* (ФОТО) slide.

сла́лом (-а) *м* slalom; **гига́нтский ~** giant slalom.

слаломи́ст (-а) *м* slalom skier.

сласте́н|а (-ы) *м/ж*: **он/она́ ~** he/she has a sweet tooth.

сла|сти́ть (-щу́, -сти́шь) *несов перех* to sweeten.

слать (шлю, шлёшь) *несов перех* to send.

слаща́в|ый (-, -а, -о) *прил* sugary.

сла́ще *сравн прил от* **сла́дкий** ♦ *сравн нареч от* **сла́дко**.

слащу́ *сов см* **сласти́ть**.

сле́ва *нареч* on the left.

слёг *итп сов см* **слечь**.

слегка́ *нареч* slightly.

след (-а; *nom pl* -ы́) *м* trace; (*колес*) track; (*перен*) sign; (*ноги*) footprint; **пре́жней уста́лости и ~á нет** all traces of my earlier tiredness have gone; **напада́ть (напа́сть** *perf*) **на чей-н ~** (*также перен*) to get on sb's trail.

сле́|довать (-жу, -дишь) *несов неперех*: ~ **за** +*instr* to follow; (*заботиться*) to take care of; (*за шпионом*) to watch; (*perf* **наследи́ть**; *грязными ногами*) to leave a trail; ~ (*impf*) **за собо́й** to take care of o.s..

сле́дование (-я) *ср* (*моде, советам итп*) following; **по́езд/авто́бус да́льнего ~я** long-distance train/bus.

сле́дователь (-я) *м* detective.

сле́довательно *вводн сл* consequently ♦ *союз* therefore.

сле́д|овать (-ую; *perf* **после́довать**) *несов неперех* (*вывод, неприятность*) to follow ♦ *безл*: **Вам ~ует поду́мать** you should think about it; **его́ ~ует за э́то наказа́ть** he should be punished for this; ~ (**после́довать** *perf*) **за кем-н/чем-н** to follow sb/sth; ~ (**после́довать** *perf*) **чему-н** (*правилам, советам*) to follow sth; **как ~ует** properly.

сле́дом *нареч*: **ходи́ть ~ за кем-н** to follow sb ♦ *предл*: ~ **за** +*instr* following.

сле́дственный *прил* investigative, investigatory.

сле́дстви|е (-я) *ср* (*последствие*) consequence;

(ЮР: *после преступления*) investigation.

сле́дующий (-ая, -ее, -ие) *прил* next ◆ *мест* following; **на ~ день** the next day; **кто ~?** who is next?

слеже́ни|е (-я) *ср* observation.

слёж|ка (-ки; *gen pl* -ек) *ж* shadowing.

слежу́ *сов см* **следи́ть**.

слез *итп сов см* **слезть**.

слез|а́ (-ы́; *nom pl* -ёзы, *dat pl* -еза́м) *ж* tear; **доводи́ть** (**довести́** *perf*) **кого́-н до ~ёз** to reduce sb to tears; **мне оби́дно до ~ёз** I'm so hurt I could cry.

слеза́|ть (-ю) *несов от* **слезть**.

слез|и́ться (*3sg* -и́тся, *3pl* -я́тся) *несов возв* (*глаза́*) to water.

слезли́в|ый (-, -а, -о) *прил* (*челове́к*) weepy; (*перен: тон, го́лос*) tearful.

слёзный *прил* lacrimal; (*жа́лобный*) pitiful.

слезоточи́в|ый *прил*: **~ газ** tear gas.

слезть (-у, -ешь; *pt* -, -ла, -ло, *impf* **слеза́ть**) *сов непepex* (**с** +*gen*) (*с де́рева*) to climb down; (*с ло́шади, с велосипе́да*) to climb off; (*разг: с авто́буса, с по́езда итп*) to get off; (: *очки́, плато́к*) to slip off; (*ко́жа, кра́ска*) to peel off.

сле́й(те) *сов см* **слить**.

сленг (-а) *м* slang.

слеп|е́нь (-ня) *м* horsefly (*мн* horseflies), cleg.

слеп|и́ть (*3sg* -и́т, *3pl* -я́т) *сов перех*: **~ глаза́ кому́-н** to blind sb.

сле|пи́ть (-плю́, -пишь) *сов от* **лепи́ть** ◆ (*impf* **слепля́ть**) *перех* to stick together

▶ **слепи́ться** (*impf* **слепля́ться**) *сов возв* to stick together.

сле́пка *итп сущ см* **сле́пок**.

слепл|ю́(сь) *сов см* **слепи́ть(ся)**.

слепля́|ть(ся) (-ю(сь)) *несов от* **слепи́ть(ся)**.

слеп|ну́ть (-у, -ешь; *perf* **осле́пнуть**) *несов непepex* to go blind.

слепня́ *итп сущ см* **слепе́нь**.

слеп|о́й (-, -а́, -о) *прил* (*также перен*) blind ◆ (-о́го; *decl like adj*) *м* blind person (*мн* people); **слепа́я кишка́** appendix (*мн* appendices); **слепо́й ме́тод печа́тания** touch-typing.

сле́п|ок (-ка) *м* cast.

слепот|а́ (-ы́) *ж* (*также перен*) blindness.

слеса́рн|ый *прил*: **~ая мастерска́я** metal workshop; **~ стано́к** lathe.

слеса́р|ь (-я; *nom pl* -я́, *gen pl* -е́й) *м* maintenance man (*мн* men).

слёт (-а) *м* (*пионе́ров*) rally.

слета́|ть (-ю) *несов от* **слете́ть** ◆ *непepex* (*на юг, на мо́ре*) to fly; (*разг: сбе́гать*) to nip

▶ **слета́ться** *несов от* **слете́ться**.

сле|те́ть (-чу́, -ти́шь) *сов непepex*: **~ (с** +*gen*) (*птица*) to fly down (from); (*разг: спесь*) to vanish (from); (: *шля́па, ребёнок*) to fall off; **вопро́с ~те́л с губ** *или* **с языка́** the question slipped out

▶ **слете́ться** (*impf* **слета́ться**) *сов возв* (*птицы*) to flock; (*мухи*) to swarm.

сл|е́чь (-я́гу, -я́жешь *итп*, -я́гут; *pt* -ёг, -егла́,

-егло́) *сов непepex* to take to one's bed.

слив (-а) *м* (*де́йствие*) discharge; (*устройство*) drain.

сли́в|а (-ы) *ж* (*де́рево*) plum (tree); (*плод*) plum.

слива́|ть(ся) (-ю(сь)) *несов от* **слить(ся)**.

сли́в|ки (-ок) *мн* (*также перен*) cream *ед*.

сли́в|ки (-ок) *мн* (*также перен*) cream *ед*.

сли́вовый *прил* plum *опред*.

сли́вок *сущ см* **сли́вки**.

сли́вочный *прил* made with cream; **сли́вочное ма́сло** butter.

сли|за́ть (-жу́, -жешь; *impf* **сли́зывать**) *сов перех* (*языко́м*) to lick off.

сли́зист|ый *прил* mucous *опред*; **сли́зистая оболо́чка** mucous membrane.

сли́зыва|ть (-ю) *несов от* **слиза́ть**.

слиз|ь (-и) *ж* mucus; (*от сы́рости, от гря́зи*) slime.

слипа́|ться (*3sg* -ется, *3pl* -ются) *несов от* **сли́пнуться** ◆ *возв* (*перен*): **у меня́ глаза́ ~ются** I can't keep my eyes open.

сли́п|нуться (*3sg* -нется, *3pl* -нутся, *pt* -ся, -лась, -лось, *impf* **слипа́ться**) *сов возв* to stick together.

сли́тка *итп сущ см* **сли́ток**.

сли́тн|ый *прил* (*звуча́ние*) unified; **~ое написа́ние** spelt as one word.

сли́т|ок (-ка) *м* (*металли́ческий*) bar; (*зо́лота, серебра́*) ingot.

сли|ть (**солью́, сольёшь**; *pt* -л, -ла́, -ло, *imper* **сле́й(те)**, *impf* **слива́ть**) *сов перех* to pour; (*вы́лить*) to pour out; (*перен: соедини́ть*) to merge

▶ **сли́ться** (*impf* **слива́ться**) *сов возв* (*ре́ки*) to flow together; (*голоса́, су́дьбы, компа́нии*) to merge.

слич|и́ть (-у́, -и́шь; *impf* **слича́ть**) *сов перех*: **~ что-н с чем-н** to check sth against sth.

сли́шком *нареч* too; **э́то уже́ ~** (*разг*) that's just too much.

слов|а́ (-) *мн*: **~ пе́сни** lyrics *мн*.

слова́к (-а) *м* Slovak.

Слова́ки|я (-и) *ж* Slovakia.

слова́рный *прил* (*рабо́та, статья́*) dictionary *опред*, lexicographic(al); (*фонд, соста́в языка́*) lexical; **слова́рный запа́с** vocabulary.

слова́р|ь (-я́) *м* (*кни́га*) dictionary; (*запа́с слов*) vocabulary.

слова́цк|ий (-ая, -ое, -ие) *прил* Slovak, Slovakian.

слова́ч|ка (-ки; *gen pl* -ек) *ж см* **слова́к**.

слове́н|ец (-ца) *м* Slovene.

Слове́ни|я (-и) *ж* Slovenia.

слове́н|ка (-ки; *gen pl* -ок) *ж см* **слове́нец**.

слове́нск|ий (-ая, -ое, -ие) *прил* Slovene, Slovenian.

слове́нца *итп сущ см* **слове́нец**.

слове́сность (-и) *ж* literature.

слове́сный *прил* oral; (*заявле́ние, проте́ст*) verbal; **слове́сный портре́т** description.

сло́вно *союз* (*как*) like; (*как бу́дто*) as if.

сло́в|о (-а; *nom pl* -а́) *ср* word; **~ в ~** word for

word; **он двух слов связа́ть не мо́жет** (*разг*)
he can't string two words together; **на слова́х**
(*переда́ть, согласи́ться*) verbally; **она́
сочу́вствует то́лько на слова́х** her sympathy
is just empty words; **со слов свиде́телей/его́
друзе́й** according to witnesses/his friends;
проси́ть (попроси́ть *perf*) **~а** (*на собра́нии*) to
ask to speak; **предоставля́ть (предоста́вить**
perf) **кому́-н ~** to allow sb to speak;
**лаборато́рия обору́дована по после́днему
~у нау́ки** the laboratory is equipped with the
latest technology; **к ~у пришло́сь** it sprang to
mind; (**одни́м**) **~м** in a word; **слов нет, ты
прав** what can I say, you're right; *см та́кже*
слова́.

словоизмене́ни|е (**-я**) *ср* inflection.
сло́вом *ввод сл* in a word.
словообразова́ни|е (**-я**) *ср* word formation.
словоохо́тлив|ый (**-, -а, -о**) *прил* loquacious.
словосочета́ни|е (**-я**) *ср* word combination.
словоупотребле́ни|е (**-я**) *ср* word usage.
словц|о́ (**-а́**) *ср* witticism; **для кра́сного ~а́** for
effect.
слог (**-а**; *nom pl* **-и**, *gen pl* **-о́в**) *м* syllable; (*стиль*)
style.
сло́ек *сущ см* **сло́йка**.
слоён|ый *прил*: **~ое те́сто** puff pastry.
сло́жен *прил см* **сло́жный**.
сложе́ни|е (**-я**) *ср* (*в матема́тике*) addition;
(*телосложе́ние*) build; (*полномо́чий,
обя́занностей*) relinquishing; (*чисел*) adding.
сложён|ный (**-, -а́, -о**) *прил*: **он хорошо́ сложён**
he is well-built.
сл|ожи́ть (**-ожу́, -о́жишь**; *impf* **скла́дывать**) *сов
перех* (*ве́щи*) to put; (*кни́ги*) to stack; (*чемода́н,
су́мку итп*) to pack; (*бума́гу, руба́шку итп*) to
fold (up); (*impf* **скла́дывать** *или* **слага́ть**;
чи́сла) to add (up); (*карти́нку*) to make; (*пе́сню,
стихи́*) to make up; **~ го́лову/ору́жие** to
lay down one's life/weapons; **~ (perf) ру́ки** to
fold one's arms; **слага́ть (~ perf) с себя́
полномо́чия/отве́тственность** to relinquish
one's authority/responsibility; **сиде́ть** (*impf*)
~ожа́ ру́ки to sit back and do nothing
► **сложи́ться** (*impf* **скла́дываться**) *сов возв*
(*коллекти́в*) to come together; (*ситуа́ция,
обстоя́тельства*) to turn out; (*хара́ктер*) to
form; (*собра́ть де́ньги*) to have a collection;
(*зонт, пала́тка*) to fold up; (*впечатле́ние*) to
form; **у нас ~ожи́лось хоро́шее впечатле́ние
о нём** we formed a good impression of him.
сло́жно *нареч* (*де́лать*) in a complicated way;
(*сложи́ться*) in a difficult way ♦ *как сказ* it's
difficult; **мне ~ поня́ть его́** I find it difficult to
understand him.
сложносокращён|ный *прил*: **~ое сло́во**
compound.
сло́жност|ь (**-и**) *ж* (*многообра́зие*) complexity;

(*зате́йливость*) intricacy; (*обы́чно мн*:
тру́дность) difficulty; **в о́бщей ~и** all in all.
сло́ж|ный (**-ен, -на́, -но**) *прил* (*де́ло,
предложе́ние, челове́к*) complex; (*узо́р*)
intricate; (*вопро́с, рабо́та*) difficult.
сло́йст|ый (**-, -а, -о**) *прил* stratified.
сло|й (**-я**; *nom pl* **-и́**) *м* layer.
сло́йк|а (**-и**; *gen pl* **-ек**) *ж* sweet pastry.
слом (**-а**) *м*: **на ~** for demolition; **дом идёт на ~**
this house is due for demolition.
слома́|ть (**-ю**) *сов от* **лома́ть**
► **слома́ться** *сов от* **лома́ться** ♦ *возв* (*перен*:
разг: *челове́к*) to break.
слом|и́ть (**-лю́, -ишь**) *сов перех*
(*сопротивле́ние, во́лю итп*) to break; (*подлеж*:
боле́знь, уста́лость) to knock out; **~я́ го́лову**
(*разг*) at breakneck speed
► **сломи́ться** *сов возв* (*перен*: *челове́к*) to
break.
слон (**-а́**) *м* elephant; (*ша́хматы*) bishop.
слонёнок (**-ёнка**; *nom pl* **-я́та**, *gen pl* **-я́т**) *м*
elephant calf (*мн* calves).
слони́х|а (**-и**) *ж* cow (*elephant*).
слоно́вый *прил* elephant *опред*; **слоно́вая
кость** ivory.
слоня́та *итп сущ см* **слонёнок**.
слоня́|ться (**-юсь**) *несов возв* (*разг*) to loaf
around.
сло́па|ть (**-ю**) *сов от* **ло́пать**.
слуг|а́ (**-и́**; *nom pl* **-и**) *м* servant.
служа́к|а (**-и**) *м* (*разг*) trouper.
служа́нк|а (**-и**; *gen pl* **-ок**) *ж* maid.
слу́жащ|ий (**-его**; *decl like adj*) *м* white collar
worker; **госуда́рственный ~** civil servant;
конто́рский ~ clerk.
слу́жб|а (**-ы**) *ж* service; (*рабо́та*) work; **срок ~ы**
durability; **Слу́жба бы́та** consumer services;
Слу́жба за́нятости ≈ Employment Service.
служе́б|ный *прил* (*дела́, обя́занности итп*)
official; (*роль, помеще́ние итп*) auxiliary; **~ое
положе́ние** rank; **служе́бное сло́во** connective
word; **служе́бная соба́ка** working dog.
служе́ни|е (**-я**) *ср* (*де́йствие*: *ро́дине*) serving;
(*РЕЛ*) service.
служи́тел|ь (**-я**) *м* (*в музе́е, в зоопа́рке*) keeper;
(*на автозапра́вке*) attendant; (*нау́ки,
иску́сства*) servant; **служи́тель це́ркви**
clergyman (*мн* clergymen).
служи́тельниц|а (**-ы**) *ж* keeper.
служ|и́ть (**-у́, -у́жишь**) *несов неперех* (*в
ба́нке, в конто́ре итп*) to work; (*в а́рмии*) to
serve ♦ *перех* (*РЕЛ*) to hear ♦ *неперех* (*соба́ка*)
to beg; (*perf* **послужи́ть**; *+instr*;
функциони́ровать) to serve as; **~** (*impf*)
ро́дине/па́ртии to serve one's country/party;
чем могу́ ~? what can I do for you?
слука́в|ить (**-лю, -ишь**) *сов от* **лука́вить**.
слух (**-а**) *м* hearing; (*музыка́льный*) ear;

(*известие*) rumour (*BRIT*), rumor (*US*); **на** ~ by hearing; **играть** (*impf*) **по слуху** to play by ear; **о нём ни слуху ни духу** there's been no word of him; **по слухам** from what people are saying.

слух|овой *прил* (*нерв, орган*) auditory; **слуховой аппарат** hearing aid.

случаен *прил см* **случайный**.

случай (-я) *м* occasion; (*подходящий момент*) chance, opportunity; (*случайность*) chance; **в** ~**е** +*gen* in the event of; **в** ~**е чего** (*разг*) if there is anything; **во всяком** ~**е** in any case; **на** ~ +*gen* in case of; **на всякий** ~ just in case; **по** ~**ю** +*gen* (*годовщины*) on the occasion of; **при** ~**е** if the opportunity arises; **несчастный** ~ accident.

случайно *нареч* accidentally, by chance ♦ *вводн сл* by any chance; **Вы**, ~, **не знаете, где здесь банк?** you don't by any chance know where there is a bank?; **не** ~ not by chance.

случайность (-и) *ж* (*chance*); **по счастливой** ~**и** by sheer luck.

случа́йный (-ен, -йна, -йно) *прил* (*встреча*) accidental, chance *опред*; (*знакомство*) casual; (*комп*) random; ~ **заработок** casual earnings.

случа́|ть (-ю) *несов от* **случить**

▸ **случа́ться** *несов от* **случиться** ♦ *возв*: **он**, ~**ется, приходит сердитый** occasionally he arrives in a temper.

случ|и́ть (-у́, -и́шь; *impf* **случа́ть**) *сов перех* to mate

▸ **случи́ться** (*impf* **случа́ться**) *сов возв* (*произойти*) to happen ♦ *безл*: **мне** ~**и́лось с ним познако́миться** I happened to become acquainted with him.

слу́шани|е (-я) *ср* (*ЮР*) hearing.

слу́шатель (-я) *м* listener; (*ПРОСВЕЩ*) student.

слу́шательниц|а (-ы) *ж см* **слу́шатель**.

слу́ша|ть (-ю) *несов перех* (*музыку, речь*) to listen to; (*ЮР*) to hear; (*курс лекций*) to attend; (*perf* **послу́шать**; *совет*) to listen to; (*perf* **вы́слушать**; *сердце, лёгкие*) to listen to; ~**йте!** (*разг*) listen!

▸ **слу́шаться** (*perf* **послу́шаться**) *несов возв*: ~**ся** +*gen* to obey; (*совета*) to follow; ~**юсь!** yes, sir!

слы|ть (-ву́, -вёшь; *pt* -л, -ла́, -ло) *несов неперех*: ~ +*instr или* **за** +*acc* to be reputed to be.

слы́хан|ный *прил*: **где э́то** ~**о?** (*разг*) whoever heard of such a thing?

слыха́|ть (*pt* -л, -ла, -ло) *несов перех* to hear; **мне ничего́ не** ~ (*разг*) I can't hear a thing.

слы́ш|ать (-у, -ишь) *несов неперех* to hear ♦ (*perf* **услы́шать**) *перех* to hear; ~ (*impf*) **о** +*prp* to hear about; **и** ~ **об э́том не хочу́** I won't hear of it; **он пло́хо** ~**ит** he's hard of hearing

▸ **слы́шаться** *несов возв* to be heard.

слы́шен *прил см* **слы́шный**.

слы́шимость (-и) *ж* (*в зале*) acoustics *мн*; (*радио, телевизора*) audibility.

слы́шно *как сказ* it can be heard; **мне ничего́ не** ~ I can't hear a thing; **о ней ничего́ не** ~ there's

no news of her; **что у Вас** ~? how are things?

слы́ш|ный (-ен, -на́, -но) *прил* (*звук, пение*) audible ♦ *как сказ* (*no full form*): **в его́ го́лосе слышна́ трево́га** anxiety can be heard in his voice.

слюд|а́ (-ы́) *ж* mica.

слюн|а́ (-ы́) *ж* saliva.

слю́нки (-ок) *мн*: **у меня́** ~ **теку́т** my mouth's watering.

слюня́в|ить (-лю, -ишь) *несов перех* (*разг*) to lick.

сля́г|у *итп сов см* **слечь**.

сля́коть (-и) *ж* slush.

сля́па|ть (-ю) *сов от* **ля́пать**.

см *сокр* (= **сантиме́тр**) cm(= *centimetre* (*BRIT*) *или centimeter* (*US*)).

см. *сокр* (= **смотри́**) v. (= *vide*,) qv (= *quod vide*).

с.м. *сокр* (= **сего́ ме́сяца**) inst. (= *instant*).

сма́з|ать (-жу, -жешь; *impf* **сма́зывать**) *сов перех* (*маслом*) to lubricate; (*разг: испортить впечатление*) to slur; **сма́зывать** (~ *perf*) **что-н ма́зью** to put ointment on sth.

сма́зк|а (-и) *ж* (*действие*) lubrication; (*вещество*) lubricant.

сма́зли́вый (-, -а, -о) *прил* (*разг*) pretty.

сма́зочный *прил* lubricating.

сма́зыва|ть (-ю) *несов от* **сма́зать**.

смак|ова́ть (-у́ю) *несов перех* (*еду*) to savour (*BRIT*), savor (*US*); (*перен: новость, книгу итп*) to relish.

смалоду́шнича|ть (-ю) *сов от* **малоду́шничать**.

смальт|а (-ы) *ж* smalto.

сманеври́р|овать (-ую) *сов от* **маневри́ровать**.

сман|и́ть (-ю́, -а́нишь; *impf* **сма́нивать**) *сов перех* (*переманить*) to lure, entice.

смастер|и́ть (-ю́, -и́шь) *сов от* **мастери́ть**.

сма́тыва|ть(ся) (-ю(сь)) *несов от* **смота́ть(ся)**.

сма́хива|ть (-ю) *несов от* **смахну́ть** ♦ *неперех* (*разг*): ~ **на** +*acc* (*походить*) to look a bit like.

смахн|у́ть (-у́, -ёшь) *сов перех* to brush off.

сма́чен *прил см* **сма́чный**.

сма́чива|ть (-ю) *несов от* **смочи́ть**.

сма́ч|ный (-ен, -на́, -но) *прил* (*разг: вкусный*) scrumptious; (*перен: слово*) juicy.

сме́жен *прил см* **сме́жный**.

сме́жник (-а) *м* (*предприятие*) related company.

сме́ж|ный (-ен, -на, -но) *прил* (*с общей границей*) adjoining, adjacent; (*производство, предприятие*) affiliated; (*наука*) related.

смекали́стый (-, -а, -о) *прил* astute.

смека́лк|а (-и) *ж* astuteness.

смека́|ть (-ю; *perf* **смекну́ть**) *несов перех* to catch onto.

смеле́|ть (-ю; *perf* **осмеле́ть**) *несов неперех* to grow bolder.

сме́ло *нареч* boldly; (*без колебаний*) confidently.

сме́лост|ь (-и) ж (*храбрость*) bravery; (*поступка, поведения*) boldness, audacity; **брать** (**взять** *perf*) **на себя́** ~ +*infin* to have the audacity to do.

сме́л|ый (-, -á, -о) *прил* (*человек, поступок*) brave; (*идея, проект*) ambitious; (*перен: нескрайний*) risqué.

смельча́к (-á) *м* brave person (*мн* people).

смелю́ *итп сов см* **смоло́ть**.

сме́н|а (-ы) ж (*руководства*) change; (*караула, одежды*) changing; (*на производстве*) shift; (*молодое поколение*) successors *мн*; (*также*: ~ **белья́**) change of sheets (*BRIT*) *или* bed-linen (*US*); **приходи́ть** (**прийти́** *perf*) **на** ~**у кому́-н/ чему́-н** to succeed sb/sth.

см|ени́ть (-еню́, -е́нишь; *impf* **сменя́ть**) *сов перех* to change; (*коллегу*) to relieve

▸ **смени́ться** (*impf* **сменя́ться**) *сов возв* (*руководство*) to change; (*радость, день*): ~**ся** +*instr* to give way to; **сменя́ться** (~**ся** *perf*) (*с* +*gen*) (*с дежурства, с вахты*) to go off duty (from).

сме́нн|ый *прил* (*работа, задание*) shift *опред*; (*колесо*) spare; ~**ое бельё** a change of sheets (*BRIT*) *или* bed-linen (*US*); (*нижнее*) a change of underwear.

сменя́ть(ся) (-ю(сь)) *несов от* **смени́ть(ся)**.

смёрзн|уться (*3sg* -ется, *3pl* -утся) *сов возв* to freeze together.

сме́р|ить (-ю, -ишь) *сов от* **ме́рить**.

смерка́|ться (*3sg* -ется, *perf* **сме́ркнуться**) *несов безл* to start to get dark.

смерте́л|ьный (-ен, -ьна, -ьно) *прил* mortal; (*рана*) fatal; (*скука, усталость*) deadly; **смерте́льный исхо́д** fatal ending; **смерте́льный слу́чай** fatality.

сме́ртен *прил см* **сме́ртный**.

сме́ртник (-а) *м* (*приговорённый к казни*) prisoner on death row; (*террорист*) kamikaze.

сме́ртность (-и) ж death-rate, mortality.

сме́ртн|ый (-ен, -на, -но) *прил* mortal; (*разг: скука*) deadly; ~ **час** hour of death; ~ **бой** (*перен*) fight to the death; **просто́й** ~ ordinary mortal; **сме́ртный пригово́р** death sentence; **сме́ртная казнь** death penalty.

смертоно́сный *прил* lethal.

смерт|ь (-и) ж death; **быть** (*impf*) **при** ~**и** to be at death's door; **умира́ть** (**умере́ть** *perf*) **свое́й сме́ртью** to die a natural death; **я до́** ~**и бою́сь** I'm scared to death.

смерч (-а) *м* tornado.

смеси́тел|ь (-я) *м* mixer.

см|еси́ть (-шу́, -сишь) *сов от* **меси́ть**.

см|ести́ (-ету́, -ете́шь; *pt* -ёл, -ела́, -ело́, *impf* **смета́ть**) *сов перех* to sweep; (*подлеж: ураган, смерч*) to sweep away.

сме|сти́ть (-щу́, -сти́шь; *impf* **смеща́ть**) *сов перех* (*уволить*) to remove; (*сдвинуть*) to shift

▸ **смести́ться** (*impf* **смеща́ться**) *сов возв* to shift.

смес|ь (-и) ж mixture; **моло́чная** ~ powdered baby milk.

сме́т|а (-ы) ж (*ЭКОН*) estimate.

смета́н|а (-ы) ж sour cream.

смета́|ть (-ю) *несов от* **смести́** ◆ *сов от* **мета́ть**.

сметли́в|ый (-, -а, -о) *прил* quick.

сме́тный *прил* estimated; **сме́тная сто́имость** estimated cost.

сме́|ть (-ю; *perf* **посме́ть**) *несов неперех*: ~ +*infin* to dare to do; **как Вы сме́ете!** how dare you!; **не смей!** don't you dare!

смету́ *итп сов см* **смести́**.

смех (-а; *part gen* -у) *м* laughter ◆ *как сказ* (*смешно*) it's ridiculous; **слу́шать э́то** – ~ it makes me laugh to hear it; **поднима́ть** (**подня́ть** *perf*) **кого́-н на** ~ to make a laughing stock of sb; **и** ~ **и грех** one can see the funny side of it.

смехотво́р|ный (-ен, -на, -но) *прил* (*смешной*) funny; (*жалкий*) ludicrous.

сме́шанный *прил* mixed.

смеша́|ть (-ю) *сов от* **меша́ть** ◆ (*impf* **сме́шивать**) *перех* (*спутать*) to mix up; ~ (*perf*) **чьи-н ка́рты** to spoil sb's plans

▸ **смеша́ться** *сов от* **меша́ться** ◆ *возв* (*смутиться*) to be taken aback; (*impf* **сме́шиваться**; *слиться*) to mingle; (*краски, цвета*) to blend; (*чувства*) to become confused.

смеше́ни|е (-я) *ср* (*стилей, чувств*) mixture.

сме́шивани|е (-я) *ср* mixing.

сме́шива|ть(ся) (-ю(сь)) *несов от* **смеша́ть(ся)**.

смеши́|ть (-у́, -и́шь; *perf* **насмеши́ть** *или* **рассмеши́ть**) *несов перех*: ~ **кого́-н** to make sb laugh.

смешка́ *итп сущ см* **смешо́к**.

смешли́в|ый (-, -а, -о) *прил* (*человек*) jolly; (*настроение*) giggly.

смешно́ *нареч* (*смотреться*) funny ◆ *как сказ* it's funny; (*глупо*) it's ludicrous; **мне не** ~ I don't find it funny; ~ **наде́яться** it's ludicrous to hope; ~ **сказа́ть, но ...** it sounds funny, but ...; **э́то про́сто** ~ that's just ridiculous.

смешн|о́й (-о́н, -на́, -но́) *прил* funny; (*требования, претензии итп*) ludicrous; **до** ~**но́го** to the point of absurdity; **дохо́дит до** ~**но́го** it's a real joke.

смешо́к (-ка́) *м* giggle.

смешо́н *прил см* **смешно́й**.

смеща́|ть(ся) (-ю(сь)) *несов от* **смести́ть(ся)**.

смеще́ни|е (-я) *ср* (*руководства*) removal; (*понятий, критериев*) shift.

смещённ|ый (-ён, -ена́, -ено́) *прил* upset; (*понятия*) disturbed.

смещу́(сь) *сов см* **смести́ть(ся)**.

сме|я́ться (-ю́сь) *несов возв* to laugh;

(*шутить*) to joke; (*perf* **посмея́ться**; *насмеха́ться*): ~ **над** +*instr* to laugh at.

СМИ *сокр* (= **Сре́дства ма́ссовой информа́ции**) the media.

смило́стив|иться (-люсь, -ишься) *сов возв*: ~ (**над** +*instr*) to take pity on.

смина́|ть (-ю) *несов от* **смять**.

сми́рен *прил см* **сми́рный**.

смире́ни|е (-я) *ср* (*покорность*) humility.

смире́н|ный (-, -на, -но) *прил* humble.

смири́тельн|ый *прил*: ~**ая руба́шка** strait-jacket.

смир|и́ть (-ю́, -и́шь; *impf* **смиря́ть**) *сов перех* to subdue

► **смир|и́ться** (*impf* **смиря́ться**) *сов возв* (*покориться*) to submit; (*примириться*): ~**ся с** +*instr* to resign o.s. to.

сми́рно *нареч* (*сидеть, вести себя*) quietly; (*ВОЕН: команда*) attention; **стоя́ть** (*impf*) **по сто́йке** ~"~" to stand to attention.

сми́р|ный (-ен, -на́, -но) *прил* docile.

смиря́|ть(ся) (-ю(сь)) *несов от* **смири́ть(ся)**.

смог (-а) *м* smog.

смог *итп сов см* **смочь**.

смогу́ *итп сов см* **смочь**.

сможешь *итп сов см* **смочь**.

смол|а́ (-ы́; *nom pl* -ы) *ж* (*дерева*) resin; (*дёготь*) tar.

смоли́стый (-, -а, -о) *прил* (*дерево*) resinous.

смо́лк|нуть (-ну, -нешь; *pt* -, -ла, -ло, *impf* **смолка́ть**) *сов непepex* (*голоса*) to fall silent; (*звуки*) to fade away.

смо́лоду *нареч* from one's youth.

смол|оти́ть (-очу́, -о́тишь) *сов от* **молоти́ть**.

смол|о́ть (-елю́, -е́лешь) *сов от* **моло́ть**.

смолочу́ *сов см* **смолоти́ть**.

смолча́|ть (-у́, -и́шь) *сов непepex* to keep quiet.

смол|ь (-и) *ж*: **чёрный как** ~ jet-black.

смонти́р|овать (-ую) *сов от* **монти́ровать**.

сморка́|ть (-ю; *perf* **вы́сморкать**) *несов перех*: ~ **нос** to blow one's nose

► **сморка́|ться** (*perf* **вы́сморкаться**) *несов возв* to blow one's nose.

сморо́дин|а (-ы) *ж*: **кра́сная** ~ (*кустарник*) redcurrant bush; (*ягоды*) redcurrants *мн*; **чёрная** ~ (*кустарник*) blackcurrant bush; (*ягоды*) blackcurrants *мн*.

сморо́|зить (-жу, -зишь) *сов перех* to say.

смо́рщенный *прил* wrinkled.

смо́рщ|ить (-у, -ишь) *сов от* **мо́рщить**

► **смо́рщ|иться** *сов от* **мо́рщиться** ♦ *возв* to become wrinkled.

смота́|ть (-ю; *impf* **сма́тывать**) *сов перех* to wind

► **смота́|ться** (*impf* **сма́тываться**) *сов возв* (*нитки*) to wind; (*разг: убежать*) to leg it; (: *быстро пойти*) to nip.

смотр (-а; *loc sg* -у́, *nom pl* -ы́) *м* presentation; (*ВОЕН*) inspection.

смо|тре́ть (-отрю́, -о́тришь; *perf* **посмотре́ть**) *несов непepex* to look ♦ *перех* (*фильм, игру*) to watch; (*газеты, почту*) to look through; (*квартиру, картину*) to look at; (*музей, выставку*) to look round; (*пациента*) to examine; (*следить*): ~ **за** +*instr* to look after; ~ (*impf*) **в/на** +*acc* to look onto; ~ (**посмотре́ть** *perf*) **на** +*acc* (*относиться*) to look at; ~**отри́те, не упади́те** watch, don't fall; ~**отрю́, ты осво́ился здесь** (*разг*) I see you've settled down here; ~**отря́ по** +*dat* depending on; **Вы хоти́те пойти́ погуля́ть?** – ~**отря́ куда́** would you like to go for a walk? – it depends where to

► **смо|тре́ться** (*perf* **посмотре́ться**) *несов возв*: ~**ся в** +*acc* (*в зеркало, в воду*) to look at o.s. in; (*разг: хорошо выглядеть*) to look good; **э́та вы́ставка** ~**о́трится легко́** this exhibition is not too demanding.

смотри́тел|ь (-я) *м* (*в музее*) attendant.

смотри́тельница (-ы) *ж см* **смотри́тель**.

смотров|о́й *прил* (*площадка*) viewing *опред*; ~**а́я ба́шня** watch tower; ~**о́е отве́рстие** peephole; **смотрово́й кабине́т** medical examination room.

смо́ч|ить (-очу́, -о́чишь; *impf* **сма́чивать**) *сов перех* to dampen.

смо́|чь (-гу́, -жешь *итп*, -гут; *pt* -г, -гла́, -гло́) *сов от* **мочь**.

смоше́нничa|ть (-ю) *сов от* **моше́нничать**.

смо́ю(сь) *итп сов см* **смы́ть(ся)**.

смрад (-а) *м* (*вонь*) stench.

смра́дный (-ен, -на, -но) *прил* stinking.

сму́гл|ый (-, -а́, -о) *прил* swarthy.

смут|а (-ы) *ж* (*социальная*) unrest; **у меня́ на душе́** ~ my soul is troubled.

сму́тен *прил см* **сму́тный**.

сму|ти́ть (-щу́, -ти́шь; *impf* **смуща́ть**) *сов перех* to embarrass

► **сму|ти́ться** (*impf* **смуща́ться**) *сов возв* to get embarrassed.

сму́т|ный (-ен, -на, -но) *прил* (*очертания, воспоминания*) vague; (*настроение, время итп*) troubled.

смуща́|ть(ся) (-ю(сь)) *несов от* **смути́ть(ся)**.

смуще́ни|е (-я) *ср* embarrassment.

смущённый *прил* embarrassed.

смущу́(сь) *сов см* **смути́ть(ся)**.

смыва́|ть(ся) (-ю(сь)) *несов от* **смы́ть(ся)**.

смыка́|ть(ся) (-ю(сь)) *несов от* **сомкну́ть(ся)**.

смысл (-а) *м* (*книги, статьи*) point; (*слов*) meaning; (*линг*) sense; **в смы́сле** +*gen* as regards; **здра́вый** ~ common sense; **прямо́й/перено́сный** ~ **сло́ва** the literal/figurative sense of a word; **какой** ~ **на э́то соглаша́ться?** what is the point of agreeing to that?; **есть** ~ **е́хать сего́дня** it makes sense to go today.

смы́сл|ить (-ю, -ишь) *несов непepex* (*разг: разбираться*): ~ **в** +*prp* to have a knack for.

смы́|ть (-о́ю, -о́ешь; *impf* **смыва́ть**) *сов перех* to wash off; (*подлеж: волна, течение*) to wash away

► **смы́|ться** (*impf* **смыва́ться**) *сов возв* to wash

off; (*разг: незаметно уйти*) to do a bunk.
смыч|Óк (-кá) *м* (*МУЗ*) bow.
смышлёный (-, -а, -о) *прил* sharp.
смягча́|ть(ся) (-ю(сь)) *несов от* смягчи́ть(ся).
смягча́ющий (-ая, -ее, -ие) *прил*: ~ие обстоя́тельства (*ЮР*) extenuating circumstances *мн*.
смягчéни|е (-я) *ср* (*действие*) softening; (: *наказания*) mitigation.
смягч|и́ть (-у́, -и́шь; *impf* смягча́ть) *сов перех* (*кожу, ткань, удар*) to soften; (*боль*) to ease; (*наказание, приговор*) to mitigate; (*человека*) to appease
▸ **смягчи́ться** (*impf* смягча́ться) *сов возв* to soften.
смятéни|е (-я) *ср* turmoil.
смять (сомну́, сомнёшь) *сов от* мять ♦ (*impf* смина́ть) *перех* (*противника, оборону*) to crush
▸ **смя́ться** *сов от* мя́ться.
сна *итп сущ см* сон.
снаб|ди́ть (-жу́, -ди́шь; *impf* снабжа́ть) *сов перех*: ~ кого́-н/что-н чем-н to supply sb/sth with sth.
снабжéни|е (-я) *ср* supply.
снабжу́ *сов см* снабди́ть.
сна́йпер (-а) *м* (*стрелок*) sniper.
снару́жи *нареч* (*покра́сить, расположи́ться*) on the outside; (*закры́ть*) from the outside.
снаря́д (-а) *м* (*ВОЕН*) shell; (*СПОРТ*) apparatus.
снаря|ди́ть (-жу́, -ди́шь; *impf* снаряжа́ть) *сов перех* to equip.
снаряжéни|е (-я) *ср* (*действие*) equipping; (*лыжное, охотничье*) equipment; (*солдата*) kit.
снаряжу́ *сов см* снаряди́ть.
снасть (-и) *ж* (*МОР: обычно мн*) rigging *только ед*; (*рыболовная*) tackle.
снача́ла *нареч* at first; (*ещё раз*) all over again.
сна́шива|ть (-ю) *несов от* сноси́ть.
СНГ *м сокр* (= Содру́жество Незави́симых Госуда́рств) CIS (= *Commonwealth of Independent States*).
снег (-а; *part gen* -у, *loc sg* -у́, *nom pl* -á) *м* snow; идёт ~ it's snowing; вы́пал ~ it's been snowing; как ~ на́ го́лову like a bolt from the blue.
снеги́р|ь (-я́) *м* bullfinch.
снегови́к (-á) *м* snowman (*мн* snowmen).
снегоочисти́тел|ь (-я) *м* snowplough (*BRIT*), snowplow (*US*).
снегопа́д (-а) *м* snowfall.
снегоубо́рочн|ый *прил*: ~ая маши́на snowplough (*BRIT*), snowplow (*US*).
снегу́роч|ка (-ки; *gen pl* -ек) *ж* Snow Maiden.
снедь (-и) *ж собир* food.
снежи́н|ка (-ки; *gen pl* -ок) *ж* snowflake.
снежка́ *итп сущ см* снежо́к.

снéжн|ый *прил* snow *опред*; ~ая зима́ snowy winter; снéжная ба́ба snowman (*мн* snowmen).
снеж|о́к (-ка́) *м* (*комок*) snowball; игра́ть (*impf*) в ~ки́ to have a snowball fight.
сн|ести́ (-есу́, -есёшь; *pt* -ёс, -есла́, -есло́) *сов от* нести́ ♦ (*impf* сноси́ть) *перех* (*отнести*) to take; (*подлеж: буря*) to carry away; (*сверху вниз*) to take down; (*перен: вытерпеть*) to take; (*дом*) to demolish
▸ **снести́сь** *сов от* нести́сь ♦ *возв* (*связаться*): ~сь с +*instr* to contact.
снижа́|ть(ся) (-ю(сь)) *несов от* сни́зить(ся).
снижéни|е (-я) *ср* (*цен итп*) lowering; (*самолёта*) descent; (*производительности итп*) reduction.
сни́|зить (-жу, -зишь; *impf* снижа́ть) *сов перех* (*цены, давление итп*) to lower; (*самолёт*) to bring down; (*скорость*) to reduce
▸ **сни́зиться** (*impf* снижа́ться) *сов возв* (*цены, производительность итп*) to fall; (*самолёт*) to descend.
снизойти́ (*как* идти́; *см* Table 18; *impf* снисходи́ть) *сов неперех*: ~ к кому́-н *или* до кого́-н to condescend to sb; он снизошёл к мое́й про́сьбе *или* до мое́й про́сьбы he condescended to grant my request.
сни́зу *нареч* (*внизу*) at the bottom; (*по направлению вверх*) from the bottom; (*перен: со стороны народа*) from the masses; ~ до́верху from top to bottom.
сни́к|нуть (-ну, -нешь; *pt* -, -ла, -ло) *сов от* ни́кнуть ♦ *неперех* to flag.
снима́|ть(ся) (-ю(сь)) *несов от* снять(ся).
сни́м|ок (-ка) *м* (*ФОТО*) snap(shot).
сниму́(сь) *итп сов см* снять(ся).
сниска́|ть (-щу́, -щешь; *impf* сниска́ть) *сов перех* to win; э́тот посту́пок ~ска́л ему́ большу́ю сла́ву this deed won him great fame.
снисходи́тельный (-ен, -ьна, -ьно) *прил* (*не строгий*) lenient; (*с оттенком высокомерия*) condescending.
снисходи́ть (-ожу́, -о́дишь) *несов от* снизойти́.
снисхождéни|е (-я) *ср* leniency.
снисхожу́ *несов см* снисходи́ть.
сни́ться (-юсь, -и́шься; *perf* присни́ться) *несов безл*: мне ~и́лся стра́шный сон I was having a terrible dream; мне ~и́лось, что я в гора́х I dreamt I was in the mountains; ты ча́сто ~и́шься мне I often dream of you.
снищу́ *итп сов см* сниска́ть.
сноб (-а) *м* snob.
сноби́зм (-а) *м* snobbery.
сно́ва *нареч* again.
снова́|ть (-у́ю) *несов неперех* (*люди*) to dash about; (*машины*) to zoom about.
сновидéни|е (-я) *ср* dream.
сногсшиба́тельный (-ен, -ьна, -ьно) *прил*

(*разг*) stunning.

сноп (-á) *м* (*с -х*) sheaf; (*перен*) shaft.

сноро́вк|а (-и) *ж* knack.

снос (-а) *м* demolition; **дом идёт на ~** the house is due for demolition; **э́тим боти́нкам сно́су нет** these boots are hard-wearing.

сноси́ть (-ошу́, -о́сишь) *несов от* снести́ ♦ (*impf* сна́шивать) *сов перех* (*износить*) to wear out.

сно́с|ка (-ки; *gen pl* -ок) *ж* footnote.

сно́с|ный (-ен, -на, -но) *прил* (*разг*) tolerable.

сно́сок *сущ см* сно́ска.

снотво́рн|ое (-ого; *decl like adj*) *ср* sleeping pill *или* tablet.

снотво́рный *прил*: **~ое сре́дство** sedative.

снох|а́ (-и́) *ж* daughter-in-law (*of husband's father*).

сноше́ни|е (-я) *ср* relations *мн*; **входи́ть (войти́** *perf***) в ~я с** +*instr* to enter into relations with.

сношу́ (*не*)*сов см* сноси́ть.

сня́ти|е (-я) *ср* removal.

снять (-иму́, -и́мешь; *impf* снима́ть) *сов перех* to take down; (*плод*) to pick; (*одежду*) to take off; (*запрет, ответственность*) to remove; (*копию*) to make; (*дом, комнату итп*) to rent; (*уволить*) to dismiss; **снима́ть (~** *perf***) фотогра́фию** to take a picture; **снима́ть (~** *perf***) фильм** to shoot a film; **снима́ть (~** *perf***) показа́ния** to take down evidence; **снима́ть (~** *perf***) урожа́й** to gather the harvest

▶ **сня́ться** (*impf* снима́ться) *сов возв* (*сфотографироваться*) to have one's photograph taken; (*покинуть: со стоянки*) to move off; (*актёр*) to appear; (*корабль*): **~я́ться с я́коря** to up anchor.

со *предл* = **с**.

соа́втор (-а) *м* coauthor.

соа́вторств|о (-а) *ср* coauthorship; **в ~е с** +*instr* in coauthorship with.

соба́к|а (-и) *ж* dog; (*разг*) rat, dog; **он на э́том ~у съел** (*разг*) he knows it inside out; **вот где ~ зары́та!** so that's what it is!

собаково́д (-а) *м* dog-breeder.

собаково́дств|о (-а) *ср* dog-breeding.

соба́чий (-ья, -ье, -ьи) *прил* (*лай, нюх*) dog's; **~ья жизнь** (*разг*) it's a dog's life; **на у́лице хо́лод ~** (*разг*) it's blooming cold outside.

соба́чник (-а) *м* (*ловящий собак*) dog-catcher; (*разг: любитель собак*) dog-lover.

собезья́нничa|ть (-ю) *сов от* обезья́нничать.

соберу́(сь) *итп сов см* собра́ть(ся).

собе́с (-а) *м сокр* (= *социа́льное обеспе́чение*) social security; (*учреждение*) ≈ social security department.

собесе́дник (-а) *м* interlocutor; **мой ~ замолча́л** the person I was telling to fell silent.

собесе́дниц|а (-ы) *ж см* собесе́дник.

собесе́дование (-я) *ср* interview.

собира́ни|е (-я) *ср* (*материала, данных итп*) collection, gathering; (*коллекционирование*) collecting; (*ягод, грибов*) picking; **~ ма́рок** *итп*

stamp *итп* collecting.

собира́телен *прил см* собира́тельный.

собира́тель (-я) *м* collector.

собира́тел|ьный (-ен, -ьна, -ьно) *прил* (*также линг*) collective.

собира́|ть (-ю) *несов от* собра́ть

▶ **собира́ться** *несов от* собра́ться ♦ *возв*: **~юсь пойти́ туда́** I'm going to go there.

собко́р (-а) *м сокр* = *со́бственный корреспонде́нт*: **э́то сообще́ние от на́шего ~а в Москве́** this report is from our own correspondent in Moscow.

собла́зн (-а) *м* temptation; **устоя́ть** (*perf*) **пе́ред ~ом** *или* **про́тив ~а** to resist temptation; **вводи́ть (ввести́** *perf*) **кого́-н в ~** to tempt sb.

соблазни́тель (-я) *м* seducer.

соблазни́тел|ьный (-ен, -ьна, -ьно) *прил* tempting; (*женщина*) seductive.

соблазни́|ть (-ю́, -и́шь; *impf* соблазня́ть) *сов перех* to seduce; (*прельстить*): **~ кого́-н чем-н** to tempt sb with sth

▶ **соблазни́ться** (*impf* соблазня́ться) *сов возв*: **~ся** +*instr*/+*infin* to be tempted by/to do.

соблюда́|ть (-ю) *несов от* соблюсти́ ♦ *перех* (*дисциплину, порядок*) to maintain; **"~йте чистоту́"** "please keep this area tidy".

соблю|сти́ (-ду́, -дёшь) *сов от* блюсти́ ♦ (*impf* соблюда́ть) *перех* (*закон, правила*) to observe.

соболе́знование (-я) *ср* condolences *мн*; **выража́ть (вы́разить** *perf*) **кому́-н ~** to express one's condolences to sb.

соболе́зн|овать (-ую) *несов неперех*: **кому́-н** to condole with sb.

со́бол|ь (-оля; *nom pl* -оля́) *м* sable.

собо́р (-а) *м* cathedral; (*съезд*) council (*of churches*).

собо́р|ный *прил* (*здание, колокол*) cathedral *опред*; **~ое постановле́ние** decree of the church council.

СОБР *сокр* (= *Сво́дный отря́д бы́строго реаги́рования*) flying squad.

собра́ни|е (-я) *ср* (*партийное, профсоюзное*) meeting; (*представителей*) assembly; (*картин итп*) collection; **собра́ние сочине́ний** collected works *мн*.

собра́н|ный (-, -на, -но) *прил* self-disciplined.

собра́|ть (-еру́, -ерёшь; *pt* -ра́л, -рала́, -ра́ло, *impf* собира́ть) *сов перех* to gather (together); (*ягоды, грибы*) to pick; (*урожай*) to gather; (*станок, приёмник итп*) to assemble; (*марки, налоги, подписи*) to collect; (*перен: мужество*) to muster up; (: *силы*) to summon; (*приготовить*): **~ кого́-н в** +*acc* (*в школу итп*) to get sb ready for; **собира́ть (~** *perf*) **чемода́н/ве́щи** to pack one's suitcase/things

▶ **собра́ться** (*impf* собира́ться) *сов возв* (*гости, делегаты*) to assemble, gather; (*в экспедицию, на урок итп*) to get ready to go; (*приготовиться*): **~ся** +*infin* to get ready to do; **собира́ться (~ся** *perf*) **с** +*instr* (*с силами, с мыслями*) to gather; **собира́ться (~ся** *perf*) **с** ду́хом to pluck up the courage; **ты куда́ ~ра́лся?** where were you going?; **то́лько ~ра́лся лечь, как зазвони́л телефо́н** I was about to go to bed when the telephone rang.

со́бственник (-а) м (*владе́лец*) owner.

со́бственниц|а (-ы) ж см **со́бственник**.

со́бственническ|ий (-ая, -ое, -ие) *прил* proprietorial.

со́бственно *част* actually ♦ *вводн сл*: ~ (**говоря́**) as a matter of fact.

собственнору́чный *прил* (*распи́ска*) own.

со́бственност|ь (-и) ж (*иму́щество*) property; (*владе́ние*) ownership; ~ **на** +*acc* right of ownership of; **быть** (*impf*) *или* **находи́ться** (*impf*) **в чьей-н ~ю** to be in sb's possession; **приобрета́ть (приобрести́** *perf*) **в ~ что-н** to become the owner of sth.

со́бственн|ый *прил* (one's) own; **по ~ому жела́нию** of one's own volition; **и́мя ~ое** proper name; **чу́вство ~ого досто́инства** self-respect; **со́бственный корреспонде́нт** см **собко́р**.

собуты́льник (-а) м (*разг: пренебр*) drinking mate (*BRIT*) *или* buddy (*US*).

собы́ти|е (-я) *ср* event.

собью́(сь) *итп сов см* **сби́ть(ся)**.

сов|а́ (-ы́; *nom pl* -ы) ж owl.

сова́ть (**сую́, суёшь;** *perf* **су́нуть**) *несов перех* to put in; ~ (**су́нуть** *perf*) **нос во что-н** to poke one's nose into sth.

▸ **сова́ться** (*perf* **су́нуться**) *несов возв* (*разг: лезть*): ~**ся вперёд** to push through; ~**ся (су́нуться** *perf*) **не в своё де́ло** to poke one's nose into other people's business.

сов|ёнок (-ёнка; *nom pl* -я́та, *gen pl* -я́т) м owlet.

соверша́ть(ся) (-ю(сь)) *несов от* **соверши́ть(ся)**.

соверше́нен *прил см* **соверше́нный**.

соверше́ни|е (-я) *ср* (*сде́лки*) conclusion; (*преступле́ния*) commission.

соверше́нно *нареч* (*игра́ть, исполня́ть*) perfectly; (*совсе́м*) absolutely, completely; **у меня́ ~ нет сил** I have absolutely no energy; **э́то ~ ве́рно** it's absolutely *или* completely true.

совершенноле́ти|е (-я) *ср*: **дости́гнуть ~я** to come of age.

совершенноле́тн|ий (-яя, -ее, -ие) *прил*: **стать ~им** to come of age.

соверше́нн|ый (-ен, -на, -но) *прил* (*безукори́зненный*) perfect; (*абсолю́тный*) absolute, complete; **соверше́нный вид** perfective aspect.

соверше́нств|о (-а) *ср* perfection; **доводи́ть (довести́** *perf*) **что-н до ~а** to do sth to perfection; **в ~е владе́ть** (*impf*) **чем-н** to have a perfect command of sth.

соверше́нств|овать (-ую; *perf* **усоверше́нствовать**) *несов перех* to improve

▸ **соверше́нствоваться** (*perf* **усоверше́нствоваться**) *несов возв*: ~**ся в** +*prp* to improve.

соверш|и́ть (-у́, -и́шь; *impf* **соверша́ть**) *сов перех* to make; (*сде́лку*) to conclude; (*преступле́ние, просту́пок итп*) to commit; (*богослуже́ние, обря́д, по́двиг*) to perform

▸ **соверши́ться** (*impf* **соверша́ться**) *сов возв* to take place.

со́вестлив|ый (-, -а, -о) *прил* conscientious.

со́вестно *как сказ*: **мне ~** +*infin* ... I am ashamed to do; **как ему́ не ~!** he ought to be ashamed of himself!

со́вест|ь (-и) ж conscience; **на ~** (*сде́ланный*) very well; **по ~и говоря́** to be honest; **поступа́ть (поступи́ть** *perf*) **по ~и** to behave as one's conscience dictates; **со споко́йной ~ю** with a clear conscience.

сове́т (-а) м advice *то́лько ед*; (*семе́йный*) discussion; (*вое́нный*) council; (*ИСТ*) Soviet; **учёный ~** academic council; **С~ Безопа́сности ООН** United Nations Security Council; **дава́ть (дать** *perf*) **кому́-н ~** to give sb advice; **держа́ть** (*impf*) ~ to hold a council.

сове́тник (-а) м (*юсти́ции итп*) councillor; (*президе́нта*) adviser.

сове́т|овать (-ую; *perf* **посове́товать**) *несов непере*: ~ **кому́-н** +*infin* to advise sb to do; ~ (*impf*) **кому́-н что-н** to recommend sth to sb

▸ **сове́товаться** (*perf* **посове́товаться**) *несов возв*: ~**ся с кем-н** (*с дру́гом*) to ask sb's advice; (*с врачо́м, с юри́стом*) to consult sb.

сове́тск|ий (-ая, -ое, -ие) *прил* Soviet.

сове́тчик (-а) м confidant(e); **в да́нном вопро́се я тебе́ не ~** I can't advise you on this subject.

совеща́ни|е (-я) *ср* (*собра́ние*) meeting; (*конфере́нция*) conference.

совеща́тельный *прил* (*о́рган, го́лос*) consultative.

совеща́ться (-юсь) *несов возв* to deliberate.

Совинформбюро́ *ср нескл сокр* (*ИСТ*) = *Сове́тское информацио́нное бюро́*.

совка́ *итп сущ см* **сово́к**.

совко́в|ый *прил*: ~**ая лопа́та** shovel.

совлада́|ть (-ю) *сов непере*: ~ **с** +*instr* to control; ~ (*perf*) **с собо́й** to control o.s.

совладе́л|ец (-ьца) м joint owner.

совладе́ни|е (-я) *ср* joint ownership.

совме́стен *прил см* **совме́стный**.

совмести́мост|ь (-и) ж compatibility.

совмести́м|ый (-, -а, -о) *прил* compatible.

совмести́тельств|о (-а) *ср*: **я рабо́таю по ~у** секретарём my second job is as a secretary.

совме|сти́ть (-щу́, -сти́шь; *impf* **совмеща́ть**) *сов перех* to combine; **он ~ща́л в себе́ учёного и администра́тора** he was both a scholar and an administrator.

совме́стно *нареч (работать, решать итп)* jointly; ~ **с** +*instr* jointly with.

совме́ст|ный (-ен, -на, -но) *прил (общий)* joint; **совме́стное предприя́тие** joint venture.

совмеща́|ть (-ю) *несов от* **совмести́ть** ♦ *перех (две должности)* to combine.

совмеще́ни|е (-я) *ср* combining.

совмещу́ *сов см* **совмести́ть**.

сов|о́к (-ка́) *м (для мусора)* dustpan; *(для муки)* scoop; *(строительный)* shovel.

совоку́пен *прил см* **совоку́пный**.

совоку́пност|ь (-и) *ж (факторов, причин)* combination; **в ~и** in total.

совоку́п|ный (-ен, -на, -но) *прил (усилие)* combined, joint.

совпада́|ть (3sg -ет, 3pl -ют) *несов от* **совпа́сть**.

совпаде́ни|е (-я) *ср (событий, обстоятельств)* coincidence; *(данных, цифр)* tallying; *(интересов, мнений)* meeting.

совпа́|сть (3sg -дёт, 3pl -ду́т, impf совпада́ть) *сов неперех (события)* to coincide; *(данные, цифры итп)* to agree; *(интересы, мнения)* to meet.

соврати́тел|ь (-я) *м* seducer.

совра|ти́ть (-щу́, -ти́шь; impf совраща́ть) *сов перех (сбить с пути)* to lead astray; *(женщину)* to seduce.

совр|а́ть (-у́, -ёшь) *сов от* **врать**.

совраща́|ть (-ю) *несов от* **соврати́ть**.

совращу́ *сов см* **соврати́ть**.

совреме́нен *прил см* **совреме́нный**.

совреме́нник (-а) *м* contemporary.

совреме́нниц|а (-ы) *ж см* **совреме́нник**.

совреме́нно *нареч (одеваться)* fashionably; *(звучать)* modern.

совреме́нност|ь (-и) *ж (взглядов, идей)* progressiveness; *(современная эпоха)* the present day.

совреме́н|ный *прил* contemporary; **(-ен, -на, -но;** *техника)* up-to-date; *(человек, идеи)* modern.

совсе́м *нареч (новый, негодный итп)* completely; *(молодой)* very; *(нисколько: не пригодный, не нужный)* totally; **не ~** *(не вполне)* not quite.

совхо́з (-а) *м сокр (= сове́тское хозя́йство)* Sovkhoz *(state farm in the Soviet Union)*.

совью́(сь) *итп сов см* **свить(ся)**.

совя́та *итп сущ см* **совёнок**.

согла́сен *прил см* **согла́сный**.

согла́си|е (-я) *ср* consent; *(в семье)* harmony, accord; **в ~и с** +*instr (с человеком)* in agreement with; **с чьего́-н ~я** with sb's consent; **дава́ть (дать** *perf)* **~ на что-н** to give one's consent to sth; **приходи́ть (прийти́** *perf)* **к ~ю** to come to an agreement; **жить** *(impf)* **в ~и** to live in harmony.

согла|си́ться (-шу́сь, -си́шься; impf соглаша́ться) *сов возв:* **~ на что-н**/+*infin* to agree to sth/to do; **~** *(perf)* **с** +*instr (с мнением, с высказыванием)* to agree with; **~** *(perf)* **на чём-н** *(раза)* to agree on sth.

согла́сно *нареч (жить, работать)* in harmony ♦ *предл:* **~** +*dat или* **с** +*instr* in accordance with.

согла́с|ный *прил:* **~ звук** consonant ♦ *(-ного; decl like adj)* *м* consonant; **(-ен, -на, -но;** *дающий согласие):* **~ на** +*acc (на условия, на ограничения)* agreeable to; **Вы ~ны (со мной)?** do you agree (with me)?; **все ~ны?** are we all agreed?; **я не ~ен** +*infin* ... I am not prepared to ....

согласова́ни|е (-я) *ср (действий, мер)* coordinating; *(обсуждение: плана)* coordination.

согласо́ван|ный (-, -на, -но) *прил (политика)* concerted; *(стратегия)* agreed.

согласо́в|ать (-ую; impf согласо́вывать) *сов перех (усилия, действия)* to coordinate; *(обговорить):* **~ что-н с** +*instr (план, цену)* to agree sth with; **~** *(perf)* **что-н с чем-н** *(спрос с предложением)* to make sth meet sth; *(прилагательное с существительным)* to make sth agree with sth.

▶ **согласова́ться** *(не)сов возв:* **~ся с** +*instr* to correspond with.

соглаша́|ться (-юсь) *несов от* **согласи́ться**.

соглаше́ни|е (-я) *ср* agreement; **приходи́ть (прийти́** *perf)* **к ~ю** to come to an agreement; **заключа́ть (заключи́ть** *perf)* **~** to conclude an agreement.

соглашу́сь *сов см* **согласи́ться**.

согн|а́ть (сгоню́, сго́нишь; pt -а́л, -ала́, -а́ло, impf сгоня́ть) *сов перех (заставить удалиться)* to drive away; *(собрать)* to round up; **сгоня́ть** *(~ perf)* **улы́бку с лица́** to wipe a smile off somebody's face.

согн|у́ть (-у́, -ёшь) *сов от* **гнуть, сгиба́ть**.

согра́жданин (-аждани́на; *nom pl* **-а́ждане,** *gen pl* **-а́ждан)** *м* fellow citizen.

согрева́ни|е (-я) *ср (воды, пищи)* heating up; *(тела)* warming up.

согре́|ть (-ю; impf согрева́ть) *сов перех (воду)* to heat up; *(землю, ноги, руки)* to warm up; *(подлеж: мысль, ласка)* to warm

▶ **согре́ться** *(impf согрева́ться)* *сов возв (вода)* to heat up; *(человек, печка)* to warm up.

согреш|и́ть (-у́, -и́шь) *сов от* **греши́ть**.

со́д|а (-ы) *ж* soda; **питьева́я ~** bicarbonate of soda.

соде́йстви|е (-я) *ср* assistance.

соде́йств|овать (-ую) *(не)сов неперех* (+*dat)* to assist.

содержа́ни|е (-я) *ср (семьи, детей)* upkeep; *(магазина, фермы)* keeping; *(книги, статьи)* contents *мн;* *(человека: под арестом)* holding; *(сахара, витаминов)* content; *(заработная плата)* allowance; *(оглавление)* contents *мн;* **о́тпуск без ~я** unpaid leave.

содержа́телен *прил см* **содержа́тельный**.

содержа́тел|ь (-я) *м (ресторана)* owner; *(магазина, пансиона)* keeper.

содержа́тел|ьный (-ен, -ьна, -ьно) *прил* (*статья, докла́д*) informative.

содержа́ть (-ержу́, -е́ржишь) *несов перех* (*дете́й, роди́телей, магази́н*) to keep; (*рестора́н*) to own; (*са́хар, оши́бки, информа́цию итп*) to contain; (*челове́ка: под аре́стом*) to hold; ~ (*impf*) что-н в чистоте́/в поря́дке to keep sth clean/in order

▸ **содержа́ться** *несов возв* (*под аре́стом*) to be held; в кни́ге ~е́ржится интере́сная информа́ция the book contains interesting information; ~ся (*impf*) в чистоте́/в поря́дке to be kept clean/in order.

содержи́м|ое (-ого) *decl like adj ср* (*ба́нки, су́мки итп*) contents *мн*.

со́довый *прил* (*раство́р*) soda *опред*.

содр|а́ть (сдеру́, сдерёшь; *pt* -а́л, -ала́, -а́ло, *impf* **сдира́ть**) *сов перех* (*слой, оде́жду*) to tear off; ~ (*perf*) ко́жу с чего́-н to skin sth; ~ (*perf*) что-н с кого́-н (*разг: до́рого взять*) to sting sb for sth.

содрога́ни|е (-я) *ср* (*стен, стёкол*) shaking; (*от бо́ли, от у́жаса*) shuddering.

содрога́ться (-ю́сь; *perf* **содрогну́ться**) *несов возв* (*сте́ны, земля́*) to shake; (*от бо́ли, от стра́ха итп*) to shudder.

содру́жеств|о (-а) *ср* (*дру́жба*) cooperation; (*сою́з*) commonwealth; **Содру́жество Незави́симых Госуда́рств** the Commonwealth of Independent States.

со́евый *прил* soya *опред*.

соедине́ни|е (-я) *ср* (*сил*) joining; (*проводо́в*) connection; (*учёбы с рабо́той*) combination; (*ме́сто соедине́ния*) contact; (*ВОЕН*) formation.

соедини́тел|ь (-я) *м* (*ЭЛЕК*) adaptor.

соедини́тельный *прил* (*про́вод, труба́*) connecting.

соедин|и́ть (-ю́, -и́шь; *impf* **соединя́ть**) *сов перех* (*си́лы, уси́лия, дета́ли*) to join; (*люде́й*) to unite; (*провода́, тру́бы, по телефо́ну*) to connect; (*установи́ть сообще́ние*) to link; (*сочета́ть*): ~ что-н с +*instr* to combine sth with; в ней ~ены́ ум и красота́ she is both clever and beautiful

▸ **соедини́ться** (*impf* **соединя́ться**) *сов возв* (*лю́ди, отря́ды*) to join together; ~ся (*perf*) с кем to make contact with sb.

сожале́ни|е (-я) *ср* (*сострада́ние*) pity; ~ (о +*prp*) (*о про́шлом, о поте́ре*) regret (about); к ~ю unfortunately; к мо́ему (вели́кому *или* глубо́кому) ~ю to my (great *или* deep) regret.

сожале́|ть (-ю) *несов неперех*: ~ (о +*prp*) (*об оши́бке, о просту́пке*) to regret.

сожгу́ *итп сов см* **сжечь.**

сожже́ни|е (-я) *ср* (*еретика́*) burning.

сожи́тел|ь (-я) *м* cohabiter.

сожи́тельниц|а (-ы) *ж см* **сожи́тель.**

сожму́(сь) *итп сов см* **сжа́ть(ся).**

сожну́ *итп сов см* **сжать.**

сожр|а́ть (-у́, -ёшь) *сов от* **жрать.**

созва́нива|ться (-юсь) *несов см* **созвони́ться.**

соз|ва́ть (-ову́, -овёшь; *pt* -ва́л, -вала́, -ва́ло, *impf* **сзыва́ть**) *сов перех* (*пригласи́ть*) to summon; (*impf* **созыва́ть**; *съезд, конфере́нцию итп*) to convene.

созве́зди|е (-я) *ср* constellation.

созвон|и́ться (-ю́сь, -и́шься; *impf* **созва́ниваться**) *сов возв*: ~ с +*instr* to phone (*BRIT*) *или* call (*US*); (*договори́ться*): нам на́до ~ we should fix something over the phone.

созву́чен *прил см* **созву́чный.**

созву́чи|е (-я) *ср* (*МУЗ*) sonority.

созву́ч|ный (-ен, -на, -но) *прил* harmonious; (*слова́*) assonant; ~но +*dat* (*соотве́тствующий*) in keeping with; ~но с +*instr* in keeping with.

созда|ва́ть(ся) (-ю́(сь), -ёшь(ся)) *несов от* **созда́ть(ся).**

созда́м(ся) *итп сов см* **созда́ть(ся).**

созда́ни|е (-я) *ср* creation; (*шко́лы*) foundation; (*челове́к, живо́тное*) creature.

созда́ст(ся) *сов см* **созда́ть(ся).**

созда́тел|ь (-я) *м* creator; (*шко́лы*) founder.

созда́тельниц|а (-ы) *ж см* **созда́тель.**

созда́ть (*как* **дать**; *см* **Table 14**; *impf* **создава́ть**) *сов перех* to create; (*шко́лу*) to found

▸ **созда́ться** (*impf* **создава́ться**) *сов возв* (*обстано́вка*) to emerge; (*впечатле́ние*) to be created.

созерца́ни|е (-я) *ср* (*рассма́тривание*) contemplation; (*душе́вное*) reflection.

созерца́|ть (-ю) *несов перех* (*рассма́тривать*) to contemplate.

созида́тельный (-ен, -ьна, -ьно) *прил* creative.

созна|ва́ть (-ю́, -ёшь) *несов от* **созна́ть ♦** *перех* to be aware of; ~ (*impf*), что ... to realize that ...

▸ **сознава́ться** *несов от* **созна́ться.**

созна́ни|е (-я) *ср* consciousness; (*вины́, до́лга*) awareness; **приходи́ть (прийти́** *perf*) **в** ~ to come round; **теря́ть (потеря́ть** *perf*) ~ to lose consciousness; он рабо́тал до поте́ри ~я he worked himself senseless.

созна́телен *прил см* **созна́тельный.**

созна́тельност|ь (-и) *ж* (*полити́ческая, социа́льная*) awareness.

созна́тел|ьный (-ен, -ьна, -ьно) *прил* (*жизнь, во́зраст*) conscious; (*отноше́ние, челове́к*) intelligent; (*обма́н, посту́пок*) deliberate, intentional.

созна́|ть (-ю; *impf* **сознава́ть**) *сов перех* (*вину́, до́лг*) to realize

▸ **созна́ться** (*impf* **сознава́ться**) *сов возв*: ~ся (в +*prp*) (*в оши́бке, в како́м-н наме́рении*) to admit (to); (*преступник*) to confess (to); **на́до ~ся** admittedly.

созову́ *итп сов см* **созва́ть**.

созрева́|ть (**-ю**) *несов неперех* = **зреть**.

созре́|ть (**-ю**) *сов от* **зреть**.

созы́в (**-а**) *м* (*съезда, собрания*) calling.

созыва́|ть (**-ю**) *несов от* **созва́ть**.

СОИ *ж сокр* (= *стратеги́ческая оборо́нная инициати́ва*) SDI (*US*) (= *Strategic Defense Initiative*).

соизмери́м|ый (**-**, **-а**, **-о**) *прил* (*величины*) proportional; (*поня́тия, це́нности*) comparable.

соизме́р|ить (**-ю**, **-ишь**; *impf* **соизмеря́ть**) *сов перех* to compare.

соиска́ни|е (**-я**) *ср*: **на ~ чего-н** pursuing sth.

соиска́тел|ь (**-я**) *м* (*приза, награды*) competitor; (*учёной степени*) candidate.

сойти́ (*как* **идти́**; *см* **Table 18**; *impf* **сходи́ть**) *сов неперех* (*с горы, с ле́стницы*) to go down; (*с доро́ги*) to leave; (*подлеж: краска, загар итп*) to come off; (*разг*): **~ +instr** (*с по́езда, с автобуса*) to get off: **~** (*perf*) **за +acc** (*за актёра, за богача*) to pass as; **сходи́ть** (**~** *perf*) **с ума́** to go mad; **фильм ~шёл с экра́на** the film is not shown anymore; **с ума́ сойдёшь** или **~** (*разг*) the mind boggles; **всё ~шло благополу́чно** everything's turned out well; **~йдёт (и так)** (*разг*) it will do (as it is); **ему́ всё схо́дит с рук** he gets away with everything

▸ **сойти́сь** (*impf* **сходи́ться**) *сов возв* (*встре́титься*) to meet; (*собра́ться*) to gather; (*ци́фры, показа́ния*) to tally; (*перен*): **~сь с +instr** (*подружи́ться*) to become friendly with; **~шли́сь на том, что ...** it was agreed that ...; **~сь** (*perf*) **во взгля́дах/во вку́сах** (*перен*) to have similar views/tastes; **сходи́ться** (**~сь** *perf*) **на цене́/усло́виях** to agree on a price/conditions; **~сь** (*perf*) **хара́ктерами** to get on.

сок (**-а**; *part gen* **-у**, *loc sg* **-ý**) *м* juice; (*также: фрукто́вый ~*) (fruit) juice.

соковыжима́л|ка (**-ки**; *gen pl* **-ок**) *ж* juice extractor.

со́кол (**-а**) *м* falcon.

соколёнок (**-ёнка**; *nom pl* **-я́та**, *gen pl* **-я́т**) *ж* falcon chick.

соколи́н|ый *прил* (*гнездо*) falcon´s *опред*; **~ая охо́та** falconry.

соколя́та *итп сущ см* **соколёнок**.

сократи́ть (**-щу́**, **-ти́шь**; *impf* **сокраща́ть**) *сов перех* (*путь, рабо́чий день, статью́*) to shorten; (*расхо́ды*) to cut down, reduce

▸ **сократи́ться** (*impf* **сокраща́ться**) *сов возв* (*расстоя́ние, сро́ки*) to be shortened; (*расхо́ды, снабже́ние*) to be reduced.

сокраще́ни|е (**-я**) *ср* (*см глаг*) shortening; cutting down, reduction; (*сокращённое назва́ние*) abbreviation; (*также:~ шта́тов*) staff reduction; **попада́ть** (**попа́сть** *perf*) **под ~** (*шта́тов*) to be made redundant.

сокращённый *прил* (*вариант те́кста*) abridged; (*рабо́чий день*) shortened; (*слово*)

abbreviated.

сокращу́(сь) *сов см* **сократи́ть(ся)**.

сокрове́нн|ый (**-ен**, **-на**, **-но**) *прил* (*мы́сли итп*) innermost; (*смысл, мечта́*) intimate.

сокро́вищ|е (**-а**) *ср* (*обычно мн: также перен*) treasure.

сокро́вищниц|а (**-ы**) *ж* (*место*) treasury; (*совоку́пность*) **~ +gen** wealth.

сокруша́|ть (**-ю**) *несов от* **сокруши́ть**

▸ **сокруша́ться** *несов возв* (*огорча́ться*) to be distressed.

сокруше́ни|е (**-я**) *ср* (*проти́вника*) destruction; (*огорче́ние*) distress.

сокруши́тельн|ый (**-ен**, **-ьна**, **-ьно**) *прил* devastating.

сокруш|и́ть (**-ý**, **-и́шь**; *impf* **сокруша́ть**) *сов перех* (*а́рмию*) to crush; (*режим*) to overthrow.

соку́рсник (**-а**) *м*: **он мой ~** he is in my year.

соку́рсниц|а (**-ы**) *ж*: **она́ моя́ ~** she is in my year.

солга́ть (**-гу́**, **-жёшь** *итп*, **-гу́т**) *сов от* **лгать**.

солда́т (**-а**) *м* soldier.

солда́тик (**-а**) *м уменьш от* **солда́т**; (*игру́шка*) toy soldier.

солда́т|ка (**-ки**; *gen pl* **-ок**) *ж* soldier's wife (*мн* wives).

солда́тск|ий (**-ая**, **-ое**, **-ие**) *прил* soldier's.

солдафо́н (**-а**) *м* (*разг: пренебр*) squaddie.

соле́ни|е (**-я**) *ср* (*огурцо́в*) pickling; (*ры́бы*) salting.

солёно|е (**-ого**; *decl like adj*) *ср* salty food.

солён|ый *прил* (*ве́тер*) salty; (*о́вощи*) pickled in brine; (*вода́*) salt *опред*; (*ры́ба*) salted; (**-он**, **-она́**, **-оно**; *пи́ща*) salty.

соле́нь|е (**-я**) *ср* (*обычно мн*) ≈ pickle.

солжёшь *итп сов см* **солга́ть**.

солида́рен *прил см* **солида́рный**.

солида́рност|ь (**-и**) *ж* solidarity.

солида́рн|ый (**-ен**, **-на**, **-но**) *прил*: **я с ним ~ен** I am on his side.

соли́дн|ый (**-ен**, **-на**, **-но**) *прил* (*постро́йка*) solid; (*зна́ния, рабо́та*) sound; (*фи́рма, специали́ст*) established; (*челове́к, мане́ры*) respectable; (*ме́бель, оде́жда*) quality; **~ во́зраст** respectable age.

соли́р|овать (**-ую**) *несов* to play a solo part.

соли́ст (**-а**) *м* soloist.

соли́ст|ка (**-ки**; *gen pl* **-ок**) *ж см* **соли́ст**.

сол|и́ть (**-ю́**, **-ишь**; *perf* **посоли́ть**) *несов перех* (*суп, ра́гу*) to salt; (*заса́ливать*) to preserve in brine.

со́лнечный *прил* (*эне́ргия, лучи́ итп*) solar; (**-ен**, **-на**, **-но**; *день, пого́да*) sunny; **со́лнечное сплете́ние** solar plexus; **со́лнечный уда́р** sunstroke; **со́лнечные очки́** sunglasses.

со́лнц|е (**-а**) *ср* sun.

солнцезащи́тный *прил*: **~ крем** suncream.

солнцепёк (**-а**) *м*: **на ~е** in a sunny spot.

солнцестоя́ни|е (**-я**) *ср* solstice.

со́ло *ср нескл нареч* solo.

солове́й (**-ья́**) *м* nightingale.

соловёть (-ю; *perf* **осоловёть**) *несов неперех* (*разг*) to become dazed.

соловьиный *прил* nightingale *опред*.

соловья *итп сущ см* **соловей**.

солод (-а) *м* malt.

соломʹ|а (-ы) *ж* straw.

соломенный *прил* (*шляпа*) straw *опред*; (*крыша*) thatched; (*цвет*) straw-coloured (*BRIT*), straw-colored (*US*).

соломин|а (-ы) *ж* straw.

соломин|ка (-ки; *gen pl* -ок) *ж уменьш от* **соломина**; (*перен*): **хвата́ться за ~ку** to clutch at straws.

соломʹ|ка (-ки; *gen pl* -ок) *ж уменьш от* **солома**; (*печенье*) long thin biscuit or bread stick.

солон *итп прил см* **солёный**.

солонʹ|ка (-ки; *gen pl* -ок) *ж* saltcellar.

солонча́к (-а́) *м* saltmarsh.

сол|ь (-и) *ж* salt; (*gen pl* -е́й; *хим*) salt; (*перен*): ~ +*gen* (*вопроса, рассказа*) point of ♦ *ср нескл* (*муз*) soh; **столо́вая ~** table salt.

со́льный *прил* solo *опред*.

солью́(сь) *итп сов см* **слить(ся)**.

соля́н|ка (-ки; *gen pl* -ок) *ж* spicy meat and vegetable soup; (*рагу*) ragout.

соляно́й *прил* (*раствор*) saline; (*промысел, залежи*) salt *опред*.

соля́нок *сущ см* **соля́нка**.

сом (-а́) *м* catfish.

Сома́ли *ср нескл* Somalia.

сомкнʹу́ть (-у́, -ёшь; *impf* **смыка́ть**) *сов перех* to close; **я глаз не ~у́л всю ночь** I didn't sleep a wink all night

▸ **сомкну́ться** (*impf* **смыка́ться**) *сов возв* to close.

сомнева́ться (-юсь) *несов возв*: ~ (**в** +*prp*) to doubt; **~юсь, что э́то пра́вда** I doubt that is true; **не ~йся приду́** don't worry, I'll come.

сомне́ние (-я) *ср* (*неуверенность*) doubt; **вне** *или* **без (вся́кого) ~я** without a doubt; **брать** (**взять** *perf*) **что-н под ~** to doubt sth.

сомни́телен *прил см* **сомни́тельный**.

сомни́тельно *как сказ* it's doubtful; ~, **что́бы он согласи́лся** it's doubtful he'll agree; **он придёт?- ~** he's coming? – it's unlikely *или* not likely.

сомни́тель|ный (-ен, -ьна, -ьно) *прил* (*дело, личность*) shady; (*предложение, знакомство*) dubious; (*комплимент, речи*) ambiguous; (*победа*) questionable.

сомну́(сь) *итп сов см* **смять(ся)**.

сон (**сна**) *м* sleep; (*сновидение*) dream; **ви́деть** (**уви́деть** *perf*) **что-н во сне** to have a dream about sth; **ви́деть** (*impf*) ~ to have a dream; **сквозь ~ слы́шать** (**услы́шать** *perf*) to hear in one's sleep; **со сна́** half-awake.

сона́т|а (-ы) *ж* sonata.

соне́т (-а) *м* sonnet.

сонли́вый *прил* sleepy.

со́нн|ый *прил* (*заспанный*) sleepy, somnolent; (*вялый*) drowsy; **~ые виде́ния** dreams.

со́нʹ|я (-и) *ж* (*животное*) dormouse (*мн* dormice) ♦ *м/ж* (*разг*) sleepyhead.

сообража́|ть (-ю) *несов от* **сообрази́ть** ♦ *неперех* (*разг*: **быть сообрази́тельным**) to be quick; (*смыслить*): ~ **в** +*prp* to be good at; **я сего́дня пло́хо ~ю** I'm slow on the uptake today.

соображе́ни|е (-я) *ср* (*суждение*) reasoning; (*обычно мн*: *мотивы*) reason; **из фина́нсовых/педагоги́ческих ~й** for financial/educational reasons.

соображу́ *сов см* **сообрази́ть**.

сообрази́тель|ный (-ен, -ьна, -ьно) *прил* bright.

сообрази́ть (-жу́, -зи́шь; *impf* **сообража́ть**) *сов неперех* to work out; **нам на́до ~, что де́лать да́льше** we've got to work out what to do next.

сообра́зно *предл*: ~ +*dat или* **с** +*instr* in accordance with.

сообра́зный *прил*: ~ **с** +*instr* in agreement with.

сообща́ *нареч* together.

сообща́|ть (-ю) *несов от* **сообщи́ть**

▸ **сообща́ться** *несов от* **сообщи́ться** ♦ *возв*: **~ся с** +*instr* (*связываться*) to communicate with.

сообще́ни|е (-я) *ср* (*действие*: *новостей, результатов*) reporting; (*по радио*) report; (*правительственное*) announcement; (*срочное*) communication; (*автобусное, почтовое*) communications *мн*; **~ об оши́бке** (*комп*) error message.

сообще́ств|о (-а) *ср* association; **в ~е с** +*instr* in association with; **мирово́е** *или* **междунаро́дное ~** international community.

сообщи́ть (-у́, -и́шь; *impf* **сообща́ть**) *сов неперех*: ~ **кому́-н о** +*prp* to inform sb of ♦ *перех* (*новости, тайну*) to tell

▸ **сообщи́ться** (*impf* **сообща́ться**) *сов возв* (+*dat*) to be communicated to.

сообщник (-а) *м* accomplice.

сообщница (-ы) *ж см* **сообщник**.

сооруди́ть (-жу́, -ди́шь; *impf* **сооружа́ть**) *сов перех* (*построить*) to erect; (*разг*: смастери́ть) to put together; (: *ужин, выпить*) to knock up.

сооружа́|ть (-ю) *несов от* **сооруди́ть**.

сооруже́ни|е (-я) *ср* (*действие*: *здания*) erection; (*крупная постройка*) structure.

сооружу́ *сов см* **сооруди́ть**.

соотве́тственно *нареч* (*как следует*) accordingly ♦ *предл*: ~ +*dat* (*обстановке*) according to; ~ **с** +*instr* in accordance with.

соотве́тственный (-, -на, -но) *прил* (*оплата*) appropriate; (*результаты*) fitting.

соотве́тстви|е (-я) *ср* (*интересов, стилей*

итп) conformity; **в ~и с** +*instr* in accordance with.

соотве́тств|овать (-ую) *несов неперех*: ~ +*dat* (*интере́сам, до́лжности итп*) to correspond with; (*тре́бованиям*) to meet; **э́то не ~ует действи́тельности** it does not correspond with reality.

соотве́тствующ|ий (-ая, -ее, -ие) *прил* appropriate; **~им о́бразом** accordingly.

сооте́чественник (-а) *м* compatriot.

сооте́чественни|ца (-ы) *ж см* **сооте́чественник**

соотн|ести́ (-есу́, -есёшь; *pt* **-ёс, -есла́, -есло́,** *impf* **соотноси́ть)** *сов перех*: ~ **что-н с чем-н** to correlate sth with sth.

соотноси́тельный (-ен, -ьна, -ьно) *прил* correlating.

соотн|оси́ть (-ошу́, -о́сишь) *несов от* **соотнести́**

▶ **соотноси́ться** *несов возв* to correlate.

соотноше́ни|е (-я) *ср* correlation.

соотношу́(сь) *несов см* **соотноси́ть(ся)**.

со́пел *сущ см* **со́пло**.

сопережива́|ть (-ю) *несов неперех* to empathize.

сопе́рник (-а) *м* rival; (*в спо́рте*) competitor.

сопе́рни|ца (-ы) *ж см* **сопе́рник**.

сопе́рнича|ть (-ю) *несов неперех*: ~ **с кем-н в чём-н** to rival sb in sth.

сопе́|ть (-лю́, -и́шь) *несов неперех* to snort.

со́п|ка (-ки; *gen pl* **-ок)** *ж* (*холм*) hill; (*вулка́н*) volcano.

со́пл|и (-е́й) *мн* (*разг*) snot *ед*.

сопли́вый *прил* (*разг: ребёнок*) snotty; **он ещё ~ мальчи́шка!** (*разг*) he's still just a young whippersnapper!

со́п|ло (-ла́; *nom pl* **-ла,** *gen pl* **-ел)** *ср* nozzle.

соплю́ *несов см* **сопе́ть**.

сопо́к *сущ см* **со́пка**.

сопостави́мый (-, -а, -о) *прил* comparable.

сопоста́в|ить (-лю, -ишь; *impf* **сопоставля́ть)** *сов перех*: ~ **что-н (с** +*instr*) to collate sth (with).

сопра́но *ср нескл* soprano.

сопреде́л|ьный (-ен, -ьна, -ьно) *прил* (*о́бласть, страна́ итп*) neighbouring *опред* (*BRIT*), neighboring *опред* (*US*); (*нау́ка, поня́тие*) related.

сопре́|ть (3sg -ет, 3pl -ют) *сов от* **преть**.

соприкаса́|ться (-юсь; *perf* **соприкосну́ться)** *несов возв* (*предме́ты, уча́стки*) to adjoin; (*интере́сы*) to cross over; ~ (**соприкосну́ться** *perf*) **с кем-н** to come into contact with sb.

сопроводи́тел|ь (-я) *м* escort.

сопроводи́тельный *прил* (*докуме́нт*) accompanying *опред*; **сопроводи́тельное письмо́** covering letter.

сопрово|ди́ть (-жу́, -ди́шь; *impf* **сопровожда́ть)** *сов перех* to accompany; (*по impf*; *допо́лнить*): ~ **что-н чем-н** to attach sth to sth.

сопровожда́|ть (-ю) *несов от* **сопроводи́ть** ◆

перех (*расска́з, пе́ние*) to accompany

▶ **сопровожда́ться** *несов возв*: ~**ся** +*instr* to be accompanied by.

сопровожде́ни|е (-я) *ср* (*де́йствие*) escorting; (*аккомпанеме́нт*) accompaniment; **в ~и** +*gen* accompanied by.

сопровожу́ *сов см* **сопроводи́ть**.

сопротивле́ни|е (-я) *ср* resistance; (*ист*) the Resistance; **оказа́ть (ока́зывать** *perf*) ~ **кому́-н** to put up resistance to sb.

сопротивля́емост|ь (-и) *ж* resistance.

сопротивля́|ться (-юсь) *несов возв* (+*dat*) to resist.

сопру́ *итп сов см* **спере́ть**.

сопряжён|ный (-, -а́, -о) *прил*: ~ **с** +*instr* (*с опа́сностями итп*) involving.

сопу́тств|овать (3sg -ует, 3pl -уют) *несов неперех* (+*dat*) to accompany.

сопью́сь *итп сов см* **спи́ться**.

сор (-а; *part gen* **-у)** *м* rubbish; **выноси́ть** (*impf*) ~ **из избы́** (*перен*) to wash one's dirty linen in public.

соразме́рен *прил см* **соразме́рный**.

соразме́р|ить (-ю, -ишь; *impf* **соразмеря́ть)** *сов перех*: ~ **что-н с чем-н** to measure sth against sth.

соразме́р|ный (-ен, -на, -но) *прил*: ~ +*dat* proportionate to; ~**но** +*dat* и́ли **с** +*instr* according to.

соразмеря́|ть (-ю) *несов от* **соразме́рить**.

сора́тник (-а) *м* comrade in arms.

сора́тни|ца (-ы) *ж см* **сора́тник**.

сорван|е́ц (-ца́) *м* (*разг*) scamp.

сорв|а́ть (-у́, -ёшь; *pt* **-а́л, -ала́, -а́ло,** *impf* **срыва́ть)** *сов перех* (*цвето́к, я́блоко*) to pick; (*дверь, кры́шу, оде́жду итп*) to tear off; (*ле́кцию, перегово́ры*) to sabotage; (*пла́ны*) to frustrate; (*разг: аплодисме́нты*) to get; (: *перен*): ~ **что-н на ком-н** (*гнев, зло́бу*) to take sth out on sb; ~ (*perf*) **го́лос** to lose one's voice

▶ **сорва́ться** (*impf* **срыва́ться**) *сов возв*: ~**ся с** +*gen* (*с пе́тель*) to come away from; (*с ле́стницы*) to fall off; (*перен: потеря́ть самооблада́ние*) to lose one's temper; (*пла́ны*) to be frustrated; (*ле́кция*) to have to be cancelled; ~**ся** (*perf*) **с ме́ста** to dash off; **у него́ срыва́лся го́лос** his voice was faltering; **он как с це́пи ~а́лся** (*пренебр*) he's gone completely berserk.

соргиниз|ова́ться (-у́юсь) *сов от* **организова́ться**.

соревнова́ни|е (-я) *ср* competition; **кома́ндные ~я** team event; **отбо́рочные ~я** elimination contests.

соревн|ова́ться (-у́юсь) *несов возв* to compete.

сориенти́р|оваться (-уюсь) *сов от* **ориенти́роваться**.

сори́н|ка (-ки; *gen pl* **-ок)** *ж* speck.

сор|и́ть (-ю́, -и́шь; *perf* **насори́ть)** *несов неперех* to make a mess; ~ (*impf*) **деньга́ми** to throw one's money about *или* around.

со́рный *прил* refuse *опред*; ~**ая трава́** weeds.

сорня́к (-а́) *м* weed.

со́рок (-а́; *см* **Table 28**) *чис* forty; **ему́ за** ~ he's over forty; *см также* **пятьдеся́т**.

соро́ка (-и) *ж* magpie; (*о болтливом человеке*) chatterbox.

сорокале́ти|е (-я) *ср* (*срок*) forty years; (*годовщина события*) fortieth anniversary.

сорокале́тн|ий (-яя, -ее, -ие) *прил* (*период*) forty-year; (*человек*) forty-year-old.

сороков|о́й (-а́я, -о́е, -ы́е) *чис* fortieth; *см также* **пятьдеся́тый**.

сороконо́ж|ка (-ки; *gen pl* -ек) *ж* centipede.

соро́ч|ка (-ки; *gen pl* -ек) *ж* (*мужская*) shirt; **ночна́я** ~ nightgown; **ни́жняя** ~ undergarment.

сорт (-а; *nom pl* -а́) *м* (*товара, продукта*) sort; (*пшеницы*) grade; **пе́рвый** ~ Grade 1; (*перен*) first rate; **това́р пе́рвого со́рта** a Grade 1 product.

сорта́мент (-а) *м* assortment.

сортиро́вальный *прил* sorting *опред*.

сортирова́ть (-у́ю) *несов перех* (*также комп*) to sort; (*по сортам, качеству*) to grade.

сортиро́в|ка (-ки; *gen pl* -ок) *ж* (*см глаг*) sorting; grading.

со́ртный *прил* ≈ Grade A *или* 1 *опред*.

сортово́й *прил* = **со́ртный**.

соса́ть (-у́, -ёшь) *несов перех* to suck; (*младенец, детёныш*) to suckle; **у меня́ ~ёт под ло́жечкой** (*разг*) I've got a sore stomach.

сосва́та|ть (-ю) *сов от* **сва́тать**.

сосе́д (-а; *nom pl* -и, *gen pl* -ей) *м* neighbour (*BRIT*), neighbor (*US*).

сосе́дн|ий (-яя, -ее, -ие) *прил* neighbouring (*BRIT*), neighboring (*US*).

сосе́дств|о (-а) *ср*: **жить по ~у** to live nearby; **в ~е с** +*instr* near.

со́сен *сущ см* **сосна́**.

соси́с|ка (-ки; *gen pl* -ок) *ж* sausage.

со́с|ка (-ки; *gen pl* -ок) *ж* (*на бутылке*) teat; (*пустышка*) dummy.

соска́ *итп сущ см* **сосо́к**.

соска́бллива|ть (-ю) *несов от* **соскобли́ть**.

соска́кива|ть (-ю) *несов от* **соскочи́ть**.

соска́льзыва|ть (-ю) *несов от* **соскользну́ть**.

соскобли́|ть (-ю́, -ишь; *impf* **соска́бливать**) *сов перех* to scrape off.

соскользну́|ть (-у́, -ёшь; *impf* **соска́льзывать**) *сов неперех* (*с горы*) to slide down; (*платок*) to slip off.

соскочи́|ть (-очу́, -о́чишь; *impf* **соска́кивать**) *сов неперех* (*с лошади, с поезда итп*) to jump off; (*с головы, с ноги*) to slip off.

соскреба́|ть (-ю) *несов от* **соскрести́**.

соскре|сти́ (-бу́, -бёшь; *pt* -ёб, -ебла́, -ебло́, *impf* **соскреба́ть**) *сов перех* to scrape away *или* off.

соску́ч|иться (-усь, -ишься) *сов возв* (*в чужом городе*) to be bored; (*затосковать*): ~ **по** +*dat* to miss.

сослага́тельн|ый *прил*: ~**ое наклоне́ние** subjunctive mood.

сосла́|ть (-шлю́, -шлёшь; *impf* **ссыла́ть**) *сов перех* to exile

▸ **сосла́ться** (*impf* **ссыла́ться**) *сов возв*: ~**ся на** +*acc* to refer to.

со́слепу *нареч* (*разг*) being unable to see properly.

сосло́ви|е (-я) *ср* social class.

сосло́вный *прил* class *опред*.

сослужи́в|ец (-ца) *м* colleague.

сослужи́виц|а (-ы) *ж см* **сослужи́вец**.

сослужи́вца *итп сущ см* **сослужи́вец**.

сослуж|и́ть (-у́, -у́жишь) *сов перех*: ~ **слу́жбу кому́-н** (*человек*) to do sb a good turn; (*вещь*) to serve sb well.

сос|на́ (-ны; *nom pl* -ны, *gen pl* -ен) *ж* pine (tree); **заблуди́ться** (*perf*) **в трёх со́снах** (*перен: разг*) to fail to solve a simple problem; **сиби́рская** ~ cedar.

сосно́вый *прил* pine *опред*.

сосн|у́ть (-у́, -ёшь) *сов неперех* to take a nap.

со́сок *сущ см* **со́ска**.

сос|о́к (-ка́) *м* nipple.

сосредота́чива|ть(ся) (-ю(сь)) *несов от* **сосредото́чить(ся)**.

сосредото́ченн|ый (-, -на, -но) *прил* (*атака, взгляд*) concentrated; (*ученик, работник*) attentive.

сосредото́ч|ить (-у, -ишь; *impf* **сосредота́чивать**) *сов перех* (*войска*) to concentrate; (*мысли, внимание*) to concentrate, focus

▸ **сосредото́читься** (*impf* **сосредота́чиваться**) *сов возв* (*войска*) to be concentrated; (*внимание*) to concentrate, focus.

соста́в (-а) *м* (*товарный, пассажирский*) train; (*классовый*) structure; ~ +*gen* (*комитета, комиссии*) members *мн* of; (*вещества*) composition of; **руководя́щий** ~ management (staff); **преподава́тельский** ~ teaching staff; **в ~е** +*gen* among(st); **входи́ть** (*impf*) **в** ~ +*gen* to be a member of; **войти́** (*perf*) **в** ~ +*gen* to become a member of; **гру́ппа верну́лась в по́лном ~е** all members of the group returned; **в ~ делега́ции вошли́** ... the delegation was made up of ...; **коми́ссия в ~е 10 челове́к** a commission consisting of 10 members; **соста́в преступле́ния** (*ЮР*) constitution of a crime.

состави́тель (-я) *м* (*словаря*) compiler; (*сборника*) editor.

соста́в|ить (-лю, -ишь; *impf* **составля́ть**) *сов перех* (*фразу*) to make; (*словарь, список*) to compile; (*план*) to draw up; (*коллекцию, мнение, впечатление*) to form; (*какую-нибудь* сумму) to constitute; (мебель) to put together; ~ (perf) себе имя to make a name for o.s.; составлять (~ perf) кому-н компанию to join sb; составлять (~ perf) себе представление о чём-н to form an impression about sth; это не ~ит большого труда it won't take a lot of effort

▶ **составиться** (impf составляться) сов возв (коллекция, хор, коллектив) to be formed; (мнение, впечатление) to form; у нас ~илось благоприятное мнение о нём we formed a good impression of him.

составление (-я) ср (словаря) compilation; (плана) drawing up; (коллекции) forming; (фразы) making.

составлю(сь) сов см составить(ся).

составлять(ся) (-ю(сь)) несов от составить(ся).

составной прил: ~ая мебель kit furniture; ~ая часть, ~ элемент component.

состарить (-ю, -ишь) сов от старить

▶ **состариться** сов возв (человек) to grow old.

состояние (-я) ср (экономическое, эмоциональное) state; (больного) condition; (собственность) capital; быть (impf) в ~и +infin to be able to do.

состоятельный (-ен, -ьна, -ьно) прил (идея, вывод итп) sound; (богатый) well-off.

состоять (-ю, -ишь) несов неперех: ~ из +gen (книга) to consist of; (квартира) to comprise; (заключаться): ~ в +prp to be; (в партии) to be a member of; (impf) +instr (директором итп) to be; проблема ~ит в том, что ... the problem is that ...

▶ **состояться** несов возв (собрание, концерт) to take place; как учёный, он не ~ялся he didn't make it as a scholar.

сострадание (-я) ср compassion.

состриг итп см состричь.

состригать (-ю) несов от состричь.

состригу итп сов см состричь.

состричь (-ю, -ишь) сов от острить.

состричь (-гу, -жёшь итп, -гут; pt -г, -гла, -гло, impf состригать) сов перех (волосы) to cut off; (шерсть) to shear off.

состроить (-ю, -ишь) сов от строить.

состряпать (-ю) несов от стряпать ♦ сов перех (перен: сделать плохо) to concoct.

состыковать(ся) (-ую(сь)) сов от стыковать(ся).

состязание (-я) ср contest.

состязаться (-юсь) несов возв to compete; ~ (impf) в беге, ~ (impf) в плавании to race; они ~лись в щедрости they were competing to show who was the most generous.

сосуд (-а) м vessel.

сосудистый прил vascular.

сосулька (-ки; gen pl -ек) ж icicle.

сосуществование (-я) ср coexistence.

сосуществовать (-ую) несов неперех to coexist.

сосчитать (-ю) сов от считать.

сот чис см сто.

сотая (-ой; decl like adj) ж: одна ~ one hundredth.

сотворение (-я) ср: ~ мира Creation.

сотворить (-ю, -ишь) сов от творить ♦ перех to create.

сотен сущ см сотня.

сотка (-ки; gen pl -ок) ж one tenth of a hectare.

соткать (-у, -ёшь) сов от ткать.

сотник (-а) м sotnik (lieutenant of Cossack troops).

сотня (-ни; gen pl -ен) ж (сто) a hundred; (деньги) one hundred roubles; (войска) Cossack squadron; ~ни людей/вопросов/писем hundreds of people/questions/letters.

соток сущ см сотка.

сотру(сь) итп сов см стереть(ся).

сотрудник (-а) м (служащий) employee; (коллега) colleague; научный ~ research worker.

сотрудница (-ы) ж см сотрудник.

сотрудничать (-ю) несов неперех (в газете, в учреждении) to work; ~ (impf) с +instr (с фирмой) to work with; (с секретными службами) to collaborate with.

сотрудничество (-а) ср (культурное, экономическое) cooperation; (в газете, в журнале) work.

сотрясать(ся) (-ю(сь)) несов от сотрясти(сь).

сотрясение (-я) ср (от взрыва, от удара) shaking; (также: ~ мозга) concussion.

сотрясти (-у, -ёшь; impf сотрясать) сов перех (стены, землю) to shake

▶ **сотрястись** (impf сотрясаться) сов возв (стены, земля) to shake.

соты (-ов) мн: (пчелиные) ~ honeycomb ед.

сотый (-ая, -ое, -ые) чис hundredth.

соус (-а) м sauce.

соусник (-а) м ≈ gravy boat.

соучастие (-я) ср complicity.

соучастник (-а) м accomplice.

соучастница (-ы) ж см соучастник.

софа (-ы; nom pl -ы) ж sofa.

София (-и) ж Sofia.

соха (-и; nom pl -и) ж wooden plough (BRIT) или plow (US).

сохнуть (-ну, -нешь; pt -, -ла, -ло, perf высохнуть) несов неперех (мокрое бельё, кожа) to dry; (perf высохнуть или засохнуть; растения, дерево) to wither; (от болезни, от переживаний) to go thin; (краска, клей) to dry; (чернила) to dry up.

сохранить (-ю, -ишь; impf сохранять) сов перех to preserve; (КОМП) to save

▶ **сохраниться** (impf сохраняться) сов возв to survive, be preserved; она хорошо ~илась (разг) she's well-preserved.

сохранность (-и) ж (груза) good condition; (вкладов, документов) security; в (полной) ~и (fully) intact.

сохраня́|ть(ся) (-ю(сь)) *несов от* **сохрани́ть(ся)**.

соцве́ти|е (-я) *ср* inflorescence.

социа́л-демокра́т (-а) *м* social democrat.

социа́л-демократи́ческ|ий (-ая, -ое, -ие) *прил* social democrat опред.

социали́зм (-а) *м* socialism.

социали́ст (-а) *м* socialist.

социалисти́ческ|ий (-ая, -ое, -ие) *прил* socialist.

социа́льный *прил* social; **социа́льная защищённость** social security.

социо́лог (-а) *м* sociologist.

социоло́ги|я (-и) *ж* sociology.

соче́льник (-а) *м* (*рождественский*) Christmas Eve; (*крещенский*) Twelfth Night.

со́чен *прил см* **со́чный**.

сочета́ни|е (-я) *ср* (*учёбы и работы*) combining; (*единство: красок, звуков*) combination.

сочета́|ть (-ю) (*не*)*сов перех* to combine

► **сочета́|ться** (*не*)*сов возв* (*соединиться*) to combine; (*гармонировать*) to match, go with; **в ней ~ются ум и доброта́** she is both kind and intelligent.

сочине́ни|е (-я) *ср* (*музыки*) composing; (*стихов*) writing; (*литературное*) work; (*музыкальное*) composition; (*ПРОСВЕЩ*) essay.

сочин|и́ть (-ю́, -и́шь; *impf* **сочиня́ть**) *сов перех* (*музыку*) to compose; (*стихи, песню*) to write; (*разг: письмо*) to concoct; (: *солгать*) to make up.

соч|и́ться (3sg -и́тся, 3pl -а́тся) *несов возв* to ooze; ~ (*impf*) **чем-н** to ooze with sth.

со́чн|ый (-ен, -на́, -но) *прил* (*плод*) juicy; (*трава*) lush; (*краски*) vibrant; (*язык*) expressive.

сочту́ *итп сов см* **счесть**.

сочу́вственн|ый (-ен, -на, -но) *прил* sympathetic.

сочу́встви|е (-я) *ср* sympathy; **встреча́ть** (**встре́тить** *perf*) **что-н с ~м** to be sympathetic to sth.

сочу́вств|овать (-ую) *несов неперех*: ~ +*dat* to sympathize with.

сочу́вствующ|ий (-его; *decl like adj*) *м* sympathizer.

сошёл(ся) *итп сов см* **сойти́(сь)**.

сошлю́(сь) *итп сов см* **сосла́ть(ся)**.

сошью́ *итп сов см* **сшить**.

сощу́р|ить(ся) (-ю(сь), -ишь(ся)) *сов от* **щу́рить(ся)**.

сою́з (-а) *м* alliance; (*республик, профессиональный*) union; (*линг*) conjunction.

сою́зник (-а) *м* ally.

сою́знически|й (-ая, -ое, -ие) *прил* ally's.

сою́зный *прил* (*государство, армия*) allied;

(*слово, связь*) conjunctive.

со́|я (-и) *ж собир* soya beans *мн*.

СП *м сокр* = **Сою́з писа́телей** ♦ *ср сокр* = **совме́стное предприя́тие**.

спаге́тти *мн нескл* spaghetti *ед*.

спад (-а) *м* (*температуры, давления*) drop; **экономи́ческий** ~ recession; **идти́** (**пойти́** *perf*) **на** ~ (*температура, давление*) to go down; (*экономика, производство*) to go into recession.

спада́|ть (3sg -ет, 3pl -ют) *несов от* **спасть** ♦ *неперех* (*волосы, складки*) to fall.

спадёт *итп сов см* **спасть**.

спа́ек *сущ см* **спа́йка**.

спазм (-а) *м* spasm.

спа́ива|ть (-ю) *несов от* **спои́ть**, **спая́ть**.

спа́|йка (-йки; *gen pl* -ек) *ж* (*действие*) soldering; (*место*) join (*from soldering*).

спа́лен *прил см* **спа́льня**.

спал|и́ть (-ю́, -и́шь) *сов от* **пали́ть**.

спа́льник (-а) *м* (*разг*) sleeping bag.

спа́льный *прил* (*место*) sleeping опред; **спа́льный ваго́н** sleeping car; **спа́льный мешо́к** sleeping bag.

спа́л|ьня (-ьни; *gen pl* -ен) *ж* (*комната*) bedroom; (*мебель*) bedroom suite.

спа́рж|а (-и) *ж* asparagus.

спар|и́ть (-ю, -ишь; *impf* **спа́ривать**) *сов перех* (*телефон*) to connect (*to a shared line*); (*вагоны, трубы*) to couple; (*собак, кошек*) to mate.

спа́рыва|ть (-ю) *несов от* **спаро́ть**.

Спас (-а) *м* (*РЕЛ*) the Day of the Saviour (*in the Orthodox Church*); (: *икона*) the Saviour.

спас(ся) *итп сов см* **спасти́(сь)**.

спаса́ни|е (-я) *ср* rescue.

спаса́тель (-я) *м* rescuer; (*судно*) lifeboat.

спаса́тельный *прил* (*станция*) rescue опред; **спаса́тельная ло́дка** lifeboat; **спаса́тельный жиле́т** lifejacket; **спаса́тельный по́яс** lifebelt.

спаса́|ть(ся) (-ю(сь)) *несов от* **спасти́(сь)**.

спасе́ни|е (-я) *ср* rescue; (*РЕЛ*) Salvation.

спаси́бо *част*: ~ (**Вам**) thank you; **большо́е ~**! thank you very much!; ~ **за по́мощь/сове́т** thanks for the help/advice; ~, **что мили́ция во́время пришла́** (*разг*) thank God the police got here on time.

спаси́телен *прил см* **спаси́тельный**.

спаси́тель (-я) *м* saviour; (*РЕЛ*) the Saviour.

спаси́тельниц|а (-ы) *ж* saviour.

спаси́тельн|ый (-ен, -ьна, -ьно) *прил* lifesaving.

спас|ова́ть (-у́ю) *сов от* **пасова́ть**.

спас|ти́ (-у́, -ёшь; *pt* -, -ла́, -ло́, *impf* **спаса́ть**) *сов перех* (*также РЕЛ*) to save; **спаса́ть** (~ *perf*) **кому́-н жизнь** to save sb's life; ~ (*perf*) **положе́ние** to rescue the situation

► **спас|ти́сь** (*impf* **спаса́ться**) *сов возв*: ~**сь** (**от** +*gen*) to escape; (*РЕЛ*) to be saved (from).

спа|сть (*3sg* -дёт, *3pl* -ду́т, *impf* спада́ть) *сов неперех* (*вода*) to drop; (*упасть вниз*): ~ с +*gen* (*одежда, покрывало*) to fall off; **жара́ к ве́черу спа́ла** the heat lessened towards evening.

спа|ть (-лю́, -ишь; *pt* -ал, -ала́, -а́ло) *несов неперех* to sleep; (*перен: разг: быть невнима́тельным*) to daydream; **ложи́ться (лечь** *perf*) ~ to go to bed; **пора́** ~ it's time for bed; ~ (*impf*) **кре́пким сном** to sleep like a log; **по́сле рабо́ты хорошо́** ~**йтся** one sleeps well after working

▸ **спа́ться** *несов возв*: **мне не** ~**йтся** I can't (get to) sleep.

спа́ян|ный (-, -на, -но) *прил* (*перен: коллектив*) unified.

спая́|ть (-ю; *impf* спа́ивать) *сов перех* (*трубы*) to weld; (*перен: сплоти́ть*) to unite.

СПБ *сокр* (= *Санкт-Петербу́рг*) St Petersburg.

СПб *сокр* = **СПБ**.

Спб *сокр* = **СПБ**.

спекта́кл|ь (-я) *м* performance.

спектр (-а) *м* (*также перен*) spectrum.

спекули́р|овать (-ую) *несов неперех* (*дефици́том*) to profiteer; (*КОММ*): ~ +*instr* (*на би́рже: це́нными бума́гами*) to speculate in; (*с ду́рными це́лями*): ~ **на** +*prp* (*на тру́дностях, на сла́бостях*) to exploit.

спекуля́нт (-а) *м* (*КОММ: биржево́й* speculator; (*дефици́том*) profiteer.

спекуляти́в|ный (-ен, -на, -но) *прил* speculative.

спекуля́ци|я (-и) *ж* (*КОММ*) speculation; (*дефици́том*) profiteering.

спеку́тся *итп сов см* **спе́чься**.

спелена́|ть (-ю) *сов от* **пелена́ть**.

спе́л|ый (-, -а́, -о) *прил* ripe.

сперва́ *нареч* (*разг: внача́ле*) (at) first.

спе́реди *нареч* in front ◆ *предл* (+*gen*) in front of.

сп|ере́ть (сопру́, сопрёшь; *pt* -ёр, -ёрла, -ёрло) *сов от* **переть**.

спе́рм|а (-ы) *ж* sperm.

спёрт|ый (-, -а, -о) *прил* (*разг: воздух*) stuffy.

спеси́в|ый (-, -а, -о) *прил* (*человек, тон*) haughty, arrogant.

спес|ь (-и) *ж* haughtiness, arrogance.

сп|еть (*3sg* -е́ет, *3pl* -е́ют, *perf* поспе́ть) *несов неперех* (*фру́кты, о́вощи*) to ripen; ◆ (-ою́, -оёшь) *сов от* **петь**

▸ **спе́ться** *сов возв* (*хор, анса́мбль*) to achieve a good sound; (*разг: пренебр*): ~**ться с** +*instr* (*с вора́ми, со спекуля́нтами*) to get in with.

спех (-а) *м*: **мне не к спе́ху** (*разг*) I'm in no hurry.

спец (-а́) *м сокр* = **специали́ст**.

спец (-а́) *м* (*разг: ма́стер, знато́к*) buff.

специализа́ци|я (-и) *ж* (*произво́дства*) specialization; (*нау́чная*) specialism.

специализи́рованный *прил* specialized.

специализи́р|оваться (-уюсь) (*не*)*сов возв*: ~ **в** +*prp или* **по** +*dat* to specialize in.

специали́ст (-а) *м*: ~ (**по** +*dat*) specialist (in).

специали́ст|ка (-ки; *gen pl* -ок) *ж см* **специали́ст**.

специа́льно *нареч* specially; (*наме́ренно*) on purpose.

специа́льност|ь (-и) *ж* (*профе́ссия*) profession; (*ПРОСВЕЩ*) main subject.

специа́льн|ый *прил* (*помеще́ние, оде́жда итп*) special; (*образова́ние*) specialist; ~ **те́рмин** technical term; **специа́льный корреспонде́нт** special correspondent.

специ́фик|а (-и) *ж* specific nature.

специфика́ци|я (-и) *ж* specification.

специфици́р|овать (-ую) (*не*)*сов перех* to specify.

специфи́чен *прил см* **специфи́чный**.

специфи́ческ|ий (-ая, -ое, -ие) *прил* specific.

специфи́чн|ый (-ен, -на, -но) *прил* = **специфи́ческий**.

спе́ци|я (-и) *ж* spice.

спецко́р (-а) *м сокр* = **специа́льный корреспонде́нт**.

спецку́рс (-а) *м сокр* = **специа́льный курс**; (*в ву́зе*) *course of lectures in a specialist field*.

спецо́вк|а (-и) *ж* (*разг*) workman's jacket.

спецоде́жд|а (-ы) *ж сокр* = **специа́льная оде́жда**) work clothes *мн*.

спе́|чься (*3sg* -чётся, *3pl* -ку́тся) *сов* = **запе́чься**.

спе́шен *прил см* **спе́шный**.

спеш|и́ть (-у́, -и́шь; *perf* поспеши́ть) *несов неперех* (*часы́*) to be fast; (*прийти́ зако́нчить*): ~ +*infin*/**с** +*instr* to be in a hurry to do/with; ~ (*impf*) **на по́езд/в шко́лу** to rush for the train/to school; **я** ~**у́** (**домо́й/на рабо́ту**) I am in a hurry (to get home/to work); **поспеши́!** hurry up; **он поспеши́л с отве́том** he gave a rash answer; ~**у́ сообщи́ть, что ...** I hasten to inform you that ...; **рабо́тать** (*impf*) **не** ~**á** to work at a relaxed pace.

спе́шк|а (-и) *ж* (*разг*) hurry, rush; **в** ~**е я забы́л ша́пку** in the rush I forgot my hat; **нет никако́й** ~ there's no hurry.

спе́шно *нареч* (*уйти́, зако́нчить*) hurriedly.

спе́ш|ный (-ен, -на, -но) *прил* (*де́ло, зада́ние*) urgent.

спива́|ться (-юсь) *несов от* **спи́ться**.

СПИД (-а) *м сокр* (= *синдро́м приобретённого иммунодефици́та*) AIDS (= *acquired immune deficiency syndrome*).

спидо́метр (-а) *м* speedometer.

спи́кер (-а) *м* speaker.

спики́р|овать (-ую) *сов от* **пики́ровать**.

спил|и́ть (-ю́, -ишь; *impf* спи́ливать) *сов перех* to saw down.

спин|а́ (-ы́; *acc sg* -у, *dat sg* -е́, *nom pl* -ы) *ж* (*челове́ка, живо́тного*) back; **за** ~**о́й у него́ бога́тая жизнь** he has lead a full life.

спи́н|ка (-ки; *gen pl* -ок) *ж уменьш от* **спина́**; (*дива́на, сту́ла итп*) back; (*крова́ти*) bedstead.

спи́ннинг (-а) *м* spinner.

спинно́й *прил* (*позвоно́к*) spinal; **спинно́й мозг**

spinal cord.

спи́нок *сущ см* **спи́нка**.

спира́ль (-и) *ж* (*линия*) spiral; (*также:*
внутрима́точная ~) coil (*contraceptive*).

спира́льный *прил* spiral.

спирт (-а; *loc sg* -у́) *м* (*технический,
медицинский*) spirit.

спиртно́е (-о́го; *decl like adj*) *ср* alcohol.

спиртно́й *прил* (*запах, раствор*) of alcohol;
спиртно́й напи́ток alcoholic drink.

списа́ние (-я) *ср* (*КОММ*) writing off; (*МОР*)
discharge.

сп|иса́ть (-ишу́, -и́шешь; *impf* **спи́сывать**) *сов
перех* to copy; (*КОММ*) to write off; (*МОР*) to
discharge; **спи́сывать** (~ *perf*) **что-н с** +*gen* to
copy sth from

► **списа́ться** (*impf* **спи́сываться**) *сов возв*
(*моряк*) to leave ship; **спи́сываться** (~ся *perf*) **с**
+*instr* (*со старым другом*) to write to.

спис|ок (-ка) *м* (*делегатов, присутствующих*)
list; (*документов, романа*) manuscript copy;
кни́га разошла́сь в ~ках the book was
distributed in handwritten copies.

спи́сыва|ть(ся) (-ю(сь)) *несов от*
списа́ть(ся).

спи́ться (сопью́сь, сопьёшься; *impf*
спива́ться) *сов возв* to take to drink.

спихн|у́ть (-у́, -ёшь; *impf* **спи́хивать**) *сов перех*
to push aside *или* down; (*разг: конкурента,
начальника*) to oust; **спи́хивать** (~ *perf*) **что-н
на кого́-н** (*разг: плохой товар,
ответственность*) to push sth onto sb.

спи́ц|а (-ы) *ж* (*для вязания*) knitting needle;
(*колеса*) spoke.

спи́чек *сущ см* **спи́чка**.

спи́чечн|ый *прил:* ~**ая коро́бка** matchbox; ~**ая
голо́вка** matchhead.

спи́чк|а (-ки; *gen pl* -ек) *ж* match; (*разг: худой
человек*) beanpole.

спишу́(сь) *итп сов см* **списа́ть(ся)**.

сплав (-а) *м* ((*не*)*металлический*) alloy; (*леса*)
floating.

спла́в|ить (-лю, -ишь; *impf* **сплавля́ть**) *сов
перех* (*металлы*) to alloy; (*лес*) to float;
(*перен: разг: избавиться*) to get rid of.

сплани́р|овать (-ую) *сов от* **плани́ровать**.

сплани́р|овать (-ую) *сов от* **плани́ровать**.

спла́чива|ть(ся) (-ю(сь)) *несов от*
сплоти́ть(ся).

сплёвыва|ть (-ю) *несов от* **сплю́нуть**.

сплести́ (-ету́, -етёшь; *pt* -ёл, -ела́, -ело́) *сов
от* **плести́** ♦ (*impf* **сплета́ть**) *перех* to plait;
(*пальцы, ноги, руки*) to intertwine

► **сплести́сь** (*impf* **сплета́ться**) *сов возв*
(*водоросли*) to be interwoven; (*руки, тела*) to
be intertwined.

сплётен *сущ см* **сплётня**.

сплете́ни|е (-я) *ср* (*лент, верёвок*) interlacing;

…то, что сплетено) tissue; (*перен: причин,
обстоятельств*) combination.

сплётник (-а) *м* gossip.

сплётни|ца (-ы) *ж см* **сплётник**.

сплётнича|ть (-ю) *несов неперех* to gossip.

сплётн|я (-ни; *gen pl* -ен) *ж* gossip; **распуска́ть**
(*impf*) ~**ни** to spread gossip; **пуска́ть** (**пусти́ть**
perf) ~**ню** to start gossip.

сплету́(сь) *итп сов см* **сплести́(сь)**.

сплеча́ *нареч* (*ударить*) straight from the
shoulder; (*разг: решать*) impulsively.

спло|ти́ть (-чу́, -ти́шь; *impf* **спла́чивать**) *сов
перех* to unite.

► **сплоти́ться** (*impf* **спла́чиваться**) *сов возв* to
unite.

сплох|ова́ть (-у́ю) *сов неперех* (*разг*) to slip up.

сплочённый *прил* united.

сплочу́(сь) *сов см* **сплоти́ть(ся)**.

сплошно́й *прил* (*стена, поток итп*)
continuous; (*грамотность, перепись*)
universal; (*разг: мучение, неудачи*) utter;
(*: восторг, маразм*) complete and utter.

сплошь *нареч* (*по всей поверхности*) all over;
(*без исключения*) completely; ~ **и ря́дом** (*разг*)
more often than not.

сплут|ова́ть (-у́ю) *сов от* **плутова́ть**.

сплы́ть (3*sg* -вёт, 3*pl* -ву́т, *impf* **сплыва́ть**) *сов
неперех* (*уплыть*) to be carried away; **был да**
~**л** (*разг*) it's gone forever

► **сплы́ться** (*impf* **сплыва́ться**) *сов возв*
(*буквы, краски итп*) to run together, merge.

сплю *несов см* **спать**.

сплю́ну|ть (-у, -ешь; *impf* **сплёвывать**) *сов
перех* to spit; (*шелуху*) to spit out.

сплю́щ|ить (-у, -ишь) *сов от* **плю́щить** ♦ (*impf*
сплю́щивать) *перех* to flatten

► **сплю́щиться** (*impf* **сплю́щиваться**) *сов возв*
to become flattened.

спля́с|ать (-яшу́, -я́шешь) *сов от* **пляса́ть**.

сподви́жник (-а) *м* loyal supporter.

сподо́б|иться (-люсь, -ишься) *сов возв:* ~
+*infin* (*разг*) to be honoured (*BRIT*) *или* honored
(*US*) to do.

спозара́нку *нареч* (*разг*) very early (*in the
morning*).

спо|и́ть (-ю́, -и́шь; *imper* -и́(те), *impf* **спа́ивать**)
сов перех: ~ **кого́-н** to get sb drunk; (*приучить
пьянствовать*) to make a drunkard of sb.

споко́ен *прил см* **споко́йный**.

споко́йно *нареч* (*жить, говорить*) quietly;
(*спать*) peacefully ♦ *как сказ безл* it's quiet; **у
меня́ на душе́** ~ I feel calm.

споко́йн|ый (-ен, -йна, -йно) *прил* (*море*) calm;
(*улица, жизнь*) quiet; (*человек, тон, беседа*)
serene; (*характер*) placid; (*цвет*) gentle,
restful; ~**йная со́весть** clear conscience.

споко́йстви|е (-я) *ср* (*в городе, в лесу*) calm,
tranquillity; (*на душе*) calm; **сохраня́ть** (*impf*) ~

to keep calm.

сполáскива|ть (-ю) *несов от* **сполоснýть**.

сполз|тú (-ý, -ёшь; *pt* **-, -лá, -лó,** *impf* **сползáть) сов неперех** to climb down; (*шапка, платок, чулки*) to slip down; (*перен: к национализму*) to slide

▶ **сползтúсь** (*impf* **сползáться**) *сов возв* to congregate.

сполнá *нареч* in full.

сполосн|ýть (-ý, -ёшь; *impf* **сполáскивать**) *сов перех* to rinse.

спóнсор (-а) *м* sponsor.

спóнсорск|ий (-ая, -ое, -ие) *прил* sponsoring *опред*.

спор (-а) *м* debate; (*имущественный*) dispute; (*спортивный*) competition; **вестú** (*impf*) **~** to have an argument; **спóру нет** there is no doubt; **нá ~** (*разг*) as a bet.

спóр|а (-ы) *ж* (*БОТ*) spore.

спорадúческ|ий (-ая, -ое, -ие) *прил* sporadic.

спóрен *прил см* **спóрный**.

спóр|ить (-ю, -ишь; *perf* **поспóрить**) *несов неперех* (*вести спор*) to argue, debate; (*держать пари*) to bet; **~** (*impf*) **с кем-н о чем-н или за что-н** (*о наследстве*) to dispute sth with sb; **~им, ты не посмéешь емý возразúть** I bet you wouldn't contradict him

▶ **спóриться** *несов возв* (*работа, дело*) to go well.

спóр|ный (-ен, -на, -но) *прил* (*дело*) disputed; (*победа, преимущество*) doubtful; **~ вопрóс** moot point.

спор|óть (-орю, -óрешь; *impf* **спáрывать**) *сов перех* to nip off.

спорт (-а) *м* sport.

спортзáл (-а) *м* sports hall, gymnasium.

спортúвный *прил* (*площадка, комментатор*) sports *опред*; (*фигура, человек*) sporty; **спортúвный костюм** tracksuit.

спортлотó *ср нескл* sports lottery.

спортсмéн (-а) *м* sportsman (*мн* sportsmen).

спортсмéн|ка (-ки; *gen pl* **-ок**) *ж* sportswoman (*мн* sportswomen).

спорттовáр|ы (-ов) *мн* sports goods *мн*.

спорхн|ýть (-ý, -ёшь) *сов неперех* to flutter off.

спóрщик (-а) *м* debater.

спóрщиц|а (-ы) *ж см* **спóрщик**.

спóрый *прил* efficient.

спóсоб (-а) *м* way.

спосóбен *прил см* **спосóбный**.

спосóбност|ь (-и) *ж* ability; (*обычно мн: талант*) aptitude *ед*; **математúческие ~и** aptitude for mathematics; **пропускнáя ~** (*дороги, метро*) capacity; **покупáтельная ~ населéния** purchasing power (of the population).

спосóб|ный (-ен, -на, -но) *прил* capable; (*талантливый*) able; **~ +infin** capable of doing; **он ~ен к математике** he has a gift for mathematics; **онá ~на на всё** she is capable of anything.

спосóбств|овать (-ую) *сов неперех*: **~ +dat** (*успеху, развитию*) to promote.

споткн|ýться (-ýсь, -ёшься; *impf* **спотыкáться**) *сов возв* (*при ходьбе, при беге*) to trip; (*при чтении*) to get stuck; (*перен: совершить проступок*) to slip up.

спохв|атúться (-ачýсь, -áтишься; *impf* **спохвáтываться**) *сов возв* (*вспомнить*) to remember suddenly; (*понять ошибку*) to realize.

спою *итп несов см* **спеть**.

спрáва *нареч* to the right; **~ от чегó-н** to the right of sth.

справедлúво *нареч* fairly, justly ♦ *как сказ*: **это ~** that's fair *или* just.

справедлúвост|ь (-и) *ж* justice; **отдáть** (*perf*) **комý-н ~** (*оценить по заслугам*) to do justice to sb; **~и рáди ...** to be fair ....

справедлúв|ый (-, -а, -о) *прил* just; (*утверждение*) correct; (*подозрение*) justified.

спрáв|ить (-лю, -ишь; *impf* **справлять**) *сов перех* (*разг: день рождения*) to celebrate; (*шубу, туфли*) to buy

▶ **спрáвиться** (*impf* **справляться**) *сов возв*: **~ся с +instr** (*с работой, с заданием*) to manage; (*с противником*) to deal with; (*с волнением, с детьми*) to cope with; (*узнавать*): **~ся о +prp** to enquire *или* ask about.

спрáв|ка (-ки; *gen pl* **-ок**) *ж* (*сведения*) information; (*документ*) certificate; **обращáться** (**обратúться** *perf*) **за ~кой** to apply for information; **наводúть** (**навестú** *perf*) **~ки** to make enquiries.

спрáвлю(сь) *сов см* **спрáвить(ся)**.

справля́|ть(ся) (-ю(сь)) *несов от* **спрáвить(ся)**.

спрáвок *сущ см* **спрáвка**.

спрáвочник (-а) *м* (*телефонный*) directory; (*грамматический*) reference book.

спрáвочный *прил* (*литература, пособие*) reference *опред*; **спрáвочное бюрó** information office *или* bureau.

спрáшива|ть (-ю) *несов от* **спросúть**

▶ **спрáшиваться** *несов от* **спросúться** ♦ *возв*: **~ется, где ты был в это врéмя** the question is, where were you at that time?

спресс|овáть (-ýю) *сов от* **прессовáть**.

спринт (-а) *м* sprint.

спрúнтер (-а) *м* sprinter.

спровá|дить (-жу, -дишь; *impf* **спровáживать**) *сов перех* (*разг*) to send off.

спровоцúр|овать (-ую) *сов от* **провоцúровать**.

спроектúр|овать (-ую) *сов от* **проектúровать**.

спрос (-а) *м*: **~ на** +*acc* (*на товары, на специалистов*) demand for; (*требование*): **~ с** +*gen* (*с родителей, с начальника*) demands *мн* on; **без спрóса** *или* **спрóсу** without permission; **с тебя ~ осóбый** there are special demands on

you; ~ **и предложе́ние** (ЭКОН) supply and
demand.
спроси́ть (-ошу́, -о́сишь; *impf* **спра́шивать**)
сов перех (*доро́гу*, *вре́мя*) to ask; (*сове́та*,
де́нег) to ask for; (*взыска́ть*): ~ **что-н с** +*gen* to
call sb to account for; (*осве́домиться*): ~
кого́-н о чём-н to ask sb about sth; **спра́шивать**
(~ *perf*) **ученика́** to question *или* test a pupil; **я**
~**оси́л, кото́рый час/когда́ по́езд** I asked what
the time was/when the train would be
▶ **спроси́ться** (*impf* **спра́шиваться**) *сов возв*:
~**ся** +*gen* или у +*gen* (у *роди́телей, у учи́теля*
итп) to ask permission of; **с нас ~о́сится за**
э́то we will be answerable for that.
спросо́нок *нареч* (*разг*) half asleep.
спрошу́(сь) *сов см* **спроси́ть(ся)**.
спрут (-а) *м* octopus.
спры́гнуть (-ну, -нешь; *impf* **спры́гивать**) *сов*
неперех: ~ **с** +*gen* to jump off.
спряга́ть (-ю; *perf* **проспряга́ть**) *несов перех*
(*ЛИНГ*) to conjugate.
спряду́ *итп сов см* **спрясть**.
спряже́ни|е (-я) *ср* (*ЛИНГ*) conjugation.
спрясть (-ду́, -дёшь; *сов см* **прясть**.
спря́тать(ся) (-чу(сь), -чешь(ся)) *сов от*
пря́тать(ся).
спугну́ть (-ну́, -нёшь; *impf* **спу́гивать**) *сов*
перех to frighten off.
спуд (-а) *м*: **держа́ть что-н под спу́дом** (*иде́ю*,
план) to keep sth back; **извлека́ть** (**извле́чь**
perf) **что-н из-под спу́да** to bring sth into the
light of day.
спуск (-а) *м* (*де́йствие: фла́га*) lowering;
(: *корабля́*) launch; (: *воды́, га́за*) draining;
(*ме́сто: к реке́, с горы́*) descent; (*в ору́жии*)
trigger; **нажима́ть** (**нажа́ть** *perf*) (**на**) ~ to pull
the trigger; **я не дал ему́ спу́ску** (*разг*) I didn't
let him off.
спуска́емый *прил*: ~ **аппара́т** (*КОСМОС*)
landing gear.
спуска́|ть (-ю) *несов от* **спусти́ть** ◆ *перех*: **я не**
~**л глаз с неё** I didn't take my eyes off her
▶ **спуска́ться** *несов от* **спусти́ться** ◆ *возв*
(*доро́га, бе́рег*) to descend, go down; (*во́лосы*,
фа́лды) to hang down.
спусково́й *прил* (*трап*) exit *опред*; (*механи́зм*)
trigger *опред*.
спусти́ть (-щу́, -стишь; *impf* **спуска́ть**) *сов*
перех to lower; (*директи́ву, план*) to send out;
(*соба́ку*) to let loose; (*газ, во́ду*) to drain; (*разг:*
зарпла́ту, насле́дство) to squander;
(*прости́ть*): ~ **что-н кому́-н** to let sb off with
sth, forgive sb for sth; ~**стя́ рукава́** (*разг:*
небре́жно) carelessly; **спуска́ть** (~ *perf*)
кора́бль (**на́ воду**) to launch a ship; **спуска́ть**
(~ *perf*) **куро́к** to pull the trigger; **спуска́ть** (~
perf) **кого́-н с ле́стницы** to kick sb downstairs;
(*вы́гнать*) to kick sb out; **у мое́й маши́ны**

~**сти́ла ши́на** my car has a flat tyre (*BRIT*) *или*
tire (*US*)
▶ **спусти́ться** (*impf* **спуска́ться**) *сов возв* to go
down; (*чулки́, ю́бка итп*) to slip down; (*тума́н*,
мгла, ночь итп) to descend.
спустя́ *нареч*: ~ **три дня/год** three days/a year
later.
спу́танный *прил* (*во́лосы, верёвки*) tangled;
(*речь*) muddled.
спу́тать(ся) (-ю(сь)) *сов от* **пу́тать(ся)**.
спу́тник (-а) *м* (*в пути́*) travelling (*BRIT*) *или*
traveling (*US*) companion; (*городо́к*) satellite
town; (*АСТРОНО́МИЯ*) satellite; (*КО́СМОС: та́кже:*
иску́сственный ~) sputnik, satellite; (*перен*): ~
+*gen* (*бе́дности, прогре́сса итп*) concomitant
of; ~ **жи́зни** (*муж*) life's companion.
спу́тниковый *прил* (*связь*) satellite *опред*;
спу́тниковое телеви́дение satellite TV.
спу́тница (-ы) *ж* (*в пути́*) travelling (*BRIT*) *или*
traveling (*US*) companion; ~ **жи́зни** (*жена́*) life's
companion.
спу́тывать (-ю; *perf* **спу́тать**) *несов перех* =
пу́тать.
спущу́(сь) *сов см* **спусти́ть(ся)**.
спя́тить (-чу, -тишь) *сов неперех* (*разг*) to go
daft.
спя́чк|а (-и) *ж* (*живо́тных*) hibernation; (*перен:*
безде́ятельность) lethargy.
спя́чу *сов см* **спя́тить**.
ср. *сокр* (= *сравни́*) cp. (= *compare*).
сраба́тыва|ть (*3sg* -ет, *3pl* -ют) *несов от*
срабо́тать.
срабо́танность (-и) *ж* harmony.
срабо́та|ть (*3sg* -ет, *3pl* -ют, *impf* **сраба́тывать**)
сов неперех to operate.
сравне́ни|е (-я) *ср* comparison; **в ~и** *или* **по ~ю**
с +*instr* compared with; **не мо́жет быть**
никако́го ~я с +*instr* there can be no comparison
with; **не поддава́ться** (*impf*) **никако́му ~ю** to
be unspeakable.
сра́внива|ть (-ю) *несов от* **сравни́ть**,
сравня́ть.
сравни́м|ый (-, -а, -о) *прил* comparable.
сравни́телен *прил см* **сравни́тельный**.
сравни́тельно *нареч* comparatively; ~ **с** +*instr*
compared to *или* with.
сравни́тельн|ый (-ен, -ьна, -ьно) *прил*
comparative; **сравни́тельная сте́пень** (*ЛИНГ*)
comparative degree.
сравни́ть (-ю́, -йшь; *impf* **сра́внивать**) *сов*
перех: ~ **что-н/кого́-н** (**с** +*instr*) to compare
sth/sb (with); (*уподо́бить*): ~ **что-н/кого́-н с**
+*instr* to compare sth/sb to
▶ **сравни́ться** *сов возв*: ~**ся с** +*instr* to compare
with.
сравня́|ть (-ю; *impf* **сра́внивать**) *сов перех*
(*расхо́д с дохо́дом*) to balance; **сра́внивать** (~
perf) **счёт** to equalize

▸ **сравня́ться** *сов возв*: ~ся с +*instr* to become the equal of.

сража́ть(ся) (-ю(сь)) *несов от* **срази́ть(ся)**.

сраже́ни|е (-я) *ср* (*битва*) battle.

срази́ть (-жу́, -зи́шь; *impf* **сража́ть**) *сов перех* (*пулей, ударом*) to slay; (*подлеж: горе, тяжёлая весть*) to crush

▸ **срази́ться** (*impf* **сража́ться**) *сов возв* to join battle.

сра́зу *нареч* (*немедленно*) straight away; (*в один приём*) (all) at once; (*рядом*) right.

срам (-а) *м* (*разг*) shame; ~ **ви́деть тако́е** it's a disgrace *или* shame.

срам|и́ть (-лю́, -и́шь; *perf* **осрами́ть**) *несов перех* (*позорить*) to shame; (*бранить*) to put to shame

▸ **срами́ться** (*perf* **осрами́ться**) *несов возв* to bring shame on o.s.

срастáни|е (-я) *ср* (*костей*) knitting.

сраст|и́сь (3sg -ётся, 3pl -у́тся, *impf* **сраста́ться**) *сов возв* (*кости*) to knit (together); (*стволы*) to grow together; (*перен: компании*) to merge.

сраще́ни|е (-я) *ср* (*костей*) knitting.

среаги́р|овать (-ую) *сов от* **реаги́ровать**.

сред|á (-ы́; *nom pl* -ы) *ж* medium; (*no pl; природная, социальная*) environment; (*артистическая, литературная*) milieu; (*acc sg* -у; *день недели*) Wednesday; *см также* **пя́тница**; **окружа́ющая** ~ environment; **охра́на окружа́ющей** ~ы́ conservation.

среди́ *предл* (+*gen*) in the middle of; (*в пределах*) in the middle of, amidst; (*в окружении*) amidst; (*в среде, в числе*) among.

средизе́мн|ый *прил*: **С**~**ое мо́ре** the Mediterranean (Sea).

среди́н|а (-ы) *ж* = **середи́на**.

среди́нный *прил* = **середи́нный**.

среднеазиа́тск|ий (-ая, -ое, -ие) *прил* Central Asian.

средневеко́вый *прил* medieval.

средневеко́вь|е (-я) *ср* the Middle Ages *мн*.

средневолно́вый *прил* medium-wave.

среднегодово́й *прил* average annual.

среднеме́сячный *прил* average monthly.

среднесу́точный *прил* average daily.

сре́дн|ий (-яя, -ее, -ие) *прил* medium; (*комната, окно итп*) middle; (*посредственный*) average; **в** ~**ем** on average; **вы́ше/ни́же** ~**его** above/below average; **он** ~**их лет** he is middle-aged; **сре́днее образова́ние** secondary education; **сре́дние века́** the Middle Ages *мн*; **сре́дний па́лец** middle finger; **сре́дняя шко́ла** secondary school.

средото́чи|е (-я) *ср* focus, centre (*BRIT*), center (*US*).

сре́дств|а (-) *мн* means *мн*; (*деньги*) means *мн*, funds *мн*; **отпуска́ть** (**отпусти́ть** *perf*) *или* **выделя́ть** (**вы́делить** *perf*) ~ **на что-н** to allocate funds to sth; **остава́ться** (**оста́ться** *perf*) **без средств** to be without means;

сре́дства произво́дства (*ЭКОН*) means of production; **сре́дства существова́ния** livelihood.

сре́дств|о (-а) *ср* means *мн*; (*лекарство*) remedy, medicine; **добива́ться** (*impf*) **чего-н все́ми** ~**ами** to use all means to get sth; **сре́дство передвиже́ния** means of conveyance; *см также* **сре́дства**.

сре́жу(сь) *итп сов см* **сре́зать(ся)**.

срез (-а) *м* (*место*) cut; (*тонкий слой*) section.

сре́з|ать (-жу, -жешь; *impf* **среза́ть**) *сов перех* (*траву, цветок*) to cut; (*разг: дотации, кредиты*) to cut off; (: *студента*) to flunk

▸ **сре́заться** (*impf* **среза́ться**) *сов возв* (*разг: студент*) to flunk.

Срете́ни|е (-я) *ср* (*РЕЛ*) Candlemas, Feast of the Purification.

срис|ова́ть (-у́ю; *impf* **срисо́вывать**) *сов перех* to copy.

срифм|ова́ть (-у́ю) *сов от* **рифмова́ть**.

сровня́ть (-ю) *сов от* **ровня́ть**.

сро́дни *предл* (+*dat*) akin to.

сродн|и́ть (-ню́, -ни́шь) *сов перех*: ~ **кого-н с** +*instr* to bring sb close to

▸ **сродни́ть** *сов возв*: ~ся с +*instr* to become close to.

сродств|о́ (-á) *ср* affinity.

сро́ду *нареч*: ~ **не ви́дел/не слы́шал** ... never in my life have I seen/heard ....

сро́|иться (3sg -ится, 3pl -я́тся) *сов от* **рои́ться**.

срок (-а; *part gen* -у) *м* (*длительность*) time, period; (*дата*) date; (*разг: тюремный*) term; **в** ~ (*во время*) in time; **после́дний** *или* **преде́льный** ~ deadline; **сро́ком на** +*acc* for a term of; **испыта́тельный** ~ trial period; ~ **произво́дства платежа́** due date; **срок го́дности** (*товара*) sell-by date; **срок де́йствия** period of validity.

сро́чен *прил см* **сро́чный**.

сро́чно *нареч* quickly, urgently.

сро́чност|ь (-и) *ж* urgency; **нет никако́й** ~**и** there's no hurry.

сро́чн|ый (-ен, -на, -но) *прил* (*дело, заказ*) urgent; (*ссуда, вклад*) fixed-term; **сро́чная телегра́мма** express telegram.

сро́ю *итп сов см* **срыть**.

сруб (-а) *м* (*место сруба*) cut; (*постройка*) log shell (*of building, well etc*).

сруба́|ть (-ю; *perf* **сруби́ть**) *несов перех* = **руби́ть**.

сруб|и́ть (-лю́, -у́бишь) *сов от* **руби́ть**.

срыв (-а) *м* (*плана итп*) disruption; (*с горы, с крыши итп*) fall; (*на экзамене итп*) failure; (*обрыв*) precipice.

срыва́ни|е (-я) *ср* picking.

срыва́|ть (-ю) *несов от* **сорва́ть, срыть**

▸ **срыва́ться** *несов от* **сорва́ться**.

срыва́ющийся (-аяся, -ееся, -иеся) *прил* (*голос*) breaking.

сры|ть (-о́ю, -о́ешь; *impf* **срыва́ть**) *сов перех*

(*насыпь, холм*) to level.

CC *м сокр* SS.

сса́дин|а (-ы) *ж* scratch.

сса|ди́ть (-жу́, -дишь; *impf* сса́живать) *сов перех* (*со стула, с колен*) to help down; (*безбилетника*) to put off.

ссо́р|а (-ы) *ж* quarrel.

ссо́р|ить (-ю, -ишь; *perf* поссо́рить) *несов перех* (*друзей, родственников*) to cause to quarrel; ~ (поссо́рить *perf*) кого́-н с +*instr* to make sb quarrel with

▶ **ссо́риться** (*perf* поссо́риться) *несов возв* to quarrel.

СССР *м сокр* (*ист.* = *Сою́з Сове́тских Социалисти́ческих Респу́блик*) USSR (= *Union of Soviet Socialist Republics*).

ссу́д|а (-ы) *ж* loan; **брать** (**взять** *perf*) ~у to take out a loan; ~ **под проце́нты** interest-bearing loan; ~ **под зало́г** loan on collateral.

ссу|ди́ть (-жу́, -дишь; *impf* ссужа́ть) *сов перех* (*де́ньги*) to lend.

ссу́дный *прил* (*операция, ведомость*) loan *опред*; **ссу́дный банк** lending bank; **ссу́дный капита́л** (*КОММ*) loan capital.

ссужа́|ть (-ю) *несов от* ссуди́ть.

ссужу́ *сов см* ссуди́ть.

ссу́т|улить(ся) (-ю(сь), -ишь(ся)) *сов от* сутулить(ся).

ссыла́|ть(ся) (-ю(сь)) *несов от* сосла́ть(ся) ◆ *возв*: ~ясь на +*acc* with reference to.

ссы́л|ка (-ки; *gen pl* -ок) *ж* exile; (*на автора, на источник*) reference; (*цитата*) quotation.

ссы́льн|ая (-ой; *decl like adj*) *ж см* ссы́льный.

ссы́льн|ый (-ого; *decl like adj*) *м* exile.

ссы́п|ать (-лю, -лешь; *impf* ссыпа́ть) *сов перех* (*насыпать*) to pour.

ст. *сокр* (= ста́нция) sta. (= *station*); (= ста́рший) Sen. (= *senior*); = ста́рый.

ста *чис см* сто.

стаби́лен *прил см* стаби́льный.

стабилиза́тор (-а) *м* (*ТЕХ*) stabilizer.

стабилиза́ци|я (-и) *ж* stabilization.

стабилизи́р|овать (-ую) (*не*)*сов перех* to stabilize

▶ **стабилизи́роваться** (*не*)*сов возв* to stabilize.

стаби́л|ьный (-ен, -ьна, -ьно) *прил* stable; **стаби́льный уче́бник** standard textbook.

ста́в|ень (-ня) *м* (*обычно мн*) shutter.

ста́в|ить (-лю, -ишь; *perf* поста́вить) *несов перех* to put; (*назначать: министром, дежурным*) to appoint; (*памятник*) to erect; (*телефон*) to install; (*парус, сроки*) to set; (*пятно, оценку*) to make; (*точку, запятую итп*) to put in; (*оперу, фильм итп*) to stage; (*выдвигать: задачу, цель*) to present; (: *вопрос*) to raise; ~ (поста́вить *perf*) де́ньги на что-н to put money on sth; ~ (поста́вить

perf) **печа́ть на что-н** to stamp sth; ~ (поста́вить *perf*) **часы́** to set a clock; ~ (поста́вить *perf*) **диа́гноз** to make a diagnosis; ~ (поста́вить *perf*) **что-н на голосова́ние** to put sth to the vote; ~ (поста́вить *perf*) **что-н кому́-н в вину́** to lay the blame for sth on sb; ~ (поста́вить *perf*) **что-н кому́-н в заслу́гу** to put sth at sb's service; ~ (поста́вить *perf*) **что-н кому́-н в досто́инство** to give sb credit for sth; ~ (поста́вить *perf*) **себе́ за пра́вило** to make it a rule; ~ (поста́вить *perf*) **кого́-н в изве́стность** to fill sb in; ~ (поста́вить *perf*) **что-н под контро́ль** to bring sth under control; **его́ здесь ни во что не ~ят** he counts for nothing here.

ста́в|ка (-ки; *gen pl* -ок) *ж* (*также КОММ*) rate; (*ВОЕН*) headquarters *мн*; (*в азартных играх*) stake; (*перен*): ~ **на** +*acc* (*расчёт*) counting on; **проце́нтные** ~ки (*КОММ*) interest rates; **ба́зовая ссу́дная** ~ base rate; **минима́льная ссу́дная** ~ minimum lending rate; **учётная** ~ (*банка*) discount rate.

ста́вленник (-а) *м* protégé.

ста́вленниц|а (-ы) *ж* protégée.

ста́влю *сов см* ста́вить.

ста́вня *итп сущ см* ста́вень.

ста́в|ок *сущ см* ста́вка.

ставри́д|а (-ы) *ж* (*ЗООЛ*) horse mackerel, scad.

стагна́ци|я (-и) *ж* stagnation.

стадио́н (-а) *м* stadium (*мн* stadia).

ста́ди|я (-и) *ж* stage.

ста́дный *прил* (*животное*) herd *опред*; (*перен: чувство*) gregarious.

ста́д|о (-а; *nom pl* -а́) *ср* (*коров*) herd; (*овец*) flock.

стаж (-а) *м* (*рабочий*) length of service; **испыта́тельный** ~ probation.

стажёр (-а) *м* probationer.

стажир|ова́ться (-у́юсь) *несов возв* to work on probation.

стажиро́в|ка (-ки; *gen pl* -ок) *ж* probationary period.

ста́ива|ть (-ю) *несов от* ста́ять.

ста́йер (-а) *м* long-distance runner.

ста́йерск|ий (-ая, -ое, -ие) *прил*: ~ая диста́нция long distance.

стака́н (-а) *м* glass; **бума́жный** ~ paper cup.

стака́нчик (-а) *м* glass; **моро́женое в** ~ах ice cream in tubs.

стакка́то *нареч* staccato.

сталагми́т (-а) *м* stalagmite.

сталакти́т (-а) *м* stalactite.

сталева́р (-а) *м* steel founder.

сталелите́йный *прил* steel-founding.

сталепла́вильный *прил* steel-smelting.

сталепрока́тный *прил* steel-rolling.

стали́йн|ый *прил*: ~ое вре́мя (*КОММ*) lay days *мн*.

сталини́зм (-а) *м* Stalinism.

ста́лкива|ть(ся) (-ю(сь)) *несов от* **столкну́ть(ся).**

сталь (-и) *ж* steel.

стально́й *прил* (кабель, рельсы, решимость) steel *опред*; (мускулы, нервы) of steel; (воля) iron *опред*; (цвет: глаза) steel-blue; (: море) steel-grey (*BRIT*), steel-gray (*US*).

стам *итп чис см* **сто.**

Стамбу́л (-а) *м* Istanbul.

стаме́с|ка (-ки; *gen pl* -ок) *ж* chisel.

стан (-а) *м* (человека) torso; (стоянка) camp; (*ТЕХ*) mill.

станда́рт (-а) *м* (также перен) standard; **по ~у** (изготовить) in line with the standard; (перен: де́йствовать) conventionally.

станда́ртен *прил см* **станда́ртный.**

стандартиза́ц|ия (-и) *ж* standardization; (личности, отношений) stereotyping.

стандартизи́р|овать (-ую) (*не)сов перех* to standardize.

станда́рт|ный (-ен, -на, -но) *прил* (детали, машина) standard; (вопросы, тема) stock.

стани́н|а (-ы) *ж* (*ТЕХ*) bed.

стани́ц|а (-ы) *ж* stanitsa (*large Cossack village*).

станка́ *итп сущ см* **стано́к.**

станко́вый *прил* (живопись) easel *опред*.

станкостро́ени|е (-я) *ср* machine-tool construction.

станкостро́ительный *прил* (завод, промышленность) machine-tool.

стан|ови́ться (-овлю́сь, -о́вишься) *несов от* **стать.**

становле́ни|е (-я) *ср* formation.

становлю́сь *несов см* **станови́ться.**

стан|о́к (-ка́) *м* (слесарный итп) machine (tool); (иску́сство) frame; (балетный) barre; **тока́рный ~** lathe.

ста́ну(сь) *итп сов см* **стать(ся).**

станцио́нный *прил* station *опред*.

ста́нци|я (-и) *ж* station; **запра́вочная ~** filling station; **телефо́нная ~** telephone exchange.

ста́пель (-я; *nom pl* -я́) *м* (*МОР*) building berth (*BRIT*), slip (*US*).

ста́плива|ть (-ю) *несов от* **стопи́ть.**

ста́птыва|ть(ся) (-ю(сь)) *несов от* **стопта́ть(ся).**

стара́ни|е (-я) *ср* effort; **при всём ~и не смогу́ тебе́ помо́чь** no matter how much I try, I can't help you.

стара́телен *прил см* **стара́тельный.**

стара́тел|ь (-я) *м* (gold) prospector.

стара́тельност|ь (-и) *ж* (*см прил*) diligence; painstakingness.

стара́тел|ьный (-ен, -ьна, -ьно) *прил* (работник, ученик) diligent; (работа, подсчёт) painstaking.

стара́|ться (-юсь; *perf* **постара́ться**) *несов возв*: **~ +*infin*** to try to do.

старе́йш|ий (-ая, -ее, -ие) *превос прил от* **ста́рый.**

старе́йшин|а (-ы) *ж* elder.

старе́ни|е (-я) *ср* ageing.

старе́|ть (-ю; *perf* **постаре́ть**) *несов неперех* (человек) to grow old(er), age; (*perf* **устаре́ть**; оборудование) to become out of date.

ста́р|ец (-ца) *м* elder; (*РЕЛ*) elderly monk.

стари́|к (-а́) *м* old man (*мн* men); **старики́** old people.

старико́вск|ий (-ая, -ое, -ие) *прил* (привычки) old people's.

старин|а́ (-ы́) *ж* (прошлое) the olden days *мн* ♦ (обращение) old man *или* chap (*BRIT*).

стари́н|ка (-и) *ж*: **по ~е** in the old way.

стари́нный *прил* ancient; (давний: друг) old.

ста́р|ить (-ю, -ишь; *perf* **соста́рить**) *несов перех* to age.

ста́р|ка (-и) *ж* (сорт водки) starka (*type of vodka*).

старо́ *как сказ*: **э́то всё ~** it's all outdated; (не ново) there's nothing new in it; **~ как мир** it's as old as the hills.

старове́р (-а) *м* (*РЕЛ*) Old Believer.

старове́р|ка (-ки; *gen pl* -ок) *ж см* **старове́р.**

старожи́л (-а) *м* old resident.

старомо́д|ный (-ен, -на, -но) *прил* old-fashioned.

старообря́д|ец (-ца) *м* (*РЕЛ*) Old Believer.

старообря́д|ка (-ки; *gen pl* -ок) *ж см* **старообря́дец.**

старообря́дца *итп сущ см* **старообря́дец.**

старообря́дчеств|о (-а) *ср* Old Belief.

старославя́нск|ий (-ая, -ое, -ие) *прил*: **старославя́нский язы́к** Old Church Slavonic.

ста́рост|а (-ы) *м* (курса) senior student; (класса: мальчик) head boy; (: девушка) head girl; (клуба) head, president; (артели) foreman (*мн* foremen).

ста́рост|ь (-и) *ж* (человека) old age; **на ~и лет** in one's old age.

старпо́м (-а) *м = ста́рший помо́щник*; (*МОР*) first mate.

старт (-а) *м* (*СПОРТ*) start; (ракеты) takeoff point; **дава́ть** (**дать** *perf*) **~** to start; **брать** (**взять** *perf*) **~** to start; (перен) to take off.

старт|ёр (-а) *м* (*АВТ*) starter.

старт|ёр (-а) *м* (*СПОРТ*) starter.

старт|ова́ть (-у́ю) (*не)сов неперех* (спортсмен) to start; (ракета) to take off.

ста́ртовый *прил* starting *опред*.

стару́х|а (-и) *ж* old woman (*мн* women).

стару́шек *сущ см* **стару́шка.**

стару́шечий (-ья, -ье, -ьи) *прил* old woman's.

стару́ш|ка (-ки; *gen pl* -ек) *ж = стару́ха.**

ста́рца *итп сущ см* **ста́рец.**

ста́рческ|ий (-ая, -ое, -ие) *прил* old person's *или* people's; **ста́рческий во́зраст** old age; **ста́рческий мара́зм** (*МЕД*) senility.

ста́рше *сравн прил от* **ста́рый** ♦ *как сказ*: **я ~ сестры́ на́ год** I am a year older than my sister; **я ~ его́ по зва́нию** I am senior to him.

старшекла́ссник (-а) *м* senior pupil.

старшекла́ссни|ца (-ы) *ж см*

старшекла́ссник.

старшеку́рсник (-а) *м* senior student.

старшеку́рсниц|а (-ы) *ж см* старшеку́рсник.

ста́рш|ий (-ая, -ее, -ие) *прил* senior *опред*; (*сестра, брат*) elder *опред* ♦ (**-его**; *decl like adj*) *м* (*группы, отделения*) senior; ~ие (*взрослые люди*) grown-ups *мн*, adults *мн*.

старшин|а́ (-ы́; *nom pl* -ы) *м* (ВОЕН) sergeant major; (*милиции*) sergeant.

старшинств|о́ (-а́) *ср* seniority; **по ~у́** by seniority.

ста́р|ый (-, -а́, -о́, -ы) *прил* old; **и стар и млад** old and young; **ста́рый стиль** (*летосчисления*) Old Style.

старь|ё (-я́) *ср собир* old things *мн*.

старьёвщик (-а) *м* junk dealer.

ста́скива|ть (-ю) *несов от* стащи́ть.

стасова́|ть (-ю) *сов от* тасова́ть.

ста́тен *прил см* ста́тный.

ста́тик|а (-и) *ж* (*наука*) statics; (*неподвижность*) stasis.

стати́ст (-а) *м* (ТЕАТР) extra.

стати́стик (-а) *м* statistician.

стати́стик|а (-и) *ж* statistics.

статисти́ческ|ий (-ая, -ое, -ие) *прил* statistical; **Центра́льное ~ое управле́ние** central statistics office.

стати́чен *прил см* стати́чный.

стати́ческ|ий (-ая, -ое, -ие) *прил* static.

стати́ч|ный (-ен, -на, -но) *прил* static.

ста́т|ный (-ен, -на, -но) *прил* stately.

ста́тус (-а) *м* status.

ста́тус-кво *м нескл* status quo.

стату́т (-а) *м* (*правила*) statute.

статуэ́т|ка (-ки; *gen pl* -ок) *ж* statuette.

стату́|я (-и) *ж* statue.

ста|ть (-ти) *ж* (*осанка*) bearing; ♦ (**-ну, -нешь**; *impf* станови́ться) *сов неперех* to stand; (*к станку, за прилавок*) to take up position; (*no impf*; *часы, завод, движение*) to stop; (*начать*): ~ +*infin* to begin *или* start doing; (*обойтись*): ~ **в** +*acc* to cost *безл* (*наличествовать*): **нас ста́ло бо́льше/тро́е** there are more/three of us; **под ~ кому́-н/чему́-н** (*подобно*) like sb/sth; **с како́й ста́ти?** (*разг*) why?; **станови́ться** (~ *perf*) +*instr* (*учителем*) to become; **его́ не ста́ло** he passed away; **не ста́ло де́нег/сил** I have no more money/energy; **с него́ ста́нет** (*разг*) that's all you can expect from him; **ста́ло быть** (*значит*) so; **во что бы то ни ста́ло** no matter what; **что с ним ста́ло?** what has become of him?; **станови́ться** (~ *perf*) **у вла́сти** to come to power; **станови́ться** (~ *perf*) **на путь чего́-н** to set out on the path of sth

► ста́ться *сов безл* (*случиться*) to happen; **мо́жет ста́ться** it is possible.

стать|я́ (-ьи́; *gen pl* -е́й) *ж* (*в газете, в сборнике*) article; (*в словаре*) entry; (*в законе, в договоре*)

paragraph, clause; (*экспорта, импорта*) type; (*КОММ: расхода, дохода*) item; **по всем ~м** (*разг*) in all respects.

стафилоко́кк (-а) *м* (МЕД) staphylococcus.

стациона́р (-а) *м* (МЕД) hospital.

ста́чек *сущ см* ста́чка.

ста́чечник (-а) *м* striker.

ста́чечниц|а (-ы) *ж см* ста́чечник.

ста́чива|ть (-ю) *несов от* сточи́ть.

ста́чк|а (-ки; *gen pl* -ек) *ж* (ЭКОН) strike.

стащ|и́ть (-у́, -ишь) *сов от* тащи́ть ♦ (*impf* ста́скивать) *перех* (*что-н сверху*) to pull down; (*что-н в подвал*) to drag down; (*сапоги, чулки*) to pull off; (*no impf*; *разг: украсть*) to nick.

ста́|я (-и) *ж* (*птиц*) flock; (*волков*) pack; (*рыб*) shoal.

ста́|ять (*3sg* -ет, *3pl* -ют, *impf* ста́ивать) *сов неперех* to melt.

ствол (-а́) *м* (*дерева*) trunk; (*ружья, пушки*) barrel.

ство́р|ка (-ки; *gen pl* -ок) *ж* door; (*ставней*) shutter; (*зеркала*) leaf.

ство́рчатый *прил* (*окно, шкаф*) double (*opening in the middle*).

стеб|ель (-ля) *м* (*цветка*) stem.

стёган|ка (-ки; *gen pl* -ок) *ж* quilted jacket.

стёганый *прил* quilted; **стёганое одея́ло** quilt.

стега́|ть (-ю; *perf* простега́ть) *несов перех* (*одеяло*) to quilt; (*no perf*; *хлыстом*) to lash.

стегн|у́ть (-у́, -ёшь) *сов перех* to lash.

стёж|ка (-ки; *gen pl* -ек) *ж* stitch.

стежо́к (-ка́) *м* stitch.

стез|я́ (-и́) *ж* path (*fig*).

стёк(ся) *итп сов см* сте́чь(ся).

стека́|ть(ся) (*3sg* -ет(ся), *3pl* -ют(ся)) *несов от* сте́чь(ся).

стекле́не́|ть (*3sg* -ет, *3pl* -ют, *perf* остеклене́ть) *несов неперех* to become glassy.

стекл|и́ть (-ю́, -и́шь; *perf* остекли́ть) *несов перех* (*окно*) to glaze.

стекл|о́ (-а́; *nom pl* стёкла, *gen pl* стёкол) *ср* glass; (*также*: **око́нное ~**) (window) pane; (*для очков*) lenses *мн* ♦ *собир* (*изделия*) glassware.

стёклыш|ко (-ка; *gen pl* -ек) *ср уменьш от* стекло́; (*осколок*) piece of glass.

стекля́нный *прил* glass; (*перен: взгляд, глаза*) glassy.

стекля́рус (-а) *м собир* glass beads *мн*.

стекля́шк|а (-ки; *gen pl* -ек) *ж* (*осколок*) piece of glass; (*пренебр: изделие*) bauble.

стёкол *сущ см* стекло́.

стеко́льный *прил* (*завод*) glass.

стеко́льщик (-а) *м* glazier.

стеку́т(ся) *итп сов см* сте́чь(ся).

сте́лек *сущ см* сте́лька.

стел|и́ть (-ю́, -ишь; *perf* постели́ть) *несов перех* (*скатерть, подстилку*) to spread out; (*perf*

настели́ть; *пол, паркет*) to lay; **~ (постели́ть** *perf*) **посте́ль** to make up a bed

▶ **стели́ться** *несов возв* (*туман*) to spread; (*perf* **постели́ться**; *разг*: приготовить постель) to get ready for bed

стелла́ж (-á) *м* shelf (*мн* shelves).

стéль|ка (-ьки; *gen pl* -ек) *ж* (*в обуви*) insole.

стелю́(сь) *итп несов см* **стла́ть(ся)**.

стемне́|ть (*3sg* -ет) *сов от* **темне́ть**.

стен|á (-ы́; *acc sg* -у, *dat sg* -é, *nom pl* -ы, *dat pl* -áм) *ж* (*также перен*) wall; **в ~х** +*gen* (*школы, учреждения*) within the confines of; **сиде́ть** (*impf*) **в четырёх ~х** to be cooped up indoors.

стена́ни|е (-я) *ср* groan.

стена́|ть (-ю) *несов неперех* to groan.

стенгазе́т|а (-ы) *ж* (= стенна́я газе́та) *newsletter displayed on wall in school or place of work.*

стенд (-а) *м* (*выставочный*) display stand; (*испытательный*) test-bed; (*для стрельбы*) rifle range.

стéндовый *прил*: **стéндовая стрельба́** target practice.

стéн|ка (-ки; *gen pl* -ок) *ж уменьш от* **стена́**; (*комнаты, желудка, также* ФУТБОЛ) wall; (*разг: мебель*) wall unit; (*ящика*) side; **прижима́ть (прижа́ть** *perf*) **кого́-н к ~ке** (*разг*) to push sb to the wall.

стенно́й *прил* wall *опред*; **стенна́я ро́спись** mural.

стеногра́мм|а (-ы) *ж* shorthand record.

стенографи́р|овать (-ую; *perf* **стенографи́ровать** *или* **застенографи́ровать**) *несов перех* to take down in shorthand.

стенографи́ст (-а) *м* shorthand typist (*BRIT*), stenographer (*US*).

стенографи́ст|ка (-ки; *gen pl* -ок) *ж см* **стенографи́ст**.

стеногра́фи|я (-и) *ж* shorthand (*BRIT*), stenography (*US*).

стéнок *сущ см* **стéнка**.

стенокарди́|я (-и) *ж* angina.

стéнопись (-и) *ж* mural painting.

стéньг|а (-и) *ж* (*МОР*) topmast.

степéнный (-ен, -на, -но) *прил* sedate.

степéн|ь (-и; *gen pl* -éй) *ж* (*также* ПРОСВЕЩ) degree; (*МАТ*) power; **в вы́сшей ~и** in the extreme; **до изве́стной** *или* **не́которой ~и** to some *или* a certain extent; **ожо́г пéрвой** *итп* **~и** first *итп* degree burn.

степно́й *прил* steppe *опред*.

степ|ь (-и; *loc sg* -и́, *gen pl* -éй) *ж* the steppe.

стéрв|а (-ы) *ж* (*груб!*) bastard (*!*); (*: женщина*) bitch (*!*).

стервенé|ть (-ю; *perf* **остервенéть**) *несов неперех* (*разг*) to get mad.

стервя́тник (-а) *м* a carrion crow.

стерёг *итп несов см* **стерéчь**.

стерегу́ *итп несов см* **стерéчь**.

стереоза́пись (-и) *ж* stereo recording.

стереозвуча́ни|е (-я) *ср* stereo (*sound*).

стереомагнитофо́н (-а) *м* stereo tape recorder.

стереопро́|игрыватель (-я) *м* stereo record player.

стереосистéм|а (-ы) *ж* stereo.

стереоти́п (-а) *м* (*ТИПОГ, перен*) stereotype.

стереоти́пный *прил* (-ен, -на, -но; *ответ, мышление итп*) stereotyped.

стерéть (**сотру́, сотрёшь;** *pt* **стёр, стёрла, стёрло,** *impf* **стира́ть**) *сов перех* (*грязь, пыль, грим*) to wipe off; (*надпись, память, различия*) to erase; **стира́ть (~** *perf*) **что-н/кого́-н в порошо́к** (*также перен*) to pulverize sth/sb; **стира́ть (~** *perf*) **с лица́ земли́** to wipe off the face of the earth

▶ **стерéться** (*impf* **стира́ться**) *сов возв* (*надпись, краска*) to be worn away; (*подошвы*) to wear down; (*перен: различия, границы*) to be erased; **стира́ться (~ся** *perf*) **в па́мяти** to become blurred.

стер|éчь (-егу́, -ежёшь *итп*, -егу́т; *pt* -ёг, -егла́, -егло́) *несов перех* to watch over; (*подстерегать*) to lie in wait for.

стéр|жень (-ня) *м* rod; (*винта*) stem; (*ось*) pivot; (*шариковой ручки*) (ink) cartridge; (*перен: политики, романа*) backbone.

стержнево́й *прил* (*осевой*) pivoted; (*перен: вопрос, проблема*) crucial.

стéржня *итп сущ см* **стéржень**.

стери́лен *прил см* **стери́льный**.

стерилиза́тор (-а) *м* sterilizer.

стерилиза́ци|я (-и) *ж* sterilization.

стерилиз|ова́ть (-у́ю) (*не)сов перех* to sterilize.

стери́льный (-ен, -ьна, -ьно) *прил* sterile, sterilized.

стéрлинг (-а) *м* (*ЭКОН*) sterling; **10 фу́нтов ~ов** 10 pounds sterling.

стéрляд|ь (-и; *gen pl* -éй) *ж* sterlet.

стерп|éть (-лю́, -ишь) *сов перех* to endure

▶ **стерпéться** *сов возв*: **~ся с** +*instr* to learn to endure.

стёртый (-, -а, -о) *прил* (*надпись*) worn; (*монета*) effaced; (*перен: фразы*) hackneyed.

стес|а́ть (-шу́, -шешь; *impf* **стёсывать**) *сов перех* (*кору*) to strip off.

стеснéни|е (-я) *ср* constraints *мн*; (*в груди*) constriction; (*смущение*) shyness.

стеснённый *прил* (*дыхание*) constricted; **в ~ых обстоя́тельствах** in financial straits.

стесни́телен *прил см* **стесни́тельный**.

стесни́тельность (-и) *ж* shyness.

стесни́тельный (-ен, -ьна, -ьно) *прил* shy.

стесн|и́ть (-ю́, -и́шь) *сов от* **тесни́ть** ◆ (*impf* **стесня́ть**) *перех* (*хозяев*) to inconvenience; (*дыхание*) to constrict; **стесня́ть (~** *perf*) **кого́-н в расхо́дах** to restrict sb's spending.

стесня́|ться (-ю́сь; *perf* **постесня́ться**) *несов возв*: **~** (+*gen*) (*женщин, незнакомых*) to be shy (of); (+*infin*; *сказать, просить итп*) to be too shy to do; ~ *(impf)* **пéред кем-н** to feel shy in sb's presence; **онá не ~ется в срéдствах** she won't stop at anything; **он не ~ется в выражéниях** he doesn't mince his words.

стёсыва|ть (-ю) *несов от* **стесáть**.

стетоскóп (-а) stethoscope.

стечéни|е (-я) *ср (нарóда)* gathering; *(случáйностей)* combination; ~ **обстоя́тельств** coincidence; **при большóм ~и нарóда** in front of a large number of people.

стечь *(3sg* **-ечёт**, *3pl* **-екýт**, *pt* **-ёк, -еклá, -еклó**, *impf* **стекáть) сов неперех**: ~ **(с +gen)** to run down (from)

▸ **стéчься** *(impf* **стекáться) сов возв** *(ручьи́, рéки)* to flow; *(лю́ди)* to congregate.

стешý *итп сов см* **стесáть**.

стúлен *прил см* **стúльный**.

стилизáци|я (-и) *ж (подражáние)* imitation; *(о произведéнии)* stylized work.

стилизóван|ный (-, -на, -но) *прил* stylized.

стилиз|овáть (-ýю) (не)сов перех to stylize.

стилистúческ|ий (-ая, -ое, -ие) *прил (приём)* stylistic.

стил|ь (-я) *м* style; *(летосчислéния)* calendar; **он в своём стúле** he's being his usual self; **6 ию́ня по стáрому/нóвому стúлю** 6th June Old Style/New Style.

стúль|ный (-ен, -ьна, -ьно) *прил* stylish; *(разг: причёска, одéжда)* snazzy.

стиля́г|а (-и) *м/ж (разг: пренебр)* fashion victim.

стúмул (-а) *м* incentive, stimulus *(мн* stimuli).

стимулúровани|е (-я) *ср* stimulation; **материáльное ~** financial incentive.

стимулúр|овать (-ую) (не)сов перех to stimulate; *(рабóту, прогрéсс)* to encourage; ~ *(impf/perf)* **рост эконóмики** to encourage economic growth.

стимуля́ци|я (-и) *ж* stimulation; *(рóдов)* induction.

стипендиáльный *прил*: ~ **фонд** scholarship fund; **стипендиáльная комúссия** grants committee.

стипéнди|я (-и) *ж (госудáрственная)* grant; *(за осóбые достижéния)* scholarship.

стипль-чéз (-а) *м (СПОРТ)* steeplechase.

стирáльный *прил*: ~ **порошóк** washing powder; **стирáльная машúна** washing machine.

стирáни|е (-я) *ср (нáдписи)* erasure; *(различий)* erosion.

стúраный *прил* washed.

стирá|ть (-ю) *несов от* **стерéть** ♦ *(perf* **выстирать** *или* **постирáть) перех** to wash

▸ **стирáться** *несов от* **стерéться**

стúр|ка (-ки; *gen pl* **-ок)** *ж* washing; **отдавáть (отдáть** *perf)* **что-н в ~ку** to put sth in for a service wash.

стúсн|уть (-у, -ешь; *impf* **стúскивать) сов перех**

(в рукé, в зубáх) to clench; *(подлеж: толпá)* to squeeze; **стúскивать (~ *perf*) когó-н в объя́тиях** to clutch sb in one's arms; ~ *(perf)* **зýбы** *(перен)* to grit one's teeth.

стих (-á) *м* verse.

стихá|ть (-ю) *несов от* **стúхнуть**.

стих|ú (-óв) *мн (поэзия)* poetry *ед*; **ромáн в ~áх** novel in verse.

стихúй|ный (-ен, -йна, -йно) *прил (сúла)* elemental; *(развúтие, становлéние)* uncontrolled; *(протéст, демонстрáции)* spontaneous; **стихúйное бéдствие** natural disaster.

стихúй|я (-и) *ж (водá, огóнь итп)* element; *(ры́нка, инфля́ции)* natural force; **борóться** *(impf)* **со ~ей** to do battle with the elements; **быть** *(impf)* **в своéй ~и** to be in one's element; **бúзнес – егó ~** business is his forte.

стúх|нуть (-ну, -нешь; *pt* **-, -ла, -ло**, *impf* **стихáть) сов неперех** to die down.

стихосложéни|е (-я) *ср* versification.

стихотворéни|е (-я) *ср* poem.

стихотвóрный *прил (произведéние)* poetic; *(парóдия)* in verse; **стихотвóрный размéр** metre *(in poetry)*.

стлать (стелю́, стéлешь; *perf* **постлáть) несов перех = стелúть**

▸ **стлáться несов возв = стелúться**.

сто (ста; *см* **Table 30)** *чис* one hundred; *(разг: мнóго)*: ~ **+gen** hundreds of; ~ **книг/столóв** a hundred books/tables; **óколо ста** about a hundred; ~ **пéрвый** hundred and first; **я увéрен на ~ процéнтов** I am one hundred percent sure; **мнóго сот** many hundreds; **нéсколько сот** several hundred.

стог (-а; *loc sg* **-ý**, *nom pl* **-á)** *м*: ~ **сéна** haystack.

стограммóвый *прил (гúря)* one-hundred-gram; ~ **стакáн** ≈ shot glass. ♦

стóек *сущ см* **стóйка** ♦ *прил см* **стóйкий**.

стóимостн|ый *прил (ЭКОН)*: ~**ые показáтели/отношéния** cost indices/relations.

стóимост|ь (-и) *ж* cost; *(цéнность)* value; ~ **по торгóвым кнúгам** *(КОММ)* book value; ~ **и фрахт** cost and freight.

стó|ить (-ю, -ишь) *несов (не)перех (+acc или +gen; дéнег)* to cost; *(усúлий, трудá итп)* to take ♦ *неперех*: ~ **+gen (внимáния, любвú)** to be worth ♦ *безл*: ~**ить +infin** to be worth doing; **кнúга ~ит 10 рублéй** the book costs 10 roubles; **дом ~ит большúе дéньги** *или* **больших дéнег** the house costs a lot of money; **на э́ту вы́ставку ~ит пойтú** it is worth going to see this exhibition; **мне ничегó не ~ит сдéлать э́то** it's no trouble for me to do it; **спасúбо! – не ~ит** thank you! – don't mention it; **чегó ~ят твоú обещáния!** what are your promises worth?; ~**ит (тóлько) захотéть/постарáться** *(об услóвии)* you only have to wish/try; ~**ит мне (тóлько)**

войти́ в дом, как сра́зу начина́ет звони́ть
телефóн the minute I come through the door the
phone starts ringing.
стойчески *нареч* stoically.
стойческ|ий (-ая, -ое, -ие) *прил* stoical.
стой(те) *несов см* **стоя́ть.**
стóйбищ|е (-а) *ср* (*кочевников*) nomad camp.
стóй|ка (-йки; *gen pl* -ек) ж (*положение тела*)
stance; (*собаки*) pose; (*подпорка*) prop;
(*прилавок*) counter; (*воротник*) stand-up collar;
стоя́ть (*impf*) **по ~йке сми́рно/во́льно** to stand
to attention/at ease; **стóйка на рука́х** handstand;
стóйка на голове́ headstand.
стóйк|ий (-ая, -ое, -ие; -ек, -йка, -йко)
прил (*человек, характер*) steadfast, resilient;
(*краска, материал*) durable, hard-wearing;
(*запах*) stubborn.
стóйко *нареч* steadfastly.
стóйкост|ь (-и) ж (*см прил*) resilience;
durability; stubborness.
стóйл|о (-а) *ср* stall (*in a stable*).
стоймя́ *нареч* upright.
стóйче *сравн прил от* **стóйкий ♦** *сравн нареч
от* **стóйко.**
сток (-а) *м* (*действие*) drainage;
(*приспособление*) drain.
Стокгóльм (-а) *м* Stockholm.
стокра́тный *прил* hundredfold.
стол (-а́) *м* table; (*письменный*) desk; (*еда*) food;
а́дресный ~ *residents' registration office*;
кру́глый ~ round table (*fig*); **сади́ться (сесть**
perf) **за ~** to sit down at the table; **за ~óм** at
table; **убира́ть (убра́ть** *perf*) **со ~á** to clear the
table; **встава́ть (встать** *perf*) **из-за ~á** to get up
from the table; **стол нахóдок** lost property
(office); **стол переговóров** negotiating table.
столб (-а́) *м* (*пограничный, указательный*) post;
(*телеграфный*) pole; (*перен: пыли, дыма*)
cloud.
столбене́|ть (-ю; *perf* **остолбене́ть**) *несов
неперех* to be rooted to the spot.
столбе́ц (-ца́) *м* column (*on page*).
стóлбик (-а) *м уменьш от* **столб;** (*бумаг*) ream;
(*цифр*) column; **ртýтный ~** mercury column;
~ом in a column.
столбня́к (-а́) *м* tetanus.
столбовóй *прил*: **~ дворяни́н** (*ИСТ*) *a member
of the old Russian nobility*; **столбова́я дорóга**
(*ИСТ*) highway.
столбца́ *итп сущ см* **столбе́ц.**
столе́ти|е (-я) *ср* (*срок*) century; (*годовщина*): **~
**+gen centenary of.
столе́тн|ий (-яя, -ее, -ие) *прил* (*период*)
hundred-year; (*старик, дерево*) hundred-year-
old.
столе́тник (-а) *м* (*БОТ*) aloe.
стóлечко *нареч* (*разг*) = **стóлько.**
стóлик (-а) *м уменьш от* **стол;** (*в ресторане, в
кафе*) table; **туале́тный ~** dressing table.
столи́ц|а (-ы) ж capital (city).
столи́чный *прил* (*газеты, жители, театры*)

of the capital; **столи́чный гóрод** capital city.
столкнове́ни|е (-я) *ср* clash; (*машин, судов*)
collision; **вооружённое ~** armed clash.
столкн|ýть (-ý, -ёшь; *impf* **ста́лкивать**) *сов
перех*: **~ (с** +gen) to push off; (*сблизить
толчком*) to push together; (*подлеж: случей, .
судьба*) to bring together; **~** (*perf*) **кого́-н в вóду**
to push sb into the water
▶ **столкн|ýться** (*impf* **ста́лкиваться**) *сов возв*
(*машины, поезда*) to collide; (*интересы,
характеры*) to clash; (*встретиться*): **~ся с**
+instr (*встречаться*) to come into contact with;
(*случайно*) to bump *или* run into; (*с
трудностями, с непониманием*) to encounter; **я
ста́лкивался с ним по рабóте** I have come into
contact with him through work.
столк|ова́ться (-ýюсь; *impf* **столкóвываться**)
сов возв: **~ (с** +instr) to come to an agreement
(with).
столóв|ая (-ой; *decl like adj*) ж (*заведение*)
canteen; (*команта*) dining room.
столóв|ка (-ки; *gen pl* -ок) ж (*разг*) canteen.
столóвый *прил* (*мебель, часы*) dining room
опред; **столóвая лóжка** (*для супа*) tablespoon;
столóвая соль table salt; **столóвое винó** table
wine; **столóвый серви́з** dinner service.
столп (-á) *м* (*обычно мн: перен*) pillar.
столп|и́ться (*3sg* -и́тся, *3pl* -я́тся) *сов возв* to
crowd.
столпотворе́ни|е (-я) *ср* chaos.
столь *нареч* so; **~ же ... скóлько ...** as ... as ....
стóлько *нареч* (*об исчисляемом количестве*)
so many; (*о неисчисляемом количестве*) so
much **♦** (**-их**) *мест* (*см нареч*) this many; this
much; **я не хочý дава́ть емý ~ де́нег** I don't
want to give him that much money; **она́ ~
пережила́!** she has been through so much!; **где
ты был ~ вре́мени?** where have you been all
this time?; **у меня́ ~ (же) де́нег/пробле́м,
скóлько (и) у тебя́** I've got as much money/as
many problems as you; **он не ~ глуп, скóлько
лени́в** he is not so much stupid as lazy.
стóлько-то *нареч* (*об исчисляемом
количестве*) X number of; (*об неисчисляемом
количестве*) X amount of; **~ сде́лано, ~
остáлось** this much has been done and this
much is left.
столя́р (-á) *м* joiner.
столя́рнича|ть (-ю) *несов неперех* (*разг*) to do
carpentry.
столя́рный *прил*: **~ая мастерка́я** joiner's;
столя́рное де́ло joinery; **столя́рные
инструме́нты** carpentry tools; **столя́рный
клей** wood glue.
стомати́т (-а) *м* mouth ulcer.
стоматóлог (-а) *м* dental surgeon.
стоматологи́ческий (-ая, -ое, -ие) *прил*
dental; **стоматологи́ческий кабине́т/
поликли́ника** dental surgery/hospital.
стоматологи|я (-и) ж dentistry.
стометрóв|ка (-ки; *gen pl* -ок) ж (*разг: СПОРТ*)

the hundred metres (BRIT) *или* meters (US).
стометро́вый *прил*: ~**ая диста́нция** one hundred metres (BRIT) *или* meters (US).
стон (-а) *м* (*см глаг*) groan; moan.
стон|а́ть (-у́, -ешь) *несов неперех* to groan; (*перен*: *жаловаться*) to moan.
стоп *межд* stop.
стоп|а́ (-ы́; *nom pl* -ы) *ж* (*в стихах*) foot; (*nom pl* -ы; ANAT) sole; **идти́ (пойти́** *perf*) **по чьим-н ~м** to follow in sb's footsteps.
стоп|и́ть (-лю́, -ишь; *impf* **ста́пливать**) *сов перех* (*дрова*) to burn up.
сто́п|ка (-ки; *gen pl* -ок) *ж* (*бумаг, писем*) pile; (*стаканчик*) glass (*for vodka etc*).
стоп-кра́н (-а) *м* emergency handle (*on train*).
стоплю́ *сов см* **стопи́ть**.
сто́пок *сущ см* **сто́пка**.
сто́пор (-а) *м* (TEX) lock.
сто́пор|ить (-ю, -ишь; *perf* **застопорить**) *несов перех* (*машину*) to stop; (*дело, работу*) to hold up; (*фиксировать*) to lock.
стопроце́нтный *прил* one-hundred percent; (*разг*: *негодяй, лгун итп*) absolute.
стоп|та́ть (-чу́, -чешь; *impf* **ста́птывать**) *сов перех* to wear out
▶ **стопта́ться** (*impf* **ста́птываться**) *сов возв* to wear out.
сторг|ова́ть(ся) (-у́ю(сь)) *сов от* **торгова́ть(ся)**.
стори́цей *нареч*: **возда́ть ~ кому́-н** to reward sb in full.
сто́рож (-а; *nom pl* -а́, *gen pl* -е́й) *м* watchman (*мн* watchmen).
сторожево́й *прил*: ~ **пост** lookout post; **сторожева́я вы́шка** watchtower; **сторожево́й ка́тер** patrol boat.
сторо́жек *сущ см* **сторо́жка**.
сторож|и́ть (-у́, -и́шь) *несов перех* (*дом, сад*) to guard; (*зверя, вора*) to lie in wait for.
сторо́ж|ка (-ки; *gen pl* -ек) *ж* hut.
сторо|на́ (-оны́; *acc sg* -ону, *dat sg* -оне́, *nom pl* -оны, *gen pl* -о́н, *dat pl* -она́м) *ж* side; (*направление*: *левая, правая*) direction; (*страна*) land; **стоя́ть** (*impf*) **в ~оне́ от** +*gen* to stand apart from; **в ~оне́** a little way off; **держа́ться** (*impf*) **в ~оне́** to keep one's distance; **в сто́рону** +*gen* towards; **смотре́ть (посмотре́ть** *perf*) **в сто́рону** to look away; **на́ ~ону** (*разг*: *продавать*) on the side; **подраба́тывать** (*impf*) **на ~оне́** (*разг*) to work on the side; **брать (взять** *perf*) **кого́-н со ~оны́** to bring sb in from outside (*fig*); **со ~оны́** +*gen* from; **со ~оны́ ма́тери/отца́** on one's mother's/father's side; **э́то о́чень любе́зно с Ва́шей ~оны́** that is very good of you; **с одно́й ~оны́ ... с друго́й ~оны́ ...** on the one hand ... on the other hand ...; **принима́ть (приня́ть** *perf*) **чью-н сто́рону** to take sb's side; **встава́ть**

(**встать** *perf*) **на чью-н сто́рону** to come out in sb's defence (BRIT) *или* defense (US); **быть** (*impf*) **на чьей-н ~оне́** to be on sb's side; **смотре́ть** (*impf*) **по ~м** to look around; (*отвлекаться*) to let one's attention wander.
сто|ро́ни́ться (-роню́сь, -ро́нишься; *perf* **посторони́ться**) *несов возв* (*дать дорогу*) to make way; (*избегать*): ~ +*gen* to avoid.
сторо́нн|ий (-яя, -ее, -ие) *прил* outside *опред*.
сторо́нник (-а) *м* supporter, advocate.
сторо́нниц|а (-ы) *ж см* **сторо́нник**.
сторубле́вый *прил* (*ассигнация*) one-hundred-rouble; (*о стоимости*) worth one hundred roubles.
стоск|ова́ться (-у́юсь) *сов возв*: ~ **по** +*dat* to miss.
сточ|и́ть (-у́, -ишь; *impf* **ста́чивать**) *сов перех* to smooth down.
сто́чн|ый *прил*: ~**ая кана́ва** gutter (*in street*); **сто́чная труба́** drainpipe; **сто́чные во́ды** effluent; **сто́чный жёлоб** gutter (*on roof*).
стошн|и́ть (-и́т) *сов от* **тошни́ть**.
сто́я *нареч* standing up.
стоя́ни|е (-я) *ср* standing.
стоя́н|ка (-ки; *gen pl* -ок) *ж* (*поезда, судна*) stop; (*автомобилей*) car park (BRIT), parking lot (US); (*геологов, путешественников*) camp; (*первобытного человека*) site; **стоя́нка такси́** taxi rank.
сто|я́ть (-ю́, -и́шь; *imper* **стой(те)**) *несов неперех* to stand; (*находиться*) to be; (*полк*) to be stationed; (*бездействовать*) to stand idle; (*сохраняться*: *цветы*) to last; (: *продукты*) to keep; (*perf* **постоя́ть**; *защищать*): ~ **за** +*acc* (*за друга, за идею*) to stand up for; **пе́ред на́ми ~ит тру́дная зада́ча/интере́сная пробле́ма** we are faced with a difficult task/interesting problem; **на бла́нке ~ит по́дпись дире́ктора** the document bears the director's signature; **по́езд ~ит здесь 15 мину́т** the train stops here for 15 minutes; **ча́йник ~ит на плите́** the kettle is on the stove; **цветы́ ~ят в ва́зе** the flowers are in the vase; **посу́да ~ит в шка́фу** the crockery is in the cupboard; ~**ла весна́/о́сень** it was spring/autumn (BRIT) *или* fall (US); **всё ле́то ~ла жара́** it was hot all through the summer; **в до́ме ~ял шум/смех** the house was full of noise/laughter; ~ (*impf*) **у вла́сти** to be in power; ~ (*impf*) **на свои́х пози́циях** to stand one's ground; **он ~ит на своём** he refuses to budge.
стоя́ч|ий (-ая, -ее, -ие) *прил* (*предложение*) standing *опред*; (*воротник*) stand-up; (*вода*) stagnant.
сто́ящ|ий (-ая, -ее, -ие) *прил* (*дело, предложение*) worthwhile; (*человек*) worthy; (*вещь*) useful.
стр. *сокр* (= **страни́ца**) pg. (= *page*).

страв|и́ть (-лю́, -ишь) *сов от* трави́ть ◆ (*impf* **стра́вливать**) *перех* to set on; **он их ~и́л** he set them on each other.

страда́ (-ы́) *ж* harvesting.

страда́л|ец (-ьца) *м* martyr.

страда́лиц|а (-ы) *ж см* **страда́лец**.

страда́льца *итп сущ см* **страда́лец**.

страда́льческий (-ая, -ое, -ие) *прил* martyred.

страда́ни|е (-я) *ср* suffering.

страда́тельный *прил*: ~ **зало́г** passive voice.

страда́|ть (-ю) *несов неперех* to suffer; (*дисциплина, грамотность итп*) to be poor; (*сочувствовать*): ~ **за** +*acc* to suffer for; (*потерпеть ущерб*): ~ **от** +*gen* (*от засухи, от инфляции итп*) to suffer as a result of; (*perf* **пострада́ть**; *поплати́ться*) to suffer; ~ (**от** +*gen*) (*от бо́ли, от го́лода*) to suffer; ~ (*impf*) +*instr* (*боле́знью, самомне́нием*) to suffer from; ~ (*impf*) **от любви́** to be lovesick.

стра́ж (-а) *м* guardian.

стра́ж|а (-и) *ж собир* guard; **быть** (*impf*) *или* **стоя́ть** (*impf*) **на ~е** +*gen* to guard; **под ~ей** in custody; **брать** (**взять** *perf*) **кого́-н под ~у** to take sb into custody; **содержа́ть** (*impf*) **кого́-н под ~ей** to remand sb in custody.

стран|а́ (-ы́; *nom pl* -ы) *ж* country; **стра́ны све́та** cardinal points (*on compass*).

стра́нен *прил см* **стра́нный**.

страни́ц|а (-ы) *ж* (*также перен*) page; (*перен: исто́рии, жи́зни*) chapter; **на ~х газе́т** in the papers.

стра́нник (-а) *м* wanderer; (*РЕЛ*) pilgrim.

стра́нниц|а (-ы) *ж см* **стра́нник**.

стра́нно *нареч* strangely ◆ *как сказ* that is strange *или* odd; **он ~ вы́глядит** he looks strange; ~, **что её ещё нет** it is strange *или* odd that she isn't here yet; **мне ~, что ...** I find it strange that ....

стра́нност|ь (-и) *ж* strangeness; (*обычно мн: челове́ка, поведе́ния*) oddity.

стра́н|ный (-ен, -на́, -но) *прил* strange; ~**ное де́ло** that's strange *или* odd.

странове́дени|е (-я) *ср* national studies *мн*.

стра́нстви|е (-я) *ср* wandering.

стра́нств|овать (-ую) *несов неперех* to wander.

Стра́сбург (-а) *м* Strasbourg.

стра́стен *прил см* **стра́стный**.

страстно́й *прил*: ~**а́я неде́ля** Holy Week.

стра́стность (-и) *ж* passion.

стра́ст|ный (-ен, -на́, -но) *прил* passionate; (*колле́кционер итп*) ardent.

страст|ь (-и) *ж* passion; (*разг: у́жас*) horror; **стра́сти разгоре́лись** passions were running high; ~ **к му́зыке/кни́гам** a passion for music/books.

страте́г (-а) *м* strategist.

стратеги́ческий (-ая, -ое, -ие) *прил* strategic.

страте́ги|я (-и) *ж* strategy.

стратосфе́р|а (-ы) *ж* stratosphere.

стра́ус (-а) *м* ostrich.

стра́усовый *прил* ostrich *опред*.

страх (-а) *м* fear; (*разг: обычно мн: стра́шное собы́тие*) horror; ~ **за дете́й/за бли́зких** fear for one's children/loved ones; ~ **сме́рти/разоблаче́ния** fear of death/exposure; ~ **пе́ред неизве́стным** fear of the unknown; **со стра́ху** in fright; **нача́льник держа́л их в стра́хе** they lived in fear of their boss; **под стра́хом сме́рти** on pain of death; **на свой ~ (и риск)** at one's own risk.

страхова́ни|е (-я) *ср* insurance; ~ **от** +*gen* insurance against; **госуда́рственное** ~ national insurance (*BRIT*); **страхова́ние жи́зни** life insurance; **страхова́ние иму́щества** property insurance.

страхова́тел|ь (-я) *м person taking out insurance*.

страх|ова́ть (-у́ю) *несов перех* (*гимна́ста*) to stand by (*to prevent sb from falling*); (*perf* **застрахова́ть**): ~ (**от** +*gen*) (*иму́щество, автомоби́ль*) to insure (against); (*от неожи́данностей*) to protect (against)

▶ **страхова́ться** (*perf* **застрахова́ться**) *несов возв*: ~**ся** (**от** +*gen*) to insure o.s. (against); (*от неожи́данностей*) to protect o.s (from).

страхо́в|ка (-ки; *gen pl* -ок) *ж* insurance; **для ~ки** to be on the safe side.

страхово́й *прил* (*фи́рма, аге́нт*) insurance *опред*; ~ **бро́кер** insurance broker; **страхово́й взнос** *или* **страхова́я пре́мия** insurance premium; **страхово́й по́лис** insurance policy.

страхо́вок *сущ см* **страхо́вка**.

страхо́вщик (-а) *м* insurer.

стра́шен *прил см* **стра́шный**.

страши́л|а (-ы) *м/ж* = **страши́лище**.

страши́лищ|е (-а; *gen pl* -) *ср* (*разг*) fright.

страш|и́ть (-у́, -и́шь) *несов перех* to frighten, scare

▶ **страши́ться** *несов возв*: ~**ся** +*gen* to be frightened *или* scared of.

стра́шно *нареч* (*крича́ть*) in a frightening way; (*разг: уста́лый, дово́льный*) terribly ◆ *как сказ* it's frightening; **мне ~** I'm frightened *или* scared; ~ **поду́мать** it's frightening to think; **он ~ дово́лен собо́й** (*разг*) he's awfully *или* terribly pleased with himself; **она́ ~ уста́ла** (*разг*) she's awfully *или* terribly tired; **она́ ~ лю́бит болта́ть** (*разг*) she really likes to chat.

стра́ш|ный (-ен, -на́, -но) *прил* terrible, awful; (*фильм, сон, путь*) terrifying; **ничего́ ~ного** it doesn't matter.

стре́ж|ень (-ня) *м* deep part (*of river*).

стреко́з|а́ (-озы́; *nom pl* -о́зы) *ж* dragonfly (*мн* dragonflies); (*ребёнок*) fidget.

стрек|ота́ть (-очу́, -о́чешь) *несов неперех* to chirp.

стрел|а́ (-ы́; *nom pl* -ы) *ж* (*для стрельбы́*) arrow; (*кра́на*) arm; (*по́езд*) express (train).

стреле́ц (-ьца́) *м* Strelets (*regular soldier of special regiment in 16th-17th century*); (*созве́здие*): **С~** Sagittarius.

стрéл|ка (-ки; *gen pl* -ок) *ж уменьш от* **стрелá**; (*часов*) hand; (*компаса, барометра*) needle; (*знак*) arrow; (*железнодорожная*) switch; (*ГЕО*) spit; (*лука*) shoot.

стрелкá *итп сущ см* **стрелóк**.

стрелкóвый *прил*: ~ **полк** infantry regiment; **стрелкóвый спорт** shooting.

стрéлок *сущ см* **стрéлка**.

стрел|óк (-кá) *м* (*ВОЕН*) rifleman (*мн* riflemen); **он хорóший** ~ he is a good shot.

стрéлочник (-а) *м* signalman (*мн* signalmen).

стрéлочни|ца (-ы) *ж см* **стрéлочник**.

стрельб|á (-ы) *ж* shooting, firing.

стрéльбищ|е (-а) *ср* shooting range.

стрельцá *итп сущ см* **стрелéц**.

стрéльчатый *прил* (*окна, свод*) arched.

стрéляный *прил* (*дичь*) shot *опред*; ~ **патрóн** spent cartridge; ~ **солдáт** *soldier who has been under fire*; ~ **воробéй** (*разг*) old hand.

стрел|я́ть (-ю) *несов неперех*: ~ (**в** +*acc*) (*в цель, во врага*) to shoot (at); (*мотор*) to backfire ♦ *перех* (*убивать: птиц*) to shoot; (*выпрашивать*) to cadge; ~ (*impf*) **из ружья́/пу́шки** to fire a rifle/canon; **у меня́ ~ет в боку́** I have a shooting pain in my side

▶ **стреля́ться** *несов возв* (*самоубийца*) to shoot o.s.; (*на дуэли*): ~**ся с** +*instr* to fight a duel with.

стремглáв *нареч* headlong.

стрéмени *итп сущ см* **стрéмя**.

стремúтельно *нареч* (*мчаться*) headlong; (*меняться*) rapidly.

стремúтельност|ь (-и) *ж* (*движений*) swiftness; (*изменений*) rapidity.

стремúтельный *прил* (*движение, бег, атака*) swift; (*человек*) energetic; (*изменения*) rapid.

стрем|úться (-лю́сь, -и́шься) *несов возв*: ~ **в** +*acc* (*в университет, на родину*) to want to go to; (*добиваться*): ~ **к** +*dat* (*к славе, к добру, к правде*) to strive for.

стремлéни|е (-я) *ср*: ~ (**к** +*dat*) striving (for).

стремлю́сь *несов см* **стремúться**.

стремнúн|а (-ы) *ж* rapid (*in river*).

стрéм|я (-ени; *как* **врéмя**; *см* **Table 4**) *ср* stirrup.

стремя́н|ка (-ки; *gen pl* -ок) *ж* step-ladder.

стрептокóкк (-а) *м* streptococcus.

стресс (-а) *м* stress.

стрéссовый *прил* (*состояние*) stressed; (*ситуация, нагрузки*) stressful.

стриг(ся) *итп несов см* **стричь(ся)**.

стригу́(сь) *итп несов см* **стричь(ся)**.

стриж (-á) *м* swift.

стрúжек *сущ см* **стрúжка**.

стрúженый *прил* shorn; (*трава*) cut; (*мальчик*) short-haired.

стрúж|ка (-ки; *gen pl* -ек) *ж* (*см глаг*) cutting; shearing; mowing; pruning; (*причёска*) haircut.

стриптúз (-а) *м* striptease.

стрихнúн (-а) *м* strychnine.

стри|чь (-гу́, -жёшь *итп*, -гу́т; *pt* -г, -гла, -гло, *perf* **постри́чь** *или* **остри́чь**) *несов перех* (*волосы, траву*) to cut; (*овцу*) to shear; (*газон*) to mow; (*кусты*) to prune; ~ (**постри́чь** *perf*) **кого́-н** to cut sb's hair; ~ (*impf*) **всех под одну́ гребёнку** to tar everyone with the same brush

▶ **стри́чься** (*perf* **постри́чься** *или* **остри́чься**) *несов возв* (*остричь себе волосы*) to cut one's hair; (*в парикмахерской*) to have one's hair cut; (*no perf*; *носить короткую стрижку*) to wear one's hair short.

стро́ганый *прил* planed.

строга́|ть (-ю; *perf* **вы́строгать**) *несов перех* to plane.

стро́г|ий (-ая, -ое, -ие; -, -á, -о) *прил* strict; (*красота, причёска, наказание, выговор*) severe; (*меры*) harsh; (*черты лица*) regular.

стро́го *нареч* (*воспитывать*) strictly; (*наказать, сказать*) severely; ~**на́строго** (*разг*) very strictly; ~ **говоря́** strictly speaking.

стро́гост|ь (-и) *ж* (*см прил*) strictness; severity; harshness; regularity; (*обычно мн*: *строгие порядки*) harsh regulation.

строево́й *прил* (*ВОЕН*: *командир*) line *опред*; **строева́я подгото́вка** drill; **строева́я часть** line unit; **строево́й лес** timber forest; **строево́й шаг** goose step.

строéк *сущ см* **стро́йка**.

стро́ен *прил см* **стро́йный**.

строéни|е (-я) *ср* (*здание*) building; (*организации, вещества*) structure.

стро́же *сравн прил от* **стро́гий** ♦ *сравн нареч от* **стро́го**.

строи́тел|ь (-я) *м* builder; (+*gen*; *нового общества*) creator of.

строи́тельный *прил* building *опред*, construction *опред*; **строи́тельный уча́сток** building site; **строи́тельные материа́лы** building materials.

строи́тельств|о (-а) *ср* (*зданий*) building, construction; (*нового общества*) building.

стро́|ить (-ю, -ишь; *perf* **вы́строить** *или* **постро́ить**) *несов перех* (*дом, дорогу, мост*) to build, construct; (*perf* **постро́ить**; *общество, быт, семью*) to create; (*фразу, мысль*) to compose; (*план, догадку*) to make; (*полк, отряд*) to draw up; ~ (**постро́ить** *perf*) **рома́н на чём-н** to base a novel on sth; ~ (**состро́ить** *perf*) (*из себя́*) **дурака́** to make o.s. out to be a fool; ~ (**состро́ить** *perf*) **гла́зки кому́-н** to make eyes at sb; ~ (**состро́ить** *perf*) **грима́сы** to make *или* pull faces.

▶ **стро́иться** (*perf* **постро́иться**) *несов возв* to build o.s. a house; (*perf* **вы́строиться**; *солдаты, пленные*) to form up; (*no perf*): ~**ся на** +*prp* (*сюжет, роман*) to be based on.

стро́|й (-я) *м* (*социальный*) system; (*языка, предложения*) structure; (*loc sg* -ю́; *ВОЕН*:

шере́нга) line; (: *похо́дный, боево́й*) formation; (: *де́йствующие войска́*) ranks мн; **входи́ть (войти́** *perf)* **в ~** (*заво́д*) to come into operation; **вводи́ть (ввести́** *perf)* **что-н в ~** (*заво́д*) to put sth into operation; **выводи́ть (вы́вести** *perf)* **что-н из стро́я** (*танк, маши́ну*) to put sth out of commission; **выходи́ть (вы́йти** *perf)* **из стро́я** to fall out; (*перен*) to break down; **~ мышле́ния** way of thinking.

стро́йка (-йки; *gen pl* -ек) ж (*зда́ния*) building; (*ме́сто*) building *или* construction site.

стройматериа́лы (-ов) *мн сокр* (= *строи́тельные материа́лы*) building materials мн.

стро́йный (-ен, -йна́, -йно) *прил* (*фигу́ра*) shapely; (*челове́к*) well-built; (*ряд, шере́нга*) orderly; (*речь, фра́за*) well-constructed; (*пе́ние*) harmonious.

строка́ (-и́; *nom pl* -и, *dat pl* -а́м) ж (*в те́ксте*) line; **кра́сная ~** new paragraph; **чита́ть** (*impf*) **ме́жду строк** to read between the lines.

стро́нуться (-усь, -ешься) *сов возв* to start moving.

строп (-а) *м* sling.

стропи́ло (-а) *ср* beam, rafter.

стропти́вый (-, -а, -о) *прил* headstrong.

строфа́ (-ы́; *nom pl* -ы, *dat pl* -а́м) ж stanza.

стро́чек *сущ см* **стро́чка**

строчи́ть (-у́, -и́шь; *perf* **прострочи́ть**) *несов перех* (*рука́в, подо́л*) to stitch; (*perf* **настрочи́ть**; *сочине́ние, статью́*) to scribble; (*no perf; перен: из автома́та*) to fire away.

стро́чка (-ки; *gen pl* -ек) ж *уменьш от* **строка́**; (*шов*) stitch.

строчно́й *прил*: **~а́я бу́ква** small *или* lower case letter.

струга́ть (-ю; *perf* **вы́стругать**) *несов перех* = **строга́ть**.

стру́ек *сущ см* **стру́йка**

стру́жка (-ки; *gen pl* -ек) ж shaving (*of wood, metal etc*).

струи́ться (*3sg* -и́тся, *3pl* -я́тся) *несов возв* (*вода́, ручеёк*) to stream; (*пот, дым*) to pour.

стру́йка (-йки; *gen pl* -ек) ж trickle.

стру́йный *прил*: **~ при́нтер** inkjet printer.

структу́ра (-ы) ж structure.

структурали́зм (-а) *м* structuralism.

структу́рный *прил* structural.

струна́ (-ы́; *nom pl* -ы) ж (*скри́пки, раке́тки*) string; (*перен: поэти́ческая*) streak.

стру́нка (-ки; *gen pl* -ок) ж string; **стать** (*perf*) *или* **вытя́гиваться (вы́тянуться** *perf)* **в ~ку** to stand to attention; **ходи́ть** (*impf*) **по ~ке у кого́-н** *или* **пе́ред кем-н** to be under sb's thumb.

стру́нный *прил* (*инструме́нт*) stringed; **стру́нный кварте́т** string quartet.

стру́нок *сущ см* **стру́нка**

струп (-а; *nom pl* -ья, *gen pl* -ьев) *м* scab.

стру́сить (-шу, -сишь) *сов от* **тру́сить**.

струхну́ть (-у́, -ёшь) *сов неперех* (*разг*) to get a fright.

стручка́ *итп сущ см* **стручо́к**.

стручко́вый *прил*: **~ пе́рец** chilli; **стручко́вая фасо́ль** runner beans мн; **стручко́вый горо́х** peas мн in the pod.

стручо́к (-ка́) *м* pod.

стру́шу *сов см* **стру́сить**.

струя́ (-и́; *nom pl* -и) ж (*воды́, во́здуха*) stream; (*перен: математи́ческая, бо́драя*) streak; **попа́сть** (*perf*) **в ~ю́** (*перен*) to fit in.

стря́пать (-ю; *perf* **состря́пать**) *несов перех* (*разг: еду́*) to cook; (: *расска́з, стихи́*) to cobble together.

стряпня́ (-и́) ж (*разг*) cooking; (*перен*) rubbish.

стрясти́ (-у́, -ёшь; *pt* -, -ла́, -ло́, *impf* **стряса́ть**) *сов перех* to shake off

► **стрясти́сь** *сов возв* (*разг*) to happen; **с ним ~ла́сь беда́** he's in trouble; **что там ~ло́сь?** what happened here?

стряхну́ть (-у́, -ёшь; *impf* **стря́хивать**) *сов перех* (*та́кже перен*) to shake off.

ст.с *сокр* (= *ста́рого сти́ля*) OS (= *Old Style*).

ст.ст. *сокр* = **ст.с.**

студене́ть (*3sg* -ет, *3pl* -ют) *несов неперех* (*зали́вное*) to gel.

студени́стый (-, -а, -о) *прил* gelatinous.

студе́нт (-а) *м* student.

студе́нтка (-ки; *gen pl* -ок) ж см **студе́нт**

студе́нческий (-ая, -ое, -ие) *прил* student *опред*; **студе́нческий биле́т** student card.

студе́нчество (-а) *ср* student days мн ♦ *собир* (*студе́нты*) students мн.

студёный (-, -а, -о) *прил* icy cold.

сту́день (-ня) *м* jellied meat.

студи́ек *сущ см* **студи́йка**

студи́ец (-йца) *м* student (*at art or drama school*).

студи́йка (-йки; *gen pl* -ек) ж см **студи́ец**

студи́йца *итп сущ см* **студи́ец**.

студи́ть (-жу́, -дишь; *perf* **остуди́ть**) *несов перех* to cool.

сту́дия (-и) ж studio; (*шко́ла*) school (*for actors, dancers, artists etc*); (*мастерска́я*) workshop.

студня *итп сущ см* **сту́день**.

стужа (-и) ж severe cold.

стужу́ *несов см* **студи́ть**.

стук (-а) *м* (*в дверь*) knock; (*маши́н, па́дающего предме́та*) thud; (*мета́лла*) thump; **входи́ть (войти́** *perf)* **без сту́ка** to enter without knocking.

сту́ка(ться) (-ю(сь)) *несов от* **сту́кнуть(ся)**

стука́ч (-а́) *м* (*разг пренебр*) grass (*informer*).

сту́кнуть (-у, -ешь) *сов неперех* (*в дверь, в окно́*) to knock; (*по столу́*) to bang; (*impf* **стука́ть**; *разг: уда́рить*) to knock ♦ *безл* (*no impf*): **мне ~уло 60** I've hit 60

► **сту́кнуться** (*impf* **стука́ться**) *сов возв* to bang o.s.

стул (-а; *nom pl* -ья, *gen pl* -ьев) *м* chair; (*no pl; физиоло́гия*) stools мн.

сту́па (-ы) ж mortar.

ступа́ть (-ю) *несов от* **ступи́ть** ♦ *неперех*

(*осторожно, медленно*) to tread; **~йте!** off you go!

ступе́нек *сущ см* **ступе́нька**.

ступе́нчат|ый (**-**, **-а**, **-о**) *прил* (*спуск, водопад*) terraced; (*процесс*) in stages.

ступе́н|ь (**-и**) *ж* step; (*gen pl* **-е́й**, *dat pl* **-я́м**; *процесса*) stage; (*МУЗ*) degree.

ступе́н|ька (**-ьки**; *gen pl* **-ек**) *ж* step.

ступ|и́ть (**-лю́**, **-ишь**; *impf* **ступа́ть**) *сов неперех* to step, tread.

ступи́ц|а (**-ы**) *ж* (*ТЕХ*) hub.

сту́п|ка (**-ки**; *gen pl* **-ок**) *ж* mortar.

ступлю́ *сов см* **ступи́ть**.

ступн|я́ (**-и́**) *ж* (*стопа*) foot (*мн* feet); (*подошва*) sole.

ступо́к *сущ см* **сту́пка**.

сту́пор (**-а**) *м* stupor.

стуч|а́ть (**-у́**, **-и́шь**; *perf* **постуча́ть**) *несов неперех* (*в дверь, в окно*) to knock; (*по столу, по доске*) to bang; (*колёса*) to rattle; (*сердце*) to thump; (*зубы*) to chatter; (*perf* **настуча́ть**; *разг: доносить*) to grass; (**у меня́**) **~и́т в виска́х** my temples are throbbing; **~ (постуча́ть** *perf*) **в окно́/в дверь** to bang on the window/door

► **стуча́ться** (*perf* **постуча́ться**) *несов возв*: **~ся (в** +*acc*) to knock (at); **~ся (постуча́ться** *perf*) **к кому́-н** to knock at sb's door.

стуш|ева́ться (**-у́юсь**; *impf* **тушева́ться**) *сов возв* to go shy.

стыд (**-а́**) *м* shame; **к ~у́ своему́** to one's shame; **сгора́ть (сгоре́ть** *perf*) **от ~а́** to burn with shame; **у тебя́ нет ни ~а́**, **ни со́вести** (*разг*) you've no shame.

стыд|и́ть (**-жу́**, **-ди́шь**; *perf* **пристыди́ть**) *несов перех* to (put to) shame

► **стыди́ться** (*perf* **постыди́ться**) *несов возв*: **~ся** +*gen*/+*infin* to be ashamed of/to do; **~ся (постыди́ться** *perf*) **кого́-н/чего́-н пе́ред кем-н** to be ashamed of sb/sth in front of sb.

стыдли́в|ый (**-**, **-а**, **-о**) *прил* bashful.

сты́дно *как сказ* it's a shame; **мне ~** I am ashamed; **мне ~ друзе́й** *или* **пе́ред друзья́ми** I'm ashamed in front of my friends; **как тебе́ не ~!** you ought to be ashamed of yourself!

стыжу́(сь) *несов см* **стыди́ть(ся)**.

стык (**-а**) *м* (*труб, рельсов*) join; (*улиц*) junction; (*перен: двух наук, двух эпох*) meeting point.

стык|ова́ть (**-у́ю**; *perf* **состыкова́ть**) *несов перех* (*рельсы, трубы*) to join; (*космос*) to dock

► **стыкова́ться** (*perf* **состыкова́ться**) *несов возв* (*космос*) to dock.

стыко́в|ка (**-ки**; *gen pl* **-ок**) *ж* docking.

сты́|нуть (**-у**, **-ешь**; *perf* **осты́нуть**) *несов неперех* = **сты́ть**.

сты́|ть (**-ну**, **-нешь**; *perf* **осты́ть**) *несов неперех* to go cold; (*perf* **просты́ть**; *мёрзнуть*) to freeze; **кровь сты́нет (в жи́лах)** the blood runs cold.

сты́ч|ка (**-ки**; *gen pl* **-ек**) *ж* (*военная*) clash; (*разг: с нача́льником, с мили́цией*) run-in.

стюа́рд (**-а**) *м* steward.

стюарде́сс|а (**-ы**) *ж* air hostess.

стяг (**-а**; *nom pl* **-и**) *м* banner.

стя́гива|ть(ся) (**-ю(сь)**) *несов от* **стяну́ть(ся)**.

стяжа́тель (**-я**) *м* taker.

стяжа́тельниц|а (**-ы**) *ж см* **стяжа́тель**.

стяжа́тельск|ий (**-ая**, **-ое**, **-ие**) *прил* grasping.

стя|ну́ть (**-у́**, **-ешь**; *impf* **стя́гивать**) *сов перех* (*пояс, шнуро́вку*) to tighten; (*войска*) to round up; (*no impf*; *разг: укра́сть*) to nick, pinch; (*перевяза́ть*): **~ что-н че́м-н** (*та́лию по́ясом*) to pull sth in with sth; (*чемода́н ремнём*) to strap sth up with sth; (*о́бувь, перча́тку*) to pull off

► **стяну́ться** (*impf* **стя́гиваться**) *сов возв* (*узел*) to tighten; (*войска*) to gather; (*разг: по́ясом*) to pull o.s. in.

СУ *ср сокр* (= *статисти́ческое управле́ние*) statistics office.

субаре́нд|а (**-ы**) *ж* sub-lease, sub-let.

суббо́т|а (**-ы**) *ж* Saturday; *см та́кже* **пя́тница**.

суббо́тн|ий (**-яя**, **-ее**, **-ие**) *прил* (*вечер, рабо́та*) Saturday *опред*; (*собы́тия*) Saturday's.

сублима́ци|я (**-и**) *ж* sublimation.

субордина́ци|я (**-и**) *ж* subordination.

субподря́д (**-а**) *м* subcontract; **заключа́ть (заключи́ть** *perf*) **~** to subcontract.

субподря́дчик (**-а**) *м* subcontractor.

субсиди́р|овать (**-ую**) (*не*)*сов перех* to subsidize.

субси́ди|я (**-и**) *ж* subsidy; **инвестицио́нные ~и** (*КОММ*) investment grant *ед*.

субстантиви́рованн|ый *прил*: **~ое прилага́тельное** substantivized adjective.

субста́нци|я (**-и**) *ж* substance.

субти́тр (**-а**) *м* subtitle.

субтро́пик|и (**-ов**) *мн* subtropics *мн*.

субъе́кт (**-а**) *м* (*индиви́д, та́кже ЮР*) individual; (*разг: о мужчи́не*) character.

субъекти́вность (**-и**) *ж* subjectivity.

субъекти́вн|ый *прил* subjective.

сувени́р (**-а**) *м* souvenir.

сувере́нен *прил см* **суверённый**.

суверените́т (**-а**) *м* sovereignty.

суверённ|ый (**-ен**, **-на**, **-но**) *прил* sovereign.

сугли́н|ок (**-ка**) *м* loam.

сугро́б (**-а**) *м* snowdrift.

сугу́бо *нареч* highly.

сугу́б|ый *прил* particular.

суд (**-а́**) *м* court session; (*о́рган*) court; (*процесс*) trial; (*мне́ние*) judgement, verdict ♦ *собир* the judges *мн*; **отдава́ть (отда́ть** *perf*) **кого́-н под ~** to prosecute sb; **подава́ть (пода́ть** *perf*) **на кого́-н в ~** to take sb to court; **предава́ть (преда́ть** *perf*) **кого́-н ~у́** (*престу́пника*) to prosecute sb; **попада́ть (попа́сть** *perf*) **под ~** to be taken to court; **встать, ~ идёт!** please stand for the court!; **на нет и ~а́ нет** oh well, that's that then.

суда́ *итп сущ см* **су́дно**.

суда́к (**-а́**) *м* pike-perch.

Суда́н (**-а**) *м* (the) Sudan.

суда́рын|**я** (**-и**; *gen pl* **-ь**) *ж* Madame.

су́дар|**ь** (**-я**) *м* Sir.

су́деб *сущ см* **судьба́**.

суде́бно-медици́нск|**ий** (**-ая, -ое, -ие**) *прил*: **суде́бно-медици́нская эксперти́за** forensics.

суде́бн|**ый** *прил* (*заседание, органы*) court *опред*; (*издержки, практика*) legal; **~ая оши́бка** miscarriage of justice; **~ое реше́ние** adjudication; **суде́бное де́ло** court case; **суде́бный исполни́тель** bailiff; **суде́бный пригово́р** sentence.

суде́йск|**ий** (**-ая, -ое, -ие**) *прил* (*ЮР*) judge's; **суде́йская колле́гия** (*ЮР*) the bench; (*СПОРТ*) panel of judges.

суде́йств|**о** (**-а**) *ср* refereeing.

су́ден *сущ см* **су́дно**.

суди́мост|**ь** (**-и**) *ж* conviction.

суди́ть (**-жу́, -дишь**) *несов перех* (*преступника*) to try; (*матч*) to referee; (*укорять*) to judge ♦ *неперех* (*на матче*) to referee; (*на соревнованиях*) to judge; **~** (*impf*) **о ком-н/чём-н** to judge sb/sth; **судя́ по** +*dat* judging by

▶ **суди́ться** *несов возв*: **~ся с кем-н** to take sb to court.

су́дн|**о** (**-а**; *nom pl* **-а́**, *gen pl* **-о́в**) *ср* vessel; (*gen pl* **-ен**; *МЕД*) bedpan.

су́дный *прил*: **~ день** Judgement Day.

судове́рф|**ь** (**-и**) *ж сокр* (= *судострои́тельная верфь*) shipyard.

судовладе́л|**ец** (**-ьца**) *м* shipowner.

судовожде́ни|**е** (**-я**) *ср* navigation.

судов|**о́й** *прил*: **~а́я кома́нда** ship's crew; **судово́й журна́л** ship's log.

судопроизво́дств|**о** (**-а**) *ср* legal proceedings *мн*.

судоремо́нтн|**ый** *прил*: **~ые мастерски́е** shipyards *мн*.

су́дорог|**а** (**-и**) *ж* (*от боли*) spasm; (*от холода, от отвращения итп*) shudder.

су́дорожн|**ый** (**-ен, -на, -но**) *прил* (*движения, плач*) convulsive; (*перен: приготовления*) feverish.

судостро́ени|**е** (**-я**) *ср* ship building.

судостро́ительный *прил* ship-building.

судохо́дный *прил* navigable; **~ кана́л** shipping canal.

судохо́дств|**о** (**-а**) *ср* navigation.

судьб|**а́** (**-ы́**; *nom pl* **-ы**, *gen pl* **-еб**) *ж* fate; (*будущее*) destiny; **~ э́той пье́сы о́чень интере́сна** this play has had a very interesting fate; **каки́ми ~ми!** fancy seeing you here!; (**нам**) **не ~ встре́титься** we are not fated to meet.

судь|**я́** (**-и́**; *nom pl* **-и**, *gen pl* **-е́й**) *ж* judge; (*СПОРТ*) referee; **я тебе́ не ~** who am I to judge

you?

суеве́рен *прил см* **суеве́рный**.

суеве́ри|**е** (**-я**) *ср* superstition.

суеве́р|**ный** (**-ен, -на, -но**) *прил* superstitious.

сует|**а́** (**-ы́**) *ж* (*житейская, мелочная*) futility; (*хлопоты*) hustle and bustle.

су́етен *прил см* **су́етный**.

суети́ться (**-чу́сь, -ти́шься**) *несов возв* to fuss (about).

суетли́в|**ый** (**-, -а, -о**) *прил* fussy; (*жизнь, работа*) busy.

су́етн|**ый** (**-ен, -на, -но**) *прил* (*интересы, желания, жизнь итп*) futile; (*человек*) superficial; (*день, жизнь*) busy.

суечу́сь *несов см* **суети́ться**.

сужа́ть (**-ю**) *несов от* **су́зить**.

сужде́ни|**е** (**-я**) *ср* (*мнение*) opinion; (*заключение*) judgement.

суждено́ *как сказ*: (**нам**) **не ~ бы́ло встре́титься** we weren't fated to meet.

су́жен|**ая** (**-ой**; *decl like adj*) *ж*: **его́ ~** his intended.

суже́ни|**е** (**-я**) *ср* (*см глаг*) narrowing; taking in.

су́жен|**ый** (**-ого**; *decl like adj*) *м*: **её ~** her intended.

сужу́(сь) *несов см* **суди́ть(ся)**.

су́зить (**-жу, -зишь**; *impf* **сужа́ть**) *сов перех* to narrow; (*платье*) to take in

▶ **су́зиться** (*impf* **сужа́ться**) *сов возв* to narrow.

су|**к** (**-ка́**; *loc sg* **-ку́**, *nom pl* **-чья**, *gen pl* **-чьев**) *м* (*дерева*) bough.

су́к|**а** (**-и**) *ж* bitch ♦ *м/ж* (*груб!: о женщине*) bitch (*!*); (*: о мужчине*) bastard (*!*); **~ин сын** (*разг*) son of a bitch (*!*).

сукн|**о́** (**-а́**; *nom pl* **-а**, *gen pl* **-он**) *ср* (*шерстяное*) felt; (*хлопчатобумажное*) coarse cloth; **класть** (**положи́ть** *perf*) **что-н под ~** (*перен*) to shelve sth.

суко́нный *прил* (*см сущ*) felt *опред*; coarse cloth *опред*.

сул|**и́ть** (**-ю́, -и́шь**; *perf* **посули́ть**) *несов перех*: **~ что-н кому́-н** (*обещать*) to promise sb sth, promise sth to sb; (*предвещать*) to bode for.

султа́н (**-а**) *м* (*монарх*) sultan; (*украшение*) plume.

сульфа́т (**-а**) *м* sulphate.

сум|**а́** (**-ы́**) *ж* (*старушечья*) (tote) bag; (*охотничья*) pouch; **ходи́ть** (*impf*) **с ~о́й** (*перен*) to go begging.

сумасбро́д (**-а**) *м* maverick.

сумасбро́ден *прил см* **сумасбро́дный**.

сумасбро́д|**ка** (**-ки**; *gen pl* **-ок**) *ж см* **сумасбро́д**.

сумасбро́дн|**ый** (**-ен, -на, -но**) *прил* (*человек, поведение*) maverick; (*идея*) madcap.

сумасбро́док *сущ см* **сумасбро́дка**.

сумасбро́дств|**о** (**-а**) *ср* (*поведение*) maverick behaviour; (*поступок*) exploit.

сумасше́дш|**ая** (**-ей**; *decl like adj*) *ж* madwoman (*мн* madwomen).

сумасше́дш|**ий** (**-ая, -ее, -ие**) *прил* mad; (*разг: успех*) amazing; (*: скорость*) lunatic ♦ (**-его**; *decl like adj*) *м* madman (*мн* madmen); **~ие**

де́ньги ridiculous amounts of money; **сумасше́дший дом** asylum; (*разг*) madhouse.

сумасше́стви|е (-я) *ср* madness, lunacy; **до ~я** like mad.

сумато́х|а (-и) *ж* chaos.

сумато́ш|ный (-ен, -на, -но) *прил* (*разг*) chaotic.

сумбу́р (-а) *м* muddle.

сумбу́р|ный (-ен, -на, -но) *прил* muddled.

су́мерек *сущ см* **су́мерки**.

су́мереч|ный (-ен, -на, -но) *прил* twilight.

су́мер|ки (-ек) *мн* twilight *ед*, dusk *ед*.

суме́|ть (-ю) *сов неперех*: ~ +*infin* to manage to do.

су́м|ка (-ки; *gen pl* -ок) *ж* bag; (*кенгуру*) pouch.

су́мм|а (-ы) *ж* sum.

сумма́р|ный (-ен, -на, -но) *прил* (*количество, затраты*) total *опред*; (*оценка, обзор, описание*) overall.

сумми́р|овать (-ую) (*не*)*сов перех* (*затраты итп*) to add up; (*информацию, данные, сказанное*) to summarize.

су́мок *сущ см* **су́мка**.

су́моч|ка (-ки; *gen pl* -ек) *ж уменьш от* **су́мка**; (*дамская, вечерняя*) handbag.

су́мрак (-а) *м* gloom.

су́мрачен *прил см* **су́мрачный**.

су́мрачно *нареч* (*посмотреть*) gloomily; (*выглядеть*) gloomy ♦ *как сказ* (*на улице, в доме*) it's gloomy; **у меня́ на душе́** ~ I have a heavy heart.

су́мрач|ный (-ен, -на, -но) *прил* (*также перен*) gloomy.

су́мчатый *прил* (*ЗООЛ*) marsupial *опред*.

сумя́тиц|а (-ы) *ж* mishmash.

сунду́к (-а́) *м* trunk, chest.

су́|нуть(ся) (-у(сь), -ешь(ся)) *сов от* **со́вать(ся)**.

суп (-а; *part gen* -у, *nom pl* -ы́) *м* soup.

суперма́ркет (-а) *м* supermarket.

суперме́н (-а) *м* superman (*мн* supermen).

супермо́дный *прил* very trendy.

суперобло́ж|ка (-ки; *gen pl* -ек) *ж* dust jacket.

су́пниц|а (-ы) *ж* soup tureen.

супру́г (-а; *nom pl* -и) *м* spouse; ~**и** husband and wife.

супру́г|а (-и) *ж* spouse.

супру́жеск|ий (-ая, -ое, -ие) *прил* marital; (*чета*) married.

супру́жеств|о (-а) *ср* matrimony.

сургу́ч (-а́) *м* sealing wax.

суро́вост|ь (-и) *ж* (*см прил*) bleakness; severity; hardship; harshness; sternness.

суро́в|ый (-, -а, -о) *прил* (*природа, зима*) bleak; (*приговор*) severe; (*жизнь*) tough; (*действительность*) harsh; (*человек, взгляд*) stern; (*no short form; ткань, нити*) coarse.

суррога́т (-а) *м* (*также перен*) substitute.

суррога́тный *прил* substitute *опред*.

суса́льн|ый *прил*: ~**ое зо́лото** gold leaf.

су́слик (-а) *м* ground squirrel (*BRIT*), gopher (*US*).

суспе́нзи|я (-и) *ж* suspension.

суста́в (-а) *м* (*АНАТ*) joint.

суста́вный *прил*: ~ **ревмати́зм** rheumatism of the joints.

сутенёр (-а) *м* pimp.

су́т|ки (-ок) *мн* twenty four hours *мн*; **кру́глые** ~ day and night.

су́толок|а (-и) *ж* hurly-burly.

су́точн|ые (-ых; *decl like adj*) *мн* subsistence allowance *ед*.

су́точный *прил* twenty-four-hour.

суту́л|ить (-ю, -ишь; *perf* **ссуту́лить**) *несов перех* to hunch

► **суту́литься** (*perf* **ссуту́литься**) *несов возв* to stoop.

суту́л|ый (-, -а, -о) *прил* stooped.

сут|ь (-и) *ж* essence; ~ **де́ла** the crux of the matter; **по су́ти (де́ла)** as a matter of fact ♦ *как сказ*: **э́то не** ~ **ва́жно** it's not all that important; **таки́е слу́чаи** ~ **гро́зное предупрежде́ние** such incidents serve as a severe warning.

суфле́ *ср нескл* soufflé.

суфлёр (-а) *м* prompter.

суфлёрск|ий (-ая, -ое, -ие) *прил*: ~**ая бу́дка** prompt box.

су́ффикс (-а) *м* suffix.

суха́р|ь (-я́) *м* cracker; (*разг: о человеке*) cold fish.

су́хо *нареч* drily ♦ *как сказ* (*о сухой погоде*) it is dry; **на у́лице** ~ it's dry outside.

сухове́й (-я) *м* hot dry wind.

сухогру́з (-а) *м* dry-cargo ship.

сухожи́ли|е (-я) *ср* tendon.

сух|о́й (-, -а́, -о) *прил* dry; (*ветка, листья*) dried; (*no short form; фрукты, овощи*) dried; **сухо́е вино́** dry wine; **сухо́е молоко́** dried milk; **сухо́й зако́н** dry law, prohibition; **сухо́й счёт** (*СПОРТ*) lockout.

сухопа́р|ый (-, -а, -о) *прил* bony.

сухопу́тный *прил* land *опред*; **сухопу́тные войска́** ground forces *мн*.

су́хост|ь (-и) *ж* dryness.

сухофру́кт|ы (-ов) *мн* dried fruit *ед*.

сухоща́в|ый (-, -а, -о) *прил* lean.

суч|о́к (-ка́) *м* twig.

су́чья *итп сущ см* **сук**.

су́ш|а (-и) *ж* (dry) land.

су́ше *сравн прил от* **сухо́й** ♦ *сравн нареч от* **су́хо**.

су́шек *сущ см* **су́шка**.

суше́ный *прил* dried.

суши́л|ка (-ки; *gen pl* -ок) *ж* (*помещение*) drying room; (*приспособление*) dryer.

суши́ть (-у́, -ишь; *perf* **вы́сушить**) *несов перех* (*бельё, одежду, сено*) to dry; (*perf* **вы́сушить**

или **засушить**; *травы итп*) to dry
▸ **сушиться** (*perf* **высушиться**) *несов* (*возв* to dry; (*человек*) to dry off.

сушка (-**ки**; *gen pl* -**ек**) *ж* (*действие*) drying; (*бублик*) small dry biscuit in the shape of a doughnut.

сушь (-**и**) *ж* dry spell.

существенно *нареч* (*улучшить, изменить*) substantially.

существенный (-, -**на**, -**но**) *прил* (*черта, качество*) essential; (*изменения*) substantial; (*замечания*) major; (*вопрос*) important.

существительное (-**ого**; *decl like adj*) *ср* (*также:* **имя** ~) noun.

существо (-**а**) *ср* (*вопроса, дела итп*) essence; (*nom pl* -**а**; *животное*) creature; (*человек*) being; **по ~у** (*говорить*) to the point; (*вводн сл*) essentially; **всем своим ~м** with one's whole being.

существование (-**я**) *ср* existence; **прекращать** (**прекратить** *perf*) ~ to cease to exist; **средства к ~ю** livelihood; **отравлять** (**отравить** *perf*) **кому-н** ~ to make sb's life a misery.

существовать (-**ую**) *несов неперех* to exist; ~ (*impf*) +*instr или* **на** +*acc* to make one's living from.

сущий (-**ая**, -**ее**, -**ие**) *прил* (*правда*) honest; (*мученик, пустяки*) utter; **она** ~ **ребёнок** she is a real baby.

сущность (-**и**) *ж* (*вопроса, проблемы*) essence; **в ~и** (*говоря*) in essence, essentially.

Суэц (-**а**) *м* Suez.

суэцкий (-**ая**, -**ое**, -**ие**) *прил*: **С~ канал** the Suez Canal.

СФ *м сокр* (= *Совет Федераций*) *upper chamber of the Russian parliament*.

сфабриковать (-**ую**) *сов от* **фабриковать**.

сфальшивить (-**лю**, -**ишь**) *сов от* **фальшивить**.

сфантазировать (-**ую**) *сов от* **фантазировать**.

сфера (-**ы**) *ж* sphere; (*производства, торговли, науки*) area; (*театральная, дипломатическая*) circles *мн*; **земная** ~ the globe; **высшие ~ы** upper echelons; **в ~е** +*gen* in the field of; **сфера обслуживания** *или* **услуг** service industry.

сферический (-**ая**, -**ое**, -**ие**) *прил* spherical.

сфинкс (-**а**) *м* sphinx.

сформировать(ся) (-**ую(сь)**) *сов от* **формировать(ся)**.

сформулировать (-**ую**) *сов от* **формулировать**.

сфотографировать(ся) (-**ую(сь)**) *сов от* **фотографировать(ся)**.

схалтурить (-**ю**, -**ишь**) *сов от* **халтурить**.

схватить (-**чу**, -**тишь**) *сов от* **хватать** ◆ (*impf* **схватывать**) *перех* (*скрепить*) to secure; (*разг: простуду*) to catch; (*мысль, смысл*) to grasp; **у меня ~тило живот** I've got stomach cramps
▸ **схватиться** *сов от* **хвататься** ◆ (*impf*

схватываться) *возв* (*борцы, оппоненты*) to lock together.

схватка (-**ки**; *gen pl* -**ок**) *ж* fight; *см также* **схватки**.

схватки (-**ок**) *мн* (*МЕД*) contractions *мн*.

схватывать(ся) (-**ю(сь)**) *несов от* **схватить(ся)**.

схвачу(сь) *сов см* **схватить(ся)**.

схема (-**ы**) *ж* (*метро, улиц*) plan; (*ЭЛЕК: радио итп*) circuit board; (*статьи итп*) outline.

схематизировать (-**ую**) (*не*)*сов перех* to schematize.

схематизм (-**а**) *м* schematism.

схематичен *прил см* **схематичный**.

схематический (-**ая**, -**ое**, -**ие**) *прил* (*ТЕХ*) diagrammatic; (*изложение*) sketchy.

схематичный (-**ен**, -**на**, -**но**) *прил* (*изложение*) sketchy.

схима (-**ы**) *ж* schema (*strict vow taken by orthodox monks*).

схимник (-**а**) *м* monk who has taken strict vows.

схитрить (-**ю**, -**ишь**) *сов от* **хитрить**.

схлестнуться (-**усь**, -**ёшься**; *impf* **схлёстываться**) *сов возв* (*разг*) to lock together.

схлопотать (-**очу**, -**очешь**) *сов перех* (*разг*): ~ **выговор** to get a telling off; **ты у меня ~очешь!** you're asking for it!

схлынуть (*3sg* -**ет**, *3pl* -**ут**) *сов неперех* (*вода*) to subside; (*толпа*) to thin out.

сход (-**а**) *м* (*с горы, с трапа*) descent.

сходен *прил см* **сходный**.

сходить (-**жу**, -**дишь**) *сов от* **ходить** ◆ *неперех* (*разг*: в театр, на прогулку) to go ◆ *несов от* **сойти**
▸ **сходиться** *несов от* **сойтись**.

сходка (-**ки**; *gen pl* -**ок**) *ж* assembly.

сходни (-**ей**) *мн* gangplank *ед*.

сходный (-**ен**, -**на**, -**но**) *прил* similar.

сходок *сущ см* **сходка**.

сходство (-**а**) *ср* similarity.

схожий (-**ая**, -**ее**, -**ие**) *прил* (*разг*) = **сходный**.

схожу(сь) (*не*)*сов см* **сходить(ся)**.

схоластика (-**и**) *ж* (*философия*) scholasticism; (*отвлечённые знания*) speculation.

схоластичный (-**ен**, -**на**, -**но**) *прил* scholastic.

схоронить (-**ю**, -**ишь**) *сов от* **хоронить**.

сцапать (-**ю**) *сов от* **цапать**.

сцедить (-**жу**, -**дишь**; *impf* **сцеживать**) *сов перех* (*жидкость, сок*) to strain off; (*грудное молоко*) to express.

сцементировать (-**ую**) *сов от* **цементировать**.

сцена (-**ы**) *ж* (*подмостки*) stage; (*эпизод: в пьесе, на улице*) scene; **сходить** (**сойти** *perf*) **со ~ы** to leave the stage; (*политик*) to fade from the scene; **устраивать** (**устроить** *perf*) ~**у** to make a scene.

сценарий (-**я**) *м* (*фильма*) script; (*вечера, праздника*) programme.

сценарист (-**а**) *м* scriptwriter.

сценичен *прил см* **сценичный**.

сцени́ческ|ий (-ая, -ое, -ие) *прил* stage *опред*; **~ое мастерство́** acting skills; **~ о́браз** dramatic character; **сцени́ческое иску́сство** dramatic art.

сцени́ч|ный (-ен, -на, -но) *прил*: **~ная пье́са** play well-suited for the theatre (*BRIT*) *или* theater (*US*).

сце́н|ка (-ки; *gen pl* -ок) *ж уменьш от* сце́на; (*зарисовка*) sketch.

сцепи́ть (-лю́, -ишь; *impf* сцепля́ть) *сов перех* (*вагоны, прицепы*) to couple; (*пальцы, руки*) to clasp

▶ **сцепи́ться (*impf* сцепля́ться) *сов возв* (*ветви*)** to be caught together; (*разг: схвати́ться*): **~ся (с +*instr*) (*дети, спорщики*)** to get into a fight (with).

сцепле́ни|е (-я) *ср* (*вагонов*) coupling; (*ТЕХ: механизм*) clutch.

сцеплю́(сь) *сов см* сцепи́ть(ся).

сцепля́ть(ся) (-ю(сь)) *несов от* сцепи́ть(ся).

сча́стли́в|ец (-ца) *м* lucky man (*мн* men).

сча́стли́вица (-ы) *ж* lucky woman (*мн* women).

сча́стли́во *нареч* (*жить, рассмеяться*) happily; **~ отде́латься (*perf*)** to have a lucky escape; **счастли́во!** all the best!; **счастли́во остава́ться!** good luck!

счастли́вца *итп сущ см* счастли́вец.

счастли́вчик (-а) *м* (*разг*) lucky devil.

счастли́в|ый (-ив, -ива, -иво) *прил* (*человек, жизнь, лицо*); (*делец, игрок, случай*) lucky; **у него́ ~ивая рука́** he's got a lucky touch; **~ивого пути́!** have a good journey!

сча́стье (-я) *ср* (*личное, семейное*) happiness; (*удача*) luck; **к ~ю** luckily, fortunately; **на на́ше ~** luckily for us; **како́е ~, что ты пришёл** how nice that you've come; **возьми́ э́то на ~** take that for good luck; **твоё ~, что ...** you're lucky that ....

счесть (сочту́, сочтёшь; *pt* счёл, сочла́, сочло́) *сов от* счита́ть ♦ *неперех*: пробле́м у меня́ не ~ I've got countless problems.

счёт (-а; *part gen* -у, *loc sg* -ý, *nom pl* -а́) *м* (*действие*) counting; (*КОММ: в банке*) account; (: *накладная*) invoice; (*ресторанный, телефонный*) bill; (*no pl; СПОРТ*) score; **в ~ +*gen*** in lieu of; **за ~ +*gen* (*фирмы*)** at the expense of; (*эффективности, внедрений итп*) due to; **на ~ кого́-н** at sb's expense; **на э́тот ~** in this respect; **быть (*impf*) на хоро́шем/плохо́м счету́ у +*gen*** to be in the good/bad books with; **у неё ка́ждая копе́йка на счету́** she counts every penny; **э́то не в ~** that doesn't count; **по большо́му ~у** having set a high standard; **име́ть (*impf*) что-н на счету́ (*победы*)** to have sth to one's name; **предъявля́ть (предъяви́ть *perf*) ~ кому́-н** to invoice sb; **принима́ть (приня́ть *perf*) что-н на свой ~** to take sth personally; **он не зна́ет ~а деньга́м** he's rolling

in money; **лицево́й ~ (*КОММ*)** personal account; **теку́щий ~ (*КОММ*)** current (*BRIT*) *или* checking (*US*) account; **~ поступле́ний (*КОММ*)** revenue account; **ссу́дный ~ (*КОММ*)** loan account; **~ ассигнова́ний (*КОММ*)** appropriation account; **счета́ креди́торов/дебито́ров (*КОММ*)** account payable/receivable; **открыва́ть (откры́ть *perf*) ~ в ба́нке** to open a bank account.

счётн|ый *прил*: ~ая коми́ссия vote counting committee; **счётная маши́на** calculator.

счётчик (-а) *м* (*человек: голосов*) counter; (*электричества, в такси*) meter.

счёт|ы (-ов) *мн* (*приспособление*) abacus; (*деловые*) dealings *мн*; **поко́нчить (*perf*) все ~ с кем-н (*рассчитаться*)** to pay off one's debts to sb; (*прекрати́ть связи*) to break off ties with sb; **сбра́сывать (сбро́сить *perf*) кого́-н/что-н со счето́в** to dismiss sb/sth; **своди́ть (свести́ *perf*) ~ с кем-н** to settle a score with sb; **у него́ с ни́ми свои́ ~** he's got his own scores to settle with them.

счи́|стить (-щу, -стишь; *impf* счища́ть) *сов перех* to clean off.

счита́л|ка (-ки; *gen pl* -ок) *ж* counting rhyme.

счи́танн|ый *прил*: ~ые дни/мину́ты only a few days/minutes; **~ое коли́чество** very few.

счита́ть (-ю) *несов неперех* to count ♦ (*perf* посчита́ть *или* сосчита́ть) *перех* (*деньги итп*) to count; (*perf* посчита́ть *или* счесть): **~ что-н/кого́-н +*instr*** to regard sth/sb as; **(посчита́ть *или* счесть *perf*) что-н необходи́мым** to consider sth (to be) necessary; **~я +*gen* (*принимая в расчёт*)** considering; **не ~я +*gen*** excluding; **~я от +*gen* или* с +*gen*** starting with; **~ (счесть *perf*) что-н/кого́-н за +*acc*** to regard sb/sth as; **я ~ю, что ...** I believe *или* think that ...

▶ **счита́ться *несов возв*: ~ся +*instr*** to be considered to be; (*уважать*): **~ся с +*instr* (с роди́телями, с другом итп*)** to be considerate to.

счи́тыва|ть (-ю; *perf* счита́ть) *несов перех* to read (*meter etc*).

счища́|ть (-ю) *несов от* счи́стить.

счи́щу *сов см* счи́стить.

США *мн сокр* (= Соединённые Шта́ты Аме́рики) USA (= United States of America).

сшиби́ть (-ý, -ёшь; *pt* -, -ла, -ло, *impf* сшиба́ть) *сов перех* (*разг: подлеж: машина*) to hit

▶ **сшиби́ться (*impf* сшиба́ться) *сов возв* (*разг*)** to get into a fight.

сшива́|ть (-ю) *несов от* сшить.

сшить (сошью́, сошьёшь; *imper* сшей(те)) *сов от* шить ♦ (*impf* сшива́ть) *перех* (*соединить шитьём*) to sew together.

съеда́|ть (-ю) *несов от* съесть.

съе́дем(ся) *сов см* съе́хать(ся).

съеде́ни|е (-я) *ср*: отдава́ть кого́-н на ~

кому́-н (та́кже перен) to leave sb at the mercy of sb.

съе́дешь(ся) итп сов см **съе́хать(ся)**.

съеди́м итп сов см **съе́сть**.

съедо́б|**ный** (**-ен, -на, -но**) прил edible.

съе́ду(сь) итп сов см **съе́хать(ся)**.

съедя́т сов см **съе́сть**.

съёж|**иться** (**-усь, -ишься**) сов от **ёжиться ♦** во́зе (от хо́лода, от стра́ха) to huddle; (ли́стья) to shrivel up.

съезд (**-а**) м (де́йствие: госте́й, делега́тов) gathering; (к реке́, в доли́ну) descent; (парти́йный) congress.

съе́зд|**ить** (**-жу, -дишь**) сов неперех (за поку́пками, к роди́телям) to go; ~ (perf) +dat (ра́за: уда́рить) to whack.

съе́здовск|**ий** (**-ая, -ое, -ие**) прил (докуме́нты, реше́ния) congress орпед.

съезжа́|ть(ся) (**-ю(сь)**) несов от **съе́хать(ся)**.

съе́зжу сов см **съе́здить**.

съём сов см **съе́сть**.

съём|**ка** (**-ки**; gen pl **-ок**) ж (ко́пии) making, taking; (ме́стности) survey; (обы́чно мн: фи́льма) shooting; (ги́пса) removal.

съёмный прил detachable.

съёмок сущ см **съёмка**.

съёмоч|**ный** прил: ~**ая площа́дка** film set; **съёмочная гру́ппа** film crew.

съёмщик (**-а**) м tennant.

съёмщиц|**а** (**-ы**) ж см **съёмщик**.

съестн|**о́й** прил: ~**ые припа́сы** food supplies мн.

съе́|**сть** (как **есть**; см Table 15; impf **есть** и́ли **съеда́ть**) сов перех (хлеб, ка́шу) to eat; (подлеж: моль, ржа́вчина) to eat away at; (: то́ска, ре́вность) to gnaw at; (impf **съеда́ть**; ра́за: де́ньги, зарпла́ту) to eat up.

съе́хать (как **е́хать**; см Table 19; impf **съезжа́ть**) сов неперех: ~ (**с** +gen) (спусти́ться: с го́рки) to go down; (плато́к) to slip; (ша́пка) to tilt; **съезжа́ть** (~ perf) (**с кварти́ры**) to move out of (one's flat); ~ (perf) **с ле́стницы** (упа́сть) to tumble down the stairs

▶ **съе́хаться** (impf **съезжа́ться**) сов возв (го́сти, делега́ты) to gather.

съехи́днича|ть (**-ю**) сов от **ехи́дничать**.

съешь сов см **съе́сть**.

съязв|**и́ть** (**-лю́, -и́шь**) сов от **язви́ть**.

сы́ворот|**ка** (**-ки**; gen pl **-ок**) ж (моло́чная) whey; (мед) serum.

сы́гранный прил well-coordinated.

сыгра́|ть (**-ю**) сов от **игра́ть**

▶ **сыгра́ться** (impf **сы́грываться**) сов возв (музыка́нты) to play well together; (спортсме́ны) to play well as a team.

сы́змала нареч from an early age.

сы́знова нареч (разг) anew.

сымити́р|**овать** (**-ую**) сов от **имити́ровать**.

сымпровизи́р|**овать** (**-ую**) сов от **импровизи́ровать**.

сын (**-а**; nom pl **-овья́**, gen pl **-ове́й**, dat pl **-овья́м**) м son; (nom pl **-ы́**, gen pl **-о́в**; перен): ~ +gen (наро́да) son of.

сынка́ итп сущ см **сыно́к**.

сыновья́ итп сущ см **сын**.

сыно́вн|**ий** (**-яя, -ее, -ие**) прил (любо́вь, долг) son's.

сыно́к (**-ка́**) м уменьш от **сын**; (как обраще́ние) son.

сы́п|**ать** (**-лю, -лешь**; imper **сы́пь(те)**) несов перех to pour ♦ неперех: ~ +instr (цита́тами, остро́тами) to pour forth with

▶ **сы́паться** несов возв (мука́, песо́к, я́блоки итп) to pour; (вопро́сы, пи́сьма итп) to pour forth; **на него́ посы́пались уда́ры со всех сторо́н** blows rained down on him from all sides.

сыпно́й прил: ~ **тиф** typhus.

сыпу́ч|**ий** (**-ая, -ее, -ие**) прил (вещество́) friable; (грунт) shifting.

сып|**ь** (**-и**) ж rash.

сыр (**-а**; part gen **-у**, nom pl **-ы́**) м cheese; **как** ~ **в ма́сле ката́ться** (impf) to live the life of Riley.

сыре́|**ть** (3sg **-ет**, 3pl **-ют**) несов неперех to get damp.

сыре́ц (**-ца́**) м: **хло́пок-**~ rough cotton; **шёлк-**~ raw silk.

сырка́ итп сущ см **сыро́к**.

сырко́в|**ый** прил: ~**ая ма́сса** cream cheese.

сы́рник (**-а**) м small thick pancake made with cream cheese.

сы́ро как сказ: **здесь** ~ it's damp here.

сыро́еж|**ка** (**-и**) ж russula.

сыр|**о́й** (**-, -а́, -о**) прил (бельё, земля́, во́здух) damp; (статья́, стихи́) rough; (no short form; мя́со, о́вощи) raw, uncooked; **сыра́я вода́** tap water.

сыро́к (**-ка́**) м: **творо́жный** ~ sweet curd cheese; **пла́вленный** ~ processed cheese.

сы́рост|**ь** (**-и**) ж dampness.

сырца́ итп сущ см **сыре́ц**.

сырь|**ё** (**-я́**) ср собир raw material.

сырьево́й прил (ресу́рсы, ба́за) raw material орпед.

сыск (**-а**) м criminal detection.

сы|**ска́ть** (**-щу́, -щешь**) сов перех (разг: отыска́ть) to find

▶ **сыска́ться** сов возв (разг: обнару́житься) to turn up.

сы́т|**ный** (**-ен, -на́, -но**) прил filling.

сыт|**ый** (**-, -а́, -о**) прил (не голо́дный) full, satisfied; (отко́рмленный) well-fed; (no short form; перен: вид, улы́бка) contented; (: меща́нство) smug; **спаси́бо, я сыт** thank you, I'm full; **я сыт по го́рло** (перен) I'm fed up.

сыч (**-а́**) м little owl; (о челове́ке) loner.

сы́щик (**-а**) м detective.

сыщу́(сь) итп сов см **сыска́ть(ся)**.

СЭВ (**-а**) м сокр (ист: = Сове́т Экономи́ческой Взаимопо́мощи) Comecon, CMEA (= Council for Mutual Economic Assistance).

СЭЗ *ж сокр* = свободная экономическая зона.
сэконо́м|ить (-лю, -ишь) *сов от* **эконо́мить.**
СЭС *м сокр* = Советский Энциклопедический Словарь.
сюда́ *нареч* here; **(и) туда́ и** ~ both here and there; **то туда́, то** ~ sometimes here, sometimes there; **ни туда́ ни** ~ neither here nor there; **туда́-**~ (*туда и обратно*) backwards and forwards; (*в разные стороны*) everywhere; **иди́** ~**!** I come here!; **э́то ещё туда́-**~ that's bearable.
сюже́т (-а) *м* plot.
сюже́тн|ый *прил*: ~**ая ли́ния** storyline; **сюже́тное разви́тие** development of the plot.
сюйт|а (-ы) *ж* (*муз*) suite.
сюрпри́з (-а) *м* surprise.
сюрреали́зм (-а) *м* surrealism.

сюрреали́ст (-а) *м* surrealist.
сюрту́к (-а́) *м* frock-coat.
сюсю́кани|е (-я) *ср* (*см глаг*) lisping; fussing.
сюсю́ка|ть (-ю) *несов неперех* (*в речи*) to lisp; (*потворствовать*): ~ **с кем-н** to fuss over sb
▶ **сюсю́каться** *несов возв*: ~**ся с кем-н** to fuss over sb.
ся́ду *итп сов см* **сесть.**
сяк *нареч*: **(и) так и** ~ *или* **то так, то** ~ (*разг*) by hook or by crook; **э́то ещё так-**~ (*разг*) it's so-so.
сяко́й *прил*: **ах ты тако́й-**~ (*разг*) you little so-and-so.
сям *нареч*: **(и) там и** ~ (*разг*) here and there; **то там, то** ~ now here, now there.

~ T, m ~

T, т *сущ нескл* (*буква*) the 19th letter of the Russian alphabet.

т *сокр* (= **тóнна**) t (= *tonne*).

т. *сокр* = **товáрищ**; (= **том**) v., vol. (= *volume*); = **ты́сяча**.

та (той) *мест см* **тот**.

табáк (**-á**; *part gen* **-ý**) *м* tobacco.

табакá *нескл*: цыплёнок ~ char-grilled chicken.

табакéр|ка (**-ки**; *gen pl* **-ок**) *ж* snuffbox.

табаковóд (**-а**) *м* tobacco grower.

табаковóдств|о (**-а**) *ср* tobacco-growing.

табáчный *прил* tobacco *опред*.

тáбел|ь (**-я**) *м* (*ПРОСВЕЩ*) school report (*BRIT*), report card (*US, SCOTTISH*); (*на работе*) *board on which employees mark their time of arrival and departure*; (*график*) chart.

таблéт|ка (**-ки**; *gen pl* **-ок**) *ж* tablet.

таблúц|а (**-ы**) *ж* table; (*СПОРТ*) (league) table; **таблúца умножéния** multiplication table.

таблúч|ка (**-ки**; *gen pl* **-ек**) *ж* (*с названием улицы*) street sign; (*экспоната*) plate; (*на двери*) nameplate.

таблó *ср нескл* (*на вокзале, в аэропорту*) (information) board; (*на стадионе*) scoreboard.

тáбор (**-а**) *м* camp.

табý *ср нескл* taboo; **налагáть** (**наложúть** *perf*) **на что-н** ~ to make a taboo of sth.

табýн (**-á**) *м* herd.

табурéт (**-а**) *м* = **табурéтка**.

табурéт|ка (**-ки**; *gen pl* **-ок**) *ж* stool.

тавтолóги|я (**-и**) *ж* tautology.

таджúк (**-а**) *м* Tajik.

Таджикистáн (**-а**) *м* Tajikistan.

таджúкск|ий (**-ая, -ое, -ие**) *прил* Tajiki.

таджúч|ка (**-ки**; *gen pl* **-ек**) *ж см* **таджúк**.

таёжный *прил* taiga *опред*.

таз (**-а**; *loc sg* **-ý**, *nom pl* **-ы́**) *м* (*сосуд*) basin; (*АНАТ*) pelvis.

тазобéдренный *прил*: ~ **сустáв** hip joint.

тáзовый *прил* (*АНАТ*) pelvic.

Таилáнд (**-а**) *м* Thailand.

таилáндец (**-ца**) *м* Thai.

таилáнд|ка (**-ки**; *gen pl* **-ок**) *ж см* **таилáндец**.

таилáндца *итп сущ см* **таилáндец**.

таúнственн|ый (**-, -на, -но**) *прил* mysterious; (*цель, намерение*) secret.

таúнств|о (**-а**) *ср* (*РЕЛ*) sacrament.

Таúти *м нескл* Tahiti.

таú|ть (**-ю, -йшь**) *несов перех* to conceal;

(*перен*): ~ **в себé** (*возможности, угрозу итп*) to conceal; ~ (*impf*) **злóбу на когó-н** to harbour (*BRIT*) *или* harbor (*US*) malice towards sb; **что грехá** ~ (*разг*) there's no point in pretending otherwise

▶ **таú|ться** *несов возв* (*скрывать что-н*) to cover up; (*опасность, неожиданность*) to lurk; **в нём** ~**йтся надéжда/злóба** he harbo(u)rs a secret hope/feeling of malice.

таитя́нск|ий (**-ая, -ое, -ие**) *прил* Tahitian.

Тайвáн|ь (**-я**) *м* Taiwan.

тайг|á (**-й**) *ж* the taiga.

тайкóм *нареч* in secret, secretly.

тайм (**-а**) *м* (*СПОРТ*) period; **пéрвый/вторóй** ~ (*ФУТБОЛ*) the first/second half.

тайм-áут (**-а**) *м* (*СПОРТ*) time-out.

тáйн|а (**-ы**) *ж* (*секрет*) secret; (*загадка*) mystery; **держáть** (*impf*) **что-н в** ~**е** to keep sth secret; **хранúть** (*impf*) ~**у** to keep a secret.

тайнúк (**-á**) *м* hiding place.

тáйный *прил* secret.

тайфýн (**-а**) *м* typhoon.

KEYWORD

так *нареч* **1** (*указательное: таким образом*) like this, this way; **дéлайте так** do it like this *или* this way; **пусть бýдет так** so be it; **так не пойдёт** that won't do; **онá всё дéлает не так** she does everything wrong

2 (*настолько*) so; **я так испугáлся, что нáчал кричáть** I was so frightened I started to shout; **всё случúлось так неожúданно!** it all happened so unexpectedly!

3 (*без последствий*) just like that; **так э́то не пройдёт** you won't get away with it

4 (*разг: без какого-н намерения*) for no (special) reason; **я сказáл э́то прóсто так** I said it for no (special) reason; **почемý ты плáчешь?** – **да так** why are you crying? – for no reason

◆ *част* **1** (*разг: ничего*) nothing; **что с тобóй?** – **так** what's wrong? – nothing

2 (*разг: усилительная*): **а онá так жáловалась!** she didn't half complain!; **так я тебé и повéрил!** I'm not falling for that!

3 (*разг: приблизительно*) about; **дня так чéрез два** in about two days

4 (*например*) for example; **поведéние у негó плохóе; так, вчерá сломáл окнó** his behaviour is bad, for example, yesterday he broke a window

5 (*да*) OK; **так, всё хорошо́/пра́вильно** OK,
that's fine/correct

◆ *союз* **1** (*в тако́м слу́чае*) then; **пло́хо себя́
чу́вствуешь, так иди́ спать** if you feel ill,
(then) go and have a sleep; **éхать, так éхать** if
we are going, (then) let's go
2 (*таки́м о́бразом*) so; **так ты поéдешь?** so,
you are going?
3 (*но*) but; **я пыта́лся его́ убеди́ть, так он не
слу́шает** I tried to convince him but he wouldn't
listen
4 (*в раздели́тельных вопро́сах*): **э́то поле́зная
кни́га, не так ли?** it's a useful book, isn't it?; **он
хоро́ший челове́к, не так ли?** he's a good
person, isn't he?; **у них есть соба́ка, не так ли?**
they have a dog, don't they?
5 (*во фра́зах*): **и так** (*и без того́ уже́*) anyway;
éсли *или* **раз так** in that case; **так и быть!** so be
it!; **так и есть** (*разг*) sure enough; **так ему́!**
serves him right!; **так себе́** (*разг*) so-so; **так как**
since; **так что** so; **так что́бы** so that.

такела́ж (-а) *м* rigging.

та́кже *союз, нареч* also; **я ~ подде́рживаю
Ва́ше предложе́ние** I too am in favour
(*BRIT*) *или* favor (*US*) of your suggestion; **мне
нра́вится ~ и Ва́ше предложе́ние** I like your
suggestion too *или* as well; **с Но́вым Го́дом! – и
Вас ~** Happy New Year! – the same to you; **a ~**
and also.

-таки *част* (*разг*: *всё же*) *emphatic particle*; **ты~
отказа́лся** so you decided to refuse then; **он~
пришёл** he did come then; **она́ пря́мо~
исхо́дит от гне́ва** she is really furious; **опя́ть~**
but having said that; **та́к~** (*разг*) so that's the
way it is.

тако́в (-á, -ó, -ы́) *как сказ* such; **~ тебé мой
совéт** that is my advice to you; **ситуа́ция
такова́, что ...** the situation is such that ...; **и
был ~** (*разг*) and we never saw him again.

таково́й *мест*: **как ~** as such.

тако́е (-óго) *ср* (*о чём-н интере́сном, ва́жном
итп*) something; **я ~ слы́шала!** I've heard
something; **~ происхо́дит!** something is going
on!; **что тут ~óго?** what is so special about that?

тако́й *мест* such; **~йе лю́ди встреча́ются
рéдко** you rarely meet such people; **до ~
стéпени** to such an extent; **~áя жара́!** such
heat!; **кто ~?** who is it?; **он сего́дня како́й-то
не ~** he is not quite himself today; **что ~óe?**
what is it?; **~-то** (*о лице́*) so-and-so; (*о
предме́те*) such-and-such.

тако́й-сяко́й *мест* (*разг*): **ах ты ~** you little
so-and-so.

та́кс|а (-ы) *ж* (*зоол*) dachshund; (*комм*) (fixed)
rate; **пла́та по ~e** fixed-rate payment.

такса́ци|я (-и) *ж* rating.

такси́ *ср нескл* taxi.

такси́р|овать (-ую) (*не*)*сов перех* (*услуги итп*)

to set a rate for.

такси́ст (-а) *м* taxi driver.

таксомото́р (-а) *м* taxicab.

таксопа́рк (-а) *м сокр* (= таксомото́рный парк)
taxi depot.

таксофо́н (-а) *м* payphone.

такт (-а) *м* (*такти́чность*) tact; (*муз*) bar (*BRIT*),
measure (*US*); (*ритм*) beat; **в ~ му́зыке** in time
with the music.

та́ктик (-а) *м* tactician.

та́ктик|а (-и) *ж* tactic; (*воен*) tactics *мн*.

такти́чен *прил см* **такти́чный**

такти́ческ|ий (-ая, -ое, -ие) *прил* tactical.

такти́чн|ый (-ен, -на, -но) *прил* tactful.

тала́нт (-а) *м* talent.

тала́нтлив|ый (-, -а, -о) *прил* talented.

талисма́н (-а) *м* charm, talisman.

та́ли|я (-и) *ж* waist; **пла́тье в ~ю** dress fitted at
the waist.

Та́ллин (-а) *м* Tallin(n).

талму́д (-а) *м* the Talmud.

тало́н (-а) *м* ticket; (*на бензи́н, на проду́кты
итп*) coupon.

та́лый *прил* (*снег, лёд*) melted.

тальк (-а) *м* talcum powder, talc.

там *нареч* there; **бу́ду ~ ско́ро** I'll be there soon;
~ посмо́трим (*разг*) we'll see; **каки́е ~
сомне́ния** (*разг*) what's there to be unsure
about?; **каки́е ~!** (*разг*) not a chance!; **я ду́мал,
что он догада́ется – куда́ уж ~!** (*разг*) I
thought he'd guess, but not a bit of it!; **что ~ ни
говори́, а мы оши́блись** whatever you say, we
still made a mistake; **и ~ и сям** (*разг*) here, there
and everywhere.

тамада́ (-ы́) *ж* (*мужчи́на*) toastmaster;
(*же́нщина*) toastmistress.

та́мбур (-а) *м section at door of train carriage*.

тамбури́н (-а) *м* (*бараба́н*) tambourin (*small
drum*); (*бу́бен*) tambourine.

тамо́жен *сущ см* **тамо́жня**

тамо́женник (-а) *м* customs officer.

тамо́женный *прил* (*досмо́тр*) customs *опред*;
тамо́женная по́шлина customs (duty).

тамо́жн|я (-ни; *gen pl* -ен) *ж* customs.

та́мпекс (-а) *м* Tampax ®.

тампо́н (-а) *м* tampon.

та́нгенс (-а) *м* (*мат*) tangent.

та́нго *ср нескл* tango.

та́н|ец (-ца) *ж* dance; *см та́кже* **та́нцы**.

танзани́йск|ий (-ая, -ое, -ие) *прил* Tanzanian.

Танзани́|я (-и) *ж* Tanzania.

тани́н (-а) *м* tannin.

танк (-а) *м* (*воен, тех*) tank.

та́нкер (-а) *м* tanker (*ship*).

танке́тк|а (-ки; *gen pl* -ок) *ж* (*обы́чно мн: о́бувь*)
wedge heel.

танки́ст (-а) *м* tank crew member.

та́нца итп сущ см **та́нец**.

танцева́льный прил dance опред; ~ **зал** dance hall.

танцева́ть (-у́ю) несов (не)перех to dance.

танцо́вщик (-а) м dancer.

танцо́вщиц|а (-ы) ж см **танцо́вщик**.

танцплоща́д|ка (-ки; gen pl -ок) ж сокр (= танцева́льная площа́дка) dance floor.

танцо́р (-а) м dancer.

та́нц|ы (-ев) мн (вечер) dance ед; **идти́ (пойти́** perf) **на** ~ to go dancing.

та́поч|ка (-ки; gen pl -ек) ж (обычно мн: домашняя) slipper; (: спортивная) plimsoll (BRIT), sneaker (US).

та́р|а (-ы) ж собир containers мн.

тараба́н|ить (-ю, -ишь) несов неперех (разг) to rap.

тараба́рщин|а (-ы) ж (разг) gobbledegook.

тарака́н (-а) м cockroach.

тара́н (-а) м (ВОЕН) ram.

тара́н|ить (-ю, -ишь; perf **протара́нить**) несов перех to ram.

таранта́с (-а) м tarantass (large springless carriage).

тара́нтул (-а) м tarantula.

тарара́м (-а) м (разг) hullaballoo.

тарато́р|ить (-ю, -ишь) несов неперех (разг) to gabble on.

тарах|те́ть (-чу́, -ти́шь) несов неперех (колёса, мотор) to rattle; (человек) to rattle on.

тара́щ|ить (-у, -ишь; perf **вы́таращить**) несов перех: ~ **глаза́ (на** +acc) to stare (at)

► **тара́щ|иться** (perf **вы́таращиться**) несов возв (разг): ~**ся (на** +acc) to gawp или gawk (at).

таре́л|ка (-ки; gen pl -ок) ж plate; **глубо́кая** ~ soup plate; **лета́ющая** ~ flying saucer; **я здесь не в свое́й** ~**ке** (разг) I feel out of place here; см также **таре́лки**.

таре́л|ки (-ок) мн (МУЗ) cymbals мн.

тари́ф (-а) м tariff.

тарифика́ци|я (-и) ж tariffing.

тарифици́р|овать (-ую) (не)сов перех (перевозки, услуги) to tariff; ~ (impf/perf) **окла́ды/нало́ги** to set the salary/tax scale.

тари́фн|ый прил: ~**ая табли́ца/се́тка** list/scale of charges.

таска́|ть (-ю) несов перех to lug; (разг: воровать) to pinch; (: одевать) to wear; ~ (impf) **с собо́й** to carry around; ~ (impf) **кого́-н за́ во́лосы** to pull sb's hair

► **таска́|ться** несов возв (по магазинам итп) to traipse around; ~**ся** (impf) **за кем-н** to trail around after sb.

Тасма́ни|я (-и) ж Tasmania.

тас|ова́ть (-у́ю; perf **стасова́ть**) несов перех to shuffle.

ТАСС м сокр (= Телегра́фное аге́нтство Сове́тского Сою́за) Tass (main news agency of the Soviet Union).

творе́ни|е (-я) ср creation.

татары итп сущ см **тата́рин**.

татуиро́в|ка (-ки; gen pl -ок) ж tattoo.

тахт|а́ (-ы́) ж divan (BRIT), ottoman (US).

та́ч|ка (-ки; gen pl -ек) ж wheelbarrow.

Ташке́нт (-а) м Tashkent.

тащ|и́ть (-у́, -ишь) несов перех (тянуть) to pull; (волочить, также перен) to drag; (нести) to haul; (perf **вы́тащить**; перен: из прогулку) to drag out; (perf **стащи́ть**; разг: красть) to nick; **он та́щит всю рабо́ту на себе́** he is lumbered with (BRIT) или has got landed with all the work

► **тащ|и́ться** несов возв (медленно ехать) to trundle along; (идти неохотно) to drag o.s. along; (волочиться: подол) to drag; **не хо́чется** ~**ся в таку́ю даль** I don't feel like traipsing all that way.

та́|ять (-ю; perf **раста́ять**) несов неперех to melt; (перен: силы, деньги) to dwindle; (: от любви, от похвал) to melt; (: от болезни) to waste away; ~ (impf) **во рту** (перен) to melt in the mouth.

Тбили́си м нескл Tbilisi.

ТВ м сокр (= **телеви́дение**) TV (= television).

тварь (-и) ж creature; (разг: пренебр) swine.

тверд|е́ть (3sg -е́т, 3pl -е́ют, perf **затверде́ть**) несов неперех (мука, также перен) to harden.

тверд|и́ть (-жу́, -ди́шь; perf **затверди́ть**) несов перех (стихотворение, урок итп) to learn by rote; ~ (impf) **о** +prp (говорить) to go on about.

твёрдо нареч (верить, сказать) firmly; (заучить, запомнить) properly; **я** ~ **зна́ю, что** ... I know for sure that ....

твердоло́б|ый (-, -а, -о) прил hard-headed.

твёрдост|ь (-и) ж firmness; (цен) stability; (воли, характера) toughness.

твёрд|ый прил (физ) solid; (-, -а́, -о; земля, предмет) hard; (решение, сторонник, тон итп) firm; (цены, ставки) stable; (порядок) set; (знания) solid; (воля, характер) tough; (линг: звук) hard, nonpalatalized; **здесь нужна́** ~**ая рука́** a firm hand is needed; **твёрдый знак** (линг) hard sign.

твердын|я (-и) ж (перен) stronghold.

твёрже сравн прил от **твёрдый** ♦ сравн нареч от **твёрдо**.

твержу́ несов см **тверди́ть**.

твид (-а) м tweed.

твист (-а) м the twist.

тво|й (-его́; f -я́, nt -ё, pl -и́; как мой; см **Table 8**) притяж мест your; **вот** ~ **чай** here is your tea; **мой оте́ц врач – а** ~? my father is a doctor – what does yours do?; **это всё** ~**ё** this is all yours; **приве́т (всем)** ~**им** say hello to your folks; **по-** ~**ему́ мне́нию** in your opinion; **как по-тво́ему?** what is your opinion?; **дава́й сде́лаем по-тво́ему** let's do it your way.

творе́ц (-ца́) м creator; **Т**~ (РЕЛ) the Creator.

твори́тельный прил: ~ **паде́ж** (линг) the instrumental (case).

Татар|ин (-а; nom pl **тата́ры**) м Tatar.

тата́р|ка (-ки; gen pl -ок) ж см **тата́рин**.

твор|и́ть (-ю́, -и́шь) *несов неперех* to create ◆ (*perf* **сотвори́ть**) *перех* (*шедевр, симфонию итп*) to create; (*perf* **натвори́ть**; *разг*) to get up to; ~ (**сотвори́ть** *perf*) **чудеса́** to work miracles; ~ (**сотвори́ть** *perf*) **добро́** to do good; ~ (*impf*) **беззако́ния** to commit unjust acts

▶ **твори́ться** *несов возв*: что тут ~и́тся? what's going on here?; с ним ~и́тся чтó-то стра́нное something strange has come over him.

творо́г (-а́; *part gen* -у́) *м* ≈ curd cheese.
творо́жник (-а) *м* curd pancake.
творо́жный *прил* curd-cheese.
творца́ *итп сущ см* **творе́ц**.
тво́рческ|ий (-ая, -ое, -ие) *прил* creative; **тво́рческий о́тпуск** sabbatical.
тво́рчеств|о (-а) *ср* creative work; (*писателя, композитора*) work; **худо́жественное** ~ artistic creativity; **наро́дное** ~ folk art.
тво|я́ (-е́й) *притяж мест см* **твой**.
ТВЧ *сокр* (= *то́ки высо́кой частоты́*) high frequency currents *мн*.
т.д. *сокр* (= **так да́лее**) etc. (= *et cetera*).
те (**тех**) *мест см* **тот**.
т.е. *сокр* (= **то есть**) i.e. (= *id est*).
теа́тр (-а) *м* theatre (*BRIT*), theater (*US*); ~ **Го́голя/Шекспи́ра** Gogol's/Shakespeare's theatrical works; ~ **вое́нных де́йствий** the theatre of operations.
театра́л (-а) *м* theatregoer (*BRIT*), theatergoer (*US*).
театрализ|ова́ть (-у́ю) (*не)сов перех* to dramatize.
театра́л|ка (-ки; *gen pl* -ок) *ж см* **театра́л**.
театра́льный *прил* (*афиша, сезон*) theatre *опред* (*BRIT*), theater *опред* (*US*); (*деятельность, жест*) theatrical; **театра́льная ка́сса** theatre box office; **театра́льная сту́дия** theatre studio; **театра́льный зал** theatre; **театра́льный институ́т** drama school.
театрове́д (-а) *м* theatre (*BRIT*) *или* theater (*US*) specialist.
тебе́ *мест см* **ты** ◆ *как част* (*разг*): **здесь** ~ **и по́мощь и понима́ние** you can get help and understanding here; **я** ~ **поспо́рю!** don't you dare to argue!; **я** ~ **дам** *или* **покажу́!** I'll show you!
теб|я́ *мест см* **ты**.
Тегера́н (-а) *м* Teheran.
теза́урус (-а) *м* thesaurus.
те́зис (-а) *м* (*идея*) thesis (*мн* theses); (: *в логике*) proposition; (*обычно мн*: *доклада*) abstract.
тёз|ка (-ки; *gen pl* -ок) *м/ж* namesake.
тёк *итп несов см* **течь**.
текст (-а) *м* text; (*песни*) words *мн*, lyrics *мн*.
тексти́л|ь (-я) *м собир* textiles *мн*.
тексти́льн|ый *прил*: ~ые изде́лия textiles; ~ая промы́шленность textile industry.
теку́т *итп несов см* **течь**.

теку́чест|ь (-и) *ж* fluidity; ~ **ка́дров** high staff turnover.
теку́ч|ий (-ая, -ее, -ие; -, -а, -е) *прил* fluid; ~ие **ка́дры** fluctuating workforce.
теку́ч|ка (-и) *ж* (*разг*) daily routine.
теку́щий (-ая, -ее, -ие) *прил* (*год*) current; (*повседневный*: *дела*) routine; ~ие **обяза́тельства** (*КОММ*) current liabilities *мн*; **теку́щие собы́тия** current affairs; **теку́щий ремо́нт** running repairs, maintenance; **теку́щий счёт** (*КОММ*) current (*BRIT*) *или* checking (*US*) account.
тел. *сокр* (= **телефо́н**) tel. (= *telephone*).
телевеща́ни|е (-я) *ср* television broadcasting.
телеви́дени|е (-я) *ср* television; **по** ~ю on television.
телевизио́нный *прил* television *опред*.
телевизио́нщик (-а) *м* broadcaster.
телеви́зор (-а) *м* television (set); **смотре́ть** (*impf*) ~ to watch television; **по** ~у on television.
теле́г|а (-и) *ж* cart.
телегра́мм|а (-ы) *ж* telegram.
телегра́ф (-а) *м* (*способ связи*) telegraph; (*учреждение*) telegraph office.
телеграфи́р|овать (-ую) (*не)сов перех* to wire.
телеграфи́ст (-а) *м* telegraphist.
телеграфи́ст|ка (-ки; *gen pl* -ок) *ж см* **телеграфи́ст**.
телегра́фный *прил* (*также перен*) telegraphic; **телегра́фное аге́нтство** news agency; **телегра́фный де́нежный перево́д** telegraphic transfer; **телегра́фный столб** telegraph pole.
теле́ж|ка (-ки; *gen pl* -ек) *ж уменьш от* **теле́га**; (*для багажа, в супермаркете*) trolley.
телезри́тел|ь (-я) *м* viewer.
телека́мер|а (-ы) *ж* television camera.
те́лекс (-а) *м* telex.
телёнок (-ёнка; *nom pl* -я́та, *gen pl* -я́т) *м* calf (*мн* calves).
телепа́ти|я (-и) *ж* telepathy.
телепереда́ч|а (-и) *ж* TV programme (*BRIT*) *или* program (*US*).
теле́сен *прил см* **теле́сный**.
телеско́п (-а) *м* telescope.
телескопи́ческ|ий (-ая, -ое, -ие) *прил* (*антенна, очки*) telescopic; (*наблюдения*) long-distance.
теле́сн|ый (-ен, -на, -но) *прил* bodily; ~ого **цве́та** flesh-coloured; **теле́сное наказа́ние** corporal punishment.
телеста́нци|я (-и) *ж* television station.
телесту́ди|я (-и) *ж* television studio.
телета́йп (-а) *м* teleprinter (*BRIT*), teletypewriter (*US*), Teletype ®.
телефо́н (-а) *м* telephone; (*разг*: *номер*) (phone) number.
телефони́ст (-а) *м* telephonist.
телефони́ст|ка (-ки; *gen pl* -ок) *ж см*

телефони́ст.

телефо́нный *прил* telephone *опред*; **телефо́нная ста́нция** telephone exchange; **телефо́нная кни́га** telephone book *или* directory.

теле́ц *сущ см* **те́льце**.

Теле́ц (-ьца́) *м (созвездие)* Taurus.

телеце́нтр (-а) *м* television centre (*BRIT*) *или* center (*US*).

тели́ться (*3sg* -ится, *3pl* -ятся, *perf* **отели́ться**) *несов возв* to calve.

тёл|ка (-ки; *gen pl* -ок) *ж* heifer.

те́л|о (-а; *nom pl* -а́) *ср* body; **небе́сные тела́** heavenly bodies; **дрожа́ть** (*impf*) **всем ~м** to tremble all over; **держа́ть** (*impf*) **кого́-н в чёрном ~е** to treat sb badly.

телогре́йка (-йки; *gen pl* -ек) *ж* body warmer.

телодвиже́ни|е (-я) *ср* movement.

тёлок *сущ см* **тёлка**.

телосложе́ни|е (-я) *ср* physique.

телохрани́тел|ь (-я) *м* bodyguard.

Тель-Ави́в (-а) *м* Tel Aviv.

тельня́ш|ка (-ки; *gen pl* -ек) *ж* sailor top.

Тельца́ *итп сущ см* **Теле́ц**.

те́льце (-ьца; *nom pl* -ьца́, *gen pl* -е́ц) *ср уменьш от* **те́ло**; *(ребёнка)* body; *(обычно мн: кровяные)* corpuscle.

теля́та *итп сущ см* **телёнок**.

теля́тин|а (-ы) *ж* veal.

теля́тник (-а) *м (помещение)* calf shed.

теля́чий (-ья, -ье, -ьи) *прил*: ~**ья ко́жа** calfskin *опред*; *(КУЛИН)* veal *опред*; ~**ьи не́жности** *(разг)* lovey-dovey behaviour; ~ **восто́рг** *(разг)* wide-eyed enthusiasm.

тем *мест см* **тот, то** ♦ *союз (+comparative)*: **чем бо́льше, ~ лу́чше** the more the better; ~ **бо́лее!** all the more so!; ~ **бо́лее что ...** especially as ...; **э́то тру́дно, ~ бо́лее для меня́** it's difficult, especially for me; ~ **лу́чше/ху́же** that's even better/worse; ~ **лу́чше для меня́** all the better for me; **не хо́чет слу́шать? ~ ху́же для него́** if he doesn't want to listen then it's his loss; ~ **не ме́нее** nevertheless; ~ **са́мым** thus.

те́м|а (-ы) *ж* subject, topic; *(МУЗ, ЛИТЕРАТУРА)* theme.

тема́тик|а (-и) *ж* theme.

темати́ческий (-ая, -ое, -ие) *прил (выставка, показ фильмов итп)* theme-based.

тембр (-а) *м* timbre.

тёмен *прил см* **тёмный**.

те́мени *итп сущ см* **те́мя**.

Те́мз|а (-ы) *ж* the Thames.

те́ми *мест см* **тот, то**.

темне́ть (*3sg* -ет, *3pl* -ют, *perf* **потемне́ть**) *несов непере́х (небо, краска)* to darken ♦ (*perf* **стемне́ть**) *безл* to get dark; *(no perf; виднеться)* to loom dark; **зимо́й ра́но ~ет** it gets dark early in winter.

темни́ть (-ю́, -и́шь) *несов непере́х (разг)* to confuse the issue.

темни́ц|а (-ы) *ж* dungeon.

темно́ *как сказ*: **на у́лице/в ко́мнате ~** it's dark outside/inside; **на душе́ у неё бы́ло ~** she felt gloomy.

темнот|а́ (-ы́) *ж* darkness; *(перен: невежество)* ignorance.

тём|ный (-ен, -на́, -но́) *прил* dark; *(смысл, теория)* obscure; *(прошлое, дела)* shady; *(невежественный: человек)* ignorant; ~**ное пятно́** *(перен)* blemish; ~**ные времена́** dark times.

темп (-а) *м* speed; *(МУЗ)* tempo; **в те́мпе** *(разг)* quickly; **ускоря́ть (ускори́ть** *perf*) ~ +*gen* to speed up

те́мпер|а (-ы) *ж* tempera.

темпера́мент (-а) *м* temperament, disposition; **он челове́к с ~ом** he is a temperamental character.

темпера́мент|ный (-ен, -на, -но) *прил (речь, исполнение, человек)* spirited.

температу́р|а (-ы) *ж* temperature; **у меня́ ~** I've got a temperature; **ходи́ть** (*impf*) **с ~ой** *(разг)* to go about with a temperature.

температу́р|ить (-ю, -ишь) *несов непере́х (разг)* to be running a temperature.

тём|я (-ени; *как* **вре́мя**; *см* **Table 4**) *ср* crown *(of the head)*.

те́нг|е (-а) *м* tenga *(currency unit of Kazakhstan)*.

тенденцио́зность (-и) *ж* bias.

тенденцио́зный *прил* bias(s)ed.

тенде́нци|я (-и) *ж*: ~ (**к** +*dat*) tendency (towards); *(предвзятость)* bias.

теневой *прил* shady; *(перен: стороны жизни)* shadowy; **теневая эконо́мика** shadow economy; **теневой кабине́т** *(ПОЛИТ)* shadow cabinet.

тенелюби́в|ый (-, -а, -о) *прил (БОТ)* shade-loving.

те́н|и (-ей) *мн (также: ~ для век)* eye shadow *ед*.

тени́стый (-, -а, -о) *прил* shady.

те́ннис (-а) *м* tennis.

тенниси́ст (-а) *м* tennis player.

тенниси́ст|ка (-ки; *gen pl* -ок) *ж см* **тенниси́ст**.

те́ннис|ка (-ки; *gen pl* -ок) *ж* polo shirt.

те́ннис|ный *прил*: ~**ая раке́тка** tennis racket; **те́ннисный корт/мяч** tennis court/ball.

те́ннисок *сущ см* **те́нниска**.

те́нор (-а; *nom pl* -а́) *м (МУЗ)* tenor.

тент (-а) *м* awning.

тен|ь (-и; *prp sg* -и́, *gen pl* -е́й) *ж (тенистое место)* shade; *(предмета, человека)* shadow; (+*gen*; *перен: волнения, печали итп)* flicker of; **отбра́сывать (отбро́сить** *perf*) ~ to cast a shadow; **держа́ться** (*impf*) **в ~й** *(перен)* to remain in the background; **броса́ть (бро́сить** *perf*) ~ **на** +*acc (перен)* to cast a slur on; **без те́ни сомне́ния** without a shadow of a doubt; **нет ни те́ни сомне́ния, что ...** there is not the slightest doubt that ...; *см также* **те́ни**.

теологи́ческий (-ая, -ое, -ие) *прил* theological.

теоло́ги|я (-и) *ж* theology.

теоре́м|а (-ы) *ж* theorem.

теоре́тик (-а) *м* theoretician.

теорети́ческ|ий (-ая, -ое, -ие) *прил* theoretical.

тео́ри|я (-и) *ж* theory.

тепе́решн|ий (-яя, -ее, -ие) *прил* (*разг*) present.

тепе́рь *нареч* (*сейчас*) now; (*в на́ше вре́мя*) nowadays ♦ *союз*: ~ **обсу́дим сле́дующий вопро́с** let us move on to the next question.

тепле́|ть (*3sg* -ет, *3pl* -ют, *perf* **потепле́ть**) *несов непереx* to get warmer; (*отноше́ния*) to become warmer.

те́пл|иться (*3sg* -ится, *3pl* -ятся) *несов возв* to flicker; **в нём ещё ~ится наде́жда** he still holds out a faint hope.

тепли́ц|а (-ы) *ж* hothouse.

тепли́чный *прил* (*расте́ние*) hothouse *опред*; (*перен*: *усло́вия*) sheltered.

тепл|о́ *нареч* warmly ♦ (-а́) *ср* (*также перен*) warmth ♦ *как сказ* it's warm; **на у́лице/в ко́мнате** ~ it's warm outside/inside; **нас** ~ **встре́тили** we were given a warm welcome; **10 гра́дусов** ~**а́** 10 degrees (centigrade); **мне** ~ I'm warm.

теплово́з (-а) *м* locomotive.

теплово́й *прил* (*лучи́, эне́ргия*) thermal; **теплово́й дви́гатель** heat engine; **теплово́й уда́р** (*МЕД*) heatstroke.

теплолюби́в|ый (-, -а, -о) *прил* (*БОТ*) heatloving.

теплообме́н (-а) *м* (*ФИЗ*) heat exchange.

теплот|а́ (-ы́) *ж* heat; (*перен*: *чувств, отноше́ний, кра́сок*) warmth.

теплохо́д (-а) *м* motor ship *или* vessel.

теплоцентра́л|ь (-и) *ж* generator plant (*supplying central heating systems*).

тёп|лый (-ел, -ла́, -ло́) *прил* warm; ~**лое месте́чко** (*разг*) cushy job; **сказа́ть** (*perf*) **кому́-н па́ру** ~**лых слов** (*разг*) to give sb a piece of one's mind.

тера́кт (-а) *м* (= **террористи́ческий акт**) act of terrorism.

терапе́вт (-а) *м* ≈ general practitioner.

терапи́|я (-и) *ж* (*МЕД*: *нау́ка*) internal medicine; (*лече́ние*) therapy; **интенси́вная** ~ intensive care.

тереб|и́ть (-лю́, -и́шь) *несов перех* (*во́лосы, бо́роду*) to twiddle; (*разг*: *надоеда́ть*) to pester.

тере́ть (**тру, трёшь**; *pt* **тёр, тёрла, тёрло**) *несов перех* to rub; (*чи́стить*) to scrub; (*о́вощи*) to grate ♦ *непереx* (*о́бувь, воротни́к*) to rub

► **тере́ться** *несов возв* (*челове́к*): ~**ся о** +*acc* to rub o.s. up against; (*перен*: *разг*): ~**ся о́коло** *или* **во́зле** +*gen* to hang around.

терза́ни|е (-я) *ср* (*обы́чно мн*: *душе́вные*) torment.

терза́|ть (-ю; *perf* **растерза́ть**) *несов перех* (*добы́чу*) to savage; (*perf* **истерза́ть**; *перен*: *упрёками, ре́вностью*) to torment

► **терза́ться** *несов возв* (+*instr*; *сомне́ниями, раска́янием*) to be racked by.

тёр|ка (-ки; *gen pl* -ок) *ж* grater.

те́рмин (-а) *м* term.

термина́л (-а) *м* terminal.

терминологи́ческ|ий (-ая, -ое, -ие) *прил*: ~ **слова́рь** specialized dictionary.

терминоло́ги|я (-и) *ж* terminology.

терми́ческ|ий (-ая, -ое, -ие) *прил* thermal.

термо́метр (-а) *м* thermometer.

те́рмос (-а) *м* Thermos®.

термоста́т (-а) *м* thermostat.

термосто́йк|ий (-ая, -ое, -ие) *прил* heatresistant.

термоя́дерный *прил* thermonuclear; **термоя́дерное ору́жие** thermonuclear weapon.

терни́ст|ый (-, -а, -о) *прил*: ~ **путь** (*перен*) difficult path.

терно́вник (-а) *м* blackthorn.

тёрок *сущ см* **тёрка**.

терпели́в|ый (-, -а, -о) *прил* patient.

терпе́ни|е (-я) *ср* patience; **выводи́ть** (**вы́вести** *perf*) **кого́-н из** ~**я** to exhaust sb's patience; ~ **у меня́ ло́пнуло** I lost my patience; **запаса́ться** (**запасти́сь** *perf*) ~**м** to call on one's reserve of patience.

терп|е́ть (-лю́, -ишь) *несов перех* (*боль, хо́лод итп*) to suffer, endure; (*perf* **потерпе́ть**; *неуда́чу*) to suffer; (*мири́ться*: *гру́бость, наглеца́ итп*) to tolerate; ~ (**потерпе́ть** *perf*) **неуда́чу/пораже́ние** to suffer failure/a defeat; ~ (**потерпе́ть** *perf*) **круше́ние** (*кора́бль*) to be wrecked; (*по́езд*) to crash; **вре́мя не те́рпит** time waits for no man; **де́ло не те́рпит отлага́тельств** this matter won't wait; ~ **не могу́ таки́х люде́й** (*разг*) I can't stand people like that; ~ **не могу́ спо́рить** I hate arguing

► **терпе́ться** *несов безл*: (**мне**) **не те́рпится** +*infin* I can't wait to do.

терпи́мост|ь (-и) *ж*: ~ (**к** +*dat*) tolerance (of).

терпи́м|ый (-, -а, -о) *прил* tolerable; (*челове́к, отноше́ние*): ~ (**к** +*dat*) tolerant (towards).

тёрп|кий (-ка, -кое, -кие; *as adv* -ок, -ка, -ко) *прил* tart.

терплю́(сь) *несов см* **терпе́ть(ся)**.

тёрпок *прил см* **тёрпкий**.

террако́т|а (-ы) *ж* terracotta.

террако́товый *прил* terracotta.

терра́с|а (-ы) *ж* (*также ГЕО*) terrace.

территориа́льный *прил* territorial.

террито́ри|я (-и) *ж* (*страны*) territory; (*шко́лы, уса́дьбы*) grounds *мн*; **о́бщая** ~ **заво́да – 100 кв миль** the plant occupies an area of 100 sq miles.

терро́р (-а) *м* terror.

терроризи́р|овать (-ую) (*не*)*сов перех* to terrorize.

террори́зм (-а) *м* terrorism.

террори́ст (-а) *м* terrorist.

террористи́ческ|ий (-ая, -ое, -ие) *прил*

terrorist *опред.*

террори́стка (-ки; *gen pl* -ок) *ж см* **террори́ст**.

тёртый *прил* (*сыр, овощи*) grated; **челове́к он ~** (*разг*) he's been around.

терье́р (-а) *м* terrier.

теря́ть (-ю; *perf* **потеря́ть**) *несов перех* to lose; **~ (потеря́ть** *perf*) **го́лову** to lose one's head; **~ (потеря́ть** *perf*) **из ви́ду** (*перестать видеть*) to lose sight of; (*не иметь сведений о*) to lose touch with; **~ (потеря́ть** *perf*) **по́чву под нога́ми** (*перен*) to lose one's way

▸ **теря́ться** (*perf* **потеря́ться**) *несов возв* to get lost; (*робеть*) to lose one's nerve; (*утрачиваться: память, уверенность*) to disappear; **~ся** (*impf*) **в дога́дках** to get caught up in conjecture.

тёс (-а) *м собир* planks *мн*.

тёсаный *прил* hewn.

теса́ть (-шу́, -шешь) *несов перех* to hew (out).

тесём|ка (-ки; *gen pl* -ок) *ж* = **тесьма́**; (*завязка*) drawstring.

те́сен *прил см* **те́сный**.

тесни́ть (-ю́, -и́шь; *perf* **потесни́ть**) *несов перех* (*друг друга в толпе*) to squeeze; (*кого-н к стене*) to press; (*противника*) to press back; (*perf* **стесни́ть;** *перен*): **~и́т в груди́** he *итп* has got a tight feeling in his chest

▸ **тесни́ться** *несов возв* (*люди: в толпе, в тесной комнате*) to be squashed together; (*мысли*) to crowd; **семья́ ~и́тся в одно́й ко́мнате** the whole family lives crammed together in one room; **в голове́ ~я́тся воспомина́ния** his *итп* mind is crowded with memories.

те́сно *нареч* (*стоять, расположить* итп) close together; (*сотрудничать*) closely ◆ *как сказ*: **в кварти́ре о́чень ~** the flat is very cramped; **мы с ним ~ знако́мы** he and I know each other very well.

теснот|а́ (-ы́) *ж* (*помещения*) cramped conditions *мн*; (*скопление людей*) crowd; (*в груди*) tightness; **в ~е́, да не в оби́де** ≈ the more the merrier.

те́с|ный (-ен, -на́, -но) *прил* (*проход*) narrow; (*помещение*) cramped; (*одежда*) tight; (*дружба, ряды*) close; **мир ~ен** it's a small world.

тест (-а) *м* test.

те́ст|о (-а) *ср* (*дрожжевое*) dough; (*слоёное, песочное*) pastry (*BRIT*), paste (*US*); (*для блинов*) batter; (*для кекса*) mixture; (*бетонное*) mix.

тест|ь (-я) *м* father-in-law, wife's father.

тесьм|а́ (-ы́) *ж* tape; (*для украшения*) trimming.

те́терев (-а) *м* black grouse.

тете́р|я (-и) *ж* (*разг*) clot; **глуха́я ~** cloth-ears; **со́нная ~** sleepyhead.

тетив|а́ (-ы́) *ж* (*лука*) bowstring.

тёт|ка (-ки; *gen pl* -ок) *ж* auntie; (*разг: пренебр: женщина*) old dear.

тетра́д|ка (-ки; *gen pl* -ок) *ж* exercise book.

тетра́д|ь (-и) *ж* exercise book; **но́тная ~**

manuscript book.

тёт|я (-и; *gen pl* -ь) *ж* aunt; (*разг: женщина*) lady.

тефте́л|и (-ей) *мн* meatballs *мн*.

тех *мест см* **те**.

Теха́с (-а) *м* Texas.

те́хник (-а) *м* technician.

те́хник|а (-и) *ж* technology; (*приёмы: музыкальная, плавания* итп) technique ◆ *собир* (*машины*) machinery; (*разг: муз*) hi-fi; **вычисли́тельная ~** (*КОМП*) computers *мн*; **те́хника безопа́сности** industrial safety.

те́хникум (-а) *м* technical college.

техни́чек *сущ см* **техни́чка**.

техни́чен *прил см* **техни́чный**.

техни́ческ|ий (-ая, -ое, -ие) *прил* technical; (*масло, волокно*) industrial; **техни́ческие нау́ки** engineering sciences; **техни́ческие сре́дства обуче́ния** educational technology; **техни́ческий осмо́тр** (*АВТ*) ≈ MOT (*BRIT*) (*annual roadworthiness check*); **техни́ческий реда́ктор** copy editor; **техни́ческое обслу́живание** maintenance, servicing.

техни́ч|ка (-ки; *gen pl* -ек) *ж* (*автомобиль*) emergency vehicle; (*уборщица*) cleaner.

техни́чн|ый (-ен, -на, -но) *прил* (*спортсмен, музыкант*) technically good.

технокра́т (-а) *м* technocrat.

техно́лог (-а) *м* technologist; (*производственного процесса*) process engineer.

технологи́ческ|ий (-ая, -ое, -ие) *прил* technological; (*не строительный*) engineering *опред*; (*не вспомогательный*) basic, major; **технологи́ческий институ́т** institute of technology.

техноло́ги|я (-и) *ж* technology.

тече́ни|е (-я) *ср* (*воды, жизни*) flow; (*поток: морское, атмосферное*) current; (*в политике, в искусстве*) trend, current; **в ~ +gen** during; **с ~м вре́мени** in the course of time; **по ~ю** with the current; **плыть** (*impf*) **по ~ю** (*перен*) to go with the flow; **про́тив ~я** against the current.

те́чк|а (-и) *ж* (*ЗООЛ*) heat; **у на́шей соба́ки ~** our dog is on *или* in heat.

те|чь (*3sg* -чёт, *3pl* -ку́т, *pt* тёк, текла́, текло́) *несов неперех* (*вода, кровь* итп) to flow; (*крыша, лодка* итп) to leak; (*перен: жизнь, время*) to go by ◆ (-чи) *ж* leak; **дава́ть** (**дать** *perf*) **~** to spring a leak.

те́ш|ить (-у, -ишь; *perf* **поте́шить**) *несов перех* to amuse; (*самолюбие*) to indulge

▸ **те́шиться** (*perf* **поте́шиться**) *несов возв*: **~ся** +*instr* (*игрушкой*) to amuse o.s. with; (*мыслью*) to console o.s. with; (*издеваться*): **~ся над** +*instr* to make fun of.

тёщ|а (-и) *ж* mother-in-law, wife's mother.

тешу́ *итп несов см* **теса́ть**.

Тибе́т (-а) *м* Tibet.

тибе́тск|ий (-ая, -ое, -ие) *прил* Tibetan.

Тибр (-а) *м* Tiber (*river*).

Тигр (-а) *м* Tigris (*river*).

тигр (-а) м tiger.

тигрёнок (-ёнка; *nom pl* -**я́та**, *gen pl* -**я́т**) м tiger cub.

тигри́ц|**а** (-ы) ж tigress.

тигро́вый *прил* tiger *опред*; **тигро́вый глаз** (*камень*) tiger's-eye.

тигря́та *итп сущ см* **тигрёнок**

тик (-а) м (*нервный*) tic; (*ткань*) ticking.

ти́кани|**е** (-я) *ср* ticking.

ти́ка|**ть** (*3sg* -**ет**, *3pl* -**ют**) *несов неперех* to tick.

ти́н|**а** (-ы) ж slime; (*перен: обывательщины итп*) mire.

тип (-а) м type; (*разг: о мужчине*) character; **ти́па** +*gen* (*разг*) sort of.

типа́ж (-á) м character type.

типи́чен *прил см* **типи́чный**.

типи́ческий (-**ая**, -**ое**, -**ие**) *прил* typical.

типи́чн|**ый** (-**ен**, -**на**, -**но**) *прил*: ~ (**для** +*gen*) typical (of).

типово́й *прил* standard-type.

типогра́фи|**я** (-и) ж press, printing house.

типогра́фск|**ий** (-**ая**, -**ое**, -**ие**) *прил* typographical; **типогра́фская кра́ска** printing ink; **типогра́фский стано́к** printing press.

типу́н (-а) м: ~ **тебе́ на язы́к!** (*разг*) don't say that!

тир (-а) м shooting gallery.

тира́д|**а** (-ы) ж tirade.

тира́ж (-á) м (*газеты*) circulation; (*книги*) printing; (*лотереи, облигаций*) drawing; **кни́га вы́шла тиражо́м в ты́сячу экземпля́ров** one thousand copies of the book were printed; **выходи́ть** (**вы́йти** *perf*) **в** ~ (*заём, облигации*) to be issued; (*книга*) to be printed; (*перен*) to fade from the scene.

тира́н (-а) м tyrant.

Тира́н|**а** (-ы) ж Tirana.

тира́н|**ить** (-**ю**, -**ишь**) *несов перех* to tyrannize.

тирани́ческий (-**ая**, -**ое**, -**ие**) *прил* tyrannical.

тирани́|**я** (-и) ж tyranny.

тире́ *ср нескл* dash.

тис (-а) м yew (tree).

ти́ска|**ть** (-**ю**) *несов перех* to squeeze.

тиск|**и́** (-**о́в**) *мн* (*ТЕХ*) vice *ед* (*BRIT*), vise *ед* (*US*); **в** ~**áx** +*gen* (*перен*) in the grip of.

тисне́ни|**е** (-**я**) *ср* (*по коже*) stamping.

ти́сненый *прил* (*переплёт*) impressed.

тита́н (-а) м (*в мифологии*) titan; (*перен: науки, мысли итп*) giant; (*хим*) titanium; (*для нагрева воды*) boiler, urn.

титани́ческий (-**ая**, -**ое**, -**ие**) *прил* titanic.

титр (-а) м (*обычно мн*) credit (*of a film*).

ти́тул (-а) м (*также комм*) title; ~ **на иму́щество** (*ЮР*) title (*to property*).

ти́тульный *прил*: ~ **лист** title page.

тиф (-а) м typhus; **брюшно́й** ~ typhoid fever.

тифо́зн|**ый** *прил*: ~**ая лихора́дка** typhoid fever ◆ (-**ого**; *decl like adj*) м typhus patient.

ти́хий (-**ая**, -**ое**, -**ие**; -, -á, -**о**) *прил* quiet;

(*течение, ход*) gentle; **Ти́хий океа́н** the Pacific (Ocean).

ти́х|**нуть** (*3sg* -**нет**, *3pl* -**нут**, *pt* -, -**ла**, -**ло**) *несов неперех* to go quiet.

ти́хо *нареч* (*говорить, жить итп*) quietly; (*идти*) slowly ◆ *как сказ*: **в до́ме** ~ the house is quiet; ~**!** (be) quiet!

тихо́н|**я** (-**и**) м/ж (*разг*) quiet operator.

ти́ше *сравн прил от* **ти́хий** ◆ *сравн нареч от* **ти́хо**; ~**!** quiet!, hush!

тишин|**а́** (-**ы́**) ж quiet.

тиш|**ь** (-**и**) ж = **тишина́**.

т.к. *сокр* = **так как**.

тка́ный *прил* woven.

тка|**нь** (-**и**) ж fabric, material; (*АНАТ*) tissue; (*перен: рассказа*) fabric.

тк|**ать** (-**у**, -**ёшь**; *perf* **сотка́ть**) *несов перех* to weave; (*паутину*) to spin.

тка́цк|**ий** (-**ая**, -**ое**, -**ие**) *прил*: ~**ое произво́дство** weaving; **тка́цкая фа́брика** mill (*for fabric production*); **тка́цкий стано́к** loom.

ткач (-á) м weaver.

ткачи́х|**а** (-**и**) ж *см* **ткач**.

ткн|**у́ть(ся)** (-**у́(сь)**, -**ёшь(ся)**) *сов от* **ты́кать(ся)**.

тлен (-а) м decay.

тлетво́рн|**ый** (-**ен**, -**на**, -**но**) *прил* pernicious.

тле|**ть** (*3sg* -**ет**, *3pl* -**ют**) *несов неперех* (*навоз, мусор*) to decay; (*дрова, угли*) to smoulder (*BRIT*), smolder (*US*); (*пламя*) to die out; (*перен: надежда*) to flicker

➤ **тле́ться** *несов возв* (*костёр, угли*) to smo(u)lder; (*надежда*) to flicker.

тл|**я** (-**и**) ж aphid.

тмин (-а) м (*БОТ*) tumin.

т.н. *сокр* = **так называ́емый**.

ТНК ж *сокр* = **транснациона́льная корпора́ция**.

то *союз* (*условный*): **е́сли** ... ~ ... if ... then ...; (*разделительный*): ~ ... ~ ... sometimes ... sometimes ...; **е́сли его́ не бу́дет там,** ~ **я не пойду́** if he isn't going to be there, (then) I'm not going; **и** ~ even; **он и** ~ **зна́ет об э́том** even he knows about it; ~ **есть** that is; ~ **и де́ло** time and again.

то (**того́**) *мест см* **тот**.

т.о. *сокр* = **таки́м о́бразом**.

-то *част* (*для выделения*): **письмо́-то ты получи́л?** did you (at least) receive the letter?; **где́-то она́ сейча́с** if only I knew where she is now; **когда́-то мы встре́тимся?** when on earth shall we meet?; **э́тот-то всё съел** this one here has eaten everything.

тобо́й *мест см* **ты**.

тобо́ю *мест* = **тобо́й**.

тов. *сокр* = **товáрищ**.

товáр (-а; *part gen* -**у**) м product; (*ЭКОН*) commodity ◆ *собир* goods *мн*.

товáрищ (-а) м (*приятель*) friend; (*по партии*)

comrade; ~ **по шкóле/рабóте** school-/
workmate.
товáрищеск|ий (**-ая, -ое, -ие**) *прил* comradely;
товáрищеский матч (*СПОРТ*) friendly (match).
товáрищество (**-а**) *ср* camaraderie; (*КОММ*)
partnership.
товáрный *прил* (*производство*) goods *опред*;
(*рынок*) commodity *опред*; **товáрная биржа**
commodity exchange; **товáрный вагóн** goods
wagon (*BRIT*), freight car (*US*); **товáрный знак**
trademark; **товáрный пóезд** goods (*BRIT*) *или*
freight (*US*) train; **товáрный склад** warehouse.
товаровéд (**-а**) *м* merchandiser.
товарообмéн (**-а**) *м* barter.
товарооборóт (**-а**) *м* turnover.
товаропроизводи́тель (**-я**) *м* (goods)
manufacturer.
тогдá *нареч* then; ~ **как** (*хотя*) while; (*при
противопоставлении*) whereas; **не хóчешь, ~
не нáдо** if you don't want to, then don't.
тогдáшн|ий (**-яя, -ее, -ие**) *прил* (*разг*): **в ~ие
временá** in those days.
тогó *мест см* **тот, то**.
тождéствен|ный (**-, -на, -но**) *прил* identical.
тóждеств|о (**-а**) *ср* (*также МАТ*) identity.
тóже *нареч* (*также*) too, as well, also ◆ *част* as
if; **я ~ пойдý** I'm going too *или* as well, I'm also
going; **~ мне поэ́т нашёлся!** as if he's a poet!;
я ~ люблю́ я́блоки I too like apples; **я идý
купáться – я ~!** I'm going swimming – me too!
той *мест см* **та**.
ток (**-а**) *м* (*ЭЛЕК*) current; (*для зерна*) threshing
floor.
токáрный *прил*: ~ **станóк** lathe.
тóкар|ь (**-я**; *nom pl* **-я́**) *м* turner.
Тóкио *м нескл* Tokyo.
токсикóз (**-а**) *м* toxicosis; (*беременной*)
hyperemesis.
токси́чный *прил см* **токси́чный**.
токси́ческ|ий (**-ая, -ое, -ие**) *прил* toxic.
токси́ч|ный (**-ен, -на, -но**) *прил* = **токси́ческий**.
толк (**-а**; *part gen* **-у**) *м* (*в рассуждениях*) sense;
(*разг: польза*) use; **рассужда́ть** (*impf*) *или*
говори́ть (*impf*) **с тóлком** to talk sense; **от негó
нет тóлку** (*разг*) he's no use; **всё бéз ~у** it's all
for nothing; **взять** (*perf*) **что-н себé в ~** (*разг*)
to get sth; **знать** (*impf*) *или* **понимáть** (*impf*) ~ **в
чём-н** to have a good understanding of sth;
сбивáть (**сбить** *perf*) **когó-н с тóлку** to confuse
sb.
толкáтел|ь (**-я**) *м*: ~ **ядрá** shot-putter.
толкá|ть (**-ю**; *perf* **толкнýть**) *несов перех* to
push; (*перен*): ~ **когó-н на** +*acc* (*подлеж:
голод*) to force sb into; (*: человек*) to put sb up
to; ~ (*impf*) **лóктем** to nudge; ~ (*impf*) **ядрó** to
put the shot; ~ (*impf*) **штáнгу** to lift weights; ~
(**толкнýть** *perf*) **речь** (*разг*) to have one's say
▶ **толкáться** *несов возв* (*в толпе*) to push
(one's way); (*разг: без дела*) to hang about *или*
around; ~**ся** (**толкнýться** *perf*) **в** +*acc* (*разг: в
дверь*) to push; (*перен: в учреждении*) to

approach.
тóлк|и (**-ов**) *мн* (*разг*) gossip *ед*.
толкнýть(ся) (**-ý(сь), -ёшь(ся)**) *сов от*
толкáть(ся).
толковáни|е (**-я**) *ср* interpretation; (*слова*)
definition.
толкова́|ть (**-ю**) *несов перех* (*явления,
события итп*) to interpret; (*разг*): ~ **что-н** +*dat*
to spell sth out to; ~ (*impf*) **с кем-н о чём-н**
(*разг*) to have a chat with sb about sth.
толкóв|ый (**-, -а, -о**) *прил* (*ученик, работник*)
intelligent; (*объяснение*) clear; **толкóвый
словáрь** dictionary with definitions.
тóлком *нареч* (*разг*) properly; **я ~ ничегó не
узнáл** I didn't manage to find anything out.
толкотн|я́ (**-и́**) *ж* (*разг: в толпе, в очереди*)
crush.
толку́(сь) *итп несов см* **толóчь(ся)**.
толку́ч|ка (**-ки**; *gen pl* **-ек**) *ж* (*разг: рынок*) flea
market; (*место скопления людей*) crush.
толóк(ся) *итп несов см* **толóчь(ся)**.
толокнó (**-á**) *ср* oatmeal.
тол|óчь (**-ку́, -чёшь** *итп*, **-ку́т**; *pt* **-óк, -клá, -клó**,
perf **истолóчь** *или* **растолóчь**) *несов перех*
(*зерна, сухари*) to pound; ~ (*impf*) **вóду в ступé**
(*разг*) to pound the air
▶ **толóчься** *несов возв* (*разг*) to crowd about
или around.
толп|á (**-ы́**; *nom pl* **-ы**) *ж* (*народа*) crowd; (*перен:
в противопоставление личности*) the crowd.
толп|и́ться (*3sg* **-и́тся**, *3pl* **-я́тся**) *несов возв* to
crowd around.
толсте́|ть (**-ю**; *perf* **потолсте́ть**) *несов неперех*
to get fatter.
толст|и́ть (*3sg* **-и́т**, *3pl* **-я́т**) *несов перех* (*разг*):
Вас ~и́т э́то плáтье that dress makes you look
fat.
толстокóж|ий (**-ая, -ее, -ие**; **-, -а, -о**) *прил*
(*также перен*) thick-skinned.
толсту́х|а (**-и**) *ж* (*разг*) = **толсту́шка**.
толсту́ш|ка (**-ки**; *gen pl* **-ек**) *ж* (*разг*) fatty.
тóлст|ый (**-, -á, -о**) *прил* thick; (*человек, ноги
итп*) fat; **тóлстая кишкá** large intestine.
толстя́к (**-á**) *м* (*разг*) fatso.
толчёный *прил* crushed.
толч|éя́ (**-и́**) *ж* (*разг*) crush.
толч|óк (**-кá**) *м* (*в спину, в грудь*) shove; (*при
торможении, при встряхивании*) jolt; (*при
землятресении*) tremor; (*перен: к работе, к
началу*) push; (*СПОРТ: штанги*) thrust; (*: ядра*)
put; (*разг: рынок*) flea market.
тóлщ|а (**-и**) *ж* (*льда, облаков*) mass.
тóлще *сравн прил от* **тóлстый**.
толщин|á (**-ы́**) *ж* (*тела, фигуры*) corpulence;
(*слоя, бревна*) thickness.
тол|ь (**-я**) *м* roofing felt.

KEYWORD

тóлько *част* **1** only; **тóлько 5 книг** only 5
books; **он читáет тóлько газéты** he only reads
newspapers
2 (+*pron*/+*adv*; *усиливает выразительность*):

зачéм тóлько я согласи́лся! why on earth did I agree!; **где тóлько он не побывáл** where has he NOT been!; **попрóбуй тóлько отказáться!** just try to refuse!; **подýмать тóлько!** imagine that!

♦ *союз* **1** (*сразу после*) as soon as; **тóлько напи́шешь, я приéду** as soon as you write, I'll come

2 (*однако, но*) only; **позвони́, тóлько разговáривай недóлго** phone (*BRIT*) *или* call (*US*), only don't talk for long

♦ *нареч* **1** (*недавно*) (only) just; **ты давнó здесь?- нет, тóлько вошлá** have you been here long? - no, I've (only) just come in

2 (*во фразах*): **тóлько лишь** (*разг*) only; **тóлько и всегó** (*разг*) that's all; **как** *или* **лишь** *или* **едвá тóлько** (*сразу после того, как*) as soon as; **не тóлько ..., но и ...** not only ... but also ...; **тóлько бы** if only; **тóлько бы знать, где он!** if only I knew where he was!; **тóлько что** only just.

том *мест см* **тот, то.**

том (-а; *nom pl* **-á**) *м* volume.

томáт (-а) *м* (*помидор*) tomato (*мн* tomatoes); (*соус*) tomato purée.

томáтный *прил*: ~ **сок/суп** tomato juice/soup.

гóмен *прил см* **тóмный.**

томи́тельный (-ен, -ьна, -ьно) *прил* tormenting.

томи́ть (-лю́, -и́шь; *perf* **истоми́ть**) *несов перех* (*расспросами, ожидáнием*) to torment

▶ **томи́ться** (*perf* **истоми́ться**) *несов возв* (*ожидáнием, жáждой*) to be tormented.

томлéние (-я) *ср* languor.

томлю́(сь) *несов см* **томи́ть(ся).**

тóмный (-ен, -на, -но) *прил* languid.

томý *мест см* **тот, то.**

тон (-а) *м* (*также МУЗ, МЕД*) tone.

тонáльность (-и) *ж* (*МУЗ*) key; (*картины*) tones *мн*; (*перен: стихотворéния*) tone.

тонзилли́т (-а) *м* tonsillitis.

тонизи́рующий (-ая, -ее, -ие) *прил* (*прогýлка, напиток*) refreshing; **~ее срéдство** tonic.

тóнкий (-кая, -кое, -кие; -ок, -кá, -ко) *прил* thin; (*фигýра, пáльцы*) slender; (*черты лица, работа, ум*) fine; (*запах, вкус*) delicate; (*обращéние, разли́чия, намёк*) subtle; (*слух*) sharp; **тóнкая кишкá** small intestine.

гóнко *нареч* (*рéзать*) thinly; (*пáхнуть*) delicately; (*намекáть, чýвствовать*) subtly; **онá ~ чýвствует мýзыку/поэ́зию** she has a fine appreciation of music/poetry.

тонкокóжий (-ая, -ее, -ие; -, -а, -о) *прил* thin-skinned.

тóнкость (-и) *ж* (*см прил*) thinness; slenderness; fineness; delicacy; subtlety; sharpness; (*частность*) detail; **до ~ей** down to the last detail; **вдавáться** (*impf*) **в ~и** to go into detail.

тóнна (-ы) *ж* tonne.

тоннáж (-а) *м* (*судна*) tonnage; (*вагóна*) capacity.

тоннéль (-я) *м* tunnel.

тóнок *прил см* **тóнкий.**

тóнус (-а) *м* (*сéрдца, ткáней*) tone; **жи́зненный ~** vitality.

тонýть (-ý, -ешь; *perf* **утонýть** *или* **потонýть**) *несов неперех* (*человéк*) to drown; (*perf* **утонýть**; *дéрево, кáмень*) to sink; (*perf* **затонýть**; *корáбль*) to sink; (*увязáть*): ~ **в** +*prp* (*в снегý, в грязи́*) to get stuck in; (*перен*: *в делáх*) to be up to one's eyes in; (*no perf*; *перен*: *в зéлени*) to get lost; (*в шýме*) to drown.

тóньше *сравн прил от* **тóнкий** ♦ *сравн нареч от* **тóнко.**

топáз (-а) *м* topaz.

тóпа|ть (-ю) *несов неперех* (*разг*: *идти́*) to go; ~ (*impf*) **ногáми** to stamp one's feet; **~й отсю́да!** (*разг*) scram!

топи́ть (-лю́, -ишь) *несов перех* (*печь*) to stoke (up); (*дом*) to warm (up); (*плáвить: мáсло, воск*) to melt; (*perf* **утопи́ть** *или* **потопи́ть**; *корáбль*) to sink; (*человéка*) to drown; (*perf* **потопи́ть**; *перен*: *дéло*) to ruin; **~ (потопи́ть** *perf*) **гóре** to drown one's sorrows

▶ **топи́ться** *несов возв* (*печь*) to burn; (*помещéние*) to be heated; (*perf* **растопи́ться**; *воск*) to melt; (*perf* **утопи́ться**; *лишить себя жизни*) to drown o.s.

тóп|ка (-и) *ж* (*дéйствие: печи*) stoking; (*часть печи*) furnace.

тóп|кий (-кая, -кое, -кие; -ок, -кá, -ко) *прил* (*дорóга, пóчва*) muddy.

топлёный *прил* (*кулин: мáсло, жир*) melted; **~ое молокó** boiled milk.

тóпливо (-а) *ср* fuel; **жи́дкое/твёрдое ~** liquid/solid fuel.

топлю́(сь) *несов см* **топи́ть(ся).**

топогрáфия (-и) *ж* topography.

тóпок *прил см* **тóпкий.**

тóполь (-я) *м* poplar.

топони́мика (-и) *ж* toponymy.

топóр (-á) *м* axe (*BRIT*), ax (*US*).

тóпорен *прил см* **топóрный.**

топóрище (-а) *ср* axe (*BRIT*) *или* ax (*US*) handle.

топóрный (-ен, -на, -но) *прил* (*перен*: *работа, стиль*) crude.

топóрщить (-у, -ишь; *perf* **встопóрщить**) *несов перех* (*разг*: *пéрья, шерсть*) to fluff up

▶ **топóрщиться** (*perf* **встопóрщиться**) *несов возв* (*разг*: *усы, хвост*) to bristle; (*плáтье, склáдки*) to puff up.

тóпот (-а) *м* clatter.

топ|тáть (-чý, -чешь; *perf* **потоптáть**) *несов перех* (*трáву*) to trample; (*пол*) to dirty

▶ **топтáться** *несов возв* (*разг*) to shift from one foot to the other; **~ся** (*impf*) **на мéсте** (*перен*) to go round in circles.

топ-топ *звукоподражание* pitter-patter.

топчáн (-á) *м* trestle bed.

топчý(сь) *итп несов см* **топтáть(ся)**.

топь (-и) *ж* marsh.

торг (-а) *м* trading.

торгáш (-á) *м* (*разг: пренебр*) money-grubber.

торгй (-óв) *мн* (*аукцион*) auction *ед*;
(*состязание*) tender *ед*.

торговáть (-ую) *несов неперех* (*перен:
совестью, убеждениями*) to forfeit; (*магазин*)
to trade; ~ (*impf*) +*instr* (*мясом, мебелью*) to
trade in; ~ (*impf*) с +*instr* to (do) trade with

▶ **торговáться** (*perf* **сторговáться**) *несов возв*
(*разг: спорить о цене*) to haggle; (*перен:
спорить*) to bicker.

торгóвец (-ца) *м* merchant; (*мелкий, уличный*)
trader.

торгóвка (-ки; *gen pl* **-ок**) *ж* (*уличная, базарная*)
trader.

торговля (-и) *ж* trade.

торгóвок *сущ см* **торгóвка**.

торгóвца *итп сущ см* **торгóвец**.

торгóвый *прил* (*договор, прибыль, барьеры*)
trade *опред*; (*судно, флот*) merchant *опред*;
торгóвая сеть retail network; **торгóвая тóчка**
retail outlet; **торгóвое представительство**
trade mission; **торгóвый рабóтник** retail
industry worker; **торгóвый центр** shopping
centre (*ВRIT*), mall (*US*).

торгпрéд (-а) *м сокр* (= *торгóвый
представитель*) head of the trade mission.

торгпрéдство (-а) *ср сокр* (= *торгóвое
представительство*) trade mission.

тореадóр (-а) *м* toreador.

торéц (-цá) *м* (*доски, книги*) butt; (*здания*) gable
end.

торжéственен *прил см* **торжéственный**.

торжéственно *нареч* (*обещать*) solemnly;
(*праздновать*) fully.

торжéственный *прил* (*день, случай*) special;
(*собрание*) celebratory; (**-ен, -на, -но**; *вид,
обстановка*) festive; (*no short form; обещание,
клятва*) solemn.

торжествó (-á) *ср* (*семейное, национальное*)
celebration; (*в голосе, в словах*) triumph; ~
+*gen* (*справедливости итп*) the triumph of.

торжествовáть (-ую; *perf* **восторжествовáть**)
несов неперех: ~ (**над** +*instr*) to triumph (over);
(*no perf; внутренно, открыто*) to rejoice.

тормáшки (-ек) *мн* (*разг*): **вверх ~ками** upside
down.

торможéние (-я) *ср* (*машины*) braking;
(*рефлексов*) inhibition.

тормóжу(сь) *несов см* **тормозить(ся)**.

тóрмоз (-а; *nom pl* **-á**) *м* brake; (*nom pl* **-ы**; *перен:
в работе*) hindrance, obstacle.

тормозить (-жý, -зишь; *perf* **затормозить**)
несов перех (*машину, поезд*) to slow down;
(*перен: движение, работу*) to hamper, impede

◆ *неперех* (*машина, поезд*) to brake

▶ **тормозиться** (*perf* **затормозиться**) *несов
возв* (*дело, работа итп*) to be hindered *или*
impeded.

тормознóй *прил* (*механизм, педаль*) brake
опред; (*БИО: рефлекс*) inhibitory; **~áя
жидкость** brake fluid.

тормошить (-ý, -ишь) *несов перех* to shake; ~
(*impf*) **когó-н за рукáв** to tug at sb's sleeve; ~
(*impf*) **когó-н** (*вопросами*) to pester sb.

торопить (-оплю, -óпишь; *perf* **поторопить**)
несов перех (*коня*) to urge on; (*ребёнка,
события*) to hurry; ~ (**поторопить** *perf*) **когó-н
с чем-н** to hurry sb with sth

▶ **торопиться** (*perf* **поторопиться**) *несов возв*
(*на поезд, в школу итп*) to hurry; (*с работой, с
выполнением*): **~ся с** +*instr* to hurry with.

тороплйвый (**-, -а, -о**) *прил* (*человек*) hasty;
(*шаг*) hurried; (*суждение, вывод*) hasty, hurried.

тороплю(сь) *несов см* **торопить(ся)**.

торпéда (-ы) *ж* torpedo (*мн* torpedoes).

торпедировать (-ую) (*не*)*сов перех* (*также
перен*) to torpedo.

торс (-а) *м* torso.

торт (-а) *м* cake.

торф (-а) *м* peat.

торцá *итп сущ см* **торéц**.

торчáть (-ý, -ишь) *несов неперех* (*вверх*) to
stick up; (*в стороны*) to stick out; (*разг: на
улице, в ресторане*) to hang around.

торчкóм *нареч* (*разг*) on end.

торшéр (-а) *м* standard lamp.

тоскá (**-й**) *ж* (*на сердце, во взгляде*) melancholy;
(*скука*) boredom; ~ **по рóдине** homesickness.

тосклйвый (**-, -а, -о**) *прил* (*настроение,
музыка итп*) melancholy; (*погода, разговор
итп*) dreary.

тосковáть (-ую) *несов неперех* to pine away; ~
(*impf*) **по** +*dat или* +*prp* to miss.

тост (-а) *м* toast; ~ **за** +*acc* toast to.

KEYWORD

тот (-гó; *f* **та**, *nt* **то**, *pl* **те**; *см* **Table 11**) *мест* **1**
that; **тот дом** that house; **та рýчка** that pen; **те
книги** those books; **по ту стóрону** on that side

2 (*указывает на ранее упомянутое*) that; **в тот
раз/день** that time/day

3 (*разг: о прошлом*) last; (: *о будущем*) next; **я
видел егó на той недéле** I saw him last week;
увидимся на той недéле we'll meet next week

4 (*в главных предложениях*): **это тот человéк,
котóрый приходил вчерá** it's the man who
came yesterday; **мы обрáдовались томý, что
он ушёл** we were pleased that he had gone

5 (*о последнем из названных лиц*): **я
посмотрéл на дрýга, тот стоял мóлча** I
looked at my friend, he stood silently

6 (*обычно с отрицанием*): **зашёл не в тот дом**
I called at the wrong house; **это всё не то** it's
not that

7 (*об одном из перечисляемых предметов*): **ни
тот, ни другóй** neither one nor the other; **тем
или иным спóсобом** by some means or other;

тот же the same; **та же маши́на, что и в про́шлый раз** the same car as last time; **он сказа́л то же са́мое** he said the same thing **8** (во фра́зах): **до того́** so; **он до того́ испуга́лся, что не мог усну́ть** he was so frightened he couldn't sleep; **мне не до того́** I have no time for that; **не то что(бы)** ... , **а** ... not so much that ... but ...; **она́ не то что(бы) глупа́, а засте́нчива** she's not so much stupid, as just shy; **к тому́ же** moreover; **с тем, что́бы** in order to; **ни с того́ ни с сего́** (разг) out of the blue; **тому́ наза́д** ago; **и тому́ подо́бное** et cetera, and so on.

тота́лен прил см **тота́льный**.
тотализа́тор (-а) м totalizer.
тоталитари́зм (-а) м totalitarianism.
тоталита́рный прил totalitarian.
тота́л|ьный (-ен, -ьна, -ьно) прил total.
то-то част (разг: вот именно) exactly, that's just it; (вот почему) that's why; (выража́ет удовлетворе́ние): **~ же** pleased to hear it; **он не сдал экза́мен – ~ он тако́й гру́стный** he didn't pass the exam – that's why he's so sad; **~ он удиви́тся!** he WILL be surprised!
то́тчас нареч immediately.
то́чек сущ см **то́чка**.
то́чен прил см **то́чный**.
точёный прил (о́стрый: нож) sharpened; (дета́ль, грань итп) turned; (перен: фигу́ра) shapely; (: черты́ лица́) fine.
то́чечный прил (ли́ния) dotted; **~ масса́ж** shiatsu, acupressure; **~ая электросва́рка** spot-welding.
точи́л|ка (-ки; gen pl -ок) ж pencil sharpener.
точи́ть (-у́, -ишь; perf наточи́ть) несов перех (нож, каранда́ш) to sharpen; (perf вы́точить) дета́ль) to turn; (no perf; подле́ж: червь, ржа́вчина) to eat away at; (перен: подле́ж: боле́знь, тоска́ итп) to drain.
то́ч|ка (-ки; gen pl -ек) ж point; (пя́тнышко) dot; (линг) full stop (BRIT), period (esp US); (де́йствие: дета́ли, каранда́ша) sharpening; **~ зре́ния** point of view; **попа́дать (попа́сть perf) в (са́мую) ~ку** to hit the bull's-eye; **дойти́** (perf) **до ~ки** (разг) to reach one's limit; **то́чка с запято́й** semicolon.
точне́е ввод сл to be exact или precise; **приходи́ ве́чером, ~, в 5 часо́в** come in the evening, at 5 o'clock to be exact или precise.
то́чно нареч exactly; (обья́снить) precisely; (подсчита́ть, перевести́) accurately ♦ част (разг: действи́тельно) precisely ♦ союз (как бу́дто) as if или though; **~ тако́й дом** exactly the same house; **он ~ так и сде́лал/сказа́л** that's exactly what he did/said; **~, он уе́хал** that's right, he's gone; **так ~!** yes, sir!; **расплака́лся, ~ ребёнок** he burst into

tears, just like a child; **он говори́л со мной, ~ я ребёнок** he talked to me as if или though I were a child.
то́чность (-и) ж (часо́в, попада́ния) accuracy; (рабо́ты) precision; **я подсчита́л затра́ты с ~ю до рубля́** I counted the expenditure right down to the last rouble; **в ~и** (разг) exactly.
то́чный (-ен, -на́, -но) прил (часы́, перево́д, попада́ние) accurate; (описа́ние, прика́з) precise; (а́дрес, ко́пия) exact; **то́чное вре́мя** exact time; **то́чные нау́ки** exact sciences.
точь-в-точь нареч (разг) just like.
тошни́ть (3sg -и́т, perf стошни́ть) несов безл: **меня́ ~и́т** I feel sick; (перен) it makes me sick; **меня́ ~и́т от твоего́ лицеме́рия** your hypocrisy makes me sick.
то́шно как сказ (перен: разг) it's nauseating или sickening.
тошнот|а́ (-ы́) ж (чу́вство) nausea; **мне э́то до ~ы́ надое́ло** I'm sick to death of it.
тошнотво́р|ный (-ен, -на, -но) прил (также перен) nauseating, sickening.
то́щий (-ая, -ее, -ие; -, -а́, -е) прил (челове́к) gaunt; (кошелёк) empty; (по́чва) poor; (расти́тельность) sparse.
т.п. сокр (= тому́ подо́бное) etc. (= et cetera).
ТПП м сокр (= Торго́во-промы́шленная пала́та) ≈ Chamber of Commerce.
тпру межд (лошадя́м) whoa.
т-р сокр = теа́тр.
трав|а́ (-ы́; nom pl -ы) ж grass; (лека́рственная) herb; **со́рная** ~ weed; **хоть ~ не расти́** (разг) he итп couldn't care less.
трави́н|ка (-ки; gen pl -ок) ж blade of grass.
трав|и́ть (-лю́, -ишь) несов перех (также перен) to poison; (perf потрави́ть; посе́вы) to damage; (perf затрави́ть; дичь) to hunt; (перен: разг: притесня́ть) to harass, hound; (perf вы́травить; узо́р) to etch
▶ **трави́ться** (perf отрави́ться) несов возв to poison o.s.
травле́ни|е (-я) ср etching.
травлю́(сь) несов см **трави́ть(ся)**.
тра́вл|я (-и) ж hunting; (демокра́тов, радика́лов) hounding.
тра́вм|а (-ы) ж (физи́ческая) injury; (психи́ческая) trauma.
травмато́лог (-а) м specialist in traumatology.
травматологи́ческ|ий (-ая, -ое, -ие) прил: **~ отде́л** casualty; **~ пункт** first-aid room.
травматоло́ги|я (-и) ж traumatology.
травми́р|овать (-ую) (не)сов перех (го́лову) to injure; (перен: гру́бостью) to traumatize.
травоя́д|ный (-ен, -на, -но) прил herbivorous.
травяни́ст|ый прил herbaceous; (-, -а, -о; луг) grassy.
травяно́й прил (насто́йка) herbal; **~ покро́в** grass.

трагéди|я (-и) ж tragedy.
траги́зм (-а) м tragedy.
трагикомéди|я (-и) ж tragicomedy.
трагикоми́ческ|ий (-ая, -ое, -ие) *прил* tragicomic.
траги́ческ|ий (-ая, -ое, -ие) *прил* tragic; ~ **актёр** (*траги́к*) tragedy actor.
траги́ч|ный (-ен, -на, -но) *прил* tragic.
традицио́н|ный (-ен, -на, -но) *прил* traditional.
тради́ци|я (-и) ж tradition; **входи́ть** (**войти́** *perf*) **в ~ю** to become a tradition.
траектóри|я (-и) ж trajectory.
тракт (-а) м (*ИСТ*) highway; **пищевари́тельный** ~ alimentary canal.
трактáт (-а) м treatise.
тракти́р (-а) м inn.
тракти́рщик (-а) м innkeeper.
тракти́рщиц|а (-ы) ж см **тракти́рщик**.
трактовáть (-ую) *несов перех* to interpret.
трактóв|ка (-ки; *gen pl* -ок) ж interpretation.
трáктор (-а) м tractor.
тракторист (-а) м tractor driver.
тракторист|ка (-ки; *gen pl* -ок) ж см **тракторист**.
трал (-а) м (*сеть*) trawl; **ми́нный** ~ minesweeping operation.
трáл|ить (-ю, -ишь; *perf* **протрáлить**) *несов перех* to trawl; ~ (**протрáлить** *perf*) **ми́ны** to sweep for mines.
трамбовáть (-ýю; *perf* **утрамбовáть**) *несов перех* to tamp.
трамвá|й (-я) м tram (*BRIT*), streetcar (*US*); **éздить/éхать** (*impf*) **на ~е** to go by tram.
трамвáй|ный *прил* tram *опред* (*BRIT*), streetcar *опред* (*US*); **~ые пути́** tramlines; **трамвáйный парк** tram *или* streetcar depot.
трампли́н (-а) м (*также перен*) springboard; **лы́жный** ~ ski jump.
транжи́р (-а) м spendthrift.
транжи́р|ить (-ю, -ишь; *perf* **растранжи́рить**) *несов перех* (*разг: де́ньги*) to blow.
транжи́р|ка (-ки; *gen pl* -ок) ж см **транжи́р**.
транзи́стор (-а) м (*усилитель*) transistor; (*радиоприёмник*) transistor (radio).
транзи́т (-а) м transit; (*о грузе*) transit goods.
транзи́тный *прил* transit *опред*.
транквилизáтор (-а) м tranquillizer (*BRIT*), tranquilizer (*US*).
транс (-а) м (*ПСИХОЛ*) trance; (*КОММ: докумéнт*) transport document; **нóмер трáнса** trans number.
трансгéнный *прил* genetically modified.
трансконтинентáльный *прил* transcontinental.
транскри́пци|я (-и) ж transcription.
трансли́р|овать (-ую) (*не*)*сов перех* to broadcast.
транслятор (-а) м (*ТЕХ*) translator.
трансля́ци|я (-и) ж (*передáчи*) transmission, broadcasting; (*передáча*) broadcast; **прямáя** ~ live broadcast.
транспарáнт (-а) м banner.
трансплантáци|я (-и) ж transplant.

трáнспорт (-а) м transport.
транспортёр (-а) м (*конвéйер*) conveyor belt; (*ВОЕН*) troop carrier.
транспорти́р|овать (-ую) (*не*)*сов перех* to transport.
транспортирóв|ка (-и) ж transportation.
трáнспортный *прил* transport *опред*.
транссексуáл (-а) м transsexual.
трансформáтор (-а) м transformer.
трансформáци|я (-и) ж transformation.
трансформи́р|овать (-ую) (*не*)*сов перех* to transform.
траншé|я (-и) ж trench.
трап (-а) м gangway; **подавáть** (**подáть** *perf*) ~ to put down the gangway.
трáпез|а (-ы) ж *communal meal in monastery*.
трáпезн|ая (-ой; *decl like adj*) ж refectory.
трапéци|я (-и) ж (*ГЕОМ*) trapezium; (*циркова́я, гимнасти́ческая*) trapeze.
трáсс|а (-ы) ж (*лы́жная*) run; (*трубопровóда, кана́ла*) route; **автомоби́льная** ~ motorway (*BRIT*), expressway (*US*); **возду́шная** ~ airway.
трассáт (-а) м (*КОММ*) drawee.
трáт|а (-ы) ж spending; **пустáя** ~ **врéмени/ дéнег** a waste of time/money.
трáт|ить (-чу, -тишь; *perf* **истрáтить** *или* **потрáтить**) *несов перех* to spend
▸ **трáт|иться** (*perf* **истрáтиться** *или* **потрáтиться**) *несов возв*: ~**ся на** +*acc* to spend a lot of money on.
трáулер (-а) м trawler.
трáур (-а) м mourning; ~ **по** +*prp* mourning for; **носи́ть** (*impf*) ~ to wear mourning.
трáур|ный *прил* (*процéссия, плáтье*) mourning *опред*; (-ен, -на, -но; *перен: обстанóвка, тон*) mournful.
трафарéт (-а) м stencil; **мы́слить** (*impf*) **по ~у** (*перен*) to think in clichés.
трафарéт|ный (-ен, -на, -но) *прил* (*рисýнок, черчéние*) stencilled; (*перен: фрáзы*) trite.
трах *межд* bang; **а он** ~ **по столу́** and he banged against the table.
трáха|ть(ся) (-ю(сь)) *несов от* **трáхнуть(ся)**.
трахé|я (-и) ж trachea.
трáхн|уть (-у, -ешь; *impf* **трáхать**) *сов непepex* (*разг: вы́стрел*) to ring out ♦ *перех* (*ударить*) to thump; (*переспáть: жéнщину*) to lay
▸ **трáхн|уться** (*impf* **трáхаться**) *сов возв* (*разг: удáриться*) to bang o.s.; (: *мужчи́на и жéнщина*) to have it off; **трáхаться** (~**ся** *perf*) **голово́й о стéнку** to bang one's head against the wall.
трáчу(сь) *несов см* **трáтить(ся)**.
трéбовани|е (-я) ср (*объяснéний, дéнег*) request; (*реши́тельное, категори́ческое*) demand; (*устáва, экзаменацио́нные*) requirement; (*докумéнт: на кни́гу*) order; ~**я** (*морáльные, эстети́ческие*) needs *мн*.
трéбовательн|ый (-ен, -ьна, -ьно) *прил* demanding; (*тон, го́лос*) peremptory.
трéб|овать (-ую; *perf* **потрéбовать**) *несов перех* (*квитáнцию*) to ask for; (*в суд, к*

начальнику) to summon; ~ **(потребовать** *perf)* **что-н/**+*infin* to demand sth/to do; ~ **(потребовать** *perf)* +*gen (сочувствия, правдивости)* to expect; *(помощи, переделки)* to need, require

▶ **требоваться** *(perf* **потребоваться)** *несов возв* to be needed *или* required.

требух|а́ (-и́) *ж* entrails *мн.*

трево́г|а (-и) *ж (волнение)* anxiety; *(на улице, в доме)* alarm; **возду́шная** ~ air-raid warning; **поднима́ть (подня́ть** *perf)* *или* **бить** *(impf)* ~**у** *(перен)* to raise the alarm.

трево́жен *прил см* **трево́жный.**

трево́ж|ить (-у, -ишь; *perf* **встрево́жить)** *несов перех (родителей, правительство)* to alarm; *(perf* **потрево́жить;** *подлеж: шум, посетители)* to disturb; *(перен: рану)* to reopen

▶ **трево́житься** *(perf* **встрево́житься)** *несов возв (за детей)* to be concerned; *(perf* **потрево́житься;** *затруднять себя)* to trouble o.s.

трево́жно *нареч (посмотреть)* anxiously ♦ *как сказ:* **на се́рдце** ~ I feel anxious; **в го́роде** ~ there is a sense of alarm in the city.

трево́ж|ный (-ен, -на, -но) *прил (голос, взгляд)* anxious; *(сведения)* alarming; ~**ное вре́мя** time of unrest; **трево́жный сигна́л** alarm.

тре́звенник (-а) *м* teetotaller.

трезве́|ть (-ю; *perf* **отрезве́ть)** *несов неперех* to sober up.

трезво́н (-а) *м (колокольный)* peal; *(разг: толки)* gossip.

трезво́н|ить (-ю, -ишь) *несов неперех (колокола)* to peal; *(телефон, звонок)* to ring; *(разг: сплетничать)* to spread gossip.

тре́звость (-и) *ж (неупотребление алкоголя)* sobriety; *(перен: взгляда, суждений)* soberness.

тре́зв|ый (-, -а́, -о) *прил (состояние, человек)* sober; *(перен: рассуждение, решение)* sensible.

трек (-а) *м* track.

грел|ь (-и) *ж* warble.

трелья́ж (-а) *м (зеркало)* triple mirror.

грём *итп чис см* **три.**

трёмста́м *итп чис см* **три́ста.**

тренажёр (-а) *м* equipment used for physical training.

гре́нер (-а) *м* coach; **гла́вный** ~ manager (*of sports team*).

тре́ни|е (-я) *ср* friction; *(обычно мн: перен)* friction *ед.*

трениров|а́ть (-у́ю; *perf* **натренирова́ть)** *несов перех* to train; *(спортсменов)* to coach.

▶ **трениров́а́ться** *(perf* **натренирова́ться)** *несов возв (спортсмен)* to train; *(ученик, работник)* to train o.s.

трениро́в|ка (-ки; *gen pl* **-ок)** *ж (памяти, лошади итп)* training; *(отдельное занятие)* training (session).

трениро́вочный *прил* training *опред;* **трениро́вочный костю́м** tracksuit.

трено́жник (-а) *м* tripod.

трёп (-а; *part gen* **-у)** *м (разг)* blethering, blathering.

трепана́ци|я (-и) *ж (МЕД)* trepanation.

трёпаный *прил (разг)* tattered.

трепа́ть (-лю́, -лешь; *perf* **потрепа́ть)** *несов перех (подлеж: ветер)* to blow about; *(по плечу)* to pat; *(перен: корабль)* to toss; *(perf* **истрепа́ть** *или* **потрепа́ть;** *разг: обувь, книги)* to wear out; (~ **(потрепа́ть** *perf)* **кого́-н за во́лосы/за у́ши** to pull sb's hair/ears; ~ **(потрепа́ть** *perf)* **не́рвы кому́-н** to wear sb's nerves down; ~ *(impf)* **языко́м** *(разг ц́ми)* to chatter

▶ **трепа́ться** *несов возв (no perf; флаги, волосы)* to be blown about; *(perf* **истрепа́ться** *или* **потрепа́ться;** *разг: одежда, обувь)* to wear out; *(perf* **потрепа́ться;** *разг: о пустяках)* to chatter.

трепа́ч (-а́) *м (разг)* chatterbox.

тре́пет (-а) *м (листьев)* quivering; *(волнение)* tremor; *(страх)* trepidation.

трепе|та́ть (-щу́, -щешь) *несов неперех (листья, флаги)* to quiver; *(от ужаса)* to quake, tremble.

тре́пет|ный (-ен, -на, -но) *прил* tremulous.

трепещу́ *итп несов см* **трепета́ть.**

треплю́(сь) *итп несов см* **трепа́ть(ся).**

трепыха́|ться (-юсь) *несов возв (разг: животное, рыба)* to wriggle; *(флаг, парус)* to flutter; *(перен: волноваться)* to be in a flutter.

треск (-а) *м (ломающихся сучьев)* snapping; *(выстрелов)* crackling; **с тре́ском прова́ливаться (провали́ться** *perf) (разг: пьеса)* to be a flop; (: *студент)* to come a cropper.

треск|а́ (-и́) *ж* cod.

тре́ска|ться (3sg* **-ется, *3pl* **-ются,** *perf* **потре́скаться)** *несов возв (земля, стекло)* to crack.

трескотн|я́ (-и́) *ж (разг: кузнечиков)* chirp; *(перен: болтовня)* chitchat.

треску́ч|ий (-ая, -ее, -ие; -, -а, -е) *прил (перен: речи, слова)* bombastic; ~ **моро́з** hard frost.

тре́сн|уть (3sg* **-ет, *3pl* **-ут)** *сов неперех (ветка)* to snap; *(стакан, кожа)* to crack; (~ **чем-н по чему́-н** *(кулаком: по столу)* to bang sth on sth ♦ *перех (разг):* ~ **кого́-н по** +*dat (по шее, по руке)* to thump sb on

▶ **тре́снуться** *сов возв (разг):* ~**ся чем-н о** +*acc* to bang sth on.

трест (-а) *м (ЭКОН)* trust.

тре́т|ий (-ья, -ье, -ьи) *чис* third; **фильм/врач** ~**ьего со́рта** a third-rate film/doctor; ~**ьего дня** the day before yesterday; **Т**~ **мир** the Third World; **тре́тий сорт** *(товара)* Grade 3 *(denoting product of inferior quality)*; **тре́тье**

лицо́ (*линг*) the third person; **тре́тья сторона́**, **тре́тьи ли́ца** third party; *см также* **пя́тый**.
трети́р|овать (-ую) *сов перех* to patronize.
трети́чный *прил* tertiary.
трет|ь (-и; *nom pl* -и, *gen pl* -**ей**) *ж* third.
тре́ть|е (-его; *decl like adj*) *ср* (*кулин*) sweet (*BRIT*), dessert.
третьекла́ссник (-а) *м pupil in third year at school* (*usually nine years old*).
третьекла́ссни|ца (-ы) *ж см* **третьекла́ссник**.
третьесо́рт|ный (-ен, -на, -но) *прил* third-rate.
тре́т|ь (-ей; *decl like adj*) *ж*: **одна́ ~** one third.
треуго́льник (-а) *м* triangle.
треуго́льный *прил* triangular.
тре́ф|ы (-) *мн* (*КАРТЫ*) clubs *мн*.
трёх *чис см* **три**.
трёхгоди́чный *прил* three-year.
трёхгодова́лый *прил* three-year-old.
трёхдне́вный *прил* three-day.
трёхкра́т|ный *прил*: **~ чемпио́н** three-times champion; **в ~ом разме́ре** threefold.
трёхле́ти|е (-я) *ср* (*срок*) three years; (*годовщина*) third anniversary.
трёхле́т|ний (-яя, -ее, -ие) *прил* (*период*) three-year; (*ребёнок*) three-year-old.
трёхме́рный *прил* 3-D, three-dimensional.
трёхме́сячный *прил* three-month; (*ребёнок*) three-month-old.
трёхнеде́льный *прил* three-week; (*ребёнок*) three-week-old.
трёхсо́т *чис см* **три́ста**.
трёхсотле́ти|е (-я) *ср* (*срок*) three hundred years; (*годовщина*) tercentenary.
трёхсотле́т|ний (-яя, -ее, -ие) *прил* (*период*) three hundred-year; (*дерево*) three hundred-year-old.
трёхсо́тый (-ая, -ое, -ые) *чис* three hundredth.
трёхста́х *чис см* **три́ста**.
трёхсторо́нн|ий (-яя, -ее, -ие) *прил* (*соглашение, союз*) trilateral.
трёхчасово́й *прил* (*операция*) three-hour; (*поезд*) three o'clock.
трёшн|а (-ки; *gen pl* -ек) *ж* (*разг*) three-rouble note.
треща́ть (-у́, -и́шь) *несов неперех* (*лёд, доски итп*) to crack; (*кузнечики*) to chip; (*пулемёты*) to crackle; (*разг*: *тараторить*) to jabber (on); **у меня́ ~и́т голова́** I've got a splitting headache; **~ (*impf*) по швам** (*также перен*) to be falling apart at the seams.
тре́щин|а (-ы) *ж* (*также перен*) crack: **дава́ть (дать** *perf*) **~у** to crack.
трещо́т|ка (-ки; *gen pl* -ок) *ж* rattle ♦ *м/ж* (*перен*: *болтун*) chatterbox.
тр|и (-ёх; *см* **Table 24**) *чис* three ♦ *нескл* (*ПРОСВЕЩ*) ≈ C (*school mark*); **ей ~ го́да** she is three (years old); **они́ живу́т в до́ме но́мер ~** they live at number three; **о́коло ~ёх** about three; **кни́га сто́ит ~ рубля́** the book costs three roubles; **~ с полови́ной часа́** three and a half hours; **сейча́с ~ часа́** it is three o'clock; **я́блоки**

продаю́тся по ~ **шту́ки** the apples are sold in threes; **дели́ть (раздели́ть** *perf*) **что-н на ~** to divide sth into three.
трибу́н|а (-ы) *ж* platform; (*стадиона*) stand.
трибуна́л (-а) *м* tribunal; **вое́нный ~** military court.
тривиа́льный (-ен, -ьна, -ьно) *прил* trivial.
тригономе́три|я (-и) *ж* trigonometry.
три́девять: **за ~ земе́ль** (*ФОЛЬКЛОР*) in far off lands.
тридеся́т|ый *прил* (*ФОЛЬКЛОР*): **в ~ом госуда́рстве** in a far off country.
тридцати́ *чис см* **три́дцать**.
тридцатиле́ти|е (-я) *ср* (*срок*) thirty years; (*годовщина события*) thirtieth anniversary.
тридцатиле́т|ний (-яя, -ее, -ие) *прил* (*период*) thirty-year; (*человек*) thirty-year-old.
тридца́т|ый (-ая, -ое, -ые) *чис* thirtieth; *см также* **пятидеся́тый**.
три́дцат|ь (-и; *как* **пять**; *см* **Table 27**) *чис* thirty; *см также* **пятьдеся́т**.
три́жды *нареч* three times; **~ два – шесть** three times two is six; **он ~ прав** he's absolutely right.
трико́ *ср нескл* leotard.
трикота́ж (-а) *м* (*ткань*) knitted fabric ♦ *собир* (*одежда*) knitwear.
трикота́жный *прил* knitted; **~ магази́н** knitwear shop.
три́лер (-а) *м* thriller.
трили́стник (-а) *м* trefoil.
триллио́н (-а) *м* trillion.
трило́ги|я (-и) *ж* trilogy.
трина́дцати *чис см* **трина́дцать**.
трина́дцат|ый (-ая, -ое, -ые) *чис* thirteenth; *см также* **пя́тый**.
трина́дцат|ь (-и; *как* **пять**; *см* **Table 27**) *чис* thirteen; *см также* **пять**.
три́|о *ср нескл* trio.
Три́поли *м нескл* Tripoli.
три́птих (-а) *м* triptych.
три́ста (**трёхсо́т**; *как* **сто**; *см* **Table 32**) *чис* three hundred; *см также* **сто**.
трито́н (-а) *м* newt.
триу́мф (-а) *м* triumph.
триумфа́льный *прил* triumphant; **триумфа́льная а́рка** triumphal arch.
тро́гательный (-ен, -ьна, -ьно) *прил* touching.
тро́га|ть (-ю; *perf* **тро́нуть**) *несов перех* (*также перен*) to touch; (*разг*: *беспокоить: вопросами*) to pester; (*подлеж: рассказ, событие*) to move ♦ *неперех* (*лошадь, повозка*) to start moving; **улы́бка тро́нула её гу́бы** a smile flickered across her lips; **седина́ тро́нула его́ во́лосы** his hair was touched with grey
► **тро́гаться** (*perf* **тро́нуться**) *несов возв* (*поезд*) to move off; (*лёд*) to (begin to) break; **~ся** (**тро́нуться** *perf*) **в путь** to set off.
тр|ое (-о́их; *см* **Table 35а**) *чис* three: *см также* **дво́е**.
троебо́рь|е (-я) *ср* triathlon.
тро́ек *сущ см* **тро́йка**.

тро́|ен *сущ см* тро́йня.

тро́йх *чис см* тро́е.

тро́иц|а (-ы) *ж* (*также*: свята́я ~) the Holy Trinity; (*праздник: также*: Т~ын день) ≈ Trinity Sunday; (*раз*: *о друзья́х*) threesome.

тро́й|ка (-йки; *gen pl* -ек) *ж* (*цифра, карта*) three; (*ПРОСВЕЩ*) ≈ C (*school mark*); (*лошадей*) troika; (*группа людей*) threesome; (*разг*: *автобус, трамвай итп*) (number) three (*bus, tram etc*); (*костюм*) three-piece suit.

тройни́к (-а́) *м* (*ЭЛЕК*) (three-way) adaptor.

тройн|о́й *прил* triple; в ~о́м разме́ре triple the size; тройно́й прыжо́к (*СПОРТ*) triple jump.

тро́йня (-йни; *gen pl* -ен) *ж* triplets *мн*.

тро́йствен|ный (-ен, -на, -но) *прил* (*связь*) threefold; (*no short form*; *ПОЛИТ*: сою́з, соглаше́ние) tripartite.

тройча́т|ка (-и) *ж* (*разг*) *mild painkiller taken for headaches etc.*

тролле́йбус (-а) *м* trolleybus.

тромб (-а) *м* blood clot.

тромбо́з (-а) *м* thrombosis.

тромбо́н (-а) *м* trombone.

трон (-а) *м* throne.

тро́н|ный *прил*: ~ зал throne room; ~ая речь royal address.

тро́н|уть (-у, -ешь) *сов от* тро́гать

▸ тро́нуться *сов от* тро́гаться ♦ *возв*: ~ся (умо́м) (*разг*) to be (a bit) touched.

тро́п|а́ (-ы́; *nom pl* -ы) *ж* pathway.

тро́пик (-а) *м*: се́верный/ю́жный ~ the tropic of Cancer/Capricorn; *см также* тро́пики.

тро́пик|и (-ов) the tropics *мн*.

тропи́н|ка (-ки; *gen pl* -ок) *ж* footpath.

тропи́ческ|ий (-ая, -ое, -ие) *прил* tropical.

трос (-а) *м* cable.

тростни́н|ка (-ки; *gen pl* -ок) *ж* (*камыша*) cane; (*травинка*) stem.

тростни́к (-а́) *м* reed; са́харный ~ sugar cane.

тро́сть (-и; *gen pl* -е́й) *ж* walking stick.

тротуа́р (-а) *м* pavement (*BRIT*), sidewalk (*US*).

трофе́й (-я) *м* trophy.

трою́родный *прил*: ~ брат second cousin (*male*); трою́родная сестра́ second cousin (*female*).

троя́к|ий (-ая, -ое, -ие; -, -а, -о) *прил* triple.

тру(сь) *итп несов см* тере́ть(ся).

труб|а́ (-ы́; *nom pl* -ы) *ж* (*газовая, водосточная итп*) pipe; (*дымовая*) chimney; (*МУЗ*) trumpet; (*АНАТ*): фалло́пиева ~ Fallopian tube; в ~у́ вылета́ть (вы́лететь *perf*) (*разг*) to go to the wall.

труба́ч (-а́) *м* trumpeter.

труб|и́ть (-лю́, -и́шь; *perf* протруби́ть) *несов неперех*: ~ в +*acc* (*МУЗ*) to blow; (*подлеж*: труба́) to sound; (*перен: разг*): ~ о +*prp* to trumpet ♦ *перех* (*сбор, отбой*) to sound.

тру́б|ка (-ки; *gen pl* -ок) *ж* tube; (*курительная*) pipe; (*телефона*) receiver; (*МЕД*) stethoscope; брать (взять *perf*) *или* поднима́ть (подня́ть *perf*) ~ку (*ТЕЛ*) to pick up the receiver; свора́чивать (сверну́ть *perf*) что-н в ~ку to roll sth into a tube.

трублю́ *несов см* труби́ть.

трубо́к *сущ см* тру́бка.

трубопрово́д (-а) *м* pipeline.

тру́бочек *сущ см* тру́бочка.

трубочи́ст (-а) *м* chimney sweep.

тру́боч|ка (-ки; *gen pl* -ек) *ж уменьш от* тру́бка; (*КУЛИН*) cream horn.

труд (-а́) *м* work; (*ЭКОН*) labour (*BRIT*), labor (*US*); (*ПРОСВЕЩ*) home economics and design; бескоры́стный ~ labo(u)r of love; брать (взять *perf*) на себя́ ~ +*infin* to take the trouble to do; без ~а́ without any difficulty; с (больши́м) ~о́м with (great) difficulty.

тру́ден *прил см* тру́дный.

труд|и́ться (-жу́сь, -дишься) *несов возв* to work hard; ~ (*impf* над +*instr* to labour (*BRIT*) *или* labor (*US*) over; не ~дитесь писа́ть мне don't bother to write.

тру́дно *как сказ* it's hard *или* difficult; у меня́ ~ с деньга́ми I've got money problems; мне ~ поня́ть э́то/найти́ вре́мя I find it hard to understand/to find the time; (мне) ~ бе́гать/ стоя́ть I have trouble running/standing up; ~ сказа́ть it's hard to say.

трудновоспиту́ем|ый (-, -а, -о) *прил*: ~ ребёнок problem child (*мн* children).

труднодосту́п|ный (-ен, -на, -но) *прил* (*горы, место*) hard to get to.

труднопроходи́м|ый (-, -а, -о) *прил* (*дорога*) almost impassable.

тру́дность (-и) *ж* difficulty.

тру́д|ный (-ен, -на́, -но) *прил* difficult.

трудов|о́й *прил* working; ~о́е законода́тельство employment legislation; ~ые дохо́ды earned income; ~ стаж working life; ~ая дисципли́на discipline in the workplace; трудова́я кни́жка employment record book; трудово́е соглаше́ние contract (of employment).

трудоёмк|ий (-ая, -кое, -кие; -ок, -ка, -ко) *прил* labour-intensive (*BRIT*), labor-intensive (*US*).

трудолюби́в|ый (-, -а, -о) *прил* hard-working, industrious.

трудоспосо́бность (-и) *ж* fitness to work; утра́та ~и disablement.

трудоспосо́бный *прил* fit to work.

трудотерапи́|я (-и) *ж* occupational therapy.

трудоустро́|ить (-ю, -ишь; *impf* трудоустра́ивать) *сов перех* to find work for.

трудоустро́йств|о (-а) *ср* placement.

трудя́щ|ийся (-аяся, -ееся, -иеся) *прил* working ♦ (*-егося; decl like adj*) *м* worker.

тру́женик (-а) *м* worker.

тру́женица (-ы) ж см **тру́женик**.
тружу́сь несов см **труди́ться**.
труп (-а) м corpse; **то́лько че́рез мой ~!** over my dead body!
тру́пп|а (-ы) ж (ТЕАТР) company.
трус (-а) м coward.
тру́сик|и (-ов) мн (женские, детские) knickers мн (BRIT), panties мн (US).
тру́с|ить (-шу, -сишь) несов неперех to get scared; **~** (impf) **пе́ред кем-н** to cower before sb.
тру́с|ить (-шу, -сишь) несов неперех to trot along ♦ перех (содержимое мешка) to shake out; (плоды: с дерева) to shake.
трусли́вый (-, -а, -о) прил cowardly.
тру́сость (-и) ж cowardice.
трусц|а́ (-ы́) ж trot; **бег ~о́й** jogging; **бе́гать** (impf) **~о́й** to jog.
трус|ы́ (-о́в) мн (бельё: обычно мужские) underpants мн; (спортивные) shorts мн.
тру́т|ень (-ня) м (ЗООЛ) drone; (перен: человек) parasite.
трух|а́ (-и́) ж dust.
трухля́вый (-, -а, -о) прил crumbly.
тру́шу несов см **тру́сить**.
трушу́ несов см **труси́ть**.
трущо́б|а (-ы) ж (бедный район) slum; (лесная) jungle (fig).
трюк (-а) м trick; (акробатический) stunt.
трюка́ч (-а́) м (в цирке) acrobat; (мошенник) fraudster.
трюм (-а) м hold (of ship).
трюмо́ ср нескл dresser (piece of furniture).
трю́фел|ь (-я; nom pl -я́) м (также конфета) truffle.
тряпи́чный прил: **~ая ку́кла** rag doll.
тря́п|ка (-ки; gen pl -ок) ж (половая, для пыли) cloth; (лоскут) rag; (перен: разг: о человеке) drip; **~ки** (разг: пренебр) rags.
тряпьё (-я́) ср собир rags мн.
тряси́н|а (-ы) ж quagmire; (перен) mire.
тря́ский (-кая, -кое, -кие; -ок, -ка, -ко) прил (вагон, машина) rickety; (дорога) bumpy.
трясогу́з|ка (-ки; gen pl -ок) ж wagtail.
тря́сок прил см **тря́ский**.
тряс|ти́ (-у́, -ёшь) несов перех to shake; (perf **вы́трясти**; ковёр, мешок) to shake down; **~** (impf) **+instr** (головой, кулаком) to shake; (гривой) to toss; **в маши́не его́ ~ёт** the car is jolting; **его́ ~ёт от стра́ха** he's shaking with fear
▸ **тряст|и́сь** несов возв (машина) to jolt; (разг: в машине, в поезде итп) to rattle along; **~сь** (impf) **пе́ред +instr** (перед начальством) to tremble before; **~сь** (impf) **над +instr** (разг: над ребёнком, над деньгами) to fret over или about; **~сь** (impf) **от сме́ха/стра́ха/хо́лода** to shake with laughter/fear/cold.
трях|ну́ть (-у́, -ёшь) сов перех to shake; **~** (perf) **старино́й** (разг) to turn the clock back.
т/с сокр (= теку́щий счёт) С/А (= current account).
т/счёт сокр = **т/с**.
тт сокр = **тома́**.
т.т. сокр = **това́рищи**.
ТУ м сокр = самолёт констру́кции А.Н.Ту́полева.
Ту м сокр = **ТУ**.
туале́т (-а) м toilet; (гардероб) outfit.
туале́тный прил: **~ая бума́га** toilet paper; **туале́тное мы́ло** toilet soap; **туале́тные принадле́жности** toiletries; **туале́тный сто́лик** dressing table.
туберкулёз (-а) м ТВ, tuberculosis.
туберкулёзный прил ТВ, tuberculosis опред.
ту́го нареч tightly; (набить) tight ♦ как сказ (разг): **(у нас) ~ с деньга́ми** money is tight (for us); **(у нас) ~ со вре́менем** we're hard-pressed for time; **дела́ иду́т ~** (разг) things aren't going too well.
тугоду́м (-а) м dimwit.
туг|о́й (-, -а́, -о) прил (струна, пружина) taut; (узел, одежда) tight; (чемодан) tightly-packed; (кошелёк) bulging; **он туг на́ ухо** (разг) he's a bit hard of hearing.
туда́ нареч there; **~ и обра́тно** there and back; **биле́т ~ и обра́тно** return (BRIT) или round-trip (US) ticket; **ни ~ ни сюда́!** (разг) it won't budge!; **~ ему́ и доро́га** (разг) that's the best place for him; **он тако́й молодо́й, а ~ же, кома́ндует** (разг) he is so young, and look at him ordering everyone around.
туда́-сюда́ нареч all over the place; (раскачиваться) backwards and forwards ♦ как сказ (разг) it's so-so.
ту́же сравн прил от **туго́й** ♦ сравн нареч от **ту́го**.
туж|и́ть (-у́, -ишь) несов неперех: **~ (о +prp)** to pine (for).
туз (-а́) м (финансовый, городской) bigwig.
тузе́м|ец (-ца) м native.
тузе́м|ка (-ки; gen pl -ок) ж см **тузе́мец**.
тузе́мный прил (население, обычай) native опред.
тузе́мок сущ см **тузе́мка**.
тузе́миц|а итп сущ см **тузе́мец**.
тук межд knock.
ту́ловищ|е (-а) ср torso.
тулу́п (-а) м (овчинный) sheepskin coat.
тума́к (-а́) м (разг) thump, whack.
тума́н (-а; part gen -у) м mist; (перен: в голове) haze.
тума́нен прил см **тума́нный**.
тума́н|ить (3sg -ит, 3pl -ят perf **затума́нить**); несов перех (подлеж: дым, дождь) to obscure; **слёзы затума́нили ей глаза́** her eyes were misty with tears; **вино́ затума́нило мне го́лову** the wine has addled my brain
▸ **тума́н|иться** (perf **затума́ниться**) несов возв to become shrouded in mist; (перен: глаза) to mist over; (: лицо) to cloud.
тума́нность (-и) ж (АСТРОНОМИЯ) nebula; (перен: в мыслях, в изложении) cloudiness.

тума́н|ный (-ен, -на, -но) *прил* (*воздух, утро*) misty; (*перен: взгляд*) dull; (: *смысл, объясне́ние*) nebulous.

ту́мб|а (-ы) *ж* (*прича́льная, у́личная*) bollard; (*для цвето́в*) stand; (*для скульпту́ры, стола́*) pedestal; **афи́шная** ~ *cylindrical advertising hoarding*.

ту́мблер (-а) *м* (*КОМП*) toggle switch.

ту́мбоч|ка (-ки; *gen pl* -ек) *ж уменьш от* ту́мба; (*ме́бель*) bedside cabinet.

ту́ндр|а (-ы) *ж* tundra.

ту́ндровый *прил* tundra *опред*.

тун|е́ц (-ца́) *м* tuna (fish).

тунея́д|ец (-ца) *м* parasite (*fig*).

тунея́дств|о (-а) *ср* parasitism.

тунея́дца *итп сущ см* тунея́дец.

Туни́с (-а) *м* (*го́род*) Tunis; (*страна́*) Tunisia.

туни́сск|ий (-ая, -ое, -ие) *прил* Tunisian.

тунне́л|ь (-я) *м* = тонне́ль.

тунца́ *итп сущ см* туне́ц.

тупе́|ть (-ю) *несов непе́рех* (*боль*) to become less acute; (*perf* отупе́ть; *разг: челове́к*) to become stupid; (*чу́вства*) to dull.

тупи́к (-а́) *м* (*у́лица*) dead end, cul-de-sac; (*для по́ездов*) siding; (*перен: в перегово́рах итп*) deadlock; **ста́вить (поста́вить** *perf*) **кого́-н в** ~ to stump sb; **стать** (*perf*) **в** ~ to be stumped; **заходи́ть (зайти́** *perf*) **в** ~ (*перегово́ры*) to reach a deadlock.

тупико́вый *прил* (*ситуа́ция*) dead-end; (*ста́нция*) at the end of the line.

туп|и́ть (-лю́, -ишь; *perf* затупи́ть) *несов пере́х* to blunt

▸ тупи́ться (*perf* затупи́ться) *несов возв* to become blunt.

тупи́ц|а (-ы) *м/ж* (*разг*) dunce.

тупли́|(сь) *несов см* тупи́ть(ся).

туп|о́й (-, -а́, -о) *прил* (*нож, каранда́ш*) blunt; (*челове́к*) stupid; (*боль, ум*) dull; (*поко́рность, страх*) blind; **тупо́й у́гол** obtuse angle.

ту́пост|ь (-и) *ж* (*челове́ка, поведе́ния*) stupidity; (*ума́*) dullness.

тур (-а) *м* (*ко́нкурса, перегово́ров, вы́боров*) round; (*в та́нце*) turn; (*ЗООЛ*) mountain goat.

тур|а́ (-ы́) *ж* (*разг: в ша́хматах*) castle.

турби́н|а (-ы) *ж* turbine.

туре́цк|ий (-ая, -ое, -ие) *прил* Turkish; ~ **язы́к** Turkish.

тури́зм (-а) *м* tourism.

тури́ст (-а) *м* tourist; (*в похо́де*) hiker.

туристи́ческ|ий (-ая, -ое, -ие) *прил* tourist *опред*.

тури́стск|ий (-ая, -ое, -ие) *прил* tourist's; ~ **маршру́т** trail; ~**ое снаряже́ние** *camping and walking equipment*.

ту́рка *итп сущ см* ту́рок.

туркме́н (-а) *м* Turkmen.

Туркме́ни|я (-и) *ж* Turkmenia.

туркме́н|ка (-ки; *gen pl* -ок) *ж см* туркме́н.

туркме́нск|ий (-ая, -ое, -ие) *прил* Turkmenian.

турне́ *ср нескл* (*ТЕАТР, СПОРТ*) tour.

турне́пс (-а) *м* turnip.

турни́к (-а́) *м* horizontal bar.

турнике́т (-а) *м* turnstile.

турни́р (-а) *м* tournament.

ту́р|ок (-ка) *м* Turk.

Ту́рци|я (-и) *ж* Turkey.

турча́н|ка (-ки; *gen pl* -ок) *ж см* ту́рок.

ту́склый (-, -а́, -о) *прил* (*стекло́*) opaque; (*лак, кра́ска, позоло́та*) matt; (*свет, стиль, взгляд*) dull.

тускне́|ть (*3sg* -ет, *3pl* -ют, *perf* потускне́ть) *несов непе́рех* (*кра́ска, тала́нт*) to fade; (*серебро́, позоло́та, кра́ски*) to tarnish.

тут *нареч* here; что ~ говори́ть! (*разг*) what is there to say?; **я** ~ **ни при чём** it has nothing to do with me; **и всё** ~ (*разг*) and that's that; **он уже́** ~ **как** ~ (*разг*) right at that moment he appeared; **не** ~-**то бы́ло** (*разг*) it wasn't to be.

ту́товый *прил*: ~**ое де́рево** mulberry tree; **ту́товый шелкопря́д** silkworm.

ту́фл|я (-ли; *nom pl* -ли, *gen pl* -ель) *ж* (*обы́чно мн*) shoe.

ту́хлый (-, -а́, -о) *прил* (*еда́*) rotten; (*за́пах*) putrid.

ту́х|нуть (*3sg* -нет, *3pl* -нут, *pt* -, -ла, -ло, *perf* поту́хнуть) *несов непе́рех* (*костёр, свет, свеча́*) to go out; (*perf* проту́хнуть; *мя́со, ры́ба*) to go off.

ту́ч|а (-и) *ж* rain cloud; (*перен: мух, стрел*) cloud; **он сего́дня, как** ~ he's been in a black mood all day.

ту́чный (-ен, -на́, -но) *прил* (*челове́к*) stout; (*по́чва*) fertile; (*трава́, луга́*) lush.

туш (-а) *м* (*МУЗ*) flourish.

ту́ш|а (-и) *ж* carcass; (*разг: о ту́чном челове́ке*) hulk.

тушева́|ть (-ю́; *perf* затушева́ть) *несов пере́х* (*рису́нок, фотогра́фию*) to shade in; (*перен: ра́зницу, противоре́чия*) to gloss over.

туш|ева́ться (-у́юсь) *несов от* стушева́ться.

тушён|ка (-ки; *gen pl* -ок) *ж* (*разг*) tinned (*BRIT*) *или* canned meat.

тушёный *прил* (*КУЛИН*) braised.

туш|и́ть (-у́, -ишь; *perf* затуши́ть *или* потуши́ть) *несов пере́х* (*свечу́, костёр, пожа́р*) to put out; (*perf* потуши́ть; *свет*) to put out; (*КУЛИН*) to braise.

тушка́нчик (-а) *м* jerboa.

туш|ь (-и) *ж* (*для рисова́ния*) Indian ink; (*для ресни́ц*) mascara.

ту́|я (-и) *ж* red cedar.

т/х *сокр* = теплохо́д.

тчк *сокр* = то́чка.

тща́тельный (-ен, -ьна, -ьно) *прил* thorough.

тщеду́ш|ный (-ен, -на, -но) *прил* feeble.

тщесла́вен *прил см* **тщесла́вный**.
тщесла́ви|е (-я) *ср* vanity.
тщесла́в|ный (-ен, -на, -но) *прил* vain.
тще́тен *прил см* **тще́тный**.
тще́тност|ь (-и) *ж* futility.
тще́т|ный (-ен, -на, -но) *прил* futile.
ты (тебя́; *см* Table 5a) *мест* you; (*разг: для усиления*): **ах ~, кака́я жа́лость!** oh, what a pity!; **быть** (*impf*) **с кем-н на ~** to be on familiar terms with sb; **вот тебе́ раз!** good grief!
ты́|кать (-чу, -чешь; *perf* ткнуть) *несов перех* (*разг: ударять*): **ты́кать что-н/кого́-н чем-н** to poke sth/sb with sth; (: *вонзать*): **ты́кать что-н в** +*acc* to stick sth into; (: *обращаться на „ты"*) *to address somebody using the informal form of "you"*; ~ (*impf*) **кого́-н но́сом во что-н** (*разг*) to rub sb's face in sth; ~ (ткнуть *perf*) **па́льцем на** +*acc* (*разг*) to point at
▸ **ты́каться** (*perf* ткну́ться) *несов возв* (*разг: суетливо двигаться*) to rush about; **~ся** (ткну́ться *perf*) **в** +*acc* (*в стену, в дверь итп*) to bang into; (*соваться*) to nuzzle.
ты́кв|а (-ы) *ж* pumpkin.
тыл (-а; *loc sg* -у́, *nom pl* -ы́) *м* (ВОЕН: *сторона, территория*) the rear; (: *вся страна*) the home front; (: *воинские организации*) rear units.
тылово́й *прил* (ВОЕН) rear.
ты́льный *прил* back; **~ая часть руки́** the back of one's hand.
тыс. *сокр* = **тысяча**
ты́сяч|а (-и; *см* Table 35) *ж чис* thousand.
тысячеле́ти|е (-я) *ср* millenium; (*годовщина*) thousandth anniversary.
тысячеле́тн|ий (-яя, -ее, -ие) *прил* (*период*) thousand-year; (*дерево*) thousand-year-old.
ты́сячн|ый *чис см* **тысяча**.
ты́сячн|ая (-ой; *decl like adj*) *ж*: **одна́ ~** one thousandth.
ты́сячн|ый (-ая, -ое, -ие) *чис* thousandth; (*толпа, армия*) of many thousands.
ты́сячу *чис см* **тысяча**.
тычи́н|ка (-ки; *gen pl* -ок) *ж* stamen.
ты́чу(сь) *итп несов см* **тыкать(ся)**.
тьм|а (-ы) *ж* (*мрак*) darkness, gloom; (*множество*) swarm.
тьфу *межд* yuk.
ТЭС *ж сокр* = **теплоэлектроста́нция**.
ТЭЦ *ж сокр* = **теплоэлектроцентра́ль**.
тюбете́йк|а (-йки; *gen pl* -ек) *ж* skullcap (*worn in Central Asia*).
тю́бик (-а) *м* tube.
ТЮЗ (-а) *м сокр* (= теа́тр ю́ного зри́теля) youth theatre (*BRIT*) *или* theater (*US*).
тюз (-а) *м сокр* = **ТЮЗ**.
тюк (-а́) *м* bale.
тю́левый *прил* tulle.
тюле́н|ь (-я) *м* (ЗООЛ) seal.
тюль (-я) *м* tulle.
тюльпа́н (-а) *м* tulip.
тюрба́н (-а) *м* turban.
тюре́мный *прил* prison *опред*; **тюре́мное**

заключе́ние imprisonment.
тюрьм|а́ (-ы́) *ж* prison; **сажа́ть (посади́ть** *perf*) **кого́-н в ~у́** to put sb in prison.
тюфя́к (-а́) *м* straw mattress; (*разг: о человеке*) wimp.
тя́вка|ть (-ю) *несов неперех* to yap.
тя́вкн|уть (-у, -ешь) *сов неперех* to yap.
тя́г|а (-и) *ж* (*в печи*) draught (*BRIT*), draft (*US*); (*насоса, пылесоса*) suction; (ТЕХ) traction; (*реактивная*) thrust; ~ **к** +*dat* (*перен*) attraction to; **на электри́ческой ~е** powered by electricity; **на ко́нной ~е** horse-drawn.
тяга́|ться (-юсь; *perf* потяга́ться) *несов возв* (*разг*): ~ **с кем-н (в** +*prp*) to compete with sb (in); ~ (**потяга́ться** *perf*) **с кем-н умо́м** to pit one's wits against sb.
тяга́ч (-а́) *м* tractor.
тя́гост|ный (-ен, -на, -но) *прил* burdensome; (*впечатления*) depressing.
тя́гост|ь (-и) *ж* (*ожидания, зависимости*) burden; (*обычно мн: войны, бедности*) hardship; (*на сердце, на душе*) heavy feeling; **быть** (*impf*) **в ~ кому́-н** to be a burden to sb.
тяготе́ни|е (-я) *ср* (ФИЗ) gravity; (*перен*): ~ **к** +*dat* attraction to.
тяготе́|ть (-ю) *несов неперех*: ~ **к** +*dat* (*к культуре, к прогрессу, к общению*) to gravitate *или* be drawn towards; (*к мнению*) to tend towards; (*перен*): ~ **над** +*instr* (*обвинение, подозрение*) to hang over; (*чья-н власть, воля*) to oppress.
тяго|ти́ть (-щу́, -ти́шь) *несов перех* to weigh (heavy) on
▸ **тяготи́ться** *несов возв* (+*instr*) to be weighed down by.
тя́гот|ы (-) *мн* hardships *мн*.
тягощу́(сь) *несов см* **тяготи́ть(ся)**.
тягу́ч|ий (-ая, -ее, -ие; -, -а, -е) *прил* (*клей, краска итп*) viscous; (*резинка, ткань*) stretchy; (*перен: речь, голос*) droning.
тя́жб|а (-ы) *ж* dispute.
тя́жек *прил см* **тя́жкий**.
тяжеле́|ть (-ю; *perf* отяжеле́ть *или* потяжеле́ть) *несов неперех* to get heavier; (*голова, ноги: от усталости*) to grow heavy.
тяжело́ *нареч* heavily; (*больной, раненый*) seriously ◆ *как сказ* (нести) it's heavy; (*понять, согласиться*) it's hard; **мне ~ здесь** I find it hard here; **больно́му ~** the patient is suffering.
тяжелоатле́т (-а) *м* weightlifter.
тяжелоатлети́ческ|ий (-ая, -ое, -ие) *прил*: **~ие соревнова́ния** weightlifting competiton.
тяжелове́с (-а) *м* (СПОРТ) heavyweight.
тяжелове́с|ный (-ен, -на, -но; *перен: речь, шутка, стиль*) laboured (*BRIT*), labored (*US*); (*архитектура*) heavy; ~ **по́езд** freight train.
тяжёл|ый (-ёл, -ела́, -ело́) *прил* heavy; (*трудный: труд, обязанность, дорога итп*) hard, tough; (*сон*) restless; (*запах*) thick;

(*воздух*) close; (*преступление, болезнь, рана*) serious; (*горестный: зрелище, день трудный*) grim; (*мрачный: мысли, настроение*) sombre (*BRIT*), somber (*US*); (*no short form*; *трудный: человек, характер*) difficult; **с ~ёлым се́рдцем** with a heavy heart; **тяжёлая атле́тика** weightlifting; **тяжёлая промы́шленность** heavy industry.

тя́жест|ь (-**и**) *ж* heaviness, weight; (*работы, задачи*) difficulty; (*болезни, раны, преступления*) seriousness, severity; (*обычно мн: тяжёлый предмет*) weight; **си́ла ~и** (*физ*) gravitational pull; **центр ~и** (*физ*) centre of gravity.

тя́ж|кий (-**кая, -кое, -кие; -ек, -ка́, -ко**) *прил* (*труд*) arduous; (*характер*) oppressive; (*зрелище*) grim; (*сомнения, подозрение, преступление*) grave.

тяну́ть (-**у́, -ешь**) *несов перех* (*канат, сеть итп*) to pull; (*вытягивать: шею, руку*) to stretch out; (*дело, разговор, заседание*) to drag out; (*напиток*) to sip (at); (*perf* **протяну́ть**; *трубопровод, кабель*) to lay; (*perf* **вы́тянуть**; *жребий, номер*) to draw ♦ *неперех*: **~ с** +*instr* (*с ответом, с решением*) to delay; (*разг*): **~ на** +*acc* (*на килограмм итп*) to weigh; **~** (**потяну́ть** *perf*) **кого́-н за́ руку** to pull at sb's arm; **~** (*impf*) **кого́-н в кино́** to tempt sb out to the cinema; **меня́ тя́нет в Петербу́рг** I want to go to Petersburg; **меня́ тя́нет ко сну** I'm feeling drowsy; **он не тя́нет на ли́дера** he is not leadership material

▸ **тяну́ться** *несов возв* to stretch; (*заседание, дни, зима итп*) to drag on; (*дым, запах*) to waft; **~ся** (*impf*) **к** +*dat* to be attracted *или* drawn to; **он тя́нется к зна́ниям** he has a thirst for knowledge; **~ся** (*impf*) **за кем-н** to try to keep up with sb.

тяну́ч|ка (-**ки**; *gen pl* -**ек**) *ж* toffee.

тя́п|ка (-**ки**; *gen pl* -**ок**) *ж* hoe.

тяп-ля́п *нареч* (*разг: пренебр*): **де́лать что-н ~** to do sth in a slapdash way.

тя́пн|уть (-**у, -ешь**) *сов неперех* (*разг: укусить*) to nip.

тя́пок *сущ см* **тя́пка**.

~ У, у ~

У, у *сущ нескл* (*буква*) the 20th letter of the Russian alphabet.

KEYWORD

у *предл* (+*gen*) **1** (*около*) by; **у окна́/стены́** by the window/wall; **у мо́ря/реки́** by the sea/river; **у вхо́да** at the entrance

2 (*обозначает орудие, место работы*) at; **сиде́ть** (*impf*) **у руля́** to sit at the helm; **стоя́ть** (*impf*) **у станка́** to stand at the workbench

3 (*обозначает обладателя чего-н*): **у меня́ есть дом/де́ти** I have a house/children; **у таки́х люде́й быва́ют интере́сные иде́и** people like that have interesting ideas; **голова́ у меня́ совсе́м разболе́лась** I have a terrible headache

4 (*обозначает объект, с которым соотносится действие*): **я живу́ у друзе́й** I live with friends; **я учи́лся у него́** I was taught by him

5 (*указывает на источник получения чего-н*) from; **я взял/попроси́л у дру́га де́нег** I got/ asked for money from a friend; **мы получи́ли разреше́ние у нача́льства** we got permission from the authorities

♦ *межд* (*выражает угрозу*) hey; (*выражает испуг, восторг*) oh; **у, негодя́й!** hey, you rascal!; **у, как высоко́!** oh, how high it is!; **у, кака́я красота́!** oh, how beautiful!

УАЗ *м сокр* = **Улья́новский автомоби́льный заво́д**; (*автомобиль*) *vehicle produced at the Ul'ianovskiy car factory*.

уба́вить (-**лю**, -**ишь**; *impf* **убавля́ть**) *сов перех* (*цену, размеры*) to reduce; (*рукава*) to shorten

► **уба́виться** (*impf* **убавля́ться**) *сов возв* (*расходы*) to decrease; (*срок*) to be reduced; (*дни*) to get shorter.

убаю́кать (-**ю**) *сов от* **баю́кать**.

убега́ть (-**ю**) *несов от* **убежа́ть**.

убегу́ *итп сов см* **убежа́ть**.

убеди́тельный (-**ен**, -**ьна**, -**ьно**) *прил* (*пример, доказательство*) convincing; (*просьба*) urgent.

убеди́ть (-**ишь**, -**и́т**; *impf* **убежда́ть**) *сов перех*: ~ **кого́-н** +*infin* to persuade sb to do; **убежда́ть** (~ *perf*) **кого́-н в чём-н** to convince sb of sth

► **убеди́ться** (*impf* **убежда́ться**) *сов возв*: ~**ся в чём-н** to be convinced of sth.

убежа́ть (*как* **бежа́ть**; *см* Table 20; *impf* **убега́ть**) *сов неперех* to run away; **молоко́ ~ло**

(*разг*) the milk has boiled over.

убежда́ть(ся) (-**ю(сь)**) *несов от* **убеди́ть(ся)**.

убежде́ние (-**я**) *ср* (*внушение*) assurance; (*взгляд*) conviction; **поддава́ться (подда́ться** *perf*) ~**ям** to give in to persuasion.

убеждённость (-**и**) *ж* (*уверенность*) assurance, conviction.

убеждённый (-**ён**, -**ена́**, -**ено́**) *прил*: ~ **в** +*prp* convinced of; (-**ён**, -**енна**, -**ённо**; *тон*) assured; (*no short form*; *католик*) convinced.

убежи́шь *итп сов см* **убежа́ть**.

убе́жище (-**а**) *ср* (*от дождя, от бомб*) shelter; **полити́ческое** ~ political asylum.

убелённый *прил*: ~ **седи́нами** silver-haired.

убере́чь (-**егу́**, -**ежёшь** *итп*, -**егу́т**; *pt* -**ёг**, -**егла́**, -**егло́**, *impf* **убере́га́ть**) *сов перех* to protect

► **убере́чься** (*impf* **убере́га́ться**) *сов возв* (*от опасности итп*) to protect o.s.; ~**ся** (*perf*) **от просту́ды** to avoid catching cold.

уберу́(сь) *итп сов см* **убра́ть(ся)**.

убива́ть (-**ю**) *несов от* **уби́ть**

► **убива́ться** *несов возв* (*разг: страдать*) to grieve; (: *на работе*) to break one's back.

уби́йственный *прил* (*оружие*) deadly; (*новость, результат*) devastating; (*разг: жара, климат*) unbearable.

уби́йство (-**а**) *ср* murder.

уби́йца (-**ы**) *м/ж* murderer.

убира́ть(ся) (-**ю(сь)**) *несов от* **убра́ть(ся)**.

уби́тая (-**ой**; *decl like adj*) *ж* dead woman (*мн* women).

уби́тый *прил* (*перен: лицо*) crushed ♦ (-**ого**; *decl like adj*) *м* dead man (*мн* men); **спит как** ~ (*перен*) he is sleeping like a log.

уби́ть (-**ью**, -**ьёшь**; *impf* **убива́ть**) *сов перех* to kill; (*совершить преступление*) to murder; (*перен: надежды, инициативу*) to destroy; ~ (*perf*) **вре́мя** (*перен*) to kill time.

ублажи́ть (-**у́**, -**и́шь**; *impf* **ублажа́ть**) *сов перех* (*разг*) to please.

убо́гий (-**ая**, -**ое**, -**ие**) *прил* (*дом, человек*) wretched; (*перен: идеи, фильм*) mediocre.

убо́жество (-**а**) *ср* (*мыслей, идей*) mediocrity; (*обстановки*) wretchedness.

убо́й (-**я**) *м* slaughter.

убо́р (-**а**) *м*: **головно́й** ~ hat.

убо́ристый (-, -**а**, -**о**) *прил* (*почерк, печать*) close, dense.

убо́рка (-**и**) *ж* (*помещения*) cleaning;

занима́ться (заня́ться *perf)* ~ to do the cleaning; ~ **урожа́я** harvest.
убо́рн|ая (-ой; *decl like adj)* ж *(артисти́ческая)* dressing-room; *(туале́т)* toilet, lavatory.
убо́рочн|ый *прил* harvesting *опред;* ~**ая маши́на** harvester.
убо́рщик (-а) *м* cleaner.
убо́рщиц|а (-и) ж см **убо́рщик.**
убра́ть (уберу́, уберёшь; *pt* **-а́л, -ала́, -а́ло,** *impf* **убира́ть)** *сов перех (унести́: ве́щи)* to take away, remove; *(поме́стить)* to put away; *(паруса́, я́корь)* to stow; *(шасси́)* to retract, draw in; *(ко́мнату)* to tidy; *(разг: пара́граф: из те́кста)* to remove; *(урожа́й)* to gather in;
▸ **убра́ть (** ~ *perf)* **со стола́** to clear the table
▸ **убра́ться (***impf* **убира́ться)** *сов возв (разг: удали́ться)* to get out; *(сде́лать убо́рку)* to clear *или* tidy up; **убира́йся отсю́да!** get lost!
убу́ду *итп сов см* **убы́ть.**
убыва́|ть (-ю) *несов от* **убы́ть.**
у́быль (-и) ж *(рабо́чей си́лы)* decrease; **идти́ (пойти́** *perf)* **на** ~ *(дни)* to get shorter; *(боле́знь, эпиде́мия)* to run its course.
убы́т|ок (-ка) *м* loss; **терпе́ть** *(impf)* *или* **нести́** *(impf)* ~**ки** to incur losses.
убы́точн|ый (-ен, -на, -но) *прил* unprofitable.
убы́ть (*как* **быть;** *см* **Table 21;** *impf* **убыва́ть)** *сов непер* to decrease; **его́ от э́того не убу́дет** he won't be any worse off for it.
убью́ *итп сов см* **уби́ть.**
уважа́ем|ый *прил* respected, esteemed; **У~ые да́мы и господа́!** Ladies and Gentlemen!
уважа́|ть (-ю) *несов перех* to respect.
уваже́ни|е (-я) *ср* respect.
уважи́тельн|ый (-ен, -ьна, -ьно) *прил (отноше́ние)* respectful; *(до́вод, причи́на)* respectable.
ува́ж|ить (-у, -ишь) *сов перех (угоди́ть)* to humour *(BRIT)*, humor *(US);* ~ *(perf)* **чью-н про́сьбу** to grant sb's request.
у́ва́л|ень (-ьня) *м* lumbering oaf.
ува́р|иться (3sg **-ится,** 3pl **-ятся,** *impf* **ува́риваться)** *сов возв (сиро́п, щи)* to boil down, reduce.
УВД *ср сокр (= Управле́ние вну́тренних дел)* administration of internal affairs within a town or region.
уве́дом|ить (-лю, -ишь; *impf* **уведомля́ть)** *сов перех* to inform.
уведомле́ни|е (-я) *ср (докуме́нт)* notification.
уве́домлю *сов см* **уве́домить.**
уведомля́|ть (-ю) *несов от* **уве́домить.**
увез|ти́ (-у́, -ёшь; *pt* **увёз, увезла́, увезло́,** *impf* **увози́ть)** *сов перех* to take away.
увекове́ч|ить (-у, -ишь) *сов перех (геро́я)* to immortalize.
увеличе́ни|е (-я) *ср* increase.

увели́чива|ть(ся) (-ю(сь)) *несов от* **увели́чить(ся).**
увеличи́тельн|ый *прил:* ~**ое стекло́** magnifying glass.
увели́ч|ить (-у, -ишь; *impf* **увели́чивать)** *сов перех* to increase; *(фотогра́фию)* to enlarge
▸ **увели́читься (***impf* **увели́чиваться)** *сов возв* to increase, be increased.
увенча́|ться (-юсь) *сов возв:* ~ **успе́хом** to result in success.
уве́ренность (-и) ж confidence; ~ **в себе́** self-confidence; **поколеба́ть** *(perf)* **чью-н** ~ **в чём-н/в том, что ...** to shake sb's conviction in sth/that ...; **я был в по́лной** ~**и, что ...** I was absolutely sure that ....
уве́ренн|ый (-, -на, -но, -ы) *прил (шаг, отве́т, го́лос)* confident; *(рука́)* sure; ~ **в** +*prp* sure of; ~ **в себе́** self-confident, sure of o.s.
уве́р|ить (-ю, -ишь; *сов от* **уверя́ть.**
уверну́|ться (-усь, -ёшься; *impf* **увёртываться)** *сов возв* to swerve; **увёртываться (~** *perf)* **от уда́ра** to dodge a blow; **увёртываться (~** *perf)* **от пря́мого отве́та** to avoid giving a straight answer.
уве́р|овать (-ую) *сов непер:* ~ **в** +*acc* to (come to) believe in.
увёртлив|ый (-, -а, -о) *прил (подви́жный)* nimble; *(перен: хи́трый)* evasive.
увёртыва|ться (-юсь) *несов от* **ув

уверну́ться.
увертю́р|а (-ы) ж overture.
уверя́|ть (-ю; *сов* **уве́рить)** *несов перех:* ~ **кого́-н/что-н (в чём-н)** to assure sb/sth (of sth); ~**ю Вас, что я был про́тив э́того** I assure you that I was against it.
увесели́тельн|ый *прил (зре́лище)* entertaining; ~**ая прогу́лка** jaunt.
уве́сист|ый (-, -а, -о) *прил* heavy.
уве|сти́ (-ду́, -дёшь; *pt* **-ёл, -ела́, -ело́,** *impf* **уводи́ть)** *сов перех* to lead off *или* away; *(разг: похи́тить)* to nick.
уве́чь|е (-я) *ср* injury; **наноси́ть (нанести́** *perf)* **кому́-н** ~ to maim sb; **получа́ть (получи́ть** *perf)* ~ to be maimed.
уве́ша|ть (-ю; *impf* **уве́шивать)** *сов перех:* ~ **кого́-н/что-н чем-н** to cover sb/sth with sth.
уве́щева|ть (-ю) *несов перех* to exhort.
увива́|ться (-юсь) *несов возв (уха́живать):* ~ **(за кем-н)** *(за же́нщиной)* to hang around (sb).
уви́|деть (-жу, -дишь) *сов от* **ви́деть** ♦ *перех* to catch sight of
▸ **уви́деться** *сов от* **ви́деться.**
увильну́|ть (-у́, -ёшь) *сов непер:* ~ **от** +*gen (разг)* to dodge; *(от отве́тственности)* to get *или* wriggle out of.
увлажн|и́ть (-ю́, -и́шь; *impf* **увлажня́ть)** *сов перех* to moisten
▸ **увлажни́ться (***impf* **увлажня́ться)** *сов возв* to become moist.

увлёк(ся) *итп сов см* увле́чь(ся).

увлека́тельный *прил* (*захватывающий*) absorbing; (-ен, -ьна, -ьно; *занимательный*) entertaining.

увлека́ть(ся) (-ю(сь)) *несов от* увле́чь(ся).

увлека́ющийся (-аяся, -ееся, -иеся) *прил* easily carried away.

увлеку́(сь) *итп сов см* увле́чь(ся).

увлече́ни|е (-я) *ср* (*влюблённость*) infatuation; ~ (+*instr*) (*работой, бадлетом*) enthusiasm *или* passion (for).

увл|е́чь (-еку́, -ечёшь *итп*, -еку́т; *pt* -ёк, -екла́, -екло́, *impf* увлека́ть) *сов перех* to lead away; (*перен*) to captivate

▶ **увле́чься** (*impf* увлека́ться) *сов возв*: ~ся +*instr* to get carried away with; (*влюбиться*) to fall for; (*шахматами итп*) to become keen on.

ув|оди́ть (-ожу́, -о́дишь) *несов от* увести́.

ув|ози́ть (-ожу́, -о́зишь) *несов от* увезти́.

увола́кива|ть (-ю) *несов от* уволо́чь.

увол|ить (-ю, -ишь; *impf* увольня́ть) *сов перех* (*с работы*) to dismiss, sack; увольня́ть (~ *perf*) в запа́с to transfer to the reserve

▶ **уво́лить|ся** (*impf* увольня́ться) *сов возв*: ~ся с рабо́ты to leave one's job.

уволо́|чь (-ку́, -чёшь *итп*, -ку́т; *pt* -к, -кла́, -кло́, *impf* увола́кивать) *сов перех* to drag away *или* off; (*разг: украсть*) to nick.

увольне́ни|е (-я) *ср* (*со службы*) dismissal; (*ВОЕН*) leave.

увольни́тельн|ая (-ой; *decl like adj*) *ж* (*ВОЕН*) leave-pass.

увольня́ть(ся) (-ю(сь)) *несов от* уво́лить(ся).

УВЧ *сокр* (= ультравысо́кая частота́) UHF (= *ultrahigh frequency*) ◆ *прил сокр* (ультравысокочасто́тный) UHF (= *ultrahigh-frequency*).

увы́ *межд* alas.

увяда́ни|е (-я) *ср* (*цветов*) withering; (*красоты*) fading.

увя́дший (-ая, -ее, -ие) *прил* (*цветок*) withered; (*красота*) faded.

увя|за́ть (-яжу́, -я́жешь; *impf* увя́зывать) *сов перех* (*вещи*) to tie up; (*перен: согласовать*) to tie in

▶ **увяза́ться** *сов возв* (*разг*): ~ся (за +*instr*) to tag along (behind).

увя́зн|уть (-у, -ешь) *сов от* вя́знуть.

увя́зыва|ть (-ю) *несов от* увяза́ть.

увя́н|уть (-у, -ешь) *сов от* вя́нуть.

угада́|ть (-ю; *impf* уга́дывать) *сов перех* to guess.

Уга́нд|а (-ы) *ж* Uganda.

уга́р (-а) *м* (*воздух*) fume-filled air; (*отравление*) carbon-monoxide poisoning; **пья́ный** ~ drunken haze.

уга́рный *прил*: ~ дым poisonous smoke; **уга́рный газ** carbon monoxide.

угаса́|ть (-ю; *perf* уга́снуть) *несов неперех* (*костёр, закат*) to die down.

уга́сн|уть (-у, -ешь) *сов от* га́снуть.

угла́ *итп сущ см* у́гол.

углево́д (-а) *м* carbohydrate.

углеводоро́д (-а) *м* hydrocarbon.

углекислот|а́ (-ы́) *ж* carbon dioxide.

углеки́слый *прил*: ~ газ carbon dioxide.

углепромы́шленность (-и) *ж* coal industry.

углеро́д (-а) *м* (*ХИМ*) carbon.

углова́тость (-и) *ж* (*лица*) angularity; (*человека, движений*) awkwardnes.

углова́тый *прил* (*лицо*) angular; (*человек, движения*) awkward.

углово́й *прил* corner *опред*; (*также*: ~ **уда́р**: *СПОРТ*) corner.

углуб|и́ть (-лю́, -и́шь; *impf* углубля́ть) *сов перех* to deepen

▶ **углуби́ться** (*impf* углубля́ться) *сов возв* (*также перен*) to deepen; **углубля́ться** (~ся *perf*) в +*acc* (*в книгу, в чтение*) to become absorbed in; ~ся (*perf*) в воспомина́ния/ мы́сли to become lost in memories/thought; ~ся (*perf*) в лес to go deep into the forest.

углубле́ни|е (-я) *ср* (*кризиса*) deepening; (*впадина*) depression.

углублённый (-ён, -ена́, -ено́) *прил* profound.

углублю́(сь) *сов см* углуби́ть(ся).

углубля́|ть(ся) (-ю(сь)) *несов от* углуби́ть(ся).

угля́ *итп сущ см* у́голь.

угля|де́ть (-жу́, -ди́шь) *сов перех* (*разг: увидеть*) to spot.

угн|а́ть (угоню́, уго́нишь; *pt* -а́л, -ала́, -а́ло, *impf* угоня́ть) *сов перех* to drive off; (*разг: украсть*) to steal; (*самолёт*) to hijack

▶ **угна́ться** *сов возв*: ~ся за +*instr* (*также перен*) to catch up with.

угнета́тель (-я) *м* oppressor.

угнета́|ть (-ю) *несов перех* (*притеснять*) to oppress; (*тяготить*) to depress.

угнете́ни|е (-я) *ср* (*народа*) oppression.

угнетённость (-и) *ж* depression.

угнетённый *прил* (*народ*) oppressed; (*МЕД*) depressed.

угова́рива|ть (-ю) *несов от* уговори́ть ◆ *перех* to try to persuade.

угово́р (-а) *м* (*обычно мн: наставление*) persuasion; (*соглашение*) agreement, arrangement; **поддава́ться** (**подда́ться** *perf*) **на** ~ы to give in to persuasion.

уговор|и́ть (-ю́, -и́шь; *impf* угова́ривать) *сов перех* to persuade.

уго́д|а (-ы) *ж*: в ~у кому́-н to please sb.

уго́ден *прил см* уго́дный.

уго|ди́ть (-жу́, -ди́шь; *impf* угожда́ть) *сов неперех*: ~ +*dat*/на +*acc* to please; (*попасть*) to end up; ~ (*perf*) под маши́ну to get run over; ~ (*perf*) ного́й в я́му to put one's foot in a hole.

уго́дливый (-, -а, -о) *прил* obsequious.

уго́дник (-а) *м* (*РЕЛ*) saint; **да́мский** ~ ladies' man.

уго́днича|ть (-ю) *несов неперех*: ~ (пе́ред

+*instr*) to fawn (on).

угóдно *част*: **что** ~ whatever you like ♦ *как сказ*: **что Вам** ~? what can I do for you?; **кто** ~ anyone; **когда/какой** ~ whenever/whichever you like; **сколько** ~ any amount; **кому** ~ **начáть?** who would like to start?; **возьмите всё, что Вам** ~ take whatever you like; **от них мóжно ожидáть чегó** ~ they might do anything.

угóдный (**-ен, -на, -но**) *прил* (+*dat*; *родителям, властям*) pleasing to.

угóдья (**-ий**) *мн*: **земéльные** ~ arable and pasture land; **лéсные** ~ forestry; **вóдные** ~ fisheries and waterways.

угождáть (**-ю**) *несов от* **угодить**.

угожý *сов см* **угодить**.

ýгол (**-лá**; *loc sg* **-лý**) *м* (ГЕОМ) angle; (*стола, дома, комнаты*) corner; **завернýть** (**завернýть** *perf*) **зá угол** to turn the corner; **за углóм** round the corner; **из-за углá** from around the corner; ~ **зрéния** perspective, standpoint; **он снимáет** ~ he's renting a tiny little place.

уголкá *сущ см* **уголóк**.

уголóвник (**-а**) *м* criminal.

уголóвный *прил* criminal *опред*; **уголóвный кóдекс** criminal code; **уголóвный престýпник** criminal; **уголóвный рóзыск** Criminal Investigation Department.

уголóвщина (**-ы**) *ж* (*разг*) crime.

уголóк (**-кá**) *м уменьш от* **ýгол**; (*место*) corner; **тихий** ~ secluded spot.

ýголь (**-лá**; *nom pl* **-ли**, *gen pl* **-лéй**) *м* coal.

угóльник (**-а**) *м* (*чертёжный*) set square.

угóльный *прил* coal.

угомониться (**-юсь, -ишься**) *сов возв* (*разг*) to quieten down.

угóн (**-а**) *м* (*самолёта*) hijacking; (*машины, коня*) theft.

угóнщик (**-а**) *м* (*самолёта*) hijacker.

угоню́(сь) *итп сов см* **угнáть(ся)**.

угонять (**-ю**) *несов от* **угнáть**.

угораздить (*3sg* **-ит**) *сов безл*: ~**ило тебя сказáть это!** what on earth made you say that?; **как это тебя** ~**ило** how on earth did you manage that?

угорéлый *прил*: **бéгать как** ~ to run around like a mad thing.

угорéть (**-ю, -ишь**) *сов неперех* to get gas-poisoning.

ýгорь (**-ря**; *nom pl* **-ри**) *м* (ЗООЛ) eel; (*на лице*) blackhead.

угостить (**-щý, -стишь**; *impf* **угощáть**) *сов перех*: ~ **когó-н чем-н** (*дома*) to offer sb sth; (*в ресторáне*) to treat sb to sth.

угощáться (**-юсь**) *несов возв*: ~**йтесь!** help yourself!

угощéние (**-я**) *ср* (*гостей*) entertaining; (*вкусное, изысканное*) food.

угощý *сов см* **угостить**.

угробить (**-лю, -ишь**) *сов от* **гробить**.

угрожáть (**-ю**) *несов неперех*: ~ **кому-н** (**чем-н**) to threaten sb (with sth); **емý** ~**ет банкрóтство** he is threatened with bankruptcy.

угрожáющий (**-ая, -ее, -ие**) *прил* threatening; (*вид*) menacing.

угрóза (**-ы**) *ж* (*обычно мн*) threat.

угрóхать (**-ю**) *сов перех* (*разг*: *деньги*) to blow; (*продукты*) to use (up).

угрызéние (**-я**) *ср*: ~**я сóвести** pangs *мн* of conscience.

угрю́мый (**-, -а, -о**) *прил* gloomy.

угря *итп сущ см* **ýгорь**.

удáбривать (**-ю**) *несов от* **удóбрить**.

удáв (**-а**) *м* boa constrictor.

удавáться (*3sg* **-ётся**, *3pl* **-ются**) *несов от* **удáться**.

удадимся *итп сов см* **удáться**.

удалéц (**-ьцá**) *м* (*разг*) hero.

удалить (**-ю, -ишь**; *impf* **удалять**) *сов перех* (*детей, посторонних*) to send away, remove; (*игрока*: *с поля*) to send off; (*пятно, занозу, орган*) to remove; (*зуб*) to extract; (*КОМП*) to delete

▸ **удалиться** (*impf* **удаляться**) *сов возв* to move away; (*перен*: *от темы*) to digress; (*в свою комнату*) to withdraw.

удалóй *прил* daring.

ýдаль (**-и**) *ж* daring.

удальцá *итп сущ см* **удалéц**.

удалять(ся) (**-ю(сь)**) *несов от* **удалить(ся)**.

удáр (**-а**) *м* blow; (*ногóй*) kick; (*звук, инсульт*) stroke; (*пульса, сéрдца*) beat; ~ **грóма** clap of thunder; **быть** (*impf*) **в** ~**е** (*разг*) to be on the ball; **стáвить** (**постáвить** *perf*) **когó-н под** ~ to put sb in a vulnerable position; **наносить** (**нанести** *perf*) ~ **кому-н** to deal a blow to sb.

ударéние (**-я**) *ср* (*также ЛИНГ*) stress.

удáрить (**-ю, -ишь**; *impf* **ударять**) *сов перех* to hit; (*подлеж*: *часы*) to strike; (: *морозы*) to set in; **ударять** (~ *perf*) **когó-н по головé/спинé** to hit sb on the head/back; **ударять** (~ *perf*) **в барабáн** to beat a drum; (*perf*) **по спекулянтам** to crack down on profiteers; **винó** ~**ило емý в гóлову** the wine has gone to his head; ~**ил гром** there was a clap of thunder; **он не** ~**ил лицóм в грязь** he didn't disgrace himself

▸ **удáриться** (*impf* **ударяться**) *сов возв* (*натолкнуться на что-н*): ~**ся о** +*acc* (*о двéрь, о стéну итп*) to bang (o.s.) against; ~**ся** (*perf*) **в пáнику** to fly into a panic; ~**ся** (*perf*) **в спорт/в наýку/в политику** to become obsessed with sport/science/politics; **он** ~**ился головóй о шкаф** he hit his head *или* against the cupboard.

удáрник (**-а**) *м* (*музыкант*) percussionist; (*ружья, пистолéта*) striker, firing pin.

уда́рный *прил (инструмент)* percussion *опред*; *(войска, труд)* shock *опред*; *(слог)* stressed; **уда́рная волна́** shock wave.

ударя́ть(ся) (-ю(сь)) *несов от* уда́рить(ся).

уда́ться (*как* дать; *см* Table 14; *impf* **удава́ться**) *сов возв (получиться: опыт, испытание)* to be successful, work; *(пирог)* to turn out well; **нам удало́сь/не удало́сь поговори́ть/зако́нчить рабо́ту** we managed/ didn't manage to talk to one another/finish the work.

уда́ч|а (-и) *ж* (good) luck; **нам вы́пала больша́я ~** we had a great stroke of luck; **жела́ю ~и!** good luck!

уда́чен *прил см* уда́чный.

уда́члив|ый (-, -а, -о) *прил* lucky.

уда́чн|ый (-ен, -на, -но) *прил* successful; *(хороший: выбор, выражение)* good.

удва́ива|ть(ся) (-ю(сь)) *несов от* удво́ить(ся).

удво́ени|е (-я) *ср* doubling.

удво́енный *прил (зарплата)* doubled; *(энергия, сила итп)* redoubled.

удво́|ить (-ю, -ишь; *impf* **удва́ивать**) *сов перех* to double; *(внимание, усилия)* to redouble

▶ **удво́иться** (*impf* **удва́иваться**) *сов возв* to double; *(усилия итп)* to be redoubled.

уде́л (-а) *м (судьба)* lot, fate.

удел|и́ть (-ю, -и́шь; *impf* **уделя́ть**) *сов перех*: ~ **что-н кому́-н/чему́-н** to devote sth to sb/sth.

уде́льный *прил*: ~ **вес** *(физ)* specific gravity.

уделя́ть (-ю) *несов от* удели́ть.

у́держ (-у) *м*: **без ~у** uncontrollably; **он не зна́ет ~у в тра́тах** he doesn't know when to stop spending.

удержа́|ть (-ержу́, -е́ржишь; *impf* **уде́рживать**) *сов перех* to restrain; *(часть зарплаты)* to deduct; *(первенство, позиции)*: ~ **(за собо́й)** to retain; ~ *(perf)* **что-н в рука́х** to hold onto sth, not let go of sth; **уде́рживать (~ *perf*) кого́-н от пое́здки** to keep sb from going on a journey; **уде́рживать (~ *perf*) кого́-н до́ма** to keep sb at home

▶ **удержа́ться** (*impf* **уде́рживаться**) *сов возв (остановить себя)* to stop *или* restrain o.s.; *(устоять: на краю обрыва)* to hang on; **~ся** *(perf)* **на нога́х** to stay on one's feet; **~ся** *(perf)* **на свои́х пози́циях** to hold one's ground; **~ся** *(perf)* **от сме́ха** to stop *или* keep o.s. from laughing; **~ся** *(perf)* **от слёз** to hold back the tears.

удеру́ *итп сов см* удра́ть.

удесятер|и́ть (-ю, -ишь) *сов перех* to increase tenfold; *(усилия)* to triple.

удешев|и́ть (-лю́, -и́шь; *impf* **удешевля́ть**) *сов перех* to make cheaper

▶ **удешеви́ться** (*impf* **удешевля́ться**) *сов возв* to get cheaper.

удешевле́ни|е (-я) *ср*: ~ **цен (на** +*acc)* reduction in the price (of).

удешевлю́(сь) *сов см* удешеви́ть(ся).

удешевля́|ть(ся) (-ю(сь)) *несов от*

удешеви́ть(ся).

удиви́телен *прил см* удиви́тельный.

удиви́тельно *нареч (красивый, вкусный)* amazingly ♦ *как сказ* it's amazing; **мне ~, что ты э́того не понима́ешь** I'm amazed that you don't understand this; ~, **как ты не простуди́лся** it's amazing that you didn't catch (a) cold; **и не ~** and no wonder.

удиви́тельн|ый (-ен, -ьна, -ьно) *прил* amazing.

удив|и́ть (-лю́, -и́шь; *impf* **удивля́ть**) *сов перех* to surprise

▶ **удиви́ться** (*impf* **удивля́ться**) *сов возв*: ~**ся** +*dat (известию, приезду итп)* to be surprised at *или* by; **я ~и́лся, что он не позвони́л** I was surprised that he didn't phone.

удивле́ни|е (-я) *ср* surprise; **к на́шему ~ю, она́ ушла́** to our surprise she left; **с ~м** with surprise; **от ~я** in surprise; **краси́вый/у́мный на ~** amazingly beautiful/clever.

удивлённый *прил* surprised.

удивлю́(сь) *сов см* удиви́ть(ся).

удивля́|ть(ся) (-ю(сь)) *несов от* удиви́ть(ся).

удил|а́ (-) *мн bit ед (of bridle)*.

уди́лищ|е (-а) *ср (часть удочки)* (fishing-)rod.

удира́|ть (-ю) *несов от* удра́ть.

уди́ть (ужу́, у́дишь) *несов неперех* to angle.

удлине́ни|е (-я) *ср (рукава)* lengthening; *(срока)* extension.

удлинённый *прил (пальто)* long; *(лицо)* elongated.

удлин|и́ть (-ю, -и́шь; *impf* **удлиня́ть**) *сов перех (рукав, пальто)* to lengthen; *(рабочий день, срок)* to extend

▶ **удлини́ться** (*impf* **удлиня́ться**) *сов возв* to grow longer.

удо́бен *прил см* удо́бный.

удо́бно *нареч (усесться, лечь)* comfortably ♦ *как сказ*: **мне ~ здесь** ~ I'm comfortable here; **мне ~ прийти́ ве́чером** it's convenient for me to come in the evening.

удо́бн|ый (-ен, -на, -но) *прил (мебель)* comfortable; *(время, формат, место)* convenient; **дожида́ться (дожда́ться** *perf)* ~**ного слу́чая** to wait for the right opportunity.

удобре́ни|е (-я) *ср (действие)* fertilizing; *(минеральное, химическое)* fertilizer.

удобр|ить (-ю, -ишь; *impf* **удобря́ть (или) уда́бривать**) *сов перех* to fertilize.

удо́бство (-а) *ср* comfort; **кварти́ра со все́ми ~ами** a flat with all (modern) conveniences.

удовлетворе́ни|е (-я) *ср* satisfaction; *(требований)* fulfilment.

удовлетворённый *прил* satisfied.

удовлетвори́телен *прил см* **удовлетвори́тельный**.

удовлетвори́тельно *нареч* satisfactorily; *(просвещ)* ≈ satisfactory (school mark).

удовлетвори́тельн|ый (-ен, -ьна, -ьно) *прил* satisfactory.

удовлетвор|и́ть (-ю́, -и́шь; *impf* **удовлетворя́ть**) *сов перех* to satisfy;

(*потребности, спрос, просьбу*) to meet;
(*жалобу*) to respond to; **удовлетворя́ть** (~ *perf*)
+*dat* (*требованиям, вкусам, правилам*) to
satisfy

▶ **удовлетвори́ться** (*impf* **удовлетворя́ться**)
сов возв: ~**ся** +*instr* to be satisfied with.

удово́льстви|**е** (-я) *ср* pleasure; **получа́ть**
(**получи́ть** *perf*) ~ **от чего́-н** to enjoy sth;
доставля́ть (**доста́вить** *perf*) **кому́-н** ~ to make
sb happy; **с** ~**м** with pleasure; **я бы с** ~**м пошёл
с Ва́ми** I would love to go with you.

удово́льств|**оваться** (-уюсь) *сов от*
дово́льствоваться.

удо́д (-а) *м* (*зоол*) hoopoe.

удо́й (-я) *м* yield (*of milk*).

удо́йлив|**ый** (-, -а, -о) *прил:* ~**ая коро́ва** good
milking cow.

удорожа́ни|**е** (-я) *ср:* ~ **проду́ктов пита́ния**
rise in food prices.

удоста́ива|**ть(ся)** (-ю(сь)) *несов от*
удосто́ить(ся).

удостовере́ни|**е** (-я) *ср* (*подписи*) verification;
(*документ*) identification (card);
удостовере́ние ли́чности identity card.

удостове́р|**ить** (-ю, -ишь; *impf* **удостоверя́ть**)
сов перех (*факт*) to verify

▶ **удостове́риться** (*impf* **удостоверя́ться**) *сов
возв:* ~**ся в** +*prp* (*в чьей-н невиновности, в
верности сообщения*) to assure o.s. of; **он**
~**ился, что она́ до́ма** he made sure that she was
at home.

удосто́|**ить** (-ю, -ишь; *impf* **удоста́ивать**) *сов
перех:* ~ **кого́-н чего́-н** to bestow sth on sb;
удоста́ивать (~ *perf*) **кого́-н свои́м визи́том** to
honour (*BRIT*) *или* honor (*US*) sb with a visit; ~
(*perf*) **кого́-н улы́бки** to bestow a smile on sb

▶ **удосто́иться** (*impf* **удоста́иваться**) *сов возв:*
~**ся** +*gen* (*награды*) to be honoured (*BRIT*) *или*
honored (*US*) with.

удосу́ж|**иться** (-усь, -ишься; *impf*
удосу́живаться) *сов возв:* ~ +*infin* to find time
to do.

у́дочек *сущ см* **у́дочка**.

удочере́ни|**е** (-я) *ср* adoption (*of daughter*).

удочер|**и́ть** (-ю, -и́шь; *impf* **удочеря́ть**) *сов
перех* to adopt (*daughter*).

у́доч|**ка** (-ки; *gen pl* -ек) *ж* (fishing-)rod; **он
попа́лся на** ~**ку** (*перен*) he fell for it;
заки́дывать (**заки́нуть** *perf*) ~**ку** (*рыболов*) to
cast; (*перен*) to put out feelers.

удр|**а́ть** (**удеру́, удерёшь**; *pt* -**а́л, -ала́, -а́ло**, *impf*
удира́ть) *сов неперех* (*разг*) to make off.

удруж|**и́ть** (-у́, -и́шь) *сов неперех:* ~ **кому́-н** to
do sb a favour (*BRIT*) *или* favor (*US*).

удручённый *прил* (*взгляд, лицо, вид*) dejected;
(-**ён, -ена́, -ено́**; *человек*) dejected, depressed.

удуш|**и́ть** (-ушу́, -у́шишь) *сов от* **души́ть** ◆
(*impf* **удуша́ть**) *перех* (*человека*) to strangle;

(*свободу*) to stifle.

уду́шливый *прил* (*газ, вещество*) suffocating;
(*жара*) stifling.

уду́шь|**е** (-я) *ср* (*no pl*) suffocation.

ужу́ *несов см* **уди́ть**.

уе́дешь *итп сов см* **уе́хать**.

уедине́ни|**е** (-я) *ср* solitude.

уединённый (-, -на, -но) *прил* (*место, остров*)
solitary.

уедин|**и́ться** (-ю́сь, -и́шься; *impf* **уединя́ться**)
сов возв to go off, withdraw.

уе́ду *итп сов см* **уе́хать**.

уе́зд (-а) *м* (*ист*) uezd (*administrative division in
pre-Revolutionary Russia*).

уезжа́й(те) *сов см* **уе́хать**.

уезжа́ть (-ю) *несов от* **уе́хать**.

УЕФА́ *м сокр* (= *Европе́йский сою́з футбо́льных
ассоциа́ций*) UEFA (= *Union of European
Football Associations*).

уе́ха|**ть** (*как* **е́хать**; *см* **Table 19**; *impf* **уезжа́ть**)
сов неперех to leave, go away; **он** ~**л в
о́тпуск/в Москву́** he has gone on holiday/to
Moscow; **мы ско́ро уезжа́ем** we are leaving
soon.

уж (-**а́**) *м* (*зоол*) grass snake ◆ *нареч* (*уже*)
already ◆ *част* (*выражает усиление*): **здесь не
так** ~ **пло́хо** it's not as bad as all that here; **э́то**
~ **о́чень до́рого** it really is too expensive.

ужа́л|**ить** (-ю, -ишь) *сов от* **жа́лить**.

у́жас (-а) *м* horror; (*страх*) terror ◆ *как сказ*
(*разг*): (**э́то**) ~! it's awful *или* terrible! ◆ *нареч:*
он ~ **како́й бога́тый** (*разг*) he's incredibly rich;
~**ы войны́** horrors of war; **прийти́** (*perf*) **в** ~ **от
чего́-н** to be horrified by sth; **к моему́** ~**у** to my
horror; **он дрожа́л от** ~**а** he was shaking in
terror; **он** ~ **как бы́стро вре́мя идёт** it's awful *или*
terrible how time flies; **ти́хий** ~! (*разг*) horror of
horrors!; **до** ~**а** (*разг*) terribly.

ужасн|**у́ть** (-у́, -ёшь; *impf* **ужаса́ть**) *сов перех* to
horrify

▶ **ужасну́ться** (*impf* **ужаса́ться**) *сов возв* to be
horrified.

ужаса́ющий (-ая, -ее, -ие) *прил* (*крик,
зре́лище*) horrific; (*запах, холод*) terrible.

ужа́сен *прил см* **ужа́сный**.

ужа́сно *нареч* (*разг: умный, краси́вый итп*)
terribly ◆ *как сказ:* **здесь сейча́с** ~ it's terrible
here now; **он чу́вствует себя́** ~ he feels
terrible.

ужа́с|**ный** (-ен, -на, -но) *прил* terrible, horrible,
awful.

у́же *сравн прил от* **у́зкий**.

уже́ *нареч, част* already; **мы не ви́делись** ~ **3
го́да** it's now 3 years since we've seen each
other; **ты же** ~ **не ма́ленький** you're not a child
any more; ~ **по э́тому мо́жно суди́ть, что ...**
one can judge from this alone that ....

ужива́|**ться** (-юсь) *несов от* **ужи́ться**.

уживу́сь *итп сов см* **ужи́ться**.

ужи́вчив|ый (-, -а, -о) *прил (человек)* easy to get along with.

ужи́м|ка (-ки; *gen pl* -ок) *ж (обычно мн)* grimace.

у́жин (-а) *м* supper.

у́жина|ть (-ю; *perf* **поу́жинать**) *несов неперех* to have supper.

ужи́|ться (-ву́сь, -вёшься; *pt* -лся, -ла́сь, -ло́сь, *impf* **ужива́ться**) *сов возв*: ~ **с ке́м-н** to get on with sb.

узако́ненный *прил (порядок, ритуал)* established.

узако́н|ить (-ю, -ишь; *impf* **узако́нивать**) *сов перех (отношения, порядок)* to legalize.

узбе́к (-а) *м* Uzbek.

Узбекиста́н (-а) *м* Uzbekistan.

узбе́кский (-ая, -ое, -ие) *прил* Uzbek; ~ **язы́к** Uzbek.

узде́ч|ка (-ки; *gen pl* -ек) *ж см* **узде́**.

узда́ (-ы́; *nom pl* -ы) *ж* bridle; **держа́ть** *(impf)* **кого́-н в** ~**é** to keep sb in check.

узде́чк|а (-и) *ж* = **узда́**.

у́здцы: **под** ~ by the bridle.

у́з|ел (-ла́) *м* knot; *(мешок)* bundle; **телефо́нный** ~ telephone exchange; **железнодоро́жный** ~ railway junction; **санита́рный** ~ bathroom and toilet; **морско́й** ~ hitch; **не́рвный** ~ ganglion; ~ **противоре́чий** a mass of contradictions.

у́зкий (-кая, -кое, -кие; -ок, -ка́, -ко) *прил* narrow; *(тесный)* tight; *(перен: человек, взгляд)* narrow-minded; ~**кая специа́льность** narrow specialism; ~ **круг друзе́й** small circle of friends.

узкоколе́йн|ый *прил*: ~**ая желе́зная доро́га** narrow-gauge railway.

узколо́бый *прил (перен)* narrow-minded.

узла́ *итп сущ см* **у́зел**.

узлова́тый (-, -а, -о) *прил* knotty.

узлов|о́й *прил (перен: вопрос, задачи)* key; ~**а́я ста́нция** junction.

узна́|ть (-ю; *impf* **узнава́ть**) *сов перех (знакомого, свою вещь итп)* to recognize; *(новости)* to find out, learn; *(познать: нужду, любовь)* to know; **я** ~**л, что ты прие́хал** I heard that you had come; **он** ~**л о состоя́нии дел** he found out how things stood.

у́зник (-а) *м* captive.

у́зок *прил см* **у́зкий**.

узо́р (-а) *м* pattern.

узо́рный *прил* = **узо́рчатый**.

узо́рчатый *прил* patterned.

у́зост|ь (-и) *ж (улиц, взглядов)* narrowness; *(платья)* tightness; *(человека)* narrow-mindedness.

узурпа́тор (-а) *м* usurper.

узурпи́р|овать (-ую) *(не)сов перех* to usurp.

у́з|ы (-) *мн (перен)* bonds *мн*.

уйду́ *итп сов см* **уйти́**.

у́йм|а (-ы) *ж (разг)*: ~ **де́нег/вре́мени** heaps *или* loads of money/time.

уйму́(сь) *итп сов см* **уня́ть(ся)**.

уйти́ (*как* **идти́**; *см* **Table 18**; *impf* **уходи́ть**) *сов неперех (человек)* to go away, leave; *(парохо́д, поезд)* to go, leave; *(молодость)* to go; *(время, годы)* to pass; *(отда́ться)*: ~ **в** +*acc (в бизнес)* to go into; *(избежать)*: ~ **от** +*gen (от опасности итп)* to get away from; *(потребоваться)*: ~ **на** +*acc (де́ньги, время)* to be spent on; **уходи́ть** (~ *perf*) **из до́ма** to leave the house; **уходи́ть** (~ *perf*) **со слу́жбы/со сце́ны** to leave one's job/the stage; **уходи́ть** *perf)* **от му́жа** to leave one's husband; **уходи́ть** (~ *perf*) **из жи́зни** to pass away; **уходи́ть** (~ *perf*) **на пе́нсию** to retire; **у нас ушло́ мно́го де́нег на поку́пки** we spent a lot of money on shopping.

укажу́ *итп сов см* **указа́ть**.

ука́з (-а) *м (президента)* decree; **он мне не** ~ *(разг)* I don't take orders from him.

указа́ни|е (-я) *ср* pointing out, indication; *(разъяснение)* instruction; (: *нача́льства)* directive; ~**я врача́** doctor's orders.

указа́тел|ь (-я) *м (дорожный)* sign; *(книга)* guide; *(список в книге)* index; *(прибор)* indicator.

указа́тельный *прил (жест)* pointing; **указа́тельное местоиме́ние** demonstrative pronoun; **указа́тельный па́лец** index finger.

указа́|ть (-жу́, -́жешь; *impf* **ука́зывать**) *сов перех* to point out; *(дорогу)* to show; *(свой адрес, интересы, срок)* to indicate; *(движением, жестом)*: ~ **на** +*acc (на дверь, на картину итп)* to point to; *(на ошибки, на недоста́тки)* to point out; ~ *(perf)* **кому́-н на дверь** *(перен)* to show sb the door.

ука́з|ка (-ки; *gen pl* -ок) *ж* pointer; **де́лать** *(сде́лать perf)* **что́-нибудь по чужо́й** ~**ке** to blindly follow somebody else's directions.

ука́зыва|ть (-ю) *несов от* **указа́ть** ♦ *неперех (свидетельствовать)*: ~ **на** +*acc (факты, цифры)* to indicate, point to.

ука́лыва|ть (-ю) *несов от* **уколо́ть**.

ука́та|ть (-ю; *impf* **ука́тывать**) *сов перех (дорогу)* to roll, flatten.

ука|ти́ть (-чу́, -́тишь) *сов перех (мяч)* to roll away; *(тачку)* to wheel away ♦ *неперех (разг: уехать)* to go off.

ука́тыва|ть (-ю) *несов от* **уката́ть**.

ука́ча|ть (-ю; *impf* **ука́чивать**) *сов перех (усыпить: ребёнка)* to rock to sleep; *(довести до тошноты)*: **его́** ~**ло (в маши́не/на парохо́де)** he got (car-/sea-)sick.

укачу́ *сов см* **укати́ть**.

укла́д (-а) *м (экон: капиталистический, феодальный)* order; ~ **жи́зни** way of life.

укла́д|ка (-и) *ж (действие: дров, рельс)* laying; *(причёска)* set.

укла́дчик (-а) *м (путей, паркета)* layer.

укла́дывани|е (-я) *ср (вещей, чемодана)* packing; *(ребёнка)* putting to bed.

укла́дыва|ть (-ю) *несов от* **уложи́ть**

▶ **укла́дываться** *несов от* **уложи́ться**,

уле́чься ♦ возв: э́то не ~ется в обы́чные
ра́мки this is out of the ordinary; э́то не ~ется
в голове́ или в созна́нии it's beyond me.
укло́н (-а) м (также перен): по́езд/доро́га
идёт под ~ the train/road is going downhill.
уклоне́ни|е (-я) ср (дороги в сторону) bending;
(от ответа, от обязанностей) evasion.
укл|они́ться (-оню́сь, -о́нишься; impf
уклоня́ться) сов возв (отстраниться: в
сторону) to swerve; (отойти от главного): ~
от +gen to dodge; (от темы, от предмета) to
digress from; (от поручения) to evade:
уклоня́ться (~ perf) от отве́та to avoid giving
an answer.
укло́нчив|ый (-, -а, -о) прил (ответ) evasive.
уклоня́|ться (-юсь) несов от уклони́ться.
уключи́н|а (-ы) ж rowlock.
уко́л (-а) м (иголкой) prick; (перен: замечание)
dig; (мед) injection: де́лать (сде́лать perf)
кому́-н ~ to give sb an injection: ~ самолю́бию
blow to one's ego.
ук|оло́ть (-олю́, -о́лешь) сов от коло́ть ♦ (impf
ука́лывать) перех (иглой, шипом) to prick;
(перен: самолюбие) to wound
▸ уколо́ться сов от коло́ться.
укомплекто́ванный прил complete.
укомплект|ова́ть (-у́ю) сов от
комплектова́ть.
уко́р (-а) м (упрёк) reproach: ~ы со́вести the
pangs of conscience: живо́й ~ кому́-н living
indictment of sb: ста́вить (поста́вить perf)
кому́-н что-н в ~ to reproach sb with sth.
укора́чива|ть(ся) (-ю(сь)) несов от
укороти́ть(ся).
укорене́ни|е (-я) ср taking root, establishment.
укорен|и́ть (-ю́, -и́шь; impf укореня́ть) сов
перех (рассаду) to allow to take root.
укорен|и́ться (3sg -и́тся, 3pl -я́тся, impf
укореня́ться) сов возв (также перен) to take
root.
укори́зн|а (-ы) ж (укор) reproach.
укори́зненно нареч reproachfully.
укори́зненн|ый (-, -на, -но) прил reproachful.
укор|и́ть (-ю́, -и́шь; impf укоря́ть) сов перех to
reproach.
укор|оти́ть (-чу́, -ти́шь; impf укора́чивать) сов
перех (платье, палку, путь) to shorten; (жизнь,
сроки) to reduce; ~ (perf) ру́ки кому́-н (перен)
to take sb down a peg
▸ укороти́ться (impf укора́чиваться) сов возв
(юбка итп) to be shortened; (сроки) to be
reduced.
укоро́ченный прил (пальто, юбка) short;
(рабочий день) reduced.
укорч|у́(сь) сов см укороти́ть(ся).
укоря́|ть (-ю) несов от укори́ть.
укоря́ющий (-ая, -ее, -ие) прил (взгляд)
reproachful.

укра́дкой нареч secretly.
украду́ итп сов см укра́сть.
Украи́н|а (-ы) ж (the) Ukraine.
украи́н|ец (-ца) м Ukrainian.
украи́н|ка (-ки; gen pl -ок) ж см украи́нец.
украи́нск|ий (-ая, -ое, -ие) прил Ukrainian; ~
язы́к Ukrainian.
украи́нца итп сущ см украи́нец.
укра́|сить (-шу, -сишь; impf украша́ть) сов
перех (комнату) to decorate; (ёлку) to decorate
(BRIT), trim (US); (речь) to embellish;
(существование, жизнь итп) to brighten
▸ укра́ситься (impf украша́ться) сов возв: ~ся
+instr (деревья, поля) to be decorated with (fig);
(жизнь, существование) to be brightened up by.
укра́|сть (-ду́, -дёшь) сов от красть.
украша́|ть (-ю) несов от укра́сить ♦ перех:
тако́е поведе́ние тебя́ не ~ет that kind of
behaviour doesn't suit you
▸ украша́ться несов от укра́ситься.
украше́ни|е (-я) ср decoration; (коллектива)
pride; (коллекции) jewel; (также: ювели́рное
~) jewellery (BRIT), jewelry (US).
укра́шу(сь) сов см укра́сить(ся).
укреп|и́ть (-лю́, -и́шь; impf укрепля́ть) сов
перех (мир, семью, организм) to strengthen;
(стену, строение) to reinforce; (город,
перевал) to fortify; укрепля́ть (~ perf)
здоро́вье to get fit(ter)
▸ укрепи́ться (impf укрепля́ться) сов возв
(нервы, организм) to become stronger;
(хозяйство, авторитет) to become
established; (здоровье) to improve;
(дисциплина) to be tightened up; ~ся (perf) в
свои́х убежде́ниях to become surer of one's
convictions; за ним ~и́лась дурна́я репута́ция
he has earned a bad reputation.
укрепле́ни|е (-я) ср (здоровья) improving;
(авторитета) reinforcement; (ВОЕН: обычно
мн) fortification.
укреплю́(сь) сов см укрепи́ть(ся).
укрепля́|ть(ся) (-ю(сь)) несов от
укрепи́ть(ся).
укрепля́ющий (-ая, -ее, -ие) прил fortifying.
укро́мный прил (уголок) secluded.
укро́п (-а) м. собир dill.
укро́пный прил dill; укро́пная вода́ (МЕД) gripe
water.
укроти́тел|ь (-я) м tamer; ~ львов lion-tamer.
укроти́тельниц|а (-ы) ж см укроти́тель.
укро|ти́ть (-щу́, -ти́шь; impf укроща́ть) сов
перех (животного, гнев, страсти) to tame;
(человека) to bring to heel.
укроще́ни|е (-я) ср (действие) taming.
укрощу́ сов см укроти́ть.
укро́ю(сь) итп сов см укры́ть(ся).
укрупне́ни|е (-я) ср enlargement.
укрупн|и́ть (-ю́, -и́шь; impf укрупня́ть) сов

перех to enlarge
► **укрупни́ться** (*impf* **укрупня́ться**) *сов возв* (*завод, производство*) to get larger; (*черты лица*) to grow more pronounced

укрыва́тельств|о (**-а**) *ср* (*преступника итп*) harbouring.

укрыва́|ть(ся) (**-ю(сь)**) *несов от* **укры́ть(ся)**.

укры́ти|е (**-я**) *ср* (*место: подземное, от бомб*) shelter.

укры́ть (**-о́ю, -о́ешь**; *impf* **укрыва́ть**) *сов перех* (*закрыть: платком, снегом*) to cover; (*спрятать: преступника*) to harbour; (: *беженца*) to shelter
► **укры́ться** (*impf* **укрыва́ться**) *сов возв* (*одеялом, платком*) to cover o.s.; (*от обстрела, от дождя*) to take cover; (*от погони*) to hide; **от моего́ взгля́да не ~ы́лось, что ...** it has not escaped my notice that ....

у́ксус (**-а**) *м* vinegar.

у́ксусный *прил* (*запах, эссенция*) vinegar *опред*; **у́ксусная кислота́** acetic acid.

уку́с (**-а**) *м* bite.

укуси́ть (**-ушу́, -у́сишь**) *сов перех* to bite.

уку́та|ть (**-ю**; *impf* **уку́тывать**) *сов перех* (*больного, шею итп*) to wrap up
► **уку́таться** (*impf* **уку́тываться**) *сов возв* to wrap o.s. up.

укушу́ *сов см* **укуси́ть**.

ул. *сокр* (= **у́лица**) St (= *street*).

ула́влива|ть (**-ю**) *несов от* **улови́ть**.

ула́|дить (**-жу, -дишь**; *impf* **ула́живать**) *сов перех* to settle
► **ула́диться** (*impf* **ула́живаться**) *сов возв* to sort o.s. out.

ула́живани|е (**-я**) *ср* (*ссоры, конфликта*) settling.

ула́жива|ть(ся) (**-ю(сь)**) *несов от* **ула́дить(ся)**.

ула́жу(сь) *сов см* **ула́дить(ся)**.

ула́мыва|ть (**-ю**) *несов от* **уломать**.

ула́н (**-а**) *м* (*ист*) uhlan (*lancer*).

Ула́н-Ба́тор (**-а**) *м* Ulan Bator.

улёгся *итп сов см* **уле́чься**.

у́ле|й (**-ья**) *м* (bee-)hive.

улете́ть (**-чу́, -ти́шь**; *impf* **улета́ть**) *сов неперех* (*птица*) to fly away; (*самолёт*) to leave; (*перен: стремительно уйти*) to fly off.

улету́ч|иться (**-усь, -ишься**; *impf* **улету́чиваться**) *сов возв* (*также перен*) to evaporate; (*перен: разг*) to vanish.

улечу́ *сов см* **улете́ть**.

уле́чься (**-ягусь, -яжешься** *итп*, **-ягутся**; *pt* **-ёгся, -егла́сь, -егло́сь**, *impf* **укла́дываться**) *сов возв* to lie down; (*по impf; пыль*) to settle; (*перен: буря, страсти, гнев*) to subside.

улизн|у́ть (**-у́, -ёшь**) *сов неперех* (*разг*) to slip away.

ули́к|а (**-и**) *ж* (piece of) evidence (*мн* evidence); **ко́свенная/пряма́я ~** circumstantial/hard evidence.

ули́т|ка (**-ки**; *gen pl* **-ок**) *ж* snail.

у́лиц|а (**-ы**) *ж* (*в городе, в селе*) street; (*перен: некультурная среда*) the gutter; **на ~е** outside; **остава́ться (оста́ться** *perf*) **на ~е** to be out on the street; **выбра́сывать (вы́бросить** *perf*) **~у** (*выселить*) to throw sb out onto the streets.

уличи́ть (**-у́, -и́шь**; *impf* **улича́ть**) *сов перех*: **~ кого́-н в чём-н** to face sb with sth.

у́личный *прил* street *опред*; **у́личное движе́ние** traffic.

уло́в (**-а**) *м* catch (*of fish*).

улови́м|ый (**-, -а, -о**) *прил*: **едва́** *или* **чуть** *или* **éле ~** barely perceptible.

уло|ви́ть (**-овлю́, -о́вишь**; *impf* **ула́вливать**) *сов перех* (*звуки, шум, запах*) to catch, detect; (*перен: мысль, связь*) to catch, grasp; **ула́вливать** (**~** *perf*) **(подходя́щий) моме́нт** to find the right moment.

уло́в|ка (**-ки**; *gen pl* **-ок**) *ж* ruse.

уловлю́ *сов см* **улови́ть**.

уло́вок *сущ см* **уло́вка**.

ул|ожи́ть (**-ожу́, -о́жишь**; *impf* **укла́дывать**) *сов перех* (*ребёнка*) to put to bed; (*вещи, чемодан*) to pack; (*волосы*) to set; (*шпалы, рельсы*) to lay; (*бельё*) to fold away; (*по impf; разг*): **~ кого́-н на ме́сте** to kill sb; **хозя́йка ~ожи́ла нас в гости́ной** our hostess put us (up) in the living room
► **уложи́ться** (*impf* **укла́дываться**) *сов возв* (*сложить вещи*) to pack; **укла́дываться (~ся** *perf*) **в сро́ки** to keep to the deadline; **~ся (**perf**) в полчаса́** to keep it down to half an hour.

улома́|ть (**-ю**; *impf* **ула́мывать**) *сов перех* (*разг*): **~ кого́-н** to talk sb round; **ула́мывать** (**~** *perf*) **кого́-н** +*infin* to talk sb into doing.

у́лоч|ка (**-ки**; *gen pl* **-ек**) *ж* lane.

улучи́ть (**-у́, -и́шь**; *impf* **улуча́ть**) *сов перех* (*момент, полчаса*) to find.

улучша́|ть (**-ю**) *несов от* **улу́чшить**.

улучше́ни|е (**-я**) *ср* improvement.

улу́чш|ить (**-у, -ишь**; *impf* **улучша́ть**) *сов перех* to improve.

улыба́|ться (**-юсь**; *perf* **улыбну́ться**) *несов возв*: **~** +*dat* to smile at; (*перен: счастье, жизнь*) to smile on; **мне не ~ется э́та рабо́та/пое́здка** this work/trip doesn't appeal to me.

улы́б|ка (**-ки**; *gen pl* **-ок**) *ж* smile.

улыбну́ться (**-у́сь, -ёшься**) *сов от* **улыба́ться**.

улы́бок *сущ см* **улы́бка**.

улы́бчив|ый (**-, -а, -о**) *прил* smiley.

ультима́тум (**-а**) *м* ultimatum; **предъявля́ть (предъяви́ть** *perf*) **кому́-н ~** to give sb an ultimatum.

ультразву́к (**-а**) *м* ultrasound.

ультразвуково́й *прил* ultrasonic.

ультрамари́н (**-а**) *м* ultramarine.

ультрафиоле́тов|ый *прил*: **~ые лучи́** ultraviolet rays *мн*.

у́лья *итп сущ см* **у́лей**.

улюлю́ка|ть (**-ю**) *несов неперех* to halloo;

(перен) to hoot (*in derision*).
улягусь *итп сов см* **улечься**.
ум (-á) *м* mind; **быть** (*impf*) **без ~á от кого-н/чего-н** to be wild about sb/sth; **в ~é** (*считать, держать*) in one's head; **в своём ~é** in one's right mind; **браться** (**взяться** *perf*) **за ~** to see sense; **сходить** (**сойти** *perf*) **с ~á** to go mad; **сводить** (**свести** *perf*) **кого-н с ~á** to drive sb mad; (*перен: увлечь*) to drive sb wild; **природный ~** native wit; **~á не приложу, куда/сколько/кто** ... I can't think where/how much/who ...; **с ~óм** (*рассудительно*) sensibly; **приходить** (**прийти** *perf*) **на ~ кому-н** to come into sb's head.
умалить (-ю, -йшь; *impf* **умалять**) *сов перех* (*значение, роль*) to diminish, belittle.
умалишённый *прил* insane.
умалчивать (-ю) *несов от* **умолчать**.
умалять (-ю) *несов от* **умалить**.
умаяться (-юсь) *сов от* **маяться**.
умелец (-ьца) *м* skilled artisan.
умело *нареч* skilfully (*BRIT*), skillfully (*US*).
умелый (-, -а, -о) *прил* (*рука, ремесленник, политик*) skilful (*BRIT*), skillful (*US*); (*работник*) able.
умельца *итп сущ см* **умелец**.
умён *прил см* **умный**.
умение (-я) *ср* ability, skill; **с ~м** (*делать что-н*) with skill.
уменьшать(ся) (-ю(сь)) *несов от* **уменьшить(ся)**.
уменьшение (-я) *ср* reduction.
уменьшительный *прил* (*суффикс*) diminutive.
уменьшить (-у, -ишь; *impf* **уменьшать**) *сов перех* to reduce; **~** (*perf*) **шаг** to slow down
▸ **уменьшиться** (*impf* **уменьшаться**) *сов возв* (*объём, опасность*) to diminish, decrease.
умеренность (-и) *ж* moderateness; (*климата*) temperate nature.
умеренный (-, -на, -но) *прил* (*аппетит, скорость, политика*) moderate; (*no short form*; *климат, характер*) temperate.
умереть (-ру, -рёшь; *pt* -ер, -ерла, -ерло, *impf* **умирать**) *сов неперех* to die; (*традиция*) to die out; **хоть ~ри, но сделай** (*разг*) do it, even if it kills you; **~** (*perf*) **от голода/рака** to die of hunger/cancer; **со смеху ~ можно** (*разг*) I could die laughing.
умерить (-ю, -ишь; *impf* **умерять**) *сов перех* (*требования, желания*) to moderate; (*гнев*) to restrain.
умертвить (-щвлю, -твишь; *impf* **умерщвлять**) *сов перех* (*также перен*) to kill.
умерщвление (-я) *ср* killing.
умерщвлю *сов см* **умертвить**.
умерщвлять (-ю) *несов от* **умертвить**.
умерять (-ю) *несов от* **умерить**.

уместить (-щу, -стишь; *impf* **умещать**) *сов перех* to fit, find room for
▸ **уместиться** (*impf* **умещаться**) *сов возв* to fit; **мы все уместимся в машину** there's room for all of us in the car; **мои вещи не ~щаются в чемодан** my things won't fit in my suitcase.
уметь (-ю) *несов неперех* can, to be able to; (*иметь способность*) to know how to; **он ~ет плавать/читать** he can swim/read; **Мария ~ет хорошо одеваться** Maria knows how to dress well.
умещать(ся) (-ю(сь)) *несов от* **уместить(ся)**.
умещу(сь) *сов см* **уместить(ся)**.
умеючи *нареч* (*разг*): **это надо делать ~** you need to have the knack (to do this).
умиление (-я) *ср* tenderness; **слёзы ~я** fond tears.
умилительный (-ен, -ьна, -ьно) *прил* touching.
умилить (-ю, -йшь; *impf* **умилять**) *сов перех* to touch
▸ **умилиться** (*impf* **умиляться**) *сов возв* to be touched.
умильный *прил* (*нежный*) touching; (*льстивый*) smarmy.
умилять(ся) (-ю(сь)) *несов от* **умилить(ся)**.
уминать (-ю) *несов от* **умять**.
умирание (-я) *ср* dying.
умирать (-ю) *несов от* **умереть** ◆ *неперех* (*перен*): **~ю, как хочу есть/спать** I'm dying for something to eat/to go to sleep; **я ~ю от скуки** I'm bored to death.
умиротворение (-я) *ср* (*сердца, души*) bringing of peace; (*агрессора*) appeasement.
умиротворённый *прил* serene, tranquil.
умиротворить (-ю, -йшь; *impf* **умиротворять**) *сов перех* (*душу*) to bring peace to; (*враждующих*) to pacify; (*агрессора*) to appease
▸ **умиротвориться** (*impf* **умиротворяться**) *сов возв* (*враждующие, спорщики итп*) to be pacified.
умнеть (-ю; *perf* **поумнеть**) *несов неперех* (*человек*) to grow wiser; (*ребёнок*) to become more intelligent; **это поможет тебе поумнеть** (*перен*) that'll teach you a lesson.
умник (-а) *м* clever boy; (*пренебр: умничающий*) clever dick, knowall.
умница (-ы) *ж* clever girl ◆ *м/ж* (*разг*): **вот ~!** good for you!, well done!; **он ~** he's a clever one.
умничать (-ю) *несов неперех* (*разг: пренебр*) to show off how clever one is, be clever; (*своевольничать*) to try to be clever.
умно *нареч* (*вести себя*) sensibly; (*говорить*) intelligently.
умножать (-ю) *несов от* **умножить**.
умножение (-я) *ср* (*см глаг*) multiplication; increase; **таблица ~я** (*МАТ*) multiplication table.

The spelling rules for Russian are shown on page xvii.

умно́ж|ить (-у, -ишь; *impf* **мно́жить** *или* **умножа́ть**) *сов перех* (МАТ) to multiply; (*доходы, опыт, сла́ву итп*) to increase; **умножа́ть** (~ *perf*) **пять на́ два** to multiply five by two
▸ **умно́житься** *сов от* **мно́житься**.
умну́ *итп сов см* **умя́ть**.
у́м|ный (-ён, -на́, -но́ *или* -но) *прил* (*челове́к*) clever, intelligent; (*лицо́*) intelligent; (*соба́ка, маши́на, прибо́р*) clever; (*ре́чи, сове́т, поли́тика*) sensible.
умозаключе́ни|е (-я) *ср* (*вы́вод*) deduction.
умозри́тельный (-ен, -ьна, -ьно) *прил* (*построе́ние, рассужде́ния*) speculative.
умол|и́ть (-ю́, -ишь; *impf* **умоля́ть**) *сов перех*: ~ **кого́-н** (+*infin*) to prevail upon sb (to do) (*by pleading*).
у́молк *м*: **без ~у** incessantly.
умо́лкн|уть (-у, -ешь; *impf* **умолка́ть**) *сов непере́х* (*го́лос, скри́пка*) to fall silent; (*смех, звон*) to stop.
умолча́ни|е (-я) *ср* (*фа́ктов*) supression, hushing up.
умолч|а́ть (-у́, -и́шь; *impf* **ума́лчивать**) *сов непере́х*: ~ **о чём-н** (*о преступле́нии, о недоста́тках итп*) to keep quiet about sth.
умоля́|ть (-ю) *несов от* **умоли́ть** ♦ *перех* to implore.
умоля́ющий (-ая, -ее, -ие) *прил* (*взгляд, го́лос*) pleading.
умонастрое́ни|е (-я) *ср* frame of mind.
умопомеша́тельств|о (-а) *ср* insanity.
умопомраче́ни|е (-я) *ср* temporary loss of one's senses; **до ~я** (*уста́ть*) terribly; (*люби́ть, влюби́ться*) madly; **рабо́тать** (*impf*)/**танцева́ть** (*impf*) **до ~я** to work/dance until one is ready to drop.
умопомрачи́тельный (-ен, -ьна, -ьно) *прил* (*разг: красота́, бога́тство*) staggering.
умо́р|а *ж нескл*: **э́то про́сто ~** (*разг*) it's hilarious.
умори́тельный (-ен, -ьна, -ьно) *прил* (*разг*) hilarious.
умор|и́ть (-ю́, -и́шь) *сов от* **мори́ть**.
умота́|ть (-ю) *сов от* **мота́ть**.
умру́ *итп сов см* **умере́ть**.
умо́ю(сь) *сов см* **умы́ть(ся)**.
у́мственно *наре́ч*: ~ **отста́лый** mentally retarded.
у́мственный *прил* (*спосо́бности*) mental; ~ **труд** brainwork.
умудр|ённый (-ён, -ена́, -ено́) *прил*: ~ **о́пытом/года́ми** wise from experience/with age.
умудр|и́ться (-ю́сь, -и́шься; *impf* **умудря́ться**) *сов возв* (*разг*) to manage; **я ~и́лся простуди́ться/опозда́ть на по́езд** I managed to catch a cold/miss the train.
умч|а́ть (-у́, -и́шь) *сов перех* to whisk off *или* away
▸ **умча́ться** *сов возв* (*ко́ни, вса́дники, де́ти*) to

dash off; (*го́ды, де́тство*) to fly by.
умыва́льник (-а) *м* washstand.
умыва́льн|ый *прил*: ~**ые принадле́жности** washing things *мн*.
умыва́ни|е (-я) *ср* washing.
умыва́|ть(ся) (-ю(сь)) *несов от* **умы́ть(ся)**.
умыкн|у́ть (-у́, -ёшь; *impf* **умыка́ть**) *сов перех* (*разг: укра́сть*) to nick; (*неве́сту*) to abduct (*as part of wedding ritual*).
у́мыс|ел (-ла) *м* intent; **де́лать** (**сде́лать** *perf*) **что-н без ~ла/с у́мыслом** to do sth without/with intent.
умы́ть (умо́ю, умо́ешь; *impf* **умыва́ть**) *сов перех* to wash
▸ **умы́ться** (*impf* **умыва́ться**) *сов возв* to wash.
умы́шленно *наре́ч* deliberately, intentionally.
умы́шленность (-и) *ж* (*посту́пка*) deliberateness; (*преступле́ния*) premeditated nature.
умы́шлен|ный (-, -на, -но) *прил* (*посту́пок*) deliberate, intentional; (*преступле́ние, уби́йство*) premeditated.
ум|я́ть (-ну́, -нёшь; *impf* **умина́ть**) *сов перех* (*снег, зе́млю*) to flatten; (*разг: съесть мно́го*) to stuff down.
унаво́|зить (-жу, -зишь) *сов от* **наво́зить**.
унасле́д|овать (-ую) *сов от* **насле́довать**.
ун|ести́ (-есу́, -есёшь; *pt* -ёс, -есла́, -есло́, *impf* **уноси́ть**) *сов перех* to take away; (*разг: укра́сть*) to carry off; (*подлеж: война́, эпиде́мия*) to claim; **ло́дку ~есло́ тече́нием** the boat drifted away; **бума́ги ~есло́ ве́тром** the papers blew away
▸ **унести́сь** (*impf* **уноси́ться**) *сов возв* (*ту́чи, ко́ни, по́езд*) to speed off; **мои́ мы́сли ~если́сь в про́шлое** his thoughts flashed back to the past; **он ~ёсся в мир фанта́зий** he was carried into the world of fantasy.
универма́г (-а) *м* (= **универса́льный магази́н**) department store.
универса́л (-а) *м* all-rounder.
универса́льность (-и) *ж* (*зна́ний*) breadth; (*средств*) universality.
универса́льный *прил* (*пробле́ма*) universal; (*образова́ние*) all-round; (*челове́к*) versatile, multitalented; (*зна́ния*) encyclopaedic (*BRIT*), encyclopedic (*US*); (*маши́на, инструме́нт*) versatile, multipurpose; ~**ое сре́дство** cure-all; ~**ая вычисли́тельная маши́на** (*КОМП*) mainframe; ~ **си́мвол** (*КОМП*) wildcard; **универса́льный магази́н** department store.
универса́м (-а) *м* supermarket.
университе́т (-а) *м* university.
университе́тский (-ая, -ое, -ие) *прил* university *опред*.
унижа́|ть(ся) (-ю(сь)) *несов от* **уни́зить(ся)**.
униже́ни|е (-я) *ср* humiliation; **идти́** (**пойти́** *perf*) **на ~** to humble o.s.
униже́н|ный (-, -на, -но) *прил* (*челове́к*) humbled; (*взгляд, про́сьба*) humble.
уни́жу(сь) *сов см* **уни́зить(ся)**.

уни зать (-ижу, -ижешь; *impf* унизывать) *сов перех* to string; (*пояс: жемчугом*) to stud.
унизителен *прил см* унизительный.
унизительность (-и) *ж* humiliation.
унизительный (-ен, -ьна, -ьно) *прил* humiliating, degrading.
унизить (-жу, -зишь; *impf* унижать) *сов перех* to humiliate; унижать (~ *perf*) себя to abase o.s.
▶ унизиться (*impf* унижаться) *сов возв*: ~ся (перед +*instr*) to abase o.s. (before).
унизывать (-ю) *несов от* унизать.
уникальный (-ен, -ьна, -ьно) *прил* unique.
уникум (-а) *м*: он настоящий ~ he's one of a kind.
унимать(ся) (-ю(сь)) *несов от* унять(ся).
унисон (-а) *м* unison; в ~ (с +*instr*) (*также перен*) in unison (with).
унитаз (-а) *м* toilet.
унификация (-и) *ж* standardization.
унифицировать (-ую) (*не*)*сов перех* to standardize.
униформа (-ы) *ж* (*одежда*) uniform.
уничижать (-ю) *несов перех* to disparage.
уничижительный (-ен, -ьна, -ьно) *прил* disparaging.
уничтожать (-ю) *несов от* уничтожить.
уничтожающий (-ая, -ее, -ие) *прил* (*огонь, удар, критика*) devastating; (*взгляд*) scathing, withering.
уничтожить (-у, -ишь; *impf* уничтожать) *сов перех* to destroy; (*насекомых, вредителей*) to exterminate; (*память о чём-н, следы*) to wipe out; (*безработицу, преступность итп*) to do away with; (*перен: унизить*) to crush.
уносить(ся) (-ошу(сь), -осишь(ся)) *несов от* унести(сь).
унтер-офицер (-а) *м* non-commissioned officer.
унция (-и) *ж* ounce.
унывать (-ю) *несов неперех* (*человек*) to be downcast *или* despondent; (*впадать в уныние*) to lose heart.
уныло *нареч* despondently.
унылый *прил* (*человек*) despondent; (*мысли*) depressing; (*природа*) cheerless, dreary.
уныние (-я) *ср* despondency.
унять (уйму, уймёшь; *pt* -л, -ла, -ло, *impf* унимать) *сов перех* (*ребёнка, хулигана*) to restrain; (*слёзы, волнение*) to suppress.
▶ уняться (*impf* униматься) *сов возв* (*ребёнок, шалун итп*) to calm down; (*буря, боль*) to die down.
упавший (-ая, -ее, -ие) *прил* (*голос*) fallen.
упад (-у) *м*: мы танцевали до ~у (*разг*) we danced till we were ready to drop; я смеялся до ~у (*разг*) I laughed my head off.
упадок (-ка) *м* decline; ~ сил exhaustion; ~ духа despondency.

упадочнический (-ая, -ое, -ие) *прил* decadent.
упаду *итп сов см* упасть.
упаковать (-ую) *сов от* паковать.
упаковка (-и) *ж* packing; (*паковочный материал*) packaging.
упаковочный *прил* packaging *опред*.
упаковывать (-ю; *perf* упаковать) *несов* = паковать ♦ *перех* (*КОМП*) to pack.
упаковщик (-а) *м* packer.
упаковщица (-ы) *ж см* упаковщик.
упасти *сов перех*: упаси Бог *или* Боже *или* Господи! God forbid!
упасть (-ду, -дёшь) *сов от* падать ♦ *неперех*: ~ в ноги кому-н to go down on one's knees to sb.
упекать (-ю) *несов от* упечь.
упеку *итп сов см* упечь.
упереть (упру, упрёшь; *pt* упёр, упёрла, упёрло, *impf* упирать) *сов перех* (*разг: украсть*) to nick, pinch; упирать (~ *perf*) что-н в +*acc* (*в стену итп*) to prop sth against
▶ упереться (*impf* упираться) *сов возв*: ~ся чем-н в +*acc* (*в землю*) to dig sth into; (*в плот*) to stick sth into; (*натолкнуться на преграду*): ~ся в +*acc* (*в ограду, в забор итп*) to come up against; (*перен: взглядом, глазами*) to stare; упираться (~ся *perf*) (на +*prp*) (*перен: разг: настоять*) to dig one's heels in.
упечь (-ку, -чёшь итп, -кут; *impf* упекать) *сов перех* (*разг: в тюрьму*) to fling.
упиваться (-юсь) *несов от* упиться.
упирать (-ю) *несов от* упереть
▶ упираться *несов от* упереться ♦ *возв* (*иметь причиной*): ~ся в +*prp* to arise from.
упитанный (-, на, -но) *прил* plump.
упиться (-ьюсь, -ьёшься; *impf* упиваться) *сов возв* (*разг: напиться допьяна*) to get very drunk; (*перен*): ~ +*instr* (*счастьем, свободой итп*) to be intoxicated by; (: *чьим-н несчастьем*) to revel in.
УПК *м сокр* (= Уголовно-процессуальный кодекс) criminal code.
уплата (-ы) *ж* payment.
уплатить (-ачу, -атишь) *сов от* платить.
уплачивать (-ю; *perf* уплатить) *несов перех* = платить.
уплачу *сов см* уплатить.
уплести (-ету, -етёшь) *сов от* уплетать.
уплетать (-ю) *несов перех* (*разг*) to tuck *или* get stuck into.
уплотнение (-я) *ср* (*почвы, снега*) compression; (*под кожей*) lump (*ANAT*).
уплотнить (-ю, -йшь; *impf* уплотнять) *сов перех* (*также перен*) to compress
▶ уплотниться (*impf* уплотняться) *сов возв* (*песок, грунт*) to become firmer; (*рабочий день, график*) to become busier.
уплыть (-ву, -вёшь; *pt* -л, -ла, -ло, *impf*

уплыва́ть) *сов непврех* (*человек, рыба итп*) to swim away *или* off; (*пароход*) to sail away *или* off; (*плавно уйти*) to float away *или* off; (*перен: пройти*) to pass; (: *разг: деньги, наследство итп*) to vanish.

упова́ни|е (-я) *ср* hope; возлага́ть (*impf*) ~я на +*acc* to set one's hopes on.

упова́|ть (-ю) *несов непврех*: ~ на +*acc* to count on.

уподо́б|ить (-лю, -ишь; *impf* уподобля́ть) *сов перех*: ~ что-н/кого́-н +*dat* to compare sth/sb to
► уподо́биться (*impf* уподобля́ться) *сов возв*: ~ся +*dat* to become like.

упое́ни|е (-я) *ср* elation; с ~м with relish.

упоённ|ый (-ён, -ена́, -ено́) *прил*: ~ +*instr* (*успехом итп*) elated by; (*счастьем*) intoxicated with.

упои́тел|ьный (-ен, -ьна, -ьно) *прил* (*воздух*) intoxicating; (*поцелуй*) rapturous.

упоко́|й (-я) *м*: моли́тва за ~ (*души́*) кого́-н prayer for sb's eternal rest.

уполз|ти́ (-у́, -ёшь; *pt* -, -ла́, -ло́) *сов непврех* (*змея*) to slither away; (*червь*) to wriggle away; (*ребёнок*) to crawl away.

уполномо́ченная (-ой; *decl like adj*) *ж см* уполномо́ченный

уполномо́ченн|ый (-ого; *decl like adj*) *м* authorized person.

уполномо́ч|ить (-у, -ишь; *impf* уполномо́чивать) *сов перех*: ~ кого́-н +*infin* to authorize sb to do.

упомина́ни|е (-я) *ср* (*см глаг*) mention; reference.

упомина́|ть (-ю) *несов от* упомяну́ть
► упомина́ться *несов непврех* (*имя, событие*) to be mentioned.

упом|яну́ть (-яну́, -я́нешь; *impf* упомина́ть) *сов* (*не*)*перех* (*назвать*): ~ +*acc или* о +*prp* to mention; (*коснуться*) to refer to.

упо́р (-а) *м* (*для ног, для рук*) rest; в ~ (*стрелять*) point-blank; (*смотреть*) intently; де́лать (сде́лать *perf*) ~ на +*prp* to put emphasis on.

упо́рно *нареч* persistently.

упо́р|ный (-ен, -на, -но) *прил* persistent; (*сопротивление*) unrelenting.

упо́рств|о (-а) *ср* persistence.

упо́рств|овать (-ую) *несов непврех* to persist *или* be persistent.

упорхн|у́ть (-у́, -ёшь) *сов непврех* (*также перен*) to flit away.

упоря́дочени|е (-я) *ср* (*корреспонденции, информации*) sorting; (*торговли, процедуры*) regulation.

упоря́доченн|ый *прил* ordered.

упоря́доч|ить (-у, -ишь; *impf* упоря́дочивать) *сов перех* to put in order; (*цены, процедуру*) to regulate
► упоря́дочиться (*impf* упоря́дочиваться) *сов возв* (*дела*) to be put in order; (*процедура*) to be regulated.

употреби́телен *прил см* употреби́тельный.

употреби́тельност|ь (-и) *ж* frequency (*of use*).

употреби́тел|ьный (-ен, -ьна, -ьно) *прил* frequently used.

употреб|и́ть (-лю, -и́шь; *impf* употребля́ть) *сов перех* to use; употребля́ть (~ *perf*) что-н в пи́щу to eat sth.

употребле́ни|е (-я) *ср* (*лекарства, наркотиков*) taking; (*алкоголя*) consumption; (*слова, термина*) usage; находи́ться (*impf*) в ~и to be in use; выходи́ть (вы́йти *perf*) из ~я (*слово*) to go out of usage; вводи́ть (ввести́ *perf*) в ~ (*слово*) to introduce; (*одежду, предмет быта*) to bring into use.

употреблю́ *сов см* употреби́ть.

употребля́|ть (-ю) *несов от* употреби́ть
► употребля́ться *несов возв* to be used.

упр. *сокр* (= управле́ние) admin (= *administration*).

упра́в|а (-ы) *ж* (*ист*) office; (*разг: мера пресечения*): иска́ть ~у to seek justice; найти́ (*perf*) ~у на кого́-н to make sure that sb is punished; на него́ нет ~ы there's no control over him.

упра́в|иться (-люсь, -ишься; *impf* управля́ться) *сов возв*: ~ с +*instr* (*разг: с делами, с уборкой*) to manage; (*с шалуном, с плохи́м учеником*) to deal with.

управле́ни|е (-я) *ср* (*судном, самолётом*) navigation; (*делами, финансами*) administration; (*оркестром, хором*) conducting; (*учреждение*) office; (*система приборов*) controls *мн*; симфо́ния испо́лнена под ~м а́втора the symphony was conducted by the composer; теря́ть (потеря́ть *perf*) ~ to lose control.

управле́нческ|ий (-ая, -ое, -ие) *прил*: ~ аппара́т ruling body.

управлю́сь *сов см* упра́виться.

управля́ем|ый (-, -а, -о) *прил*: ~ая раке́та guided missile; ~ (с по́мощью) меню́ (*комп*) menu-driven.

управля́|ть (-ю) *несов непврех*: ~ +*instr* (*автомобилем*) to drive; (*судном*) to navigate; (*конём*) to ride; (*государством*) to govern; (*учреждением, фирмой итп*) to manage; (*оркестром, хором*) to conduct
► управля́ться *несов от* упра́виться.

управля́ющ|ий (-его; *decl like adj*) *м* (*хозяйством*) manager; (*имением, поместьем*) bailiff.

упражне́ни|е (-я) *ср* (*мускулов, памяти*) exercising; (*грамматические, гимнастические*) exercise.

упражня́|ть (-ю) *несов перех* to exercise
► упражня́ться *несов возв* to practise.

упраздн|и́ть (-ю́, -и́шь; *impf* упраздня́ть) *сов перех* to abolish.

упра́шива|ть (-ю) *несов от* упроси́ть.

упрёк (-а) *м* reproach; броса́ть (бро́сить *perf*) ~ кому́-н to reproach sb; ста́вить (поста́вить *perf*) **что-н в ~ кому-н** to hold sth against sb.

упрека|ть (-ю; *perf* **упрекнуть**) *несов перех*: ~ **кого-н (в** +*prp*) to reproach sb (for).

упр|осить (-ошу, -осишь; *impf* **упрашивать**) *сов перех*: ~ **кого-н** +*infin* to persuade sb to do.

упро|стить (-щу, -стишь; *impf* **упрощать**) *сов перех* to simplify; (*сделать слишком простым*) to oversimplify

▶ **упроститься** (*impf* **упрощаться**) *сов возв* to become simpler.

упрочени|е (-я) *ср* consolidation.

упроч|ить (-у, -ишь; *impf* **упрочивать**) *сов перех* to consolidate

▶ **упрочиться** (*impf* **упрочиваться**) *сов возв* (*работник*) to establish o.s.; (*положение, позиции*) to be consolidated; (*перен*): **за ним ~илась репутация хорошего редактора** his reputation as a good editor was established.

упрошу *сов см* **упросить**.

упроща|ть(ся) (-ю(сь)) *несов от* **упростить(ся)**.

упрощени|е (-я) *ср* simplification.

упрощённый *прил* (*простой*) simplified; (*излишне простой*) oversimplified.

упрощу(сь) *сов см* **упростить(ся)**.

упру(сь) *итп сов см* **упереть(ся)**.

упруг|ий (-ая, -ое, -ие; -, -а, -о) *прил* (*пружина, тело*) elastic; (*походка, движения*) bouncy, springy.

упругост|ь (-и) *ж* (*пружины, мышц*) elasticity; (*походки*) springiness.

упря|жка (-ки; *gen pl* -ек) *ж* team (*of horses, dogs etc*); (*упряжь*) harness.

упряж|ь (-и) *ж* (*no pl*) harness.

упря́м|ец (-ца) *м* stubborn person (*мн* people).

упря́м|иться (-люсь, -ишься) *несов возв* to be obstinate *или* stubborn.

упря́миц|а (-ы) *ж см* **упря́мец**.

упря́мо *нареч* (*сказать*) obstinately, stubbornly; (*искать*) persistently.

упря́мств|о (-а) *ср* obstinacy, stubbornness.

упря́мца *итп сущ см* **упря́мец**.

упря́м|ый (-, -а, -о) *прил* obstinate, stubborn; (*поиски, стремление*) persistent.

упря́|тать (-чу, -чешь) *сов перех* (*разг*) to put away.

упуска|ть (-ю; *perf* **упустить**) *несов перех* (*мяч*) to let go of; (*момент, случай*) to miss; ~ **(упустить** *perf*) **из виду** to overlook.

уп|устить (-ущу, -устишь) *сов от* **упускать**.

упущени|е (-я) *ср* omission.

упыр|ь (-я) *м* vampire.

упью́сь *итп сов см* **упиться**.

ура́ *межд* hooray, hurrah; **на ~** (*с энтузиазмом*) enthusiastically; (*без подготовки*) just like that.

уравнени|е (-я) *ср* (*сил*) equalization; (*МАТ*) equation.

уравнива|ть (-ю) *несов от* **уравнять**,

уровнять.

уравни|ловка (-и) *ж* (*разг: пренебр*) equal rewarding regardless of contribution.

уравнове́|сить (-шу, -сишь; *impf* **уравнове́шивать**) *сов перех* to balance

▶ **уравнове́ситься** (*impf* **уравнове́шиваться**) *сов возв* (*чаши весов*) to balance; (*силы*) to be counterbalanced.

уравнове́шенность (-и) *ж* composure.

уравнове́шен|ный (-, -на, -но) *прил* balanced, steady.

уравнове́шива|ть(ся) (-ю(сь)) *несов от* **уравнове́сить(ся)**.

уравнове́шу(сь) *сов см* **уравнове́сить(ся)**.

уравня́|ть (-ю; *impf* **ура́внивать**) *сов перех* (*размеры, доли итп*) to make equal; **ура́внивать (~** *perf*) **кого-н в права́х с кем-н** to give sb the same rights as sb.

урага́н (-а) *м* hurricane; (*перен: страстей*) storm.

урага́нный *прил*: ~ **ве́тер** gale.

Уралма́ш (-а) *м сокр* = **Ура́льский машинострои́тельный заво́д**.

ура́н (-а) *м* uranium; (*планета*): **У~** Uranus.

ура́новый *прил* uranium.

ура-патрио́т (-а) *м* (*пренебр*) jingoist.

ура-патриоти́зм (-а) *м* jingoism.

урбаниза́ци|я (-и) *ж* urbanization.

урв|а́ть (-у́, -ёшь; *impf* **урыва́ть**) *сов перех* (*разг: материальные блага*) to grab; (: *время*) to snatch.

урегули́ровани|е (-я) *ср* settlement.

урегули́р|овать (-ую) *сов от* **регули́ровать** ♦ *перех* (*отношения*) to put to rights; (*конфликт*) to settle.

уре́жу *итп сов см* **уре́зать**.

уре́занный *прил* (*демокра́тия, свобо́да*) limited.

уре́|зать (-жу, -жешь; *impf* **уреза́ть**) *сов перех* (*расходы, штаты*) to cut down.

урезо́н|ить (-ю, -ишь; *impf* **урезо́нивать**) *сов перех*: ~ **кого-н** (*разг*) to make sb see reason.

уреми́|я (-и) *ж* uraemia (*BRIT*), uremia (*US*).

уре́тр|а (-ы) *ж* urethra.

у́рн|а (-ы) *ж* (*погреба́льная*) urn; (*для мусора, для окурков*) bin; **избира́тельная ~** ballot box.

у́ров|ень (-ня) *м* level; (*техники*) standard; (*зарплаты, доходов*) rate; **в ~ с** +*instr* on a level with; **на ~не земли́** at ground level; **встре́ча на вы́сшем ~не** summit meeting; **вы́ше/ни́же ~ня мо́ря** above/below sea level; **моя́ рабо́та была́ на ~не** my work was up to standard; **у́ровень жи́зни** living standard.

уровня́|ть (-ю; *impf* **ура́внивать**) *сов перех* (*дорогу, зе́млю*) to level.

уро́д (-а) *м* person with a deformity; (*нра́вственный*) monster.

уро́дин|а (-ы) *м/ж* ugly person (*мн* people).

уро|ди́ться (-жу́сь, -ди́шься) *сов возв* (*пшеница*) to give a good yield; ~ (*perf*) **в кого́-н** (*в де́да, в отца́* итп) to take after sb.

уро́д|ка (-ки; *gen pl* -ок) *ж см* уро́д.

уро́дливост|ь (-и) *ж* (*см прил*) deformity; distortion; ugliness.

уро́длив|ый (-, -а, -о) *прил* (*с уро́дством*) deformed; (*представле́ние*) distorted; (*безобра́зный*) ugly.

уро́д|овать (-ую; *perf* изуро́довать) *несов перех* (*кале́чить*) to deform; (*де́лать некраси́вым*) to make ugly; (*созна́ние*) to distort; (*ду́шу, мо́лодёжь*) to corrupt.

уро́дств|о (-а) *ср* (*физи́ческий недоста́ток*) deformity; (*некраси́вая вне́шность*) ugliness.

урожа́|й (-я) *м* (*зерна́, карто́феля* итп) harvest; (*большо́е коли́чество*) abundance; **снима́ть (снять** *perf***) и́ли собира́ть (собра́ть** *perf***)** ~ to gather the harvest; **убира́ть (убра́ть** *perf***)** ~ to take in the harvest.

урожа́йност|ь (-и) *ж* yield.

урожа́йный *прил* (*год*) productive.

урождённая *прил* née.

уроже́н|ец (-ца) *м* native.

урожу́сь *сов см* уроди́ться.

уро́к (-а) *м* lesson; (*зада́ние*) task; (*обы́чно мн: дома́шняя рабо́та*) homework *ед*; **де́лать (сде́лать** *perf***)** ~**и** to do one's homework; **э́то послу́жит тебе́ хоро́шим** ~**ом** let it be a (good) lesson to you; **брать** (*impf*) ~**и чего́-н у кого́-н** to take lessons in sth from sb; **дава́ть** (*impf*) ~ to give a lesson; **дава́ть** (*impf*) ~**и где́-нибудь/ кому́-н** to teach somewhere/sb.

уро́лог (-а) *м* urologist.

урологи́ческ|ий (-ая, -ое, -ие) *прил* urological.

уроло́ги|я (-и) *ж* urology.

уро́н (-а) *м* (*поте́ри*) losses *мн*; **нести́ (понести́** *perf***)** ~ to suffer losses; **наноси́ть (нанести́** *perf***) кому́-н** ~ to inflict loss on sb.

уро́н|ить (-оню́, -о́нишь) *сов от* роня́ть.

уро́чищ|е (-а) *ср* natural boundary.

Уругва́|й (-я) *м* Uruguay.

уругва́йск|ий (-ая, -ое, -ие) *прил* Uruguayan.

урча́ни|е (-я) *ср* (*воды́*) gurgling; (*соба́ки*) growling; (*ко́шки*) purring.

урча́|ть (-у́, -и́шь) *несов неперех* (*вода́*) to gurgle; (*тигр*) to growl; (*ко́шка*) to purr; **у меня́** ~**ит в желу́дке** my tummy's rumbling.

урыва́|ть (-ю) *несов от* урва́ть.

уры́вками *нареч* at odd times.

урю́к (-а) *м собир* dried apricots *мн*.

ус (-а) *м* whisker; *см та́кже* усы́.

усади́ть (-ажу́, -а́дишь; *impf* уса́живать) *сов перех*: ~ **госте́й** to show the guests to their seats; (*заста́вить де́лать*): ~ **кого́-н за что-н**/+*infin* to sit sb down to sth/to do; **уса́живать** (~ *perf*) **сад цвета́ми** to plant the garden with lots of flowers.

уса́дьб|а (-ы) *ж* (*поме́щичья*) country estate; (*крестья́нская*) farmstead.

уса́жива|ть (-ю) *несов от* усади́ть

▸ уса́живаться *несов от* усе́сться.

усажу́ *сов см* усади́ть.

уса́т|ый (-, -а, -о) *прил*: ~ **мужчи́на** man with a moustache; ~ **кот** cat with whiskers.

усва́ива|ть (-ю) *несов от* усво́ить.

усвое́ни|е (-я) *ср* (*уро́ка, нау́ки*) mastering; (*пи́щи*) assimilation.

усво́|ить (-ю, -ишь; *impf* усва́ивать) *сов перех* (*привы́чку*) to acquire; (*уро́к*) to master; (*пи́щу, лека́рство*) to assimilate.

усвоя́емост|ь (-и) *ж* assimilability.

усёк итп *сов см* усе́чь.

усека́|ть (-ю) *несов от* усе́чь.

усеку́ итп *сов см* усе́чь.

усе́рден *прил см* усе́рдный.

усе́рди|е (-я) *ср* diligence.

усе́рдн|ый (-ен, -на, -но) *прил* diligent.

усе́рдств|овать (-ую) *несов неперех* to make an effort.

усе́сться (-я́дусь, -я́дешься; *pt* -е́лся, -е́лась, -е́лось, *impf* уса́живаться) *сов возв* to settle down; (*заня́ться чем-н*): ~ **за** +*acc* (*за рабо́ту, за письмо́*) to sit down to.

усе́|чь (-ку́, -че́шь итп, -ку́т; *pt* -ёк, -екла́, -екло́, *impf* усека́ть) *сов перех* (*укороти́ть*) to truncate; (*разг: поня́ть*) to catch on to.

усе́|ять (-ю) *сов перех* (*по́ле, не́бо*) to cover

▸ усе́яться *сов возв*: ~**ся** +*instr* to be dotted *или* strewn with; (*цвета́ми*) to be full of.

усиде́|ть (-жу́, -ди́шь) *сов неперех* (*оста́ться сиде́ть*) to stay sitting; (*не упа́сть*) to stay in one's seat; **он е́ле** ~**де́л на ме́сте** he could hardly sit still; **он не мог** ~ **до́ма** he couldn't just sit at home.

уси́дчивост|ь (-и) *ж* assiduity.

уси́дчив|ый (-, -а, -о) *прил* assiduous.

усижу́ *сов см* усиде́ть.

у́сик|и (-ов; *nom sg* -) *мн* (*ма́ленькие усы́*) small moustache *ед*; (*у расте́ний*) tendril *ед*; (*у членистоно́гих*) feelers *мн*.

уси́ленн|ый *прил* (*охра́на*) reinforced; (*про́сьбы, напомина́ния*) persistent; (*внима́ние*) increased; ~**ое пита́ние** high calorie diet.

уси́лива|ть(ся) (-ю(сь)) *несов от* уси́лить(ся).

уси́ли|е (-я) *ср* effort; (*физи́ческое*) exertion; **де́лать (сде́лать** *perf***)** ~ **над собо́й** to force o.s.

уси́лит|ель (-я) *м* amplifier.

уси́лительный *прил* amplifying.

уси́л|ить (-ю, -ишь; *impf* уси́ливать) *сов перех* to intensify; (*охра́ну*) to reinforce; (*внима́ние*) to increase; (*звук*) to amplify

▸ уси́литься (*impf* уси́ливаться) *сов возв* (*ве́тер*) to get stronger; (*сопротивле́ние*) to intensify; (*волне́ние*) to increase.

уска́ка|ть (-ачу́, -а́чешь) *сов неперех* (*ко́ни*) to gallop away *или* off; (*перен: разг: челове́к*) to whizz off.

ускользну́|ть (-у́, -ёшь; *impf* ускольза́ть) *сов неперех* (*ры́ба, змея́* итп) to slip off; (*перен*): ~ **из** +*gen*/**от** +*gen* to slip out of/away from; **ускольза́ть** (~ *perf*) **от чьего́-н внима́ния** to escape sb's attention.

ускоре́ни|е (-я) *ср* acceleration; (*шага*) quickening.

ускоренный *прил* (*шаг*) quickened; (*дыхание, пульс, темпы*) accelerated; ~ **курс** crash course.

ускори́тел|ь (-я) *м* accelerator; **раке́тный** ~ rocket booster.

уско́р|ить (-ю, -ишь; *impf* **ускоря́ть**) *сов перех* (*шаги*) to quicken; (*ход механизма, прогресс*) to accelerate; (*выздоровление, отъезд*) to be speeded up

► **ускори́ться** (*impf* **ускоря́ться**) *сов возв* (*ход поезда*) to accelerate; (*шаги*) to quicken; (*отъезд, решение вопроса*) to speed up.

услáвлива|ться (-юсь) *несов от* **усло́виться**.

услáд|а (-ы) *ж* delight, joy.

услад|и́ть (-жу́, -ди́шь; *impf* **услажда́ть**) *сов перех* (*слух, зрение*) to delight

► **услади́ться** (*impf* **услажда́ться**) *сов возв*: ~**ся** +*instr* (*зрелищем, ароматом*) to delight in.

усл|а́ть (ушлю́, ушлёшь; *impf* **усыла́ть**) *сов перех* (*курьера, слуг*) to dispatch; (*на каторгу*) to send away.

услед|и́ть (-жу́, -ди́шь) *сов неперех*: ~ **за** +*instr* (*за ребёнком*) to keep an eye on; (*за ходом разговора*) to follow.

усло́вен *прил см* **усло́вный**.

усло́ви|е (-я) *ср* condition; (*договора, платежа*) term; (*соглашение*) agreement; (*обычно мн: поступления в институт, приёма на работу*) requirement; **ста́вить** (**поста́вить** *perf*) **что-н** ~**м** to make sth a condition; **при** ~**и хоро́шей пого́ды** on the condition that the weather is good; **при** ~**и, что он согласи́тся** on the condition *или* provided that he agrees; *см также* **усло́вия**.

усло́в|иться (-люсь, -ишься; *impf* **усла́вливаться**) *сов возв*: ~ **о** +*prp* (*договориться*) to agree on.

усло́ви|я (-й) *мн* (*природные*) conditions *мн*; (*задачи, теоремы*) factors *мн*; (*пользования чем-н, какого-н режима*) terms *мн*; **жили́щные** ~ housing; ~ **труда́** working conditions; **в** ~**х** +*gen* in an atmosphere of; **по** ~**м догово́ра** on the terms of the agreement; **на льго́тных** ~**х** on special terms; **на сле́дующих** ~**х** on the following conditions; **для рабо́ты здесь – все** ~ (*разг*) everything you need for working here is laid on.

усло́вленный *прил* agreed.

усло́влюсь *сов см* **усло́виться**.

усло́вност|ь (-и) *ж* conditional nature; (*обычай*) convention.

усло́в|ный (-ен, -на, -но) *прил* (*срок, согласие итп*) conditional; (*знак, сигнал*) code *опред*; (*линия*) imaginary; (*no short form; линг*) conditional; **усло́вный рефле́кс** conditional reflex; **усло́вный срок** suspended sentence.

усложн|и́ть (-ю́, -и́шь; *impf* **усложня́ть**) *сов перех* to complicate

► **усложни́ться** (*impf* **усложня́ться**) *сов возв* to get more complicated.

услу́г|а (-и) *ж* (*одолжение*) favour (*BRIT*), favor (*US*); (*обычно мн: облуживание*) service; **коммуна́льные** ~**и** public utilities; **бюро́ (до́брых) услу́г** domestic services agency; **к Ва́шим** ~**м**! at your service!; **ока́зывать** (**оказа́ть** *perf*) **кому́-н** ~**у** to do sb a good turn.

услуже́ни|е (-я) *ср*: **быть в** ~**х** (**у** +*gen*) to be in service (with).

услуж|и́ть (-ужу́, -у́жишь) *сов неперех*: ~ **кому́-н** to do sb a good turn.

услу́жлив|ый (-, -а, -о) *прил* obliging.

услы́ш|ать (-у, -ишь) *сов от* **слы́шать**.

усма́трива|ть (-ю) *несов от* **усмотре́ть**.

усмехн|у́ться (-у́сь, -ёшься; *impf* **усмеха́ться**) *сов возв* to smile slightly.

усме́шк|а (-и) *ж* slight smile; **зла́я** ~ sneer.

усмире́ни|е (-я) *ср* (*тигра*) taming; (*страстей, мятежа*) suppression.

усмир|и́ть (-ю́, -и́шь; *impf* **усмиря́ть**) *сов перех* (*льва*) to tame; (*детей*) to discipline; (*страсти, мятеж, восстание*) to suppress

► **усмири́ться** (*impf* **усмиря́ться**) *сов возв* (*лев*) to become tame; (*дети*) to calm down.

усмотре́ни|е (-я) *ср* discretion; **предоставля́ть** (**предоста́вить** *perf*) **на** ~ **нача́льства** to be left to the management's discretion; **де́йствовать** (*impf*) **по своему́** ~**ю** to use one's own discretion *или* judgement; **на Ва́ше** ~ at your discretion.

усм|отре́ть (-отрю́, -о́тришь; *impf* **усма́тривать**) *сов перех* (*разг*) to spot; (*счесть*): ~ **что-н в** +*prp* to see sth in ♦ *неперех* (*разг: уследить*): ~ **за** +*instr* to keep an eye on.

усна|сти́ть (-щу́, -сти́шь; *impf* **уснаща́ть**) *сов перех*: ~ **что-н чем-н** to pepper sth with sth.

усн|у́ть (-у́, -ёшь; *impf* **засну́ть**) *сов неперех* (*заснуть*) to fall asleep, to go to sleep; ~ (*perf*) **наве́ки** *или* **ве́чным сном** to go to one's eternal rest.

усоверше́нствовани|е (-я) *ср* improvement, refinement.

усоверше́нств|овать(ся) (-ую(сь)) *сов от* **соверше́нствовать(ся)**.

усо́ве|стить (-щу, -стишь; *impf* **усо́вещивать**) *сов перех*: ~ **кого́-н** to make sb (feel) ashamed.

усомн|и́ться (-ю́сь, -и́шься) *сов возв*: ~ **в** +*prp* to doubt.

усо́пша|я (-ей; *decl like adj*) *ж см* **усо́пший**.

усо́пш|ий (-его; *decl like adj*) *м* deceased.

усо́хн|уть (-у, -ешь; *impf* **усыха́ть**) *сов неперех* (*также перен*) to shrivel (up); (*шерсть*) to shrink.

успева́емост|ь (-и) *ж* performance (*in studies*).

успева́|ть (-ю) *несов от* **успе́ть** ♦ *неперех* to make progress (*in one's studies*).

успе́ется *сов безл* there's no hurry *или* rush.

Успе́ни|е (-я) *ср* the Assumption.

успе́|ть (-ю; *impf* **успева́ть**) *сов неперех* (*сделать что-н в срок*) to manage; (*прийти вовремя*) to *или* make it in time; **я не ~л э́то сде́лать, как ... I'd** hardly done it when ...; **не ~л огляну́ться, как он уже́ ушёл I** hardly had time to blink before he'd already gone.

успе́х (-а) *м* success; (*обычно мн: в спо́рте, в учёбе*) achievement; **как Ва́ши ~и?** how are you doing?; **с ~ом** (*успешно*) successfully; (*без затруднений*) easily; **добива́ться (доби́ться** *perf*) **~а** to achieve success; **с тем же ~ом** just as well.

успе́шно *нареч* successfully.

успе́ш|ный (-ен, -на, -но) *прил* successful.

успока́ива|ть(ся) (-ю(сь)) *несов от* **успоко́ить(ся)**.

успоко́ени|е (-я) *ср* (*боли, совести*) easing; (*плачущего*) pacifying; **э́ти мы́сли принесли́ ей ~** these thoughts brought her peace of mind.

успоко́енност|ь (-и) *ж* complacency.

успокои́тельн|ое (-ого; *decl like adj*) *ср* sedative.

успокои́тельный *прил* (*известие, ответ*) calming, soothing; (*лекарство*) sedative *опред*.

успоко́|ить (-ю, -ишь; *impf* **успока́ивать**) *сов перех* to calm (down); (*совесть*) to ease; (*боль*) to soothe

▸ **успоко́иться** (*impf* **успока́иваться**) *сов возв* (*человек*) to calm down; (*море*) to calm; (*боль, совесть, волнения*) to be eased; (*ветер*) to drop; **успока́иваться (~ся** *perf*) **на дости́гнутом** to be content with one's achievements; **он не ~ился, пока́ не раскры́ли всё де́ло** he couldn't rest until they'd uncovered the whole business.

уст|а́ (-) *мн* lips *мн*; **в его́ ~х э́то звучи́т стра́нно** it sounds strange coming from him; **из уст в ~** by word of mouth; **из пе́рвых уст** from the horse's mouth; **э́то у всех на ~х** it's on everyone's lips.

уста́в (-а) *м* (*партийный*) rules *мн*; (*воинский*) regulations *мн*; (*корпорации*) statute; **~ акционе́рной компа́нии** (*КОММ*) articles of association.

устава́|ть (-ю, -ёшь) *несов от* **уста́ть**.

уста́в|ить (-лю, -ишь; *impf* **уставля́ть**) *сов перех* (*разместить*) to place, put; (*занять*): **~ что-н чем-н** (*стол*) to cover sth with; (*полку*) to fill sth with; (*разг: устремить*): **~ что-н в** +*acc* to fix sth on

▸ **уста́виться** (*impf* **уставля́ться**) *сов возв* (*разг*): **~ся на/в** +*acc* (*на собеседника, в сте́ну*) to gaze at.

уста́вный *прил* statutory; **уста́вный капита́л** (*КОММ*) authorized capital.

уста́ло *нареч* wearily.

уста́лост|ь (-и) *ж* tiredness, fatigue.

уста́лый *прил* tired, weary.

у́стал|ь (-и) *ж*: **без** *или* **не зна́я ~и** tirelessly, indefatigably.

устан|ови́ть (-овлю́, -о́вишь; *impf* **устана́вливать**) *сов перех* to establish; (*размер оплаты, сроки*) to set; (*прибор, машину*) to install; **устана́вливать (~** *perf*) **реко́рд** to set a record

▸ **установи́ться** (*impf* **устана́вливаться**) *сов возв* to be established; (*погода*) to become settled; (*характер*) to be formed.

устано́вк|а (-и) *ж* installation; (*директива*) directive; (*цель*) objective.

установлю́(сь) *сов см* **установи́ть(ся)**.

уста́ну *итп сов см* **уста́ть**.

устаре́|ть (-ю) *сов от* **старе́ть** ◆ (*impf* **устарева́ть**) *неперех* (*оборудование*) to become obsolete.

уста́|ть (-ну, -нешь; *impf* **устава́ть**) *сов неперех* to get tired.

уст|ла́ть (-елю́, -е́лешь; *impf* **устила́ть**) *сов перех*: **~ что-н (чем-н)** to cover sth (with sth).

у́стный *прил* (*экзамен*) oral; (*обещание, приказ*) verbal; **у́стная речь** spoken language.

усто́|й (-я) *м* (*опора*) support; **~и** (*основы*) foundations.

усто́йчивост|ь (-и) *ж* stability.

усто́йчив|ый (-, -а, -о) *прил* (*также перен*) stable; (*лестница*) steady; **усто́йчивое (сло́во)сочета́ние** set phrase.

усто|я́ть (-ю́, -и́шь) *сов неперех* (*не упасть*) to remain standing; (*в споре, в борьбе итп*) to stand one's ground; (*не поддаться*) to resist; **~** (*perf*) **на нога́х** to keep one's balance

▸ **устоя́ться** *сов возв* (*характер*) to be formed; (*жидкость*) to settle; (*взгляды*) to become fixed.

устра́ива|ть(ся) (-ю(сь)) *несов от* **устро́ить(ся)**.

устран|и́ть (-ю́, -и́шь; *impf* **устраня́ть**) *сов перех* (*препятствие*) to remove; (*недостатки, соперника*) to eliminate; (*работника*) to dismiss

▸ **устрани́ться** (*impf* **устраня́ться**) *сов возв* to resign.

устраша́|ть(ся) (-ю(сь)) *несов от* **устраши́ть(ся)**.

устраша́ющий (-ая, -ее, -ие) *прил* frightening.

устраш|и́ть (-у́, -и́шь; *impf* **устраша́ть**) *сов перех* to frighten

▸ **устраши́ться** (*impf* **устраша́ться**) *сов возв*: **~ся** +*gen* to be frightened of.

устрем|и́ть (-лю́, -и́шь; *impf* **устремля́ть**) *сов перех* (*удар, глаза итп*) to direct; (*внимание, помыслы*) to focus

▸ **устреми́ться** (*impf* **устремля́ться**) *сов возв*: **~ся на** +*acc* (*конница, толпа*) to charge at; (*перен: внимание, мысли*) to be focused on; (*взгляд, глаза*) to be fixed on.

устремле́ни|е (-я) *ср* aspiration.

устремлённост|ь (-и) *ж* tendency.

устремлю́(сь) *сов см* **устреми́ть(ся)**.

устремля́|ть(ся) (-ю(сь)) *несов от* **устреми́ть(ся)**.

у́стриц|а (-ы) *ж* oyster.

у́стричный *прил* oyster.

устро́ен|ный (-, -а, -о) *прил (жизнь)* ordered; *(квартира)* habitable.

устро́итель (-я) *м* organizer.

устро́|ить (-ю, -ишь; *impf* устра́ивать) *сов перех (жизнь, дела)* to organize; *(спектакль, выставку)* to arrange; *(подлеж: предложение, цена)* to suit; устра́ивать (~ *perf)* кого́-н на рабо́ту/кварти́ру to help sb find work/a flat; устра́ивать (~ *perf)* сканда́л to make a scene; э́то меня́ ~ит that suits me

▸ устро́иться *(impf* устра́иваться) *сов возв (расположиться)* to settle down; *(прийти в поря́док)* to work out; устра́иваться (~ся *perf)* на рабо́ту to get a job; он ~ился на заво́д he got a job in a factory.

устро́йств|о (-а) *ср (действие: выставки)* organization; (: *на рабо́ту)* operation; *(дома, прибора)* construction; *(государственное, общественное)* structure; *(техническое)* device, mechanism; ~ опти́ческого счи́тывания си́мволов *(комп)* optical character reader.

усту́п (-а) *м* ledge.

уступ|и́ть (-плю́, -у́пишь; *impf* уступа́ть) *сов перех:* ~ что-н кому́-н to give sth up for sb ♦ *непере*х: ~ кому́-н/чему́-н *(сильному, силе, желанию итп)* to give in to sb/sth; уступа́ть (~ *perf)* в +*prp (в силе, в уме)* to be inferior in; уступа́ть (~ *perf)* доро́гу кому́-н to make way for sb; он ~упи́л мне кни́гу за 10 рубле́й he let me have the book for 10 roubles.

усту́п|ка (-ки; *gen pl* -ок) *ж (компромисс)* compromise; *(силе, врагу)* surrender; *(скидка)* discount; пойти́ *(perf)* на ~ку to compromise.

уступлю́ *сов см* уступи́ть.

усту́пок *сущ см* усту́пка.

усту́пчив|ый (-, -а, -о) *прил* compliant.

устыд|и́ть (-жу́, -ди́шь) *сов перех* to shame

▸ устыди́ться *сов возв:* ~ся +*gen* to be ashamed of.

у́сть|е (-я) *ср (реки)* mouth; *(шахты)* entrance.

усугуб|и́ть (-лю, -ишь; *impf* усугубля́ть) *сов перех (вину, опасность)* to increase; *(болезнь, положение итп)* to aggravate

▸ усугуб|и́ться *(impf* усугубля́ться) *сов возв (вина)* to increase; *(страдания, болезнь)* to be aggravated.

усу́шк|а (-и) *ж (зерна)* loss of weight *(through drying)*.

ус|ы́ (-о́в) *мн (у человека)* moustache *ед*; *(у животных)* whiskers *мн*; он (и) в ус (себе́) не ду́ет *(разг)* he's completely unruffled; на ус мота́ть (намота́ть *perf)* что-н *(разг)* to take good note of sth; са́ми с ~а́ми *(разг)* we weren't born yesterday.

усыла́|ть (-ю) *несов от* усла́ть.

усынов|и́ть (-лю́, -и́шь; *impf* усыновля́ть) *сов перех* to adopt *(son)*.

усыновле́ни|е (-я) *ср* adoption *(son)*.

усыновлю́ *сов см* усынови́ть.

усыновля́|ть (-ю) *несов от* усынови́ть.

усыпа́льниц|а (-ы) *ж* burial chamber.

усы́п|ать (-лю, -лешь; *impf* усыпа́ть) *сов перех:* ~ что-н чем-н *(путь, дорогу)* to scatter sth with sth.

усып|и́ть (-лю́, -и́шь; *impf* усыпля́ть) *сов перех (больного)* to anaesthetize *(ВRIТ)*, anesthetize *(US)*; *(ребёнка)* to lull to sleep; *(перен: внимание, бдительность)* to weaken; *(больную собаку итп)* to put to sleep; он ~и́л меня́ свои́ми ску́чными разгово́рами his boring conversation sent me to sleep.

усы́плю *итп сов см* усы́пать.

усыплю́ *сов см* усыпи́ть.

усыпля́|ть (-ю) *несов от* усыпи́ть.

усыха́|ть (-ю) *несов от* усо́хнуть.

уся́дусь *итп сов см* усе́сться.

ута|и́ть (-ю́, -и́шь; *impf* ута́ивать) *сов перех (правду)* to keep secret; *(деньги, документы)* to appropriate.

ута́й|ка (-и) *ж: без ~и (разг)* openly.

ута́ивать (-ю) *несов от* утаи́ть.

ута́щ|ить (-ащу́, -а́щешь; *impf* ута́скивать) *сов перех (унести)* to drag away *или* off; *(разг: украсть)* to make off with.

у́твар|ь (-и) *ж собир* utensils *мн*.

утверди́тельный (-ен, -ьна, -ьно) *прил (также линг)* affirmative.

утвер|ди́ть (-жу́, -ди́шь; *impf* утвержда́ть) *сов перех (проект, график)* to approve; *(господство, демократию итп)* to establish; ~ *(perf)* кого́-н в подозре́ниях to confirm sb's suspicions; ~ *(perf)* кого́-н в до́лжности to approve sb's appointment to office; ~ *(perf)* кого́-н в мне́нии/наме́рении to strengthen sb's conviction/intention

▸ утверди́ться *(impf* утвержда́ться) *сов возв* to be established; *(увериться):* ~ся в +*prp (в намерении)* to become convinced of.

утвержда́|ть (-ю) *несов от* утверди́ть ♦ *перех (правильность, достоверность)* to maintain; он ~л, что ничего́ не зна́ет he maintained that he didn't know anything

▸ утвержда́ться *несов от* утверди́ться.

утвержде́ни|е (-я) *ср (см глаг)* approval; establishment; *(правильное, интересное)* statement.

утвержу́(сь) *сов см* утверди́ть(ся).

утёк *итп сов см* уте́чь.

утека́|ть (*3sg* -ет, *3pl* -ют) *несов от* уте́чь.

утеку́т *итп сов см* уте́чь.

утёнок (-ёнка; *nom pl* -я́та, *gen pl* -я́т) *м* duckling.

утеплённый *прил (гараж)* insulated; *(обувь)* lined.

утепл|и́ть (-ю́, -и́шь; *impf* утепля́ть) *сов перех* to insulate.

ут|ере́ть (-ру́, -ре́шь; pt -ёр, -ёрла, -ёрло, impf
утира́ть) сов перех (пот) to wipe off; (слёзы)
to wipe away; (лицо, нос) to wipe; ~ (perf) нос
кому́-н (перен: разг) to show sb what's what
► утере́ться (impf утира́ться) сов возв to wipe
one's face; (нос) to wipe one's nose.
уте́р|я (-и) ж loss.
утеря́|ть (-ю) сов от теря́ть.
утёс (-а) м cliff.
уте́ч|ка (-и) ж (также перен) leak; (кадров)
turnover; уте́чка мозго́в brain drain.
ут|е́чь (3sg -ечёт, 3pl -еку́т, pt -ёк, -екла́, -екло́,
impf утека́ть) сов неперех (вода, газ) to leak;
(годы) to go by, pass; (информация) to be
leaked.
утеша́|ть(ся) (-ю(сь)) несов от уте́шить(ся).
утеше́ни|е (-я) ср (плачущего) comforting; (о
чём-н утешающем) consolation.
уте́ш|ить (-у, -ишь; impf утеша́ть) сов перех
(плачущего, несчастного) to comfort, console;
(подлеж: мысль, успехи детей) to comfort
► уте́шиться (impf утеша́ться) сов возв to cheer
up.
утилиза́ци|я (-и) ж recycling.
утилизи́р|овать (-ую) (не)сов перех to recycle.
утилита́р|ный (-ен, -на, -но) прил (взгляды)
utilitarian; (знания) practical.
утиль (-я) м собир recyclable waste.
ути́|ный прил (гнездо) duck's; (яйцо, охота)
duck опред.
утира́|ть(ся) (-ю(сь)) несов от утере́ть(ся).
утих|ну́ть (-у, -нешь; impf утиха́ть) сов неперех
(спор) to calm down; (гром, звон) to die away;
(ветер) to drop; (вьюга) to die down.
утихоми́р|ить (-ю, -ишь; impf утихоми́ривать)
сов перех to pacify
► утихоми́риться (impf утихоми́риваться)
сов возв to calm down.
у́т|ка (-ки; gen pl -ок) ж duck; (ложный слух)
canard; (сосуд) bedpan; пуска́ть (пусти́ть perf)
~ку to spread a false rumour (BRIT) или rumor
(US).
уткн|у́ть (-у́, -ёшь) сов перех (разг: подбородок)
to bury; ~ (perf) нос в +acc to bury one's nose in;
~ (perf) глаза́ в зе́млю to fix one's eyes on the
ground
► уткну́ться сов возв (разг): ~ся в +acc (в
книгу, в газету) to bury one's nose in; она́
~у́лась голово́й в поду́шку she buried her face
in the pillow.
утконо́с (-а) м duck-billed platypus (мн
platypus).
у́тлый прил (лодка) decrepit.
у́ток сущ см у́тка.
утол|и́ть (-ю́, -и́шь; impf утоля́ть) сов перех
(жажду) to quench; (голод, любопытство) to
satisfy; (боль) to ease.
утол|сти́ть (-щу́, -сти́шь; impf утолща́ть) сов
перех to thicken.
утолще́ни|е (-я) ср widening.
утолщу́ сов см утолсти́ть.

утоля́|ть (-ю) несов от утоли́ть.
утоми́тель|ный (-ен, -ьна, -ьно) прил tedious,
tiresome; (ребёнок) tiring.
утом|и́ть (-лю́, -и́шь; impf утомля́ть) сов перех
to tire
► утоми́ться (impf утомля́ться) сов возв to get
tired.
утомле́ни|е (-я) ср tiredness, fatigue.
утомлю́(сь) сов см утоми́ть(ся).
утомля́емость (-и) ж (также ТЕХ) fatigue.
утомля́|ть(ся) (-ю(сь)) несов от утоми́ть(ся).
ут|о́нуть (-ону́, -о́нешь) сов от тону́ть.
утончённость (-и) ж refinement.
утончён|ный (-, -на, -но) прил refined.
утонч|и́ть (-у́, -и́шь) сов перех (нитку) to make
thinner
► утончи́ться сов возв (вкусы, восприятие) to
become refined.
утопа́|ть (-ю) несов неперех (тонуть) to drown;
(перен): ~ в +prp (в кружевах, в цветах) to be
smothered in; (в роскоши, в разврате) to
wallow in.
утопи́ст (-а) м utopian.
утоп|и́ть(ся) (-оплю́(сь), -о́пишь(ся)) сов от
топи́ть(ся).
утопи́чен прил см утопи́чный.
утопи́ческий (-ая, -ое, -ие) прил utopian.
утопи́|чный (-чен, -чна, -чно) прил utopian.
уто́пи|я (-и) ж utopia.
уто́пленник (-а) м drowned man (мн men).
уто́пленни|ца (-ы) ж drowned woman (мн
women).
утоплю́(сь) сов см утопи́ть(ся).
ут|опта́ть (-опчу́, -о́пчешь; impf ута́птывать)
сов перех to stamp down.
уточне́ни|е (-я) ср elaboration; вноси́ть
(внести́ perf) ~я в +acc to elaborate on.
уточн|и́ть (-ю́, -и́шь; impf уточня́ть) сов перех
(пункт договора, выводы) to elaborate on;
(сведения, факты) to clarify.
утрамб|ова́ть (-у́ю) сов от трамбова́ть.
утра́т|а (-ы) ж loss; ~ трудоспосо́бности
disablement; понести́ (perf) ~у to suffer a loss.
утра́|тить (-чу, -тишь; impf утра́чивать) сов
перех (потерять) to lose; ~ (perf) си́лу
(документ итп) to become invalid.
у́тренн|ий (-яя, -ее, -ие) прил morning опред;
(событие, известие) this morning's.
у́тренник (-а) м matinée; (с участием детей)
children's party.
утри́рованный прил exaggerated.
утри́р|овать (-ую) (не)сов перех to exaggerate.
у́тр|о (-а́; nom pl -а, gen pl -, dat pl -ам) ср morning;
до утра́ till morning; с утра́ since this morning;
дава́й встре́тимся с утра́ let's meet in the
morning; с утра́ до́ ночи from morn till night;
до́брое ~!, с до́брым ~м! good morning!; на
~ next morning; по утра́м in the mornings; под
~, к утру́ in the early hours of the morning.
утро́б|а (-ы) ж (материнская) womb; (брюхо)
belly.

утро́бный *прил* (БИО) f(o)etal; (*истошный*)
hollow.

утро́|**ить** (-ю, -ишь) *сов перех* to treble, triple
▶ **утро́иться** *сов возв* to treble, triple.

у́тром *нареч* in the morning; **ра́но ~** early in the
morning.

утру́(сь) *итп сов см* **утере́ть(ся)**.

утружда́|**ть** (-ю) *несов перех*: **~ кого́-н чем-н** to
trouble sb with sth; **не ~йте себя́** don't trouble
yourself
▶ **утружда́ться** *несов возв* to trouble o.s.

утру́ск|**а** (-и) *ж* spillage.

утря|**сти́** (-су́, -сёшь; *impf* **утряса́ть**) *сов
перех* (*перен: разг: вопрос, проблему*) to settle;
(*муку́*) to shake down
▶ **утрясти́сь** *сов возв* (*разг*) to settle.

уты́|**кать** (-чу, -чешь; *impf* **утыка́ть**) *сов перех*:
~ что-н чем-н to stick sth into sth.

утю́г (-а́) *м* iron (*appliance*).

утю́ж|**ить** (-у, -ишь; *perf* **вы́утюжить** *или*
отутю́жить) *несов перех* to iron.

утяжел|**и́ть** (-ю́, -и́шь; *impf* **утяжеля́ть**) *сов
перех* to make heavier, increase the weight of.

утя́та *итп сущ см* **утёнок**.

утя́тин|**а** (-ы) *ж* (*мясо*) duck.

уф *межд*: **~!** phew!

ух *межд*: **~!** ooh!

ух|**а́** (-и́) *ж* fish broth.

уха́б (-а) *м* pothole.

уха́бист|**ый** (-, -а, -о) *прил*: **~ая доро́га** road
full of potholes.

ухажёр (-а) *м* (*разг*) admirer.

уха́живани|**е** (-я) *ср* courting.

уха́жива|**ть** (-ю) *несов неперех*: **~ за** +*instr* (*за
больным, за ранеными*) to nurse; (*за цветами,
за садом*) to tend; (*за женщиной*) to court.

у́ханье (-я) *ср* (*no pl*) hooting.

у́ха|**ть** (-ю) *несов от* **у́хнуть**.

ухва́т (-а) *м* oven fork.

ухва|**ти́ть** (-ачу́, -а́тишь; *impf* **ухва́тывать**) *сов
перех* (*человека: за руку, за рукав*) to get hold
of; (*перен: идею, смысл*) to grasp
▶ **ухвати́ться** (*impf* **ухва́тываться**) *сов возв*:
~ся за +*acc* (*за перила, за руку*) to grab hold of;
(*за дело, за мысль*) to latch onto; (*за
предложение*) to jump at.

ухва́т|**ки** (-ок) *мн* manners *мн*.

ухва́тыва|**ть(ся)** (-ю(сь)) *несов от*
ухвати́ть(ся).

ухвачу́(сь) *сов см* **ухвати́ть(ся)**.

ухитр|**и́ться** (-ю́сь, -и́шься; *impf* **ухитря́ться**)
сов возв = **умудри́ться**.

ухищре́ни|**е** (-я) *ср* (*уловка*) trick; **прибега́ть
(прибе́гнуть** *perf*) **к ра́зным ~ям** to resort to
various tricks.

ухищрённ|**ый** *прил* crafty.

ухищр|**я́ться** (-я́юсь) *несов возв* to contrive.

ухло́па|**ть** (-ю; *impf* **ухло́пывать**) *сов перех*

(*разг: истра́тить*) to blow.

ухмы́лк|**а** (-и) *ж* (*разг*) smirk.

ухмыл|**я́ться** (-я́юсь; *perf* **ухмыльну́ться**) *несов
возв* (*разг*) to smirk.

у́хн|**уть** (-у, -ешь; *impf* **у́хать**) *сов неперех*
(*снаряд*) to thud; (*гром*) to rumble; (*филин,
сова*) to hoot; (*разг: упа́сть*) to come a cropper
♦ *перех* (*разг: все де́ньги*) to blow; (*: ка́мень*)
to hurl; **~ (*perf*) кулако́м по столу́** to bang one's
fist down on the table.

у́х|**о** (-а; *nom pl* **у́ши**, *gen pl* **уше́й**) *ср* ear; (*у
ша́пки*) flap; **говори́ть (сказа́ть** *perf*) **что-н
кому́-н на́ ухо** to whisper sth in sb's ear; **не
вида́ть тебе́ де́нег как свои́х уше́й** (*разг*)
you've got no chance of getting the money;
слу́шать (*impf*) **во все у́ши** to be all ears;
слы́шать (услы́шать *perf*) **что-н кра́ем ~а** *или*
одни́м ~м to listen to sth with half an ear; **по́
уши влюби́ться** (*perf*) **в кого́-н** (*разг*) to fall
head over heels in love with sb; **уши́ вя́нут от
твои́х шу́ток** your jokes make me sick.

ухо́д (-а) *м* (*со службы, из семьи́*) leaving; (*от
пого́ни, от реа́льности*) escape; (*в
монасты́рь*) retreat; (*с собра́ния, со сце́ны*)
exit; (*за больны́м, за ребёнком*) care; **~ в
отста́вку** resignation; **~ на пе́нсию** retirement.

ухо|**ди́ть** (-ожу́, -о́дишь) *несов от* **уйти́** ♦
неперех (*простира́ться*) to extend.

ухо́женный *прил* (*лицо́, ру́ки*) well-looked-
after; (*сад*) well-kept; (*ло́шадь, челове́к*) well-
groomed.

ухо́жу *несов см* **уходи́ть**.

ухудша́|**ть(ся)** (-ю(сь)) *несов от*
уху́дшить(ся).

ухудше́ни|**е** (-я) *ср* deterioration, worsening.

уху́дш|**ить** (-у, -ишь; *impf* **ухудша́ть**) *сов перех*
to make worse
▶ **уху́дшиться** (*impf* **ухудша́ться**) *сов возв* to
get worse, deteriorate.

уцеле́|**ть** (-ю) *сов неперех* to survive.

уценённый *прил* reduced.

уцен|**и́ть** (-ю́, -е́нишь; *impf* **уце́нивать**) *сов
перех* to reduce (the price of).

уце́н|**ка** (-ки; *gen pl* -ок) *ж* reduction.

уцеп|**и́ть** (-лю́, -е́пишь) *сов перех* to hook
▶ **уцепи́ться** *сов возв* (**ухвати́ться**): **~ся за**
+*acc* (*за руку*) to get hold of; (*за предложе́ние,
за возмо́жность*) to jump at.

уча́ств|**овать** (-ую) *сов неперех*: **~ в** +*prp* (*в
собра́нии, в спекта́кле*) to take part in; (*в
предприя́тии, в при́былях*) to have a share in.

уча́сти|**е** (-я) *ср* (*в собра́нии, в спекта́кле итп*)
participation; (*в предприя́тии, в при́былях*)
share; (*родственное, дружеское*) concern;
принима́ть (приня́ть *perf*) **~ в** +*prp* to take part
in; **принима́ть (приня́ть** *perf*) **~ в ком-н** to
show concern for sb.

уча|**сти́ть** (-щу́, -сти́шь; *impf* **учаща́ть**) *сов* *перех* (*шаг*) to quicken; (*контакты, встречи*) to make more frequent

▶ **участи́ться** (*impf* **учаща́ться**) *сов возв* (*пульс, дыхание*) to quicken; (*столкновения, контакты*) to become more frequent.

уча́стка *сущ см* **уча́сток**.

участко́в|ый *прил* local ♦ (**-ого**; *decl like adj*) *м* (*разг*) local policeman (*мн* policemen); (*также:* ~ **врач**) local GP *или* doctor; (*также:* ~ **инспе́ктор**) local policeman (*мн* policemen).

уча́стливо *нареч* sympathetically.

уча́стливый *прил* sympathetic.

уча́стник (**-а**) *м* (*кружка, экспедиции*) member; (*восстания, репетиции, переговоров*) participant; ~ **соревнова́ния** competitor, contestant; ~ **вы́ставки** exhibitor; ~ **войны́** (war) veteran.

уча́стница (**-ы**) *ж см* **уча́стник**.

уча́ст|ок (**-ка**) *м* (*земли, кожи итп*) area; (*дороги, реки, фронта*) stretch; (*врачебный*) catchment area; (*приусадебный, земельный*) plot; (*строительный*) site; (*работы, деятельности*) field; **избира́тельный** ~ polling station; **садо́вый** ~ allotment.

у́часть (**-и**) *ж* lot; **его́ пости́гла стра́шная** ~ fate dealt him a terrible blow.

учаща́|ть(ся) (**-ю(сь)**) *несов от* **участи́ть(ся)**.

уча́щаяся (**-ейся**; *decl like adj*) *ж см* **уча́щийся**.

уча́щийся (**-егося**; *decl like adj*) *м* (*школы*) pupil; (*училища*) student.

учащу́(сь) *сов см* **участи́ть(ся)**.

учёб|а (**-ы**) *ж* studies *мн*.

уче́бник (**-а**) *м* textbook; ~ **исто́рии** *или* **по исто́рии** history textbook.

уче́бный *прил* (*работа*) academic; (*процесс, фильм*) educational; (*стрельба*) practice; (*бой*) mock; (*мастерская, судно*) training *опред*; (*методы*) teaching *опред*; **уче́бная програ́мма** curriculum; **уче́бное заведе́ние** educational establishment; **уче́бный год** academic year; **уче́бный план** course outline; **уче́бный о́тпуск** block release.

учёл *итп см* **уче́сть**.

учён|ая (**-ой**; *decl like adj*) *ж см* **учёный**.

уче́ни|е (**-я**) *ср* (*в школе, в вузе*) study; (*теория*) teachings *мн*; *см также* **уче́ния**.

учени|к (**-а́**) *м* (*школы*) pupil; (*училища*) student; (*мастера*) apprentice; (*последователь*) follower.

учени́ц|а (**-ы**) *ж см* **учени́к**.

учени́ческий (**-ая, -ое, -ие**) *прил* (*дневник, тетради*) school *опред*; (*перен: рассуждение, работа*) primitive.

учени́честв|о (**-а**) *ср* (*у мастера*) apprenticeship; **го́ды** ~**а** schooldays *мн*.

уче́ни|я (**-й**) *мн* exercises *мн*.

учёност|ь (**-и**) *ж* learning.

учён|ый *прил* (*спор, круги*) academic; (*разг: опытом, каким-л событием*) educated; (*труды*) scholarly; (*кот, собака*) trained; (-, **-а, -о**; *человек*) learned, scholarly ♦ (**-ого**; *decl like*

adj) *м* (*научный работник*) academic, scholar; (: *в области точных и естественных наук*) scientist; **учёное зва́ние** academic title; **учёный сове́т** academic council.

уч|е́сть (**-ту́, -тёшь**; *pt* **-ёл, -ла́, -ло́**, *impf* **учи́тывать**) *сов перех* (*обстоятельства, сложности*) to take into account; (*материал, имущество*) to make an inventory of; (*присутствующих*) to make a list of; ~**ти́те, что** ... bear in mind that ...; ~ (*perf*) **ве́ксель** to discount a bill.

уч|ёт (**-а**) *м* (*потребностей, обстоятельств*) consideration; (*товара*) stock-taking; (*военный, медицинский*) registration; (*векселей*) discount; (*затрат, поступлений*) record; **бухга́лтерский** ~ (*учебный предмет*) accountancy; (*практическая деятельность*) bookkeeping; **брать** (**взять** *perf*) **на** ~ to register; **вести́** (*impf*) ~ to keep a record; **с** ~**ом всех обстоя́тельств** bearing in mind all the circumstances; **с** ~**ом сезо́нных колеба́ний** allowing for seasonal fluctuations.

учётн|ый *прил*: ~**ая ка́рточка** registration form; ~**ая кни́га** record book; ~ **проце́нт** (*комм*) rate of discount; ~ **дом** (*комм*) discount house.

учи́лищ|е (**-а**) *ср* college; **профессиона́льно-техни́ческое** ~ technical college.

учин|и́ть (**-ю́, -и́шь**; *impf* **учиня́ть**) *сов перех* (*драку*) to start; **учиня́ть** (~ *perf*) **сканда́л** to make a scene.

учи́тел|ь (**-я**; *nom pl* **-я́**) *м* (*школьный*) teacher; (*nom pl* **-и**; *мудрости*) master.

учи́тельница (**-ы**) *ж* teacher.

учи́тельск|ая (**-ой**; *decl like adj*) *ж* staffroom.

учи́тельств|о (**-а**) *ср* (*профессия*) teaching ♦ *собир* (*учителя*) teachers *мн*.

учи́тельств|овать (**-ую**) *несов неперех* to teach, work as a teacher.

учи́тыва|ть (**-ю**) *несов от* **уче́сть**.

уч|и́ть (**-у́, -ишь**; *perf* **вы́учить**) *несов перех* (*урок, роль*) to learn; (*perf* **вы́учить** *или* **научи́ть** *или* **обучи́ть**): ~ **кого́-н чему́-н** /+*infin* to teach sb sth/to do; **исто́рия/э́та тео́рия у́чит, что** ... history/this theory teaches that ...

▶ **учи́ться** *несов возв* (*в школе, училище*) to study; (*perf* **вы́учиться** *или* **научи́ться**): **получи́ть навыки** /+*infin*) ~**ся чему́-н** /+*infin* to learn sth/to do.

учреди́тел|ь (**-я**) *м* founder.

учреди́тельница (**-ы**) *ж см* **учреди́тель**.

учреди́тельн|ый *прил*: ~**ое собра́ние** inaugural meeting.

учре|ди́ть (**-жу́, -ди́шь**; *impf* **учрежда́ть**) *сов перех* (*фонд, банк*) to set up; (*контроль, порядок*) to introduce.

учрежде́ни|е (**-я**) *ср* (*фонда, организации итп*) setting up; (*контроля*) introduction; (*научное, исследовательское*) establishment; (*финансовое, общественное*) institution; (*страховое*) agency.

учрежу́ *сов см* **учреди́ть**.

учти́вость (-и) ж courtesy.

учти́в|ый (-, -а, -о) *прил* courteous, civil.

учту́ *итп сов см* **уче́сть**.

учу́|ять (-ю, -ешь) *сов перех (разг: собака)* to sniff; (: *перен: человек*) to sense.

уша́н|ка (-ки; *gen pl* -ок) ж *cap with ear-flaps*.

уша́ст|ый (-, -а, -о) *прил:* ~ **ма́льчик** boy with big ears.

уша́т (-а) м tub.

у́шек *сущ см* **у́шко**.

ушёл *сов см* **уйти́**.

у́ши *итп сущ см* **у́хо**.

уши́б (-а) м bruise.

ушиб|и́ть (-у́, -ёшь; *pt* -, -ла, -ло, *impf* **ушиба́ть**) *сов перех* to bang

▸ **ушиби́ться** *сов возв* to bang o.s.

уш|и́ть (-ью, -ьёшь; *impf* **ушива́ть**) *сов перех (сделать уже)* to take in; (*сделать короче*) to shorten, take up.

у́ш|ко (-ка; *nom pl* -ки, *gen pl* -ек) *ср уменьш от* **у́хо**; (*медали*) eyelet; (*иголки*) eye.

ушла́ *итп сов см* **уйти́**.

у́шлый *прил* smart.

ушлю́ *итп сов см* **усла́ть**.

ушни́к (-а́) м (*разг*) ear specialist.

ушн|о́й *прил* ear *опред;* ~**а́я боль** earache; ~**а́я ра́ковина** (*АНАТ*) auricle.

ушью́ *итп сов см* **уши́ть**.

уще́ль|е (-ья; *gen pl* -ий) *ср* gorge, ravine.

ущем|и́ть (-лю́, -и́шь; *impf* **ущемля́ть**) *сов перех (права, возможности)* to limit; (*палец*) to trap; **ущемля́ть (**~ *perf*) **чьё-н самолю́бие** to hurt *или* wound sb's pride.

ущемле́ни|е (-я) *ср (прав, возможностей)*

limitation; ~ **чьего́-н самолю́бия** wound to sb's pride.

ущемлённый *прил (самолюбие, гордость)* wounded; (*права*) limited.

ущемлю́ *сов см* **ущеми́ть**.

ущемля́|ть (-ю) *несов от* **ущеми́ть**.

ущёрб (-а) м (*материальный*) loss; (*здоровью*) detriment; **в** ~ +*dat* to the detriment of; **на** ~**е** on the wane; **наноси́ть (нанести́** *perf*) *или* **причиня́ть (причини́ть** *perf*) ~ **кому́-н/чему́-н** to inflict loss on sb/sth.

ущёрбен *прил см* **ущёрбный**.

ущёрбност|ь (-и) ж (*см прил*) waning; abnormality.

ущёрб|ный *прил (луна)* waning; (-ен, -на, -но; *характер, психика*) abnormal.

ущипн|у́ть (-у́, -ёшь) *сов перех* to nip, pinch.

Уэ́льс (-а) м Wales.

уэ́льск|ий (-ая, -ое, -ие) *прил* Welsh; ~ **язы́к** Welsh.

ую́т (-а) м comfort, cosiness.

ую́тен *прил см* **ую́тный**.

ую́тно *нареч (расположиться)* comfortably ♦ *как сказ:* **здесь** ~ it's cosy here; **мне здесь** ~ I feel comfortable here.

ую́т|ный (-ен, -на, -но) *прил* cosy.

уязви́мост|ь (-и) ж vulnerability.

уязви́м|ый (-, -а, -о) *прил* vulnerable; ~**ое ме́сто** weak spot.

уязв|и́ть (-лю́, -и́шь) *сов перех* to wound, hurt.

уясне́ни|е (-я) *ср* clarification.

уясн|и́ть (-ю́, -и́шь; *impf* **уясня́ть**) *сов перех (смысл, значение)* to comprehend; **уясня́ть (**~ *perf*) **(себе́)** to clarify for o.s.

~ Ф, ф ~

Ф, ф *сущ нескл (буква)* the 21st letter of the Russian alphabet.

фа *ср нескл (МУЗ)* fa.

фа́брик|а (-и) *ж* factory; *(ткацкая, бумажная)* mill.

фабрик|ова́ть (-у́ю; *perf* **сфабрикова́ть**) *несов перех (перен)* to fabricate.

фабри́чный *прил* factory *опред*; **фабри́чная ма́рка** trademark.

фа́бул|а (-ы) *ж* plot.

фавори́т (-а) *м (также СПОРТ)* the favourite (*BRIT*) *или* favorite (*US*).

фавори́т|ка (-ки; *gen pl* -ок) *ж см* **фавори́т**.

фаго́т (-а) *м* bassoon.

фа́з|а (-ы) *ж* phase; *(работы, строительства)* stage.

фаза́н (-а) *м* pheasant.

файл (-а) *м (КОМП)* file.

фак. *сокр* (= **факульте́т**) Fac. (= *Faculty*).

фа́кел (-а) *м* torch; *(дыма, выбросов)* column.

факс (-а) *м* fax; **посыла́ть (посла́ть** *perf*) ~ to send a fax.

факси́миле *ср нескл* facsimile.

факси́мильный *прил* facsimile *опред*.

факт (-а) *м* fact; **ста́вить (поста́вить** *perf*) **кого́-н пе́ред фа́ктом** to present sb with a fait accompli; **го́лые фа́кты** the bare facts; ~ **тот, что** ... (*разг*) the fact of the matter is that ....

факти́чески *нареч* actually, in fact.

факти́ческ|ий (-ая, -ое, -ие) *прил (материал, данные)* factual; *(руководитель, положение дел)* real, actual.

фа́ктор (-а) *м* factor.

факту́р|а (-ы) *ж* texture; *(КОММ)* invoice.

факультати́в (-а) *м* optional *или* elective course.

факультати́в|ный (-ен, -на, -но) *прил* optional, elective.

факульте́т (-а) *м* faculty.

фала́нг|а (-и) *ж (АНАТ, ВОЕН)* phalanx.

фа́лд|а (-ы) *ж* tail *(of coat)*; *(складка)* crease.

фальсифика́тор (-а) *м* falsifier.

фальсифика́ци|я (-и) *ж* falsification.

фальсифици́р|овать (-ую) *(не)сов перех* to falsify.

фальста́рт (-а) *м (СПОРТ)* false start.

фальце́т (-а) *м* falsetto.

фальши́в|ить (-лю, -ишь; *perf* **сфальши́вить**) *несов неперех (петь)* to sing out of tune; *(играть)* to play out of tune; *(лицемерить)* to pretend, put on an act.

фальши́в|ка (-ки; *gen pl* -ок) *ж (разг)* forgery.

фальши́влю *несов см* **фальши́вить**.

фальши́вок *сущ см* **фальши́вка**.

фальшивомоне́тчик (-а) *м* counterfeiter.

фальшивомоне́тчиц|а (-ы) *ж см* **фальшивомоне́тчик**.

фальши́в|ый *прил (документ, паспорт)* false, forged; *(монета, банкнот)* counterfeit; *(пение, инструмент)* out of tune; *(борода, улыбка, нота)* false; (-, -а, -о; *игра актёра)* unnatural, artificial; *(человек, поведение)* insincere.

фальшь (-и) *ж* insincerity.

фами́ли|я (-и) *ж* surname; *(королевская, старинная)* family; **де́вичья** ~ maiden name; **как Ва́ша** ~? what is your surname?; **моя́** ~ **Серо́в** my surname is Serov.

фами́льный *прил* family *опред*.

фамилья́рен *прил см* **фамилья́рный**.

фамилья́рнича|ть (-ю) *несов неперех*: ~ **(с** +*instr*) to be too familiar (with).

фамилья́р|ный (-ен, -на, -но) *прил* over(ly)-familiar.

фанати́зм (-а) *м* fanaticism.

фана́тик (-а) *м (также перен)* fanatic.

фанати́ч|ный (-ен, -на, -но) *прил* fanatical.

фане́р|а (-ы) *ж (для облицовки)* veneer; *(древесный материал)* plywood.

фане́рный *прил* plywood *опред*.

фант (-а) *м* forfeit.

фантазёр (-а) *м* dreamer.

фантазёр|ка (-ки; *gen pl* -ок) *ж см* **фантазёр**.

фантази́р|овать (-ую) *несов неперех (мечтать)* to dream; *(выдумывать)* to make up stories.

фанта́зи|я (-и) *ж (художника, писателя)* imagination; *(мечта)* fantasy; *(выдумка)* fib; *(МУЗ)* fantasia.

фанта́ст (-а) *м* writer of fantasy; *(научный)* science-fiction writer.

фанта́стик|а (-и) *ж (сказок, преданий)* fantastic element ♦ *собир (ЛИТЕРАТУРА)* fantasy; **нау́чная** ~ science fiction; **э́то** ~! *(разг)* it's incredible!

фантасти́ческ|ий (-ая, -ое, -ие) *прил* fantastic; *(причудливый)* fantastical; *(проект)* fantastic, far-fetched.

фа́нтик (-а) *м* wrapper.

фанфа́р|а (-ы) *ж (инструмент)* bugle; *(обычно*

мн: сигнал) fanfare.
ФАО сокр FAO (= *Food and Agriculture Organization*).
фа́р|а (-ы) ж (АВТ, АВИА) light; **пере́дние ~ы** headlights, headlamps; **за́дние ~ы** rear lights (БРИТ), taillights или taillamps (US).
фарао́н (-а) м pharaoh.
фарва́тер (-а) м (МОР) fairway, channel.
Фаренге́йт (-а) м Fahrenheit; **70 гра́дусов по ~у** 70 degrees Fahrenheit.
фаре́рск|ий (-ая, -ое, -ие) прил: **Ф~ие острова́** the Faroe Islands, the Faroes.
фаринги́т (-а) м pharyngitis.
фарисе́|й (-я) м Pharisee.
фарисе́йств|о (-а) ср hypocrisy.
фармаколо́ги|я (-и) ж pharmacology.
фармаце́вт (-а) м chemist, pharmacist.
фарс (-а) м farce.
фа́ртук (-а) м apron.
фарфо́р (-а) м, собир porcelain, china.
фарфо́ровый прил porcelain, china.
фарцо́вщик (-а) м (разг) *illegal trader who sells imported goods to Russians*.
фарцо́вщиц|а (-ы) ж см **фарцо́вщик**.
фарш (-а) м stuffing, forcemeat; (мясной) mince, minced или ground (US) meat.
фарширо́ванный прил (КУЛИН) stuffed.
фарширова́ть (-у́ю; perf **зафарширова́ть**) несов перех to stuff.
ФАС сокр f.a.s. (= *free alongside ship*).
фас (-а) м (ФОТО) front.
фаса́д (-а) м (лицевая сторона) facade, front; **за́дний ~** back; **боково́й ~** side.
фасова́ть (-у́ю; perf **расфасова́ть**) несов перех to prepack.
фасо́в|ка (-и) ж packing.
фасо́вочн|ый прил (цех, машина) packing опред; **~ая бума́га** wrapping paper.
фасо́л|ь (-и) ж (растение) bean plant ♦ собир (БОТ; семена) beans мн; **кра́сная ~** kidney beans мн.
фасо́н (-а) м style.
фат|а́ (-ы́) ж veil.
фата́л|ьный (-ен, -ьна, -ьно) прил fatal, fateful.
фа́ун|а (-ы) ж fauna.
фаши́зм (-а) м fascism.
фаши́ст (-а) м fascist.
фаши́стск|ий (-ая, -ое, -ие) прил fascist.
фая́нс (-а) м (материал) faïence ♦ собир (изделия) faïence, glazed earthenware.
фая́нсовый прил (посуда, изделия) glazed earthenware опред.
ФБР ср сокр (= *Федера́льное бюро́ расследований (США)*) FBI (= *Federal Bureau of Investigation*).
февра́л|ь (-я́) м February; см также **октя́брь**.
февра́льск|ий (-ая, -ое, -ие) прил February опред.

федера́льный прил federal; **Федера́льное бюро́ рассле́дований** Federal Bureau of Investigation; **Федера́льное собра́ние** (ПОЛИТ) the Federal Assembly (*upper house of the Russian parliament*).
федерати́вный прил federal.
федера́ци|я (-и) ж federation; **Росси́йская Ф~** the Russian Federation; **Сове́т Ф~й** *upper chamber of the Russian parliament*.
фее́ри|я (-и) ж magic show.
фейерве́рк (-а) м firework.
фе́льдшер (-а) м medical assistant.
фельето́н (-а) м satirical article.
фемини́ст|ка (-ки; gen pl -ок) ж feminist.
фен (-а) м hairdryer.
фено́мен (-а) м phenomenon (мн phenomena).
феномена́л|ьный (-ен, -ьна, -ьно) прил phenomenal.
феода́л (-а) м feudal lord.
феодали́зм (-а) м feudalism.
феода́льный прил feudal.
ферз|ь (-я́) м (ШАХМАТЫ) queen.
фе́рм|а (-ы) ж farm.
ферме́нт (-а) м ferment, enzyme.
фе́рмер (-а) м farmer.
фе́рмерск|ий (-ая, -ое, -ие) прил: **~ое хозя́йство** farm.
фестива́л|ь (-я) м festival.
фетр (-а) м felt.
фе́тровый прил felt.
фехтова́льщик (-а) м fencer.
фехтова́льщиц|а (-ы) ж см **фехтова́льщик**.
фехтова́ни|е (-я) ср (СПОРТ) fencing.
фешене́бел|ьный (-ен, -ьна, -ьно) прил fashionable.
фе́|я (-и) ж fairy.
фи межд: **~! ugh!**
фиа́л|ка (-ки; gen pl -ок) ж violet.
фиа́ско ср нескл fiasco; **терпе́ть (потерпе́ть** perf) **~** to suffer an embarrassment.
фи́г|а (-и) ж (БОТ) fig; (разг) fig (*gesture of refusal*); **ни фига́ не полу́чишь (от них)** (разг) you won't get a thing out of them; **иди́ на́ фиг** (разг) get lost, clear off.
фи́говый прил fig опред.
фиго́вый прил (разг) lousy, rotten.
фигу́р|а (-ы) ж (ГЕОМ, перен) figure; (ШАХМАТЫ) (chess)piece; **фигу́ра вы́сшего пилота́жа** aerobatic figure.
фигура́л|ьный (-ен, -ьна, -ьно) прил figurative.
фигури́р|овать (-ую) несов неперех (присутствовать) to be present; (имя, тема) to figure; **~** (*impf*) **на суде́ в ка́честве свиде́теля** to appear as a witness.
фигури́ст (-а) м figure skater.
фигури́ст|ка (-ки; gen pl -ок) ж см **фигури́ст**.
фигу́р|ка (-ки; gen pl -ок) ж (скульптура) figurine, statuette; (обычно мн: игра́льная) piece.

фигу́рный *прил (резьба)* figured; *(СПОРТ)*
figure *опред*; **фигу́рное ката́ние** figure skating;
фигу́рные ско́бки curly *или* brace brackets.
фигу́рок *сущ см* **фигу́рка**.
Фи́джи *ср нескл* Fiji.
фи́зик (-а) *м* physicist.
фи́зик|а (-и) *ж* physics.
физио́лог (-а) *м* physiologist.
физиологи́ческ|ий (-ая, -ое, -ие) *прил*
physiological.
физиоло́ги|я (-и) *ж* physiology.
физионо́ми|я (-и) *ж (разг)* face.
физиотерапе́вт (-а) *м* physiotherapist.
физиотерапевти́ческ|ий (-ая, -ое, -ие) *прил*
physiotherapy *опред*.
физиотерапи́|я (-и) *ж* physiotherapy.
физи́ческ|ий (-ая, -ое, -ие) *прил (также СПОРТ,
ФИЗ)* physical; *(труд)* manual; **физи́ческая
культу́ра** physical education; **физи́ческие
упражне́ния** physical exercise *ед*; **физи́ческое
лицо́** *(ЮР)* individual; **физи́ческое наси́лие**
physical violence.
физкульту́р|а (-ы) *ж сокр* (= *физи́ческая
культу́ра*) PE (= *physical education*).
физма́т (-а) *м сокр* = *физико-математи́ческий
факульте́т*.
фикс *м*: **иде́я ~** idée fixe.
фикса́ж (-а) *м (ФОТО)* fixer.
фикса́ци|я (-и) *ж (ТЕХ)* clamping; *(ФОТО)* fixing.
фикси́р|овать (-ую; *perf* **зафикси́ровать**)
несов перех (события, факты, показания) to
record, chronicle; *(срок, дату, цены)* to fix, set;
(внимание, взгляд) to fix; *(груз, тормоз)* to
clamp, fix.
фикти́в|ный (-ен, -на, -но) *прил* fictitious;
фикти́вный брак *(ЮР)* marriage of
convenience.
фи́кус (-а) *м* ficus; *(каучуконосный)* rubber
plant.
фи́кци|я (-и) *ж* fiction.
филармо́ни|я (-и) *ж (зал)* concert hall;
(организация) philharmonic society.
филатели́ст (-а) *м* philatelist.
филе́ *ср нескл (сорт мяса)* fillet.
филиа́л (-а) *м* branch.
филигра́н|ный (-ен, -на, -но) *прил (изделия,
орнамент)* filigree; *(перен: работа)* intricate.
фи́лин (-а) *м* eagle owl.
филиппи́н|ец (-ца) *м* Filipino.
филиппи́н|ка (-ки; *gen pl* -ок) *ж см*
филиппи́нец.
филиппи́нск|ий (-ая, -ое, -ие) *прил* Filipino,
Philippine.
филиппи́нца *итп сущ см* **филиппи́нец**.
Филиппи́н|ы (-) *мн* the Philippines *мн*.
фило́лог (-а) *м* philologist (*specialist in
languages and literature*).
филологи́ческ|ий (-ая, -ое, -ие) *прил*
philological; **филологи́ческий факульте́т**
faculty of philology.
филоло́ги|я (-и) *ж* philology (*study of language

and literature).
фило́н|ить (-ю, -ишь) *несов неперех (разг)* to
skive.
фило́соф (-а) *м* philosopher.
филосо́фи|я (-и) *ж* philosophy.
филфа́к (-а) *м сокр* = *филологи́ческий
факульте́т*.
фильм (-а) *м* film; **сего́дня идёт хоро́ший ~**
there's a good film on today.
фильмоско́п (-а) *м* slide projector.
фильтр (-а) *м* filter.
фильтр|ова́ть (-у́ю; *perf* **профильтрова́ть**)
несов перех to filter.
фин. *сокр* (= **фина́нсовый**) fin. (= *financial*).
фина́л (-а) *м (спектакля, концерта)* finale;
(СПОРТ) final; **выходи́ть (вы́йти** *perf*) **в ~** to
reach the final.
фина́льный *прил (также СПОРТ, КОММ)* final
опред.
финанси́ровани|е (-я) *ср* financing.
финанси́р|овать (-ую) *несов перех* to finance.
финанси́ст (-а) *м (предприниматель)*
financier; *(специалист)* specialist in financial
matters.
фина́нсовый *прил* financial; *(год)* fiscal;
(отдел, инспектор, комиссия) finance *опред*; ~
институ́т institute of finance; ~ **отчёт** financial
statement.
фина́нс|ы (-ов) *мн* finances *мн*; *(деньги)* cash
ед; **Министе́рство ~ов** ≈ the Treasury *(BRIT)*, ≈
the Treasury Department *или* Department of the
Treasury *(US)*.
фи́ник (-а) *м (плод)* date; *(дерево)* date palm.
финифт|ь (-и) *ж, собир* decorated Russian
enamel.
фи́ниш (-а) *м (СПОРТ)* finish; **приходи́ть
(прийти́** *perf*) **к ~y** to reach the finish.
финиши́р|овать (-ую) *(не)сов неперех* to
finish, come in.
фи́нишн|ый *прил* finishing *опред*; **выходи́ть
(вы́йти** *perf*) **на ~ую пряму́ю** to reach the final
straight; *(перен)* to be on the home straight; **~ая
черта́/ле́нточка** finishing line/tape.
фи́н|ка (-ки; *gen pl* -ок) *ж см* **финн**; *(разг: нож)*
Finnish knife.
Финля́нди|я (-и) *ж* Finland.
финн (-а) *м* Finn.
фи́нок *сущ см* **фи́нка**.
фи́нск|ий (-ая, -ое, -ие) *прил* Finnish; ~ **язы́к**
Finnish; **Фи́нский зали́в** Gulf of Finland.
финт (-а́) *м (СПОРТ)* feint; *(разг: уловка)* trick.
финт|и́ть (-чу́, -ти́шь) *несов неперех (разг)* to
be tricky.
Ф.И.О. *сокр* (= *фами́лия, и́мя, о́тчество*)
surname, first name, patronymic.
ф.и.о. *сокр* = **Ф.И.О.**.
фиоле́товый *прил* purple.
фи́рм|а (-ы) *ж* firm; *(разг: модная вещь)* quality;
секре́т ~ы *(разг)* trade secret.
фи́рменный *прил (марка, ресторан)* firm's,
company *опред*; *(магазин)* chain *опред*; *(разг:

джинсы, юбка, костюм итп) quality опред (usually of imported brand names); **фи́рменный знак** brand name.

фиста́шк|а (-и) ж pistachio.

фити́л|ь (-я́) м wick; *(взрывных устройств)* fuse.

ФИФА́ ж сокр (= *Междунаро́дная федера́ция футбо́ла)* FIFA (= *Fédération Internationale de Football Association).*

фи́ф|а (-ы) ж *(разг)* bimbo, dolly bird.

фи́шк|а (-ки; *gen pl* -ек) ж counter, chip.

флаг (-а) м flag.

фла́гман (-а) м *(командующий)* flag officer; *(корабль)* flagship.

флагшто́к (-а) м flagpole.

флажо́к (-ка́) ж flag.

флако́н (-а) м bottle.

флама́ндец (-ца) м Fleming.

флама́нд|ка (-ки; *gen pl* -ок) ж см **флама́ндец**.

флама́ндск|ий (-ая, -ое, -ие) прил Flemish; ~ **язы́к** Flemish.

флама́ндца итп сущ см **флама́ндец**.

флами́нго м нескл flamingo.

фланг (-а) м flank.

Фла́ндри|я (-и) ж Flanders.

флане́левый прил flannel.

флане́л|ь (-и) ж flannel.

флегма́тик (-а) м: **он ~** he is phlegmatic.

флегмати́ч|ный (-ен, -на, -но) прил phlegmatic.

флейт|а (-ы) ж flute.

флейти́ст (-а) м flautist.

фле́кси|я (-и) ж inflection.

флекти́вный прил inflected.

фли́гел|ь (-я) м *(АРХИТ)* wing.

флирт (-а) м flirtation.

флирт|ова́ть (-у́ю) несов неперех: ~ *(с +instr)* to flirt (with).

флокс (-а) м phlox.

флома́стер (-а) м felt-tip (pen).

фло́р|а (-ы) ж flora.

флоренти́йск|ий (-ая, -ое, -ие) прил Florentine.

Флоре́нци|я (-и) ж Florence.

флот (-а) м *(ВОЕН)* navy; *(МОР)* fleet.

флоти́ли|я (-и) ж flotilla.

флю́гер (-а) м wind gauge; *(на башне)* weather vane.

флюи́д|ы (-ов) мн *(разг)* vibes мн.

флюорогра́фи|я (-и) ж fluorography.

флюс (-а) м (dental) abscess, gumboil.

фля́г|а (-и) ж *(для воды, спирта)* flask; *(для молока, для сметаны)* churn.

ФНО м сокр (= *Фронт национа́льного освобожде́ния)* NLF (= *National Liberation Front).*

ФОБ сокр (= *фра́нко-борт)* f.o.b. (= *free on board).*

фойе́ ср нескл foyer.

фокстерье́р (-а) м fox terrier.

фокстро́т (-а) м foxtrot.

фо́кус (-а) м trick; *(ТЕХ, перен)* focus; **выки́дывать (вы́кинуть** perf**) ~** *(перен: разг)* to start some nonsense.

фо́кусник (-а) м conjurer.

фолкле́ндск|ий (-ая, -ое, -ие) прил: Ф~**ие острова́** the Falkland Islands, the Falklands.

фольг|а́ (-и́) ж foil.

фолькло́р (-а) м folklore.

фолькло́рный прил *(фестиваль, ансамбль)* folk опред.

фон (-а) м background; **на фо́не чего́-н** against a background of sth; **на фо́не кого́-н** next to sb, compared to sb.

фона́р|ь (-я́) м *(уличный)* lamp; *(карманный)* torch; *(разг: синяк)* black eye, shiner; **ему́ всё до фонаря́** *(разг)* he doesn't give a toss about anything.

фонд (-а) м *(организация)* fund, foundation; *(денежные средства, запас)* fund; *(жилищный, семенной, земельный)* resources мн; **фо́нды** *(ценные бумаги)* stocks; **уставно́й ~** *(КОММ)* authorized capital.

фо́ндов|ый прил: ~**ая би́ржа** stock exchange.

фоне́тик|а (-и) ж phonetics.

фоногра́мм|а (-ы) ж recording; **петь (спеть** perf**) под ~у** to mime to a recording.

фоноло́ги|я (-и) ж phonology.

фоноте́к|а (-и) ж record and tape collection.

фонта́н (-а) м fountain; *(нефти)* gusher.

фо́р|а (-ы) ж: **дать кому́-н ~у** *(разг)* to give sb a start *или* an advantage; *(перен: разг)* to be miles better than sb.

фо́рвард (-а) м forward.

форе́л|ь (-и) ж trout.

фо́рм|а (-ы) ж *(также ЛИНГ)* form; *(одежда)* uniform; *(ТЕХ)* mould; *(КУЛИН)* (cake) tin *(BRIT)* *или* pan *(US)*; **быть** *(impf)* **в ~е** to be in good form; см также **фо́рмы**.

форма́лен прил см **форма́льный**.

формали́зм (-а) м *(в искусстве, в науке)* formalism; ~ **в рабо́те** bureaucratic attitude to work.

формали́ст (-а) м *(бюрократ)* bureaucrat.

формали́стик|а (-и) ж bureaucracy.

форма́льно нареч *(относиться)* formally; ~ **он прав** factually he's right.

форма́льност|ь (-и) ж formality.

форма́льный (-ен, -ьна, -ьно) прил *(отношение, подход)* bureaucratic; *(ответ)* nominal; *(no short form; согласие, метод, логика)* formal.

форма́т (-а) м format.

формати́р|овать (-ую) *(не)сов перех (КОМП)* to format.

форма́ци|я (-и) ж *(общественная)* structure; **челове́к но́вой ~и** forward-thinking person.

фо́рменн|ый *прил (безобразие, негодяй)* absolute; **~ бланк** official form; **фо́рменная оде́жда** uniform.

формирова́ни|е (-я) *ср* formation; **вое́нное ~** military unit.

формир|ова́ть (-у́ю; *perf* **сформирова́ть)** *несов перех* to form

▶ **формирова́ться** *(perf* **сформирова́ться)** *несов возв* to form.

фо́рмул|а (-ы) *ж* formula.

формули́р|овать (-ую; *perf* **сформули́ровать)** *несов перех* to formulate.

формули́ро́в|ка (-ки; *gen pl* **-ок)** *ж (мысли, предложения)* formulation; *(определение)* definition.

формуля́р (-а) *м* library ticket *или* card.

фо́рм|ы (-) *мн (разг)* curves *мн*.

форпо́ст (-а) *м (ВОЕН)* outpost; *(перен: демократии, науки)* stronghold.

форс (-а) *м (разг)* swank.

форси́р|овать (-ую) *(не)сов перех* to force.

фор|си́ть (-шу́, -си́шь) *несов неперех (разг)* to show off.

форсу́н|ка (-ки; *gen pl* **-ок)** *ж (двигателя)* fuel injector.

форт (-а; *loc sg* **-у́,** *nom pl* **-ы́)** *м* fort.

фортепья́нный *прил* piano *опред*.

фортепья́но *ср нескл* piano.

фо́рточ|ка (-ки; *gen pl* **-ек)** *ж hinged, upper pane for ventilation.*

форту́н|а (-ы) *ж* fortune.

фо́рум (-а) *м* forum.

форшу́ *несов см* **форси́ть.**

фосфа́т (-а) *м (обычно мн)* phosphate.

фо́сфор (-а) *м* phosphorous.

фо́то *ср нескл (разг)* photo.

фотоаппара́т (-а) *м* camera.

фотоателье́ *ср нескл* photographic *или* photographer's studio.

фотобума́г|а (-и) *ж* photographic paper.

фотогени́чный (-ен, -на, -но) *прил* photogenic.

фото́граф (-а) *м* photographer.

фотографи́р|овать (-ую; *perf* **сфотографи́ровать)** *несов перех* to photograph

▶ **фотографи́роваться** *(perf* **сфотографи́роваться)** *несов возв* to have one's photo(graph) taken.

фотогра́фи|я (-и) *ж (занятие)* photography; *(снимок)* photograph; *(учреждение)* photographer's studio.

фотока́рточ|ка (-ки; *gen pl* **-ек)** *ж* photo.

фоторо́бот (-а) *м* Photofit®.

фотоси́нтез (-а) *м* photosynthesis.

фототелегра́мм|а (-ы) *ж* phototelegram.

фотоэлеме́нт (-а) *м* photocell.

фрагме́нт (-а) *м (фильма, спектакля)* excerpt; *(древних сосудов итп)* fragment.

фрагмента́р|ный (-ен, -на, -но) *прил* fragmentary.

фра́з|а (-ы) *ж* phrase.

фразеоло́ги|я (-и) *ж (линг)* phraseology; *(пустословие)* rhetoric.

фрак (-а) *м* tail coat, tails *мн*.

фракцио́нный *прил* factional.

фра́кци|я (-и) *ж* faction.

франк (-а) *м* franc.

фра́нко *прил неизм (КОММ):* **~ вдоль бо́рта су́дна** free alongside ship; **~-железнодоро́жный ваго́н** free on rail.

Фра́нкфурт (-а) *м* Frankfurt.

франт (-а) *м* dandy.

Фра́нци|я (-и) *ж* France.

францу́жен|ка (-ки; *gen pl* **-ок)** *ж* Frenchwoman *(мн* Frenchwomen).

францу́з (-а) *м* Frenchman *(мн* Frenchmen).

францу́зск|ий (-ая, -ое, -ие) *прил* French; **~ язы́к** French.

франши́з|а (-ы) *ж (КОММ)* franchise; **держа́тель/предостави́тель ~ы** franchisee/franchiser.

фрахт (-а) *м* freight; **~, упла́чиваемый по прибы́тие (КОММ)** freight inward; **~, упла́чиваемый в порту́ вы́грузки (КОММ)** freight forward.

фрахт|ова́ть (-у́ю; *perf* **зафрахтова́ть)** *несов перех* to charter.

ФРГ *ж сокр (ИСТ:* = Федерати́вная Респу́блика Герма́нии) FRG (= *Federal Republic of Germany).*

фрега́т (-а) *м* frigate.

фре́йлин|а (-ы) *ж* lady-in-waiting *(мн* ladies-in-waiting).

фре́с|ка (-ки; *gen pl* **-ок)** *ж* fresco.

фриво́льность (-и) *ж* frivolity.

фриво́ль|ный (-ен, -ьна, -ьно) *прил* frivolous.

фриз (-а) *м* frieze.

фрикаде́ль|ка (-ьки; *gen pl* **-ек)** *ж* meatball.

фронт (-а; *nom pl* **-ы́)** *м* front; **рабо́тать** *(impf)* **на два фро́нта** *(перен)* to do two things at the same time.

фронта́л|ьный (-ен, -ьна, -ьно) *прил (ВОЕН)* frontal; *(перен)* по́лный, general.

фронтиспи́с (-а) *м* frontispiece.

фронтови́к (-а́) *м* front line soldier; *(ветеран)* war veteran.

фронто́н (-а) *м (АРХИТ)* pediment.

фрукт (-а) *м (БОТ)* fruit; *(разг · пренебр: человек)* suspicious character.

фрукто́вый *прил* fruit *опред*.

фрукто́з|а (-ы) *ж* fructose.

ФСК *ж сокр* (= Федера́льная слу́жба контрразве́дки) *Russian counterespionage intelligence service.*

фтор (-а) *м* fluorin(e).

фу *межд* ~! ugh!

фу́г|а (-и) *ж* fugue.

фу́кси|я (-и) *ж* fuchsia.

фуже́р (-а) *м* wineglass; *(для шампанского)* flute.

фунда́мент (-а) *м (СТРОИТ)* foundation, base; *(перен: семьи, науки)* foundation, basis.

фундамента́льный (-ен, -ьна, -ьно) *прил* (*здание, мост*) sound, solid; (*перен: знания, труд*) profound; ~**ьные нау́ки** basic science.

фунду́к (-а́) *м* (*кустарник*) hazel; (*плод*) hazelnut.

фуникулёр (-а) *м* funicular railway.

функциона́льный (-ен, -ьна, -ьно) *прил* functional; **функциона́льная кла́виша** (*КОМП*) function key.

функционе́р (-а) *м* official, functionary.

функциони́ровать (-ую) *несов неперех* to function.

фу́нкция (-и) *ж* function; (*круг обязанностей*) function, duties *мн*.

фунт (-а) *м* pound.

фура́ж (-а́) *м* fodder.

фура́жка (-ки; *gen pl* -ек) *ж* cap; (*ВОЕН*) forage cap.

фурго́н (-а) *м* (*АВТ*) van; (*конная повозка*) (covered) wagon.

фу́рия (-и) *ж* (*разг*) virago.

фуро́р (-а) *м* furore; **производи́ть** (**произвести́** *perf*) ~ to create a furore.

фуру́нкул (-а) *м* boil.

фут (-а) *м* foot.

футбо́л (-а) *м* football (*BRIT*), soccer; **америка́нский** ~ (American) football.

футболи́ст (-а) *м* footballer (*BRIT*), soccer player.

футбо́лка (-ки; *gen pl* -ок) *ж* T-shirt, tee shirt.

футбо́льный *прил* football *опред*, soccer *опред*; **футбо́льный мяч** football.

футля́р (-а) *м* case.

фуфа́йка (-йки; *gen pl* -ек) *ж* (*ватник*) padded jacket; (*вязаная рубашка*) jersey.

фы́ркать (-ю) *несов неперех* (*животное*) to snort; (*разг: смеяться*) to snort with laughter; (: *брюзжать*) to complain.

фы́ркнуть (-у, -ешь) *сов неперех* (*животное*) to give a snort; (*разг: издать смешок*) to snort with laughter.

фырча́ть (-у́, -и́шь) *несов неперех* (*разг*) to snort; (*брюзжать*) to whinge.

фью́черсы (-ов) *мн* (*КОММ*) futures *мн*.

~ X, x ~

X, x *сущ нескл (буква) the 22nd letter of the Russian alphabet.*

ха́кер (-а) *м* hacker.

ха́ки *прил неизм, ср нескл* khaki.

хала́т (-а) *м (домашний)* dressing gown; **ба́нный ~** bathrobe.

хала́тен *прил см* хала́тный.

хала́тность (-и) *ж* negligence.

хала́тный (-ен, -на, -но) *прил* negligent.

халв|а́ (-ы́) *ж* halva.

халту́р|а (-ы) *ж (разг: плохая работа)* shoddy work; (: *работа на стороне)* moonlighting.

халту́р|ить (-ю, -ишь; *perf* схалту́рить) *несов неперех (разг)* to cut corners; (*no perf*, *разг: работать на стороне)* to moonlight.

хам (-а) *м (разг)* brute, lout.

хамелео́н (-а) *м (также перен)* chameleon.

хаме́|ть (-ю; *perf* охаме́ть) *несов неперех* to become impudent.

хам|и́ть (-лю́, -и́шь; *perf* нахами́ть) *несов неперех: ~ (+dat) (разг)* to be cheeky (BRIT) *или* rude (US) (to).

ха́м|ка (-ки; *gen pl* -ок) *ж (разг)* hussy.

хамлю́ *сов см* хами́ть.

ха́мок *сущ см* ха́мка.

ха́мск|ий (-ая, -ое, -ие) *прил (разг)* brutish, loutish.

ха́мств|о (-а) *ср* rudeness.

хан (-а) *м* khan.

хандр|а́ (-ы́) *ж* depression.

хандр|и́ть (-ю, -и́шь) *несов неперех* to feel down.

ханж|а́ (-и́; *gen pl* -е́й) *м/ж* prude, prig.

ха́нжеств|о (-а) *ср* prudishness, priggishness.

Хано́|й (-я) *м* Hanoi.

ха́ос (-а) *м* chaos.

хаоти́чен *прил см* хаоти́чный.

хаоти́ческ|ий (-ая, -ое, -ие) *прил* chaotic.

хаоти́чн|ый (-ен, -на, -но) *прил* = хаоти́ческий.

ха́па|ть (-ю, -ешь) *несов перех (разг: хватать)* to grab at; (: *присваивать)* to swipe.

хара́ктер (-а) *м* nature; (*человека)* personality; **он челове́к с ~ом** he has a lot of character; **выде́рживать (вы́держать** *perf*) **~** to hold firm.

хара́ктерен *прил см* хара́ктерный.

характериз|ова́ть (-у́ю) *несов перех* to be typical of, (*perf* охарактеризова́ть; *персонаж, эпоху итп)* to characterize; **его́ ~у́ет доброта́** he is a kind person

▶ **характеризова́ться** *несов возв (+instr)* to be characterized by.

характери́сти|ка (-и) *ж (документ)* (character) reference; (*описание)* description.

характе́р|ный (-ен, -на, -но) *прил (внешность, поведение)* distinctive; (*свойственный)*: (**для** +*gen*) characteristic (of); (*no short form*; *обычаи. танцы итп)* typical; **для него́ ~ пери́оды депре́ссии** he tends to go through bouts of depression.

ха́рка|ть (-ю) *несов неперех (+instr; кровью, слизью)* to cough up.

ха́рти|я (-и) *ж (документ)* charter.

харч (-а; *nom pl* -и́, *gen pl* -е́й) *м (обычно мн: разг)* grub *ед*, chow *ед*.

харчо́ *ср нескл* spicy Georgian meat and vegetable soup.

ха́р|я (-и) *ж (разг)* mug (*face)*.

ха́т|а (-ы) *ж* cottage (*in Southern Russia and Ukraine)*; **моя́ ~ с кра́ю** *(разг)* it's nothing to do with me.

ха-ха́ *межд* ha-ha.

хачапу́ри *ср нескл* flat Georgian cheese pie.

ха́я|ть (-ю) *несов перех (разг)* to slag off.

х/б *сокр* = хлопчатобума́жный.

хвал|а́ (-ы́) *ж* praise.

хвале́бный *прил* complimentary.

хвалёный *прил* celebrated.

хвал|и́ть (-ю́, -ишь; *perf* похвали́ть) *несов перех* to praise

▶ **хвали́ться** (*perf* похвали́ться) *несов возв: ~ся (+instr) (разг)* to show off (about).

хва́ста|ться (-юсь; *perf* похва́статься) *несов возв: ~ (+instr)* to boast (about).

хвастли́в|ый (-, -а, -о) *прил* boastful.

хвастовств|о́ (-а́) *ср* boasting.

хвасту́н (-а́) *м (разг)* show-off.

хвасту́н|ья (-ьи; *gen pl* -ий) *ж см* хвасту́н.

хвата́|ть (-ю; *perf* схвати́ть) *несов перех* to grab (hold of); (*преступника)* to arrest; (*разг: простуду, насморк)* to catch; (: *плохую отме́тку, оплеу́ху)* to get ◆ (*perf* хвати́ть) *безл* (+*gen*; *денег, времени итп)* to have enough; **мне ~ет де́нег на еду́** I've got enough to buy food; **его́ не хвати́ло на э́то** he wasn't up to it; **он ~л всё подря́д** *(разг)* he grabbed whatever he could; **~** (*impf*) **за́ душу** to tug at one's heartstrings; **~** (**схвати́ть** *perf*) **что-н на лету́** to grasp sth in an instant; **э́того ещё не ~ло!**

(*разг*) as if that wasn't enough!; **не ~ет то́лько, что́бы он отказа́лся** (*разг*) now all we need is for him to refuse

▶ **хвата́ться** (*perf* **схвати́ться**) *несов возв*: **~ся за** +*acc* (*за се́рдце*) to clutch at: (*за дверь, за ору́жие*) to grab; **~ся** (*impf*) **за всё сра́зу** (*разг*) to try to do everything at once; **~ся (схвати́ться** *perf*) **за соло́минку** to clutch at straws; **~ся (схвати́ться** *perf*) **за́ го́лову** (*перен*) to panic.

хвати́ть (**-чу́, -тишь**) *сов от* **хвата́ть** ◆ *перех* (*разг*): **~ по рю́мочке/ча́йку** to have a quick drink/cuppa; (+*gen*: *беды, горя*) to suffer; (*разг*: *уда́рить*) to whack, thump ◆ *безл* (*разг*): **хва́тит!** that's enough!; **его́ ~ти́л парали́ч** he was paralysed; **её ~ти́л уда́р** she had a stroke; **он ~ти́л меня́ по голове́** he thumped me on the head; **он ~ти́л кулако́м по столу́** he banged on the table with his fist; **хва́тит спо́ров** *или* **спо́рить!** (*разг*) that's enough of this arguing!; **~** (*perf*) **че́рез край** to go too far; **с меня́ хва́тит!** I've had enough!

▶ **хвати́ться** *сов возв* (*разг*): **~ся чего́-н/ кого́-н** to notice that sth/sb is gone.

хва́т|ка (**-ки**; *gen pl* **-ок**) *ж* grip; (*перен: ло́вкость*) skill; **делова́я ~** business acumen; **вцепля́ться (вцепи́ться** *perf*) **в что-н/кого́-н мёртвой ~кой** (*также перен*) to cling onto sth/sb for dear life.

хвать *как сказ* (*разг*) **он меня́ ~ по голове́** he whacked me right in the head; **я поверну́лся, и ~ – нет кошелька́** I turned round and my purse (*BRIT*) *или* wallet (*US*) had vanished.

хвачу́(сь) *сов см* **хвати́ть(ся)**.

х-во *сокр* = **хозя́йство**.

хво́йный *прил* coniferous; **хво́йное де́рево** conifer.

хвора́ть (**-ю**) *несов неперех* to feel poorly (*BRIT*), to feel sick (*US*).

хво́рост (**-а**; *part gen* **-у**) *м собир* firewood; (*кули́н*) sugar-coated strips of dough fried in oil.

хворости́н|а (**-ы**) *ж* switch.

хво́рый *прил* (*разг*) ill.

хворь (**-и**) *ж* ailment.

хвост (**-а́**) *м* tail; (*по́езда*) tail end; (*перен: пы́ли, зева́к итп*) trail; (*разг: о́чередь*) queue (*BRIT*), line (*US*); (*: по матема́тике итп*) an exam which has to be taken again.

хво́стик (**-а**) *м* (*мы́ши, реди́ски*) tail; **ему́ 50 с ~ом** (*разг*) he's just over 50.

хвостов|о́й *прил* tail *опред*; **~а́я часть** (*самолёта, по́езда*) the tail end.

хвощ (**-а́**) *м* (*бот*) horsetail.

хво́|я (**-и**) *ж собир* needles *мн* (*of a conifer*).

ХДС *м сокр* (= **Христиа́нско-демократи́ческий сою́з**) CDU (= *Christian Democratic Union*).

хек (**-а**) *м* whiting.

хе́кер (**-а**) *м* (*комп*) hacker.

Хе́льсинки *м нескл* Helsinki.

хе́рес (**-а**; *part gen* **-у**) *м* sherry.

хи́жин|а (**-ы**) *ж* hut.

хи́л|ый (**-, -á, -о**) *прил* (*мужчи́на, рука́*) puny; (*расте́ние, ребёнок*) sickly; (*дом, постро́йка*) rickety.

хи́мик (**-а**) *м* chemist.

химика́т (**-а**) *м* chemical.

химиотерапи́|я (**-и**) *ж* chemotherapy.

хими́ческ|ий (**-ая, -ое, -ие**) *прил* chemical *опред*; (*факульте́т. кабине́т*) chemistry *опред*; **хими́ческий каранда́ш** *graphite pencil which writes in purple when moistened*.

хи́ми|я (**-и**) *ж* chemistry; **бытова́я ~** household chemicals *мн*.

химчи́ст|ка (**-ки**; *gen pl* **-ок**) *ж сокр* = **хими́ческая чи́стка**; (*проце́сс*) dry-cleaning; (*пункт приёма*) dry-cleaner('s).

хини́н (**-а**) *м* quinine.

хи́ппи *м нескл* hippie.

хире́|ть (**-ю**) *perf* **захире́ть**) *несов неперех* (*челове́к*) to waste away; (*расте́ние*) to wither; (*перен: тво́рчество, тала́нт*) to dry up.

хирома́нти|я (**-и**) *ж* palmistry.

Хироси́м|а (**-ы**) *ж* Hiroshima.

хиру́рг (**-а**) *м* surgeon.

хирурги́ческ|ий (**-ая, -ое, -ие**) *прил* surgical; (*больно́й, кли́ника*) surgery *опред*.

хирурги́|я (**-и**) *ж* surgery.

хит (**-а**) *м* (*муз*) hit.

хитёр *прил см* **хи́трый**.

хитре́ц (**-а́**) *м* cunning devil.

хитр|и́ть (**-ю́, -и́шь**; *perf* **схитри́ть**) *несов неперех* to act slyly.

хи́тро *нареч* cunningly; (*сде́ланный*) intricately.

хи́трост|ь (**-и**) *ж* slyness; (*уло́вка*) cunning.

хитроу́ми|е (**-я**) *ср* ingenuity.

хитроу́м|ный (**-ен, -на, -но**) *прил* ingenious.

хи́тр|ый (**-ёр, -ра́, -ро**) *прил* sly, cunning; (*изобрета́тельный*) cunning; (*замыслова́тый*) intricate.

хихи́ка|ть (**-ю**) *несов неперех* (*разг*) to giggle; (*: смея́ться исподти́шка*) to snigger.

хи́щен *прил см* **хи́щный**.

хище́ни|е (**-я**) *ср* misappropriation.

хи́щник (**-а**) *м* (*также перен*) predator.

хи́щниц|а (**-ы**) *ж* (*перен*) predator.

хи́щническ|ий (**-ая, -ое, -ие**) *прил* (*поли́тика, инсти́нкт*) predatory; (*истребле́ние ле́са, охо́та*) ruthless; (*испо́льзование ресу́рсов*) rapacious.

хи́щн|ый (**-ен, -на, -но**) *прил* (*также перен*) predatory; (*делец, торга́ш*) cutthroat; **~ная пти́ца** bird of prey.

хладнокро́вен *прил см* **хладнокро́вный**.

хладнокро́ви|е (**-я**) *ср* composure.

хладнокро́в|ный (**-ен, -на, -но**) *прил* composed; (*уби́йство итп*) cold-blooded.

хлам (**-а**) *м собир* (*также перен*) junk.

хлеб (**-а**) *м* bread; (*зерно́*) grain; (*nom pl* **-ы́**;

формовой, круглый) loaf (мн loaves); (nom pl -á; озимые, яровые) cereal; зарабáтывать (impf) на ~ to earn a crust; ~ насýщный bread and butter (fig); ~соль bread and salt (traditionally offered to guests as a symbol of hospitality).

хлебáть (-ю) несов перех (разг) to slurp.

хлебéц (-цá) м loaf; хрустя́щие ~цы̌ ≈ crispbreads.

хлéбница (-ы) ж bread basket; (для хранения) bread bin.

хлебнýть (-ý, -ёшь) сов перех (разг: чай итп) to take a gulp of; ~ (perf) гóря to see a lot of sorrow.

хлéбный прил bread опред; (злак, растение) corn опред; (край, поле) fertile; (разг: местечко) well-paid; э́то год был ~ we had a good harvest this year; ~ые дрóжжи baker's yeast.

хлебобýлочный прил: ~ые издéлия bread products мн.

хлебозавóд (-а) м bakery.

хлеборéзка (-и; gen pl -ок) ж bread slicer.

хлеборóб (-а) м harvester.

хлеборóдный прил (край, земля) fertile; э́тот год был ~ we had a good harvest this year.

хлебосóльный прил hospitable.

хлебцá итп сущ см хлебéц.

хлев (-а; loc sg -ý, nom pl -á) м cowshed; (перен: разг) pigsty.

хлестáть (-ещý, -éщешь) несов перех (ремнём, кнутóм) to whip; (по лицу, по щекам) to slap; (разг: водку, пиво) to knock back ♦ неперех (дождь) to lash down; (вода, кровь) to gush; (пули) to rain down; вóлны ~естáли о борт лóдки the waves lashed against the side of the boat.

хлёсткий (-кая, -кое, -кие; -ок, -кá, -ко) прил (перен) scathing.

хлестнýть (-ý, -ёшь) сов перех to whip; (по щеке) to slap.

хлёсток прил см хлёсткий.

хлещý итп несов см хлестáть.

хли́пкий (-ая, -ое, -ие) прил (разг: здоровье) poor; (: человек, земля) weedy; (: стол, строение) wobbly.

хлоп как сказ (разг): он меня́ ~ по спинé he whacked me right in the back; он ~ на кровáть he flopped onto the bed.

хлóпать (-ю) несов перех (ладóнью) to slap; (кнутóм) to lash ♦ неперех (+instr; дверью, крышкой) to slam; (+dat; артисту, певцу) to clap; (хлопушка, выстрел) to go bang; ~ (impf) ушáми/глазáми (разг) to look stupid/baffled.

хлóпка сущ см хлопóк.

хлопкá сущ см хлопóк.

хлопковóдство (-а) ср cotton growing.

хлóпковый прил cotton.

хлопнýть (-у, -ешь) сов перех (по спине) to slap ♦ неперех (в ладони) to clap; (дверь) to slam shut; (хлопушка, выстрел) to go bang; (+instr; дверью) to slam; (кнутóм) to crack.

хлопóк (-ка) м cotton.

хлопóк (-кá) м (удар в ладоши) clap; (выстрела, кнута) crack; (по спине, по затылку) slap.

хлопотáть (-очý, -óчешь) несов неперех (по дому, по хозяйству) to busy o.s.; (добиваться): ~ о +prp (о разрешении, о пособии итп) to be busy trying to get; ~ (impf) о ком-н или за кого-н to trouble o.s. on sb's behalf.

хлопотли́вый (-, -а, -о) прил (человек) busy; (дело, обязанности) troublesome.

хлопóтный прил (разг) troublesome.

хлопóты (-óт; dat pl -отам) мн (по хозяйству, по дому итп) things мн to do; (о ком-н) effort ед, trouble ед; все мои́ ~ бы́ли напрáсны all of my efforts were in vain; хлопóт пóлон рот he итп has troubles galore.

хлопочý итп несов см хлопотáть.

хлопýшка (-ки; gen pl -ек) ж (для мух) fly swatter; (игрушка) (Christmas) cracker.

хлопчáтник (-а) м (бот: растение) cotton.

хлопчатобумáжный прил cotton.

хлóпья (-ев) мн (снега, мыла) flakes мн; (ваты, овчины) clumps мн; кукурýзные ~ cornflakes.

хлор (-а) м chlorine.

хлóрка (-и) ж (разг) bleaching powder.

хлóрный прил: ~ая и́звесть bleaching powder; хлóрная кислотá hydrochloric acid.

хлы́нуть (3sg -ет, 3pl -ут) сов неперех to flood; (перен: мысли, воспоминания) to flood back.

хлыст (-á) м whip.

хлыщ (-á) м playboy.

хлюпать (-ю) несов неперех (разг) to squelch; ~ (impf) нóсом to sniff.

хля́стик (-а) м half-belt.

хмелéть (-ю) несов неперех to be drunk; ~ (impf) от счáстья/свобóды to be drunk with happiness/freedom.

хмель (-я) м (бот) hops мн; (опьянение) drunkenness; во ~ю̌ drunk.

хмельнóй прил drunken; (напиток) alcoholic; (воздух, запах) intoxicating.

хмýрить (-ю, -ишь; perf нахмýрить) несов перех (лоб, брови) to furrow

► хмýриться несов возв to frown; (небо) to become overcast; (погода, день) to turn gloomy.

хмýро нареч gloomily ♦ как сказ: сегóдня на ýлице ~ it's very gloomy outside; у негó на душé ~ he's feeling very gloomy.

хмýрый прил gloomy.

хмы́кать (-ю) несов неперех (разг) to say "hmm" as a sign of surprise, annoyance etc.

хмы́кнуть (-у, -ешь) сов неперех to say "hmm" as a sign of surprise, annoyance etc.

хна (-ы) ж henna.

хны́кать (-ю) несов неперех (разг: плакать) to whimper; (перен: жаловаться) to whine.

хóбби ср нескл hobby.

хóбот (-а) м (слона) trunk.

хоботóк (-кá) м (насекомого) proboscis.

ход (-а; part gen -у, loc sg -ý) м (поезда, машины,

руля, поршня) movement; (*событий, дела итп*) course; (*часов, двигателя*) working; (*КАРТЫ*) go; (*маневр, также ШАХМАТЫ*) move; (*возможность*) chance; (*вход*) entrance; (*туннель*) passage; **в хо́де** +gen in the course of; ~ **мы́слей** train of thought; **идти́ (пойти́** perf) **в** ~ to come into use; **пуска́ть (пусти́ть** perf) **что-н в** ~ (*механизм*) to bring into use; (*слово, тип одежды*) to popularize; **быть** (*impf*) **в (большо́м)** ~**у́** to be (very) popular; **на** ~**у́** (*есть, разгова́ривать*) on the move; (*делать замечания, шутить*) in passing; **с хо́ду** straight off; **он с хо́ду взбежа́л на ле́стницу** he ran straight upstairs; **до до́ма три часа́** ~**у́** it's three hours' walk to the house; **дава́ть (дать** perf) ~ **де́лу** to set things in motion; **дава́ть (дать** perf) ~ **но́вым лю́дям/ме́тодам** to give new people/ methods a chance; **дава́ть (дать** perf) **за́дний** ~ (*АВТ*) to reverse; (*человек*) to retreat; **знать** (*impf*) **все** ~**ы́ и вы́ходы** to know all the ins and outs; **де́ло идёт свои́м хо́дом** events are taking their natural course; **по хо́ду де́ла** during the course of events; **чей** ~? (*в игре*) whose go is it?

хода́тайство (-а) *ср* petition; **подава́ть (пода́ть** perf) ~ to submit a petition.

хода́тайствовать (-ую; *perf* **походата́йствовать**) *несов неперех*: ~ **о чём-н/за кого́-н** to petition for sth/on sb's behalf.

хо́дики (-ов) *мн* wall clock *ед*.

ходи́ть (-жу́, -дишь) *несов неперех* to walk; (*по магазинам, в гости, в кино итп*) to go (*on foot*); (*поезд, автобус итп*) to go; (*слухи, грипп*) to go round; (*часы*) to work; (+*instr: тузом итп*) to play; (*конём, пешкой итп*) to move; (*носить*): ~ **в** +*prp* (*в пальто, в сапога́х итп*) to wear; (*ухаживать*): ~ **за кем-н** to look after sb.

хо́дкий (-кая, -кое, -кие; -ок, -ка́, -ко) *прил* (*разг: машина*) speedy; (: *товар*) popular.

ходово́й *прил* popular.

ходо́к *прил см* **хо́дкий**.

ходо́к (-а́) *м*: **он хоро́ший** ~ he's a good walker; **туда́ я бо́льше не** ~ (*разг*) I'm not going there again.

ходу́ля (-и; *gen pl* -ей) *ж* (*обычно мн*) stilt.

ходуно́м *нареч*: **ходи́ть** ~ (*разг*) to shake.

ходьба́ (-ы́) *ж* walking; **полчаса́** ~**ы́** half an hour's walk.

ходя́чий (-ая, -ее, -ие) *прил* trendy; (*избитый*) hackneyed; (*больной*) able to walk; **он** ~**ая доброде́тель** he is a paragon of virtue.

хожде́ние (-я) *ср* walking; (*слухов*) circulation; **име́ть** (*impf*) ~ (*валюта*) to be in circulation; (*выражение, товар*) to be popular.

хожу́ *несов см* **ходи́ть**.

хозрасчёт (-а) *м* (= *хозя́йственный расчёт*) *system of management based on self-financing and self- governing principles.*

хозрасчётн|**ый** *прил*: ~**ое предприя́тие** self-financing, self-governing enterprise.

хозя́ева *итп сущ см* **хозя́ин**.

хозя́ек *сущ см* **хозя́йка**.

хозя́|ин (-ина; *nom pl* -**ева**, *gen pl* -**ев**) *м* (*владелец*) owner; (*сдающий жильё*) landlord; (*пользующийся наёмным трудом*) employer; (*принимающий гостей*) host; (*ведущий хозяйство*) manager; (*перен: положения, своей судьбы*) master.

хозя́|йка (-**йки**; *gen pl* -**ек**) *ж* (*владелица*) owner; (*сдающая жильё*) landlady; (*принимающая гостей*) hostess; (*разг: жена*) missus, old lady; **дома́шняя** ~ housewife.

хозя́йнича|**ть** (-**ю**) *несов неперех* (*в доме, на кухне*) to be in charge; (*командовать*) to be bossy.

хозя́йский (-ая, -ое, -ие) *прил*: (**это**) **де́ло** ~**ое** (*разг*) have it your own way.

хозя́йственник (-а) *м* manager.

хозя́йственный *прил* (*деятельность, управление*) economic *опред*; (*постройка, инвентарь*) domestic *опред*; (*человек*) thrifty; **хозя́йственные това́ры** hardware; **хозя́йственный магази́н** hardware shop.

хозя́йств|**о** (-а) *ср* (*ЭКОН*) economy; (*производственная единица*) enterprise; (*оборудование*) equipment; (*предметы быта*) household goods *мн*; **городско́е/наро́дное** ~ urban/national economy; **дома́шнее** ~ housekeeping; **вести́** (*impf*) ~ to run the house.

хозя́йств|**овать** (-**ую**) *несов неперех*: ~ **на предприя́тии/фи́рме** to manage an enterprise/firm; **он уме́ло** ~**ует** he is a good manager.

хоккеи́ст (-а) *м* hockey player.

хокке́й (-я) *м* hockey; ~ **с ша́йбой/на траве́** ice/field hockey.

хокке́йный *прил* hockey *опред*.

хо́лдинг (-а) *м* (*КОММ*) holding.

хо́лдингов|**ый** *прил*: ~**ая компа́ния** holding company.

хо́леный *прил* (*человек, лошадь*) well-groomed; (*лицо, руки*) elegant.

холёный *прил* = **хо́леный**.

холе́р|**а** (-**ы**) *ж* (*МЕД*) cholera.

холестери́н (-а) *м* cholesterol.

холл (-а) *м* (*театра, гостиницы*) foyer, lobby; (*в квартире, в доме*) hall.

холм (-а́) *м* hill.

хо́лмик (-а) *м* hillock.

холми́стый (-, -а, -о) *прил* hilly.

хо́лод (-а; *nom pl* -а́) *м* cold; (*осенний, зимний*) cold weather; (*перен: равнодушие*) coldness; (*озно́б*) cold shiver.

холода́|ть (*3sg* -ет, *perf* **похолода́ть**) *несов безл* to turn cold.

хо́лоден *прил см* **холо́дный**.

холоде́|ть (-**ю**; *perf* **похолоде́ть**) *несов неперех* (*руки, ноги*) to get cold; (*от страха, при смерти*) to go cold.

холодéц (**-цá**) *м* meat in aspic.

холодúльник (**-а**) *м* (*домашний*) fridge, refrigerator; (*промышленный*) refrigerator; **двухкáмерный ~** fridge-freezer.

хóлодно *нареч* coldly ♦ *как сказ* it's cold; (+*dat*): **мне** *итп* **~** I'm *итп* cold; **на ýлице сегóдня ~** it's cold outside today.

холóдный (**-оден, -однá, -одно**) *прил* cold; **эта кýртка ~óдная** this jacket isn't very warm; **холóдная войнá** cold war; **холóдное орýжие** side arms *мн*.

холодцá *итп сущ см* **холодéц**.

холостóй (**хóлост**) *прил* (*мужчина*) unmarried, single; (*no short form*; **выстрел, патрон**) blank; **рабóтать** (*impf*) **на ~óм ходý** (*АВТ, ТЕХ*) to idle, tick over; **~ прогóн** dry run.

холостя́к (**-á**) *м* bachelor.

холу́й (**-я**) *м* sycophant.

холст (**-á**) *м* canvas.

хомýт (**-á**) *м* (*коня*) harness collar; (*ТЕХ*) clamp; (*перен*) bind; **повéсить** (*perf*) *или* **надéть** (*perf*) **себé ~ на шéю** to weigh o.s. down.

хомя́к (**-á**) *м* hamster.

хор (**-а**) *м* choir; (*перен*) chorus.

хорвáт (**-а**) *м* Croatian.

Хорвáтия (**-и**) *ж* Croatia.

хорвáтка (**-ки**; *gen pl* **-ок**) *ж см* **хорвáт**.

хорвáтский (**-ая, -ое, -ие**) *прил* Croatian.

хорёк (**-ькá**) *м* ferret.

хореóграф (**-а**) *м* choreographer.

хореогрáфия (**-и**) *ж* choreography.

хорúст (**-а**) *м* chorister.

хорúстка (**-ки**; *gen pl* **-ок**) *ж см* **хорúст**.

хормéйстер (**-а**) *м* choirmaster.

хоровóд (**-а**) *м* round dance.

хоровóй *прил* choral.

хóром *нареч* in unison.

хорóмы (**-**) *мн* mansion *ед*.

хорóнить (**-оню, -óнишь**; *perf* **похоронúть**) *несов перех* to bury.

хорохóриться (**-юсь, -ишься**) *несов возв* (*разг*) to brag.

хорóшенький (**-ая, -ое, -ие**) *прил* (*симпатичный*) pretty; (*разг: плохой*) fine, nice.

хорóшенько *нареч* well (*разг*) properly.

хорошéть (**-ю**; *perf* **похорошéть**) *несов неперех* to become more attractive.

хорóший (**-ая, -ее, -ие**; **-, -á, -о**) *прил* good; **он хорóш (собóю)** he's good-looking; **хорóш друг!** (*разг*) a fine friend!; **всегó ~его!** all the best!

хорошó *нареч* well ♦ *как сказ* it's good; (+*dat*): **мне ~** I feel good ♦ *част, вводн сл* okay, all right ♦ *ср нескл* (*ПРОСВЕЩ*) ≈ good (*school mark*); **~ отдыхáть (отдохнýть** *perf*) to have a good rest; **на мóре ~** it's nice by the sea; **мне здесь ~** I like it here; **~, я соглáсен** okay, I agree; **ну, ~!** (*разг: выражение угрозы*) right then!; **~ бы поéсть/поспáть** (*разг*) I wouldn't

mind a bite to eat/getting some sleep.

хóры (**-ов**) *мн* (*в церкви, в большом зале*) gallery *ед*.

хорькá *итп сущ см* **хорёк**.

хот-дóг (**-а**) *м* hot dog.

хотéть (*см* **Table 16**) *несов перех*: **~ +***infin* to want to do; **как ~тúте** (*как вам угодно*) as you wish; (*а всё-таки*) no matter what you say; **хóчешь не хóчешь** whether you like it or not; **~** (*impf*) **есть/пить** to be hungry/thirsty

► **хотéться** *несов безл* (+*infin*): **мне** *итп* **хóчется плáкать/есть** I *итп* feel like crying/something to eat; **мне хóчется чáю** I feel like some tea.

KEYWORD

хоть *союз* **1** (*несмотря на то, что*) (al)though; **хоть я и обúжен, я помогý тебé** although I am hurt, I will help you

2 (*до такой степени, что*) even if; **не соглашáется, хоть до утрá просú** he won't agree, even if you ask all night; **хоть умрú, а дéнег достáнь** get hold of some money, even if it kills you; **хоть убéй, не могý пойтú на это** I couldn't do that to save my life; **хоть..., хоть** either ..., or; **езжáй хоть сегóдня, хоть чéрез мéсяц** go either today, or in a month's time
♦ *част* **1** (*служит для усиления*) at least; **подвезú егó хоть до стáнции** take him to the station at least; **поймú хоть ты** you of all people should understand

2 (*разг: например*) for example; **взять хоть Мáрию**: **онá же всё врéмя рабóтает** take Maria for example, she works all the time

3 (*во фразах*): **хоть бы** at least; **хоть бы ты емý позвонúл!** you could at least phone him!; **хоть бы закóнчить сегóдня!** if only we could get finished today!; **хоть кто** anyone; **хоть какóй** any; **емý хоть бы что** it doesn't bother him; **хоть кудá!** (*разг*) excellent!; **хоть бы и так!** so what!

хотя́ *союз* although; **~ и** even though; **~ бы** at least; **он срáзу всё пóнял, ~ и не знал подрóбностей** even without knowing the details, he was able to understand at once; **возьмúте ~ бы примéр Áнглии** take England for example.

хотя́т(ся) *несов см* **хотéть(ся)**.

хохлá *итп сущ см* **хохóл**.

хохломá (**-ы́**) *ж* khokhloma (*traditional wooden articles decorated in red, gold and black*).

хóхма (**-ы**) *ж* (*разг*) joke; (*что-н смешное*) laugh.

хохóл (**-лá**) *м* (*клок волос*) tuft of hair; (*разг: пренебр*) Ukrainian.

хóхот (**-а**) *м* guffaw; (*шакала*) laugh.

хохотáть (**-очý, -óчешь**) *несов неперех* to laugh (loudly); (*филин, шакал*) to laugh; **~** (*impf*) **над** +*instr* to laugh at; **я ~отáл до слёз** I laughed till the tears ran down my face.

хочý(сь) *итп несов см* **хотéть(ся)**.

храбре́ц (-á) *м* brave person (*мн* people).
храбри́ться (-ю́сь, -и́шься) *несов возв* (*разг*) to try to appear brave.
хра́бро *нареч* bravely.
хра́брость (-и) *ж* bravery, courage.
хра́бр|ый (-, -á, -о) *прил* brave, courageous.
храм (-а) *м* (*РЕЛ*) temple.
хране́ни|е (-я) *ср* (*денег*) keeping; ~ **ору́жия** possession of firearms; **ка́мера для ~я багажа́** left-luggage office (*BRIT*), checkroom (*US*); **сдава́ть** (**сдать** *perf*) **ве́щи на** ~ to put things in for safekeeping.
храни́лищ|е (-а) *ср* store.
храни́тел|ь (-я) *м* curator, keeper.
хран|и́ть (-ю́, -и́шь) *несов перех* to keep; (*границы, достоинство*) to protect; (*традиции*) to preserve; ~ (*impf*) **что-н в та́йне** to keep sth secret
▸ **храни́ться** *несов возв* to be kept.
храп (-а) *м* (*во сне*) snoring.
храп|е́ть (-лю́, -и́шь) *несов неперех* (*человек*) to snore; (*лошадь*) to snort.
хреб|е́т (-та́) *м* (*АНАТ*) spine; (*разг: спина*) back; (*ГЕО*) ridge.
хребто́вый *прил* (*позвонки*) spinal; (*перевал, гряда*) mountain *опред*.
хрен (-а) *м* (*БОТ, КУЛИН*) horseradish; (*груб!*) willy (*!*); ~ **его́ зна́ет** (*разг*) who the hell knows; **ста́рый** ~ (*разг*) old fool.
хрено́вый *прил* (*БОТ, КУЛИН*) horseradish *опред*; (*груб!*) crappy (*!*) (*BRIT*), lousy (*US*).
хрестомати́йный *прил* (*идея, образ*) basic.
хрестома́ти|я (-и) *ж* study aid, reader.
хризанте́м|а (-ы) *ж* chrysanthemum.
хрип (-а) *м* wheezing; **предсме́ртный** ~ dying gasp.
хрип|е́ть (-лю́, -и́шь) *несов неперех* (*лошадь, больной*) to wheeze; (*пластинка*) to crackle.
хри́пл|ый (-, -á, -о) *прил* (*голос*) hoarse; (*гармонь, звук*) wheezing.
хриплю́ *несов см* **хрипе́ть**
хри́пн|уть (-у, -ешь; *perf* **охри́пнуть**) *несов неперех* to become *или* grow hoarse.
хрипот|а́ (-ы́) *ж* hoarseness.
христиан|и́н (-ани́на; *nom pl* -а́не, *gen pl* -а́н) *м* Christian.
христиа́н|ка (-ки; *gen pl* -ок) *ж см* **христиани́н**.
христиа́нск|ий (-ая, -ое, -ие) *прил* Christian.
христиа́нств|о (-а) *ср* Christianity.
Христ|о́с (-а́) *м* Christ; ~**á ра́ди** (*разг*) for Christ's sake.
хром (-а) *м* (*ХИМ*) chrome; (*краска*) chrome yellow; (*кожа*) box calf.
хрома́|ть (-ю) *несов неперех* to limp; (*перен: разг: знания, дисциплина*) to be weak; **моя́ матема́тика** ~**ет** (*разг*) my maths is pretty shaky.
хро́мовый *прил* (*ХИМ*) chrome; (*кожа, сапоги*

итп) box-calf.
хром|о́й (-, -á, -о) *прил* lame; (*перен: разг: стол итп*) wobbly.
хромосо́м|а (-ы) *ж* chromosome.
хромот|а́ (-ы́) *ж* limp.
хро́ник (-а) *м* (*разг*) bad case.
хро́ник|а (-и) *ж* chronicle; (*КИНО*) film chronicle.
хроника́льный *прил* chronicle *опред*.
хроникёр (-а) *м* (*журналист*) reporter.
хрони́ческ|ий (-ая, -ое, -ие) *прил* chronic.
хронологи́ческ|ий (-ая, -ое, -ие) *прил* chronological; **в** ~**ой после́довательности** in chronological order.
хроноло́ги|я (-и) *ж* chronology.
хронометра́ж (-а) *м* time-keeping.
хру́п|кий (-кая, -кое, -кие; -ок, -ка́, -ко) *прил* (*лёд, стекло итп*) fragile; (*печенье, кости*) brittle; (*перен: фигура, девушка*) delicate; (: *здоровье, организм*) frail.
хру́пкость (-и) *ж* (*см прил*) fragility; brittleness; delicacy; frailty.
хру́пок *прил см* **хру́пкий**.
хруст (-а) *м* crunch.
хруста́лик (-а) *м* (*АНАТ*) lens.
хруста́л|ь (-я́) *м, собир* crystal; **го́рный** ~ rock crystal.
хруста́льный *прил* crystal *опред*; (*перен: лёд, звон*) crystal clear.
хру|сте́ть (-щу́, -сти́шь) *несов неперех* to crunch; (+*instr*; *редиской, сахаром итп*) to crunch.
хрустя́щ|ий (-ая, -ее, -ие) *прил* crunchy; (*скатерть, бельё*) crisp; **хрустя́щий карто́фель** potato crisps (*BRIT*) *или* chips (*US*) *мн*.
хрущу́ *несов см* **хрусте́ть**.
хрю́ка|ть (-ю) *несов неперех* to grunt.
хрящ (-á) *м* (*АНАТ*) cartilage.
ХСС *м сокр* (= **Христиа́нско-социалисти́ческий сою́з**) CSU (= *Christian Socialist Union*).
худе́|ть (-ю) *несов неперех* to grow thin; (*быть на дие́те*) to slim.
худо́жественный *прил* artistic; (*школа, выставка*) art *опред*; **худо́жественная литерату́ра** fiction; **худо́жественная самоде́ятельность** amateur art and performance; **худо́жественный сало́н** (*выставка*) art exhibition; (*магазин*) ≈ craft shop; **худо́жественный фильм** feature film.
худо́жеств|о (-а) *ср*: **акаде́мия худо́жеств** art school.
худо́жник (-а) *м* artist.
худо́жниц|а (-ы) *ж см* **худо́жник**.
худ|о́й (-, -á, -о) *прил* thin; (*разг: плохой*) bad; (: *дырявый*) full of holes; **на** ~ **коне́ц** if the worst comes to the worst (*BRIT*), in the worst case scenario (*US*).
худоща́в|ый (-, -а, -о) *прил* thin.

The spelling rules for Russian are shown on page xvii.

хýдш|ее (-его; *decl like adj*) *ср* the worst.

хýдш|ий (-ая, -ее, -ие) *превос прил* the worst опред.

хýже *сравн прил, нареч* worse.

хуй (-я) *м* (*груб!*) cock (*!*), prick (*!*)

хулигáн (-а) *м* hooligan.

хулигáн|ить (-ю, -ишь; *perf* **нахулигáнить**) *несов неперех* to act like a hooligan.

хулигáн|ка (-ки; *gen pl* -**ок**) *ж см* **хулигáн**.

хулигáнск|ий (-ая, -ое, -ие) *прил*: ~ **постýпок** act of hooliganism; ~**ое поведéние** hooliganism.

хулигáнств|о (-а) *ср* hooliganism.

хулиганьё (-я) *ср собир* hooligans *мн*, yobs *мн* (*BRIT*).

хули́ть (-ю, -ишь) *несов перех* (*порочить*) to abuse.

хýнт|а (-ы) *ж* (*ПОЛИТ*) junta.

хурм|á (-ы́) *ж* (*дерево*) persimmon tree; (*плод*) persimmon, sharon fruit.

хýтор (-а) *м* (*ферма*) farmstead; (*селение*) village (*in Southern Russia and the Ukraine*).

хуторя́н|ин (-ина; *nom pl* -**е**, *gen pl* -) *м* (*владелец хутора*) farmer; (*житель хутора*) villager.

хуторя́н|ка (-ки; *gen pl* -**ок**) *ж см* **хуторя́нин**.

~ Ц, ц ~

Ц, ц *сущ нескл (буква)* the 23rd letter of the Russian alphabet.

ц. *сокр* (= **центр**) ctr. (= *centre*); = **цена́**.

ца́па|ть (-ю) *несов перех (когтями, зубами)* to seize; *(perf* **сца́пать**; *разг)* to snatch, grab.

ца́п|ля (-ли; *gen pl* **-ель)** *ж* heron.

ца́пн|уть (-у, -ешь) *сов перех* to seize; *(разг)* to snatch, grab.

цара́панье (-я) *ср* scratching.

цара́па|ть (-ю; *perf* **оцара́пать)** *несов перех (раздирать)* to scratch; *(perf* **нацара́пать**; *разг:* *писать)* to scribble

▸ **цара́паться** *(perf* **оцара́паться)** *несов возв* to scratch; *(no perf; друг друга)* to scratch one another.

цара́пин|а (-ы) *ж* scratch.

царе́вен *сущ см* **царе́вна**.

царе́вич (-а) *м* tsarevich *(son of the tsar)*.

царе́в|на (-ны; *gen pl* **-ен)** *ж* tsarevna *(daughter of the tsar)*.

цари́зм (-а) *м* tsarism.

цар|и́ть (-ю́, -и́шь) *несов неперех (также перен)* to reign.

цари́ц|а (-ы) *ж* tsarina *(wife of the tsar)*, empress; *(перен: бала, моды)* queen.

ца́рск|ий (-ая, -ое, -ие) *прил (двор, указ, семья)* tsar's, royal; *(режим, правительство)* tsarist; *(перен: роскошь, прием)* regal.

ца́рствен|ный (-, -на, -но) *прил* regal.

ца́рств|о (-а) *ср (государство)* tsardom; *(царствование)* reign; *(перен: любви, природы)* realm; **живо́тное/расти́тельное ~** the animal/plant kingdom.

ца́рствование (-я) *ср* reign.

ца́рств|овать (-ую) *несов неперех (также перен)* to reign.

цар|ь (-я́) *м* tsar; *(перен)* king; **без ~я́ в голове́** *(разг)* completely daft.

ЦБ *м сокр* = **центра́льный банк**.

ЦБНТИ *ср сокр* = **Центра́льное бюро́ нау́чно-техни́ческой информа́ции**.

цве|сти́ (-ту́, -тёшь) *несов неперех (БОТ)* to blossom, flower; *(перен: страна, человек)* to flourish; **~** *(impf)* **здоро́вьем/от ра́дости** to be bursting with health/joy.

цвет (-а; *nom pl* **-á)** *м (окраска)* colour *(BRIT)*, color *(US)*; *(part gen* **-у**, *loc sg* **-у́**; *БОТ)* blossom; **~ о́бщества** the cream of society; **во цве́те лет** in the prime of life.

цвета́с|тый (-, -а, -о) *прил* colourful *(BRIT)*, colorful *(US)*.

цвете́ни|е (-я) *ср* blossoming.

цвети́с|тый (-, -а, -о) *прил (узор)* floral; *(луг, поле)* flower-covered; *(речь, стиль)* flowery.

цветка́ *итп сущ см* **цвето́к**.

цветни́к (-á) *м* flowerbed.

цветн|о́й *прил (карандаш)* coloured *(BRIT)*, colored *(US)*; *(одежда)* colourful *(BRIT)*, colorful *(US)*; *(фотография, фильм)* colour *(BRIT)*, color *(US)* ◆ *(-о́го; decl like adj)* *м (человек)* colo(u)red: **цветна́я капу́ста** cauliflower: **цветно́й телеви́зор** colo(u)r television: **цветны́е мета́ллы** non-ferrous metals.

цвет|о́к (-ка́; *nom pl* **-ки́)** *м* flower *(reproductive part of a plant)*; *(nom pl* **-ы́)** flower *(bloom)*; *(комнатный)* plant.

цветому́зык|а (-и) *ж* son et lumière, sound-and-light show *(US)*.

цвето́чник (-а) *м* florist.

цвето́чниц|а (-ы) *ж см* **цвето́чник**.

цвето́чный *прил* flower *опред*; *(духи)* flower-scented; **цвето́чный горшо́к** flowerpot; **цвето́чный магази́н** florist's.

цвету́ *итп несов см* **цвести́**.

цвету́щ|ий (-ая, -ее, -ие) *прил (вид, женщина)* blossoming; *(область, экономика)* flourishing.

ЦГА́ЛИ *м сокр* = **Центра́льный госуда́рственный архи́в литерату́ры и иску́сства**.

ЦГИА́ *м сокр* = **Центра́льный госуда́рственный истори́ческий архи́в**.

це|ди́ть (-жу́, -дишь; *perf* **процеди́ть)** *несов перех (молоко, отвар)* to strain; *(no perf; заливить: в бутылку)* to siphon; *(perf* **процеди́ть**; *перен: слова)* to force out.

це́др|а (-ы) *ж* (dried) peel.

цежу́ *несов см* **цеди́ть**.

Цейло́н (-а) *м* Ceylon.

цейло́нск|ий (-ая, -ое, -ие) *прил* Ceylonese.

цейтно́т (-а) *м:* **быть в ~е** *(ШАХМАТЫ)* to be in time-trouble; *(перен: разг)* to be pushed for time.

целе́бен *прил см* **целе́бный**.

целе́бност|ь (-и) *ж* healing *или* medicinal properties *мн*.

целе́б|ный (-ен, -на, -но) *прил* medicinal; *(воздух)* healthy.

целево́й *прил (задание, установка)* special; *(финансирование, ссуды)* for a specified purpose; **~ ры́нок** *(КОММ)* target market.

це́лен *прил см* **це́льный**.

целенапра́вленност|ь (-и) *ж* single-mindedness.

целенапра́вленный *прил* single-minded.

целесообра́зен *прил см* **целесообра́зный**.

целесообра́зно *нареч* expediently ♦ *как сказ* it makes sense; **~ заверши́ть рабо́ту сейча́с** it makes sense to finish the work now.

целесообра́зност|ь (-и) *ж* expediency.

целесообра́з|ный (-ен, -на, -но) *прил* expedient.

целеустремлён|ный (-, -на, -но) *прил* purposeful.

целико́м *нареч:* **проглоти́ть/съесть что-н ~** to swallow/eat sth whole; *(перен: без ограничений)* wholly, entirely.

целин|а́ (-ы́) *ж (также перен)* virgin territory; **сне́жная ~** virgin snow.

цели́нный *прил (земля)* virgin *опред*.

цели́тел|ьный (-ен, -ьна, -ьно) *прил (бальзам)* medicinal; *(действие, свойство)* healing *опред*; *(воздух)* healthy.

це́л|ить (-ю, -ишь; *perf* **наце́лить)** *несов непрех:* **~ в** *+acc* to aim at; *(перен: в начальники)* to have one's sights set on

▶ **це́литься** *(perf* **наце́литься)** *несов возв:* **~ся в** *+acc* to (take) aim at; **~ся (наце́литься** *perf)* *+infin (разг)* to aim to do.

целлофа́н (-а) *м* cellophane®.

целлофа́новый *прил* cellophane® *опред*.

целлуло́ид (-а) *м* celluloid.

целлюло́з|а (-ы) *ж* cellulose.

цел|ова́ть (-у́ю; *perf* **поцелова́ть)** *несов перех* to kiss

▶ **целова́ться** *(perf* **поцелова́ться)** *несов возв* to kiss (each other).

це́л|ое (-ого; *decl like adj)* *ср* whole; *(МАТ)* integer; **еди́ное ~** unified whole.

целому́дрен|ный (-, -на, -но) *прил* chaste.

целому́дри|е (-я) *ср (девственность)* chastity; *(нравственность)* chasteness.

це́лостен *прил см* **це́лостный**.

це́лостност|ь (-и) *ж* integrity.

це́лост|ный (-ен, -на, -но) *прил* integrated.

це́лост|ь (-и) *ж (машины, предмета)* safety; *(денег, инвестиций)* security, safety; **в ~и и сохра́нности** in one piece; **сохран|я́ть (сохрани́ть** *perf)* **что-н в ~и** to keep sth safe.

це́л|ый *прил* whole, entire; *(-, -а́, -о; неповреждённый: машина, оборудование итп)* intact, undamaged; *(: одежда)* undamaged; **в ~ом (целико́м)** as a whole; *(в общем)* on the whole; **~ и невреди́мый** safe and sound; **~ ряд**

+gen pl a whole range of; **це́лое число́** *(МАТ)* whole number.

цель (-и) *ж (при стрельбе)* target; *(перен)* aim, goal; **с це́лью** *+infin* with the object *или* aim of doing; **с це́лью** *+gen* for; **в це́лях** *+gen* for the purpose of; **в воспита́тельных/рекла́мных це́лях** for education/publicity purposes.

це́льност|ь (-и) *ж* integrity, completeness.

це́л|ьный (-ен, -ьна, -ьно; характер, произведение) *прил (кусок, камень)* solid; *(-ен, -ьна,* complete; *(теория)* integrated; **~ьное молоко́** full-cream milk.

цеме́нт (-а) *м* cement.

цементи́р|овать (-ую; *perf* **зацементи́ровать)** *несов перех* to cement; *(perf* **сцементи́ровать;** *перен)* to cement.

цеме́нтный *прил* cement *опред*.

цен|а́ (-ы́; *acc sg* **-у,** *dat sg* **-е́,** *nom pl* **-ы)** *ж* price; *(перен: суждения, человека)* value; **~о́ю** *+gen* at the expense of; **таки́е лю́ди/кни́ги в ~е́** such people/books are highly prized; **ему́ ~ы́ нет** he is invaluable; **~ продавца́** *(КОММ)* offer price; **торго́вая ~** *(КОММ)* trade price.

це́нен *прил см* **це́нный**.

ценз (-а) *м* requirement.

це́нзор (-а) *м* censor.

цензу́р|а (-ы) *ж* censorship.

цензу́р|ный *прил* censorship *опред*; *(-ен, -на, -но; присто́йный)* acceptable.

цени́тел|ь (-я) *м* judge *(of art, character etc)*.

цени́тельни|ца (-ы) *ж см* **цени́тель**.

цен|и́ть (-ю́, -ишь) *несов перех (дорожи́ть)* to value; *(помощь, совет)* to appreciate; *(разг: назнача́ть цену)* to name a price for

▶ **цени́ться** *несов непрех* to be (highly) valued.

це́нник (-а) *м (бирка)* price tag; *(список)* price list.

це́нност|ь (-и) *ж* value; *(обычно мн: духовные, культурные)* treasure; **~и** valuables; **материа́льные ~и** commodities.

це́н|ный (-ен, -на, -но) *прил* valuable; *(no short form; посылка, письмо)* registered; **це́нные бума́ги** *(КОММ)* securities *мн*.

ценообразова́ни|е (-я) *ср* price formation.

цент (-а) *м* cent.

це́нтнер (-а) *м* centner *(100kg)*.

центр (-а) *м* centre *(BRIT)*, center *(US)*; **в це́нтре внима́ния** in the limelight; **торго́вый центр** shopping centre *(BRIT) или* mall *(US)*.

централи́зм (-а) *м* centralism.

централиз|ова́ть (-у́ю; *(не)сов перех* to centralize.

центра́льный *прил* central; **~ проце́ссор** *(КОМП)* central processing unit; **центра́льная пре́сса** the national press; **центра́льное отопле́ние** central heating.

центрово́й *прил:* **~ напада́ющий/круг** centre forward/circle ♦ *(-о́го; decl like adj)* *м (в баскетбо́ле)* centre *(BRIT)*, center *(US)*; *(в футбо́ле)* midfielder.

цепене́|ть (-ю; *perf* **оцепене́ть)** *несов непрех*

(от ужаса, от страха) to freeze; ~ **(оцепенéть** *perf*) **от хóлода** to be frozen stiff.
цéп|кий (-кая, -кое, -кие; -ок, -ка, -ко) *прил* tenacious.
цепля́|ться (-юсь) *несов возв:* ~ **за** +*acc (также перен)* to cling *или* hang on to; ~ *(impf)* **рукавóм/ногóй за что-н** to catch one's sleeve/leg on sth; ~ *(impf)* **к чемý-н** *(перен: разг)* to pick up on sth.
цепнóй *прил* chain *опред;* **цепнáя реáкция** chain reaction; **цепнáя собáка** guard dog; **цепнóй мост** drawbridge.
цепpóк *прил см* **цéпкий.**
цепóч|ка (-ки; *gen pl* **-ек)** *ж (тонкая цепь)* chain; *(машин, людéй)* line; *(предложений)* string; **идти́** *(impf)* ~**кой** to walk in single file.
цеп|ь (-и; *loc sg* **-й)** *ж (также перен)* chain; *(элек)* circuit; **гóрная** ~ mountain range; **сажáть (посади́ть** *perf*) **когó-н на** ~ to chain sb up; **закóвывать (заковáть** *perf*) **когó-н в цéпи** to put sb in chains.
церемóнен *прил см* **церемóнный.**
церемóн|иться (-юсь, -ишься) *несов возв (стесняться)* to stand on ceremony; *(быть снисходительным):* ~ **с кем-н** to be too soft on sb.
церемóни|я (-и) *ж* ceremony; **без** ~**й** without ceremony.
церемóн|ный (-ен, -на, -но) *прил* ceremonious.
цéркви *итп сущ см* **цéрковь.**
церкóвник (-а) *м* clergyman *(мн* clergymen).
церковнослужи́тель (-я) *м* junior churchman *(мн* churchmen).
церкóвный *прил* church *опред.*
цéрк|овь (-ви; *instr sg* **-овью;** *nom pl* **-ви,** *gen pl* **-вéй)** *ж* church.
цех (-а; *loc sg* **-ý,** *nom pl* **-á)** *м* (work)shop *(in factory).*
цивилизáци|я (-и) *ж* civilization.
цивилизóванно *нареч* in a civilized manner.
цивилизóван|ный (-, -на, -но) *прил* civilized.
цивилизовáть (-ýю) *(не)сов перех* to civilize.
цигéй|ка (-и) *ж* beaver lamb.
цигéйковый *прил* beaver-lamb.
цикл (-а) *м* cycle; *(лекций, концертов итп)* series.
цикламéн (-а) *м* cyclamen.
цикли́чен *прил см* **цикли́чный.**
цикли́ческ|ий (-ая, -ое, -ие) *прил* cyclical.
цикли́ч|ный (-ен, -на, -но) *прил* = **цикли́ческий.**
циклóн (-а) *м* cyclone.
цикóри|й (-я) *м* chicory.
цили́ндр (-а) *м* cylinder; *(шляпа)* top hat.
цилиндри́ческ|ий (-ая, -ое, -ие) *прил* cylindrical.
цинг|á (-и́) *ж* scurvy.
цини́зм (-а) *м* cynicism.
цини́к (-а) *м* cynic.
цини́чен *прил см* **цини́чный.**
цини́чност|ь (-и) *ж* cynicism.

цини́ч|ный (-ен, -на, -но) *прил* cynical.
цинк (-а) *м* zinc.
ци́нковый *прил* zinc.
цирк (-а) *м* circus; *(разг: смешное событие)* farce.
циркá|ч (-á) *м (разг)* circus performer.
циркóвой *прил* circus *опред.*
циркули́р|овать (3sg -ует, 3pl -уют) *несов неперех* to circulate.
ци́ркул|ь (-я) *м* (a pair of) compasses.
циркуля́р (-а) *м* circular.
циркуля́ци|я (-и) *ж* circulation.
циррóз (-а) *м* cirrhosis.
цистéрн|а (-ы) *ж (резервуар)* cistern; *(автомобиль)* tanker; *(вагон)* tank wagon *(BRIT)* *или* car *(US).*
цитадéл|ь (-и) *ж (также перен)* citadel.
цитáт|а (-ы) *ж* quote, quotation.
цити́р|овать (-ую; *perf* **процити́ровать)** *несов перех* to quote.
ци́трус (-а) *м (обычно мн)* citrus fruit.
ци́трусовый *прил* citrus *опред.*
циферблáт (-а) *м* dial; *(на часах)* face.
ци́фр|а (-ы) *ж* number; *(арабские, римские)* numeral; *(обычно мн: расчет)* figure.
цифровóй *прил* numerical.
ЦК *м сокр* = **Центрáльный Комитéт.**
цóка|ть (-ю) *несов неперех (языком)* to tut; *(каблуки, копыта)* to clatter.
ЦП *сокр (= центрáльный процéссор)* CPU *(= central processing unit).*
ЦПКиО *м сокр (= Центрáльный парк культýры и óтдыха)* park used for recreational purposes.
ЦПКО *м сокр* = **ЦПКиО.**
ЦРУ *ср сокр (= Центрáльное разве́дывательное управлéние (США))* CIA *(= Central Intelligence Agency).*
ЦСДФ *ж сокр* = **Центрáльная стýдия документáльных фи́льмов.**
ЦСКА *м сокр* = **Центрáльный спорти́вный клуб áрмии.**
ЦСУ *ср сокр* = **Центрáльное статисти́ческое управлéние.**
ЦТ *ср сокр* = **Центрáльное телеви́дение.**
цукáт (-а) *м* candied fruit.
ЦУМ (-а) *м сокр* = **центрáльный универсáльный магази́н.**
цум (-а) *м сокр* = **ЦУМ.**
цунáми *ср нескл* tidal wave.
цыгáн (-а; *nom pl* **-е)** *м* gypsy.
цыгáн|ка (-ки; *gen pl* **-ок)** *ж см* **цыгáн.**
цыгáнск|ий (-ая, -ое, -ие) *прил* gypsy *опред.*
цы́ка|ть (-ю) *несов неперех (разг):* ~ **на** +*acc* to snap at.
цыплён|ок (-ёнка; *nom pl* **-я́та,** *gen pl* **-я́т)** *м* chick.
цыпля́ч|ий (-ая, -ее, -ие) *прил* chicken *опред;* *(перен: шея, руки)* scrawny.
цы́поч|ки (-ек) *мн:* **на** ~**ках** on tiptoe; **вставáть (встать** *perf*) **на** ~ to stand on tiptoe.
Цюрих (-а) *м* Zürich.

~ Ч, ч ~

Ч, ч *сущ нескл (буква)* the 24th letter of the Russian alphabet.

ча́вка|ть (-ю) *несов неперех* to chomp; *(перен: по грязи)* to squelch.

чад (-а; *loc sg* **-у́)** *м* fumes *мн*.

ча|ди́ть (-жу́, -ди́шь; *perf* **начади́ть)** *несов неперех* to give off fumes.

ча́д|о (-а) *ср* offspring *(мн* offspring*)*.

чадр|а́ (-ы́) *ж* yashmak.

чаевы́|е (-ы́х; *decl like adj)* мн tip *ед*; **дава́ть (дать** *perf)* **кому́-н** ~ to tip sb.

чаево́д (-а) *м* tea-grower.

чаево́дств|о (-а) *ср* tea-growing.

ча́ек *сущ см* **ча́йка.**

чаепи́ти|е (-я) *ср (занятие)* tea-drinking; *(событие)* tea-party.

чажу́ *несов см* **чади́ть.**

ча́йн|ка (-ки; *gen pl* **-ок)** *ж* tea leaf.

ча|й (-я; *part gen* **-ю,** *nom pl* **-й)** *м* tea; **зава́ривать (завари́ть** *perf)* ~ to make tea; **за ча́ем** over a cup of tea; **ча́шка ча́я** a cup of tea; **дава́ть (дать** *perf)* **кому́-н на** ~ to give sb a tip.

ча́йк|а (-йки; *gen pl* **-ек)** *ж* (sea)gull.

ча́йн|ая (-ой; *decl like adj)* ж tearoom, teashop.

ча́йник (-а) *м* kettle; *(для заварки)* teapot.

ча́йн|ый *прил (плантация)* tea *опред*; **ча́йная ло́жка** teaspoon; **ча́йный серви́з** tea service *или* set.

чалм|а́ (-ы́) *ж* turban.

чан (-а) *м (деревянный)* vat; *(металлический)* tank.

ча́р|ка (-ки; *gen pl* **-ок)** *ж* chalice.

чар|ова́ть (-у́ю) *несов перех (красотой)* to charm; *(умом)* to captivate.

чароде́ек *сущ см* **чароде́йка.**

чароде́|й (-я) *м* sorcerer.

чароде́|йка (-йки; *gen pl* **-ек)** *ж* sorceress.

ча́рок *сущ см* **ча́рка.**

ча́ртер (-а) *м (КОММ)* charter.

ча́ртерный *прил* charter *опред*.

ча́р|ы (-) *мн (обаяние)* charms *мн*; *(волшебство)* magic *ед*.

час (-а́; *nom pl* **-ы́)** *м* hour; **академи́ческий** ~ *(ПРОСВЕЩ)* ≈ period; **кото́рый** ~? what time is it?; **сейча́с 3** ~**а́ но́чи/дня** it's 3 o'clock in the morning/afternoon; **в 9** ~**о́в утра́/ве́чера** at 9 o'clock in the morning/evening; **стоя́ть** *(impf)* **на** ~**а́х** to stand guard; **по** ~**а́м** by the clock; ~ **от** ~**у не ле́гче** it gets worse by the hour; **в**

до́брый ~! Godspeed!; **с ча́су на** ~ any moment; **он помо́г мне в тру́дный** ~ he helped me in my hour of need; *см также* **часы́.**

часо́в|ня (-ни; *gen pl* **-ен)** *ж* chapel.

часово́|й *прил (лекция, перерыв итп)* one-hour; *(поезд)* one o'clock; *(механизм: ручных часов)* watch *опред*; *(: стенных часов)* clock *опред* ♦ **(-о́го;** *decl like adj)* м sentry; ~**я стре́лка** the small hand; ~**я опла́та** payment by the hour; **часово́й по́яс** time zone.

часовщи́к (-а́) *м* watchmaker.

ча́сом *нареч (разг: иногда)* the odd time ♦ *вводн сл (разг: случайно)* by any chance.

часосло́в (-а) *м (РЕЛ)* Book of Hours.

часте́нько *нареч (разг)* many's the time.

части́ц|а (-ы) *ж (маленькая часть)* fragment; *(ФИЗ, ЛИНГ)* particle; *(перен: правды)* grain.

части́чен *прил см* **части́чный.**

части́чно *нареч* partly.

части́чный (-ен, -на, -но) *прил* partial.

ча́стник (-а) *м (разг: предприниматель)* entrepreneur; *(собственник)* proprietor.

частновладе́льческ|ий (-ая, -ое, -ие) *прил* privately owned.

ча́стн|ое (-ого; *decl like adj)* ср quotient.

ча́стность (-и) *ж (деталь)* detail; **в** ~**и** in particular.

ча́стный *прил* private; *(нехарактерный)* certain; **в** ~**ых рука́х** in private hands; ~ **слу́чай** isolated case; **ча́стная со́бственность** private property; **ча́стное лицо́** individual; **ча́стный капита́л** *(ЭКОН)* private capital; **ча́стный со́бственник** private owner; **ча́стная акционе́рная компа́ния** private limited company.

ча́сто *нареч (много раз)* often; *(тесно)* close together.

частоко́л (-а) *м* palings *мн*.

част|ота́ (-оты́) *ж (повторяемость)* frequency; *(nom pl* **-о́ты;** *ТЕХ)* frequency.

частотность (-и) *ж* frequency.

часту́ш|ка (-ки; *gen pl* **-ек)** *ж traditional humorous folk song.*

ча́стый *прил* frequent; *(сито)* fine; *(лес, ряд предметов)* dense.

част|ь (-и; *gen pl* **-е́й,** *dat pl* **-я́м)** *ж* part; *(симфонии)* movement; *(отдел)* department; *(ВОЕН)* unit; **хозя́йственная** ~ supply department; **уче́бная** ~ academic studies office;

по ча́сти +*gen* when it comes to; **э́то не по мое́й ча́сти** this is not my department; **разрыва́ться** (*impf*) **на ча́сти** to have lots on the go at once; **её рву́т на ча́сти** she is in constant demand; **часть** part of speech; **часть све́та** continent.

ча́стью *нареч* partly.

час|ы́ (**-о́в**) *мн* (*карманные*) watch *ед*; (*стенные*) clock *ед*.

ча́хл|ый (**-**, **-а**, **-о**) *прил* (*цветок*) withered; (*человек*) sickly.

ча́х|нуть (**-ну**, **-нешь**; *pt* **-**, **-ла**, **-ло**, *perf* **зача́хнуть**) *несов неперех* (*растения*) to wither; (*человек, животное*) to fade away.

чахо́тк|а (**-и**) *ж* consumption.

ча́ш|а (**-и**) *ж* bowl; (*весов*) pan; **у них дом – по́лная ~** they've got everything imaginable in their house; **~ терпе́ния перепо́лнилась** this is the last straw.

ча́шек *сущ см* **ча́шка**.

ча́шеч|ка (**-ки**; *gen pl* **-ек**) *ж уменьш от* **ча́шка**; (*БОТ*) calyx; **коле́нная ~** kneecap.

ча́ш|ка (**-ки**; *gen pl* **-ек**) *ж* cup; (*весов*) pan.

ча́щ|а (**-и**) *ж* (*лес*) thick forest.

ча́ще *сравн прил от* **ча́стый** ◆ *сравн нареч от* **ча́сто**.

ча́яни|е (**-я**) *ср* (*обычно мн*) aspiration.

ча́|ять (**-ю**) *несов перех*: **он в ней души́ не ~ет** he dotes on her.

чванли́в|ый (**-**, **-а**, **-о**) *прил* conceited.

чва́нств|о (**-а**) *ср* conceit.

чебуре́к (**-а**) *м ≈* meat pasty.

чего́ *мест см* **что**.

чей (**чьего́**; *см* **Table 7**; *f* **чья**, *nt* **чьё**, *pl* **чьи**) *мест* whose; **~ э́то ребёнок?** whose child is this?; **~ бы то ни́ был** no matter whose it is.

чей-либо (**чьего́-либо**; *как* **чей**; *см* **Table 7**; *f* **чья́-либо**, *nt* **чьё-либо**, *pl* **чьи́-либо**) *мест* = **чей-нибудь**.

чей-нибудь (**чьего́-нибудь**; *как* **чей**; *см* **Table 7**; *f* **чья́-нибудь**, *nt* **чьё-нибудь**, *pl* **чьи́-нибудь**) *мест* anyone's.

чей-то (**чьего́-то**; *как* **чей**; *см* **Table 7**; *f* **чья́-то**, *nt* **чьё-то**, *pl* **чьи́-то**) *мест* someone's, somebody's.

чек (**-а**) *м* (*банковский*) cheque (*BRIT*), check (*US*); (*товарный, кассовый*) receipt; **выбива́ть** (**вы́бить** *perf*) **~** to issue a receipt (*to be presented as proof of payment in Russian shops*).

Чека́ *ж сокр* (*ИСТ*: = **Чрезвыча́йная коми́ссия по борьбе́ с контрреволю́цией и сабота́жем**) Cheka (*state security police in Soviet Russia from 1918–1922*).

чека́н|ить (**-ю**, **-ишь**; *perf* **отчека́нить**) *несов перех* (*монеты*) to mint; (*узор*) to enchase; **~** (**отчека́нить** *perf*) **слова́** to enunciate one's words.

чека́н|ка (**-и**) *ж* (*монет*) minting; (*изделие*) enchased object.

чеки́ст (**-а**) *м* (*ИСТ*) Cheka officer.

че́ковый *прил* cheque *опред* (*BRIT*), check *опред* (*US*); **че́ковая кни́жка** cheque book.

чёл|ка (**-ки**; *gen pl* **-ок**) *ж* (*человека*) fringe (*BRIT*), bangs *мн* (*US*); (*лошади*) forelock.

челно́к (**-а́**) *м* (*лодка*) dugout; (*швейный*) shuttle.

челно́чный *прил* shuttle *опред*.

челове́к (**-а**; *nom pl* **лю́ди**, *gen pl* **люде́й**) *м* human (being); (*некто, личность*) person (*мн* people); **два/три/четы́ре ~а** two/three/four people; **пять/шесть** *итп* **~** five/six *итп* people; **будь ~ом, помоги́ нам!** (*разг*) be a sport and give us a hand!; **вот ~!** (*разг*) what a character!

челове́ко-де́нь (**-ня**; *gen pl* **-ней**) *м* man-day.

человеколю́би|е (**-я**) *ср* philanthropy.

человеконенави́стник (**-а**) *м* misanthrope.

человеконенави́стническ|ий (**-ая**, **-ое**, **-ие**) *прил* misanthropic.

челове́ко-час (**-а**) *м* man-hour.

челове́чен *прил см* **челове́чный**.

челове́ческ|ий (**-ая**, **-ое**, **-ие**) *прил* human *опред*; (*человечный*) humane; **по-~и** in a humane way.

челове́честв|о (**-а**) *ср* humanity, mankind.

челове́ч|ный (**-ен**, **-на**, **-но**) *прил* humane.

чёлок *сущ см* **чёлка**.

че́люст|ь (**-и**) *ж* (*АНАТ*) jaw.

Челя́бинск (**-а**) *м* Chelyabinsk.

чем *мест см* **что** ◆ *союз* than; (*разг: вместо того чтобы*) instead of; **бо́льше ~ де́сять челове́к** more than ten people; **~ спо́рить, дава́й спро́сим кого́-нибудь** instead of arguing, let's ask someone; **~ бо́льше/ра́ньше** *итп*, **тем лу́чше** the bigger/earlier *итп*, the better.

чемода́н (**-а**) *м* suitcase; **сиде́ть** (*impf*) **на ~ах** (*перен: разг*) to have one's bags packed.

чемпио́н (**-а**) *м* champion; **~ по те́ннису** tennis champion.

чемпиона́т (**-а**) *м* championship; **~ страны́ по хокке́ю** national hockey championships.

чемпио́н|ка (**-ки**; *gen pl* **-ок**) *ж см* **чемпио́н**.

чему́ *мест см* **что**.

чепе́ *ср нескл* (*разг*) crisis.

чепух|а́ (**-и́**) *ж* (*разг*) rubbish (*BRIT*), garbage (*US*).

че́пчик (**-а**) *м* bonnet (*hat*).

че́рв|и (**-е́й**) *мн* (*КАРТЫ*) hearts *мн*.

черви́в|ый (**-**, **-а**, **-о**) *прил* maggoty.

черво́н|ец (**-ца**) *м* (*разг: 10 рублей*) ten roubles.

черво́нный *прил* (*КАРТЫ*): **~ая да́ма/деся́тка** the queen/ten of hearts.

черво́нца *итп сущ см* **черво́нец**.

черв|ь (**-я́**; *gen pl* **-е́й**) *м* worm; (*личинка*) maggot.

червя́к (**-а́**) *м* worm.

червя́чный *прил* (*ТЕХ*) worm *опред*.

черда́к (**-а́**) *м* attic, loft.

черда́чный *прил* attic *опред*.

черёд *м* (*разг*) turn; **всё идёт свои́м чередо́м**

everything is going as normal.

череда́ (-ы́) ж (людей) stream; (событий) sequence.

череду́|ова́ть (-ю) несов перех: ~ что-н с +instr to alternate sth with

▸ **череду́|ова́ться** несов возв to alternate; ~ся (impf) с +instr to take turns with.

KEYWORD

че́рез предл (+acc) **1** (поперёк) across, over; **мост че́рез кана́л/ре́ку** the bridge across или over the canal/river; **переходи́ть (перейти́** perf) **че́рез доро́гу** to cross the road

2 (сквозь) through; **он влез че́рез окно́** he climbed through the window; **че́рез лу́пу** through a magnifying glass

3 (поверх) over; **он переле́з че́рез забо́р** he climbed over the fence; **де́ти пры́гают че́рез верёвку** the children are jumping over a rope

4 (спустя) in; **че́рез час** in an hour('s time); **че́рез ме́сяц/год** in a month('s)/year('s) (time)

5 (минуя какое-н пространство): **че́рез три кварта́ла – ста́нция** the station is three blocks away

6 (при помощи) via; **он переда́л письмо́ че́рез знако́мого** he sent the letter via a friend

7 (при повторении действия) every; **принима́йте табле́тки че́рез ка́ждый час** take the tablets every hour.

черёмух|а (-и) ж bird cherry.

че́рен прил см **чёрный**.

черен|о́к (-ка́) м (рукоятка) handle; (бот) cutting.

че́реп (-а) м skull.

черепа́х|а (-и) ж tortoise; (морская) turtle.

черепа́ховый прил (суп) turtle; (гребень) tortoiseshell.

черепа́ш|ий (-ья, -ье, -ьи) прил tortoise's; (морской) turtle's; **идти́** (impf) ~ьим ша́гом to go at a snail's pace.

черепи́ц|а (-ы) ж tile ◆ собир tiles мн.

черепи́чный прил tiled.

черепка́ сущ см **черепо́к**.

черепно́й прил skull опред; **черепна́я коро́бка** cranium.

череп|о́к (-ка́) м pottery fragment.

чересчу́р нареч far too; **э́то уж** ~! that's just too much!

чере́ш|ня (-ни; gen pl -ен) ж (дерево) cherry (tree); (плод) cherry.

черка́|ть (-ю; perf **начерка́ть**) несов перех (разг) to draw lines on; (зачёркивать) to cross out.

черкну́|ть (-у́, -ёшь) сов перех (разг: написать) to scribble.

черне́|ть (-ю; perf **почерне́ть**) несов неперех (становиться чёрным) to turn black; (no perf; виднеться) to show black.

черни́к|а (-и) ж (кустарник) bilberry (bush) ◆ собир bilberries мн.

черни́л|а (-) мн ink ед.

черни́льниц|а (-ы) ж inkwell.

черни́льный прил ink опред; **черни́льный каранда́ш** graphite pencil which writes in purple when moistened.

черни́|ть (-ю́, -и́шь; perf **начерни́ть**) несов перех (брови) to tint; (perf **очерни́ть**; имя, репутацию) to tarnish; (no perf; сталь, серебро) to tarnish.

чёрно-бе́лый прил black-and-white.

чернобу́рк|а (-и) ж (разг: мех) silver fox.

черно-бу́р|ый прил: ~ая лиса́ silver fox.

чернови́к (-а́) м draft.

чернов|о́й прил draft; ~а́я рабо́та rough work.

черноволо́с|ый (-, -а, -о) прил black-haired.

черного́р|ец (-ца) м Montenegrin.

Черного́ри|я (-и) ж Montenegro.

черного́р|ка (-ки; gen pl -ок) ж см **черного́рец**.

черного́рск|ий (-ая, -ое, -ие) прил Montenegrin.

черного́рца итп сущ см **черного́рец**.

чернозём (-а) м black earth.

чернокож|ий (-ая, -ее, -ие) прил black (person) ◆ (-его; decl like adj) м black (person) (мн people).

чернорабо́ч|ий (-его; decl like adj) м unskilled worker.

черносли́в (-а) м собир prunes мн.

чернот|а́ (-ы́) ж blackness.

чёр|ный (-ен, -на́, -но́) прил black; (мрачный) gloomy; (no short form; преступный) wicked; (задний) back опред; **держа́ть** (impf) **кого́-н в** ~ном те́ле to treat sb badly; ~ным по бе́лому in black and white; ~ная рабо́та dirty work; **чёрные мета́ллы** ferrous metals; **чёрный ко́фе** black coffee; **чёрный ры́нок** black market; **чёрный нал** profits from the shadow economy.

че́рпа|ть (-ю) несов перех (жидкость) to ladle; (песок) to scoop (up); (перен: знания, силы) to derive.

черпну́|ть (-у́, -ёшь) сов перех (жидкость) to ladle; (песок) to scoop (up).

черстве́|ть (-ю; perf **зачерстве́ть**) несов неперех (хлеб) to go stale; (perf **очерстве́ть**; человек, душа) to harden.

чёрств|ый (-, -а́, -о) прил (хлеб) stale; (человек, душа) hard.

чёрт (-а; nom pl **че́рти**, gen pl **черте́й**) м (дьявол) devil; **у него́ де́нег до** ~а (разг) he's rolling in money; **иди́ к** ~у! (разг) go to hell!; **к** ~у! reply to a wish of good luck; **ни черта́** not a thing; ~ **меня́ дёрнул** I don't know what got into me; **чем** ~ **не шу́тит** you never know; ~ **возьми́** или **побери́** или **подери́!** (разг) damn it!; ~ **его́ зна́ет!** (разг) God knows!; ~ **зна́ет что!** (разг) it's outrageous!; **он мо́жет** ~ **зна́ет, что наде́лать** it's frightening to think what he might do; ~ **с ним!** (разг) to hell with him!; **он дал тебе́ де́нег? –** ~**а с два!** (разг) did he give you any money? – like hell he did!

черт|а́ (-ы́) ж (линия) line; (граница) limit; (признак) trait; **в о́бщих** ~х in general terms; см также **черты́**.

чертёж (-á) м draft.

чертёжник (-a) м draughtsman (*BRIT*) (*мн* draughtsmen), draftsman (*US*) (*мн* draftsmen).

чертёжный *прил* drawing *опред*.

чер|тить (-чý, -тишь; *perf* **начертить**) *несов перех* (линию) to draw; (план, график) to draw up.

чёртов (-a, -o, -ы) *прил* (*разг*: холод, работа *итп*) damn(ed); **чёртова дюжина** baker's dozen.

чертóвски *нареч* (*разг*) dreadfully: **я ~ гóлоден** I'm ravenous.

чертóвск|ий (-ая, -oe, -ие) *прил* (*разг*) damn (ed).

чертополóх (-a) м thistle.

чёрточ|ка (-ки; *gen pl* -ек) ж уменьш от **чертá**; (дефис) hyphen; **это слóво пишется чéрез ~ку** this word is written with a hyphen.

черт|ы́ (-) *мн* (*также:* ~ **лицá**) features *мн*.

черчéни|е (-я) *ср* (действие) drawing; (*ПРОСВЕЩ*) technical drawing.

черчý *несов см* **чертить**.

чеса́ть (-шý, -шешь; *perf* **почеса́ть**) *несов перех* (спину) to scratch; (*no perf*; *разг*: гребнем) to comb; (: щёткой) to brush; ~ (*impf*) **язы́к** или **языкóм** to natter

▶ **чеса́ться** (*perf* **почеса́ться**) *несов возв* to scratch o.s.; (*no perf*; зудеть) to itch; **он и не чéшется** (*разг*) he doesn't lift a finger; **у меня́ рýки ~шýтся** +*infin* (*разг*) I'm itching to do.

чеснóк (-á) м garlic.

чесóтк|а (-и) ж (*МЕД*) scabies.

чéствовани|е (-я) *ср* (действие) honouring (*BRIT*), honoring (*US*).

чéств|овать (-ую) *несов перех* to honour (*BRIT*), honor (*US*).

чéстен *прил см* **чéстный**.

чéстно *нареч* honestly ♦ *как сказ*: **так бýдет ~** that'll be fair.

чéстность (-и) ж honesty.

чéстн|ый (-ен, -нá, -но) *прил* honest; (безупречный) upright; **~ное имя** good name; **~ное слóво** honest to God; **держа́ться** (*impf*) **на ~ном слóве** (*разг*) to hang by a thread.

честолюб|ец (-ца) м ambitious person (*мн* people).

честолюби́в|ый (-, -a, -o) *прил* (человек, план) ambitious.

честолюби|е (-я) *ср* ambition.

честолю́бца *итп сущ см* **честолю́бец**.

честь (-и) ж honour (*BRIT*), honor (*US*); (*loc sg* -и́; почёт) glory; **в ~** +*gen* in hono(u)r of; **к чéсти когó-н** to sb's credit; **дéлать** (*impf*) ~ **комý-н** to do sb credit; (оказывать уважение) to do sb an hono(u)r; **отдава́ть** (**отда́ть** *perf*) **комý-н ~** to salute sb; **выходи́ть** (**вы́йти** *perf*) **с чéстью из чегó-н** to come out of sth with one's hono(u)r intact; **порá и ~ знать** (*разг*) it is time to wind up.

четá (-ы́) ж couple; **он мне не ~** he is no match for me.

четвéрг (-á) м Thursday; *см также* **вторник**.

четверéнь|ки (-ек) *мн*: **встава́ть** (**встать** *perf*) **на ~** to go down on all fours; **ходи́ть** (*impf*) **на ~ьках** to move on all fours.

четвёр|ка (-ки; *gen pl* -ок) ж (цифра, карта) four; (*ПРОСВЕЩ*) ≈ B (*school mark*); (группа людéй) foursome; (*разг*: автóбус, трамвáй *итп*) (number) four (*bus, tram etc*).

четверня́ (-и́; *gen pl* -éй) ж quadruplets *мн*.

чéтвер|о (*см* Table 36a: -ы́х) *чис* four; *см также* **двóе**.

четвёрок *сущ см* **четвёрка**.

четверокла́ссник (-a) м *pupil in fourth year at school* (*usually ten years old*).

четверокла́ссниц|а (-ы) ж *см* **четверокла́ссник**.

четвероно́г|ий (-ая, -oe, -ие) *прил* four-legged.

четверости́ши|е (-я) *ср* quatrain.

четвёрт|ая (-ой; *decl like adj*) ж: **одна́ ~** one quarter.

четверт|ова́ть (-у́ю) *несов перех* to quarter (*at execution*).

четвёрт|ый (-ая, -oe, -ые) *чис* fourth; **сейча́с ~ час** it's after four; *см также* **пя́тый**.

чéтверть (-и) ж quarter; (*МУЗ*) crotchet (*BRIT*), quarter note (*US*); (*ПРОСВЕЩ*) term.

четвертьфина́л (-a) м (*СПОРТ*) quarter final.

четверы́м *итп чис см* **чéтверо**.

чёт|кий (-кая, -кое, -кие; -ок, -ка́, -ко) *прил* clear; (движения, шаг) precise.

чёткость (-и) ж (*см прил*) clarity; precision.

чётный *прил* (число) even.

чёток *сущ см* **чёткий**.

четы́р|е (-ёх; *instr sg* -ьмя́; *см* Table 25) *чис* (цифра, число) four; (*ПРОСВЕЩ*) ≈ B (*school mark*); **ей ~ гóда** she is four (years old); **они́ живýт в дóме нóмер ~** they live at number four; **óколо четырёх** about four; **книга стóит ~ рубля́** the book costs four roubles; **~ с половиной часá** four and a half hours; **сейча́с ~ часá** it is four o'clock; **я́блоки продаю́тся по ~ штýки** the apples are sold in fours; **дели́ть** (**раздели́ть** *perf*) **что-н на ~** to divide sth into four.

четы́реста (-ёхсóт; *см* Table 33) *чис* four hundred; *см также* **стó**.

четырёх *чис см* **четы́ре**.

четырёхдне́вный *прил* four-day.

четырёхкра́тн|ый *прил*: ~ **чемпио́н** four-times champion; **в ~ом разме́ре** fourfold.

четырёхле́ти|е (-я) *ср* (срок) four years; (годовщина) fourth anniversary.

четырёхле́тн|ий (-яя, -ее, -ие) *прил* (период) four-year; (ребёнок) four-year-old.

четырёхме́сячный *прил* four-month;

(*ребёнок*) four-month-old.

четырёхнедельный *прил* four-week; (*ребёнок*) four-week-old.

четырёхсот *чис см* **четыреста**.

четырёхсотлетие (-я) *ср* (*срок*) four hundred years; (*годовщина*) quartercentenary.

четырёхсотлетний (-яя, -ее, -ие) *прил* (*период*) four-hundred-year; (*дерево*) four-hundred-year-old.

четырёхсотый (-ая, -ое, -ые) *чис* four-hundredth.

четырёхстах *чис см* **четыреста**.

четырёхугольник (-а) *м* quadrangle.

четырёхугольный *прил* quadrangular.

четырёхчасовой *прил* (*рабочий день*) four-hour; (*поезд*) four o'clock.

четырнадцатый (-ая, -ое, -ые) *чис* fourteenth; *см также* **пятый**.

четырнадцать (-и; *как* пять; *см* **Table 27**) *чис* fourteen; *см также* **пять**.

четырьмя *чис см* **четыре**.

четырьмястами *чис см* **четыреста**.

чех (-а) *м* Czech.

чехарда (-ы) *ж* (*разг: игра*) leapfrog; (*перен: путаница*) muddle.

Чехия (-и) *ж* the Czech Republic.

чехол (-ла) *м* (*для мебели*) cover; (*для гитары, для оружия*) case.

Чехословакия (-и) *ж* (*ист*) Czechoslovakia.

чечевица (-ы) *ж* lentil ♦ *собир* lentils *мн*.

чеченец (-ца) *м* Chechen.

чеченка (-ки; *gen pl* -ок) *ж см* **чеченец**.

чеченца *итп сущ см* **чеченец**.

чечётка (-и) *ж* tap dance.

Чечня (-и) *ж* Chechenia, Chechnya.

чешка (-ки; *gen pl* -ек) *ж см* **чех**.

чешский (-ая, -ое, -ие) *прил* Czech; ~ **язык** Czech.

чешу(сь) *итп несов см* **чесать(ся)**.

чешуйка (-и) *ж* scale.

чешуйчатый *прил* scaly.

чешуя (-и) *ж собир* scales *мн*.

чибис (-а) *м* lapwing.

чиж (-а) *м* siskin.

чизбургер (-а) *м* cheeseburger.

Чикаго *м нескл* Chicago.

Чили *ср нескл* Chile.

чилийский (-ая, -ое, -ие) *прил* Chilean.

чин (-а; *nom pl* -ы) *м* rank; **повышать** (**повысить** *perf*) **кого-н в чине** to promote sb to a higher rank.

чинить (-ю, -ишь; *perf* **починить**) *несов перех* to mend, repair; (*perf* **очинить**; *карандаш*) to sharpen; (-ю, -йшь; *perf* **учинить**; *насилие, произвол*) to commit; (*no perf*; *препятствия*) to create.

чиновник (-а) *м* (*служащий*) official; (*бюрократ*) bureaucrat.

чиновнический (-ая, -ое, -ие) *прил* (*должность*) official; (*аппарат*) bureaucratic.

чипсы (-ов) *мн* crisps *мн*.

чирикать (-ю) *несов неперех* to twitter.

чиркать (-ю) *несов неперех*: ~ **спичкой** to strike a match.

чиркнуть (-у, -ешь) *сов неперех* to strike.

чисел *сущ см* **число**.

численность (-и) *ж* (*армии*) numbers *мн*; (*учащихся*) number; ~ **населения** population.

численный *прил* (*количественный*) numerical; **численное превосходство** numerical advantage; **численный состав** (*армии*) total numbers *мн*.

числитель (-я) *м* numerator.

числительное (-ого; *decl like adj*) *ср* numeral.

числиться (-юсь, -ишься) *несов возв* (*в организации*) to be registered; ~ (*impf*) +*instr* (*больным, должником итп*) to be registered as; **он** ~**ится директором фирмы** he's officially the director of the firm; **за ним** ~**ится долг** he owes some money; **в списке его фамилия не** ~**ится** his name is not on the list.

число (-ла; *nom pl* -ла, *gen pl* -ел) *ср* number; (*день месяца*) date; **единственное** ~ singular; **множественное** ~ plural; **быть** (*impf*) **в** ~**ле** +*gen* to be among(st); **какое сегодня** ~? what is the date today?; **приеду в первых числах марта** I am coming at the beginning of March; **отмечать** (**отметить** *perf*) **что-н задним** ~**м** to backdate sth; **узнавать** (**узнать** *perf*) **задним** ~**м** (*разг*) to find out later; **в том** ~**ле** including; **ошибкам нет** ~**ла** there are countless mistakes.

числовой *прил*: ~**ое программное управление** (*комп*) numerically programmed (*BRIT*) *или* programed (*US*) control.

чистилище (-а) *ср* purgatory.

чистить (-щу, -стишь; *perf* **вычистить** *или* **почистить**) *несов перех* to clean; (*зубы*) to brush, clean; (*perf* **почистить**; *яблоко, картошку*) to peel; (*рыбу*) to scale; (*perf* **очистить**; *дно реки*) to dredge; (*сад*) to clean up; (*perf* **обчистить**; *разг: кассу, человека*) to clean out.

чистка (-ки; *gen pl* -ок) *ж* (*действие*) cleaning; (: *овощей*) peeling; (*в партии*) purge.

чисто *нареч* (*только*) purely; (*убранный, сделанный*) neatly ♦ *как сказ*: **в доме** ~ the house is clean.

чистовик (-а) *м* fair copy.

чистовой *прил* fair.

чисток *сущ см* **чистка**.

чистокровный *прил* pure-breed; ~**ая лошадь** thoroughbred.

чистоплотен *прил см* **чистоплотный**.

чистоплотность (-и) *ж* cleanliness.

чистоплотный (-ен, -на, -но) *прил* clean; (*перен: порядочный*) decent.

чистопробный *прил* (*золото*) pure.

чистосердечный (-ен, -на, -но) *прил* sincere.

чистота (-ы) *ж* (*воздуха, спирта, раствора*) purity; **у него в доме всегда** ~ his house is always extremely clean.

чистый (-, -а, -о) *прил* (*одежда, комната*) clean; (*любовь, сердце, человек*) pure and innocent;

(*совесть, небо, произношение*) clear; (*золото, спирт*) pure; (*язык*) proper; (*no short form; прибыль, вес*) net; (*совпадение, случайность*) pure; **выводи́ть (вы́вести** *perf*) **кого́-н на ~ую во́ду** (*разоблачить*) to expose sb.
читáльный *прил*: ~ **зал** reading room.
читáтел|**ь** (-**я**) *м* reader.
читáтельни|**ца** (-**ы**) *ж см* **читáтель**.
читáть (-**ю**) *несов перех* to read; (*декламировать*) to recite; (*курс*) to teach; (*лекцию*) to give.
чихáть (-**ю**) *perf* **чихну́ть**) *несов неперех* to sneeze; (*разг: мотор*) to splutter: **ему́ ~ на прáвила/свои́х роди́телей** he doesn't give a damn about the rules/his parents.
чи́ще *сравн прил от* **чи́стый** ♦ *сравн нареч от* **чи́сто**.
чи́щу *несов см* **чи́стить**.
ЧК *ж сокр* = **Чекá**.
член (-**а**) *м* member; (*обычно мн: конечности*) limb; **половóй ~** penis; **~ предложéния** part of a sentence.
член|**и́ть** (-**ю́, -и́шь**) *perf* **расчлени́ть**) *несов перех* to break up.
членкóр (-**а**) *м сокр* = **член-корреспондéнт**.
член-корреспондéнт (-**а, -а**) *м* (*звание*) *academic title junior to academician.*
членораздéльный (-**ен, -ьна, -ьно**) *прил* intelligible.
члéнск|**ий** (-**ая, -ое, -ие**) *прил* membership.
члéнств|**о** (-**а**) *ср* membership.
ЧМ *сокр* (= *частóтная модуляция*) FM (= *frequency modulation*).
чóка|**ться** (-**юсь**; *perf* **чóкнуться**) *несов возв* to clink glasses (*during a toast*).
чóкнут|**ый** (-**, -а, -о**) *прил* (*разг: человек*) barmy, crazy.
чóкнуться (-**усь, -ешься**) *сов от* **чóкаться**.
чóпор|**ный** (-**ен, -на, -но**) *прил* prim.
ЧП *ср сокр* = **чрезвычáйное происшéствие**.
ЧПУ *ср сокр* = **числовóе прогрáммное управлéние**.
чрезвычáен *прил см* **чрезвычáйный**.
чрезвычáйно *нареч* extremely.
чрезвычáй|**ный** (-**ен, -йна, -йно**) *прил* (*исключительный*) extraordinary; (*no short form; экстренный*) emergency *опред*;
чрезвычáйный и полномóчный посóл ambassador extraordinary and plenipotentiary; **чрезвычáйное положéние** state of emergency; **чрезвычáйное происшéствие** crisis.
чрезмéр|**ный** (-**ен, -на, -но**) *прил* excessive.
чтéни|**е** (-**я**) *ср* reading; *см также* **чтéния**.
чтéни|**я** (-**й**) *мн* course *ед* of lectures.
чтец (-**á**) *м* reader.
чт|**ить** (*см* **Table 17**) *несов перех* to honour (*BRIT*), honor (*US*).

KEYWORD

что (**чегó**; *см* **Table 6**) *мест* **1**
(*вопросительное*) what; **что ты скáзал?** what did you say?; **что с тобóй?** what's the matter (with you)?; **что Вы говори́те?** you don't say!; **к чему́** *или* **на что тебé э́то?** what do you need it for?
2 (*относительное*) which; **онá не поздорóвалась, что бы́ло мне неприя́тно** she did not say hello, which was unpleasant for me; **что ни говори́** ... whatever you say ...
3 (*столько сколько*): **онá закричáла что бы́ло сил** she shouted with her all might
4 (*который*) that; **дéрево, что растёт у дóма** the tree that grows by the house
5 (*разг: что-нибудь*) anything; **éсли что случи́тся** if anything happens, should anything happen; **в слу́чае чегó** if anything crops up; **чуть что – срáзу скажи́ мне** get in touch at the slightest thing
♦ *нареч* (*почему*) why; **что ты грусти́шь?** why are you sad?; **мне не хóчется идти́ – что так?** I don't feel like going – why's that?
♦ *союз* **1** (*при сообщении, высказывании*): **я знáю, что нáдо дéлать** I know what must be done; **я знáю, что он приéдет** I know that he will come; **стрáнно то, что он молчи́т** it is strange that he remains silent; **что ни день, то нóвые проблéмы** there isn't a day without new problems
2 (*во фразах*): **а что?** (*разг*) why (do you ask)?; **к чему́** (*зачем*) why; **нé за что!** not at all! (*BRIT*), you're welcome! (*US*); **ни за что!** (*разг*) no way!; **ни за что ни про что** (*разг*) for no (good) reason; **что ты!** (*при возражении*) what!; **я здесь ни при чём** it has nothing to do with me; **э́то тут ни при чём** that's beside the point; **чегó там!** forget it!; **что ж** (*да*) oh well; **что за чепухá?** what kind of nonsense is this!; **сáмый что ни на есть лу́чший/óпытный** best/most experienced there is; **что к чему́** (*разг*) what's what; **поéхали, что ли?** (*разг*) shall we go or not?

чтоб *союз* = **чтóбы**.

KEYWORD

чтóбы *союз*: **чтóбы** +*infin* (*выражает цель*) in order *или* so as to do; **я бу́ду рабóтать нóчью, чтóбы сдать сочинéние зáвтра** I will work at night in order *или* so as to hand in the composition tomorrow
♦ *союз* (+*pt*) **1** (*выражает цель*) so that; **учи́тель говори́т мéдленно, чтóбы мы всё понимáли** the teacher speaks slowly so that we understand everything
2 (*выражает желательность*): **я хочу́, чтóбы онá пришлá** I want her to come
3 (*выражает возможность*): **не мóжет быть,**

что́бы он так поступи́л it can't be possible that he should have acted like that

♦ *част 1 (выражает пожелание):* **что́бы она́ заболе́ла!** I hope she gets ill!

2 *(выражает требование):* **что́бы я его́ здесь бо́льше не ви́дел!** I hope (that) I never see him here again!

что́-либо (чего́-либо; *как* что; *см* **Table 6**) *мест* = **что́-нибудь.**

что́-нибудь (чего́-нибудь; *как* что; *см* **Table 6**) *мест (в утвердительных предложениях)* something; *(в вопросительных предложениях)* anything; **скажи́ ~** say something; **есть ~ интере́сное?** is there anything interesting?

что́-то (чего́-то; *как* что; *см* **Table 6**) *мест* something; *(приблизительно)* something like ♦ *нареч (разг: почему-то)* somehow; **он получи́л ~ о́коло ста пи́сем** he got something like a hundred letters; **~ не по́мню тако́го** somehow I don't remember that.

чуб (-а́) *м* forelock.

чува́ш (-а́) *м* Chuvash.

чува́шек *сущ см* **чува́шка.**

Чува́ши|я (-и) *ж* Chuvashia.

чува́ш|ка (-ки; *gen pl* -ек) *ж см* **чува́ш.**

чу́вствен|ный (-, -на, -но) *прил (удовольствие, любовь итп)* sensual; *(no short form; восприятия)* sensory.

чувстви́телен *прил см* **чувстви́тельный.**

чувстви́тельность (-и) *ж* sensitivity; *(стихов, музыки)* sentimentality.

чувстви́тель|ный (-, -на, -ьно) *прил* sensitive; *(стихи, музыка)* sentimental; *(удар)* heavy; *(оскорбление)* deep; *(потери)* considerable.

чу́вств|о (-а) *ср (эмоция, ощущение)* feeling; *(+gen: юмора, долга, ответственности)* sense of; **лиша́ться (лиши́ться** *perf)* **чувств** to faint, lose consciousness; **приводи́ть (привести́** *perf)* **кого́-н в ~** to bring sb round.

чу́вств|овать (-ую; *perf* **почу́вствовать)** *несов перех* to feel; *(присутствие, опасность)* to sense; **~** *(impf)* **себя́ хорошо́/пло́хо/нело́вко** to feel good/bad/awkward

▶ **чу́вствоваться** *несов возв (жара, усталость)* to be felt; **~уется, что он волну́ется** you can tell he's worried.

чугу́н (-а́) *м* cast iron.

чугу́нный *прил* cast-iron.

чуда́к (-а́) *м* eccentric.

чу́ден *прил см* **чу́дный.**

чуде́н *прил см* **чудно́й.**

чудеса́ *итп сущ от* **чу́до.**

чуде́сен *прил см* **чуде́сный.**

чуде́сно *нареч* wonderfully ♦ *как сказ* it's wonderful.

чуде́с|ный (-ен, -на, -но) *прил (необычный)* miraculous; *(очень хороший)* marvellous (BRIT), marvelous (US), wonderful.

чуди́ть (2sg -и́шь, 3sg -и́т) *несов неперех* to behave oddly.

чу́ди|ться (3sg -ится, 3pl -ятся, *perf* **почу́диться)** *несов возв (+dat)* to appear.

чу́дище (-а) *ср* monster.

чудно́й (-ён, -на́, -но́) *прил (разг)* odd.

чу́дный (-ен, -на, -но) *прил (великолепный)* marvellous (BRIT), marvelous (US).

чу́д|о (-а; *nom pl* -еса́) *ср* miracle.

чудо́вище (-а) *ср* monster.

чудо́вищ|ный (-ен, -на, -но) *прил (преступление, факт)* monstrous; *(перен: ураган, мороз)* terrible.

чудоде́йствен|ный (-ен, -на, -но) *прил (средство)* miraculous.

чу́дом *нареч (спастись)* by a miracle.

чужа́к (-а́) *м* stranger.

чужби́н|а (-ы) *ж* foreign country.

чужда́|ться (-юсь) *несов возв:* **~ +gen** *(также перен)* to shun.

чу́жд|ый (-, -а́, -о) *прил (взгляды, ценности)* alien; **~ +gen** devoid of; **ему́ чужда́ за́висть** he is devoid of envy.

чужезе́м|ец (-ца) *м* stranger.

чужезе́мный *прил* from foreign parts.

чужезе́мца *итп сущ см* **чужезе́мец.**

чужеро́дный *прил (элемент)* alien.

чуж|о́й *прил (принадлежащий другому)* someone *или* somebody else's; *(речь, обычай)* foreign; *(человек)* strange ♦ *(-о́го; decl like adj)* *м* stranger; **под ~им и́менем** under an assumed name.

чу́кч|а (-и) *м/ж нескл* Chukchi.

чула́н (-а) *м* storeroom.

чул|о́к (-ка́; *gen pl* -о́к, *dat pl* -ка́м) *м (обычно мн)* stocking.

чум|а́ (-ы́) *ж* plague.

чума́з|ый (-, -а, -о) *прил (разг)* mucky.

чур *межд (разг):* **~ я пе́рвый!** mind out, I'm first!; **~ меня́!** get away from me! *(to keep evil at bay)*

чурба́н (-а) *м (деревянный)* block; *(разг: пренебр: человек)* blockhead.

чу́т|кий (-кая, -кое, -кие, -ок, -ка́, -ко) *прил* sensitive; *(натура)* sympathetic; **~ сон** light sleep.

чу́ткость (-и) *ж (см прил)* sensitivity; sympathy.

чу́ток *прил см* **чу́ткий.**

чу́точ|ка (-и) *ж (разг):* **~у** a bit; **ни ~и** not a bit.

чуть *нареч (разг: едва)* hardly; *(немного)* a little ♦ *союз (как только)* as soon as; **~ (бы́ло) не** almost, nearly; **~ ли не** almost certainly; **~ что** *(разг)* at the slightest thing.

чуть|ё (-я́) *ср (у животных)* scent; *(у людей)* intuition.

чу́чел|о (-а) *ср (также перен)* scarecrow; **~ живо́тного/пти́цы** stuffed animal/bird.

чушь (-и) *ж (разг)* rubbish (BRIT), garbage (US).

чу́|ять (-ю) *несов перех (также перен)* to scent; **я ног под собо́й не ~ю** I'm walking on air; *(от усталости)* my legs are giving way beneath me.

чьё (чьего́) *мест см* **чей.**

чьи (чьих) *мест см* **чей.**

чья (чьей) *мест см* **чей.**

~ Ш, ш ~

Ш, ш *сущ нескл (буква)* the 25th letter of the Russian alphabet.

ш *сокр* (= **широта́**) w. (= *width*).

ш. *сокр* (= **шту́ка**) ea. (= *each*).

шаба́ш (-а) *м* Sabbath.

шаба́ш *част (кончено)* that's enough.

шабло́н (-а) *м (ТЕХ)* pattern, gauge; *(перен: в речи, в письме)* cliché.

шабло́н|ный *прил (об инструменте, о чертеже)* pattern *опред*; (-ен, -на, -но; *перен: фраза, ответ)* trite.

шаг (-а; *part gen* -у, *loc sg* -у́, *nom pl* -и́) *м (также перен)* step; **на ка́ждом ~у́** *(перен)* continually; **~ за ша́гом** step by step; **ша́гу не даю́т ступи́ть** *(перен)* one has no freedom of action; **прибавля́ть (приба́вить** *perf)* **ша́гу** to quicken one's pace; **предпринима́ть (предприня́ть** *perf)* **но́вые ~и** to take a new initiative; **я услы́шал ~и** I heard footsteps.

шага́ть (-ю) *несов неперех* to march; *(делать шаг)* to step; **~й отсю́да!** *(разг)* get lost!

шагну́ть (-у́, -ёшь) *сов неперех* to step, take a step; **~** *(perf)* **вперёд** *(также перен)* to take a step forward.

ша́гом *нареч (идти)* at a walk, at walking pace; **~ марш!** *(ВОЕН)* quick march!

ша́ек *сущ см* **ша́йка.**

ша́йб|а (-ы) *ж (ТЕХ: прокладка)* spacer; (: *болта)* washer; *(СПОРТ)* puck.

ша́йка (-йки; *gen pl* -ек) *ж (бандитская)* gang.

шака́л (-а) *м* jackal.

шала́нд|а (-ы) *ж* scow, barge.

шала́ш (-а́) *м* hut *(made of branches)*.

ша́левый *прил:* **~ платок** shawl; **ша́левый воротни́к** shawl collar.

шале́ть (-ю; *perf* **ошале́ть**) *несов неперех (разг)* to go crazy; **~ (ошале́ть** *perf)* **от ра́дости** to go mad with joy.

шали́ть (-ю, -ишь) *несов неперех (дети)* to be mischievous; *(разг: мотор, сердце)* to play up.

шаловли́вый (-, -а, -о) *прил (ребёнок)* mischievous; *(тон, глаза)* playful.

шалопа́й (-я) *м (разг)* loafer, skiver.

ша́лост|ь (-и) *ж (проказа)* mischief.

шалу́н (-а́) *м* mischievous boy.

шалу́нья (-ьи; *gen pl* -ий) *ж* mischievous girl.

шалфе́й (-я) *м (БОТ)* sage.

шаль (-и) *ж* shawl.

шально́й *прил (разг)* wild; *(пуля)* stray; *(деньги)* easy.

шаля́й-валя́й *нареч (разг: небрежно)* any(old) how.

шама́н (-а) *м (колдун)* shaman.

шама́н|ка (-ки; *gen pl* -ок) *ж см* **шама́н.**

ша́мка|ть (-ю) *несов неперех* to mumble.

шампа́нск|ое (-ого; *decl like adj)* *ср* champagne.

шампиньо́н (-а) *м (БОТ)* (field) mushroom.

шампу́н|ь (-я) *м* shampoo.

шампу́р (-а) *м* skewer.

шанс (-а) *м* chance; **~ на что-н** chance of sth.

шансоне́т|ка (-ки; *gen pl* -ок) *ж см* **шансонье́.**

шансонье́ *м нескл* singer.

шанта́ж (-а́) *м* blackmail.

шантажи́р|овать (-ую) *несов перех* to blackmail.

шантажи́ст (-а) *м* blackmailer.

шантажи́ст|ка (-ки; *gen pl* -ок) *ж см* **шантажи́ст.**

шантрапа́ (-ы́) *м/ж собир (разг)* yobs *мн.*

Шанха́й (-я) *м* Shanghai.

ша́п|ка (-ки; *gen pl* -ок) *ж (на голову)* hat; *(перен: снежная)* cap; *(заголовок)* headline; **по ~ке дава́ть (дать** *perf)* +*dat (перен: разг)* to punish; **по ~ке получа́ть (получи́ть** *perf)* *(разг)* to be punished; **на воре́ ~ гори́т** he's given the game away.

ша́почн|ый *прил* a hat; **~ое знако́мство** nodding acquaintance; **приходи́ть (прийти́** *perf)* **к ~ому разбо́ру** *(перен)* to miss the bus.

шар (-а; *nom pl* -ы́) *м (ГЕОМ)* sphere; *(кегли, билья́рдный итп)* ball; **возду́шный ~** balloon; **земно́й ~** the Earth; **в до́ме хоть ~о́м покати́** the house is completely empty.

шара́д|а (-ы) *ж* charade.

шара́хн|уть (-у, -ешь; *impf* **шара́хать**) *сов (не)перех (разг)* : **~** +*acc или* +*instr (ударять)* to thump

▶ **шара́хнуться** *(impf* **шара́хаться**) *сов возв (разг: отпрянуть)* to leap back; (: *удариться)* : **~ся о** +*acc* to bang into.

шара́шкин *прил:* **~а конто́ра** dodgy enterprise; *(несолидное учреждение)* pathetic place.

шарж (-а) *м* caricature.

шаржи́р|овать (-ую) *несов перех* to caricature.

шáрик (-а) *м уменьш от* **шар**; (*АНАТ*): **кровянóй** ~ blood corpuscle.

шáриков|**ый** *прил* (*подшипник*) ball *опред*; ~**ая рýчка** ballpoint pen.

шарикоподшúпник (-а) *м* (*ТЕХ*) ball bearing.

шáр|**ить** (-ю, -ишь) *несов неперех* (*разг*) to grope; ~ (*impf*) **глазáми** to sweep; ~ (*impf*) **по** (**чужúм**) **кармáнам** (*разг*) to pick pockets.

шáркан|**ье** (-я) *ср* shuffling.

шáрка|**ть** (-ю) *несов неперех*: ~ +*instr* to shuffle.

шáркн|**уть** (-у, -ешь) *сов неперех*: ~ **ногóй** to click one's heels.

шарлатáн (-а) *м* charlatan.

шарлатáн|**ка** (-ки; *gen pl* -ок) *ж см* **шарлатáн**.

шарлатáнств|**о** (-а) *ср* charlatanism.

шарлóт|**ка** (-ки; *gen pl* -ок) *ж* (*КУЛИН*) charlotte.

шарм (-а) *м* (*обаяние*) charm.

шармáн|**ка** (-ки; *gen pl* -ок) *ж* (*МУЗ*) barrel organ.

шарнúр (-а) *м* (*ТЕХ*) hinge; (*АВТ*) (suspension) joint.

шаровáр|**ы** (-) *мн* baggy trousers *мн*.

шаровúдн|**ый** (-ен, -на, -но) *прил* spherical.

шаровóй *прил* (*ГЕОМ*) spherical; ~ **клáпан** ball valve; **шаровáя мóлния** (*ГЕО*) fireball, globe lightning.

шарообрáзн|**ый** (-ен, -на, -но) *прил* = **шаровúдный**.

шарф (-а) *м* scarf.

шассú *ср нескл* (*самолёта*) landing gear; (*автомобиля*) chassis.

шáста|**ть** (-ю) *несов неперех* (*разг*) to mooch about.

шатáни|**е** (-я) *ср* (*хождение*) mooching about; (*раскачивание*) swaying; (*перен: идейные*) vacillation.

шата|**ть** (-ю) *несов перех* (*раскачивать*) to rock; **меня** ~**ет от устáлости** I am reeling with tiredness

▶ **шатáться** *несов возв* (*зуб*) to be loose *или* wobbly; (*столб*) to shake; (*от усталости*) to reel, stagger; (*разг: по городу, по улицам итп*) to mooch about.

шатéн (-а) *м man with auburn hair.*

шатёр (-á) *м* tent.

шáт|**кий** (-кая, -кое, -кие; -ок, -ка, -ко) *прил* (*стул*) wobbly, rickety; (*перен: положение*) precarious; (*: доводы*) shaky.

шáткост|**ь** (-и) *ж* (*см прил*) wobbliness; precariousness; shakiness.

шатн|**ýть** (-ý, -ёшь) *сов перех* (*столб*) to shake

▶ **шатнýться** *сов возв* (*столб*) to be unsteady; (*от усталости*) to reel.

шáток *прил см* **шáткий**.

шатрá *итп сущ см* **шатёр**.

шатрóв|**ый** *прил* (*крыша, купол*) hipped; **шатрóвая архитектýра** hipped architecture.

шатýн (-á) *м* (*ТЕХ*) connecting rod.

шáфер (-а) *м* best man (*мн* men).

шафрáн (-а) *м* (*БОТ*) saffron.

шах (-а) *м* (*монарх*) shah; (*в шахматах*) check.

шахматúст (-а) *м* chess player.

шахматúст|**ка** (-ки; *gen pl* -ок) *ж см* **шахматúст**.

шáхматн|**ый** *прил* (*кружок, чемпионат*) chess *опред*; (*порядок, рисунок*) staggered; **шáхматная доскá** chessboard.

шáхмат|**ы** (-) *мн* (*игра*) chess *ед*; (*фигуры*) chessmen *мн*.

шáхт|**а** (-ы) *ж* (*выработка*) mine, pit; (*предприятие*) mine; (*лифта*) shaft.

шахтёр (-а) *м* miner.

шáшек *сущ см* **шáшки**.

шашúст (-а) *м* draughts (*BRIT*) *или* checkers (*US*) player.

шашúст|**ка** (-ки; *gen pl* -ок) *ж см* **шашúст**.

шáш|**ка** (-и) *ж* (*игральная*) draught (*BRIT*), checker (*US*); (*взрывчатка*) blasting cartridge; (*оружие*) sabre (*BRIT*), saber (*US*); *см также* **шáшки**.

шáш|**ки** (-ек) *мн* (*игра*) draughts *мн* (*BRIT*), checkers *мн* (*US*).

шашлýк (-á) *м* shashlik, kebab.

шашлы́чн|**ая** (-ой; *decl like adj*) *ж* kebab-house.

шáшн|**и** (-ей) *мн* (*разг*) affair *ед*.

шва *итп сущ см* **шов**.

швáбр|**а** (-ы) *ж* mop.

швáркн|**уть** (-у, -ешь; *impf* **швáркать**) *сов перех* (*разг*) to hurl.

швартóв (-а) *м* (*МОР*) mooring line; **отдавáть** (**отдáть** *perf*) ~**ы** to cast off.

швартóва|**ть** (-ю; *perf* **пришвартовáть** *или* **ошвартовáть**) *несов перех* (*МОР*) to moor.

швед (-а) *м* Swede.

швéд|**ка** (-ки; *gen pl* -ок) *ж см* **швед**.

швéдск|**ий** (-ая, -ое, -ие) *прил* Swedish; ~ **язы́к** Swedish.

швéйн|**ый** *прил* (*машина, нитки*) sewing *опред*; (*фабрика*) clothing *опред*.

швейцáр (-а) *м* doorman (*мн* doormen).

швейцáр|**ец** (-ца) *м* Swiss.

Швейцáри|**я** (-и) *ж* Switzerland.

швейцáр|**ка** (-ки; *gen pl* -ок) *ж см* **швейцáрец**.

швейцáрск|**ий** (-ая, -ое, -ие) *прил* Swiss.

швейцáрца *итп сущ см* **швейцáрец**.

Швéци|**я** (-и) *ж* Sweden.

швея́ (-и) *ж* seamstress.

швырн|**ýть** (-ý, -ёшь) *сов* (*не*)*перех*: ~ +*acc или* +*instr* to hurl.

швыря́|**ть** (-ю) *несов перех* to hurl, fling; ~ (*impf*) **дéньги** *или* **деньгáми** (*разг*) to throw one's money about

▶ **швыря́ться** *несов возв* (*разг*) to throw at each other; (*перен*): ~**ся** +*instr* (*людьми*) to treat lightly; ~**ся** (*impf*) **деньгáми** (*разг*) to throw one's money about.

шевел|**úть** (-ю́, -ишь; *perf* **пошевелúть**) *несов перех* (*сено*) to turn over; (*подлеж: ветер*) to stir ◆ *неперех*: ~ +*instr* (*пальцами, губами*) to move; ~ (**пошевелúть** *perf*) **мозгáми** (*перен: разг*) to use one's head

▶ **шевелúться** (*perf* **пошевелúться**) *несов возв* to stir; ~**úсь!** (*разг*) get a move on!

шевельн|**ýть** (-ý, -ёшь) *сов неперех*: ~ +*instr*

(пальцами, плечом) to move
▶ **шевельну́ться** *сов возв* to stir.
шевелю́р|а (-ы) *ж* (head of) hair.
шевро́н (-а) *м (нашивка)* chevron, long-service stripe.
шеде́вр (-а) *м* masterpiece.
ше́ек *сущ см* **ше́йка**.
шезло́нг (-а) *м* deckchair.
ше́йк|а (-йки; *gen pl* -ек) *ж уменьш от* **ше́я**; *(рельса, гильзы)* neck; **ше́йка ма́тки** *(АНАТ)* cervix.
ше́йный *прил (мышца)* neck *опред; (позвонок)* cervical; ~ **плато́к** neckerchief.
шейх (-а) *м* sheikh.
шёл *несов см* **идти́**.
ше́лест (-а) *м* rustle.
шелест|е́ть (-и́шь) *несов неперех* to rustle.
шёлк (-а; *nom pl* -а́) *м* silk.
шелкови́ст|ый (-, -а, -о) *прил (гладкий)* silky.
шелкови́чный *прил:* ~ **червь** silkworm.
шелково́дств|о (-а) *ср* sericulture, silkworm breeding.
шёлковый *прил (нить, одежда)* silk; *(перен: разг: человек)* meek.
шелкопря́д (-а) *м* silkworm.
шелкопряди́льный *прил* silk-spinning.
шелоткáцк|ий (-ая, -ое, -ие) *прил* silk-weaving.
шелохн|у́ть (-у́, -ёшь) *сов перех* to stir, agitate
▶ **шелохну́ться** *сов возв* to stir, move.
шелух|а́ (-и́) *ж (картофельная)* skin, peel; *(гороховая)* pod; *(семечек)* chaff; *(перен)* dross.
шелуше́ни|е (-я) *ср (зерна)* shelling; *(кожи)* peeling.
шелуш|и́ть (-у́, -и́шь) *несов перех* to shell
▶ **шелуши́ться** *несов возв* to peel.
ше́льм|а (-ы) *м/ж (разг)* rascal.
шельф (-а) *м (ГЕО)* shelf.
шепеля́в|ить (-лю, -ишь) *несов неперех* to lisp.
шепеля́в|ый (-, -а, -о) *прил (человек, речь)* lisping.
шепн|у́ть (-у́, -ёшь) *сов перех* to whisper.
шёпот (-а) *м* whisper; *(перен: ручья, листьев)* murmuring.
шёпотом *нареч (сказать, подсказать)* in a whisper.
шепта́ни|е (-я) *ср (см глаг)* whispering; murmuring.
шеп|та́ть (-чу́, -чешь) *несов перех* to whisper ♦ *неперех (перен: ручей, листья)* to murmur
▶ **шепта́ться** *несов возв* to whisper to each other.
шербе́т (-а) *м* sherbet.
шере́нг|а (-и) *ж (солдат)* rank; *(машин)* line.
шери́ф (-а) *м* sheriff.
шерохова́тост|ь (-и) *ж (см прил)* roughness; uneveness; *(шероховатое место)* rough area.

шерохова́т|ый (-, -а, -о) *прил (доска, кожа)* rough; *(перен: изложение)* uneven.
шерсти́нк|а (-ки; *gen pl* -ок) *ж* strand of wool.
шерстопряди́льный *прил* wool-spinning.
шерст|ь (-и) *ж (животного)* hair; *(пряжа, ткань)* wool.
шерстяно́й *прил (пряжа, ткань)* woollen *(BRIT)*, woolen *(US)*.
шерша́в|ый (-, -а, -о) *прил (руки, ткань)* rough.
шест (-á) *м* pole; **прыжо́к с** ~**óм** pole vault.
шест|áя (-óй; *decl like adj)* ж:* **одна́** ~ one sixth.
ше́стви|е (-я) *ср* procession.
ше́ств|овать (-ую) *несов неперех* to walk in procession.
шестерён|ка (-ки; *gen pl* -ок) *ж (ТЕХ)* gear (wheel).
шестёр|ка (-и) *ж (цифра, карта)* six; *(шлюпка)* six-oar boat; *(группа из шести)* group of six; *(разг: автобус, трамвай итп)* (number) six *(bus, tram etc)*.
ше́стер|о (-ы́х; *см* **Table 36b**) *чис* six; *см также* **дво́е**.
шести́ *чис см* **шесть**.
шести́десяти *чис см* **шестьдеся́т**.
шестидесятиле́ти|е (-я) *ср (срок)* sixty years *мн; (годовщина события)* sixtieth anniversary.
шестидесятиле́т|ний (-яя, -ее, -ие) *прил (период)* sixty-year; *(юбилей)* sixtieth; *(человек)* sixty-year-old.
шестидеся́т|ый (-ая, -ое, -ые) *чис* sixtieth; *см также* **пятидеся́тый**.
шестидне́вный *прил* six-day.
шестикла́ссник (-а) *м pupil in sixth year at school (usually twelve years old)*.
шестикла́ссниц|а (-ы) *ж см* **шестикла́ссник**.
шестикра́т|ный (-ая, -ое, -ые) *прил* six-times champion; **в** ~**ом разме́ре** sixfold.
шестиле́ти|е (-я) *ср (срок)* six years; *(годовщина)* sixth anniversary.
шестиле́т|ний (-яя, -ее, -ие) *прил (отсутствие)* six-year; *(ребёнок)* six-year-old.
шестиме́сячный *прил* six-month; *(ребёнок)* six-month-old.
шестинеде́льный *прил* six-week; *(ребёнок)* six-week-old.
шестисо́т *чис см* **шестьсо́т**.
шестисотле́ти|е (-я) *ср (срок)* six hundred years *мн; (годовщина)* six hundredth anniversary, sexcentenary.
шестисотле́т|ний (-яя, -ее, -ие) *прил (период)* six hundred-year; *(дерево)* six hundred-year-old.
шестисо́т|ый (-ая, -ое, -ые) *чис* six-hundredth.
шестиуго́льник (-а) *м* hexagon.
шестичасово́й *прил (рабочий день)* six-hour; *(поезд)* six-o'clock.
шестна́дцати *чис см* **шестна́дцать**.
шестна́дцат|ый (-ая, -ое, -ые) *чис* sixteenth; *см*

также **пя́тый**.

шестнáдцат|ь (**-и**; *как* **пять**; *см* **Table 27**) *чис* sixteen; *см также* **пять**.

шест|óй (**-áя, -óе, -ы́е**) *чис* sixth; *см также* **пя́тый**.

шест|ь (**-и́**; *как* **пять**; *см* **Table 27**) *чис* six; *см также* **пять**.

шестьдеся́т (**-и́десяти**; *как* **пятьдеся́т**; *см* **Table 29**) *чис* sixty; *см также* **пятьдеся́т**.

шест|ьсóт (**-исóт**; *как* **пятьсóт**; *см* **Table 34**) *чис* six hundred; *см также* **сто**.

шестью *нареч* six times.

шестью *чис см* **шесть**.

шестьюстáми *чис см* **шестьсóт**.

шетлáндск|ий (**-ая, -ое, -ие**) *прил*: **Ш~ие островá** Shetland Islands.

шеф (**-а**) *м* (*полиции*) chief; (*разг: начальник*) boss; (*обычно мн: детского дома*) patron.

шéфск|ий (**-ая, -ое, -ие**) *прил* (*помощь*) patronal.

шéфств|о (**-а**) *ср*: **~ над** +*instr* patronage of.

шéфств|овать (**-ую**) *несов неперех*: **~ над** +*instr* to be patron of.

ше|я (**-и**) *ж* (*АНАТ*) neck; **на свою ~ю** (*разг*) to our loss; **сидéть** (*impf*) *или* **висéть** (*impf*) **у когó-н на ~е** to live off sb; **гнать** (*impf*) **когó-н в ~ю** (*разг*) to throw sb out on his *итп* ear.

шúбко *нареч* terribly.

шúворот (**-а**) *м* (*разг*): **за ~** by the collar; **~-навы́ворот** back to front.

шизофрéник (**-а**) *м* schizophrenic.

шизофрéни|я (**-и**) *ж* schizophrenia.

шик (**-а**; *part gen* **-у**) *м* chic, stylishness.

шикáрен *прил см* **шикáрный**.

шикáрно *нареч* (*разг: жить*) in style; (*обставленный*) stylishly ♦ *как сказ*: **в гости́нице ~** the hotel is stylish.

шикáрн|ый (**-ен, -на, -но**) *прил* (*разг*) smart, stylish.

шúка|ть (**-ю**) *несов неперех* (*разг*): **~ на когó-н** to hush sb.

шúкн|уть (**-у, -ешь**) *сов неперех*: **~ на когó-н** to hush sb.

шик|овáть (**-ýю**) *несов неперех* (*разг*) to show off.

шúллинг (**-а**) *м* (*денежная единица*) shilling.

шúл|о (**-а**; *nom pl* **-ья**, *gen pl* **-ьев**) *ср* awl.

шимпанзé *м нескл* chimpanzee.

шúн|а (**-ы**) *ж* (*АВТ*) tyre (*BRIT*), tire (*US*); (*МЕД*) splint.

шинéл|ь (**-и**) *ж* (*солдатская*) greatcoat, overcoat.

шинковáни|е (**-я**) *ср* shredding.

шинк|овáть (**-ýю**; *perf* **нашинковáть**) *несов перех* (*овощи*) to shred.

шиньóн (**-а**) *м* chignon.

шип (**-á**) *м* (*растения*) thorn; (*соединительный*) tenon, tongue; (*на колесе*) stud; (*на ботинке*) spike.

шипéни|е (**-я**) *ср* hissing.

шип|éть (**-лю́, -úшь**) *несов неперех* (*также*

разг) to hiss; (*шампанское, газировка*) to fizz.

шипóвк|и (**-ок**) *мн* (*СПОРТ*) spikes *мн*.

шипóвник (**-а**) *м* (*куст*) wild rose; (*плод*) (rose)hip; (*настой*) rosehip drink.

шипóвок *сущ см* **шипóвки**.

шипýч|ий (**-ая, -ее, -ее; -, -á, -е**) *прил* fizzy; (*вино*) sparkling.

шипя́щ|ий (**-ая, -ее, -ие**) *прил* (*линг*) sibilant *опред*.

шúре *сравн прил от* **широ́кий** ♦ *сравн нареч от* **широко́**.

ширин|á (**-ы́**) *ж* width; **доро́жка метр ~о́й** *или* **в ~ý** a path a metre (*BRIT*) *или* meter (*US*) wide.

ширúнк|а (**-ки**; *gen pl* **-ок**) *ж* (*брюк*) fly.

шúр|иться (*3sg* **-ится**, *3pl* **-ятся**) *несов возв* (*дела*) to expand; (*движение*) to grow.

шúрм|а (**-ы**) *ж* (*также перен*) screen.

широ́к|ий (**-ая, -ое, -ие; -, -á, -ó**) *прил* wide; (*степи, фронт, планы*) extensive; (*перен: общественность, публика*) general; (*: смысл, интерпретация*) broad; (*: масштабы*) large; (*: натура, жест*) generous; (*: образ жизни*) grand; **товáры ~ого потреблéния** (*ЭКОН*) consumer goods; **жить** (*impf*) **на ~ую но́гу** to live in grand style; **широ́кий экра́н** (*КИНО*) wide screen.

широко́ *нареч* (*раскинуться*) widely; (*улыбаться, интерпретировать*) broadly; (*жить*) in grand style; **~ раскрыва́ть** (**раскры́ть** *perf*) **глазá** to open one's eyes wide; (*перен*) to be amazed.

широковещáтельн|ый (**-ен, -ьна, -ьно**) *прил* broadcasting *опред*; **широковещáтельная сеть** (*КОМП*) broadcast network.

широкоплéч|ий (**-ая, -ее, -ие; -, -а, -е**) *прил* (*человек*) broad-shouldered.

широкопо́л|ый (*шляпа*) wide-brimmed; (*пальто*) with a full skirt.

широкоформáтный *прил* (*экран*) wide-format.

широкофюзеля́жный *прил* (*самолёт*) wide-bodied.

широкоэкрáнный *прил* (*фильм*) wide-screen.

широт|á (**-оты́**) *ж* breadth; (*nom pl* **-óты**; *ГЕО*) latitude.

ширпотрéб (**-а**) *м сокр* = **широ́кое потреблéние**; (*разг: о товарах*) consumer goods *мн*; (*: о плохом товаре*) low-quality goods *мн*.

шир|ь (**-и**) *ж* expanse; **развора́чиваться** (**развернýться** *perf*) **во всю ~** (*перен*) to develop to one's full potential.

шúто-кры́то *нареч* (*разг*): **всё ~** it's all being kept under wraps.

шúтый *прил* embroidered.

шить (**шью, шьёшь**; *perf* **сшить**) *несов перех* (*платье итп*) to sew ♦ *неперех*: **~** +*instr* (*шёлком итп*) to embroider.

шить|ё (**-я́**) *ср* (*см глаг*) sewing; embroidery.

шúфер (**-а**) *м* (*натуральный*) slate; (*СТРОИТ*) corrugated asbestos board.

шифóн (**-а**) *м* chiffon.

шифоньéр (**-а**) *м* wardrobe.

шифр (-а) *м* (*для секретного письма*) code, cipher; (*книги, документа*) pressmark.

шифровáльщик (-а) *м* cipher-clerk; (*расшифровывающий*) code cracker.

шифровáть (-ýю; *perf* **зашифровáть**) *несов перех* (*донесение*) to encode, encipher.

шифрóвка (-ки; *gen pl* -ок) *ж* (*см глаг*) encoding, enciphering; (*сообщение*) coded message.

шиш (-á) *м разг: кукиш*) fig (*rude gesture*); **ни ~á** (*разг*) damn all; **~ ты от меня полýчишь** (*разг*) you'll get damn all from me; **на какие ~й?** (*разг*) who's paying?

шишка (-ки; *gen pl* -ек) *ж* (*БОТ*) cone; (*на лбу*) bump, lump; (*разг: важный человек*) bigwig.

шишковáтый (-, -а, -о) *прил* (*руки*) knobbly; (*лоб*) lumpy; (*доска*) rough.

шкалá (-ы́; *nom pl* -ы) *ж* scale; (*приёмника*) dial.

шкатýлка (-ки; *gen pl* -ок) *ж* casket; **музыкáльная ~** musical box.

шкаф (-а; *loc sg* -ý, *nom pl* -ы́) *м* (*для одежды*) wardrobe; (*для посуды*) cupboard; (*ТЕХ: сушильный итп*) oven; **духовóй ~** airing cupboard; **книжный ~** bookcase.

шквал (-а) *м* (*ветер*) squall; **~ +gen** (*оваций, огня*) burst of.

шквáльный *прил* (*ветер*) squally; (*огонь*) heavy.

шкив (-а) *м* (*ТЕХ*) pulley.

шкипер (-а) *м* (*МОР*) skipper.

шкирка (-и) *ж*: **брать когó-н за ~у** (*разг*) to take sb by the scruff of the neck; (*перен*) to twist sb's arm.

шкóла (-ы) *ж* school; (*милиции*) college, academy; (*выучка*) education, training; (*СПОРТ*) training; **высшая ~** higher education; **начáльная ~** primary (*BRIT*) *или* elementary (*US*) school; **срéдняя ~** secondary (*BRIT*) *или* high (*US*) school.

шкóла-интернáт (-ы, -а) *м* boarding school.

шкóльник (-а) *м* schoolboy.

шкóльница (-ы) *ж* schoolgirl.

шкóльный *прил* (*здание*) school *опред*; **шкóльные гóды** schooldays; **шкóльный вóзраст** school age; **шкóльный учéбник** school book; **шкóльный учúтель** school teacher.

шкýра (-ы) *ж* (*животного*) fur; (*убитого животного*) skin; (: *обработанная*) hide ♦ *м/ж* (*разг: продажный человек*) self-seeker; **быть** (*impf*) **в чьей-н ~е** to be in sb's shoes (*fig*); **спасáть** (*impf*) **свою ~у** (*разг*) to save one's (own) skin; **на своéй ~е узнáть** (*perf*) (*разг*) to experience first-hand.

шкýрить (-ю, -ишь) *несов перех* (*шлифовать*) to sand(paper).

шкýрка (-и) *ж уменьш от* **шкýра**; (*разг: плода*) rind, peel; (*абразив*) sandpaper.

шкýрник (-а) *м* (*разг: пренебр*) self-seeker.

шкýрный *прил* (*интересы*) selfish.

шла *несов см* **идтú**.

шлагбáум (-а) *м* barrier.

шлак (-а) *м* (*ТЕХ*) slag.

шлакобетóнный *прил* (*панель, кирпич*) slag-concrete.

шланг (-а) *м* hose.

шлейф (-а) *м* (*платья*) train; (*дыма*) trail.

шлем (-а) *м* helmet.

шлёпанец (-ца) *м* (*разг: обычно мн*) bedroom slipper.

шлёпать (-ю) *несов перех* (*бить*) to slap ♦ *неперех*: **~ по** +*acc* (*по полу*) to shuffle; (*по воде*) to splash

▶ **шлёпаться** (*perf* **шлёпнуться**) *несов возв* (*разг*) to plop.

шли *несов см* **идтú**.

шлифовáльный *прил* (*ТЕХ*) grinding *опред*.

шлифовáть (-ýю; *perf* **отшлифовáть**) *несов перех* (*ТЕХ*) to grind; (*перен: стиль*) to polish.

шлифóвка (-и) *ж* (*детали*) grinding.

шлúца (-ы) *ж* (*ТЕХ*) spline; (*юбки*) slit.

шло *несов см* **идтú**.

шлю *итп несов см* **слать**.

шлюз (-а) *м* (*на канале*) lock; (*на реке*) sluice.

шлюпка (-ки; *gen pl* -ок) *ж* (*МОР*) dinghy; **спасáтельная ~** lifeboat.

шлюха (-и) *ж* (*разг*) tart.

шлягер (-а) *м* (*МУЗ*) hit.

шляпа (-ы) *ж* hat ♦ *м/ж* (*перен: разг: человек*) wimp; **дéло в ~е** (*разг*) it's in the bag.

шляпка (-ки; *gen pl* -ок) *ж* hat; (*гвоздя*) head; (*гриба*) cap.

шляпник (-а) *м* (*мужской*) hatter; (*женский*) milliner.

шляпный *прил* hat *опред*.

шляпок *сущ см* **шляпка**.

шляться (-юсь) *несов возв* (*разг*) to mooch about.

шмель (-я́) *м* bumblebee.

шмóтки (-ок) *мн* (*разг*) clobber *ед*.

шмыгáть (-ю) *несов неперех* (*разг: шнырять*) to rush; (*исчезнуть*) to slip, dart; **~ нóсом** to sniff.

шмыгнýть (-ý, -ёшь) *сов неперех* (*быстро пройти*) to dart, nip; (*исчезнуть*) to slip, dart.

шмякнуть (-у, -ешь; *impf* **шмякать**) *сов перех* (*разг: бросить*) to thump down

▶ **шмякнуться** (*impf* **шмякаться**) *сов возв* (*разг: упасть*) to topple over.

шницель (-я) *м* (*кулин*) schnitzel.

шнур (-á) *м* (*верёвка*) cord; (*телефонный, лампы*) flex.

шнурóк *итп сущ см* **шнурóк**.

шнуровáть (-ýю; *perf* **зашнуровáть**) *несов перех* (*ботинки*) to lace (up); (*perf* **прошнуровáть**; *прошивать шнуром*) to tie, bind.

шнуро́вк|а (-и) ж (см глаг) lacing up; tying, binding; (на одежде, на обуви) lacing.

шнур|о́к (-ка́) м (ботинка) lace.

шныря́|ть (-ю) несов неперех (разг: в толпе, по улицам) to dash about; **он ~л глаза́ми** (перен: разг) his eyes darted about.

шов (шва) м (швейный) seam; (хирургический) stitch, suture; (намёточный, тамбурный итп) stitch; (кровельный) joint, seam; **сварно́й ~** joint weld, weld seam; **накла́дывать (наложи́ть** perf)/**снима́ть (снять** perf) **швы** (МЕД) to put in/take out stitches; **треща́ть** (impf) **по всем швам** (перен: разг) to fall apart at the seams; **ру́ки по швам** stand at attention.

шовини́зм (-а) м chauvinism.

шовини́ст (-а) м chauvinist.

шовинисти́ческ|ий (-ая, -ое, -ие) прил chauvinist.

шок (-а) м (МЕД, перен) shock.

шоки́р|овать (-ую) (не)сов перех to shock.

шо́ков|ый прил: **~ое состоя́ние** state of shock; **шо́ковая терапи́я** (МЕД, перен) shock therapy.

шокола́д (-а) м chocolate; (напиток) (hot) chocolate.

шокола́д|ка (-ки; gen pl **-ок)** ж (разг) bar of chocolate.

шокола́дн|ый прил (конфета) chocolate; (цвет) chocolate-brown; **~ая пли́тка** bar of chocolate.

шокола́док сущ см шокола́дка.

шо́мпол (-а) м (ВОЕН) cleaning rod.

шо́рох (-а) м rustle.

шорт-лист (-а) м short list.

шо́рт|ы (-) мн shorts мн.

шоссе́ ср нескл highway.

шоссе́йн|ый прил: **~ая доро́га** highway.

шотла́нд|ец (-ца) м Scotsman (мн Scotsmen).

Шотла́нди|я (-и) ж Scotland.

шотла́нд|ка (-ки; gen pl **-ок)** ж Scotswoman (мн Scotswomen); (ткань) tartan (BRIT), plaid (US).

шотла́ндск|ий (-ая, -ое, -ие) прил Scottish, Scots.

шотла́ндца итп сущ см шотла́ндец.

шо́у ср нескл (также перен) show.

шофёр (-а) м driver.

шпа́г|а (-и) ж sword.

шпага́т (-а) м (бечёвка) string, twine; (СПОРТ) the splits.

шпажи́ст (-а) м (СПОРТ) fencer.

шпажи́ст|ка (-ки; gen pl **-ок)** ж см шпажи́ст.

шпакл|ева́ть (-ю́ю; perf **зашпаклева́ть)** несов перех (трещины, дыры) to fill.

шпаклёвк|а (-и) ж (действие) filling; (замазка) filler.

шпа́л|а (-ы) ж sleeper (RAIL).

шпале́р|а (-ы) ж (обои) handpainted wallpaper; (для растений) trellis.

шпан|а́ (-ы́) ж собир (разг) rabble.

шпарга́л|ка (-ки; gen pl **-ок)** ж (разг: для экзаменов) crib.

шпа́р|ить (-ю, -ишь) несов неперех (разг): **~ на**

гита́ре to play away on the guitar; **~** (impf) **по-англи́йски** (разг) to speak fluent English; **~** (impf) **по у́лице** (разг) to rush along the street.

шпа́тел|ь (-я) м (для шпаклёвки, для краски) palette knife (мн knives); (МЕД) spatula.

шпиг|ова́ть (-у́ю; perf **нашпигова́ть)** несов перех (мясо) to lard.

шпик (-а; part gen **-у)** м (сало) lard; (разг: сыщик) detective.

шпи́лек сущ см шпи́лька.

шпиль (-я) м spire.

шпи́л|ька (-ьки; gen pl **-ек)** ж (для волос) hairpin; (для шляпы) hatpin; (каблук) stiletto (heel); (перен: разг: замечание) dig; **ту́фли на ~ьке** stilettos.

шпина́т (-а) м spinach.

шпингале́т (-а) м (на окне) catch; (разг: о мальчишке) little boy.

шпио́н (-а) м spy.

шпиона́ж (-а) м espionage.

шпио́н|ить (-ю, -ишь) несов неперех (разг) to spy; **~** (impf) **за** +instr (за женой) to spy on.

Шпицбе́рген (-а) м Spitzbergen.

шпо́р|а (-ы) ж spur.

шприц (-а) м syringe.

шпро́т|ы (-ов) мн sprats мн.

шпу́ль|ка (-и) ж spool, bobbin.

шрам (-а) м (на теле) scar.

шрапне́л|ь (-и) ж (ВОЕН) shrapnel только ед.

Шри-Ла́нк|а (-и) ж Sri Lanka.

шрифт (-а; nom pl **-ы́)** м type, print; **жи́рный/ курси́вный ~** bold/italic type; **набо́рный ~** (ТИПОГ) printing type.

шт. сокр = **шту́ка.**

штаб (-а; nom pl **-ы́)** м headquarters мн; (люди) staff.

шта́бел|ь (-я; nom pl **-я́)** м (дров) stack.

штаб-кварти́р|а (-ы) ж (ВОЕН) headquarters мн.

штабн|о́й прил (разведка, офицер) staff опред.

штаке́тник (-а) м (ограда) palings мн.

штамп (-а) м (печать) stamp; (перен: в речи) cliché; (ТЕХ) die, stamp.

штамп|ова́ть (-у́ю; perf **проштампова́ть)** несов перех (справки, документы) to stamp; (perf **отштампова́ть;** детали) to punch, press; (no perf; решения, ответы) to rubber-stamp.

штампо́вочный прил (ТЕХ) punching опред, pressing опред.

шта́нг|а (-и) ж (СПОРТ: в тяжёлой атлетике) weight; (: ворот) post.

штангенци́ркул|ь (-я) м (ТЕХ) sliding calipers мн, slide gauge.

штанги́ст (-а) м (СПОРТ) weightlifter.

штанда́рт (-а) м (ВОЕН) standard.

штани́н|а (-ы) ж (разг) trouser leg.

штан|ы́ (-о́в) мн trousers мн.

шта́пел|ь (-я) м (ткань) viscose manufactured to resemble cotton.

шта́пельный прил (ткань, платье) made with viscose manufactured to resemble cotton.

штат (-а) м (государства) state; (работники)

staff; (положение) staff regulations мн; э́та до́лжность полага́ется по шта́ту this job is stipulated by the regulations; зачисля́ть (зачи́слить perf) кого-н в ~ to take sb onto the staff.

штати́в (-а) м (ФОТО) tripod; (микроскопа) stand.

шта́тный прил (сотрудник) permanent; шта́тная до́лжность (АДМИН) established post; шта́тное расписа́ние (АДМИН) staff register.

шта́тский (-ая, -ое, -ие) прил (одежда) civilian опред ♦ (-ого; decl like adj) м civilian.

шта́тское (-ого; decl like adj) ср civilian clothes мн, civvies мн (inf).

ште́мпель (-я) м: почто́вый ~ postmark.

ште́псель (-я) м (ЭЛЕК) plug.

ште́псельный прил: ~ая розе́тка electric socket.

штибле́ты (-) мн lace-up boots мн.

штилево́й прил (погода) calm.

штиль (-я) м (МОР) calm.

штифт (-а́) м (ТЕХ) pin.

што́льня (-ьни; gen pl -ен) ж (ГЕО) gallery.

што́паный прил darned.

што́пать (-ю; perf зашто́пать) несов перех to darn.

што́пка (-и) ж (действие) darning; (нитки) darning thread; (разг: зашто́панное место) darn.

што́пор (-а) м corkscrew.

што́ра (-ы) ж drapery; (поднимающаяся) blind.

шторм (-а) м gale.

шторми́ть (3sg -и́т) несов неперех (море) to be rough; сего́дня ~и́т it is rough today.

штормо́вка (-ки; gen pl -ок) ж oilskin coat.

штормово́й прил (погода) stormy; (ветер) gale-force; штормово́е предупрежде́ние (МОР) gale warning.

штормо́вок сущ см штормо́вка

штраф (-а) м (денежный) fine; (СПОРТ) punishment; накла́дывать (наложи́ть perf) ~ на +acc to impose a fine on.

штрафни́к (-а́) м (СПОРТ) player who has been sent off; скаме́йка штрафнико́в penalty box (in ice-hockey).

штрафно́й прил penal ♦ (-о́го; decl like adj) м (СПОРТ: также: ~ уда́р) penalty (kick); штрафно́е очко́ (СПОРТ) penalty point.

штрафова́ть (-у́ю; perf оштрафова́ть) несов перех to fine; (СПОРТ) to penalize.

штрейкбре́хер (-а) м strikebreaker, blackleg.

штрек (-а) м (ГЕО) drift.

штрих (-а́) м (черта) stroke; (частность) feature.

штрихова́ть (-у́ю; perf заштрихова́ть) несов перех (рисунок) to shade.

штуди́ровать (-ую; perf проштуди́ровать) несов перех to study.

што́тка (-и) ж (отдельный предмет) item; (разг: трудная, забавная) thing; (: проделка) trick; вот так ~! (разг) what do you know!

штукату́р (-а) м plasterer.

штукату́рить (-ю, -ишь; perf отштукату́рить или оштукату́рить) несов перех to plaster.

штукату́рка (-и) ж (действие) plastering; (раствор) plaster; (на стене) plaster, stucco.

штукату́рный прил (работы) plaster опред.

штуко́вина (-ы) ж (разг) thing.

штурва́л (-а) м (судна, комбайна) wheel; (самолёта) controls мн.

штурва́льный прил steering опред.

штурм (-а) м (ВОЕН) storm; (перен: горной верши́ны) conquest; брать (взять perf) что-н штурмом to take sth by storm.

штурма́н (-а) м (МОР, АВИА) navigator.

штурма́нский (-ая, -ое, -ие) прил navigator's.

штурмова́ть (-у́ю) несов перех (ВОЕН) to storm; (перен) to conquer.

шту́чный прил (товар, изделие) sold by the piece; (работа, оплата) piece опред.

штык (-а́) м (ВОЕН) bayonet; принима́ть (приня́ть perf) или встреча́ть (встре́тить perf) что-н/кого-н в ~и́ (перен) to give sth/sb a hostile reception; как ~ (разг) on the dot.

штыково́й прил (атака) bayonet опред; штыкова́я лопа́та sharp-bladed spade.

штырь (-я́) м (ТЕХ) pin, pintle.

шу́ба (-ы) ж (меховая) fur coat; (разг: животного) coat; селёдка под ~ой (КУЛИН) herring served with an elaborate topping.

шу́лер (-а) м cardsharper.

шум (-а; part gen -у) м (звук) noise; (перен: ажиотаж) stir, sensation; (МЕД) murmur; (разг: ссора) row, racket; (суета) bustle, fuss; вызыва́ть (вы́звать perf) или наде́лать (perf) ~ to cause a sensation.

шу́мен прил см шу́мный.

шуме́ть (-лю́, -и́шь) несов неперех to make a noise; (разглашать) to create a scene; (ссориться) to kick up a row; у меня́ ~и́т в голове́/в уша́х I have a buzzing in my head/ears.

шуми́ха (-и) ж (разг: пренебр: толки) sensation, stir; поднима́ть (подня́ть perf) ~у вокру́г чего-н to create a sensation around sth; газе́тная ~ sensation created by the press.

шумли́вый (-, -а, -о) прил noisy.

шумлю́ несов см шуме́ть.

шумно́ нареч noisily ♦ как ска́з it is noisy.

шу́мный (-ен, -на́, -но) прил noisy; (разговор, компания) loud; (оживлённый: улица, залы итп) bustling; (перен: успех) sensational.

шумо́вка (-ки; gen pl -ок) ж perforated spoon.

шумово́й прил (оформление) sound опред.

шумо́вок сущ см шумо́вка.

шумо́к м (разг): под ~ (разг) on the quiet.

шу́рин (-а) *м* brother-in-law, wife's brother.

шуру́п (-а) *м* (*ТЕХ*) screw.

шурш|а́ть (-у́, -и́шь) *несов неперех* to rustle.

шу́ры-му́ры *мн нескл* (*разг*) love affairs *мн*.

шу́стрый (-, -а́, -о) *прил* (*разг*) nimble.

шут (-а́) *м* (*придворный*) jester; (*разг: человек*) fool, clown; ~ горо́ховый (*разг*) buffoon; ~ с ним (*разг*) forget it.

шу|ти́ть (-чу́, -тишь) *perf* пошути́ть) *несов неперех* to joke; (*смеяться*): ~ над +*instr* to make fun of; (*no perf*; *пренебрегать*): ~ +*instr* (*здоровьем*) to disregard; ~ (*impf*) с огнём (*перен*) to play with fire; чем чёрт не шу́тит! (*разг*) anything might happen!

шу́т|ка (-ки; *gen pl* -ок) *ж* joke; без ~ок joking apart, seriously; кро́ме ~ок, ты пра́вда согла́сен? joking apart *или* seriously, do you really agree?; не на ~ку (*рассердился, испугался итп*) in earnest; сказа́ть (*perf*) что-н в ~ку to say sth as a joke; ~ки пло́хи с

кем-н/чем-н sb/sth is not to be trifled with.

шутли́в|ый (-, -а, -о) *прил* (*человек, тон, замечание*) humourous (*BRIT*), humorous (*US*); (*настроение*) light-hearted.

шутни́к (-а́) *м* joker.

шутовск|о́й *прил*: ~и́е вы́ходки buffoonery; ~ колпа́к jester's cap.

шутовство́ (-а́) *ср* buffoonery.

шу́ток *сущ см* шу́тка.

шу́точ|ный (-ен, -на, -но) *прил* (*рассказ*) comic, funny; э́то де́ло не ~ное it's no laughing matter.

шутя́ *нареч* (*разг: без труда*) easily.

шучу́ *несов см* шути́ть.

шу́шер|а (-ы) *ж собир* (*разг*) riffraff.

шушу́ка|ться (-юсь) *несов возв*: ~ (с +*instr*) to whisper (to).

шху́н|а (-ы) *ж* (*МОР*) schooner.

ш-ш *межд* sh.

шью *итп несов см* шить.

~ Щ, щ ~

Щ, щ *сущ нескл (буква)* the 26th letter of the Russian alphabet.

щаве́л|ь (-я́) *м* sorrel.

щади́ть (-жу́, -ди́шь; *perf* **пощади́ть**) *несов перех* to spare; **он на ~дя́щем режи́ме** (*МЕД*) he's not allowed to exert himself.

щам *итп сущ см* **щи**.

щебёнк|а (-и) *ж* = **щебень**.

ще́б|ень (-ня) *м* (*СТРОИТ*) ballast.

ще́бет (-а) *м* twitter.

щебета́ть (-ечу́, -е́чешь) *несов неперех (также перен*) to twitter.

ще́бня *итп сущ см* **щебень**.

щег|о́л (-ла́) *м* goldfinch.

щеголева́т|ый (-, -а, -о) *прил (одежда)* fancy; (*мужчина*) stylish.

щёгол|ь (-я) *м* dandy.

щегольну́|ть (-ý, -ёшь) *сов неперех:* ~ +*instr* to show off.

щегольско́й *прил* stylish.

щегольств|о́ (-а́) *ср* dandyism.

щеголя́|ть (-ю) *несов неперех* to dress up; ~ (*impf*) +*instr* to show off; ~ (*impf*) **в** +*prp* to rig o.s. out in.

ще́дрост|ь (-и) *ж* generosity.

ще́др|ый (-, -á, -о) *прил* generous; (*природа*) lush; (*климат*) fertile; ~ **на** +*acc* generous with.

щей *сущ см* **щи**.

щек|а́ (щеки́; *nom pl* **щёки**, *gen pl* **щёк**, *dat pl* **щека́м**) *ж* cheek; **за о́бе щеки́ есть** (*impf*) **или упи́сывать** (*impf*) (*разг*) to gobble one's food up *или* down.

щеко́лд|а (-ы) *ж* latch.

щекот|а́ть (-очу́, -о́чешь; *perf* **пощекота́ть**) *несов неперех (пятки итп*) to tickle; ~ (*impf*) **кому́-н не́рвы** to excite sb; **у меня́ ~о́чет в го́рле/носу́** I've got a tickle in my throat/nose.

щеко́тк|а (-и) *ж* tickling.

щекотли́в|ый (-, -а, -о) *прил (вопрос итп*) delicate.

щеко́тно *как сказ:* **мне ~** it's tickling me; **здесь ~ ходи́ть босико́м** it's ticklish going barefoot here.

щекочу́ *итп несов см* **щекота́ть**.

щёлк|а (-и) *ж* small hole.

щёлка|ть (-ю) *несов перех (человека*) to flick; (*орехи, семечки*) to crack (open) ♦ *неперех:* ~ +*instr (языком*) to click; (*кнутом*) to crack.

щёлкну|ть (-у, -ешь) *сов неперех* to click; (*хлыстом*) to crack.

щелочно́й *прил* alkaline.

щёлоч|ь (-и) *ж* alkali.

щелч|о́к (-ка́) *м* flick; (*звук*) click; (*перен: оскорбление*) jibe.

щел|ь (-и; *loc sg* -и́, *gen pl* -е́й) *ж (отверстие*) crack; (*ТЕХ*) slit; **смотрова́я ~** vision slit.

щем|и́ть (*3sg* -и́т, *3pl* -я́т) *несов перех (перен: тревожить*) to trouble ♦ *безл (ныть*): **~и́т в боку́** his *итп* side is aching; **~и́т в груди́** his *итп* heart is heavy.

щемя́щ|ий (-ая, -ее, -ие) *прил* aching.

щен|и́ться (*3sg* -и́тся, *3pl* -я́тся, *perf* **ощени́ться**) *несов возв (собака*) to have pups; (*волчица, лиса*) to have cubs.

щен|о́к (-ка́; *nom pl* -я́та, *gen pl* -я́т) *м (собаки*) pup; (*лисы, волчицы*) cub; (*перен: разг*) whippersnapper.

щепети́лен *прил см* **щепети́льный**.

щепети́льност|ь (-и) *ж (в отношениях, денежных делах*) scrupulousness.

щепети́л|ьный (-ен, -ьна, -ьно) *прил* scrupulous.

ще́п|ка (-ки; *gen pl* -ок) *ж* splinter; (*для растопки*): **~ки** chippings *мн*; **худо́й как ~** thin as a rake.

щепо́т|ка (-ки; *gen pl* -ок) *ж (соли, табака*) pinch.

щерба́т|ый (-, -а, -о) *прил (рот*) gap-toothed; (*лицо*) pock-marked.

щерби́н|а (-ы) *ж (на лице, на коже*) pock-mark; (*во рту*) gap (between teeth); (*на посуде*) chink.

щети́н|а (-ы) *ж (животных, щётки*) bristle; (*у мужчины*) stubble.

щети́нист|ый (-, -а, -о) *прил (жёсткий*) bristly; (*небритый*) stubbly.

щети́н|иться (*3sg* -ится, *3pl* -ятся, *perf* **ощети́ниться**) *несов возв (также перен*) to bristle.

щёт|ка (-ки; *gen pl* -ок) *ж* brush; **зубна́я ~** toothbrush; **~ для воло́с** hairbrush.

щи (щей; *dat pl* **щам**) *мн* cabbage soup *ед*; **ки́слые ~** sour cabbage soup; **зелёные ~** sorrel soup.

щи́колот|ка (-ки; *gen pl* -ок) ж ankle.
щип|а́ть (-лю́, -лешь) *несов перех* (*защемлять до боли*) to nip, pinch; (*no perf*; *подлеж*: *мороз*) to bite; (: *специя, кислое*) to sting; (*perf* **ощипа́ть**; *волосы, курицу*) to pluck
▸ **щипа́ться** *несов возв* (*разг*) to nip, pinch.
щипка́ *итп сущ см* **щипо́к**.
щипко́вый *прил* (*муз*): ~ **инструме́нт** plucked (*BRIT*) *или* picked (*US*) instrument.
щиплю́(сь) *итп несов см* **щипа́ть(ся)**.
щипн|у́ть (-у́, -ёшь) *сов перех* to nip, pinch.
щипо́к (-ка́) *м* nip, pinch.
щипц|ы́ (-о́в) *мн*: **ками́нные** ~ tongs *мн*; **кузне́чные** ~ pliers *мн*; **хирурги́ческие** ~ forceps *мн*; ~ **для са́хара** sugar-tongs *мн*.
щи́пчик|и (-ов) *мн уменьш от* **щипцы́**; (*для ногтей, бровей*) tweezers *мн*.
щит (-а́) *м* shield; (*фанерный, металлический*

итп) barrier; (*рекламный, баскетбольный*) board; (*TEX*) panel; ~ **управле́ния** control panel.
щитови́дн|ый *прил*: ~**ая железа́** thyroid gland.
щу́к|а (-и) *ж* pike (*мн* pike).
щуп (-а) *м* (*TEX*) probe.
щу́пал|ьце (-ьца; *nom pl* -ьца, *gen pl* -ец) *ср* (*осьминога*) tentacle; (*насекомых*) feeler.
щу́па|ть (-ю; *perf* **пощу́пать**) *несов перех* (*опухоль, пульс*) to feel for; (*карманы*) to grope in.
щу́пл|ый (-, -а́, -о) *прил* (*разг*) puny.
щу́р|ить (-ю, -ишь; *perf* **сощу́рить**) *несов перех*: ~ **глаза́** to screw up one's eyes
▸ **щу́риться** (*perf* **сощу́риться**) *несов возв* (*от солнца*) to squint.
щу́чий (-ья, -ье, -ьи) *прил*: по ~**ьему веле́нью** (as if) by magic.

~ Э, э ~

Э, э *сущ нескл (буква)* the 30th letter of the Russian alphabet.

э *межд (выражает недоумение)* er ..., um ...; *(выражает решимость)* oh; **э, нет, я не пойду!** oh, no, I'm not going!

эбони́т (-а) *м* vulcanite, ebonite.

эвакуацио́нный *прил (пункт)* evacuation *опред*; *(госпиталь)* evacuee *опред*.

эвакуа́ци|я (-и) *ж* evacuation.

эвакуи́р|овать (-ую) *(не)сов перех* to evacuate
▶ **эвакуи́роваться** *(не)сов возв* to be evacuated.

Эвере́ст (-а) *м* Mount Everest.

эвкали́пт (-а) *м* eucalyptus.

эвкали́птов|ый *прил:* ~**ое ма́сло** eucalyptus oil.

ЭВМ *ж сокр (= электро́нная вычисли́тельная маши́на)* computer.

эволюциони́р|овать (-ую) *(не)сов неперех* to evolve.

эволюцио́нный *прил* evolutionary.

эволю́ци|я (-и) *ж* evolution.

эвфеми́зм (-а) *м* euphemism.

эвфемисти́ческ|ий (-ая, -ое, -ие) *прил* euphemistic.

эги́д|а (-ы) *ж:* **под** ~**ой** +*gen* under the aegis of.

эгои́зм (-а) *м* egoism.

эгои́ст (-а) *м* egoist.

эгоисти́чен *прил см* **эгоисти́чный.**

эгоисти́ческ|ий (-ая, -ое, -ие) *прил* egotistic-(al).

эгоисти́ч|ный (-ен, -на, -но) *прил* = **эгоисти́ческий.**

эгои́ст|ка (-ки; *gen pl* -ок) *ж см* **эгои́ст.**

эгоцентри́ст (-а) *м:* **он настоя́щий** ~ he is very egocentric.

эдельве́йс (-а) *м* edelweiss.

Эдинбу́рг (-а) *м* Edinburgh.

эй *межд (разг)* hey; ~, **кто идёт?** hey, who's there?

Эй-би-си *м сокр (= Америка́нская радиовеща́тельная компа́ния)* ABC (= American Broadcasting Company).

Эквадо́р (-а) *м* Ecuador.

эквадо́рск|ий (-ая, -ое, -ие) *прил* Ecuadorian.

эква́тор (-а) *м* equator.

экваториа́льный *прил* equatorial.

эквивале́нт (-а) *м* equivalent.

эквивале́нт|ный (-ен, -на, -но) *прил* equivalent.

эквилибри́стик|а (-и) *ж* tightrope walking.

ЭКГ *ж сокр* (= **электрокардиогра́мма**) ECG (= electrocardiogram).

экзальта́ци|я (-и) *ж* exhilaration.

экзальти́рован|ный (-, -на, -но) *прил* exhilarated.

экза́мен (-а) *м:* ~ (**по** +*dat*) *(по истории, по языку)* exam(ination) (in); *(для получения звания, должности):* ~ **на перево́дчика** translator's test; *(перен):* ~ (**на** +*acc*) test (of); **выпускны́е** ~**ы** Finals *мн;* **сдава́ть** (*impf*) ~ to sit (*BRIT*) *или* take an exam(ination); **сдать** (*perf*) *или* **выде́рживать** (**вы́держать** *perf*) ~ to pass an exam(ination); **прова́ливать** (**провали́ть** *perf*) ~ to fail an exam(ination); **принима́ть** (**приня́ть** *perf*) ~ to hold an exam(ination).

экзамена́тор (-а) *м* examiner.

экзаменацио́нный *прил (комиссия, сессия)* examination *опред;* **экзаменацио́нный биле́т** exam(ination) paper.

экзамен|ова́ть (-у́ю; *perf* **проэкзаменова́ть**) *несов перех* to examine.

экзе́м|а (-ы) *ж* eczema.

экземпля́р (-а) *м (рукописи, документа)* copy; *(животного, растения)* specimen; **в двух/трёх** ~**ах** in duplicate/triplicate.

экзистенциали́зм (-а) *м* existentialism.

экзо́тик|а (-и) *ж* exotica *мн.*

экзоти́чен *прил см* **экзоти́чный.**

экзоти́ческ|ий (-ая, -ое, -ие) *прил (растение, страна)* exotic.

экзоти́ч|ный (-ен, -на, -но) *прил (наряд, декорации)* exotic.

э́к|ий (-ая, -ое, -ие; -а, -о, -и) *мест:* ~**ая незада́ча!** what a nuisance!; ~ **ты стра́нный** what a strange one you are!

экипа́ж (-а) *м (коляска)* carriage; *(команда)* crew.

экипир|ова́ть (-у́ю) *(не)сов перех (бойцов, экспедицию)* to equip.

экипиро́в|ка (-и) *ж (действие)* equipping; *(снаряжение)* equipment.

экологи́ческий (**-ая, -ое, -ие**) *прил* ecological.
эколо́ги|я (**-и**) *ж* ecology.
эконо́мен *прил см* **эконо́мный**.
эконо́ми|ка (**-и**) *ж* (*страны, региона*) economy; (*наука*) economics.
эконо́мист (**-а**) *м* economist.
эконо́м|ить (**-лю, -ишь**; *perf* **сэконо́мить**) *несов перех* (*энергию, деньги*) to save; (*выгадывать*): ~ **на** +*prp* to economize *или* save on.
эконо́мичен *прил см* **эконо́мичный**.
экономи́ческий (**-ая, -ое, -ие**) *прил* economic.
эконо́мичный (**-ен, -на, -но**) *прил* economical.
эконо́ми|я (**-и**) *ж* (*в работе, в использовании чего-н*) economy; (*выгода*): ~ +*prp* (*в топливе, в ресурсах*) economizing in; **соблюда́ть** (*impf*) ~**ю** to economize; **полити́ческая** ~ political economy.
эконо́м|ка (**-ки**; *gen pl* **-ок**) *ж* housekeeper.
эконо́млю *несов см* **эконо́мить**.
эконо́м|ный (**-ен, -на, -но**) *прил* (*хозяин*) thrifty; (*метод*) economical.
эконо́мок *сущ см* **эконо́мка**.
экосисте́м|а (**-ы**) *ж* ecosystem.
экра́н (**-а**) *м* screen.
экраниза́ци|я (**-и**) *ж* screen adaptation.
экранизи́р|овать (**-ую**) (*не*)*сов перех* to screen.
экра́н|ный *прил*: ~**ая па́мять** (*КОМП*) screen memory; ~**ое редакти́рование** (*КОМП*) screen editing.
экс- *префикс* ex-; ~**чемпио́н** ex-champion.
экскава́тор (**-а**) *м* excavator, digger.
экскава́торщик (**-а**) *м* excavator operator.
эксклюзи́вный *прил* exclusive.
э́кскурс (**-а**) *м* excursus, digression.
экскурса́нт (**-а**) *м* tour group member.
экскурсио́нный *прил* excursion *опред*.
экску́рси|я (**-и**) *ж* (*посещение*) excursion; (*группа*) party.
экскурсово́д (**-а**) *м* guide.
экспанси́вный (**-ен, -на, -но**) *прил* enthusiastic.
экспа́нси|я (**-и**) *ж* (*полит*) expansion.
экспеди́тор (**-а**) *м* shipping agent.
экспеди́ци|я (**-и**) *ж* (*научная, студенческая*) field work; (*группа людей*) expedition; (*газетная*) dispatch.
экспериме́нт (**-а**) *м* experiment.
эксперимента́льный *прил* experimental.
эксперименти́р|овать (**-ую**) *несов неперех*: ~ (**над** *или* **с** +*instr*) to experiment (on *или* with).
экспе́рт (**-а**) *м* expert.
экспертИ́з|а (**-ы**) *ж* (*медицинская*) medical assessment; (*судебная*) legal evaluation.
экспе́ртный *прил* expert *опред*.
эксплуата́тор (**-а**) *м* exploiter.
эксплуата́ци|я (**-и**) *ж* (*человека, ресурсов*) exploitation; (*машин, месторождений*) utilization; **сдава́ть** (**сдать** *perf*) **что-н в** ~**ю** to put sth into commission.
эксплуати́р|овать (**-ую**) *несов перех* to exploit; (*машины, дороги*) to use.

экспози́ци|я (**-и**) *ж* (*музейная*) exhibition; (*фото*) exposure.
экспона́т (**-а**) *м* exhibit.
экспони́р|овать (**-ую**) (*не*)*сов перех* to exhibit.
э́кспорт (**-а**) *м* export; **на** ~ for export.
экспортёр (**-а**) *м* exporter.
экспорти́р|овать (**-ую**) *несов перех* to export.
э́кспортный *прил* (*товар*) exported; (*правила*) export *опред*.
экспре́сс (**-а**) *м* (*транспорт*) express.
экспресси́в|ный (**-ен, -на, -но**) *прил* expressive.
экспре́сси|я (**-и**) *ж* expression.
экспро́мт (**-а**) *м* impromptu.
экспро́мтом *нареч* spontaneously.
экста́з (**-а**) *м* ecstasy.
экстенси́в|ный (**-ен, -на, -но**) *прил* extensive.
экстравага́нтный (**-ен, -на, -но**) *прил* extravagant.
экстра́кт (**-а**) *м* extract.
экстраордина́рный (**-ен, -на, -но**) *прил* extraordinary.
экстрасе́нс (**-а**) *м* psychic.
экстрема́ль|ный (**-ен, -ьна, -ьно**) *прил* extreme.
экстреми́зм (**-а**) *м* extremism.
экстреми́ст (**-а**) *м* extremist.
экстреми́стский (**-ая, -ое, -ие**) *прил* extremist.
э́кстрен|ный (**-ен, -на, -но**) *прил* (*отъезд, вызов*) urgent; (*расходы, заседание*) emergency *опред*.
эксце́нтрик (**-а**) *м* eccentric.
эксцентри́чен *прил см* **эксцентри́чный**.
эксцентри́ческий (**-ая, -ое, -ие**) *прил* eccentric.
эксцентри́чный (**-ен, -на, -но**) *прил* eccentric.
эксце́сс (**-а**) *м* excess.
ЭКЮ́ *сокр* ECU (= *European Currency Unit*).
эла́стик (**-а**) *м* stretchy material.
эласти́чный (**-ен, -на, -но**) *прил* (*материал*) stretchy; (*походка*) springy.
элева́тор (**-а**) *м* (*с.-х.*) grain store *или* elevator (*US*); (*ТЕХ*) elevator.
элега́нтный (**-ен, -на, -но**) *прил* elegant.
эле́ги|я (**-и**) *ж* elegy.
электриз|ова́ть (**-у́ю**; *perf* **наэлектризова́ть**) *несов перех* (*физ*) to electrify; (*перен: человека, атмосферу*) to stir up.
эле́ктрик (**-а**) *м* electrician.
электрифика́ци|я (**-и**) *ж* electrification.
электрифици́р|овать (**-ую**) (*не*)*сов перех* to connect an electricity supply to.
электри́чек *сущ см* **электри́чка**.
электри́ческий (**-ая, -ое, -ие**) *прил* electric.
электри́честв|о (**-а**) *ср* (*энергия*) electricity; (*освещение*) light; **зажига́ть** (**зажёчь** *perf*) ~ to turn on the light.
электри́ч|ка (**-ки**; *gen pl* **-ек**) *ж* electric train.
электробыто́в|ой *прил*: ~**ые прибо́ры** electrical appliances.
электрово́з (**-а**) *м* electric locomotive.
электрогита́р|а (**-ы**) *ж* electric guitar.

электро́д (-а) *м* electrode.
электрокардиогра́мм|а (-ы) *ж* electrocardiogram.
электромонтёр (-а) *м* electrician.
электромото́р (-а) *м* electric motor.
электро́н (-а) *м* electron.
электро́ник|а (-и) *ж* electronics *мн*.
электро́нн|ый *прил*: ~ **микроско́п** electron microscope; ~**ая доска́ объявле́ний** (*КОМП*) bulletin board; ~**ая по́чта** (*КОМП*) electronic mail; ~**ая табли́ца** (*КОМП*) spreadsheet; **электро́нная вычисли́тельная маши́на** computer.
электропереда́ч|а (-и) *ж* power transmission; **ли́ния** ~**и** power line.
электропо́езд (-а) *м* electric train.
электроприбо́р (-а) *м* electrical device.
электропрово́дк|а (-и) *ж* (electrical) wiring.
электропрово́дность (-и) *ж* conductivity.
электросва́рк|а (-и) *ж* (electric) welding.
электроста́нци|я (-и) *ж* (electric) power station.
электроте́хник (-а) *м* electrical engineer.
электроте́хник|а (-и) *ж* electrical engineering.
электроэне́рги|я (-и) *ж* electric power.
элеме́нт (-а) *м* (*также хим. ЭЛЕК*) element; **престу́пные** ~**ы** criminal element; **прогресси́вные** ~**ы о́бщества** progressive elements in society.
элемента́р|ный *прил* (*также физ*) elementary; (-ен, -на, -но; *правила. условия*) basic.
эликси́р (-а) *м* elixir.
эли́т|а (-ы) *ж собир* elite.
элита́рный *прил* elite.
э́ллипс (-а) *м* ellipse.
эл|ь (-я) *м* ale.
Э́льб|а (-ы) *ж* (*остров*) Elba; (*река*) Elbe.
Эльза́с (-а) *м* Alsace.
эльза́сск|ий (-ая, -ое, -ие) *прил* Alsatian.
эльф (-а) *м* elf.
эма́левый *прил* enamel.
эмали́рованный *прил* enamelled.
эмали́р|ова́ть (-у́ю) *несов перех* to enamel.
эма́л|ь (-и) *ж* enamel.
эмансипа́ци|я (-и) *ж* emancipation.
эмансипи́рованный *прил* emancipated.
эмба́рго *ср нескл* embargo; **налага́ть** (**наложи́ть** *perf*) ~ **на** +*acc* to place an embargo on.
эмбле́м|а (-ы) *ж* emblem.
эмбриоло́ги|я (-и) *ж* embryology.
эмбрио́н (-а) *м* embryo.
эмигра́нт (-а) *м* emigrant.
эмигра́нтск|ий (-ая, -ое, -ие) *прил* (*поселение*) emigrant *опред*; (*литература*) emigré *опред*.
эмиграцио́нный *прил* emigration *опред*.
эмигра́ци|я (-и) *ж* emigration ♦ *собир* emigrants *мн*.
эмигри́р|овать (-ую) (*не*)*сов неперех* to emigrate.
эмоциона́л|ьный (-ен, -ьна, -ьно) *прил* emotional.
эмо́ци|я (-и) *ж* emotion.
эму́льси|я (-и) *ж* emulsion.
эмфати́ческ|ий (-ая, -ое, -ие) *прил* emphatic.
эндокри́нн|ый *прил* (*ФИЗИОЛОГИЯ*) endocrine; ~**ые же́лезы** endocrine glands.
эндокриноло́ги|я (-и) *ж* endocrinology.
энерге́тик|а (-и) *ж* (*отдел физики*) energetics; (*промышленность*) power industry; (*наука*) power engineering.
энергети́ческ|ий (-ая, -ое, -ие) *прил* (*проблемы, ресурсы*) energy *опред*; **энергети́ческий кри́зис** energy crisis.
энерги́|чный (-ен, -на, -но) *прил* (*человек, движения*) energetic; (*меры*) effective.
эне́рги|я (-и) *ж* energy.
энергонезави́сим|ый *прил*: ~**ая па́мять** (*КОМП*) nonvolatile memory.
э́нн|ый *прил*: ~**ое число́/коли́чество вре́мени** X number/amount of time; **в** ~ **раз** yet again; **в** ~**ой сте́пени** to the nth degree.
энтузиа́зм (-а) *м* enthusiasm.
энтузиа́ст (-а) *м* enthusiast.
энциклопеди́ческ|ий (-ая, -ое, -ие) *прил* (*ум*) encyclopaedic (*BRIT*), encyclopedic (*US*); **энциклопеди́ческий слова́рь** encyclopaedia (*BRIT*), encyclopedia (*US*).
энциклопе́ди|я (-и) *ж* encyclopaedia (*BRIT*), encyclopedia (*US*).
эпигра́мм|а (-ы) *ж* epigram.
эпи́граф (-а) *м* epigraph.
эпиде́ми|я (-и) *ж* epidemic.
эпизо́д (-а) *м* episode.
эпизоди́ческ|ий (-ая, -ое, -ие) *прил* (*случай, факт*) random.
эпизоди́чный *прил* = **эпизоди́ческий**.
эпиле́пси|я (-и) *ж* epilepsy.
эпиле́птик (-а) *м* epileptic.
эпило́г (-а) *м* epilogue (*BRIT*), epilog (*US*).
эпистоля́рный *прил* epistolary.
эпи́тет (-а) *м* epithet.
эпице́нтр (-а) *м* epicentre (*BRIT*), epicenter (*US*).
эпи́ческ|ий (-ая, -ое, -ие) *прил* epic.
эполе́т|а (-ы) *ж* (*обычно мн*) epaulette.
эпопе́|я (-и) *ж* epic.
э́пос (-а) *м* epic literature.
эпо́х|а (-и) *ж* epoch.
эпоха́л|ьный (-ен, -на, -но) *прил* epoch-making.
э́р|а (-ы) *ж* era; **1-ый век на́шей** ~**ы/до на́шей** ~**ы** the first century AD/BC.
эре́кци|я (-и) *ж* (*АНАТ*) erection.
эрза́ц (-а) *м* substitute.
Эритре́|я (-и) *ж* Eritrea.
эритроци́т (-а) *м* erythrocyte, red blood cell.
эро́зи|я (-и) *ж* erosion.
эро́тик|а (-и) *ж* erotica *мн*.

эроти́ческ|ий (-ая, -ое, -ие) *прил* erotic.
Эр-Рия́д (-а) *м* Riyadh.
эруди́рован|ный (-, -на, -но) *прил* erudite.
эруди́т (-а) *м*: **он настоя́щий ~** he knows an enormous amount.
эруди́ци|я (-и) *ж* erudition.
эска́др|а (-ы) *ж* squadron (*navy*).
эскадри́ль|я (-и) *ж* squadron (*air force*).
эскадро́н (-а) *м* squadron (*army*).
эскала́тор (-а) *м* escalator.
эскала́ци|я (-и) *ж* escalation.
эскало́п (-а) *м* escalope.
эски́з (-а) *м* (*к карти́не*) sketch; (*к прое́кту*) draft.
эскимо́ *ср нескл* choc-ice, Eskimo (*US*).
эскимо́с (-а) *м* Eskimo.
эскимо́с|ка (-ки; *gen pl* -ок) *ж см* **эскимо́с**.
эско́рт (-а) *м* escort.
эсми́н|ец (-ца) *м* (= **эска́дренный миноно́сец**) destroyer.
эссе́ *ср нескл* essay.
эссе́нци|я (-и) *ж* essence.
эстака́д|а (-ы) *ж* (*на автомагистра́ли*) flyover (*BRIT*), overpass; (*на желе́зной доро́ге*) viaduct; (*на при́стани*) pier.
эста́мп (-а) *м* (*ИСКУССТВО*) print.
эстафе́т|а (-ы) *ж* (*СПОРТ*) relay (race); (: *па́лочка*) baton.
эсте́ти|ка (-и) *ж* aesthetics.
эстети́чен *прил см* **эстети́чный**.
эстети́ческ|ий (-ая, -ое, -ие) *прил* aesthetic.
эстети́ч|ный (-ен, -на, -но) *прил* aesthetic.
эсто́н|ец (-ца) *м* Estonian.
Эсто́ни|я (-и) *ж* Estonia.
эсто́н|ка (-ки; *gen pl* -ок) *ж см* **эсто́нец**.
эсто́нск|ий (-ая, -ое, -ие) *прил* Estonian; **~ язы́к** Estonian.
эсто́нца *итп сущ см* **эсто́нец**.
эстра́д|а (-ы) *ж* (*для орке́стра*) platform; (*вид иску́сства*) variety.
эстра́дный *прил*: **~ конце́рт** variety show; **~ арти́ст** variety performer.
эт|а (-ой) *мест см* **э́тот**.
эта́ж (-á) *м* floor, storey (*BRIT*), story (*US*); **пе́рвый/второ́й/тре́тий ~** ground/first/second floor (*BRIT*), first/second/third floor (*US*).
этажёр|ка (-ки; *gen pl* -ок) *ж* (stack of) shelves.
э́так *нареч* (*разг*: *таки́м о́бразом*) in such a way
 ♦ *вводн сл* (*приблизи́тельно*): **~ 25 лет** 25 years or so; **у нас ничего́ не полу́чится** we won't get anywhere this way; **и так и ~** (*разг*) this way and that (way).
э́так|ий (-ая, -ое, -ие) *мест* (*разг*) such.
этало́н (-а) *м* (*ве́са, ме́ры*) standard; (*перен*: *красоты́, благоро́дства итп*) model; **брать** (**взять** *perf*) **что-н за ~** to use sth as a standard.
эта́п (-а) *м* (*разви́тия, рабо́ты*) stage; (*го́нки*) lap; **ссы́льный ~** stopping point (*for deported convicts*); **отправля́ть** (*impf*) **~ом** *или* **по ~у** to deport (*under convoy*).
эта́п|ный *прил* (*рабо́та, произведе́ние*)

prominent; **~ое собы́тие** an event of great significance.
э́ти (-их) *мест см* **э́тот**.
э́ти|ка (-и) *ж* ethics.
этике́т (-а) *м* etiquette.
этике́т|ка (-ки; *gen pl* -ок) *ж* label.
эти́л (-а) *м* ethyl.
эти́ловый *прил* ethyl *опред*.
э́тим *мест см* **э́тот**, **э́то**, **э́ти**.
э́тими *мест см* **э́ти**.
этимоло́ги|я (-и) *ж* etymology.
эти́ч|ный (-ен, -на, -но) *прил* ethical.
этни́ческ|ий (-ая, -ое, -ие) *прил* ethnic.
этнографи́ческ|ий (-ая, -ое, -ие) *прил* ethnographic.
этногра́фи|я (-и) *ж* ethnography.

KEYWORD

э́то (-ого; *см* **Table 10**) *мест* **1** (*указа́тельное*) this; **на́до успе́ть к ве́черу; э́то бу́дет тру́дно** we need to finish by this evening, this will be difficult; **он на всё соглаша́ется; э́то о́чень стра́нно** he is agreeing to everything, this is most strange
2 (*свя́зка в сказу́емом*) **любо́вь – э́то проще́ние** love is forgiveness
3 (*как подлежа́щее*): **с кем ты разгова́ривал? – э́то была́ моя́ сестра́** who were you talking to? – that was my sister; **как э́то произошло́?** how did it happen?
4 (*для усиле́ния*): **э́то он во всём винова́т** he is the one who is to blame for everything; **э́то они́ нас подвели́** they are the ones who let us down
 ♦ *част* **1** (*слу́жит для усиле́ния*): **кто э́то звони́л?** who was it who phoned (*BRIT*) *или* called (*US*)?; **о чём э́то ты так беспоко́ишься?** what is it that you are so worried about?
2 (*указа́тельная*): **э́то ты так крича́л?** was it you who called out?

KEYWORD

э́тот (-ого; *f* **э́та**, *nt* **э́то**, *pl* **э́ти**; *см* **Table 10**) *мест* **1** (*указа́тельное: о бли́зком предме́те*) this; (: *о бли́зких предме́тах*) these; **э́тот дом** this house; **э́ти кни́ги** these books
2 (*о да́нном вре́мени*) this; **э́тот год осо́бенно тру́дный** this year is particularly hard; **в э́ти дни я при́нял реше́ние** in the last few days I have come to a decision; **э́тот са́мый** that very
3 (*о чём-то то́лько что упомя́нутом*) this; **он ложи́лся в 10 часо́в ве́чера; э́та привы́чка меня́ всегда́ удивля́ла** he used to go to bed at 10 pm, this habit always amazed me
 ♦ *ср* (*как сущ: об одно́м предме́те*) this one; (: *о мно́гих предме́тах*) these ones; **дай мне вот э́ти** give me these ones; **э́тот не всё спосо́бен** this one is capable of anything; **при э́том** in addition.

этю́д (-а) *м* (*ИСКУССТВО*) sketch; (*ЛИТЕРАТУРА*) study; (*МУЗ*) étude; (*ша́хматный*) problem.
эфеме́р|ный (-ен, -на, -но) *прил* ephemeral.
эфе́с (-а) *м* (*шпа́ги, са́бли*) hilt.

эфио́п (-а) *м* Ethiopian.
Эфио́пи|я (-и) *ж* Ethiopia.
эфио́п|ка (-ки; *gen pl* -ок) *ж см* **эфио́п**.
эфио́пск|ий (-ая, -ое, -ие) *прил* Ethiopian.
эфи́р (-а) *м* (*хим*) ether; (*воздушное пространство*) air; **выходи́ть** (**вы́йти** *perf*) **в** ~ to go on the air; **прямо́й** ~ live broadcast.
эфи́рн|ый *прил*: ~**ое ма́сло** essential oil; ~**ое вре́мя** airtime.
эффе́кт (-а) *м* effect; (*обычно мн*: *шумовы́е, световы́е*) effects *мн*; **экономи́ческий** ~ economic result; **производи́ть** (**произвести́** *perf*) ~ **на** +*acc* to have an effect on; **дава́ть** (**дать** *perf*) **жела́емый** ~ to have the desired

effect.
эффе́ктен *прил см* **эффе́ктный**.
эффекти́вен *прил см* **эффекти́вный**.
эффекти́вность (-и) *ж* effectiveness.
эффекти́в|ный (-ен, -на, -но) *прил* effective.
эффе́кт|ный (-ен, -на, -но) *прил* (*одежда*) striking; (*речь*) impressive.
эх *межд* (*разг*) oh; ~ **ты, лентя́й** ! oh, you're such a lazybones!
э́х|о (-а) *ср* echo (*мн* echoes).
эшафо́т (-а) *м* scaffold; **всходи́ть** (**взойти́** *perf*) **на** ~ to mount the scaffold.
эшело́н (-а) *м* echelon; (*поезд*) special train; ~**ы вла́сти** echelons of power.

~ Ю, ю ~

Ю, ю *сущ нескл* (*буква*) the 31st letter of the Russian alphabet.

ю. *сокр* (= **юг**) S (= *South*); (= **южный**) S (= *South*).

юа́нь (**-я**) *м* yuan (*мн* yuan).

ЮАР *ж сокр* (= Южно-Африка́нская Респу́блика) RSA (= *Republic of South Africa*).

юбиле́й (**-я**) *м* (*годовщина*) anniversary; (*празднование*) jubilee.

юбиле́йный *прил* (*торжество*) anniversary *опред*; (*монета, значок итп*) jubilee *опред*.

юбиля́р (**-а**) *м*: **учёный-/заво́д-~** scientist/ factory whose anniversary is being celebrated.

ю́б|ка (**-ки**; *gen pl* **-ок**) *ж* skirt; **держа́ться** (*impf*) **за чью-н ~ку** (*разг*) to be tied to sb's apron strings.

ювели́р (**-а**) *м* jeweller (*BRIT*), jeweler (*US*).

ювели́рный *прил* jewellery *опред* (*BRIT*), jewelery *опред* (*US*); (*перен: работа, точность*) painstaking; **~ые изде́лия** jewel(l) ery; **~ магази́н** jeweller's (*BRIT*) *или* jeweler's (*US*) (shop).

юг (**-а**) *м* south; **на ю́ге страны́** in the south of the country; **к ю́гу от го́рода** to the south of the town.

ю́го-восто́к (**-а**) *м* south-east.

ю́го-за́пад (**-а**) *м* south-west.

Югосла́ви|я (**-и**) *ж* (*ИСТ*) Yugoslavia.

южа́н|ин (**-ина**; *nom pl* **-е**, *gen pl* **-**) *м* southerner.

южа́н|ка (**-ки**; *gen pl* **-ок**) *ж см* **южа́нин**.

ю́жный *прил* southern; **Ю́жная Коре́я** South Korea; **Ю́жный по́люс** the South Pole.

юл|а́ (**-ы́**) *ж* (*игрушка*) (spinning) top ♦ *м/ж* (*перен: разг*) fidget.

юл|и́ть (**-ю́, -и́шь**) *несов неперех* (*разг: суетиться*) to fidget; (: *хитрить*) to be shifty; **~** (*impf*) **пе́ред** +*instr* (*заискивать*) to play up to.

ю́мор (**-а**) *м* humour (*BRIT*), humor (*US*).

юморе́с|ка (**-ки**; *gen pl* **-ок**) *ж* (*МУЗ*) humoresque; (*ЛИТЕРАТУРА*) short comedy.

юмори́ст (**-а**) *м* (*автор*) humorist; (*шутливый человек*) comedian.

юмори́стик|а (**-и**) *ж* (*ЛИТЕРАТУРА*) humour (*BRIT*), humor (*US*).

юмори́ст|ка (**-ки**; *gen pl* **-ок**) *ж* comedienne.

юмористи́ческий (**-ая, -ое, -ие**) *прил* humorous; **~ журна́л** satirical magazine.

ю́нг|а (**-и**) *м* (*младший матрос*) cabin boy; trainee sailor.

ЮНЕ́СКО *ср сокр* UNESCO (= *United Nations*

Educational Scientific and Cultural Organization).

юне́ц (**-ца́**) *м* (*разг: юноша*) youth.

юнио́р (**-а**) *м* junior.

ЮНИСЕ́Ф *м сокр* UNICEF (= *United Nations (International) Children's (Emergency) Fund*).

ю́нкер (**-а**; *nom pl* **-а́**) *м* (*ИСТ*) cadet.

ю́нкерский (**-ая, -ое, -ие**) *прил* cadet *опред*; **~ое учи́лище** military school.

ю́ност|ь (**-и**) *ж* youth ♦ *собир* (*юношество*) young people *мн*; **в ~и он был любозна́телен** in his youth he was greedy for knowledge.

ю́нош|а (**-и**; *nom pl* **-и**, *gen pl* **-ей**) *м* young man (*мн* men).

ю́ношеский (**-ая, -ое, -ие**) *прил* youthful; (*журнал*) young person's; (*организация, клуб*) youth; **~ие го́ды** youth.

ю́ношеств|о (**-а**) *ср собир* young people *мн*; (*юность*) youth.

юнца́ *итп сущ см* **юне́ц**.

ю́н|ый (**-, -а́, -о**) *прил* (*молодой*) young; (*силы, задор*) youthful; **теа́тр ~ого зри́теля** children's theatre (*BRIT*) *или* theater (*US*).

ЮПИ́ *м сокр* UPI (= *United Press International*).

юпи́тер (**-а**) *м* (*прибор*) floodlight; **Ю~** Jupiter).

юриди́чески *нареч*: **~ обяза́тельный** legally binding.

юриди́ческий (**-ая, -ое, -ие**) *прил* (*сила*) juridical; (*образование*) legal; **~ факульте́т** law faculty; **юриди́ческая консульта́ция** ≈ legal advice office; **юриди́ческое лицо́** body corporate.

юрисди́кци|я (**-и**) *ж* (*ЮР*) jurisdiction; **подлежа́ть** (*impf*) **чьей-н ~и** to come under sb's jurisdiction.

юрисконсу́льт (**-а**) *м* legal adviser.

юриспруде́нци|я (**-и**) *ж* (*правоведение*) jurisprudence; (*практика юриста*) law.

юри́ст (**-а**) *м* lawyer.

ю́р|кий (**-кая, -кое, -кие; -ок, -ка́, -ко**) *прил* nimble.

юркну́ть (**-у, -ешь**) *сов неперех* to scurry away.

юро́дивый (**-ого**; *разг*) crazy ♦ (**-ого**; *decl like adj*) *м* (*РЕЛ*) holy fool.

юро́дств|овать (**-ую**) *несов неперех* (*перен*) to behave like a lunatic.

ю́рок *прил см* **ю́ркий**.

ю́рский (**-ая, -ое, -ие**) *прил* (*ГЕО*) Jurassic.

ю́рт|а (**-ы**) *ж* yurt (*skin tent used by nomads in*

Central Asia and Siberia).
ЮСИА *м сокр* USIA (= *United States Information Agency*).
юсти́ция (**-и**) *ж* (*правовые учреждения*) the judiciary; **Министе́рство ~и** the Ministry of

Justice.
юти́ться (**-чу́сь, -ти́шься**) *несов неперех* (*располагаться*) to huddle together; (*иметь приют*) to live in cramped conditions.

~ Я, я ~

Я, я сущ нескл (буква) the 32nd letter of the Russian alphabet.

я (меня; см Table 5a) мест I ♦ сущ нескл (личность) the self, the ego; **~ тебя́** или **тебе́!** (разг: угроза) I'll teach you!; **не ~ бу́ду, е́сли не ...** (разг) I'll be damned if I don't ...; **второ́е "я"** alter ego.

я́беда (-ы) м/ж sneak.

я́бедник (-а) м = **я́беда**.

я́бедничать (-ю; perf **наябедничать**) несов неперех: **~ на** +acc (разг) to tell tales about.

я́блоко (-а; nom pl -и) ср apple; **глазно́е ~** eyeball; **в ~ах** (о масти лошадей) dappled; **~у не́где упа́сть** (перен) there's not enough room to swing a cat.

я́блоневый прил (цвет) apple-green; **~ая ве́тка** branch of an apple tree.

я́блоня (-и) ж apple tree.

я́блочко (-а) ср уменьш от **я́блоко**; (на мишени) bull's-eye.

я́блочный прил apple опред.

я́вен прил см **я́вный**.

яви́ться (-лю́сь, -ишься; impf **явля́ться**) сов возв (в суд) to appear; (на службу) to report; (домой, в гости) to arrive; (мысль, образ) to arise; **явля́ться** (~ perf) +instr (причиной, следствием) to turn out to be.

я́вка (-ки; gen pl -ок) ж (действие: в суд, на допрос) appearance; (: на интервью итп) attendance; (место: конспираторов) secret meeting place.

явле́ние (-я) ср phenomenon (мн phenomena); (событие) occurrence; (ТЕАТР) scene; (РЕЛ) manifestation.

явлю́сь сов см **яви́ться**.

явля́ться (-юсь) несов от **яви́ться** ♦ возв: **~** +instr to be.

я́вно нареч (очевидно) obviously.

я́вный (-ен, -на, -но) прил (вражда, благосклонность) overt; (ложь, лесть итп) obvious.

я́вок сущ см **я́вка**.

я́вочный прил; **~ая кварти́ра** secret meeting place; **~ пункт** (ВОЕН) reporting point; **~ым поря́дком** without permission; **я́вочный лист** attendance sheet.

я́вственный (-, -на, -но) прил (звук) distinct; (сознание, понимание итп) clear.

я́вствовать (3sg -ует) несов неперех to be obvious; **из показа́ний ~ует, что он невино́вен** from the evidence it is obvious that he is innocent.

явь (-и) ж reality.

яга́ (-и́) ж Baba-Yaga (witch in Russian folk tales).

я́гель (-я) м Iceland moss.

ягнёнок (-ёнка; nom pl -я́та, gen pl -я́т) м lamb.

ягни́ться (3sg -ится, 3pl -ятся, perf **оягни́ться**) несов возв to lamb.

ягня́та итп сущ см **ягнёнок**.

я́года (-ы) ж berry; **одного́ по́ля ~** kindred spirit.

ягоди́ца (-ы) ж buttock.

я́годник (-а) м (место) berry patch; (кустарник) berry bush; (разг: сборщик) berry picker.

я́годный прил berry опред.

ягуа́р (-а) м jaguar.

яд (-а; part gen -у) м poison.

я́дер сущ см **ядро́**.

я́дерный прил nuclear.

я́дерщик (-а) м (разг) nuclear physicist.

ядови́тый (-, -а, -о) прил poisonous; (перен: человек, слова) venomous.

ядохимика́т (-а) м (обычно мн) chemical (used as weedkiller or pesticide).

ядрёный (-, -а, -о) прил (яблоко) juicy; (перен: воздух) fresh; (: мороз) hard.

ядро́ (-á; nom pl -ра, gen pl -ер) ср nucleus; (ореха) kernel; (Земли, древесины) core; (ВОЕН) projectile; (СПОРТ) shot; **толка́ние ~ра́** (СПОРТ) shot put.

яз. сокр (= **язы́к**) lang. (= language).

я́зва (-ы) ж (МЕД) ulcer; (перен: общества) evil ♦ м/ж (перен: разг) sarcastic person (мн people); **я́зва желу́дка** stomach ulcer.

я́звенный прил: **~ая боле́знь** stomach ulcer.

язви́тельный (-ен, -ьна, -ьно) прил scathing.

язви́ть (-лю́, -ишь; perf **съязви́ть**) несов неперех (+dat) to speak sharply to; **~ (съязви́ть** perf) **на чей-н счёт** to be scathing at sb's expense.

язы́к (-á) м tongue; (русский, разговорный итп) language; (ВОЕН: разг) prisoner captured for information; **держа́ть** (impf) **~ за зуба́ми** (разг) to hold one's tongue; **вопро́с (был) у него́ на ~е** (разг) the question was on the tip of his tongue; **прикуси́ть** (perf) **~** (разг) to bite one's tongue; **тяну́ть** *(perf)* **кого́-н за** ~ *(разг)* to make sb talk; ~ **не повернётся сказа́ть/попроси́ть** *(разг)* I could not bring myself to say/ask; **владе́ть** *(impf)* **языко́м** to speak a language; **находи́ть (найти́** *perf)* **о́бщий** ~ to find a common language; ~ **программи́рования** **высо́кого/ни́зкого у́ровня** *(КОМП)* high-level/low-level language; ~ **ассе́мблера** *(КОМП)* assembly language.

языка́с|тый (-, -а, -о) *прил (человек)* sharp-tongued.

языков|е́д (-а) *м* linguist.

языкове́дени|е (-я) *ср* linguistics.

языков|о́й *прил (факультет, система)* language *опред*; ~**о́е пра́вило** rule of a language.

языкозна́ни|е (-я) *ср* linguistics.

язы́ческ|ий (-ая, -ое, -ие) *прил* pagan *опред*.

язы́честв|о (-а) *ср* paganism.

язычка́ *итп сущ см* **язычо́к**.

язы́чник (-а) *м* pagan.

язы́чниц|а (-ы) *ж см* **язы́чник**.

язы́ч|о́к (-ка́) *м уменьш от* **язы́к**; *(АНАТ)* uvula; *(боти́нка)* tongue; *(замка́)* catch.

яйка́ *сущ см* **яйцо́**.

яй́ч|ко (-ка; gen pl -ек) *ср уменьш от* **яйцо́**; *(АНАТ)* testicle.

яи́чник (-а) *м* ovary.

яи́чниц|а (-ы) *ж* fried eggs *мн*.

яи́чный *прил:* ~ **бело́к** egg white; ~**ая скорлупа́** eggshell.

яйцеви́д|ный (-ен, -на, -но) *прил* egg-shaped.

яйцево́д (-а) *м* oviduct.

яйцекле́т|ка (-ки; gen pl -ок) *ж* ovule.

яйцо́ (яйца́; nom pl яйца, gen pl яи́ц, dat pl я́йцам) *ср* egg; *(АНАТ)* ovum; ~ **всмя́тку/вкруту́ю** soft-boiled/hard-boiled egg.

ЯК (-а) *м сокр = самолёт констру́кции А С. Яковлева.*

Як (-а) *м сокр =* **ЯК**.

як (-а) *м* yak.

я́кобы *союз (будто бы)* that ♦ *част* supposedly; **он утвержда́ет,** ~ **ничего́ не зна́ет** he claims that he doesn't know anything; **он предлага́ет** ~ **вы́годную сде́лку** he is supposedly proposing a good deal.

я́корный *прил* anchor *опред*.

я́кор|ь (-я; nom pl -я́) *м (МОР)* anchor; **броса́ть (бро́сить** *perf)* ~ to cast anchor; **стоя́ть** *(impf)* **на** ~**е** to ride at anchor; **снима́ться (сня́ться** *perf)* **с** ~**я** to weigh anchor.

яку́т (-а) *м* Yakut.

Яку́ти|я (-и) *ж* Yakutia.

яку́т|ка (-ки; gen pl -ок) *ж см* **яку́т**.

якша́|ться (-юсь) *несов возв:* ~ **с** +*instr* to consort with.

Я́лт|а (-ы) *ж* Yalta.

я́м|а (-ы) *ж (в земле́)* pit; *(разг: впа́дина)* hollow;

рыть *(impf)* ~**у кому́-н** to lay a trap for sb; **возду́шная** ~ air pocket; **оркестро́вая** ~ orchestra pit.

Яма́йк|а (-и) *ж* Jamaica.

яма́йск|ий (-ая, -ое, -ие) *прил* Jamaican.

я́моч|ка (-ки; gen pl -ек) *ж* dimple.

ямщи́к (-а́) *м* coachman *(мн* coachmen).

январ|ь (-я́) *м* January; *см также* **октя́брь**.

янта́рный *прил* amber *опред*.

янта́р|ь (-я́) *м* amber.

япо́н|ец (-ца) *м* Japanese.

Япо́ни|я (-и) *ж* Japan.

япо́нк|а (-и; gen pl -ок) *ж см* **япо́нец**.

япо́нск|ий (-ая, -ое, -ие) *прил* Japanese; ~ **язы́к** Japanese.

япо́нца *итп сущ см* **япо́нец**.

ярд (-а) *м* yard.

я́рк|ий (-ая, -кое, -кие; -ок, -ка́, -ко) *прил* bright; *(перен: человек, речь)* brilliant; (*: тала́нт)* outstanding.

я́ркост|ь (-и) *ж (цве́та, кра́ски)* brightness; *(челове́ка, ре́чи)* brilliance.

ярлы́к (-а́) *м* label; **ему́ накле́или** ~ **реакционе́ра** he was labelled as a reactionary.

я́рмар|ка (-ки; gen pl -ок) *ж* fair; **междунаро́дная** ~ international trade fair.

ярм|о́ (-а́) *ср (также перен)* yoke.

яров|о́й *прил (зла́ки)* spring *опред*; ~**о́е по́ле** field sown with spring crops.

я́рок *прил см* **я́ркий**.

я́рост|ный (-ен, -на, -но) *прил (взгляд, слова́)* furious; *(пере́н: ата́ка, кри́тика)* fierce.

я́рост|ь (-и) *ж* fury; **приходи́ть (прийти́** *perf)* **в** ~ to fly into a rage.

я́рус (-а) *м (в зри́тельном за́ле)* circle; *(ряд)* tier; *(ГЕО)* layer.

я́рый *прил (пре́данный)* ardent.

я́сен *прил см* **я́сный**.

я́сен|ь (-я) *м* ash (tree).

я́сл|и (-ей) *мн (для скота́)* trough *ед*; *(также:* **де́тские** ~) crèche, day nursery *(ВНГ)*.

ясне́|ть (3sg -ет, 3pl -ют) *несов неперех* to clear, become clear.

я́сно *нареч* clearly ♦ *как сказ (о пого́де)* it's fine; *(поня́тно)* it's clear; **я** ~ **выража́юсь?** do I make myself clear?; **на у́лице сего́дня** ~ it's fine outside today; **тепе́рь мне всё** ~ it's all clear to me now; ~, **что он недово́лен** it's clear that he's not happy; **с ним всё** ~ nothing more needs to be said about him.

яснови́дени|е (-я) *ср* clairvoyance.

яснови́д|ец (-ца) *м* clairvoyant.

яснови́дящ|ий (-ая, -ее, -ие) *прил (человек)* clairvoyant *опред* ♦ *(-его; decl like adj)* **м** clairvoyant.

я́сност|ь (-и) *ж* clarity; **вноси́ть (внести́** *perf)* ~ **в что-н** to clarify sth.

я́с|ный (-ен, -на́, -но) *прил* clear.

я́стреб (-а) м (ЗООЛ) hawk.

ястреби́н|ый прил (клюв) hawk's; ~**ая охо́та**
falconry; ~ **нос** (перен) hooked nose.

я́хонт (-а) м (рубин) ruby; (сапфир) sapphire.

я́хт|а (-ы) ж yacht.

яхт-клу́б (-а) м yacht club.

яхтсме́н (-а) м yachtsman (мн yachtsmen).

яче́|йка (-йки; gen pl -ек) ж (сотовая,
партийная) cell; (профсоюзная) branch; (для
почты) pigeonhole; **яче́йка па́мяти** (КОМП)
memory cell.

ячме́нный прил barley опред.

ячме́н|ь (-я́) м (С -х) barley; (МЕД) sty(e).

я́чневый прил crushed-barley.

я́шм|а (-ы) ж jasper.

я́щериц|а (-ы) ж lizard.

я́щик (-а) м (вместилище: большой) chest;
(: маленький) box; (в письменном столе итп)
drawer; (также: **мусо́рный** ~) dustbin (BRIT),
garbage can (US); **почто́вый** ~ (домашний)
letter box (BRIT), mailbox (US); (уличный: как
адрес) post office box; (: об учреждении)
secret plant, institution etc; (: ТЕЛ) the box;
откла́дывать (отложи́ть perf**) что-н в до́лгий
~** (перен) to shelve sth.

я́щур (-а) м (болезнь) foot-and-mouth disease.

GUIDE TO RUSSIAN GRAMMAR

It is not the purpose of this grammar section to attempt to give an exhaustive treatment of Russian grammar. Instead it is intended to outline the basic grammatical principles and to draw the user's attention to the most commonly encountered irregular forms.

NOUNS

1 Gender

A Russian noun has either masculine, feminine or neuter gender. In most cases it is grammatically determinable by its ending:

дом *m*
картина *f*
кресло *nt*

Gender of nouns is significant since, for example, it determines the ending of a qualifying adjective:

большой дом
большая картина
большое кресло

1.1 Masculine noun categories

I) All nouns ending in a hard consonant eg. кот, собор, адрес or in -й eg. крематорий, музей.

II) Some nouns ending in -а/-я which are natural masculine nouns eg.мужчина, дядя and masculine first names eg. Саша.

III) Numerous nouns ending in a soft sign, including:
      i) natural masculines eg. парень, король.
      ii) months of the year eg. июль.

1.2 Feminine noun categories

I) The majority of nouns ending in -а/-я, eg. дорога, комната, тётя.

II) The majority of nouns ending in a soft sign, including:
      i) natural feminines eg. мать
      ii) all nouns ending in -жь,-чь,-шь,-щь,-знь,-мь,-пь,-фь.
      iii) most nouns ending in -сть,-бь,-вь,-дь,-зь,-сь,-ть.

1.3 Neuter noun categories

a) Almost all nouns ending in -о eg. окно
b) Almost all nouns ending in -е eg. солнце
c) Nouns ending in -ё eg. копьё.
d) Nouns ending in -мя eg. время, племя.
e) Most indeclinable loan words eg. виски, радио (a notable exception being кофе, which is masculine).

2 Declension

There are three declension patterns for nouns. The first covers most masculine and ne[uter] nouns, the second most feminine nouns and the third is specific to feminine nouns endin[g in] a soft sign. For the first declension pattern hard-ending masculine and neuter nouns [(eg. мост, óзеро) have the genitive singular ending -a, whereas soft-ending masculine [and] neuter nouns (eg. крематóрий, гость, гóре) have the genitive ending -я. Similarly [the] second declension pattern has a split between hard-ending feminine nouns (eg. лáм[па] which have the genitive singular ending -ы, and soft-ending feminine nouns (eg. бáш[ня] which have the genitive ending -и. All nouns in the third declension pattern, as they [are] soft-ending, have the genitive ending -и.

The genitive singular declension generally sets the pattern for the other oblique cases [of a] noun, ie. whether these will be hard- or soft-ending. The general pattern followed in all t[he] declensions is illustrated by the following table, using specific noun examples:

[NB. The table does not, of course, cover all the variations in declension or stress that e[...]

| | | Singular | | | | | | Plural | | | |
Nom	Acc	Gen	Dat	Instr	Prp	Nom	Acc	Gen	Dat	Instr	P
Masculine											
завóд	~	~а	~у	~ом	~е	~ы	~ы	~ов	~ам	~ами	~
музéй	~й	~я	~ю	~ем	~е	~и	~и	~ев	~ям	~ями	~
гость	~я	~я	~ю	~ем	~е	~и	~éй	~éй	~я́м	~я́ми	~
писáтель	~я	~я	~ю	~ем	~е	~и	~ей	~ей	~ям	~ями	~
двигатель	~ь	~я	~ю	~ем	~е	~и	~и	~ей	~ям	~ями	~
Neuter											
мéсто	~о	~а	~у	~ом	~е	~á	~á	~	~áм	~áми	~
пóле	~е	~я	~ю	~ем	~е	~я́	~я́	~éй	~я́м	~я́ми	~
здáние	~е	~я	~ю	~ем	~и	~я	~я	~й	~ям	~ями	~
Feminine											
лáмпа	~у	~ы	~е	~ой	~е	~ы	~ы	~	~ам	~ами	~
бáшня	~ню	~ни	~не	~ней	~не	~ни	~ни	~ен	~ням	~нями	~
пóвесть	~ь	~и	~и	~ью	~и	~и	~и	~éй	~ям	~ями	~
стáнция	~ю	~и	~и	~ей	~и	~и	~и	~й	~ям	~ями	~

One particularly important rule to bear in mind is that the accusative case of ani[mate] masculine singular nouns and of all animate plural nouns is identical with the genitive.

3 Stress patterns

Stress varies a great deal from one Russian noun to the next, and even oblique cases [of a] particular noun frequently differ from each other in this respect.

Nouns ending in unstressed -a/-я and in -ия/-ие do not undergo any stress changes.

Fixed stem-stress is found in first declension masculine nouns such as стул, му[зéй,] локомотúв, in nouns with medial stress, in nouns of three or more syllables, and in n[ouns] with unstressed prefixes or suffixes.

Fixed end-stress is found in many hard-ending and soft-ending first declension masculine nouns such as стол, дождь, словарь, as well as in almost all nouns with the stressed suffixes -áк/-я́к,-áч,-éж, -ёж,-и́к,-и́ч,-у́н,-у́х.

A shift of stress from the stem in the singular to the end in the plural is found in first declension masculine nouns such as мост and сад, as well as in many nouns with nominative plural endings -ья́,-á/-я́. A similar stress shift occurs in neuter nouns such as дéло and мéсто. The reverse happens (ie. a shift of stress from the end in the singular to the stem in the plural) in other neuter nouns eg. письмó, винó, окнó. This is also true for many second declension feminine nouns eg. войнá, игрá, странá and others which undergo a vowel mutation in the stress change eg. женá » жёны, сестрá » сёстры.

Irregularity of stress pattern is greatest in end-stressed second declension feminine nouns, where the following patterns are possible: the accusative singular and nominative/accusative plural have stem stress eg. рукá, ногá, сторонá, or only the nominative/accusative plural have stem stress eg. губá, волнá. Alternatively, stem stress may be confined to: the singular accusative and all plural forms, as in the case of водá, ценá, стенá; all plural forms with the exception of the genitive and animate accusative, as in the case of семья́, судья́; the accusative singular and all plural forms excepting the genitive, as in the case of земля́.

2 ADJECTIVES

Russian adjectives generally have a long (attributive) form eg. вéжливый, вéжливая, вéжливое, вéжливые and a short (predicative) form eg. вéжлив, вéжлива, вéжливо, вéжливы.

1 Long form

Russian long adjectives are mostly used attributively and the majority have hard endings, the first vowel of the ending being -ы,-а or -о. The declension of such adjectives is seen as the regular one for the purposes of this dictionary. Thus, adjectives such as стáрый decline as follows:

	m	f	nt	pl
Nom	стáрый	стáрая	стáрое	стáрые
Acc	~ый/~ого	~ую	~ое	~ые/~ых
Gen	~ого	~ой	~ого	~ых
Dat	~ому	~ой	~ому	~ым
Instr	~ым	~ой	~ым	~ыми
Prp	о ~ом	о ~ой	о ~ом	о ~ых

(NB. The alternative forms of the accusative are animate and identical with the genitive. The feminine instrumental ending -ою also exists)

End-stressed adjectives with hard endings, eg. живóй, decline similarly, with the only difference being the masculine nominative singular and inanimate accusative singular, where the ending -óй replaces -ый. Alternative endings are determined by Russian spelling rules, according to which и replaces ы after г,к,х,ж,ч,ш,щ, and е replaces an unstressed о after ж,ч,ш,щ and ц. Thus, a stem-stressed adjective such as глáдкий declines as follows:

	m	*f*	*nt*	*pl*
Nom	гла́дк|ий	гла́дк|ая	гла́дк|ое	гла́дк|ие
Acc	~ий/~ого	~ую	~ое	~ие/~их
Gen	~ого	~ой	~ого	~их
Dat	~ому	~ой	~ому	~им
Instr	~им	~ой	~им	~ими
Prp	о ~ом	о ~ой	о ~ом	о ~их

(NB. The alternative forms of the accusative are animate and identical with the genitive. feminine instrumental ending -ою also exists)

End-stressed adjectives such as большо́й decline similarly, with only the mascul\ nominative and inanimate accusative singular differing in that they have the ending instead of -ий. In stem-stressed adjectives such as хоро́ший, however, the declensions as follows:

	m	*f*	*nt*	*pl*
Nom	хоро́ш|ий	хоро́ш|ая	хоро́ш|ее	хоро́ш|ие
Acc	~ий/~его	~ую	~ее	~ие/~их
Gen	~его	~ей	~его	~их
Dat	~ему	~ей	~ему	~им
Instr	~им	~ей	~им	~ими
Prp	о ~ем	о ~ей	о ~ем	о ~их

(NB. The alternative forms of the accusative are animate and identical with the genitive. feminine instrumental ending -ею also exists)

Soft-ending adjectives, ie. those ending in -ний, decline differently again. Thus, adjecti such as осе́нний or сосе́дний decline as follows:

	m	*f*	*nt*	*pl*
Nom	осе́нн|ий	осе́нн|яя	осе́нн|ее	осе́нн|ие
Acc	~ий/~его	~юю	~ее	~ие/~их
Gen	~его	~ей	~его	~их
Dat	~ему	~ей	~ему	~им
Instr	~им	~ей	~им	~ими
Prp	о ~ем	о ~ей	о ~ем	о ~их

(NB. The alternative forms of the accusative are animate and, therefore, identical with genitive. The feminine instrumental ending -ею also exists)

1.1 Possessive adjectives

These follow one of two declension patterns. Possessive adjectives like соба́чий де́вичий decline as follows:

	m	*f*	*nt*	*pl*
Nom	соба́ч|ий	соба́ч|ья	соба́ч|ье	соба́ч|ьи
Acc	~ий/~ьего	~ью	~ье	~ьи/~ьих
Gen	~ьего	~ьей	~ьего	~ьих
Dat	~ьему	~ьей	~ьему	~ьим
Instr	~ьим	~ьей	~ьим	~ьими
Prp	о ~ьем	о ~ьей	о ~ьем	о ~ьих

(NB. The alternative forms of the accusative are animate and identical with the genitive.

feminine instrumental ending -ьею also exists. The ordinal numeral тре́тий declines according to the above table)

In addition, there are those possessive adjectives formed by adding the suffixes -ин,-нин or -ов to the stems of nouns. This form is mainly used with reference to particular family members, eg. ма́мин, му́жнин, де́дов, but can also be derived from the familiar forms of first names, eg. Ле́нин, Са́шин. These decline as follows:

	m	f	nt	pl
Nom	Са́шин	Са́шина	Са́шино	Са́шины
Acc	~/~ого	~у	~о	~ы/~ых
Gen	~ого	~ой	~ого	~ых
Dat	~у	~ой	~у	~ым
Instr	~ым	~ой	~ым	~ыми
Prp	o ~ом	o ~ой	o ~ом	o ~ых

(NB. The alternative forms of the accusative are animate and identical with the genitive. The feminine instrumental ending -ою also exists)

Note that the animate accusative/genitive rule which affects nouns also applies to long adjectives.

1.2 Usage

Long adjectives are typically used attributively, for example:

на у́лице стои́т **бе́лая** маши́на "a white car is parked on the street"

or showing the use of the accusative case:

он во́дит **бе́лую** маши́ну "he drives a white car"

Long adjectives may be used predicatively when they denote characteristics inherent to the nouns they refer to.

э́та у́лица – **дли́нная** "this street is long"
э́тот груз – **тяжёлый** "this load is heavy"

2 Short adjectives

Short adjectives can be derived from most long adjectives. They are formed by replacing the long-form endings with contracted ones eg. ве́жливый. This declines as follows:

	Long Form	Short Form
m	ве́жливый	ве́жлив
f	~ая	~a
nt	~ое	~o
pl	~ые	~ы

The masculine short form of many adjectives requires a buffer vowel (e,o or ё) to be inserted between the last two consonants or to replace a soft sign. Thus, ва́жный has masculine short form ва́жен, ви́дный has ви́ден, лёгкий лёгок, у́мный умён etc. Masculine short forms of adjectives ending in -енный (ie. unstressed) generally have -ен endings, whereas those in -ённый (ie. stressed) are replaced by the short form -ёнен.

Short-form adjectives have either fixed stem stress, eg. ве́жлив, ве́жлива, ве́жливо, ве́жливы, end stress in feminine, neuter and plural, eg. хоро́ш, хороша́, хорошо́,

хоро́ший, end stress in the feminine, eg. жив, жива́, жи́во, жи́вы, or end stress in
feminine and plural, eg. ви́ден, видна́, ви́дно, видны́.

2.1 Usage

In contrast to the predicative use of long adjectives, the short form on the whole is used w
talking about a temporary state. For example, он **плох** "he is poorly" contrasts with с
плохо́й "he is bad".

3 VERBS

1 Conjugation

Russian verbs can be divided into two groups, according to their endings when conjuga
The two groups are often referred to as "first-conjugation" and "second-conjugation" ve
and the following examples – one from either group – show the pattern of endi
encountered in the present-tense conjugations of verbs from each group:

	1st Conjugation	*2nd Conjugation*
	рабо́тать	говори́ть
я	рабо́таю	говорю́
ты	рабо́таешь	говори́шь
он/она́	рабо́тает	говори́т
мы	рабо́таем	говори́м
вы	рабо́таете	говори́те
они́	рабо́тают	говоря́т

1.1 First-conjugation verbs

These include verbs with infinitive endings in -ать (eg. рабо́тать: see above), in -ять
стреля́ть: стреля́ю,стреля́ешь etc), in -овать/-евать (eg. интересова́ть: интер
у́ю,интересу́ешь etc), in -уть (eg. махну́ть: махну́,махнёшь etc), in -авать
узнава́ть: узнаю́,узнаёшь etc), in -ыть (eg. мыть: мо́ю,мо́ешь etc), and
-зть,-оть,-сть and -ти, as well as monosyllabic verbs in -ить (eg. шить: шью,шьё
etc). Note how under stress e is replaced by ё.

Many first-conjugation verbs – generally those with end-stressed infinitives – unde
consonant mutation in conjugation, which is frequently accompanied by a stress shift fi
the end to the stem after the first person singular; this is the general pattern for stress char
within the conjugation of first-conjugation verbs. For example:

	писа́ть	иска́ть
я	пишу́	ищу́
ты	пи́шешь	и́щешь
он/она́	пи́шет	и́щет
мы	пи́шем	и́щем
вы	пи́шете	и́щете
они́	пи́шут	и́щут

Stress change does not occur in first-conjugation verbs where the stress falls on the ster
the infinitive, eg. пла́кать: пла́чу, пла́чешь etc, and дви́гать: дви́жу,дви́жешь etc.

1.2 Second-conjugation verbs

These include most verbs with infinitive endings in -ить (the main exception being the monosyllabic ones), many verbs in -еть, some in -ать and two in -ять (боя́ться and стоя́ть).

Note that y replaces ю and a replaces я after ж,ч,ш, or щ. Thus, смотре́ть conjugates: смотрю́,смо́тришь,...смо́трят, whereas слы́шать conjugates: слы́шу,слы́шишь,...слы́шат.

As with first-conjugation verbs, stress change in second-conjugation verbs that are end-stressed in the infinitive is often accompanied by a consonant change in conjunction, eg. плати́ть: плачу́,пла́тишь,...пла́тят and суди́ть: сужу́,су́дишь,...су́дят. However, this mutation applies consistently only to the first person singular of second-conjugation verbs in -ить and -еть. Furthermore, the addition of л in the first person singular of verbs with the stem ending in п, б, в, ф and м is a salient feature of the second conjugation, eg. люби́ть: люблю́,лю́бишь,...лю́бят and корми́ть: кормлю́, ко́рмишь,...ко́рмят. In fact, a consonant change of one form or other, in the first person singular, is found in all second conjugation verbs in -ить whose stems end in -б,-в,-д,-з,-с,-т and -ф, and those in -еть and -ить whose stems end in -м,-п, and -ст.

2 Past Tense

The past tense for most Russian verbs, including all those with infinitive endings in -сть and -ть, is formed by replacing the infinitive ending by -л,-ла,-ло,-ли, giving the masculine, feminine, neuter and plural forms respectively.

For example:

infinitive	*past tense*
молча́ть	он молча́л
	она́ молча́ла
	оно́ молча́ло
	они́ молча́ли
укра́сть	он укра́л
	она́ укра́ла
	оно́ укра́ло
	они́ укра́ли
звони́ть	он звони́л
	она́ звони́ла
	оно́ звони́ло
	они́ звони́ли

The singular past tense always reflects the gender of the subject, so that even after the personal pronouns я and ты the gender is always marked, eg. я сказа́л (masculine subject)
я сказа́ла (feminine subject)

Verbs with infinitives ending in -ереть,-зть,-чь, and many in -ти have no -л in the masculine past tense, eg. умере́ть (у́мер,умерла́), лезть (лез,ле́зла), мочь (мог,могла́), нести́ (нёс,несла́). This is also the case with some verbs in -нуть, привы́кнуть (привы́к, привы́кла).

The verb быть, while not used in the present tense, is encountered frequently in the past tense:

был, была́, бы́ло, бы́ли

Note the stress changes when used in the negative, ie. preceded by не:

не́ был, не была́, не́ было, не́ были

3 Imperative Mood

The imperative mood has two forms – the familiar and the formal - which are use
accordance with the mode of address (ie. the familiar ты or the formal Вы) appropria
any given situation. The formal imperative is obtained by simply adding -те to the end o
familiar form. The familiar imperative is formed by replacing the third person plural en
of a verb by -й where it is directly preceded by a vowel, eg.:

де́лать (*infin*) » де́лают (*3rd person pl*) » де́лай(те) (*imperative*)

similarly:

чита́ть » чита́ют » чита́й(те)

Alternatively, -и(те) replaces the third person plural ending where this is directly prece
by a consonant and the verb has mobile or end stress in conjunction, eg.:

подчеркну́ть » подчеркну́т » подчеркни́(те)
держа́ть » де́ржат » держи́(те)

The imperative ending -ь(те) replaces the third person plural ending where this is dire
preceded by no more than one consonant and the verb has fixed stem stress in conjugat
eg.:

поста́вить » поста́вят » поста́вь(те)
оде́ть » оде́нут » оде́нь(те)

Note: stress in imperative forms is identical to that of the first person singular.

- дава́|ть and its compounds have imperative -й(те).
- пить has imperative пей(те) (compare петь which has imperative по́й(те)). б
  вить, лить and шить also form the imperative like пить.
- the imperative of быть is бу́дь(те).

4 Aspect

The majority of Russian verbs have two verb aspects, the **imperfective** for conveying
frequency of an action or describing a **process**, and the **perfective** for emphasis o
single action or a **result**. It follows that the perfective can only be used in the past
future, while the imperfective can also be used in the present tense.

Aspectual pairs can be differentiated either by the presence of a prefix in the perfec
aspect, eg. сде́лать (cf imperfective де́лать), by the presence of a suffix in the imperfec
aspect, eg. пока́зывать (cf perfective показа́ть), or by a change in conjugation,
perfective ко́нчить (2nd conjugation) and its imperfective counterpart конча́ть
conjugation).

It should be noted, though, that some aspectual pairs do not follow this pattern, for insta
those that derive from different roots, eg. говори́ть (*impf*)/сказа́ть (*perf*), бр
(*impf*)/взять (*perf*). Then there are a minority of verbs which exist in one aspect only,
сто́ить (*impf*), while some verbs incorporate the two aspects in one form, eg. иссле́дов
(*impf/perf*).

pect also has a bearing on the use of the imperative mood, where, generally speaking, the rfective aspect is used in positive commands (ie. telling someone to do something), while imperfective is used in negative commands (ie. telling someone not to do something), in er words where the imperative form is preceded by "не".

~ *A, a* ~

A, a [eɪ] *n* (*letter*) 1-ая бу́ква англи́йского
алфави́та; (*SCOL: mark*) ≈ отли́чно; **~ road**
(*BRIT: AUT*) шоссе́ *nt ind* (пе́рвой катего́рии);
~ shares (*BRIT: STOCK EXCHANGE*) а́кции *fpl* с
ограни́ченным пра́вом го́лоса; **from ~ to Z**
от "а" до "я".
A [eɪ] *n* (*MUS*) ля *nt ind*.

KEYWORD

a [eɪ] (*before vowel or silent h* **an**) *indef art*: **1: a book**
кни́га; **an apple** я́блоко; **she's a student** она́
студе́нтка
2 (*instead of the number "one"*): **a week ago**
неде́лю наза́д; **a hundred/thousand** *etc*
pounds сто/ты́сяча *etc* фу́нтов
3 (*in expressing time*) в +*acc*; **3 a day/week** 3 в
день/неде́лю; **10 km an hour** 10 км в час
4 (*in expressing prices*): **30p a kilo** 30 пе́нсов
килогра́мм; **£5 a person** с ка́ждого 5 фу́нтов.

---

a. *abbr* = **acre**.
AA *n abbr* (*BRIT:* = *Automobile Association*)
Автомоби́льная ассоциа́ция; (*US:* =
Associate in/of Arts) член ассоциа́ции
рабо́тников иску́сства; (= *Alcoholics
Anonymous*) о́бщество анони́много
излече́ния от алкоголи́зма; (= *anti-aircraft*)
противовозду́шный.
AAA *n abbr* (= *American Automobile
Association*) Америка́нская автомоби́льная
ассоциа́ция; (*BRIT:* = *Amateur Athletics
Association*) Люби́тельская ассоциа́ция
лёгкой атле́тики.
A & R *n abbr* (*MUS:* = *artists and repertoire*)
исполни́тели и репертуа́р.
AAUP *n abbr* = *American Association of
University Professors*.
AB *abbr* (*BRIT*) = **able-bodied seaman**; (*CANADA*)
= *Alberta*.
abaci ['æbəsaɪ] *npl of* **abacus**.
aback [ə'bæk] *adv*: **I was taken ~** я был
поражён.
abacus ['æbəkəs] (*pl* **abaci**) *n* счёты *pl*.
abandon [ə'bændən] *vt* (*person*) покида́ть
(покину́ть *perf*); (*car*) броса́ть (бро́сить* *perf*);
(*search, research*) прекраща́ть (прекрати́ть*
perf); (*idea, hope*) отка́зываться (отказа́ться*

perf) от +*gen* ◆ *n* (*wild behaviour*): **with ~**
самозабве́нно; **to ~ ship** покида́ть
(покину́ть *perf*) кора́бль.
abandoned [ə'bændənd] *adj* поки́нутый;
(*unrestrained*) безу́держный.
abase [ə'beɪs] *vt*: **to ~ o.s. (before)** унижа́ться
(уни́зиться* *perf*) (пе́ред +*instr*).
abashed [ə'bæʃt] *adj* смущённый* (смущён).
abate [ə'beɪt] *vi* (*storm*) утиха́ть (ути́хнуть*
perf); (*anger, terror*) ослабева́ть (ослабе́ть*
perf).
abatement [ə'beɪtmənt] *n*: **noise ~** сниже́ние
у́ровня шу́ма.
abattoir ['æbətwɑ:'] *n* (*BRIT*) скотобо́йня.
abbey ['æbɪ] *n* абба́тство.
abbot ['æbət] *n* абба́т.
abbreviate [ə'bri:vɪeɪt] *vt* (*essay, word*)
сокраща́ть (сократи́ть* *perf*).
abbreviation [əbri:vɪ'eɪʃən] *n* сокраще́ние.
ABC *n abbr* = *American Broadcasting Company*.
abdicate ['æbdɪkeɪt] *vt* (*responsibility, right*)
слага́ть (сложи́ть *perf*) с себя́ ◆ *vi* (*monarch*)
отрека́ться (отре́чься* *perf*) от престо́ла.
abdication [æbdɪ'keɪʃən] *n* (*see vb*)
скла́дывание; отрече́ние от престо́ла.
abdomen ['æbdəmɛn] *n* брюшна́я по́лость *f*,
живо́т.
abdominal [æb'dɔmɪnl] *adj* брюшно́й; **~ pain**
бо́ли *fpl* в брюшно́й по́лости *or* в животе́.
abduct [æb'dʌkt] *vt* похища́ть (похи́тить* *perf*).
abduction [æb'dʌkʃən] *n* похище́ние.
Aberdeen [æbə'di:n] *n* Аберди́н.
Aberdonian [æbə'dəunɪən] *adj* аберди́нский ◆ *n*
аберди́нец(-нка).
aberration [æbə'reɪʃən] *n* аберра́ция,
отклоне́ние (от но́рмы); **in a moment of
mental ~** в мину́ту помраче́ния рассу́дка.
abet [ə'bɛt] *vt see* **aid**.
abeyance [ə'beɪəns] *n*: **in ~**
приостано́вленный (приостано́влен).
abhor [əb'hɔ:'] *vt* испы́тывать (*impf*)
отвраще́ние к +*dat*.
abhorrent [əb'hɔrənt] *adj* отврати́тельный*
(отврати́телен).
abide [ə'baɪd] *vt*: **I can't ~ it/him** я э́того/его́ не
выношу́

---

* marks translations which have irregular inflections. The Russian-English side of the dictionary gives inflectional information.

▶ **abide by** vt fus (law, decision) соблюда́ть (соблюсти́* perf).
abiding [ə'baɪdɪŋ] adj неослабева́ющий.
ability [ə'bɪlɪtɪ] n (capacity) спосо́бность f; (talent, skill) спосо́бности fpl; **to the best of my ~** в ме́ру мои́х спосо́бностей.
abject ['æbdʒɛkt] adj (poverty, coward) жа́лкий*; (apology) уни́женный*.
ablaze [ə'bleɪz] adj (building etc) в огне́; **the city was ~ with light** го́род был за́лит огня́ми.
able ['eɪbl] adj (capable) спосо́бный* (спосо́бен); (skilled) уме́лый (уме́л); **he is/ was ~ to ...** он спосо́бен/был спосо́бен +infin ....
able-bodied ['eɪbl'bɔdɪd] adj (person) кре́пкий*; **~ seaman** (BRIT) матро́с пе́рвого кла́сса.
ablutions [ə'blu:ʃənz] npl омове́ние ntsg.
ably ['eɪblɪ] adv (skilfully) уме́ло.
ABM n abbr (= anti-ballistic missile) ≈ ЗУРС= зени́тный управля́емый реакти́вный снаря́д.
abnormal [æb'nɔ:ml] adj ненорма́льный* (ненорма́лен).
abnormality [æbnɔ:'mælɪtɪ] n ненорма́льность f, анома́лия.
aboard [ə'bɔ:d] prep (position: NAUT, AVIAT) на борту́ +gen; (: train, bus) в +prp; (motion: NAUT, AVIAT) на борт +gen; (: train, bus) в +acc
♦ adv: **to climb ~** (ship) сади́ться (сесть* perf) на кора́бль; (train) сади́ться (сесть* perf) в/на по́езд.
abode [ə'bəud] n (LAW): **of no fixed ~** без постоя́нного местожи́тельства.
abolish [ə'bɔlɪʃ] vt отменя́ть (отмени́ть* perf).
abolition [æbə'lɪʃən] n отме́на.
abominable [ə'bɔmɪnəbl] adj отврати́тельный* (отврати́телен).
abominably [ə'bɔmɪnəblɪ] adv отврати́тельно.
aborigine [æbə'rɪdʒɪnɪ] n абориге́н(ка).
abort [ə'bɔ:t] vt (plan, activity) прекраща́ть (прекрати́ть* perf); (COMPUT) прерыва́ть (прерва́ть* perf); (MED): **to ~ a baby** де́лать (сде́лать perf) або́рт.
abortion [ə'bɔ:ʃən] n (MED) або́рт; **to have an ~** де́лать (сде́лать perf) або́рт.
abortionist [ə'bɔ:ʃənɪst] n челове́к, де́лающий подпо́льные або́рты.
abortive [ə'bɔ:tɪv] adj неуда́чный* (неуда́чен).
abound [ə'baund] vi быть* (impf) в изоби́лии; **to ~ in** or **with** изоби́ловать (impf) +instr.

KEYWORD

about [ə'baut] adv **1** (approximately: referring to time, price etc) приблизи́тельно +acc, приме́рно +acc, о́коло +gen; **it will take me about 3 hours** э́то займёт у меня́ приме́рно or приблизи́тельно 3 часа́; **at about 2 (o'clock)** приблизи́тельно or приме́рно в 2 (часа́), часа́ в 2, о́коло двух (часо́в); **I've just about finished** я почти́ зако́нчил
2 (approximately: referring to height, size etc) приме́рно +nom, приблизи́тельно +nom; **the room is about 10 metres wide** ко́мната

приме́рно or приблизи́тельно 10 ме́тров в ширину́; **she is about your height/age** она́ приме́рно or приблизи́тельно Ва́шего ро́ста/во́зраста
3 (referring to place) повсю́ду; **to leave things lying about** разбра́сывать (разброса́ть perf) ве́щи повсю́ду; **to run/walk etc about** бе́гать (impf)/ходи́ть* (impf) etc
4: **to be about to do** собира́ться (собра́ться* perf) +infin; **he was about to go to bed** он собра́лся лечь спать
♦ prep **1** (relating to) о(б) +prp; **a book about London** кни́га о Ло́ндоне; **what is it about?** о чём э́то?; **we talked about it** мы говори́ли or разгова́ривали об э́том; **what** or **how about doing this?** как насчёт того́, что́бы +infin?
2 (referring to place) по +dat; **to walk about the town** ходи́ть* (impf) по го́роду; **her clothes were scattered about the room** её оде́жда была́ разбро́сана по ко́мнате.

---

about-face [ə'baut'feɪs] n (MIL) поворо́т круго́м; (fig) поворо́т на 180 гра́дусов.
about-turn [ə'baut'tə:n] n = **about-face**.
above [ə'bʌv] adv (higher up) наверху́; (greater, more) вы́ше, свы́ше ♦ prep (higher than) над +instr; (: in rank etc) вы́ше +gen; (: in number) свы́ше +gen, бо́лее +gen; **from ~** све́рху; **costing ~ £10** сто́ящий свы́ше £10; **~ the knees** вы́ше коле́н; **mentioned ~** вышеупомя́нутый; **he's not ~ a bit of blackmail** он не погнуша́ется шантажо́м; **~ suspicion/criticism** вне подозре́ния/кри́тики; **~ all** пре́жде всего́.
above board adj че́стный* (че́стен), откры́тый (откры́т).
abrasion [ə'breɪʒən] n тре́ние; (on skin) сса́дина.
abrasive [ə'breɪzɪv] adj (substance) абрази́вный; (manner) жёсткий* (жёсток).
abreast [ə'brɛst] adv (people, vehicles) в ряд; **three ~** по́ тро́е в ряд; **to keep ~ of** (fig) быть* (impf) в ку́рсе +gen.
abridge [ə'brɪdʒ] vt (novel, play) сокраща́ть (сократи́ть* perf).
abroad [ə'brɔ:d] adv (to be) за грани́цей or рубежо́м; (to go) за грани́цу or рубе́ж; (from abroad) из-за грани́цы or рубежа́; **there is a rumour ~ that ...** (fig) хо́дит слух, что ....
abrupt [ə'brʌpt] adj (action, ending etc) внеза́пный* (внеза́пен); (person, manner) ре́зкий* (ре́зок).
abruptly [ə'brʌptlɪ] adv (leave, end) внеза́пно; (speak) ре́зко.
abscess ['æbsɪs] n абсце́сс.
abscond [əb'skɔnd] vi (thief): **to ~ with** скрыва́ться (скры́ться* perf) с +instr; (prisoner): **to ~ (from)** сбега́ть (сбежа́ть* perf) (из +gen).
abseil [ə'bseɪl] vi спуска́ться (спусти́ться* perf) при по́мощи кана́та.
absence ['æbsəns] n (of person, thing)

отсу́тствие; **in the ~ of** (*person*) в отсу́тствие +*gen*; (*thing*) при отсу́тствии +*gen*; **~ without leave** (*MIL*) самово́льная отлу́чка.
absent [*adj* 'æbsənt, *vb* æb'sɛnt] *adj* отсу́тствующий* ♦ *vt*: **to ~ o.s.** отлуча́ться (отлучи́ться *perf*).
absentee [æbsən'ti:] *n* отсу́тствующий*(-ая) *m(f) adj*.
absenteeism [æbsən'ti:ɪzəm] *n* прогу́лы *mpl*.
absent-minded ['æbsənt'maɪndɪd] *adj* рассе́янный* (рассе́ян).
absent-mindedly ['æbsənt'maɪndɪdlɪ] *adv* рассе́янно.
absent-mindedness ['æbsənt'maɪndɪdnɪs] *n* рассе́янность *f*.
absolute ['æbsəlu:t] *adj* абсолю́тный*.
absolutely [æbsə'lu:tlɪ] *adv* (*totally*) абсолю́тно, соверше́нно; (*certainly*) безусло́вно.
absolute monopoly *n* абсолю́тная монопо́лия.
absolution [æbsə'lu:ʃən] *n* (*REL*) отпуще́ние грехо́в.
absolve [əb'zɔlv] *vt*: **to ~ sb (from sth)** отпуска́ть (отпусти́ть* *perf*) кому́-н (что-н).
absorb [əb'zɔ:b] *vt* (*liquid, information*) впи́тывать (впита́ть *perf*); (*light, business*) поглоща́ть (поглоти́ть* *perf*); (*changes, effects*) воспринима́ть (восприня́ть* *perf*); **he is ~ed in a book** он поглощён кни́гой.
absorbent [əb'zɔ:bənt] *adj* гигроскопи́чный.
absorbent cotton *n* (*US*) гигроскопи́ческая ва́та.
absorbing [əb'zɔ:bɪŋ] *adj* (*book, film etc*) увлека́тельный* (увлека́телен).
absorption [əb'sɔ:pʃən] *n* (*see vt*) впи́тывание; поглоще́ние; восприя́тие; (*interest*) увлечённость *f*.
abstain [əb'steɪn] *vi*: **to ~ (from)** возде́рживаться (воздержа́ться* *perf*) (от +*gen*).
abstemious [əb'sti:mɪəs] *adj* (*person*) возде́ржанный* (возде́ржан).
abstention [əb'stɛnʃən] *n* (*refusal to vote*) неуча́стие в голосова́нии.
abstinence ['æbstɪnəns] *n* воздержа́ние.
abstract [*adj, n* 'æbstrækt, *vb* æb'strækt] *adj* абстра́ктный*; (*idea, quality*) отвлечённый ♦ *n* (*summary*) аннота́ция; (*of dissertation*) рефера́т ♦ *vt* (*remove*) извлека́ть (извле́чь* *perf*); (*summarize*) анноти́ровать (проанноти́ровать *perf*).
abstruse [æb'stru:s] *adj* замыслова́тый.
absurd [əb'sə:d] *adj* абсу́рдный* (абсу́рден), неле́пый (неле́п).
absurdity [əb'sə:dɪtɪ] *n* абсу́рдность *f*, неле́пость *f*.
ABTA ['æbtə] *n abbr* = Association of British

Travel Agents.
Abu Dhabi ['æbu:'dɑ:bɪ] *n* Абу́-Да́би.
abundance [ə'bʌndəns] *n* изоби́лие; **in ~** в изоби́лии.
abundant [ə'bʌndənt] *adj* изоби́льный* (изоби́лен).
abundantly [ə'bʌndəntlɪ] *adv* в изоби́лии; **~ clear/obvious** соверше́нно я́сно/очеви́дно.
abuse [*n* ə'bju:s, *vb* ə'bju:z] *n* (*insults*) брань *f*; (*ill-treatment*) жесто́кое обраще́ние; (*misuse of power, drugs etc*) злоупотребле́ние ♦ *vt* (*insult*) оскорбля́ть (оскорби́ть* *perf*); (*ill-treat*) жесто́ко обраща́ться (*impf*) с +*instr*; (*misuse*) злоупотребля́ть (злоупотреби́ть* *perf*) +*instr*; **this system is open to ~** э́той систе́мой легко́ злоупотребля́ть.
abuser [ə'bju:zə'] *n*: **drug ~** наркома́н; **child ~** челове́к, подверга́ющий дете́й физи́ческому и́ли сексуа́льному наси́лию.
abusive [ə'bju:sɪv] *adj* (*person*) гру́бый (груб); **~ language** брань *f*.
abysmal [ə'bɪzməl] *adj* (*performance, failure*) плаче́вный* (плаче́вен); (*ignorance etc*) вопию́щий* (вопию́щ).
abysmally [ə'bɪzməlɪ] *adv* (*see adj*) плаче́вно; вопию́ще.
abyss [ə'bɪs] *n* про́пасть *f*.
AC *abbr* = **alternating current**; (*US*: = *athletic club*) легкоатлети́ческий клуб.
a/c *abbr* (*COMM*) = **account**; (= *account current*) теку́щий* счёт*.
academic [ækə'dɛmɪk] *adj* (*system, standards*) академи́ческий*; (*qualifications*) учёный; (*work, books*) нау́чный*; (*person, child*) интеллектуа́льный*; (*pej: issue*) академи́чный (академи́чен) ♦ *n* учёный(-ая) *m(f) adj*.
academic year *n* (*in school*) уче́бный год*; (*in higher education*) академи́ческий* год*.
academy [ə'kædəmɪ] *n* (*learned body*) акаде́мия; (*school*) учи́лище; (: *in Scotland*) сре́дняя шко́ла; **~ of music** консервато́рия; **military/naval ~** вое́нная/вое́нно-морска́я акаде́мия.
ACAS ['eɪkæs] *n abbr* (*BRIT*: = *Advisory, Conciliation and Arbitration Service*) слу́жба юриди́ческих консульта́ций и арбитра́жа.
accede [æk'si:d] *vi*: **to ~ to** (*request*) удовлетворя́ть (удовлетвори́ть *perf*); (*opinion, contention*) соглаша́ться (согласи́ться* *perf*) с +*instr*.
accelerate [æk'sɛləreɪt] *vt* (*process*) ускоря́ть (уско́рить *perf*) ♦ *vi* (*AUT*) разгоня́ться (разогна́ться *perf*).
acceleration [æksɛlə'reɪʃən] *n* (*see vb*) ускоре́ние; разго́н.
accelerator [æk'sɛləreɪtə'] *n* акселера́тор.
accent ['æksɛnt] *n* акце́нт; (*stress mark*) знак

ударе́ния; **to speak with an Irish ~** говори́ть (*impf*) с ирла́ндским акце́нтом; **to have a strong ~** име́ть (*impf*) си́льный акце́нт.
accented [æk'sɛntɪd] *adj* с акце́нтом; **heavily ~** с си́льным акце́нтом.
accentuate [æk'sɛntjueɪt] *vt* (*syllable*) акценти́ровать (*impf/perf*), проставля́ть (проста́вить *perf*) ударе́ние на +*acc*; (*need, difference*) подчёркивать (подчеркну́ть *perf*).
accept [ək'sɛpt] *vt* (*gift, proposal etc*) принима́ть (приня́ть* *perf*); (*fact, situation, risk*) мири́ться (примири́ться *perf*) с +*instr*; (*responsibility, blame*) принима́ть (приня́ть* *perf*) на себя́.
acceptable [ək'sɛptəbl] *adj* прие́млемый (прие́млем).
acceptance [ək'sɛptəns] *n* (*of gift, offer etc*) приня́тие; (*of fact, situation*) прия́тие; **to meet with general ~** находи́ть* (найти́* *perf*) всео́бщее одобре́ние.
access [ˈæksɛs] *n* до́ступ ♦ *vt* (*COMPUT*) испо́льзовать (*impf/perf*) до́ступ к +*dat*; (: *data*) обраща́ться (обрати́ться* *perf*) к +*dat*; **to have ~ to** (*child*) име́ть (*impf*) возмо́жность обще́ния с +*instr*; **the burglars gained ~ through a window** взло́мщики прони́кли че́рез окно́.
accessible [æk'sɛsəbl] *adj* досту́пный*.
accession [æk'sɛʃən] *n* прихо́д к вла́сти; (*of king*) вступле́ние на престо́л; (*to library*) поступле́ние.
accessory [æk'sɛsərɪ] *n* (*COMM, TECH, AUT*) принадле́жность *f*; (*LAW*): **~ to** соуча́стник(-ица) +*gen*; **accessories** *npl* (*DRESS*) аксессуа́ры *mpl*; **toilet accessories** (*BRIT*) туале́тные принадле́жности *fpl*.
access road *n* подъездно́й путь* *m*.
access time *n* (*COMPUT*) вре́мя* *nt* до́ступа.
accident [ˈæksɪdənt] *n* (*chance event*) случа́йность *f*; (*mishap, disaster*) несча́стный слу́чай, ава́рия; **to meet with** *or* **to have an ~** попада́ть (попа́сть *perf*) в ава́рию *or* катастро́фу; **he had an ~** с ним произошёл несча́стный слу́чай; **by ~** (*unintentionally*) неча́янно; (*by chance*) случа́йно.
accidental [æksɪ'dɛntl] *adj* случа́йный* (случа́ен).
accidentally [æksɪ'dɛntəlɪ] *adv* случа́йно, неча́янно.
accident insurance *n* страхова́ние от несча́стных слу́чаев.
accident-prone [ˈæksɪdənt'prəun] *adj* невезу́чий; **he is ~** его́ пресле́дуют несча́стья.
acclaim [ə'kleɪm] *n* призна́ние ♦ *vt*: **he was ~ed for his achievements** он получи́л призна́ние за свои́ достиже́ния.
acclamation [æklə'meɪʃən] *n* (*approval*) бу́рное *or* шу́мное одобре́ние; (*applause*) бу́рные аплодисме́нты *mpl*.

acclimate [ə'klaɪmət] *vt* (*US*) = **acclimatize**.
acclimatize [ə'klaɪmətaɪz] (*US* **acclimate**) *vt*: **become ~d (to)** (*surroundings*) акклиматизи́роваться (*impf/perf*) (в +*prp*), осва́иваться (осво́иться *perf*) (в +*prp*); (*heat, cold*) привыка́ть (привы́кнуть* *perf*) (к +*dat*).
accolade [ˈækəleɪd] *n* по́честь *f*.
accommodate [ə'kɔmədeɪt] *vt* (*subj: person*) предоставля́ть (предоста́вить* *perf*) жильё +*dat*; (: *car, hotel etc*) вмеща́ть (вмести́ть* *perf*); (*oblige, help*) ока́зывать (оказа́ть* *perf*) услу́гу +*dat*; **to ~ one's plans to** приспоса́бливать (приспосо́бить* *perf*) свои́ пла́ны к +*dat*.
accommodating [ə'kɔmədeɪtɪŋ] *adj* услу́жливый (услу́жлив).
accommodation [əkɔmə'deɪʃən] *n* (*to live in*) жильё; (*to work in*) помеще́ние; **~s** *npl* (*US: lodgings*) жильё *ntsg*; **"accommodation to let"** (*living*) "сдаётся жильё"; (*office*) "сдаётся помеще́ние"; **they have ~ for 500** они́ мо́гут размести́ть 500 челове́к; **the hall has seating ~ for 600** (*BRIT*) зал рассчи́тан на 600 мест; **do you have any ~?** (*for yourself*) Вам есть где жить?; (*for me*) Вы предоставля́ете жильё?
accompaniment [ə'kʌmpənɪmənt] *n* сопровожде́ние; (*MUS*) аккомпанеме́нт.
accompanist [ə'kʌmpənɪst] *n* аккомпаниа́тор.
accompany [ə'kʌmpənɪ] *vt* (*escort, go along with*) сопровожда́ть (сопроводи́ть* *perf*); (*MUS*) аккомпани́ровать (*impf*) +*dat*.
accomplice [ə'kʌmplɪs] *n* соуча́стник(-ица), соо́бщник(-ица).
accomplish [ə'kʌmplɪʃ] *vt* (*task*) заверша́ть (заверши́ть *perf*); (*goal*) достига́ть (дости́гнуть* *or* дости́чь* *perf*) +*gen*.
accomplished [ə'kʌmplɪʃt] *adj* (*person*) тала́нтливый (тала́нтлив); (*performance*) соверше́нный* (соверше́нен).
accomplishment [ə'kʌmplɪʃmənt] *n* (*completion, bringing about*) заверше́ние; (*achievement*) достиже́ние; (*skill: usu pl*) уме́ние.
accord [ə'kɔːd] *n* соглаше́ние ♦ *vt* ока́зывать (оказа́ть* *perf*); **of his own ~** по со́бственному жела́нию; **of its own ~** сам по себе́; **with one ~** единоду́шно; (*movement*) как по кома́нде; **he and I are in ~ on this issue** мы с ним в согла́сии на э́тот счёт *or* по э́тому по́воду.
accordance [ə'kɔːdəns] *n*: **in ~ with** в согла́сии *or* соотве́тствии с +*instr*.
according [ə'kɔːdɪŋ] *prep*: **~ to** согла́сно +*dat*; **~ to plan** по пла́ну.
accordingly [ə'kɔːdɪŋlɪ] *adv* (*appropriately*) соотве́тствующим о́бразом; (*as a result*) соотве́тственно.
accordion [ə'kɔːdɪən] *n* аккордео́н.
accost [ə'kɔst] *vt* пристава́ть* (приста́ть* *perf*) к +*dat*.
account [ə'kaunt] *n* (*bill*) счёт*; (*monthly*

account) ежемéсячный счёт; (*in bank*) (расчётный) счёт; (*report*) отчёт; ~s *npl* (*COMM*) счетá* *mpl*; (*books*) бухгáлтерские кнúги *fpl*; **"account payee only"** (*BRIT*) "подлежúт уплáте тóлько на счёт получáтеля"; **to keep an ~ of** вестú* (*impf*) счёт* +*gen or* +*dat*; **to bring sb to ~ for sth** призывáть (призвáть* *perf*) когó-н к отвéту за что-н; **by all ~s** по всем свéдениям; **of no ~** не вáжно; **on ~** в крéдит; **to pay £5 on ~** платúть* (заплатúть* *perf*) £5 в задáток; **to buy sth on ~** покупáть (купúть* *perf*) что-н в крéдит; **on no ~** ни в кóем слýчае; **on ~ of** по причúне +*gen*; **to take into ~, take ~ of** принимáть (приня́ть* *perf*) в расчёт

▶ **account for** *vt fus* (*money spent, expenses*) отчúтываться (отчитáться *perf*) за +*acc*; (*absence, failure*) объясня́ть (объяснúть *perf*); (*represent*) составля́ть (состáвить* *perf*); **all the children were ~ed for** все дéти бы́ли на мéсте; **four people are still not ~ed for** не досчитáлись четырёх человéк.

accountability [ə'kauntə'bılıtı] *n* отчётность *f*.

accountable [ə'kauntəbl] *adj* подотчётный* (подотчётен); **to be ~ to sb for sth** отвечáть (*impf*) за что-н пéред кем-н.

accountancy [ə'kauntənsı] *n* бухгалтéрия.

accountant [ə'kauntənt] *n* бухгáлтер.

account executive *n* делопроизводúтель *m*.

accounting [ə'kauntıŋ] *n* бухгáлтерское дéло*.

accounting period *n* отчётный перúод.

account number *n* (*at bank etc*) нóмер* счёта.

account payable *n* счёт кредитóров (*в балáнсе*).

account receivable *n* счёт дебитóров (*в балáнсе*).

accredited [ə'krɛdıtıd] *adj* (*agent etc*) аккредитóванный.

accretion [ə'kri:ʃən] *n* (*process*) нарастáние; (*layer*) нарóст.

accrue [ə'kru:] *vi* (*mount up*) нарастáть (нарастú* *perf*); **to ~ to** доставáться* (достáться* *perf*) +*dat*.

accrued charges *npl* нарóсшие процéнты *mpl*.

accrued interest *n* нарóсшие процéнты *mpl*.

accumulate [ə'kju:mjuleıt] *vt* накáпливать (накопúть* *perf*) ◆ *vi* накáпливаться (накопúться* *perf*).

accumulation [əkju:mju'leıʃən] *n* накоплéние.

accuracy ['ækjurəsı] *n* тóчность *f*.

accurate ['ækjurıt] *adj* тóчный* (тóчен); (*person, device*) аккурáтный* (аккурáтен); (*shot*) мéткий*.

accurately ['ækjurıtlı] *adv* тóчно; (*shoot*) мéтко.

accusation [ækju'zeıʃən] *n* обвинéние.

accusative [ə'kju:zətıv] *n* (*LING*) винúтельный падéж*.

accuse [ə'kju:z] *vt*: **to ~ sb (of sth)** обвиня́ть (обвинúть *perf*) когó-н (в чём-н).

accused [ə'kju:zd] *n* (*LAW*): **the ~** обвиня́емый(-ая) *m(f) adj*.

accuser [ə'kju:zəʳ] *n* обвинúтель *m*.

accusing [ə'kju:zıŋ] *adj* обвиня́ющий.

accustom [ə'kʌstəm] *vt* приучáть (приучúть* *perf*); **to ~ o.s. to sth** приучáться (приучúться *perf*) *or* привыкáть (привы́кнуть* *perf*) к чемý-н.

accustomed [ə'kʌstəmd] *adj* (*usual*) привы́чный*; **to be ~ to working late/to the heat** я привы́к рабóтать пóздно/к жарé.

AC/DC *abbr* (= *alternating current/direct current*) перемéнный ток/постоя́нный ток.

ACE [eıs] *n abbr* = *American Council on Education*.

ace [eıs] *n* (*CARDS*) туз; (*TENNIS*) вы́игрыш с подáчи.

acerbic [ə'sə:bık] *adj* (*remark*) éдкий* (éдок).

acetate ['æsıteıt] *n* ацетáт.

ache [eık] *n* боль *f* ◆ *vi* (*be painful*) болéть (*impf*); (*yearn*): **to ~ to do** томúться* (*impf*) желáнием +*infin*; **I've got stomach ~ or a stomach ~** у меня́ болúт живóт; **I'm aching all over** у меня́ всё тéло нóет; **my head ~s** у меня́ болúт головá.

achieve [ə'tʃi:v] *vt* (*aim, result*) достигáть (достúгнуть* *or* достúчь* *perf*) +*gen*; (*success, victory*) добивáться (добúться* *perf*) +*gen*.

achievement [ə'tʃi:vmənt] *n* достижéние.

Achilles heel [ə'kılı:z-] *n* Ахиллéсова пятá.

acid ['æsıd] *adj* (*CHEM: soil etc*) кислóтный*; (*taste*) кúслый* ◆ *n* (*CHEM*) кислотá*; (*inf: DRUGS*) ЛСД (*наркóтик*).

acid house *adj* áсид хáус (*стиль поп-мýзыки*).

acidic [ə'sıdık] *adj* кúслый* (кисел).

acidity [ə'sıdıtı] *n* кислóтность *f*.

acid rain *n* кислóтный* дождь* *m*.

acid test *n* прóбный кáмень* *m*.

acknowledge [ək'nɔlıdʒ] *vt* (*letter etc: also: ~ receipt of*) подтвержда́ть (подтвердúть* *perf*) получéние +*gen*; (*fact, situation*) признавáть* (призна́ть* *perf*).

acknowledgement [ək'nɔlıdʒmənt] *n* (*of letter etc*) подтверждéние получéния; **~s** *npl* (*in book*) выражéние *ntsg* благодáрности (*в предислóвии кнúги*).

ACLU *n abbr* = *American Civil Liberties Union*.

acme ['ækmı] *n* верх*, вершúна.

acne ['æknı] *n* угрú* *mpl*, прыщú *mpl*.

acorn ['eıkɔ:n] *n* жёлудь *m*.

acoustic [ə'ku:stık] *adj* (*guitar etc*) акустúческий*.

acoustic coupler *n* (*COMPUT*) акустúческий* соединúтель *m*.

acoustics [ə'ku:stıks] *n* (*science*) акýстика ◆ *npl* (*of hall, room*) акýстика *fsg*.

---

* marks translations which have irregular inflections. The Russian-English side of the dictionary gives inflectional information.

acquaint [ə'kweınt] *vt:* **to ~ sb with sth** (*inform*) ознако́мить* (*perf*) кого́-н с чем-н; **I am/was ~ed with** (*person, fact*) я знако́м/был знако́м с +*instr.*

acquaintance [ə'kweıntəns] *n* (*person*) знако́мый(-ая) *m(f) adj;* (*with person, subject*) знако́мство; **to make sb's ~** познако́миться* (*perf*) с кем-н.

acquiesce [ækwı'ɛs] *vi:* **to ~ to** соглаша́ться (согласи́ться* *perf*) на +*acc.*

acquire [ə'kwaıəʳ] *vt* приобрета́ть (приобрести́* *perf*).

acquired [ə'kwaıəd] *adj* приобретённый; **it's an ~ taste** к э́тому на́до привы́кнуть.

acquisition [ækwı'zıʃən] *n* приобрете́ние.

acquisitive [ə'kwızıtıv] *adj* (*greedy*) приобрета́тельский.

acquit [ə'kwıt] *vt* (*LAW*) опра́вдывать (оправда́ть *perf*); **to ~ o.s. well** хорошо́ проявля́ть (прояви́ть* *perf*) себя́.

acquittal [ə'kwıtl] *n* оправда́ние.

acre ['eıkəʳ] *n* акр.

acreage ['eıkərıdʒ] *n* пло́щадь* *f* в а́крах.

acrid ['ækrıd] *adj* е́дкий* (е́док).

acrimonious [ækrı'məunıəs] *adj* язви́тельный* (язви́телен).

acrimony ['ækrımənı] *n* язви́тельность *f.*

acrobat ['ækrəbæt] *n* акроба́т.

acrobatic [ækrə'bætık] *adj* (*movement, display*) акробати́ческий; (*person*) ги́бкий* (ги́бок) и ло́вкий* (ло́вок).

acrobatics [ækrə'bætıks] *npl* акроба́тика *fsg.*

acronym ['ækrənım] *n* бу́квенная аббревиату́ра.

Acropolis [ə'krɔpəlıs] *n:* **the ~** (*GEO*) Акро́поль *m.*

across [ə'krɔs] *prep* (*from one side to the other of*) че́рез +*acc;* (*on the other side of*) на друго́й стороне́ +*gen;* (*crosswise over*) поперёк +*gen* ♦ *adv* на ту́ ог другу́ю сто́рону; (*measurement: width*) ширино́й; **to walk ~ the road** переходи́ть* (перейти́* *perf*) доро́гу; **to take sb ~ the road** переводи́ть* (перевести́* *perf*) кого́-н че́рез доро́гу; **a road ~ the wood** доро́га че́рез лес; **the lake is 12 km ~** ширина́ о́зера – 12 км; **~ from** напро́тив +*gen;* **to get sth ~ (to sb)** втолко́вывать (втолкова́ть *perf*) что-н (кому́-н).

acrylic [ə'krılık] *adj* акри́ловый ♦ *n* акри́л; **~s** *npl* (*ART*) акри́ловые кра́ски *fpl.*

ACT *n abbr* = **American College Test.**

act [ækt] *n* (*action, also LAW*) акт; (*deed*) посту́пок*; (*of play*) де́йствие, акт; (*in music-hall etc*) но́мер* ♦ *vi* (*do sth, take action*) де́йствовать* (*impf*); (*behave*) вести́* (*impf*) себя́; (*have effect*) де́йствовать (поде́йствовать *perf*); (*THEAT*) игра́ть (сыгра́ть *perf*); (*pretend*) разы́грывать (разыгра́ть *perf*) ♦ *vt* (*part*) игра́ть (сыгра́ть *perf*); **it's only an ~** э́то всего́ лишь игра́; **~ of God** (*LAW*) стихи́йное бе́дствие; **in the ~ of в** проце́ссе +*gen;* **to catch sb in the ~** пойма́ть (*perf*) кого́-н на ме́сте преступле́ния; **to ~ as** де́йствовать* (*impf*) в ка́честве +*gen;* **it ~s as a deterrent** э́то де́йствует в ка́честве сде́рживающей си́лы; **~ing in my capacity as chairman, I ...** выступа́я в ка́честве председа́теля, я ...; **to ~ the fool** (*BRIT*) валя́ть (сваля́ть *perf*) дурака́

▶ **act on** *vt:* **to ~ on sth** де́йствовать (поде́йствовать *perf*) на что-н

▶ **act out** *vt* (*event*) разы́грывать (разыгра́ть *perf*); (*fantasies*) выплёскивать (вы́плеснуть *perf*).

acting ['æktıŋ] *adj:* **~ manager/director** исполня́ющий обя́занности управля́ющего/дире́ктора ♦ *n* (*activity, profession*) актёрская профе́ссия.

action ['ækʃən] *n* (*deed*) де́йствие; (*motion*) движе́ние; (*MIL*) вое́нные де́йствия *ntpl;* (*LAW*) иск; **to bring an ~ against sb** (*LAW*) предъявля́ть (предъяви́ть* *perf*) иск кому́-н; **he was killed in ~** (*MIL*) он был уби́т в бою́; **she/the machine was out of ~ for a week** она́/маши́на вы́шла из стро́я на неде́лю; **to take ~** принима́ть (приня́ть* *perf*) ме́ры; **to put a plan into ~** реализо́вывать (реализова́ть *perf*) план.

action replay *n* (*TV*) повторе́ние ка́дра (*ча́сто* заме́дленное).

activate ['æktıveıt] *vt* (*mechanism*) приводи́ть* (привести́* *perf*) в де́йствие; (*CHEM*) активи́ровать (*impf/perf*); (*PHYS*) де́лать (сде́лать *perf*) радиоакти́вным.

active ['æktıv] *adj* (*person, life*) акти́вный* (акти́вен); (*volcano*) де́йствующий*; **to play an ~ part in** игра́ть (сыгра́ть *perf*) акти́вную роль в +*prp.*

active duty *n* (*US: MIL*) де́йствующая а́рмия.

actively ['æktıvlı] *adv* (*participate*) акти́вно; (*discourage, dislike*) си́льно.

active partner *n* (*COMM*) гла́вный партнёр с ограни́ченной (иму́щественной) отве́тственностью.

active service *n* (*BRIT: MIL*) де́йствующая а́рмия.

active suspension *n* автомати́ческая систе́ма амортиза́ции го́ночного автомоби́ля, реаги́рующая на ка́чество пове́рхности.

activist ['æktıvıst] *n* активи́ст(ка).

activity [æk'tıvıtı] *n* (*being active*) акти́вность *f;* (*action*) де́ятельность *f;* (*pastime, pursuit*) заня́тие.

actor ['æktəʳ] *n* актёр.

actress ['æktrıs] *n* актри́са.

actual ['æktjuəl] *adj* (*real*) действи́тельный* (действи́телен); (*emphatic use*): **the ~ work hasn't begun yet** сама́ рабо́та ещё не начала́сь.

actually ['æktjuəlı] *adv* (*really*) действи́тельно; (*in fact*) факти́чески, на са́мом де́ле; (*even*) да́же.

actuary ['æktjuərɪ] *n* (COMM) актуа́рий.

actuate ['æktjueɪt] *vt* приводи́ть* (привести́* *perf*) в де́йствие.

acuity [ə'kju:ɪtɪ] *n* острота́.

acumen ['ækjumən] *n* сообрази́тельность *f*: **business** ~ делова́я хва́тка*.

acupuncture ['ækjupʌŋktʃə'] *n* иглоука́лывание, акупункту́ра.

acute [ə'kju:t] *adj* (*illness, mind, angle*) о́стрый* (остр); (*anxiety*) си́льный*; (*person, observer*) проница́тельный* (проница́телен); (*LING*): ~ **accent** аку́т.

AD *adv abbr* (= *Anno Domini*) н.э.= *на́шей э́ры* ♦ *n abbr* (US: MIL) = **active duty**.

ad [æd] *n abbr* (*inf*) = **advertisement**.

adage ['ædɪdʒ] *n* погово́рка*.

adamant ['ædəmənt] *adj* непрекло́нный* (непрекло́нен).

Adam's apple ['ædəmz-] *n* ада́мово я́блоко*, кады́к*.

adapt [ə'dæpt] *vt* (*alter, change*) приспоса́бливать {or} приспособля́ть (приспосо́бить* *perf*) ♦ *vi*: **to** ~ **(to)** приспоса́бливаться *or* приспособля́ться (приспосо́биться* *perf*) *or* адапти́роваться (*impf/perf*) (к +*dat*).

adaptability [ədæptə'bɪlɪtɪ] *n* приспособля́емость *f*.

adaptable [ə'dæptəbl] *adj* (*device*) приспособля́емый; (*person*) легко́ приспоса́бливающийся.

adaptation [ædæp'teɪʃən] *n* (*of story, novel etc*) переложе́ние; (*of machine, equipment etc*) приспособле́ние.

adapter [ə'dæptə'] *n* (ELEC) ада́птер, переходни́к.

adaptor [ə'dæptə'] *n* = **adapter**.

ADC *n abbr* (MIL) = **aide-de-camp**; (US: = *Aid to Dependent Children*) по́мощь нужда́ющимся де́тям.

add [æd] *vt* (*to a collection etc*) прибавля́ть (приба́вить* *perf*); (*comment etc*) добавля́ть (доба́вить* *perf*); (*figures: also:* ~ **up**) скла́дывать (сложи́ть* *perf*), сумми́ровать (*impf/perf*) ♦ *vi*: **to** ~ **to** (*increase*) увели́чивать (увели́чить *perf*)

▶ **add on** *vt*: ~ **on (to)** прибавля́ть (приба́вить* *perf*) (к +*dat*)

▶ **add up** *vt* скла́дывать (сложи́ть *perf*) в +*acc* ♦ *vi* (*fig*): **it doesn't** ~ **up** концы́ не схо́дятся; **it doesn't** ~ **up to much** (*fig*) э́то не впечатля́ет.

addenda [ə'dɛndə] *npl of* **addendum**.

addendum [ə'dɛndəm] (*pl* **addenda**) *n* приложе́ние.

adder ['ædə'] *n* гадю́ка.

addict ['ædɪkt] *n* (*also:* **drug** ~) наркома́н; (*enthusiast*) фана́тик.

addicted [ə'dɪktɪd] *adj*: **to be** ~ **to** (*drugs, drink etc*) пристрасти́ться* (*perf*) к +*dat*; (*fig*): **he's** ~ **to football/golf** он зая́длый люби́тель футбо́ла/го́льфа.

addiction [ə'dɪkʃən] *n* пристра́стие; **drug** ~ наркома́ния.

addictive [ə'dɪktɪv] *adj* (*drug*) вызыва́ющий* привыка́ние; (*activity*) захва́тывающий*.

adding machine ['ædɪŋ-] *n* счётная маши́на.

Addis Ababa ['ædɪs'æbəbə] *n* (GEO) Аддис-Абе́ба *f*.

addition [ə'dɪʃən] *n* (MATH) сложе́ние; (*thing added*) добавле́ние; (*to collection*) пополне́ние; **in** ~ вдоба́вок; **in** ~ **to** в дополне́ние к +*dat*.

additional [ə'dɪʃənl] *adj* дополни́тельный*.

additive ['ædɪtɪv] *n* доба́вка*.

addled ['ædld] *adj* (BRIT: *egg*) ту́хлый*; **his brain is** ~ он сбит с то́лку.

address [ə'drɛs] *n* а́дрес*; (*speech*) речь* *f* ♦ *vt* (*letter, parcel*) адресова́ть (*impf/perf*); (*person, problem*) обраща́ться (обрати́ться* *perf*) к +*dat*; **form of** ~ фо́рма обраще́ния; **absolute/relative** ~ (COMPUT) абсолю́тный/относи́тельный а́дрес; **to** ~ **o.s. to** обраща́ться (обрати́ться* *perf*) к +*dat*.

address book *n* записна́я кни́жка.

addressee [ædrɛ'si:] *n* адреса́т.

Aden ['eɪdən] *n*: **Gulf of** ~ А́денский зали́в.

adenoids ['ædɪnɔɪdz] *npl* адено́иды *mpl*.

adept ['ædɛpt] *adj*: ~ **at** иску́сный* (иску́сен) в +*prp*.

adequacy ['ædɪkwəsɪ] *n* (*in quantity*) доста́точность *f*; (*in quality*) адеква́тность *f*.

adequate ['ædɪkwɪt] *adj* (*sufficient*) доста́точный (доста́точен); (*satisfactory*) удовлетвори́тельный (удовлетвори́телен), адеква́тный* (адеква́тен).

adequately ['ædɪkwɪtlɪ] *adv* адеква́тно.

adhere [əd'hɪə'] *vi*: **to** ~ **to** прилипа́ть (прили́пнуть* *perf*) к +*dat*; (*fig*) приде́рживаться (*impf*) +*gen*.

adhesion [əd'hi:ʒən] *n* прилипа́ние; (*fig*) приве́рженность *f*.

adhesive [əd'hi:zɪv] *adj* кле́йкий* ♦ *n* клей*.

adhesive tape *n* (BRIT) кле́йкая ле́нта; (US: MED) лейкопла́стырь *m*.

ad hoc [æd'hɔk] *adj* (*decision*) момента́льный; (*committee*) со́зданный на ме́сте ♦ *adv* (*decide, appoint*) тут же.

ad infinitum ['ædɪnfɪ'naɪtəm] *adv* до бесконе́чности.

adjacent [ə'dʒeɪsənt] *adj*: ~ **(to)** сме́жный* (сме́жен) (с +*instr*).

adjective ['ædʒɛktɪv] *n* прилага́тельное *nt adj*.

adjoining [ə'dʒɔɪnɪŋ] *adj* (*room*) сме́жный.

adjourn [ə'dʒə:n] *vt* откла́дывать (отложи́ть*

---

* marks translations which have irregular inflections The Russian-English side of the dictionary gives inflectional information

perf) ◆ *vi*: **the meeting ~ed** собра́ние бы́ло
отло́жено; **to ~ a meeting till the following
week** отложи́ть* *(perf)* заседа́ние до
сле́дующей неде́ли; **they ~ed to the
restaurant** *(BRIT: inf)* они́ перебра́лись в
рестора́н.

adjournment [ə'dʒɜ:nmənt] *n (period)*
переры́в.

Adjt. *abbr (MIL)* = **adjutant**.

adjudicate [ə'dʒu:dɪkeɪt] *vt (claim)*
рассма́тривать (рассмотре́ть* *perf)*;
(competition) суди́ть* *(impf)* ◆ *vi* суди́ть* *(impf)*.

adjudication [ədʒu:dɪ'keɪʃən] *n (LAW)* реше́ние
суда́.

adjudicator [ə'dʒu:dɪkeɪtə'] *n* судья́* *m/f*.

adjust [ə'dʒʌst] *vt (plans, views)*
приспоса́бливать (приспосо́бить* *perf)*;
(clothing) поправля́ть (попра́вить* *perf)*;
(mechanism) регули́ровать
(отрегули́ровать* *perf)* ◆ *vi*: **to ~ (to)**
приспоса́бливаться (приспосо́биться* *perf)*
(к +*dat)*.

adjustable [ə'dʒʌstəbl] *adj* регули́руемый.

adjuster [ə'dʒʌstə'] *n see* **loss**.

adjustment [ə'dʒʌstmənt] *n (to surroundings)*
адапта́ция; *(of prices, wages)*
регули́рование; **to make ~s** to вноси́ть*
(внести́* *perf)* измене́ния в +*acc*.

adjutant ['ædʒətənt] *n* адъюта́нт.

ad-lib [æd'lɪb] *vti* импровизи́ровать
(сымпровизи́ровать* *perf)* ◆ *adv*: **ad lib** *(speak)*
экспро́мтом.

adman ['ædmæn] *irreg n (inf)* реклами́ст.

admin ['ædmɪn] *n abbr (inf)* = **administration**.

administer [əd'mɪnɪstə'] *vt (country,
department)* управля́ть *(impf)* +*instr*,
руководи́ть* *(impf)* +*instr*; *(justice)*
отправля́ть *(impf)*; *(test)* проводи́ть*
(провести́* *perf)*; *(drug)* вводи́ть* (ввести́*
perf).

administration [ədmɪnɪs'treɪʃən] *n
(management)* администра́ция; **the A~** *(US)*
прави́тельство; **the Clinton A~**
администра́ция Кли́нтона.

administrative [əd'mɪnɪstrətɪv] *adj* админи-
страти́вный.

administrator [əd'mɪnɪstreɪtə'] *n* админи-
стра́тор.

admirable ['ædmərəbl] *adj (quality)*
восхити́тельный* (восхити́телен); *(action)*
замеча́тельный* (замеча́телен).

admiral ['ædmərəl] *n* адмира́л.

Admiralty ['ædmərəltɪ] *n (BRIT)*: **the ~** *(also: the
~ Board)* ≈ адмиралте́йство *(вое́нно-морско́е
ве́домство)*.

admiration [ædmə'reɪʃən] *n* восхище́ние; **I have
great ~ for her** она́ вызыва́ет у меня́
большо́е восхище́ние.

admire [əd'maɪə'] *vt (respect, appreciate)*
восхища́ться (восхити́ться *perf)* +*instr*; *(gaze
at)* любова́ться *(impf)* +*instr*.

admirer [əd'maɪərə'] *n* покло́нник(-ица).

admiring [əd'maɪərɪŋ] *adj* восхищённый
(восхищён), восто́рженный* (восто́ржен).

admissible [əd'mɪsəbl] *adj* прие́млемый
(прие́млем), допусти́мый* (допусти́м); **it is
~ evidence** э́то мо́жет быть* при́нято в
ка́честве доказа́тельства.

admission [əd'mɪʃən] *n (admittance)* до́пуск;
(entry fee) входна́я пла́та; *(confession)*
призна́ние; **to gain ~ to** *(official permission)*
получа́ть (получи́ть* *perf)* до́пуск в/на +*acc*;
"admission free", **"free ~"** "вход
свобо́дный"; **by his own ~** по его́
со́бственному призна́нию.

admit [əd'mɪt] *vt (confess, accept)* признава́ть*
(призна́ть* *perf)*; *(permit to enter)* впуска́ть
(впусти́ть* *perf)*; *(to club, organization)*
принима́ть (приня́ть* *perf)*; *(to hospital)*
госпитализи́ровать *(impf/perf)*; **"children not
~ted"** "де́тям вход воспрещён"; **this ticket
~s two** э́тот биле́т на́ два лица́

▶ **admit of** *vt fus (allow)* допуска́ть *(impf)*

▶ **admit to** *vt fus (murder etc)* сознава́ться*
(созна́ться *perf)* в +*prp*.

admittance [əd'mɪtəns] *n* до́пуск; **no ~** вход
воспрещён.

admittedly [əd'mɪtɪdlɪ] *adv*: **~ it is not easy**
призна́ться, э́то не легко́.

admonish [əd'mɒnɪʃ] *vt* де́лать (сде́лать *perf)*
внуше́ние +*dat*; *(LAW)* де́лать (сде́лать *perf)*
предупрежде́ние +*dat*.

ad nauseam [æd'nɔ:sɪæm] *adv* бесконе́чно.

ado [ə'du:] *n*: **without (any) more ~** без
дальне́йших церемо́ний.

adolescence [ædəu'lɛsns] *n* подро́стковый
во́зраст.

adolescent [ædəu'lɛsnt] *adj* подро́стковый ◆ *n*
подро́сток*.

adopt [ə'dɒpt] *vt (son)* усыновля́ть
(усынови́ть* *perf)*; *(daughter)* удочеря́ть
(удочери́ть* *perf)*; *(policy)* приде́рживаться
(impf) +*gen*; **to ~ sb as a candidate** выдвига́ть
(вы́двинуть *perf)* кого́-н в кандида́ты.

adopted [ə'dɒptɪd] *adj (child)* приёмный.

adoption [ə'dɒpʃən] *n (see vb)* усыновле́ние;
удочере́ние; приня́тие.

adoptive [ə'dɒptɪv] *adj (parent)* приёмный.

adorable [ə'dɔ:rəbl] *adj* преле́стный*
(преле́стен).

adoration [ædə'reɪʃən] *n (of person)* обожа́ние.

adore [ə'dɔ:'] *vt* обожа́ть *(impf)*.

adoring [ə'dɔ:rɪŋ] *adj* обожа́ющий.

adoringly [ə'dɔ:rɪŋlɪ] *adv* с обожа́нием.

adorn [ə'dɔ:n] *vt* украша́ть (укра́сить* *perf)*.

adornment [ə'dɔ:nmənt] *n* украше́ние.

ADP *n abbr* = **automatic data processing**.

adrenalin [ə'drɛnəlɪn] *n* адренали́н; **to get the
~ going** дава́ть* (дать* *perf)* заря́д эне́ргии.

Adriatic [eɪdrɪ'ætɪk] *n*: **the ~** Адриа́тика.

adrift [ə'drɪft] *adv (NAUT)*: **to be ~** дрейфова́ть
(impf); *(fig)* плыть* *(impf)* по тече́нию; **to go ~**

(*plans etc*) расстра́иваться (расстро́иться *perf*); **to come ~** (*boat*) лечь* *(perf)* в дрейф; (*fastening*) расслабля́ться (рассла́биться *perf*).

adroit [əˈdrɔɪt] *adj* ло́вкий* (ло́вок).

adroitly [əˈdrɔɪtlɪ] *adv* ло́вко.

ADT *abbr* (*US*) = Atlantic Daylight Time.

adulation [ædjuˈleɪʃən] *n* обожа́ние.

adult [ˈædʌlt] *n* взро́слый(-ая) *m adj* ♦ *adj* (*grown-up*) взро́слый; (*for adults*) для взро́слых.

adult education *n* образова́ние для взро́слых.

adulterate [əˈdʌltəreɪt] *vt* (*food, drink: with additives*) по́ртить* (испо́ртить* *perf*) (*доба́вками*); (: *with water*) разбавля́ть (разба́вить* *perf*).

adulterer [əˈdʌltərə*] *n* неве́рный муж.

adulteress [əˈdʌltərɪs] *n* неве́рная жена́.

adultery [əˈdʌltərɪ] *n* супру́жеская неве́рность *f*.

adulthood [ˈædʌlthud] *n* зре́лый во́зраст.

advance [ədˈvɑːns] *n* (*progress*) успе́х; (*MIL*) наступле́ние; (*movement*) продвиже́ние; (*money*) ава́нс ♦ *adj* (*booking*) предвари́тельный ♦ *vt* (*theory, idea*) выдвига́ть (вы́двинуть *perf*) ♦ *vi* (*move forward: also fig*) продвига́ться (продви́нуться *perf*) вперёд; (*MIL*) наступа́ть (*impf*); **in ~** предвари́тельно, зара́нее; **to make ~s (to sb)** заи́грывать (*impf*) (с кем-н); **to give sb ~ notice** *or* **~ warning (of sth)** предупрежда́ть (предупреди́ть* *perf*) кого́-н зара́нее (о чём-н); **to ~ sb money** плати́ть* (заплати́ть* *perf*) кому́-н ава́нсом; **we ~d 20 km** мы продви́нулись на 20 кило ме́тров.

advanced [ədˈvɑːnst] *adj* (*studies, course*) для продви́нутого у́ровня; (*child, country*) разви́то́й* (ра́звит); (*ideas, views*) прогресси́вный* (прогресси́вен); **~ maths** вы́сшая матема́тика; **a man of ~ years** *or* **~ in years** челове́к прекло́нного во́зраста.

advancement [ədˈvɑːnsmənt] *n* (*of science*) прогре́сс; (*in job, rank*) продвиже́ние (по слу́жбе).

advancing [ədˈvɑːnsɪŋ] *adj* надвига́ющийся.

advantage [ədˈvɑːntɪdʒ] *n* преиму́щество; (*TENNIS*) "бо́льше"; **to take ~ of** (*person*) испо́льзовать (*perf*); (*sb's hospitality*) злоупотребля́ть (злоупотреби́ть* *perf*) +*instr*; (*opportunity*) воспо́льзоваться (*perf*) +*instr*; **to our/his ~** в на́ших/его́ интере́сах; **to turn sth to one's ~** обраща́ть (обрати́ть* *perf*) что-н в свою́ по́льзу.

advantageous [ædvənˈteɪdʒəs] *adj* (*position, situation*) вы́годный* (вы́годен); **it's ~ to us** нам э́то вы́годно.

advent [ˈædvənt] *n* появле́ние; (*REL*): **A~** *ме́сяц до Рождества́*.

Advent calendar *n* календа́рь *с две́рцами на ка́ждый день ме́сяца до Рождества́.*

adventure [ədˈvɛntʃə*] *n* (*exciting event*) приключе́ние; **to look for ~** иска́ть* (*impf*) приключе́ний.

adventure playground *n* де́тский городо́к.

adventurous [ədˈvɛntʃərəs] *adj* (*action*) риско́ванный (риско́ван); (*person*) сме́лый (смел); **an ~ life** жизнь по́лная приключе́ний.

adverb [ˈædvəːb] *n* наре́чие.

adversarial [ædvəˈsɛərɪəl] *adj* противо бо́рствующий, вражде́бный.

adversary [ˈædvəsərɪ] *n* проти́вник(-ница).

adverse [ˈædvəːs] *adj* неблагоприя́тный; **in ~ circumstances** при неблагоприя́тных обстоя́тельствах.

adversity [ədˈvəːsɪtɪ] *n* бе́дствие, невзго́да.

advert [ˈædvəːt] *n abbr* (*BRIT*) = **advertisement**.

advertise [ˈædvətaɪz] *vti* реклами́ровать (*impf*); **to ~ on television/in a newspaper** дава́ть* (дать* *perf*) объявле́ние по телеви́дению/в газе́ту; **to ~ a job** объявля́ть (объяви́ть* *perf*) ко́нкурс на ме́сто; **to ~ for staff/ accommodation** дава́ть* (дать* *perf*) объявле́ние, что тре́буются рабо́тники/ тре́буется жильё.

advertisement [ədˈvəːtɪsmənt] *n* рекла́ма; (*in classified ads*) объявле́ние.

advertiser [ˈædvətaɪzə*] *n* (*professional*) реклами́ст(ка); (*in newspaper, on television etc*) рекламода́тель *m*.

advertising [ˈædvətaɪzɪŋ] *n* рекла́ма.

advertising agency *n* рекла́мное аге́нтство.

advertising campaign *n* рекла́мная кампа́ния.

advice [ədˈvaɪs] *n* сове́т; (*notification*) уведомле́ние; **a piece of ~** сове́т; **to ask sb for ~** (*friend*) сове́товаться (посове́товаться *perf*) с кем-н; (*professional*) обраща́ться (обрати́ться* *perf*) (за сове́том) к кому́-н; **to take legal ~** обраща́ться (обрати́ться* *perf*) (за сове́том) к юри́сту.

advice note *n* (*BRIT*) извеще́ние.

advisable [ədˈvaɪzəbl] *adj* целесообра́зный* (целесообра́зен).

advise [ədˈvaɪz] *vt* сове́товать (посове́товать *perf*) +*dat*; (*professionally*) консульти́ровать (проконсульти́ровать *perf*) +*gen*; (*inform*): **to ~ sb of sth** извеща́ть (извести́ть* *perf*) кого́-н о чём-н; **to ~ (sb) against doing** отсове́товать (*perf*) (кому́-н) +*impf infin*; **you would be well-/ill-~d to go** Вам бы сле́довало пойти́/ не сле́довало ходи́ть ....

advisedly [ədˈvaɪzɪdlɪ] *adv* наме́ренно.

adviser [ədˈvaɪzə*] *n* сове́тник, консульта́нт;

---

* marks translations which have irregular inflections. The Russian-English side of the dictionary gives inflectional information.

legal ~ юрисконсульт.
advisor [əd'vaizə⁷] *n* = **adviser**.
advisory [əd'vaizəri] *adj* (*body, role*)
консультативный; **in an** ~ **capacity** в
качестве советника *or* консультанта.
advocate [*vb* 'ædvəkeit, *n* 'ædvəkit] *vt*
выступать (*impf*) за +*acc* ♦ *n* (*LAW*) защитник,
адвокат; (*supporter*): ~ **of** сторонник(-ица)
+*gen*.
advt. *abbr* = **advertisement**.
AEA *n abbr* (*BRIT: = Atomic Energy Authority*)
Управление атомной энергии.
AEC *n abbr* (*US: = Atomic Energy Commission*)
Комиссия по атомной энергии.
AEEU *n abbr* (*BRIT*) = *Amalgamated Engineering
and Electrical Union*.
Aegean [i:'dʒi:ən] *n*: **the** ~ Эгейское море.
aegis ['i:dʒis] *n*: **under the** ~ **of** под
эгидой +*gen*.
aeon ['i:ən] *n*: **for** ~**s** целую вечность.
aerial ['ɛəriəl] *n* антенна ♦ *adj* воздушный*; ~
photography аэрофотосъёмка.
aerobatics ['ɛərəu'bætiks] *npl* высший*
пилотаж *msg*.
aerobics [ɛə'rəubiks] *n* аэробика.
aerodrome ['ɛərədrəum] *n* (*BRIT*) аэродром.
aerodynamic ['ɛərəudai'næmik] *adj*
аэродинамический*.
aeronautics [ɛərə'nɔ:tiks] *n* аэронавтика.
aeroplane ['ɛərəplein] *n* (*BRIT*) самолёт.
aerosol ['ɛərəsɔl] *n* аэрозоль *m*.
aerospace industry ['ɛərəuspeis-] *n*
аэро-космическая промышленность *f*.
aesthetic [i:s'θɛtik] *adj* эстетический*.
aesthetically [i:s'θɛtikli] *adv* эстетически.
afar [ə'fɑ:⁷] *adv*: **from** ~ издалека.
AFB *n abbr* (*US*) = *Air Force Base*.
AFDC *n abbr* (*US*) = *Aid to Families with
Dependent Children*.
affable ['æfəbl] *adj* (*person*) добродушный*
(добродушен); (*behaviour*)
доброжелательный* (доброжелателен).
affair [ə'fɛə⁷] *n* (*matter*) дело*; (*also: love* ~)
роман; ~**s** *npl* (*business*) дела* *ntpl*.
affect [ə'fɛkt] *vt* (*influence*) действовать
(подействовать *perf*) на +*acc*, влиять
(повлиять *perf*) на +*acc*; (*afflict*) поражать
(поразить* *perf*); (*move deeply*) трогать
(тронуть *perf*); (*feign*) подделывать
(подделать *perf*); **to** ~ **an American accent**
говорить (*impf*) с деланным американским
акцентом.
affectation [æfɛk'teiʃən] *n* (*in manner, speech*)
наигранность *f*.
affected [ə'fɛktid] *adj* (*person*) претенциозный*
(претенциозен); (*manner*) деланный.
affection [ə'fɛkʃən] *n* привязанность *f*.
affectionate [ə'fɛkʃənit] *adj* нежный*.
affectionately [ə'fɛkʃənitli] *adv* нежно.
affidavit [æfi'deivit] *n* (*LAW*) письменное
свидетельство, аффидавит.
affiliated [ə'filieitid] *adj* (*company*) дочерний*;

to be ~ **to** (*body*) являться (*impf*) филиалом
+*gen*.
affinity [ə'finiti] *n*: **to have an** ~ **with** (*bond*)
ощущать (ощутить* *perf*) близость с +*instr*;
(*resemblance*) обнаруживать (обнаружить
perf) родство с +*instr*.
affirm [ə'fə:m] *vt* утверждать (утвердить* *perf*).
affirmation [æfə'meiʃən] *n* (*of facts*)
подтверждение; (*of ideas*) утверждение.
affirmative [ə'fə:mətiv] *adj* утвердительный*
♦ *n*: **in the** ~ утвердительно.
affix [ə'fiks] *vt* прикреплять (прикрепить* *perf*).
afflict [ə'flikt] *vt* постигать (постичь* *perf*); **to
be** ~**ed by** (*illness*) страдать (*impf*) от +*gen*.
affliction [ə'flikʃən] *n* несчастье.
affluence ['æfluəns] *n* благосостояние.
affluent ['æfluənt] *adj* благополучный*
(благополучен); **the** ~ **society** общество
благосостояния.
afford [ə'fɔ:d] *vt* позволять (*perf*) себе;
(*provide*) предоставлять (предоставить*
perf); **I can't** ~ **it** мне это не по карману; **can
we** ~ **a car?** мы можем себе позволить
купить машину?; **I can't** ~ **the time** мне
время не позволяет.
affordable [ə'fɔ:dəbl] *adj* доступный по цене.
affray [ə'frei] *n* (*BRIT: LAW*) драка в
общественном месте.
affront [ə'frʌnt] *n* оскорбление.
affronted [ə'frʌntid] *adj* оскорблённый
(оскорблён).
Afghan ['æfgæn] *adj* афганский* ♦ *n*
афганец*(-нка).
Afghanistan [æf'gænistæn] *n* Афганистан.
afield [ə'fi:ld] *adv*: **far** ~ вдалеке, вдали; **from
far** ~ издалека.
AFL-CIO *n abbr* = *American Federation of Labor
and Congress of Industrial Organizations*.
afloat [ə'fləut] *adv* (*floating*) на плаву; **to stay** ~
(*fig*) держаться (*impf*) на поверхности; **to
keep a business** ~ не давать (дать* *perf*)
потонуть предприятию.
afoot [ə'fut] *adv*: **there is something** ~ что-то
затевается.
aforementioned [ə'fɔ:mɛnʃənd] *adj*
вышеупомянутый.
aforesaid [ə'fɔ:sɛd] *adj* вышеупомянутый.
afraid [ə'freid] *adj* (*frightened*) испуганный
(испуган); **to be** ~ **of sth/sb/of doing** бояться*
(*impf*) чего-н/кого-н/+*infin*; **to be** ~ **to** бояться
(побояться *perf*) +*infin*; **I am** ~ **that** (*apology*)
боюсь, что; **I am** ~ **that I'll be late** боюсь, что
я опоздаю; **I am** ~ **so/not** боюсь, что да/нет.
afresh [ə'frɛʃ] *adv* заново.
Africa ['æfrikə] *n* Африка.
African ['æfrikən] *adj* африканский* ♦ *n*
африканец*(-нка).
Afrikaans [æfri'kɑ:ns] *n* (*язык*) африкаанс.
Afrikaner [æfri'kɑ:nə⁷] *n* африканер (*уроженец
Южной Африки голландского
происхождения*).

Afro-American ['æfrəuə'mɛrɪkən] *adj* афро-американский*.

Afro-Caribbean ['æfrəkærɪ'bi:ən] *adj* афро-карибский.

AFT *n abbr* (*US*) = *American Federation of Teachers.*

after ['ɑ:ftə'] *prep* (*time*) после +*gen*, спустя +*acc*; (*place, order*) за +*instr*; (*style, technique*) в стиле +*gen* ♦ *adv* потом, после ♦ *conj* после того как; ~ **dinner** после обеда; **the day ~ tomorrow** послезавтра; ~ **three years they divorced** спустя три года они развелись; **what/who are you ~?** что/кто Вам нужно/нужен?; **the police are ~ him** его разыскивает полиция; **to name sb ~ sb** называть (назвать* *perf*) кого-н в честь кого-н; **it's twenty ~ eight** (*US*) сейчас двадцать минут девятого; **to ask ~ sb** справляться (справиться* *perf*) о ком-н; ~ **all** в конце концов; ~ **you!** после Вас!; ~ **he left** после того, как он ушёл; ~ **having done this** сделав это.

afterbirth ['ɑ:ftəbə:θ] *n* послед.

aftercare ['ɑ:ftəkɛə'] *n* (*BRIT: MED*) уход за выздоравливающим.

after-effects ['ɑ:ftərɪfɛkts] *npl* последствия *ntpl*.

afterlife ['ɑ:ftəlaɪf] *n* загробная жизнь *f*.

aftermath ['ɑ:ftəmɑ:θ] *n* последствия *ntpl*; **in the ~ of** после +*gen*.

afternoon ['ɑ:ftə'nu:n] *n* вторая половина дня; **in the ~** днём; **good ~!** (*goodbye*) до свидания!; (*hello*) добрый день!

afters ['ɑ:ftəz] *n* (*inf: dessert*): **for ~** на третье *or* десерт.

after-sales service [ɑ:ftə'seɪlz-] *n* (*BRIT*) гарантированное техобслуживание.

after-shave (lotion) ['ɑ:ftəʃeɪv-] *n* одеколон после бритья.

aftershock ['ɑ:ftəʃɔk] *n* толчок* (*после основного землетрясения*).

aftertaste ['ɑ:ftəteɪst] *n* привкус.

afterthought ['ɑ:ftəθɔ:t] *n*: **as an ~** машинально.

afterward ['ɑ:ftəwəd] *adv* (*US*) = **afterwards.**

afterwards ['ɑ:ftəwədz] (*US* **afterward**) *adv* позже, потом.

again [ə'gɛn] *adv* (*once more*) ещё раз, снова; (*repeatedly*) опять; **I won't see him/go there ~** я больше не увижу его/пойду туда; **to do sth ~** делать (сделать *perf*) что-н ещё раз *or* снова; **to begin ~** начать* (*perf*) сначала; **to see ~** смотреть* (посмотреть* *perf*) *or* видеть* (увидеть* *perf*) ещё раз; **he opened the door ~** он опять *or* снова открыл дверь; ~ **and** снова и снова; **now and ~** время от времени.

against [ə'gɛnst] *prep* (*lean*) к +*dat*; (*hit, rub*) о +*acc*; (*standing*) у +*gen*; (*in opposition to*)

против +*gen*; (*at odds with*) вопреки +*dat*; (*compared to*) по сравнению с +*instr*; ~ **a blue background** на синем фоне; (**as**) ~ в сравнении с +*instr*.

age [eɪdʒ] *n* (*of person*) возраст; (*period in history*) век* ♦ *vi* (*person*) стареть (постареть *perf*) ♦ *vt* (*subj: hairstyle, dress*) старить (*impf*); **what ~ is he?** сколько ему лет?; **he is 20 years of ~** ему двадцать лет; **under ~** несовершеннолетний*; **to come of ~** достигать (достичь* *perf*) совершеннолетия; **it's been ~s since I saw you** я не видел Вас целую вечность.

aged[1] ['eɪdʒd] *adj*: **a boy ~ ten** мальчик десяти лет.

aged[2] ['eɪdʒɪd] *npl*: **the ~** престарелые *pl adj*.

age group *n* возрастная группа; **the forty to fifty ~ ~** люди возрастом от сорока до пятидесяти лет.

ageing ['eɪdʒɪŋ] *adj* стареющий ♦ *n* старение.

ageless ['eɪdʒlɪs] *adj* (*building, ritual*) вечный* (вечен).

age limit *n* возрастной предел.

agency ['eɪdʒənsɪ] *n* (*COMM*) агентство, бюро *nt ind*; (*government body*) управление; **through** *or* **by the ~ of** при посредстве +*gen*.

agenda [ə'dʒɛndə] *n* (*of meeting*) повестка* (дня); **on the ~** на повестке (дня).

agent ['eɪdʒənt] *n* (*representative, spy*) агент; (*COMM*) посредник; (*CHEM*) реактив; (*fig*) фактор.

aggravate ['ægrəveɪt] *vt* (*situation*) усугублять (усугубить* *perf*); (*person*) раздражать (раздражить *perf*).

aggravating ['ægrəveɪtɪŋ] *adj*: **his behaviour is ~** его поведение раздражает меня.

aggravation [ægrə'veɪʃən] *n* (*see vt*) усугубление; раздражение.

aggregate ['ægrɪgɪt] *n* (*total*) совокупность *f* ♦ *vt* группировать (сгруппировать *perf*) в +*acc*.

aggression [ə'grɛʃən] *n* агрессия.

aggressive [ə'grɛsɪv] *adj* (*belligerent*) агрессивный* (агрессивен); (*assertive*) напористый (напорист).

aggressiveness [ə'grɛsɪvnɪs] *n* агрессивность *f*.

aggressor [ə'grɛsə'] *n* агрессор.

aggrieved [ə'gri:vd] *adj* огорчённый* (огорчён).

aggro ['ægrəu] *n* (*inf: aggressive behaviour*) напряжёнка; (*difficulties*) возня.

aghast [ə'gɑ:st] *adj*: **to be ~ at** быть* (*impf*) в ужасе от +*gen*.

agile ['ædʒaɪl] *adj* (*person*) проворный* (проворен); (*mind*) живой*.

agility [ə'dʒɪlɪtɪ] *n* подвижность *f*; **mental ~** живость *f* ума.

agitate ['ædʒɪteɪt] *vt* (*person*) возбуждать

---

* marks translations which have irregular inflections. The Russian-English side of the dictionary gives inflectional information.

(возбуди́ть• *perf*); (*liquid*) взба́лтывать (взболта́ть *perf*) ♦ *vi*: **to ~ for/against** агити́ровать (сагити́ровать *perf*) за +*acc*/ про́тив +*gen*.

agitated [ˈædʒɪteɪtɪd] *adj* возбуждённый• (возбуждён), взволно́ванный (взволно́ван).

agitator [ˈædʒɪteɪtə] *n* агита́тор.

AGM *n abbr* (= *annual general meeting*) ежего́дное о́бщее собра́ние.

agnostic [ægˈnɒstɪk] *n* агно́стик.

ago [əˈgəu] *adv*: **two days ~** два дня наза́д; **not long ~** неда́вно; **as long ~ as 1960** ещё в 1960 году́; **how long ~?** как давно́?

agog [əˈgɒg] *adj* (*excited*) взволно́ванный (взволно́ван); **to be (all) ~** (*with anticipation*) сгора́ть (*impf*) от нетерпе́ния.

agonize [ˈægənaɪz] *vi*: **he ~d over the problem** он му́чился над пробле́мой.

agonizing [ˈægənaɪzɪŋ] *adj* мучи́тельный• (мучи́телен).

agony [ˈægənɪ] *n* (*pain*) мучи́тельная боль *f*; (*torment*) му́ка, муче́ние; **to be in ~** му́читься (*impf*) от бо́ли.

agony aunt *n* психо́лог "по́чты дове́рия", отвеча́ющий на вопро́сы чита́телей.

agony column *n* ру́брика "по́чта дове́рия".

agree [əˈgriː] *vt* согласо́вывать (согласова́ть *perf*) ♦ *vi*: **to ~ with** (*have same opinion*) соглаша́ться (согласи́ться *perf*) с +*instr*; (*correspond*) согласова́ться (*impf/perf*) с +*instr*; **to ~ that** согласи́ться• (*perf*), что; **it was ~d that ...** бы́ло решено́, что ...; **the price is still to be ~d** це́ну всё ещё на́до согласова́ть; **I ~ (with you)** я согла́сен (с Ва́ми); **to ~ (with)** (*LING*) согласо́вывать (согласова́ть• *perf*) (с +*instr*); **garlic doesn't ~ with me** я не переношу́ чеснока́; **to ~ on sth** догова́риваться (договори́ться *perf*) о чём-н; **they ~d on this** они́ сошли́сь на э́том; **they ~d on going/on a price** они́ договор-и́лись пойти́/о цене́; **to ~ to sth/to do** соглаша́ться (согласи́ться• *perf*) на что-н/+*infin*.

agreeable [əˈgriːəbl] *adj* (*pleasant*) прия́тный• (прия́тен); (*willing*) согла́сен; **are you ~ to this?** Вы согла́сны на э́то?

agreed [əˈgriːd] *adj* усло́вленный (усло́влен).

agreement [əˈgriːmənt] *n* (*consent*) согла́сие; (*arrangement*) соглаше́ние, догово́р; **in ~ with** в согла́сии с +*instr*; **we are in complete ~** ме́жду на́ми по́лное согла́сие; **by mutual ~** по взаи́мному соглаше́нию.

agricultural [ægrɪˈkʌltʃərəl] *adj* се́льско-хозя́йственный; **~ land** земе́льные уго́дья *ntpl*.

agriculture [ˈægrɪkʌltʃə] *n* се́льское хозя́йство.

aground [əˈgraund] *adv*: **to run ~** сади́ться• (сесть• *perf*) на мель.

ahead [əˈhɛd] *adv* впереди́; (*direction*) вперёд; **~ of** (*more advanced than*) впереди́ +*gen*;

(*earlier than*) ра́ньше +*gen*; **~ of time** *or* **schedule** досро́чно; **go right** *or* **straight ~** иди́те вперёд *or* пря́мо; **go ~!** (*permission*) дава́йте!; **they were (right) ~ of us** они́ бы́ли (пря́мо) пе́ред на́ми.

AI *n abbr* (= *Amnesty International*) Междунаро́дная амни́стия; (*COMPUT*) = **artificial intelligence**.

AIB *n abbr* (*BRIT*) = *Accident Investigation Bureau*.

AID *n abbr* (= *artificial insemination by donor*) иску́сственное оплодотворе́ние се́менем до́нора; (*US*) = *Agency for International Development*.

aid [eɪd] *n* (*assistance*) по́мощь *f*; (*device*) приспособле́ние ♦ *vt* помога́ть (помо́чь• *perf*) +*dat*; **with the ~ of** при по́мощи +*gen*; **in ~ of** в по́мощь +*dat*; **to ~ and abet** (*LAW*) подстрека́ть (*impf*); *see also* **hearing**.

aide [eɪd] *n* помо́щник.

aide-de-camp [ˈeɪddəˈkɒŋ] *n* адъюта́нт.

AIDS [eɪdz] *n abbr* (= *acquired immune deficiency syndrome*) СПИД= *синдро́м приобретённого иммунодефици́та*.

AIH *n abbr* (= *artificial insemination by husband*) иску́сственное оплодотворе́ние се́менем му́жа.

ailing [ˈeɪlɪŋ] *adj* больно́й• (бо́лен); **an ~ economy** эконо́мика прише́дшая в упа́док.

ailment [ˈeɪlmənt] *n* неду́г.

aim [eɪm] *n* (*objective*) цель *f* ♦ *vi* (*also*: **take ~**) це́литься (наце́литься *perf*) ♦ *vt*: **to ~ (at)** (*gun, camera*) наводи́ть• (навести́• *perf*) (на +*acc*); (*missile, blow*) це́лить (*impf*) *or* наце́ливать (наце́лить *perf*) (на +*acc*); (*remark*) направля́ть (напра́вить• *perf*) (на +*acc*); **to ~ at** це́литься (*impf*) в +*acc*, прице́ливаться (прице́литься *perf*) в +*acc*; (*fig*) стреми́ться• (*impf*) к +*dat*; **to ~ to do** ста́вить• (поста́вить• *perf*) свое́й це́лью +*infin*; **he has a good ~** он ме́ткий стрело́к.

aimless [ˈeɪmlɪs] *adj* бесце́льный• (бесце́лен).

aimlessly [ˈeɪmlɪslɪ] *adv* бесце́льно.

ain't [eɪnt] (*inf*) = **am not**, **aren't**, **isn't**; *see* **be**.

air [ɛəʳ] *n* во́здух; (*tune*) моти́в; (*appearance*) вид• ♦ *vt* (*room, bedclothes*) прове́тривать (прове́трить *perf*); (*views*) обнаро́довать (*perf*) ♦ *cpd* (*currents, attack etc*) возду́шный; **to throw sth into the ~** подбра́сывать (подбро́сить• *perf*) что-н в во́здух; **by ~** самолётом; **everything's still very much in the ~** всё до сих пор виси́т в во́здухе; **on the ~** в эфи́ре; **to go on the ~** выходи́ть• (вы́йти• *perf*) в эфи́р.

airbag [ˈɛəbæg] *n возду́шная поду́шка, надува́ющаяся автомати́чески ме́жду рулём и шофёром, в слу́чае ава́рии.*

air base *n* авиаба́за.

airbed [ˈɛəbɛd] *n* (*BRIT*) надувно́й матра́с.

airborne [ˈɛəbɔːn] *adj* возду́шный• (возду́шен); (*troops*) возду́шно-деса́нтный; (*particles*) лету́чий•; **as soon as the plane was**

~ как то́лько самолёт подня́лся в во́здух.

air cargo *n* возду́шный груз.

air-conditioned ['ɛəkən'dɪʃənd] *adj* кондициони́рованный.

air conditioning *n* кондициони́рование.

air-cooled ['ɛəku:ld] *adj* охлажда́емый во́здухом.

aircraft ['ɛəkrɑːft] *n inv* самолёт.

aircraft carrier *n* авиано́сец*.

air cushion *n* возду́шная поду́шка*.

airfield ['ɛəfi:ld] *n* аэродро́м.

Air Force *n* Вое́нно-Возду́шные Си́лы *fpl*.

air freight *n* авиагру́з.

air freshener *n* освежи́тель *m* во́здуха.

air gun *n* духово́е ружьё*.

air hostess *n* (*BRIT*) бортпроводни́ца, стюарде́сса.

airily ['ɛərɪlɪ] *adv* с лёгкостью, небре́жно.

airing ['ɛərɪŋ] *n*: **to give an ~ to** (*ideas, views etc*) обнаро́довать (*perf*).

air letter *n* (*BRIT*) письмо́* а́виа.

airlift ['ɛəlɪft] *n* возду́шная перебро́ска ♦ *vt* перебра́сывать (перебро́сить* *perf*) по во́здуху.

airline ['ɛəlaɪn] *n* авиакомпа́ния.

airliner ['ɛəlaɪnəʳ] *n* пассажи́рский* (авиа)ла́йнер.

airlock ['ɛəlɔk] *n* возду́шная про́бка.

air mail *n*: **by ~ ~** авиапо́чтой.

air mattress *n* надувно́й матра́с.

airplane ['ɛəpleɪn] *n* (*US*) самолёт.

air pocket *n* возду́шная я́ма.

airport ['ɛəpɔːt] *n* аэропо́рт.

air rage *n* агресси́вное поведе́ние на борт самолёта.

air raid *n* возду́шный налёт.

air rifle *n* пневмати́ческая винто́вка.

airsick ['ɛəsɪk] *adj*: **to be ~** страда́ть (*impf*) возду́шной боле́знью.

airspace ['ɛəspeɪs] *n* возду́шное простра́нство.

airspeed ['ɛəspiːd] *n* возду́шная ско́рость *f*, ско́рость *f* в во́здухе.

airstrip ['ɛəstrɪp] *n* взлётно-поса́дочная полоса́*.

air terminal *n* аэровокза́л.

airtight ['ɛətaɪt] *adj* гермети́ческий.

air time *n* вре́мя* *nt* в эфи́ре.

air-traffic control ['ɛətræfɪk-] *n* возду́шно-диспе́тчерская слу́жба.

air-traffic controller *n* возду́шный диспе́тчер.

airway ['ɛəweɪ] *n* возду́шная тра́сса.

air waybill *n* тра́нспортная накладна́я для авиагру́за.

airy ['ɛərɪ] *adj* просто́рный* (просто́рен); (*manner*) беспе́чный* (беспе́чен).

aisle [aɪl] *n* прохо́д.

ajar [ə'dʒɑːʳ] *adj* приоткры́тый (приоткры́т).

AK *abbr* (*US*: *POST*) = Alaska.

aka *abbr* (= *also known as*) изве́стный та́кже под и́менем.

akin [ə'kɪn] *adj*: ~ **to** сродни́ +*dat*.

AL (*US*: *POST*) *abbr* = Alabama.

ALA *n abbr* = American Library Association.

alabaster ['æləbɑːstəʳ] *n* алеба́стр.

à la carte [ɑːlɑː'kɑːt] *adv*: **dinner ~ ~ ~** обе́д с зака́зом блюд по меню́.

alacrity [ə'lækrɪtɪ] *n* гото́вность *f*; **with ~** с гото́вностью.

alarm [ə'lɑːm] *n* (*anxiety*) трево́га; (*device*) сигнализа́ция ♦ *vt* (*person*) трево́жить (встрево́жить *perf*); (*car, house*) устана́вливать (установи́ть* *perf*) сигнализа́цию в +*prp*.

alarm call *n*: **I would like an ~ ~ for 6 a.m.** позвони́те, пожа́луйста, в 6 часо́в и разбуди́те меня́.

alarm clock *n* буди́льник.

alarmed [ə'lɑːmd] *adj* встрево́женный* (встрево́жен); **his car is ~** у него́ в маши́не сигнализа́ция.

alarming [ə'lɑːmɪŋ] *adj* трево́жный* (трево́жен).

alarmist [ə'lɑːmɪst] *n* паникёр(ша).

alas [ə'læs] *excl* увы.

Alaska [ə'læskə] *n* Аля́ска.

Albania [æl'beɪnɪə] *n* Алба́ния.

Albanian [æl'beɪnɪən] *adj* алба́нский* ♦ *n* алба́нец*(-нка); (*LING*) алба́нский* язы́к*.

albatross ['ælbətrɔs] *n* (*ZOOL*) альбатро́с.

albeit [ɔːl'biːɪt] *conj* хотя́ и.

album ['ælbəm] *n* альбо́м.

albumen ['ælbjumɪn] *n* бело́к*.

alchemy ['ælkɪmɪ] *n* алхи́мия.

alcohol ['ælkəhɔl] *n* алкого́ль *m*.

alcohol-free ['ælkəhɔl'friː] *adj* безалкого́льный.

alcoholic [ælkə'hɔlɪk] *adj* алкого́льный ♦ *n* алкого́лик(-и́чка).

alcoholism ['ælkəhɔlɪzəm] *n* алкоголи́зм.

alcove ['ælkəuv] *n* алько́в.

alderman ['ɔːldəmən] *irreg n* глава́ муниципалите́та.

ale [eɪl] *n* пи́во (*пригото́вленное без хме́ля*).

alert [ə'ləːt] *adj* (*attentive*) внима́тельный (внима́телен); (*to danger*) бди́тельный* (бди́телен) ♦ *n* (*alarm*) трево́га ♦ *vt* (*police etc*) предупрежда́ть (предупреди́ть* *perf*); **to be on the ~** (*also MIL*) быть* (*impf*) начеку́; **to ~ sb to sth** предупрежда́ть (предупреди́ть *perf*) кого́-н о чём-н; **to ~ sb to the dangers of sth** предостерега́ть (предостере́чь* *perf*) кого́-н от опа́сности чего́-н.

Aleutian Islands [ə'luːʃən-] *npl* Алеу́тские острова́ *mpl*.

Alexandria [ælɪg'zɑːndrɪə] *n* Александри́я.

alfresco [æl'frɛskəu] *adj, adv* под откры́тым

небом.
algebra ['ældʒɪbrə] *n* а́лгебра.
Algeria [æl'dʒɪərɪə] *n* Алжи́р.
Algerian [æl'dʒɪərɪən] *adj* алжи́рский* ♦ *n* алжи́рец*(-рка).
Algiers [æl'dʒɪəz] *n* Алжи́р (*го́род*).
algorithm ['ælgərɪðəm] *n* алгори́тм.
alias ['eɪlɪəs] *n* (*of criminal*) вы́мышленное и́мя* *nt*; (*of writer*) псевдони́м ♦ *adv*: ~ **John Green** он же Джон Грин.
alibi ['ælɪbaɪ] *n* а́либи *nt ind*.
alien ['eɪlɪən] *n* (*foreigner*) иностра́нец*(-нка); (*extraterrestrial*) инопланетя́нин*(-я́нка) ♦ *adj*: ~ (**to**) чу́ждый* (чужд) (+*dat*); **pity was ~ to his nature** чу́вство жа́лости ему́ бы́ло чу́ждо.
alienate ['eɪlɪəneɪt] *vt* (*person*) отчужда́ть (*impf*), отта́лкивать (оттолкну́ть *perf*).
alienation [eɪlɪə'neɪʃən] *n* отчужде́ние.
alight [ə'laɪt] *adj*: **to be** ~ горе́ть (*impf*); (*eyes, face*) сия́ть (*impf*) ♦ *adv*: **to set** ~ поджига́ть (поджечь* *perf*) ♦ *vi*: **to** ~ **on** опуска́ться (опусти́ться* *perf*) на +*acc*; ~ **from** (*boat*) сходи́ть* (сойти́* *perf*) с +*gen*; (*bus, train*) выходи́ть* (вы́йти* *perf*) из +*gen*.
align [ə'laɪn] *vt* (*objects*) выра́внивать (вы́ровнять *perf*); **to** ~ **o.s. with** присоединя́ться (присоедини́ться *perf*) к +*dat*.
alignment [ə'laɪnmənt] *n* сою́з; (*POL*) алья́нс; **out of** ~ неро́вно.
alike [ə'laɪk] *adj* одина́ковый (одина́ков) ♦ *adv* одина́ково; **they look** ~ они́ похо́жи друг на дру́га; **winter and summer** ~ и зимо́й и ле́том.
alimony ['ælɪmənɪ] *n* алиме́нты* *pl*.
alive [ə'laɪv] *adj* жив; (*place*) оживлённый*; (*active: person*) живо́й*; ~ **with** по́лон +*gen*; **to be** ~ **to sth** осознава́ть (осозна́ть *perf*) что-н.
alkali ['ælkəlaɪ] *n* ще́лочь* *f*.
alkaline ['ælkəlaɪn] *adj* щелочно́й.

KEYWORD

all [ɔ:l] *adj* весь* (*f* вся, *nt* всё, *pl* все); **all day** весь день* *m*; **all night** всю ночь* *f*; **all men are equal** все лю́ди равны́; **all five stayed** все пя́теро оста́лись; **all the books** все кни́ги; **all the time** всё вре́мя; **all his life** всю свою́ жизнь

♦ *pron* **1** всё; **I ate it all; I ate all of it** я всё съел; **all of us stayed** мы все оста́лись; **we all sat down** мы все се́ли; **is that all?** э́то всё?; (*in shop*) всё?

2 (*in phrases*): **above all** пре́жде всего́; **after all** в конце́ концо́в; **all in all** в це́лом *or* о́бщем; **not at all** (*in answer to question*) совсе́м нет, ничу́ть нет; (*in answer to thanks*) не́ за что; **I'm not at all tired** я совсе́м не уста́л

♦ *adv* совсе́м; **I am all alone** я совсе́м оди́н; **I did it all by myself** я всё сде́лал сам; **it's not as hard as all that** э́то совсе́м не так уж тру́дно; **all the more/the better** тем бо́лее/лу́чше; **I**

have all but finished я почти́ что зако́нчил; **the score is two all** счёт-два два.

allay [ə'leɪ] *vt* (*fears etc*) разве́ивать (разве́ять *perf*).
all clear *n* отбо́й.
allegation [ælɪ'geɪʃən] *n* обвине́ние; **according to his ~s** согла́сно его́ утвержде́ниям.
allege [ə'ledʒ] *vt* (*claim*) утвержда́ть (*impf*); **he is ~d to have said that** ... утвержда́ют, что он сказа́л что ....
alleged [ə'ledʒd] *adj* подозрева́емый.
allegedly [ə'ledʒɪdlɪ] *adv* я́кобы.
allegiance [ə'li:dʒəns] *n* (*to people*) ве́рность *f*; (*to ideas*) приве́рженность *f*.
allegory ['ælɪgərɪ] *n* аллего́рия.
all-embracing ['ɔ:lɪm'breɪsɪŋ] *adj* всеобъе́млющий* (всеобъе́млющ).
allergic [ə'lə:dʒɪk] *adj* аллерги́ческий*; **he is ~ to** у него́ аллерги́я на +*acc*; (*fig*) он не выно́сит +*gen*.
allergy ['ælədʒɪ] *n* (*MED*) аллерги́я.
alleviate [ə'li:vɪeɪt] *vt* облегча́ть (облегчи́ть *perf*).
alley ['ælɪ] *n* (*street*) переу́лок*.
alleyway ['ælɪweɪ] *n* прое́улок*.
alliance [ə'laɪəns] *n* сою́з; (*POL*) алья́нс.
allied ['ælaɪd] *adj* (*POL, MIL*) сою́зный; (*industries*) сме́жный.
alligator ['ælɪgeɪtə'] *n* аллига́тор.
all-important ['ɔ:lɪm'pɔ:tnt] *adj* суще́ственный.
all-in ['ɔ:lɪn] *adj* (*BRIT: cost*) о́бщий*; **it cost me £100** ~ в о́бщей сло́жности мне э́то сто́ило £100.
all-in wrestling *n* во́льная борьба́.
alliteration [əlɪtə'reɪʃən] *n* аллитера́ция.
all-night ['ɔ:l'naɪt] *adj* (*café, cinema*) ночно́й.
allocate ['æləkeɪt] *vt* (*money, time, room*) выделя́ть (вы́делить *perf*); (*tasks*) поруча́ть (поручи́ть* *perf*).
allocation [æləu'keɪʃən] *n* (*of responsibilty*) распределе́ние; (*of resources*) выделе́ние; (*of money*) ассигнова́ние.
allot [ə'lɔt] *vt*: **to** ~ (**to**) отводи́ть* (отвести́* *perf*) (+*dat*); **in the ~ted time** в отведённое вре́мя.
allotment [ə'lɔtmənt] *n* (*share*) до́ля*; (*garden*) (земе́льный) уча́сток*.
all-out ['ɔ:laut] *adj* (*effort*) максима́льный; (*attack*) масси́рованный; (*strike*) всеобщий* ♦ *adv* по́лностью; **to go all out (for)** по́лностью выкла́дываться (вы́ложиться *perf*) (для +*gen*).
allow [ə'lau] *vt* (*permit*) разреша́ть (разреши́ть *perf*); (*claim, goal*) признава́ть* (призна́ть *perf*) действи́тельным; (*set aside: sum*) выделя́ть (вы́делить *perf*); (*concede*): **to ~ that** допуска́ть (допусти́ть* *perf*), что; **to ~ sb to do** разреша́ть (разреши́ть *perf*) *or* позволя́ть (позво́лить *perf*) кому́-н +*infin*; **he was ~ed to** ... ему́ бы́ло разрешено́ +*infin* ...; **smoking is not ~ed** кури́ть воспреща́ется *or*

запреща́ется; **we must ~ 3 days for the journey** мы должны́ оста́вить три дня на доро́гу
▸ **allow for** *vt fus* учи́тывать (уче́сть* *perf*), принима́ть (приня́ть* *perf*) в расчёт.
allowance [ə'lauəns] *n* (*company expenses*) де́ньги* *pl* на расхо́ды; (*pocket money*) карма́нные де́ньги; (*welfare payment*) посо́бие; (*tax allowance*) нало́говая ски́дка*; **to make ~s for sb/sth** де́лать (сде́лать *perf*) ски́дку для кого́-н/на что-н.
alloy ['ælɔɪ] *n* сплав.
all right *adv* хорошо́, норма́льно; (*as answer: in agreement*) хорошо́, ла́дно ♦ *adj* неплохо́й*, норма́льный; **is everything ~~?** всё норма́льно *or* в поря́дке?; **are you ~~?** как Вы (себя́ чу́вствуете)?; **do you like him? – he's ~ ~** он Вам нра́вится? – ничего́.
all-rounder [ɔ:l'raundə'] *n* универса́л.
allspice ['ɔ:lspaɪs] *n* души́стый пе́рец*.
all-time ['ɔ:l'taɪm] *adj* (*record*) непревзойдённый; **inflation is at an ~ low** инфля́ция на небыва́ло ни́зком у́ровне.
allude [ə'lu:d] *vi:* **to ~ to** намека́ть (намекну́ть *perf*) на +*acc*.
alluring [ə'ljuərɪŋ] *adj* соблазни́тельный* (соблазни́телен).
allusion [ə'lu:ʒn] *n:* ~ **(to)** намёк (на +*acc*); (*LITERATURE*) аллю́зия (на +*acc*).
alluvium [ə'lu:vɪəm] *n* аллю́вий.
ally [*n* 'ælaɪ, *vb* ə'laɪ] *n* сою́зник ♦ *vt:* **to ~ o.s. with** объединя́ться (объедини́ться *perf*) с +*instr*.
Alma-Ata [ælmɑ:ə'tɑ:] *n* А́лма-Ата́ *f ind*.
almighty [ɔ:l'maɪtɪ] *adj* (*omnipotent*) всемогу́щий* (всемогу́щ); (*tremendous*) колосса́льный.
almond ['ɑ:mənd] *n* минда́ль* *m*.
almost ['ɔ:lməust] *adv* почти́; (*all but*) чуть *or* едва́ не; **he ~ fell** он чуть не упа́л.
alms [ɑ:mz] *npl* ми́лостыня *fsg*, подая́ние *ntsg*.
aloft [ə'lɔft] *adv* (*hold, carry*) над голово́й.
alone [ə'ləun] *adj, adv* оди́н (одна́); **to leave sb/sth ~** оставля́ть (оста́вить* *perf*) кого́-н/что-н в поко́е; **let ~ ...** не говоря́ уже́ о +*prp* ....
along [ə'lɔŋ] *prep* (*motion*) по +*dat*, вдоль +*gen*; (*position*) вдоль +*gen* ♦ *adv:* **is he coming ~ (with us)?** он идёт с на́ми?; **he was limping ~** он шёл хрома́я; ~ **with** вме́сте с +*instr*; **all ~** с са́мого нача́ла.
alongside [ə'lɔŋ'saɪd] *prep* (*position*) ря́дом с +*instr*, вдоль +*gen*; (*motion*) к +*dat* ♦ *adv* ря́дом; **we brought our boat ~** мы причали́ли ло́дку.
aloof [ə'lu:f] *adj* отрешённый (отрешён) ♦ *adv:* **to stand ~** держа́ться (*impf*) в стороне́.
aloofness [ə'lu:fnɪs] *n* отрешённость *f*.

aloud [ə'laud] *adv* (*read, speak*) вслух.
alphabet ['ælfəbɛt] *n* алфави́т.
alphabetical [ælfə'bɛtɪkl] *adj* алфави́тный; **in ~ order** в алфави́тном поря́дке.
alphanumeric ['ælfənju:'mɛrɪk] *adj* алфави́тно-цифрово́й.
alpine ['ælpaɪn] *adj* высокого́рный, альпи́йский*.
Alps [ælps] *npl:* **the ~** А́льпы* *pl*.
already [ɔ:l'rɛdɪ] *adv* уже́.
alright ['ɔ:l'raɪt] *adv* (*BRIT*) = **all right**.
Alsace ['ælsæs] *n* Эльза́с.
Alsatian [æl'seɪʃən] *n* (*BRIT: dog*) неме́цкая овча́рка*; (*person*) эльза́сец(-ска).
also ['ɔ:lsəu] *adv* (*referring to subject*) та́кже, то́же; (*referring to object*) та́кже; (*moreover*) кро́ме того́, к тому́ же; **he ~ likes apples** он та́кже *or* то́же лю́бит я́блоки; **he likes apples ~** он лю́бит та́кже я́блоки.
altar ['ɔltə'] *n* алта́рь* *m*.
alter ['ɔltə'] *vt* изменя́ть (измени́ть* *perf*) ♦ *vi* изменя́ться (измени́ться* *perf*).
alteration [ɔltə'reɪʃən] *n* измене́ние; ~**s** *npl* (*SEWING*) переде́лки *fpl*; **to make ~s to a building** перестра́ивать (перестро́ить *perf*) зда́ние.
altercation [ɔltə'keɪʃən] *n* препира́тельство.
alternate [*adj* ɔl'tə:nɪt, *vb* 'ɔltə:neɪt] *adj* чередующийся; (*US: alternative*) альтернати́вный ♦ *vi:* **to ~ (with)** чередова́ться (*impf*) (с +*instr*); **on ~ days** че́рез день.
alternately [ɔl'tə:nɪtlɪ] *adv* попереме́нно.
alternating current ['ɔltə:neɪtɪŋ-] *n* переме́нный ток*.
alternative [ɔl'tə:nətɪv] *adj* альтернати́вный ♦ *n* альтернати́ва.
alternatively [ɔl'tə:nətɪvlɪ] *adv:* ~ **one could ...** кро́ме того́ мо́жно ....
alternative medicine *n* альтернати́вная *or* нетрадицио́нная медици́на.
alternator ['ɔltə:neɪtə'] *n* (*AUT*) генера́тор переме́нного то́ка.
although [ɔ:l'ðəu] *conj* хотя́.
altitude ['æltɪtju:d] *n* (*of plane*) высота́*; (*of place*) высота́ над у́ровнем мо́ря.
alto ['æltəu] *n* (*female*) контра́льто *nt ind*; (*male*) альт*.
altogether [ɔ:ltə'gɛðə'] *adv* (*completely*) соверше́нно; (*in all*) в о́бщем, в о́бщей сло́жности; **how much is that ~?** ско́лько бу́дет в о́бщей сло́жности?
altruism ['æltruɪzəm] *n* альтруи́зм.
altruistic [æltru'ɪstɪk] *adj* (*action*) альтруисти́ческий; (*person*) альтруисти́чный (альтруисти́чен).
aluminium [ælju'mɪnɪəm] *n* (*BRIT*) алюми́ний.

---

aluminum [ə'lu:mɪnəm] *n* (*US*) = **aluminium**.
always ['ɔ:lweɪz] *adv* всегда́.
Alzheimer's disease ['æltshaɪməz-] *n* боле́знь *f* Альцхе́ймера.
AM *abbr* (= *amplitude modulation*) амплиту́дная модуля́ция; (= *Assembly Member*) член ассамбле́и.
am [æm] *vb see* **be**.
a.m. *adv abbr* (= *ante meridiem*) до полу́дня.
AMA *n abbr* = *American Medical Association*.
amalgam [ə'mælgəm] *n* амальга́ма.
amalgamate [ə'mælgəmeɪt] *vi* слива́ться (сли́ться *perf*) ◆ *vt* слива́ть (слить *perf*).
amalgamation [əmælgə'meɪʃən] *n* (*of companies*) слия́ние.
amass [ə'mæs] *vt* нака́пливать (накопи́ть* *perf*).
amateur ['æmətə*] *n* люби́тель *m*; ~ **sport/ dramatics** люби́тельский* спорт/теа́тр; ~ **photographer** фото́граф-люби́тель *m*.
amateurish ['æmətərɪʃ] *adj* (*work, efforts*) непрофессиона́льный (непрофессиона́лен).
amaze [ə'meɪz] *vt* поража́ть (порази́ть* *perf*), изумля́ть (изуми́ть* *perf*); **I was ~d (at)** я был поражён (+*instr*).
amazement [ə'meɪzmənt] *n* изумле́ние.
amazing [ə'meɪzɪŋ] *adj* (*surprising*) порази́тельный* (порази́телен); (*fantastic*) изуми́тельный* (изуми́телен), замеча́тельный* (замеча́телен).
amazingly [ə'meɪzɪŋlɪ] *adv* порази́тельно.
Amazon ['æməzən] *n* (*river*) Амазо́нка; (*woman*) амазо́нка*; **the ~ basin** бассе́йн реки́ Амазо́нки; **the ~ jungle** джу́нгли *pl* Амазо́нки.
Amazonian [æmə'zəunɪən] *adj* амазо́нский.
ambassador [æm'bæsədə*] *n* посо́л*.
amber ['æmbə*] *n* янта́рь* *m*; **the lights were at ~** на светофо́ре был жёлтый свет.
ambidextrous [æmbɪ'dɛkstrəs] *adj* одина́ково владе́ющий пра́вой и ле́вой руко́й.
ambience ['æmbɪəns] *n* атмосфе́ра.
ambiguity [æmbɪ'gjuːtɪ] *n* двусмы́сленность *f*, нея́сность *f*.
ambiguous [æm'bɪgjuəs] *adj* двусмы́сленный, нея́сный*.
ambition [æm'bɪʃən] *n* (*quality: positive*) честолю́бие; (: *negative*) амби́ция; (*aim*) цель *f*; **to achieve one's ~** достига́ть (дости́чь* *perf*) свое́й це́ли.
ambitious [æm'bɪʃəs] *adj* честолюби́вый (честолюби́в); амбицио́зный* (амбицио́зен).
ambivalence [æm'bɪvələns] *n* (*indecision*) дво́йственное отноше́ние; (*ambiguity*) несоотве́тствия *ntpl*.
ambivalent [æm'bɪvələnt] *adj* (*attitude*) дво́йственный (дво́йствен); (*person*) противоречи́вый (противоречи́в).
amble ['æmbl] *vi* прогу́ливаться (прогуля́ться *perf*).

ambulance ['æmbjuləns] *n* ско́рая по́мощь *f*.
ambulanceman ['æmbjulənsmən] *irreg n* фе́льдшер ско́рой по́мощи.
ambush ['æmbuʃ] *n* заса́да ◆ *vt* устра́ивать (устро́ить* *perf*) заса́ду +*dat*.
ameba [ə'mi:bə] *n* (*US*) = **amoeba**.
ameliorate [ə'mi:lɪəreɪt] *vt* (*situation*) улучша́ть (улу́чшить *perf*).
amen ['ɑ:'mɛn] *excl* ами́нь.
amenable [ə'mi:nəbl] *adj*: ~ **to** пода́тливый (пода́тлив) на +*acc*; **he's ~ to advice** он прислу́шивается к сове́там; ~ **to the law** отве́тственный (отве́тствен) пе́ред зако́ном.
amend [ə'mɛnd] *vt* пересма́тривать (пересмотре́ть *perf*); (*habits*) исправля́ть (испра́вить* *perf*) ◆ *vi* исправля́ться (испра́виться* *perf*) ◆ *n*: **to make ~s** загла́живать (загла́дить* *perf*) вину́.
amendment [ə'mɛndmənt] *n* попра́вка*.
amenities [ə'mi:nɪtɪz] *npl* удо́бства *ntpl*.
amenity [ə'mi:nɪtɪ] *n* удо́бство.
America [ə'mɛrɪkə] *n* Аме́рика.
American [ə'mɛrɪkən] *adj* америка́нский* ◆ *n* америка́нец*(-нка).
americanize [ə'mɛrɪkənaɪz] *vt* американизи́ровать (*impf/perf*).
amethyst ['æmɪθɪst] *n* амети́ст.
Amex ['æmɛks] *n abbr* = *American Stock Exchange*.
amiable ['eɪmɪəbl] *adj* дружелю́бный* (дружелю́бен).
amiably ['eɪmɪəblɪ] *adv* дружелю́бно.
amicable ['æmɪkəbl] *adj* (*relationship*) дру́жеский*; (*divorce*) ми́рный* (ми́рен).
amicably ['æmɪkəblɪ] *adv* по-дру́жески, ми́рно.
amid(st) [ə'mɪd(st)] *prep* посреди́ +*gen*.
amiss [ə'mɪs] *adj, adv*: **to take sth ~** оши́бочно истолко́вывать (истолкова́ть* *perf*) что-н; **there's something ~** что-то нела́дно.
ammeter ['æmɪtə*] *n* ампермет́р.
ammo ['æməu] *n abbr* (*inf*) = **ammunition**.
ammonia [ə'məunɪə] *n* (*gas*) аммиа́к; (*liquid*) нашаты́рный спирт*.
ammunition [æmju'nɪʃən] *n* (*MIL*) боеприпа́сы *pl*; (*for gun*) патро́ны *mpl*; (*fig*) ору́жие.
ammunition dump *n* склад боеприпа́сов.
amnesia [æm'ni:zɪə] *n* амнези́я, утра́та па́мяти.
amnesty ['æmnɪstɪ] *n* амни́стия; **to grant an ~ to** объявля́ть (объяви́ть* *perf*) амни́стию +*dat*.
amoeba [ə'mi:bə] (*US* **ameba**) *n* амёба.
amok [ə'mɔk] *adv*: **to run ~** (*people*) беснова́ться (*impf*); (*animals*) беси́ться* (взбеси́ться *perf*).
among(st) [ə'mʌŋ(st)] *prep* среди́ +*gen*; (*between*) ме́жду +*instr*.
amoral [æ'mɔrəl] *adj* безнра́вственный* (безнра́вственен), амора́льный* (амора́лен).
amorous ['æmərəs] *adj* любо́вный.

amorphous [ə'mɔ:fəs] *adj* амо́рфный*
(амо́рфен).
amortization [əmɔ:tai'zeiʃn] *n* (*COMM*)
амортиза́ция.
amount [ə'maunt] *n* коли́чество; (*sum of
money*) су́мма ◆ *vi*: **to ~ to** (*total*) составля́ть
(соста́вить* *perf*); **this ~s to a refusal** э́то
равноси́льно отка́зу; **the total ~** (*of money*)
о́бщая су́мма.
amp(ère) ['æmp(εə')] *n* ампе́р*; **a 13 amp plug**
ви́лка в 13 ампе́р.
ampersand ['æmpəsænd] *n* знак "&"
(*обозначающий "и"*).
amphetamine [æm'fεtəmi:n] *n* амфетами́н.
amphibian [æm'fibiən] *n* амфи́бия,
земново́дное живо́тное *nt adj*.
amphibious [æm'fibiəs] *adj* (*animal*)
земново́дный; (*vehicle*) амфи́бийный; **~
tank** танк-амфи́бия.
amphitheatre ['æmfiθiətə'] (*US* **amphitheater**) *n*
амфитеа́тр.
ample ['æmpl] *adj* (*large*) большо́й; (*abundant*)
оби́льный* (оби́лен); (*enough*) доста́точный
(доста́точен); **to have ~ time/room** име́ть
(*impf*) доста́точно вре́мени/ме́ста; **this is ~**
э́того вполне́ доста́точно.
amplifier ['æmplifaiə'] *n* усили́тель *m*.
amplify ['æmplifai] *vt* уси́ливать (уси́лить
perf).
amply ['æmpli] *adv* вполне́.
ampoule ['æmpu:l] (*US* **ampule**) *n* а́мпула.
amputate ['æmpjuteit] *vt* ампути́ровать (*impf/
perf*).
amputation [æmpju'teiʃən] *n* ампута́ция.
amputee [æmpju'ti:] *n* инвали́д.
Amsterdam ['æmstədæm] *n* Амстерда́м.
amt *abbr* (= **amount**) кол-во= *коли́чество*.
amuck [ə'mʌk] *adv* = **amok**.
amuse [ə'mju:z] *vt* развлека́ть (развле́чь* *perf*);
to ~ o.s. with sth заня́ться (*perf*) *or*
развлека́ться (развле́чься* *perf*) чем-н; **he
was ~d at this** его́ э́то позаба́вило; **he was
not ~d** ему́ бы́ло не до сме́ха.
amusement [ə'mju:zmənt] *n* (*mirth*)
удово́льствие; (*pastime*) развлече́ние; **much
to my ~** к моему́ осо́бенному
удово́льствию.
amusement arcade *n* павильо́н с игровы́ми
аппара́тами.
amusement park *n* луна-парк.
amusing [ə'mju:ziŋ] *adj* заба́вный* (заба́вен),
занима́тельный* (занима́телен).
an [æn] *indef art see* **a**.
ANA *n abbr* = **American Newspaper Association**;
American Nurses Association.
anachronism [ə'nækrənizəm] *n* анахрони́зм.
anaemia [ə'ni:miə] (*US* **anemia**) *n* анеми́я,
малокро́вие.

anaemic [ə'ni:mik] (*US* **anemic**) *adj* (*MED, fig*)
анеми́чный* (анеми́чен).
anaesthetic [ænis'θεtik] (*US* **anesthetic**) *n*
нарко́з; **under the ~** под нарко́зом; **local/
general ~** ме́стный/о́бщий* нарко́з.
anaesthetist [æ'ni:sθitist] (*US* **anesthetist**) *n*
анестезио́лог.
anagram ['ænəgræm] *n* анагра́мма.
anal ['einl] *adj* ана́льный, заднепрохо́дный.
analgesic [ænæl'dʒi:sik] *adj* обезбо́ливающий*
◆ *n* обезбо́ливающее сре́дство.
analog ['ænələg] *adj* = **analogue**.
analogous [ə'næləgəs] *adj* аналоги́чный*
(аналоги́чен).
analogue ['ænələg] *adj* (*computer*)
ана́логовый.
analogy [ə'nælədʒi] *n* анало́гия; **to draw an ~
between** проводи́ть* (провести́* *perf*)
анало́гию ме́жду +*instr*; **by ~** по анало́гии.
analyse ['ænəlaiz] (*US* **analyze**) *vt*
анализи́ровать (проанализи́ровать *perf*);
(*PSYCH*): **to ~ sb** подверга́ть (подве́ргнуть*
perf) кого́-н психоана́лизу.
analyses [ə'næləsi:z] *npl of* **analysis**.
analysis [ə'næləsis] (*pl* **analyses**) *n* ана́лиз;
(*PSYCH*) психоана́лиз; **in the last ~** в
коне́чном ито́ге.
analyst ['ænəlist] *n* (*political*) коммента́тор;
(*financial, economic*) экспе́рт; (*US:
psychiatrist*) психиа́тр.
analytic(al) [ænə'litik(l)] *adj* аналити́ческий.
analyze ['ænəlaiz] *vt* (*US*) = **analyse**.
anarchic [æ'na:kik] *adj* анархи́ческий.
anarchist ['ænəkist] *adj* анархи́ческий ◆ *n*
анархи́ст.
anarchy ['ænəki] *n* ана́рхия.
anathema [ə'næθimə] *n*: **that is ~ to him** для
него́ э́то ана́фема.
anatomical [ænə'tɔmikl] *adj* анатоми́ческий.
anatomy [ə'nætəmi] *n* анато́мия; (*body*)
органи́зм.
ANC *n abbr* (= *African National Congress*)
АНК= *Африка́нский* *национа́льный
конгре́сс*.
ancestor ['ænsistə'] *n* пре́док*.
ancestral [æn'sεstrəl] *adj* родово́й; **~ home**
родово́е поме́стье.
ancestry ['ænsistri] *n* происхожде́ние.
anchor ['æŋkə'] *n* я́корь *m* ◆ *vi* (*also:* **to drop ~**)
броса́ть (бро́сить* *perf*) я́корь; **to weigh ~**
поднима́ть (подня́ть* *perf*) я́корь.
anchorage ['æŋkəridʒ] *n* я́корная стоя́нка*.
anchor man *n* веду́щий* *m adj* (програ́ммы).
anchovy ['æntʃəvi] *n* анчо́ус.
ancient ['einʃənt] *adj* (*civilization, person*)
дре́вний*; (*monument*) стари́нный.
ancient monument *n* па́мятник старины́.
ancillary [æn'siləri] *adj* подсо́бный.

---

* marks translations which have irregular inflections. The Russian-English side of the dictionary gives inflectional information.

and [ænd] *conj* и; (*with pronouns*) с +*instr*;
you ~ I мы с Ва́ми; my father ~ I мы с отцо́м;
bread ~ butter хлеб с ма́слом; ~ so on и так
да́лее; try ~ come постара́йтесь прийти́; he
talked ~ talked он всё говори́л и говори́л.

Andes ['ændi:z] *npl:* the ~ А́нды *pl*.

Andorra [æn'dɔ:rə] *n* Андо́рра.

anecdote ['ænɪkdəut] *n* заба́вная исто́рия.

anemia *etc n* (*US*) = anaemia *etc*.

anemone [ə'nɛmənɪ] *n* ве́треница, анемо́на.

anesthetic *etc* (*US*) = anaesthetic *etc*.

anew [ə'nju:] *adv* за́ново.

angel ['eɪndʒəl] *n* а́нгел.

angel dust *n* (*drug*) „а́нгельская пыль" *f*.

angelic [æn'dʒɛlɪk] *adj* а́нгельский*.

anger ['æŋgə^r] *n* гнев, возмуще́ние ♦ *vt*
серди́ть* (рассерди́ть* *perf*), возмуща́ть
(возмути́ть* *perf*).

angina [æn'dʒaɪnə] *n* грудна́я жа́ба.

angle ['æŋgl] *n* (*corner*) у́гол*; (*viewpoint*): from
their ~ с их то́чки зре́ния ♦ *vi:* to ~ for
(*invitation*) напра́шиваться (напроси́ться*
perf) на +*acc* ♦ *vt:* the idea is/was ~d towards *or*
to иде́я рассчи́тана/была́ рассчи́тана на
+*acc*.

angler ['æŋglə^r] *n* рыболо́в.

Anglican ['æŋglɪkən] *adj* англика́нский* ♦ *n*
англика́нец(-а́нка).

anglicize ['æŋglɪsaɪz] *vt* англизи́ровать (*impf*).

angling ['æŋglɪŋ] *n* ры́бная ло́вля.

Anglo- ['æŋgləu] *prefix* а́нгло-.

Anglo-Saxon ['æŋgləu'sæksən] *adj* а́нгло-
саксо́нский; (*LING*) древнеангли́йский ♦ *n*
англоса́кс; (*LING*) древнеангли́йский язы́к*.

Angola [æŋ'gəulə] *n* Анго́ла.

Angolan [æŋ'gəulən] *adj* анго́льский* ♦ *n*
анго́лец*(-лка*).

angrily ['æŋgrɪlɪ] *adv* серди́то, гне́вно.

angry ['æŋgrɪ] *adj* серди́тый (серди́т),
гне́вный* (гне́вен); (*wound*) воспалённый
(воспалён); to be ~ with sb/at sth серди́ться*
(*impf*) *or* зли́ться (*impf*) на кого́-н/что-н; to get
~ серди́ться* (рассерди́ться* *perf*), зли́ться
(разозли́ться *perf*); he gets ~ easily его́ легко́
рассерди́ть; to make sb ~ серди́ть*
(рассерди́ть* *perf*) *or* злить (разозли́ть *perf*)
кого́-н.

anguish ['æŋgwɪʃ] *n* му́ка.

anguished ['æŋgwɪʃt] *adj* страда́льческий*.

angular ['æŋgjulə^r] *adj* (*person, features*)
углова́тый (углова́т).

animal ['ænɪməl] *n* живо́тное *nt adj*; (*wild
animal*) зверь *m*; (*pej: person*) зверь,
живо́тное ♦ *adj* живо́тный*.

animal rights [-raɪts] *npl* права́ *ntpl* живо́тных;
the ~ ~ movement движе́ние за права́
живо́тных.

animate [*vb* 'ænɪmeɪt, *adj* 'ænɪmɪt] *vt* оживля́ть
(оживи́ть* *perf*) ♦ *adj* живо́й*; (*LING*)
одушевлённый.

animated ['ænɪmeɪtɪd] *adj* оживлённый*

animation ['ænɪ'meɪʃən] *n* (*CINEMA*)
мультиплика́ция; (*enthusiasm*) оживле́ние.

animosity [ænɪ'mɔsɪtɪ] *n* враждебность *f*.

aniseed ['ænɪsi:d] *n* ани́с ♦ *adj* ани́совый.

Ankara ['æŋkərə] *n* Анкара́.

ankle ['æŋkl] *n* лоды́жка*.

ankle sock *n* носо́к*.

annex ['ænɛks] *n* (*also:* ~e: *BRIT*) пристро́йка;
(: *separate building*) отде́льный ко́рпус ♦ *vt*
аннекси́ровать (*impf/perf*).

annexation [ænɛk'seɪʃən] *n* анне́ксия.

annihilate [ə'naɪəleɪt] *vt* уничтожа́ть
(уничто́жить *perf*).

annihilation [ənaɪə'leɪʃən] *n* уничтоже́ние.

anniversary [ænɪ'və:sərɪ] *n* годовщи́на.

Anno Domini ['ænəu'dɔmɪnaɪ] *adv* на́шей э́ры.

annotate ['ænəuteɪt] *vt* составля́ть (соста́вить
perf) коммента́рий на +*acc*.

announce [ə'nauns] *vt* (*decision, engagement*)
объявля́ть (объяви́ть* *perf*) (о +*prp*); (*birth,
death etc*) извеща́ть (извести́ть* *perf*) о +*prp*;
he ~d that he wasn't going он заяви́л, что не
пойдёт.

announcement [ə'naunsmənt] *n* объявле́ние;
(*in newspaper etc*) сообще́ние; (*in letter etc*)
извеще́ние; I'd like to make an ~ я бы хоте́л
сде́лать заявле́ние.

announcer [ə'naunsə^r] *n* (*RADIO, TV*) ди́ктор.

annoy [ə'nɔɪ] *vt* раздража́ть (раздражи́ть
perf); I am ~ed with him он меня́ раздража́ет;
don't get ~ed! не раздража́йтесь *or*
серди́тесь!

annoyance [ə'nɔɪəns] *n* (*feeling*) раздраже́ние,
доса́да.

annoyed [ə'nɔɪd] *adj* раздражённый*
(раздражён).

annoying [ə'nɔɪɪŋ] *adj* (*noise*) раздража́ющий;
(*mistake, event*) доса́дный* (доса́ден); he is ~
он меня́ раздража́ет.

annual ['ænjuəl] *adj* (*meeting*) ежего́дный;
(*income*) годово́й ♦ *n* (*BOT*) одноле́тнее
расте́ние; (*book*) ежего́дник.

annual general meeting *n* (*BRIT*) ежего́дное
о́бщее собра́ние.

annually ['ænjuəlɪ] *adv* ежего́дно.

annual report *n* годово́й отчёт.

annuity [ə'nju:ɪtɪ] *n* ре́нта; life ~ пожи́зненная
ре́нта.

annul [ə'nʌl] *vt* (*contract*) аннули́ровать (*impf/
perf*); (*marriage*) расторга́ть (расто́ргнуть*
perf); (*law*) отменя́ть (отмени́ть* *perf*).

annulment [ə'nʌlmənt] *n* (*see vt*)
аннули́рование; расторже́ние; отме́на.

annum ['ænəm] *n see* per.

Annunciation [ənʌnsɪ'eɪʃən] *n* Благове́щение.

anode ['ænəud] *n* ано́д.

anodyne ['ænədaɪn] *n* успока́ивающее
сре́дство ♦ *adj* нейтра́льный* (нейтра́лен).

anoint [ə'nɔɪnt] *vt* пома́зывать (пома́зать*

okeáн.

anomalous [ə'nɔmələs] *adj* аномáльный* (аномáлен).

anomaly [ə'nɔmələ] *n* аномáлия.

anon. [ə'nɔn] *abbr* = **anonymous**.

anonymity [ænə'nɪmɪtɪ] *n* анонúмность *f*.

anonymous [ə'nɔnɪməs] *adj* анонúмный* (анонúмен); (*place*) безлúкий* (безлúк); **to remain ~** сохранять (сохранúть *perf*) анонúмность.

anorak ['ænəræk] *n* кýртка* с капюшóном.

anorexia [ænə'rɛksɪə] *n* анорéксия.

anorexic [ænə'rɛksɪk] *adj*: **she is ~** онá страдáет анорéксией.

another [ə'nʌðə*] *pron* другóй ♦ *adj*: **~ book** (*additional*) ещё однá кнúга; (*different*) другáя кнúга; **I waited ~ week** я подождáл ещё однý недéлю; **~ drink?** Вам ещё налúть?; **in ~ 5 years** ещё чéрез 5 лет; *see also* **one**.

ANSI *n abbr* (= *American National Standards Institute*) Институт америкáнских национáльных стандáртов.

answer ['ɑ:nsə*] *n* отвéт; (*to problem*) решéние ♦ *vi* отвечáть (отвéтить* *perf*) ♦ *vt* (*letter, question*) отвечáть (отвéтить* *perf*) на +*acc*; (*person*) отвечáть (отвéтить* *perf*) +*dat*; **in ~ to your letter** в отвéт на Вáше письмó; **to ~ the phone** подходúть* (подойтú* *perf*) к телефóну; **to ~ the bell** *or* **the door** открывáть (открыть* *perf*) дверь; **our prayers were ~ed** нáши молúтвы были услышаны

▸ **answer back** *vi* огрызáться (*impf*)

▸ **answer for** *vt fus* отвечáть (отвéтить* *perf*) за +*acc*

▸ **answer to** *vt fus* (*description*) соотвéтствовать (*impf*) +*dat*.

answerable ['ɑ:nsərəbl] *adj*: **~ to sb for sth** отвéтственный пéред кем-н за что-н; **I am ~ to no-one** я не отвечáю ни пéред кем.

answering machine ['ɑ:nsərɪŋ-] *n* автоотвéтчик.

ant [ænt] *n* муравéй*.

ANTA *n abbr* = *American National Theater and Academy*.

antagonism [æn'tægənɪzəm] *n* антагонúзм.

antagonist [æn'tægənɪst] *n* протúвник.

antagonistic [æntægə'nɪstɪk] *adj* (*feelings*) враждéбный* (враждéбен); **he is ~ to the government** он враждéбен по отношéнию к прáвительству.

antagonize [æn'tægənaɪz] *vt*: **to ~ sb** вызывáть (вызвать* *perf*) чьё-н враждéбное отношéние.

Antarctic [ænt'ɑ:ktɪk] *n*: **the ~** Антáрктика.

Antarctica [ænt'ɑ:ktɪkə] *n* Антáрктида.

Antarctic Circle *n*: **the ~ ~** Южный полярный круг.

Antarctic Ocean *n*: **the ~ ~** Антарктúческий*

ante ['æntɪ] *n*: **to up the ~** повышáть (повысить* *perf*) стáвку.

ante... ['æntɪ] *prefix* до..., пред....

anteater ['ænti:tə*] *n* муравьéд.

antecedent [æntɪ'si:dənt] *n* предшéственник; (*ancestor*) прéдок*.

antechamber ['æntɪtʃeɪmbə*] *n* передняя *f adj*, прихóжая *f adj*.

antelope ['æntɪləup] *n* антилóпа.

antenatal ['æntɪ'neɪtl] *adj* дородовóй.

antenatal clinic *n* ≈ жéнская консультáция.

antenna [æn'tɛnə] (*pl* **~e**) *n* ýсик; (*TV*) антéнна.

antennae [æn'tɛni:] *npl of* **antenna**.

anteroom ['æntɪrum] *n* приёмная *f adj*.

anthem ['ænθəm] *n*: **national ~** госудáрственный гимн.

ant hill *n* муравéйник.

anthology [æn'θɔlədʒɪ] *n* антолóгия.

anthropologist [ænθrə'pɔlədʒɪst] *n* антропóлог.

anthropology [ænθrə'pɔlədʒɪ] *n* антрополóгия.

anti... ['æntɪ] *prefix* áнти..., прóтиво....

anti-aircraft ['æntɪ'ɛəkrɑ:ft] *adj* (*missile*) противовоздýшный.

anti-aircraft defence *n* противовоздýшная оборóна.

antiballistic ['æntɪbə'lɪstɪk] *adj* (*missile*) антибаллистúческий.

antibiotic ['æntɪbaɪ'ɔtɪk] *n* (*MED*) антибиóтик.

antibody ['æntɪbɔdɪ] *n* антитéло*.

anticipate [æn'tɪsɪpeɪt] *vt* (*expect*) ожидáть (*impf*) +*gen*; (*foresee*) предвúдеть (*impf/perf*); (*look forward to*) предвкушáть (*impf*); (*forestall*) предвосхищáть (предвосхúтить* *perf*); **this is worse than I ~d** это хýже, чем я ожидáл; **as ~d** как предполагáлось.

anticipation [æntɪsɪ'peɪʃən] *n* (*expectation*) ожидáние; (*eagerness*) предвкушéние; **thanking you in ~** зарáнее благодарю Вас.

anticlimax ['æntɪ'klaɪmæks] *n* разочаровáние.

anticlockwise ['æntɪ'klɔkwaɪz] *adv* (*BRIT*) прóтив часовóй стрéлки.

antics ['æntɪks] *npl* (*of animal, child*) шáлости *fpl*; (*of politicians etc*) выходки *pl*.

anticyclone ['æntɪ'saɪkləun] *n* антициклóн.

antidepressant ['æntɪdɪ'prɛsənt] *n* антидепрессáнт.

antidote ['æntɪdəut] *n* (*also fig*) противоядие.

antifreeze ['æntɪfri:z] *n* антифрúз.

antihistamine ['æntɪ'hɪstəmɪn] *n* антигистамúн.

Antilles [æn'tɪliz] *npl*: **the ~** Антúльские островá *mpl*.

antipathy [æn'tɪpəθɪ] *n* антипáтия.

antiperspirant ['æntɪ'pə:spɪrənt] *n* дезодорáнт.

Antipodean [æntɪpə'di:ən] *adj* антипóдный

---

* marks translations which have irregular inflections. The Russian-English side of the dictionary gives inflectional information.

(*обычно о жителях Австралии и Новой Зеландии*).

Antipodes [æn'tɪpədɪːz] *npl:* **the ~** Австралия и Новая Зеландия.

antiquarian [æntɪ'kwɛərɪən] *n* антиквар ◆ *adj:* **~ bookshop** букинистический* магазин.

antiquated ['æntɪkweɪtɪd] *adj* устарелый.

antique [æn'tiːk] *n* предмет старины ◆ *adj* (*furniture etc*) антикварный*; (*pre-medieval*) античный.

antique dealer *n* антиквар.

antique shop *n* антикварный магазин.

antiquity [æn'tɪkwɪtɪ] *n* античность *f*.

anti-Semitic ['æntɪsɪ'mɪtɪk] *adj* анти-семитский*.

anti-Semitism ['æntɪ'sɛmɪtɪzəm] *n* анти-семитизм.

antiseptic [æntɪ'sɛptɪk] *n* антисептик ◆ *adj* антисептический*.

antisocial ['æntɪ'səuʃəl] *adj* (*behaviour*) антиобщественный*; (*person*) необщительный* (необщителен).

antitank ['æntɪ'tæŋk] *adj* противотанковый.

antitheses [æn'tɪθɪsɪːz] *npl of* **antithesis**.

antithesis [æn'tɪθɪsɪs] (*pl* **antitheses**) *n* антитеза.

antitrust ['æntɪ'trʌst] *adj:* **~ legislation** антимонопольное законодательство.

antlers ['æntləz] *npl* (оленьи) рога* *mpl*.

Antwerp ['æntwəːp] *n* Антверпен.

anus ['eməs] *n* задний* проход.

anvil ['ænvɪl] *n* наковальня.

anxiety [æŋ'zaɪətɪ] *n* (*also MED*) тревога; **~ to do** стремление +*infin*.

anxious ['æŋkʃəs] *adj* (*person*) беспокойный* (беспокоен); (*expression*) озабоченный* (озабочен); (*worrying*) тревожный* (тревожен); (*keen*): **she is ~ to do** она очень хочет +*infin*; **to be ~ about** беспокоиться (*impf*) о +*prp*; **I'm very ~ about you** я очень беспокоюсь за Вас.

anxiously ['æŋkʃəslɪ] *adv* беспокойно, тревожно.

┌─ **KEYWORD** ─────────────────────────┐

any ['ɛnɪ] *adj* **1** (*in questions etc*): **have you any butter/children?** у Вас есть масло/дети?; **do you have any questions/doubts?** у Вас есть какие-нибудь вопросы/сомнения?; **if there are any tickets left** если ещё остались билеты

2 (*with negative*): **I haven't any bread/books** у меня нет хлеба/книг; **I didn't buy/read any newspapers** я не купил/не читал газеты

3 (*no matter which*) любой; **any colour will do** любой цвет пойдёт; **choose any book you like** выбирайте любую книгу, какая Вам понравится

4 (*in phrases*): **in any case** в любом случае; **any day now** сейчас в любой день; **at any moment** в любой момент; **at any rate** во всяком случае; (*anyhow*) так или иначе; **any time** (*at any moment*) в любой момент;

(*whenever*) в любое время; (*in answer to thanks*) не за что; **I need some black leather boots – have you any?** мне нужны чёрные кожаные сапоги – у Вас такие есть?; **I have run out of sugar, you don't have any?** у меня кончился сахар, у Вас не найдётся немного?

◆ *pron* **1** (*in questions etc*): **I need some money, have you got any?** мне нужны деньги, у Вас они есть?; **can any of you sing?** кто-нибудь из Вас умеет петь?

2 (*with negative*) ни один (*f* одна, *nt* одно, *pl* одни); **I haven't any (of those)** у меня таких нет

3 (*no matter which one(s)*) любой; **take any you like** возьмите то, что Вам нравится

◆ *adv* **1** (*in questions etc*): **do you want any more soup/sandwiches?** хотите ещё супа/бутерброды?; **are you feeling any better?** Вам хоть сколько-нибудь лучше?

2 (*with negative*): **I can't hear him any more** я больше его не слышу; **don't wait any longer** не ждите больше; **he isn't any better** ему нисколько *or* ничуть не лучше.

└──────────────────────────────────────┘

anybody ['ɛnɪbɔdɪ] *pron* = **anyone**.

anyhow ['ɛnɪhau] *adv* (*at any rate*) так или иначе; (*haphazardly*): **the work is done ~** работа сделана кое-как *or* как попало; **I shall go ~** я так или иначе пойду; **she leaves things just ~** она разбрасывает вещи как попало.

anyone ['ɛnɪwʌn] *pron* (*in questions etc*) кто-нибудь; (*with negative*) никто; (*no matter who*) кто угодно, любой, всякий*; **can you see ~?** Вы видите кого-нибудь?; **I can't see ~** я никого не вижу; **~ could do it** кто угодно *or* любой *or* всякий* может это сделать; **you can invite ~** Вы можете пригласить кого угодно.

anyplace ['ɛnɪpleɪs] *adv* (*US*) = **anywhere**.

┌─ **KEYWORD** ─────────────────────────┐

anything ['ɛnɪθɪŋ] *pron* **1** (*in questions etc*) что-нибудь; **can you see anything?** Вы видите что-нибудь?

2 (*with negative*) ничего; **I can't see anything** я ничего не вижу

3 (*no matter what*) (всё,) что угодно; **anything (at all) will do** всё, (что угодно) подойдёт; **he'll eat anything** он ест всё, что ему ни дай.

└──────────────────────────────────────┘

anyway ['ɛnɪweɪ] *adv* (*at any rate*) всё равно; (*besides*) всё равно, в любом случае; **I will be there ~** я всё равно там буду; **~, I couldn't stay even if I wanted to** всё равно *or* в любом случае, я не мог бы остаться, даже если бы я захотел; **why are you phoning, ~?** а что Вы звоните?

┌─ **KEYWORD** ─────────────────────────┐

anywhere ['ɛnɪwɛə] *adv* **1** (*in questions etc: position*) где-нибудь; (: *motion*) куда-нибудь; **can you see him anywhere?** Вы его где-нибудь видите?; **did you walk anywhere yesterday?** Вы вчера куда-нибудь ходили? **2** (with negative: position) нигде; (: motion) никуда; **I can't see him anywhere** я нигде его не вижу; **I'm not walking anywhere today** сегодня я никуда не иду **3** (no matter where: position) где угодно; (: motion) куда угодно; **anywhere in the world** где угодно в мире; **put the books down anywhere** положите книги куда угодно.

Anzac ['ænzæk] n abbr = Australia-New Zealand Army Corps.

apace [ə'peɪs] adv стремительно.

apart [ə'pɑːt] adv (position) в стороне; (motion) в сторону; (separately) раздельно, врозь; **they are ten miles/a long way ~** они находятся на расстоянии десяти миль/на большом расстоянии друг от друга; **they are living ~** они живут врозь; **they jumped ~** они отпрыгнули в стороны; **with one's legs ~** с расставленными ногами; **to take ~** разбирать (разобрать* perf) (на части); **from ~** кроме +gen.

apartheid [ə'pɑːteɪt] n апартейд.

apartment [ə'pɑːtmənt] n (US) квартира; (room) комната.

apartment building n (US) многоквартирный дом*.

apathetic [æpə'θɛtɪk] adj апатичный* (апатичен).

apathy ['æpəθɪ] n апатия.

APB n abbr (US: = all points bulletin) ≈ сигнал всем постам.

ape [eɪp] n (ZOOL) человекообразная обезьяна ♦ vt копировать (скопировать perf).

Apennines ['æpənaɪnz] npl: **the ~** Апеннины pl.

aperitif [ə'pɛrɪtiːf] n аперитив.

aperture ['æpətjuə] n отверстие; (PHOT) диафрагма.

apex ['eɪpɛks] n (also fig) вершина.

aphid ['æfɪd] n тля*.

aphorism ['æfərɪzəm] n афоризм.

aphrodisiac [æfrəu'dɪzɪæk] n средство, возбуждающее половое влечение ♦ adj возбуждающий* половое влечение.

API n abbr = American Press Institute.

apiece [ə'piːs] adv (each person) на каждого; (each thing) за штуку.

aplomb [ə'plɔm] n апломб.

APO n abbr (US) = Army Post Office.

apocalypse [ə'pɔkəlɪps] n (end of world) конец* света; (destruction) катастрофа.

apolitical [eɪpə'lɪtɪkl] adj аполитичный* (аполитичен).

apologetic [əpɔlə'dʒɛtɪk] adj (tone) извиняющийся*; (person, expression) виноватый; **an ~ letter** письмо* с

извинениями; **he's very ~ about ...** он приносит свои извинения за +acc ....

apologize [ə'pɔlədʒaɪz] vi: **to ~ (for sth to sb)** извиняться (извиниться perf) (за что-н перед кем-н).

apology [ə'pɔlədʒɪ] n извинение; **to send one's apologies** извиняться (извиниться* perf) за своё отсутствие; **please accept my apologies** пожалуйста, примите мои извинения.

apoplectic [æpə'plɛktɪk] adj (MED) апоплексический; (fig): **~ with rage** разъярённый (разъярён).

apoplexy ['æpəplɛksɪ] n апоплексия.

apostle [ə'pɔsl] n апостол.

apostrophe [ə'pɔstrəfɪ] n апостроф.

apotheosis [əpɔθɪ'əusɪs] n (deification) обожествление; (fig) апофеоз.

appal [ə'pɔːl] vt ужасать (ужаснуть perf); **to be ~led by** ужасаться (ужаснуться perf) +dat.

Appalachian Mountains [æpə'leɪʃən-] npl: **the ~ ~** Аппалачи pl.

appalling [ə'pɔːlɪŋ] adj (awful) ужасный* (ужасен); (shocking) ужасающий*; **she's an ~ cook** она ужасно готовит.

apparatus [æpə'reɪtəs] n аппаратура; (in gymnasium) (гимнастический) снаряд; (of organization) аппарат.

apparel [ə'pærl] n (esp US) одеяние.

apparent [ə'pærənt] adj (seeming) видимый; (obvious) очевидный* (очевиден); **it is ~ that ...** очевидно, что ...

apparently [ə'pærəntlɪ] adv по всей видимости.

apparition [æpə'rɪʃən] n видение, призрак.

appeal [ə'piːl] vi (LAW) апеллировать (impf/perf), подавать* (подать* perf) апелляцию ♦ n (attraction) привлекательность f; (plea) призыв; (LAW) апелляция, обжалование; **to ~ (to sb) for** (help, funds) обращаться (обратиться* perf) (к кому-н) за +instr; (calm, order) призывать (призвать* perf) (кого-н) к +dat; **to ~ to** (be attractive to) привлекать (привлечь* perf), нравиться (понравиться perf) +dat; **to ~ to sb for mercy** взывать (воззвать* perf) к кому-н о милосердии; **the idea doesn't ~ to me** эта идея не привлекает меня; **right of ~** право на апелляцию or на обжалование; **on ~** (LAW) на апелляции.

appealing [ə'piːlɪŋ] adj (attractive) привлекательный* (привлекателен); (touching) трогательный* (трогателен); (pleading) умоляющий*.

appear [ə'pɪə] vi (come into view, develop) появляться (появиться* perf); (seem) казаться* (показаться* perf); (be published) выходить* (выйти* perf); **to ~ in court** представать* (предстать* perf) перед судом; **to ~ on TV** выступать* (выступить* perf) по

---

* marks translations which have irregular inflections. The Russian-English side of the dictionary gives inflectional information.

телеви́дению; **to ~ in "Hamlet"** игра́ть
(сыгра́ть *perf*) в "Га́млете"; **it would ~ that ...**
похо́же (на то), что ....
appearance [ə'pɪərəns] *n* (*arrival*) появле́ние;
(*look, aspect*) вне́шность *f*; (*in public, on TV*)
выступле́ние; **to put in** *or* **make an ~**
появля́ться (появи́ться* *perf*); **cast in** *or* **by
order of ~** (*THEAT*) соста́в исполни́телей в
поря́дке появле́ния; **to keep up ~s**
соблюда́ть (соблюсти́* *perf*) прили́чия; **to** *or*
by all ~s су́дя по всему́.
appease [ə'piːz] *vt* (*person, country*)
умиротворя́ть (умиротвори́ть *perf*).
appeasement [ə'piːzmənt] *n* (*POL*)
умиротворе́ние.
append [ə'pɛnd] *vt* (*COMPUT*) добавля́ть
(доба́вить* *perf*) (в коне́ц), присоединя́ть
(присоедини́ть *perf*).
appendage [ə'pɛndɪdʒ] *n* прида́ток*.
appendices [ə'pɛndɪsiːz] *npl of* **appendix**.
appendicitis [əpɛndɪ'saɪtɪs] *n* аппендици́т.
appendix [ə'pɛndɪks] (*pl* **appendices**) *n*
приложе́ние; (*ANAT*) аппе́ндикс; **he had his ~
out** ему́ вы́резали аппендици́т.
appetite ['æpɪtaɪt] *n* аппети́т; (*fig*) страсть* *f*;
that walk has given me an ~ по́сле прогу́лки
у меня́ разыгра́лся аппети́т.
appetizer ['æpɪtaɪzə'] *n* (*food*) заку́ска*; (*drink*)
аперити́в.
appetizing ['æpɪtaɪzɪŋ] *adj* (*smell*) аппети́тный.
applaud [ə'plɔːd] *vi* (*clap*) аплоди́ровать (*impf*),
рукоплеска́ть* (*impf*) ♦ *vt* аплоди́ровать (*impf*)
+*dat*, рукоплеска́ть* (*impf*) +*dat*; (*praise*)
одобря́ть (одо́брить *perf*).
applause [ə'plɔːz] *n* (*clapping*) аплодисме́нты
pl.
apple ['æpl] *n* я́блоко*; **he's the ~ of her eye**
она́ в нём души́ не ча́ет.
apple tree *n* я́блоня.
apple turnover *n* шарло́тка.
appliance [ə'plaɪəns] *n* (*electrical, domestic*)
прибо́р.
applicable [ə'plɪkəbl] *adj*: ~ **(to)** примени́мый
(примени́м) (к +*dat*); **the law is ~ from
January** зако́н вступа́ет в си́лу с января́.
applicant ['æplɪkənt] *n* (*for job, scholarship*)
кандида́т; (*for college*) абитурие́нт.
application [æplɪ'keɪʃən] *n* (*for a job, a grant etc*)
заявле́ние; (*hard work*) стара́ние; (*of cream,
paint*) нанесе́ние; **on ~** (*of rule, knowledge*) по
зая́вке; (*of methods*) примене́ние.
application form *n* заявле́ние-анке́та.
application program *n* (*COMPUT*) прикладна́я
програ́мма.
applications package *n* (*COMPUT*) паке́т
прикладны́х програ́мм.
applied [ə'plaɪd] *adj* (*science, art*) прикладно́й.
apply [ə'plaɪ] *vt* (*paint, makeup*) наноси́ть*
(нанести́* *perf*); (*bandage*) накла́дывать
(наложи́ть *perf*); (*theory, law*) применя́ть
(примени́ть* *perf*) ♦ *vi*: **to ~ to** (*be applicable*)

применя́ться (*impf*) к +*dat*; (*ask*) обраща́ться
(обрати́ться* *perf*) (с про́сьбой) к +*dat*; **to ~
the brakes** нажима́ть (нажа́ть* *perf*) на
тормоза́; **to ~ o.s. to** сосредота́чиваться
(сосредото́читься *perf*) на +*prp*; **to ~ for a
grant/job** подава́ть* (пода́ть* *perf*) заявле́ние
на стипе́ндию/о приёме на рабо́ту.
appoint [ə'pɔɪnt] *vt* назнача́ть (назна́чить *perf*).
appointed [ə'pɔɪntɪd] *adj*: **at the ~ time** в
назна́ченное вре́мя*.
appointee [əpɔɪn'tiː] *n* получи́вший(-ая) *m(f)*
adj назначе́ние.
appointment [ə'pɔɪntmənt] *n* (*of person*)
назначе́ние; (*post*) до́лжность* *f*; (*arranged
meeting*) приём; **to make an ~** (**with sb**)
назнача́ть (назна́чить *perf*) (кому́-н) встре́чу
or свида́ние; **I have an ~ with the director/the
doctor** я запи́сан на приём к мини́стру/к
врачу́; **to make an ~ with the hairdresser/
doctor** записа́ться* (*perf*) в парикма́херскую/
на приём к врачу́; **by ~** по за́писи.
apportion [ə'pɔːʃən] *vt* распределя́ть
(распредели́ть *perf*); **to ~ sth to sb** наделя́ть
(надели́ть *perf*) кого́-н чем-н; **to ~ blame to
sb** возлага́ть (возложи́ть *perf*) вину́ на
кого́-н.
apposition [æpə'zɪʃən] *n* приложе́ние.
appraisal [ə'preɪzl] *n* оце́нка*.
appraise [ə'preɪz] *vt* оце́нивать (оцени́ть*
perf).
appreciable [ə'priːʃəbl] *adj* значи́тельный.
appreciably [ə'priːʃəblɪ] *adv* заме́тно,
ощути́мо.
appreciate [ə'priːʃɪeɪt] *vt* (*value*) цени́ть* (*impf*);
(*understand*) понима́ть (поня́ть* *perf*) ♦ *vi*
(*COMM*) повыша́ться (повы́ситься* *perf*) в
цене́; **I ~ your help** я благода́рен Вам за
по́мощь; **he ~s good cooking/opera** он
цени́тель хоро́шей ку́хни/о́перы.
appreciation [əpriːʃɪ'eɪʃən] *n* (*understanding*)
понима́ние; (*gratitude*) призна́тельность *f*;
(*COMM*) повыше́ние сто́имости.
appreciative [ə'priːʃɪətɪv] *adj* (*person, audience*)
призна́тельный* (призна́телен); (*comment*)
одобри́тельный* (одобри́телен).
apprehend [æprɪ'hɛnd] *vt* (*arrest*) заде́рживать
(задержа́ть* *perf*); (*understand*) понима́ть
(поня́ть* *perf*).
apprehension [æprɪ'hɛnʃən] *n* опасе́ние; (*of
criminal*) задержа́ние.
apprehensive [æprɪ'hɛnsɪv] *adj* (*glance etc*)
опа́сливый; **to be ~ about sth** опаса́ться
(*impf*) за что-н.
apprentice [ə'prɛntɪs] *n* подмастерье*, учени́к*
♦ *vt*: **to be ~d to sb** быть (*impf*) в уче́нии у
кого́-н.
apprenticeship [ə'prɛntɪsʃɪp] *n* (*also fig*)
учени́чество; **to serve one's ~** проходи́ть*
(пройти́ *perf*) обуче́ние.
appro. ['æprəu] *abbr* (*BRIT*: *inf*: *COMM*:) =
approval): **on ~** на про́бу.

approach [ə'prəʊtʃ] *vi* приближа́ться
(прибли́зиться* *perf*) ♦ *vt* (*ask, apply to*)
обраща́ться (обрати́ться* *perf*) к +*dat*; (*come
to*) приближа́ться (прибли́зиться* *perf*) к
+*dat*; (*consider*) подходи́ть* (подойти́* *perf*) к
+*dat* ♦ *n* (*advance: also fig*) приближе́ние;
(*access: on foot*) подхо́д; (: *by transport*)
подъе́зд; (*to problem, situation*) подхо́д; **to ~
sb about sth** обраща́ться (обрати́ться* *perf*) к
кому́-н с предложе́нием о чём-н.
approachable [ə'prəʊtʃəbl] *adj* (*person, place*)
досту́пный* (досту́пен).
approach road *n* подъездно́й путь* *m*.
approbation [æprə'beɪʃən] *n* одобре́ние.
appropriate [*adj* ə'prəʊprɪɪt, *vb* ə'prəʊprɪeɪt] *adj*
(*behaviour*) подоба́ющий*; (*remarks*)
уме́стный; (*tools*) подходя́щий* ♦ *vt*
присва́ивать (присво́ить* *perf*); **it would not
be ~ for me to comment** бы́ло бы неуме́стно
с мое́й стороны́ комменти́ровать; **it is not ~
for you to behave like that** Вам не подоба́ет
вести́ себя́ так.
appropriately [ə'prəʊprɪɪtlɪ] *adv* подоба́ющим
or соотве́тствующим о́бразом.
appropriation [əprəʊprɪ'eɪʃən] *n* присвое́ние.
appropriation account *n* счёт ассигнова́ний.
approval [ə'pruːvəl] *n* одобре́ние; (*permission*)
согла́сие; **to meet with sb's ~** получа́ть
(получи́ть* *perf*) чьё-н одобре́ние; **on ~**
(*COMM*) на про́бу.
approve [ə'pruːv] *vt* (*motion, decision*)
одобря́ть (одо́брить* *perf*); (*publication,
product*) утвержда́ть (утверди́ть* *perf*)
▸ **approve of** *vt fus* одобря́ть (одо́брить *perf*).
approved school [ə'pruːvd-] *n* (*BRIT: formerly*)
исправи́тельная шко́ла.
approvingly [ə'pruːvɪŋlɪ] *adv* одобри́тельно.
approx. *abbr* = **approximately**.
approximate [*adj* ə'prɒksɪmɪt, *vb* ə'prɒksɪmeɪt]
adj приблизи́тельный (приблизи́телен) ♦ *vi*:
to ~ to приближа́ться (прибли́зиться* *perf*) к
+*dat*.
approximately [ə'prɒksɪmɪtlɪ] *adv* приблиз-
и́тельно.
approximation [əprɒksɪ'meɪʃən] *n* приближ-
е́ние.
APR *n abbr* (= *annual percentage rate*) годова́я
проце́нтная ста́вка.
Apr. *abbr* = **April**.
apricot ['eɪprɪkɔt] *n* абрико́с.
April ['eɪprəl] *n* апре́ль *m*; **~ fool!** пе́рвое
Апре́ля – никому́ не ве́рю!; *see also* **July**.
April Fool's Day *n* день *m* дурако́в.
apron ['eɪprən] *n* пере́дник, фа́ртук; (*AVIAT*)
площа́дка пе́ред анга́ром.
apse [æps] *n* апси́да.
APT *n abbr* (*BRIT*: = *advanced passenger train*)
пассажи́рский* суперэкспре́сс.

apt [æpt] *adj* (*suitable: comment, description etc*)
уда́чный* (уда́чен), уме́стный (уме́стен); **~
to do** скло́нный +*infin*.
Apt. *abbr* (= *apartment*) кв.= кварти́ра.
aptitude ['æptɪtjuːd] *n* скло́нность *f*.
aptitude test *n* тест на выявле́ние
скло́нностей.
aptly ['æptlɪ] *adv* уме́стно; (*accurately*) то́чно.
aqualung ['ækwəlʌŋ] *n* аквала́нг.
aquarium [ə'kwɛərɪəm] *n* аква́риум.
Aquarius [ə'kwɛərɪəs] *n* Водоле́й; **he is ~** он –
Водоле́й.
aquatic [ə'kwætɪk] *adj* во́дный.
aqueduct ['ækwɪdʌkt] *n* акведу́к.
AR *abbr* (*US: POST*) = *Arkansas*.
ARA *n abbr* (*BRIT*) = *Associate of the Royal
Academy*.
Arab ['ærəb] *adj* ара́бский* ♦ *n* ара́б(ка).
Arabia [ə'reɪbɪə] *n* Ара́вия.
Arabian [ə'reɪbɪən] *adj* ара́бский*.
Arabian Desert *n*: **the ~ ~** Арави́йская
пусты́ня.
Arabian Sea *n*: **the ~ ~** Арави́йское мо́ре*.
Arabic ['ærəbɪk] *adj* ара́бский* ♦ *n* ара́бский
язы́к*.
arable ['ærəbl] *adj* (*land*) па́хотный; (*farm*)
полево́дческий.
Aral Sea ['ærəl-] *n* Ара́льское мо́ре.
ARAM *n abbr* (*BRIT*) = *Associate of the Royal
Academy of Music*.
arbiter ['ɑːbɪtə'] *n* арби́тр (*в спо́ре*).
arbitrary ['ɑːbɪtrən] *adj* произво́льный*
(произво́лен).
arbitrate ['ɑːbɪtreɪt] *vi* выноси́ть* (вы́нести*
perf) трете́йское реше́ние.
arbitration [ɑːbɪ'treɪʃən] *n* (*of quarrel*)
трете́йский суд*; (*INDUSTRY*) арбитра́ж; **the
dispute went to ~** спор пе́редан в арбитра́ж.
arbitrator ['ɑːbɪtreɪtə'] *n* трете́йский судья́*,
арби́тр.
ARC *n abbr* = *American Red Cross*.
arc [ɑːk] *n* (*also MATH*) дуга́*.
arcade [ɑː'keɪd] *n* (*round a square*) арка́да;
(*shopping mall*) пасса́ж.
arch [ɑːtʃ] *n* а́рка*, свод; (*of foot*) свод ♦ *vt*
(*back*) выгиба́ть (вы́гнуть* *perf*) ♦ *adj* (*playful*)
игри́вый; (*knowing*) многозначи́тельный ♦
prefix а́рхи-.
archaeological [ɑːkɪə'lɔdʒɪkl] (*US
archeological*) *adj* археологи́ческий*.
archaeologist [ɑːkɪ'ɔlədʒɪst] (*US archeologist*) *n*
архео́лог.
archaeology [ɑːkɪ'ɔlədʒɪ] (*US archeology*) *n*
археоло́гия.
archaic [ɑː'keɪɪk] *adj* архаи́ческий.
Archangel ['ɑːkeɪndʒəl] *n* Арха́нгельск.
archangel ['ɑːkeɪndʒəl] *n* арха́нгел.
archbishop [ɑːtʃ'bɪʃəp] *n* архиепи́скоп.

---

* marks translations which have irregular inflections. The Russian-English side of the dictionary gives inflectional information.

arch-enemy [ˈɑːtʃˈɛnəmɪ] n заклятый враг*.
archeology etc [ɑːkɪˈɔlədʒɪ] (US) = **archaeology** etc.
archery [ˈɑːtʃərɪ] n стрельба* из лука.
archetypal [ˈɑːkɪtaɪpəl] adj типичный*.
archetype [ˈɑːkɪtaɪp] n образец.
archipelago [ɑːkɪˈpɛlɪgəu] n архипелаг.
architect [ˈɑːkɪtɛkt] n (of building) архитектор.
architectural [ɑːkɪˈtɛktʃərəl] adj архитектурный.
architecture [ˈɑːkɪtɛktʃəʳ] n архитектура.
archive [ˈɑːkaɪvz] n архив.
archive file n (COMPUT) архивный файл.
archives [ˈɑːkaɪvz] npl архив msg.
archivist [ˈɑːkɪvɪst] n архивариус.
archway [ˈɑːtʃweɪ] n арочный проход.
ARCM n abbr (BRIT) = Associate of the Royal College of Music.
Arctic [ˈɑːktɪk] adj арктический* ♦ n: the ~ Арктика.
Arctic Circle n: the ~~ Северный Полярный круг.
Arctic Ocean n: the ~~ Северный Ледовитый океан.
ARD n abbr (US: MED: = acute respiratory disease) ОРЗ= острое респираторное заболевание.
ardent [ˈɑːdənt] adj пылкий* (пылок).
ardour [ˈɑːdəʳ] (US ardor) n пыл*.
arduous [ˈɑːdjuəs] adj тяжёлый* (тяжёл).
are [ɑːʳ] vb see be.
area [ˈɛərɪə] n (of country, knowledge) область f; (part: of place) участок*; (: of room) часть f; (GEOM etc) площадь* f; in the London ~ в районе Лондона.
area code n код зоны.
arena [əˈriːnə] n (also fig) арена.
aren't [ɑːnt] = are not; see be.
Argentina [ɑːdʒənˈtiːnə] n Аргентина.
Argentinian [ɑːdʒənˈtɪnɪən] adj аргентинский* ♦ n аргентинец*(-инка*).
arguable [ˈɑːgjuəbl] adj спорный* (спорен); it is ~ whether this is necessary нужно ли это – вопрос спорный; it is ~ that ... можно утверждать, что ....
arguably [ˈɑːgjuəblɪ] adv возможно; he is ~ the best in his profession можно утверждать, что он лучший специалист в своей области.
argue [ˈɑːgjuː] vi (quarrel) ссориться (поссориться perf); (reason) доказывать (доказать* perf) ♦ vt обсуждать (обсудить* perf); to ~ that ... доказывать (доказать* perf), что ...; to ~ about sth спорить (поспорить perf) о чём-н; to ~ for/against sth приводить* (привести* perf) доводы в пользу/против чего-н.
argument [ˈɑːgjumənt] n (quarrel) ссора; (reasons) аргумент, довод; (debate) обсуждение, спор*; ~ for/against аргумент or довод в пользу/против +gen.
argumentative [ɑːgjuˈmɛntətɪv] adj (person) конфликтный; (voice) вызывающий*.

aria [ˈɑːrɪə] n ария.
ARIBA n abbr (BRIT) = Associate of the Royal Institute of British Architects.
arid [ˈærɪd] adj безводный* (безводен); (fig) сухой.
aridity [əˈrɪdɪtɪ] n сухость f.
Aries [ˈɛərɪz] n Овен*; he is ~ он – Овен.
arise [əˈraɪz] (pt arose, pp arisen) vi (occur) возникать (возникнуть* perf); to ~ from возникать (возникнуть* perf) вследствие +gen; should the need ~ если возникнет необходимость.
arisen [əˈrɪzn] pp of arise.
aristocracy [ærɪsˈtɔkrəsɪ] n аристократия.
aristocrat [ˈærɪstəkræt] n аристократ(ка*).
aristocratic [ærɪstəˈkrætɪk] adj (family) аристократический*; (features) аристократичный.
arithmetic [əˈrɪθmətɪk] n (MATH) арифметика; (calculation) подсчёт.
arithmetical [ærɪθˈmɛtɪkl] adj арифметический*.
ark [ɑːk] n: Noah's A~ Ноев ковчег.
arm [ɑːm] n рука*; (of chair) ручка*; (of clothing) рукав*; (of organization) подразделение ♦ vt вооружать (вооружить* perf); ~s npl (MIL) вооружение ntsg; (HERALDRY) герб*; ~ in ~ под руку.
armaments [ˈɑːməmənts] npl вооружение sg.
armband [ˈɑːmbænd] n нарукавная повязка.
armchair [ˈɑːmtʃɛəʳ] n кресло*.
armed [ɑːmd] adj вооружённый (вооружён); the ~ forces вооружённые силы.
armed robbery n вооружённый грабёж*.
Armenia [ɑːˈmiːnɪə] n Армения.
Armenian [ɑːˈmiːnɪən] adj армянский* ♦ n армянин*(-нка); (LING) армянский* язык*.
armful [ˈɑːmful] n охапка.
armistice [ˈɑːmɪstɪs] n перемирие.
armor etc (US) = **armour** etc.
armour [ˈɑːməʳ] (US armor) n (also: suit of ~) доспехи mpl; (also: ~plating) броня; (tanks) бронесилы fpl.
armoured car [ˈɑːməd-] n бронемашина.
armoury [ˈɑːmərɪ] n (also fig) арсенал.
armpit [ˈɑːmpɪt] n подмышка*.
armrest [ˈɑːmrɛst] n подлокотник.
arms control [ɑːmz-] n контроль m вооружений.
arms race n: the ~~ гонка вооружений.
army [ˈɑːmɪ] n (also fig) армия.
aroma [əˈrəumə] n аромат.
aromatherapy [ərəumə'θɛrəpɪ] n ароматерапия.
aromatic [ærəˈmætɪk] adj ароматный* (ароматен).
arose [əˈrəuz] pt of arise.
around [əˈraund] adv вокруг ♦ prep (encircling) вокруг +gen; (near, about) около +gen; is he ~? он здесь?; ~ £5/3 o'clock около £5/3 часов; ~ here здесь поблизости.

arousal [əˈrauzəl] *n* возбуждёние.
arouse [əˈrauz] *vt* (*sleeping person*) будить*
(разбудить* *perf*); (*interest, passions*)
возбуждать (возбудить* *perf*).
arpeggio [ɑːˈpɛdʒɪəu] *n* арпёджио *nt ind*.
arrange [əˈreɪndʒ] *vt* (*organize*) устраивать
(устроить *perf*); (*put in order*) расставлять
(расставить *perf*); (*MUS*) аранжировать (*impf/
perf*) ♦ *vi*: **we have ~d for a car to pick you up**
мы договорились, чтобы машина заёхала
за Вами; **it was ~d that ...** было условлено,
что ...; **to ~ to do** уславливаться
(условиться* *perf*) +*infin*, договариваться
(договориться* *perf*) +*infin*.
arrangement [əˈreɪndʒmənt] *n* (*agreement*)
договорённость *f*; (*MUS*) аранжировка*;
(*order, layout*) расположёние; **~s** *npl*
(*preparations, plans*) приготовлёния *ntpl*; **to
come to an ~ with sb** приходить* (прийти*
perf) к соглашёнию с кем-н; **home deliveries
by ~** доставка на дом по договорённости;
I'll make ~s for you to be met я договорюсь,
чтобы Вас встрётили.
arrant [ˈærənt] *adj* отъявленный.
array [əˈreɪ] *n* (*MATH, COMPUT*) массив; **~ of**
масса +*gen*, множество +*gen*.
arrears [əˈrɪəz] *npl* задолженность *fsg*; **to be in
~ with one's rent** иметь (*impf*)
задолженность по квартплате.
arrest [əˈrɛst] *vt* (*criminal*) арестовывать
(арестовать *perf*); (*sb's attention*)
приковывать (приковать *perf*) ♦ *n* арёст,
задержание; **under ~** под арёстом.
arresting [əˈrɛstɪŋ] *adj* поразительный.
arrival [əˈraɪvl] *n* прибытие; (*COMM*) привоз;
new ~ (*person*) новичок*; (*baby*)
новорождённый(-ая) *m(f) adj*.
arrive [əˈraɪv] *vi* (*traveller*) прибывать
(прибыть* *perf*); (*letter, news*) приходить*
(прийти* *perf*); (*baby*) рождаться (родиться*
perf)
▸ **arrive at** *vt fus* (*fig*) приходить* (прийти* *perf*)
к +*dat*.
arrogance [ˈærəgəns] *n* высокомёрие.
arrogant [ˈærəgənt] *adj* высокомёрный*
(высокомёрен).
arrow [ˈærəu] *n* (*weapon*) стрела*; (*sign*)
стрёлка*.
arse [ɑːs] *n* (*BRIT: infl*) жопа (*!*)
arsenal [ˈɑːsɪnl] *n* арсенал.
arsenic [ˈɑːsnɪk] *n* мышьяк*.
arson [ˈɑːsn] *n* поджог.
art [ɑːt] *n* (*also fig*) искусство; (*also: Fine A~*)
изобразительное искусство; **A~s** *npl*
гуманитарные науки *fpl*; **work of ~**
произведёние искусства.
artefact [ˈɑːtɪfækt] *n* художественное издёлие,
подёлка.

arterial [ɑːˈtɪərɪəl] *adj* (*ANAT*) артериальный; **~
road** магистраль *f*.
artery [ˈɑːtərɪ] *n* (*also fig*) артёрия.
artful [ˈɑːtful] *adj* ловкий*.
art gallery *n* (*national*) картинная галерёя;
(*private*) галерёя.
arthritic [ɑːˈθrɪtɪk] *adj* артритический*.
arthritis [ɑːˈθraɪtɪs] *n* артрит.
artichoke [ˈɑːtɪtʃəuk] *n* (*also: globe ~*)
артишок; (*also: Jerusalem ~*) земляная
груша.
article [ˈɑːtɪkl] *n* (*object, item*) предмёт; (*LING*)
артикль *m*; (*in newspaper*) статья*; (*in
document*) пункт; **~s** *npl* (*BRIT: LAW*) курс
профессиональной подготовки адвокатов; **~
of clothing** предмёт одёжды.
articles of association *npl* (*COMM*) устав
акционёрной компании.
articulate [*adj* ɑːˈtɪkjulɪt, *vb* ɑːˈtɪkjuleɪt] *adj*
(*speech, writing*) вразумительный*
(вразумителен) ♦ *vt* (*fears, ideas*) выражать
(выразить* *perf*) ♦ *vi*: **to ~ well/badly** чётко/
нечётко выговаривать (выговорить *perf*);
she is very ~ она чётко *or* ясно выражает
свои мысли.
articulated lorry *n* (*BRIT*) грузовик* с
прицёпом.
artifice [ˈɑːtɪfɪs] *n* (*trick*) приём; (*skill*)
искусность *f*.
artificial [ɑːtɪˈfɪʃəl] *adj* искусственный*;
(*affected*) неестёственный* (неестёствен).
artificial insemination [-ɪnsɛmɪˈneɪʃən] *n*
искусственное оплодотворёние.
artificial intelligence *n* искусственный
интеллёкт.
artificial respiration *n* искусственное
дыхание.
artillery [ɑːˈtɪlərɪ] *n* (*MIL: corps*) артиллёрия.
artisan [ˈɑːtɪzæn] *n* ремёсленник(-ица).
artist [ˈɑːtɪst] *n* художник(-ица); (*performer*)
артист(ка).
artistic [ɑːˈtɪstɪk] *adj* художественный; **an ~
person** художественная личность *f*.
artistry [ˈɑːtɪstrɪ] *n* мастерство.
artless [ˈɑːtlɪs] *adj* безыскусный (безыскусен).
art school *n* художественное училище.
artwork [ˈɑːtwəːk] *n* оформлёние.
ARV *n abbr* (*BIBLE*: = *American Revised Version*)
американский *вариант Библии.*
AS *n abbr* (*US*: = *Associate in/of Science*) член
ассоциации научных работников ♦ *abbr*
(*POST*) = *American Samoa.*

KEYWORD

as [æz] *conj* **1** (*referring to time*) когда; **as the
years went by** с годами; **he came in as I was
leaving** он вошёл, когда я уходил; **as from
tomorrow** с завтрашнего дня
2 (*in comparisons*): **as big as** такой же

---

* marks translations which have irregular inflections. The Russian-English side of the dictionary gives inflectional information.

большо́й, как; **twice as big as** в два ра́за бо́льше, чем; **as white as snow** бе́лый как снег; **as much money/many books as** сто́лько же де́нег/книг, ско́лько; **as soon as** как то́лько; **as soon as possible** как мо́жно скоре́е

3 (*since, because*) поско́льку, так как

4 (*referring to manner, way*) как; **do as you wish** де́лайте, как хоти́те; **as she said** она́ сказа́ла

5 (*concerning*) **as for** *or* **to** что каса́ется +*gen*:

6: **as if** *or* **though** так, как бу́дто бы; **he looked as if he had been ill** он вы́глядел так, как бу́дто бы он был бо́лен

♦ *prep* (*in the capacity of*): **he works as a driver/ waiter** он рабо́тает шофёром/официа́нтом; **as chairman of the company, he ...** как глава́ компа́нии, он ...; *see also* **long, same, such, well**.

ASA *n abbr* (= *American Standards Association*) Америка́нская ассоциа́ция станда́ртов.

a.s.a.p. *adv abbr* (= *as soon as possible*) как мо́жно скоре́е.

asbestos [æz'bɛstəs] *n* асбе́ст.

ascend [ə'sɛnd] *vt* (*hill*) восходи́ть* (взойти́* *perf*) на +*acc*; (*stairs*) всходи́ть* (взойти́* *perf*) по +*dat*; (*throne*) взойти́* (*perf*) на +*acc*.

ascendancy [ə'sɛndənsɪ] *n* госпо́дство; **~ over sb** госпо́дство над кем-н.

ascendant [ə'sɛndənt] *n*: **to be in the ~** госпо́дствовать (*impf*).

ascension [ə'sɛnʃən] *n*: **the A~** (*REL*) Вознесе́ние.

Ascension Island *n* О́стров Вознесе́ния.

ascent [ə'sɛnt] *n* (*slope*) подъём; (*climb*) восхожде́ние.

ascertain [æsə'teɪn] *vt* устана́вливать (установи́ть* *perf*).

ascetic [ə'sɛtɪk] *adj* аскети́ческий*.

asceticism [ə'sɛtɪsɪzəm] *n* аскети́зм.

ASCII ['æskiː] *n* (*COMPUT*: = *American Standard Code for Information Interchange*) *америка́нский станда́ртный код для обме́на информа́цией*.

ascribe [ə'skraɪb] *vt*: **to ~ sth to** припи́сывать (приписа́ть* *perf*) что-н +*dat*.

ASCU *n abbr* (*US*) = *Association of State Colleges and Universities*.

ASEAN ['æsiæn] *n abbr* (= *Association of South-East Asian Nations*) АСЕА́Н.

ASH [æʃ] *n abbr* (*BRIT*: = *Action on Smoking and Health*) О́бщество борьбы́ с куре́нием.

ash [æʃ] *n* (*of fire*) зола́, пе́пел*; (*of cigarette*) пе́пел; (*wood, tree*) я́сень *m*.

ashamed [ə'ʃeɪmd] *adj*: **to be ~ (of)** стыди́ться (*impf*) (+*gen*); **I'm ~ of ...** мне сты́дно +*gen* ...; **I'm ~ of myself for having done that** мне сты́дно, что я сде́лал э́то.

ashen ['æʃən] *adj* (*face*) мёртвенно-бле́дный*.

Ashkhabad [aʃxa'bat] *n* Ашхаба́д.

ashore [ə'ʃɔː'] *adv* (*be*) на берегу́; (*swim, go*) на бе́рег.

ashtray ['æʃtreɪ] *n* пе́пельница.

Ash Wednesday *n* пе́рвый день* *m* Вели́кого Поста́.

Asia ['eɪʃə] *n* А́зия.

Asia Minor *n* Ма́лая А́зия.

Asian ['eɪʃən] *adj* азиа́тский* ♦ *n* азиа́т(ка*).

Asiatic [eɪsɪ'ætɪk] *adj* азиа́тский*.

aside [ə'saɪd] *adv* в сто́рону ♦ *n* ре́плика ♦ *prep*: **~ from** поми́мо +*gen*; **to brush objections ~** отмета́ть (отмести́* *perf*) возраже́ния в сто́рону.

ask [ɑːsk] *vt* (*inquire*) спра́шивать (спроси́ть* *perf*); (*invite*) звать (позва́ть* *perf*); **to ~ sb for sth/sb to do** проси́ть* (попроси́ть* *perf*) у кого́-н/кого́-н +*infin*; **to ~ sb the time** спра́шивать (спроси́ть* *perf*) кого́-н, кото́рый час; **to ~ sb about sth** спра́шивать (спроси́ть* *perf*) кого́-н о чём-н; **to ~ about the price** спра́шивать (спроси́ть* *perf*) о цене́; **to ~ (sb) a question** задава́ть* (зада́ть* *perf*) (кому́-н) вопро́с; **to ~ sb out to dinner** приглаша́ть (пригласи́ть* *perf*) кого́-н в рестора́н

▶ **ask after** *vt fus* (*person*) справля́ться (справи́ться* *perf*) о +*prp*

▶ **ask for** *vt fus* (*request*) проси́ть* (попроси́ть* *perf*); (*look for: trouble*) напра́шиваться (напроси́ться* *perf*) на +*acc*; **he's just ~ing for trouble** *or* **for it** он про́сто напра́шивается на неприя́тности.

askance [ə'skɑːns] *adv*: **to look ~ at sb/sth** смотре́ть* (посмотре́ть* *perf*) на кого́-н/ что-н ко́со.

askew [ə'skjuː] *adv* (*clothes*) кри́во, ко́со.

asking price ['ɑːskɪŋ-] *n*: **the ~ ~** запра́шиваемая цена́*.

asleep [ə'sliːp] *adj* спя́щий; **to be ~** спать* (*impf*); **to fall ~** засыпа́ть (засну́ть *perf*).

ASLEF ['æzlɛf] *n abbr* (*BRIT*) = *Associated Society of Locomotive Engineers and Firemen*.

asp [æsp] *n* а́спид.

asparagus [əs'pærəgəs] *n* спа́ржа.

asparagus tips *npl* спа́ржевые голо́вки* *fpl*.

ASPCA *n abbr* (= *American Society for the Prevention of Cruelty to Animals*) Америка́нское о́бщество защи́ты живо́тных.

aspect ['æspɛkt] *n* (*element*) аспе́кт, сторона́*; (*quality, air*) вид*; **a room with a southern ~** ко́мната с ви́дом на юг.

aspersions [əs'pəːʃənz] *npl*: **to cast ~ on** (*integrity, ability*) ста́вить* (поста́вить* *perf*) под сомне́ние; (*person*) очерня́ть (очерни́ть* *perf*).

asphalt ['æsfælt] *n* асфа́льт.

asphyxiate [æs'fɪksɪeɪt] *vt* души́ть* (задуши́ть* *perf*).

asphyxiation [æsfɪksɪ'eɪʃən] *n* удуше́ние.

aspirate [*vt* 'æspəreɪt, *adj* 'æspərɪt] *vt*

произноси́ть* (произнести́* *perf*) с
придыха́нием ◆ *adj* придыха́тельный.
aspirations [æspə'reɪʃənz] *npl*
устремле́ния *ntpl*.
aspire [əs'paɪə²] *vi*: **to ~ to** стреми́ться* (*impf*) к
+*dat*.
aspirin ['æsprɪn] *n* аспири́н.
aspiring [əs'paɪərɪŋ] *adj* начина́ющий*.
ass [æs] *n* (*also fig*) осёл*; (*US*: *inf*!) жо́па (!)
assail [ə'seɪl] *vt* (*person*) напада́ть (напа́сть*
perf) на +*acc*; (*fig*): **he was ~ed by doubts** его́
одоле́ли сомне́ния.
assailant [ə'seɪlənt] *n*: **his/her ~** напа́вший(-ая)
m(f) adj на него́/неё.
assassin [ə'sæsɪn] *n* полити́ческий* уби́йца *m/f*.
assassinate [ə'sæsɪneɪt] *vt* соверша́ть
(соверши́ть *perf*) покуше́ние на +*acc*.
assassination [əsæsɪ'neɪʃən] *n* полити́ческое
уби́йство.
assault [ə'sɔːlt] *n* нападе́ние; (*MIL*, *fig*) ата́ка ◆
vt напада́ть (напа́сть* *perf*) на +*acc*; (*MIL*)
атакова́ть (*impf/perf*); (*sexually*) соверша́ть
(соверши́ть *perf*) сексуа́льное
посяга́тельство на +*acc*; **~ and battery**
оскорбле́ние де́йствием.
assemble [ə'sɛmbl] *vt* собира́ть (собра́ть* *perf*)
◆ *vi* собира́ться (собра́ться* *perf*).
assembly [ə'sɛmblɪ] *n* (*meeting*) собра́ние;
(*institution*) ассамбле́я, законода́тельное
собра́ние; (*construction*) сбо́рка; **General A~
of the UN** Генера́льная Ассамбле́я ООН.
assembly language *n* (*COMPUT*) язы́к*
ассе́мблера.
assembly line *n* сбо́рочный конве́йер.
assent [ə'sɛnt] *n* согла́сие ◆ *vi*: **to ~ (to)**
соглаша́ться (согласи́ться* *perf*) (на +*acc*).
assert [ə'sɜːt] *vt* (*opinion, authority*)
утвержда́ть (утверди́ть* *perf*); (*rights,
innocence*) отста́ивать (отстоя́ть *perf*); **to ~
o.s.** самоутвержда́ться (самоутверди́ться*
perf).
assertion [ə'sɜːʃən] *n* (*claim*) утвержде́ние.
assertive [ə'sɜːtɪv] *adj* самоуве́ренный
(самоуве́рен).
assess [ə'sɛs] *vt* оце́нивать (оцени́ть* *perf*); **to
~ for tax** оцени́ть (*perf*) сто́имость для це́лей
налогообложе́ния.
assessment [ə'sɛsmənt] *n*: **~ (of)** оце́нка*
(+*gen*); **tax ~** оце́нка сто́имости в це́лях
налогообложе́ния.
assessor [ə'sɛsə²] *n* (*LAW*) экспе́рт-
(-консульта́нт).
asset ['æsɛt] *n* (*useful quality*) досто́инство; **~s**
npl (*property, funds*) акти́вы *mpl*; (*COMM*)
акти́в *msg* бала́нса; **he's an ~ to the company**
он представля́ет собо́й большу́ю це́нность
для компа́нии.
asset-stripping ['æsɛt'strɪpɪŋ] *n* (*COMM*)
распрода́жа неприбыльных акти́вов (*при*

поглоще́нии одно́й компа́нии друго́й).
assiduous [ə'sɪdjuəs] *adj* (*care, work*)
усе́рдный* (усе́рден).
assign [ə'saɪn] *vt* (*task*) поруча́ть (поручи́ть*
perf), предпи́сывать (предписа́ть* *perf*);
(*significance*) придава́ть* (прида́ть* *perf*);
(*resources, role*) предназнача́ть
(предназна́чить *perf*); **to ~ a date for a
meeting** назнача́ть (назна́чить *perf*) да́ту
заседа́ния.
assignment [ə'saɪnmənt] *n* (*task*) предписа́ние;
(*SCOL*) зада́ние.
assimilate [ə'sɪmɪleɪt] *vt* (*ideas*) усва́ивать
(усво́ить *perf*); (*immigrants*): **to be ~d**
ассимили́роваться (*impf/perf*).
assimilation [əsɪmɪ'leɪʃən] *n* усвое́ние; (*of
immigrants etc*) ассимиля́ция.
assist [ə'sɪst] *vt* помога́ть (помо́чь* *perf*) +*dat*;
(*financially*) соде́йствовать (*impf/perf*) +*dat*.
assistance [ə'sɪstəns] *n* по́мощь *f*; (*financial*)
соде́йствие.
assistant [ə'sɪstənt] *n* помо́щник(-ица); (*in
office etc*) ассисте́нт(ка); (*BRIT*: *also*: **shop ~**)
продаве́ц*(-вщи́ца); **laboratory ~**
лабора́нт(ка).
assistant manager *n* замести́тель *m*
заве́дующего.
assizes [ə'saɪzɪz] *npl* (*BRIT*: *LAW*) выездна́я
се́ссия суда́ прися́жных.
associate [*n, adj* ə'səuʃɪt, *vb* ə'səuʃɪeɪt] *n*
(*colleague*) колле́га *m/f*, партнёр ◆ *adj*
(*member, director, professor*)
ассоции́рованный ◆ *vt* (*mentally*)
ассоции́ровать (*impf/perf*); **to ~ with sb**
обща́ться (*impf*) с кем-н.
associated company [ə'səuʃɪeɪtɪd-] *n* доче́рнее
предприя́тие.
association [əsəusɪ'eɪʃən] *n* (*group, PSYCH*)
ассоциа́ция; (*involvement*) связь* *f*; **in ~ with**
в сотру́дничестве с +*instr*.
association football *n* футбо́л.
assorted [ə'sɔːtɪd] *adj* разнообра́зный*; **hats in
~ sizes** шля́пы ра́зных разме́ров.
assortment [ə'sɔːtmənt] *n* (*of clothes, colours*)
ассортиме́нт; (*of books, people*) подбо́р.
Asst. *abbr* (= **assistant**) ассисте́нт.
assuage [ə'sweɪdʒ] *vt* (*grief, pain*) смягча́ть
(смягчи́ть *perf*); (*thirst, hunger*) утоля́ть
(утоли́ть *perf*).
assume [ə'sjuːm] *vt* (*suppose*) предполага́ть
(предположи́ть* *perf*), допуска́ть
(допусти́ть* *perf*); (*responsibilities*) брать*
(взять* *perf*) на себя́; (*command, appearance,
air*) принима́ть (приня́ть* *perf*); (*power*)
брать* (взять* *perf*).
assumed name [ə'sjuːmd-] *n* вы́мышленное
и́мя* *nt*.
assumption [ə'sʌmpʃən] *n* (*supposition*)
предположе́ние; (*of control, responsibility*)

принятие на себя́; ~ **of power** прихо́д к
вла́сти; **on the** ~ **that** ... предполага́я, что ....

assurance [əˈʃuərəns] *n* (*promise*) завере́ние;
(*confidence*) уве́ренность *f*; (*insurance*)
страхова́ние; **I can give you no** ~**s** я не могу́
дать Вам никаки́х гара́нтий.

assure [əˈʃuəˈ] *vt* (*reassure*) уверя́ть (уве́рить
perf), заверя́ть (заве́рить *perf*); (*guarantee*)
обеспе́чивать (обеспе́чить *perf*).

assured [əˈʃuəd] *adj* (*voice*) уве́ренный*
(уве́рен); (*success*) несомне́нный*
(несомне́нен).

AST *abbr* (*US*) = *Atlantic Standard Time.*

asterisk [ˈæstərɪsk] *n* звёздочка* (*знак* "*").

astern [əˈstəːn] *adv* (*NAUT: on ship: position*) на
корме́; (: *motion*) на корму́; (*behind ship*) за
кормо́й; **to move** ~ идти́* (*impf*) за́дним
хо́дом.

asteroid [ˈæstərɔɪd] *n* астеро́ид.

asthma [ˈæsmə] *n* а́стма.

asthmatic [æsˈmætɪk] *adj* (*breathing*)
астмати́ческий* ♦ *n* астма́тик; ~ **attack**
при́ступ а́стмы.

astigmatism [əˈstɪgmətɪzəm] *n* астигмати́зм.

astir [əˈstəːˈ] *adv* на нога́х.

astonish [əˈstɔnɪʃ] *vt* изумля́ть (изуми́ть* *perf*),
поража́ть (порази́ть* *perf*).

astonishing [əˈstɔnɪʃɪŋ] *adj* порази́тельный*
(порази́телен); **I find it** ~ **that** ... меня́
поража́ет, что ....

astonishingly [əˈstɔnɪʃɪŋlɪ] *adv* порази́тельно;
the play, ~, **was successful** порази́тельным
о́бразом пье́са была́ уда́чной.

astonishment [əˈstɔnɪʃmənt] *n* удивле́ние,
изумле́ние; **to my** ~ к моему́ изумле́нию.

astound [əˈstaund] *vt* поража́ть (порази́ть*
perf), изумля́ть (изуми́ть* *perf*).

astounded [əˈstaundɪd] *adj* поражённый
(поражён), изумлённый (изумлён).

astounding [əˈstaundɪŋ] *adj* порази́тельный*
(порази́телен), изуми́тельный*
(изуми́телен).

astray [əˈstreɪ] *adv*: **to go** ~ (*letter*) затеря́ться
(*perf*); (*fig*) сбива́ться (сби́ться* *perf*) с пути́;
to lead ~ (*fig*) сбива́ть (сбить* *perf*) с пути́; **to
go** ~ **in one's calculations** сбива́ться
(сби́ться* *perf*) со счёта.

astride [əˈstraɪd] *prep* верхо́м на +*prp* ♦ *adv*
верхо́м.

astringent [əsˈtrɪndʒənt] *adj* вя́жущий* ♦ *n*
вя́жущее вещество́.

astrologer [əsˈtrɔlədʒəˈ] *n* астро́лог.

astrology [əsˈtrɔlədʒɪ] *n* астроло́гия.

astronaut [ˈæstrənɔːt] *n* астрона́вт,
космона́вт.

astronomer [əsˈtrɔnəməˈ] *n* астроно́м.

astronomical [æstrəˈnɔmɪkl] *adj* (*also fig*)
астрономи́ческий*.

astronomy [əsˈtrɔnəmɪ] *n* астроно́мия.

astrophysics [ˈæstrəuˈfɪzɪks] *n* астрофи́зика.

astute [əsˈtjuːt] *adj* (*person*) проница́тельный*

(проница́телен); (*decision*) дальнови́дный*
(дальнови́ден).

asunder [əˈsʌndəˈ] *adv*: **to tear** ~ разрыва́ть
(разорва́ть* *perf*) на куски́.

ASV *n abbr* (*BIBLE*: = *American Standard Version*)
америка́нский станда́ртный вариа́нт
Би́блии.

asylum [əˈsaɪləm] *n* (*refuge*) убе́жище; (*mental
hospital*) сумасше́дший* дом*; **to seek
political** ~ иска́ть* (*perf*) полити́ческого
убе́жища.

asymmetrical [eɪsɪˈmɛtrɪkl] *adj*
ассиметри́чный* (ассиметри́чен).

┌─────────────────────────────────────┐
│ **KEYWORD** │
└─────────────────────────────────────┘

at [æt] *prep* **1** (*referring to position*) в/на +*prp*; **at
the top** наверху́; **at home** до́ма; **at school** в
шко́ле; **at the theatre** в теа́тре; **at the baker's**
в бу́лочной; **at a concert** на конце́рте; **at the
station** на ста́нции; **they are sitting at the
table** они́ сидя́т за столо́м; **at my friend's
(house)** у моего́ дру́га; **at the doctor's** у врача́
2 (*referring to direction*) в/на +*acc*; **to look at
sb/sth** смотре́ть (посмотре́ть *perf*) на
кого́-н/что-н; **to throw sth at sb** (*several
objects*) броса́ться (*impf*) чем-н в кого́-н; (*one
object*) броса́ть (бро́сить* *perf*) что-н в
кого́-н

3 (*referring to time*): **at four o'clock** в четы́ре
часа́; **at half past two** в полови́не тре́тьего; **at
a quarter to two** без че́тверти два; **at a
quarter past two** в че́тверть тре́тьего; **at
dawn** на заре́; **at night** но́чью; **at Christmas**
на Рождество́; **at lunch** за обе́дом; **at times**
времена́ми

4 (*referring to rates*): **at £1 a kilo** по фу́нту за
килогра́мм; **two at a time** по два за раз; **at
fifty km/h** со ско́ростью пятьдеся́т км/ч; **at
full speed** на по́лной ско́рости

5 (*referring to manner*): **at a stroke** одни́м
ма́хом; **at peace** в ми́ре

6 (*referring to activity*): **to be at home/work**
быть (*impf*) до́ма/на рабо́те; **to play at
cowboys** игра́ть (*impf*) в ковбо́и; **to be good at
doing sth** хорошо́ уме́ть (*impf*) что-н де́лать
(*impf*)

7 (*referring to cause*): **shocked/surprised/
annoyed at sth** шоки́рован/удивлён*/
раздражён* чем-н; **I am surprised at you** Вы
меня́ удивля́ете; **I stayed at his suggestion** я
оста́лся по его́ предложе́нию.

ate [eɪt] *pt of* **eat.**

atheism [ˈeɪθɪːzəm] *n* атеи́зм.

atheist [ˈeɪθɪɪst] *n* атеи́ст(ка*).

Athenian [əˈθiːnɪən] *adj* афи́нский ♦ *n*
афиня́нин(-нка).

Athens [ˈæθɪnz] *n* Афи́ны* *pl.*

athlete [ˈæθliːt] *n* спортсме́н(ка*).

athletic [æθˈlɛtɪk] *adj* спорти́вный; (*physique*)
атлети́ческий*.

athletics [æθˈlɛtɪks] *n* лёгкая атле́тика.

Atlantic [ət'læntɪk] *adj* атланти́ческий* ♦ *n*: **the ~ (Ocean)** Атланти́ческий* океа́н.
atlas ['ætləs] *n* а́тлас.
Atlas Mountains *npl*: **the ~ ~** Атла́сские го́ры* *fpl*.
ATM *abbr* (= *Automated Telling Machine*) банкома́т.
atmosphere ['ætməsfɪəʳ] *n* атмосфе́ра; (*air*) во́здух.
atmospheric [ætməs'fɛrɪk] *adj* атмосфе́рный.
atmospherics [ætməs'fɛrɪks] *npl* (*RADIO*) атмосфе́рные поме́хи *fpl*.
atoll ['ætɔl] *n* ато́лл.
atom ['ætəm] *n* а́том.
atomic [ə'tɔmɪk] *adj* а́томный.
atom(ic) bomb *n* а́томная бо́мба.
atomizer ['ætəmaɪzəʳ] *n* (*for perfume*) пульвериза́тор.
atone [ə'təun] *vi*: **to ~ for** искупа́ть (искупи́ть* *perf*).
atonement [ə'təunmənt] *n* искупле́ние.
ATP *n abbr* = *Association of Tennis Professionals*.
atrocious [ə'trəuʃəs] *adj* ужа́сный* (ужа́сен).
atrocity [ə'trɔsɪtɪ] *n* (*act*) зве́рство.
atrophy ['ætrəfɪ] *n* атрофи́я ♦ *vt* атрофи́ровать (*impf/perf*) ♦ *vi* атрофи́роваться (*impf/perf*).
attach [ə'tætʃ] *vt* прикрепля́ть (прикрепи́ть* *perf*); (*document, letter*) прилага́ть (приложи́ть* *perf*); **he is/was ~ed to** (*fond of*) он привя́зан/был привя́зан к +*dat*; (*connected with*) он свя́зан/был свя́зан с +*instr*; **to ~ importance to** придава́ть (прида́ть* *perf*) значе́ние +*dat*; **the ~ed letter** прилага́емое письмо́.
attaché [ə'tæʃeɪ] *n* атташе́ *m ind*.
attaché case *n* диплома́т (*портфе́ль*).
attachment [ə'tætʃmənt] *n* (*fastening*) крепле́ние; (*device*) приспособле́ние, наса́дка; (*love*): **~ (to sb)** привя́занность *f* (к кому́-н).
attack [ə'tæk] *vt* (*MIL, fig*) атакова́ть (*impf/perf*); (*assault*) напада́ть (напа́сть* *perf*) на +*acc*; (*tackle: problem*) бра́ться* (взя́ться* *perf*) энерги́чно за +*acc* ♦ *n* (*criticism, MIL*) ата́ка; (*assault*) нападе́ние; (*of illness*) при́ступ*; **heart ~** серде́чный при́ступ.
attacker [ə'tækəʳ] *n*: **his/her ~** напа́вший(-ая) *m(f) adj* на него́/неё.
attain [ə'teɪn] *vt* (*happiness, success*) достига́ть (дости́гнуть* *or* дости́чь* *perf*) +*gen*, добива́ться (доби́ться* *perf*) +*gen*; (*knowledge*) приобрета́ть (приобрести́* *perf*).
attainments [ə'teɪnmənts] *npl* достиже́ния *ntp*.
attempt [ə'tɛmpt] *n* (*try*) попы́тка* ♦ *vt* (*try*) пыта́ться (попыта́ться* *perf*) +*infin*; **to make an ~ on sb's life** соверша́ть (соверши́ть* *perf*) покуше́ние на чью-н жизнь; **he made no ~ to help** он соверше́нно не попыта́лся помо́чь.
attempted [ə'tɛmptɪd] *adj*: **~ murder**

покуше́ние на жизнь; **~ suicide** попы́тка* самоуби́йства; **~ burglary** попы́тка* ограбле́ния.
attend [ə'tɛnd] *vt* (*school, church, lectures*) посеща́ть (*impf*); (*patient*) уха́живать (*impf*) за +*instr*; (*course*) слу́шать (прослу́шать *perf*); (*meeting, talk*) прису́тствовать (*impf*) на +*prp*
► **attend to** *vt fus* (*needs, patient*) занима́ться (заня́ться* *perf*) +*instr*; (*customer*) обслу́живать (обслужи́ть *perf*).
attendance [ə'tɛndəns] *n* прису́тствие; (*in school*) посеща́емость *f*; (*SPORT: gate*) коли́чество боле́льщиков на ма́тче.
attendant [ə'tɛndənt] *n* сопровожда́ющий(-ая) *m(f) adj*; (*in garage etc*) служи́тель(ница) *m(f)* ♦ *adj* (*dangers, risks*) сопу́тствующий.
attention [ə'tɛnʃən] *n* (*concentration*) внима́ние; (*care*) ухо́д ♦ *excl* (*MIL*) сми́рно; **~s** *npl* (*acts of courtesy*) зна́ки *mpl* внима́ния; **for the ~ of ...** (*ADMIN*) к све́дению +*gen*; **it has come to my ~ that ...** мне ста́ло изве́стно, что ...; **to stand to/at ~** (*MIL*) стоя́ть (*impf*) по сто́йке "сми́рно".
attentive [ə'tɛntɪv] *adj* (*audience*) внима́тельный (внима́телен); (*polite*) предупреди́тельный* (предупреди́телен); (*kind*) забо́тливый (забо́тлив).
attentively [ə'tɛntɪvlɪ] *adv* внима́тельно, забо́тливо.
attenuate [ə'tɛnjueɪt] *vt* ослабля́ть (осла́бить* *perf*) ♦ *vi* ослабля́ться (осла́биться* *perf*).
attest [ə'tɛst] *vi*: **to ~ to** (*demonstrate*) свиде́тельствовать (*impf*) о +*prp*; (*LAW*) свиде́тельствовать (засвиде́тельствовать *perf*).
attic ['ætɪk] *n* (*living space*) манса́рда; (*storage space*) черда́к*.
attire [ə'taɪəʳ] *n* одея́ние.
attitude ['ætɪtjuːd] *n* (*view, behaviour*): **~ (to or towards)** отноше́ние (к +*dat*); (*posture*) по́за.
attorney [ə'təːnɪ] *n* (*US: lawyer*) юри́ст; (*having proxy*) дове́ренный(-ая) *m(f) adj*; **power of ~** дове́ренность *f*.
Attorney General *n* (*BRIT*) мини́стр юсти́ции; (*US*) Генера́льный прокуро́р.
attract [ə'trækt] *vt* привлека́ть (привле́чь* *perf*)
attraction [ə'trækʃən] *n* (*charm, appeal*) привлека́тельность *f*; (*usu pl: amusements*) аттракцио́ны *mpl*; (*PHYS*) притяже́ние; (*fig: towards sb, sth*) влече́ние.
attractive [ə'træktɪv] *adj* привлека́тельный* (привлека́телен).
attribute [*n* 'ætrɪbjuːt, *vb* ə'trɪbjuːt] *n* при́знак, атрибу́т ♦ *vt*: **to ~ sth to** (*cause*) относи́ть* (отнести́* *perf*) что-н за счёт +*gen*; (*painting, quality*) припи́сывать (приписа́ть* *perf*) что-н +*dat*.
attribution [ætrɪ'bjuːʃən] *n* припи́сывание.

---

* marks translations which have irregular inflections. The Russian-English side of the dictionary gives inflectional information.

attrition [ə'trɪʃən] n: **war of** ~ война* на изнуре́ние.
Atty. Gen. abbr = **Attorney General.**
ATV n abbr (= all terrain vehicle) вездехо́д.
atypical [ei'tɪpɪkl] adj нетипи́чный (нетипи́чен).
aubergine ['əubəʒiːn] n (vegetable) баклажа́н; (colour) тёмно-лило́вый.
auburn ['ɔːbən] adj (hair) тёмно-ры́жий*.
auction ['ɔːkʃən] n (also: **sale by** ~) аукцио́н ♦ vt продава́ть (прода́ть* perf) с аукцио́на.
auctioneer [ɔːkʃə'nɪəʳ] n аукциони́ст.
auction room n аукцио́нный зал.
audacious [ɔː'deɪʃəs] adj (behaviour) де́рзкий* (де́рзок).
audacity [ɔː'dæsɪtɪ] n де́рзость f.
audible ['ɔːdɪbl] adj слы́шный* (слы́шен).
audience ['ɔːdɪəns] n аудито́рия, пу́блика; (with queen etc) аудие́нция.
audio typist ['ɔːdɪəu-] n фономашини́стка.
audiovisual ['ɔːdɪəu'vɪzjuəl] adj (materials, equipment) а́удио-визуа́льный*.
audiovisual aids ['ɔːdɪəu'vɪzjuəl-] npl техни́ческие сре́дства ntpl обуче́ния.
audit ['ɔːdɪt] vt (COMM) проводи́ть* (провести́* perf) реви́зию +gen ♦ n реви́зия, ауди́т.
audition [ɔː'dɪʃən] n (CINEMA, THEAT etc) прослу́шивание ♦ vi: **to** ~ **(for)** проходи́ть* (пройти́* perf) прослу́шивание (на +acc).
auditor ['ɔːdɪtəʳ] n реви́зия, ауди́тор.
auditorium [ɔːdɪ'tɔːrɪəm] n зал.
Aug. abbr = **August.**
augment [ɔːg'mɛnt] vt (income etc) увели́чивать (увели́чить perf).
augur ['ɔːgəʳ] vi: **it** ~**s well** э́то хоро́шее предзнаменова́ние.
August ['ɔːgəst] n а́вгуст; see also **July.**
august [ɔː'gʌst] adj (figure, building) вели́чественный*.
aunt [ɑːnt] n тётя*.
auntie ['ɑːntɪ] n dimin of **aunt.**
aunty ['ɑːntɪ] n dimin of **aunt.**
au pair ['əu'pɛəʳ] n (also: ~ ~ **girl**) молода́я ня́ня-иностра́нка, живу́щая в семье́.
aura ['ɔːrə] n (fig: air) орео́л.
auspices ['ɔːspɪsɪz] npl: **under the** ~ **of** под эги́дой +gen.
auspicious [ɔːs'pɪʃəs] adj благоприя́тный.
austere [ɔs'tɪəʳ] adj (room etc) стро́гий*; (person, manner) суро́вый (суро́в).
austerity [ɔs'tɛrɪtɪ] n (simplicity) стро́гость f; (ECON: hardship) лише́ния ntpl.
Australasia [ɔːstrə'leɪzɪə] n Австра́лия и Но́вая Зела́ндия.
Australasian [ɔːstrə'leɪzɪən] adj австра́ло-азиа́тский*.
Australia [ɔs'treɪlɪə] n Австра́лия.
Australian [ɔs'treɪlɪən] adj австрали́йский* ♦ n австрали́ец*(-и́йка).
Austria ['ɔstrɪə] n А́встрия.
Austrian ['ɔstrɪən] adj австри́йский* ♦ n

австри́ец*(-и́йка).
AUT n abbr (BRIT) = Association of University Teachers.
authentic [ɔː'θɛntɪk] adj по́длинный*.
authenticate [ɔː'θɛntɪkeɪt] vt (удостове́рить perf) по́длинность +gen.
authenticity [ɔːθɛn'tɪsɪtɪ] n по́длинность f.
author ['ɔːθəʳ] n (of text, plan) а́втор; (profession) писа́тель*(ница).
authoritarian [ɔːθɔrɪ'tɛərɪən] adj (attitudes, conduct) авторита́рный* (авторита́рен).
authoritative [ɔː'θɔrɪtətɪv] adj авторите́тный* (авторите́тен).
authority [ɔː'θɔrɪtɪ] n (power) власть f; (government body) управле́ние; (expert) авторите́т; (official permission) полномо́чие; **the authorities** npl (ruling body) вла́сти* fpl; **to have the** ~ **to do** име́ть (impf) полномо́чия +infin.
authorization [ɔːθəraɪ'zeɪʃən] n: ~ **(for)** са́нкция (на +acc).
authorize ['ɔːθəraɪz] vt санкциони́ровать (impf/perf); **to** ~ **sb to do** уполномо́чивать (уполномо́чить perf) кого́-н +infin.
authorized capital ['ɔːθəraɪzd-] n (COMM) уста́вный капита́л.
authorship ['ɔːθəʃɪp] n а́вторство.
autistic [ɔː'tɪstɪk] adj (person) страда́ющий аути́змом.
auto ['ɔːtəu] n (US: inf) авто́ nt ind.
autobiographical ['ɔːtəbaɪə'græfɪkl] adj автобиографи́ческий*.
autobiography [ɔːtəbaɪ'ɔgrəfɪ] n автобиогра́фия.
autocracy [ɔː'tɔkrəsɪ] n автокра́тия.
autocratic [ɔːtə'krætɪk] adj автократи́ческий.
Autocue® [ɔː'təukjuː] n телесуфлёр.
autograph ['ɔːtəgrɑːf] n автогра́ф ♦ vt надпи́сывать (надписа́ть* perf).
auto-immune [ɔːtəu'mjuːn] adj аутоимму́нный.
automat ['ɔːtəmæt] n (vending machine) автома́т; (US: place) кафе́-автома́т.
automata [ɔː'tɔmətə] npl of **automaton.**
automate ['ɔːtəmeɪt] vt автоматизи́ровать (impf/perf).
automated ['ɔːtəmeɪtɪd] adj автоматизи́рованный.
automatic [ɔːtə'mætɪk] adj автомати́ческий* ♦ n (US: gun) (самозаря́дный) пистоле́т; (car) автомоби́ль m с автомати́ческим переключе́нием скоросте́й; (washing machine) стира́льная маши́на-автома́т.
automatically [ɔːtə'mætɪklɪ] adv автомати́чески.
automatic data processing n автомати́ческая обрабо́тка да́нных.
automation [ɔːtə'meɪʃən] n автоматиза́ция.
automaton [ɔː'tɔmətən] n (pl **automata**) n автома́т.
automobile ['ɔːtəməbiːl] n (US) автомоби́ль m.

autonomous [ɔ:'tɔnəməs] *adj* (*region*)
автоно́мный* (автоно́мен); (*person,
organization*) самостоя́тельный*
(самостоя́телен).
autonomy [ɔ:'tɔnəmɪ] *n* (*of organization, country
etc*) автоно́мия, самостоя́тельность *f*.
autopsy ['ɔ:tɔpsɪ] *n* вскры́тие (*трупа*).
autumn ['ɔ:təm] *n* о́сень *f*; **in** ~ о́сенью.
autumnal [ɔ:'tʌmnəl] *adj* осе́нний*.
auxiliary [ɔ:g'zɪlɪərɪ] *adj* вспомога́тельный ♦ *n*
помо́щник.
AV *n abbr* (*BIBLE*: = *Authorized Version*) *перево́д
Би́блии, при́нятый в англика́нской це́ркви* ♦
abbr = **audiovisual**.
Av. *abbr* = **avenue**.
avail [ə'veɪl] *vt*: **to** ~ **o.s. of** воспо́льзоваться
(*perf*) +*instr* ♦ *n*: **to no** ~ напра́сно.
availability [əveɪlə'bɪlɪtɪ] *n* (*supply*) нали́чие.
available [ə'veɪləbl] *adj* (*article, service*)
име́ющийся в нали́чии, досту́пный*
(досту́пен); (*person, time*) свобо́дный*
(свобо́ден); **every** ~ **means** все досту́пные
сре́дства; **is the manager** ~? заве́дующий *m
adj* свобо́ден?; **to make sth** ~ **to sb**
предоставля́ть (предоста́вить* *perf*) что-н
кому́-н.
avalanche ['ævəla:nʃ] *n* (*also fig*) лави́на.
avant-garde ['ævɑ̃ŋ'ga:d] *adj*
авангарди́стский*.
avarice ['ævərɪs] *n* а́лчность *f*.
avaricious [ævə'rɪʃəs] *adj* а́лчный* (а́лчен).
avdp. *abbr* (= *avoirdupois*) *систе́ма едини́ц
ве́са, испо́льзуемая в англоязы́чных
стра́нах*.
Ave. *abbr* = **avenue**.
avenge [ə'vɛndʒ] *vt* мстить* (отомсти́ть* *perf*)
за +*acc*.
avenue ['ævənju:] *n* (*street*) у́лица; (*drive*)
алле́я; (*means, solution*) путь* *m*.
average ['ævərɪdʒ] *n* сре́днее *nt adj* ♦ *adj*
сре́дний* ♦ *vt* достига́ть (дости́чь* *perf*) в
сре́днем +*gen*, составля́ть (соста́вить* *perf*) в
сре́днем; **on** ~ в сре́днем; **above/below (the)**
~ вы́ше/ни́же сре́днего у́ровня
▶ **average out** *vi*: **to** ~ **out at** равня́ться (*impf*) в
сре́днем +*dat*.
averse [ə'və:s] *adj*: **to be** ~ **to sth/doing** быть*
(*impf*) про́тив чего́-н/того́, что́бы +*infin*; **I
wouldn't be** ~ **to a drink** я непро́чь что́-
нибудь вы́пить.
aversion [ə'və:ʃən] *n* неприя́знь *f*; **to have an** ~
to sb/sth испы́тывать (*impf*) неприя́знь к
кому́-н/чему́-н.
avert [ə'və:t] *vt* (*accident, war*) предотвраща́ть
(предотврати́ть* *perf*); (*blow, eyes*)
отводи́ть* (отвести́* *perf*).
aviary ['eɪvɪərɪ] *n* пти́чий* вольёр.
aviation [eɪvɪ'eɪʃən] *n* авиа́ция.

avid ['ævɪd] *adj* (*supporter, viewer*) стра́стный.
avidly ['ævɪdlɪ] *adv* стра́стно.
avocado [ævə'ka:dəu] *n* (*also:* ~ **pear**: *BRIT*)
авока́до *nt ind*.
avoid [ə'vɔɪd] *vt* избега́ть* (избежа́ть* *perf*).
avoidable [ə'vɔɪdəbl] *adj* (*death, accident*)
предотврати́мый.
avoidance [ə'vɔɪdəns] *n*: ~ **(of)** (*of tax, issue*)
уклоне́ние (от +*gen*).
avowed [ə'vaud] *adj* откры́тый.
AVP *n abbr* (*US*: = *assistant vice-president*)
помо́щник ви́це-президе́нта.
avuncular [ə'vʌŋkjulə] *adj* (*expression, tone*)
оте́ческий*; (*person*) забо́тливый.
AWACS ['eɪwæks] *n abbr* (= *airborne warning
and control system*) АВАКС (*авиацио́нная
систе́ма да́льнего радиолокацио́нного
обнаруже́ния и управле́ния*).
await [ə'weɪt] *vt* ожида́ть (*impf*) +*gen*; ~**ing
delivery** (*COMM*) отпра́вка предстои́т; **long**
~**ed** долгожда́нный.
awake [ə'weɪk] (*pt* **awoke**, *pp* **awoken** *or*
awaked) *vt* буди́ть* (разбуди́ть* *perf*) ♦ *vi*
просыпа́ться (просну́ться *perf*) ♦ *adj*: **he is** ~
он просну́лся; **to be** ~ **to** (*dangers,
possibilities*) сознава́ть* (*impf*); **he was still** ~
он ещё не спал.
awakening [ə'weɪknɪŋ] *n* (*also fig*)
пробужде́ние.
award [ə'wɔ:d] *n* награ́да; (*LAW*) возмеще́ние
♦ *vt* награжда́ть (награди́ть* *perf*); (*LAW*)
присужда́ть (присуди́ть* *perf*).
aware [ə'wɛə] *adj*: **to be** ~ **(of)** (*realize*)
сознава́ть (*impf*) (+*acc*); **to become** ~ **of/that**
осознава́ть* (осозна́ть *perf*) +*acc*/, что;
politically/socially ~ полити́чески/социа́льно
созна́тельный; **I am fully** ~ **that** я по́лностью
созна́ю, что.
awareness [ə'wɛənɪs] *n* осозна́ние; **to develop
people's** ~ **of** развива́ть (разви́ть* *perf*)
обще́ственное осозна́ние +*gen*.
awash [ə'wɔʃ] *adj* зато́пленный; (*fig*): ~ **with**
наводнённый (наводнён) +*instr*.
away [ə'weɪ] *adv* (*movement*) в сто́рону;
(*position*) в стороне́, поо́даль; (*far away*)
далеко́; (*in time*): **the holidays are two weeks**
~ до кани́кул (оста́лось) две неде́ли; ~ **from**
(*movement*) от +*gen*; (*position*) поо́даль от
+*gen*; **two kilometres** ~ **from the town** в двух
киломе́трах от го́рода; **two hours** ~ **by car** в
двух часа́х езды́ на маши́не; **he's** ~ **for a
week** он в отъе́зде на неде́лю; **he's** ~ **in Milan**
он в отъе́зде в Мила́не; (*remove*) забира́ть (забра́ть* *perf*) (у +*gen*);
(*subtract*) отнима́ть (отня́ть* *perf*) (от +*gen*);
he is working ~ он продолжа́ет рабо́тать; **to
fade** ~ (*colour*) выцвета́ть (вы́цвести* *perf*);
(*enthusiasm, light*) угаса́ть (уга́снуть *perf*).

---

* marks translations which have irregular inflections. The Russian-English side of the dictionary gives inflectional information.

away game n (SPORT) игра́ на вы́езде.
awe [ɔ:] n благогове́ние.
awe-inspiring ['ɔ:mspaɪərɪŋ] adj (person, thing) внуша́ющий благогове́ние.
awesome ['ɔ:səm] adj = awe-inspiring.
awestruck ['ɔ:strʌk] adj охва́ченный (охва́чен) благогове́нием.
awful ['ɔ:fəl] adj ужа́сный* (ужа́сен); an ~ lot (of) ужа́сно мно́го (+gen).
awfully ['ɔ:fəlɪ] adv ужа́сно.
awhile [ə'waɪl] adv недо́лго, како́е-то вре́мя; wait ~ подожди́те немно́го.
awkward ['ɔ:kwəd] adj (clumsy) неуклю́жий* (неуклю́ж); (inconvenient) неудо́бный* (неудо́бен); (embarrassing) нело́вкий*.
awkwardness ['ɔ:kwədnɪs] n (see adj) неуклю́жесть f; неудо́бство; нело́вкость f.
awl [ɔ:l] n ши́ло*.
awning ['ɔ:nɪŋ] n (of tent) наве́с; (of shop, hotel) тент.
awoke [ə'wəuk] pt of awake.
awoken [ə'wəukən] pp of awake.
AWOL ['eɪwɔl] abbr (MIL: = absent without leave) (находя́щийся) в самово́льной отлу́чке.
awry [ə'raɪ] adv (crooked) кри́во, ко́со; to go ~ (plan) спу́тываться (спу́таться perf).
axe [æks] (US ax) n топо́р* ♦ vt (employee) увольня́ть (уво́лить perf); (project etc)

урéзывать (урéзать* perf); (jobs) сокраща́ть (сократи́ть* perf); **to have an ~ to grind** (fig) име́ть (impf) коры́стные побужде́ния.
axes[1] ['æksɪz] npl of ax(e).
axes[2] ['æksi:z] npl of axis.
axiom ['æksɪəm] n аксио́ма.
axiomatic [æksɪəu'mætɪk] adj аксиомати́чный (аксиомати́чен).
axis ['æksɪs] (pl axes) n ось* f.
axle ['æksl] n (also: ~tree: AUT) ось* f.
aye [aɪ] excl да; **the ~s** npl голосу́ющие "за".
AYH n abbr = American Youth Hostels.
AZ abbr (US: POST) = Arizona.
azalea [ə'zeɪlɪə] n аза́лия.
Azerbaijan [[ae]zəbaɪ'dʒɑ:n] n Азербайджа́н.
Azerbaijani [[ae]zəbaɪ'dʒɑ:nɪ] n (person) азербайджа́нец*(-а́нка*); (LING) азербайджа́нский* язы́к* ♦ adj азербайджа́нский*.
Azores [ə'zɔ:z] npl: **the ~** Азо́рские острова́ mpl.
Azov ['ɑ:zɔv] n: **Sea of ~** Азо́вское мо́ре.
AZT n abbr (= azidothymidine) аздотимиди́н.
Aztec ['æztɛk] n ацте́к ♦ adj: ~ **civilization/art** цивилиза́ция/иску́сство ацте́ков.
azure ['eɪʒəʳ] adj лазу́рный.

~ B, b ~

B, b [bi:] *n* (*letter*) 2-áя бýква англи́йского
алфави́та; (*SCOL: mark*) ≈ хорошо́; **~ road**
(*BRIT: AUT*) шоссе́ *nt ind* (второ́й катего́рии).
B [bi:] *n* (*MUS*) си *nt ind.*
b. *abbr* (= **born**) род.= роди́лся.
BA *n abbr* (= *Bachelor of Arts*) бакала́вр
гуманита́рных нау́к; (= *British Academy*)
Брита́нская акаде́мия (*гуманита́рных
нау́к*).
babble ['bæbl] *vi* лепета́ть• (залепета́ть• *perf*) ◆
n: **a ~ of voices** го́мон голосо́в.
babe [beɪb] *n* (*inf*) детка•, кро́шка•.
baboon [bə'bu:n] *n* бабуи́н.
baby ['beɪbɪ] *n* ребёнок•; (*US: inf*) детка•.
baby carriage *n* (*US*) коля́ска•.
baby grand *n* (*also*: **~ ~ piano**) кабине́тный
роя́ль *m*.
babyhood ['beɪbɪhud] *n* младе́нчество.
babyish ['beɪbɪʃ] *adj* де́тский•.
baby-minder ['beɪbɪ'maɪndə•] *n* (*BRIT*) ня́ня•
(*присма́тривающая за детьми́ у себя́ до́ма*).
baby-sit ['beɪbɪsɪt] *vi* смотре́ть (*impf*) за
детьми́.
baby-sitter ['beɪbɪsɪtə•] *n* приходя́щая ня́ня•.
bachelor ['bætʃələ•] *n* холостя́к•; **B~ of Arts/
Science** ≈ бакала́вр гуманита́рных/
есте́ственных нау́к; **B~ of Arts/Science
degree** ≈ сте́пень *f* бакала́вра
гуманита́рных/есте́ственных нау́к.
bachelorhood ['bætʃələhud] *n* холостя́цкая
жизнь *f.*
bachelor party *n* (*US*) мальчи́шник.

───────────────
KEYWORD
───────────────
back [bæk] *n* 1 (*of person, animal*) спина́; **the
back of the hand** ты́льная сторона́ ладо́ни;
he has his back to the wall (*fig*) он прижа́т к
сте́нке
2 (*of house, car etc*) за́дняя часть *f*; (*of chair*)
спи́нка•; (*of page*) обра́тная сторона́,
оборо́т; (*back cover: of book*) оборо́т; **back to
front** за́дом наперёд; **to break the back of a
job** (*BRIT*) выполня́ть (вы́полнить *perf*)
гла́вную часть рабо́ты; **at the back** (*of
crowd*) в за́дних ряда́х; (*of book*) в конце́
3 (*FOOTBALL*) защи́тник
◆ *vt* **1** (*candidate: also*: **back up**)

подде́рживать (поддержа́ть *perf*)
2 (*financially: person*) финанси́ровать (*impf*),
ока́зывать (оказа́ть *perf*) фина́нсовую
подде́ржку; (: *horse*) ста́вить• (поста́вить•
perf) на +*acc*
3 (*car*): **he backed the car into the garage** он
дал за́дний ход и поста́вил маши́ну в гара́ж
◆ *vi* (*car etc: also*: **back up**) дава́ть• (дать• *perf*)
за́дний ход
◆ *adv* **1** (*not forward*) обра́тно, наза́д; **he ran
back** он побежа́л обра́тно *or* наза́д
2 (*returned*): **he's back** он верну́лся; **when will
you be back?** когда́ Вы вернётесь?
3 (*restitution*): **to throw the ball back** кида́ть
(ки́нуть *perf*) мяч обра́тно; **can I have the pen
back?** верни́те мне ру́чку, пожа́луйста
4 (*again*): **to call back** (*TEL*) перезва́нивать
(перезвони́ть *perf*); (*visit again*) заходи́ть
(зайти́ *perf*) ещё раз
◆ *cpd* **1** (*payment*) за́дним число́м
2 (*AUT: seat, wheels*) за́дний•; (*room, garden*)
вну́тренний•; **to take a back seat** (*fig*)
станови́ться• (стать• *perf*) пасси́вным
наблюда́телем
▶ **back down** *vi* отступа́ть (отступи́ть• *perf*)
▶ **back on to** *vt fus*: **the house backs on to a park**
дом выхо́дит за́дним фаса́дом в парк
▶ **back out** *vi* (*of promise*) отступа́ться
(отступи́ться• *perf*)
▶ **back up** *vt* (*person, theory etc*) подде́рживать
(поддержа́ть• *perf*); (*COMPUT*) резерви́ровать
(*impf/perf*).

backache ['bækeɪk] *n* простре́лы *mpl*, боль *f* в
пояснице.
backbencher ['bæk'bentʃə•] *n* (*BRIT*)
"заднескаме́ечник".
backbiting ['bækbaɪtɪŋ] *n* злосло́вие.
backbone ['bækbəun] *n* позвоно́чник; **he's the
~ of the organization** на нём де́ржится вся
организа́ция.
backchat ['bæktʃæt] *n* (*BRIT: inf*)
препира́тельство.
backcloth ['bækklɔθ] *n* (*BRIT: THEAT*) за́дник.
backcomb ['bækkəum] *vt* (*BRIT*) начёсывать
(начеса́ть• *perf*).

---

* marks translations which have irregular inflections. The Russian-English side of the dictionary gives inflectional information.

backdate [bæk'deɪt] *vt (pay rise)* проводи́ть•
(провести́• *perf*) за́дним число́м; *(letter)*
помеча́ть (поме́тить• *perf*) за́дним число́м;
~**d pay rise (of 20%)** повыше́ние зарпла́ты
за́дним число́м (на 20%).
backdrop ['bækdrɒp] *n* = **backcloth**.
backer ['bækə'] *n (COMM)* финанси́рующая
сторона́•.
backfire [bæk'faɪə'] *vi (AUT)* дава́ть• (дать• *perf*)
обра́тную вспы́шку; **his plan** ~**d** его́ план
оберну́лся про́тив него́.
backgammon ['bækgæmən] *n* триктра́к.
background ['bækgraund] *n (of picture)*
за́дний• план; *(of events)* предысто́рия;
(COMPUT) фон; *(experience)* о́пыт ♦ *cpd (noise,
music)* посторо́нний•; **he's from a working
class** ~ он из рабо́чей семьи́; **against a** ~ **of ...**
на фо́не +*gen* ...; ~ **reading (on)**
дополни́тельное чте́ние (по +*dat*).
backhand ['bækhænd] *n (TENNIS)* уда́р сле́ва.
backhanded ['bæk'hændɪd] *adj (fig)*
двусмы́сленный (двусмы́слен).
backhander ['bæk'hændə'] *n (BRIT: inf)* взя́тка•.
backing ['bækɪŋ] *n (support)* подде́ржка•;
(COMM) финанси́рование; *(MUS)*
сопровожде́ние.
back issue *n* ста́рый но́мер•.
backlash ['bæklæʃ] *n (fig)* обра́тная реа́кция.
backlog ['bæklɒg] *n*: ~ **of work** невы́полненная
рабо́та.
back number *n* = **back issue**.
backpack ['bækpæk] *n* рюкза́к•.
backpacker ['bækpækə'] *n молодо́й челове́к,
путеше́ствующий с рюкзако́м.*
back pay *n* пла́та за́дним число́м.
backpedal ['bækpɛdl] *vi (fig)* идти́• (пойти́•
perf) на попя́тный.
backseat driver ['bæksi:t-] *n* пассажи́р,
даю́щий сове́ты шофёру.
backside ['bæksaɪd] *n (inf)* зад•.
backslash ['bækslæʃ] *n* коса́я черта́ вле́во.
backslide ['bækslaɪd] *vi* принима́ться
(приня́ться *perf)* за ста́рое.
backspace ['bækspeɪs] *vi* реверси́ровать *(impf/
perf).*
backstage [bæk'steɪdʒ] *adv* за кули́сами.
backstreet ['bækstri:t] *n* окра́ина ♦ *cpd:* ~
abortionist *челове́к, де́лающий подпо́льные
або́рты.*
backstroke ['bækstrəuk] *n* пла́вание на спине́;
to do the ~ пла́вать *(impf)* на спине́.
backtrack ['bæktræk] *vi (fig)* идти́• (пойти́• *perf)*
на попя́тный.
backup ['bækʌp] *adj (train, plane)*
дополни́тельный•; *(COMPUT)* резе́рвный ♦ *n
(support)* подде́ржка•; *(also:* ~ **disk)**
дублика́т ги́бкого ди́ска.
backward ['bækwəd] *adj (movement)*
обра́тный; *(person, country)* отста́лый.
backwards ['bækwədz] *adv* наза́д; *(in reverse
order)* наоборо́т; *(fall)* на́взничь; **to know sth**

~ *or (US)* ~ **and forwards** знать *(impf)* что-н
вдоль и поперёк; **to walk** ~ пя́титься•
(попя́титься• *perf).*
backwater ['bækwɔ:tə'] *n (fig)* боло́то.
backyard [bæk'jɑ:d] *n (of house)* за́дний•
двор•.
bacon ['beɪkən] *n* беко́н.
bacteria [bæk'tɪərɪə] *npl* бакте́рии *fpl.*
bacteriology [bæktɪərɪ'ɔlədʒɪ] *n*
бактериоло́гия.
bad [bæd] *adj* плохо́й•; *(mistake)* серьёзный;
(injury, crash) тяжёлый• (тяжёл); *(food)*
ту́хлый•; **his** ~ **leg** его́ больна́я нога́; **to go** ~
(food) ту́хнуть (проту́хнуть *perf)*, по́ртиться•
(испо́ртиться• *perf); (milk)* скиса́ть (ски́снуть
perf); **she's having a** ~ **time of it** у неё тяжёлый
пери́од; **I feel** ~ **about it** я чу́вствую себя́
винова́тым; **in** ~ **faith** неи́скренне.
bad debt *n* спи́санный долг *(по
несостоя́тельности должника́).*
baddy ['bædɪ] *n (inf)* плохо́й• *m adj (в кни́ге,
фи́льме).*
bade [bæd] *pt of* **bid**.
badge [bædʒ] *n* значо́к•; *(of policeman)* бля́ха;
(sew-on) наши́вка; *(fig)* си́мвол.
badger ['bædʒə'] *n* барсу́к ♦ *vt* пристава́ть•
(приста́ть• *perf)* к +*dat.*
badly ['bædlɪ] *adv* пло́хо; ~ **wounded** тяжело́
ра́неный; **he needs it** ~ он си́льно в э́том
нужда́ется; **to be** ~ **off (for money)** нужда́ться
(impf) (в деньга́х).
bad-mannered ['bæd'mænəd] *adj*
невоспи́танный.
badminton ['bædmɪntən] *n* бадминто́н.
bad-tempered ['bæd'tɛmpəd] *adj (by nature)*
вспы́льчивый (вспы́льчив),
раздражи́тельный (раздражи́телен); *(on
one occasion)* раздражённый (раздражён).
baffle ['bæfl] *vt* озада́чивать (озада́чить *perf).*
baffling ['bæflɪŋ] *adj:* **I find his behaviour** ~ его́
поведе́ние меня́ озада́чивает.
bag [bæg] *n* су́мка; *(paper, plastic)* паке́т;
(handbag) су́мочка•; *(satchel)* ра́нец•; *(case)*
портфе́ль *m; (of hunter)* ягдта́ш; *(pej:
woman)* карга́; ~**s of** *(inf)* у́йма +*gen;* **to pack
one's** ~**s** собира́ть (собра́ть• *perf)* чемода́ны;
~**s under the eyes** мешки́ под глаза́ми.
bagful ['bægful] *n (of flour etc)* (по́лный) паке́т;
(of shopping) (по́лная) су́мка•.
baggage ['bægɪdʒ] *n (US)* бага́ж•.
baggage car *n (US)* бага́жный ваго́н.
baggage claim *n (US)* вы́дача багажа́.
baggy ['bægɪ] *adj* мешкова́тый.
Baghdad [bæg'dæd] *n* Багда́д.
bag lady *n (esp US)* городска́я бродя́жка.
bagpipes ['bægpaɪps] *npl* волы́нка *fsg.*
bag-snatcher ['bægsnætʃə'] *n (BRIT)* вор•,
выхва́тывающий су́мки.
Bahamas [bə'hɑ:məz] *npl:* **the** ~ Бага́мские
острова́ *mpl.*
Bahrain [bɑ:'reɪn] *n* Бахре́йн.

Baikal [baɪˈkɑːl] *n*: **Lake** ~ Байкáл.
bail [beɪl] *n* (*payment*) залóг ◆ *vt* (*also*: **to grant**
~ **to**) выпускáть (вы́пустить* *perf*) под залóг;
he was released on ~ он был вы́пущен на
порýки
▶ **bail out** *vt* (*LAW*) плати́ть* (заплати́ть* *perf*)
залóговую сýмму за +*acc*; (*boat*)
вычéрпывать (вы́черпать *perf*) вóду из +*gen*;
(*firm, friend*) выручáть (вы́ручить *perf*) ◆ *vi*
выбрáсываться (вы́броситься* *perf*) с
парашю́том.
bailiff [ˈbeɪlɪf] *n* (*LAW*: *BRIT*) судéбный
исполни́тель *m*; (: *US*) помóщник шери́фа;
(*BRIT*: *of estate*) управля́ющий(-ая) *m(f) adj*
имéнием.
bait [beɪt] *n* (*for fish*) нажи́вка*; (*for animal,
criminal*) примáнка* ◆ *vt* (*hook, trap*)
наживля́ть (наживи́ть* *perf*); (*person*)
дразни́ть* (*impf*).
baize [beɪz] *n* (зелёное) сукнó.
bake [beɪk] *vt* печь* (испéчь* *perf*); (*clay etc*)
обжигáть (обжéчь* *perf*) ◆ *vi* (*bread etc*)
пéчься* (испéчься* *perf*); (*make cakes etc*)
печь* (испéчь* *perf*) пироги́.
baked beans [beɪkt-] *npl* консерви́рованная
фасóль *fsg*.
baker [ˈbeɪkəʳ] *n* пéкарь* *m*; (*also*: **the ~'s**)
бýлочная *f adj*.
baker's dozen *n* чёртова дю́жина.
bakery [ˈbeɪkərɪ] *n* (*factory*) пекáрня*; (*shop*)
бýлочная *f adj*.
baking [ˈbeɪkɪŋ] *n* вы́печка ◆ *adj* (*inf*): **it's** ~ **hot
today** сегóдня печёт; **she does her** ~ **once a
week** онá печёт раз в недéлю.
baking powder *n* разрыхли́тель *m*.
baking tin *n* (*for cake, meat*) фóрма.
baking tray *n* проти́вень* *m*.
Baku [baˈku] *n* Бакý *m ind*.
balaclava [bæləˈklɑːvə] *n* (*also*: ~ **helmet**)
вя́заный шлем.
balance [ˈbæləns] *n* (*equilibrium*) равновéсие;
(*COMM*: *in account*) балáнс; (: *remainder*)
остáток*; (*scales*) весы́ *pl* ◆ *vt* (*budget,
account*) баланси́ровать (сбаланси́ровать
perf); (*make equal*) уравновéшивать
(уравновéсить* *perf*); **on** ~ по зрéлом
размышлéнии; ~ **of trade/payments**
торгóвый/платёжный балáнс; ~ **carried
forward** балáнс к перенóсу; ~ **brought
forward** балáнс с перенóса; **to** ~ **the books**
баланси́ровать (сбаланси́ровать *perf*)
кни́ги; **to** ~ **the pros and cons** взвéшивать
(взвéсить* *perf*) все за и прóтив.
balanced [ˈbælənst] *adj* (*report*) взвéшенный
(взвéшен); (*diet*) сбаланси́рованный
(сбаланси́рован); (*personality*)
уравновéшенный.
balance sheet *n* свóдный балáнс.

balcony [ˈbælkənɪ] *n* балкóн.
bald [bɔːld] *adj* (*head*) лы́сый*; (*tyre*) стёртый;
(*statement*) прямóй*.
baldness [ˈbɔːldnɪs] *n* лы́сина.
bale [beɪl] *n* (*of hay etc*) тюк*; (*of papers etc*)
ки́па
▶ **bale out** *vti see* **bail out**.
Balearic Islands [bælɪˈærɪk-] *npl*: **the** ~ ~
Балéрские островá *mpl*.
baleful [ˈbeɪlful] *adj* (*glance*) зловéщий*
(зловéщ).
balk [bɔːk] *vi*: **he** ~**ed at the idea** емý прети́ла
э́та идéя; (*subj*: *horse*): **to** ~ (**at**) заартáчиться
(*perf*) (пéред +*instr*).
Balkan [ˈbɔːlkən] *adj* балкáнский; **the** ~**s** *npl*
Балкáны *pl*.
ball [bɔːl] *n* (*for football*) мяч*; (*for tennis, golf*)
мя́чик; (*of wool, string*) клубóк*; (*dance*)
бал*; **to set the** ~ **rolling** (*fig*) пускáть
(пусти́ть* *perf*) дéло в ход; **to play** ~ (**with sb**)
(*fig*) подыгрывать (подыгрáть *perf*)
(комý-н); **to be on the** ~ (*fig*) быть* (*impf*) на
конé; **the** ~ **is in their court** (*fig*) óчередь за
ни́ми.
ballad [ˈbæləd] *n* баллáда.
ballast [ˈbæləst] *n* баллáст.
ball bearing *n* шáрик подши́пника.
ballcock [ˈbɔːlkɔk] *n* шаровóй клáпан.
ballerina [bæləˈriːnə] *n* балери́на.
ballet [ˈbæleɪ] *n* балéт.
ballet dancer *n* арти́ст(ка) балéта.
ballistic [bəˈlɪstɪk] *adj* баллисти́ческий*.
ballistic missile *n* баллисти́ческий* снаря́д.
ballistics [bəˈlɪstɪks] *n* балли́стика.
balloon [bəˈluːn] *n* воздýшный шар; (*also*: **hot
air** ~) аэростáт; (*in comic strip*) кóнтур, в
котóрый впи́сываются рéплики герóев
кóмиксов.
balloonist [bəˈluːnɪst] *n* воздухоплáватель *m*.
ballot [ˈbælət] *n* голосовáние, баллотирóвка*.
ballot box *n* избирáтельная ýрна.
ballot paper *n* избирáтельный бюллетéнь *m*.
ballpark [ˈbɔːlpɑːk] *n* (*US*) бейсбóльное пóле.
ballpark figure *n* (*inf*) приблизи́тельный
подсчёт.
ballpoint (pen) [ˈbɔːlpɔɪnt(-)] *n* шáриковая
рýчка*.
ballroom [ˈbɔːlrum] *n* бáльный зал.
balls [bɔːlz] *npl* (*inf!*) я́йца* *ntpl* (*!*); (: *nonsense*)
фигня́ *fsg* (*!*)
balm [bɑːm] *n* бальзáм.
balmy [ˈbɑːmɪ] *adj* (*breeze*) ласкáющий
(ласкáющ); (*day*) прия́тный* (прия́тен);
(*BRIT*: *inf*) = **barmy**.
BALPA [ˈbælpə] *n abbr* = **British Airline Pilots'
Association**.
balsam [ˈbɔːlsəm] *n* бальзáм.
balsa (wood) [ˈbɔːlsə-] *n* бáльзовое дéрево*.

---

* marks translations which have irregular inflections. The Russian-English side of the dictionary gives inflectional information.

Baltic [bɔ:ltɪk] n: **the ~** Балтийское Море ♦ adj: **the ~ States** прибалтийские государства ntpl.

balustrade [bæləs'treɪd] n балюстрада.

bamboo [bæm'bu:] n бамбук.

bamboozle [bæm'bu:zl] vt (inf) одурачивать (одурачить perf).

ban [bæn] vt (prohibit) запрещать (запретить* perf); (suspend, exclude) отстранять (отстранить perf) ♦ n (prohibition) запрет; (suspension): **~ from** отстранение от +gen; **he was ~ned from driving** (BRIT) у него отобрали водительские права.

banal [bə'nɑ:l] adj (remark, idea etc) банальный* (банален).

banana [bə'nɑ:nə] n банан.

band [bænd] n (group: of people, rock musicians) группа; (: of jazz, military musicians) оркестр; (strip: of light, colour) полоса*; (: of cloth) лента; (range) диапазон
► **band together** vi объединяться (объединиться perf).

bandage ['bændɪdʒ] n повязка* ♦ vt (wound, leg) бинтовать (забинтовать perf); (person) перевязывать (перевязать* perf).

Bandaid® ['bændeɪd] n (US) пластырь m.

bandit ['bændɪt] n бандит.

bandstand ['bændstænd] n эстрада.

bandwagon ['bændwægən] n: **to jump on the ~** примкнуть (perf) к сильной стороне or модному течению.

bandy ['bændɪ] vt (jokes, ideas) перебрасываться (переброситься* perf) +instr
► **bandy about** vt бесконечно упоминать (impf).

bandy-legged ['bændɪ'lɛgɪd] adj (person) кривоногий*.

bane [beɪn] n: **it/he is the ~ of my life** это/он несчастье моей жизни.

bang [bæŋ] n (of gun, explosion) выстрел; (blow) удар ♦ excl бах ♦ vt (door) хлопать (хлопнуть perf) +instr; (one's head etc) ударять (ударить perf) ♦ vi (door) захлопываться (захлопнуться perf); (fireworks) хлопать (impf) ♦ adv: **~ on time** (BRIT: inf) как раз во время; **to ~ at the door** колотить* (impf) в дверь; **to ~ into sth** сталкиваться (столкнуться perf) с чем-н.

banger ['bæŋə] n (BRIT: inf: also: **old ~**) драндулет; (: sausage) сарделька*; (: firework) хлопушка.

Bangkok [bæŋ'kɔk] n Бангкок.

Bangladesh [bæŋglə'dɛʃ] n Бангладеш.

Bangladeshi [bæŋglə'dɛʃɪ] n (person) бангладешец(-ешка*) ♦ adj бангладешский.

bangle ['bæŋgl] n браслет.

bangs [bæŋz] npl (US) чёлка* fsg.

banish ['bænɪʃ] vt высылать (выслать* perf).

banister ['bænɪstə] n (usu pl) перила pl.

banjo ['bændʒəu] (pl **~es** or **~s**) n банджо nt ind.

bank [bæŋk] n банк; (of river, lake) берег*; (of earth) насыпь f; (of switches) панель f ♦ vi (AVIAT) крениться (накрениться perf); (COMM): **they ~ with Pitt's** они держат деньги в банке Питт
► **bank on** vt fus полагаться (положиться* perf) на +acc.

bank account n банковский* счёт.

bank balance n количество денег на банковском счету.

bank card n банковская карточка*.

bank charges npl (BRIT) плата, взимаемая банком за услуги.

bank draft n банковская тратта.

banker ['bæŋkə] n банкир.

banker's card n (BRIT) = **bank card**.

banker's order n (BRIT) банковское поручение.

Bank Giro n Жиро nt ind банк.

bank holiday n (BRIT) нерабочий* день m (обычно понедельник).

banking ['bæŋkɪŋ] n банковское дело*.

banking hours npl часы mpl работы банка.

bank loan n банковский* заём*.

bank manager n управляющий(-ая) m(f) adj банком.

banknote ['bæŋknəut] n банкнот.

bank rate n учётная ставка* банка.

bankroll ['bæŋkrəul] vt обеспечивать (обеспечить perf) деньгами ♦ n (esp US) финансовые ресурсы pl.

bankrupt ['bæŋkrʌpt] adj обанкротившийся ♦ n банкрот; **to go ~** обанкротиться* (perf); **I am ~** я – банкрот.

bankruptcy ['bæŋkrʌptsɪ] n (COMM, fig) банкротство, несостоятельность f.

bank statement n выписка* с банковского счёта.

banner ['bænə] n транспарант.

banner headline n (газетная) шапка*.

bannister ['bænɪstə] n = **banister**.

banns [bænz] npl оглашение в церкви имён вступающих в брак.

banquet ['bæŋkwɪt] n банкет.

bantamweight ['bæntəmweɪt] n (BOXING) боксёр лёгкого веса*.

banter ['bæntə] n подшучивание.

BAOR n abbr = British Army of the Rhine.

baptism ['bæptɪzəm] n крещение.

Baptist ['bæptɪst] n баптист(ка).

baptize [bæp'taɪz] vt крестить* (окрестить* perf).

bar [bɑ:'] n (pub) бар; (counter) стойка; (rod) прут; (cake: of soap) брусок*; (: of chocolate) плитка*; (obstacle) преграда; (prohibition) запрет*; (MUS) такт ♦ vt (door, way) загораживать (загородить* perf); (road) преграждать (преградить perf); (person) не допускать (допустить* perf); (activity) запрещать (запретить* perf); **~s** npl (on window etc) решётка fsg; **behind ~s** за решёткой; **the B~** адвокатура; **~ none** без исключе́ния.

Barbados [bɑː'beɪdɔs] *n* Барба́дос.
barbaric [bɑː'bærɪk] *adj* ва́рварский*.
barbarous ['bɑːbərəs] *adj* ва́рварский*.
barbecue ['bɑːbɪkjuː] *n* барбекю́ *nt ind*.
barbed wire ['bɑːbd-] *n* колю́чая про́волока.
barber ['bɑːbəʳ] *n* парикма́хер.
barbiturate [bɑː'bɪtjurɪt] *n* барбитура́т.
Barcelona [bɑːsə'ləunə] *n* Барсело́на.
bar chart *n* гистогра́мма.
bar code *n* штрихово́й код.
bare [bɛəʳ] *adj (body)* го́лый*, обнажённый (обнажён); *(trees)* оголённый (оголён) ◆ *vt (one's body)* обнажа́ть (обнажи́ть *perf*); *(teeth)* ска́лить (оска́лить *perf*); **in** *or* **with ~ feet** босико́м; **the ~ essentials** предме́ты *mpl* пе́рвой необходи́мости; **~ minimum** то́лько ми́нимум; **to ~ one's soul** раскрыва́ть (раскры́ть* *perf*) свою́ ду́шу.
bareback ['bɛəbæk] *adv* без седла́.
barefaced ['bɛəfeɪst] *adj* бессты́дный*.
barefoot ['bɛəfut] *adj* босо́й* (бос) ◆ *adv* босико́м.
bareheaded [bɛə'hɛdɪd] *adj, adv* с непокры́той голово́й.
barely ['bɛəlɪ] *adv* едва́.
Barents Sea ['bærənts-] *n*: **the ~ ~** Ба́ренцево мо́ре.
bargain ['bɑːgɪn] *n* сде́лка*; *(good buy)* вы́годная поку́пка* ◆ *vi*: **to ~ (with sb)** торгова́ться (сторгова́ться *perf*) (с кем-н); **into the ~** в прида́чу
▸ **bargain for** *vt fus*: **he got more than he ~ed for** он получи́л бо́льше, чем ожида́л.
bargaining ['bɑːgənɪŋ] *n* торг.
bargaining position *n* пози́ция, с кото́рой предъявля́ются тре́бования и усло́вия сде́лки и́ли догово́ра.
barge [bɑːdʒ] *n* ба́ржа
▸ **barge in** *vi (enter)* вва́ливаться (ввали́ться* *perf*); *(interrupt)* влеза́ть (влезть* *perf*)
▸ **barge into** *vt fus (person)* ната́лкиваться (натолкну́ться *perf*) на +*acc*.
bargepole ['bɑːdʒpəul] *n*: **I wouldn't touch him with a ~** я к э́тому на пу́шечный вы́стрел не подойду́.
baritone ['bærɪtəun] *n* барито́н.
barium meal ['bɛərɪəm-] *n* ба́риевая миксту́ра.
bark [bɑːk] *n (of tree)* кора́; *(of dog)* лай ◆ *vi (dog)* ла́ять *(impf)*; **she's ~ing up the wrong tree** она́ обраща́ется не по а́дресу.
barley ['bɑːlɪ] *n* ячме́нь *m*.
barley sugar *n ≈* леденёц*.
barmaid ['bɑːmeɪd] *n* буфе́тчица.
barman ['bɑːmən] *irreg n* ба́рмен.
barmy ['bɑːmɪ] *adj (BRIT: inf: person)* чо́кнутый; *(: idea)* неле́пый.

barn [bɑːn] *n* амба́р.
barn owl *n* сипу́ха.
barnacle ['bɑːnəkl] *n* моллю́ск.
barometer [bə'rɔmɪtəʳ] *n* баро́метр.
baron ['bærən] *n* баро́н; *(of press, industry)* магна́т.
baroness ['bærənɪs] *n* бароне́сса.
baronet ['bærənɪt] *n* бароне́т.
barracking ['bærəkɪŋ] *n* вы́крики *mpl*, неодобри́тельные во́згласы *mpl*.
barracks ['bærəks] *npl (MIL)* каза́рма *fsg*.
barrage ['bɑːrɑːʒ] *n (MIL)* загради́тельный ого́нь *m*; *(dam)* да́мба; *(fig)* лави́на.
barrel ['bærəl] *n (of wine, beer)* бо́чка*; *(of oil)* барре́ль *m*; *(of gun)* ствол*.
barrel organ *n* шарма́нка*.
barren ['bærən] *adj (land)* беспло́дный* (беспло́ден).
barricade [bærɪ'keɪd] *n* баррика́да ◆ *vt* баррикади́ровать (забаррикади́ровать *perf*); **to ~ o.s. in** баррикади́роваться (забаррикади́роваться *perf*).
barrier ['bærɪəʳ] *n (at entrance)* барье́р; *(at frontier)* шлагба́ум; *(BRIT: also ~)* предохрани́тельный барьер на шоссе́ и доро́гах; *(fig: to progress etc)* препя́тствие; *(: to communication)* поме́ха.
barrier cream *n (BRIT)* защи́тный крем.
barring ['bɑːrɪŋ] *prep* за исключе́нием +*gen*.
barrister ['bærɪstəʳ] *n (BRIT)* адвока́т.
barrow ['bærəu] *n (also: wheelbarrow)* та́чка*; *(cart)* двухколёсная теле́жка*.
bar stool *n* высо́кое сиде́нье во́зле сто́йки ба́ра.
Bart. *abbr (BRIT.* = baronet*)* бароне́т.
bartender ['bɑːtɛndəʳ] *n (US)* ба́рмен.
barter ['bɑːtəʳ] *vi* производи́ть* (произвести́* *perf*) ба́ртерный обме́н ◆ *n* ба́ртер.
base [beɪs] *n* основа́ние; *(of monument etc)* постаме́нт; *(of make up)* осно́ва; *(MIL)* ба́за; *(for organization)* местонахожде́ние ◆ *adj* ни́зкий* (ни́зок) ◆ *vt*: **to ~ sth on** *(opinion, belief)* осно́вывать *(impf)* что-н на +*prp*; **to be ~d at** бази́роваться *(impf)* в/на +*prp*; **the film is ~d on the book** фильм осно́ван на кни́ге; **I'm ~d in London for now** сейча́с я бази́руюсь в Ло́ндоне *(inf)*; **a Paris-~d firm** фи́рма бази́рующаяся в Пари́же; **computer-~d teaching** обуче́ние при по́мощи компью́теров.
baseball ['beɪsbɔːl] *n* бейсбо́л.
baseboard ['beɪsbɔːd] *n (US)* пли́нтус.
base camp *n* ба́зовый ла́герь* *m*.
Basel [bɑːl] *n* = **Basle**.
baseline ['beɪslaɪn] *n (SPORT)* ли́ния пода́чи; *(starting point)* исхо́дная черта́.
basement ['beɪsmənt] *n* подва́л.
base rate *n* тари́фная ста́вка.

---

* marks translations which have irregular inflections. The Russian-English side of the dictionary gives inflectional information.

bases[1] ['beɪsɪz] npl of **base**.
bases[2] ['beɪsi:z] npl of **basis**.
bash [bæʃ] (inf) vt колоти́ть* (поколоти́ть*
  perf) ♦ n: **I'll have a ~ (at it)** (BRIT) я попыта́юсь
  ▶ **bash up** vt (car) разбива́ть (разби́ть* perf);
  (BRIT: person) избива́ть (изби́ть* perf).
bashful ['bæʃful] adj засте́нчивый (засте́нчив).
bashing ['bæʃɪŋ] n (inf): union-~ я́ростные
  напа́дки на профсою́зы.
BASIC ['beɪsɪk] n (COMPUT) Бэ́йсик.
basic ['beɪsɪk] adj (fundamental)
  фундамента́льный; (elementary)
  нача́льный; (primitive) элемента́рный
  (элемента́рен).
basically ['beɪsɪklɪ] adv по существу́; (on the
  whole) в основно́м.
basic rate n ба́зисная ста́вка.
basics ['beɪsɪks] npl: **the ~** осно́вы fpl.
basil ['bæzl] n базили́к.
basin ['beɪsn] n (also: **washbasin**) ра́ковина;
  (BRIT: for food) ми́ска*; (GEO) бассе́йн.
basis ['beɪsɪs] (pl **bases**) n основа́ние; **on a part-
  time ~** на непо́лной ста́вке; **on a trial ~** на
  испыта́тельный срок; **on the ~ of what
  you've said** на осно́ве ска́занного Ва́ми.
bask [bɑːsk] vi: **to ~ in the sun** гре́ться (impf) на
  со́лнце.
basket ['bɑːskɪt] n корзи́на.
basketball ['bɑːskɪtbɔːl] n баскетбо́л.
basketball player n баскетболи́ст(ка).
Basle [bɑːl] n Ба́зель m.
Basque [bæsk] adj ба́скский ♦ n баск.
bass [beɪs] n бас* ♦ adj ба́ссовый.
bass clef n ба́совый ключ*.
bassoon [bə'suːn] n фаго́т.
bastard ['bɑːstəd] n внебра́чный ребёнок*;
  (inf!) ублю́док* (!)
baste [beɪst] vt (CULIN) полива́ть (поли́ть* perf)
  жи́ром и со́ком; (SEWING) смётывать
  (смета́ть* perf).
bastion ['bæstɪən] n (fig) опло́т.
bat [bæt] n (ZOOL) летучая мышь f; (SPORT)
  бита́*; (BRIT: TABLE TENNIS) раке́тка* ♦ vt: **he
  didn't ~ an eyelid** он и гла́зом не моргну́л;
  off one's own ~ по со́бственному почи́ну.
batch [bætʃ] n (of bread) вы́печка*; (of papers
  etc) па́чка*; (of applicants, goods) па́ртия.
batch processing n (COMPUT) паке́тная
  обрабо́тка (да́нных).
bated ['beɪtɪd] adj: **with ~ breath** затаи́в
  дыха́ние.
bath [bɑːθ] n ва́нна ♦ vt купа́ть (вы́купать
  perf); **to have a ~** принима́ть (приня́ть* perf)
  ва́нну; see also **baths**.
bathe [beɪð] vi (swim) купа́ться (impf); (US: have
  a bath) принима́ть (приня́ть* perf) ва́нну ♦ vt
  (wound) промыва́ть (промы́ть* perf).
bather ['beɪðə'] n купа́льщик(-ица).
bathing ['beɪðɪŋ] n купа́ние.
bathing cap n купа́льная ша́почка*.
bathing costume (US **bathing suit**) n

купа́льный костю́м.
bath mat n ко́врик для ва́нной.
bathrobe ['bɑːθrəub] n купа́льный хала́т.
bathroom ['bɑːθrum] n ва́нная f adj.
baths [bɑːðz] npl (also: **swimming ~**)
  пла́вательный бассе́йн msg.
bath towel n ба́нное полоте́нце.
bathtub ['bɑːθtʌb] n ва́нна.
batman ['bætmən] irreg n (BRIT) денщи́к.
baton ['bætən] n (MUS) дирижёрская па́лочка*;
  (ATHLETICS) эстафе́тная па́лочка*; (POLICE)
  дуби́нка*.
battalion [bə'tælɪən] n батальо́н.
batten ['bætn] n (CARPENTRY) ре́йка; (NAUT) ре́я
  ▶ **batten down** vt (NAUT): **to ~ down the
  hatches** задра́ивать (задра́ить perf) лю́ки.
batter ['bætə'] vt (child, wife) бить (изби́ть*
  perf); (subj: wind, rain) бить* (поби́ть* perf) ♦ n
  (CULIN) жи́дкое те́сто.
battered ['bætəd] adj (hat) потрёпанный
  (потрёпан); (pan) покорёженный (покорё-
  жен); **~ wife** подверга́емая побо́ям жена́*.
battering ram ['bætərɪŋ-] n тара́н.
battery ['bætərɪ] n (of torch etc) батаре́йка*;
  (AUT) аккумуля́тор; (of tests, reporters) ряд*.
battery charger n заря́дное устро́йство
  (батаре́и).
battery farm n птицефа́брика.
battery hens npl инкуба́торные ку́ры mpl.
battle ['bætl] n би́тва, бой ♦ vi боро́ться*
  (impf), сража́ться (impf); **that's half the ~** э́то
  уже́ пол де́ла; **it's a** or **we're fighting a losing ~**
  (fig) э́то безнадёжная борьба́, мы ведём
  безнадёжную борьбу́.
battle dress n похо́дная фо́рма.
battlefield ['bætlfiːld] n по́ле* би́твы or бо́я.
battlements ['bætlmənts] npl сте́ны* fpl с
  бойни́цами.
battleship ['bætlʃɪp] n вое́нный кора́бль* m.
batty ['bætɪ] adj (inf) чо́кнутый (чо́кнут).
bauble ['bɔːbl] n безделу́шка*.
baud [bɔːd] n (COMPUT) бод.
baud rate n (COMPUT) ско́рость f переда́чи в
  бо́дах*.
baulk [bɔːlk] vi = **balk**.
bauxite ['bɔːksaɪt] n бокси́т.
Bavaria [bə'vɛərɪə] n Бава́рия.
Bavarian [bə'vɛərɪən] adj бава́рский* ♦ n
  бава́рец(-рка).
bawdy ['bɔːdɪ] adj (joke, song) скабрёзный*
  (скабрёзен).
bawl [bɔːl] vi ора́ть* (заора́ть* perf).
bay [beɪ] n зали́в; (smaller) бу́хта; (horse)
  гнеда́я ло́шадь f; **parking ~** (BRIT) ме́сто*
  парко́вки; **loading ~** погру́зочная
  площа́дка*; **to hold sb at ~** держа́ть (impf)
  кого́-н на расстоя́нии.
bay leaf n лавро́вый лист*.
bayonet ['beɪənɪt] n штык*.
bay tree n ла́вровое де́рево*.
bay window n э́ркер.

bazaar [bəˈzɑːʔ] n (*market*) база́р, ры́нок*; (*fete*) благотвори́тельный база́р.

bazooka [bəˈzuːkə] n базу́ка, гранатомёт.

BB n abbr (*BRIT:* = *Boys' Brigade*) = отря́д бойска́утов.

B & B n abbr = **bed and breakfast.**

b & b n abbr = **B & B.**

BBC n abbr (= *British Broadcasting Corporation*) Би-Би-Си nt ind.

BC adv abbr (= *before Christ*) до рождества́ Христо́ва ♦ abbr (*CANADA*) = *British Columbia.*

BCG n abbr (= *Bacillus Calmette-Guérin*) БЦЖ.

BD n abbr (= *Bachelor of Divinity*) бакала́вр богосло́вия.

B/D abbr = **bank draft.**

BDS n abbr (= *Bachelor of Dental Surgery*) бакала́вр стоматоло́гии.

KEYWORD

---

be [biː] (*pt* was, were, *pp* been) aux vb **1** (*with present participle: forming continuous tenses*): **what are you doing?** что Вы де́лаете?; **it is raining** идёт дождь; **they're working tomorrow** они́ рабо́тают за́втра; **the house is being built** дом стро́ится/стро́ят; **I've been waiting for you for ages** я жду Вас уже́ це́лую ве́чность

2 (*with pp: forming passives*): **he was killed** он был уби́т; **the box had been opened** я́щик открыва́ли; **the thief was nowhere to be seen** во́ра нигде́ не́ было ви́дно

3 (*in tag questions*) пра́вда, да; **she's back again, is she?** она́ верну́лась, да?; **she is pretty, isn't she?** она́ хоро́шенькая, пра́вда?

4 (*to +infin*): **the house is to be sold** дом бу́дет про́дан; **you're to be congratulated for all your work** Вы бу́дете отме́чены за всю ва́шу рабо́ту; **he's not to open it** он не до́лжен открыва́ть э́то

♦ vb **1** (*+ complement: in present tense*): **he is English** он англича́нин; (*in past/future tense*) быть (*impf*) +*instr* or +*nom*; **he was a doctor** он был врачо́м; **she is going to be very tall** она́ бу́дет о́чень высо́кая or высо́кой; **he is going to be an actor** он бу́дет актёром; **I'm tired** я уста́л; **I was hot/cold** мне бы́ло жа́рко/хо́лодно; **two and two are four** два́жды два – четы́ре; **she's tall/pretty** она́ высо́кая/симпати́чная; **be careful!** бу́дьте осторо́жны!; **be quiet!** ти́ше!

2 (*of health*): **how are you feeling?** как Вы себя́ чу́вствуете?; **he's very ill** он о́чень бо́лен; **I'm better now** мне сейча́с лу́чше

3 (*of age*): **how old are you?** ско́лько Вам лет?; **I'm sixteen (years old)** мне шестна́дцать (лет); **I was only 5 (years old) then** мне тогда́ бы́ло всего́ 5 (лет)

4 (*cost*): **how much is/was the wine?** ско́лько

сто́ит/сто́ило вино́?; **that'll be £5.75, please** с Вас £5.75, пожа́луйста

♦ vi **1** (*exist*) быть (*impf*); **there are people who...** есть лю́ди, кото́рые...; **there is one drug that...** есть одно́ лека́рство, кото́рое...; **is there a God?** Бог есть на све́те?

2 (*occur*) быва́ть (*impf*); **there are frequent accidents on this road** на э́той доро́ге ча́сто быва́ют ава́рии; **be that as it may** как бы то ни́ было; **so be it** так и бы́ть, быть по сему́

3 (*referring to place*): **I won't be here tomorrow** меня́ здесь за́втра не бу́дет; **Edinburgh is in Scotland** Эдинбу́рг нахо́дится в Шотла́ндии; **the book is on the table** кни́га на столе́; **there are pictures on the wall** на стене́ карти́ны; **there is someone in the house** в до́ме кто-то есть; **we've been here for ages** мы здесь уже́ о́чень давно́

4 (*referring to movement*) быть (*impf*); **where have you been?** где Вы бы́ли?; **I've been to the post office** я был на по́чте

♦ impers vb **1** (*referring to time*): **it's five o'clock (now)** сейча́с пять часо́в; **it's the 28th of April (today)** сего́дня 28-ое апре́ля

2 (*referring to distance, weather: in present tense*): **it's 10 km to the village** до дере́вни 10 км; (: *in past/future tense*) быть (*impf*); **it's too hot/cold (today)** сего́дня сли́шком жа́рко/хо́лодно; **it was very windy yesterday** вчера́ бы́ло о́чень ве́трено; **it will be sunny tomorrow** за́втра бу́дет со́лнечно

3 (*emphatic*): **it's (only) me/the postman** э́то я/почтальо́н; **it was Maria who paid the bill** счёт оплати́ла Мари́я.

B/E abbr = **bill of exchange.**

beach [biːtʃ] n (*stony*) бе́рег* мо́ря; (*sandy*) пляж ♦ vt (*boat*) выта́скивать (вы́тащить *perf*) на бе́рег.

beach buggy n пля́жный вездехо́д.

beachcomber [ˈbiːtʃkəumə] n бич*.

beachwear [ˈbiːtʃwɛəʔ] n пля́жная оде́жда.

beacon [ˈbiːkən] n (*lighthouse*) мая́к*; (*marker*) сигна́льный ого́нь* m; (*also:* radio ~) радиома́як*.

bead [biːd] n бу́сина; (*of sweat*) ка́пля*; ~**s** npl (*necklace*) бу́сы pl.

beady [ˈbiːdɪ] adj: ~ **eyes** глаза́-буси́нки mpl.

beagle [ˈbiːɡl] n го́нчая f adj (соба́ка).

beak [biːk] n клюв.

beaker [ˈbiːkəʔ] n (*cup*) пластма́ссовый стака́н.

beam [biːm] n (*ARCHIT*) ба́лка*; (*of light*) луч*; (*RADIO*) радиосигна́л ♦ vi (*smile*) сия́ть (*impf*) ♦ vt (*signal*) передава́ть* (переда́ть* *perf*); **to drive on full or main or (US) high ~** е́хать (*impf*) с включёнными да́льними фа́рами.

beaming [ˈbiːmɪŋ] adj сия́ющий*.

---

bean [bi:n] *n* боб*; **French** ~ фасо́ль *f no pl*; **runner** ~ фасо́ль о́гненная; **coffee** ~ кофе́йное зерно́.

beanpole ['bi:npəul] *n* (*inf*) каланча́* (*высо́кий челове́к*).

beansprouts ['bi:nsprauts] *npl* побе́ги *mpl* бобо́в.

bear [bɛə^r] (*pt* **bore**, *pp* **borne**) *n* медве́дь(-дица) *m(f)*; (*STOCK EXCHANGE*) “медве́дь” (*спекуля́нт, игра́ющий на пониже́ние ку́рса*) ♦ *vt* (*responsibility, cost*) нести́* (понести́* *perf*); (*weight*) нести́* (*impf*); (*examination, scrutiny*) выде́рживать (вы́держать* *perf*); (*situation, person*) выноси́ть* (вы́нести* *perf*); (*traces, signs*) нести́* (*impf*) на себе́; (*children*) рожда́ть (роди́ть* *perf*); (*fruit*) приноси́ть* (принести́* *perf*); (*COMM*): **to** ~ **interest** приноси́ть* (принести́* *perf*) проце́нты ♦ *vi*: **to** ~ **right/left** (*AUT*) держа́ться (*impf*) пра́вого/ле́вого поворо́та; **to** ~ **the responsibility of** нести́* (понести́* *perf*) отве́тственность за +*acc*; **to** ~ **comparison with** выде́рживать (вы́держать *perf*) сравне́ние с +*instr*; **I can't** ~ **him** я его́ не выношу́; **the road** ~**s to the right/left** доро́га идёт впра́во/вле́во; **to bring pressure to** ~ **on sb** ока́зывать (оказа́ть* *perf*) давле́ние на кого́-н

▶ **bear out** *vt* подде́рживать (поддержа́ть *perf*)

▶ **bear up** *vi* держа́ться (*impf*); **he bore up well** он держа́лся молодцо́м

▶ **bear with** *fus* терпе́ть (*impf*) с +*instr*; ~ **with me a minute** потерпи́те мину́ту.

bearable ['bɛərəbl] *adj* терпи́мый (терпи́м).

beard [bɪəd] *n* борода́*.

bearded ['bɪədɪd] *adj* борода́тый.

bearer ['bɛərə^r] *n* (*of letter*) пода́тель(ница) *m(f)*; (*of news*) ве́стник; (*of cheque, passport etc*) владе́лец*, предъяви́тель *m*; (*of title*) носи́тель(ница) *m(f)*.

bearing ['bɛərɪŋ] *n* (*manner*) мане́ра держа́ть себя́; (*connection*) отноше́ние; (*TECH*) подши́пник; ~**s** *npl* (*also:* **ball** ~**s**) ша́рики *mpl* подши́пника; **to take a** ~ ориенти́роваться (*impf/perf*); **to get one's** ~**s** ориенти́роваться (сориенти́роваться *perf*).

beast [bi:st] *n* (*also inf*) зверь* *m*.

beastly ['bi:stlɪ] *adj* ужа́сный (ужа́сен), жу́ткий (жу́ток).

beat [bi:t] (*pt* **beat**, *pp* **beaten**) *n* (*of heart*) бие́ние; (*MUS: rhythm*) ритм; (: *in bar*) такт; (*POLICE*) уча́сток ♦ *vt* (*wife, child*) бить* (поби́ть* *perf*); (*eggs etc*) взбива́ть (взби́ть* *perf*); (*opponent, record*) побива́ть (поби́ть* *perf*); (*drum*) бить* (*impf*) в +*acc* ♦ *vi* (*heart*) би́ться* (*impf*); (*rain, wind*) стуча́ть (*impf*); **to** ~ **time** отбива́ть (*impf*) такт; ~ **it!** (*inf*) кати́сь!; **that** ~**s everything** э́то превосхо́дит всё; **to** ~ **about the bush** ходи́ть (*impf*) вокру́г да о́коло; **off the** ~**en track** по непроторённому пути́

▶ **beat down** *vt* (*door*) выла́мывать (вы́ломать *perf*); (*price*) сбива́ть (сбить* *perf*); (*seller*) добива́ться (доби́ться* *perf*) ски́дки у +*gen* ♦ *vi* (*rain*) хлеста́ть* (*impf*); (*sun*) пали́ть (*impf*)

▶ **beat off** *vt* отбива́ть (отби́ть* *perf*)

▶ **beat up** *vt* (*person*) избива́ть (изби́ть* *perf*); (*eggs etc*) взбива́ть (взби́ть* *perf*).

beaten ['bi:tn] *pp of* **beat**.

beater ['bi:tə^r] *n* ве́нчик.

beating ['bi:tɪŋ] *n* (*thrashing*) по́рка*; **to take a** ~ (*fig*) терпе́ть* (потерпе́ть* *perf*) пораже́ние.

beat-up ['bi:tʌp] *adj* (*inf*) искорёженный (искорёжен).

beautician [bju:'tɪʃən] *n* космети́чка*.

beautiful ['bju:tɪful] *adj* (*woman, place*) краси́вый (краси́в); (*day, experience*) прекра́сный* (прекра́сен).

beautifully ['bju:tɪflɪ] *adv* (*play, sing etc*) краси́во, прекра́сно; (*quiet, empty etc*) замеча́тельно.

beautify ['bju:tɪfaɪ] *vt* украша́ть (украси́ть* *perf*).

beauty ['bju:tɪ] *n* красота́*; (*woman*) краса́вица; **the** ~ **of it is that ...** (*fig*) пре́лесть *f* э́того в том, что ....

beauty contest *n* ко́нкурс красоты́.

beauty queen *n* короле́ва красоты́.

beauty salon *n* сало́н красоты́.

beauty sleep *n* сон до полу́ночи, по пове́рию де́лающий челове́ка молоды́м и здоро́вым.

beauty spot *n* (*BRIT: TOURISM*) живопи́сная ме́стность *f*.

beaver ['bi:və^r] *n* (*ZOOL*) бобр*.

becalmed [bɪ'kɑ:md] *adj* заштиле́вший.

became [bɪ'keɪm] *pt of* **become**.

because [bɪ'kɔz] *conj* потому́ что; (*since, as*) так как; ~ **of** (*illness etc*) из-за +*gen*.

beck [bɛk] *n*: **to be at sb's** ~ **and call** быть* (*impf*) у кого́-н на побегу́шках.

beckon ['bɛkən] *vt* (*also:* ~ **to**) мани́ть* (помани́ть* *perf*) ♦ *vi* (*fame, glory*) мани́ть* (*impf*).

become [bɪ'kʌm] (*irreg: like* **come**) *vi* станови́ться* (стать* *perf*) +*instr*; **to** ~ **fat** толсте́ть (потолсте́ть *perf*); **to** ~ **thin** худе́ть (похуде́ть *perf*); **to** ~ **angry** серди́ться* (рассерди́ться* *perf*); **it became known that** ста́ло изве́стно, что; **what has** ~ **of him?** что с ним ста́лось?

becoming [bɪ'kʌmɪŋ] *adj* (*behaviour*) прили́чествующий; (*clothes*): **your dress is** ~ э́то пла́тье Вам к лицу́.

BECTU *n abbr* (*BRIT*) = **Broadcasting Entertainment Cinematographic and Theatre Union.**

BEd *n abbr* (= *Bachelor of Education*) бакала́вр педаго́гики.

bed [bɛd] *n* крова́ть *f*; (*of coal, clay*) пласт*; (*of river, sea*) дно*; (*of flowers*) клу́мба; **to go to** ~ ложи́ться (лечь* *perf*) спать

▶ **bed down** vi располага́ться
(расположи́ться* perf) на ночле́г.
bed and breakfast n ма́ленькая ча́стная
гости́ница с за́втраком; (terms) ночле́г и
за́втрак.
bedbug ['bɛdbʌɡ] n клоп*.
bedclothes ['bɛdkləʊðz] npl посте́льное бельё
ntsg.
bedding ['bɛdɪŋ] n посте́льные
принадле́жности fpl.
bedevil [bɪ'dɛvl] vt (person) опу́тывать
(опу́тать perf); (plans) спу́тывать (спу́тать
perf); **to be ~led by** вя́знуть (увя́знуть perf) в
+prp.
bedfellow ['bɛdfɛləʊ] n: **they are strange ~s**
(fig) они́ стра́нная па́ра.
bedlam ['bɛdləm] n бедла́м.
bedpan ['bɛdpæn] n (подкладно́е) су́дно*.
bedpost ['bɛdpəʊst] n сто́лбик крова́тного
по́лога.
bedraggled [bɪ'dræɡld] adj (person, clothes)
потрёпанный (потрёпан); (hair)
всклоко́ченный (всклоко́чен).
bedridden ['bɛdrɪdn] adj прико́ванный
(прико́ван) к посте́ли.
bedrock ['bɛdrɒk] n (fig) краеуго́льный
ка́мень* m; (GEO) материко́вая поро́да.
bedroom ['bɛdrum] n спа́льня*.
Beds abbr (BRIT: POST) = Bedfordshire.
bed settee n дива́н-крова́ть f.
bedside ['bɛdsaɪd] n: **at sb's ~** у посте́ли
кого́-н ♦ cpd (lamp, cabinet) прикрова́тный.
bedsit(ter) ['bɛdsɪt(ə')] n (BRIT) ко́мната,
соединя́ющая в себе́ спа́льню, гости́ную и
иногда́ ку́хню.
bedspread ['bɛdsprɛd] n покрыва́ло.
bedtime ['bɛdtaɪm] n вре́мя* nt ложи́ться
спать; **it's ~** пора́ (ложи́ться) спать.
bee [bi:] n пчела́*; **to have a ~ in one's bonnet
about sth** помеша́ться (impf) на чём-н.
beech [bi:tʃ] n бук.
beef [bi:f] n говя́дина; **roast ~** ро́стбиф
▶ **beef up** vt (inf: support) придава́ть (прида́ть*
perf) си́лы +dat; (: essay) напо́лнить (perf)
+instr.
beefburger ['bi:fbə:ɡə'] n говя́жья котле́та,
га́мбургер.
Beefeater ['bi:fi:tə'] n лейб-гварде́ец охра́ны
Та́уэра в Ло́ндоне.
beehive ['bi:haɪv] n у́лей*.
beekeeping ['bi:ki:pɪŋ] n пчелово́дство.
beeline ['bi:laɪn] n: **to make a ~ for** мча́ться
(помча́ться perf) пря́мо в +acc.
been [bi:n] pp of **be**.
beep [bi:p] n гудо́к* ♦ vi сигна́лить
(просигна́лить perf).
beer [bɪə'] n пи́во.
beer belly n (inf) брю́хо.

beer can n ба́нка из-под пи́ва.
beet [bi:t] n (vegetable) кормова́я свёкла; (US:
also: **red ~**) свёкла.
beetle ['bi:tl] n жук*.
beetroot ['bi:tru:t] n (BRIT) свёкла no pl.
befall [bɪ'fɔ:l] (irreg: like **fall**) vt выпада́ть
(вы́пасть* perf) +dat.
befit [bɪ'fɪt] vt прили́чествовать (impf) +dat.
before [bɪ'fɔ:'] prep пе́ред +instr, до +gen ♦ conj
до того́ or пе́ред тем, как ♦ adv (time)
ра́ньше, пре́жде; (space) впереди́; **the day ~
yesterday** позавчера́; **do this ~ you forget**
сде́лайте э́то пока́ Вы не забы́ли; **~ going**
пе́ред ухо́дом; **~ she goes** до того́ or пе́ред
тем, как она́ уйдёт; **the week ~** неде́лю
наза́д, на про́шлой неде́ле; **I've never seen it
~** я никогда́ э́того ра́ньше не ви́дел.
beforehand [bɪ'fɔ:hænd] adv зара́нее.
befriend [bɪ'frɛnd] vt подружи́ться (perf) с
+instr.
befuddled [bɪ'fʌdld] adj одурма́ненный
(одурма́нен).
beg [bɛg] vi ни́щенствовать (impf) ♦ vt (also: ~
for: food, money) проси́ть* (impf);
(: forgiveness, mercy etc) умоля́ть (умоли́ть
perf) о +prp; **to ~ sb to do** умоля́ть (умоли́ть
perf) кого́-н +infin; **I ~ your pardon**
(apologizing) прошу́ проще́ния; (not hearing)
прости́те, не расслы́шал; **to ~ the question**
счита́ть (счесть* perf) спо́рный вопро́с
решённым; **to ~ a favour of sb** проси́ть*
(попроси́ть* perf) об одолже́нии у кого́-н.
began [bɪ'ɡæn] pt of **begin**.
beggar ['bɛɡə'] n ни́щий*(-ая) m(f) adj.
begin [bɪ'ɡɪn] (pt **began**, pp **begun**) vt начина́ть
(нача́ть* perf) ♦ vi начина́ться (нача́ться*
perf); **to ~ doing** or **to do** начина́ть (нача́ть*
perf) +impf infin; **~ning (from) Monday** начина́я
с понеде́льника; **I can't ~** не зна́ю, как Вас благодари́ть; **we'll have soup
to ~ with** мы начнём с су́па; **to ~ with, I'd like
to know ...** для нача́ла, я бы хоте́л знать ....
beginner [bɪ'ɡɪnə'] n начина́ющий*(-ая) m(f)
adj.
beginning [bɪ'ɡɪnɪŋ] n нача́ло; **right from the ~**
с са́мого нача́ла.
begrudge [bɪ'ɡrʌdʒ] vt: **he ~s me my success** он
зави́дует моему́ успе́ху.
beguile [bɪ'ɡaɪl] vt соблазня́ть (соблазни́ть
perf).
beguiling [bɪ'ɡaɪlɪŋ] adj соблазни́тельный,
зама́нчивый.
begun [bɪ'ɡʌn] pp of **begin**.
behalf [bɪ'hɑ:f] n: **on** or **(US) in ~ of** от и́мени
+gen; (for benefit of) ра́ди +gen, в интере́сах
+gen; **on my/his ~** от моего́/его́ и́мени.
behave [bɪ'heɪv] vi вести́* (impf) себя́; (well:
also: ~ **o.s.**) вести́* (impf) себя́ хорошо́.

---

* marks translations which have irregular inflections. The Russian-English side of the dictionary gives inflectional information.

behaviour [bɪˈheɪvjəʳ] (*US* **behavior**) *n*
поведе́ние.
behead [bɪˈhɛd] *vt* обезгла́вливать
(обезгла́вить* *perf*).
beheld [bɪˈhɛld] *pt, pp of* **behold**.
behind [bɪˈhaɪnd] *prep* (*at the back of*) за +*instr*,
позади́ +*gen*; (*supporting*) за +*instr*; (*lower in
rank etc*) ни́же +*gen* ♦ *adv* сза́ди, позади́ ♦ *n*
(*buttocks*) зад*; ~ **the scenes** за кули́сами;
we're ~ them in technology мы отста́ли от
них в техноло́гии; **to be ~ schedule**
отстава́ть* (отста́ть* *perf*) от гра́фика; **to
leave sth ~** (*forget*) оставля́ть (оста́вить*
perf) что-н.
behold [bɪˈhəʊld] (*irreg: like* **hold**) *vt* узре́ть
(*perf*).
beige [beɪʒ] *adj* бе́жевый.
Beijing [ˈbeɪˈdʒɪŋ] *n* Пеки́н.
being [ˈbiːɪŋ] *n* (*creature*) существо́*;
(*existence*) существова́ние; **to come into ~**
возника́ть (возни́кнуть* *perf*).
Beirut [beɪˈruːt] *n* Бейру́т.
Belarus [bɛləˈrus] *n* Белару́сь *f*.
belated [bɪˈleɪtɪd] *adj* запозда́лый.
belch [bɛltʃ] *vi* отры́гивать (отрыгну́ть *perf*) ♦
vt (*also: ~* **out**) изверга́ть (изве́ргнуть* *perf*).
beleaguered [bɪˈliːgɪd] *adj* (*also fig*)
осаждённый (осаждён*); (*army*)
окружённый*.
Belfast [ˈbɛlfɑːst] *n* Бе́лфаст.
belfry [ˈbɛlfrɪ] *n* коло́кольня*.
Belgian [ˈbɛldʒən] *adj* бельги́йский* ♦ *n*
бельги́ец*(-и́йка).
Belgium [ˈbɛldʒəm] *n* Бе́льгия.
Belgrade [bɛlˈgreɪd] *n* Белгра́д.
belie [bɪˈlaɪ] *vt* (*give false impression of*) дава́ть*
(дать* *perf*) неве́рное представле́ние о +*prp*;
(*disprove*) опроверга́ть (опрове́ргнуть *perf*).
belief [bɪˈliːf] *n* (*conviction*) убежде́ние; (*trust,
faith*) ве́ра; **it's beyond ~** это невероя́тно; **in
the ~ that** полага́я, что.
believable [bɪˈliːvəbl] *adj* правдоподо́бный*
(правдоподо́бен).
believe [bɪˈliːv] *vt* ве́рить (пове́рить *perf*) +*dat
or* в(о) +*acc* ♦ *vi* ве́рить (*impf*); **to ~ in** ве́рить
(пове́рить *perf*) в +*acc*; **I don't ~ in corporal
punishment** я не ве́рю в теле́сные
наказа́ния; **he is ~d to be abroad** полага́ют,
что он за грани́цей.
believer [bɪˈliːvəʳ] *n* сторо́нник(-ица); (*REL*)
ве́рующий*(-ая) *m(f) adj*; **she's a great ~ in
healthy eating** она́ — сторо́нница здоро́вого
пита́ния.
belittle [bɪˈlɪtl] *vt* преуменьша́ть
(преуме́ньшить *perf*), уничижа́ть (*impf*).
Belize [bɛˈliːz] *n* Бели́з.
bell [bɛl] *n* ко́локол*; (*small*) колоко́льчик; (*on
door*) звоно́к*; **that rings a ~** я что́-то
припомина́ю.
bell-bottoms [ˈbɛlbɔtəmz] *npl* брю́ки клёш *pl*.
bellboy [ˈbɛlbɔɪ] *n* (*BRIT*) коридо́рный *m adj*.

bellhop [ˈbɛlhɔp] *n* (*US*) = **bellboy**.
belligerence [bɪˈlɪdʒərəns] *n* вои́нственность *f*.
belligerent [bɪˈlɪdʒərənt] *adj* (*person, attitude*)
вои́нственный (вои́нствен).
bellow [ˈbɛləʊ] *vi* реве́ть* (*impf*) ♦ *vt* (*orders*)
прореве́ть* (*perf*).
bellows [ˈbɛləʊz] *npl* (*for fire*) меха́ *mpl*.
bell push *n* (*BRIT*) звоно́к*.
belly [ˈbɛlɪ] *n* брю́хо*.
bellyache [ˈbɛlɪeɪk] (*inf*) *n* бо́ли *fpl* в животе́ ♦
vi ныть* (*impf*).
bellybutton [ˈbɛlɪbʌtn] *n* пупо́к*.
bellyful [ˈbɛlɪful] *n*: **I've had a ~ of it** я сыт по
го́рло э́тим.
belong [bɪˈlɔŋ] *vi*: **to ~ to** принадлежа́ть (*impf*)
+*dat*; (*club etc*) состоя́ть (*impf*) в +*prp*; **this
book ~s here** ме́сто э́той кни́ги здесь.
belongings [bɪˈlɔŋɪŋz] *npl* ве́щи* *fpl*; **personal ~**
ли́чные принадле́жности *fpl*.
Belorussia [bɛləʊˈrʌʃə] *n* Белору́ссия.
Belorussian [bɛləʊˈrʌʃən] *n* (*person*)
белору́с(ка*); (*LING*) белору́сский* язы́к* ♦
adj белору́сский*.
beloved [bɪˈlʌvɪd] *adj* люби́мый ♦ *n*
возлю́бленный(-ая) *m(f) adj*.
below [bɪˈləʊ] *prep* (*position*) под(о) +*instr*;
(*motion*) под(о) +*acc*; (*less than*) ни́же +*gen* ♦
adv (*position*) внизу́; (*motion*) вниз;
temperatures ~ normal температу́ры ни́же
норма́льных; **see ~** смотри́те ни́же.
belt [bɛlt] *n* (*leather etc*) реме́нь* *m*; (*cloth*)
по́яс*; (*of land*) по́яс*, зо́на; (*TECH*)
приводно́й реме́нь* ♦ *vt* (*thrash*) поро́ть*
(вы́пороть *perf*) ♦ *vi* (*BRIT: inf*): **to ~ along** *or*
down the road жа́рить (*impf*) по доро́ге;
industrial ~ индустриа́льная зо́на
▸ **belt out** *vt* горла́нить (*impf*)
▸ **belt up** *vi* (*inf: BRIT*) заткну́ться (*perf*); (*: AUT*)
застёгиваться (застегну́ться *perf*).
beltway [ˈbɛltweɪ] *n* (*US: AUT*) кольцева́я
доро́га; (*motorway*) кольцева́я скоростна́я
автомагистра́ль *f*.
bemoan [bɪˈməʊn] *vt* опла́кивать (опла́кать*
perf).
bemused [bɪˈmjuːzd] *adj* озада́ченный.
bench [bɛntʃ] *n* скамья́*; (*in workshop*)
верста́к*; (*in laboratory*) лаборато́рный
стол*; (*BRIT: POL*) места́ па́ртий в
Парла́менте; **the B~** (*LAW*) суде́йская
колле́гия.
benchmark [ˈbɛntʃmɑːk] *n* крите́рий.
bend [bɛnd] (*pt, pp* **bent**) *vt* (*pipe, leg etc*) гнуть
(согну́ть *perf*), сгиба́ть (*impf*) ♦ *vi* (*person*)
гну́ться (согну́ться *perf*) ♦ *n* (*BRIT: in road*)
поворо́т; (*in pipe*) изги́б; (*in river*) излу́чина;
~s *npl* (*MED*): **the ~s** кессо́нная боле́знь *fsg*
▸ **bend down** *vi* наклоня́ться (наклони́ться*
perf), нагиба́ться (нагну́ться *perf*).
▸ **bend over** *vt fus* (*book, child*) склоня́ться
(склони́ться* *perf*) над +*instr*; (*fence*)
перегиба́ться (перегну́ться *perf*) че́рез +*acc*.

beneath [bɪˈniːθ] *prep* (*position*) под +*instr*; (*motion*) под(о) +*acc*; (*unworthy of*) ни́же +*gen* ♦ *adv* внизу́.

benefactor [ˈbɛnɪfæktə'] *n* (*to person*) благоде́тель *m*; (*to institution*) благотвори́тель *m*.

benefactress [ˈbɛnɪfæktrɪs] *n* благоде́тельница; благотвори́тельница.

beneficial [bɛnɪˈfɪʃəl] *adj*: ~ (**to**) благотво́рный* (благотво́рен) (для +*gen*).

beneficiary [bɛnɪˈfɪʃərɪ] *n* (LAW) бенефициа́рий.

benefit [ˈbɛnɪfɪt] *n* (*advantage*) вы́года; (*money*) посо́бие; (*also*: ~ **concert**) благотвори́тельный конце́рт; (*also*: ~ **match**) благотвори́тельный матч ♦ *vt* приноси́ть* (принести́* *perf*) по́льзу +*dat* ♦ *vi*: **he'll ~ from it** он полу́чит от э́того вы́году.

Benelux [ˈbɛnɪlʌks] *n* Бенилю́кс.

benevolent [bɪˈnɛvələnt] *adj* (*person*) доброжела́тельный* (доброжела́телен); (*organization*) благотвори́тельный* (благотвори́телен).

BEng *n abbr* (= *Bachelor of Engineering*) ≈ бакала́вр инжене́рного де́ла.

Bengal [bɛnˈɡɔːl] *n*: **Bay of ~** Бенга́льский зали́в.

Bengali [bɛnˈɡɔːlɪ] *n* (*person*) бенга́лец*(-а́лка*); (LING) бенга́льский язы́к* ♦ *adj* бенга́льский.

benign [bɪˈnaɪn] *adj* добросерде́чный* (добросерде́чен); (MED) доброка́чественный.

bent [bɛnt] *pt, pp of* **bend** ♦ *adj* (*wire, pipe*) погну́тый; (*inf: dishonest*) жуликова́тый (жуликова́т); (: *pej: homosexual*): **he is** ~ он голубо́й ♦ *n*: **a ~ for** скло́нность *f* к +*dat*; **he is** ~ **on doing** он реши́тельно настро́ен +*infin*.

bequeath [bɪˈkwiːð] *vt* завеща́ть (*impf/perf*).

bequest [bɪˈkwɛst] *n* насле́дство.

bereaved [bɪˈriːvd] *adj* поне́сший тяжёлую утра́ту ♦ *n*: **the** ~ друзья́ *mpl* и ро́дственники *mpl* поко́йного.

bereavement [bɪˈriːvmənt] *n* тяжёлая утра́та.

bereft [bɪˈrɛft] *adj*: ~ **of** лишённый (лишён) +*gen*.

beret [ˈbɛreɪ] *n* бере́т.

Bering Sea [ˈbeɪrɪŋ-] *n*: **the ~ ~** Бе́рингово мо́ре.

berk [bəːk] *n* (*inf: pej*) крети́н, деби́л.

Berks *abbr* (BRIT: POST) = **Berkshire**.

Berlin [bəːˈlɪn] *n* Берли́н; **East/West ~** (*formerly*) Восто́чный/За́падный Берли́н.

Bermuda [bəːˈmjuːdə] *n* Берму́дские острова́ *mpl*.

Bermuda shorts *npl* берму́ды *pl*.

Bern [bəːn] *n* Берн.

berry [ˈbɛrɪ] *n* я́года.

berserk [bəˈsəːk] *adj*: **to go** ~ разъяря́ться (разъяри́ться *perf*).

berth [bəːθ] *n* (*bed: in caravan*) ко́йка*; (: *on ship*) каю́та; (: *on train*) по́лка*; (*mooring*) прича́л ♦ *vi* прича́ливать (прича́лить *perf*); **to give sb/sth a wide** ~ обходи́ть* (обойти́* *perf*) кого́-н/что-н за версту́.

beseech [bɪˈsiːtʃ] (*pt, pp* **besought**) *vt* моли́ть* (*impf*).

beset [bɪˈsɛt] (*pt, pp* **beset**) *vt*: **we have been** ~ **with problems** нас одолева́ли пробле́мы.

beside [bɪˈsaɪd] *prep* ря́дом с +*instr*, о́коло +*gen*, у +*gen*; (*compared with*) ря́дом с +*instr*; **to be** ~ **o.s. (with)** быть* (*impf*) вне себя́ (от +*gen*); **that's** ~ **the point** э́то к де́лу не отно́сится.

besides [bɪˈsaɪdz] *adv* кро́ме того́ ♦ *prep* кро́ме +*gen*, поми́мо +*gen*.

besiege [bɪˈsiːdʒ] *vt* (*also fig*) осажда́ть (осади́ть* *perf*).

besmirch [bɪˈsməːtʃ] *vt* очерня́ть (очерни́ть *perf*).

besotted [bɪˈsɔtɪd] *adj* (BRIT): ~ **with** опьянённый (опьянён) +*instr*.

besought [bɪˈsɔːt] *pt, pp of* **beseech**.

bespectacled [bɪˈspɛktɪkld] *adj* в очка́х.

bespoke [bɪˈspəuk] *adj* (BRIT) поши́тый (поши́т); ~ **tailor** портно́й, рабо́тающий на зака́з.

best [bɛst] *adj* лу́чший* ♦ *adv* лу́чше всего́; **the ~ thing to do is** ... лу́чше всего́ +*infin* ...; **the ~ part of** (*quantity*) бо́льшая часть +*gen*; **at** ~ в лу́чшем слу́чае; **to make the ~ of sth** испо́льзовать (*impf*) что-н наилу́чшим о́бразом; **to do one's** ~ де́лать (сде́лать *perf*) всё возмо́жное; **to the ~ of my knowledge** наско́лько мне изве́стно; **to the ~ of my ability** в ме́ру мои́х спосо́бностей; **he's not exactly patient at the ~ of times** он не отлича́ется осо́бым терпе́нием.

bestial [ˈbɛstɪəl] *adj* ско́тский*.

best man *n* ша́фер*.

bestow [bɪˈstəu] *vt*: **to** ~ **sth on sb** (*title*) дарова́ть (*impf/perf*) что-н кому́-н; (*affection*) ода́ривать (одари́ть *perf*) кого́-н чем-н.

bestseller [ˈbɛstˈsɛlə'] *n* бестсе́ллер.

bet [bɛt] (*pt, pp* **bet** *or* **betted**) *n* (*wager*) пари́ *nt ind*; (*in gambling*) ста́вка ♦ *vi* (*wager*) держа́ть (*impf*) пари́; (*expect, guess*) би́ться* (*impf*) об закла́д ♦ *vt*: **to** ~ **sb sth** би́ться* (поби́ться* *perf*) об закла́д с кем-н на чём-н, спо́рить (поспо́рить *perf*) с кем-н на что-н; **it's a safe** ~ (*fig*) э́то ве́рное де́ло; **to** ~ **money on sth** ста́вить* (поста́вить* *perf*) де́ньги на что-н.

Bethlehem [ˈbɛθlɪhɛm] *n* Вифлее́м.

betray [bɪˈtreɪ] *vt* (*friends*) предава́ть* (преда́ть* *perf*); (*trust*) обма́нывать (обману́ть* *perf*); (*emotion*) выдава́ть* (вы́дать* *perf*).

---

* marks translations which have irregular inflections. The Russian-English side of the dictionary gives inflectional information

betrayal [bɪ'treɪəl] *n* преда́тельство.
better ['bɛtə'] *adj* лу́чший* ◆ *adv* лу́чше ◆ *vt* (*score*) улучша́ть (улу́чшить *perf*) ◆ *n*: **to get the ~ of** бра́ть* (взять* *perf*) верх над +*instr*; **I feel ~** я чу́вствую себя́ лу́чше; **to get ~** (*MED*) поправля́ться (попра́виться* *perf*); **that's ~!** вот так(-то) лу́чше!; **I had ~ go** мне лу́чше уйти́; **he thought ~ of it** он переду́мал; **a change for the ~** измене́ние к лу́чшему.
better off *adj* (*wealthier*) бо́лее состоя́тельный* (состоя́телен); (*more comfortable etc*) лу́чше; (*fig*): **you'd be ~ ~ this way** так Вам бу́дет лу́чше.
betting ['bɛtɪŋ] *n* пари́ *nt ind*.
betting shop *n* (*BRIT*) ме́сто, где де́лают ста́вки.
between [bɪ'twi:n] *prep* ме́жду +*instr* ◆ *adv*: **in ~** ме́жду тем; **the road ~ here and London** доро́га отсю́да до Ло́ндона; **we only had £5 ~ us** у нас на двои́х бы́ло всего́ £5.
bevel ['bɛvəl] *n* (*also:* **~ edge**) скос.
bevelled ['bɛvəld] *adj*: **a ~ edge** ско́шенный край*.
beverage ['bɛvərɪdʒ] *n* напи́ток*.
bevy ['bɛvɪ] *n*: **a ~ of** (*people*) гру́ппа +*gen*; (*things*) ряд +*gen*.
bewail [bɪ'weɪl] *vt* скорбе́ть (*impf*) о +*prp*.
beware [bɪ'wɛə'] *vi*: **to ~ (of)** остерега́ться (остере́чься* *perf*) (+*gen*); **"beware of the dog"** "осторо́жно, (зла́я) соба́ка".
bewildered [bɪ'wɪldəd] *adj* изумлённый (изумлён).
bewildering [bɪ'wɪldrɪŋ] *adj* изуми́тельный* (изуми́телен).
bewitching [bɪ'wɪtʃɪŋ] *adj* (*smile, person*) чару́ющий.
beyond [bɪ'jɔnd] *prep* (*position*) за +*instr*; (*motion*) за +*acc*; (*understanding*) вы́ше +*gen*; (*expectations*) сверх +*gen*; (*age*) бо́льше +*gen*; (*date*) по́сле +*gen* ◆ *adv* (*position*) вдали́; (*motion*) вда́ль; **~ doubt** вне сомне́ния; **it's ~ repair** э́то невозмо́жно почини́ть; **it's ~ me** э́то вы́ше моего́ понима́ния.
b/f *abbr* (*COMM*. = brought forward) перенесённый на сле́дующую страни́цу.
BFPO *n abbr* = British Forces Post Office.
bhp *n abbr* (*AUT*. = brake horsepower) эффекти́вная мо́щность дви́гателя вну́треннего сгора́ния в лошади́ных си́лах.
bi... [baɪ] *prefix* би..., дву(х)....
biannual [baɪ'ænjuəl] *adj* выходя́щий два ра́за в год.
bias ['baɪəs] *n* (*against*) предубежде́ние; (*towards*) пристра́стие.
bias(s)ed ['baɪəst] *adj* (*jury*) пристра́стный* (пристра́стен); (*judgement*) предвзя́тый (предвзя́т); **he is/was ~ against** он предубеждён/был предубеждён про́тив +*gen*.
bib [bɪb] *n* (*child's*) нагру́дник.
Bible ['baɪbl] *n* Би́блия.

biblical ['bɪblɪkl] *adj* библе́йский*.
bibliography [bɪblɪ'ɔgrəfɪ] *n* библиогра́фия.
bicarbonate of soda [baɪ'kɑ:bənɪt-] *n* питьева́я *or* пищева́я со́да.
bicentenary [baɪsɛn'ti:nərɪ] *n* двухсотле́тие.
bicentennial [baɪsɛn'tɛnɪəl] *n* (*US*) = **bicentenary**.
biceps ['baɪsɛps] *n* би́цепс.
bicker ['bɪkə'] *vi* препира́ться (*impf*).
bickering ['bɪkərɪŋ] *n* препира́тельство.
bicycle ['baɪsɪkl] *n* велосипе́д.
bicycle path *n* велосипе́дная доро́жка.
bicycle pump *n* велосипе́дный насо́с.
bicycle track *n* велотре́к.
bid [bɪd] (*pt* **bade** *or* **bid**, *pp* **bid(den)**) *n* (*at auction*) предложе́ние цены́; (*in tender*) зая́вка*; (*attempt*) попы́тка* ◆ *vt* (*offer*) предлага́ть (предложи́ть* *perf*) ◆ *vi*: **to ~ for** (*at auction*) предлага́ть (предложи́ть* *perf*) це́ну за +*acc*; (*CARDS*) объявля́ть (объяви́ть* *perf*) (*масть или коли́чество взя́ток*); **to ~ sb good day** здоро́ваться (поздоро́ваться *perf*) с кем-н.
bidden ['bɪdn] *pp of* **bid**.
bidder ['bɪdə'] *n*: **the highest ~** лицо́, предлага́ющее наивы́сшую це́ну.
bidding ['bɪdɪŋ] *n* (*at auction*) предложе́ние цены́, торги́ *pl*; (*command*): **to do sb's ~** исполня́ть (испо́лнить *perf*) чьи-н приказа́ния.
bide [baɪd] *vt*: **to ~ one's time** дожида́ться (дожда́ться *perf*) своего́ ча́са.
bidet ['bi:deɪ] *n* биде́ *nt ind*.
bidirectional ['baɪdɪ'rɛkʃənl] *adj* (*COMPUT*: *printing*) двунапра́вленный; (: *drive*) реверси́вный.
biennial [baɪ'ɛnɪəl] *adj* происходя́щий раз в два го́да ◆ *n* двухле́тник.
bier [bɪə'] *n* катафа́лк.
bifocals [baɪ'fəuklz] *npl* бифока́льные очки́ *pl*.
big [bɪg] *adj* большо́й; (*important*) ва́жный* (ва́жен); (*bulky*) кру́пный*; (*older*: *brother, sister*) ста́рший*; **to do things in a ~ way** де́лать (сде́лать *perf*) что-н с широ́ким разма́хом.
bigamist ['bɪgəmɪst] *n* (*man*) двоеже́нец*.
bigamous ['bɪgəməs] *adj* бига́мный.
bigamy ['bɪgəmɪ] *n* бига́мия.
big dipper [-'dɪpə'] *n* аттракцио́н "америка́нские го́ры".
big end *n* больша́я голо́вка (шатуна́).
biggish ['bɪgɪʃ] *adj* дово́льно большо́й *or* кру́пный.
bigheaded ['bɪg'hɛdɪd] *adj* зано́счивый (зано́счив).
big-hearted ['bɪg'hɑ:tɪd] *adj* великоду́шный* (великоду́шен).
bigot ['bɪgət] *n* фана́тик.
bigoted ['bɪgətɪd] *adj* фанати́чный* (фанати́чен).
bigotry ['bɪgətrɪ] *n* фанати́зм.

big toe *n* большо́й па́лец* ноги́.
big top *n* ку́пол* ци́рка.
big wheel *n* колесо́* обозре́ния.
bigwig ['bɪgwɪg] *n* (*inf*) (ва́жная) ши́шка*.
bike [baɪk] *n* (*bicycle*) ве́лик; (*motorcycle*) мотоци́кл.
bikini [bɪ'ki:nɪ] *n* бики́ни *nt ind*.
bilateral [baɪ'lætərl] *adj* двусторо́нний*.
bile [baɪl] *n* жёлчь *f*; (*fig*) жёлчность *f*.
bilingual [baɪ'lɪŋgwəl] *adj* двуязы́чный*.
bilious ['bɪlɪəs] *adj* (*also fig*) тошнотво́рный (тошнотво́рен).
bill [bɪl] *n* (*invoice*) счёт*; (*POL*) законопрое́кт; (*US: banknote*) банкно́та; (*beak*) клюв ◆ *vt* (*item*) реклами́ровать (*impf/perf*); (*customer*) присыла́ть (присла́ть* *perf*) счёт +*dat*; "**post no ~s**" "помеща́ть афи́ши воспреща́ется"; **to fit** *or* **fill the ~** (*fig*) отвеча́ть (*impf*) всем тре́бованиям; **on the ~** (*THEAT*) в афи́шах *or* програ́мме; **~ of exchange** ве́ксель* *m*; **~ of fare** меню́ *nt ind*; **~ of lading** коносаме́нт, (тра́нспортная) накладна́я *f adj*; **~ of sale** ку́пчая *f adj*.
billboard ['bɪlbɔ:d] *n* доска́ объявле́ний.
billet ['bɪlɪt] *n* (*MIL*) кварти́ры *fpl* ◆ *vt* расквартиро́вывать (расквартирова́ть *perf*).
billfold ['bɪlfəuld] *n* (*US*) бума́жник.
billiards ['bɪljədz] *n* билья́рд.
billion ['bɪljən] *n* (*BRIT*) биллио́н; (*US*) миллиа́рд.
billow ['bɪləu] *n* (*of smoke, steam*) клуб ◆ *vi* (*smoke*) клуби́ться (*impf*); (*sail*) надува́ться (наду́ться* *perf*).
billy goat ['bɪlɪ-] *n* козёл*.
bimbo ['bɪmbəu] *n* (*inf*) ку́кла (*хоро́шенькая, но не у́мная же́нщина*).
bin [bɪn] *n* (*BRIT: also:* **rubbish ~**) му́сорное ведро́*; (*container*) я́щик.
binary ['baɪnərɪ] *adj* (*MATH, COMPUT*) дво́ичный, бина́рный.
bind [baɪnd] (*pt, pp* **bound**) *vt* (*tie*) привя́зывать (привяза́ть* *perf*); (*tie together: hands and feet*) свя́зывать (связа́ть* *perf*); (*oblige*) обя́зывать (обяза́ть* *perf*); (*book*) переплета́ть (переплести́* *perf*) ◆ *n* (*inf*) обу́за
▶ **bind over** *vt* (*LAW*) обя́зывать (обяза́ть* *perf*)
▶ **bind up** *vt* (*wound*) перевя́зывать (перевяза́ть* *perf*); **he is/was bound up in** (*work etc*) он вовлечён/был вовлечён в +*acc*; **he is/was bound up with** (*person*) он свя́зан/был свя́зан с +*instr*.
binder ['baɪndə*'*] *n* (*file*) скоросшива́тель *m*.
binding ['baɪndɪŋ] *adj* обя́зывающий ◆ *n* (*of book*) переплёт.
binge [bɪndʒ] *n* (*inf*): **to go on a ~** (*drink a lot*) пья́нствовать (*impf*).
bingo ['bɪŋgəu] *n* лото́ *nt ind*.
bin-liner ['bɪnlaɪnə*'*] *n* мешо́к* для му́сора.

binoculars [bɪ'nɔkjuləz] *npl* бино́кль *msg*.
bio... [baɪəu] *prefix* био...; **~chemistry** биохи́мия.
biodegradable ['baɪəudɪ'greɪdəbl] *adj* биологи́чески разложи́мый (разложи́м).
biodiversity ['baɪəudaɪ'və:sɪtɪ] *n* биолог- и́ческое разнообра́зие.
biographer [baɪ'ɔgrəfə*'*] *n* био́граф.
biographic(al) [baɪə'græfɪk(l)] *adj* биографи́ческий.
biography [baɪ'ɔgrəfɪ] *n* биогра́фия.
biological [baɪə'lɔdʒɪkl] *adj* (*science*) биологи́ческий; (*warfare*) бактериолог- и́ческий*; (*washing powder*) содержа́щий* биопрепара́ты.
biological clock *n* биологи́ческие часы́ *pl*; **to upset sb's ~** ~ наруша́ть (нару́шить *perf*) чей-н режи́м.
biologist [baɪ'ɔlədʒɪst] *n* био́лог.
biology [baɪ'ɔlədʒɪ] *n* биоло́гия.
biophysics ['baɪəu'fɪzɪks] *n* биофи́зика.
biopic ['baɪəupɪk] *n* (*inf*) биографи́ческий фильм.
biopsy ['baɪɔpsɪ] *n* биопси́я.
biosphere ['baɪəsfɪə*'*] *n* биосфе́ра.
biotechnology ['baɪəutɛk'nɔlədʒɪ] *n* биотехноло́гия.
biped ['baɪpɛd] *n* двуно́гое *nt adj*.
birch [bə:tʃ] *n* берёза.
bird [bə:d] *n* пти́ца; (*BRIT: inf: girl*) деви́ца.
bird of prey *n* хи́щная пти́ца.
bird's-eye view ['bə:dzaɪ-] *n* (*aerial view*) вид* с высоты́ пти́чьего полёта; (*overview*) о́бщая карти́на.
bird-watcher ['bə:dwɔtʃə*'*] *n* орнито́лог- люби́тель *m*.
Birmingham ['bə:mɪŋəm] *n* Бирминге́м.
Biro® ['baɪərəu] *n* ша́риковая ру́чка*.
birth [bə:θ] *n* рожде́ние; **to give ~ to** рожа́ть (роди́ть* *perf*).
birth certificate *n* свиде́тельство о рожде́нии.
birth control *n* (*policy*) контро́ль *m* рожда́емости; (*methods*) противо- зача́точные ме́ры *fpl*.
birthday ['bə:θdeɪ] *n* день* *m* рожде́ния ◆ *cpd* ко дню рожде́ния; *see also* **happy**.
birthmark ['bə:θmɑ:k] *n* (*large*) роди́мое пятно́; (*small*) ро́динка*.
birthplace ['bə:θpleɪs] *n* (*also fig*) ро́дина.
birth rate *n* рожда́емость *f*.
Biscay ['bɪskeɪ] *n*: **the Bay of ~** Биска́йский зали́в.
biscuit ['bɪskɪt] *n* (*BRIT*) пече́нье; (*US*) ≈ кекс.
bisect [baɪ'sɛkt] *vt* (*MATH*) дели́ть* (раздели́ть* *perf*).
bisexual ['baɪ'sɛksjuəl] *adj* бисексуа́льный* (бисексуа́лен).
bishop ['bɪʃəp] *n* (*REL*) епи́скоп; (*CHESS*) слон*.

---

* marks translations which have irregular inflections. The Russian-English side of the dictionary gives inflectional information.

bistro ['bi:strəu] *n* бистро́ *nt ind.*

bit [bɪt] *pt of* **bite ♦** *n* (*piece*) кусо́к*, кусо́чек*; (*of tool*) сверло́*; (*COMPUT*) бит; (*of horse*) удила́* *pl*; (*US: coin*) (ме́лкая) моне́та; **a ~ of** немно́го +*gen*; **a ~ dangerous** слегка́ опа́сный; **~ by ~** ма́ло-пома́лу; **to come to ~s** разла́мываться (разлома́ться* *perf*); **bring all your ~s and pieces** принеси́те все Ва́ши пожи́тки; **to do one's ~** вноси́ть* (внести́* *perf*) свой вклад.

bitch [bɪtʃ] *n* (*also inf!*) су́ка (*also !*)

bitching ['bɪtʃɪŋ] *n* хула́.

bite [baɪt] (*pt* **bit**, *pp* **bitten**) *vt* куса́ть (укуси́ть* *perf*) ♦ *vi* куса́ться (*impf*) ♦ *n* (*insect bite*) уку́с; **to ~ one's nails** куса́ть (*impf*) но́гти; **let's have a ~ (to eat)** (*inf*) дава́йте переку́сим; **he had a ~ of cake** он откуси́л кусо́к пирога́.

biting ['baɪtɪŋ] *adj* (*wind*) прони́зывающий; (*wit*) язви́тельный* (язви́телен).

bit part *n* проходна́я роль *f*.

bitten ['bɪtn] *pp of* **bite**.

bitter ['bɪtə'] *adj* го́рький*; (*wind*) прони́зывающий; (*struggle*) ожесточённый ♦ *n* (*BRIT*) пи́во с горькова́тым при́вкусом; **to the ~ end** до са́мого конца́.

bitterly ['bɪtəlɪ] *adv* го́рько; (*oppose, criticize*) ожесточённо; (*jealous*) ужа́сно; **it's ~ cold today** сего́дня прони́зывающий хо́лод.

bitterness ['bɪtənɪs] *n* (*anger*) го́речь *f*, ожесточённость *f*; (*taste*) го́речь.

bittersweet ['bɪtəswi:t] *adj* горькова́то-сла́дкий*.

bitty ['bɪtɪ] *adj* (*BRIT: inf*) неро́вный* (неро́вен).

bitumen ['bɪtjumɪn] *n* би́тум.

bivouac ['bɪvuæk] *n* бива́к.

bizarre [bɪ'zɑ:'] *adj* стра́нный, причу́дливый.

bk *abbr* = **bank**, **book**.

BL *n abbr* (= *Bachelor of Law*) ≈ бакала́вр правове́дения; (= *Bachelor of Letters*) ≈ бакала́вр литературове́дения; (*US:* = *Bachelor of Literature*) ≈ бакала́вр литературове́дения.

bl *abbr* (= *bill of lading*) ≈ тра́нспортная накладна́я *f adj*.

blab [blæb] *vi* (*inf*) проба́лтываться (проболта́ться *perf*).

black [blæk] *adj* чёрный*; (*tea, coffee*) без молока́; (*person*) черноко́жий* ♦ *n* (*colour*) чёрный цвет, чёрное *nt adj*; (*person*): **B~** негр(итя́нка) ♦ *vt* (*BRIT: INDUSTRY*) бойкоти́ровать (*impf/perf*); **to give sb a ~ eye** подбива́ть (подби́ть* *perf*) кому́-н глаз; **~ and blue** в синяка́х; **there it is in ~ and white** (*fig*) вот оно́, чёрным по бе́лому напи́сано; **to be in the ~** име́ть (*impf*) де́ньги в ба́нке
  ► **black out** *vi* па́дать (упа́сть* *perf*) в о́бморок.

black belt *n* (*JUDO*) чёрный по́яс*; (*US: area*) ю́жные райо́ны США, в кото́рых преоблада́ет негритя́нское населе́ние.

blackberry ['blækbərɪ] *n* ежеви́ка *no pl*.

blackbird ['blækbə:d] *n* (чёрный) дрозд*.

blackboard ['blækbɔ:d] *n* кла́ссная доска́*.

black box *n* (*AVIAT*) чёрный я́щик.

black coffee *n* чёрный ко́фе *m ind.*

Black Country *n* (*BRIT*): **the ~ ~** индустриа́льные райо́ны Се́веро-За́падной А́нглии.

blackcurrant ['blæk'kʌrənt] *n* чёрная сморо́дина.

black economy *n*: **the ~ ~** теневáя эконо́мика.

blacken ['blækn] *vt* (*fig*) черни́ть (очерни́ть* *perf*).

black eye *n* синя́к* *or* фона́рь* *m* под гла́зом.

Black Forest *n*: **the ~ ~** Шварцва́льд.

blackhead ['blækhɛd] *n* у́горь* *m*.

black hole *n* чёрная дыра́*.

black ice *n* гололе́дица.

blackjack ['blækdʒæk] *n* (*CARDS*) блэкджéк*; (*US: truncheon*) дуби́нка.

blackleg ['blæklɛg] *n* (*BRIT: INDUSTRY*) штрейкбрéхер.

blacklist ['blæklɪst] *n* чёрный спи́сок* ♦ *vt* (*person*) заноси́ть* (занести́* *perf*) в чёрный спи́сок.

blackmail ['blækmeɪl] *n* шанта́ж ♦ *vt* шантажи́ровать (*impf*).

blackmailer ['blækmeɪlə'] *n* шантажи́ст.

black market *n* чёрный ры́нок*.

blackout ['blækaut] *n* (*in wartime*) затемне́ние; (*ELEC*) обесто́чивание*; (*TV, RADIO*) приостановле́ние переда́ч; (*MED*) о́бморок.

black pepper *n* чёрный пе́рец*.

Black Sea *n*: **the ~ ~** Чёрное мо́ре.

black sheep *n* (*fig*) парши́вая овца́*.

blacksmith ['blæksmɪθ] *n* кузне́ц*.

black spot *n* (*AUT*) ги́блое ме́сто*; (*ECON*) мёртвая зо́на.

bladder ['blædə'] *n* (*ANAT*) мочево́й пузы́рь* *m*.

blade [bleɪd] *n* ле́звие; (*of oar, propeller*) ло́пасть* *f*; **a ~ of grass** трави́нка*.

blame [bleɪm] *n* вина́* ♦ *vt*: **to ~ sb for sth** вини́ть (*impf*) кого́-н в чём-н; **he is/was to ~ (for sth)** он винова́т *or* винова́н/был винова́т *or* вино́вен (в чём-н); **who's to ~?** кого́ сле́дует в э́том вини́ть?; **I'm not to ~** э́то не моя́ вина́.

blameless ['bleɪmlɪs] *adj* (*person*) невино́вный, безупре́чный.

blanch [blɑ:ntʃ] *vi* беле́ть (побеле́ть *perf*) ♦ *vt* (*CULIN*) обва́ривать (обвари́ть* *perf*) кипятко́м.

blancmange [blə'mɒnʒ] *n* бланманже́ *nt ind.*

bland [blænd] *adj* (*taste, food*) пре́сный (пре́сен).

blank [blæŋk] *adj* (*paper*) чи́стый* (чист); (*look*) безуча́стный* (безуча́стен) ♦ *n* (*of memory*) пробе́л; (*on form*) про́пуск; (*for gun*) холосто́й патро́н; **we drew a ~** (*fig*) мы оста́лись ни с чем.

blank cheque *n* незапо́лненный чек; **to give sb a ~ ~** (*fig*) предоставля́ть (предоста́вить*

perf) кому́-н карт-бланш.
blanket ['blæŋkɪt] *n* одея́ло; (*of snow*) покро́в;
(*of fog*) пелена́ ♦ *adj* всеобъе́млющий*.
blanket cover *n* (*INSURANCE*) бла́нковый *or*
блок по́лис.
blare [blɛə'] *vi* реве́ть (*impf*)
► **blare out** *vi* пропеве́ть *(perf)*.
blarney ['blɑːnɪ] *n* лесть *f*.
blasé ['blɑːzeɪ] *adj* валья́жный.
blaspheme [blæs'fiːm] *vi* богоху́льствовать
(*impf*), святота́тствовать (*impf*).
blasphemous ['blæsfɪməs] *adj* (*words*)
богоху́льный; **a ~ person** богоху́льник.
blasphemy ['blæsfɪmɪ] *n* богоху́льство,
святота́тство.
blast [blɑːst] *n* (*of wind*) поры́в; (*of air, steam*)
волна́*; (*of whistle*) пронзи́тельный свист;
(*explosion*) взрыв ♦ *vt* (*blow up*) взрыва́ть
(взорва́ть* *perf*) ♦ *excl* (*BRIT: inf*) пропади́ (всё)
про́падом; **at full ~** (*play music etc*) на
по́лную мо́щность
► **blast off** *vi* взлета́ть (взлете́ть* *perf*),
взмыва́ть (взмыть* *perf*).
blast furnace *n* до́менная печь* *f*.
blast-off ['blɑːstɔf] *n* старт.
blatant ['bleɪtənt] *adj* я́вный (я́вен),
неприкры́тый.
blatantly ['bleɪtəntlɪ] *adv* я́вно, неприкры́то;
it's ~ obvious э́то абсолю́тно я́сно.
blaze [bleɪz] *n* (*fire*) пла́мя* *nt*; (*of colour*)
полыха́ние; (*of glory*) сия́ние ♦ *vi* (*fire*)
пыла́ть (*impf*); (*guns*) пали́ть (*impf*); (*fig: eyes*)
сверка́ть (*impf*) ♦ *vt*: **to ~ a trail** прокла́га́ть
(проложи́ть* *perf*) путь; **in a ~ of publicity** в
газе́тной шуми́хе.
blazer ['bleɪzə'] *n* фо́рменная ку́ртка.
bleach [bliːtʃ] *n* (*also*: **household ~**)
отбе́ливатель *m* ♦ *vt* (*fabric*) отбе́ливать
(отбели́ть* *perf*); (*hair*) обесцве́чивать
(обесцве́тить* *perf*).
bleached [bliːtʃt] *adj* (*hair*) обесцве́ченный
(обесцве́чен).
bleachers ['bliːtʃəz] *npl* (*US: SPORT*) откры́тая
трибу́на *fsg*.
bleak [bliːk] *adj* (*weather, expression*) уны́лый
(уны́л); (*prospect*) безра́достный*
(безра́достен).
bleary-eyed ['blɪərɪ'aɪd] *adj* с воспалёнными
глаза́ми.
bleat [bliːt] *vi* (*animal*) бле́ять (забле́ять *perf*) ♦
n (*of animal*) бле́яние.
bled [blɛd] *pt, pp of* **bleed**.
bleed [bliːd] (*pt, pp* **bled**) *vi* кровото́чить (*impf*);
(*colour*) течь* (поте́чь* *perf*) ♦ *vt* (*brakes,
radiator*) опорожня́ть (опорожни́ть *perf*); **my
nose is ~ing** у меня́ идёт кровь из но́са.
bleep [bliːp] *n* сигна́л; (*TEL*) гудо́к* ♦ *vi*
сигна́лить (просигна́лить *perf*) ♦ *vt* (*doctor*)

вызыва́ть (вы́звать* *perf*).
bleeper ['bliːpə'] *n* переносна́я ра́ция.
blemish ['blɛmɪʃ] *n* пятно́*.
blend [blɛnd] *n* (*of tea, whisky*) буке́т ♦ *vt*
(*CULIN*) сме́шивать (смеша́ть *perf*); (*colours,
styles etc*) сочета́ть (*impf*) ♦ *vi* (*also:* **~ in**)
сочета́ться (*impf*), слива́ться (сли́ться* *perf*).
blender ['blɛndə'] *n* смеси́тель *m*, ми́ксер.
bless [blɛs] (*pt, pp* **blessed** *or* **blest**) *vt* (*REL*)
благословля́ть (благослови́ть* *perf*); **he is
~ed with** Бог награди́л его́ +*instr*; **~ you!**
бу́дьте здоро́вы!
blessed ['blɛsɪd] *adj* блаже́нный; **it rains every
~ day** (*inf*) дождь идёт ка́ждый Бо́жий день.
blessing ['blɛsɪŋ] *n* благослове́ние; (*godsend*)
бо́жий дар, благода́ть *f*; **to count one's ~s** не
гневи́ть (*impf*) Бо́га, не ропта́ть (*impf*)
по́пусту на судьбу́; **it was a ~ in disguise** ≈ не
бы́ло бы сча́стья, да несча́стье помогло́.
blest [blɛst] *pt, pp of* **bless**.
blew [bluː] *pt of* **blow**.
blight [blaɪt] *vt* губи́ть* (погуби́ть* *perf*) ♦ *n* (*of
plants*) головня́*.
blimey ['blaɪmɪ] *excl* (*BRIT: inf*) чтоб мне
провали́ться.
blind [blaɪnd] *adj* слепо́й* ♦ *n* што́ра; (*also:*
Venetian ~) жалюзи́ *pl ind* ♦ *vt* ослепля́ть
(ослепи́ть* *perf*); **the ~ npl** (*blind people*)
слепы́е *pl adj*; **to be ~ (to)** (*fig*) не ви́деть*
(*impf*) (+*acc*); **to turn a ~ eye (on *or* to)**
закрыва́ть (закры́ть* *perf*) глаза́ (на +*acc*).
blind alley *n* (*fig*) тупи́к.
blind corner *n* (*BRIT*) непросма́триваюшийся
поворо́т.
blind date *n* свида́ние с незнако́мцем.
blinders ['blaɪndəz] *npl* (*US*) = **blinkers**.
blindfold ['blaɪndfəuld] *n* повя́зка ♦ *adv*
вслепу́ю ♦ *vt* завя́зывать (завяза́ть* *perf*)
глаза́ +*dat*.
blinding ['blaɪndɪŋ] *adj* ослепля́ющий
(ослепля́ющ), слепя́щий; (*fig*)
ослепи́тельный (ослепи́телен).
blindly ['blaɪndlɪ] *adv* (*without seeing*) вслепу́ю.
(*without thinking*) сле́по.
blindness ['blaɪndnɪs] *n* слепота́; (*fig*)
ослепле́ние.
blind spot *n* (*AUT*) опа́сное ме́сто*; (*fig*) сла́бое
ме́сто*.
blink [blɪŋk] *vi* (*person, animal*) морга́ть (*impf*;
(*light*) мига́ть (*impf*) ♦ *n*: **the TV's on the ~** (*inf*)
телеви́зор барахли́т.
blinkers ['blɪŋkəz] *npl* шо́ры *fpl*.
blinking ['blɪŋkɪŋ] *adj* (*BRIT: inf*): **this ~ weather**
прокля́тая пого́да.
blip [blɪp] *n* вспы́шка* (*на экра́не*); (*scientific*)
отражённый и́мпульс.
bliss [blɪs] *n* блаже́нство.
blissful ['blɪsful] *adj* блаже́нный (блаже́н);

(*event*) счастли́вый (сча́стлив); in ~
ignorance в счастли́вом неве́дении.
blissfully ['blɪsfəlɪ] *adv* блаже́нно; ~ **happy**
бесконе́чно счастли́вый; ~ **unaware of ...** в
счастли́вом неве́дении о +*prp* ....
blister ['blɪstə'] *n* (*on skin*) волды́рь* *m*; (*in
paint, rubber*) пузы́рь* *m* ♦ *vi* (*paint*)
пузыри́ться (*impf*).
blithely ['blaɪðlɪ] *adv* беспе́чно.
blithering ['blɪðərɪŋ] *adj* (*inf*): this ~ **idiot** э́тот
зако́нченный дура́к.
BLit(t) *n abbr* = *Bachelor of Literature, Bachelor
of Letters*.
blitz [blɪts] *n* (*MIL*) бомбёжка*; to have a ~ on
sth (*fig*) нава́ливаться (навали́ться* *perf*) на
что-н.
blizzard ['blɪzəd] *n* вью́га.
BLM *n abbr* (*US*) = *Bureau of Land Management*.
bloated ['bləʊtɪd] *adj* (*face, stomach*) взду́тый
(взду́т); **I feel** ~ я весь разду́лся.
blob [blɔb] *n* (*of glue, paint*) сгу́сток*; (*indistinct
shape*) сму́тное очерта́ние.
bloc [blɔk] *n* блок; the Eastern ~ (*formerly*)
стра́ны Восто́чного бло́ка.
block [blɔk] *n* (*of buildings*) кварта́л; (*of stone
etc*) плита́*; (*in pipe etc*) про́бка; (*toy*) ку́бик
♦ *vt* (*entrance, road*) загора́живать
(загороди́ть* *perf*); (*progress*)
препя́тствовать (*impf*); (*COMPUT*)
блоки́ровать (*impf/perf*); ~ **of flats** (*BRIT*)
многокварти́рный дом*; three ~s **from here**
че́рез три у́лицы; **mental** ~ прова́л па́мяти;
~ **and tackle** лебёдка*; to ~ sb's **way**
прегражда́ть (прегради́ть* *perf*) кому́-н
доро́гу
▸ **block up** *vt* затыка́ть (заткну́ть *perf*) ♦ *vi*
засоря́ться (засори́ться *perf*); my **nose is** ~**ed**
up у меня́ нос заложи́ло.
blockade [blɔ'keɪd] *n* блока́да ♦ *vt*
блоки́ровать (заблоки́ровать *perf*).
blockage ['blɔkɪdʒ] *n* блоки́рование.
block booking *n* группова́я бронь *f*.
blockbuster ['blɔkbʌstə'] *n* боеви́к*.
block capitals *npl* печа́тные бу́квы *fpl*.
blockhead ['blɔkhɛd] *n* (*inf*) болва́н.
block letters *npl* печа́тные бу́квы *fpl*.
block release *n* (*BRIT*) уче́бный о́тпуск.
block vote *n* (*BRIT*) представи́тельное
голосова́ние.
bloke [bləʊk] *n* (*BRIT: inf*) па́рень* *m*.
blond(e) [blɔnd] *adj* белоку́рый (белоку́р) ♦ *n*:
blonde (*woman*) блонди́нка*.
blood [blʌd] *n* кровь* *f*; new ~ (*fig*) све́жие
си́лы *fpl*.
blood bank *n* храни́лище кро́ви.
bloodbath ['blʌdbɑːθ] *n* бо́йня.
blood count *n* о́бщий* ана́лиз кро́ви.
bloodcurdling ['blʌdkəːdlɪŋ] *adj* ледени́щий*
кровь.
blood donor *n* до́нор.
blood group *n* гру́ппа кро́ви.

bloodhound ['blʌdhaund] *n* ище́йка*.
bloodless ['blʌdlɪs] *adj* бескро́вный*
(бескро́вен).
bloodletting ['blʌdlɛtɪŋ] *n* кровопуска́ние;
(*fig*) кровопроли́тие.
blood poisoning *n* зараже́ние кро́ви.
blood pressure *n* кровяно́е давле́ние; **he has
high/low** ~ ~ у него́ высо́кое/ни́зкое
давле́ние.
bloodshed ['blʌdʃɛd] *n* кровопроли́тие.
bloodshot ['blʌdʃɔt] *adj* (*eyes*) нали́тый
кро́вью.
blood sport *n* охо́та (*как вид спо́рта*).
bloodstained ['blʌdsteɪnd] *adj* запя́тнанный
кро́вью.
bloodstream ['blʌdstriːm] *n* кровообраще́ние.
blood test *n* ана́лиз кро́ви.
bloodthirsty ['blʌdθəːstɪ] *adj* кровожа́дный*
(кровожа́ден).
blood transfusion *n* перелива́ние кро́ви.
blood type *n* гру́ппа кро́ви.
blood vessel *n* кровено́сный сосу́д.
bloody ['blʌdɪ] *adj* (*battle*) крова́вый; (*nose*)
окрова́вленный (окрова́влен); (*BRIT: infl*):
this ~ **weather** э́та прокля́тая пого́да (!); ~
strong/good (*infl*) ужа́сно си́льный/
хоро́ший*.
bloody-minded ['blʌdɪ'maɪndɪd] *adj* (*BRIT: inf*)
по́длый (подл).
bloom [bluːm] *n* (*BOT*) цвето́к ♦ *vi* (*BOT*) цвести́*
(*impf*); (*talent, person*) расцвета́ть (расцвести́*
perf); to be in ~ быть* (*impf*) в цвету́, цвести́*
(*impf*).
blooming ['bluːmɪŋ] *adj* (*BRIT: inf*): this ~
weather э́та чёртова пого́да.
blossom ['blɔsəm] *n* цвет ♦ *vi* цвести́* (*impf*);
(*fig*): to ~ **into** расцвести́* (*perf*) в +*acc*.
blot [blɔt] *n* (*on text*) кля́кса; (*on name etc*)
пятно́* ♦ *vt* (*with ink etc*) ста́вить* (поста́вить*
perf) кля́ксу на +*acc*; to be a ~ **on the
landscape** по́ртить* (*impf*) вид; to ~ **one's copy
book** (*fig*) мара́ть (замара́ть *perf*) свою́
репута́цию
▸ **blot out** *vt* (*view*) заслоня́ть (заслони́ть *perf*);
(*memory*) уничтожа́ть (уничто́жить *perf*).
blotchy ['blɔtʃɪ] *adj* (*complexion*) пятни́стый
(пятни́ст).
blotter ['blɔtə'] *n* бюва́р.
blotting paper ['blɔtɪŋ-] *n* промока́тельная
бума́га.
blotto ['blɔtəu] *adj* (*inf*) пья́ный (пьян) в
сте́льку.
blouse [blauz] *n* блу́за, блу́зка*.
blow [bləu] (*pt* **blew**, *pp* **blown**) *n* (*also fig*) уда́р
♦ *vi* (*wind, person*) дуть (поду́ть *perf*); (*fuse*)
перегора́ть (перегоре́ть *perf*) ♦ *vt* (*subj: wind*)
гнать* (*impf*); (*instrument*) дуть (*impf*) в +*acc*;
to ~ **one's nose** сморка́ться (вы́сморкаться
perf); to ~ **a whistle** свисте́ть (просвисте́ть
perf) в свисто́к; to come to ~s доходи́ть*
(дойти́* *perf*) до дра́ки

▶ **blow away** *vt* сдува́ть (сдуть *perf*) ◆ *vi* уноси́ться* (унести́сь* *perf*)

▶ **blow down** *vt* вали́ть* (повали́ть* *perf*)

▶ **blow off** *vt* сдува́ть (сдуть *perf*) ◆ *vi* слета́ть (слете́ть* *perf*); (*NAUT*): **the ship was ~n off course** кора́бль снесло́ с ку́рса

▶ **blow out** *vi* га́снуть* (пога́снуть *perf*)

▶ **blow over** *vi* (*storm, crisis*) проходи́ть* (пройти́* *perf*)

▶ **blow up** *vi* (*storm, crisis*) разража́ться (разрази́ться* *perf*) ◆ *vt* (*bridge*) взрыва́ть (взорва́ть* *perf*); (*tyre*) надува́ть (наду́ть *perf*); (*PHOT*) увели́чивать (увели́чить *perf*).

blow-dry ['bləudraɪ] *n* укла́дка воло́с фе́ном ◆ *vt* укла́дывать (уложи́ть* *perf*) во́лосы фе́ном.

blowlamp ['bləulæmp] *n* (*BRIT*) пая́льная ла́мпа.

blown [bləun] *pp of* **blow**.

blow-out ['bləuaut] *n* (*of tyre*) разры́в; (*of oil well*) проры́в; (*inf*: *big meal*) кутёж*.

blowtorch ['bləutɔ:tʃ] *n* = **blowlamp**.

blow-up ['bləuʌp] *n* увели́ченный сни́мок*.

blowzy ['blauzɪ] *adj* (*BRIT*) обрю́зглый.

BLS *n abbr* (*US*) = **Bureau of Labor Statistics**.

blubber ['blʌbə'] *n* вы́топленный жир ◆ *vi* (*pej*) реве́ть* (зареве́ть* *perf*).

bludgeon ['blʌdʒən] *vt* бить* (изби́ть* *perf*) дуби́нкой; (*fig*): **to ~ sb into doing** заставля́ть (заста́вить* *perf*) кого́-н из-под па́лки +*infin*.

blue [blu:] *adj* (*colour. light*) голубо́й; (: *dark*) си́ний*; (*depressed*) гру́стный, пода́вленный; ~**s** *npl* (*MUS*):**the ~s** блюз *msg*; ~ **film** поха́бный фильм; (**only**) **once in a ~ moon** раз в сто лет; **out of the ~** (*fig*) как с не́ба свали́ться.

blue baby *n* синю́шный младе́нец*.

bluebell ['blu:bɛl] *n* колоко́льчик.

bluebottle ['blu:bɔtl] *n* наво́зная му́ха.

blue cheese *n* сыр* ти́па рокфо́р.

blue-chip ['blu:tʃɪp] *adj*: ~ **investment/shares** вложе́ния/а́кции с высо́кими дивиде́ндами.

blue-collar worker ['blu:kɔlə'-] *n* заводско́й рабо́чий*(-ая) *m(f)* *adj*.

blue jeans *npl* джи́нсы *pl*.

blueprint ['blu:prɪnt] *n* (*fig*): **a ~ (for)** прое́кт (+*gen*).

bluff [blʌf] *vi* (*pretend, threaten*) блефова́ть (*impf*) ◆ *n* блеф; (*GEO*) утёс; **to call sb's ~** заставля́ть (заста́вить* *perf*) кого́-н раскры́ть ка́рты.

blunder ['blʌndə'] *n* про́мах ◆ *vi* (*make mistake*) допуска́ть (допусти́ть* *perf*) про́мах; **to ~ into sb/sth** натыка́ться (наткну́ться *perf*) на кого́-н/что-н.

blunt [blʌnt] *adj* тупо́й* (туп*); (*person*) прямолине́йный* (прямолине́ен); (*talk*) открове́нный* (открове́нен) ◆ *vt* (*chisel etc*) затупля́ть (затупи́ть* *perf*); (*feelings*) тупи́ть (притупи́ть* *perf*); ~ **instrument** (*LAW*) тупо́е ору́дие.

bluntly ['blʌntlɪ] *adv* пря́мо.

bluntness ['blʌntnɪs] *n* прямолине́йность *f*.

blur [blə:'] *n* сму́тное очерта́ние; (*memory*) сму́тное воспомина́ние ◆ *vt* (*vision*) затума́нивать (затума́нить *perf*); (*distinction*) стере́ть* (стира́ть *perf*).

blurb [blə:b] *n* (*about book etc*) рекла́ма.

blurred [blə:d] *adj* стёртый, сму́тный.

blurt out [blə:t-] *vt* выпа́ливать (вы́палить *perf*).

blush [blʌʃ] *vi* красне́ть (покрасне́ть *perf*) ◆ *n* румя́нец*.

blusher ['blʌʃə'] *n* румя́на *pl*.

bluster ['blʌstə'] *n* взрыв гне́ва ◆ *vi* разбушева́ться* (*perf*).

blustering ['blʌstərɪŋ] *adj* (*person*) бу́йный* (бу́ен); (*tone etc*) громогла́сный* (громогла́сен).

blustery ['blʌstərɪ] *adj* ве́треный.

Blvd *abbr* = **boulevard**.

BM *n abbr* = **British Museum**; (= *Bachelor of Medicine*) ≈ бакала́вр медици́ны.

BMA *n abbr* = **British Medical Association**.

BMJ *n abbr* = **British Medical Journal**.

BMus *n abbr* (= *Bachelor of Music*) ≈ бакала́вр музыковеде́ния.

BMX *n abbr* (= *bicycle motorcross*) велосипе́дные го́нки *pl*; ~ **bike** *ма́рка велосипе́да*.

BNP *n abbr* (= *British National Party*) Брита́нская национа́льная па́ртия.

BO *n abbr* (*inf*: = *body odour*): **he has ~** от него́ па́хнет по́том; (*US*) = **box office**.

boar [bɔ:'] *n* бо́ров; (*wild pig*) каба́н*.

board [bɔ:d] *n* доска́*; (*cardboard*) карто́н; (*committee*) комите́т; (*in firm*) правле́ние ◆ *vt* (*ship*) сади́ться* (сесть* *perf*) на +*acc*; (*train*) сади́ться* (сесть* *perf*) в/на +*acc*; **on ~** (*NAUT, AVIAT*) на борту́; **full ~** (*BRIT*) по́лный пансио́н; **half ~** (*BRIT*) пансио́н с за́втраком и у́жином; ~ **and lodging** прожива́ние и пита́ние; **the plan went by the ~** (*fig*) план был вы́брошен за́ борт; **above ~** (*fig*) зако́нным о́бразом; **across the ~** (*fig*) по всем кате́гориям.

▶ **board up** *vt* забива́ть (заби́ть* *perf*), закола́чивать (заколоти́ть* *perf*).

boarder ['bɔ:də'] *n* (*SCOL*) учени́к*(-и́ца) шко́лы-интерна́та.

board game *n* насто́льная игра́*.

boarding card ['bɔ:dɪŋ-] *n* (*AVIAT, NAUT*) = **boarding pass**.

boarding house *n* пансио́н.

---

* marks translations which have irregular inflections. The Russian-English side of the dictionary gives inflectional information.

boarding party n спецгру́ппа тамо́женников и́ли полице́йских, проводя́щая инспе́кцию судо́в, подозрева́емых в прово́зе контраба́нды и нарко́тиков.

boarding pass n поса́дочный тало́н.

boarding school n шко́ла-интерна́т.

board meeting n совеща́ние правле́ния.

board room n зал заседа́ний.

boardwalk ['bɔ:dwɔ:k] n (US) доща́тый насти́л.

boast [bəust] vt горди́ться (impf) +instr ♦ vi: **to ~ (about** or **of)** хва́статься (похва́статься perf) (+instr).

boastful ['bəustful] adj хвастли́вый (хвастли́в).

boastfulness ['bəustfulnɪs] n хвастовство́.

boat [bəut] n (small) ло́дка*; (large) кора́бль* m; **to go by ~** плыть* (поплы́ть* perf); **to be in the same ~** (fig) быть* (impf) това́рищами по несча́стью.

boater ['bəutə'] n соло́менная шля́па.

boating ['bəutɪŋ] n ката́ние на ло́дке.

boatswain ['bəusn] n бо́цман.

bob [bɔb] vi (boat: also: ~ **up and down)** пока́чиваться (impf) ♦ n (BRIT: inf) = **shilling**
► **bob up** vi выска́кивать (вы́скочить perf).

bobbin ['bɔbɪn] n шпу́лька.

bobby ['bɔbɪ] n (BRIT: inf) мент.

bobsleigh ['bɔbsleɪ] n бо́бслей.

bode [bəud] vi: **to ~ well/ill** предвеща́ть (impf) or сули́ть (impf) хоро́шее/недо́брое.

bodice ['bɔdɪs] n корса́ж.

bodily ['bɔdɪlɪ] adj физи́ческий* ♦ adv целико́м.

body ['bɔdɪ] n те́ло*; (torso) ту́ловище; (of speech, document) основна́я часть* f; (of car) ко́рпус; (of plane) фюзеля́ж; (fig: group) гру́ппа; (: organization) о́рган, организа́ция; (of information) ма́сса; (of wine) консисте́нция; (also: ~ **stocking)** сви́тер-гольф (по ти́пу закры́того купа́льника), трико́ nt ind; **ruling ~** о́рган правле́ния; **in a ~** в по́лном соста́ве.

body blow n сокруши́тельный уда́р.

body-building ['bɔdɪ'bɪldɪŋ] n бо́ди-би́лдинг, атлети́зм.

body-double ['bɔdɪdʌbl] n актёр, снима́ющийся в обнажённом ви́де вме́сто веду́щего актёра.

bodyguard ['bɔdɪgɑ:d] n телохрани́тель m.

body language n язы́к* же́стов.

body repairs npl ремо́нт ко́рпуса.

body search n ли́чный досмо́тр.

bodywork ['bɔdɪwɜ:k] n ко́рпус.

boffin ['bɔfɪn] n (BRIT: inf) спец.

bog [bɔg] n (GEO) боло́то, тряси́на ♦ vt: **to get ~ged down in** (fig) вя́знуть (увя́знуть perf) в +prp.

bogey ['bəugɪ] n (worry) пу́гало; (also: ~ **man)** бу́ка m/f.

boggle ['bɔgl] vi: **the mind ~s** уму́ непостижи́мо.

bogie ['bəugɪ] n (RAIL) двухо́сная теле́жка*.

Bogotá [bəugə'tɑ:] n Богота́.

bogus ['bəugəs] adj (claim) фикти́вный* (фикти́вен); (person) сомни́тельный (сомни́телен).

Bohemia [bəu'hi:mɪə] n Боге́мия.

Bohemian [bəu'hi:mɪən] adj (GEO) боге́мский ♦ n богеме́ц(ка); (non-conformist: also: **b~**) представи́тель(ница) m(f) боге́мы.

boil [bɔɪl] vt (water) кипяти́ть* (вскипяти́ть* perf); (eggs, potatoes etc) вари́ть (свари́ть perf), отва́ривать (отвари́ть perf) ♦ vi (also fig) кипе́ть* (вскипе́ть* perf) ♦ n фуру́нкул; **to come to the** (BRIT) or **a** (US) ~ вскипе́ть* (perf)
► **boil down to** vt fus (fig) своди́ться (свести́сь* perf) к +dat
► **boil over** vi (milk) убега́ть (убежа́ть* perf); (potatoes) выкипа́ть (impf).

boiled egg [bɔɪld-] n варёное яйцо́*.

boiled potatoes npl варёная карто́шка fsg.

boiler ['bɔɪlə'] n (device) парово́й котёл*, бо́йлер.

boiler suit n (BRIT) комбинезо́н.

boiling ['bɔɪlɪŋ] adj: **I'm ~** (hot) (inf) я запа́рился; **it's ~** (of weather) жара́!, жари́ща!

boiling point n (of liquid) то́чка кипе́ния.

boisterous ['bɔɪstərəs] adj разбитно́й.

bold [bəuld] adj (brave) сме́лый* (смел); (pej: cheeky) на́глый (нагл); (pattern, colours) бро́ский* (бро́сок).

boldly ['bəuldlɪ] adv (bravely) сме́ло; (impudently) на́гло.

boldness ['bəuldnɪs] n (see adv) сме́лость f; на́глость f.

bold type n жи́рный шрифт.

Bolivia [bə'lɪvɪə] n Боли́вия.

Bolivian [bə'lɪvɪən] adj боливи́йский ♦ n боливи́ец(-и́йка).

bollard ['bɔləd] n (BRIT: AUT) ту́мба; (: NAUT) швартова́я ту́мба.

bolshy ['bɔlʃɪ] adj (BRIT: inf) агресси́вный* (агресси́вен), вои́нственный.

bolster ['bəulstə'] n ва́лик
► **bolster up** vt подкрепля́ть (подкрепи́ть* perf).

bolt [bəult] n (lock) засо́в; (with nut) болт* ♦ vt (lock) запира́ть (запере́ть* perf) на засо́в; (also: ~ **together)** скрепля́ть (скрепи́ть* perf) болта́ми; (devour) загла́тывать (заглотну́ть* perf) ♦ vi (run away) понести́сь* (perf) ♦ adv: ~ **upright** вы́тянувшись в стру́нку; **a ~ of lightning** разря́д мо́лнии; **a ~ from the blue** (fig) гром среди́ я́сного не́ба.

bomb [bɔm] n бо́мба ♦ vt бомби́ть* (impf).

bombard [bɔm'bɑ:d] vt (MIL, fig) бомбардирова́ть (impf).

bombardment [bɔm'bɑ:dmənt] n бомбардиро́вка.

bombastic [bɔm'bæstɪk] adj претенцио́зный* (претенцио́зен).

bomb disposal *n*: ~ ~ **unit** отря́д сапёров; ~ ~ **expert** сапёр.
bomber ['bɔmə'] *n* (*AVIAT*) бомбардиро́вщик; (*person*) террори́ст.
bombing ['bɔmɪŋ] *n* бомбардиро́вка, бомбёжка.
bombshell ['bɔmʃɛl] *n* (*fig*): **my sacking was a real ~** изве́стие о моём увольне́нии произвело́ эффе́кт разорва́вшейся бо́мбы.
bomb site *n* разбомблённый уча́сток*.
bona fide ['bəunə'faɪdɪ] *adj* (*traveller etc*) по́длинный*; (*offer*) настоя́щий*.
bonanza [bə'nænzə] *n* золото́е дно.
bond [bɔnd] *n* у́зы *pl*; (*binding promise*) обяза́тельство; (*FINANCE*) облига́ция; (*COMM*): **goods in ~** това́ры, неопла́ченные по́шлиной.
bondage ['bɔndɪdʒ] *n* (*slavery*) нево́ля.
bonded goods ['bɔndɪd-] *npl* храня́щиеся това́ры *mpl* на тамо́женных скла́дах.
bonded warehouse *n* тамо́женный склад (*для това́ров неопла́ченных по́шлиной*).
bone [bəun] *n* кость* *f* ♦ *vt* о̄ целя́ть (отдели́ть* *perf*) от косте́й; **I've got a ~ to pick with you** у меня́ к тебе́ прете́нзия.
bone china *n* костяно́й фарфо́р.
bone-dry ['bəun'draɪ] *adj* соверше́нно сухо́й*.
bone idle *adj* пра́здный* (пра́зден); **he is ~ ~** он безде́льник.
bone marrow *n* ко́стный мозг.
boner ['bəunə'] *n* (*US*) про́мах*.
bonfire ['bɔnfaɪə'] *n* костёр*.
bonk [bɔŋk] (*inf*) *vt* тра́хать (тра́хнуть *perf*) ♦ *vi* тра́хаться (тра́хнуться *perf*).
bonkers ['bɔŋkəz] *adj* (*inf*) чо́кнутый.
Bonn [bɔn] *n* Бонн.
bonnet ['bɔnɪt] *n* (*hat*) ка́пор; (*BRIT*: *of car*) капо́т.
bonny ['bɔnɪ] *adj* (*esp SCOTTISH*) краси́вый (краси́в).
bonus ['bəunəs] *n* (*payment*) пре́мия; (*on wages*) премиа́льные *pl adj*; (*fig*) дополни́тельное преиму́щество.
bony ['bəunɪ] *adj* (*person, fingers*) костля́вый (костля́в); (*meat, fish*) кости́стый.
boo [bu:] *excl* фу ♦ *vt* освисты́вать (освиста́ть* *perf*).
boob [bu:b] *n* (*inf*: *breast*) грудь *f*; (*BRIT*: *mistake*) глу́пость *f*.
booby prize ['bu:bɪ-] *n* приз* проигра́вшему игроку́.
booby trap *n* (*MIL*) ми́на-лову́шка*; (*fig*) лову́шка*.
booby-trapped ['bu:bɪtræpt] *adj*: **a ~ car** маши́на с подло́женной ми́ной.
book [buk] *n* кни́га; (*of stamps, tickets*) кни́жечка* ♦ *vt* (*ticket, table*) зака́зывать (заказа́ть* *perf*); (*seat, room*) брони́ровать (заброни́ровать *perf*); (*subj*: *policeman, referee*) штрафова́ть (оштрафова́ть *perf*); **~s** *npl* (*COMM*: *accounts*) бухга́лтерские кни́ги *fpl*; **to keep the ~s** вести́* (*impf*) бухга́лтерские кни́ги; **by the ~** согла́сно инстру́кции; **to throw the ~ at sb** обвиня́ть (обвини́ть *perf*) кого́-н во всех сме́ртных греха́х
▸ **book in** *vi* (*BRIT*: *at hotel*) регистри́роваться (зарегистри́роваться *perf*)
▸ **book up** *vt*: **all seats are ~ed up** все биле́ты про́даны; **the hotel is ~ed up** в гости́нице нет мест; **I'm ~ed up that week** у меня́ э́та неде́ля по́лностью за́нята.
bookable ['bukəbl] *adj*: **all seats are ~** все биле́ты по предвари́тельным зака́зам.
bookcase ['bukkeɪs] *n* кни́жный шкаф*.
book end *n* книгодержа́тель *m*.
booking ['bukɪŋ] *n* (*BRIT*) зака́з.
booking office *n* (*BRIT*) биле́тная ка́сса.
book-keeping ['buk'ki:pɪŋ] *n* бухгалте́рия, счетово́дство.
booklet ['buklɪt] *n* брошю́ра.
bookmaker ['bukmeɪkə'] *n* букме́кер.
bookseller ['buksɛlə'] *n* книготорго́вец*.
bookshelf ['bukʃɛlf] *n* кни́жная по́лка.
bookshop ['bukʃɔp] *n* кни́жный магази́н.
bookstall ['bukstɔ:l] *n* кни́жный кио́ск.
book store *n* = **bookshop**.
book token *n* пода́рочный тало́н на поку́пку кни́ги.
book value *n* сто́имость *f* по торго́вым кни́гам.
bookworm ['bukwə:m] *n* кни́жный червь *m*.
boom [bu:m] *n* (*noise*) ро́кот; (*growth*: *in population etc*) бы́стрый рост; (*ECON*) бум ♦ *vi* (*guns, thunder*) грохота́ть* (прогрохота́ть* *perf*); (*voice*) рокота́ть* (пророкота́ть* *perf*); (*business*) процвета́ть (*impf*).
boomerang ['bu:məræŋ] *n* бумера́нг ♦ *vi*: **to ~ on sb** верну́ться (*perf*) к кому́-н бумера́нгом.
boom town *n* го́род, процвета́ющий во вре́мя экономи́ческого подъёма.
boon [bu:n] *n* бла́го.
boorish ['buərɪʃ] *adj* неотёсанный (неотёсан).
boost [bu:st] *n* (*to confidence etc*) толчо́к*, сти́мул ♦ *vt* стимули́ровать (*impf*), дава́ть* (дать* *perf*) толчо́к +*dat*; **to give a ~ to sb's spirits** *or* **to sb** окрыля́ть (окрыли́ть *perf*) кого́-н.
booster ['bu:stə'] *n* (*MED*) повто́рная приви́вка*; (*TV, ELEC*) усили́тель *m*; (*also:* ~ **rocket**) раке́та-носи́тель *m*.
booster cushion *n* сиде́нье для дете́й в маши́не.
boot [bu:t] *n* (*for winter*) сапо́г*; (*for football*) бу́тса; (*for walking*) боти́нок*; (*BRIT*: *of car*) бага́жник ♦ *vt* (*COMPUT*) загружа́ть (загрузи́ть* *perf*); ... **to ~** (*in addition*) ... в

---

* marks translations which have irregular inflections. The Russian-English side of the dictionary gives inflectional information.

прида́чу; **to give sb the ~** (inf) вы́турить (perf) кого́-н.
booth [bu:ð] n (at fair) ларёк*; (TEL, for voting) бу́дка*.
bootleg ['bu:tlɛg] adj контраба́ндный.
bootlegger ['bu:tlɛgə'] n контрабанди́ст.
booty ['bu:ti] n трофе́и mpl.
booze [bu:z] (inf) n вы́пивка ♦ vi выпива́ть (impf).
boozer ['bu:zə'] n (BRIT: inf: pub) пивну́шка*; **he's a real ~** (inf) он настоя́щий* пьянчу́га.
border ['bɔ:də'] n (of a country) грани́ца; (for flowers) бордю́р; (on cloth etc) кайма́* ♦ vt (road, river etc) окаймля́ть (окайми́ть* perf); (another country: also: ~ on) грани́чить (impf) с +instr; **B~s** n: **the B~s** райо́н на грани́це ме́жду А́нглией и Шотла́ндией
▶ **border on** vt fus (fig) грани́чить (impf) с +instr.
borderline ['bɔ:dəlaɪn] n: **on the ~** на гра́ни.
borderline case n промежу́точный слу́чай.
bore [bɔ:'] pt of **bear** ♦ vt (hole) сверли́ть (просверли́ть perf); (well, tunnel) бури́ть (пробури́ть* perf); (person) наску́чить (perf) +dat ♦ n (person) зану́да m/f; (of gun) кана́л ствола́, кали́бр; **to be ~d** скуча́ть (impf); **he's ~d to tears** or **~d to death** or **~d stiff** ему́ смерте́льно ску́чно.
boredom ['bɔ:dəm] n (condition) ску́ка; (boring quality) зану́дство.
boring ['bɔ:rɪŋ] adj ску́чный*.
born [bɔ:n] adj рождённый; **to be ~** рожда́ться (роди́ться* perf); **I was ~ in 1960** я роди́лся в 1960 году́; **~ blind** слепорождённый; **a ~ comedian** прирождённый ко́мик.
born-again [bɔ:nə'gɛn] adj: **~ Christian** новообращённый(-ая) христиа́нин*(-а́нка).
borne [bɔ:n] pp of **bear**.
Borneo ['bɔ:nɪəu] n Борне́о m ind.
borough ['bʌrə] n администрати́вный о́круг*.
borrow ['bɔrəu] vt: **to ~ sth from sb** занима́ть (заня́ть* perf) что-н у кого́-н; **to ~ books from the library** брать* (взять* perf) кни́ги в библиоте́ке; **may I ~ your car?** мо́жно взять на вре́мя Ва́шу маши́ну?
borrower ['bɔrəuə'] n заёмщик.
borrowing ['bɔrəuɪŋ] n (word, custom) заи́мствование; (of money) заём*.
borstal ['bɔ:stl] n (BRIT) исправи́тельная коло́ния для несовершенноле́тних престу́пников.
Bosnia ['bɔznɪə] n Бо́сния; **~-Herzegovina** Бо́сния-Герцегови́на.
Bosnian ['bɔznɪən] n босни́ец(-и́йка).
bosom ['buzəm] n грудь* f; (fig: of family) ло́но.
bosom friend n закады́чный друг*.
Bosphorus ['bɔsfərəs] n: **the ~** Босфо́р.
boss [bɔs] n (employer) хозя́ин*(-я́йка), босс; (leader) ли́дер, вожа́к ♦ vt (also: ~ around, ~ about) распоряжа́ться (impf), кома́ндовать (impf) +instr; **stop ~ing everyone about!**

переста́нь все́ми кома́ндовать!
bossy ['bɔsɪ] adj вла́стный (вла́стен).
bosun ['bəusn] n бо́цман.
botanical [bə'tænɪkl] adj ботани́ческий.
botanist ['bɔtənɪst] n бота́ник.
botany ['bɔtənɪ] n бота́ника.
botch [bɔtʃ] vt (also: ~ up) состря́пать (perf).
both [bəuθ] adj, pron о́ба* (f о́бе*) ♦ adv: ~ **A and B** и А, и Б; **~ (of them)** о́ба (они́); **~ of us went, we ~ went** мы о́ба пошли́; **they sell ~ meat and poultry** они́ торгу́ют и мя́сом, и пти́цей.
bother ['bɔðə'] vt (worry) беспоко́ить (обеспоко́ить perf); (disturb) беспоко́ить (побеспоко́ить perf) ♦ vi (also: ~ o.s.) беспоко́иться (impf) ♦ n (trouble) беспоко́йство; (nuisance) хло́поты* pl ♦ excl: ~! чёрт возьми́!; **to ~ doing** брать* (взять* perf) на себя́ труд +infin; **I'm sorry to ~ you** извини́те за беспоко́йство; **please don't ~** пожа́луйста, не беспоко́йтесь; **don't ~!** не на́до!; **it is a ~ to have to do** э́то так хло́потно +infin; **it's no ~** э́то меня́ не затрудни́т; **I can't be ~ed** мне лень.
Botswana [bɔt'swɑ:nə] n Ботсва́на.
bottle ['bɔtl] n буты́лка*; (for baby) рожо́к*; (BRIT: inf: courage) сме́лость f ♦ vt (beer, wine) разлива́ть (разли́ть* perf) по буты́лкам; (fruit) консерви́ровать (законсерви́ровать perf); ~ **of wine/milk** буты́лка* вина́/молока́; **wine/milk ~** буты́лка* из-под вина́/молока́
▶ **bottle up** vt скрыва́ть (скрыть* perf).
bottle bank n контейнер для стекля́нной та́ры.
bottle-fed ['bɔtlfɛd] adj: ~ **baby** иску́сственник.
bottleneck ['bɔtlnɛk] n (AUT) у́зкий* езд; (fig) зато́р.
bottle-opener ['bɔtləupnə'] n штопор.
bottom ['bɔtəm] n (of container, sea etc) дно* (ANAT) зад*; (of page, list) низ*; (of class) неуспева́ющий*(-ая) m(f) adj; (of mountain etc) подно́жие ♦ adj (lowest) ни́жний*; (last) после́дний*; **at the ~ of** на дне +gen; **to get to the ~ of sth** (fig) добира́ться (добра́ться* perf) до су́ти чего́-н.
bottomless ['bɔtəmlɪs] adj (funds, store) бездо́нный* (бездо́нен).
bottom line n суть f де́ла.
botulism ['bɔtjulɪzəm] n ботули́зм.
bough [bau] n сук*.
bought [bɔ:t] pt, pp of **buy**.
boulder ['bəuldə'] n валу́н*.
boulevard ['bu:ləvɑ:d] n бульва́р.
bounce [bauns] vi (ball) отска́кивать (отскочи́ть perf); (cheque) верну́ться (perf) (о че́ке, ввиду́ отсу́тствия де́нег на счету́) ♦ vt (ball) ударя́ть (уда́рить* perf); (signal) отража́ть (отрази́ть* perf) ♦ n (of ball) отско́к; **he's got plenty of ~** (fig) он о́чень живо́й.

bouncer ['baunsə'] n (inf) вышибáла m.
bouncy castle ['baunsı-] n надувнóй
воздýшный зáмок.
bound [baund] pt, pp of **bind** ◆ n (leap) прыжóк*,
скачóк* ◆ vi (leap) прыгать (прыгнуть perf) ◆
vt (border) служить (impf) границей +gen ◆ adj:
he is ~ by law to ... егó обязывает закóн
+infin...; **~s** npl (limits) предéлы mpl; **he is/was
~ to do** он обязан/был обязан +infin; **he's ~
to come** он обязáтельно or непремéнно
придёт; **~ for** направляющийся* в/на +acc;
this area is out of ~s (fig: place) это мéсто
является запрéтным.
boundary ['baundrı] n граница.
boundless ['baundlıs] adj безграничный*
(безгранúчен).
bountiful ['bauntıful] adj (person) щéдрый*
(щедр); (supply) обúльный* (обúлен).
bounty ['bauntı] n (generosity) щéдрость f;
(reward) вознаграждéние.
bounty hunter n охóтник за наградóй.
bouquet ['bukeı] n букéт.
bourbon ['buəbən] n (US: also: ~ **whiskey**)
кукурýзное вúски nt ind, бурбóн.
bourgeois ['buəʒwɑː] adj буржуáзный* ◆ n
буржуá m ind.
bout [baut] n (of illness) прúступ; (of activity)
всплéск; (BOXING etc) схвáтка*.
boutique [buːˈtiːk] n бутúк.
bow[1] [bəu] n (knot) бант; (weapon) лук; (MUS)
смычóк.
bow[2] [bau] n (of the head, body) поклóн; (NAUT:
also: ~s) нос ◆ vi (with head, body) клáняться
(поклонúться* perf); (yield): **to ~ to** or **before**
поддавáться* (поддáться* perf) +dat or на
+acc; **to ~ to the inevitable** покоряться
(покорúться perf) неизбéжно.
bowels ['bauəlz] npl кишéчник msg; (of the
earth etc) нéдра pl.
bowl [bəul] n мúска*, чáша; (for washing) таз*;
(ball) шар*; (of pipe) голóвка*; (US: stadium)
арéна ◆ vi подавáть* (подáть* perf) мяч
► **bowl over** vt (fig) сбивáть (сбить* perf).
bow-legged ['bəuˈlɛgıd] adj кривонóгий*.
bowler ['bəulə'] n бóулер, подающий мяч;
(BRIT: also: ~ **hat**) котелóк*.
bowling ['bəulıŋ] n (game) кегельбáн.
bowling alley n кегельбáн.
bowling green n площáдка* для игры в
шары.
bowls [bəulz] n игрá* в шары.
bow tie [bəu-] n бáбочка*.
box [bɔks] n ящик, корóбка*; (also: **cardboard
~**) картóнная корóбка*; (THEAT) лóжа; (BRIT
AUT) разграничúтельная лúния; (ADMIN: or
form) графá* ◆ vt (put in a box) упакóвывать
(упаковáть perf) в корóбку; (SPORT) ударять
(удáрить perf) ◆ vi (SPORT) боксúровать

(impf); **what's on the ~?** (inf: TV) что сегóдня
по ящику?; **to ~ sb's ears** надирáть
(надрáть* perf) комý-н ýши
► **box in** vt окружáть (окружúть perf)
► **box off** vt отгорáживать (отгородúть* perf).
boxer ['bɔksə'] n боксёр.
box file n ящик для хранéния докумéнтов.
boxing ['bɔksıŋ] n бокс.
Boxing Day n (BRIT) день пóсле Рождествá.
boxing gloves npl боксёрские перчáтки*
fpl.
boxing ring n ринг.
box number n нóмер* абонéнтского ящика.
box office n театрáльная кáсса.
boxroom ['bɔksrum] n чулáн.
boy [bɔı] n мáльчик; (son) сынóк*.
boycott ['bɔıkɔt] n бойкóт ◆ vt бойкотúровать
(impf/perf).
boyfriend ['bɔıfrɛnd] n друг*.
boyish ['bɔıʃ] adj мальчúшеский*.
boy scout n бойскáут.
Bp abbr = **bishop**.
BR abbr = **British Rail**.
bra [brɑː] n лúфчик.
brace [breıs] n (on leg) шúна; (on teeth)
пластúнки pl; (tool) коловорóт; (also: ~
bracket) скóбка* ◆ vt (knees, shoulders)
напрягáть (напрячь* perf); **~s** npl (BRIT: for
trousers) подтяжки* pl; **to ~ o.s.** (for shock)
собирáться (собрáться* perf) с дýхом.
bracelet ['breıslıt] n браслéт.
bracing ['breısıŋ] adj бодрящий.
bracken ['brækən] n орляк.
bracket ['brækıt] n (TECH) кронштéйн; (group,
range) категóрия; (also: **brace** ~) скóбка*;
(also: **round** ~) крýглая скóбка*; (also: **square**
~) квадрáтная скóбка* ◆ vt (fig: also: ~
together) группировáть (сгруппировáть
perf); (word, phrase) заключáть (заключúть
perf) в скóбки; **income** ~ ýровень m дохóда;
in ~**s** в скóбках.
brackish ['brækıʃ] adj солоновáтый
(солоновáт).
brag [bræg] vi хвáстаться (похвáстаться perf).
braid [breıd] n (for clothes etc) тесьмá; (of hair)
косá*.
Braille [breıl] n шрифт Брáйля.
brain [breın] n (ANAT, fig) мозг*; ~**s** npl (CULIN)
мозгú mpl; (intelligence) мозгú mpl,
сообразúтельность f; **he's got** ~**s** он пáрень
с головóй.
brainchild ['breıntʃaıld] n дéтище.
braindead ['breındɛd] adj: **the patient was** ~ у
пациéнта наступила биологúческая смерть
brain drain n: **the** ~ ~ утéчка мозгóв.
brainless ['breınlıs] adj безмóзглый.
brainstorm ['breınstɔːm] n (fig) умопо-
мрачéние; (US: brainwave) озарéние

brainwash ['breɪnwɒʃ] *vt* промыва́ть
(промы́ть* *perf*) мозги́ +*dat*.
brainwave ['breɪnweɪv] *n* озаре́ние; **he had a ~**
на него́ нашло́ озаре́ние.
brainy ['breɪnɪ] *adj* мозгови́тый.
braise [breɪz] *vt* туши́ть* (потуши́ть* *perf*).
brake [breɪk] *n* (*also fig*) то́рмоз* ♦ *vi*
тормози́ть* (затормози́ть* *perf*).
brake fluid *n* тормозна́я жи́дкость *f*.
brake light *n* тормозно́й сигна́л.
brake pedal *n* педа́ль *f* то́рмоза, тормоза́*
mpl.
bramble ['bræmbl] *n* ежеви́ка.
bran [bræn] *n* о́труби *pl*.
branch [brɑːntʃ] *n* (*of tree*) ве́тка*, ветвь* *f*;
(*fig: of family, organization*) ве́твь*;
(*COMM: of bank, company etc*) филиа́л ♦ *vi*
разветвля́ться (разветви́ться* *perf*).
▶ **branch out** *vi* (*fig*) разветвля́ться
(разветви́ться* *perf*).
branch line *n* (железнодоро́жная) ве́тка*.
branch manager *n* дире́ктор* филиа́ла.
brand [brænd] *n* (*also: ~ name*) фи́рменная
ма́рка*; (*fig: type*) сорт* ♦ *vt* клейми́ть*
(заклейми́ть* *perf*); (*fig: pej*): **to ~ sb a**
communist *etc* клейми́ть* (заклейми́ть* *perf*)
кого́-н коммуни́стом *etc*.
brandish ['brændɪʃ] *vt* разма́хивать (*impf*)
+*instr*; (*weapon*) потряса́ть (*impf*) +*instr*.
brand name *n* фи́рменная ма́рка.
brand-new ['brænd'njuː] *adj* соверше́нно
но́вый*.
brandy ['brændɪ] *n* бре́нди *nt ind*, конья́к*.
brash [bræʃ] *adj* наха́льный* (наха́лен).
Brasilia [brə'zɪlɪə] *n* Брази́лия.
brass [brɑːs] *n* (*metal*) лату́нь *f*; **the ~** (*MUS*)
духовы́е инструме́нты *mpl*.
brass band *n* духово́й орке́стр.
brassiere ['bræsɪə'] *n* бюстга́льтер.
brass tacks *npl*: **to get down to ~ ~** доходи́ть*
(дойти́* *perf*) до су́ти.
brassy ['brɑːsɪ] *adj* (*colour*) ме́дный; (*sound*)
ре́зкий*; (*behaviour*) вызыва́ющий*.
brat [bræt] *n* (*pej*) отро́дье*.
Bratislava [bræti'slɑːvə] *n* Братисла́ва.
bravado [brə'vɑːdəu] *n* брава́да.
brave [breɪv] *adj* сме́лый (смел), хра́брый
(храбр) ♦ *n* инде́йский во́ин ♦ *vt* сме́ло *or*
хра́бро встреча́ть (встре́тить* *perf*).
bravely ['breɪvlɪ] *adv* сме́ло, хра́бро.
bravery ['breɪvərɪ] *n* сме́лость *f*, хра́брость *f*.
bravo [brɑː'vəu] *excl* бра́во.
brawl [brɔːl] *n* дра́ка ♦ *vi* дра́ться* (подра́ться*
perf).
brawn [brɔːn] *n* (*strength*) му́скулы *mpl*; (*meat*)
зельц, сту́день *m*.
brawny ['brɔːnɪ] *adj* мускули́стый
(мускули́ст).
bray [breɪ] *vi* (*donkey*) реве́ть* (*impf*) ♦ *n* рёв
осла́.
brazen ['breɪzn] *adj* (*woman*) бессты́жий

(бессты́ж); (*lie, accusation*) на́глый (нагл) ♦
vt: **to ~ it out** выкру́чиваться (вы́крутиться*
perf).
brazier ['breɪzɪə'] *n* жаро́вня*.
Brazil [brə'zɪl] *n* Брази́лия.
Brazilian [brə'zɪljən] *adj* брази́льский* ♦ *n*
брази́лец*(-лья́нка*).
Brazil nut *n* америка́нский* оре́х.
breach [briːtʃ] *vt* (*defence, wall*) пробива́ть
(проби́ть* *perf*) брешь в +*acc* ♦ *n* (*gap*) брешь
f; (*estrangement*) разры́в; **~ of contract**
наруше́ние догово́ра; **~ of the peace**
наруше́ние обще́ственного поря́дка; **~ of**
trust злоупотребле́ние дове́рием.
bread [brɛd] *n* хлеб; (*inf: money*) ба́бки *fpl*; **to**
earn one's daily ~ зараба́тывать
(зарабо́тать *perf*) на хлеб *or* на жизнь; **to**
know which side one's ~ is buttered (on)
знать (*impf*) свою́ вы́году.
bread and butter *n* хлеб с ма́слом; (*fig*) хлеб
насу́щный, жи́зненная осно́ва.
breadbin ['brɛdbɪn] *n* (*BRIT*) хле́бница.
breadboard ['brɛdbɔːd] *n* хле́бная доска́*;
(*COMPUT*) маке́т, маке́тная пла́та.
breadbox ['brɛdbɔks] *n* (*US*) хле́бница.
breadcrumbs ['brɛdkrʌmz] *npl* кро́шки* *fpl*;
(*CULIN*) паниро́вочные сухари́ *mpl*.
breadline ['brɛdlaɪn] *n*: **on the ~** за черто́й
бе́дности.
breadth [brɛtθ] *n* (*of cloth etc*) ширина́; (*fig: of*
knowledge, subject) широта́.
breadwinner ['brɛdwɪnə'] *n* корми́лец*(-лица).
break [breɪk] (*pt* **broke**, *pp* **broken**) *vt* (*cup, glass*)
разбива́ть (разби́ть* *perf*); (*leg, arm*) лома́ть
(слома́ть *perf*); (*promise, law*) наруша́ть
(нару́шить *perf*); (*record*) побива́ть (поби́ть*
perf) ♦ *vi* (*crockery*) разбива́ться (разби́ться
perf); (*storm*) разрази́ться (*perf*); (*weather*)
по́ртиться (испо́ртиться* *perf*); (*dawn*)
бре́зжить (забре́зжить *perf*); (*story, news*)
сообща́ть (сообщи́ть *perf*) ♦ *n* (*gap*) пробе́л;
(*fracture*) перело́м; (*rest*) переды́шка*;
(*interval*) переры́в; (*playtime*) переме́на;
(*chance*) шанс; (*holiday*) о́тпуск*, о́тдых; **to ~**
the news to sb сообща́ть (сообщи́ть *perf*)
кому́-н но́вость; **~ even** (*COMM*)
зако́нчить (*perf*) без убы́тка; **to ~ with sb**
порыва́ть (порва́ть* *perf*) с кем-н; **to ~ free** *or*
loose вырыва́ться* (*perf*) на свобо́ду; **to take a**
~ (*few minutes*) де́лать (сде́лать *perf*)
небольшо́й переры́в; (*holiday*) брать*
(взять* *perf*) о́тпуск; **without a ~** без
переры́ва; **a lucky ~** счастли́вый слу́чай.
▶ **break down** *vt* (*figures etc*) разбива́ть
(разби́ть* *perf*) по статья́м; (*door etc*)
взла́мывать (взлома́ть *perf*) ♦ *vi* (*machine,*
car) лома́ться (слома́ться *perf*); (*resistance*)
быть* (*impf*) сло́мленным(-ой); (*person*)
сломи́ться (*perf*); (*talks*) срыва́ться
(сорва́ться* *perf*).
▶ **break in** *vt* (*horse*) обу́здывать (обузда́ть

perf) ◆ *vi* (*burglar*) вламываться (вломиться *perf*); (*interrupt*) вмешиваться (вмешаться *perf*)

▶ **break into** *vt fus* (*house*) вламываться (вломиться* *perf*) в +*acc*

▶ **break off** *vi* (*branch*) отламываться (отломиться* *perf*); (*speaker*) прерываться (прерваться* *perf*) ◆ *vt* (*talks*) прерывать (прервать* *perf*); (*engagement*) расторгать (расторгнуть *perf*)

▶ **break open** *vt* взламывать (взломать *perf*)

▶ **break out** *vi* (*begin*) разражаться (разразиться* *perf*); (*escape*) сбегать (сбежать* *perf*); **to ~ out in spots/a rash** покрываться (покрыться* *perf*) прыщами/сыпью

▶ **break through** *vt fus* прорываться (прорваться* *perf*) сквозь +*acc* ◆ *vi*: **the sun broke through** солнце пробилось сквозь тучи

▶ **break up** *vi* (*ship*) разбиваться (разбиться* *perf*); (*crowd, meeting*) расходиться* (разойтись* *perf*); (*marriage, partnership*) распадаться (распасться *perf*); (*SCOL*) закрываться (закрыться* *perf*) на каникулы ◆ *vt* (*rocks etc*) разламывать (разломить* *perf*); (*journey*) прерывать (прервать* *perf*); (*fight etc*) прекращать (прекратить* *perf*); (*meeting*) распускать (распустить* *perf*); (*marriage*) разбивать (разбить* *perf*).

breakable ['breɪkəbl] *adj* хрупкий* (хрупок), ломкий* (ломок) ◆ *n*: **~s** хрупкие предметы *mpl*.

breakage ['breɪkɪdʒ] *n* (*act of breaking*) поломка*; (*object*) бой; **to pay for ~s** платить* (заплатить* *perf*) за бой.

breakaway ['breɪkəweɪ] *adj* (*group etc*) отделившийся, отколовшийся.

break-dancing ['breɪkdɑːnsɪŋ] *n* брейк.

breakdown ['breɪkdaun] *n* (*AUT*) небольшая авария; (*in communications*) нарушение; (*of marriage*) распад; (*of statistics*) разбивка*; (*also*: **nervous ~**) нервный срыв.

breakdown service *n* (*BRIT*) аварийная служба.

breakdown van *n* (*BRIT*) фургон аварийной службы.

breaker ['breɪkə'] *n* вал*.

breakeven ['breɪk'iːvn] *cpd*: **~ chart** график рентабельности; **~ point** точка* безубыточности.

breakfast ['brɛkfəst] *n* завтрак ◆ *vi* завтракать (позавтракать *perf*).

breakfast cereal *n* крупа для завтрака.

break-in ['breɪkɪn] *n* взлом.

breaking and entering ['breɪkɪŋən'ɛntrɪŋ] *n* (*LAW*) вторжение со взломом.

breaking point *n* предел.

breakthrough ['breɪkθruː] *n* (*fig: in technology*) переломное открытие.

break-up ['breɪkʌp] *n* (*of partnership, marriage*) распад.

break-up value *n* (*COMM*) ликвидационная стоимость *f*.

breakwater ['breɪkwɔːtə'] *n* волнорез, мол*.

breast [brɛst] *n* грудь* *f*; (*of meat*) грудинка; (*of poultry*) белое мясо.

breast-feed ['brɛstfiːd] (*irreg: like* feed) *vt* кормить* (покормить* *perf*) грудью ◆ *vi* кормить (*impf*) (грудью).

breast pocket *n* (*of jacket etc*) нагрудный карман.

breast-stroke ['brɛststrəuk] *n* брасс.

breath [brɛθ] *n* вдох; (*breathing*) дыхание; **to go out for a ~ of air** выходить* (выйти* *perf*) подышать *or* на свежий воздух; **to be out of ~** запыхиваться (запыхаться *perf*); **to get one's ~ back** отдышаться (*perf*).

breathalyse ['brɛθəlaɪz] *vt* проверять (проверить *perf*) дыхание на алкоголь.

Breathalyser® ['brɛθəlaɪzə'] *n* спиртометр.

breathe [briːð] *vt* вдыхать (вдохнуть *perf*) ◆ *vi* дышать* (*impf*); **I won't ~ a word about it** я словом не обмолвлюсь об этом

▶ **breathe in** *vt* вдыхать (вдохнуть *perf*) ◆ *vi* делать (сделать *perf*) вдох

▶ **breathe out** *vt* выдыхать (выдохнуть *perf*) ◆ *vi* делать (сделать *perf*) выдох.

breather ['briːðə'] *n* передышка*.

breathing ['briːðɪŋ] *n* дыхание.

breathing space *n* (*fig*) передышка*.

breathless ['brɛθlɪs] *adj* (*from exertion*) запыхавшийся; (*after illness*) с затруднённым дыханием; **he was ~ with excitement** у него перехватило дыхание от волнения.

breathtaking ['brɛθteɪkɪŋ] *adj* захватывающий* дух.

breath test *n* дыхательная проба.

bred [brɛd] *pt, pp of* **breed**.

-bred [brɛd] *suffix*: **well/ill-~** хорошо/плохо воспитанный* (воспитан).

breed [briːd] (*pt, pp* bred) *vt* (*animals, plants*) разводить* (развести* *perf*); (*fig: give rise to*) порождать (породить* *perf*) ◆ *vi* размножаться (*impf*) ◆ *n* (*ZOOL*) порода; (*type, class*) сорт*, род*.

breeder ['briːdə'] *n* (*person*) селекционер; (*PHYS: also:* **~ reactor**) реактор-размножитель *m*; **cattle ~** скотовод.

breeding ['briːdɪŋ] *n* воспитание.

breeding ground *n* место* размножения; (*fig*) рассадник.

breeze [briːz] *n* бриз.

breeze block ['briːzblɔk] *n* (*BRIT*) шлакобетонный кирпич.

breezy ['briːzɪ] *adj* (*manner, tone*) оживлённый

(оживлён); (*weather*) прохла́дный*
(прохла́ден).
Bremen ['breɪmən] *n* Бре́мен.
Breton ['brɛtən] *adj* брето́нский ♦ *n*
брето́нец*(-нка*).
brevity ['brevɪtɪ] *n* кра́ткость *f*.
brew [bruː] *vt* (*tea*) зава́ривать (завари́ть*
perf); (*beer*) вари́ть* (свари́ть* *perf*) ♦ *vi* (*tea*)
зава́риваться (завари́ться *perf*); (*beer*)
броди́ть* (вы́бродить* *perf*); (*storm*)
надвига́ться (надви́нуться *perf*); (*fig: trouble*)
назрева́ть (назре́ть *perf*).
brewer ['bruːə'] *n* пивова́р.
brewery ['bruːərɪ] *n* пивова́ренный заво́д.
briar ['braɪə'] *n* (*thorny bush*) колю́чий*
куста́рник; (*wild rose*) шипо́вник.
bribe [braɪb] *n* взя́тка*, по́дкуп ♦ *vt* (*person*)
подкупа́ть (подкупи́ть* *perf*), дава́ть* (дать*
perf) взя́тку; **to ~ sb to do** подкупа́ть
(подкупи́ть* *perf*) кого́-н +*infin*.
bribery ['braɪbərɪ] *n* по́дкуп.
bric-a-brac ['brɪkəbræk] *n* безделу́шки* *fpl*.
brick [brɪk] *n* кирпи́ч*; (*of ice cream*) брике́т.
bricklayer ['brɪkleɪə'] *n* ка́менщик.
brickwork ['brɪkwəːk] *n* (*кирпи́чная*) кла́дка.
bridal ['braɪdl] *adj* подвене́чный, сва́дебный.
bride [braɪd] *n* неве́ста.
bridegroom ['braɪdɡruːm] *n* жени́х*.
bridesmaid ['braɪdzmeɪd] *n* подру́жка*
неве́сты.
bridge [brɪdʒ] *n* (*TECH, ARCHIT, DENTISTRY*) мост*;
(*NAUT*) капита́нский мо́стик; (*CARDS*)
бридж; (*of nose*) перено́сица ♦ *vt* (*fig: gap,
gulf*) преодолева́ть (преодоле́ть *perf*); **to ~ a
river** стро́ить (постро́ить *perf*) мост че́рез
ре́ку.
bridging loan ['brɪdʒɪŋ-] *n* (*BRIT: COMM*)
промежу́точный заём.
bridle ['braɪdl] *n* узде́чка*, узда́ ♦ *vt* (*horse*)
взну́здывать (взнузда́ть *perf*) ♦ *vi*: **to ~ at**
взвива́ться (взви́ться* *perf*) на дыбы́,
возмуща́ться (возмути́ться* *perf*).
bridle path *n* верхова́я тропа́*.
brief [briːf] *adj* (*period of time*) коро́ткий*
(ко́роток); (*description*) кра́ткий* (кра́ток) ♦
n (*LAW*) изложе́ние де́ла; (*task*) зада́ние ♦ *vt*
(*inform*) знако́мить* (ознако́мить* *perf*) с
+*instr*; (*MIL etc*): **to ~ sb** (*about*)
инструкти́ровать (проинструкти́ровать
perf) кого́-н (о +*prp*); **~s** *npl* (*for men*) трусы́ *pl*;
(*for women*) тру́сики *pl*; **in ~** ... вкра́тце ....
briefcase ['briːfkeɪs] *n* портфе́ль *m*.
briefing ['briːfɪŋ] *n* инструкта́ж; (*PRESS*)
бри́финг.
briefly ['briːflɪ] *adv* (*glance, smile*) бе́гло; (*visit*)
на коро́ткое вре́мя; (*explain*) вкра́тце; **to
glimpse ~** броса́ть (бро́сить* *perf*) бе́глый
взгляд.
Brig. *abbr* = **brigadier**.
brigade [brɪ'ɡeɪd] *n* (*MIL*) брига́да.
brigadier [brɪɡə'dɪə'] *n* бригади́р.

bright [braɪt] *adj* (*light, colour*) я́ркий* (я́рок);
(*room, future*) све́тлый* (све́тел); (*clever:
person, idea*) блестя́щий*; (*lively: person*)
живо́й*, весёлый*; **to look on the ~ side**
ви́деть* (*impf*) све́тлую сто́рону.
brighten ['braɪtn] *vt* (*also: ~ up: room, event*)
оживля́ть (оживи́ть* *perf*); (: *person*)
ра́довать (обра́довать *perf*) ♦ *vi* (*weather*)
проясня́ться (проясни́ться *perf*); (*person*)
оживля́ться (оживи́ться* *perf*); (*face*)
светле́ть (просветле́ть *perf*); (*prospects*)
улучша́ться (улу́чшиться *perf*).
brightly ['braɪtlɪ] *adv* (*shine*) я́рко; (*smile, talk*)
ра́достно.
brill [brɪl] (*inf*) *adj* здо́рово.
brilliance ['brɪljəns] *n* блеск, я́ркость *f*; (*fig: of
person*) генина́льность *f*.
brilliant ['brɪljənt] *adj* блестя́щий* (блестя́щ);
(*sunshine, light*) я́ркий* (я́рок); (*inf: holiday
etc*) великоле́пный* (великоле́пен).
brilliantly ['brɪljəntlɪ] *adv* (*see adj*) блестя́ще;
я́рко.
brim [brɪm] *n* (*of cup*) край; (*of hat*) поля́ *ntpl*.
brimful ['brɪm'ful] *adj*: **~ (of)** по́лный (по́лон)
до краёв (+*gen*); (*fig*) перепо́лненный
(перепо́лнен) (+*instr*).
brine [braɪn] *n* (*CULIN*) рассо́л.
bring [brɪŋ] (*pt, pp* **brought**) *vt* (*thing*)
приноси́ть* (принести́* *perf*); (*person: on foot*)
приводи́ть* (привести́* *perf*); (: *by transport*)
привози́ть* (привезти́* *perf*); (*fig: satisfaction,
trouble*) доставля́ть (доста́вить* *perf*); **to ~
sth to an end** поко́нчить (*perf*) с чем-н; **I can't
~ myself to tell him** я не могу́ заста́вить себя́
сообщи́ть ему́
▶ **bring about** *vt* (*cause: unintentionally*)
вызыва́ть (вы́звать* *perf*), порожда́ть
(породи́ть *perf*); (: *intentionally*)
осуществля́ть (осуществи́ть* *perf*)
▶ **bring back** *vt* (*restore*) возрожда́ть
(возроди́ть* *perf*); (*return*) возвраща́ть
(возврати́ть* *perf*), верну́ть (*perf*)
▶ **bring down** *vt* (*government*) сверга́ть
(све́ргнуть* *perf*); (*plane*) сбива́ть (сбить*
perf); (*price*) снижа́ть (сни́зить* *perf*)
▶ **bring forward** *vt* (*meeting*) переноси́ть*
(перенести́* *perf*) на бо́лее ра́нний срок;
(*proposal*) выдвига́ть (вы́двинуть* *perf*);
(*BOOKKEEPING*) переноси́ть* (перенести́* *perf*)
на сле́дующую страни́цу
▶ **bring in** *vt* (*money*) приноси́ть* (принести́*
perf); (*person, legislation*) вводи́ть* (ввести́*
perf); (*verdict*) выноси́ть* (вы́нести* *perf*)
▶ **bring off** *vt* (*task, plan*) исполня́ть
(испо́лнить *perf*); (*deal*) заключа́ть
(заключи́ть *perf*)
▶ **bring out** *vt* вынима́ть (вы́нуть *perf*);
(*meaning*) выявля́ть (вы́явить *perf*);
(*publish*) выпуска́ть (вы́пустить *perf*)
▶ **bring round** *vt* (*MED*) приводи́ть* (привести́*
perf) в чу́вство

▸ **bring up** vt (carry up) приноси́ть* (принести́* perf) наве́рх; (educate) воспи́тывать (воспита́ть perf); (question) поднима́ть (подня́ть* perf); (vomit): **he brought up his food** его́ стошни́ло.

bring and buy sale n благотвори́тельная перепрода́жа веще́й ме́жду её организа́торами.

brink [brɪŋk] n (of disaster, war etc) грань f; **on the ~ of doing** чуть не +infin; **she was on the ~ of tears** она́ е́ле сде́рживала слёзы.

brisk [brɪsk] adj (tone) отры́вистый (отры́вист); (person, trade) оживлённый* (оживлён); **business is ~** дела́ иду́т по́лным хо́дом.

bristle ['brɪsl] n щети́на ♦ vi (in anger) щети́ниться (ощети́ниться perf); **bristling with** по́лный (по́лон) +instr or +gen.

bristly ['brɪslɪ] adj щети́нистый; **your chin's all ~** у тебя́ подборо́док щети́нистый.

Brit [brɪt] n abbr (inf: = British person) брита́нец*(-нка*).

Britain ['brɪtən] n (also: **Great ~**) Брита́ния; **in ~** в Брита́нии.

British ['brɪtɪʃ] adj брита́нский*; **the ~** npl брита́нцы* mpl.

British Isles npl: **the ~~** Брита́нские острова́* mpl.

British Rail n Брита́нская желе́зная доро́га.

British Summer Time n Брита́нское ле́тнее вре́мя* nt.

Briton ['brɪtən] n брита́нец*(-нка*).

Brittany ['brɪtənɪ] n Брета́нь f.

brittle ['brɪtl] adj хру́пкий* (хру́пок), ло́мкий* (ло́мок).

Bro. abbr (REL) = **brother**.

broach [brəutʃ] vt (subject) поднима́ть (подня́ть perf) вопро́с о +prp.

broad [brɔːd] adj (wide) широ́кий* (широ́к); (general) о́бщий*; (strong) си́льный* ♦ n (US: inf) ба́ба; **in ~ daylight** средь бе́ла дня; **~ hint** прозра́чный намёк.

broad bean n фасо́ль f no pl.

broadcast ['brɔːdkɑːst] (pt, pp **broadcast**) n (RADIO) (радио)переда́ча; (TV) (теле)-переда́ча ♦ vt (RADIO) передава́ть* (переда́ть* perf) по ра́дио, транслировать (impf); (TV) передава́ть* (переда́ть* perf) по телеви́дению, транслировать (impf) ♦ vi трансли́роваться (impf).

broadcaster ['brɔːdkɑːstə'] n (RADIO) ра́дио-журнали́ст; (TV) теле-журнали́ст.

broadcasting ['brɔːdkɑːstɪŋ] n (RADIO) радиовеща́ние; (TV) телевеща́ние.

broadcasting station n (RADIO) радиоста́нция; (TV) телеста́нция.

broaden ['brɔːdn] vt расширя́ть (расши́рить perf) ♦ vi расширя́ться (расши́риться perf); **to**

~ one's horizons расширя́ть (расши́рить perf) свой кругозо́р.

broadly ['brɔːdlɪ] adv вообще́.

broad-minded ['brɔːd'maɪndɪd] adj с широ́кими взгля́дами.

broadsheet ['brɔːdʃiːt] n (advertisement) рекла́мный плака́т or рекла́мная афи́ша; (newspaper) газе́та, отпеча́танная на одно́м развёрнутом листе́ бума́ги.

broccoli ['brɒkəlɪ] n бро́кколи nt ind.

brochure ['brəuʃjuə'] n брошю́ра.

brogue [brəug] n (accent) провинциа́льный акце́нт (осо́бенно ирла́ндский или шотла́ндский); (shoe) башма́к.

broil [brɔɪl] vt жа́рить (зажа́рить perf).

broiler ['brɔɪlə'] n бро́йлер.

broke [brəuk] pt of **break** ♦ adj (inf) прогоре́вший; **to go ~** прогора́ть (прогоре́ть perf).

broken ['brəukn] pp of **break** ♦ adj (window, cup etc) разби́тый (разби́т); (machine) сло́манный (сло́ман); (promise, vow) нару́шенный (нару́шен); **a ~ leg** сло́манная нога́*; **a ~ marriage** распа́вшийся брак; **a ~ home** неблагополу́чная семья́*; **in ~ English/Russian** на ло́маном англи́йском/ру́сском.

broken-down ['brəukn'daun] adj (car) сло́манный (сло́ман); (house) полу-разру́шенный.

broken-hearted ['brəukn'hɑːtɪd] adj уби́тый го́рем, с разби́тым се́рдцем.

broker ['brəukə'] n (COMM: in shares) бро́кер; (: in insurance) страхово́й аге́нт.

brokerage ['brəukrɪdʒ] n (COMM: commission) брокера́ж; (: business) бро́керское аге́нтство.

brolly ['brɒlɪ] n (BRIT: inf) зонт.

bronchitis [brɒŋ'kaɪtɪs] n бронхи́т.

bronze [brɒnz] n (metal) бро́нза; (sculpture) бро́нзовая скульпту́ра.

bronzed [brɒnzd] adj (person, body) загоре́лый, бро́нзовый f.

brooch [brəutʃ] n брошь f.

brood [bruːd] n вы́водок* ♦ vi (hen) сиде́ть* (impf) на я́йцах; (person) размышля́ть (impf)

▸ **brood on** or **over** vt fus грусти́ть* (impf) or размышля́ть (impf) о +prp.

broody ['bruːdɪ] adj (thoughtful, moody) угрю́мый (угрю́м); **~ hen** насе́дка*.

brook [bruk] n руче́й*.

broom [brum] n метла́*; (BOT) раки́тник.

broomstick ['brumstɪk] n (broom handle) ру́чка метлы́.

Bros. abbr (COMM: = **brothers**) бра́тья* mpl.

broth [brɒθ] n похлёбка*.

brothel ['brɒθl] n публи́чный дом*, борде́ль m.

brother ['brʌðə'] n (also REL) брат*; (in association) собра́т*.

brotherhood ['brʌðəhud] *n* бра́тство.
brother-in-law ['brʌðərın'lɔ:] *n* (*sister's husband*) зять* *m*; (*wife's brother*) шу́рин*; (*husband's brother*) де́верь* *m*.
brotherly ['brʌðəlı] *adj* бра́тский*.
brought [brɔ:t] *pt, pp of* **bring**.
brought forward *adj* перенесённый на сле́дующую страни́цу.
brow [brau] *n* (*forehead*) лоб*, чело́*; (*also:* **eyebrow**) бровь *f*; (*of hill*) гре́бень *m*.
browbeat ['braubi:t] *vt*: **to ~ sb (into doing)** запу́гивать (запуга́ть *perf*) кого́-н (для того́, что́бы +*infin*).
brown [braun] *adj* кори́чневый; (*hair*) кашта́новый; (*eyes*) ка́рий*; (*tanned*) загоре́лый ♦ *n* (*colour*) кори́чневый цвет ♦ *vt* (*CULIN*) подрумя́нивать (подрумя́нить *perf*); **to go ~** (*person*) загора́ть (загоре́ть *perf*); (*leaves*) желте́ть (пожелте́ть *perf*).
brown bread *n* чёрный хлеб.
Brownie ['braunı] *n* (*also:* ~ **Guide**) *мла́дшая де́вочка-ска́ут*.
brownie ['braunı] *n* (*US: cake*) *шокола́дное пиро́жное с оре́хами*.
brown paper *n* обёрточная бума́га.
brown rice *n* неочи́щенный рис.
brown sugar *n* неочи́щенный са́хар.
browse [brauz] *vi* (*in shop*) рассма́тривать (*impf*), разгля́дывать (*impf*); (*animal*) пита́ться (*impf*) подно́жным ко́рмом ♦ *n*: **to have a ~ (around)** рассма́тривать (*impf*) *or* разгля́дывать (*impf*); **to ~ through a book** проли́стывать (пролиста́ть *perf*) кни́гу.
browser ['brauzə*] *n* (*COMPUT*) бра́узер.
bruise [bru:z] *n* (*on face etc*) синя́к*; (*on fruit*) вмя́тина ♦ *vt* ушиба́ть (ушиби́ть* *perf*); (*fruit*) помя́ть* (*perf*) ♦ *vi* (*fruit*) помя́ться* (*perf*).
bruising ['bru:zıŋ] *n* синяки́* *mpl*.
Brummie ['brʌmı] *n* (*inf*) бирмингеме́ц(-емка).
brunch [brʌntʃ] *n* по́здний за́втрак.
brunette [bru:'nɛt] *n* брюне́тка*.
brunt [brʌnt] *n*: **to bear the ~ of** принима́ть (приня́ть* *perf*) на себя́ основно́й уда́р +*gen*.
brush [brʌʃ] *n* (*for cleaning*) щётка*; (*for painting*) кисть* *f*; (*for shaving*) помазо́к*; (*quarrel*) столкнове́ние ♦ *vt* (*sweep*) подмета́ть (подмести́* *perf*); (*groom*) чи́стить* (почи́стить* *perf*) щёткой; (*also:* ~ **against**) слегка́ задева́ть (заде́ть* *perf*); **to have a ~ with sb** (*verbally*) вздо́рить (повздо́рить *perf*) с ке́м-н; (*physically*) дра́ться* (подра́ться* *perf*) с ке́м-н; **to have a ~ with the police** име́ть (*impf*) столкнове́ние с поли́цией
► **brush aside** *vt* (*criticism, emotion*) отмета́ть (отмести́ *perf*)
► **brush past** *vt* проноси́ться* (пронести́сь* *perf*) ми́мо +*gen*
► **brush up** *vt* (*subject, language*) шлифова́ть (отшлифова́ть *perf*); (*knowledge*) освежа́ть (освежи́ть *perf*).

brushed [brʌʃt] *adj* (*steel, chrome etc*) ма́товый; (*nylon, denim etc*) ворси́стый.
brush-off ['brʌʃɔf] *n* (*inf*): **to give sb the ~** отбрива́ть (отбри́ть* *perf*) кого́-н.
brushwood ['brʌʃwud] *n* хво́рост.
brusque [bru:sk] *adj* бесцеремо́нный*.
Brussels ['brʌslz] *n* Брюссе́ль *m*.
Brussels sprout *n* брюссе́льская капу́ста.
brutal ['bru:tl] *adj* (*person*) жесто́кий*; (*actions*) зве́рский*; (*honesty, frankness*) жёсткий*.
brutality [bru:'tælıtı] *n* (*see adj*) жесто́кость *f*; зве́рство.
brutalize ['bru:təlaız] *vt* ожесточа́ть (ожесточи́ть *perf*).
brute [bru:t] *n* зверь* *m* ♦ *adj*: **by ~ force** грубо́й си́лой.
brutish ['bru:tıʃ] *adj* зве́рский*, ско́тский*.
BS *n abbr* (*US:* = *Bachelor of Science*) ≈ бакала́вр есте́ственных нау́к.
bs *abbr* = **bill of sale**.
BSA *n abbr* (= *Boy Scouts of America*) Сою́з америка́нских бойска́утов.
BSE *n abbr* (= *bovine spongiform encephalopathy*) энцефалопа́тия кру́пного рога́того скота́.
BSc *abbr* (= *Bachelor of Science*) ≈ бакала́вр есте́ственных нау́к.
BSI *n abbr* (= *British Standards Institution*) Брита́нский* институ́т станда́ртов.
BST *abbr* = *British Summer Time*.
Bt. *abbr* (*BRIT*) = **Bart**.
btu *n abbr* (= *British thermal unit*) брита́нская теплова́я едини́ца.
bubble ['bʌbl] *n* пузы́рь* *m* ♦ *vi* (*liquid*) пе́ниться (вспе́ниться *perf*); (*fig*): **to ~ with laughter** залива́ться (*impf*) сме́хом.
bubble bath *n* пе́нистая ва́нна.
bubble gum *n* жева́тельная рези́нка (*образу́ющая пузыри́*).
bubblejet printer ['bʌbldʒɛt-] *n* *тип компью́терного при́нтера*.
bubble pack *n* бли́стерная упако́вка*.
bubbly ['bʌblı] *adj* (*inf: girl*) живо́й; (*mineral water*) шипу́чий*, газиро́ванный ♦ *n* (*inf*) шипу́чка*.
Bucharest [bu:kə'rɛst] *n* Бухаре́ст.
buck [bʌk] *n* (*rabbit*) кро́лик; (*deer*) саме́ц оле́ня; (*US: inf*) бакс ♦ *vi* (*horse*) брыка́ться (*impf*); **to pass the ~ (to sb)** перекла́дывать (переложи́ть *perf*) отве́тственность (на кого́-н)
► **buck up** *vi* (*cheer up*) встряхну́ться (*perf*); (*hurry up*) пошеве́ливаться (*impf*) ♦ *vt*: **to ~ one's ideas up** исправля́ться (испра́виться* *perf*).
bucket ['bʌkıt] *n* ведро́* ♦ *vi* (*BRIT: inf*): **the rain is ~ing (down)** дождь льёт как из ведра́.
buckle ['bʌkl] *n* пря́жка* ♦ *vt* (*shoe, belt*) застёгивать (застегну́ть *perf*); (*wheel*) деформи́ровать (*impf/perf*) ♦ *vi* (*wheel*) деформи́роваться (*impf/perf*); (*bridge,*

support) прогибáться (прогнýться *perf*);
(*knees, legs*) подгибáться (подогнýться *perf*)
▶ **buckle down** *vi*: to ~ down (to sth) засéсть*
(*perf*) (за что-н).

Bucks [bʌks] *abbr* (*BRIT: POST*) = Buckingham-
shire.

bud [bʌd] *n* (*of tree*) пóчка*; (*of flower*) бутóн ◆
vi (*flower*) распускáться (распустúться* *perf*);
the trees are ~ding на дерéвьях
распускáются пóчки; **to nip in the ~**
пресекáть (пресéчь* *perf*) в кóрне.

Budapest [bjuːdəˈpɛst] *n* Будапéшт.

Buddha [ˈbudə] *n* Бýдда *m*.

Buddhism [ˈbudɪzəm] *n* буддúзм.

Buddhist [ˈbudɪst] *adj* буддúйский ◆ *n*
буддúст.

budding [ˈbʌdɪŋ] *adj* подаю́щий надéжды.

buddy [ˈbʌdɪ] *n* (*US*) прия́тель *m*.

budge [bʌdʒ] *vt* (*object*) сдвигáть (сдвúнуть
perf) (с мéста); (*fig: person*) заставля́ть
(застáвить* *perf*) уступúть* ◆ *vi* сдвúнуться
(*perf*) (с мéста).

budgerigar [ˈbʌdʒərɪgɑː] *n* волнúстый
попугáйчик.

budget [ˈbʌdʒɪt] *n* бюджéт ◆ *vi*: to ~ for sth
ассигновáть (*impf/perf*) *or* откла́дывать
(отложúть *perf*) дéньги на что-н; **I'm on a
tight ~** у меня́ тýго с фина́нсами; **she works
out her ~ every month** она́ рассчúтывает
свой бюджéт кáждый мéсяц.

budgie [ˈbʌdʒɪ] *n* = **budgerigar**.

Buenos Aires [ˈbwɛməsˈaɪrɪz] *n* Буэ́нос-Áйрес.

buff [bʌf] *adj* корúчневый ◆ *n* (*inf: enthusiast*)
знатóк*.

buffalo [ˈbʌfələu] (*pl ~ or ~es*) *n* (*BRIT*) бýйвол;
(*US: bison*) бизóн.

buffer [ˈbʌfə] *n* бýфер*.

buffering [ˈbʌfərɪŋ] *n* (*COMPUT*) буферизáция,
испóльзование бýфера.

buffer state *n* бýферное госудáрство.

buffer zone *n* бýферная зóна.

buffet[1] [ˈbufeɪ] *n* (*BRIT: in station*) буфéт; (*food*)
швéдский* стол*.

buffet[2] [ˈbʌfɪt] *vt* (*subj: wind, sea*) трепáть
(*perf*), швыря́ть (*impf*).

buffet car *n* (*BRIT: RAIL*) вагóн-рестора́н.

buffet lunch *n* швéдский* стол*.

buffoon [bəˈfuːn] *n* фигля́р.

bug [bʌg] *n* (*esp US: insect*) насекóмое *nt adj*;
(*COMPUT: of program*) ошúбка*; (*fig: germ*)
вúрус, зарáза; (*hidden microphone*)
микрофóн, подслýшивающее устрóйство ◆
vt (*inf: annoy*) раздражáть (раздражúть *perf*);
(: *bother*) надоедáть (надоéсть* *perf*) +*dat*;
(*room etc*) прослýшивать (*impf*); **I've got the
travel ~** (*fig*) я помéшан на путешéствиях.

bugbear [ˈbʌgbɛə] *n* проблéма.

bugger [ˈbʌgə] (*inf!*) *n* свóлочь *m/f* (*!*) ◆ *vb*: ~

off! катúсь отсю́да! (*!*); ~ **(it)!** твою́ мать! (*!*)

buggy [ˈbʌgɪ] *n* (*also: baby ~*) складна́я
дéтская коля́ска*.

bugle [ˈbjuːgl] *n* горн.

build [bɪld] (*pt, pp* **built**) *n* (*of person*)
телосложéние ◆ *vt* стрóить (пострóить *perf*)
▶ **build on** *vt fus* (*fig*) пóльзоваться
(воспóльзоваться *perf*) +*instr*
▶ **build up** *vt* (*forces, production*) нара́щивать
(*impf*); (*morale*) укрепля́ть (укрепúть* *perf*);
(*stocks*) нака́пливать (накопúть* *perf*);
(*business*) создава́ть* (созда́ть* *perf*); **don't ~
your hopes up too soon** не ра́дуйтесь ра́ньше
врéмени.

builder [ˈbɪldə] *n* стрóитель *m*.

building [ˈbɪldɪŋ] *n* (*industry, construction*)
стрóительство; (*structure*) строéние; (:
residential, offices) зда́ние.

building contractor *n* стройтельный
подря́дчик.

building industry *n* стройтельная
промы́шленность *f*.

building site *n* стройтельный уча́сток*.

building society *n* (*BRIT*) ≈
стройтельно-сберега́тельная ка́сса.

building trade *n* = **building industry**.

build-up [ˈbɪldʌp] *n* (*of gas etc*) скопле́ние;
(*publicity*) to **give sb/sth a good ~**
обеспéчивать (обеспéчить *perf*) комý-н/
чемý-н хорóшую реклáму.

built [bɪlt] *pt, pp of* **build** ◆ *adj*: **~-in** встрóенный;
well-~ person хорошó сложённый* человéк.

built-in obsolescence [ˈbɪltɪn-] *n*
заплани́рованное устарева́ние.

built-up area [ˈbɪltʌp-] *n* застрóенный райóн.

bulb [bʌlb] *n* (*BOT*) лýковица; (*ELEC*) ла́мпа,
ла́мпочка*.

bulbous [ˈbʌlbəs] *adj* пуза́тый (пуза́т); (*nose*)
тóлстый (толст).

Bulgaria [bʌlˈgɛərɪə] *n* Болга́рия.

Bulgarian [bʌlˈgɛərɪən] *adj* болга́рский* ◆ *n*
болга́рин*(-рка*); (*LING*) болга́рский*
язы́к*.

bulge [bʌldʒ] *n* (*bump*) вы́пуклость *f*; (*in birth
rate*) врéменное увеличéние ◆ *vi* (*stomach*)
выпя́чиваться (вы́пятиться* *perf*); (*pocket,
file*) треща́ть (*impf*) по швам; **her purse is
bulging with money** её кошелёк наби́т
деньга́ми.

bulimia [bəˈlɪmɪə] *n* булими́я.

bulimic [bəˈliːmɪk] *adj*: **she is ~** она́ страда́ет
булими́ей.

bulk [bʌlk] *n* грома́да; **in ~** óптом; **the ~ of**
бóльшая ча́сть +*gen*.

bulk buying [-ˈbaɪɪŋ] *n* оптóвая заку́пка*.

bulk carrier *n* грузовóе сýдно, сухогрýз.

bulkhead [ˈbʌlkhɛd] *n* перегорóдка.

bulky [ˈbʌlkɪ] *adj* громóздкий* (громóздок).

---

* marks translations which have irregular inflections. The Russian-English side of the dictionary gives inflectional information.

bull [bul] n (ZOOL) бык*; (male: whale) самéц* китá; (: elephant) слон; (STOCK EXCHANGE) спекулянт, играющий* на повышéние на бирже; (REL) бýлла.

bulldog ['buldɔg] n бульдóг.

bulldoze ['buldəuz] vt (flatten) расчищáть (расчистить* perf) бульдóзером; (knock down) ломáть (сломáть perf) бульдóзером; **I was ~d into it** (fig: inf) меня застáвили сдéлать это.

bulldozer ['buldəuzə'] n бульдóзер.

bullet ['bulɪt] n пýля.

bulletin ['bulɪtɪn] n: **news ~** свóдка* новостéй; (journal) бюллетéнь m.

bulletin board n (COMPUT) электрóнная доскá объявлéний.

bulletproof ['bulɪtpru:f] adj пуленепробивáемый.

bullfight ['bulfaɪt] n бой* быкóв.

bullfighter ['bulfaɪtə'] n тореадóр.

bullfighting ['bulfaɪtɪŋ] n бой быкóв.

bullion ['buljən] n слитóк*.

bullock ['bulək] n вол*.

bullring ['bulrɪŋ] n арéна (на котóрой происхóдит бой быкóв).

bull's-eye ['bulzaɪ] n (on a target) яблоко* мишéни.

bullshit ['bulʃɪt] (inf!) n бред (собáчий) (!) ♦ vt нести* (impf) бред (!)

bully ['bulɪ] n задира m/f ♦ vt травить* (затравить* perf); (frighten) запýгивать (запугáть perf).

bullying ['bulɪɪŋ] n трáвля, запýгивание.

bum [bʌm] n (inf: backside) зáдница; (esp US: tramp) бродяга m/f; (: good-for-nothing) бездéльник

► **bum around** vi (inf) шатáться (impf)

bumblebee ['bʌmblbi:] n шмель* m.

bumf [bʌmf] n (inf) бумáжки* fpl.

bump [bʌmp] n (minor accident) столкновéние; (jolt) толчóк: (swelling) шишка; (on road) ухáб ♦ vt (strike) ударять (удáрить perf); (dent) помять* (perf); **he ~ed his head on the door** он удáрился о стýкнулся головóй о дверь

► **bump along** vi трястись* (impf) по +dat

► **bump into** vt fus натáлкиваться (натолкнуться perf) на +acc.

bumper ['bʌmpə'] n (AUT) бáмпер ♦ adj: **~ crop** or **harvest** небывáлый урожáй.

bumper cars npl (US) аттракциóнный электромобиль m.

bumper sticker n наклéйка на бáмпер.

bumph [bʌmf] n = **bumf**.

bumptious ['bʌmpʃəs] adj самоувéренный (самоувéрен).

bumpy ['bʌmpɪ] adj ухáбистый; **it was a ~ flight** нас всю дорóгу трясло.

bun [bʌn] n (CULIN) сдóбная бýлка*; (of hair) ýзел*.

bunch [bʌntʃ] n (of flowers) букéт*; (of keys) свя́зка*; (of bananas) гроздь f; (of people) компáния; **~es** npl (in hair) хвóстики mpl; **~ of grapes** гроздь or кисть* f виногрáда.

bundle ['bʌndl] n (of clothes) ýзел*; (of sticks) вязáнка*; (of papers) пáчка* ♦ vt (also: **~ up**) связывать (связáть perf) в ýзел; (put): **to ~ sth/sb into** затáлкивать (затолкнуть perf) что-н/кого-н в +acc

► **bundle off** vt отсылáть (отослáть* perf)

► **bundle out** vt быстро уходить* (уйти* perf).

bun fight n (BRIT: inf: official function) банкéт; (: tea party) чаепитие.

bung [bʌŋ] n прóбка* ♦ vt (BRIT: throw) запихивать (запихáть perf); (also: **~ up**: pipe, hole) затыкáть (заткнуть perf); **my nose is ~ed up** у меня залóжен нос.

bungalow ['bʌŋgələu] n бунгáло nt ind.

bungee jumping ['bʌndʒi:'dʒʌmpɪŋ] n прыжки́ с высоты́ вниз головóй, в котóрых человéк привя́зан за нóги к эласти́чному кана́ту.

bungle ['bʌŋgl] vt завáливать (завали́ть perf).

bunion ['bʌnjən] n натóптыш.

bunk [bʌŋk] n (bed) кóйка.

bunk beds npl двухъя́русная кровáть fsg.

bunker ['bʌŋkə'] n бýнкер*; (GOLF) я́ма с пескóм (на пóле для гóльфа).

bunny ['bʌnɪ] n (also: **~ rabbit**) зáйчик.

bunny girl n (BRIT) официáнтка ночнóго клýба, в облегáющем костю́ме с крóличьим хвостóм и ушáми.

bunny hill n (US: SKIING) лягушáтник.

bunting ['bʌntɪŋ] n флажки́ mpl.

buoy [bɔɪ] n буй*, бáкен

► **buoy up** vt (fig) подбáдривать (подбодри́ть perf).

buoyancy ['bɔɪənsɪ] n плавýчесть f.

buoyant ['bɔɪənt] adj (ship) плавýчий*; (economy, market) оживлённый* (оживлён); (prices, currency) твёрдый; (fig: person) жизнерáдостный* (жизнерáдостен).

burden ['bə:dn] n (responsibility) брéмя* nt; (load) нóша ♦ vt (trouble): **to ~ sb with** обременять (обремени́ть perf) когó-н +instr; **to be a ~ to sb** быть* (impf) в тя́гость комý-н.

bureau ['bjuərəu] (pl **~x**) n (BRIT) бюрó nt ind; (US) комóд.

bureaucracy [bjuə'rɔkrəsɪ] n (POL, COMM) бюрокрáтия; (system) бюрократи́зм.

bureaucrat ['bjuərəkræt] n бюрокрáт.

bureaucratic [bjuərə'krætɪk] adj бюрократи́ческий.

bureaux ['bjuərəuz] npl of **bureau**.

burgeon ['bə:dʒən] vi (fig) расцветáть (расцвести́* perf).

burger ['bə:gə'] n бýргер.

burglar ['bə:glə'] n взлóмщик.

burglar alarm n сигнализáция.

burglarize ['bə:gləraɪz] vt (US) совершáть (соверши́ть perf) крáжу со взлóмом.

burglary ['bə:glərɪ] n (crime) крáжа со взлóмом; (act) взлом.

burgle ['bə:gl] *vt* соверша́ть (соверши́ть *perf*) кра́жу со взло́мом.

Burgundy ['bə:gəndɪ] *n* (*GEO*) Бургу́ндия.

burial ['bɛrɪəl] *n* погребе́ние, по́хороны *pl*.

burial ground *n* ме́сто* погребе́ния.

burlesque [bə:'lɛsk] *n* паро́дия.

burly ['bə:lɪ] *adj* дю́жий.

Burma ['bə:mə] *n* Би́рма.

Burmese [bə:'mi:z] *adj* бирма́нский ♦ *n inv* бирма́нец*(-нка*); (*LING*) бирма́нский язы́к*.

burn [bə:n] (*pt, pp* **burned** *or* **burnt**) *vt* жечь* (сжечь* *perf*), сжига́ть (сжечь* *perf*); (*arson*) поджига́ть (подже́чь* *perf*) ♦ *vi* (*house, wood*) горе́ть (сгоре́ть *perf*), сгора́ть (сгоре́ть *perf*); (*cakes*) подгора́ть (подгоре́ть *perf*) ♦ *n* ожо́г; **the cigarette ~t a hole in her dress** сигаре́та прожгла́ ды́рку в её пла́тье; **she always ~s the meat** у неё всегда́ подгора́ет мя́со; **I've ~t myself!** я обжёгся!

▶ **burn down** *vt* сжига́ть (сжечь* *perf*) дотла́

▶ **burn out** *vt*: **to ~ o.s. out** выма́тываться (вы́мотаться *perf*); **the fire ~t itself out** ого́нь догоре́л.

burner ['bə:nə'] *n* горе́лка*.

burning ['bə:nɪŋ] *adj* (*building, forest*) горя́щий*; (*sand, desert*) раскалённый; (*issue, ambition*) жгу́чий*.

burnish ['bə:nɪʃ] *vt* полирова́ть (отполирова́ть *perf*).

burnt [bə:nt] *pt, pp of* **burn**.

burnt sugar *n* (*BRIT*) жжёный са́хар.

burp [bə:p] *n* отры́жка* ♦ *vi*: **to ~ a baby** вызыва́ть (вы́звать* *perf*) отры́жку у ребёнка ♦ *vi* отры́гивать (отрыгну́ть *perf*).

burrow ['bʌrəu] *n* нора́* ♦ *vi* (*dig*) рыть* (вы́рыть* *perf*) нору́; (*rummage*) ры́ться* (*impf*).

bursar ['bə:sə'] *n* казначе́й.

bursary ['bə:sərɪ] *n* (*BRIT*) стипе́ндия.

burst [bə:st] (*pt, pp* **burst**) *vt* (*bag etc*) разрыва́ть (разорва́ть* *perf*) ♦ *vi* (*pipe*) прорыва́ться (прорва́ться* *perf*); (*tyre, balloon*) ло́паться (ло́пнуть *perf*) ♦ *n* (*of gunfire*) залп; (*of shelling*) разры́в; (*also: ~ pipe*) проры́в; **the river has ~ its banks** река́ вы́шла из берего́в; **to ~ into flames** вспы́хивать (вспы́хнуть *perf*); **to ~ into tears** распла́каться* (*perf*); **to ~ out laughing** расхохота́ться* (*perf*); **to ~ into a room** врыва́ться (ворва́ться* *perf*) в ко́мнату; **~ blood vessel** разо́рванный кровено́сный сосу́д; **the room is/was ~ing with people** ко́мната наби́та/была́ наби́та до отка́за людьми́; **to be ~ing with** (*pride, anger*) раздува́ться (разду́ться* *perf*) +*gen*; **a ~ of energy/enthusiasm** прили́в эне́ргии/энтузиа́зма; **~ of laughter/applause** взрыв сме́ха/рукоплеска́ний; **~ of machine gun fire** пулемётная о́чередь *f*

▶ **burst into** *vt fus* (*room*) врыва́ться (ворва́ться* *perf*)

▶ **burst open** *vi* (*door etc*) распа́хиваться (распахну́ться *perf*).

bury ['bɛrɪ] *vt* (*object*) зарыва́ть (зары́ть* *perf*), зака́пывать (закопа́ть *perf*); (*person*) хорони́ть* (похорони́ть* *perf*); **many people were buried in the rubble** мно́го люде́й бы́ло зары́то под обло́мками; **to ~ one's face in one's hands** пря́тать* (спря́тать* *perf*) лицо́ в ладо́ни; **to ~ one's head in the sand** (*fig*) зарыва́ть (зары́ть* *perf*) го́лову в песо́к; **to ~ the hatchet** (*fig*) забыва́ть (забы́ть* *perf*) раздо́ры, мири́ться (помири́ться *perf*).

bus [bʌs] *n* авто́бус; (*double decker*) (двухэта́жный) авто́бус.

bus boy *n* (*US*) помо́щник официа́нта, убира́ющий гря́зную посу́ду со стола́.

bush [buʃ] *n* куст*; (*scrubland*) простра́нства, покры́тые куста́рниками (в Австра́лии и *m.п.*); **to beat about the ~** ходи́ть* (*impf*) вокру́г да о́коло.

bushed [buʃt] *adj* (*inf*) вы́мотанный (вы́мотан).

bushel ['buʃl] *n* бу́шель *m*.

bush fire *n* лесно́й пожа́р.

bushy ['buʃɪ] *adj* (*tail*) пуши́стый (пуши́ст); (*hair, eyebrows*) густо́й* (густ); (*plant*) кусти́стый.

busily ['bɪzɪlɪ] *adv* (*actively*) делови́то, энерги́чно; **to be ~ doing sth** энерги́чно занима́ться (*impf*) чем-н.

business ['bɪznɪs] *n* (*matter*) де́ло*; (*trading*) би́знес; (*firm*) предприя́тие, фи́рма; (*occupation*) заня́тие; **to be away on ~** быть (*impf*) в командиро́вке; **I'm here on ~** я здесь по де́лу; **he's in the insurance/transport ~** он рабо́тает в страхово́м/тра́нспортном би́знесе; **to do ~ with sb** вести́ (*impf*) дела́ с кем-н; **it's my ~ to ...** э́то моя́ обя́занность +*infin* ...; **it's none of my ~** э́то не моё де́ло; **he means ~** он серьёзно настро́ен.

business address *n* а́дрес* фи́рмы.

business card *n* визи́тная ка́рточка*.

businesslike ['bɪznɪslaɪk] *adj* делови́тый (делови́т).

businessman ['bɪznɪsmən] *irreg n* бизнесме́н.

business trip *n* командиро́вка*.

businesswoman ['bɪznɪswumən] *irreg n* же́нщина-бизнесме́н, делова́я же́нщина.

busker ['bʌskə'] *n* (*BRIT*) у́личный музыка́нт.

bus lane *n* (*BRIT*) *часть доро́ги, отведённая для движе́ния авто́бусов.*

bus shelter *n* авто́бусная остано́вка (с наве́сом).

bus station *n* авто́бусная ста́нция, автовокза́л.

bus-stop ['bʌsstɔp] *n* авто́бусная остано́вка*.

bust [bʌst] n (ANAT) бюст, грудь* f; (measurement) объём груди́; (sculpture) бюст ♦ adj (inf: broken) сло́манный (сло́ман) ♦ vt (inf: arrest) накрыва́ть (накры́ть* perf); **to go ~** (company etc) прогора́ть (прогоре́ть perf), вылета́ть (вы́лететь* perf) в трубу́.

bustle ['bʌsl] n (activity) суматóха, суетá ♦ vi (person) суети́ться* (impf).

bustling ['bʌslɪŋ] adj (place) оживлённый, шу́мный*.

bust-up ['bʌstʌp] n (BRIT: inf) сканда́л, ссо́ра.

BUSWE n abbr (BRIT) = British Union of Social Work Employees.

busty ['bʌstɪ] adj (inf) груда́стый (груда́ст).

busy ['bɪzɪ] adj (person) занято́й; (street) оживлённый (оживлён), шу́мный* (шу́мен); (TEL): **the line is ~** ли́ния занята́ ♦ vt: **to ~ o.s. with** занима́ть (заня́ть* perf) себя́ +instr, занима́ться (заня́ться* perf) +instr; **he's a ~ man** (normally) он занятóй челове́к; **he's ~** (temporarily) он за́нят; **it's usually a very ~ shop** в э́том магази́не обы́чно мно́го наро́ду.

busybody ['bɪzɪbɔdɪ] n: **he is a ~** он суёт нос в чужи́е дела́.

busy signal n (US: TEL) коро́ткие гудки́ mpl.

but [bʌt] conj **1** (yet) но; (: in contrast) a; **he's not very bright, but he's hard-working** он не о́чень умён, но усе́рден; **I'm tired but Paul isn't** я уста́л, а Па́вел не уста́л

2 (however) но; **I'd love to come, but I'm busy** я бы с удово́льствием пришёл, но я за́нят

3 (showing disagreement, surprise etc) но; **but that's fantastic!** но э́то же потряса́юще!

♦ prep (apart from, except): **no-one but him can do it** никто́, кро́ме него́, не мо́жет э́то сде́лать; **nothing but trouble/bad luck** сплошны́е неприя́тности/неуда́чи; **but for you/your help** е́сли бы не Вы/ва́ша по́мощь; **I'll do anything but that** я сде́лаю всё, что уго́дно, но то́лько не э́то

♦ adv (just, only): **she's but a child** она́ всего́ лишь ребёнок; **had I but known** е́сли бы то́лько я знал; **I can but try** но я, коне́чно, могу́ попро́бовать; **the work is all but finished** рабо́та почти́ зако́нчена.

butane ['bju:tem] n (also: ~ **gas**) бута́н.

butch [butʃ] adj (pej: woman) мужеподо́бный* (мужеподо́бен); **he's very ~** он (настоя́щий) мужи́к.

butcher ['butʃə] n мясни́к*; (pej: murderer) пала́ч* ♦ vt (cattle) бить* (заби́ть* perf), ре́зать* (заре́зать* perf); (prisoners) выреза́ть* (вы́резать* perf).

butcher's (shop) ['butʃəz-] n мяснóй магази́н.

butler ['bʌtlə²] n дворе́цкий m adj.

butt [bʌt] n (large barrel) бóчка*; (thick end) утолщённый коне́ц*; (of rifle) прикла́д; (of pistol) рукоя́тка; (of cigarette) окýрок*; (BRIT:

of teasing) посме́шище; (: of criticism) предме́т; (US: inf!) за́дница (!) ♦ vt (subj: goat) бода́ть (impf)

▶ **butt in** vi встрева́ть (встрять* perf).

butter ['bʌtə²] n (сли́вочное) ма́сло* ♦ vt (bread) нама́зывать (нама́зать* perf) (сли́вочным) ма́слом.

buttercup ['bʌtəkʌp] n лю́тик.

butter dish n маслёнка*.

butterfingers ['bʌtəfɪŋgəz] n (inf) растя́па m/f.

butterfly ['bʌtəflaɪ] n ба́бочка*; (also: ~ **stroke**) баттерфля́й.

buttocks ['bʌtəks] npl я́годицы fpl.

button ['bʌtn] n (on clothes) пу́говица; (on machine) кно́пка*; (US: badge) значо́к* ♦ vt (also: ~ **up**) застёгивать (застегну́ть perf).

buttonhole ['bʌtnhəul] n петля́*, петли́ца ♦ vt: **to ~ sb** пристава́ть (приста́ть* perf) к кому́-н с разгово́рами.

buttress ['bʌtrɪs] n контрфо́рс.

buxom ['bʌksəm] adj (woman) полногру́дый (полногру́д).

buy [baɪ] (pt, pp **bought**) vt покупа́ть (купи́ть* perf); (COMM) приобрета́ть (приобрести́* perf) ♦ n поку́пка*; **to ~ sb sth/sth from sb** покупа́ть (купи́ть* perf) кому́-н что-н/что-н у кого́-н; **to ~ sb a drink** покупа́ть (купи́ть* perf) кому́-н вы́пить что́-нибудь; **that was a good/bad ~** э́то была́ уда́чная/неуда́чная поку́пка

▶ **buy back** vt выкупа́ть (вы́купить* perf)

▶ **buy in** vt (BRIT) закупа́ть (закупи́ть* perf)

▶ **buy into** vt fus (BRIT) покупа́ть (купи́ть* perf) часть +gen, входи́ть (войти́* perf) в до́лю с +instr

▶ **buy off** vt подкупа́ть (подкупи́ть* perf)

▶ **buy out** vt выкупа́ть (вы́купить* perf)

▶ **buy up** vt скупа́ть (скупи́ть* perf).

buyer ['baɪə²] n покупа́тель(ница) m(f); (COMM) заку́пщик(-ица).

buyer's market ['baɪəz-] n ры́нок, вы́годный для покупа́теля.

buy-out ['baɪaut] n: **management ~** вы́куп ча́стной фи́рмы у её владе́льца чле́нами администра́ции, рабо́тающими на фи́рме.

buzz [bʌz] n жужжа́ние ♦ vi (insect, saw) жужжа́ть* (прожужжа́ть* perf); (inf: place) гуде́ть* (impf) ♦ vt (call on intercom) звони́ть (позвони́ть perf) по вну́треннему телефо́ну; (with buzzer) звони́ть (позвони́ть perf); (AVIAT) соверша́ть (соверши́ть perf) бре́ющий полёт над +instr; **to give sb a ~** (inf: TEL) звя́кнуть (perf) кому́-н; **my head is ~ing** у меня́ голова́ гуди́т

▶ **buzz off** vi (inf) отва́ливать (отвали́ть* perf).

buzzard ['bʌzəd] n каню́к*, сары́ч*.

buzzer ['bʌzə²] n зу́ммер, звоно́к.

buzz word n (inf) мо́дное словцо́*.

by [baɪ] prep **1** (referring to cause, agent): **he was killed by lightning** он был уби́т мо́лнией; **a**

painting by Van Gogh карти́на Ван Го́га; **it's by Shakespeare** э́то Шекспи́р
2 (*referring to manner, means*): **by bus/train** на авто́бусе/по́езде, авто́бусом/по́ездом; **by car** на маши́не; **by phone** по телефо́ну; **to pay by cheque** плати́ть* (заплати́ть* *perf*) че́ком; **by moonlight** при све́те луны́; **by candlelight** при свеча́х; **by working constantly, he...** благодаря́ тому́, что он рабо́тал без остано́вки, он...
3 (*via, through*) че́рез +*acc*; **by land/sea** по су́ше/мо́рю; **by the back door** че́рез за́днюю дверь
4 (*close to*) о́коло +*gen*, у +*gen*; **the house is by the river** дом* нахо́дится о́коло *or* у реки́; **a holiday by the sea** о́тпуск на мо́ре
5 (*past*) ми́мо +*gen*; **she rushed by me** она́ пронесла́сь ми́мо меня́
6 (*not later than*) к +*dat*; **by four o'clock** к четырём часа́м; **by the time I got here it was too late** к тому́ вре́мени, когда́ я добра́лся сюда́, бы́ло сли́шком по́здно
7 (*during*): **by day** днём; **by night** но́чью
8 (*amount*): **to sell by the kilo/metre** продава́ть* (*impf*) в килогра́ммах/ме́трах; **she is paid by the hour** у неё почасова́я опла́та
9 (*MATH, measure*) на +*acc*; **to divide/multiply by three** дели́ть* (раздели́ть* *perf*)/умножа́ть (умно́жить *perf*) на три; **a room three metres by four** ко́мната разме́ром три ме́тра на четы́ре
10 (*according to*) по +*dat*; **to play by the rules** игра́ть (*impf*) по пра́вилам; **it's all right by me** я не возража́ю; **by law** по зако́нам
11: (**all**) **by oneself** (*alone*) (соверше́нно) оди́н (*f* одна́, *nt* одно́, *pl* одни́); (*unaided*) сам (*f* сама́, *nt* само́, *pl* сами́); **I did it all by myself** я сде́лал всё сам; **he was standing by himself in the corner** он стоя́л в углу́ оди́н/сам по себе́
12: **by the way** кста́ти; **this wasn't my idea by the way** кста́ти *or* ме́жду про́чим, э́то была́ не моя́ иде́я
♦ *adv* **1** *see* **go, pass** *etc*
2: **by and by** вско́ре; **by and large** в це́лом.

bye(-bye) ['baɪ('baɪ)] *excl* пока́, всего́.
by(e)-law ['baɪlɔ:] *n* постановле́ние ме́стной вла́сти.
by-election ['baɪlɛkʃən] *n* (*BRIT*) дополни́тельные вы́боры *mpl*.
Byelorussia [bjɛləʊ'rʌʃə] *n* Белору́ссия.
bygone ['baɪgɔn] *adj* мину́вший* ♦ *n*: **let ~s be ~s** что бы́ло, то прошло́.
bypass ['baɪpɑ:s] *n* (*AUT*) объе́зд; (*MED*) обходно́е шунти́рование (*обычно в кардиохирурги́и*) ♦ *vt* (*town*) объезжа́ть (объе́хать* *perf*); (*fig*) обходи́ть* (обойти́* *perf*).
by-product ['baɪprɔdʌkt] *n* (*of industrial process*) побо́чный проду́кт; (*of situation*) побо́чный результа́т.
byre ['baɪəʳ] *n* (*BRIT*) коро́вник.
bystander ['baɪstændəʳ] *n* свиде́тель(ница) *m(f)*, прохо́жий(-ая) *m(f) adj*.
byte [baɪt] *n* (*COMPUT*) байт.
byway ['baɪweɪ] *n* (*in country*) просёлочная доро́га; (*in city*) у́лочка.
byword ['baɪwə:d] *n*: **to be a ~ for** быть* (*impf*) олицетворе́нием *or* си́мволом +*gen*.
by-your-leave ['baɪjɔ:'li:v] *n*: **without so much as a ~** без вся́кого разреше́ния.

~ C, c ~

C, c [si:] n (letter) 3-ья бу́ква англи́йского алфави́та; (SCOL: mark) ≈ удовлетвори́тельный.

C [si:] n (MUS) до nt ind.

C. abbr = **Celsius, centigrade**.

c abbr (= century) в.= век; (= circa) о́коло +gen; (US etc.= cents) це́нты mpl.

CA n abbr (BRIT) = **chartered accountant** ♦ abbr = **Central America**; (US: POST) = California.

ca. abbr (= circa) о́коло +gen.

c/a abbr (COMM) = **capital account, credit account, current account**.

CAA n abbr (BRIT: = Civil Aviation Authority) Управле́ние гражда́нской авиа́ции; (US) = Civil Aeronautics Authority.

CAB n abbr (BRIT: = Citizens' Advice Bureau) бюро́, даю́щее беспла́тные сове́ты по широ́кому спе́ктру пробле́м.

cab [kæb] n такси́ nt ind; (of truck etc) каби́на; (horse-drawn) экипа́ж, кэб.

cabaret ['kæbəreɪ] n кабаре́ nt ind.

cabbage ['kæbɪdʒ] n капу́ста.

cabbie ['kæbɪ] n такси́ст.

cab driver n шофёр такси́.

cabin ['kæbɪn] n (on ship) каю́та; (on plane) каби́на; (house) хи́жина.

cabin cruiser n пассажи́рский ка́тер*.

cabinet ['kæbɪnɪt] n шкаф*; (also: **display** ~) го́рка; (POL) кабине́т (мини́стров).

cabinet-maker ['kæbɪnɪt'meɪkə'] n красноде́ревщик.

cabinet minister n член кабине́та мини́стров.

cable ['keɪbl] n (strong rope) кана́т; (metal) трос; (ELEC, TEL, TV) ка́бель m; (also: ~gram) каблогра́мма, телегра́мма ♦ vt (message) телеграфи́ровать (impf/perf); (money) посыла́ть (посла́ть* perf) телегра́фом.

cable car n кана́тная доро́га.

cable railway n фуникулёр.

cable television n ка́бельное телеви́дение.

cache [kæʃ] n та́йный склад; **a** ~ **of food** запа́с продово́льствия.

cackle ['kækl] vi (person) хихи́кать (impf); (hen) куда́хтать (impf).

cacti ['kæktaɪ] npl of **cactus**.

cactus ['kæktəs] n (pl **cacti**) n ка́ктус.

CAD n abbr (= computer-aided design) автоматизи́рованное проекти́рование.

caddie ['kædɪ] n (GOLF) подру́чный m adj игрока́ в гольф.

caddy ['kædɪ] n = **caddie**.

cadence ['keɪdəns] n (of voice) интона́ция.

cadet [kə'dɛt] n курса́нт; **police** ~ курса́нт полице́йской шко́лы.

cadge [kædʒ] vt (inf): **to** ~ **(from or off)** выкля́нчивать (вы́клянчить perf) (у +gen).

cadger ['kædʒə'] n (BRIT: inf) попроша́йка m/f.

cadre ['kædrɪ] n ка́дры mpl.

Caesarean [si:'zɛərɪən] n (also: ~ **section**) ке́сарево сече́ние.

CAF abbr (BRIT: = cost and freight) КАФ (сто́имость и фрахт).

café ['kæfeɪ] n кафе́ nt ind.

cafeteria [kæfɪ'tɪərɪə] n кафете́рий.

caffein(e) ['kæfi:n] n кофеи́н.

cage [keɪdʒ] n (of animal) кле́тка; (of lift) каби́на ♦ vt сажа́ть (посади́ть* perf) в кле́тку.

cagey ['keɪdʒɪ] adj (inf: person) скры́тный* (скры́тен); (: answer) укло́нчивый (укло́нчив).

cagoule [kə'gu:l] n дождеви́к.

cahoots [kə'hu:ts] npl: **to be in** ~ **with sb** быть* (impf) в сго́воре с кем-н.

CAI n abbr (= computer-aided instruction) автоматизи́рованное обуче́ние.

Cairo ['kaɪərəu] n Каи́р.

cajole [kə'dʒəul] vt: **to** ~ **sb** склоня́ть (склони́ть perf) ле́стью кого́-н.

cake [keɪk] n (large) торт; (small) пиро́жное nt adj; (of soap) брусо́к*; **it's a piece of** ~ (inf) э́то пустяко́вое де́ло*; **his books sell like hot** ~**s** его́ кни́ги иду́т на расхва́т.

caked [keɪkt] adj: ~ **with** облеплённый +instr.

cake shop n бу́лочная-конди́терская f adj.

calamine lotion ['kæləmaɪn-] n каками́нный лосьо́н.

calamitous [kə'læmɪtəs] adj бе́дственный.

calamity [kə'læmɪtɪ] n бе́дствие.

calcium ['kælsɪəm] n ка́льций.

calculate ['kælkjuleɪt] vt (work out: numbers, cost) подсчи́тывать (подсчита́ть perf); (: distance) вычисля́ть (вы́числить perf); (estimate) рассчи́тывать (рассчита́ть perf)

► **calculate on** vt fus: **to** ~ **on sth** рассчи́тывать (impf) на что-н.

calculated ['kælkjuleɪtɪd] adj наме́ренный (наме́рен); **a** ~ **risk** созна́тельный риск.

calculating ['kælkjuleɪtɪŋ] *adj* расчётливый (расчётлив).

calculation [kælkju'leɪʃən] *n* (*see vb*) подсчёт; вычисление; расчёт.

calculator ['kælkjuleɪtəʳ] *n* калькулятор.

calculus ['kælkjuləs] *n* исчисление; **integral/differential ~** интегральное/дифференциальное исчисление.

Calcutta [kæl'kʌtə] *n* Калькутта.

calendar ['kæləndəʳ] *n* календарь* *m* ♦ *cpd*: **~ month/year** календарный месяц*/год*.

calf [kɑːf] (*pl* **calves**) *n* (*of cow*) телёнок*; (*of elephant, seal*) детёныш; (*also:* **~skin**) телячья кожа; (*ANAT*) икра*.

caliber ['kælɪbəʳ] (*US*) *n* = **calibre**.

calibrate ['kælɪbreɪt] *vt* калибровать (*impf*).

calibre ['kælɪbəʳ] (*US* **caliber**) *n* калибр.

calico ['kælɪkəu] *n* (*BRIT*) миткаль* *m*; (*US*) ситец*.

California [kælɪ'fɔːnɪə] *n* Калифорния.

calipers ['kælɪpəz] (*US*) *npl* = **callipers**.

call [kɔːl] *vt* (*name, label*) называть (назвать* *perf*); (*TEL*) звонить (позвонить *perf*) +*dat*; (*summon*) вызывать (вызвать* *perf*); (*arrange*) созывать (созвать* *perf*); (*announce*) объявлять (объявить* *perf*) ♦ *vi* (*shout*) кричать (крикнуть *perf*) звонить (позвонить *perf*); (*visit: also:* **~ in**, **~ round**) заходить* (зайти* *perf*) ♦ *n* (*shout, cry*) крик; (*TEL*) звонок*; (*visit*) посещение; (*demand*) призыв; (*summons: for flight*) объявление; (*fig: lure*) зов*; **she is ~ed Suzanne** её зовут Сюзанна; **the mountain is ~ed Ben Nevis** эта гора называется Бен Невис; **to ~ sb as a witness** призывать (призвать* *perf*) кого-н в свидетели; **who is ~ing?** (*TEL*) кто звонит?; **London ~ing** (*RADIO*) говорит Лондон; **please give me a ~ at 7** позвоните мне, пожалуйста, в 7 часов*; **to make a ~** звонить (позвонить *perf*); **to pay a ~ on sb** навещать (навестить* *perf*) кого-н; **there's not much ~ for these items** на эти предметы нет большого спроса; **to be on ~** (*nurse, doctor*) дежурить (*impf*); (*army, fire brigade*) быть* (*impf*) наготове

▶ **call at** *vt fus* (*subj: ship*) заходить* (зайти* *perf*) в +*prp*; (: *train*) останавливаться (остановиться* *perf*) в +*prp*

▶ **call back** *vi* (*return*) заходить* (зайти* *perf*) опять; (*TEL*) перезванивать (перезвонить *perf*) ♦ *vt* (*TEL*) перезванивать (перезвонить *perf*) +*dat*

▶ **call for** *vt fus* (*demand*) призывать (призвать* *perf*) к +*dat*; (*fetch*) заходить* (зайти* *perf*) за +*instr*

▶ **call in** *vt* (*doctor*) вызывать (вызвать* *perf*) ♦ *vi* (*visit*) заходить* (зайти* *perf*); **to ~ sth in** (*books, stock*) отзывать (отозвать* *perf*)

▶ **call off** *vt* отменять (отменить* *perf*); **the strike was ~ed off** забастовка была отменена

▶ **call on** *vt fus* (*visit*) заходить* (зайти* *perf*) к +*dat*; (*appeal to*) призывать (призвать* *perf*) к +*dat*; (*request*): **to ~ on sb to do** призывать (призвать* *perf*) кого-н +*infin*

▶ **call out** *vi* кричать (крикнуть *perf*) ♦ *vt* (*doctor, police*) вызывать (вызвать* *perf*)

▶ **call up** *vt* (*MIL*) призывать (призвать* *perf*) (в армию); (*TEL*) звонить (позвонить *perf*) +*dat*.

Callanetics® [kælə'netɪks] *n* калланетика (*вид оздоровительной гимнастики*).

call box *n* (*BRIT*) телефонная будка.

call centre *n* центр приёма коммерческих итп звонков в большом объёме.

caller ['kɔːləʳ] *n* (*visitor*) посетитель(ница) *m(f)*; (*TEL*) звонящий(-ая) *m(f) adj*; **hold the line, ~!** не кладите трубку!

call girl *n* проститутка* (*которую вызывают по телефону*).

call-in ['kɔːlɪn] *n* (*US*) программа „Звоните-отвечаем".

calling ['kɔːlɪŋ] *n* призвание.

calling card *n* (*US*) визитная карточка*.

callipers ['kælɪpəz] (*US* **calipers**) *npl* (*MATH*) штангенциркуль *msg*.

callous ['kæləs] *adj* (*heartless*) бездушный (бездушен), жестокий.

callousness ['kæləsnɪs] *n* бездушие.

callow ['kæləu] *adj*: **~ youth** птенец*.

calm [kɑːm] *adj* спокойный* (спокоен); (*place*) тихий*; (*weather*) безветренный ♦ *n* тишина, покой; (*at sea*) штиль *m* ♦ *vt* успокаивать (успокоить *perf*)

▶ **calm down** *vt* (*person, animal*) успокаивать (успокоить *perf*) ♦ *vi* (*person*) успокаиваться (успокоиться *perf*).

calmly ['kɑːmlɪ] *adv* спокойно.

calmness ['kɑːmnɪs] *n* спокойствие.

Calor gas® ['kælə'-] *n* фирменная марка баллонного газа.

calorie ['kælərɪ] *n* калория; **low-~ product** низкокалорийный продукт.

calve [kɑːv] *vi* (*cow*) телиться* (отелиться* *perf*); (*elephant, seal*) рождать (родить* *perf*) детёныша.

calves [kɑːvz] *npl of* **calf**.

CAM *n abbr* (= *computer-aided manufacturing*) автоматизированное производство.

camber ['kæmbəʳ] *n* поперечный уклон.

Cambodia [kæm'bəudɪə] *n* Камбоджа.

Cambodian [kæm'bəudɪən] *adj* камбоджийский* ♦ *n* камбоджиец(-ийка).

Cambridge ['keɪmbrɪdʒ] *n* Кембридж.

Cambs *abbr* (*BRIT: POST*) = **Cambridgeshire**.

camcorder ['kæmkɔːdəʳ] *n* видеокамера.

came [keɪm] *pt of* **come**.

---

* marks translations which have irregular inflections. The Russian-English side of the dictionary gives inflectional information.

camel ['kæməl] *n* верблю́д.
cameo ['kæmɪəʊ] *n* (*jewellery*) каме́я; (*THEAT, LITERATURE*) миниатю́ра.
camera ['kæmərə] *n* (*PHOT*) фотоаппара́т; (*also:* **cine ~, movie ~**) кинока́мера; (*TV*) телека́мера; **35 mm ~** кинока́мера для 35-мм плёнки; **in ~** (*LAW*) при закры́тых дверя́х.
cameraman ['kæmərəmæn] *irreg n* (*CINEMA*) (кино)опера́тор; (*TV*) (теле)опера́тор.
Cameroon [kæmə'ruːn] *n* Камеру́н.
Cameroun [kæmə'ruːn] *n* = **Cameroon**.
camomile ['kæməmaɪl] *n* рома́шка; **~ tea** рома́шковый чай*.
camouflage ['kæməflɑːʒ] *n* (*MIL*) камуфля́ж, маскиро́вка; (*ZOOL*) защи́тная окра́ска ◆ *vt* (*also MIL*) маскирова́ть (замаскирова́ть *perf*).
camp [kæmp] *n* ла́герь* *m*; (*MIL*) вое́нный городо́к* ◆ *vi* (*set up camp*) разбива́ть (разби́ть* *perf*) ла́герь; (*go camping*) жить* (*impf*) в пала́тках ◆ *adj* (*effeminate*) женоподо́бный.
campaign [kæm'peɪn] *n* кампа́ния ◆ *vi:* **to ~ (for/against)** вести́* (*impf*) кампа́нию (за +*acc*/ про́тив +*gen*).
campaigner [kæm'peɪnə'] *n:* **~ (for/against)** боре́ц* (за +*acc*/про́тив +*gen*).
camp bed *n* (*BRIT*) раскладу́шка*.
camper ['kæmpə'] *n* (*person*) тури́ст(ка) (*живу́щий* в пала́тке*); (*vehicle*) фурго́н (*обору́дованный для похо́дной жи́зни*).
camping ['kæmpɪŋ] *n* ке́мпинг; **to go ~** отправля́ться (отпра́виться* *perf*) в похо́д.
camping site *n* = **camp site**.
camp site *n* ке́мпинг.
campus ['kæmpəs] *n* университе́тский* *or* студе́нческий* городо́к*.
camshaft ['kæmʃɑːft] *n* кулачко́вый вал*.
can[1] [kæn] *n* (*for foodstuffs*) консе́рвная ба́нка; (*for oil, beer*) ба́нка ◆ *vt* консерви́ровать (законсерви́ровать *perf*); **a ~ of beer** ба́нка пи́ва; **he had to carry the ~** (*BRIT: inf*) ему́ пришло́сь за всё отдува́ться.

KEYWORD

can[2] (*negative* **cannot, can't**, *conditional, pt* **could**) *aux vb* **1** (*be able to*) мочь* (смочь* *perf*); **you can do it (if you try)** Вы смо́жете э́то сде́лать(, е́сли Вы постара́етесь); **I'll help you all I can** я помогу́ Вам всем, чем могу́; **I can't go on any longer** я бо́льше не могу́; **I can't see/hear you** я не ви́жу/слы́шу Вас; **she couldn't sleep that night** в ту ночь она́ не могла́ усну́ть
2 (*know how to*) уме́ть (*impf*); **I can swim** я уме́ю пла́вать; **can you speak Russian?** Вы говори́те *or* уме́ете говори́ть по-ру́сски?
3 (*may*) мо́жно; **can I use your phone?** мо́жно от Вас позвони́ть?; **could I have a word with you?** мо́жно с Ва́ми поговори́ть?; **you can smoke if you like** Вы мо́жете кури́ть, е́сли хоти́те; **can I help you with that?** могу́ я Вам

в э́том помо́чь?
4 (*expressing disbelief, puzzlement*): **it can't be true!** не мо́жет быть!; **what CAN he want?** что ему́ ну́жно?
5 (*expressing possibility, suggestion etc*): **he could be in the library** он мо́жет быть в библиоте́ке, возмо́жно, он в библиоте́ке; **she could have been delayed** возмо́жно, её что-то задержа́ло.

Canada ['kænədə] *n* Кана́да.
Canadian [kə'neɪdɪən] *adj* кана́дский* ◆ *n* кана́дец*(-дка*).
canal [kə'næl] *n* кана́л.
Canaries [kə'nɛərɪz] *npl* = **Canary Islands**.
canary [kə'nɛərɪ] *n* канаре́йка*.
Canary Islands *npl:* **the ~ ~** Кана́рские острова́ *mpl*.
Canberra ['kænbərə] *n* Канбе́рра.
cancel ['kænsəl] *vt* отменя́ть (отмени́ть* *perf*); (*contract, cheque, visa*) аннули́ровать (*impf/ perf*); (*words, figures*) вычёркивать (вы́черкнуть *perf*); (*stamp*) погаша́ть (погаси́ть* *perf*)
▸ **cancel out** *vt* нейтрализова́ть (*impf/perf*); **they ~ each other out** они́ нейтрализу́ют друг дру́га.
cancellation [kænsə'leɪʃən] *n* отме́на, аннули́рование.
cancer ['kænsə'] *n* (*MED*) рак; (*fig*) бич; **C~** (*ASTROLOGY*) Рак; **he is C~** он – Рак.
cancerous ['kænsrəs] *adj* ра́ковый.
cancer patient *n* ра́ковый(-ая) больно́й(-а́я) *m(f) adj*.
cancer research *n* онкологи́ческие иссле́дования *ntpl*.
C and F *abbr* (*BRIT: COMM*) = **CAF**.
candid ['kændɪd] *adj* и́скренний* (и́скренен), чистосерде́чный* (чистосерде́чен).
candidacy ['kændɪdəsɪ] *n* кандидату́ра.
candidate ['kændɪdeɪt] *n* (*for job*) претенде́нт; (*in exam*) экзамену́емый(-ая) *m(f) adj*; (*POL*) кандида́т.
candidature ['kændɪdətʃə'] (*BRIT*) *n* = **candidacy**.
candied ['kændɪd] *adj:* **~ fruit** цука́ты *mpl*; **~ apple** (*US*) я́блочный цука́т.
candle ['kændl] *n* свеча́*; (*smaller*) све́чка*.
candleholder ['kændlhəʊldə'] *n* = **candlestick**.
candlelight ['kændllaɪt] *n:* **by ~** при свеча́х.
candlestick ['kændlstɪk] *n* подсве́чник.
candour ['kændə'] (*US* **candor**) *n* и́скренность *f*.
candy ['kændɪ] *n* (*also:* **sugar~**) караме́ль *f*, ледене́ц*; (*US*) конфе́та.
candyfloss ['kændɪflɔs] *n* (*BRIT*) са́харная ва́та.
candy store *n* (*US*) конди́терская *f adj*.
cane [keɪn] *n* (*BOT*) тростни́к*; (*stick*) ро́зга*; (*for walking*) трость* *f* ◆ *vt* (*BRIT*) нака́зывать (наказа́ть* *perf*) ро́згами.
canine ['keɪnaɪn] *adj* соба́чий*.
canister ['kænɪstə'] *n* (*for tea etc*) жестяна́я ба́нка*; (*pressurized container*) балло́н; (*of chemicals etc*) кани́стра.

cannabis ['kænəbɪs] *n* гаши́ш; (*also:* ~ **plant**) конопля́.

canned [kænd] *adj* (*fruit, vegetables etc*) консерви́рованный; (*inf: music*) в за́писи; (*BRIT: inf: drink*) ба́ночный; (: *drunk*) наклю́кавшийся.

cannibal ['kænɪbəl] *n* (*animal*) канниба́л; (*person*) канниба́л, людое́д.

cannibalism ['kænɪbəlɪzəm] *n* каннибали́зм, людое́дство.

cannon ['kænən] (*pl* ~ *or* ~**s**) *n* (*gun*) пу́шка*.

cannonball ['kænənbɔːl] *n* пу́шечное ядро́*.

cannon fodder *n* пу́шечное мя́со.

cannot ['kænɔt] = **can not**; *see* **can²**.

canny ['kænɪ] *adj* смека́листый (смека́лист).

canoe [kə'nuː] *n* (*boat*) челно́к*; (*for competition*) кано́э *nt ind*.

canoeing [kə'nuːɪŋ] *n* гре́бля на кано́э.

canon ['kænən] *n* (*clergyman*) кано́ник; (*rule*) кано́н; (*standard*) крите́рий.

canonize ['kænənaɪz] *vt* канонизи́ровать (*impf/ perf*).

can-opener ['kænəupnə'] *n* консе́рвный нож* *or* ключ*.

canopy ['kænəpɪ] *n* (*above bed etc*) балдахи́н, по́лог; (*of leaves etc*) свод.

cant [kænt] *n* ха́нжество.

can't [kænt] = **can not**; *see* **can²**.

Cantab. *abbr* (*BRIT: in degree titles*) = *Cantabrigiensis*.

cantankerous [kæn'tæŋkərəs] *adj* сварли́вый (сварли́в), приди́рчивый (приди́рчив).

canteen [kæn'tiːn] *n* столо́вая *f adj*; (*mobile*) похо́дная ку́хня*; (*BRIT*): ~ **of cutlery** похо́дный я́щик со столо́выми принадле́жностями.

canter ['kæntə'] *vi* е́здить*/е́хать* (*impf*) лёгким гало́пом ♦ *n* лёгкий* гало́п.

cantilever ['kæntɪliːvə'] *n* консо́ль *f*, кронште́йн; ~ **bridge** консо́льный мост*.

canvas ['kænvəs] *n* (*fabric, also ART*) холст*; (*for tents*) брезе́нт; (*NAUT*) паруси́на ♦ *adj* (*shoes, bag*) паруси́новый; **under** ~ (*camping*) в пала́тках.

canvass ['kænvəs] *vi*: **to** ~ **for** агити́ровать (*impf/perf*) за +*acc* ♦ *vt* (*opinions*) собира́ть (*impf*).

canvasser ['kænvəsə'] *n* агита́тор.

canvassing ['kænvəsɪŋ] *n* предвы́борная агита́ция.

canyon ['kænjən] *n* каньо́н.

CAP *n abbr* (= *Common Agricultural Policy*) о́бщая сельскохозя́йственная поли́тика (*в страна́х Общего ры́нка*).

cap [kæp] *n* (*hat*) ке́пка*; (*of uniform*) фура́жка*; (*of pen*) колпачо́к*; (*of bottle*) кры́шка*; (*also:* **Dutch** ~: *contraceptive*) колпачо́к*; (*for toy gun*) писто́н; (*FOOTBALL*) футбо́льный игро́к,

кото́рый получа́ет ке́пку как знак отли́чия ♦ *vt* (*outdo*) превосходи́ть* (превзойти́* *perf*); (*SPORT*): **he was** ~**ped ten times** он игра́л в сбо́рной кома́нде страны́ де́сять раз: **swimming** ~ купа́льная ша́почка; **to be** ~**ped with** уве́нчиваться (увенча́ться *perf*) +*instr*; **and to** ~ **it all, he** ... в доверше́ние ко всему́, он ....

capability [keɪpə'bɪlɪtɪ] *n* (*competence*) спосо́бность *f*; (*MIL*) потенциа́л.

capable ['keɪpəbl] *adj* (*person*) спосо́бный* (спосо́бен); ~ **of sth/doing** (*person, object*) спосо́бен к чему́-н/+*infin*.

capacious [kə'peɪʃəs] *adj* вмести́тельный* (вмести́телен).

capacity [kə'pæsɪtɪ] *n* (*of container*) ёмкость *f*; (*of ship, theatre etc*) вмести́тельность *f*; (*of lift*) подъёмная спосо́бность *f*; (*of person: capability*) спосо́бность; (: *role*) роль* *f*; (*of factory*) произво́дственная мо́щность *f*; **filled to** ~ запо́лнен до преде́ла; **in his** ~ **as** в ро́ли +*gen*; **in an advisory** ~ в ро́ли сове́тника; **this work is beyond my** ~ э́та рабо́та вне мое́й компете́нции; **to work at full** ~ рабо́тать (*impf*) на по́лную мо́щность.

cape [keɪp] *n* (*GEO*) мыс*; (*cloak*) плащ.

Cape of Good Hope *n*: **the** ~ ~ ~ ~ Мыс До́брой Наде́жды.

caper ['keɪpə'] *n* (*CULIN: usu pl*) ка́персы *mpl*; (*prank*) ро́зыгрыш.

Cape Town *n* Кейпта́ун.

capita ['kæpɪtə] *see* **per capita**.

capital ['kæpɪtl] *n* (*also:* ~ **city**) столи́ца; (*money*) капита́л; (*also:* ~ **letter**) загла́вная бу́ква.

capital account *n* бала́нс движе́ния капита́ла.

capital allowance *n* *нало́говая ски́дка, свя́занная с инвести́циями в основно́й капита́л*.

capital assets *npl* основно́й капита́л *msg*, основны́е фо́нды *mpl*.

capital employed *n* применя́емый капита́л.

capital expenditure *n* капиталовложе́ние.

capital gains tax *n* нало́г на реализо́ванный приро́ст капита́ла.

capital goods *npl* капита́льные това́ры *mpl*, сре́дства *ntpl* произво́дства.

capital-intensive ['kæpɪtlɪn'tɛnsɪv] *adj* капиталоёмкий.

capital investment *n* капиталовложе́ние.

capitalism ['kæpɪtəlɪzəm] *n* капитали́зм.

capitalist ['kæpɪtəlɪst] *adj* капиталисти́ческий* ♦ *n* капитали́ст.

capitalize ['kæpɪtəlaɪz] *vt* (*COMM*) капитализи́ровать (*impf/perf*) ♦ *vi*: **to** ~ **on** извлека́ть (извле́чь* *perf*) вы́году из +*gen*.

capital punishment *n* сме́ртная казнь *f*.

---

capital transfer tax *n* (*BRIT*) нало́г на перево́д капита́ла.

Capitol ['kæpɪtl] *n*: **the ~** Капито́лий.

capitulate [kə'pɪtjuleɪt] *vi*: **to ~ (to)** капитули́ровать (*impf/perf*) (пе́ред +*instr*).

capitulation [kəpɪtju'leɪʃən] *n* капитуля́ция.

capricious [kə'prɪʃəs] *adj* (*person*) капри́зный* (капри́зен), прихотли́вый (прихотли́в).

Capricorn ['kæprɪkɔ:n] *n* (*ASTROLOGY*) Козеро́г; **he is ~** он – Козеро́г.

caps [kæps] *abbr* = **capital letters**.

capsize [kæp'saɪz] *vt* опроки́дывать (опроки́нуть *perf*) ♦ *vi* опроки́дываться (опроки́нуться *perf*).

capstan ['kæpstən] *n* (*NAUT*) кабеста́н.

capsule ['kæpsju:l] *n* ка́псула.

Capt. *abbr* (*MIL*) = **captain**.

captain ['kæptɪn] *n* (*of ship, plane*) команди́р; (*of team, army*) капита́н ♦ *vt* (*ship*) кома́ндовать (*impf*) +*instr*; (*team*) явля́ться (*impf*) капита́ном +*gen*.

caption ['kæpʃən] *n* по́дпись *f*.

captivate ['kæptɪveɪt] *vt* пленя́ть (плени́ть *perf*).

captive ['kæptɪv] *adj* пле́нный ♦ *n* пле́нник(-ица).

captivity [kæp'tɪvɪtɪ] *n* плен*; **in ~** (*animal*) в нево́ле; (*person*) в плену́.

captor ['kæptə] *n* (*unlawful*) похити́тель(ница) *m(f)*; (*lawful*) взя́вший(-ая) *m(f) adj* в плен; **his ~s** взя́вшие его́ в плен.

capture ['kæptʃə] *vt* (*animal*) лови́ть* (пойма́ть *perf*); (*person, city, also* COMM) захва́тывать (захвати́ть* *perf*); (*attention*) прико́вывать (прикова́ть *perf*) ♦ *n* (*of person, town etc*) захва́т; (*of animal*) пои́мка*; (*COMPUT*): **data ~** сбор информа́ции; **to ~ the screen** (*COMPUT*) фикси́ровать (зафикси́ровать *perf*) изображе́ние с экра́на.

car [kɑ:ʳ] *n* автомоби́ль *m*, маши́на; (*RAIL*) ваго́н; **by ~** на автомоби́ле *or* маши́не; **dining ~** (*BRIT*) ваго́н-рестора́н.

Caracas [kə'rækəs] *n* Кара́кас.

carafe [kə'ræf] *n* графи́н.

caramel ['kærəməl] *n* (*sweet*) караме́ль *f*; (*burnt sugar*) жжёный са́хар*.

carat ['kærət] *n* (*of diamond, gold*) кара́т; **24 ~ gold** чи́стое зо́лото.

caravan ['kærəvæn] *n* (*BRIT*) жило́й-автоприце́п; (*in desert*) карава́н.

caravan site *n* (*BRIT*) *пло́щадка для сто́янки жилы́х-автоприце́пов*.

caraway ['kærəweɪ] *n*: **~ seeds** тмин *msg*.

carbohydrate [kɑ:bəu'haɪdreɪt] *n* углево́д.

carbolic acid [kɑ:'bɔlɪk-] *n* карбо́ловая кислота́.

car bomb *n* бо́мба, подло́женная в *or* под маши́ну.

carbon ['kɑ:bən] *n* углеро́д.

carbonated ['kɑ:bəneɪtɪd] *adj* (*drink*) газиро́ванный.

carbon copy *n* ко́пия (*сде́ланная под копи́рку*).

carbon dioxide *n* двуо́кись *f* углеро́да.

carbon monoxide [mɔ'nɔksaɪd] *n* моноки́сд углеро́да.

carbon paper *n* копирова́льная бума́га, копи́рка.

carbon ribbon *n* ле́нта (*для пи́шущей маши́нки или при́нтера*).

car boot sale *n* *барахо́лка, на кото́рой това́р продаётся с маши́н.*

carburettor [kɑ:bju'rɛtəʳ] (*US* **carburetor**) *n* карбюра́тор.

carcass ['kɑ:kəs] *n* ту́ша.

carcinogenic [kɑ:sɪnə'dʒɛnɪk] *adj* канцероге́нный.

card [kɑ:d] *n* (*material*) карто́н; (*also:* **record ~**) ка́рточка*; (*also:* **membership ~**) чле́нский* биле́т; (*also:* **playing ~**) (игра́льная) ка́рта; (*also:* **greetings ~**) открытка; (*also:* **visiting ~, business ~**) визи́тная ка́рточка*; **to play ~s** игра́ть (*impf*) в ка́рты.

cardamom ['kɑ:dəməm] *n* кардамо́н.

cardboard ['kɑ:dbɔ:d] *n* карто́н.

cardboard box *n* карто́нная коро́бка*.

cardboard city *n* (*inf*) *райо́н го́рода, за́нятый бездо́мными, живу́щими в карто́нных я́щиках.*

card-carrying ['kɑ:d'kærɪŋ] *adj*: **~ member** *полнопра́вный член полити́ческой организа́ции.*

card game *n* игра́* в ка́рты.

cardiac ['kɑ:dɪæk] *adj* серде́чный; (*unit*) кардиологи́ческий*.

Cardiff ['kɑ:dɪf] *n* Ка́рдифф.

cardigan ['kɑ:dɪgən] *n* жаке́т (*вя́заный*).

cardinal ['kɑ:dɪnl] *adj* (*also:* **~ number**) коли́чественное числи́тельное *nt adj*; (*sin*) сме́ртный; (*principle, importance*) кардина́льный ♦ *n* кардина́л.

card index *n* картоте́ка.

cardsharp ['kɑ:dʃɑ:p] *n* шу́лер*.

card vote *n* (*BRIT*) манда́тное голосова́ние.

CARE [kɛəʳ] *n abbr* = *Cooperative for American Relief Everywhere*.

care [kɛəʳ] *n* (*worry*) забо́та; (*of the ill*) ухо́д; (*attention*) внима́ние ♦ *vi*: **to ~ about** (*person, animal*) забо́титься* (позабо́титься* *perf*) о +*prp*; **in sb's ~** на чьём-н попече́нии; **the child has been taken into ~** ребёнок был взят в де́тский дом; **"handle with ~"** "не кантова́ть"; **to take ~ (to do)** позабо́титься (*perf*) (+*infin*); **to take ~ of** (*patient, child etc*) забо́титься* (позабо́титься* *perf*) о +*prp*; (*problem, situation*) занима́ться (заня́ться* *perf*) +*instr*; **~ of** для переда́чи +*dat*; **he ~s about environmental issues** его́ волну́ют пробле́мы защиты́ окружа́ющей среды́; **would you ~ to/for ...?** не хоти́те ли +*infin/*+*acc*; **I wouldn't ~ to repeat the experience** мне бы не хоте́лось испыта́ть э́то сно́ва; **I**

don't ~ мне всё равно́; **I couldn't** ~ **less** мне наплева́ть
▶ **care for** *vt fus* (*look after*) забо́титься* (позабо́титься* *perf*) о +*prp*; (*like*): **he ~s for her** он неравноду́шен к ней.
career [kə'rɪə^r] *n* карье́ра ♦ *vi* мча́ться* (помча́ться* *perf*); **my school** ~ (*life*) мои́ шко́льные го́ды.
career girl *n* = **career woman**.
careers officer [kə'rɪəz-] *n* консульта́нт по профессиона́льной ориента́ции.
career woman *irreg n* делова́я же́нщина.
carefree ['kɛəfriː] *adj* беззабо́тный* (беззабо́тен).
careful ['kɛəful] *adj* (*cautious*) осторо́жный* (осторо́жен); (*thorough*) тща́тельный* (тща́телен); (**be**) ~! осторо́жно!, береги́сь!; **he is/was** ~ **with his money** он эконо́мен/был эконо́мен.
carefully ['kɛəfəlɪ] *adv* (*see adj*) осторо́жно; тща́тельно.
careless ['kɛəlɪs] *adj* (*negligent*) невнима́тельный* (невнима́телен); (*casual: remark*) небре́жный* (небре́жен); (*untroubled*) беззабо́тный* (беззабо́тен).
carelessly ['kɛəlɪslɪ] *adv* (*see adj*) невнима́тельно; небре́жно; беззабо́тно.
carelessness ['kɛəlɪsnɪs] *n* (*negligence*) невнима́тельность *f*; (*casualness*) небре́жность *f*; (*lack of concern*) беззабо́тность *f*.
carer ['kɛərə^r] *n* челове́к, уха́живающий за больны́ми, престаре́лыми и т.п.
caress [kə'rɛs] *n* ла́ска* ♦ *vt* ласка́ть (*impf*).
caretaker ['kɛəteɪkə^r] *n* (*of building*) завхо́з.
caretaker government *n* (*BRIT*) вре́менное прави́тельство.
car ferry *n* автомоби́льный паро́м.
cargo ['kɑːgəu] (*pl* ~**es**) *n* груз.
cargo boat *n* грузово́е су́дно*.
cargo plane *n* грузово́й самолёт.
car hire *n* (*BRIT*) прока́т автомоби́лей.
Caribbean [kærɪ'biːən] *adj* кари́бский ♦ *n*: **the** ~ (**Sea**) Кари́бское мо́ре*.
caricature ['kærɪkətjuə^r] *n* карикату́ра; ~ **of the truth** карикату́ра на пра́вду.
caring ['kɛərɪŋ] *adj* забо́тливый (забо́тлив).
carjack [kɑː'dʒæk] *n* домкра́т.
carnage ['kɑːnɪdʒ] *n* резня́.
carnal ['kɑːnl] *adj* пло́тский*.
carnation [kɑː'neɪʃən] *n* гвозди́ка.
carnival ['kɑːnɪvl] *n* карнава́л; (*US: funfair*) аттракцио́нный городо́к*.
carnivorous [kɑː'nɪvərəs] *adj* (*animal*) плотоя́дный*; (*plant*) насекомоя́дный*.
carol ['kærəl] *n* (*also:* **Christmas** ~) Рожде́ственский* гимн.
carouse [kə'rauz] *vi* бра́жничать (*impf*).

carousel [kærə'sɛl] *n* (*US*) карусе́ль *f*.
carp [kɑːp] *n* карп
▶ **carp at** *vt fus* придира́ться (придра́ться* *perf*) к +*dat*.
car park *n* (*BRIT*) автостоя́нка*.
Carpathian Mountains [kɑː'peɪθɪən-] *npl* Карпа́ты *pl*.
carpenter ['kɑːpɪntə^r] *n* пло́тник.
carpentry ['kɑːpɪntrɪ] *n* пло́тницкое де́ло.
carpet ['kɑːpɪt] *n* (*also fig*) ковёр*; (*of snow*) покро́в ♦ *vt* (*room*) устила́ть (устла́ть* *perf*) ковра́ми; **fitted** ~ (*BRIT*) ковро́вое покры́тие.
carpet bombing *n* ковро́вое бомбомета́ние.
carpet slippers *npl* шлёпанцы *mpl*.
carpet sweeper [-'swiːpə^r] *n* щётка для ковра́.
car phone *n* ра́дио-телефо́н (*в маши́не*).
carport ['kɑːpɔːt] *n* наве́с для маши́ны.
car rental *n* прока́т автомоби́лей.
carriage ['kærɪdʒ] *n* (*BRIT: RAIL*) (пассажи́рский*) ваго́н; (*horse-drawn*) экипа́ж; (*of goods*) перево́зка; (*of typewriter*) каре́тка*; (*transport costs*) сто́имость *f* перево́зки; ~ **forward** сто́имость перево́зки подлежи́т опла́те получа́телем; ~ **free** перево́зка осуществля́ется беспла́тно; ~ **inwards** су́мма, опла́чиваемая покупа́телем за доста́вку полу́ченного гру́за; ~ **outwards** су́мма, предста́вленная продавцо́м к опла́те на покры́тие расхо́дов по доста́вке; ~ **paid** за перево́зку упла́чено.
carriage return *n* перево́д каре́тки.
carriageway ['kærɪdʒweɪ] *n* (*BRIT*) прое́зжая часть *f* доро́ги.
carrier ['kærɪə^r] *n* (*transporter*) транспорти́ровщик; (*MED*) носи́тель *m*.
carrier bag *n* (*BRIT*) паке́тик (*для поку́пок*).
carrier pigeon *n* почто́вый го́лубь* *m*.
carrion ['kærɪən] *n* па́даль *f*.
carrot ['kærət] *n* морко́вь *f*; (*fig*): ~ **and stick policy** поли́тика кнута́ и пря́ника.
carry ['kærɪ] *vt* (*take*) носи́ть*/нести́* (*impf*); (*transport*) вози́ть*/везти́* (*impf*); (*a motion, bill*) проводи́ть* (провести́* *perf*); (*involve*) влечь* (повле́чь* *perf*); (*MED*) переноси́ть* (*impf*); (*have: picture, slogan*) содержа́ть* (*impf*) ♦ *vi* (*sound*) передава́ться* (*impf*); **he carries the virus** он носи́тель ви́руса; **this loan carries 10% interest per annum** э́тот заём предоставля́ется под 10% годовы́х; **to get carried away (by)** (*fig*) увлека́ться (увле́чься* *perf*) (+*instr*)
▶ **carry forward** *vt* (*also COMM*) переноси́ть* (перенести́* *perf*) на другу́ю страни́цу
▶ **carry on** *vi* (*continue*) продолжа́ться (продо́лжиться* *perf*); (*inf: make a fuss*) заводи́ться* (завести́сь* *perf*) ♦ *vt* продолжа́ть (продо́лжить *perf*); **to** ~ **on with sth/doing** продолжа́ть (продо́лжить *perf*) что-н/+*impf*

---

* marks translations which have irregular inflections. The Russian-English side of the dictionary gives inflectional information.

infin

► **carry out** *vt* (*orders*) выполнять (выполнить *perf*), исполнять (исполнить *perf*); (*investigation*) проводить* (провести* *perf*); (*threat*) осуществлять (осуществить* *perf*).

carrycot ['kærɪkɔt] *n* (*BRIT*) переносная колыбель *f*.

carry-on ['kærɪ'ɔn] *n* (*inf: fuss*) суматоха, суета; (: *annoying behaviour*) капризы *mpl*; **I've had enough of your ~!** надоели мне твои капризы!; **what a ~!** какая суматоха *or* суета!

cart [kɑːt] *n* телега, повозка; (*handcart*) тележка* ♦ *vt* (*inf: people, objects*) таскать/ тащить* (*impf*).

carte blanche ['kɑːt'blɒnʃ] *n*: **to give sb ~ ~** предоставлять (предоставить* *perf*) кому-н полную свободу действий.

cartel [kɑː'tɛl] *n* картель *m*.

cartilage ['kɑːtɪlɪdʒ] *n* хрящ*.

cartographer [kɑː'tɔgrəfə'] *n* картограф.

cartography [kɑː'tɔgrəfɪ] *n* картография.

carton ['kɑːtən] *n* (*large box*) картонная коробка*; (*container*) пакет.

cartoon [kɑː'tuːn] *n* (*drawing*) карикатура; (*BRIT: comic strip*) комикс; (*TV*) мультфильм= *мультипликационный фильм*.

cartoonist [kɑː'tuːnɪst] *n* карикатурист(ка).

cartridge ['kɑːtrɪdʒ] *n* (*for gun*) гильза; (*for camera*) кассета с фотоплёнкой; (*music tape*) кассета; (*of record-player*) головка*; (*of pen*) (чернильный) баллончик; (*of printer*) картридж.

cartwheel ['kɑːtwiːl] *n* колесо* телеги; **to turn a ~** делать (сделать *perf*) колесо.

carve [kɑːv] *vt* (*meat*) нарезать (нарезать* *perf*); (*initials, design*) вырезать (вырезать* *perf*); (*wood, stone*) вырезать (*impf*)

► **carve up** *vt* (*land, property*) раздроблять (раздробить* *perf*); (*meat*) разрезать (разрезать* *perf*).

carving ['kɑːvɪŋ] *n* (*object*) резное изделие; (*design*) резьба; (*art*) искусство резьбы.

carving knife *n* разделочный нож*.

car wash *n* мойка автомобилей.

Casablanca [kæsə'blæŋkə] *n* Касабланка.

cascade [kæs'keɪd] *n* (*waterfall*) каскад ♦ *vi* (*water*) низвергаться (*impf*); (*hair*) ниспадать (*impf*).

case [keɪs] *n* (*instance, problem*) случай; (*MED: patient*) больной(-ая) *m(f) adj*; (*LAW*) (судебное) дело*; (*criminal investigation*) расследование; (*for spectacles etc*) футляр; (*BRIT: also: suitcase*) чемодан; (*of wine etc*) ящик (*содержащий* 12 *бутылок*); (*TYP*): **lower/upper ~** нижний/верхний* регистр; **to have a good ~** иметь (*impf*) убедительные доводы; **there's a strong ~ for reform** есть все основания для проведения реформы; **in ~ (of)** (*fire, emergency*) в случае (+*gen*); **in ~ he** comes в случае, если он придёт; **in any ~** во всяком случае; **just in ~** на всякий* случай.

case history *n* (*MED*) история болезни.

case study *n* изучение конкретного случая.

cash [kæʃ] *n* наличные *pl adj* (деньги) ♦ *vt*: **to ~ a cheque** обменивать (обменять *perf*) чек на деньги; **to pay (in) ~** платить* (заплатить* *perf*) наличными; **~ on delivery** наложенный платёж; **~ with order** оплата при совершении заказа

► **cash in** *vt* получать (получить* *perf*) деньги по +*dat*

► **cash in on** *vt fus* использовать (*impf*) в своих интересах.

cash account *n* наличный счёт*.

cash-and-carry [kæʃən'kærɪ] *n* мелкооптовый магазин*.

cash-book ['kæʃbuk] *n* кассовая книга.

cash box *n* коробка для хранения кассы.

cash card *n* (*BRIT*) *карточка для получения наличных из автомата*.

cash cow *n* (*enterprise*) хлебное дело*; (*product*) золотое дно*.

cash crop *n* товарная культура.

cash desk *n* (*BRIT*) касса.

cash discount *n* скидка с цены товара в случае уплаты наличными.

cash dispenser *n* (*BRIT*) банкомат.

cashew [kæ'ʃuː] *n* (*also: ~ nut*) орех кешью *m ind*.

cash flow *n* движение денежной наличности.

cashier [kæ'ʃɪə'] *n* кассир.

cashmere ['kæʃmɪə'] *n* (*wool, jersey*) кашемир.

cash point *n* банкомат.

cash price *n* цена товара при продаже за наличные.

cash register *n* кассовый аппарат.

cash reserves *npl* кассовый резерв *msg*.

cash sale *n* продажа за наличные *pl adj*.

casing ['keɪsɪŋ] *n* оболочка*, футляр.

casino [kə'siːnəu] *n* казино *nt ind*.

cask [kɑːsk] *n* бочонок*.

casket ['kɑːskɪt] *n* шкатулка; (*US: coffin*) гроб*.

Caspian Sea ['kæspɪən-] *n* (*GEO*): **the ~ ~** Каспийское море*.

casserole ['kæsərəul] *n* рагу *nt ind*; (*also: ~ dish*) латка*.

cassette [kæ'sɛt] *n* кассета.

cassette deck *n* кассетный магнитофон (*стационарный*).

cassette player *n* кассетный плейер.

cassette recorder *n* кассетный магнитофон (*портативный*).

cast [kɑːst] (*pt, pp* **cast**) *vt* (*light, shadow, glance*) бросать (бросить* *perf*); (*net, fishing line*) забрасывать (забросить* *perf*); (*doubts*) сеять (посеять *perf*); (*spell*) околдовывать (околдовать *perf*); (*skin*) сбрасывать (сбросить* *perf*); (*statue*) отливать (отлить*

perf) ♦ *vi (FISHING)* забрасывать (забросить*
perf) сети ♦ *n (THEAT)* состав (исполнителей);
(mould) форма *(для отливки); (also:* **plaster**
~) гипсовый слепок*; **to ~ one's vote (for sb)**
отдавать* (отдать* *perf)* свой голос (за
кого-н); **to ~ sb as Hamlet** *(THEAT)* назначать
(назначить *perf)* кого-н на роль Гамлета;
the ~ was full of celebrities в спектакле
играло много знаменитостей
▶ **cast aside** *vt* отвергать (отвергнуть *perf)*
▶ **cast off** *vi (NAUT)* отчаливать (отчалить
perf); (KNITTING) сбрасывать (сбросить* *perf)*
петлю ♦ *vt (KNITTING)* сбрасывать (сбросить*
perf) (петлю)
▶ **cast on** *vi (KNITTING)* набирать (набрать*
perf) петли ♦ *vt* набирать (набрать* *perf)*
(петли).
castaway ['kɑ:stəweɪ] *n попавший после
кораблекрушения на необитаемый остров.*
caste [kɑ:st] *n* каста; **the ~ system** кастовая
система.
caster sugar ['kɑ:stə-] *n (BRIT)* сахарная пудра.
casting vote ['kɑ:stɪŋ-] *n (BRIT)* решающий*
голос *(при равном числе голосов "за" и
"против").*
cast iron *n* чугун* ♦ *adj:* ~~~ *(fig)* железный.
castle ['kɑ:sl] *n* замок*; *(fortified)* крепость *f;
(CHESS)* ладья*, тура.
cast-offs ['kɑ:stɔfs] *npl* обноски *mpl.*
castor ['kɑ:stə] *n (wheel)* ролик.
castor oil *n* касторовое масло.
castrate [kæs'treɪt] *vt* кастрировать *(impf/perf).*
casual ['kæʒjul] *adj (meeting)* случайный*
(случаен); (attitude) небрежный* (небрежен);
(clothes) повседневный; **to do ~ work** делать
(impf) случайную работу; ~ **wear**
повседневная одежда.
casual labour *n* временные работники *mpl.*
casually ['kæʒjulɪ] *adv (behave)* небрежно;
(dress) повседневно; *(by chance)* случайно;
he was ~ dressed он был одет в повсе-
дневную одежду.
casualty ['kæʒjultɪ] *n (sb injured)*
пострадавший(-ая) *m(f) adj; (sb killed, victim)*
жертва; *(MED: department)* травматология;
heavy casualties тяжёлые потери *fpl.*
casualty ward *n (BRIT)* травматологическое
отделение.
cat [kæt] *n (pet)* кошка*; *(tomcat)* кот; **big ~s**
кошачьи *pl adj.*
catacombs ['kætəku:mz] *npl* катакомбы *fpl.*
catalogue ['kætəlɔg] *(US* **catalog)** *n* каталог; *(of
events, faults)* перечень *m* ♦ *vt (books,
collection)* каталогизировать *(impf/perf);
(events)* перечислять (перечислить *perf).*
catalyst ['kætəlɪst] *n (CHEM, fig)* катализатор.
catalytic converter [kætə'lɪtɪk kən'və:tə] *n
(AUT)* каталитический нейтрализатор.

catapult ['kætəpʌlt] *n (BRIT)* рогатка*; *(MIL)*
катапульта ♦ *vi* катапультироваться *(impf/
perf)* ♦ *vt* катапультировать *(impf/perf).*
cataract ['kætərækt] *n* катаракта.
catarrh [kə'tɑ:'] *n* катар.
catastrophe [kə'tæstrəfɪ] *n* катастрофа.
catastrophic [kætə'strɔfɪk] *adj*
катастрофический*.
catcall ['kætkɔ:l] *n* освистывание.
catch [kætʃ] *(pt, pp* **caught)** *vt* ловить* (поймать
perf); (bus etc) садиться (сесть* *perf)* на +*acc;
(breath)* затаивать (затаить *perf); (attention)*
привлекать (привлечь* *perf); (hit)* ударять
(ударить *perf); (hear)* улавливать (уловить*
perf); (illness) подхватывать (подхватить*
perf); (person) заставать (застать* *perf)* ♦ *vi
(become trapped)* застревать (застрять *perf)*
♦ *n (of fish)* улов; *(criminal caught)*
задержанный(-ая) *m(f) adj; (of ball)* захват;
(hidden problem) подвох; *(of lock)* защёлка;
(game) пятнашки *pl;* **to ~ sb's attention** *or* **eye**
привлекать (привлечь* *perf)* чьё-н внимание;
to ~ sight of увидеть* *(perf);* **to ~ fire**
загореться* *perf.*
▶ **catch on** *vi (grow popular)* приживаться
(прижиться* *perf); (understand):* **to ~ on (to
sth)** понимать (понять* *perf)* (что-н)
▶ **catch out** *vt (BRIT: fig)* ловить* (поймать *perf)*
▶ **catch up** *vi (fig)* нагонять (нагнать* *perf)* ♦ *vt
(also:* ~ **up with)** догонять (догнать* *perf).*
catching ['kætʃɪŋ] *adj (fig)* заразительный*;
(MED) заразный*.
catchment area ['kætʃmənt-] *n (BRIT: of school
etc)* микрорайон; *(GEO)* бассейн.
catch phrase *n* модное выражение.
catch-22 ['kætʃtwentɪ'tu:] *n:* **it's a ~ situation**
это безвыходная ситуация.
catchy ['kætʃɪ] *adj* легко запоминающийся.
catechism ['kætɪkɪzəm] *n* катехизис.
categoric(al) [kætɪ'gɔrɪk(l)] *adj*
категорический*.
categorize ['kætɪgəraɪz] *vt (classify)*
классифицировать *(impf/perf).*
category ['kætɪgərɪ] *n* категория.
cater ['keɪtə] *vi (provide food):* **to ~ (for)**
организовывать (организовать *perf)*
питание *(для +gen)*
▶ **cater for** *vt fus (BRIT: needs, tastes)*
удовлетворять (удовлетворить *perf);
(: readers, consumers)* обслуживать
(обслужить* *perf).*
caterer ['keɪtərə'] *n* организатор питания.
catering ['keɪtərɪŋ] *n (trade, business)*
общественное питание.
caterpillar ['kætəpɪlə'] *n* гусеница ♦ *cpd
(vehicle)* гусеничный*.
caterpillar track *n* гусеница *(TEX)*
cat flap *n* кошачий* лаз* *(в двери),* кошачья

две́рца.

cathedral [kə'θiːdrəl] *n* собо́р.

cathode ['kæθəud] *n* като́д.

cathode-ray tube [kæθəud'reɪ-] *n* электроннолучева́я тру́бка*.

Catholic ['kæθəlɪk] *adj* католи́ческий* ◆ *n* като́лик(-и́чка).

catholic *adj* (*tastes, interests*) разносторо́нний*.

CAT scanner *n abbr* (*MED*: = *computerized axial tomography scanner*) аксиа́льный компью́терный томо́граф.

Catseye® ['kæts'aɪ] *n* (*BRIT*: *AUT*) "коша́чий глаз" (*вмонти́рованный в доро́гу отража́тель све́та фар*).

catsup ['kætsəp] *n* (*US*) ке́тчуп.

cattle ['kætl] *npl* скот* *msg*.

catty ['kætɪ] *adj* ехи́дный*.

catwalk ['kætwɔːk] *n* помо́ст *or* эстра́да (*для демонстра́ции моде́лей оде́жды*).

Caucasian [kɔː'keɪzɪən] *adj* кавка́зский ◆ *n* кавка́зец*(-зка).

Caucasus ['kɔːkəsəs] *n* Кавка́з.

caucus ['kɔːkəs] *n* (*POL*: *group*) влия́тельная группиро́вка внутри́ па́ртии; (: *US*) предвы́борный ми́тинг сторо́нников па́ртии.

caught [kɔːt] *pt, pp of* **catch**.

cauliflower ['kɔlɪflauə'] *n* цветна́я капу́ста.

cause [kɔːz] *n* (*reason*) причи́на; (*aim*) де́ло* ◆ *vt* явля́ться (яви́ться* *perf*) причи́ной +*gen*; **there is no ~ for concern** нет причи́н для беспоко́йства; **to ~ sb trouble/harm** причиня́ть (причини́ть* *perf*) кому́-н неприя́тности/вред; **to ~ sb to do** (*force*) заставля́ть (заста́вить* *perf*) кого́-н +*infin*.

causeway ['kɔːzweɪ] *n* доро́га (*проло́женная че́рез то́пкое ме́сто*).

caustic ['kɔːstɪk] *adj* каусти́ческий*; (*fig*) е́дкий*.

cauterize ['kɔːtəraɪz] *vt* прижига́ть (прижёчь* *perf*).

caution ['kɔːʃən] *n* осторо́жность *f*; (*warning*) предупрежде́ние, предостереже́ние ◆ *vt* предупрежда́ть (предупреди́ть *perf*).

cautious ['kɔːʃəs] *adj* осторо́жный* (осторо́жен).

cautiously ['kɔːʃəslɪ] *adv* осторо́жно.

cautiousness ['kɔːʃəsnɪs] *n* осторо́жность *f*.

cavalier [kævə'lɪə'] *adj* надме́нный*, пренебрежи́тельный.

cavalry ['kævəlrɪ] *n* кавале́рия; (*mechanized*) мотопехо́та.

cave [keɪv] *n* пеще́ра ◆ *vi*: **to go caving** занима́ться (*impf*) спелеоло́гией

► **cave in** *vi* (*roof etc*) обва́ливаться (обвали́ться *perf*); (*inf*: *give in*) сдава́ться* (сда́ться* *perf*).

caveman ['keɪvmæn] *irreg n* пеще́рный челове́к*.

cavern ['kævən] *n* пеще́ра.

caviar(e) ['kævɪɑː'] *n* икра́*.

cavity ['kævɪtɪ] *n* по́лость* *f*; (*in tooth*) дупло́*.

cavity wall insulation *n* двойна́я стена́ с изоля́цией.

cavort [kə'vɔːt] *vi* скака́ть* (*impf*).

cayenne [keɪ'ɛn] *n* (*also*: ~ **pepper**) кра́сный стручко́вый пе́рец.

CB *n abbr* (= *Citizens' Band (Radio)*) диапазо́н часто́т люби́тельской радиосвя́зи; (*BRIT*: = *Companion of (the Order of) the Bath*) кавале́р о́рдена Ба́ни.

CBC *n abbr* = *Canadian Broadcasting Corporation*.

CBE *n abbr* (*BRIT*: = *Companion of (the Order of) the British Empire*) кавале́р о́рдена Брита́нской Импе́рии.

CBI *n abbr* (= *Confederation of British Industries*) Конфеде́рация брита́нской промы́шленности.

CBS *n abbr* (*US*) = *Columbia Broadcasting System*.

CC *abbr* (*BRIT*: = *county council*) ≈ сове́т гра́фства.

cc *abbr* (= *cubic centimetre*) куби́ческий* сантиме́тр; = **carbon copy**.

CCA *n abbr* (*US*: = *Circuit Court of Appeals*) Окружно́й апелляцио́нный суд.

CCTV *n abbr* = **closed-circuit television**.

CCU *n abbr* (*US*: = *coronary care unit*) отделе́ние интенси́вной терапи́и для больны́х с о́строй серде́чной недоста́точностью.

CD *abbr* (*BRIT*: = *Corps Diplomatique*) ≈ дипко́рпус= *дипломати́ческий ко́рпус* ◆ *n abbr* (*MIL*: *BRIT*: = *Civil Defence (Corps)*) гражда́нская оборо́на; (: *US*: = *Civil Defense*) гражда́нская оборо́на; = **compact disc**; ~ **player** прои́грыватель *m* для компа́кт-ди́сков. '

CDC *n abbr* (*US*) = *Center for Disease Control*.

CD-I *n abbr* (= *compact disc interactive*) компа́ктный диск-интеракти́вный (*устро́йство, позволя́ющее передава́ть содержа́ние компа́ктного ди́ска на телеэкра́н*).

Cdr. *abbr* (*MIL*) = **commander**.

CD-ROM *abbr* (= *compact disc read-only memory*) па́мять, счи́тывающая информа́цию с компа́кт-ди́ска.

CDT *abbr* (*US*) = *Central Daylight Time*.

cease [siːs] *vt* прекраща́ть (прекрати́ть* *perf*) ◆ *vi* прекраща́ться (прекрати́ться* *perf*).

cease-fire ['siːsfaɪə'] *n* прекраще́ние огня́.

ceaseless ['siːslɪs] *adj* непреры́вный*.

CED *n abbr* (*US*) = *Committee for Economic Development*.

cedar ['siːdə'] *n* кедр.

cede [siːd] *vt* уступа́ть (уступи́ть* *perf*).

cedilla [sɪ'dɪlə] *n* седи́ль *m* (*орфографи́ческий знак*).

CEEB *n abbr* (*US*) = *College Entry Examination Board*.

Ceefax ['siːfæks] *n информацио́нная слу́жба*

БиБиСи, *осуществляемая путём вывода на экран телевизора информации, классифицированной по различным направлениям.*

ceilidh ['keɪlɪ] *n* вечер народной музыки.

ceiling ['si:lɪŋ] *n* (*also fig*) потолок*.

celebrate ['sɛlɪbreɪt] *vt* праздновать (отпраздновать *perf*) ♦ *vi* веселиться (повеселиться *perf*); **to ~ mass** отправлять (*impf*) церковную службу.

celebrated ['sɛlɪbreɪtɪd] *adj* знаменитый (знаменит).

celebration [sɛlɪ'breɪʃən] *n* (*event*) праздник; (*of anniversary etc*) празднование.

celebrity [sɪ'lɛbrɪtɪ] *n* знаменитость *f*.

celeriac [sə'lɛrɪæk] *n* корнеплод сельдерея.

celery ['sɛlərɪ] *n* сельдерей.

celestial [sɪ'lɛstɪəl] *adj* небесный.

celibacy ['sɛlɪbəsɪ] *n* сексуальное воздержание; (*unmarried state*) безбрачие.

cell [sɛl] *n* (*in prison*) камера; (*in monastery*) келья*; (*of revolutionaries etc*) ячейка*; (*BIO*) клетка*; (*ELEC*) элемент.

cellar ['sɛlə'] *n* подвал; (*also:* **wine ~**) винный погреб*.

cellist ['tʃɛlɪst] *n* виолончелист(ка).

cello ['tʃɛləu] *n* виолончель *f*.

cellophane ['sɛləfeɪn] *n* целлофан.

cellphone ['sɛlfəun] *n* портативный телефон.

cellular ['sɛljulə'] *adj* (*BIO*) клеточный; (*fabrics*) сетчатый.

celluloid ['sɛljulɔɪd] *n* целлулоид.

cellulose ['sɛljuləus] *n* клетчатка, целлюлоза.

Celsius ['sɛlsɪəs] *adj*: **30 degrees ~** 30 градусов по Цельсию.

Celt [kɛlt] *n* кельт.

Celtic ['kɛltɪk] *adj* кельтский* ♦ *n* (*LING*) кельтский* язык*.

cement [sə'mɛnt] *n* цемент; (*glue*) клей* ♦ *vt* (*also fig*) цементировать (*impf/perf*); (*stick, glue*): **to ~ to** приклеивать (приклеить *perf*) *or* прикреплять (прикрепить* *perf*) к +*dat.*

cement mixer *n* бетономешалка*.

cemetery ['sɛmɪtrɪ] *n* кладбище.

cenotaph ['sɛnətɑ:f] *n* памятник погибшим солдатам.

censor ['sɛnsə'] *n* цензор ♦ *vt* подвергать (подвергнуть* *perf*) цензуре.

censorship ['sɛnsəʃɪp] *n* цензура.

censure ['sɛnʃə'] *vt* осуждать (осудить* *perf*), порицать (*impf*) *n* осуждение, порицание.

census ['sɛnsəs] *n* (*of population*) перепись *f.*

cent [sɛnt] *n* (*US etc: coin*) цент; *see also* **per.**

centenary [sɛn'ti:nərɪ] *n* столетие.

centennial [sɛn'tɛnɪəl] *n* (*US*) столетие.

center *etc n* (*US*) = **centre** *etc.*

centigrade ['sɛntɪgreɪd] *adj*: **30 degrees ~** 30 градусов по Цельсию.

centilitre ['sɛntɪli:tə'] (*US* **centiliter**) *n* центилитр.

centimetre ['sɛntɪmi:tə'] (*US* **centimeter**) *n* сантиметр.

centipede ['sɛntɪpi:d] *n* многоножка*.

central ['sɛntrəl] *adj* центральный*; **this flat is very ~** эта квартира расположена близко к центру города.

Central African Republic *n* Центрально-Африканская республика.

Central America *n* Центральная Америка.

central heating *n* центральное отопление.

centralize ['sɛntrəlaɪz] *vt* централизовать (*impf/perf*).

central processing unit *n* центральный процессор.

central reservation *n* (*BRIT: AUT*) разделительная полоса.

centre ['sɛntə'] (*US* **center**) *n* центр ♦ *vt* (*PHOT, TYP*) центрировать (*impf/perf*); (*SPORT: ball*) подавать* (подать* *perf*) в центр поля; (*concentrate on*): **to ~ (on)** сосредоточиваться (сосредоточиться *perf*) (на +*prp*); **to ~ sth on** сосредоточивать (сосредоточить *perf*) что-н на +*acc.*

centrefold ['sɛntəfəuld] (*US* **centerfold**) *n* центральная вкладка*.

centre forward *n* (*SPORT*) центральный нападающий* *m adj*, центр-форвард.

centre half *n* (*SPORT*) центральный полузащитник.

centrepiece ['sɛntəpi:s] (*US* **centerpiece**) *n* декоративный предмет, выставленный посередине стола, полки итд; (*fig*) главное украшение.

centre spread *n* (*BRIT: PRESS*) разворот.

centre-stage [sɛntə'steɪdʒ] *n* центр сцены.

centrifugal [sɛn'trɪfjugl] *adj* (*PHYS*) центробежный.

centrifuge ['sɛntrɪfju:ʒ] *n* центрифуга.

century ['sɛntjurɪ] *n* век*; (*CRICKET*) сто очков; **twentieth ~** двадцатый век; **in the twentieth ~** в двадцатом веке.

CEO *n abbr* (*US: = chief executive officer*) главный администратор.

ceramic [sɪ'ræmɪk] *adj* керамический*.

ceramics [sɪ'ræmɪks] *npl* керамика *fsg.*

cereal ['si:rɪəl] *n* (*plant, crop*): **~s** зерновые *pl adj*; (*also:* **breakfast ~**) хлопья *pl* к завтраку.

cerebral ['sɛrɪbrəl] *adj* (*MED*) мозговой, церебральный; (*intellectual*) умозрительный* (умозрителен); **~ palsy** церебральный паралич.

ceremonial [sɛrɪ'məunɪəl] *n* церемониал ♦ *adj* обрядовый.

ceremony ['sɛrɪmənɪ] *n* церемония; (*behaviour*) церемонии *fpl*; **with ~** со всеми

---

* marks translations which have irregular inflections. The Russian-English side of the dictionary gives inflectional information.

формáльностями; **to stand on** ~ настáивать (настоя́ть* *perf*) на соблюдéнии формáльностей.

cert [sə:t] *n* (*BRIT: inf*): **it's a dead** ~ э́то дéло вéрное.

certain ['sə:tən] *adj* (*sure*): **I'm** ~ (*that*) я увéрен (что); (*particular*): ~ **days** определённые дни; (*some*): **a** ~ **pleasure** нéкоторое удовóльствие; **it's** ~ (*that*) несомнéнно (что); **in** ~ **circumstances** при определённых обстоя́тельствах; **a** ~ **Mr Smith** нéкий Ми́стер Смит; **to make** ~ **of/that** удостоверя́ться (удостовéриться *perf*) в +*prp*/что; **for** ~ наверняка́.

certainly ['sə:tənlɪ] *adv* (*undoubtedly*) несомнéнно; (*of course*) конéчно.

certainty ['sə:təntɪ] *n* (*assurance*) увéренность *f*; (*inevitability*) несомнéнность *f*.

certificate [sə'tɪfɪkɪt] *n* (*doctor's etc*) спрáвка; (*diploma*) диплóм; **birth** ~ свидéтельство рождéнии; **marriage** ~ свидéтельство о заключéнии брáка.

certified letter ['sə:tɪfaɪd-] *n* (*US*) гаранти́рованное письмó.

certified mail *n* (*US*) гаранти́рованная пóчта.

certified public accountant *n* (*US*) бухгáлтер *вы́сшей квалифика́ции*.

certify ['sə:tɪfaɪ] *vt* (*fact*) удостоверя́ть (удостовéрить *perf*); (*after studies*) выдавáть* (вы́дать* *perf*) диплóм +*dat*; (*also:* ~ **insane**) признавáть* (призна́ть* *perf*) душевнобольны́м(-ой); **he is a certified lawyer** он дипломи́рованный юри́ст.

cervical ['sə:vɪkl] *adj*: ~ **cancer** рак шéйки мáтки; ~ **smear** мазóк* с шéйки мáтки.

cervix ['sə:vɪks] *n* шéйка мáтки.

Cesarean [si:'zɛərɪən] *adj*, *n* (*US*) = **Caesarean**.

cessation [sə'seɪʃən] *n* прекращéние.

cesspit ['sespɪt] *n* выгребнáя я́ма.

CET *abbr* (= *Central European Time*) центральноевропéйское врéмя* *nt*.

Ceylon [sɪ'lɔn] *n* Цейлóн.

cf. *abbr* = **compare**.

c/f *abbr* (*COMM:* = *carried forward*) перенесенó на слéдующую страни́цу.

CFC *n abbr* (= *chlorofluorocarbon*) хлор-фтороуглерóд.

CG *n abbr* (*US*) = **coastguard**.

cg *abbr* (= *centigram*) сантигрáмм.

CH *n abbr* (*BRIT:* = *Companion of Honour*) кавалéр óрдена.

ch. *abbr* (= **chapter**) гл. = *глава́*.

c.h. *abbr* (*BRIT*) = **central heating**.

Chad [tʃæd] *n* Чад.

chafe [tʃeɪf] *vt* (*rub*) натирáть (натерéть *perf*) ♦ *vi* (*fig*): **to** ~ **at/under** раздражáться (*impf*) из-за +*gen*.

chaffinch ['tʃæfɪntʃ] *n* зя́блик.

chagrin ['ʃægrɪn] *n* (*annoyance*) доса́да; (*disappointment*) огорчéние.

chain [tʃeɪn] *n* (*also fig*) цепь* *f*; (*decorative, on*

bicycle) цепóчка*; (*of shops, hotels*) сеть* *f*; (*of events, ideas*) верени́ца ♦ *vt* (*also:* ~ **up**: *person*) прикóвывать (прикова́ть *perf*); (*dog*) сажáть (посади́ть* *perf*) на цепь; **a** ~ **of mountains** гóрная цепь.

chain reaction *n* цепнáя реáкция.

chain-smoke ['tʃeɪnsməuk] *vi* кури́ть* (*impf*) однý сигарéту за другóй.

chain store *n* филиáл (*магази́на*).

chair [tʃɛə'] *n* стул*; (*also: armchair*) крéсло*; (*of university*) кáфедра; (*of meeting: also:* ~**person**) председáтель *m* ♦ *vt* председáтельствовать (*impf*) на +*prp*; **the** ~ (*US: also:* **the electric** ~) электри́ческий* стул*; **to take the** ~ председáтельствовать (*impf*).

chair lift *n* канáтный подъёмник.

chairman ['tʃɛəmən] *irreg n* председáтель *m*; (*BRIT: of company*) президéнт.

chairperson ['tʃɛəpə:sn] *n* председáтель *m*.

chairwoman ['tʃɛəwumən] *irreg n* председáтель *m*.

chalet ['ʃæleɪ] *n* ≈ коттéдж.

chalice ['tʃælɪs] *n* (*REL*) поти́р.

chalk [tʃɔ:k] *n* мел*

▸ **chalk up** *vt* (*fig: success etc*) заноси́ть* (занести́* *perf*) в спи́сок свои́х достижéний.

challenge ['tʃælɪndʒ] *n* вы́зов; (*challenging task*) испытáние ♦ *vt* (*rival: also SPORT*) бросáть (брóсить* *perf*) вы́зов +*dat*; (*authority, right etc*) оспáривать (оспóрить *perf*); **to** ~ **sb to sth** вызывáть (вы́звать* *perf*) когó-н на что-н.

challenger ['tʃælɪndʒə'] *n* (*in sport*) претендéнт(ка).

challenging ['tʃælɪndʒɪŋ] *adj* (*task*) трýдный* (трýден); (*tone, look*) вызывáющий*; **this work is very** ~ э́та рабóта трéбует большóй отдáчи.

chamber ['tʃeɪmbə'] *n* (*room*) кáмера; (*POL*) палáта; (*BRIT: LAW: usu pl*) адвокáтская контóра; ~ **of commerce** Торгóвая Палáта.

chambermaid ['tʃeɪmbəmeɪd] *n* гóрничная *f adj*.

chamber music *n* кáмерная мýзыка.

chamber pot *n* ночнóй горшóк*.

chameleon [kə'mi:lɪən] *n* хамелеóн.

chamois ['ʃæmwa:] *n* (*ZOOL*) сéрна; (*also:* ~ **leather**) зáмша.

champagne [ʃæm'peɪn] *n* шампáнское *nt adj*.

champers ['ʃæmpəz] *n* (*inf*) шампáнское *nt adj*.

champion ['tʃæmpɪən] *n* (*SPORT*) чемпиóн; (*of cause*) побóрник(-ица); (*of person*) защи́тник(-ица) ♦ *vt* защищáть (защити́ть* *perf*).

championship ['tʃæmpɪənʃɪp] *n* (*contest*) чемпионáт; (*title*) звáние чемпиóна.

chance [tʃɑ:ns] *n* (*hope, possibility*) шанс; (*opportunity*) возмóжность *f*; (*risk*) риск ♦ *vt* (*risk*) рискова́ть (*impf*) +*instr* ♦ *adj* случáйный; **the** ~**s are that ...** все шáнсы за то, что ...;

there is little ~ of his coming маловероятно, что он придёт; **to take a ~** рискнуть *(perf)*; **by ~** случайно; **to leave to ~** оставлять (оставить* *perf*) на волю случая; **it's the ~ of a lifetime** такая возможность представляется раз в жизни; **to ~ it** рискнуть *(perf)*; **to ~ to overhear/see** *(happen)* случайно подслушать *(perf)*/увидеть *(perf)*
▶ **chance (up)on** *vt fus* случайно наткнуться *(perf)* на *+acc.*

chancel ['tʃɑ:nsəl] *n* алтарная часть *f.*

chancellor ['tʃɑ:nsələ'] *n* (*POL*) канцлер; (*BRIT: of university*) почётный ректор (*номинальный пост*).

Chancellor of the Exchequer *n* (*BRIT*) канцлер казначейства (*министр финансов*).

chancy ['tʃɑ:nsɪ] *adj* рискованный (рискован).

chandelier [ʃændə'lɪə'] *n* люстра.

change [tʃeɪndʒ] *vt* менять (поменять *perf*); (*wheel, bulb etc*) заменять (заменить* *perf*); (*job, address*) сменять (сменить* *perf*); (*money: to different currency*) обменивать (обменять *perf*); (: *for smaller notes or coins*) разменивать (разменять *perf*) ♦ *vi* (*alter*) меняться (*impf*), изменяться (измениться* *perf*); (*one's clothes*) переодеваться (переодеться* *perf*); (*change trains, buses*) делать (сделать *perf*) пересадку ♦ *n* (*alteration*) изменение; (*difference*) перемена; (*replacement*) смена; (*coins: also:* **small or loose ~**) мелочь *f*; (*money returned*) сдача; **to ~ sb into** превращать (превратить* *perf*) кого-н в *+acc*; **to ~ one's mind** передумывать (передумать *perf*); **to ~ gear** (*AUT*) переключать (переключить *perf*) скорость; **to ~ a baby's nappy** перепелёнывать (перепеленать *perf*) ребёнка; **to ~ into** (*be transformed*) превращаться (превратиться* *perf*) в *+acc*; **a ~ of clothes** смена одежды; **to give sb ~ for** *or* **of ten pounds** давать* (дать* *perf*) кому-н сдачу с десяти фунтов; **keep the ~** сдачи не надо; **for a ~** для разнообразия.

changeable ['tʃeɪndʒəbl] *adj* (*weather, mood*) изменчивый (изменчив); (*person*) непостоянный* (непостоянен).

change machine *n* размéнный автомат.

changeover ['tʃeɪndʒəʊvə'] *n*: **~ (to)** (*to new system*) переход (к *+dat*).

changing ['tʃeɪndʒɪŋ] *adj* (*world*) изменяющийся; (*colours*) меняющийся.

changing room *n* (*BRIT: in shop*) примерочная *f adj*; (: *SPORT*) раздевалка*.

channel ['tʃænl] *n* канал; (*for shipping*) трасса; (*groove*) жёлоб ♦ *vt*: **to ~ into** (*money, interest*) направлять (направить* *perf*) на *+acc*; **through the usual ~s** через обычные каналы; **~s of communication** каналы связи; **green/red ~** зелёный/красный канал (*при*

таможенном контроле); **the (English) C~** Ла-Манш; **the C~ Islands** Нормандские острова *mpl.*

Channel Tunnel *n* туннель *m* под Ла-Маншем.

chant [tʃɑ:nt] *n* (*of crowd, fans etc*) скандирование; (*REL: song*) пение ♦ *vti* (*shout*) скандировать (*impf*); **the demonstrators ~ed their disapproval** демонстранты хором выражали неодобрение.

chaos ['keɪɔs] *n* хаос.

chaos theory *n*: **the ~~** теория хаоса.

chaotic [keɪ'ɔtɪk] *adj* (*mess, situation*) хаотичный* (хаотичен).

chap [tʃæp] *n* (*BRIT: inf*) парень* *m*; (*term of address*): **old ~** старина *m*, старик.

chapel ['tʃæpl] *n* (*in church*) придел; (*in hospital, prison, school etc*) часовня; (*BRIT: also:* **non-conformist ~**) протестантская нон-конформистская церковь*; (: *of trade union*) отделение профсоюза полиграфистов.

chaperone ['ʃæpərəʊn] *n* (*for woman*) компаньонка ♦ *vt* сопровождать (сопроводить* *perf*).

chaplain ['tʃæplɪn] *n* капеллан.

chapped [tʃæpt] *adj* (*skin, lips etc*) потрескавшийся.

chapter ['tʃæptə'] *n* (*of book*) глава*; (*of life, history*) страница; **a ~ of accidents** череда неудач.

char [tʃɑ:'] *vt* (*burn*) обугливать (обуглить *perf*) ♦ *vi* (*BRIT*) работать (*impf*) уборщицей ♦ *n* (*BRIT*) = **charlady.**

character ['kærɪktə'] *n* (*personality*) личность *f*; (*nature, strength of character*) характер; (*in novel, film*) персонаж; (*eccentric*) оригинал; (*letter, symbol*) знак; (: *COMPUT*) символ; **a person of good ~** достойный человек.

character code *n* (*COMPUT*) код символа.

characteristic ['kærɪktə'rɪstɪk] *n* характерная черта ♦ *adj*: **~ (of)** характерный* (характерен) (для *+gen*); **it is ~ of him** это характерно для него.

characterize ['kærɪktəraɪz] *vt* (*typify*) характеризовать (*impf/perf*); (*describe*): **to ~ (as)** характеризовать* (*impf/perf*) (как); **to be ~d by** характеризоваться (*impf*) *+instr.*

charade [ʃə'rɑ:d] *n* шарада; (*fig*) комедия.

charcoal ['tʃɑ:kəʊl] *n* (*fuel*) древесный уголь* *m*; (*for drawing*) уголь.

charge [tʃɑ:dʒ] *n* (*fee*) плата; (*LAW: accusation*) обвинение; (*responsibility*) ответственность *f*; (*of gun, battery*) заряд; (*MIL: attack*) атака ♦ *vi* (*also MIL*) атаковать (*impf/perf*); (*rush*) кидаться (кинуться *perf*), бросаться (броситься *perf*) ♦ *vt* (*battery, gun*) заряжать

(заряди́ть* perf); (LAW: accuse): to ~ sb with обвиня́ть (обвини́ть perf) кого́-н в +prp; (entrust) поруча́ть (поручи́ть* perf) кому́-н +acc; ~s npl (bank charges) де́нежный,сбор msg; (telephone charges) телефо́нный тари́ф msg; labour ~s сто́имость fsg рабо́чей си́лы; to reverse the ~s (TEL) звони́ть (impf) по колле́кту; is there a ~? за э́то ну́жно плати́ть?; at no extra ~ без дополни́тельной опла́ты; free of ~ беспла́тно; to take ~ of (child) брать* (взять* perf) на попече́ние; (company) брать* (взять* perf) на себя́ руково́дство +instr; to be in ~ of отвеча́ть (impf) за +acc; who's in ~ here? кто здесь гла́вный?; to ~ (sb) (for) (demand fee) проси́ть* (попроси́ть* perf) (у кого́-н) пла́ту (за +acc); they ~d us £10 for the meal с нас взя́ли £10 за еду́; how much do you ~ for? ско́лько Вы про́сите за +acc?; to ~ an expense (up) to sb's account переводи́ть* (перевести́* perf) расхо́ды на чей-н счёт.

charge account n креди́т по откры́тому счёту.

charge card n креди́тная ка́рточка* (определённого магази́на).

chargé d'affaires [ʃɑːʒeɪ dæˈfɛə] n пове́ренный* m adj в дела́х.

charge hand n (BRIT) ма́стер* (на произво́дстве).

charger [ˈtʃɑːdʒə'] n (also: battery ~) заря́дное устро́йство; (warhorse) боево́й конь m.

chariot [ˈtʃærɪət] n колесни́ца.

charisma [kæˈrɪsmə] n обая́ние.

charitable [ˈtʃærɪtəbl] adj (organization) благотвори́тельный; (person) милосе́рдный* (милосе́рден).

charity [ˈtʃærɪtɪ] n (organization) благотвори́тельная организа́ция; (kindness) милосе́рдие; (money, gifts) ми́лостыня.

charlady [ˈtʃɑːleɪdɪ] n (BRIT) убо́рщица.

charlatan [ˈʃɑːlətən] n шарлата́н.

charm [tʃɑːm] n (attractiveness) обая́ние, очарова́ние; (spell) заклина́ние; (talisman) амуле́т; (on bracelet etc) брело́к ♦ vt (please, delight) очаро́вывать (очарова́ть perf).

charm bracelet n брасле́т с брелка́ми.

charming [ˈtʃɑːmɪŋ] adj очарова́тельный* (очарова́телен).

chart [tʃɑːt] n (graph, diagram) гра́фик; (NAUT) навигацио́нная ка́рта; (ASTRONOMY) ка́рта звёздного не́ба; (weather chart) синопти́ческая ка́рта ♦ vt (put on map) наноси́ть* (нанести́* perf) на ка́рту; (keep track of) фикси́ровать (impf); ~s npl (hit parade) хит-пара́д msg; to be in the ~s (record) быть в спи́ске наибо́лее популя́рных ди́сков.

charter [ˈtʃɑːtə'] vt (plane, ship etc) фрахтова́ть (зафрахтова́ть perf) ♦ n (of company) уста́в; (document, constitution) ха́ртия; on ~ (plane,

train etc) по ча́ртеру.

chartered accountant [ˈtʃɑːtəd-] n (BRIT) бухга́лтер вы́сшей квалифика́ции.

charter flight n ча́ртерный рейс.

charwoman [ˈtʃɑːwumən] irreg n = charlady.

chary [ˈtʃɛərɪ] adj: to be ~ of остерега́ться (impf) +gen.

chase [tʃeɪs] vt (pursue: also fig) гна́ться*/ гоня́ться (impf) за +instr ♦ n пого́ня; to ~ away or off прогоня́ть (прогна́ть* perf)
► **chase down** vt (US) = chase up
► **chase up** vt (BRIT: information) разы́скивать (разыска́ть* perf); (: person: remind) напомина́ть (напо́мнить perf) +dat.

chasm [ˈkæzəm] n (GEO) уще́лье; (between people) про́пасть f.

chassis [ˈʃæsɪ] n шасси́ nt ind.

chaste [tʃeɪst] adj (person, relationship etc) целому́дренный*.

chastened [ˈtʃeɪsnd] adj присты́женный (присты́жен).

chastening [ˈtʃeɪsnɪŋ] adj (sobering) отрезвля́ющий.

chastise [tʃæsˈtaɪz] vt отчи́тывать (отчита́ть perf).

chastity [ˈtʃæstɪtɪ] n целому́дрие.

chat [tʃæt] vi болта́ть (поболта́ть perf) ♦ n бесе́да; idle ~ болтовня́
► **chat up** vt (BRIT: inf) зайгрывать (impf) с +instr.

chatline [ˈtʃætlaɪn] n телефо́нная слу́жба, предоставля́ющая собесе́дника.

chat show n (BRIT) ≈ шóу с уча́стием знамени́тостей.

chattel [ˈtʃætl] n see goods.

chatter [ˈtʃætə'] vi (person, monkey, parrot) треща́ть (impf); (magpie) стрекота́ть* (impf); (teeth) стуча́ть (impf) ♦ n (of people) болтовня́; (of birds, animals) трескотня́; my teeth are ~ing я стучу́ зуба́ми.

chatterbox [ˈtʃætəbɔks] n (inf) трещо́тка.

chattering classes [ˈtʃætərɪŋ ˈklɑːsɪz] npl: the ~ ~ псевдоинтеллиге́нция, лю́бящая обсужда́ть совреме́нные полити́ческие и обще́ственные пробле́мы.

chatty [ˈtʃætɪ] adj (letter) живо́й; (person) говорли́вый (говорли́в).

chauffeur [ˈʃəufə'] n (персона́льный) шофёр.

chauvinism [ˈʃəuvɪnɪzəm] n (also: male ~) мужско́й шовини́зм; (nationalism) шовини́зм.

chauvinist [ˈʃəuvɪnɪst] n (also: male ~) шовини́ст.

chauvinistic [ʃəuvɪˈnɪstɪk] adj (ideas, views) шовинисти́ческий.

ChE abbr = chemical engineer.

cheap [tʃiːp] adj (also fig) дешёвый*; (reduced) со ски́дкой ♦ adv: to buy/sell sth ~ дёшево покупа́ть (купи́ть* perf)/продава́ть* (прода́ть* perf) что-н.

cheapen [ˈtʃiːpn] vt (person) унижа́ть

(уни́зить* *perf*).
cheaper ['tʃiːpə'] *adj* деше́вле.
cheaply ['tʃiːplɪ] *adv* дёшево.
cheap money *n*: ~ ~ **policy** ситуа́ция, когда́ вла́сти стремя́тся стимули́ровать экономи́ческий рост с по́мощью ни́зких проце́нтных ста́вок, „дешёвые де́ньги".
cheat [tʃiːt] *vi* (*at cards*) жу́льничать (*impf*); (*in exam*) спи́сывать (списа́ть* *perf*) ♦ *n* (*person*) жу́лик ♦ *vt*: **to** ~ **sb** (**out of £10**) наду́ть (*perf*) кого́-н (на £10); **to** ~ **on sb** (*inf*: *husband, wife etc*) изменя́ть (измени́ть* *perf*) кому́-н.
cheating ['tʃiːtɪŋ] *n* жу́льничество, надува́тельство.
check [tʃɛk] *vt* проверя́ть (прове́рить *perf*); (*halt*) приостана́вливать (приостанови́ть* *perf*); (*restrain*) сде́рживать (сдержа́ть* *perf*); (*US*: *items on list*) отмеча́ть (отме́тить* *perf*) ♦ *vi* проверя́ть (прове́рить *perf*) ♦ *n* (*inspection*) прове́рка*; (*US*: *bill*) счёт*; (: *COMM*) = **cheque**; (*pattern*: *usu pl*) кле́тка* ♦ *adj* (*cloth, skirt*) кле́тчатый; **to** ~ **with sb** посове́товаться (*perf*) с кем-н; **to keep a** ~ **on sb/sth** контроли́ровать (*impf*) кого́-н/что-н; **to act as a** ~ **on** (*curb*) явля́ться (яви́ться* *perf*) ме́рой контро́ля +*gen*
▶ **check in** *vi* (*at hotel, airport*) регистри́роваться (зарегистри́роваться *perf*) ♦ *vt* (*luggage*) сдава́ть* (сдать* *perf*)
▶ **check off** *vt* (*items on list etc*) отмеча́ть (отме́тить* *perf*)
▶ **check out** *vi* (*of hotel*) выпи́сываться (вы́писаться* *perf*) ♦ *vt* (*investigate*: *story*) проверя́ть (прове́рить *perf*); (: *building*) прочёсывать (прочеса́ть *perf*)
▶ **check up** *vi*: **to** ~ **up on sb/sth** наводи́ть (навести́* *perf*) спра́вки о ком-н/чём-н.
checkered ['tʃɛkəd] *adj* (*US*) = **chequered**.
checkers ['tʃɛkəz] *npl* (*US*: *draughts*) ша́шки *pl*.
check guarantee card (*US*) = **cheque card**.
check-in (desk) ['tʃɛkɪn-] *n* (*at airport*) сто́йка регистра́ции.
checking account ['tʃɛkɪŋ-] *n* (*US*: *current account*) теку́щий* счёт*.
check list *n* контро́льный спи́сок*.
checkmate ['tʃɛkmeɪt] *n* (*CHESS*) мат.
checkout ['tʃɛkaut] *n* (*in shop*) контро́ль *m*. ка́сса.
checkpoint ['tʃɛkpɔɪnt] *n* (*on border*) контро́льно-пропускно́й пункт.
checkroom ['tʃɛkrum] *n* (*US*) ка́мера хране́ния.
checkup ['tʃɛkʌp] *n* (*MED*) осмо́тр.
cheek [tʃiːk] *n* (*ANAT*) щека́*; (*impudence*) на́глость *f*; (*nerve*) де́рзость *f*.
cheekbone ['tʃiːkbəun] *n* скула́*.
cheeky ['tʃiːkɪ] *adj* наха́льный* (наха́лен), на́глый (нагл).

cheep [tʃiːp] *vi* пища́ть (*impf*) ♦ *n* писк.
cheer [tʃɪə'] *vt* (*encourage*) приве́тствовать (поприве́тствовать *perf*); (*gladden*) обод ря́ть (обод ри́ть *perf*) ♦ *vi* одобри́тельно восклица́ть (*impf*); ~**s** *npl* (*of crowd*: *of welcome*) приве́тственные во́згласы *mpl*; (: *of approval*) одобри́тельные во́згласы *mpl*; ~**s!** (*toast*) (за) Ва́ше здоро́вье!
▶ **cheer on** *vt* обод ря́ть (обод ри́ть *perf*)
▶ **cheer up** *vi* развесели́ться (*perf*), повеселе́ть (*perf*) ♦ *vt* (*person*) развесели́ть (*perf*); ~ **up!** не грусти́(те)!
cheerful ['tʃɪəful] *adj* весёлый* (ве́сел).
cheerfulness ['tʃɪəfulnɪs] *n* весёлость *f*.
cheerio [tʃɪərɪ'əu] *excl* (*BRIT*) пока́!
cheerleader ['tʃɪəliːdə'] *n* заводи́ла (*де́вушка, подстрека́ющая боле́льщиков на спорти́вных состяза́ниях*).
cheerless ['tʃɪəlɪs] *adj* уны́лый* (уны́л).
cheese [tʃiːz] *n* сыр*.
cheeseboard ['tʃiːzbɔːd] *n* доска́* для сы́ра; (*with cheese on it*) доска́* с сы́ром.
cheeseburger ['tʃiːzbəːgə'] *n* чи́збургер.
cheesecake ['tʃiːzkeɪk] *n* ≈ творо́жный кекс.
cheetah ['tʃiːtə] *n* гепа́рд.
chef [ʃɛf] *n* шеф-по́вар*.
chemical ['kɛmɪkl] *adj* хими́ческий* ♦ *n* химика́т; (*in laboratory*) реакти́в.
chemical engineering *n* хими́ческая техноло́гия.
chemist ['kɛmɪst] *n* (*BRIT*: *pharmacist*) фармаце́вт; (*scientist*) хи́мик.
chemistry ['kɛmɪstrɪ] *n* хи́мия.
chemist's (shop) ['kɛmɪsts-] *n* (*BRIT*) апте́ка.
chemotherapy [kiːməu'θɛrəpɪ] *n* химотерапи́я.
cheque [tʃɛk] *n* (*BRIT*) чек; **to pay by** ~ плати́ть* (заплати́ть* *perf*) че́ком.
chequebook ['tʃɛkbuk] *n* (*BRIT*) че́ковая кни́жка.
cheque card *n* (*BRIT*) ка́рточка, подтвержда́ющая платёжеспосо́бность владе́льца.
chequered ['tʃɛkəd] (*US* **checkered**) *adj* (*fig*: *career*) пёстрый.
cherish ['tʃɛrɪʃ] *vt* леле́ять (взлеле́ять *perf*).
cheroot [ʃə'ruːt] *n* сига́ра (*с уплощёнными конца́ми*).
cherry ['tʃɛrɪ] *n* (*fruit, tree*) чере́шня*; (: *sour variety*) ви́шня.
chervil ['tʃəːvɪl] *n* купы́рь *m*.
Ches *abbr* (*BRIT*: *POST*) = **Cheshire**.
chess [tʃɛs] *n* ша́хматы *pl*.
chessboard ['tʃɛsbɔːd] *n* ша́хматная доска́*.
chessman ['tʃɛsmən] *irreg n* ша́хматная фигу́ра.
chess player *n* шахмати́ст.
chest [tʃɛst] *n* (*ANAT*) грудь* *f*; (*box*) сунду́к*;

I'm glad I got it off my ~ (*inf*) я рад, что облегчи́л ду́шу.
chest measurement *n* окру́жность *f* груди́.
chestnut ['tʃɛsnʌt] *n* кашта́н ◆ *adj* (*hair*) кашта́новый; (*horse*) гнедо́й.
chest of drawers *n* комо́д.
chesty ['tʃæsti] *adj* грудно́й.
chew [tʃu:] *vt* (*food*) жева́ть (*impf*); (*nails*) грызть* (*impf*); (*a hole*) прогрыза́ть (прогры́зть* *perf*).
chewing gum ['tʃu:ɪŋ-] *n* жева́тельная рези́нка.
chic [ʃi:k] *adj* шика́рный*, элега́нтный* (элега́нтен).
Chicago [ʃɪ'kɑ:geu] *n* Чика́го *m ind*.
chick [tʃɪk] *n* (*of hen*) цыплёнок*; (*of wild bird*) птене́ц*; (*inf: girl*) пта́шка.
chicken ['tʃɪkɪn] *n* (*bird, meat*) ку́рица; (*inf: coward*) труси́шка *m/f*
► **chicken out** *vi* (*inf*) тру́сить (стру́сить* *perf*);
he ~ed out of going он стру́сил и не пошёл.
chicken feed *n* (*fig*) гроши́ *mpl*.
chickenpox ['tʃɪkɪnpɔks] *n* ветря́нка.
chickpeas ['tʃɪkpi:z] *npl* туре́цкий горо́х* *msg*.
chicory ['tʃɪkərɪ] *n* цико́рий.
chide [tʃaɪd] *vt* (*person*): **to ~ sb (for)** брани́ть (вы́бранить* *perf*) кого́-н (за +*acc*).
chief [tʃi:f] *n* (*of tribe*) вождь* *m*; (*of organization, department*) нача́льник ◆ *adj* гла́вный, основно́й.
chief constable *n* (*BRIT*) нача́льник поли́ции.
chief executive (*US* **chief executive officer**) *n* гла́вный исполни́тельный дире́ктор.
chiefly ['tʃi:flɪ] *adv* гла́вным о́бразом.
Chief of Staff *n* (*MIL*) нача́льник шта́ба.
chiffon ['ʃɪfɔn] *n* шифо́н.
chilblain ['tʃɪlbleɪn] *n* обморо́женное ме́сто* (на па́льцах).
child [tʃaɪld] (*pl* **~ren**) *n* ребёнок*; (*fig*): **~ (of)** дитя́ (+*gen*); **do you have any ~ren?** у Вас есть де́ти?
child benefit *n* (*BRIT*) де́нежное посо́бие на ребёнка.
childbirth ['tʃaɪldbə:θ] *n* ро́ды *pl*.
childhood ['tʃaɪldhud] *n* де́тство.
childish ['tʃaɪldɪʃ] *adj* (*games, attitude*) ребя́ческий*; (*person*) ребя́чливый (ребя́лчив).
childless ['tʃaɪldlɪs] *adj* безде́тный* (безде́тен).
childlike ['tʃaɪldlaɪk] *adj* (*smile, figure*) де́тский*.
child minder *n* (*BRIT*) ня́ня.
child prodigy *n* вундерки́нд.
children ['tʃɪldrən] *npl of* **child**.
children's home *n* ['tʃɪldrənz-] *n* де́тский* дом*.
child's play ['tʃaɪldz-] *n*: **it was ~ ~** (*fig*) э́то бы́ло пустяко́вое де́ло.
Chile ['tʃɪlɪ] *n* Чи́ли *nt ind*.
Chilean ['tʃɪlɪən] *adj* чили́йский* ◆ *n* чили́ец(-и́йка).
chili ['tʃɪlɪ] *n* (*US*) = **chilli**.

chill [tʃɪl] *n* (*coldness*) прохла́да; (*MED*) простуда ◆ *adj* холо́дный* ◆ *vt* (*food, drinks*) охлажда́ть (охлади́ть* *perf*); **to catch a ~** простуди́ться (простуди́ться* *perf*); **his words sent a ~ down my spine** от его́ слов у меня́ пробежа́л холодо́к по спине́; **a ~ reminder** (*fig*) злове́щее предзнаменова́ние; **I'm ~ed to the bone** я промёрз до косте́й; **"serve ~ed"** "подава́ть в охлаждённом ви́де"
► **chill out** *vi* (*inf*) кайфова́ть (*impf*).
chilli ['tʃɪlɪ] (*US* **chili**) *n* (*CULIN*) кра́сный стручко́вый пе́рец*.
chilling ['tʃɪlɪŋ] *adj* (*wind*) прохла́дный* (прохла́ден), холо́дный* (хо́лоден); (*tale*) ужаса́ющий*.
chilly ['tʃɪlɪ] *adj* (*weather*) холо́дный, промо́зглый; (*response, person*) холо́дный* (хо́лоден); **to feel ~** зя́бнуть* (*impf*).
chime [tʃaɪm] *n* (*of bell*) звон; (*of clock*) бой* ◆ *vi* (*bell*) звони́ть (*impf*); (*clock*) бить* (проби́ть* *perf*).
chimney ['tʃɪmnɪ] *n* (дымова́я) труба́.
chimney sweep *n* трубочи́ст.
chimpanzee [tʃɪmpæn'zi:] *n* шимпанзе́ *m ind*.
chin [tʃɪn] *n* подборо́док*.
China ['tʃaɪnə] *n* Кита́й.
china ['tʃaɪnə] *n* фарфо́р.
Chinese [tʃaɪ'ni:z] *adj* кита́йский* ◆ *n inv* (*person*) кита́ец(-а́янка); (*LING*) кита́йский* язы́к*.
chink [tʃɪŋk] *n* (*crack*) щель* *f*; (*clink*) звя́канье.
chintz [tʃɪnts] *n* набивно́й си́тец.
chinwag ['tʃɪnwæg] *n* (*inf*) дру́жеская болтовня́; **we had a good ~** мы хорошо́ поболта́ли.
chip [tʃɪp] *n* (*of wood*) ще́пка*; (*of glass, stone*) оско́лок*; (*in glass, cup etc*) щерби́нка; (*in gambling*) фи́шка; (*COMPUT: also: microchip*) микросхе́ма ◆ *vt* (*cup, plate*) обива́ть (оби́ть* *perf*); **~s** *npl* (*BRIT: CULIN*) карто́фель *msg*-фри; (*US: also: potato ~s*) чи́псы *mpl*; **when the ~s are down** (*fig*) когда́ уда́ча отверне́тся
► **chip in** *vi* (*inf: contribute*) сбра́сываться (сбро́ситься* *perf*); (*: interrupt*) встрева́ть (встрять *perf*).
chipboard ['tʃɪpbɔ:d] *n* древесно-стру́жечная плита́.
chipmunk ['tʃɪpmʌŋk] *n* бурунду́к.
chippings ['tʃɪpɪŋz] *npl*: **loose ~** ще́пки* *fpl*.
chiropodist [kɪ'rɔpədɪst] *n* (*BRIT*) мозо́льный опера́тор *m/f*.
chiropody [kɪ'rɔpədɪ] *n* (*BRIT*) ухо́д за нога́ми.
chirp [tʃə:p] *vi* (*bird*) чири́кать (*impf*); (*cricket, grasshopper*) стрекота́ть* (*impf*).
chirpy ['tʃə:pɪ] *adj* (*inf*) жизнера́достный* (жизнера́достен).
chisel ['tʃɪzl] *n* (*for wood*) долото́; (*for stone*) зуби́ло; (*of sculptor*) резе́ц*.
chit [tʃɪt] *n* (*note*) запи́ска*; (*receipt*) распи́ска.
chitchat ['tʃɪttʃæt] *n* болтовня́.

chivalrous ['ʃɪvəlrəs] adj галáнтный*
(галáнтен).
chivalry ['ʃɪvəlrɪ] n галáнтность f.
chives [tʃaɪvz] npl лук-резáнец msg.
chloride ['klɔːraɪd] n хлорúд.
chlorinate ['klɔːrɪneɪt] vt хлорúровать (impf).
chlorine ['klɔːriːn] n хлор.
chock [tʃɔk] n (AUT, AVIAT) тормознáя
колóдка*.
chock-a-block ['tʃɔkə'blɔk] adj биткóм
набúтый (набúт).
chock-full [tʃɔk'ful] adj = **chock-a-block**.
chocolate ['tʃɔklɪt] n шоколáд; (sweet)
шоколáдная конфéта ♦ cpd шоколáдный.
choice [tʃɔɪs] n (selection) вы́бор ♦ adj (cut of
meat, fruit etc) отбóрный; **this is a possible ~**
э́то возмóжный вариáнт; **by** or **from ~**
добровóльно; **a wide ~** большóй вы́бор; **to
have first ~** выбирáть (вы́брать* perf)
пéрвым; **I have no ~, but/but to** у меня́ нет
другóго вы́хода крóме +gen/крóме как
+infin.
choir ['kwaɪə'] n хор*; (area of church) хóры pl.
choirboy ['kwaɪə'bɔɪ] n пéвчий* m adj.
choke [tʃəuk] vi (on food, drink) давúться*
(подавúться* perf); (with smoke, anger)
задыхáться (задохнýться perf) ♦ vt (strangle)
душúть* (задушúть* or удушúть* perf) ♦ n
(AUT) воздýшная заслóнка*; **~d (with)**
(blocked) засорённый (засорён) (+instr).
cholera ['kɔlərə] n холéра.
cholesterol [kə'lɛstərɔl] n холестерúн; **high/
low ~** с высóким/нúзким содержáнием
холестерúна.
choose [tʃuːz] (pt **chose**, pp **chosen**) vt
выбирáть (вы́брать perf); (elect) избирáть
(избрáть* perf) ♦ vi: **to ~ between/from**
выбирáть (вы́брать* perf) мéжду +instr/из
+gen; **to ~ to do** решáть (решúть perf) +infin.
choosy ['tʃuːzɪ] adj привередлúвый
(привередлúв); **he is ~ about his food** он
привередлúв в едé.
chop [tʃɔp] vt (wood) рубúть* (нарубúть* perf);
(also: ~ up: vegetables, meat) рéзать*
(нарéзать* or порéзать* perf) ♦ n (CULIN) ≈
отбивнáя (котлéта); **~s** npl (inf: jaws): **to lick
one's ~s** облúзываться (облизáться* perf);
he got the ~ (BRIT: inf) егó вы́гнали с рабóты
► **chop down** vt (tree) рубúть* (срубúть* perf).
chopper ['tʃɔpə'] n (helicopter) вертолёт.
choppy ['tʃɔpɪ] adj (sea) неспокóйный*
(неспокóен).
chopsticks ['tʃɔpstɪks] npl пáлочки fpl для
еды́.
choral ['kɔːrəl] adj хоровóй; (in church)
хорáльный.
chord [kɔːd] n (MUS) аккóрд; (MATH) хóрда.
chore [tʃɔː'] n (domestic task) рабóта по дóму;

(routine task) повседнéвная обя́занность f;
household ~s домáшние хлóпоты.
choreographer [kɔrɪ'ɔgrəfə'] n хореóграф; (of
ballet) балетмéйстер*.
choreography [kɔrɪ'ɔgrəfɪ] n хореогрáфия.
chorister ['kɔrɪstə'] n пéвчий* m adj, хорúст.
chortle ['tʃɔːtl] vi хохотáть* (impf).
chorus ['kɔːrəs] n (choir, song, also fig) хор*;
(church song) хорáл; (refrain) припéв; **in ~**
хóром.
chose [tʃəuz] pt of **choose**.
chosen ['tʃəuzn] pp of **choose**.
chow [tʃau] n (dog) чáу-чáу m/f ind.
chowder ['tʃaudə'] n ≈ похлёбка.
Christ [kraɪst] n Христóс.
christen ['krɪsn] vt крестúть* (окрестúть* perf);
(with nickname) окрестúть* (perf) +instr.
christening ['krɪsnɪŋ] n крещéние.
Christian ['krɪstɪən] adj христиáнский* ♦ n
христианúн*(-áнка).
Christianity [krɪstɪ'ænɪtɪ] n христиáнство.
Christian name n úмя* nt.
Christmas ['krɪsməs] n Рождествó; **Happy** or
Merry ~! Счастлúвого Рождествá!
Christmas card n рождéственская откры́тка*.
Christmas Day n день m Рождествá.
Christmas Eve n сочéльник.
Christmas Island n óстров* Рождествá.
Christmas tree n рождéственская ёлка*.
chrome [krəum] n = **chromium**.
chromium ['krəumɪəm] n хром; (also: ~
plating) хромúрование.
chromosome ['krəuməsəum] n хромосóма.
chronic ['krɔnɪk] adj хронúческий*.
chronicle ['krɔnɪkl] n (of events) хрóника.
chronological [krɔnə'lɔdʒɪkl] adj (order)
хронологúческий.
chrysanthemum [krɪ'sænθəməm] n
хризантéма.
chubby ['tʃʌbɪ] adj пýхлый*.
chuck [tʃʌk] (inf) vt швыря́ть (швырнýть perf);
(BRIT: also: ~ up, ~ in: job, girlfriend) бросáть
(брóсить* perf)
► **chuck out** vt (person, rubbish) вышвы́ривать
(вы́швырнуть perf).
chuckle ['tʃʌkl] vi посмéиваться (impf); **"Yes",
he ~d** Да, – сказáл он, посмéиваясь.
chuffed [tʃʌft] adj (inf) довóльный* (довóлен).
chug [tʃʌg] vi пыхтéть* (impf); (also: ~ along)
пыхтéть* (пропыхтéть* perf).
chum [tʃʌm] n (inf: friend) закады́чный друг*.
chump [tʃʌmp] n (inf) болвáн.
chunk [tʃʌŋk] n (of meat) кусóк*; (of bread)
лóмоть m.
chunky ['tʃʌŋkɪ] adj (furniture etc) громóздкий*
(громóздок); (person) коренáстый
(коренáст); (knitwear) тóлстый.
church [tʃəːtʃ] n цéрковь* f; **the C~ of England**

Англика́нская Це́рковь*.
churchyard ['tʃə:tʃɑ:d] *n* пого́ст.
churlish ['tʃə:lɪʃ] *adj* гру́бый (груб).
churn [tʃə:n] *n* (*machine*) маслобо́йка; (*also:* **milk ~**) бидо́н
▶ **churn out** *vt* производи́ть* (произвести́* *perf*) в большо́м коли́честве.
chute [ʃu:t] *n* (*also:* **rubbish ~**) мусоропрово́д; (*for parcels etc*) жёлоб*; (*BRIT*: *slide*) го́рка*.
chutney ['tʃʌtnɪ] *n* ча́тни *nt ind* (*индийская припра́ва*).
CIA *n abbr* (*US:* = *Central Intelligence Agency*) ЦРУ.
cicada [sɪ'kɑ:də] *n* цика́да.
CID *n abbr* (*BRIT*: = *Criminal Investigation Department*) Уголо́вный ро́зыск.
cider ['saɪdə'] *n* сидр.
c.i.f. *abbr* (*COMM*: = *cost, insurance and freight*) СИФ (*сто́имость, страхова́ние, фрахт*).
cigar [sɪ'gɑ:'] *n* сига́ра.
cigarette [sɪgə'rɛt] *n* сигаре́та.
cigarette case *n* портсига́р.
cigarette end *n* оку́рок*.
cigarette holder *n* мундшту́к*.
C-in-C *abbr* (*MIL*: = *commander in chief*) главнокома́ндующий*.
cinch [sɪntʃ] *n* (*inf*): **it's a ~** э́то пустя́к.
Cinderella [sɪndə'rɛlə] *n* 3о́лушка.
cinders ['sɪndəz] *npl* зола́ *fsg*.
cine camera ['sɪnɪ-] *n* (*BRIT*) кинока́мера.
cine film *n* (*BRIT*) киноплёнка*.
cinema ['sɪnəmə] *n* кинотеа́тр; (*film-making*) кинематогра́фия.
cine projector *n* (*BRIT*) кинопрое́ктор.
cinnamon ['sɪnəmən] *n* кори́ца.
cipher ['saɪfə'] *n* шифр; (*fig*) пе́шка*; **a letter in ~** зашифро́ванное письмо́.
circa ['sə:kə] *prep* о́коло +*gen*.
circle ['sə:kl] *n* круг*; (*THEAT*) балко́н; (*of trees*) кольцо́ ◆ *vi* (*bird, plane*) кружи́ть* (*impf*) ◆ *vt* (*move round*) дви́гаться* (*impf*) вокру́г +*gen*; (*surround*) окружа́ть (окружи́ть *perf*); **to form a ~** встава́ть* (встать* *perf*) в круг.
circuit ['sə:kɪt] *n* (*ELEC*) цепь *f*; (*tour*) турне́ *nt ind*; (*track*) трек; (*lap*) зае́зд.
circuit board *n* монта́жная пла́та.
circuitous [sə:'kjuɪtəs] *adj* око́льный.
circular ['sə:kjulə'] *adj* (*plate, pond etc*) кру́глый*; (*route*) окружно́й; (*argument*) несконча́емый ◆ *n* (*letter*) циркуля́р; (*advertisement*) проспе́кт.
circulate ['sə:kjuleɪt] *vi* (*blood, traffic*) циркули́ровать (*impf*); (*news, rumour etc*) передава́ться* (переда́ться* *perf*) ◆ *vt* передава́ть* (переда́ть* *perf*); **to ~ amongst the guests** переходи́ть (*impf*) от одного́ го́стя к друго́му.
circulating capital [sə:kju'leɪtɪŋ-] *n* оборо́тный капита́л.
circulation [sə:kju'leɪʃən] *n* (*of newspaper*) тира́ж*; (*MED*) кровообраще́ние; (*of money*)

обраще́ние; (*of air, traffic*) циркуля́ция.
circumcise ['sə:kəmsaɪz] *vt* обреза́ть (обре́зать* *perf*) (*РЕЛ*).
circumference [sə'kʌmfərəns] *n* окру́жность *f*.
circumflex ['sə:kəmflɛks] *n* (*also:* **~ accent**) циркумфле́кс.
circumscribe ['sə:kəmskraɪb] *vt* (*GEOM*) впи́сывать (вписа́ть* *perf*) в окру́жность; (*fig*) ограни́чивать (ограни́чить *perf*).
circumspect ['sə:kəmspɛkt] *adj* осмотри́тельный* (осмотри́телен).
circumstances ['sə:kəmstənsɪz] *npl* обстоя́тельства *ntpl*; **in** *or* **under the ~** в да́нных обстоя́тельствах; **under no ~** ни в ко́ем слу́чае.
circumstantial [sə:kəm'stænʃl] *adj* обстоя́тельный* (обстоя́телен); **~ evidence** ко́свенные ули́ки *fpl*.
circumvent [sə:kəm'vɛnt] *vt* обходи́ть* (обойти́* *perf*).
circus ['sə:kəs] *n* цирк; (*also:* **C~**: *in place names*) ≈ пло́щадь *f*.
cirrhosis [sɪ'rəusɪs] *n* цирро́з.
CIS *n abbr* (= *Commonwealth of Independent States*) СНГ = *Содру́жество Незави́симых Госуда́рств*.
cissy ['sɪsɪ] *n* (*boy*) девчо́нка*; (*girl*) не́женка*.
cistern ['sɪstən] *n* (*water tank*) цисте́рна; (*of toilet*) бачо́к.
citation [saɪ'teɪʃən] *n* (*from book etc*) цита́та; (*for bravery etc*) благода́рность *f*; (*US: LAW*) пове́стка (*в суд*).
cite [saɪt] *vt* (*quote*) цити́ровать (процити́ровать *perf*); (*LAW*) вызыва́ть (вы́звать* *perf*) в суд.
citizen ['sɪtɪzn] *n* (*of a country*) граждани́н*(-а́нка); (*of town*) жи́тель(ница) *m(f)*.
Citizens' Advice Bureau ['sɪtɪznz-] *n* бюро́, даю́щее беспла́тные сове́ты по широ́кому кру́гу вопро́сов.
citizenship ['sɪtɪznʃɪp] *n* (*of a country*) гражда́нство.
citric acid ['sɪtrɪk-] *n* лимо́нная кислота́*.
citrus fruit ['sɪtrəs-] *n* ци́трус.
city ['sɪtɪ] *n* го́род*; **the C~** Си́ти *nt ind*.
city centre *n* центр (го́рода).
City Hall *n* ра́туша.
civic ['sɪvɪk] *adj* муниципа́льный*; (*duties, pride*) гражда́нский*.
civic centre *n* (*BRIT*) ≈ Дом* Культу́ры.
civil ['sɪvɪl] *adj* гражда́нский*; (*authorities*) госуда́рственный; (*polite*) учти́вый (учти́в).
Civil Aviation Authority *n* (*BRIT*) Управле́ние гражда́нской авиа́ции.
civil defence *n* гражда́нская оборо́на.
civil disobedience *n* гражда́нское неповинове́ние.
civil engineer *n* инжене́р-строи́тель *m*.
civil engineering *n* гражда́нское строи́тельство.

civilian [sɪ'vɪlɪən] *adj* (*life*) обще́ственный ♦ *n* ми́рный(-ая) жи́тель(ница) *m(f)*; ~ **casualties** же́ртвы среди́ ми́рного населе́ния.

civilization [sɪvɪlaɪ'zeɪʃən] *n* цивилиза́ция.

civilized ['sɪvɪlaɪzd] *adj* (*society*) цивилизо́ванный; (*person*) культу́рный; (*place*) комфорта́бельный.

civil law *n* Гражда́нское пра́во.

civil liberties *npl* гражда́нские свобо́ды *fpl*.

civil rights *npl* гражда́нские права́ *ntpl*.

civil servant *n* госуда́рственный слу́жащий* *m adj*.

Civil Service *n* госуда́рственная слу́жба.

civil war *n* гражда́нская война́*.

civvies ['sɪvɪz] *npl* (*inf*) циви́льная оде́жда *fsg*.

cl *abbr* = **centilitre**.

clad [klæd] *adj*: ~ **(in)** облачённый (облачён) (в +*acc*).

claim [kleɪm] *vt* (*responsibility, credit*) припи́сывать (приписа́ть* *perf*) себе́; (*rights, inheritance*) претендова́ть (*impf*) *or* притяза́ть (*impf*) на +*acc*; (*compensation, damages*) тре́бовать (потре́бовать *perf*) ♦ *vi* (*for insurance*) де́лать (сде́лать *perf*) страхову́ю зая́вку ♦ *n* (*assertion*) утвержде́ние; (*for compensation, pension*) тре́бование; (*right*) пра́во; (*to inheritance, land*) прете́нзия, притяза́ние; (*for expenses*) зая́вка; **to ~ (that)** *or* **to be** (*assert*) утвержда́ть (*impf*), что; (**insurance**) ~ страхова́я зая́вка; **to put in a ~ for** (*expenses*) подава́ть* (пода́ть* *perf*) зая́вку на +*acc*.

claimant ['kleɪmənt] *n* (*LAW*) претенде́нт; (*ADMIN*) пода́тель(ница) *m(f)* заявле́ния.

claim form *n* бланк заявле́ния.

clairvoyant [klɛə'vɔɪənt] *n* яснови́дец*(-дица).

clam [klæm] *n* двухство́рчатый моллю́ск ► **clam up** *vi* (*inf*) уходи́ть* (уйти́* *perf*) в себя́.

clamber ['klæmbəʳ] *vi* кара́бкаться (вскара́бкаться *perf*).

clammy ['klæmɪ] *adj* (*hands*) ли́пкий*; (*weather*) ду́шный*.

clamour ['klæməʳ] (*US* **clamor**) *n* (*noise*) гул; (*protest*) ро́пот ♦ *vi*: **to ~ for** шу́мно тре́бовать (*impf*) +*gen*.

clamp [klæmp] *n* зажи́м ♦ *vt* зажима́ть (зажа́ть* *perf*) ► **clamp down on** *vt fus* повести́* (*perf*) наступле́ние про́тив +*gen*.

clampdown ['klæmpdaun] *n*: ~ **(on)** стро́гие ме́ры *fpl* (про́тив +*gen*); **there was a ~ on drug dealing in the area** в райо́не прикры́ли торго́влю нарко́тиками.

clan [klæn] *n* клан.

clandestine [klæn'dɛstɪn] *adj* подпо́льный.

clang [klæŋ] *vi* (*bell*) звене́ть (*impf*); (*metal object*) ля́згать (*impf*) ♦ *n* (*see vi*) звон; лязг.

clanger ['klæŋəʳ] *n* (*inf*) ля́псус.

clansman ['klænzmən] *irreg n* член кла́на.

clap [klæp] *vi* хло́пать (*impf*) ♦ *vt*: **to ~ one's hands** хло́пать (*impf*) в ладо́ши; **a ~ of thunder** уда́р гро́ма.

clapping ['klæpɪŋ] *n* хлопки́ *mpl*, аплодисме́нты *fpl*.

claptrap ['klæptræp] *n* (*inf*) белиберда́.

claret ['klærət] *n* бордо́ *nt ind*.

clarification [klærɪfɪ'keɪʃən] *n* (*fig*) разъясне́ние.

clarify ['klærɪfaɪ] *vt* (*fig*) разъясня́ть (разъясни́ть *perf*).

clarinet [klærɪ'nɛt] *n* кларне́т.

clarity ['klærɪtɪ] *n* (*of explanation, thought*) я́сность *f*.

clash [klæʃ] *n* столкнове́ние; (*of events etc*) совпаде́ние; (*of metal objects*) звя́канье ♦ *vi* (*gangs*) име́ть (*impf*) столкнове́ние; (*political opponents*) вступа́ть (вступи́ть* *perf*) в столкнове́ние; (*beliefs*) ста́лкиваться (столкну́ться *perf*); (*colours*) не совмеща́ться (*impf*); (*events etc*) совпада́ть (совпа́сть* *perf*) (по вре́мени); (*metal objects*) звя́кать (*impf*).

clasp [klɑːsp] *n* (*hold*) хва́тка*; (*of necklace, bag*) застёжка* ♦ *vt* сжима́ть (сжать* *perf*).

class [klɑːs] *n* (*in school, society*) класс; (*lesson*) уро́к; (*of goods: type*) разря́д; (: *quality*) сорт ♦ *adj* кла́ссовый ♦ *vt* классифици́ровать (*impf* *perf*).

class-conscious ['klɑːs'kɔnʃəs] *adj* (*person*) осознаю́щий кла́ссовое разли́чие.

class-consciousness ['klɑːs'kɔnʃəsnɪs] *n* кла́ссовое созна́ние.

classic ['klæsɪk] *adj* класси́ческий* ♦ *n* (*film, novel etc*) класси́ческое произведе́ние; (*author*) кла́ссик; **C~s** *npl* (*SCOL*) класси́ческая филоло́гия *fsg*.

classical ['klæsɪkl] *adj* класси́ческий*.

classification [klæsɪfɪ'keɪʃən] *n* классифика́ция; (*category*) разря́д.

classified ['klæsɪfaɪd] *adj* засекре́ченный.

classified advertisement *n* объявле́ния под ру́брикой.

classify ['klæsɪfaɪ] *vt* классифици́ровать (*impf* *perf*).

classless ['klɑːslɪs] *adj* бескла́ссовый.

classmate ['klɑːsmeɪt] *n* однокла́ссник(-ица).

classroom ['klɑːsrum] *n* класс.

classy ['klɑːsɪ] *adj* (*inf*: *car, flat*) кла́ссный.

clatter ['klætəʳ] *n* (*of dishes etc*) звя́канье; (*of hooves*) цо́канье ♦ *vi* (*see n*) звя́кать (*impf*); цо́кать (*impf*).

clause [klɔːz] *n* (*LAW*) пункт; (*LING*): **principal/subordinate ~** гла́вное/прида́точное предложе́ние.

claustrophobia [klɔːstrə'fəubɪə] *n* клаустрофо́бия.

claustrophobic [klɔːstrə'fəubɪk] *adj*: **she is ~**

она страдáет клаустрофóбией, у неё
клаустрофóбия.

claw [klɔ:] n (of animal, bird) кóготь* m;
(of lobster) клешня*
► **claw at** vt fus цепля́ться (impf) за +acc.

clay [kleɪ] n гли́на.

clean [kli:n] adj чи́стый*; (fight) чéстный*;
(reputation) незапя́тнанный (незапя́тан);
(joke) прили́чный* (прили́чен); (edge,
fracture) рóвный* (рóвен) ♦ vt (hands, face)
мыть (вы́мыть* perf); (car, cooker) чи́стить*
(почи́стить* perf) ♦ adv: **he ~ forgot** он
на́чисто забы́л; **~ driving licence** or (US)
record чи́стые води́тельские права́ ntpl; **to ~
one's teeth** (BRIT) чи́стить* (почи́стить perf)
зу́бы; **the thief got ~ away** вóра и след
простыл; **to come ~** (inf) выкла́дывать
(вы́ложить perf) всё начистую
► **clean off** vt (wash) смыва́ть (смыть* perf);
(brush, dust etc) счища́ть (счи́стить* perf)
► **clean out** vt (cupboard etc) вычища́ть
(вы́чистить* perf); (inf: person) обчища́ть
(обчи́стить* perf)
► **clean up** vt (room) убира́ть (убра́ть* perf);
(child) мыть* (помы́ть* perf); (fig) проводи́ть*
(провести́* perf) чи́стку в +prp ♦ vi убира́ться
(убра́ться* perf); (fig) загреба́ть (загрести́*
perf) больши́е дéньги; **to ~ up after sb/sth**
убира́ть (убра́ть* perf) за кем-н/чем-н.

clean-cut ['kli:n'kʌt] adj (person) опря́тный*
(опря́тен); (situation) я́сный* (я́сен).

cleaner ['kli:nə'] n (person) убóрщик(-ица);
(substance) мóющее срéдство.

cleaner's ['kli:nəz] n (also: dry ~) химчи́стка*.

cleaning ['kli:nɪŋ] n убóрка*.

cleaning lady n убóрщица.

cleanliness ['klɛnlɪnɪs] n чистоплóтность f.

cleanly ['kli:nlɪ] adv чи́сто.

cleanse [klɛnz] vt (purify) очища́ть (очи́стить*
perf); (face) мыть* (вы́мыть* perf); (cut)
промыва́ть (промы́ть* perf).

cleanser ['klɛnzə'] n (for face) очища́ющий
лосьóн.

clean-shaven ['kli:n'ʃeɪvn] adj чи́сто
вы́бритый.

cleansing department ['klɛnzɪŋ-] n (BRIT)
санита́рное управлéние.

clean sweep n: **to make a ~ ~** (in tournaments)
забира́ть (забра́ть* perf) все призы́.

cleanup ['kli:nʌp] n (of house, room) убóрка*;
(of river, air) очи́стка.

clear [klɪə'] adj я́сный* (я́сен); (report,
argument) я́сный* (я́сен), поня́тный*;
(footprint) чёткий*; (writing) разбóрчивый;
(majority) подавля́ющий*; (glass, water)
прозра́чный* (прозра́чен); (road) свобóдный*
(свобóден); (conscience, profit) чи́стый* ♦ vt
(space, room) освобожда́ть (освободи́ть* perf);
(ground) расчища́ть (расчи́стить* perf); (weeds,
slums) убира́ть (убра́ть* perf); (suspect)

оправдывать (оправда́ть perf); (fence etc)
брать* (взять* perf); (goods) распродава́ть
(распрода́ть* perf) ♦ vi (sky) проясня́ться
(проясни́ться perf); (fog, smoke)
рассéиваться (рассéяться perf); (room etc)
обезлю́деть (perf) ♦ adv: ~ **of** (trouble, ground)
пода́льше от +gen ♦ n: **he is/was in the ~** (out
of debt) он свобóден/был свобóден от
долгóв; **to be in the ~** (free of suspicion)
быть* (impf) вне подозрéния; (out of danger)
быть* (impf) вне опа́сности; **have I made
myself ~?** я я́сно вы́разился?; **to make it ~ to
sb that ...** дава́ть* (дать* perf) комý-н поня́ть,
что ...; **I have a ~ day tomorrow** (BRIT) у меня́
за́втра свобóдный день; **to ~ the table**
убира́ть (убра́ть* perf) со стола́; **to ~ one's
throat** прочища́ть (прочи́стить* perf) гóрло;
to ~ a cheque выпла́чивать (вы́платить* perf)
дéньги по чéку; **to ~ a profit** получа́ть
(получи́ть* perf) чи́стую при́быль; **to keep ~
of sb/sth** держа́ться* (impf) пода́льше от
когó-н/чегó-н
► **clear off** vi (inf: leave) убира́ться (убра́ться*
perf)
► **clear up** vt (room) убира́ть (убра́ть* perf);
(mystery, problem) разреша́ть (разреши́ть
perf) ♦ vi убира́ться (убра́ться* perf); (illness)
проходи́ть* (пройти́* perf); (weather)
проясня́ться (проясни́ться perf).

clearance ['klɪərəns] n (removal) расчи́стка*;
(permission) разрешéние; (above vehicle)
габари́тная высота́*.

clearance sale n распрода́жа.

clear-cut ['klɪə'kʌt] adj (decision, issue) я́сный*
(я́сен); (division) чёткий*.

clearing ['klɪərɪŋ] n поля́на; (BRIT: COMM)
кли́ринг.

clearing bank n (BRIT) кли́ринговый банк.

clearing house n кли́ринговая пала́та.

clearly ['klɪəlɪ] adv (distinctly) я́сно, отчётливо;
(obviously) я́вно, очеви́дно; (coherently)
я́сно, поня́тно.

clearway ['klɪəweɪ] n (BRIT) автодорóга, где
останóвка тра́нспорта запрещена́.

cleavage ['kli:vɪdʒ] n я́мка*.

cleaver ['kli:və'] n (for meat) топóрик.

clef [klɛf] n (MUS) ключ*.

cleft [klɛft] n рассéлина.

cleft palate n за́ячья губа́.

clemency ['klɛmənsɪ] n милосéрдие.

clement ['klɛmənt] adj мя́гкий*.

clench [klɛntʃ] vt сжима́ть (сжать* perf).

clergy ['klə:dʒɪ] n духовéнство.

clergyman ['klə:dʒɪmən] irreg n свящéнник,
свящéннослужи́тель m.

clerical ['klɛrɪkl] adj (job, error) канцеля́рский*;
(skills) секрета́рский*; (REL) церкóвный*.

clerk [klɑ:k, (US) klə:rk] n (BRIT: office worker)
клерк, делопроизводи́тель*(ница) m(f); (US:
sales person) продавéц*(-вщи́ца).

Clerk of Court n секрета́рь* m суда́.

clever ['klɛvə'] *adj* (*intelligent*) ýмный (умён); (*deft, crafty*) лóвкий* (лóвок).
cleverly ['klɛvəlɪ] *adv* лóвко.
clew [klu:] *n* (*US*) = **clue**.
cliché ['kli:ʃeɪ] *n* клишé *nt ind*, штамп.
click [klɪk] *vt* (*tongue, heels*) щёлкать (щёлкнуть *perf*) +*instr* ◆ *vi* (*device, switch etc*) щёлкать (щёлкнуть *perf*); (*COMPUT*): **to ~ on the mouse** нажимáть (нажáть* *perf*) на мышь.
client ['klaɪənt] *n* клиéнт.
clientele [kli:ā:n'tɛl] *n* клиентýра.
cliff [klɪf] *n* скалá*, утёс.
cliffhanger ['klɪfhæŋə'] *n* (*TV, also fig*) напряжённый момéнт.
climactic [klaɪ'mæktɪk] *adj* кульминациóнный.
climate ['klaɪmɪt] *n* (*weather, fig*) клúмат; **~ of opinion** состоя́ние обще́ственного мне́ния.
climax ['klaɪmæks] *n* кульминáция, апофеóз; (*during sex*) оргáзм.
climb [klaɪm] *vi* (*sun*) поднимáться (подня́ться* *perf*); (*plant*) вúться (*impf*); (*plane*) набирáть (набрáть* *perf*) высотý; (*prices, shares*) поднимáться (подня́ться* *perf*) ◆ *vt* (*stairs, ladder*) взбирáться (взобрáться* *perf*) по +*prp*; (*tree, hill*) взбирáться (взобрáться* *perf*) *or* поднимáться (подня́ться* *perf*) на +*acc* ◆ *n* подъём; **to ~ over a wall** перелезáть (перелéзть* *perf*) чéрез стéну
▸ **climb down** *vi* (*fig*) уступáть (уступúть* *perf*).
climb-down ['klaɪmdaun] *n* (*BRIT*) устýпка*.
climber ['klaɪmə'] *n* (*mountaineer*) альпинúст(ка*); (*plant*) выющееся растéние.
climbing ['klaɪmɪŋ] *n* альпинúзм.
clinch [klɪntʃ] *vt* (*deal*) заключáть (заключúть *perf*); (*argument*) разрешáть (разрешúть *perf*).
clincher ['klɪntʃə'] *n* решáющий* дóвод.
cling [klɪŋ] (*pt, pp* **clung**) *vi* (*clothes, dress*) облегáть (*impf*); **to ~ to** (*mother, support*) вцепля́ться (вцепúться* *perf*) в +*acc*; (*idea, belief*) цепля́ться (*impf*) за +*acc*.
clingfilm ['klɪŋfɪlm] *n* обёрточная плёнка для продýктов.
clinic ['klɪnɪk] *n* (*medical centre*) клúника; (*session*) консультáция.
clinical ['klɪnɪkl] *adj* (*MED*) клинúческий*; (*fig: attitude*) бесстрáстный (бесстрáстен); (*: room*) стерúльный.
clink [klɪŋk] *vi* звенéть (*impf*) ◆ *vt* (*glasses*) чóкаться (чóкнуться *perf*) +*instr*.
clip [klɪp] *n* (*also:* **paper ~**) скрéпка*; (*BRIT: also:* **bulldog ~**) зажúм; (*for hair*) закóлка*; (*TV, CINEMA*) клип ◆ *vt* (*fasten*) прикрепля́ть (прикрепúть* *perf*); (*also:* **~ together**: *papers*) скрепля́ть (скрепúть* *perf*); (*cut*) подстригáть (подстрúчь* *perf*).
clippers ['klɪpəz] *npl* (*for gardening*) секáтор *msg*; (*also:* **nail ~**) щúпчики *pl*.

clipping ['klɪpɪŋ] *n* (*PRESS*) вы́резка*.
clique [kli:k] *n* клúка.
clitoris ['klɪtərɪs] *n* клúтор.
cloak [kləuk] *n* (*cape*) плащ* ◆ *vt* (*fig: in mist*) окýтывать (окýтать *perf*); **~ed in** окýтанный (окýтан) +*instr*.
cloakroom ['kləukrum] *n* (*for coats*) гардерóб; (*BRIT: toilet*) убóрная *f adj*.
clobber ['klɔbə'] (*inf*) *n* монáтки *pl* ◆ *vt* (*hit*) колошмáтить* (исколошмáтить* *perf*); (*defeat*) бить* (побúть* *perf*).
clock [klɔk] *n* часы́ *pl*; (*of taxi*) счётчик; **to sleep/work round the ~** спать* (*impf*)/ рабóтать (*impf*) крýглые сýтки; **this car has 30,000 miles on the ~** наéздила 30,000 миль; **to work against the ~** рабóтать (*impf*) наперегонки со врéменем
▸ **clock in** *vi* (*BRIT: for work*) отмечáться (отмéтиться* *perf*) (*приходя́ на рабóту*)
▸ **clock off** *vi* (*BRIT: from work*) отмечáться (отмéтиться* *perf*) (*уходя́ с рабóты*)
▸ **clock on** *vi* (*BRIT*) = **clock in**
▸ **clock out** *vi* (*BRIT*) = **clock off**
▸ **clock up** *vt* (*debts*) накáпливать (накопúть* *perf*); (*miles*) накрýчивать (накрутúть* *perf*); (*hours*) набирáть (набрáть* *perf*).
clockwise ['klɔkwaɪz] *adv* по часовóй стрéлке.
clockwork ['klɔkwə:k] *n* завóд ◆ *adj* (*toy*) заводнóй.
clog [klɔg] *n* сабó* *nt ind* ◆ *vt* (*drain*) засоря́ть (засорúть *perf*) ◆ *vi* (*also:* **~ up**: *sink*) засоря́ться (засорúться *perf*); **my nose is ~ged (up)** у меня́ залóжен нос.
cloister ['klɔɪstə'] *n* перистúль *m*.
clone [kləun] *n* (*BIO*) клон.
close¹ [kləus] *adj* (*near*) блúзкий* (блúзок); (*writing*) убóристый (убóрист); (*contact, ties*) тéсный* (тéсен); (*watch, attention*) прúстальный* (прúстален); (*weather, room*) дýшный* (дýшен) ◆ *adv* блúзко; **~ to** (*near*) блúзкий* (блúзок) к +*dat*; **~ to** *or* **on** (*almost*) блúзко к +*dat*; **~ by** *or* **at hand** ря́дом; **how ~ is Edinburgh to Glasgow?** как блúзко от Эдинбýрга нахóдится Глáзго?; **a ~ friend** блúзкий* друг*; **a ~ contest** борьбá на рáвных; **I had a ~ shave** (*fig*) я был на волосóк от этого; **to keep a ~ eye on sb/sth** внимáтельно следúть (*impf*) за +*instr*; **at ~ quarters** на блúзком расстоя́нии.
close² [kləuz] *vt* (*shut*) закрывáть (закры́ть* *perf*); (*finalize*) заключáть (заключúть *perf*); (*end*) завершáть (завершúть *perf*) ◆ *vi* (*shut*) закрывáться (закры́ться* *perf*); (*end*) завершáться (завершúться *perf*) ◆ *n* конéц*; **to bring sth to a ~** завершáть (завершúть *perf*) что-н
▸ **close down** *vt* закрывáть (закры́ть* *perf*) ◆ *vi* закрывáться (закры́ться* *perf*)

---

* marks translations which have irregular inflections. The Russian-English side of the dictionary gives inflectional information.

▶ **close in** vi (night, fog) опускаться (опуститься* perf); (hunters): **to ~ in (on sb/sth)** окружать (окружить perf) (кого-н/что-н); **the days are closing in** дни становятся короче

▶ **close off** vt (area) огораживать (огородить* perf); (road) блокировать (impf/perf).

closed [kləuzd] adj закрытый (закрыт).

closed-circuit [ˈkləuzdˈsəːkɪt] adj: ~ **television** замкнутая телевизионная система.

closed shop n (union) предприятие, на котором работают только члены определённого профсоюза.

close-knit [ˈkləusˈnɪt] adj сплочённый (сплочён).

closely [ˈkləuslɪ] adv (watch, examine) пристально; (connected, related) тесно; **he ~ resembles his father** он очень похож на отца; **we are ~ related** мы близкие родственники; **a ~ guarded secret** тщательно оберегаемый секрет.

close season [ˈkləus-] n закрытый сезон.

closet [ˈklɔzɪt] n (cupboard) шкаф*; (room) чулан.

close-up [ˈkləusʌp] n (PHOT) крупный план.

closing [ˈkləuzɪŋ] adj (stages, remarks) заключительный.

closing price n (COMM) последняя цена or ставка*.

closing time n время* nt закрытия (бара).

closure [ˈkləuʒə³] n (of factory) закрытие; (of road) блокирование.

clot [klɔt] n (of blood etc) сгусток*; (inf) балда m/f ♦ vi (blood) сворачиваться (свернуться perf).

cloth [klɔθ] n (material) ткань f; (for cleaning etc) тряпка*; (BRIT: also: **teacloth**) кухонное полотенце*; (also: **tablecloth**) скатерть* f.

clothe [kləuð] vt одевать (одеть* perf).

clothes [kləuðz] npl одежда fsg; **to put one's ~ on** одеваться (одеться* perf); **to take one's ~ off** раздеваться (раздеться* perf); **to change one's ~** переодеваться (переодеться* perf).

clothes brush n одёжная щётка*.

clothesline [ˈkləuðzlam] n бельевая верёвка*.

clothes peg (US **clothes pin**) n прищепка*.

clothing [ˈkləuðɪŋ] n = **clothes**.

clotted cream [ˈklɔtɪd-] n (BRIT) густые сливки pl.

cloud [klaud] n облако* ♦ vt (liquid) мутить* (замутить* perf); **every ~ has a silver lining** нет худа без добра; **to ~ the issue** запутывать (запутать perf) дело

▶ **cloud over** vi (sky) покрываться (покрыться* perf) облаками; (face) туманиться (затуманиться perf).

cloudburst [ˈklaudbəːst] n ливень* m.

cloud-cuckoo-land [klaudˈkukuːlænd] n (BRIT): **he is living in ~** он живёт в безоблачном царстве.

cloudy [ˈklaudɪ] adj (sky) облачный* (облачен); (liquid) мутный* (мутен).

clout [klaut] vt (inf) долбануть (perf) ♦ n (fig) влияние.

clove [kləuv] n гвоздика; **~ of garlic** долька чеснока.

clover [ˈkləuvə³] n клевер.

cloverleaf [ˈkləuvəliːf] n лист* клевера; (AUT) клеверный лист* (о конструкции пересечения автомобильных дорог).

clown [klaun] n клоун ♦ vi (also: ~ **about**, ~ **around**) паясничать (impf).

cloying [ˈklɔɪŋ] adj (taste, smell) приторный* (приторен).

club [klʌb] n (society, place) клуб; (weapon) дубинка; (implement: also: **golf ~**) клюшка* ♦ vt (hit) избивать (избить* perf) ♦ vi: **to ~ together** складываться (сложиться* perf); **~s** npl (CARDS) трефы fpl; **king of ~s** трефовый король m.

club car n (US: RAIL) вагон-ресторан.

club class n особый класс (в самолётах).

clubhouse [ˈklʌbhaus] n спортивный клуб (здание).

club soda n содовая вода.

cluck [klʌk] vi (hen) кудахтать* (impf).

clue [kluː] n ключ*; (for police) улика; **I haven't a ~** я понятия не имею.

clued-up [kluːdʌp] (US **clued in**) adj (inf): **to be ~** быть (impf) в курсе (дел).

clueless [ˈkluːlɪs] adj без понятия.

clump [klʌmp] n (of trees, plants) заросли fpl; (of buildings) скопление.

clumsy [ˈklʌmzɪ] adj (person, movement) неуклюжий* (неуклюж); (object) неудобный (неудобен).

clung [klʌŋ] pt, pp of **cling**.

cluster [ˈklʌstə³] n (of people, stars) скопление; (of flowers) пучок* ♦ vi (people) сгрудиться (perf); (things) скапливаться (скопиться* perf).

clutch [klʌtʃ] n (grip) хватка; (AUT) сцепление ♦ vt сжимать (сжать* perf) ♦ vi: **to ~ at** цепляться (impf) за +acc; **he has me in his ~es** я у него в руках.

clutter [ˈklʌtə³] vt (also: ~ **up**: room, table) захламлять (захламить* perf) ♦ n хлам.

CM abbr (US: POST) = North Mariana Islands.

cm abbr (= centimetre) см = сантиметр.

CNAA n abbr (BRIT) = Council for National Academic Awards.

CND n abbr = Campaign for Nuclear Disarmament.

CO n abbr = commanding officer; (BRIT: = Commonwealth Office) отдел по делам наций британского Содружества ♦ abbr (US: POST) = Colorado.

Co. abbr = company, county.

c/o abbr (= care of) для передачи +dat.

coach [kəutʃ] n (bus) автобус; (horse-drawn) карета; (of train) вагон; (SPORT) тренер; (SCOL) репетитор ♦ vt (SPORT) тренировать

(натренировáть *perf*); (*SCOL*): to ~ sb for sth
готóвить* (подготóвить* *perf*) когó-н к
чемý-н.
coach trip *n* автóбусная экскýрсия.
coagulate [kəu'ægjuleɪt] *vi* (*blood*)
свóрáчиваться (свернýться *perf*); (*paint*)
сгущáться (сгустúться* *perf*).
coal [kəul] *n* ýголь* *m*.
coalface ['kəulfeɪs] *n* забóй.
coalfield ['kəulfiːld] *n* каменноýгольный
бассéйн.
coalition [kəuə'lɪʃən] *n* (*also POL*) коалúция.
coalman ['kəulmən] *irreg n* ýгольщик.
coalmine ['kəulmaɪn] *n* ýгольная шáхта.
coal miner *n* шахтёр.
coal mining *n* добыча ýгля.
coarse [kɔːs] *adj* грýбый*; (*hair*) жёсткий*;
(*salt, sand etc*) крýпный*.
coast [kəust] *n* бéрег*; (*area*) побережье ♦ *vi*
(*car etc*) катúться* (покатúться* *perf*) по
инéрции.
coastal ['kəustl] *adj* прибрéжный; (*services*)
береговóй.
coaster ['kəustə'] *n* (*NAUT*) каботáжное сýдно*;
(*for glass*) подстáвка* для стакáна.
coastguard ['kəustɡɑːd] *n* (*officer*) офицéр
береговóй слýжбы; **the ~ (service)** береговáя
слýжба.
coastline ['kəustlaɪn] *n* береговáя лúния.
coat [kəut] *n* пальтó *nt ind*; (*on animal: fur*) мех*;
(: *wool*) шерсть*; (*of paint*) слой* ♦ *vt*
покрывáть (покрыть* *perf*).
coat hanger *n* вéшалка*.
coating ['kəutɪŋ] *n* слой.
coat of arms *n* герб*.
coauthor ['kəu'ɔːθə'] *n* соáвтор.
coax [kəuks] *vt* уговáривать (уговорúть *perf*)
лáской.
cob [kɔb] *n see* **corn**.
cobbler ['kɔblə'] *n* сапóжник.
cobbles ['kɔblz] *npl* булыжники *mpl*.
cobblestones ['kɔblstəunz] *npl* = **cobbles**.
COBOL ['kəubɔl] *n* КОБÓЛ.
cobra ['kəubrə] *n* кóбра.
cobweb ['kɔbwɛb] *n* паутúна.
cocaine [kə'keɪn] *n* кокаúн.
cock [kɔk] *n* (*rooster*) петýх*; (*male bird*) самéц*
♦ *vt* (*gun*) взводúть* (взвестú* *perf*); **to ~ one's
ears** (*fig*) навострúть (*perf*) ýши.
cock-a-hoop [kɔkə'huːp] *adj*: **to be ~** балдéть
(*impf*).
cockerel ['kɔkərl] *n* петýх*.
cockeyed ['kɔkaɪd] *adj* (*fig*) дурáцкий*.
cockle ['kɔkl] *n* моллюск.
cockney ['kɔknɪ] *n* (*person*) кóкни *m/f ind*
(*урожéнец райóна Ист-Энд в Лóндоне*);
(*LING*) кóкни *m ind* (*диалéкт урожéнцев
Ист-Энда*).

cockpit ['kɔkpɪt] *n* кабúна.
cockroach ['kɔkrəutʃ] *n* таракáн.
cocktail ['kɔkteɪl] *n* (*drink*) коктéйль *m*; (*with
fruit, prawns etc*) салáт, закýска.
cocktail cabinet *n* бар (*в сервáнте*).
cocktail party *n* приём.
cocktail shaker [-'ʃeɪkə'] *n* мúксер.
cockup ['kɔkʌp] *n* (*inf!*) лáжа, прокóл.
cocky ['kɔkɪ] *adj* дéрзкий* (дéрзок),
задúристый (задúрист).
cocoa ['kəukəu] *n* какáо *nt ind*.
coconut ['kəukənʌt] *n* (*fruit*) кокóсовый орéх;
(*flesh*) кокóс.
cocoon [kə'kuːn] *n* (*of butterfly*) кóкон; (*fig*)
оболóчка.
COD *abbr* (= *cash on delivery*) налóженный
платёж; (*US*: = *collect on delivery*)
налóженный платёж.
cod [kɔd] *n* трескá *f no pl*.
code [kəud] *n* (*of behaviour*) кóдекс; (*cipher,
TEL*) код; **post** ~ почтóвый úндекс; ~ **of
practice** свод прáвил (*профессионáльной
дéятельности*).
codeine ['kəudiːn] *n* кодеúн.
codger ['kɔdʒə'] *n* чудáк*.
codicil ['kɔdɪsɪl] *n* (*LAW*) дополнúтельный
парáграф завещáния.
codify ['kəudɪfaɪ] *vt* кодифицúровать (*impf/perf*).
cod-liver oil ['kɔdlɪvə-] *n* рыбий* жир*.
co-driver ['kəu'draɪvə'] *n* (*in race*) штýрман; (*of
lorry*) смéнный водúтель.
co-ed ['kəu'ɛd] *adj abbr* (*SCOL*) = **coeducational** ♦
n abbr (*US*: *female student*) студéнтка (*в
учéбных заведéниях смéшанного тúпа*);
(*BRIT*: *school*) смéшанная шкóла.
coeducational ['kəuɛdju'keɪʃənl] *adj* (*school*)
смéшанный.
coerce [kəu'əːs] *vt* принуждáть (принýдить*
perf).
coercion [kəu'əːʃən] *n* принуждéние.
coexistence ['kəuɪɡ'zɪstəns] *n*
сосуществовáние.
C. of C. *n abbr* (= *chamber of commerce*)
Торгóвая палáта.
C of E *abbr* = **Church of England**.
coffee ['kɔfɪ] *n* кóфе *m ind*; **black ~** чёрный
кóфе; **white ~** кóфе с молокóм; ~ **with cream**
кóфе со слúвками.
coffee bar *n* (*BRIT*) кофéйня.
coffee beans *npl* кофéйные зёрна *ntpl*.
coffee break *n* перерыв на кóфе.
coffee cake *n* (*US*) торт к кóфе.
coffee cup *n* кофéйная чáшка*.
coffeepot ['kɔfɪpɔt] *n* кофéйник.
coffee table *n* кофéйный стóлик.
coffin ['kɔfɪn] *n* гроб*.
C of I *abbr* = **Church of Ireland**.
C of S *abbr* = **Church of Scotland**.

---

* marks translations which have irregular inflections. The Russian-English side of the dictionary gives inflectional information.

cog [kɔg] *n* (*wheel*) зубча́тое колесо́*; (*tooth*) зубе́ц*.

cogent ['kəudʒənt] *adj* внуши́тельный* (внуши́телен).

cognac ['kɔnjæk] *n* конья́к*.

cogwheel ['kɔgwiːl] *n* зу́бчатое колесо́*.

cohabit [kəu'hæbɪt] *vi*: **to ~ (with sb)** сожи́тельствовать (*impf*) (с кем-н).

coherent [kəu'hɪərənt] *adj* свя́зный; **she was very ~** её речь была́ о́чень свя́зной.

cohesion [kəu'hiːʒən] *n* це́льность *f*.

cohesive [kə'hiːsɪv] *adj* (*fig*) це́льный* (це́лен).

COI *n abbr* (*BRIT*: = *Central Office of Information*) Центра́льное управле́ние информа́ции.

coil [kɔɪl] *n* (*of rope, wire*) мото́к*; (*one loop*) вито́к*; (*of smoke*) кольцо́*; (*AUT*) кату́шка*; (*contraceptive*) спира́ль *f* ♦ *vt* (*rope*) сма́тывать (смота́ть *perf*).

coin [kɔɪn] *n* моне́та ♦ *vt* (*phrase*) приду́мывать (приду́мать *perf*).

coinage ['kɔɪnɪdʒ] *n* (*money*) де́нежные зна́ки *mpl*; (*system*) де́нежная систе́ма; (*LING*) неологи́зм.

coin box *n* (*BRIT*) телефо́н-автома́т.

coincide [kəun'saɪd] *vi* совпада́ть (совпа́сть* *perf*).

coincidence [kəu'ɪnsɪdəns] *n* совпаде́ние.

coin-operated ['kɔɪn'ɔpəreɪtɪd] *adj*: **~ machine** автома́т.

Coke® [kəuk] *n* (*drink*) ко́ка-ко́ла; **I would like a ~, please** да́йте пожа́луйста ко́ка-ко́лу.

coke [kəuk] *n* (*coal*) кокс.

Col. *abbr* = **colonel**.

COLA *n abbr* (*US*: = *cost-of-living adjustment*) индекса́ция зарабо́тной пла́ты.

colander ['kɔləndə'] *n* (*CULIN*) дуршла́г.

cold [kəuld] *adj* холо́дный* ♦ *n* хо́лод; (*MED*) просту́да; **it's ~** хо́лодно; **I am** *or* **feel ~** мне хо́лодно; **the wall is ~** э́та стена́ холо́дная; **to catch ~** *or* **a ~** простужа́ться (простуди́ться* *perf*); **in ~ blood** хладнокро́вно; **to have ~ feet** (*fig*) тру́сить* (стру́сить* *perf*); **I gave her the ~ shoulder** я был неприве́тлив с ней.

cold-blooded ['kəuld'blʌdɪd] *adj* (*ZOOL*) холоднокро́вный (холоднокро́вен); (*callous*) хладнокро́вный* (хладнокро́вен).

cold cream *n* кольд крем.

coldly ['kəuldlɪ] *adv* хо́лодно.

cold-shoulder [kəuld'ʃəuldə'] *vt* относи́ться* (отнести́сь* *perf*) неприве́тливо к +*dat*.

cold sore *n* лихора́дка* (*на губе́ и́ли носу́*).

cold sweat *n* холо́дный пот.

cold turkey *n* (*inf*): **he is going through ~ ~** у него́ ло́мка.

cold war *n*: **the ~ ~** холо́дная война́.

coleslaw ['kəulslɔː] *n капу́стный сала́т с майоне́зом*.

colic ['kɔlɪk] *n* ко́лики *pl*.

colicky ['kɔlɪkɪ] *adj* страда́ющий ко́ликами.

collaborate [kə'læbəreɪt] *vi* сотру́дничать

(*impf*).

collaboration [kəlæbə'reɪʃən] *n* сотру́дничество.

collaborator [kə'læbəreɪtə'] *n* (*on book etc*) соа́втор; (*with enemy*) коллаборациони́ст.

collage [kɔ'lɑːʒ] *n* (*ART*) колла́ж.

collagen ['kɔlədʒən] *n* коллаге́н.

collapse [kə'læps] *vi* (*building, system, plans*) ру́шиться (ру́хнуть *perf*); (*table etc*) скла́дываться (сложи́ться *perf*); (*company*) разоря́ться (разори́ться *perf*); (*government*) развали́ваться (развали́ться *perf*); (*resistance*) сломи́ться (*perf*); (*MED: person*) свали́ться (*perf*) ♦ *n* (*of building*) обва́л; (*of system, plans*) круше́ние; (*of company*) разоре́ние; (*of government*) паде́ние; (*MED*) упа́док сил, колла́пс; **a ~d lung** колла́пс лёгкого.

collapsible [kə'læpsəbl] *adj* складно́й.

collar ['kɔlə'] *n* (*of shirt etc*) воротни́к*; (*of dog etc*) оше́йник; (*TECH*) ше́йка* ♦ *vt* (*inf: physically*) схва́тывать (схвати́ть* *perf*); (*to speak to*) заде́рживать (задержа́ть* *perf*).

collarbone ['kɔləbəun] *n* ключи́ца.

collate [kə'leɪt] *vt* сопоставля́ть (сопоста́вить* *perf*).

collateral [kə'lætərl] *n* (*COMM*) обеспече́ние креди́та.

collateral damage *n* сопу́тствующее разруше́ние.

collation [kə'leɪʃən] *n* сопоставле́ние, сличе́ние; (*CULIN*): **a cold ~** холо́дный буфе́т.

colleague ['kɔliːg] *n* колле́га *m/f*.

collect [kə'lɛkt] *vt* (*gather*) собира́ть (собра́ть* *perf*); (*stamps etc*) коллекциони́ровать (*impf*); (*BRIT: on foot*) заходи́ть* (зайти́* *perf*) за +*instr*; (*: by vehicle*) заезжа́ть* (зае́хать* *perf*) за +*instr*; (*debts etc*) взы́скивать (взыска́ть* *perf*); (*mail*) забира́ть (забра́ть* *perf*) ♦ *vi* (*crowd*) собира́ться (собра́ться* *perf*); **to call ~** (*US*) звони́ть (*impf*) по колле́кту; **to ~ one's thoughts** собира́ться (собра́ться *perf*) с мы́слями; **~ on delivery** (*US*) нало́женный платёж.

collected [kə'lɛktɪd] *adj*: **~ works** собра́ние сочине́ний.

collection [kə'lɛkʃən] *n* (*of stamps etc*) колле́кция; (*of poems etc*) сбо́рник; (*for charity, also REL*) поже́ртвования *ntpl*; (*of mail*) вы́емка.

collective [kə'lɛktɪv] *adj* коллекти́вный ♦ *n* коллекти́в.

collective bargaining *n переговоры между предпринимателем и профсоюзами об оплате труда рабочих*.

collector [kə'lɛktə'] *n* (*of stamps etc*) коллекционе́р; (*of taxes etc*) сбо́рщик(-ица); (*of cash*) инкасса́тор; **~'s item** *or* **piece** *вещь, представляющая интерес для коллекционера*.

college ['kɔlɪdʒ] *n* (*of university*) ко́лледж; (*of*

technology etc) институ́т; **to go to** ~
поступа́ть (поступи́ть* *perf*) в институ́т; ~ **of
education** уче́бное заведе́ние.
collide [kə'laɪd] *vi* (*cars, people*) ста́лкиваться
(столкну́ться *perf*); **to** ~ **with sth**
ната́лкиваться (натолкну́ться *perf*) на что-н.
collie ['kɒlɪ] *n* ко́лли *m ind*.
colliery ['kɒlɪərɪ] *n* (*BRIT*) у́гольная ша́хта.
collision [kə'lɪʒən] *n* (*of vehicles*)
столкнове́ние; **to be on a** ~ **course**
находи́ться* (*impf*) на пути́, веду́щем к
столкнове́нию; (*fig*) вставать* (встать* *perf*)
на путь конфронта́ции.
collision damage waiver *n страхо́вка,
освобождающая от вы́платы компенса́ции
за поврежде́ние взя́той напрока́т маши́ны.*
colloquial [kə'ləukwɪəl] *adj* разгово́рный.
collusion [kə'lu:ʒən] *n* (*collaboration*) сго́вор; **in**
~ **with** в сго́воре с +*instr*.
Cologne [kə'ləun] *n* Кёльн.
cologne [kə'ləun] *n* (*also:* **eau de** ~) одеколо́н.
Colombia [kə'lɒmbɪə] *n* Колу́мбия.
Colombian [kə'lɒmbɪən] *adj* колумби́йский* ♦
n колумби́ец(-и́йка).
colon ['kəulən] *n* (*LING*) двоето́чие; (*ANAT*)
пряма́я кишка́.
colonel ['kɔ:nl] *n* полко́вник.
colonial [kə'ləunɪəl] *adj* колониа́льный.
colonize ['kɒlənaɪz] *vt* (*country etc*)
колонизи́ровать (*impf/perf*).
colony ['kɒlənɪ] *n* (*of people, animals*) коло́ния.
color *etc* (*US*) = **colour** *etc*.
Colorado beetle [kɒlə'rɑːdəu-] *n* колора́дский
жук*.
colossal [kə'lɒsl] *adj* колосса́льный*
(колосса́лен).
colour ['kʌlə] (*US* **color**) *n* цвет*; (*of spectacle
etc*) кра́сочность *f* ♦ *vt* (*paint*) раскра́шивать
(раскра́сить* *perf*); (*dye*) кра́сить*
(покра́сить* *perf*); (*fig: judgement etc*)
окра́шивать (окра́сить* *perf*) ♦ *vi* (*blush*)
красне́ть (покрасне́ть *perf*) ♦ *cpd* цветно́й; ~**s**
npl (*of club etc*) эмбле́ма *fsg*; (*MIL*) флаг *msg*;
skin ~ цвет ко́жи; **in** ~ в цве́те; **with flying** ~**s**
с триу́мфом
  ▶ **colour in** *vt* раскра́шивать (раскра́сить*
  perf).
colour bar *n* ра́совый барье́р.
colour-blind ['kʌləblaɪnd] *adj*: **he is** ~ он
дальто́ник.
coloured ['kʌləd] *adj* цветно́й.
colour film *n* цветна́я плёнка.
colourful ['kʌləful] *adj* (*cloth*) цвети́стый
(цвети́ст); (*story*) кра́сочный* (кра́сочен);
(*personality*) я́ркий*.
colouring ['kʌlərɪŋ] *n* (*complexion*) цвет лица́;
(*in food*) краси́тель *m*.
colour scheme *n* цветова́я га́мма.

colour supplement *n* (*BRIT: PRESS*)
иллюстри́рованное приложе́ние.
colour television *n* цветно́й телеви́зор.
colt [kəult] *n* жеребёнок*.
column ['kɒləm] *n* (*of people, also ARCHIT*)
коло́нна; (*of smoke*) столб*; (*PRESS*)
ру́брика; **the editorial** ~ реда́кторская
статья́*.
columnist ['kɒləmnɪst] *n* (*PRESS*) обозрева́тель
m.
coma ['kəumə] *n* (*MED*): **to be in a** ~
находи́ться* (*impf*) в ко́ме.
comb [kəum] *n* (*for hair*) расчёска; (:
ornamental) гре́бень* *m* ♦ *vt* (*hair*)
расчёсывать (расчеса́ть* *perf*); (*area*)
прочёсывать (прочеса́ть* *perf*).
combat [*n* 'kɒmbæt, *vt* kəm'bæt] *n* (*fighting*)
бой*; (*battle*) би́тва ♦ *vt* боро́ться* (*impf*)
про́тив +*gen*.
combination [kɒmbɪ'neɪʃən] *n* (*mixture*)
сочета́ние, комбина́ция; (*code*) код.
combination lock *n* замо́к* с ши́фром.
combine [*vb* kəm'baɪn, *n* 'kɒmbaɪn] *vt*
комбини́ровать (скомбини́ровать *perf*) ♦ *vi*
(*groups*) объединя́ться (объедини́ться *perf*);
(*CHEM*) вступа́ть (вступи́ть* *perf*) в
соедине́ние ♦ *n* (*ECON*) объедине́ние; (*also:* ~
harvester) комба́йн; **to** ~ **sth with sth**
(*qualities*) сочета́ть *perf* что-н с чем-н;
(*activities*) совмеща́ть (совмести́ть* *perf*)
что-н с чем-н; **a** ~**d effort** совме́стное
уси́лие.
combo ['kɒmbəu] *n* (*JAZZ*) ко́мбо*.
combustible [kəm'bʌstɪbl] *adj* горю́чий*.
combustion [kəm'bʌstʃən] *n* (*act*) сгора́ние;
(*process*) горе́ние.

KEYWORD

come [kʌm] (*pt* came, *pp* come) *vi* 1 (*move
towards: on foot*) подходи́ть* (подойти́* *perf*);
(: *by transport*) подъезжа́ть (подъе́хать* *perf*);
they came to a river (*on foot*) они́ подошли́ к
реке́; (*by transport*) они́ подъе́хали к реке́; **he
came running up to us** он подбежа́л к нам; **to
come running** подбега́ть (подбежа́ть* *perf*)
2 (*arrive: on foot*) приходи́ть* (прийти́* *perf*);
(: *by transport*) приезжа́ть (прие́хать* *perf*); **to
come home** (*on foot*) приходи́ть* (прийти́*
perf) домо́й; (*by transport*) приезжа́ть
(прие́хать* *perf*) домо́й; **he came running to
tell us** он прибежа́л сказа́ть нам; **are you
coming to my party?** Вы придёте ко мне на
вечери́нку?; **I've only come for an hour** я
зашёл то́лько на час
3 (*reach: power, decision, conclusion*): **to come
to** прийти́* (прийти́* *perf*) к +*dat*; **the bill
came to £40** счёт был £40; **her hair came to
her waist** у неё бы́ли во́лосы до по́яса
4 (*occur*): **an idea came to me** мне в го́лову

---

* marks translations which have irregular inflections. The Russian-English side of the dictionary gives inflectional information.

пришла идея

5 (*be, become*): **to come into being** возникать (возникнуть *perf*); **to come loose** отходить* (отойти* *perf*); **I've come to like him** он стал мне нравиться

► **come about** *vi*: **how did it come about?** каким образом это получилось?; **it came about through...** это получилось из-за +*gen*

► **come across** *vt fus* наталкиваться (натолкнуться *perf*) на +*acc*
   ♦ *vi*: **to come across well/badly** производить* (произвести* *perf*) хорошее/плохое впечатление

► **come along** *vi* (*pupil, work*) продвигаться (продвинуться *perf*); **come along!** идёмте!, пошли!

► **come apart** *vi* (*break*) ломаться (сломаться *perf*); (*can be dismantled*) разбираться (*impf*); (*tear*) рваться* (разорваться* *perf*)

► **come away** *vi* (*leave*) уходить* (уйти* *perf*); (*to become detached*) отходить* (отойти* *perf*)

► **come back** *vi* (*return*) возвращаться (вернуться *perf*); (*inf*): **can I come back to you on that one?** я ещё обращусь к Вам по этому вопросу, ладно?

► **come by** *vt fus* (*acquire*) доставать* (достать* *perf*)

► **come down** *vi* (*price*) понижаться (понизиться* *perf*); **the tree came down in the storm** дерево снесло бурей; **the building will have to come down soon** здание должны скоро снести

► **come forward** *vi* (*volunteer*) вызываться (вызваться* *perf*)

► **come from** *vt fus* (*place, source etc*): **she comes from India** она из Индии

► **come in** *vi* (*person*) входить* (войти* *perf*); (*on deal etc*): **to come in on** вступать (вступить* *perf*) в +*acc*; **where does he come in?** в чём состоит его роль?

► **come in for** *vt fus* подвергаться (подвергнуться* *perf*) +*dat*

► **come into** *vt fus* (*fashion*) входить* (войти* *perf*) в +*acc*; (*be involved in*) играть (*impf*) роль в +*prp*; **to come into money** получать (получить* *perf*) большую сумму денег

► **come off** *vi* (*button*) отрываться (оторваться *perf*); (*handle*) отламываться (отломаться* *perf*); (*can be taken off*) сниматься (*impf*); (*attempt*) удаваться* (удаться* *perf*)

► **come on** *vi* (*pupil*) делать (сделать *perf*) успехи; (*work etc*) продвигаться (*impf*); (*lights etc*) включаться (включиться* *perf*); **come on!** (ну,) давайте!

► **come out** *vi* (*fact*) становиться (стать* *perf*) известным(-ой); (*book, sun*) выходить* (выйти* *perf*); (*stain*) сходить* (сойти* *perf*); (*person*) выходить* (выйти* *perf*); (*workers*): **to come out on strike** выходить* (выйти* *perf*)

на забастовку

► **come over** *vt fus*: **I don't know what's come over him!** я не знаю, что с ним такое!

► **come round** *vi* (*MED*) очнуться (*perf*), приходить* (прийти* *perf*) в себя

► **come through** *vt fus* (*survive*) пережить* (*perf*); (: *operation*) переносить* (перенести* *perf*)
   ♦ *vi*: **his visa came through yesterday** его виза пришла вчера

► **come to** *vi* (*MED*) очнуться (*perf*), приходить* (прийти* *perf*) в себя
   ♦ *vt fus*: **how much does it come to?** сколько это всё будет?

► **come under** *vt fus*: **to come under (the heading)** идти* (*impf*) под заголовком; **to come under criticism from ...** подвергаться (подвергнуться *perf*) критике со стороны +*gen* ...; **he has come under pressure from his boss** начальник оказывал на него давление

► **come up** *vi* (*sun*) всходить* (взойти* *perf*); (*approach: event*) приближаться (*impf*); (*arise: questions*) вставать* (встать* *perf*); (*to be mentioned*) быть (*impf*) затронутым; **I can't come with you, something important has come up** я не смогу пойти с тобой, у меня возникло важное дело

► **come up against** *vt fus* наталкиваться (натолкнуться *perf*) на +*acc*

► **come up to** *vt fus*: **the film didn't come up to our expectations** фильм не оправдал наши ожидания

► **come up with** *vt fus* (*idea, solution*) придумывать (придумать *perf*); (*money*) находить (найти* *perf*)

► **come upon** *vt fus* наталкиваться (натолкнуться *perf*) на +*acc*.

comeback ['kʌmbæk] *n* (*reaction*) язвительный ответ; (*response*) возражение; **to make a ~** (*of actor etc*) обретать (обрести* *perf*) новую популярность.

Comecon ['kɔmikɔn] *n abbr* (= *Council for Mutual Economic Aid*) ≈ СЭВ= *Совет Экономической Взаимопомощи*.

comedian [kə'mi:dɪən] *n* комик.

comedienne [kəmi:dɪ'ɛn] *n* комическая актриса.

comedown ['kʌmdaun] *n* (*inf: humiliation*) унижение; (: *demotion*) понижение.

comedy ['kɔmɪdɪ] *n* (*play, film*) комедия; (*humour*) комизм.

comet ['kɔmɪt] *n* комета.

comeuppance [kʌm'ʌpəns] *n*: **to get one's ~** получать (получить* *perf*) по заслугам.

comfort ['kʌmfət] *n* (*well-being*) комфорт; (*solace*) утешение; (*relief*) облегчение ♦ *vt* утешать (утешить *perf*); **~s** *npl* (*luxuries*) удобства *ntpl*.

comfortable ['kʌmfətəbl] *adj* (*furniture, room*)

удо́бный* (удо́бен), комфорта́бельный* (комфорта́белен); (*walk etc*) лёгкий*; (*majority*) прили́чный* (прили́чен); **to be ~** (*person: physically*) чу́вствовать (*impf*) себя́ удо́бно; (: *financially*) жить (*impf*) в доста́тке; (*patient*) чу́вствовать (*impf*) себя́ норма́льно; **I don't feel very ~ about it** я чу́вствую себя́ нело́вко в да́нном слу́чае; **make yourself ~** располага́йтесь поудо́бнее.
comfortably ['kʌmfətəblɪ] *adv* удо́бно.
comforter ['kʌmfətəʳ] *n* (*US*) со́ска-пусты́шка*.
comfort station *n* (*US*) обще́ственный туале́т.
comic ['kɒmɪk] *adj* коми́ческий*, смешно́й ◆ *n* (*comedian*) ко́мик; (*BRIT: magazine*) ко́микс.
comical ['kɒmɪkl] *adj* смешно́й* (смешо́н), коми́чный* (коми́чен).
comic strip *n* ко́микс (*се́рия рису́нков*).
coming ['kʌmɪŋ] *n* прибы́тие ◆ *adj* (*approaching*) приближа́ющийся; (*next*) сле́дующий*; (*future*) бу́дущий*; **in the ~ weeks** в тече́ние сле́дующих неде́ль.
coming(s) and going(s) *n(pl)* прихо́д *msg* и ухо́д *msg*.
Comintern ['kɒmɪntə:n] *n* (*POL*) Коминте́рн.
comma ['kɒmə] *n* (*LING*) запята́я *f adj*.
command [kə'mɑ:nd] *n* (*order*) кома́нда; (*control*) контро́ль *m*; (*MIL*) кома́ндование; (*mastery*) владе́ние; (*COMPUT*) кома́нда, директи́ва ◆ *vt* (*troops*) кома́ндовать (*impf*) +*instr*; (*be able to get*) располага́ть (*impf*) +*instr*; (*deserve*) заслу́живать (*impf*) +*gen*; **to be in ~ of** (*situation*) владе́ть (овладе́ть *perf*) +*instr*; **to take ~ of** (*MIL*) принима́ть (приня́ть* *perf*) кома́ндование +*instr*; **to have at one's ~** (*resources etc*) име́ть (*impf*) в своём распоряже́нии; **he has a good ~ of English** он хорошо́ владе́ет англи́йским языко́м; **to ~ sb to do** прика́зывать (приказа́ть* *perf*) кому́-н +*infin*.
commandant ['kɒməndænt] *n* коменда́нт.
command economy *n* кома́ндная эконо́мика.
commandeer [kɒmən'dɪəʳ] *vt* (*requisition*) реквизи́ровать (*impf/perf*); (*fig*) присва́ивать (присво́ить *perf*).
commander [kə'mɑ:ndəʳ] *n* (*MIL: of troops*) кома́ндующий *m adj*; (: *of batallion*) команди́р.
commander in chief *n* главнокома́ндующий *m adj*.
commanding [kə'mɑ:ndɪŋ] *adj* (*appearance*) внуши́тельный*; (*voice etc*) вла́стный*; (*situation*) госпо́дствующий*.
commanding officer *n* команди́р.
commandment [kə'mɑ:ndmənt] *n* за́поведь *f*.
command module *n* (*SPACE*) кома́ндный отсе́к корабля́.
commando [kə'mɑ:ndəu] *n* (*group*) деса́нтные

войска́ *ntpl*; (*soldier*) деса́нтник.
commemorate [kə'mɛmәreɪt] *vt* (*with statue etc*) увекове́чивать (увекове́чить *perf*); (*with celebration etc*) отмеча́ть (отме́тить* *perf*).
commemoration [kəmɛmə'reɪʃən] *n* ознаменова́ние.
commemorative [kə'mɛmәrәtɪv] *adj* (*stamp*) юбиле́йный*; (*plaque*) мемориа́льный.
commence [kə'mɛns] *vt* приступа́ть (приступи́ть* *perf*) к +*dat* ◆ *vi* начина́ться (нача́ться* *perf*).
commend [kə'mɛnd] *vt* хвали́ть* (похвали́ть* *perf*); (*recommend*): **to ~ sth to sb** рекомендова́ть (порекомендова́ть *perf*) что-н кому́-н.
commendable [kə'mɛndəbl] *adj* похва́льный* (похва́лен).
commendation [kɒmɛn'deɪʃən] *n* благода́рность *f*.
commensurate [kə'mɛnʃərɪt] *adj*: **~ with** соразме́рный* (соразме́рен) +*dat* or с +*instr*.
comment ['kɒmɛnt] *n* (*remark*) замеча́ние; (*on situation*) коммента́рий ◆ *vi*: **to ~ (on)** комменти́ровать (прокомменти́ровать *perf*) (+*acc*); **to ~ that** поясня́ть (поясни́ть *perf*), что; **"no ~"** "возде́рживаюсь от коммента́риев".
commentary ['kɒməntərɪ] *n* репорта́ж; (*book, article*) коммента́рий.
commentator ['kɒmənteɪtəʳ] *n* (*TV, RADIO*) коммента́тор; (*sports*) ~ спорти́вный коммента́тор.
commerce ['kɒmə:s] *n* комме́рция.
commercial [kə'mə:ʃl] *adj* (*organization*) комме́рческий*; (*success, failure*) фина́нсовый ◆ *n* (*TV, RADIO*) рекла́ма.
commercial bank *n* комме́рческий* банк.
commercial break *n* рекла́мная па́уза.
commercial college *n* институ́т комме́рции.
commercialism [kə'mə:ʃəlɪzəm] *n* меркантили́зм.
commercialized [kə'mə:ʃəlaɪzd] *adj* (*pej*) поста́вленный на комме́рческую но́гу.
commercial radio *n* комме́рческое ра́дио.
commercial television *n* комме́рческое телеви́дение.
commercial traveller *n* коммивояжёр.
commercial vehicle *n* комме́рческий тра́нспорт.
commiserate [kə'mɪzəreɪt] *vi*: **to ~ with** сочу́вствовать (посочу́вствовать *perf*) +*dat*.
commission [kə'mɪʃən] *n* (*order for work*) зака́з; (*COMM*) комиссио́нные *pl adj*, комиссио́нное вознагражде́ние; (*committee*) коми́ссия; (*MIL*) офице́рский* чин ◆ *vt* (*order*) зака́зывать (заказа́ть* *perf*); (*MIL*) присва́ивать (присво́ить *perf*) офице́рский* чин +*dat*; **out of ~** (*NAUT*) не приго́дный

(пригоден) к плаванию; (*machine*)
неисправный* (неисправен); **I get 10%** ~ я
получаю 10% комиссионных; ~ **of inquiry**
следственная комиссия; **to** ~ **sb to do**
sth поручать (поручить* *perf*) кому-н +*infin*; **to** ~
sth from sb заказывать (заказать* *perf*) что-н
кому-н.

commissionaire [kəmɪʃə'nɛə'] *n* (*BRIT*)
швейцар.

commissioner [kə'mɪʃənə'] *n*: (**police**) ~
полицейский* комиссар.

commit [kə'mɪt] *vt* (*crime*) совершать
(совершить *perf*); (*money*) выделять
(выделить *perf*); (*entrust*) вверять (вверить
perf); **to** ~ **o.s.** принимать (принять* *perf*) на
себя обязательства; **to** ~ **suicide** совершать
(совершить *perf*) самоубийство; **to** ~ **to**
writing записывать (записать* *perf*); **to** ~ **to**
memory запоминать (запомнить *perf*); **to** ~
sb for trial отдавать* (отдать* *perf*) кого-н
под суд.

commitment [kə'mɪtmənt] *n* (*belief*)
преданность *f*; (*obligation*) обязательство.

committed [kə'mɪtɪd] *adj* (*supporter*)
приверженный (привержен).

committee [kə'mɪtɪ] *n* комитет; **to be on a** ~
входить* (*impf*) в состав комитета.

committee meeting *n* заседание комитета.

commodity [kə'mɔdɪtɪ] *n* (*saleable item*) товар;
(*food*) продукт.

commodity exchange *n* товарная биржа.

common ['kɔmən] *adj* (*shared*) общий*; (*usual,
ordinary*) обычный; (*vulgar*) вульгарный*
(вульгарен) ♦ *n* общественный луг*; **the C**~**s**
npl (*also*: **the House of C**~**s**: *BRIT*) Палата *fsg*
Общин; **to have sth in** ~ (**with sb**) иметь (*impf*)
что-н общее (с кем-н); **in** ~ **use** в широком
употреблении; **it's** ~ **knowledge that**
общеизвестно, что; **to** *or* **for the** ~ **good** для
всеобщего блага.

common cold *n* обыкновенная простуда.

common denominator *n* (*MATH*) общий*
знаменатель *m*; (*characteristic*) общая черта;
(*attitude*) общее* мнение.

commoner ['kɔmənə'] *n* простолюдин.

common ground *n* (*fig*) точки *fpl*
соприкосновения.

common land *n* общественная земля*.

common law *n* обычное право.

common-law ['kɔmənlɔ:] *adj* гражданский*.

commonly ['kɔmənlɪ] *adv* обычно.

Common Market *n*: **the** ~ ~ Общий* рынок*.

commonplace ['kɔmənpleɪs] *adj* обычный,
обыденный.

common room *n* комната отдыха (*для
студентов, учителей и т.д.*).

common sense *n* здравый смысл.

Commonwealth ['kɔmənwelθ] *n* (*BRIT*): **the** ~
Содружество.

commotion [kə'məuʃən] *n* суматоха.

communal ['kɔmju:nl] *adj* (*shared*) общий*;

(*life*) общественный; **a** ~ **flat** коммунальная
квартира.

commune [*n* 'kɔmju:n, *vi* kə'mju:n] *n* коммуна
♦ *vi*: **to** ~ **with** общаться (*impf*) с +*instr*.

communicate [kə'mju:nɪkeɪt] *vt* передавать*
(передать* *perf*) ♦ *vi*: **to** ~ (**with**) общаться
(*impf*) (с +*instr*); **to** ~ (**by letter**) обращаться
(обратиться* *perf*) письменно.

communication [kəmju:nɪ'keɪʃən] *n* (*process*)
коммуникация; (*letter etc*) сообщение.

communication cord *n* (*BRIT*) аварийный
сигнал "стоп".

communications network [kəmju:nɪ'keɪʃənz-]
n система коммуникаций.

communications satellite *n* спутник связи.

communicative [kə'mju:nɪkətɪv] *adj* (*person*)
общительный* (общителен).

communion [kə'mju:nɪən] *n* (*also*: **Holy C**~)
Святое Причастие.

communiqué [kə'mju:nɪkeɪ] *n* коммюнике *nt*
ind.

communism ['kɔmjunɪzəm] *n* коммунизм.

communist ['kɔmjunɪst] *adj* коммунист-
ический* ♦ *n* коммунист(ка).

community [kə'mju:nɪtɪ] *n* (*public*)
общественность *f*; (*within larger group*)
община; **the business** ~ деловые круги *mpl*.

community centre *n* ≈ общественный центр.

community charge *n* (*BRIT*: *formerly*)
подушный налог.

community chest *n* (*US*) объединённый
благотворительный фонд.

community health centre *n* районная
поликлиника.

community home *n* (*BRIT*: *for children*)
детский* дом.

community service *n* трудовая повинность *f*
(*как форма наказания*).

community spirit *n* чувство общности *or*
товарищества.

commutation ticket [kəmju:'teɪʃən-] *n* (*US*)
сезонный билет.

commute [kə'mju:t] *vi* (*to work*) ездить на
работу из пригорода в город ♦ *vt* (*LAW*)
смягчать (смягчить *perf*) наказание.

commuter [kə'mju:tə'] *n* человек, который
ездит на работу из пригорода в город; ~
train пригородный поезд.

compact [*adj* kəm'pækt, *n* 'kɔmpækt] *adj*
компактный* (компактен) ♦ *n* (*also*: **powder**
~) пудреница.

compact disc *n* компакт-диск.

compact-disc player [kɔmpækt'dɪsk-] *n*
проигрыватель *m* для компакт-дисков.

companion [kəm'pænjən] *n* спутник(-ица).

companionship [kəm'pænjənʃɪp] *n* общение.

companionway [kəm'pænjənweɪ] *n* (*NAUT*)
трап.

company ['kʌmpənɪ] *n* (*COMM*) компания;
(*THEAT*) труппа; (*MIL*) рота; (*companionship*)
компания, общество; **he's good** ~ его

общество приятно; **we have** ~ у нас гости;
to keep sb ~ составлять (составить* *perf*)
кому-н компанию; **to part** ~ **with**
расходиться* (разойтись* *perf*) с +*instr*; **Smith
and C**~ Смит и Компания.
company car *n* служебная машина.
company director *n* директор* компании.
company secretary *n* (*BRIT*) секретарь* *m(f)*
фирмы.
comparable ['kɔmpərəbl] *adj* (*size*) сравнимый
(сравним); (*style*) сопоставимый
(сопоставим); (*car, property etc*) подобный*
(подобен).
comparative [kəm'pærətɪv] *adj* (*also* LING)
сравнительный; (*relative*) относительный
(относителен).
comparatively [kəm'pærətɪvlɪ] *adv* (*relatively*)
относительно.
compare [kəm'pɛə'] *vt*: **to ~ sb/sth with** *or* **to**
(*liken*) сравнивать (сравнить *perf*) кого-н/
что-н с +*instr*; (*set side by side*) сопоставлять
(сопоставить* *perf*) кого-н/что-н с +*instr* ♦ *vi*:
to ~ (with) соотноситься (*impf*) (с +*instr*); **how
do the prices ~?** как соотносятся цены?; ~**d
with** *or* **to** по сравнению *or* в сравнении с
+*instr*.
comparison [kəm'pærɪsn] *n* (*see vt*) сравнение;
сопоставление; **in ~ (with)** по сравнению *or*
в сравнении (с +*instr*).
compartment [kəm'pɑːtmənt] *n* (*RAIL*) купе *nt
ind*; (*section*) отделение.
compass ['kʌmpəs] *n* (*instrument*) компас; (*fig*)
диапазон; ~**es** *npl* (*also*: **pair of** ~**es**) циркуль
msg; **beyond the** ~ **of** за пределами +*gen*;
within the ~ **of** в пределах +*gen*.
compassion [kəm'pæʃən] *n* сострадание.
compassionate [kəm'pæʃənɪt] *adj*
сострадательный (сострадателен); **on** ~
grounds по состоянию здоровья; ~ **leave**
отпуск по семейным обстоятельствам.
compatibility [kəmpætɪ'bɪlɪtɪ] *n*
совместимость *f*.
compatible [kəm'pætɪbl] *adj* (*also* COMPUT)
совместимый (совместим).
compel [kəm'pɛl] *vt* вынуждать (вынудить*
perf).
compelling [kəm'pɛlɪŋ] *adj* (*fig: argument*)
убедительный* (убедителен); (: *reason*)
настоятельный.
compendium [kəm'pɛndɪəm] *n* (*summary*)
резюме *nt ind*.
compensate ['kɔmpənseɪt] *vt*: **to ~ sb for sth**
компенсировать (*impf/perf*) кому-н что-н ♦ *vi*:
to ~ for (*loss, distress etc*) компенсировать
(*impf/perf*).
compensation [kɔmpən'seɪʃən] *n*
компенсация; (*money*) денежная
компенсация.

compère ['kɔmpɛə'] *n* (*TV, RADIO*)
ведущий*(-ая) *m(f)* *adj*.
compete [kəm'piːt] *vi* (*in contest etc*)
соревноваться (*impf*); **to ~ (with)** (*companies*)
конкурировать (*impf*) (с +*instr*); (*rivals*)
соперничать (*impf*) (с +*instr*); **to ~ (with one
another)** (*theories etc*) соперничать (*impf*)
друг с другом.
competence ['kɔmpɪtəns] *n* компетенция.
competent ['kɔmpɪtənt] *adj* (*person*)
компетентный* (компетентен); (*piece of
work*) искусный.
competing [kəm'piːtɪŋ] *adj* (*firms*)
конкурирующий; (*claims, explanations*)
разноречивый (разноречив).
competition [kɔmpɪ'tɪʃən] *n* (*contest*)
соревнование; (*between firms*) конкуренция;
(*between rivals*) соперничество; **to be in ~
with** конкурировать (*impf*) с +*instr*.
competitive [kəm'pɛtɪtɪv] *adj* (*industry*)
основанный на конкуренции; (*person*)
честолюбивый (честолюбив);
(*price etc*) конкурентноспособный*
(конкурентноспособен); (*sport*)
состязательный.
competitive examination *n* конкурс.
competitor [kəm'pɛtɪtə'] *n* (*rival*) соперник,
конкурент; (*in musical competition*)
конкурсант; (*participant*) участник(-ица)
соревнования.
compile [kəm'paɪl] *vt* составлять (составить*
perf).
complacency [kəm'pleɪsnsɪ] *n* безмятежность
f.
complacent [kəm'pleɪsnt] *adj* безмятежный
(безмятежен).
complain [kəm'pleɪn] *vi*: **to ~ (about)**
жаловаться (пожаловаться *perf*) (на +*acc*); **to
~ of a pain** жаловаться (пожаловаться *perf*)
на боль.
complaint [kəm'pleɪnt] *n* жалоба; **to make a ~
against** подавать (подать* *perf*) жалобу на
+*acc*.
complement [*n* 'kɔmplɪmənt, *vb* 'kɔmplɪmɛnt] *n*
(*supplement*) дополнение; (*ship's crew*)
экипаж ♦ *vt* (*enhance*) дополнять (*impf*); **to
have a full ~ of** иметь (*impf*) полный
комплект +*gen*.
complementary [kɔmplɪ'mɛntərɪ] *adj*: **they are
~ (to one another)** они дополняют друг
друга.
complete [kəm'pliːt] *adj* полный*; (*finished*)
завершённый (завершён) ♦ *vt* (*building, task*)
завершать (завершить *perf*); (*set etc*)
комплектовать (укомплектовать *perf*); (*a
form*) заполнять (заполнить *perf*); **it's a ~
disaster** это полный провал.
completely [kəm'pliːtlɪ] *adv* полностью,

---

* marks translations which have irregular inflections. The Russian-English side of the dictionary gives inflectional information.

совершённо.

completion [kəm'pli:ʃən] n (of building) завершёние; (of contract) совершёние; **to be nearing ~** блйзиться (impf) к завершёнию; **on ~** по завершёнии.

complex ['kɔmplɛks] adj слóжный*, кóмплексный ◆ n (also PSYCH) кóмплекс.

complexion [kəm'plɛkʃən] n (of face) цвет* лицá; (nature) харáктер.

complexity [kəm'plɛksɪtɪ] n слóжность f.

compliance [kəm'plaɪəns] n (submission) послушáние; (agreement) соглáсие; **~ with** слéдование +dat; **in ~ with** в соотвéтствии с +instr.

compliant [kəm'plaɪənt] adj послýшный* (послýшен).

complicate ['kɔmplɪkeɪt] vt усложнять (усложнйть perf).

complicated ['kɔmplɪkeɪtɪd] adj слóжный* (слóжен).

complication [kɔmplɪ'keɪʃən] n (also MED) осложнéние.

complicity [kəm'plɪsɪtɪ] n соучáстие.

compliment [n 'kɔmplɪmənt, vb 'kɔmplɪmɛnt] n комплимéнт, хвалá ◆ vt хвалйть (похвалйть perf); **~s** npl (regards) привéты mpl; **to ~ sb, pay sb a ~** дéлать (сдéлать perf) комý-н комплимéнт; **to ~ sb (on sth or on doing)** поздравлять (поздрáвить* perf) когó-н (с чем-н).

complimentary [kɔmplɪ'mɛntərɪ] adj (remark) лéстный* (лéстен); (ticket etc) дáрственный.

compliments slip n фúрменный бланк для неофициáльных запúсок.

comply [kəm'plaɪ] vi: **to ~ (with)** подчиняться (подчинйться perf) (+dat).

component [kəm'pəunənt] adj составнóй ◆ n компонéнт.

compose [kəm'pəuz] vt (write) сочинять (сочинйть perf); (form): **to be ~d of** состоять (impf) из +gen; **to ~ o.s.** успокáиваться (успокóиться perf).

composed [kəm'pəuzd] adj спокóйный* (спокóен).

composer [kəm'pəuzə'] n композúтор.

composite ['kɔmpəzɪt] adj составнóй; (BOT) сложноцвéтный; (MATH) слóжный.

composition [kɔmpə'zɪʃən] n (structure) состáв; (essay) сочинéние; (MUS) композúция.

compositor [kəm'pɔzɪtə'] n набóрщик.

compos mentis ['kɔmpɔs 'mɛntɪs] adj вменяемый (вменяем).

compost ['kɔmpɔst] n компóст; (also: **potting ~**) удóбренная земля.

composure [kəm'pəuʒə'] n самооблáдание.

compound [n, adj 'kɔmpaund, vt kəm'paund] n (CHEM) соединéние; (enclosure) укреплённый кóмплекс; (LING) слóжное слóво* ◆ adj слóжный ◆ vt (problem etc) осложнять (осложнйть perf).

compound fracture n открытый перелóм.

compound interest n слóжные процéнты pl.

comprehend [kɔmprɪ'hɛnd] vt постигáть (постúгнуть or постúчь* perf).

comprehension [kɔmprɪ'hɛnʃən] n понимáние.

comprehensive [kɔmprɪ'hɛnsɪv] adj исчéрпывающий (исчéрпывающ) ◆ n = **comprehensive school**; **~ insurance** всеобъéмлющее страховáние.

comprehensive school n (BRIT) срéдняя шкóла.

compress [vt kəm'prɛs, n 'kɔmprɛs] vt (air) сжимáть (сжать* perf); (cotton, paper) прессовáть (спрессовáть perf); (text etc) сокращáть (сократúть* perf) ◆ n компрéсс.

compressed air [kəm'prɛst-] n сжáтый вóздух.

compression [kəm'prɛʃən] n (of air) сжáтие; (of text) сокращéние.

comprise [kəm'praɪz] vt (also: **be ~d of**) включáть (impf) в себя, состоять (impf) из +gen; (constitute) составлять (состáвить* perf).

compromise ['kɔmprəmaɪz] n компромúсс ◆ vt компрометúровать (скомпрометúровать perf) ◆ vi (make concessions) идтú* (пойтú* perf) на компромúсс ◆ cpd компромúссный.

compulsion [kəm'pʌlʃən] n (desire) влечéние; (force) принуждéние; **under ~** по принуждéнию.

compulsive [kəm'pʌlsɪv] adj (gambler etc) безрассýдный; (behaviour) маниакáльный; (reading etc) захвáтывающий* (захвáтывающ); **he's a ~ liar** он неисправúмый лгун.

compulsory [kəm'pʌlsərɪ] adj (attendance) обязáтельный* (обязáтелен); (redundancy) принудúтельный (принудúтелен).

compulsory purchase n обязáтельная покýпка*.

compunction [kəm'pʌŋkʃən] n раскáяние; **to have no ~ about doing** дéлать (сдéлать perf) что-н без всякого сожалéния.

computer [kəm'pju:tə'] n компьютер ◆ cpd компьютерный; **the process is done by ~** процéсс выполняется при пóмощи компьютера.

computer game n компьютерная игрá*.

computerization [kəmpju:təraɪ'zeɪʃən] n компьютеризáция.

computerize [kəm'pju:təraɪz] vt компьютеризовáть (impf/perf); **to ~ information** обрабáтывать (обрабóтать perf) информáцию на компьютере.

computer literate adj: **to be ~ ~** умéть (impf) пóльзоваться компьютером.

computer peripheral n периферúйное устрóйство (компьютера).

computer programmer n программúст.

computer programming n программúрование.

computer science n электрóнно-

вычисли́тельная нау́ка.
computer scientist *n* специали́ст в о́бласти ЭВМ.

computing [kəm'pju:tɪŋ] *n* (*activity*) рабо́та на компью́тере; (*science*) электро́нно-вычисли́тельная нау́ка; **I've never done any ~** я никогда́ не рабо́тал на компью́тере.

comrade ['kɔmrɪd] *n* (POL, MIL) сора́тник; (*friend*) това́рищ.

comradeship ['kɔmrɪdʃɪp] *n* това́рищество.

Comsat® ['kɔmsæt] *n abbr* = **communications satellite**.

con [kɔn] *vt* надува́ть (наду́ть *perf*) ♦ *n* (*trick*) обма́н; **to ~ sb into doing** обма́ном заставля́ть (заста́вить* *perf*) кого́-н +*infin*.

concave ['kɔnkeɪv] *adj* (*mirror etc*) во́гнутый; (*cheeks*) впа́лый.

conceal [kən'si:l] *vt* (*hide*) укрыва́ть (укры́ть* *perf*); (*keep back*) скрыва́ть (скрыть* *perf*).

concede [kən'si:d] *vt* признава́ть* (призна́ть *perf*) ♦ *vi* (*admit error*) признава́ться (призна́ться *perf*); (*admit defeat*) сдава́ться* (сда́ться* *perf*).

conceit [kən'si:t] *n* высокоме́рие.

conceited [kən'si:tɪd] *adj* высокоме́рный.

conceivable [kən'si:vəbl] *adj* мы́слимый (мы́слим); **it is ~ that** ... вполне́ допусти́мо, что ....

conceivably [kən'si:vəblɪ] *adv*: **he may ~ be right** возмо́жно, что он прав.

conceive [kən'si:v] *vt* (*child*) зача́ть* (*perf*); (*idea*) заду́мывать (заду́мать *perf*) ♦ *vi* (BIO) забере́менеть (*perf*); **to ~ of sth** представля́ть (предста́вить* *perf*) что-н.

concentrate ['kɔnsəntreɪt] *vi* сосредо-то́чиваться (сосредото́читься *perf*), концентри́роваться (сконцентри́роваться *perf*) ♦ *vt*: **to ~ (on)** (*energies etc*) сосредото́чивать (сосредото́чить *perf*) *or* концентри́ровать (сконцентри́ровать *perf*) (на +*prp*).

concentration [kɔnsən'treɪʃən] *n* сосредото́чение, концентра́ция; (*attention*) сосредото́ченность *f*; (CHEM) концентра́ция.

concentration camp *n* концентрацио́нный ла́герь* *m*.

concentric [kɔn'sɛntrɪk] *adj* концентри́ческий*.

concept ['kɔnsɛpt] *n* поня́тие.

conception [kən'sɛpʃən] *n* (*idea*) конце́пция; (BIO) зача́тие.

concern [kən'sə:n] *n* (*affair*) де́ло*; (*worry*) озабо́ченность *f*; (COMM) предприя́тие ♦ *vt* (*worry*) беспоко́ить (*impf*); (*involve*) вовлека́ть (вовле́чь* *perf*); (*relate to*) каса́ться (*impf*) +*gen*; **to be ~ed (about)** беспоко́иться (*impf*) (о +*prp*); **"to whom it may ~"** "надлежа́щему лицу́"; **as far as I am ~ed** что каса́ется меня́; **the department ~ed** (*relevant*)

отде́л, о кото́ром идёт речь; (*involved*) отде́л, кото́рый э́тим занима́ется.

concerning [kən'sə:nɪŋ] *prep* относи́тельно +*gen*.

concert ['kɔnsət] *n* конце́рт; **to be in ~** (MUS) дава́ть* (*impf*) конце́рт; **in ~ with** (*activities etc*) совме́стно *or* во взаимоде́йствии с +*instr*.

concerted [kən'sə:tɪd] *adj* совме́стный.

concert hall *n* конце́ртный зал.

concertina [kɔnsə'ti:nə] *n* гармо́ника ♦ *vi* (*fig*) скла́дываться (сложи́ться* *perf*) гармо́никой.

concerto [kən'tʃə:təu] *n* (MUS) конце́рт; **piano/violin ~** конце́рт для фортепья́но/скри́пки с орке́стром.

concession [kən'sɛʃən] *n* (*compromise*) усту́пка*; (*right*) конце́ссия; (*for pensioners, the unemployed*) льго́та; **tax ~** нало́говая ски́дка*.

concessionaire [kənsɛʃə'nɛəˈ] *n* концессионе́р.

concessionary [kən'sɛʃənrɪ] *adj* льго́тный.

conciliation [kənsɪlɪ'eɪʃən] *n* примире́ние.

conciliatory [kən'sɪlɪətrɪ] *adj* примири́тельный* (примири́телен).

concise [kən'saɪs] *adj* кра́ткий*.

conclave ['kɔnkleɪv] *n* та́йное совеща́ние; (REL) конкла́в.

conclude [kən'klu:d] *vt* (*speech, chapter*) зака́нчивать (зако́нчить *perf*); (*treaty, deal etc*) заключа́ть (заключи́ть *perf*); (*decide*) приходи́ть* (прийти́* *perf*) к заключе́нию *or* вы́воду ♦ *vi* (*speaker*) заключа́ть (заключи́ть *perf*) речь; (*events*): **to ~ (with)** заверша́ться (заверши́ться *perf*) (+*instr*); **"that," he ~d, "is why we did it"** "вот почему́, – заключи́л он, – мы сде́лали э́то"; **I ~ that** ... я прихожу́ к заключе́нию, что ....

concluding [kən'klu:dɪŋ] *adj* заключи́тельный.

conclusion [kən'klu:ʒən] *n* заключе́ние; (*of speech*) оконча́ние; (*of events*) заверше́ние; **to come to the ~ that** приходи́ть* (прийти́* *perf*) к заключе́нию, что ....

conclusive [kən'klu:sɪv] *adj* (*evidence*) неопроверж́ймый (неопроверж́йм); (*defeat*) оконча́тельный* (оконча́телен).

concoct [kən'kɔkt] *vt* (*excuse*) приду́мывать (приду́мать *perf*); (*meal*) гото́вить* (пригото́вить* *perf*).

concoction [kən'kɔkʃən] *n* смесь *f*.

concord ['kɔnkɔ:d] *n* (*harmony*) согла́сие; (*treaty*) соглаше́ние.

concourse ['kɔnkɔ:s] *n* (*hall*) вестибю́ль *m*; (*crowd*) стече́ние.

concrete ['kɔnkri:t] *n* бето́н ♦ *adj* бето́нный; (*fig*) конкре́тный* (конкре́тен).

concrete mixer *n* бетономеша́лка.

concur [kən'kə:ˈ] *vi* (*events*) совпада́ть

(совпасть* perf); **to ~ (with)** соглашаться (согласиться* perf) (с +instr).

concurrently [kən'kʌrntlɪ] adv одновременно.

concussion [kən'kʌʃən] n сотрясение мозга.

condemn [kən'dɛm] vt осуждать (осудить* perf); (building) браковать (забраковать perf).

condemnation [kɔndɛm'neɪʃən] n (criticism) осуждение.

condensation [kɔndɛn'seɪʃən] n конденсация.

condense [kən'dɛns] vi конденсироваться (impf/perf) ◆ vt сжимать (сжать* perf).

condensed milk [kən'dɛnst-] n сгущённое молоко.

condescend [kɔndɪ'sɛnd] vi вести (impf) себя снисходительно; **to ~ to do** соизволять (соизволить perf) +infin.

condescending [kɔndɪ'sɛndɪŋ] adj снисходительный* (снисходителен).

condition [kən'dɪʃən] n (requirement) условие ◆ vt (person) формировать (сформировать perf); (hair, skin) обрабатывать (обработать perf); **~s** npl (circumstances) обстоятельства ntpl; **in good/poor ~** в хорошем/плохом состоянии; **a heart ~** болезнь f сердца; **weather ~s** погодные условия; **~s of sale** условия продажи; **on ~ that** при условии, что.

conditional [kən'dɪʃənl] adj условный; **to be ~ upon** зависеть* (impf/perf) от +gen.

conditioner [kən'dɪʃənə'] n (for hair) бальзам; (for fabrics) смягчающий* раствор.

condo ['kɔndəu] n abbr (US: inf) = **condominium**.

condolences [kən'dəulənsɪz] npl соболезнования ntpl.

condom ['kɔndəm] n презерватив.

condominium [kɔndə'mɪnɪəm] n (US: building) кооперативный многоквартирный дом; (: rooms) кооперативная квартира.

condone [kən'dəun] vt мириться (примириться perf) с +instr.

conducive [kən'dju:sɪv] adj: **~ to** способствующий +dat.

conduct [n 'kɔndʌkt, vt kən'dʌkt] n (of person) поведение ◆ vt (survey etc) проводить* (провести* perf); (MUS) дирижировать (impf); (PHYS) проводить* (impf); **to ~ o.s. (behave)** вести* (повести* perf) себя.

conducted tour [kən'dʌktɪd-] n (of museum etc) экскурсия с гидом.

conductor [kən'dʌktə'] n (MUS) дирижёр; (US: RAIL) контролёр; (PHYS) проводник*; (on bus) кондуктор.

conductress [kən'dʌktrɪs] n кондуктор.

conduit ['kɔndjuɪt] n (ELEC) труба для электропроводки; (TECH) трубопровод.

cone [kəun] n (shape) конус; (on road) конусообразное дорожное заграждение; (BOT) шишка*; (CULIN) вафельная трубочка* (для мороженого).

confectioner [kən'fɛkʃənə'] n кондитер.

confectioner's (shop) [kən'fɛkʃənəz-] n кондитерская f adj.

confectionery [kən'fɛkʃənrɪ] n кондитерские изделия ntpl.

confederate [kən'fɛdrɪt] adj конфедеративный ◆ n (pej) сообщник; (US) конфедерат.

confederation [kənfɛdə'reɪʃən] n конфедерация.

confer [kən'fə:'] vi совещаться (impf) ◆ vt: **to ~ sth (on sb)** (honour) оказывать (оказать* perf) что-н (кому-н); (degree) присуждать (присудить* perf) что-н (кому-н); (advantage) давать* (дать* perf) что-н (кому-н); **to ~ (with sb about sth)** совещаться (impf) (с кем-н о чём-н).

conference ['kɔnfərəns] n конференция; **to be in ~** быть* (impf) на совещании.

conference room n зал заседаний, конференцзал.

confess [kən'fɛs] vt (guilt, ignorance) признавать* (признать perf); (sin) исповедоваться (исповедаться perf) в +prp; (crime) сознаваться* (сознаться perf) в +prp ◆ vi (admit to crime) признаваться* (признаться perf); **to ~ to sth** сознаваться* (сознаться perf) в чём-н; **I must ~ that I didn't enjoy it at all** должен признаться, мне это совершенно не понравилось.

confession [kən'fɛʃən] n признание; (REL) исповедь f; **to make a ~** делать (сделать perf) признание.

confessor [kən'fɛsə'] n исповедник.

confetti [kən'fɛtɪ] n конфетти nt ind.

confide [kən'faɪd] vi: **to ~ in** доверяться (довериться perf) +dat.

confidence ['kɔnfɪdns] n (faith) уверенность f; (self-assurance) уверенность в себе; (secret) секрет; **I have ~ in him** я уверен в нём; **she has (every) ~ that** она полностью уверена в том, что; **motion of no ~** выражение недоверия; **in ~** конфиденциально; **to tell sb sth in strict ~** рассказать* (perf) кому-н что-н строго конфиденциально.

confidence trick n мошенничество.

confident ['kɔnfɪdənt] adj (positive) уверенный (уверен); (self-assured) уверенный (уверен) в себе.

confidential [kɔnfɪ'dɛnʃəl] adj (report etc) конфиденциальный* (конфиденциален); (tone) доверительный (доверителен); (secretary) пользующийся доверием.

confidentiality [kɔnfɪdɛnʃɪ'ælɪtɪ] n конфиденциальность f.

configuration [kənfɪgju'reɪʃən] n (also COMPUT) конфигурация.

confine [kən'faɪn] vt (lock up) запирать (запереть* perf); (limit): **to ~ (to)** ограничивать (ограничить perf) (+instr); **to ~ o.s. to sth** ограничиваться (ограничиться perf) чем-н.

confined [kən'faɪnd] adj закрытый.
confinement [kən'faɪnmənt] n (тюрéмное)
заключéние; (*MED*) рóды pl.
confines ['kɔnfaɪnz] npl (*also fig*) предéлы mpl.
confirm [kən'fɜːm] vt подтверждáть
(подтвердúть* perf); **to be ~ed** (*REL*) получáть
(получúть* perf) конфирмáцию.
confirmation [kɔnfə'meɪʃən] n
подтверждéние; (*REL*) конфирмáция.
confirmed [kən'fɜːmd] adj убеждённый.
confiscate ['kɔnfɪskeɪt] vt конфискóвывать
(конфисковáть perf).
confiscation [kɔnfɪs'keɪʃən] n конфискáция.
conflagration [kɔnflə'greɪʃən] n пожáрище.
conflict [n 'kɔnflɪkt, vi kən'flɪkt] n конфлúкт; (*of
interests*) столкновéние ♦ vi противорéчить
(*impf*) друг дрýгу; **to ~ with sth**
противорéчить (*impf*) чемý-н.
conflicting [kən'flɪktɪŋ] adj (*reports*)
противорéчивый (противорéчив); (*interests*)
противополóжный (противополóжен).
conform [kən'fɔːm] vi: **to ~ (to)** подчинáться
(подчинúться perf) (+dat).
conformist [kən'fɔːmɪst] n конформúст.
confound [kən'faund] vt (*confuse*) озадáчивать
(озадáчить perf); (*amaze*) поражáть
(поразúть* perf).
confounded [kən'faundɪd] adj (*nuisance*)
проклятый; (*idiot*) закóнченный.
confront [kən'frʌnt] vt (*problems*)
стáлкиваться (столкнýться perf) с +instr;
(*enemy*) противостоять (*impf*) +dat.
confrontation [kɔnfrən'teɪʃən] n
конфронтáция.
confuse [kən'fjuːz] vt (*perplex, complicate*)
запýтывать (запýтать perf); (*mix up: two
things, people etc*) пýтать (спýтать perf).
confused [kən'fjuːzd] adj (*person*)
озадáченный (озадáчен); (*situation*)
запýтанный (запýтан); **to get ~**
запýтываться (запýтаться perf).
confusing [kən'fjuːzɪŋ] adj запýтанный.
confusion [kən'fjuːʒən] n (*mix-up*) пýтаница;
(*perplexity*) замешáтельство; (*disorder*)
беспорядок.
congeal [kən'dʒiːl] vi (*blood*) запекáться
(запéчься* perf); (*sauce, fat*) застывáть
(застыть* perf).
congenial [kən'dʒiːnɪəl] adj (*atmosphere*)
благоприятный* (благоприятен); (*person*)
рóдственный; (*place, job etc*) подходящий*.
congenital [kən'dʒɛnɪtl] adj (*MED*)
врождённый.
conger eel ['kɔŋgər-] n морскóй ýгорь* m.
congested [kən'dʒɛstɪd] adj (*road*)
перегрýженный (перегрýжен); (*area*)
перенаселённый (перенаселён); (*MED*)
застóйный.

congestion [kən'dʒɛstʃən] n (*of road*)
перегрýженность f; (*of area*)
перенаселённость f; (*MED*) застóй.
conglomerate [kən'glɔmərɪt] n (*COMM*)
конгломерáт.
conglomeration [kənglɔmə'reɪʃən] n
конгломерáция.
Congo ['kɔŋgəu] n Кóнго ind.
congratulate [kən'grætjuleɪt] vt: **to ~ sb (on)**
поздравлять (поздрáвить* perf) когó-н (с
+instr).
congratulations [kəngrætju'leɪʃənz] npl
поздравлéния ntpl; **~ (on)** (*from one person*)
поздравляю (с +instr); (*from several people*)
поздравляем (с +instr).
congregate ['kɔŋgrɪgeɪt] vi собирáться
(собрáться* perf).
congregation [kɔŋgrɪ'geɪʃən] n прихожáне*
mpl.
congress ['kɔŋgrɛs] n (*conference*) конгрéсс;
(*US*): **C~** конгрéсс США.
congressman ['kɔŋgrɛsmən] irreg n (*US*)
конгрессмéн.
congresswoman ['kɔŋgrɛswumən] irreg n (*US*)
конгрессмéн.
conical ['kɔnɪkl] adj конúческий*.
conifer ['kɔnɪfər] n хвóйное дéрево*.
coniferous [kə'nɪfərəs] adj хвóйный.
conjecture [kən'dʒɛktʃər] n предположéние ♦ vi
предполагáть (предположúть perf).
conjugal ['kɔndʒugl] adj супрýжеский*.
conjugate ['kɔndʒugeɪt] vt (*LING*) спрягáть
(проспрягáть perf).
conjugation [kɔndʒə'geɪʃən] n (*LING*)
спряжéние.
conjunction [kən'dʒʌŋkʃən] n (*LING*) сою́з; **in ~
with** совмéстно с +instr.
conjunctivitis [kəndʒʌŋktɪ'vaɪtɪs] n (*MED*)
конъюнктивúт.
conjure ['kʌndʒər] vt (*fig*) создавáть* (создáть*
perf) из ничегó ♦ vi (*magician*) покáзывать
(показáть* perf) фóкусы
▶ **conjure up** vt (*ghost*) вызывáть* (вýзвать*
perf); (*memories*) пробуждáть (пробудúть*
perf).
conjurer ['kʌndʒərər] n фóкусник.
conjuring trick ['kʌndʒərɪŋ-] n фóкус.
conker ['kɔŋkər] n (*BRIT*) кóнский* каштáн.
conk out [kɔŋk-] vi (*inf*) сдыхáть (сдóхнуть
perf).
con man irreg n мошéнник.
connect [kə'nɛkt] vt (*ELEC*) подсоединять
(подсоединúть perf); (*TEL: subscriber*)
подключáть (подключúть perf); (*fig:
associate*) связывать (связáть* perf) ♦ vi: **to ~
with** согласóвываться (согласовáться perf)
по расписáнию с +instr; **to ~ sb/sth (to)** (*also
TEL*) соединять (соединúть perf) когó-н/что-н

---

* marks translations which have irregular inflections. The Russian-English side of the dictionary gives inflectional information.

(c +*instr*); **he is/was ~ed with** он свя́зан/был свя́зан с +*instr*; **I am trying to ~ you** (*TEL*) я пыта́юсь нала́дить связь.

connection [kə'nɛkʃən] *n* (*also fig, ELEC*) связь* *f*; (*train etc*) переса́дка*; (*TEL*: *caller*) соедине́ние; (: *subscriber*) подключе́ние; **in ~ with** в связи́ с +*instr*; **what is the ~ between them?** кака́я связь ме́жду ни́ми?; **business ~s** делов́ые свя́зи; **to miss one's ~** опа́здывать (опозда́ть *perf*) на переса́дку; **to get one's ~** де́лать (сде́лать *perf*) переса́дку.

connexion [kə'nɛkʃən] *n* (*BRIT*) = **connection**.

conning tower ['kɔnɪŋ-] *n* (*NAUT*) рубка*.

connive [kə'naɪv] *vi*: **to ~ at** потво́рствовать (*impf*) +*dat*.

connoisseur [kɔnɪ'səː'] *n* знато́к*.

connotation [kɔnə'teɪʃən] *n* коннота́ция.

connubial [kə'njuːbɪəl] *adj* бра́чный.

conquer ['kɔŋkə'] *vt* (*MIL*) завоёвывать (завоева́ть* *perf*); (*overcome*) поборо́ть* (*perf*).

conqueror ['kɔŋkərə'] *n* завоева́тель *m*.

conquest ['kɔŋkwɛst] *n* (*MIL*) завоева́ние; (*prize*) побе́да; (*of space*) покоре́ние.

cons [kɔnz] *npl see* **convenience, pro**.

conscience ['kɔnʃəns] *n* со́весть *f*; **he has a guilty/clear ~** у него́ со́весть нечиста́/чиста́; **in all ~** по со́вести.

conscientious [kɔnʃɪ'ɛnʃəs] *adj* добро-со́вестный* (добросо́вестен).

conscientious objector *n* отка́зывающийся *от призы́ва в а́рмию по убежде́нию.*

conscious ['kɔnʃəs] *adj* (*deliberate*) созна́тельный (созна́телен); (*aware*): **to be ~ of sth/that** сознава́ть* (*impf*) что-н/, что; (*awake*): **the patient was ~** пацие́нт находи́лся в созна́нии; **to become ~ of sth/ that** осознава́ть (осозна́ть *perf*) что-н/, что.

consciousness ['kɔnʃəsnɪs] *n* (*also MED*) созна́ние; (*of society etc*) самосозна́ние; **to lose ~** теря́ть (потеря́ть *perf*) созна́ние; **to regain ~** приходи́ть* (прийти́* *perf*) в созна́ние.

conscript ['kɔnskrɪpt] *n* призывни́к*, новобра́нец*.

conscription [kən'skrɪpʃən] *n* во́инская пови́нность *f*.

consecrate ['kɔnsɪkreɪt] *vt* (*building etc*) освяща́ть (освяти́ть* *perf*).

consecutive [kən'sɛkjutɪv] *adj*: **on three ~ occasions** в трёх слу́чаях подря́д; **on three ~ days** три дня подря́д.

consensus [kən'sɛnsəs] *n* (*medical, scientific*) еди́ное мне́ние; **~ (of opinion)** консе́нсус.

consent [kən'sɛnt] *n* согла́сие ♦ *vi*: **to ~ to** соглаша́ться (согласи́ться* *perf*) на +*acc*; **age of ~** совершенноле́тие; **by common ~** с о́бщего согла́сия.

consenting [kən'sɛntɪŋ] *adj*: **~ adult** совершенноле́тний*(-яя) *m(f) adj.*

consequence ['kɔnsɪkwəns] *n* (*result*) сле́дствие; (*significance*): **of ~** значи́тельный (значи́телен); **it's of little ~** э́то не име́ет большо́го значе́ния; **in ~** (*consequently*) всле́дствие.

consequently ['kɔnsɪkwəntlɪ] *adv* сле́довательно.

conservation [kɔnsə'veɪʃən] *n* (*preservation*) сохране́ние; (*also: nature ~*) охра́на приро́ды, природоохра́на; **energy ~** эконо́мия эне́ргии.

conservationist [kɔnsə'veɪʃnɪst] *n* эко́лог(ист).

conservative [kən'səːvətɪv] *adj* (*person*) консервати́вный*; (*estimate*) скро́мный*; (*BRIT*): **C~** консервати́вный ♦ *n* (*BRIT*): **C~** консерва́тор.

conservatory [kən'səːvətrɪ] *n* застеклённая вера́нда; (*MUS*) консервато́рия.

conserve [kən'səːv] *vt* (*preserve*) сохраня́ть (сохрани́ть *perf*); (*energy*) рациона́льно испо́льзовать (*impf*) ♦ *n* варе́нье*.

consider [kən'sɪdə'] *vt* (*believe*) счита́ть (посчита́ть *perf*); (*study*) рассма́тривать (рассмотре́ть* *perf*); (*take into account*) учи́тывать (уче́сть* *perf*); (*regard*): **to ~ that ...** полага́ть (*impf*), что ...; **to ~ sth** поду́мывать (*impf*) о чём-н; **they ~ themselves to be superior** они́ счита́ют себя́ в́ыше; **she ~ed it a disaster** она́ счита́ла, что э́то катастро́фа; **~ yourself lucky** счита́йте, что Вам повезло́; **all things ~ed** приня́в всё во внима́ние.

considerable [kən'sɪdərəbl] *adj* значи́тельный* (значи́телен).

considerably [kən'sɪdərəblɪ] *adv* (*improve, deteriorate etc*) значи́тельно; (*bigger, smaller etc*) гора́здо.

considerate [kən'sɪdərɪt] *adj* (*person*) забо́тливый (забо́тлив); (*action*) внима́тельный (внима́телен).

consideration [kənsɪdə'reɪʃən] *n* (*deliberation*) рассмотре́ние, обду́мывание; (*factor*) соображе́ние; (*thoughtfulness*) внима́ние; (*reward*) вознагражде́ние; **out of ~ for** из уваже́ния к +*dat*; **to take sth into ~** принима́ть (приня́ть *perf*) что-н во внима́ние; **under ~** на рассмотре́нии; **my first ~ is my family** я пре́жде всего́ забо́чусь о свое́й семье́.

considered [kən'sɪdəd] *adj* (*approach, answer*) обду́манный; **it is my ~ opinion that ...** у меня́ сложи́лось мне́ние, что ....

considering [kən'sɪdərɪŋ] *prep* учи́тывая +*acc* ♦ **~ (that)** учи́тывая (, что).

consign [kən'saɪn] *vt* (*send: goods*) отправля́ть (отпра́вить* *perf*); **to ~ to** (*thing: to place*) забра́сывать (забро́сить* *perf*) в +*acc*; (*person: to sb's care*) поруча́ть (поручи́ть *perf*) +*dat*; (: *to poverty*) обрека́ть (обре́чь* *perf*) на +*acc*.

consignee [kɔnsaɪ'niː] *n* грузополуча́тель *m*.

consignment [kən'saɪnmənt] *n* (*COMM*) па́ртия.

consignment note *n* (*COMM*) тра́нспортная накладна́я *f adj*.
consignor [kən'saɪnə^r] *n* грузоотправи́тель *m*.
consist [kən'sɪst] *vi*: **to ~ of** состоя́ть (*impf*) из +*gen*.
consistency [kən'sɪstənsɪ] *n* (*of actions etc*) после́довательность *f*; (*of yoghurt etc*) консисте́нция.
consistent [kən'sɪstənt] *adj* (*person, argument*) после́довательный* (после́довате́лен); **~ with** соотве́тствующий* +*dat*.
consolation [kɔnsə'leɪʃən] *n* утеше́ние.
console [*vt* kən'səul, *n* 'kɔnsəul] *vt* утеша́ть (уте́шить *perf*) ♦ *n* (*panel*) пане́ль *f*.
consolidate [kən'sɔlɪdeɪt] *vt* (*position, power*) укрепля́ть (укрепи́ть* *perf*).
consolidated balance sheet [kən'sɔlɪdeɪtɪd-] *n* сво́дный бала́нсовый отчёт.
consols ['kɔnsɔlz] *npl* (*BRIT*) консо́ли *fpl* (*прави́тельственные облига́ции*).
consommé [kən'sɔmeɪ] *n* прозра́чный бульо́н*.
consonant ['kɔnsənənt] *n* согла́сный *m adj*.
consort [*n* 'kɔnsɔːt, *vb* kən'sɔːt] *n* супру́г(а) ♦ *vi*: **to ~ with sb** свя́зываться (связа́ться* *perf*) с кем-н; **prince ~** принц-консо́рт, супру́г ца́рствующей короле́вы.
consortium [kən'sɔːtɪəm] *n* консо́рциум.
conspicuous [kən'spɪkjuəs] *adj* (*person, feature*) заме́тный* (заме́тен); **to make o.s. ~** обраща́ть (обрати́ть* *perf*) на себя́ внима́ние.
conspiracy [kən'spɪrəsɪ] *n* за́говор.
conspiratorial [kən'spɪrə'tɔːrɪəl] *adj* загово́рщический.
conspire [kən'spaɪə^r] *vi* (*people*) устра́ивать (устро́ить *perf*) за́говор; **circumstances ~d against us** обстоя́тельства скла́дывались про́тив нас.
constable ['kʌnstəbl] (*BRIT*) *n* полице́йский *m adj*; **chief ~** нача́льник поли́ции.
constabulary [kən'stæbjulərɪ] *n* (*BRIT*) поли́ция.
constant ['kɔnstənt] *adj* (*continuous*) постоя́нный*; (*fixed*) неизме́нный*.
constantly ['kɔnstəntlɪ] *adv* (*continually*) постоя́нно.
constellation [kɔnstə'leɪʃən] *n* (*ASTRONOMY*) созве́здие.
consternation [kɔnstə'neɪʃən] *n* смяте́ние.
constipated ['kɔnstɪpeɪtɪd] *adj*: **he/she is ~** у него́/неё запо́р.
constipation [kɔnstɪ'peɪʃən] *n* запо́р.
constituency [kən'stɪtjuənsɪ] *n* (*area*) избира́тельный о́круг*; (*electors*) избира́тели *mpl* о́круга.
constituency party *n* ме́стная парти́йная организа́ция.
constituent [kən'stɪtjuənt] *n* (*POL*)

избира́тель(ница) *m(f)*; (*component*) компоне́нт.
constitute ['kɔnstɪtjuːt] *vt* (*represent*) явля́ться (яви́ться* *perf*) +*instr*; (*make up*) составля́ть (соста́вить* *perf*).
constitution [kɔnstɪ'tjuːʃən] *n* (*of country*) конститу́ция; (*of organization*) уста́в; (*health*) органи́зм; (*of committee etc*) строе́ние.
constitutional [kɔnstɪ'tjuːʃənl] *adj* конституцио́нный; **~ monarchy** конституцио́нная мона́рхия.
constrain [kən'streɪn] *vt* (*force*) вынужда́ть (вы́нудить* *perf*); (*limit*) сде́рживать (сдержа́ть *perf*).
constrained [kən'streɪnd] *adj* принуждённый*.
constraint [kən'streɪnt] *n* (*restriction*) ограниче́ние; (*compulsion*) принужде́ние; (*embarrassment*) стесне́ние.
constrict [kən'strɪkt] *vt* (*squeeze*) сжима́ть (сжать* *perf*); (*limit*) стесня́ть (стесни́ть *perf*).
constriction [kən'strɪkʃən] *n* (*in throat*) стесне́ние; (*restriction*) ограниче́ние.
construct [kən'strʌkt] *vt* (*build*) сооружа́ть (сооруди́ть* *perf*); (*formulate*) стро́ить (постро́ить *perf*).
construction [kən'strʌkʃən] *n* (*of building etc*) сооруже́ние; (*structure*) констру́кция; (*fig: interpretation*) истолкова́ние; **the building is under ~** зда́ние стро́ится.
construction industry *n* строи́тельная промы́шленность *f*.
constructive [kən'strʌktɪv] *adj* конструкти́вный* (конструкти́вен).
construe [kən'struː] *vt* истолко́вывать (истолкова́ть *perf*).
consul ['kɔnsl] *n* ко́нсул.
consulate ['kɔnsjulɪt] *n* ко́нсульство.
consult [kən'sʌlt] *vt* (*friend*) сове́товаться (посове́товаться *perf*) с +*instr*; (*book, map etc*) справля́ться (спра́виться* *perf*) с +*instr*; **to ~ sb (about sth)** (*doctor etc*) консульти́роваться (проконсульти́роваться *perf*) с кем-н (о чём-н).
consultancy [kən'sʌltənsɪ] *n* (*company*) консульти́рующая фи́рма; (*MED*) до́лжность *f* врача́-консульта́нта.
consultant [kən'sʌltənt] *n* (*MED*) врач-консульта́нт; (*other specialist*) консульта́нт ♦ *cpd*: **~ engineer/paediatrician** инжене́р-/педиа́тр-консульта́нт; **legal ~** юрисконсу́льт; **management ~** консульта́нт по ме́неджменту.
consultation [kɔnsəl'teɪʃən] *n* (*MED*) консульта́ция; (*discussion*) совеща́ние; (*LAW*) юриди́ческая консульта́ция; **in ~ with** с по́мощью +*gen*.
consultative [kən'sʌltətɪv] *adj* консультати́вный.

---

* marks translations which have irregular inflections. The Russian-English side of the dictionary gives inflectional information.

consulting room [kən'sʌltɪŋ-] *n* (*BRIT*)
врачéбный кабинéт.

consume [kən'sju:m] *vt* (*food, drink*)
потреблять (потребить* *perf*); (*fuel, energy
etc*) расхóдовать (израсхóдовать *perf*); (*subj:
emotion, fire etc*) охвáтывать (охватить*
perf).

consumer [kən'sju:mə*] *n* (*COMM, also of gas etc*)
потребитель *m*.

consumer credit *n* потребительский* кредит.

consumer durables *npl* потребительские
товáры *mpl* длительного пóльзования.

consumer goods *npl* потребительские
товáры *mpl*.

consumerism [kən'sju:mərɪzəm] *n* защита
прав потребителей.

consumer society *n* óбщество потреблéния.

consummate ['kɔnsʌmeɪt] *vt* (*marriage,
ambition etc*) осуществлять (осуществить*
perf).

consumption [kən'sʌmpʃən] *n* потреблéние;
(*amount consumed*) расхóд; (*MED*)
туберкулёз лёгких; **not fit for human ~** не
гóден к потреблéнию.

cont. *abbr* (= *continued*): **~ on** продолжéние на
+*prp*.

contact ['kɔntækt] *n* (*communication*) контáкт;
(*touch*) соприкосновéние; (*person*)
деловóй(-áя) знакóмый(-ая) *m(f) adj* ♦ *vt*
связываться (связáться* *perf*) с +*instr*; **to
lose/be in ~ with sb/sth** терять (потерять
perf)/поддéрживать (impf) контáкт с кем-н/
чем-н; **business ~s** деловые связи.

contact lenses *npl* контáктные линзы *fpl*.

contagious [kən'teɪdʒəs] *adj* (*disease*)
зарáзный* (зарáзен); (*fig*) заразительный*
(заразителен).

contain [kən'teɪn] *vt* (*hold*) вмещáть
(вместить* *perf*); (*include*) содержáть* (impf);
(*curb*) сдéрживать (сдержáть* *perf*); **to ~ o.s.**
сдéрживаться (сдержáться* *perf*).

container [kən'teɪnə*] *n* (*also COMM*) контéйнер
♦ *cpd* (*ship, lorry etc*) контéйнерный.

containerization [kənteɪnəraɪ'zeɪʃən] *n*
упакóвка* грýзов в контéйнеры.

containerize [kən'teɪnəraɪz] *vt* осуществлять
(осуществить* *perf*) контéйнерные
перевóзки.

contaminate [kən'tæmɪneɪt] *vt* загрязнять
(загрязнить *perf*).

contamination [kəntæmɪ'neɪʃən] *n*
загрязнéние.

cont'd *abbr* (= *continued*): **~ on** продолжéние
на +*prp*; **to be ~** продолжéние слéдует.

contemplate ['kɔntəmpleɪt] *vt* (*consider*)
размышлять (impf) о +*prp*; (*look at*)
созерцáть (impf).

contemplation [kɔntəm'pleɪʃən] *n* (*see vb*)
размышлéние; созерцáние.

contemporary [kən'tɛmpərərɪ] *adj* (*present-day*)
современный*; (*belonging to same time*)

относящийся к томý врéмени ♦ *n*
совремéнник(-ица); **Samuel Pepys and his
contemporaries** Самюéль Пипс и егó
совремéнники.

contempt [kən'tɛmpt] *n* презрéние; **~ of court**
оскорблéние судá; **to have ~ for sb/sth, to
hold sb/sth in ~** презирáть (impf) когó-н/
что-н.

contemptible [kən'tɛmptəbl] *adj* (*conduct*)
презрéнный.

contemptuous [kən'tɛmptjuəs] *adj*
презрительный* (презрителен).

contend [kən'tɛnd] *vt*: **to ~ that** утверждáть
(impf), что ♦ *vi* (*struggle*): **to ~ with** (*problem
etc*) борóться* (impf) с +*instr*; (*compete*): **to ~
for** (*power etc*) борóться* (impf) за +*acc*; **to
have to ~ with** стáлкиваться (столкнýться
perf) с +*instr*; **he has a lot to ~ with** емý
прихóдится справляться со мнóгим.

contender [kən'tɛndə*] *n* претендéнт(ка).

content [*n* 'kɔntɛnt, *adj, vt* kən'tɛnt] *n*
содержáние ♦ *adj* довóльный* (довóлен) ♦ *vt*
(*satisfy*) удовлетворять (удовлетворить*
perf); **~s** *npl* (*of bottle etc*) содержимое *ntsg adj*;
(*of book*) содержáние *ntsg*; (**table of**) **~s**
оглавлéние; **she is ~ with her life** онá
довóльна жизнью; **to ~ o.s. with sth**
довóльствоваться (impf) чем-н.

contented [kən'tɛntɪd] *adj* довóльный*
(довóлен).

contentedly [kən'tɛntɪdlɪ] *adv* довóльно,
удовлетворённо.

contention [kən'tɛnʃən] *n* (*assertion*)
утверждéние; (*argument*) разноглáсие; **bone
of ~** яблоко* раздóра.

contentious [kən'tɛnʃəs] *adj* спóрный*
(спóрен).

contentment [kən'tɛntmənt] *n* удовлетворённость *f*.

contest [*n* 'kɔntɛst, *vt* kən'tɛst] *n* (*competition:
sport*) соревновáние; (: *beauty*) кóнкурс; (*for
power etc*) борьбá* ♦ *vt* (*statement, decision,
LAW*) оспáривать (оспóрить *perf*); (*compete
for*) борóться* (impf) за +*acc*; (*election,
competition*) борóться* (impf) на +*prp*.

contestant [kən'tɛstənt] *n* (*in competition*)
учáстник(-ница); (*in fight*)
противник(-ница).

context ['kɔntɛkst] *n* контéкст; **in ~** в
контéксте; **out of ~** вне контéкста.

continent ['kɔntɪnənt] *n* континéнт, материк;
the C~ (*BRIT*) Еврóпа (*крóме Британских
островóв*); **on the C~** в Еврóпе (*крóме
британских островóв*).

continental [kɔntɪ'nɛntl] (*BRIT*) *adj*
европéйский* ♦ *n* европéец*(-éйка).

continental breakfast *n* европéйский*
зáвтрак (*лёгкий зáвтрак из кóфе и бýлочки*).

continental quilt *n* (*BRIT*) стёганое одеяло.

contingency [kən'tɪndʒənsɪ] *n* возмóжность *f*.

contingency plan *n* план дéйствий на слýчай

непредвиденных обстоятельств.
contingent [kən'tındʒənt] *n* (*also* MIL)
контингéнт ♦ *adj*: **to be ~ upon** зави́сеть*
(*impf*) от +*gen*.
continual [kən'tınjuəl] *adj* непреры́вный*.
continually [kən'tınjuəlı] *adv* непреры́вно,
постоя́нно.
continuation [kəntınju'eıʃən] *n* продолже́ние.
continue [kən'tınju:] *vi* (*carry on*)
продолжа́ться (*impf*); (*after interruption: talk*)
продолжа́ться (продо́лжиться *perf*);
(: *person*) продолжа́ть (продо́лжить *perf*) ♦ *vt*
продолжа́ть (продо́лжить *perf*); **to ~ to do**
продолжа́ть (продо́лжить *perf*) +*impf infin*; **to
be ~d** продолже́ние сле́дует; **~d on page 10**
продолже́ние на страни́це 10.
continuing education [kən'tınjuıŋ-] *n* ку́рсы
mpl вече́рнего обуче́ния.
continuity [kɒntı'nju:ıtı] *n* (*in management*)
прее́мственность *f*; (*TV, CINEMA*)
непреры́вность *f* (*телевизио́нных програ́мм
и фи́льмов*); **~ announcer** ди́ктор,
заполня́ющий пробе́лы; **~ department** *отде́л,
обеспе́чивающий непреры́вность
телевизио́нных програ́мм.*
continuous [kən'tınjuəs] *adj* (*process, growth
etc*) непреры́вный*; (*line*) сплошно́й; (*LING*)
дли́тельный*; **~ performance** (*CINEMA*) пока́з
кинофи́льма без переры́ва ме́жду сеа́нсами.
continuously [kən'tınjuəslı] *adv* (*repeatedly*)
неоднокра́тно, постоя́нно; (*uninterruptedly*)
непреры́вно.
continuous stationery *n* (*COMPUT*) руло́нная
бума́га (*для печа́тающего устро́йства*).
contort [kən'tɔ:t] *vt* (*body*) искривля́ть
(искриви́ть* *perf*); (*face*) криви́ть* (скриви́ть*
perf).
contortion [kən'tɔ:ʃən] *n* искривле́ние.
contortionist [kən'tɔ:ʃənıst] *n*
пласти́ческий*(-ая) акроба́т(ка).
contour ['kɒntuə'] *n* (*also:* **~ line**) ко́нтурная
ли́ния; (*outline: usu pl*) ко́нтур.
contraband ['kɒntrəbænd] *n* контраба́нда ♦ *adj*
контраба́ндный.
contraception [kɒntrə'sɛpʃən] *n* пред-
упрежде́ние бере́менности.
contraceptive [kɒntrə'sɛptıv] *adj* противо-
зача́точный ♦ *n* противозача́точное
сре́дство, контрацепти́в.
contract [*n, cpd* 'kɒntrækt, *vb* kən'trækt] *n* (*LAW,
COMM*) догово́р, контра́кт ♦ *vi* (*become
smaller*) сжима́ться (сжа́ться* *perf*) ♦ *vt*
(*illness*) заболева́ть (заболе́ть *perf*) +*instr* ♦
cpd (*price, date*) догово́рный; **~ of
employment** служе́бный контра́кт; **~ of
service** *догово́р ме́жду компа́нией и
руководя́щим сотру́дником*; **to ~ to do**
(*COMM*) обя́зывать (обяза́ть *perf*) +*infin*; **~**

work рабо́та по контра́кту
▶ **contract in** *vi* (*BRIT*) официа́льно заявля́ть
(заяви́ть* *perf*) о жела́нии уча́ствовать в +*prp*
▶ **contract out** *vi* (*BRIT*) официа́льно
отка́зываться (отказа́ться* *perf*) от уча́стия
в +*prp*.
contraction [kən'trækʃən] *n* (*of metal*) сжа́тие;
(*LING*) сокраще́ние; (*MED*) родова́я поту́га.
contractor [kən'træktə'] *n* подря́дчик.
contractual [kən'træktʃuəl] *adj* (*agreement etc*)
догово́рный.
contradict [kɒntrə'dıkt] *vt* (*person*) возража́ть
(возрази́ть* *perf*) +*dat*; (*statement*) возража́ть
(возрази́ть* *perf*) на +*acc*; (*be contrary to*)
противоре́чить (*impf*) +*dat*.
contradiction [kɒntrə'dıkʃən] *n* противоре́чие;
to be in ~ with находи́ться* (*impf*) в
противоре́чии с +*instr*; **a ~ in terms**
логи́ческое противоре́чие.
contradictory [kɒntrə'dıktərı] *adj*
противоре́чивый (противоречи́в).
contralto [kən'træltəu] *n* (*MUS*) контра́льто *nt
ind*.
contraption [kən'træpʃən] *n* дура́цкая вещь *f*.
contrary[1] ['kɒntrərı] *adj* (*opposite, different*)
противополо́жный*; (*unfavourable*)
неблагоприя́тный ♦ *n* противополо́жность
f; **~ to what we thought** в противо-
поло́жность тому́, что мы ду́мали; **on the ~**
напро́тив, наоборо́т; **unless you hear to the
~** е́сли не бу́дет други́х инстру́кций.
contrary[2] [kən'trɛərı] *adj* своенра́вный*.
contrast [*n* 'kɒntrɑ:st, *vt* kən'trɑ:st] *n* (*difference*)
контра́ст ♦ *vt* сопоставля́ть (сопоста́вить*
perf); **in ~ to** *or* **with** по контра́сту с +*instr*.
contrasting [kən'trɑ:stıŋ] *adj* (*colours*)
контрасти́рующий; (*attitudes, views*)
противополо́жный.
contravene [kɒntrə'vi:n] *vt* преступа́ть
(преступи́ть* *perf*).
contravention [kɒntrə'vɛnʃən] *n*: **in ~ of** в
наруше́ние +*gen*.
contribute [kən'trıbju:t] *vi* (*give*) де́лать
(сде́лать *perf*) вклад ♦ *vt* (*money, an article*)
вноси́ть* (внести́* *perf*); **to ~ to** (*to charity*)
же́ртвовать (поже́ртвовать *perf*) на +*acc or*
для +*gen*; (*to newspaper*) писа́ть* (написа́ть*
perf) для +*gen*; (*to discussion*) уча́ствовать
(*impf*) в +*prp*; (*to problem*) усугубля́ть
(усугуби́ть* *perf*).
contribution [kɒntrı'bju:ʃən] *n* (*donation*)
поже́ртвование; (*BRIT: for social security*)
взнос; (*to debate, campaign*) вклад; (*to
journal*) публика́ция.
contributor [kən'trıbjutə'] *n* (*to appeal*)
же́ртвователь *m*; (*to newspaper*) а́втор.
contributory [kən'trıbjutərı] *adj*
спосо́бствующий; **it was a ~ factor in ...** э́то

---

* marks translations which have irregular inflections. The Russian-English side of the dictionary gives inflectional information.

явилось одним из способствующих
факторов в ....
contributory pension scheme n (BRIT)
пенсионный договор, по которому работник
принимает частичное участие в
формировании своей будущей пенсии.
contrite ['kɔntraɪt] adj (person) виноватый; **she
looked ~** у неё был виноватый вид.
contrivance [kən'traɪvəns] n (scheme) уловка;
(device) приспособление.
contrive [kən'traɪv] vt (meeting) затевать
(затеять perf) ♦ vi: **to ~ to do** ухитряться
(ухитриться perf) +infin.
control [kən'trəul] vt контролировать (impf) ♦ n
(of country, organization) контроль m; (of
oneself) самообладание; (also: ~ **group**)
контрольная группа; **~s** npl (of vehicle)
рычаги mpl управления; (on radio etc) ручки
fpl настройки; **to ~ o.s.** сохранять
(сохранить perf) самообладание; **to take ~ of**
брать (взять* perf) в свои руки управление
+instr; (COMM) брать* (взять* perf) под
контроль +acc; **to be in ~ of** контролировать
(impf); **under ~** спокойный; **everything is
under ~** всё под контролем; **out of ~**
неуправляемый; **the car went out of ~**
машина потеряла управление;
circumstances beyond our ~ не зависящие от
нас обстоятельства; **governmental ~s**
государственный контроль msg.
control key n управляющая клавиша,
клавиша управления.
controller [kən'trəulə*] n (head) руководитель
m.
controlling interest [kən'trəulɪŋ-] n (COMM)
контрольный пакет акций.
control panel n пульт управления.
control point n контрольный пункт.
control room n (NAUT, MIL) пункт управления;
(RADIO, TV) аппаратная f adj.
control tower n контрольно-диспетчерский*
пункт.
control unit n (COMPUT) блок управления.
controversial [kɔntrə'və:ʃl] adj (topic etc)
спорный* (спорен); (person, writer)
неоднозначный* (неоднозначен).
controversy ['kɔntrəvə:sɪ] n дискуссия, спор.
conurbation [kɔnə'beɪʃən] n агломерация.
convalesce [kɔnvə'lɛs] vi выздоравливать
(выздороветь perf).
convalescence [kɔnvə'lɛsns] n вы-
здоровление.
convalescent [kɔnvə'lɛsnt] n вы-
здоравливающий*(-ая)m(f) adj ♦ adj: ~ **home**
санаторий; ~ **leave** отпуск* по
выздоровлению.
convector [kən'vɛktə*] n (also: ~ **heater**)
конвектор.
convene [kən'vi:n] vt (meeting) созывать
(созвать* perf) ♦ vi (parliament etc)
собираться (собраться* perf).

convener [kən'vi:nə*] n (ADMIN) человек,
ответственный за подготовку и созыв
собрания, заседания итп.
convenience [kən'vi:nɪəns] n удобство; **at your
~** когда or как Вам будет удобно; **at your
earliest ~** при первой возможности; **a flat
with all modern ~s** or (BRIT) **all mod cons**
квартира со всеми удобствами.
convenience foods npl пищевые
полуфабрикаты.
convenient [kən'vi:nɪənt] adj удобный*
(удобен); **if it is ~ to you** если Вам удобно.
conveniently [kən'vi:nɪəntlɪ] adv (happen) как
раз; (situated) удобно.
convenor [kən'vi:nə*] n = **convener**.
convent ['kɔnvənt] n (REL) (женский*)
монастырь* m.
convention [kən'vɛnʃən] n (custom)
условность f; (conference) конференция;
(agreement) конвенция; (in art, literature)
приём.
conventional [kən'vɛnʃənl] adj обычный.
convent school n монастырская школа.
converge [kən'və:dʒ] vi (roads) сходиться*
(сойтись* perf); (people) съезжаться
(съехаться* perf); (ideas) совпадать
(совпасть* perf).
conversant [kən'və:snt] adj: **he is/was ~ with**
он сведущ/был сведущ в +prp.
conversation [kɔnvə'seɪʃən] n беседа,
разговор; **to have a ~ with sb** разговаривать
(impf) or беседовать (perf) с кем-н.
conversational [kɔnvə'seɪʃənl] adj
разговорный; (COMPUT) диалоговый.
conversationalist [kɔnvə'seɪʃnəlɪst] n: **a good ~**
интересный(-ая) собеседник(-ница).
converse [n 'kɔnvə:s, vb kən'və:s] n (of
statement) противоположность f ♦ vi: **to ~
(with sb) (about sth)** беседовать
(побеседовать perf) (с кем-н) (о чём-н).
conversely [kən'və:slɪ] adv наоборот.
conversion [kən'və:ʃən] n (of weights) перевод;
(of substances) превращение; (of currency,
REL) обращение; (BRIT: of house)
перестройка; (RUGBY) один из приёмов
получения очков.
conversion table n таблица преобразования.
convert [vt kən'və:t, n 'kɔnvə:t] vt (person: REL,
POL) обращать (обратить* perf); (building,
vehicle) преобразовывать (преобразовать
perf); (COMM) переводить (перевести* perf) ♦
n (REL, POL) новообращённый(-ая)m(f) adj; **to
~ sth into** превращать (превратить* perf)
что-н в +acc.
convertible [kən'və:təbl] adj (currency)
конвертируемый ♦ n автомобиль m с
откидным верхом; ~ **loan stock** (COMM)
конвертабельные акции.
convex ['kɔnvɛks] adj выпуклый.
convey [kən'veɪ] vt (information, idea, thanks)
передавать* (передать* perf); (cargo, person)

перевози́ть* (перевезти́* *perf*).
conveyance [kən'veɪəns] *n* (*of goods*)
перево́зка*; (*vehicle*) тра́нспортное
сре́дство.
conveyancing [kən'veɪənsɪŋ] *n* (*LAW*)
*состав.іе́ние нотариа́льного а́кта о
переда́че прав на недви́жимость.*
conveyor belt [kən'veɪə'-] *n* конве́йер.
convict [*vt* kən'vɪkt, *n* 'kɔnvɪkt] *vt* осужда́ть
(осуди́ть* *perf*) ♦ *n* ка́торжник.
conviction [kən'vɪkʃən] *n* (*belief*) убежде́ние;
(*certainty*) убеждённость *f*; (*LAW: decision*)
осужде́ние; (*previous*) суди́мость *f*.
convince [kən'vɪns] *vt* (*assure*) уверя́ть
(уве́рить *perf*); (*persuade*) убежда́ть
(убеди́ть* *perf*); **to ~ sb (of sth/that)** убежда́ть
(убеди́ть* *perf*) кого́-н (в чём-н/, что).
convinced [kən'vɪnst] *adj*: **~ of/that**
убеждённый в +*prp*/, что.
convincing [kən'vɪnsɪŋ] *adj* убеди́тельный*
(убеди́телен).
convincingly [kən'vɪnsɪŋlɪ] *adv* убеди́тельно.
convivial [kən'vɪvɪəl] *adj* (*atmosphere*)
дру́жеский*; (*person*) дружелю́бный*
(дружелю́бен).
convoluted ['kɔnvəlu:tɪd] *adj* замыслова́тый
(замылова́т).
convoy ['kɔnvɔɪ] *n* (*of trucks*) коло́нна; (*of
ships*) конво́й.
convulse [kən'vʌls] *vt*: **to be ~d with laughter/
pain** содрога́ться (*impf*) от сме́ха/бо́ли.
convulsion [kən'vʌlʃən] *n* су́дорога,
конву́льсия.
coo [ku:] *vi* (*dove, person*) воркова́ть (*impf*).
cook [kuk] *vt* (*food*) гото́вить* (пригото́вить*
perf) ♦ *vi* (*person*) гото́вить* (*impf*); (*food*)
гото́виться* (*impf*) ♦ *n* по́вар*
  ► **cook up** *vt* (*inf*) стря́пать (состря́пать *perf*).
cookbook ['kukbuk] *n* пова́ренная *or*
кулина́рная кни́га.
cook-chill ['kuktʃɪl] *adj*: **~ food** заморо́женные
полуфабрика́ты *mpl*.
cooker ['kukə'] *n* (*stove*) плита́*.
cookery ['kukərɪ] *n* кулинари́я.
cookery book *n* (*BRIT*) = **cookbook**.
cookie ['kukɪ] *n* (*US*) пече́нье*.
cooking ['kukɪŋ] *n* гото́вка ♦ *cpd* (*apples,
chocolate*) испо́льзуемый в кулина́рии; **her
~ is very good** она́ хорошо́ гото́вит; **Italian ~**
италья́нская ку́хня; **~ utensils** кухо́нные
принадле́жности.
cookout ['kukaut] *n* (*US*) *пригото́вление пищи
на откры́том во́здухе.*
cool [ku:l] *adj* (*temperature, drink etc*)
прохла́дный*; (*dress, clothes*) лёгкий*
(лёгок); (*person: calm, unemotional*)
невозмути́мый (невозмути́м); (: *unfriendly*)
холо́дный* (хо́лоден) ♦ *vt* (*tea, room*)

охлажда́ть (охлади́ть* *perf*) ♦ *vi* (*water, air*)
остыва́ть (осты́ть* *perf*); **it's ~** прохла́дно; **to
keep sth ~** *or* **in a ~ place** держа́ть* (*impf*)
что-н в прохла́дном ме́сте; **to keep one's ~**
сохраня́ть (сохрани́ть *perf*) хладнокро́вие;
to lose one's ~ теря́ть (потеря́ть *perf*)
самооблада́ние.
  ► **cool down** *vi* остыва́ть (осты́ть* *perf*);
(*situation*) нормализова́ться (*impf/perf*).
coolant ['ku:lənt] *n* хладоаге́нт.
cool box (*US* **cooler**) *n* холоди́льный я́щик.
cooler ['ku:lə'] *n* (*US*) = **cool box**.
cooling ['ku:lɪŋ] *n* охлажде́ние ♦ *adj*
прохлади́тельный, освежа́ющий
(освежа́ющ).
cooling tower *n* гради́рня*.
coolly ['ku:lɪ] *adv* (*calmly*) невозмути́мо;
(*coldly*) хо́лодно.
coolness ['ku:lnɪs] *n* (*see adj*) прохла́да;
лёгкость *f*; невозмути́мость *f*; хо́лодность *f*.
coop [ku:p] *n* кле́тка* ♦ *vt*: **to ~ up** (*fig*)
запира́ть (запере́ть* *perf*).
co-op ['kəuɔp] *n abbr* (= *cooperative (society)*)
кооперати́вное о́бщество.
cooperate [kəu'ɔpəreɪt] *vi* (*collaborate*)
сотру́дничать (*impf*); (*assist*) соде́йствовать
(*impf*); **to ~ with sb** сотру́дничать (*impf*) с
кем-н.
cooperation [kəuɔpə'reɪʃən] *n* (*see vb*)
коопера́ция, сотру́дничество; соде́йствие.
cooperative [kəu'ɔpərətɪv] *adj* кооперати́вный
♦ *n* кооперати́в; **he is very ~** он всегда́ гото́в
оказа́ть по́мощь.
coopt [kəu'ɔpt] *vt*: **to ~ sb onto a committee**
коопти́ровать (*impf/perf*) кого́-н в чле́ны
комите́та.
coordinate [*vt* kəu'ɔ:dɪneɪt, *n* kəu'ɔdɪnət] *vt*
(*activity, attack*) согласо́вывать (согласова́ть
perf); (*movements*) координи́ровать (*impf/perf*)
♦ *n* (*MATH*) координа́та; **~s** *npl* (*clothes*)
*предме́ты оде́жды, составля́ющие оди́н
анса́мбль.*
coordination [kəuɔ:dɪ'neɪʃən] *n* координа́ция.
co-ownership ['kəu'əunəʃɪp] *n* совме́стное
владе́ние.
cop [kɔp] *n* (*inf*) мент.
cope [kəup] *vi*: **to ~ with** справля́ться
(спра́виться* *perf*) с +*instr*.
Copenhagen ['kəupn'heɪgən] *n* Копенга́ген.
copier ['kɔpɪə'] *n* (*also:* **photocopier**)
(фо́то)копирова́льная маши́на.
co-pilot ['kəu'paɪlət] *n* второ́й пило́т.
copious ['kəupɪəs] *adj* оби́льный* (оби́лен).
copper ['kɔpə'] *n* (*metal*) медь *f*; (*BRIT: inf*)
мент; **~s** *npl* (*small change*) медяки́*
mpl.
coppice ['kɔpɪs] *n* ро́щица.
copse [kɔps] *n* = **coppice**.

copulate ['kɔpjuleɪt] *vi* совокупля́ться (совокупи́ться *perf*).

copy ['kɔpɪ] *n* (*duplicate*) ко́пия; (*of book etc*) экземпля́р; (*material: for printing*) пи́сьменный экземпля́р, ру́копись *f* ♦ *vt* (*person, idea, text*) копи́ровать (скопи́ровать *perf*); **to make good ~** (*PRESS*) составля́ть (соста́вить* *perf*) хоро́ший материа́л (для печа́ти)

► **copy out** (*text*) копи́ровать (скопи́ровать *perf*)

► **copy down** (*text*) копи́ровать (скопи́ровать *perf*)

copycat ['kɔpɪkæt] *n* (*inf*) обезья́на *m/f*.

copyright ['kɔpɪraɪt] *n* а́вторское пра́во*; **~ reserved** а́вторское пра́во сохранено́.

copy typist *n* машини́стка*.

copywriter ['kɔpɪraɪtə'] *n* реклами́ст.

coral ['kɔrəl] *n* кора́лл.

coral reef *n* кора́лловый риф.

Coral Sea *n*: **the ~ ~** Кора́лловое мо́ре*.

cord [kɔːd] *n* (*string*) верёвка*; (*ELEC*) шнур*; (*fabric*) вельве́т; **~s** *npl* (*trousers*) вельве́товые брю́ки *pl*.

cordial ['kɔːdɪəl] *adj* (*friendly*) серде́чный* ♦ *n* (*BRIT*) фрукто́вый напи́ток*.

cordless ['kɔːdlɪs] *adj* переносно́й.

cordon ['kɔːdn] *n* кордо́н, оцепле́ние

► **cordon off** *vt* оцепля́ть (оцепи́ть* *perf*).

cordon bleu ['kɔːdɔn 'bləː] *adj* (*cookery, cook*) вы́сшего кла́сса (*о кулина́рном иску́сстве*).

corduroy ['kɔːdərɔɪ] *n* вельве́т*.

CORE [kɔː'] *n abbr* (*US*) = Congress of Racial Equality.

core [kɔː'] *n* (*of fruit, organization*) сердцеви́на; (*of earth*) ядро́*; (*of nuclear reactor*) серде́чник; (*of problem*) суть *f* ♦ *vt* выреза́ть (вы́резать* *perf*) сердцеви́ну +*gen*; **rotten to the ~** (*fig*) прогни́вший до основа́ния.

Corfu [kɔː'fuː] *n* Ко́рфу *m ind*.

coriander [kɔrɪ'ændə'] *n* (*spice*) ки́нза, кориа́ндр.

cork [kɔːk] *n* про́бка*.

corkage ['kɔːkɪdʒ] *n дополни́тельная опла́та в ресто́ране за отку́поривание и пода́чу принесённого с собо́й вина́*.

corked [kɔːkt] (*US corky*) *adj* пропа́хший про́бкой.

corkscrew ['kɔːkskruː] *n* што́пор.

corky ['kɔːkɪ] *adj* (*US*) = corked.

cormorant ['kɔːmərənt] *n* бакла́н.

Corn *abbr* (*BRIT: POST*) = Cornwall.

corn [kɔːn] *n* (*BRIT*) зерно́; (*US: maize*) кукуру́за; (*on foot*) мозо́ль *f*; **~ on the cob** поча́ток* кукуру́зы.

cornea ['kɔːnɪə] *n* рогова́я оболо́чка*.

corned beef ['kɔːnd-] *n* консерви́рованная говя́дина.

corner ['kɔːnə'] *n* у́гол*; (*SPORT: also: ~ kick*) углово́й *m adj* (уда́р*) ♦ *vt* (*trap*) загоня́ть (загна́ть* *perf*) в у́гол; (*COMM: market*)

приобрета́ть (приобрести́* *perf*) контро́ль над +*instr* ♦ *vi* (*in car*) де́лать (сде́лать *perf*) поворо́т; **to cut ~s** (*fig*) среза́ть (*impf*) углы́.

corner flag *n* углово́й флажо́к*.

corner kick *n* углово́й уда́р.

cornerstone ['kɔːnəstəun] *n* (*fig*) крае-уго́льный ка́мень* *m*.

cornet ['kɔːnɪt] *n* (*MUS*) корне́т; (*BRIT: of ice-cream*) моро́женое в ва́фельной тру́бочке.

cornflakes ['kɔːnfleɪks] *npl* кукуру́зные хло́пья* *pl*.

cornflour ['kɔːnflauə'] *n* (*BRIT*) кукуру́зная мука́.

cornice ['kɔːnɪs] *n* карни́з.

Cornish ['kɔːnɪʃ] *adj* корнуэ́льский.

corn oil *n* кукуру́зное ма́сло*.

cornstarch ['kɔːnstɑːtʃ] *n* (*US*) = cornflour.

cornucopia [kɔːnju'kəupɪə] *n* рог* изоби́лия.

Cornwall ['kɔːnwəl] *n* Ко́рнуолл.

corny ['kɔːnɪ] *adj* (*inf*) пло́ский* (пло́сок).

corollary [kə'rɔlərɪ] *n* сле́дствие.

coronary ['kɔrənərɪ] *n* (*also: ~ thrombosis*) корона́рный тромбо́з.

coronation [kɔrə'neɪʃən] *n* корона́ция.

coroner ['kɔrənə'] *n* (*LAW*) ко́ронер (*судья́, рассле́дующий причи́ны сме́рти, происше́дшей при подозри́тельных обстоя́тельствах*).

coronet ['kɔrənɪt] *n* диаде́ма.

Corp. *abbr* = corporation; (*MIL*) = corporal.

corporal ['kɔːpərl] *n* капра́л ♦ *adj*: **~ punishment** теле́сное наказа́ние.

corporate ['kɔːpərɪt] *adj* (*COMM*) корпорацио́нный; (*ownership, effort*) о́бщий*; (*identity*) корпорати́вный.

corporate hospitality *n спецобслу́живание и привиле́гии, ока́зываемые корпора́цией осо́бо ва́жным и́ли це́нным клие́нтам*.

corporation [kɔːpə'reɪʃən] *n* (*COMM*) корпора́ция; (*of town*) муниципалите́т*.

corporation tax *n* корпорацио́нный нало́г.

corps [kɔː'] (*pl ~*) *n* (*also MIL*) ко́рпус*; **the press ~** корреспонде́нтский ко́рпус.

corpse [kɔːps] *n* труп.

corpuscle ['kɔːpʌsl] *n* (*BIO*) те́льце* (*кровяны́е*).

corral [kə'rɑːl] *n* заго́н.

correct [kə'rɛkt] *adj* (*accurate*) пра́вильный* (пра́вилен); (*proper*) соотве́тствующий* ♦ *vt* (*mistake, fault*) исправля́ть (испра́вить* *perf*); (*exam*) проверя́ть (прове́рить *perf*); **you are ~** Вы пра́вы.

correction [kə'rɛkʃən] *n* (*act of correcting*) исправле́ние; (*mistake corrected*) попра́вка*; (*of proofs*) корректу́ра.

correctly [kə'rɛktlɪ] *adv* пра́вильно.

correlate ['kɔrɪleɪt] *vt* соотноси́ть* (соотнести́* *perf*) ♦ *vi*: **to ~ with** соотноси́ться* (*impf*) or коррели́ровать (*impf*) с +*instr*.

correlation [kɔrɪ'leɪʃən] *n* соотноше́ние, корреля́ция.

correspond [kɔrɪs'pɔnd] *vi*: **to ~ (with)** (*write*)

переписываться (impf) (с +instr); (tally)
согласовываться (impf) (с +instr); (equate): to
~ (to) соответствовать (impf) (+dat).

correspondence ['kɔrɪs'pɒndəns] n (letters)
корреспонденция, переписка; (relationship)
соотношение.

correspondence course n заочный курс.

correspondent [kɔrɪs'pɒndənt] n (PRESS)
корреспондент(ка).

corresponding [kɔrɪs'pɒndɪŋ] adj
соответствующий*.

corridor ['kɒrɪdɔ:'] n (in building etc) коридор;
(in train) проход.

corroborate [kə'rɒbəreɪt] vt подтверждать
(подтвердить* perf).

corrode [kə'rəud] vt (metal) разъедать
(разъесть* perf) ◆ vi (metal) ржаветь
(заржаветь perf).

corrosion [kə'rəuʒən] n (damage) ржавчина;
(process) коррозия.

corrosive [kə'rəuzɪv] adj коррозийный.

corrugated ['kɒrəgeɪtɪd] adj рифлёный.

corrugated iron n рифлёное железо.

corrupt [kə'rʌpt] adj (person) продажный*
(продажен), коррумпированный; (COMPUT)
испорченный, искажённый ◆ vt развращать
(развратить* perf); (COMPUT) искажать
(исказить* perf); ~ **practices** бесчестные
приёмы.

corruption [kə'rʌpʃən] n (see adj) коррупция,
продажность f; искажение.

corset ['kɔ:sɪt] n (also MED) корсет.

Corsica ['kɔ:sɪkə] n Корсика.

Corsican ['kɔ:sɪkən] adj корсиканский ◆ n
корсиканец*(-нка*).

cortège [kɔ:'teɪʒ] n (also: funeral ~) процессия.

cortisone ['kɔ:tɪzəun] n кортизон.

coruscating ['kɒrəskeɪtɪŋ] adj сверкающий.

c.o.s. abbr (= cash on shipment) оплата
наличными при отправке.

cosh [kɒʃ] n (BRIT) дубинка*.

cosignatory ['kəu'sɪgnətərɪ] n одна из сторон,
подписывающих документ.

cosiness ['kəuzɪnɪs] n уют.

cos lettuce ['kɒs-] n латук (салат).

cosmetic [kɒz'mɛtɪk] n (usu pl) косметика ◆ adj
(fig) косметический*; ~ **surgery**
косметическая хирургия.

cosmic ['kɒzmɪk] adj космический*.

cosmonaut ['kɒzmənɔ:t] n космонавт.

cosmopolitan [kɒzmə'pɒlɪtn] adj (place)
космополитический.

cosmos ['kɒzmɒs] n: the ~ космос.

cosset ['kɒsɪt] vt баловать (избаловать perf).

cost [kɒst] (pt, pp cost) n стоимость f; (fig) цена*
◆ vt (be priced at) стоить (impf); (pt, pp costed;
find out cost of) оценивать (оценить perf)
стоимость +gen; ~**s** npl (COMM) расходы mpl;

(LAW) судебные издержки* fpl; **how much
does it ~?** сколько это стоит?; **it ~s £5/too
much** это стоит £5/слишком дорого; **what
will it ~ to have it repaired?** сколько будет
стоить ремонт?; **to ~ sb time/effort** стоить
(impf) кому-н времени/усилий; **it ~ him his
life/job** это стоило ему жизни/работы; **the ~
of living** стоимость жизни; **to sell/buy at ~**
продавать* (продать* perf)/покупать
(купить* perf) по себестоимости; **at all ~s**
любой ценой.

cost accountant n бухгалтер (ведущий учёт
затрат).

co-star ['kəustɑ:'] n партнёр (главной роли).

Costa Rica ['kɒstə'ri:kə] n Коста-Рика.

cost-benefit analysis ['kɒstbɛnɪfɪt-] n анализ
издержек и прибыли.

cost centre n счёт, фиксирующий
производственные издержки.

cost control n контроль m за уровнем
издержек.

cost-effective ['kɒstɪ'fɛktɪv] adj выгодный*
(выгоден); (COMM) рентабельный.

cost-effectiveness ['kɒstɪ'fɛktɪvnɪs] n (see adj)
выгодность f; рентабельность f.

costing ['kɒstɪŋ] n (COMM) оценка стоимости.

costly ['kɒstlɪ] adj (expensive) дорогой*
(дорог); (in time, effort) дорогостоящий.

cost of living n стоимость f жизни.

cost price n (BRIT) себестоимость f; **to sell/buy
at ~ ~** продавать* (продать* perf)/покупать
(купить* perf) по себестоимости.

costume ['kɒstju:m] n костюм; (BRIT: also:
swimming ~) купальник, купальный
костюм.

costume jewellery n бижутерия.

cosy ['kəuzɪ] (US cozy) adj (room, atmosphere)
уютный* (уютен); (bed) удобный* (удобен);
(scarf, gloves) тёплый*; (person)
заботливый; (chat, evening) приятный*
(приятен).

cot [kɒt] n (BRIT: for baby) детская кроватка*;
(US: camp bed) койка*.

cot death n внезапная смерть здорового
грудного ребёнка во сне.

Cotswolds ['kɒtswəuldz] npl: the ~ Котсволд
msg.

cottage ['kɒtɪdʒ] n коттедж.

cottage cheese n творог.

cottage industry n надомный труд*.

cottage pie n запеканка из мяса и
картофеля.

cotton ['kɒtn] n (fabric) хлопок*,
хлопчатобумажная ткань f; (plant)
хлопчатник; (thread) (швейная) нитка*; ~
dress etc хлопчатобумажное платье* etc
▶ **cotton on** vi (inf): **he has ~ed on to the fact
that ...** до него дошло, что ....

---

* marks translations which have irregular inflections. The Russian-English side of the dictionary gives inflectional information.

cotton candy n (US) сáхарная вáта.
cotton wool n (BRIT) вáта.
couch [kautʃ] n тахтá, дивáн; (for patients) кушéтка* ◆ vt излагáть (изложи́ть* perf).
couchette [kuːˈʃɛt] n спáльное мéсто*, пóлка*.
couch pota̱to n лежебóка m/f.
cough [kɔf] vi (person) кáшлять (impf); (engine) тарахтéть (impf) ◆ n кáшель m.
cough drop n таблéтка* от кáшля.
cough mixture n микстýра от кáшля.
cough syrup n = cough mixture.
could [kud] pt of **can²**.
couldn't ['kudnt] = could not; see **can²**.
council ['kaunsl] n совéт; **city** or **town** ~ городскóй совéт, муниципалитéт; **C~ of Europe** Совéт Европéйского Сообщества.
council estate n (BRIT) жилóй массúв, принадлежáщий муниципалитéту.
council house n (BRIT) дом, принадлежáщий муниципалитéту.
council housing n (BRIT) жильё, принадлежáщее муниципалитéту и сдавáемое в арéнду.
councillor ['kaunslə*] n ≈ член муниципалитéта.
council tax n муниципáльный налóг.
counsel ['kaunsl] n (advice) совéт; (lawyer) адвокáт, юрискóнсульт ◆ vt: **to ~ sth/sb to do** совéтовать (посовéтовать perf) что-н/ кому́-н +infin; ~ **for the defence** защи́тник; ~ **for the prosecution** обвини́тель m.
counsellor ['kaunslə*] n (advisor) совéтник; (US: lawyer) адвокáт.
count [kaunt] vt (add up) считáть (посчитáть perf); (include) считáть (impf) ◆ vi пересчи́тывать (пересчитáть perf); (qualify) считáться (impf); (matter) имéть (impf) значéние ◆ n (of things, people) подсчёт; (level) ýровень* m; (nobleman) граф; **to ~ (up) to 10** считáть (посчитáть perf) до 10; **not ~ing the children** не считáя детéй; **10 ~ing him 10**, считáя егó; **to ~ the cost of** оцéнивать (оцени́ть* perf) стóимость +gen; **it ~s for very little** это имéет óчень мáленькое значéние; ~ **yourself lucky** считáйте, что Вам повезлó; **to keep/lose ~ of sth** вести́* (impf)/ терять (потеря́ть perf) счёт чегó-н
▶ **count on** vt fus рассчи́тывать (impf) на +acc; **to ~ on doing** рассчи́тывать (impf) +infin
▶ **count up** vt подсчи́тывать (подсчитáть perf).
countdown ['kauntdaun] n счёт в обрáтном направлéнии.
countenance ['kauntɪnəns] n лицó* ◆ vt одобря́ть (одóбрить perf).
counter ['kauntə*] n (in shop, café) прилáвок*; (in bank, post office) стóйка*; (in game) фи́шка*; (TECH) счётчик ◆ vt (oppose) опровергáть (опровéргнуть perf); (blow) отражáть (отрази́ть perf) ◆ adv: ~ **to** в противовéс +dat; **to buy under the ~** (fig) покупáть (купи́ть* perf) из-под прилáвка; **to**

~ **sth with sth** противостоя́ть (impf/perf) чему́-н чем-н.
counteract ['kauntər'ækt] vt (effect etc) противодéйствовать (impf) +dat; (poison etc) нейтрализовáть (impf/perf), обезврéживать (обезврéдить* perf).
counterattack ['kauntərə'tæk] n контратáка ◆ vi контратаковáть (impf/perf).
counterbalance ['kauntə'bæləns] vt уравновéшивать (уравновéсить* perf).
counterclockwise ['kauntə'klɔkwaɪz] adv прóтив часовóй стрéлки.
counterespionage ['kauntər'ɛspɪənɑːʒ] n контрразвéдка*.
counterfeit ['kauntəfɪt] n поддéлка* ◆ vt поддéлывать (поддéлать perf) ◆ adj (coin) фальши́вый.
counterfoil ['kauntəfɔɪl] n (of cheque, money order) корешóк*.
counterintelligence ['kauntərɪn'tɛlɪdʒəns] n контрразвéдка*.
countermand ['kauntəmɑːnd] vt (order) отменя́ть (отмени́ть* perf).
countermeasure ['kauntəmɛʒə*] n контрмéра.
counteroffensive ['kauntərə'fɛnsɪv] n контрнаступлéние.
counterpane ['kauntəpeɪn] n покрывáло.
counterpart ['kauntəpɑːt] n (of person) коллéга m/f; (of document etc) кóпия.
counterproductive ['kauntəprə'dʌktɪv] adj непродукти́вный* (непродукти́вен).
counterproposal ['kauntəprə'pəuzl] n встрéчное предложéние.
countersign ['kauntəsaɪn] vt заверя́ть (завéрить perf), засвидéтельствовать (perf).
countersink ['kauntəsɪŋk] vt зенковáть (impf).
countess ['kauntɪs] n графи́ня.
countless ['kauntlɪs] adj несчётный*, бесчи́сленный.
countrified ['kʌntrɪfaɪd] adj деревéнский*.
country ['kʌntrɪ] n (state, nation) странá*; (native land) рóдина; (rural area) дерéвня*; (region) райóн; **in the** ~ в дерéвне; **mountainous** ~ гори́стая мéстность f.
country and western (music) n кáнтри nt ind.
country dancing n (BRIT) нарóдные тáнцы mpl.
country house n зáгородный дом*, ≈ дáча.
countryman ['kʌntrɪmən] irreg n (compatriot) земля́к*, соотéчественник; (country dweller) деревéнский* or сéльский* жи́тель m.
countryside ['kʌntrɪsaɪd] n сéльская мéстность f.
countrywide ['kʌntrɪ'waɪd] adj обще-национáльный ◆ adv по всéй странé.
county ['kauntɪ] n грáфство.
county council n ≈ областнóй совéт, совéт грáфства.
county town n (BRIT) глáвный гóрод* грáфства.
coup [kuː] (pl ~s) n (also: ~ **d'état**)

государственный переворо́т; (*fig*)
переворо́т.
coupé [kuː'peɪ] *n* (*AUT*) *закры́тый автомоби́ль
с двумя́ дверя́ми и накло́нным ку́зовом.*
couple ['kʌpl] *n* (*married couple*) супру́ги *pl*; (*of
people, things*) па́ра ♦ *vt* (*ideas, names*)
свя́зывать (связа́ть* *perf*); (*machinery*)
сцепля́ть (сцепи́ть* *perf*); **a ~ of** (*two, a few*)
па́ра +*gen*.
couplet ['kʌplɪt] *n* двусти́шие.
coupling ['kʌplɪŋ] *n* (*RAIL*) сцепле́ние.
coupon ['kuːpɔn] *n* (*voucher*) купо́н;
(*detachable form*) тало́н; (*COMM*) отрывно́й
бланк.
courage ['kʌrɪdʒ] *n* сме́лость *f*, хра́брость *f*,
му́жество.
courageous [kə'reɪdʒəs] *adj* сме́лый* (смел),
хра́брый (храбр), му́жественный
(му́жествен).
courgette [kuə'ʒɛt] *n* (*BRIT*) молодо́й кабачо́к*.
courier ['kurɪə'] *n* (*messenger*) курье́р; (*for
tourists*) руководи́тель *m* гру́ппы.
course [kɔːs] *n* (*SCOL, MED, NAUT*) курс; (*of
events, time etc*) ход; (*of argument, action*)
направле́ние; (*of river*) тече́ние; (*part of
meal*): **first/next/last ~** пе́рвое/второ́е/
сла́дкое блю́до; **~ of lectures/treatment** курс
ле́кций/лече́ния; **in the ~ of the next few days**
в тече́ние сле́дующих не́скольких дней; **in
due ~** в своё вре́мя; **~ (of action)** ли́ния
поведе́ния; **the best ~ would be ...** лу́чшим
вы́ходом бы́ло бы ...; **we have no other ~ but
to ...** у нас нет друго́го вы́хода, кроме как ...;
of ~ (*naturally*) коне́чно; (*certainly*)
безусло́вно; **of ~!** коне́чно!; **(no) of ~ not!**
(нет,) коне́чно, нет!; **golf ~** *по́ле для игры́ в
гольф.*
court [kɔːt] *n* (*LAW*) суд*; (*SPORT*) корт; (*royal*)
двор* ♦ *vt* (*woman*) уха́живать (*impf*) за +*instr*;
(*fig: favour*) добива́ться (доби́ться* *perf*)
+*gen*; (: *death, disaster*) заи́грывать (*impf*) с
+*instr*; **to settle out of ~** приходи́ть* (прийти́*
perf) к соглаше́нию без суде́бного
разбира́тельства; **to take sb to ~** подава́ть*
(пода́ть* *perf*) на кого́-н в суд.
courteous ['kɜːtɪəs] *adj* ве́жливый (ве́жлив).
courtesan [kɔːtɪ'zæn] *n* куртиза́нка*.
courtesy ['kɜːtəsɪ] *n* ве́жливость *f*; (**by**) **~ of**
благодаря́ любе́зности +*gen*.
courtesy light *n ла́мпочка в сало́не
автомоби́ля.*
courthouse ['kɔːthaus] *n* (*US*) зда́ние суда́.
courtier ['kɔːtɪə'] *n* придво́рный *m adj*.
court martial (*pl* **~s ~**) *n* вое́нный трибуна́л.
court of appeal (*pl* **~s ~ ~**) *n* апелляцио́нный
суд*.
court of inquiry (*pl* **~s ~ ~**) *n* сле́дственная
коми́ссия.

courtroom ['kɔːtrum] *n* зал суда́.
court shoe *n* ло́дочки *pl*.
courtyard ['kɔːtjɑːd] *n* вну́тренний* двор*.
cousin ['kʌzn] *n* (*relative: male*) неродно́й
брат*; (: *female*) неродна́я сестра́*; **first ~**
(*male*) двою́родный брат*; (*female*)
двою́родная сестра́*.
cove [kəuv] *n* (*bay*) бу́хточка*.
covenant ['kʌvənənt] *n* (*promise*)
обяза́тельство ♦ *vt*: **to ~ £200 per year to
charity** обя́зываться (обяза́ться* *perf*)
перечисля́ть £200 в год в благо-
твори́тельный фонд.
Coventry ['kɔvəntrɪ] *n*: **send sb to ~** (*fig*)
бойкоти́ровать (*impf/perf*) кого́-н.
cover ['kʌvə'] *vt* (*protect, hide*) закрыва́ть
(закры́ть* *perf*), укрыва́ть (укры́ть* *perf*);
(*distance*) покрыва́ть (покры́ть* *perf*); (*MIL*)
прикрыва́ть (прикры́ть* *perf*); (*INSURANCE*)
предусма́тривать (предусмотре́ть* *perf*);
(*topic*) рассма́тривать (рассмотре́ть* *perf*);
(*include*) охва́тывать (охвати́ть* *perf*);
(*PRESS*) освеща́ть (освети́ть* *perf*) ♦ *n* (*for
furniture, machinery etc*) чехо́л*; (*of book,
magazine*) обло́жка*; (*shelter*) укры́тие;
(*INSURANCE*) покры́тие; (*MIL*) прикры́тие;
(*fig*) прикры́тие; **~s** *npl* (*bedclothes*)
посте́льные принадле́жности *fpl*; **he was ~ed
in** *or* **with** (*mud*) он был весь в +*prp*; **to take ~**
укрыва́ться (укры́ться* *perf*); **under ~** в
укры́тии; **under ~ of darkness** под покро́вом
темноты́; **under separate ~** (*COMM*) в
отде́льном паке́те; **£10 will ~ my expenses**
£10 покро́ют мои́ расхо́ды
 ► **cover up** *vt* (*protect, hide*) закрыва́ть
(закры́ть* *perf*); (*fig: facts, feelings*) скрыва́ть
(скрыть* *perf*) ♦ *vi* (*fig*): **to ~ up for sb**
покрыва́ть (покры́ть* *perf*) кого́-н.
coverage ['kʌvərɪdʒ] *n* (*TV, PRESS*) освеще́ние;
television ~ of the conference освеще́ние
конфере́нции по телеви́дению; **to give full ~
to** дава́ть* (дать* *perf*) по́лное освеще́ние
+*gen*.
coveralls ['kʌvərɔːlz] *npl* (*US*) рабо́чий*
комбинезо́н *msg*.
cover charge *n* (*in restaurant*) наце́нка.
covering ['kʌvərɪŋ] *n* (*layer*) пласт*; (*of snow,
dust etc*) слой*; (*on floor*) насти́л.
covering letter (*US* **cover letter**) *n*
сопроводи́тельное письмо́*.
cover note *n докуме́нт, удостоверя́ющий
факт страхова́ния.*
cover price *n цена́, ука́занная на обло́жке.*
covert ['kʌvət] *adj* (*threat*) скры́тый; (*attack*)
неожи́данный*; **she gave me a ~ glance** она́
укра́дкой на меня́ посмотре́ла.
cover-up ['kʌvərʌp] *n* ши́рма, прикры́тие.
covet ['kʌvɪt] *vt* жа́ждать (*impf*) +*gen*.

cow [kau] *n* (*also inf!*) коро́ва (*also !*) ◆ *vt* запу́гивать (запуга́ть *perf*).
coward ['kauəd] *n* трус(и́ха).
cowardice ['kauədıs] *n* тру́сость *f*.
cowardly ['kauədlı] *adj* трусли́вый (трусли́в).
cowboy ['kaubɔı] *n* (*in US*) ковбо́й; (*pej: tradesman*) шаба́шник.
cow elephant *n* слони́ха.
cower ['kauə'] *vi* съёживаться (съёжиться *perf*).
cow shed *n* коро́вник.
cowslip ['kauslıp] *n* первоцве́т (настоя́щий* or весе́нний*).
cox [kɔks] *n abbr* = **coxswain**.
coxswain ['kɔksn] *n* (*ROWING*) старшина́ (байда́рки).
coy [kɔı] *adj* (*shy*) засте́нчивый (засте́нчив).
coyote [kɔı'əutı] *n* койо́т.
cozy ['kəuzı] *adj* (*US*) = **cosy**.
CP *n abbr* = Communist Party.
cp. *abbr* (= **compare**) ср.= сравни́.
c/p *abbr* (*BRIT*: = carriage paid) с опла́ченной доста́вкой.
CPA *n abbr* (*US*) = certified public accountant.
CPI *n abbr* (= Consumer Price Index) и́ндекс потреби́тельских цен.
Cpl. *abbr* (*MIL*) = corporal.
CP/M *n abbr* (= Central Program for Microprocessors) СРМ (*операцио́нная систе́ма для микроЭВМ*).
c.p.s. *abbr* (*COMPUT, TYP*: = characters per second) зна́ков в секу́нду.
CPSA *n abbr* (*BRIT*: = Civil and Public Services Association.
CPU *n abbr* (*COMPUT*) (= central processing unit) ЦП= *центра́льный проце́ссор*.
cr. *abbr* = credit, creditor.
crab [kræb] *n* краб.
crab apple *n* ди́кое я́блоко*.
crack [kræk] *n* (*noise*) треск; (*gap*) щель* *f*; (*in bone, dish, wall*) тре́щина; (*joke*) хо́хма; (*DRUGS*) крэк (*фо́рма кока́ина*) ◆ *vt* (*whip, twig*) щёлкать (щёлкнуть *perf*) +*instr*; (*bone, dish etc*) раска́лывать (расколо́ть* *perf*); (*nut*) коло́ть* (расколо́ть* *perf*); (*problem*) реша́ть (реши́ть *perf*); (*code*) разга́дывать (разгада́ть *perf*); (*joke*) отпуска́ть (отпусти́ть* *perf*) ◆ *adj* первокла́ссный*; **at the ~ of dawn** на заре́; **to have a ~ (at sth)** (*inf*) пыта́ться (попыта́ться *perf*) свои́ си́лы (в чём-н); **to get ~ing** (*inf*) пошеве́ливаться (*impf*)
▸ **crack down on** *vt fus* расправля́ться (distинсправиться* *perf*) с +*instr*
▸ **crack up** *vi* (*with laughter*) пры́скать (пры́снуть *perf*) со́ смеху; **she ~ed up** (*under strain*) у неё был не́рвный срыв.
crackdown ['krækdaun] *n*: ~ **(on)** распра́ва (с +*instr*).
cracked [krækt] *adj* (*inf*) сло́манный (сло́ман).
cracker ['krækə'] *n* (*biscuit*) кре́кер; (*Christmas cracker*) хлопу́шка*; (*firework*) шути́ха; **a ~ of**

a goal (*BRIT*: *inf*) сногсшиба́тельный гол; **she's a ~** (*BRIT*: *inf*) она́ сногсшиба́тельная же́нщина; **he's ~s** (*BRIT*: *inf*) он спя́тил.
crackle ['krækl] *vi* потре́скивать (*impf*).
crackling ['kræklıŋ] *n* треск; (*of pork*) шква́рки* *fpl*.
crackpot ['krækpɔt] *n* (*inf*) полоу́мный(-ая) *m(f)* *adj* ◆ *adj* полоу́мный.
cradle ['kreıdl] *n* (*for baby*) колыбе́ль *f* ◆ *vt* прижима́ть (*impf*) к груди́.
craft [krɑːft] *n* (*skill*) мастерство́; (*trade*) ремесло́*; (*boat*: *pl inv*) кора́бль* *f*.
craftsman ['krɑːftsmən] *irreg n* (*artisan*) реме́сленник.
craftsmanship ['krɑːftsmənʃıp] *n* (*quality*) вы́делка; (*skill*) мастерство́.
crafty ['krɑːftı] *adj* лука́вый (лука́в).
crag [kræg] *n* уте́с.
craggy ['krægı] *adj* (*mountain, cliff*) отве́сный*; (*face*) с ре́зкими черта́ми.
cram [kræm] *vi* (*for exams*) зубри́ть (вы́зубрить *perf*) ◆ *vt* (*fill*): **to ~ sth with** набива́ть (наби́ть* *perf*) что-н +*instr*; (*put*): **to ~ sth into** вти́скивать (вти́снуть *perf*) что-н в +*acc*.
cramming ['kræmıŋ] *n* зубрёжка.
cramp [kræmp] *n* су́дорога ◆ *vt* стесня́ть (стесни́ть *perf*).
cramped [kræmpt] *adj* (*accommodation*) те́сный (те́сен).
crampon ['kræmpən] *n* (*CLIMBING*) клещи́ *pl*.
cranberry ['krænbərı] *n* клю́ква.
crane [kreın] *n* (*machine*) (подъёмный) кран; (*bird*) жура́вль* *m* ◆ *vt*: **to ~ one's neck** вытя́гивать (вы́тянуть *perf*) ше́ю ◆ *vi*: **to ~ forward** высо́вываться (вы́сунуться *perf*).
crania ['kreınıə] *npl of* **cranium**.
cranium ['kreınıəm] (*pl* **crania**) *n* че́реп*.
crank [kræŋk] *n* (*person*) чуда́к*; (*handle*) заводна́я рукоя́тка.
crankshaft ['kræŋkʃɑːft] *n* коле́нчатый вал*.
cranky ['kræŋkı] *adj* чудакова́тый (чудакова́т).
cranny ['krænı] *n see* **nook**.
crap [kræp] (*inf!*) *n* дерьмо́ (!) ◆ *vi* срать* (*impf*) (!); **to have a ~** посра́ть* (*perf*) (!)
crappy ['kræpı] *adj* (*inf!*) дерьмо́вый (!)
crash [kræʃ] *n* (*noise*) гро́хот; (*of car*) ава́рия; (*of plane, train*) круше́ние; (*COMM*) крах ◆ *vt* (*car, plane*) разбива́ть (разби́ть* *perf*) ◆ *vi* (*car, plane*) разбива́ться (разби́ться* *perf*); (*two cars*) ста́лкиваться (столкну́ться *perf*); (*COMM*) потерпе́ть* (*perf*) крах; **to ~ into** вреза́ться (вре́заться* *perf*) в +*acc*; **he ~ed the car into a wall** он вре́зался на маши́не в сте́ну.
crash barrier *n* (*BRIT*) предохрани́тельный барье́р (на доро́ге).
crash course *n* интенси́вный курс.
crash helmet *n* защи́тный шлем.
crash landing *n* вы́нужденная поса́дка*.

crass [kræs] *adj* тупо́й (туп).
crate [kreɪt] *n* (*box*) деревя́нный я́щик; (*for bottles*) упако́вочный я́щик (*для буты́лок*); (*inf: car*) драндуле́т.
crater ['kreɪtə'] *n* (*of volcano*) кра́тер; (*of bomb blast*) воро́нка*.
cravat [krə'væt] *n* ше́йный плато́к*.
crave [kreɪv] *vti*: **to ~ sth** *or* **for sth** жа́ждать (*impf*) чего́-н.
craven ['kreɪvən] *adj* трусли́вый (трусли́в).
craving ['kreɪvɪŋ] *n*: **~ (for)** жа́жда (+*gen*).
crawl [krɔ:l] *vi* по́лзать/ползти́* (*impf*); (*inf: grovel*) пресмыка́ться (*impf*) ♦ *n* (*SWIMMING*) кроль *f*; **to ~ to sb** (*inf*) пресмыка́ться (*impf*) пе́ред кем-н; **I was driving along at a ~** моя́ маши́на е́ле ползла́.
crayfish ['kreɪfɪʃ] *n inv* (*freshwater*) речно́й рак; (*saltwater*) лангу́ст.
crayon ['kreɪən] *n* цветно́й мело́к*.
craze [kreɪz] *n* пова́льное увлече́ние.
crazed [kreɪzd] *adj* (*look, person*) безу́мный*; (*pottery etc*) потре́скавшийся.
crazy ['kreɪzɪ] *adj* сумасше́дший*; (*inf*): **he's ~ about skiing** (*inf*) он поме́шан на лы́жах; **to go ~** помеша́ться (*perf*).
crazy paving *n* (*BRIT*) насти́л из ка́менных плит разли́чной фо́рмы.
creak [kri:k] *vi* скрипе́ть* (*impf*).
cream [kri:m] *n* (*of milk*) сли́вки* *pl*; (*made artificially*) (иску́сственные) сли́вки*; (*cosmetic*) крем ♦ *adj* (*colour*) кре́мовый; **whipped ~** взби́тые сли́вки*; **soured ~** смета́на; **the ~ of society** сли́вки* о́бщества
▸ **cream off** *vt* (*fig: best talents*) отбира́ть (отобра́ть* *perf*); (*part of profits*) снима́ть (*impf*) пе́нки.
cream cake *n* пиро́жное *nt adj* с кре́мом.
cream cheese *n* сли́вочный сыр*.
creamery ['kri:mərɪ] *n* (*shop*) моло́чный магази́н; (*factory*) маслобо́йный заво́д.
creamy ['kri:mɪ] *adj* (*colour*) кре́мовый; (*taste*) сли́вочный.
crease [kri:s] *n* (*fold*) скла́дка*; (: *in trousers*) стре́лка*; (*wrinkle: in dress, on brow*) морщи́на ♦ *vt* мять* (помя́ть* *perf*) ♦ *vi* мя́ться* (помя́ться* *perf*).
crease-resistant ['kri:srɪzɪstənt] *adj* немну́щийся*.
create [kri:'eɪt] *vt* (*cause to happen, exist*) твори́ть (сотвори́ть *perf*), порожда́ть (породи́ть* *perf*); (*produce: impression*) создава́ть* (созда́ть* *perf*).
creation [kri:'eɪʃən] *n* созда́ние; (*REL*) сотворе́ние.
creative [kri:'eɪtɪv] *adj* (*artistic*) тво́рческий*; (*inventive*) изобрета́тельный* (изобрета́телен).
creativity [kri:eɪ'tɪvɪtɪ] *n* тво́рчество.

creator [kri:'eɪtə'] *n* созда́тель *m*.
creature ['kri:tʃə'] *n* (*animal*) существо́; (*person*) созда́ние.
creature comforts [- 'kʌmfəts] *npl* удо́бства *ntpl*.
crèche [krɛʃ] *n* (де́тские) я́сли *pl*.
credence ['kri:dns] *n*: **to lend** *or* **give ~ to** придава́ть* (прида́ть* *perf*) правдоподо́бность +*dat*.
credentials [krɪ'dɛnʃlz] *npl* (*references*) квалифика́ция *fsg*, достиже́ния *ntpl*; (*identity papers*) рекоменда́ция, рекоменда́тельное письмо́.
credibility [krɛdɪ'bɪlɪtɪ] *n* (*of fact*) правдоподо́бность *f*; (*of person*) авторите́т.
credible ['krɛdɪbl] *adj* (*thing*) вероя́тный* (вероя́тен), правдоподо́бный* (правдоподо́бен); (*person*) авторите́тный* (авторите́тен).
credit ['krɛdɪt] *n* (*COMM*) креди́т; (*recognition*) до́лжное *nt adj*; (*SCOL*) курс, необходи́мый для получе́ния дипло́ма ♦ *adj* (*COMM*) прихо́дный ♦ *vt* (*COMM*) кредитова́ть (*impf/perf*); (*believe: also*: **give ~ to**) ве́рить (пове́рить* *perf*) +*dat*; **~s** *npl* (*CINEMA, TV*) (вступи́тельные) ти́тры *mpl*; **he is/was in ~** он платёжеспосо́бен/был платёжеспосо́бен; **on ~** в креди́т; **to sb's ~** к чьей-н чести; **to take the ~ for** припи́сывать (приписа́ть* *perf*) себе́ +*acc*; **it does him ~** э́то де́лает ему́ честь; **he's a ~ to his family** он де́лает честь свое́й семье́; **to ~ sb with sth** (*fig*) припи́сывать (приписа́ть* *perf*) кому́-н что-н; **to ~ £5 to sb** вноси́ть* (внести́* *perf*) £5 на чей-н счёт.
creditable ['krɛdɪtəbl] *adj* (*behaviour*) досто́йный*; (*mark*) похва́льный* (похва́лен).
credit account *n* креди́тный счёт (*в отде́льном магази́не*).
credit agency *n* (*BRIT*) креди́тно-информацио́нное бюро́.
credit balance *n* креди́тный оста́ток* на счёте.
credit bureau *n* (*US*) = **credit agency**
credit card *n* креди́тная ка́рточка*.
credit control *n* (*ECON*) креди́тный контро́ль *m*.
credit facilities *npl* креди́тный лими́т (*креди́тной ка́рточки заёмщика*).
credit limit *n* креди́тный лими́т (*в примене́нию к индивидуа́льному заёмщику или определя́емый креди́тной ли́нией ба́нка*).
credit note *n* (*BRIT*) докуме́нт, позволя́ющий купи́ть това́р взаме́н неиспра́вного.
creditor ['krɛdɪtə'] *n* кредито́р.
credit transfer *n* креди́тный перево́д, жи́ро.
creditworthy ['krɛdɪtwə:ðɪ] *adj* кредитоспосо́бный*.

---

* marks translations which have irregular inflections. The Russian-English side of the dictionary gives inflectional information.

credulity [krɪ'dju:lɪtɪ] n доверчивость f.
creed [kri:d] n (REL) вероучение.
creek [kri:k] n узкий залив; (US) ручей*; **to be up the ~** (inf) влипнуть (perf) в историю.
creel [kri:l] n (also: lobster ~) клетка для ловли лангустов.
creep [kri:p] (pt, pp **crept**) vi (person, animal) красться* (impf); (plant) виться* (impf) ♦ n (inf) подхалим(ка); **it gives me the ~s** от этого у меня мороз по коже подирает; **to ~ up on sb** подкрадываться (подкрасться* perf) к кому-н.
creeper ['kri:pəʳ] n ползучее растение.
creepers ['kri:pəz] npl (US) ползунки pl.
creepy ['kri:pɪ] adj жуткий*.
creepy-crawly ['kri:pɪ'krɔ:lɪ] n (inf) букашка*.
cremate [krɪ'meɪt] vt кремировать (impf/perf).
cremation [krɪ'meɪʃən] n кремация.
crematoria [krɛmə'tɔ:rɪə] npl of **crematorium**.
crematorium [krɛmə'tɔ:rɪəm] (pl **crematoria**) n крематорий.
creosote ['krɪəsəut] n креозот.
crêpe [kreɪp] n (fabric) креп; (rubber) сорт каучука.
crêpe bandage n (BRIT) эластичная повязка*.
crêpe paper n крепированная бумага.
crêpe sole n каучуковая подошва.
crept [krɛpt] pt, pp of **creep**.
crescendo [krɪ'ʃɛndəu] n (MUS) крещендо nt ind; **the noise reached a ~** шум нарастал крещендо.
crescent ['krɛsnt] n (shape) полумесяц; (street) серпообразная улица.
cress [krɛs] n кресс-салат.
crest [krɛst] n (of hill) гребень* m; (of bird) хохолок*, гребешок*; (coat of arms) герб.
crestfallen ['krɛstfɔ:lən] adj удручённый (удручён); **he looked ~** у него был удручённый вид.
Crete [kri:t] n Крит.
crevasse [krɪ'væs] n расселина or расщелина (в леднике).
crevice ['krɛvɪs] n щель f.
crew [kru:] n (NAUT, AVIAT) экипаж; (TV, CINEMA) съёмочная группа; (gang) компания.
crew cut n ёжик; **to have a ~~** стричься (постричься* perf) под ёжик.
crew neck n вырез под горло.
crib [krɪb] n (cot) детская кроватка*; (REL) ясли pl ♦ vt (inf) сдувать (сдуть* perf).
cribbage ['krɪbɪdʒ] n криббидж.
crick [krɪk] n (in back) болезненный спазм; **~ in the neck** вывих шейного позвонка.
cricket ['krɪkɪt] n (game) крикет; (insect) сверчок*.
cricketer ['krɪkɪtəʳ] n игрок* в крикет.
crime [kraɪm] n (also fig) преступление; (illegal activity) преступность f; **petty ~** мелкое хулиганство.
Crimea [kraɪ'mɪə] n: **the ~** Крым.
crime wave n волна* преступности.
criminal ['krɪmɪnl] n преступник*(-ица) ♦ adj

(illegal) криминальный, уголовный; (morally wrong) преступный*; **~ law** уголовное право; **C~ Investigation Department** Уголовный розыск.
criminal code n уголовный кодекс.
crimp [krɪmp] vt (fabric) гофрировать (impf/ perf); (pastry) защипывать (защипнуть perf); (hair) завивать (завить* perf).
crimson ['krɪmzn] adj малиновый, тёмно-красный*.
cringe [krɪndʒ] vi съёживаться (съёжиться perf).
crinkle ['krɪŋkl] vt мять* (измять* perf).
cripple ['krɪpl] n калека m/f ♦ vt (person) калечить (искалечить perf); (ship, plane) повреждать (повредить* perf); (production, exports) наносить* (нанести* perf) вред +dat; **~d with rheumatism** искалеченный ревматизмом.
crippling ['krɪplɪŋ] adj (disease) ведущий* к инвалидности; (taxation, debts) разорительный (разорителен).
crises ['kraɪsi:z] npl of **crisis**.
crisis ['kraɪsɪs] (pl **crises**) n кризис.
crisp [krɪsp] adj (vegetables) хрустящий*; (weather) свежий* (свеж); (reply) чёткий* (чёток).
crisps [krɪsps] npl (BRIT) чипсы pl.
crisscross ['krɪskrɔs] adj перекрёстный ♦ vt пересекать (пересечь* perf).
criteria [kraɪ'tɪərɪə] npl of **criterion**.
criterion [kraɪ'tɪərɪən] (pl **criteria**) n критерий.
critic ['krɪtɪk] n критик.
critical ['krɪtɪkl] adj (time, situation, analysis) критический*; (person, opinion) критичный* (критичен); **he is ~** (MED) он в критическом состоянии; **she is ~ of him/the system** она критична по отношению к нему/системе.
critically ['krɪtɪklɪ] adv (speak, look) критически; (ill) опасно; (examine) критично.
criticism ['krɪtɪsɪzəm] n критика; (of book, play) критический* разбор.
criticize ['krɪtɪsaɪz] vt (find fault with) критиковать (impf).
critique [krɪ'ti:k] n критический* анализ.
croak [krəuk] vi (frog) квакать (impf); (bird) каркать (impf); (person) хрипеть (impf ♦ n (see vi) кваканье; карканье; хрип.
Croatia [krəu'eɪʃə] n Хорватия.
Croatian [krəu'eɪʃən] n (person) хорват(ка*) ♦ adj хорватский*.
crochet ['krəuʃeɪ] n вязание крючком.
crock [krɔk] n глиняный кувшин; (inf: also: old ~) развалина.
crockery ['krɔkərɪ] n глиняная or фаянсовая посуда.
crocodile ['krɔkədaɪl] n крокодил.
crocus ['krəukəs] n шафран.
croft [krɔft] n (BRIT: small farm) хутор*.
crofter ['krɔftəʳ] n (BRIT) хуторянин(-нка*).

crone [krəun] *n* карга́.
crony ['krəunɪ] *n* (*inf*) дружо́к.
crook [kruk] *n* (*criminal*) жу́лик; (*of shepherd*) по́сох; **the ~ of the arm** вну́тренний* сгиб ло́ктя.
crooked ['krukɪd] *adj* криво́й* (крив); (*dishonest*) нече́стный*.
crop [krɔp] *n* (*produce grown*) (сельскохозя́йственная) культу́ра; (*amount produced: cereals etc*) урожа́й; (: *honey, herbs*) сбор; (*also:* **riding ~**) плеть *f*; (*of bird*) зоб* ◆ *vt* (*hair*) ко́ротко подстрига́ть (подстри́чь* *perf*); (*subj: animal*) щипа́ть* (*impf*)
▶ **crop up** *vi* неожи́данно возника́ть (возни́кнуть* *perf*).
crop circle *n* круг непоня́тного происхожде́ния на зерново́м по́ле.
cropper ['krɔpə'] *n* (*inf*): **to come a ~** (*fail*) сади́ться* (сесть *perf*) в лу́жу *or* в кало́шу; (*fall*) шлёпаться (шлёпнуться *perf*).
crop spraying [-'spreɪɪŋ] *n* опры́скивание посе́вов.
croquet ['krəukeɪ] *n* (*BRIT*) кроке́т.
croquette [krə'kɛt] *n* (*CULIN*) кроке́ты *pl*.
cross [krɔs] *n* (*shape, also REL*) крест; (*mark*) кре́стик; (*BIO*) по́месь *f*; (*BOT*) гибри́д ◆ *vt* (*street, room etc*) пересека́ть (пересе́чь* *perf*), переходи́ть* (перейти́* *perf*); (*cheque*) кросси́ровать (*impf/perf*); (*BIO, BOT, also arms etc*) скре́щивать (скрести́ть* *perf*); (*thwart: person, plan*) препя́тствовать* (*impf*) +*dat* ◆ *adj* серди́тый ◆ *vi*: **the boat ~es from ... to ...** кора́бль плывёт из +*gen* ... в +*acc*...; **to ~ o.s.** крести́ться* (перекрести́ться* *perf*); **we have a ~ed line** (*BRIT: TEL*) кто́-то подсоедини́лся к на́шей ли́нии; **they've got their lines** *or* **wires ~ed** (*fig*) они́ совсе́м запу́тались; **the thought did not ~ my mind** э́та мысль не приходи́ла мне в го́лову; **to be/get ~ with sb (about sth)** серди́ться (*impf*)/рассерди́ться* *perf* на кого́-н (из-за чего́-н)
▶ **cross out** *vt* вычёркивать (вы́черкнуть *perf*).
crossbar ['krɔsbɑ:'] *n* (*FOOTBALL*) перекла́дина; (*on bicycle*) попере́чная пла́нка.
crossbow ['krɔsbəu] *n* самостре́л, арбале́т.
crossbreed ['krɔsbri:d] *n* по́месь *f*.
cross-Channel ferry ['krɔs'tʃænl-] *n* паро́м че́рез Ла-Ма́нш.
crosscheck ['krɔstʃɛk] *n* перепрове́рка ◆ *vt* перепроверя́ть (перепрове́рить *perf*).
cross-country (race) ['krɔs'kʌntrɪ-] *n* бег по пересечённой ме́стности.
cross-dressing [krɔs'drɛsɪŋ] *n* переодева́ние в оде́жду противополо́жного по́ла.
cross-examination ['krɔsɪgzæmɪ'neɪʃən] *n* перекрёстный допро́с.

cross-examine ['krɔsɪg'zæmɪn] *vt* (*LAW*) подверга́ть (подве́ргнуть* *perf*) перекрёстному допро́су.
cross-eyed ['krɔsaɪd] *adj* косогла́зый.
crossfire ['krɔsfaɪə'] *n* перекрёстный ого́нь* *m*; **to get caught in the ~** (*MIL*) оказа́ться (*perf*) под перекрёстным огнём; (*fig*) оказа́ться (*perf*) ме́жду двух огне́й.
crossing ['krɔsɪŋ] *n* (*sea passage*) перепра́ва; (*also:* **pedestrian ~**) перехо́д.
crossing guard *n* (*US*) регулиро́вщик движе́ния, кото́рый обеспе́чивает безопа́сный перехо́д у́лицы шко́льниками.
cross-purposes ['krɔs'pə:pəsɪz] *npl*: **to be at ~ with sb** не находи́ть* (*impf*) о́бщего языка́ с ке́м-н; **we're (talking) at ~** мы говори́м о ра́зных веща́х.
cross-question ['krɔs'kwɛstʃən] *vt* подверга́ть (подве́ргнуть *perf*) перекрёстному допро́су.
cross-reference ['krɔs'rɛfrəns] *n* перекрёстная ссы́лка*.
crossroads ['krɔsrəudz] *n* перекрёсток*.
cross section *n* (*of population*) про́филь *m*; (*of object*) попере́чное сече́ние; (*BIO*) попере́чный разре́з *or* срез.
crosswalk ['krɔswɔ:k] *n* (*US*) перехо́д.
crosswind ['krɔswɪnd] *n* боково́й ве́тер*.
crosswise ['krɔswaɪz] *adv* крест-на́крест.
crossword ['krɔswə:d] *n* кроссво́рд.
crotch [krɔtʃ] *n* (*ANAT*) проме́жность *f*; **the trousers are tight in the ~** брю́ки жмут в шагу́.
crotchet ['krɔtʃɪt] *n* четвертна́я но́та.
crotchety ['krɔtʃɪtɪ] *adj* раздражи́тельный* (раздражи́телен), брюзгли́вый (брюзгли́в).
crouch [krautʃ] *vi* (*person, animal*) приседа́ть (присе́сть* *perf*).
croup [kru:p] *n* круп.
croupier ['kru:pɪə'] *n* крупье́ *m ind*.
crouton ['kru:tɔn] *n* грено́к*.
crow [krəu] *n* (*bird*) воро́на; (*of cock*) кукаре́канье ◆ *vi* (*cock*) кукаре́кать (*impf*); (*fig: boast*): **to ~ about** хва́статься (*impf*) +*instr*.
crowbar ['krəubɑ:'] *n* лом*.
crowd [kraud] *n* толпа́*; (*clique*) компа́ния ◆ *vt* (*fill*) заполня́ть (запо́лнить *perf*); (*cram*): **to ~ sb/sth into sth** набива́ть (наби́ть* *perf*) что́-н кем-н/чем-н ◆ *vi* (*gather*): **to ~ round** толпи́ться (*impf*); (*cram*): **to ~ into sth** набива́ться (наби́ться* *perf*) в что́-н; **~s of people** то́лпы люде́й.
crowded ['kraudɪd] *adj* (*overpopulated*) перенаселённый (перенаселён); (*full*): **the room was ~** ко́мната была́ полна́ наро́ду; **~ with** по́лный* +*gen*, напо́лненный +*instr*.

---

* marks translations which have irregular inflections. The Russian-English side of the dictionary gives inflectional information.

crowd scene n массо́вка*, ма́ссовая сце́на.

crown [kraun] n (of monarch) коро́на; (of head) маку́шка; (of hill) верши́на; (of tooth) коро́нка*; (of hat) тулья́* ♦ vt (monarch) коронова́ть (impf/perf); (tooth) ста́вить* (поста́вить* perf) коро́нку на +acc; (fig) венча́ть (увенча́ть perf); **the C~** (monarchy) коро́на; **and to ~ it all ...** (fig) и в довершéние всего́ ....

crown court n (BRIT) коро́нный суд (в отли́чие от магистрату́р с постоя́нными судья́ми и прися́жными заседа́телями).

crowning ['kraunɪŋ] adj блиста́тельный*.

crown jewels npl короле́вские рега́лии fpl.

crown prince n кронпри́нц.

crow's-feet ['krəuzfi:t] npl гуси́ные ла́пки* fpl, морщи́нки* fpl (в уголка́х глаз).

crow's-nest ['krəuznɛst] n (NAUT) воро́нье гнездо́.

crucial ['kru:ʃl] adj (event, moment) реша́ющий*; (work) ва́жный* (ва́жен); ~ **to** ва́жный (ва́жен) для +gen.

crucifix ['kru:sɪfɪks] n распя́тие.

crucifixion [kru:sɪ'fɪkʃən] n распя́тие на кресте́.

crucify ['kru:sɪfaɪ] vt (also fig) распина́ть (распя́ть* perf).

crude [kru:d] adj (materials) сыро́й*; (fig: basic) примити́вный* (примити́вен); (: vulgar) гру́бый* (груб).

crude (oil) n сыра́я нефть f.

cruel ['kruəl] adj жесто́кий* (жесто́к).

cruelty ['kruəltɪ] n жесто́кость f.

cruet ['kru:ɪt] n судо́к*.

cruise [kru:z] n (on ship) круи́з ♦ vi (ship, aircraft) крейси́ровать (impf).

cruise missile n управля́емый снаря́д с я́дерной боеголо́вкой.

cruiser ['kru:zə'] n (motorboat) ка́тер*; (warship) кре́йсер*.

cruising speed ['kru:zɪŋ-] n сре́дняя (экономи́ческая) ско́рость f.

crumb [krʌm] n (of bread, cake) кро́шка*; (fig: of information) обры́вок; (: of sympathy, hope) крупи́ца.

crumble ['krʌmbl] vt (bread, biscuit etc) кроши́ть* (раскроши́ть* perf) ♦ vi осыпа́ться (осы́паться* perf); (fig) ру́шиться (impf), ру́хнуть (perf).

crumbly ['krʌmblɪ] adj рассы́пчатый.

crummy ['krʌmɪ] adj (inf) задри́панный.

crumpet ['krʌmpɪt] n ≈ блин.

crumple ['krʌmpl] vt мять* (измя́ть* perf).

crunch [krʌntʃ] vt (food etc) грызть* (сгрызть* perf) ♦ vi (stones, glass etc) скрипе́ть* (impf), хрусте́ть* (impf) ♦ n (fig): **the ~** крити́ческий* or реша́ющий* моме́нт; **if it comes to the ~** éсли насту́пит крити́ческий моме́нт; **when the ~ comes** когда́ насту́пит крити́ческий моме́нт.

crunchy ['krʌntʃɪ] adj хрустя́щий*.

crusade [kru:'seɪd] n (campaign) кресто́вый похо́д ♦ vi (fig): **to ~ for/against** боро́ться* (impf) за +acc/про́тив +gen.

crusader [kru:'seɪdə'] n крестоно́сец*; (fig): ~ **(for)** боре́ц* (за +acc).

crush [krʌʃ] vt (squash) выжима́ть (вы́жать* perf); (: grapes) дави́ть* (impf); (crumple) мять* (смять* perf); (grind: garlic, ice) размельча́ть (размельчи́ть perf); (defeat) сокруша́ть (сокруши́ть perf); (devastate) уничтожа́ть (уничто́жить perf) ♦ n (crowd) да́вка; (infatuation): **to have a ~ on sb** сходи́ть* (сойти́* perf) с ума́ по кому́-н; (drink): **lemon ~** лимо́нный напи́ток*.

crush barrier n (BRIT) огражде́ние (сде́рживающее толпу́).

crushing ['krʌʃɪŋ] adj сокруши́тельный*.

crust [krʌst] n ко́рка*; (of earth) кора́.

crustacean [krʌs'teɪʃən] n ракообра́зное nt adj (живо́тное).

crusty ['krʌstɪ] adj хрустя́щий*; (fig) раздражи́тельный* (раздражи́телен); (bread) ко́рочкой; (old gentleman) жёлчный.

crutch [krʌtʃ] n (MED) косты́ль* m; (support, TECH) опо́ра; (ANAT, in garment) see **crotch**.

crux [krʌks] n суть f.

cry [kraɪ] vi (weep) пла́кать* (impf); (also: ~ out) крича́ть* (impf) ♦ n крик; **what are you ~ing about?** почему́ Вы пла́чете?; **he began to ~** он запла́кал or на́чал пла́кать; **to ~ for help** звать* (позва́ть* perf) на по́мощь; **she cried out suddenly in pain** она́ вскри́кнула от бо́ли; **she had a good ~** она́ вы́плакалась; **it's a far ~ from ...** (fig) э́то си́льно отлича́ется от +gen

▸ **cry off** vi (inf) отка́зываться (отказа́ться* perf).

crying ['kraɪɪŋ] adj (fig: need) о́стрый*; **it's a ~ shame** э́то весьма́ приско́рбно.

crypt [krɪpt] n склеп.

cryptic ['krɪptɪk] adj (remark) зага́дочный* (зага́дочен); (clue) зашифро́ванный.

crystal ['krɪstl] n (mineral) го́рный хруста́ль* m; (glass) хруста́ль*; (CHEM) криста́лл.

crystal clear adj (water, air) криста́льно чи́стый*; (sound, idea) соверше́нно я́сный.

crystallize ['krɪstəlaɪz] vt (opinion etc) формирова́ть (сформирова́ть perf) ♦ vi (sugar etc) кристаллизова́ться (impf/perf); ~**d fruits** (BRIT) заса́харенные фру́кты.

CSA n abbr = Confederate States of America.

CSC n abbr (= Civil Service Commission) Коми́ссия гражда́нской слу́жбы.

CSE n abbr (BRIT: formerly: = Certificate of Secondary Education) аттеста́т о сре́днем образова́нии.

CS gas n (BRIT) слезоточи́вый газ*.

CST abbr (US) = Central Standard Time.

CT abbr (US: POST) = Connecticut.

ct abbr = carat.

CTC n abbr (BRIT: = city technology college)

техникум.

cu. *abbr* (= **cubic**) куб.= *кубический*.

cub [kʌb] *n* детёныш; (*also*: ~ **scout**) член *младшего отряда бойскаутов*.

Cuba ['kju:bə] *n* Куба.

Cuban ['kju:bən] *adj* кубинский* ♦ *n* кубинец*(-нка*).

cubbyhole ['kʌbɪhəul] *n* закуток*.

cube [kju:b] *n* (*also MATH*) куб* ♦ *vt* возводить* (возвести* *perf*) в куб; **the ~ of 4 is 64** 4 в кубе равняется 64.

cube root *n* кубический* корень* *m*.

cubic ['kju:bɪk] *adj* кубический*; ~ **metre** *etc* кубический* метр *etc*.

cubic capacity *n* кубический* объём.

cubicle ['kju:bɪkl] *n* (*at pool*) кабинка*; (*in hospital*) бокс.

cuckoo ['kuku:] *n* кукушка*.

cuckoo clock *n* часы *pl* с кукушкой.

cucumber ['kju:kʌmbə'] *n* огурец*.

cud [kʌd] *n*: **to chew the** ~ жевать* (*impf*) жвачку.

cuddle ['kʌdl] *vt* обнимать (обнять* *perf*) ♦ *vi* обниматься (обняться* *perf*) ♦ *n* ласка.

cuddly ['kʌdlɪ] *adj* миленький*.

cudgel ['kʌdʒl] *n* дубина ♦ *vt*: **to** ~ **one's brains about sth** ломать (*impf*) голову над чем-н.

cue [kju:] *n* (*SNOOKER etc*) кий*; (*THEAT etc*) реплика.

cuff [kʌf] *n* (*of sleeve*) манжета; (*US: of trousers*) отворот; (*blow*) шлепок* ♦ *vt* (*hit*) шлёпать (шлёпнуть *perf*); **off the** ~ экспромтом.

cuff links *npl* запонки* *fpl*.

cu. in. *abbr* (= **cubic inches**) кубические дюймы.

cuisine [kwɪ'zi:n] *n* кухня* (*кушанья*).

cul-de-sac ['kʌldəsæk] *n* (*road*) тупик*.

culinary ['kʌlɪnərɪ] *adj* кулинарный.

cull [kʌl] *vt* (*story, idea*) отбирать (отобрать* *perf*); (*animals*) отбраковывать (отбраковать* *perf*) ♦ *n* отбраковка*.

culminate ['kʌlmɪneɪt] *vi*: **to** ~ **in** завершаться (завершиться *perf*) +*instr*.

culmination [kʌlmɪ'neɪʃən] *n* кульминация.

culottes [kju:'lɒts] *npl* юбка-брюки *pl*.

culpable ['kʌlpəbl] *adj*: ~ (**of**) виновный (виновен) (в +*prp*).

culprit ['kʌlprɪt] *n* (*of crime*) виновник(-ница).

cult [kʌlt] *n* (*also REL*) культ.

cult figure *n* кумир.

cultivate ['kʌltɪveɪt] *vt* (*crop, feeling*) культивировать (*impf*); (*land*) возделывать (*impf*); (*person*) обхаживать (*impf*).

cultivation [kʌltɪ'veɪʃən] *n* (*AGR*) культивация.

cultural ['kʌltʃərəl] *adj* культурный.

culture ['kʌltʃə'] *n* (*also BIO*) культура.

cultured ['kʌltʃəd] *adj* (*individual*) культурный; (*pearl*) культивированный.

cumbersome ['kʌmbəsəm] *adj* (*object, process*) громоздкий* (громоздок).

cumin ['kʌmɪn] *n* (*spice*) тмин*.

cumulative ['kju:mjulətɪv] *adj* (*effect, result*) суммарный; (*process*) нарастающий.

cunning ['kʌnɪŋ] *n* хитрость *f* ♦ *adj* (*crafty*) хитрый* (хитёр).

cunt [kʌnt] *n* (*inf!*) пизда (*!*)

cup [kʌp] *n* чашка*; (*as prize*) кубок*; (*of bra*) чашечка*; **a** ~ **of tea** чашка* чая.

cupboard ['kʌbəd] *n* шкаф*; (*built-in*) стенной шкаф*.

cup final *n* (*BRIT: SPORT*) финал розыгрыша кубка.

cupful ['kʌpful] *n* полная чашка*.

cupid ['kju:pɪd] *n* (*figurine*) путти *pl ind*; **C~** Купидон, Амур.

cupidity [kju:'pɪdɪtɪ] *n* алчность *f*.

cupola ['kju:pələ] *n* купол*.

cuppa ['kʌpə] (*inf*) *n* чашка чая.

cup tie *n* (*BRIT: SPORT*) кубковый матч.

curable ['kjuərəbl] *adj* излечимый (излечим*).

curate ['kjuərɪt] *n* викарий.

curator [kjuə'reɪtə'] *n* (*in museum*) хранитель *m*.

curb [kə:b] *vt* (*powers, expenditure*) обуздывать (обуздать *perf*); (*person*) сдерживать (сдержать* *perf*) ♦ *n* ограничение; (*US*) бордюр (*тротуара*).

curd cheese [kə:d-] *n* творог*.

curdle ['kə:dl] *vi* (*milk*) свёртываться (свернуться *perf*).

curds [kə:dz] *npl* простокваша *fsg*.

cure [kjuə'] *vt* (*illness, patient*) вылечивать (вылечить *perf*); (*CULIN*) обрабатывать (обработать *perf*); (*problem*) устранять (устранить *perf*) ♦ *n* (*MED*) лекарство; (*solution*) средство; **~d of sth** вылечиться (*perf*) *or* излечиться* (*perf*) от чего-н.

cure-all ['kjuərɔ:l] *n* (*also fig*) панацея.

curfew ['kə:fju:] *n* комендантский* час*.

curio ['kjuərɪəu] *n* редкая антикварная вещь* *f*.

curiosity [kjuərɪ'ɒsɪtɪ] *n* (*see adj*) любознательность *f*; любопытство.

curious ['kjuərɪəs] *adj* (*interested*) любознательный* (любознателен); (*nosy, strange*) любопытный* (любопытен); **I'm ~ about him** он меня интересует.

curiously ['kjuərɪəslɪ] *adv* странно; (*inquisitively*) с любопытством; ~ **enough**, ... как ни странно, ...

curl [kə:l] *n* (*of hair*) локон, завиток; (*of smoke etc*) кольцо* ♦ *vt* (*hair: loosely*) завивать (завить* *perf*); (: *tightly*) закручивать (закрутить* *perf*) ♦ *vi* (*hair*) виться* (*impf*); (*smoke*) клубиться (*impf*)

▶ **curl up** *vi* сворачиваться (свернуться *perf*); **to ~ up into a ball** сворачиваться (свернуться *perf*) клубком.

---

* marks translations which have irregular inflections. The Russian-English side of the dictionary gives inflectional information.

curler ['kə:lə'] n бигуди ntpl ind; (SPORT) игрок в кэрлинг.

curlew ['kə:lu:] n большой кроншнеп.

curling ['kə:lɪŋ] n (SPORT) кэрлинг (игра на льду, в которой игроки сбивают цель при помощи специальных камней).

curling tongs (US **curling irons**) npl щипцы pl для завивки.

curly ['kə:lɪ] adj вьющийся; (tightly curled) кудрявый.

currant ['kʌrnt] n (dried grape) изюминка; (bush, fruit) смородинка; ~s (dried grapes) изюм msg; (fruit) смородина fsg.

currency ['kʌrnsɪ] n (system) деньги pl в обращении; (money) валюта; to gain ~ (fig) получать (получить perf) распространение.

current ['kʌrnt] n (of air, water) струя*, поток; (ELEC) ток*; (of opinion) направление ♦ adj (present) текущий*, современный; (accepted) общепринятый; **direct/alternating** ~ постоянный/переменный ток*; **the ~ issue of a magazine** текущий* номер* журнала; **this word is in ~ use** это слово является общепринятым.

current account n (BRIT) текущий* счёт*.

current affairs npl текущие события ntpl.

current assets npl текущие оборотные активы mpl.

current liabilities npl текущие обязательства ntpl.

currently ['kʌrntlɪ] adv в данный or настоящий момент.

curricula [kə'rɪkjulə] npl of **curriculum**.

curriculum [kə'rɪkjuləm] (pl ~s or **curricula**) n (SCOL) учебный план.

curriculum vitae [-'vi:taɪ] n автобиография (обычно пишущаяся при поступлении на учёбу или работу *).

curry ['kʌrɪ] n блюдо, с кэрри ♦ vt: to ~ favour with заискивать (impf) перед +instr.

curry powder n порошок* кэрри nt ind.

curse [kə:s] vi (swear) ругаться (impf) ♦ vt проклинать (проклясть* perf) ♦ n (spell, problem) проклятие; (swearword) ругательство.

cursor ['kə:sə'] n курсор.

cursory ['kə:sərɪ] adj (glance, examination) беглый.

curt [kə:t] adj резкий*.

curtail [kə:'teɪl] vt (freedom, rights) ограничивать (ограничить perf); (expenses, visit) сокращать (сократить* perf).

curtain ['kə:tn] n (light) занавеска*; (heavy, also THEAT) занавес; to draw the ~s (together) задёргивать (задёрнуть perf) занавески; (apart) отдёргивать (отдёрнуть perf) занавески.

curtain call n (THEAT) поклоны mpl; **they took four** ~ ~s их вызывали четыре раза.

curts(e)y ['kə:tsɪ] vi делать (сделать perf) реверанс, приседать (присесть* perf) в

реверансе ♦ n реверанс.

curvature ['kə:vətʃə'] n (of the earth) кривизна; (of curve) изгиб; (of spine) искривление.

curve [kə:v] n изгиб ♦ vi изгибаться (изогнуться perf) ♦ vt сгибать (согнуть perf), изгибать (изогнуть perf).

curved [kə:vd] adj изогнутый, согнутый.

cushion ['kuʃən] n подушка* ♦ vt (collision, effect) смягчать (смягчить perf); (seat) подкладывать (подложить perf) подушку под +acc.

cushy ['kuʃɪ] adj (inf): **a ~ job** тёпленькое местечко*; **to have a ~ time** бить* (impf) баклуши.

cussed ['kʌsɪd] adj упрямый (упрям).

custard ['kʌstəd] n заварной крем.

custard powder n (BRIT) заварной крем (порошок).

custodial [kʌs'təudɪəl] adj: ~ **care** опекунство; **he was given a ~ sentence** он был приговорён к тюремному заключению.

custodian [kʌs'təudɪən] n попечитель m.

custody ['kʌstədɪ] n (of child) опека; (for offenders) содержание под стражей, заключение; **to take into ~** (suspect) брать* (взять* perf) под стражу, арестовывать (арестовать perf); **he was remanded in ~** он был оставлен под стражей; **in the ~ of** под опекой +gen; **the mother has ~ of the children** дети находятся под опекой матери.

custom ['kʌstəm] n (traditional) традиция; (convention) обычай; (habit) привычка*; **we get a lot of ~ from the locals** большая часть наших покупателей or нашей клиентуры – местные жители.

customary ['kʌstəmərɪ] adj обычный*, традиционный; **it is ~ to** принято +infin.

custom-built ['kʌstəm'bɪlt] adj изготовленный на заказ.

customer ['kʌstəmə'] n (of shop) покупатель*(ница) m(f); (of small business) клиент; (of large company) заказчик; **he's an awkward ~** (inf) он трудный тип.

customer profile n профиль m покупателя.

customized ['kʌstəmaɪzd] adj изготовленный на заказ.

custom-made ['kʌstəm'meɪd] adj изготовленный на заказ.

customs ['kʌstəmz] npl таможня fsg; **to go through (the) ~** проходить* (пройти* perf) таможенный досмотр.

Customs and Excise n (BRIT) таможенно-акцизное управление.

customs officer n таможенник.

cut [kʌt] (pt, pp **cut**) vt (bread, meat) резать* (разрезать* perf); (hand, knee) резать* (порезать* perf); (grass, hair) стричь* (постричь* perf); (text, spending, supply) урезывать (урезать* perf); (prices) снижать (снизить* perf); (cloth) кроить (раскроить perf); (inf: lecture, appointment) прогуливать

(прогуля́ть *perf*) ♦ *vi* (*knife, scissors*) ре́зать*
(*impf*); (*lines*) пересека́ться (пересе́чься* *perf*)
♦ *n* (*in skin*) поре́з; (*in salary, spending etc*)
сниже́ние; (*of meat*) кусо́к*; (*of garment*)
покро́й; (*of jewel*) отде́лка*; **she is ~ting a
tooth** у неё прореза́ется зуб; **to ~ one's finger**
ре́зать (поре́зать* *perf*) па́лец*; **to get one's
hair ~** стри́чься* (постри́чься* *perf*); **to ~ sth
short** прерыва́ть (прерва́ть* *perf*) что-н; **to ~
sb short** обрыва́ть (оборва́ть* *perf*) кого́-н; **to
~ sb dead** соверше́нно игнори́ровать (*impf/
perf*) кого́-н; **cold ~s** (*US*) холо́дные мясны́е
заку́ски*; **we had a power ~** у нас
отключи́лось электри́чество

▶ **cut back** *vt* (*plants*) подреза́ть (подре́зать*
perf); (*production, expenditure*) сокраща́ть
(сократи́ть* *perf*)

▶ **cut down** *vt* (*tree*) сруба́ть (сруби́ть* *perf*);
(*consumption*) сокраща́ть (сократи́ть* *perf*);
to ~ sb down to size (*fig*) поста́вить* (*perf*)
кого́-н на ме́сто

▶ **cut down on** *vt fus*: **to ~ down on smoking/
drinking** ме́ньше кури́ть (*impf*)/пить (*impf*)

▶ **cut in** *vi* (*AUT*) пересека́ть (пересе́чь* *perf*)
путь; (*interrupt*): **to ~ in on** вме́шиваться
(вмеша́ться *perf*) в +*acc*

▶ **cut off** *vt* (*also fig*) отреза́ть (отре́зать* *perf*);
(*water, electricity*) отключа́ть (отключи́ть*
perf); (*food*) прекраща́ть (прекрати́ть* *perf*)
снабже́ние +*gen*; (*TEL*) разъединя́ть
(разъедини́ть *perf*); **we've been ~ off** (*TEL*) нас
разъедини́ли

▶ **cut out** *vt* (*remove*) выреза́ть (вы́резать*
perf); (*stop*) прекраща́ть (прекрати́ть* *perf*)

▶ **cut up** *vt* (*pieces*) разреза́ть (разре́зать* *perf*); **it really
~ me up** (*inf*) э́то о́чень подкоси́ло меня́; **she
still feels ~ up about her sister's death** (*inf*)
она́ всё ещё не опра́вилась по́сле сме́рти
свое́й сестры́.

cut-and-dried ['kʌtən'draɪd] *adj* (*answer,
solution*) гото́вый.

cut-and-dry ['kʌtən'draɪ] *adj* = **cut-and-dried**.

cutaway ['kʌtəweɪ] *n* (*coat*) визи́тка*; (*of
machine, engine etc*): **a ~ model** моде́ль *f* в
разре́зе; (*CINEMA, TV*) вста́вка*.

cutback ['kʌtbæk] *n* сокраще́ние.

cute [kju:t] *adj* (*sweet*) ми́лый (мил),
преле́стный* (преле́стен); (*clever*) у́мный
(умён).

cut glass *n* гранёное стекло́*.

cuticle ['kju:tɪkl] *n* (*of nail*) ко́жица; **~ remover**
жи́дкость и́ли крем размягча́ющий и
уничтожа́ющий ко́жицу вокру́г ногтево́й
лу́нки.

cutlery ['kʌtlərɪ] *n* столо́вый прибо́р.

cutlet ['kʌtlɪt] *n* котле́та.

cutoff ['kʌtɔf] *n* (*also:* **~ point**) преде́л ♦ *cpd*: **~
date** преде́льный срок.

cutoff switch *n* автомати́ческий*
выключа́тель *m*.

cutout ['kʌtaut] *n* (*switch*) автомати́ческий*
выключа́тель *m*; (*shape*) вы́резанная
фигу́ра; (*paper figure*) апплика́ция.

cut-price ['kʌt'praɪs] (*US* **cut-rate**) *adj* по
сни́женной цене́.

cut-rate ['kʌt'reɪt] *adj* (*US*) = **cut-price**.

cutthroat ['kʌtθrəut] *n* головоре́з* ♦ *adj* (*fig*)
беспоща́дный; **~ competition** жёсткая
конкуре́нция.

cutting ['kʌtɪŋ] *adj* (*edge*) о́стрый*; (*remark etc*)
язви́тельный* ♦ *n* (*BRIT: PRESS*) вы́резка*;
(: *RAIL*) вы́емка*; (*from plant*) черено́к*.

cutting edge *n* острие́.

cuttlefish ['kʌtlfɪʃ] *n* карака́тица.

CV *n abbr* = **curriculum vitae**.

C & W *n abbr* = **country and western** (*music*).

c.w.o. *abbr* (*COMM.* = *cash with order*) вы́дача
това́ра по нали́чному расчёту.

cwt. *abbr* = **hundredweight**.

cyanide ['saɪənaɪd] *n* циа́н, циани́стый ка́лий.

cybernetics [saɪbə'nɛtɪks] *n* киберне́тика.

cyclamen ['sɪkləmən] *n* (*BOT*) цикламе́н.

cycle ['saɪkl] *n* (*bicycle*) велосипе́д; (*series, also
TECH*) цикл ♦ *vi* е́здить* (*impf*) на велосипе́де.

cycle race *n* велого́нка*.

cycle rack *n* металли́ческая ра́ма для
стоя́нки велосипе́дов.

cycling ['saɪklɪŋ] *n* езда́ на велосипе́де; (*in
competition*) велоспо́рт; **to go on a ~ holiday**
(*BRIT*) е́хать (пое́хать* *perf*) в о́тпуск на
велосипе́де.

cyclist ['saɪklɪst] *n* велосипеди́ст.

cyclone ['saɪkləun] *n* цикло́н.

cygnet ['sɪgnɪt] *n* (*ZOOL*) лебедёнок*.

cylinder ['sɪlɪndə'] *n* (*also TECH*) цили́ндр; (*of
gas*) балло́н; **a five ~ engine**
пятицили́ндровый дви́гатель *m*.

cylinder head *n* кры́шка* цили́ндра.

cylinder-head gasket ['sɪlɪndəhɛd-] *n*
прокла́дка* кры́шки цили́ндра.

cymbals ['sɪmblz] *npl* (*MUS*) таре́лки* *fpl*.

cynic ['sɪnɪk] *n* ци́ник.

cynical ['sɪnɪkl] *adj* цини́чный* (цини́чен).

cynicism ['sɪnɪsɪzəm] *n* цини́зм.

CYO *n abbr* (*US*) = **Catholic Youth Organization**.

cypress ['saɪprɪs] *n* (*tree*) кипари́с.

Cypriot ['sɪprɪət] *adj* ки́прский ♦ *n*
киприо́т(ка*).

Cyprus ['saɪprəs] *n* Кипр.

cyst [sɪst] *n* киста́.

cystitis [sɪs'taɪtɪs] *n* цисти́т.

CZ *n abbr* (*US*) = **Canal Zone**.

czar [zɑ:'] *n* царь *m*.

Czech [tʃɛk] *adj* че́шский ♦ *n* чех (че́шка*);
(*LING*) че́шский* язы́к*.

Czech Republic *n* Че́шская Респу́блика.

---

* marks translations which have irregular inflections. The Russian-English side of the dictionary gives inflectional information.

~ D, d ~

D, d [di:] n (letter) 4-ая буква английского алфавита; (SCOL) ≈ неудовлетворительно.
D [di:] n (MUS) ре.
D abbr (US: POL) = **democrat(ic)**.
d abbr (BRIT: formerly) = **penny**.
d. abbr = **died**.
DA n abbr (US) = **district attorney**.
dab [dæb] vt (eyes, wound) просушивать (просушить perf); (paint, cream) наносить* (нанести* perf) ♦ n мазок*; **she's a ~ hand at sth/doing** она дока в чём-н/+infin
▸ **dab at** vt fus просушивать (просушить perf).
dabble ['dæbl] vi: **to ~ in** (politics, antiques etc) баловаться (impf) +instr.
dachshund ['dækshund] n такса.
dad [dæd] n (inf) папа m, папочка* m.
daddy ['dædɪ] n (inf) = **dad**.
daddy-longlegs [dædɪ'lɔŋlɛgz] n (inf) долгоножка*.
daffodil ['dæfədɪl] n нарцисс.
daft [dɑ:ft] adj (ideas) дурацкий*; (person) чокнутый, ненормальный; **to be ~ about sb/sth** рехнуться (perf) на ком-н/чём-н.
dagger ['dægə'] n кинжал; **to be at ~s drawn with sb** быть* (impf) на ножах с кем-н; **to look ~s at sb** пронзать (пронзить* perf) кого-н злобным взглядом.
dahlia ['deɪljə] n георгин.
daily ['deɪlɪ] adj (dose) суточный; (routine) повседневный; (wages) дневной ♦ n (also: ~ **paper**) ежедневная газета; (BRIT: also: ~ **help**) приходящая домработница ♦ adv ежедневно; **twice ~** два раза or дважды в день.
dainty ['deɪntɪ] adj изящный* (изящен).
dairy ['dɛərɪ] n (BRIT: shop) молочный магазин; (company) ≈ молочная фирма; (on farm: for making butter) маслодельня*; (: for making cheese) сыроварня* ♦ cpd молочный.
dairy farm n молочная ферма.
dairy products npl молочные продукты mpl.
dairy store n (US) молочный магазин.
dais ['deɪs] n помост.
daisy ['deɪzɪ] n маргаритка*.
daisywheel ['deɪzɪwi:l] n лепестковый шрифтоноситель m.
daisywheel printer n (COMPUT) лепестковый принтер.
Dakar ['dækə'] n Дакар.

dale [deɪl] n (BRIT) долина.
dally ['dælɪ] vi болтаться (impf) без дела; **to ~ with** (idea, plan) носиться* (impf) с +instr.
dalmatian [dæl'meɪʃən] n далматский дог.
dam [dæm] n (on river) дамба; (reservoir) водохранилище ♦ vt перекрывать (перекрыть* perf) дамбой.
damage ['dæmɪdʒ] n (harm) ущерб; (dents etc) повреждение; (fig) вред ♦ vt (object) повреждать (повредить perf); (reputation, economy) наносить (нанести perf) урон +dat; ~**s** npl (LAW) компенсация fsg; ~ **to property** имущественный ущерб; **to pay £5,000 in** ~**s** выплачивать (выплатить* perf) компенсацию в размере £5.000.
damaging ['dæmɪdʒɪŋ] adj: ~ **(to)** вредный* (для +gen).
Damascus [də'mɑ:skəs] n Дамаск.
dame [deɪm] n (US: inf) баба; (THEAT) комическая старуха; (title): **D~ Леди** f ind.
damn [dæm] vt (condemn) осуждать (осудить* perf); (curse at) проклинать (проклясть* perf) ♦ adj (inf: also: ~**ed**) проклятый ♦ n (inf): **I don't give a ~** мне плевать; ~ **(it)!** чёрт возьми or побери!; ~ **good** (inf) чертовски хороший.
damnable ['dæmnəbl] adj отвратный* (отвратен).
damnation [dæm'neɪʃən] n, excl (REL: also inf) проклятие.
damning ['dæmɪŋ] adj изобличительный.
damp [dæmp] adj (building, wall) сырой*; (cloth) влажный* ♦ n сырость f ♦ vt (also: ~**en**: cloth etc) смачивать (смочить* perf); (: enthusiasm etc) охлаждать (охладить* perf).
dampcourse ['dæmpkɔ:s] n гидроизоляция.
damper ['dæmpə'] n (MUS) демпфер; (of fire) заслонка*; **to put a ~ on** (fig: atmosphere) портить* (испортить* perf); (enthusiasm) охлаждать (охладить* perf).
dampness ['dæmpnɪs] n сырость f.
damson ['dæmzən] n (fruit) тернослива.
dance [dɑ:ns] n танец; (social event) танцы* mpl ♦ vi танцевать (impf); **to ~ about** скакать* (impf).
dance hall n танцевальный зал.
dancer ['dɑ:nsə'] n (for pleasure) танцор(ка*); (professional) танцовщик(-ица).

dancing ['dɑ:nsɪŋ] *n* та́нец.
D and C *n abbr* (*MED*: = *dilation and curettage*) расшире́ние ше́йки ма́тки и выска́бливание.
dandelion ['dændɪlaɪən] *n* одува́нчик.
dandruff ['dændrəf] *n* пе́рхоть *f*.
dandy ['dændɪ] *n* де́нди *m ind*, щёголь *m* ♦ *adj* (*US*: *inf*) кла́ссный.
Dane [deɪn] *n* датча́нин*(-а́нка*).
danger ['deɪndʒə'] *n* опа́сность *f*; **there is a ~ of** ... есть *or* существу́ет опа́сность +*gen* ...; **"danger!"** "опа́сно!"; **in/out of ~** в/вне опа́сности; **he is in ~ of losing his job** ему́ грози́т поте́ря рабо́ты.
danger list *n*: **on the ~ ~** (*MED*) в спи́ске *or* числе́ осо́бо тяжёлых больны́х.
dangerous ['deɪndʒrəs] *adj* опа́сный* (опа́сен).
dangerously ['deɪndʒrəslɪ] *adv* с ри́ском; **~ close (to)** в опа́сной бли́зости (к +*dat*); **he is ~ ill** он опа́сно бо́лен.
danger zone *n* опа́сная зо́на.
dangle ['dæŋgl] *vt* болта́ть (*impf*) +*instr* ♦ *vi* болта́ться (*impf*).
Danish ['deɪnɪʃ] *adj* да́тский* ♦ *n* (*LING*) да́тский* язы́к*; **the ~** *npl* датча́не.
Danish pastry *n* пиро́жное *nt adj* по-да́тски (*с откры́той начи́нкой из фру́ктов и́ли оре́хов*).
dank [dæŋk] *adj* сыро́й*.
Danube ['dænju:b] *n*: **the ~** Дуна́й.
dapper ['dæpə'] *adj* щеголева́тый (щеголева́т).
Dardanelles [dɑ:də'nɛlz] *npl*: **the ~** Дардане́ллы *pl*.
dare [dɛə'] *vt*: **to ~ sb to do** вызыва́ть (вы́звать* *perf*) кого́-н +*infin* ♦ *vi*: **to ~ (to) do** сметь (посме́ть *perf*) +*infin*; **I ~n't tell him** (*BRIT*) я не могу́ осме́литься сказа́ть ему́; **how ~ you say that!** как Вы сме́ете так говори́ть!; **I ~ say** сме́ю заме́тить.
daredevil ['dɛədɛvl] *n* сорвиголова́* *m/f*.
Dar es Salaam ['dɑ:rɛssə'lɑ:m] *n* Да́р-эс-Сала́м.
daring ['dɛərɪŋ] *adj* (*audacious*) де́рзкий* (де́рзок); (*bold*) сме́лый* (смел) ♦ *n* де́рзость *f*.
dark [dɑ:k] *adj* тёмный* (тёмен); (*complexion*) сму́глый*; (*fig: deed*) чёрный ♦ *n*: **in the ~** в темноте́; **~ blue** *etc* тёмно-си́ний* *etc*; **it is getting ~** темне́ет; **it is ~** темно́; **~ chocolate** чёрный шокола́д*; **to be in the ~ about** (*fig*) быть* (*impf*) в неве́дении относи́тельно +*gen*; **after ~** по́сле наступле́ния темноты́.
Dark Ages *npl*: **the ~ ~** ра́ннее средневеко́вье *ntsg.*
darken [dɑ:kn] *vt* затемня́ть (затемни́ть *perf*) ♦ *vi* (*sky, room*) темне́ть (потемне́ть *perf*).
dark glasses *npl* тёмные очки́ *pl*.
dark horse *n* тёмная лоша́дка*.

darkly ['dɑ:klɪ] *adv* мра́чно.
darkness ['dɑ:knɪs] *n* темнота́.
darkroom ['dɑ:krum] *n* тёмная ко́мната, прояви́тельная лаборато́рия.
darling ['dɑ:lɪŋ] *adj* (*child, spouse*) люби́мый ♦ *n* дорого́й(-а́я) *m(f) adj*; (*favourite*): **he is the ~ of** он л|оби́мец +*gen*; **she is a ~** она́ пре́лесть *f*.
darn [dɑ:n] *vt* што́пать (зашто́пать *perf*).
dart [dɑ:t] *n* (*in game*) стре́лка* (*для игры́ в да́рт*); (*in sewing*) вы́тачка* ♦ *vi*: **to (make a) ~ towards** броса́ться (бро́ситься* *perf*) навстре́чу +*dat*; **to ~ along** промча́ться (*perf*); **to ~ away** умча́ться (*perf*).
dartboard ['dɑ:tbɔ:d] *n* мише́нь *f* в да́рте.
darts [dɑ:ts] *n* дарт.
dash [dæʃ] *n* (*drop*) ка́пелька*; (*pinch*) щепо́тка*; (*sign*) тире́ *nt ind*; (*rush*) рыво́к* ♦ *vt* (*throw*) швыря́ть (швырну́ть *perf*); (*shatter: hopes*) разруша́ть (разру́шить *perf*), разбива́ть (разби́ть* *perf*) ♦ *vi*: **to ~ towards** рвану́ться (*perf*) к +*dat*; **we'll have to make a ~ for the house** мы должны́ бежа́ть к до́му
▸ **dash away** *vi* умча́ться (*perf*)
▸ **dash off** *vi* = **dash away**.
dashboard ['dæʃbɔ:d] *n* (*AUT*) прибо́рная пане́ль *f*.
dashing ['dæʃɪŋ] *adj* шика́рный* (шика́рен).
dastardly ['dæstədlɪ] *adj* по́длый*, ме́рзкий*.
DAT *n abbr* (= *digital audio tape*) дискретизи́рованная аудиокассе́та.
data ['deɪtə] *npl* да́нные *pl adj*.
database ['deɪtəbeɪs] *n* ба́за да́нных.
data capture *n* сбор да́нных.
data processing *n* обрабо́тка да́нных.
data transmission *n* переда́ча да́нных.
date [deɪt] *n* (*day*) число́*, да́та; (*with friend*) свида́ние; (*fruit*) фи́ник ♦ *vt* дати́ровать (*impf/perf*); (*person*) встреча́ться (*impf*) с +*instr*; **what's the ~ today?** како́е сего́дня число́?; **~ of birth** да́та рожде́ния; **the closing ~ for applications is** ... срок пода́чи заявле́ний истека́ет +*gen* ...; **to ~** на сего́дняшний* день; **out of ~** (*old-fashioned*) устаре́лый (устаре́л); (*expired*) просро́ченный (просро́чен); **up to ~** совреме́нный; **to bring up to ~** (*method*) обновля́ть (обнови́ть* *perf*); (*correspondence, information*) пополня́ть (попо́лнить *perf*); (*person*) вводи́ть* (ввести́* *perf*) в курс де́ла; **letter ~d 5th July** *or* (*US*) **July 5th** письмо́, дати́рованное 5-ым ию́ля.
dated ['deɪtɪd] *adj* устаре́лый.
dateline ['deɪtlaɪn] *n* указа́ние ме́ста и да́ты (*опи́сываемого собы́тия*).
date rape *n* изнаси́лование во вре́мя свида́ния.
date stamp *n* календа́рный штемпель* *m*.
dative ['deɪtɪv] *n* (*also: ~ case*) да́тельный паде́ж*.
daub [dɔ:b] *vt* разма́зывать (разма́зать* *perf*);

---

* marks translations which have irregular inflections. The Russian-English side of the dictionary gives inflectional information.

(*wall, face*): **to ~ with** ма́зать* (нама́зать* *perf*) +*instr*.
daughter ['dɔːtə] *n* дочь* *f*.
daughter-in-law ['dɔːtərınlɔː] *n* неве́стка*, сноха́*.
daunt [dɔːnt] *vt* страши́ть (*impf*).
daunting ['dɔːntıŋ] *adj* устраша́ющий*.
dauntless ['dɔːntlıs] *adj* бесстра́шный* (бесстра́шен).
dawdle ['dɔːdl] *vi* копа́ться (*impf*), вози́ться* (*impf*); **to ~ over one's work** вози́ться* (*impf*) с рабо́той.
dawn [dɔːn] *n* (*of day*) рассве́т; (*of period, situation*) заря́ ♦ *vi* рассвета́ть (рассвести́* *perf*), света́ть (*impf*); (*fig*): **it ~ed on him that ...** его́ осени́ло, что ...; **from ~ to dusk** с рассве́та до зака́та, от зари́ до зари́.
dawn chorus *n* (*BRIT*) пе́ние птиц на рассве́те.
day [deı] *n* (*period*) су́тки *pl*, день* *m*; (*daylight*) день*; (*working day*) рабо́чий* день*; (*heyday*) вре́мя *nt*; **the ~ before** накану́не; **the ~ after** на сле́дующий* день; **the ~ after tomorrow** послеза́втра; **the ~ before yesterday** позавчера́; **the following ~** на сле́дующий* день; **the ~ that ...** в тот день, когда́ ...; **~ by ~** ка́ждый день; **~ after ~** изо дня́ в день; **by ~** днём; **he is paid by the ~** ему́ пла́тят поде́нно; **I have a ~ off tomorrow** за́втра у меня́ отгу́л; **to work an 8 hour ~** рабо́тать (*impf*) 8 часо́в в день; **these ~s, in the present ~** в на́ши дни, в настоя́щее вре́мя.
daybook ['deıbuk] *n* (*BRIT*: *ADMIN*) журна́л.
dayboy ['deıbɔı] *n* приходя́щий учени́к* (*в интерна́те*).
daybreak ['deıbreık] *n* рассве́т.
day-care centre ['deıkɛə-] *n* (*BRIT*) дневно́й центр по ухо́ду за больны́ми и престаре́лыми.
daydream ['deıdriːm] *vi* предава́ться (*impf*) мечта́ниям, гре́зить* (*impf*) ♦ *n* мечта́ние, гре́за.
daygirl ['deıgəːl] *n* приходя́щая учени́ца (*в интерна́те*).
daylight ['deılaıt] *n* дневно́й свет*.
daylight robbery *n* грабёж средь бе́ла дня.
Daylight Saving Time *n* (*US*) ле́тнее вре́мя* *nt*.
day release *n*: **to be on ~ ~** находи́ться на дневны́х ку́рсах по повыше́нию квалифика́ции.
day return *n* (*BRIT*) обра́тный биле́т (*действи́тельный в тече́ние одного́ дня*).
day shift *n* дневна́я сме́на.
daytime ['deıtaım] *n* день* *m*.
day-to-day ['deıtə'deı] *adj* (*life, organization*) повседне́вный*, ежедне́вный; **on a ~ basis** ежедне́вно.
day trip *n* однодне́вная экску́рсия.
day-tripper ['deı'trıpə'] *n* челове́к на однодне́вной экску́рсии.
daze [deız] *vt* (*stun*) ошеломля́ть (ошеломи́ть*

perf); (*subj*: *drug*) тума́нить (затума́нить *perf*) созна́ние +*dat*; (: *blow*) ошеломля́ть (ошеломи́ть *perf*) ♦ *n*: **in a ~** как в тума́не.
dazed [deızd] *adj* ошеломлённый.
dazzle ['dæzl] *vt* (*bewitch*) завора́живать (заворожи́ть *perf*); (*blind*) ослепля́ть (ослепи́ть* *perf*).
dazzling ['dæzlıŋ] *adj* (*also fig*) ослепи́тельный* (ослепи́телен).
DC *abbr* = **direct current**; (*US*: *POST*) = **District of Columbia**.
DD *n abbr* (= *Doctor of Divinity*) ≈ до́ктор богосло́вия.
dd. *abbr* (*COMM*) = **delivered**.
D/D *abbr* = **direct debit**.
D-day ['diːdeı] *n* пе́рвый день генера́льного сраже́ния.
DDS *n abbr* (*US*: = *Doctor of Dental Surgery*) до́ктор стоматоло́гии.
DDT *n abbr* (= *dichlorodiphenyltrichloroethane*) ДДТ= *дихлордифени́л трихлорэта́н*.
DE *abbr* (*US*: *POST*) = **Delaware**.
DEA *n abbr* (*US*: = *Drug Enforcement Administration*) Управле́ние по соблюде́нию зако́нов о нарко́тиках.
deacon ['diːkən] *n* дья́кон*.
dead [dɛd] *adj* (*person, place, flowers*) мёртвый* (мёртв); (*silence*) мёртвый*; (*arm, leg*) онеме́лый; (*centre*) са́мый ♦ *adv* (*completely*) внеза́пно; (*inf*: *directly*) пря́мо ♦ *npl*: **the ~** мёртвые *pl adj*; (*in an accident, war*) поги́бшие *pl adj*; **the battery is ~** батаре́йка се́ла; **the telephone is ~** телефо́н отключи́лся; **to shoot sb ~** застрели́ть* (*perf*) кого́-н; **~ on time** то́чно во́время; **to stop ~** (*person*) остана́вливаться (останови́ться* *perf*) как вко́панный; **~ tired** смерте́льно уста́лый* (уста́л); **the line has gone ~** телефо́н замолча́л.
dead-beat ['dɛdbiːt] *adj* смерте́льно уста́вший, соверше́нно вы́мотанный (вы́мотан).
deaden [dɛdn] *vt* (*pain, sound*) заглуша́ть (заглуши́ть *perf*).
dead end *n* тупи́к*.
dead-end ['dɛdɛnd] *adj*: **a ~ job** бесперспекти́вная рабо́та.
dead heat *n*: **to finish in a ~ ~** приходи́ть* (прийти́* *perf*) к фи́нишу одновреме́нно.
dead-letter office [dɛd'lɛtə-] *n* отде́л невостре́бованной и́ли недоста́вленной корреспонде́нции.
deadline ['dɛdlaın] *n* после́дний *or* преде́льный срок; **to work to a ~** рабо́тать (*impf*) в ра́мках ограни́ченного сро́ка.
deadlock ['dɛdlɔk] *n* тупи́к; **the meeting ended in ~** собра́ние зашло́ в тупи́к.
dead loss *n* (*inf*): **she is a ~ ~** она́ никчёмна.
deadly ['dɛdlı] *adj* (*poison, weapon*) смертоно́сный* (смертоно́сен); (*insult*) смерте́льный* (смерте́лен); (*accuracy*)

ги́бельный ♦ *adv* (*dull*) смерте́льно.
deadpan ['dɛdpæn] *adj* невозмути́мый
(невозмути́м).
Dead Sea *n*: the ~ ~ Мёртвое мо́ре.
dead season *n* мёртвый сезо́н.
deaf [dɛf] *adj* (*totally*) глухо́й* (глух); (*partially*)
тугоу́хий (тугоу́х); **to turn a ~ ear to sth**
игнори́ровать *(impf)* что-н.
deaf aid *n* (*BRIT*) слухово́й аппара́т.
deaf-and-dumb ['dɛfən'dʌm] *adj* глухонемо́й;
~ **alphabet** алфави́т для глухонемы́х.
deafen [dɛfn] *vt* оглуша́ть (оглуши́ть *perf*).
deafening ['dɛfnɪŋ] *adj* оглуши́тельный*
(оглуши́телен).
deaf-mute ['dɛfmjuːt] *n* глухонемо́й(-а́я) *m(f)*
adj.
deafness ['dɛfnɪs] *n* глухота́.
deal [diːl] (*pt, pp* dealt) *n* (*agreement*) сде́лка* ♦
vt (*blow*) наноси́ть* (нанести́* *perf*); (*cards*)
сдава́ть (сдать* *perf*); **to strike a ~ with sb**
заключа́ть (заключи́ть *perf*) сде́лку с кем-н;
it's a ~! (*inf*) по рука́м!; **he got a fair/bad ~
from them** с ним обошли́сь че́стно/
нече́стно; **a good ~ (of)** мно́го (+*gen*); **a great
~ (of)** о́чень мно́го (+*gen*)
▶ **deal in** *vt fus* (*COMM*) торгова́ть *(impf)* +*instr*;
(*drugs*) занима́ться *(impf)* прода́жей +*gen*
▶ **deal with** *vt fus* (*person, company*) име́ть
(impf) де́ло с +*instr*; (*problem*) реша́ть
(реши́ть *perf*); (*subject*) занима́ться
(заня́ться* *perf*) +*instr*.
dealer ['diːlə'] *n* (*COMM*) торго́вец*; (*also*: **art ~**)
ди́лер; (*CARDS*) сдаю́щий(-ая) *m(f) adj* ка́рты,
банкомёт; **drug ~** наркоделе́ц.
dealership ['diːləʃɪp] *n* (*COMM*) аге́нтство (*по
прода́же проду́кции определённой фи́рмы*).
dealings ['diːlɪŋz] *npl* (*transactions*) опера́ции
fpl; (*in business*) дела́ *ntpl*.
dealt [dɛlt] *pt, pp of* **deal**.
dean [diːn] *n* (*REL*) настоя́тель *m*; (*SCOL*) дека́н.
dear [dɪə'] *adj* (*person*) дорого́й*, ми́лый*;
(*expensive*) дорого́й* ♦ *n*: (**my**) ~ (*to man,
boy*) дорого́й (мой); (*to woman, girl*)
дорога́я (моя́) ♦ *excl*: ~ **me!** о, Го́споди!; **D~
Sir** уважа́емый господи́н; **D~ Madam**
уважа́емая госпожа́; **D~ Mr Smith** дорого́й
or уважа́емый ми́стер Смит; **D~ Mrs Smith**
дорога́я *or* уважа́емая ми́ссис Смит.
dearly ['dɪəlɪ] *adv* (*love*) о́чень; (*pay*) до́рого.
dear money *n* (*COMM*) „дороги́е де́ньги" *pl*.
dearth [dəːθ] *n*: **a ~ of** нехва́тка +*gen*,
недоста́ток* +*gen*.
death [dɛθ] *n* смерть* *f*.
deathbed ['dɛθbɛd] *n*: **to be on one's ~** быть*
(impf) на сме́ртном одре́.
death certificate *n* свиде́тельство о сме́рти.
deathly ['dɛθlɪ] *adj* (*colour*) смерте́льный*;
(*silence*) мёртвый ♦ *adv* смерте́льно.

death penalty *n* сме́ртная казнь *f*.
death rate *n* сме́ртность *f*.
death row [-rəu] *n* ка́меры *fpl* сме́ртников;
prisoners on ~ ~ заключённые *pl adj*,
ожида́ющие сме́ртной ка́зни.
death sentence *n* сме́ртный пригово́р.
death toll *n* число́* поги́бших.
deathtrap ['dɛθtræp] *n* ги́блое ме́сто*.
deb [dɛb] *n abbr* (*inf*) = **debutante**.
debacle [deɪˈbɑːkl] *n* (*defeat*) разгро́м; (*failure*)
фиа́ско *nt ind*.
debar [dɪˈbɑː] *vt*: **to ~ sb from doing** лиша́ть
(лиши́ть *perf*) кого́-н возмо́жности +*infin*; **to
~ sb from a club** изгоня́ть (изгна́ть* *perf*)
кого́-н из клу́ба.
debase [dɪˈbeɪs] *vt* (*value, quality*) снижа́ть
(сни́зить *perf*); (*person*) унижа́ть (уни́зить*
perf); **to ~ o.s.** унижа́ться (уни́зиться*
perf).
debatable [dɪˈbeɪtəbl] *adj* спо́рный*; **it is ~
whether he can come** смо́жет ли он прийти́ –
вопро́с спо́рный.
debate [dɪˈbeɪt] *n* деба́ты *pl* ♦ *vt* (*topic*)
обсужда́ть (обсуди́ть* *perf*); (*course of action*)
обду́мывать (обду́мать *perf*); **he ~d whether
to stay** он размышля́л, сле́дует ли оста́ться.
debauchery [dɪˈbɔːtʃərɪ] *n* (*drunkenness etc*)
распу́щенность *f*.
debenture [dɪˈbɛntʃə'] *n* (*bond*) це́нная бума́га;
~ **capital** ссу́да, обеспе́ченная
фикси́рованными и́ли други́ми акти́вами
компа́нии.
debilitate [dɪˈbɪlɪteɪt] *vt* истоща́ть (истощи́ть
perf).
debilitating [dɪˈbɪlɪteɪtɪŋ] *adj* изнури́тельный*
(изнури́телен).
debit ['dɛbɪt] *n* дебе́т ♦ *vt*: **to ~ a sum to sb** *or* **to
sb's account** дебетова́ть *(impf/perf)* су́мму с
кого́-н *or* с чьего́-н счёта; *see also* **direct
debit**.
debit balance *n* дебето́вый оста́ток*.
debit note *n* дебето́вое ави́зо.
debonair [dɛbəˈnɛə'] *adj* гала́нтный.
debrief [diːˈbriːf] *vt* опра́шивать (опроси́ть*
perf).
debriefing [diːˈbriːfɪŋ] *n* расспро́с.
debris ['dɛbriː] *n* (*rubble*) обло́мки *mpl*,
разва́лины *fpl*.
debt [dɛt] *n* (*sum*) долг*; (*state of owing money*)
задо́лженность *f*; **to be in ~** быть* *(impf)* в
долгу́; **bad ~** безнадёжный долг*.
debt collector *n* челове́к, взы́скивающий
долги́.
debtor ['dɛtə'] *n* должни́к*.
debug ['diːˈbʌg] *vt* отла́живать (отла́дить*
perf).
debunk [diːˈbʌŋk] *vt* (*claim*) опроверга́ть
(опрове́ргнуть *perf*); (*person, institution*,

---

myth) развенчивать (развенчать *perf*).

début ['deɪbju:] *n* дебют.

debutante ['dɛbjutænt] *n девушка, выходящая в (высший) свет.*

Dec. *abbr* = **December.**

decade ['dɛkeɪd] *n* десятилетие.

decadence ['dɛkədəns] *n* упадок*.

decadent ['dɛkədənt] *adj* (*sentiments*) упадочнический*; (*class*) упадочный.

de-caff ['di:kæf] (*inf*) *adj* без кофеина ◆ *n* кофе без кофеина.

decaffeinated [dɪ'kæfɪneɪtɪd] *adj* без кофеина.

decamp [dɪ'kæmp] *vi* (*inf*) удирать (удрать* *perf*).

decant [dɪ'kænt] *vt* переливать (перелить* *perf*).

decanter [dɪ'kæntə'] *n* графин.

decarbonize [di:'kɑ:bənaɪz] *vt* очищать (очистить* *perf*) от нагара.

decathlon [dɪ'kæθlən] *n* десятиборье.

decay [dɪ'keɪ] *n* разрушение; (*of society*) разложение ◆ *vi* (*body, leaves, society etc*) разлагаться (разложиться* *perf*); (*teeth*) разрушаться (разрушиться* *perf*).

decease [dɪ'si:s] *n* (*LAW*): **upon your** ~ по Вашей кончине.

deceased [dɪ'si:st] *n*: **the** ~ покойный(-ая) *m(f) adj*.

deceit [dɪ'si:t] *n* обман.

deceitful [dɪ'si:tful] *adj* лживый (лжив).

deceive [dɪ'si:v] *vt* обманывать (обмануть* *perf*); **to** ~ **o.s.** обманываться (обмануться* *perf*).

decelerate [di:'sɛləreɪt] *vi* замедлять (замедлить *perf*) скорость.

December [dɪ'sɛmbə'] *n* декабрь* *m*; *see also* **July.**

decency ['di:sənsɪ] *n* (*propriety*) благопристойность *f*; (*kindness*) порядочность *f*.

decent ['di:sənt] *adj* (*wages, meal, sleep*) приличный* (прилично); (*interval, behaviour, person*) порядочный (порядочен); **we expect you to do the** ~ **thing** мы ожидаем, что Вы поступите порядочно; **they were very** ~ **about it** они отреагировали на это очень благородно; **it was very** ~ **of him** это было очень порядочно с его стороны; **are you** ~? Вы прилично одеты?

decently ['di:səntlɪ] *adv* (*respectably*) прилично; (*kindly*) порядочно.

decentralization ['di:sɛntrəlaɪ'zeɪʃən] *n* децентрализация.

decentralize [di:'sɛntrəlaɪz] *vt* децентрализовать (*impf/perf*).

deception [dɪ'sɛpʃən] *n* обман.

deceptive [dɪ'sɛptɪv] *adj* обманчивый* (обманчив).

decibel ['dɛsɪbɛl] *n* децибел.

decide [dɪ'saɪd] *vt* (*person: persuade*) убеждать (убедить* *perf*); (*settle*) решать (решить* *perf*) ◆ *vi*: **to** ~ **to do/that** решать (решить* *perf*) +*infin*/, что; **to** ~ **on sth** останавливаться (остановиться* *perf*) на чём-н; **to** ~ **on doing/against doing** решать (решить* *perf*) +*infin*/не +*infin*.

decided [dɪ'saɪdɪd] *adj* (*character*) решительный* (решителен); (*views, opinions*) определённый; (*dangers, improvement*) несомненный* (несомненен).

decidedly [dɪ'saɪdɪdlɪ] *adv* (*distinctly*) несомненно; (*emphatically*) решительно.

deciding [dɪ'saɪdɪŋ] *adj* решающий*.

deciduous [dɪ'sɪdjuəs] *adj* лиственадный.

decimal ['dɛsɪməl] *adj* десятичный ◆ *n* десятичная дробь *f*; **to three** ~ **places** с точностью до третьего знака.

decimalize ['dɛsɪmələɪz] *vt* (*BRIT*) переводить* (перевести* *perf*) в метрическую систему мер.

decimal point *n* точка* *or* запятая *f adj* (*отделяющая целое от дроби*).

decimate ['dɛsɪmeɪt] *vt* истреблять (истребить* *perf*).

decipher [dɪ'saɪfə'] *vt* (*message etc: enigmatic*) расшифровывать (расшифровать *perf*); (: *illegible*) разбирать (разобрать* *perf*).

decision [dɪ'sɪʒən] *n* решение; (*decisiveness*) решимость *f*; **to make a** ~ принимать (принять* *perf*) решение.

decisive [dɪ'saɪsɪv] *adj* решительный* (решителен).

deck [dɛk] *n* (*NAUT*) палуба; (*of cards*) колода; (*also*: **record** ~) проигрыватель *m*; (*of bus*): **top** ~ верхний* этаж*; **to go up on** ~ подниматься (подняться* *perf*) на палубу; **below** ~ под палубой; **cassette** ~ кассетная дека.

deck chair *n* шезлонг.

deck hand *n* матрос.

declaration [dɛklə'reɪʃən] *n* (*statement*) декларация; (*public announcement*) заявление.

declare [dɪ'klɛə'] *vt* (*state*) объявлять (объявить* *perf*); (*for tax*) декларировать (*impf/perf*).

declassify [di:'klæsɪfaɪ] *vt* рассекречивать (рассекретить* *perf*).

decline [dɪ'klaɪn] *n* (*drop*) падение; (*lessening*) уменьшение; (*decay*) упадок* ◆ *vt* (*invitation*) отклонять (отклонить* *perf*) ◆ *vi* (*strength*) падать (*impf*); (*business*) приходить* (прийти* *perf*) в упадок; ~ **in living standards** снижение уровня жизни; **to be in** *or* **on the** ~ быть* (*impf*) в упадке.

declutch ['di:'klʌtʃ] *vi* выключать (выключить *perf*) сцепление.

decode ['di:'kəud] *vt* (*message*) декодировать (*impf/perf*), расшифровывать (расшифровать *perf*).

decoder [di:'kəudə'] *n* (*person*) человек, обращающийся к словарю с целью понять

смысл слова в иностранном языке;
(*machine*) декодер.
decompose [di:kəm'pəuz] *vi* разлагаться
(разложиться* *perf*).
decomposition [di:kɔmpə'zıʃən] *n*
разложение.
decompression [di:kəm'prɛʃən] *n*
декомпрессия.
decompression chamber *n*
декомпрессионная камера.
decongestant [di:kən'dʒɛstənt] *n*
сосудосужающее средство.
decontaminate [di:kən'tæmıneıt] *vt*
обеззараживать (обеззаразить* *perf*).
decontrol [di:kən'trəul] *vt* освобождать
(освободить* *perf*) от (государственного)
контроля.
décor ['deıkɔ:'] *n* (*in house*) отделка*; (*THEAT*)
декорация.
decorate ['dɛkəreıt] *vt* (*room etc*) отделывать
(отделать *perf*); (*adorn*): **to ~ (with)** украшать
(украсить* *perf*) +*instr*.
decoration [dɛkə'reıʃən] *n* (*on tree, dress etc*)
украшение; (*of room*) отделка*; (*medal*)
награда.
decorative ['dɛkərətıv] *adj* декоративный*.
decorator ['dɛkəreıtə'] *n* обойщик; **painter and
~** маляр и обойщик, отделочник.
decorum [dı'kɔ:rəm] *n* благопристойность *f*,
декорум.
decoy ['di:kɔı] *n* приманка*.
decrease ['di:kri:s] *vt* уменьшать (уменьшить
perf) ◆ *vi* уменьшаться (уменьшиться *perf*) ◆
n: ~ (**in**) уменьшение (+*gen*); **to be on the ~**
идти* (пойти* *perf*) на убыль.
decreasing [di:'kri:sıŋ] *adj* уменьшающийся.
decree [dı'kri:] *n* (*ADMIN, LAW*) постановление;
(*POL, REL*) указ ◆ *vt:* **to ~ (that)** (*ADMIN, LAW*)
постановлять (постановить* *perf*)(, что).
decree absolute *n* окончательное решение о
разводе.
decree nisi [-'naısaı] *n* условно-
окончательное решение суда о разводе.
decrepit [dı'krɛpıt] *adj* дряхлый* (дряхл).
decry [dı'kraı] *vt* порицать (*impf*).
dedicate ['dɛdıkeıt] *vt:* **to ~ to** посвящать
(посвятить* *perf*) +*dat*.
dedicated ['dɛdıkeıtıd] *adj* (*person*)
преданный* (предан); (*COMPUT*)
выделенный, назначенный: ~ **word
processor** специализированный процессор
для обработки текстов.
dedication [dɛdı'keıʃən] *n* (*devotion*)
преданность *f*; (*in book etc*) посвящение.
deduce [dı'dju:s] *vt:* **to ~ that** заключать
(заключить *perf*), что.
deduct [dı'dʌkt] *vt* вычитать (вычесть* *perf*); **to
~ sth (from)** (*from wage etc*) вычитать

(вычесть* *perf*) что-н (из +*gen*).
deduction [dı'dʌkʃən] *n* (*conclusion*)
умозаключение; (*subtraction*) вычитание;
(*amount*) вычет.
deed [di:d] *n* (*feat*) деяние, поступок*; (*LAW*)
акт; ~ **of covenant** акт о передаче.
deem [di:m] *vt* (*formal*) полагать (*impf*); **to ~ it
wise to do** полагать (*impf*) целесообразным
+*infin*.
deep [di:p] *adj* глубокий* (глубок); (*voice*)
низкий* (низок) ◆ *adv:* **the spectators stood 20
~** зрители стояли в 20 рядов; **the lake is 4
metres ~** глубина озера – 4 метра; **knee-~ in
water** по колено в воде; **he took a ~ breath**
он сделал глубокий вздох; ~ **blue** тёмно-
синий*.
deepen ['di:pn] *vt* (*hole etc*) углублять
(углубить* *perf*) ◆ *vi* (*crisis, mystery*)
углубляться (углубиться* *perf*).
deepfreeze ['di:p'fri:z] *n* морозильная
камера.
deep-fry ['di:p'fraı] *vt* жарить (зажарить *perf*)
во фритюре.
deeply ['di:plı] *adv* глубоко.
deep-rooted ['di:p'ru:tıd] *adj* (*prejudice*)
глубоко укоренившийся; (*affection*)
глубокий* (глубок); (*habit*) закоренелый
(закоренел).
deep-sea ['di:p'si:] *cpd* (*fishing*)
глубоководный*; ~ **diver** водолаз.
deep-seated ['di:p'si:tıd] *adj* укоренившийся.
deep-set ['di:p'sɛt] *adj* глубоко посаженный
(посажен).
deer [dıə'] *n inv* олень *m*; (*red*) ~ благородный
олень; (*roe*) ~ косуля; (*fallow*) ~ лань *f*.
deerskin ['dıəskın] *n* замша.
deerstalker ['dıəstɔ:kə'] *n* (*hat*) треух.
deface [dı'feıs] *vt* обезображивать
(обезобразить* *perf*).
defamation [dɛfə'meıʃən] *n* клевета,
диффамация.
defamatory [dı'fæmətrı] *adj* клеветнический*.
default [dı'fɔ:lt] *n* (*COMPUT: also:* ~ **value**)
значение по умолчанию ◆ *vi:* **to ~ on a debt**
не выплачивать (выплатить* *perf*) долг; **by ~**
(*win*) за неявкой противника.
defaulter [dı'fɔ:ltə'] *n* неплательщик.
default option *n* (*COMPUT*) параметр *or*
вариант, выбираемый по умолчанию.
defeat [dı'fi:t] *n* поражение ◆ *vt* наносить*
(нанести* *perf*) поражение +*dat*.
defeatism [dı'fi:tızəm] *n* пораженчество.
defeatist [dı'fi:tıst] *adj* пораженческий ◆ *n*
пораженец*.
defecate ['dɛfəkeıt] *vi* испражняться
(испражниться* *perf*).
defect ['di:fɛkt] *n* (*of product*) дефект; (*of plan,
society*) недостаток* ◆ *vi:* **to ~ to the enemy**

---

* marks translations which have irregular inflections. The Russian–English side of the dictionary gives inflectional information

перебега́ть (перебежа́ть* *perf*) на сто́рону врага́; **physical/mental** ~ физи́ческий*/ у́мственный недоста́ток*.

defective [dɪ'fɛktɪv] *adj* (*goods*) дефе́ктный (дефе́ктен).

defector [dɪ'fɛktə^r] *n* перебе́жчик(-ица).

defence [dɪ'fɛns] (*US* **defense**) *n* (*protection, justification*) защи́та; (*MIL*) оборо́на; **in** ~ **of** в защи́ту +*gen*; **witness for the** ~ свиде́тель *m* защи́ты; **the Ministry of D**~ Министе́рство оборо́ны; **the Department of Defense** (*US*) Департа́мент по оборо́не.

defenceless [dɪ'fɛnslɪs] *adj* беззащи́тный* (беззащи́тен).

defend [dɪ'fɛnd] *vt* (*also SPORT*) защища́ть (защити́ть* *perf*); (*LAW*) защища́ть (*impf*).

defendant [dɪ'fɛndənt] *n* (*in criminal case*) подсуди́мый(-ая) *m(f) adj*, обвиня́емый(-ая) *m(f) adj*; (*in civil case*) отве́тчик(-ица).

defender [dɪ'fɛndə^r] *n* (*also fig*) защи́тник(-ица); (*SPORT*) защи́тник.

defending champion [dɪ'fɛndɪŋ-] *n* чемпио́н, *защища́ющий своё зва́ние.*

defending counsel *n* адвока́т отве́тчика.

defense *etc* (*US*) = **defence** *etc.*

defensive [dɪ'fɛnsɪv] *adj* (*weapons, measures*) оборони́тельный; (*behaviour, manner*) вызыва́ющий* ◆ *n*: **he was on the** ~ он был гото́в к оборо́не.

defer [dɪ'fə:^r] *vt* отсро́чивать (отсро́чить *perf*).

deference ['dɛfərəns] *n* почте́ние; **out of** *or* **in** ~ **to** из почте́ния к +*dat*.

deferential [dɛfə'rɛnʃəl] *adj* почти́тельный* (почти́телен).

deferred creditor [dɪ'fə:d-] *n* кредито́р, получи́вший отсро́чку.

defiance [dɪ'faɪəns] *n* вы́зов; **in** ~ **of** вопреки́ +*dat*.

defiant [dɪ'faɪənt] *adj* (*person, reply*) де́рзкий* (де́рзок); (*tone*) вызыва́ющий*.

defiantly [dɪ'faɪəntlɪ] *adv* де́рзко, вызыва́юще.

deficiency [dɪ'fɪʃənsɪ] *n* (*lack*) нехва́тка*; (*inadequacy*) недоста́ток*; (*COMM*) дефици́т.

deficiency disease *n* авитамино́з.

deficient [dɪ'fɪʃənt] *adj* (*inadequate*) несоверше́нный* (несоверше́нен); (*lacking*): **to be** ~ **in** испы́тывать (*impf*) недоста́ток в +*prp*.

deficit ['dɛfɪsɪt] *n* (*COMM*) дефици́т.

defile [dɪ'faɪl] *vt* оскверня́ть (оскверни́ть *perf*) ◆ *n* уще́лье*.

define [dɪ'faɪn] *vt* (*limits etc*) определя́ть (определи́ть *perf*); (*word etc*) дава́ть* (дать* *perf*) определе́ние +*dat*.

definite ['dɛfɪnɪt] *adj* определённый* (определён); **he was** ~ **about it** его́ мне́ние на э́тот счёт бы́ло определённым.

definite article *n* определённый арти́кль *m*.

definitely ['dɛfɪnɪtlɪ] *adv* (*positively*) определённо; (*certainly*) несомне́нно.

definition [dɛfɪ'nɪʃən] *n* (*of word*) определе́ние;

(*of photograph etc*) чёткость *f*.

definitive [dɪ'fɪnɪtɪv] *adj* оконча́тельный* (оконча́телен).

deflate [di:'fleɪt] *vt* (*tyre, balloon*) спуска́ть (спусти́ть* *perf*); (*person*) сбива́ть (сбить* *perf*) спесь с +*gen*; (*ECON*): **to** ~ **the money supply** осуществля́ть (осуществи́ть* *perf*) дефля́цию.

deflation [di:'fleɪʃən] *n* (*ECON*) дефля́ция.

deflationary [di:'fleɪʃənrɪ] *adj* дефляцио́нный.

deflect [dɪ'flɛkt] *vt* (*criticism, shot*) отклоня́ть (отклони́ть* *perf*); (*attention*) отвлека́ть (отвле́чь* *perf*).

defog ['di:'fɔg] *vt* (*US*) устраня́ть (устрани́ть *perf*) запотева́ние +*gen*.

defogger ['di:'fɔgə^r] *n* (*US: AUT*) *устро́йство, устраня́ющее запотева́ние стекла́.*

deform [dɪ'fɔ:m] *vt* (*damage*) деформи́ровать (*impf/perf*); (*distort*) искажа́ть (искази́ть* *perf*).

deformed [dɪ'fɔ:md] *adj* (*see vt*) деформи́рованный (деформи́рован); искажённый (искажён).

deformity [dɪ'fɔ:mɪtɪ] *n* (*distorted part*) физи́ческий* недоста́ток; (*condition*) деформа́ция.

defraud [dɪ'frɔ:d] *vt*: **to** ~ **sb of sth** обма́ном лиша́ть (лиши́ть* *perf*) кого́-н чего́-н.

defray [dɪ'freɪ] *vt*: **to** ~ **sb's expenses** возмеща́ть (возмести́ть* *perf*) чьи-н расхо́ды.

defrost [di:'frɔst] *vt* (*fridge, food*) разморя́живать (разморо́зить* *perf*); (*windscreen*) очища́ть (очи́стить* *perf*) ото льда́.

defroster [di:'frɔstə^r] *n* (*US: demister*) дефро́стер.

deft [dɛft] *adj* ло́вкий* (ло́вок).

defunct [dɪ'fʌŋkt] *adj* безде́йственный (безде́йствен).

defuse [di:'fju:z] *vt* (*also fig*) разряжа́ть (разряди́ть* *perf*).

defy [dɪ'faɪ] *vt* (*resist*) оспа́ривать (оспо́рить *perf*); (*fig: description, explanation*) не поддава́ться* (*impf*) +*dat*; (*challenge*): **to** ~ **sb to do** призыва́ть (призва́ть* *perf*) кого́-н +*infin*.

degenerate [*vb* dɪ'dʒɛnəreɪt, *adj* dɪ'dʒɛnərɪt] *vi* ухудша́ться (уху́дшиться *perf*), дегради́ровать (*impf/perf*) ◆ *adj* растле́нный.

degradation [dɛgrə'deɪʃən] *n* деграда́ция.

degrade [dɪ'greɪd] *vt* (*debase: person*) унижа́ть (уни́зить* *perf*); (*worsen*) ухудша́ть (уху́дшить *perf*).

degrading [dɪ'greɪdɪŋ] *adj* унизи́тельный* (унизи́телен).

degree [dɪ'gri:] *n* (*extent*) сте́пень* *f*; (*unit of measurement*) гра́дус; (*SCOL*) (учёная) сте́пень*; **10** ~**s below (zero)** 10 гра́дусов ни́же нуля́; **a considerable** ~ **of risk** значи́тельная сте́пень* ри́ска; **by** ~**s** постепе́нно; **to some** ~, **to a certain** ~

до не́которой сте́пени.
dehydrated [diːˈhaɪˈdreɪtɪd] *adj* (*MED*)
обезво́женный (обезво́жен); (*milk, eggs*)
порошко́вый.
dehydration [diːhaɪˈdreɪʃən] *n* обезво́живание.
de-ice [ˈdiːˈaɪs] *vt* удаля́ть (удали́ть *perf*)
обледене́ние +*gen*.
de-icer [ˈdiːˈaɪsəʳ] *n* антиобледени́тель *m*.
deign [deɪn] *vi*: **to ~ to do** соизволя́ть
(соизво́лить *perf*) +*infin*.
deity [ˈdiːɪtɪ] *n* божество́*.
déjà vu [deɪʒɑːˈvuː] *n* чу́вство узнава́ния в
незнако́мом ме́сте; **I had a sense of ~ ~** у
меня́ бы́ло тако́е чу́вство, бу́дто э́то уже́
бы́ло.
dejected [dɪˈdʒɛktɪd] *adj* уны́лый.
dejection [dɪˈdʒɛkʃən] *n* уны́ние.
del. *abbr* = **delete**.
delay [dɪˈleɪ] *vt* (*decision, ceremony etc*)
откла́дывать (отложи́ть* *perf*); (*person,
plane etc*) заде́рживать (задержа́ть* *perf*) ♦ *vi*
ме́длить (*impf*) ♦ *n* заде́ржка*; **to be ~ed**
заде́рживаться (*impf*); **without ~** без
отлага́тельств.
delayed-action [dɪˈleɪdˈækʃən] *adj*: **~ device**
приспособле́ние с регули́руемой заде́ржкой
де́йствия.
delectable [dɪˈlɛktəbl] *adj* (*person*)
притяга́тельный* (притяга́телен); (*food*)
ла́комый (ла́ком).
delegate [*n* ˈdɛlɪgɪt, *vt* ˈdɛlɪgeɪt] *n* делега́т ♦ *vt*
(*person*) делеги́ровать (*impf/perf*); (*task*)
поруча́ть (поручи́ть *perf*); **to ~ sth to sb/sb to
do** поруча́ть (поручи́ть *perf*) что-н кому́-н/
кому́-н +*infin*.
delegation [dɛlɪˈgeɪʃən] *n* (*group*) делега́ция;
(*by manager, leader*) переда́ча.
delete [dɪˈliːt] *vt* вычёркивать (вы́черкнуть
perf); (*COMPUT*) удаля́ть (удали́ть *perf*).
Delhi [ˈdɛlɪ] *n* Де́ли *m ind*.
deli [ˈdɛlɪ] (*inf*) *n* магази́н деликате́сов.
deliberate [*adj* dɪˈlɪbərɪt, *vi* dɪˈlɪbəreɪt] *adj*
(*intentional*) наме́ренный* (наме́рен); (*slow*)
неторопли́вый (неторопли́в) ♦ *vi*
обду́мывать (обду́мать *perf*).
deliberately [dɪˈlɪbərɪtlɪ] *adv* (*see adj*)
наме́ренно, наро́чно; неторопли́во.
deliberation [dɪlɪbəˈreɪʃən] *n* (*consideration*)
размышле́ние; (*usu pl*: *discussion*)
обсужде́ние.
delicacy [ˈdɛlɪkəsɪ] *n* то́нкость *f*; (*food*)
деликате́с.
delicate [ˈdɛlɪkɪt] *adj* то́нкий* (то́нок); (*colour*)
не́жный (не́жен); (*approach, problem*)
делика́тный* (делика́тен); (*health*) хру́пкий*
(хру́пок).
delicately [ˈdɛlɪkɪtlɪ] *adv* то́нко.
delicatessen [dɛlɪkəˈtɛsn] *n* магази́н

деликате́сов.
delicious [dɪˈlɪʃəs] *adj* (*food*) о́чень вку́сный*
(вку́сен); (*smell, feeling, person*)
восхити́тельный* (восхити́телен).
delight [dɪˈlaɪt] *n* (*feeling*) восто́рг; (*person,
experience etc*) пре́лесть *f* ♦ *vt* ра́довать
(пора́довать *perf*); **to take (a) ~ in** находи́ть*
(найти́* *perf*) удово́льствие в +*prp*; **her son
was her ~** она́ души́ не ча́яла в своём сы́не;
she was a ~ to interview брать (*impf*) у неё
интервью́ бы́ло и́стинным удово́льствием;
the ~s of country life пре́лести дереве́нской
жи́зни.
delighted [dɪˈlaɪtɪd] *adj*: **(to be) ~ (at** *or* **with)**
(быть (*impf*)) в восто́рге (от +*gen*); **he was ~
to see her** он был рад ви́деть её; **I'd be ~ to
help** я с ра́достью помогу́; **I am ~ to meet
you** о́чень прия́тно познако́миться.
delightful [dɪˈlaɪtful] *adj* восхити́тельный*
(восхити́телен).
delimit [diːˈlɪmɪt] *vt* определя́ть (определи́ть
perf) грани́цы +*gen*.
delineate [dɪˈlɪnɪeɪt] *vt* оче́рчивать (очерти́ть*
perf).
delinquency [dɪˈlɪŋkwənsɪ] *n*
правонаруше́ние.
delinquent [dɪˈlɪŋkwənt] *adj* престу́пный ♦ *n*
несовершеннолéтний(-яя)
правонаруши́тель(ница) *m(f)*.
delirious [dɪˈlɪrɪəs] *adj*: **to be ~ (with fever)**
быть* (*impf*) в бреду́; (*with excitement*) быть*
(*impf*) в забытьи́.
delirium [dɪˈlɪrɪəm] *n* (*MED*) бреди́.
deliver [dɪˈlɪvəʳ] *vt* (*goods*) доставля́ть
(доста́вить* *perf*); (*letter*) вруча́ть (вручи́ть
perf); (*message*) передава́ть* (переда́ть* *perf*);
(*speech*) произноси́ть* (произнести́* *perf*);
(*blow*) наноси́ть* (нанести́* *perf*); (*baby*)
принима́ть (приня́ть* *perf*); (*warning,
ultimatum*) предъявля́ть (предъяви́ть* *perf*);
(*person*): **to ~ (from)** избавля́ть (изба́вить*
perf) (от +*gen*); **to ~ the goods** (*fig*) выполня́ть
(вы́полнить *perf*) обе́щанное.
deliverance [dɪˈlɪvrəns] *n* избавле́ние.
delivery [dɪˈlɪvərɪ] *n* (*of goods*) доста́вка*; (*of
speaker*) стиль *m* изложе́ния; (*MED*) ро́ды *pl*;
to take ~ of получа́ть (получи́ть* *perf*).
delivery note *n* тра́нспортная накладна́я *f adj*.
delivery van (*US* **delivery truck**) *n* автофурго́н
для доста́вки това́ров.
delouse [ˈdiːˈlaus] *vt* избавля́ть (изба́вить*
perf) от вше́й. .
delta [ˈdɛltə] *n* (*GEO*) де́льта.
delude [dɪˈluːd] *vt* вводи́ть* (ввести́* *perf*) в
заблужде́ние; **to ~ o.s.** заблужда́ться (*impf*).
deluge [ˈdɛljuːdʒ] *n* ли́вень *m*; (*fig*) лави́на.
delusion [dɪˈluːʒən] *n* заблужде́ние; **he has ~s
of grandeur** у него́ ма́ния вели́чия.

de luxe [dəˈlʌks] *adj* роскóшный* (роскóшен); **a ~ ~ car/hotel** маши́на/гости́ница люкс.

delve [dɛlv] *vi*: **to ~ into** (*subject*) углубля́ться (углуби́ться* *perf*) в +*acc*; (*handbag etc*) ры́ться* (*impf*) в +*acc*.

Dem. *abbr* (*US*: *POL*) = **democrat(ic)**.

demagogue [ˈdɛmǝgɔg] *n* демагóг.

demand [dɪˈmɑːnd] *vt* трéбовать (потрéбовать *perf*) +*gen* ♦ *n* (*request, claim*) трéбование; (*ECON*): **~ (for)** спрос (на +*acc*); **to ~ sth (from** *or* **of sb)** трéбовать (потрéбовать *perf*) чегó-н (от когó-н); **to be in ~** (*commodity*) пóльзоваться (*impf*) спрóсом; **specialists are in great ~** на специали́стов большóй спрос; **on ~** (*available, payable*) по трéбованию.

demand draft *n* (*COMM*) вéксель, *опла́чиваемый при предъявлéнии.*

demanding [dɪˈmɑːndɪŋ] *adj* (*boss, parents*) трéбовательный (трéбователен); (*child*) трýдный; (*work: involving responsibility*) отвéтственный; (: *requiring effort*) тяжёлый.

demarcation [diːmɑːˈkeɪʃən] *n* разграничéние.

demarcation dispute *n* (*INDUSTRY*) *разноглáсие по пóводу разделéния труда́.*

demean [dɪˈmiːn] *vt*: **to ~ o.s.** унижа́ться (уни́зиться *perf*).

demeanour [dɪˈmiːnǝʳ] (*US* **demeanor**) *n* манéра поведéния.

demented [dɪˈmɛntɪd] *adj* (*person*) помéшанный* (помéшан).

demilitarized zone [diːˈmɪlɪtǝraɪzd-] *n* (*MIL*) демилитаризóванная зóна.

demise [dɪˈmaɪz] *n* упáдок; (*death*) кончи́на.

demist [diːˈmɪst] *vt* (*BRIT*: *AUT*): **to ~ the windscreen** суши́ть обогревáтелем *запотéвшее лобовóе стеклó.*

demister [diːˈmɪstǝʳ] *n* (*BRIT*: *AUT*) обогревáтель *для сýшки запотéвших стёкол.*

demiveg [ˈdɛmɪvɛdʒ] *n* полу-вегетариáнец*(-нка*).

demo [ˈdɛmǝu] *n abbr* (*inf*) = **demonstration**.

demob [diːˈmɔb] *vt* (*MIL*: *inf*) демобилизовáть (*impf/perf*).

demobilize [diːˈmǝubɪlaɪz] *vt* (*MIL*) демобилизовáть (*impf/perf*).

democracy [dɪˈmɔkrǝsɪ] *n* (*system*) демокрáтия; (*country*) демократи́ческая странá*.

democrat [ˈdɛmǝkræt] *n* демокрáт; **D~** (*US*) член пáртии демокрáтов.

democratic [dɛmǝˈkrætɪk] *adj* демократи́ческий*; **D~ Party** (*US*) пáртия демокрáтов.

demography [dɪˈmɔgrǝfɪ] *n* демогрáфия.

demolish [dɪˈmɔlɪʃ] *vt* (*building*) сноси́ть* (снести́* *perf*); (*argument*) разгроми́ть* (*perf*).

demolition [dɛmǝˈlɪʃǝn] *n* (*of building*) снос; (*of argument*) разгрóм.

demon [ˈdiːmǝn] *n* дéмон ♦ *adj* (*skilled*) гениáльный* (гениáлен).

demonstrate [ˈdɛmǝnstreɪt] *vt* демонстри́ровать (продемонстри́ровать *perf*) ♦ *vi* (*POL*): **to ~ (for/against)** демонстри́ровать (*impf*) (за +*acc*/прóтив +*gen*).

demonstration [dɛmǝnˈstreɪʃǝn] *n* демонстрáция; **to hold a ~** (*POL*) проводи́ть* (провести́* *perf*) демонстрáцию.

demonstrative [dɪˈmɔnstrǝtɪv] *adj* (*LING*) указáтельный; **she's very ~** онá открыто выражáет свои чýвства.

demonstrator [ˈdɛmǝnstreɪtǝʳ] *n* (*POL*) демонстрáнт; (*sales person*) демонстрáтор.

demoralize [dɪˈmɔrǝlaɪz] *vt* деморализовáть (*impf/perf*).

demote [dɪˈmǝut] *vt* понижáть (пони́зить* *perf*) в дóлжности.

demotion [dɪˈmǝuʃǝn] *n* понижéние в дóлжности.

demur [dɪˈmǝːʳ] *vi* (*formal*) возражáть (возрази́ть* *perf*) ♦ *n*: **without ~** без возражéний; **they ~red at his suggestion** они возрази́ли на егó предложéние.

demure [dɪˈmjuǝʳ] *adj* (*smile, person*) чи́нный; (*dress*) скрóмный* (скрóмен).

demurrage [dɪˈmʌrɪdʒ] *n* (*COMM*) *плáта за простóй сýдна.*

den [dɛn] *n* (*of animal, person*) лóгово; (*of thieves*) прито́н.

denationalization [ˈdiːnæʃǝnalaɪˈzeɪʃǝn] *n* денационализáция.

denationalize [diːˈnæʃǝnǝlaɪz] *vt* денационализи́ровать (*impf/perf*).

denatured alcohol [diːˈneɪtʃǝd-] *n* (*US*) денатурáт.

denial [dɪˈnaɪǝl] *n* отрицáние; (*refusal*) откáз.

denier [ˈdɛnɪǝʳ] *n* (*of tights, stockings*) деньé *nt ind*.

denigrate [ˈdɛnɪgreɪt] *vt* принижáть (прини́зить* *perf*).

denim [ˈdɛnɪm] *n* джи́нсовая ткань *f*; **~s** *npl* (*jeans*) джи́нсы *pl*.

denim jacket *n* джи́нсовая кýртка*.

denizen [ˈdɛnɪzn] *n* (*inhabitant*) обитáтель(ница) *m(f)*.

Denmark [ˈdɛnmɑːk] *n* Дáния.

denomination [dɪnɔmɪˈneɪʃǝn] *n* (*of money*) достóинство; (*REL*) конфéссия.

denominator [dɪˈnɔmɪneɪtǝʳ] *n* (*MATH*) знаменáтель *m*.

denote [dɪˈnǝut] *vt* (*indicate*) укáзывать (указáть* *perf*) на +*acc*; (*represent*) обозначáть (обознáчить *perf*).

denounce [dɪˈnauns] *vt* (*condemn*) осуждáть (осуди́ть* *perf*); (*give information against*) доноси́ть* (донести́* *perf*) на +*acc*.

dense [dɛns] *adj* (*crowd*) плóтный*; (*smoke, foliage etc*) густóй* (густ); (*inf*: *person*) тупóй* (туп).

densely [ˈdɛnslɪ] *adv*: **~ populated** гýсто населённый; **~ wooded** покрытый (покрыт) густы́м ле́сом.

density ['dɛnsɪtɪ] *n* (*of population: also* PHYS) пло́тность *f*; **single/double-~ disk** (COMPUT) диск с одина́рной/двойно́й пло́тностью.

dent [dɛnt] *n* (*in metal*) вмя́тина ♦ *vt* (*also:* **make a ~ in**: *car etc*) оставля́ть (оста́вить* *perf*) вмя́тину в +*acc*; (*ego*) удари́ть (*perf*) по +*dat*.

dental ['dɛntl] *adj* зубно́й.

dental floss [-flɒs] *n* нить для чи́стки межзу́бных промежу́тков.

dental surgeon *n* зубно́й врач*, стомато́лог.

dentifrice ['dɛntɪfrɪs] *n* (MED: *paste*) зубна́я па́ста, (: *powder*) зубно́й порошо́к*.

dentist ['dɛntɪst] *n* зубно́й врач*, стомато́лог; (*also:* **~'s surgery**) зубовраче́бный кабине́т, стоматологи́ческий* кабине́т.

dentistry ['dɛntɪstrɪ] *n* стоматоло́гия.

dentures ['dɛntʃəz] *npl* зубно́й проте́з *sg*.

denuded [di:'nju:dɪd] *adj* оголённый (оголён); **~ of** (*fig*) лишённый (лишён) +*gen*.

denunciation [dɪnʌnsɪ'eɪʃən] *n* (*accusation*) обличе́ние; (*condemnation*) осужде́ние.

deny [dɪ'naɪ] *vt* (*refute*) отрица́ть (*impf*); (*allegation*) отверга́ть (отве́ргнуть *perf*); (*disown*) отрека́ться (отре́чься* *perf*) от +*gen*; (*refuse*): **to ~ sb sth** отка́зывать (отказа́ть* *perf*) кому́-н в чём-л; **he denies having said it** он отрица́ет, что он э́то сказа́л.

deodorant [di:'əudərənt] *n* дезодора́нт.

depart [dɪ'pɑ:t] *vi* (*person*) отбыва́ть (отбы́ть* *perf*); (*bus, train*) отправля́ться (отпра́виться* *perf*); (*plane*) улета́ть (улете́ть* *perf*); **to ~ from** (*fig*) отклоня́ться (отклони́ться* *perf*) от +*gen*.

departed [dɪ'pɑ:tɪd] *adj* поко́йный ♦ *n* поко́йный(-ая) *m(f) adj*, у́мерший*(-ая) *m(f) adj*.

department [dɪ'pɑ:tmənt] *n* (*in shop*) отде́л; (*in university, school*) отделе́ние; (*POL*) ве́домство, департа́мент; **D~ of Trade and Industry** Министе́рство торго́вли и промы́шленности; **that's not my ~** (*fig*) я не специали́ст в э́том де́ле; **D~ of State** (US) Госуда́рственный департа́мент.

departmental [di:pɑ:t'mɛntl] *adj* (COMM, ADMIN): **~ meeting/activities** собра́ние/ де́ятельность *f* отде́ла; **~ manager** заве́дующий*(-ая) *m(f) adj* отде́лом.

department store *n* универса́льный магази́н.

departure [dɪ'pɑ:tʃə] *n* (*of visitor etc*) отъе́зд; (*of employee*) ухо́д; (*of bus, train*) отправле́ние; (*of plane*) отлёт; (*fig*): **~ from** отклоне́ние от +*gen*; **a new ~** но́вое направле́ние.

departure lounge *n* (*at airport*) зал отлёта.

depend [dɪ'pɛnd] *vi*: **to ~ on** зави́сеть* (*impf*) от +*gen*; (*trust*) полага́ться (положи́ться* *perf*) на +*acc*; **it ~s** смотря́ по обстоя́тельствам,

как полу́чится; **~ing on the outcome** ... в зави́симости от исхо́да ....

dependable [dɪ'pɛndəbl] *adj* надёжный* (надёжен).

dependant [dɪ'pɛndənt] *n* иждиве́нец(-нка).

dependence [dɪ'pɛndəns] *n* зави́симость *f*.

dependent [dɪ'pɛndənt] *adj*: **~ (on)** зави́симый (зави́сим) (от +*gen*) ♦ *n* = **dependant**.

depict [dɪ'pɪkt] *vt* изобража́ть (изобрази́ть* *perf*).

depilatory [dɪ'pɪlətrɪ] *n* (*also:* **~ cream**) крем для удале́ния воло́с.

depleted [dɪ'pli:tɪd] *adj* истощённый* (истощён).

deplorable [dɪ'plɔ:rəbl] *adj* (*conditions*) плаче́вный* (плаче́вен); (*behaviour*) возмути́тельный* (возмути́телен).

deplore [dɪ'plɔ:'] *vt* (*condemn*) негодова́ть (*impf*) по по́воду +*gen*.

deploy [dɪ'plɔɪ] *vt* (*troops*) дислоци́ровать (*impf/perf*).

depopulate [di:'pɔpjuleɪt] *vt* обезлю́дить (*perf*).

depopulation ['di:pɔpju'leɪʃən] *n* опустоше́ние.

deport [dɪ'pɔ:t] *vt* депорти́ровать (*impf/perf*), высыла́ть (вы́слать* *perf*).

deportation [di:pɔ:'teɪʃən] *n* депорта́ция, вы́сылка*.

deportation order *n* (LAW) прика́з о депорта́ции.

deportee [di:pɔ:'ti:] *n* депорти́рованный(-ая) *m(f) adj*.

deportment [dɪ'pɔ:tmənt] *n* оса́нка.

depose [dɪ'pəuz] *vt* (*remove*) смеща́ть (смести́ть* *perf*); (*overthrow*) низлага́ть (низложи́ть* *perf*).

deposit [dɪ'pɔzɪt] *n* (*in account*) депози́т, вклад; (*down payment*) пе́рвый взнос, зада́ток*; (: *when hiring, renting*) зало́г*; (*on bottle etc*) сто́имость *f* посу́ды; (CHEM) оса́док*; (*of ore, oil*) за́лежь *f* ♦ *vt* (*money*) помеща́ть (помести́ть* *perf*); (*subj: river: sand, silt etc*) намыва́ть (намы́ть* *perf*); (*case, bag*) сдава́ть (сдать* *perf*); **to put down a ~ of £50** дава́ть (дать* *perf*) зада́ток £50.

deposit account *n* депози́тный счёт*.

depositor [dɪ'pɔzɪtə'] *n* вкла́дчик* *m/f*.

depository [dɪ'pɔzɪtərɪ] *n* (*person*) дове́ренное лицо́*; (*place*) храни́лище.

depot ['dɛpəu] *n* (*storehouse*) склад; (*for buses*) парк; (*for trains*) депо́ *nt ind*; (US: *station*) ста́нция.

depraved [dɪ'preɪvd] *adj* развращённый (развращён).

depravity [dɪ'prævɪtɪ] *n* развращённость *f*.

deprecate ['dɛprɪkeɪt] *vt* порица́ть (*impf*).

deprecating ['dɛprɪkeɪtɪŋ] *adj* неодобри́тельный* (неодобри́телен).

---

* marks translations which have irregular inflections. The Russian-English side of the dictionary gives inflectional information.

depreciate [dɪˈpriːʃɪeɪt] *vi* обесце́ниваться (обесце́ниться *perf*).
depreciation [dɪpriːʃɪˈeɪʃən] *n* обесце́нивание.
depress [dɪˈprɛs] *vt* (PSYCH) подавля́ть (*impf*), угнета́ть (*impf*); (*prices, profits*) снижа́ть (сни́зить *perf*); (*lever, pedal*) нажима́ть (нажа́ть* *perf*) на +*acc*.
depressant [dɪˈprɛsnt] *n* (MED) депресса́нт, успокои́тельное сре́дство.
depressed [dɪˈprɛst] *adj* (*person*) пода́вленный* (пода́влен), угнетённый* (угнетён); (*prices*) сни́женный* (*industry*): **to be ~** находи́ться* (*impf*) в состоя́нии спа́да; **to get ~** впада́ть (впасть* *perf*) в депре́ссию; **~ area** райо́н, находя́щийся в состоя́нии экономи́ческого упа́дка.
depressing [dɪˈprɛsɪŋ] *adj* (*time*) тяжёлый; (*news, outlook*) удруча́ющий.
depression [dɪˈprɛʃən] *n* (PSYCH, ECON) депре́ссия; (METEOROLOGY) о́бласть *f* ни́зкого давле́ния; (*hollow*) углубле́ние; (: *in landscape*) впа́дина.
deprivation [dɛprɪˈveɪʃən] *n* (*poverty*) нужда́; (*depriving*) лише́ние.
deprive [dɪˈpraɪv] *vt*: **to ~ sb of** лиша́ть (лиши́ть* *perf*) кого́-н +*gen*.
deprived [dɪˈpraɪvd] *adj* (*area, family*) бе́дный* (бе́ден), обездо́ленный; **~ child** обездо́ленный ребёнок.
dept. *abbr* = **department**.
depth [dɛpθ] *n* глубина́*; **in the ~s of despair/a crisis** в глубо́ком отча́янии/кри́зисе; **in the ~s of winter** глубо́кой зимо́й; **at a ~ of three metres** на глубине́ трёх ме́тров; **to be out of one's ~** (*in water*) не достава́ть* (*impf*) до дна; **I'm out of my ~ with this job** мне э́та рабо́та не по плечу́; **to study sth in ~** изуча́ть (изучи́ть* *perf*) что-н углублённо.
depth charge *n* глуби́нная бо́мба.
deputation [dɛpjuˈteɪʃən] *n* депута́ция.
deputize [ˈdɛpjutaɪz] *vi*: **to ~ for sb** замеща́ть (*impf*) кого́-н.
deputy [ˈdɛpjutɪ] *n* замести́тель *m*; (POL) депута́т; (US: also: **~ sheriff**) исполня́ющий обя́занности шери́фа ◆ *cpd*: **~ leader/chairman** замести́тель ли́дера/председа́теля; **~ head** (BRIT: SCOL) замести́тель дире́ктора.
derail [dɪˈreɪl] *vt*: **to be ~ed** сходи́ть* (сойти́* *perf*) с ре́льсов.
derailment [dɪˈreɪlmənt] *n*: **the cause of the ~ is unknown** причи́на, по кото́рой по́езд сошёл с ре́льсов, неизве́стна.
deranged [dɪˈreɪndʒd] *adj* (*person*) психи́чески больно́й; **he is ~** он психи́чески бо́лен.
derby [ˈdɑːrbɪ] *n* (US: *bowler hat*) котело́к.
Derbys *abbr* (BRIT: POST) = **Derbyshire**.
deregulate [dɪˈrɛɡjuleɪt] *vt* (INDUSTRY) ослабля́ть (осла́бить* *perf*) госуда́рственное регули́рование +*gen*.
deregulation [dɪˈrɛɡjuˈleɪʃən] *n* ослабле́ние

госуда́рственного контро́ля.
derelict [ˈdɛrɪlɪkt] *adj* забро́шенный* (забро́шен).
deride [dɪˈraɪd] *vt* насмеха́ться (*impf*) над +*instr*.
derision [dɪˈrɪʒən] *n* презре́ние.
derisive [dɪˈraɪsɪv] *adj* презри́тельный* (презри́телен).
derisory [dɪˈraɪsərɪ] *adj* (*ridiculous*) смехотво́рный* (смехотво́рен); (*derisive*) презри́тельный* (презри́телен).
derivation [dɛrɪˈveɪʃən] *n* происхожде́ние.
derivative [dɪˈrɪvətɪv] *n* (CHEM) дерива́т; (LING) произво́дное сло́во, дерива́т ◆ *adj* (*word, form*) произво́дный; (*not original*) неоригина́льный* (неоригина́лен).
derive [dɪˈraɪv] *vt* (*get*): **to ~ (from)** (*pleasure*) получа́ть (получи́ть* *perf*) (от +*gen*); (*benefit*) извлека́ть (извле́чь* *perf*) (из +*gen*) ◆ *vi* (*originate in*): **to ~ from** происходи́ть* (*impf*) от +*gen*.
derived demand [dɪˈraɪvd-] *n* ко́свенный *or* произво́дственный спрос.
dermatitis [dəːməˈtaɪtɪs] *n* дермати́т.
dermatology [dəːməˈtɔlədʒɪ] *n* дерматоло́гия.
derogatory [dɪˈrɔɡətərɪ] *adj* пренебрежи́тельный* (пренебрежи́телен).
derrick [ˈdɛrɪk] *n* (*on ship*) де́ррик; (*on well*) бурова́я вы́шка*.
derv [dəːv] *n* (BRIT: AUT) ди́зельное то́пливо.
DES *n abbr* (BRIT: *formerly*: = *Department of Education and Science*) Министе́рство просвеще́ния и нау́ки.
desalination [diːsælɪˈneɪʃən] *n* опресне́ние.
descend [dɪˈsɛnd] *vt* (*stairs*) спуска́ться (спусти́ться* *perf*) по +*dat*; (*hill*) спуска́ться (спусти́ться* *perf*) с +*gen* ◆ *vi* (*go down*) спуска́ться (спусти́ться* *perf*); **to ~ from** (*family, person*) происходи́ть* (*impf*) из +*gen*; **to ~ to** (*lying, begging etc*) опуска́ться (опусти́ться* *perf*) до +*gen*; **in ~ing order of importance** в нисходя́щем поря́дке
▶ **descend on** *vt fus* (*subj: enemy, misfortune*) обру́шиваться (обру́шиться *perf*) на +*acc*; (: *gloom, darkness*) опуска́ться (опусти́ться* *perf*) на +*acc*; (: *silence*) воцаря́ться (воцари́ться *perf*) на +*acc*; **visitors ~ed (up)on us** к нам нагря́нули го́сти.
descendant [dɪˈsɛndənt] *n* пото́мок*.
descent [dɪˈsɛnt] *n* спуск; (AVIAT) сниже́ние; (*origin*) происхожде́ние.
describe [dɪsˈkraɪb] *vt* опи́сывать (описа́ть* *perf*).
description [dɪsˈkrɪpʃən] *n* описа́ние; (*sort*) род*; **of every ~** всевозмо́жного ро́да.
descriptive [dɪsˈkrɪptɪv] *adj* описа́тельный.
desecrate [ˈdɛsɪkreɪt] *vt* оскверня́ть (оскверни́ть *perf*).
desegregate [diːˈsɛɡrɪɡeɪt] *vt*: **to ~ a society/school** ликвиди́ровать (*impf/perf*) сегрега́цию в о́бществе/шко́ле.
desert [*n* ˈdɛzət, *vb* dɪˈzəːt] *n* (*also fig*) пусты́ня ◆

vt покида́ть (поки́нуть *perf*) ♦ *vi* (*MIL*) дезерти́ровать *(impf/perf)*; *see also* **deserts**.

deserter [dɪ'zə:təʳ] *n* (*MIL*) дезерти́р.

desertion [dɪ'zə:ʃən] *n* (*MIL*) дезерти́рство; (*LAW*) оставле́ние.

desert island *n* необита́емый о́стров*.

deserts [dɪ'zə:ts] *npl*: **to get one's just ~** получа́ть (получи́ть *perf*) по заслу́гам.

deserve [dɪ'zə:v] *vt* заслу́живать (заслужи́ть* *perf*).

deservedly [dɪ'zə:vɪdlɪ] *adv* заслу́женно.

deserving [dɪ'zə:vɪŋ] *adj* досто́йный*.

desiccated ['dɛsɪkeɪtɪd] *adj* (*coconut*) сушёный.

design [dɪ'zaɪn] *n* диза́йн; (*process: of dress*) модели́рование; (*sketch: of building*) прое́кт; (*type: of appliance etc*) моде́ль *f*; (*pattern*) рису́нок*; (*intention*) за́мысел* ♦ *vt* (*house, kitchen*) проекти́ровать (спроекти́ровать *perf*); (*product, test*) разраба́тывать (разрабо́тать *perf*); **to have ~s on** име́ть *(impf)* ви́ды на +*acc*; **by ~** с у́мыслом.

designate [*vt* 'dɛzɪgneɪt, *adj* 'dɛzɪgnɪt] *vt* (*nominate*) назнача́ть (назна́чить *perf*); (*indicate*) обознача́ть (обозна́чить *perf*) ♦ *adj*: **minister ~** назна́ченный мини́стр (*до вступле́ния в до́лжность*).

designation [dɛzɪg'neɪʃən] *n* (*description, name*) обозначе́ние.

designer [dɪ'zaɪnəʳ] *n* (*ART*) дизайнер; (*of program*) разрабо́тчик; (*of building*) проекти́ровщик; (*of machine*) констру́ктор; (*also*: **fashion ~**) моделье́р ♦ *adj* (*clothes*) моде́льный; **~ label** фи́рменный знак (модельера).

desirability [dɪzaɪərə'bɪlɪtɪ] *n*: **the ~ of** жела́тельность *f* +*gen*.

desirable [dɪ'zaɪərəbl] *adj* (*proper*) жела́тельный* (жела́телен); (*attractive*) привлека́тельный* (привлека́телен); **it is ~ that** жела́тельно, что́бы.

desire [dɪ'zaɪəʳ] *n* жела́ние ♦ *vt* (*want*) жела́ть *(impf)*; **to ~ to do/that** жела́ть *(impf)* +*infin*/, что́бы.

desirous [dɪ'zaɪərəs] *adj*: **to be ~ of doing** жела́ть *(impf)* +*infin*.

desist [dɪ'zɪst] *vi*: **to ~ (from)** возде́рживаться (воздержа́ться *perf*) (от +*gen*)

desk [dɛsk] *n* (*in office, study*) (пи́сьменный) стол*; (*for pupil*) па́рта; (*in hotel, at airport*) сто́йка*; (*BRIT: also*: **cash~**) ка́сса.

desk job *n* канцеля́рская рабо́та.

desktop ['dɛsktɔp] *adj* насто́льный.

desktop publishing *n* (*COMPUT*) насто́льное изда́тельство, насто́льная типогра́фия.

desolate ['dɛsəlɪt] *adj* (*place*) забро́шенный*; (*person*) поки́нутый.

desolation [dɛsə'leɪʃən] *n* (*action*) опустоше́ние; (*quality*) опустошённость *f*.

despair [dɪs'pɛəʳ] *n* отча́яние ♦ *vi*: **to ~ of sth/ doing** отча́иваться (отча́яться *perf*) в +*prp*/+*infin*; **to be in ~** быть* *(impf)* в отча́янии.

despatch [dɪs'pætʃ] *n, vt* = **dispatch**.

desperate ['dɛspərɪt] *adj* (*action, situation*) отча́янный* (отча́ян); (*criminal*) отъя́вленный; (*person*): **he/she is ~** он/она́ в отча́янии; **to be ~ to do** жа́ждать *(impf)* +*infin*; **to be ~ for money** стра́шно нужда́ться *(impf)* в деньга́х.

desperately ['dɛspərɪtlɪ] *adv* отча́янно; (*very*) чрезвыча́йно.

desperation [dɛspə'reɪʃən] *n* отча́яние; **in (sheer) ~** в (по́лном) отча́янии.

despicable [dɪs'pɪkəbl] *adj* презре́нный* (презре́нен).

despise [dɪs'paɪz] *vt* презира́ть *(impf)*.

despite [dɪs'paɪt] *prep* несмотря́ на +*acc*.

despondent [dɪs'pɔndənt] *adj* уны́лый (уны́л).

despot ['dɛspɔt] *n* де́спот.

dessert [dɪ'zə:t] *n* десе́рт.

dessertspoon [dɪ'zə:tspu:n] *n* десе́ртная ло́жка*.

destabilize [di:'steɪbɪlaɪz] *vt* (*also fig*) дестабилизи́ровать *(impf/perf)*.

destination [dɛstɪ'neɪʃən] *n* (*of traveller*) цель *f*; (*of mail*) ме́сто* назначе́ния.

destined [dɪs'tɪnd] *adj*: **he/she is ~ to do** ему́/ей суждено́ +*infin*; **to be ~ for** предназнача́ться *(impf)* для +*gen*.

destiny ['dɛstɪnɪ] *n* судьба́*.

destitute ['dɛstɪtju:t] *adj* (*person*) обездо́ленный (обездо́лен).

destroy [dɪs'trɔɪ] *vt* (*also fig*) уничтожа́ть (уничто́жить *perf*), разруша́ть (разру́шить *perf*); (*kill: pet*) усыпля́ть (усыпи́ть* *perf*); (: *farm animal*) забива́ть (заби́ть* *perf*).

destroyer [dɪs'trɔɪəʳ] *n* (*NAUT*) миноно́сец*.

destruction [dɪs'trʌkʃən] *n* уничтоже́ние, разруше́ние; (*fig: of reputation etc*) ги́бель *f*.

destructive [dɪs'trʌktɪv] *adj* (*capacity, force*) разруши́тельный; (*criticism*) деструкти́вный; (*emotion*) губи́тельный* (губи́телен); (*child*): **he's very ~** он всё лома́ет.

desultory ['dɛsəltərɪ] *adj* (*attempt*) сла́бый (слаб); (*reading, work*) беспоря́дочный (беспоря́дочен).

detach [dɪ'tætʃ] *vt* снима́ть (снять* *perf*); (*unstick*) отделя́ть (отдели́ть *perf*).

detachable [dɪ'tætʃəbl] *adj* съёмный

detached [dɪ'tætʃt] *adj* (*objective*) беспристра́стный* (беспристра́стен); **~ house** особня́к*.

detachment [dɪ'tætʃmənt] *n* (*aloofness*) отдалённость *f*; (*MIL*) отря́д.

detail ['di:teɪl] *n* дета́ль *f*, подро́бность *f* ♦ *vt* (*list*) перечисля́ть (перечи́слить *perf*); **in ~**

---

* marks translations which have irregular inflections. The Russian-English side of the dictionary gives inflectional information.

подробно, в деталях; **to go into ~s**
вдаваться *(impf)* в детали *or* подробности.
detailed ['di:teild] *adj* детальный* (детален),
подробный* (подробен).
detain [dɪ'teɪn] *vt (delay, confine)* задерживать
(задержать* *perf*); **to ~ in hospital** оставлять
(оставить* *perf*) в больнице.
detainee [di:teɪ'ni:] *n (POL)* узник(-ица).
detect [dɪ'tɛkt] *vt (sense)* чувствовать
(почувствовать *perf*); *(discover)*
обнаруживать (обнаружить *perf*).
detection [dɪ'tɛkʃən] *n (discovery)*
обнаружение; **crime ~** раскрытие
преступлений; **the criminal escaped ~**
преступник не обнаружен; **the mistake
escaped ~** ошибка осталась незамеченной.
detective [dɪ'tɛktɪv] *n (POLICE)* сыщик,
детектив.
detective story *n* детектив.
detector [dɪ'tɛktə'] *n (TECH)* детектор.
détente [deɪ'tɑ:nt] *n (POL)* разрядка.
detention [dɪ'tɛnʃən] *n (arrest)* задержание;
(imprisonment) содержание под стражей;
(SCOL): **to give sb ~** оставлять (оставить*
perf) кого-н после уроков.
deter [dɪ'tə:'] *vt* сдерживать (сдержать *perf*).
detergent [dɪ'tə:dʒənt] *n* моющее средство.
deteriorate [dɪ'tɪərɪəreɪt] *vi* ухудшаться
(ухудшиться *perf*).
deterioration [dɪtɪərɪə'reɪʃən] *n* ухудшение.
determination [dɪtə:mɪ'neɪʃən] *n (resolve)*
решимость *f*; *(establishment)* установление.
determine [dɪ'tə:mɪn] *vt (find out)*
устанавливать (установить* *perf*); *(establish,
dictate)* определять (определить *perf*); **to ~
that** *(establish)* устанавливать (установить*
perf), что; **to ~ to do** *(decide)* решать (решить
perf) +*infin*.
determined [dɪ'tə:mɪnd] *adj (person, effort)*
решительный* (решителен); *(quantity)*
определённый*; **~ to do** полный (полон*)
решимости +*infin*.
deterrence [dɪ'tɛrəns] *n* сдерживание.
deterrent [dɪ'tɛrənt] *n* средство сдерживания,
сдерживающее средство; **nuclear ~**
средство ядерного сдерживания; **to act as a
~** являться (явиться* *perf*) средством
сдерживания.
detest [dɪ'tɛst] *vt* ненавидеть* *(impf)*.
detestable [dɪ'tɛstəbl] *adj* отвратительный*
(отвратителен).
detonate ['dɛtəneɪt] *vi* взрываться
(взорваться* *perf*) ♦ *vt* взрывать (взорвать*
perf).
detonator ['dɛtəneɪtə'] *n* детонатор.
detour ['di:tuə'] *n (in vehicle, also US)* объезд;
(on foot) обход; **to make a ~** *(in vehicle)*
ехать* (поехать* *perf*) в объезд; *(on foot)*
идти* (пойти* *perf*) в обход.
detract [dɪ'trækt] *vi*: **to ~ from** умалять
(умалить *perf*).

detractor [dɪ'træktə'] *n* недоброжелатель *m*.
detriment ['dɛtrɪmənt] *n*: **to the ~ of** в ущерб
+*dat*; **without ~ to** без ущерба для +*gen*.
detrimental [dɛtrɪ'mɛntl] *adj*: **~ to** вредный*
(вреден) для +*gen*.
deuce [dju:s] *n (TENNIS)* „ровно".
devaluation [dɪvælju'eɪʃən] *n (ECON)*
девальвация.
devalue ['di:'vælju:] *vt (currency)*
обесценивать (обесценить *perf*); *(person,
work)* недооценивать (недооценить *perf*).
devastate ['dɛvəsteɪt] *vt* опустошать
(опустошить *perf*); *(fig)*: **she is ~d by** она
потрясена +*instr*.
devastating ['dɛvəsteɪtɪŋ] *adj (weapon, storm)*
разрушительный* (разрушителен); *(news,
effect)* сокрушительный.
devastation [dɛvəs'teɪʃən] *n* разрушение,
опустошение.
develop [dɪ'vɛləp] *vt (idea, industry)* развивать
(развить* *perf*); *(plan, resource)*
разрабатывать (разработать *perf*); *(land)*
застраивать (застроить *perf*); *(PHOT)*
проявлять (проявить* *perf*); *(disease)*
заболевать (заболеть *perf*) +*instr* ♦ *vi (evolve,
advance)* развиваться (развиться* *perf*);
(appear) проявляться (проявиться* *perf*); **the
machine ~ed a fault** в машине возникли
неполадки; **to ~ a taste for sth**
пристраститься* *(perf)* к чему-н; **to ~ into**
превращаться (превратиться* *perf*) в +*acc*.
developer [dɪ'vɛləpə'] *n (also*: **property ~**:
company) строительная фирма; (: *person)*
разработчик.
developing country [dɪ'vɛləpɪŋ-] *n*
развивающаяся страна*.
development [dɪ'vɛləpmənt] *n* развитие; *(of
resources)* разработка; *(of land)* застройка;
housing ~ жилищный комплекс.
development area *n* территория, на
*развитие которой направлены
дополнительные правительственные
средства.*
deviant ['di:vɪənt] *adj* отклоняющийся от
нормы.
deviate ['di:vɪeɪt] *vi*: **to ~ (from)** отклоняться
(отклониться *perf*) (от +*gen*).
deviation [di:vɪ'eɪʃən] *n*: **~ (from)** отклонение
(от +*gen*).
device [dɪ'vaɪs] *n* устройство, прибор; *(ploy,
stratagem)* средство; **explosive ~** взрывчатое
устройство.
devil ['dɛvl] *n* дьявол, чёрт*; **go on, be a ~!**
давай, позволь себе!; **talk of the ~!** лёгок* на
помине!
devilish ['dɛvlɪʃ] *adj* дьявольский*.
devil's advocate [dɛvlz-] *n* провокатор.
devious ['di:vɪəs] *adj* лукавый (лукав); *(route,
path)* извилистый (извилист).
devise [dɪ'vaɪz] *vt* разрабатывать
(разработать *perf*).

devoid [dɪ'vɔɪd] *adj*: ~ **of** лишённый (лишён) +*gen*.

devolution [di:və'lu:ʃən] *n* (*POL*) переда́ча вла́сти (*ме́стным о́рганам*).

devolve [dɪ'vɔlv] *vt* (*power, duty etc*) передава́ть* (переда́ть* *perf*) ♦ *vi*: **to** ~ **(up)on** переходи́ть* (перейти́* *perf*) к +*dat*.

devote [dɪ'vəut] *vt*: **to** ~ **sth to** посвяща́ть (посвяти́ть* *perf*) что-н +*dat*.

devoted [dɪ'vəutɪd] *adj* (*admirer, partner*) пре́данный* (пре́дан); (*service, friendship*) ве́рный*; **he is** ~ **to her** он пре́дан ей; **his book is** ~ **to the history of Scotland** его́ кни́га посвящена́ исто́рии Шотла́ндии.

devotee [dɛvəu'ti:] *n* (*fan*) приве́рженец*; (*REL*) правове́рный(-ая) *m(f) adj*.

devotion [dɪ'vəuʃən] *n* пре́данность *f*; (*REL*) поклоне́ние.

devour [dɪ'vauə'] *vt* (*also fig*) пожира́ть (пожра́ть* *perf*).

devout [dɪ'vaut] *adj* (*REL*) благочести́вый (благочести́в).

dew [dju:] *n* роса́*.

dexterity [dɛks'tɛrɪtɪ] *n* (*manual*) ло́вкость *f*; (*mental*) сообрази́тельность *f*.

dext(e)rous ['dɛkstrəs] *adj* (*see n*) ло́вкий* (ло́вок); сообрази́тельный* (сообрази́телен).

dg *abbr* (= *decigram*) децигра́мм.

DH *n abbr* (*BRIT*: = *Department of Health*) Министе́рство здравоохране́ния.

Dhaka ['dækə] *n* Да́ка.

DHSS *n abbr* (*BRIT: formerly*: = *Department of Health and Social Security*) Министе́рство здравоохране́ния и социа́льного обеспе́чения.

diabetes [daɪə'bi:ti:z] *n* диабе́т.

diabetic [daɪə'bɛtɪk] *n* диабе́тик ♦ *adj* диабети́ческий.

diabolical [daɪə'bɔlɪkl] *adj* дья́вольский*; (*inf*: *dreadful*) жу́ткий*.

diaeresis [daɪ'ɛrɪsɪs] *n* диере́за.

diagnose [daɪəg'nəuz] *vt* (*illness*) диагности́ровать (*impf/perf*); (*problem*) определя́ть (определи́ть *perf*).

diagnoses [daɪəg'nəusi:z] *npl of* **diagnosis**.

diagnosis [daɪəg'nəusɪs] (*pl* **diagnoses**) *n* диа́гноз.

diagonal [daɪ'ægənl] *adj* диагона́льный ♦ *n* (*MATH*) диагона́ль *f*.

diagram ['daɪəgræm] *n* схе́ма.

dial ['daɪəl] *n* (*of clock*) цифербла́т; (*of indicator*) шкала́; (*of phone*) диск; (*of radio*) регуля́тор настро́йки ♦ *vt* (*number*) набира́ть (набра́ть* *perf*); **to** ~ **a wrong number** не туда́ попада́ть (попа́сть* *perf*); **can I** ~ **London direct?** могу́ я набра́ть Ло́ндон по автома́ту?

dial. *abbr* = **dialect.**

dial code *n* (*US*) = **dialling code.**

dialect ['daɪəlɛkt] *n* диале́кт.

dialling code ['daɪəlɪŋ-] (*US* **dial code**) *n* код; **the** ~~ **for London** код Ло́ндона.

dialling tone (*US* **dial tone**) *n* непреры́вный гудо́к*.

dialogue ['daɪəlɔg] (*US* **dialog**) *n* диало́г.

dial tone *n* (*US*) = **dialling tone.**

dialysis [daɪ'ælɪsɪs] *n* (*MED*) диа́лиз.

diameter [daɪ'æmɪtə'] *n* диа́метр.

diametrically [daɪə'mɛtrɪklɪ] *adv*: ~ **opposed (to)** диаметра́льно противополо́жный* (противополо́жен) (+*dat*).

diamond ['daɪəmənd] *n* алма́з; (*cut diamond*) бриллиа́нт; (*shape*) ромб; ~**s** *npl* (*CARDS*) бу́бны* *fpl*.

diamond ring *n* бриллиа́нтовое кольцо́*.

diaper ['daɪəpə'] *n* (*US*) подгу́зник.

diaphragm ['daɪəfræm] *n* диафра́гма.

diarrhoea [daɪə'ri:ə] (*US* **diarrhea**) *n* поно́с.

diary ['daɪərɪ] *n* (*journal*) дневни́к*; (*engagements book*) записна́я кни́жка*; **to keep a** ~ вести́* (*impf*) дневни́к.

diatribe ['daɪətraɪb] *n* ре́зкая кри́тика.

dice [daɪs] *npl of* **die**; (*in game*) ку́бик; (*game*) ко́сти* *fpl* ♦ *vt* (*CULIN*) ре́зать (нареза́ть* *perf*) ку́биками.

dicey ['daɪsɪ] *adj* (*inf*): **it's a bit** ~ э́то немно́го риско́ванно.

dichotomy [daɪ'kɔtəmɪ] *n* дихотоми́я.

dickhead ['dɪkhɛd] *n* (*inf*) муда́к.

Dictaphone® ['dɪktəfəun] *n* диктофо́н.

dictate [dɪk'teɪt] *vt* диктова́ть (продиктова́ть *perf*) ♦ *n* веле́ние ♦ *vi*: **to** ~ **to** диктова́ть (продиктова́ть *perf*) +*dat*; **the** ~**s of** веле́ние +*gen*; **I won't be** ~**d to by him** я не позво́лю, что́бы он мне диктова́л.

dictation [dɪk'teɪʃən] *n* (*of letter*) дикто́вка*; (*SCOL*) дикта́нт; **at** ~ **speed** со ско́ростью дикто́вки.

dictator [dɪk'teɪtə'] *n* дикта́тор.

dictatorship [dɪk'teɪtəʃɪp] *n* диктату́ра.

diction ['dɪkʃən] *n* ди́кция.

dictionary ['dɪkʃənrɪ] *n* слова́рь* *m*.

did [dɪd] *pt of* **do**.

didactic [daɪ'dæktɪk] *adj* дидакти́ческий*, поучи́тельный* (поучи́телен).

diddle ['dɪdl] *vt* (*inf*) надува́ть (наду́ть* *perf*).

didn't ['dɪdnt] = **did not**.

die [daɪ] *n* (*pl* **dice**; *in game*) игра́льная кость* *f*; (*pl* ~**s**; *TECH*) ма́трица, штамп ♦ *vi* (*person, emotion*) умира́ть (умере́ть* *perf*); (*smile, light*) угаса́ть (уга́снуть* *perf*); **to** ~ **of** *or* **from** умира́ть (умере́ть* *perf*) от +*gen*; **to be dying** умира́ть (*impf*); **to be dying for sth/to do** до́ смерти хоте́ть* (*impf*) чего́-н/+*infin*

▶ **die away** *vi* (*sound*) замира́ть (замере́ть*

---

* marks translations which have irregular inflections. The Russian-English side of the dictionary gives inflectional information.

perf); (*light*) угасáть (угáснуть* *perf*)

▶ **die down** *vi* (*wind, noise*) утихáть (утихнуть* *perf*); (*fire*) потухáть (потухнуть* *perf*); (*excitement*) улéчься* (*perf*)

▶ **die out** *vi* (*species*) умирáть (умерéть* *perf*); (*species*) вымирáть (вымереть* *perf*).

diehard ['daɪhɑ:d] *n* ретрогрáд ♦ *adj* непреклóнный.

diesel ['di:zl] *n* дизель* *m*; (*also:* ~ **oil**) дизельное тóпливо.

diesel engine *n* дизельный мотóр.

diet ['daɪət] *n* диéта ♦ *vi* (*also:* **be on a** ~) быть* (*impf*) на диéте; **to live on a** ~ **of** питáться (*impf*) одним(-óй) +*instr*.

dietician [daɪə'tɪʃən] *n* диетóлог.

differ ['dɪfə'] *vi*: **to** ~ (**from**) отличáться (*impf*) (от +*gen*); (*disagree*): **to** ~ **about** расходиться* (разойтись* *perf*) в вопрóсе +*gen*; **we agreed to** ~ кáждый из нас остáлся при своём мнéнии.

difference ['dɪfrəns] *n* (*dissimilarity*) разлиⅽиие; (: *in size, age*) рáзница; (*disagreement*) разноглáсие; **it makes no** ~ **to me** мне всё равнó; **a** ~ **of opinion** расхождéние во мнéниях; **to settle one's** ~**s** улáживать (улáдить* *perf*) разноглáсия.

different ['dɪfrənt] *adj* (*other*) другóй, инóй; (*various*) разлиⅽиый, рáзный; **to be** ~ **from** отличáться (*impf*) от +*gen*.

differential [dɪfə'renʃəl] *n* (MATH) дифференциáл; (BRIT: *in wages*) рáзница в тарифах.

differentiate [dɪfə'renʃieɪt] *vi*: **to** ~ (**between**) проводить* (провести* *perf*) разлиⅽиие (мéжду +*instr*) ♦ *vt*: **to** ~ **from** отличáть (отличить* *perf*) от +*gen*.

differently ['dɪfrəntlɪ] *adv* (*otherwise*) инáче, по-другóму; (*in different ways*) по-рáзному.

difficult ['dɪfɪkəlt] *adj* трудный* (трýден); (*person*) тяжёлый; ~ **to understand/see** трýдно понять/видеть.

difficulty ['dɪfɪkəltɪ] *n* трýдность *f*, затруднéние; **to have difficulties** испытывать (испытáть* *perf*) трýдности; **to be in difficulties** находиться* (*impf*) в трýдном положéнии.

diffidence ['dɪfɪdəns] *n* застéнчивость *f*.

diffident ['dɪfɪdənt] *adj* застéнчивый (застéнчив).

diffuse [*vt* dɪ'fju:z, *adj* dɪ'fju:s] *vt* (*information*) распространять (распространить* *perf*) ♦ *adj* (*idea, sense*) расплыⅽиатый (расплывчат); (*light*) рассéянный*.

dig [dɪg] (*pt, pp* **dug**) *vt* (*hole*) копáть (выкопать* *perf*), рыть* (вырыть* *perf*); (*garden*) вскáпывать (вскопáть* *perf*) ♦ *n* (*prod*) толчóк*; (*archaeological excavation*) раскóпки* *fpl*; (*remark*): **to have a** ~ **at sb** подкáлывать (подколóть* *perf*) когó-н; **to** ~ **one's nails/claws into sth** впивáться (впиться* *perf*) ногтями/когтями во что-н

▶ **dig in** *vi* (*inf*: *eat*): **to** ~ **in** (**to**) налегáть

(налéчь* *perf*) (на +*acc*) ♦ *vt*: **to** ~ **in** (**to**) (*compost*) вкáпывать (вкопáть *perf*) (в +*acc*); (*knife*) вонзáть (вонзить* *perf*) (в +*acc*); **to** ~ **in one's heels** (*fig*) упирáться (упереться* *perf*)

▶ **dig into** *vt fus* (*snow, soil*) зарывáть (зарыть* *perf*), закáпывать (закопáть* *perf*); **to** ~ **into one's savings** начáть (*perf*) трáтить сбережéния; **to** ~ **into one's pockets** (**for sth**) запускáть (запустить* *perf*) рукý в кармáн (за чем-н)

▶ **dig out** *vt* (*from snow, earth*) откáпывать (откопáть *perf*)

▶ **dig up** *vt* (*plant*) выкáпывать (выкопать *perf*); (*information*) раскáпывать (раскопáть *perf*).

digest [*vt* daɪ'dʒɛst, *n* 'daɪdʒɛst] *vt* (*food*) перевáривать (переварить* *perf*); (*facts*) усвáивать (усвóить *perf*) ♦ *n* (*book*) сбóрник, дайджéст.

digestible [dɪ'dʒɛstəbl] *adj* удобоваримый (удобоварим).

digestion [dɪ'dʒɛstʃən] *n* пищеварéние.

digestive [dɪ'dʒɛstɪv] *adj* пищеварительный ♦ *n* (*also:* ~ **biscuit**) печéнье из муки грýбого помóла.

digit ['dɪdʒɪt] *n* (*number*) цифра; (*finger*) пáлец*.

digital ['dɪdʒɪtl] *adj*: ~ **watch** электрóнные часы* *mpl*; ~ **recording** электрóнная зáпись*.

digital camera *n* цифровáя кáмера.

digital compact cassette *n* оцифрóванная компáктная кассéта.

digital computer *n* электрóнно-вычислительная машина*.

digital TV *n* цифровóе телевидéние.

dignified ['dɪgnɪfaɪd] *adj* пóлный* (пóлон) достóинства.

dignitary ['dɪgnɪtərɪ] *n* высокопостáвленное лицó*.

dignity ['dɪgnɪtɪ] *n* достóинство.

digress [daɪ'grɛs] *vi*: **to** ~ (**from**) отступáть (отступить* *perf*) (от +*gen*).

digression [daɪ'grɛʃən] *n* отступлéние.

digs [dɪgz] *npl* (BRIT: *inf*) жилище.

dike [daɪk] *n* = **dyke**.

dilapidated [dɪ'læpɪdeɪtɪd] *adj* вéтхий*.

dilate [daɪ'leɪt] *vi* расширяться (расшириться* *perf*) ♦ *vt* расширять (расширить* *perf*).

dilatory ['dɪlətərɪ] *adj* (*influence*) замедляющий; (*person*) медлительный* (медлителен).

dilemma [daɪ'lɛmə] *n* дилéмма; **to be in a** ~ стоять* (*impf*) пéред дилéммой.

diligence ['dɪlɪdʒəns] *n* усéрдие, прилежáние.

diligent ['dɪlɪdʒənt] *adj* (*worker*) усéрдный* (усéрден), прилéжный* (прилéжен); (*work*) тщáтельный* (тщáтелен).

dill [dɪl] *n* укрóп*; (*seed*) укрóпное сéмя*.

dilly-dally ['dɪlɪ'dælɪ] *vi* мéшкать (*impf*).

dilute [daɪ'lu:t] *vt* (*liquid*) разбавлять (разбáвить* *perf*); (*belief, principle*) ослаблять (ослáбить* *perf*) ♦ *adj*

разба́вленный (разба́влен).
dim [dɪm] *adj* (*outline, feeling, memory*)
сму́тный* (сму́тен); (*light*) ту́склый* (тускл);
(*room*) пло́хо освещённый (освещён);
(*eyesight*) сла́бый* (слаб); (*future, prospects*)
мра́чный* (мра́чен); (*inf: person*) тупо́й*
(туп) ◆ *vt* (*also US: light*) приглуша́ть
(приглуши́ть* *perf*); **to take a ~ view of sth**
неодобри́тельно смотре́ть* (*impf*) на что-н.
dime [daɪm] *n* (*US*) десятице́нтовая моне́та.
dimension [daɪˈmɛnʃən] *n* (*measurement*)
измере́ние; (*also pl: scale, size*) разме́ры *mpl*;
(*aspect*) аспе́кт.
diminish [dɪˈmɪnɪʃ] *vi* уменьша́ться
(уме́ньшиться *perf*) ◆ *vt* (*belittle*) принижа́ть
(прини́зить* *perf*).
diminished [dɪˈmɪnɪʃt] *adj*: **~ responsibility**
(*LAW*) ограни́ченная отве́тственность *f*.
diminutive [dɪˈmɪnjʊtɪv] *adj* кро́шечный ◆ *n*
(*LING*) уменьши́тельно-ласка́тельное сло́во.
dimly [ˈdɪmlɪ] *adv* (*glow, illuminate*) ту́скло;
(*see, remember*) сму́тно.
dimmer [ˈdɪmə^r] *n* (*also: ~ switch*) регуля́тор
освещённости.
dimmers [ˈdɪməz] *npl* (*US: dipped headlights*)
бли́жний свет *msg* фар; (*parking lights*)
стоя́ночный свет *msg*.
dimple [ˈdɪmpl] *n* я́мочка*.
dim-witted [ˈdɪmˈwɪtɪd] *adj* (*inf*) тупоу́мный*
(тупоу́мен).
din [dɪn] *n* гро́хот ◆ *vt* (*inf*): **to ~ sth into sb**
вда́лбливать (вдолби́ть* *perf*) что-н в
кого́-н.
dine [daɪn] *vi* обе́дать (пообе́дать *perf*).
diner [ˈdaɪnə^r] *n* (*person*) обе́дающий(-ая) *m(f)*
adj; (*US*) дешёвый рестора́нчик.
dinghy [ˈdɪŋgɪ] *n* (*also: sailing ~*) шлю́пка*;
(*also: rubber ~*) надувна́я ло́дка.
dingy [ˈdɪndʒɪ] *adj* (*streets, room*) мра́чный*
(мра́чен); (*clothes, curtains etc*) ве́тхий,
замы́зганный.
dining car [ˈdaɪnɪŋ-] *n* (*BRIT*) ваго́н-рестора́н.
dining room *n* столо́вая *f adj*.
dinner [ˈdɪnə^r] *n* (*evening meal*) у́жин; (*lunch,
banquet*) обе́д.
dinner jacket *n* смо́кинг.
dinner party *n* зва́ный обе́д.
dinner service *n* столо́вый серви́з.
dinner time *n* (*midday*) обе́денное вре́мя* *nt*;
(*evening*) вре́мя* у́жина.
dinosaur [ˈdaɪnəsɔː^r] *n* диноза́вр.
dint [dɪnt] *n*: **by ~ of** посре́дством +*gen*.
diocese [ˈdaɪəsɪs] *n* епа́рхия.
dioxide [daɪˈɔksaɪd] *n* двуо́кись *f*.
dip [dɪp] *n* (*slope*) укло́н; (*depression*) впа́дина;
(*CULIN*) со́ус*; (*AGR: for sheep*)
дезинфици́рующий раство́р ◆ *vt* (*immerse*)
погружа́ть (погрузи́ть* *perf*), окуна́ть

(окуну́ть *perf*); (: *in liquid*) обма́кивать
(обмакну́ть *perf*); (*BRIT: AUT: lights*) приглу-
ша́ть (приглуши́ть* *perf*) ◆ *vi* (*ground, road*)
идти́* (пойти́* *perf*) под укло́н; **to go for a ~ in
the sea** окуна́ться (окуну́ться *perf*) в мо́ре.
Dip. *abbr* (*BRIT*) = **diploma**.
diphtheria [dɪfˈθɪərɪə] *n* дифтери́т.
diphthong [ˈdɪfθɔŋ] *n* дифто́нг.
diploma [dɪˈpləumə] *n* дипло́м.
diplomacy [dɪˈpləuməsɪ] *n* диплома́тия.
diplomat [ˈdɪpləmæt] *n* диплома́т.
diplomatic [dɪpləˈmætɪk] *adj* (*POL*)
дипломати́ческий*; (*tactful*)
дипломати́чный* (дипломати́чен); **to break
off ~ relations (with)** (*POL*) разрыва́ть
(разорва́ть* *perf*) дипломати́ческие
отноше́ния (с +*instr*).
diplomatic corps *n* дипломати́ческий*
ко́рпус*.
diplomatic immunity *n* дипломати́ческая
неприкоснове́нность *f*.
dip stick *n* (*BRIT: AUT*) щуп для измере́ния
у́ровня ма́сла.
dip switch *n* (*BRIT: AUT*) переключа́тель *m*
све́та фар.
dire [daɪə^r] *adj* (*consequences*) злове́щий*;
(*poverty, situation*) жу́ткий*.
direct [daɪˈrɛkt] *adj* прямо́й ◆ *adv* пря́мо ◆ *vt*
(*company, project etc*) руководи́ть* (*impf*)
+*instr*; (*play, film, programme*) ста́вить*
(поста́вить* *perf*); (*letter*): **to ~ to** направля́ть
(напра́вить* *perf*) +*dat*; (*attention, remark*): **to
~ (towards or at)** направля́ть (напра́вить*
perf) (на +*acc*); (*order*): **to ~ sb to do** веле́ть
(*impf*) кому́-н +*infin*; **can you ~ me to ...?** Вы не
ука́жете, где нахо́дится ...?
direct access *n* (*COMPUT*) прямо́й до́ступ.
direct cost *n* (*COMM*) прямы́е затра́ты *fpl*.
direct current *n* постоя́нный ток.
direct debit *n* (*BRIT: COMM*) прямо́е
дебетова́ние.
direct dialling *n* автомати́ческая телефо́нная
связь *f*.
direct hit *n* (*MIL*) прямо́е попада́ние.
direction [dɪˈrɛkʃən] *n* (*way*) направле́ние; (*TV,
CINEMA*) постано́вка; **~s** *npl* (*instructions*)
указа́ния *ntpl*; **to have a good sense of ~**
хорошо́ ориенти́роваться (*impf/perf*); **~s for
use** инстру́кция (по эксплуата́ции); **to ask for
~s (to)** спра́шивать (спроси́ть* *perf*) доро́гу
(к +*dat*); **in the ~ of** в направле́нии +*gen*.
directional [dɪˈrɛkʃənl] *adj* (*TECH*)
напра́вленный.
directive [dɪˈrɛktɪv] *n* (*POL, ADMIN*) директи́ва,
постановле́ние; **a government ~**
прави́тельственное постановле́ние.
direct labour *n* (*BRIT*) постоя́нная рабо́чая
си́ла.

---

* marks translations which have irregular inflections. The Russian-English side of the dictionary gives inflectional information.

directly [dɪ'rɛktlɪ] *adv* пря́мо; (*at once*) сейча́с же; (*as soon as*) как то́лько.

direct mail *n* прода́жа това́ров по по́чте.

direct-mail shot [dɪ'rɛkt'meɪl-] *n* (*BRIT*) почто́вая рекла́ма.

directness [daɪ'rɛktnɪs] *n* прямота́.

director [dɪ'rɛktə'] *n* (*COMM*) дире́ктор*; (*of project*) руководи́тель(ница) *m(f)*; (*TV, RADIO, CINEMA*) режиссёр.

Director of Public Prosecutions *n* (*BRIT*) Гла́вный прокуро́р.

directory [dɪ'rɛktərɪ] *n* (*also COMPUT*) спра́вочник; (*also: street* ~) указа́тель *m*.

directory enquiries (*US* **directory assistance**) *n* (телефо́нная) спра́вочная *f adj*.

dirt [də:t] *n* грязь* *f*; **to treat sb like** ~ ни во что́ не ста́вить (*impf*) кого́-н.

dirt-cheap ['də:t'tʃi:p] *adv* по дешёвке.

dirt road *n* грунтова́я доро́га.

dirty ['də:tɪ] *adj* гря́зный* ♦ *vt* па́чкать (испа́чкать *perf*).

dirty trick *n* зла́я шу́тка*.

disability [dɪsə'bɪlɪtɪ] *n* (*physical*) инвали́дность *f no pl*; (*mental*) у́мственная неполноце́нность *f*; **physical disabilities** физи́ческие недоста́тки.

disability allowance *n* посо́бие по инвали́дности.

disable [dɪs'eɪbl] *vt* (*subj: illness, accident*) кале́чить (искале́чить *perf*); (*tank, gun*) выводи́ть* (вы́вести* *perf*) из стро́я.

disabled [dɪs'eɪbld] *adj* (*mentally*) у́мственно неполноце́нный; (*physically*): ~ **person** инвали́д ♦ *npl*: **the** ~ инвали́ды *mpl*.

disabuse [dɪsə'bju:z] *vt*: **to** ~ **sb (of)** разуверя́ть (разуве́рить *perf*) кого́-н в (+*prp*).

disadvantage [dɪsəd'vɑ:ntɪdʒ] *n* недоста́ток*; **to be at a** ~ быть* (*impf*) в невы́годном положе́нии.

disadvantaged [dɪsəd'vɑ:ntɪdʒd] *adj* (*person, region*) обездо́ленный* (обездо́лен).

disadvantageous [dɪsædvə:n'teɪdʒəs] *adj* невы́годный* (невы́годен).

disaffected [dɪsə'fɛktɪd] *adj* разочаров-а́вшийся.

disaffection [dɪsə'fɛkʃən] *n*: ~ (**with**) поте́ря дове́рия (к +*dat*).

disagree [dɪsə'gri:] *vi* (*differ*) расходи́ться* (разойти́сь* *perf*); (*be against, think otherwise*): **to** ~ (**with**) не соглаша́ться (согласи́ться* *perf*) (с +*instr*); **I** ~ **with you** я с Ва́ми не согла́сен; **we** ~ **on many things** мы во мно́гом расхо́димся; **garlic** ~**s with me** я пло́хо переношу́ чесно́к.

disagreeable [dɪsə'gri:əbl] *adj* неприя́тный* (неприя́тен).

disagreement [dɪsə'gri:mənt] *n* (*lack of consensus, argument*) разногла́сие; (*opposition*): ~ **with sb/sth** несогла́сие с кем-н/чем-н; **to have a** ~ **with sb** име́ть (*impf*) разногла́сие с кем-н.

disallow ['dɪsə'lau] *vt* (*appeal*) отклоня́ть (отклони́ть *perf*); (*goal*) не засчи́тывать (засчита́ть *perf*).

disappear [dɪsə'pɪə'] *vi* исчеза́ть (исче́знуть* *perf*).

disappearance [dɪsə'pɪərəns] *n* исчезнове́ние.

disappoint [dɪsə'pɔɪnt] *vt* разочаро́вывать (разочарова́ть *perf*).

disappointed [dɪsə'pɔɪntɪd] *adj* разочаро́ванный* (разочаро́ван).

disappointing [dɪsə'pɔɪntɪŋ] *adj*: **the film is rather** ~ э́тот фильм разочаро́вывает; **the election results were** ~ **for the Democrats** демокра́ты бы́ли разочаро́ваны результа́тами вы́боров.

disappointment [dɪsə'pɔɪntmənt] *n* разочарова́ние.

disapproval [dɪsə'pru:vəl] *n* неодобре́ние.

disapprove [dɪsə'pru:v] *vi*: **to** ~ (**of**) не одобря́ть (*impf*) (+*acc*).

disapproving [dɪsə'pru:vɪŋ] *adj* неодобри́тельный* (неодобри́телен).

disarm [dɪs'ɑ:m] *vt* (*MIL*) разоружа́ть (разоружи́ть *perf*); (*fig*) обезору́живать (обезору́жить *perf*) ♦ *vi* разоружа́ться (разоружи́ться *perf*).

disarmament [dɪs'ɑ:məmənt] *n* разоруже́ние.

disarming [dɪs'ɑ:mɪŋ] *adj* обезору́живающий.

disarray [dɪsə'reɪ] *n*: **in** ~ (*army, organization, thoughts*) в смяте́нии; (*hair, clothes*) в беспоря́дке; **to throw into** ~ приводи́ть* (привести́* *perf*) в смяте́ние.

disaster [dɪ'zɑ:stə'] *n* (*natural*) бе́дствие; (*man-made, also fig*) катастро́фа.

disaster area *n* (*also fig*) зо́на бе́дствия.

disastrous [dɪ'zɑ:strəs] *adj* губи́тельный* (губи́телен).

disband [dɪs'bænd] *vt* распуска́ть (распусти́ть* *perf*) ♦ *vi* расформиро́вываться (расформирова́ться *perf*).

disbelief ['dɪsbə'li:f] *n* неве́рие; **in** ~ в недоуме́нии.

disbelieve ['dɪsbə'li:v] *vt* (*person*) не ве́рить (*impf*) +*dat*; (*story*) не ве́рить (*impf*) +*dat or* в +*acc*; **I don't** ~ **you** я не могу́ сказа́ть, что не ве́рю Вам.

disc [dɪsk] *n* (*ANAT*) межпозвоно́чный хрящ*; (*record*) диск; (*COMPUT*) = **disk**.

disc. *abbr* (*COMM*) = **discount**.

discard [dɪs'kɑ:d] *vt* (*old things*) выбра́сывать (вы́бросить* *perf*); (*idea, plan*) отбра́сывать (отбро́сить* *perf*).

disc brake *n* ди́сковый то́рмоз*.

discern [dɪ'sə:n] *vt* (*see*) различа́ть (различи́ть *perf*); (*identify*) определя́ть (определи́ть *perf*).

discernible [dɪ'sə:nəbl] *adj* различи́мый.

discerning [dɪ'sə:nɪŋ] *adj* разбо́рчивый (разбо́рчив); **he has** ~ **tastes** у него́ то́нкий вкус.

discharge [*vt* dɪs'tʃɑ:dʒ, *n* 'dɪstʃɑ:dʒ] *vt* (*duties*) выполня́ть (вы́полнить *perf*); (*debt*)

распла́чиваться (расплати́ться* *perf*) с +*instr*;
(*waste*) выбра́сывать (вы́бросить* *perf*);
(*ELEC*) разряжа́ть (разряди́ть* *perf*); (*pus etc*)
выделя́ть (*impf*); (*patient*) выпи́сывать
(вы́писать* *perf*); (*employee*) увольня́ть
(уво́лить *perf*); (*soldier*) демобилизова́ть
(*impf/perf*); (*defendant*) опра́вдывать
(оправда́ть *perf*) ♦ *n* (*CHEM, MED*) выделе́ние;
(*ELEC*) разря́д; (*of patient*) вы́писка; (*of
employee*) увольне́ние; (*of soldier*)
демобилиза́ция; (*of defendant*) оправда́ние;
to ~ a gun разряжа́ть (разряди́ть* *perf*)
ружьё.
discharged bankrupt [dɪsˈtʃɑːdʒd-] *n лицо́,
восстано́вленное в права́х по́сле
банкро́тства.*
disciple [dɪˈsaɪpl] *n* (*REL*) апо́стол; (*fig*)
учени́к*(-и́ца).
disciplinary [ˈdɪsɪplɪnərɪ] *adj* (*code, measures*)
дисциплина́рный; **~ problems** пробле́мы с
дисципли́ной; **to take ~ action against sb**
принима́ть (приня́ть* *perf*) дисциплина́рные
ме́ры к кому́-н.
discipline [ˈdɪsɪplɪn] *n* дисципли́на ♦ *vt* (*train*)
дисциплини́ровать (*impf/perf*); (*punish*)
налага́ть (наложи́ть* *perf*) дисциплина́рное
взыска́ние на +*acc*; **to ~ o.s. to do** приуча́ться
(приучи́ться* *perf*) +*impf infin*.
disc jockey *n* диск-жоке́й.
disclaim [dɪsˈkleɪm] *vt* отрица́ть (*impf*).
disclaimer [dɪsˈkleɪməʳ] *n* отка́з от
отве́тственности; **to issue a ~** обнаро́довать
(*perf*) отка́з *or* отрече́ние от отве́тств-
енности.
disclose [dɪsˈkləuz] *vt* раскрыва́ть (раскры́ть*
perf).
disclosure [dɪsˈkləuʒəʳ] *n* раскры́тие.
disco [ˈdɪskəu] *n abbr* = **discotheque**.
discolour [dɪsˈkʌləʳ] (*US* **discolor**) *vt*
обесцве́чивать (обесцве́тить* *perf*) ♦ *vi*
обесцве́чиваться (обесцве́титься* *perf*).
discolouration [dɪskʌləˈreɪʃən] (*US*
discoloration) *n* обесцве́чивание.
discoloured [dɪsˈkʌləd] (*US* **discolored**) *adj*
вы́цветший.
discomfort [dɪsˈkʌmfət] *n* (*unease*) нело́вкость
f; (*pain etc*) недомога́ние.
disconcert [dɪskənˈsəːt] *vt* смуща́ть (смути́ть*
perf).
disconcerting [dɪskənˈsəːtɪŋ] *adj*
вызыва́ющий* чу́вство нело́вкости.
disconnect [dɪskəˈnɛkt] *vt* (*pipe, telephone*)
разъединя́ть (разъедини́ть *perf*); (*ELEC,
RADIO*) отключа́ть (отключи́ть *perf*).
disconnected [dɪskəˈnɛktɪd] *adj* (*speech,
thoughts*) бессвя́зный* (бессвя́зен).
disconsolate [dɪsˈkɔnsəlɪt] *adj* неуте́шный*
(неуте́шен), безуте́шный* (безуте́шен).

discontent [dɪskənˈtɛnt] *n* недово́льство.
discontented [dɪskənˈtɛntɪd] *adj*: **~ (with)**
недово́льный* (недово́лен) (+*instr*).
discontinue [dɪskənˈtɪnjuː] *vt* прекраща́ть
(прекрати́ть* *perf*); **"discontinued"** (*COMM*)
"сня́то с произво́дства".
discord [ˈdɪskɔːd] *n* разла́д; (*MUS*) диссона́нс.
discordant [dɪsˈkɔːdənt] *adj* (*fig: note*)
несогласу́ющийся; (*MUS*) диссон-
и́рующий.
discotheque [ˈdɪskəutɛk] *n* дискоте́ка.
discount [*n* ˈdɪskaunt, *vt* dɪsˈkaunt] *n* ски́дка* ♦ *vt*
(*COMM*) снижа́ть (сни́зить* *perf*) це́ну на +*acc*;
(*idea, fact*) не принима́ть (приня́ть* *perf*) в
расчёт; **to give sb a ~ on sth** де́лать (сде́лать
perf) кому́-н ски́дку на что-н; **~ for cash**
ски́дка* при усло́вии опла́ты нали́чными; **at
a ~** со ски́дкой.
discount house *n* (*esp BRIT: FINANCE*) учётный
дом*; (*esp US: also*: **discount store**) *магази́н,
торгу́ющий по сни́женным це́нам.*
discount rate *n* сни́женная цена́.
discourage [dɪsˈkʌrɪdʒ] *vt* (*dishearten*)
отбива́ть (отби́ть* *perf*) жела́ние у +*gen*;
(*advise against*): **to ~ sb from doing**
отгова́ривать (отговори́ть *perf*) кого́-н
+*infin*.
discouragement [dɪsˈkʌrɪdʒmənt] *n* (*feeling*)
разочарова́ние; **to act as a ~ to sb** отбива́ть
(отби́ть* *perf*) охо́ту у кого́-н *or* +*infin or* к
+*dat*.
discouraging [dɪsˈkʌrɪdʒɪŋ] *adj* удруча́ющий.
discourteous [dɪsˈkəːtɪəs] *adj* нелюбе́зный*
(нелюбе́зен).
discover [dɪsˈkʌvəʳ] *vt* обнару́живать
(обнару́жить *perf*).
discovery [dɪsˈkʌvərɪ] *n* (*of object etc*)
откры́тие; (*object etc found*)
обнаруже́ние.
discredit [dɪsˈkrɛdɪt] *vt* дискредити́ровать
(*impf/perf*) ♦ *n*: **it is to his ~ that he ...** его́
дискредити́рует то, что он ....
discreet [dɪsˈkriːt] *adj* (*tactful*) такти́чный*
(такти́чен); (*careful*) осмотри́тельный*
(осмотри́телен); (*barely noticeable*)
непримѐтный* (примѐтен).
discreetly [dɪsˈkriːtlɪ] *adv* (*see adj*) такти́чно;
осмотри́тельно; незаметно.
discrepancy [dɪsˈkrɛpənsɪ] *n* расхожде́ние.
discretion [dɪsˈkrɛʃən] *n* (*tact*) такти́чность *f*; **at
the ~ of** на усмотре́ние +*gen*; **use your (own)
~** поступа́йте по своему́ усмотре́нию.
discretionary [dɪsˈkrɛʃənrɪ] *adj* (*powers etc*)
дискрецио́нный.
discriminate [dɪsˈkrɪmɪneɪt] *vi*: **to ~ between**
различа́ть (различи́ть *perf*); **to ~ against**
дискримини́ровать (*impf/perf*).
discriminating [dɪsˈkrɪmɪneɪtɪŋ] *adj* (*discerning*)

---

* marks translations which have irregular inflections. The Russian-English side of the dictionary gives inflectional information.

разбо́рчивый (разбо́рчив); (*tax etc*)
дифференциа́льный.

discrimination [dɪskrɪmɪ'neɪʃən] *n* (*bias*)
дискримина́ция; (*discernment*)
разбо́рчивость *f*; **racial ~** ра́совая
дискримина́ция; **sexual ~** дискримина́ция
по полово́му при́знаку.

discus ['dɪskəs] *n* (*object*) диск; (*event*)
мета́ние ди́ска.

discuss [dɪs'kʌs] *vt* обсужда́ть (обсуди́ть*
perf).

discussion [dɪs'kʌʃən] *n* (*talk*) обсужде́ние;
(*debate*) диску́ссия; **the matter is under ~**
э́тот вопро́с обсужда́ется.

disdain [dɪs'deɪn] *n* презре́ние ♦ *vt* презира́ть
(*impf*) ♦ *vi*: **to ~ to do** счита́ть (посчита́ть *perf*)
ни́же своего́ досто́инства +*infin*.

disease [dɪ'ziːz] *n* боле́знь *f*.

diseased [dɪ'ziːzd] *adj* (*also fig*) больно́й*
(бо́лен).

disembark [dɪsɪm'bɑːk] *vt* (*goods*) выгружа́ть
(вы́грузить* *perf*); (*passengers*) выса́живать
(вы́садить* *perf*) ♦ *vi* выса́живаться
(вы́садиться* *perf*).

disembarkation [dɪsɛmbɑː'keɪʃən] *n* (*see vt*)
вы́грузка*; вы́садка*.

disembodied ['dɪsɪm'bɔdɪd] *adj* (*limb, head*)
отчленённый; (*voice*) бестеле́сный.

disembowel ['dɪsɪm'bauəl] *vt* потроши́ть
(вы́потрошить *perf*).

disenchanted ['dɪsɪn'tʃɑːntɪd] *adj*: **~ (with)**
разочаро́ванный* (разочаро́ван) (+*instr*).

disenfranchise ['dɪsɪn'fræntʃaɪz] *vt* (*POL*)
лиша́ть (лиши́ть *perf*) избира́тельных прав;
(*COMM*) лиша́ть (лиши́ть *perf*) франши́зы.

disengage [dɪsɪn'geɪdʒ] *vt* (*TECH*) расцепля́ть
(расцепи́ть* *perf*); (*AUT*): **to ~ the clutch**
выключа́ть (вы́ключить *perf*) сцепле́ние.

disengagement [dɪsɪn'geɪdʒmənt] *n*
освобожде́ние; **military ~** вы́вод войск.

disentangle [dɪsɪn'tæŋgl] *vt* (*from wreckage*)
высвобожда́ть (вы́свободить* *perf*); (*wool,
wire*) распу́тывать (распу́тать *perf*); **to ~ o.s.
(from)** выпу́тываться (вы́путаться *perf*) (из
+*gen*).

disfavour [dɪs'feɪvə] (*US* **disfavor**) *n* неми́лость
f.

disfigure [dɪs'fɪgə] *vt* уро́довать (изуро́довать
perf).

disgorge [dɪs'gɔːdʒ] *vt* (*subj: river*)
выбра́сывать (вы́бросить* *perf*); (:
building, vehicle) изверга́ть (изве́ргнуть*
perf).

disgrace [dɪs'greɪs] *n* позо́р ♦ *vt* позо́рить
(опозо́рить *perf*).

disgraceful [dɪs'greɪsful] *adj* позо́рный*
(позо́рен).

disgruntled [dɪs'grʌntld] *adj* недово́льный*
(недово́лен).

disguise [dɪs'gaɪz] *n* (*make-up, costume*)
маскиро́вка*; (*art*) гримиро́вка, маскиро́вка

♦ *vt* (*object*) маскирова́ть (замаскирова́ть
perf); (*feelings*) скрыва́ть (скрыть* *perf*);
(*person*): **to ~ (as)** (*dress up*) переодева́ть
(переоде́ть* *perf*) (+*instr*); (*make up*)
гримирова́ть (загримирова́ть *perf*) (под
+*acc*); **in ~** (*person*) переоде́тый; **to ~ o.s. as**
переодева́ться (переоде́ться* *perf*) +*instr*;
there's no disguising the fact that ... нельзя́
скрыть того́, что ....

disgust [dɪs'gʌst] *n* отвраще́ние ♦ *vt* внуша́ть
(внуши́ть *perf*) отвраще́ние +*dat*; **she walked
off in ~** она́ ушла́ в знак проте́ста.

disgusting [dɪs'gʌstɪŋ] *adj* отврати́тельный*
(отврати́телен).

dish [dɪʃ] *n* (*plate, food*) блю́до; (*also: satellite
~*) параболи́ческая анте́нна; **to do** *or* **wash
the ~es** мыть* (вы́мыть* *perf*) посу́ду

► **dish out** *vt* (*money, advice etc*) раздава́ть*
(разда́ть* *perf*); (*food*) раскла́дывать
(разложи́ть* *perf*) (по таре́лкам)

► **dish up** *vt* (*food*) подава́ть* (пода́ть* *perf*) к
столу́; (*inf: facts*) преподноси́ть*
(преподнести́* *perf*).

dishcloth ['dɪʃklɔθ] *n* тря́пка* для мытья́
посу́ды.

dishearten [dɪs'hɑːtn] *vt* приводи́ть*
(привести́* *perf*) в уны́ние.

dishevelled [dɪ'ʃevəld] (*US* **disheveled**) *adj*
растрёпанный* (растрёпан).

dishonest [dɪs'ɔnɪst] *adj* нече́стный*
(нече́стен).

dishonesty [dɪs'ɔnɪstɪ] *n* нече́стность *f*.

dishonour [dɪs'ɔnə] (*US* **dishonor**) *n* бесче́стье.

dishonourable [dɪs'ɔnərəbl] *adj* бесче́стный*
(бесче́стен).

dish soap *n* (*US*) хозя́йственное мы́ло*.

dishtowel ['dɪʃtauəl] *n* (*esp US*) ку́хонное *or*
посу́дное полоте́нце*.

dishwasher ['dɪʃwɔʃə] *n* (*machine*)
посудомо́ечная маши́на.

dishy [dɪʃɪ] *adj* (*inf*): **~ bloke** клёвый па́рень *m*.

disillusion [dɪsɪ'luːʒən] *vt* разочаро́вывать
(разочарова́ть *perf*) ♦ *n* разочарова́ние; **to
become ~ed (with)** разочаро́вываться
(разочарова́ться *perf*) ι в +*prp*).

disillusionment [dɪsɪ'luːʒənmənt] *n*
разочарова́ние.

disincentive [dɪsɪn'sɛntɪv] *n* сде́рживающее
обстоя́тельство; **to be a ~ to sb** явля́ться
(*impf*) сде́рживающим обстоя́тельством для
кого́-н.

disinclined [dɪsɪn'klaɪnd] *adj*: **I am ~ to do it** мне
не хо́чется э́то де́лать.

disinfect [dɪsɪn'fɛkt] *vt* дезинфици́ровать (*impf
perf*).

disinfectant [dɪsɪn'fɛktənt] *n* дезинфиц-
и́рующее сре́дство.

disinflation [dɪsɪn'fleɪʃən] *n* (*ECON*) дез-
инфля́ция.

disinformation [dɪsɪnfə'meɪʃən] *n*
дезинформа́ция.

disingenuous [dısın'dʒɛnjuəs] *adj*
неискренний* (неискренен).
disinherit [dısın'hɛrıt] *vt*: **to ~ sb** лишáть
(лишúть *perf*) когó-н наслéдства.
disintegrate [dıs'ıntıgreıt] *vi* (*break up*)
распадáться (распáсться* *perf*) на чáсти;
(*decay*) разлагáться (разложúться* *perf*).
disinterested [dıs'ıntrəstıd] *adj* (*impartial*)
бескорýстный* (бескорýстен).
disjointed [dıs'dʒɔıntıd] *adj* бессвязный*
(бессвязен).
disk [dısk] *n* (*COMPUT*) диск; **single-/double-
sided ~** односторóнний/двустóрóнний
диск.
disk drive *n* дисковóд.
diskette [dıs'kɛt] *n* (*US*) = **disk**.
disk operating system *n* дúсковая
операциóнная систéма.
dislike [dıs'laık] *n* (*feeling*) неприязнь *f*; (*usu pl*:
object of dislike) нелюбúмая вещь *f* ◆ *vt* не
любúть* (*impf*) +*gen*; **to take a ~ to sb/sth**
невзлюбúть* (*perf*) когó-н/чтó-н; **I ~ the idea**
мне не нрáвится эта идéя; **he ~s cooking** он
не любúт готóвить.
dislocate ['dısləkeıt] *vt* вúвихнуть (*perf*); **he has
~d his shoulder** он вúвихнул плечó.
dislodge [dıs'lɔdʒ] *vt* смещáть (сместúть* *perf*).
disloyal [dıs'lɔıəl] *adj*: **~ (to)** невéрный*
(невéрен) (+*dat*).
dismal ['dızml] *adj* унúлый (унúл), мрáчный*
(мрáчен); **a ~ failure** жáлкий провáл.
dismantle [dıs'mæntl] *vt* разбирáть
(разобрáть* *perf*).
dismast [dıs'mɑ:st] *vt* (*NAUT*) снимáть (снять*
perf) мáчты с +*gen*.
dismay [dıs'meı] *n* смятéние ◆ *vt* приводúть*
(привестú* *perf*) в смятéние; **much to my ~** к
моемý смятéнию; **he gasped in ~** он áхнул в
смятéнии.
dismiss [dıs'mıs] *vt* (*worker*) увольнять
(увóлить *perf*); (*pupils, soldiers*) распускáть
(распустúть *perf*); (*LAW: case*) прекращáть
(прекратúть* *perf*); (*possibility, idea*)
отбрáсывать (отбрóсить* *perf*).
dismissal [dıs'mısl] *n* (*sacking*) увольнéние.
dismount [dıs'maunt] *vi* (*from horse*)
спéшиваться (спéшиться *perf*); (*from bicycle*)
слезáть (слезть *perf*).
disobedience [dısə'bi:dıəns] *n* непослушáние.
disobedient [dısə'bi:dıənt] *adj* непослýшный*
(непослýшен).
disobey [dısə'beı] *vt* не слýшаться
(послýшаться *perf*).
disorder [dıs'ɔ:də] *n* беспорядок*; (*MED*)
расстрóйство; **civil ~** социáльные
беспорядки.
disorderly [dıs'ɔ:dəlı] *adj* (*room etc*)
беспорядочный; (*meeting*)

неорганизóванный* (неорганизóван);
(*behaviour*) бесчúнствующий.
disorderly conduct *n* нарушéние
общéственного порядка.
disorganize [dıs'ɔ:gənaız] *vt* дезорганизовáть
(*impf/perf*).
disorganized [dıs'ɔ:gənaızd] *adj*
неорганизóванный.
disorientated [dıs'ɔ:rıɛnteıtıd] *adj* лишённый
(лишён) чýвства ориентáции.
disown [dıs'əun] *vt* (*action*) откáзываться
(отказáться* *perf*) от +*gen*; (*person*)
отрекáться (отрéчься* *perf*) от +*gen*.
disparaging [dıs'pærıdʒın] *adj* пренебрéж-
úтельный* (пренебрежúтелен); **to be ~ about
sb/sth** относúться* (отнестúсь* *perf*)
пренебрежúтельно к комý-н/чемý-н.
disparate ['dıspərıt] *adj* несравнúмый.
disparity [dıs'pærıtı] *n* нерáвенство.
dispassionate [dıs'pæʃənət] *adj* бесстрáстный*
(бесстрáстен).
dispatch [dıs'pætʃ] *vt* (*send*) отправлять
(отпрáвить* *perf*); (*deal with*) раздéлываться
(раздéлаться *perf*) с +*instr*; (*kill*) покóнчить
(*perf*) с +*instr* ◆ *n* (*sending*) отпрáвка; (*PRESS*)
сообщéние; (*MIL*) донесéние.
dispatch department *n* отдéл отпрáвки.
dispatch rider *n* (*MIL*) мотоциклúст связи.
dispel [dıs'pɛl] *vt* рассéивать (рассéять *perf*).
dispensary [dıs'pɛnsərı] *n* аптéка.
dispensation [dıspən'seıʃən] *n* (*of justice,
treatment*) осуществлéние; (*permission*):
(*special*) **~** осóбое разрешéние.
dispense [dıs'pɛns] *vt* (*medicines*)
приготовлять (приготóвить* *perf*) и
отпускáть (отпустúть* *perf*); (*charity, advice*)
раздавáть (раздáть* *perf*); **to ~ justice**
отправлять (*impf*) правосýдие
▶ **dispense with** *vt fus* (*do without*)
обходúться* (обойтúсь* *perf*) без +*gen*; (*make
unnecessary*) освобождáть (освободúть*
perf) от необходúмости +*gen*.
dispenser [dıs'pɛnsə] *n* (*machine*) торгóвый
автомáт.
dispensing chemist [dıs'pɛnsın-] *n* (*BRIT: shop*)
аптéка.
dispersal [dıs'pə:sl] *n* рассéивание.
disperse [dıs'pə:s] *vt* (*objects*) рассéивать
(рассéять *perf*); (*crowd*) разгонять (разо-
гнáть* *perf*); (*knowledge*) распространять
(распространúть *perf*) ◆ *vi* (*crowd, clouds*)
рассéиваться (рассéяться *perf*).
dispirited [dıs'pırıtıd] *adj* удручённый*
(удручён).
displace [dıs'pleıs] *vt* замещáть (заместúть*
perf).
displaced person [dıs'pleıst-] *n* перемещённое
лицó*.

---

displacement [dɪs'pleɪsmənt] *n* замещéние; (*PHYS*) вытеснéние.

display [dɪs'pleɪ] *n* демонстрáция; (*exhibition*) выставка*; (*pej: bad manners*) выставлéние напокáз*; (*COMPUT, TECH*) дисплéй ♦ *vt* (*emotion, quality*) выкáзывать (выказать* *perf*); (*goods, exhibits*) выставлять (выставить* *perf*) напокáз); (*results, departure times*) покáзывать (показáть* *perf*); **on ~** (*exhibits*) на выставке; (*goods in window*) на витрине.

display advertising *n* витринно-выставочная реклáма.

displease [dɪs'pliːz] *vt* раздражáть (раздражить *perf*).

displeased [dɪs'pliːzd] *adj*: **~ with** раздражённый* (раздражён) +*instr*.

displeasure [dɪs'plɛʒə*] *n* неудовóльствие.

disposable [dɪs'pəuzəbl] *adj* (*lighter, bottle*) однорáзового употреблéния*; (*syringe*) однорáзовый; **~ income** дохóд, котóрым населéние располагáет пóсле уплáты налóгов.

disposable nappy *n* (*BRIT*) однорáзовая пелёнка*.

disposal [dɪs'pəuzl] *n* (*of goods for sale*) реализáция, (*of property etc: by selling*) распродáжа; (: *by giving away*) удалéние; (*of rubbish*) удалéние; **to have sth at one's ~** располагáть (*impf*) чем-н; **to put sth at sb's ~** предоставлять (предостáвить* *perf*) что-н в чьё-н распоряжéние.

dispose [dɪs'pəuz] *vi*: **~ of** (*body, unwanted goods*) избавляться (избáвиться* *perf*) от +*gen*; (*problem, task*) управляться (упрáвиться* *perf*) с +*instr*; (*COMM: stock*) реализóвывать (реализовáть* *perf*).

disposed [dɪs'pəuzd] *adj*: **I am ~ to do** я настрóен +*infin*; **to be well ~ towards sb** хорошó относиться* (*impf*) к комý-н.

disposition [dɪspə'zɪʃən] *n* (*nature*) нрав; (*inclination*) склóнность *f*.

dispossess ['dɪspə'zɛs] *vt*: **to ~ sb (of)** лишáть (лишить* *perf*) когó-н (+*gen*).

disproportion [dɪsprə'pɔːʃən] *n* диспропóрция.

disproportionate [dɪsprə'pɔːʃənət] *adj* (*excessive*) непропорционáльно большóй; **our income is ~ to our expenditure** нáши дохóды не соизмеримы с нáшими расхóдами.

disprove [dɪs'pruːv] *vt* опровергáть (опровéргнуть* *perf*).

dispute [dɪs'pjuːt] *n* (*domestic*) ссóра; (*POL, MIL, INDUSTRY*) спор; (*LAW*) тяжба ♦ *vt* оспáривать (оспóрить *perf*); **to be in** *or* **under ~** (*matter*) опротестóвываться (*impf*); (*territory*) оспáриваться (*impf*).

disqualification [dɪskwɔlɪfɪ'keɪʃən] *n*: **~ from sth** лишéние прáва на учáстие в чём-н; **~ from driving** (*BRIT*) лишéние водительских прав.

disqualify [dɪs'kwɔlɪfaɪ] *vt* (*SPORT*) дисквалифицировать (*impf/perf*); **to ~ sb for sth/from doing** (*status, situation*) лишáть (лишить *perf*) когó-н прáва на учáстие в чём-н/+*infin*; (*authority*) лишáть (лишить *perf*) +*gen*; **to ~ sb from driving** (*BRIT*) лишáть (лишить *perf*) когó-н водительских прав.

disquiet [dɪs'kwaɪət] *n* беспокóйство.

disquieting [dɪs'kwaɪətɪŋ] *adj* тревóжный* (тревóжен).

disregard [dɪsrɪ'gɑːd] *vt* пренебрегáть (пренебрéчь* *perf*) ♦ *n*: **~ (for)** пренебрежéние (к +*dat*).

disrepair ['dɪsrɪ'pɛə*] *n*: **to fall into ~** приходить* (прийти* *perf*) в негóдность.

disreputable [dɪs'rɛpjutəbl] *adj* (*person, behaviour*) недостóйный.

disrepute ['dɪsrɪ'pjuːt] *n* дурнáя слáва; **to fall into ~** приобретáть (приобрести* *perf*) дурнýю слáву; **to bring sb/sth into ~** навлекáть (навлéчь* *perf*) на когó-н/что-н дурнýю слáву.

disrespectful [dɪsrɪ'spɛktful] *adj* непочтительный* (непочтителен).

disrupt [dɪs'rʌpt] *vt* нарушáть (нарýшить *perf*).

disruption [dɪs'rʌpʃən] *n* (*interruption*) нарушéние; (*disturbance*) социáльные беспорядки *mpl*.

disruptive [dɪs'rʌptɪv] *adj* (*influence*) подрывнóй; (*action*) разрушительный.

dissatisfaction [dɪssætɪs'fækʃən] *n* недовóльство, неудовлетворённость *f*.

dissatisfied [dɪs'sætɪsfaɪd] *adj*: **~ (with)** недовóльный* (недовóлен) (+*instr*).

dissect [dɪ'sɛkt] *vt* (*ANAT*) вскрывáть (вскрыть* *perf*); (*theory, article*) анализировать (проанализировать *perf*).

disseminate [dɪ'sɛmɪneɪt] *vt* распространять (распространить *perf*).

dissent [dɪ'sɛnt] *n* инакомыслие; **~ from the party line** отхóд от партийной линии.

dissenter [dɪ'sɛntə*] *n* (*REL, POL*) инакомыслящий*(-ая) *m(f)* adj.

dissertation [dɪsə'teɪʃən] *n* диссертáция.

disservice [dɪs'səːvɪs] *n*: **to do sb a ~** окáзывать (оказáть* *perf*) комý-н плохýю услýгу.

dissident ['dɪsɪdnt] *adj* (*faction, voice*) диссидéнтский ♦ *n* (*POL, REL*) диссидéнт.

dissimilar [dɪ'sɪmɪlə*] *adj*: **~ (to)** несхóдный (с +*instr*); **this is not ~ to ...** это схóдно с +*instr* ....

dissipate ['dɪsɪpeɪt] *vt* (*heat, clouds*) рассéивать (рассéять *perf*); (*money, effort*) растрáчивать (растрáтить* *perf*).

dissipated ['dɪsɪpeɪtɪd] *adj* (*debauched*) распýщенный* (распýщен).

dissociate [dɪ'səuʃɪeɪt] *vt*: **to ~ from** отделять (отделить* *perf*) от +*gen*; **to ~ o.s. from** отмежёвываться (отмежевáться *perf*) от +*gen*.

dissolute ['dɪsəluːt] *adj* развратный* (разврáтен).

dissolution [dɪsə'luːʃən] *n* (*of parliament,*

organization) ро́спуск; (*of marriage*)
расторже́ние.

dissolve [dɪ'zɔlv] *vt* (*substance*) растворя́ть
(раствори́ть *perf*); (*organization, parliament*)
распуска́ть (распусти́ть* *perf*); (*marriage*)
расторга́ть (расто́ргнуть* *perf*) ◆ *vi*
растворя́ться (раствори́ться *perf*); **to ~ in(to)
tears** залива́ться (зали́ться* *perf*) слеза́ми.

dissuade [dɪ'sweɪd] *vt*: **to ~ sb (from sth)**
отгова́ривать (отговори́ть *perf*) кого́-н (от
чего́-н).

distaff ['dɪstɑ:f] *n*: **on the ~ side** по же́нской
ли́нии.

distance ['dɪstns] *n* (*in space*) расстоя́ние; (*in
sport*) диста́нция; (*in time*) отдалённость *f*;
(*reserve*) сде́ржанность *f* ◆ *vt*: **to ~ o.s. (from)**
отдаля́ться (отдали́ться *perf*) (от +*gen*); **in
the ~** вдалеке́, вдали́; **from a ~** издалека́,
и́здали; **what's the ~ to London?** каково́
расстоя́ние до Ло́ндона; **into the ~** вдаль;
it's within walking ~ туда́ мо́жно дойти́
пешко́м; **the town is some ~ from the sea**
го́род нахо́дится в не́котором отдале́нии
от мо́ря; **at a ~ of two metres** на расстоя́нии
двух ме́тров; **keep your ~**! соблюда́йте
диста́нцию!; **to keep sb at a ~** держа́ть (*impf*)
кого́-н на расстоя́нии.

distant ['dɪstnt] *adj* (*place, time*) далёкий*;
(*relative*) да́льний*; (*manner*) сде́ржанный*;
in the ~ past/future в далёком про́шлом/-
бу́душем.

distaste [dɪs'teɪst] *n* неприя́знь *f*.

distasteful [dɪs'teɪstful] *adj* неприя́тный*
(неприя́тен).

Dist. Atty. *abbr* (*US*) = **district attorney.**

distemper [dɪs'tempə'] *n* (*paint*) те́мпера;
(*disease: of dogs*) (соба́чья) чума́.

distend [dɪs'tend] *vt* расширя́ть (расши́рить
perf), раздува́ть (разду́ть *perf*) ◆ *vi*
раздува́ться (разду́ться *perf*).

distended [dɪs'tendɪd] *adj* (*stomach*) взду́тый.

distil [dɪs'tɪl] (*US* **distill**) *vt* (*water*)
дистилли́ровать (*impf/perf*); (*whisky*)
перегоня́ть (перегна́ть* *perf*); (*information
etc*) извлека́ть (извле́чь* *perf*).

distillery [dɪs'tɪlərɪ] *n* спи́рто-во́дочный заво́д.

distinct [dɪs'tɪŋkt] *adj* (*clear*) отчётливый
(отчётлив); (*unmistakable*) определённый;
(*different*): **~ (from)** отли́чный* (отли́чен) (от
+*gen*); **as ~ from** в отли́чие от +*gen*.

distinction [dɪs'tɪŋkʃən] *n* (*difference*) отли́чие;
(*honour*) честь *f*; (*in exam*) ≈ "отли́чно"; **to
draw a ~ between** проводи́ть* (провести́*
perf) разли́чие ме́жду +*instr*; **to pass an exam
with ~** сдава́ть* (сдать* *perf*) экза́мен на
отли́чно; **he is a writer of ~** он выдаю́щийся
писа́тель.

distinctive [dɪs'tɪŋktɪv] *adj* (*voice, walk etc*)

своеобра́зный* (своеобра́зен),
характе́рный* (характе́рен); (*feature*)
отличи́тельный.

distinctly [dɪs'tɪŋktlɪ] *adv* (*remember, specify*)
отчётливо; (*unhappy, better*) определённо.

distinguish [dɪs'tɪŋgwɪʃ] *vt* различа́ть
(различи́ть *perf*); **to ~ (between)** проводи́ть*
(провести́* *perf*) разли́чие (ме́жду +*instr*); **to ~
o.s.** отлича́ться (отличи́ться *perf*).

distinguished [dɪs'tɪŋgwɪʃt] *adj* (*eminent*)
выдаю́щийся*; (*in appearance*)
благоро́дный* (благоро́ден).

distinguishing [dɪs'tɪŋgwɪʃɪŋ] *adj* (*feature*)
отличи́тельный.

distort [dɪs'tɔ:t] *vt* искажа́ть (искази́ть* *perf*).

distortion [dɪs'tɔ:ʃən] *n* искаже́ние.

distract [dɪs'trækt] *vt* отвлека́ть (отвле́чь* *perf*).

distracted [dɪs'træktɪd] *adj* (*dreaming*)
невнима́тельный* (невнима́телен); (*look*)
отсу́тствующий*; (*anxious*) встрево́женный*
(встрево́жен).

distraction [dɪs'trækʃən] *n* (*inattention*)
отвлече́ние; (*confusion*) пу́таница;
(*amusement*) развлече́ние; **to drive sb to ~**
доводи́ть* (довести́* *perf*) кого́-н до
безу́мия.

distraught [dɪs'trɔ:t] *adj*: **~ (with)** (*pain, worry*)
обезу́мевший (от +*gen*).

distress [dɪs'tres] *n* (*extreme worry, hardship*)
отча́яние; (*through pain*) страда́ние ◆ *vt*
огорча́ть (огорчи́ть *perf*); **the ship is in ~**
кора́бль те́рпит бе́дствие; **he is in ~** он в
бе́дственном положе́нии; **~ed area** (*BRIT*)
райо́н бе́дствия.

distressing [dɪs'tresɪŋ] *adj* огорчи́тельный*
(огорчи́телен).

distress signal *n* сигна́л бе́дствия.

distribute [dɪs'trɪbju:t] *vt* (*leaflets, prizes etc*)
раздава́ть* (разда́ть* *perf*); (*profits, weight*)
распределя́ть (распредели́ть* *perf*).

distribution [dɪstrɪ'bju:ʃən] *n* (*of goods*)
распростране́ние; (*of profits, weight*)
распределе́ние.

distribution cost *n* изде́ржки* *fpl* обраще́ния.

distributor [dɪs'trɪbjutə'] *n* (*COMM*)
дистрибью́тер; (*AUT, TECH*) распредели́тель
m зажига́ния.

district ['dɪstrɪkt] *n* райо́н.

district attorney *n* (*US*) ≈ окружно́й
прокуро́р.

district council *n* (*BRIT*) райо́нный сове́т.

district nurse *n* (*BRIT*) участко́вая медсестра́*.

distrust [dɪs'trʌst] *n* недове́рие ◆ *vt* не
доверя́ть (*impf*) +*dat*.

distrustful [dɪs'trʌstful] *adj*: **~ (of)**
недове́рчивый (недове́рчив) (к +*dat*).

disturb [dɪs'tə:b] *vt* (*person*) беспоко́ить
(побеспоко́ить *perf*); (*interrupt: thoughts,*

---

* marks translations which have irregular inflections. The Russian-English side of the dictionary gives inflectional information.

peace etc) меша́ть (помеша́ть perf) +dat;
(disorganize) наруша́ть (нару́шить perf);
sorry to ~ you извини́те за беспоко́йство.

disturbance [dɪs'tə:bəns] n расстро́йство;
(political etc) волне́ние ntpl; (violent event)
беспоря́дки mpl; (of mind) расстро́йство; (by
drunks etc) наруше́ние (обще́ственного)
поря́дка; **to cause a ~** (in street etc) вызыва́ть
(вы́звать* perf) беспоря́дки; **~ of the peace**
наруше́ние обще́ственного поря́дка.

disturbed [dɪs'tə:bd] adj (person: upset)
расстро́енный* (расстро́ен); (childhood)
неспоко́йный; **mentally ~** душевнобольно́й;
emotionally ~ психи́чески неуравно-
ве́шенный.

disturbing [dɪs'tə:bɪŋ] adj трево́жный*
(трево́жен).

disuse [dɪs'ju:s] n: **to fall into ~** выходи́ть*
(вы́йти* perf) из употребле́ния.

disused [dɪs'ju:zd] adj забро́шенный*
(забро́шен).

ditch [dɪtʃ] n ров, кана́ва; (for irrigation) кана́л
♦ vt (inf: person, car) броса́ть (бро́сить* perf);
(: plan) забра́сывать (забро́сить* perf).

dither [ˈdɪðəʳ] vi колеба́ться* (impf).

ditto [ˈdɪtəu] adv так же.

divan [dɪˈvæn] n (also: ~ **bed**) тахта́.

dive [daɪv] n (from board) прыжо́к* (в во́ду);
(underwater) ныря́ние; (of submarine)
погруже́ние; (pej: place) забега́ловка ♦ vi
ныря́ть (impf); (submarine) погружа́ться
(погрузи́ться* perf); **to ~ into** (bag, drawer etc)
запуска́ть (запусти́ть* perf) ру́ку в +acc;
(shop, car etc) ныря́ть (нырну́ть perf) в +acc.

diver [ˈdaɪvəʳ] n водола́з.

diverge [daɪˈvə:dʒ] vi расходи́ться (разойти́сь*
perf).

divergent [daɪˈvə:dʒənt] adj расходя́щийся*.

diverse [daɪˈvə:s] adj разнообра́зный*
(разнообра́зен).

diversification [daɪvə:sɪfɪˈkeɪʃən] n
диверсифика́ция.

diversify [daɪˈvə:sɪfaɪ] vi разнообра́зить* (impf);
(COMM) расширя́ть (расши́рить perf) вы́бор.

diversion [daɪˈvə:ʃən] n (BRIT: AUT) объе́зд; (of
attention, funds) отвлече́ние.

diversionary [daɪˈvə:ʃənrɪ] adj диверсио́нный.

diversity [daɪˈvə:sɪtɪ] n разнообра́зие,
многообра́зие.

divert [daɪˈvə:t] vt (funds, attention) отвлека́ть
(отвле́чь* perf); (traffic) отводи́ть* (отвести́*
perf).

divest [daɪˈvɛst] vt: **to ~ sb of** лиша́ть (лиши́ть
perf) кого́-н +gen.

divide [dɪˈvaɪd] vt (separate) разделя́ть
(раздели́ть* perf); (MATH) дели́ть*
(раздели́ть* perf); (share out) дели́ть*
(подели́ть* perf) ♦ vi (cells etc) дели́ться*
(раздели́ться* perf); (road) разделя́ться
(раздели́ться* perf); (people, groups)
дели́ться* or разделя́ться (раздели́ться* perf)

♦ n расхожде́ние; **to ~ (between** or **among)**
дели́ть* (подели́ть* perf) (ме́жду +instr); **40
~d by 5** 40 раздели́ть на 5

▶ **divide out** vt: **to ~ out (between** or **among)**
разделя́ть (раздели́ть* perf) (ме́жду +instr).

divided [dɪˈvaɪdɪd] adj (fig: country, couple)
разделённый* (разделён); **opinions were ~**
мне́ния раздели́лись.

divided highway n (US) шоссе́ nt ind.

dividend [ˈdɪvɪdɛnd] n (COMM) дивиде́нд; (fig):
to pay ~s окупа́ться (окупи́ться perf).

dividend cover n (COMM) покры́тие
дивиде́нда.

dividers [dɪˈvaɪdəz] npl (MATH, TECH)
раздели́тельный ци́ркуль msg.

divine [dɪˈvaɪn] adj (also fig) боже́ственный ♦ vt
(future, truth) уга́дывать (раздели́ть* perf);
(water, metal) иска́ть (impf).

diving [ˈdaɪvɪŋ] n ныря́ние; (SPORT) прыжки́
mpl в во́ду.

diving board n вы́шка* (для прыжко́в в во́ду).

diving suit n гидрокостю́м.

divinity [dɪˈvɪnɪtɪ] n (holiness) боже́ственность
f; (god) божество́*; (SCOL) богосло́вие.

divisible [dɪˈvɪzəbl] adj (MATH): **~ (by)** дели́мый
(на +acc); **to be ~ into** подразделя́ться (impf)
на +acc.

division [dɪˈvɪʒən] n (also MATH) деле́ние;
(sharing out) разделе́ние; (disagreement)
разногла́сие; (BRIT: POL) парла́ментское
голосова́ние, соверша́емое в ра́зных
ко́мнатах; (COMM) подразделе́ние,
отделе́ние; (MIL) диви́зия; (SPORT) ли́га; **~ of
labour** разделе́ние труда́.

divisive [dɪˈvaɪsɪv] adj (tactics, system etc)
вызыва́ющий* разногла́сия.

divorce [dɪˈvɔ:s] n разво́д ♦ vt (spouse)
разводи́ться* (развести́сь* perf) с +instr;
(dissociate) отделя́ть (отдели́ть* perf).

divorced [dɪˈvɔ:st] adj разведённый*
(разведён).

divorcee [dɪvɔ:ˈsi:] n разведённый(-ая) m(f) adj.

divot [ˈdɪvət] n вы́рванный кусо́к* дёрна.

divulge [daɪˈvʌldʒ] vt разглаша́ть
(разгласи́ть* perf).

DIY n abbr (BRIT) = **do-it-yourself**.

dizziness [ˈdɪzɪnɪs] n головокруже́ние.

dizzy [ˈdɪzɪ] adj (height) головокружи́тельный;
~ turn or **spell** при́ступ головокруже́ния; **I
feel ~** у меня́ кру́жится голова́; **to make sb ~**
приводи́ть (привести́* perf) кого́-н в
смяте́ние.

DJ n abbr = **disc jockey**.

d.j. n abbr = **dinner jacket**.

Djakarta [dʒəˈkɑ:tə] n Джака́рта.

DJIA n abbr (US: = Dow-Jones Industrial
Average) и́ндекс Доу Джо́нса.

dl abbr (= decilitre) децили́тр.

DLit(t) n abbr (= Doctor of Literature, Doctor of
Letters) до́ктор филоло́гии.

DLO n abbr (= dead-letter office) Отде́л

недоста́вленной корреспонде́нции.

dm *n abbr* (= *decimetre*) дм= *дециме́тр*.

DMus *n abbr* (= *Doctor of Music*) до́ктор музыкове́дения.

DMZ *n abbr* (= *demilitarized zone*) демилитаризо́ванная зо́на.

DNA *n abbr* (= *deoxyribonucleic acid*) ДНК= *дезоксирибонуклеи́новая кислота́*.

Dnieper ['dniːpə'] *n*: **the ~** Днепр.

KEYWORD
---

do [duː] (*pt* **did**, *pp* **done**) *aux vb* **1** (*in negative constructions and questions*); **I don't understand** я не понима́ю; **she doesn't want it** она́ не хо́чет э́то; **didn't you know?** ра́зве Вы не зна́ли?; **what do you think?** как Вы ду́маете?

2 (*for emphasis*) да; **she does look rather pale** да, она́ вы́глядит о́чень бле́дной; **oh do shut up!** да, замолчи́те же!

3 (*in polite expressions*) пожа́луйста; **do sit down/help yourself** пожа́луйста, сади́тесь/-угоща́йтесь; **do take care!** пожа́луйста, береги́те себя́!

4 (*used to avoid repeating vb*): **she swims better than I do** она́ пла́вает лу́чше меня́ *or* чем я; **do you read/buy newspapers? – yes, I do/no, I don't** Вы чита́ете/покупа́ете газе́ты? – да, (чита́ю/покупа́ю)/нет, (не чита́ю/-покупа́ю); **she lives in Glasgow – so do I** она́ живёт в Гла́зго – и, я то́же; **he didn't like it and neither did we** ни ему́, ни нам э́то не понра́вилось; **who made this mess? – I did** кто здесь насори́л? – я; **he asked me to help him and I did** он попроси́л меня́ помо́чь ему́, что я и сде́лал

5 (*in question tags*) ве́рно, ведь; **you like him, don't you?** он Вам нра́вится, ве́рно?, он ведь Вам нра́вится; **I don't know him, do I?** я ведь его́ не зна́ю

♦ *vt* **1** де́лать (сде́лать *perf*); **what are you doing tonight?** что Вы де́лаете сего́дня ве́чером?; **I've got nothing to do** мне не́чего де́лать; **what can I do for you?** чем я могу́ Вам помо́чь?; **we're doing "Othello" at school** (*studying*) мы прохо́дим "Оте́лло" в шко́ле; (*performing*) мы ста́вим "Оте́лло" в шко́ле; **to do one's teeth** чи́стить* (почи́стить* *perf*) зу́бы; **to do one's hair** причёсываться (причеса́ться *perf*); **to do the washing-up** мыть (помы́ть *perf*) посу́ду

2 (*AUT etc*): **the car was doing 100 (km/h)** маши́на шла со ско́ростью 100 км/ч; **we've done 200 km already** мы уже́ прое́хали 200 км; **he can do 100 mph in that car** на э́той маши́не он мо́жет е́хать со ско́ростью 100 миль в час

♦ *vi* **1** (*act, behave*) де́лать (сде́лать *perf*); **do**

as I do де́лайте, как я; **you did well to react so quickly** Вы молоде́ц, что так бы́стро среаги́ровали

2 (*get on, fare*): **he's doing well/badly at school** он хорошо́/пло́хо у́чится; **the firm is doing well** дела́ в фи́рме иду́т успе́шно; **how do you do?** о́чень прия́тно

3 (*be suitable*) подходи́ть (подойти́ *perf*); **will it do?** э́то подойдёт?

4 (*be sufficient*) хвата́ть (хвати́ть *perf*) +*gen*; **will ten pounds do?** десяти́ фу́нтов хва́тит?; **that'll do** ла́дно, хорошо́; **that'll do!** (*in annoyance*) дово́льно!, хва́тит!; **to make do (with)** обходи́ться (обойти́сь *perf*) (+*instr*)

♦ *n* (*inf*): **we're having a bit of a do on Saturday** у нас бу́дет вечери́нка в суббо́ту; **it was a formal do** э́то был официа́льный приём

► **do away with** *vt fus* (*kill*) прико́нчить (*perf*); (*abolish*) поко́нчить (*perf*) с +*instr*

► **do for** *vt fus* (*BRIT: inf*) убира́ть (*impf*) у +*gen*

► **do up** *vt* (*laces*) завя́зывать (завяза́ть* *perf*); (*dress, buttons*) застёгивать (застегну́ть *perf*); (*room, house*) ремонти́ровать* (отремонти́ровать* *perf*)

► **do with** *vt fus*: **I could do with a drink** я бы вы́пил чего́-нибудь; **I could do with some help** по́мощь мне бы не помеша́ла; **what has it got to do with you?** како́е э́то к Вам име́ет отноше́ние?; **I won't have anything to do with it** я не жела́ю име́ть к э́тому никако́го отноше́ния; **it has to do with money** э́то каса́ется де́нег

► **do without** *vt fus* обходи́ться* (обойти́сь* *perf*) без +*gen*; **if you're late for tea then you'll do without** е́сли Вы опозда́ете, то оста́нетесь без ча́я.

---

do. *abbr* = *ditto*.

DOA *abbr* (= *dead on arrival*): **he was ~** по прибы́тии в больни́цу он был мёртв.

d.o.b. *abbr* = *date of birth*.

doc [dɔk] *n* (*inf*) до́ктор.

docile ['dəusaɪl] *adj* кро́ткий* (кро́ток*).

dock [dɔk] *n* (*NAUT*) док; (*LAW*) скамья́ подсуди́мых; (*BOT*) щаве́ль* *m* ♦ *vi* (*NAUT*) прича́ливать (прича́лить *perf*); (*SPACE*) стыкова́ться (состыкова́ться *perf*) ♦ *vt*: **they ~ed a third of his wages** они́ удержа́ли треть его́ зарпла́ты; **~s** *npl* (*NAUT*) док, верфь *f*.

dock dues [-djuːz] *npl* (*COMM*) пла́та за по́льзование до́ком.

docker ['dɔkə'] *n* до́кер.

docket ['dɔkɪt] *n* (*ADMIN, COMM: certificate*) квита́нция; (*on parcel*) о́пись *f*.

dockyard ['dɔkjaːd] *n* док, верфь *f*.

doctor ['dɔktə'] *n* (*MED*) врач*; (*SCOL*) до́ктор* ♦ *vt*: **I ~ed his coffee with arsenic** я подмеша́л в его́ ко́фе мышья́к; **~'s office** (*US*) враче́бный

кабине́т.

doctorate ['dɔktərɪt] *n* (*thesis*) до́кторская рабо́та; (*degree*) до́кторская сте́пень* *f*.

Doctor of Philosophy *n* (*degree, person*) до́ктор филосо́фии *or* филосо́фских нау́к.

doctrine ['dɔktrɪn] *n* доктри́на.

docudrama ['dɔkjudrɑːmə] *n* фи́льм и́ли програ́мма, в осно́ву кото́рых вошли́ реа́льные собы́тия.

document [*n* 'dɔkjumənt, *vb* 'dɔkjumɛnt] *n* докуме́нт ♦ *vt* документи́ровать (*impf/perf*).

documentary [dɔkju'mɛntərɪ] *adj* документа́льный ♦ *n* (*TV, CINEMA*) документа́льный фи́льм.

documentation [dɔkjumən'teɪʃən] *n* (*also COMPUT*) документа́ция.

DOD *n abbr* (*US*: = *Department of Defense*) Департа́мент оборо́ны.

doddering ['dɔdərɪŋ] *adj* дря́хлый* (дряхл).

doddery ['dɔdərɪ] *adj* = **doddering**.

doddle ['dɔdl] *n* (*inf*) пустя́к, па́ра пустяко́в.

Dodecanese [dəudɪkə'niːz] *n*: **the ~ (Islands)** Додеканэ́зские острова́* *mpl*.

dodge [dɔdʒ] *n* (*trick*) уве́ртка*, уло́вка ♦ *vt* увёртываться (уверну́ться *perf*) от +*gen* ♦ *vi* увёртываться (уверну́ться *perf*); (*SPORT*) де́лать (сде́лать *perf*) обма́нное движе́ние; **to ~ out of the way** отска́кивать (отскочи́ть* *perf*) в сто́рону; **to ~ through the traffic** лави́ровать (*impf*) в пото́ке маши́н.

dodgems ['dɔdʒəmz] *npl* (*BRIT*) аттракцио́нный электромоби́ль *msg*.

dodgy ['dɔdʒɪ] *adj* (*inf*: *plan*) риско́ванный* (риско́ван); (: *person*): **~ character** подозри́тельный тип.

DOE *n abbr* (*BRIT*: = *Department of the Environment*) Департа́мент охра́ны окружа́ющей среды́; (*US*: = *Department of Energy*) Департа́мент энерге́тики.

doe [dəu] *n* (*deer*) са́мка* оле́ня; (*rabbit*) са́мка* кро́лика.

does [dʌz] *vb see* **do**.

doesn't ['dʌznt] = **does not**.

dog [dɔg] *n* соба́ка ♦ *vt* пресле́довать (*impf*); **to go to the ~s** (*fig*) приходи́ть* (прийти́* *perf*) в упа́док.

dog biscuits *npl* гале́ты *fpl* для соба́к.

dog collar *n* оше́йник; (*REL*) высо́кий жёсткий воротни́к у свяще́нников.

dog-eared ['dɔgɪəd] *adj* потрёпанный* (потрёпан).

dog food *n* корм* для соба́к.

dogged ['dɔgɪd] *adj* упо́рный.

doggy bag ['dɔgɪ-] *n* паке́т, в кото́ром посети́тели рестора́на мо́гут унести́ объе́дки.

dogma ['dɔgmə] *n* до́гма.

dogmatic [dɔg'mætɪk] *adj* догмати́ческий*.

do-gooder [du:'gudə'] *n* (*pej*) благо-де́тель(ница) *m(f)*.

dogsbody ['dɔgzbɔdɪ] *n* (*BRIT*: *inf*) иша́к*.

doily ['dɔɪlɪ] *n* ажу́рная *or* кружевна́я салфе́точка.

doing ['duːɪŋ] *n*: **this is your ~** э́то твои́х рук де́ло.

doings ['duːɪŋz] *npl* (*activities*) де́йствия *ntpl*.

do-it-yourself ['duːɪtjɔː'sɛlf] *n* сде́лай сам.

doldrums ['dɔldrəmz] *npl*: **to be in the ~** (*person*) хандри́ть (*impf*); (*business*) находи́ться (*impf*) в упа́дке.

▶ **dole out** *vt* (*food, money*) раздава́ть* (разда́ть* *perf*).

doleful ['dəulful] *adj* ско́рбный* (ско́рбен).

doll [dɔl] *n* (*also US*: *inf*) ку́кла*.

dolled up *adj* (*inf*) разря́женный (разря́жен).

dollar ['dɔlə'] *n* до́ллар.

dollar area *n* до́лларовая зо́на.

dollop ['dɔləp] *n*: **a ~ (of)** ло́жка (+*gen*).

dolly ['dɔlɪ] *n* ку́кла.

Dolomites ['dɔləmaɪts] *npl*: **the ~** Доломи́товые А́льпы *fpl*.

dolphin ['dɔlfɪn] *n* дельфи́н.

domain [də'meɪn] *n* (*sphere*) сфе́ра; (*empire*) владе́ние.

dome [dəum] *n* ку́пол*.

domestic [də'mɛstɪk] *adj* дома́шний*; (*trade, politics*) вну́тренний*; (*happiness*) семе́йный.

domesticated [də'mɛstɪkeɪtɪd] *adj* (*animal*) одома́шненный; (*person*) домови́тый (домови́т); **he's very ~** он о́чень домови́тый.

domesticity [dəumɛs'tɪsɪtɪ] *n* дома́шняя жизнь *f*.

domestic servant *n* прислу́га.

domicile ['dɔmɪsaɪl] *n* (*LAW, ADMIN*) ме́сто* жи́тельства.

dominant ['dɔmɪnənt] *adj* (*share, role*) преоблада́ющий, домини́рующий; (*partner*) вла́стный* (вла́стен).

dominate ['dɔmɪneɪt] *vt* домини́ровать (*impf*) над +*instr*.

domination [dɔmɪ'neɪʃən] *n* преоблада́ние, домини́рование.

domineering [dɔmɪ'nɪərɪŋ] *adj* вла́стный* (вла́стен).

Dominican Republic [də'mɪnɪkən-] *n*: **the ~ ~** Доминика́нская Респу́блика.

dominion [də'mɪnɪən] *n* (*territory*) доминио́н; (*authority*): **to have ~ over** владыче́ствовать (*impf*) над +*instr*.

domino ['dɔmɪnəu] (*pl* **~es**) *n* домино́ *nt ind*.

domino effect *n* цепна́я реа́кция.

dominoes ['dɔmɪnəuz] *n* (*game*) домино́ *nt ind*.

don [dɔn] *n* (*BRIT*: *SCOL*) преподава́тель(ница) *m(f)* ♦ *vt* (*clothing*) надева́ть (наде́ть* *perf*).

donate [də'neɪt] *vt*: **to ~ (to)** же́ртвовать (поже́ртвовать *perf*) (+*dat* *or* на +*acc*).

donation [də'neɪʃən] *n* поже́ртвование.

done [dʌn] *pp of* **do**.

donkey ['dɔŋkɪ] *n* осёл*, иша́к.

donkey-work ['dɒŋkɪwə:k] n (BRIT: inf) ишачья работа.
donor ['dəunəʳ] n (MED: of blood, heart etc) донор; (to charity) жёртвователь(ница) m(f).
donor card n донорская карточка.
don't [dəunt] = **do not**.
donut ['dəunʌt] n (US) = **doughnut**.
doodle ['du:dl] vi чиркать (impf) ♦ n каракули* fpl.
doom [du:m] n рок ♦ vt: **the plan was ~ed to failure** план был обречён на провал.
doomsday ['du:mzdeɪ] n страшный суд*.
door [dɔ:ʳ] n дверь* f; **to go from ~ to ~** ходить* (impf) от дома к дому.
doorbell ['dɔ:bɛl] n (дверной) звонок*.
door handle n дверная ручка*; (of car) ручка* двери.
doorman ['dɔ:mən] irreg n (in hotel) швейцар; (in block of flats) привратник.
doormat ['dɔ:mæt] n (mat) половик*; (inf: person) тряпка* m/f.
doorpost ['dɔ:pəust] n дверной косяк*.
doorstep ['dɔ:stɛp] n порог; **on the ~** на пороге.
door-to-door ['dɔ:tə'dɔ:ʳ] adj: **~ salesman** агент, сбывающий товары и различные виды услуг непосредственно в домах потребителей; **~ selling** продажа вразнос.
doorway ['dɔ:weɪ] n дверной проём; **in the ~** в дверях.
dope [dəup] n (inf: drug) наркотик; (: in sport) допинг; (: person) придурок*; (: information) секретная информация ♦ vt (horse, person) вводить* (ввести* perf) наркотик +dat.
dopey ['dəupɪ] adj (inf: groggy) одурманенный; (: stupid) одурелый.
dormant ['dɔ:mənt] adj (plant) покоящийся; (volcano) спящий; (idea, report etc): **to lie ~** бездействовать (impf).
dormer ['dɔ:məʳ] n (also: **~ window**) мансардное окно*.
dormice ['dɔ:maɪs] npl of **dormouse**.
dormitory ['dɔ:mɪtrɪ] n (room) общая спальня*; (US: building) общежитие.
dormouse ['dɔ:maus] (pl **dormice**) n соня.
Dors abbr (BRIT: POST) = **Dorset**.
DOS [dɒs] n abbr (COMPUT: = disk operating system) ДОС= дисковая операционная система.
dosage ['dəusɪdʒ] n доза.
dose [dəus] n доза; (BRIT: bout) приступ ♦ vt: **to ~ o.s. with** принимать (принять* perf); **I had a ~ of flu last week** на прошлой неделе у меня был грипп.
dosh [dɒʃ] n (inf) бабки pl.
dosser ['dɒsəʳ] (inf) n (tramp) бомж; (layabout) разгильдяй.
doss house ['dɒs-] n (BRIT: inf) ночлёжка*.

dossier ['dɒsɪeɪ] n досьё nt ind.
DOT n abbr (US: = Department of Transportation) департамент путей сообщения.
dot [dɒt] n точка*; (speck) пятнышко* ♦ vt: **~ted with** усеянный (усеян) +instr; **on the ~** минута в минуту.
dote [dəut]: **to ~ on** vt fus души не чаять (impf) в +prp.
dot-matrix printer [dɒt'meɪtrɪks-] n (COMPUT) матричный принтер.
dotted line ['dɒtɪd-] n пунктирная линия; **to sign on the ~ ~** (fig) окончательно соглашаться (согласиться perf).
dotty ['dɒtɪ] adj (inf) тронутый.
double ['dʌbl] adj двойной ♦ adv: **to cost ~** стоить (impf) вдвое дороже ♦ n двойник* ♦ vt удваивать (удвоить perf); (fold in two) складывать (сложить* perf) вдвое ♦ vi (increase) удваиваться (удвоиться perf); **to ~ as** (person) совмещать (impf) обязанности +gen; (object) служить* (impf) одновременно +instr; **he ~s as a servant in this play** он также исполняет роль слуги в этом спектакле; **on the ~**, (BRIT) **at the ~** бегом; **~ five two six (5526)** (TEL) пятьдесят пять двадцать шесть; **it's spelt with a ~ "l"** пишется с двумя „л"
▸ **double back** vi разворачиваться (развернуться perf) и идти* (пойти* perf) назад
▸ **double up** vi (bend over) скорчиваться (скорчиться perf); (share room) делить (impf).
double bass n контрабас.
double bed n двуспальная кровать f.
double bend n (BRIT) извилистая дорога.
double blind n эксперимент, в котором исследуемый объект неизвестен ни экспериментаторам, ни экспериментируемым (в маркетинге).
double-breasted ['dʌbl'brɛstɪd] adj двубортный.
double-check ['dʌbl'tʃɛk] vti перепроверять (перепроверить perf).
double-click ['dʌbl'klɪk] vt (COMPUT) дважды нажимать (нажать* perf) на+acc.
double cream (BRIT) n густые сливки* pl.
double-cross ['dʌbl'krɒs] vt надувать (надуть perf).
double-decker ['dʌbl'dɛkəʳ] n (also: **double-decker bus**) двухэтажный автобус.
double exposure n (PHOT) двойная экспозиция.
double glazing [-'gleɪzɪŋ] n (BRIT) двойные рамы fpl.
double indemnity n (US) выплата страховой суммы в двойном размере.
double-page spread ['dʌblpeɪdʒ-] n двойной разворот (газеты, журнала).
double parking n парковка вторым рядом.

---

* marks translations which have irregular inflections. The Russian-English side of the dictionary gives inflectional information.

double room *n* (*in hotel*) двухме́стный но́мер*; (*in house*) больша́я ко́мната.
doubles ['dʌblz] *n* (*TENNIS*) па́ры *fpl*.
double time *n* двойна́я опла́та.
double whammy [-'wæmɪ] *n* двойно́й уда́р.
doubly ['dʌblɪ] *adv* вдвойне́.
doubt [daut] *n* сомне́ние ◆ *vt* сомнева́ться (*impf*); (*mistrust*) сомнева́ться (*impf*) в +*prp*. не доверя́ть (*impf*) +*dat*; **without (a)** ~ без сомне́ния; **I ~ it (very much)** я (о́чень) сомнева́юсь; **I ~ if** *or* **whether she'll come** я сомнева́юсь, что она́ придёт; **I don't ~ that** ... я не сомнева́юсь, что ....
doubtful ['dautful] *adj* сомни́тельный; **to be ~ about sth** сомнева́ться (*impf*) насчёт чего-н; **I'm a bit ~** я не́сколько сомнева́юсь; **it's ~ whether** ... сомни́тельно, что ....
doubtless ['dautlɪs] *adv* несомне́нно.
dough [dəu] *n* те́сто; (*inf: money*) ба́бки* *fpl*.
doughnut ['dəunʌt] (*US* **donut**) *n* по́нчик.
dour [duər] *adj* суро́вый* (суро́в).
douse [dauz] *vt*: **to ~ (with)** облива́ть (обли́ть* *perf*) (+*instr*) ◆ *vt* (*extinguish*) туши́ть (потуши́ть *perf*), гаси́ть (погаси́ть *perf*).
dove [dʌv] *n* го́лубь *m*.
Dover ['dəuvər] *n* Дувр; **Straits of ~** Па-де-Кале́ *m ind*.
dovetail ['dʌvteɪl] *vi* (*fig*) совпада́ть (совпа́сть* *perf*); (*schedules*) дополня́ть (допо́лнить *perf*) друг дру́га ◆ *n* (*TECH*): ~ **joint** ла́сточкин хвост*.
dowager ['dauədʒər] *n* престаре́лая све́тская да́ма; **the ~ duchess** вдо́вствующая герцоги́ня.
dowdy ['daudɪ] *adj* неказистый* (неказист).
Dow-Jones average ['dau'dʒəunz-] *n* (*US*) и́ндекс веду́щих монопо́лий До́у Джо́нса.
down [daun] *n* пух*; (*hill*) холм* ◆ *adv* (*motion*) вниз; (*position*) внизу́ ◆ *prep* (*towards lower level*) (вниз) с +*gen* or по +*dat*; (*movement along*) (вдоль) по +*dat* ◆ *vt* (*inf: drink*) прогла́тывать (проглоти́ть* *perf*); ~ **there** вот там; ~ **here** вот здесь; **the price of meat is ~** цена́ на мя́со упа́ла; **I've got it ~ somewhere** у меня́ где́-то э́то запи́сано; **to pay £2 ~** плати́ть* (заплати́ть* *perf*) пе́рвый взнос £2; **England is two goals ~** А́нглия проигрывает на два очка́; **to ~ tools** (*BRIT*) прекраща́ть (прекрати́ть *perf*) рабо́ту; ~ **with the government!** доло́й прави́тельство!
down-and-out ['daunəndaut] *n* бродя́га, бездо́мный(-ая) *m(f) adj*.
down-at-heel ['daunət'hi:l] *adj* (*shoes etc*) сто́птанный (сто́птан); (*appearance, person*) потрёпанный* (потрёпан).
downbeat ['daunbi:t] *n* (*MUS*) си́льная до́ля ◆ *adj* небре́жный* (небре́жен).
downcast ['daunka:st] *adj* (*person*) пода́вленный (пода́влен); (*eyes*) опу́щенный (опу́щен).
downer ['daunər] *n* (*inf: drug*) успокои́тельное

nt *adj*; **to be on a ~** (*depressed*) быть* (*impf*) в депре́ссии.
downfall ['daunfɔ:l] *n* паде́ние; (*from drinking, gambling etc*) ги́бель *f*.
downgrade ['daungreɪd] *vt*: **he was ~d** его́ пони́зили.
downhearted ['daun'hɑ:tɪd] *adj* упа́вший* ду́хом.
downhill ['daun'hɪl] *n* (*also:* ~ **race**: *SKIING*) скоростно́й спуск ◆ *adv* (*face, look*) вниз; **to go ~** (*person*) идти́* (пойти́* *perf*) под го́ру; (*road*) идти́* (пойти́* *perf*) под укло́н; (*car*) е́хать* (пое́хать* *perf*) под го́ру; (*fig: person*) кати́ться (покати́ться *perf*) по накло́нной пло́скости; (: *business*) идти́* (пойти́* *perf*) под го́ру *or* под укло́н.
Downing Street ['daunɪŋ-] *n* (*BRIT: POL*) Да́унинг Стрит.
download ['daunləud] *vt* (*COMPUT*) загружа́ть (загрузи́ть* *perf*) (*в па́мять*).
down-market ['daun'mɑ:kɪt] *adj* (*product*) дешёвый.
down payment *n* пе́рвый взнос.
downplay ['daunpleɪ] *vt* (*US*) преуменьша́ть (преуме́ньшить *perf*).
downpour ['daunpɔ:'] *n* ли́вень* *m*.
downright ['daunraɪt] *adj* я́вный; (*refusal*) по́лный ◆ *adv* соверше́нно.
Downs [daunz] *npl* (*BRIT: GEO*): **the ~** Да́унз (*известко́вые холмы́ на ю́ге А́нглии*).
Down's syndrome [daunz-] *n* синдро́м Да́уна.
downstairs ['daun'stɛəz] *adv* (*position*) внизу́; (*motion*) вниз.
downstream ['daunstri:m] *adv* вниз по тече́нию.
downtime ['dauntaɪm] *n* просто́й.
down-to-earth ['dauntu'ə:θ] *adj* (*person*) просто́й; (*solution*) практи́чный* (практи́чен).
downtown ['daun'taun] *adv* (*position*) в це́нтре; (*motion*) в центр ◆ *adj* (*US*): ~ **Chicago** центр Чика́го.
downtrodden ['dauntrɔdn] *adj* (*person*) заби́тый (заби́т).
down under *adv* (*BRIT: inf: Australia etc*) друго́й коне́ц све́та (*Австра́лия и Но́вая Зела́ндия*); **he lives ~** ~ он живёт на друго́м конце́ све́та.
downward ['daunwəd] *adj* напра́вленный вниз ◆ *adv* вниз; **a ~ trend** понижа́тельная тенде́нция.
downwards ['daunwədz] *adv* = **downward**.
dowry ['dauri] *n* прида́ное *nt adj*.
doz. *abbr* = **dozen**.
doze [dəuz] *vi* дрема́ть* (*impf*)
► **doze off** *vi* задрема́ть* (*perf*).
dozen ['dʌzn] *n* дю́жина; **a ~ books** дю́жина книг; **80 pence a ~** 80 пе́нсов за дю́жину; **~s of** деся́тки +*gen*.
DPh *n abbr* (= *Doctor of Philosophy*) до́ктор

философии.
DPhil *n abbr* (= *Doctor of Philosophy*) до́ктор философии.
DPP *n abbr* (*BRIT*: = *Director of Public Prosecutions*) Генера́льный прокуро́р.
DPT *n abbr* (= *diphtheria, pertussis, tetanus*) коклю́шно-дифтери́йно-столбня́чная вакци́на.
DPW *n abbr* (*US*: = *Department of Public Works*) Департа́мент обще́ственного строи́тельства.
Dr *abbr* = **doctor.**
Dr. *abbr* (*in street names*) = **Drive.**
dr *abbr* (*COMM*) = **debtor.**
drab [dræb] *adj* (*weather, building, clothes*) се́рый (сер), уны́лый (уны́л).
draft [drɑ:ft] *n* (*first version*) чернови́к•, набро́сок•; (*POL: of bill*) прое́кт; (*COMM*) тра́тта; (*US: MIL*) призы́в ♦ *vt* (*plan*) составля́ть (соста́вить• *perf*); (*write roughly*) писа́ть• (написа́ть• *perf*) на́черно; *see also* **draught.**
draftsman ['drɑ:ftsmən] *irreg n* (*US*) = **draughtsman.**
draftsmanship ['drɑ:ftsmənʃɪp] *n* (*US*) = **draughtsmanship.**
drag [dræg] *vt* тащи́ть• (*impf*); (*lake, pond*) прочёсывать (прочеса́ть• *perf*) ♦ *vi* (*time, a concert etc*) тяну́ться• (*impf*) ♦ *n* (*inf: person*) обу́за; (: *task*) бре́мя• *nt*; (*NAUT, AVIAT*) лобово́е сопротивле́ние; **in** ~ в костю́ме же́нщины (*о мужчи́не*)
► **drag away** *vt*: **to** ~ **sb away (from)** отта́скивать (оттащи́ть• *perf*) кого́-н (от +*gen*)
► **drag on** *vi* тяну́ться• (*impf*).
dragnet ['drægnɛt] *n* нево́д•, бре́день• *m*; (*fig*) обла́ва.
dragon ['drægn] *n* драко́н.
dragonfly ['drægənflaɪ] *n* стрекоза́•.
dragoon [drə'gu:n] *n* драгу́н• ♦ *vt*: **to** ~ **sb into sth** (*BRIT*) втя́гивать (втяну́ть• *perf*) кого́-н во что-н.
drain [dreɪn] *n* (*in street*) водосто́к, водоотво́д; (*on resources, manpower*) уте́чка•; (*on health, energy*) расхо́д ♦ *vt* (*land, glass etc*) осуша́ть (осуши́ть• *perf*); (*vegetables*) слива́ть (слить• *perf*) ♦ *vi* (*liquid*) стека́ть (стечь• *perf*); **I feel** ~**ed** я истощён; **I feel** ~**ed of emotion** у меня́ истощи́лись эмо́ции.
drainage ['dreɪnɪdʒ] *n* (*system*) канализа́ция; (*process*) дрена́ж, осуше́ние.
drainboard ['dreɪnbɔ:d] *n* (*US*) = **draining board.**
draining board ['dreɪnɪŋ-] (*US* **drainboard**) *n* су́шка•.
drainpipe ['dreɪnpaɪp] *n* водосто́чная труба́•.
drake [dreɪk] *n* се́лезень• *m.*
dram [dræm] *n* (*SCOTTISH: drink*) глото́к• (*о*

спиртно́м).
drama ['drɑ:mə] *n* (*also fig*) дра́ма.
dramatic [drə'mætɪk] *adj* драмати́ческий•; (*increase etc*) ре́зкий•; (*change*) рази́тельный.
dramatically [drə'mætɪklɪ] *adv* драмати́чески; (*increase, change*) ре́зко.
dramatist ['dræmətɪst] *n* драмату́рг.
dramatize ['dræmətaɪz] *vt* (*exaggerate*) драматизи́ровать (*impf/perf*); (*adapt: for TV, cinema*) инсцени́ровать (*impf/perf*).
drank [dræŋk] *pt of* **drink.**
drape [dreɪp] *vt* драпирова́ть (задрапирова́ть• *perf*).
drapes [dreɪps] *npl* (*US: curtains*) занаве́ски• *fpl.*
drastic ['dræstɪk] *adj* (*measure*) реши́тельный• (реши́телен); (*change*) коренно́й.
drastically ['dræstɪklɪ] *adv* (*change*) коренны́м о́бразом; (*reduce*) ре́зко.
draught [drɑ:ft] (*US* **draft**) *n* (*of air*) сквозня́к•; (*NAUT*) оса́дка•; (*of chimney*) тя́га; **on** ~ (*beer*) из бо́чки.
draught beer *n* бо́чковое пи́во.
draughtboard ['drɑ:ftbɔ:d] *n* (*BRIT*) ша́шечная доска́•.
draughts [drɑ:fts] *n* (*BRIT*) ша́шки• *pl.*
draughtsman ['drɑ:ftsmən] *irreg* (*US* **draftsman**) *n* чертёжник(-ица).
draughtsmanship ['drɑ:ftsmənʃɪp] (*US* **draftsmanship**) *n* черче́ние; (*art*) иску́сство черче́ния.
draw [drɔ:] (*pt* **drew**, *pp* **drawn**) *vt* (*ART*) рисова́ть (*impf*); (*TECH*) черти́ть• (*impf*); (*pull: cart*) тащи́ть• (*impf*); (: *curtains*) задёргивать (задёрнуть• *perf*); (*gun, tooth*) вырыва́ть (вы́рвать• *perf*); (*attention*) привлека́ть (привле́чь• *perf*); (*crowd*) собира́ть (собра́ть• *perf*); (*money*) снима́ть (снять• *perf*); (*wages*) получа́ть (получи́ть• *perf*) ♦ *vi* (*SPORT*) игра́ть (сыгра́ть *perf*) в ничью́ ♦ *n* (*SPORT*) ничья́•; (*lottery*) лотере́я; (: *of teams*) жеребьёвка•; **to** ~ **near** приближа́ться (прибли́зиться• *perf*); **to** ~ **to a close** подходи́ть• (подойти́• *perf*) к концу́; **to** ~ **a conclusion** де́лать (сде́лать *perf*) вы́вод; **to** ~ **a comparison between** проводи́ть• (провести́• *perf*) сравне́ние ме́жду +*instr*
► **draw back** *vi*: **to** ~ **back (from)** отпря́нуть (*perf*) (от +*gen*)
► **draw in** *vi* (*BRIT*: *car*) остана́вливаться (останови́ться• *perf*); (: *train*) подъезжа́ть (подъе́хать• *perf*); (*nights*) станови́ться• (стать• *perf*) длинне́е
► **draw on** *vt* испо́льзовать (*impf/perf*)
► **draw out** *vi* (*lengthen*) растя́гивать (растяну́ть• *perf*) ♦ *vt* (*money*) снима́ть (снять• *perf*)
► **draw up** *vi* (*train, bus etc*) подъезжа́ть

---

* marks translations which have irregular inflections. The Russian-English side of the dictionary gives inflectional information.

(подъе́хать* perf) ♦ vt (chair etc) придвига́ть (придви́нуть perf); (document) составля́ть (соста́вить* perf).

drawback ['drɔːbæk] n недоста́ток*.

drawbridge ['drɔːbrɪdʒ] n подъёмный or разводно́й мост*.

drawee [drɔː'iː] n трасса́т.

drawer [drɔː'] n я́щик.

drawing ['drɔːɪŋ] n (picture) рису́нок*; (act) рисова́ние.

drawing board n чертёжная доска́*; **to go back to the ~ ~** (fig) всё начина́ть (нача́ть* perf) снача́ла.

drawing pin n (BRIT) (канцеля́рская) кно́пка*.

drawing room n гости́ная f adj.

drawl [drɔːl] n протя́жное произноше́ние ♦ vi протя́гивать (протяну́ть* perf).

drawn [drɔːn] pp of **draw** ♦ adj изму́ченный* (изму́чен).

drawstring ['drɔːstrɪŋ] n шнур* (кото́рый продёрнут во что́-нибудь).

dread [drɛd] n у́жас ♦ vt боя́ться (impf) +gen.

dreadful ['drɛdful] adj ужа́сный*; **I feel ~!** я ужа́сно себя́ чу́вствую!

dream [driːm] n (pt, pp **dreamed** or **dreamt**) n сон*; (ambition) мечта́ ♦ vt: **I must have ~t it** мне, наве́рное, э́то присни́лось ♦ vi ви́деть (impf) сон*; (wish) мечта́ть (impf); **I had a ~ about you** ты мне присни́лся; **sweet ~s!** прия́тных сновиде́ний!

▸ **dream up** vt выду́мывать (вы́думать perf).

dreamer ['driːmə'] n (fig) мечта́тель*(ница) m(f).

dreamt [drɛmt] pt, pp of **dream**.

dream world n: **to live in a ~ ~** жить* (impf) в приду́манном ми́ре.

dreamy ['driːmɪ] adj (expression, person) мечта́тельный* (мечта́телен); (music) убаю́кивающий.

dreary ['drɪərɪ] adj тоскли́вый (тоскли́в).

dredge [drɛdʒ] vt драги́ровать (impf/perf).

▸ **dredge up** vt драги́ровать (impf/perf); (fig: facts) выта́скивать (вы́тащить perf).

dredger ['drɛdʒə'] n (ship) землечерпа́лка, дра́га; (BRIT: also: **sugar ~**) сосу́д с ма́ленькими ды́рочками в кры́шке для са́хара.

dregs [drɛgz] npl муть* fsg; **~ of society** отбро́сы о́бщества.

drench [drɛntʃ] vt: **to be ~ed** мо́кнуть (промо́кнуть* perf): **~ed to the skin** наскво́зь промо́кший.

Dresden ['drɛzdən] n Дре́зден.

dress [drɛs] n (frock) пла́тье*; (no pl: clothing) оде́жда ♦ vt одева́ть (оде́ть* perf); (wound) перевя́зывать (перевяза́ть* perf) ♦ vi одева́ться (оде́ться* perf); **she ~es very well** она́ о́чень хорошо́ одева́ется; **to ~ a shop window** оформля́ть (офо́рмить* perf) витри́ну; **to get ~ed** одева́ться (оде́ться* perf)

▸ **dress up** vi наряжа́ться (наряди́ться* perf).

dress circle n (BRIT) бельэта́ж.

dress designer n модельє́р.

dresser ['drɛsə'] n (BRIT) ку́хонный шкаф*; (US: chest of drawers) туале́тный сто́лик; (also: **window ~**) оформи́тель(ница) m(f) витри́н.

dressing ['drɛsɪŋ] n (MED) повя́зка*; (: process) перевя́зка*; (CULIN) запра́вка*.

dressing gown n (BRIT) хала́т.

dressing room n (THEAT) артисти́ческая убо́рная f adj; (SPORT) раздева́лка*.

dressing table n туале́тный сто́лик.

dressmaker ['drɛsmeɪkə'] n портни́ха.

dressmaking ['drɛsmeɪkɪŋ] n поши́в же́нского пла́тья.

dress rehearsal n генера́льная репети́ция.

dressy ['drɛsɪ] adj (inf) наря́дный* (наря́ден).

drew [druː] pt of **draw**.

dribble ['drɪbl] vi (liquid) ка́пать* (impf); (baby) пуска́ть (пусти́ть* perf) слю́ни; (SPORT) вести́* (impf) мяч ♦ vt (ball) вести́* (impf).

dried [draɪd] adj (fruit) сушёный*; (milk) сухо́й.

drier ['draɪə'] n = **dryer**.

drift [drɪft] n (of current etc) ско́рость* f; (of snow) зано́с, сугро́б; (meaning) смысл ♦ vi (boat) дрейфова́ть (impf); **sand/snow had ~ed over the road** доро́гу занесло́ песко́м/сне́гом; **to let things ~** пуска́ть (пусти́ть* perf) всё на самотёк; **to ~ apart** расходи́ться (разойти́сь* perf); **I get or catch your ~** я понима́ю куда́ Вы кло́ните.

drifter ['drɪftə'] n (person) бродя́га m/f.

driftwood ['drɪftwud] n пла́вник.

drill [drɪl] n (drill bit) сверло́*; (machine) дрель f; (: for mining etc) бура́в*; (MIL) уче́ние ♦ vt (hole) сверли́ть (просверли́ть* perf); (troops) муштрова́ть (вы́муштровать perf); (pupils) ната́скивать (натаска́ть perf) ♦ vi (for oil) бури́ть (impf).

drilling ['drɪlɪŋ] n (for oil) буре́ние.

drilling rig n бурова́я устано́вка*.

drily ['draɪlɪ] adv = **dryly**.

drink [drɪŋk] n (pt **drank**, pp **drunk**) n напи́ток*; (alcoholic drink) (спиртно́й) напи́ток*; (sip) глото́к* ♦ vt пить* (вы́пить* perf) ♦ vi пить* (impf); **to have a ~** попи́ть* (perf); (alcohol) вы́пить* (perf); **a ~ of water** глото́к* воды́; (glassful) стака́н воды́; **would you like something to ~?** хоти́те чего́-нибудь вы́пить?: **we had ~s before lunch** мы вы́пили пе́ред обе́дом

▸ **drink in** vt упива́ться (impf) +instr.

drinkable ['drɪŋkəbl] adj (water) питьево́й; (palatable: wine etc) неплохо́й (непло́х), прия́тный* (прия́тен).

drink-driving ['drɪŋk'draɪvɪŋ] n вожде́ние в нетре́звом состоя́нии ♦ cpd: **they are running a ~ campaign** они́ веду́т кампа́нию про́тив води́телей, садя́щихся за руль в нетре́звом состоя́нии

drinker ['drɪŋkə'] n (of alcohol) пью́щий*(-ая)

m(f) adj.

drinking ['drɪŋkɪŋ] *n* питьё*; **there was a lot of ~ at the party** на вечери́нке мно́го пи́ли.

drinking fountain *n* питьево́й фонта́нчик.

drinking water *n* питьева́я вода́*.

drip [drɪp] *n* ка́панье; *(one drip)* ка́пля*; *(MED)* ка́пельница ◆ *vi (water, rain)* ка́пать* *(impf)*; **the tap is ~ping** кран течёт; **the washing is ~ping** с белья́ ка́пает.

drip-dry ['drɪp'draɪ] *adj:* **~ material** ткань, кото́рой даю́т стечь по́сле сти́рки и кото́рую не гла́дят.

drip-feed ['drɪpfi:d] *vt (MED)* влива́ть (влить* *perf)* че́рез ка́пельницу ◆ *n:* **to be on a ~** быть* *(impf)* на ка́пельнице.

dripping ['drɪpɪŋ] *n (CULIN)* (то́плёный) жир ◆ *adj (very wet)* мо́крый (мокр); **I'm ~** с меня́ течёт; **~ wet** соверше́нно мо́крый (мокр).

drive [draɪv] *(pt* **drove***, pp* **driven***) n (journey)* пое́здка*; *(also:* **~way***)* подъе́зд; *(energy)* напо́ристость *f*; *(campaign)* кампа́ния; *(FOOTBALL)* уда́р; *(TENNIS)* дра́йв; *(COMPUT: also: disk~)* дисково́д; *(in street names):* **Rose D~** Ро́уз Драйв ◆ *vt (vehicle)* води́ть*/вести́* *(impf)*; *(TECH: machine, motor, wheel)* приводи́ть* (привести́* *perf)* в движе́ние; *(animal)* гнать* *(impf)*; *(ball)* ударя́ть (уда́рить *perf)* (пло́ско); *(nail, stake etc):* **to ~ sth into sth** вбива́ть (вбить* *perf)* что-н во что-н ◆ *vi (AUT: at controls)* води́ть*/вести́* *(impf)* (маши́ну); *(travel)* е́здить*/е́хать* *(impf)*; **to go for a ~** пое́хать *(perf)* поката́ться; **the town is three hours' ~ from London** го́род в трёх часа́х езды́ от Ло́ндона; **right-/left-hand ~** *(AUT)* пра́во-/левосторо́ннее управле́ние; **front-/rear-wheel ~** *(AUT)* приво́д на пере́дние/за́дние колёса; **economy ~** борьба́ за эконо́мию; **he ~s a taxi** он во́дит такси́; **to ~ at 50 km an hour** е́здить*/е́хать* *(impf)* со ско́ростью 50 км в час; **to ~ sb home/to the airport** отвози́ть* (отвезти́* *perf)* кого́-н домо́й/в аэропо́рт; **to ~ sb mad** своди́ть* (свести́* *perf)* кого́-н с ума́; **to ~ sb to sth** доводи́ть* (довести́* *perf)* кого́-н до чего́-н; **what are you driving at?** куда́ Вы кло́ните?

▶ **drive off** *vt (repel)* отбра́сывать (отбро́сить* *perf)*

▶ **drive out** *vt (force to leave)* вытесня́ть (вы́теснить *perf)*; *(person, animal, evil)* выгоня́ть (вы́гнать *perf)*.

drive-by shooting ['draɪvbaɪ-] *n* стрельба́ из дви́жущегося автомоби́ля.

drive-in ['draɪvɪn] *n (esp US: restaurant)* кафе́, где мо́жно купи́ть еду́ не выходя́ из маши́ны.

drivel ['drɪvl] *n (inf)* чушь *f*.

driven ['drɪvn] *pp of* **drive**.

driver ['draɪvəʳ] *n* води́тель *m*; *(of train)*

машини́ст.

driver's license ['draɪvəz-] *n (US)* води́тельские права́ *nt pl*.

driveway ['draɪvweɪ] *n* подъе́зд.

driving ['draɪvɪŋ] *n* вожде́ние ◆ *adj:* **~ rain** проливно́й дождь* *m*; **~ snow** мете́ль *f*.

driving belt *n* приводно́й реме́нь* *m*.

driving force *n* дви́жущая си́ла.

driving instructor *n* инстру́ктор* по вожде́нию.

driving lesson *n* уро́к по вожде́нию.

driving licence *n (BRIT)* води́тельские права́ *ntpl*.

driving mirror *n* зе́ркало за́днего ви́да.

driving school *n* автошко́ла.

driving test *n* экза́мен по вожде́нию.

drizzle ['drɪzl] *n* моро́ся́щий дождь* *m* ◆ *vi* мороси́ть *(impf)*.

droll [drəul] *adj* заба́вный.

dromedary ['drɒmədərɪ] *n* одного́рбый верблю́д, дромеда́р.

drone [drəun] *n (noise)* гуде́ние; *(male bee)* тру́тень* *m* ◆ *vi (bee)* жужжа́ть *(impf)*; *(engine etc)* гуде́ть *(impf)*; *(also:* **~ on***)* бубни́ть *(impf)*.

drool [dru:l] *vi:* **he is ~ing** у него́ теку́т слю́ни; **to ~ over sth/sb** *(inf)* роня́ть *(impf)* слю́ни по по́воду чего́-н/кого́-н.

droop [dru:p] *vi (flower, head)* поника́ть (пони́кнуть *perf)*; *(shoulders)* ссуту́литься *(perf)*.

drop [drɒp] *n (of water)* ка́пля*; *(reduction)* паде́ние; *(fall: distance)* расстоя́ние *(све́рху вниз)*; *(: in salary)* сниже́ние; *(also:* **parachute ~***)* сбра́сывание на парашю́те *(продово́льствия, боеприпа́сов)* ◆ *vt (allow to fall: object)* роня́ть (урони́ть* *perf)*; *(eyes)* опуска́ть (опусти́ть* *perf)*; *(voice, price)* понижа́ть (пони́зить* *perf)*; *(set down from car)* выса́живать (вы́садить* *perf)*; *(exclude)* исключа́ть (исключи́ть *perf)* ◆ *vi* па́дать (упа́сть* *perf)*; *(wind)* стиха́ть (сти́хнуть* *perf)*; **~s** *npl (MED)* ка́пли *fpl*; **cough ~s** леденцы́ от ка́шля; **there is a 30 ft ~ from the window to the ground** высота́ от окна́ до земли́ 30 фу́тов; **there's been a ~ of 10% in profits** при́быль упа́ла на 10%; **to ~ anchor** броса́ть (бро́сить* *perf)* я́корь; **to ~ sb a line** черкну́ть* *(perf)* кому́-н не́сколько стро́чек

▶ **drop in** *vi (inf):* **to ~ in on sb** загля́дывать (загляну́ть* *perf)* к кому́-н

▶ **drop off** *vi (go to sleep)* засыпа́ть (засну́ть *perf)* ◆ *vt (passenger)* выса́живать (вы́садить* *perf)*

▶ **drop out** *vi (of game, agreement)* выходи́ть* (вы́йти* *perf)*; **to ~ out of college** броса́ть (бро́сить* *perf)* ко́лледж.

droplet ['drɒplɪt] *n* ка́пелька*.

drop-out ['drɒpaut] *n (from society)*

отщепе́нец*(-нка*); (*SCOL*) недоу́чка* *m/f*.
dropper ['drɔpə'] *n* пипе́тка*.
droppings ['drɔpɪŋz] *npl* помёт *msg*.
dross [drɔs] *n* шлак; (*rubbish*) му́сор.
drought [draut] *n* за́суха.
drove [drəuv] *pt of* **drive** ♦ *n*: ~**s of people** то́лпы *fpl* люде́й.
drown [draun] *vt* топи́ть* (утопи́ть* *perf*); (*also*: ~ **out**: *sound, voice*) заглуша́ть (заглуши́ть *perf*) ♦ *vi* тону́ть* (утону́ть* *perf*).
drowse [drauz] *vi* дрема́ть* (*impf*).
drowsy ['drauzɪ] *adj* со́нный.
drudge [drʌdʒ] *n* (*person*) рабо́тяга *m/f*.
drudgery ['drʌdʒərɪ] *n* тяжёлая, ну́дная рабо́та; **housework is sheer** ~ рабо́та по до́му – тяжёлый труд.
drug [drʌg] *n* (*MED*) лека́рство; (*narcotic*) нарко́тик ♦ *vt* (*person, animal*) вводи́ть* (ввести́* *perf*) нарко́тик +*dat*; **to be on** ~**s** быть* (*impf*) на нарко́тиках; **hard/soft** ~**s** си́льные/сла́бые нарко́тики.
drug addict *n* наркома́н.
druggist ['drʌgɪst] *n* (*US*) апте́карь *m*.
drug peddler *n* торго́вец* нарко́тиками.
drugstore ['drʌgstɔ:'] *n* (*US*) апте́ка (*иногда с небольши́м кафе́*).
drum [drʌm] *n* бараба́н; (*for oil*) бо́чка* ♦ *vi* бараба́нить (*impf*); ~**s** *npl* (*kit*) уда́рные инструме́нты *mpl*
  ▸ **drum up** *vt* (*support*) призыва́ть (призва́ть* *perf*).
drummer ['drʌmə'] *n* (*with military band*) бараба́нщик; (*in rock group*) уда́рник.
drum roll *n* бараба́нный бой*.
drumstick ['drʌmstɪk] *n* бараба́нная па́лочка*; (*of chicken*) но́жка*.
drunk [drʌŋk] *pp of* **drink** ♦ *adj* пья́ный* ♦ *n* пья́ный*(-ая) *m(f) adj*; (*also*: ~**ard**) пья́ница *m/f*; **to get** ~ напива́ться (напи́ться* *perf*); ~ **driving** вожде́ние в нетре́звом состоя́нии.
drunken ['drʌŋkən] *adj* пья́ный* (пьян); ~ **driving** вожде́ние в нетре́звом состоя́нии.
drunkenness ['drʌŋkənnɪs] *n* пья́нство.
dry [draɪ] *adj* (*also fig*) сухо́й* (сух); (*lake, riverbed*) вы́сохший; (*humour*) сде́ржанный* (сде́ржан); (*lecture, subject*) ску́чный* (ску́чен) ♦ *vt* (*clothes, ground*) суши́ть* (вы́сушить *perf*); (*surface*) вытира́ть (вы́тереть* *perf*) ♦ *vi* (*paint, washing*) со́хнуть (вы́сохнуть *perf*); **on** ~ **land** на су́ше; **to** ~ **one's hands/eyes** вытира́ть (вы́тереть* *perf*) ру́ки/глаза́; **to** ~ **one's hair** (*with towel*) вытира́ть (вы́тереть* *perf*) во́лосы; (*with hairdryer*) суши́ть* (вы́сушить *perf*) во́лосы; **to** ~ **the dishes** вытира́ть (вы́тереть* *perf*) посу́ду
  ▸ **dry up** *vi* (*river, well*) высыха́ть (вы́сохнуть* *perf*); (*resources, speaker*) иссяка́ть (исся́кнуть* *perf*).
dry clean *vt* чи́стить* (почи́стить* *perf*) (*в химчи́стке*).

dry cleaner *n* рабо́тник химчи́стки.
dry-cleaner's ['draɪ'kli:nəz] *n* химчи́стка*.
dry-cleaning ['draɪ'kli:nɪŋ] *n* хими́ческая чи́стка.
dry dock *n* (*NAUT*) сухо́й док.
dryer ['draɪə'] *n* (*for clothes*) суши́лка*.
dry goods *npl* (*US*) галантере́я *fsg* и тка́ни *fpl*.
dry ice *n* сухо́й* лёд*.
dryly ['draɪlɪ] *adv* ирони́чно.
dryness ['draɪnɪs] *n* су́хость *f*.
dry rot *n* суха́я гниль *f* (*боле́знь древеси́ны*).
dry run *n* (*fig: inf*) холосто́й прого́н.
dry ski slope *n* склон с иску́сственным покры́тием.
DSc *n abbr* (= *Doctor of Science*) до́ктор естествозна́ния.
DSS *n abbr* (*BRIT*: = *Department of Social Security*) Министе́рство социа́льного обеспе́чения.
DST *abbr* (*US*: = *Daylight Saving Time*) ле́тнее вре́мя* *nt*.
DT *n abbr* (*COMPUT*: = *data transmission*) переда́ча да́нных.
DTI *n abbr* (*BRIT*: = *Department of Trade and Industry*) Министе́рство промы́шленности и торго́вли.
DTP *n abbr* = **desktop publishing**.
DT's *npl abbr* (*inf*: = *delirium tremens*) бе́лая горя́чка; **to have the** ~ страда́ть (*impf*) бе́лой горя́чкой.
dual ['djuəl] *adj* двойно́й; (*function, number*) двойственный.
dual carriageway *n* (*BRIT*) шоссе́ *nt ind*.
dual nationality *n* двойно́е гражда́нство.
dual-purpose ['djuəl'pə:pəs] *adj* двойно́го назначе́ния.
dubbed [dʌbd] *adj* (*CINEMA*) дубли́рованный (дубли́рован); (*nicknamed*) про́званный (про́зван).
dubious ['dju:bɪəs] *adj* сомни́тельный; **I'm very** ~ **about it** у меня́ серьёзные сомне́ния на э́тот счёт.
Dublin ['dʌblɪn] *n* Ду́блин.
Dubliner ['dʌblɪnə'] *n* ду́блинец*(-нка*).
duchess ['dʌtʃɪs] *n* герцоги́ня.
duck [dʌk] *n* у́тка* ♦ *vi* (*also*: ~ **down**) пригиба́ться (пригну́ться *perf*) ♦ *vt* (*blow*) увёртываться (уверну́ться *perf*) от +*gen*; (*responsibility etc*) уви́ливать (увильну́ть *perf*) от +*gen*.
duckling ['dʌklɪŋ] *n* утёнок*.
duct [dʌkt] *n* (*ELEC*) ка́бельный кана́л; (*TECH*) трубопрово́д; (*ANAT*) прото́к, кана́л.
dud [dʌd] *adj* (*object, tool*) бесполе́зный* (бесполе́зен); (*grenade*) неразорва́вшийся; (*BRIT: cheque*) недействи́тельный ♦ *n* (*note, coin*) подде́лка*.
due [dju:] *adj* (*expected*) предполага́емый; (*attention, consideration*) до́лжный; (*owed*): **I am** ~ **£20** мне должны́ *or* причита́ется £20 ♦ *n*: **to give sb his** (*or* **her**) ~ отдава́ть*

(отда́ть* *perf*) кому́-н до́лжное ♦ *adv*: ~ **north** пря́мо на се́вер; ~**s** *npl* (*for club, union*) взно́сы *mpl*; (*in harbour*) порто́вые сбо́ры *mpl*; **in ~ course** в своё вре́мя; ~ **to** из-за +*gen*; **he is ~ to go** он до́лжен идти́; **the rent is ~ on the 30th** за кварти́ру должно́ быть* запла́чено 30-ого числа́; **the train is ~ at 8** по́езд до́лжен прийти́ в 8 часо́в; **she is ~ back tomorrow** она́ должна́ верну́ться за́втра; **I am ~ 6 days' leave** мне причита́ется 6 свобо́дных дней.

due date *n* срок произво́дства платежа́.

duel ['dju:əl] *n* дуэ́ль *f*; (*fig*) поеди́нок.

duet [dju:'ɛt] *n* дуэ́т.

duff [dʌf] *adj* (*BRIT*: *inf*) дрянно́й*
▸ **duff up** *vt* (*inf*) колошма́тить* (исколошма́тить* *perf*).

duffel bag ['dʌfl-] *n* су́мка-мешо́к*.

duffel coat *n* шерстяно́е пальто́ с капюшо́ном.

duffer ['dʌfə'] *n* (*inf*) тупи́ца *m/f*.

dug [dʌg] *pt, pp of* **dig**.

dugout ['dʌgaut] *n* (*canoe*) челно́к; (*shelter*) земля́нка.

duke [dju:k] *n* ге́рцог.

dull [dʌl] *adj* (*light, colour*) ту́склый* (ту́скл); (*weather, day*) се́рый* (сер); (*sound*) глухо́й* (глух); (*pain, wit*) тупо́й* (туп); (*event*) ску́чный* (ску́чен) ♦ *vt* притупля́ть (притупи́ть* *perf*).

duly ['dju:lɪ] *adv* (*properly*) до́лжным о́бразом; (*on time*) своевре́менно.

dumb [dʌm] *adj* (*mute*) немо́й*; (*inf*: *pej*: *stupid*: *person*) тупо́й*; (: *idea*) дура́цкий*; **to be struck ~** онеме́ть (*perf*).

dumbbell ['dʌmbɛl] *n* (*SPORT*) ганте́ль *f*.

dumbfounded [dʌm'faundɪd] *adj* ошеломлённый (ошесломлён).

dummy ['dʌmɪ] *n* (*tailor's model*) манеке́н; (*TECH*) маке́т; (*COMM*) моде́ль *f*; (*SPORT*) обма́нный приём; (*BRIT*: *for baby*) со́ска*, пусты́шка* ♦ *adj* (*bullet*) холосто́й*; (*firm*) фикти́вный.

dummy run *n* испыта́тельный прого́н.

dump [dʌmp] *n* (*also*: **rubbish ~**) сва́лка*; (*inf*: *pej*: *place*) дыра́*; (*MIL*) полево́й склад ♦ *vt* (*put down*) сва́ливать (свали́ть* *perf*), выбра́сывать (вы́бросить* *perf*); (*car*) броса́ть (бро́сить* *perf*); (*COMPUT*: *data*) выгружа́ть (вы́грузить* *perf*), сбра́сывать (сбро́сить* *perf*); **to be down in the ~s** (*inf*) хандри́ть (*impf*); **"no ~ing"** "сва́лка му́сора запрещена́".

dumpling ['dʌmplɪŋ] *n* (*CULIN*) клёцка*.

dumpy ['dʌmpɪ] *adj* кря́жистый* (кря́жист).

dunce [dʌns] *n* тупи́ца *m/f*.

Dundee [dʌn'di:] *n* Данди́ *m ind*.

Dundonian [dʌn'dəunɪən] *adj* го́рода Данди́ ♦

n жи́тель(ница) *m(f)* го́рода Данди́.

dune [dju:n] *n* дю́на.

dung [dʌŋ] *n* наво́з*.

dungarees [dʌŋgə'ri:z] *npl* комбинезо́н *msg*.

dungeon ['dʌndʒən] *n* темни́ца.

dunk [dʌŋk] *vt* мака́ть (макну́ть *perf*).

Dunkirk [dʌn'kə:k] *n* Данке́рк.

duo ['dju:əu] *n* дуэ́т.

duodenal [dju:əu'di:nl] *adj* дуодена́льный; ~ **ulcer** я́зва двенадцатипе́рстной кишки́.

duodenum [dju:əu'di:nəm] *n* двенадцатипе́рстная кишка́.

dupe [dju:p] *n* проста́к*, простофи́ля* *m/f* ♦ *vt* надува́ть (наду́ть* *perf*).

duplex ['dju:plɛks] *n* (*US*: *also*: ~ **house**) одна́ из часте́й двухкварти́рного до́ма; (*also*: ~ **apartment**) двухэта́жная кварти́ра.

duplicate [*n, adj* 'dju:plɪkət, *vt* 'dju:plɪkeɪt] *n* (*of document, key etc*) дублика́т, ко́пия ♦ *adj* (*key, copy etc*) запасно́й ♦ *vt* копи́ровать (скопи́ровать *perf*); (*repeat*) дубли́ровать (продубли́ровать *perf*); **in ~** в двойно́м экземпля́ре.

duplicating machine ['dju:plɪkeɪtɪŋ-] *n* копирова́льная маши́на.

duplicator ['dju:plɪkeɪtə'] *n* копирова́льная маши́на.

duplicity [dju:'plɪsɪtɪ] *n* двули́чие.

Dur *abbr* (*BRIT*: *POST*) = **Durham**.

durability [djuərə'bɪlɪtɪ] *n* про́чность *f*.

durable ['djuərəbl] *adj* про́чный.

duration [dju'reɪʃən] *n* продолжи́тельность *f*.

duress [djuə'rɛs] *n*: **under ~** под давле́нием.

Durex® ['djuərɛks] *n* (*BRIT*) ма́рка презервати́ва.

during ['djuərɪŋ] *prep* (*in the course of*) во вре́мя +*gen*, в тече́ние +*gen*; (*from beginning to end*) в тече́ние +*gen*.

Dushanbe [du:'ʃɑ:nbɪ] *n* Душанбе́ *m ind*.

dusk [dʌsk] *n* су́мерки *pl*.

dusky ['dʌskɪ] *adj* (*light*) су́меречный*; (*room*) тёмный*.

dust [dʌst] *n* пыль* *f* ♦ *vt* вытира́ть (вы́тереть* *perf*) пыль с +*gen*; (*cake etc*): **to ~ with** посыпа́ть (посы́пать* *perf*) +*instr*
▸ **dust off** *vt* (*also fig*) стря́хивать (стряхну́ть *perf*) пыль с +*gen*.

dustbin ['dʌstbɪn] *n* (*BRIT*) му́сорное ведро́*.

dustbin liner *n* целофа́новая прокла́дка для му́сорного ведра́.

duster ['dʌstə'] *n* (*cloth*) тря́пка* для пы́ли.

dust jacket *n* суперобло́жка*.

dustman ['dʌstmən] *irreg n* (*BRIT*) му́сорщик.

dustpan ['dʌstpæn] *n* сово́к* для му́сора.

dusty ['dʌstɪ] *adj* пы́льный*.

Dutch [dʌtʃ] *adj* голла́ндский* ♦ *n* (*LING*) голла́ндский* язы́к*; **the ~** *npl* (*people*) голла́ндцы* *mpl*; **they decided to go ~** (*inf*) они́ реши́ли, что ка́ждый пла́тит за себя́.

Dutch auction *n* "голла́ндский* аукцио́н" (*аукцио́н со сниже́нием цен, пока́ не найдётся покупа́тель*).

Dutchman ['dʌtʃmən] *irreg n* голла́ндец*.

Dutchwoman ['dʌtʃwumən] *irreg n* голла́ндка*.

dutiable ['dju:tɪəbl] *adj* (*COMM: goods*) облага́емый по́шлиной.

dutiful ['dju:tɪful] *adj* (*son, daughter*) послу́шный* (послу́шен); (*husband, wife*) поко́рный* (поко́рен); (*employee*) исполни́тельный* (исполни́телен).

duty ['dju:tɪ] *n* (*responsibility*) обя́занность *f*; (*obligation*) долг; (*tax*) по́шлина; **duties** *npl* (*functions*) обя́занности *fpl*; **to make it one's ~ to do** счита́ть (посчита́ть *perf*) свои́м до́лгом +*infin*; **to pay ~ on sth** плати́ть* (заплати́ть* *perf*) по́шлину за что-н; **on ~** на дежу́рстве; **off ~** вне слу́жбы.

duty-free ['dju:tɪ'fri:] *adj* беспо́шлинный; **~ shop** магази́н това́ров не облага́емых по́шлиной.

duty officer *n* (*MIL*) дежу́рный офице́р.

duvet ['du:veɪ] *n* (*BRIT*) пухо́вое одея́ло.

DV *abbr* (= *Deo volente*) Бог даст.

DVD *abbr* (= *digital video disc*) цифрово́й диск.

DVLA *n abbr* (*BRIT*) = *Driver and Vehicle Licensing Authority.*

DVLC *n abbr* (*BRIT*) = *Driver and Vehicle Licensing Centre.*

DVM *n abbr* (*US*: = *Doctor of Veterinary Medicine*) до́ктор ветерина́рных нау́к.

dwarf [dwɔ:f] (*pl* **dwarves**) *n* ка́рлик ◆ *vt* де́лать (сде́лать *perf*) кро́хотным.

dwarves [dwɔ:vz] *npl of* **dwarf**.

dwell [dwɛl] (*pt, pp* **dwelt**) *vi* прожива́ть (прожи́ть* *perf*)

▶ **dwell on** *vt fus* заде́рживаться (задержа́ться* *perf*) на +*prp*.

dweller ['dwɛlə'] *n* жи́тель(ница) *m(f)*, обита́тель(ница) *m(f)*; **city ~** городско́й(-а́я) жи́тель(ница).

dwelling ['dwɛlɪŋ] *n* (*house*) жили́ще.

dwelt [dwɛlt] *pt, pp of* **dwell**.

dwindle ['dwɪndl] *vi* (*interest, attendance*) сокраща́ться (сократи́ться* *perf*).

dwindling ['dwɪndlɪŋ] *adj* (*strength, interest*) убыва́ющий; (*resources, supplies*) сокраща́ющийся.

dye [daɪ] *n* (*for hair, cloth*) краси́тель *m*, кра́ска* ◆ *vt* кра́сить* (покра́сить* *perf*).

dyestuffs ['daɪstʌfs] *npl* краси́тели *mpl*.

dying ['daɪŋ] *adj* умира́ющий; (*moments, words*) предсме́ртный.

dyke [daɪk] *n* (*BRIT: wall*) да́мба; (*channel*) кана́ва; (*causeway*) на́сыпь *f*.

dynamic [daɪ'næmɪk] *adj* (*leader, force*) динами́чный.

dynamics [daɪ'næmɪks] *n or npl* (*TECH*) дина́мика *fsg*.

dynamite ['daɪnəmaɪt] *n* динами́т ◆ *vt* взрыва́ть (взорва́ть* *perf*) динами́том.

dynamo ['daɪnəməu] *n* (*ELEC*) дина́мо-маши́на.

dynasty ['dɪnəstɪ] *n* дина́стия.

dysentery ['dɪsntrɪ] *n* дизентери́я.

dyslexia [dɪs'lɛksɪə] *n* дисле́ксия.

dyslexic [dɪs'lɛksɪk] *adj* дислекти́ческий ◆ *n* дисле́ктик.

dyspepsia [dɪs'pɛpsɪə] *n* диспепси́я.

~ E, e ~

E, e [i:] n (*letter*) 5-ая бу́ква англи́йского алфави́та; (*SCOL: mark*) ≈ о́чень пло́хо.

E [i:] n (*MUS*) ми nt ind.

E abbr (= **east**) B= восто́к ♦ n abbr (= *Ecstasy*) "Экста́з" (*нарко́тик*).

E111 n abbr (*also:* **form** ~) спра́вка, обеспе́чивающая медици́нскую по́мощь за преде́лами Великобрита́нии.

ea. abbr = **each**.

E.A. n abbr (*US*) = educational age.

each [i:tʃ] adj ка́ждый ♦ pron (*each one*) ка́ждый; ~ **other** друг дру́га; **they hate** ~ **other** они́ ненави́дят друг дру́га; **they don't talk to** ~ **other** они́ не разгова́ривают друг с дру́гом; **they think about** ~ **other** они́ ду́мают друг о дру́ге; **they are jealous of** ~ **other** они́ зави́дуют друг дру́гу; ~ **day** ка́ждый день; **they have two books** ~ у ка́ждого из них по две кни́ги; **they cost £5** ~ они́ сто́ят £5 шту́ка *or* за шту́ку; ~ **of us** ка́ждый из нас.

eager [ˈiːɡə] adj (*keen*) нетерпели́во ожида́ющий; **to be** ~ **for** жа́ждать (*impf*) +gen; **he is** ~ **to** ... он по́лон жела́ния +infin ....

eagerly [ˈiːɡəlɪ] adv с воодушевле́нием; (*awaited*) с нетерпе́нием.

eagle [ˈiːɡl] n орёл*.

ear [ɪə] n (*ANAT*) у́хо*; (*of corn*) ко́лос*; **up to one's** ~**s in debt/work/paint** по́ у́ши в долга́х/в рабо́те/в кра́ске; **to give sb a thick** ~ дать* (*perf*) кому́-н в у́хо; **we'll play it by** ~ (*fig*) мы посмо́трим по ситуа́ции.

earache [ˈɪəreɪk] n боль f в у́хе; **I have** ~ у меня́ боли́т у́хо.

eardrum [ˈɪədrʌm] n бараба́нная перепо́нка*.

earful [ˈɪəful] n (*inf*): **to give sb an** ~ устра́ивать (устро́ить *perf*) разно́с кому́-н.

earl [ə:l] n (*BRIT*) граф.

earlier [ˈə:lɪə] adj бо́лее ра́нний ♦ adv ра́ньше; **I can't come any** ~ я не могу́ прийти́ ра́ньше.

early [ˈə:lɪ] adv ра́но ♦ adj ра́нний*; (*death, departure*) преждевре́менный*; (*quick: reply*) незамедли́тельный; (*Christians, settlers*) пе́рвый; ~ **in the morning** ра́но у́тром; **to have an** ~ **night** ра́но ложи́ться (лечь* *perf*) спать; **in the** ~ **spring,** ~ **in the spring** ра́нней весно́й; **in the** ~ **19th century,** ~ **in the 19th century** в нача́ле 19-го ве́ка; **you need to take the** ~ **train** Вам на́до е́хать* ра́нним по́ездом; **you're** ~! Вы пришли́ ра́но!; **she's in her** ~ **forties** ей немно́го за со́рок; **at your earliest convenience** в ближа́йшее удо́бное для Вас вре́мя.

early retirement n: **to take** ~ ~ ра́но уходи́ть* (уйти́* *perf*) на пе́нсию.

early warning system n (*MIL*) систе́ма ра́ннего предупрежде́ния.

earmark [ˈɪəmɑːk] vt: **to** ~ **for** (*funds*) предназнача́ть (предназна́чить *perf*) для +gen.

earn [ə:n] vt (*salary*) зараба́тывать (зарабо́тать *perf*); (*interest*) приноси́ть* (принести́* *perf*); (*praise*) заслу́живать (заслужи́ть* *perf*); **to** ~ **one's living** зараба́тывать (*impf*) на жизнь; **this** ~**ed him much praise, he** ~**ed much praise for this** э́то принесло́ ему́ мно́го похва́л, он заслужи́л мно́го похва́л за э́то; **he's** ~**ed his rest/reward** он заслужи́л свой о́тдых/свою́ награ́ду.

earned income [ə:nd-] n (*COMM*) трудово́й дохо́д.

earnest [ˈə:nɪst] adj (*person, manner*) серьёзный* (серьёзен); (*wish, desire*) и́скренний* ♦ n (*also:* ~ **money**) зада́ток*; **in** ~ всерьёз; **work on the tunnel soon began in** ~ рабо́та по прокла́дке тунне́ля вско́ре начала́сь всерьёз; **is he in** ~ **about these proposals?** всерьёз ли он говори́т об э́тих предложе́ниях?

earnings [ˈə:nɪŋz] npl (*personal*) за́работок* msg; (*of company etc*) при́быль fsg.

ear nose and throat specialist n (*MED*) отоларинго́лог, врач* у́хо-го́рло-но́с.

earphones [ˈɪəfəunz] npl нау́шники mpl.

earplugs [ˈɪəplʌgz] npl заты́чки fpl для уше́й.

earring [ˈɪərɪŋ] n серьга́*.

earshot [ˈɪəʃɔt] n: **within/out of** ~ в преде́лах/вне преде́лов слы́шимости.

earth [ə:θ] n земля́*; (*BRIT: ELEC*) заземле́ние; (*of fox*) нора́* ♦ vt (*BRIT: ELEC*) заземля́ть (заземли́ть *perf*); **E**~ (*planet*) Земля́*.

---

* marks translations which have irregular inflections. The Russian-English side of the dictionary gives inflectional information.

earthenware ['ə:θnwɛə'] *n* керамика, гончарные изделия *pl* ◆ *adj* глиняный.

earthly ['ə:θlɪ] *adj* земной; ~ **paradise** земной рай*; **there is no ~ reason to think ...** нет ни малейшей причины думать ....

earthquake ['ə:θkweɪk] *n* землетрясение.

earthshattering ['ə:θʃætərɪŋ] *adj* (*surprising*) потрясающий* (потрясающ).

earth tremor *n* подземный толчок*.

earthworks ['ə:θwə:ks] *npl* земляные работы *fpl*.

earthworm ['ə:θwə:m] *n* земляной червь* *m*.

earthy ['ə:θɪ] *adj* (*humour*) грубоватый (грубоват).

earwig ['ɪəwɪg] *n* уховёртка*.

ease [i:z] *n* лёгкость *f*; (*comfort*) покой* ◆ *vt* (*pain*) облегчать (облегчить *perf*); (*problem*) уменьшать (уменьшить *perf*); (*tension*) ослаблять (ослабить* *perf*); (*loosen: grip, belt*) отпускать (отпустить* *perf*) ◆ *vi* (*situation*) упрощаться (упроститься* *perf*); (*pain, grief, grip*) слабеть (ослабеть *perf*); (*rain, snow*) становиться* (стать* *perf*) тише; **to ~ sth into sth** вставлять (вставить* *perf*) что-н в что-н; **to ~ sth out of sth** выдвигать (выдвинуть *perf*) что-н из чего-н; **to ~ o.s. into** опускаться (опуститься *perf*) в +*acc*; **at ~!** (*MIL*) вольно!; **with ~** с лёгкостью; **life of ~** жизнь в покое и довольстве

► **ease off** *vi* становиться* (стать* *perf*) тише; (*slow down*) замедляться (замедлиться *perf*)

► **ease up** *vi* = **ease off**.

easel ['i:zl] *n* мольберт.

easily ['i:zɪlɪ] *adv* легко; (*in a relaxed manner*) непринуждённо; (*without doubt*) несомненно.

easiness ['i:zɪnɪs] *n* лёгкость *f*; (*of manner*) непринуждённость *f*.

east [i:st] *n* восток ◆ *adj* восточный ◆ *adv* на восток; **the E~** Восток.

Easter ['i:stə'] *n* пасха ◆ *adj* пасхальный.

Easter egg *n* (*painted*) пасхальное яйцо*; (*chocolate*) шоколадное пасхальное яйцо*.

Easter Island *n* остров Пасхи.

easterly ['i:stəlɪ] *adj* восточный.

Easter Monday *n* ≈ Светлый понедельник.

eastern ['i:stən] *adj* восточный; (*POL*) восточно-европейский; **E~ Europe** Восточная Европа; **the E~ bloc** (*formerly*) Восточно-Европейский* блок.

Easter Sunday *n* ≈ Светлое *or* Христово воскресенье.

East Germany *n* (*formerly*) Восточная Германия.

eastward(s) ['i:stwəd(z)] *adv* на восток.

easy ['i:zɪ] *adj* лёгкий*; (*manner*) непринуждённый* ◆ *adv*: **to take it** *or* **things ~** не напрягаться (*impf*); (*not worry*) не волноваться (*impf*); **payment on ~ terms** (*COMM*) платёж* на лёгких условиях; **that's easier said than done** легче сказать, чем

сделать; **I'm ~** (*inf*) мне всё равно.

easy chair *n* удобное кресло*.

easy-going ['i:zɪ'gəuɪŋ] *adj* с лёгким характером.

easy touch *n* (*inf*): **she is an ~ ~** её легко убедить.

eat [i:t] (*pt* **ate**, *pp* **eaten**) *vt* есть* (съесть* *perf*) ◆ *vi* есть* (*impf*)

► **eat away** *vt* (*rock, metal*) разъедать (разъесть* *perf*); (*savings*) съедать (съесть* *perf*)

► **eat away at** *vt fus* = **eat away**

► **eat into** *vt fus* = **eat away**

► **eat out** *vi* есть* (*impf*) в ресторане

► **eat up** *vt* (*food*) доедать (доесть* *perf*); **it ~s up electricity** это потребляет много электроэнергии.

eatable ['i:təbl] *adj* съедобный*.

eaten ['i:tn] *pp of* **eat**.

eau de Cologne ['əudəkə'ləun] *n* одеколон*.

eaves [i:vz] *npl* (*of house*) карниз *msg*.

eavesdrop ['i:vzdrɔp] *vi*: **to ~ (on)** подслушивать (подслушать *perf*).

ebb [ɛb] *n* отлив ◆ *vi* (*tide, sea*) отливать (*impf*); (*fig: also: ~ away*) угасать (угаснуть *perf*); **the ~ and flow** отлив и прилив; **to be at a low ~** (*fig*) находиться* (*impf*) в состоянии упадка.

ebb tide *n* отлив.

ebony ['ɛbənɪ] *n* эбеновое *or* чёрное дерево.

ebullient [ɪ'bʌlɪənt] *adj* полный* (полон) энтузиазма.

EC *n abbr* (= *European Community*) ЕС = *Европейское сообщество или союз*.

ECB *n abbr* (= *European Central Bank*) Европейский центральный банк.

eccentric [ɪk'sɛntrɪk] *adj* (*choice, views*) эксцентричный* ◆ *n* эксцентричный человек*.

ecclesiastic(al) [ɪkli:zɪ'æstɪk(l)] *adj* духовный*.

ECG *n abbr* = **electrocardiogram**.

echo ['ɛkəu] (*pl* **~es**) *n* эхо *no pl* ◆ *vt* (*repeat*) вторить (*impf*) +*dat* ◆ *vi* (*sound*) отдаваться* (*impf*); **the room ~ed with her laughter** в комнате раздавался её смех.

éclair ['eɪklɛə'] *n* эклер.

eclipse [ɪ'klɪps] *n* затмение ◆ *vt* (*also fig*) затмевать (затмить* *perf*).

ECM *n abbr* (*US*: = *European Common Market*) Общий* рынок*.

eco- ['i:kəu] *prefix* эко-.

eco-friendly ['i:kəu'frɛndlɪ] *adj* экологически безопасный* (безопасен).

ecological [i:kə'lɔdʒɪkəl] *adj* экологический*.

ecologist [ɪ'kɔlədʒɪst] *n* эколог.

ecology [ɪ'kɔlədʒɪ] *n* (*SCOL*) экология; (*environment*) окружающая среда.

economic [i:kə'nɔmɪk] *adj* экономический*; (*profitable*) рентабельный* (рентабелен).

economical [i:kə'nɔmɪkl] *adj* (*cheap to run*) экономичный* (экономичен); (*thrifty*) экономный*.

economically [i:kə'nɔmɪklɪ] *adv* экономно;

(*regarding economics*) экономически.
economics [i:kə'nɔmɪks] *n* экономика ♦ *npl* (*of project, situation*) экономический* расчёт *msg*.
economic warfare *n* экономическая война.
economist [ɪ'kɔnəmɪst] *n* экономист.
economize [ɪ'kɔnəmaɪz] *vi* экономить* (сэкономить* *perf*).
economy [ɪ'kɔnəmɪ] *n* экономика, хозяйство; (*financial prudence*) экономия; **economies of scale** (*COMM*) экономичность за счёт крупных объёмов операций.
economy class *n* (*AVIAT*) *наиболее дешёвые посадочные места*.
economy size *n* (*COMM*) *большая упаковка какого-либо товара, стоящая дешевле, чем маленькая*.
ecosystem ['i:kəʊsɪstəm] *n* экосистема.
ECSC *n abbr* (= *European Coal & Steel Community*) *европейское сообщество производителей угля и стали*.
ecstasy ['ɛkstəsɪ] *n* экстаз; **to go into ecstasies over** впадать (впасть* *perf*) в экстаз от +*gen*; **in ecstasy** в экстазе.
ecstatic [ɛks'tætɪk] *adj* восторженный*.
ECT *n abbr* = **electroconvulsive therapy**.
ECU *n abbr* (= *European Currency Unit*) экю *ind*.
Ecuador ['ɛkwədɔ:'] *n* Эквадор.
ecumenical [i:kju'mɛnɪkl] *adj* вселенский.
eczema ['ɛksɪmə] *n* экзема.
eddy ['ɛdɪ] *n* (*of water*) водоворот; (*of air*) вихрь *m*.
edge [ɛdʒ] *n* край*; (*of knife etc*) остриё* ♦ *vt* (*trim*) окаймлять (окаймить* *perf*) ♦ *vi*: **to ~ forward** медленно продвигаться (продвинуться *perf*); **on ~** (*fig*) = **edgy**; **to have the ~ on** иметь (*impf*) преимущество перед +*instr*; **to ~ past** протиснуться (*perf*); **to ~ away from** отходить* (отойти* *perf*) бочком от +*gen*; **to ~ up** (*COMM*) незначительно изменяться.
edgeways ['ɛdʒweɪz] *adv*: **he couldn't get a word in** = он не мог словечка ввернуть *or* слова вставить.
edging ['ɛdʒɪŋ] *n* кайма*.
edgy ['ɛdʒɪ] *adj* (*nervous, agitated*) раздражённый*.
edible ['ɛdɪbl] *adj* съедобный* (съедобен).
edict ['i:dɪkt] *n* указ.
edifice ['ɛdɪfɪs] *n* величественное здание.
edifying ['ɛdɪfaɪɪŋ] *adj* поучительный* (поучителен).
Edinburgh ['ɛdɪnbərə] *n* Эдинбург.
edit ['ɛdɪt] *vt* (*text, newspaper, COMPUT*) редактировать (отредактировать *perf*); (*book*) готовить* (подготовить* *perf*) к печати; (*film, broadcast*) монтировать (смонтировать *perf*).

edition [ɪ'dɪʃən] *n* (*of book*) издание; (*of newspaper, TV programme*) выпуск.
editor ['ɛdɪtə'] *n* редактор*; **foreign/political ~** (*PRESS*) редактор* отдела зарубёжных новостей/политики.
editorial [ɛdɪ'tɔ:rɪəl] *adj* редакционный ♦ *n* передовица, передовая статья*.
EDP *n abbr* (*COMPUT*) = **electronic data processing**.
EDT *abbr* (*US*) = *Eastern Daylight Time*.
educate ['ɛdjukeɪt] *vt* (*teach*) давать* (дать* *perf*) образование +*dat*; (*instruct*) просвещать (просветить* *perf*); **to be ~d at ...** получать (получить *perf*) образование в +*prp*.
educated guess ['ɛdjukeɪtɪd-] *n* догадка располагающего предварительной информацией.
education [ɛdju'keɪʃən] *n* (*schooling*) образование; (*teaching*) обучение; (*knowledge*) образованность *f*; **primary or** (*US*) **elementary/secondary ~** начальное/среднее образование.
educational [ɛdju'keɪʃənl] *adj* (*institution*) учебный; (*staff*) преподавательский; (*policy, practice*) учебный, воспитательный; (*toy*) обучающий; **~ system** система образования; **~ technology** технические средства обучения.
Edwardian [ɛd'wɔ:dɪən] *adj* эпохи английского короля Эдуарда VII.
EE *abbr* = **electrical engineer**.
EEC *n abbr* (= *European Economic Community*) ЕЭС= *Европейское экономическое сообщество*.
EEG *n abbr* = **electroencephalogram**.
eel [i:l] *n* угорь* *m*.
EENT *n abbr* (*US: MED*: = *eye, ear, nose and throat*) ≈ ухо-горло-нос.
EEOC *n abbr* (*US*: = *Equal Employment Opportunity Commission*) *комиссия равных возможностей при найме на работу*.
eerie ['ɪərɪ] *adj* жуткий*.
EET *abbr* (= *Eastern European Time*) восточноевропейское время* *nt*.
efface [ɪ'feɪs] *vt* (*erase*) стирать (стереть* *perf*); **to ~ o.s.** держаться* (*impf*) в тени.
effect [ɪ'fɛkt] *n* (*result*) эффект, последствие; (*impression*) впечатление, эффект ♦ *vt* (*carry out*) производить* (произвести* *perf*); **~s** *npl* (*property*) имущество *ntsg*; (*THEAT, CINEMA*) эффекты *mpl*; **to take ~** (*drug*) действовать (подействовать *perf*); (*law*) вступать (вступить* *perf*) в силу; **to put into ~** осуществлять (осуществить* *perf*); **to have an ~ on sb/sth** действовать (подействовать *perf*) на кого-н/что-н; **in ~** в сущности; **his letter is to the ~ that ...** суть его письма заключается в том, что ....

---

effective [ɪ'fɛktɪv] *adj* (*successful*) эффекти́вный* (эффекти́вен); (*actual*) действи́тельный*; **to become ~** (*LAW*) входи́ть* (войти́* *perf*) в си́лу; **~ date** да́та вступле́ния в си́лу.

effectively [ɪ'fɛktɪvlɪ] *adv* (*successfully*) эффекти́вно; (*in reality*) факти́чески.

effectiveness [ɪ'fɛktɪvnɪs] *n* (*success*) эффекти́вность *f*.

effeminate [ɪ'fɛmɪnɪt] *adj* женоподо́бный* (женоподо́бен).

effervescent [ɛfə'vɛsnt] *adj* (*drink*) шипу́чий*.

efficacy ['ɛfɪkəsɪ] *n* эффекти́вность *f*.

efficiency [ɪ'fɪʃənsɪ] *n* (*see adj*) эффекти́вность *f*; делови́тость *f*.

efficiency apartment *n* (*US*) кварти́ра, соединя́ющая в себе́ спа́льню, гости́ную и иногда́ ку́хню.

efficient [ɪ'fɪʃənt] *adj* (*organization, method, machine*) эффекти́вный* (эффекти́вен); (*person*) делови́тый.

efficiently [ɪ'fɪʃəntlɪ] *adv* эффекти́вно.

effigy ['ɛfɪdʒɪ] *n* (*dummy*) чу́чело; (*image*) изображе́ние.

effluent ['ɛfluənt] *n* сток, жи́дкие отхо́ды *mpl*.

effort ['ɛfət] *n* (*attempt*) попы́тка*; (*exertion, concerted attempt*) уси́лие; **to make an ~ to do** прикла́дывать (приложи́ть* *perf*) уси́лия, что́бы +*infin*.

effortless ['ɛfətlɪs] *adj* (*achievement*) не тре́бующий уси́лий; (*style*) лёгкий*.

effrontery [ɪ'frʌntərɪ] *n* наха́льство, на́глость *f*; **to have the ~ to do** име́ть (*impf*) наха́льство *or* на́глость, что́бы +*infin*.

effusive [ɪ'fju:sɪv] *adj* экспанси́вный*.

EFL *n abbr* (*SCOL*) = *English as a Foreign Language*.

EFTA ['ɛftə] *n abbr* (= *European Free Trade Association*) ЕАСТ= *Европе́йская ассоциа́ция свобо́дной торго́вли*.

e.g. *adv abbr* (*for example*: = *exempli gratia*) наприме́р.

egalitarian [ɪgælɪ'tɛərɪən] *adj* эгалита́рный ♦ *n* (*person*) побо́рник(-ица) равнопра́вия.

egg [ɛg] *n* яйцо́; **hard-boiled/soft-boiled ~** яйцо́ вкруту́ю/всмя́тку

▶ **egg on** *vt* (*encourage*) подстрека́ть (подстрекну́ть *perf*).

egg cup *n* рю́мка* для яйца́.

eggplant ['ɛgplɑ:nt] *n* (*esp US*) баклажа́н*.

eggshell ['ɛgʃɛl] *n* яи́чная скорлупа́* ♦ *adj* (*paint*) ма́товый.

egg timer *n* та́ймер.

egg white *n* яи́чный бело́к*.

egg yolk *n* яи́чный желто́к*.

ego ['i:gəu] *n* (*self-esteem*) самолю́бие.

egoism ['ɛgəuɪzəm] *n* эго́йзм.

egoist ['ɛgəuɪst] *n* эго́йст(ка*).

egotism ['ɛgəutɪzəm] *n* эготи́зм.

egotist ['ɛgəutɪst] *n* эготи́ст(ка*).

ego trip *n* (*pej*) самоублаже́ние.

Egypt ['i:dʒɪpt] *n* Еги́пет*.

Egyptian [ɪ'dʒɪpʃən] *adj* еги́петский* ♦ *n* египтя́нин*(-я́нка*).

eiderdown ['aɪdədaun] *n* (*quilt*) ва́тное одея́ло.

eight [eɪt] *n* во́семь*; *see also* **five**.

eighteen [eɪ'ti:n] *n* восемна́дцать*; *see also* **five**.

eighteenth [eɪ'ti:nθ] *adj* восемна́дцатый; *see also* **fifth**.

eighth [eɪtθ] *adj* восьмо́й ♦ *n* (*fraction*) восьма́я *f adj*; *see also* **fifth**.

eightieth ['eɪtɪəθ] *adj* восьмидеся́тый; *see also* **fifth**.

eighty ['eɪtɪ] *n* во́семьдесят*; *see also* **fifty**.

Eire ['ɛərə] *n* Эйре *nt ind*.

EIS *n abbr* = *Educational Institute of Scotland*.

either ['aɪðə'] *adj* (*one or other*) любо́й (из двух); (*both, each*) ка́ждый ♦ *adv* та́кже ♦ *pron*: **~ (of them)** любо́й (из них) ♦ *conj*: **~ yes or no** ли́бо "да", ли́бо "нет"; **on ~ side** на обе́их сторона́х; **I don't smoke – I don't ~** я не курю́ – я то́же; **I don't like ~** мне не нра́вится ни то, ни друго́е; **there was no sound from ~ of the flats** не́ было зву́ка ни из одно́й из кварти́р; **I haven't seen ~** я не ви́дел ни того́, ни друго́го.

ejaculation [ɪdʒækju'leɪʃən] *n* (*PHYSIOL*) эякуля́ция.

eject [ɪ'dʒɛkt] *vt* выбра́сывать (вы́бросить* *perf*); (*tenant*) выселя́ть (вы́селить *perf*); (*gate-crasher*) выгоня́ть (вы́гнать* *perf*) ♦ *vi* (*pilot*) катапульти́роваться (*impf/perf*).

ejector seat [ɪ'dʒɛktə-] *n* (*AVIAT*) катапульти́руемое кре́сло*.

Ekaterinburg [jɪkətɪrɪn'burk] *n* Екатеринбу́рг.

eke [i:k] *vi*: **to ~ out** (*income*) растя́гивать (растяну́ть *perf*); **to ~ out a living from** существова́ть (*impf*) за счёт +*gen*.

EKG *n abbr* (*US*) = **electrocardiogram**.

el [ɛl] *n abbr* (*US*: *inf*: = *elevated railroad*) надзе́мная желе́зная доро́га.

elaborate [*adj* ɪ'læbərɪt, *vb* ɪ'læbəreɪt] *adj* сло́жный* ♦ *vt* (*expand*) развива́ть (разви́ть* *perf*); (*refine*) тща́тельно разраба́тывать (разрабо́тать *perf*) ♦ *vi*: **to ~ on** (*idea, plan etc*) рассма́тривать (рассмотре́ть* *perf*) в деталя́х.

elapse [ɪ'læps] *vi* (*time*) проходи́ть* (пройти́* *perf*).

elastic [ɪ'læstɪk] *n* (*material*) рези́нка ♦ *adj* (*stretchy*) эласти́чный* (эласти́чен); (*adaptable*) ги́бкий* (ги́бок).

elastic band *n* (*BRIT*) рези́нка*.

elasticity [ɪlæs'tɪsɪtɪ] *n* эласти́чность *f*.

elated [ɪ'leɪtɪd] *adj*: **to be ~** быть* (*impf*) в припо́днятом настрое́нии.

elation [ɪ'leɪʃən] *n* припо́днятое настрое́ние.

elbow ['ɛlbəu] *n* ло́коть* *m* ♦ *vt*: **to ~ one's way through the crowd** прота́лкиваться (*impf*) в толпе́.

elbow grease *n*: **a lot of ~ ~ is required** придётся хороше́нько потруди́ться.

elbowroom ['ɛlbəʊrʊm] *n* простóр.
elder ['ɛldə'] *adj* (*brother, sister etc*) стáрший* ♦ *n* (*tree*) бузинá; (*older person*): ~s стáршие *pl adj*.
elderly ['ɛldəlɪ] *adj* пожилóй; **the** ~ *npl* стáрые лю́ди *pl*, престарéлые *pl adj*.
elder statesman *irreg n* заслýженный полити́ческий* дéятель *m*.
eldest ['ɛldɪst] *adj* (*child*) (сáмый) стáрший* ♦ *n* стáрший*(-ая) *m(f) adj*.
elect [ɪ'lɛkt] *vt* избирáть (избрáть* *perf*) ♦ *adj*: **the president** ~ и́збранный президéнт; **to** ~ **to do** (*choose*) предпочитáть (предпочéсть* *perf*) +*infin*.
election [ɪ'lɛkʃən] *n* (*voting*) вы́боры *pl*; (*installation*) избрáние; **to hold an** ~ проводи́ть* (провести́* *perf*) вы́боры.
election campaign *n* избирáтельная кампáния.
electioneering [ɪlɛkʃə'nɪərɪŋ] *n* агитáция.
elector [ɪ'lɛktə'] *n* избирáтель(ница) *m(f)*.
electoral [ɪ'lɛktərəl] *adj* избирáтельный.
electoral college *n* коллéгия вы́борщиков.
electorate [ɪ'lɛktərɪt] *n*: **the** ~ избирáтели *mpl*.
electric [ɪ'lɛktrɪk] *adj* электри́ческий*.
electrical [ɪ'lɛktrɪkl] *adj* электри́ческий*; ~ **failure** отключéние тóка.
electrical engineer *n* инженéр-элéктрик.
electric blanket *n* одеялó-грéлка*.
electric chair *n* (*US*) электри́ческий* стул*.
electric cooker *n* электри́ческая плитá*.
electric current *n* электри́ческий* ток.
electric fire *n* (*BRIT*) электри́ческий* камéн.
electrician [ɪlɛk'trɪʃən] *n* электромонтёр, элéктрик.
electricity [ɪlɛk'trɪsɪtɪ] *n* электри́чество ♦ *cpd* электри́ческий*; **to switch on/off the** ~ подключáть (подключи́ть *perf*)/отключáть (отключи́ть *perf*) электри́чество; ~ **bill** счёт* за электри́чество.
electricity board *n* (*BRIT*) управлéние по электрификáции.
electric light *n* электри́ческий* свет.
electric shock *n* удáр тóком.
electrify [ɪ'lɛktrɪfaɪ] *vt* (*fence, rail network*) электрифици́ровать (*impf/perf*); (*thrill*) электризовáть (наэлектризовáть *perf*).
electro... [ɪ'lɛktrəʊ] *prefix* элéктро....
electrocardiogram [ɪ'lɛktrə'kɑ:dɪəgræm] *n* электрокардиогрáмма.
electroconvulsive therapy [ɪ'lɛktrəkən'vʌlsɪv-] *n* электротóковая терапи́я.
electrocute [ɪ'lɛktrəkju:t] *vt* (*person: kill*) убивáть (уби́ть* *perf*) электри́ческим тóком; (: *injure*) ударя́ть (удáрить *perf*) электри́ческим тóком.
electrode [ɪ'lɛktrəʊd] *n* электрóд.

electroencephalogram [ɪ'lɛktrəʊɛn'sɛfələgræm] *n* электро-энцефалогрáмма.
electrolysis [ɪlɛk'trɒlɪsɪs] *n* электрóлиз.
electromagnetic [ɪ'lɛktrəmæg'nɛtɪk] *adj* электромагни́тный.
electron [ɪ'lɛktrɒn] *n* электрóн.
electronic [ɪlɛk'trɒnɪk] *adj* электрóнный
electronic data processing *n* электрóнная обрабóтка информáции.
electronic mail *n* (*COMPUT*) электрóнная пóчта.
electronics [ɪlɛk'trɒnɪks] *n* электрóника.
electron microscope *n* электрóнный микроскóп.
electroplated [ɪ'lɛktrə'pleɪtɪd] *adj* покры́тый *метáллом с пóмощью электрóлиза*.
electrotherapy [ɪ'lɛktrə'θɛrəpɪ] *n* электро-терапи́я.
elegance ['ɛlɪgəns] *n* элегáнтность *f*.
elegant ['ɛlɪgənt] *adj* элегáнтный* (элегáнтен).
element ['ɛlɪmənt] *n* (*also* CHEM) элемéнт; (*of heater, kettle etc*) электронагревáтельный элемéнт; **the** ~**s** *npl* стихи́я *fsg*; **you are in your** ~ Вы в своéй стихи́и.
elementary [ɛlɪ'mɛntərɪ] *adj* элементáрный* (элементáрен); (*school, education*) начáльный.
elephant ['ɛlɪfənt] *n* слон*(и́ха).
elevate ['ɛlɪveɪt] *vt* (*in rank*) повышáть (повы́сить* *perf*); (*in importance*) возводи́ть* (возвести́* *perf*); (*physically*) поднимáть (подня́ть* *perf*).
elevated railroad ['ɛlɪveɪtɪd-] *n* (*US*) надзéмная желéзная дорóга.
elevation [ɛlɪ'veɪʃən] *n* (*see vb*) повышéние; возведéние; подня́тие; (*height*) высотá*; (*ARCHIT*) фасáд.
elevator ['ɛlɪveɪtə'] *n* (*US*) лифт; (*in warehouse etc*) грузоподъёмник.
eleven [ɪ'lɛvn] *n* оди́ннадцать*; *see also* **five**.
elevenses [ɪ'lɛvnzɪz] *npl* (*BRIT*) лёгкий зáвтрак *óколо оди́ннадцати часóв утрá*.
eleventh [ɪ'lɛvnθ] *adj* оди́ннадцатый; **at the** ~ **hour** в послéднюю минýту; *see also* **fifth**.
elf [ɛlf] (*pl* **elves**) *n* эльф.
elicit [ɪ'lɪsɪt] *vt*: **to** ~ (**from**) (*information*) извлекáть (извлéчь* *perf*) (из +*gen*); (*response, reaction*) вызывáть (вы́звать* *perf*) (от +*gen*); **to** ~ **a reply** добивáться (доби́ться* *perf*) отвéта; **to** ~ **applause from the audience** вызывáть (вы́звать* *perf*) аплодисмéнты аудитóрии.
eligible ['ɛlɪdʒəbl] *adj* (*for marriage*) подходя́щий*; **to be** ~ **for sth** (*qualified, suitable*) быть* (*impf*) подходя́щей кандидатýрой для чегó-н; **to be** ~ **for a pension** имéть (*impf*) прáво на пéнсию.

---

eliminate [ɪˈlɪmɪneɪt] *vt* ликвиди́ровать *(impf/ perf)*, исключа́ть (исключи́ть *perf*); (*candidate, team, contestant*) отсе́ивать (отсе́ять *perf*); **they were ~d in the first round** они́ бы́ли отсе́яны на пе́рвом ту́ре.

elimination [ɪlɪmɪˈneɪʃən] *n* ликвида́ция, исключе́ние; (*of team, candidate*) устране́ние; **by process of ~** путём исключе́ния *or* ликвида́ции.

élite [eɪˈliːt] *n* эли́та.

élitist [eɪˈliːtɪst] *adj* (*pej*) элита́рный.

elixir [ɪˈlɪksəˈ] *n* эликси́р.

Elizabethan [ɪlɪzəˈbiːθən] *adj* (*house, music, period*) эпо́хи короле́вы Елизаве́ты.

ellipse [ɪˈlɪps] *n* (*MATH*) э́ллипс.

elliptical [ɪˈlɪptɪkl] *adj* (*MATH*) эллипти́ческий.

elm [ɛlm] *n* вяз.

elocution [ɛləˈkjuːʃən] *n* ора́торское иску́сство.

elongated [ˈiːlɔŋɡeɪtɪd] *adj* удлинённый* (удлинён).

elope [ɪˈləup] *vi*: **to ~ (with)** та́йно сбежа́ть* (*perf*) (с +*instr*).

elopement [ɪˈləupmənt] *n* та́йное бе́гство.

eloquence [ˈɛləkwəns] *n* (*see adj*) краснор́ечие; я́ркость *f*.

eloquent [ˈɛləkwənt] *adj* (*description, person*) краснор́ечивый; (*speech*) я́ркий*.

El Salvador [ɛlˈsælvədɔːˈ] *n* Сальвадо́р.

else [ɛls] *adv* (*other*) ещё; **nothing ~** бо́льше ничего́; **somewhere ~** (*be*) где́-нибудь ещё; (*go*) куда́-нибудь ещё; (*come from*) отку́да-то ещё; **everywhere ~** везде́; **where ~?** (*position*) где ещё?; (*motion*) куда́ ещё?; **is there anything ~ I can do to help?** я могу́ чём-нибудь ещё помо́чь?; **there was little ~ to do** почти́ не́чем бы́ло заня́ться; **everyone ~** все остальны́е; **nobody ~ spoke** бо́льше никто́ не выступа́л; **or ~ ...** не то (бу́дет ху́же) ....

elsewhere [ɛlsˈwɛəˈ] *adv* (*be*) где́-нибудь ещё (*в друго́м ме́сте*); (*go*) куда́-нибудь ещё (*в друго́е ме́сто*).

ELT *n abbr* (*SCOL*) = **English Language Teaching**.

elucidate [ɪˈluːsɪdeɪt] *vt* разъясня́ть (разъясни́ть *perf*).

elude [ɪˈluːd] *vt* (*captor, capture*) ускольза́ть (ускользну́ть *perf*) от +*gen*; (*subj: fact, idea*): **to ~ sb** не приходи́ть (*impf*) кому́-н на ум.

elusive [ɪˈluːsɪv] *adj* (*person, animal*) неулови́мый; (*quality*) не поддаю́щийся описа́нию; **he's very ~** он о́чень за́мкнутый.

elves [ɛlvz] *npl of* **elf**.

emaciated [ɪˈmeɪsɪeɪtɪd] *adj* (*person, animal*) истощённый*.

E-mail *n abbr* (= *electronic mail*) электро́нная по́чта.

emanate [ˈɛməneɪt] *vi*: **to ~ from** исходи́ть (*impf*) от +*gen*.

emancipate [ɪˈmænsɪpeɪt] *vt* освобожда́ть (освободи́ть* *perf*), эмансипи́ровать (*impf/ perf*).

emancipation [ɪmænsɪˈpeɪʃən] *n* освобожде́ние, эмансипа́ция.

emasculate [ɪˈmæskjuleɪt] *vt* (*weaken*) ослабля́ть (осла́бить* *perf*).

embalm [ɪmˈbɑːm] *vt* бальзами́ровать (забальзами́ровать *perf*).

embankment [ɪmˈbæŋkmənt] *n* (*of road, railway*) на́сыпь *f*; (*of river*) на́бережная *f adj*.

embargo [ɪmˈbɑːɡəu] (*pl* **~es**) *n* эмба́рго *nt ind* ♦ *vt* запреща́ть (запрети́ть* *perf*); **to put** *or* **impose** *or* **place an ~ on sth** накла́дывать (наложи́ть* *perf*) эмба́рго на что-н; **to lift an ~ from** снима́ть (снять* *perf*) эмба́рго с +*gen*.

embark [ɪmˈbɑːk] *vi*: **to ~ (on)** (*ship*) грузи́ться* (погрузи́ться* *perf*) (на +*acc*); **to ~ on** (*journey*) отправля́ться (отпра́виться* *perf*) в +*acc*; (*task, course of action*) предпринима́ть (предприня́ть* *perf*).

embarkation [ɛmbɑːˈkeɪʃən] *n* (*of people*) поса́дка; (*of cargo*) погру́зка.

embarkation card *n* поса́дочный тало́н.

embarrass [ɪmˈbærəs] *vt* смуща́ть (смути́ть* *perf*); (*politician, government*) затрудня́ть (затрудни́ть* *perf*).

embarrassed [ɪmˈbærəst] *adj* (*laugh, silence*) смущённый*; **to be ~** смуща́ться (смути́ться* *perf*).

embarrassing [ɪmˈbærəsɪŋ] *adj* вызыва́ющий смуще́ние, щекотли́вый.

embarrassment [ɪmˈbærəsmənt] *n* (*feeling*) смуще́ние; (*problem*) стыд*.

embassy [ˈɛmbəsɪ] *n* посо́льство; **the French E~** Францу́зское посо́льство, посо́льство Фра́нции.

embedded [ɪmˈbɛdɪd] *adj* (*object*) заде́ланный; (*attitude, belief*) устоя́вшийся.

embellish [ɪmˈbɛlɪʃ] *vt* (*story*) приукра́шивать (приукра́сить* *perf*); (*place, dress*): **~ed with** укра́шенный +*instr*.

embers [ˈɛmbəz] *npl* тле́ющие уголькú *mpl*.

embezzle [ɪmˈbɛzl] *vt* присва́ивать (присво́ить *perf*).

embezzlement [ɪmˈbɛzlmənt] *n* растра́та.

embezzler [ɪmˈbɛzləˈ] *n* растра́тчик(-ица).

embitter [ɪmˈbɪtəˈ] *vt* (*fig*) озлобля́ть (озло́бить* *perf*).

embittered [ɪmˈbɪtəd] *adj* (*person*) озло́бленный*.

emblem [ˈɛmbləm] *n* эмбле́ма.

embodiment [ɪmˈbɔdɪmənt] *n*: **she is the ~ of** она́ – воплоще́ние +*gen*.

embody [ɪmˈbɔdɪ] *vt* (*incarnate*) воплоща́ть (воплоти́ть* *perf*); (*include, contain*) содержа́ть (*impf*) (в себе́).

embolden [ɪmˈbəuldn] *vt* ободря́ть (ободри́ть *perf*).

embolism [ˈɛmbəlɪzəm] *n* эмболи́я.

embossed [ɪmˈbɔst] *adj* (*design, word*) рельéфный*; **~ with his initials** с рельéфными инициáлами.

embrace [ɪmˈbreɪs] *vt* обнима́ть (обня́ть* *perf*); (*include*) охва́тывать (охвати́ть* *perf*) ♦ *vi* обнима́ться (*impf*) ♦ *n* объя́тие.

embroider [ɪmˈbrɔɪdəʳ] *vt* (*cloth*) вышива́ть (вы́шить* *perf*); (*fig: story*) приукра́шивать (приукра́сить* *perf*).

embroidery [ɪmˈbrɔɪdərɪ] *n* (*stitching*) вы́шивка; (*activity*) вышива́ние.

embroil [ɪmˈbrɔɪl] *vt*: **to become ~ed** (**in sth**) ока́зываться (оказа́ться* *perf*) вовлечённым(-ой) (во что-н).

embryo [ˈɛmbrɪəu] *n* (BIO) эмбрио́н; (*fig*) заро́дыш.

emend [ɪˈmɛnd] *vt* (*text*) исправля́ть (испра́вить* *perf*).

emerald [ˈɛmərəld] *n* изумру́д.

emerge [ɪˈmɜːdʒ] *vi* (*fact*) всплыва́ть (всплыть* *perf*); (*new industry, society*) появля́ться (появи́ться* *perf*); **to ~ from** (*from room, imprisonment*) выходи́ть* (вы́йти* *perf*) из +*gen*; (*from sleep*) пробужда́ться (пробуди́ться* *perf*) от +*gen*; **it ~s that** (BRIT) вы́яснилось, что.

emergence [ɪˈmɜːdʒəns] *n* (*of new idea etc*) появле́ние.

emergency [ɪˈmɜːdʒənsɪ] *n* (*crisis*) кра́йняя необходи́мость *f* ♦ *cpd*: **~ repair** сро́чный ремо́нт; **in an ~** в слу́чае опа́сности; **state of ~** чрезвыча́йное положе́ние; **~ talks** экстренные перегово́ры.

emergency cord *n* (US) ≈ стоп-кра́н.
emergency exit *n* запасно́й вы́ход.
emergency landing *n* (AVIAT) вы́нужденная поса́дка.
emergency lane *n* (US: AUT) авари́йная полоса́*.
emergency road service *n* (US) авари́йная доро́жная слу́жба.
emergency services *npl*: **the ~ ~** авари́йная слу́жба *fsg*.
emergency stop *n* (BRIT: AUT) внеза́пная остано́вка (*в крити́ческой ситуа́ции*).

emergent [ɪˈmɜːdʒənt] *adj* (*nation, group*) получи́вший незави́симость, образова́вшийся; **an ~ industrial class** зая́вивший о себе́ промы́шленный класс.

emeritus [ɪˈmɛrɪtəs] *adj*: **professor ~** заслу́женный профе́ссор в отста́вке.

emery board [ˈɛmərɪ-] *n* пи́лка для ногте́й (*покры́тая кору́ндом*).

emery paper *n* нажда́чная бума́га.
emetic [ɪˈmɛtɪk] *n* (MED) рво́тное *nt adj*.
emigrant [ˈɛmɪɡrənt] *n* эмигра́нт(ка*).
emigrate [ˈɛmɪɡreɪt] *vi* эмигри́ровать (*impf/perf*).
emigration [ɛmɪˈɡreɪʃən] *n* эмигра́ция.
émigré [ˈɛmɪɡreɪ] *n* полити́ческий* эмигра́нт(ка).

eminence [ˈɛmɪnəns] *n* (*importance*) знамени́тость *f*.

eminent [ˈɛmɪnənt] *adj* (*scientist, writer*) знамени́тый (знамени́т).

eminently [ˈɛmɪnəntlɪ] *adv* (*practical etc*) весьма́.

emirate [ˈɛmɪrɪt] *n* эмира́т.

emission [ɪˈmɪʃən] *n* (*of gas, heat*) выделе́ние *nt no pl*; (*of light, radiation*) излуче́ние.

emit [ɪˈmɪt] *vt* (*smoke, smell*) испуска́ть (испусти́ть* *perf*); (*sound*) издава́ть* (изда́ть* *perf*); (*light, heat*) излуча́ть (*impf*).

emolument [ɪˈmɔljumənt] *n* (*usu pl*) дохо́д; (*fee*) вознагражде́ние; (*salary*) жа́лованье*.

emotion [ɪˈməuʃən] *n* чу́вство; (*as opposed to reason*) эмо́ция.

emotional [ɪˈməuʃənl] *adj* эмоциона́льный* (эмоциона́лен); (*issue*) волну́ющий.

emotionally [ɪˈməuʃnəlɪ] *adv* (*behave, speak*) эмоциона́льно; **~ disturbed** эмоциона́льно неуравнове́шенный*.

emotive [ɪˈməutɪv] *adj* (*subject, language*) вызыва́ющий эмо́ции, эмоциона́льно волну́ющий; **~ power** эмоциона́льная си́ла.

empathy [ˈɛmpəθɪ] *n* сочу́вствие; **to feel ~ with sb** сочу́вствовать (*impf*) кому́-н.

emperor [ˈɛmpərəʳ] *n* импера́тор.
emphases [ˈɛmfəsiːz] *npl of* **emphasis**.
emphasis [ˈɛmfəsɪs] (*pl* **emphases**) *n* значе́ние; (*in speaking*) ударе́ние, акце́нт; **to lay** *or* **place ~ on sth** (*fig*) подчёркивать (подчеркну́ть* *perf*) что-н; **the ~ is on reading** наибо́льшее значе́ние придаётся чте́нию.

emphasize [ˈɛmfəsaɪz] *vt* подчёркивать (подчеркну́ть* *perf*); **I must ~ that ...** я до́лжен подчеркну́ть, что ....

emphatic [ɛmˈfætɪk] *adj* (*statement, denial*) убеди́тельный* (убеди́телен); (*person, manner*) насто́йчивый; **to be ~ about sth** насто́йчиво убежда́ть (*impf*) в чем-н.

emphatically [ɛmˈfætɪklɪ] *adv* насто́йчиво; (*certainly*) убеди́тельно.

emphysema [ɛmfɪˈsiːmə] *n* эмфизе́ма.
empire [ˈɛmpaɪəʳ] *n* (*also fig*) импе́рия.
empirical [ɛmˈpɪrɪkl] *adj* (*knowledge, study*) эмпири́ческий.

employ [ɪmˈplɔɪ] *vt* (*workforce, person*) нанима́ть (наня́ть* *perf*), трудоустра́ивать (трудоустро́ить* *perf*), дава́ть* (дать* *perf*) рабо́ту +*dat*; (*tool, weapon*) применя́ть (примени́ть* *perf*); **he's ~ed in a bank** он рабо́тает в ба́нке.

employee [ɪmplɔɪˈiː] *n* рабо́тник.
employer [ɪmˈplɔɪəʳ] *n* работода́тель *m*.
employment [ɪmˈplɔɪmənt] *n* рабо́та; **to find ~** трудоустра́иваться (трудоустро́иться *perf*); **without ~** без рабо́ты; **place of ~** ме́сто

рабо́ты.

employment agency *n* бюро́ *nt ind* по трудоустро́йству.

employment exchange *n* (*BRIT: formerly*) би́ржа труда́.

empower [ɪm'pauəʳ] *vt*: **to ~ sb to do** уполномо́чивать (уполномо́чить *perf*) кого́-н +*infin*.

empress ['ɛmprɪs] *n* императри́ца.

empties ['ɛmptɪz] *npl* (*bottles*) та́ра *fsg*.

emptiness ['ɛmptɪnɪs] *n* пустота́.

empty ['ɛmptɪ] *adj* (*also fig*) пусто́й* ◆ *vt* (*container*) опорожня́ть (опорожни́ть *perf*); (*place, house etc*) опустоша́ть (опустоши́ть *perf*) ◆ *vi* (*house, container*) пусте́ть (опусте́ть *perf*); (*liquid*) вытека́ть (вы́течь* *perf*); **on an ~ stomach** на пусто́й желу́док; **to ~ into** (*river*) впада́ть (*impf*) в +*acc*.

empty-handed ['ɛmptɪ'hændɪd] *adj* с пусты́ми рука́ми; **he returned ~** он верну́лся с пусты́ми рука́ми.

empty-headed ['ɛmptɪ'hɛdɪd] *adj* (*person*) пустоголо́вый.

EMS *n abbr* (= *European Monetary System*) ЕВС = *Европейская валютная система*.

EMT *n abbr* = *emergency medical technician*.

EMU *n abbr* = *economic and monetary union*.

emu ['iːmjuː] *n* э́му *m ind*.

emulate ['ɛmjuleɪt] *vt* (*hero, idol*) подража́ть (*impf*) +*dat*.

emulsion [ɪ'mʌlʃən] *n* (*liquid*) эму́льсия; (*also:* **~ paint**) эму́льсия, эмульсио́нная кра́ска*.

enable [ɪ'neɪbl] *vt* (*make possible*) спосо́бствовать (*impf*) +*dat*; **to ~ sb to do** (*permit, allow*) дава́ть* (дать* *perf*) возмо́жность кому́-н +*infin*.

enact [ɪ'nækt] *vt* (*law*) вводи́ть* (ввести́* *perf*); (*play*) ста́вить* (поста́вить* *perf*); (*role*) игра́ть (сыгра́ть *perf*).

enamel [ɪ'næməl] *n* эма́ль *f*; (*also:* **~ paint**) эма́ль, эма́левая кра́ска*.

enamoured [ɪ'næməd] (*US* **enamored**) *adj*: **to be ~ of** (*pastime, idea, belief*) пита́ть (*impf*) сла́бость к +*dat*.

encampment [ɪn'kæmpmənt] *n* бивуа́к.

encased [ɪn'keɪst] *adj*: **~ in** (*in plaster, armour*) зако́ванный в +*acc*; (*in shell*) заключённый в +*acc*.

encash [ɪn'kæʃ] *vt* инкасси́ровать (*impf/perf*).

enchant [ɪn'tʃɑːnt] *vt* (*delight*) очаро́вывать (очарова́ть *perf*).

enchanted [ɪn'tʃɑːntɪd] *adj* (*under a spell*) заколдо́ванный, зачаро́ванный.

enchanting [ɪn'tʃɑːntɪŋ] *adj* обворож-и́тельный* (обворожи́телен).

encircle [ɪn'sɜːkl] *vt* (*place, prisoner*) окружа́ть (окружи́ть *perf*).

encl. *abbr* (*on letters etc*): = **enclosed, enclosure** приложе́ние.

enclave ['ɛnkleɪv] *n*: **an ~ of** анкла́в +*gen*, о́стров +*gen*.

enclose [ɪn'kləuz] *vt* (*land, space*) огора́живать (огороди́ть* *perf*); (*object*) заключа́ть (заключи́ть *perf*); (*letter etc*): **to ~ (with)** прилага́ть (приложи́ть *perf*) (к +*dat*); **please find ~d a cheque for £100** здесь прилага́ется чек на £100.

enclosure [ɪn'kləuʒəʳ] *n* (*area of land*) огоро́женное ме́сто*; (*in letter etc*) приложе́ние.

encoder [ɪn'kəudəʳ] *n* (*COMPUT*) коди́рующее устро́йство, ко́дер.

encompass [ɪn'kʌmpəs] *vt* (*include*) охва́тывать (охвати́ть* *perf*).

encore [ɔŋ'kɔː'] *excl* бис ◆ *n*: **as an ~** на бис.

encounter [ɪn'kauntəʳ] *n* встре́ча; (*problem*) столкнове́ние ◆ *vt* (*person*) встреча́ться (встре́титься *perf*) с +*instr*; (*new experience, problem*) ста́лкиваться (столкну́ться *perf*) с +*instr*.

encourage [ɪn'kʌrɪdʒ] *vt* поощря́ть (поощри́ть *perf*); (*growth*) спосо́бствовать (*impf*) +*dat*; **to ~ sb to do** убежда́ть (*impf*) кого́-н +*infin*.

encouragement [ɪn'kʌrɪdʒmənt] *n* (*see vt*) поощре́ние; подде́ржка.

encouraging [ɪn'kʌrɪdʒɪŋ] *adj* (*situation, meeting, news*) обнадёживающий.

encroach [ɪn'krəutʃ] *vi*: **to ~ (up)on** (*rights, property, time*) покуша́ться (покуси́ться* *perf*) *or* посяга́ть (посягну́ть *perf*) на +*acc*.

encrusted [ɪn'krʌstɪd] *adj*: **~ with** покры́тый +*instr*.

encumber [ɪn'kʌmbəʳ] *vt*: **~ed with** (*suitcase, baggage etc*) загромождённый (загроможд́ён) +*instr*; (*debts*) обременённый (обремен́ён) +*instr*.

encyclop(a)edia [ɛnsaɪkləu'piːdɪə] *n* энциклопе́дия.

end [ɛnd] *n* коне́ц*; (*of town*) часть *f*; (*aim*) цель *f* ◆ *vt* (*also:* **bring to an ~**, **put an ~ to**) зака́нчивать (зако́нчить *perf*), прекраща́ть (прекрати́ть* *perf*) ◆ *vi* (*situation, activity, period etc*) конча́ться (ко́нчиться *perf*); **from ~ to ~** с нача́ла до конца́; **to come to an ~** подходи́ть* (подойти́* *perf*) к концу́, конча́ться (ко́нчиться *perf*); **to be at an ~** зака́нчиваться (зако́нчиться *perf*); **in the ~** в конце́ концо́в; **on ~** (*object*) стоймя́; **to stand on ~** (*hair*) стоя́ть (стать* *perf*) ды́бом; **for hours on ~** часа́ми; **for 5 hours on ~** 5 часо́в подря́д; **at the ~ of the street** в конце́ у́лицы; **at the ~ of the day** (*BRIT: fig*) в конце́ концо́в; **to this ~**, **with this ~ in view** с э́той це́лью.

▶ **end up** *vi*: **to ~ up in** (*place*) конча́ть (ко́нчить *perf*) в +*prp*; **we ~ed up taking a taxi** мы ко́нчили тем, что взя́ли такси́.

endanger [ɪn'deɪndʒəʳ] *vt* подверга́ть (подве́ргнуть* *perf*) опа́сности; **an ~ed species** вымира́ющий вид.

endear [ɪn'dɪəʳ] *vt*: **to ~ o.s. to sb** внуша́ть (внуши́ть *perf*) кому́-н симпа́тию к себе́.

endearing [ɪn'dɪərɪŋ] *adj* (*personality, conduct*)

покоря́ющий.

endearment [ɪn'dɪəmənt] *n*: **to whisper ~s**
ше́пта́ть* (*impf*) ла́сковые слова́; **term of ~**
ла́сковое сло́во.

endeavour [ɪn'dɛvəʳ] (*US* **endeavor**) *n* (*attempt*)
попы́тка*; (*effort*) стара́ние ♦ *vi*: **to ~ to do**
(*attempt*) стара́ться (постара́ться *perf*) +*infin*;
(*strive*) стреми́ться* (*impf*) +*infin*.

endemic [ɛn'dɛmɪk] *adj* энデми́ческий.

ending ['ɛndɪŋ] *n* (*of book, play etc*) коне́ц*;
(*LING*) оконча́ние.

endive ['ɛndaɪv] *n* (*curly*) энди́вый сала́т;
(*chicory*) цико́рный сала́т.

endless ['ɛndlɪs] *adj* бесконе́чный*
(бесконе́чен); (*forest, beach*) бескра́йний;
(*patience, resources*) беспреде́льный*
(беспреде́лен); (*possibilities*)
неограни́ченный* (неограни́чен).

endorse [ɪn'dɔ:s] *vt* (*cheque, document*)
распи́сываться (расписа́ться* *perf*) на +*prp*;
(*approve: proposal, candidate*) подде́рживать
(поддержа́ть* *perf*).

endorsee [ɪndɔ:'si:] *n* индосса́т.

endorsement [ɪn'dɔ:smənt] *n* индоссаме́нт;
(*BRIT: on driving licence*) отме́тка*; (*approval*)
подде́ржка.

endorser [ɪn'dɔ:səʳ] *n* индосса́нт.

endow [ɪn'dau] *vt* (*provide with money*)
обеспе́чивать (обеспе́чить *perf*); **~ed with**
(*talent, quality*) наделённый (наделён) +*instr*.

endowment [ɪn'daumənt] *n* (*money*)
поже́ртвование (*для обеспечения
ежего́дным дохо́дом*); (*quality*) спосо́бности
fpl.

endowment mortgage *n ипоте́чная ссу́да в
сочета́нии со страхова́нием жи́зни.*

endowment policy *n по́лис, включа́ющий
страхова́ние жи́зни.*

end product *n* (*INDUSTRY*) коне́чный проду́кт;
(*fig*) результа́т.

end result *n* коне́чный результа́т.

endurable [ɪn'djuərəbl] *adj* терпи́мый.

endurance [ɪn'djuərəns] *n* выно́сливость *f*.

endurance test *n* испыта́ние на про́чность.

endure [ɪn'djuəʳ] *vt* (*bear*) переноси́ть*
(перенести́* *perf*) ♦ *vi* (*last*) выде́рживать
(вы́держать *perf*) (*испыта́ние вре́менем*).

enduring [ɪn'djuərɪŋ] *adj* (*lasting*) про́чный*
(про́чен).

end user *n* (*COMPUT*) коне́чный по́льзователь
m.

enema ['ɛnɪmə] *n* (*MED*) кли́зма.

enemy ['ɛnəmɪ] *adj* (*forces, strategy*)
неприя́тельский, вра́жеский ♦ *n* враг*;
(*opponent*) проти́вник; (*MIL*) враг*,
неприя́тель *m*; **to make an ~ of sb** нажива́ть
(нажи́ть* *perf*) врага́ в ком-н.

energetic [ɛnə'dʒɛtɪk] *adj* энерги́чный*

(энерги́чен).

energy ['ɛnədʒɪ] *n* эне́ргия; **Department of E~**
Управле́ние по энергоснабже́нию.

energy crisis *n* энергети́ческий* кри́зис.

energy-saving ['ɛnədʒɪ'seɪvɪŋ] *adj* (*device*)
сокраща́ющий расхо́д эне́ргии; **~ policy**
поли́тика эконо́мии эне́ргии.

enervating ['ɛnəveɪtɪŋ] *adj* обесси́ливающий,
отнима́ющий си́лы.

enforce [ɪn'fɔ:s] *vt* (*law*) следи́ть* (*impf*) за
соблюде́нием +*gen*.

enforced [ɪn'fɔ:st] *adj* (*inactivity,
unemployment*) вы́нужденный.

enfranchise [ɪn'fræntʃaɪz] *vt* предоставля́ть
(предоста́вить* *perf*) избира́тельные права́
+*dat*.

engage [ɪn'geɪdʒ] *vt* (*attention, interest*)
привлека́ть (привле́чь* *perf*); (*employ*)
нанима́ть (наня́ть* *perf*); (*AUT: clutch*)
зацепля́ть (зацепи́ть* *perf*); (*MIL: enemy*)
вступа́ть (вступи́ть* *perf*) в бой с +*instr* ♦ *vi*
(*TECH*) входи́ть* (войти́* *perf*) в зацепле́ние;
to ~ in занима́ться (заня́ться* *perf*) +*instr*; **to
~ sb in conversation** вовлека́ть (вовле́чь*
perf) кого́-н в разгово́р.

engaged [ɪn'geɪdʒd] *adj* обручённый
(обручён); (*BRIT: busy*) за́нят; **~ to** обручён с
+*instr*; **to get ~** обручи́ться (*perf*); **he is ~ in
research** он занима́ется иссле́дованием.

engaged tone *n* (*BRIT: TEL*) гудки́ *pl* "за́нято".

engagement [ɪn'geɪdʒmənt] *n* (*appointment*)
договорённость *f*; (*hiring*) контра́кт; (*to
marry*) обруче́ние; (*MIL*) бой*; **I have a
previous ~** у меня́ уже́ есть договорённость.

engagement ring *n* обруча́льное кольцо́*.

engaging [ɪn'geɪdʒɪŋ] *adj* привлека́тельный*
(привлека́телен).

engender [ɪn'dʒɛndəʳ] *vt* порожда́ть
(породи́ть* *perf*).

engine ['ɛndʒɪn] *n* (*AUT*) дви́гатель *m*, мото́р;
(*RAIL*) локомоти́в.

engine driver *n* (*BRIT*) машини́ст.

engineer [ɛndʒɪ'nɪəʳ] *n* (*designer*) инжене́р; (*for
repairs, also NAUT*) меха́ник; (*US: RAIL*)
машини́ст; **civil ~** инжене́р-строи́тель *m*;
mechanical ~ инжене́р-меха́ник.

engineering [ɛndʒɪ'nɪərɪŋ] *n* (*science*)
инжене́рное де́ло; (*design*) техни́ческий
диза́йн; (*construction: of roads, ships*)
строи́тельство; (*of cars, machines*)
произво́дство ♦ *cpd*: **~ works** *or* **factory**
машинострои́тельный заво́д.

engine failure *n* отка́з дви́гателя.

engine trouble *n* неиспра́вность *f* дви́гателя.

England ['ɪŋglənd] *n* А́нглия.

English ['ɪŋglɪʃ] *adj* англи́йский* ♦ *n* (*LING*)
англи́йский язы́к*; **the ~** *npl* (*people*)
англича́не* *mpl*; **an ~ speaker**

англоговоря́щий(-ая) *m(f) adj.*
English Channel *n*: **the ~~** Ла-Ма́нш.
Englishman ['ɪŋglɪʃmən] *irreg n* англича́нин*.
English-speaking ['ɪŋglɪʃ'spiːkɪŋ] *adj*
англоговоря́щий.
Englishwoman ['ɪŋglɪʃwumən] *irreg n*
англича́нка*.
engrave [ɪn'greɪv] *vt* гравирова́ть
(вы́гравировать *perf*).
engraving [ɪn'greɪvɪŋ] *n* гравю́ра.
engrossed [ɪn'grəust] *adj*: **~ in** поглощённый
(поглощён) *+instr*.
engulf [ɪn'gʌlf] *vt (subj: water)* поглоща́ть
(поглоти́ть* *perf*); (: *panic, fear, fire*)
охва́тывать (охвати́ть* *perf*).
enhance [ɪn'hɑːns] *vt (enjoyment)* увели́чивать
(увели́чить *perf*); (*beauty, reputation*)
улучша́ть (улу́чшить *perf*).
enigma [ɪ'nɪgmə] *n* зага́дка.
enigmatic [ɛnɪg'mætɪk] *adj* зага́дочный*
(зага́дочен).
enjoy [ɪn'dʒɔɪ] *vt* люби́ть (*impf*); (*have benefit
of*) облада́ть (*impf*) *+instr*; **to ~ o.s.** хорошо́
проводи́ть* (провести́* *perf*) вре́мя; **I ~
dancing** я люблю́ танцева́ть.
enjoyable [ɪn'dʒɔɪəbl] *adj* прия́тный*
(прия́тен).
enjoyment [ɪn'dʒɔɪmənt] *n (feeling of pleasure)*
удово́льствие.
enlarge [ɪn'lɑːdʒ] *vt* увели́чивать (увели́чить
perf) ♦ *vi*: **to ~ on** распространя́ться (*impf*) о
+prp.
enlarged [ɪn'lɑːdʒd] *adj (edition)*
дополненный; (*MED, PHOT*) увели́ченный
(увели́чен).
enlargement [ɪn'lɑːdʒmənt] *n (PHOT)*
увеличе́ние.
enlighten [ɪn'laɪtn] *vt* просвеща́ть
(просвети́ть* *perf*).
enlightened [ɪn'laɪtnd] *adj* просвещённый.
enlightening [ɪn'laɪtnɪŋ] *adj* просвеща́ющий.
enlightenment [ɪn'laɪtnmənt] *n*: **the E~**
Просвеще́ние.
enlist [ɪn'lɪst] *vt (person)* вербова́ть
(завербова́ть *perf*); (*support*) заруча́ться
(заручи́ться *perf*) *+instr* ♦ *vi*: **to ~ in** (*army,
navy etc*) идти́* (пойти́* *perf*) в *+acc*; **~ed man**
(*US: MIL*) военнослу́жащий* *m adj (рядово́го
или сержа́нтского соста́ва*).
enliven [ɪn'laɪvn] *vt (events)* оживля́ть
(оживи́ть* *perf*); (*people*) подбодря́ть
(подбодри́ть *perf*).
enmity ['ɛnmɪtɪ] *n* вражде́бность *f*.
ennoble [ɪ'nəubl] *vt* возводи́ть* (возвести́* *perf*)
в ти́тул; (*fig*) облагора́живать
(облагоро́дить* *perf*).
enormity [ɪ'nɔːmɪtɪ] *n (of problem, danger)*
величина́.
enormous [ɪ'nɔːməs] *adj* грома́дный*
(грома́ден).
enormously [ɪ'nɔːməslɪ] *adv* чрезвыча́йно.

enough [ɪ'nʌf] *adj (time, books, people etc)*
доста́точно *+gen* ♦ *pron* доста́точно ♦ *adv*: **big
~** доста́точно большо́й; **I've had ~!** с меня́
хва́тит!; **have you got ~ work to do?** у Вас
доста́точно рабо́ты?; **have you had ~ to eat?**
Вы нае́лись?; **that's ~, thanks** доста́точно,
спаси́бо; **I've had ~ of him** он мне надое́л; **he
has not worked ~** он недоста́точно рабо́тал;
will five pounds be ~? пяти́ фу́нтов бу́дет
доста́точно?; **I do not have ~ money to buy it**
у меня́ не хвата́ет де́нег, что́бы купи́ть э́то;
it's hot ~ as it is и так дово́льно жа́рко; **he
was kind ~ to lend me the money** он был
насто́лько добр, что́бы одолжи́ть мне
де́ньги; **~!** дово́льно!; **strangely** *or* **oddly ~** …
как э́то ни стра́нно ….
enquire [ɪn'kwaɪə'] *vti* = **inquire**.
enrage [ɪn'reɪdʒ] *vt* беси́ть* (взбеси́ть* *perf*).
enrich [ɪn'rɪtʃ] *vt* обогаща́ть (обогати́ть *perf*).
enrol [ɪn'rəul] (*US* **enroll**) *vt (subj: administrator)*
зачисля́ть (зачи́слить *perf*); (: *parents etc*)
запи́сывать (записа́ть* *perf*) ♦ *vi (see vt)*
зачисля́ться (зачи́слиться *perf*);
запи́сываться (записа́ться* *perf*).
enrolment [ɪn'rəulmənt] *n (US* **enrollment**) *n*
(*registration*) зачисле́ние; (*for course, club*)
за́пись *f*.
en route [ɔn'ruːt] *adv* по пути́; **~~ for** *or* **to/
from** по пути́ в *+acc*/из *+gen*.
ensconce [ɪn'skɔns] *vt*: **to ~ o.s. in**
устра́иваться (устро́иться *perf*) в *+prp*.
ensemble [ɔn'sɔmbl] *n* анса́мбль *m*.
enshrine [ɪn'ʃraɪn] *vt (belief, right)* храни́ть
(*impf*); **to be ~d in** сохраня́ться (сохрани́ться
perf) в *+prp*.
ensue [ɪn'sjuː] *vi* сле́довать (после́довать *perf*);
a terrible argument ~d (за э́тим)
после́довала ужа́сная ссо́ра.
ensuing [ɪn'sjuːɪŋ] *adj* после́дующий*.
ensure [ɪn'ʃuə'] *vt* обеспе́чивать (обеспе́чить
perf); **to ~ that** обеспе́чивать (обеспе́чить
perf), что.
ENT *n abbr (MED*: = *Ear, Nose and Throat*)
у́хо-го́рло-нос.
entail [ɪn'teɪl] *vt* влечь* (повле́чь* *perf*) за
собо́й.
entangled [ɪn'tæŋgld] *adj*: **to become ~ (in)** (*in
net, rope etc*) запу́тываться (запу́таться *perf*)
(в *+prp*).
enter ['ɛntə'] *vt (room, building)* входи́ть*
(войти́* *perf*) в *+acc*; (*university, college*)
поступа́ть (поступи́ть* *perf*) в *+acc*; (*club,
profession, contest*) вступа́ть (вступи́ть* *perf*)
в *+acc*; (*in book*) запи́сывать (записа́ть* *perf*);
(*COMPUT*) вводи́ть* (ввести́* *perf*) ♦ *vi*
входи́ть* (войти́* *perf*); **I ~ed my son in the
marathon** я по́дал зая́вку на включе́ние
моего́ сы́на в марафо́н
▸ **enter for** *vt fus (competition, examination)*
подава́ть* (пода́ть* *perf*) зая́вку на уча́стие в
+prp

▶ **enter into** *vt fus (discussion, correspondence, agreement)* вступа́ть (вступи́ть* *perf*) в +*acc*
▶ **enter (up)on** *vt fus (career, policy)* начина́ть (нача́ть* *perf*).

enteritis [ɛntə'raɪtɪs] *n* энтери́т.

enterprise ['ɛntəpraɪz] *n (company, undertaking)* предприя́тие; *(initiative)* предприи́мчивость *f*; **free/private ~** свобо́дное/ча́стное предпринима́тельство.

enterprising ['ɛntəpraɪzɪŋ] *adj (person)* предприи́мчивый (предприи́мчив); *(scheme)* предпринима́тельский*.

entertain [ɛntə'teɪn] *vt (amuse)* развлека́ть (развле́чь* *perf*); *(play host to)* принима́ть (приня́ть* *perf*); *(idea)* разду́мывать *(impf)* над +*instr*.

entertainer [ɛntə'teɪnəʳ] *n* веду́щий*(-ая) *m(f)* *adj* развлека́тельной програ́ммы.

entertaining [ɛntə'teɪnɪŋ] *adj* занима́тельный* (занима́телен), развлека́тельный ◆ *n*: **we do a lot of ~** мы ча́сто приглаша́ем к себе́ госте́й.

entertainment [ɛntə'teɪnmənt] *n (amusement)* развлече́ние; *(show)* представле́ние.

entertainment allowance *n* сре́дства на представи́тельские расхо́ды.

enthral [ɪn'θrɔ:l] *(US* **enthrall)** *vt* приводи́ть* (привести́* *perf*) в восто́рг.

enthralled [ɪn'θrɔ:ld] *adj* увлечённый (увлечён); **he was ~ by** *or* **with the book** он был увлечён кни́гой.

enthralling [ɪn'θrɔ:lɪŋ] *adj* увлека́тельный* (увлека́телен).

enthuse [ɪn'θu:z] *vi*: **to ~ about** *or* **over** приходи́ть* (прийти́* *perf*) в восто́рг от +*gen*.

enthusiasm [ɪn'θu:zɪæzəm] *n* энтузиа́зм.

enthusiast [ɪn'θu:zɪæst] *n* энтузиа́ст; **a jazz** *etc* **~** энтузиа́ст джа́за *etc*.

enthusiastic [ɪnθu:zɪ'æstɪk] *adj* по́лный* (по́лон) энтузиа́зма; *(response, reception)* восто́рженный; **he is ~ about** он по́лон энтузиа́зма по по́воду +*gen*.

entice [ɪn'taɪs] *vt (lure)* зама́нивать (замани́ть* *perf*); *(tempt)* соблазня́ть (соблазни́ть *perf*).

enticing [ɪn'taɪsɪŋ] *adj (offer, food)* соблазни́тельный.

entire [ɪn'taɪəʳ] *adj* весь*.

entirely [ɪn'taɪəlɪ] *adv* по́лностью; *(for emphasis)* соверше́нно; **~ different** соверше́нно разли́чный.

entirety [ɪn'taɪərətɪ] *n*: **in its ~** весь целико́м.

entitle [ɪn'taɪtl] *vt*: **to ~ sb to sth/to do** дава́ть* (дать* *perf*) пра́во кому́-н что-н/+*infin*.

entitled [ɪn'taɪtld] *adj (book, film etc)* озагла́вленный; **to be ~ to sth/to do** име́ть *(impf)* пра́во на что-н/на то, что́бы +*infin*.

entity ['ɛntɪtɪ] *n (еди́ная) су́щность *f*; **a**

separate ~ *(person)* отде́льная ли́чность.

entourage [ɔntu'ra:ʒ] *n* антура́ж, окруже́ние.

entrails ['ɛntreɪlz] *npl* вну́тренности *fpl*.

entrance [*n* 'ɛntrns, *vt* ɪn'trɑ:ns] *n (way in)* вход; *(arrival)* вступле́ние, появле́ние; *(THEAT)* вы́ход (на сце́ну) ◆ *vt (enchant)* очаро́вывать (очарова́ть *perf*); **to gain ~ to** *(university)* поступа́ть (поступи́ть* *perf*) в +*acc*; *(profession)* получа́ть (получи́ть *perf*) до́ступ к +*dat*; **to make an ~** появля́ться (появи́ться* *perf*).

entrance examination *n* вступи́тельный экза́мен.

entrance fee *n (for museum etc)* входна́я пла́та.

entrance ramp *n (US: AUT)* въезд на автостра́ду.

entrancing [ɪn'trɑ:nsɪŋ] *adj* восхити́тельный* (восхити́телен).

entrant ['ɛntrnt] *n* уча́стник(-ица).

entreat [ɛn'tri:t] *vt (implore)*: **to ~ sb to do** умоля́ть (умоли́ть *perf*) кого́-н +*infin*.

entreaty [ɛn'tri:tɪ] *n* мольба́.

entrée ['ɔntreɪ] *n (CULIN: main course)* гла́вное блю́до.

entrenched [ɛn'trɛntʃt] *adj (ideas etc)* укорени́вшийся.

entrepreneur ['ɔntrəprə'nə:ʳ] *n* предпринима́тель(ница) *m(f)*.

entrepreneurial ['ɔntrəprə'nə:rɪəl] *adj* предпринима́тельский*.

entrust [ɪn'trʌst] *vt (possessions, task)*: **to ~ sth to sb** доверя́ть (дове́рить *perf*) что-н кому́-н; **to ~ sb with sth** *(task)* возлага́ть (возложи́ть* *perf*) на кого́-н что-н.

entry ['ɛntrɪ] *n (way in)* вход; *(in register, account book)* за́пись *f*; *(in reference book)* статья́*; *(in competition: participants)* число́ уча́стников; *(arrival: in country)* въезд; (: *in room)* вход; **"no ~"** *(to room, building)* "нет вхо́да"; *(AUT)* "нет въе́зда"; **single/double ~ book-keeping** *(COMM)* проста́я/двойна́я бухгалте́рия.

entry form *n* зая́вка* на уча́стие.

entry phone *n (BRIT)* домофо́н.

entwine [ɪn'twaɪn] *vt*: **to ~ (with)** переплета́ть (переплести́* *perf*) (с +*instr*).

enumerate [ɪ'nju:məreɪt] *vt* перечисля́ть (перечи́слить *perf*).

enunciate [ɪ'nʌnsɪeɪt] *vt (word)* произноси́ть* (произнести́* *perf*); *(principle, plan etc)* излага́ть (изложи́ть* *perf*).

envelop [ɪn'vɛləp] *vt (cover, enclose)* облега́ть (обле́чь* *perf*).

envelope ['ɛnvələup] *n* конве́рт.

enviable ['ɛnvɪəbl] *adj* зави́дный* (зави́ден).

envious ['ɛnvɪəs] *adj* зави́стливый (зави́стлив); **to be ~ of sth/sb** зави́довать

---

* marks translations which have irregular inflections. The Russian-English side of the dictionary gives inflectional information.

(impf) чему́-н/кому́-н.

environment [ɪn'vaɪərnmənt] *n* среда́; **the ~** окружа́ющая среда́; **Department of the E~** *(BRIT)* отде́л охра́ны окружа́ющей среды́.

environmental [ɪnvaɪərn'mɛntl] *adj* свя́занный с окружа́ющей средо́й, экологи́ческий*; **children respond to ~ stimuli** де́ти реаги́руют на сти́мулы предлага́емые средо́й; **~ studies** эколо́гия.

environmentalist [ɪnvaɪərn'mɛntlɪst] *n* сторо́нник(-ица) защи́ты окружа́ющей среды́.

environmentally [ɪnvaɪərn'mɛntlɪ] *adv* экологи́чески.

Environmental Protection Agency *n (US)* аге́нтство по охра́не окружа́ющей среды́.

envisage [ɪn'vɪzɪdʒ] *vt (foresee)* предви́деть* *(impf)*; **I ~ that** ... я предви́жу, что ....

envision [ɪn'vɪʒən] *vt (US)* = **envisage**.

envoy ['ɛnvɔɪ] *n* посла́нник.

envy ['ɛnvɪ] *n* за́висть *f* ◆ *vt* зави́довать (позави́довать *perf*) +*dat*; **to ~ sb sth** зави́довать (позави́довать *perf*) кому́-н из-за чего́-н.

enzyme ['ɛnzaɪm] *n (BIO, MED)* энзи́м.

EPA *n abbr (US: = Environmental Protection Agency)* аге́нтство по охра́не окружа́ющей среды́.

ephemeral [ɪ'fɛmərl] *adj* эфеме́рный* (эфеме́рен).

epic ['ɛpɪk] *n* эпопе́я; *(poem)* эпи́ческая поэ́ма ◆ *adj (journey)* эпоха́льный* (эпоха́лен).

epicentre ['ɛpɪsɛntə'] *(US* **epicenter**) *n* эпице́нтр.

epidemic [ɛpɪ'dɛmɪk] *n* эпиде́мия.

epigram ['ɛpɪgræm] *n* эпигра́мма.

epilepsy ['ɛpɪlɛpsɪ] *n* эпиле́псия.

epileptic [ɛpɪ'lɛptɪk] *adj* эпилепти́ческий ◆ *n* эпиле́птик.

epilogue ['ɛpɪlɔg] *n* эпило́г.

Epiphany [ɪ'pɪfənɪ] *n* Богоявле́ние, Креще́ние.

episcopal [ɪ'pɪskəpl] *adj (REL)* епи́скопский; **the E~ Church** Епископа́льная Це́рковь*.

episode ['ɛpɪsəud] *n* эпизо́д.

epistle [ɪ'pɪsl] *n* посла́ние.

epitaph ['ɛpɪtɑːf] *n* эпита́фия.

epithet ['ɛpɪθɛt] *n* эпи́тет.

epitome [ɪ'pɪtəmɪ] *n* воплоще́ние.

epitomize [ɪ'pɪtəmaɪz] *vt* воплоща́ть (воплоти́ть* *perf*).

epoch ['iːpɔk] *n* эпо́ха.

epoch-making ['iːpɔkmeɪkɪŋ] *adj* эпоха́льный* (эпоха́лен).

eponymous [ɪ'pɔnɪməs] *adj*: **~ hero** геро́й, и́менем кото́рого назва́но произведе́ние.

EPOS *n abbr (= electronic point of sale)* электро́нное счи́тывание информа́ции с това́рных этике́ток.

equable ['ɛkwəbl] *adj* ро́вный* (ро́вен).

equal ['iːkwl] *adj* ра́вный* (ра́вен); *(intensity, quality)* одина́ковый ◆ *n* ра́вный(-ая) *m(f) adj*

◆ *vt (number)* равня́ться *(impf)* +*dat*; *(quality)* не уступа́ть (уступи́ть* *perf*) +*dat or* по +*dat*; **they are roughly ~ in size** они́ приме́рно равны́ по разме́ру; **the number of exports should be ~ to imports** коли́чество э́кспорта должно́ быть* равно́ коли́честву и́мпорта; **he is ~ to** *(task)* он мо́жет спра́виться с +*instr*.

Equal Employment Opportunity Commission *n (US)* = **Equal Opportunities Commission**.

equality [iː'kwɔlɪtɪ] *n* ра́венство, равнопра́вие; **~ of opportunity** ра́венство возмо́жностей.

equalize ['iːkwəlaɪz] *vt* ура́внивать (уравня́ть *perf*) ◆ *vi (SPORT)* сра́внивать (сравня́ть *perf*) счёт.

equally ['iːkwəlɪ] *adv (share etc)* равно́; *(good, bad)* одина́ково; **they are ~ clever** они́ в ра́вной сте́пени умны́.

Equal Opportunities Commission *(US* **Equal Employment Opportunity Commission**) *n* коми́ссия ра́вных возмо́жностей при на́йме на рабо́ту.

equal(s) sign *n* знак ра́венства.

equanimity [ɛkwə'nɪmɪtɪ] *n (calm)* хладнокро́вие; **with ~** хладнокро́вно.

equate [ɪ'kweɪt] *vt*: **to ~ sth with sth, ~ sth to sth** прира́внивать (приравня́ть *perf*) что-н чему́-н.

equation [ɪ'kweɪʒən] *n (MATH)* уравне́ние.

equator [ɪ'kweɪtə'] *n* эква́тор.

equatorial [ɛkwə'tɔːrɪəl] *adj* экваториа́льный.

Equatorial Guinea *n* Экваториа́льная Гвине́я.

equestrian [ɪ'kwɛstrɪən] *adj* ко́нный ◆ *n* вса́дник(-ица).

equilibrium [iːkwɪ'lɪbrɪəm] *n* равнове́сие.

equinox ['iːkwɪnɔks] *n* равноде́нствие; **the spring/autumn ~** весе́ннее/осе́ннее равноде́нствие.

equip [ɪ'kwɪp] *vt*: **to ~ (with)** *(person, army)* снаряжа́ть (снаряди́ть* *perf*) (+*instr*); *(room, car etc)* обору́довать *(impf/perf)* (+*instr*); **to ~ sb for** *(prepare)* гото́вить* (подгото́вить* *perf*) кого́-н к +*dat*.

equipment [ɪ'kwɪpmənt] *n* обору́дование.

equitable ['ɛkwɪtəbl] *adj* справедли́вый (справедли́в).

equities ['ɛkwɪtɪz] *npl (BRIT)* обыкнове́нные а́кции *fpl*.

equity ['ɛkwɪtɪ] *n* справедли́вость *f*.

equity capital *n* капита́л в фо́рме а́кций.

equivalent [ɪ'kwɪvələnt] *n* эквивале́нт ◆ *adj*: **~ (to)** эквивале́нтный* (эквивале́нтен) (+*dat*); **it is ~ to** э́то эквивале́нтно +*dat*.

equivocal [ɪ'kwɪvəkl] *adj (ambiguous)* двусмы́сленный* (двусмы́слен); *(open to suspicion)* сомни́тельный* (сомни́телен).

equivocate [ɪ'kwɪvəkeɪt] *vi* говори́ть *(impf)* двусмы́сленно.

equivocation [ɪkwɪvə'keɪʃən] *n* укло́нчивость *f*.

ER *abbr* (*BRIT*) = Elizabeth Regina.

ERA *n abbr* (*US*: *POL*: = Equal Rights Amendment) попра́вка о ра́вных права́х (*к конститу́ции США*).

era ['ɪərə] *n* э́ра.

eradicate [ɪ'rædɪkeɪt] *vt* искореня́ть (искорени́ть *perf*).

erase [ɪ'reɪz] *vt* стира́ть (стере́ть* *perf*).

eraser [ɪ'reɪzəʳ] *n* рези́нка*, ла́стик для стира́ния.

erect [ɪ'rɛkt] *adj* (*posture*) прямо́й* (прям), вертика́льный* (вертика́лен); (*tail, ears*) по́днятый (по́днят) ♦ *vt* (*build*) возводи́ть* (возвести́* *perf*); (*assemble*) ста́вить* (поста́вить* *perf*).

erection [ɪ'rɛkʃən] *n* возведе́ние; (*of ten' machinery*) устано́вка*; (*PHYSIOL*) эре́кция.

ergonomics [ə:gə'nɔmɪks] *n* эргоно́мика.

ERISA *n abbr* (*US*) = Employee Retirement Income Security Act.

ERM *n abbr* (= Exchange Rate Mechanism) МВК = *механи́зм валю́тных ку́рсов*.

ermine ['ə:mɪn] *n* горноста́й.

ERNIE ['ə:nɪ] *n abbr* (*BRIT*: = Electronic Random Number Indicator Equipment) *ЭВМ, определя́ющая вы́игрышные номера́ госуда́рственного вы́игрышного за́йма.*

erode [ɪ'rəud] *vt* (*soil, rock*: *subj*: *wind*) выве́тривать (вы́ветрить *perf*); (: *water*) размыва́ть (размы́ть* *perf*); (*metal*) разъеда́ть (разъе́сть* *perf*); (*confidence, power*) подрыва́ть (подорва́ть* *perf*).

erogenous [ɪ'rɔdʒənəs] *adj* эроге́нный.

erosion [ɪ'rəuʒən] *n* эро́зия.

erotic [ɪ'rɔtɪk] *adj* эроти́ческий*.

eroticism [ɪ'rɔtɪsɪzəm] *n* эроти́зм.

err [ə:ʳ] *vi* допуска́ть (допусти́ть* *perf*) оши́бку; **to ~ on the side of ...** склоня́ться (*impf*) к +*dat*
....

errand ['ɛrənd] *n* поруче́ние; **to run ~s** выполня́ть (*impf*) поруче́ния; **~ of mercy** пое́здка* с до́брой ми́ссией.

erratic [ɪ'rætɪk] *adj* (*attempts*) беспоря́дочный* (беспоря́дочен); (*behaviour*) сумасбро́дный* (сумасбро́ден).

erroneous [ɪ'rəunɪəs] *adj* оши́бочный* (оши́бочен).

error ['ɛrəʳ] *n* оши́бка*; **typing ~** опеча́тка*; **spelling ~** орфографи́ческая оши́бка*; **in ~** по оши́бке; **~s and omissions excepted** не счита́я оши́бок и про́пусков.

error message *n* (*COMPUT*) сообще́ние об оши́бке.

erstwhile ['ə:stwaɪl] *adj* бы́вший*.

erudite ['ɛrjudaɪt] *adj* (*person*) эруди́рованный* (эруди́рован).

erupt [ɪ'rʌpt] *vi* (*war, crisis*) разража́ться (разрази́ться* *perf*); **the volcano ~ed**

произошло́ изверже́ние вулка́на.

eruption [ɪ'rʌpʃən] *n* (*of volcano*) изверже́ние; (*of fighting*) взры́в.

ESA *n abbr* (= European Space Agency) ЕКА= *Европе́йское косми́ческое аге́нтство.*

escalate ['ɛskəleɪt] *vi* обостря́ться (обостри́ться *perf*).

escalation [ɛskə'leɪʃən] *n* обостре́ние, эскала́ция.

escalation clause *n огово́рка о скользя́щих це́нах и́ли скользя́щей зарпла́те.*

escalator ['ɛskəleɪtəʳ] *n* эскала́тор.

escapade [ɛskə'peɪd] *n* (*adventure*) эскапа́да, авантю́ра.

escape [ɪs'keɪp] *n* (*from prison*) побе́г; (*from person*) избега́ние; (*TECH*) вы́ход; (*of gas*) выделе́ние, вы́пуск ♦ *vi* (*get away*) убега́ть (убежа́ть* *perf*); (*from jail*) бежа́ть* (*impf/perf*); (*leak*) утека́ть (уте́чь* *perf*), дава́ть* (дать* *perf*) уте́чку ♦ *vt* (*avoid*: *consequences etc*) избега́ть (избежа́ть* *perf*) +*gen*; (*elude*): **his name ~s me** его́ и́мя вы́пало у меня́ из па́мяти; **to ~ from** (*place*) сбега́ть (сбежа́ть* *perf*) *or* убега́ть (убежа́ть* *perf*) из/от +*gen*; (*person*) сбега́ть (сбежа́ть* *perf*) *or* убега́ть (убежа́ть* *perf*) от +*gen*; **he ~d with minor injuries** он отде́лался лёгкими тра́вмами; **to ~ to** (*another place*) сбега́ть (сбежа́ть* *perf*) *or* убега́ть (убежа́ть* *perf*) в/на +*prp*; **to ~ to safety** скрыва́ться (скры́ться* *perf*) в безопа́сном ме́сте; **to ~ notice** ускольза́ть (ускользну́ть *perf*) незаме́ченным.

escape artist *n* трюка́ч.

escape clause *n пункт догово́ра, иеба́вляющий сто́рону от отве́тственности.*

escapee [ɪskeɪ'pi:] *n* сбежа́вший(-ая) *m(f) adj*.

escape hatch *n* авари́йный люк.

escape key *n* (*COMPUT*) кла́виша вы́хода.

escape route *n* (*from fire*) запасно́й (пожа́рный) вы́ход; (*of prisoners etc*) маршру́т побе́га.

escapism [ɪs'keɪpɪzəm] *n* бе́гство от действи́тельности, эскапи́зм.

escapist [ɪs'keɪpɪst] *adj* (*literature*) уводя́щий от пробле́м жи́зни, эскапи́стский.

escapologist [ɛskə'pɔlədʒɪst] *n* (*BRIT*) = escape artist.

escarpment [ɪs'kɑ:pmənt] *n* отко́с.

eschew [ɪs'tʃu:] *vt* (*company, violence*) сторони́ться (*impf*) +*gen*.

escort [*n* 'ɛskɔ:t, *vt* ɪs'kɔ:t] *n* (*companion*: *male*) сопровожда́ющий *m adj*; (: *female*) сопровожда́ющая *f adj*; (*MIL, POLICE*) конво́й ♦ *vt* сопровожда́ть (*impf*); **his/her ~** его́/её сопровожда́ющий(-ая).

escort agency *n* бюро́ *nt ind* по на́йму

---

* marks translations which have irregular inflections. The Russian-English side of the dictionary gives inflectional information.

сопровождающих.

Eskimo ['ɛskɪməu] *n* эскимос(ка*).

ESL *n abbr* (*SCOL*) = *English as a Second Language.*

esophagus [i:'sɔfəgəs] *n* (*US*) = **oesophagus.**

esoteric [ɛsə'tɛrɪk] *adj* эзотерический.

ESP *n abbr* = **extrasensory perception;** (*SCOL*) = *English for Special Purposes.*

esp. *abbr* = **especially.**

especially [ɪs'pɛʃlɪ] *adv* особенно.

espionage ['ɛspɪənɑːʒ] *n* шпионаж.

esplanade [ɛsplə'neɪd] *n* эспланада.

espouse [ɪs'pauz] *vt* (*policy, idea*) (целиком) отдаваться* (отдаться* *perf*) +*dat*, поддерживать (поддержать* *perf*).

Esq. *abbr* = **Esquire.**

Esquire [ɪs'kwaɪəˈ] *n*: **J. Brown,** ~ Дж. Браун, эсквайр.

essay ['ɛseɪ] *n* (*SCOL*) сочинение; (*LITERATURE*) очерк.

essence ['ɛsns] *n* сущность *f*; (*CULIN*) эссенция; **in** ~ в сущности; **speed is of the** ~ всё дело в скорости.

essential [ɪ'sɛnʃl] *adj* (*vital*) существенно необходимый* (необходим); (*basic*) основной ♦ *n* (*see adj*) существенно необходимая вещь *f*; основное *nt adj*; **it is** ~ **that** существенно важно, чтобы.

essentially [ɪ'sɛnʃəlɪ] *adv* в сущности.

EST *abbr* (*US*) = *Eastern Standard Time.*

est. *abbr* = *established; estimate(d).*

establish [ɪs'tæblɪʃ] *vt* (*organization*) учреждать (учредить* *perf*); (*facts, contact*) устанавливать (установить* *perf*); (*reputation*) утверждать (утвердить* *perf*) за собой.

established [ɪs'tæblɪʃt] *adj* (*business*) солидный; (*custom, practice*) признанный.

establishment [ɪs'tæblɪʃmənt] *n* (*see vb*) учреждение; установление; утверждение; (*shop etc*) заведение; **the E~** истеблишмент

estate [ɪs'teɪt] *n* (*land*) поместье*; (*BRIT: also*: **housing** ~) жилой комплекс; (*LAW*) состояние.

estate agency *n* (*BRIT*) агентство по продаже недвижимости.

estate agent *n* (*BRIT*) агент по продаже недвижимости.

estate car *n* (*BRIT*) автомобиль *m*-пикап.

esteem [ɪs'tiːm] *n*: **to hold sb in high** ~ относиться* (отнестись* *perf*) к кому-н с большим почтением.

esthetic [ɪs'θɛtɪk] *adj* (*US*) = **aesthetic.**

estimate [*vb* 'ɛstɪmeɪt, *n* 'ɛstɪmət] *vt* (*reckon, calculate*) предварительно подсчитывать (подсчитать* *perf*); (: *chances*) оценивать (оценить* *perf*) ♦ *n* (*calculation*) подсчёт; (*assessment*) оценка*; (*builder's etc*) смета ♦ *vi* (*BRIT*: *COMM*): **to** ~ **for** составлять (составить* *perf*) смету +*gen*; **I** ~ **that** я полагаю, что; **to give sb an** ~ давать* (дать*

perf) кому-н оценку стоимости; **at a rough** ~ по грубым подсчётам.

estimation [ɛstɪ'meɪʃən] *n* (*opinion*) оценка*; (*calculation*) подсчёт; **in my** ~ по моим подсчётам.

estimator ['ɛstɪmeɪtəˈ] *n* оценщик.

Estonia [ɛs'təunɪə] *n* Эстония.

Estonian [ɛs'təunɪən] *n* (*person*) эстонец*-(-онка*); (*LING*) эстонский* язык* ♦ *adj* эстонский*.

estranged [ɪs'treɪndʒd] *adj* (*from spouse, family*) отчуждённый* (отчуждён); **his** ~ **wife** ушедшая от него жена; **he is** ~ **from his wife** он разошёлся с женой.

estrangement [ɪs'treɪndʒmənt] *n* отчуждение.

estrogen ['iːstrəudʒən] *n* (*US*) = **oestrogen.**

estuary ['ɛstjuərɪ] *n* устье*.

ET *n abbr* (*BRIT*: = *Employment Training*) профессиональная подготовка ♦ *abbr* (*US*) = *Eastern Time.*

ETA *n abbr* (= *estimated time of arrival*) ожидаемое время* *nt* прибытия.

et al. *abbr* (*and others*: = *et alii*) и другие.

etc. *abbr* (= *et cetera*) и т.д.= *и так далее.*

etch [ɛtʃ] *vt* (*surface*) гравировать (выгравировать *perf*); (*design*): **to** ~ **(on)** травить* (вытравить* *perf*) (на +*prp*); **it will be** ~**ed on my memory** это запечатлеется в моей памяти.

etching ['ɛtʃɪŋ] *n* (*craft*) гравировка*; (*product*) гравюра, офорт.

ETD *n abbr* (= *estimated time of departure*) ожидаемое время* *nt* отправления.

eternal [ɪ'təːnl] *adj* вечный* (вечен).

eternity [ɪ'təːnɪtɪ] *n* вечность *f*.

ether ['iːθəˈ] *n* эфир*.

ethereal [ɪ'θɪərɪəl] *adj* (*delicate*) эфирный.

ethical ['ɛθɪkl] *adj* (*relating to ethics*) этический*; (*morally right*) этичный* (этичен).

ethics ['ɛθɪks] *n, npl* этика *fsg.*

Ethiopia [iːθɪ'əupɪə] *n* Эфиопия.

Ethiopian [iːθɪ'əupɪən] *adj* эфиопский* ♦ *n* эфиоп(ка).

ethnic ['ɛθnɪk] *adj* этнический*.

ethnic cleansing *n* этническая чистка*.

ethnology [ɛθ'nɔlədʒɪ] *n* этнология.

ethos ['iːθɔs] *n* этос.

etiquette ['ɛtɪkɛt] *n* этикет.

ETV *n abbr* (*US*) = *Educational Television.*

etymology [ɛtɪ'mɔlədʒɪ] *n* этимология.

eucalyptus [juːkə'lɪptəs] *n* эвкалипт.

Eucharist ['juːkərɪst] *n* (*REL*): **the** ~ евхаристия, причастие.

eulogy ['juːlədʒɪ] *n* восхваление.

euphemism ['juːfəmɪzəm] *n* эвфемизм.

euphemistic [juːfə'mɪstɪk] *adj* эвфемистический*.

euphoria [juː'fɔːrɪə] *n* эйфория.

Eurasia [juə'reɪʃə] *n* Евразия.

Eurasian [juə'reɪʃən] *adj* евразийский ♦ *n* евразиец* (ийка*).

Euratom [juə'rætəm] *n abbr* (= *European Atomic Energy Community*) Европейский* комитет по атомной энергии.
euro ['juərəu] *n* евро *ind.*
Euro- ['juərəu] *prefix* евро-.
eurocheque ['juərəutʃɛk] *n* еврочек.
Eurocrat ['juərəukræt] *n служащий в организации Европейского Сообщества.*
Eurodollar ['juərəudɔlə'] *n* евродоллар.
Euroland ['juərəulænd] *n* (*inf*) Евроленд.
Europe ['juərəp] *n* Европа.
European [juərə'pi:ən] *adj* европейский* ♦ *n* европеец(-ейка).
European Community *n*: the ~ ~ Европейское Сообщество.
European Court of Justice *n*: the ~ ~ ~ ~ Европейский* Суд*.
European Economic Community *n*: the ~ ~ ~ Европейское Экономическое Сообщество.
Euro-sceptic ['juərəuskɛptɪk] *n* евроскептик.
euthanasia [ju:θə'neɪzɪə] *n* эвтаназия.
evacuate [ɪ'vækjueɪt] *vt* (*people*) эвакуировать (*impf/perf*); (*place*) очищать (очистить* *perf*).
evacuation [ɪvækju'eɪʃən] *n* (*see vb*) эвакуация; очистка*.
evacuee [ɪvækju'i:] *n* эвакуированный(-ая) *m(f) adj.*
evade [ɪ'veɪd] *vt* (*duties, question*) уклоняться (уклониться* *perf*) от +*gen*; (*person*) избегать (*impf*) +*gen.*
evaluate [ɪ'væljueɪt] *vt* оценивать (оценить* *perf*).
evangelical [i:væn'dʒɛlɪkl] *adj* евангел- ический*.
evangelist [ɪ'vændʒəlɪst] *n* евангелист.
evangelize [ɪ'vændʒəlaɪz] *vi* проповедовать (*impf*) евангелизм.
evaporate [ɪ'væpəreɪt] *vi* испаряться (испариться* *perf*); (*feeling, attitude*) пропадать (пропасть* *perf*).
evaporated milk [ɪ'væpəreɪtɪd-] *n* сгущённое молоко (*без сахара*).
evaporation [ɪvæpə'reɪʃən] *n* испарение.
evasion [ɪ'veɪʒən] *n* (*of responsibility, tax etc*) уклонение.
evasive [ɪ'veɪsɪv] *adj* (*reply, action*) уклончивый (уклончив).
eve [i:v] *n*: **on the ~ of** накануне +*gen*; **Christmas E~** канун Рождества; **New Year's E~** канун Нового года.
even ['i:vn] *adj* (*level, smooth*) ровный* (ровен); (*equal*) равный* (равен); (*number*) чётный ♦ *adv* даже; **~ if** даже если; **~ though** хотя и; **~ more** ещё больше; **he loves her ~ more** он любит её ещё больше; **the work is going ~ better/faster** работа идёт ещё лучше/быстрее; **~ so** всё же; **not ~** даже не; **~ he was there** даже он там был; **~ on Sundays** даже по воскресеньям; **I am ~ more likely to leave now** теперь даже ещё более вероятно, что я уеду; **to break ~** *работать на уровне самоокупаемости (но без дохода*); **to get ~ with sb** (*inf*) расквитаться (*perf*) с кем-н
▶ **even out** *vt* выравнивать (выровнять *perf*) ♦ *vi* выравниваться (выровняться *perf*).
even-handed ['i:vnhændɪd] *adj* беспристрастный* (беспристрастен).
evening ['i:vnɪŋ] *n* вечер*; **in the ~** вечером; **this ~** сегодня вечером; **tomorrow/yesterday ~** завтра/вчера вечером.
evening class *n* вечерние курсы *mpl.*
evening dress *n* (*no pl: formal clothes*) вечерний туалет*; (*gown*) вечернее платье*.
evenly ['i:vnlɪ] *adv* (*distribute*) равномерно; (*divide, breathe*) ровно.
evensong ['i:vnsɔŋ] *n* вечерня*.
event [ɪ'vɛnt] *n* (*occurrence*) событие; (*SPORT: competition*) соревнование, вид; **in the normal course of ~s** при нормальном течении событий; **in the ~ of** в случае +*gen*; **in the ~** в конечном счёте; **at all ~s** (*BRIT*), **in any ~** во всяком случае.
eventful [ɪ'vɛntful] *adj* насыщенный* (насыщен) событиями.
eventing [ɪ'vɛntɪŋ] *n* (*HORSE-RIDING*) *участие в ряде состязаний по верховой езде.*
eventual [ɪ'vɛntʃuəl] *adj* (*outcome, goal*) конечный.
eventuality [ɪvɛntʃu'ælɪtɪ] *n* (*possibility*) возможность *f.*
eventually [ɪ'vɛntʃuəlɪ] *adv* в конце концов.
ever ['ɛvə'] *adv* (*always*) всегда; (*at any time*) когда-либо, когда-нибудь; **why ~ not?** почему же нет?; **the best ~** самый лучший*; **have you ~ been to Russia?** Вы когда-нибудь были в России?; **for ~** навсегда; **hardly ~** почти никогда; **I hardly ~ read** я почти никогда не читаю; **better than ~** лучше чем бы то ни было *or* чем когда-либо; **~ since** с тех пор, как; **~ since that day** с того дня; **~ so pretty** ужасно симпатичная; **thank you ~ so much** я Вам так благодарен; **yours ~** (*BRIT: in letters*) преданный Вам.
Everest ['ɛvərɪst] *n* (*GEO: also:* **Mount ~**) Эверест.
evergreen ['ɛvəgri:n] *n* вечнозелёный.
everlasting [ɛvə'lɑ:stɪŋ] *adj* (*love, life etc*) вечный* (вечен).

KEYWORD

every ['ɛvrɪ] *adj* **1** (*each*) каждый; **every child will receive a present** каждый ребёнок получит подарок; **every one of them** каждый из них; **every shop in the town was closed** все

магази́ны в го́роде бы́ли закры́ты
2 (*all possible*): **I gave you every assistance** я помо́г Вам, всем чем то́лько мо́жно; **I tried every option** я испро́бовал я все пути́; **I have every confidence in him** я в нём соверше́нно уве́рен; **we wish you every success** мы жела́ем Вам вся́ческого успе́ха; **he's every bit as clever/stupid as his brother** он столь же умён/глуп, как и его́ брат
3 (*showing recurrence*) ка́ждый; **every week** ка́ждую неде́лю; **every other car** ка́ждая втора́я маши́на; **she visits me every third/ other day** она́ прихо́дит ко мне ка́ждые два дня/че́рез день; **every now and then** вре́мя от вре́мени.

everybody ['ɛvrɪbɔdɪ] *pron* (*each*) ка́ждый; (*all*) все *pl*; ~ **knows about it** об э́том ка́ждый зна́ет; ~ **else** все остальны́е.
everyday ['ɛvrɪdeɪ] *adj* (*daily*) ежедне́вный; (*common*) повседне́вный*.
everyone ['ɛvrɪwʌn] *pron* = **everybody**.
everything ['ɛvrɪθɪŋ] *pron* всё; ~ **is ready** всё гото́во; **he did** ~ **possible** он сде́лал всё возмо́жное; **you think of** ~ Вы ду́маете обо всём; **I don't agree with** ~ **he says** я не согла́сен со всем, что он говори́т.
everywhere ['ɛvrɪwɛə'] *adv* везде́, повсю́ду; ~ **you go you meet** ... куда́ ни пойдёшь, везде́ *or* повсю́ду встреча́ешь ....
evict [ɪ'vɪkt] *vt* выселя́ть (вы́селить *perf*).
eviction [ɪ'vɪkʃən] *n* выселе́ние.
eviction notice *n* предупрежде́ние о выселе́нии.
eviction order *n* прика́з о выселе́нии.
evidence ['ɛvɪdns] *n* (*proof*) доказа́тельство; (*testimony*) показа́ние; (*indication*) при́знаки *mpl*; **to give** ~ дава́ть* (дать* *perf*) (свиде́тельские) показа́ния; **to show** ~ **of** проявля́ть (прояви́ть* *perf*) при́знаки +*gen*; **in** ~ (*obvious*) заме́тен.
evident ['ɛvɪdnt] *adj* заме́тный* (заме́тен).
evidently ['ɛvɪdntlɪ] *adv* очеви́дно.
evil ['iːvl] *adj* (*person, spirit*) злой* (зол); (*system, influence*) дурно́й* ♦ *n* зло.
evocative [ɪ'vɔkətɪv] *adj* (*description, music*) *навева́ющий чу́вства и воспомина́ния*.
evoke [ɪ'vəuk] *vt* вызыва́ть (вы́звать* *perf*).
evolution [iːvə'luːʃən] *n* эволю́ция.
evolve [ɪ'vɔlv] *vt* развива́ть (разви́ть* *perf*) ♦ *vi* (*animal, plant*) эволюциони́ровать (*impf/perf*); (*plan, idea*) развива́ться (разви́ться* *perf*).
ewe [juː] *n* овца́*.
ewer ['juːə'] *n* кувши́н*.
ex- [ɛks] *prefix* (*former*) экс-, бы́вший*; (*out of*): **the price ex works** цена́ с предприя́тия.
exacerbate [ɛks'æsəbeɪt] *vt* (*situation, pain*) обостря́ть (обостри́ть *perf*).
exact [ɪg'zækt] *adj* то́чный* (то́чен) ♦ *vt*: **to** ~ **sth from** (*obedience*) тре́бовать (потре́бовать *perf*) чего́-н от +*gen*; (*payment*) взы́скивать (взыска́ть* *perf*) что-н с +*gen*.

exacting [ɪg'zæktɪŋ] *adj* (*task*) тру́дный*; (*person*) взыска́тельный* (взыска́телен).
exactly [ɪg'zæktlɪ] *adv* то́чно; ~! вот и́менно!
exaggerate [ɪg'zædʒəreɪt] *vti* преувели́чивать (преувели́чить *perf*).
exaggerated [ɪg'zædʒəreɪtɪd] *adj* преувели́ченный (преувели́чен).
exaggeration [ɪgzædʒə'reɪʃən] *n* преувеличе́ние.
exalt [ɪg'zɔːlt] *vt* превозноси́ть* (превознести́* *perf*).
exalted [ɪg'zɔːltɪd] *adj* (*prominent*) высо́кий* (высо́к); (*elated*) восто́рженный* (восто́ржен).
exam [ɪg'zæm] *n abbr* = **examination**.
examination [ɪgzæmɪ'neɪʃən] *n* (*inspection*) изуче́ние; (*plan*) рассмотре́ние; (*SCOL*) экза́мен; (*LAW*) допро́с; (*MED*) осмо́тр; **to take** *or* (*BRIT*) **sit an** ~ сдава́ть* (сдать* *perf*) экза́мен; **the matter is under** ~ де́ло нахо́дится на рассмотре́нии.
examine [ɪg'zæmɪn] *vt* (*scrutinize*) смотре́ть (посмотре́ть *perf*) на +*acc*; (*inspect*) осма́тривать (осмотре́ть *perf*); (*plan*) рассма́тривать (рассмотре́ть *perf*); (*SCOL*) экзаменова́ть (проэкзаменова́ть *perf*); (*LAW*) допра́шивать (допроси́ть* *perf*); (*MED*) осма́тривать (осмотре́ть* *perf*).
examiner [ɪg'zæmɪnə'] *n* (*SCOL*) экзамена́тор.
example [ɪg'zɑːmpl] *n* приме́р*; **for** ~ наприме́р; **to set a good/bad** ~ подава́ть* (пода́ть* *perf*) хоро́ший*/плохо́й приме́р.
exasperate [ɪg'zɑːspəreɪt] *vt* изма́тывать (измота́ть *perf*); ~**d by** *or* **with** изму́ченный +*instr*.
exasperating [ɪg'zɑːspəreɪtɪŋ] *adj* раздража́ющий.
exasperation [ɪgzɑːspə'reɪʃən] *n* раздраже́ние; **in** ~ в раздраже́нии.
excavate ['ɛkskəveɪt] *vt* (*site*) раска́пывать (раскопа́ть *perf*); (*hole*) выка́пывать (вы́копать *perf*) ♦ *vi* производи́ть* (произвести́* *perf*) раско́пки.
excavation [ɛkskə'veɪʃən] *n* (*activity*) раска́пывание; (*archeological dig*): ~**s** раско́пки *fpl*.
excavator ['ɛkskəveɪtə'] *n* экскава́тор.
exceed [ɪk'siːd] *vt* превыша́ть (превы́сить* *perf*); (*hopes*) превосходи́ть* (превзойти́* *perf*).
exceedingly [ɪk'siːdɪŋlɪ] *adv* чрезвыча́йно.
excel [ɪk'sɛl] *vt* превосходи́ть* (превзойти́* *perf*) ♦ *vi*: **to** ~ (**in** *or* **at**) отлича́ться (отличи́ться *perf*) (в +*prp*); **to** ~ **o.s.** (*BRIT*) превосходи́ть* (превзойти́* *perf*) самого́ себя́.
excellence ['ɛksələns] *n* (*in sport, business*) мастерство́; (*superiority*) превосхо́дство.
Excellency ['ɛksələnsɪ] *n*: **His** ~ его́ Превосходи́тельство.
excellent ['ɛksələnt] *adj* отли́чный* (отли́чен),

превосхо́дный* (превосхо́ден) ◆ *excl*: ~!
отли́чно!, превосхо́дно!

except [ɪkˈsɛpt] *prep* (*also*: ~ **for**) кро́ме +*gen* ◆
vt: **to ~ sb (from)** исключа́ть (исключи́ть *perf*)
кого́-н (из +*gen*); ~ **if/when** кро́ме *or* за
исключе́нием тех слу́чаев е́сли/когда́; ~ **that**
кро́ме того́, что.

excepting [ɪkˈsɛptɪŋ] *prep* за исключе́нием
+*gen*.

exception [ɪkˈsɛpʃən] *n* исключе́ние; **to take ~
to** обижа́ться (оби́деться* *perf*) на +*acc*; **with
the ~ of** за исключе́нием +*gen*.

exceptional [ɪkˈsɛpʃənl] *adj* исключи́тельный*
(исключи́телен).

excerpt [ˈɛksəːpt] *n* отры́вок*.

excess [ɪkˈsɛs] *n* изби́ток*; (*INSURANCE*)
превыше́ние; ~**es** *npl* (*of cruelty etc*) эксце́ссы
mpl, кра́йности *fpl*; **an ~ of** £15, **a** £15 ~
изли́шек* в £15; **in ~ of** сверх +*gen*, свы́ше
+*gen*; **to drink to ~** пить (*impf*) сверх ме́ры.

excess baggage *n* изли́шек* багажа́.

excess fare *n* (*BRIT*) допла́та (*за биле́т*).

excessive [ɪkˈsɛsɪv] *adj* чрезме́рный*
(чрезме́рен).

excess supply *n* избы́точное предложе́ние.

exchange [ɪksˈtʃeɪndʒ] *n* (*conversation*) обме́н
мне́ниями; (*argument*) перепа́лка*; (*also*:
telephone ~) коммута́тор ◆ *vt*: **to ~ (for)**
(*goods etc*) обме́нивать (обменя́ть *perf*) (на
+*acc*); ~ (**of**) обме́н (+*instr*); **in ~ for** в обме́н
на +*acc*; **foreign ~** валю́тная би́ржа.

exchange control *n* валю́тный контро́ль *m*.

exchange market *n* валю́тный ры́нок*.

exchange rate *n* валю́тный *or* обме́нный
курс.

Exchequer [ɪksˈtʃɛkəʳ] *n* (*BRIT*): **the ~**
казначе́йство.

excisable [ɪkˈsaɪzəbl] *adj* (*goods*) облага́емый
акци́зным сбо́ром.

excise [*n* ˈɛksaɪz, *vt* ɛkˈsaɪz] *n* акци́з, акци́зный
сбор ◆ *vt* (*remove*) выреза́ть (вы́резать* *perf*).

excise duties *npl* акци́зный сбор *msg*.

excitable [ɪkˈsaɪtəbl] *adj* (*легко́*) возбуди́мый.

excite [ɪkˈsaɪt] *vt* возбужда́ть (возбуди́ть* *perf*);
(*stimulate*) заинтересо́вывать
(заинтересова́ть *perf*); **to get ~d** волнова́ться
(взволнова́ться *perf*).

excitement [ɪkˈsaɪtmənt] *n* (*agitation*)
возбужде́ние; (*exhilaration*) оживле́ние.

exciting [ɪkˈsaɪtɪŋ] *adj* восхити́тельный.

excl. *abbr* = **excluding**, **exclusive (of)**.

exclaim [ɪksˈkleɪm] *vi* восклица́ть
(воскли́кнуть *perf*).

exclamation [ɛkskləˈmeɪʃən] *n* восклица́ние.

exclamation mark *n* восклица́тельный знак.

exclude [ɪksˈkluːd] *vt* исключа́ть (исключи́ть
perf).

excluding [ɪksˈkluːdɪŋ] *prep* исключа́я +*acc*.

exclusion [ɪksˈkluːʒən] *n* исключе́ние; **to the ~
of** исключа́я +*acc*.

exclusion clause *n* статья́* об исключе́ниях.

exclusion zone *n* запре́тная зо́на.

exclusive [ɪksˈkluːsɪv] *adj* (*select*)
недосту́пный* (недосту́пен), для
и́збранных; (*use*) исключи́тельный*
(исключи́телен); (*interview*) уника́льный*
(уника́лен) ◆ *n* (*PRESS*) эксклюзи́вный
материа́л (*напеча́танный то́лько в одно́й
газе́те*) ◆ *adv*: ~ **of** (*COMM*) не счита́я +*gen*;
mutually ~ взаимоисключа́ющие; ~ **of
postage** без сто́имости почто́вых расхо́дов; ~
from the 1st to the 15th March ~ с 1-ого до
15-ого ма́рта, включи́тельно; ~ **of tax** не
счита́я нало́га.

exclusively [ɪksˈkluːsɪvlɪ] *adv* исключи́тельно.

exclusive rights *npl* исключи́тельные права́
ntpl.

excommunicate [ɛkskəˈmjuːnɪkeɪt] *vt*
отлуча́ть (отлучи́ть *perf*) от це́ркви.

excrement [ˈɛkskrəmənt] *n* экскреме́нты *mpl*.

excruciating [ɪksˈkruːʃɪeɪtɪŋ] *adj* мучи́тельный*
(мучи́телен).

excursion [ɪksˈkəːʃən] *n* экску́рсия.

excursion ticket *n* дешёвый биле́т на
коро́ткую экску́рсию.

excusable [ɪksˈkjuːzəbl] *adj* прости́тельный*
(прости́телен).

excuse [*n* ɪksˈkjuːs, *vt* ɪksˈkjuːz] *n* оправда́ние ◆
vt (*justify*) опра́вдывать (оправда́ть *perf*);
(*forgive*) проща́ть (прости́ть* *perf*); **to make
~s for sb** находи́ть* (найти́* *perf*) оправда́ние
кому́-н; **that's no ~!** э́то не причи́на!; **to ~ sb
from sth/doing** освобожда́ть (освободи́ть*
perf) кого́-н от чего́-н/от того́, что́бы +*infin*;
~ **me!** (*attracting attention*) извини́те!,
прости́те!; (*as apology*) извини́те *or*
прости́те (меня́)!; **if you will ~ me, I have to ...**
Вы прости́те, мне на́до ...; **to ~ o.s. for sth/
for having done sth** извиня́ться (извини́ться
perf) за что-н/за то, что сде́лал что-н.

ex-directory [ˈɛksdɪˈrɛktərɪ] *adj* (*BRIT: number*)
не включённый (включён) в телефо́нный
спра́вочник; **she's ~** её но́мер не включён в
телефо́нный спра́вочник.

execrable [ˈɛksɪkrəbl] *adj* отврати́тельный*
(отврати́телен).

execute [ˈɛksɪkjuːt] *vt* (*kill*) казни́ть (*impf/perf*);
(*carry out, perform*) выполня́ть (вы́полнить
perf).

execution [ɛksɪˈkjuːʃən] *n* (*see vb*) казнь *f*;
выполне́ние.

executioner [ɛksɪˈkjuːʃnəʳ] *n* пала́ч*.

executive [ɪgˈzɛkjutɪv] *n* (*person*)
руководи́тель *m*; (*committee*)
исполни́тельный о́рган ◆ *adj* (*board, role*)
руководя́щий*; (*secretary*) отве́тственный;

---

* marks translations which have irregular inflections. The Russian-English side of the dictionary gives inflectional information.

(*car, plane, chair, toys*) для руководя́щих рабо́тников.

executive director n дире́ктор*-распоряди́тель m.

executor [ɪɡ'zɛkjutəʳ] n (*LAW*) исполни́тель m.

exemplary [ɪɡ'zɛmpləɪ] adj приме́рный* (приме́рен).

exemplify [ɪɡ'zɛmplɪfaɪ] vt (*typify*) служи́ть* (послужи́ть perf) приме́ром +gen; (*illustrate*) поясня́ть (поясни́ть perf) приме́ром.

exempt [ɪɡ'zɛmpt] adj: ~ **from** освобожд-ённый (освобождён) от +gen ♦ vt: **to** ~ **sb from** освобожда́ть (освободи́ть* perf) кого́-н от +gen.

exemption [ɪɡ'zɛmpʃən] n освобожде́ние.

exercise ['ɛksəsaɪz] n (*no pl*) гимна́стика; (*keep-fit*) заря́дка*; (*SCOL, MUS*) упражне́ние; (*of authority etc*) проявле́ние ♦ vt (*patience, authority*) проявля́ть (прояви́ть* perf); (*right*) осуществля́ть (осуществи́ть* perf); (*dog*) выгу́ливать (impf); (*mind*) занима́ть (impf) ♦ vi (*also:* **to take** ~) упражня́ться (impf); **military** ~**s** вое́нные уче́ния; **you need more** ~ Вам на́до бо́льше дви́гаться.

exercise bike n велосипе́д-тренажёр.

exercise book n тетра́дь f.

exert [ɪɡ'zəːt] vt (*influence, pressure*) ока́зывать (оказа́ть* perf); (*authority*) применя́ть (примени́ть* perf); **to** ~ **o.s.** напряга́ться (напря́чься* perf).

exertion [ɪɡ'zəːʃən] n (*effort*) уси́лие; (*strain*) напряже́ние.

ex gratia ['ɛks'greɪʃə] adj: ~~ **payment** де́нежное вознагражде́ние.

exhale [ɛks'heɪl] vti выдыха́ть (вы́дохнуть perf).

exhaust [ɪɡ'zɔːst] n (*also:* ~ **pipe**) выхлопна́я труба́; (*fumes*) выхлопны́е га́зы mpl ♦ vt (*person*) изнуря́ть (изнури́ть perf); (*money, resources etc*) истоща́ть (истощи́ть perf); (*topic*) исче́рпывать (исче́рпать perf); **to** ~ **o.s.** доводи́ть* (довести́* perf) себя́ до изнеможе́ния or изнуре́ния.

exhausted [ɪɡ'zɔːstɪd] adj (*person*) изнурённый* (изнурён), изнеможённый* (изнеможён).

exhausting [ɪɡ'zɔːstɪŋ] adj изнури́тельный* (изнури́телен).

exhaustion [ɪɡ'zɔːstʃən] n (*tiredness*) изнеможе́ние; **nervous** ~ не́рвное истоще́ние.

exhaustive [ɪɡ'zɔːstɪv] adj исче́рпывающий*.

exhibit [ɪɡ'zɪbɪt] n экспона́т; (*LAW*) веще́ственное доказа́тельство ♦ vt (*paintings*) экспони́ровать (impf/perf); (*quality, emotion*) проявля́ть (прояви́ть* perf).

exhibition [ɛksɪ'bɪʃən] n (*of paintings etc*) вы́ставка*; (*of ability, emotion*) проявле́ние; **to make an** ~ **of o.s.** выставля́ть (вы́ставить* perf) себя́ на посме́шище.

exhibitionist [ɛksɪ'bɪʃənɪst] n эксгибициони́ст;

(*show-off*): **he's a real** ~ он всё де́лает напока́з.

exhibitor [ɪɡ'zɪbɪtəʳ] n экспоне́нт.

exhilarating [ɪɡ'zɪləreɪtɪŋ] adj волну́ющий.

exhilaration [ɪɡzɪlə'reɪʃən] n взволно́ванность f.

exhort [ɪɡ'zɔːt] vt: **to** ~ **sb to do** увещева́ть (impf) кого́-н +infin.

exile ['ɛksaɪl] n (*banishment*) ссы́лка*, изгна́ние; (*person*) ссы́льный(-ая) m(f) adj, изгна́нник ♦ vt ссыла́ть (сосла́ть* perf); (*abroad*) высыла́ть (вы́слать* perf); **in** ~ в ссы́лке or изгна́нии.

exist [ɪɡ'zɪst] vi существова́ть (impf).

existence [ɪɡ'zɪstəns] n существова́ние; **to be in** ~ существова́ть (impf).

existentialism [ɛgzɪs'tenʃlɪzəm] n экзистенциали́зм.

existing [ɪɡ'zɪstɪŋ] adj существу́ющий.

exit ['ɛksɪt] n (*way out*) вы́ход; (*on motorway*) вы́езд; (*departure*) ухо́д ♦ vi (*THEAT*) уходи́ть* (уйти́* perf); (*COMPUT*) выходи́ть* (вы́йти* perf); (*leave*): **to** ~ **from** (*room*) выходи́ть* (вы́йти* perf) из +gen; (*motorway*) съезжа́ть (съе́хать* perf) с +gen.

exit poll n предвари́тельный подсчёт голосо́в.

exit ramp n (*US: AUT*) съезд с автостра́ды.

exit visa n выездна́я ви́за.

exodus ['ɛksədəs] n ма́ссовое бе́гство; **the** ~ **to the cities** ма́ссовое переселе́ние в города́.

ex officio ['ɛksə'fɪʃɪəu] adv по до́лжности.

exonerate [ɪɡ'zɔnəreɪt] vt: **to** ~ **sb from guilt/ responsibility** снима́ть (снять* perf) с кого́-н обвине́ние/отве́тственность.

exorbitant [ɪɡ'zɔːbɪtnt] adj непоме́рный* (непоме́рен).

exorcize ['ɛksɔːsaɪz] vt (*person, place*) изгоня́ть (изгна́ть* perf) дья́вола из +gen; (*spirit*) изгоня́ть (изгна́ть* perf).

exotic [ɪɡ'zɔtɪk] adj экзоти́ческий*.

expand [ɪks'pænd] vt (*area, business, influence*) расширя́ть (расши́рить perf); (*numbers*) увели́чивать (увели́чить perf) ♦ vi (*gas, metal, business*) расширя́ться (расши́риться perf); (*population*) увели́чиваться (увели́читься perf); **to** ~ **on** (*story, idea etc*) подро́бно разъясня́ть (разъясни́ть perf).

expanse [ɪks'pæns] n: **an** ~ **of sea/sky** морско́й/ небе́сный просто́р.

expansion [ɪks'pænʃən] n расшире́ние; (*of population*) увеличе́ние; (*of economy*) рост.

expansionism [ɪks'pænʃənɪzəm] n (*ECON*) экспансиони́зм.

expansionist [ɪks'pænʃənɪst] adj (*policy*) экспансиони́стский.

expatriate [ɛks'pætrɪət] n эмигра́нт(ка*).

expect [ɪks'pɛkt] vt (*anticipate, hope for, await*) ожида́ть (impf); (*baby*) ждать (impf); (*suppose*) полага́ть (impf) ♦ vi: **to be** ~**ing** (*be pregnant*) ждать* (impf) ребёнка; **he** ~**s me to**

finish by Tuesday он ожида́ет, что я зако́нчу
ко вто́рнику; **to ~ to do** рассчи́тывать *(impf)*
+*infin*; **as ~ed** как и ожида́лось; **I ~ so** я
полага́ю.

expectancy [ɪks'pɛktənsɪ] *n* предвкуше́ние; **life
~** сре́дняя продолжи́тельность *f* жи́зни.

expectant [ɪks'pɛktənt] *adj (silence, crowd)*
выжида́ющий.

expectantly [ɪks'pɛktəntlɪ] *adv* с наде́ждой.

expectant mother *n* бере́менная же́нщина.

expectation [ɛkspɛk'teɪʃən] *n (hope)*
ожида́ние; **in ~ of** в ожида́нии +*gen*; **contrary
to** *or* **against all ~(s)** вопреки́ всем
ожида́ниям; **to come** *or* **live up to sb's ~s**
опра́вдывать (оправда́ть *perf*) чьи-н
ожида́ния.

expedience [ɪks'pi:dɪəns] *n* = **expediency**.

expediency [ɪks'pi:dɪənsɪ] *n* вы́года; **for the
sake of ~** ра́ди вы́годы.

expedient [ɪks'pi:dɪənt] *adj* целесообра́зный*
(целесообра́зен) ♦ *n* уло́вка.

expedite ['ɛkspədaɪt] *vt* ускоря́ть (уско́рить
perf).

expedition [ɛkspə'dɪʃən] *n* экспеди́ция; *(for
shopping etc)* похо́д.

expeditionary force [ɛkspə'dɪʃənrɪ-] *n*
экспедицио́нные войска́* *pl*.

expeditious [ɛkspə'dɪʃəs] *adj* эффекти́вный*
(эффекти́вен).

expel [ɪks'pɛl] *vt (person: from school,
organization)* исключа́ть (исключи́ть *perf*);
(: *from place)* изгоня́ть (изгна́ть* *perf*);
(substance: from body etc) выводи́ть*
(вы́вести* *perf*).

expend [ɪks'pɛnd] *vt* расхо́довать
(израсхо́довать *perf*), тра́тить* (затра́тить*
perf).

expendable [ɪks'pɛndəbl] *adj (resources)*
подлежа́щий списа́нию; **he is entirely ~** его́
мо́жно сбро́сить со счёта.

expenditure [ɪks'pɛndɪtʃəʳ] *n (money spent)*
затра́ты *fpl*; *(of money)* расхо́дование; *(of
energy, time)* затра́та.

expense [ɪks'pɛns] *n (cost)* сто́имость *f*; **~s** *npl*
(travelling expenses etc) расхо́ды *mpl*;
(expenditure) затра́ты *fpl*; **at the ~ of** за счёт
+*gen*; **to go to the ~ of doing** тра́титься*
(потра́титься* *perf*) +*infin*; **at great/little ~** с
больши́ми/небольши́ми затра́тами.

expense account *n* счёт подотчётных сумм.

expensive [ɪks'pɛnsɪv] *adj* дорого́й* (до́рог); **to
be ~** до́рого сто́ить *(impf)*; **to have ~ tastes**
име́ть *(impf)* вкус к дороги́м веща́м.

experience [ɪks'pɪərɪəns] *n (in job, of situation)*
о́пыт; *(event, activity)* слу́чай; (: *difficult,
painful)* испыта́ние; *(of emotion)*
пережива́ние ♦ *vt* испы́тывать (испыта́ть
perf), пережива́ть (пережи́ть* *perf*); **to know**

by *or* **from ~** знать *(impf)* по о́пыту; **to learn by
~** учи́ться *(impf)* на о́пыте.

experienced [ɪks'pɪərɪənst] *adj* о́пытный*
(о́пытен).

experiment [ɪks'pɛrɪmənt] *n* экспериме́нт,
о́пыт ♦ *vi*: **to ~ (with/on)**
эксперименти́ровать *(impf)* (с +*instr*/на +*prp*);
to carry out *or* **perform an ~** проводи́ть*
(провести́* *perf*) экспериме́нт; **as an ~** в
ка́честве экспериме́нта; **to ~ with a new
vaccine** проводи́ть* (провести́* *perf*) о́пыты с
но́вой вакци́ной.

experimental [ɪkspɛrɪ'mɛntl] *adj (methods,
ideas)* эксперимента́льный; *(tests)* про́бный;
at the ~ stage на ста́дии экспериме́нта.

expert ['ɛkspə:t] *n* экспе́рт, специали́ст ♦ *adj
(person)* уме́лый; **~ opinion/advice** мне́ние/
сове́т экспе́рта *or* специали́ста; **an ~ on sth**
специали́ст по чему́-н; **she is ~ at resolving
disputes** она́ прекра́сно уме́ет разреша́ть
спо́ры; **~ witness** *(LAW)* суде́бный экспе́рт.

expertise [ɛkspə:'ti:z] *n* зна́ния *ntpl* и о́пыт.

expire [ɪks'paɪəʳ] *vi* истека́ть (исте́чь* *perf*); **my
passport ~s in January** срок де́йствия моего́
па́спорта истека́ет в январе́.

expiry [ɪks'paɪərɪ] *n* истече́ние сро́ка.

expiry date *n* да́та истече́ния сро́ка.

explain [ɪks'pleɪn] *vt* объясня́ть (объясни́ть
perf)

► **explain away** *vt (mistake, situation)*
находи́ть* (найти́* *perf*) оправда́ние +*gen*.

explanation [ɛksplə'neɪʃən] *n* объясне́ние; **to
find an ~ for sth** находи́ть* (найти́* *perf*)
объясне́ние чему́-н.

explanatory [ɪks'plænətrɪ] *adj (comment etc)*
объясни́тельный; **~ notes** примеча́ния *ntpl*.

expletive [ɪks'pli:tɪv] *n* бра́нное сло́во*,
руга́тельство.

explicable [ɪks'plɪkəbl] *adj* объясни́мый; **for no
~ reason** по необъясни́мой причи́не.

explicit [ɪks'plɪsɪt] *adj* я́вный* (я́вен); *(sex,
violence)* открове́нный.

explode [ɪks'pləud] *vi (bomb, person)*
взрыва́ться (взорва́ться* *perf*); *(population)*
ре́зко возраста́ть (возрасти́* *perf*) ♦ *vt (bomb)*
взрыва́ть (взорва́ть* *perf*); *(myth, theory)*
опроверга́ть* (опрове́ргнуть* *perf*); **to ~ with
laughter** разража́ться (разрази́ться* *perf*)
сме́хом.

exploit [*vt* ɪks'plɔɪt, *n* 'ɛksplɔɪt] *vt (resources, also
pej: person, idea)* эксплуати́ровать *(impf)*;
(opportunity) испо́льзовать *(impf/perf)* ♦ *n*
по́двиг.

exploitation [ɛksplɔɪ'teɪʃən] *n (see vb)*
эксплуата́ция; испо́льзование.

exploration [ɛksplə'reɪʃən] *n (of place)*
иссле́дование; *(of idea)* изуче́ние.

exploratory [ɪks'plɔrətrɪ] *adj (expedition)*

---

* marks translations which have irregular inflections. The Russian-English side of the dictionary gives inflectional information.

исследовательский*; (*talks, operation*) предварительный.

explore [ɪksˈplɔː] *vt* (*place*) исследовать (*impf/ perf*); (*with hands etc*) ощупывать (ощупать *perf*); (*idea, suggestion*) изучать (изучить* *perf*).

explorer [ɪksˈplɔːrə] *n* исследователь(ница) *m(f)*.

explosion [ɪksˈpləuʒən] *n* взрыв; **population ~** демографический* взрыв.

explosive [ɪksˈpləusɪv] *adj* (*device, effect*) взрывной; (*situation*) взрывоопасный* (взрывоопасен) ♦ *n* (*substance*) взрывчатое вещество*; (*device*) взрывное устройство; **he has an ~ temper** он очень вспыльчивый.

exponent [ɪksˈpəunənt] *n* (*of idea, theory*) сторонник(-ица); (*of skill, activity*) мастер; (*MATH*) показатель *m* степени.

exponential [ɛkspəuˈnɛnʃl] *adj* (*growth*) стремительный* (стремителен); (*MATH*) экспоненциальный ♦ *n* (*MATH*) экспонента.

export [*n, cpd* ˈɛkspɔːt, *vt* ɛksˈpɔːt] *n* (*process*) экспорт, вывоз; (*product*) предмет экспорта ♦ *vt* экспортировать (*impf/perf*), вывозить* (вывезти* *perf*) ♦ *cpd* (*duty, licence*) экспортный.

exportation [ɛkspɔːˈteɪʃən] *n* экспортирование.

exporter [ɛksˈpɔːtə] *n* экспортёр.

expose [ɪksˈpəuz] *vt* (*object*) обнажать (обнажить* *perf*); (*truth, plot*) раскрывать (раскрыть* *perf*); (*person*) разоблачать (разоблачить* *perf*); (*PHOT*) экспонировать (*impf/perf*); **to ~ sb to sth** подвергать (подвергнуть* *perf*) кого-н чему-н; **to ~ o.s.** (*LAW*) демонстрировать (*impf*) половые органы.

exposé [ɛksˈpəuzeɪ] *n* разоблачение.

exposed [ɪksˈpəuzd] *adj* (*wire*) оголённый; (*place*): **~ (to)** открытый (открыт) (+*dat*).

exposition [ɛkspəˈzɪʃən] *n* (*explanation*) изложение; (*exhibition*) экспозиция.

exposure [ɪksˈpəuʒə] *n* (*of culprit*) разоблачение; (*PHOT*) экспозиция, выдержка; (: *shot*) кадр; **~ to radiation** пребывание под воздействием радиации; **to suffer/die from ~** (*MED*) страдать (пострадать *perf*)/умирать (умереть* *perf*) от переохлаждения.

exposure meter *n* (*PHOT*) экспонометр.

expound [ɪksˈpaund] *vt* излагать (изложить* *perf*).

express [ɪksˈprɛs] *adj* (*clear*) чёткий*; (*BRIT: service*) срочный* ♦ *n* (*train, coach etc*) экспресс ♦ *adv* (*send*) экспрессом ♦ *vt* выражать (выразить* *perf*); **to ~ o.s.** выражать (выразить* *perf*) себя.

expression [ɪksˈprɛʃən] *n* выражение; (*expressiveness*) выразительность *f*.

expressionism [ɪksˈprɛʃənɪzəm] *n* экспрессионизм.

expressive [ɪksˈprɛsɪv] *adj* выразительный* (выразителен).

expressly [ɪksˈprɛslɪ] *adv* (*clearly*) определённо; (*intentionally*) специально.

expressway [ɪksˈprɛsweɪ] *n* (*esp US*) скоростная автострада.

expropriate [ɛksˈprəuprɪeɪt] *vt* (*money, property*) экспроприировать (*impf/perf*).

expulsion [ɪksˈpʌlʃən] *n* (*from school*) исключение; (*from country*) изгнание; (*of substance*) вывод.

expurgate [ˈɛkspəːgeɪt] *vt*: **to ~ a text** вычёркивать (вычеркнуть *perf*) нежелательные места из текста; **the ~d version** вариант с купюрами.

exquisite [ɛksˈkwɪzɪt] *adj* (*face, lace, taste, workmanship*) изысканный* (изыскан); (*pain, pleasure*) острый.

exquisitely [ɛksˈkwɪzɪtlɪ] *adv* (*dressed, polite, carved*) изысканно; (*sensitive*) обострённо.

ex-serviceman [ˈɛksˈsəːvɪsmən] *irreg n* бывший* военнослужащий* *m adj*.

ext. *abbr* (*TEL*) = **extension**.

extemporize [ɪksˈtɛmpəraɪz] *vi* импровизировать (*impf*).

extend [ɪksˈtɛnd] *vt* (*visit, deadline*) продлевать (продлить *perf*); (*building*) расширять (расширить *perf*); (*arm, hand*) протягивать (протянуть* *perf*); (*offer*) оказывать (оказать* *perf*); (*credit, help*) предоставлять (предоставить* *perf*) ♦ *vi* (*land, road*) простираться (*impf*); (*period*) продолжаться (продолжиться *perf*); **to ~ an invitation to sb** приглашать (пригласить* *perf*) кого-н.

extension [ɪksˈtɛnʃən] *n* (*of time*) продление; (*of campaign, rights*) расширение; (*of building*) пристройка*; (*of road*) продолжение; (*ELEC*) удлинитель *m*; (*TEL: in house*) параллельный телефон; (: *in office*) добавочный телефон; **~ 3718** (*TEL*) добавочный (номер) 3718.

extension cable *n* удлинитель *m*.

extension lead *n* = **extension cable**.

extensive [ɪksˈtɛnsɪv] *adj* обширный* (обширен); **~ damage** значительный ущерб.

extensively [ɪksˈtɛnsɪvlɪ] *adv*: **he has travelled ~** он много путешествовал.

extent [ɪksˈtɛnt] *n* (*size: of area etc*) протяжённость *f*; (: *of problem etc*) масштаб; (*degree: of damage, loss*) размер; **to some ~** до некоторой степени; **to a large ~** в значительной степени; **to go to the ~ of ...** доходить (дойти* *perf*) до того, что ...; **to such an ~ that ...** до такой степени, что ...; **what ~?** до какой степени?

extenuating [ɪksˈtɛnjueɪtɪŋ] *adj*: **~ circumstances** смягчающие обстоятельства *ntpl*.

exterior [ɛksˈtɪərɪə] *adj* (*drain, light, paint*) наружный; (*world*) внешний ♦ *n* (*outside*) внешняя сторона*; (*appearance*) внешность *f*.

exterminate [ɪks'tə:mɪneɪt] *vt* истребля́ть
(истреби́ть* *perf*).
extermination [ɪkstə:mɪ'neɪʃən] *n*
истребле́ние.
external [ɛks'tə:nl] *adj* вне́шний*; **the ~s** *npl*
вне́шняя сторона́* *sg*; **"for ~ use only"** "для
нару́жного употребле́ния"; **~ affairs** (*POL*)
вне́шняя поли́тика*; **~ evidence**
свиде́тельство со стороны́.
externally [ɛks'tə:nəlɪ] *adv* вне́шне.
extinct [ɪks'tɪŋkt] *adj* (*animal*) вы́мерший;
(*plant*) исче́знувший; (*volcano*) поту́хший; **to
become ~** вымира́ть (вы́мереть* *perf*).
extinction [ɪks'tɪŋkʃən] *n* (*see adj*) вымира́ние;
исчезнове́ние.
extinguish [ɪks'tɪŋgwɪʃ] *vt* (*fire*) туши́ть*
(потуши́ть* *perf*); (*light*) гаси́ть* (погаси́ть*
perf); (*memory, hope*) уничтожа́ть
(уничто́жить *perf*).
extinguisher [ɪks'tɪŋgwɪʃəʳ] *n* (*also:* **fire ~**)
огнетуши́тель *m*.
extol [ɪks'təul] (*US* **extoll**) *vt* превозноси́ть*
(превознести́* *perf*).
extort [ɪks'tɔ:t] *vt*: **to ~ sth (from)** вымога́ть
(*impf*) что-н (у +*gen*).
extortion [ɪks'tɔ:ʃən] *n* вымога́тельство.
extortionate [ɪks'tɔ:ʃnɪt] *adj* (*price*) граб-
и́тельский*; (*demands*) вымога́тельский.
extra ['ɛkstrə] *adj* (*additional*)
дополни́тельный; (*spare*) ли́шний ◆ *adv* (*in
addition*) дополни́тельно; (*especially*)
осо́бенно ◆ *n* (*luxury*) изли́шество;
(*surcharge*) допла́та; (*CINEMA*) стати́ст(ка*);
wine will cost ~ за вино́ ну́жно бу́дет
заплати́ть отде́льно; **the room charge does
not include ~s** цена́ но́мера не включа́ет
пла́ту за дополни́тельные услу́ги и
удо́бства.
extra... ['ɛkstrə] *prefix* экстра..., особо...,
сверх....
extract [*vt* ɪks'trækt, *n* 'ɛkstrækt] *vt* (*tooth*)
удаля́ть (удали́ть* *perf*); (*mineral*) добыва́ть
(добы́ть* *perf*); (*money, promise*) вытя́гивать
(вы́тянуть *perf*) ◆ *n* (*from novel, recording*)
отры́вок*; (*CULIN*) экстра́кт; **to ~ sth (from)**
извлека́ть (извле́чь* *perf*) что-н (из +*gen*).
extraction [ɪks'trækʃən] *n* (*of object*)
извлече́ние; (*of tooth*) удале́ние; (*of minerals
etc*) добы́ча; (*descent*): **of Scottish ~**
шотла́ндец(-дка) по происхожде́нию.
extractor fan [ɪks'træktə-] *n* вытяжно́е
устро́йство, вентиля́тор.
extracurricular ['ɛkstrəkə'rɪkjuləʳ] *adj*
внекла́ссный, внеуче́бный.
extradite ['ɛkstrədaɪt] *vt*: **to ~ sb to/from**
выдава́ть (вы́дать* *perf*) кого́-н +*dat*/из +*gen*.
extradition [ɛkstrə'dɪʃən] *n* вы́дача
(*престу́пника*) ◆ *cpd*: **~ order/treaty** про́сьба/

соглаше́ние о вы́даче.
extramarital ['ɛkstrə'mærɪtl] *adj* внебра́чный.
extramural ['ɛkstrə'mjuərl] *adj* зао́чный.
extraneous [ɛks'treɪnɪəs] *adj* посторо́нний*.
extraordinary [ɪks'trɔ:dnrɪ] *adj* незауря́дный*
(незауря́ден), необыча́йный* (необыча́ен);
(*meeting*) чрезвыча́йный; **the ~ thing is that**
... са́мое удиви́тельное в том, что ....
extraordinary general meeting *n*
чрезвыча́йное о́бщее собра́ние.
extrapolation [ɛkstræpə'leɪʃən] *n*
экстраполя́ция.
extrasensory perception ['ɛkstrə'sɛnsərɪ-] *n*
сверхчу́вственное *or* экстрасе́нсорное
восприя́тие.
extra time *n* дополни́тельное вре́мя* *nt*.
extravagance [ɪks'trævəgəns] *n* (*of behaviour*)
экстравага́нтность *f*; (*with money*)
расточи́тельство.
extravagant [ɪks'trævəgənt] *adj* (*lavish*)
экстравага́нтный* (экстравага́нтен);
(*wasteful: person*) расточи́тельный*
(расточи́телен); (*: machine*) неэконо́мный*
(неэконо́мен); (*wild: ideas, claims*)
сумасбро́дный* (сумасбро́ден).
extreme [ɪks'tri:m] *adj* кра́йний*; (*heat, cold*)
сильне́йший ◆ *n* (*of behaviour*) кра́йность *f*;
the ~ right/left (*POL*) кра́йне пра́вые *pl adj*/
ле́вые *pl adj*; **~s of temperature** перепа́ды
температу́ры.
extremely [ɪks'tri:mlɪ] *adv* кра́йне.
extremist [ɪks'tri:mɪst] *n* экстреми́ст(ка*) ◆ *adj*
экстреми́стский.
extremities [ɪks'trɛmɪtɪz] *npl* (*ANAT*)
коне́чности *fpl*.
extremity [ɪks'trɛmɪtɪ] *n* коне́чность *f*; (*of
situation*) кра́йность *f*.
extricate ['ɛkstrɪkeɪt] *vt*: **to ~ sb/sth (from)**
высвобожда́ть (вы́свободить* *perf*) кого́-н/
что-н (из +*gen*); **to ~ o.s. (from)**
выпу́тываться (вы́путаться *perf*) (из +*gen*).
extrovert ['ɛkstrəvə:t] *n* экстрове́рт.
exuberance [ɪg'zju:bərns] *n* экспанси́вность *f*.
exuberant [ɪg'zju:bərnt] *adj* (*person, behaviour*)
экспанси́вный* (экспанси́вен); (*imagination*)
бу́йный* (бу́ен).
exude [ɪg'zju:d] *vt* (*confidence, enthusiasm*)
источа́ть (*impf*); (*liquid*) выделя́ть (вы́делить
perf); (*smell*) издава́ть* (*impf*).
exult [ɪg'zʌlt] *vi* (*rejoice*): **to ~ (in)** ликова́ть*
(*impf*) (по по́воду +*gen*).
exultant [ɪg'zʌltənt] *adj* лику́ющий,
торжеству́ющий; **to be ~** ликова́ть (*impf*),
торжествова́ть (*impf*).
exultation [ɛgzʌl'teɪʃən] *n* экзальта́ция,
ликова́ние.
eye [aɪ] *n* (*ANAT*) глаз*; (*of needle*) у́шко* ◆ *vt*
разгля́дывать (разгляде́ть* *perf*); **to keep an**

---

* marks translations which have irregular inflections. The Russian-English side of the dictionary gives inflectional information.

~ **on** (*person, object*) присма́тривать
(присмотре́ть* *perf*) за +*instr*; (*time*) следи́ть*
(*impf*) за +*instr*; **in the public** ~ на виду́, в
це́нтре внима́ния; **to have an ~ for sth** знать
(*impf*) толк в чём-н; **with an ~ to doing** (*BRIT*) с
расчётом +*infin*; **as far as the ~ can see**
наско́лько мо́жно охвати́ть взгля́дом;
there's more to this than meets the ~ э́то не
так про́сто, как ка́жется на пе́рвый взгляд.
eyeball ['aɪbɔːl] *n* глазно́е я́блоко*.
eyebath ['aɪbɑːθ] *n* (*BRIT*) глазна́я ва́нночка*.
eyebrow ['aɪbrau] *n* бровь* *f*.
eyebrow pencil *n* каранда́ш* для брове́й.
eye-catching ['aɪkætʃɪŋ] *adj* броса́ющийся в
глаза́.
eyecup ['aɪkʌp] *n* (*US*) = **eyebath**.
eye drops *npl* глазны́е ка́пли *fpl*.
eyeful ['aɪful] *n*: **an ~ of sand/dust** по́лные
глаза́ песка́*/пы́ли; **to get an ~ of sb/sth** (*inf*)
разгляде́ть* (*perf*) кого́-н/что-н.
eyeglass ['aɪglɑːs] *n* моно́кль *m*.
eyelash ['aɪlæʃ] *n* ресни́ца.
eyelet ['aɪlɪt] *n* фесто́н.

eye level *n*: **at ~~** на у́ровне глаз.
eyelevel ['aɪlɛvl] *adj* (*grill*) располо́женный на
у́ровне глаз.
eyelid ['aɪlɪd] *n* ве́ко*.
eyeliner ['aɪlaɪnə'] *n* каранда́ш* для глаз.
eye-opener ['aɪəupnə'] *n* открове́ние.
eye shadow *n* те́ни* *fpl* (для век).
eyesight ['aɪsaɪt] *n* зре́ние.
eyesore ['aɪsɔː'] *n*: **that building is a real ~** э́то
зда́ние как бельмо́ на глазу́.
eyestrain ['aɪstreɪn] *n* чрезме́рное напряже́ние
глаз.
eyeteeth ['aɪtiːθ] *npl of* **eyetooth**.
eyetooth ['aɪtuːθ] (*pl* **eyeteeth**) *n* глазно́й зуб;
to give one's eyeteeth for sth/to do
же́ртвовать (поже́ртвовать *perf*) всем за
что-н/за то, что́бы +*infin*.
eyewash ['aɪwɔʃ] *n* примо́чка* для глаз; (*fig*:
inf) очковтира́тельство.
eyewitness ['aiwitnis] *n* очеви́дец* ♦ *cpd*: **an ~**
account свиде́тельство очеви́дца.
eyrie ['ɪərɪ] *n* (*nest*) орли́ное гнездо́*.

~ F, f ~

F, f [ɛf] n (letter) 6-ая бу́ква англи́йского
алфави́та.

F [ɛf] n (MUS) фа.

F abbr = **Fahrenheit**.

FA n abbr (BRIT: = Football Association)
Футбо́льная ассоциа́ция.

FAA n abbr (US: = Federal Aviation
Administration) Федера́льное управле́ние
авиа́цией.

fable ['feɪbl] n ба́сня*.

fabric ['fæbrɪk] n (cloth) ткань f; (of society)
структу́ра; (of building) констру́кция.

fabricate ['fæbrɪkeɪt] vt (make up) фабрикова́ть
(сфабрикова́ть perf); (make) производи́ть*
(произвести́* perf).

fabrication [fæbrɪ'keɪʃən] n (lie) фабрика́ция;
(making) произво́дство.

fabric ribbon n (for typewriter) печа́тная
ле́нта.

fabulous ['fæbjuləs] adj (extraordinary)
невероя́тный* (невероя́тен); (mythical)
ска́зочный*; (inf: super) ска́зочный*
(ска́зочен).

façade [fə'saːd] n фаса́д; (fig: pretence)
ви́димость f; **a ~ of gaiety/indifference** фаса́д
весе́лья/равноду́шия.

face [feɪs] n (of person, organization) лицо́*;
(grimace) грима́са; (of clock) цифербла́т; (of
mountain, cliff) склон; (of building) фаса́д; (of
surface: of cube etc) сторона́* ♦ vt (fact)
признава́ть* (призна́ть* perf); **the house is
facing the sea** дом обращён к мо́рю; **he was
facing the door** он был обращён лицо́м к
двери́; **we are facing difficulties** нам
предстоя́т тру́дности; **~ down** лицо́м вниз;
to lose/save ~ теря́ть (потеря́ть perf)/спаса́ть
(спасти́* perf) репута́цию; **to make or pull a ~**
де́лать (сде́лать perf) грима́су; **in the ~ of**
(difficulties etc) несмотря́ на +acc; **on the ~ of
it** на пе́рвый взгляд; **~ to ~ (with)** (with
person, problem) лицо́м к лицу́ (с +instr); **to ~
the fact that ...** признава́ть* (призна́ть* perf)
тот факт, что ...

▸ **face up to** vt fus (obligations, responsibility)
признава́ть* (призна́ть* perf); (difficulties)
справля́ться (спра́виться* perf) с +instr.

face cloth n (BRIT) махро́вая салфе́тка (для
обтира́ния лица́).

face cream n крем* для лица́.

faceless ['feɪslɪs] adj безли́кий*.

face-lift ['feɪslɪft] n подтя́жка* ко́жи на лице́;
(of building etc) облицо́вка*.

face powder n пу́дра для лица́.

face-saving ['feɪs'seɪvɪŋ] adj для спасе́ния
репута́ции.

facet ['fæsɪt] n (also fig) грань f.

facetious [fə'siːʃəs] adj остроу́мный.

face to face adv лицо́м к лицу́.

face value n номина́льная сто́имость f; **to
take sth at ~ ~** (fig) принима́ть (приня́ть*
perf) что-н за чи́стую моне́ту.

facia ['feɪʃə] n = **fascia**.

facial ['feɪʃl] n космети́ческая обрабо́тка лица́
♦ adj: **~ expression** выраже́ние лица́; **~ hair**
во́лосы, расту́щие на лице́.

facile ['fæsaɪl] adj пове́рхностный*.

facilitate [fə'sɪlɪteɪt] vt спосо́бствовать (impf/
perf) +dat.

facilities npl (buildings) помеще́ние ntsg;
(equipment) обору́дование ntsg; **credit ~**
креди́тный лими́т (креди́тной ка́рточки
заёмщика); **cooking ~** усло́вия npl для
приготовле́ния пи́щи.

facility [fə'sɪlɪtɪ] n (feature) приспособле́ние;
(service) услу́га; (aptitude): **to have a ~ for**
име́ть (impf) спосо́бности к +dat.

facing ['feɪsɪŋ] prep (opposite) напро́тив +gen ♦
n (SEWING) отде́лка*.

facsimile [fæk'sɪmɪlɪ] n факси́миле nt ind;
(machine, document) факс.

fact [fækt] n факт; **in ~** факти́чески; **to know for
a ~ that ...** знать (impf) наверняка́, что ...; **the
~ (of the matter) is that ...** де́ло в том, что ...;
the ~s of life (sex) полова́я сторона́ жи́зни;
(fig) реа́льности fpl жи́зни.

fact-finding ['fæktfaɪndɪŋ] adj для
рассле́дования фа́ктов.

faction ['fækʃən] n (group) фра́кция.

factor ['fæktə] n фа́ктор; (COMM)
комиссионе́р; (: agent) аге́нт; **safety ~**
фа́ктор безопа́сности; **human ~**
челове́ческий* фа́ктор.

---

* marks translations which have irregular inflections. The Russian-English side of the dictionary gives inflectional information.

factory ['fæktərɪ] *n* (*for textiles etc*) фа́брика; (*for machinery etc*) заво́д.
factory farming *n* (*BRIT*) веде́ние животново́дства промы́шленными ме́тодами.
factory floor *n* (*fig: workers*) рабо́чие *pl adj* у станка́.
factory ship *n* плаву́чая фа́брика.
factual ['fæktjuəl] *adj* факти́ческий*.
faculty ['fækəltɪ] *n* спосо́бность *f*; (*of university*) факульте́т; (*US: teaching staff*) профе́ссорско-преподава́тельский соста́в.
fad [fæd] *n* причу́да.
fade [feɪd] *vi* (*colour*) выцвета́ть (вы́цвести* *perf*); (*light*) угаса́ть (уга́снуть* *perf*); (*sound*) замира́ть (замере́ть* *perf*); (*flower*) вя́нуть* (завя́нуть* *perf*); (*hope, smile*) угаса́ть (уга́снуть* *perf*); (*memory*) сгла́живаться (сгла́диться* *perf*)
▶ **fade in** *vt*: **to ~ the picture/sound in** постепе́нно увели́чивать (*impf*) чёткость изображе́ния/си́лу зву́ка.
▶ **fade out** *vt*: **to ~ the picture/sound out** постепе́нно уменьша́ть (*impf*) чёткость изображе́ния/си́лу зву́ка.
faeces ['fi:si:z] (*US* **feces**) *npl* фека́лии *fpl*.
fag [fæg] (*inf*) *n* (*BRIT: cigarette*) сигаре́та; (*US: pej: homosexual*) го́мик; (*BRIT: chore*): **what a ~!** ну и работёнка!
Fahrenheit ['færənhaɪt] *n* Фаренге́йт.
fail [feɪl] *vt* (*exam, candidate*) прова́ливать (провали́ть* *perf*); (*subj: person, memory*) изменя́ть (измени́ть *perf*) +*dat*, подводи́ть (подвести́ *perf*); (: *courage*) покида́ть (поки́нуть *perf*) ♦ *vi* (*candidate, attempt*) прова́ливаться (провали́ться* *perf*); (*brakes*) отка́зывать (отказа́ть* *perf*); **my eyesight/ health is ~ing** у меня́ слабе́ет зре́ние/ здоро́вье; **to ~ to do** не смочь* (*perf*) +*infin*; **without ~** обяза́тельно; **the light is ~ing** смерка́ется.
failing ['feɪlɪŋ] *n* недоста́ток* ♦ *prep* за неиме́нием +*gen*; **~ that** за неиме́нием э́того.
fail-safe ['feɪlseɪf] *adj* (*device*) предохрани́тельный.
failure ['feɪljə*] *n* неуда́ча; (*mechanical*) поврежде́ние*; (*of crops*) неурожа́й; (*in exam*) прова́л; (*person*) неуда́чник(-ица); **his ~ to complete the work** то, что он не смог вы́полнить рабо́ту; **the evening was a complete ~** ве́чер был по́лным прова́лом.
faint [feɪnt] *adj* сла́бый* (слаб); (*recollection*) сму́тный* (смутен); (*mark*) едва́ заме́тный* (заме́тен); (*breeze, trace*) лёгкий* ♦ *n* (*MED*) о́бморок ♦ *vi* (*MED*) па́дать (упа́сть* *perf*) в о́бморок; **to feel ~** чу́вствовать (почу́вствовать *perf*) сла́бость.
faintest ['feɪntɪst] *adj* мале́йший*; **I haven't the ~ idea** я не име́ю ни мале́йшего поня́тия.
faint-hearted ['feɪnt'hɑ:tɪd] *adj* малоду́шный* (малоду́шен).

faintly ['feɪntlɪ] *adv* (*a bit*) сла́бо; (*hardly*) едва́.
fair [fɛə*] *adj* (*person, decision*) справедли́вый (справедли́в); (*size, number*) значи́тельный; (*chance, guess*) хоро́ший*; (*skin, hair*) све́тлый* (све́тел); (*weather*) хоро́ший*, я́сный* ♦ *n* (*also*: **trade ~**) я́рмарка*; (*BRIT: also*: **funfair**) аттракцио́ны *mpl* ♦ *adv*: **to play ~** вести́* (*impf*) дела́ разу́мно *or* че́стно; **it's not ~!** э́то нече́стно!; **a ~ amount of money** значи́тельная су́мма де́нег; **a ~ amount of success** значи́тельный успе́х; **I had a pretty ~ idea** была́ дово́льно хоро́шая иде́я; **~ wear and tear** обосно́ванный изно́с.
fair copy *n* чистово́й экземпля́р.
fair game *n*: **he is ~ ~** он зако́нная добы́ча.
fairground ['fɛəgraund] *n* лу́на-парк.
fair-haired [fɛə'hɛəd] *adj* светловоло́сый (светловоло́с).
fairly ['fɛəlɪ] *adv* (*justly*) справедли́во; (*quite*) дово́льно; **I'm ~ sure** я почти́ уве́рен.
fairness ['fɛənɪs] *n* (*justice*) справедли́вость *f*; **in all ~** со всей справедли́востью.
fair play *n* че́стная игра́.
fairway ['fɛəweɪ] *n* (*GOLF*): **the ~** *травяни́стая доро́жка ме́жду лу́нками в го́льфе.*
fairy ['fɛərɪ] *n* фе́я.
fairy godmother *n* до́брая волше́бница.
fairy lights *npl* (*BRIT*) электри́ческая гирля́нда *fsg*.
fairy tale *n* ска́зка*.
faith [feɪθ] *n* (*also REL*) ве́ра; **to have ~ in sb/sth** ве́рить (*impf*) в кого́-н/что-н.
faithful ['feɪθful] *adj*: **~ (to)** ве́рный* (ве́рен) (+*dat*).
faithfully ['feɪθfəlɪ] *adv* ве́рно.
faith healer *n* зна́харь(-рка*) *m(f)*.
fake [feɪk] *n* (*painting, document*) подде́лка*; (*person*) притво́рщик(-ица) ♦ *adj* фальши́вый, подде́льный ♦ *vt* (*painting, document*) подде́лывать (подде́лать *perf*); (*illness, emotion*) симули́ровать (*impf*); **his illness is a ~** его́ боле́знь – симуля́ция.
falcon ['fɔ:lkən] *n* со́кол.
Falkland Islands ['fɔ:lklənd-] *npl*: **the ~ ~** Фолкле́ндские острова́* *mpl*.
fall [fɔ:l] (*pt* **fell**, *pp* **fallen**) *n* паде́ние; (*US: autumn*) о́сень *f* ♦ *vi* па́дать (упа́сть* *perf*); (*government, country*) пасть* (*perf*); (*rain, snow*) выпада́ть (вы́пасть* *perf*); (*silence, hush, night*) наступа́ть (наступи́ть* *perf*); (*sadness*) охва́тывать (охвати́ть *perf*); **~s** *npl* (*waterfall*) водопа́д*; **a ~ of snow** снегопа́д; **a ~ of earth** обва́л; **to ~ flat** (*plan*) не удава́ться* (уда́ться* *perf*); (*joke*) не име́ть (*impf*) успе́ха; **to ~ flat (on one's face)** па́дать (упа́сть* *perf*) ничко́м; **to ~ in love (with sb/ sth)** влюбля́ться (влюби́ться* *perf*) (в кого́-н/ во что-н); **to ~ short of (sb's expectations)** не опра́вдывать (оправда́ть *perf*) (чьих-н ожида́ний); **a lot of rain/snow fell yesterday** вчера́ вы́пало мно́го сне́га/дождя́; **darkness/**

night fell наступи́ла темнота́/ночь
▸ **fall apart** *vi* разва́ливаться (развали́ться*
perf); (*inf*: *emotionally*) расскле́иваться
(расскле́иться *perf*)
▸ **fall back** *vt fus* (*MIL*) отступа́ть (отступи́ть*
perf)
▸ **fall back on** *vt fus* прибега́ть (прибе́гнуть*
perf) к +*dat*; **to have sth to ~ back on** (*money,
job etc*) име́ть (*impf*) что-н в запа́се
▸ **fall behind** *vi* отстава́ть* (отста́ть* *perf*); **to ~
behind with the payments** просро́чивать
(просро́чить *perf*) платежи́
▸ **fall down** *vi* (*person*) па́дать (упа́сть* *perf*);
(*building*) ру́шиться (ру́хнуть *perf*)
▸ **fall for** *vt fus* (*trick etc*) попада́ться
(попа́сться* *perf*) на +*acc*; (*story*) ве́рить
(пове́рить *perf*) +*dat*; (*person*) влюбля́ться
(влюби́ться* *perf*) в +*acc*
▸ **fall in** *vi* (*roof*) обва́ливаться (обвали́ться
perf); (*MIL*) стро́иться (постро́иться *perf*)
▸ **fall in with** *vt fus* (*sb's plans etc*) соглаша́ться
(согласи́ться* *perf*) с +*instr*
▸ **fall off** *vi* па́дать (упа́сть* *perf*)
▸ **fall out** *vi* (*hair, teeth*) выпада́ть (вы́пасть*
perf); (*friends etc*): **to ~ out with sb** ссо́риться
(поссо́риться *perf*) с кем-н
▸ **fall over** *vi* па́дать (упа́сть* *perf*) ♦ *vt*: **to ~
over o.s. to do** лезть* (вы́лезть* *perf*) из ко́жи
вон, что́бы +*infin*
▸ **fall through** *vi* (*plan*) прова́ливаться
(провали́ться* *perf*).
fallacy ['fæləsɪ] *n* (*misconception*)
заблужде́ние.
fall-back ['fɔːlbæk] *adj*: **~ position** пози́ция для
отступле́ния.
fallen ['fɔːlən] *pp of* **fall**.
fallible ['fæləbl] *adj* спосо́бный* (спосо́бен)
ошиба́ться (ошиби́ться *perf*).
falling ['fɔːlɪŋ] *adj*: **~ market** (*COMM*)
понижа́тельная ры́ночная конъюнкту́ра.
falling off *n* сниже́ние.
falling out *n* размо́лвка.
Fallopian tube [fə'ləupɪən-] *n* фалло́пиевы
тру́бы *fpl*.
fallout ['fɔːlaut] *n* радиоакти́вные оса́дки *pl*.
fallout shelter *n* убе́жище от радиоакти́вных
оса́дков.
fallow ['fæləu] *adj* (*land, field*) парово́й.
false [fɔːls] *adj* (*untrue, wrong*) ло́жный*
(ло́жен); (*insincere, artificial*) фальши́вый
(фальши́в); **~ imprisonment** незако́нное
лише́ние свобо́ды.
false alarm *n* ло́жная трево́га.
falsehood ['fɔːlshud] *n* ложь* *f*.
falsely ['fɔːlslɪ] *adv* (*accuse*) ло́жно.
false pretences *npl*: **under ~ ~** под ло́жным
предло́гом.
false teeth *npl* (*BRIT*) иску́сственные зу́бы* *mpl*.

falsify ['fɔːlsɪfaɪ] *vt* фальсифици́ровать (*impf/
perf*), подде́лывать (подде́лать *perf*).
falter ['fɔːltə'] *vi* (*engine*) ка́шлять (*impf*);
(*person: hesitate*) замя́ться* (*perf*); (: *in
speech*) запина́ться (запну́ться *perf*); (: *while
moving*) спотыка́ться (споткну́ться *perf*).
fame [feɪm] *n* сла́ва.
familiar [fə'mɪlɪə'] *adj* (*well-known*) знако́мый
(знако́м); (*intimate*) дру́жеский*; **he is/was ~
with** (*subject*) он знако́м/был знако́м с +*instr*;
to make o.s. ~ with sth знако́миться*
(ознако́миться* *perf*) с чем-н; **to be on ~
terms with sb** быть* (*impf*) в прия́тельских *or*
дру́жеских отноше́ниях с кем-н.
familiarity [fəmɪlɪ'ærɪtɪ] *n* (*knowledge*) зна́ние;
(*informality*) фамилья́рность *f*.
familiarize [fə'mɪlɪəraɪz] *vt*: **to ~ o.s. with sth**
ознакомля́ться (ознако́миться* *perf*) с
чем-н.
family ['fæmɪlɪ] *n* семья́*; (*children*) де́ти* *pl*.
family business *n* семе́йный би́знес.
family credit *n* де́нежное посо́бие,
выпла́чиваемое госуда́рством се́мьям с
ни́зким у́ровнем дохо́дов.
family doctor *n* семе́йный врач*.
family life *n* семе́йная жизнь *f*.
family man *n* семьяни́н*, семе́йный челове́к*.
family planning *n* плани́рование семьи́; **~ ~
clinic** ≈ же́нская консульта́ция.
family tree *n* родосло́вное де́рево*.
famine ['fæmɪn] *n* го́лод*.
famished ['fæmɪʃt] (*inf*) *adj* голо́дный; **I'm ~** я
умира́ю с го́лоду.
famous ['feɪməs] *adj* знамени́тый (знамени́т).
famously ['feɪməslɪ] *adv* (*get on*) великоле́пно.
fan [fæn] *n* (*folding*) ве́ер*; (*ELEC*) вентиля́тор;
(*of famous person*) покло́нник(-ица), фэн; (*of
sports team*) боле́льщик(-ица) ♦ *vt* (*face*)
обма́хивать (обмахну́ть *perf*); (*fire, quarrel*)
раздува́ть (разду́ть *perf*)
▸ **fan out** *vi* (*people*) развёртываться
(разверну́ться *perf*) ве́ером; (*roads*)
расходи́ться* (разойти́сь* *perf*) ве́ером.
fanatic [fə'nætɪk] *n* (*extremist*) фана́тик.
fanatical [fə'nætɪkl] *adj* (*support, dedication*)
фанати́ческий (фанати́чен).
fan belt *n* (*AUT*) вентиля́торный реме́нь* *m*.
fan club *n* клуб покло́нников, фэн-клуб.
fanciful ['fænsɪful] *adj* причу́дливый
(причу́длив).
fancy ['fænsɪ] *n* (*whim*) при́хоть *f*; (*imagination*)
воображе́ние; (*fantasy*) фанта́зия ♦ *adj*
изы́сканный ♦ *vt* (*feel like, want*) хоте́ть*
(захоте́ть* *perf*); (*imagine*) вообража́ть
(вообрази́ть* *perf*); (*think*) ду́мать (*impf*); **to
take a ~ to** увлека́ться (увле́чься* *perf*) +*instr*;
when the ~ takes him когда́ ему́ взду́мается;
the idea took *or* **caught my ~** иде́я пришла́сь

мне по вку́су; **to ~ that** ду́мать *(impf)*, что; **he fancies her** *(inf)* она́ ему́ нра́вится; **~ that!** предста́вьте себе́.

fancy dress *n* маскара́дный костю́м.

fancy-dress ball ['fænsɪdrɛs-] *n* костю́м-и́рованный бал*.

fancy goods *npl* украше́ния *ntpl (обычно для до́ма)*.

fanfare ['fænfɛəʳ] *n* фанфа́ра.

fanfold paper ['fænfəuld-] *n* перфори́рованная *or* фальцо́ванная бума́га.

fang [fæŋ] *n* клык*; *(of snake)* ядови́тый зуб*.

fan heater *m (BRIT)* электрообогрева́тель *m (нагнета́ющий тёплый во́здух при по́мощи вентиля́тора)*.

fanlight ['fænlaɪt] *n* веерообра́зное окно́ над две́рью.

fanny ['fænɪ] *n (inf)* за́дница.

fantasize ['fæntəsaɪz] *vi* фантази́ровать *(impf)*.

fantastic [fæn'tæstɪk] *adj* фантасти́ческий*; **that's ~!** э́то фанта́стика!

fantasy ['fæntəsɪ] *n* фанта́зия.

fanzine ['fænzi:n] *n* журна́л или газе́та, самоде́ятельно издава́емый покло́нниками поп-гру́ппы, телепрогра́ммы, спо́рта итп.

FAO *n abbr (= Food and Agriculture Organization)* ФАО *(продово́льственная и сельскохозя́йственная организа́ция ООН)*.

f.a.q. *abbr (= free alongside quay)* фра́нко на́бережная.

far [fɑːʳ] *adj (distant)* да́льний* ◆ *adv (a long way)* далеко́; *(much)* гора́здо; **at the ~ end** в да́льнем конце́; **at the ~ side** на друго́й стороне́; **the ~ left/right** *(POL)* кра́йне ле́вый/пра́вый; **~ away, ~ off** далеко́; **~ better** гора́здо лу́чше; **he was ~ from poor** он был далеко́ *or* отню́дь не бе́ден; **by ~** намно́го; **is it ~ to London?** далеко́ ли до Ло́ндона?; **it's not ~ from here** э́то недалеко́ отсю́да; **go as ~ as the post office** дойди́те до по́чты; **as ~ back as the 13th century** ещё в 13-ом ве́ке; **as ~ as I know** наско́лько мне изве́стно; **as ~ as possible** наско́лько возмо́жно; **how ~?** *(distance)* как далеко́?; *(to what extent)* наско́лько?; **how ~ have you got with your work?** наско́лько Вы продви́нулись в свое́й рабо́те?

faraway ['fɑːrəweɪ] *adj (place)* да́льний*, далёкий*; *(look)* отсу́тствующий*.

farce [fɑːs] *n (also fig)* фарс.

farcical ['fɑːsɪkl] *adj (fig)* неле́пый.

fare [fɛəʳ] *n (on trains, buses)* пла́та за прое́зд; *(in taxi)* сто́имость *f* прое́зда; *(: passenger)* пассажи́р; *(food)* еда́ ◆ *vi*: **how did you ~?** как успе́хи?; **half/full ~** полсто́имости/по́лная сто́имость прое́зда; **bus/train ~** пла́та за прое́зд в авто́бусе/на по́езде; **they ~ better than we do under the present system** с ни́ми обраща́ются лу́чше, чем с на́ми при ны́нешней систе́ме; **they ~d well/badly in the recent elections** им повезло́/не повезло́ на неда́вних вы́борах.

Far East *n*: **the ~~** Да́льний* Восто́к.

farewell [fɛə'wɛl] *excl* проща́йте ◆ *n* проща́ние ◆ *cpd (party etc)* проща́льный.

far-fetched ['fɑː'fɛtʃt] *adj* неправдоподо́бный, невероя́тный.

farm [fɑːm] *n* фе́рма ◆ *vt (land)* обраба́тывать (обрабо́тать *perf)*.
▶ **farm out** *vt* отдава́ть* (отда́ть* *perf)*.

farmer ['fɑːməʳ] *n* фе́рмер.

farm hand *n* рабо́тник(-ица) фе́рмы.

farmhouse ['fɑːmhaus] *n* фе́рмерский дом*.

farming ['fɑːmɪŋ] *n (agriculture)* се́льское хозя́йство; *(of crops)* выра́щивание; *(of animals)* разведе́ние; **sheep ~** разведе́ние ове́ц, овцево́дство; **intensive ~** интенси́вное веде́ние се́льского хозя́йства.

farm labourer *n* рабо́тник на фе́рме.

farmland ['fɑːmlænd] *n* се́льско-хозя́йственные уго́дья* *ntpl*.

farm produce *n* проду́кты *mpl* се́льского хозя́йства.

farm worker *n* = farm hand.

farmyard ['fɑːmjɑːd] *n* фе́рмерский двор*.

Faroe Islands ['fɛərəu-] *npl*: **the ~~** Фаре́рские острова́* *mpl*.

Faroes ['fɛərəuz] *npl* = Faroe Islands.

far-reaching ['fɑː'riːtʃɪŋ] *adj (reform)* далеко́ иду́щий*; *(effect)* глубо́кий*.

far-sighted ['fɑː'saɪtɪd] *adj (US)* дальнозо́ркий* (дальнозо́рок); *(fig)* дальнови́дный* (дальнови́ден); **he is ~** *(US)* у него́ дальнозо́ркость.

fart [fɑːt] *(inf!)* *vi* перде́ть* (пёрнуть *perf)* (!) ◆ *n* перде́ние (!)

farther ['fɑːðəʳ] *adv* да́льше ◆ *adj* бо́лее да́льний*, далёкий*.

farthest ['fɑːðɪst] *superl of* far.

f.a.s. *abbr (BRIT: = free alongside ship)* ФАС *(свобо́дно вдоль бо́рта су́дна)*.

fascia ['feɪʃə] *n (AUT)* пане́ль *f*.

fascinate ['fæsɪneɪt] *vt* захва́тывать (захвати́ть* *perf)*; *(subj: person)* очаро́вывать (очарова́ть* *perf)*.

fascinating ['fæsɪneɪtɪŋ] *adj (story)* захва́тывающий*; *(person)* очарова́тельный* (очарова́телен).

fascination [fæsɪ'neɪʃən] *n* очарова́ние.

fascism ['fæʃɪzəm] *n (POL)* фаши́зм.

fascist ['fæʃɪst] *adj* фаши́стский* ◆ *n* фаши́ст(ка).

fashion ['fæʃən] *n (trend)* мо́да; *(fashion industry)* инду́стрия мо́ды ◆ *vt (make)* мастери́ть (смастери́ть *perf)*; **in/out of ~** в/не в мо́де; **in an animated ~** оживлённо; **in a friendly ~** по-дру́жески; **he did it after a ~** он сде́лал э́то ко́е-ка́к; **in the Greek ~** в гре́ческом сти́ле.

fashionable ['fæʃnəbl] *adj* мо́дный* (мо́ден).

fashion designer *n* модельер.

fashion show *n* пока́з *or* демонстра́ция мод.

fast [fɑ:st] *adv* (*quickly*) бы́стро; (*firmly*: *stick*) про́чно; (: *hold*) кре́пко ◆ *n* (*REL*) пост* ◆ *vi* (*REL*) пости́ться* (*impf*) ◆ *adj* бы́стрый* (быстр); (*progress*) стреми́тельный*; (*car*) скоростно́й; (*dye, colour*) про́чный; (*clock*): **to be ~** спеши́ть (*impf*); **he is ~ asleep** он кре́пко спит; **as ~ as possible** как мо́жно быстре́е; **to make a boat ~** (*BRIT*) кре́пко привяза́ть* (*perf*) ло́дку; **my watch is 5 minutes ~** мои́ часы́ спеша́т на 5 мину́т.

fasten ['fɑ:sn] *vt* закрепля́ть (закрепи́ть* *perf*); (*door*) запира́ть (запере́ть* *perf*); (*shoe*) завя́зывать (завяза́ть* *perf*); (*coat, dress*) застёгивать (застегну́ть *perf*); (*seat belt*) пристёгивать (пристегну́ть *perf*) ◆ *vi* (*coat, belt*) застёгиваться (застегну́ться *perf*); (*door*) запира́ться (запере́ться* *perf*)

▸ **fasten (up)on** *vt fus* (*idea etc*) сосредото́чиваться (сосредото́читься *perf*) на +*acc*.

fastener ['fɑ:snə'] *n* (*for clothing*) застёжка*.

fastening ['fɑ:snɪŋ] *n* = **fastener**.

fast food *n* быстроприготавливаемая еда́ ◆ *cpd*: **~~ restaurant** рестора́н быстро-приготавливаемой еды́.

fastidious [fæs'tɪdɪəs] *adj* (*fussy*) скрупулёзный* (скрупулёзен).

fast lane *n* (*BRIT*: *AUT*): **the ~ ~** скоростно́й ряд*.

fat [fæt] *adj* то́лстый* (толст); (*inf*: *profit*) соли́дный* ◆ *n* жир*; **that's a ~ lot of use to us** (*inf*) нам э́то нигде́ не на́до; **to live off the ~ of the land** как сыр в ма́сле ката́ться (*impf*).

fatal ['feɪtl] *adj* (*mistake*) фата́льный* (фата́лен), роково́й; (*injury, illness*) смерте́льный* (смерте́лен).

fatalistic [feɪtə'lɪstɪk] *adj* (*attitude*) фаталисти́ческий.

fatality [fə'tælɪtɪ] *n* (*death*) смерте́льный слу́чай.

fatally ['feɪtəlɪ] *adv* (*injured*) смерте́льно; (*flawed*) фата́льно, роковы́м о́бразом.

fate [feɪt] *n* судьба́*, рок; **to meet one's ~** находи́ть* (найти́* *perf*) свой коне́ц.

fated ['feɪtɪd] *adj* обречённый* (обречён); **it seemed ~** каза́лось, э́тому бы́ло сужде́но случи́ться.

fateful ['feɪtful] *adj* роково́й.

fat-free ['fæt'fri:] *adj* обезжи́ренный.

father ['fɑ:ðə'] *n* оте́ц*.

Father Christmas *n* ≈ Дед Моро́з.

fatherhood ['fɑ:ðəhud] *n* отцо́вство.

father-in-law ['fɑ:ðərənlɔ:] *n* (*wife's father*) свёкор*; (*husband's father*) тесть *m*.

fatherland ['fɑ:ðəlænd] *n* оте́чество.

fatherly ['fɑ:ðəlɪ] *adj* оте́ческий*.

fathom ['fæðəm] *n* (*NAUT*) фа́том, морска́я са́жень *f* ◆ *vt* (*understand*: *also*: **~ out**)

постига́ть (пости́чь* *perf*).

fatigue [fə'ti:g] *n* утомле́ние; **~s** *npl* (*MIL*) солда́тская рабо́чая оде́жда *fsg*; **metal ~** уста́лость *f* мета́лла.

fatness ['fætnɪs] *n* (*of person*) полнота́; (*of wallet*) толщина́.

fatten ['fætn] *vt* (*animal*) отка́рмливать (откорми́ть* *perf*) ◆ *vi* жире́ть (разжире́ть *perf*); **chocolate is ~ing** от шокола́да толсте́ют.

fatty ['fætɪ] *adj* (*food*) жи́рный* ◆ *n* (*inf*) толстя́к*.

fatuous ['fætjuəs] *adj* бессмы́сленный*.

faucet ['fɔ:sɪt] *n* (*US*) (водопрово́дный) кран.

fault [fɔ:lt] *n* (*blame*) вина́*; (*defect*: *in person*) недоста́ток*; (: *in machine*) дефе́кт; (*GEO*) разло́м; (*TENNIS*) оши́бка* при пода́че ◆ *vt* (*criticize*) придира́ться (*impf*) к +*dat*; **it's my ~** э́то моя́ вина́; **to find ~ with** придира́ться (придра́ться* *perf*) к +*dat*; **I am at ~** я винова́т; **if my memory is not at ~** е́сли мне не изменя́ет па́мять; **generous to a ~** чрезме́рно ще́дрый*.

faultless ['fɔ:ltlɪs] *adj* безупре́чный* (безупре́чен).

faulty ['fɔ:ltɪ] *adj* (*goods*) испо́рченный*; (*machine*) повреждённый.

fauna ['fɔ:nə] *n* фа́уна.

faux pas ['fəu'pɑ:] *n inv* неве́рный шаг*.

favour ['feɪvə'] (*US* **favor**) *n* (*approval*) расположе́ние; (*help*) одолже́ние ◆ *vt* (*prefer*: *solution*) ока́зывать (оказа́ть* *perf*) предпочте́ние +*dat*; (: *pupil etc*) выделя́ть (вы́делить *perf*); (*assist*) благоприя́тствовать (*impf*) +*dat*; **to ask a ~ of sb** проси́ть* (попроси́ть* *perf*) кого́-н об одолже́нии; **to do sb a ~** ока́зывать (оказа́ть* *perf*) кому́-н услу́гу; **in ~ of** в по́льзу +*gen*; **to be in ~ of sth/doing** быть* (*impf*) за что-н/за то, что́бы +*infin*; **to find ~ with sb** (*subj*: *person*) завоёвывать (завоева́ть* *perf*) расположе́ние кого́-н; (: *suggestion*) находи́ть* (найти́* *perf*) подде́ржку у кого́-н.

favourable ['feɪvrəbl] (*US* **favorable**) *adj* благоприя́тный* (благоприя́тен).

favourably ['feɪvrəblɪ] (*US* **favorably**) *adv* (*react*) положи́тельно, благоприя́тно; **to compare ~ with** выи́грывать (*impf*) в сравне́нии с +*instr*.

favourite ['feɪvrɪt] (*US* **favorite**) *adj* люби́мый ◆ *n* (*of teacher, parent*) люби́мец*; (*SPORT*) фавори́т.

favouritism ['feɪvrɪtɪzəm] (*US* **favoritism**) *n* фавори́зм.

fawn [fɔ:n] *n* молодо́й оле́нь *m* ◆ *adj* (*also*: **~-coloured**) желтова́то-кори́чневый ◆ *vi*: **to ~ (up)on** заи́скивать (*impf*) пе́ред +*instr*.

fax [fæks] *n* факс ◆ *vt* (*letter, document*)

посылáть (послáть* perf) фáксом.
FBI n abbr (US: = Federal Bureau of Investigation)
ФБР= Федерáльное бюрó расслéдований.
FCC n abbr (US: = Federal Communications
Commission) Федерáльная комúссия свя́зи.
FCO n abbr (BRIT: = Foreign and Commonwealth
Office) Министéрство инострáнных дел и
сношéний со стрáнами Британского
содрýжества.
FD n abbr (US) = **fire department**.
FDA n abbr (US: = Food and Drug Administration)
управлéние по контрóлю за продýктами и
медикамéнтами.
FE abbr (= Further Education) ≈ профессионáльно-
технúческое образовáние.
fear [fɪəʳ] n страх; (less strong) боя́знь f;
(worry) опасéние ♦ vt боя́ться (impf) +gen ♦ vi
боя́ться (impf); **to ~ for** боя́ться (impf) за +acc;
to ~ that боя́ться (impf), что; **~ of heights**
боя́знь высоты́; **for ~ of missing my flight** (in
case) боя́сь опоздáть на самолёт.
fearful ['fɪəful] adj (person) боязлúвый
(боязлúв); (sight) ужасáющий*; (risk, noise)
стрáшный* (стрáшен); **to be ~ of**
страшúться (impf) +gen.
fearfully ['fɪəfəlɪ] adv (timidly) боязлúво; (inf:
very) ужáсно.
fearless ['fɪəlɪs] adj бесстрáшный*
(бесстрáшен).
fearsome ['fɪəsəm] adj (opponent)
внушáющий страх; (sight) устрашáющий.
feasibility [fiːzə'bɪlɪtɪ] n (of plan)
осуществúмость f.
feasibility study n тéхнико-экономúческое
обоснóвание.
feasible ['fiːzəbl] adj осуществúмый
(осуществúм).
feast [fiːst] n (banquet) пир*; (REL: also: ~ **day**)
прáздник ♦ vi пировáть (impf); **to ~ on**
лáкомиться* (impf) +instr; **to ~ one's eyes on**
sth любовáться (impf) чем-н.
feat [fiːt] n пóдвиг.
feather ['fɛðəʳ] n перó* ♦ cpd перьевóй ♦ vt: **to ~**
one's nest набивáть (набúть* perf) себé
кармáн; **~ bed** перúна.
featherweight ['fɛðəweɪt] n (BOXING) боксёр
полулёгкого вéса.
feature ['fiːtʃəʳ] n чертá, осóбенность f; (of
landscape) осóбенность; (PRESS) óчерк; (TV,
RADIO) передáча ♦ vi: **to ~ in** фигурúровать
(impf) в +prp ♦ vi: **the film ~s 2 famous actors** в
фúльме снимáются 2 извéстных актёра; **~s**
npl (of face) чертú fpl; **a film featuring ...**
фильм с учáстием +gen...; **his article ~d in all**
the newspapers егó статья́ фигурúровала во
всех газéтах; **a special ~ on sth/sb**
специáльная передáча о чём-н/ком-н.
feature film n худóжественный фильм.
featureless ['fiːtʃəlɪs] adj невырáзительный*
(невырáзителен).

Feb. abbr = **February**.
February ['fɛbruərɪ] n феврáль* m; see also **July**.
feces ['fiːsiːz] npl (US) = **faeces**.
feckless ['fɛklɪs] adj безотвéтственный.
Fed abbr (US) = **federal, federation**.
fed [fɛd] pt, pp of **feed**.
Fed. n abbr (US: inf. = Federal Reserve Board)
совéт, управля́ющий федерáльной резéрвной
систéмой.
federal ['fɛdərəl] adj федерáльный.
Federal Republic of Germany n
Федератúвная Респýблика Гермáнии.
Federal Reserve Board n (US) Федерáльное
резéрвное правлéние.
Federal Trade Commission n (US)
Федерáльная торгóвая комúссия.
federation [fɛdə'reɪʃən] n федерáция.
fed up adj: **he is ~~** емý надоéло.
fee [fiː] n плáта; (of doctor, lawyer) плáта,
гонорáр; **school ~s** плáта за обучéние;
entrance ~ входнáя плáта; **membership ~**
члéнский взнос; **for a small ~** за небольшóе
вознаграждéние.
feeble ['fiːbl] adj хúлый (хил); (joke) слáбый.
feeble-minded ['fiːbl'maɪndɪd] adj
слабоýмный.
feed [fiːd] (pt, pp **fed**) n (feeding) кормлéние;
(fodder) корм*; (on printer) загрýзка* ♦ vt
кормúть* (накормúть* perf); **to ~ sth into sth**
(data, information) загружáть (загрузúть*
perf) что-н во что-н; (material) подавáть*
(подáть* perf) что-н во что-н
▶ **feed back** vt (results) подавáть* (подáть*
perf) обрáтно
▶ **feed on** vt fus питáться (impf) +instr.
feedback ['fiːdbæk] n (response) обрáтная
связь f; (from person) óтзыв.
feeding bottle ['fiːdɪŋ-] n (BRIT) бутúлочка*
(для кормлéния младéнца).
feel [fiːl] (pt, pp **felt**) n ощущéние ♦ vt (touch)
трóгать (потрóгать perf); (experience)
чýвствовать (impf); (think, believe): **to ~ (that)**
считáть (impf) (, что); **to get the ~ of sth**
освáиваться (освóиться perf) с чем-н; **I ~ that**
you ought to do it я считáю, что Вы должны́
это сдéлать; **he ~s hungry** он гóлоден; **she**
~s cold ей хóлодно; **to ~ lonely/better**
чýвствовать (impf) себя́ одинóким/лýчше; **I**
don't ~ well я плóхо себя́ чýвствую; **he ~s**
sorry for me емý меня́ жáлко or жаль; **the**
material ~s soft/like velvet этот материáл на
óщупь мя́гкий/как бáрхат; **it ~s colder here**
здесь холоднéе; **I ~ like ...** (want) мне хóчется
...; **I'm still ~ing my way** я всё ещё освáиваюсь
or присмáтриваюсь
▶ **feel about** vi: **to ~ about for sth** искáть (impf)
что-н на óщупь; **to ~ about or around in one's**
pocket for шáрить (пошáрить perf) в
кармáне в пóисках +gen
▶ **feel around** vi = **feel about**.
feeler ['fiːləʳ] n (of insect) ýсик, щýпальце*;

to put out a ~ *or* **~s** (*fig*) зондировать
(прозондировать *perf*) почву.
feeling ['fi:lɪŋ] *n* (*emotion, impression*)
чувство; (*physical sensation*) ощущение; **~s
ran high** страсти разгорелись; **what are your
~s about the matter?** каково Ваше
отношение к этому вопросу?; **I have a ~ that
...** у меня такое ощущение, что ...; **my ~ is
that ...** по-моему мнению ...; **to hurt sb's ~s**
задевать (задеть* *perf*) чьи-н чувства.
fee-paying ['fi:peɪɪŋ] *adj*: **~ school** платная
школа; **~ student** студент, платящий за
обучение.
feet [fi:t] *npl of* **foot**.
feign [feɪn] *vt* (*injury, interest*) симулировать
(*impf/perf*).
feigned [feɪnd] *adj* притворный* (притворен).
feint [feɪnt] *n* (*of paper*) линовка; **a pad of
narrow ~** блокнот в узкую линейку.
felicitous [fɪ'lɪsɪtəs] *adj* удачный* (удачен).
feline ['fi:laɪn] *adj* кошачий*.
fell [fɛl] *pt of* **fall** ♦ *vt* валить (свалить *perf*) ♦ *n*
(*BRIT*) *гора, холм или болото в названиях* ♦
adj: **in one ~ swoop** одним махом; **the ~s** *npl*
(*moorland*) болотистая местность *fsg*.
fellow ['fɛləu] *n* (*man*) парень *m*; (*comrade*)
товарищ; (*of learned society*)
действительный член; (*of university*) член
совета ♦ *cpd*: **their ~ prisoners/students** их
сокамерники/сокурсники; **his ~ workers** его
товарищи по работе.
fellow citizens *npl* сограждане* *mpl*.
fellow countryman *irreg n* соотечественник.
fellow men *npl* ближние *pl adj*.
fellowship ['fɛləuʃɪp] *n* (*comradeship*)
содружество; (*society*) членство; (*SCOL*)
стипендия аспиранта (*звание члена совета
колледжа или научного общества*).
fell-walking ['fɛlwɔ:kɪŋ] *n* (*BRIT*) хождение по
горам, болотистой местности итп.
felon ['fɛlən] *n* (*LAW*) уголовный преступник.
felony ['fɛlənɪ] *n* (*LAW*) уголовное
преступление.
felt [fɛlt] *pt, pp of* **feel** ♦ *n* (*fabric*) фетр.
felt-tip pen ['fɛltɪp-] *n* фломастер.
female ['fi:meɪl] *n* (*also pej*) самка ♦ *adj* (*sex,
character, profession*) женский*; (*child*)
женского пола; (*ELEC*) охватывающий; **~
suffrage** избирательное право для женщин;
male and ~ students студенты и студентки.
female impersonator *n* (*THEAT*) актёр,
играющий женщин.
Femidom® ['fɛmɪdɒm] *n* фемидом (*женский
презерватив*).
feminine ['fɛmɪnɪn] *adj* (*clothes, behaviour*)
женственный* (женственен); (*LING*)
женского рода ♦ *n* (*LING*) женский* род.
femininity [fɛmɪ'nɪnɪtɪ] *n* женственность *f*.

feminism ['fɛmɪnɪzəm] *n* феминизм.
feminist ['fɛmɪnɪst] *n* феминист(ка).
fen [fɛn] (*BRIT*) *n* (*marsh*) болото; **the F~s**
*низкая болотистая местность в
Кеймбредшире и Линкольншире*.
fence [fɛns] *n* (*barrier*) забор, изгородь *f*;
(*SPORT*) препятствие ♦ *vt* (*also: ~ in*)
огораживать (огородить* *perf*) ♦ *vi* (*SPORT*)
фехтовать (*impf*); **to sit on the ~** (*fig*)
занимать (*impf*) выжидательную позицию в
споре.
fencing ['fɛnsɪŋ] *n* (*SPORT*) фехтование.
fend [fɛnd] *vi*: **to ~ for o.s.** заботиться*
(позаботиться* *perf*) о себе
▸ **fend off** *vt* отражать (отразить* *perf*).
fender ['fɛndə'] *n* (*of fireplace*) каминная
решётка*; (*on boat*) кранец*; (*US: of car*)
крыло*.
fennel ['fɛnl] *n* фенхель *m* обыкновенный,
сладкий* укроп*.
ferment [*n* 'fə:mɛnt, *vi* fə'mɛnt] *n* (*unrest*)
брожение ♦ *vi* бродить* (*impf*).
fermentation [fə:mɛn'teɪʃən] *n* брожение.
fern [fə:n] *n* папоротник.
ferocious [fə'rəuʃəs] *adj* (*animal*) свирепый
(свиреп); (*behaviour*) дикий* (дик);
(*competition, opposition, criticism*) жестокий*
(жесток); (*heat*) ужасный* (ужасен).
ferocity [fə'rɒsɪtɪ] *n* жестокость *f*; (*of
opposition*) ярость *f*; **the ~ of the sun**
невыносимое пекло.
ferret ['fɛrɪt] *n* хорёк*
▸ **ferret about** *vi* шарить (*impf*)
▸ **ferret around** *vi* = **ferret about**
▸ **ferret out** *vt* выведывать (выведать *perf*).
ferry ['fɛrɪ] *n* (*also: ~boat*) паром ♦ *vt*
перевозить* (перевезти* *perf*); **to ~ sth/sb
across** *or* **over** переправлять (переправить
perf) что-н/кого-н.
ferryman ['fɛrɪmən] *irreg n* паромщик.
fertile ['fə:taɪl] *adj* (*land, soil*) плодородный*
(плодороден); (*imagination*) богатый
(богат); (*woman*) способная к зачатию; **~
period** плодотворный период.
fertility [fə'tɪlɪtɪ] *n* (*see adj*) плодородие;
богатство; способность *f* к зачатию.
fertility drug *n* препарат от бесплодия.
fertilization [fə:tɪlaɪ'zeɪʃən] *n* (*of egg*)
оплодотворение.
fertilize ['fə:tɪlaɪz] *vt* (*land*) удобрять
(удобрить* *perf*); (*egg*) оплодотворять
(оплодотворить* *perf*); (*plant*) опылять
(опылить* *perf*).
fertilizer ['fə:tɪlaɪzə'] *n* удобрение.
fervent ['fə:vənt] *adj* (*admirer, belief*) пылкий*.
fervour ['fə:və'] (*US* **fervor**) *n* пыл*.
fester ['fɛstə'] *vi* (*wound*) гноиться
(загноиться* *perf*); (*insult, row*) разрастаться

(разрости́сь* perf).

festival ['fɛstɪvəl] n (REL) пра́здник; (ART, MUS) фестива́ль m.

festive ['fɛstɪv] adj (mood, atmosphere) пра́здничный* (пра́здничен); **the ~ season** (BRIT) свя́тки* pl.

festivities [fɛs'tɪvɪtɪz] npl пра́зднества ntpl.

festoon [fɛs'tu:n] vt: **to ~ with** украша́ть (укра́сить* perf) +instr.

fetch [fɛtʃ] vt (object) приноси́ть* (принести́* perf); (person) приводи́ть* (привести́* perf); (by transport) привози́ть* (привезти́* perf); **would you ~ me a jug of water please?** принеси́те мне, пожа́луйста, кувши́н воды́; **how much did the book ~?** ско́лько Вы вы́ручили за кни́гу?; **his pictures ~ very high prices** его́ карти́ны продаю́тся по высо́ким це́нам

► **fetch up** vi (BRIT) оказа́ться* (perf).

fetching ['fɛtʃɪŋ] adj преле́стный* (преле́стен).

fête [feɪt] n благотвори́тельный пра́здник-база́р.

fetid ['fɛtɪd] adj воню́чий*.

fetish ['fɛtɪʃ] n (also fig) фети́ш*.

fetter ['fɛtə*] vt (person) зако́вывать (закова́ть perf); (horse) спу́тывать (спу́тать perf); (fig) ско́вывать (скова́ть perf).

fetters ['fɛtəz] npl (also fig) око́вы pl.

fettle ['fɛtl] n (BRIT): **in fine ~** (person) в прекра́сной фо́рме.

fetus ['fi:təs] n (US) = **foetus**.

feud [fju:d] n вражда́ ♦ vi враждова́ть (impf); **a family ~** фами́льная вражда́.

feudal ['fju:dl] adj феода́льный.

feudalism ['fju:dlɪzəm] n феодали́зм.

fever ['fi:və*] n (temperature) жар; (disease) лихора́дка*; **he has a ~** у него́ жар.

feverish ['fi:vərɪʃ] adj (also fig) лихора́дочный* (лихора́дочен); (person: with excitement) возбуждённый* (возбуждён); **he is ~** у него́ жар, его́ лихора́дит.

few [fju:] adj (not many) немно́гие; (several): **a ~** (number) не́сколько +gen; (some) не́которые pl adj ♦ pron: **(a) ~** немно́гие pl adj; **a ~ more** ещё не́сколько; **for a ~ days** на не́сколько дней; **with a ~ of them** с не́которыми из них; **they were ~** их бы́ло ма́ло or немно́го; **~ succeed** немно́гим удаётся; **very ~ survive** о́чень немно́гие выжива́ют; **I know a ~** я зна́ю не́скольких; **a good ~** дово́льно мно́гие; **quite a ~** дово́льно мно́го; **in the next ~ days** в ближа́йшие не́сколько дней; **in the past ~ days** за после́дние не́сколько дней; **every ~ days/months** че́рез ка́ждые не́сколько дней/ме́сяцев.

fewer ['fju:ə*] adj ме́ньше +gen; **they are ~** их ме́ньше; **there are ~ buses on Sundays** по воскресе́ньям хо́дит ме́ньше авто́бусов.

fewest ['fju:ɪst] adj ме́ньше всего́ +gen.

FFA n abbr = Future Farmers of America.

FH n abbr (BRIT) = fire hydrant.

FHA n abbr (US) = Federal Housing Administration.

fiancé [fɪ'ɑ̃:ŋseɪ] n жени́х*.

fiancée [fɪ'ɑ̃:ŋseɪ] n неве́ста.

fiasco [fɪ'æskəu] n фиа́ско nt ind.

fib [fɪb] n враньё nt no pl; **to tell ~s** привира́ть (привра́ть* perf); **a few small ~s don't hurt** немно́жко привра́ть не повреди́т.

fibre ['faɪbə*] (US fiber) n волокно́*; (dietary) клетча́тка.

fibreboard ['faɪbəbɔ:d] (US fiberboard) n фи́бровый карто́н*.

fibreglass ['faɪbəglɑ:s] (US fiberglass) n стекловолокно́.

fibrositis [faɪbrə'saɪtɪs] n фиброз.

FICA n abbr (US) = Federal Insurance Contributions Act.

fickle ['fɪkl] adj непостоя́нный* (непостоя́нен).

fiction ['fɪkʃən] n (LITERATURE) худо́жественная литерату́ра; (invention) вы́мысел*; (lie) вы́думка*.

fictional ['fɪkʃənl] adj (character, event) вы́мышленный (вы́мышлен); (relating to fiction) беллетристи́ческий.

fictionalize ['fɪkʃnəlaɪz] vt беллетризи́ровать (impf/perf).

fictitious [fɪk'tɪʃəs] adj (false, invented) фикти́вный* (фикти́вен); (character, event) вы́мышленный* (вы́мышлен).

fiddle ['fɪdl] n (MUS) скри́пка*; (swindle) обма́н ♦ vt (BRIT: accounts) подде́лывать (подде́лать perf); **tax ~** махина́ции с нало́гами; **to work a ~** моше́нничать (смоше́нничать perf)

► **fiddle with** vt fus верте́ть* (impf) в рука́х.

fiddler ['fɪdlə*] n скрипа́ч*(ка*).

fiddly ['fɪdlɪ] adj (task) трудновыполни́мый; (object) неудо́бный в обраще́нии.

fidelity [fɪ'dɛlɪtɪ] n ве́рность f; (accuracy) то́чность f.

fidget ['fɪdʒɪt] vi ёрзать (impf).

fidgety ['fɪdʒɪtɪ] adj беспоко́йный* (беспоко́ен).

fiduciary [fɪ'dju:ʃɪərɪ] n (LAW) дове́ренное лицо́*.

field [fi:ld] n (also ELEC, COMPUT) по́ле; (SPORT) по́ле, площа́дка*; (fig: area of interest) о́бласть* f ♦ cpd (study, trip, scientist etc) полево́й; **the ~** (competitors, entrants) уча́стники mpl состяза́ния; **they lead the ~** (COMM) они́ веду́щие в свое́й о́бласти.

field day n: **to have a ~ ~** (fig) пра́здновать (impf), торжествова́ть (impf).

field glasses npl полево́й бино́кль msg.

field hospital n полево́й го́спиталь m.

field marshal n фельдма́ршал.

field work n полевы́е иссле́дования ntpl; (GEO) рабо́та в по́ле.

fiend [fi:nd] n злоде́й.

fiendish ['fi:ndɪʃ] adj дья́вольский*.

fierce [fɪəs] *adj* (*animal, person, look*) свире́пый; (*fighting*) я́ростный; (*loyalty*) горя́чий* (горя́ч); (*enemy, cold, hatred*) лю́тый (лют); (*wind, heat, storm*) стра́шный* (стра́шен).

fiery ['faɪərɪ] *adj* (*burning*) жгу́чий*; (*sunset*) о́гненный; (*taste*) обжига́ющий; (*temperament*) горя́чий* (горя́ч); **~ red** о́гненно-кра́сный.

FIFA ['fi:fə] *n abbr* (= *Fédération Internationale de Football Association*) ФИФА.

fifteen [fɪf'ti:n] *n* пятна́дцать*; *see also* **five**.

fifteenth [fɪf'ti:nθ] *adj* пятна́дцатый; *see also* **fifth**.

fifth [fɪfθ] *adj* пя́тый ♦ *n* (*fraction*) пя́тая *f adj*; (*AUT: also:* **~ gear**) пя́тая ско́рость *f*; **he came ~ in the competition** он за́нял пя́тое ме́сто в соревнова́нии; **~ form** (*BRIT: SCOL*) пя́тый класс; **I was (the) ~ to arrive** я пришёл пя́тым; **Henry the F~** Ге́нрих Пя́тый; **the ~ of July, July the ~** пя́тое ию́ля; **I wrote to him on the ~** я написа́л ему́ пя́того числа́.

fifth column *n* пя́тая коло́нна.

fiftieth ['fɪftɪɪθ] *adj* пятидеся́тый; *see also* **fifth**.

fifty ['fɪftɪ] *n* пятьдеся́т*; **there are about ~ people here** здесь о́коло пяти́десяти челове́к; **he'll be ~ (years old) next week** на сле́дующей неде́ле ему́ бу́дет пятьдеся́т (лет); **he's about ~** ему́ о́коло пяти́десяти; **the Fifties (1950s)** пятидеся́тые го́ды; **he is in his fifties** ему́ за пятьдеся́т лет; **the temperature was in the fifties** температу́ра была́ вы́ше пяти́десяти гра́дусов; **to do ~ (miles per hour)** (*AUT*) е́хать (*impf*) со ско́ростью пятьдеся́т миль в час.

fifty-fifty ['fɪftɪ'fɪftɪ] *adj* (*deal, split*) ра́вный* ♦ *adv* попола́м, по́ровну; **to share ~ with sb** дели́ть* (раздели́ть* *perf*) попола́м с кем-н; **to have a ~ chance (of success)** име́ть (*impf*) ра́вные ша́нсы (на успе́х).

fig [fɪg] *n* инжи́р*.

fight [faɪt] (*pt, pp* **fought**) *n* дра́ка; (*MIL*) бой*; (*campaign, struggle*) борьба́ ♦ *vt* (*person*) дра́ться* (подра́ться* *perf*) с +*instr*; (*MIL*) воева́ть* (*impf*) с +*instr*; (*illness, problem, emotion*) боро́ться* (*impf*) с +*instr*; (*POL: election*) уча́ствовать (*impf*) в +*prp*; (*LAW: case*) защища́ть (*impf*) ♦ *vi* (*people*) дра́ться* (*impf*); (*MIL*) воева́ть* (*impf*); **to put up a ~** упо́рно сопротивля́ться (*impf*); **to ~ one's way through a crowd/the undergrowth** прокла́дывать (*impf*) себе́ доро́гу че́рез толпу́/за́росли; **to ~ with sb** дра́ться* (*impf*) с кем-н; **to ~ (for/against)** боро́ться* (*impf*) (за +*acc*/про́тив +*gen*)

▸ **fight back** *vi* защища́ться (защити́ться *perf*); (*SPORT, after illness*) верну́ть (*perf*) себе́ спорти́вную фо́рму ♦ *vt fus* (*tears, fear etc*) сде́рживать (сдержа́ть* *perf*)

▸ **fight down** *vt* (*urge, emotion*) подавля́ть (подави́ть* *perf*)

▸ **fight off** *vt* (*attacker*) отбива́ть (отби́ть* *perf*); (*sleep*) отгоня́ть (отогна́ть* *perf*)

▸ **fight out** *vt*: **to ~ it out** отста́ивать (отстоя́ть* *perf*) что́-нибудь в борьбе́.

fighter ['faɪtə'] *n* (*also fig*) боре́ц*; (*MIL: soldier*) бое́ц*; (: *plane*) истреби́тель *m*.

fighter pilot *n* лётчик-истреби́тель *m*.

fighting ['faɪtɪŋ] *n* (*battle*) бой*; (*brawl*) дра́ка.

figment ['fɪgmənt] *n*: **a ~ of the imagination** плод* воображе́ния.

figurative ['fɪgjʊrətɪv] *adj* (*style*) о́бразный*; (*sense*) перено́сный.

figure ['fɪgə'] *n* (*shape, body, also GEOM*) фигу́ра; (*number*) ци́фра; (*personality*) ли́чность *f* ♦ *vt* (*US: think*) счита́ть (*impf*) ♦ *vi* (*appear*) фигури́ровать (*impf*); **to put a ~ on** назнача́ть (назна́чить *perf*) це́ну +*gen or* на +*acc*; **public ~** изве́стная ли́чность

▸ **figure out** *vt* понима́ть (поня́ть* *perf*); (*cost*) подсчи́тывать (подсчита́ть *perf*).

figurehead ['fɪgəhɛd] *n* (*NAUT*) фигу́ра на носу́ корабля́; (*pej: leader*) номина́льный глава́ *m*.

figure of speech *n* фигу́ра ре́чи.

figure skating *n* фигу́рное ката́ние.

Fiji (Islands) ['fi:dʒi:-] *n(pl)* Фи́джи *ntpl ind*.

filament ['fɪləmənt] *n* (*ELEC, TECH*) нить *f* нака́ла; (*BIO*) тычи́ночная нить.

filch [fɪltʃ] *vt* (*inf*) стяну́ть (*perf*).

file [faɪl] *n* (*dossier*) де́ло*; (*in cabinet*) картоте́ка; (*folder*) скоросшива́тель *m*; (: *for loose leaf*) па́пка*; (*COMPUT*) файл; (*row*) коло́нна; (*tool*) напи́льник ♦ *vt* (*papers, document*) подшива́ть (подши́ть* *perf*); (*in card index*) вноси́ть* (внести́* *perf*); (*LAW: claim*) подава́ть* (пода́ть* *perf*); (*wood, fingernails*) шлифова́ть (отшлифова́ть *perf*) ♦ *vi*: **to ~ in/out/past** входи́ть* (войти́* *perf*)/выходи́ть* (вы́йти* *perf*)/проходи́ть* (пройти́* *perf*) коло́нной; **to ~ in single ~** в коло́нну по одному́; **to ~ a suit against sb** подава́ть* (пода́ть* *perf*) в суд на кого́-н; **to ~ for divorce** подава́ть* (пода́ть* *perf*) на разво́д.

filename ['faɪlneɪm] *n* (*COMPUT*) и́мя* *nt* фа́йла.

filibuster ['fɪlɪbʌstə'] *n* (*esp US: POL*) *n* (*also:* **~er**) обструкциони́ст ♦ *vi* тормози́ть (*impf*) приня́тие зако́на путём обстру́кции.

filing ['faɪlɪŋ] *n* (*ADMIN*) систематиза́ция.

filing cabinet *n* картоте́чный шкаф*, шкаф* с картоте́кой.

filing clerk *n* делопроизводи́тель *m*.

Filipino [fɪlɪ'pi:nəu] *n* филиппи́нец*(-нка*); (*LING*) филиппи́нский язы́к*.

fill [fɪl] *vi* (*room, hall*) наполня́ться

---

* marks translations which have irregular inflections. The Russian-English side of the dictionary gives inflectional information.

(напо́лниться *perf*) ♦ *vt* (*tooth*) пломбирова́ть (запломбирова́ть *perf*); (*vacancy*) заполня́ть (запо́лнить *perf*); (*need*) удовлетворя́ть (удовлетвори́ть *perf*) ♦ *n*: **to eat one's ~** наеда́ться (нае́сться* *perf*); **to ~ (with)** (*container*) наполня́ть (напо́лнить *perf*) (+*instr*); (*space, area*) заполня́ть (запо́лнить *perf*) (+*instr*)

▶ **fill in** *vt* (*cavity, form*) заполня́ть (запо́лнить *perf*); (*time*) корота́ть (*impf*) ♦ *vi*: **to ~ in for sb** замеща́ть (*impf*) кого́-н вре́менно; **to ~ sb in** (*inf*) вводи́ть* (ввести́* *perf*) кого́-н в курс де́ла

▶ **fill out** *vt* (*form, receipt*) заполня́ть (запо́лнить *perf*)

▶ **fill up** *vt* (*container*) наполня́ть (напо́лнить *perf*); (*space*) заполня́ть (запо́лнить *perf*) ♦ *vi* (*AUT*) заправля́ться (запра́виться* *perf*); **~ it up, please** (*AUT*) запра́вьте мне маши́ну, пожа́луйста.

fillet ['fɪlɪt] *n* филе́ *nt ind* ♦ *vt* отделя́ть (отдели́ть *perf*) от косте́й.

fillet steak *n* вы́резка.

filling ['fɪlɪŋ] *n* (*for tooth*) пло́мба; (*of pie*) начи́нка; (*of layer cake*) просло́йка.

filling station *n* запра́вочная ста́нция.

fillip ['fɪlɪp] *n* (*fig*) толчо́к.

filly ['fɪlɪ] *n* молода́я кобы́ла.

film [fɪlm] *n* (*CINEMA*) фи́льм; (*PHOT, COMM*) плёнка*; (*of powder, liquid etc*) то́нкий* слой ♦ *vti* снима́ть (снять *perf*).

film star *n* кинозвезда́* *m/f*.

film strip *n* диафи́льм.

film studio *n* киносту́дия.

Filofax® ['faɪleufæks] *n* записна́я кни́жка и́ли дневни́к.

filter ['fɪltə'] *n* фильтр ♦ *vt* (*liquid*) фильтрова́ть (профильтрова́ть *perf*)

▶ **filter in** *vi* (*news*) проса́чиваться (просочи́ться *perf*)

▶ **filter through** *vi* = **filter in**.

filter coffee *n* ко́фе то́нкого помо́ла для кофева́рок с фи́льтром.

filter lane *n* (*BRIT: AUT*) полоса́, по кото́рой на́до е́хать, что́бы поверну́ть по указа́нию стре́лки светофо́ра.

filter tip *n* фильтр (*сигаре́ты*).

filter-tipped ['fɪltə'tɪpt] *adj* с фи́льтром.

filth [fɪlθ] *n* грязь *f*; (*fig: on TV etc*) непристо́йность *f*.

filthy ['fɪlθɪ] *adj* гря́зный* (гря́зен); (*fig*) ме́рзкий* (ме́рзок).

fin [fɪn] *n* (*of fish*) плавни́к*; (*TECH: of rocket*) стабилиза́тор.

final ['faɪnl] *adj* (*last*) после́дний*; (*SPORT*) фина́льный; (*ultimate*) заключи́тельный; (*definitive*) окончательный* ♦ *n* (*SPORT*) фина́л; **~s** *npl* (*SCOL*) выпускны́е экза́мены *mpl*.

final demand *n* (*for bill etc*) окончательное требование.

final dividend *n* окончательный дивиде́нд.

finale [fɪ'nɑːlɪ] *n* фина́л.

finalist ['faɪnəlɪst] *n* финали́ст.

finality [faɪ'nælɪtɪ] *n* окончательность *f*; **to speak with an air of ~** говори́ть (*impf*) то́ном, не допуска́ющим возраже́ния.

finalize ['faɪnəlaɪz] *vt* (*arrangements, plans*) окончательно уточня́ть (уточни́ть *perf*).

finally ['faɪnəlɪ] *adv* (*eventually*) в конце́ концо́в; (*lastly*) наконе́ц; (*irrevocably*) окончательно.

finance [faɪ'næns] *n* фина́нсы *pl* ♦ *vt* (*back, fund*) финанси́ровать (*impf/perf*); **~s** *npl* (*personal finances*) фина́нсы *pl*.

financial [faɪ'nænʃəl] *adj* (*difficulties, venture*) фина́нсовый; **~ statement** фина́нсовый отчёт.

financially [faɪ'nænʃəlɪ] *adv* в фина́нсовом отноше́нии.

financial management *n* фина́нсовое руково́дство.

financial year *n* фина́нсовый год*.

financier [faɪ'nænsɪə'] *n* финанси́ст.

find [faɪnd] (*pt, pp* **found**) *vt* находи́ть* (найти́* *perf*); (*discover*) обнару́живать (обнару́жить *perf*) ♦ *n* нахо́дка*; **to ~ sb at home** застава́ть* (заста́ть* *perf*) кого́-н до́ма; **to ~ sb guilty** (*LAW*) признава́ть* (призна́ть* *perf*) кого́-н вино́вным(-ой)

▶ **find out** *vt* (*fact, truth*) узнава́ть* (узна́ть* *perf*); (*person*) разоблача́ть (разоблачи́ть *perf*) ♦ *vi*: **to ~ out about** узнава́ть* (узна́ть* *perf*) о +*prp*.

findings ['faɪndɪŋz] *npl* (*LAW*) заключе́ние *ntsg*; (*in research*) результа́ты *mpl*.

fine [faɪn] *adj* (*quality, performance etc*) прекра́сный* (прекра́сен); (*hair, features*) то́нкий*; (*sand, powder, detail*) ме́лкий*; (*adjustment*) то́чный* ♦ *adv* (*well*) прекра́сно; (*small*) ме́лко ♦ *n* штраф ♦ *vt* штрафова́ть (оштрафова́ть *perf*); **he's ~** (*ill*) он чу́вствует себя́ хорошо́; (*without problems*) у него́ всё в поря́дке; **the weather is ~** пого́да хоро́шая; **to cut it ~** (*of time*) оставля́ть (оста́вить* *perf*) сли́шком ма́ло вре́мени; **you're doing ~** у Вас всё в поря́дке.

fine arts *npl* изя́щные иску́сства *nt pl*.

finely ['faɪnlɪ] *adv* (*splendidly*) превосхо́дно; (*chop*) ме́лко; (*adjust: instrument*) то́нко.

fine print *n* напи́санное *or* напеча́танное ме́лким шри́фтом.

finery ['faɪnərɪ] *n* (*dress*) наря́д; (*jewellery*) украше́ния *ntpl*.

finesse [fɪ'nɛs] *n* то́нкость *f*, изя́щество.

fine-tooth comb ['faɪntuː θ-] *n*: **to go through sth with a ~ ~** (*fig*) скрупулёзно изуча́ть (изучи́ть* *perf*) что-н.

finger ['fɪŋgə'] *n* па́лец* ♦ *vt* тро́гать (потро́гать *perf*); **little ~** мизи́нец*; **index ~** указа́тельный па́лец*.

fingernail ['fɪŋgəneɪl] *n* но́готь *m* (*на руке́*).

fingerprint ['fɪŋgəprɪnt] *n* отпеча́ток* па́льца ◆ *vt* (*person*) брать* (взять* *perf*) отпеча́тки па́льцев у +*gen*.
fingerstall ['fɪŋgəstɔːl] *n* напа́льчник.
fingertip ['fɪŋgətɪp] *n* ко́нчик па́льца; **to have sth at one's ~s** (*at one's disposal*) име́ть (*impf*) что-н под руко́й; (*know well*) знать* (*impf*) что-н как свои́ пять па́льцев.
finicky ['fɪnɪkɪ] *adj* привере́дливый (привере́длив).
finish ['fɪnɪʃ] *n* коне́ц*; (*SPORT*) фи́ниш; (*polish etc*) отде́лка* ◆ *vt* зака́нчивать (зако́нчить *perf*), конча́ть (ко́нчить *perf*) ◆ *vi* зака́нчиваться (зако́нчиться *perf*); (*person*) зака́нчивать (зако́нчить *perf*); **have you ~ed?** Вы уже́ зако́нчили?; **to ~ doing** конча́ть (ко́нчить *perf*) +*infin*; **he ~ed third** (*in race etc*) он зако́нчил тре́тьим; **to ~ with sth** поко́нчить (*perf*) с чем-н; **she's ~ed with him** у неё с ним всё ко́нчено
▸ **finish off** *vt* (*complete*) зака́нчивать (зако́нчить *perf*); (*kill*) прика́нчивать (прико́нчить *perf*)
▸ **finish up** *vt* (*food*) доеда́ть (дое́сть* *perf*); (*drink*) допива́ть (допи́ть* *perf*) ◆ *vi* (*end up*) конча́ть (ко́нчить *perf*).
finished ['fɪnɪʃt] *adj* (*product*) отде́ланный (отде́лан); (*performance*) отто́ченный (отто́чен); (*inf: tired*) измо́танный (измо́тан).
finishing line ['fɪnɪʃɪŋ-] *n* (*SPORT*) фи́нишная черта́.
finishing school *n частный женский пансион.*
finishing touches *npl* после́дние штрихи́* *mpl*.
finite ['faɪnaɪt] *adj* (*time, space*) ограни́ченный* (ограни́чен), коне́чный* (коне́чен); (*verb*) ли́чный.
Finland ['fɪnlənd] *n* Финля́ндия; **Gulf of ~** Фи́нский зали́в.
Finn [fɪn] *n* финн (фи́нка).
Finnish ['fɪnɪʃ] *adj* фи́нский* ◆ *n* фи́нский язы́к*.
fiord [fjɔːd] *n* = **fjord**.
fir [fəːʳ] *n* ель *f*.
fire ['faɪəʳ] *n* (*flames*) пла́мя* *nt*; (*in hearth*) ого́нь* *m*; (*accidental*) пожа́р; (*bonfire*) костёр* ◆ *vt* (*shoot: gun, cannon etc*) вы́стрелить (*perf*) из +*gen*; (*stimulate: imagination etc*) разжига́ть (разже́чь* *perf*); (*inf: dismiss*) увольня́ть (уво́лить *perf*) ◆ *vi* (*shoot*) вы́стрелить (*perf*); **the house is on ~** дом* гори́т; **to set ~ to sth, set sth on ~** поджига́ть (подже́чь* *perf*) что-н; **the house is insured against ~** дом* застрахо́ван на слу́чай пожа́ра; **electric ~** электро-обогрева́тель *m*; **to come under ~ (from)** (*fig*) ока́зываться (оказа́ться* *perf*) под

обстре́лом (со стороны́ +*gen*); **to be under ~** быть* (*impf*) под обстре́лом; **to ~ a gun** стреля́ть (вы́стрелить *perf*) из пу́шки.
fire alarm *n* пожа́рная сигнализа́ция.
firearm ['faɪərɑːm] *n* огнестре́льное ору́жие *nt no pl*.
fire brigade *n* пожа́рная кома́нда.
fire chief *n* нача́льник пожа́рной кома́нды.
fire department *n* (*US*) = **fire brigade**.
fire door *n* пожа́рная дверь* *f*.
fire drill *n* пожа́рное уче́ние.
fire engine *n* пожа́рная маши́на.
fire escape *n* пожа́рная ле́стница.
fire-extinguisher ['faɪərɪk'stɪŋgwɪʃəʳ] *n* огнетуши́тель *m*.
fireguard ['faɪəgɑːd] *n* (*BRIT*) ками́нная решётка*.
fire hazard *n*: **that's a ~ ~** э́то огнеопа́сно.
fire hydrant *n* пожа́рный насо́с.
fire insurance *n* страхова́ние на слу́чай пожа́ра.
fireman ['faɪəmən] *irreg n* пожа́рный *m adj*, пожа́рник.
fireplace ['faɪəpleɪs] *n* ками́н.
fireplug ['faɪəplʌg] *n* (*US*) = **fire hydrant**.
fire practice *n* = **fire drill**.
fireproof ['faɪəpruːf] *adj* (*objects*) несгора́емый; (*materials*) огнеупо́рный*.
fire regulations *npl* пра́вила *ntpl* пожа́рной безопа́сности.
fire screen *n* (*decorative*) ками́нный экра́н; (*for protection*) противопожа́рное загражде́ние.
fireside ['faɪəsaɪd] *n*: **by the ~** (*indoors*) у ками́на.
fire station *n* пожа́рное депо́ *nt ind*.
firewood ['faɪəwud] *n* дрова́ *pl*.
fireworks ['faɪəwəːks] *npl* фейерве́рк *msg*; (*display*) фейерве́рк *msg*, салю́т *msg*.
firing line ['faɪərɪŋ-] *n* ли́ния огня́; **to be in the ~ ~** (*fig*) находи́ться* (*impf*) на ли́нии огня́.
firing squad *n* расстре́льная кома́нда.
firm [fəːm] *adj* (*ground, decision, faith*) твёрдый* (твёрд); (*mattress*) жёсткий*; (*grasp, body, muscles*) кре́пкий* (кре́пок); (*offer*) оконча́тельный* (оконча́телен) ◆ *n* фи́рма; **to be a ~ believer in sth** твёрдо ве́рить (*impf*) во что-н.
firmly ['fəːmlɪ] *adv* (*believe, stand*) твёрдо; (*grasp, shake hands*) кре́пко.
firmness ['fəːmnɪs] *n* (*of ground, decision, faith*) твёрдость *f*; (*of mattress*) жёсткость *f*; (*of grip, hold*) кре́пость *f*.
first [fəːst] *adj* пе́рвый* ◆ *adv* (*before all others*) пе́рвый; (*before other things*) снача́ла; (*when listing reasons etc*) во-пе́рвых; (*for the first time*) впервы́е ◆ *n* (*person: in race*) пе́рвый(-ая) *m(f) adj*; (*AUT: also: ~* **gear**)

пе́рвая ско́рость *f*; (*BRIT: SCOL: degree*) дипло́м пе́рвой сте́пени; **the ~ of January** пе́рвое января́; **at** ~ снача́ла; **~ of all** пре́жде всего́; **in the ~ instance** в пе́рвую о́чередь; **I'll do it ~ thing (tomorrow)** я сде́лаю э́то за́втра в пе́рвую о́чередь; **from the very ~** с са́мого нача́ла; *see also* **fifth**.

first aid *n* пе́рвая по́мощь *f*.

first-aid kit [fə:st'eɪd-] *n* паке́т пе́рвой по́мощи.

first-class ['fə:st'klɑ:s] *adj* пе́рвого кла́сса; (*excellent*) первокла́ссный ◆ *adv* пе́рвым кла́ссом.

first-hand ['fə:st'hænd] *adj* (*experience, knowledge*) ли́чный; **a ~ account** расска́з очеви́дца.

first lady *n* (*US*) пе́рвая ле́ди *f ind*; **the ~ ~ of** **jazz** короле́ва джа́за.

firstly ['fə:stlɪ] *adv* во-пе́рвых.

first name *n* и́мя* *nt*.

first night *n* (*THEAT*) премье́ра.

first-rate ['fə:st'reɪt] *adj* первокла́ссный*; (*liar*) отме́нный.

first-time buyer ['fə:sttaɪm-] *n* челове́к, впервы́е покупа́ющий дом и́ли кварти́ру.

fir tree *n* ель *f*.

FIS *n abbr* (*BRIT.* = *Family Income Supplement*) дополне́ние к семе́йному дохо́ду (*посо́бие для малоиму́щих*).

fiscal ['fɪskl] *adj* фиска́льный; **~ year** фиска́льный *or* фина́нсовый год.

fish [fɪʃ] *n inv* ры́ба ◆ *vt* (*river, area*) лови́ть* (*impf*) ры́бу в +*prp* ◆ *vi* (*commercially*) занима́ться (*impf*) рыболо́вством; (*as sport, hobby*) занима́ться (*impf*) ры́бной ло́влей; **to go ~ing** ходи́ть*/идти́* (пойти́* *perf*) на рыба́лку

▶ **fish out** *vt* (*from water*) выу́живать (вы́удить* *perf*); (*from box etc*) выта́скивать (вы́тащить *perf*).

fishbone ['fɪʃbəun] *n* ры́бья кость* *f*.

fish cake *n* ры́бная котле́та.

fisherman ['fɪʃəmən] *irreg n* рыба́к*.

fishery ['fɪʃərɪ] *n* (*fishing ground*) ры́бные места́ *ntpl*; (*fish farm*) рыбово́дческое хозя́йство.

fish factory *n* (*BRIT*) рыбозаво́д.

fish farm *n* рыбово́дческая фе́рма.

fish fingers *npl* (*BRIT*) ры́бные па́лочки* *fpl*.

fish hook *n* рыболо́вный крючо́к*.

fishing boat ['fɪʃɪn-] *n* рыболо́вное су́дно*.

fishing line *n* (*on rod*) ле́са*.

fishing net *n* рыболо́вная сеть *f*.

fishing rod *n* у́дочка*.

fishing tackle *n* рыболо́вная снасть *f*.

fish market *n* ры́бный ры́нок*.

fishmonger ['fɪʃmʌŋgə[r]] *n* (*esp BRIT*) торго́вец* ры́бой.

fishmonger's (shop) ['fɪʃmʌŋgəz-] *n* (*esp BRIT*) ры́бный магази́н.

fish slice *n* (*BRIT*) лопа́точка для

перевора́чивания ры́бы на сковороде́.

fish sticks *npl* (*US*) = **fish fingers**.

fishy ['fɪʃɪ] *adj* (*inf: tale, story etc*) сомни́тельный.

fission ['fɪʃən] *n* расщепле́ние; **atomic** *or* **nuclear ~** а́томное *or* я́дерное расщепле́ние.

fissure ['fɪʃə[r]] *n* (*in rock*) расще́лина; (*in ground*) щель* *f*, тре́щина.

fist [fɪst] *n* кула́к*.

fistfight ['fɪstfaɪt] *n* дра́ка, кула́чный бой*.

fit [fɪt] *adj* (*suitable*) приго́дный* (приго́ден); (*healthy*) в хоро́шей фо́рме ◆ *vt* (*be the right size for*) быть* (*impf*) впо́ру +*dat*, подходи́ть* (подойти́* *perf*) по разме́ру +*dat*; (*adjust to the right size*) подгоня́ть (подогна́ть* *perf*); (: *clothes*) примеря́ть (приме́рить *perf*); (*match: facts, description*) соотве́тствовать (*impf*) +*dat*; (*put in: kitchen etc*) устана́вливать (установи́ть* *perf*); (*equip*) обору́довать (*impf*); (*suit: person*) подходи́ть (подойти́* *perf*) +*dat* ◆ *vi* (*clothes*) подходи́ть* (подойти́* *perf*) по разме́ру, быть* (*impf*) впо́ру; (*parts*) подходи́ть* (подойти́* *perf*) ◆ *n* (*MED*) припа́док*; (*of coughing, giggles*) при́ступ; **~ to do** (*ready*) гото́вый (гото́в) +*infin*; **~ to keep** приго́дный (приго́ден) для хране́ния; **~ for** (*suitable for*) приго́дный (приго́ден) для +*gen*; **to keep ~** сохраня́ть (*impf*) фо́рму; **~ for work** го́дный (го́ден) к рабо́те; **she's** **not ~ to be a teacher** рабо́та учи́теля ей не подхо́дит; **do as you think** *or* **see ~** де́лайте так, как Вы счита́ете ну́жным; **the suit ~s** **her** костю́м сиди́т на ней хорошо́; **to ~ into** входи́ть* (войти́* *perf*) в +*acc*; **a ~ of anger** при́ступ гне́ва; **a ~ of pride** поры́в го́рдости; **he had a ~** (*MED*) у него́ был припа́док; **he** **nearly had a ~ when he learned about it** (*fig:* *inf*) его́ чуть уда́р не хвати́л когда́ он об э́том узна́л; **this dress is a good ~** э́то пла́тье хорошо́ сиди́т; **by ~s and starts** уры́вками

▶ **fit in** *vi* (*person, object*) вписыва́ться (вписа́ться* *perf*) ◆ *vt* (*fig: appointment, visitor*) находи́ть* (найти́* *perf*) вре́мя для +*gen*; **to ~** **in with sb's plans** совпада́ть (совпа́сть* *perf*) с чьи́ми-н пла́нами.

fitful ['fɪtful] *adj* (*sleep*) преры́вистый (преры́вист).

fitment ['fɪtmənt] *n* (*in room, cabin*) предме́т обстано́вки, обору́дование.

fitness ['fɪtnɪs] *n* (*MED*) состоя́ние здоро́вья.

fitted carpet *n* ковро́вое покры́тие.

fitted cupboards *npl* встро́енные шкафы́ *mpl*.

fitted kitchen *n* (*BRIT*) по́лностью обору́дованная ку́хня.

fitter ['fɪtə[r]] *n* (*of machinery*) меха́ник; (*of* *equipment*) устано́вщик.

fitting ['fɪtɪn] *adj* (*thanks*) надлежа́щий* ◆ *n* (*of* *dress*) приме́рка*; (*of piece of equipment*) устано́вка; **~s** *npl* (*in building*) обстано́вка *fsg*.

fitting room *n* (*in shop*) приме́рочная *f adj*.

five [faɪv] *n* пять*; **she is ~ (years) old** ей пять
лет; **they live at number 5/at 5 Green Street**
они живу́т в до́ме но́мер 5/в до́ме но́мер 5
по Зелёной у́лице; **there are ~ of us** нас
пя́теро; **all ~ of them came** все пя́теро
пришли́; **about ~** о́коло пяти́; **the book costs
~ pounds** кни́га сто́ит пять фу́нтов; **~ and a
half/quarter** пять с полови́ной/и одна́
че́тверть; **it's ~ (o'clock)** сейча́с пять часо́в;
to divide sth into ~ дели́ть (раздели́ть *perf*)
что-н на пять; **they are sold in ~s** они́
продаю́тся по пять.

five-day week ['faɪvdeɪ-] *n* пятидне́вная
рабо́чая неде́ля.

fiver ['faɪvə'] *n* (*inf: money: BRIT*) пять фу́нтов;
(: *US*) пять до́лларов.

fix [fɪks] *vt* (*sort out, arrange: amount*)
устана́вливать (установи́ть* *perf*); (: *date*)
назнача́ть (назна́чить *perf*); (*mend*)
нала́живать (нала́дить* *perf*); (*inf: meal,
drink*) организова́ть (*impf/perf*); (: *game etc*)
подстра́ивать (подстро́ить *perf*) ◆ *n* (*inf*): **to
be in a ~** быть* (*impf*) в тру́дном положе́нии;
to ~ sth to (*attach*) прикрепля́ть (прикрепи́ть
perf) что-н к +*dat*; **to ~ one's eyes on**
остана́вливать (останови́ть* *perf*) глаза́ на
+*prp*; **to ~ one's attention on**
сосредота́чивать (сосредото́чить *perf*)
внима́ние на +*prp*; **the fight was a ~** (*inf*)
исхо́д поеди́нка был предрешён

▶ **fix up** *vt* (*meeting*) устра́ивать (устро́ить
perf); **to ~ sb up with sth** устра́ивать
(устро́ить *perf*) кому́-н что-н.

fixation [fɪk'seɪʃən] *n* помеша́тельство; (*fig*):
she has a ~ about cleanliness чистота́ – её
пу́нктик.

fixative ['fɪksətɪv] *n* фиксати́в.

fixed [fɪkst] *adj* (*price*) твёрдый*; (*amount*)
устано́вленный; (*ideas*) навя́зчивый; (*smile*)
засты́вший*; **there's a ~ charge** существу́ет
устано́вленная пла́та; **how are you ~ for
money?** как у тебя́ с деньга́ми?

fixed assets *npl* недви́жимое иму́щество *ntsg*.

fixed charge *n* (*COMM*) постоя́нные изде́ржки*
pl.

fixed-price contract [['fɪkstpraɪs-]] *n* контра́кт
с фикси́рованной цено́й.

fixture ['fɪkstʃə'] *n* (*fitting*) обору́дование;
(*SPORT*) назна́ченный матч.

fizz [fɪz] *vi* (*drink*) шипе́ть (*impf*).

fizzle out ['fɪzl-] *vi* (*event*) ока́нчиваться
(око́нчиться *perf*) неуда́чей; (*interest*)
угаса́ть (уга́снуть* *perf*); (*plan*)
прова́ливаться (провали́ться *perf*).

fizzy ['fɪzɪ] *adj* (*drink*) шипу́чий*,
газиро́ванный.

fjord [fjɔ:d] *n* фьорд, фио́рд.

FL *abbr* (*US: POST*) = **Florida**.

flabbergasted ['flæbəgɑ:stɪd] *adj* изумлённый
(изумлён).

flabby ['flæbɪ] *adj* дря́блый*.

flag [flæg] *n* флаг; (*for signalling*) флажо́к*;
(*also:* ~**stone**) ка́менная плита́* ◆ *vi* (*person*)
выдыха́ться (вы́дохнуться *perf*); (*spirits*)
пропада́ть* (пропа́сть* *perf*); **~ of
convenience** "удо́бный" флаг (*пла́вание под
кото́рым явля́ется осо́бенно вы́годным*); **to
~ down** (*taxi, car etc*) остана́вливать
(останови́ть* *perf*).

flagging ['flægɪŋ] *adj*: **~ spirits** упа́док ду́ха.

flagon ['flægən] *n* буты́ль *f*; (*for cider, wine*)
кувши́н.

flagpole ['flægpəul] *n* флагшто́к.

flagrant ['fleɪgrənt] *adj* (*injustice*) вопию́щий*.

flagship ['flægʃɪp] *n* (*also fig*) фла́гман.

flagstone ['flægstəun] *n* ка́менная плита́.

flag stop *n* (*US: for bus*) остано́вка* по
тре́бованию.

flair [flɛə'] *n* (*style*) стиль *m*; (*talent*): **a ~ for**
скло́нность *f* к +*dat*; **political ~**
полити́ческий* тала́нт.

flak [flæk] *n* (*MIL*) зени́тная артилле́рия; (*inf:
criticism*) нахлобу́чка*.

flake [fleɪk] *n* (*of snow, soap powder, cereal*)
хло́пья* *pl*; (*of rust, paint*) слой ◆ *vi* (*also:* ~
off: *enamel*) лупи́ться (облупи́ться *perf*);
(: *paint*) тре́скаться (потре́скаться *perf*);
(*skin*) шелуши́ться (*impf*)

▶ **flake out** *vi* (*inf: person*) отключа́ться
(отключи́ться *perf*).

flaky ['fleɪkɪ] *adj* (*paintwork*) облу́пленный;
(*skin*) шелуша́щийся.

flaky pastry *n* слоёное те́сто.

flamboyant [flæm'bɔɪənt] *adj* (*dress, design*)
бро́ский (бро́сок); (*person*) колори́тный*
(колори́тен).

flame [fleɪm] *n* (*of fire*) пла́мя* *nt*; **to burst into
~s** вспы́хнуть (*perf*); **to be in ~s** пыла́ть (*impf*);
an old ~ (*inf*) ста́рая страсть.

flaming ['fleɪmɪ[ŋg]] *adj* (*inf*) дья́вольский*.

flamingo [flə'mɪŋgəu] *n* флами́нго *m ind*.

flammable ['flæməbl] *adj* легко́
воспламеня́ющийся.

flan [flæn] *n* (*BRIT*) откры́тый кру́глый пиро́г*.

Flanders ['flɑ:ndəz] *n* Фла́ндрия.

flange [flændʒ] *n* кро́мка.

flank [flæŋk] *n* (*of animal*) бок*; (*of army*) фланг
◆ *vt* окаймля́ть (*impf*); **~ed by** ме́жду +*instr*.

flannel ['flænl] *n* (*fabric*) флане́ль *f*; (*BRIT: also:
face* ~) махро́вая салфе́тка для лица́; **~s** *npl*
(*trousers*) флане́левые брю́ки; **to give sb
some ~** (*BRIT: inf*) моро́чить (*impf*) кому́-н
го́лову.

flannelette [flænə'lɛt] *n* ба́йка.

flap [flæp] *n* (*of envelope*) оттворо́т; (*of pocket*)
кла́пан; (*of jacket*) пола́* ◆ *vt* (*arms*) маха́ть*

---

* marks translations which have irregular inflections. The Russian-English side of the dictionary gives inflectional information

(impf) +instr; (*wings*) хло́пать (impf) +instr ♦ vi (*sail, flag*) колыха́ться* (impf); (inf: *also*: **be in a ~**) волнова́ться (impf).

flapjack ['flæpdʒæk] n (US: *pancake*) ола́дья*; (BRIT: *biscuit*) овся́ное пече́нье*.

flare [flɛəʳ] n (*signal*) сигна́льная раке́та; (in *skirt etc*) клёш

▸ **flare up** vi (*fire*) вспы́хивать (вспы́хнуть perf) я́рким пла́менем; (fig: *person, fighting, trouble*) вспы́хивать (вспы́хнуть perf).

flared ['flɛəd] adj: **~ trousers** брю́ки-клёш; **~ skirt** ю́бка-клёш.

flash [flæʃ] n (*of light, also* PHOT) вспы́шка*; (*also*: **news ~**) "мо́лния"; (US: *torch*) фона́рик ♦ vt (*light*) (внеза́пно) освеща́ть (освети́ть* perf); (*send: news, message*) посыла́ть (посла́ть* perf) мо́лнией; (*look*) мета́ть* (метну́ть perf) ♦ vi (*lightning, light, eyes*) сверка́ть (сверкну́ть perf); (*light on ambulance etc*) мига́ть (impf); **in a ~** мгнове́нно; **quick as a ~** с быстрото́й мо́лнии; **~ of inspiration** поры́в вдохнове́ния; **to ~ one's headlights** сигна́лить (просигна́лить perf); **to ~ a smile at sb** улыба́ться (улыбну́ться perf) мимохо́дом кому́-н; **the thought ~ed through his mind** у него́ промелькну́ла мысль; **to ~ by** or **past** (*person*) мча́ться (промча́ться perf) ми́мо +gen.

flashback ['flæʃbæk] n (CINEMA) ретроспекти́вный кадр.

flashbulb ['flæʃbʌlb] n фотовспы́шка*, ла́мпа-вспы́шка*.

flash card n (SCOL) ка́рточка со сло́вом и́ли бу́квой, испо́льзуемая при обуче́нии чте́нию.

flashcube ['flæʃkjuːb] n фотовспы́шка.

flasher ['flæʃəʳ] n (AUT) указа́тель m поворо́та; (inf: *man*) эксгибициони́ст.

flashlight ['flæʃlaɪt] n фона́рь* m, прожёктор.

flash point n (fig): **to be at ~ ~** находи́ться* (impf) на гра́ни взры́ва.

flashy ['flæʃɪ] adj (pej) крича́щий*.

flask [flɑːsk] n (*bottle*) фля́жка*; (CHEM) ко́лба; (*also*: **vacuum ~**) те́рмос.

flat [flæt] adj (*surface*) пло́ский*; (*tyre*) спу́щенный; (*battery*) се́вший; (*beer*) вы́дохшийся; (*refusal, denial*) категори́ческий*; (MUS: *note*) бемо́льный; (*voice*) одното́нный; (*rate, fee*) еди́ный (еди́н) ♦ n (BRIT: *apartment*) кварти́ра; (AUT: *also*: **~ tyre**) спу́щенная ши́на; (MUS) бемо́ль m; **to work ~ out** выкла́дываться (impf) по́лностью, рабо́тать (impf) на изно́с; **~ rate of pay** еди́ная ста́вка.

flat-footed ['flæt'futɪd] adj: **he is ~** у него́ плоскосто́пие.

flatly ['flætlɪ] adv (*deny*) на́чисто; (*refuse*) наотре́з.

flatmate ['flætmeɪt] n (BRIT) сосе́д*(ка*) по кварти́ре.

flatness ['flætnɪs] n (*of land*) ро́вность f.

flat-screen ['flætskriːn] adj: **~ TV set** телеви́зор с пло́ским экра́ном.

flatten ['flætn] vt (*also*: **~ out**) выра́внивать (вы́ровнять perf); (*building*) сноси́ть* (снести́* perf); (*crop*) побива́ть (поби́ть* perf); (*city*) сравня́ть (perf) с землёй; (fig: inf: *person*) разбива́ть (разби́ть* perf) в пух и прах; **to ~ o.s. against a wall/door** etc пло́тно прижима́ться (прижа́ться* perf) к стене́/две́ри etc.

flatter ['flætəʳ] vt льсти́ть* (польсти́ть* perf) +dat.

flatterer ['flætərəʳ] n льстец́*.

flattering ['flætərɪŋ] adj (*comment*) ле́стный* (ле́стен); (*clothes*): **that dress is very ~** э́то пла́тье скрыва́ет все недоста́тки.

flattery ['flætərɪ] n лесть f.

flatulence ['flætjuləns] n (MED) метеори́зм.

flaunt [flɔːnt] vt щеголя́ть (impf) +instr.

flavour ['fleɪvəʳ] (US **flavor**) vt (*soups etc*) приправля́ть (припра́вить* perf) ♦ n (*of food, drink*) вкус; (*of ice-cream etc*) сорт*; (fig): **music with an African ~** му́зыка с африка́нскими моти́вами or в африка́нском сти́ле; **strawberry-~ed** с клубни́чным при́вкусом; **to give** or **add ~ to** придава́ть* (прида́ть* perf) вкус +dat.

flavouring ['fleɪvərɪŋ] n аромати́ческое вещество́.

flaw [flɔː] n (*in argument, character*) недоста́ток*, изъя́н; (*in cloth, glass*) дефе́кт.

flawless ['flɔːlɪs] adj безупре́чный*.

flax [flæks] n лён*.

flaxen ['flæksən] adj (*hair*) льняно́й.

flea [fliː] n блоха́*.

flea market n барахо́лка*.

fleck [flɛk] n (*mark*) кра́пинка* ♦ vt: **to ~ (with)** забры́згивать (perf) (+instr); **brown ~ed with white** кори́чневый в бе́лую кра́пинку.

fled [flɛd] pt, pp of **flee**.

fledg(e)ling ['flɛdʒlɪŋ] n (опери́вшийся) птене́ц*.

flee [fliː] (pt, pp **fled**) vt (*danger, famine*) бежа́ть* (impf) от +gen; (*country*) бежа́ть* (impf/perf) из +gen ♦ vi (*refugees, escapees*) спаса́ться (impf) бе́гством.

fleece [fliːs] n (*sheep's coat*) руно́*; (*sheep's wool*) ове́чья шерсть f ♦ vt (inf: *cheat*) обира́ть (обобра́ть* perf).

fleecy ['fliːsɪ] adj пуши́стый.

fleet [fliːt] n (*of ships*) флот*; (*of lorries, cars*) парк.

fleeting ['fliːtɪŋ] adj мимолётный*.

Flemish ['flɛmɪʃ] adj флама́ндский* ♦ n (LING) флама́ндский* язы́к*; **the ~** npl (GEO) Флама́ндцы* mpl.

flesh [flɛʃ] n (ANAT) плоть f; (*skin*) те́ло; (*of fruit*) мя́коть f

▸ **flesh out** vt излага́ть (изложи́ть* perf) во всех дета́лях.

flesh wound [-wuːnd] n пове́рхностная ра́на.

183

flew [flu:] *pt of* **fly**.

flex [flɛks] *n* гибкий* шнур* ◆ *vt* (*leg, muscles*) разминать (размять* *perf*).

flexibility [flɛksɪ'bɪlɪtɪ] *n* гибкость *f*.

flexible ['flɛksəbl] *adj* гибкий*.

flexitime ['flɛksɪtaɪm] *n* гибкий* график (*рабочего дня*).

flick [flɪk] *n* щелчок* ◆ *vt* (*with finger*) смахивать (смахнуть* *perf*); (*ash*) стряхивать (стряхнуть* *perf*); (*towel, whip*) хлестнуть (*perf*) +*instr*; (*switch*) щёлкнуть (*perf*) +*instr*; ~**s** (*inf*) киношка *fsg*

▶ **flick through** *vt fus* просматривать (просмотреть* *perf*).

flicker ['flɪkə'] *vi* (*light, flame*) мерцать (*impf*); (*eyelids*) трепетать (*impf*) ◆ *n* (*of light*) мерцание; (*of pain, fear*) вспышка*; (*of suspicion, doubt*) тень *f*; (*of interest, hope*) проблеск; (*of eyelid*) трепетание.

flick knife *n* (*BRIT*) кнопочный нож.

flier ['flaɪə'] *n* (*pilot*) лётчик.

flight [flaɪt] *n* полёт; (*escape*) бегство; (*of steps*) пролёт (*лестницы*); **to take** ~ обращаться (обратиться* *perf*) в бегство; **to put to** ~ обращать (обратить* *perf*) в бегство.

flight attendant *n* (*US*) стюард(есса).

flight crew *n* экипаж самолёта.

flight deck *n* (*AVIAT*) кабина экипажа; (*NAUT*) взлётно-посадочная полоса на палубе.

flight path *n* (*of plane*) курс полёта; (*of rocket*) траектория полёта.

flight recorder *n* "чёрный ящик".

flimsy ['flɪmzɪ] *adj* (*shoes, clothes*) лёгкий*; (*building, structure*) непрочный*; (*excuse, evidence*) слабый*.

flinch [flɪntʃ] *vi* (*in pain, shock*) вздрагивать (вздрогнуть* *perf*); **to** ~ **from** (*unpleasant duty*) уклоняться (уклониться* *perf*) от +*gen*.

fling [flɪŋ] (*pt, pp* **flung**) *vt* (*throw*) швырять (швырнуть* *perf*) ◆ *n* (*love affair*) роман; **to** ~ **one's arms around sb's neck** обнимать (обнять* *perf*) кого-н за шею; **to** ~ **o.s.** (*move quickly*) кидаться (кинуться* *perf*), бросаться (броситься* *perf*).

flint [flɪnt] *n* кремень* *m*.

flip [flɪp] *vt* (*switch*) щёлкать (щёлкнуть *perf*) +*instr*; (*coin*) подбрасывать (подбросить* *perf*) щелчком; (*US: pancake*) подбрасывать (подбросить* *perf*) ◆ *vi*: **to** ~ **for sth** (*US*) бросать (бросить* *perf*) монету

▶ **flip through** *vt fus* просматривать (просмотреть* *perf*).

flippant ['flɪpənt] *adj* несерьёзный*.

flipper ['flɪpə'] *n* (*of seal etc*) плавник*; (*for swimming*) ласт*.

flip side *n* оборот.

flirt [flɜːt] *vi* (*with person*) флиртовать (*impf*),

зайгрывать (*impf*); (*with idea*) зайгрывать (*impf*) ◆ *n* кокетка*, любитель(ница) *m(f)* пофлиртовать.

flirtation [flɜː'teɪʃən] *n* флирт.

flit [flɪt] *vi* (*birds*) перелетать (перелететь* *perf*); (*butterfly*) порхать (*impf*); (*expression, smile*) мелькать (*impf*).

float [fləʊt] *n* (*for fishing*) поплавок*; (*for swimming*) пенопластовая доска для обучающихся плавать; (*lorry*) украшенная платформа на колёсах в праздничной процессии; (*money*) разменные деньги *pl* ◆ *vi* (*object: on water*) плавать (*impf*), держаться (*impf*) на поверхности; (*swimmer*) плыть* (*impf*); (*sound, smell, cloud*) плыть* (*impf*); (*paper*) летать (*impf*); (*COMM: currency*) свободно колебаться* (*impf*) ◆ *vt* (*idea, plan*) пускать (пустить* *perf*) в ход; **to** ~ **currency** вводить (ввести* *perf*) плавающий валютный курс; **to** ~ **a company** выпускать (выпустить* *perf*) акции компании через биржу

▶ **float around** *vi* (*idea, rumour*) носиться* (*impf*) в воздухе; (*person, object*) плавать (*impf*).

flock [flɒk] *n* (*of sheep*) стадо; (*of birds*) стая; (*REL*) паства ◆ *vi*: **to** ~ **to** (*place, event*) стекаться (стечься *perf*) в +*prp*.

floe [fləʊ] *n* (*also:* **ice** ~) плавучая льдина.

flog [flɒg] *vt* (*whip*) сечь* (высечь* *perf*); (*inf: sell*) сплавлять (сплавить* *perf*).

flood [flʌd] *n* (*of water*) наводнение; (*of letters, imports etc*) поток ◆ *vt* (*subj: water*) заливать (залить* *perf*); (: *people*) наводнять (наводнить* *perf*); (*AUT: carburettor*) наполнять (наполнить* *perf*) ◆ *vi* (*place*) наполняться (наполниться *perf*) водой; (*people, goods*): **to** ~ **into** хлынуть (*perf*) в/на +*acc*; **the river is in** ~ река вышла из берегов; **to** ~ **the market with** (*COMM*) наводнять (наводнить *perf*) рынок +*instr*.

flooding ['flʌdɪŋ] *n* наводнение.

floodlight ['flʌdlaɪt] *n* прожектор* ◆ *vt* (*area*) освещать (осветить* *perf*) прожектором.

floodlit ['flʌdlɪt] *pt, pp of* **floodlight** ◆ *adj* освещённый прожектором.

flood tide *n* прилив.

flood water *n* паводковые воды *fpl*.

floor [flɔː'] *n* (*of room*) пол; (*storey*) этаж*; (*of sea, valley*) дно* ◆ *vt* (*subj: blow*) валить* (повалить* *perf*) на пол, сбивать (сбить* *perf*) с ног; (: *question, remark*) сражать (сразить* *perf*); **on the** ~ на полу; **ground** *or* (*US*) **first** ~ первый этаж*; **first** *or* (*US*) **second** ~ второй этаж*; **top** ~ последний* этаж*; **to take the** ~ (*fig*) брать* (взять* *perf*) слово; **to have the** ~ (*speaker*) получать (получить* *perf*) слово.

---

* marks translations which have irregular inflections. The Russian-English side of the dictionary gives inflectional information.

floorboard ['flɔ:bɔ:d] n половѝца.
flooring ['flɔ:rɪŋ] n (floor) пол*; (material to make floor) настѝл; (covering) настѝлка полóв.
floor lamp n (US) торшéр.
floor show n (in nightclub) развлекáтельная прогрáмма.
floorwalker ['flɔ:wɔ:kə'] n (esp US) дежýрный администрáтор магазѝна.
floozy ['flu:zɪ] n (inf) шлю́ха.
flop [flɔp] n (failure) провáл ◆ vi (fail) провáливаться (провалѝться* perf); (fall: into chair, onto floor etc) шлёпаться (шлёпнуться perf).
floppy ['flɔpɪ] adj свисáющий, отвѝслый ◆ n (also: ~ disk) гѝбкий* диск, дискéта, флóппи-диск; ~ hat шля́па с отвѝслыми поля́ми.
flora ['flɔ:rə] n флóра.
floral ['flɔ:rl] adj (pattern) цветѝстый.
Florence ['flɔrəns] n Флорéнция.
Florentine ['flɔrəntaɪn] adj флорентѝйский*.
florid ['flɔrɪd] adj (style) цветѝстый; (complexion) крáсный*.
florist ['flɔrɪst] n торгóвец* цветáми; (female) цветóчница.
florist's (shop) ['flɔrɪsts-] n цветóчный магазѝн.
flotation [fləu'teɪʃən] n (of shares) свобóдная продáжа; (of company) распродáжа áкций компáнии.
flotsam ['flɔtsəm] n (also: ~ and jetsam: rubbish) мýсор; (: people) бродя́ги pl.
flounce [flauns] n (frill) обóрка*
► **flounce out** vi: **she ~d out of the room** онá брóсилась вон из кóмнаты.
flounder ['flaundə'] vi (in water) барáхтаться (impf); (fig) спотыкáться (impf), пýтаться (impf) ◆ n (ZOOL) кáмбала.
flour ['flauə'] n мукá.
flourish ['flʌrɪʃ] vi (business) процветáть (impf); (plant) пы́шно растѝ* (impf) ◆ vt (document, handkerchief) размáхивать (impf) +instr ◆ n (in writing) завитýшка; (bold gesture): **with a ~** демонстратѝвно.
flourishing ['flʌrɪʃɪŋ] adj (company, trade) процветáющий.
flout [flaut] vt (law, rules) пренебрегáть (пренебрéчь* perf).
flow [fləu] n (of blood, river) течéние; (ELEC) потóк; (of traffic, orders, information) потóк; (of tide) прилѝв ◆ vi течь* (impf); (clothes, hair) ниспадáть (impf), пáдать (impf).
flow chart n блок-схéма.
flow diagram n = **flow chart**.
flower ['flauə'] n цветóк* ◆ vi (plant, tree) цвестѝ* (impf); ~**s** цветы́; **in ~** в цветý.
flowerbed ['flauəbɛd] n клýмба.
flowerpot ['flauəpɔt] n цветóчный горшóк*.
flowery ['flauərɪ] adj (perfume) цветóчный; (pattern, speech) цветѝстый.

flown [fləun] pp of **fly**.
flu [flu:] n (MED) грипп*.
fluctuate ['flʌktjueɪt] vi (price, rate, temperature) колебáться* (impf); (opinions, attitudes) меня́ться (impf).
fluctuation [flʌktju'eɪʃən] n: ~ (in) колебáние (в +prp).
flue [flu:] n дымохóд.
fluency ['flu:ənsɪ] n бéглость f; **his ~ in Russian** егó бéглость в рýсском языкé.
fluent ['flu:ənt] adj (linguist) бéгло говоря́щий; (speech, writing etc) бéглый, плáвный*; **he's a ~ speaker** он óчень красноречѝв; **he's a ~ reader** он бы́стро читáет; **he speaks ~ Russian, he's ~ in Russian** он свобóдно or бéгло говорѝт по-рýсски.
fluently ['flu:əntlɪ] adv (speak) бéгло; (read, write) свобóдно.
fluff [flʌf] n (on jacket, carpet) ворс; (fur, down) пух* ◆ vt (inf: do badly: lines) спýтать (спýтать perf; (: exam) завáливать (завалѝть* perf); (also: ~ out: hair) взбивáть (взбить* perf); (: feathers) распушáть (распушѝть perf).
fluffy ['flʌfɪ] adj пушѝстый; ~ **toy** мя́гкая игрýшка*.
fluid ['flu:ɪd] adj (movement) текýчий*; (situation, arrangement) переменчѝвый (переменчѝв); (opinion) неустóйчивый (неустóйчив) ◆ n жѝдкость f.
fluid ounce n (BRIT: = 0.028l; 0.05 pints) жѝдкая ýнция.
fluke [flu:k] n (inf) везéние.
flummox ['flʌməks] vt сбивáть (сбить* perf) с тóлку.
flung [flʌŋ] pt, pp of **fling**.
flunky ['flʌŋkɪ] n лакéй.
fluorescent [fluə'rɛsnt] adj (dial, light) флюоресцѝрующий; (paint) флюорес-цéнтный.
fluoride ['fluəraɪd] n фторѝд.
fluorine ['fluəri:n] n фтор.
flurry ['flʌrɪ] n (of wind) поры́в; **snow ~** снéжный вихрь m; **a ~ of activity** бýрная дéятельность f; **a ~ of excitement** бýрное возбуждéние.
flush [flʌʃ] n (on face) румя́нец*; (fig: of youth, beauty etc) расцвéт ◆ vt (drains, pipe) промывáть (промы́ть* perf) ◆ vi (become red: face) зардéться (perf) ◆ adj: ~ **with** (level) на однóм ýровне с +instr; ~ **against** вплоть до +gen; **in the first ~ of youth/freedom** в упоéнии мóлодостью/свобóдой; **hot ~es** (BRIT: MED) прилѝвы крóви; **to ~ the toilet** спускáть (спустѝть* perf) вóду в туалéте
► **flush out** vt (game, birds) вспýгивать (вспугнýть perf); (criminal) спýгивать (спугнýть perf).
flushed ['flʌʃt] adj раскраснéвшийся.
fluster ['flʌstə'] vt (person) смущáть (смутѝть* perf) ◆ n: **in a ~** в смущéнии.
flustered ['flʌstəd] adj смущённый* (смущён).

185

flute [fluːt] n флéйта.
fluted ['fluːtɪd] adj рифлёный, гофрирóванный.
flutter ['flʌtə'] n (of wings) взмах; (of panic, excitement) трéпет ◆ vi (bird) взмáхивать (impf) крылья́ми; (person) метáться* (impf).
flux [flʌks] n: **in a state of** ~ в состоя́нии непрерывного изменéния.
fly [flaɪ] (pt **flew**, pp **flown**) n (insect) мýха; (on trousers: also: **flies**) ширúнка ◆ vt (plane) водúть/вестú* (impf); (passengers, cargo) перевозúть* (перевезтú* perf); (distances) пролетáть (пролетéть perf), преодолевáть (преодолéть perf); (kite) запускáть (запустúть* perf) ◆ vi (also fig) летáть/летéть (impf); (escape) спасáться (спастúсь* perf) бéгством, сбегáть (сбежáть perf); (flag) развевáться (impf); **to** ~ **open** распáхиваться (распахнýться perf); **to** ~ **off the handle** (inf) срывáться (сорвáться perf); **pieces of metal went** ~**ing everywhere** оскóлки метáлла полетéли во все стóроны; **she came** ~**ing into the room** онá влетéла в кóмнату; **her glasses flew off** у неё слетéли очкú
► **fly away** vi улетáть (улетéть perf)
► **fly in** vi (plane, person) прилетáть (прилетéть* perf)
► **fly off** vi = **fly away**
► **fly out** vi (person, plane) вылетáть (вы́лететь* perf).
fly-fishing ['flaɪfɪʃɪŋ] n ужéние на блеснý.
flying ['flaɪɪŋ] n (activity) лётное дéло; (action) полёт ◆ adj: **a** ~ **visit** крáткий* визúт; **he doesn't like** ~ он не лю́бит летáть самолётом; **with** ~ **colours** блестя́ще.
flying buttress n áрочный контрфóрс.
flying picket n грýппа профсою́зных агитáторов, объезжáющая фáбрики с цéлью убедúть рабóчих приня́ть учáстие в забастóвке.
flying saucer n летáющая тарéлка*.
flying squad n отря́д бы́строго реагúрования.
flying start n: **to get off to a** ~ ~ начинáть (начáть* perf) óчень успéшно.
flyleaf ['flaɪliːf] n фóрзац.
flyover ['flaɪəuvə'] n (BRIT: overpass) эстакáда.
fly-past ['flaɪpɑːst] n воздýшный парáд.
fly sheet n (for tent) навéс.
flyweight ['flaɪweɪt] n боксёр лёгкой весовóй категóрии.
flywheel ['flaɪwiːl] n маховóе колесó*.
FM abbr (BRIT: MIL) = **field marshal**; (RADIO: = frequency modulation) ЧМ= частóтная модуля́ция.
FMB n abbr (US) = Federal Maritime Board.
FMCS n abbr (US: = Federal Mediation and Conciliation Services) слýжба

посрéдничества мéжду предпринимáтелями и рабóчими.
FO n abbr (BRIT) = **Foreign Office**.
foal [fəul] n жеребёнок*.
foam [fəum] n пéна; (also: ~ **rubber**) пенорезúна ◆ vi пéниться (impf).
fob [fɔb] n (also: **watch** ~) цепóчка* для кармáнных часóв ◆ vt: **to** ~ **sb off (with sth)** всýчивать (всучúть perf) or подсóвывать (подсýнуть perf) комý-н что-н.
f.o.b. abbr (COMM. = free on board) ФОБ= фрáнко-бóрт.
foc abbr (COMM: BRIT: = free of charge) беcплáтно.
focal point ['fəukl-] n средотóчие; (PHOT) фокáльная тóчка.
focus ['fəukəs] (pl ~**es**) n (PHOT) фóкус; (of attention, interest, argument) центр ◆ vt (camera) настрáивать* (настрóить* perf); (light rays) фокусúровать (сфокусúровать perf) ◆ vi: **to** ~ **(on)** (PHOT) настрáиваться (настрóиться perf) (на +acc); (fig): **to** ~ **on** сосредотáчиваться (сосредотóчиться perf) на +prp; **in** ~ в фóкусе; **out of** ~ не в фóкусе.
fodder ['fɔdə'] n корм*.
FOE n abbr (= Friends of the Earth) ОДЗ= Óбщество "Друзья́ Землú"; (US: = Fraternal Order of Eagles) Брáтский óрден орлóв.
foe [fəu] n нéдруг.
foetus ['fiːtəs] (US **fetus**) n плод, зарóдыш.
fog [fɔg] n тумáн.
fogbound ['fɔgbaund] adj закры́тый úли задéржанный из-за тумáна.
foggy ['fɔgɪ] adj тумáнный* (тумáнен); **it's** ~ стоúт тумáн.
fog lamp (US **fog light**) n (AUT) фáра для тумáна.
foible ['fɔɪbl] n причýда.
foil [fɔɪl] vt (plan) расстрáивать (расстрóить* perf); (attempt, attack) срывáть (сорвáть* perf) ◆ n (metal) фольгá; (FENCING) рапúра; **to act as a** ~ **to** (fig) служúть* (impf) контрáстом +dat.
foist [fɔɪst] vt: **to** ~ **sth on sb** навя́зывать (навязáть* perf) что-н комý-н.
fold [fəuld] n (crease) склáдка*; (: in paper) сгиб; (AGR) загóн; (fig) лóно ◆ vt (clothes, paper) склáдывать (сложúть* perf); (arms) скрéщивать (скрестúть* perf) ◆ vi (business) свóрачиваться (свернýться perf)
► **fold up** vi склáдываться (сложúться* perf); (business) свóрачиваться (свернýться perf) ◆ vt (object) склáдывать (сложúть* perf).
folder ['fəuldə'] n (for papers) пáпка*, скоросшивáтель m; (: binder) пáпка* (с металлúческим зажúмом); (brochure) брошю́ра.
folding ['fəuldɪŋ] adj (chair, bed) складнóй.

* marks translations which have irregular inflections. The Russian-English side of the dictionary gives inflectional information.

foliage ['fəʊlɪdʒ] *n* листва.
folk [fəʊk] *npl* люди *pl*, народ* *msg* ◆ *cpd* (*art, music*) народный; ~s *npl* (*inf: relatives*) близкие *pl adj*.
folklore ['fəʊklɔ:'] *n* фольклор.
folk music *n* народная музыка.
folk song *n* народная песня*.
follow ['fɒləʊ] *vt* (*leader, person*) следовать (последовать *perf*) за +*instr*; (*example, advice*) следовать (последовать *perf*) +*dat*; (*event, story*) следить* (*impf*) за +*instr*; (*route, path*) держаться* (*impf*) +*gen*; (*with eyes*) провожать (проводить* *perf*) взглядом ◆ *vi* следовать (последовать *perf*); **to ~ in sb's footsteps** идти* (пойти* *perf*) по чьим-н стопам; **I don't quite ~ you** я не совсем Вас понимаю; **to ~ sb's advice** следовать (последовать *perf*) чьему-н совету; **I left the room, and he ~ed** я вышел из комнаты и он последовал за мной; **it ~s that he** ... отсюда следует, что он ...; **to ~ suit** (*fig*) следовать (последовать *perf*) примеру
▶ **follow on** *vi* (*continue*): **to ~ on from** следовать (последовать *perf*) за +*instr*
▶ **follow out** *vt* (*idea, plan*) приводить* (привести* *perf*) в исполнение
▶ **follow through** *vt* = **follow out**
▶ **follow up** *vt* (*letter, offer*) рассматривать (рассмотреть* *perf*); (*case*) расследовать (*impf*).
follower ['fɒləʊə'] *n* (*of person*) последователь(ница) *m(f)*; (*of belief*) сторонник(-ица).
following ['fɒləʊɪŋ] *adj* следующий* ◆ *n* (*followers*) сторонники *mpl*; **a large ~** много сторонников.
follow-up ['fɒləʊʌp] *n* продолжение ◆ *adj* (*treatment, survey*) последующий*.
folly ['fɒlɪ] *n* (*foolishness*) *f*, (*building*) декоративное парковое сооружение.
fond [fɒnd] *adj* (*smile, look, parents*) ласковый* (ласков); (*memory*) приятный* (приятен); (*hopes, dreams*) тщетный* (тщетен); **to be ~ of** любить* (*impf*); **she's ~ of swimming** она любит плавать.
fondle ['fɒndl] *vt* ласкать (*impf*).
fondly ['fɒndlɪ] *adv* (*lovingly*) ласково; (*naively*) наивно; **he ~ believed that** ... он наивно верил, что ....
fondness ['fɒndnɪs] *n* любовь* *f*; **a special ~ for** особенная любовь к +*dat*.
font [fɒnt] *n* (*in church*) купель *f*; (*TYP*) комплект (шрифта).
food [fu:d] *n* еда, пища.
food chain *n* пищевой симбиоз.
food mixer *n* миксер.
food poisoning *n* пищевое отравление.
food processor *n* кухонный комбайн.
food stamp *n* продуктовый талон.
foodstuffs ['fu:dstʌfs] *npl* продукты *mpl* питания.

fool [fu:l] *n* (*male*) дурак*; (*female*) дура; (*CULIN*) сладкое блюдо из сливок и фруктов *vt* (*deceive*) обманывать (обмануть* *perf*), одурачивать (одурачить *perf*) ◆ *vi* (*be silly*) дурачиться (*impf*); **to make a ~ of** (*ridicule*) выставлять (выставить* *perf*) кого-н на посмешище; (*trick*) одурачивать (одурачить *perf*) кого-н; **to make a ~ of o.s.** ставить* (поставить* *perf*) себя в глупое положение; **you can't ~ me** меня не проведёте
▶ **fool about** *vi* (*pej: waste time*) валять (*impf*) дурака; (*behave foolishly*) дурачиться *perf*
▶ **fool around** *vi* = **fool about**.
foolhardy ['fu:lhɑ:dɪ] *adj* безрассудный* (безрассуден)
foolish ['fu:lɪʃ] *adj* (*stupid*) глупый* (глуп); (*rash*) опрометчивый (опрометчив).
foolishly ['fu:lɪʃlɪ] *adv* (*see adj*) глупо; опрометчиво.
foolishness ['fu:lɪʃnɪs] *n* дурачество.
foolproof ['fu:lpru:f] *adj* (*plan*) надёжный* (надёжен).
foolscap ['fu:lskæp] *n* бумага формата: 34 см x 43 см.
foot [fut] *n* (*pl* **feet**) (*of person*) нога*, ступня; (*of animal*) нога*; (*of bed*) конец*; (*of cliff*) подножие; (*measure*) фут; (*of page, stairs etc*) низ ◆ *vt*: **to ~ the bill** платить* (*perf*); **on ~** пешком; **at the ~ of the page/stairs** внизу страницы/лестницы; **to find one's feet** (*fig*) вставать* (встать* *perf*) на ноги; **to put one's ~ down** (*AUT*) нажимать (нажать* *perf*) на педаль; (*assert authority*) занимать (занять* *perf*) твёрдую позицию.
footage ['futɪdʒ] *n* (*CINEMA: material*) кадры *mpl*; (: *length*) ≈ метраж.
foot-and-mouth [futən'maʊθ] *n* (*also: ~ disease*) ящур.
football ['futbɔ:l] *n* (*ball*) футбольный мяч*; (*sport: BRIT*) футбол; (: *US*) американский* футбол.
footballer ['futbɔ:lə'] *n* (*BRIT*) футболист.
football ground *n* футбольное поле.
football match *n* (*BRIT*) футбольный матч.
football player *n* футболист.
foot brake *n* ножной тормоз*.
footbridge ['futbrɪdʒ] *n* пешеходный мост*.
foothills ['futhɪlz] *npl* предгорья* *ntpl*.
foothold ['futhəʊld] *n* опора; (*fig*): **to get a ~** укрепляться (укрепиться* *perf*), утвердиться* (*perf*).
footing ['futɪŋ] *n* (*fig: basis, relationship*) основа; **to be on a friendly ~** быть* (*impf*) на дружеской ноге; **to lose one's ~** (*fall*) терять (потерять *perf*) опору; **on an equal ~** на равных (основаниях).
footlights ['futlaɪts] *npl* огни *mpl* рампы.
footman ['futmən] *irreg n* лакей.
footnote ['futnəʊt] *n* сноска*.
footpath ['futpɑ:θ] *n* тропинка*, дорожка*; (*in street*) тротуар.

footprint ['futprɪnt] n след*, отпечаток ноги.
footrest ['futrɛst] n скамеечка* для ног.
footsie ['futsɪ] n: **to play ~ with sb** толкать (толкнуть perf) ножкой кого-н.
footsore ['futsɔː] adj: **I am ~** у меня болят ноги.
footstep ['futstɛp] n (sound) шаг*; (footprint) след*; (fig): **to follow in sb's ~s** идти (пойти* perf) по чьим-н стопам.
footwear ['futwɛə] n обувь f.
footwork ['futwəːk] n фигуры fpl (движения ног в танце).

<hr>

KEYWORD

for [fɔː] prep **1** (indicating destination, intention): **the train for London/Paris** поезд в Лондон/Париж; **he left for Rome/work** он уехал в Рим/на работу; **when does the train for Moscow leave?** когда отправляется поезд на Москву?; **he went for the paper/the doctor** он пошёл за газетой/врачом; **is this for me?** это мне or для меня?; **there's a letter for you** Вам письмо; **it's time for lunch/bed** пора обедать (impf)/спать (impf)

2 (indicating purpose) для +gen; **what's it for?** для чего это?; **give it to me – what for?** дайте это мне – зачём?; **to pray for forgiveness** молить* (impf) о прощении; **to pray for peace** молиться* (impf) о мире

3 (on behalf of, representing): **to speak for sb** говорить (impf) от лица кого-н; **MP for Brighton** представляющий Брайтон; **he works for the government** он на государственной службе; **he works for a local firm** он работает в местной фирме; **I'll ask him for you** я спрошу его от вашего имени; **to do sth for sb** (on behalf of) делать (сделать perf) что-н за кого-н

4 (because of) из-за +gen; **for lack of funds** из-за отсутствия средств; **for this reason** по этой причине; **for some reason, for whatever reason** почему-то; **for fear of being criticized** боясь критики; **to be famous for sth** быть (impf) известным чем-н

5 (with regard to): **it's cold for July** для июля сейчас холодно; **he's tall for fourteen/for his age** для четырнадцати лет/для своего возраста он высокий; **a gift for languages** способности к языкам; **for everyone who voted yes, 50 voted no** на каждый голос „за", приходилось 50 голосов „против"

6 (in exchange for, in favour of) за +acc; **I sold it for £5** я продал это за £5; **I'm all for it** я целиком и полностью за это

7 (referring to distance): **there are roadworks for five miles** дорожные работы на протяжении пяти миль; **to stretch for miles** простираться (impf) на много миль; **we**

walked for miles/for ten miles мы прошли много миль/десять миль

8 (referring to time) на +acc; (: in past): **he was away for 2 years** он был в отъезде 2 года; **she will be away for a month** она уезжает на месяц; **can you do it for tomorrow?** Вы можете сделать это на завтра; **it hasn't rained for 3 weeks** уже 3 недели не было дождя; **for hours** часами

9 (with infinite clause): **it is not for me to decide** не мне решать; **there is still time for you to do it** у Вас ещё есть время сделать это; **for this to be possible** ... чтобы это осуществить ...

10 (in spite of) несмотря на +acc; **for all his complaints** несмотря на все его жалобы

11 (in phrases): **for the first/last time** в первый/последний раз; **for the time being** пока

◆ conj (rather formal) ибо.

<hr>

f.o.r. abbr (COMM: = free on rail) франко-вагон.
forage ['fɔrɪdʒ] n корм ◆ vi: **to ~ for sth** рыскать* (impf) поискать чего-н.
forage cap n фуражка, пилотка.
foray ['fɔreɪ] n (raid) набег.
forbad(e) [fə'bæd] pt of **forbid**.
forbearing [fɔː'bɛərɪŋ] adj сдержанный.
forbid [fə'bɪd] (pt forbad(e), pp forbidden) vt запрещать (запретить* perf); **to ~ sb to do** запрещать (запретить* perf) кому-н +infin.
forbidden [fə'bɪdn] pp of **forbid** ◆ adj (entry, activity) запрещённый* (запрещён); (place) запретный; **it's ~ to** ... запрещено +infin ....
forbidding [fə'bɪdɪŋ] adj (look etc) неприязненный; (prospect) мучительный* (мучителен).
force [fɔːs] n (also PHYS) сила; (influence) воздействие ◆ vt (compel) заставлять (заставить* perf), принуждать (принудить* perf); (push) толкать (толкнуть perf); (break open) взламывать (взломать perf); **the F~s** npl (BRIT: MIL) вооружённые силы fpl; **in ~** в большом числе; **to come into ~** вступать (вступить* perf) в силу; **to join ~s** объединять (объединить perf) усилия; **it's a ~ wind** сила ветра – пять баллов; **the sales ~** (COMM) торговые агенты; **to ~ o.s. to do** заставлять (заставить* perf) себя +infin; **to ~ sb to do** заставлять (заставить* perf) or вынуждать (вынудить* perf) кого-н +infin

▶ **force back** vt (enemy) отражать (отразить* perf); (crowd, tears) сдерживать (сдержать* perf)
▶ **force down** vt (food) есть* (съесть* perf) с трудом.
forced [fɔːst] adj (landing) вынужденный; (smile) натянутый (натянут); **~ labour** принудительный труд.

force-feed ['fɔːsfiːd] *vt* наси́льно корми́ть* (*impf*).
forceful ['fɔːsful] *adj* си́льный* (силён).
forceps ['fɔːsɛps] *npl* щипцы́ *pl*.
forcible ['fɔːsəbl] *adj* (*action*) наси́льственный; (*reminder, lesson*) убеди́тельный.
forcibly ['fɔːsəblɪ] *adv* (*remove*) наси́льно; (*express*) с си́лой.
ford [fɔːd] *n* (*in river*) брод* ♦ *vt* переходи́ть* (перейти́* *perf*) вброд.
fore [fɔː*] *n*: **to come to the ~** выдвига́ться (вы́двинуться *perf*).
forearm ['fɔːrɑːm] *n* предпле́чье*.
forebear ['fɔːbɛə*] *n* пре́док*.
foreboding [fɔː'bəudɪŋ] *n* предчу́вствие.
forecast ['fɔːkɑːst] (*irreg: like* **cast**) *n* прогно́з ♦ *vt* (*predict*) предска́зывать (предсказа́ть* *perf*).
foreclose [fɔː'kləuz] *vt* (*LAW: also:* ~ **on**) лиша́ть (лиши́ть *perf*) прав со́бственности.
foreclosure [fɔː'kləuʒə*] *n* (*COMM*) лише́ние прав со́бственности.
forecourt ['fɔːkɔːt] *n* (*of garage*) пере́дняя площа́дка.
forefathers ['fɔːfɑːðəz] *npl* пре́дки* *mpl*.
forefinger ['fɔːfɪŋɡə*] *n* указа́тельный па́лец*.
forefront ['fɔːfrʌnt] *n*: **in** *or* **at the ~ of** (*industry, movement*) в аванга́рде +*gen*.
forego [fɔː'ɡəu] (*irreg: like* **go**) *vt* поступа́ться (поступи́ться* *perf*) +*instr*.
foregoing [fɔː'ɡəuɪŋ] *adj* предше́ствующий* ♦ *n*: **the ~** вышеупомя́нутое *nt adj*.
foregone ['fɔːɡɔn] *adj*: **it's a ~ conclusion** э́то предрешённый исхо́д.
foreground ['fɔːɡraund] *n* (*also COMPUT*) пере́дний* план.
forehand ['fɔːhænd] *n* (*TENNIS*) уда́р спра́ва.
forehead ['fɔrɪd] *n* лоб*.
foreign ['fɔrɪn] *adj* (*person, language*) иностра́нный; (*country*) зарубе́жный; (*trade*) вне́шний*; (*object*) посторо́нний*.
foreign body *n* иноро́дное те́ло.
foreign currency *n* иностра́нная валю́та.
foreigner ['fɔrɪnə*] *n* иностра́нец*(-нка*).
foreign exchange *n* (*system*) обме́н валю́ты; (*money*) валю́та.
foreign-exchange market [fɔrɪnɪks'tʃeɪndʒ-] *n* валю́тный ры́нок*.
foreign-exchange rate *n* валю́тный курс.
foreign investment *n* иностра́нные капиталовложе́ния *ntpl*.
foreign minister *n* мини́стр иностра́нных дел.
Foreign Office *n* (*BRIT*) министе́рство иностра́нных дел.
Foreign Secretary *n* (*BRIT*) мини́стр иностра́нных дел.
foreleg ['fɔːlɛɡ] *n* (*of animal*) пере́дняя нога́*.
foreman ['fɔːmən] *irreg n* (*in factory, on building site etc*) ма́стер*; (*of jury*) старшина́ *m* присяжных.

foremost ['fɔːməust] *adj* (*most important*) наибо́лее ва́жный* ♦ *adv*: **first and ~** в пе́рвую о́чередь, пре́жде всего́.
forename ['fɔːneɪm] *n* и́мя* *nt*.
forensic [fə'rɛnsɪk] *adj* (*medicine, test*) суде́бный*; ~ **expert** специали́ст по суде́бной медици́не.
foreplay ['fɔːpleɪ] *n* возбужда́ющие ла́ски *fpl*.
forerunner ['fɔːrʌnə*] *n* предше́ственник(-ница).
foresee [fɔː'siː] (*irreg: like* **see**) *vt* предви́деть* (*impf/perf*).
foreseeable [fɔː'siːəbl] *adj* предви́димый; **in the ~ future** в обозри́мом бу́дущем.
foreseen [fɔː'siːn] *pp of* **foresee**.
foreshadow [fɔː'ʃædəu] *vt* (*event*) предзнаменова́ть (*impf*).
foreshore ['fɔːʃɔː*] *n* берегова́я полоса́, затопля́емая прили́вом.
foreshortened [fɔː'ʃɔːtnd] *adj* (*figure, scene*) в ра́курсе.
foresight ['fɔːsaɪt] *n* предусмотри́тельность *f*.
foreskin ['fɔːskɪn] *n* кра́йняя плоть *f*.
forest ['fɔrɪst] *n* лес*.
forestall [fɔː'stɔːl] *vt* (*person*) приостана́вливать (приостанови́ть* *perf*); (*discussion*) опережа́ть (опереди́ть* *perf*).
forestry ['fɔrɪstrɪ] *n* лесово́дство, лесни́чество.
foretaste ['fɔːteɪst] *n*: **a ~ of** представле́ние о +*prp*.
foretell [fɔː'tɛl] (*irreg: like* **tell**) *vt* предска́зывать (предсказа́ть* *perf*).
forethought ['fɔːθɔːt] *n* предусмотри́тельность *f*.
foretold [fɔː'təuld] *pt, pp of* **foretell**.
forever [fə'rɛvə*] *adv* (*for good*) навсегда́; (*endlessly*) ве́чно; **that time has gone ~** то вре́мя ушло́ навсегда́; **it will last ~** э́то бу́дет дли́ться ве́чно; **you're ~ finding difficulties** Вы ве́чно нахо́дите тру́дности.
forewarn [fɔː'wɔːn] *vt* предупрежда́ть (предупреди́ть* *perf*).
foreword ['fɔːwəːd] *n* (*in book*) предисло́вие.
forfeit ['fɔːfɪt] *n* (*penalty*) штраф ♦ *vt* (*right, friendship etc*) теря́ть (потеря́ть *perf*); (*one's happiness, health*) поплати́ться* (*perf*) +*instr*.
forgave [fə'ɡeɪv] *pt of* **forgive**.
forge [fɔːdʒ] *n* ку́зница ♦ *vt* (*signature, money*) подде́лывать (подде́лать *perf*); (*metal*) кова́ть (*impf*); **to ~ documents/a will** подде́лывать (подде́лать *perf*) докуме́нты/завеща́ние
▶ **forge ahead** *vi* (*country, person*) вырыва́ться (вы́рваться* *perf*) вперёд.
forger ['fɔːdʒə*] *n* (*of documents, paintings*) подде́лыватель *m*; (*of money*) фальшивомоне́тчик.
forgery ['fɔːdʒərɪ] *n* подде́лка*.
forget [fə'ɡɛt] (*pt* **forgot**, *pp* **forgotten**) *vt* забыва́ть (забы́ть* *perf*); (*appointment*) забыва́ть (забы́ть* *perf*) о +*prp* ♦ *vi* забыва́ть

(забы́ть* *perf*); **to ~ o.s.** забы́ться* *(perf)*.
forgetful [fə'gɛtful] *adj* (*person*) забы́вчивый
(забы́вчив); **~ of** забы́в о *+prp*.
forgetfulness [fə'gɛtfulnɪs] *n* забы́вчивость *f*;
(*oblivion*) забве́ние.
forget-me-not [fə'gɛtmɪnɔt] *n* незабу́дка*.
forgive [fə'gɪv] (*pt* **forgave**, *pp* **forgiven**) *vt*
(*pardon*) проща́ть (прости́ть* *perf*) *+dat or*
+gen; **to ~ sb for sth** (*excuse*) проща́ть
(прости́ть* *perf*) кому́-н *or* кого́-н за что-н; **I
forgave him for doing it** я прости́л ему́ *or* его́
за то, что он э́то сде́лал; **~ my ignorance, but**
... прости́те моё неве́жество, но ...; **they
could be ~n for thinking that** ... их мо́жно
прости́ть за то, что они́ ду́мают, что ....
forgiven [fə'gɪvn] *pp of* **forgive**.
forgiveness [fə'gɪvnɪs] *n* проще́ние.
forgiving [fə'gɪvɪŋ] *adj* великоду́шный*
(великоду́шен).
forgo [fɔː'gəu] *vt* = **forego**.
forgot [fə'gɔt] *pt of* **forget**.
forgotten [fə'gɔtn] *pp of* **forget**.
fork [fɔːk] *n* ви́лка*; (*for gardening*) ви́лы *pl*; (*in
road*) развилка*; (*in railway*) стык; (*in river,
tree*) разветвле́ние ◆ *vi* (*road*) разветвля́ться
(impf)
▶ **fork out** (*inf*) ◆ *vt* выкла́дывать (вы́ложить*
perf) ◆ *vi* раскоше́ливаться (раскоши́ться
perf).
forked [fɔːkt] *adj* (*lightning*) зигзагообра́зный.
fork-lift truck ['fɔːklɪft-] *n* грузоподъёмник.
forlorn [fə'lɔːn] *adj* (*person*) несча́стный;
(*place*) поки́нутый; (*hope, attempt*) сла́бый.
form [fɔːm] *n* (*type*) вид; (*shape*) фо́рма; (*SCOL*)
класс; (*questionnaire*) бланк ◆ *vt* (*make*)
образо́вывать (образова́ть *perf*); (*set up:
organization, group*) формирова́ть
(сформирова́ть *perf*); (*idea, habit*)
выраба́тывать (вы́работать *perf*); **in the ~ of**
в фо́рме *+gen*; **to be in good ~** (*SPORT, fig*)
быть* *(impf)* в хоро́шей фо́рме; **in top ~** в
лу́чшей фо́рме; **on ~** в фо́рме; **to ~ part of
sth** явля́ться (яви́ться* *perf*) ча́стью чего́-н; **I
~ed a good impression of her** у меня́
созда́лось хоро́шее впечатле́ние о ней.
formal ['fɔːml] *adj* форма́льный*; (*statement*)
форма́льный* (форма́лен); (*person,
behaviour*) церемо́нный* (церемо́нен);
(*occasion, dinner*) официа́льный*
(официа́лен); (*garden*) англи́йский*; **~
clothes** официа́льная оде́жда; **~
dress** (*evening dress*) вече́рняя оде́жда.
formalities [fɔː'mælɪtɪz] *npl* форма́льности *fpl*.
formality [fɔː'mælɪtɪ] *n* форма́льность *f*; (*of
person, behaviour*) церемо́нность *f*; (*of
occasion*) официа́льность *f*.
formalize ['fɔːməlaɪz] *vt* (*plan, arrangement*)
оформля́ть (офо́рмить* *perf*).

formally ['fɔːməlɪ] *adv* форма́льно; (*behave*)
церемо́нно; **to be ~ invited** получа́ть
(получи́ть* *perf*) официа́льное приглаше́ние.
format ['fɔːmæt] *n* (*form, style*) форма́т ◆ *vt*
(*COMPUT: disk*) формати́ровать *(impf/perf)*.
formation [fɔː'meɪʃən] *n* формирова́ние; (*of
rocks*) форма́ция; (*of clouds*) скопле́ние.
formative ['fɔːmətɪv] *adj*: **in his ~ years** в го́ды
формирова́ния его́ хара́ктера.
former ['fɔːmə] *adj* (*one-time*) бы́вший*;
(*earlier*) пре́жний*; **the ~ ... the latter ...**
пе́рвый ... после́дний*; **the ~ president**
бы́вший* президе́нт.
formerly ['fɔːməlɪ] *adv* ра́ньше, до э́того.
form feed *n* (*on printer*) пода́ча страни́ц.
Formica® [fɔː'maɪkə] *n* формайка
(*огнеупо́рная пластма́сса*).
formidable ['fɔːmɪdəbl] *adj* (*task*) чрезвыча́йно
тру́дный* (тру́ден); (*opponent*) гро́зный*
(гро́зен).
formula ['fɔːmjulə] (*pl* **~e** *or* **~s**) *n* (*MATH, CHEM*)
фо́рмула; (*plan*) схе́ма; **F~ One** (*AUT*)
обозначе́ние го́ночной маши́ны.
formulae ['fɔːmjuliː] *npl of* **formula**.
formulae ['fɔːmjuleɪt] *vt* (*plan, strategy*)
выраба́тывать (вы́работать *perf*),
разраба́тывать (разрабо́тать *perf*); (*opinion,
thought*) формули́ровать (сформули́ровать
perf).
fornicate ['fɔːnɪkeɪt] *vi* прелюбоде́йствовать
(impf).
forsake [fə'seɪk] (*pt* **forsook**, *pp* **forsaken**) *vt*
(*abandon*) покида́ть (поки́нуть *perf*).
forsaken [fə'seɪkən] *pp of* **forsake**.
forsook [fə'suk] *pt of* **forsake**.
fort [fɔːt] *n* кре́пость *f*, форт*; **to hold the ~** (*fig*)
стоя́ть *(impf)* на стра́же.
forte ['fɔːtɪ] *n* (*strength*) си́льная сторона́.
forth [fɔːθ] *adv* (*out*): **to go ~** идти́* *(impf)*
вперёд; **to send ~** посла́ть* *(perf)*; **to go back
and ~** ходи́ть* *(impf)* взад и вперёд; **to bring ~**
вынима́ть (вы́нуть *perf*); **and so ~** и так
да́лее.
forthcoming [fɔːθ'kʌmɪŋ] *adj* предстоя́щий;
(*person*) общи́тельный; **to be ~** (*help,
evidence*) ожида́ться *(impf)*, появля́ться
(impf).
forthright ['fɔːθraɪt] *adj* (*condemnation,
opposition*) прямо́й.
forthwith ['fɔːθ'wɪθ] *adv* то́тчас.
fortieth ['fɔːtɪθ] *adj* сороково́й*; *see also* **fifth**.
fortification [fɔːtɪfɪ'keɪʃən] *n* (*MIL*) укрепле́ние.
fortified wine ['fɔːtɪfaɪd-] *n* креплёное вино́*.
fortify ['fɔːtɪfaɪ] *vt* (*city*) укрепля́ть (укрепи́ть*
perf); (*person*) придава́ть* (прида́ть* *perf*)
си́лы *+dat*.
fortitude ['fɔːtɪtjuːd] *n* сто́йкость *f*.
fortnight ['fɔːtnaɪt] (*BRIT*) *n* две неде́ли; **it's a ~**

---

* marks translations which have irregular inflections. The Russian-English side of the dictionary gives inflectional information.

since ... прошло две недели с тех пор, как ....

fortnightly ['fɔ:tnaɪtlɪ] *adv* раз в две недели ♦ *adj*: ~ **magazine** журнал, выходящий раз в две недели.

FORTRAN ['fɔ:træn] *n* ФОРТРАН.

fortress ['fɔ:trɪs] *n* крепость *f*.

fortuitous [fɔ:'tju:ɪtəs] *adj* случайный* (случаен).

fortunate ['fɔ:tʃənɪt] *adj* (*person*) счастливый* (счастлив); (*event*) счастливый*; **he is/was** ~ ему везёт/повезло; **he is** ~ **to have** ... ему хорошо, что у него есть ...; **it is** ~ **that** ... удачно, что ....

fortunately ['fɔ:tʃənɪtlɪ] *adv* к счастью.

fortune ['fɔ:tʃən] *n* (*wealth*) состояние; (*also*: **good** ~) счастье, удача; **bad** *or* **ill** ~ несчастье, неудача; **to make a** ~ наживать (нажить* *perf*) себе состояние; **to tell sb's** ~ гадать (*impf*) кому-н, предсказывать (предсказать* *perf*) чью-н судьбу.

fortune-teller ['fɔ:tʃəntɛlə'] *n* гадалка, предсказатель(ница) *m(f)*.

forty ['fɔ:tɪ] *n* сорок*; *see also* **fifty**.

forum ['fɔ:rəm] *n* форум.

forward ['fɔ:wəd] *adv* вперёд ♦ *n* (*SPORT*) нападающий*(-ая) *m(f)* *adj* ♦ *vt* (*letter, parcel*) пересылать (переслать* *perf*); (*career*) продвигать (продвинуть *perf*) ♦ *adj* (*position*) передний*; (*not shy*) дерзкий* (дерзок); (*COMM: delivery, sales*) заблаговременный; **to move** ~ (*progress*) продвигаться (продвинуться *perf*); "**please** ~", „перешлите адресату"; ~ **movement** движение вперёд; ~ **planning** предварительное планирование.

forward contract *n* форвардный *or* срочный контракт.

forward rate *n* форвардный *or* срочный валютный курс, по которому заключается срочная валютная сделка.

forwards ['fɔ:wədz] *adv* вперёд.

fossil ['fɔsl] *n* окаменелость *f*, ископаемое *nt adj*.

fossil fuel *n* окаменелое топливо.

foster ['fɔstə'] *vt* (*child*) брать* (взять* *perf*) на воспитание; (*activity*) поощрять (*impf*); (*hope*) питать (*impf*); **to** ~ **an idea** вынашивать (*impf*) мысль.

foster child *n* приёмный ребёнок*.

foster mother *n* приёмная мать* *f*.

fought [fɔ:t] *pt, pp of* **fight**.

foul [faul] *adj* отвратительный* (отвратителен); (*language*) непристойный* (непристоен); (*temper*) гневливый (гневлив) ♦ *n* (*SPORT*) нарушение* ♦ *vt* гадить* (загадить* *perf*); (*SPORT*) нарушать (нарушить *perf*) правила против +*gen*; (*entangle: anchor, propeller*) опутывать (опутать *perf*).

foul play *n* (*LAW*) преступные действия *ntpl*: ~ ~ **is not suspected** нет подозрений о преступных действиях.

found [faund] *pt, pp of* **find** ♦ *vt* (*establish*) основывать (основать *perf*).

foundation [faun'deɪʃən] *n* (*act*) основание; (*base*) основа; (*fig*) основа, устои *mpl*; (*organization*) общество; (*also*: ~ **cream**) крем под макияж; ~**s** *npl* (*of building*) фундамент *msg*; **the rumours are without** ~ слухи не имеют оснований; **to lay the** ~**s** (*fig*) закладывать (заложить* *perf*) основы.

foundation stone *n* краеугольный камень* *m*.

founder ['faundə'] *n* (*of firm, college*) основатель(ница) *m(f)* ♦ *vi* (*ship*) идти* (пойти* *perf*) ко дну.

founder member *n* член-учредитель(ница) *m(f)*.

founding fathers ['faundɪŋ-] *npl* (*esp US*) основоположники *mpl*.

foundry ['faundrɪ] *n* литейная *f adj*, литейный цех.

fount [faunt] *n* источник; (*TYP*) комплект шрифта.

fountain ['fauntɪn] *n* фонтан.

fountain pen *n* чернильная ручка*.

four [fɔ:'] *n* четыре*; **on all** ~**s** на четвереньках; *see also* **five**.

four-letter word ['fɔ:lɛtə-] *n* ≈ мат.

four-poster ['fɔ:'pəustə'] *n* (*also*: ~ **bed**) кровать *f* с пологом.

foursome ['fɔ:səm] *n* четвёрка*.

fourteen ['fɔ:'ti:n] *n* четырнадцать*; *see also* **five**.

fourteenth ['fɔ:'ti:nθ] *adj* четырнадцатый*; *see also* **fifth**.

fourth ['fɔ:θ] *adj* четвёртый ♦ *n* (*AUT: also*: ~ **gear**) четвёртая скорость *f*; *see also* **fifth**.

four-wheel drive ['fɔ:wi:l-] *n* (*AUT*) внедорожник; **with** ~ ~ с приводом на четыре колеса.

fowl [faul] *n* птица; (*wild*) дичь *f*.

fox [fɔks] *n* лиса* ♦ *vt* озадачивать (озадачить *perf*).

foxglove ['fɔksglʌv] *n* (*BOT*) наперстянка*.

fox-hunting ['fɔkshʌntɪŋ] *n* охота на лис.

foxtrot ['fɔkstrɔt] *n* (*dance*) фокстрот.

foxy ['fɔksɪ] *adj*: ~ **lady** шикарная женщина.

foyer ['fɔɪeɪ] *n* фойе *nt ind*.

FPA *n abbr* (*BRIT*: = *Family Planning Association*) *организация, обеспечивающая консультации по планированию семьи.*

Fr. *abbr* (*REL*) = **father**, **friar**.

fr. *abbr* = **franc**.

fracas ['fræka:] *n* скандал.

fraction ['frækʃən] *n* (*portion*) небольшая часть *f*; (*MATH*) дробь *f*; **a** ~ **of a second** доля секунды.

fractionally ['frækʃnəlɪ] *adv*: ~ **smaller** *etc* незначительно меньше *etc*.

fractious ['frækʃəs] *adj* капризный* (капризен); **she was** ~ она капризничала.

fracture ['fræktʃəʳ] n (of bone) перело́м ♦ vt (bone) лома́ть (слома́ть perf).

fragile ['frædʒaɪl] adj (object) хру́пкий* (хру́пок).

fragment ['frægmənt] n фрагме́нт; (of stone, glass) оско́лок*, обло́мок*.

fragmentary ['frægməntərɪ] adj (evidence, knowledge) отры́вочный* (отры́вочен).

fragrance ['freɪgrəns] n благоуха́ние.

fragrant ['freɪgrənt] adj души́стый (души́ст).

frail [freɪl] adj (person) сла́бый* (слаб); (structure) хру́пкий* (хру́пок), непро́чный* (непро́чен).

frame [freɪm] n (of building, structure) карка́с; (of car, human, animal) о́стов; (of picture, door, window) ра́ма; (of spectacles: also: ~s) опра́ва ♦ vt обрамля́ть (обра́мить* perf); (reply, law, theory) формули́ровать (сформули́ровать perf); ~ of mind настрое́ние; to ~ sb (inf) подста́вить* (perf) кого́-н.

framework ['freɪmwəːk] n (structure) карка́с; (fig) ра́мки fpl.

France [frɑːns] n Фра́нция.

franchise ['fræntʃaɪz] n (POL) пра́во го́лоса; (COMM) франши́за.

franchisee [fræntʃaɪˈziː] n держа́тель m франши́зы.

franchiser ['fræntʃaɪzəʳ] n предостави́тель m франши́зы.

frank [fræŋk] adj (discussion, person) открове́нный* (открове́нен); (look) откры́тый ♦ vt (letter) франки́ровать (зафранки́ровать perf).

Frankfurt ['fræŋkfəːt] n Фра́нкфурт.

frankfurter ['fræŋkfəːtəʳ] n соси́ска*.

franking machine ['fræŋkɪŋ-] n франкирова́льная маши́на.

frankly ['fræŋklɪ] adv открове́нно.

frankness ['fræŋknɪs] n открове́нность f.

frantic ['fræntɪk] adj (distraught) обезу́мевший; (hectic) сумато́шный*; (desperate: need, desire) безу́мный*; (: cry) неи́стовый; we were ~ with worry мы обезу́мели от волне́ния.

frantically ['fræntɪklɪ] adv отча́янно.

fraternal [frəˈtəːnl] adj бра́тский*.

fraternity [frəˈtəːnɪtɪ] n (feeling) бра́тство; (club) содру́жество.

fraternize ['frætənaɪz] vi обща́ться (impf).

fraud [frɔːd] n (crime) моше́нничество; (person) моше́нник.

fraudulent ['frɔːdjulənt] adj (scheme, claim) моше́ннический*.

fraught [frɔːt] adj (person) не́рвный* (не́рвен); (situation): ~ with (danger, problems) чрева́тый (чрева́т) +instr.

fray [freɪ] vi обтрёпываться (обтрепа́ться perf)

♦ n (battle, fight): the ~ бой, дра́ка; tempers were ~ed все бы́ли на гра́ни срыва; her nerves were ~ed у неё бы́ли истрёпаны не́рвы; to return to the ~ сно́ва ри́нуться (perf) в бой or дра́ку.

FRB n abbr (US: = Federal Reserve Board) Федера́льное резе́рвное правле́ние.

FRCM n abbr (BRIT) = Fellow of the Royal College of Music.

FRCO n abbr (BRIT) = Fellow of the Royal College of Organists.

FRCP n abbr (BRIT) = Fellow of the Royal College of Physicians.

FRCS n abbr (BRIT) = Fellow of the Royal College of Surgeons.

freak [friːk] adj (event, accident) стра́нный ♦ n (person: in appearance) уро́дец*(-дица), вы́родок* m/f; (: in attitude, behaviour): he is a ~ он со стра́нностями; (pej: fanatic): she's an aerobics ~ она́ помеша́лась на аэро́бике

▶ **freak out** vi (inf: on drugs) входи́ть* (войти́* perf) в раж.

freakish ['friːkɪʃ] adj стра́нный.

freckle ['frekl] n весну́шка*.

freckled ['frekld] adj весну́шчатый.

free [friː] adj свобо́дный* (свобо́ден); (costing nothing) беспла́тный* (беспла́тен) ♦ vt (prisoner etc) освобожда́ть (освободи́ть* perf), выпуска́ть (вы́пустить* perf) (на свобо́ду); (jammed object) высвобожда́ть (вы́свободить* perf), выта́скивать (вы́тащить perf); to give sb a ~ hand предоставля́ть (предоста́вить* perf) кому́-н свобо́ду де́йствий; ~ and easy непринуждённый; admission ~ свобо́дный вход; ~ (of charge), for ~ беспла́тно; ~ alongside ship фра́нко вдоль бо́рта су́дна; ~ of tax освобождённый от упла́ты нало́гов; ~ on rail фра́нко – железнодоро́жный ваго́н

free agent n: he's a ~ ~ он сам себе́ хозя́ин.

freebie ['friːbɪ] n (inf: gift) пода́рок*.

freedom ['friːdəm] n свобо́да.

freedom fighter n бое́ц* за свобо́ду.

freedom of association n свобо́да объедине́ния в ассоциа́ции.

free enterprise n свобо́дное предпринима́тельство.

Freefone® ['friːfəun] n систе́ма, позволя́ющая звони́ть беспла́тно в определённые организа́ции.

free-for-all ['friːfərɔːl] n (fight) потасо́вка.

free gift n пода́рок*.

freehold ['friːhəuld] n (of property) по́лное пра́во на владе́ние.

free kick n (FOOTBALL) свобо́дный уда́р.

freelance ['friːlɑːns] adj внешта́тный, рабо́тающий по договора́м.

freelance work n рабо́та по контра́кту or

договорáм.

freeloader ['fri:ləudə'] *n* (*pej*) дармоéд(ка*).

freely ['fri:lɪ] *adv* (*without restriction*) свобóдно; (*liberally*) обúльно; **drugs are ~ available in the city** наркóтики мóжно легкó достáть в гóроде.

free-market economy ['fri:'mɑ:kɪt-] *n* рýночная эконóмика.

Freemason ['fri:meɪsn] *n* масóн.

Freemasonry ['fri:meɪsnrɪ] *n* масóнство.

Freepost® ['fri:pəust] *n* (*BRIT*) бесплáтная пóчта.

free-range ['fri:'reɪndʒ] *adj*: ~ **eggs** *яйца от кур свобóдно-вýгульного содержáния*.

free sample *n* бесплáтный образéц*.

freesia ['fri:zɪə] *n* фрéзия.

free speech *n* свобóда слóва.

freestyle ['fri:staɪl] *n* (*in swimming*) кроль *m*.

free trade *n* неогранúченная беспóшлинная торгóвля.

freeway ['fri:weɪ] *n* (*US: AUT*) скоростнáя автострáда.

freewheel [fri:'wi:l] *vi* (*on bicycle*) катúться* (покатúться* *perf*); (*in car*) идтú* (пойтú* *perf*) свобóдным хóдом.

free will *n* свобóда вóли; **of one's own ~ ~** по дóброй вóле.

freeze [fri:z] (*pt* **froze**, *pp* **frozen**) *vi* (*weather*) холодáть (похолодáть *perf*); (*liquid, pipe, person*) замерзáть (замёрзнуть* *perf*); (*person: stop moving*) застывáть (застýть* *perf*) ♦ *vt* морáживать (заморóзить* *perf*) ♦ *n* (*weather*) зáморозки *pl*; (*on arms, wages*) морáживание; **it's freezing** óчень хóлодно

▸ **freeze over** *vi* замерзáть (замёрзнуть* *perf*)

▸ **freeze up** *vi* замерзáть (замёрзнуть* *perf*).

freeze-dried ['fri:zdraɪd] *adj* обрабóтанный мéтодом заморáживания-высýшивания.

freeze-dry ['fri:zdraɪ] *vt* быстро заморáживать и затéм высýшивать в вáкуме.

freezer ['fri:zə'] *n* морозúльник.

freezing ['fri:zɪŋ] *adj*: ~ (**cold**) ледянóй ♦ *n*: **3 degrees below** ~ мúнус 3 грáдуса, 3 грáдуса морóза; **I'm** ~ я замёрз.

freezing point *n* температýра замерзáния.

freight [freɪt] *n* фрахт; ~ **forward** фрахт уплáчиваемый в портý вýгрузки; ~ **inward** фрахт, уплáчиваемый по прибýтии.

freight car *n* (*US*) товáрный вагóн.

freighter ['freɪtə'] *n* (*NAUT*) грузовóе сýдно*; (*AVIAT*) грузовóй самолёт.

freight forwarder [-'fɔ:wədə'] *n* экспедúтор.

freight train *n* (*US*) товáрный пóезд*.

French [frentʃ] *adj* францýзский* ♦ *n* (*LING*) францýзский язýк*; **the** ~ *npl* (*people*) францýзы *mpl*.

French bean *n* (*BRIT*) стручкóвая фасóль *f*.

French Canadian *n* франкоязýчный(-ая) канáдец*(-дка).

French-Canadian [frentʃkə'neɪdjən] *adj*

франко-канáдский*.

French dressing *n* сóус для салáта из растúтельного мáсла и ýксуса.

French fried potatoes *npl* чúпсы *mpl*.

French fries [-fraɪz] *npl* (*US*) = **French fried potatoes**.

French Guiana [-gaɪ'ænə] *n* Францýзская Гвиáна.

Frenchman ['frentʃmən] *irreg n* францýз.

French Riviera *n*: **the** ~ ~ Францýзская Ривьéра.

French stick *n* длúнный батóн.

French window *n* двуствóрчатое окнó до пóла.

Frenchwoman ['frentʃwumən] *irreg n* францýженка*.

frenetic [frə'nɛtɪk] *adj* лихорáдочный* (лихорáдочен).

frenzied ['frenzɪd] *adj* (*person*) бéшеный, взбешённый; (*behaviour*) нейстовый.

frenzy ['frenzɪ] *n* (*of violence*) бéшенство, нейстовство; ~ **of joy** безýмная рáдость; ~ **of excitement** безýмное возбуждéние; **to drive sb into a** ~ доводúть* (довестú* *perf*) когó-н до бéшенства, приводúть* (привестú* *perf*) когó-н в бéшенство; **to be in a** ~ быть* (*impf*) в бéшенстве.

frequency ['fri:kwənsɪ] *n* (*also RADIO*) частотá*.

frequency modulation *n* частóтная модулýция.

frequent [*adj* 'fri:kwənt, *vt* frɪ'kwɛnt] *adj* чáстый ♦ *vt* (*pub, restaurant*) посещáть (посетúть* *perf*).

frequently ['fri:kwəntlɪ] *adv* (*often*) чáсто.

fresco ['freskəu] *n* фрéска*.

fresh [frɛʃ] *adj* свéжий* (свеж); (*instructions, approach*) нóвый* (нов); (*cheeky: person*) нахáльный* (нахáлен), фамильýрный* (фамильýрен); **to make a** ~ **start** начáть* *perf* зáново; ~ **in one's mind** свежó в пáмяти.

freshen ['freʃən] *vi* (*wind, air*) свежéть (*impf*)

▸ **freshen up** *vi* (*person*) освежáться (освежúться *perf*).

freshener ['freʃnə'] *n*: **skin** ~ лосьóн для освежéния кóжи; **air** ~ освежúтель *m* вóздуха.

fresher ['freʃə'] *n* (*BRIT: inf*) первокýрсник.

freshly ['freʃlɪ] *adv*: ~ **made** свéжеприготóвленный; ~ **painted** свéжепокрáшенный.

freshman ['freʃmən] *irreg n* (*US*) = **fresher**.

freshness ['freʃnɪs] *n* свéжесть *f*.

freshwater ['freʃwɔ:tə'] *adj* (*lake*) прéсный; (*fish*) пресновóдный.

fret [frɛt] *vi* волновáться (*impf*).

fretful ['frɛtful] *adj* (*child*) беспокóйный*.

Freudian ['frɔɪdɪən] *adj* фрейдúстский; ~ **slip** оговóрка по Фрéйду.

FRG *n abbr* (= *Federal Republic of Germany*) ФРГ= *Федератúвная Респýблика Гермáнии.*

Fri. *abbr* = **Friday**.
friar ['fraɪə'] *n* монáх.
friction ['frɪkʃən] *n* трéние; (*fig*) трéния *ntpl*.
friction feed *n* (*on printer*) подáча бумáги с пóмощью вáлика.
Friday ['fraɪdɪ] *n* пя́тница; *see also* **Tuesday**.
fridge [frɪdʒ] *n* (*BRIT*) холодильник.
fridge-freezer ['frɪdʒ'fri:zə'] *n* холодильник с большóй морозильной кáмерой.
fried [fraɪd] *pt, pp of* **fry** ♦ *adj* жáреный.
friend [frɛnd] *n* (*male*) друг*; (*female*) подрýга; **to make ~s with** подружиться (*perf*) с +*instr*.
friendliness ['frɛndlɪnɪs] *n* (*of person*) дружелю́бие.
friendly ['frɛndlɪ] *adj* (*person, smile etc*) дружелю́бный* (дружелю́бен); (*government, country*) дрýжественный* (дрýжествен); (*place, restaurant*) прия́тный* (прия́тен); (*game, match*) товáрищеский* ♦ *n* (*also:* ~ **match**) товáрищеская встрéча; **to be ~ with** дружить* (*impf*) с +*instr*; **to be ~ to sb** относиться* (отнестись* *perf*) к комý-н дружелю́бно.
friendly fire *n* огóнь* *m* со своих пози́ций.
friendly society *n* óбщество *or* кáсса взаимопóмощи.
friendship ['frɛndʃɪp] *n* дрýжба.
frieze [fri:z] *n* фриз, бордю́р.
frigate ['frɪgɪt] *n* фрегáт.
fright [fraɪt] *n* испýг; **to take ~** испугáться (*perf*); **she looks a ~** она вы́глядит как пýгало.
frighten ['fraɪtn] *vt* пугáть (испугáть *or* напугáть *perf*).
► **frighten away** *vt* (*birds, children etc*) спýгивать (спугнýть *perf*).
► **frighten off** *vt* = **frighten away**.
frightened ['fraɪtnd] *adj* (*afraid*) испýганный* (испýган); **I am ~** я бою́сь; **to be ~ (of)** боя́ться (*impf*) (+*gen*); **he is ~ by change** егó пугáют изменéния.
frightening ['fraɪtnɪŋ] *adj* (*experience, prospect*) стрáшный.
frightful ['fraɪtful] *adj* (*dreadful*) кошмáрный* (кошмáрен), ужáсный* (ужáсен).
frightfully ['fraɪtfəlɪ] *adv* ужáсно; **I'm ~ sorry** мне ужáсно сты́дно.
frigid ['frɪdʒɪd] *adj* (*woman*) фриги́дный.
frigidity [frɪ'dʒɪdɪtɪ] *n* фриги́дность *f*.
frill [frɪl] *n* (*of dress, shirt*) обóрка*; **without ~s** (*fig*) без прикрáс.
frilly ['frɪlɪ] *adj* с обóрками.
fringe [frɪndʒ] *n* (*BRIT: of hair*) чёлка*; (*on shawl, lampshade etc*) бахромá*; (*of forest etc*) край*, окрáина, (*fig: of activity, organization etc*) периферия.
fringe benefits *npl* дополнительные льгóты *fpl*.
fringe theatre *n* эксперимéнтальный теáтр.

Frisbee® ['frɪzbɪ] *n* фрисби *m ind*.
frisk [frɪsk] *vt* (*search*) обы́скивать (обыскáть* *perf*) ♦ *vi* (*animal*) резви́ться (порезви́ться *perf*).
frisky ['frɪskɪ] *adj* игри́вый (игри́в).
fritter ['frɪtə'] *n* (*CULIN*) лóмтик чегó-нибудь, обжáренный в кипя́щем мáсле
► **fritter away** *vt* (*money*) растрáчивать (растрáтить* *perf*); (*time*) пóпусту теря́ть (потеря́ть *perf*).
frivolity [frɪ'vɔlɪtɪ] *n* легкомы́слие.
frivolous ['frɪvələs] *adj* (*conduct, person*) легкомы́сленный* (легкомы́слен); (*object, activity*) пустя́чный.
frizzy ['frɪzɪ] *adj* (*hair*) курчáвый, мéлко-вью́щийся.
fro [frəu] *adv*: **to and ~** тудá-сюдá.
frock [frɔk] *n* плáтье*.
frog [frɔg] *n* лягýшка*; **to have a ~ in one's throat** хрипéть* (*impf*).
frogman ['frɔgmən] *irreg n* водолáз, ныря́льщик.
frogmarch ['frɔgmɑːtʃ] *vt* (*BRIT*): **to ~ sb in/out** втáскивать (втащить *perf*)/выта́скивать (вы́тащить *perf*) когó-н зá руки лицóм вниз.
frolic ['frɔlɪk] *vi* (*animals, children*) весели́ться (*impf*) ♦ *n* весéлье*.

KEYWORD

from [frɔm] *prep* **1** (*indicating starting place, origin etc*): **where do you come from?** откýда Вы?; **from London to Glasgow** из Лóндона в Глáзго; **a letter from my sister** письмó от моéй сестры́; **a quotation from Dickens** цитáта из Ди́ккенса; **to drink from the bottle** пить* (*impf*) из буты́лки
2 (*indicating movement: from inside*) из +*gen*; (: *away from*) от +*gen*; (: *off*) с(о) +*gen*; (: *from behind*) из-за +*gen*; **she ran from the house** она вы́бежала из дóма; **the car drove away from the house** маши́на отъéхала от дóма; **he took the magazine from the table** он взял журнáл со столá; **they got up from the table** они встáли из-за столá
3 (*indicating time*) с +*gen*; **from two o'clock to** *or* **until** *or* **till three** с двух (часóв) до трёх (часóв); **from January (to August)** с января́ (по áвгуст)
4 (*indicating distance: position*) от +*gen*; (: *motion*) до +*gen*; **the hotel is 1 km from the beach** оте́ль нахóдится в киломéтре от пля́жа; **we're still a long way from home** нам ещё далекó до дóма
5 (*indicating price, number etc: range*) от +*gen*; (: *change*) с +*gen*; **prices range from £10 to £50** цéны от £10 до £50; **the interest rate was increased from nine per cent to ten per cent** процéнты на вклáды повы́сили с девяти́ до десяти́ (процéнтов)

---

6 (indicating difference) от +gen; **to be different from sb/sth** отлича́ться (impf) от кого́-н/чего́-н

7 (because of, on the basis of): **from what he says** из того́, что он говори́л; **from what I understand** наско́лько я зна́ю; **to act from conviction** де́йствовать* (impf) по убежде́нию; **he is weak from hunger** он осла́б от го́лода.

frond [frɒnd] n ветвь f; **palm** ~ лист* па́льмы.

front [frʌnt] n (of house, also fig) фаса́д; (of dress) пе́ред; (of train, car) пере́дняя часть f; (promenade: also: **sea** ~) на́бережная f adj; (MIL, METEOROLOGY) фронт* ♦ adj пере́дний* ♦ vi: **to** ~ **onto sth** выходи́ть* (impf) фаса́дом на что-н; **in** ~ вперёд; **in** ~ **of** пе́ред +instr; **on the political** ~ на полити́ческом фро́нте.

frontage ['frʌntɪdʒ] n фаса́д.

frontal ['frʌntl] adj (attack) лобово́й, фронта́льный; ~ **view** вид спе́реди.

front bench n (POL: BRIT) мини́стры пра́вящей па́ртии и руководи́тели па́ртии оппози́ции.

front desk n (US: in hotel) сто́йка администра́тора; (: in doctor's surgery) регистрату́ра.

front door n входна́я дверь* f.

frontier ['frʌntɪəʳ] n грани́ца.

frontispiece ['frʌntɪspiːs] n фронтиспи́с.

front page n пе́рвая страни́ца (газе́ты).

front room n гости́ная f adj.

frontrunner ['frʌntrʌnəʳ] n (fig) претенде́нт.

front-wheel drive ['frʌntwiːl-] n (AUT) пере́дний* при́вод.

frost [frɒst] n моро́з; (also: **hoarfrost**) и́ней.

frostbite ['frɒstbaɪt] n обмороже́ние.

frosted ['frɒstɪd] adj (glass) ма́товый; (esp US: cake) глазиро́ванный.

frosting ['frɒstɪŋ] n (esp US: on cake) глазу́рь f.

frosty ['frɒstɪ] adj (weather, night) моро́зный* (моро́зен); (welcome, look) ледяно́й; (window) покры́тый (покры́т) и́неем, замёрзший.

froth ['frɒθ] n (on liquid) пе́на.

frothy ['frɒθɪ] adj (liquid) пе́нистый.

frown [fraun] n нахму́ренный взгляд ♦ vi хму́риться (нахму́риться perf)

► **frown on** vt fus (fig) смотре́ть* (impf) с неодобре́нием на +acc.

froze [frəuz] pt of **freeze**.

frozen ['frəuzn] pp of **freeze** ♦ adj (food) моро́женый; (COMM: assets) заморо́женный.

FRS n abbr (BRIT) = Fellow of the Royal Society; (US: = Federal Reserve System) Федера́льная резе́рвная систе́ма.

frugal ['fruːgl] adj (person) бережли́вый (бережли́в); (meal) ску́дный* (ску́ден).

fruit [fruːt] n inv (AGR) фрукт; (BOT) плод; (fig: results) плоды́ mpl.

fruiterer ['fruːtərəʳ] n торго́вец* фру́ктами.

fruit fly n фрукто́вая му́шка*.

fruitful ['fruːtful] adj плодотво́рный* (плодотво́рен).

fruition [fruː'ɪʃən] n: **to come to** ~ осуществля́ться (осуществи́ться perf), реализо́вываться (реализова́ться perf).

fruit juice n фрукто́вый сок.

fruitless ['fruːtlɪs] adj (fig) беспло́дный* (беспло́ден).

fruit machine n (BRIT) игрово́й автома́т.

fruit salad n фрукто́вый сала́т.

fruity ['fruːtɪ] adj фрукто́вый; (voice, laugh) зы́чный* (зы́чен).

frump [frʌmp] n (woman) замухры́шка.

frustrate [frʌs'treɪt] vt (person) расстра́ивать (расстро́ить perf); (plan, attempt) срыва́ть (сорва́ть perf).

frustrated [frʌs'treɪtɪd] adj (person) неудовлетворённый (неудовлетворён); (plan, attempt) со́рванный (со́рван); ~ **artist/poet** неуда́вшийся худо́жник/поэ́т.

frustrating [frʌs'treɪtɪŋ] adj (day) неуда́чный* (неуда́чен); **I find this job very** ~ я о́чень неудовлетворён э́той рабо́той.

frustration [frʌs'treɪʃən] n (irritation) доса́да; (thwarting) круше́ние.

fry [fraɪ] (pt, pp **fried**) vt жа́рить (пожа́рить or поджа́рить perf); see also **small**.

frying pan ['fraɪɪŋ-] (US **fry-pan**) n сковорода́*.

fry-pan ['fraɪpæn] n (US) = **frying pan**.

FT n abbr (BRIT) = Financial Times; **the** ~ **index** фо́ндовый и́ндекс „Файнэ́ншел Таймс".

ft. abbr = **feet**, **foot**.

FTC n abbr (US: = Federal Trade Commission) Федера́льная торго́вая коми́ссия.

FTSE 100 Index n (COMM) показа́тель состоя́ния фо́ндовой би́ржи, публику́емый в газе́те „Файнэ́ншел Таймс".

fuchsia ['fjuːʃə] n фу́ксия.

fuck [fʌk] (inf!) vti тра́хать (impf) (!); ~ **off!** иди́ на фиг! (!)

fuddled ['fʌdld] adj одурма́ненный.

fuddy-duddy ['fʌdɪdʌdɪ] n (pej) ста́рый зану́да m.

fudge [fʌdʒ] n ≈ сли́вочная пома́дка ♦ vt (issue, problem) уклоня́ться (уклони́ться perf) от +gen.

fuel ['fjuəl] n (for heating) то́пливо; (for plane, car) горю́чее nt adj ♦ vt (furnace etc) топи́ть* (impf); (aircraft, ship) заправля́ть (запра́вить* perf).

fuel oil n мазу́т.

fuel pump n то́пливный насо́с.

fuel tank n то́пливный бак; (in car) бензоба́к.

fug [fʌg] n (BRIT) духота́.

fugitive ['fjuːdʒɪtɪv] n бегле́ц*(-ля́нка*).

fulfil [ful'fɪl] (US **fulfill**) vt (function) исполня́ть (испо́лнить perf); (ambition) реализо́вывать (реализова́ть perf).

fulfilled [ful'fɪld] adj (person) состоя́вшийся; (life) напо́лненный.

fulfilment [ful'fɪlmənt] (US **fulfillment**) n (of

promise, desire) исполне́ние; (*satisfaction*) удовлетворе́ние; (*of ambitions*) реализа́ция.

full [ful] *adj* по́лный* (по́лон); (*skirt*) широ́кий*; (*life*) напо́лненный; (*maximum*) **at ~ volume/power** на по́лную гро́мкость/ мо́щность ◆ *adv*: **to know ~ well that** прекра́сно знать (*impf*), что; **I'm ~ (up)** я сыт; **he is ~ of enthusiasm/hope** он по́лон энтузиа́зма/наде́жды; **~ details** все дета́ли; **~ marks** отли́чные оце́нки; **at ~ speed** на по́лной ско́рости; **a ~ two hours** це́лых два часа́; **in ~** полностью́.

fullback ['fulbæk] *n* (*SPORT*) защи́тник.

full-blooded ['ful'blʌdɪd] *adj* энерги́чный*.

full board *n*: **hotel with ~ ~** гости́ница с трёхразовым пита́нием.

full-cream ['ful'kri:m] *adj*: **~ milk** (*BRIT*) несня́тое молоко́.

full employment *n* по́лная за́нятость *f*.

full-grown ['ful'grəun] *adj* (*animal, person*) взро́слый; (*plant*) вы́росший.

full-length ['ful'leŋθ] *adj* (*film, novel*) полнометра́жный; (*coat*) дли́нный; (*portrait*) во весь рост.

full moon *n* по́лная луна́*.

fullness ['fulnɪs] *n*: **in the ~ of time** по проше́ствии вре́мени.

full-page ['fulpeɪdʒ] *adj* (*advertisement, picture*) на всю страни́цу.

full-scale ['fulskeɪl] *adj* (*model*) в натура́льную величину́; (*attack, war, search*) широко-масшта́бный.

full-sized ['ful'saɪzd] *adj* (*portrait*) в по́лную величину́.

full stop *n* (*BRIT*) то́чка*.

full-time ['ful'taɪm] *adj, adv* (*study*) на дне́вном отделе́нии; (*work*) на по́лной ста́вке, на по́лную ста́вку.

fully ['fulɪ] *adv* (*completely*) по́лностью, вполне́; (*at least*): **~ as big as** по кра́йней ме́ре тако́й же величины́, как.

fully fledged [-'fledʒd] *adj* (*teacher, barrister*) вполне́ сложи́вшийся; (*citizen, member*) полнопра́вный*; (*bird*) опери́вшийся.

fully-paid share ['fulpeɪd-] *n* по́лностью опла́ченная а́кция.

fulsome ['fulsəm] *adj* (*praise*) чрезме́рный.

fumble ['fʌmbl] *vi*: **to ~ with** (*catch, key*) вози́ться (*impf*) с +*instr* ◆ *vt*: **to ~ the ball** неуклю́же стара́ться (*impf*) пойма́ть (*perf*) мяч; **to ~ in** (*pocket*) ры́ться (*impf*) в +*prp*; **she ~d for the switch in the dark** она́ шари́ла в темноте́ в по́исках выключа́теля.

fume [fju:m] *vi* дыми́ть (*impf*); **he was fuming** он был разъярён.

fumes [fju:mz] *npl* пары́ *mpl*, испаре́ния *ntpl*.

fumigate ['fju:mɪgeɪt] *vt* оку́ривать (окури́ть* *perf*).

fun [fʌn] *n*: **what ~!** как ве́село!; **to have ~** весели́ться (повесели́ться *perf*); **he's good ~ (to be with)** с ним ве́село; **for ~** для заба́вы; **it's not much ~** э́то дово́льно ску́чно; **to make ~ of** подшу́чивать (подшути́ть *perf*) над +*instr*; **to poke ~ at** насмеха́ться (*impf*) над +*instr*.

function ['fʌŋkʃən] *n* (*also MATH*) фу́нкция; (*product*) произво́дная *f adj*; (*social occasion*) прие́м ◆ *vi* (*operate*) функциони́ровать (*impf*); **to ~ as** выполня́ть (вы́полнить *perf*) *or* исполня́ть (испо́лнить *perf*) фу́нкции +*gen*.

functional ['fʌŋkʃənl] *adj* (*operational*) де́йствующий*; (*practical*) функциона́льный.

function key *n* (*COMPUT*) функциона́льная кла́виша.

fund [fʌnd] *n* (*of money*) фонд; (*of knowledge etc*) запа́с; **~s** *npl* (*money*) (де́нежные) сре́дства *ntpl*, фо́нды *mpl*.

fundamental [fʌndə'mentl] *adj* фундамента́льный*.

fundamentalism [fʌndə'mentəlɪzəm] *n* фундаментали́зм.

fundamentalist [fʌndə'mentəlɪst] *n* фундаментали́ст.

fundamentally [fʌndə'mentəlɪ] *adv* в свое́й осно́ве; **they are ~ different** они́ коренны́м о́бразом различа́ются.

fundamentals [fʌndə'mentlz] *npl* осно́вы *fpl*.

funding ['fʌndɪŋ] *n* финанси́рование.

fund raising [-reɪzɪŋ] *n* сбор средств.

funeral ['fju:nərəl] *n* по́хороны* *pl*.

funeral director *n* распоряди́тель *m* на похорона́х.

funeral parlour *n* похоро́нное бюро́ *nt ind*.

funeral service *n* панихи́да.

funereal [fju:'nɪərɪəl] *adj* тра́урный.

funfair ['fʌnfɛə'] *n* (*BRIT*) я́рмарка*.

fungi ['fʌŋgaɪ] *npl of* **fungus**.

fungus ['fʌŋgəs] (*pl* **fungi**) *n* (*plant*) гриб*; (*mould*) пле́сень *f*.

funicular [fju:'nɪkjulə'] *n* (*also*: **~ railway**) фуникулёр.

funky ['fʌŋkɪ] *adj* *о му́зыке с си́льным синкопи́рованным ри́тмом*; (*inf*) клёвый.

funnel ['fʌnl] *n* (*for pouring*) воро́нка*; (*of ship*) труба́*.

funnily ['fʌnɪlɪ] *adv* (*strangely*) стра́нно; **~ enough** как ни стра́нно.

funny ['fʌnɪ] *adj* (*comical*) смешно́й* (смешо́н); (*amusing*) заба́вный* (заба́вен); (*strange*) стра́нный* (стра́нен), чудно́й.

funny bone *n* (*inf*) локтева́я кость *f*.

fun run *n* благотвори́тельный пробе́г.

fur [fə:'] *n* мех*; (*BRIT*: *in kettle*) на́кипь *f*.

fur coat *n* мехова́я шу́ба.

furious ['fjuərɪəs] *adj* (*person*) взбешённый (взбешён); (*exchange, argument*) бу́рный*

(бу́рен); (*effort, speed*) нейстовый; **I am ~
with her** я о́чень серди́т на неё.
furiously ['fjuərɪəslɪ] *adv* нейстово.
furl [fə:l] *vt* свёртывать (сверну́ть *perf*).
furlong ['fə:lɒŋ] *n 201.2 ме́тра в ко́нных
ска́чках.*
furlough ['fə:ləu] *n* (*MIL*) увольне́ние.
furnace ['fə:nɪs] *n* печь *f*.
furnish ['fə:nɪʃ] *vt* (*room, building*) обставля́ть
(обста́вить* *perf*); (*supply*): **to ~ sb with sth**
предоставля́ть (предоста́вить* *perf*) что-н
кому́-н; **~ed flat** *or* (*US*) **apartment**
меблиро́ванная кварти́ра.
furnishings ['fə:nɪʃɪŋz] *npl* обстано́вка *fsg.*
furniture ['fə:nɪtʃə'] *n* ме́бель *f*; **piece of ~**
предме́т ме́бели.
*furniture polish n сре́дство для полиро́вки
ме́бели.*
furore [fjuə'rɔ:rɪ] *n* (*protests*) негодова́ние.
furrier ['fʌrɪə'] *n* (*fur seller*) меховщи́к*;
(*artisan*) скорня́к*.
furrow ['fʌrəu] *n* борозда́* ♦ *vt*: **to ~ one's brow**
хму́рить (нахму́рить *perf*) бро́ви.
furry ['fə:rɪ] *adj* пуши́стый (пуши́ст).
further ['fə:ðə'] *adj* (*additional*)
дополни́тельный ♦ *adv* (*farther*) да́льше;
(*moreover*) бо́лее того́ ♦ *vt* (*career, project*)
соде́йствовать (*impf/perf*) +*dat*; **until ~ notice**
впредь до дальне́йшего уведомле́ния; **how
much ~ is it to the station?** ско́лько ещё до
вокза́ла?; **~ to your letter of ...** (*formal*)
ссыла́ясь на Ва́ше письмо́ от +*gen* ...; **to ~
one's interests** пресле́довать (*impf*) свои́
интере́сы.
further education *n* (*BRIT*) дальне́йшее
обуче́ние (*не включа́я вы́сшее образова́ние*).
furthermore [fə:ðə'mɔ:'] *adv* (*moreover*) бо́лее
того́.
furthermost ['fə:ðəməust] *adj* са́мый
да́льний*.
furthest ['fə:ðɪst] *superl of* **far**.
furtive ['fə:tɪv] *adj*: **~ glance/movement** взгляд/
движе́ние укра́дкой.
furtively ['fə:tɪvlɪ] *adv* укра́дкой.
fury ['fjuərɪ] *n* (*anger, rage*) я́рость *f*,
бе́шенство; **to be in a ~** быть* (*impf*) в
бе́шенстве *or* в я́рости.
fuse [fju:z] (*US* **fuze**) *n* (*ELEC*) предохрани́тель
m; (*for bomb*) фити́ль* *m* ♦ *vt* (*metal*) пла́вить*
(распла́вить* *perf*); (*ideas, systems*) слива́ть
(слить* *perf*) ♦ *vi* (*see vt*) пла́виться

(распла́виться *perf*); слива́ться (сли́ться
perf); **a ~ has blown** предохрани́тель
перегоре́л; **to ~ the lights** (*BRIT*) вызыва́ть
(вы́звать* *perf*) коро́ткое замыка́ние.
fuse box *n* блок предохрани́телей.
fuselage ['fju:zəlɑ:ʒ] *n* фюзеля́ж.
fuse wire *n* пла́вкая про́волока (*для
предохрани́телей*).
fusillade [fju:zɪ'leɪd] *n* залп.
fusion ['fju:ʒən] *n* (*of ideas, qualities*) слия́ние;
(*also*: **nuclear ~**) я́дерный си́нтез.
fuss [fʌs] *n* (*excitement*) сумато́ха; (*anxiety*)
суета́; (*trouble*) шум ♦ *vi* суети́ться* (*impf*) ♦ *vt*
надоеда́ть (*impf*) +*dat*; **to make** *or* **kick up a ~**
поднима́ть (подня́ть* *perf*) шум; **to make a ~
of sb** носи́ться* (*impf*) с кем-н
▶ **fuss over** *vt fus* (*person*) трясти́сь* (*impf*) над
+*instr*.
fusspot ['fʌspɒt] *n* (*inf*) хлопоту́н(ья).
fussy ['fʌsɪ] *adj* (*nervous*) суетли́вый; (*choosy*)
ме́лочный (ме́лочен), су́етный; (*clothes,
room*) вы́чурный*; **I'm not ~** мне всё равно́.
fusty ['fʌstɪ] *adj* (*pej: archaic*) старомо́дный*
(старомо́ден); (*musty*) за́тхлый.
futile ['fju:taɪl] *adj* (*attempt*) тще́тный*
(тще́тен); (*comment, existence*) беспло́дный*
(беспло́ден).
futility [fju:'tɪlɪtɪ] *n* (*see adj*) тще́тность *f*;
беспло́дность *f*.
futon ['fu:tɒn] *n* фу́тон (*япо́нский матра́с*).
future ['fju:tʃə'] *adj* бу́дущий* ♦ *n* бу́дущее *nt*
adj; (*LING*: *also*: **~ tense**) бу́дущее вре́мя* *nt*;
~s *npl* (*COMM*) фью́черсы *pl*, фью́черский
това́р *msg* (*с согласо́ванной дато́й
прода́жи*); **in (the) ~** в бу́дущем; **be more
careful in ~** в бу́дущем бу́дьте осторо́жнее;
in the near/immediate ~ в недалёком/
ближа́йшем бу́дущем.
futuristic [fju:tʃə'rɪstɪk] *adj* футуристи́ческий.
fuze [fju:z] (*US*) = **fuse**.
fuzz [fʌz] *n* (*inf: police*): **the ~** менты́ *mpl*.
fuzzy ['fʌzɪ] *adj* (*thoughts, also PHOT*)
расплы́вчатый (расплы́вчат); (*hair*)
кудря́вый (кудря́в).
fwd. *abbr* = **forward**.
f-word ['ɛfwə:d] *n*: **the ~** ≈ сло́во на́ три
бу́квы.
fwy *abbr* (*US*) = **freeway**.
FY *abbr* = **fiscal year**.
FYI *abbr* (= *for your information*) к Ва́шему
све́дению.

~ *G, g* ~

G, g [dʒi:] *n* (*letter*) 7-áя бýква англи́йского алфави́та.

G [dʒi:] *n* (*MUS*) соль *nt ind*.

G *n abbr* (*BRIT: SCOL*) = **good**; (*US: CINEMA*: = **general (audience)**) фильм, приго́дный для пока́за всем возрастны́м гру́ппам; (*PHYS*): **G-force** си́ла тя́жести.

g. *abbr* (= **gram**) г= *грамм*; (*PHYS*) = **gravity**.

G7 *n abbr* (*POL*: = **Group of Seven**) „больша́я семёрка".

GA *n abbr* (*US: POST*) = **Georgia**.

gab [gæb] *n* (*inf*): **he has the gift of the** ~ у него́ хорошо́ подве́шен язы́к.

gabble ['gæbl] *vi* тарато́рить (протарато́рить (*perf*)).

gaberdine [gæbə'di:n] *n* сукно́*, габарди́н.

gable ['geɪbl] *n* фронто́н.

Gabon [gə'bɔn] *n* Габо́н.

gad about [gæd-] *vi* (*inf*) болта́ться (*impf*) без де́ла.

gadget ['gædʒɪt] *n* приспособле́ние.

gadgetry ['gædʒɪtrɪ] *n* приспособле́ния *ntpl*.

Gaelic ['geɪlɪk] *adj* гэ́льский ♦ *n* (*LING*) гэ́льский язы́к*.

gaff [gæf] *n* (*NAUT*) га́фель *m*; (*inf: nonsense*): **he made a real** ~ он тако́е ля́пнул.

gaffe [gæf] *n* опло́шность *f*.

gaffer ['gæfəʳ] (*inf*) *n* (*supervisor*) старшо́й *m adj*; (*fellow*) стари́к*.

gag [gæg] *n* (*on mouth*) кляп; (*joke*) хо́хма ♦ *vt* вставля́ть (вста́вить* *perf*) кляп +*dat*, завя́зывать (завяза́ть* *perf*) рот +*dat*; (*fig*) затыка́ть (заткну́ть *perf*) рот +*dat* ♦ *vi*: **the smell made him** ~ у него́ го́рло перехвати́ло от за́паха.

gaga ['ɡɑːɡɑː] *adj*: **he is** ~ у него́ не все до́ма.

gage [geɪdʒ] *n*, *vt* (*US*) = **gauge**.

gaiety ['geɪɪtɪ] *n* весе́лье.

gaily ['geɪlɪ] *adv* ве́село; (*coloured*) я́рко.

gain [geɪn] *n* (*increase*) увеличе́ние; (*profit*) при́быль *f* ♦ *vt* (*confidence, experience*) приобрета́ть (приобрести́* *perf*); (*speed*) набира́ть (набра́ть* *perf*) ♦ *vi* (*clock, watch*) спеши́ть (*impf*); (*benefit*): **to** ~ **from sth** извлека́ть (извле́чь* *perf*) по́льзу из чего́-н; **to do sth for** ~ де́лать (сде́лать *perf*) что-н

ра́ди вы́годы; **what will you** ~ **by that?** чего́ Вы э́тим добьётесь?; **to** ~ **ground** получа́ть (получи́ть *perf*) большо́е распростране́ние; **to** ~ **3 pounds (in weight)** попра́виться (*perf*) на 3 фу́нта; **to** ~ **on sb** догоня́ть (догна́ть* *perf*) кого́-н.

gainful ['geɪnful] *adj* (*employment*) вы́годный* (вы́годен).

gainfully ['geɪnfəlɪ-] *adv*: ~ **employed** по опла́чиваемой рабо́те.

gainsay [geɪn'seɪ] (*irreg: like* **say**) *vt* отрица́ть (*impf*).

gait [geɪt] *n* по́ступь *f*; **to walk with a slow/ confident** ~ идти́* (*impf*) ме́дленной/ уве́ренной по́ступью.

gala ['ɡɑːlə] *n* (*festival*) пра́зднество; **swimming** ~ пра́здник на воде́.

Galapagos Islands [gə'læpəgəs-] *npl*: **the** ~ ~ Галапаго́сские острова́* *mpl*.

galaxy ['gæləksɪ] *n* гала́ктика.

gale [geɪl] *n* (*wind*) си́льный ве́тер*; ~ **force ten** поры́вы ве́тра в де́сять ба́ллов.

gall [gɔ:l] *n* (*ANAT*) жёлчь *f*; (*fig: impudence*) на́глость *f* ♦ *vt* раздража́ть (*impf*).

gall. *abbr* = **gallon**.

gallant ['gælənt] *adj* (*brave*) до́блестный*; (*chivalrous*) гала́нтный*.

gallantry ['gæləntrɪ] *n* (*see adj*) до́блесть *f*; гала́нтность *f*.

gall bladder *n* жёлчный пузы́рь* *m*.

galleon ['gælɪən] *n* галео́н.

gallery ['gælərɪ] *n* (*also: art* ~) галере́я; (*in hall, church, theatre*) балко́н.

galley ['gælɪ] *n* (*ship's kitchen*) ка́мбуз; (*ship*) гале́ра; (*PUBLISHING: also:* ~ **proof**) гра́нка*.

Gallic ['gælɪk] *adj* га́лльский.

galling ['gɔːlɪŋ] *adj* раздража́ющий.

gallon ['gæln] *n* галло́н (*4.5 ли́тра*).

gallop ['gæləp] *n* гало́п ♦ *vi* (*horse*) скака́ть (*impf*) (гало́пом), галопи́ровать (*impf*); (*person*) носи́ться*/нести́сь* (*impf*); ~**ing inflation** галопи́рующая инфля́ция.

gallows ['gæləuz] *n* ви́селица.

gallstone ['gɔ:lstəun] *n* жёлчный ка́мень* *m*.

Gallup Poll ['gæləp-] *n* опро́с Гэ́лопа.

---

* marks translations which have irregular inflections The Russian-English side of the dictionary gives inflectional information

galore [gə'lɔː'] *adv* в изоби́лии.
galvanize ['gælvənaɪz] *vt* (*person*) возбужда́ть (возбуди́ть* *perf*); (*support*) обеспе́чивать (обеспе́чить *perf*); **to ~ sb into action** побужда́ть (побуди́ть* *perf*) кого́-н к де́йствию.
Gambia ['gæmbɪə] *n* Га́мбия.
gambit ['gæmbɪt] *n* (*fig*): (**opening**) ~ пе́рвый ход.
gamble ['gæmbl] *n* риск, риско́ванное предприя́тие ♦ *vt* (*money*) ста́вить* (поста́вить* *perf*) ♦ *vi* (*take a risk*) рискова́ть (рискну́ть *perf*); (*bet*) игра́ть (*impf*) в аза́ртные и́гры; **to ~ on the Stock Exchange** игра́ть (*impf*) на би́рже; **to ~ on sth** (*also fig*) де́лать (сде́лать *perf*) ста́вку на что-н.
gambler ['gæmblə'] *n* игро́к*.
gambling ['gæmblɪŋ] *n* аза́ртные и́гры *fpl*.
gambol ['gæmbl] *vi* резви́ться* (*impf*).
game [geɪm] *n* игра́*; (*match*) матч; (*esp TENNIS*) гейм; (*also*: **board ~**) насто́льная игра́; (*CULIN, HUNTING*) дичь *f* ♦ *adj* (*willing*): ~ (**for**) гото́вый (гото́в) (на +*acc*); **~s** *npl* (*SCOL*) спорти́вные и́гры *fpl*; **a ~ of football/tennis** футбо́льный/те́ннисный матч; **a ~ of chess** ша́хматная па́ртия; **big ~** (*lions, tigers etc*) кру́пный зверь.
game bird *n* перна́тая дичь *f*.
gamekeeper ['geɪmkiːpə'] *n* е́герь *m*.
gamely ['geɪmlɪ] *adv* хра́бро.
game reserve *n* охо́тничий* запове́дник.
games console ['geɪmz-] *n панель управления компьютерными играми.*
gamesmanship ['geɪmzmənʃɪp] *n* трюка́чество.
gaming ['geɪmɪŋ] *n* аза́ртные и́гры *fpl*.
gammon ['gæmən] *n* (*bacon*) о́корок*; (*ham*) ветчина́.
gamut ['gæmət] *n* (*range*) га́мма; **to run the ~ of emotions** пережива́ть (пережи́ть* *perf*) це́лую га́мму эмо́ций.
gander ['gændə'] *n* гусь* *m*.
gang [gæŋ] *n* ба́нда; (*of friends*) компа́ния; (*of workmen*) кома́нда
▸ **gang up** *vi*: **to ~ up on sb** ополча́ться (ополчи́ться *perf*) на *or* про́тив кого́-н.
Ganges ['gændʒiːz] *n*: **the ~** Ганг.
gangland ['gæŋlænd] *adj* (*boss, killers*) мафио́зный.
gangling ['gæŋglɪŋ] *adj* долговя́зый (долговя́з).
gangly ['gæŋglɪ] (*inf*) *adj* = **gangling**.
gangplank ['gæŋplæŋk] *n* трап.
gangrene ['gæŋgriːn] *n* гангре́на.
gangster ['gæŋstə'] *n* га́нгстер.
gangway ['gæŋweɪ] *n* (*from ship*) трап; (*BRIT: in cinema, bus etc*) прохо́д.
gantry ['gæntrɪ] *n* (*for crane*) порта́л; (*for railway signal*) сигна́льный мо́стик; (*for rocket*) раке́тная устано́вка.
GAO *n abbr* (*US*: = *General Accounting Office*)

Центра́льное фина́нсово-контро́льное управле́ние.
gaol *etc* [dʒeɪl] (*BRIT*) = **jail** *etc*.
gap [gæp] *n* (*space*) промежу́ток*; (: *between teeth*) щербина; (: *in time*) интерва́л; (: *in market, records etc*) пробе́л; (*difference*) расхожде́ния *ntpl*; **generation ~** разногла́сия ме́жду поколе́ниями.
gape [geɪp] *vi* (*person*) рази́нуть (*perf*) рот от удивле́ния; (*hole*) зия́ть (*perf*); (*shirt*) распа́хиваться (распахну́ться *perf*).
gaping ['geɪpɪŋ] *adj* (*hole*) зия́ющий; (*shirt*) распа́хнутый (распа́хнут).
garage ['gærɑːʒ] *n* гара́ж; (*petrol station*) запра́вочная ста́нция, бензоколо́нка*.
garb [gɑːb] *n* оде́жда.
garbage ['gɑːbɪdʒ] *n* (*US: rubbish*) му́сор*; (*inf: nonsense*) ерунда́; (*fig: film, book*) дрянь *f*.
garbage can *n* (*US*) помо́йный я́щик.
garbage collector *n* (*US*) му́сорщик.
garbage disposal (unit) *n* (*US*) мусоро-прово́д.
garbage truck *n* (*US*) мусороубо́рочная маши́на.
garbled ['gɑːbld] *adj* (*account, message*) запу́танный* (запу́тан).
garden ['gɑːdn] *n* сад ♦ *vi* занима́ться (заня́ться* *perf*) садово́дством; **~s** *npl* (*park*) парк *msg*; (*in street names*): **Rose G~s** Ро́уз Га́рденз; **she was busy ~ing** она́ рабо́тала в саду́.
garden centre *n* магази́н садо́вых принадле́жностей.
garden city *n* го́род*-сад*, зелёный го́род*.
gardener ['gɑːdnə'] *n* садово́д; (*employee*) садо́вник(-ица).
gardening ['gɑːdnɪŋ] *n* садово́дство.
gargle ['gɑːgl] *vi* полоска́ть* (прополоска́ть* *perf*) го́рло ♦ *n* полоска́ние.
gargoyle ['gɑːgɔɪl] *n* (*ARCHIT*) химе́ра.
garish ['gɛərɪʃ] *adj* (*light*) ре́жущий глаз; (*dress, colour*) крича́щий.
garland ['gɑːlənd] *n* гирля́нда.
garlic ['gɑːlɪk] *n* чесно́к*.
garment ['gɑːmənt] *n* (*dress etc*) предме́т оде́жды.
garner ['gɑːnə'] *vt* добыва́ть (добы́ть* *perf*).
garnish ['gɑːnɪʃ] *vt* украша́ть (укра́сить* *perf*).
garret ['gærɪt] *n* камо́рка*.
garrison ['gærɪsn] *n* гарнизо́н.
garrulous ['gærjuləs] *adj* болтли́вый, говорли́вый.
garter ['gɑːtə'] *n* подвя́зка*.
garter belt *n* (*US*) по́яс* (*с подвя́зками*).
gas [gæs] *n* газ*; (*US: gasoline*) бензи́н*; (*as anaesthetic*) ингаляцио́нный анесте́тик ♦ *vt* (*kill*) удуша́ть (удуши́ть *perf*) га́зом; (*MIL*) отравля́ть (отрави́ть* *perf*) га́зом.
gas cooker *n* (*BRIT*) га́зовая плита́*.
gas cylinder *n* га́зовый балло́н.
gaseous ['gæsɪəs] *adj* газообра́зный.

gas fire n (BRIT) газовый камин.
gas-fired ['gæsfaɪəd] adj газовый, работающий на газе.
gash [gæʃ] n (wound) глубокая рана; (cut, slash) глубокий порез ♦ vt (person) наносить* (нанести* perf) глубокую рану +dat; (object) распарывать (распороть perf); наносить* (нанести* perf) глубокий порез +dat.
gasket ['gæskɪt] n (AUT) прокладка*.
gas mask n противогаз.
gas meter n газовый счётчик.
gasoline ['gæsəliːn] n (US) бензин*.
gasp [gɑːsp] n (breath) вдох ♦ vi (pant) тяжело дышать* (impf); (in surprise) издавать* (издать* perf) вздох; I am ~ing for a smoke я умираю от желания курить
▶ **gasp out** vt выпаливать (выпалить perf).
gas ring n конфорка*.
gas station n (US) заправочная станция, бензоколонка*.
gas stove n (cooker) газовая плита*.
gassy ['gæsɪ] adj (beer etc) газированный* (газирован).
gas tank n бензобак.
gastric ['gæstrɪk] adj желудочный.
gastric ulcer n язва желудка.
gastroenteritis ['gæstrəuentə'raɪtɪs] n гастроэнтерит.
gastronomy [gæs'trɒnəmɪ] n кулинарное искусство.
gasworks ['gæswɜːks] n газовый завод.
gate [geɪt] n (single) калитка*; (double) ворота mpl; (at airport) выход; (of lock, level crossing etc) шлагбаум.
gateau ['gætəu] (pl ~x) n торт.
gateaux ['gætəuz] npl of **gateau**.
gate-crash ['geɪtkræʃ] vt (BRIT) to ~ a party приходить* (прийти* perf) на вечеринку без приглашения.
gate-crasher ['geɪtkræʃə'] n (to party) незваный гость m.
gatehouse ['geɪthaus] n сторожка* у ворот.
gateway ['geɪtweɪ] n (also fig) ворота mpl.
gather ['gæðə'] vt собирать (собрать* perf); (understand) полагать (impf); (SEWING) собирать (собрать* perf) в складки ♦ vi собираться (собраться* perf); (clouds) скапливаться (скопиться* perf); (dust) собираться (собраться* perf), оседать (осесть* perf); to ~ from sb выяснять (выяснить perf) у кого-н; I ~ that ... я полагаю, что ...; as far as I can ~ насколько я понимаю; to ~ speed набирать (набрать* perf) скорость.
gathering ['gæðərɪŋ] n собрание.
GATT [gæt] n abbr (= General Agreement on Tariffs and Trade) ГАТТ (Генеральное

соглашение по тарифам и торговле).
gauche [gəuʃ] adj неловкий*.
gaudy ['gɔːdɪ] adj пёстрый*.
gauge [geɪdʒ] n (instrument) измерительный прибор; (RAIL) ширина колеи ♦ vt (amount, quantity) измерять (измерить perf); (fig: feelings, character etc) оценивать (оценить* perf), получать (получить* perf) представление о +prp; **petrol** ~, **fuel** ~, (US) **gas** ~ указатель m уровня бензина; **to** ~ **the right moment** выбирать (выбрать* perf) подходящий момент.
Gaul [gɔːl] n (country) Галлия; (person) галл.
gaunt [gɔːnt] adj (haggard) изможденный* (изможден); (bare, stark) угрюмый* (угрюм).
gauntlet ['gɔːntlɪt] n перчатка*; (fig): **to run the** ~ подвергаться (подвергнуться perf) нападкам; **to throw down the** ~ бросать (бросить* perf) перчатку.
gauze [gɔːz] n (fabric) марля.
gave [geɪv] pt of **give**.
gavel ['gævl] n молоток (председателя собрания, судьи или аукциониста).
gawk [gɔːk] vi (inf): **to** ~ **at** таращить (вытаращить perf) глаза на +acc.
gawky ['gɔːkɪ] adj неотёсанный* (неотёсан).
gawp [gɔːp] vi: **to** ~ **at** таращить (вытаращить perf) глаза на +acc.
gay [geɪ] adj (cheerful) весёлый* (весел); (homosexual): **he is** ~ он голубой or гомосексуалист; ~ **bar** бар гомосексуалистов or голубых.
gaze [geɪz] n (look, stare) (пристальный) взгляд ♦ vi: **to** ~ **at sth** глядеть* (impf) на что-н.
gazelle [gə'zɛl] n газель f.
gazette [gə'zɛt] n (newspaper) газета; (official publication) орган.
gazetteer [gæzə'tɪə'] n географический справочник.
gazumping [gə'zʌmpɪŋ] n (BRIT: pej) увеличение цены дома в последний момент.
gazundering [gə'zʌndərɪŋ] n (BRIT: pej) понижение предложенной цены на покупку дома до подписания контракта.
GB abbr = **Great Britain**.
GBH n abbr (BRIT: LAW: = grievous bodily harm) тяжёлые телесные повреждения ntpl.
GC n abbr (BRIT: = George Cross) ≈ Георгиевский крест.
GCE n abbr (BRIT: = General Certificate of Education) ≈ аттестат о среднем образовании.
GCHQ n abbr (BRIT: = Government Communications Headquarters) Главный штаб служб правительственной связи.
GCSE n abbr (BRIT: = General Certificate of

---

* marks translations which have irregular inflections. The Russian-English side of the dictionary gives inflectional information.

Secondary Education) ≈ аттеста́т о сре́днем образова́нии.

Gdansk [gdænsk] *n* Гда́ньск.

Gdns. *abbr* (*in street names*) = **Gardens.**

GDP *n abbr* (= **gross domestic product**) ВВП= *валово́й вну́тренний проду́кт.*

GDR *n abbr* (*formerly*: = **German Democratic Republic**) ГДР= *Герма́нская Демократи́ческая Респу́блика.*

gear [gɪə'] *n* (*equipment, belongings etc*) принадле́жности *fpl*; (*for hunting*) снаряже́ние; (*for fishing*) сна́сти *fpl*; (*TECH*) зубча́тое колесо́; (*AUT*) ско́рость *f* ♦ *vt* (*fig*): **to ~ sth to** приспоса́бливать (приспосо́бить' *perf*) что-н к +*dat*; **top** *or* (*US*) **high/low/bottom ~** вы́сшая/ни́зкая/са́мая ма́лая переда́ча *or* ско́рость; **in ~** на переда́че *or* ско́рости, включённый (включён); **out of ~** не на переда́че *or* ско́рости, невключённый (невключён); **our service is ~ed to meet the needs of the disabled** на́ши услу́ги напра́влены на удовлетворе́ние потре́бностей инвали́дов

▶ **gear up** *vi*: **to ~ up (to do)** гото́виться' (пригото́виться' *or* подгото́виться' *perf*) (+*infin*) ♦ *vt*: **to ~ o.s. up (to do)** гото́вить' (пригото́вить' *or* подгото́вить' *perf*) себя́ (+*infin*).

gearbox ['gɪəbɔks] *n* коро́бка' переда́ч *or* скоросте́й.

gear lever (*US* **gear shift**) *n* переключа́тель *m* скоросте́й.

GED *n abbr* (*US: SCOL*) = **general educational development.**

geek [gi:k] *n* (*inf*) приду́рок'.

geese [gi:s] *npl of* **goose.**

geezer ['gi:zə'] *n* (*inf*) чува́к.

Geiger counter ['gaɪgə-] *n* счётчик Ге́йгера (*для измере́ния радиоакти́вности*).

gel [dʒɛl] *n* (*also CHEM*) гель *m*.

gelatin(e) ['dʒɛləti:n] *n* желати́н'.

gelignite ['dʒɛlɪgnaɪt] *n* гелигни́т.

gem [dʒɛm] *n* (*stone*) драгоце́нный ка́мень *m*, самоцве́т; (*fig*) сокро́вище.

Gemini ['dʒɛmɪnaɪ] *n* Близнецы́ *mpl*; **he is ~** он – Близне́ц.

gen [dʒɛn] *n* (*BRIT: inf*): **to give sb the ~ on sth** опи́сывать (описа́ть' *perf*) кому́-н что-н в о́бщих черта́х.

Gen. *abbr* (*MIL*) = **general.**

gen. *abbr* = **general, generally.**

gender ['dʒɛndə'] *n* (*sex*) пол; (*LING*) род.

gene [dʒi:n] *n* ген.

genealogy [dʒi:nɪ'ælədʒɪ] *n* генеало́гия.

general ['dʒɛnərl] *n* (*MIL*) генера́л ♦ *adj* о́бщий'; (*widespread: movement, interest*) всео́бщий'; **in ~** в о́бщем; **the ~ public** широ́кая пу́блика; **~ audit** (*COMM*) аудито́рская прове́рка.

general anaesthetic *n* о́бщий' нарко́з.

general delivery *n* (*US*) по́чта „до

востре́бования".

general election *n* всео́бщие вы́боры *mpl*.

generalization ['dʒɛnrəlaɪ'zeɪʃən] *n* обобще́ние.

generalize ['dʒɛnrəlaɪz] *vi* обобща́ть (обобщи́ть *perf*).

generally ['dʒɛnrəlɪ] *adv* вообще́; (+*vb*) обы́чно; **it is ~ accepted that ...** обы́чно счита́ется, что ...; **to become ~ available** станови́ться' (стать' *perf*) обще-досту́пным(-ой).

general manager *n* гла́вный управля́ющий' *m adj*.

general practitioner *n* врач о́бщей пра́ктики.

general strike *n* всео́бщая забасто́вка'.

generate ['dʒɛnəreɪt] *vt* (*power, electricity*) производи́ть' (произвести́' *perf*); (*excitement, interest*) вызыва́ть (вы́звать' *perf*); (*jobs*) создава́ть' (созда́ть' *perf*).

generation [dʒɛnə'reɪʃən] *n* поколе́ние; (*of electricity etc*) генери́рование; **for ~s** из поколе́ния в поколе́ние.

generator ['dʒɛnəreɪtə'] *n* генера́тор.

generic [dʒɪ'nɛrɪk] *adj* о́бщий'.

generosity [dʒɛnə'rɔsɪtɪ] *n* ще́дрость *f*; (*of spirit*) великоду́шие.

generous ['dʒɛnərəs] *adj* (*person: lavish*) ще́дрый (щедр); (: *unselfish*) великоду́шный' (великоду́шен); (*amount of money*) изря́дный.

genesis ['dʒɛnɪsɪs] *n* ге́незис, исто́ки *mpl*; **the ~ of an idea** возникнове́ние иде́и.

genetic [dʒɪ'nɛtɪk] *adj* генети́ческий', ге́нный.

genetically modified [dʒɪ'nɛtɪkəlɪ'mɔdɪfaɪd] *adj* генети́чески модифици́рованный, трансге́нный.

genetic engineering *n* ге́нная инжене́рия.

genetic fingerprinting [-'fɪŋgəprɪntɪŋ] *n* установле́ние ли́чности челове́ка по его́ генети́ческим осо́бенностям (*по ДНК*).

genetics [dʒɪ'nɛtɪks] *n* гене́тика.

Geneva [dʒɪ'ni:və] *n* Жене́ва.

genial ['dʒi:nɪəl] *adj* (*smile, expression etc*) приве́тливый; (*host*) раду́шный'; (*climate*) мя́гкий'.

genitals ['dʒɛnɪtlz] *npl* половы́е о́рганы *mpl*.

genitive ['dʒɛnɪtɪv] *n* роди́тельный паде́ж'.

genius ['dʒi:nɪəs] *n* тала́нт; (*person*) ге́ний.

Genoa ['dʒɛnəuə] *n* Ге́нуя.

genocide ['dʒɛnəusaɪd] *n* геноци́д.

Genoese [dʒɛnəu'i:z] *adj* генуэ́зский ♦ *n inv* генуэ́зец'(-зка').

gent [dʒɛnt] *n abbr* (*BRIT: inf*) = **gentleman.**

genteel [dʒɛn'ti:l] *adj* (*family*) благоро́дный', благоро́дного происхожде́ния; (*person*) све́тский'.

gentle ['dʒɛntl] *adj* не́жный' (не́жен); (*movement, breeze, landscape, nature*) мя́гкий' (мя́гок); **a ~ hint** то́нкий' намёк.

gentleman ['dʒɛntlmən] *irreg n* (*man*) джентльме́н; (*referring to social position*) дворяни́н*; ~'s **agreement** джентльме́нское соглаше́ние.

gentlemanly ['dʒɛntlmənlɪ] *adj* джентльме́нский.

gentleness ['dʒɛntlnɪs] *n* (*see adj*) не́жность *f*; мя́гкость *f*.

gently ['dʒɛntlɪ] *adv* (*smile, treat*) не́жно; (*curve, slope, move*) мя́гко; (*speak*) ла́сково.

gentry ['dʒɛntrɪ] *n inv*: **the** ~ дворя́нство.

gents [dʒɛnts] *n*: **the** ~ мужска́я убо́рная *f adj*.

genuine ['dʒɛnjuɪn] *adj* (*person, feeling*) и́скренний*; (*painting etc*) по́длинный*.

genuinely ['dʒɛnjuɪnlɪ] *adv* (*sincerely*) и́скренне; (*truly*) по-настоя́щему.

geographer [dʒɪ'ɔgrəfə˞] *n* гео́граф.

geographic(al) [dʒɪə'græfɪk(l)] *adj* географи́ческий.

geography [dʒɪ'ɔgrəfɪ] *n* геогра́фия.

geological [dʒɪə'lɔdʒɪkl] *adj* геологи́ческий.

geologist [dʒɪ'ɔlədʒɪst] *n* гео́лог.

geology [dʒɪ'ɔlədʒɪ] *n* геоло́гия.

geometric(al) [dʒɪə'mɛtrɪk(l)] *adj* геометри́ческий.

geometry [dʒɪ'ɔmɪtrɪ] *n* геоме́трия.

Geordie ['dʒɔːdɪ] *n* (*GEO: inf*) *урожéнец гóрода Нюкасл в Англии.*

Georgia ['dʒɔːdʒə] *n* Гру́зия.

Georgian ['dʒɔːdʒən] *adj* грузи́нский* ◆ *n* грузи́н(ка*); (*LING*) грузи́нский* язы́к*.

geranium [dʒɪ'reɪnɪəm] *n* гера́нь *f*.

geriatric [dʒɛrɪ'ætrɪk] *adj* гериатри́ческий ◆ *n* дря́хлый стари́к.

germ [dʒɜːm] *n* (*MED*) микро́б; (*BOT, fig*) зача́ток; **the** ~ **of an idea** заро́дыш иде́и.

German ['dʒɜːmən] *adj* неме́цкий* ◆ *n* неме́ц*(-мка*); (*LING*) неме́цкий* язы́к*.

German Democratic Republic *n* (*formerly*) Герма́нская Демократи́ческая Респу́блика.

germane [dʒɜː'meɪn] *adj*: ~ **to** релева́нтный для +*gen*.

German measles *n* (*BRIT*) красну́ха.

Germany ['dʒɜːmənɪ] *n* Герма́ния.

germinate ['dʒɜːmɪneɪt] *vi* (*BOT*) прораста́ть (прорасти́* *perf*); (*fig*) дава́ть (дать* *perf*) ростки́.

germination [dʒɜːmɪ'neɪʃən] *n* (*BOT*) прораста́ние.

germ warfare *n* бактериологи́ческая война́.

gerrymandering ['dʒɛrɪmændərɪŋ] *n изменéние грани́ц избирáтельных округóв с цéлью дать преиму́щество определённой полити́ческой пáртии.*

gestation [dʒɛs'teɪʃən] *n* созрева́ние плода́.

gesticulate [dʒɛs'tɪkjuleɪt] *vi* жестикули́ровать (*impf*).

gesture ['dʒɛstjə˞] *n* (*movement, token*) жест; **as a** ~ **of friendship** в знак дру́жбы.

KEYWORD

get [gɛt] (*pt, pp* **got**; *US*) (*pp* **gotten**) *vi* **1** (*become, be*): **it's getting late** стано́вится* (*impf*) по́здно; **to get old** старе́ть (постаре́ть *perf*); **to get tired** устава́ть* (уста́ть* *perf*); **to get cold** мёрзнуть (замёрзнуть *perf*); **to get annoyed easily** ча́сто раздража́ться (*impf*); **he was getting bored** ему́ ста́ло ску́чно; **he gets drunk quickly** он бы́стро пьяне́ет; **he gets drunk every weekend** он напива́ется ка́ждый выходно́й; **he got killed** его́ уби́ли; **when do I get paid?** когда́ мне запла́тят?

2 (*go*): **to get to/from** добира́ться (добра́ться* *perf*) до +*gen*/от +*gen*; **to get home** приходи́ть* (прийти́* *perf*) домо́й; **how did you get here/there?** как Вы сюда́/туда́ добра́лись?

3 (*begin*): **to get to know sb** (*become acquainted*) познако́миться* (*perf*) с кем-н; **to get to know sb well** бли́зко познако́миться* (*perf*) с кем-н; **I'm getting to like him** он начина́ет мне нра́виться; **let's get started** дава́йте начнём

◆ *modal aux vb*: **you've got to do it** Вы должны́ это сде́лать (*perf*)

◆ *vt*: **1**: **to get sth done** сде́лать (*perf*) что-н; **to get the washing done** постира́ть (*perf*); **to get the dishes done** помы́ть* (*perf*) *or* вы́мыть (*perf*) посу́ду; **to get the car started** *or* **to start** завести́* (*perf*) маши́ну; **to get sb to do** заставля́ть (заста́вить* *perf*) кого́-н +*infin*; **to get sb ready** собра́ть* (*perf*) кого́-н; **to get sth ready** пригото́вить* (*perf*) что-н; **to get sb drunk** напои́ть* (*perf*) кого́-н; **she got me into trouble** я влип с ней в неприя́тности

2 (*obtain: permission, results*) получа́ть (получи́ть* *perf*); (: *money*) достава́ть* (доста́ть* *perf*); (*find: job, flat*) находи́ть* (найти́* *perf*); (*person: call*) звать* (позва́ть* *perf*); (: *pick up*) забира́ть (забра́ть* *perf*); (*call out: doctor, plumber etc*) вызыва́ть (вы́звать* *perf*); (*object: carry*) приноси́ть* (принести́* *perf*); (: *buy*) покупа́ть (купи́ть* *perf*); **I'll get the car** я схожу́ за маши́ной; **can I get you something to drink?** что Вам мо́жно предложи́ть (*perf*)

3 (*receive*) получа́ть (получи́ть* *perf*); **to get a reputation for sth** зарабо́тать (*perf*) дурну́ю репута́цию чем-н; **what did you get for your birthday?** что Вам подари́ли на день рожде́ния?

4 (*grab*) хвата́ть (схвати́ть* *perf*); (*hit*): **the bullet got him in the leg** пу́ля попа́ла ему́ в но́гу; **I'll get you there somehow** я Вас как-нибудь туда́ доста́влю; **do you think we'll get the piano through the door?** как Вы ду́маете, пиани́но пройдёт че́рез дверь?; **we must get him to hospital** мы должны́ отвезти́

---

* marks translations which have irregular inflections. The Russian-English side of the dictionary gives inflectional information.

его в больницу; **I'll get the book to you
tomorrow** за́втра кни́га бу́дет у Вас
5 (*catch, take*): **we got a taxi** мы взя́ли такси́;
did she get her plane? она́ успе́ла на
самолёт?; **what train are you getting?** каки́м
по́ездом Вы е́дете?; **where do I get the train?**
где мне сади́ться на по́езд?
6 (*understand*) понима́ть (поня́ть* *perf*);
(*hear*) расслы́шать (*perf*); (**do you) get it?** (*inf*)
поня́тно?; **I've got it!** тепе́рь поня́тно!; **I'm
sorry, I didn't get your name** прости́те, я не
расслы́шал Ва́ше и́мя
7 (*have, possess*): **how many children have you
got?** ско́лько у Вас дете́й?; **I've got very little
time** у меня́ о́чень ма́ло вре́мени
► **get about** *vi* (*after illness*) ходи́ть* (*impf*);
(*news*) распространя́ться (рас-
простани́ться *perf*); **I don't get about much
now** (*go to places*) тепе́рь я ма́ло где быва́ю
► **get across** *vt* (*subj: speaker*) объясня́ть
(объясни́ть *perf*); **it's important to get this
message across to them** ва́жно, что́бы они́
э́то по́няли
► **get along** *vi* (*agree*) ла́дить* (*impf*) с +*instr*;
(*manage*) = **get by**; **I'd better be getting along**
мне пора́
► **get around** *vt* = **get round**
► **get at** *vt fus* (*criticize*) придира́ться
(придра́ться* *perf*) к +*dat*; (*reach*)
дотя́гиваться (дотяну́ться* *perf*) до +*gen*;
what are you getting at? что Вы хоти́те э́тим
сказа́ть?
► **get away** *vi* (*leave*) уходи́ть (уйти́* *perf*); (*on
holiday*) уезжа́ть (уе́хать* *perf*); (*escape*)
убега́ть (*impf*)
► **get away with** *vt fus*: **he always gets away
with it** ему́ всё схо́дит с рук; **he'll never get
away with it!** э́то ему́ да́ром не пройдёт!
► **get back** *vi* (*return*) возвраща́ться
(верну́ться *perf*)
   ♦ *vt* (*book, car*) получа́ть (получи́ть* *perf*)
обра́тно *or* наза́д; **get back!** отойди́те!
► **get back at** *vt fus* (*inf*): **I'll get back at you (for
that)** ты у меня́ (за э́то) полу́чишь
► **to get back to** *vt fus* (*return to*) возвраща́ться
(возврати́ться *perf*) к +*dat*; (*contact again*)
свя́зываться (связа́ться* *perf*) с +*instr*; **to get back to sleep**
сно́ва засыпа́ть (засну́ть *perf*)
► **get by** *vi* (*pass: on foot*) проходи́ть (пройти́*
perf); (*manage*) = **to get by without**
обходи́ться (обойти́сь* *perf*) без +*gen*; **I can/
will get by** (*with little food, money*) мне
хвата́ет/хва́тит; **I can get by in Dutch** я могу́
объясни́ться по-голла́ндски
► **get down** *vi*: **to get down from** слеза́ть
(слезть* *perf*) с +*gen*
   ♦ *vt* (*depress*) де́йствовать* (*impf*)
угнета́юще; (*write*) запи́сывать (записа́ть*
perf); (*swallow*) впи́хивать (впихну́ть *perf*) в
себя́; **to get down on your hands and knees**
встава́ть (встать* *perf*) на четвере́ньки

► **get down to** *vt fus* (*work, business*) сади́ться*
(засе́сть* *perf*) *or* бра́ться* (взя́ться* *perf*) за +*acc*
► **get in** *vi* (*train*) прибыва́ть (прибы́ть* *perf*),
приходи́ть (прийти́* *perf*); (*arrive home: on
foot*) приходи́ть (прийти́* *perf*); (*by transport*)
приезжа́ть (прие́хать* *perf*); (*be elected*): **he
got in by ten votes** его́ избра́ли
большинство́м в де́сять голосо́в; **as soon as
the bus pulled up we all got in** как то́лько
авто́бус подошёл, мы се́ли в него́; **we
queued for a long time for the concert but
couldn't get in** мы до́лго стоя́ли в о́череди,
но так и не попа́ли на конце́рт
   ♦ *vt* (*harvest*) собира́ть (собра́ть* *perf*); (*coal,
supplies*) загота́вливать (загото́вить* *perf*);
(*shopping*) закупа́ть (закупи́ть* *perf*); (*into
conversation*) вставля́ть (вста́вить* *perf*)
► **get into** *vt fus* (*building*) входи́ть* (войти́*
perf) в +*acc*; (*subj: train*) прибыва́ть
(прибы́ть* *perf*) в/на +*acc*; (*vehicle*) сади́ться*
(сесть* *perf*) в +*acc*; (*clothes*) влеза́ть (влезть*
perf) в +*acc*; (*fight, argument*) вступа́ть
(вступи́ть* *perf*) в +*acc*; (*university, college*)
поступа́ть (поступи́ть* *perf*) в +*acc*; **to get into
bed** ложи́ться (лечь* *perf*) в посте́ль; **I can't
get into this skirt** э́та ю́бка не налеза́ет на
меня́; **she has got into the habit of going for a
walk before breakfast** у неё вошло́ в
привы́чку выходи́ть гуля́ть до за́втрака
► **get off** *vi* (*escape*): **to get off lightly/with sth**
отде́лываться (отде́латься *perf*) легко́/чем-н
   ♦ *vt* (*clothes*) снима́ть (снять* *perf*); (*stain*)
выводи́ть* (вы́вести* *perf*); (*letter etc*)
отправля́ть (отпра́вить* *perf*); (*day, time*): **we
got 2 days/2 weeks off last month** у нас бы́ло
два выходны́х дня/две свобо́дные неде́ли в
про́шлом ме́сяце
   ♦ *vt fus* (*train, bus*) сходи́ть* (сойти́* *perf*) с
+*gen*; (*horse, bicycle*) слеза́ть (слезть* *perf*) с
+*gen*; **to get off and walk** (*bicycle*) слеза́ть
(слезть* *perf*) и идти́* (пойти́* *perf*) пешко́м;
you should get off at the next station Вам
на́до сойти́ (*perf*) на сле́дующей ста́нции; **to
get off to a good/poor start** (*fig*) с бле́ском/
пло́хо начина́ть (нача́ть* *perf*); **I'd better be
getting off** (*departing*) мне пора́
► **get on** *vi* (*age*) старе́ть (*impf*); (*progress*): **how
are you getting on?** у тебя́ подвига́ется
де́ло?; **to get on (with)** (*agree*) ла́дить (*impf*)
(с +*instr*); (*manage*) справля́ться
(спра́виться* *perf*) (с +*instr*)
   ♦ *vt fus* (*train, bus*) сади́ться* (сесть* *perf*) в
+*acc*; (*horse, bicycle*) сади́ться* (сесть* *perf*) на
+*acc*; **time is getting on** вре́мя идёт
► **get on to** *vt fus* (*BRIT: from one subject to
another*) переходи́ть* (перейти́* *perf*) +*instr*;
(*person*) свя́зываться (связа́ться* *perf*) с
+*instr*; **how did we get on to this?** как мы к
э́тому пришли́
► **get out** *vi* (*leave: building, vehicle*) выходи́ть*
(вы́йти* *perf*); (*by transport*) выезжа́ть

(вы́ехать* *perf*); (: *city*) уезжа́ть (уе́хать* *perf*); (*socialize*) выбира́ться (вы́браться* *perf*) из до́ма

♦ *vt* (*stain*) выводи́ть* (вы́вести* *perf*); (*object*) достава́ть (доста́ть* *perf*); (*report*) публикова́ть* (опубликова́ть* *perf*); **get out!** убира́йся!; **the news got out that...** ста́ло изве́стно, что...; **the news got out in the end** но́вости разошли́сь в конце́ концо́в

▶ **get out of** *vt fus* (*duty etc*) отде́лываться (отде́латься *perf*) от +*gen*

♦ *vt* (*pleasure, satisfaction*) получа́ть (получи́ть* *perf*) от +*gen*; (*money*): **to get out (of)** (*from bank*) брать* (взять* *perf*) (в +*prp*); (*from account*) снима́ть (снять* *perf*) с +*gen*; **I couldn't get a word out of him** я не мог и сло́ва доби́ться от него́

▶ **get over** *vt fus* (*illness*) поправля́ться (попра́виться* *perf*)

♦ *vt*: **to get sth over with** зако́нчить (*perf*) что-н; **to get the message over that...** объясни́ть (*perf*), что...; **let's get it over with!** дава́йте поко́нчим с э́тим де́лом!

▶ **get round** *vt fus* (*law, rule*) обходи́ть* (обойти́* *perf*); (*fig: person*) добива́ться (доби́ться* *perf*) своего́ от +*gen*

▶ **get round to** *vt fus*: **to get round to doing** собира́ться (собра́ться* *perf*) +*infin*; **I'll get around to it some day** когда́-н я доберу́сь до э́того

▶ **get through** *vi* (*TEL*) дозвони́ться (*perf*)

♦ *vt fus* (*work, book*) зака́нчивать (зако́нчить *perf*)

▶ **get through to** *vt fus* (*TEL*) дозвони́ться (*perf*) до +*gen*

▶ **get together** *vi* (*several people*) собира́ться (собра́ться* *perf*); (*two people*) встреча́ться (встре́титься* *perf*)

♦ *vt* (*people*) собира́ть (собра́ть *perf*); (*project, plan etc*) составля́ть (соста́вить* *perf*)

▶ **get up** *vi* вставать* (встать* *perf*)

♦ *vt* (*person*) поднима́ть (подня́ть* *perf*); **I can't get up any enthusiasm for it** у меня́ не возника́ет энтузиа́зма на э́тот счёт

▶ **get up to** *vt fus* (*BRIT: prank etc*) занима́ться (заня́ться* *perf*) +*instr*; **they're always getting up to mischief** они́ всегда́ проказничают.

getaway ['gɛtəweɪ] *n*: **to make a** *or* **one's ~** бежа́ть (*impf*).

getaway car *n* маши́на, испо́льзованная при побе́ге.

get-together ['gɛttəgɛðə'] *n* (*meeting*) неофициа́льное собра́ние; (*party*) вечери́нка*.

get-up ['gɛtʌp] *n* (*inf*) наря́д.

get-well card [gɛt'wɛl-] *n* откры́тка* с

пожела́ниями выздоровле́ния.

geyser ['giːzə'] *n* ге́йзер; (*BRIT: water heater*) га́зовая коло́нка*.

Ghana ['gɑːnə] *n* Га́на.

Ghanaian [gɑː'neɪən] *adj* га́нский ♦ *n* жи́тель(ница) *m(f)* Га́ны.

ghastly ['gɑːstlɪ] *adj* (*horrible: person, situation*) ужа́сный* (ужа́сен), отврати́тельный* (отврати́телен); (: *building, appearance, behaviour*) безобра́зный* (безобра́зен); (*pale: complexion*) ме́ртвенно-бле́дный* (ме́ртвенно-бле́ден); (*ill*): **you look ~!** Вы ужа́сно вы́глядите!

gherkin ['gɜːkɪn] *n* ме́лкий огуре́ц для маринова́ния.

ghetto ['gɛtəʊ] *n* ге́тто *nt ind*.

ghetto blaster [-'blɑːstə'] *n* переносно́й радиомагнитофо́н.

ghost [gəʊst] *n* (*spirit*) привиде́ние, при́зрак ♦ *vt* явля́ться (яви́ться* *perf*) та́йным а́втором +*gen*; **to give up the ~** (*fig*) приказа́ть* (*perf*) до́лго жить.

ghost town *n* забро́шенный го́род.

ghostwriter ['gəʊstraɪtə'] *n* та́йный а́втор, писа́тель-неви́димка *m*.

ghoul [guːl] *n* (*ghost*) вурдала́к.

ghoulish ['guːlɪʃ] *adj* (*tastes etc*) ме́рзкий* (ме́рзок).

GHQ *n abbr* (*MIL*) = **general headquarters**.

GI *n abbr* (*US: inf*) = **government issue**.

giant ['dʒaɪənt] *n* (*in myths, stories*) велика́н; (*fig: large company etc*) гига́нт ♦ *adj* огро́мный.

giant killers *npl* кома́нда без и́мени, оде́рживающая побе́ды над кома́ндами мирово́го кла́сса.

gibber ['dʒɪbə'] *vi* говори́ть (проговори́ть *perf*) невня́тно.

gibberish ['dʒɪbərɪʃ] *n* тараба́рщина.

gibe [dʒaɪb] *n* насме́шка* ♦ *vi*: **to ~ at** смея́ться (*impf*) *or* издева́ться (*impf*) над +*instr*.

giblets ['dʒɪblɪts] *npl* (*of chicken etc*) потроха́* *mpl*.

Gibraltar [dʒɪ'brɔːltə'] *n* Гибралта́р.

giddiness ['gɪdɪnɪs] *n* головокруже́ние.

giddy ['gɪdɪ] *adj* (*height*) головокружи́тельный* (головокружи́телен); (*dizzy*): **I feel ~** у меня́ кру́жится голова́; **~ with success** опьянённый (опьянён) успе́хом.

gift [gɪft] *n* (*present*) пода́рок*; (*donation*) дар*; (*COMM: also*: **free ~**) беспла́тный пода́рок*; (*ability*) дар*, тала́нт; **to have a ~ for sth** облада́ть (*impf*) тала́нтом чего́-н.

gifted ['gɪftɪd] *adj* одарённый*.

gift token *n* пода́рочный купо́н.

gift voucher *n* = **gift token**.

gig [gɪg] *n* (*inf*: *concert*) конце́рт (*рок- или*

поп-группы).

gigabyte ['dʒɪgəbaɪt] *n единица измерения мощности памяти компьютера.*

gigantic [dʒaɪ'gæntɪk] *adj* гигантский*.

giggle ['gɪgl] *vi* хихикать *(impf)* ◆ *n*: **it was just a ~** I это был просто смех!; **to do sth for a ~** делать (сделать *perf*) что-н для смеха.

GIGO ['gaɪgəu] *abbr (COMPUT. inf. = garbage in, garbage out)* МЗМП= *мякину заложишь – мякину получишь.*

gild [gɪld] *vt* золотить* (позолотить* *perf*).

gill [dʒɪl] *n мера жидкости.*

gills [gɪlz] *npl (of fish)* жабры *fpl*.

gilt [gɪlt] *adj* позолоченный ◆ *n* позолота; **~s** *npl (COMM)* = **gilt-edged securities**.

gilt-edged ['gɪltedʒd] *adj*: **~** золотообразные ценные бумаги *fpl (o надёжных акциях)*.

gimlet ['gɪmlɪt] *n* буравчик.

gimmick ['gɪmɪk] *n (sales)* уловка; *(electoral)* трюк.

gin [dʒɪn] *n* джин *(можжевёловая водка)*.

ginger ['dʒɪndʒə'] *n (spice)* имбирь* *m* ◆ *adj (in colour)* рыжий*.

ginger ale *n* имбирный эль.

ginger beer *n* имбирное пиво.

gingerbread ['dʒɪndʒəbrɛd] *n (cake)* ≈ коврижка, имбирный пирог*; *(biscuit)* ≈ пряник, имбирное печенье*.

ginger group *n (BRIT)* группа членов организации, настаивающая на более решительных действиях.

ginger-haired ['dʒɪndʒə'hɛəd] *adj* рыжеволосый.

gingerly ['dʒɪndʒəlɪ] *adv* опасливо.

gingham ['gɪŋəm] *n хлопчатобумажная ткань в клетку.*

ginseng ['dʒɪnsɛŋ] *n женьшень* *m*.

gipsy ['dʒɪpsɪ] *n* цыган(ка*).

gipsy caravan *n* цыганская кибитка.

giraffe [dʒɪ'rɑːf] *n* жираф.

girder ['gə:də'] *n* металлическая балка*.

girdle ['gə:dl] *n (corset)* корсет ◆ *vt (encircle)* опоясывать (опоясать* *perf*).

girl [gə:l] *n (child)* девочка*; *(young unmarried woman)* девушка*; *(daughter)* дочка*; **this is my little ~** это моя дочка; **an English ~** англичанка*.

girlfriend ['gə:lfrɛnd] *n (of girl)* подруга; *(of boy)* девушка*, подруга.

Girl Guide *n* девочка*-скаут *f*.

girlish ['gə:lɪʃ] *adj* девичий*.

Girl Scout *n (US)* = **Girl Guide**.

Giro ['dʒaɪrəu] *n*: **the National ~** *(BRIT)* способ перевода денег через банк или по почте.

giro ['dʒaɪrəu] *n (bank giro)* перевод денег через банк; *(post office giro)* перевод денег через почту; *(BRIT: welfare cheque)* чек, по которому получают пособия по безработице.

girth [gə:θ] *n (circumference)* окружность *f*; *(of*

horse) подпруга.

gist [dʒɪst] *n (of speech, programme)* суть *f*.

KEYWORD

give [gɪv] *(pt* **gave**, *pp* **given**) *vt* **1** *(hand over)*: **to give sb sth** *or* **sth to sb** давать* (дать* *perf*) кому-н что-н; **they gave her a book for her birthday** они подарили ей книгу на день рождения

2 *(used with noun to replace a verb)*: **to give a sigh** вздохнуть *(perf)*; **to give a push** толкнуть *(perf)*; **to give a shrug** передёрнуть *(perf)* плечами; **to give a speech** выступать (выступить* *perf*) с речью; **to give a lecture** читать (прочитать* *perf*) лекцию; **to give three cheers** трижды кричать (прокричать* *perf*) „ура"

3 *(tell, deliver: news)* сообщать (сообщить* *perf*); *(advice)* давать* (дать* *perf*); **could you give him a message for me please? tell him that...** передайте ему, пожалуйста, от меня, что...; **I've got a message to give you from your brother** я тебе должен что-то передать от твоего брата; **let me give you some advice** разрешите мне дать Вам совет; **he gave me his new address over the phone** он дал мне свой новый адрес по телефону

4: **to give sb sth** *(clothing, food, right)* давать* (дать* *perf*) кому-н что-н; *(title)* присваивать (присвоить* *perf*) кому-н что-н; *(honour, responsibility)* возлагать (возложить* *perf*) на кого-н что-н; **to give sb a surprise** удивить* (*perf*) кого-н; **that's given me an idea** это навело меня на мысль

5 *(dedicate: one's life)* отдавать (отдать* *perf*); *(allow: time, attention)* уделять (уделить* *perf*); **you'll need to give me more time** Вы должны дать мне больше времени; **she gave it all her attention** она отнеслась к этому с большим вниманием

6 *(organize)*: **to give a party** устраивать (устроить* *perf*) вечер, приглашать (пригласить* *perf*) гостей; **to give a dinner** *etc* давать* (дать* *perf*) обед

◆ *vi* **1** *(stretch: fabric)* растягиваться (растянуться* *perf*)

2 *(break, collapse)* = **give way**

▶ **give away** *vt (money, object)* отдавать* (отдать* *perf*); *(betray: secret, information)* выдавать* (выдать* *perf*); (: *person*) выдавать* (выдать* *perf*); *(bride)* отдавать* *(impf)* замуж

▶ **give back** *vt* отдавать* (отдать* *perf*) обратно

▶ **give in** *vi (yield)* сдаваться* (сдаться* *perf*) ◆ *vt (essay etc)* сдавать* (сдать* *perf*)

▶ **give off** *vt fus (smoke)* дымить* *(impf)*; **the radiator/coal fire gives off a lot of heat** от батареи/камина идёт тепло

▶ **give out** *vt (distribute)* раздавать* (раздать* *perf*); *(make known)* объявлять (объявить*

perf)
♦ *vi* (*be exhausted*) конча́ться (ко́нчиться *perf*); (*fail*) лома́ться (слома́ться *perf*)
▶ **give up** *vi* (*stop trying*) сдава́ться* (сда́ться* *perf*)
♦ *vt* (*job, boyfriend, habit*) броса́ть (бро́сить* *perf*); (*idea, hope*) оставля́ть (оста́вить* *perf*); **to give up smoking** броса́ть (бро́сить* *perf*) кури́ть; **to give o.s. up** сдава́ться* (сда́ться* *perf*)
▶ **give way** *vi* (*rope, ladder etc*) не вы́держивать (вы́держать *perf*); (*wall, roof*) обва́ливаться (обвали́ться* *perf*); (*chair, floor*) прола́мываться (проломи́ться* *perf*); (*BRIT: AUT*) уступа́ть (уступи́ть* *perf*) доро́гу; **his legs gave way beneath him** его́ но́ги подогну́лись; **to give way (to)** (*to demands*) уступа́ть (уступи́ть* *perf*) +*dat*.

give-and-take ['gɪvənd'teɪk] *n* ги́бкость *f*, свобо́да.
giveaway ['gɪvəweɪ] (*inf*) *n*: **her expression was a ~** выраже́ние (её) лица́ вы́дало её ♦ *adj*: ~ **prices** даровы́е це́ны; **the exam was a ~!** экза́мен был ерундо́вый!
given ['gɪvn] *pp of* **give** ♦ *adj* да́нный ♦ *conj*: ~ **the circumstances ...** с учётом обстоя́тельств ..., учи́тывая обстоя́тельства ...; ~ **that** учи́тывая, что.
glacial ['gleɪsɪəl] *adj* (*also fig*) ледяно́й.
glacier ['glæsɪə'] *n* ледни́к*.
glad [glæd] *adj*: **I am ~** я рад; **I was ~ of his help** я был рад его́ по́мощи.
gladden ['glædn] *vt* (*heart*) ра́довать (пора́довать *perf*); (*person*) обра́довать (*perf*); **it ~ed his heart to see her well again** у него́ пора́довалось се́рдце, когда́ он уви́дел, что ей ста́ло лу́чше.
glade [gleɪd] *n* поля́на.
gladioli [glædɪ'əʊlaɪ] *npl* гладио́лусы *mpl*.
gladly ['glædlɪ] *adv* (*willingly*) с ра́достью.
glamorous ['glæmərəs] *adj* очарова́тельный* (очарова́телен).
glamour ['glæmə'] *n* очарова́ние.
glance [glɑːns] *n* (*look*) взгляд ♦ *vi*: **to ~ at** взгля́дывать (взгляну́ть* *perf*) на +*acc*
▶ **glance off** *vt fus* отска́кивать (отскочи́ть* *perf*) от +*gen*.
glancing ['glɑːnsɪŋ] *adj* (*blow*) боково́й.
gland [glænd] *n* железа́*.
glandular ['glændjulə'] *adj*: ~ **fever** (*BRIT*) (инфекцио́нный) мононуклео́з.
glare [glɛə'] *n* (*angry*) свире́пый взгляд; (*hostile*) вражде́бный взгляд; (*of light*) ослепи́тельное сия́ние ♦ *vi* (*light*) ослепи́тельно сия́ть (*impf*); **she lives in the full ~ of publicity** все подро́бности её жи́зни стано́вятся достоя́нием пре́ссы; **to ~ at**

свире́по *or* при́стально смотре́ть* (посмотре́ть* *perf*) на +*acc*.
glaring ['glɛərɪŋ] *adj* (*mistake*) я́вный, очеви́дный.
Glasgow ['glɑːzgəu] *n* Гла́зго *m ind*.
glasnost ['glæznɒst] *n* гла́сность *f*.
glass [glɑːs] *n* (*substance*) стекло́; (*container, contents*) стака́н; ~**es** *npl* (*spectacles*) очки́ *ntpl*.
glass-blowing ['glɑːsbləuɪŋ] *n* стеклоду́вное де́ло.
glass fibre *n* стекловолокно́.
glasshouse ['glɑːshaus] *n* тепли́ца, парни́к.
glassware ['glɑːswɛə'] *n* стекля́нная посу́да.
glassy ['glɑːsɪ] *adj* (*eyes, stare*) безжи́зненный* (безжи́зен).
Glaswegian [glæs'wiːdʒən] *adj* гла́зговский ♦ *n* жи́тель(ница) *m(f)* Гла́зго.
glaze [gleɪz] *vt* (*window*) застекля́ть (застекли́ть *perf*); (*pottery*) покрыва́ть (покры́ть* *perf*) глазу́рью ♦ *n* (*on pottery*) глазу́рь *f*.
glazed [gleɪzd] *adj* (*eyes*) му́тный*, ту́склый*; (*pottery*) покры́тый глазу́рью.
glazier ['gleɪzɪə'] *n* стеко́льщик.
gleam [gliːm] *vi* сия́ть (засия́ть *perf*) ♦ *n*: **a ~ of hope** луч* наде́жды.
gleaming ['gliːmɪŋ] *adj* сия́ющий*.
glean [gliːn] *vt* (*information*) добыва́ть (добы́ть* *perf*), собира́ть (собра́ть* *perf*).
glee [gliː] *n* (*joy*) ликова́ние.
gleeful ['gliːful] *adj* лику́ющий.
glen [glɛn] *n* (*SCOTTISH, IRISH*) доли́на реки́.
glib [glɪb] *adj* (*person*) болтли́вый (болтли́в); (*promise, response*) бо́йкий* (бо́ек).
glibly ['glɪblɪ] *adv* (*talk, answer*) бо́йко.
glide [glaɪd] *vi* скользи́ть* (*impf*); (*AVIAT*) плани́ровать (*impf*); (*bird*) пари́ть (*impf*) ♦ *n* скольже́ние.
glider ['glaɪdə'] *n* (*AVIAT*) планёр.
gliding ['glaɪdɪŋ] *n* (*AVIAT*) плани́рование.
glimmer ['glɪmə'] *n* (*of light*) мерца́ние; (*of interest, hope*) про́блеск ♦ *vi* (*light*) мерца́ть (*impf*).
glimpse [glɪmps] *n* мимолётное впечатле́ние ♦ *vt* ви́деть (уви́деть *perf*) ме́льком; **to catch a ~ of** уви́деть* (*perf*) ме́льком.
glint [glɪnt] *vi* блесте́ть* (блесну́ть *perf*), сверка́ть (сверкну́ть *perf*) ♦ *n* (*of metal, light*) блеск, сверка́ние; (*in eyes*) блеск.
glisten ['glɪsn] *vi* (*with sweat, rain etc*) блесте́ть* (*impf*).
glitter ['glɪtə'] *vi* сверка́ть (сверкну́ть *perf*) ♦ *n* сверка́ние.
glittering ['glɪtərɪŋ] *adj* (*eyes, career*) блестя́щий*; (*stars*) сия́ющий*; (*diamonds*) сверка́ющий.
glitz [glɪts] *n* (*inf*) блеск.

---

* marks translations which have irregular inflections. The Russian–English side of the dictionary gives inflectional information.

gloat [glǝut] vi: **to ~ (over)** злора́дствовать (impf) (над +instr).

global ['glǝubl] adj (interest, attention) всео́бщий*; (overall: picture) о́бщий*.

global warming [-'wɔ:mɪŋ] n всеми́рное or глоба́льное потепле́ние.

globe [glǝub] n (world) земно́й шар*; (model of world) гло́бус; (shape) шар*.

globetrotter ['glǝubtrɒtǝ'] n путеше́ственник(-ица).

globule ['glɒbju:l] n ка́пля*.

gloom [glu:m] n (dark) мрак; (sadness) уны́ние.

gloomily ['glu:mɪlɪ] adv уны́ло.

gloomy ['glu:mɪ] adj мра́чный.

glorification [glɔ:rɪfɪ'keɪʃǝn] n прославле́ние; **the ~ of war** прославле́ние войны́.

glorified ['glɔ:rɪfaɪd] adj: **she is merely a ~ secretary** она́ по су́ти де́ла про́сто секрета́рша.

glorify ['glɔ:rɪfaɪ] vt (praise) прославля́ть (просла́вить* perf).

glorious ['glɔ:rɪǝs] adj (sunshine, weather) великоле́пный* (великоле́пен); (victory) сла́вный; (future) прекра́сный (прекра́сен).

glory ['glɔ:rɪ] n (prestige) сла́ва; (splendour) великоле́пие ♦ vi: **to ~ in** упива́ться (impf) +instr.

glory hole n (inf) кладо́вка.

Glos abbr (BRIT: POST) = Gloucestershire.

gloss [glɒs] n блеск; (also: ~ **paint**) лак*
▶ **gloss over** vt fus зама́зывать (зама́зать perf).

glossary ['glɒsǝrɪ] n глосса́рий.

glossy ['glɒsɪ] adj (photograph, magazine) гля́нцевый; (hair) блестя́щий ♦ n (also: ~ **magazine**) журна́л в гля́нцевой обло́жке.

glove [glʌv] n перча́тка*.

glove compartment n (AUT) перча́точный я́щик, барда́чо́к* (разг).

glow [glǝu] vi (embers, stars) свети́ться (impf); (face, eyes) горе́ть (impf) ♦ n (of eyes, stars) свет; (of face) румя́нец*.

glower ['glauǝ'] vi: **to ~ at sb** смотре́ть* (посмотре́ть* perf) с негодова́нием на кого́-н.

glowing ['glǝuɪŋ] adj (fire) я́рко светя́щийся; (complexion) румя́ный; (fig) блестя́щий*.

glow-worm ['glǝuwǝ:m] n светлячо́к*.

glucose ['glu:kǝus] n глюко́за.

glue [glu:] n клей* ♦ vt: **to ~ sth onto sth** прикле́ивать (прикле́ить perf) что-н на что-н.

glue-sniffing ['glu:snɪfɪŋ] n токсикома́ния.

glum [glʌm] adj мра́чный*.

glut [glʌt] n переизбы́ток* ♦ vt: **to be ~ted (with)** (market, economy etc) быть* (impf) зава́ленным*(+instr).

glutinous ['glu:tɪnǝs] adj кле́йкий*.

glutton ['glʌtn] n обжо́ра m/f; **he is a ~ for work** он охо́ч до рабо́ты; **he is a ~ for punishment** он жа́ден до рабо́ты.

gluttonous ['glʌtǝnǝs] adj (person, habits) ненасы́тный* (ненасы́тен).

gluttony ['glʌtǝnɪ] n ненасы́тность f.

glycerin(e) ['glɪsǝri:n] n глицери́н*.

GM adj abbr = **genetically modified**.

gm abbr (= gram) г= грамм.

GMAT n abbr (US) = Graduate Management Admissions Test.

GMB n abbr (BRIT) = General Municipal and Boilermakers (Union).

GMO n abbr (= genetically modified organism) трансге́нный органи́зм.

GMT abbr (= Greenwich Mean Time) сре́днее вре́мя* nt по Гри́нвичу.

gnarled [nɑ:ld] adj (tree) сучкова́тый (сучкова́т); (hand) скрю́ченный (скрю́чен).

gnash [næʃ] vt: **to ~ one's teeth** скрежета́ть* (impf) зуба́ми.

gnat [næt] n мо́шка*.

gnaw [nɔ:] vt грызть* (impf) ♦ vi (doubts, suspicions): **to ~ at** терза́ть (impf).

gnome [nǝum] n гном.

GNP n abbr (= gross national product) ВНП= валово́й национа́льный проду́кт.

KEYWORD

---

go [gǝu] (pt **went**, pp **gone**, pl **goes**) vi **1** (move: on foot) ходи́ть*/идти́* (пойти́* perf); (travel: by transport) е́здить*/е́хать (пое́хать* perf); **she went into the kitchen** она́ пошла́ на ку́хню; **he often goes to China** он ча́сто е́здит в Кита́й; **they are going to the theatre tonight** сего́дня ве́чером они́ иду́т в теа́тр
2 (depart: on foot) уходи́ть* (уйти́* perf); (: by plane) улета́ть (улете́ть* perf); (: by train, car) уезжа́ть (уе́хать* perf); **the plane goes at 6am** самолёт улета́ет в 6 часо́в утра́; **the train/ bus goes at 6pm** по́езд/авто́бус ухо́дит в 6 часо́в; **now I must go** тепе́рь я до́лжен идти́
3 (attend): **to go to** ходи́ть* (impf) в/на +acc; **she went to university in Aberdeen** она́ учи́лась в Абердн́нском университе́те; **she doesn't go to lectures** она́ не хо́дит на ле́кции
4 (take part in an activity) ходи́ть*/идти́* (пойти́* perf)
5 (work): **is your watch going** ва́ши часы́ иду́т?; **the clock stopped going** часы́ останови́лись; **the bell went just then** зазвони́л звоно́к; **the tape recorder was still going** магнитофо́н не был вы́ключен
6 (become): **to go pale** бледне́ть (побледне́ть perf); **to go mouldy** пле́сневеть (запле́сневеть perf)
7 (be sold): **the books went for £10** кни́ги бы́ли про́даны за £10
8 (fit, suit): **to go with** подходи́ть* (подойти́* perf) к +dat
9 (be about to, intend to) собира́ться (собра́ться* perf) +infin
10 (time: slowly) тяну́ться (impf); (quickly) проходи́ть* (пройти́* perf)
11 (event, activity) проходи́ть* (пройти́* perf);

how did it go? ну как всё прошло?
12 (*be given*): **the job is to go to someone else** рабóту должны отдáть комý-то другóму; **the proceeds will go to charity** прибыль пойдёт на благотворительные цéли
13 (*break etc*): **the fuse went** предохранитель *m* перегорéл; **the leg of the chair went** нóжка стýла сломáлась
14 (*be placed*): **the milk goes in the fridge** молокó нýжно постáвить в холодильник; **where does this cup go?** кудá постáвить эту чáшку?; **the suitcase goes on top of the wardrobe** чемодáн обычно лежит на шкафý
◆ *n* **1** (*try*): **to have a go (at sth/at doing sth)** прóбовать* (попрóбовать* *perf*) (что-н/+*perf infin*)
2 (*turn*): **whose go is it?** (*in board games*) чей ход?; (*in sports*) чья (сейчáс) óчередь?
3 (*move*): **to be on the go** быть (*impf*) на ногáх
▶ **go about** *vi* (*also:* **go around**: *rumour*) ходить* (*impf*)
◆ *vt fus*: **to go about one's business** занимáться (заняться* *perf*) своими делáми; **how do I go about (doing) this?** как мне это сдéлать?
▶ **go after** *vt fus* (*person*) бежáть (побежáть *perf*) (вдогóнку) за +*instr*; **to go after a job** стремиться* (*impf*) получить рабóту
▶ **go against** *vt fus* (*subj: decision, verdict*): **to go against sb** быть (*impf*) не в чью-н пóльзу
▶ **go ahead** *vi* (*proceed*) продвигáться (продвинуться *perf*); (*event*): **to go ahead with** (*project*) приступить* (*perf*) к +*dat*; **may I begin? – yes, go ahead!** мóжно начáть? – да, пожáлуйста!
▶ **go along** *vi* идти (пойти* *perf*); **I went along with him/his decision** (*agree with*) я не стал противиться емý/его решéнию; **to go along with sb** (*accompany*) идти (пойти* *perf*) с кем-н
▶ **go away** *vi* (*leave: on foot*) уходить* (уйти* *perf*); (: *by transport*) уезжáть (уéхать* *perf*); **go away and think about it for a while** пойди и подýмай немнóжко на этот счёт
▶ **go back** *vi* (*return*) возвращáться (вернýться* *perf*); (*go again: on foot*) идти* (пойти* *perf*) ещё раз *or* опять; (: *by transport*) éхать* (поéхать* *perf*) ещё раз *or* опять; **we went back into the house** мы пошли обрáтно в дом; **I am never going back to her house again** я никогдá бóльше не пойдý к ней; **to go back to** (*date from*) относиться (*impf*) к +*dat*
▶ **go back on** *vt fus* (*promise, word*) не сдéрживать (сдержáть* *perf*) +*gen*
▶ **go by** *vi* (*years, time*) проходить* (пройти* *perf*)
◆ *vt fus* (*book, rule*) дéлать (сдéлать *perf*) всё по +*dat*; **as time goes by** ... врéмя идёт, и ...

▶ **go down** *vi* (*descend*) спускáться (спуститься* *perf*); (*ship*) тонýть* (затонýть* *perf*); (*sun*) заходить* (зайти* *perf*); (*prices, temperature*) пáдать (упáсть* *perf*); (*swelling*) спадáть (спасть* *perf*)
◆ *vt fus* (*stairs, ladder*) спускáться (спуститься* *perf*) с +*gen*; **that should go down well with him** это емý должнó понрáвится; **he went to London/to see his sister** он поéхал в Лóндон/в гóсти к своéй сестрé
▶ **go for** *vt fus* (*fetch: paper, doctor*) идти* (пойти* *perf*) за +*instr*; (*choose, like*) любить* (*impf*); (*attack*) набрáсываться (набрóситься* *perf*) на +*acc*; **that goes for me too** и я тóже
▶ **go in** *vi* (*enter*) входить* (войти* *perf*); **it's time to go in** порá заходить
▶ **go in for** *vt fus* принимáть (принять* *perf*) учáстие в +*prp*; (*take up*) заняться* (*perf*) +*instr*
▶ **go into** *vt fus* (*enter*) входить* (войти* *perf*) в +*acc*; (*investigate*) рассмáтривать (рассмотрéть* *perf*); (*take up*) заняться* (*perf*) +*instr*; **to go into detail** вдавáться* (*impf*) в подрóбности
▶ **go off** *vi* (*leave: on foot*) уходить* (уйти* *perf*); (: *by transport*) уезжáть (уéхать* *perf*); (*food*) пóртиться* (испóртиться* *perf*); (*bomb*) взрывáться (взорвáться* *perf*); (*gun*) выстрелить (*perf*); (*alarm*) звонить (зазвонить *perf*); (*event*) проходить* (пройти* *perf*); (*lights*) выключáться (выключиться *perf*)
◆ *vt fus* разлюбить* (*perf*); **to go off to sleep** засыпáть (заснýть *perf*)
▶ **go on** *vi*: **to go on (doing)** (*continue*) продолжáть (*impf*) (+*infin*); (*happen*: *discussion, argument*) идти* (*impf*); **life goes on** жизнь продолжáется; **what's going on here?** что здесь происхóдит?; **we don't have enough evidence/information to go on** у нас нет достáточных доказáтельств/ информáции
▶ **go on at** *vt fus* пристáвать* (*impf*) к +*dat*
▶ **go on with** *vt fus* продолжáть (продóлжить* *perf*)
▶ **go out** *vi* (*fire, light*) гáснуть* (погáснуть* *perf*); (*single person*) выходить* (выйти* *perf*) из +*gen*; **are you going out tonight?** (*for entertainment*) Вы сегóдня вéчером куда-нибудь идёте?
▶ **go over** *vi* идти* (пойти* *perf*)
◆ *vt fus* (*check*) просмáтривать (просмотрéть* *perf*); **to go over sth in one's mind** повторять (повторить *perf*) что-н в умé
▶ **go round** *vi* (*circulate*) ходить* (*impf*); (*revolve*) вращáться (*impf*); (*suffice*) хватáть (хватить *perf*) на всех; (*visit*): **to go round (to sb's)** заходить* (зайти* *perf*) (к комý-н);

(make a detour): **to go round (by)** *(on foot)*
идти́* (пойти́* *perf*) круго́м (че́рез +*acc*); *(by transport)* е́хать (пое́хать *perf*) круго́м (че́рез +*acc*)

▶ **go through** *vt fus (town etc: on foot)*
проходи́ть* (пройти́* *perf*) че́рез +*acc*; (: *by transport*) проезжа́ть (прое́хать* *perf*) че́рез +*acc*; *(files, papers)* просма́тривать (просмотре́ть* *perf*); *(aloud: list)* чита́ть (прочита́ть *perf*); *(practice)* проде́лывать (проде́лать *perf*)

▶ **go through with** *vt fus (plan, crime)*
осуществля́ть (осуществи́ть* *perf*); **I couldn't go through with it** я не мог осуществи́ть э́то

▶ **go under** *vi (also fig)* идти́* (пойти́* *perf*) под во́ду

▶ **go up** *vi (ascend)* поднима́ться (подня́ться* *perf*); *(price, level)* расти́* (вы́расти* *perf*); *(buildings)* выраста́ть (вы́расти* *perf*); **to go up in flames** загора́ться *(impf)*

▶ **go with** *vt fus (match)* подходи́ть* (подойти́* *perf*) к +*dat*

▶ **go without** *vt fus (treats)* остава́ться* (оста́ться* *perf*) без +*gen*; **I can go without food for 24 hours** я могу́ су́тки не есть.

goad [gəud] *vt (person)* подстрека́ть *(impf)*
▶ **goad on** *vt (person)* подгоня́ть *(impf)*.
go-ahead ['gəuɛhɛd] *adj* предприи́мчивый (предприи́мчив) ♦ *n (for project)* добро́; **to give sb the ~** дава́ть* (дать* *perf*) кому́-н добро́.
goal [gəul] *n (SPORT)* гол; (: *goal posts*) воро́та *mpl*; *(aim)* цель *f*; **to score a ~** забива́ть (заби́ть* *perf*) гол.
goal difference *n* ра́зница мяче́й.
goalie ['gəulı] *n (inf)* врата́рь* *m*, голки́пер.
goalkeeper ['gəulkiːpəʳ] *n* врата́рь* *m*, голки́пер.
goal post *n* боковая шта́нга, сто́йка* воро́т.
goat [gəut] *n (billy)* козёл*; *(nanny)* коза́.
gobble ['gɔbl] *vt (also: ~ down, ~ up)* ло́пать (сло́пать *perf*), жрать (сожра́ть* *perf*).
go-between ['gəubɪtwiːn] *n* посре́дник(-ица).
Gobi Desert ['gəubɪ-] *n:* **the ~ ~** пусты́ня Го́би.
goblet ['gɔblıt] *n* ку́бок*.
goblin ['gɔblın] *n* го́блин.
gobsmacked ['gɔbsmækt] *adj:* **I was ~** *(inf)* я соверше́нно обалде́л.
go-cart ['gəukaːt] *n* карт.
God [gɔd] *n* Бог ♦ *excl* Го́споди!, о Бо́же!
god [gɔd] *n (MYTHOLOGY, fig)* божество́*, бог*.
god-awful [gɔd'ɔːfəl] *adj (inf!)* жу́ткий*, кошма́рный*.
godchild ['gɔdtʃaɪld] *n* кре́стник(-ица).
goddam ['gɔddæm] *adj (inf!)* прокля́тый *(!)*
goddamned ['gɔddæmd] *adj (inf!)* прокля́тый.
goddaughter ['gɔddɔːtəʳ] *n* кре́стница.
goddess ['gɔdıs] *n* боги́ня.
godfather ['gɔdfaːðəʳ] *n* кре́стный оте́ц*.
God-fearing ['gɔdfıərıŋ] *adj* богобоя́зненный.

godforsaken ['gɔdfəseɪkən] *adj* забы́тый Бо́гом, забро́шенный*.
godmother ['gɔdmʌðəʳ] *n* кре́стная мать* *f*.
godparent ['gɔdpɛərənt] *n* кре́стный(-ая) *m(f) adj*.
godsend ['gɔdsɛnd] *n* благода́ть *f*.
godson ['gɔdsʌn] *n* кре́стник.
goes [gəuz] *vb see* **go**.
gofer ['gəufəʳ] *n (inf)* ма́льчик на побегу́шках.
go-getter ['gəugɛtəʳ] *n* предприи́мчивый челове́к*.
goggle ['gɔgl] *vi (inf):* **to ~ at** тара́щиться (вы́тараща́ться *perf*) на +*acc*.
goggles ['gɔglz] *npl* защи́тные очки́ *ntpl*.
going ['gəuıŋ] *n (conditions):* **the ~** обстоя́тельства *ntpl* ♦ *adj:* **the ~ rate** существу́ющие расце́нки *fpl*; **this book is heavy ~** э́та кни́га тру́дно чита́ется; **it was hard ~** понача́лу приходи́лось тру́дно; **a ~ concern** де́йствующее предприя́тие.
going-over [gəuıŋ'əuvəʳ] *n (inf: examination)* осмо́тр; *(physical attack)* трёпка.
goings-on ['gəuıŋz'ɔn] *npl (inf)* дела́ *ntpl*.
go-kart ['gəukaːt] *n =* **go-cart**.
gold [gəuld] *n* зо́лото; *(SPORT: also: ~ medal)* зо́лото, золота́я меда́ль *f* ♦ *adj* золото́й; **~ reserves** золоты́е запа́с.
golden ['gəuldən] *adj (made of gold)* золото́й; *(gold in colour)* золоти́стый; *(opportunity, future)* прекра́сный*.
golden age *n* золото́й век*.
golden handshake *n (BRIT)* де́нежное вознагражде́ние при ухо́де на пе́нсию.
golden rule *n* золото́е пра́вило.
goldfish ['gəuldfıʃ] *n* золота́я ры́бка*.
gold leaf *n* суса́льное зо́лото.
gold medal *n (SPORT)* золота́я меда́ль *f*.
gold mine *n* золото́й при́иск *or* рудни́к*; *(fig)* золото́е дно*.
gold-plated ['gəuld'pleıtıd] *adj* позоло́ченный.
goldsmith ['gəuldsmıθ] *n* золоты́х дел ма́стер*.
gold standard *n* золото́й станда́рт.
golf [gɔlf] *n* гольф.
golf ball *n* мяч для игры́ в гольф; *(on typewriter)* металли́ческий шар с бу́квами в электри́ческой печа́тной маши́нке.
golf club *n (organization)* клуб люби́телей игры́ в гольф; *(stick)* клю́шка* для игры́ в гольф.
golf course *n* по́ле для игры́ в гольф.
golfer ['gɔlfəʳ] *n* игро́к* в гольф.
golfing ['gɔlfıŋ] *adj* для игры́ в гольф.
gondola ['gɔndələ] *n* гондо́ла.
gondolier [gɔndə'lıəʳ] *n* гондолье́р.
gone [gɔn] *pp of* **go** ♦ *adj* уе́хавший, уше́дший.
goner ['gɔnəʳ] *n (inf):* **I was a ~** со мной бы́ло всё поко́нчено.
gong [gɔŋ] *n* гонг.
good [gud] *adj* хоро́ший*; *(pleasant)* прия́тный*; *(kind)* до́брый*; *(morally correct)* пра́вильный* ♦ *n (virtue)* добро́; *(benefit)*

по́льза; **~s** *npl* (COMM) това́ры *mpl*; **~l** хорошо́!; **to be ~ at** име́ть (*impf*) спосо́бности к +*dat*; **to be ~ for** (*useful*) быть° (*impf*) поле́зным(-ой) для +*dat*; **it's a ~ for you** э́то Вам поле́зно (для здоро́вья); **it's a ~ thing you were there** хорошо́, что Вы бы́ли там; **she is ~ with children** она́ уме́ет обраща́ться с детьми́; **she is ~ with her hands** у неё золоты́е ру́ки; **to feel ~** чу́вствовать (*impf*) себя́ хорошо́; **it's ~ to see you** о́чень прия́тно Вас ви́деть; **would you be ~ enough to ...?** не бу́дете ли Вы так добры́ +*perf infin* ...?; **that's very ~ of you** э́то о́чень ми́ло с Ва́шей стороны́; **is this any ~?** (*will it do?*) э́то пойдёт?; (*what's it like?*) понра́вилось ли э́то Вам?; **a ~ deal (of)** большо́е коли́чество (+*gen*); **a ~ many** мно́го +*gen*; **to take a ~ look** смотре́ть° (посмотре́ть° *perf*) хороше́нько; **a ~ while ago** о́чень давно́; **to make ~** (*damage*) ремонти́ровать (отремонти́ровать *perf*); (*loss*) восполня́ть (воспо́лнить *perf*); **~ afternoon/evening!** до́брый день/ве́чер!; **~ morning!** до́брое у́тро!; **~ night!** (*on leaving*) до свида́ния!; (*on going to bed*) споко́йной *or* до́брой но́чи!; **he's up to no ~** он заду́мал что́-то (плохо́е); **for the common ~** для о́бщего бла́га; **it's no ~ complaining** что то́лку жа́ловаться; **for ~** навсегда́; **~s and chattels** ли́чные ве́щи°.

goodbye [gud'baɪ] *excl* до свида́ния; **to say ~ (to)** проща́ться (попроща́ться *perf*) (с +*instr*).

good-for-nothing ['gudfənʌθɪŋ] *adj* никуды́шний.

Good Friday *n* Страстна́я пя́тница.

good-humoured ['gud'hju:məd] (*US* **good-humored**) *adj* (*person*) доброду́шный°; (*remark, joke*) до́брый°.

good-looking ['gud'lukɪŋ] *adj* краси́вый.

good-natured ['gud'neɪtʃəd] *adj* (*person*) доброду́шный°; (*pet*) послу́шный; (*discussion*) споко́йный°.

goodness ['gudnɪs] *n* доброта́; **for ~ sake!** ра́ди Бо́га!; **~ gracious!** Го́споди!

goods train *n* (BRIT) това́рный по́езд°.

goodwill [gud'wɪl] *n* (*of person*) доброжела́тельность *f*; (COMM) прести́ж фи́рмы.

goody-goody ['gudɪgudɪ] *n* (*pej*) па́инька° *m/f*.

gooey ['gu:ɪ] (*inf*) *adj* ли́пкий° (ли́пок).

goose [gu:s] (*pl* **geese**) *n* (*male*) гусь° *m*; (*female*) гусы́ня.

gooseberry ['guzbərɪ] *n* крыжо́вник *no pl*; **he is playing ~** (BRIT) он тре́тий ли́шний.

goose flesh *n* = **goose pimples**.

goose pimples *npl* гуси́ная ко́жа *fsg*.

goose step *n* (MIL) гуси́ный шаг.

GOP *n abbr* (*US: POL: inf.* = Grand Old Party)

неофициа́льное назва́ние Республика́нской па́ртии США.

gopher ['gəufə°] *n* го́фер (*колумби́йский су́слик*).

gore [gɔ:°] *vt* бода́ть (забода́ть *perf*) ◆ *n* (*запёкшаяся*) кровь *f*.

gorge [gɔ:dʒ] *n* тесни́на, (*у́зкое*) уще́лье° ◆ *vt*: **to ~ o.s. (on)** наеда́ться (нае́сться° *perf*) (+*gen*).

gorgeous ['gɔ:dʒəs] *adj* великоле́пный, прекра́сный.

gorilla [gə'rɪlə] *n* гори́лла.

gormless ['gɔ:mlɪs] *adj* (BRIT: *inf*) тупо́й°.

gorse [gɔ:s] *n* (BOT) утёсник.

gory ['gɔ:rɪ] *adj* (*details*) крова́вый; (*situation*) кровопроли́тный°.

go-slow ['gəu'sləu] *n* (BRIT) сниже́ние те́мпа рабо́ты (*как вид забасто́вки*).

gospel ['gɔspl] *n* (REL) ева́нгелие; (*doctrine*) про́поведь *f*.

gossamer ['gɔsəmə°] *n* (*cobweb*) паути́нка; (*light fabric*) газ.

gossip ['gɔsɪp] *n* (*rumours*) спле́тня°; (*chat*) разгово́ры *mpl*; (*person*) спле́тник(-ица) ◆ *vi* болта́ть (поболта́ть *perf*); **a piece of ~** спле́тня°, слух.

gossip column *n* коло́нка° све́тской хро́ники.

got [gɔt] *pt, pp of* **get**.

Gothic ['gɔθɪk] *adj* готи́ческий°.

gotten ['gɔtn] *pp* (*US*) *of* **get**.

gouge [gaudʒ] *vt* (*also: ~ out: hole etc*) выда́лбливать (вы́долбить° *perf*); (: *initials*) выреза́ть (вы́резать° *perf*); **to ~ sb's eyes out** выка́лывать (вы́колоть° *perf*) кому́-н глаза́.

gourd [guəd] *n* ты́ква.

gourmet ['guəmeɪ] *n* гурма́н.

gout [gaut] *n* (MED) пода́гра.

govern ['gʌvən] *vt* (*country, also* LING) управля́ть (*impf*) +*instr*; (*event, conduct*) руководи́ть° (*impf*) +*instr*.

governess ['gʌvənɪs] *n* гуверна́нтка°.

governing ['gʌvənɪŋ] *adj* (POL) пра́вящий°, руководя́щий°.

governing body *n* (*of party*) руководя́щий° о́рган; (*of university*) о́рган управле́ния.

government ['gʌvnmənt] *n* (*act of governing*) управле́ние; (*governing body*) прави́тельство ◆ *cpd* прави́тельственный°; **local ~** ме́стное самоуправле́ние.

governmental [gʌvn'mɛntl] *adj* прави́тельственный°.

government housing *n* (*US*) жили́щный ко́мплекс, постро́енный на госуда́рственные сре́дства.

government stock *n* прави́тельственные облига́ции и це́нные бума́ги.

governor ['gʌvənə°] *n* (*of state, colony*) губерна́тор; (*of bank, school, hospital*)

---

* marks translations which have irregular inflections. The Russian-English side of the dictionary gives inflectional information.

дире́ктор*; (BRIT: of prison) нача́льник.
Govt abbr = **government**.
gown [gaun] n (dress) пла́тье*; (of teacher: BRIT: of judge) ма́нтия.
GP n abbr = **general practitioner**.
GPO n abbr (BRIT: formerly) = General Post Office; (US) Government Printing Office.
gr. abbr (COMM) = **gross**.
grab [græb] vt (seize, also fig) хвата́ть (схвати́ть* perf); (food) перехва́тывать (перехвати́ть* perf); (sleep) урыва́ть (урва́ть* perf) ♦ vi: **to ~ at** хвата́ться (ухвати́ться* perf) за +acc.
grace [greɪs] n гра́ция; (REL) моли́тва (пе́ред едо́й) ♦ vt (honour) удоста́ивать (удосто́ить perf); (adorn) украша́ть (укра́сить* perf); **5 days' ~** 5 дней отсро́чки; **with (a) good ~** любе́зно, с досто́инством; **with (a) bad ~** нелюбе́зно, без досто́инства; **his sense of humour is his saving ~** его́ спаса́ет чу́вство ю́мора; **to say ~** моли́ться* (помоли́ться* perf) пе́ред едо́й.
graceful ['greɪsful] adj (animal, person) грацио́зный*; (style, shape) изя́щный*; (refusal, behaviour) досто́йный*.
gracious ['greɪʃəs] adj (person, smile) любе́зный*; (house) прекра́сный*; (living) краси́вый ♦ excl: **(good) ~!** Бо́же мой!
gradation [grə'deɪʃən] n града́ция.
grade [greɪd] n (COMM: quality) сорт*; (in hierarchy) ранг; (SCOL: mark) оце́нка*; (US: school year) класс; (: gradient) укло́н ♦ vt (rank, class) распределя́ть (распредели́ть perf); (products) сортирова́ть (рассортирова́ть perf); **to make the ~** (fig) добива́ться (доби́ться* perf) своего́ or успе́ха.
grade crossing n (US) железнодоро́жный перее́зд.
grade school n (US) нача́льная шко́ла.
gradient ['greɪdɪənt] n (of hill) укло́н; (GEOM) градие́нт.
gradual ['grædjuəl] adj постепе́нный*.
gradually ['grædjuəlɪ] adv постепе́нно.
graduate [n 'grædjuɪt, vi 'grædjueɪt] n выпускни́к*(-и́ца) ♦ vi: **to ~ from** зака́нчивать (зако́нчить perf); **I ~d last year** я зако́нчил университе́т в про́шлом году́.
graduated pension ['grædjueɪtɪd-] n пе́нсия, увели́чивающаяся в зави́симости от ста́жа рабо́ты.
graduation [grædju'eɪʃən] n (ceremony: at university) церемо́ния вруче́ния дипло́ма; (: US) ≈ церемо́ния вруче́ния аттеста́та.
graffiti [grə'fi:tɪ] n, npl граффи́ти nt ind.
graft [grɑ:ft] n (AGR) приви́вка*; (MED) переса́дка* (ко́жи и́ли ко́стной тка́ни); (BRIT: inf: hard work) тяжёлая рабо́та; (bribery) взя́точничество ♦ vt: **to ~** (onto) (AGR, also fig) привива́ть (приви́ть* perf) (к +dat); (MED) переса́живать (пересади́ть* perf)

(на +acc).
grain [greɪn] n (seed) зерно́*; (no pl: cereals) хле́бные зла́ки mpl; (US: corn) зерно́; (of sand) песчи́нка*; (of salt) крупи́ца; (of wood) волокно́*; **however much it goes against the ~, I ...** (fig) как бы э́то ни противоре́чило мои́м при́нципам, я ....
gram [græm] n грамм.
grammar ['græmə] n грамма́тика; (book) уче́бник грамма́тики.
grammar school n (BRIT) сре́дняя шко́ла (для одарённых дете́й).
grammatical [grə'mætɪkl] adj граммати́ческий*.
gramme [græm] n = **gram**.
gramophone ['græməfəun] n (BRIT) граммофо́н.
granary ['grænərɪ] n амба́р; (larger) зернохрани́лище.
Granary bread or **loaf®** n хлеб и́ли буха́нка из муки́ кру́пного помо́ла с це́лыми зёрнами внутри́.
grand [grænd] (pl ~) adj грандио́зный*; (gesture) вели́чественный*; (inf: wonderful) великоле́пный*, восхити́тельный* ♦ n (inf) ты́сяча.
grandchild ['græntʃaɪld] (pl ~ren) n внук(-у́чка*).
grandchildren ['græntʃɪldrən] npl of **grandchild**.
granddad ['grændæd] n (inf) де́душка* m.
granddaughter ['grændɔ:tə'] n вну́чка*.
grandeur ['grændjə'] n великоле́пие.
grandfather ['grændfɑ:ðə'] n де́душка* m.
grandiose ['grændɪəus] adj грандио́зный*.
grand jury n (US) прися́жные, реша́ющие вопро́с о преда́нии суду́.
grandma ['grænmɑ:] n (inf) ба́бушка*.
grandmother ['grænmʌðə'] n ба́бушка*.
grandpa ['grænpɑ:] n (inf) = **granddad**.
grandparents ['grændpɛərənts] npl де́душка* m и ба́бушка*.
grand piano n роя́ль m.
Grand Prix ['grɑ̃:'pri:] n гран-при́ m ind.
grandson ['grænsʌn] n внук.
grandstand ['grændstænd] n (SPORT) центра́льная трибу́на.
grand total n о́бщая су́мма.
granite ['grænɪt] n грани́т.
granny ['grænɪ] n (inf) ба́бушка*.
grant [grɑ:nt] vt (money, visa) выдава́ть* (вы́дать* perf); (pension) назнача́ть (назна́чить perf); (request) удовлетворя́ть (удовлетвори́ть perf); (admit) признава́ть* (призна́ть* perf) ♦ n (SCOL) стипе́ндия; (ADMIN) субси́дия; **to take sb/sth for ~ed** принима́ть (приня́ть* perf) кого́-н/что́-н как до́лжное; **to ~ that** признава́ть* (призна́ть* perf), что.
granulated sugar ['grænjuleɪtɪd-] n са́харный песо́к*.
granule ['grænjuːl] n (of coffee) гра́нула; (of

salt) крупи́ца.

grape [greɪp] *n* виногра́д* *no pl*; **a bunch of ~s** кисть* *f or* гроздь* *f* виногра́да.

grapefruit ['greɪpfruːt] (*pl ~ or ~s*) *n* грейпфру́т.

grapevine ['greɪpvaɪn] *n* виногра́дная лоза́*; **I heard on the ~ that** ... я слы́шал, что ..., говоря́т, что ....

graph [grɑːf] *n* (*diagram*) гра́фик.

graphic ['græfɪk] *adj* (*account, description*) я́ркий*; (*design*) изобрази́тельный; **~ art** гра́фика; *see also* **graphics**.

graphic designer *n* худо́жник-оформи́тель *m*.

graphic equalizer *n* графи́ческий* выра́вниватель *m*.

graphics ['græfɪks] *n* гра́фика ◆ *npl* рису́нки *mpl*.

graphite ['græfaɪt] *n* графи́т.

graph paper *n* миллиметро́вка.

grapple ['græpl] *vi*: **to ~ with sb** схва́тываться (схвати́ться* *perf*) с кем-н; **to ~ with a problem** би́ться* (*impf*) над пробле́мой.

grasp [grɑːsp] *vt* (*also fig*) схва́тывать (схвати́ть* *perf*) ◆ *n* (*grip*) хва́тка; (*understanding*) понима́ние; **the vase slipped from my ~** ва́за вы́скользнула из мои́х рук; **success was now within his ~** успе́х был тепе́рь в его́ рука́х; **to have a good ~ of sth** (*fig*) хорошо́ разбира́ться (*impf*) в чём-н
▸ **grasp at** *vt fus* (*rope etc*) хвата́ться (ухвати́ться* *perf*) за +*acc*; (*fig: opportunity*) цепля́ться (уцепи́ться* *perf*) за +*acc*.

grasping ['grɑːspɪŋ] *adj* (*greedy*) жа́дный*.

grass [grɑːs] *n* трава́*; (*lawn*) газо́н; (*BRIT. inf: informer*) стука́ч*; (: *ex-terrorist*) доно́счик.

grasshopper ['grɑːshɒpəʳ] *n* кузне́чик.

grass-roots ['grɑːsruːts] *adj* (*support*) низово́й; (*member*) рядово́й.

grass snake *n* уж*.

grassy ['grɑːsɪ] *adj* (*bank, slope*) травяни́стый.

grate [greɪt] *n* ками́нная решётка* ◆ *vt* (*CULIN*) тере́ть* (натере́ть* *perf*) ◆ *vi* (*metal, chalk*): **to ~ (on)** скрипе́ть* (*impf*) (по +*dat*).

grateful ['greɪtful] *adj* (*person*) благода́рный* (благода́рен); **~ thanks** и́скренняя благода́рность.

gratefully ['greɪtfəlɪ] *adv* благода́рно.

grater ['greɪtəʳ] *n* тёрка*.

gratification [grætɪfɪ'keɪʃən] *n* удовлетворе́ние.

gratify ['grætɪfaɪ] *vt* (*person*) ра́довать (пора́довать *perf*); (*whim, desire*) удовлетворя́ть (удовлетвори́ть *perf*).

gratifying ['grætɪfaɪɪŋ] *adj* (*pleasing*) прия́тный* (прия́тен).

grating ['greɪtɪŋ] *n* решётка* ◆ *adj* (*noise*) ре́зкий*.

gratitude ['grætɪtjuːd] *n* благода́рность *f*.

gratuitous [grə'tjuːɪtəs] *adj* (*violence, cruelty*) бессмы́сленный* (бессмы́слен).

gratuity [grə'tjuːɪtɪ] *n* (*tip*) чаевы́е *pl adj*.

grave [greɪv] *n* моги́ла ◆ *adj* серьёзный* (серьёзен); (*mistake*) роково́й.

grave digger *n* моги́льщик.

gravel ['grævl] *n* гра́вий.

gravely ['greɪvlɪ] *adv* серьёзно; **~ ill** тяжело́ больно́й* (бо́лен).

gravestone ['greɪvstəun] *n* надгро́бие.

graveyard ['greɪvjɑːd] *n* кла́дбище.

gravitas ['grævɪtæs] *n* многозначи́тельность *f*.

gravitate ['grævɪteɪt] *vi*: **to ~ towards** стреми́ться* (*impf*) *or* тяну́ться* (*impf*) к +*dat*.

gravity ['grævɪtɪ] *n* (*PHYS*) си́ла тя́жести; (*seriousness*) серьёзность *f*.

gravy ['greɪvɪ] *n* (*meat juices*) подли́вка; (*sauce*) со́ус*.

gravy boat *n* со́усник.

gravy train *n* (*inf*): **to ride the ~ ~** име́ть (*impf*) лёгкий за́работок.

gray [greɪ] *adj* (*US*) = **grey**.

graze [greɪz] *vi* пасти́сь* (*impf*) ◆ *vt* (*touch lightly*) задева́ть (заде́ть* *perf*); (*scrape*) цара́пать (оцара́пать *perf*) ◆ *n* цара́пина.

grazing ['greɪzɪŋ] *n* (*pasture*) па́стбище.

grease [griːs] *n* (*lubricant*) сма́зка*; (*fat*) жир* ◆ *vt* сма́зывать (сма́зать* *perf*); **to ~ sb's palm** (*fig*) дава́ть* (дать* *perf*) кому́-н взя́тку.

grease gun *n* сма́зочный шприц.

greasepaint ['griːspeɪnt] *n* (театра́льный) грим.

greaseproof paper ['griːspruːf-] *n* (*BRIT*) жиронепроница́емая бума́га.

greasy ['griːsɪ] *adj* жи́рный*; (*clothes*) заса́ленный* (заса́лен); (*BRIT: road, surface*) ско́льзкий*.

great [greɪt] *adj* (*large*) большо́й*; (*heat, pain*) си́льный*; (*city, man*) вели́кий*; (*inf: terrific*) замеча́тельный*; **they're ~ friends** они́ больши́е друзья́; **we had a ~ time** мы замеча́тельно провели́ вре́мя; **it was ~!** э́то бы́ло замеча́тельно *or* здо́рово!; **the ~ thing is that** ... са́мое гла́вное то, что ....

Great Barrier Reef *n*: **the ~ ~ ~** Большо́й Барье́рный риф.

Great Britain *n* Великобрита́ния.

greater ['greɪtəʳ] *adj*: **~ Calcutta** больша́я Кальку́тта; **G~ Manchester** большо́й Манче́стер.

great-grandchild [greɪt'græntʃaɪld] (*pl ~ren*) *n* пра́внук*(-учка*).

great-grandchildren [greɪt'græntʃɪldrən] *npl of* **great-grandchild**.

great-grandfather [greɪt'grænfɑːðəʳ] *n* праде́душка* *m*.

great-grandmother [greɪt'grænmʌðəʳ] *n*

---

* marks translations which have irregular inflections. The Russian-English side of the dictionary gives inflectional information.

прабáбушка*.

Great Lakes *npl*: **the ~ ~** Большúе Озёра *ntpl*.

greatly ['greɪtlɪ] *adv* óчень; (*influenced*) в значúтельной стéпени.

greatness ['greɪtnɪs] *n* (*importance*) велúчие.

Grecian ['griːʃən] *adj* грéческий*.

Greece [griːs] *n* Грéция.

greed [griːd] *n* (*greediness*) жáдность *f*; (*for power, wealth*) жáжда.

greedily ['griːdɪlɪ] *adv* жáдно.

greedy ['griːdɪ] *adj* жáдный* (жáден).

Greek [griːk] *adj* грéческий ♦ *n* (*person*) грек (гречáнка*); (*LING*) грéческий язы́к*; **ancient/ modern ~** древнегрéческий*/совремéнный грéческий язы́к*.

green [griːn] *adj* зелёный ♦ *n* (*colour*) зелёный цвет; (*stretch of grass*) лужáйка*; (*on golf course*) площáдка вокрýг лýнки, покры́тая травóй; (*also*: **village ~**) газóн в цéнтре дерéвни; **~s** *npl* (*vegetables*) óвощи *mpl*; (*POL*) :**the G~s** зелёные *pl adj*; **the G~ Party** пáртия зелёных; **he has ~ fingers** *or* (*US*) **a ~ thumb** (*fig*) что он ни посáдит, всё у негó растёт; **to give sb the ~ light** давáть* (дать* *perf*) комý-н зелёную ýлицу.

green belt *n* (*round town*) зелёная зóна, зелёный пóяс*.

green card *n* (*BRIT: AUT*) зелёная кáрточка (*для страхóвки автомобúля за рубежóм*); (*US: ADMIN*) зелёная кáрточка (*необходúмая для трудоустрóйства*).

greenery ['griːnərɪ] *n* зéлень *f*.

greenfly ['griːnflaɪ] *n* (*BRIT*) тля.

greengage ['griːngeɪdʒ] *n* слúва-венчéрка.

greengrocer ['griːngrəʊsə'] *n* (*BRIT*) зеленщúк* (*продавéц овощéй и фрýктов*).

greenhouse ['griːnhaʊs] *n* теплúца.

greenhouse effect *n*: **the ~ ~** парникóвый эффéкт.

greenhouse gas *n* одúн из гáзов, вызывáющий теплúчный эффéкт.

greenish ['griːnɪʃ] *adj* зеленовáтый.

Greenland ['griːnlənd] *n* Гренлáндия.

Greenlander ['griːnləndə'] *n* жúтель(ница) *m(f)* Гренлáндии.

green pepper *n* зелёный пéрец*.

greet [griːt] *vt* (*person*) привéтствовать* (попривéтствовать *perf*), здорóваться (поздорóваться *perf*); (*receive: news*) встречáть (встрéтить* *perf*).

greeting ['griːtɪŋ] *n* (*welcome*) привéтствие; **Christmas/birthday ~s** поздравля́ю с Рождествóм/с днём рождéния; **Season's ~s** поздравля́ю с Рождествóм и Нóвым гóдом.

greeting(s) card *n* поздравúтельная откры́тка*.

gregarious [grə'gɛərɪəs] *adj* общúтельный* (общúтелен).

Grenada [grə'neɪdə] *n* Гренáда.

grenade [grə'neɪd] *n* (*also*: **hand ~**) гранáта.

grew [gruː] *pt of* **grow**.

grey [greɪ] (*US* **gray**) *adj* сéрый* (сер); (*hair*) седóй; (*dismal*) мрáчный* (мрáчен); **to go ~** седéть (поседéть *perf*).

grey-haired [greɪ'hɛəd] *adj* седóй*.

greyhound ['greɪhaʊnd] *n* борзáя *f adj*.

grid [grɪd] *n* (*pattern*) сéтка*, сеть *f*; (*grating*) решётка*; (*ELEC*) энергосистéма; (*US: AUT*) решётка радиáтора.

griddle [grɪdl] *n* (*on cooker*) плóский металлúческий диск, испóльзуемый как сковородá.

gridiron ['grɪdaɪən] *n* решётка грúля.

gridlock ['grɪdlɔk] *n* (*US: of traffic etc*) затóр.

grief [griːf] *n* гóре; **to come to ~** (*plan*) рýшиться (рýхнуть *perf*); (*person*) терпéть* (потерпéть* *perf*) неудáчу; **good ~**! Бóже мой!

grievance ['griːvəns] *n* (*complaint*) жáлоба.

grieve [griːv] *vi* горевáть* (*impf*) ♦ *vt* огорчáть (огорчúть *perf*); **to ~ for** горевáть (*impf*) о +*prp*.

grievous ['griːvəs] *adj* (*mistake, injury*) серьёзный*; (*shock*) сúльный.

grievous bodily harm *n* (*LAW*) тяжёлые телéсные поврежде́ния *ntpl*.

grill [grɪl] *n* (*on cooker*) гриль *m*; (*grilled food*: *also*: **mixed ~**) жáренные на грúле продýкты *mpl*; (*restaurant*) = **grillroom** ♦ *vt* (*BRIT*) жáрить (пожáрить *perf*) (на грúле); (*inf: question*) допрáшивать (допросúть* *perf*) с пристрáстием.

grille [grɪl] *n* решётка*; (*AUT*) *решётка радиáтора*.

grillroom ['grɪlrum] *n* ≈ гриль-бар.

grim [grɪm] *adj* (*place, person*) мрáчный* (мрáчен); (*situation*) тяжёлый* (тяжёл).

grimace [grɪ'meɪs] *n* гримáса ♦ *vi* гримáсничать (*impf*).

grime [graɪm] *n* (*from soot, smoke*) кóпоть *f*; (*from mud*) грязь *f*.

grimy ['graɪmɪ] *adj* (*dirty*) гря́зный* (гря́зен).

grin [grɪn] *n* ухмы́лка* ♦ *vi*: **to ~ (at)** (широкó) улыбáться (улыбнýться *perf*) (+*dat*).

grind [graɪnd] (*pt, pp* **ground**) *vt* (*coffee, pepper etc*) молóть (смолóть* *perf*); (*US: meat*) пропускáть (пропустúть* *perf*) чéрез мясорýбку; (*make sharp: knife etc*) точúть* (наточúть* *perf*); (*polish: gem, lens*) шлифовáть (отшлифовáть* *perf*) ♦ *vi* (*car gears*) скрежетáть* (*impf*) ♦ *n* (*work*) изнурúтельная рабóта; **to ~ one's teeth** скрежетáть* (*impf*) зубáми; **to ~ one's heel into the ground** вдáвливать (вдавúть* *perf*) каблýк в зéмлю; **to ~ to a halt** (*vehicle*) останáвливаться (останóвиться* *perf*) с ля́згом; (*fig*) застóпориться (*perf*); **the daily ~** (*inf*) рутúна бýдней.

grinder ['graɪndə'] *n* (*for coffee*) кофемóлка*; (*for waste disposal etc*) дробúлка*.

grindstone ['graɪndstəun] *n*: **to keep one's nose**

to the ~ рабо́тать *(impf)* без переды́шки.
grip [grɪp] *n (of person)* хва́тка; (: *control, grasp)* схва́тывание; *(of tyre)* сцепле́ние; *(handle)* ру́чка*; *(holdall)* доро́жная су́мка* ◆ *vt (object)* схва́тывать (схвати́ть* *perf)*; *(audience, attention)* захва́тывать (захвати́ть* *perf)*; **to come to ~s with** *(problem, difficulty)* бра́ться* (взя́ться* *perf)* за реше́ние +*gen*; **to ~ the road** *(car)* име́ть *(impf)* хоро́шее сцепле́ние с доро́гой; **to lose one's ~** *(tyres)* стира́ться (стере́ться* *perf)*; *(shoes)* изна́шиваться (износи́ться* *perf)*; *(fig)* теря́ть (потеря́ть *perf)* хва́тку.
gripe [graɪp] *n (inf: complaint)* жа́лоба ◆ *vi (inf)* ворча́ть *(impf)*; **the ~s** *(MED)* ко́лики *pl*.
gripping ['grɪpɪŋ] *adj* захва́тывающий*.
grisly ['grɪzlɪ] *adj* ужа́сный*.
grist [grɪst] *n (fig)*: **it's all ~ to the mill** э́то принесёт по́льзу.
gristle ['grɪsl] *n (on meat)* хрящ*.
grit [grɪt] *n (sand)* песо́к*; *(stone)* гра́вий; *(determination, courage)* вы́держка ◆ *vt (road)* посыпа́ть (посы́пать* *perf)* гра́вием; ~**s** *npl (US)* дроблёная кукуру́за *fsg*; **to ~ one's teeth** сти́скивать (сти́снуть *perf)* зу́бы; **I've got a piece of ~ in my eye** мне в глаз попа́ла сори́нка.
grizzle ['grɪzl] *vi (BRIT)* хны́кать* *(impf)*.
grizzly ['grɪzlɪ] *n (also: ~ bear)* гри́зли *m ind*.
groan [grəʊn] *n (of person)* стон ◆ *vi (person: in pain)* стона́ть* *(impf)*; (: *in disapproval)* тяжело́ вздыха́ть (вздохну́ть *perf)*; *(tree, floorboard)* скрипе́ть *(impf)*.
grocer ['grəʊsə'] *n* бакале́йщик.
groceries ['grəʊsərɪz] *npl* бакале́я *fsg*.
grocer's (shop) *n* бакале́йный магази́н.
grog [grɒg] *n (drink)* грог*.
groggy ['grɒgɪ] *adj*: **I feel ~** у меня́ подка́шиваются но́ги.
groin [grɔɪn] *n* пах*.
groom [gru:m] *n (for horse)* ко́нюх; *(also: bridegroom)* жени́х* ◆ *vt (horse)* уха́живать *(impf)* за +*instr*; *(fig)*: **to ~ sb for** *(job)* гото́вить* (пригото́вить* *perf)* кого́-н к +*dat*; **well-~ed** *(person)* ухо́женный* (ухо́жен).
groove [gru:v] *n* желобо́к*; *(habit)* рути́на.
grope [grəʊp] *vi*: **to ~ for** иска́ть* *(impf)* о́щупью; *(fig)* нащу́пывать *(impf)*; **to ~ one's way to** дви́гаться *(impf)* о́щупью к +*dat*.
gross [grəʊs] *adj (vulgar)* вульга́рный*; *(flagrant: neglect, injustice)* вопию́щий*; *(COMM: income)* валово́й ◆ *n inv (twelve dozen)* гросс *(12 дю́жин)* ◆ *vt (COMM)*: **to ~ £500,000** получа́ть (получи́ть* *perf)* о́бщую при́быль в £500.000; ~ **weight** вес бру́тто.
gross domestic product *n* валово́й вну́тренний* проду́кт.
grossly ['grəʊslɪ] *adv (greatly)* чрезме́рно.

gross national product *n* валово́й национа́льный проду́кт.
gross profit *n* валова́я при́быль *f*.
gross sales *npl* валово́й объём *msg* прода́жи.
grotesque [grə'tɛsk] *adj* гроте́скный*.
grotto ['grɒtəʊ] *n* грот.
grotty ['grɒtɪ] *adj (inf: dreadful)* парши́вый (парши́в).
grouch [graʊtʃ] *(inf) vi* брюзжа́ть *(impf)* ◆ *n (person)* брюзга́ *m/f*.
ground [graʊnd] *pt, pp of* **grind** ◆ *n (earth, land)* земля́*; *(floor)* пол; *(SPORT)* по́ле; *(US: also: ~ wire)* заземле́ние; *(reason: usu pl)* основа́ние ◆ *vt (US: ELEC)* заземля́ть (заземли́ть *perf)* ◆ *adj (coffee etc)* мо́лотый ◆ *vi (ship)* сади́ться* (сесть* *perf)* на мель; ~**s** *npl (of coffee)* гу́ща *fsg*; **school ~s** пришко́льный уча́сток*; **sports ~** спорти́вная площа́дка*; **on the ~** на земле́; **to the ~** *(burnt)* дотла́; **below ~** под землёй; **to gain ~** продвига́ться (продви́нуться *perf)* вперёд; **to lose ~** отступа́ть (отступи́ть* *perf)*; **common ~** вопро́с, в кото́ром спо́рящие сто́роны схо́дятся; **on the ~s that** на том основа́нии, что; **the plane was ~ed by the fog** самолёт не мог подня́ться в во́здух из-за тума́на.
ground cloth *n (US)* = **groundsheet**.
ground control *n (AVIAT, SPACE)* слу́жбы *fpl* назе́много контро́ля *or* управле́ния.
ground floor *n* пе́рвый эта́ж*.
grounding ['graʊndɪŋ] *n (in education)* подгото́вка.
groundless ['graʊndlɪs] *adj* беспо́чвенный*, необосно́ванный*.
groundnut ['graʊndnʌt] *n* земляно́й оре́х.
ground rent *n (BRIT)* земе́льная ре́нта.
ground rule *n* основно́е пра́вило.
groundsheet ['graʊndʃi:t] *n (BRIT)* водонепроница́емая ткань *f (испо́льзуемая в похо́дах для подкла́дки под спа́льные мешки́)*.
groundskeeper ['graʊndzki:pə'] *n (US)* = **groundsman**.
groundsman ['graʊndzmən] *irreg n (SPORT)* слу́жащий стадио́на и́ли па́рка подде́рживающий поря́док.
ground staff *n (AVIAT)* назе́мный персона́л.
ground swell *n*: ~ ~ **of opinion (against)** нараста́ющее чу́вство проте́ста (про́тив +*gen*).
ground-to-air ['graʊntu'ɛə'] *adj* противовозду́шный.
ground-to-ground ['graʊntə'graʊnd] *adj*: ~ **missile** управля́емая раке́та кла́сса „земля́-земля́".
groundwork ['graʊndwə:k] *n (preparation)* фунда́мент, осно́ва.
group [gru:p] *n* гру́ппа ◆ *vt (also: ~ together*:

people, things etc) группирова́ть
(сгруппирова́ть perf) ♦ vi (also: ~ **together**)
группирова́ться (сгруппирова́ться perf).
groupie ['gru:pɪ] n деви́ца из антура́жа (non-
гру́ппы, певца́ итп).
group therapy n группова́я терапи́я.
grouse [graus] n inv (bird) (шотла́ндская)
куропа́тка* ♦ vi (complain) ворча́ть (impf).
grove [grəuv] n ро́ща.
grovel ['grɔvl] vi (crawl) по́лзать (impf); (fig): to
~ **(before)** заи́скивать (impf) (пе́ред +instr).
grow [grəu] (pt **grew**, pp **grown**) vi расти́*
(вы́расти* perf); (increase) увели́чиваться
(увели́читься perf); (become): to ~ **rich/weak**
станови́ться* (стать* perf) бога́тым(-ой)/
сла́бым(-ой) ♦ vt (roses, vegetables)
выра́щивать (вы́растить* perf); (beard, hair)
отра́щивать (отрасти́ть* perf); to ~ **(out of** or
from) (city, society) вырасти́ть (вы́расти* perf)
(из +gen); (idea, plan) возника́ть (возни́кнуть
perf) (из +gen); to ~ **tired of waiting** устава́ть*
(уста́ть* perf) от ожида́ния
► **grow apart** vi (fig) отдаля́ться (отдали́ться
perf) друг от дру́га
► **grow away from** vt fus (fig) отдаля́ться
(отдали́ться perf) от +gen
► **grow on** vt fus: **that painting is ~ing on me** э́та
карти́на нра́вится мне всё бо́льше
► **grow out of** vt fus (clothes) выраста́ть
(вы́расти* perf) из +gen; (habit) перераста́ть
(перерасти́* perf); **he'll ~ out of it** он
перерастёт э́то
► **grow up** vi (child) расти́* (вы́расти* perf),
взросле́ть (повзросле́ть perf); (develop: idea,
friendship) возника́ть (возни́кнуть perf).
grower ['grəuə] n (BOT) садово́д; **lily/rose ~**
садово́д, разводя́щий ли́лии/ро́зы.
growing ['grəuɪŋ] adj (increasing) расту́щий: ~
pains (MED) невралги́ческие и́ли
ревмати́ческие бо́ли в де́тском во́зрасте;
(fig) боле́знь f ро́ста.
growl [graul] vi (dog) рыча́ть (зарыча́ть perf);
(person) рыча́ть (прорыча́ть perf).
grown [grəun] pp of **grow**.
grown-up [grəun'ʌp] n (adult) взро́слый(-ая)
m(f) adj ♦ adj (son, daughter) взро́слый.
growth [grəuθ] n (development) рост;
(increase) приро́ст; (of weeds) за́росли fpl; (of
beard) щети́на; (MED) о́пухоль f.
growth rate n темп ро́ста.
grub [grʌb] n (larva) личи́нка*; (inf: food)
жратва́ ♦ vi: to ~ **about** or **around (for)**
ры́ться* (impf) (в по́исках +gen).
grubby ['grʌbɪ] adj (also fig) гря́зный* (гря́зен).
grudge [grʌdʒ] n (grievance) недово́льство ♦
vt: to ~ **sb sth** жале́ть (пожале́ть perf) что-н
для кого́-н; **to bear sb a ~** быть* (impf) на
кого́-н в оби́де.
grudging ['grʌdʒɪŋ] adj (respect, silence)
вы́нужденный; (praise) скупо́й.
grudgingly ['grʌdʒɪŋlɪ] adv неохо́тно.

gruelling ['gruəlɪŋ] (US **grueling**) adj
изнури́тельный* (изнури́телен), тяжёлый*
(тяжёл).
gruesome ['gru:səm] adj (tale, scene) жу́ткий*.
gruff [grʌf] adj (voice) хри́плый* (хрипл);
(manner) ре́зкий* (ре́зок).
grumble ['grʌmbl] vi ворча́ть (impf).
grumpy ['grʌmpɪ] adj сварли́вый (сварли́в).
grunge [grʌndʒ] n стиль m грю́ндж.
grunt [grʌnt] vi (pig) хрю́кать (хрю́кнуть perf);
(person) бурча́ть (бу́ркнуть perf) ♦ n (see vb)
хрю́канье; бурча́ние.
G-string ['dʒi:strɪŋ] n (garment) тип
откры́тых пла́вок.
GSUSA n abbr (= Girl Scouts of the United States
of America) организа́ция де́вочек-ска́утов
США.
GT abbr (AUT: = gran turismo) дорого́й
двухме́стный закры́тый автомоби́ль.
GU abbr (US: POST) = Guam.
guarantee [gærən'ti:] n (assurance)
поручи́тельство; (COMM: warranty) гара́нтия
♦ vt гаранти́ровать (impf/perf); **he can't ~**
(that) he'll come он не мо́жет поручи́ться за
то, что он придёт.
guarantor [gærən'tɔ:] n (COMM) поручи́тель
(ница) m(f).
guard [gɑ:d] n (one person) часово́й;
охра́нник; (squad) охра́на; (MIL) карау́л;
(BOXING, FENCING) оборони́тельная сто́йка;
(BRIT: RAIL) проводни́к*(-и́ца); (on machine)
предохрани́тельное устро́йство; (also:
fireguard) предохрани́тельная решётка*
(пе́ред ками́ном) ♦ vt (prisoner) охраня́ть
(impf); (secret) храни́ть (сохрани́ть perf);
(place, person): to ~ **(against)** охраня́ть (impf)
(от +gen); **to be on one's ~** быть* (impf)
насторо́же or начеку́
► **guard against** vt fus (prevent: disease,
damage etc) предохраня́ть (impf) от +gen.
guard dog n сторожева́я соба́ка.
guarded ['gɑ:dɪd] adj (statement, reply)
осторо́жный* (осторо́жен).
guardian ['gɑ:dɪən] n (LAW: of minor) опеку́н*;
(defender) защи́тник*(-ица).
guardrail ['gɑ:dreɪl] n пери́ла pl.
guard's van n (BRIT: RAIL) бага́жный ваго́н.
Guatemala [gwɑ:tɪ'mɑ:lə] n Гватема́ла.
Guatemalan [gwɑ:tɪ'mɑ:lən] adj
гватема́льский.
Guernsey ['gə:nzɪ] n Ге́рнси.
guerrilla [gə'rɪlə] n партиза́н*(ка*).
guerrilla warfare n партиза́нская война́*.
guess [gɛs] vt (estimate: number etc) счита́ть
(подсчита́ть perf) приблизи́тельно;
(: distance) рассчи́тывать (рассчита́ть perf)
приблизи́тельно; (correct answer)
уга́дывать (угада́ть perf) ♦ vi дога́дываться
(impf) ♦ n (attempt at correct answer) дога́дка;
to take or **have a ~** отга́дывать (отгада́ть
perf); **my ~ is that ...** мне сдаётся, что ...; **I ~ ...**

(*US*) мне ка́жется ...; **I ~ you're right** Вы, наве́рное, пра́вы; **to keep sb ~ing** держа́ть* (*impf*) кого́-н в неве́дении.

guesstimate ['gɛstɪmɪt] *n* (*inf*) прики́дка.

guesswork ['gɛswəːk] *n* (*speculation*) дога́дки *fpl*, предположе́ния *ntpl*; **I got the answer by ~** я угада́л отве́т.

guest [gɛst] *n* (*visitor*) гость*(я) *m(f)*; (*in hotel*) постоя́лец*, прожива́ющий(-ая) *m(f) adj*; **be my ~** (*inf*) пожа́луйста.

guesthouse ['gɛsthaus] *n* пансио́н.

guest room *n* ко́мната для госте́й.

guff [gʌf] *n* (*inf*) трёп.

guffaw [gʌ'fɔ:] *vi* гогота́ть* (*impf*) ♦ *n* го́гот.

guidance ['gaɪdəns] *n* (*advice*) сове́т; **under the ~ of** с по́мощью +*gen*, под руково́дством +*gen*; **vocational ~** сове́т по профориента́ции; **marriage ~** *сове́т по вопро́сам семьи́ и бра́ка*.

guide [gaɪd] *n* (*in museum, on tour*) гид, экскурсово́д; (*mountain guide*) проводни́к*; (*also:~book*) путеводи́тель *m*; (*handbook*) руково́дство; (*BRIT: also: Girl G~*) де́вочка*-ска́ут *f* ♦ *vt* (*show around*) води́ть* (*impf*), вести́* (провести́* *perf*); (*direct*) направля́ть (напра́вить* *perf*); **to be ~d by sb/sth** (*fig*) руково́дствоваться (*impf*) чьим-н сове́том/ чем-н.

guidebook ['gaɪdbuk] *n* путеводи́тель *m*.

guided missile *n* управля́емая раке́та.

guide dog *n* соба́ка-поводы́рь* *f*.

guidelines ['gaɪdlaɪnz] *npl* директи́ва *fsg*.

guild [gɪld] *n* ассоциа́ция; (*HISTORY*) ги́льдия.

guildhall ['gɪldhɔ:l] *n* (*BRIT: in London*): **the G~** Ги́льдхолл (*зда́ние ра́туши ло́ндонского Си́ти*).

guile [gaɪl] *n* хи́трость *f*.

guileless ['gaɪlɪs] *adj* бесхи́тростный*.

guillotine ['gɪləti:n] *n* гильоти́на; (*for paper*) ре́зальная маши́на.

guilt [gɪlt] *n* (*remorse*) вина́; (*culpability*) вино́вность *f*.

guilty ['gɪltɪ] *adj* (*person, expression*) винова́тый; (*of crime*) вино́вный*; (*secret*) позо́рный*; **to plead ~/not guilty** признава́ть* (призна́ть* *perf*) себя́ вино́вным(-ой)/невино́вным(-ой); **to feel ~ about sth** чу́вствовать (*impf*) себя́ винова́тым(-ой) в чём-н.

Guinea ['gɪnɪ] *n*: **Republic of ~** Гвине́я.

guinea ['gɪnɪ] *n* (*BRIT*) гине́я.

guinea pig *n* (*animal*) морска́я сви́нка*; (*fig*) „подо́пытный кро́лик".

guise [gaɪz] *n*: **in** *or* **under the ~ of** под ви́дом +*gen*.

guitar [gɪ'tɑ:'] *n* гита́ра.

guitarist [gɪ'tɑ:rɪst] *n* гитари́ст(ка).

gulch [gʌltʃ] *n* (*US*) (у́зкое) уще́лье*.

gulf [gʌlf] *n* (*GEO*) зали́в; (*also fig*) про́пасть *f*; **the (Persian) G~** Перси́дский* зали́в.

Gulf States *npl*: **the ~ ~** стра́ны *fpl* Перси́дского зали́ва.

Gulf Stream *n*: **the ~ ~** Гольфстри́м.

gull [gʌl] *n* ча́йка*.

gullet ['gʌlɪt] *n* пищево́д.

gullibility [gʌlɪ'bɪlɪtɪ] *n* легкове́рие.

gullible ['gʌlɪbl] *adj* (*naive, trusting*) легкове́рный* (легкове́рен).

gully ['gʌlɪ] *n* (*ravine*) глубо́кий* овра́г.

gulp [gʌlp] *vi* (*swallow: from nerves, excitement*) сгла́тывать (сглотну́ть *perf*) не́рвно ♦ *vt* (*also: ~ down: food, drink*) прогла́тывать (проглоти́ть* *perf*) ♦ *n*: **to drink at one ~** вы́пить* (*perf*) за́лпом.

gum [gʌm] *n* (*ANAT*) десна́*; (*glue*) клей*; (*sweet: also: ~drop*) желе́йный мармела́д (*конфе́та*); (*also: chewing-~*) жева́тельная рези́нка*, жва́чка* (*разг*) ♦ *vt* (*stick*): **to ~ (together)** скле́ивать (скле́ить *perf*)

▶ **gum up** *vt*: **to ~ up the works** (*inf*) засто́порить (*perf*) рабо́ту.

gumboots ['gʌmbu:ts] *npl* (*BRIT*) рези́новые сапоги́* *mpl*.

gumption ['gʌmpʃən] *n* (*sense, wit*) сообрази́тельность *f*, нахо́дчивость *f*.

gumtree ['gʌmtri:] *n*: **to be up a ~** (*fig: inf*) попада́ть (попа́сть* *perf*) впроса́к.

gun [gʌn] *n* (*revolver, pistol*) пистоле́т; (*rifle, airgun*) ружьё*; (*cannon*) пу́шка* ♦ *vt* (*also: ~ down*) расстре́ливать (расстреля́ть *perf*), застрели́ть* (*perf*); **to stick to one's ~s** (*fig*) не скла́дывать (сложи́ть* *perf*) ору́жия.

gunboat ['gʌnbəut] *n* канонёрская ло́дка*.

gun dog *n* охо́тничья соба́ка.

gunfire ['gʌnfaɪə'] *n* оруди́йный ого́нь* *m*.

gung ho [gʌŋ həu] *adj* (*inf*) безрассу́дный*, фанати́чный.

gunk [gʌŋk] *n* (*inf*) га́дость *f*.

gunman ['gʌnmən] *irreg n* вооружённый банди́т.

gunner ['gʌnə'] *n* (*MIL*) артиллери́ст.

gunpoint ['gʌnpɔɪnt] *n*: **at ~** под ду́лом пистоле́та, под прице́лом.

gunpowder ['gʌnpaudə'] *n* по́рох*.

gunrunner ['gʌnrʌnə'] *n* контрабанди́ст, торгу́ющий ору́жием.

gunrunning ['gʌnrʌnɪŋ] *n* контраба́нда ору́жием.

gunshot ['gʌnʃɔt] *n* вы́стрел.

gunsmith ['gʌnsmɪθ] *n* оруже́йный ма́стер*.

gurgle ['gə:gl] *vi* (*baby*) гу́кать (*impf*); (*water*) журча́ть (*impf*).

guru ['guru:] *n* (*REL*) гуру́ *m ind*; (*fig*) духо́вный наста́вник.

gush [gʌʃ] *vi* хлы́нуть (*perf*); (*enthuse*) захлёбываться (захлебну́ться *perf*) от восто́рга ♦ *n* (*of water etc*) пото́к.

gushing [ˈgʌʃɪŋ] *adj* (*female*) восто́рженный* (восто́ржен); (*admiration, reverence*) неуёмный* (неуёмен).

gusset [ˈgʌsɪt] *n* клин*.

gust [gʌst] *n* (*of wind*) поры́в.

gusto [ˈgʌstəu] *n*: **with** ~ (*eat*) с удово́льствием; (*work*) с жа́ром.

gusty [ˈgʌstɪ] *adj* (*wind*) поры́вистый (поры́вист); (*day*) ве́треный (ве́трен).

gut [gʌt] *n* кишка́*; (*MUS, SPORT*) струна́* (*из кишо́к живо́тных*) ♦ *vt* (*poultry, fish*) потроши́ть (вы́потрошить *perf*); (*building*) удаля́ть все вну́тренние ча́сти до́ма; ~**s** *npl* (*ANAT*) кишки́* *fpl*, вну́тренности *fpl*; (*inf: courage*) му́жество *ntsg*; **the house was** ~**ted by fire** дом сгоре́л по́лностью; **to hate sb's** ~**s** (*inf*) не принима́ть (приня́ть* *perf*) кого́-н на́ дух, смерте́льно ненави́деть* (*impf*) кого́-н.

gut reaction *n* инстинкти́вная реа́кция.

gutsy [ˈgʌtsɪ] (*inf*) *adj* напо́ристый.

gutted [ˈgʌtɪd] (*inf*) *adj*: **I was** ~ (*very disappointed*) я был соверше́нно уби́т.

gutter [ˈgʌtə*] *n* (*in street*) сто́чная кана́ва; (*of roof*) водосто́чный жёлоб*.

gutter press (*inf: pej*) *n* бульва́рная пре́сса.

guttural [ˈgʌtərl] *adj* гортанный*.

guy [gaɪ] *n* (*inf: man*) па́рень* *m*; (*also:* ~**rope**) шнуры́ *mpl* для натя́гивания пала́тки; (*effigy of Guy Fawkes*) изображе́ние Гая Фо́кса, сжига́емое 5 ноября́.

Guyana [gaɪˈænə] *n* Гайа́на.

guzzle [ˈgʌzl] *vt* (*drink*) пить* (вы́пить* *perf*) с жа́дностью; (*food*) есть* (съесть* *perf*) с жа́дностью.

gym [dʒɪm] *n* (*also:* ~**nasium**) гимнасти́ческий зал; (*also:* ~**nastics**) гимна́стика.

gymkhana [dʒɪmˈkɑːnə] *n* конноспорти́вные состяза́ния *ntpl*.

gymnasium [dʒɪmˈneɪzɪəm] *n* гимнасти́ческий зал.

gymnast [ˈdʒɪmnæst] *n* гимна́ст(ка*).

gymnastics [dʒɪmˈnæstɪks] *n* гимна́стика.

gym shoes *npl* спорти́вные та́почки* *fpl*.

gymslip [ˈdʒɪmslɪp] *n* (*BRIT: tunic*) шко́льное пла́тье без рукаво́в.

gynaecologist [gaɪnɪˈkɔlədʒɪst] (*US* **gynecologist**) *n* гинеко́лог.

gynaecology [gaɪnəˈkɔlədʒɪ] (*US* **gynecology**) *n* гинеколо́гия.

gypsy [ˈdʒɪpsɪ] *n* = **gipsy**.

gyrate [dʒaɪˈreɪt] *vi* (*revolve*) враща́ться (*impf*) по кру́гу.

gyroscope [ˈdʒaɪərəskəup] *n* гироско́п.

~ H, h ~

H, h [eɪtʃ] n (letter) 8-áя бу́ква англи́йского алфави́та.

habeas corpus ['heɪbɪəs'kɔ:pəs] n (LAW) Ха́беас Ко́рпус (закон о неприкосновенности личности).

haberdashery [hæbə'dæʃərɪ] n (BRIT) галантере́йные това́ры mpl.

habit ['hæbɪt] n (custom) привы́чка*; (addiction) пристра́стие; (REL: costume) облаче́ние; **to get out of the ~ of doing** отвыка́ть (отвы́кнуть* perf) +infin; **to get into the ~ of doing** привыка́ть (привы́кнуть perf) +infin; **to be in the ~ of doing** име́ть (impf) обыкнове́ние +infin.

habitable ['hæbɪtəbl] adj (house etc) приго́дный* для жилья́.

habitat ['hæbɪtæt] n (BOT, ZOOL) есте́ственная среда́* обита́ния.

habitation [hæbɪ'teɪʃən] n (house etc) жили́ще; **fit for human ~** приго́дный* для жилья́.

habitual [hə'bɪtjuəl] adj (action) привы́чный* (привы́чен); (drinker) запо́йный; (liar) отъя́вленный.

habitually [hə'bɪtjuəlɪ] adv (late, untidy) обы́чно.

hack [hæk] vt (cut, slice) отруба́ть (отруби́ть perf) ♦ n (pej: writer) писа́ка* m/f; (horse) ло́шадь, сдава́емая напрока́т для верхово́й езды́ ♦ vi: **to ~ into** (COMPUT) нелега́льно входи́ть* (войти́* perf) в +acc.

hacker ['hækə'] n (COMPUT) хэ́кер.

hackles ['hæklz] npl: **to make sb's ~ rise** (fig) приводи́ть* (привести́ perf) в состоя́ние раздраже́ния.

hackney cab ['hæknɪ-] n наёмный экипа́ж.

hackneyed ['hæknɪd] adj изби́тый.

hacksaw ['hæksɔ:] n ножо́вка.

had [hæd] pt, pp of **have**.

haddock ['hædək] (pl ~ or ~s) n треска́; **smoked ~** копчёная треска́.

hadn't ['hædnt] = **had not**.

haematology ['hi:mə'tɔlədʒɪ] (US **hematology**) n гематоло́гия.

haemoglobin ['hi:mə'gləubɪn] (US **hemoglobin**) n гемоглоби́н.

haemophilia ['hi:mə'fɪlɪə] (US **hemophilia**) n

гемофили́я.

haemorrhage ['hɛmərɪdʒ] (US **hemorrage**) n кровотече́ние; **brain ~** кровоизлия́ние (в мозг).

haemorrhoids ['hɛmərɔɪdz] (US **hemorroids**) npl геморро́й msg.

hag [hæg] n (woman) карга́; (witch) ве́дьма.

haggard ['hægəd] adj (face, look) измождённый*.

haggis ['hægɪs] n (SCOTTISH) ха́ггис (шотландское блюдо из бараньей или телячьей требухи с овсяной крупой и специями).

haggle ['hægl] vi (bargain) торгова́ться (сторгова́ться perf); **to ~ over** спо́рить (impf) о +prp.

haggling ['hæglɪŋ] n торго́вля.

Hague [heɪg] n: **The ~** (GEO) Гаа́га.

hail [heɪl] n (also fig) град ♦ vt (call) оклика́ть (окли́кнуть perf); (flag down) подзыва́ть (подозва́ть* perf); (acclaim) превозноси́ть* (превознести́* perf) ♦ vi: **it's ~ing** идёт град; **he ~s from Scotland** он ро́дом из Шотла́ндии.

hailstone ['heɪlstəun] n гра́дина.

hailstorm ['heɪlstɔ:m] n гроза́* с гра́дом.

hair [hɛə'] n во́лосы* pl; (of animal) шерсть f; (single hair) во́лос*; **to do one's ~** причёсываться (причеса́ться* perf); **to miss by a ~'s breadth** (fig) чуть-чу́ть промахну́ться (perf).

hairbrush ['hɛəbrʌʃ] n щётка* для воло́с.

haircut ['hɛəkʌt] n стри́жка*.

hairdo ['hɛədu:] n причёска*.

hairdresser ['hɛədrɛsə'] n парикма́хер.

hairdresser's ['hɛədrɛsəz] n парикма́херская f adj.

hair dryer n фен.

-haired [hɛəd] suffix: **fair/long-~** светло-/ длинноволо́сый*.

hairgrip ['hɛəgrɪp] n невиди́мка.

hairline ['hɛəlaɪn] n ли́ния воло́с.

hairline fracture n тре́щина.

hairnet ['hɛənɛt] n се́тка* для воло́с.

hair oil n ма́сло* для воло́с.

hairpiece ['hɛəpi:s] n накладны́е во́лосы* mpl.

---

* marks translations which have irregular inflections. The Russian-English side of the dictionary gives inflectional information.

hairpin ['hɛəpɪn] n шпи́лька*.
hairpin bend (US **hairpin curve**) n круто́й
поворо́т.
hair-raising ['hɛəreɪzɪŋ] adj (experience, tale)
жу́ткий*.
hair remover n (cream) крем для удале́ния
воло́с.
hair slide n зако́лка* для воло́с.
hair spray n лак для воло́с.
hairstyle ['hɛəstaɪl] n причёска*.
hairy ['hɛərɪ] adj (person) волоса́тый; (animal)
мохна́тый (мохна́т); (inf: situation)
риско́ванный*.
Haiti ['heɪtɪ] n Гаи́ти m ind.
hake [heɪk] (pl ~ or ~s) n серебри́стый хек.
halcyon ['hælsɪən] adj: ~ **days** безмяте́жные
дни.
hale [heɪl] adj: ~ **and hearty** здоро́вый*
(здоро́в) и бо́дрый* (бодр).
half [hɑːf] (pl **halves**) n полови́на; (also: ~ **pint**:
of beer etc) полпи́нты f; (RAIL, bus) биле́т за
полцены́ ♦ adv (empty, closed, open, asleep)
наполови́ну; **first/second** ~ (SPORT) пе́рвый/
второ́й тайм; **one and a** ~ (with m nouns)
полтора́ +gen sg; (with f nouns) полторы́ +gen
sg; **three and a** ~ три с полови́ной; ~**-an-hour**
полчаса́* m; **a dozen (of)** полдю́жины* f
(+gen); ~ **a pound (of)** полфу́нта m (+gen); **a**
week and a ~ полторы́* f неде́ли; ~ **(of)**
полови́на (+gen); ~ **the amount of** полови́на
+gen; **to cut sth in** ~ разреза́ть (разре́зать*
perf) что-н попола́м; ~ **past three** полови́на
четвёртого; **to go halves (with sb)** дели́ть*
(подели́ть* perf) попола́м (с кем-н); **she never**
does things by halves она́ никогда́ не
остана́вливается на полпути́; **he's too clever**
by ~ он чересчу́р уж у́мный; ~ **empty/closed**
наполови́ну пусто́й*/закры́тый; **a** ~ **bottle**
(of) полбуты́лки (+gen).
half-baked ['hɑːf'beɪkt] adj (idea, scheme)
непроду́манный.
half board n пансио́н с за́втраком и у́жином.
half-breed ['hɑːfbriːd] n = **half-caste**.
half-brother ['hɑːfbrʌðə'] n (with same mother)
единоутро́бный брат*; (with same father)
единокро́вный брат*.
half-caste ['hɑːfkɑːst] n челове́к сме́шанной
ра́сы.
half-day [hɑːf'deɪ] n коро́ткий* день* m.
half-hearted ['hɑːf'hɑːtɪd] adj лени́вый.
half-hour [hɑːf'auə'] n полчаса́* m.
half-life ['hɑːflaɪf] n (TECH) пери́од
полураспа́да.
half-mast ['hɑːf'mɑːst] adv: **at** ~ (flag)
приспу́щенный (приспу́щен).
halfpenny ['heɪpnɪ] n (BRIT) полпе́нса* m.
half-price ['hɑːf'praɪs] adj, adv за полцены́.
half-sister ['hɑːfsɪstə'] n (with same mother)
единоутро́бная сестра́*; (with same father)
единокро́вная сестра́*.
half term n (BRIT: SCOL) кани́кулы в середи́не

шко́льного триме́стра.
half-timbered [hɑːf'tɪmbəd] adj деревя́нно-
кирпи́чный.
half-time [hɑːf'taɪm] n (SPORT) переры́в ме́жду
та́ймами.
halfway ['hɑːf'weɪ] adv на полпути́; **I am**
prepared to meet you ~ (fig) я гото́в пойти́
Вам навстре́чу.
halfway house n дом* на полпути́; (fig)
середи́на.
halfwit ['hɑːfwɪt] n приду́рок*,
полоу́мный(-ая) m(f) adj.
half-yearly [hɑːf'jɪəlɪ] adv раз в полго́да ♦ adj
полугодово́й.
halibut ['hælɪbət] n inv па́лтус.
halitosis [hælɪ'təusɪs] n дурно́й за́пах изо рта́.
hall [hɔːl] n (entrance way) прихо́жая f adj;
(corridor) коридо́р; (mansion) уса́дьба; (for
concerts, meetings etc) зал; **to live in** ~**s** (BRIT:
students) жить* (impf) в общежи́тии.
hallmark ['hɔːlmɑːk] n про́ба; (fig)
отличи́тельная черта́*.
hallo [hə'ləu] excl = **hello**.
hall of residence (pl ~**s** ~ ~) n (BRIT)
общежи́тие.
hallowed ['hæləud] adj (REL) свято́й*; (fig:
respected, revered) почита́емый.
Hallowe'en ['hæləu'iːn] n кану́н Дня всех
святы́х.
hallucination [həluːsɪ'neɪʃən] n галлюцина́ция.
hallucinogenic [həluːsɪnəu'dʒɛnɪk] adj
галлюцинато́рный.
hallway ['hɔːlweɪ] n (entrance hall) прихо́жая f
adj.
halo ['heɪləu] n (REL) нимб; (circle of light)
орео́л.
halt [hɔːlt] n остано́вка ♦ vt остана́вливать
(останови́ть* perf) ♦ vi остана́вливаться
(останови́ться* perf); **to call a** ~ **to sth** (fig)
дава́ть* (дать* perf) отбо́й чему́-н.
halter ['hɔːltə'] n (for horse) по́вод*.
halterneck ['hɔːltənɛk] adj: ~ **dress** пла́тье с
откры́той спино́й и завя́зками вокру́г ше́и.
halve [hɑːv] vt (reduce) сокраща́ть
(сократи́ть* perf) наполови́ну; (divide)
дели́ть* (раздели́ть* perf) попола́м.
halves [hɑːvz] pl of **half**.
ham [hæm] n ветчина́*; (inf: also: **radio** ~)
радиолюби́тель m; (: actor) безда́рный(-ая)
актёр(-три́са) ♦ vt: **to** ~ **it up** переи́грывать
(переигра́ть perf).
Hamburg ['hæmbəːg] n Га́мбург.
hamburger ['hæmbəːgə'] n га́мбургер.
ham-fisted ['hæm'fɪstɪd] adj нело́вкий*.
ham-handed ['hæm'hændɪd] adj = **ham-fisted**.
hamlet ['hæmlɪt] n дереву́шка*.
hammer ['hæmə'] n молото́к*, мо́лот ♦ vi (on
door etc) колоти́ть* (impf) ♦ vt (criticize
severely) критикова́ть (раскритикова́ть
perf); (nail): **to** ~ **in** забива́ть (заби́ть* perf),
вбива́ть (вбить* perf); (fig: force): **to** ~ **sth into**

sb вда́лбливать (вдолби́ть* perf) что-н кому́-н

▶ **hammer out** vt (metal) расплю́щивать (расплю́щить perf); (fig: solution, agreement) выраба́тывать (вы́работать perf).

hammock ['hæmək] n (on ship) ко́йка*; (in garden) гама́к*.

hamper ['hæmpər] vt меша́ть (помеша́ть perf) +dat ♦ n (basket) больша́я корзи́на с кры́шкой.

hamster ['hæmstə'] n хомя́к*.

hamstring ['hæmstriŋ] n (ANAT) подколе́нное сухожи́лие ♦ vt (restrict) ограни́чивать (ограни́чить perf).

hand [hænd] n (ANAT) рука́*, кисть* f руки́; (of clock) стре́лка*; (handwriting) по́черк; (worker) рабо́чий* m adj; (of cards) ка́рты fpl (находя́щиеся на рука́х у игрока́); (measurement: of horse) ладо́нь f (ме́ра при измере́нии ро́ста ло́шади) ♦ vt (pass) передава́ть* (переда́ть* perf); (give) вруча́ть (вручи́ть perf); **to give** or **lend sb a ~** помога́ть (помо́чь* perf) кому́-н; **at ~** под руко́й; **by ~** вручну́ю; **in ~** (time) в распоряже́нии; (situation) под контро́лем; **the job in ~** теку́щее де́ло; **on ~** (person, services etc) в распоряже́нии; **to get out of ~** (child) отбива́ться (отби́ться* perf) от рук; (situation) выходи́ть* (вы́йти* perf) из-под контро́ля; **to dismiss out of ~** отве́ргнуть (perf) сра́зу; **I have the information to ~** я располага́ю информа́цией; **on the one ~** ..., **on the other ~** ... с одно́й стороны́ ..., с друго́й стороны́; **to force sb's ~** заставля́ть (заста́вить* perf) кого́-н раскры́ть свои́ ка́рты; **he has a free ~** у него́ развя́заны ру́ки; **to change ~s** (be sold etc) переходи́ть* (перейти́* perf) из рук в ру́ки; **to have in one's ~** (fig) держа́ть* (impf) под контро́лем; **~s off!** ру́ки прочь!

▶ **hand down** vt (knowledge, possessions) передава́ть* (переда́ть* perf); (LAW: judgement, sentence) выноси́ть* (вы́нести* perf)

▶ **hand in** vt (essay, work) сдава́ть* (сдать* perf)

▶ **hand out** vt раздава́ть* (разда́ть* perf)

▶ **hand over** vt передава́ть* (переда́ть* perf)

▶ **hand round** vt (BRIT) раздава́ть* (разда́ть* perf); (subj: hostess) разноси́ть* (разнести́* perf).

handbag ['hændbæg] n (да́мская) су́мочка*.

hand baggage n ручно́й бага́ж*.

handball ['hændbɔːl] n гандбо́л.

hand basin n таз*.

handbook ['hændbuk] n руково́дство.

handbrake ['hændbreɪk] n ручно́й то́рмоз*.

h & c abbr (BRIT) = hot and cold (water).

hand cream n крем для рук.

handcuff ['hændkʌf] vt надева́ть (наде́ть* perf) нару́чники +dat or на +acc.

handcuffs ['hændkʌfs] npl нару́чники mpl.

handful ['hændful] n горсть* f, (fig: of people) го́рстка*.

hand-held ['hænd'hɛld] adj ручно́й.

handicap ['hændɪkæp] n (disability) физи́ческая неполноце́нность f, (disadvantage) препя́тствие; (SPORT) гандика́п ♦ vt препя́тствовать (воспрепя́тствовать perf) +dat; **mentally/physically ~ped** у́мственно/ физи́чески неполноце́нный.

handicraft ['hændɪkrɑːft] n рукоде́лие; (objects) изде́лие ручно́й рабо́ты.

handiwork ['hændɪwɜːk] n ручны́е изде́лия ntpl; **this looks like his ~** (pej) похо́же, что э́то его́ рук де́ло.

handkerchief ['hæŋkətʃɪf] n носово́й плато́к*.

handle ['hændl] n ру́чка*; (CB RADIO: name) про́звище ♦ vt (touch) держа́ть* (impf) в рука́х; (deal with) справля́ться (спра́виться* perf) с +instr; (treat: people) обраща́ться (impf) с +instr; **to fly off the ~** (inf) срыва́ться (сорва́ться* perf); **to get a ~ on a problem** (inf) бра́ться* (взя́ться* perf) за реше́ние пробле́мы; **"handle with care"** „обраща́ться осторо́жно".

handlebar(s) ['hændlbɑː(z)] n(pl) руль* msg (велосипе́да и́ли мотоци́кла).

handling ['hændlɪŋ] n: **~ of** (of situation, problem etc) подхо́д к +dat; (luggage) обраще́ние с +instr; (LAW) веде́ние +gen.

handling charges npl (COMM) пла́та fsg за услу́ги.

hand luggage n ручно́й бага́ж*.

handmade ['hænd'meɪd] adj ручно́й рабо́ты; **it's ~** э́то – ручна́я рабо́та.

hand-out ['hændaut] n (money, clothing, food) благотвори́тельная по́мощь f, (publicity leaflet) рекла́мный листо́к*; (summary: of lecture) проспе́кт.

hand-picked ['hænd'pɪkt] adj (produce) со́бранный вручну́ю; (staff etc) специа́льно подо́бранный.

handrail ['hændreɪl] n пери́ла pl.

handset ['hændsɛt] n телефо́нная тру́бка*.

handshake ['hændʃeɪk] n рукопожа́тие.

handsome ['hænsəm] adj (man) краси́вый (краси́в); (woman) интере́сный (интере́сен); (building) внуши́тельный*; (gift) ще́дрый (щедр); (fig: profit, return) внуши́тельный* (внуши́телен).

hands-on ['hændz'ɔn] adj практи́ческий*.

handstand ['hændstænd] n: **to do a ~** де́лать (сде́лать perf) сто́йку на рука́х.

hand-to-mouth ['hændtə'mauθ] adj: **they live a ~ existence** они́ живу́т впро́голодь.

handwriting ['hændraɪtɪŋ] n по́черк.

---

* marks translations which have irregular inflections. The Russian-English side of the dictionary gives inflectional information.

handwritten ['hændrɪtn] *adj* напи́санный от руки́.

handy ['hændɪ] *adj* (*useful*) удо́бный*; (*skilful*) ло́вкий*; (*close at hand*) побли́зости; **to come in** ~ пригожда́ться* (пригоди́ться* *perf*).

handyman ['hændɪmæn] *irreg n* (*at home*) ма́стер* на все ру́ки; (*in hotel etc*) подру́чный *m adj*.

hang [hæŋ] (*pt, pp* **hung**) *vt* ве́шать (пове́сить* *perf*); (*pt, pp* **hanged**; *execute*) ве́шать (пове́сить* *perf*) ♦ *vi* висе́ть* (*impf*) ♦ *n*: **to get the** ~ **of sth** (*inf*) разбира́ться (разобра́ться* *perf*) в чём-н; **to** ~ **one's head** ве́шать (пове́сить* *perf*) го́лову

▸ **hang about** *vi* слоня́ться (*impf*)

▸ **hang around** *vi* = **hang about**

▸ **hang back** *vi* (*hesitate*): **to** ~ **back (from doing)** быть* (*impf*) в нереши́тельности (+*infin*)

▸ **hang on** *vi* (*wait*) подожда́ть* (*impf*) ♦ *vt fus* (*depend on*) зави́сеть (*impf*) от +*gen*; **to** ~ **on to** (*keep hold of*) цепля́ться (*impf*) за +*acc*; (*keep*) держа́ть (*impf*) у себя́

▸ **hang out** *vt* (*washing*) выве́шивать (вы́весить* *perf*) ♦ *vi* высо́вываться (вы́сунуться *perf*); **this is where the students always** ~ **out** (*inf*) студе́нты всегда́ там ока́лачиваются

▸ **hang together** *vi* (*argument*) быть* (*impf*) убеди́тельным(-ой)

▸ **hang up** *vi* (*TEL*) ве́шать (пове́сить* *perf*) тру́бку ♦ *vt* ве́шать (пове́сить* *perf*).

hangar ['hæŋə'] *n* анга́р.

hangdog ['hæŋdɔg] *adj* (*look, expression*) винова́тый.

hanger ['hæŋə'] *n* (*for clothes*) ве́шалка*.

hanger-on [hæŋər'ɔn] *n* прихлеба́тель(ница) *m(f)*.

hang-glider ['hæŋɡlaɪdə'] *n* (*craft*) дельтапла́н; (*pilot*) дельтапланери́ст.

hang-gliding ['hæŋɡlaɪdɪŋ] *n* дельта-планери́зм.

hanging ['hæŋɪŋ] *n* (*execution*) пове́шение; (*for wall*) портье́ра.

hangman ['hæŋmən] *irreg n* пала́ч*.

hangover ['hæŋəʊvə'] *n* (*after drinking*) похме́лье; (*from past*) пережи́ток*.

hang-up ['hæŋʌp] *n* (*inhibition*) ко́мплекс.

hank [hæŋk] *n* мото́к*.

hanker ['hæŋkə'] *vi*: **to** ~ **after** (*desire, long for*) мечта́ть (*impf*) о +*prp*.

hankering ['hæŋkərɪŋ] *n*: **I have a** ~ **for a beer** мне бы сейча́с пи́ва.

hankie ['hæŋkɪ] *n abbr* = **handkerchief**.

hanky ['hæŋkɪ] *n abbr* = **handkerchief**.

Hanoi [hæ'nɔɪ] *n* Хано́й.

Hants *abbr* (*BRIT: POST*) = Hampshire.

haphazard [hæp'hæzəd] *adj* бессисте́мный*.

hapless ['hæplɪs] *adj* несча́стный*.

happen ['hæpən] *vi* случа́ться (случи́ться *perf*); (*произойти́* (произойти́* *perf*); (*chance*): **I** ~**ed to meet him in the park** я случа́йно встре́тил его́ в па́рке; **as it** ~**s** кста́ти; **what's** ~**ing?** что происхо́дит?; **she** ~**ed to be free** она́ оказа́лась свобо́дной; **if anything** ~**ed to him** е́сли с ним что-н случи́тся

▸ **happen (up)on** *vt fus* натыка́ться (наткну́ться *perf*) на +*acc*.

happening ['hæpnɪŋ] *n* слу́чай.

happily ['hæpɪlɪ] *adv* (*luckily*) к сча́стью; (*cheerfully*) ра́достно.

happiness ['hæpɪnɪs] *n* сча́стье.

happy ['hæpɪ] *adj* (*pleased*) счастли́вый (счастли́в); (*cheerful*) весёлый* (ве́сел); (*apt*) уда́чный* (уда́чен); **I am** ~ **(with it)** (*content*) я дово́лен (э́тим); **he is always** ~ **to help** (*willing*) он всегда́ с удово́льствием помога́ет; ~ **birthday!** с днём рожде́ния!

happy-go-lucky ['hæpɪɡəʊ'lʌkɪ] *adj* беспе́чный* (беспе́чен).

happy hour *n вре́мя, в тече́ние кото́рого спиртны́е напи́тки в ба́рах продаю́тся по сни́женным це́нам.*

harangue [hə'ræŋ] *vt* (*audience, class*) увещева́ть (*impf*).

harass ['hærəs] *vt* изводи́ть* (извести́* *perf*).

harassed ['hærəst] *adj* (*person*) изнурённый* (изнурён).

harassment ['hærəsmənt] *n* пресле́дование; **sexual** ~ сексуа́льное пресле́дование.

harbour ['hɑːbə'] (*US* **harbor**) *n* га́вань *f* ♦ *vt* (*hope, fear etc*) зата́ивать (зата́ить *perf*); (*criminal, fugitive*) укрыва́ть (укры́ть* *perf*); **to** ~ **a grudge against sb** держа́ть* (*impf*) зло на кого́-н.

harbour dues *npl* порто́вые сбо́ры *mpl*.

harbour master *n* нача́льник по́рта.

hard [hɑːd] *adj* (*surface, object*) твёрдый (твёрд); (*question, problem*) тру́дный* (тру́ден); (*work, life*) тяжёлый (тяжёл); (*person*) суро́вый (суро́в); (*facts, evidence*) неопроверж́имый (неопроверж́им); (*drink*) кре́пкий* (кре́пок); (*drugs*) си́льный* ♦ *adv*: **to work** ~ мно́го и усе́рдно рабо́тать (*impf*); ~ **luck!** не везёт!; **no** ~ **feelings!** не держи́те зла!; **I don't have any** ~ **feelings** я не держу́ зла; **he is** ~ **of hearing** он туг на́ ухо; **to think** ~ хорошо́ поду́мать (*perf*); **to try** ~ **to win** упо́рно добива́ться (*impf*) побе́ды; **to look** ~ **at** смотре́ть* (посмотре́ть* *perf*) при́стально на +*acc*; **I felt** ~ **done by** я почу́вствовал, что со мной обошли́сь несправедли́во; **I find it** ~ **to believe that ...** мне тру́дно пове́рить, что ...

hard-and-fast ['hɑːdən'fɑːst] *adj* неукосни́т-ельный*.

hardback ['hɑːdbæk] *n* (*book*) кни́га в твёрдом переплёте.

hardboard ['hɑːdbɔːd] *n* древе́сно-стру́жечная плита́.

hard-boiled egg ['hɑːd'bɔɪld-] *n* яйцо́*

вкруту́ю.

hard cash *n* нали́чные де́ньги* *pl*.

hard copy *n* (*COMPUT*) печа́тная ко́пия, распеча́тка.

hard core *n* (*of group*) гру́ппа пре́данных сторо́нников.

hard-core ['hɑ:d'kɔ:ʳ] *adj* (*pornography*) преде́льно открове́нный*; (*supporters*) ве́рный*.

hard court *n* (*TENNIS*) твёрдый корт.

hard disk *n* (*COMPUT*) жёсткий* диск.

harden ['hɑ:dn] *vt* (*substance*) де́лать (сде́лать *perf*) твёрдым(-ой); (*attitude, person*) ожесточа́ть (ожесточи́ть *perf*) ◆ *vi* (*substance*) твёрдеть (затверде́ть *perf*); (*attitude, person*) ожесточа́ться (ожесточи́ться *perf*).

hardened ['hɑ:dnd] *adj* (*criminal*) закорене́лый; **to be ~ to sth** быть* (*impf*) нечувстви́тельным(-ой) к чему́-н.

hardening ['hɑ:dnɪŋ] *n* зака́ливание; (*of opposition*) усиле́ние.

hard graft *n*: **by sheer ~ ~** то́лько благодаря́ упо́рной рабо́те.

hard-headed ['hɑ:d'hɛdɪd] *adj* (*businessman*) расчётливый (расчётлив).

hardhearted ['hɑ:d'hɑ:tɪd] *adj* бессерде́чный* (бессерде́чен).

hard-hitting ['hɑ:d'hɪtɪŋ] *adj* (*report, speech, article*) бью́щий напрями́к.

hard labour *n* (*punishment*) принуди́тельные рабо́ты *fpl*.

hardliner [hɑ:d'laɪnəʳ] *n* сторо́нник(-ица) жёсткой ли́нии (*в поли́тике*).

hard-luck story ['hɑ:dlʌk-] *n* жа́лостливая исто́рия.

hardly ['hɑ:dlɪ] *adv* (*scarcely*) едва́; (*no sooner*) как то́лько; (*harshly*) суро́во; **~ anywhere/ ever** почти́ нигде́/никогда́; **it's ~ the case** э́то не тот слу́чай; **I ~ think so** я так не ду́маю; **I can ~ believe it** я с трудо́м могу́ пове́рить в э́то.

hard-nosed [hɑ:d'nəuzd] *adj* трézвый.

hard-pressed [hɑ:d'prɛst] *adj*: **I am ~ for time/ money** у меня́ ту́го со вре́менем/деньга́ми.

hard sell *n* (*COMM*) уси́ленное реклами́рование това́ров.

hardship ['hɑ:dʃɪp] *n* (*difficulty*) тру́дности *fpl*.

hard shoulder *n* (*BRIT: AUT*) обо́чина с твёрдым покры́тием, на кото́рой разрешена́ остано́вка тра́нспорта.

hard up *adj* (*inf*) на мели́.

hardware ['hɑ:dwɛəʳ] *n* скобяны́е изде́лия *ntpl*; (*COMPUT*) обору́дование, аппарату́ра; (*MIL*) вое́нная те́хника.

hardware shop *n* магази́н скобяны́х изде́лий.

hard-wearing [hɑ:d'wɛərɪŋ] *adj* (*clothes, shoes*)

кре́пкий* (кре́пок).

hard-won [hɑ:d'wʌn] *adj* с трудо́м завоёванный (завоёван); (*victory*) с трудо́м оде́ржанный (оде́ржан).

hard-working [hɑ:d'wə:kɪŋ] *adj* (*employee, student*) усе́рдный* (усе́рден).

hardy ['hɑ:dɪ] *adj* (*animals, people*) выно́сливый (выно́слив); (*plant*) морозоусто́йчивый (морозоусто́йчив).

hare [hɛəʳ] *n* за́яц*.

harebrained ['hɛəbreɪnd] *adj* (*scheme, idea*) несура́зный* (несура́зен).

harelip ['hɛəlɪp] *n* за́ячья губа́*.

harem [hɑ:'ri:m] *n* гаре́м.

hark back [hɑ:k-] *vi*: **to ~ ~ to** (*be reminiscent of*) напомина́ть (напо́мнить *perf*) о +*prp*; (*remember*) вспомина́ть (вспо́мнить *perf*) о +*prp*.

harm [hɑ:m] *n* (*injury*) теле́сное поврежде́ние; (*damage*) уще́рб ◆ *vt* (*thing*) поврежда́ть (повреди́ть* *perf*); (*person*) наноси́ть* (нанести́* *perf*) вред +*dat*; **to mean no ~** не хоте́ть* (*impf*) оби́деть; **to come to no ~** зако́нчиться (*perf*) благополу́чно; **out of ~'s way** от греха́ пода́льше; **there's no ~ in trying** попы́тка – не пы́тка.

harmful ['hɑ:mful] *adj* (*toxin, influence etc*) вре́дный* (вре́ден).

harmless [hɑ:mlɪs] *adj* (*animal, person*) безоби́дный* (безоби́ден); (*joke, activity*) неви́нный* (неви́нен).

harmonic [hɑ:'mɔnɪk] *adj* гармони́ческий.

harmonica [hɑ:'mɔnɪkə] *n* губна́я гармо́ника.

harmonics [hɑ:'mɔnɪks] *npl* гармо́ния *fsg*.

harmonious [hɑ:'məunɪəs] *adj* гармони́чный* (гармони́чен).

harmonium [hɑ:'məunɪəm] *n* фисгармо́ния.

harmonize ['hɑ:mənaɪz] *vi* (*MUS*) гармони́ровать (*impf*); (*colours, ideas*): **to ~ (with)** гармони́ровать (*impf*) (с +*instr*).

harmony ['hɑ:mənɪ] *n* (*accord*) гармо́ния; (*MUS*) созву́чие.

harness ['hɑ:nɪs] *n* (*for horse*) у́пряжь *f*; (*for child*) постро́мки* *fpl*; (*safety harness*) привязны́е ремни́ *mpl* ◆ *vt* (*horse, dog*) запряга́ть (запря́чь* *perf*); (*resources, energy etc*) обу́здывать (обузда́ть *perf*).

harp [hɑ:p] *n* а́рфа ◆ *vi*: **to ~ on about** (*pej*) заводи́ть* (завести́* *perf*) волы́нку о +*prp*.

harpist ['hɑ:pɪst] *n* арфи́ст(ка*).

harpoon [hɑ:'pu:n] *n* гарпу́н*.

harpsichord ['hɑ:psɪkɔ:d] *n* клавеси́н.

harried ['hærɪd] *adj* заму́ченный (заму́чен).

harrow ['hærəu] *n* (*AGR*) борона́.

harrowing ['hærəuɪŋ] *adj* душераздира́ющий*.

harry ['hærɪ] *vt* изводи́ть* (извести́* *perf*).

harsh [hɑ:ʃ] *adj* (*sound, light, criticism*) ре́зкий* (ре́зок); (*person*) жёсткий* (жёсток);

---

* marks translations which have irregular inflections. The Russian-English side of the dictionary gives inflectional information

(*remark*) стро́гий* (строг); (*life, winter*)
суро́вый (суро́в).

harshly ['hɑːʃlɪ] *adv* (*criticize*) ре́зко; (*mark, speak*) стро́го; (*act*) жёстко.

harshness ['hɑːʃnɪs] *n* (*see adj*) ре́зкость *f*;
жёсткость *f*; стро́гость *f*; суро́вость *f*.

harvest ['hɑːvɪst] *n* (*harvest time*) жа́тва; (*of barley, fruit etc*) урожа́й ♦ *vt* убира́ть (убра́ть *perf*).

harvester ['hɑːvɪstə'] *n* (*machine: also:* **combine** ~) комба́йн.

has [hæz] *vb see* **have**.

has-been ['hæzbiːn] *n* (*inf: person*): **he's/she's a** ~ его́/её вре́мя прошло́.

hash [hæʃ] *n* (*CULIN*) мясно́е рагу́ *nt ind*; (*fig: mess*): **to make a** ~ **of sth** запа́рывать (запоро́ть *perf*) что-н.

hash [hæʃ] *n abbr* (*inf*) = **hashish**.

hashish ['hæʃɪʃ] *n* гаши́ш.

hasn't ['hæznt] = **has not**.

hassle ['hæsl] (*inf*) *n* моро́ка ♦ *vt* надоеда́ть (*impf*) +*dat*.

haste [heɪst] *n* спе́шка; **in** ~ в спе́шке; **to make** ~ (**to do**) торопи́ться (поторопи́ться *perf*) (+*infin*).

hasten ['heɪsn] *vt* (*speed up*) торопи́ть* (поторопи́ть* *perf*) ♦ *vi* (*hurry*): **to** ~ **to do** торопи́ться* (поторопи́ться* *perf*) +*infin*; **I** ~ **to add ...** спешу́ доба́вить ...; **she** ~**ed back to the house** она́ поспеши́ла обра́тно к до́му.

hastily ['heɪstɪlɪ] *adv* (*hurriedly*) поспе́шно; (*rashly*) опроме́тчиво.

hasty ['heɪstɪ] *adj* (*hurried*) поспе́шный* (поспе́шен); (*rash*) опроме́тчивый (опроме́тчив).

hat [hæt] *n* шля́па; (*woolly, furry*) ша́пка*; **to keep sth under one's** ~ держа́ть* (*impf*) что-н в секре́те.

hatbox ['hætbɔks] *n* шля́пная коро́бка*.

hatch [hætʃ] *n* (*NAUT: also:* ~**way**) люк; (*also:* **service** ~) разда́точное *or* буфе́тное окно́* ♦ *vi* (*also:* ~ **out**: *chick, egg*) вылупля́ться (вы́лупиться* *perf*) ♦ *vt* (*egg, chick etc*) выси́живать (вы́сидеть* *perf*); (*plot*) вына́шивать (вы́носить* *perf*).

hatchback ['hætʃbæk] *n* (*AUT*) маши́на-пика́п *f*.

hatchet ['hætʃɪt] *n* (*axe*) топо́рик; **to bury the** ~ мири́ться (помири́ться *perf*).

hatchet job (*inf*) *n* напа́дки* *pl*; **to do a** ~ ~ **on sb** разноси́ть* (разнести́* *perf*) кого́-н в пух и прах.

hatchet man *n* (*US: inf*) наёмник.

hate [heɪt] *vt* ненави́деть* (*impf*) ♦ *n* не́нависть *f*; **to** ~ **to do** *or* **doing** ненави́деть* (*impf*) +*infin*; **I** ~ **to trouble you, but ...** мне о́чень не хо́чется беспоко́ить Вас, но ....

hateful ['heɪtful] *adj* ненави́стный* (ненави́стен).

hatred ['heɪtrɪd] *n* не́нависть *f*.

hat trick *n* (*SPORT, also fig*) побе́да три ра́за подря́д.

haughty ['hɔːtɪ] *adj* надме́нный*.

haul [hɔːl] *vt* (*pull*) таска́ть/тащи́ть* (*impf*); (*transport*) перевози́ть* (перевезти́* *perf*) ♦ *n* (*of stolen goods etc*) добы́ча; (*of fish*) уло́в; **he** ~**ed himself out of the pool** он с трудо́м вы́брался из бассе́йна.

haulage ['hɔːlɪdʒ] *n* перево́зка.

haulage contractor *n* (*BRIT: COMM: firm*) фи́рма, производя́щая перево́зки; (: *person*) руководи́тель *m* фи́рмы, производя́щей перево́зки.

hauler ['hɔːlə'] *n* (*US*) = **haulage contractor**.

haulier ['hɔːlɪə'] *n* (*BRIT*) руководи́тель *m* фи́рмы, производя́щей перево́зки.

haunch [hɔːntʃ] *n* бедро́*; (*of meat*) бе́дренная часть* *f*.

haunt [hɔːnt] *n* (*of crooks*) прито́н; (*in childhood etc*) люби́мое ме́сто* ♦ *vt* (*subj: problem, memory, fear*) пресле́довать (*impf*); **to** ~ **sb/a house** явля́ться (яви́ться* *perf*) кому́-н/в до́ме.

haunted ['hɔːntɪd] *adj* (*expression, look*) встрево́женный* (встрево́жен); **a** ~ **house** дом* с привиде́ниями; **this house is** ~ в э́том до́ме есть привиде́ния.

haunting ['hɔːntɪŋ] *adj* (*sight, music*) пресле́дующий.

Havana [hə'vænə] *n* Гава́на.

KEYWORD
---

have [hæv] (*pt, pp* **had**) *aux vb*: **1**: **to have arrived** прие́хать (*perf*); **have you already eaten?** ты уже́ пое́л?; **he has been kind to me** он прояви́л доброту́ по отноше́нию ко мне; **he has been promoted** он получи́л повыше́ние по слу́жбе; **has he told you?** он Вам сказа́л?; **having finished** *or* **when he had finished, he went to bed** зако́нчив *or* когда́ он зако́нчил, он пошёл спать

2 (*in tag questions*): **you've done it, haven't you?** Вы сде́лали э́то, да?; **he hasn't done it, has he?** он ведь э́то не сде́лал, ве́рно?

3 (*in short answers and questions*): **you've made a mistake – no I haven't/so I have** Вы оши́блись – нет, не оши́бся/да, оши́бся; **we haven't paid – yes we have!** мы не заплати́ли – нет, заплати́ли!; **I've been there before, have you?** я там был, а Вы?

♦ *modal aux vb* (*be obliged*): **to have (got) to do** быть (*impf*) до́лжным(-о́й) +*infin*; **I have (got) to finish this work** я до́лжен зако́нчить э́ту рабо́ту; **you haven't to tell her** Вы не должны́ говори́ть ей; **I haven't got** *or* **I don't have to wear glasses** я могу́ не носи́ть очки́; **this has to be a mistake** э́то, наверняка́, оши́бка

♦ *vt* **1** (*possess*): **I** *etc* **have** у меня́ *etc*; **he has (got) blue eyes/dark hair** у него́ голубы́е глаза́/тёмные во́лосы; **do you have** *or* **have you got a car/phone?** у Вас есть маши́на/телефо́н?

2 (*referring to meals etc*): **to have breakfast** за́втракать (поза́втракать *perf*); **to have**

dinner обéдать (пообéдать *perf*); **to have a cigarette** выкýривать (вы́курить *perf*) сигарéту; **to have a glass of wine** выпивáть (вы́пить* *perf*) стакáн винá
3 (*receive, obtain etc*): **may I have your address?** Вы мне мóжете дать свой áдрес?; **you can have the book for £5** э́та кни́га вáша за £5; **I must have it by tomorrow** э́то должнó быть у меня́ к зáвтрашнему дню; **she is having a baby in March** у неё в мáрте бýдет ребёнок
4 (*maintain, allow*): **he will have it that he is right** он настáивает на том, что он прав; **I won't have it!** я э́того не допущý!
5: I am having my television repaired мне должны́ почини́ть телеви́зор; **to have sb do** попроси́ть* (*perf*) когó-н +*infin*; **he soon had them all laughing/working** они́ у негó все тут же стáли смея́ться/рабóтать
6 (*experience, suffer*): **I have flu/a headache** у меня́ грипп/боли́т головá; **to have a cold** простужáться (простуди́ться* *perf*); **she had her bag stolen** у неё украли сýмку; **he had an operation** емý сдéлали операцию
7 (+*n*): **to have a swim** плáвать (поплáвать *perf*); **to have a rest** отдыхáть (отдохнýть *perf*); **let's have a look** давáйте посмóтрим; **we are having a meeting/party tomorrow** зáвтра у нас бýдет собрáние/бýдут гóсти; **let me have a try** дáйте мне попрóбовать
8 (*inf. dupe*) провести́* (*perf*); **he's been had** его́ провели́; **to have sb on** (*BRIT: inf*) води́ть* (*impf*) когó-н зá нос
▸ **have in** *vt* (*inf*): **he has got it in for me** у негó прóтив меня́ зуб
▸ **have on** *vt*: **have you anything on tomorrow?** у Вас есть на зáвтра каки́е-нибудь плáны?; **I don't have any money on me** у меня́ нет при себé дéнег; **he had a black sweater on** на нём был чёрный сви́тер
▸ **have out** *vt*: **to have it out with sb** объясня́ться (объясни́ться* *perf*) с кем-н; **she had her tooth out** ей удали́ли зуб; **she had her tonsils/appendix out** ей вы́резали глáнды/аппендици́т.

haven ['heɪvn] *n* гáвань *f*; (*fig*) убéжище.
haven't ['hævnt] = **have not**.
haversack ['hævəsæk] *n* (*of hiker*) рюкзáк*; (*of soldier*) рáнец*.
haves [hævz] *npl* (*inf*): **the ~ and have-nots** имýщие *pl adj* и неимýщие *pl adj*.
havoc ['hævək] *n* (*chaos*) хáос; **to play ~ with** (*plans etc*) игрáть (*impf*) злы́е шýтки над +*instr*.
Hawaii [hə'waɪi:] *n* Гавáйи *m ind*.
Hawaiian [hə'waɪjən] *adj* гавáйский ◆ *n* гавáец*(-áйка*); (*LING*) гавáйский язы́к*.

hawk [hɔ:k] *n* я́стреб*.
hawker ['hɔ:kə'] *n* (*COMM*) ýличный(-ая) торгóвец*(-вка*).
hawkish ['hɔ:kɪʃ] *adj* хи́щный.
hawthorn ['hɔ:θɔ:n] *n* боя́рышник.
hay [heɪ] *n* сéно.
hay fever *n* сеннáя лихорáдка*.
haystack ['heɪstæk] *n* стог* сéна; **it's like looking for a needle in a ~** э́то как искáть иго́лку в стóге сéна.
haywire ['heɪwaɪə'] (*inf*) *adj*: **to go ~** (*machine*) барахли́ть (забарахли́ть *perf*); (*plans*) нарушáться (нарýшиться *perf*).
hazard ['hæzəd] *n* (*danger*) опáсность *f* ◆ *vt* (*risk*): **to ~ a guess** осмéливаться (осмéлиться *perf*) предположи́ть; **it's a health ~** э́то опáсно для здорóвья; **smoking is a fire ~** курéние мóжет служи́ть причи́ной пожáра.
hazard lights *npl* = **hazard warning lights**.
hazardous ['hæzədəs] *adj* опáсный* (опáсен).
hazard pay *n* (*US*) дополни́тельная плáта за труд в опáсных услóвиях.
hazard warning lights *npl* (*AUT*) авари́йные огни́ *mpl*.
haze [heɪz] *n* ды́мка*; **heat ~** мáрево.
hazel ['heɪzl] *n* лещи́на ◆ *adj* (*eyes*) зеленовáто-кáрий*.
hazelnut ['heɪzlnʌt] *n* леснóй орéх.
hazy ['heɪzɪ] *adj* тумáнный* (тумáнен); **I'm rather ~ about the details** у меня́ довóльно смýтное представлéние о подрóбностях.
H-bomb ['eɪtʃbɒm] *n* водорóдная бóмба.
HE *abbr* (*REL, DIPLOMACY*: = *His/Her Excellency*) Егó/Её Превосходи́тельство; = *high explosive*.
he [hi:] *pron* он.
head [hɛd] *n* (*ANAT*) головá*; (*mind*) ум*; (*of list, queue*) начáло; (*of table*) главá; (*of company, organization*) руководи́тель(ница) *m(f)*; (*of school*) дирéктор*; (*on tape recorder etc*) головка ◆ *vt* (*list, queue*) стоя́ть (*impf*) пéрвым(-ой) в +*prp*; (*group, company*) возглавля́ть (возглáвить* *perf*); **~s or tails** ≈ орёл или рéшка; **~ over heels in love** влюблён пó уши; **to ~ a ball** забивáть (заби́ть* *perf*) мяч головóй; **£10 a or per ~** по £10 кáждому *or* на кáждого; **to sit at the ~ of the table** сидéть* (сесть* *perf*) во главé столá; **he has a ~ for business** у негó есть спосóбности к би́знесу; **I have no ~ for heights** у меня́ крýжится головá от высоты́; **to come to a ~** (*fig: situation etc*) доходи́ть (дойти́* *perf*) до крити́ческой тóчки; **let's put our ~s together** давáйте обсýдим э́то вмéсте; **to say sth off the top of one's ~** говори́ть (сказáть* *perf*) что-н не задýмываясь; **on your own ~ be it!** пусть это бýдет на Вáшей сóвести!; **to bite**

---

* marks translations which have irregular inflections. The Russian-English side of the dictionary gives inflectional information.

or **snap sb's ~ off** огрыза́ться (огрызну́ться *perf*) кому́-н, гру́бо обрыва́ть (обры́ть* *perf*) кого́-н; **to go to sb's ~** (*alcohol*) ударя́ть (уда́рить *perf*) кому́-н в го́лову; (*success, power*) кружи́ть (вскружи́ть *perf*) кому́-н го́лову; **to keep/lose one's ~** не теря́ть (потеря́ть *perf*)/теря́ть (потеря́ть *perf*) го́лову; **I can't make ~ nor tail of this** я ничего́ не могу́ поня́ть в э́том; **he's off his ~!** (*inf*) он рехну́лся!

▶ **head for** *vt fus* (*place*) направля́ться (напра́виться* *perf*) в/на +*acc* or к +*dat*; (*disaster*) обрека́ть (обре́чь* *perf*) себя́ на +*acc*

▶ **head off** *vt* (*threat, danger*) отводи́ть* (отвести́* *perf*).

headache ['hɛdeɪk] *n* головна́я боль* *f*; (*fig: problem*) неприя́тность *f*; **I've got a ~** у меня́ боли́т голова́.

headband ['hɛdbænd] *n* о́бруч* для воло́с.

headboard ['hɛdbɔːd] *n* спи́нка* крова́ти.

head cold *n* на́сморк.

headdress ['hɛddrɛs] *n* головно́е украше́ние.

headed notepaper ['hɛdɪd-] *n* бланк; (*personal*) *бланк для письма́ со шта́мпом отправи́теля*.

header ['hɛdə'] *n* (*BRIT: inf: FOOTBALL*) уда́р голово́й.

headfirst ['hɛd'fəːst] *adv* (*dive, fall*) голово́й вниз; (*rush*) сломя́ го́лову.

headgear ['hɛdgɪə'] *n* головно́й убо́р.

head-hunt ['hɛdhʌnt] *vi* сма́нивать (смани́ть* *perf*) лу́чших специали́стов ♦ *vt* сма́нивать (смани́ть *perf*).

head-hunter ['hɛdhʌntə'] *n* (*COMM*) *челове́к, кото́рый перема́нивает сотру́дников из одно́й фи́рмы в другу́ю*.

heading ['hɛdɪŋ] *n* (*of chapter, article*) заголо́вок*.

headlamp ['hɛdlæmp] *n* (*BRIT*) = **headlight**.

headland ['hɛdlənd] *n* мыс*.

headlight ['hɛdlaɪt] *n* фа́ра.

headline ['hɛdlaɪn] *n* (*PRESS, TV, RADIO*) заголо́вок*.

headlong ['hɛdlɔŋ] *adv* (*headfirst*) голово́й вперёд; (*hastily*) опроме́тчиво.

headmaster [hɛd'mɑːstə'] *n* дире́ктор* шко́лы.

headmistress [hɛd'mɪstrɪs] *n* дире́ктор* шко́лы.

head office *n* (*of company etc*) дире́кция.

head of state (*pl* **~s of ~**) *n* глава́* госуда́рства.

head-on [hɛd'ɔn] *adj* (*collision, confrontation*) лобово́й ♦ *adv* но́сом к но́су.

headphones ['hɛdfəunz] *npl* нау́шники *mpl*.

headquarters ['hɛdkwɔːtəz] *npl* (*of company, organization*) гла́вное управле́ние *ntsg*; (*MIL*) штаб-кварти́ра *fsg*.

headrest ['hɛdrɛst] *n* подголо́вник.

headroom ['hɛdrum] *n* (*in car*) вну́тренняя высота́ (*ку́зова*); (*under bridge*) просве́т.

headscarf ['hɛdskɑːf] *n* косы́нка*; (*square*) головно́й плато́к*.

headset ['hɛdsɛt] *n* = **headphones**.

head start *n*: **to have/get a ~ ~** име́ть (*impf*)/получа́ть (получи́ть* *perf*) исхо́дное преиму́щество.

headstone ['hɛdstəun] *n* (*on grave*) надгро́бный ка́мень* *m*.

headstrong ['hɛdstrɔŋ] *adj* упо́рный* (упо́рен).

head teacher *n* дире́ктор* шко́лы.

head waiter *n* (*in restaurant*) гла́вный официа́нт.

headway ['hɛdweɪ] *n*: **to make ~** продвига́ться (продви́нуться *perf*) вперёд.

headwind ['hɛdwɪnd] *n* встре́чный ве́тер*.

heady ['hɛdɪ] *adj* (*experience, time*) головокружи́тельный; (*drink*) хмельно́й; (*atmosphere*) взбудора́женный.

heal [hiːl] *vt* (*patient*) изле́чивать (излечи́ть* *perf*); (*injury*) изъявля́ть (зажи́ть* *perf*); (*damage*) восстана́вливать (восстанови́ть* *perf*) ♦ *vi* (*injury*) зажива́ть (зажи́ть *perf*); (*damage*) восстана́вливаться (восстанови́ться* *perf*).

health [hɛlθ] *n* (*also MED*) здоро́вье; **good ~** кре́пкое здоро́вье.

health care *n* здравоохране́ние.

health centre *n* (*BRIT*) поликли́ника.

health food *n* здоро́вая пи́ща.

health-food shop ['hɛlθfuːd-] *n* магази́н здоро́вого пита́ния.

health hazard *n* опа́сность *f* для здоро́вья.

Health Service *n* (*BRIT*): **the ~ ~** слу́жба здравоохране́ния.

healthy ['hɛlθɪ] *adj* (*person*) здоро́вый (здоро́в); (*economy, appetite*) здоро́вый; (*pursuit, pastime*) поле́зный* (поле́зен); (*profit*) доста́точно хоро́ший*; **it's not ~ to drink too much** сли́шком мно́го пить – вре́дно для здоро́вья.

heap [hiːp] *n* (*small*) ку́ча; (*large*) гру́да ♦ *vt* (*stones, sand*): **to ~ (up)** сва́ливать (свали́ть* *perf*) в ку́чу; (*plate, sink*): **to ~ with sth** наполня́ть (напо́лнить *perf*) чем-н; (*food, books*): **to ~ sth on** нава́ливать (навали́ть* *perf*) что-н на +*acc*; **~s of** (*inf*) ку́ча *fsg* +*gen*; **to ~ favours/praise/gifts on sb** осыпа́ть (осы́пать* *perf*) кого́-н ми́лостями/похвала́ми/пода́рками.

hear [hɪə'] (*pt, pp* **heard**) *vt* слы́шать (услы́шать *perf*); (*lecture, concert*) слу́шать (*impf*); (*LAW: case*) слу́шать (*impf*); **to ~ about** слы́шать (услы́шать *perf*) о +*prp*; **did you ~ about the move?** Вы слы́шали о перее́зде?; **to ~ from sb** слы́шать (услы́шать *perf*) от кого́-н; **I can't ~ you** Вас не слы́шно; **I've never ~d of that book** я никогда́ не слы́шал об э́той кни́ге; **I wouldn't ~ of it!** я и слы́шать об э́том не хочу́!

▶ **hear out** *vt* выслу́шивать (вы́слушать *perf*).

heard [həːd] *pt, pp of* **hear**.

hearing ['hɪərɪŋ] n (*sense*) слух; (*LAW, POL*) слушание; **she is a bit hard of ~** она тугова́та на́ ухо; **within/out of ~ distance** в преде́лах/за преде́лами слы́шимости; **to give sb a (fair) ~** (*perf*) дать* кому́-н вы́сказаться.

hearing aid n слухово́й аппара́т.

hearsay ['hɪəseɪ] n слух; **by ~** по слу́хам.

hearse [hə:s] n катафа́лк.

heart [hɑ:t] n се́рдце*; (*of lettuce*) сердцеви́на; (*of problem, matter*) суть *f*; **~s** npl (*CARDS*) че́рви* *fpl*; **to lose/take ~** пасть* (*perf*)/не па́дать (*impf*) ду́хом; **at ~** в глубине́ души́; **(off) by ~** наизу́сть; **he has a weak ~** у него́ сла́бое се́рдце; **to set one's ~ on sth/on doing** стреми́ться* (*impf*) всей душо́й к чему́-н/+infin; **to pour one's ~ out to sb** излива́ть (изли́ть* *perf*) кому́-н ду́шу; **he's a man after my own ~** он мне по́ се́рдцу; **the ~ of the matter** суть де́ла.

heartache ['hɑ:teɪk] n серде́чная боль *f*.

heart attack n серде́чный при́ступ.

heartbeat ['hɑ:tbi:t] n (*one pulsation*) серде́чное сокраще́ние; (*rhythm*) сердцебие́ние.

heartbreak ['hɑ:tbreɪk] n большо́е го́ре.

heartbreaking ['hɑ:tbreɪkɪŋ] adj душераздира́ющий* (душераздира́ющ).

heartbroken ['hɑ:tbrəukən] adj: **he is ~** (*sad*) он уби́т го́рем.

heartburn ['hɑ:tbə:n] n изжо́га.

-hearted ['hɑ:tɪd] suffix: **kind-~** добросерде́чный.

hearten ['hɑ:tn] vt воодушевля́ть (воодушеви́ть* *perf*).

heart failure n (*resulting in death*) остано́вка се́рдца.

heartfelt ['hɑ:tfɛlt] adj и́скренний*.

hearth [hɑ:θ] n оча́г*.

heartily ['hɑ:tɪlɪ] adv (*thank, welcome*) серде́чно; (*dislike*) всем се́рдцем; **to laugh ~** смея́ться (*impf*) от души́.

heartland ['hɑ:tlænd] n (*of country*) се́рдце; **Britain's industrial ~** промы́шленный центр Брита́нии.

heartless ['hɑ:tlɪs] adj бессерде́чный* (бессерде́чен).

heartstrings ['hɑ:tstrɪŋz] npl душе́вные стру́ны* *ntpl*; **the film really tugs at your ~** фильм берёт за́ душу.

heartthrob ['hɑ:tθrɔb] n сердцее́д.

heart-to-heart ['hɑ:t'tə'hɑ:t] adj серде́чный; **to have a ~** говори́ть (*impf*) по душа́м.

heart transplant n переса́дка* се́рдца.

heartwarming ['hɑ:twɔ:mɪŋ] adj (*sight*) тро́гательный* (тро́гателен).

hearty ['hɑ:tɪ] adj (*person, laugh*) весёлый* (ве́сел); (*welcome, support*) серде́чный; (*appetite*) здоро́вый; (*dislike*) глубо́кий*.

heat [hi:t] n тепло́; (*extreme*) жар*; (*of weather*) жара́; (*temperature*) температу́ра; (*excitement*) пыл*; (*also*: **qualifying ~**: *in race etc*) забе́г; (: *in swimming*) заплы́в; (*ZOOL*): **our dog is in** *or* (*US*) **on ~** у на́шей соба́ки те́чка ♦ vt (*water, food*) греть *or* нагрева́ть (нагре́ть *perf*); (*house*) ота́пливать (отопи́ть* *perf*)

▶ **heat up** vi (*water, house*) согрева́ться (согре́ться *perf*) ♦ vt (*food, water*) подогрева́ть (подогре́ть *perf*); (*room*) обогрева́ть (обогре́ть *perf*); (*engine*) разогрева́ть (разогре́ть *perf*).

heated ['hi:tɪd] adj ота́пливаемый; (*argument*) горя́чий*; (*pool*) обогрева́емый.

heater ['hi:tə'] n обогрева́тель m.

heath [hi:θ] n (*BRIT*) (ве́ресковая) пу́стошь *f*.

heathen ['hi:ðn] n язы́чник(-ица).

heather ['hɛðə'] n ве́реск.

heating ['hi:tɪŋ] n отопле́ние.

heat-resistant ['hi:trɪzɪstənt] adj жаропро́чный* (жаропро́чен), термосто́йкий* (термосто́ек).

heat-seeking ['hi:tsi:kɪŋ] adj теплоула́вливающий.

heatstroke ['hi:tstrəuk] n теплово́й уда́р.

heat wave ['hi:tweɪv] n пери́од си́льной жары́.

heave [hi:v] vt (*pull*) вытя́гивать (вы́тянуть *perf*); (*push*) толка́ть (толкну́ть *perf*); (*lift*) взва́ливать (взвали́ть *perf*); (*throw*) швыря́ть (швырну́ть *perf*) ♦ vi (*chest*) вздыма́ться (*impf*); (*retch*) чу́вствовать (почу́вствовать *perf*) тошноту́ ♦ n (*upwards*) подъём; (*sideways*) рыво́к; **to ~ a sigh** глубоко́ вздохну́ть (*perf*)

▶ **heave to** ♦ (*pt, pp* **hove**) vi (*NAUT*) ложи́ться (лечь* *perf*) в дрейф.

heaven ['hɛvn] n (*also fig*) рай*; **thank ~(s)!** сла́ва Бо́гу!; **~ forbid!** Бо́же упаси́!; **for ~'s sake!** ра́ди Бо́га!

heavenly ['hɛvnlɪ] adj небе́сный; (*fig*) ра́йский*.

heaven-sent [hɛvn'sɛnt] adj благода́тный* (благода́тен).

heavily ['hɛvɪlɪ] adv (*fall, sigh*) тяжело́; (*drink, smoke, depend*) си́льно; (*sleep*) кре́пко; (*say*) ве́ско (ве́со́м).

heavy ['hɛvɪ] adj тяжёлый* (тяжёл); (*rain, blow, fall*) си́льный* (си́лен); (*breathing, sleep*) тяжёлый*; (*build: of person*) грузный; (*sea*) бу́рный* (бу́рен); **he is a ~ drinker/smoker** он мно́го пьёт/ку́рит; **the work is ~ going** рабо́та идёт тяжело́; **he is ~ going** с ним тру́дно име́ть де́ло.

heavy cream n (*US*) жи́рные сли́вки* *pl*.

heavy-duty ['hɛvɪ'dju:tɪ] adj сверхпро́чный*.

heavy goods vehicle n (*BRIT*) грузови́к, перевозя́щий тяжёлые гру́зы.

---

heavy-handed ['hɛvɪ'hændɪd] *adj* властный*
(властен).

heavy industry *n* тяжёлая промышленность
f.

heavy metal *n* (*MUS*) хэви метал, (тяжёлый)
металл.

heavy-set ['hɛvɪ'sɛt] *adj* (*esp US*) коренастый
(коренаст).

heavy user *n* лицо/компания, покупающее/-ая
большие партии определённого товара.

heavyweight ['hɛvɪweɪt] *n* боксёр тяжёлого
веса.

Hebrew ['hiːbruː] *adj* древнееврейский ♦ *n*
(*LING*: *ancient*) древнееврейский язык*;
(*modern*) иврит.

Hebrides ['hɛbrɪdiːz] *npl*: **the ~** Гебридские
острова* *mpl*.

heck [hɛk] *excl* (*inf*) чёрт.

heckle ['hɛkl] *vt* перебивать (перебить* *perf*).

heckler ['hɛklə'] *n*: **there were several ~s in the
audience** некоторые люди в зале
перебивали.

hectare ['hɛktɑː'] *n* (*BRIT*) гектар.

hectic ['hɛktɪk] *adj* (*day*) суматошный*
(суматошен); (*actions, activities*)
лихорадочный* (лихорадочен).

hector ['hɛktə'] *vt* запугивать (запугать *perf*).

he'd [hiːd] = **he would, he had**.

hedge [hɛdʒ] *n* живая изгородь *f* ♦ *vi* (*stall*)
увиливать (увильнуть *perf*) ♦ *vt*: **to ~ one's
bets** подстраховываться (подстраховаться
perf); **as a ~ against inflation** как страховка от
инфляции

▸ **hedge in** *vt* ограничивать (ограничить *perf*).

hedgehog ['hɛdʒhɔg] *n* ёж*.

hedgerow ['hɛdʒrəu] *n* живая изгородь *f*.

hedonism ['hiːdənɪzəm] *n* гедонизм.

heed [hiːd] *vt* (*also*: **take ~ of**) принимать
(принять* *perf*) во внимание ♦ *n*: **to pay (no) ~
to, take (no) ~ of** (не) принимать (принять*
perf) во внимание.

heedless ['hiːdlɪs] *adj*: **~ of** не обращая
внимания на +*acc*.

heel [hiːl] *n* (*of foot*) пятка*; (*of shoe*) каблук* ♦
vt (*shoe*) подбивать (подбить* *perf*); **to bring
to ~** (*dog*) заставлять (заставить* *perf*) идти
or стоять рядом; (*person*) подчинять
(подчинить *perf*); **to take to one's ~s** (*inf*)
пускаться (пуститься* *perf*) наутёк.

hefty ['hɛftɪ] *adj* (*person, object*) здоровенный;
(*profit, fine*) изрядный*.

heifer ['hɛfə'] *n* тёлка*.

height [haɪt] *n* (*of tree, of plane*) высота*; (*of
person*) рост; (*of power*) вершина; (*of
mountain*) возвышенность *f*; (*of season*)
разгар; (*of luxury, taste*) верх; **what ~ are
you?** какой у Вас рост?; **of average ~**
среднего роста; **to be afraid of ~s** бояться
(*impf*) высоты; **it's the ~ of fashion** это верх
моды; **at the ~ of the tourist season** в разгар
туристического сезона.

heighten ['haɪtn] *vt* усиливать (усилить *perf*).

heinous ['heɪnəs] *adj* (*crime*) чудовищный.

heir [ɛə'] *n* наследник.

heir apparent *n* прямой наследник.

heiress ['ɛərɛs] *n* наследница.

heirloom ['ɛəluːm] *n* семейная реликвия.

heist [haɪst] *n* (*US*: *inf*) грабёж*.

held [hɛld] *pt, pp* *of* **hold**.

helicopter ['hɛlɪkɔptə'] *n* вертолёт.

heliport ['hɛlɪpɔːt] *n* вертодром.

helium ['hiːlɪəm] *n* гелий.

hell [hɛl] *n* (*also fig*) ад*; **~!** (*inf*) чёрт!; **a** *or* **one
~ of a mess** (*inf*) кошмарный беспорядок*; **a**
or **one ~ of a party** (*inf*) классная вечеринка.

he'll [hiːl] = **he will, he shall**; *see* **will**.

hellish ['hɛlɪʃ] *adj* (*inf*: *awful*) кошмарный*
(кошмарен).

hello [hə'ləu] *excl* здравствуйте; (*informal*)
привет; (*TEL*: *on answering*) алло; (*to attract
attention*) эй; (*in surprise*): **~!, what's this!** эй
(что это!).

helm [hɛlm] *n* (*NAUT*) руль* *m*; **man at the ~** (*fig*)
рулевой *m adj*; **at the ~ of** у кормила +*gen*.

helmet ['hɛlmɪt] *n* (*of policeman, miner*) каска*;
(*also*: **crash ~**) шлем.

helmsman ['hɛlmzmən] *n* рулевой *m adj*.

help [hɛlp] *n* помощь *f*; (*charwoman*) прислуга
♦ *vt* помогать (помочь* *perf*) +*dat*; **with the ~
of** (*person*) с помощью +*gen*; (*tool*) при
помощи +*gen*; **can I be of (any) ~?** я могу Вам
чем-нибудь помочь?; **~! I** помогите!; **can I ~
you?** (*in shop*) чем могу быть* полезен?; **~
yourself** угощайтесь; **he can't ~ it** он ничего
не может поделать с этим; **I can't ~ thinking
that ...** я не могу не думать, что ....

helper ['hɛlpə'] *n* помощник(-ица).

helpful ['hɛlpful] *adj* полезный* (полезен).

helping ['hɛlpɪŋ] *n* порция.

helping hand *n*: **to lend a ~ ~** протягивать
(протянуть *perf*) руку помощи.

helpless ['hɛlplɪs] *adj* беспомощный*
(беспомощен).

helplessly ['hɛlplɪslɪ] *adv* беспомощно.

helpline ['hɛlplaɪn] *n* телефон доверия.

Helsinki ['hɛlsɪŋkɪ] *n* Хельсинки *m ind*.

helter-skelter ['hɛltə'skɛltə'] *n* (*BRIT*)
спиральная горка (*аттракцион*).

hem [hɛm] *n* (*of dress*) подол; (*of curtains*) низ
♦ *vt* подшивать (подшить* *perf*)

▸ **hem in** *vt* плотно окружать (окружить *perf*);
city life made him feel ~med in жизнь в
городе стесняла его.

hematology ['hiːmə'tɔlədʒɪ] *n* (*US*) =
haematology.

hemisphere ['hɛmɪsfɪə'] *n* полушарие.

hemlock ['hɛmlɔk] *n* (*BOT*) болиголов.

hemoglobin ['hiːmə'gləubɪn] *n* (*US*) =
haemoglobin.

hemophilia ['hiːmə'fɪlɪə] *n* (*US*) = **haemophilia**.

hemorrhage ['hɛmərɪdʒ] *n* (*US*) = **haemorrhage**.

hemorrhoids ['hɛmərɔɪdz] *npl* (*US*) =

haemorrhoids.

hemp [hɛmp] *n* конопля.

hen [hɛn] *n* (*chicken*) курица*; (*female bird*) самка*.

hence [hɛns] *adv* (*therefore*) следовательно; (*from now*): **2 years** ~ (*formal*) по истечении двух лет.

henceforth [hɛns'fɔː θ] *adv* впредь.

henchman ['hɛntʃmən] *irreg n* приспешник.

henna ['hɛnə] *n* хна.

hen party *n* (*inf*) девичник.

henpecked ['hɛnpɛkt] *adj* (*husband*) покорный* (покорен).

hepatitis [hɛpə'taɪtɪs] *n* гепатит.

her [hɜː'] *pron* (*direct*) её; (*indirect*) ей; (*after prep*: +*instr*, +*dat*, +*prp*) ней; (: +*gen*) неё; *see also* **me** ♦ *adj* её; (*referring to subject of sentence*) свой; *see also* **my**.

herald ['hɛrəld] *n* (*precursor*) предвестник ♦ *vt* (*event*) предвещать (*impf*).

heraldic [hɛ'rældɪk] *adj* геральдический.

heraldry ['hɛrəldrɪ] *n* (*study*) геральдика; (*coat of arms*) герб.

herb [hɜːb] *n* (*BOT, CULIN*) трава*; (*MED*) лекарственная трава*; ~**s** *npl* (*CULIN*) зелень *fsg*.

herbaceous [hɜː'beɪʃəs] *adj*: ~ **plant** цветочное растение; ~ **border** клумба.

herbal ['hɜːbl] *adj*: ~ **medicine** лечение травами; ~ **remedy** лекарство из трав; ~ **tea** чай* из трав.

herbicide ['hɜːbɪsaɪd] *n* гербицид.

herd [hɜːd] *n* стадо* ♦ *vt* (*drive: animals, people*) гнать* (*impf*); (*gather*) сгонять (согнать* *perf*).

here [hɪə'] *adv* (*location*) здесь; (*destination*) сюда; (*departure point*): **from** ~ отсюда; (*at this point: in past*) тут; "**here!**" (*present*) „здесь!"; ~ **is** ..., ~ **are** ... вот ...; ~ **you are** (*giving*) вот, пожалуйста; **where are my keys?** ~ **we are!** (*finding sth*) где мой ключи? вот они!; ~**'s my sister** вот моя сестра; ~ **she comes** вот она идёт; **come** ~**!** идите сюда!; **she left** ~ **yesterday** она уехала отсюда вчера; ~ **and there** (*location*) там и сям; (*motion*) туда и сюда; "**here's to** ...**!**" (*toast*) „за +*acc* ...!".

hereabouts ['hɪərə'bauts] *adv* поблизости.

hereafter [hɪər'ɑːftə'] *adv* в дальнейшем.

hereby [hɪə'baɪ] *adv* (*formal: in letter*): **we** ~ **acknowledge** ... настоящим подтверждаем ....

hereditary [hɪ'rɛdɪtrɪ] *adj* наследственный.

heredity [hɪ'rɛdɪtɪ] *n* наследственность *f*.

heresy ['hɛrəsɪ] *n* ересь *f*.

heretic ['hɛrətɪk] *n* еретик*(-ичка*).

heretical [hɪ'rɛtɪkl] *adj* еретический*.

herewith [hɪə'wɪð] *adv* (*formal: letter*): **please find enclosed** ~ ... при сём прилагается ....

heritage ['hɛrɪtɪdʒ] *n* наследие; **our national** ~

наше национальное богатство.

hermetically [hɜː'mɛtɪklɪ] *adv*: ~ **sealed** герметически закрытый.

hermit ['hɜːmɪt] *n* отшельник(-ица).

hernia ['hɜːnɪə] *n* грыжа.

hero ['hɪərəu] (*pl* ~**es**) *n* герой.

heroic [hɪ'rəuɪk] *adj* геройческий*.

heroin ['hɛrəuɪn] *n* героин.

heroin addict *n* наркоман (*принимающий героин*).

heroine ['hɛrəuɪn] *n* героиня.

heroism ['hɛrəuɪzəm] *n* геройзм.

heron ['hɛrən] *n* цапля*.

hero worship *n* культ героя.

herring ['hɛrɪŋ] *n* (*ZOOL*) сельдь* *f*; (*CULIN*) селёдка.

hers [hɜːz] *pron* её; (*referring to subject of sentence*) свой; *see also* **mine**[1].

herself [hɜː'sɛlf] *pron* (*reflexive, after prep*: +*acc*, +*gen*) себя; (: +*dat*, +*prp*) себе; (: +*instr*) собой; (*emphatic*) сама; (*alone*): **by** ~ одна; *see also* **myself**.

Herts *abbr* (*BRIT: POST*) = Hertfordshire.

he's [hiːz] = **he is**, **he has**; *see* **be**, **have**.

hesitant ['hɛzɪtənt] *adj* нерешительный* (нерешителен); **to be** ~ **about doing** не решаться (*impf*) *or* колебаться* (*impf*) +*infin*.

hesitate ['hɛzɪteɪt] *vi* (*pause*) колебаться* (поколебаться* *perf*); (*be unwilling*) не решаться (*impf*); **to** ~ (**about/to do**) не решаться (*impf*) (на +*acc*/+*infin*); **don't** ~ **to see a doctor if you are worried** Вы обеспокоены (этим), без колебаний обратитесь к врачу.

hesitation [hɛzɪ'teɪʃən] *n* (*pause*) колебание; **I have no** ~ **in saying (that)** ... я говорю не колеблясь(, что) ....

hessian ['hɛsɪən] *n* мешковина.

heterogeneous ['hɛtərə'dʒiːnɪəs] *adj* разнородный* (разнороден).

heterosexual ['hɛtərəu'sɛksjuəl] *adj* гетеросексуальный ♦ *n* гетеросексуальный человек*.

het up [hɛt-] *adj* (*inf*): **to get** ~ ~ (**about**) заводиться* (завестись* *perf*) (из-за +*gen*).

HEW *n abbr* (*US*) = Department of Health, Education and Welfare.

hew [hjuː] (*pp* **hewed** *or* **hewn**) *vt* (*stone*) выдалбливать (выдолбить* *perf*); (*wood*) вырубать (вырубить* *perf*).

hewn [hjuːn] *pp of* **hew**.

hex [hɛks] (*US*) *n* колдунья*, ведьма ♦ *vt* заворажывать (заворожить* *perf*).

hexagon ['hɛksəgɔn] *n* шестиугольник.

hexagonal [hɛk'sægənl] *adj* шестиугольный.

hey [heɪ] *excl* эй.

heyday ['heɪdeɪ] *n*: **the** ~ **of** расцвет +*gen*.

HF *n abbr* (= high frequency) ВЧ= высокая

частота́.

HGV n abbr (BRIT: = heavy goods vehicle) грузово́й автомоби́ль m.

HI abbr (US: POST) = Hawaii.

hi [haɪ] excl (as greeting) приве́т; (to attract attention) эй.

hiatus [haɪˈeɪtəs] n (in activity) пробе́л; (in conversation) па́уза.

hibernate [ˈhaɪbəneɪt] vi впада́ть (впасть* perf) в зи́мнюю спя́чку.

hibernation [haɪbəˈneɪʃən] n зи́мняя спя́чка.

hick [hɪk] n (US: inf: pej) дереве́нщина m/f.

hiccough etc = **hiccup** etc.

hiccup [ˈhɪkʌp] vi ика́ть (impf).

hiccups [ˈhɪkʌps] npl ико́та fsg; **she's got (the) ~** у неё ико́та.

hid [hɪd] pt of **hide**.

hidden [ˈhɪdn] pp of **hide** ♦ adj: **there are no ~ extras** здесь нет скры́тых доба́вочных расхо́дов; **there is a ~ agenda** за э́тим что-то кро́ется.

hide [haɪd] (pt **hid**, pp **hidden**) n (skin) шку́ра; (of birdwatcher) укры́тие ♦ vt (object, person) пря́тать* (спря́тать* perf); (feeling, information) скрыва́ть (скрыть* perf); (sun, view) закрыва́ть (закры́ть* perf) ♦ vi: **to ~ (from sb)** пря́таться* (спря́таться* perf) (от кого́-н); **to ~ sth (from sb)** (object, person) пря́тать* (спря́тать* perf) что-н (от кого́-н); (information) скрыва́ть (скрыть* perf) что-н (от кого́-н).

hide-and-seek [ˈhaɪdənˈsiːk] n пря́тки* fpl.

hideaway [ˈhaɪdəweɪ] n убе́жище.

hideous [ˈhɪdɪəs] adj (painting, conditions) жу́ткий (жу́ток); (face) омерзи́тельный* (омерзи́телен).

hideously [ˈhɪdɪəslɪ] adv (ugly) омерзи́тельно; (difficult) жу́тко.

hide-out [ˈhaɪdaut] n укры́тие; (of criminals) ло́говище.

hiding [ˈhaɪdɪŋ] n (beating) по́рка*; (concealed): **to be in ~** скрыва́ться (impf).

hiding place n (for person) укры́тие; (for money etc) тайни́к*, потайно́е ме́сто*.

hierarchy [ˈhaɪərɑːkɪ] n иера́рхия.

hieroglyphic [haɪərəˈɡlɪfɪk] adj иероглифи́ческий.

hieroglyphics [haɪərəˈɡlɪfɪks] npl иеро́глифы mpl.

hi-fi [ˈhaɪfaɪ] n abbr (= high fidelity) высо́кая ве́рность звуковоспроизведе́ния ♦ adj (equipment, system): **~ equipment** аппарату́ра с высо́кой ве́рностью звуковоспроизведе́ния.

higgledy-piggledy [ˈhɪɡldɪˈpɪɡldɪ] (inf) adj беспоря́дочный* (беспоря́дочен) ♦ adv ко́е-ка́к, беспоря́дочно.

high [haɪ] adj высо́кий* (высо́к); (wind) си́льный*; (BRIT: meat) вы́держанный (вы́держан) ♦ adv (climb, aim etc) высо́ко ♦ n: **exports have reached a new ~** э́кспорт дости́г но́вой высоты́; **the building is 20 m ~** высота́ зда́ния – 20 м; **to be ~** (inf: on drugs, drink) кайфова́ть (impf); **~ risk** высо́кая сте́пень f ри́ска; **~ in the air** (position) высо́ко в во́здухе; (motion) высоко́ в во́здух; **to pay a ~ price for sth** плати́ть* (заплати́ть* perf) высо́кую це́ну за что-н; **it's ~ time you learned how to do it** Вам давно́ пора́ научи́ться де́лать э́то.

highball [ˈhaɪbɔːl] n (US) ви́ски с со́довой и льдом (в высо́ком стака́не).

highboy [ˈhaɪbɔɪ] n (US) высо́кий комо́д.

highbrow [ˈhaɪbrau] adj (subjects) учёный; (person) интеллектуа́льный* (интеллектуа́лен).

highchair [ˈhaɪtʃɛəʳ] n высо́кий сту́льчик (для ма́леньких дете́й).

high-class [ˈhaɪˈklɑːs] adj (hotel, performance) первокла́ссный, высо́кого кла́сса; (neighbourhood) прести́жный* (прести́жен).

High Court n (BRIT): **the ~ ~** ≈ Верхо́вный суд*.

higher [ˈhaɪəʳ] adj вы́сший ♦ adv вы́ше.

higher education n вы́сшее образова́ние.

highfalutin [haɪfəˈluːtɪn] adj (inf) высоко-па́рный* (высокопа́рен).

high finance n: **the world of ~ ~** мир вы́сших фина́нсовых круго́в.

high-five [haɪˈfaɪv] n пятерня́ (хлопо́к ладо́нью по чьей-нибудь ладо́ни).

high-flier [haɪˈflaɪəʳ] n пти́ца высо́кого полёта.

high-flying [haɪˈflaɪɪŋ] adj (person) честолюби́вый; (lifestyle) шика́рный.

high-handed [haɪˈhændɪd] adj (decision, person) своево́льный* (своеволен).

high-heeled [haɪˈhiːld] adj на высо́ком каблуке́.

high heels npl ту́фли fpl на высо́ком каблуке́.

high jump n прыжо́к* в высоту́.

Highlands [ˈhaɪləndz] npl: **the ~** Высокого́рья ntpl (Шотла́ндии).

high-level [ˈhaɪlɛvl] adj (talks etc) на вы́сшем у́ровне; **~ language** (COMPUT) язы́к* высо́кого у́ровня.

highlight [ˈhaɪlaɪt] n (of event) кульмина́ция ♦ vt (problem, need) выявля́ть (вы́явить* perf); **~s** npl (in hair) пря́ди fpl; **the match ~s were shown on TV** кульмина́ционные моме́нты ма́тча бы́ли пока́заны по телеви́дению.

highlighter [ˈhaɪlaɪtəʳ] n (also: **~ pen**) флома́стер (для выделе́ния часте́й те́кста).

highly [ˈhaɪlɪ] adv о́чень; (paid) высоко́; **to speak ~ of** высоко́ отзыва́ться (отозва́ться* perf) о +prp; **to think ~ of** быть* (impf) высо́кого мне́ния о +prp.

highly strung adj нерво́зный* (нерво́зен).

High Mass n торже́ственная ме́сса.

highness [ˈhaɪnɪs] n: **Her/His H~** Её/Его́ Высо́чество.

high-pitched [haɪˈpɪtʃt] adj пронзи́тельный* (пронзи́телен).

high point n кульмина́ция.

high-powered ['haɪ'pauəd] adj (*engine*)
мо́щный*; (*job*) отве́тственный; (*course,
person*) высо́кого у́ровня.
high-pressure ['haɪprɛʃə'] adj высо́кого
давле́ния.
high-rise ['haɪraɪz] adj (*buildings, flats*)
высо́тный.
high school n (*BRIT*) сре́дняя шко́ла (*для
11-18ти ле́тних*); (*US*) сре́дняя шко́ла (*для
15-18ти летних*).
high season n (*BRIT*) разга́р сезо́на.
high spirits npl припо́днятое настрое́ние ntsg.
high street n (*BRIT*) центра́льная у́лица.
high-strung ['haɪ'strʌŋ] adj (*US*) = **highly
strung**.
high tide n прили́в.
highway ['haɪweɪ] n (*US: between towns, states*)
шоссе́ nt ind, автостра́да; (*main road*)
автостра́да.
Highway Code n (*BRIT*) ≈ пра́вила ntpl
доро́жного движе́ния.
highwayman ['haɪweɪmən] irreg n разбо́йник с
большо́й доро́ги.
hijack ['haɪdʒæk] vt угоня́ть (угна́ть* perf); (*fig*)
перехва́тывать (перехвати́ть* perf) ♦ n (*also:
~ing*) уго́н.
hijacker ['haɪdʒækə'] n уго́нщик.
hike [haɪk] vi ходи́ть*/идти́* (*impf*) в похо́д ♦ vt
(*inf: prices*) взви́нчивать (взвинти́ть* perf) ♦
n: **to go for a ~** идти́* (пойти́* perf) на
дли́тельную прогу́лку; (*inf*): **a ~ in prices**
скачо́к* цен.
hiker ['haɪkə'] n тури́ст(ка).
hiking ['haɪkɪŋ] n: **to go ~** ходи́ть*/идти́* (*impf*)
в похо́д.
hilarious [hɪ'lɛərɪəs] adj чрезвыча́йно
смешно́й (смешо́н).
hilarity [hɪ'lærɪtɪ] n бу́йное весе́лье.
hill [hɪl] n (*small*) холм*; (*fairly high*)
(небольша́я) гора́*; (*slope*) склон; (*on road*)
подъём.
hillbilly ['hɪlbɪlɪ] n (*US*) го́рец*; (: *pej*)
дереве́нщина m/f.
hillock ['hɪlək] n пригоро́к*.
hillside ['hɪlsaɪd] n склон.
hill start n (*AUT*) заво́д и управле́ние
автомоби́лей на подъёме.
hilltop ['hɪltɔp] n верши́на (*холма́, горы́*).
hilly ['hɪlɪ] adj холми́стый (холми́ст).
hilt [hɪlt] n рукоя́тка*; **to back sb to the ~**
подде́рживать (*impf*) кого́-н по́лностью.
him [hɪm] pron (*direct*) его́; (*indirect*) ему́; (*after
prep: +gen*) него́; (: *+dat*) ему́; (: *+instr*) ним;
(: *+prp*) нём; *see also* **me**.
Himalayas [hɪmə'leɪəz] npl: **the ~** Гимала́и* pl.
himself [hɪm'sɛlf] pron (*reflexive, after prep:
+acc, +gen*) себя́; (: *+dat, +prp*) себе́; (: *+instr*)
собо́й; (*emphatic*) сам; (*alone*): **by ~** оди́н; *see*

also **myself.**
hind [haɪnd] adj за́дний* ♦ n са́мка* оле́ня.
hinder ['hɪndə'] vt (*progress, movement*)
препя́тствовать (воспрепя́тствовать perf) or
меша́ть (помеша́ть perf) +dat; **to ~ sb from
doing** меша́ть (помеша́ть perf) кому́-н +infin.
hindquarters ['haɪnd'kwɔ:təz] npl (*of animal*)
зад msg.
hindrance ['hɪndrəns] n (*nuisance, interruption*)
поме́ха.
hindsight ['haɪndsaɪt] n: **with ~** ретроспект-
и́вным взгля́дом.
Hindu ['hɪndu:] adj инду́сский.
hinge [hɪndʒ] n (*on door*) петля́* ♦ vi (*fig*): **to ~
on** зави́сеть (*impf*) от +gen.
hint [hɪnt] n (*suggestion*) намёк; (*tip*) сове́т;
(*sign, glimmer*) подо́бие ♦ vt: **to ~ that**
намека́ть (намекну́ть perf) что ♦ vi: **to ~ at**
намека́ть (намекну́ть perf) на +acc; **to drop a
~** оброни́ть* (perf) намёк; **to give sb a ~**
подска́зывать (подсказа́ть* perf) кому́-н;
white with a ~ of pink бе́лый с намёком на
ро́зовый.
hip [hɪp] n бедро́*.
hip flask n набе́дренная фля́га.
hip hop n *стиль поп-му́зыки*.
hippie ['hɪpɪ] n хи́ппи m/f ind.
hippo ['hɪpəu] n гиппопота́м.
hip pocket n за́дний карма́н.
hippopotami [hɪpə'pɔtəmaɪ] npl of
hippopotamus.
hippopotamus [hɪpə'pɔtəməs] (pl **~es** or
hippopotami) n гиппопота́м.
hippy ['hɪpɪ] n = **hippie**.
hire ['haɪə'] vt (*BRIT: car, equipment*) брать*
(взять* perf) напрока́т; (*venue*) снима́ть
(снять* perf), арендова́ть (*impf/perf*); (*worker*)
нанима́ть (наня́ть* perf) ♦ n (*BRIT: of car*)
прока́т; (*venue*) аре́нда; **for ~** напрока́т; **on
~** взя́тый напрока́т
▶ **hire out** vt (*car, equipment*) дава́ть* (дать*
perf) напрока́т; (*venue*) сдава́ть (сдать* perf)
внаём.
hire(d) car n (*BRIT*) маши́на, взя́тая напрока́т.
hire-purchase [haɪə'pə:tʃɪs] n (*BRIT*): **to buy sth
on ~** покупа́ть (купи́ть* perf) что-н в
рассро́чку.
Hiroshima [hɪ'rɔʃɪmə] n Хироси́ма.
his [hɪz] adj его́; (*referring to subject of
sentence*) свой; *see also* **my** ♦ pron его́; *see also*
mine[1].
hiss [hɪs] vi (*snake, gas, fat*) шипе́ть* (*impf*);
(*person, audience*) освисты́вать (освиста́ть*
perf), ши́кать (оши́кать perf) ♦ n (*see vb*)
шипе́ние; свист, ши́канье.
histogram ['hɪstəgræm] n гистогра́мма.
historian [hɪ'stɔ:rɪən] n исто́рик.
historic [hɪ'stɔrɪk] adj (*agreement, achievement*)

истори́ческий*.

historical [hɪ'stɔrɪkl] *adj* (*event, film*)
истори́ческий*.

history ['hɪstərɪ] *n* исто́рия; **medical ~** (*of
patient*) исто́рия боле́зни; **there's a long ~ of
illness in his family** боле́знь передава́лась в
его́ семье́ по насле́дству.

hit [hɪt] (*pt* **hit**) *vt* ударя́ть (уда́рить *perf*);
(*reach: target*) попада́ть (попа́сть* *perf*) в
+*acc*; (*collide with: car*) ста́лкиваться
(столкну́ться *perf*) с +*instr*; (*affect: person,
services*) ударя́ть (уда́рить *perf*) по +*dat* ♦ *n*
(*knock*) уда́р; (*success*): **the play was a big ~**
пье́са по́льзовалась больши́м успе́хом; **to ~
it off (with sb)** (*inf*) найти́* (*perf*) о́бщий язы́к
(с кем-н); **to ~ the headlines** попа́сть* (*perf*) на
пе́рвые страни́цы газе́т; **to ~ the road** (*inf*)
отправля́ться (отпра́виться* *perf*) в путь;
he'll ~ the roof when he finds out about it (*inf*)
он всё здесь разнесёт, когда́ узна́ет об э́том
► **hit back** *vi*: **to ~ back at sb** (*in fight, argument*)
наноси́ть* (нанести́* *perf*) отве́тный уда́р
кому́-н
► **hit out at** *vt fus* (*also fig*) набра́сываться
(набро́ситься* *perf*) на +*acc*
► **hit (up)on** *vt fus* (*answer, solution etc*)
оты́скивать (отыска́ть* *perf*).

hit and miss *adj* (*unpredictable*) непред-
ска́зуемый (непредска́зуем).

hit-and-run driver ['hɪtən'rʌn-] *n* води́тель,
кото́рый, сбив пешехо́да, уезжа́ет с ме́ста
происше́ствия.

hitch [hɪtʃ] *vt* (*also: ~ up: trousers, skirt*)
подтя́гивать (подтяну́ть* *perf*) ♦ *n* (*difficulty*)
поме́ха; **to ~ sth to** (*fasten*) привя́зывать
(привяза́ть* *perf*) что-н к +*dat*; (*hook*)
прицепля́ть (прицепи́ть* *perf*) что-н к +*dat*; **to
~ a lift** лови́ть* (пойма́ть *perf*) попу́тку;
technical ~ техни́ческая неувя́зка*
► **hitch up** *vt* (*horse, cart*) запряга́ть (запря́чь*
perf); *see also* **hitch**.

hitchhike ['hɪtʃhaɪk] *vi* е́здить*/е́хать*
(пое́хать* *perf*) автосто́пом.

hitchhiker ['hɪtʃhaɪkə*] *n* путеше́ственник
(-ица) автосто́пом.

hi-tech ['haɪ'tɛk] *adj* высокотехни́ческий.

hitherto [hɪðə'tu:] *adv* (*formal*) до настоя́щего
вре́мени.

hit list *n* спи́сок* наме́ченных жертв.

hit man *irreg n* наёмный уби́йца *m*.

hit-or-miss ['hɪtə'mɪs] *adj* сде́ланный (сде́лан)
науга́д; (*casual*) сде́ланный как попа́ло *or*
ко́е-как; (*unpredictable*) непредска́зуемый
(непредска́зуем); **it's ~ whether I'll be able to
come** тру́дно предсказа́ть, смогу́ ли я
прийти́.

hit parade *n* (*formerly*) хит-пара́д.

HIV *n abbr* (= *human immunodeficiency virus*)
ВИЧ= *ви́рус иммунодефици́та челове́ка*;
~~negative с отрица́тельной реа́кцией на
ВИЧ; **~~positive** с положи́тельной реа́кцией

на ВИЧ.

hive [haɪv] *n* (*of bees*) у́лей*; (*fig*): **Moscow is a
~ of activity** жизнь в Москве́ кипи́т
► **hive off** *vt* отделя́ть (отдели́ть* *perf*).

hl *abbr* (= *hectolitre*) гектоли́тр.

HM *abbr* (= *His/Her Majesty*) Его́/Её
Вели́чество.

HMG *abbr* (BRIT) = *His (or Her) Majesty's
Government*.

HMI *n abbr* (BRIT: SCOL) = *His (or Her) Majesty's
Inspector*.

HMO *n abbr* (US) = *health maintenance
organization*.

HMS *abbr* (BRIT) = *His (or Her) Majesty's Ship*.

HMSO *n abbr* (BRIT) = *His (or Her) Majesty's
Stationery Office*.

HNC *n abbr* (BRIT: = *Higher National Certificate*)
*свиде́тельство о сре́днем техни́ческом
образова́нии*.

HND *n abbr* (BRIT: = *Higher National Diploma*)
*дипло́м о сре́днем техни́ческом
образова́нии*.

hoard [hɔ:d] *n* (*of food*) (та́йный) запа́с; (*of
treasure*) клад ♦ *vt* (*provisions*) запаса́ть
(запасти́* *perf*); (*money*) копи́ть* (скопи́ть*
perf).

hoarding ['hɔ:dɪŋ] *n* (BRIT) рекла́мный щит*.

hoarfrost ['hɔ:frɔst] *n* и́ней.

hoarse [hɔ:s] *adj* (*voice*) хри́плый* (хрипл).

hoax [həʊks] *n* (*trick*) мистифика́ция; (*false
alarm*) ло́жная трево́га.

hob [hɔb] *n* ве́рхняя часть плиты́ с
конфо́рками.

hobble ['hɔbl] *vi* ковыля́ть (*impf*).

hobby ['hɔbɪ] *n* хо́бби *nt ind*.

hobbyhorse ['hɔbɪhɔ:s] *n* (*fig*) люби́мый
конёк*; **he is on his ~** он сел на своего́
люби́мого конька́.

hobnail boot ['hɔbneɪl-] *n* подко́ванный
сапо́г.

hobnob ['hɔbnɔb] *vi* (*inf*): **to ~ with** води́ться
(*impf*) с +*instr*.

hobo ['həʊbəʊ] *n* (US) бродя́га *m/f*.

hock [hɔk] *n* (BRIT: *wine*) рейнве́йн; (*of horse*)
скака́тельный суста́в ♦ *vt* (*inf*) закла́дывать
(заложи́ть *perf*); **to be in ~** (*inf: person*) быть*
(*impf*) в долга́х; (: *object*) быть* (*impf*) в
закла́де.

hockey ['hɔkɪ] *n* хокке́й (на траве́).

hocus-pocus ['həʊkəs'pəʊkəs] *n* (*trickery*)
очковтира́тельство; (*words: of magician*)
фо́кус-по́кус; (*jargon*) белиберда́.

hod [hɔd] *n* лото́к* (*для перено́ски кирпиче́й*).

hodgepodge ['hɔdʒpɔdʒ] *n* (US) = **hotchpotch**.

hoe [həʊ] *n* моты́га, тя́пка* ♦ *vt* моты́жить
(*impf*).

hog [hɔg] *n* бо́ров ♦ *vt* (*inf: road, telephone*)
завладева́ть (завладе́ть *perf*) +*instr*; **to go the
whole ~** (*inf*) гуля́ть (*impf*) на всю кату́шку.

Hogmanay [hɔgmə'neɪ] *n* (SCOTTISH) кану́н
Но́вого го́да.

hogwash ['hɔgwɔʃ] *n* (*inf*) чушь *f*.

hoist [hɔɪst] *n* подъёмник, лебёдка* ◆ *vt* поднима́ть (подня́ть* *perf*); **to ~ sth on to one's shoulders** взва́ливать (взвали́ть* *perf*) что-н на пле́чи.

hoity-toity [hɔɪtɪ'tɔɪtɪ] *adj* (*inf: pej*) кичли́вый (кичли́в).

hold [həuld] (*pt, pp* held) *vt* (*grip*) держа́ть* (*impf*); (*contain*) вмеща́ть (вмести́ть* *perf*); (*power, qualification*) облада́ть (*impf*) +*instr*; (*opinion*) приде́рживаться (*impf*) +*gen*; (*post*) занима́ть (заня́ть* *perf*); (*conversation, meeting*) вести́* (провести́* *perf*); (*party*) устра́ивать (устро́ить *perf*); (*detain*) держа́ть* (*impf*) ◆ *vi* (*withstand pressure*) выде́рживать (вы́держать *perf*); (*be valid*) остава́ться (оста́ться* *perf*) в си́ле; (*weather*) держа́ться* (продержа́ться* *perf*) ◆ *n* (*grasp*) захва́т; (*NAUT*) трюм; (*AVIAT*) грузово́й отсе́к; **to ~ one's head up** высоко́ держа́ть* (*impf*) го́лову; **to ~ sb hostage** держа́ть* (*impf*) кого́-н в ка́честве зало́жника(-ицы); **~ the line!** (*TEL*) не кла́ди́те тру́бку!; **to ~ one's own** не ударя́ть (уда́рить *perf*) лицо́м в грязь; **he ~s you responsible for her death** он счита́ет тебя́ вино́вным в её сме́рти; **~ it!** подожди́те!; **he ~s the view that ...** он приде́рживается того́ мне́ния, что ...; **to ~ firm** *or* **fast** кре́пко держа́ться* (*impf*); **~ still, ~ steady** не дви́гайтесь; **if my luck ~s ...** е́сли мне бу́дет продолжа́ть везти́ ...; **I don't ~ with ...** я не одобря́ю ...; **to get ~ of** (*obtain*) достава́ть* (доста́ть* *perf*); **to get ~ of o.s.** сде́рживать (сдержа́ть *perf*) себя́, сде́рживаться (сдержа́ться *perf*); **to catch** *or* **grab ~ of** хвата́ться (схвати́ться* *perf*) за +*acc*; **to have a ~ over sb** держа́ть (*impf*) кого́-н в рука́х

► **hold back** *vt* (*thing*) приде́рживать (придержа́ть* *perf*); (*person*) уде́рживать (удержа́ть* *perf*); (*information*) скрыва́ть (скрыть* *perf*)

► **hold down** *vt* (*person*) уде́рживать (удержа́ть* *perf*); **to ~ down a job** уде́рживаться (удержа́ться* *perf*) на рабо́те

► **hold forth** *vi*: **to ~ forth (on** *or* **about)** увлечённо говори́ть (*impf*) (о +*prp*)

► **hold off** *vt* (*enemy*) сде́рживать (сдержа́ть* *perf*) ◆ *vi* (*weather*): **if the rain ~s off** е́сли не пойдёт дождь

► **hold on** *vi* (*hang on*) держа́ться* (*impf*); (*wait*) ждать* (подожда́ть* *perf*); **~ on!** (*TEL*) не ве́шайте тру́бку!

► **hold on to** *vt fus* (*for support*) держа́ться* (*impf*) за +*acc*; (*keep: an object*) приде́рживать (придержа́ть *perf*); (: *beliefs*) сохраня́ть (сохрани́ть *perf*)

► **hold out** *vt* (*hand*) протя́гивать (протяну́ть

perf); (*hope, prospect*) сохраня́ть (сохрани́ть *perf*) ◆ *vi* (*resist*) держа́ться (продержа́ться *perf*)

► **hold over** *vt* (*meeting*) откла́дывать (отложи́ть* *perf*)

► **hold up** *vt* (*raise*) поднима́ть (подня́ть* *perf*); (*support*) подде́рживать (поддержа́ть* *perf*); (*delay*) заде́рживать (задержа́ть* *perf*); (*rob*) гра́бить* (огра́бить* *perf*).

holdall ['həuldɔːl] *n* (*BRIT*) доро́жная су́мка*.

holder ['həuldə'] *n* (*container*) держа́тель *m*; (*of ticket, record*) облада́тель(ница) *m(f)*; **post ~** занима́ющий(-ая) *m(f) adj* пост; **title ~** нося́щий(-ая) *m(f) adj* ти́тул.

holding ['həuldɪŋ] *n* (*share*) вклад; (*farm*) уча́сток* земли́ ◆ *adj*: **~ operation/tactic** опера́ция/та́ктика сде́рживания.

holding company *n* хо́лдинг-компа́ния.

hold-up ['həuldʌp] *n* (*robbery*) ограбле́ние*; (*delay*) заде́ржка*; (*BRIT: in traffic*) про́бка*.

hole [həul] *n* (*in wall*) дыра́*; (*in road*) я́ма; (*burrow*) нора́*; (*in clothing*) ды́рка*; (*in argument*) брешь *f*; (*inf: place*) дыра́* ◆ *vt* (*ship, building*) пробива́ть (проби́ть* *perf*); **~ in the heart** поро́к се́рдца; **to pick ~s (in)** находи́ть* (найти́* *perf*) сла́бое ме́сто (в +*prp*)

► **hole up** *vi* уединя́ться (уедини́ться *perf*).

holiday ['hɔlɪdeɪ] *n* (*BRIT: from school*) кани́кулы *mpl*; (: *from work*) о́тпуск*; (*day off*) выходно́й день *m*; (*also:* **public ~**) пра́здник; **on ~** (*from school*) на кани́кулах; (*from work*) в о́тпуске; **tomorrow is a (public) ~** за́втра – пра́здник.

holiday camp *n* (*for children*) молодёжный ла́герь *m*; (*BRIT: also:* **holiday centre**) ба́за о́тдыха.

holiday-maker ['hɔlɪdeɪmeɪkə'] *n* (*BRIT*) отпускни́к(-и́ца), отдыха́ющий*(-ая) *m(f) adj*.

holiday pay *n* отпускны́е *pl adj*.

holiday resort *n* куро́рт.

holiday season *n* куро́ртный сезо́н.

holiness ['həulɪnɪs] *n* свя́тость *f*.

holistic [həu'lɪstɪk] *adj* це́лостный.

Holland ['hɔlənd] *n* Голла́ндия.

holler ['hɔlə'] *n* (*inf*) ора́ть (заора́ть *perf*).

hollow ['hɔləu] *adj* (*container*) по́лый; (*log, tree*) дупли́стый; (*cheeks*) впа́лый (впал); (*eyes*) вва́лившийся; (*laugh*) неи́скренний* (неи́скренен); (*claim, sound*) пусто́й* (пуст); (*doctrine, opinion*) пове́рхностный (пове́рхностен) ◆ *n* (*in ground*) впа́дина; (*in tree*) дупло́* ◆ *vt*: **to ~ out** выка́пывать (вы́копать *perf*).

holly ['hɔlɪ] *n* остроли́ст.

hollyhock ['hɔlɪhɔk] *n* алте́й ро́зовый.

Hollywood ['hɔlɪwud] *n* Голливу́д.

holocaust ['hɔləkɔːst] *n* (*nuclear*) истребле́ние;

(*Jewish*) холокóст.

hologram ['hɔləgræm] *n* гологрáмма.

hols [hɔlz] (*inf*) *npl* (*for students, pupils etc*) канúкулы *pl*; (*for workers*) óтпуск* *msg*.

holster ['həulstə^r] *n* кобурá*.

holy ['həulɪ] *adj* святóй* (свят).

Holy Communion *n* Святóе Причáстие.

Holy Father *n* Егó святéйшество *m* (*пáпа рúмский*).

Holy Ghost *n* святóй дух.

Holy Land *n*: **the ~ ~** святáя земля*.

holy orders *npl* духóвный сан *msg*.

Holy Spirit *n* = **Holy Ghost**.

homage ['hɔmɪdʒ] *n* почтéние; **to pay ~ to** воздавáть* (воздáть* *perf*) пóчести +*dat*.

home [həum] *n* (*house, institution, family*) дом*; (*area, country*) рóдина ♦ *cpd* (*domestic*) домáшний*; (*ECON, POL*) внýтренний*; (*SPORT*): **~ team** хозя́ева* *mpl* пóля ♦ *adv* (*go, come*) домóй; (*right in*) в цель *or* тóчку; **at ~** (*house*) дóма; (*country*) на рóдине; (*in situation*) как у себя́ дóма; **make yourself at ~** чýвствуйте себя́ как дóма; **to make one's ~ somewhere** поселя́ться (поселúться *perf*) где́-то; **the ~ of free enterprise/jazz** *etc* рóдина свобóдного предпринимáтельства/джáза *etc*; **a ~ from ~** вторóй дом; **match/win ~ and dry** цел и невредúм; **to bring sth ~ to sb** доводúть* (довестú* *perf*) что-н до чьегó-н сознáния

▸ **home in on** *vt fus* (*subj: missile*) осуществля́ть (осуществúть* *perf*) самонаведéние на +*acc*.

home address *n* домáшний* áдрес*.

home-brew [həum'bru:] *n* домáшнее пúво.

homecoming ['həumkʌmɪŋ] *n* возвращéние домóй.

home computer *n* домáшний компью́тер.

Home Counties *npl* (*BRIT*): **the ~ ~** грáфства прилегáющие к Лóндону.

home economics *n* домовóдство.

home ground *n*: **to be on ~ ~** (*in place*) чýвствовать (*impf*) себя́ как дóма.

home-grown ['həumgrəun] *adj* (*from garden*) домáшний*; (*not foreign*) отéчественный.

home help *n* рабóтник собеса оказывающий пóмощь по дóму больны́м и престарéлым

homeland ['həumlænd] *n* рóдина.

homeless ['həumlɪs] *adj* (*family, refugee*) бездóмный* (бездóмен) ♦ *npl*: **the ~** бездóмные *pl adj*.

home loan *n* бáнковская ссýда на покýпку дóма.

homely ['həumlɪ] *adj* простóй* (прост), ую́тный* (ую́тен).

home-made [həum'meid] *adj* (*food*) домáшний*; (*bomb*) самодéльный.

Home Office *n* (*BRIT*): **the ~ ~** ≈ Министéрство внýтренних дел.

homeopathy *etc* (*US*) = **homoeopathy** *etc*

home page *n* (*COMPUT*) странúца в Интернéте, домáшняя странúца.

home rule *n* самоуправлéние.

Home Secretary *n* (*BRIT*) ≈ минúстр внýтренних дел.

homesick ['həumsɪk] *adj*: **to be ~** (*for family*) скучáть (*impf*) по дóму; (*for country*) скучáть по рóдине.

homestead ['həumstɛd] *n* усáдьба.

home stretch *n* (*of race*) фúнишная прямáя.

home town *n* роднóй гóрод*.

home truth *n*: **he needs to learn some ~ ~s** емý порá объяснúть, что к чемý.

homeward ['həumwəd] *adj* (*journey*) обрáтный ♦ *adv*: **~(s)** домóй.

homework ['həumwə:k] *n* домáшняя рабóта, домáшнее задáние.

homicidal [hɔmɪ'saɪdl] *adj* предрасполóженный к убúйству.

homicide ['hɔmɪsaɪd] *n* (*esp US*) убúйство.

homily ['hɔmɪlɪ] *n* (*tirade*) тирáда; (*sermon*) нравоучéние.

homing ['həumɪŋ] *adj*: **~ device** голóвка* самонаведéния; **~ pigeon** почтóвый гóлубь* *m*.

homoeopath ['həumɪəupæθ] (*US* **homeopath**) *n* гомеопáт.

homoeopathy [həumɪ'ɔpəθɪ] (*US* **homeopathy**) *n* гомеопáтия.

homogeneous [hɔməu'dʒi:nɪəs] *adj* однорóдный* (однорóден).

homogenize [hə'mɔdʒənaɪz] *vt* гомогенизúровать (*impf/perf*).

homosexual [hɔməu'sɛksjuəl] *adj* гомосексуáльный ♦ *n* гомосексуалúст(ка*).

Hon. *abbr* = **honorary**, **honourable**.

Honduras [hɔn'djuərəs] *n* Гондурáс.

hone [həun] *n* точúльный кáмень* *m* ♦ *vt* точúть (наточúть *perf*); (*TECH*) хонинговáть (*impf/perf*); (*fig*) оттáчивать (отточúть* *perf*).

honest ['ɔnɪst] *adj* чéстный* (чéстен); **to be quite ~ (with you)** ... чéстно говоря́, ...

honestly ['ɔnɪstlɪ] *adv* чéстно.

honesty ['ɔnɪstɪ] *n* чéстность *f*.

honey ['hʌnɪ] *n* мёд*; (*esp US: inf: darling*) мúлый*(-ая) *m(f) adj*, голýбчик.

honeycomb ['hʌnɪkəum] *n* (*пчелúные*) сóты *fpl*; (*pattern*) шестиугóльный мозáичный узóр ♦ *vt*: **to ~ with** кишéть (*impf*) +*instr*.

honeymoon ['hʌnɪmu:n] *n* медóвый мéсяц.

honeysuckle ['hʌnɪsʌkl] *n* жúмолость *f*.

Hong Kong ['hɔŋ'kɔŋ] *n* Гонкóнг.

honk [hɔŋk] *vi* (*AUT*) гудéть* (прогудéть* *perf*).

Honolulu [hɔnə'lu:lu:] *n* Гонолýлу *m ind*.

honor *etc* (*US*) = **honour** *etc*.

honorary ['ɔnərərɪ] *adj* почётный* (почётен).

honour ['ɔnə^r] (*US* **honor**) *vt* (*person*) почитáть (*impf*), чтить* (*impf*); (*commitment*) выполня́ть (вы́полнить *perf*) ♦ *n* (*pride*) честь *f*; (*tribute, distinction*) пóчесть *f*; **in ~ of** в честь +*gen*.

honourable ['ɔnərəbl] *adj* благорóдный* (благорóден); (*BRIT: POL*) уважáемый (*о* членах парламента).

honour-bound ['ɔnə'baund] *adj*: **he is ~ to keep his word** сдержать слово является для него делом чести.

honours degree ['ɔnəz-] *n* учёная степень *f* (обычно бакалавра).

honours list *n* (*BRIT*) список* представленных к награде.

Hons. *abbr* (*SCOL*) = **honours degree**.

hood [hud] *n* капюшон; (*AUT. BRIT: folding roof*) откидной верх*; (: *US: bonnet*) капот; (*of cooker*) вытяжной колпак.

hooded ['hudɪd] *adj* (*robber*) в маске; (*jacket*) с капюшоном.

hoodlum ['hu:dləm] *n* (*inf*) громила *m*.

hoodwink ['hudwɪŋk] *vt* (*inf*) одурачивать (одурачить *perf*).

hoof [hu:f] (*pl* **hooves**) *n* копыто.

hook [huk] *n* крючок* ♦ *vt* прицеплять (прицепить* *perf*); (*fish*) поймать (*perf*) (на крючок); **by ~ or by crook** всеми правдами и неправдами; **he is ~ed on her/sweets** (*inf*) он помешан на ней/конфетах; **to get ~ed (on)** (*on drugs*) пристраститься* *perf* (к +*dat*)

▶ **hook up** *vt* (*dress*) застёгивать (застегнуть *perf*) на крючок; (*COMPUT, TV*): **to ~ up to the main network** подключать (подключить* *perf*) к центральной сети.

hook and eye (*pl* **~s ~ ~s**) *n* крючок* и петля* (на одежде).

hooligan ['hu:lɪgən] *n* хулиган.

hooliganism ['hu:lɪgənɪzəm] *n* хулиганство.

hoop [hu:p] *n* обруч*; (*for croquet*) ворота *pl*.

hooray [hu:'reɪ] *excl* = **hurrah**.

hoot [hu:t] *vi* (*AUT: horn*) гудеть* (прогудеть* *perf*); (*siren*) выть (*impf*); (*owl*) ухать (*impf*); (*laugh, jeer*) улюлюкать (*impf*) ♦ *vt* (*horn*) гудеть* (прогудеть* *perf*) в +*acc* ♦ *n* (*see vi*) гудок*; вой; уханье; улюлюканье; **to ~ with laughter** разражаться (разразиться* *perf*) оглушительным смехом.

hooter ['hu:tə'] *n* (*BRIT*) гудок*.

hoover® ['hu:və'] (*BRIT*) *n* пылесос ♦ *vt* пылесосить (пропылесосить *perf*).

hooves [hu:vz] *npl of* **hoof**.

hop [hɔp] *vi* скакать* (*impf*) на одной ноге; (*bird*) скакать (*impf*) ♦ *n* скачок*.

hope [həup] *vti* надеяться (*impf*) ♦ *n* надежда; **to ~ that/to do** надеяться (*impf*), что/+*infin*; **I ~ so/not** надеюсь, что да/нет; **to ~ for the best** надеяться (*impf*) на лучшее; **I have no ~ of sth/doing** у меня нет никакой надежды на что-н/+*infin*; **in the ~ of/that** в надежде на +*acc*/что.

hopeful ['həupful] *adj* (*person*) полный* (полон) надежд; (*situation etc*) обнадёживающий; **to be ~ of sth** надеяться (*impf*) на что-н; **I'm ~ that she'll manage to**

come я надеюсь, что она сможет прийти.

hopefully ['həupfulɪ] *adv* (*expectantly*) с надеждой; (*one hopes*): **~, he'll come back** будем надеяться, что он вернётся.

hopeless ['həuplɪs] *adj* (*situation, person*) безнадёжный* (безнадёжен); (*incorrigible*) неисправимый (неисправим); **I'm ~ at names** я не в состоянии запоминать имена.

hopper ['hɔpə'] *n* бункер*.

hops [hɔps] *npl* хмель *msg*.

horde [hɔ:d] *n* полчище.

horizon [hə'raɪzn] *n* горизонт.

horizontal [hɔrɪ'zɔntl] *adj* горизонтальный* (горизонтален).

hormone ['hɔ:məun] *n* гормон.

hormone replacement therapy *n* гормональная терапия.

horn [hɔ:n] *n* (*of animal*) рог*; (*also: French ~*) валторна; (*AUT*) гудок*.

horned [hɔ:nd] *adj* рогатый.

hornet ['hɔ:nɪt] *n* (*insect*) шершень* *m*.

horn-rimmed ['hɔ:n'rɪmd] *adj*: **~ spectacles** очки в роговой оправе.

horny ['hɔ:nɪ] *adj* (*inf: aroused*) (сексуально) возбуждённый* (возбуждён).

horoscope ['hɔrəskəup] *n* гороскоп.

horrendous [hə'rɛndəs] *adj* ужасающий*.

horrible ['hɔrɪbl] *adj* ужасный* (ужасен).

horrid ['hɔrɪd] *adj* противный* (противен), мерзкий* (мерзок).

horrific [hə'rɪfɪk] *adj* ужасный* (ужасен); **it was simply ~** это было просто ужасно.

horrify ['hɔrɪfaɪ] *vt* ужасать (ужаснуть *perf*).

horrifying ['hɔrɪfaɪɪŋ] *adj* ужасающий*.

horror ['hɔrə'] *n* (*alarm*) ужас; (*abhorrence*) отвращение; (*of war*) ужасы *mpl*.

horror film *n* фильм ужасов.

horror-stricken ['hɔrəstrɪkn] *adj* = **horror-struck**.

horror-struck ['hɔrəstrʌk] *adj* объятый (объят) ужасом.

hors d'oeuvre [ɔ:'də:vrə] *n* закуска*.

horse [hɔ:s] *n* лошадь* *f*; (*male*) конь* *m*.

horseback ['hɔ:sbæk] *adj* верховой ♦ *adv*: **on ~** верхом; **police on ~** конная полиция.

horsebox ['hɔ:sbɔks] *n* (*BRIT*) вагон для лошадей.

horse chestnut *n* конский* каштан.

horse-drawn ['hɔ:sdrɔ:n] *adj* конный; (*transport*) гужевой.

horsefly ['hɔ:sflaɪ] *n* слепень* *m*.

horseman ['hɔ:smən] *irreg n* всадник.

horsemanship ['hɔ:smənʃɪp] *n* искусство верховой езды.

horseplay ['hɔ:spleɪ] *n* возня.

horsepower ['hɔ:spauə'] *n* лошадиная сила; **a 30 ~ engine** двигатель *m* мощностью в 30 лошадиных сил.

---

* marks translations which have irregular inflections. The Russian-English side of the dictionary gives inflectional information.

horse racing n скáчки* *fpl.*
horseradish ['hɔːsrædɪʃ] n хрен*.
horseshoe ['hɔːsʃuː] n подкóва.
horse show n соревновáния по вы́ездке.
horse trading n закули́сные сдéлки *fpl.*
horse trials *npl* = **horse show.**
horsewhip ['hɔːswɪp] n хлыст* ♦ *vt* хлестáть* (отхлестáть* *perf*).
horsewoman ['hɔːswʊmən] *irreg* n вcáдница.
horsey ['hɔːsɪ] *adj* (*person*) увлекáющийся* лошадьми́; (*features*) лошади́ный.
horticulture ['hɔːtɪkʌltʃə'] n садовóдство.
hose [hauz] n (*also: ~pipe*) шланг
► **hose down** *vt* полив́ать (поли́ть *perf*) из шлáнга.
hosepipe ['hauzpaɪp] n шланг.
hosiery ['hauzɪərɪ] n чулóчные издéлия *ntpl.*
hospice ['hɔspɪs] n больни́ца (*для безнадёжно больны́х*).
hospitable ['hɔspɪtəbl] *adj* (*person, behaviour*) гостеприи́мный* (гостеприи́мен); (*climate*) благоприя́тный* (благоприя́тен).
hospital ['hɔspɪtl] n больни́ца; **to be in ~** *or* (*US*) **in the ~** лежáть* (*impf*) в больни́це.
hospitality [hɔspɪ'tælɪtɪ] n гостеприи́мство.
hospitalize ['hɔspɪtəlaɪz] *vt* госпитализи́ровать (*impf/perf*).
host [həust] n (*at party, dinner*) хозя́ин*; (*TV, RADIO*) веду́щий* *m adj* ♦ *adj* (*country, organization*) принимáющий ♦ *vt* (*programme*) вести́* (*impf*); (*event*) проводи́ть* (провести́* *perf*); **the H~** (*REL*) просвирá*; **a ~ of** мáсса +*gen*, мнóжество +*gen.*
hostage ['hɔstɪdʒ] n зало́жник(-ица); **he was taken/held ~** его́ взя́ли/держáли в кáчестве зало́жника.
hostel ['hɔstl] n общежи́тие; (*for homeless*) прию́т; (*also: youth ~*) молодёжная гости́ница.
hostelling ['hɔstlɪŋ] n: **to go (youth) ~** путешéствовать (*impf*), останáвливаясь в молодёжных гости́ницах.
hostess ['həustɪs] n (*at party, dinner etc*) хозя́йка*; (*BRIT: also: air ~*) стюардéсса; (*TV, RADIO*) веду́щая *f adj*; (*in club, restaurant*) жéнщина, развлекáющая посети́телей нóчного клу́ба, рестoрáна *итп.*
hostile ['hɔstaɪl] *adj* (*person, attitude*) враждéбный* (враждéбен); (*conditions, environment*) неблагоприя́тный* (неблагоприя́тен); (*troops*) врáжеский; **~ to** *or* **towards** враждéбный* (враждéбен) по отношéнию к +*dat.*
hostility [hɔ'stɪlɪtɪ] n враждéбность *f*;
hostilities *npl* (*fighting*) вoéнные дéйствия *ntpl.*
hot [hɔt] *adj* (*object, temper, argument etc*) горя́чий* (горя́ч); (*weather*) жáркий*; (*spicy: food*) óстрый* (остр); **she is ~** ей жáрко; **it's ~** (*weather*) жáрко; **I'm not too ~ on**

mathematics я не óчень разбирáюсь в матемáтике
► **hot up** *vi* (*BRIT: inf: situation*) накаля́ться (накали́ться *perf*); (*: party*) разгорáться (разгорéться *perf*) ♦ *vt* (*engine*) разогревáть (разогрéть* *perf*); (*pace*) ускоря́ть (ускóрить *perf*).
hot air n (*fig*) пустослóвие, болтовня́.
hot-air balloon [hɔt'ɛə-] n воздýшный шар*.
hotbed ['hɔtbɛd] n (*fig*) рассáдник.
hot-blooded [hɔt'blʌdɪd] *adj* пы́лкий* (пы́лок).
hotchpotch ['hɔtʃpɔtʃ] n (*BRIT*) сбóрная соля́нка (*тáкже перен*).
hot dog n ≈ соси́ска* в бýлке.
hotel [hau'tɛl] n гости́ница, отéль *m.*
hotelier [hau'tɛlɪə'] n (*owner*) владéлец* (-éлица) гости́ницы; (*manager*) администрáтор гости́ницы.
hot flush n (*esp BRIT*) прили́в.
hotel industry n гости́ничный би́знес.
hotel room n гости́ничный нóмер*.
hotfoot ['hɔtfut] *adv* (*inf*) стремглáв.
hothead ['hɔthɛd] n (*inf*) горя́чая головá*.
hot-headed [hɔt'hɛdɪd] *adj* (*person*) поры́вистый (поры́вист); (*remark*) необдýманный (необдýман).
hothouse ['hɔthaus] n оранжерéя, тепли́ца.
hot line n (*POL*) прямáя телефóнная связь *мéжду прави́тельствами рáзных стран.*
hotly ['hɔtlɪ] *adv* горячó.
hotplate ['hɔtpleɪt] n конфóрка*.
hotpot ['hɔtpɔt] n (*BRIT*) жаркóе *nt adj.*
hot potato n (*inf*) больнóй вопрóс.
hot seat n (*inf*): **to be in the ~ ~** занимáть (заня́ть* *perf*) отвéтственный пост.
hot spot n (*war zone*) горя́чая тóчка*.
hot spring n горя́чий* истóчник.
hot stuff n (*inf: woman*) красóтка*; (*: film, book*) клáссная вещь *f.*
hot-tempered ['hɔt'tɛmpəd] *adj* вспы́льчивый (вспы́льчив).
hot-water bottle [hɔt'wɔːtə-] n грéлка*.
hound [haund] *vt* трави́ть* (затрави́ть* *perf*) ♦ n (*dog*) гóнчая *f adj.*
hour ['auə'] n час*; **at 60 miles an** *or* **per ~ со** скóростью 60 миль в час; **24 ~ job** круглосýточная рабóта; **I am paid by the ~ я** получáю почасовýю оплáту.
hourly ['auəlɪ] *adj* (*rate*) почасовóй; (*service*) ежечáсный ♦ *adv* (*each hour*) ежечáсно; (*soon*) с чáсу на час.
house [n haus, *vt* hauz] n дом*; (*company*) фи́рма; (*THEAT*) зал* ♦ *vt* (*person*) сели́ть (посели́ть *perf*); (*collection*) размещáть (размести́ть* *perf*); **at my ~** у меня́ дóма; **to my ~** ко мне домóй; **the H~ of Commons/ Lords** (*BRIT*) палáта óбщин/лóрдов; **the H~ (of Representatives)** (*US*) палáта предстáвителей; **the H~s of Parliament** здáние *ntsg* парлáмента; **on the ~** (*inf*) бесплáтно.
house arrest n домáшний* арéст.

houseboat ['hausbəut] *n* плавучий* дом*.
housebound ['hausbaund] *adj*: **she is** ~ она́ не
мо́жет выходи́ть из до́ма.
housebreaking ['hausbreɪkɪŋ] *n* грабёж со
взло́мом.
house-broken ['hausbrəukn] *adj* (*US*) = **house-
trained**.
housecoat ['hauskəut] *n* дома́шний* хала́т.
household ['haushəuld] *n* (*home, inhabitants*)
дом*; ~ **name** (*brand*) изве́стная ма́рка*;
(*person*) широко́ изве́стная ли́чность *f*.
householder ['haushəuldə'] *n* домовладе́лец*.
house-hunting ['haushʌntɪŋ] *n*: **to go** ~
занима́ться (заня́ться* *perf*) по́исками до́ма.
housekeeper ['hauski:pə'] *n* эконо́мка*.
housekeeping ['hauski:pɪŋ] *n* (*work*)
дома́шние дела́ *ntpl*; (*also:* ~ **money**) де́ньги*
pl на хозя́йственные ну́жды.
houseman ['hausmən] *irreg n* (*BRIT*) врач-
стажёр, интерн.
house-owner ['hausəunə'] *n* домовладе́лец*
(-лица).
house-party ['hauspɑ:tɪ] *n приглашение в
гости с ночёвкой*.
house plant *n* комнатное расте́ние.
house-proud ['hauspraud] *adj* домови́тый
(домови́т).
house-to-house ['haustə'haus] *adj*: **to make** ~
enquiries проводи́ть* (провести́* *perf*)
поквартирный опро́с.
house-train ['haustreɪn] *vt*: **to** ~ **a pet** приуча́ть
(приучи́ть* *perf*) дома́шнего живо́тного не
га́дить в до́ме.
house-trained ['haustreɪnd] *adj* (*BRIT*): **our dog
is fully** ~ на́ша соба́ка приу́чена к туале́ту.
house-warming ['hauswɔ:mɪŋ] *n* (*also:* ~
party) новосе́лье*.
housewife ['hauswaɪf] *irreg n* дома́шняя
хозя́йка*, домохозя́йка.
housework ['hauswə:k] *n* дома́шнее
хозя́йство.
housing ['hauzɪŋ] *n* жили́ще, жильё;
(*provision*) жили́щное снабже́ние; (*TECH*)
ко́рпус, кожу́х* ◆ *cpd* жили́щный; ~ **shortage**
недоста́ток жилья́.
housing association *n* (*BRIT*) ассоциа́ция
домовладе́льцев (*предоставля́ющая жильё
по бо́лее вы́годным це́нам*).
housing benefit *n де́нежное пособие не-
иму́щим се́мьям по вы́плате кварти́рной пла́ты*.
housing conditions *npl* жили́щные усло́вия.
housing development *n* = **housing estate**.
housing estate (*US* **housing project**) *n* жили́щ-
ный ко́мплекс; (*larger*) жило́й масси́в.
housing project *n* (*US*) = **housing estate**.
hove [həuv] *pt, pp of* **heave**.
hovel ['hɔvl] *n* лачу́га.
hover ['hɔvə'] *vi* (*bird, insect*) пари́ть (*impf*);

(*person*) мя́ться (*impf*); **to** ~ **round sb**
увива́ться (*impf*) вокру́г кого́-н.
hovercraft ['hɔvəkrɑ:ft] *n* су́дно на возду́шной
поду́шке.
hoverport ['hɔvəpɔ:t] *n* порт для су́ден на
возду́шной поду́шке.

KEYWORD

how [hau] *adv* **1** (*in what way*) как; **to know how
to do** знать *perf*, как +*infin*, уме́ть (*impf*) +*infin*;
how did you like the film? как Вам
понра́вился фильм?; **how are you?** как дела́?
2 ско́лько; **how much milk/many people?**
ско́лько молока́/челове́к?; **how long have
you been here?** ско́лько Вы уже́ здесь?; **how
old are you?** ско́лько Вам лет?; **how tall is he?**
како́го он ро́ста?; **how lovely/awful!** как
чуде́сно/ужа́сно!

however [hau'ɛvə'] *conj* одна́ко ◆ *adv* (*no
matter how*) как бы ... ни; (*in questions*) как
же; ~ **did you find me?** как же Вы меня́
нашли́?
howl [haul] *vi* (*animal, wind*) выть* (*impf*); (*baby,
person*) реве́ть* (*impf*) ◆ *n* (*see vb*) вой*; рёв.
howler ['haulə'] *n* (*inf: mistake*) ля́псус.
howling ['haulɪŋ] *adj* невероя́тный*
(невероя́тен), фантасти́ческий*.
HP *n abbr* (*BRIT*) = **hire-purchase**.
h.p. *abbr* (*AUT*) (= **horsepower**) л.с.=
лошади́ная си́ла.
HQ *abbr* = **headquarters**.
HR *n abbr* (*US: POL*: = *House of Representatives*)
пала́та представи́телей.
HRH *abbr* (*BRIT*: = *His/Her Royal Highness*) Его́/
Её Короле́вское Высо́чество.
hr(s) *abbr* = **hour(s)**.
HS *abbr* (*US*) = **high school**.
HST *abbr* (*US*) = *Hawaiian Standard Time*.
HTML *n abbr* (= *hypertext markup language*)
гипертекст.
hub [hʌb] *n* (*of wheel*) ступи́ца; (*fig*)
средото́чие.
hubbub ['hʌbʌb] *n* гам, го́мон.
hubcap ['hʌbkæp] *n* (*AUT*) покры́шка.
HUD *n abbr* (*US*) = *Department of Housing and
Urban Development*.
huddle ['hʌdl] *vi*: **to** ~ **together** прижима́ться
(прижа́ться* *perf*) друг к дру́гу ◆ *n*: **to lie in a**
~ лежа́ть* (*impf*) в ку́че.
hue [hju:] *n* тон, отте́нок*.
hue and cry *n* шум; (*pej*) шуми́ха.
huff [hʌf] *n*: **he's in a** ~ он оби́жен ◆ *vi*: **to** ~ **and
puff** (*also fig*) пыхте́ть* (*impf*).
huffy ['hʌfɪ] *adj* (*inf*) наду́тый (наду́т).
hug [hʌg] *vt* (*person*) обнима́ть (обня́ть* *perf*);
(*thing*) обхва́тывать (обхвати́ть* *perf*) ◆ *n*
объя́тие; **to give sb a** ~ обнима́ть (обня́ть*
perf) кого́-н.

---

* marks translations which have irregular inflections. The Russian-English side of the dictionary gives inflectional information.

huge [hju:dʒ] *adj* огро́мный* (огро́мен), грома́дный* (грома́ден).

hugely ['hju:dʒlɪ] *adv* чрезвыча́йно.

hulk [hʌlk] *n* (NAUT) ко́рпус* (затону́вшего корабля́); (building, person) грома́дина.*

hulking ['hʌlkɪŋ] *adj* здорове́нный; **a ~ great oaf** у́валень *m*.

hull [hʌl] *n* (NAUT) ко́рпус; (of seeds) шелуха́; (of strawberries) ча́шечка ♦ *vt* (fruit) лущи́ть (облущи́ть *perf*).

hullabal(l)oo ['hʌləbə'lu:] *n* (inf) шуми́ха.

hullo [hə'ləu] *excl* = **hello**.

hum [hʌm] *vt* напева́ть (impf) (без слов) ♦ *vi* (person) напева́ть (impf); (machine) гуде́ть* (прогуде́ть* *perf*); (insect) жужжа́ть (impf) ♦ *n* (of wires) гуде́ние; (of voices, machines) гул.

human ['hju:mən] *adj* челове́ческий* ♦ *n* (also: ~ **being**) челове́к*.

humane [hju:'meɪn] *adj* (treatment) челове́чный* (челове́чен); (slaughter) гума́нный* (гума́нен).

humanely [hju:'meɪnlɪ] *adv* по-челове́чески, гума́нно.

humanism ['hju:mənɪzəm] *n* гумани́зм.

humanitarian [hju:mænɪ'tɛərɪən] *adj* (aid) гуманита́рный; (principles) гума́нный*.

humanity [hju:'mænɪtɪ] *n* (mankind) челове́чество; (humaneness) челове́чность *f*, гума́нность *f*; (human nature) челове́ческая суть *f*; **the humanities** *npl* гума́нитарные нау́ки *fpl*.

humanly ['hju:mənlɪ] *adv*: **it's not ~ possible** э́то вне челове́ческих возмо́жностей; **it is ~ possible** э́то в преде́лах челове́ческих возмо́жностей.

humanoid ['hju:mənɔɪd] *adj* человеко-подо́бный* ♦ *n* гумано́ид.

human relations *npl* (COMM) обще́ственные отноше́ния *ntpl*.

human rights *npl* права́ *ntpl* челове́ка.

humble ['hʌmbl] *adj* (modest, simple) скро́мный* (скро́мен) ♦ *vt* сбива́ть (сбить* *perf*) спесь с +*gen*.

humbly ['hʌmblɪ] *adv* скро́мно, смире́нно.

humbug ['hʌmbʌg] *n* (of statement) надува́тельство; (BRIT: sweet) чёрно-бе́лый мя́тный ледене́ц.

humdrum ['hʌmdrʌm] *adj* ну́дный* (ну́ден).

humid ['hju:mɪd] *adj* вла́жный* (вла́жен).

humidifier [hju:'mɪdɪfaɪə'] *n* увлажни́тель *m* во́здуха.

humidity [hju:'mɪdɪtɪ] *n* вла́жность *f*.

humiliate [hju:'mɪlɪeɪt] *vt* унижа́ть (уни́зить* *perf*).

humiliating [hju:'mɪlɪeɪtɪŋ] *adj* унизи́тельный* (унизи́телен).

humiliation [hju:mɪlɪ'eɪʃən] *n* униже́ние.

humility [hju:'mɪlɪtɪ] *n* (modesty) скро́мность *f*; (humbleness) смире́ние.

humming bird ['hʌmɪŋ-] *n* коли́бри *m/f ind*.

humor *etc* (US) = **humour** *etc*.

humorist ['hju:mərɪst] *n* юмори́ст(ка*).

humorous ['hju:mərəs] *adj* (book) юмористи́ческий*; (remark) шутли́вый (шутли́в); (person) с ю́мором.

humour ['hju:mə'] (US **humor**) *n* ю́мор; (mood) настрое́ние ♦ *vt* ублажа́ть (ублажи́ть *perf*); **sense of ~** чу́вство ю́мора; **to be in good/ bad ~** быть* (impf) в хоро́шем/плохо́м настрое́нии.

humourless ['hju:məlɪs] *adj* лишённый (лишён) чу́вства ю́мора.

hump [hʌmp] *n* (in ground) буго́р*; (on back) горб*.

humpbacked ['hʌmpbækt] *adj*: ~ **bridge** горба́тый мост.

humus ['hju:məs] *n* перегно́й.

hunch [hʌntʃ] *n* (premonition) дога́дка*; **I have a ~ that** ... я предчу́вствую, что ....

hunchback ['hʌntʃbæk] *n* горбу́н*(ья*).

hunched [hʌntʃt] *adj* суту́лый (суту́л).

hundred ['hʌndrəd] *n* сто*; **a** or **one ~ books/ people/dollars** сто* книг/люде́й/до́лларов; **about a ~** о́коло ста; **~ and first** сто* пе́рвый; **to live to be a ~** жить* (дожи́ть* *perf*) до ста лет; **~s of** со́тни* +*gen* +*pl*: **people came in their ~s** or **by the ~** пришли́ со́тни люде́й; **I'm a ~ per cent sure** я уве́рен на сто проце́нтов.

hundredth ['hʌndrədθ] *adj* со́тый ♦ *n* (fraction) одна́ со́тая *f adj*.

hundredweight ['hʌndrɪdweɪt] *n* (BRIT) ме́ра ве́са, равня́ющаяся 50.8 килогра́ммов; (US) ме́ра ве́са, равня́ющаяся 45.3 килогра́ммов.

hung [hʌŋ] *pt, pp of* **hang**.

Hungarian [hʌŋ'gɛərɪən] *adj* венге́рский* ♦ *n* венгр(-ге́рка*); (LING) венге́рский* язык*.

Hungary ['hʌŋgərɪ] *n* Ве́нгрия.

hunger ['hʌŋgə'] *n* го́лод* ♦ *vi*: **to ~ for** жа́ждать* (impf) +*gen*.

hunger strike *n* голодо́вка*.

hung over *adj* (inf): **I'm feeling ~ ~** у меня́ похме́лье.

hungrily ['hʌŋgrəlɪ] *adv* (also fig) жа́дно.

hungry ['hʌŋgrɪ] *adj* голо́дный* (го́лоден); (keen): **~ for** жа́ждущий +*gen*; **he is ~** он го́лоден; **to go ~** голода́ть (impf).

hung up *adj* (inf): **to be ~ ~ about** or **on** зацикли́ваться (зацикли́ться *perf*) на +*prp*.

hunk [hʌŋk] *n* (большо́й) кусо́к*; (of bread) ломо́ть* *m*; (inf: man) краса́вчик.

hunt [hʌnt] *vt* (animal) охо́титься* (impf) на +*acc*; (criminal) охо́титься* (impf) за +*instr* ♦ *vi* (SPORT) о .охо́титься* (impf) ♦ *n* охо́та; (for criminal) ро́зыск; **to ~ (for)** (search) иска́ть* (impf)

▶ **hunt down** *vt* высле́живать (вы́следить* *perf*).

hunter ['hʌntə'] *n* охо́тник(-ица).

hunting ['hʌntɪŋ] *n* охо́та.

hurdle ['hə:dl] *n* (difficulty) препя́тствие; (SPORT) препя́тствие, барье́р.

hurl [hə:l] *vt* (object) швыря́ть (швырну́ть *perf*);

to ~ abuse *or* **insults at sb** осыпа́ть (осы́пать *perf*) кого́-н ру́ганью.
hurling ['hə:lɪŋ] *n* (*SPORT*) ирла́ндский* хокке́й на траве́.
hurly-burly ['hə:lɪ'bə:lɪ] *n* сумато́ха.
hurrah [hu'rɑ] *excl* ура́.
hurray [hu'reɪ] *excl* = **hurrah.**
hurricane ['hʌrɪkən] *n* урага́н.
hurried ['hʌrɪd] *adj* поспе́шный* (поспе́шен).
hurriedly ['hʌrɪdlɪ] *adv* поспе́шно.

hurry ['hʌrɪ] *n* спе́шка ♦ *vi* спеши́ть (поспеши́ть *perf*), торопи́ться* (потороп́ться* *perf*) ♦ *vt* (*person*) подгоня́ть (подогна́ть* *perf*), торопи́ть* (поторопи́ть* *perf*); (*work*) ускоря́ть (уско́рить *perf*); **to be in a ~** спеши́ть (*impf*); **to do sth in a ~** де́лать (сде́лать *perf*) что-н в спе́шке; **there's no ~** нет никако́й спе́шки; **what's the ~?** почему́ така́я спе́шка?; **to ~ in/out** поспе́шно входи́ть (войти́* *perf*)/выходи́ть (вы́йти* *perf*); **they hurried to help him** они́ поспеши́ли ему́ на по́мощь; **to ~ home** спеши́ть (поспеши́ть *perf*) домо́й
► **hurry along** *vi* поспе́шно проходи́ть* (пройти́* *perf*)
► **hurry away** *vi* поспе́шно уходи́ть* (уйти́* *perf*)
► **hurry off** *vi* = **hurry away**
► **hurry up** *vt* (*person*) подгоня́ть (подогна́ть* *perf*), торопи́ть* (поторопи́ть* *perf*); (*process*) ускоря́ть (уско́рить *perf*) ♦ *vi* торопи́ться* (поторопи́ться* *perf*); **~ up!** поторопи́сь!

hurt [hə:t] (*pt, pp* **hurt**) *vt* (*also fig*) причиня́ть (причини́ть *perf*) боль +*dat*; (*injure*) ушиба́ть (ушиби́ть* *perf*); (*offend*) обижа́ть (оби́деть* *perf*); (*chances, reputation*) поврежда́ть (повреди́ть* *perf*) ♦ *vi* (*be painful*) боле́ть (*impf*) ♦ *adj* (*offended*) оби́женный* (оби́жен); (*injured*) уши́бленный (уши́блен); **to ~ o.s.** ушиба́ться (ушиби́ться *perf*); **I've ~ my arm** я уши́б ру́ку; **where does it ~?** где боли́т?; **nobody was ~ in the crash** в ава́рии никто́ не пострада́л.
hurtful ['hə:tful] *adj* оби́дный* (оби́ден).
hurtle ['hə:tl] *vi*: **to ~ past** проноси́ться* (пронести́сь* *perf*); **to ~ down** ска́тываться (скати́ться* *perf*).
husband ['hʌzbənd] *n* муж*.
hush [hʌʃ] *n* тишина́ ♦ *vt* заставля́ть (заста́вить* *perf*) замолча́ть; **~!** ти́хо!, ти́ше!
► **hush up** *vt* (*scandal*) замина́ть (замя́ть* *perf*).
hushed [hʌʃt] *adj* (*place*) ти́хий* (тих); (*voice*) приглушённый (приглушён).
hush-hush [hʌʃ'hʌʃ] *adj* (*inf*) сугу́бо секре́тный* (секре́тен).
husk [hʌsk] *n* шелуха́.
husky ['hʌskɪ] *adj* (*voice*) хри́плый* (хрипл) ♦ *n* ездова́я соба́ка.

hustings ['hʌstɪŋz] *npl* (*BRIT: POL*) пред-вы́борные собра́ния *ntpl*.
hustle ['hʌsl] *vt* (*hurry*) подта́лкивать (подтолкну́ть *perf*) ♦ *n*: **~ and bustle** сумато́ха.
hut [hʌt] *n* (*house*) избу́шка*, хи́жина; (*shed*) сара́й.
hutch [hʌtʃ] *n* кле́тка* (*для кро́ликов итп*).
hyacinth ['haɪəsɪnθ] *n* гиаци́нт.
hybrid ['haɪbrɪd] *n* (*BIO*) гибри́д; (*fig*) смесь *f* ♦ *adj* (*see n*) гибри́дный; сме́шанный.
hydrant ['haɪdrənt] *n* (*also: fire ~*) ≈ пожа́рный кран.
hydraulic [haɪ'drɔ:lɪk] *adj* гидравли́ческий*.
hydraulics [haɪ'drɔ:lɪks] *n* гидра́влика.
hydrochloric acid ['haɪdrəu'klɔrɪk-] *n* соля́ная кислота́.
hydroelectric ['haɪdrəuɪ'lɛktrɪk] *adj* гидро-электри́ческий.
hydrofoil ['haɪdrəfɔɪl] *n* су́дно на подво́дных кры́льях.
hydrogen ['haɪdrədʒən] *n* водоро́д.
hydrogen bomb *n* водоро́дная бо́мба.
hydrophobia ['haɪdrə'fəubɪə] *n* водобоя́знь *f*.
hydroplane ['haɪdrəpleɪn] *n* (*boat*) гли́ссер; (*plane*) гидросамолёт ♦ *vi* (*boat*) глисси́ровать (*impf*).
hyena [haɪ'i:nə] *n* гие́на.
hygiene ['haɪdʒi:n] *n* гигие́на.
hygienic [haɪ'dʒi:nɪk] *adj* (*product*) гигиени́ческий*; (*habits*) гигиени́чный* (гигиени́чен).
hymn [hɪm] *n* церко́вный гимн.
hype [haɪp] *n* (*inf*) ажиота́ж.
hyperactive ['haɪpər'æktɪv] *adj* (*MED*) гиперакти́вный.
hyper-inflation ['haɪpərɪn'fleɪʃən] *n* гипер-инфля́ция.
hypermarket ['haɪpəmɑ:kɪt] *n* (*BRIT*) кру́пный универса́м.
hypertension ['haɪpə'tɛnʃən] *n* гипертони́я.
hyphen ['haɪfn] *n* дефи́с.
hyphenated ['haɪfəneɪtɪd] *adj*: **this word is ~** э́то сло́во пи́шется че́рез дефи́с.
hypnosis [hɪp'nəusɪs] *n* гипно́з.
hypnotic [hɪp'nɔtɪk] *adj* (*trance etc*) гипноти́ческий.
hypnotism ['hɪpnətɪzəm] *n* гипноти́зм.
hypnotist ['hɪpnətɪst] *n* гипноти́зёр.
hypnotize ['hɪpnətaɪz] *vt* (*also fig*) гипнотизи́ровать (загипнотизи́ровать *perf*).
hypoallergenic ['haɪpəuælə'dʒɛnɪk] *adj* не вызыва́ющий* аллерги́ческой реа́кции.
hypochondriac [haɪpə'kɔndrɪæk] *n* ипохо́ндрик.
hypocrisy [hɪ'pɔkrɪsɪ] *n* лицеме́рие.
hypocrite ['hɪpəkrɪt] *n* лицеме́р(ка*).
hypocritical [hɪpə'krɪtɪkl] *adj* лицеме́рный*

(лицемéрен).

hypodermic [haɪpə'də:mɪk] *adj* подкóжный ♦ *n* (*also:* ~ **syringe**) шприц для подкóжных инъéкций.

hypotenuse [haɪ'pɔtɪnju:z] *n* гипотенýза.

hypothermia [haɪpə'θə:mɪə] *n* гипотермѝя.

hypotheses [haɪ'pɔθɪsi:z] *npl of* **hypothesis**.

hypothesis [haɪ'pɔθɪsɪs] (*pl* **hypotheses**) *n* гипóтеза.

hypothesize [haɪ'pɔθɪsaɪz] *vi* предполагáть (предположѝть* *perf*).

hypothetic(al) [haɪpəu'θεtɪk(l)] *adj* гипотетѝческий*.

hysterectomy [hɪstə'rεktəmɪ] *n* удалéние мáтки.

hysteria [hɪ'stɪərɪə] *n* истерѝя.

hysterical [hɪ'stεrɪkl] *adj* (*uncontrolled*) истерѝческий*; (*funny*) морѝтельный* (уморѝтелен); **to become** ~ впадáть (впасть* *perf*) в истéрику.

hysterically [hɪ'stεrɪklɪ] *adv* истерѝчески; ~ **funny** óчень смешнóй* (смешóн).

hysterics [hɪ'stεrɪks] *npl*: **to be in** *or* **have** ~ быть* (*impf*) в истéрике.

Hz *abbr* (= *hertz*) Гц= *герц*.

~ I, i ~

I, i [aɪ] *n* (*letter*) 9-ая бу́ква англи́йского алфави́та.
I [aɪ] *pron* я.
I *abbr* (= **island, isle**) о.= о́стров.
IA *abbr* (*US: POST*) = **Iowa**.
IAEA *n abbr* = **International Atomic Energy Agency**.
IBA *n abbr* (*BRIT*) = **Independent Broadcasting Authority**.
Iberian [aɪˈbɪərɪən] *adj*: **the ~ Peninsula** Пирене́йский полуо́стров.
IBEW *n abbr* (*US*) = **International Brotherhood of Electrical Workers**.
ib(id) *abbr* (*from the same source*: = *ibidem*) там же.
i/c *abbr* (*BRIT*) = **in charge**.
ICBM *n abbr* (= *intercontinental ballistic missile*) МБР= *межконтинента́льная баллисти́ческая раке́та.*
ICC *n abbr* = **International Chamber of Commerce**; (*US*: = *Interstate Commerce Commission*) Коми́ссия по торго́вле ме́жду шта́тами.
ice [aɪs] *n* лёд*; (*portion of ice cream*) моро́женое *nt adj* ♦ *vt* (*cake*) покрыва́ть (покры́ть* *perf*) глазу́рью; **to put sth on ~** (*fig*) заморо́зить* (*perf*) что-н
▶ **ice over** *vi* (*road, window etc*) обледене́ть (*perf*), покрыва́ться (покры́ться* *perf*) льдом
▶ **ice up** *vi* = **ice over**.
Ice Age *n* леднико́вый пери́од.
ice axe *n* ледору́б.
iceberg [ˈaɪsbəːg] *n* а́йсберг; **the tip of the ~** (*fig*) верху́шка а́йсберга.
icebox [ˈaɪsbɔks] *n* (*US: fridge*) холоди́льник; (*BRIT: compartment*) морози́льник; (*insulated box*) су́мка-холоди́льник *f*.
ice breaker *n* ледоко́л.
ice bucket *n* ведёрко* со льдом.
ice-cap [ˈaɪskæp] *n* леднико́вый покро́в.
ice-cold [aɪsˈkəuld] *adj* ледяно́й.
ice cream *n* моро́женое *nt adj*.
ice-cream soda [ˈaɪskriːm-] *n* со́довая вода́ с моро́женым.
ice cube *n* ку́бик льда.
iced [aɪst] *adj* (*cake*) покры́тый глазу́рью; ~

tea холо́дный чай со льдом; ~ **beer** холо́дное пи́во.
ice hockey *n* (*SPORT*) хокке́й (*на льду*).
Iceland [ˈaɪslənd] *n* Исла́ндия.
Icelander [ˈaɪsləndə*] *n* исла́ндец*(-дка*).
Icelandic [aɪsˈlændɪk] *adj* исла́ндский* ♦ *n* (*LING*) исла́ндский* язы́к*.
ice lolly *n* (*BRIT*) фрукто́вое моро́женое на па́лочке.
ice pick *n* топо́рик для льда.
ice rink *n* като́к*.
ice-skate [ˈaɪsskeɪt] *n* конёк* ♦ *vi* ката́ться (*impf*) на конька́х.
ice-skating [ˈaɪsskeɪtɪŋ] *n* (*SPORT*) ката́ние на конька́х.
icicle [ˈaɪsɪkl] *n* сосу́лька*.
icing [ˈaɪsɪŋ] *n* (*on cake*) глазу́рь *f*; (*on window etc*) обледене́ние.
icing sugar *n* (*BRIT*) са́харная пу́дра для приготовле́ния глазу́ри.
ICJ *n abbr* = **International Court of Justice**.
icon [ˈaɪkɔn] *n* (*REL*) ико́на.
ICR *n abbr* (*US*) = **Institute for Cancer Research**.
ICU *n abbr* (*MED*: = *intensive care unit*) отделе́ние интенси́вной терапи́и.
icy [ˈaɪsɪ] *adj* (*cold*) ледяно́й; (*covered in ice*) покры́тый (покры́т*) льдом.
ID *abbr* (*US: POST*) = **Idaho**.
I'd [aɪd] = **I would, I had**.
ID card *n* = **identity card**.
IDD *n abbr* (*BRIT: TEL*: = *international direct dialling*) пряма́я междунаро́дная связь *f*.
idea [aɪˈdɪə] *n* (*scheme, opinion*) иде́я; (*notion*) представле́ние; (*objective*) зада́ча; **good ~!** прекра́сная иде́я!; **to have an ~ that** подозрева́ть (*impf*) что; **I haven't the least ~** я не име́ю ни мале́йшего представле́ния.
ideal [aɪˈdɪəl] *n* идеа́л ♦ *adj* идеа́льный* (идеа́лен).
idealist [aɪˈdɪəlɪst] *n* идеали́ст(ка*).
ideally [aɪˈdɪəlɪ] *adv* идеа́льно; ~ **the work should be done by tomorrow** в идеа́ле, рабо́та должна́ бы́ть зако́нчена к за́втрашнему дню; **she's ~ suited for the job** она́ идеа́льно подхо́дит для э́той рабо́ты.
identical [aɪˈdɛntɪkl] *adj* одина́ковый

(одинáков), идентúчный* (идентúчен).

identification [aɪdɛntɪfɪ'keɪʃən] *n* определéние; (*process*) выявлéние; (*of person, dead body*) опознáние; **(means of)** ~ удостоверéние лúчности.

identify [aɪ'dɛntɪfaɪ] *vt* (*recognize*) определять (определúть *perf*); (: *person*) узнавáть* (узнáть* *perf*); (: *body*) опознавáть* (опознáть* *perf*); (*distinguish*) отличáть (отличúть *perf*); **he is identified with radical politics** он отличáется радикáльными политúческими взглядами.

Identikit® [aɪ'dɛntɪkɪt] *n*: ~ **(picture)** *портрéт-рóбот престýпника, состáвленный по опиcáнию свидéтелей.*

identity [aɪ'dɛntɪtɪ] *n* (*of person, suspect etc*) лúчность *f*; (*of group, culture, nation etc*) самосознáние.

identity card *n* удостоверéние лúчности.

identity papers *npl* докумéнты *mpl*, удостоверяющие лúчности.

identity parade *n* (BRIT) *процедýра опознáния подозревáемого в грýппе людéй.*

ideological [aɪdɪə'lɒdʒɪkl] *adj* идеологúческий*.

ideology [aɪdɪ'ɒlədʒɪ] *n* идеолóгия.

idiocy ['ɪdɪəsɪ] *n* идиотúзм.

idiom ['ɪdɪəm] *n* (*style*) стиль *m*; (*phrase*) идиóма.

idiomatic [ɪdɪə'mætɪk] *adj* идиоматúчный* (идиоматúчен).

idiosyncrasy [ɪdɪəu'sɪŋkrəsɪ] *n* (*foible*) особенность *f*, характéрная чертá.

idiosyncratic [ɪdɪəsɪŋ'krætɪk] *adj* индивидуáльный* (индивидуáлен), особенный.

idiot ['ɪdɪət] *n* идиóт(ка*).

idiotic [ɪdɪ'ɒtɪk] *adj* идиóтский*.

idle ['aɪdl] *adj* прáздный; (*lazy*) ленúвый (ленúв); (*unemployed*) безрабóтный; (*machinery, factory*) бездéйствующий ♦ *vi* (*machine*) простáивать (*impf*); (*engine*) рабóтать (*impf*) на холостóм ходý; **to be** ~ бездéйствовать (*impf*); **to lie** ~ быть* (*impf*) неиспóльзованным(-ой); **an** ~ **hour** час досýга

▸ **idle away** *vt*: **to** ~ **away the time** коротáть (*impf*) врéмя.

idle capacity *n* неиспóльзуемая произвóдственная мóщность *f*.

idle money *n* неинвестúрованные дéньги* *pl*.

idleness ['aɪdlnɪs] *n* (*inactivity*) бездéлье; (*laziness*) лень *f*.

idler ['aɪdlə'] *n* бездéльник(-ица), лентя́й(ка*).

idle time *n* (COMM) простóй.

idly ['aɪdlɪ] *adv* прáздно, ленúво.

idol ['aɪdl] *n* (*hero*) кумúр; (REL) úдол.

idolize ['aɪdəlaɪz] *vt* боготворúть (*impf*).

idyllic [ɪ'dɪlɪk] *adj* (*place, holiday*) идиллúческий*.

i.e. *abbr* (*that is:* = *id est*) т.е.= *то есть*.

KEYWORD

if [ɪf] *conj* **1** (*conditional use*) éсли; **if I finish early today, I will ring you** éсли я закóнчу рáно сегóдня, я тебé позвоню́; **if I were you (I would …)** на Вáшем мéсте (я бы …)
2 (*whenever*) когдá
3 (*although*): **(even) if** (дáже) éсли; **I'll get it done, even if it takes all night** я сдéлаю э́то, éсли дáже э́то займёт у меня́ всю ночь; **I like it, (even) if you don't** хоть Вам и не нрáвится э́то, а мне (всё равнó) нрáвится
4 (*whether*) ли; **I don't know if he is here** я не знáю, здесь ли он; **ask him if he can stay** спросúте, смóжет ли он остáться
5: **if so/not** éсли да/нет; **if only** éсли тóлько; **if only I could** éсли бы я тóлько мог; *see also* **as**.

iffy ['ɪfɪ] *adj* (*inf: scheme, suggestion*) подозрúтельный; **I'm feeling a bit** ~ **today** я сегóдня фигóво себя́ чýвствую.

igloo ['ɪɡluː] *n* úглу *nt ind* (*жилúще эскимóсов*).

ignite [ɪɡ'naɪt] *vt* (*set fire to*) зажигáть (зажéчь* *perf*) ♦ *vi* воспламеня́ться (воспламенúться *perf*), загорáться (загорéться *perf*).

ignition [ɪɡ'nɪʃən] *n* (AUT) зажигáние; **to switch on/off the** ~ включáть (включúть *perf*)/ выключáть (вы́ключить *perf*) зажигáние.

ignition key *n* (AUT) ключ* зажигáния.

ignoble [ɪɡ'nəubl] *adj* недостóйный* (недостóен).

ignominious [ɪɡnə'mɪnɪəs] *adj* позóрный* (позóрен).

ignoramus [ɪɡnə'reɪməs] *n* невéжда *m/f*.

ignorance ['ɪɡnərəns] *n* невéжество; ~ **of the facts** незнáние фáктов; **to keep sb in** ~ **of sth** держáть* (*impf*) когó-н в невéдении по пóводу чегó-н.

ignorant ['ɪɡnərənt] *adj* (*uninformed, unaware*) несвéдущий* (несвéдущ); (*badly educated*) невéжественный* (невéжествен); **to be** ~ **of** (*subject, events etc*) быть* (*impf*) неосведомлённым(-ой) относúтельно +*gen*.

ignore [ɪɡ'nɔː'] *vt* (*pay no attention to*) игнорúровать* (*impf/perf*); (*fail to take into account*) упускáть (упустúть* *perf*) из вúду.

ikon ['aɪkɒn] *n* = **icon**.

IL *abbr* (US: POST) = **Illinois**.

ILA *n abbr* (US) = **International Longshore Association**.

I'll [aɪl] = **I will, I shall**.

ill [ɪl] *adj* (*child etc*) больнóй*; (*harmful: effects*) дурнóй ♦ *n* (*evil*) зло; (*trouble*) бедá ♦ *adv*: **to speak/think** ~ **(of sb)** плóхо говорúть (*impf*)/ дýмать (*impf*) (о ком-н); **he is** ~ он бóлен; **to be taken** ~ заболевáть (заболéть *perf*).

ill-advised [ɪləd'vaɪzd] *adj* опромéтчивый (опромéтчив).

ill-at-ease [ɪlət'iːz] *adj* (*awkward, uncomfortable*) нелóвкий*.

ill-considered [ɪlkən'sɪdəd] *adj* необдýманный* (необдýман).

ill-disposed [ɪldɪsˈpəuzd] adj: **to be ~ towards sb/sth** недоброжела́тельно относи́ться˙ (*impf*) к кому́-н/чему́-н.

illegal [ɪˈliːgl] adj нелега́льный˙ (нелега́лен), незако́нный˙ (незако́нен).

illegally [ɪˈliːgəlɪ] adv нелега́льно, незако́нно.

illegible [ɪˈlɛdʒɪbl] adj неразбо́рчивый (неразбо́рчив).

illegitimate [ɪlɪˈdʒɪtɪmət] adj (*child*) внебра́чный; (*activity, treaty*) незако́нный˙ (незако́нен).

ill-fated [ɪlˈfeɪtɪd] adj (*doomed*) злополу́чный˙ (злополу́чен).

ill-favoured [ɪlˈfeɪvəd] (*US* **ill-favored**) adj некраси́вый (некраси́в).

ill feeling n неприя́знь f.

ill-gotten [ˈɪlgɔtn] adj: **~ gains** добы́тый нече́стным путём дохо́д.

ill-health [ɪlˈhɛlθ] n плохо́е здоро́вье.

illicit [ɪˈlɪsɪt] adj незако́нный˙ (незако́нен).

ill-informed [ɪlɪnˈfɔːmd] adj неосведомлённый˙ (неосведомлён).

illiterate [ɪˈlɪtərət] adj негра́мотный˙ (негра́мотен).

ill-mannered [ɪlˈmænəd] adj невоспи́танный˙ (невоспи́тан), неве́жливый (неве́жлив).

illness [ˈɪlnɪs] n боле́знь f.

illogical [ɪˈlɔdʒɪkl] adj нелоги́чный˙ (нелоги́чен).

ill-suited [ɪlˈsuːtɪd] adj: **they are ~** они́ не подхо́дят друг к дру́гу; **he is ~ to the job** он не годи́тся для э́той рабо́ты.

ill-timed [ɪlˈtaɪmd] adj несвоевре́менный˙ (несвоевре́мен); **her comments were ~** её замеча́ния бы́ли не к ме́сту.

ill-treat [ɪlˈtriːt] vt пло́хо обраща́ться (*impf*) с +*instr*.

ill-treatment [ɪlˈtriːtmənt] n жесто́кость f.

illuminate [ɪˈluːmɪneɪt] vt (*light up*) освеща́ть (освети́ть˙ *perf*).

illuminated sign [ɪˈluːmɪneɪtɪd-] n освещённая вы́веска˙.

illuminating [ɪˈluːmɪneɪtɪŋ] adj (*report, book etc*) разъясня́ющий; (*person*) просвещённый˙ (просвещён), познава́тельный˙ (познава́телен).

illumination [ɪluːmɪˈneɪʃən] n (*lighting*) освеще́ние; **~s** npl (*decorative lights*) иллюмина́ция fsg.

illusion [ɪˈluːʒən] n (*false idea*) иллю́зия; (*trick*) фо́кус; **to be under the ~ that** ... находи́ться (*impf*) под впечатле́нием, что ....

illusive [ɪˈluːsɪv] adj = **illusory**.

illusory [ɪˈluːsərɪ] adj иллюзо́рный˙ (иллюзо́рен), обма́нчивый (обма́нчив).

illustrate [ˈɪləstreɪt] vt иллюстри́ровать (проиллюстри́ровать *perf*).

illustration [ɪləˈstreɪʃən] n (*example, picture*) иллюстра́ция; (*act*) иллюстри́рование.

illustrator [ˈɪləstreɪtə˹] n иллюстра́тор.

illustrious [ɪˈlʌstrɪəs] adj (*career*) блестя́щий˙ (блестя́щ); (*predecessor, partner*) просла́вленный˙ (просла́влен).

ill will n неприя́знь f.

ILO n abbr = **International Labour Organization**.

ILWU n abbr (*US*) = **International Longshoremen's and Warehousemen's Union**.

I'm [aɪm] = **I am**.

image [ˈɪmɪdʒ] n (*picture*) о́браз; (*public face*) и́мидж; (*reflection*) отраже́ние.

imagery [ˈɪmɪdʒərɪ] n (*ART, LITERATURE*) о́бразность f, о́бразный мир.

imaginable [ɪˈmædʒɪnəbl] adj вообрази́мый; **we've tried every ~ solution** мы перепро́бовали все вообрази́мые реше́ния; **she had the prettiest hair ~** у неё бы́ли невообрази́мо краси́вые во́лосы.

imaginary [ɪˈmædʒɪnərɪ] adj (*creature, land*) вообража́емый; (*danger, illness*) мни́мый.

imagination [ɪmædʒɪˈneɪʃən] n воображе́ние; (*illusion*) фанта́зия; **it's just your ~** э́то про́сто плод Ва́шего воображе́ния.

imaginative [ɪˈmædʒɪnətɪv] adj (*person*) облада́ющий бога́тым *or* тво́рческим воображе́нием; (*solution*) хитроу́мный˙ (хитроу́мен).

imagine [ɪˈmædʒɪn] vt (*visualize*) представля́ть (предста́вить˙ *perf*) (себе́), воображать (вообрази́ть˙ *perf*); (*dream*) вообража́ть (вообрази́ть˙ *perf*); (*suppose*) полага́ть (*impf*).

imbalance [ɪmˈbæləns] n несоотве́тствие, неравнове́сие.

imbecile [ˈɪmbəsiːl] n ненорма́льный(-ая) m(f) adj.

imbue [ɪmˈbjuː] vt: **to ~ sb with sth** вдохновля́ть (вдохнови́ть˙ *perf*) кого́-н чем-л; **to ~ sth with sth** наполня́ть (напо́лнить *perf*) что-н чем-н.

IMF n abbr (= *International Monetary Fund*) МВФ= *Междунаро́дный валю́тный фонд*.

imitate [ˈɪmɪteɪt] vt (*copy*) копи́ровать (скопи́ровать *perf*); (*mimic*) подража́ть (*impf*) +*dat*, имити́ровать (*impf*).

imitation [ɪmɪˈteɪʃən] n (*see vb*) копи́рование; подража́ние; (*instance*) имита́ция.

imitator [ˈɪmɪteɪtə˹] n подража́тель(ница) m(f).

immaculate [ɪˈmækjulət] adj безупре́чный˙ (безупре́чен); (*REL*) непоро́чный.

immaterial [ɪməˈtɪərɪəl] adj (*unimportant*) несуще́ственный˙ (несуще́ственен).

immature [ɪməˈtjuə˹] adj (*fruit*) неспе́лый (неспе́л); (*cheese*) незре́лый; (*organism*) недоразви́вшийся; (*person*) незре́лый (незре́л).

immaturity [ɪməˈtjuərɪtɪ] n незре́лость f.

immeasurable [ɪˈmɛʒrəbl] adj неизмери́мый

˙ marks translations which have irregular inflections. The Russian-English side of the dictionary gives inflectional information.

(неизмери́м).

immediacy [ɪ'mi:dɪəsɪ] n (of events etc) непосре́дственность f; (of needs) безотлага́тельность f.

immediate [ɪ'mi:dɪət] adj (reaction, answer) неме́дленный, мгнове́нный; (pressing: need) безотлага́тельный* (безотлага́телен); (nearest: neighbourhood, family etc) ближа́йший*.

immediately [ɪ'mi:dɪətlɪ] adv (at once) неме́дленно; (directly) непосре́дственно; ~ next to непосре́дственно ря́дом с +instr.

immense [ɪ'mɛns] adj (huge: size) необъя́тный* (необъя́тен); (: progress, importance) огро́мный* (огро́мен).

immensely [ɪ'mɛnslɪ] adv (grateful etc) бесконе́чно; (difficult) необыча́йно; I enjoyed it ~ мне э́то о́чень понра́вилось.

immensity [ɪ'mɛnsɪtɪ] n необъя́тность f.

immerse [ɪ'mɜːs] vt (submerge) погружа́ть (погрузи́ть* perf); to ~ sth in погружа́ть (погрузи́ть* perf) что-н в +acc; to be ~d in (fig) быть* (impf) погружённым(-ой) в +acc.

immersion heater [ɪ'mɜː'ʃən-] n (BRIT) бо́йлер.

immigrant ['ɪmɪgrənt] n иммигра́нт(ка*).

immigration [ɪmɪ'greɪʃən] n (process) иммигра́ция; (also: ~ control: at airport etc) пограни́чный контро́ль m ♦ cpd: ~ laws зако́ны mpl об иммигра́ции; ~ authorities пограни́чная слу́жба.

imminent ['ɪmɪnənt] adj (arrival, departure) немину́емый (немину́ем).

immobile [ɪ'məubaɪl] adj неподви́жный* (неподви́жен).

immobilize [ɪ'məubɪlaɪz] vt (person, machine) остана́вливать (останови́ть* perf), свя́зывать (связа́ть perf).

immoderate [ɪ'mɔdərət] adj неуме́ренный* (неуме́рен).

immodest [ɪ'mɔdɪst] adj нескро́мный* (нескро́мен).

immoral [ɪ'mɔrl] adj амора́льный* (амора́лен), безнра́вственный* (безнра́вственен).

immorality [ɪmə'rælɪtɪ] n амора́льность f, безнра́вственность f.

immortal [ɪ'mɔːtl] adj (also fig) бессме́ртный* (бессме́ртен).

immortality [ɪmɔː'tælɪtɪ] n бессме́ртие.

immortalize [ɪ'mɔːtlaɪz] vt увекове́чивать (увекове́чить perf).

immovable [ɪ'muːvəbl] adj (object) неподви́жный* (неподви́жен); (opinion) неизме́нный* (неизме́нен).

immune [ɪ'mjuːn] adj: ~ (to) (disease) облада́ющий иммуните́том (к +dat); he is ~ to ... (flattery, criticism etc) он неподве́ржен влия́нию +gen ....

immune system n имму́нная систе́ма.

immunity [ɪ'mjuːnɪtɪ] n (to disease) иммуните́т; (to criticism) невос-

прии́мчивость f; (of diplomat, from prosecution) неприкоснове́нность f.

immunization [ɪmjunaɪ'zeɪʃən] n иммуниза́ция, приви́вка*.

immunize ['ɪmjunaɪz] vt (MED): to ~ (against) привива́ть (приви́ть* perf) (про́тив +gen).

imp [ɪmp] n бесёнок*.

impact ['ɪmpækt] n (of bullet) моме́нт попада́ния; (of crash) уда́р; (of law, measure) возде́йствие.

impair [ɪm'pɛə'] vt (vision, judgement) ослабля́ть (осла́бить* perf).

impaired [ɪm'pɛəd] adj осла́бленный (осла́блен).

impale [ɪm'peɪl] vt нака́лывать (наколо́ть* perf); to ~ sth on наса́живать (насади́ть* perf) что-н на +acc.

impart [ɪm'pɑːt] vt: to ~ (to) (information) передава́ть* (переда́ть* perf) (+dat); (flavour) придава́ть* (прида́ть* perf) (+dat).

impartial [ɪm'pɑːʃl] adj беспристра́стный* (беспристра́стен).

impartiality [ɪmpɑːʃɪ'ælɪtɪ] n беспристра́стие.

impassable [ɪm'pɑːsəbl] adj непроходи́мый* (непроходи́м).

impasse [æm'pɑːs] n тупи́к*; to reach an ~ зайти́* (perf) в тупи́к.

impassive [ɪm'pæsɪv] adj бесстра́стный* (бесстра́стен).

impatience [ɪm'peɪʃəns] n нетерпели́вость f.

impatient [ɪm'peɪʃənt] adj нетерпели́вый (нетерпели́в); to get or grow ~ начина́ть (нача́ть* perf) теря́ть терпе́ние; she was ~ to leave ей не терпе́лось уйти́.

impatiently [ɪm'peɪʃəntlɪ] adv нетерпели́во.

impeach [ɪm'piːtʃ] vt привлека́ть (привле́чь* perf) к отве́тственности.

impeachment [ɪm'piːtʃmənt] n привлече́ние к отве́тственности.

impeccable [ɪm'pɛkəbl] adj безупре́чный* (безупре́чен).

impecunious [ɪmpɪ'kjuːnɪəs] adj (formal) нужда́ющийся.

impede [ɪm'piːd] vt затрудня́ть (затрудни́ть* perf).

impediment [ɪm'pɛdɪmənt] n (obstacle) препя́тствие; speech ~ дефе́кт ре́чи.

impel [ɪm'pɛl] vt: to ~ sb to do вынужда́ть (вы́нудить* perf) кого́-н +infin.

impending [ɪm'pɛndɪŋ] adj надвига́ющийся.

impenetrable [ɪm'pɛnɪtrəbl] adj (jungle, fortress) непроходи́мый (непроходи́м); (look, expression) непроница́емый (непроница́ем); (darkness, fog) непрогля́дный* (непрогля́ден); (fig: law, text) недосту́пный* (недосту́пен) (для понима́ния).

imperative [ɪm'pɛrətɪv] adj (tone) вла́стный* (вла́стен); (need etc) настоя́тельный* (настоя́телен) ♦ n (LING) повели́тельное наклоне́ние; it is ~ that ... необходи́мо, чтобы ....

imperceptible [ɪmpə'sɛptɪbl] *adj* незаметный*
(назаметен).

imperfect [ɪm'pəːfɪkt] *adj* (*system etc*)
несовершённый* (несовершёнен); (*goods*)
дефёктный ♦ *n* (*LING: also:* ~ **tense**)
имперфёкт.

imperfection [ɪmpə:'fɛkʃən] *n* (*failing*)
недостаток*; (*blemish*) изъян.

imperial [ɪm'pɪərɪəl] *adj* (*history, power*)
импёрский*; (*BRIT: measure*): ~ **system**
британская система меры и веса.

imperialism [ɪm'pɪərɪəlɪzəm] *n* империализм.

imperil [ɪm'pɛrɪl] *vt* подвергать (подвёргнуть*
perf) опасности.

imperious [ɪm'pɪərɪəs] *adj* (*person*) властный*
(властен).

impersonal [ɪm'pəːsənl] *adj* (*organization,
place*) безликий*.

impersonate [ɪm'pəːsəneɪt] *vt* (*pass o.s. off as*)
выдавать* (выдать *perf*) себя за +*acc*; (*THEAT*)
изображать (изобразить* *perf*).

impersonation [ɪmpəːsə'neɪʃən] *n*
изображёние; (*LAW*) самозванство; (*THEAT*)
исполнёние роли.

impertinent [ɪm'pəːtɪnənt] *adj* (*pupil, question*)
дёрзкий* (дёрзок), нахальный* (нахален).

imperturbable [ɪmpə'təːbəbl] *adj* невоз-
мутимый (невозмутим).

impervious [ɪm'pəːvɪəs] *adj* (*fig*): **he is** ~ **to** ... на
него не дёйствует ....

impetuous [ɪm'pɛtjuəs] *adj* порывистый
(порывист).

impetus ['ɪmpətəs] *n* (*momentum*) инёрция;
(*fig*) стимул.

impinge [ɪm'pɪndʒ]: **to** ~ **on** *vt fus* (*person*)
посягать (посягнуть *perf*) на +*acc*; (*rights*)
попирать (попрать* *perf*).

impish ['ɪmpɪʃ] *adj* озорной.

implacable [ɪm'plækəbl] *adj* непримиримый
(непримирим).

implant [ɪm'plɑːnt] *vt* (*MED*) пересаживать
(пересадить* *perf*); (*fig: idea, principle*)
внушать (внушить *perf*).

implausible [ɪm'plɔːzɪbl] *adj* неправдоподобный* (неправдоподобен).

implement [*vt* 'ɪmplɪmɛnt, *n* 'ɪmplɪmənt] *vt* (*plan,
regulation*) проводить* (провести* *perf*) в
жизнь ♦ *n*: **gardening** ~ садовый
инструмёнт; **farming** ~**s** сельско-
хозяйственные орудия; **cooking** ~**s**
кухонные принадлёжности.

implicate ['ɪmplɪkeɪt] *vt* (*in crime, error*)
вовлекать (вовлёчь* *perf*).

implication [ɪmplɪ'keɪʃən] *n* (*inference*) вывод;
(*involvement*) причастность *f*; **by** ~ судя по
всему.

implicit [ɪm'plɪsɪt] *adj* (*inferred*) подраз-

умевающийся; (*unquestioning*)
безоговорочный.

implicitly [ɪm'plɪsɪtlɪ] *adv* (*totally*)
безоговорочно.

implore [ɪm'plɔː'] *vt* (*beg*) умолять (*impf*); **to** ~
sb to do умолять (*impf*) кого-н +*infin*.

imply [ɪm'plaɪ] *vt* (*hint*) намекать (намекнуть
perf) на +*acc*; (*mean*) подразумевать (*impf*).

impolite [ɪmpə'laɪt] *adj* (*rude, offensive*)
невёжливый (невёжлив).

imponderable [ɪm'pɔndərəbl] *adj* неуловимый
(неуловим) ♦ *n* вещь, не поддающаяся
определёнию.

import [*vb* ɪm'pɔːt, *n, cpd* 'ɪmpɔːt] *vt*
импортировать (*impf/perf*), ввозить* (ввезти*
perf) ♦ *n* (*article*) импортируемый товар;
(*importation*) импорт ♦ *cpd*: ~ **duty** пошлина
на ввоз; ~ **licence** лицёнзия на ввоз; ~ **quota**
импортная квота.

importance [ɪm'pɔːtns] *n* важность *f*; **it is of
great/little** ~ это очень/не очень важно.

important [ɪm'pɔːtnt] *adj* важный* (важен);
(*influential: person*) важный*; **it's not** ~ это
неважно.

importantly [ɪm'pɔːtntlɪ] *adv* важно; **but more**
~ ... но ещё важнёе ..., но самое главное ....

importation [ɪmpɔː'teɪʃən] *n* импорт.

imported [ɪm'pɔːtɪd] *adj* импортный.

importer [ɪm'pɔːtə'] *n* импортёр.

impose [ɪm'pəuz] *vt* (*sanctions, restrictions,
discipline etc*) налагать (наложить* *perf*) ♦ *vi*:
to ~ **on sb** навязываться (навязаться* *perf*)
кому-н.

imposing [ɪm'pəuzɪŋ] *adj* внушительный*
(внушителен), величественный*
(величествен).

imposition [ɪmpə'zɪʃən] *n* (*of tax etc*)
обложёние; **to be an** ~ **on sb** быть* (*impf*)
обузой кому-н.

impossibility [ɪmpɔsə'bɪlɪtɪ] *n* невозможность
f.

impossible [ɪm'pɔsɪbl] *adj* (*task, demand,
person*) невозможный* (невозможен);
(*situation*) невероятный* (невероятен); **it's** ~
for me to leave now я не могу сейчас уйти.

impossibly [ɪm'pɔsɪblɪ] *adj* невозможно.

imposter [ɪm'pɔstə'] *n* = impostor.

impostor [ɪm'pɔstə'] *n* самозванец*(-нка*).

impotence ['ɪmpətns] *n* бессилие; (*MED*)
импотёнция.

impotent ['ɪmpətnt] *adj* бессильный*
(бессилен); (*MED*) импотёнтный*
(импотёнтен).

impound [ɪm'paund] *vt* конфисковывать
(конфисковать* *perf*).

impoverished [ɪm'pɔvərɪʃt] *adj* (*country*)
обеднёвший*.

impracticable [ɪm'præktɪkəbl] *adj*

---

* marks translations which have irregular inflections. The Russian-English side of the dictionary gives inflectional information.

неосуществимый (неосуществим).
impractical [ɪmˈpræktɪkl] *adj* (*plan etc*)
нереальный* (нереален); (*person*)
непрактичный* (непрактичен).
imprecise [ɪmprɪˈsaɪs] *adj* неточный*
(неточен).
impregnable [ɪmˈprɛgnəbl] *adj* (*castle, fortress*)
неприступный* (неприступен); (*fig: person*)
неуязвимый (неуязвим).
impregnate [ˈɪmprɛgneɪt] *vt* (*saturate*)
пропитывать (пропитать *perf*); (*fertilize*)
оплодотворять (оплодотворить *perf*).
impresario [ɪmprɪˈsɑːrɪəʊ] *n* импресарио *m ind*.
impress [ɪmˈprɛs] *vt* (*person*) производить*
(произвести* *perf*) впечатление на +*acc*;
(*mark*) отпечатывать (отпечатать *perf*); **to ~
sth on sb** внушать (внушить *perf*) что-н
кому-н.
impression [ɪmˈprɛʃən] *n* впечатление; (*of
stamp, seal*) отпечаток; (*imitation*)
имитация; **to make a good/bad ~ on sb**
производить* (произвести* *perf*) хорошее/
плохое впечатление на кого-н; **he is under
the ~ that** ... у него создалось впечатление,
что ....
impressionable [ɪmˈprɛʃnəbl] *adj*
впечатлительный* (впечатлителен).
impressionist [ɪmˈprɛʃənɪst] *n* (*ART*)
импрессионист; (*entertainer*) имитатор.
impressive [ɪmˈprɛsɪv] *adj* впечатляющий.
imprest system [ˈɪmprɛst-] *n* система
денежного аванса.
imprint [ˈɪmprɪnt] *n* отпечаток*; (*PUBLISHING*)
выходные данные *pl adj*; (: *label*) печать на
переплёте с именем владельца или
издателя.
imprinted [ɪmˈprɪntɪd] *adj*: **~ on** (*surface*)
отпечатавшийся в/на +*prp*; (*memory*)
запечатлённый (запечатлён) в +*prp*.
imprison [ɪmˈprɪzn] *vt* (*criminal*) заключать
(заключить *perf*) в тюрьму.
imprisonment [ɪmˈprɪznmənt] *n* (тюремное)
заключение.
improbable [ɪmˈprɔbəbl] *adj* (*outcome*)
маловероятный* (маловероятен); (*story*)
неправдоподобный* (неправдоподобен).
impromptu [ɪmˈprɔmptjuː] *adj* (*celebration,
party*) импровизированный
(импровизирован); (*tactics*) неплановый.
improper [ɪmˈprɔpəʳ] *adj* (*unsuitable: conduct*)
неуместный* (неуместен); (: *procedure*)
неправильный* (неправилен); (*dishonest:
activities*) незаконный* (незаконен).
impropriety [ɪmprəˈpraɪətɪ] *n* (*indecency*)
неприличие; **the ~ of his conduct**
непристойность *f* его поведения.
improve [ɪmˈpruːv] *vt* улучшать (улучшить
perf) ♦ *vi* улучшаться (улучшиться *perf*);
(*pupil*) становиться* (стать* *perf*) лучше;
(*patient*) начинать (начать *perf*)
выздоравливать

▶ **improve (up)on** *vt fus* (*work, achievement etc*)
делать (сделать *perf*) лучше.
improvement [ɪmˈpruːvmənt] *n*: **~ (in)**
улучшение (+*gen*); **to make ~s to** вносить*
(внести* *perf*) улучшения в +*acc*.
improvisation [ɪmprəvaɪˈzeɪʃən] *n* (*THEAT*)
импровизация.
improvise [ˈɪmprəvaɪz] *vt* (*meal*) наскоро
готовить* (приготовить* *perf*); (*bed, shelter*)
наскоро устраивать (устроить *perf*) ♦ *vi*
(*THEAT, MUS*) импровизировать
(сымпровизировать *perf*).
imprudence [ɪmˈpruːdns] *n* неблагоразумное
поведение.
imprudent [ɪmˈpruːdnt] *adj* неблагоразумный*
(неблагоразумен); **it would be ~ of you to
insult him** оскорбить его будет
неблагоразумием с Вашей стороны.
impudent [ˈɪmpjudnt] *adj* наглый* (нагл).
impugn [ɪmˈpjuːn] *vt* подвергать
(подвергнуть* *perf*) сомнению.
impulse [ˈɪmpʌls] *n* (*urge*) порыв; (*ELEC*)
импульс; **to act on ~** поддаваться*
(поддаться* *perf*) порыву.
impulse buy *n* случайная покупка*.
impulsive [ɪmˈpʌlsɪv] *adj* (*purchase*) случайный* (случаен); (*person*) импульсивный*
(импульсивен); (*gesture*) порывистый
(порывист).
impunity [ɪmˈpjuːnɪtɪ] *n*: **with ~** безнаказанно.
impure [ɪmˈpjuəʳ] *adj* нечистый (нечист);
(*sinful*) непристойный* (непристоен).
impurity [ɪmˈpjuərɪtɪ] *n* (*foreign substance*)
примесь *f*.
IN *abbr* (*US: POST*) = Indiana.

KEYWORD

in [ɪn] *prep* **1** (*indicating place, position*) в/на
+*prp*; **in the house/garden** в доме/саду; **in the
street/Ukraine/north** на улице/Украине/
севере; **in London/Canada** в Лондоне/
Канаде; **in the country** загородом; **in town** в
городе; **in here** здесь; **in there** там
2 (*indicating motion*) в +*acc*; **in the house/
room** в дом/комнату
3 (*indicating time: during*) в +*prp*; **in spring/
summer/autumn/winter** весной/летом/
осенью/зимой; **in the morning/afternoon/
evening** утром/днём/вечером; **they often
play cards in the evening** они часто играют в
карты по вечерам; **at 4 o'clock in the
afternoon** в 4 часа дня
4 (*indicating time: in the space of*) за +*acc*; (:
after a period of) через +*acc*; **I did it in 3 hours** я
сделал это за 3 часа; **I'll see you in 2 weeks**
увидимся через 2 недели
5 (*indicating manner etc*): **in a loud/quiet voice**
громким/тихим голосом; **in English/Russian**
по-английски/по-русски, на английском/
русском языке; **the boy in the blue shirt**
мальчик в голубой рубашке
6 (*indicating circumstances*): **in the sun** на

со́лнце; **in the rain** под дождём; **in the shade** в тени́; **there has been a change in public opinion** обще́ственное мне́ние перемени́лось; **a rise in prices** повыше́ние цен

7 (*indicating mood, state*) в +*prp*

8 (*with ratios, numbers*): **one in ten households have a second car** одна́ из десяти́ семе́й име́ет втору́ю маши́ну; **20 pence in the pound** 20 пе́нсов с фу́нта; **they lined up in twos** они́ вы́строились по́ дво́е; **a gradient of one in five** укло́н оди́н к пяти́

9 (*referring to people, works*): **the disease is common in children** э́то заболева́ние ча́сто встреча́ется у дете́й; **in Dickens** у Ди́ккенса; **you have a good friend in him** он тебе́ хоро́ший друг

10 (*indicating profession etc*): **to be in teaching** рабо́тать (*impf*) учи́телем; **to be in publishing** занима́ться (*impf*) изда́тельским де́лом; **to be in the army** быть* (*impf*) в а́рмии

11 (*after superlative*) в +*prp*; **the best doctor in the city** лу́чший* врач в го́роде

12 (*with present participle*): **in saying this** говоря́ э́то; **in behaving like this, she ...** поступа́я таки́м о́бразом, она́ ...

♦ *adv*: **to be in** (*train, ship, plane*) прибы́ть* (*perf*); (*in fashion*) быть* (*impf*) в мо́де; **is he in today? – yes, he's in/no, he's not in** (*at work*) он сего́дня на рабо́те? – да, он на рабо́те/нет, его́ сего́дня нет; (*at home*) он сего́дня до́ма? – да, он до́ма/нет, его́ сего́дня нет; **he wasn't in yesterday** его́ вчера́ не́ было; **he'll be in later today** он бу́дет сего́дня по́зже; **to ask sb in** предложи́ть* (*perf*) кому́-н зайти́; **to run/walk** *etc* **in** вбега́ть (вбежа́ть* *perf*)/входи́ть* (войти́* *perf*) *etc*

♦ *n*: **to know all the ins and outs** знать (*impf*) все ходы́.

in. *abbr* = **inch.**

inability [ɪnə'bɪlɪtɪ] *n* (*incapacity*): ~ **(to do)** неспосо́бность *f* (+*infin*).

inaccessible [ɪnək'sɛsɪbl] *adj* (*also fig*) недосту́пный* (недосту́пен).

inaccuracy [ɪn'ækjurəsɪ] *n* (*quality*) нето́чность *f*; (*mistake*) оши́бка*.

inaccurate [ɪn'ækjurət] *adj* нето́чный* (нето́чен).

inaction [ɪn'ækʃən] *n* безде́йствие.

inactive [ɪn'æktɪv] *adj* (*person*) бездея́тельный* (безде́ятелен), пасси́вный* (пасси́вен); (*animal*) пасси́вный* (пасси́вен); (*volcano*) поту́хший.

inactivity [ɪnæk'tɪvɪtɪ] *n* (*idleness*) безде́ятельность *f*.

inadequacy [ɪn'ædɪkwəsɪ] *n* недоста́точность *f*; (*of person*) неполноце́нность *f*.

inadequate [ɪn'ædɪkwət] *adj* (*income, amount, preparation*) недоста́точный* (недоста́точен); (*reply*) неадеква́тный* (неадеква́тен); (*work, result*) неудовлетвори́тельный* (неудовлетвори́телен); (*person*) неполноце́нный (неполноце́н).

inadmissible [ɪnəd'mɪsəbl] *adj* недопусти́мый (недопусти́м); (*LAW: evidence*) неприе́млемый (неприе́млем).

inadvertently [ɪnəd'və:tntlɪ] *adv* неумы́шленно.

inadvisable [ɪnəd'vaɪzəbl] *adj* (*course of action*) нецелесообра́зный* (нецелесообра́зен); **it is ~ to ...** не рекоменду́ется +*infin* ....

inane [ɪ'neɪn] *adj* (*smile*) глу́пый* (глуп); (*remark etc*) бессмы́сленный* (бессмы́слен).

inanimate [ɪn'ænɪmət] *adj* (*object*) неодушевлённый* (неодушевлён).

inapplicable [ɪn'æplɪkəbl] *adj* (*description, comment*) неподходя́щий*; (*rule*) неприменѝмый (неприменѝм).

inappropriate [ɪnə'prəʊprɪət] *adj* (*unsuitable*) неподходя́щий*; (*improper*) неуме́стный* (неуме́стен).

inapt [ɪn'æpt] *adj* неуме́стный* (неуме́стен).

inarticulate [ɪnɑ:'tɪkjulət] *adj* (*person*) косноязы́чный* (косноязы́чен); (*speech*) невня́тный* (невня́тен).

inasmuch as [ɪnəz'mʌtʃ-] *adv* (*in that*) посто́льку поско́льку; (*insofar as*) насто́лько наско́лько.

inattention [ɪnə'tɛnʃən] *n* невнима́ние.

inattentive [ɪnə'tɛntɪv] *adj* невнима́тельный* (невнима́телен).

inaudible [ɪn'ɔ:dɪbl] *adj* неслы́шный* (неслы́шен).

inaugural [ɪ'nɔ:gjurəl] *adj* (*speech*) вступи́тельный; (*meeting*) пе́рвый.

inaugurate [ɪ'nɔ:gjureɪt] *vt* (*president, official*) вводи́ть* (ввести́* *perf*) в до́лжность; (*system, measure*) вводи́ть* (ввести́* *perf*); (*organization*) открыва́ть (откры́ть* *perf*).

inauguration [ɪnɔ:gju'reɪʃən] *n* (*see vb*) вступле́ние в до́лжность; введе́ние; откры́тие.

inauspicious [ɪnɔ:s'pɪʃəs] *adj* (*occasion*) неблагоприя́тный* (неблагоприя́тен).

in-between [ɪnbɪ'twi:n] *adj* (*intermediate*) промежу́точный; ~ **stage** промежу́точная ста́дия.

inborn [ɪn'bɔ:n] *adj* врождённый, приро́дный.

inbred [ɪn'brɛd] *adj* (*quality*) врождённый, приро́дный; **an ~ family** семья́, в кото́рой *де́ти рождены́ от роди́телей, состоя́щих в кро́вном родстве́*.

inbreeding [ɪn'bri:dɪŋ] *n* (*among animals*) ро́дственное спа́ривание; (*among people*) узкоро́дственные бра́чные отноше́ния *ntpl*.

---

* marks translations which have irregular inflections. The Russian-English side of the dictionary gives inflectional information.

inbuilt [ɪn'bɪlt] *adj* (*quality, feeling etc*)
врождённый.

Inc. *abbr* = **incorporated**.

Inca ['ɪŋkə] *adj*: **the ~** *or* **~n civilization** инки *fpl*.

incalculable [ɪn'kælkjuləbl] *adj* (*effect*)
огро́мный* (огро́мен); (*loss*) неисчисли́мый
(неисчисли́м); (*consequences*) непред-
ви́денный.

incapable [ɪn'keɪpəbl] *adj* (*helpless*) бес-
по́мощный* (беспо́мощен); (*unable to*): **~ of
sth/doing** неспосо́бный* (неспосо́бен) на
что-н/+*infin*.

incapacitate [ɪnkə'pæsɪteɪt] *vt*: **to ~ sb**
выводи́ть* (вы́вести* *perf*) кого́-н из стро́я;
to ~ sb for work де́лать (сде́лать *perf*) кого́-н
нетрудоспосо́бным(-ой).

incapacitated [ɪnkə'pæsɪteɪtɪd] *adj* (*LAW*)
лишённый (лишён) пра́ва.

incapacity [ɪnkə'pæsɪtɪ] *n* (*weakness*)
беспо́мощность *f*; (*inability*) неспосо́бность
f.

incarcerate [ɪn'kɑːsəreɪt] *vt* заключа́ть
(заключи́ть *perf*) в тюрьму́.

incarnate [ɪn'kɑːnɪt] *adj* воплощённый
(воплощён), олицетворённый
(олицетворён); **evil ~** воплоще́ние *or*
олицетворе́ние зла.

incarnation [ɪnkɑː'neɪʃən] *n* воплоще́ние,
олицетворе́ние; (*REL*) инкарна́ция.

incendiary [ɪn'sɛndɪərɪ] *adj* (*device, bomb*)
зажига́тельный.

incense [*n* 'ɪnsɛns, *vt* ɪn'sɛns] *n* (*also REL*) ла́дан
♦ *vt* (*anger*) приводи́ть* (привести́* *perf*) в
я́рость.

incense burner *n* кури́льница.

incentive [ɪn'sɛntɪv] *n* (*inducement*) сти́мул ♦
cpd: **~ scheme** систе́ма поощре́ния; **~ bonus**
материа́льное поощре́ние.

inception [ɪn'sɛpʃən] *n* (*of institution*)
откры́тие, основа́ние; (*of activity*) нача́ло.

incessant [ɪn'sɛsnt] *adj* бесконе́чный*
(бесконе́чен), постоя́нный* (постоя́нен).

incessantly [ɪn'sɛsntlɪ] *adv* бесконе́чно,
постоя́нно.

incest ['ɪnsɛst] *n* кровосмеше́ние.

inch [ɪntʃ] *n* (*measurement*) дюйм; **he was
within an ~ of succeeding** он был уже́ бли́зок
к успе́ху; **to be within an ~ of one's life** быть*
(*impf*) на́ волосо́к от сме́рти; **he didn't give an
~** (*fig: back down, yield*) он не уступи́л ни на
йо́ту

▸ **inch forward** *vi* ме́дленно тро́гаться
(тро́нуться *perf*) с ме́ста.

incidence ['ɪnsɪdns] *n* (*of crime, disease*)
чи́сленность *f*.

incident ['ɪnsɪdnt] *n* (*event*) слу́чай; (*MIL*)
инциде́нт; **without ~** без происше́ствий.

incidental [ɪnsɪ'dɛntl] *adj* (*additional,
supplementary*) дополни́тельный; **these
duties are ~ to the job** э́ти обя́занности
сопряжены́ с рабо́той; **ills ~ to old age**

недýги, прису́щие ста́рости; **~ expenses**
побо́чные расхо́ды.

incidentally [ɪnsɪ'dɛntəlɪ] *adv* (*by the way*)
кста́ти, ме́жду про́чим.

incidental music *n* (*CINEMA*) му́зыка к
кинофи́льму.

incident room *n* диспе́тчерская *f adj* (*в
полице́йском управле́нии*).

incinerate [ɪn'sɪnəreɪt] *vt* (*rubbish, paper etc*)
сжига́ть (сжечь* *perf*).

incinerator [ɪn'sɪnəreɪtə'] *n* мусоросжига́тель
m.

incipient [ɪn'sɪpɪənt] *adj* (*baldness*)
начина́ющийся*; (*madness*) в нача́льной
ста́дии.

incision [ɪn'sɪʒən] *n* (*also MED*) разре́з.

incisive [ɪn'saɪsɪv] *adj* (*comment*) о́стрый*
(остёр), ре́зкий* (ре́зок); (*criticism*) ре́зкий*
(ре́зок).

incisor [ɪn'saɪzə'] *n* резе́ц*.

incite [ɪn'saɪt] *vt* (*rioters*) подстрека́ть
(подстрекну́ть *perf*); (*violence, hatred*)
вызыва́ть (вы́звать* *perf*).

incl. *abbr* = **including**, **inclusive (of)**.

inclement [ɪn'klɛmənt] *adj* (*weather*)
нена́стный* (нена́стен).

inclination [ɪnklɪ'neɪʃən] *n* (*tendency*)
скло́нность *f*; (*disposition, desire*) жела́ние.

incline [*n* 'ɪnklaɪn, *vb* ɪn'klaɪn] *n* (*slope*) укло́н,
накло́н ♦ *vt* (*bend: head*) наклоня́ть
(наклони́ть* *perf*) ♦ *vi* (*surface*) наклоня́ться
(наклони́ться* *perf*); **to be ~d to sth/to do**
быть* (*impf*) скло́нным(-ой) к чему́-н/+*infin*;
to be well ~d towards sb быть* (*impf*)
благоскло́нным(-ой) к кому́-н.

include [ɪn'kluːd] *vt* включа́ть (включи́ть *perf*);
to be ~d (in) быть* (*impf*) включённым(-ой) (в
+*acc*); **to ~ sth in the price** включа́ть
(включи́ть *perf*) в це́ну.

including [ɪn'kluːdɪŋ] *prep* включа́я +*acc*; **~
service charge** включа́я пла́ту за
обслу́живание.

inclusion [ɪn'kluːʒən] *n* включе́ние.

inclusive [ɪn'kluːsɪv] *adj* (*price, terms*)
включа́ющий в себя́ все услу́ги; **~ of**
включа́я +*acc*; **from March 1st to 5th ~** с 1-ого
до 5-ое ма́рта включи́тельно.

incognito [ɪnkɔg'niːtəu] *adv* инко́гнито.

incoherent [ɪnkəu'hɪərənt] *adj* (*argument*)
непосле́довательный* (непосле́дователен);
(*speech*) несвя́зный* (несвя́зен); (*person*)
косноязы́чный* (косноязы́чен).

income ['ɪnkʌm] *n* (*earned*) за́работок*; (*from
property, investment*) дохо́д; **gross/net ~**
валово́й/чи́стый дохо́д; **~ and expenditure
account** прихо́дно-расхо́дный счёт*; **high/
low ~ bracket** гру́ппа населе́ния с высо́ким/
ни́зким дохо́дом.

income support *n* де́нежное посо́бие.

income tax *n* подохо́дный нало́г ♦ *cpd* (*COMM*)
нало́говый.

incoming ['ɪnkʌmɪŋ] *adj* (*flight, passenger*) прибыва́ющий; (*call*) поступа́ющий; (*mail*) входя́щий; (*government*) новои́збранный; (*official*) вступа́ющий в до́лжность; ~ **tide** прили́в.

incommunicado ['ɪnkəmjunɪ'kɑːdəu] *adj*: **to hold sb** ~ держа́ть* (*impf*) кого́-н взаперти́.

incomparable [ɪn'kɔmpərəbl] *adj* несравне́нный*.

incompatible [ɪnkəm'pætɪbl] *adj* (*lifestyles*) соверше́нно ра́зный; (*systems, aims*) несовмести́мый (несовмести́м); **they are** ~ они́ соверше́нно ра́зные.

incompetence [ɪn'kɔmpɪtns] *n* некомпете́нтность *f*.

incompetent [ɪn'kɔmpɪtnt] *adj* (*person*) некомпете́нтный* (некомпете́нтен); (*work*) неуме́лый (неуме́л).

incomplete [ɪnkəm'pliːt] *adj* (*unfinished*) незако́нченный* (незако́нчен); (*partial*) непо́лный (непо́лон).

incomprehensible [ɪnkɔmprɪ'hɛnsɪbl] *adj* непоня́тный* (непоня́тен).

inconceivable [ɪnkən'siːvəbl] *adj* немы́слимый (немы́слим); **it is** ~ **that** ... немы́слимо, что ....

inconclusive [ɪnkən'kluːsɪv] *adj* (*evidence*) недоста́точный* (недоста́точен); (*result*) неоконча́тельный* (неоконча́телен); (*argument*) неубеди́тельный* (неубеди́телен); **the experiment was** ~ экспериме́нт не дал определённых результа́тов; **the discussion was** ~ диску́ссия зако́нчилась ниче́м.

incongruous [ɪn'kɔŋgruəs] *adj* (*strange*) неле́пый (неле́п); (*inappropriate*) неуме́стный* (неуме́стен).

inconsequential [ɪnkɔnsɪ'kwɛnʃl] *adj* несуще́ственный* (несуще́ственен), незначи́тельный* (незначи́телен).

inconsiderable [ɪnkən'sɪdərəbl] *adj*: **not** ~ значи́тельный* (значи́телен).

inconsiderate [ɪnkən'sɪdərət] *adj* (*person*) не счита́ющийся ни с ке́м; (*action*) безду́мный* (безду́мен); ~ **towards** невнима́тельный к +*dat*.

inconsistency [ɪnkən'sɪstənsɪ] *n* (*of behaviour*) непосле́довательность *f*; (*of statement*) противоречи́вость *f*.

inconsistent [ɪnkən'sɪstnt] *adj* (*behaviour, person*) непосле́довательный* (непосле́дователен); (*work*) неро́вный* (неро́вен); (*statement*) противоречи́вый (противоречи́в); ~ **with** (*beliefs, values*) несовмести́мый (несовмести́м) с +*instr*.

inconsolable [ɪnkən'səuləbl] *adj* безуте́шный* (безуте́шен).

inconspicuous [ɪnkən'spɪkjuəs] *adj* незаме́т-ный* (незаме́тен), непримéтный* (непримéтен); **to make o.s.** ~ стара́ться (постара́ться *perf*) не привлека́ть к себе́ внима́ния.

incontinence [ɪn'kɔntɪnəns] *n* (*MED*) недержа́ние (*мочи́ или ка́ла*).

incontinent [ɪn'kɔntɪnənt] *adj* (*MED*) страда́ющий недержа́нием (*мочи́ или ка́ла*).

inconvenience [ɪnkən'viːnjəns] *n* (*problem*) неудо́бство; (*trouble*) беспоко́йство ♦ *vt* причиня́ть (причини́ть *perf*) неудо́бство +*dat*; **don't** ~ **yourself** не утружда́йте себя́; **sorry about the** ~ извини́те за причинённое неудо́бство.

inconvenient [ɪnkən'viːnjənt] *adj* неудо́бный* (неудо́бен); (*visitor*) прише́дший не ко вре́мени; **that time is very** ~ **for me** э́то о́чень неудо́бное для меня́ вре́мя.

incorporate [ɪn'kɔːpəreɪt] *vt* (*contain*) содержа́ть* (*impf*); **to** ~ (**into**) включа́ть (включи́ть *perf*) (в +*acc*); **safety features have been** ~**d in the design** предохрани́тельные устро́йства бы́ли внесены́ в прое́кт; **the coat of arms** ~**s three lions** на гербе́ изображены́ три льва́.

incorporated company [ɪn'kɔːpəreɪtɪd-] *n* (*US*) компа́ния, зарегистри́рованная как корпора́ция.

incorrect [ɪnkə'rɛkt] *adj* неве́рный* (неве́рен), непра́вильный* (непра́вилен).

incorrigible [ɪn'kɔrɪdʒɪbl] *adj* (*liar, crook*) неисправи́мый (неисправи́м).

incorruptible [ɪnkə'rʌptɪbl] *adj* (*not open to bribes*) неподку́пный* (неподку́пен).

increase [*n* 'ɪnkriːs, *vb* ɪn'kriːs] *n*: ~ (**in**), ~ (**of**) увеличе́ние (+*gen*) ♦ *vi* увели́чиваться (увели́читься *perf*) ♦ *vt* увели́чивать (увели́чить *perf*); (*price*) поднима́ть (подня́ть* *perf*); (*knowledge*) расширя́ть (расши́рить *perf*); **an** ~ **of 5%** увеличе́ние на 5%; **to be on the** ~ увели́чиваться (*impf*), расти́* (*impf*).

increasing [ɪn'kriːsɪŋ] *adj* увели́чивающийся, возраста́ющий.

increasingly [ɪn'kriːsɪŋlɪ] *adv* (*more intensely*) всё бо́лее; (*more often*) всё ча́ще.

incredible [ɪn'krɛdɪbl] *adj* (*unbelievable*) неправдоподо́бный* (неправдоподо́бен), невероя́тный* (невероя́тен); (*enormous*) невероя́тный* (невероя́тен); (*amazing, wonderful*) потряса́ющий* (потряса́ющ); **it was an** ~ **experience** э́то бы́ло потряса́юще.

incredulity [ɪnkrɪ'djuːlɪtɪ] *n* недове́рие.

incredulous [ɪn'krɛdjuləs] *adj* недове́рчивый (недове́рчив).

increment ['ɪnkrɪmənt] *n* (*in salary*) приба́вка*.

incriminate [ɪn'krɪmɪneɪt] *vt* изоблича́ть (изобличи́ть *perf*).

---

* marks translations which have irregular inflections. The Russian-English side of the dictionary gives inflectional information.

incriminating [ɪnˈkrɪmɪneɪtɪŋ] *adj* изоблич-а́ющий.

incrusted [ɪnˈkrʌstɪd] *adj* = **encrusted**.

incubate [ˈɪnkjubeɪt] *vt* (*egg*) высиживать (вы́сидеть° *perf*) ◆ *vi* (*chickens*) вылупля́ться (вы́лупиться *perf*); (*disease*) развива́ться (разви́ться° *perf*).

incubation [ɪnkjuˈbeɪʃən] *n* (*by bird*) выведе́ние цыпля́т; (*of illness*) инкубацио́нный пери́од.

incubation period *n* инкубацио́нный пери́од.

incubator [ˈɪnkjubeɪtə°] *n* (*for babies*) инкуба́тор.

inculcate [ˈɪnkʌlkeɪt] *vt*: **to ~ sth in sb** внуша́ть (внуши́ть *perf*) что-н кому́-н.

incumbent [ɪnˈkʌmbənt] *n* (*official*) отве́тственное лицо́° ◆ *adj*: **it is ~ on him to ...** он обя́зан +*infin* ....

incur [ɪnˈkɜː°] *vt* (*expenses, loss*) нести́° (понести́° *perf*); (*debt*) наде́лать (*perf*) +*gen*; (*disapproval, anger*) навлека́ть (навле́чь° *perf*) на себя́.

incurable [ɪnˈkjuərəbl] *adj* (*disease*) неизлечи́мый (неизлечи́м).

incursion [ɪnˈkɜːʃən] *n* (*MIL*) вторже́ние.

indebted [ɪnˈdetɪd] *adj*: **to be ~ to sb** (*grateful*) быть° (*impf*) обя́занным(-ой) кому́-н.

indecency [ɪnˈdiːsnsɪ] *n* непристо́йность *f*.

indecent [ɪnˈdiːsnt] *adj* непристо́йный° (непристо́ен); (*haste*) неприли́чный° (неприли́чен).

indecent assault *n* (*BRIT*) (сексуа́льное) оскорбле́ние де́йствием.

indecent exposure *n* обнаже́ние половы́х о́рганов.

indecipherable [ɪndɪˈsaɪfərəbl] *adj* (*writing*) неразбо́рчивый (неразбо́рчив); (*expression, glance etc*) зага́дочный° (зага́дочен).

indecision [ɪndɪˈsɪʒn] *n* нереши́тельность *f*.

indecisive [ɪndɪˈsaɪsɪv] *adj* нереши́тельный° (нереши́телен).

indeed [ɪnˈdiːd] *adv* (*certainly*) коне́чно, безусло́вно; (*in fact, furthermore*) на са́мом де́ле; (*rather*) скоре́е да́же; **I'm upset, ~ shocked** я расстро́ен, пожа́луй да́же шоки́рован; **this book is very interesting ~** э́та кни́га чрезвыча́йно интере́сная; **thank you very much ~** большо́е Вам спаси́бо; **he is ~ very talented** он и впра́вду *or* на са́мом де́ле о́чень тала́нтлив; **yes ~!** ну коне́чно!

indefatigable [ɪndɪˈfætɪgəbl] *adj* (*person*) неутоми́мый (неутоми́м); (*rhythm, pulse etc*) неослабева́ющий.

indefensible [ɪndɪˈfensɪbl] *adj* (*conduct*) непрости́тельный° (непрости́телен).

indefinable [ɪndɪˈfaɪnəbl] *adj* (*quality*) не поддаю́щийся определе́нию.

indefinite [ɪnˈdefɪnɪt] *adj* (*answer, view*) неопределённый° (неопределён); (*period, number*) неограни́ченный° (неограни́чен).

indefinite article *n* (*LING*) неопределённый арти́кль *m*.

indefinitely [ɪnˈdefɪnɪtlɪ] *adv* (*continue, wait*) бесконе́чно; (*be closed, postponed*) на неопределённое вре́мя.

indelible [ɪnˈdelɪbl] *adj* (*mark, stain: on clothes*) неотсти́рывающийся; (: *on hands, furniture*) несмыва́емый; (*fig: memory, impact*) неизглади́мый.

indelicate [ɪnˈdelɪkɪt] *adj* нетакти́чный° (нетакти́чен).

indemnify [ɪnˈdemnɪfaɪ] *vt* (*COMM*) гарант-и́ровать (*impf*) возмеще́ние убы́тков +*dat*.

indemnity [ɪnˈdemnɪtɪ] *n* (*insurance*) гара́нтия возмеще́ния убы́тков; (*compensation*) возмеще́ние.

indent [ɪnˈdent] *vt* (*line of text*) писа́ть° (написа́ть° *perf*) с кра́сной строки́.

indentation [ɪndenˈteɪʃən] *n* углубле́ние; (*TYP*) абза́ц; (*on metal*) зазу́брина.

indenture [ɪnˈdentʃə°] *n* догово́р° (*ме́жду подмастерьем и́ли ученико́м и хозя́ином*).

independence [ɪndɪˈpendns] *n* незави́симость *f*.

independent [ɪndɪˈpendnt] *adj* незави́симый (незави́сим).

independently [ɪndɪˈpendntlɪ] *adv* незави́симо; **~ of** незави́симо от +*gen*.

in-depth [ˈɪndepθ] *adj* дета́льный, глубо́кий°.

indescribable [ɪndɪsˈkraɪbəbl] *adj* неописуемый (неопису́ем).

indestructible [ɪndɪsˈtrʌktəbl] *adj* (*object*) неразруши́мый (неразруши́м); (*friendship, alliance*) неруши́мый (неруши́м); (*army*) непобеди́мый (непобеди́м).

indeterminate [ɪndɪˈtɜːmɪnɪt] *adj* неопред-елённый° (неопределён).

index [ˈɪndeks] (*pl* **~es**) *n* (*in book*) (слова́рь°-)указа́тель *m*; (*in library etc*) катало́г; (*pl* **indices**; *MATH*) показа́тель° *msg*.

index card *n* (карто́течная) ка́рточка°.

indexed [ˈɪndekst] *adj* (*US*) = **index-linked**.

index finger *n* указа́тельный па́лец°.

index-linked [ˈɪndeksˈlɪŋkt] *adj* (*income, payment*) изменя́ющийся в соотве́тствии с и́ндексом инфля́ции.

India [ˈɪndɪə] *n* Индия.

Indian [ˈɪndɪən] *adj* инди́йский° ◆ *n* инди́ец° (индиа́нка°); **Red ~** инде́ец° (индиа́нка°).

Indian Ocean *n*: **the ~ ~** Инди́йский° океа́н.

Indian Summer *n* инде́йское *or* ба́бье ле́то.

India paper *n* кита́йская бума́га.

India rubber *n* рези́на, каучу́к.

indicate [ˈɪndɪkeɪt] *vt* (*point to: also fig*) ука́зывать (указа́ть° *perf*) на +*acc*; (*mention*) дава́ть° (дать° *perf*) знать о +*prp* ◆ *vi*: **to ~ that** (*show*) пока́зывать (показа́ть° *perf*), что; (*BRIT: AUT*): **to ~ left/right** включа́ть (включи́ть *perf*) ле́вый/пра́вый указа́тель поворо́та.

indication [ɪndɪˈkeɪʃən] *n* знак; **all the ~s are that ...** всё ука́зывает на то, что ....

indicative [ɪnˈdɪkətɪv] *n* (*LING*) изъяви́тельное

наклоне́ние ♦ *adj*: **to be ~ of** свиде́тельствовать *(impf)* о +*prp*, ука́зывать *(impf)* на +*acc*.

indicator ['ɪndɪkeɪtəʳ] *n* (*marker, signal*) указа́тель *m*; (*AUT*) указа́тель поворо́та; (*fig*) показа́тель *m*.

indices ['ɪndɪsiːz] *npl of* **index**.

indict [ɪn'daɪt] *vt* (*LAW*) предъявля́ть (предъяви́ть* *perf*) обвине́ние +*dat*.

indictable [ɪn'daɪtəbl] *adj* подлежа́щий уголо́вному рассмотре́нию; **~ offence** уголо́вное преступле́ние.

indictment [ɪn'daɪtmənt] *n* (*denunciation*) осужде́ние; (*charge*) обвини́тельный акт.

indie ['ɪndɪ] *adj* (*music, chart etc*) *вы́пущенный ма́ленькой незави́симой сту́дией звукоза́писи.*

indifference [ɪn'dɪfrəns] *n* (*lack of interest*) безразли́чие, равноду́шие.

indifferent [ɪn'dɪfrənt] *adj* безразли́чный* (безразли́чен), равноду́шный* (равноду́шен); (*mediocre*) посре́дственный* (посре́дствен).

indigenous [ɪn'dɪdʒɪnəs] *adj* (*wildlife, population*) коренно́й; (*culture*) ме́стный.

indigestible [ɪndɪ'dʒɛstɪbl] *adj* тру́дно перева́риваемый (перева́риваем).

indigestion [ɪndɪ'dʒɛstʃən] *n* расстро́йство желу́дка.

indignant [ɪn'dɪgnənt] *adj* возмущённый* (возмущён); **to be ~ at sth/with sb** быть* *(impf)* возмущённым(-ой) чем-н/кем-н.

indignation [ɪndɪg'neɪʃən] *n* возмуще́ние, негодова́ние.

indignity [ɪn'dɪgnɪtɪ] *n* униже́ние.

indigo ['ɪndɪgəʊ] *n* (*colour*) инди́го *nt ind*.

indirect [ɪndɪ'rɛkt] *adj* (*way, route*) око́льный, обхо́дный; (*answer*) укло́нчивый (укло́нчив); (*effect*) побо́чный; (*LING*): **~ object** ко́свенное дополне́ние.

indirectly [ɪndɪ'rɛktlɪ] *adv* ко́свенно.

indiscreet [ɪndɪs'kriːt] *adj* неосмотри́тельный* (неосмотри́телен), неблагоразу́мный* (неблагоразу́мен).

indiscretion [ɪndɪs'krɛʃən] *n* неосмотри́тель-ность *f*; (*indiscreet act*) неблагоразу́мный посту́пок*.

indiscriminate [ɪndɪs'krɪmɪnət] *adj* (*bombing*) беспоря́дочный* (беспоря́дочен); (*taste, reader, love*) неразбо́рчивый (неразбо́рчив); (*criticism*) огу́льный.

indispensable [ɪndɪs'pɛnsəbl] *adj* (*object*) необходи́мый (необходи́м); (*person*) незамени́мый (незамени́м).

indisposed [ɪndɪs'pəʊzd] *adj* (*unwell*) нездоро́вый (нездоро́в).

indisputable [ɪndɪs'pjuːtəbl] *adj* (*undeniable*) неоспори́мый (неоспори́м).

indistinct [ɪndɪs'tɪŋkt] *adj* (*image, noise*) нея́сный* (нея́сен); (*memory*) сму́тный* (сму́тен).

indistinguishable [ɪndɪs'tɪŋgwɪʃəbl] *adj*: **~ from** неотличи́мый (неотличи́м) от +*gen*.

individual [ɪndɪ'vɪdjuəl] *n* (*person*) ли́чность *f*, индиви́дуум ♦ *adj* (*personal*) индивид-уа́льный* (индивидуа́лен), ли́чный; (*single*) отде́льный; (*particular: characteristic*) своеобра́зный* (своеобра́зен), индивидуа́льный* (индивидуа́лен); **certain ~s** не́которые лю́ди.

individualist [ɪndɪ'vɪdjuəlɪst] *n* индивид-уали́ст(ка*).

individuality [ɪndɪvɪdju'ælɪtɪ] *n* индивид-уа́льность *f*.

individually [ɪndɪ'vɪdjuəlɪ] *adv* отде́льно; **he is ~ responsible** он несёт ли́чную отве́тственность; **we'll help each of you ~** мы помо́жем ка́ждому из Вас.

indivisible [ɪndɪ'vɪzɪbl] *adj* недели́мый (недели́м).

Indo-China ['ɪndəʊ'tʃaɪnə] *n* Индокита́й.

indoctrinate [ɪn'dɔktrɪneɪt] *vt* подверга́ть (подве́ргнуть* *perf*) идеологи́ческой обрабо́тке.

indoctrination [ɪndɔktrɪ'neɪʃən] *n* идеолог-и́ческая обрабо́тка.

indolence ['ɪndələns] *n* ле́ность *f*.

indolent ['ɪndələnt] *adj* лени́вый (лени́в).

Indonesia [ɪndə'niːzɪə] *n* Индоне́зия.

Indonesian [ɪndə'niːzɪən] *adj* индонези́йский* ♦ *n* индонези́ец*(-и́йка*).

indoor ['ɪndɔː'] *adj* (*plant, games for children*) ко́мнатный; (*swimming pool*) закры́тый; **~ games** спорти́вные и́гры в закры́том помеще́нии.

indoors [ɪn'dɔːz] *adv* (*go*) в помеще́ние; (*be*) в помеще́нии; **he stayed ~ all morning** он проси́дел до́ма всё у́тро.

indubitable [ɪn'djuːbɪtəbl] *adj* несомне́нный* (несомне́нен).

indubitably [ɪn'djuːbɪtəblɪ] *adv* несомне́нно.

induce [ɪn'djuːs] *vt* (*bring about*) вызыва́ть (вы́звать* *perf*); (*persuade*) побужда́ть (побуди́ть* *perf*); (*MED: birth*) стимули́ровать *(impf/perf)*; **to ~ sb to do** побужда́ть (побуди́ть* *perf*) кого́-н +*infin*.

inducement [ɪn'djuːsmənt] *n* (*incentive*) сти́мул; (*pej: bribe*) по́дкуп.

induct [ɪn'dʌkt] *vt* назнача́ть (назна́чить *perf*) на до́лжность; (*fig*) посвяща́ть (посвяти́ть* *perf*) в(о) +*acc*.

induction [ɪn'dʌkʃən] *n* (*MED: of birth*) стимуля́ция.

induction course *n* (*BRIT*) вво́дный курс.

indulge [ɪn'dʌldʒ] *vt* (*desire, whim etc*) потво́рствовать *(impf)* +*dat*, потака́ть *(impf)*

+*dat*; (*person, child*) баловáть (избаловáть *perf*) ♦ *vi*: **to ~ in** баловáться (побаловáться *perf*) +*instr*.

indulgence [ɪn'dʌldʒəns] *n* (*pleasure*) прихоть *f*; (*leniency*) потвóрство.

indulgent [ɪn'dʌldʒənt] *adj* (*smile*) снисходительный* (снисходителен); **he has very ~ parents** егó родители (во всём) емý потакáют.

industrial [ɪn'dʌstrɪəl] *adj* индустриáльный, промышленный; **~ accident** несчáстный слýчай на произвóдстве.

industrial action *n* забастóвка.

industrial design *n* промышленный дизáйн.

industrial estate *n* (*BRIT*) промышленный кóмплекс.

industrialist [ɪn'dʌstrɪəlɪst] *n* промышленник.

industrialize [ɪn'dʌstrɪəlaɪz] *vt* (*country*) индустриализировать (*impf/perf*).

industrial park *n* (*US*) = **industrial estate**.

industrial relations *npl* произвóдственные отношéния *ntpl*.

industrial tribunal *n* (*BRIT*) суд, занимáющийся рассмотрéнием произвóдственных конфликтов.

industrial unrest *n* (*BRIT*) рабóчие волнéния *ntpl*.

industrious [ɪn'dʌstrɪəs] *adj* трудолюбивый (трудолюбив).

industry ['ɪndəstrɪ] *n* (*manufacturing*) индустрия, промышленность *f no pl*; (*diligence*) трудолюбие; **industries** óтрасли *pl* промышленности; **the oil/textile ~** нефтянáя/текстильная промышленность.

inebriated [ɪ'niːbrɪeɪtɪd] *adj* нетрéзвый (нетрéзв).

inedible [ɪn'ɛdɪbl] *adj* несъедóбный* (несъедóбен).

ineffective [ɪnɪ'fɛktɪv] *adj* неэффективный* (неэффективен).

ineffectual [ɪnɪ'fɛktʃuəl] *adj* = **ineffective**.

inefficiency [ɪnɪ'fɪʃənsɪ] *n* неэффективность *f*; непроизводительность *f*.

inefficient [ɪnɪ'fɪʃənt] *adj* неэффективный* (неэффективен); (*machine*) непроизводительный* (непроизводителен).

inelegant [ɪn'ɛlɪɡənt] *adj* неэлегáнтный* (неэлегáнтен).

ineligible [ɪn'ɛlɪdʒɪbl] *adj* (*candidate*) неподходящий*; **to be ~ for sth** не имéть (*impf*) прáво на что-н.

inept [ɪ'nɛpt] *adj* (*management etc*) неумéлый (неумéл).

ineptitude [ɪ'nɛptɪtjuːd] *n* неумéние, неумéлость *f*.

inequality [ɪnɪ'kwɔlɪtɪ] *n* (*of system*) нерáвенство; (*of amount, share*) рáзница.

inequitable [ɪn'ɛkwɪtəbl] *adj* несправедливый (несправедлив).

inert [ɪ'nɜːt] *adj* (*immobile*) неподвижный* (неподвижен); (*gas*) инéртный.

inertia [ɪ'nɜːʃə] *n* (*laziness*) инéртность *f*; (*PHYS*) инéрция.

inertia-reel seat belt [ɪ'nɜːʃə'riːl-] *n* инерциóнный ремéнь* *m* безопáсности.

inescapable [ɪnɪ'skeɪpəbl] *adj* неизбéжный* (неизбéжен).

inessential [ɪnɪ'sɛnʃl] *adj* несущéственный* (несущéственен).

inessentials [ɪnɪ'sɛnʃlz] *npl* рóскошь *fsg*.

inestimable [ɪn'ɛstɪməbl] *adj* (*value*) неоценимый (неоцéним); (*cost*) неподдающийся* оцéнке.

inevitability [ɪnɛvɪtə'bɪlɪtɪ] *n* неизбéжность *f*; **the ~ of change** неизбéжность изменéний; **it is an ~** это неизбéжность.

inevitable [ɪn'ɛvɪtəbl] *adj* неизбéжный* (неизбéжен).

inevitably [ɪn'ɛvɪtəblɪ] *adv* неизбéжно; **as ~ happens, ...** как это неизбéжно случáется, ...

inexact [ɪnɪɡ'zækt] *adj* нетóчный* (нетóчен).

inexcusable [ɪnɪks'kjuːzəbl] *adj* непростительный* (непростителен).

inexhaustible [ɪnɪɡ'zɔːstɪbl] *adj* (*wealth, resources*) неисчерпáемый (неисчерпáем).

inexorable [ɪn'ɛksərəbl] *adj* (*progress*) неотвратимый (неотвратим); (*decline*) неумолимый (неумолим).

inexpensive [ɪnɪk'spɛnsɪv] *adj* недорогóй* (недóрог).

inexperience [ɪnɪk'spɪərɪəns] *n* неóпытность *f*.

inexperienced [ɪnɪk'spɪərɪənst] *adj* неóпытный* (неóпытен); **to be ~ in sth** не имéть (*impf*) óпыта в чём-н.

inexplicable [ɪnɪk'splɪkəbl] *adj* необъяснимый (необъясним).

inexpressible [ɪnɪk'sprɛsɪbl] *adj* невыразимый (невырази́м).

inextricable [ɪnɪk'strɪkəbl] *adj* (*union, knot, tangle*) неразрывный* (неразрывен); (*dilemma*) безвыходный* (безвыходен).

inextricably [ɪnɪk'strɪkəblɪ] *adv* неразрывно.

infallibility [ɪnfælə'bɪlɪtɪ] *n* непогрешимость *f*.

infallible [ɪn'fælɪbl] *adj* (*person*) непогрешимый (непогрешим); (*guide*) надёжный* (надёжен).

infamous ['ɪnfəməs] *adj* бесчéстный* (бесчéстен).

infamy ['ɪnfəmɪ] *n* бесчéстие.

infancy ['ɪnfənsɪ] *n* (*of person*) младéнчество; (*of movement, firm*) пери́од становлéния.

infant ['ɪnfənt] *n* (*baby*) младéнец*; (*young child*) ребёнок* ♦ *cpd* дéтский*.

infantile ['ɪnfəntaɪl] *adj* (*disease*) дéтский*; (*childish*) инфантильный* (инфантилен).

infantry ['ɪnfəntrɪ] *n* пехóта.

infantryman ['ɪnfəntrɪmən] *irreg* *n* пехотинец*.

infant school *n* (*BRIT*) ≈ начáльная шкóла (*для детéй от 5-и до 7-и лет*).

infatuated [ɪn'fætjueɪtɪd] *adj*: **~ with** увлечённый (увлечён) +*instr*; **to become ~ with** увлекáться (увлéчься* *perf*) +*instr*.

infatuation [ɪnfætjuˈeɪʃən] *n* увлече́ние*.
infect [ɪnˈfɛkt] *vt (also fig)* заража́ть (зарази́ть* *perf*); **to become ~ed** (*wound*) заража́ться (зарази́ться* *perf*).
infection [ɪnˈfɛkʃən] *n* инфе́кция.
infectious [ɪnˈfɛkʃəs] *adj (person, animal)* зара́зный (зара́зен); (*disease*) инфекцио́нный; (*fig*) зарази́тельный*
infer [ɪnˈfəː] *vt (deduce)* заключа́ть (заключи́ть *perf*); (*imply*) подразумева́ть (*impf*).
inference [ˈɪnfərəns] *n (deduction)* заключе́ние; (*implication*) вы́вод.
inferior [ɪnˈfɪərɪə] *adj (position, status)* подчинённый; (*goods*) ни́зкого ка́чества ♦ *n* (*subordinate*) подчинённый(-ая) *m(f) adj*; (*junior*) мла́дший по чи́ну; **to feel ~ (to)** ощуща́ть (ощути́ть* *perf*) свою́ неполноце́нность (по сравне́нию с +*instr*); **he is ~ to me in rank** он ни́же меня́ по до́лжности; **the second model is ~ to the first** втора́я моде́ль уступа́ет пе́рвой по ка́честву.
inferiority [ɪnfɪərɪˈɔrətɪ] *n (of position, status)* подчинённое положе́ние; (*of goods*) низкосо́ртность *f*.
inferiority complex *n* ко́мплекс неполноце́нности.
infernal [ɪnˈfəːnl] *adj* а́дский*.
inferno [ɪnˈfəːnəu] *n (also fig)* ад.
infertile [ɪnˈfəːtaɪl] *adj (soil)* неплодоро́дный* (неплодоро́ден); (*person, animal*) бесплóдный (беспло́ден).
infertility [ɪnfəːˈtɪlɪtɪ] *n (see adj)* неплодоро́дность *f*; беспло́дие.
infested [ɪnˈfɛstɪd] *adj*: **the house is ~ with rats** дом киши́т кры́сами.
infidelity [ɪnfɪˈdɛlɪtɪ] *n* неве́рность *f*.
infighting [ˈɪnfaɪtɪŋ] *n* вну́тренний* конфли́кт.
infiltrate [ˈɪnfɪltreɪt] *vt* проника́ть (прони́кнуть* *perf*) в +*acc*.
infinite [ˈɪnfɪnɪt] *adj* бесконе́чный* (бесконе́чен); (*resources*) несме́тный* (несме́тен).
infinitely [ˈɪnfɪnɪtlɪ] *adv* бесконе́чно.
infinitesimal [ɪnfɪnɪˈtɛsɪməl] *adj* бесконе́чно ма́лый* (мал).
infinitive [ɪnˈfɪnɪtɪv] *n* инфинити́в, неопределённая фо́рма глаго́ла.
infinity [ɪnˈfɪnɪtɪ] *n* бесконе́чность *f*.
infirm [ɪnˈfəːm] *adj* не́мощный* (не́мощен).
infirmary [ɪnˈfəːmərɪ] *n* больни́ца.
infirmity [ɪnˈfəːmɪtɪ] *n* не́мощь *f*.
inflame [ɪnˈfleɪm] *vt (person, crowd)* распаля́ть (распали́ть* *perf*); (*situation, emotions*) накаля́ть (накали́ть* *perf*).
inflamed [ɪnˈfleɪmd] *adj (throat, appendix)* воспалённый (воспалён).
inflammable [ɪnˈflæməbl] *adj (fabric)* легко́

воспламеня́ющийся; (*chemical*) горю́чий* (горю́ч).
inflammation [ɪnfləˈmeɪʃən] *n* воспале́ние.
inflammatory [ɪnˈflæmətərɪ] *adj (speech)* подстрека́тельский.
inflatable [ɪnˈfleɪtəbl] *adj* надувно́й.
inflate [ɪnˈfleɪt] *vt (tyre)* нака́чивать (накача́ть *perf*); (*balloon*) надува́ть (наду́ть *perf*); (*price*) вздува́ть (вздуть *perf*); (*expectation, position, ideas*) раздува́ть (разду́ть *perf*).
inflated [ɪnˈfleɪtɪd] *adj (style)* напы́щенный* (напы́щен); (*prices*) вздутый (вздут).
inflation [ɪnˈfleɪʃən] *n (ECON)* инфля́ция.
inflationary [ɪnˈfleɪʃənərɪ] *adj* инфляцио́нный.
inflationist [ɪnˈfleɪʃənɪst] *n* сторо́нник(-ица) поли́тики инфля́ции.
inflexible [ɪnˈflɛksɪbl] *adj (rule, timetable)* жёсткий (жёсток); (*person*) неги́бкий* (неги́бок).
inflict [ɪnˈflɪkt] *vt*: **to ~ sth on sb** причиня́ть (причини́ть *perf*) что-н кому́-н; (*penalty*) налага́ть (наложи́ть *perf*) что-н на кого́-н.
infliction [ɪnˈflɪkʃən] *n (of pain)* причине́ние; (*of penalty*) наложе́ние.
in-flight [ˈɪnflaɪt] *adj (meal, entertainment)* на борту́ самолёта; **~ refuelling** дозапра́вка в полёте.
inflow [ˈɪnfləu] *n* прито́к.
influence [ˈɪnfluəns] *n (power)* влия́ние; (*effect*) возде́йствие ♦ *vt (person, situation, choice etc)* влия́ть (повлия́ть *perf*) на +*acc*, ока́зывать (оказа́ть* *perf*) влия́ние на +*acc*; **under the ~ of alcohol** под возде́йствием алкого́ля.
influential [ɪnfluˈɛnʃl] *adj* влия́тельный* (влия́телен).
influenza [ɪnfluˈɛnzə] *n* грипп.
influx [ˈɪnflʌks] *n (of people, funds)* прито́к.
inform [ɪnˈfɔːm] *vt*: **to ~ sb of sth** (*tell*) сообща́ть (сообщи́ть *perf*) кому́-н о чём-н, информи́ровать (проинформи́ровать *perf*) кого́-н о чём-н ♦ *vi*: **to ~ on sb** доноси́ть* (донести́* *perf*) на кого́-н.
informal [ɪnˈfɔːml] *adj (visit, meeting, invitation)* неофициа́льный* (неофициа́лен); (*manner, discussion*) непринуждённый* (непринуждён); (*clothes*) бу́дничный, повседне́вный* (повседне́вен); (*language*) разгово́рный.
informality [ɪnfɔːˈmælɪtɪ] *n* непринуждённость *f*.
informally [ɪnˈfɔːməlɪ] *adv* неофициа́льно; (*discuss*) непринуждённо; (*dress*) бу́днично; (*invite*) без церемо́ний.
informant [ɪnˈfɔːmənt] *n (source)* информа́нт.
information [ɪnfəˈmeɪʃən] *n* информа́ция; **to get ~ on** получа́ть (получи́ть* *perf*) информа́цию о +*prp*; **a piece of ~** сообще́ние; **for your ~** к Ва́шему све́дению.

---

* marks translations which have irregular inflections. The Russian-English side of the dictionary gives inflectional information.

information bureau n = **information office**.
information office n спра́вочное бюро́ nt ind.
information processing n обрабо́тка
информа́ции.
information retrieval n (COMPUT) по́иск
информа́ции, информацио́нный по́иск.
information science n информа́тика.
information technology n информацио́нная
техноло́гия.
informative [ɪn'fɔ:mətɪv] adj содержа́тельный*
(содержа́телен).
informed [ɪn'fɔ:md] adj осведомлённый*
(осведомлён), информи́рованный*
(информи́рован); **well/ill ~** хорошо́/пло́хо
информи́рованный (информи́рован); **an ~
guess** обосно́ванная дога́дка*.
informer [ɪn'fɔ:mə°] n (also: **police ~**)
осведоми́тель(ница) m(f).
infra dig ['ɪnfrə'dɪg] adj abbr (inf: = beneath one's
dignity: = infra dignitatem) ни́же чьего́-н
досто́инства.
infrared [ɪnfrə'rɛd] adj инфракра́сный.
infrastructure ['ɪnfrəstrʌktʃə°] n
инфраструкту́ра.
infrequent [ɪn'fri:kwənt] adj ре́дкий* (ре́док).
infringe [ɪn'frɪndʒ] vt (law) преступа́ть
(преступи́ть perf) ♦ vi: **to ~ on** (rights)
ущемля́ть (ущеми́ть* perf), посяга́ть
(посягну́ть perf) на +acc.
infringement [ɪn'frɪndʒmənt] n (see vb)
наруше́ние; ущемле́ние, посяга́тельство.
infuriate [ɪn'fjuərɪeɪt] vt (person) приводи́ть*
(привести́* perf) в я́рость or бе́шенство,
беси́ть* (взбеси́ть* perf).
infuriating [ɪn'fjuərɪeɪtɪŋ] adj приводя́щий в
я́рость or бе́шенство; **the noise is ~** шум
приво́дит меня́ etc в я́рость.
infuse [ɪn'fju:z] vt (tea, herbs) наста́ивать
(настоя́ть perf); (person): **to ~ sb with sth**
вселя́ть (всели́ть perf) что-н в кого́-н.
infusion [ɪn'fju:ʒən] n (tea) настойка*.
ingenious [ɪn'dʒi:njəs] adj хитроу́мный*
(хитроу́мен); (person) изобрета́тельный*
(изобрета́телен).
ingenuity [ɪndʒɪ'nju:ɪtɪ] n хитроу́мность f; (of
person) изобрета́тельность f.
ingenuous [ɪn'dʒɛnjuəs] adj бесхи́тростный*
(бесхи́тростен).
ingot ['ɪŋgət] n сли́ток*.
ingrained [ɪn'greɪnd] adj закоренелый.
ingratiate [ɪn'greɪʃɪeɪt] vt: **to ~ o.s. with**
заи́скивать (impf) пе́ред +instr.
ingratiating [ɪn'greɪʃɪeɪtɪŋ] adj (smile, speech)
заи́скивающий*; (person) льсти́вый
(льстив).
ingratitude [ɪn'grætɪtju:d] n неблагода́р-
ность f.
ingredient [ɪn'gri:dɪənt] n (CULIN) ингредие́нт;
(of situation) составна́я часть f.
ingrowing ['ɪngrəuɪŋ] adj: **~ toenail**
враста́ющий но́готь* m (на па́льце ноги́).

inhabit [ɪn'hæbɪt] vt населя́ть (impf).
inhabitant [ɪn'hæbɪtnt] n жи́тель(ница) m(f).
inhale [ɪn'heɪl] vt вдыха́ть (вдохну́ть* perf) ♦ vi
вдыха́ть (вдо́хнуть* perf); (when smoking)
затя́гиваться (затяну́ться* perf).
inhaler [ɪn'heɪlə°] n ингаля́тор.
inherent [ɪn'hɪərənt] adj (laziness)
прирождённый; **~ in** or **to** сво́йственный*
(сво́йствен) +dat, прису́щий* (прису́щ) +dat.
inherently [ɪn'hɪərəntlɪ] adv (easy, difficult) по
приро́де; (lazy) по нату́ре.
inherit [ɪn'hɛrɪt] vt насле́довать (impf/perf),
унасле́довать (perf).
inheritance [ɪn'hɛrɪtəns] n насле́дство;
(cultural, political etc) насле́дие; **right of ~**
пра́во насле́дования.
inhibit [ɪn'hɪbɪt] vt (impulse) ско́вывать
(скова́ть perf); (growth) заде́рживать
(задержа́ть* perf).
inhibited [ɪn'hɪbɪtɪd] adj (see vb) ско́ванный*
(ско́ван); заде́ржанный*.
inhibiting [ɪn'hɪbɪtɪŋ] adj (situation)
ско́вывающий; (factor) препя́тствующий.
inhibition [ɪnhɪ'bɪʃən] n (see vb) ско́ванность f
no pl; заде́ржка*.
inhospitable [ɪnhɔs'pɪtəbl] adj (person)
негостеприи́мный* (негостеприи́мен);
(place) неприве́тливый (неприве́тлив).
inhuman [ɪn'hju:mən] adj (behaviour)
бесчелове́чный* (бесчелове́чен);
(appearance) нечелове́ческий*.
inhumane [ɪnhju:'meɪn] adj негума́нный*
(негума́нен).
inimitable [ɪ'nɪmɪtəbl] adj неподража́емый
(неподража́ем).
iniquitous [ɪ'nɪkwɪtəs] adj (see n) чудо́вищный*
(чудо́вищен); чудо́вищно несправедли́вый
(несправедли́в).
iniquity [ɪ'nɪkwɪtɪ] n (wickedness) чудо́вищ-
ность f; (injustice) несправедли́вость f.
initial [ɪ'nɪʃl] adj первонача́льный, нача́льный
♦ n (also: **~ letter**) нача́льная бу́ква ♦ vt
ста́вить* (поста́вить* perf) инициа́лы на
+prp; **~s** npl инициа́лы mpl.
initialize [ɪ'nɪʃəlaɪz] vt (COMPUT) инициализи́-
́ровать (impf/perf).
initially [ɪ'nɪʃəlɪ] adv (at first) внача́ле, снача́ла;
(first) первонача́льно.
initiate [ɪ'nɪʃɪeɪt] vt (talks, process) класть*
(положи́ть perf) нача́ло +dat; (new member)
посвяща́ть (посвяти́ть* perf); **to ~ sb into a
secret** посвяща́ть (посвяти́ть* perf) кого́-н в
та́йну; **to ~ proceedings against sb**
возбужда́ть (возбуди́ть* perf) де́ло про́тив
кого́-н.
initiation [ɪnɪʃɪ'eɪʃən] n (beginning) основа́ние;
(into secret etc) посвяще́ние; **~ ceremony**
церемо́ния посвяще́ния.
initiative [ɪ'nɪʃətɪv] n (move) инициати́ва,
начина́ние; (enterprise) инициати́вность f; **to
take the ~** брать* (взять* perf) на себя́

инициати́ву.
inject [ɪn'dʒɛkt] vt (drugs, poison) вводи́ть*
(ввести́* perf); (patient): **to ~ sb with sth**
де́лать (сде́лать perf) уко́л or инъе́кцию
чего́-н кому́-н; (money): **to ~ into** влива́ть
(влить* perf) в +acc.
injection [ɪn'dʒɛkʃən] n уко́л, инъе́кция; (of
money) влива́ние; **to give an ~** де́лать
(сде́лать perf) уко́л or инъе́кцию; **I had an ~**
мне сде́лали уко́л.
injudicious [ɪndʒu'dɪʃəs] adj неразу́мный*
(неразу́мен).
injunction [ɪn'dʒʌŋkʃən] n (LAW) (суде́бный)
запре́т.
injure ['ɪndʒər] vt (person, limb, feelings) ра́нить
(impf/perf); (reputation) поврежда́ть
(повреди́ть* perf); **to ~ o.s.** пора́ниться (perf),
ушиба́ться (ушиби́ться* perf).
injured ['ɪndʒəd] adj (see vb) ра́неный;
повреждённый (повреждён); уши́бленный
(уши́блен); **~ party** (LAW) потерпе́вшая
сторона́*.
injurious [ɪn'dʒuərɪəs] adj: **~ to** вре́дный*
(вре́ден) для +gen, губи́тельный*
(губи́телен) для +gen.
injury ['ɪndʒərɪ] n поврежде́ние; (more serious)
ране́ние; (industrial, sports) тра́вма; (to
reputation, feelings) оскорбле́ние; **to escape
without ~** избега́ть (избежа́ть* perf)
ране́ний.
injury time n (SPORT) доба́вочное вре́мя* nt.
injustice [ɪn'dʒʌstɪs] n несправедли́вость f; **you
do me an ~** Вы ко мне несправедли́вы.
ink [ɪŋk] n (in pen) черни́ла pl; (for printing)
типогра́фская кра́ска*.
ink-jet printer ['ɪŋkdʒɛt-] n (COMPUT)
стру́йный при́нтер.
inkling ['ɪŋklɪŋ] n (idea, clue): **to have an ~ of**
име́ть (impf) поня́тие о +prp.
ink pad n штемпельная поду́шечка*.
inky ['ɪŋkɪ] adj (blackness, sky) черни́льный;
(fingers) запа́чканный (запа́чкан)
черни́лами.
inlaid ['ɪnleɪd] adj: **~ (with)** инкрусти́рованный
(инкрусти́рован) (+instr).
inland ['ɪnlənd] adj вну́тренний* ♦ adv (travel)
вглубь.
Inland Revenue n (BRIT) ≈ Гла́вное нало́говое
управле́ние.
in-laws ['ɪnlɔːz] npl родня́ со стороны́ му́жа
и́ли жены́.
inlet ['ɪnlɛt] n (у́зкий) зали́в.
inlet pipe n впускна́я труба́*.
inmate ['ɪnmeɪt] n (of prison)
заключённый(-ая) m(f); (of asylum)
пацие́нт(ка*).
inmost ['ɪnməust] adj сокрове́ннейший*.
inn [ɪn] n тракти́р.

innards ['ɪnədz] npl (inf) вну́тренности fpl.
innate [ɪ'neɪt] adj врождённый.
inner ['ɪnər] adj вну́тренний*.
inner city n центра́льная часть* f го́рода.
innermost ['ɪnəməust] adj = **inmost**.
inner tube n ка́мера (ши́ны).
innings ['ɪnɪŋz] n серия атаку́ющих ударо́в в
кри́кете; **he's had a good ~** (BRIT: inf) он
прожи́л до́лгую и счастли́вую жизнь.
innocence ['ɪnəsns] n (LAW) невино́вность f;
(naivety) неви́нность f.
innocent ['ɪnəsnt] adj (also LAW) невино́вный*
(невино́вен); (naive) неви́нный* (неви́нен).
innocuous [ɪ'nɔkjuəs] adj (substance)
безвре́дный* (безвре́ден); (remarks)
безоби́дный* (безоби́ден).
innovation [ɪnəu'veɪʃən] n но́вшество.
innuendo [ɪnju'ɛndəu] (pl **~es**) n инсинуа́ция.
innumerable [ɪ'njuːmrəbl] adj бесчи́сленный*
(бесчи́слен).
inoculate [ɪ'nɔkjuleɪt] vt: **to ~ sb against sth**
де́лать (сде́лать perf) кому́-н приви́вку
про́тив чего́-н; **to ~ sb with sth** привива́ть
(приви́ть* perf) кому́-н что-н.
inoculation [ɪnɔkju'leɪʃən] n приви́вка*.
inoffensive [ɪnə'fɛnsɪv] adj безоби́дный*
(безоби́ден).
inopportune [ɪn'ɔpətjuːn] adj (moment)
неподходя́щий*; (event) несвоевре́менный*
(несвоевре́менен).
inordinate [ɪ'nɔːdɪnət] adj необыча́йный*
(необыча́ен).
inordinately [ɪ'nɔːdɪnətlɪ] adv необыча́йно.
inorganic [ɪnɔː'gænɪk] adj неоргани́ческий*.
inpatient ['ɪnpeɪʃənt] n стациона́рный(-ая)
больно́й(-а́я) m(f) adj.
input ['ɪnput] n (resources, money) вложе́ние;
(COMPUT) ввод ♦ vt (COMPUT): **to ~ (into)**
вводи́ть* (ввести́* perf) (в +acc).
inquest ['ɪnkwɛst] n (on sb's death) (суде́бное)
рассле́дование.
inquire [ɪn'kwaɪər] vt спра́шивать (спроси́ть*
perf) ♦ vi: **to ~ (about)** справля́ться
(спра́виться* perf) (о +prp); **to ~ when/where**
справля́ться (спра́виться* perf) когда́/где; **he
~d whether he could go** он спроси́л, мо́жет
ли он идти́
► **inquire after** vt fus спра́шивать (спроси́ть*
perf) о +prp
► **inquire into** vt fus рассле́довать (impf/perf).
inquiring [ɪn'kwaɪərɪŋ] adj пытли́вый.
inquiry [ɪn'kwaɪərɪ] n (question) вопро́с; (: more
official) запро́с; (investigation)
рассле́дование; (: LAW) сле́дствие; **to make
inquiries about sth** наводи́ть* (навести́* perf)
спра́вки о чём-н; **to hold an ~ into sth** вести́*
(impf) рассле́дование чего́-н.
inquiry desk n (BRIT) спра́вочный стол*.

---

* marks translations which have irregular inflections. The Russian-English side of the dictionary gives inflectional information.

inquiry office *n* (BRIT) спра́вочное бюро́ *nt ind.*
inquisition [ɪnkwɪˈzɪʃən] *n* сле́дствие *no pl;*
(REL): **the I~** Инквизи́ция.
inquisitive [ɪnˈkwɪzɪtɪv] *adj* любопы́тный*
(любопы́тен).
inroads [ˈɪnrəudz] *npl:* **to make ~ into** (savings,
resources) тра́тить* (потра́тить* perf).
ins *abbr* = **inches**.
ins and outs [ˈɪnzənˈauts] *npl:* **to know all the ~
~~** знать (impf) все хо́ды.
insane [ɪnˈseɪn] *adj* (foolish, crazy) безу́мный*
(безу́мен); (PSYCH) душевнобольно́й.
insanitary [ɪnˈsænɪtərɪ] *adj* антисанита́рный*
(антисанита́рен).
insanity [ɪnˈsænɪtɪ] *n* (also fig) безу́мие,
сумасше́ствие.
insatiable [ɪnˈseɪʃəbl] *adj* ненасы́тный*
(ненасы́тен).
inscribe [ɪnˈskraɪb] *vt* надпи́сывать
(надписа́ть* perf).
inscription [ɪnˈskrɪpʃən] *n* на́дпись *f.*
inscrutable [ɪnˈskruːtəbl] *adj* зага́дочный*
(зага́дочен).
inseam measurement [ˈɪnsiːm-] *n* (US) =
inside leg measurement.
insect [ˈɪnsɛkt] *n* насеко́мое *nt adj.*
insect bite *n* уку́с насеко́мого.
insecticide [ɪnˈsɛktɪsaɪd] *n* инсектици́д.
insect repellent *n* сре́дство от насеко́мых.
insecure [ɪnsɪˈkjuəʳ] *adj* (structure, border)
ненадёжный* (ненадёжен); (person)
неуве́ренный* (неуве́рен) в себе́.
insecurity [ɪnsɪˈkjuərɪtɪ] *n* (see adj)
ненадёжность *f;* неуве́ренность *f* в себе́.
insemination [ɪnsɛmɪˈneɪʃən] *n:* **artificial ~**
иску́сственное оплодотворе́ние.
insensible [ɪnˈsɛnsɪbl] *adj* (unconscious) без
созна́ния; (unable to feel): **~ to**
нечувстви́тельный* (нечувстви́телен) к +dat;
(unaware): **~ of** не осознаю́щий +gen.
insensitive [ɪnˈsɛnsɪtɪv] *adj* бесчу́вственный*
(бесчу́вствен).
insensitivity [ɪnsɛnsɪˈtɪvɪtɪ] *n* (of person)
бесчу́вственность *f.*
inseparable [ɪnˈsɛprəbl] *adj* (ideas, elements)
нераздели́мый (нераздели́м); (friends)
неразлу́чный* (неразлу́чен).
insert [vt ɪnˈsəːt, n ˈɪnsəːt] *vt:* **to ~** (into)
вставля́ть (вста́вить* perf) (в +acc); (piece of
paper) вкла́дывать (вложи́ть* perf) ◆ *n*
вкла́дыш, вкла́дка.
insertion [ɪnˈsəːʃən] *n* (in book, file) вста́вка*;
(of needle) введе́ние; (of peg) вбива́ние.
in-service [ˈɪnˈsəːvɪs] *adj:* **~ training**
произво́дственное обуче́ние.
inshore [ɪnˈʃɔːʳ] *adj* (fishing, waters) при-
бре́жный ◆ *adv* (be) у бе́рега; (go) к бе́регу.
inside [ˈɪnsaɪd] *n* вну́тренняя часть* *f;* (of coat
etc) изна́нка; (of road: BRIT) ле́вая сторона́;
(: US, Europe etc) пра́вая сторона́ ◆ *adj*
вну́тренний* ◆ *adv* (go) внутрь; (be) внутри́ ◆

prep (position) внутри́ +gen; (motion) внутрь
+gen; (of time): **~ ten minutes** в преде́лах
де́сяти мину́т; **~s** *npl* (inf: stomach)
вну́тренности *fpl.*
inside forward *n* (FOOTBALL) полусре́дний
нападаю́щий* *m adj.*
inside information *n* информа́ция,
полу́ченная из вну́тренних исто́чников.
inside lane *n* (AUT: BRIT) ле́вый ряд*; (: US,
Europe etc) пра́вый ряд*.
inside leg measurement *n* (BRIT) вну́тренняя*
длина́ ноги́.
inside out *adv* (be, wear, turn) наизна́нку;
(know) вдоль и поперёк.
insider [ɪnˈsaɪdəʳ] *n* свой челове́к; (COMM)
инса́йдер.
insider dealing *n* (STOCK EXCHANGE)
незако́нное испо́льзование делово́й
информа́ции при сде́лках на би́рже.
insider trading *n* = **insider dealing.**
inside story *n* информа́ция из пе́рвых рук.
insidious [ɪnˈsɪdɪəs] *adj* кова́рный* (кова́рен).
insight [ˈɪnsaɪt] *n:* **~** (into) понима́ние *no pl*
(+gen); **to gain** (an) **~ into sth** вника́ть
(вни́кнуть perf) в что-н.
insignia [ɪnˈsɪgnɪə] *n inv* зна́ки *mpl* отли́чия.
insignificant [ɪnsɪgˈnɪfɪknt] *adj*
незначи́тельный* (незначи́телен).
insincere [ɪnsɪnˈsɪəʳ] *adj* нейскренний*
(нейскренен).
insincerity [ɪnsɪnˈsɛrɪtɪ] *n* нейскренность *f.*
insinuate [ɪnˈsɪnjueɪt] *vt* намека́ть (намекну́ть*
perf) на +acc.
insinuation [ɪnsɪnjuˈeɪʃən] *n* инсинуа́ция.
insipid [ɪnˈsɪpɪd] *adj* (person) бесцве́тный*
(бесцве́тен); (colour) блёклый; (food, drink)
пре́сный* (пре́сен).
insist [ɪnˈsɪst] *vi:* **to ~** (on) наста́ивать
(настоя́ть perf) (на +prp); **to ~ that** (demand)
наста́ивать (настоя́ть perf) на том, что́бы
+past tense; (claim) наста́ивать (настоя́ть perf)
на том, что.
insistence [ɪnˈsɪstəns] *n* настоя́ние; **at his ~** по
его́ настоя́нию.
insistent [ɪnˈsɪstənt] *adj* насто́йчивый
(насто́йчив).
insofar as [ɪnsəuˈfɑːʳ-] *adv* поско́льку.
insole [ˈɪnsəul] *n* сте́лька*.
insolence [ˈɪnsələns] *n* на́глость *f.*
insolent [ˈɪnsələnt] *adj* (attitude, remark)
на́глый* (нагл).
insoluble [ɪnˈsɔljubl] *adj* неразреши́мый
(неразреши́м).
insolvency [ɪnˈsɔlvənsɪ] *n* неплатёже-
спосо́бность *f.*
insolvent [ɪnˈsɔlvənt] *adj* неплатёже-
спосо́бный* (неплатёжеспосо́бен).
insomnia [ɪnˈsɔmnɪə] *n* бессо́нница.
insomniac [ɪnˈsɔmnɪæk] *n* страда́ющий(-ая)
m(f) adj бессо́нницей.
inspect [ɪnˈspɛkt] *vt* (premises, equipment)

осма́тривать (осмотре́ть* *perf*); (*BRIT: ticket, luggage*) проверя́ть (прове́рить *perf*).

inspection [ɪn'spɛkʃən] *n* (*see vb*) осмо́тр; прове́рка*.

inspector [ɪn'spɛktəʳ] *n* (*ADMIN, POLICE*) инспе́ктор*; (*BRIT: on buses, trains*) контролёр.

inspiration [ɪnspə'reɪʃən] *n* вдохнове́ние.

inspire [ɪn'spaɪəʳ] *vt* (*workers, troops*) вдохновля́ть (вдохнови́ть* *perf*); **to ~ sth (in sb)** внуша́ть (внуши́ть *perf*) что-н (кому́-н).

inspired [ɪn'spaɪəd] *adj* (*writer etc*) вдохновлённый (вдохновлён); (*book*) вдохнове́нный (вдохнове́нен); **in an ~ moment** в моме́нт вдохнове́ния.

inspiring [ɪn'spaɪərɪŋ] *adj* вдохновля́ющий*.

inst. *abbr* (*BRIT: COMM:* = *instant*) с.м.= *сего́ ме́сяца.*

instability [ɪnstə'bɪlɪtɪ] *n* нестаби́льность *f*.

install [ɪn'stɔ:l] *vt* (*machine*) устана́вливать (установи́ть* *perf*); (*official*) ста́вить* (поста́вить* *perf*).

installation [ɪnstə'leɪʃən] *n* (*of machine, plant*) устано́вка; (*MIL*) объе́кт.

installment plan *n* (*US*) рассро́чка.

instalment [ɪn'stɔ:lmənt] (*US* **installment**) *n* (*of payment*) взнос; (*of story, TV serial*) часть* *f*; **to pay in ~s** плати́ть* (заплати́ть* *perf*) в рассро́чку.

instance ['ɪnstəns] *n* (*example*) приме́р; **for ~** наприме́р; **in this** *or* **that ~** в да́нном слу́чае; **in many ~s** во мно́гих слу́чаях; **in the first ~** в пе́рвую о́чередь.

instant ['ɪnstənt] *n* мгнове́ние, миг ◆ *adj* (*reaction, success*) мгнове́нный* (мгнове́нен); **come here this ~!** иди́ сюда́ сию́ мину́ту!; **the 10th ~** (*COMM, ADMIN*) 10-ое число́ сего́ ме́сяца; **~ coffee** раствори́мый ко́фе; **~ food** пищево́й концентра́т.

instantaneous [ɪnstən'teɪnɪəs] *adj* (*immediate*) мгнове́нный* (мгнове́нен).

instantly ['ɪnstəntlɪ] *adv* неме́дленно, сра́зу.

instant replay *n* (*TV*) повто́р.

instead [ɪn'stɛd] *adv* взаме́н ◆ *prep*: **~ of** вме́сто +*gen*, взаме́н +*gen*; **~ of sb** вме́сто кого́-н.

instep ['ɪnstɛp] *n* подъём (*ноги́, ту́фли*).

instigate ['ɪnstɪgeɪt] *vt* (*rebellion, strike etc*) подстрека́ть (*impf*) к +*dat*; **to ~ talks** дава́ть* (дать* *perf*) толчо́к перегово́рам.

instigation [ɪnstɪ'geɪʃən] *n* подстрека́тельство; **at my ~** по мое́й инициати́ве.

instil [ɪn'stɪl] *vt*: **to ~ sth in(to) sb** (*confidence, fear etc*) вселя́ть (всели́ть *perf*) что-н в кого́-н.

instinct ['ɪnstɪŋkt] *n* инсти́нкт; **by ~** инстинкти́вно; **maternal ~** матери́нский инсти́нкт.

instinctive [ɪn'stɪŋktɪv] *adj* инстинкти́вный*

(инстинкти́вен).

instinctively [ɪn'stɪŋktɪvlɪ] *adv* инстинкти́вно.

institute ['ɪnstɪtjuːt] *n* (*for research, teaching*) институ́т; (*professional body*) ассоциа́ция ◆ *vt* (*system, rule*) учрежда́ть (учреди́ть* *perf*); (*inquiry*) назнача́ть (назна́чить *perf*); **to ~ proceedings (against)** возбужда́ть (возбуди́ть* *perf*) суде́бное де́ло (про́тив +*gen*).

institution [ɪnstɪ'tjuːʃən] *n* учрежде́ние; (*custom, tradition*) институ́т.

institutional [ɪnstɪ'tjuːʃənl] *adj* (*value, quality etc*) закреплённый (закреплён); (*education*) осуществля́емый кру́пными учрежде́ниями; **~ care** попече́ние (*осуществля́емое учрежде́ниями*); **~ reform** рефо́рма социа́льных учрежде́ний.

instruct [ɪn'strʌkt] *vt*: **to ~ sb in sth** обуча́ть (обучи́ть* *perf*) кого́-н чему́-н; **to ~ sb to do** поруча́ть (поручи́ть* *perf*) кому́-н +*infin*.

instruction [ɪn'strʌkʃən] *n* (*teaching*) обуче́ние ◆ *cpd*: **~ manual**, **~ leaflet** инстру́кция; **~s** *npl* (*orders*) указа́ния *ntpl*; **~s (for use)** инстру́кция *or* руково́дство (по примене́нию).

instructive [ɪn'strʌktɪv] *adj* поучи́тельный* (поучи́телен).

instructor [ɪn'strʌktəʳ] *n* преподава́тель(ница) *m(f)*; (*for skiing, driving etc*) инстру́ктор*.

instrument ['ɪnstrumənt] *n* инструме́нт.

instrumental [ɪnstru'mɛntl] *adj* (*MUS*) инструмента́льный; (*important*): **to be ~ in** игра́ть (сыгра́ть *perf*) суще́ственную роль в +*prp*.

instrumentalist [ɪnstru'mɛntəlɪst] *n* инструментали́ст.

instrument panel *n* прибо́рная пане́ль *f*.

insubordination [ɪnsəbɔːdə'neɪʃən] *n* неповинове́ние.

insufferable [ɪn'sʌfrəbl] *adj* невыноси́мый (невыноси́м).

insufficient [ɪnsə'fɪʃənt] *adj* недоста́точный* (недоста́точен).

insufficiently [ɪnsə'fɪʃəntlɪ] *adv* недоста́точно.

insular ['ɪnsjuləʳ] *adj* ограни́ченный* (ограни́чен).

insulate ['ɪnsjuleɪt] *vt* (*protect: person, group, also ELEC*) изоли́ровать (*impf/perf*); (*against cold*) утепля́ть (утепли́ть *perf*); (*against sound*) (зву́ко)изоли́ровать (*impf/perf*).

insulating tape *n* (*BRIT*) изоляцио́нная ле́нта.

insulation [ɪnsju'leɪʃən] *n* (*see vb*) изоля́ция; (тепло)изоля́ция; (зву́ко)изоля́ция.

insulator ['ɪnsjuleɪtəʳ] *n* (*material*) изоля́тор.

insulin ['ɪnsjulɪn] *n* инсули́н.

insult [*vt* ɪn'sʌlt, *n* 'ɪnsʌlt] *vt* оскорбля́ть (оскорби́ть* *perf*) ◆ *n* оскорбле́ние.

---

* marks translations which have irregular inflections. The Russian-English side of the dictionary gives inflectional information.

insulting [ɪn'sʌltɪŋ] *adj* оскорби́тельный* (оскорби́телен).

insuperable [ɪn'sjuːprəbl] *adj* непреодоли́мый (непреодоли́м).

insurance [ɪn'ʃuərəns] *n* страхова́ние; **life/fire** ~ страхова́ние жи́зни/на слу́чай пожа́ра; **to take out** ~ **(against)** брать* (взять* *perf*) страхо́вку (от +*gen*).

insurance agent *n* страхово́й аге́нт.

insurance broker *n* страхово́й бро́кер.

insurance policy *n* страхово́й по́лис.

insurance premium *n* страхова́я пре́мия.

insure [ɪn'ʃuə'] *vt*: **to** ~ **(against)** страхова́ть (застрахова́ть *perf*) (от +*gen*); **to** ~ **(o.s.) against** страхова́ться (застрахова́ться *perf*) от +*gen*; **the car is** ~**d for £5,000** маши́на застрахо́вана на су́мму в £5.000.

insured [ɪn'ʃuəd] *n*: **the** ~ страхова́тель(ница) *m(f)*.

insurer [ɪn'ʃuərə'] *n* (*insurance company*) страхо́вщик.

insurgent [ɪn'sɜːdʒənt] *adj* восста́вший ◆ *n* повста́нец*.

insurmountable [ɪnsə'mauntəbl] *adj* непреодоли́мый (непреодоли́м).

insurrection [ɪnsə'rɛkʃən] *n* восста́ние.

intact [ɪn'tækt] *adj* (*whole*) нетро́нутый (нетро́нут); (*unharmed*) неповреждённый (неповреждён).

intake ['ɪnteɪk] *n* (*of food, drink*) потребле́ние; (*of air*) поглоще́ние; (*BRIT: of pupils, recruits*) набо́р.

intangible [ɪn'tændʒɪbl] *adj* неощути́мый (неощути́м).

integer ['ɪntɪdʒə'] *n* це́лое число́*.

integral ['ɪntɪɡrəl] *adj* (*feature, element*) неотъе́млемый (неотъе́млем) ◆ *n* (*MATH*) интегра́л.

integrate ['ɪntɪɡreɪt] *vt* интегри́ровать (*impf/ perf*) ◆ *vi* (*groups, individuals*) объединя́ться (объедини́ться *perf*).

integrated circuit ['ɪntɪɡreɪtɪd-] *n* (*COMPUT*) интегра́льная схе́ма.

integration [ɪntɪ'ɡreɪʃən] *n* интегра́ция; **racial** ~ ра́совая интегра́ция.

integrity [ɪn'tɛɡrɪtɪ] *n* (*morality*) че́стность *f*, поря́дочность *f*; (*wholeness*) це́лостность *f*

intellect ['ɪntəlɛkt] *n* интелле́кт.

intellectual [ɪntə'lɛktjuəl] *adj* интеллектуа́льный* (интеллектуа́лен) ◆ *n* интеллектуа́л.

intelligence [ɪn'tɛlɪdʒəns] *n* (*cleverness*) ум*; (*thinking power*) у́мственные спосо́бности *fpl*; (*MIL etc*) разве́дка.

intelligence quotient *n* коэффицие́нт у́мственного разви́тия.

intelligence service *n* разве́дывательная слу́жба.

intelligence test *n* тест. *определя́ющий у́ровень у́мственных спосо́бностей*.

intelligent [ɪn'tɛlɪdʒənt] *adj* у́мный* (умён);

(*animal*) разу́мный* (разу́мен).

intelligently [ɪn'tɛlɪdʒəntlɪ] *adv* умно́.

intelligentsia [ɪntɛlɪ'dʒɛntsɪə] *n*: **the** ~ интеллиге́нция.

intelligible [ɪn'tɛlɪdʒɪbl] *adj* поня́тный* (поня́тен).

intemperate [ɪn'tɛmpərət] *adj* несде́ржанный* (несде́ржан).

intend [ɪn'tɛnd] *vt*: **to** ~ **sth for** предназнача́ть (предназна́чить *perf*) что-н для +*gen*; **to** ~ **to do** намерева́ться (*impf*) +*infin*.

intended [ɪn'tɛndɪd] *adj* (*effect, route*) заплани́рованный (заплани́рован); (*victim*) предполага́емый (предполага́ем); (*insult*) преднаме́ренный* (преднаме́рен).

intense [ɪn'tɛns] *adj* (*heat, emotion*) си́льный* (силён); (*look*) напряжённый*; (*noise, activity*) интенси́вный* (интенси́вен); **she is very** ~ она́ всё о́чень серьёзно воспринима́ет.

intensely [ɪn'tɛnslɪ] *adv* (*see adj*) си́льно; напряжённо.

intensify [ɪn'tɛnsɪfaɪ] *vt* уси́ливать (уси́лить *perf*).

intensity [ɪn'tɛnsɪtɪ] *n* (*of effort, sun*) интенси́вность *f*; (*of look*) напряжённость *f*.

intensive [ɪn'tɛnsɪv] *adj* интенси́вный* (интенси́вен).

intensive care *n* интенси́вная терапи́я.

intensive care unit *n* отделе́ние интенси́вной терапи́и.

intent [ɪn'tɛnt] *n* (*also LAW*) наме́рение ◆ *adj*: ~ **(on)** сосредото́ченный* (сосредото́чен) (на +*prp*); **to all** ~**s and purposes** что бы там ни́ бы́ло; **to be** ~ **on doing** (*determined*) стреми́ться* (*impf*) +*infin*.

intention [ɪn'tɛnʃən] *n* наме́рение.

intentional [ɪn'tɛnʃənl] *adj* наме́ренный (наме́рен); (*LAW*) преднаме́ренный* (преднаме́рен).

intentionally [ɪn'tɛnʃnəlɪ] *adv* (*see adj*) наме́ренно; преднаме́ренно.

intently [ɪn'tɛntlɪ] *adv* при́стально.

inter [ɪn'tɜː'] *vt* погреба́ть (погрести́* *perf*).

interact [ɪntər'ækt] *vi*: **to** ~ **(with)** взаимоде́йствовать (*impf*) (с +*instr*).

interaction [ɪntər'ækʃən] *n* взаимоде́йствие.

interactive [ɪntər'æktɪv] *adj* взаимо- де́йствующий; (*COMPUT*) интеракти́вный, диало́говый.

intercede [ɪntə'siːd] *vi*: **to** ~ **(with sb/on behalf of sb)** хода́тайствовать (*impf*) (пе́ред кем-н/ за кого́-н).

intercept [ɪntə'sɛpt] *vt* перехва́тывать (перехвати́ть* *perf*).

interception [ɪntə'sɛpʃən] *n* перехва́т.

interchange ['ɪntətʃeɪndʒ] *n* (*on motorway*) тра́нспортная развя́зка*; ~ **(of)** (*exchange*) обме́н (+*instr*).

interchangeable [ɪntə'tʃeɪndʒəbl] *adj* взаимозаменя́емый (взаимозаменя́ем).

intercity [ɪntə'sɪtɪ] *adj* междугоро́дный.

intercom ['ɪntəkɔm] *n* селе́ктор.
interconnect [ɪntəkə'nɛkt] *vi* соединя́ться (*impf*) (ме́жду собо́й).
intercontinental ['ɪntəkɔntɪ'nɛntl] *adj* межконтинента́льный.
intercourse ['ɪntəkɔːs] *n* (*sexual*) полово́е сноше́ние; (*social, verbal*) обще́ние.
interdependence [ɪntədɪ'pɛndəns] *n* взаимозави́симость *f*.
interdependent [ɪntədɪ'pɛndənt] *adj* взаимозави́симый (взаимозави́сим).
interest ['ɪntrɪst] *n*: ~ **(in)** интере́с (к +*dat*); (*COMM: in company*) до́ля*; (: *sum of money*) проце́нты *mpl* ♦ *vt* интересова́ть (*impf*); **compound/simple** ~ сло́жные/просты́е проце́нты *mpl*; **it is in our** ~**s** (*to our advantage*) э́то в на́ших интере́сах; **British** ~**s in the Middle East** брита́нские интере́сы на Бли́жнем Восто́ке; **his main** ~ **is history** его́ основно́й интере́с – э́то исто́рия.
interested ['ɪntrɪstɪd] *adj* заинтересо́ванный (заинтересо́ван); **to be** ~ **(in sth)** (*music etc*) интересова́ться (*impf*) (чем-н); **they are** ~ **in increasing production** они́ заинтересо́ваны в увеличе́нии производи́тельности; **she is** ~ **in becoming a nurse** она́ хо́чет стать медсестро́й.
interest-free ['ɪntrɪst'friː] *adj* беспроце́нтный ♦ *adv* без упла́ты проце́нтов.
interesting ['ɪntrɪstɪŋ] *adj* интере́сный* (интере́сен).
interest rate *n* проце́нтная ста́вка*.
interface ['ɪntəfeɪs] *n* (*COMPUT*) интерфе́йс; (*area of contact*): ~ **between technology and design** соприкоснове́ние техноло́гии с диза́йном.
interfere [ɪntə'fɪəʳ] *vi*: **to** ~ **in** вме́шиваться (вмеша́ться *perf*) в +*acc*; **to** ~ **with** (*object*) тро́гать (*impf*); (*plans, career, duty, decision*) меша́ть (помеша́ть *perf*) +*dat*; **don't** ~ не вме́шивайтесь.
interference [ɪntə'fɪərəns] *n* вмеша́тельство; (*RADIO, TV*) поме́хи *fpl*.
interfering [ɪntə'fɪərɪŋ] *adj* назо́йливый (назо́йлив).
interim ['ɪntərɪm] *adj* (*POL*) вре́менный; (*report*) промежу́точный ♦ *n*: **in the** ~ тем вре́менем.
interim dividend *n* промежу́точный дивиде́нд.
interior [ɪn'tɪərɪəʳ] *n* (*of building*) интерье́р; (*of car, box etc*) вну́тренность *f*; (*of country*) глуби́нные райо́ны *mpl* ♦ *adj* (*door, room etc*) вну́тренний*; ~ **minister/department** мини́стр/департа́мент вну́тренних дел.
interior decorator *n* худо́жник(-ица) по интерье́ру.
interior designer *n* диза́йнер интерье́ра.
interjection [ɪntə'dʒɛkʃən] *n* перебива́ющий во́зглас; (*LING*) междоме́тие.

interlock [ɪntə'lɔk] *vi* сцепля́ться (сцепи́ться* *perf*).
interloper ['ɪntələupəʳ] *n* наруши́тель *m*.
interlude ['ɪntəluːd] *n* переры́в; (*THEAT*) антра́кт.
intermarry [ɪntə'mærɪ] *vi* вступа́ть (вступи́ть* *perf*) в сме́шанный брак.
intermediary [ɪntə'miːdɪərɪ] *n* посре́дник (-ица).
intermediate [ɪntə'miːdɪət] *adj* (*stage*) промежу́точный; ~ **student** студе́нт сре́дней ступе́ни обуче́ния.
interment [ɪn'təːmənt] *n* погребе́ние.
interminable [ɪn'təːmɪnəbl] *adj* бесконе́чный* (бесконе́чен).
intermission [ɪntə'mɪʃən] *n* переры́в.
intermittent [ɪntə'mɪtnt] *adj* периоди́ческий*.
intermittently [ɪntə'mɪtntlɪ] *adv* периоди́чески.
intern [*vt* ɪn'təːn, *n* 'ɪntəːn] *vt* интерни́ровать (*impf/perf*) ♦ *n* (*US: MED*) врач-стажёр.
internal [ɪn'təːnl] *adj* вну́тренний*.
internally [ɪn'təːnəlɪ] *adv*: **"not to be taken** ~**"** „внутрь не принима́ть".
Internal Revenue Service *n* (*US*) ≈ Гла́вное нало́говое управле́ние.
international [ɪntə'næʃənl] *adj* междунаро́дный ♦ *n* (*BRIT. SPORT. also*: ~ **match**) междунаро́дная встре́ча.
International Atomic Energy Agency *n* Междунаро́дное аге́нтство по а́томной эне́ргии.
International Chamber of Commerce *n* Междунаро́дная торго́вая пала́та.
International Court of Justice *n* Междунаро́дный суд*.
International Date Line *n* ли́ния переме́ны дат.
International Labour Organization *n* Междунаро́дная организа́ция труда́.
internationally [ɪntə'næʃnəlɪ] *adv* в междунаро́дном масшта́бе.
International Monetary Fund *n* Междунаро́дный валю́тный фонд.
international relations *npl* междунаро́дные отноше́ния *ntpl*.
internecine [ɪntə'niːsaɪn] *adj* междоусо́бный.
internee [ɪntəː'niː] *n* интерни́рованный(-ая) *m(f) adj*.
Internet ['ɪntə.net] *n*: **the** ~ Интерне́т, Сеть *f*.
internment [ɪn'təːnmənt] *n* интерни́рование.
interplay ['ɪntəpleɪ] *n*: ~ **(of** *or* **between)** взаимоде́йствие (+*gen*).
Interpol ['ɪntəpɔl] *n* Интерпо́л.
interpret [ɪn'təːprɪt] *vt* (*explain*) интерпрети́ровать (*impf/perf*), толкова́ть (*impf*); (*translate*) переводи́ть* (перевести́* *perf*) (у́стно) ♦ *vi* переводи́ть* (перевести́* *perf*)

---

* marks translations which have irregular inflections. The Russian-English side of the dictionary gives inflectional information.

(*ýстно*).
interpretation [ɪntə:prɪ'teɪʃən] *n*
интерпретáция, толковáние.
interpreter [ɪn'tə:prɪtəʳ] *n* перевóдчик(-ица).
interpreting [ɪn'tə:prɪtɪŋ] *n* (*ýстный*) перевóд.
interrelated [ɪntərɪ'leɪtɪd] *adj* взаимо-
свя́занный (взаимосвя́зан).
interrogate [ɪn'tɛrəugeɪt] *vt* допрáшивать
(допроси́ть* *perf*).
interrogation [ɪntɛrəu'geɪʃən] *n* допрóс.
interrogative [ɪntə'rɔgətɪv] *adj* (*LING*)
вопроси́тельный.
interrogator [ɪn'tɛrəgeɪtəʳ] *n* слéдователь *m*.
interrupt [ɪntə'rʌpt] *vti* прерывáть (прервáть*
perf).
interruption [ɪntə'rʌpʃən] *n* (*act*) прерывáние; **I
hate ~s when I'm working** я ненави́жу, когдá
меня́ прерывáют во врéмя рабóты.
intersect [ɪntə'sɛkt] *vi* пересекáться (пере-
сéчься* *perf*) ♦ *vt* пересекáть (пересéчь* *perf*).
intersection [ɪntə'sɛkʃən] *n* (*of roads*)
пересечéние; (*MATH*) тóчка* пересечéния.
intersperse [ɪntə'spə:s] *vt*: **to ~ with**
перемежáть (*impf*) с +*instr*.
intertwine [ɪntə'twaɪn] *vi* переплетáться
(переплести́сь* *perf*).
interval ['ɪntəvl] *n* (*also MUS*) интервáл; (*BRIT:
SPORT*) перерýв; (: *THEAT*) антрáкт; **bright ~s**
(*in weather*) проснéния *ntpl*; **at ~s** врéмя от
врéмени.
intervene [ɪntə'vi:n] *vi* (*in conversation,
situation*) вмéшиваться (вмешáться *perf*);
(*event*) мешáть (помешáть *perf*); (*time*)
проходи́ть* (пройти́* *perf*).
intervening [ɪntə'vi:nɪŋ] *adj* (*period*) промежýточный.
intervention [ɪntə'vɛnʃən] *n* (*interference*)
вмешáтельство; (*mediation*)
посрéдничество; **military ~** воéнная
интервéнция.
interview ['ɪntəvju:] *n* (*for job*) собесéдование;
(*RADIO, TV etc*) интервью́ *nt ind* ♦ *vt* (*see n*)
проводи́ть* (провести́* *perf*) собесéдование с
+*instr*; интервью́и́ровать (*impf/perf*), брать*
(взять* *perf*) интервью́ у +*gen*; **to give an ~**
давáть* (дать* *perf*) интервью́.
interviewee [ɪntəvju'i:] *n* интервью́и́руемый
(-ая) *m(f) adj*.
interviewer ['ɪntəvjuəʳ] *n* (*of candidate*)
проводя́щий(-ая) *m(f) adj* собесéдование;
(*RADIO, TV etc*) интервьюéр.
intestate [ɪn'tɛsteɪt] *adj*: **to die ~** скончáться
(*perf*), не остáвив завещáния.
intestinal [ɪn'tɛstɪnl] *adj* кишéчный.
intestine [ɪn'tɛstɪn] *n* кишкá*; **large/small ~**
тóлстая/тóнкая кишкá; **~s** кишéчник *msg*.
intimacy ['ɪntɪməsɪ] *n* инти́мность *f*.
intimate [*adj* 'ɪntɪmət, *vt* 'ɪntɪmeɪt] *adj* (*very
close*) бли́зкий* (бли́зок); (*relationship,
conversation, atmosphere*) инти́мный*
(инти́мен); (*knowledge*) глубóкий* (глубóк)

♦ *vt* намекáть (намекнýть *perf*) на +*acc*; **to ~
that** намекáть (намекнýть *perf*), что.
intimately ['ɪntɪmətlɪ] *adv* (*see adj*) инти́мно;
глубокó.
intimation [ɪntɪ'meɪʃən] *n* намёк.
intimidate [ɪn'tɪmɪdeɪt] *vt* запýгивать
(запугáть *perf*).
intimidation [ɪntɪmɪ'deɪʃən] *n* запýгивание.

KEYWORD
---

into ['ɪntu] *prep* **1** (*indicating motion or direction*)
в/на +*acc*; **into the house/garden** в дом/сад;
into the post office/factory на пóчту/фáбрику;
research into cancer исслéдования *ntpl* в
óбласти рáковых заболевáний; **he worked
late into the night** он рабóтал до пóздней
нóчи
2 (*indicating change of condition, result*): **she
has translated the letter into Russian** онá
переведá письмó на рýсский язы́к; **the vase
broke into pieces** вáза разби́лась вдрéбезги
or на кусóчки; **they got into trouble for it** им
попáло за э́то; **he lapsed into silence** он
погрузи́лся в молчáние; **to burst into tears**
расплáкаться* (*perf*); **to burst into flames**
загорéться (загорéться* *perf*).

intolerable [ɪn'tɔlərəbl] *adj* нетерпи́мый
(нетерпи́м), невыноси́мый (невыноси́м).
intolerance [ɪn'tɔlərns] *n* нетерпи́мость *f*.
intolerant [ɪn'tɔlərnt] *adj*: **~ (of)** нетерпи́мый
(нетерпи́м) (к +*dat*).
intonation [ɪntəu'neɪʃən] *n* интонáция.
intoxicated [ɪn'tɔksɪkeɪtɪd] *adj* (*drunk*)
опьянéвший; (*fig*) опьянённый (опьянён).
intoxication [ɪntɔksɪ'keɪʃən] *n* (*also fig*)
опьянéние.
intractable [ɪn'træktəbl] *adj* (*person, temper*)
неподáтливый (неподáтлив); (*problem*)
трудноразреши́мый (трудноразреши́м);
(*illness*) трудноизлечи́мый (трудно-
излечи́м).
intranet ['ɪntrənet] *n* интранéт.
intransigence [ɪn'trænsɪdʒəns] *n* упóрство.
intransigent [ɪn'trænsɪdʒənt] *adj* упóрный*
(упóрен).
intransitive [ɪn'trænsɪtɪv] *adj* (*LING*)
непереходный.
intrauterine device ['ɪntrə'ju:təraɪn-] *n*
внутримáточное противозачáточное
срéдство.
intravenous [ɪntrə'vi:nəs] *adj* внутривéнный.
in-tray ['ɪntreɪ] *n* (*in office*) корзи́на для
входя́щих бумáг.
intrepid [ɪn'trɛpɪd] *adj* неустраши́мый
(неустраши́м).
intricacy ['ɪntrɪkəsɪ] *n* (*of situation*) слóжность
f; (*of pattern, design*) замыслловáтость *f*.
intricate ['ɪntrɪkət] *adj* замыслловáтый
(замыслловáт).
intrigue [ɪn'tri:g] *n* интри́га ♦ *vt* интриговáть
(заинтриговáть *perf*).

intriguing [ɪnˈtriːgɪŋ] *adj (fascinating)*
интригу́ющий.
intrinsic [ɪnˈtrɪnsɪk] *adj* неотъе́млемый
(неотъе́млем).
introduce [ɪntrəˈdjuːs] *vt (new idea, measure
etc)* вводи́ть* (ввести́* *perf*); *(speaker, TV show
etc)* представля́ть (предста́вить* *perf*); **to ~
sb (to sb)** представля́ть (предста́вить* *perf*)
кого́-н (кому́-н); **to ~ sb to** *(pastime,
technique)* знако́мить* (познако́мить* *perf*)
кого́-н с +*instr*; **may I ~ ...?** разреши́те Вам
предста́вить ....
introduction [ɪntrəˈdʌkʃən] *n* введе́ние; *(to
person, new experience)* знако́мство; **a letter
of ~** рекоменда́тельное письмо́*.
introductory [ɪntrəˈdʌktərɪ] *adj (lesson)*
вступи́тельный; **~ remarks** вступи́тельные
замеча́ния; **an ~ offer** предвари́тельная
цена́*.
introspection [ɪntrəʊˈspɛkʃən] *n* самоана́лиз.
introspective [ɪntrəʊˈspɛktɪv] *adj*
самосозерца́тельный.
introvert [ˈɪntrəʊvəːt] *n* интрове́рт.
introverted [ˈɪntrəʊvəːtɪd] *adj* само-
углублённый (самоуглублён).
intrude [ɪnˈtruːd] *vi*: **to ~ (on)** вторга́ться
(вто́ргнуться* *perf*) (в/на +*acc*); **am I
intruding?** я не помеша́ю?
intruder [ɪnˈtruːdəʳ] *n*: **there is an ~ in our house**
к нам в дом кто-то вто́ргся.
intrusion [ɪnˈtruːʒən] *n* вторже́ние.
intrusive [ɪnˈtruːsɪv] *adj* назо́йливый
(назо́йлив).
intuition [ɪntjuːˈɪʃən] *n* интуи́ция.
intuitive [ɪnˈtjuːɪtɪv] *adj* интуити́вный*
(интуити́вен).
inundate [ˈɪnʌndeɪt] *vt*: **to ~ with** *(calls, letters
etc)* зава́ливать (завали́ть* *perf*) +*instr*;
Moscow is ~d with visitors Москва́
наводнена́ прие́зжими.
inure [ɪnˈjʊəʳ] *vt*: **to ~ o.s. to** приуча́ть
(приучи́ть* *perf*) себя́ к +*dat*.
invade [ɪnˈveɪd] *vt (MIL)* вторга́ться
(вто́ргнуться* *perf*) в +*acc*; *(fig: subj: people,
animals etc)* наводня́ть (наводни́ть* *perf*).
invader [ɪnˈveɪdəʳ] *n (MIL)* захва́тчик.
invalid [*n* ˈɪnvəlɪd, *adj* ɪnˈvælɪd] *n (MED)* инвали́д
♦ *adj (not valid)* недействи́тельный*
(недействи́телен).
invalidate [ɪnˈvælɪdeɪt] *vt (argument, result etc)*
дока́зывать (доказа́ть* *perf*) несостоя́тель-
ность *f* +*gen*; *(law, marriage, election)* де́лать
(сде́лать *perf*) недействи́тельным.
invaluable [ɪnˈvæljuəbl] *adj (person, thing)*
неоцени́мый (неоцени́м).
invariable [ɪnˈvɛərɪəbl] *adj (amount, result,
routine)* неизме́нный* (неизме́нен).
invariably [ɪnˈvɛərɪəblɪ] *adv* неизме́нно; **she is**

~ late она неизме́нно опа́здывает.
invasion [ɪnˈveɪʒən] *n (MIL)* вторже́ние; *(fig)*
посяга́тельство; **an ~ of privacy** вторже́ние в
ли́чную жизнь.
invective [ɪnˈvɛktɪv] *n* оскорбле́ние.
inveigle [ɪnˈviːgl] *vt*: **to ~ sb into sth** вовлека́ть
(вовле́чь* *perf*) кого́-н во что́-н.
invent [ɪnˈvɛnt] *vt (machine, game, phrase etc)*
изобрета́ть (изобрести́* *perf*); *(fabricate: lie,
excuse)* выду́мывать (вы́думать *perf*).
invention [ɪnˈvɛnʃən] *n* изобрете́ние; *(untrue
story)* вы́думка.
inventive [ɪnˈvɛntɪv] *adj (person)*
изобрета́тельный* (изобрета́телен).
inventiveness [ɪnˈvɛntɪvnɪs] *n*
изобрета́тельность *f*.
inventor [ɪnˈvɛntəʳ] *n (of machines, systems)*
изобрета́тель *m*.
inventory [ˈɪnvəntrɪ] *n (of house, ship etc)*
(инвентаризацио́нная) о́пись.
inventory control *n (COMM)* управле́ние
запа́сами.
inverse [ɪnˈvəːs] *adj (relationship)* обра́тный; **in
~ proportion to** в обра́тной пропорциона́ль-
ности к +*dat*.
invert [ɪnˈvəːt] *vt (turn upside down)*
перевора́чивать (переверну́ть *perf*).
invertebrate [ɪnˈvəːtɪbrət] *n* беспозвоно́чное *nt
adj*.
inverted commas [ɪnˈvəːtɪd-] *npl (BRIT: LING)*
кавы́чки *fpl*.
invest [ɪnˈvɛst] *vt (money)* инвести́ровать*
(impf/perf) в(о) +*acc*; *(fig: time, energy)*
вкла́дывать (вложи́ть* *perf*) ♦ *vi*: **~ in** *(COMM)*
помеща́ть (помести́ть* *perf*) капита́л в +*acc*;
(fig: sth useful) вкла́дывать (вложи́ть* *perf*)
де́ньги в +*acc*; **to ~ sb with sth** облека́ть
(обле́чь* *perf*) кого́-н чем-н.
investigate [ɪnˈvɛstɪgeɪt] *vt (accident, crime)*
рассле́довать* *(impf/perf)*; *(person)*
иссле́довать* *(impf/perf)*.
investigation [ɪnvɛstɪˈgeɪʃən] *n* рассле́дование.
investigative [ɪnˈvɛstɪgeɪtɪv] *adj*: **~ journalism**
журнали́стское рассле́дование.
investigator [ɪnˈvɛstɪgeɪtəʳ] *n (of events, people
etc)* иссле́дователь(ница) *m(f)*; **private ~**
ча́стный сле́дователь *m*.
investiture [ɪnˈvɛstɪtʃəʳ] *n (of chancellor)*
введе́ние в до́лжность *f*; *(of prince)*
пожа́лование зва́ния.
investment [ɪnˈvɛstmənt] *n (activity)*
инвести́рование; *(amount of money)*
инвести́ция, вклад.
investment grant *n (COMM)* инвестицио́нные
субси́дии *fpl*.
investment income *n (COMM)* дохо́д с
инвести́ций.
investment portfolio *n (COMM)* портфе́ль *m*

це́нных бума́г.

investment trust *n* (*COMM*) инвестицио́нный
трест.

investor [ɪn'vɛstə^r] *n* (*COMM*) инве́стор,
вкла́дчик.

inveterate [ɪn'vɛtərət] *adj* (*liar, cheat etc*)
неисправи́мый (неисправи́м); (*smoker*)
зая́длый; (*dislike etc*) да́вний*.

invidious [ɪn'vɪdɪəs] *adj* (*task, job*) неприя́тный*
(неприя́тен); (*comparison, decision*)
несправедли́вый (несправедли́в).

invigilator [ɪn'vɪdʒɪleɪtə^r] *n* (*in exam*)
экзамена́тор, следя́щий за тем, что́бы
студе́нты не спи́сывали во вре́мя экза́менов.

invigorating [ɪn'vɪgəreɪtɪŋ] *adj* (*air*) бодря́щий
(бодря́щ); (*experience*) воодушевля́ющий.

invincible [ɪn'vɪnsɪbl] *adj* (*army, team*)
непобеди́мый (непобеди́м); (*belief,
conviction*) неукроти́мый (неукроти́м).

inviolate [ɪn'vaɪələt] *adj* ненару́шенный
(ненару́шен).

invisible [ɪn'vɪzɪbl] *adj* неви́димый (неви́дим)
♦ *cpd* (*COMM: exports, earnings, assets*)
неви́димый.

invisible mending *n* худо́жественная
што́пка.

invitation [ɪnvɪ'teɪʃən] *n* приглаше́ние; **by ~
only** то́лько по приглаше́нию; **at sb's ~** по
приглаше́нию кого́-н.

invite [ɪn'vaɪt] *vt* (*to party, meal, meeting etc*)
приглаша́ть (пригласи́ть* *perf*); (*discussion,
criticism*) побужда́ть (побуди́ть* *perf*); **to ~ sb
to do** предлага́ть (предложи́ть* *perf*) кому́-н
+*infin*; **to ~ sb to dinner** приглаша́ть
(пригласи́ть* *perf*) кого́-н на обе́д
▶ **invite out** *vt* приглаша́ть (пригласи́ть* *perf*).

inviting [ɪn'vaɪtɪŋ] *adj* (*attractive, desirable*)
соблазни́тельный* (соблазни́телен).

invoice ['ɪnvɔɪs] *n* (*COMM*) счёт, факту́ра ♦ *vt*
выпи́сывать (вы́писать* *perf*) счёт *or*
факту́ру +*dat*; **to ~ sb for goods** выпи́сывать
(вы́писать* *perf*) счёт *or* факту́ру кому́-н за
това́ры.

invoke [ɪn'vəuk] *vt* (*law, principle*) обраща́ться
(обрати́ться* *perf*) к +*dat*; (*feelings, memories
etc*) взыва́ть (воззва́ть* *perf*) к +*dat*.

involuntary [ɪn'vɔləntrɪ] *adj* (*action, reflex etc*)
непроизво́льный* (непроизво́лен).

involve [ɪn'vɔlv] *vt* (*person, thing: include, use*)
вовлека́ть (вовле́чь* *perf*); (: *concern, affect*)
включа́ть (включи́ть* *perf*); **to ~ sb (in sth)**
вовлека́ть (вовле́чь* *perf*) кого́-н (во
что-н).

involved [ɪn'vɔlvd] *adj* (*complicated*)
запу́танный* (запу́тан); (*thing required: in
task, situation etc*) включённый (включён); **to
be ~ in** (*in activity etc*) быть* (*impf*)
вовлечённым(-ой) в(о) +*acc*; **to feel ~** быть*
(*impf*) вовлечённым; **to become ~ with sb**
(*socially*) свя́зываться (связа́ться *perf*) с
кем-н; (*emotionally*) увлека́ться (увле́чься*

perf) кем-н.

involvement [ɪn'vɔlvmənt] *n* (*participation*)
прича́стность *f*; (*concern, enthusiasm*)
вовлечённость *f*; (*relationship*) связь *f*.

invulnerable [ɪn'vʌlnərəbl] *adj* (*person, ship,
building etc*) неуязви́мый (неуязви́м).

inward ['ɪnwəd] *adj* (*thought, feeling*)
вну́тренний*; (*movement*) напра́вленный
внутрь ♦ *adv* = **inwards**.

inwardly ['ɪnwədlɪ] *adv* внутри́.

inwards ['ɪnwədz] *adv* (*move, face*) внутрь.

I/O *abbr* (*COMPUT*. = *input/output*) ввод-вы́вод.

IOC *n abbr* = *International Olympic Committee*.

iodine ['aɪəudiːn] *n* йод.

IOM *abbr* (*BRIT: POST*) = *Isle of Man*.

ion ['aɪən] *n* (*ELEC*) ио́н.

Ionian Sea [aɪ'əunɪən-] *n*: **the ~ ~** Иони́ческое
мо́ре.

ioniser ['aɪənaɪzə^r] *n* иониэи́рующая
устано́вка*.

iota [aɪ'əutə] *n* йо́та.

IOU *n abbr* (= *I owe you*) просте́йший долгово́й
докуме́нт.

IOW *abbr* (*BRIT: POST*) = *Isle of Wight*.

IPA *n abbr* (= *International Phonetic Alphabet*)
Междунаро́дная систе́ма транскри́пции.

IQ *n abbr* (= *intelligence quotient*) коэффицие́нт
у́мственного разви́тия.

IRA *n abbr* (= *Irish Republican Army*) ИРА=
Ирла́ндская респу́бликанская а́рмия; (*US*) =
individual retirement account.

Iran [ɪ'rɑːn] *n* Ира́н.

Iranian [ɪ'reɪnɪən] *adj* ира́нский* ♦ *n*
ира́нец(-нка).

Iraq [ɪ'rɑːk] *n* Ира́к.

Iraqi [ɪ'rɑːkɪ] *adj* ира́кский* ♦ *n* жи́тель(ница)
m(f) Ира́ка.

irascible [ɪ'ræsɪbl] *adj* (*person*) вспы́льчивый
(вспы́льчив).

irate [aɪ'reɪt] *adj* (*person, letter etc*)
разгне́ванный* (разгне́ван).

Ireland ['aɪələnd] *n* Ирла́ндия; **the Republic of
~** Ирла́ндская Респу́блика.

iris ['aɪrɪs] (*pl* **~es**) *n* (*ANAT*) ра́дужная
оболо́чка* (гла́за); (*BOT*) и́рис.

Irish ['aɪrɪʃ] *adj* ирла́ндский*; **the ~** ирла́ндцы.

Irishman ['aɪrɪʃmən] *irreg n* ирла́ндец*.

Irish Sea *n*: **the ~ ~** Ирла́ндское мо́ре.

Irishwoman ['aɪrɪʃwumən] *irreg n* ирла́ндка.

irk [əːk] *vt* (*person*) раздража́ть (*impf*).

irksome ['əːksəm] *adj* надое́дливый
(надое́длив).

IRN *n abbr* = *Independent Radio News*.

IRO *n abbr* (*US*) = *International Refugee
Organization*.

iron ['aɪən] *n* (*metal*) желе́зо *no pl*; (*for clothes*)
утю́г ♦ *cpd* желе́зный ♦ *vt* (*clothes*) гла́дить*
(погла́дить* *perf*).

▶ **iron out** *vt* (*fig: problems*) ула́живать
(ула́дить* *perf*).

Iron Curtain *n* (*POL: formerly*): **the ~ ~**

желе́зный за́навес.

iron foundry *n* чугунолите́йный цех.

ironic(al) [aɪ'rɒnɪk(l)] *adj* ирони́ческий.

ironically [aɪ'rɒnɪklɪ] *adv* (*say, enquire etc*) ирони́чно; ~, **the intelligence chief was the last to find out** иро́ния в том, что шеф разве́дки узна́л после́дним.

ironing ['aɪənɪŋ] *n* (*activity*) гла́женье; (*clothes*) бельё для гла́женья.

ironing board *n* гла́дильная доска́.

iron lung *n* (*MED*) аппара́т (для) иску́сственного дыха́ния.

ironmonger ['aɪənmʌŋgəʳ] *n* (*BRIT*) торго́вец скобяны́ми изде́лиями.

ironmonger's (shop) ['aɪənmʌŋgəz-] *n* магази́н скобяны́х изде́лий.

iron ore *n* желе́зная руда́.

irons ['aɪəns] *npl* (*chains*) кандалы́ *pl*; **to clap sb in** ~ зако́вывать (закова́ть *perf*) кого́-н в кандалы́.

ironworks ['aɪənwɔːks] *n* чугунолите́йный заво́д.

irony ['aɪrənɪ] *n* иро́ния.

irrational [ɪ'ræʃənl] *adj* (*feelings, behaviour*) нерациона́льный* (нерациона́лен), неразу́мный* (неразу́мен).

irreconcilable [ɪrɛkən'saɪləbl] *adj* (*ideas, conflict*) непримири́мый (непримири́м).

irredeemable [ɪrɪ'diːməbl] *adj* (*COMM*) не подлежа́щий погаше́нию *or* вы́купу; (*fault, character*) неисправи́мый (неисправи́м).

irrefutable [ɪrɪ'fjuːtəbl] *adj* (*fact, argument*) неопровержи́мый (неопровержи́м).

irregular [ɪ'rɛgjuləʳ] *adj* (*surface*) неро́вный* (неро́вен); (*pattern*) непра́вильной фо́рмы; (*action, event*) нерегуля́рный* (нерегуля́рен); (*behaviour*) распу́щенный; (*LING: verb etc*) непра́вильный.

irregularity [ɪrɛgju'lærɪtɪ] *n* (*see adj*) неро́вность *f*; непра́вильность *f*; нерегуля́рность *f*; распу́щенность *f*.

irrelevance [ɪ'rɛləvəns] *n* неуме́стность *f*.

irrelevant [ɪ'rɛləvənt] *adj* неуме́стный.

irreligious [ɪrɪ'lɪdʒəs] *adj* неве́рующий*.

irreparable [ɪ'rɛprəbl] *adj* (*harm, damage etc*) непоправи́мый (непоправи́м).

irreplaceable [ɪrɪ'pleɪsəbl] *adj* (*antique, wedding ring etc*) незамени́мый (незамени́м).

irrepressible [ɪrɪ'prɛsəbl] *adj* (*person, good humour etc*) неудержи́мый (неудержи́м).

irreproachable [ɪrɪ'prəutʃəbl] *adj* (*behaviour, character*) безупре́чный* (безупре́чен).

irresistible [ɪrɪ'zɪstɪbl] *adj* (*urge, desire*) непреодоли́мый (непреодоли́м); (*person, thing*) неотрази́мый (неотрази́м).

irresolute [ɪ'rɛzəluːt] *adj* (*person*) нереши́тельный* (нереши́телен).

irrespective [ɪrɪ'spɛktɪv] *prep*: ~ **of** незави́симо от +*gen*.

irresponsible [ɪrɪ'spɒnsɪbl] *adj* (*person, action*) безотве́тственный* (безотве́тствен).

irretrievable [ɪrɪ'triːvəbl] *adj* (*object*) безвозвра́тный* (безвозвра́тен); (*loss, damage*) непоправи́мый (непоправи́м).

irreverent [ɪ'rɛvərnt] *adj* (*person, comment etc*) непочти́тельный* (непочти́телен).

irrevocable [ɪ'rɛvəkəbl] *adj* (*action, decision*) бесповоро́тный* (бесповоро́тен).

irrigate ['ɪrɪgeɪt] *vt* ороша́ть (ороси́ть* *perf*).

irrigation [ɪrɪ'geɪʃən] *n* (*AGR*) ороше́ние, иррига́ция.

irritable ['ɪrɪtəbl] *adj* раздражи́тельный* (раздражи́телен).

irritant ['ɪrɪtənt] *n* раздражи́тель *m*.

irritate ['ɪrɪteɪt] *vt* (*also MED*) раздража́ть (раздражи́ть *perf*).

irritating ['ɪrɪteɪtɪŋ] *adj* раздража́ющий.

irritation [ɪrɪ'teɪʃən] *n* (*also MED*) раздраже́ние; (*annoying thing*) раздража́ющий фа́ктор.

IRS *n abbr* (*US*) = **Internal Revenue Service**.

is [ɪz] *vb see* **be**.

ISA *n abbr* (= *Individual Savings Account*) Индивидуа́льный сберега́тельный счёт.

ISBN *n abbr* (= *International Standard Book Number*) ISBN.

ISDN *abbr* (= *integrated services digital network*) Цифрова́я сеть с ко́мплексными услу́гами.

Islam ['ɪzlɑːm] *n* (*REL*) исла́м; (*Islamic countries*) мусульма́нские стра́ны *fpl*.

Islamic [ɪz'læmɪk] *adj* мусульма́нский*.

island ['aɪlənd] *n* о́стров*; (*also:* **traffic** ~) острово́к безопа́сности.

islander ['aɪləndəʳ] *n* островитя́нин*(-нка).

isle [aɪl] *n* о́стров*.

isn't ['ɪznt] = **is not**.

isobar ['aɪsəubɑːʳ] *n* изоба́ра.

isolate ['aɪsəleɪt] *vt* изоли́ровать* (*impf/perf*); (*substance*) выделя́ть (вы́делить *perf*).

isolated ['aɪsəleɪtɪd] *adj* (*place, person*) изоли́рованный* (изоли́рован); (*incident*) отде́льный.

isolation [aɪsə'leɪʃən] *n* изоля́ция.

isolationism [aɪsə'leɪʃənɪzəm] *n* изоляциони́зм.

isotope ['aɪsəutəup] *n* (*PHYS*) изото́п.

ISP *abbr* (= *Internet service provider*) компа́ния-прова́йдер, предоставля́ющая до́ступ к Сеть.

Israel ['ɪzreɪl] *n* Изра́иль *m*.

Israeli [ɪz'reɪlɪ] *adj* изра́ильский* ♦ *n* (*person*) израильтя́нин*(-нка).

issue ['ɪʃuː] *n* (*problem, subject*) вопро́с; (*most important part*) суть *f*; (*of book, stamps etc*) вы́пуск; (*LAW, old: offspring*) пото́мок* ♦ *vt* (*statement, newspaper*) издава́ть* (изда́ть* *perf*); (*rations, equipment, documents*) выдава́ть* (вы́дать* *perf*) ♦ *vi*: **to** ~ **from**

---

* marks translations which have irregular inflections. The Russian-English side of the dictionary gives inflectional information.

(*liquid, gas*) вытека́ть (вы́течь* *perf*) из +*gen*;
(*sound, smell*) исходи́ть* (*impf*) из/от +*gen*; **to
be at** ~ быть* (*impf*) предме́том обсужде́ния;
to avoid the ~ обходи́ть* (обойти́* *perf*) суть
де́ла; **to confuse** *or* **obscure the** ~ затемня́ть
(затемни́ть *perf*) суть вопро́са; **to** ~ **sth to sb**
выдава́ть* (вы́дать* *perf*) что-н кому́-н; **to** ~
sb with sth снабжа́ть (снабди́ть* *perf*) кого́-н
чем-н; **to take** ~ **with sb** (**over**) начина́ть
(нача́ть* *perf*) спо́рить с кем-н (о +*prp*); **to
make an** ~ **of sth** де́лать (сде́лать *perf*)
исто́рию из чего́-н.

issued capital ['ıʃuːd-] *n* (*COMM*) вы́пущенный
акционе́рный капита́л.

Istanbul [ɪstæn'buːl] *n* Стамбу́л.

isthmus ['ɪsməs] *n* переше́ек.

IT *n abbr* = **information technology**.

KEYWORD
---

it [ɪt] *pron* **1** (*specific subject*) он (*f* она́, *nt* оно́);
(*direct object*) его́ (*f* её); (*indirect object*) ему́ (*f*
ей); (*after prep*: +*gen*) его́ (*f* её); (: +*dat*) ему́ (*f*
ей); (: +*instr*) им (*f* ей); (: +*prp*) нём (*f* ней);
where is your car? – **it's in the garage** где
Ва́ша маши́на? – она́ в гараже́; **I like this hat,
whose is it?** мне нра́вится э́та шля́па, чья
она́?; **have you got the dictionary with you?** –
no, **I gave it to Mary** у Вас с собо́й словарь? –
нет, я дал его́ Мэ́ри; **this pen is fine, I wrote
with it yesterday** э́та ру́чка рабо́тает, я писа́л
е́ю вчера́

2 э́то; (: *indirect object*) э́тому; **what kind of
car is it?** – **it's a Lada** кака́я э́то маши́на? – э́то
Ла́да; **who is it?** – **it's me** кто э́то? – э́то я

3 (*after prep*: +*gen*) э́того; (: +*dat*) э́тому;
(: +*instr*) э́тим; (: +*prp*) э́том; **I spoke to him
about it** я говори́л с ним об э́том; **that's just
it!** вот и́менно!; **why is it that** ... почему́ же
тогда́ ...; **what is it?** (*what's wrong*) что
тако́е?; **that's it for today** на сего́дня всё

4 (*impersonal*): **it's raining** идёт дождь; **it's
cold today** сего́дня хо́лодно; **it's interesting
that** ... интере́сно, что ...; **it's 6 o'clock** сейча́с
6 часо́в; **it's the 10th of August** сего́дня 10-ое
а́вгуста.

ITA *n abbr* (*BRIT*: = *initial teaching alphabet*)

алфави́т, испо́льзуемый при обуче́нии
чте́нию.

Italian [ı'tæljən] *adj* италья́нский* ♦ *n* (*person*)
италья́нец(-нка); (*LING*) италья́нский* язы́к*;
the ~**s** италья́нцы.

italics [ı'tælıks] *npl* (*TYP*) курси́в *msg*.

Italy ['ıtəlı] *n* Ита́лия.

itch [ıtʃ] *n* (*irritation*) зуд ♦ *vi* (*part of body*)
чеса́ться* (*impf*); **I am** ~**ing all over** у меня́ всё
че́шется; **he was** ~**ing to know our secret** ему́
не терпе́лось узна́ть наш секре́т.

itchy ['ıtʃı] *adj* (*skin*) зудя́щий; **I feel all** ~ у
меня́ всё че́шется; **my back is** ~ у меня́
че́шется спина́.

it'd ['ıtd] = **it had**, **it would**.

item ['aɪtəm] *n* (*one thing: of list, collection*)
предме́т; (*on agenda*) пункт; (*also*: **news** ~)
сообще́ние; ~**s of clothing** предме́ты
оде́жды.

itemize ['aɪtəmaɪz] *vt* (*list*) составля́ть
(соста́вить* *perf*) спи́сок +*gen*.

itemized bill ['aɪtəmaɪzd-] *n* счёт с указа́нием
сто́имости ка́ждой ве́щи и́ли ка́ждого ви́да
услу́г.

itinerant [ı'tınərənt] *adj* (*labourer, salesman,
priest etc*) стра́нствующий.

itinerary [aɪ'tınərərɪ] *n* маршру́т.

it'll ['ıtl] = **it shall**, **it will**.

ITN *n abbr* (*BRIT*: *TV*) = **Independent Television
News**.

its [ıts] *adj* его́/её; свой/своя́/своё; *see also* **my** ♦
pron его́/её; свой/своя́/своё; *see also* **mine**[1].

it's [ıts] = **it has**, **it is**.

itself [ɪt'self] *pron* (*reflexive*) себя́*; (*emphatic*)
он сам/она́ сама́/оно́ само́.

ITV *n abbr* (*BRIT*: *TV*) = **Independent Television**.

IUD *n abbr* (= *intrauterine device*) внутри-
ма́точное противозача́точное сре́дство.

I've [aɪv] = **I have**.

ivory ['aɪvərɪ] *n* (*substance*) слоно́вая кость* *f*;
(*colour*) цвет слоно́вой ко́сти.

Ivory Coast *n* Бе́рег Слоно́вой Ко́сти.

ivory tower *n* (*fig*) ба́шня из слоно́вой ко́сти.

ivy ['aɪvɪ] *n* (*BOT*) плющ*.

Ivy League *n* (*US*: *SCOL*) гру́ппа старе́йших
университе́тов США.

~ J, j ~

J, j [dʒeɪ] n (letter) 10-ая буква английского алфавита.
JA n abbr = judge advocate.
J/A abbr = joint account.
jab [dʒæb] vt (with finger, stick etc) тыкать* (ткнуть* perf) ♦ n (BRIT: inf: MED) укол ♦ vi: to ~ at стучать (impf) по +dat; to ~ sth into sth втыкать* (воткнуть* perf) что-н в что-н.
jack [dʒæk] n (AUT) домкрат; (SPORT) малый шар, служащий мишенью для игроков в шары; (CARDS) валет
▶ **jack in** vt (inf) завязывать (завязать* perf) с +instr
▶ **jack up** vt (AUT) поднимать (поднять* perf) домкратом.
jackal ['dʒækl] n шакал.
jackass ['dʒækæs] n (also fig) осёл*.
jackdaw ['dʒækdɔ:] n галка*.
jacket ['dʒækɪt] n (of suit) пиджак*; (casual) куртка*; (of book) суперобложка; **potatoes in their ~s, jacket potatoes** картошка в мундире.
jack-in-the-box ['dʒækɪnðəbɔks] n чёртик в табакерке.
jackknife ['dʒæknaɪf] n складной нож* ♦ vi: **the lorry ~d** грузовик заносило.
jack of all trades n: **he's a ~ ~ ~ ~** он мастер на все руки.
jack plug n штеккер.
jackpot ['dʒækpɔt] n куш; **to hit the ~** (fig) срывать (сорвать* perf) куш.
jacuzzi [dʒə'ku:zɪ] n „джакузи" m ind (ванна, в которой под напором циркулирует вода).
jade [dʒeɪd] n нефрит.
jaded ['dʒeɪdɪd] adj утомлённый (утомлён) и равнодушный (равнодушен).
JAG n abbr (= Judge Advocate General) главный правительственный советник по военно-юридическим вопросам.
jagged ['dʒægɪd] adj зубчатый.
jaguar ['dʒægjuə] n ягуар.
jail [dʒeɪl] n тюрьма* ♦ vt заключать (заключить* perf) в тюрьму.
jailbird ['dʒeɪlbə:d] n (inf) уголовник.
jailbreak ['dʒeɪlbreɪk] n побег из тюрьмы.
jalopy [dʒə'lɔpɪ] n (inf) драндулет.

jam [dʒæm] n (preserve) джем; (conserve) варенье; (also: traffic ~) пробка* ♦ vt (passage) забивать (забить* perf); (mechanism) заклинивать (заклинить perf); (RADIO) глушить (заглушить* perf) ♦ vi (drawer) застревать (застрять* perf); (mechanism): **the engine/rifle has ~med** заело or заклинило мотор/ружьё; **I'm in a real ~** (inf: difficulty) я (здорово) влип; **to get sb out of a ~** (inf) помогать (помочь perf) кому-н выбраться из переделки; **to ~ sth into sth** запихивать (запихнуть* perf) что-н во что-н; **the telephone lines are ~med** все линии (связи) перегружены.
Jamaica [dʒə'meɪkə] n Ямайка.
Jamaican [dʒə'meɪkən] adj ямайский* ♦ n житель(ница) m(f) Ямайки.
jamb ['dʒæm] n косяк*.
jamboree [dʒæmbə'ri:] n гулянье*.
jam-packed [dʒæm'pækt] adj: ~ **(with)** битком набитый (набит) (+instr).
jam session n джем-сейшен.
Jan. abbr = January.
jangle ['dʒæŋgl] vi (keys, bracelets etc) бренчать (impf).
janitor ['dʒænɪtə] n (caretaker) вахтёр(ша).
January ['dʒænjuəri] n январь* m; see also **July**.
Japan [dʒə'pæn] n Япония.
Japanese [dʒæpə'ni:z] adj японский* ♦ n inv (person) японец*(-нка*); (LING) японский* язык*.
jar [dʒɑ:] n банка* ♦ vi (sound) резать* (impf) слух; (colours) резать* (impf) глаза ♦ vt (fig) потрясать (потрясти* perf).
jargon ['dʒɑ:gən] n жаргон.
jarring ['dʒɑ:rɪŋ] adj (sound) режущий ухо; (colour) режущий глаз.
Jas. abbr = James.
jasmine ['dʒæzmɪn] n жасмин.
jaundice ['dʒɔ:ndɪs] n желтуха.
jaundiced ['dʒɔ:ndɪst] adj: **he has a very ~ view of politics** он смотрит на политику весьма пессимистически.
jaunt [dʒɔ:nt] n вылазка*.
jaunty ['dʒɔ:ntɪ] adj (tone, step) бойкий*.
Java ['dʒɑ:və] n Ява.

---

* marks translations which have irregular inflections. The Russian-English side of the dictionary gives inflectional information.

javelin ['dʒævlɪn] *n* копьё*.

jaw [dʒɔː] *n* чéлюсть* *f*.

jawbone ['dʒɔːbəun] *n* челюстнáя кость* *f*.

jay [dʒeɪ] *n* сóйка*.

jaywalker ['dʒeɪwɔːkə*] *n* недисциплинúрованный пешехóд.

jazz [dʒæz] *n* джаз
▶ **jazz up** (*inf*) ◆ *vt* (*party, image etc*) оживля́ть (оживи́ть* *perf*); (*food*) придава́ть* (прида́ть* *perf*) пика́нтность +*dat*.

jazz band *n* джáзовый оркéстр, джаз-банд.

JCB® *n* (колёсный) экскавáтор.

JCS *n abbr* (*US*: = *Joint Chiefs of Staff*) Комитéт начáльников штабóв.

JD *n abbr* (*US*: = *Doctor of Laws*) дóктор правовéдения; (= *Justice Department*) Министéрство юстúции.

jealous ['dʒɛləs] *adj* ревнúвый (ревнúв); **to be ~ of** (*possessive*) ревновáть (*impf*) к +*dat*; (*envious*) завúдовать (*impf*) +*dat*.

jealously ['dʒɛləslɪ] *adv* (*enviously*) ревнúво; (*watchfully*) рéвностно.

jealousy ['dʒɛləsɪ] *n* (*resentment*) рéвность *f*; (*envy*) зáвисть *f*.

jeans [dʒiːnz] *npl* джúнсы *pl*.

Jeep® [dʒiːp] *n* джип.

jeer [dʒɪə*] *vi*: **to ~** (**at**) (*mock, scoff*) насмехáться (*impf*) (над +*instr*), высмéивать (вы́смеять *perf*).

jeering ['dʒɪərɪŋ] *adj* насмéшливый ◆ *n* насмéшки* *fpl*.

jeers ['dʒɪəz] *npl* улюлю́канье *ntsg*.

jelly ['dʒɛlɪ] *n* желé *nt ind*; (*US*) джем.

jellyfish ['dʒɛlɪfɪʃ] *n* медýза.

jeopardize ['dʒɛpədaɪz] *vt* подвергáть (подвéргнуть* *perf*) опáсности, стáвить* (постáвить* *perf*) под угрóзу.

jeopardy ['dʒɛpədɪ] *n*: **to be in ~** бы́ть* (*impf*) в опáсности.

jerk [dʒɜːk] *n* (*jolt*) толчóк*, рывóк*; (*inf: idiot*) болвáн ◆ *vt* дёргать (дёрнуть *perf*), рванýть (*perf*) ◆ *vi* дёргаться (дёрнуться *perf*); **the car ~ed to a halt** машúна рéзко затормозúла.

jerkin ['dʒɜːkɪn] *n* безрукáвка.

jerky ['dʒɜːkɪ] *adj* сýдорожный (сýдорожен).

jerry-built ['dʒɛrɪbɪlt] *adj* пострóенный (пострóен) кóе-кáк *or* на скóрую рýку.

jerry can ['dʒɛrɪ-] *n* канúстра.

Jersey ['dʒɜːzɪ] *n* Джéрси *nt ind*.

jersey ['dʒɜːzɪ] *n* (*pullover*) свúтер; (*fabric*) джерсú *nt ind*.

Jerusalem [dʒə'ruːsləm] *n* Иерусалúм.

jest [dʒɛst] *n* шýтка.

jester ['dʒɛstə*] *n* (*HISTORY*) шут*.

Jesus ['dʒiːzəs] *n* (*REL*) Иисýс; **~ Christ** Иисýс Христóс.

jet [dʒɛt] *n* (*of gas, liquid*) струя́*; (*AVIAT*) реактúвный самолёт; (*MINERALOGY*) гагáт.

jet-black ['dʒɛt'blæk] *adj* (*hair*) чёрный как смоль; (*eyes*) агáтовый.

jet engine *n* реактúвный двúгатель *m*.

jet lag *n* нарушéние сýточного режúма органúзма пóсле длúтельного полёта.

jet-propelled ['dʒɛt'prəpeld] *adj* реактúвный.

jetsam ['dʒɛtsəm] *n* плавнúк.

jet-setter ['dʒɛtsɛtə*] *n* человéк, разъезжáющий по свéту.

jettison ['dʒɛtɪsn] *vt* выбрáсывать (вы́бросить* *perf*) за борт.

jetty ['dʒɛtɪ] *n* причáл.

Jew [dʒuː] *n* еврéй(ка*).

jewel ['dʒuːəl] *n* (*also fig*) драгоцéнный кáмень* *m*; (*in watch*) кáмень.

jeweller ['dʒuːələ*] (*US* **jeweler**) *n* ювелúр.

jeweller's (shop) *n* ювелúрный магазúн.

jewellery ['dʒuːəlrɪ] (*US* **jewelry**) *n* драгоцéнности *fpl*.

Jewess ['dʒuːɪs] *n* еврéйка, жидóвка (*пренебр*).

Jewish ['dʒuːɪʃ] *adj* еврéйский*.

JFK *n abbr* (*US*) = *John Fitzgerald Kennedy International Airport*.

jib [dʒɪb] *n* (*NAUT*) клúвер*; (*of crane*) стрелá* ◆ *vi* (*horse*) упирáться (уперéться* *perf*), артáчиться (*impf*); **to ~ at doing** наотрéз отказáться (*perf*) +*infin*.

jibe [dʒaɪb] *n* = **gibe**.

jiffy ['dʒɪfɪ] *n* (*inf*): **in a ~** мúгом.

jig [dʒɪg] *n* джúга.

jigsaw ['dʒɪgsɔː] *n* (*also*: **~ puzzle**) головолóмка (*в вúде картúны, кусóчки котóрой нýжно сложúть вмéсте*); (*tool*) ажýрная пилá*.

jilt [dʒɪlt] *vt* (*person*) бросáть (брóсить* *perf*).

jingle ['dʒɪŋgl] *n* (*for advert*) корóткая незамыславáтая мелóдия в реклáме ◆ *vi* звенéть (*impf*).

jingoism ['dʒɪŋgəuɪzəm] *n* ура-патриотúзм.

jinx [dʒɪŋks] *n* (*inf*): **he is a ~** у негó дурнóй глаз.

jitters ['dʒɪtəz] *npl* (*inf*): **she's got the ~** её трясёт.

jittery ['dʒɪtərɪ] *adj* (*inf*) нéрвный* (нéрвен).

jiujitsu [dʒuː'dʒɪtsuː] *n* джúу-джúтсу *nt ind*.

job [dʒɔb] *n* (*employment*) рабóта; (*task*) дéло*; (*inf: difficulty*): **I had a ~ getting here!** я с трудóм добрáлся сюдá!; **it's not my ~** это не моё дéло; **a part-time/full-time ~** рабóта на почасовóй/пóлной стáвке; **he's only doing his ~** он всегó-нáвсего выполня́ет свои обя́занности; **it's a good ~ that** ... хорошó ещё, что ...; **just the ~!** сáмое то!

jobber ['dʒɔbə*] *n* (*BRIT*) джóббер.

jobbing ['dʒɔbɪŋ] *adj* (*BRIT*): **~ workman** шабáшник.

Jobcentre ['dʒɔbsɛntə*] *n* (*BRIT*) бюрó *nt ind* по трудоустрóйству.

job creation scheme *n* прогрáмма зáнятости.

job description *n* описáние служéбных обя́занностей.

jobless ['dʒɔblɪs] *adj* безрабóтный*; **the ~** *npl* безрабóтные *pl adj*.

job lot *n* па́ртия дешёвых това́ров, продаю́щихся о́птом.
job satisfaction *n* удовлетворённость *f* рабо́той.
job security *n* гара́нтия рабо́ты.
job sharing *n* *ситуа́ция, когда́ два челове́ка де́лят рабо́чее ме́сто*.
job specification *n* пе́речень *m* служе́бных обя́занностей.
jock [dʒɔk] *n* (*US: inf*) спортсме́н.
jockey ['dʒɔkɪ] *n* жоке́й ♦ *vi*: **to ~ for position** сопе́рничать (*impf*).
jockey box *n* (*US: AUT*) перча́точный я́щик, барда́чок (*разг*).
jocular ['dʒɔkjulə⁷] *adj* (*person*) весёлый* (ве́сел); (*remark*) шутли́вый (шутли́в).
jog [dʒɔg] *vt* толка́ть (толкну́ть *perf*) ♦ *vi* бе́гать (*impf*) трусцо́й; **to ~ sb's memory** подстёгивать (подстегну́ть *perf*) чью-н па́мять
▶ **jog along** *vi* ме́дленно продвига́ться (*impf*).
jogger ['dʒɔgə⁷] *n* бегу́н* (*трусцо́й*).
jogging ['dʒɔgɪŋ] *n* бег трусцо́й.
Johannesburg [dʒəu'hænɪsbə:g] *n* Йоха́ннесбург.
john [dʒɔn] *n* (*inf. US*) туале́т.
join [dʒɔɪn] *vt* (*queue*) встава́ть (встать* *perf*) в +*acc*; (*organization*) вступа́ть (вступи́ть* *perf*) в +*acc*; (*put together: things, places*) соединя́ть (соедини́ть *perf*); (*meet: group of people*) присоединя́ться (присоедини́ться *perf*) к +*dat* ♦ *vi* (*rivers*) слива́ться (сли́ться* *perf*); (*roads*) сходи́ться (сойти́сь* *perf*) ♦ *n* сочлене́ние; **to ~ forces (with)** (*fig*) объединя́ть (объедини́ть *perf*) уси́лия (с +*instr*); **will you ~ us for dinner?** не хоти́те с на́ми поу́жинать?; **I'll ~ you later** я присоединю́сь к Вам по́зже
▶ **join in** *vi* присоединя́ться (присоедини́ться *perf*) ♦ *vt fus* (*work, discussion etc*) принима́ть (приня́ть* *perf*) уча́стие в +*prp*
▶ **join up** *vi* (*meet*) соединя́ться (соедини́ться *perf*); (*MIL*) поступа́ть (поступи́ть* *perf*) на вое́нную слу́жбу.
joiner ['dʒɔɪnə⁷] *n* (*BRIT*) столя́р*.
joinery ['dʒɔɪnərɪ] *n* (*BRIT*) столя́рное ремесло́*.
joint [dʒɔɪnt] *n* (*TECH*) соедине́ние, стык; (*ANAT*) суста́в; (*BRIT: CULIN*) кусо́к* (*мя́са*); (*inf: place*) прито́н; (: *of cannabis*) скру́тка с марихуа́ной ♦ *adj* совме́стный.
joint account *n* совме́стный счёт (*в ба́нке*).
jointly ['dʒɔɪntlɪ] *adv* совме́стно.
joint owners *npl* совладе́льцы *mpl*.
joint ownership *n* совме́стное владе́ние.
joint-stock bank ['dʒɔɪntstɔk-] *n* акционе́рный банк.
joint-stock company *n* акционе́рная компа́ния.

joint venture *n* совме́стное предприя́тие.
joist [dʒɔɪst] *n* ба́лка*.
joke [dʒəuk] *n* (*gag*) шу́тка*, анекдо́т; (*also:* **practical ~**) ро́зыгрыш ♦ *vi* шути́ть* (пошути́ть* *perf*); **to play a ~ on** шути́ть* (пошути́ть* *perf*) над +*instr*, сыгра́ть (*perf*) шу́тку с +*instr*.
joker ['dʒəukə⁷] *n* (*person*) шу́тник; (*CARDS*) джо́кер.
joking ['dʒəukɪŋ] *adj* (*remark*) шу́точный.
jokingly ['dʒəukɪŋlɪ] *adv* в шу́тку.
jollity ['dʒɔlɪtɪ] *n* жизнера́достность *f*.
jolly ['dʒɔlɪ] *adj* (*merry*) весёлый* (ве́сел) ♦ *adv* (*BRIT: inf*) о́чень ♦ *vt* (*BRIT*): **to ~ sb along** ободря́ть (*impf*) кого́-н; **~ good!** о́чень хорошо́!, здо́рово!
jolt [dʒəult] *n* (*jerk*) толчо́к*; (*shock*) потрясе́ние ♦ *vt* (*physically*) тряхну́ть *or* встря́хивать (встряхну́ть *perf*); (*emotionally*) потряса́ть (потрясти́* *perf*).
Jordan [dʒɔ:dən] *n* (*country*) Иорда́ния; (*river*) Иорда́н.
Jordanian [dʒɔ:'deɪnɪən] *adj* иорда́нский* ♦ *n* иорда́нец*(-нка).
joss stick [dʒɔs-] *n* аромати́ческая па́лочка*.
jostle ['dʒɔsl] *vt* (*subj: passers-by etc*) толка́ть (толкну́ть *perf*), раста́лкивать (растолка́ть *perf*) ♦ *vi* толка́ться (*impf*).
jot [dʒɔt] *n*: **not one ~** ни ка́пли, ниско́лько
▶ **jot down** *vt* помеча́ть (поме́тить* *perf*).
jotter ['dʒɔtə⁷] *n* (*BRIT*) блокно́т.
journal [dʒə:nl] *n* (*periodical*) журна́л; (*diary*) дневни́к*.
journalese [dʒə:nə'li:z] *n* (*pej*) газе́тный штамп.
journalism ['dʒə:nəlɪzəm] *n* журнали́стика.
journalist ['dʒə:nəlɪst] *n* журнали́ст(ка)*.
journey ['dʒə:nɪ] *n* (*trip, route*) пое́здка*; (*distance covered*) путь* *m*, доро́га ♦ *vi* путеше́ствовать (*impf*); **a five-hour ~** пятичасова́я пое́здка; **return ~** обра́тный путь*, обра́тная доро́га.
jovial ['dʒəuvɪəl] *adj* бо́дрый, жизнера́достный.
jowl [dʒaul] *n* че́люсть* *f*.
joy [dʒɔɪ] *n* ра́дость *f*.
joyful ['dʒɔɪful] *adj* ра́достный* (ра́достен).
joyride ['dʒɔɪraɪd] *n* ката́ние на укра́денной маши́не.
joyrider ['dʒɔɪraɪdə⁷] *n* челове́к, кото́рый угоня́ет маши́ны и ката́ется на них.
joyriding ['dʒɔɪraɪdɪŋ] *n* езда́ (*обы́чно на угна́нном автомоби́ле*).
joystick ['dʒɔɪstɪk] *n* (*AVIAT*) рыча́г* управле́ния; (*COMPUT*) джо́йстик.
JP *n abbr* = **Justice of the Peace**.
Jr. *abbr* (*in names*) = **junior**.
JTPA *n abbr* (*US*) = **Job Training Partnership Act**.

---

* marks translations which have irregular inflections. The Russian-English side of the dictionary gives inflectional information.

jubilant ['dʒu:bɪlnt] *adj* ликующий.
jubilation [dʒu:bɪ'leɪʃən] *n* ликование.
jubilee ['dʒu:bɪli:] *n* (*anniversary*) юбилей; **silver/golden ~** 25-летний/50-летний юбилей.
judge [dʒʌdʒ] *n* судья* *m* ♦ *vt* (*LAW*) выносить* (вынести* *perf*) приговор; (*competition, person etc*) судить* (*impf*); (*consider, estimate*) оценивать (оценить* *perf*) ♦ *vi*: **judging** or **to ~ by his expression** судя по его выражению; **she's a good ~ of character** она хорошо разбирается в людях; **I'll be the ~ of that** ну это уж мне судить; **I ~d it necessary to inform him** я посчитал нужным сообщить ему об этом; **as far as I can ~** насколько я могу судить.
judge advocate *n* (*MIL*) военный прокурор.
judg(e)ment ['dʒʌdʒmənt] *n* (*LAW*) приговор, решение суда; (*view*) суждение; (*discernment*) рассудительность *f*; **in my ~** по моему мнению; **to pass ~ (on)** (*LAW*) выносить* (вынести* *perf*) решение (о +*prp*); (*fig*) судить* (*impf*) (о +*prp*).
judicial [dʒu:'dɪʃl] *adj* (*LAW*) судебный; (*fig*) рассудительный* (рассудителен); **~ review** судебное разбирательство.
judiciary [dʒu:'dɪʃɪərɪ] *n*: **the ~** судебные органы *mpl*.
judicious [dʒu:'dɪʃəs] *adj* благоразумный* (благоразумен).
judo ['dʒu:dəu] *n* дзюдо *nt ind*.
jug [dʒʌg] *n* кувшин.
jugged hare ['dʒʌgd-] *n* (*BRIT*) ≈ жаркое *nt adj* из зайца.
juggernaut ['dʒʌgənɔ:t] *n* (*BRIT*) многотонный грузовик*.
juggle ['dʒʌgl] *vi* (*also fig*) жонглировать (*impf*) ♦ *vt* (*fig*) жонглировать (*impf*) +*instr*; **to ~ with sth** жонглировать (*impf*) чем-н.
juggler ['dʒʌglə'] *n* жонглёр.
Jugoslav *etc* ['ju:gəu'slɑ:v] = **Yugoslav** *etc*.
jugular ['dʒʌgjulə'] *adj* (*also*: **~ vein**) яремная вена.
juice [dʒu:s] *n* сок*; (*inf*: *petrol*) бензин.
juicy ['dʒu:sɪ] *adj* сочный* (сочен).
jukebox ['dʒu:kbɔks] *n* музыкальный автомат.
Jul. *abbr* = **July**.
July [dʒu:'laɪ] *n* июль *m*; **the first of ~** первое июля; **on the eleventh of ~** одиннадцатого июля; **in the month of ~** в июле месяце; **at the beginning/end of ~** в начале/конце июля; **in the middle of ~** в середине июля; **during ~** в течение июля; **in ~** в июле; **~ of next year** в июле следующего года; **each** or **every ~** каждый июль; **~ was wet this year** в этом году июль был дождливым.
jumble ['dʒʌmbl] *n* нагромождение; (*BRIT*: *items for sale*) старьё ♦ *vt* (*also*: **~ up**) перемешивать (перемешать *perf*).
jumble sale *n* (*BRIT*) благотворительная распродажа подержанных вещей.
jumbo ['dʒʌmbəu] *n* (*also*: **~ jet**) реактивный аэробус.
jumbo-size ['dʒʌmbəusaɪz] *adj* гигантский*.
jump [dʒʌmp] *vi* прыгать (прыгнуть *perf*); (*start*) подпрыгивать (подпрыгнуть *perf*); (*increase*) подскакивать (подскочить* *perf*) ♦ *vt* (*fence*) перепрыгивать (перепрыгнуть *perf*), перескакивать (перескочить* *perf*) ♦ *n* прыжок*; (*increase*) скачок*; **to ~ the queue** (*BRIT*) идти* (пойти* *perf*) без очереди
► **jump about** *vi* спрыгивать (спрыгнуть *perf*)
► **jump at** *vt fus* (*seize*) ухватываться (ухватиться *perf*) за +*acc*
► **jump down** *vi* спрыгивать (спрыгнуть *perf*)
► **jump up** *vi* (*from a seat*) вскакивать (вскочить* *perf*); (*into the air*) подпрыгивать (подпрыгнуть *perf*).
jumped-up ['dʒʌmptʌp] *adj* (*BRIT*: *pej*): **~ office boy** выскочка *m*.
jumper ['dʒʌmpə'] *n* (*BRIT*: *pullover*) свитер, джемпер; (*US*: *dress*) сарафан; (*SPORT*) прыгун*(ья*).
jumper cables *npl* (*US*) = **jump leads**.
jump leads *npl* (*BRIT*) провод большого сечения (*для пуска двигателя*).
jump-start ['dʒʌmpstɑ:t] *vt*: **to ~ a car** подталкивать (подтолкнуть *perf*) машину, чтобы завести её.
jump suit *n* комбинезон.
jumpy ['dʒʌmpɪ] *adj* нервный.
Jun. *abbr* = **June**.
junction ['dʒʌŋkʃən] *n* (*BRIT*: *of roads*) пересечение; (*RAIL*) узел*.
juncture ['dʒʌŋktʃə'] *n*: **at this ~** в данный момент.
June [dʒu:n] *n* июнь *m*; *see also* **July**.
jungle ['dʒʌŋgl] *n* (*also fig*) джунгли *pl*.
junior ['dʒu:nɪə'] *adj* младший* ♦ *n* младший*(-ая) *m(f) adj*; **he's ~ to me (by 2 years), he's my ~ (by 2 years)** он младше меня (на 2 года); **he's ~ to me** (*seniority*) он мой подчинённый.
junior executive *n* младший* руководящий работник.
junior high school *n* (*US*) ≈ неполная средняя школа.
junior minister *n* (*BRIT*) младший* министр.
junior partner *n* младший* партнёр.
junior school *n* (*BRIT*) *школа для детей в возрасте от 7 до 11 лет*.
junior sizes *npl* детские размеры *mpl*.
juniper ['dʒu:nɪpə'] *n*: **~ berry** можжевельник.
junk [dʒʌŋk] *n* барахло, хлам; (*ship*) джонка* ♦ *vt* (*inf*) выкидывать (выкинуть *perf*).
junk bond *n* *облигации, обещающие высокие проценты, но не дающие гарантий*.
junket ['dʒʌŋkɪt] *n* (*CULIN*) *сладкое молочное блюдо*; (*US*: *inf*: *pej*): **to go on a ~** прокатиться* (*perf*) за казённый счёт.
junk food *n* *еда, содержащая мало*

питáтельных вещéств.
junkie ['dʒʌŋkɪ] *n* (*inf*) наркомáн.
junk mail *n незапрóшенная реклáма,
достáвляемая по пóчте.*
junk room *n* чулáн.
junk shop *n* лáвка* старьёвщика.
Junr *abbr* (*in names*) = **junior.**
junta ['dʒʌntə] *n* хýнта.
Jupiter ['dʒu:pɪtə'] *n* Юпúтер.
jurisdiction [dʒuəns'dɪkʃən] *n* (*LAW*)
юрисдúкция; (*ADMIN*) сфéра полномóчий; **it
is within/outside my** ~ э́то вхóдит/не вхóдит
в мой полномóчия.
jurisprudence [dʒuəns'pru:dəns] *n*
юриспрудéнция.
juror ['dʒuərə'] *n* присяжный заседáтель *m.*
jury ['dʒuərɪ] *n* присяжные *pl adj* (заседáтели).
jury box *n* скамья* присяжных.
juryman ['dʒuənmən] *irreg n* = **juror.**
just [dʒʌst] *adj* справедлúвый (справедлúв) ♦
adv (*exactly*) как раз, úменно; (*only*) тóлько;
(*barely*) едвá; **he's ~ left/done it** он тóлько
что ушёл/э́то сдéлал; **~ as I expected** как я и
ожидáл; **it's ~ right** э́то как раз то, что нáдо;
~ two o'clock рóвно два часá; **we were ~
going** *or* **about to go** мы как раз собирáлись
уходúть; **I was ~ about to phone** я ужé
собрáлся позвонúть; **she's ~ as clever as you**
она столь же умнá, как и ты; **it's ~ as well
(that)** ... дáже и хорошó, (что) ...; **~ as he was
leaving** как раз когдá он собрáлся уходúть;
~ before Christmas пéред сáмым
Рождествóм; **there was ~ enough petrol** едвá
хватúло бензúна; **~ here** вот здесь; **he (only)
~ missed** он чуть не попáл; **it's ~ me** э́то
(тóлько) я; **it's ~ a mistake** э́то прóсто
ошúбка; **~ listen!** ты тóлько послýшай!; **~
ask someone the way** прóсто спросú у когó-
нибудь дорóгу; **not ~ now** тóлько не сейчáс;

~ a minute!, ~ one moment! подождúте!,
⟨однý⟩ минýту!
justice ['dʒʌstɪs] *n* (*LAW*: *system*) правосýдие;
(*rightness*) справедлúвость *f*, (*US*: *judge*)
судья* *m*; **Lord Chief J~** (*BRIT*) второ́й по
значéнию судья́ в британской системе
правосýдия; **to do ~ to** (*fig*: *task, meal, person*)
отдавáть* (отдáть* *perf*) дóлжное +*dat.*
Justice of the Peace *n* (*BRIT*) мировóй судья*
m.
justifiable [dʒʌstɪ'faɪəbl] *adj* опрáвданный*
(опрáвдан), обоснóванный (обоснóван).
justifiably [dʒʌstɪ'faɪəblɪ] *adv* опрáвданно,
обоснóванно.
justification [dʒʌstɪfɪ'keɪʃən] *n* (*of action*)
оправдáние; (*reason*) основáние; (*TYP*)
вырáвнивание строкú.
justify ['dʒʌstɪfaɪ] *vt* опрáвдывать (оправдáть
perf); (*text*) вырáвнивать (вы́ровнять *perf*); **to
~ o.s.** опрáвдываться (оправдáться *perf*); **to
be justified in doing** имéть (*impf*) все
основáния +*infin.*
justly ['dʒʌstlɪ] *adv* справедлúво.
jut [dʒʌt] *vi* (*also*: **~ out**) выступáть (*impf*).
jute [dʒu:t] *n* джут.
juvenile ['dʒu:vənaɪl] *n* (*LAW, ADMIN*)
подрóсток*, несовершеннолéтний*(-яя) *m(f)*
adj ♦ *adj* (*humour, mentality*) дéтский*.
juvenile court *n* суд для несовершеннолéтних.
juvenile delinquency *n* престýпность *f* средú
несовершеннолéтних.
juvenile delinquent *n* несовершеннолéтний*(-яя) правонарушúтель(-ница) *m(f).*
juxtapose ['dʒʌkstəpəuz] *vt* сопоставлять
(сопостáвить* *perf*).
juxtaposition ['dʒʌkstəpə'zɪʃən] *n*
сопоставлéние.

~ K, k ~

K, k [keɪ] *n* (*letter*) 11-ая бу́ква англи́йского
алфави́та.
K *abbr* = **one thousand**; (*COMPUT*) (= **kilobyte**)
К = килоба́йт; (*BRIT: in titles*) = **knight**.
Kabul ['kɑːbul] *n* Кабу́л.
kaftan ['kæftæn] *n* кафта́н.
Kalahari Desert [kælə'hɑːrɪ-] *n*: **the ~ ~**
пусты́ня Калаха́ри.
kale [keɪl] *n* капу́ста кормова́я.
kaleidoscope [kə'laɪdəskəup] *n* калейдоско́п.
kamikaze [kæmɪ'kɑːzɪ] *n* камика́дзе *m ind*,
лётчик-сме́ртник.
Kampala [kæm'pɑːlə] *n* Кампа́ла.
Kampuchea [kæmpu'tʃɪə] *n* Кампучи́я.
Kampuchean [kæmpu'tʃɪən] *adj*
кампучи́йский*.
kangaroo [kæŋgə'ruː] *n* кенгуру́ *m ind*.
kaput [kə'put] (*inf*) *adj*: **the TV is ~!** телеви́зору
капу́т!
karaoke [kɑːrə'əukɪ] *n* карио́ки *ind*
(*самодеятельное пение под запись
профессионального ансамбля*).
karate [kə'rɑːtɪ] *n* карате́ *nt ind*.
Kashmir [kæʃ'mɪə*] *n* Кашми́р.
kayak ['kaɪæk] *n* кая́к*.
Kazakh ['kæzæk] *n* (*person*) каза́х(-а́шка*);
(*LING*) каза́хский* язы́к* ♦ *adj* каза́хский*.
Kazakhstan [kæzæk'stɑːn] *n* Казахста́н.
KC *n abbr* (*BRIT: LAW*: = **King's Counsel**)
короле́вский* адвока́т (*адвокатский ранг*).
kd *abbr* (*US: COMM*: = **knocked down**) в
разо́бранном ви́де.
kebab [kə'bæb] *n* шашлы́к*.
keel [kiːl] *n* киль *m*; **on an even ~** (*fig*) в
состоя́нии стаби́льности
▸ **keel over** *vi* опроки́дываться
(опроки́нуться *perf*).
keen [kiːn] *adj* о́стрый; (*eager*) стра́стный*
(стра́стен), увлечённый; **to be ~ to do** *or* **on
doing** о́чень хоте́ть* (*impf*) +*infin*; **to be ~ on
sth** увлека́ться (*impf*) чем-н; **he is ~ on her** он
увлечён е́ю; **I'm not ~ on going** мне не о́чень
хо́чется идти́; **~ competition** напряжённая
конкуре́нтная борьба́.
keenly ['kiːnlɪ] *adv* (*enthusiastically*) увлечённо;
(*intently*) при́стально; **to feel sth ~** глубоко́
пережива́ть (*impf*) что-н.
keenness ['kiːnnɪs] *n* (*eagerness*)
увлечённость *f*; **~ to do** стремле́ние +*infin*.

keep [kiːp] (*pt, pp* **kept**) *vt* (*receipt, money*)
оставля́ть (оста́вить* *perf*) себе́; (*store*)
храни́ть (*impf*); (*preserve*) сохраня́ть
(сохрани́ть *perf*); (*house, garden, shop, family*)
содержа́ть (*impf*); (*prisoner, chickens, bees*)
держа́ть* (*impf*); (*accounts, diary*) вести́* (*impf*);
(*promise*) сде́рживать (сдержа́ть* *perf*) ♦ *vi* (*in
a certain state or place*) остава́ться*
(оста́ться* *perf*); (*food*) сохраня́ться (*impf*);
(*continue*): **to ~ doing** продолжа́ть (*impf*)
+*impf infin* ♦ *n* (*of castle*) центра́льная ба́шня*;
(*food etc*): **he has enough for his ~** ему́
доста́точно на прожи́тие; **he kept the job** он
сохрани́л э́ту рабо́ту; **where do you ~ the
salt?** где у Вас соль?; **he tries to ~ her happy**
он де́лает всё для того́, что́бы она́ была́
дово́льна; **to ~ the house tidy** содержа́ть*
(*impf*) дом в поря́дке; **to ~ sb waiting**
заставля́ть (заста́вить* *perf*) кого́-н ждать;
to ~ sb from doing не дава́ть* (дать* *perf*)
кому́-н +*infin*; **to ~ an appointment** прийти́*
(*perf*) в назна́ченное вре́мя; **to ~ a record**
вести́* (*impf*) учёт; **to ~ sth to o.s.** держа́ть
(*impf*) что-н при себе́; **to ~ sth (back) from sb**
скрыва́ть (скрыть* *perf*) что-н от кого́-н; **to
~ sth from happening** не дава́ть* (дать* *perf*)
чему́-н случи́ться; **to ~ time** (*clock*) идти́*
(*impf*) то́чно
▸ **keep away** *vi*: **to ~ sth/sb away from sb/sth**
держа́ть (*impf*) что-н/кого́-н пода́льше от
кого́-н/чего́-н ♦ *vi*: **to ~ away (from)**
держа́ться* (*impf*) пода́льше (от +*gen*)
▸ **keep back** *vt* (*crowds, tears*) сде́рживать
(сдержа́ть* *perf*); (*money*) уде́рживать
(удержа́ть* *perf*) ♦ *vi* держа́ться* (*impf*) на
расстоя́нии
▸ **keep down** *vt* (*prices, spending*) сде́рживать
(сдержа́ть* *perf*); (*retain*): **she can't ~ her food
down** что бы она́ ни съе́ла, её всё вре́мя
рвёт ♦ *vi*: **~ down!** ложи́сь!
▸ **keep in** *vt* (*person*) держа́ть (*impf*) до́ма ♦ *vi*
(*inf*): **to ~ in with sb** подде́рживать (*impf*)
хоро́шие отноше́ния с кем-н
▸ **keep off** *vt* (*hold back*) не подпуска́ть
(подпусти́ть* *perf*); (*abstain*) избега́ть (*impf*)
+*gen* ♦ *vi* держа́ться* (*impf*) в стороне́; **"keep
off the grass"** „по газо́нам не ходи́ть"; **~
your hands off** рука́ми не тро́гать
▸ **keep on** *vi*: **to ~ on doing** продолжа́ть (*impf*)

+*impf infin*; **to ~ on (about sth)** не переставая
говорить *(impf)* (о чём-н)
► **keep out** *vt* не впускать (впустить* *perf*);
"**keep out**" „посторонним вход воспрещён"
► **keep up** *vt (payments, standards)*
поддерживать *(impf)* ◆ *vi*: **to ~ up (with)** *(pace)*
поспевать (поспеть *perf*) (за +*instr*); *(level)*
идти* *(impf)* в ногу (с +*instr*).
keeper ['ki:pə^r] *n (of zoo, park)* смотритель
(ница) *m(f)*.
keep fit *n* аэробика.
keeping ['ki:pɪŋ] *n (care)* присмотр; **I'll leave
this in your ~** оставляю это под Вашим
присмотром; **in ~ with** в соответствии с
+*instr*; **out of ~ with** несовместимый
(несовместим) с +*instr*.
keeps [ki:ps] *n*: **for ~** *(inf)* на совсем.
keepsake ['ki:pseɪk] *n* памятный подарок.
keg [kɛg] *n* бочонок*; **~ beer** бочковое пиво.
kennel ['kɛnl] *n* конура*.
kennels ['kɛnlz] *npl* гостиница *fsg or* платный
приют *msg* для собак.
Kenya ['kɛnjə] *n* Кения.
Kenyan ['kɛnjən] *adj* кенийский* ◆ *n*
кениец*(-ийка*).
kept [kɛpt] *pt, pp of* **keep**.
kerb [kə:b] *n (BRIT)* бордюр.
kerb crawler [-'krɔ:lə^r] *n шофёр, выбирающий
себе проституток из окна медленно
ползущего автомобиля*.
kernel ['kə:nl] *n (of nut)* ядро*; *(of idea)* суть *f*.
kerosene ['kɛrəsi:n] *n* керосин.
kestrel ['kɛstrəl] *n* пустельга*.
ketchup ['kɛtʃəp] *n* кетчуп.
kettle ['kɛtl] *n* чайник.
kettledrum ['kɛtldrʌm] *n* литавра.
key [ki:] *n* ключ*; *(MUS)* тональность *f*; *(of
piano, computer)* клавиша(а) ◆ *cpd (issue etc)*
ключевой ◆ *vt (also: ~ in)* набирать
(набрать* *perf*) на клавиатуре.
keyboard ['ki:bɔ:d] *n* клавиатура.
keyboarder ['ki:bɔ:də^r] *n* машинист(ка),
оператор клавиатуры.
keyed up [ki:d'-] *adj*: **he was all ~ ~** он был
очень взвинчен.
keyhole ['ki:həul] *n* замочная скважина.
keyhole surgery *n полостная операция,
осуществляемая через минимальный
разрез*.
keynote ['ki:nəut] *n (MUS)* тоника; *(of speech)*
лейтмотив.
keypad ['ki:pæd] *n (COMPUT)* (малая)
клавиатура, клавишная панель *f*.
keyring ['ki:rɪŋ] *n* брелок*.
keystroke ['ki:strəuk] *n (COMPUT)* нажатие
клавиши.
kg *abbr* (= **kilogram(me)**) кг= *килограмм*.
KGB *n abbr (POL: formerly)* КГБ.

khaki ['kɑ:kɪ] *n, adj* хаки *nt, adj ind*.
kHz *abbr* (= **kilohertz**) кГц= *килогерц*.
kibbutz [kɪ'buts] *n* киббуц.
kick [kɪk] *vt (person, table)* ударять (ударить
perf) ногой; *(ball)* ударять (ударить *perf*)
ногой по +*dat*; *(inf: habit, addiction)* побороть
(perf) ◆ *vi (horse)* лягаться *(impf)* ◆ *n* удар; *(of
rifle)* отдача; *(thrill: inf)*: **he does it for ~s** он
делает это, чтобы пощекотать себе нервы
► **kick around** *vi (inf)* валяться *(impf)*
► **kick off** *vi*: **the match ~s off at 3pm** матч
начинается в 3 часа *(в футболе)*.
kickoff ['kɪkɔf] *n* начало (футбольного)
матча.
kick-start ['kɪkstɑ:t] *n (also: ~er: BRIT)* ножной
стартёр.
kid [kɪd] *n (inf: child)* ребёнок*; *(goat)*
козлёнок*; *(leather)* лайка ◆ *vt (inf)* водить*
(impf) за нос, дурачить *(impf)*; **~ brother**
младший* братишка* *m*; **~ sister** младшая
сестрёнка*; **you're ~ding!** ты шутишь!
kid gloves *n*: **to handle sb with ~ ~** бережно
обращаться* с кем-н.
kidnap ['kɪdnæp] *vt* похищать (похитить* *perf*).
kidnapper ['kɪdnæpə^r] *n* похититель(ница)
m(f).
kidnapping ['kɪdnæpɪŋ] *n* похищение.
kidney ['kɪdnɪ] *n (MED)* почка*; *(CULIN)* почки
fpl.
kidney bean *n* красная фасоль *f no pl*.
kidney machine *n* искусственная почка*.
Kiev ['ki:ɛf] *n* Киев.
Kilimanjaro [kɪlɪmən'dʒɑ:rəu] *n*: **Mount ~** гора
Килиманджаро *nt ind*.
kill [kɪl] *vt* убивать (убить* *perf*); *(proposal)*
губить (загубить *perf*); *(rumour)* пресекать
(пресечь* *perf*) ◆ *n (prey)* добыча; **to ~ time**
(inf) убивать (убить* *perf*) время; **to ~ s.o.**
покончить *(perf)* с собой; **to be ~ed** *(in war,
accident)* погибать (погибнуть* *perf*); **to ~
o.s. to do** *(fig)* надрываться *(impf)*, чтобы
+*perf infin*; **to ~ o.s. (laughing)** помирать *(impf)*
(со смеху)
► **kill off** *vt (also fig)* уничтожать (уничтожить
perf).
killer ['kɪlə^r] *n* убийца *m/f*.
killer instinct *n* смертельная *or* мёртвая
хватка.
killing ['kɪlɪŋ] *n* убийство; *(profit)*: **to make a ~**
(inf) срывать (сорвать* *perf*) куш.
killjoy ['kɪldʒɔɪ] *n*: **don't be such a ~!** не
отравляй другим удовольствие!
kiln [kɪln] *n* печь* *(для обжига)*.
kilo ['ki:ləu] *n* кило *nt ind*.
kilobyte ['ki:ləubaɪt] *n* килобайт.
kilogram(me) ['kɪləugræm] *n* килограмм.
kilohertz ['kɪləuhə:ts] *n inv* килогерц.
kilometre ['kɪləmi:tə^r] *(US* **kilometer***) n*

---

* marks translations which have irregular inflections. The Russian-English side of the dictionary gives inflectional information.

киломе́тр.
kilowatt ['kɪləuwɔt] *n* килова́тт.
kilt [kɪlt] *n* шотла́ндская ю́бка*.
kilter ['kɪltə'] *n*: **out of** ~ в беспоря́дке.
kimono [kɪ'məunəu] *n* кимоно́ *nt ind*.
kin [kɪn] *n see* **kith, next**.
kind [kaɪnd] *adj* до́брый* (добр) ♦ *n* род*; **would you be** ~ **enough** *or* **so** ~ **as to ...?** не бу́дете ли Вы так добры́ *or* любе́зны *+perf infin* ...?; **it's very** ~ **of you to help me** о́чень любе́зно с Ва́шей стороны́, что Вы мне помогли́; **he seemed** ~ **of unhappy** он был вро́де бы недово́лен; **in** ~ (*COMM*) това́рами и услу́гами; **a** ~ **of** род +*gen*; **two of a** ~ две ве́щи одного́ ти́па; **what** ~ **of person is he?** что он за челове́к?; **she has a strange** ~ **of smile** у неё стра́нная улы́бка.
kindergarten ['kɪndəgɑ:tn] *n* де́тский сад*.
kind-hearted [kaɪnd'hɑ:tɪd] *adj* до́брый* (добр), добросерде́чный* (добрсерде́чен).
kindle ['kɪndl] *vt* (*also fig*) разжига́ть (разже́чь* *perf*).
kindling ['kɪndlɪŋ] *n* ще́пки* *fpl*, расто́пка.
kindly ['kaɪndlɪ] *adj* (*smile*) до́брый* (добр); (*person, tone*) доброжела́тельный* (доброжела́телен) ♦ *adv* (*smile, behave*) любе́зно, доброжела́тельно; **will you** ~ **...** бу́дьте добры́ ...; **he didn't take it** ~ он был далеко́ не рад э́тому.
kindness ['kaɪndnɪs] *n* (*quality*) доброта́; (*act*) любе́зность *f*.
kindred ['kɪndrɪd] *adj*: ~ **spirit** ро́дственная душа́*.
kinetic [kɪ'nɛtɪk] *adj* кинети́ческий*.
king [kɪŋ] *n* коро́ль* *m*.
kingdom ['kɪŋdəm] *n* короле́вство; **the animal/ plant** ~ живо́тное/расти́тельное ца́рство.
kingfisher ['kɪŋfɪʃə'] *n* зиморо́док*.
kingpin ['kɪŋpɪn] *n* (*TECH*) шкво́рень* *m*; (*fig*) ва́жная ши́шка*.
king-size(d) ['kɪŋsaɪz(d)] *adj* са́мого большо́го разме́ра.
kink [kɪŋk] *n* (*in rope*) у́зел; (*in hair*) завито́к*; (*in character*) причу́да, стра́нность *f*.
kinky ['kɪŋkɪ] *adj* (*inf*) поро́чный* (поро́чен).
kinship ['kɪnʃɪp] *n* родство́.
kinsman ['kɪnzmən] *irreg n* ро́дич.
kinswoman ['kɪnzwumən] *irreg n* кро́вная ро́дственница.
kiosk ['ki:ɔsk] *n* кио́ск; (*BRIT: TEL*) телефо́нная бу́дка*; (*also*: **newspaper** ~) газе́тный кио́ск.
kipper ['kɪpə'] *n* ≈ копчёная селёдка*.
Kirghiz ['kə:gɪz] *n* (*person*) кирги́з(ка*); (*LING*) кирги́зский* язы́к* ♦ *adj* кирги́зский*.
Kirghizia [kə:'gɪzɪə] *n* Кирги́зия.
Kishinev [kɪʃi'njɔf] *n* Кишинёв.
kiss [kɪs] *n* поцелу́й ♦ *vt* целова́ть (поцелова́ть* *perf*) ♦ *vi* целова́ться (поцелова́ться *perf*); **to** ~ **sb goodbye** целова́ть (поцелова́ть *perf*) кого́-н на проща́ние.
kissagram ['kɪsəgr[+e]m] *n* сюрпри́зная доста́вка поздравле́ний, сопровожда́ющаяся поцелу́ем доста́вщика и́ли доста́вщицы.
kiss of life *n* (*BRIT*): **the** ~ ~ ~ иску́сственное дыха́ние.
kit [kɪt] *n* (*also: sports* ~) костю́м; (*equipment*) снаряже́ние; (*set of tools*) набо́р; (*for assembly*) компле́кт.
▶ **kit out** *vt* (*BRIT*) снаряжа́ть (снаряди́ть* *perf*).
kitbag ['kɪtbæg] *n* вещмешо́к*= вещево́й мешо́к.
kitchen ['kɪtʃɪn] *n* ку́хня*.
kitchen garden *n* огоро́д.
kitchen sink *n* (ку́хонная) мо́йка* *or* ра́ковина.
kitchen unit *n* (*BRIT*) ку́хонный шкаф.
kitchenware ['kɪtʃɪnwɛə'] *n* ку́хонные принадле́жности *fpl*, (ку́хонная) у́тварь *f*.
kite [kaɪt] *n* (*toy*) возду́шный змей; (*ZOOL*) ко́ршун.
kith [kɪθ] *n*: ~ **and kin** родны́е *pl adj* и бли́зкие *pl adj*.
kitten ['kɪtn] *n* котёнок*.
kitty ['kɪtɪ] *n* (*pool of money*) о́бщая ка́сса.
kiwi ['ki:wi:] *n* ки́ви *f ind*.
KKK *n abbr* (*US*: = *Ku Klux Klan*) ку-клукс-кла́н.
Kleenex® ['kli:nɛks] *n inv* бума́жный носово́й плато́к*.
kleptomaniac [klɛptəu'meɪnɪæk] *n* клептома́н(ка*).
km *abbr* (= **kilometre**) км= *киломе́тр*.
km/h *abbr* (= **kilometres per hour**) км/ч= *киломе́тров в час*.
knack [næk] *n*: **he has the** ~ **of imitating other people** он о́чень ло́вко имити́рует други́х люде́й; **there's a** ~ **to doing this** тут есть оди́н секре́т *or* осо́бая хи́трость.
knackered ['nækəd] *adj* (*inf: tired*) вы́мотанный (вы́мотан).
knapsack ['næpsæk] *n* (небольшо́й) рюкза́к.
knead [ni:d] *vt* меси́ть* (смеси́ть* *perf*).
knee [ni:] *n* коле́но.
kneecap ['ni:kæp] *n* коле́нная ча́шечка*.
kneecapping ['ni:kæpɪŋ] *n* вы́стрел по коле́нной ча́шечке (*фо́рма ме́сти, применя́емая террори́стами*).
knee-deep ['ni:'di:p] *adj, adv* по коле́но.
knee-jerk ['ni:dʒə:k] *n* коле́нный рефле́кс ♦ *adj*: ~ **reaction** (*fig*) рефле́кс.
kneel [ni:l] (*pt, pp* **knelt**) *vi* (*also*: ~ **down**: *action*) встава́ть* (встать* *perf*) на коле́ни; (: *state*) стоя́ть (*impf*) на коле́нях.
kneepad ['ni:pæd] *n* наколе́нник.
knell [nɛl] *n* погреба́льный звон; (*fig*) коне́ц*.
knelt [nɛlt] *pt, pp of* **kneel**.
knew [nju:] *pt of* **know**.
knickers ['nɪkəz] *npl* (*BRIT*) (же́нские) тру́сики *mpl*.
knick-knacks ['nɪknæks] *npl* безделу́шки* *fpl*.
knife [naɪf] (*pl* **knives**) *n* нож* ♦ *vt* ра́нить (*impf*) ножо́м.

knight [naɪt] *n* ры́царь *m*; (*CHESS*) конь* *m*.
knighthood ['naɪthud] *n* (*BRIT*) ры́царство
(*полученное за заслуги перед страной*).
knit [nɪt] *vt* (*garment*) вяза́ть (связа́ть *perf*) ♦ *vi*
(*with wool etc*) вяза́ть (*impf*); (*bones*)
сраста́ться (срасти́сь* *perf*); **to ~ one's brows**
хму́рить (нахму́рить *perf*) бро́ви.
knitted ['nɪtɪd] *adj* (*garment*) вя́заный.
knitting ['nɪtɪŋ] *n* вяза́нье.
knitting machine *n* вяза́льная маши́на.
knitting needle *n* вяза́льная спи́ца.
knitting pattern *n* вя́зка*.
knitwear ['nɪtwɛəʳ] *n* трикота́ж.
knives [naɪvz] *npl of* **knife**.
knob [nɔb] *n* (*of door*) ру́чка*; (*on radio etc*)
кно́пка*; (*of stick*) набалда́шник; **a ~ of butter**
(*BRIT*) кусо́чек (сли́вочного) ма́сла.
knobbly ['nɔblɪ] (*US* **knobby**) *adj* (*surface*)
бугри́стый (бугри́ст); (*hand*) узлова́тый
(узлова́т); (*knee*) шишкова́тый.
knobby ['nɔbɪ] *adj* (*US*) = **knobbly**.
knock [nɔk] *vt* (*strike*) ударя́ть (уда́рить *perf*);
(*bump into*) ста́лкиваться (столкну́ться *perf*)
с +*instr*; (*inf: criticize*) критикова́ть (*impf*) ♦ *vi*
(*engine*) стуча́ть (*impf*) ♦ *n* (*blow, bump*) уда́р,
толчо́к*; (*on door*) стук; **to ~ a nail into sth**
вбива́ть (вбить* *perf*) гвоздь во что-н; **to ~**
some sense into sb учи́ть* (научи́ть* *perf*)
кого́-н уму́-ра́зуму; **he ~ed at *or* on the door**
он постуча́л в дверь
▶ **knock about** (*inf*) ♦ *vt* (*hit*) колоти́ть*
(поколоти́ть* *perf*) ♦ *vi* (*travel*) шата́ться
(*impf*) по све́ту; (*hang out*): **~ about (with)**
води́ться (*impf*) (с +*instr*)
▶ **knock around** *vti* = **knock about**
▶ **knock back** *vt* (*inf: drink*) пропуска́ть
(пропусти́ть* *perf*)
▶ **knock down** *vt* (*person, price*) сбива́ть
(сбить* *perf*); (*building*) сноси́ть (снести́* *perf*)
▶ **knock off** *vi* (*inf: finish*) закругля́ться
(закругли́ться *perf*) ♦ *vt* (*from price*) сба́влять
(сба́вить* *perf*); (*inf: steal*) стяну́ть* (*perf*)
▶ **knock out** *vt* (*subj: person, drug*) оглуша́ть
(оглуши́ть *perf*); (*BOXING*) нокаути́ровать
(*perf*); (*defeat*) выбива́ть (вы́бить* *perf*)
▶ **knock over** *vt* (*person, object*) сбива́ть
(сбить* *perf*).
knockdown ['nɔkdaun] *adj*: **~ price** сни́женная
цена́.
knocker ['nɔkəʳ] *n* дверно́й молото́к*.
knocking ['nɔkɪŋ] *n* стук.
knock-kneed [nɔk'niːd] *adj* с вы́вернутыми
внутрь коле́нями.
knockout ['nɔkaut] *n* (*BOXING*) нока́ут ♦ *cpd*
(*competition*) отбо́рочный.
knock-up ['nɔkʌp] *n* (*TENNIS*): **to have a ~**
размина́ться (размя́ться* *perf*).
knot [nɔt] *n* (*also NAUT*) у́зел*; (*in wood*) сучо́к*

♦ *vt* завя́зывать (завяза́ть* *perf*) узло́м; **to**
tie/untie a ~ завя́зывать (завяза́ть* *perf*)/
развя́зывать (развяза́ть* *perf*) у́зел.
knotty ['nɔtɪ] *adj* (*fig*) запу́танный.
know [nəu] (*pt* **knew**, *pp* **known**) *vt* (*facts,*
people) знать (*impf*); **to ~ how to do** уме́ть
(*impf*) +*infin*; **to ~ about *or* of sth/sb** знать (*impf*)
о чём-н/ком-н; **to get to ~ sth** (*news*)
узнава́ть* (узна́ть* *perf*) что-н; **to get to ~ sb**
(*more intimately*) узнава́ть* (узна́ть* *perf*)
кого́-н побли́же; (*get acquainted*)
знако́миться* (познако́миться* *perf*) с кем-н;
to get to ~ about узна́ть (*perf*) о +*prp*; **as far as**
I ~ наско́лько мне изве́стно; **yes, I ~** да,
зна́ю; **I don't ~** не зна́ю.
know-all ['nəuɔːl] *n* (*BRIT: pej*) всезна́йка* *m/f*.
know-how ['nəuhau] *n* но́у-ха́у *nt ind*.
knowing ['nəuɪŋ] *adj* (*look*) понима́ющий.
knowingly ['nəuɪŋlɪ] *adv* (*purposely*)
созна́тельно; (*smile, look*) понима́юще.
know-it-all ['nəuɪtɔːl] *n* (*US*) = **know-all**.
knowledge ['nɔlɪdʒ] *n* (*abstract concept*)
зна́ние; (*things learnt*) зна́ния *ntpl*;
(*awareness*) представле́ние; **to have no ~ of**
не име́ть (*impf*) никако́го представле́ния о
+*prp*; **not to my ~** наско́лько мне изве́стно –
нет; **without my ~** без моего́ ве́дома; **to have**
a working ~ of Russian непло́хо владе́ть
(*impf*) ру́сским (языко́м); **it is common ~ that**
... общеизве́стно, что ...; **it has come to my ~**
that ... мне ста́ло изве́стно, что ....
knowledgeable ['nɔlɪdʒəbl] *adj* знающий*; **he**
is very ~ about art он большо́й знато́к
иску́сства.
known [nəun] *pp of* **know** ♦ *adj* (*thief, facts*)
изве́стный* (изве́стен).
knuckle ['nʌkl] *n* костя́шка*
▶ **knuckle down** *vi* бра́ться* (взя́ться* *perf*) за
де́ло
▶ **knuckle under** *vi* (*inf*) подчиня́ться
(подчини́ться *perf*).
knuckleduster ['nʌkldʌstəʳ] *n* касте́т.
KO *n abbr* (= *knockout*) нока́ут ♦ *vt*
нокаути́ровать (*impf/perf*).
koala [kəu'ɑːlə] *n* (*also: ~ bear*) коа́ла *f ind*.
kook [kuːk] *n* (*US*) поме́шанный(-ая) *m(f) adj*.
Koran [kɔ'rɑːn] *n*: **the ~** Кора́н.
Korea [kə'rɪə] *n* Коре́я; **North/South ~**
Се́верная/Ю́жная Коре́я.
Korean [kə'rɪən] *adj* коре́йский* ♦ *n*
коре́ец*(-е́йнка*).
kosher ['kəuʃəʳ] *adj* (*food*) коше́рный.
Kosovo ['kɔsɔvəu] *n* Ко́сово.
Kosovan ['kɔsɔvən] *n* косова́р(-ка).
Kosovar ['kɔsɔvɑːʳ] *n* = **Kosovan**.
kowtow ['kau'tau] *vi*: **to ~ to sb** заи́скивать
(*impf*) *or* уго́дничать (*impf*) пе́ред кем-н.
Kremlin ['krɛmlɪn] *n*: **the ~** Кремль* *m*.

---

* marks translations which have irregular inflections. The Russian-English side of the dictionary gives inflectional information.

KS *abbr* (*US*: *POST*) = Kansas.
Kt *abbr* (*BRIT*: *in titles*) = **knight**.
Kuala Lumpur [ˈkwɑːləˈlumpuəʳ] *n*
  Куала-Лумпу́р.
kudos [ˈkjuːdɔs] *n* прести́жность *f*.
Kurd [kəːd] *n* курд(ка*).

Kuwait [kuˈweɪt] *n* Куве́йт.
Kuwaiti [kuˈweɪtɪ] *adj* куве́йтский ♦ *n*
  жи́тель(ница) *m(f)* Куве́йта.
kW *abbr* (= **kilowatt**) кВт= *килова́тт*.
KY *abbr* (*US*: *POST*) = Kentucky.

~ L, l ~

L, l [ɛl] *n* (*letter*) 12-ая бу́ква англи́йского алфави́та.
L *abbr* (*BRIT: AUT* = *learner*) уче́бная *f adj*; (= **lake**) о.= *о́зеро*; = **large, left.**
l. *abbr* (= **litre**) л= *литр.*
LA *n abbr* (*US*) = *Los Angeles* ◆ *abbr* (*POST*) = *Louisiana.*
lab [læb] *n abbr* = **laboratory.**
label ['leɪbl] *n* этике́тка*, ярлы́к; (*on suitcase*) би́рка*; (*also:* **record** ~) знак фи́рмы грамза́писи ◆ *vt* (*suitcase*) прикрепля́ть (прикрепи́ть* *perf*) би́рку к +*dat*; (*merchandise*) прикрепля́ть (прикрепи́ть* *perf*) ярлы́к на +*acc*; (*fig*) накле́ивать (накле́ить *perf*) ярлы́к на +*acc.*
labor *etc* ['leɪbə*ʳ*] *n* (*US*) = **labour** *etc.*
laboratory [lə'bɒrətərɪ] *n* лаборато́рия.
Labor Day *n* (*US*) День* *m* Труда́.
laborious [lə'bɔːrɪəs] *adj* трудоёмкий* (трудоёмок).
labor union *n* (*US*) профсою́з.
labour ['leɪbə*ʳ*] (*US* **labor**) *n* (*work*) труд*; (*workforce*) рабо́чая си́ла; (*MED*): **to be in** ~ рожа́ть (*impf*) ◆ *vi*: **to** ~ (**at sth**) труди́ться* (*impf*) (над чем-н) ◆ *vi*: **to** ~ **the point** входи́ть* (*impf*) в изли́шние подро́бности; **L~, the L~ Party** (*BRIT*) лейбори́сты *mpl*, Лейбори́стская Па́ртия; **hard** ~ ка́торжные рабо́ты *pl.*
labour camp *n* исправи́тельно-трудово́й ла́герь* *m.*
labour cost *n* сто́имость *f* рабо́чей си́лы.
labour dispute *n* трудово́й конфли́кт.
laboured ['leɪbəd] *adj* (*breathing, movement*) затруднённый (затруднён); (*style, joke*) вы́мученный (вы́мучен).
labourer ['leɪbərə*ʳ*] *n* (неквалифици́рованный) рабо́чий *m adj*; **farm** ~ се́льско-хозя́йственный рабо́чий.
labour force *n* рабо́чая си́ла.
labour-intensive [leɪbərɪn'tɛnsɪv] *adj* трудоёмкий* (трудоёмок).
labour market *n* ры́нок* труда́.
labour pains *npl* родовы́е схва́тки *fpl.*
labour relations *npl* трудовы́е отноше́ния *ntpl.*
labour-saving ['leɪbəseɪvɪŋ] *adj* облегча́ющий труд.
labour unrest *n* рабо́чие волне́ния *ntpl.*
laburnum [lə'bəːnəm] *n* (*BOT*) золото́й дождь* *m.*
labyrinth ['læbɪrɪnθ] *n* лабири́нт.
lace [leɪs] *n* (*fabric*) кру́жево*; (*of shoe*) шнуро́к* ◆ *vt* (*shoe: also:* ~ **up**) шнурова́ть (зашнурова́ть *perf*); **I** ~**d his coffee with arsenic** я подмеша́л в его́ ко́фе мышья́к.
lacemaking ['leɪsmeɪkɪŋ] *n* плете́ние кру́жев.
lacerate ['læsəreɪt] *vt* раздира́ть (разодра́ть* *perf*).
laceration [læsə'reɪʃən] *n* рва́ная ра́на.
lace-up ['leɪsʌp] *adj* шнуро́ванный.
lack [læk] *n* (*absence*) отсу́тствие; (*shortage*) недоста́ток*, нехва́тка ◆ *vt*: **she** ~**ed self-confidence** ей не хвата́ло *or* не достава́ло уве́ренности в себе́; **he is** ~**ing in experience** ему́ не хвата́ет *or* не достаёт о́пыта; **through** *or* **for** ~ **of** из-за недоста́тка +*gen.*
lackadaisical [lækə'deɪzɪkl] *adj* вя́лый (вял).
lackey ['lækɪ] *n* (*pej*) лаке́й.
lacklustre ['læklʌstə*ʳ*] (*US* **lackluster**) *adj* ту́склый* (ту́скл).
laconic [lə'kɒnɪk] *adj* лакони́чный* (лакони́чен).
lacquer ['lækə*ʳ*] *n* лак*.
lacrosse [lə'krɒs] *n* (*SPORT*) лакро́сс.
lacy ['leɪsɪ] *adj* кружевно́й.
lad [læd] *n* па́рень* *m.*
ladder ['lædə*ʳ*] *n* (*also fig*) ле́стница; (*BRIT: in tights*) спусти́вшиеся пе́тли *fpl* ◆ *vti*: **I've** ~**ed my tights, my tights have** ~**ed** у меня́ пе́тли на колго́тках спусти́лись.
laden ['leɪdn] *adj*: **to be** ~ (**with**) ломи́ться (*impf*) от +*gen*; (*person*): ~ (**with**) нагру́женный (нагру́жен) (+*instr*); **fully** ~ по́лностью нагру́женный; **the trees were** ~ **with fruit** дере́вья ломи́лись от плодо́в.
ladle ['leɪdl] *n* поло́вник ◆ *vt* (*soup, stew*) разлива́ть (разли́ть* *perf*)
▸ **ladle out** *vt* (*advice, money*) раздава́ть* (разда́ть* *perf*) напра́во и нале́во.
Ladoga ['lɑːdəgə] *n*: **Lake** ~ Ла́дожское о́зеро.
lady ['leɪdɪ] *n* да́ма; (*BRIT: title*) ле́ди *f ind*; **ladies and gentlemen ...** да́мы и господа́ ...; **young** ~

молодáя жéнщина; (*younger*) дéвушка*; **old ~** пожилáя жéнщина; **the ladies' (room)** жéнский туалéт.
ladybird ['leɪdɪbəːd] *n* бóжья корóвка.
ladybug ['leɪdɪbʌg] *n* (*US*) = **ladybird**.
lady-in-waiting ['leɪdɪn'weɪtɪŋ] *n* фрéйлина.
lady-killer ['leɪdɪkɪlə'] *n* (*fig*) сердцеéд.
ladylike ['leɪdɪlaɪk] *adj* элегáнтный* (элегáнтен).
ladyship ['leɪdɪʃɪp] *n*: **your ~** Вáша мúлость *f*.
lag [læg] *n* (*period of time*) задéржка ◆ *vi* (*also*: **~ behind:** *person*) тащúться* (*impf*) (позадú); (: *trade, investment*) отставáть* (отстáть* *perf*) ◆ *vt* (*pipes etc*) покрывáть (покрýть* *perf*) теплоизоляцией; **old ~** (*inf: prisoner*) рецидивúст; **to ~ behind** (*trade, development*) отставáть* (отстáть* *perf*) от +*gen*.
lager ['laːgə'] *n* свéтлое пúво.
lager lout *n* (*inf*) пьяная шпанá *f no pl*.
lagging ['lægɪŋ] *n* (*for pipes*) теплоизоляция.
lagoon [lə'guːn] *n* лагýна.
Lagos ['leɪgɔs] *n* Лáгос.
laid [leɪd] *pt, pp of* **lay**.
laid-back [leɪd'bæk] *adj* (*inf*) спокóйный* (спокóен).
laid up *adj*: **~ ~ (with)** прикóванный (прикóван) к постéли (+*instr*).
lain [leɪn] *pp of* **lie**.
lair [lɛə'] *n* лóгово, лóговище.
laissez faire [lɛseɪ'fɛə'] *n* (*ECON*) экономúческое невмешáтельство.
laity ['leɪətɪ] *n or npl* (*REL*) миряне *mpl*; (*non-professionals*) не профессионáлы *mpl*.
lake [leɪk] *n* óзеро*.
Lake District *n* (*BRIT*): **the ~ ~** Озёрный край.
lamb [læm] *n* (*ZOOL*) ягнёнок*; (*CULIN*) (молодáя) барáнина.
lambada [læm'baːdə] *n* ламбáда.
lamb chop *n* барáнья котлéта.
lambskin ['læmskɪn] *n* овчúна.
lambswool ['læmzwul] *n* поярок* ◆ *cpd* поярковый.
lame [leɪm] *adj* (*person, animal*) хромóй* (хром); (*excuse, argument*) слáбый* (слаб).
lame duck *n* неудáчник(-ица).
lamely ['leɪmlɪ] *adv* неубедúтельно.
lament [lə'mɛnt] *n* плач ◆ *vt* оплáкивать (оплáкать* *perf*).
lamentable ['læməntəbl] *adj* плачéвный* (плачéвен).
laminated ['læmɪneɪtɪd] *adj* (*layered*) слоúстый; (*plastic coated*) с плáстиковым покрытием.
lamp [læmp] *n* (*electric, gas, oil*) лáмпа; (*street lamp*) фонáрь* *m*.
lamplight ['læmplaɪt] *n*: **by ~** (*indoors*) при свéте лáмпы.
lampoon [læm'puːn] *n* пáсквиль *m* ◆ *vt* писáть* (написáть* *perf*) пáсквиль на +*acc*.
lamppost ['læmppəust] *n* (*BRIT*) фонáрный столб*.
lampshade ['læmpʃeɪd] *n* абажýр.

lance [laːns] *n* пúка ◆ *vt* (*MED*) вскрывáть (вскрыть* *perf*).
lance corporal *n* (*BRIT*) млáдший* капрáл.
lancet ['laːnsɪt] *n* ланцéт.
Lancs [læŋks] *abbr* (*BRIT: POST*) = **Lancashire**.
land [lænd] *n* земля*; (*not sea*) сýша; (*country*) странá* ◆ *vi* (*from ship*) высáживаться (высадиться* *perf*); (*AVIAT*) приземляться (приземлúться* *perf*); (*fig: arrive unexpectedly*) очутúться* (*perf*) ◆ *vt* (*plane*) посадúть* (*perf*); (*passengers*) высáживать (высадить* *perf*); (*goods*) выгружáть (выгрузить* *perf*); **to own ~** владéть (*impf*) землёй; **to go by ~** éхать*/éздить* (*impf*) по сýше; **he always ~s on his feet** (*fig*) в концé концóв емý везёт; **she ~ed (herself) a good job** (*inf*) онá добúлась хорóшей рабóты; **to ~ sb with sth** (*inf*) навáливать (навалúть* *perf*) что-н на когó-н
▸ **land up** *vi*: **to ~ up (in/at)** очутúться* (*perf*) (в/на +*prp*).
landed gentry ['lændɪd-] *n* землевладéльческая аристокрáтия.
landfill site ['lændfɪl-] *n* мéсто захоронéния отхóдов.
landing ['lændɪŋ] *n* (*of house*) лéстничная площáдка*; (*of plane*) посáдка*, приземлéние.
landing card *n* кáрта, заполняемая прибывáющими в странý инострáнцами.
landing craft *n inv* десáнтное сýдно*.
landing gear *n* (*AVIAT*) шассú *nt ind*.
landing stage *n* прúстань* *f*.
landing strip *n* взлётно-посáдочная полосá*.
landlady ['lændleɪdɪ] *n* (*of house, flat*) домовладéлица, хозяйка*; (*of pub*) хозяйка*.
landlocked ['lændlɔkt] *adj* без выхода к мóрю.
landlord ['lændlɔːd] *n* (*of house, flat*) домовладéлец*, хозяин*; (*of pub*) хозяин*.
landlubber ['lændlʌbə'] *n*: **to be a ~** не любúть (*impf*) путешéствовать мóрем.
landmark ['lændmaːk] *n* (*назéмный*) ориентúр; (*fig*) вéха.
landowner ['lændəunə'] *n* землевладéлец (-лица).
landscape ['lænskeɪp] *n* (*view, painting*) пейзáж; (*terrain*) ландшáфт ◆ *vt*: **to ~ an area** (*искýсственно*) создавáть* (создáть* *perf*) ландшáфт.
landscape architect *n* = **landscape gardener**.
landscape gardener *n* ландшáфтный архитéктор.
landscape painting *n* (*picture*) пейзáж; (*art*) пейзáжная жúвопись *f*.
landslide ['lændslaɪd] *n* (*GEO*) óползень* *m*; (*POL: also: ~ victory*) решúтельная побéда.
lane [leɪn] *n* (*in country*) тропúнка*; (*in town*) переýлок*; (*of carriageway*) полосá; (*SPORT*) дорóжка*; **shipping ~** морскáя трáсса.
language ['læŋgwɪdʒ] *n* язык*; **bad ~** сквернослóвие.

language laboratory *n* лингафо́нный
кабине́т.
languid ['læŋgwɪd] *adj* то́мный* (то́мен).
languish ['læŋgwɪʃ] *vi* (*person*) томи́ться*
(истоми́ться* *perf*); (*project, case*) тяну́ться*
(*impf*).
lank [læŋk] *adj* (*hair*) дли́нный* и са́льный*.
lanky ['læŋkɪ] *adj* долгови́зый (долгови́з).
lanolin(e) ['lænəlɪn] *n* ланоли́н.
lantern ['læntən] *n* фона́рь* *m*.
Laos [laus] *n* Лаóс.
lap [læp] *n* коле́ни* *ntpl*; (*SPORT*) круг* ◆ *vt* (*also:*
~ **up**) лака́ть (вы́лакать *perf*) ◆ *vi* (*water*)
плеска́ться* (*impf*); **in his/my** ~ у него́/меня́
на коле́нях
▶ **lap up** *vt* (*fig: flattery*) упива́ться (упи́ться*
perf) +*instr*.
La Paz [læ'pæz] *n* Ла-Па́с.
lapdog ['læpdɔg] *n* боло́нка*.
lapel [lə'pɛl] *n* ла́цкан.
Lapland ['læplænd] *n* Лапла́ндия.
Lapp [læp] *adj* лапла́ндский ◆ *n* (*person*)
лапла́ндец*(-дка), саа́м(ка); (*LING*) саа́мский
язы́к*.
lapse [læps] *n* (*bad behaviour*) про́мах*; (*of
time*) промежу́ток*; (*of concentration*) поте́ря
◆ *vi* (*law, membership*) теря́ть (потеря́ть *perf*)
си́лу; **memory** ~ прова́л в па́мяти; **to** ~ **into
bad habits** усва́ивать (усво́ить *perf*) дурны́е
привы́чки.
lap-top ['læptɔp] *n:* ~ **computer** портати́вный
компью́тер.
larceny ['lɑːsənɪ] *n* (*esp US*) воровство́.
larch [lɑːtʃ] *n* ли́ственница.
lard [lɑːd] *n* свино́й жир*.
larder ['lɑːdə⁷] *n* кладова́я *f adj*.
large [lɑːdʒ] *adj* большо́й; (*major*) кру́пный*;
to make ~**r** увели́чивать (увели́чить *perf*);
this coat is too ~ **for me** э́то пальто́ мне
велико́; **a** ~ **number of people** большо́е число́
люде́й; **on a** ~ **scale** в кру́пном масшта́бе; **at**
~ (*as a whole*) в це́лом; (*at liberty*) на во́ле; **by
and** ~ вообще́.
largely ['lɑːdʒlɪ] *adv* по бо́льшей ча́сти; ~
because ... в основно́м, потому́ что ....
large-scale ['lɑːdʒ'skeɪl] *adj*
крупномасшта́бный.
largesse [lɑː'ʒɛs] *n* ще́дрость* *f*.
lark [lɑːk] *n* (*bird*) жа́воронок*; (*BRIT: inf: joke*)
прока́за
▶ **lark about** *vi* (*BRIT: inf*) прока́зничать
(напрока́зничать *perf*).
larva ['lɑːvə] (*pl* ~**e**) *n* личи́нка.
larvae ['lɑːviː] *npl of* **larva**.
laryngitis [lærɪn'dʒaɪtɪs] *n* ларинги́т.
larynx ['lærɪŋks] *n* горта́нь *f*.
lasagne [lə'zænjə] *n* лаза́нья (*италья́нское
блю́до*).

lascivious [lə'sɪvɪəs] *adj* похотли́вый
(похотли́в).
laser ['leɪzə⁷] *n* ла́зер.
laser beam *n* ла́зерный луч*.
laser printer *n* ла́зерный при́нтер.
lash [læʃ] *n* (*eyelash*) ресни́ца; (*of whip*) уда́р
(*хлыста́*) ◆ *vt* (*whip*) хлеста́ть* (*impf*), стега́ть
(*impf*); (*also:* ~ **against**: *subj: rain, wind*)
хлеста́ть* (*impf*) о +*acc*; (*tie*): **to** ~ **to**
привя́зывать (привяза́ть* *perf*) к +*dat*; **to** ~
together свя́зывать (связа́ть* *perf*)
▶ **lash down** *vt* привя́зывать (привяза́ть* *perf*)
◆ *vi* (*rain*) хлеста́ть* (*impf*)
▶ **lash out** *vi:* **to** ~ **out at** (*also fig*)
наки́дываться (наки́нуться *perf*) на +*acc*; **to** ~
out (on sth) (*inf*) разоря́ться (разори́ться
perf) (на что-н).
lashing ['læʃɪŋ] *n:* ~**s of** (*BRIT: inf: cream etc*)
ку́ча +*gen*.
lass [læs] *n* (*BRIT: girl*) де́вочка*; (: *young
woman*) де́вушка*.
lasso [læ'suː] *n* лассо́ *nt ind*, арка́н ◆ *vt*
арка́нить (заарка́нить *perf*).
last [lɑːst] *adj* (*most recent*) про́шлый; (*final*)
после́дний ◆ *adv* в после́дний раз; (*finally*) в
конце́ ◆ *vi* (*continue*) дли́ться (продли́ться
perf), продолжа́ться (продо́лжиться* *perf*);
(*keep: thing*) сохраня́ться (сохрани́ться *perf*);
(: *person*) держа́ться (продержа́ться* *perf*);
(*suffice*): **we had enough money to** ~ **us** нам
хвати́ло де́нег; ~ **year** в про́шлом году́; ~
week на про́шлой неде́ле; ~ **night** (*early*)
вчера́ ве́чером; (*late*) про́шлой но́чью; **at** ~
наконе́ц; ~ **but one** предпосле́дний*; **the** ~
time в после́дний раз; **the film** ~**s (for) 2 hours**
фильм дли́тся 2 часа́.
last-ditch ['lɑːst'dɪtʃ] *adj* (*attempt*) отча́янный.
lasting ['lɑːstɪŋ] *adj* (*friendship*)
продолжи́тельный* (продолжи́телен),
дли́тельный* (дли́телен); (*solution*)
долговре́менный* (долговре́менен).
lastly ['lɑːstlɪ] *adv* наконе́ц.
last-minute ['lɑːstmɪnɪt] *adj* (*attempt*)
сде́ланный в после́днюю мину́ту; (*details,
meeting*) после́дний*.
latch [lætʃ] *n* (*on gate*) задви́жка*; (*on front
door*) замо́к* *m*; **to leave the door on the** ~
оставля́ть (оста́вить* *perf*) замо́к на
предохрани́теле
▶ **latch on to** *vt fus* (*person*) прилипа́ть
(прили́пнуть *perf*) к +*dat*; (*idea*)
привя́зываться (привяза́ться* *perf*) к +*dat*.
latchkey ['lætʃkiː] *n* ключ от замка́ (*к входно́й
две́ри*).
latchkey child *n* ребёнок, находя́щийся до́ма в
то вре́мя когда́ роди́тели рабо́тают.
late [leɪt] *adj* (*far on in time, process, work etc*)
по́здний*; (*former*) бы́вший*; (*dead*)

---

* marks translations which have irregular inflections. The Russian-English side of the dictionary gives inflectional information.

поко́йный ♦ *adv* по́здно; (*behind time*) с опозда́нием; **to be ~** опа́здывать (опозда́ть *perf*); **I was 10 minutes ~** я опозда́л на 10 мину́т; **in the ~ 1970s** к концу́ семидеся́тых годо́в; **he is in his ~ thirties** ему́ далеко́ за три́дцать; **in ~ May** в конце́ ма́я; **to work ~** рабо́тать (*impf*) допоздна́; **~ in life** в пожило́м во́зрасте; **of ~** в после́днее вре́мя.

latecomer ['leɪtkʌməʳ] *n* опозда́вший(-ая)*m(f) adj*.

lately ['leɪtlɪ] *adv* в после́днее вре́мя.

lateness ['leɪtnɪs] *n* опозда́ние; **owing to the ~ of the hour** из-за по́зднего ча́са.

latent ['leɪtnt] *adj* скры́тый (скрыт); **~ defect** скры́тый дефе́кт.

later ['leɪtəʳ] *adj* (*time, date*) бо́лее по́здний*; (*meeting, version*) после́дующий* ♦ *adv* по́зже, поздне́е; **~ on** в после́дствии, пото́м; **he arrived ~ than me** он пришёл по́зже меня́.

lateral ['lætərl] *adj* боково́й; **~ thinking** нестанда́ртное мы́шление.

latest ['leɪtɪst] *adj* са́мый по́здний*; (*most recent*) (са́мый) но́вый *or* после́дний*; (*news*) после́дний*; **at the ~** са́мое по́зднее.

latex ['leɪtɛks] *n* ла́текс.

lathe [leɪð] *n* тока́рный стано́к*.

lather ['lɑːðəʳ] *n* (мы́льная) пе́на ♦ *vt* мы́лить (намы́лить *perf*).

Latin ['lætɪn] *n* (*LING*) лати́нский* язы́к*; (*person*) жи́тель(ница) *m(f)* ю́жной Евро́пы ♦ *adj*: **~ languages** рома́нские языки́; **~ countries** стра́ны ю́жной Евро́пы.

Latin America *n* Лати́нская Аме́рика.

Latin American *adj* латиноамерика́нский ♦ *n* латиноамерика́нец*(-а́нка*).

latitude ['lætɪtjuːd] *n* (*GEO*) широта́*; (*fig*) свобо́да.

latrine [lə'triːn] *n* отхо́жее ме́сто*.

latter ['lætəʳ] *adj* после́дний* ♦ *n*: **the ~** после́дний*(-яя) *m(f) adj*; **the ~ part of the week** втора́я полови́на неде́ли.

latter-day ['lætədeɪ] *adj* совреме́нный.

latterly ['lætəlɪ] *adv* неда́вно, в после́днее вре́мя.

lattice ['lætɪs] *n* решётка*.

lattice window *n* решётчатое окно́*.

Latvia ['lætvɪə] *n* Ла́твия.

Latvian ['lætvɪən] *adj* латви́йский ♦ *n* латы́ш(ка); (*LING*) латы́шский язы́к*.

laudable ['lɔːdəbl] *adj* похва́льный* (похва́лен).

laudatory ['lɔːdətrɪ] *adj* хвале́бный* (хвале́бен).

laugh [lɑːf] *n* смех* ♦ *vi* смея́ться* (*impf*); **(to do sth) for a ~** (де́лать (*impf*) что-н) для сме́ха.

▶ **laugh at** *vt fus* смея́ться* (посмея́ться *perf*) над +*instr*

▶ **laugh off** *vt*: **to ~ sth off** отде́лываться (отде́латься *perf*) от чего́-н шу́ткой.

laughable ['lɑːfəbl] *adj* смехотво́рный*

(смехотво́рен).

laughing gas ['lɑːfɪŋ-] *n* веселя́щий газ*.

laughing matter *n*: **this is no ~ ~** э́то де́ло нешу́точное.

laughing stock *n* посме́шище; **to be the ~ ~ of** служи́ть (*impf*) посме́шищем для +*gen*.

laughter ['lɑːftəʳ] *n* смех*.

launch [lɔːntʃ] *n* (*of rocket, product*) за́пуск; (*motorboat*) мото́рный ка́тер* ♦ *vt* (*ship*) спуска́ть (спусти́ть* *perf*) на́ воду; (*rocket*) запуска́ть (запусти́ть* *perf*); (*campaign, attack*) начина́ть (нача́ть* *perf*); (*product*) пуска́ть (пусти́ть* *perf*) в прода́жу

▶ **launch into** *vt fus* (*speech, activity*) пуска́ться (пусти́ться* *perf*) в +*acc*

▶ **launch out** *vi*: **to ~ out into** бра́ться* (взя́ться* *perf*) за +*acc*.

launching ['lɔːntʃɪŋ] *n* (*of ship*) спуск (на́ воду); (*of rocket, product*) за́пуск; (*of campaign, attack*) нача́ло.

launch(ing) pad *n* ста́ртовая площа́дка*.

launder ['lɔːndəʳ] *vt* (*clothes, sheets*) стира́ть (вы́стирать *perf*); (*money*) отмыва́ть (отмы́ть* *perf*).

Launderette® [lɔːn'drɛt] *n* (*BRIT*) пра́чечная *f adj* самообслу́живания.

Laundromat® ['lɔːndrəmæt] *n* (*US*) = **Launderette®**.

laundry ['lɔːndrɪ] *n* (*washing*) сти́рка; (*place*) пра́чечная *f adj*; **to do the ~** стира́ть (вы́стирать *perf*).

laureate ['lɔːrɪət] *adj see* **poet laureate**

laurel ['lɔrl] *n* (*tree*) лавр, ла́вровое де́рево; **to rest on one's ~s** почива́ть (почи́ть* *perf*) на ла́врах.

Lausanne [ləu'zæn] *n* Лоза́нна.

lava ['lɑːvə] *n* ла́ва.

lavatory ['lævətərɪ] *n* туале́т.

lavatory paper *n* туале́тная бума́га.

lavender ['lævəndəʳ] *n* лава́нда.

lavish ['lævɪʃ] *adj* (*amount, hospitality*) ще́дрый* (щедр); (*meal*) оби́льный* (оби́лен); (*surroundings*) пы́шный* (пы́шен); (*person*): **~ with** ще́дрый* (щедр) на +*acc* ♦ *vt*: **to ~ sth on sb** осыпа́ть (осы́пать* *perf*) кого́-н чем-н.

lavishly ['lævɪʃlɪ] *adv* (*generously*) ще́дро; (*sumptuously*) пы́шно.

law [lɔː] *n* зако́н; (*professions*): **(the) ~** юриспруде́нция; (*SCOL*) пра́во; **it's against the ~** э́то противозако́нно; **to study ~** изуча́ть (*impf*) пра́во; **to go to ~** обраща́ться (обрати́ться* *perf*) в суд; **to break the ~** наруша́ть (нару́шить *perf*) зако́н.

law-abiding ['lɔː'əbaɪdɪŋ] *adj* законопослу́шный.

law and order *n* правопоря́док*.

lawbreaker ['lɔːbreɪkəʳ] *n* правонаруши́тель-(ница) *m(f)*.

law court *n* суд*.

lawful ['lɔːful] *adj* зако́нный.

lawfully ['lɔːfəlɪ] *adv* зако́нно.
lawless ['lɔːlɪs] *adj* (*action*) беззако́нный.
Law Lord *n* (*BRIT*) член пала́ты ло́рдов, состоя́щий в апелляцио́нном суде́.
lawmaker ['lɔːmeɪkəʳ] *n* законода́тель(ница) *m(f)*.
lawn [lɔːn] *n* газо́н.
lawn mower ['lɔːnməuəʳ] *n* газонокоси́лка*.
lawn tennis *n* те́ннис (*на травяно́м ко́рте*).
law school *n* (*US*) юриди́ческий институ́т.
law student *n* студе́нт(ка) юриди́ческого факульте́та.
lawsuit ['lɔːsuːt] *n* суде́бный иск.
lawyer ['lɔːjəʳ] *n* (*solicitor, barrister*) адвока́т; (*legal specialist*) юри́ст.
lax [læks] *adj* (*discipline, standards*) нестро́гий (нестро́г); (*morals, behaviour*) распу́щенный (распу́щен).
laxative ['læksətɪv] *n* слаби́тельное *nt adj*.
laxity ['læksɪtɪ] *n* небре́жность *f*; (*moral*) распу́щенность *f*.
lay [leɪ] (*pt, pp* laid) *pt of* lie ♦ *adj* (*REL*) мирско́й; (*not expert*) непрофессиона́льный ♦ *vt* (*place*) класть* (положи́ть* *perf*); (*table*) накрыва́ть (накры́ть* *perf*) (на +*acc*); (*carpet*) стлать (настла́ть *or* настели́ть* *perf*); (*cable*) прокла́дывать (проложи́ть* *perf*); (*plans*) составля́ть (соста́вить* *perf*); (*trap*) ста́вить* (поста́вить* *perf*); (: *fig*) подстра́ивать (подстро́ить *perf*); (*egg*) откла́дывать (отложи́ть *perf*); **to ~ facts/proposals before sb** излага́ть (изложи́ть* *perf*) фа́кты/ предложе́ния пе́ред кем-н; **to ~ one's hands on sth** (*inf*) достава́ть* (доста́ть* *perf*) что-н; **to get laid** (*inf!*) тра́хаться (тра́хнуться *perf*) (*!*)
▶ **lay aside** *vt* откла́дывать (отложи́ть* *perf*)
▶ **lay by** *vt* = lay aside
▶ **lay down** *vt* (*object*) класть* (положи́ть* *perf*); (*rules, laws*) устана́вливать (установи́ть* *perf*); (*weapons*) скла́дывать (сложи́ть* *perf*); **to ~ down the law** прика́зывать (*impf*); **to ~ down one's life** положи́ть* (*perf*) жизнь
▶ **lay in** *vt* (*supplies*) запаса́ть (запасти́* *perf*)
▶ **lay into** *vt fus* (*also fig*) набра́сываться (набро́ситься* *perf*) на +*acc*
▶ **lay off** *vt* (*workers*) увольня́ть (уво́лить *perf*)
▶ **lay on** *vt* (*meal, entertainment*) устра́ивать (устро́ить *perf*); (*water, gas*) прокла́дывать (проложи́ть* *perf*); (*paint*) наноси́ть* (нанести́* *perf*)
▶ **lay out** *vt* раскла́дывать (разложи́ть* *perf*); (*inf*): **to ~ out money on sth** выкла́дывать (вы́ложить* *perf*) де́ньги на что-н
▶ **lay up** *vt* (*ship*) ста́вить* (поста́вить* *perf*) на прико́л; (*sick person*): **to be laid up with** валя́ться (*impf*) с +*instr*; **the car was laid up all**

year маши́на простоя́ла весь год.
layabout ['leɪəbaut] *n* (*inf*) безде́льник(-ица).
lay-by ['leɪbaɪ] *n* (*BRIT*) площа́дка для вре́менной стоя́нки (*на автодоро́ге*).
lay days *npl* (*NAUT*) сталийное вре́мя* *ntsg*.
layer ['leɪəʳ] *n* слой*.
layette [leɪˈet] *n* прида́ное *nt adj* (*для новорождённого*).
layman ['leɪmən] *irreg n* (*non-expert*) неспециали́ст.
lay-off ['leɪɔf] *n* увольне́ние.
layout ['leɪaut] *n* (*of garden, building*) планиро́вка*; (*of page*) компано́вка*.
laze [leɪz] *vi* (*also: ~ about*) безде́льничать (*impf*); **to ~ about in bed/the sun** не́житься (*impf*) в посте́ли/на со́лнце.
laziness ['leɪzɪnɪs] *n* лень *f*.
lazy ['leɪzɪ] *adj* лени́вый (лени́в).
LB *n abbr* (*CANADA*) = Labrador.
lb. *abbr* (= *pound (weight)*) фунт.
lbw *abbr* (*CRICKET*) = leg before wicket.
LC *n abbr* (*US*) = Library of Congress.
lc *abbr* (*TYP*: = *lower case*) строчна́я бу́ква.
L/C *abbr* (= *letter of credit*) аккредити́в.
LCD *n abbr* = liquid crystal display.
Ld *abbr* (*BRIT*: *in titles*) = lord.
LDS *n abbr* (*BRIT*: = *Licentiate in Dental Surgery*) лице́нзия на стоматологи́ческую пра́ктику ♦ *abbr* (= *Latter-day Saints*) „Святы́е после́днего дня" (*официа́льное назва́ние се́кты мормо́нов*).
LEA *n abbr* (*BRIT*: = *Local Education Authority*) ме́стное управле́ние по дела́м просвеще́ния.
lead¹ [liːd] (*pt, pp* led) *n* (*front position*) пе́рвенство, ли́дерство; (*clue*) нить *f*; (*in play, film*) гла́вная роль *f*; (*for dog*) поводо́к*; (*ELEC*) про́вод* ♦ *vt* (*competition, market*) лиди́ровать (*impf*) в +*prp*; (*opponent*) опережа́ть (*impf*); (*person, group: guide*) вести́* (повести́* *perf*); (*activity, organization etc*) руководи́ть* (*impf*) +*instr*, возглавля́ть (возгла́вить* *perf*) ♦ *vi* (*road, pipe etc*) вести́* (*impf*); (*SPORT*) лиди́ровать (*impf*); **to take the ~** (*SPORT*) выходи́ть* (вы́йти* *perf*) вперёд; (*fig*) брать* (взять* *perf*) на себя́ веду́щую роль; **to ~ the way** (*also fig*) ука́зывать (указа́ть* *perf*) путь; **to ~ sb astray** вводи́ть* (ввести́* *perf*) кого́-н в заблужде́ние; **to ~ sb to do** приводи́ть* (привести́* *perf*) кого́-н к чему́-н; **to ~ sb to believe that ...** дава́ть* (дать* *perf*) кому́-н поня́ть, что ...; **to ~ an interesting life** вести́* (*impf*) интере́сную жизнь; **to ~ an orchestra** (*BRIT*) исполня́ть (испо́лнить *perf*) пе́рвую скри́пку
▶ **lead away** *vt* уводи́ть* (увести́* *perf*)
▶ **lead back** *vt* приводи́ть* (привести́* *perf*) обра́тно
▶ **lead into** *vt fus* вводи́ть* (ввести́* *perf*) в +*acc*

---

* marks translations which have irregular inflections. The Russian-English side of the dictionary gives inflectional information.

▶ **lead off** *vi* (*in game, conversation*) начинáть (начáть* *perf*); (*road, corridor*) отходи́ть* (*impf*) ◆ *vt fus* отходи́ть* (*impf*) от +*gen*

▶ **lead on** *vt* (*tease*) води́ть* (*impf*) зá нос

▶ **lead out of** *vt fus* выводи́ть* (вы́вести* *perf*) из +*gen*

▶ **lead to** *vt fus* вести́* (привести́* *perf*) к +*dat*

▶ **lead up to** *vt fus* (*events*) приводи́ть* (привести́* *perf*) к +*dat*; (*topic*) подводи́ть* (подводи́ть* *perf*) к +*dat*.

lead² [lɛd] *n* (*metal*) свинéц*; (*in pencil*) графи́т.

leaded ['lɛdɪd] *adj* (*window, glass*) со свинцóвыми креплéниями; (*petrol*) содержáщий свинéц.

leaden ['lɛdn] *adj* (*sky, sea*) свинцóвый; (*movements*) скóванный (скóван).

leader ['liːdə'] *n* (*of group, SPORT*) ли́дер; (*in newspaper*) передовáя статья́; **the L~ of the House of Commons/Lords**) (*BRIT*) *представи́тель прáвящей пáртии в палáте Общи́н/Лóрдов, наделённый осóбыми полномóчиями.*

leadership ['liːdəʃɪp] *n* (*position, process*) руковóдство; (*quality*) ли́дерские кáчества *ntpl.*

lead-free ['lɛdfriː] *adj* (*petrol*) не содержáщий свинцá.

leading ['liːdɪŋ] *adj* (*most important*) веду́щий*; (*first, front*) передний*; (*winning*) лиди́рующий; ~ **role** (*in film, play*) глáвная роль *f.*

leading lady *n* (*THEAT*) исполни́тельница глáвной рóли.

leading light *n* (*person*) свети́ло.

leading man *irreg n* (*THEAT*) исполни́тель *m* глáвной рóли.

leading question *n* наводя́щий* вопрóс.

lead pencil [lɛd-] *n* графи́тный карандáш*.

lead poisoning [lɛd-] *n* отравлéние свинцóм.

lead singer [liːd-] *n* соли́ст(ка).

lead time [liːd-] *n* (*COMM*) врéмя* *ntsg* реализáции закáза.

lead-up ['liːdʌp] *n*: **in the ~ to** незадóлго до +*gen.*

leaf [liːf] (*pl* **leaves**) *n* (*BOT, of book*) лист*; (*of table*) откиднáя доскá* ◆ *vi*: **to ~ through** листáть (пролистáть* *perf*); **to turn over a new ~** начáть* (*perf*) нóвую жизнь; **to take a ~ out of sb's book** слéдовать (послéдовать *perf*) примéру когó-н.

leaflet ['liːflɪt] *n* листóвка*.

leafy ['liːfɪ] *adj* (*trees, vegetables*) покры́тый (покры́т) листвóй; (*place*) зелёный* (зéлен).

league [liːg] *n* ли́га; **to be in ~ with sb** быть* (*impf*) в сгóворе с кем-н.

league table *n* (*BRIT: SPORT*) табли́ца результáтов спортклу́бов однóй из лиг; (*fig: of wages, prices*) сравни́тельная табли́ца.

leak [liːk] *n* (*hole*) течь *f*; (*seepage*) утéчка*; (*fig*): (**information**) ~ утéчка* информáции ◆

vi (*pipe, roof, shoes*) протекáть (протéчь* *perf*); (*ship*) давáть* (дать* *perf*) течь; (*liquid, gas*) просáчиваться (просочи́ться *perf*) ◆ *vt* (*information*) разглашáть (разгласи́ть* *perf*).

▶ **leak out** *vi* (*liquid*) вытекáть (вы́течь* *perf*); (*information*) просáчиваться (просочи́ться *perf*).

leakage ['liːkɪdʒ] *n* утéчка*.

leaky ['liːkɪ] *adj* (*roof etc*) дыря́вый, прохуди́вшийся.

lean [liːn] (*pt, pp* **leaned** *or* **leant**) *adj* (*person*) поджáрый (поджáр); (*meat*) пóстный (*period*) скýдный* (скýден) ◆ *vi*: **to ~ sth on** *or* **against sth** прислоня́ть (прислони́ть *perf*) что-н к чему́-н ◆ *vi*: **to ~ (forward/back)** наклоня́ться (наклони́ться* *perf*) (вперёд/назáд); **to ~ against** (*wall*) прислоня́ться (прислони́ться *perf*) к +*dat*; (*person*) опирáться (оперéться* *perf*) на +*acc*; **to ~ on** (*chair*) опирáться (оперéться* *perf*) о +*acc*; (*rely on*) опирáться (оперéться* *perf*) на +*acc*; (*pressurize*) нажимáть (нажáть* *perf*) на +*acc*; **to ~ towards** (*idea, belief*) склоня́ться (склони́ться* *perf*) к +*dat*

▶ **lean out** *vi*: **to ~ out (of)** высóвываться (вы́сунуться *perf*) (из +*gen*)

▶ **lean over** *vi* наклоня́ться (наклони́ться* *perf*).

leaning ['liːnɪŋ] *n*: ~ **(towards)** склóнность *f* (к +*dat*).

leant [lɛnt] *pt, pp of* **lean.**

lean-to ['liːntuː] *n* пристрóйка*.

leap [liːp] (*pt, pp* **leaped** *or* **leapt**) *n* прыжóк*, скачóк*; (*increase*) скачóк* ◆ *vi* пры́гать (пры́гнуть *perf*); (*price, number*) подскáкивать (подскочи́ть *perf*); **to ~ at** (*offer, opportunity*) ухвати́ться* (*perf*) за +*acc*; **to ~ to one's feet** вскáкивать (вскочи́ть *perf*) нá ноги

▶ **leap up** *vi* подпры́гивать (подпры́гнуть *perf*).

leapfrog ['liːpfrɔg] *n* чехардá.

leapt [lɛpt] *pt, pp of* **leap.**

leap year *n* високóсный год*.

learn [ləːn] (*pt, pp* **learned** *or* **learnt**) *vt* (*skill*) учи́ться* (научи́ться* *perf*) +*dat*; (*facts, poem*) учи́ть* (вы́учить* *perf*) ◆ *vi* учи́ться* (*impf*); **to ~ about** *or* **of/that ...** (*hear, read*) узнавáть* (узнáть* *perf*) о +*prp/*, что ...; **to ~ about sth** (*study*) изучáть (изучи́ть* *perf*) что-н; **to ~ (how) to do** учи́ться* (научи́ться* *perf*) +*impf infin.*

learned ['ləːnɪd] *adj* учёный*.

learner ['ləːnə'] *n* учени́к*(-и́ца*).

learning ['ləːnɪŋ] *n* учёность *f*; **person of ~** учёный человéк.

learnt [ləːnt] *pt, pp of* **learn.**

lease [liːs] *n* арéндный договóр ◆ *vt*: **to ~ sth (to sb)** сдавáть* (сдать* *perf*) что-н в арéнду (комý-н); **to ~ sth from sb** арендовáть (*impf/perf*) *or* брать* (взять* *perf*) в арéнду у когó-н;

on ~ (to sb) сда́нный (сдан) в аре́нду (кому́-н)

► **lease back** vt сдава́ть (сдать* perf) в аре́нду пре́жнему владе́льцу (для мобилиза́ции де́нежных средств)

leaseback ['li:sbæk] n сда́ча со́бственности в аре́нду её пре́жнему владе́льцу.

leasehold ['li:shəuld] n (also: ~ **property**) арендо́ванная со́бственность f ♦ adj арендо́ванный (арендо́ван).

leash [li:ʃ] n поводо́к*.

least [li:st] adj: **the** ~ (+noun: smallest) наиме́ньший*; (: slightest) мале́йший* ♦ adv (+vb) ме́ньше всего́; (+adj): **the** ~ наиме́нее; **the** ~ **possible effort** наиме́ньшее уси́лие; **I don't have the** ~ **idea about it** я не име́ю ни мале́йшего представле́ния об э́том; **at** ~ по кра́йней ме́ре; **you could at** ~ **have written** Вы могли́ бы по кра́йней ме́ре написа́ть; **not in the** ~ совсе́м нет; (+vb, +adj) совсе́м or во́все не.

leather ['lɛðə'] n ко́жа.

leather goods npl ко́жаные изде́лия ntpl.

leave [li:v] (pt, pp **left**) vt оставля́ть (оста́вить* perf); (go away from: on foot) уходи́ть* (уйти́* perf) из +gen; (: by transport) уезжа́ть (уе́хать* perf) из +gen; (party, committee) выходи́ть* (вы́йти* perf) из +gen ♦ vi (on foot) уходи́ть* (уйти́* perf); (by transport) уезжа́ть (уе́хать* perf); (bus, train) уходи́ть* (уйти́* perf) ♦ n о́тпуск*; **to** ~ **sth to sb** (money, property) оставля́ть (оста́вить* perf) что-н кому́-н; (responsibility) оставля́ть (оста́вить* perf) что-н под чью-н отве́тственность; **to be left (over)** оставля́ться (оста́ться* perf); **to take one's** ~ **of sb** проща́ться (попроща́ться perf) с кем-н; **on** ~ в о́тпуске

► **leave behind** vt оставля́ть (оста́вить* perf)

► **leave off** vt (heating, light) не включа́ть (включи́ть perf) ♦ vi (stop: inf) отстава́ть* (отста́ть* perf); **he left the lid off** он не положи́л кры́шку

► **leave on** vt (coat) не снима́ть (снять* perf); (light, heating) оставля́ть (оста́вить* perf)

► **leave out** vt (omit) пропуска́ть (пропусти́ть* perf); **he was left out** его́ пропусти́ли.

leave of absence n о́тпуск без содержа́ния.

leaves [li:vz] npl of **leaf**.

Lebanese [lɛbə'ni:z] adj лива́нский* ♦ n inv лива́нец(-нка).

Lebanon ['lɛbənən] n Лива́н.

lecherous ['lɛtʃərəs] adj развра́тный* (развра́тен).

lectern ['lɛktə:n] n ка́федра.

lecture ['lɛktʃə'] n ле́кция ♦ vi чита́ть (impf) ле́кции ♦ vt (scold): **to** ~ **sb** on or **about sth** чита́ть (impf) кому́-н ле́кцию по по́воду чего́-н; **to give a** ~ **on** чита́ть (прочита́ть perf) ле́кцию о +prp.

lecture hall n аудито́рия, лекцио́нный зал.

lecturer ['lɛktʃərə'] n (BRIT: at university) преподава́тель(ница) m(f); (speaker) ле́ктор.

LED n abbr (ELEC: = light-emitting diode) СИД= светоизлуча́ющий дио́д.

led [lɛd] pt, pp of **lead**[1].

ledge [lɛdʒ] n (of mountain) вы́ступ; (of window) подоко́нник; (on wall) по́лка*.

ledger ['lɛdʒə'] n расхо́дно-прихо́дная кни́га.

lee [li:] n (shelter) покро́в.

leech [li:tʃ] n (also fig) пия́вка*.

leek [li:k] n лук-поре́й no pl.

leer [lɪə'] vi: **to** ~ **at sb** похотли́во смотре́ть (посмотре́ть perf) на кого́-н.

leeward ['li:wəd] (NAUT) adj подве́тренный ♦ adv с подве́тренной стороны́ ♦ n подве́тренная сторона́*; **to** ~ на подве́тренную сто́рону.

leeway ['li:weɪ] n (fig): **to allow o.s. some** ~ дава́ть* (дать* perf) себе́ свобо́ду; **we have a lot of** ~ **to make up** нам ну́жно мно́гое наверста́ть.

left [lɛft] pt, pp of **leave** ♦ adj (remaining) оста́вшийся; (of direction, position) ле́вый ♦ n ле́вая сторона́* ♦ adv (motion): **(to the)** ~ нале́во; (position): **(on the)** ~ сле́ва; **the L**~ (POL) ле́вые pl adj.

left-hand drive ['lɛfthænd-] adj (AUT) с рулём на ле́вой стороне́.

left-handed [lɛft'hændɪd] adj: **he/she is** ~ он/ она́ левша́.

left-hand side n: **the** ~ ~ ле́вая сторона́.

leftie ['lɛftɪ] n (inf: pej: BRIT: left winger) ле́вый(-ая) m/f adj.

leftist ['lɛftɪst] n ле́вый(-ая) m(f) adj ♦ adj ле́вый.

left-luggage (office) [lɛft'lʌgɪdʒ(-)] n (BRIT) ка́мера хране́ния.

leftovers ['lɛftəuvəz] npl оста́тки mpl.

left-wing ['lɛft'wɪŋ] adj (POL) ле́вый.

left-winger ['lɛft'wɪŋə'] n (BRIT: POL) ле́вый(-ая) m(f) adj, представи́тель m ле́вого крыла́.

lefty ['lɛftɪ] n = **leftie**.

leg [lɛg] n (ANAT, also CULIN: of lamb) нога́*; (of insect, furniture, also CULIN: of chicken) но́жка*; (also: trouser ~) штани́на; (of journey, race) эта́п; **to stretch one's** ~**s** размина́ть (размя́ть* perf) но́ги.

legacy ['lɛgəsɪ] n (in will) насле́дство; (fig) насле́дие.

legal ['li:gl] adj (advice, requirement) юриди́ческий*; (system, action) суде́бный; (lawful) зако́нный (зако́нен); **to take** ~ **action** or **proceedings against sb** возбужда́ть (возбуди́ть* perf) суде́бное де́ло про́тив кого́-н.

legal adviser n юрисконсу́льт.

---

legal holiday n (US) неприсутственный день* m.

legality [lɪˈgælɪtɪ] n законность f.

legalize [ˈliːgəlaɪz] vt узаконивать (узаконить* perf); (party, group) легализовать (impf/perf).

legally [ˈliːgəlɪ] adv юридически; (act) законно; (by law) по закону; ~ **binding** юридически обязательный* (обязателен).

legal tender n законное средство платежа (обычно о бумажных и металлических деньгах).

legatee [lɛgəˈtiː] n наследник.

legation [lɪˈgeɪʃən] n миссия, представительство.

legend [ˈlɛdʒənd] n (story) легенда; (person) легендарная личность f.

legendary [ˈlɛdʒəndərɪ] adj легендарный* (легендарен).

-legged [ˈlɛgɪd] suffix -ногий*.

leggy [ˈlɛgɪ] adj длинноногий* (длинноног).

leggings [ˈlɛgɪŋz] npl лосины fpl.

legibility [lɛdʒɪˈbɪlɪtɪ] n разборчивость f.

legible [ˈlɛdʒəbl] adj разборчивый (разборчив).

legibly [ˈlɛdʒəblɪ] adv разборчиво.

legion [ˈliːdʒən] n легион ◆ adj (numerous): **their problems are** ~ у них легион проблем.

legionnaire [liːdʒəˈnɛəˈ] n легионер.

legionnaire's disease n болезнь f „легионеров".

legislate [ˈlɛdʒɪsleɪt] vi издавать* (издать* perf) закон(ы).

legislation [lɛdʒɪsˈleɪʃən] n законодательство.

legislative [ˈlɛdʒɪslətɪv] adj (POL) законодательный.

legislator [ˈlɛdʒɪsleɪtəˈ] n (POL) законодатель m.

legislature [ˈlɛdʒɪslətʃəˈ] n законодательные органы mpl.

legitimacy [lɪˈdʒɪtɪməsɪ] n законность f.

legitimate [lɪˈdʒɪtɪmət] adj законный* (законен).

legitimize [lɪˈdʒɪtɪmaɪz] vt узаконивать (узаконить perf).

legless [ˈlɛglɪs] adj (without legs) безногий* (безног); (very drunk: inf: BRIT) пьяный в стельку.

legroom [ˈlɛgruːm] n (in car etc) пространство для ног.

Leics abbr (BRIT: POST) = **Leicestershire.**

Leipzig [ˈlaɪpsɪg] n Лейпциг.

leisure [ˈlɛʒəˈ] n (also: ~ **time**) досуг, свободное время* nt; **to do sth at (one's)** ~ делать (сделать perf) что-н не спеша.

leisure centre n спортивно-оздоровительный комплекс.

leisurely [ˈlɛʒəlɪ] adj неторопливый (неторопл́ив).

leisure suit n спортивный костюм.

lemon [ˈlɛmən] n лимон ◆ adj лимонный.

lemonade [lɛməˈneɪd] n лимонад.

lemon cheese n = **lemon curd.**

lemon curd n (CULIN) сладкое лимонное повидло.

lemon juice n лимонный сок*.

lemon squeezer n (ручная) соковыжималка*.

lemon tea n чай* с лимоном.

lend [lɛnd] (pt, pp **lent**) vt: **to ~ sth to sb, ~ sb sth** одалживать (одолжить perf) что-н кому-н; **it ~s itself to ...** это поддаётся +dat ...; **to ~ sb a hand** выручать (выручить perf) кого-н.

lender [ˈlɛndəˈ] n кредитор.

lending library [ˈlɛndɪŋ-] n библиотека, выдающая книги на дом.

length [lɛŋθ] n (measurement) длина; (distance) протяжённость f; (piece: of wood, cloth etc) кусок*; (duration) продолжительность f; (of book) объём; **2 metres in** ~ длиной в 2 метра; **he walked the (whole)** ~ **of the island** он прошёл через весь остров; **I swam three ~s** я проплыл три длины плавательного бассейна; **at** ~ (at last) наконец; (for a long time) долго; **to lie full** ~ растягиваться (растянуться* perf) во весь рост; **to go to any ~(s) to do** прикладывать (приложить* perf) все усилия чтобы +perf infin.

lengthen [ˈlɛŋθn] vt удлинять (удлинить perf) ◆ vi удлиняться (удлиниться perf).

lengthways [ˈlɛŋθweɪz] adv вдоль.

lengthy [ˈlɛŋθɪ] adj (text) длинный* (длинен); (meeting) продолжительный* (продолжителен); (explanation) долгий*.

leniency [ˈliːnɪənsɪ] n мягкость f.

lenient [ˈliːnɪənt] adj мягкий* (мягок).

leniently [ˈliːnɪəntlɪ] adv мягко.

Leningrad [ˈlɛnɪngræd] n Ленинград.

lens [lɛnz] n (of spectacles, camera) линза; (of telescope) объектив.

Lent [lɛnt] n Великий* пост*.

lent [lɛnt] pt, pp of **lend.**

lentil [ˈlɛntl] n чечевица no pl.

Leo [ˈliːəu] n Лев*; **he is** ~ он – Лев.

leopard [ˈlɛpəd] n леопард.

leotard [ˈliːətɑːd] n трико nt ind.

leper [ˈlɛpəˈ] n прокажённый(-ая) m(f) adj.

leper colony n лепрозорий.

leprosy [ˈlɛprəsɪ] n проказа.

lesbian [ˈlɛzbɪən] adj лесбийский ◆ n лесбиянка*.

lesion [ˈliːʒən] n повреждение.

Lesotho [lɪˈsuːtuː] n Лесото.

less [lɛs] adj (in size, degree, amount) меньше; (in quality) менее ◆ adv меньше ◆ prep: ~ **tax/10% discount** минус налог/скидка на 10%; ~ **than half** меньше половины; ~ **than ever** меньше, чем когда-либо; ~ **and** ~ всё меньше и меньше; **the** ~ ... **the more** ... чем меньше ..., тем больше ...; **the Prime Minister, no** ~ никто иной как премьер-министр.

lessee [lɛˈsiː] n (of premises) съёмщик; (of land) арендатор.

lessen ['lɛsn] vt уменьша́ть (уме́ньшить perf).
♦ vi уменьша́ться (уме́ньшиться perf).
lesser ['lɛsəʳ] adj ме́ньший*; **to a ~ extent** в
ме́ньшей сте́пени.
lesson ['lɛsn] n (also fig) уро́к; **to teach sb a ~**
(fig) проучи́ть* (perf) кого́-н.
lessor ['lɛsɔːʳ] n лицо́, сдаю́щее со́бствен-
ность в аре́нду.
lest [lɛst] conj: ~ **you (should) forget** что́бы Вы
не забы́ли.
let [lɛt] (pt, pp **let**) vt (BRIT: lease) сдава́ть*
(сдать* perf) (внаём); (allow): **to ~ sb do**
разреша́ть (разреши́ть perf) or позволя́ть
(позво́лить perf) кому́-н +infin; ~ **me try**
да́йте я попро́бую; ~ **him come** пусть он
придёт; **to ~ sb know about ...** дава́ть* (дать*
perf) кому́-н знать o +prp ...; ~'s **go** пошли́,
пойдёмте; **"to ~"** „сдаётся внаём"; **to ~ go of**
отпуска́ть (отпусти́ть* perf); ~ **go!** (от)пусти́!;
to ~ sth drop роня́ть (урони́ть* perf) что-н; **to**
~ **o.s. go** (relax) расслабля́ться
(рассла́биться* perf); (neglect o.s.)
опуска́ться (опусти́ться* perf)
▶ **let down** vt (tyre etc) спуска́ть (спусти́ть*
perf); (fig: person) подводи́ть* (подвести́*
perf); (hair) распуска́ть (распусти́ть* perf);
(dress, hem) отпуска́ть (отпусти́ть* perf)
▶ **let in** vt (water, air) пропуска́ть (пропусти́ть*
perf); (person) впуска́ть (впусти́ть* perf)
▶ **let off** vt (culprit, schoolchildren) отпуска́ть
(отпусти́ть* perf); (bomb) взрыва́ть
(взорва́ть* perf); (gun) выстре́ливать
(вы́стрелить perf) из +gen; (smell) испуска́ть
(испусти́ть* perf); **to ~ off steam** (inf)
выпуска́ть (вы́пустить* perf) пар
▶ **let on** vi проговори́ваться (проговори́ться
perf)
▶ **let out** vt (person, dog, water, air) выпуска́ть
(вы́пустить* perf); (passenger) выса́живать
(вы́садить* perf); (sound) издава́ть* (изда́ть*
perf); (house, room) сдава́ть* (сдать* perf)
▶ **let up** vi (cease) переставать* (переста́ть*
perf); (diminish) ослабева́ть (ослабе́ть perf).
letdown ['lɛtdaun] n разочарова́ние.
lethal ['liːθl] adj (weapon, chemical)
смертоно́сный (смертоно́сен); (dose)
смерте́льный* (смерте́лен).
lethargic [lɛ'θɑːdʒɪk] adj вя́лый* (вял),
со́нный* (со́нен).
lethargy ['lɛθədʒɪ] n вя́лость f.
letter ['lɛtəʳ] n (correspondence) письмо́*; (of
alphabet) бу́ква; **small/capital ~** строчна́я/
прописна́я бу́ква.
letter bomb n бо́мба, при́сланная по по́чте.
letter box n (BRIT) почто́вый я́щик.
letterhead ['lɛtəhɛd] n ша́пка (в письме́).
lettering ['lɛtərɪŋ] n шрифт.
letter of credit n аккредити́в.

letter opener n нож для разреза́ния бума́ги.
letterpress ['lɛtəprɛs] n (method) высо́кая
печа́ть f.
letter quality n (of printer) ка́чество печа́ти.
letters patent npl пате́нт.
lettuce ['lɛtɪs] n сала́т* лату́к.
let-up ['lɛtʌp] n ослабле́ние.
leukaemia [luː'kiːmɪə] (US **leukemia**) n
белокро́вие, лейкеми́я.
level ['lɛvl] adj (flat) ро́вный* (ро́вен) ♦ n
у́ровень m; (also: spirit ~) ватерпа́с ♦ vt
(land) ровня́ть (сровня́ть perf); (building)
сровня́ть (perf) c землёй ♦ vi (inf): **to ~ with**
sb объясня́ться (объясни́ться perf) c кем-н
начистоту́ ♦ adv: **to draw ~ with** (person,
vehicle) поравня́ться (perf) c +instr; **to be ~**
with быть* (impf) на одно́м у́ровне c +instr;
"A" ~s (BRIT: exams) выпускны́е экза́мены (в
сре́дней шко́ле); (: qualification)
квалифика́ция, получа́емая при успе́шной
сда́че выпускно́го экза́мена; **on the ~** (inf)
че́стный* (че́стен); **to ~ a gun at sb** наводи́ть*
(навести́* perf) ружьё на кого́-н; **to ~ an**
accusation/a criticism at or against sb
направля́ть (напра́вить* perf) обвине́ние/
кри́тику про́тив кого́-н
▶ **level off** vi (prices etc) выра́вниваться
(вы́ровняться* perf)
▶ **level out** vi = **level off**.
level crossing n (BRIT) железнодоро́жный
перее́зд.
level-headed [lɛvl'hɛdɪd] adj уравнове́шенный
(уравнове́шен).
levelling ['lɛvlɪŋ] n выра́внивание.
level playing field n ра́вные пози́ции fpl.
lever ['liːvəʳ] n (also fig) рыча́г*; (bar) лом ♦ vt:
to ~ up/out поднима́ть (подня́ть perf)/
тащи́ть (вы́тащить perf) c уси́лием.
leverage ['liːvərɪdʒ] n рыча́жная си́ла; (fig:
influence) влия́ние.
levity ['lɛvɪtɪ] n легкомы́слие.
levy ['lɛvɪ] n нало́г ♦ vt взима́ть (impf).
lewd [luːd] adj (look) похотли́вый (похотли́в);
(remark) непристо́йный* (непристо́ен).
lexicographer [lɛksi'kɔgrəfəʳ] n лексико́граф.
lexicography [lɛksi'kɔgrəfɪ] n лексикогра́фия.
LI abbr (US) = **Long Island**.
liability [laɪə'bɪlətɪ] n (LAW: responsibility)
отве́тственность f; (person, thing) обу́за m/f;
liabilities npl (COMM) обяза́тельства ntpl.
liable ['laɪəbl] (LAW) adj (responsible): ~ **for** (for
actions) отве́тственный (отве́тствен) за
+acc; (legally responsible) подсу́дный*
(подсу́ден) за +acc; (subject): ~ **to**
подлежа́щий +dat; **to be ~ for** нести́* (impf)
отве́тственность за +acc; **to be ~ to**
подлежа́ть (impf) +dat; **he's ~ to take offence**
возмо́жно, что он оби́дится.

---

* marks translations which have irregular inflections. The Russian-English side of the dictionary gives inflectional information.

liaise [li:'eɪz] *vi*: **to ~ (with)** кооперироваться (скооперироваться *perf*) (с +*instr*).

liaison [li:'eɪzɒn] *n* (*cooperation*) координация; (*sexual*) связь *f*.

liar ['laɪə'] *n* лжец*, лгун*(ья).

libel ['laɪbl] *n* клевета ♦ *vt* клеветать* (оклеветать* *perf*).

libellous ['laɪbləs], (*US* **libelous**) *adj* (*comment etc*) клеветнический*.

liberal ['lɪbərl] *adj* (*tolerant, also* POL) либеральный* (либерален); (*large, generous*) щедрый; **~ with** щедрый* (щедр) на +*acc* ♦ *n* (*tolerant person*) либерал; (POL): **L~** либерал.

liberalize ['lɪbərəlaɪz] *vt* либерализовать (*impf*/ *perf*).

liberally ['lɪbrəlɪ] *adv* (*see adj*) либерально; щедро.

Liberal Democrat *n* либерал-демократ; **the ~ ~s** (*party*) партия Либерал-демократов.

liberal-minded ['lɪbərl'maɪndɪd] *adj* либерально-настроенный (либерально-настроен).

liberate ['lɪbəreɪt] *vt* освобождать (освободить* *perf*).

liberation [lɪbə'reɪʃən] *n* освобождение.

Liberia [laɪ'bɪərɪə] *n* Либерия.

Liberian [laɪ'bɪərɪən] *adj* либерийский ♦ *n* либериец*(-ийка*).

liberty ['lɪbətɪ] *n* свобода; **to be at ~** (*criminal*) быть* (*impf*) на свободе; **I'm not at ~ to comment** я не волен комментировать; **to take the ~ of doing** позволять (позволить* *perf*) себе +*infin*.

libido [lɪ'bi:dəu] *n* либидо *nt ind*.

Libra ['li:brə] *n* Весы *pl*; **he is ~** он – Весы.

librarian [laɪ'brɛərɪən] *n* библиотекарь *m*.

library ['laɪbrərɪ] *n* библиотека.

library book *n* библиотечная книга.

libretto [lɪ'brɛtəu] *n* либретто *nt ind*.

Libya ['lɪbɪə] *n* Ливия.

Libyan ['lɪbɪən] *adj* ливийский ♦ *n* ливиец*(-ийка*).

lice [laɪs] *npl of* **louse**.

licence ['laɪsns] (*US* **license**) *n* (*permit*) лицензия; (AUT: *also*: **driving ~**) (водительские) права *ntpl*; (*freedom*) вольность *f*; **under ~** (COMM) по лицензии.

license ['laɪsns] *n* (*US*) = **licence** ♦ *vt* выдавать* (выдать* *perf*) лицензию на +*acc*.

licensed ['laɪsnst] *adj* (*car etc*) зарегистрированный (зарегистрирован); (*restaurant*) с лицензией на продажу спиртных напитков.

licensed trade *n организации, торгующие алкогольными напитками*.

licensee [laɪsn'si:] *n* держатель *m* лицензии.

license plate *n* (*US*) номерной знак (*на автомобиле*).

licensing hours ['laɪsnsɪŋ] *npl* (BRIT) *часы, в которые разрешена торговля спиртными напитками*.

licentious [laɪ'sɛnʃəs] *adj* распущенный (распущен).

lichen ['laɪkən] *n* лишайник.

lick [lɪk] *vt* (*stamp, fingers etc*) лизать* (*impf*), облизывать (облизать* *perf*); (*inf: defeat*) положить* (*perf*) на лопатки ♦ *n*: **to give sth a ~** лизнуть (*perf*) что-н; **to give sth a ~ of paint** подкрашивать (подкрасить* *perf*) что-н; **to one's lips** облизываться (облизаться* *perf*); (*fig*) облизываться (*impf*).

licorice ['lɪkərɪs] *n* (*US*) = **liquorice**.

lid [lɪd] *n* крышка*; (*also*: **eyelid**) веко; **to take the ~ off sth** (*fig person*) вытаскивать (вытащить* *perf*) что-н на свет божий.

lido ['laɪdəu] *n* (BRIT: *pool*) бассейн на открытом воздухе.

lie [laɪ] (*pt* **lay**, *pp* **lain**) *vi* (*be horizontal*) лежать* (*impf*); (*be situated*) лежать* (*impf*), находиться* (*impf*); (*problem, cause*) заключаться (*impf*); (*be untruthful*) (*pt, pp* **lied**) лгать (солгать* *perf*), врать (соврать* *perf*) ♦ *n* (*untrue statement*) ложь* *f no pl*; **to ~ or be lying in first/last place** быть* (*impf*) на первом/ последнем месте; **to ~ low** (*fig*) пережидать (переждать* *perf*); **to tell ~s** говорить (*impf*) неправду

▶ **lie about** *vi* валяться (*impf*)

▶ **lie around** *vi* = **lie about**

▶ **lie back** *vi* откидываться (откинуться *perf*); (*fig*) успокаиваться (успокоиться *perf*)

▶ **lie down** *vi* ложиться (лечь* *perf*); **to be lying down** лежать* (*impf*)

▶ **lie up** *vi* (*hide*) скрываться (скрыться* *perf*).

Liechtenstein ['lɪktənstaɪn] *n* Лихтенштейн.

lie detector *n* детектор лжи.

lie-down ['laɪdaun] *n* (BRIT): **to have a ~** полежать* (*perf*).

lie-in ['laɪɪn] *n* (BRIT): **to have a ~** вставать* (встать* *perf*) попозже.

lieu [lu:]: **in ~ of** *prep* вместо +*gen*.

Lieut. *abbr* (MIL) = **lieutenant**.

lieutenant [lɛf'tɛnənt], (*US*) lu:'tɛnənt] *n* лейтенант.

lieutenant colonel *n* подполковник.

life [laɪf] (*pl* **lives**) *n* жизнь *f no pl*; **true to ~** правдоподобный* (правдоподобен); **to paint from ~** писать* (написать* *perf*) с натуры; **to be sent to prison for ~** получать (получить* *perf*) пожизненное заключение; **to come to ~** (*fig: person*) оживать (ожить* *perf*); (: *party*) оживляться (оживиться* *perf*).

life annuity *n* пожизненный аннуитет.

life assurance *n* (BRIT) = **life insurance**.

life belt *n* (BRIT) спасательный круг*.

lifeblood ['laɪfblʌd] *n* (*fig*) жизненная основа.

lifeboat ['laɪfbəut] *n* (*rescue launch*) спасательное судно*; (*on ship*) спасательная шлюпка.

life buoy *n* = **life belt**.

life expectancy *n* продолжительность *f* жизни.

lifeguard ['laɪfgɑːd] n спаса́тель(ница) m(f).
life imprisonment n пожи́зненное
    заключе́ние.
life insurance n страхова́ние жи́зни.
life jacket n спаса́тельный жиле́т.
lifeless ['laɪflɪs] adj (also fig) безжи́зненный
    (безжи́знен).
lifelike ['laɪflaɪk] adj (model, robot) как живо́й;
    (performance) реалисти́чный*
    (реалисти́чен).
lifeline ['laɪflaɪn] n (fig) сре́дство вы́живания;
    (rope) спаса́тельный кана́т.
lifelong ['laɪflɔŋ] adj (friend, habit)
    неизме́нный; **it was a ~ ambition of his** э́то
    бы́ло мечто́й всей его́ жи́зни.
life preserver n (US) = **life belt, life jacket**.
lifer ['laɪfə'] n бессро́чник(-ица).
life raft n спаса́тельный плот*.
life-saver ['laɪfseɪvə'] n спасе́ние.
life science n есте́ственные нау́ки fpl.
life sentence n пригово́р к пожи́зненному
    заключе́нию.
life-size(d) ['laɪfsaɪz(d)] adj в натура́льную
    величину́.
life span n (of living thing) продолж-
    и́тельность f жи́зни; (of product) срок*
    слу́жбы; (of idea, organization)
    долгове́чность f.
lifestyle ['laɪfstaɪl] n о́браз жи́зни.
life-support system ['laɪfsəpɔːt-] n систе́ма
    жизнеобеспече́ния.
lifetime ['laɪftaɪm] n (of person) жизнь f; (of
    institution) вре́мя* nt существова́ния; **the
    chance of a ~** уника́льный шанс.
lift [lɪft] vt поднима́ть (подня́ть* perf); (ban,
    sanctions) снима́ть (снять* perf); (inf: steal)
    тащи́ть (стащи́ть* perf) ◆ vi (fog)
    рассе́иваться (рассе́яться perf) ◆ n (BRIT)
    лифт; **to give sb a ~** (BRIT: AUT) подвози́ть*
    (подвезти́* perf) кого́-н
▸ **lift in** vt (goods, people) ввози́ть* (ввезти́*
    perf) самолётом
▸ **lift off** vi (rocket) отрыва́ться (оторва́ться*
    perf) от земли́, стартова́ть (impf/perf)
▸ **lift out** vt (goods, people) вывози́ть*
    (вы́везти* perf) самолётом
▸ **lift up** vt (object, person) поднима́ть
    (подня́ть* perf).
liftoff ['lɪftɔf] n старт.
ligament ['lɪgəmənt] n (ANAT) свя́зка*.
light [laɪt] (pt, pp lit) n свет*; (AUT) фа́ра ◆ vt
    (candle, cigarette, fire) зажига́ть (заже́чь*
    perf); (place) освеща́ть (освети́ть* perf) ◆ adj
    (pale, bright) све́тлый* (све́тел); (not heavy)
    лёгкий* (лёгок) ◆ adv (travel) налегке́; **~s** npl
    (also: **traffic ~s**) светофо́р msg; **to turn the ~
    on/off** включа́ть (включи́ть perf)/выключа́ть
    (вы́ключить perf) свет; **have you got a ~?** (for

cigarette) мо́жно у Вас прикури́ть?; **to come
    to ~** выясня́ться (вы́ясниться perf); **to cast** or
    shed or **throw ~ on** пролива́ть (проли́ть* perf)
    свет на +acc; **in the ~ of** (discussions, new
    evidence) в све́те +gen; **to make ~ of** не
    заостря́ть (impf) внима́ние на +acc; **the house
    is lit by electricity** дом освещён
    электри́чеством
▸ **light up** vi (face) светле́ть (просветле́ть perf)
    ◆ vt (illuminate) освеща́ть (освети́ть* perf).
light bulb n ла́мпочка*.
lighten ['laɪtn] vi (become less dark) светле́ть
    (посветле́ть perf) ◆ vt (make less heavy)
    облегча́ть (облегчи́ть perf).
lighter ['laɪtə'] n (also: cigarette ~) зажига́лка*;
    (boat) ли́хтер.
light-fingered [laɪt'fɪŋgəd] adj нечи́стый*
    (нечи́ст) на́ руку.
light-headed [laɪt'hɛdɪd] adj: **she felt ~** у неё
    кружи́лась голова́.
light-hearted [laɪt'hɑːtɪd] adj (person)
    беспе́чный* (беспе́чен); (question, remark)
    несерьёзный* (несерьёзен).
lighthouse ['laɪthaus] n мая́к*.
lighting ['laɪtɪŋ] n освеще́ние.
lighting-up time [laɪtɪŋ'ʌp-] n вре́мя* nt
    включе́ния у́личного освеще́ния.
lightly ['laɪtlɪ] adv (touch, kiss) слегка́; (eat,
    treat) легко́; (sleep) неглубоко́; **to get off ~**
    легко́ отде́лываться (отде́латься perf).
light meter n экспоно́метр.
lightness ['laɪtnɪs] n (in weight) лёгкость f.
lightning ['laɪtnɪŋ] n мо́лния ◆ adj (rapid)
    молниено́сный* (молниено́сен).
lightning conductor n (BRIT) громоотво́д.
lightning rod n (US) = **lightning conductor**.
light pen n прибо́р, счи́тывающий штрихово́й
    код.
lightship ['laɪtʃɪp] n плаву́чий* мая́к*.
lightweight ['laɪtweɪt] adj (suit) лёгкий* ◆ n
    (BOXING) бо́ксер лёгкого ве́са.
light year n светово́й год*.
like [laɪk] prep как +acc; (similar to) похо́жий на
    +acc ◆ adj подо́бный (подо́бен) ◆ vt (sweets,
    reading) люби́ть* (impf); (find attractive,
    acceptable): **I ~ him** он мне нра́вится ◆ n: **and
    the ~** тому́ подо́бное; **to be** or **look ~**
    походи́ть* (impf) на +acc; **he looks ~ his father**
    он похо́ж на своего́ отца́; **what does she look
    ~?** как она́ вы́глядит?; **what's he ~?** что он
    за челове́к?; **what's the weather ~?** кака́я
    сего́дня пого́да?; **something ~ that** что́-то в
    э́том ро́де; **I feel ~ a drink** я хочу́ что́-нибудь
    вы́пить; **there's nothing ~ ...** ничто́ не мо́жет
    сравни́ться с +instr ...; **do it ~ this** де́лайте
    (сде́лайте perf) э́то так; **that's just ~ him**
    (typical) э́то на него́ похо́же; **it is nothing ~ ...**
    э́то совсе́м не то, что ...; **I would ~, I'd ~** мне

хотелось бы, я бы хотел; **would you ~ a coffee?** хотите кофе?; **I ~d him** он мне понравился; **I don't ~ his behaviour** мне не нравится его поведение; **if you ~** если хотите; **his ~s and dislikes** его вкусы.
likeable ['laɪkəbl] *adj* симпатичный* (симпатичен).
likelihood ['laɪklɪhud] *n* вероятность *f*; **in all ~** по всей вероятности; **there is every ~ that ...** очень вероятно, что ....
likely ['laɪklɪ] *adj* вероятный* (вероятен); **she is ~ to agree** она вероятно согласится; **not ~!** (*inf*) ни за что!
like-minded ['laɪk'maɪndɪd] *adj:* **a ~ person** единомышленник; **~ friends/colleagues** друзья/коллеги – единомышленники.
liken ['laɪkən] *vt:* **to ~ sth/sb to** уподоблять (уподобить* *perf*) что-н/кого-н +*dat*.
likeness ['laɪknɪs] *n* сходство; **the portrait is a good ~ of her** портрет обнаруживает большое сходство с ней.
likewise ['laɪkwaɪz] *adv* также; **to do ~** поступать (поступить* *perf*) таким же образом.
liking ['laɪkɪŋ] *n:* **~ (for)** (*person*) симпатия (к +*dat*); (*thing*) вкус (к +*dat*); **to be to sb's ~** быть* (*impf*) *or* приходиться* (прийтись* *perf*) кому-н по вкусу; **I took an instant ~ to him** он мне сразу понравился.
lilac ['laɪlək] *n* сирень *f no pl* ♦ *adj* сиреневый.
Lilo® ['laɪləu] *n* надувной резиновый матрац.
lilt [lɪlt] *n* (*in voice*) переливы *mpl*.
lilting ['lɪltɪŋ] *adj* (*voice*) мелодичный* (мелодичен).
lily ['lɪlɪ] *n* лилия.
lily of the valley *n* ландыш.
Lima ['li:mə] *n* Лима.
limb [lɪm] *n* (*ANAT*) конечность *f*; (*of tree*) ветвь *f*; **to be out on a ~** быть* (*impf*) *or* находиться* (*impf*) в критическом положении.
limber up ['lɪmbə'-] *vi* разминаться (размяться* *perf*).
limbo ['lɪmbəu] *n:* **to be in ~** (*fig*) находиться* (*impf*) в состоянии неопределённости.
lime [laɪm] *n* (*fruit*) лайм; (*tree*) липа*; (*also:* **~ juice**) сок лайма; (*chemical*) известь *f*; (*rock*) известняк*.
limelight ['laɪmlaɪt] *n:* **to be in the ~** быть* (*impf*) в центре внимания.
limerick ['lɪmərɪk] *n* лимерик (*юмористическое пятистрочное стихотворение*).
limestone ['laɪmstəun] *n* известняк*.
limit ['lɪmɪt] *n* предел; (*restriction*) лимит, ограничение ♦ *vt* (*production, expense etc*) лимитировать (*impf/perf*), ограничивать (ограничить *perf*); **speed ~** предельная скорость *f*; **within ~s** в пределах допустимого; **that's the ~!** это переходит все границы!

limitation [lɪmɪ'teɪʃən] *n* ограничение; **~s** *npl* недостатки *mpl*.
limited ['lɪmɪtɪd] *adj* ограниченный (ограничен); **to be ~ to** ограничиваться (ограничиться *perf*) +*instr*.
limited edition *n* малотиражное издание.
limited (liability) company *n* (*BRIT*) компания с ограниченной ответственностью.
limitless ['lɪmɪtlɪs] *adj* беспредельный* (беспределен).
limousine ['lɪməzi:n] *n* лимузин.
limp [lɪmp] *vi* хромать (*impf*) ♦ *adj* (*person, limb*) бессильный* (бессилен); (*material*) мягкий* (мягок) ♦ *n:* **to have a ~** хромать (*impf*).
limpet ['lɪmpɪt] *n* блюдечко* (*моллюск*).
limpid ['lɪmpɪd] *adj* прозрачный* (прозрачен).
limply ['lɪmplɪ] *adv* (*lie*) бессильно; (*fall*) мягко.
linchpin ['lɪntʃpɪn] *n* опора.
Lincs [lɪŋks] *abbr* (*BRIT: POST*) = Lincolnshire.
line [laɪn] *n* (*also TEL, RAIL*) линия; (*row*) ряд*; (*US: queue*) очередь *f*; (*of writing, song*) строка*, строчка*; (*wrinkle*) морщина; (*rope*) верёвка*; (*for fishing*) леска*; (*wire*) провод; (*route*) маршрут; (*fig: attitude, policy*) линия; (*: of thought, reasoning*) ход; (*of business, work*) область *f*; (*of product(s)*) модель *f*, тип ♦ *vt* (*stand along*) выстраиваться (выстроиться *perf*) вдоль +*gen*; (*clothing*) подбивать (подбить* *perf*); (*container*) выкладывать (выложить* *perf*) изнутри; **hold the ~ please!** (*TEL*) пожалуйста, не кладите трубку!; **to cut in ~** (*US*) идти* (пойти* *perf*) без очереди; **to stand in ~** (*in a row*) стоять (*impf*) в шеренге *or* ряд; **in ~ with** (*in keeping with*) в соответствии с +*instr*; **to bring sth into ~ with sth** приводить* (привести* *perf*) что-н в соответствие с чем-н; **on the right ~s** на верном пути; **to draw the ~ at sth** ограничиваться (ограничиться *perf*) чем-н; **he is in ~ for a pay rise** он скоро должен получить повышение зарплаты; **the streets are ~d with trees** улицы обсажены деревьями; **the walls were ~d with pictures** стены были завешены картинами
▶ **line up** *vi* выстраиваться (выстроиться *perf*) ♦ *vt* (*place in order*) выстраивать (выстроить *perf*); (*prepare*) подготавливать (подготовить* *perf*); **she has a new job ~d up** она устроилась на новую работу.
linear ['lɪnɪə] *adj* линейный*.
lined [laɪnd] *adj* (*paper*) линованный*; (*face*) морщинистый (морщинист); (*skirt, jacket*) на подкладке, с подкладкой.
line editing *n* (*COMPUT*) построчное редактирование.
line feed *n* (*COMPUT*) перевод *or* прогон строки.
lineman ['laɪnmən] *n* (*US: workman*) инженер телефонной связи; (*: SPORT*) боковой судья.
linen ['lɪnɪn] *n* (*material*) лён*; (*sheets etc*)

бельё.
line printer n (COMPUT) постро́чно-печата́ющее устро́йство, устро́йство постро́чной печа́ти.
liner ['laɪnə^r] n (ship) ла́йнер; (also: **bin** ~) целофа́новый мешо́к для му́сорного ведра́.
linesman ['laɪnzmən] irreg n судья́* m на ли́нии.
line-up ['laɪnʌp] n (also: **team** ~) соста́в кома́нды; (at event) соста́в уча́стников; (US: queue) о́чередь* f; (identity parade) опозна́ние (престу́пника).
linger ['lɪŋgə^r] vi (smell, tradition) уде́рживаться (удержа́ться* perf); (person) заде́рживаться (задержа́ться* perf).
lingerie ['lænʒəri:] n же́нское ни́жнее бельё.
lingering ['lɪŋgərɪŋ] adj (sense, feeling, doubt) усто́йчивый.
lingo ['lɪŋgəu] (pl ~es) n (inf: language) (иностра́нный) язы́к.
linguist ['lɪŋgwɪst] n (language specialist) лингви́ст; **he is a good** ~ (speaks several languages) он спосо́бен к языка́м.
linguistic [lɪŋ'gwɪstɪk] adj лингвисти́ческий*.
linguistics [lɪŋ'gwɪstɪks] n языкозна́ние, лингви́стика.
liniment ['lɪnɪmənt] n жи́дкая мазь f.
lining ['laɪnɪŋ] n (cloth) подкла́дка*; (TECH) прокла́дка*; (of stomach etc) вы́стилка.
link [lɪŋk] n связь f; (of a chain) звено́* ♦ vt (join) соединя́ть (соедини́ть perf); (associate): **to** ~ **with** or **to** свя́зывать (связа́ть* perf) с +instr; ~**s** npl (GOLF) по́ле для игры́ в гольф; **rail** ~ железнодоро́жная связь
  ▶ **link up** vt (machines, systems) соединя́ть (соедини́ть perf) ♦ vi соединя́ться (соедини́ться perf).
linkup ['lɪŋkʌp] n соедине́ние; (of spaceships) стыко́вка*; (RADIO, TV) свя́зка*, связна́я часть* f; (⌐etween studios: RADIO) радиомо́ст; (: TV) телемо́ст.
lino ['laɪnəu] n = linoleum.
linoleum [lɪ'nəulɪəm] n лино́леум.
linseed oil ['lɪnsi:d-] n льняно́е ма́сло.
lint [lɪnt] n ма́рля.
lintel ['lɪntl] n при́толока.
lion ['laɪən] n лев*.
lion cub n львёнок*.
lioness ['laɪənɪs] n льви́ца.
lip [lɪp] n (ANAT) губа́*; (of container) край*; (inf: insolence) гру́бости fpl.
liposome ['lɪpəusəum] n липосо́ма.
liposuction ['lɪpəusʌkʃən] n липоса́кция, отса́сывание жирово́й тка́ни.
lip-read ['lɪpri:d] vi чита́ть (impf) с губ.
lip salve n мазь f для смягче́ния губ.
lip service n: **to pay** ~ ~ **to sth** признава́ть* (призна́ть perf) что-н то́лько на слова́х.
lipstick ['lɪpstɪk] n губна́я пома́да.

liquefy ['lɪkwɪfaɪ] vt превраща́ть (преврати́ть* perf) в жи́дкость ♦ vi переходи́ть* (перейти́* perf) в жи́дкое состоя́ние.
liqueur [lɪ'kjuə^r] n ликёр.
liquid ['lɪkwɪd] n жи́дкость f ♦ adj жи́дкий* (жидо́к).
liquid assets npl ликви́дные акти́вы mpl.
liquidate ['lɪkwɪdeɪt] vt ликвиди́ровать (impf/perf).
liquidation [lɪkwɪ'deɪʃən] n ликвида́ция; **to go into** ~ ликвиди́роваться (impf).
liquidation sale n (US) распрода́жа иму́щества ликвиди́рованного предприя́тия.
liquidator ['lɪkwɪdeɪtə^r] n ликвида́тор.
liquid crystal display n жидкокристалли́ческий индика́тор.
liquidity [lɪ'kwɪdɪtɪ] n ликви́дность f.
liquidize ['lɪkwɪdaɪz] vt пропуска́ть (пропусти́ть* perf) че́рез ми́ксер.
liquidizer ['lɪkwɪdaɪzə^r] n ми́ксер, смеси́тель m.
liquor ['lɪkə^r] n (esp US) спиртно́е nt adj, спиртно́й напи́ток*.
liquorice ['lɪkərɪs] n (BRIT: sweet) лакри́ца.
liquor store n (US) ви́нно-во́дочный магази́н.
Lisbon ['lɪzbən] n Лиссабо́н.
lisp [lɪsp] n шепеля́вость f ♦ vi шепеля́вить* (impf).
lissom(e) ['lɪsəm] adj изя́щный* (изя́щен).
list [lɪst] n (also COMPUT) спи́сок* ♦ vt (enumerate) перечисля́ть (перечи́слить perf); (write down) составля́ть (соста́вить* perf) спи́сок +gen; (put on list) включа́ть (включи́ть* perf) в спи́сок ♦ vi (ship) крени́ться (накрени́ться perf).
listed building n (BRIT) зда́ние, охраня́емое госуда́рством.
listed company n официа́льно зарегистри́рованная компа́ния.
listen ['lɪsn] vi: **to** ~ (**to sb/sth**) слу́шать (impf) (кого́-н/что-н); **to** ~ **to sb** or **sb's advice** слу́шать (послу́шать perf) кого́-н; **I'm** ~**ing** out for him я прислу́шиваюсь, не идёт ли он; ~! послу́шайте!
listener ['lɪsnə^r] n слу́шатель(ница) m(f); (RADIO) радиослу́шатель(ница) m(f).
listeria [lɪs'tɪərɪə] n листе́рия.
listing [lɪstɪŋ] n (COMPUT) распеча́тка, ли́стинг.
listless ['lɪstlɪs] adj вя́лый (вял).
listlessly ['lɪstlɪslɪ] adv вя́ло.
list price n прейскура́нтная цена́*.
lit [lɪt] pt, pp of light.
litany ['lɪtənɪ] n (REL: Catholic) лита́ния; (: Orthodox) ектенья́*; (list) моното́нное перечисле́ние.
liter ['li:tə^r] n (US) = litre.
literacy ['lɪtərəsɪ] n гра́мотность f.
literacy campaign n борьба́ с

неграмотностью.

literal ['lɪtərl] *adj* буквальный* (буквален).

literally ['lɪtrəlɪ] *adv* буквально.

literary ['lɪtərərɪ] *adj* литературный*.

literate ['lɪtərət] *adj* (*able to read and write*) грамотный* (грамотен); (*educated*) образованный (образован).

literature ['lɪtrɪtʃə*] *n* литература.

lithe [laɪð] *adj* гибкий* (гибок).

lithograph ['lɪθəgrɑ:f] *n* литография.

lithography [lɪ'θɒgrəfɪ] *n* литография.

Lithuania [lɪθju'eɪnɪə] *n* Литва.

Lithuanian [lɪθju'eɪnɪən] *adj* литовский* ♦ *n* (*person*) литовец*(-вка*); (*LING*) литовский язык.

litigation [lɪtɪ'geɪʃən] *n* тяжба.

litmus paper ['lɪtməs-] *n* лакмусовая бумага.

litre ['li:tə*] (*US* **liter**) *n* литр.

litter ['lɪtə*] *n* (*rubbish*) мусор; (*young animals*) помёт.

litter bin *n* (*BRIT*) урна (*для мусора*).

litterbug ['lɪtəbʌg] *n* (*inf*) человек, который сорит в общественных местах.

littered ['lɪtəd] *adj*: ~ **with** заваленный (завален) +*instr*.

litter lout *n* (*inf*) = **litterbug**.

little ['lɪtl] *adj* (*small, young*) маленький*; (*younger*) младший*; (*short*) короткий* ♦ *adv* мало; **a ~ (bit)** немного; **I have ~ time/money** у меня мало времени/денег; **to make ~ of** не заостять (*impf*) внимание на +*prp*; **~ by ~** мало-помалу, понемногу.

little finger *n* мизинец* (*на руке*).

little-known ['lɪtl'nəun] *adj* малоизвестный* (малоизвестен).

liturgy ['lɪtədʒɪ] *n* литургия.

live [*vb* lɪv, *adj* laɪv] *vi* жить* (*impf*) ♦ *adj* (*animal, plant*) живой*; (*broadcast*) прямой*; (*performance*) перед публикой; (*ELEC*) под напряжением; (*bullet*) боевой*; (*bomb*) не взорвавшийся; **to ~ with sb** жить* (*impf*) с кем-н; **he ~d to (be) a hundred** он прожил до ста лет

▸ **live down** *vt* заглаживать (загладить* *perf*)

▸ **live for** *vt* жить* (*impf*) для +*gen*

▸ **live in** *vi*: **most students ~ in** большинство студентов живёт в общежитии

▸ **live off** *vt fus* (*survive on*): **we ~d off fish** мы жили на одной рыбе; (*pej: parents etc*) жить* (*impf*) за счёт +*gen*

▸ **live on** *vt fus* (*food*) жить* (*impf*) на одном(-ой) +*prp*; (*salary*) жить* (*impf*) на +*acc*

▸ **live out** *vi*: **postgraduates usually ~ out** аспиранты обычно не живут в общежитии ♦ *vt*: **to ~ out one's days** *or* **life** проживать (прожить* *perf*) остаток своей жизни

▸ **live together** *vi* жить* (*impf*) вместе

▸ **live up** *vt*: **to ~ it up** (*inf*) жить* (*impf*) широко

▸ **live up to** *vt fus* оправдывать (оправдать* *perf*).

live-in ['lɪvɪn] *adj*: ~ **lover** сожитель(ница) *m(f)*;

they have a ~ nanny с ними живёт няня.

livelihood ['laɪvlɪhud] *n* средства *ntpl* к существованию.

liveliness ['laɪvlɪnɪs] *n* живость *f*.

lively ['laɪvlɪ] *adj* (*person, book, interest, mind*) живой*; (*place, event*) оживлённый (оживлён).

liven up ['laɪvn-] *vt* (*person*) ободрять (ободрить perf); (*discussion, evening*) оживлять (оживить* perf) ♦ *vi* оживляться (оживиться* perf).

liver ['lɪvə*] *n* (*ANAT*) печень *f*; (*CULIN*) печёнка.

liverish ['lɪvərɪʃ] *adj*: **he is feeling ~** его подташнивает.

Liverpool ['lɪvəpu:l] *n* Ливерпуль *m*.

Liverpudlian [lɪvə'pʌdlɪən] *adj* ливерпульский ♦ *n* ливерпулец*(-лька*).

livery ['lɪvərɪ] *n* (*of servant*) ливрея.

lives [laɪvz] *npl of* **life**.

livestock ['laɪvstɔk] *n* скот*.

live wire *n* (*inf*): **he's a real ~~** он ужасно заводной.

livid ['lɪvɪd] *adj* (*colour*) серовато-синий*; (*inf: furious*): **she was ~** она была в ярости.

living ['lɪvɪŋ] *adj* живой* ♦ *n*: **to earn** *or* **make a ~** зарабатывать (заработать perf) на жизнь; **within ~ memory** на памяти живущих; **the cost of ~** стоимость *f* жизни.

living conditions *npl* условия *ntpl* жизни.

living expenses *npl* расходы *mpl* на жизнь.

living room *n* гостиная *f adj*.

living standards *npl* жизненный уровень* *msg*.

living wage *n* прожиточный минимум.

lizard ['lɪzəd] *n* ящерица.

Ljubljana [lu:'bljɑ:nə] *n* Любляна.

llama ['lɑ:mə] *n* лама (*ЗООЛ*).

LLB *n abbr* (= *Bachelor of Laws*) ≈ бакалавр правоведения.

LLD *n abbr* (= *Doctor of Laws*) ≈ доктор правоведения.

LMT *abbr* (*US*) = *Local Mean Time*.

load [ləud] *n* (*of person, animal*) ноша; (*of vehicle*) груз; (*weight, also* ELEC, TECH) нагрузка* ♦ *vt* (*also:* ~ **up**: *cargo, goods*) грузить* (погрузить* perf); (*COMPUT*) загружать (загрузить* perf); (*gun, camera*) заряжать (зарядить* perf); (*tape recorder*) ставить* (поставить* perf) кассету в +*prp*; **to ~ (with)** (*also:* ~ **up**: *vehicle, ship*) нагружать (нагрузить* perf) (+*instr*); **~s of, a ~ of** (*inf*) куча +*gen*; **a ~ of rubbish** (*inf*) сплошная чепуха.

loaded ['ləudɪd] *adj* (*gun*) заряженный (заряжен); (*dice*) утяжелённый (утяжелён); (*vehicle*): ~ **(with)** нагруженный (нагружен) (+*instr*); (*inf*): **he's ~** у него куча денег; ~ **question** вопрос с подвохом.

loading bay ['ləudɪŋ-] *n* погрузочная площадка*.

loaf [ləuf] (*pl* **loaves**) *n* буханка* ♦ *vi* (*also:* ~ **about** *or* **around**: *inf*) болтаться (*impf*) без

де́ла; **use your ~!** (*inf*) шевели́те мозга́ми!
loam [ləum] *n* сугли́нок*.

loan [ləun] *n* заём*; (*money*) ссу́да* ◆ *vt* дава́ть*
(дать* *perf*) взаймы́; (*money*) ссужа́ть
(ссуди́ть* *perf*); **to take sth on ~** брать*
(взять* *perf*) что́-н на вре́мя.

loan account *n* ссу́дный счёт*.

loan capital *n* заёмный *or* ссу́дный капита́л.

loan shark *n* (*inf*: *pej*) ростовщи́к,
заимода́вец*.

loath [ləuθ] *adj*: **he is ~ to** ... ему́ о́чень не
хо́чется +*infin* ....

loathe [ləuð] *vt* ненави́деть* (*impf*).

loathing ['ləuðɪŋ] *n* отвраще́ние, омерзе́ние.

loathsome ['ləuðsəm] *adj* отврати́тельный*
(отврати́телен), омерзи́тельный*
(омерзи́телен).

loaves [ləuvz] *npl of* **loaf.**

lob [lɔb] *vt* (*ball*) перебра́сывать (перебро́сить*
perf).

lobby ['lɔbɪ] *n* (*of building*) вестибю́ль *m*;
(*pressure group*) ло́бби *nt ind* ◆ *vt* (*politician*)
склоня́ть (склони́ть *perf*) на свою́ сто́рону.

lobbyist ['lɔbɪɪst] *n* лобби́ст.

lobe [ləub] *n* (*of ear*) мо́чка*.

lobster ['lɔbstə'] *n* ома́р.

lobster pot *n* ве́рша* для ома́ров.

local ['ləukl] *adj* ме́стный ◆ *n* (*BRIT: inf*): **this is
my ~** э́то мой люби́мый ме́стный паб; **the
~s** *npl* ме́стные жи́тели *mpl*.

local anaesthetic *n* ме́стный нарко́з.

local authority *n* ме́стные вла́сти* *fpl*.

local call *n* (*TEL*) ме́стный (телефо́нный)
разгово́р.

locale [ləu'ka:l] *n* ме́сто*.

local government *n* ме́стные вла́сти*
fpl.

locality [ləu'kælɪtɪ] *n* ме́стность *f*.

localize ['ləukəlaɪz] *vt* (*limit*) локализова́ть
(*impf/perf*).

locally ['ləukəlɪ] *adv* (*live*) побли́зости; (*solve
problems*) на места́х.

locate [ləu'keɪt] *vt* определя́ть (определи́ть
perf) местонахожде́ние +*gen*; (*situate*): **to be
~d in** находи́ться* (*impf*) в *or* на +*prp*.

location [ləu'keɪʃən] *n* (*place*)
местонахожде́ние; (*finding*): **~ (of)** лока́ция
(+*gen*); **on ~** (*CINEMA*) на нату́ре.

loch [lɔx] *n* (*SCOTTISH*) о́зеро*.

lock [lɔk] *n* (*on door etc*) замо́к*; (*on canal*)
шлюз; (*of hair*) ло́кон ◆ *vt* запира́ть
(запере́ть* *perf*); (*immobilize*) фикси́ровать
(зафикси́ровать *perf*) ◆ *vi* (*door*) запира́ться
(запере́ться* *perf*); (*jaw, mechanism*)
смыка́ться (сомкну́ться *perf*); (*wheels*)
тормози́ть* (затормози́ть* *perf*); **the steering
wheel was on full ~** (*AUT*) руль был повёрнут
до отка́за; **~, stock and barrel** всё целико́м

▸ **lock away** *vt* (*valuables*) пря́тать* (спря́тать*
perf) под замо́к; (*criminal*) заключа́ть
(заключи́ть *perf*) под стра́жу

▸ **lock in** *vt*: **to ~ sb in** запира́ть (запере́ть* *perf*)
кого́-н

▸ **lock out** *vt* (*person*) запира́ть (запере́ть* *perf*)
дверь и не впуска́ть (впусти́ть* *perf*);
(*INDUSTRY*) объявля́ть (объяви́ть* *perf*)
лока́ут +*dat*

▸ **lock up** *vt* (*criminal, mental patient*)
упря́тывать (упря́тать* *perf*); (*house*)
запира́ть (запере́ть* *perf*) ◆ *vi* запира́ться
(запере́ться* *perf*).

locker ['lɔkə'] *n* шка́фчик.

locker room *n* раздева́лка*.

locket ['lɔkɪt] *n* медальо́н.

lockjaw ['lɔkdʒɔ:] *n* (*trismus*) тризм; (*tetanus*)
столбня́к.

lockout ['lɔkaut] *n* (*INDUSTRY*) лока́ут.

locksmith ['lɔksmɪθ] *n* сле́сарь* *m*.

lockup ['lɔkʌp] *n* (*jail*) куту́зка*; (*BRIT: also:*
lock-up garage) гара́ж.

locomotive [ləukə'məutɪv] *n* локомоти́в.

locum ['ləukəm] *n* (*MED*) врач, *вре́менно
замеща́ющий друго́го врача́.*

locust ['ləukəst] *n* саранча́* *f no pl*.

lodge [lɔdʒ] *n* привра́тницкая *f adj*; (*also:
hunting ~*) охо́тничий* дом*; (*also: masonic
~*) масо́нская ло́жа ◆ *vt* (*complaint*)
подава́ть* (пода́ть* *perf*) ◆ *vi* (*bullet*)
застрева́ть (застря́ть* *perf*); (*person*): **to ~
(with)** (*вре́менно*) жить* (*impf*) на кварти́ре (у
+*gen*).

lodger ['lɔdʒə'] *n* кварти́рант(ка).

lodging ['lɔdʒɪŋ] *n* (*вре́менное*) жильё.

lodging house *n* меблиро́ванные ко́мнаты
fpl.

lodgings ['lɔdʒɪŋz] *npl* кварти́ра *fsg*.

loft [lɔft] *n* черда́к*.

lofty ['lɔftɪ] *adj* (*high*) высо́кий* (высо́к);
(*noble*) возвы́шенный (возвы́шен); (*self-
important*) высокоме́рный* (высокоме́рен).

log [lɔg] *n abbr* = **logarithm.**

log [lɔg] *n* (*piece of wood*) бревно́*; (: *for fire*)
поле́но*; (*account*) журна́л* ◆ *vt* (*event, fact*)
регистри́ровать (зарегистри́ровать *perf*)

▸ **log in** *vi* (*COMPUT*) входи́ть* (войти́* *perf*) в
систе́му

▸ **log into** *vt fus* (*COMPUT*) входи́ть* (войти́* *perf*)
в +*acc*

▸ **log off** *vi* (*COMPUT*) выходи́ть* (вы́йти* *perf*)
из систе́мы

▸ **log on** *vi* = **log in**

▸ **log out** *vi* = **log off.**

logarithm ['lɔgərɪðm] *n* логари́фм.

logbook ['lɔgbuk] *n* (*NAUT*) ва́хтенный
журна́л; (*AVIAT*) бортово́й журна́л; (*of car,
lorry*) формуля́р; (*of events, movement of*

---

* marks translations which have irregular inflections. The Russian-English side of the dictionary gives inflectional information.

goods) журна́л.
log fire *n* дровяно́й ками́н.
logger ['lɔgə'] *n* лесору́б.
loggerheads ['lɔgəhedz] *npl*: **to be at ~ (with)** конфликтова́ть *(impf)* (с +*instr*).
logic ['lɔdʒɪk] *n* ло́гика.
logical ['lɔdʒɪkl] *adj* (*based on logic*) логи́ческий*; (*reasonable*) логи́чный* (логи́чен).
logically ['lɔdʒɪkəlɪ] *adv* (*see adj*) логи́чески; логи́чно.
logistics [lɔ'dʒɪstɪks] *npl* организа́ция *fsg*.
log jam ['lɔgdʒæm] *n* (*fig*) тупи́к.
logo ['ləugəu] *n* эмбле́ма.
loin [lɔɪn] *n* (*of meat*) филе́йная часть* *f*; **~s** *npl* (*ANAT*) чре́сла *pl*.
loincloth ['lɔɪnklɔθ] *n* набе́дренная повя́зка*.
Loire [lwɑ:] *n*: **the ~** Луа́ра.
loiter ['lɔɪtə'] *vi* слоня́ться *(impf)*.
loll [lɔl] *vi* (*person: also: ~ about*) разва́ливаться (развали́ться* *perf*); (*head, tongue*) све́шиваться (све́ситься* *perf*).
lollipop ['lɔlɪpɔp] *n* леденёц* на па́лочке ◆ *cpd*: **~ man/lady** (*BRIT*) регулиро́вщик/ *регулиро́вщица движе́ния, кото́рый обеспе́чивает безопа́сный перехо́д у́лицы шко́льниками*.
lollop ['lɔləp] *vi* бе́гать/бежа́ть* *(impf)* вперева́лку.
lolly ['lɔlɪ] *n* (*inf: lollipop*) леденёц на па́лочке; (*: also*: **ice ~**) моро́женое на па́лочке; (*: money*) деньжа́та *pl*.
London ['lʌndən] *n* Ло́ндон.
Londoner ['lʌndənə'] *n* ло́ндонец*(-донка).
lone [ləun] *adj* (*person, parent*) одино́кий*; (*thing*) еди́нственный.
loneliness ['ləunlɪnɪs] *n* одино́чество.
lonely ['ləunlɪ] *adj* (*person, childhood*) одино́кий* (одино́к); (*place*) уединённый (уединён).
lonely hearts *n* одино́кие сердца́ *nt pl*.
lone parent *n* (*father*) оте́ц*-одино́чка; (*mother*) мать* *f*-одино́чка.
loner ['ləunə'] *n* одино́чка* *m/f*.
long [lɔŋ] *adj* (*in time*) до́лгий* (до́лог); (*road, book*) дли́нный* (дли́нен); (*clothes*) дли́нен ◆ *adv* (*see adj*) до́лго; дли́нно ◆ *vi*: **to ~ for sth/to do** жа́ждать *(impf)* чего́-н/+*infin*; **in the ~ run** в коне́чном ито́ге; **so** *or* **as ~ as you don't mind** е́сли то́лько Вы не возража́ете; **don't be ~!** не заде́рживайтесь!; **how ~ is the street?** какова́ длина́ э́той у́лицы?; **how ~ is the lesson?** ско́лько дли́тся уро́к?; **6 metres ~** длино́й в 6 ме́тров; **6 months ~** продолжи́тельностью в 6 ме́сяцев; **all night (long)** всю ночь (напролёт); **he no ~er comes** он бо́льше не прихо́дит; **~ ago** давно́; **~ before** задо́лго до +*gen*; **~ after** до́лгое вре́мя по́сле +*gen*; **before ~** вско́ре; **at ~ last** наконе́ц; **the ~ and the short of it is that ...** коро́че говоря́ ....

long-distance [lɔŋ'dɪstəns] *adj* (*travel*) да́льний* (да́лен); **~ race** забе́г на дли́нную диста́нцию; **~ runner** бегу́н на дли́нные диста́нции.
long-distance call *n* (*within same country*) междугоро́дный (телефо́нный) разгово́р; (*international*) междунаро́дный (телефо́нный) разгово́р.
longevity [lɔn'dʒevɪtɪ] *n* (*of person*) долголе́тие; (*of scheme, marriage etc*) долгове́чность *f*.
long-haired ['lɔŋ'hɛəd] *adj* (*person*) длинноволо́сый (длинноволо́с); (*animal*) длинношёрстый.
longhand ['lɔŋhænd] *n*: **in ~** (*write*) от руки́.
longing ['lɔŋɪŋ] *n*: **~ (for)** тоска́ (по +*dat*).
longingly ['lɔŋɪŋlɪ] *adv* с тоско́й.
longitude ['lɔŋgɪtjuːd] *n* долгота́*.
long johns [-dʒɔnz] *npl* кальсо́ны* *pl*.
long jump *n* прыжо́к* в длину́.
long-life ['lɔŋlaɪf] *adj* (*milk etc*) консерви́рованный; (*battery*) продлённого де́йствия.
long-lost ['lɔŋlɔst] *adj* (*relative etc*) давно́ утра́ченный (утра́чен) *or* поте́рянный (поте́рян).
long-playing record ['lɔŋpleɪŋ-] *n* долгоигра́ющая пласти́нка*.
long-range ['lɔŋ'reɪndʒ] *adj* (*plan, forecast*) долгосро́чный* (долгосро́чен); (*missile*) дальноб́ойный.
longshoreman ['lɔŋʃɔːmən] *n* (*US*) порто́вый гру́зчик.
long-sighted ['lɔŋ'saɪtɪd] *adj* дальнозо́ркий* (дальнозо́рок).
long-standing ['lɔŋ'stændɪŋ] *adj* долголе́тний.
long-suffering [lɔŋ'sʌfərɪŋ] *adj* много-страда́льный* (многострада́лен).
long-term ['lɔŋtəːm] *adj* долгосро́чный* (долгосро́чен).
long wave *n* (*RADIO*) дли́нные во́лны *fpl*.
long-winded [lɔŋ'wɪndɪd] *adj* многосло́вный* (многосло́вен).
loo [luː] *n* (*BRIT: inf*) туале́т.
loofah ['luːfə] *n* люфа́ (гу́бка).
look [luk] *vi* (*see*) смотре́ть* (посмотре́ть* *perf*); (*glance*) взгляну́ть (*perf*); (*seem, appear*) вы́глядеть* *(impf)* ◆ *n* (*glance*) взгляд; (*appearance*) вид; (*expression*) выраже́ние; **~s** *npl*: **good ~s** краси́вая вне́шность *fsg*; **to ~ south/(out) onto the sea** (*face*) выходи́ть* *(impf)* на юг/на мо́ре; **~ (here)!** (*expressing annoyance*) послу́шайте!; **~!** (*expressing surprise*) смотри́те!; **to ~ like sb/sth** походи́ть* *(impf)* на кого́-н/что-н; **the wall ~s about 4 metres long** похо́же, что длина́ э́той стены́ 4 ме́тра; **everything ~s all right to me** мне ка́жется, что всё в поря́дке; **it ~s as if** he's not coming похо́же, что он не придёт; **to ~ ahead** смотре́ть* (посмотре́ть* *perf*) вперёд; **to have a ~** посмотре́ть* (*perf*),

взгляну́ть *(perf)*; to ~ around осма́триваться (осмотре́ться* *perf)*; to have a ~ at sth *(glance at)* взгляну́ть* *(perf)* на что-н; *(study)* рассма́тривать (рассмотре́ть* *(perf))* что-н; to have a ~ for sth иска́ть* (поиска́ть* *perf)* что-н; you can't tell by ~s alone нельзя́ суди́ть то́лько по вне́шности

► look after *vt fus (care for)* ула́живать *(impf)* за +*instr*; *(deal with)* забо́титься* *(impf)* о +*prp*

► look (a)round *vt fus (castle, museum etc)* осма́тривать (осмотре́ть* *perf)*

► look at *vt fus (see)* смотре́ть* (посмотре́ть* *perf)* на +*acc*; *(study)* рассма́тривать (рассмотре́ть* *perf)*; *(read quickly)* просма́тривать (просмотре́ть* *perf)*

► look back *vi (turn around)*: to ~ back (at sth/ sb) огля́дываться (огляну́ться* *perf)* (на что-н/кого́-н); to ~ back (at *or* on the past) огля́дываться (огляну́ться* *perf)* (на про́шлое)

► look down on *vt fus (fig)* смотре́ть* *(impf)* свысока́ на +*acc*

► look for *vt fus* иска́ть* (поиска́ть* *perf)*

► look forward *vt fus*: to ~ forward to sth ждать *(impf)* чего́-н с нетерпе́нием; *(in letters)*: we ~ forward to hearing from you (с нетерпе́нием) ждём Ва́шего отве́та

► look in *vi*: to ~ in on sb загля́дывать (загляну́ть* *perf)* к кому́-н

► look into *vt fus* рассле́довать *(impf/perf)*

► look on *vi (watch)* наблюда́ть *(impf)*

► look out *vi (beware)*: to ~ out (for) остерега́ться *(impf)* (+*gen)*; *(glance out)*: to ~ out (of) выгля́дывать (вы́глянуть *perf)* (в +*acc)*

► look out for *vt fus (search for)* стара́ться (постара́ться *perf)* найти́

► look over *vt (essay)* просма́тривать (просмотре́ть* *perf)*; *(town, building)* осма́тривать (осмотре́ть* *perf)*; *(person)* проверя́ть (прове́рить *perf)*

► look round *vi* осма́триваться (осмотре́ться* *perf)*

► look through *vt fus (papers)* просма́тривать (просмотре́ть* *perf)*; *(window)* смотре́ть* (посмотре́ть* *perf)* в +*acc*

► look to *vt fus (rely on)* ждать* *(impf)* от +*gen*

► look up *vi (with eyes)* поднима́ть (подня́ть* *perf)* глаза́; *(situation)* идти́* *(impf)* к лу́чшему ◆ *vt (piece of information)* посмотре́ть* *(perf)*

► look up to *vt fus* почита́ть *(impf)*.

lookalike ['lʊkəlaɪk] *n* двойни́к*.

look-in ['lʊkɪn] *n*: to get a ~ *(inf)* получи́ть* *(perf)* свой кусо́к пирога́; I couldn't get a ~ *(in conversation)* я не мог вста́вить сло́ва.

lookout ['lʊkaʊt] *n (person)* наблюда́тель (ница) *m(f)*; *(point)* наблюда́тельный пункт; to be on the ~ быть* *(impf)* начеку́ or

насторо́же; to be on the ~ for sth присма́тривать *(impf)* что-н.
LOOM *n abbr (US: = Loyal Order of Moose)* та́йное о́бщество.
loom [luːm] *vi (also: ~ up: object)* нея́сно вырисо́вываться *(impf)*; *(event)* надвига́ться *(impf)* ◆ *n* тка́цкий* стано́к*.
loony ['luːnɪ] *(inf) adj* чо́кнутый ◆ *n* чо́кнутый(-ая) *m(f) adj*.
loop [luːp] *n (also* COMPUT*)* пе́тля*; *(contraceptive)* спира́ль *f* ◆ *vt*: to ~ sth round sth (завяза́ть* *perf)* что-н пе́тлей вокру́г чего́-н.
loophole ['luːphəʊl] *n* лазе́йка*.
loose [luːs] *adj* свобо́дный* (свобо́ден); *(knot, grip)* сла́бый (слаб); *(hair)* распу́щенный (распу́щен); *(definition, translation)* приблизи́тельный* (приблизи́телен); *(weave)* непло́тный* (непло́тен); *(promiscuous)* распу́щенный; *(ELEC)*: ~ connection сла́бый конта́кт ◆ *n*: to be on the ~ быть* *(impf)* в бега́х; the handle is ~ ру́чка расша́талась; to set ~ *(prisoner)* освобожда́ть (освободи́ть* *perf)*; *(unleash)* высвобожда́ть (вы́свободить* *perf)*; to come ~ расша́тываться (расшата́ться *perf)*.
loose change *n* ме́лочь *f*.
loose chippings *npl (on road)* щебёнка *fsg*.
loose end *n*: to be at a ~ ~ *or (US)* at ~ ~s шата́ться *(impf)* без де́ла; to tie up (the) ~ ~s заверши́ть (заверши́ть *perf)* все ме́лочи.
loose-fitting ['luːsfɪtɪŋ] *adj* просто́рный* (просто́рен).
loose-leaf ['luːsliːf] *adj* отрывно́й.
loose-limbed [luːs'lɪmd] *adj* ги́бкий* (ги́бок).
loosely ['luːslɪ] *adv (freely)* свобо́дно; *(vaguely)* приблизи́тельно.
loosely-knit ['luːslɪ'nɪt] *adj* ре́дко свя́занный.
loosen ['luːsn] *vt (belt, screw, grip)* ослабля́ть (осла́бить* *perf)*; *(by shaking)* расша́тывать (расшата́ть *perf)*
► loosen up *vi (before game)* разогрева́ться (разогре́ться *perf)*; *(inf: relax)* расслабля́ться (рассла́биться* *perf)*.
loot [luːt] *n (inf)* награ́бленное *nt adj* ◆ *vt (shops, homes)* разграбля́ть (разгра́бить* *perf)*.
looter ['luːtə*] *n (during riot)* граби́тель(ница) *m(f)*; *(during war)* мародёр.
looting ['luːtɪŋ] *n* разграбле́ние; *(during war)* мародёрство.
lop off [lɔp-] *vt (branches etc)* отреза́ть (отре́зать* *perf)*.
lopsided ['lɔp'saɪdɪd] *adj* кривобо́кий (кривобо́к); *(smile)* криво́й* (крив).
lord [lɔːd] *n (BRIT: peer)* лорд; *(REL)*: the L~ Госпо́дь* *m*; my L~ *(to bishop, noble, judge)* мило́рд; good L~! Бо́же мой!; the (House of) L~s *(BRIT)* пала́та ло́рдов.

---

* marks translations which have irregular inflections. The Russian-English side of the dictionary gives inflectional information.

lordly ['lɔ:dlɪ] *adj* ба́рственный.
lordship ['lɔ:dʃɪp] *n*: **your L~** Ва́ша све́тлость *f*.
lore [lɔ:ʳ] *n* преда́ния *ntpl*.
lorry ['lɒrɪ] *n* (*BRIT*) грузови́к*.
lorry driver *n* (*BRIT*) води́тель *m* грузовика́.
Los Angeles [lɒs 'ændʒɪli:z] *n* Лос-А́нджелес.
lose [lu:z] (*pt, pp* **lost**) *vt* теря́ть (потеря́ть *perf*); (*contest, argument*) прои́грывать (проигра́ть *perf*); (*pursuers*) избавля́ться (изба́виться* *perf*) от +*gen* ♦ *vi* (*in contest, argument*) прои́грывать (проигра́ть *perf*); **to ~ (time)** (*clock*) отстава́ть* (отста́ть* *perf*); **to ~ sight of sth** теря́ть (потеря́ть *perf*) из ви́ду что-н; (*fig*) упуска́ть (упусти́ть* *perf*) из ви́ду что-н.
loser ['lu:zəʳ] *n* (*in contest*) проигра́вший(-ая) *m(f) adj*; (*inf: failure*) неуда́чник(-ица) *m(f)*; **to be a good/bad ~** уме́ть (*impf*)/не уме́ть досто́йно прои́грывать (*impf*).
loss [lɒs] *n* поте́ря; (*sense of bereavement*) утра́та; (*COMM*) **to make a ~** терпе́ть* (потерпе́ть* *perf*) убы́ток; **to sell sth at a ~** продава́ть* (прода́ть* *perf*) что-н в убы́ток; **heavy ~es** тяжёлые поте́ри *fpl*; **to cut one's ~es** сокраща́ть (сократи́ть* *perf*) поте́ри; **to be at a ~** теря́ться (растеря́ться *perf*); **to be at a ~ for words** не найти́сь* (*perf*), что сказа́ть.
loss adjuster *n* специали́ст по оце́нке убы́тков.
loss leader *n* това́р, *продава́емый в убы́ток для привлече́ния покупа́телей*.
lost [lɒst] *pt, pp of* **lose** ♦ *adj* (*person, animal*) пропа́вший; (*object*) потеря́нный (потеря́н); **to get ~** заблуди́ться* (*perf*); **get ~!** (*inf*) прова́ливай!; **he was ~ in thought** он был погружён в свои́ мы́сли.
lost and found *n* (*US*) стол *or* бюро́ *nt ind* нахо́док.
lost cause *n* прои́гранное де́ло*.
lost property *n* потеря́нные ве́щи *fpl*; (*BRIT: also: ~ office*) стол *or* бюро́ *nt ind* нахо́док.
lot [lɒt] *n* (*of people, goods*) па́ртия; (*at auction*) лот; (*destiny*) у́часть *f*; (*esp US: ground*) (земе́льный) уча́сток*; (*large number, amount*): **a ~ (of)** мно́го (+*gen*); **the ~** (*everything*) всё; **~s of ...** мно́го +*gen* ...; **I see a ~ of him** мы с ним ча́сто ви́димся; **I read/don't read a ~** я мно́го/ма́ло чита́ю; **a ~ bigger/louder/more expensive** намно́го *or* гора́здо бо́льше/гро́мче/доро́же; **to draw ~s (for sth)** тяну́ть* (*impf*) жре́бий (для чего́-н).
lotion ['ləuʃən] *n* (*for skin, hair*) лосьо́н.
lottery ['lɒtərɪ] *n* лотере́я.
loud [laud] *adj* (*noise, voice, laugh*) гро́мкий* (гро́мок); (*support, condemnation*) шу́мный* (шу́мен); (*clothes*) крича́щий* ♦ *adv* гро́мко; **out ~** вслух.
loud-hailer [laud'heɪləʳ] *n* (*BRIT*) ру́пор.
loudly ['laudlɪ] *adv* (*see adj*) гро́мко; шу́мно.
loudmouthed ['laudmauθt] *adj* горла́стый (горла́ст).
loudspeaker [laud'spi:kəʳ] *n* громко-

говори́тель *m*.
lounge [laundʒ] *n* (*in house, hotel*) гости́ная *f adj*; (*at airport*) зал ожида́ния; (*BRIT: also: ~ bar*) часть *f* ба́ра, *где посети́тели сидя́т* ♦ *vi* (*in chair*) развали́ться (*perf*)
► **lounge about** *vi* болта́ться (*impf*) (без де́ла)
► **lounge around** *vi* = **lounge about**.
lounge suit *n* (*BRIT*) пиджа́чный костю́м.
louse [laus] (*pl* **lice**) *n* (*insect*) вошь *f*
► **louse up** *vt* (*inf*) напо́ртить* (*perf*) +*dat*.
lousy ['lauzɪ] *adj* (*inf: bad quality*) парши́вый; (: *ill*): **to feel ~** чу́вствовать (*impf*) себя́ парши́во.
lout [laut] *n* (*inf*) хам.
louvre ['lu:vəʳ] (*US* **louver**) *n* жалюзи́ *nt ind*.
lovable ['lʌvəbl] *adj* ми́лый* (мил).
love [lʌv] *vt* люби́ть* (*impf*) ♦ *n*: **~ (for)** любо́вь *f* (к +*dat*); **to ~ to do** люби́ть* (*impf*) +*infin*; **I ~ chocolate** я люблю́ шокола́д; **I'd ~ to come** я с удово́льствием пришёл бы; **"love (from) Anne"** (*in letter*) „лю́бящая Вас А́нна"; **to fall in ~ with** влюбля́ться (влюби́ться* *perf*) в +*acc*; **he is in ~ with her** он в неё влюблён; **to make ~** занима́ться (заня́ться* *perf*) любо́вью; **~ at first sight** любо́вь* с пе́рвого взгля́да; **to send one's ~ to sb** передава́ть* (переда́ть* *perf*) приве́т кому́-н; **"fifteen ~"** (*TENNIS*) „пятна́дцать – ноль".
love affair *n* рома́н.
love child *n* дитя́* *nt* любви́.
loved ones ['lʌvdwʌnz] *npl* люби́мые *pl adj*.
love-hate relationship ['lʌvheɪt-] *n* любо́вь *f*-не́нависть *f*.
love letter *n* любо́вное письмо́*.
love life *n* инти́мная жизнь *f*.
lovely ['lʌvlɪ] *adj* (*beautiful*) краси́вый (краси́в); (*delightful*) чуде́сный* (чуде́сен).
lover ['lʌvəʳ] *n* (*sexual partner*) любо́вник (-ица) *m(f)*; (*person in love*) влюблённый(-ая)*m(f) adj*; **a ~ of art/music** люби́тель(ница) *m(f)* иску́сства/му́зыки.
lovesick ['lʌvsɪk] *adj* томи́мый любо́вью; **to be ~** томи́ться* (*impf*) от любви́.
love song *n* любо́вная пе́сня*.
loving ['lʌvɪŋ] *adj* (*person*) любя́щий*, не́жный* (не́жен); (*actions*) не́жный* (не́жен).
low [ləu] *adj* ни́зкий* (ни́зок); (*sound: quiet*) ти́хий* (тих); (*depressed*) пода́вленный (пода́влен); (*ill*) нездоро́вый (нездоро́в) ♦ *adv* (*sing: deeply*) ни́зким го́лосом; (: *quietly*) ти́хо; (*fly*) ни́зко ♦ *n* (*METEOROLOGY*) ни́зкое давле́ние; **we are (running) ~ on milk** у нас остаётся ма́ло молока́; **to reach a new** *or* **an all-time ~** (*morale, profits*) опуска́ться (опусти́ться* *perf*) на небыва́ло ни́зкий у́ровень.
low-alcohol ['ləu'ælkəhɒl] *adj*: **~ wine/beer** вино́/пи́во с ни́зким содержа́нием алкого́ля.
lowbrow ['ləubrau] *adj* низкопро́бный.
low-calorie ['ləu'kælərɪ] *adj* низко-

калори́йный* (низкокалори́ен).
low-cut ['ləukʌt] *adj* с глубо́ким вы́резом.
lowdown ['ləudaun] *n* (*inf*): **to give sb the ~ on sth** раскрыва́ть (раскры́ть* *perf*) пе́ред кем-н всю подного́тную чего́-н.
lower ['ləuəʳ] *adj* (*bottom: of two things*) ни́жний*; (*less important*) ни́зший* ♦ *vt* (*object*) спуска́ть (спусти́ть* *perf*); (*level, price*) снижа́ть (сни́зить* *perf*); (*voice*) понижа́ть (пони́зить* *perf*); (*eyes*) опуска́ть (опусти́ть* *perf*).
low-fat ['ləu'fæt] *adj* обезжи́ренный (обезжи́рен).
low-key ['ləu'ki:] *adj* сде́ржанный (сде́ржан).
lowlands ['ləuləndz] *npl* ни́зменность *fsg*.
low-level language ['ləulɛvl-] *n* (*COMPUT*) язы́к* программи́рования ни́зкого у́ровня.
low-loader ['ləuləudəʳ] *n* автомоби́ль *m* с погру́зочным приспособле́нием.
lowly ['ləulɪ] *adj* (*position, origin*) ни́зкий* (ни́зок).
low-lying [ləu'laɪŋ] *adj* ни́зменный.
low-paid [ləu'peɪd] *adj* низкоопла́чиваемый (низкоопла́чиваем).
low-rise ['ləuraɪz] *adj* ни́зкий* (ни́зок).
low-tech ['ləutɛk] *adj*: **their office is very ~** у них в о́фисе техноло́гия на о́чень ни́зком у́ровне.
loyal ['lɔɪəl] *adj* ве́рный* (ве́рен); (*POL*) лоя́льный* (лоя́лен).
loyalist ['lɔɪəlɪst] *n* лояли́ст(ка).
loyalty ['lɔɪəltɪ] *n* ве́рность *f*; (*POL*) лоя́льность *f*; **~ card** ≈ диско́нтная ка́рта.
lozenge ['lɔzɪndʒ] *n* (*shape*) ромб; (*pastille*): **throat ~** табле́тка* от ка́шля.
LP *n abbr* = **long-playing record**.
L-plate ['ɛlpleɪt] *n* (*BRIT*) *знак на маши́не, обознача́ющий "учени́к"*
LPN *n abbr* (*US*) = **Licensed Practical Nurse**.
LRAM *n abbr* (*BRIT*) = **Licentiate of the Royal Academy of Music**.
LSAT *n abbr* (*US*) = **Law School Admissions Test**.
LSD *n abbr* (= *lysergic acid diethylamide*) ЛСД; (*BRIT*: = *pounds, shillings and pence*) *фу́нты, ши́ллинги и пе́нсы*.
LSE *n abbr* (*BRIT*) = **London School of Economics**.
LT *abbr* (*ELEC*: = *low tension*) ни́зкое напряже́ние.
Lt *abbr* (*MIL*) = **lieutenant**.
Ltd *abbr* (*COMM*) = **limited (liability) company**.
lubricant ['lu:brɪkənt] *n* сма́зка, лубрика́тор.
lubricate ['lu:brɪkeɪt] *vt* сма́зывать (сма́зать* *perf*).
lucid ['lu:sɪd] *adj* (*writing, speech*) я́сный* (я́сен); (*thinking*): **I'm not feeling very ~ today** я сего́дня пло́хо сообража́ю.
lucidity [lu:'sɪdɪtɪ] *n* я́сность *f*.
luck [lʌk] *n* (*also: good* ~) уда́ча; **bad ~**

неуда́ча; **good ~!** уда́чи (Вам)!; **bad** *or* **hard** *or* **tough ~!** не повезло́!; **we are in ~/out of ~** нам везёт/не везёт; **to push one's ~** искуша́ть (*impf*) судьбу́.
luckily ['lʌkɪlɪ] *adv* к сча́стью.
luckless ['lʌklɪs] *adj* невезу́чий (невезу́ч).
lucky ['lʌkɪ] *adj* (*situation, event, object*) счастли́вый; (*person*) уда́чливый (уда́члив); **he is ~ at cards/in love** ему́ везёт в ка́ртах/любви́; **how did you manage it? – I was ~** как Вам э́то удало́сь? – мне повезло́.
lucrative ['lu:krətɪv] *adj* (*profitable*) при́быльный* (при́былен), дохо́дный* (дохо́ден); (*job*) высокоопла́чиваемый.
ludicrous ['lu:dɪkrəs] *adj* смехотво́рный* (смехотво́рен).
ludo ['lu:dəu] *n настольная игра́ с фи́шками и броса́нием косте́й*.
lug [lʌg] *vt* (*inf*) воло́чь* (*impf*).
luggage ['lʌgɪdʒ] *n* бага́ж*.
luggage car *n* = **luggage van**.
luggage rack *n* (*in train*) бага́жная по́лка.
luggage van *n* (*BRIT*) бага́жный ваго́н.
lugubrious [lu'gu:brɪəs] *adj* ско́рбный* (ско́рбен).
lukewarm ['lu:kwɔ:m] *adj* (*liquid*) слегка́ тёплый; (*reaction*) прохла́дный* (прохла́ден).
lull [lʌl] *n* зати́шье ♦ *vt*: **to ~ sb to sleep** убаю́кивать (убаю́кать *perf*) кого́-н; **to ~ sb into a false sense of security** усыпля́ть (усыпи́ть* *perf*) чью-о бди́тельность.
lullaby ['lʌləbaɪ] *n* колыбе́льная *f adj*.
lumbago [lʌm'beɪgəu] *n* люмба́го *nt ind*.
lumber ['lʌmbəʳ] *n* (*esp US: wood*) лесоматериа́лы *mpl*; (*junk*) ру́хлядь *f* ♦ *vi*: **to ~ about/along** *etc* тащи́ться (*impf*)
▶ **lumber with** *vt*: **to ~ sb with sth** навя́зывать (навяза́ть* *perf*) кому́-н что-н; **he was ~ed with all the work** ему́ навяза́ли всю рабо́ту.
lumberjack ['lʌmbədʒæk] *n* лесору́б.
lumber room *n* (*BRIT*) чула́н.
lumberyard ['lʌmbəjɑ:d] *n* (*US*) склад лесоматериа́лов.
luminous ['lu:mɪnəs] *adj* (*fabric, colour*) блестя́щий*; (*digit, star*) светя́щийся.
lump [lʌmp] *n* (*of clay, snow*) кусо́к; (*of butter, sugar etc*) кусо́к*; (*swelling*) ши́шка; (*growth*) о́пухоль *f* ♦ *vt*: **to ~ together** меша́ть (смеша́ть* *perf*) в (одну́) ку́чу; **a ~ sum** единовре́менно выпла́чиваемая су́мма.
lumpy ['lʌmpɪ] *adj* (*sauce*) комкова́тый; (*bed*) бугри́стый (бугри́ст).
lunacy ['lu:nəsɪ] *n* (*fig*) безу́мие; (*mental illness*) помеша́тельство.
lunar ['lu:nəʳ] *adj* лу́нный*.
lunatic ['lu:nətɪk] *adj* (*behaviour*) безу́мный* (безу́мен) ♦ *n* (*also fig*) сумасше́дший*(-ая)

---

* marks translations which have irregular inflections. The Russian-English side of the dictionary gives inflectional information.

m(f) adj.
lunatic asylum *n* сумасше́дший* дом*.
lunatic fringe *n*: **the ~ ~** ку́чка фана́тиков.
lunch [lʌntʃ] *n* обе́д ♦ *vi* обе́дать (пообе́дать *perf*).
lunch break *n* переры́в на обе́д, обе́денный переры́в.
luncheon ['lʌntʃən] *n* (*formal meal*) за́втрак.
luncheon meat *n* свина́я тушёнка.
luncheon voucher *n* (*BRIT*) тало́н на обе́д.
lunch hour *n* = **lunch break**.
lunch time *n* обе́денное вре́мя* *nt*.
lung [lʌŋ] *n* лёгкое *nt adj*; **~ cancer** рак лёгких.
lunge [lʌndʒ] *vi* (*also*: **~ forward**) рвану́ться (*perf*); (*SPORT*) де́лать (сде́лать *perf*) вы́пад; **to ~ at** ри́нуться (*perf*) на +*acc*; (*SPORT*) де́лать (сде́лать *perf*) вы́пад про́тив +*gen*.
lupin ['lu:pɪn] *n* (*BOT*) люпи́н.
lurch [lə:tʃ] *vi* (*person*) покачну́ться (*perf*); (*vehicle*) рвану́ть (*perf*); (*ship*): **to ~ sideways** крени́ться* (накрени́ться* *perf*) ♦ *n* (*of ship*) крен; (*of vehicle*) бросо́к*; **the car ~ed forward** маши́ну бро́сило вперёд; **to leave sb in the ~** (*inf*) броса́ть (бро́сить* *perf*) кого́-н в беде́.
lure [luəʳ] *n* прима́нка ♦ *vt* зама́нивать (замани́ть* *perf*); **to ~ sb away from** отвлека́ть (отвле́чь* *perf*) кого́-н от +*gen*.
lurid ['luərɪd] *adj* (*garish*) аляпова́тый (аляпова́т).
lurk [lə:k] *vi* (*animal, person, also fig*) таи́ться (*impf*).
luscious ['lʌʃəs] *adj* (*person, thing*) притяга́тельный* (притяга́телен); (*food*) со́чный* (со́чен).
lush [lʌʃ] *adj* (*fields, gardens*) пы́шный* (пы́шен); (*restaurant, lifestyle*) роско́шный* (роско́шен).
lust [lʌst] *n* (*sexual desire*) по́хоть *f*; (*greed*): **~ (for)** жа́жда (к +*dat*)

▶ **lust after** *vt fus* (*desire sexually*) испы́тывать (испыта́ть *perf*) вожделе́ние к +*dat*; (*crave*) жа́ждать* (*impf*) +*gen*
▶ **lust for** *vt fus* = **lust after**.
lustful ['lʌstful] *adj* похотли́вый (похотли́в).
lustre ['lʌstəʳ] (*US* **luster**) *n* блеск.
lusty ['lʌstɪ] *adj* по́лный* (по́лон) жи́зни и здоро́вья.
lute [lu:t] *n* лю́тня*.
luvvie ['lʌvɪ] *n* (*inf*) дорогу́ша *m/f*.
luvvy ['lʌvɪ] *n* = **luvvie**.
Luxembourg ['lʌksəmbə:g] *n* Люксембу́рг.
luxuriant [lʌg'zjuərɪənt] *adj* (*plants, gardens*) бу́йный* (бу́ен); (*hair*) пы́шный* (пы́шен).
luxuriate [lʌg'zjuərɪeɪt] *vi*: **to ~ in** наслажда́ться (наслади́ться* *perf*) +*instr*.
luxurious [lʌg'zjuərɪəs] *adj* роско́шный* (роско́шен).
luxury ['lʌkʃərɪ] *n* (*great comfort*) ро́скошь *f*; (*treat*) роско́шество ♦ *cpd* роско́шный.
luxury tax *n* нало́г на предме́ты ро́скоши.
LV *n abbr* = **luncheon voucher**.
Lvov [ljvof] *n* Льво́в.
LW *abbr* (*RADIO*) (= **long wave**) ДВ= *дли́нные во́лны*.
lycra® ['laɪkrə] *n* синтети́ческий эласти́чный материа́л, испо́льзуемый при изготовле́нии трикота́жной оде́жды.
lying ['laɪŋ] *n* ложь *f* ♦ *adj* лжи́вый.
lynch [lɪntʃ] *vt* линчева́ть* (*impf/perf*).
lynx [lɪŋks] *n* (*ZOOL*) рысь *f*.
Lyon ['li:ɔ̃] *n* Лио́н.
lyric ['lɪrɪk] *adj*: **~ poetry** ли́рика, лири́ческая поэ́зия.
lyrical ['lɪrɪkl] *adj* (*poem*) лири́ческий*; (*fig: praise, comment*) восто́рженный (восто́ржен).
lyricism ['lɪrɪsɪzəm] *n* лири́зм.
lyrics ['lɪrɪks] *npl* слова́ *ntpl or* текст *msg* (*пе́сни*).

~ *M, m* ~

M, m [ɛm] *n* (*letter*) 13-ая бу́ква англи́йского алфави́та.

M *n abbr* (*BRIT.* = *motorway*) автомагистра́ль *f* ◆ *abbr* = **medium**.

m. *abbr* (= **metre**) м= *метр*; = **mile, million**.

MA *n abbr* (= *Master of Arts*) ≈ маги́стр гуманита́рных нау́к; (= *military academy*) Вое́нная акаде́мия ◆ *abbr* (*US: POST*) = *Massachusetts*.

mac [mæk] *n* (*BRIT. inf*) макинто́ш.

macabre [mə'kɑ:brə] *adj* жу́ткий* (жу́ток).

macaroni [mækə'rəʊnɪ] *n* макаро́ны* *pl*.

macaroon [mækə'ru:n] *n* минда́льное безе́ *nt ind*.

mace [meɪs] *n* (*weapon*) булава́*; (*ceremonial*) жезл*; (*spice*) муска́т.

Macedonia [mæsɪ'dəʊnɪə] *n* Македо́ния.

Macedonian [mæsɪ'dəʊnɪən] *adj* македо́нский*.

machinations [mækɪ'neɪʃənz] *npl* (*plot*) ко́зни* *pl*; (*scheme*) махина́ция *fsg*.

machine [mə'ʃi:n] *n* (*also fig*) маши́на ◆ *vt* (*TECH*) подверга́ть (подве́ргнуть* *perf*) маши́нной обрабо́тке; (*dress etc*) шить* (сшить* *perf*) на маши́не.

machine code *n* (*COMPUT*) маши́нный код.

machine gun *n* пулемёт.

machine language *n* (*COMPUT*) маши́нный язы́к*.

machine readable *adj* (*COMPUT*) маши́но-чита́емый.

machinery [mə'ʃi:nərɪ] *n* обору́дование; (*of government*) механи́зм.

machine shop *n* механи́ческий* цех*.

machine tool *n* стано́к*.

machine washable *adj* (*garment*) приго́дный к маши́нной сти́рке.

machinist [mə'ʃi:nɪst] *n* стано́чник(-ица).

macho ['mætʃəʊ] *adj* мужи́цкий.

mackerel ['mækrl] *n inv* ску́мбрия.

mackintosh ['mækɪntɔʃ] *n* (*BRIT*) макинто́ш.

macro... ['mækrəʊ] *prefix* ма́кро....

macroeconomics ['mækrəʊiːkə'nɔmɪks] *npl* макроэконо́мика *fsg*.

mad [mæd] *adj* (*also fig*) сумасше́дший*, поме́шанный (поме́шан); (*angry*) бе́шеный; (*keen*): **he is ~ about** он поме́шан на +*prp*; **to**

go ~ (*insane*) сходи́ть* (сойти́* *perf*) с ума́; (*angry*) беси́ться* (взбеси́ться* *perf*).

Madagascar [mædə'gæskə'] *n* Мадагаска́р.

madam ['mædəm] *n* (*form of address*) мада́м *f ind*, госпожа́; **yes, ~** да, мада́м; **Dear M~** (*in formal letter*) уважа́емая госпожа́; **M~ Chairman** госпожа́ председа́тель.

madcap ['mædkæp] *adj* сумасбро́дный*.

mad cow disease *n* (*inf*) энцефалопа́тия кру́пного рога́того скота́.

madden ['mædn] *vt* (*make angry*) беси́ть* (взбеси́ть* *perf*).

maddening ['mædnɪŋ] *adj* невыноси́мый (невыноси́м).

made [meɪd] *pt, pp of* **make**.

Madeira [mə'dɪərə] *n* (*GEO*) Маде́йра; (*wine*) маде́ра.

made-to-measure ['meɪdtə'meʒə'] *adj* (*BRIT*) индивидуа́льного поши́ва.

madhouse ['mædhaʊs] *n* (*inf: asylum*) сумасше́дший* дом*, психу́шка*; (*state of uproar*) сумасше́дший дом.

madly ['mædlɪ] *adv* безу́мно; **she is ~ in love with him** она́ безу́мно влюблена́ в него́; **to fall ~ in love with sb** безу́мно влюби́ться* (*perf*) в кого́-н.

madman ['mædmən] *irreg n* сумасше́дший* *m adj*.

madness ['mædnɪs] *n* (*insanity*) безу́мие, сумасше́ствие; (*foolishness*) безу́мие.

Madrid [mə'drɪd] *n* Мадри́д.

madwoman ['mædwʊmən] *irreg n* сумасше́дшая* *f adj*.

Mafia ['mæfɪə] *n*: **the ~** ма́фия.

mag [mæg] *n abbr* (*BRIT: inf*) = **magazine**.

magazine [mægə'zi:n] *n* журна́л; (*RADIO*) радиожурна́л; (*TV*) тележурна́л; (*MIL: store*) склад боеприпа́сов; (: *of firearm*) магази́н.

maggot ['mægət] *n* личи́нка* му́хи.

magic ['mædʒɪk] *n* ма́гия; (*conjuring*) фо́кусы *mpl* ◆ *adj* (*powers, ritual*) маги́ческий*; (*fig: place, moment, experience*) волше́бный* (волше́бен); **~ wand** волше́бная па́лочка*.

magical ['mædʒɪkl] *adj* (*powers, ritual*) маги́ческий*; (*experience, evening*) волше́бный* (волше́бен).

---

magician [mə'dʒɪʃən] n (*wizard*) маг; (*conjurer*) фо́кусник.

magistrate ['mædʒɪstreɪt] n (*LAW*) мирово́й судья́* m.

magistrates' court n магистрату́ра.

magnanimous [mæg'nænɪməs] adj великоду́шный* (великоду́шен).

magnate ['mægneɪt] n магна́т.

magnesium [mæg'ni:zɪəm] n ма́гний.

magnet ['mægnɪt] n магни́т.

magnetic [mæg'nɛtɪk] adj магни́тный; (*personality*) притяга́тельный* (притяга́телен).

magnetic disk n (*COMPUT*) магни́тный диск.

magnetic tape n магни́тная плёнка*.

magnetism ['mægnɪtɪzəm] n магнети́зм.

magnetize ['mægnɪtaɪz] vt намагни́чивать (намагни́тить* perf).

magnification [mægnɪfɪ'keɪʃən] n увеличе́ние.

magnificence [mæg'nɪfɪsns] n великоле́пие.

magnificent [mæg'nɪfɪsnt] adj великоле́пный* (великоле́пен).

magnify ['mægnɪfaɪ] vt увели́чивать (увели́чить perf); (*sound*) уси́ливать (уси́лить perf); (*exaggerate*) преувели́чивать (преувели́чить perf).

magnifying glass ['mægnɪfaɪŋ-] n увеличи́тельное стекло́*, лу́па.

magnitude ['mægnɪtju:d] n (*size*) величина́; (*importance*) масшта́б.

magnolia [mæg'nəʊlɪə] n магно́лия.

magpie ['mægpaɪ] n соро́ка.

mahogany [mə'hɔgənɪ] n кра́сное де́рево ♦ cpd кра́сного де́рева.

maid [meɪd] n (*in private house*) служа́нка*; (*in hotel*) го́рничная f adj; **old ~** (*pej*) ста́рая де́ва.

maiden ['meɪdn] n (*literary*) де́ва ♦ adj (*aunt etc*) незаму́жняя; (*speech, voyage*) пе́рвый.

maiden name n де́вичья фами́лия.

mail [meɪl] n по́чта ♦ vt отправля́ть (отпра́вить* perf) по по́чте; **by ~** по по́чте.

mailbox ['meɪlbɔks] n (*US: letter box, also COMPUT*) почто́вый я́щик.

mailing list ['meɪlɪŋ-] n спи́сок* адреса́тов.

mailman ['meɪlmæn] irreg n (*US*) почтальо́н.

mail order n систе́ма зака́за това́ров по по́чте ♦ cpd: **~~ catalogue** катало́г торго́во-посы́лочной фи́рмы; **~~ firm** торго́во-посы́лочная фи́рма.

mailshot ['meɪlʃɔt] n рассы́лка объявле́ний по по́чте.

mail train n почто́вый по́езд*.

mail truck n (*US*) почто́вый фурго́н.

mail van n (*BRIT: AUT*) почто́вый фурго́н; (: *RAIL*) почто́вый ваго́н.

maim [meɪm] vt кале́чить (искале́чить perf).

main [meɪn] adj (*reason, point, door*) гла́вный ♦ n (*pipe*): **gas/water ~** газопрово́дная/ водопрово́дная магистра́ль f; **the ~s** npl сеть fsg; **~ meal** обе́д; **in the ~** в основно́м.

main course n основно́е or второ́е блю́до.

mainframe ['meɪnfreɪm] n (*COMPUT*) (универса́льная) вычисли́тельная маши́на.

mainland ['meɪnlənd] n: **the ~** матери́к, больша́я земля́*.

main line n (*RAIL*) железнодоро́жная магистра́ль f.

mainline ['meɪnlaɪn] adj (*RAIL: station*) магистра́льный ♦ vt (*DRUGS*) вка́лывать (вколо́ть* perf) ♦ vi (*DRUGS*) коло́ться* (impf).

mainly ['meɪnlɪ] adv гла́вным о́бразом.

main road n шоссе́ nt ind; (*in town, village*) гла́вная у́лица.

mainstay ['meɪnsteɪ] n гла́вная опо́ра.

mainstream ['meɪnstri:m] n госпо́дствующая тенде́нция ♦ adj госпо́дствующий*.

maintain [meɪn'teɪn] vt (*friendship, system, momentum*) подде́рживать (поддержа́ть* perf); (*dependant*) содержа́ть* (impf); (*building*) обслу́живать (impf); (*affirm: belief, opinion*) утвержда́ть (impf); **to ~ (that ...)** утвержда́ть (impf) (, что ...).

maintenance ['meɪntənəns] n (*see vb*) подде́ржание; содержа́ние; обслу́живание; утвержде́ние; (*LAW: alimony*) алиме́нты* pl.

maintenance contract n контра́кт по обслу́живанию.

maintenance grant n стипе́ндия.

maintenance order n (*LAW*) постановле́ние о вы́плате алиме́нтов.

maisonette [meɪzə'nɛt] n (*BRIT*) двухэта́жная кварти́ра.

maize [meɪz] n кукуру́за, маи́с.

Maj. abbr (*MIL*) = **major**.

majestic [mə'dʒɛstɪk] adj вели́чественный* (вели́чествен).

majesty ['mædʒɪstɪ] n (*sovereignty*) короле́в-ская власть f; (*splendour*) вели́чественность f; (*form of address*): **Your M~** Ва́ше Вели́чество.

major ['meɪdʒəʳ] n (*MIL*) майо́р ♦ adj (*important*) гла́вный; (*MUS*) мажо́рный ♦ vi (*US: SCOL*): **to ~ in** специализи́роваться (impf/perf) в +prp; **a ~ operation** (*also fig*) кру́пная опера́ция.

Majorca [mə'jɔːkə] n Мальо́рка, Майо́рка.

major general n генера́л-майо́р.

majority [mə'dʒɔrɪtɪ] n большинство́ ♦ cpd: **~ verdict** пригово́р, вы́несенный большинство́м (голосо́в); **~ (share)holding** контро́льный паке́т а́кций.

make [meɪk] (pt, pp **made**) vt де́лать (сде́лать perf); (*clothes*) шить* (сшить* perf); (*manufacture*) изготовля́ть (изгото́вить* perf); (*meal*) гото́вить* (пригото́вить* perf); (*money*) зараба́тывать (зарабо́тать perf) ♦ n (*brand*) ма́рка*; **to ~ sb do** (*force*) заставля́ть (заста́вить* perf) кого́-н +infin; **two and two ~ four** (*equal*) два плюс два — четы́ре; **to ~ sb unhappy** расстра́ивать (расстро́ить perf) кого́-н; **to ~ a noise** шуме́ть* (impf); **to ~ the bed** стели́ть* (постели́ть* perf) посте́ль; **to ~**

a fool of sb де́лать (сде́лать *perf*) из кого́-н
дурака́; **to ~ a profit** получа́ть (получи́ть*
perf) при́быль; **to ~ a loss** нести́* (понести́*
perf) убы́ток; **to ~ it** (*succeed*) преуспева́ть
(преуспе́ть* *perf*); (*arrive*) успева́ть (успе́ть*
perf); **what time do you ~ it?** ско́лько на
ва́ших (часа́х)?; **let's ~ it Monday** дава́йте
договори́мся на понеде́льник; **to ~ good ♦** *vi*
(*succeed*) преуспева́ть (преуспе́ть* *perf*) **♦** *vt*
(*deficit*) возмеща́ть (возмести́ть* *perf*);
(*damage*) исправля́ть (испра́вить* *perf*); **to ~
do with/without** обходи́ться* (обойти́сь*
perf) +*instr*/без +*gen*

► **make for** *vt fus* (*place*) направля́ться
(напра́виться* *perf*) к +*dat*/в +*acc*
► **make off** *vi* (*escape*) скрыва́ться (скры́ться*
perf)
► **make out** *vt* (*decipher*) разбира́ть
(разобра́ть* *perf*); (*see*) различа́ть
(различи́ть* *perf*); (*write out*) выпи́сывать
(вы́писать* *perf*); (*claim*) утвержда́ть (*impf*);
(*understand*) разбира́ться (разобра́ться*
perf) в +*prp*; (*claim, imply*) де́лать (сде́лать
perf) вид; **to ~ out a case for sth**
обосно́вывать (обоснова́ть *perf*) что-н
► **make over** *vt* (*assign*): **to ~ over (to)**
передава́ть* (переда́ть* *perf*) (+*dat*)
► **make up** *vt fus* (*constitute*) составля́ть
(соста́вить* *perf*) **♦** *vt* (*invent*) выду́мывать
(вы́думать *perf*); (*prepare: bed, parcel*)
гото́вить* (пригото́вить* *perf*); (*with
cosmetics*) де́лать (сде́лать *perf*) макия́ж +*dat*
♦ *vi* (*after quarrel*) мири́ться (помири́ться*
perf); (*with cosmetics*): **to ~ (o.s.) up** де́лать
(сде́лать *perf*) макия́ж; **to be made up of**
состоя́ть (*impf*) из +*gen*
► **make up for** *vt fus* (*mistake, misdemeanour*)
загла́живать (загла́дить* *perf*); (*loss*)
восполня́ть (воспо́лнить *perf*); **to ~ up for
lost time** навёрстывать (наверста́ть *perf*)
упу́щенное вре́мя.

make-believe ['meɪkbɪliːv] *n* фанта́зии *fpl*; **a
world of ~** мир фанта́зий; **it's just ~** э́то –
про́сто фанта́зия.

maker ['meɪkə^r] *n* (*of programme, film*)
созда́тель(ница) *m(f)*; (*of goods*)
изготови́тель *m*.

makeshift ['meɪkʃɪft] *adj* (*temporary*)
вре́менный.

make-up ['meɪkʌp] *n* косме́тика, макия́ж;
(*THEAT*) грим.

make-up bag *n* косме́тичка*.

make-up remover *n* сре́дство для сня́тия
макия́жа.

making ['meɪkɪŋ] *n* (*of programme*) созда́ние;
(*of goods*) изготовле́ние; (*fig*): **in the ~** в
проце́ссе созда́ния; **to have the ~s of** име́ть
(*impf*) зада́тки +*gen*; **the problem is of your**

own ~ пробле́ма Ва́ми же и со́здана.

maladjusted [mælə'dʒʌstɪd] *adj* (*child*)
трудновоспиту́емый.

maladroit [mælə'drɔɪt] *adj* (*behaviour*)
неуме́лый (неуме́л); (*comment*) беста́ктный*
(беста́ктен).

malaise [mæ'leɪz] *n* (*of society*) неду́г.

malaria [mə'lɛərɪə] *n* маляри́я.

Malawi [mə'lɑːwɪ] *n* Мала́ви *nt ind*.

Malay [mə'leɪ] *adj* мала́йский **♦** *n* (*person*)
мала́ец*(-а́йка*); (*LING*) мала́йский* язы́к*.

Malaya [mə'leɪə] *n* Мала́йя.

Malayan [mə'leɪən] *adj, n* = **Malay**.

Malaysia [mə'leɪzɪə] *n* Мала́йзия.

Malaysian [mə'leɪzɪən] *adj* малайзи́йский **♦** *n*
малайзи́ец*(-и́йка*).

Maldives ['mɔːldaɪvz] *npl*: **the ~** Мальди́вские
острова́* *mpl*.

male [meɪl] *n* (*human*) мужчи́на *m*; (*animal*)
саме́ц* **♦** *adj* (*sex, attitude*) мужско́й; (*child
etc*) мужско́го по́ла; (*ELEC*) охва́тываемый;
~ and female students студе́нты: ю́ноши и
де́вушки*.

male chauvinist *n*: **he's a ~ ~** он о́чень
пренебрежи́тельно отно́сится к же́нщинам.

male nurse *n* медбра́т*.

malevolence [mə'lɛvələns] *n* (*act*) злодея́ние;
(*feeling*) зло́ба.

malevolent [mə'lɛvələnt] *adj* зло́бный*
(зло́бен).

malformed [mæl'fɔːmd] *adj* непра́вильно
сформирова́вшийся.

malfunction [mæl'fʌŋkʃən] *n* неиспра́вность *f*.

Mali ['mɑːli] *n* Мали́ *nt ind*.

Malian ['mɑːlɪən] *adj* мали́йский **♦** *n*
мали́ец*(-и́йка*).

malice ['mælɪs] *n* зло́ба.

malicious [mə'lɪʃəs] *adj* (*person, gossip*)
зло́бный* (зло́бен), злой* (зол); (*LAW*)
злонаме́ренный (злонаме́рен).

malign [mə'laɪn] *vt* клевета́ть* (оклевета́ть*
perf) **♦** *adj* па́губный* (па́губен).

malignant [mə'lɪgnənt] *adj* (*MED*)
злока́чественный*; (*behaviour, intention*)
зло́стный* (зло́стен).

malingerer [mə'lɪŋgərə^r] *n* симуля́нт(ка*).

mall [mɔːl] *n* (*also*: **shopping ~**) = торго́вый
центр.

malleable ['mælɪəbl] *adj* (*clay, substance*)
пода́тливый (пода́тлив); (*person*)
поко́рный* (поко́рен).

mallet ['mælɪt] *n* деревя́нный молото́к*.

malnutrition [mælnjuː'trɪʃən] *n* недоеда́ние.

malpractice [mæl'præktɪs] *n* злоупотребле́ние
служе́бным положе́нием.

malt [mɔːlt] *n* (*grain*) со́лод*; (*also*: **~ whisky**)
солодо́вое ви́ски *nt ind*.

Malta ['mɔːltə] *n* Ма́льта.

---

* marks translations which have irregular inflections. The Russian-English side of the dictionary gives inflectional information.

Maltese [mɔːˈtiːz] *adj* мальти́йский* ♦ *n inv*
мальти́ец*(-и́йка*); (*LING*) мальти́йский*
язы́к*.

maltreat [mælˈtriːt] *vt* пло́хо обраща́ться (*impf*)
с +*instr*.

mammal [ˈmæml] *n* млекопита́ющее *nt adj*.

mammoth [ˈmæməθ] *n* ма́монт ♦ *adj* (*task*)
колосса́льный* (колосса́лен).

man [mæn] (*pl* **men**) *n* (*adult male*) мужчи́на *m*;
(*person, mankind*) челове́к*; (*CHESS*) фигу́ра ♦
vt (*machine*) обслу́живать (*impf*); (*post*)
занима́ть (заня́ть* *perf*); (*NAUT*): **to ~ a ship**
набира́ть (набра́ть* *perf*) кома́нду корабля́;
an old ~ стари́к*; **~ and wife** муж и жена́.

manage [ˈmænɪdʒ] *vi* (*get by*) обходи́ться*
(обойти́сь* *perf*) ♦ *vt* (*business, organization*)
руководи́ть* (*impf*) +*instr*, управля́ть (*impf*)
+*instr*; (*shop, restaurant*) заве́довать (*impf*)
+*instr*; (*economy*) управля́ть (*impf*) +*instr*;
(*control*) кома́ндовать (*impf*) +*instr*; (*workload,
task*) справля́ться (*impf*) с +*instr*; **to ~ without
sb/sth** обходи́ться* (обойти́сь* *perf*) без
кого́-н/чего́-н; **I ~d to convince him** мне
удало́сь убеди́ть его́; **I ~d to finish in time** я
успе́л зако́нчить во́время.

manageable [ˈmænɪdʒəbl] *adj* (*task*)
выполни́мый (выполни́м); (*number, size*)
удо́бный.

management [ˈmænɪdʒmənt] *n* (*body*)
руково́дство; (*act*): **~ (of)** управле́ние
(+*instr*); "**under new ~**" "под но́вым
руково́дством".

management accounting *n* управле́нческий*
учёт.

management consultant *n* консульта́нт по
вопро́сам ме́неджмента.

manager [ˈmænɪdʒə*] *n* (*of business,
organization*) управля́ющий* *m adj*;
ме́неджер; (*of estate*) управля́ющий*; (*of
shop*) заве́дующий*(-ая) *m(f) adj*; (*of pop star*)
ме́неджер; (*SPORT*) гла́вный тре́нер; **sales ~**
нача́льник по сбы́ту.

manageress [mænɪdʒəˈrɛs] *n* (*of shop*)
заве́дующая *f adj*.

managerial [mænɪˈdʒɪərɪəl] *adj* (*role*)
управле́нческий*; **~ staff** управле́нческий*
аппара́т; **~ decisions** реше́ния, при́нятые
руково́дством.

managing director [ˈmænɪdʒɪŋ-] *n*
дире́ктор*-распоряди́тель *m*.

Managua [məˈnɑːgwə] *n* Мана́гуа.

Manchester [ˈmæntʃɪstə*] *n* Манче́стер.

Manchuria [mænˈtʃuərɪə] *n* Маньчжу́рия.

Mancunian [mænˈkjuːnɪən] *n* жи́тель(ница)
m(f) Манче́стера.

mandarin [ˈmændərɪn] *n* (*also:* **~ orange**)
мандари́н; (*BRIT: POL*) кру́пный чино́вник;
(*LING*): **M~** (*Chinese*) мандари́нское наре́чие
кита́йского языка́.

mandate [ˈmændeɪt] *n* (*POL: from electorate*)
полномо́чие; (: *from UN etc*) манда́т; (*task*)

поруче́ние.

mandatory [ˈmændətərɪ] *adj* обяза́тельный*
(обяза́телен).

mandolin(e) [ˈmændəlɪn] *n* мандоли́на.

mane [meɪn] *n* гри́ва.

maneuver *etc* (*US*) = **manoeuvre** *etc*.

manfully [ˈmænfəlɪ] *adv* му́жественно.

manganese [mæŋgəˈniːz] *n* ма́рганец*.

mangetout [ˈmɔnʒˈtuː] *n* стручко́вый горо́х
(*со съедо́бными стру́чками*).

mangle [ˈmæŋgl] *vt* корёжить (искорёжить
perf) ♦ *n* пресс для отжима́ния белья́.

mango [ˈmæŋgəu] (*pl* **~es**) *n* ма́нго *nt ind*.

mangrove [ˈmæŋgrəuv] *n* ма́нгровое де́рево*.

mangy [ˈmeɪndʒɪ] *adj* (*diseased*) парши́вый
(парши́в); (*scruffy*) обле́злый (обле́зл).

manhandle [ˈmænhændl] *vt* (*mistreat*) гру́бо
обраща́ться (*impf*) с +*instr*; (*move by hand*)
приводи́ть* (привести́* *perf*) в де́йствие
вручну́ю.

manhole [ˈmænhəul] *n* люк.

manhood [ˈmænhud] *n* (*state*) возмужа́лость *f*;
(*age*) зре́лость *f*.

man-hour [ˈmænauə*] *n* челове́ко-час*.

manhunt [ˈmænhʌnt] *n* ро́зыск.

mania [ˈmeɪnɪə] *n* (*also PSYCH*) ма́ния.

maniac [ˈmeɪnɪæk] *n* (*also fig*) манья́к; **he's a
football ~** он стра́стный люби́тель футбо́ла.

manic [ˈmænɪk] *adj* безу́мный* (безу́мен).

manic-depressive [ˈmænɪkdɪˈprɛsɪv] *adj*
маниака́льно-депресси́вный* ♦ *n* челове́к,
страда́ющий маниака́льно-депресси́вным
психо́зом.

manicure [ˈmænɪkjuə*] *n* маникю́р ♦ *vt* (*person*)
де́лать (сде́лать *perf*) маникю́р +*dat*.

manicure set *n* маникю́рный набо́р.

manifest [ˈmænɪfest] *vt* проявля́ть (прояви́ть*
perf) ♦ *adj* очеви́дный* (очеви́ден), я́вный*
(я́вен) ♦ *n* (*NAUT*) деклара́ция (судово́го
гру́за); (*AVIAT*) манифе́ст.

manifestation [mænɪfɛsˈteɪʃən] *n*: **a ~ of**
проявле́ние +*gen*.

manifesto [mænɪˈfestəu] *n* манифе́ст.

manifold [ˈmænɪfəuld] *adj* многообра́зный*
(многообра́зен) ♦ *n* (*AUT*): **exhaust ~**
выхлопно́й колле́ктор.

Manila [məˈnɪlə] *n* Мани́ла.

manila [məˈnɪlə] *adj*: **~ paper** пло́тная
кори́чневая бума́га.

manipulate [məˈnɪpjuleɪt] *vt* манипули́ровать
(*impf*) +*instr*.

manipulation [mənɪpjuˈleɪʃən] *n* манипуля́ция.

mankind [mænˈkaɪnd] *n* челове́чество.

manliness [ˈmænlɪnɪs] *n* му́жественность *f*.

manly [ˈmænlɪ] *adj* му́жественный*
(му́жествен).

man-made [ˈmænˈmeɪd] *adj* иску́сственный*.

manna [ˈmænə] *n* ма́нна небе́сная.

mannequin [ˈmænɪkɪn] *n* (*dummy*) манеке́н;
(*fashion model*) манеке́нщица.

manner [ˈmænə*] *n* (*way*) о́браз; (*behaviour*)

манéра; ~**s** *npl* манéры *fpl*; **bad ~s** плохи́е
манéры; **all ~ of things/people**
всевозмóжные вéщи/лю́ди; **in a ~ of
speaking** в некотóром рóде.
mannerism ['mænərɪzəm] *n* осóбенность *f*
манéра.
mannerly ['mænəlɪ] *adj* учти́вый (учти́в).
manning ['mænɪŋ] *n* набóр рабóчей си́лы.
manoeuvrable [mə'nu:vrəbl] (*US* **maneuvrable**)
adj манёвренный.
manoeuvre [mə'nu:vəʳ] (*US* **maneuver**) *vt*
(*move*) умéло передвигáть (передви́нуть
perf); (*manipulate*) маневри́ровать (*impf*) +*instr*
♦ *vi* маневри́ровать (*impf*) ♦ *n* манёвр; ~**s** *npl*
(*MIL*) манёвры *mpl*; **to ~ sb into doing**
подводи́ть* (подвести́* *perf*) когó-н к томý,
чтóбы сдéлал чтó-н.
manor ['mænəʳ] *n* (*also:* ~ **house**) усáдебный
дом*.
manpower ['mænpauəʳ] *n* рабóчая си́ла.
manservant ['mænsə:vənt] (*pl* **menservants**) *n*
слугá* *m*.
mansion ['mænʃən] *n* особня́к*.
manslaughter ['mænslɔ:təʳ] *n*
непредумы́шленное уби́йство.
mantelpiece ['mæntlpi:s] *n* ками́нная доскá*.
mantle ['mæntl] *n* (*cloak*) мáнтия; (*fig:
covering*) покрóв.
man-to-man ['mæntə'mæn] *adj* мужскóй ♦ *adv*
по-мужски́, как мужчи́на с мужчи́ной.
manual ['mænjuəl] *adj* ручнóй ♦ *n* (*book*)
посóбие; ~ **worker** чернорабóчий*(-ая) *m(f)*
adj.
manufacture [mænju'fæktʃəʳ] *vt* (*goods*)
изготовля́ть (изготóвить* *perf*),
производи́ть* (произвести́* *perf*) ♦ *n*
изготовлéние, произвóдство.
manufactured goods *npl* промы́шленные
товáры *mpl*.
manufacturer [mænju'fæktʃərəʳ] *n*
изготови́тель *m*, производи́тель *m*.
manufacturing [mænju'fæktʃərɪŋ] *n*
изготовлéние, произвóдство.
manure [mə'njuəʳ] *n* навóз.
manuscript ['mænjuskrɪpt] *n* (*author's draft*)
рýкопись *f*; (*old document*) манускри́пт,
рýкопись.
many ['mɛnɪ] *adj* (*a lot of*) мнóго +*gen* ♦ *pron*
(*several*) мнóгие; **a great ~** óчень мнóго +*gen*,
мнóжество +*gen*; **how ~?** скóлько?; **how ~
people/times?** скóлько людéй/раз?; **too ~
difficulties** сли́шком мнóго трýдностей;
twice as ~ вдвóе бóльше, в два рáза
бóльше; ~ **a time** мнóго раз; **in ~ cases** во
мнóгих слýчаях; ~ **of us** мнóгие из нас.
Maori ['mauri] *n* мáори *m/f ind*.
map [mæp] *n* кáрта; (*of town*) план ♦ *vt*
составля́ть (состáвить* *perf*) кáрту +*gen*

▸ **map out** *vt* (*plan*) составля́ть (состáвить*
perf); (*task, holiday, career*) плани́ровать
(*impf*).
maple ['meɪpl] *n* клён ♦ *cpd* кленóвый.
mar [mɑ:ʳ] *vt* пóртить* (испóртить* *perf*).
Mar. *abbr* = **March.**
marathon ['mærəθən] *n* марафóн ♦ *adj* (*fig*)
марафóнский.
marathon runner *n* марафóнец*.
marauder [mə'rɔ:dəʳ] *n* мародёр.
marble ['mɑ:bl] *n* (*stone*) мрáмор; (*toy*)
стекля́нный шáрик ♦ *adj* мрáморный.
marbles ['mɑ:blz] *n* (*game*) дéтская игрá* в
стекля́нные шáрики.
March [mɑ:tʃ] *n* март; *see also* **July.**
march [mɑ:tʃ] *vi* маршировáть
(промаршировáть *perf*); (*protesters*)
проходи́ть* (пройти́* *perf*) мáршем ♦ *n* марш
♦ *vt*: **to ~ sb out of** выдворя́ть (вы́дворить
perf) когó-н из +*gen*; **to ~ out of**
демонстрати́вно выходи́ть* (вы́йти* *perf*) из
+*gen*; **to ~ into** реши́тельно входи́ть* (войти́*
perf) в +*acc*.
marcher ['mɑ:tʃəʳ] *n* (*demonstrator*)
учáстник*(-ица) мáрша.
marching orders ['mɑ:tʃɪŋ-] *npl*: **to give sb his
~ ~** увольня́ть (уволи́ть *perf*) когó-н.
march past *n* (*MIL*) строевóй смотр.
mare [mɛəʳ] *n* кобы́ла.
marge [mɑ:dʒ] *n abbr* (*BRIT: inf*) = **margarine.**
margarine [mɑ:dʒə'ri:n] *n* маргари́н.
margin ['mɑ:dʒɪn] *n* (*on page*) поля́ *ntpl*; (*of
group*) перифери́я; (*of area*) край*;
(*difference: of victory*) преимýщество; (: *of
defeat*) меньшинствó; (*also:* **profit ~**) чи́стая
при́быль *f no pl*; **safety ~** запáс прóчности; ~
of error предéл допусти́мой погрéшности;
they won by a ~ of five votes они́ победи́ли с
большинствóм в пять голосóв.
marginal ['mɑ:dʒɪnl] *adj* незначи́тельный*
(незначи́телен) ♦ *n* (*also:* ~ **seat** *or*
constituency: *BRIT: POL*) избирáтельный
*учáсток где прáвящая пáртия имéет
незначи́тельное большинствó голосóв*.
marginally ['mɑ:dʒɪnəlɪ] *adv* незначи́тельно.
marigold ['mærɪgəuld] *n* (*BOT*) ноготки́ *mpl*.
marijuana [mærɪ'wɑ:nə] *n* марихуáна.
marina [mə'ri:nə] *n* мари́на *or* при́стань* *f* для
яхт.
marinade [mærɪ'neɪd] *n* маринáд ♦ *vt* =
marinate.
marinate ['mærɪneɪt] *vt* мариновáть
(замариновáть *perf*).
marine [mə'ri:n] *adj* морскóй; (*engineer*)
судовóй ♦ *n* (*BRIT*) слýжащий* *m adj*
воéнно-морскóго флóта; (*US*) морскóй
пехоти́нец*.
marine insurance *n* морскóе страховáние.

marital ['mærɪtl] *adj* супру́жеский*; ~ **status** семе́йное положе́ние.

maritime ['mærɪtaɪm] *adj* морско́й; ~ **law** морско́е пра́во.

Mariupol [marɪˈupəlj] *n* Мариу́поль *m*.

marjoram ['mɑ:dʒərəm] *n* души́ца, майора́н.

mark [mɑ:k] *n* (*written symbol*) значо́к*, поме́тка*; (*stain*) пятно́*; (*trace*) след*; (*of friendship, respect*) знак; (*BRIT: SCOL*) отме́тка*, оце́нка*; (*level*) отме́тка*; (*currency*) ма́рка* ♦ *vt* (*with pen*) помеча́ть (поме́тить* *perf*); (*subj: shoes, tyres*) оставля́ть (оста́вить* *perf*) след на +*prp*; (*furniture etc*) поврежда́ть (повреди́ть* *perf*); (*clothes, carpet*) ста́вить* (поста́вить* *perf*) пятно́ на +*prp*; (*place, time*) ука́зывать (указа́ть* *perf*); (*characterize*) отмеча́ть (отме́тить* *perf*); (*BRIT: SCOL*) проверя́ть (прове́рить *perf*); (*SPORT: player*) блоки́ровать (*impf*); **punctuation** ~ знак препина́ния; **M~ 2/3** (*BRIT: TECH*) второ́го/ тре́тьего вы́пуска; **up to the** ~ на высоте́; **to be quick off the** ~ **to do** (*fig*) не заме́длить (*perf*) +*infin*; **to** ~ **the price on sth** (поста́вить* *perf*) це́ну на чём-н; **to** ~ **time** (*MIL*) марширова́ть (*impf*) на ме́сте; (*fig*) топта́ться* (*impf*)

▶ **mark down** *vt* (*price*) снижа́ть (сни́зить* *perf*); (*goods*) уце́нивать (уцени́ть* *perf*)

▶ **mark off** *vt* (*tick off*) отмеча́ть (отме́тить* *perf*)

▶ **mark out** *vt* (*area, road*) размеча́ть (разме́тить* *perf*); (*person*) выделя́ть (вы́делить *perf*)

▶ **mark up** *vt* (*price*) повыша́ть (повы́сить* *perf*).

marked [mɑ:kt] *adj* заме́тный* (заме́тен).

markedly ['mɑ:kɪdlɪ] *adv* заме́тно.

marker ['mɑ:kə'] *n* (*sign*) знак; (*bookmark*) закла́дка*; (*pen*) флома́стер.

market ['mɑ:kɪt] *n* (*also COMM*) ры́нок ♦ *vt* выпуска́ть (вы́пустить* *perf*) в прода́жу; **to be on the** ~ быть* (*impf*) в прода́же; **on the open** ~ в свобо́дной прода́же; **to play the** ~ игра́ть (*impf*) на би́рже.

marketable ['mɑ:kɪtəbl] *adj* по́льзующийся спро́сом; **to be** ~ по́льзоваться (*impf*) спро́сом.

market analysis *n* ана́лиз ры́нка.

market day *n* база́рный день* *m*.

market demand *n* ры́ночный спрос.

market economy *n* ры́ночная эконо́мика.

market forces *npl* ры́ночные си́лы *fpl*.

market garden *n* (*BRIT*) огоро́д (*для выра́щивания овоще́й на прода́жу*).

marketing ['mɑ:kɪtɪŋ] *n* ма́ркетинг.

marketing manager *n* ме́неджер по ма́ркетингу.

marketplace ['mɑ:kɪtpleɪs] *n* ры́ночная *or* база́рная пло́щадь* *f*; (*COMM*) ры́нок*.

market price *n* ры́ночная цена́.

market research *n* иссле́дование ры́нка.

market value *n* ры́ночная сто́имость *f*.

marking ['mɑ:kɪŋ] *n* (*on animal*) расцве́тка; (*on road*) разме́тка.

marksman ['mɑ:ksmən] *irreg n* ме́ткий* стрело́к*.

marksmanship ['mɑ:ksmənʃɪp] *n* ме́ткая стрельба́.

mark-up ['mɑ:kʌp] *n* (*margin*) ра́зница (*ме́жду себесто́имостью и прода́жной цено́й*); (*increase*) наце́нка*.

marmalade ['mɑ:məleɪd] *n* джем (*ци́трусовый*).

maroon [məˈru:n] *adj* бордо́вый ♦ *vi*: **we were ~ed** мы бы́ли отре́заны от вне́шнего ми́ра; (*fig*) мы бы́ли в изоля́ции.

marquee [mɑ:ˈki:] *n* марки́за, пала́точный павильо́н, шатёр.

marquess ['mɑ:kwɪs] *n* (*BRIT*) марки́з.

marquis ['mɑ:kwɪs] *n* = **marquess**.

Marrakech [mærəˈkɛʃ] *n* = **Marrakesh**.

Marrakesh [mærəˈkɛʃ] *n* Марраке́ш.

marriage ['mærɪdʒ] *n* брак; (*wedding*) сва́дьба*.

marriage bureau *nt ind* бюро́ *nt ind* знако́мств.

marriage certificate *n* свиде́тельство о бра́ке.

marriage guidance (*US* **marriage counselling**) *n* консульта́ция по вопро́сам семьи́ и бра́ка.

marriage of convenience *n* фикти́вный брак.

married ['mærɪd] *adj* (*man*) жена́тый (жена́т); (*woman*) заму́жняя (*couple*) жена́ты (жена́ты); (*life*) супру́жеский*; **he is** ~ **to** он жена́т на +*prp*; **she is** ~ **to** она́ за́мужем за +*instr*; **they are** ~ они́ жена́ты.

marrow ['mærəu] *n* (*vegetable*) кабачо́к*; (*also*: **bone** ~) ко́стный мозг.

marry ['mærɪ] *vt* (*subj: man*) жени́ться* (*impf/ perf*) на +*prp*; (: *woman*) выходи́ть* (вы́йти* *perf*) за́муж за +*acc*; (*also*: ~ **off**: *son*) жени́ть* (*impf/perf*); (: *daughter*) выдава́ть* (вы́дать* *perf*) за́муж; (*priest*) венча́ть (обвенча́ть *perf*) ♦ *vi* (*get married: man*) жени́ться (*impf*); (: *woman*) выходи́ть* (вы́йти* *perf*) за́муж; (: *couple*) жени́ться (пожени́ться *perf*).

Mars [mɑ:z] *n* Марс.

Marseilles [mɑ:ˈseɪlz] *n* Марсе́ль *m*.

marsh [mɑ:ʃ] *n* боло́то; **salt** ~ солонча́ковое боло́то.

marshal ['mɑ:ʃl] *n* (*MIL*) ма́ршал; (*at public event*) распоряди́тель(ница) *m(f)* ♦ *vt* (*thoughts, support*) упоря́дочить (*perf*); (*soldiers*) выстра́ивать (вы́строить *perf*); **police/fire** ~ (*US*) нача́льник полице́йского уча́стка/пожа́рной ча́сти.

marshalling yard ['mɑ:ʃlɪŋ-] *n* (*RAIL*) сортиро́вочная ста́нция.

marshmallow [mɑ:ʃˈmæləu] *n* (*BOT*) мушмула́*; (*sweet*) ≈ зефи́р.

marshy ['mɑ:ʃɪ] *adj* боло́тистый (боло́тист).

marsupial [mɑ:ˈsu:pɪəl] *n* су́мчатое *nt adj*

(живо́тное) ◆ *adj* су́мчатый.
marten ['mɑ:tɪn] *n* куни́ца.
martial ['mɑ:ʃl] *adj* вое́нный.
martial art *n* боево́е иску́сство.
martial law *n* вое́нное положе́ние.
Martian ['mɑ:ʃən] *n* марсиа́нин*(-а́нка*).
martin ['mɑ:tɪn] *n*: **house/sand** ~ городска́я/
берегова́я ла́сточка*.
martyr ['mɑ:təˡ] *n* му́ченик(-ица) ◆ *vt* му́чить
(замучить *perf*).
martyrdom ['mɑ:tədəm] *n* му́ченичество.
marvel ['mɑ:vl] *n* чу́до* ◆ *vi*: **to** ~ **(at)**
восхища́ться (восхити́ться* *perf*) (+*instr*).
marvellous ['mɑ:vləs] (*US* **marvelous**) *adj*
восхити́тельный* (восхити́телен),
изуми́тельный* (изуми́телен).
Marxism ['mɑ:ksɪzm] *n* маркси́зм.
Marxist ['mɑ:ksɪst] *adj* маркси́стский ◆ *n*
маркси́ст(ка*).
marzipan ['mɑ:zɪpæn] *n* марципа́н.
mascara [mæsˈkɑ:rə] *n* тушь *f* для ресни́ц.
mascot ['mæskət] *n* талисма́н.
masculine ['mæskjulɪn] *adj* мужско́й; (*woman*)
мужеподо́бный* (мужеподо́бен); ~ **noun/
pronoun** существи́тельное/местоиме́ние
мужско́го ро́да.
masculinity [mæskjuˈlɪnɪtɪ] *n* му́жественность
f.
MASH [mæʃ] *n abbr* (*US*: = *mobile army surgical
hospital*) ≈ ППГ= *полевой подвижный
госпиталь*.
mash [mæʃ] *vt* де́лать (сде́лать *perf*) пюре́ из
+*gen*.
mashed potatoes [mæʃt-] *npl* карто́фельное
пюре́ *nt ind*.
mask [mɑ:sk] *n* ма́ска* ◆ *vt* (*face*) закрыва́ть
(закры́ть* *perf*); (*feelings*) маскирова́ть (*impf*).
masking tape ['mɑ:skɪŋ-] *n* кле́йкая ле́нта.
masochism ['mæsəukɪzəm] *n* мазохи́зм.
masochist ['mæsəukɪst] *n* мазохи́ст(ка*).
mason ['meɪsn] *n* (*also: stone* ~) ка́менщик;
(*also: freemason*) масо́н.
masonic [məˈsɔnɪk] *adj* масо́нский*.
masonry ['meɪsnrɪ] *n* (*stonework*) (ка́менная)
кла́дка.
masquerade [mæskəˈreɪd] *n* маскара́д ◆ *vi*: **to**
~ **as** выдава́ть* себя́ за +*acc*.
mass [mæs] *n* (*also PHYS*) ма́сса; (*REL*:
Orthodox) обе́дня*; (: *Catholic*) ме́сса ◆ *cpd*
ма́ссовый ◆ *vi* сосредото́чиваться
(сосредото́читься *perf*); **the** ~**es** *npl*
(наро́дные) ма́ссы *fpl*; **to go to M**~ идти́*
(пойти́* *perf*) к обе́дне/ме́ссе; ~**es of** (*inf*)
ма́сса *fsg* +*gen*, у́йма *fsg* +*gen*.
massacre ['mæsəkəˡ] *n* ма́ссовое уби́йство ◆ *vt*
зве́рски убива́ть (уби́ть* *perf*).
massage ['mæsɑ:ʒ] *n* масса́ж ◆ *vt* (*rub*)
масси́ровать (*impf*).

masseur [mæˈsə:ˡ] *n* массажи́ст.
masseuse [mæˈsə:z] *n* массажи́стка*.
massive ['mæsɪv] *adj* (*furniture, person*)
масси́вный* (масси́вен); (*support, changes*)
огро́мный* (огро́мен).
mass market *n* ма́ссовый спрос.
mass media *n inv* сре́дства *ntpl* ма́ссовой
информа́ции.
mass meeting *n* ма́ссовый ми́тинг.
mass-produce ['mæsprəˈdju:s] *vt* ма́ссово
производи́ть* (произвести́* *perf*).
mass production *n* ма́ссовое произво́дство.
mast [mɑ:st] *n* ма́чта.
mastectomy [mæsˈtɛktəmɪ] *n* мастэктоми́я.
master ['mɑ:stəˡ] *n* (*also fig*) хозя́ин*; (*BRIT*:
SCOL) учи́тель* *m*; (*expert*) ма́стер ◆ *cpd*
(*baker, craftsman*) уме́лый ◆ *vt* (*control*)
владе́ть (овладе́ть *perf*) +*instr*; (*learn,
understand*) овладева́ть (овладе́ть *perf*)
+*instr*; **M**~ **Smith** (*title for boys*) господи́н *or*
ма́стер Смит; **M**~**'s degree** сте́пень *f*
маги́стра; **M**~ **of Arts/Science** маги́стр
гуманита́рных/есте́ственных нау́к; **M**~ **of
Ceremonies** церемоний ме́йстер.
master disk *n* (*COMPUT*) оригина́л ди́ска.
masterful ['mɑ:stəful] *adj* вла́стный*
(вла́стен).
master key *n* (универса́льная) отмы́чка
(*подходящий ко всем дверям здания*).
masterly ['mɑ:stəlɪ] *adj* ма́стерский.
mastermind ['mɑ:stəmaɪnd] *n* (*of plan*)
созда́тель(ница) *m(f)* ◆ *vt* разраба́тывать
(разрабо́тать *perf*).
masterpiece ['mɑ:stəpi:s] *n* шеде́вр.
master plan *n* генера́льный план.
masterstroke ['mɑ:stəstrəuk] *n* гениа́льный
ход*.
mastery ['mɑ:stərɪ] *n* (*excellence: skill*)
мастерство́; ~ **of** (*skill, language*) владе́ние
+*instr*.
mastiff ['mæstɪf] *n* (*dog*) ма́стифф.
masturbate ['mæstəbeɪt] *vi* мастурби́ровать
(*impf*).
masturbation [mæstəˈbeɪʃən] *n* мастурба́ция.
mat [mæt] *n* ко́врик; (*also: doormat*) дверно́й
ко́врик; (*also: table* ~) подста́вка* ◆ *adj* =
matt.
match [mætʃ] *n* спи́чка; (*SPORT*) матч; (*equal*)
ро́вня *m/f* ◆ *vt* (*subj: colours*) сочета́ться (*impf*)
с +*instr*; (*equal*) сравни́ться (*perf*) с +*instr*;
(*correspond to*) соотве́тствовать (*impf*) +*dat* ◆
vi (*colours, materials*) сочета́ться (*impf*); **to be
a good** ~ (*colours, clothes*) сочета́ться (*impf*);
they make *or* **are a good** ~ они́ хоро́шая па́ра;
I'm no ~ **for him** я ему́ не ро́вня; **to** ~ **sth (up)
with sth** (*pair*) подбира́ть (подобра́ть* *perf*)
что-н к чему́-н
▸ **match up** *vi* совпада́ть (совпа́сть* *perf*).

matchbox ['mætʃbɒks] *n* спи́чечная коро́бка*.
matching ['mætʃɪŋ] *adj* (*clothes, colours*) сочета́ющийся.
matchless ['mætʃlɪs] *adj* несравне́нный* (несравнён).
mate [meɪt] *n* (*inf: friend*) друг* (подру́га); (*animal*) саме́ц*(-мка*); (*workman's assistant*) подру́чный *m adj*; (*NAUT*) помо́щник (*капита́на*) ♦ *vi* спа́риваться (спа́риться *perf*).
material [mə'tɪərɪəl] *n* (*substance, information*) материа́л; (*cloth*) материа́л, ткань *f* ♦ *adj* (*possessions, existence*) материа́льный*; (*evidence*) веще́ственный*; ~**s** *npl* принадле́жности *fpl*; **building** ~**s** строи́тельные материа́лы; **reading** ~ материа́л для чте́ния.
materialistic [mətɪərɪə'lɪstɪk] *adj* (*person etc*) материалисти́ческий.
materialize [mə'tɪərɪəlaɪz] *vi* материализова́ться (*impf/perf*), осуществля́ться (осуществи́ться* *perf*).
maternal [mə'tə:nl] *adj* матери́нский*.
maternity [mə'tə:nɪtɪ] *n* матери́нство ♦ *cpd* (*hospital, ward*) роди́льный; ~ **care** ухо́д за рожени́цами.
maternity benefit *n* декре́тные *pl adj*.
maternity dress *n* пла́тье* для бере́менной (же́нщины).
maternity hospital *n* роди́льный дом*, роддо́м*.
maternity leave *n* декре́тный о́тпуск.
matey ['meɪtɪ] *adj* (*BRIT: inf*) дружелю́бный* (дружелю́бен).
math [mæθ] *n abbr* (*US*) = **mathematics**.
mathematical [mæθə'mætɪkl] *adj* математи́ческий*.
mathematician [mæθəmə'tɪʃən] *n* матема́тик.
mathematics [mæθə'mætɪks] *n* матема́тика.
maths [mæθs] *n abbr* (*BRIT*) = **mathematics**.
matinée ['mætɪneɪ] *n* (*CINEMA*) дневно́й сеа́нс; (*THEAT*) дневно́й спекта́кль *m*.
mating ['meɪtɪŋ] *n* спа́ривание, слу́чка.
mating call *n* бра́чный призы́в.
mating season *n* бра́чный сезо́н.
matriarchal [meɪtrɪ'ɑ:kl] *adj* матриарха́льный.
matrices ['meɪtrɪsi:z] *npl of* **matrix**.
matriculation [mətrɪkju'leɪʃən] *n* (*enrolment*) зачисле́ние в университе́т.
matrimonial [mætrɪ'məunɪəl] *adj* матримониа́льный, бра́чный.
matrimony ['mætrɪmənɪ] *n* супру́жество.
matrix ['meɪtrɪks] (*pl* **matrices**) *n* ма́трица.
matron ['meɪtrən] *n* (*in hospital*) ста́ршая медсестра́*; (*in school*) (шко́льная) медсестра́*.
matronly ['meɪtrənlɪ] *adj* пы́шный* (пы́шен).
matt [mæt] *adj* ма́товый.
matted ['mætɪd] *adj* (*hair*) спу́танный (спу́тан).
matter ['mætə'] *n* де́ло*, вопро́с; (*PHYS*) мате́рия; (*substance, material*) вещество́*;

(*MED: pus*) гной ♦ *vi* име́ть (*impf*) значе́ние; ~**s** *npl* (*affairs, situation*) дела́ *ntpl*; **printed** ~ печа́тный материа́л; **reading** ~ (*BRIT*) материа́л для чте́ния; **what's the ~?** в чём де́ло?; **no** ~ **what** несмотря́ ни на что́, что́ бы то ни́ бы́ло; **that's another** ~ э́то друго́е де́ло; **as a** ~ **of course** как само́ собо́й разуме́ющееся; **as a** ~ **of fact** со́бственно говоря́; **it's a** ~ **of habit** э́то де́ло привы́чки; **it doesn't** ~ э́то не ва́жно.
matter-of-fact ['mætərəv'fækt] *adj* безразли́чный* (безразли́чен).
matting ['mætɪŋ] *n* цино́вка; **rush** ~ камышо́вая цино́вка.
mattress ['mætrɪs] *n* матра́с, матра́ц.
mature [mə'tjuə'] *adj* (*person*) зре́лый* (зрел); (*cheese, wine*) вы́держанный* (вы́держан) ♦ *vi* (*develop*) развива́ться (разви́ться* *perf*); (*grow up*) взросле́ть (повзросле́ть *perf*); (*cheese*) зреть *or* созрева́ть (созре́ть *perf*); (*wine*) выста́иваться (вы́стояться *perf*); (*COMM*): **this policy is due to** ~ **next year** в сле́дующем году́ начина́ются вы́платы по э́тому по́лису.
mature student *n* студе́нт, начина́ющий вы́сшее образова́ние в во́зрасте 23 лет и́ли ста́рше.
maturity [mə'tjuərɪtɪ] *n* зре́лость *f*.
maudlin ['mɔ:dlɪn] *adj* плакси́вый (плакси́в), слезли́вый (слезли́в).
maul [mɔ:l] *vt* (*physically*) терза́ть (растерза́ть *perf*).
Mauritania [mɔ:rɪ'teɪnɪə] *n* Маврита́ния.
Mauritius [mə'rɪʃəs] *n* Маври́кий.
mausoleum [mɔ:sə'lɪəm] *n* мавзоле́й.
mauve [məuv] *adj* сире́невый.
maverick ['mævrɪk] *n* индивидуали́ст.
mawkish ['mɔ:kɪʃ] *adj* слаща́вый (слаща́в).
max. *abbr* (= **maximum**) макс(им)., масима́ль.
maxim ['mæksɪm] *n* ма́ксима.
maxima ['mæksɪmə] *npl of* **maximum**.
maximize ['mæksɪmaɪz] *vt* максима́льно увели́чивать (увели́чить *perf*).
maximum ['mæksɪməm] (*pl* **maxima** *or* ~**s**) *adj* максима́льный* (максима́лен) ♦ *n* ма́ксимум.
May [meɪ] *n* май; *see also* **July**.
may [meɪ] (*conditional* **might**) *vi* (*indicating possibility*): **I** ~ **go to Russia** я, мо́жет быть, пое́ду в Росси́ю; (*indicating permission*): ~ **I smoke/sit here** мо́жно закури́ть/здесь присе́сть; (*indicating wishes*): ~ **God bless you!** да благослови́т Вас Бог!; **it** ~ **or might rain** мо́жет пойти́ дождь; **he might be there** возмо́жно, что он там; **you might like to try** мо́жет быть, Вы хоти́те попро́бовать; **you** ~ **or might as well go now** мо́жете, пожа́луй, уйти́ сейча́с; **come what** ~ будь что бу́дет.
maybe ['meɪbi:] *adv* мо́жет быть; ~ **he'll ...**

мо́жет быть, он +*infin* ...; ~ **not** мо́жет быть,
нет.
mayday ['meɪdeɪ] *n* сигна́л бе́дствия.
May Day *n* Пе́рвое Ма́я.
mayhem ['meɪhɛm] *n* погро́м.
mayonnaise [meɪə'neɪz] *n* майоне́з.
mayor [mɛəˈ] *n* мэр.
mayoress ['mɛərɛs] *n* (*partner*) жена́* мэ́ра.
maypole ['meɪpəul] *n* укра́шенный цвета́ми
столб.
maze [meɪz] *n* (*labyrinth*) лабири́нт; (*puzzle*)
головоло́мка*; (*of ideas*) пу́таница.
MB *abbr* (*COMPUT*) (= **megabyte**) M=
мегаба́йт; (*CANADA*) = Manitoba.
MBA *n abbr* (= Master of Business
Administration) маги́стрская сте́пень по
менеджме́нту.
MBBS *n abbr* (*BRIT*: = Bachelor of Medicine and
Surgery) бакала́вр медици́нских нау́к и
хирурги́и.
MBChB *n abbr* (*BRIT*: = Bachelor of Medicine and
Surgery) бакала́вр медици́нских нау́к и
хирурги́и.
MBE *n abbr* (*BRIT*) = Member of the Order of the
British Empire.
MC *n abbr* = Master of Ceremonies.
MCAT *n abbr* (*US*) = Medical College Admissions
Test.
MCP *n abbr* (*BRIT*: inf) = male chauvinist pig.
MD *n abbr* (= Doctor of Medicine) до́ктор
медици́ны *or* медици́нских нау́к; (*COMM*) =
managing director ♦ abbr (*US*: POST) =
Maryland.
MDT *abbr* (*US*) = Mountain Daylight Time.
ME *n abbr* (*US*: = medical examiner)
суде́бно-медици́нский экспе́рт; (*MED*: =
myalgic encephalomyelitis) миалги́ческий
энцефаломиели́т ♦ abbr (*US*: POST) = Maine.

┌─────────────┐
│ **KEYWORD** │
└─────────────┘

me [mi:] *pron* **1** (*direct*) меня́; **he loves me** он
лю́бит меня́; **it's me** э́то я
2 (*indirect*) мне; **give me them** *or* **them to me**
да́йте их мне
3 (*after prep*: +*gen*) меня́; (: +*dat*, +*prp*) мне;
(: +*instr*) мной; **it's for me** (*on answering
phone*) э́то мне *or* для меня́; **this kind of work
is not for me** э́та рабо́та не для меня́
4 (*referring to subject of sentence*: *after prep*:
+*gen*) себя́; (: +*dat*) себе́; (: +*instr*) собо́й;
(: +*prp*) себе́; **I took him with me** я взял его́ с
собо́й.

meadow ['mɛdəu] *n* луг*.
meagre [mi:gəˈ] (*US* **meager**) *adj* ску́дный*
(ску́ден).
meal [mi:l] *n* еда́ *no pl*; (*afternoon*) обе́д;
(*evening*) у́жин; (*flour*) мука́ гру́бого
помо́ла; **during ~s** во вре́мя еды́; **to go out**

for a ~ (*in the evening*) у́жинать (поу́жинать
perf) в рестора́не; **to eat 3 ~s a day** есть* (*impf*)
3 ра́за в день; **to make a ~ of sth**
безоснова́тельно усложня́ть (усложни́ть
perf) что-н.
meals on wheels *npl* доста́вка обе́дов на́ дом
инвали́дам и престаре́лым.
meal time *n* вре́мя* *nt* еды́; **during ~ ~s** во
вре́мя еды́, за едо́й.
mealy-mouthed ['mi:lɪmauðd] *adj* чрезме́рно
делика́тный* (делика́тен) в вы́боре слов.
mean [mi:n] (*pt, pp* **meant**) *adj* (*miserly*) скупо́й*
(скуп); (*unkind*) по́длый* (подл); (*US*: inf:
animal) зло́бный* (зло́бен); (*shabby*) убо́гий*
(убо́г); (*average*) сре́дний ♦ *vt* (*signify*)
зна́чить (*impf*), означа́ть (*impf*); (*refer to*)
име́ть (*impf*) в виду́ ♦ *n* (*average*) середи́на;
~s *npl* (*way*) спо́соб *msg*, сре́дство *ntsg*;
(*money*) сре́дства *ntpl*; **by ~s of** посре́дством
+*gen*, с по́мощью +*gen*; **by all ~s!**
пожа́луйста!; **do you ~ it?** Вы говори́те об
э́том всерьёз?, Вы э́то серьёзно?; **what do
you ~?** что Вы име́ете в виду́?; **to ~ to do**
(*intend*) намерева́ться (*impf*) +*infin*; **to be ~t
for sb/sth** предназнача́ться (*impf*) кому́-н/
чему́-н.
meander [mɪ'ændəˈ] *vi* (*river*) извива́ться (*impf*);
(*person*) броди́ть* (*impf*).
meaning ['mi:nɪŋ] *n* (*purpose, value*) смысл;
(*definition*) значе́ние; **this word has two ~s**
э́то сло́во име́ет два значе́ния; **his words
have no ~** его́ слова́ не име́ют смы́сла.
meaningful ['mi:nɪŋful] *adj* (*result, occasion*)
значи́тельный* (значи́телен); (*explanation*)
вразуми́тельный* (вразуми́телен); (*glance,
remark*) многозначи́тельный*
(многозначи́телен); (*relationship*)
серьёзный* (серьёзен).
meaningless ['mi:nɪŋlɪs] *adj* бессмы́сленный
(бессмы́слен).
meanness ['mi:nnɪs] *n* (*with money*) ску́пость
f, (*unkindness*) по́длость *f*; (*shabbiness*)
убо́гость *f*.
means test [mi:nz-] *n* (*ADMIN*) прове́рка*
дохо́дов (*при получе́нии социа́льного
посо́бия*).
meant [mɛnt] *pt, pp of* **mean**.
meantime ['mi:ntaɪm] *adv* (*also:* in the ~) тем
вре́менем, ме́жду тем.
meanwhile ['mi:nwaɪl] *adv* = meantime.
measles ['mi:zlz] *n* корь *f*.
measly ['mi:zlɪ] *adj* (*inf*) жа́лкий*.
measurable ['mɛʒərəbl] *adj* измери́мый
(измери́м).
measure ['mɛʒəˈ] *vt* измеря́ть (изме́рить *perf*)
♦ *n* (*action, amount*) ме́ра; (*of whisky etc*)
по́рция; (*also:* tape ~) руле́тка*, сантиме́тр;
(*of achievement*) мери́ло; (*of performance*)

---

* marks translations which have irregular inflections. The Russian-English side of the dictionary gives inflectional information.

критерий ♦ *vi*: **the room ~s 10 feet by 20** площадь этой комнаты 10 футов на 20; **in some/great ~** (*extent*) в какой-то/ значительной мере; **a litre ~** (*vessel*) литровый сосуд; **to take ~s (to do)** принимать (принять* *perf*) меры (чтобы* +*infin*)

▶ **measure up** *vi*: **to ~ up to** (*to standard*) отвечать (*impf*) +*dat*; (*to expectations*) оправдывать (оправдать* *perf*).

measured ['mɛʒəd] *adj* (*tone*) сдержанный* (сдержан); (*step*) размеренный* (размерен); (*opinion*) взвешенный (взвешен).

measurement ['mɛʒəmənt] *n* размер; (*process*) измерение; **chest/hip ~** объём груди/бёдер.

measurements ['mɛʒəmənts] *npl* размеры *mpl*; **to take sb's ~** снимать (снять* *perf*) с кого-н мерки.

meat [mi:t] *n* мясо; **cold ~s** (*BRIT*) холодные мясные закуски* *fpl*; **crab ~** мясо краба.

meatball ['mi:tbɔ:l] *n* фрикаделька*.

meat pie *n* пирог* с мясом.

meaty ['mi:tɪ] *adj* (*hand, face*) мясистый (мясист); (*stew*) мясной; (*discussion*) содержательный* (содержателен).

Mecca ['mɛkə] *n* (*also fig*) Мекка.

mechanic [mɪ'kænɪk] *n* механик.

mechanical [mɪ'kænɪkl] *adj* механический*.

mechanical engineering *n* машиностроение.

mechanics [mɪ'kænɪks] *n* (*PHYS*) механика ♦ *npl* (*of reading, government*) механика *fsg*.

mechanism ['mɛkənɪzəm] *n* механизм.

mechanization [mɛkənaɪ'zeɪʃən] *n* механизация.

mechanize ['mɛkənaɪz] *vt* механизировать (*impf/perf*) ♦ *vi* проводить* (провести* *perf*) механизацию.

MEd *n abbr* (= *Master of Education*) магистр педагогических наук.

medal ['mɛdl] *n* медаль *f*.

medalist ['mɛdlɪst] *n* (*US*) = **medallist**.

medallion [mɪ'dælɪən] *n* медальон.

medallist ['mɛdlɪst] (*US* **medalist**) *n* медалист(ка*).

meddle ['mɛdl] *vi*: **to ~ in** вмешиваться (вмешаться *perf*) в +*acc*; **to ~ with sth** вторгаться (вторгнуться *perf*) в что-н.

meddlesome ['mɛdlsəm] *adj* назойливый (назойлив).

media ['mi:dɪə] *n or npl*: **the ~** средства *ntpl* массовой информации ♦ *npl see* **medium**.

mediaeval [mɛdɪ'i:vl] *adj* = **medieval**.

median ['mi:dɪən] *n* медиана.

median strip ['mi:dɪən-] *n* (*US*) разделительная полоса (*автострады*).

media research *n* исследование *or* опрос средствами массовой информации.

mediate ['mi:dɪeɪt] *vi* (*arbitrate*) посредничать (*impf*).

mediation [mi:dɪ'eɪʃən] *n* посредничество.

mediator ['mi:dɪeɪtə'] *n* посредник(-ица).

Medicaid ['mɛdɪkeɪd] *n* (*US*) *государственная программа, субсидирующая медицинское обслуживание малоимущей части населения.*

medical ['mɛdɪkl] *adj* медицинский ♦ *n* (*examination*) медосмотр= *медицинский* *осмотр.*

medical certificate *n* медицинская справка*.

medical examiner *n* (*US*) судебно-медицинский эксперт.

medical student *n* студент – медик.

Medicare ['mɛdɪkɛə'] *n* (*US*) *государственная программа медицинского страхования для людей в возрасте от 65 лет и старше.*

medicated ['mɛdɪkeɪtɪd] *adj* содержащий лекарственное вещество.

medication [mɛdɪ'keɪʃən] *n* лекарство, лекарственный препарат; **to be on ~** проходить* (пройти* *perf*) лекарственную терапию.

medicinal [mɛ'dɪsɪnl] *adj* (*substance, qualities*) лекарственный; (*purposes, reasons*) лечебный.

medicine ['mɛdsɪn] *n* (*science*) медицина; (*drug*) лекарство.

medicine ball *n* (*SPORT*) = гиря.

medicine chest *n* аптечка*.

medicine man *n* знахарь *m*.

medieval [mɛdɪ'i:vl] *adj* средневековый.

mediocre [mi:dɪ'əukə'] *adj* заурядный* (зауряден), посредственный* (посредствен).

mediocrity [mi:dɪ'ɔkrɪtɪ] *n* заурядность *f*, посредственность *f*.

meditate ['mɛdɪteɪt] *vi* размышлять (*impf*); (*REL*) заниматься (заняться* *perf*) медитацией.

meditation [mɛdɪ'teɪʃən] *n* (*see vb*) размышление; медитация.

Mediterranean [mɛdɪtə'reɪnɪən] *adj* средиземноморский; **the ~ (Sea)** Средиземное море.

medium ['mi:dɪəm] (*pl* **media** *or* **~s**) *adj* средний* ♦ *n* (*means*) средство; (*substance*) материал; (*environment*) среда; (*pl* **~s**; *person*) медиум; **a happy ~** золотая середина.

medium-dry ['mi:dɪəm'draɪ] *adj* полусухой.

medium-sized ['mi:dɪəm'saɪzd] *adj* (*tin etc*) средней величины.

medium wave *n* (*RADIO*) средние волны *fpl*.

medley ['mɛdlɪ] *n* (*mixture*) смесь *f*; (*MUS*) попурри *r ind*.

meek [mi:k] *adj* кроткий* (кроток).

meet [mi:t] (*pt, pp* **met**) *vt* (*friend, opponent etc*) встречать (встретить* *perf*); (*obligations*) выполнять (выполнить *perf*); (*problem*) сталкиваться (столкнуться *perf*) с +*instr*; (*need*) удовлетворять (удовлетворить *perf*); (*expenses, bill*) оплачивать (оплатить* *perf*) ♦ *vi* (*people*) встречаться (встретиться* *perf*);

(*lines, roads*) пересека́ться (пересе́чься* *perf*)
♦ *n* (*BRIT: hunting*) сбор; (*US: SPORT*) встре́ча;
pleased to ~ you! рад (с Ва́ми)
познако́миться!, о́чень прия́тно!
▸ **meet up** *vi*: **to ~ up with sb** сходи́ться*
(сойти́сь* *perf*) с кем-н
▸ **meet with** *vt fus* (*difficulty*) ста́лкиваться
(столкну́ться *perf*) с +*instr*; (*success*)
по́льзоваться (*impf*) +*instr*; (*approval*)
находи́ть* (найти́* *perf*).
meeting ['mi:tɪŋ] *n* встре́ча; (*of club,
committee etc*) собра́ние; (*POL: also:* **mass ~**)
ми́тинг; **she's at a ~** она́ на заседа́нии; **to call
a ~** созыва́ть (созва́ть* *perf*) собра́ние.
meeting place *n* ме́сто* встре́чи.
megabyte ['mɛgəbaɪt] *n* мегаба́йт.
megadrive ['mɛgədraɪv] *n* ме́гадрайв (*игрова́я
систе́ма*).
megalomania [mɛgələ'meɪnɪə] *n* ма́ния
вели́чия.
megaphone ['mɛgəfəʊn] *n* мегафо́н.
megawatt ['mɛgəwɔt] *n* мегава́тт.
melancholy ['mɛlənkəlɪ] *n* меланхо́лия ♦ *adj*
(*smile*) меланхоли́ческий; (*person*)
меланхоли́чный* (меланхоли́чен).
Melbourne ['mɛlbən] *n* Ме́льбурн.
mellow ['mɛləʊ] *adj* (*sound, colour, light*)
бархати́стый (бархати́ст); (*taste*) мя́гкий*
(мя́гок); (*stone, building*) приобре́тший с
года́ми гла́дкую пове́рхность и мя́гкий цвет
♦ *vi* (*person*) смягча́ться (смягчи́ться *perf*).
melodious [mɪ'ləʊdɪəs] *adj* мелоди́чный*
(мелоди́чен).
melodrama ['mɛləʊdrɑ:mə] *n* мелодра́ма.
melodramatic [mɛlədrə'mætɪk] *adj* (*situation*)
мелодрамати́ческий; (*behaviour, person*)
мелодрамати́чный* (мелодрамати́чен).
melody ['mɛlədɪ] *n* мело́дия.
melon ['mɛlən] *n* ды́ня.
melt [mɛlt] *vi* (*metal*) пла́виться* (рас-
пла́виться* *perf*); (*snow, butter, also fig*) та́ять
(раста́ять *perf*) ♦ *vt* (*metal*) пла́вить*
(распла́вить* *perf*); (*snow, butter*) топи́ть*
(растопи́ть* *perf*)
▸ **melt down** *vt* (*metal*) расплавля́ть
(распла́вить* *perf*).
meltdown ['mɛltdaun] *n* (*in nuclear reactor*)
расплавле́ние сте́ржня (*в а́томном
реа́кторе*).
melting point ['mɛltɪŋ-] *n* то́чка* плавле́ния.
melting pot *n* (*fig*) смеше́ние; **to be in the ~ ~**
вари́ться* (*impf*) в одно́м котле́.
member ['mɛmbə'] *n* (*also ANAT*) член ♦ *cpd*: **~
country** *or* **state** госуда́рство-член; **M~ of
Parliament** (*BRIT*) член парла́мента.
membership ['mɛmbəʃɪp] *n* (*members*) чле́ны
mpl; (*status*) чле́нство; (*number of members*)
число́* чле́нов.

membership card *n* чле́нский* биле́т.
membrane ['mɛmbreɪn] *n* мембра́на.
memento [mə'mɛntəʊ] *n* сувени́р.
memo ['mɛməʊ] *n* (*ADMIN: report*) докладна́я
запи́ска; (: *instruction*) отноше́ние, запи́ска.
memoir ['mɛmwɑ:'] *n* биографи́ческий о́черк.
memoirs ['mɛmwɑ:z] *npl* мемуа́ры *pl*.
memo pad *n* записна́я кни́жка.
memorable ['mɛmərəbl] *adj* па́мятный*
(па́мятен).
memoranda [mɛmə'rændə] *npl of*
memorandum.
memorandum [mɛmə'rændəm] (*pl*
memoranda) *n* мемора́ндум.
memorial [mɪ'mɔ:rɪəl] *n* па́мятник ♦ *cpd*
(*service*) мемориа́льный; ... **M~ Prize** пре́мия
и́мени +*gen* ....
Memorial Day *n* (*US*) *30 мáя – день пáмяти
погибших*.
memorize ['mɛməraɪz] *vt* зау́чивать (заучи́ть
perf) (наизу́сть).
memory ['mɛmərɪ] *n* (*ability to remember*)
па́мять *f no pl*; (*COMPUT*) па́мять *f*,
запомина́ющее устро́йство; (*recollection*)
воспомина́ние; **in ~ of** в па́мять +*gen*; **I have a
good/bad ~** у меня́ хоро́шая/плоха́я
па́мять; **loss of ~** поте́ря па́мяти.
men [mɛn] *npl of* **man**.
menace ['mɛnɪs] *n* (*threat*) угро́за; (*nuisance*)
наказа́ние ♦ *vt* угрожа́ть (*impf*) +*dat*, грози́ть*
(*impf*) +*dat*; **a public ~** угро́за о́бществу.
menacing ['mɛnɪsɪŋ] *adj* угрожа́ющий*
(угрожа́ющ).
menagerie [mɪ'nædʒərɪ] *n* звери́нец.
mend [mɛnd] *vt* ремонти́ровать
(отремонти́ровать *perf*), чини́ть* (почини́ть*
perf); (*clothes*) чини́ть* (почини́ть* *perf*) ♦ *n*: **to
be on the ~** идти́* (*impf*) на попра́вку; **to ~
one's ways** исправля́ться (испра́виться*
perf).
mending ['mɛndɪŋ] *n* (*of machine etc*) ремо́нт;
(*of clothes*) почи́нка.
menial ['mi:nɪəl] *adj* (*work, tasks*) чёрный.
meningitis [mɛnɪn'dʒaɪtɪs] *n* менинги́т.
menopause ['mɛnəʊpɔ:z] *n*: **the ~**
климактери́ческий пери́од, кли́макс.
menservants ['mɛnsə:vənts] *npl of* **manservant**.
men's room *n* (*US*): **the ~ ~** мужска́я
раздева́лка.
menstrual ['mɛnstruəl] *adj* менструа́льный.
menstruate ['mɛnstrueɪt] *vi* менструи́ровать
(*impf*).
menstruation [mɛnstru'eɪʃən] *n* менструа́ция.
menswear ['mɛnzwɛə'] *n* мужска́я оде́жда.
mental ['mɛntl] *adj* (*ability, exhaustion*)
у́мственный; (*image*) мы́сленный; (*illness*)
душе́вный, психи́ческий; (*arithmetic,
calculation*) в уме́; **~ healthcare** забо́та о

душевнобольны́х.
mental hospital *n* психиатри́ческая
больни́ца.
mentality [mɛn'tælɪtɪ] *n* менталите́т,
умонастрое́ние; (*way of thinking*) склад ума́.
mentally ['mɛntlɪ] *adv* (*see adj*) у́мственно;
мы́сленно; ~ **ill** душевнобольно́й.
mentally handicapped *adj* у́мственно
отста́лый.
menthol ['mɛnθɒl] *n* менто́л.
mention ['mɛnʃən] *n* упомина́ние ♦ *vt*
упомина́ть (упомяну́ть* *perf*); **don't ~ it!**
ничего́!, не́ за что!; **I need hardly ~ that** ...
вряд ли сто́ит упомина́ть, что ...; **not to ~** ...,
without ~ing ... не говоря́ уж о +*prp* ....
mentor ['mɛntɔ:'] *n* наста́вник.
menu ['mɛnju:] *n* (*also COMPUT*) меню́ *nt ind*.
menu-driven ['mɛnju:drɪvn] *adj* (*COMPUT*)
управля́емый меню́.
MEP *n abbr* (*BRIT*: = *Member of the European
Parliament*) член Европе́йского парла́мента.
mercantile ['mə:kəntaɪl] *adj* (*society, law*)
торго́вый.
mercenary ['mə:sɪnərɪ] *adj* коры́стный*
(коры́стен) ♦ *n* (*soldier*) наёмник.
merchandise ['mə:tʃəndaɪz] *n* това́ры *mpl*.
merchandiser ['mə:tʃəndaɪzə'] *n* торго́вец*.
merchant ['mə:tʃənt] *n* (*trader*) торго́вец*,
купе́ц* (*ИСТ*); **timber/wine ~** торго́вец*
ле́сом/вино́м.
merchant bank *n* (*BRIT*) торго́вый банк.
merchantman ['mə:tʃəntmən] *irreg n* торго́вое
су́дно*.
Merchant Navy (*US* **merchant marine**) *n*
торго́вый флот.
merciful ['mə:sɪful] *adj* (*person*) милосе́рдный*
(милосе́рден); (*fortunate*) благо́й.
mercifully ['mə:sɪflɪ] *adv* милосе́рдно;
(*fortunately*) к сча́стью.
merciless ['mə:sɪlɪs] *adj* беспоща́дный*
(беспоща́ден).
mercurial [mə:'kjuərɪəl] *adj* изме́нчивый
(изме́нчив).
mercury ['mə:kjurɪ] *n* ртуть *f*; (*planet*): **M~**
Мерку́рий.
mercy ['mə:sɪ] *n* милосе́рдие; **to have ~ on sb**
проявля́ть (прояви́ть* *perf*) милосе́рдие к
кому́-н; **to be at sb's ~** быть* (*impf*) *or*
находи́ться* (*impf*) во вла́сти кого́-н.
mercy killing *n* уби́йство из милосе́рдия.
mere [mɪə'] *adj*: **she's a ~ child** она́ всего́ лишь
ребёнок*; **his ~ presence irritates her** само́ его́
прису́тствие раздража́ет её; **by a ~ chance**
по чи́стой случа́йности.
merely ['mɪəlɪ] *adv* (*simply*) про́сто; (*just*)
то́лько.
merge [mə:dʒ] *vt* (*also COMPUT*) слива́ть
(слить* *perf*), объединя́ть (объедини́ть* *perf*)
♦ *vi* (*also COMM*) слива́ться (сли́ться* *perf*);
(*roads*) сходи́ться* (сойти́сь* *perf*).
merger ['mə:dʒə'] *n* (*COMM*) слия́ние.

meridian [mə'rɪdɪən] *n* меридиа́н.
meringue [mə'ræŋ] *n* безе́ *nt ind*.
merit ['mɛrɪt] *n* (*worth, value*) досто́инство ♦ *vt*
заслу́живать (заслужи́ть* *perf*); **to judge sth
on its ~s** оце́нивать (оцени́ть *perf*) что-н по
досто́инству.
meritocracy [mɛrɪ'tɔkrəsɪ] *n* о́бщество, в
кото́ром положе́ние челове́ка определя́ется
его́ спосо́бностями.
mermaid ['mə:meɪd] *n* руса́лка*.
merrily ['mɛrɪlɪ] *adv* ве́село.
merriment ['mɛrɪmənt] *n* весе́лье.
merry ['mɛrɪ] *adj* весёлый* (ве́сел); **M~
Christmas!** С Рождество́м!
merry-go-round ['mɛrɪgəuraund] *n* карусе́ль *f*.
mesh [mɛʃ] *n* (*net*) сеть *f*; **wire ~** про́волочная
се́тка.
mesmerize ['mɛzməraɪz] *vt* гипнотизи́ровать
(загипнотизи́ровать *perf*).
mess [mɛs] *n* (*muddle: in room*) беспоря́док*; (:
of situation) неразбери́ха; (*dirt*) грязь* *f*; (*MIL*)
столо́вая *f adj*; **to be in a ~** (*untidy*) быть*
(*impf*) в беспоря́дке; **to get o.s. into a ~** (*inf*)
влипа́ть (вли́пнуть* *perf*); **my life is in a real ~**
(*inf*) у меня́ в жи́зни всё идёт вверх дном
▸ **mess about** *vi* (*inf: fool around*) дура́читься
(*impf*), валя́ть (*impf*) дурака́
▸ **mess about with** *vt fus* (*inf: play around with*)
вози́ться* (*impf*) с +*instr*
▸ **mess around** *vi* (*inf*) = **mess about**
▸ **mess around with** *vt fus* (*inf*) = **mess about
with**
▸ **mess up** *vt* (*spoil*) по́ртить* (испо́ртить*
perf); (*dirty*) па́чкать (испа́чкать *perf*).
message ['mɛsɪdʒ] *n* (*piece of information*)
сообще́ние; (*note*) запи́ска*; (*of play, book*)
иде́я; **to leave sb a ~** (*note*) оставля́ть
(оста́вить* *perf*) кому́-н запи́ску; **can I give
him a ~?** ему́ что́-нибудь переда́ть?; **he got
the ~** (*fig: inf*) до него́ дошло́.
message switching [-'swɪtʃɪŋ] *n* (*COMPUT*)
коммута́ция сообще́ний.
messenger ['mɛsɪndʒə'] *n* курье́р, посы́льный
m adj.
Messiah [mɪ'saɪə] *n* Месси́я *m*.
Messrs *abbr* (*on letters*: = *messieurs*) гг.=
господа́.
Messrs. *abbr* = **Messrs**.
messy ['mɛsɪ] *adj* (*untidy*) неу́бранный
(неу́бран); (*dirty*) гря́зный* (гря́зен).
Met [mɛt] *n abbr* (*US*) = *Metropolitan Opera*
met [mɛt] *pt, pp of* **meet**.
met *adj abbr* = *meteorological*: **the M~ Office**
метеоце́нтр.
metabolism [mɛ'tæbəlɪzəm] *n* метаболи́зм,
обме́н веще́ств.
metal ['mɛtl] *n* мета́лл.
metal fatigue *n* уста́лость *f* мета́лла.
metalled ['mɛtld] *adj*: ~ **road** доро́га, с
щебёночным покры́тием.
metallic [mɪ'tælɪk] *adj* металли́ческий*.

metallurgy [mɛ'tælədʒɪ] *n* металлургия.
metalwork ['mɛtlwə:k] *n* работа по металлу.
metamorphoses [mɛtə'mɔ:fəsi:z] *npl of*
metamorphosis.
metamorphosis [mɛtə'mɔ:fəsɪs] (*pl*
metamorphoses) *n* метаморфоза.
metaphor ['mɛtəfə'] *n* метафора.
metaphorical [mɛtə'fɔrɪkl] *adj*
метафорический.
metaphysics [mɛtə'fɪzɪks] *n* метафизика.
meteor ['mi:tɪə'] *n* метеор.
meteoric [mi:tɪ'ɔrɪk] *adj* (*fig*) метеорический.
meteorite ['mi:tɪəraɪt] *n* метеорит.
meteorological [mi:tɪərə'lɔdʒɪkl] *adj*
метеорологический.
meteorology [mi:tɪə'rɔlədʒɪ] *n* метеорология.
mete out [mi:t-] *vt* отмерять (отмерить *perf*).
meter ['mi:tə'] *n* (*instrument*) счётчик; (*US: unit*)
= **metre**.
methane ['mi:θeɪn] *n* метан.
method ['mɛθəd] *n* (*way*) метод, способ; ~ **of**
payment способ оплаты.
methodical [mɪ'θɔdɪkl] *adj* методичный*
(методичен).
Methodist ['mɛθədɪst] *n* (*REL*) методист(ка*).
methodology [mɛθə'dɔlədʒɪ] *n* методология.
meths [mɛθs] *n* (*BRIT: inf*) = **methylated spirit.**
methylated spirit ['mɛθɪleɪtɪd-] *n* (*BRIT*)
денатурат.
meticulous [mɪ'tɪkjuləs] *adj* тщательный*
(тщателен).
metre ['mi:tə'] (*US* **meter**) *n* метр.
metric ['mɛtrɪk] *adj* метрический*; **to go** ~
переходить* (перейти* *perf*) на метрическую
систему мер.
metrical ['mɛtrɪkl] *adj* метрический*.
metrication [mɛtrɪ'keɪʃən] *n* введение
метрической системы мер.
metric system *n* метрическая система мер.
metric ton *n* (метрическая) тонна.
metronome ['mɛtrənəum] *n* метроном.
metropolis [mɪ'trɔpəlɪs] *n* столица.
metropolitan [mɛtrə'pɔlɪtn] *adj* столичный.
Metropolitan Police *n* (*BRIT*): **the ~ ~**
Лондонская полиция.
mettle ['mɛtl] *n*: **to show one's** ~ проявлять
(проявить* *perf*) (свой) характер.
mew [mju:] *vi* мяукать (*impf*).
mews [mju:z] *n* (*BRIT*) *переулок в жилое*
помещение.
Mexican ['mɛksɪkən] *adj* мексиканский* ♦ *n.*
мексиканец*(-нка*).
Mexico ['mɛksɪkəu] *n* Мексика.
Mexico City *n* Мехико *m ind.*
mezzanine ['mɛtsəni:n] *n* (*also:* ~ **floor**)
мезонин, полуэтаж.
MFA *n abbr* (*US:* = *Master of Fine Arts*) магистр
искусств.
mfr *abbr* = **manufacture, manufacturer.**

mg *abbr* (= *milligram(me)*) мг.= *миллиграмм.*
Mgr *abbr* (= *Monseigneur, Monsignor*)
монсеньёр; (*COMM*) = **manager.**
MHR *n abbr* (*US:* = *Member of the House of*
Representatives) член палаты
представителей.
MHz *abbr* (= *megahertz*) МГц = *мегагерц.*
MI *abbr* (*US: POST*) = *Michigan.*
MI5 *n abbr* (*BRIT:* = *Military Intelligence 5*)
внешняя разведка Великобритании.
MI6 *n abbr* (*BRIT:* = *Military Intelligence 6*)
внутренняя разведка Великобритании.
MIA *abbr* (*MIL:* = *missing in action*) пропавший
без вести.
miaow [mi:'au] *vi* мяукать (*impf*).
mice [maɪs] *npl of* **mouse.**
micro... ['maɪkrəu] *prefix* микро....
microbe ['maɪkrəub] *n* микроб.
microbiology [maɪkrəbaɪ'ɔlədʒɪ] *n* микро-
биология.
microchip ['maɪkrəutʃɪp] *n* микрочип.
micro(computer) ['maɪkrəu(kəm'pju:tə')] *n*
микрокомпьютер.
microcosm ['maɪkrəukɔzəm] *n* микрокосмос,
микрокосм.
microeconomics ['maɪkrəui:kə'nɔmɪks] *n*
микроэкономика.
microelectronics ['maɪkrəuɪlɛk'trɔnɪks] *n*
микроэлектроника.
microfiche ['maɪkrəufi:ʃ] *n* микрофиша.
microfilm ['maɪkrəufɪlm] *n* микрофильм,
микроплёнка*.
microlight ['maɪkrəulaɪt] *n* сверхлёгкий
самолёт.
micrometer [maɪ'krɔmɪtə'] *n* микрометр.
microphone ['maɪkrəfəun] *n* микрофон.
microprocessor ['maɪkrəu'prəusesə'] *n*
микропроцессор.
microscope ['maɪkrəskəup] *n* микроскоп;
under the ~ под микроскопом.
microscopic [maɪkrə'skɔpɪk] *adj* микро-
скопический*.
microsurgery [maɪkrəusə:dʒərɪ] *n* микро-
хирургия.
microwave ['maɪkrəuweɪv] *n* (*also:* ~ **oven**)
микроволновая печь* *f.*
mid [mɪd] *adj*: **in** ~ **May/afternoon** в середине
мая/дня; **in** ~ **air** в воздухе; **he's in his** ~
thirties ему за тридцать.
midday [mɪd'deɪ] *n* полдень* *m.*
middle ['mɪdl] *n* середина; (*waist*) пояс* ♦ *adj*
средний*; **in the** ~ **of the night** посреди ночи;
I'm in the ~ **of reading it** я как раз сейчас это
читаю.
middle age *n* средний возраст.
middle-aged [mɪdl'eɪdʒd] *adj* средних лет.
Middle Ages *npl*: **the ~ ~** средние века* *mpl.*
middle class *n*: **the ~ ~** средний* класс.

---

middle-class [mɪdl'klɑ:s] adj принадлежащий к среднему классу.

middle classes npl = **middle class**.

Middle East n: **the ~ ~** Ближний* Восток.

middleman ['mɪdlmæn] irreg n посредник.

middle management n среднее руководящее звено.

middle name n второе имя* nt.

middle-of-the-road ['mɪdləvðə'rəud] adj (politician) умеренный*; (music) лёгкий*.

middleweight ['mɪdlweɪt] n (BOXING) боксёр среднего веса.

middling ['mɪdlɪŋ] adj средний*.

Middx abbr (BRIT: POST) = **Middlesex**.

midge [mɪdʒ] n мошка*.

midget ['mɪdʒɪt] n карлик(-ица).

midi system ['mɪdɪ-] n МИДИ (электронный контроль для синтезаторов).

Midlands ['mɪdləndz] npl: **the ~** Центральные районы mpl Англии.

midnight ['mɪdnaɪt] n полночь* f ♦ cpd (party, feast) полночный; **at ~** в полночь.

midriff ['mɪdrɪf] n живот.

midst [mɪdst] n: **in the ~ of** посреди +gen.

midsummer [mɪd'sʌmə'] n середина лета; **M~'s Day** день* m летнего солнцестояния.

midway [mɪd'weɪ] adv: **~ (between)** на полпути (между +instr); **~ through** в середине +gen; **to turn back ~** вернуться (perf) с полпути.

midweek [mɪd'wi:k] adj, adv в середине недели.

midwife ['mɪdwaɪf] (pl **midwives**) n акушерка*.

midwifery ['mɪdwɪfərɪ] n акушерство.

midwinter [mɪd'wɪntə'] n середина зимы.

midwives ['mɪdwaɪvz] npl of **midwife**.

miffed [mɪft] adj (inf) обиженный (обижен).

might [maɪt] vb see **may** ♦ n (power) мощь f.

mighty ['maɪtɪ] adj мощный* (мощен).

migraine ['mi:greɪn] n мигрень f.

migrant ['maɪgrənt] adj (bird) перелётный ♦ n (bird) перелётная птица; (animal) мигрирующее животное nt adj; (person) переселенец*(-нка*); **~ worker** рабочий*-мигрант.

migrate [maɪ'greɪt] vi мигрировать (impf/perf).

migration [maɪ'greɪʃən] n миграция.

mike [maɪk] n abbr = **microphone**.

Milan [mɪ'læn] n Милан.

mild [maɪld] adj (character, climate, taste, reproach) мягкий* (мягок); (infection, illness) лёгкий* (лёгок); (interest) незначительный* (незначителен).

mildew ['mɪldju:] n плесень f.

mildly ['maɪldlɪ] adv (see adj) мягко; легко; слегка; **to put it ~** мягко говоря.

mildness ['maɪldnɪs] n (see adj) мягкость f; лёгкость f; незначительность f.

mile [maɪl] n миля*; **this car does 30 ~s to the gallon** этот автомобиль затрачивает галлон бензина каждый 30 миль; **~s better**

(inf) намного лучше.

mileage ['maɪlɪdʒ] n (number of miles) пробег в милях; (distance) расстояние в милях.

mileage allowance n покрытие дорожных расходов (в расчёте на каждую милю).

mileometer [maɪ'lɔmɪtə'] n счётчик (пройденных миль).

milestone ['maɪlstəun] n ≈ километровый столб; (fig) веха.

milieu ['mi:ljə:] n среда*.

militant ['mɪlɪtnt] adj воинствующий ♦ n радикал.

militarism ['mɪlɪtərɪzəm] n милитаризм.

militaristic [mɪlɪtə'rɪstɪk] adj милитаристический.

military ['mɪlɪtərɪ] adj военный ♦ n: **the ~** военные pl adj.

military police n военная полиция.

military service n военная служба.

militate ['mɪlɪteɪt] vi: **to ~ against** препятствовать (impf) +dat.

militia [mɪ'lɪʃə] n (MIL) (народное) ополчение.

milk [mɪlk] n молоко ♦ vt (cow) доить* (подоить* perf); (fig: situation, person) эксплуатировать (impf).

milk chocolate n молочный шоколад.

milk float n (BRIT) молочный фургон.

milking ['mɪlkɪŋ] n доение.

milkman ['mɪlkmən] irreg n разносчик молока.

milk shake n молочный коктейль m.

milk tooth n молочный зуб*.

milk truck n (US) = **milk float**.

milky ['mɪlkɪ] adj молочный.

Milky Way n: **the ~ ~** Млечный путь* m.

mill [mɪl] n (windmill) мельница; (factory: making cloth) фабрика; (: making steel) завод; (also: **coffee ~**) кофемолка* ♦ vt молоть* (смолоть* perf) ♦ vi (also: **~ about**) толочься* (impf).

millennia [mɪ'lɛnɪə] npl of **millennium**.

millennium [mɪ'lɛnɪəm] (pl **~s** or **millennia**) n тысячелетие; **~ bug** Проблема 2000 (года).

miller ['mɪlə'] n мельник.

millet ['mɪlɪt] n пшено.

milli... ['mɪlɪ] prefix милли....

milligram(me) ['mɪlɪgræm] (US **milligram**) n миллиграм.

millilitre ['mɪlɪli:tə'] (US **milliliter**) n миллилитр.

millimetre ['mɪlɪmi:tə'] (US **millimeter**) n миллиметр.

millinery ['mɪlɪnərɪ] n дамские шляпы fpl.

million ['mɪljən] n миллион.

millionaire [mɪljə'nɛə'] n миллионер.

millipede ['mɪlɪpi:d] n тысяченожка*.

millstone ['mɪlstəun] n (fig): **a ~ around one's neck** камень m на шее.

millwheel ['mɪlwi:l] n мельничное колесо*.

milometer [maɪ'lɔmɪtə'] n = **mileometer**.

mime [maɪm] n (art) пантомима; (also: **~ artist**) мим ♦ vt изображать (изобразить* perf) жестами.

mimic ['mɪmɪk] *n* пароди́ст ♦ *vt (subj: comedian)* пароди́ровать *(impf/perf)*; *(animal, person)* имити́ровать *(impf)*.
mimicry ['mɪmɪkrɪ] *n* имита́ция.
Min. *abbr (BRIT: POL)* = **ministry**.
min. *abbr* (= **minute**) мин(.)= *мину́та*; (= **minimum**) мин.= *минима́льный*.
minaret [mɪnə'rɛt] *n* минаре́т.
mince [mɪns] *vt (meat)* пропуска́ть (пропусти́ть* *perf)* че́рез мясору́бку ♦ *vi (in walking)* семени́ть *(impf)* ♦ *n (BRIT)* (мясно́й) фарш; **he doesn't ~ (his) words** он не выбира́ет выраже́ний.
mincemeat ['mɪnsmiːt] *n (BRIT: fruit)* начи́нка из сухофру́ктов *(для пирожко́в)*; *(US: meat)* (мясно́й) фарш; **to make ~ of sb** разбива́ть (разби́ть* *perf)* кого́-н в пух и прах.
mince pie *n (BRIT: sweet) пирожо́к* с начи́нкой из сухофру́ктов.
mincer ['mɪnsə^r] *n* мясору́бка*.
mincing ['mɪnsɪŋ] *adj (walk)* семеня́щий; *(voice)* жема́нный* (жема́нен).
mind [maɪnd] *n (intellect)* ум*; *(thoughts)* голова́* ♦ *vt (look after)* смотре́ть* *(impf)* за *+instr; (object to)*: **I don't ~ the noise** меня́ не беспоко́ит шум; **to be out of one's ~** быть* *(impf)* не в своём уме́; **it's constantly on my ~** э́то не выхо́дит у меня́ из головы́; **to keep** *or* **bear sth in ~** по́мнить *(impf)* что-н, име́ть *(impf)* что-н в виду́; **to make up one's ~** реша́ться (реши́ться *perf)*; **to change one's ~** переду́мывать (переду́мать *perf)*; **to my ~** ... *(opinion)* по моему́ мне́нию ...; **to be in two ~s about sth** сомнева́ться *(impf)* в чём-н; **to have in ~ to do** намерева́ться *(impf)* +*infin*; **I have somebody in ~** у меня́ есть ко́е-кто на приме́те; **it went right out of my ~** э́то совсе́м вы́летело у меня́ из головы́; **to bring** *or* **call to ~** напомина́ть (напо́мнить *perf)* о +*prp*; **she doesn't ~ the cold** она́ не бои́тся хо́лода; **do you ~ if ...?** Вы не возража́ете, е́сли ...?; **I don't ~** мне всё равно́; **~ you, ...** име́йте в виду́ ...; **never ~!** ничего́!; **"mind the step"** "осторо́жно, не споткни́тесь".
mind-boggling ['maɪndbɒglɪŋ] *adj (inf)* уму́ непостижи́мый.
-minded ['maɪndɪd] *adj*: **fair-~** справедли́вый (справедли́в); **an industrially-~ nation** наро́д, скло́нный к индустриа́льной де́ятельности.
minder ['maɪndə^r] *n (childminder)* ня́ня*; *(inf: bodyguard)* телохрани́тель *m*.
mindful ['maɪndful] *adj*: **to be ~ of** име́ть *(impf)* в виду́.
mindless ['maɪndlɪs] *adj (violence)* безду́мный* (безду́мен); *(job)* механи́ческий*.

┌─────────────┐
│ **KEYWORD** │
└─────────────┘

mine¹ [maɪn] *pron* **1** мой; **that book is mine** э́та

кни́га моя́, э́то моя́ кни́га; **this is mine** э́то моё; **an uncle of mine** мой дя́дя
2 *(referring back to subject)* свой; **may I borrow your pen? I have forgotten mine** мо́жно взять Ва́шу ру́чку? я забы́л свою́.

mine² [maɪn] *n (coal)* ша́хта; *(gold, diamonds)* при́иск; *(copper, tin)* рудни́к; *(explosive)* ми́на ♦ *vt (coal)* добыва́ть (добы́ть* *perf)*; *(beach)* мини́ровать (замини́ровать *perf)*.
mine detector *n* миноиска́тель *m*.
minefield ['maɪnfiːld] *n (also fig)* ми́нное по́ле*.
miner ['maɪnə^r] *n* шахтёр.
mineral ['mɪnərəl] *n (crystalline)* минера́л; *(ore)* поле́зное ископа́емое *nt adj* ♦ *adj* минера́льный; **~s** *npl (BRIT: soft drinks)* прохлади́тельные напи́тки *mpl*.
mineralogy [mɪnə'rælədʒɪ] *n* минерало́гия.
mineral water *n* минера́льная вода́.
minesweeper ['maɪnswiːpə^r] *n* ми́нный тра́льщик.
mingle ['mɪŋgl] *vi*: **to ~ with** сме́шиваться (смеша́ться *perf)* с +*instr*.
mingy ['mɪndʒɪ] *adj (inf: person)* прижи́мистый (прижи́мист); *(: amount)* ми́зерный* (ми́зерен).
mini... ['mɪnɪ] *prefix* мини....
miniature ['mɪnətʃə^r] *adj* миниатю́рный* (миниатю́рен) ♦ *n* миниатю́ра.
minibus ['mɪnɪbʌs] *n* микроавто́бус.
minicab ['mɪnɪkæb] *n (BRIT)* такси́ *nt ind*.
minicomputer ['mɪnɪkəm'pjuːtə^r] *n* мини-компью́тер.
Minidisc® ['mɪnɪdɪsk] *n* ми́нидиск.
minim ['mɪnɪm] *n* полови́нная но́та.
minima ['mɪnɪmə] *npl of* **minimum**.
minimal ['mɪnɪml] *adj* минима́льный* (минима́лен).
minimalist ['mɪnɪməlɪst] *adj* минималѝст(-ка).
minimize ['mɪnɪmaɪz] *vt (reduce)* своди́ть* (свести́* *perf)* к ми́нимуму; *(play down)* преуменьша́ть (преуме́ньшить *perf)*.
minimum ['mɪnɪməm] *(pl* **minima**) *n* ми́нимум ♦ *adj* минима́льный; **to reduce to a ~** своди́ть* (свести́* *perf)* к ми́нимуму; **~ wage** минима́льная зарпла́та.
minimum lending rate *n* минима́льная ссу́дная ста́вка.
mining ['maɪnɪŋ] *n (process)* добы́ча; *(science)* го́рное де́ло; *(industry)* у́гольная промы́шленность *f* ♦ *cpd (industry)* горнодобыва́ющий*; *(region)* шахтёрский.
minion ['mɪnjən] *n (pej)* подчинённый *m adj*.
mini-series ['mɪnɪsɪəriːz] *n* минисериа́л.
miniskirt ['mɪnɪskəːt] *n* ми́ни ю́бка*.
minister ['mɪnɪstə^r] *n (BRIT: POL)* мини́стр; *(REL)* свяще́нник ♦ *vi*: **to ~ to** служи́ть *(impf)* +*dat*.
ministerial [mɪnɪs'tɪərɪəl] *adj (BRIT: POL)* министе́рский*; **~ post** пост мини́стра.

---

* marks translations which have irregular inflections. The Russian-English side of the dictionary gives inflectional information.

ministry ['mınıstrı] n (BRIT: POL) министе́рство; (REL): **to go into the ~** принима́ть (приня́ть* perf) духо́вный сан.
Ministry of Defence n Министе́рство оборо́ны.
mink [mıŋk] n но́рка*.
mink coat n но́рковая шу́ба.
minnow ['mınəu] n песка́рь m
minor ['maınə'] adj (injuries, poet) незначи́тельный; (repairs) ме́лкий*; (MUS) мино́рный ♦ n (LAW) несовершенноле́тний* (-яя) m(f) adj.
Minorca [mı'nɔːkə] n Мино́рка.
minority [maı'nɔrıtı] n меньшинство́*; **to be in a ~** быть* (impf) в меньшинстве́; **~ interest** (COMM) неконтро́льный паке́т а́кций.
Minsk [mınsk] n Минск.
minster ['mınstə'] n собо́р.
minstrel ['mınstrəl] n менестре́ль m.
mint [mınt] n (BOT) мя́та; (sweet) мя́тная конфе́та ♦ vt (coins) чека́нить (отчека́нить perf); **the (Royal) M~**, (US) **the (US) M~** ≈ Моне́тный двор; **in ~ condition** как но́венький*.
mint sauce n со́ус из мя́ты.
minuet [mınju'ɛt] n менуэ́т.
minus ['maınəs] n (also: **~ sign**) ми́нус ♦ prep: **12 ~ 6 equals 6** 12 ми́нус 6 равня́ется 6; (temperature): **~ 24 (degrees)** ми́нус 24 гра́дуса.
minuscule ['mınəskjuːl] adj кро́хотный* (кро́хотен), кро́шечный* (кро́шечен).
minute¹ [maı'njuːt] adj (search) тща́тельный; **in ~ detail** до мале́йших подро́бностей.
minute² ['mınıt] n (also fig) мину́та; (official record) за́пись f; **~s** npl (of meeting) протоко́л msg; **it's five ~s past three** сейча́с пять мину́т четвёртого ...; **wait a ~**!, **just a ~**! подожди́те мину́точку!; **up to the ~** (fashion, news) са́мый после́дний*; (technology) нове́йший; **at the last ~** в после́днюю мину́ту.
minute book n кни́га протоко́лов.
minute hand n мину́тная стре́лка*.
minutely [maı'njuːtlı] adv (by a small amount) едва́ заме́тно; (in detail) подро́бно, подро́бнейшим о́бразом.
minutiae [mı'njuːʃiː] npl мельча́йшие дета́ли fpl.
miracle ['mırəkl] n чу́до*.
miraculous [mı'rækjuləs] adj чуде́сный* (чуде́сен).
mirage ['mırɑːʒ] n мира́ж.
mire ['maıə'] n тряси́на.
mirror ['mırə'] n зе́ркало*; (also: **hand-~**) зе́ркальце ♦ vt отража́ть (отрази́ть* perf).
mirror image n зерка́льное отраже́ние.
mirth [mɜːθ] n весе́лье.
misadventure [mısəd'vɛntʃə'] n злоключе́ние; **death by ~** (BRIT) смерть* f в результа́те несча́стного слу́чая.
misanthropist [mı'zænθrəpıst] n мизантро́п.

misapply [mısə'plaı] vt непра́вильно применя́ть (примени́ть perf).
misapprehension ['mısæprı'hɛnʃən] n ло́жное представле́ние.
misappropriate [mısə'prəuprıeıt] vt незако́нно присва́ивать (присво́ить perf).
misappropriation ['mısəprəuprı'eıʃən] n назако́нное присвое́ние.
misbehave [mısbı'heıv] vi пло́хо себя́ вести́* (impf).
misbehaviour [mısbı'heıvjə'] (US **misbehavior**) n плохо́е поведе́ние.
misc. abbr = **miscellaneous**.
miscalculate [mıs'kælkjuleıt] vt неве́рно оце́нивать (оцени́ть perf) ♦ vi просчи́тываться (просчита́ться perf).
miscalculation ['mıskælkju'leıʃən] n просчёт.
miscarriage ['mıskærıdʒ] n (MED) вы́кидыш; (LAW): **~ of justice** суде́бная оши́бка.
miscarry [mıs'kærı] vi (plans) не удава́ться* (уда́ться* perf); **she miscarried** у неё был вы́кидыш.
miscellaneous [mısı'leınıəs] adj (collection, group) разноро́дный* (разноро́ден); (subjects, items) разнообра́зный* (разнообра́зен); **~ expenses** ме́лкие расхо́ды; **~ files** ра́зное nt adj.
mischance [mıs'tʃɑːns] n (misfortune) невезе́ние; **by (some) ~** по несча́стной случа́йности.
mischief ['mıstʃıf] n (naughtiness, playfulness) озо́рство; (maliciousness) зло; **to get into ~** прока́зничать (напрока́зничать perf); **to do sb a ~** причиня́ть (причини́ть perf) кому́-н зло.
mischievous ['mıstʃıvəs] adj (naughty, playful) озорно́й; (malicious) зло́бный.
misconception ['mıskən'sɛpʃən] n ло́жное представле́ние.
misconduct [mıs'kɔndʌkt] n дурно́е поведе́ние; **professional ~** наруше́ние профессиона́льной э́тики.
misconstrue [mıskən'struː] vt неве́рно истолко́вывать (истолкова́ть* perf).
miscount [mıs'kaunt] vt неве́рно счита́ть (сосчита́ть perf) ♦ vi ошиба́ться (ошиби́ться* perf) в подсчётах.
misdemeanour [mısdı'miːnə'] (US **misdemeanor**) n просту́пок*.
misdirect [mısdı'rɛkt] vt (person) оши́бочно направля́ть (напра́вить* perf); (letter) непра́вильно адресова́ть (impf/perf).
miser ['maızə'] n скря́га m/f.
miserable ['mızərəbl] adj (unhappy: person, expression) несча́стный* (несча́стен); (unpleasant: weather, person) скве́рный* (скве́рен); (donation, conditions) жа́лкий* (жа́лок); (failure) позо́рный*; **to feel ~** чу́вствовать (impf) себя́ о́чень пло́хо; **she looked ~** у неё был несча́стный вид.
miserably ['mızərəblı] adv (live, pay) ску́дно;

(*smile*) жа́лко; (*small*) ничто́жно; (*fail*) позо́рно.

miserly ['maɪzəlɪ] *adj* (*person*) скупо́й• (скуп); (*amount*) ми́зерный• (ми́зерен).

misery ['mɪzərɪ] *n* (*unhappiness*) невзго́да; (*pain*) страда́ние; (*wretchedness*) бе́дственное положе́ние.

misfire [mɪs'faɪə'] *vi* (*plan*) прова́ливаться (провали́ться *perf*); (*car engine*) пропуска́ть (пропусти́ть• *perf*) вспы́шку.

misfit ['mɪsfɪt] *n* (*person*): **he was a ~ in our community** он не подходи́л к на́шему о́бществу.

misfortune [mɪs'fɔ:tʃən] *n* несча́стье•.

misgiving [mɪs'gɪvɪŋ] *n* опасе́ния *ntpl*; **I have ~s about it** у меня́ есть опасе́ния на э́тот счёт.

misguided [mɪs'gaɪdɪd] *adj* (*person*) неве́рно ориенти́рованный (ориенти́рован); (*ideas*) оши́бочный• (оши́бочен).

mishandle [mɪs'hændl] *vt* (*problem, situation*) не справля́ться (спра́виться• *perf*) с +*instr*.

mishap ['mɪshæp] *n* неприя́тность *f*.

mishear [mɪs'hɪə'] *vt* (*irreg: like* **hear**) не расслы́шать (*perf*) ◆ *vi* ослы́шаться (*perf*).

misheard [mɪs'hə:d] *pt, pp of* **mishear**.

mishmash ['mɪʃmæʃ] *n* (*inf*) неразбери́ха.

misinform [mɪsɪn'fɔ:m] *vt* неве́рно информи́ровать (проинформи́ровать *perf*); (*deliberately*) дезинформи́ровать (*impf/perf*).

misinterpret [mɪsɪn'tə:prɪt] *vt* неве́рно интерпрети́ровать (*impf/perf*) *or* истолко́вывать (истолкова́ть *perf*).

misinterpretation ['mɪsɪntə:prɪ'teɪʃən] *n* неве́рная интерпрета́ция.

misjudge [mɪs'dʒʌdʒ] *vt* неве́рно оце́нивать (оцени́ть *perf*).

mislay [mɪs'leɪ] *irreg vt* (*lose*) дева́ть (подева́ть *perf*).

mislead [mɪs'li:d] (*irreg: like* **lead**¹) *vt* вводи́ть• (ввести́• *perf*) в заблужде́ние.

misleading [mɪs'li:dɪŋ] *adj* обма́нчивый (обма́нчив).

misled [mɪs'lɛd] *pt, pp of* **mislead**.

mismanage [mɪs'mænɪdʒ] *vt* (*business, institution*) неуме́ло руководи́ть• (*impf*) +*instr*; (*problem, situation*) неуме́ло справля́ться (спра́виться• *perf*) с +*instr*.

mismanagement [mɪs'mænɪdʒmənt] *n* (*of company*) неуме́лое руково́дство; (*of situation*) неуме́лое реше́ние.

misnomer [mɪs'nəumə'] *n* непра́вильное назва́ние.

misogynist [mɪ'sɔdʒɪnɪst] *n* женоненави́стник.

misplace [mɪs'pleɪs] *vt* (*lose*) дева́ть (подева́ть *perf*).

misplaced [mɪs'pleɪst] *adj* (*unwarranted*) неуме́стный• (неуме́стен).

misprint ['mɪsprɪnt] *n* опеча́тка•.

mispronounce [mɪsprə'nauns] *vt* непра́вильно произноси́ть• (произнести́• *perf*).

misquote ['mɪs'kwəut] *vt* неве́рно цити́ровать (процити́ровать *perf*).

misread [mɪs'ri:d] *irreg vt* непра́вильно чита́ть (прочита́ть *or* проче́сть• *perf*).

misrepresent [mɪsrɛprɪ'zɛnt] *vt* преподноси́ть• (преподнести́• *perf*) в ло́жном све́те.

misrepresentation [mɪsrɛprɪzɛn'teɪʃən] *n* искаже́ние; (*LAW*) умы́шленный обма́н.

Miss [mɪs] *n* мисс *f ind*; **Dear ~ Smith** (*formal*) Госпожа́ Смит; (*informal*) Мисс Смит.

miss [mɪs] *vt* (*train, bus, class etc*) пропуска́ть (пропусти́ть• *perf*); (*fail to hit*) не попада́ть (попа́сть• *perf*) в +*acc*; (*notice loss of: money etc*) обнару́живать (обнару́жить *perf*) пропа́жу +*gen*; (*pine for*) скуча́ть (*impf*) по +*dat*; (*chance, opportunity*) упуска́ть (упусти́ть• *perf*) ◆ *vi* (*subj: person*) промахну́ться (промахну́ться• *perf*); (: *missile, object*) не достига́ть (дости́чь• *or* дости́гнуть• *perf*) це́ли ◆ *n* (*failure to hit*) про́мах; **you can't ~ my house** мой дом невозмо́жно не заме́тить; **the bus just ~ed the wall** авто́бус чуть не вре́зался в сте́ну; **I ~ him** я скуча́ю по нему́; **nobody will ~ us** никто́ не заме́тит, что нас нет; **you're ~ing the point** Вы не понима́ете су́ти де́ла

▶ **miss out** *vt* (*BRIT*) пропуска́ть (пропусти́ть• *perf*)

▶ **miss out on** *vt fus* (*fun, party*) пропуска́ть (пропусти́ть• *perf*); (*chance, bargain*) упуска́ть (упусти́ть• *perf*).

missal ['mɪsl] *n* моли́твенник.

misshapen [mɪs'ʃeɪpən] *adj* деформи́рованный (деформи́рован).

missile ['mɪsaɪl] *n* (*MIL*) раке́та; (*projectile*): **demonstrators threw ~s at the police** демонстра́нты забра́сывали поли́цию разли́чными предме́тами.

missile base *n* раке́тная ба́за.

missile launcher [-'lɔ:ntʃə'] *n* раке́тная пускова́я устано́вка•.

missing ['mɪsɪŋ] *adj* (*lost*) пропа́вший; (*removed: tooth, wheel*) недостаю́щий•; (*absent*): **who is ~ today?** кто сего́дня отсу́тствует?; **to be ~, go ~** пропада́ть (пропа́сть• *perf*) бе́з вести; **~ person** пропа́вший(-ая) *m(f) adj* бе́з вести.

mission ['mɪʃən] *n* (*also POL, REL*) ми́ссия; (*MIL*) зада́ние; **on a ~ to sb** с ми́ссией к кому́-н.

missionary ['mɪʃənrɪ] *n* миссионе́р(ка•).

Mississippi [mɪsɪ'sɪpɪ] *n*: **the ~** Миссиси́пи *f ind*.

missive ['mɪsɪv] *n* посла́ние.

misspell ['mɪs'spɛl] (*irreg: like* **spell**) *vt* писа́ть• (написа́ть• *perf*) с оши́бками.

misspent ['mɪs'spɛnt] *adj*: **a ~ youth**

растра́ченная ю́ность *f*.

mist [mɪst] *n* (*heavy*) тума́н; (*light*) ды́мка ◆ *vi* (*also:* ~ **over**: *eyes*) затума́ниваться (затума́ниться *perf*); (*BRIT*: *also:* ~ **over** *or* **up**: *windows*) запотева́ть (запоте́ть *perf*).

mistake [mɪsˈteɪk] (*irreg: like* **take**) *n* оши́бка* ◆ *vt* (*be wrong about*) ошиба́ться (ошиби́ться* *perf*) в +*prp*; (*intentions*) непра́вильно понима́ть (поня́ть* *perf*); **by** ~ по оши́бке; **to make a** ~ ошиба́ться (ошиби́ться* *perf*), де́лать (сде́лать *perf*) оши́бку; **to make a** ~ **about sb/sth** ошиба́ться (ошиби́ться* *perf*) в ком-н/чём-н; **to** ~ **A for B** принима́ть (приня́ть* *perf*) А за Б.

mistaken [mɪsˈteɪkən] *pp of* **mistake** ◆ *adj* оши́бочный* (оши́бочен); **to be** ~ ошиба́ться (ошиби́ться* *perf*).

mistaken identity *n*: **a case of** ~ ~ слу́чай оши́бочного опозна́ния.

mistakenly [mɪsˈteɪkənlɪ] *adv* оши́бочно.

mister [ˈmɪstəʳ] *n* (*inf*) дя́дя *m* (*обраще́ние*); *see* **Mr**.

mistletoe [ˈmɪsltəu] *n* (*BOT*) оме́ла.

mistook [mɪsˈtuk] *pt of* **mistake**.

mistranslation [mɪstrænsˈleɪʃən] *n* непра́вильный перево́д.

mistreat [mɪsˈtriːt] *vt* пло́хо обраща́ться (*impf*) с +*instr*.

mistress [ˈmɪstrɪs] *n* (*lover*) любо́вница; (*also fig*) хозя́йка*; (*BRIT*: *SCOL*) учи́тельница.

mistrust [mɪsˈtrʌst] *vt* не доверя́ть (*impf*) +*dat*, испы́тывать (испыта́ть *perf*) недове́рие к +*dat* ◆ *n*: ~ (**of**) недове́рие (к +*dat*).

mistrustful [mɪsˈtrʌstful] *adj* недове́рчивый (недове́рчив); **to be** ~ **of** не доверя́ть (*impf*) +*dat*.

misty [ˈmɪstɪ] *adj* (*day*) тума́нный* (тума́нен); (*eyes*) затума́ненный (затума́нен); (*glasses, window*) запоте́вший*.

misty-eyed [ˈmɪstɪˈaɪd] *adj* (*girl*) с глаза́ми по́лными слёз; (*fig: girl*) с затума́ненным взгля́дом.

misunderstand [mɪsʌndəˈstænd] (*irreg: like* **understand**) *vt* непра́вильно понима́ть (поня́ть* *perf*) ◆ *vi* не понима́ть (поня́ть* *perf*).

misunderstanding [ˈmɪsʌndəˈstændɪŋ] *n* недоразуме́ние.

misunderstood [mɪsʌndəˈstud] *pt, pp of* **misunderstand**.

misuse [*n* mɪsˈjuːs, *vb* mɪsˈjuːz] *n* (*of power, funds*) злоупотребле́ние; (*of word*) непра́вильное употребле́ние ◆ *vt* (*see n*) злоупотребля́ть (злоупотреби́ть* *perf*) +*instr*; непра́вильно употребля́ть (употреби́ть* *perf*).

MIT *n abbr* (*US*) = *Massachusetts Institute of Technology*.

mite [maɪt] *n* (*small quantity*) ка́пля*; (*BRIT*: *small child*) кро́шка* *m/f*.

miter [ˈmaɪtəʳ] *n* (*US*) = **mitre**.

mitigate [ˈmɪtɪgeɪt] *vt* смягча́ть (смягчи́ть *perf*); **mitigating circumstances** смягча́ющие обстоя́тельства.

mitigation [mɪtɪˈgeɪʃən] *n* смягче́ние; **in** ~ (*LAW*) в оправда́ние.

mitre [ˈmaɪtəʳ] (*US* **miter**) *n* ми́тра; (*also:* ~ **joint**) соедине́ние в ус.

mitt [mɪt] *n* (*inf*) = **mitten**.

mitten [ˈmɪtn] *n* ва́режка*, рукави́ца.

mix [mɪks] *vt* (*cake, cement*) заме́шивать (замеси́ть* *perf*) ◆ *n* смесь *f* ◆ *vi* (*people*): **to** ~ (**with**) обща́ться (*impf*) (с +*instr*); **to** ~ **sth** (**with sth**) сме́шивать (смеша́ть *perf*) что-н (с чем-н); **to** ~ **business with pleasure** сочета́ть (*impf*) прия́тное с поле́зным; **cake** ~ гото́вая смесь для то́рта

▶ **mix in** *vt* (*eggs etc*) вме́шивать (вмеша́ть *perf*)

▶ **mix up** *vt* (*combine*) переме́шивать (перемеша́ть *perf*); (*confuse*: *people*) пу́тать (спу́тать *perf*); (*: things*) пу́тать (перепу́тать *perf*); **to get** ~**ed up in sth** впу́тываться (впу́таться *perf*) во что-н; **he's** ~**ed up in this business too** он то́же заме́шан в э́том де́ле.

mixed [mɪkst] *adj* сме́шанный.

mixed-ability [ˈmɪkstəˈbɪlɪtɪ] *adj* с ра́зными спосо́бностями.

mixed bag *n* (*of people*) разноше́рстная гру́ппа; (*of activities*) всего́ понемно́жку.

mixed blessing *n*: **it was a** ~ ~ нет ху́да без добра́.

mixed doubles *npl* (*TENNIS etc*) игра́ *fsg* сме́шанных пар.

mixed economy *n* сме́шанная эконо́мика.

mixed grill *n* (*BRIT*) *ассорти́ из жа́реного мя́са и овоще́й*.

mixed marriage *n* сме́шанный брак.

mixed-up [ˈmɪkstʌp] *adj* (*confused*) сби́тый (сбит) с то́лку.

mixer [ˈmɪksəʳ] *n* (*for food*) ми́ксер; (*for drinks*) смеси́тель *m*; (*person*): **she is a good** ~ она́ о́чень общи́тельна.

mixer tap *n* кран со смеси́телем.

mixture [ˈmɪkstʃəʳ] *n* смесь *f*; (*MED*) миксту́ра.

mix-up [ˈmɪksʌp] *n* пу́таница.

Mk *abbr* (*BRIT*: *TECH*) = **mark**.

mk *abbr* (*COMM*) = **mark**.

mkt *abbr* = **market**.

MLitt *n abbr* (= *Master of Literature, Master of Letters*) ≈ маги́стр литературове́дения.

MLR *n abbr* (*BRIT*: = *minimum lending rate*) минима́льная ссу́дная ста́вка.

mm *abbr* (= *millimetre*) мм= *миллиме́тр*.

MN *abbr* (*BRIT*) = *Merchant Navy*; (*US*: *POST*) = *Minnesota*.

MO *n abbr* = *medical officer*; (*US*: *inf*.= *modus operandi*) при́нцип рабо́ты ◆ *abbr* (*US*: *POST*) = *Missouri*.

m.o. *abbr* = *money order*.

moan [məun] *n* (*cry*) стон ◆ *vi* (*inf*: *complain*): **to** ~ (**about**) ныть* (*impf*) (о +*prp*).

moaner [ˈməunəʳ] *n* (*inf*: *pej*) ны́тик*.

moat [məut] *n* ров*.
mob [mɔb] *n* толпа*; (*inf: group of friends*) компания ♦ *vt* осаждать (осадить* *perf*).
mobile ['məubaɪl] *adj* подвижный* (подвижен); (*population, forces*) мобильный* (мобилен) ♦ *n* (*decoration*) подвесное декоративное украшение; **applicants must be** ~ кандидаты должны быть готовы к смене местожительства.
mobile home *n* дом* на колёсах.
mobile phone *n* портативный телефон.
mobile shop *n* (*BRIT*) автолавка*.
mobility [məu'bɪlɪtɪ] *n* (*see adj*) подвижность *f*; мобильность *f*; (*of applicant*) готовность *f* менять местожительство.
mobility allowance *n* (*BRIT*) пособие, *выплачиваемое инвалидам для покрытия дополнительных дорожных расходов*.
mobilize ['məubɪlaɪz] *vt* мобилизовать (*impf/perf*) ♦ *vi* мобилизоваться (*impf/perf*).
moccasin ['mɔkəsɪn] *n* мокасин.
mock [mɔk] *vt* (*ridicule*) издеваться (*impf*) над +*instr*; (*laugh at*) насмехаться (*impf*) над +*instr* ♦ *adj* (*fake*) ложный* (ложен); (: *emotion*) притворный; ~ (**exam**) (*BRIT*) пробный экзамен (*для подготовки к основному*); ~ **battle** инсценировка боя.
mockery ['mɔkərɪ] *n* издевательство; **to make a ~ of sb/sth** выставлять (выставить* *perf*) кого-н/что-н на посмешище.
mocking ['mɔkɪŋ] *adj* издевательский*.
mockingbird ['mɔkɪŋbə:d] *n* пересмешник.
mock-up ['mɔkʌp] *n* макет.
MOD *n abbr* (*BRIT*: = *Ministry of Defence*) Министерство обороны.
mod cons ['mɔd'kɔnz] *npl abbr* (*BRIT*: = *modern conveniences*) современные удобства *ntpl*.
mode [məud] *n* (*form: of life*) образ; (: *of transport*) вид; (*COMPUT*) режим.
model ['mɔdl] *n* модель *f*, макет; (*also: fashion* ~) манекенщик(-ица); (*also: artist's* ~) натурщик(-ица) ♦ *adj* (*small scale*) модельный; (*ideal*) образцовый ♦ *vt* (*clothes*) демонстрировать (*impf/perf*); (*with clay etc*) лепить* (вылепить* *perf*) ♦ *vi* (*for designer, photographer*) позировать (*impf*); **to ~ o.s. on** (*copy*) копировать (*impf*).
modeller ['mɔdlə'] (*US* **modeler**) *n* (*model maker*) моделист(ка*).
model railway *n* макет железной дороги.
modem ['məudɛm] *n* (*COMPUT*) модем.
moderate [*adj, n* 'mɔdərət, *vb* 'mɔdəreɪt] *adj* (*views, amount*) умеренный* (умерен); (*change*) незначительный ♦ *n* человек* умеренных взглядов ♦ *vt* умерять (умерить *perf*) ♦ *vi* (*storm, wind etc*) утихать (утихнуть* *perf*).
moderately ['mɔdərətlɪ] *adv* (*act*) умеренно; ~

expensive/pleased довольно дорого/рад; ~ **priced** по умеренной цене.
moderation [mɔdə'reɪʃən] *n* умеренность *f*; **in** ~ в умеренных количествах.
moderator ['mɔdəreɪtə'] *n* (*mediator*) посредник; (*chairman*) председатель *m*.
modern ['mɔdən] *adj* современный; ~ **languages** современные языки *mpl*.
modernization [mɔdənaɪ'zeɪʃən] *n* модернизация.
modernize ['mɔdənaɪz] *vt* модернизировать (*impf/perf*).
modest ['mɔdɪst] *adj* скромный* (скромен).
modestly ['mɔdɪstlɪ] *adv* скромно.
modesty ['mɔdɪstɪ] *n* скромность *f*.
modicum ['mɔdɪkəm] *n*: **a ~ of** толика +*gen*.
modification [mɔdɪfɪ'keɪʃən] *n* (*of vehicle, engine*) модификация; (*of plan*) видоизменение; **to make ~s to** вносить* (внести* *perf*) видоизменения в +*acc*.
modify ['mɔdɪfaɪ] *vt* (*see n*) модифицировать (*impf/perf*); видоизменять (видоизменить *perf*).
modish ['məudɪʃ] *adj* модный* (моден).
Mods [mɔdz] *n abbr* (*BRIT*: *SCOL*: = (*Honour*) *Moderations*) экзамен, *позволяющий перейти на курс, необходимый для получения степени бакалавра в Оксфордском университете*.
modular ['mɔdjulə'] *adj* (*filing, unit*) модульный.
modulate ['mɔdjuleɪt] *vt* (*voice*) модулировать (*impf*).
modulation [mɔdju'leɪʃən] *n* (*MUS, RADIO*) модуляция.
module ['mɔdju:l] *n* модуль *m*; (*SPACE*) отсек; (*BRIT*: *SCOL*) курс.
modus operandi ['məudəsɔpə'rændi:] *n* принцип работы.
Mogadishu [mɔgə'dɪʃu:] *n* Могадишу *m ind*.
mogul ['məugl] *n* (*fig*) магнат.
MOH *n abbr* (*BRIT*) = *Medical Officer of Health*.
mohair ['məuhɛə'] *n* мохер.
Mohammed [mə'hæmɛd] *n* Магомет.
moist [mɔɪst] *adj* влажный* (влажен).
moisten ['mɔɪsn] *vt* (*lips*) увлажнять (увлажнить *perf*); (: *with tongue*) облизывать (облизать *perf*); (*sponge*) мочить* (намочить* *perf*).
moisture ['mɔɪstʃə'] *n* влага.
moisturize ['mɔɪstʃəraɪz] *vt* увлажнять (увлажнить *perf*).
moisturizer ['mɔɪstʃəraɪzə'] *n* увлажняющий крем.
molar ['məulə'] *n* коренной зуб*.
molasses [məu'læsɪz] *n* патока.
mold *etc* [məuld] (*US*) = **mould** *etc*.
Moldavian [mɔl'deɪvɪən] *n* (*person*)

молдова́нин*(-а́нка*) ◆ *adj* молдо́вский.
Moldova [mɔlˈdəʊvə] *n* Молдо́ва.
mole [məʊl] *n* (*spot*) ро́динка*; (*ZOOL*) крот*; (*spy*) доно́счик(-ица), стука́ч*(ка).
molecular [məʊˈlɛkjʊlə*] *adj* молекуля́рный.
molecule [ˈmɔlɪkjuːl] *n* моле́кула.
molehill [ˈməʊlhɪl] *n* крото́вая нора́*.
molest [məˈlɛst] *vt* (*assault sexually*) надруга́ться (*perf*) над +*instr*; (*harass*) трави́ть* (затрави́ть* *perf*).
mollusc [ˈmɔləsk] *n* моллю́ск.
mollycoddle [ˈmɔlɪkɔdl] *vt* трясти́сь* (*impf*) над +*instr*.
Molotov cocktail [ˈmɔlətɔf-] *n* кокте́йль *m* Мо́лотова (*буты́лка с зажига́тельной сме́сью*).
molt [məʊlt] *vi* (*US*) = **moult**.
molten [ˈməʊltən] *adj* распла́вленный.
mom [mɔm] *n* (*US*) = **mum**.
moment [ˈməʊmənt] *n* моме́нт, мгнове́ние; (*PHYS*) моме́нт; **for a ~** на мгнове́ние *or* мину́ту; **at that ~** в э́тот моме́нт; **at the ~** в настоя́щий* моме́нт; **for the ~** пока́; **in a ~** че́рез мину́ту; (**at**) **any ~** (**now**) в любо́й моме́нт; **"one ~ please"** „одну́ мину́точку".
momentarily [ˈməʊməntrɪlɪ] *adv* на мгнове́ние; (*US: very soon*) в любо́й моме́нт.
momentary [ˈməʊməntərɪ] *adj* (*brief*) мгнове́нный.
momentous [məʊˈmɛntəs] *adj* важне́йший.
momentum [məʊˈmɛntəm] *n* (*PHYS*) и́мпульс; (*fig*) дви́жущая си́ла; **to gather** *or* **gain ~** набира́ть (набра́ть* *perf*) си́лу.
mommy [ˈmɔmɪ] *n* (*US: mother*) = **mummy**.
Mon. *abbr* = **Monday**.
Monaco [ˈmɔnəkəʊ] *n* Мона́ко *nt ind*.
monarch [ˈmɔnək] *n* мона́рх.
monarchist [ˈmɔnəkɪst] *n* монархи́ст(ка*).
monarchy [ˈmɔnəkɪ] *n* мона́рхия.
monastery [ˈmɔnəstərɪ] *n* монасты́рь* *m*.
monastic [məˈnæstɪk] *adj* (*vows, order, also fig*) мона́шеский*; (*building*) монасты́рский.
Monday [ˈmʌndɪ] *n* понеде́льник; *see also* **Tuesday**.
Monegasque [mɔnəˈgæsk] *adj* мона́кский ◆ *n* жи́тель(ница) *m(f)* Мона́ко.
monetarist [ˈmʌnɪtərɪst] *n* монетари́ст ◆ *adj* монетари́стский.
monetary [ˈmʌnɪtərɪ] *adj* де́нежный.
money [ˈmʌnɪ] *n* де́ньги* *pl*; **to make ~** (*person*) зараба́тывать (зарабо́тать* *perf*); (*business*) приноси́ть* (принести́* *perf*) дохо́д; **danger ~** (*BRIT*) надба́вка за вре́дность; **I've got no ~ left** у меня́ совсе́м не оста́лось де́нег.
moneyed [ˈmʌnɪd] *adj* де́нежный.
moneylender [ˈmʌnɪlɛndə*] *n* ростовщи́к*.
money-maker [ˈmʌnɪmeɪkə*] *n* (*person*) кру́пный деле́ц*; (*project, investment*) при́быльное де́ло.
moneymaking [ˈmʌnɪmeɪkɪŋ] *adj* при́быльный.

money market *n* де́нежный ры́нок*.
money order *n* де́нежный перево́д.
money-spinner [ˈmʌnɪspɪnə*] *n* (*inf*): **this business/idea will be a real ~** э́тот би́знес/э́та иде́я бу́дет де́лать больши́е де́ньги.
money supply *n* де́нежная ма́сса.
Mongol [ˈmɔŋgəl] *n* (*LING*) монго́льский* язы́к*; (*HISTORY*): **the ~s** монго́ло-тата́ры.
mongol [ˈmɔŋgəl] *n* (*pej*) челове́к, страда́ющий боле́знью Да́уна.
Mongolia [mɔŋˈgəʊlɪə] *n* Монго́лия.
Mongolian [mɔŋˈgəʊlɪən] *adj* монго́льский* ◆ *n* (*person*) монго́л(ка*); (*LING*) монго́льский* язы́к*.
mongoose [ˈmɔŋguːs] *n* мангу́ст.
mongrel [ˈmʌŋgrəl] *n* дворня́га.
monitor [ˈmɔnɪtə*] *n* монито́р ◆ *vt* (*broadcasts*) контроли́ровать (*impf*); (*heartbeat, pulse*) наблюда́ть (*impf*) за +*instr*; (*progress*) следи́ть* (*impf*) за +*instr*; (*foreign station*) прослу́шивать (*impf*).
monk [mʌŋk] *n* мона́х.
monkey [ˈmʌŋkɪ] *n* обезья́на.
monkey business *n* (*inf*) проде́лки* *fpl*.
monkey nut *n* (*BRIT*) ара́хис *no pl*.
monkey tricks *npl* = **monkey business**.
monkey wrench *n* разводно́й га́ечный ключ*.
mono [ˈmɔnəʊ] *adj* (*recording*) мо́но *ind*.
monochrome [ˈmɔnəkrəʊm] *adj* черно-бе́лый; (*COMPUT*) монохро́мный.
monogamous [mɔˈnɔgəməs] *adj* монога́мный* (монога́мен).
monogamy [mɔˈnɔgəmɪ] *n* монога́мия, единобра́чие.
monogram [ˈmɔnəgræm] *n* моногра́мма.
monolith [ˈmɔnəlɪθ] *n* моноли́т.
monolithic [mɔnəˈlɪθɪk] *adj* моноли́тный.
monologue [ˈmɔnəlɔg] *n* моноло́г.
monoplane [ˈmɔnəpleɪn] *n* монопла́н.
monopolist [məˈnɔpəlɪst] *n* монополи́ст.
monopolize [məˈnɔpəlaɪz] *vt* (*ECON*) монополизи́ровать (*impf/perf*); (*place, conversation*) завладева́ть (завладе́ть *perf*) +*instr*; (*person*) захва́тывать (захвати́ть* *perf*).
monopoly [məˈnɔpəlɪ] *n* (*also ECON*) монопо́лия; **Monopolies and Mergers Commission** (*BRIT*) Коми́ссия по монопо́лиям и слия́ниям.
monorail [ˈmɔnəʊreɪl] *n* моноре́льсовая доро́га.
monosodium glutamate [mɔnəˈsəʊdɪəm ˈgluːtəmeɪt] *n* глутамина́т на́трия.
monosyllabic [mɔnəsɪˈlæbɪk] *adj* (*word*) односло́жный; (*person*) немногосло́вный*.
monosyllable [ˈmɔnəsɪləbl] *n* односло́жное сло́во*.
monotone [ˈmɔnətəʊn] *n*: **to speak in a ~** говори́ть (*impf*) моното́нно.
monotonous [məˈnɔtənəs] *adj* (*life, job etc*)

однообра́зный* (однообра́зен); (*voice, sound*) моното́нный* (моното́нен).
monotony [mə'nɔtənɪ] *n* (*see adj*) однообра́зие; моното́нность *f*.
monsoon [mɔn'su:n] *n* муссо́н.
monster ['mɔnstə'] *n* (*also fig*) чудо́вище, монстр.
monstrosity [mɔn'strɔsɪtɪ] *n* (*object, building*) чу́дище, монстр.
monstrous ['mɔnstrəs] *adj* чудо́вищный* (чудо́вищен).
montage [mɔn'tɑ:ʒ] *n* монта́ж.
Mont Blanc [mɔ̃ blɑ̃] *n* Монбла́н.
Montenegrin [mɔntə'ni:grɪn] *n* черного́рец*(-о́рка*) ◆ *adj* черного́рский*.
Montenegro [mɔntə'ni:grəu] *n* Черного́рия.
month [mʌnθ] *n* ме́сяц; **every ~** ка́ждый ме́сяц; **300 dollars a ~** 300 до́лларов в ме́сяц.
monthly ['mʌnθlɪ] *adj* ежеме́сячный; (*ticket*) ме́сячный ◆ *adv* ежеме́сячно; **twice ~** два́жды в ме́сяц.
Montreal [mɔntrɪ'ɔ:l] *n* Монреа́ль *m*.
monument ['mɔnjumənt] *n* (*memorial*) па́мятник, монуме́нт; (*historical building*) па́мятник.
monumental [mɔnju'mɛntl] *adj* (*building, book*) монумента́льный* (монумента́лен); (*storm, row*) колосса́льный.
moo [mu:] *vi* мыча́ть* (*impf*).
mood [mu:d] *n* настрое́ние; (*of group, crowd*) настро́й; **to be in a good/bad ~** быть* (*impf*) в хоро́шем/плохо́м настрое́нии; **I'm in the ~ for a drink/to watch TV** у меня́ есть настрое́ние вы́пить/смотре́ть телеви́зор.
moodily ['mu:dɪlɪ] *adv* мра́чно, угрю́мо.
moody ['mu:dɪ] *adj* (*sullen*) угрю́мый (угрю́м); (*temperamental*): **she is a very ~ person** у неё о́чень переме́нчивое настрое́ние.
moon [mu:n] *n* луна́*.
moonlight ['mu:nlaɪt] *n* лу́нный свет ◆ *vi* (*inf*) рабо́тать (*impf*) на стороне́.
moonlighting ['mu:nlaɪtɪŋ] *n* (*inf*) рабо́та по совмести́тельству.
moonlit ['mu:nlɪt] *adj*: **a ~ night** лу́нная ночь*.
moonshot ['mu:nʃɔt] *n* полёт на Луну́.
moor [muə'] *n* ве́ресковая пу́стошь *f* ◆ *vt* (*ship*) пришварто́вывать (пришвартова́ть *perf*) ◆ *vi* пришварто́вываться (пришвартова́ться *perf*).
mooring ['muərɪŋ] *n* прича́л; **~s** *npl* (*chains*) швартов́ые це́пи* *fpl*.
Moorish ['muərɪʃ] *adj* маврита́нский.
moorland ['muələnd] *n* ве́ресковая пу́стошь *f*.
moose [mu:s] *n inv* лось* *m*.
moot [mu:t] *vt*: **it was ~ed that ...** бы́ло предло́жено, что ... ◆ *adj*: **~ point** спо́рный вопро́с.
mop [mɔp] *n* (*for floor*) шва́бра; (*for dishes*)

щётка*; (*of hair*) копна́ ◆ *vt* (*floor*) мыть* (вы́мыть* *or* помы́ть* *perf*) (шва́брой); (*eyes, face*) вытира́ть (вы́тереть* *perf*)
▶ **mop up** *vt* (*liquid*) вытира́ть (вы́тереть* *perf*).
mope [məup] *vi* хандри́ть (*impf*)
▶ **mope about** *vi* слоня́ться (*impf*)
▶ **mope around** *vi* = **mope about**.
moped ['məupɛd] *n* мопе́д.
moquette [mɔ'kɛt] *n* ≈ плюш.
MOR *adj abbr* (*MUS*: = *middle-of-the-road*) лёгкий*.
moral ['mɔrl] *adj* нра́вственный, мора́льный; (*person*) нра́вственный* (нра́вственен) ◆ *n* (*of story*) мора́ль *f*; **~s** *npl* нра́вы *mpl*; **~ support/dilemma/victory** мора́льная подде́ржка/диле́мма/побе́да; **~ courage** душе́вное му́жество.
morale [mɔ'rɑ:l] *n* мора́льный дух.
morality [mɔ'rælɪt] *n* нра́вственность *f*.
moralize ['mɔrəlaɪz] *vi*: **to ~ (about)** морализи́ровать (*impf*) (о *+prp*).
morally ['mɔrəlɪ] *adv* (*wrong, responsible*) мора́льно; (*live, behave*) нра́вственно.
moral victory *n* мора́льная побе́да.
morass [mə'ræs] *n* (*also fig*) тряси́на.
moratorium [mɔrə'tɔ:rɪəm] *n* морато́рий.
morbid ['mɔ:bɪd] *adj* (*imagination*) ненорма́льный; (*ideas*) жу́ткий*.

━━━━━━ **KEYWORD** ━━━━━━

more [mɔ:'] *adj* **1** (*greater in number etc*) бо́льше *+gen*; **I have more friends than enemies** у меня́ бо́льше друзе́й, чем враго́в **2** (*additional*) ещё; **do you want (some) more tea?** хоти́те ещё ча́ю?; **is there any more wine?** ещё есть вино́?; **I have no** *or* **I don't have any more money** у меня́ бо́льше нет де́нег; **it'll take a few more weeks** э́то займёт ещё не́сколько неде́ль
◆ *pron* **1** (*greater amount*): **more than ten** бо́льше десяти́; **we've sold more than a hundred tickets** мы прода́ли бо́лее ста биле́тов; **it cost more than we expected** э́то сто́ит бо́льше, чем мы ожида́ли
2 (*further or additional amount*): **is there any more?** ещё есть?; **there's no more** бо́льше ничего́ нет; **a little more** ещё немно́го *or* чуть-чу́ть; **many/much more** намно́го/ гора́здо бо́льше
◆ *adv* **1** (*+vb*) бо́льше; **I like this one more** мне э́то бо́льше нра́вится
2 (*+adj*): **more dangerous/difficult** *etc* (**than**) бо́лее опа́сный/тру́дный *etc*, (чем)
3 (*+adv*): **more economically** (**than**) бо́лее эконо́мично (чем); **more easily/quickly** (**than**) ле́гче/быстре́е (чем); **he became more and more excited/friendly** он станови́лся всё бо́лее и бо́лее возбуждённым/ дружелю́бным; **he grew to like her more and**

more она́ нра́вилась ему́ всё бо́льше и бо́льше; **more or less** бо́лее и́ли ме́нее; **it should cost £500, more or less** э́то должно́ сто́ить приблизи́тельно £500; **she is more beautiful than ever** она́ прекра́снее, чем когда́-либо; **he loved her more than ever** он люби́л её бо́льше, чем когда́-либо; **the more ..., the better** чем бо́льше ..., тем лу́чше; **once more** ещё раз; **I'd like to see more of you** хоте́лось бы поча́ще Вас ви́деть.

moreover [mɔː'rəuvəʳ] *adv* бо́лее того́.
morgue [mɔːg] *n* морг.
MORI ['mɔːrɪ] *n abbr* (*BRIT*: = Market & Opinion Research Institute) нау́чно-иссле́довательский институ́т изуче́ния ры́нка и обще́ственного мне́ния.
moribund ['mɔrɪbʌnd] *adj* (*industry*) отжи́вший своё.
Mormon ['mɔːmən] *n* мормо́н(ка•).
morning ['mɔːnɪŋ] *n* у́тро•; (*between midnight and 3 a.m.*) ночь *f* ♦ *cpd* (*paper, sun, walk*) у́тренний•; **in the ~** у́тром; **3 o'clock in the ~** 3 часа́ но́чи; **7 o'clock in the ~** 7 часо́в утра́; **this ~** сего́дня у́тром.
morning-after pill ['mɔːnɪŋ'ɑːftə-] *n* противозача́точная табле́тка (*обы́чно принима́ется по́сле се́кса*).
morning sickness *n* у́тренняя тошнота́ (*у бере́менных*).
Moroccan [mə'rɔkən] *adj* моро́кка́нский ♦ *n* моро́кка́нец•(-нка•).
Morocco [mə'rɔkəu] *n* Моро́кко *nt ind.*
moron ['mɔːrɔn] *n* (*inf*) крети́н(ка•).
moronic [mə'rɔnɪk] *adj* (*inf*) крети́нский.
morose [mə'rəus] *adj* (*miserable*) угрю́мый (угрю́м).
morphine ['mɔːfiːn] *n* мо́рфий.
morris dancing ['mɔrɪs-] *n* (*BRIT*) мо́ррис (*наро́дный англи́йский та́нец*).
Morse [mɔːs] *n* (*also:* ~ **code**) а́збука Мо́рзе.
morsel ['mɔːsl] *n* (*of food*) кусо́чек•.
mortal ['mɔːtl] *adj* (*human*) сме́ртный• (сме́ртен); (*deadly*) сме́ртный (сме́ртелен); (*sin*) сме́ртный ♦ *n*: **mere ~** просто́й(-а́я) сме́ртный(-ая) *m(f) adj*; **~ remains** бре́нные оста́нки.
mortality [mɔː'tælɪtɪ] *n* (*death*) сме́ртность *f*.
mortality rate *n* сме́ртность *f*.
mortar ['mɔːtəʳ] *n* (*cannon*) миноме́т; (*cement*) цеме́нтный раство́р; (*bowl*) сту́пка•.
mortgage ['mɔːgɪdʒ] *n* ипоте́чный креди́т, ипоте́чная ссу́да ♦ *vt* закла́дывать (заложи́ть• *perf*); **to take out a ~** брать• (взять• *perf*) ипоте́чный креди́т.
mortgage company *n* (*US*) ипоте́чная компа́ния.
mortgagee [mɔːgə'dʒiː] *n* кредито́р (*при ипоте́чном креди́те*).
mortgagor ['mɔːgədʒəʳ] *n* заёмщик (*при ипоте́чном креди́те*).

mortician [mɔː'tɪʃən] *n* (*US*) рабо́тник похоро́нного бюро́.
mortified ['mɔːtɪfaɪd] *adj*: **to be ~** быть• (*impf*) в сме́ртельном у́жасе.
mortify ['mɔːtɪfaɪ] *vt* приводи́ть• (привести́• *perf*) в по́лный у́жас.
mortise lock ['mɔːtɪs-] *n* врезно́й замо́к•.
mortuary ['mɔːtjuərɪ] *n* морг (*при больни́це*), поко́йницкая *f adj*.
mosaic [məu'zeɪɪk] *n* моза́ика.
Moscow ['mɔskəu] *n* Москва́.
Moslem ['mɔzləm] *adj, n* = **Muslim**.
mosque [mɔsk] *n* мече́ть *f*.
mosquito [mɔs'kiːtəu] (*pl* ~**es**) *n* кома́р•.
mosquito net *n* моски́тная се́тка•.
moss [mɔs] *n* мох•.
mossy ['mɔsɪ] *adj* (*ground, wall*) поро́сший мхом.

KEYWORD

most [məust] *adj* **1** (*almost all: countable nouns*) большинство́ +*gen*; (: *uncountable and collective nouns*) по бо́льшей ча́сти; **most people/cars** большинство́ люде́й/маши́н; **most milk** молоко́, по бо́льшей ча́сти; **in most cases** в большинстве́ слу́чаев
2 (*largest, greatest*): **who has the most money?** у кого́ бо́льше всего́ де́нег?; **this book has attracted the most interest among the critics** э́та кни́га вы́звала наибо́льший интере́с у кри́тиков
♦ *pron* (*greatest quantity, number: countable nouns*) большинство́; (: *uncountable and collective nouns*) бо́льшая часть *f*; **most of the houses/her friends** большинство́ домо́в/её друзе́й; **most of the cake** бо́льшая часть то́рта; **do the most you can** де́лайте всё, что мо́жете; **I ate the most** я съел бо́льше всех; **to make the most of sth** максима́льно испо́льзовать (*impf*) что-н; **at the (very) most** са́мое бо́льшее
♦ *adv* (+*vb*) бо́льше всего́; (+*adv*) исключи́тельно; **the most interesting/ expensive** наибо́лее *or* са́мый интере́сный/ дорого́й; **I liked him the most** он понра́вился мне бо́льше всех; **what do you value most, wealth or health?** что Вы бо́льше це́ните, бога́тство и́ли здоро́вье?

---

mostly ['məustlɪ] *adv* в основно́м, гла́вным о́бразом.
MOT *n abbr* (*BRIT*: = Ministry of Transport) Министе́рство тра́нспорта; ~ (**test**) техосмо́тр= техни́ческий осмо́тр.
motel [məu'tɛl] *n* моте́ль *m*.
moth [mɔθ] *n* мотылёк•; (*also:* **clothes** ~) моль *f no pl*.
mothballs ['mɔθbɔːlz] *npl* нафтали́новые ша́рики *mpl*.
moth-eaten ['mɔθiːtn] *adj* (*also fig*) изъе́денный (изъе́ден).
mother ['mʌðəʳ] *n* мать• *f* ♦ *vt* (*raise*)

выра́щивать (вы́растить* *perf*); (*pamper*)
ня́нчиться (*impf*) с +*instr* ◆ *adj*: ~ **country**
ро́дина; ~ **company** матери́нская компа́ния.
motherboard ['mʌðəbɔːd] *n* (*COMPUT*)
объедини́тельная пла́та.
motherhood ['mʌðəhud] *n* матери́нство.
mother-in-law ['mʌðərɪnlɔː] *n* (*wife's mother*)
тёща; (*husband's mother*) свекро́вь *f*.
motherly ['mʌðəlɪ] *adj* матери́нский*.
mother-of-pearl ['mʌðərəv'pɜːl] *n* перламу́тр
◆ *adj* перламу́тровый.
Mother's Day *n* пра́здник посвящённый
матеря́м.
mother's help *n* ня́ня.
mother-to-be ['mʌðətə'biː] *n* бу́дущая мать* *f*.
mother tongue *n* родно́й язы́к*.
mothproof ['mɔθpruːf] *adj* (*fabric etc*)
молесто́йкий.
motif [məu'tiːf] *n* (*design*) орна́мент; (*theme*)
моти́в.
motion ['məuʃən] *n* (*movement, gesture*)
движе́ние; (*proposal*) предложе́ние; (*BRIT:
bowel movement*) стул *no pl* ◆ *vti*: **he ~ed (to)
her to sit down** он жёстом предложи́л ей
сесть; **to be in** ~ быть* (*impf*) в движе́нии; **to
set in** ~ приводи́ть* (привести́* *perf*) в
де́йствие; **to go through the ~s** (*fig:
formalities*) исполня́ть (испо́лнить *perf*)
форма́льности.
motionless ['məuʃənlɪs] *adj* неподви́жный*
(неподви́жен).
motion picture *n* кинокарти́на.
motivate ['məutɪveɪt] *vt* (*act, decision*)
мотиви́ровать (*impf*); (*person*)
заинтересо́вывать (заинтересова́ть *perf*); **he
is ~d by ambition** им дви́жет честолю́бие.
motivated ['məutɪveɪtɪd] *adj* (*enthusiastic*)
заинтересо́ванный (заинтересо́ван);
(*impelled*): ~ **by envy/greed** движи́мый
чу́вством за́висти/жа́дности.
motivation [məutɪ'veɪʃən] *n* (*drive*)
целеустремлённость *f*.
motivational research *n* иссле́дование
мотива́ций.
motive ['məutɪv] *n* моти́в, побужде́ние ◆ *adj*: ~
power *or* **force** дви́жущая си́ла; **from the best
(of)** ~**s** из лу́чших побужде́ний.
motley ['mɔtlɪ] *adj* пёстрый* (пёстр).
motor ['məutə'] *n* (*also BRIT: inf*) мото́р ◆ *cpd*
(*industry, trade*) автомоби́льный.
motorbike ['məutəbaɪk] *n* мотоци́кл.
motorboat ['məutəbəut] *n* мото́рная ло́дка*.
motorcade ['məutəkeɪd] *n* корте́ж
автомоби́лей.
motorcar ['məutəkɑː] *n* (*BRIT*) автомоби́ль *m*.
motorcoach ['məutəkəutʃ] *n* (*BRIT*) авто́бус.
motorcycle ['məutəsaɪkl] *n* мотоци́кл.
motorcycle racing *n* мотого́нки* *fpl*.

motorcyclist ['məutəsaɪklɪst] *n*
мотоцикли́ст(ка*).
motoring ['məutərɪŋ] (*BRIT*) *n* езда́ на
автомоби́ле ◆ *cpd*: ~ **accident**
автомоби́льная ава́рия; ~ **offence**
наруше́ние пра́вил доро́жного движе́ния;
we went on a ~ holiday in France мы провели́
о́тпуск путеше́ствуя по Фра́нции на
маши́не.
motorist ['məutərɪst] *n* автомобили́ст.
motorized ['məutəraɪzd] *adj*: ~ **transport**
автотра́нспорт; ~ **vehicle** автомаши́на; ~
regiment моторизо́ванный полк*.
motor oil *n* мото́рное ма́сло.
motor racing *n* (*BRIT*) автого́нки* *fpl*=
автомоби́льные го́нки.
motor scooter *n* мотморо́ллер.
motor vehicle *n* автомаши́на.
motorway ['məutəweɪ] *n* (*BRIT*)
автомагистра́ль *f*, автостра́да.
mottled ['mɔtld] *adj* пятни́стый.
motto ['mɔtəu] *n* (*pl* **~es**) деви́з.
mould [məuld] (*US* **mold**) *n* (*cast*) фо́рма;
(*mildew*) пле́сень *f* ◆ *vt* (*substance*) лепи́ть*
(слепи́ть* *or* вы́лепить* *perf*); (*fig: opinion,
character*) формирова́ть (сформирова́ть
perf).
moulder ['məuldə'] *vi* разлага́ться
(разложи́ться* *perf*).
moulding ['məuldɪŋ] *n* (*ARCHIT*) лепно́е
украше́ние.
mouldy ['məuldɪ] *adj* (*food*) заплесневе́лый;
(*smell*) за́тхлый (за́тхл).
moult [məult] (*US* **molt**) *vi* линя́ть (*impf*).
mound [maund] *n* (*hillock*) холм, приго́рок*;
(*heap*) ку́ча.
mount [maunt] *n* (*horse*) ло́шадь* *f*; (*for picture,
photograph*) паспарту́ *nt ind* ◆ *vt* (*horse*)
сади́ться* (сесть* *perf*) на +*acc*; (*exhibition,
display*) устра́ивать (устро́ить *perf*); (*jewel*)
оправля́ть (опра́вить* *perf*); (*picture*)
обрамля́ть (обрами́ть* *perf*; (*staircase*)
восходи́ть* (взойти́* *perf*) по +*dat*; (*attack*)
предпринима́ть (предприня́ть* *perf*) ◆ *vi*
(*increase*) расти́* (*impf*); (*get on a horse*)
сади́ться* (сесть* *perf*) на ло́шадь; **M~
Ararat/Kilimanjaro** гора́ Арара́т/
Килиманджа́ро
▶ **mount up** *vi* (*bills, costs*) нака́пливаться
(накопи́ться* *perf*).
mountain ['mauntɪn] *n* (*also fig*) гора́* ◆ *cpd*
го́рный; **to make a ~ out of a molehill** де́лать
(сде́лать *perf*) из му́хи слона́.
mountain bike *n* велосипе́д, приспосо́бленный
*для испо́льзования на пересечённой
ме́стности*.
mountaineer [mauntɪ'nɪə'] *n* альпини́ст(ка*).
mountaineering [mauntɪ'nɪərɪŋ] *n* альпини́зм;

---

to go ~ ходи́ть* *(impf)* в го́ры.
mountainous ['mauntɪnəs] *adj* гори́стый (гори́ст).
mountain range *n* го́рная цепь* *f*.
mountain rescue team *n* горноспаса́тельный отря́д.
mountainside ['mauntɪnsaɪd] *n* склон горы́.
mounted ['mauntɪd] *adj* (*on horseback*) ко́нный.
Mount Everest *n* гора́ Эвере́ст.
mourn [mɔ:n] *vt* опла́кивать *(impf)* ♦ *vi*: **to** ~ **for** скорбе́ть *(impf)* по +*dat or* о +*prp*.
mourner ['mɔ:nə*] *n* прису́тствующий(-ая) *m(f) adj* на похорона́х.
mournful ['mɔ:nful] *adj* (*sad*) ско́рбный* (ско́рбен).
mourning ['mɔ:nɪŋ] *n* тра́ур; **in** ~ в тра́уре.
mouse [maus] (*pl* **mice**) *n* (*also fig, COMPUT*) мышь* *f*; ~ **mat** *or* **pad** ко́врик для мы́ши.
mousetrap ['maustræp] *n* мышело́вка*.
moussaka [mu'sɑ:kə] *n* мусса́ка (*гре́ческое блю́до*).
mousse [mu:s] *n* мусс.
moustache [məs'tɑ:ʃ] (*US* **mustache**) *n* усы́ *mpl*.
mousy ['mausɪ] *adj* (*hair*) мыши́ного цве́та.
mouth [mauθ] (*pl* ~**s**) *n* (*of cave, hole*) вход; (*of river*) у́стье*; (*of bottle*) го́рлышко*.
mouthful ['mauθful] *n* (*of food*) кусо́чек*; (*of drink*) глото́к*.
mouth organ *n* губна́я гармо́шка*.
mouthpiece ['mauθpi:s] *n* (*of musical instrument*) мундштук*; (*of telephone*) микрофо́н; (*spokesman, newspaper*) глаша́тай.
mouth-to-mouth ['mauθtə'mauθ] *adj*: ~ **resuscitation** иску́сственное дыха́ние.
mouthwash ['mauθwɔʃ] *n* жи́дкость *f* для полоска́ния рта.
mouthwatering ['mauθwɔ:tərɪŋ] *adj* о́чень аппети́тный* (аппети́тен).
movable ['mu:vəbl] *adj* подвижно́й; **Easter is a** ~ **feast** в ра́зные го́ды Па́сха прихо́дится на ра́зные числа.
move [mu:v] *n* (*movement*) движе́ние; (*in game*) ход*; (*change: of house*) перее́зд; (: *of job*) перехо́д (*на другу́ю рабо́ту*) ♦ *vt* передвига́ть (передви́нуть *perf*); (*piece: in game*) ходи́ть* (пойти́* *perf*) +*instr*; (*part of body*) дви́гать (дви́нуть *perf*) +*instr*; (*person: emotionally*) тро́гать (тро́нуть *perf*), растро́гать *(perf)*; (*resolution etc*) предлага́ть (предложи́ть* *perf*) ♦ *vi* дви́гаться (дви́нуться *perf*); (*in game*) де́лать (сде́лать *perf*) ход; (*of things*) дви́гаться *(impf)*; (*also*: ~ **house**) переезжа́ть (перее́хать* *perf*); **get a** ~ **on!** потора́пливайтесь!; **to** ~ **to a new job** переходи́ть* (перейти́* *perf*) на но́вую рабо́ту; **to** ~ **sb to sth** подви́гнуть* *(perf)* кого́-н на что-н; **to** ~ **towards** дви́гаться (дви́нуться *perf*) к +*dat*
▶ **move about** *vi* (*change position*)

передвига́ться (передви́нуться *perf*); (*travel, change residence*) переезжа́ть *(impf)* с ме́ста на ме́сто; (*change job*) переходи́ть* *(impf)* с рабо́ты на рабо́ту
▶ **move along** *vi* проходи́ть* (пройти́* *perf*)
▶ **move around** *vi* = **move about**
▶ **move away** *vi*: **to** ~ **away (from)** (*leave*) уезжа́ть (уе́хать* *perf*) (из +*gen*); (*step away*) отходи́ть* (отойти́* *perf*) (от +*gen*)
▶ **move back** *vi* переезжа́ть (перее́хать* *perf*) обра́тно
▶ **move forward** *vi* продвига́ться (продви́нуться *perf*)
▶ **move in** *vi* (*police, soldiers*) входи́ть* (войти́* *perf*); **to** ~ **in(to)** (*house*) въезжа́ть (въе́хать* *perf*) (в +*acc*)
▶ **move off** *vi* отъезжа́ть (отъе́хать* *perf*)
▶ **move on** *vi* (*leave*) направля́ться (напра́виться* *perf*) да́льше ♦ *vt* (*onlookers*) продвига́ть (продви́нуть *perf*)
▶ **move out** *vi* (*of house*) выезжа́ть (вы́ехать* *perf*)
▶ **move over** *vi* (*to make room*) подвига́ться (подви́нуться *perf*)
▶ **move up** *vi* (*be promoted*) продвига́ться (продви́нуться *perf*).
moveable ['mu:vəbl] *adj* = **movable**.
movement ['mu:vmənt] *n* (*action, also POL, REL*) движе́ние; (*between two fixed points*) передвиже́ние; (*transportation: of goods etc*) перево́зка*; (*shift: in attitude, policy*) сдвиг; (*MUS*) часть* *f*.
mover ['mu:və*] *n* (*of proposal*) инициа́тор.
movie ['mu:vɪ] *n* фильм, кинофи́льм; **to go to the** ~**s** ходи́ть*/идти́* (пойти́* *perf*) в кино́.
movie camera *n* кинока́мера.
moviegoer ['mu:vɪɡəuə*] *n* (*US*) кинолюби́тель *m*.
moving ['mu:vɪŋ] *adj* (*emotional*) тро́гательный* (тро́гателен); (*mobile*) подви́жный* (подви́жен); (*spirit, force*) дви́жущий ♦ *n* (*US*) перее́зд.
mow [məu] (*pt* **mowed**, *pp* **mowed** *or* **mown**) *vt* (*grass*) подстрига́ть (подстри́чь* *perf*); (*hay*) коси́ть* (скоси́ть* *perf*)
▶ **mow down** *vt* (*kill*) коси́ть* (скоси́ть* *perf*).
mower ['məuə*] *n* коси́лка*.
mown [məun] *pp of* **mow**.
Mozambique [məuzəm'bi:k] *n* Мозамби́к.
MP *n abbr* (= *Member of Parliament*) член парла́мента; (= *Military Police*) вое́нная поли́ция; (*CANADA* = *Mounted Police*) ко́нная поли́ция.
mpg *n abbr* = *miles per gallon*.
mph *n abbr* = *miles per hour*.
MPhil *n abbr* (= *Master of Philosophy*) ≈ маги́стр филосо́фии.
MPS *n abbr* (*BRIT*) = *Member of the Pharmaceutical Society*.
Mr ['mɪstə*] (*US* **Mr.**) *n*: ~ **Smith** (*informal*) ми́стер Смит; (*formal*) г-н Смит= *господи́н*

Смит.

MRC *n abbr* (*BRIT*) = *Medical Research Council.*

MRCP *n abbr* (*BRIT*) = *Member of the Royal College of Physicians.*

MRCS *n abbr* (*BRIT*) = *Member of the Royal College of Surgeons.*

Mrs ['mɪsɪz] (*US* **Mrs.**) *n*: ~ **Smith** (*informal*) мйссис Смит; (*formal*) г-жа Смит= *госпожа Смит.*

Ms [mɪz] (*US* **Ms.**) *n* (= *Miss or Mrs*): ~ **Smith** г-жа Смит= *госпожа Смит.*

MS *n abbr* = **multiple sclerosis**; (*US*: = *Master of Science*) ≈ магистр естественных наук ♦ *abbr* (*US*: *POST*) = *Mississippi.*

MS. *n abbr* = **manuscript.**

MSA *n abbr* (*US*: = *Master of Science in Agriculture*) ≈ магистр сельско-хозяйственных наук.

MSc *n abbr* (= *Master of Science*) ≈ магистр естественных наук.

MSG *n abbr* = *monosodium glutamate.*

MSP *n abbr* = (*Member of the Scottish Parliament*) член шотландского парламента.

MST *abbr* (*US*) = *Mountain Standard Time.*

MSW *n abbr* (*US*: = *Master of Social Work*) ≈ магистр социологии.

MT *n abbr* (*COMPUT, LING*: = *machine translation*) МП= *машинный перевод* ♦ *abbr* (*US*: *POST*) = *Montana.*

Mt *abbr* (*GEO*) = *mount.*

MTV *n abbr* (*US*) = *music television.*

KEYWORD

much [mʌtʃ] *adj* (*time, money, effort*) много +*gen*; **we haven't got much time/money** у нас не так много времени/денег; **how much money/time do you need?** сколько денег/времени Вам нужно?; **he's spent so much money today** он сегодня потратил столько денег; **I have as much money as you (do)** у меня столько же денег, сколько у Вас; **I don't have as much time as you do** у меня нет столько времени, сколько у Вас
♦ *pron*: **there isn't much to do here** здесь нечего делать; **much is still unclear** многое ещё неясно; **much has been gained from our discussions** наша дискуссия дала большие результаты *or* многое; **how much does it cost? – too much** сколько это стоит? – слишком дорого; **how much is it?** почём это?
♦ *adv* **1** (*greatly, a great deal*): **thank you very much** большое спасибо; **we are very much looking forward to your visit** мы очень ждём Вашего приезда; **he is very much a gentleman/politician** он настоящий джентльмен/политик; **however much he tries** сколько бы он ни старался; **I try to help**

as much as possible *or* **as much as I can** я стараюсь помогать как можно больше *or* сколько могу; **I read as much as ever** я читаю столько же, сколько прежде; **he is as much a member of the family as you** он такой же член семьи, как и Вы
2 (*by far*) намного, гораздо; **I'm much better now** мне намного *or* гораздо лучше; **it's much the biggest publishing company in Europe** это самое крупное издательство в Европе
3 (*almost*) почти; **the view from my window today is much as it was 10 years ago** вид из моего окна сегодня сейчас почти такой же, как и 10 лет назад; **how are you feeling? – much the same** как Вы себя чувствуете? – всё так же.

---

muck [mʌk] *n* (*dirt*) грязь* *f*; (*manure*) навоз
► **muck about** *vi* (*inf*) валять (*impf*) дурака; (*tinker*): **to ~ about with** возиться* (*impf*) с +*instr*
► **muck around** *vi* = **muck about**
► **muck in** *vi* (*inf*) впрягаться (впрячься* *perf*)
► **muck out** *vt* (*stable*) выгребать (выгрести* *perf*) навоз из +*gen*
► **muck up** *vt* (*inf*) заваливать (завалить* *perf*).
muckraking ['mʌkreɪkɪŋ] *n* (*fig: inf*) копание в грязном белье.
mucky ['mʌkɪ] *adj* грязный* (грязен).
mucus ['mju:kəs] *n* слизь *f*.
mud [mʌd] *n* грязь* *f*.
muddle ['mʌdl] *n* (*mess*) беспорядок*; (*mix-up*) неразбериха, путаница ♦ *vt* (*also:* ~ **up**: *person*) запутывать (запутать *perf*); (: *things*) перемешивать (перемешать *perf*); (: *story, names*) путать (перепутать *perf*); **to get in(to) a** ~ (*while explaining etc*) запутываться (запутаться *perf*); **I'm in a real** ~ я совершенно запутался
► **muddle along** *vi* справляться (*impf*) кое-как
► **muddle through** *vi* выкарабкиваться (выкарабкаться *perf*).
muddleheaded [mʌdl'hɛdɪd] *adj* бестолковый (бестолков).
muddy ['mʌdɪ] *adj* грязный* (грязен).
mud flats *npl* илистые участки *mpl* (*вскрывающиеся во время отлива*).
mudguard ['mʌdgɑ:d] *n* (*on vehicle*) крыло*.
mudpack ['mʌdpæk] *n* грязевая маска*.
mudslinging ['mʌdslɪŋɪŋ] *n* (*fig*) поливание грязью.
muesli ['mju:zlɪ] *n* смесь овсяных хлопьев и сухофруктов.
muffin ['mʌfɪn] *n* (*BRIT*) (сдобная) булочка; (*US*) кекс.
muffle ['mʌfl] *vt* (*sound*) приглушать (приглушить *perf*); (*against cold: also:* ~ **up**)

закутывать (закутать *perf*).
muffled ['mʌfld] *adj* (*see vb*) приглушённый
(приглушён); (*also:* ~ **up**) закутанный.
muffler ['mʌfləʳ] *n* (*US: AUT*) глушитель *m*;
(*scarf*) шарф.
mufti ['mʌftɪ] *n*: **in** ~ в штатском.
mug [mʌg] *n* кружка*; (*inf: face*) морда; (: *fool*)
дурак* (дура) ♦ *vt* (*assault*) грабить*
(ограбить* *perf*) (*на улице*); **it's a** ~'s **game**
(*BRIT: inf*) это никчёмное дело
▶ **mug up** *vt* (*BRIT: inf: also:* ~ **up on**) зубрить*
(вызубрить *perf*).
mugger ['mʌgəʳ] *n* уличный грабитель *m*.
mugging ['mʌgɪŋ] *n* грабёж* (*на улице*).
muggins ['mʌgɪnz] *n* (*inf*) простак*.
muggy ['mʌgɪ] *adj* душный* (душен).
mug shot *n* (*inf*) фотография
подозреваемого в преступлении.
mulatto [mjuː'lætəu] (*pl* ~**es**) *n* мулат(ка*).
mulberry ['mʌlbrɪ] *n* (*fruit*) тутовая ягода;
(*tree*) тутовое дерево*, шелковица.
mule [mjuːl] *n* (*ZOOL*) мул.
mulled wine [mʌld-] *n* глинтвейн.
mullioned ['mʌlɪənd] *adj* (*ARCHIT*): ~ **window**
окно сп средником.
mull over [mʌl-] *vt* размышлять (*impf*) над
+*instr*.
multi... [['mʌltɪ]] *prefix* много..., мульти....
multiaccess ['mʌltɪ'æksɛs] *adj* (*COMPUT*)
многопользовательский*.
multicoloured ['mʌltɪkʌləd] (*US* **multicolored**)
adj многоцветный* (многоцветен).
multifarious [mʌltɪ'fɛərɪəs] *adj*
многообразный* (многообразен).
multilateral [mʌltɪ'lætərl] *adj*
многосторонний*.
multilevel ['mʌltɪlɛvl] *adj* (*US*) = **multistorey**.
multimillionaire [mʌltɪmɪljə'nɛəʳ] *n*
мультимиллионер.
multinational [mʌltɪ'næʃənl] *adj*
международный ♦ *n* международная
корпорация.
multiple ['mʌltɪpl] *adj* (*injuries*) много-
численный; (*interests*) разнообразный*
(разнообразен) ♦ *n* (*MATH*) кратное число*;
(*BRIT: also:* ~ **store**) филиал сети (*магазинов*);
~ **collision** столкновение нескольких
автомобилей.
multiple-choice ['mʌltɪpltʃɔɪs] *adj*: ~ (**exam**)
тест на выбор, правильного ответа из
нескольких предложенных вариантов.
multiple sclerosis *n* рассеянный склероз.
multiplication [mʌltɪplɪ'keɪʃən] *n* умножение.
multiplication table *n* таблица умножения.
multiplicity [mʌltɪ'plɪsɪtɪ] *n*: **a** ~ **of** множество
+*gen*.
multiply ['mʌltɪplaɪ] *vt* умножать (умножить
perf) ♦ *vi* размножаться (размножиться *perf*).
multiracial [mʌltɪ'reɪʃl] *adj* много-
национальный* (многонационален).
multistorey ['mʌltɪ'stɔːrɪ] *adj* (*BRIT*)

многоэтажный.
multitude ['mʌltɪtjuːd] *n* (*crowd*) массы *fpl*;
(*large number*): **a** ~ **of** множество +*gen*.
mum [mʌm] (*BRIT: inf*) *n* мама ♦ *adj*: **to keep** ~
about sth помалкивать (*impf*) о чём-н;
"mum's the word!" „молчу!".
mumble ['mʌmbl] *vt* бормотать*
(пробормотать* *perf*) ♦ *vi* бормотать (*impf*).
mumbo jumbo ['mʌmbəu-] *n* (*inf*)
тарабарщина.
mummify ['mʌmɪfaɪ] *vt* мумифицировать
(*impf/perf*).
mummy ['mʌmɪ] *n* (*BRIT: inf: mother*) мама;
(*embalmed corpse*) мумия.
mumps [mʌmps] *n* свинка.
munch [mʌntʃ] *vti* (*chew*) жевать (*impf*).
mundane [mʌn'deɪn] *adj* обыденный
(обыден).
Munich ['mjuːnɪk] *n* Мюнхен.
municipal [mjuː'nɪsɪpl] *adj* муниципальный.
municipality [mjuːnɪsɪ'pælɪtɪ] *n* город*;
(*authority*) муниципалитет.
munitions [mjuː'nɪʃənz] *npl* боеприпасы *mpl*.
mural ['mjuərl] *n* настенная роспись *f*, фреска.
murder ['məːdəʳ] *n* убийство (*умышленное*) ♦
vt (*kill*) убивать (убить* *perf*) (*умышленно*);
(*fig: inf*) угробить* (*perf*); **to commit** ~
совершать (совершить *perf*) убийство.
murderer ['məːdərəʳ] *n* убийца *m/f*.
murderess ['məːdərɪs] *n* убийца *m/f*.
murderous ['məːdərəs] *adj* (*dictator, regime*)
кровавый; (*look*) убийственный; (*attack*)
смертоносный* (смертоносен); ~ **tendencies**
склонность *f* к убийству.
murk [məːk] *n* мгла.
murky ['məːkɪ] *adj* (*street, night*) мрачный*
(мрачен); (*water*) мутный* (мутен).
murmur ['məːməʳ] *n* (*of voices, waves*) ропот;
(*of wind*) шелест ♦ *vti* шептать* (*impf*); **heart** ~
шумы *mpl* в сердце.
MusB(ac) *n abbr* (= *Bachelor of Music*)
бакалавр музыковедения.
muscle ['mʌsl] *n* (*ANAT*) мышца, мускул; (*fig:
strength*) сила.
▶ **muscle in** *vi* пролезать (пролезть* *perf*).
Muscovite ['mʌskəvaɪt] *n* москвич*(ка*).
muscular ['mʌskjulə] *adj* (*pain, injury*)
мышечный; (*person, build*) мускулистый
(мускулист).
muscular dystrophy *adj* мускульная
дистрофия.
MusD(oc) *n abbr* (= *Doctor of Music*) доктор
музыковедения.
muse [mjuːz] *vi* размышлять (*impf*) ♦ *n* муза.
museum [mjuː'zɪəm] *n* музей.
mush [mʌʃ] *n* месиво; (*pej*) масса.
mushroom ['mʌʃrum] *n* гриб* ♦ *vi* (*fig*) быстро
разрастаться (разрастись* *perf*).
mushroom cloud *n* атомный гриб*.
mushy ['mʌʃɪ] *adj* разварившийся, как каша;
(*inf. pej: story, fiction*) слащавый (слащав); ~

peas горо́шек.

music ['mjuːzɪk] *n* му́зыка; **sheet** ~ но́ты *fpl.*

musical ['mjuːzɪkl] *adj (career, skills)* музыка́льный; *(person)* музыка́льный* (музыка́лен); *(sound, tune)* мелоди́чный* (мелоди́чен) ♦ *n (show, film)* мю́зикл.

music(al) box *n* музыка́льная шкату́лка*.

musical chairs *n* ≈ тре́тий ли́шний* *m adj* (игра́).

musical instrument *n* музыка́льный инструме́нт.

music centre *n* де́ка с прои́грывателем и магнитофо́ном.

music hall *n (BRIT: vaudeville)* мю́зик-холл.

musician [mjuːˈzɪʃən] *n* музыка́нт.

music stand *n* пюпи́тр.

musk [mʌsk] *n* му́скус.

musket ['mʌskɪt] *n* мушке́т.

muskrat ['mʌskræt] *n* онда́тра.

musk rose *n* му́скусная ро́за.

Muslim ['mʌzlɪm] *n* мусульма́нин*(-нка*) ♦ *adj* мусульма́нский*.

muslin ['mʌzlɪn] *n* ма́рля.

musquash ['mʌskwɒʃ] *n* = **muskrat.**

mussel ['mʌsl] *n* ми́дия.

must [mʌst] *n (necessity)* необходи́мость *f* ♦ *aux vb (necessity)*: **I** ~ **do it** я до́лжен э́то сде́лать; *(probability)*: **he** ~ **be there by now** он до́лжен уже́ там быть; **it's (simply) a** ~ э́то про́сто необходи́мость; **you** ~ **come and see me soon** Вы обяза́тельно должны́ ско́ро ко мне зайти́; **why** ~ **he behave so badly?** отчего́ он так пло́хо себя́ ведёт?; **I** ~ **have made a mistake** я, должно́ быть, оши́бся.

mustache ['mʌstæʃ] *n (US)* = **moustache.**

mustard ['mʌstəd] *n* горчи́ца.

mustard gas *n* ипри́т, горчи́чный газ.

muster ['mʌstə'] *vt (support, energy)* собира́ть (собра́ть* *perf)*; *(troops)* набира́ть (набра́ть* *perf)*; *(also:* ~ **up: strength, courage)** набира́ться (набра́ться* *perf)* +gen.

mustiness ['mʌstɪnɪs] *n* за́тхлость *f.*

mustn't ['mʌsnt] = **must not.**

musty ['mʌstɪ] *adj (smell)* за́тхлый (затхл).

mutant ['mjuːtənt] *n* мута́нт.

mutate [mjuːˈteɪt] *vi (BIO)* мути́ровать *(impf).*

mutation [mjuːˈteɪʃən] *n (BIO)* мута́ция; *(change)* преобразова́ния *ntpl.*

mute [mjuːt] *adj (silent)* безмо́лвный* (безмо́лвен) ♦ *n (MUS)* сурди́нка.

muted ['mjuːtɪd] *adj (reaction, criticism)* сде́ржанный* (сде́ржан); *(colour, noise)* приглушённый (приглушён); ~ **strings** стру́ны под сурди́нкой.

mutilate ['mjuːtɪleɪt] *vt (person)* уве́чить (изуве́чить *perf)*; *(thing)* уро́довать (изуро́довать *perf).*

mutilation [mjuːtɪˈleɪʃən] *n (injury)* уве́чье*; *(maiming)* нанесе́ние уве́чья.

mutinous ['mjuːtɪnəs] *adj (troops, attitude)* мяте́жный*.

mutiny ['mjuːtɪnɪ] *n* мяте́ж*, бунт ♦ *vi* бунтова́ть *(impf).*

mutter ['mʌtə'] *vti* бормота́ть* *(impf).*

mutton ['mʌtn] *n* бара́нина.

mutual ['mjuːtʃuəl] *adj (feeling)* взаи́мный* (взаи́мен); *(help)* взаи́мный; *(friend, interest)* о́бщий*; ~ **understanding** взаимопонима́ние; ~ **aid** взаимопо́мощь *f.*

mutually ['mjuːtʃuəlɪ] *adv* взаи́мно; ~ **beneficial** взаимовы́годный* (взаимовы́годен).

Muzak® ['mjuːzæk] *n* бессодержа́тельная лёгкая му́зыка, испо́льзуемая в магази́нах и рестора́нах как фон.

muzzle ['mʌzl] *n (mouth: of dog)* мо́рда; *(: of gun)* ду́ло; *(guard: for dog)* намо́рдник ♦ *vt (dog)* надева́ть (наде́ть* *perf)* намо́рдник на +acc; *(fig: press, person)* затыка́ть (заткну́ть *perf)* рот +dat.

MV *abbr* = **motor vessel.**

MVP *n abbr (US: SPORT:* = **most valuable player)** са́мый це́нный игро́к.

MW *abbr (RADIO)* (= **medium wave)** СВ= сре́дние во́лны.

my [maɪ] *adj* **1** *(with objects, possessions)* мой; **this is my house/car** э́то мой дом/моя́ маши́на; **is this my pen or yours?** э́то моя́ ру́чка или ва́ша?
2 *(with parts of the body etc)*: **I've washed my hair/cut my finger** я помы́л го́лову/поре́зал па́лец
3 *(referring to subject of sentence)* свой; **I've lost my key** я потеря́л свой ключ.

myopic [maɪˈɒpɪk] *adj (also fig)* близору́кий* (близору́к).

myriad ['mɪrɪəd] *n* мириа́ды *mpl.*

myrrh [mɜː'] *n* ми́рра.

myself [maɪˈsɛlf] *pron* **1** *(reflexive)*: **I've hurt myself** я уши́бся; **I consider myself clever** я счита́ю себя́ у́мным
2 *(complement)*: **she's the same age as myself** она́ одного́ во́зраста со мной
3 *(after prep: +gen)* себя́; *(: +dat, +prp)* себе́; *(: +instr)* собо́й; **I wanted to keep the book for myself** я хоте́л оста́вить кни́гу себе́; **I sometimes talk to myself** иногда́ я сам с собо́й разгова́риваю; **(all) by myself** *(alone)* сам; **I made it all by myself** я всё э́то сде́лал сам; **I myself chose the flowers** я сам выбира́л цветы́.

mysterious [mɪsˈtɪərɪəs] *adj* таи́нственный* (таи́нствен).

mysteriously [mɪsˈtɪərɪəslɪ] *adv (disappear, die)*

таинственно; (*smile*) загадочно.
mystery ['mɪstərɪ] *n* (*strangeness*) тайна;
  (*puzzle*) загадка* ◆ *cpd* (*tour, guest, voice*)
  загадочный.
mystery story *n* детектив.
mystic ['mɪstɪk] *n* мистик ◆ *adj* мистический.
mystical ['mɪstɪkl] *adj* = **mystic**.
mystify ['mɪstɪfaɪ] *vt* (*perplex*) озадачивать

(озадачить *perf*).
mystique [mɪs'tiːk] *n* мистика.
myth [mɪθ] *n* миф.
mythical ['mɪθɪkl] *adj* (*also fig*) мифический*.
mythological [mɪθə'lɔdʒɪkl] *adj*
  мифологический.
mythology [mɪ'θɔlədʒɪ] *n* мифология.

~ *N, n* ~

N, n [ɛn] *n* (*letter*) 14-ая бу́ква англи́йского алфави́та.

N *abbr* (= *north*) С= се́вер.

NA *n abbr* (*US*: = *Narcotics Anonymous*) о́бщество анони́много излече́ния от наркома́нии; = *National Academy*.

n/a *abbr* (= *not applicable*) не применя́ется; (*COMM etc*: = *no account*) счёт отсу́тствует.

NAACP *n abbr* (*US*) = *National Association for the Advancement of Colored People*.

NAAFI ['næfɪ] *n abbr* (*BRIT*: = *Navy, Army & Air Force Institute*) Институ́т а́рмии, вое́нно-морско́го и вое́нно-возду́шного фло́та.

NACU *n abbr* (*US*) = *National Association of Colleges and Universities*.

nadir ['neɪdɪəʳ] *n* (*ASTRONOMY*) нади́р; (*fig*) ни́зшая то́чка.

nag [næg] *vt* (*scold*) пили́ть* (*impf*) ◆ *vi*: **to ~ at** ныть (*impf*) (из-за +*gen*) ◆ *n* (*pej: horse*) кля́ча; (: *person*): **she's an awful ~** она́ жу́ткая зану́да.

nagging ['nægɪŋ] *adj* (*pain*) ною́щий; (*suspicion, doubt*) неотвя́зный.

nail [neɪl] *n* (*on finger etc*) но́готь* *m*; (*metal*) гвоздь* *m* ◆ *vt* (*inf: catch*) засту́кивать (засту́кать *perf*); **to ~ sth to sth** прибива́ть (приби́ть* *perf*) что-н к чему́-н; **to ~ sb down to doing** (*inf*) прижима́ть (прижа́ть* *perf*) кого́-н к сте́нке и заста́вить* +*infin*.

nailbrush ['neɪlbrʌʃ] *n* щёточка* для ногте́й.

nailfile ['neɪlfaɪl] *n* пи́лка* (*для ногте́й*).

nail polish *n* лак для ногте́й.

nail polish remover *n* жи́дкость *f* для сня́тия ла́ка.

nail scissors *npl* маникю́рные но́жницы *pl*.

nail varnish *n* (*BRIT*) = *nail polish*.

Nairobi [naɪ'rəubɪ] *n* Найро́би *m ind*.

naive [naɪ'iːv] *adj* наи́вный* (наи́вен).

naiveté [naɪ'iːvteɪ] *n* = *naivety*.

naivety [naɪ'iːvtɪ] *n* наи́вность *f*.

naked ['neɪkɪd] *adj* (*also fig*) го́лый* (гол); (*anger*) не скрыва́емый; **with the ~ eye** невооружённым гла́зом.

nakedness ['neɪkɪdnɪs] *n* нагота́.

NAM *n abbr* (*US*) = *National Association of Manufacturers*.

name [neɪm] *n* (*of person*) и́мя* *nt*; (*of place, object, species*) назва́ние; (*of pet*) кли́чка* ◆ *vt* называ́ть (назва́ть* *perf*); **what's your ~?** как Вас зову́т?; **my ~ is Peter** меня́ зову́т Пи́тер; **what's the ~ of this place?** как называ́ется э́то ме́сто?; **by ~** по и́мени; **in the ~ of** во и́мя +*gen*; **to give one's ~ and address** (*to police etc*) дава́ть* (дать* *perf*) своё и́мя и а́дрес; **to make a ~ for o.s.** создава́ть* (созда́ть* *perf*) себе́ и́мя; **to get (o.s.) a bad ~** зараба́тывать (зарабо́тать *(perf)*) себе́ дурну́ю репута́цию; **to call sb ~s** обзыва́ть (обозва́ть* *perf*) кого́-н.

name-dropping ['neɪmdrɔpɪŋ] *n* упомина́ние изве́стных имён.

nameless ['neɪmlɪs] *adj* (*unknown*) безымя́нный* (безымя́нен); (*anonymous*) неизве́стный* (неизве́стен).

namely ['neɪmlɪ] *adv* а и́менно.

nameplate ['neɪmpleɪt] *n* табли́чка* (*с и́менем*).

namesake ['neɪmseɪk] *n* тёзка* *m/f*.

Namibia [nə'mɪbɪə] *n* Нами́бия.

nan bread [nɑː-] *n* инди́йский* хлеб в фо́рме лепёшки.

nanny ['nænɪ] *n* ня́ня.

nanny goat *n* коза́*.

nap [næp] *n* коро́ткий сон; (*of fabric*) ворс ◆ *vi*: **he was caught ~ping** (*fig*) его́ заста́ли врасплёх; **to have** *or* **take a ~** вздремну́ть *(perf)*.

NAPA *n abbr* (*US*) = *National Association of Performing Artists*.

napalm ['neɪpɑːm] *n* напа́лм.

nape [neɪp] *n*: **~ of the neck** за́дняя часть *f* ше́и.

napkin ['næpkɪn] *n* (*also:* **table ~**) салфе́тка*.

Naples ['neɪplz] *n* Неа́поль *m*.

Napoleonic [nəpəulɪ'ɔnɪk] *adj* наполео́новский.

nappy ['næpɪ] *n* (*BRIT*) подгу́зник.

nappy liner *n* (*BRIT*) прокла́дка для подгу́зника.

nappy rash *n* (*BRIT*) потни́ца.

narcissi [nɑː'sɪsaɪ] *npl of* **narcissus**.

narcissistic [nɑːsɪ'sɪstɪk] *adj* самовлюблённый.

narcissus [nɑː'sɪsəs] (*pl* **narcissi**) *n* (*BOT*)
нарци́сс.
narcotic [nɑː'kɔtɪk] *adj* наркоти́ческий ♦ *n*
(*MED*) снотво́рное *nt adj*; ~**s** *npl* (*drugs*)
нарко́тики *mpl*.
nark [nɑːk] *vt* (*BRIT: inf*) раздража́ть
(раздражи́ть *perf*).
narrate [nə'reɪt] *vt* (*story, novel*) расска́зывать
(рассказа́ть* *perf*); **to ~ a film/programme**
чита́ть (*impf*) текст фи́льма/переда́чи.
narration [nə'reɪʃən] *n* повествова́ние.
narrative ['nærətɪv] *n* исто́рия.
narrator [nə'reɪtə'] *n* (*in book*)
расска́зчик(-ица); (*in film*) ди́ктор.
narrow ['nærəʊ] *adj* (*also fig*) у́зкий* (у́зок);
(*majority, advantage*) незначи́тельный*
(незначи́телен) ♦ *vi* (*road*) сужа́ться
(су́зиться* *perf*); (*gap, difference*)
уменьша́ться (уме́ньшиться *perf*) ♦ *vt*: **to ~**
sth down to своди́ть* (свести́* *perf*) что-н к
+*dat*; **to have a ~ escape** едва́ спасти́сь* (*perf*).
narrow-gauge ['nærəʊgeɪdʒ] *adj* (*RAIL*)
узкоколе́йный.
narrowly ['nærəʊlɪ] *adv* (*miss*) чуть не;
(*interpret*) у́зко; **he only ~ avoided injury/**
defeat он чуть не покале́чился/проигра́л; **he**
only ~ missed the target он почти́ попа́л в
цель.
narrow-minded [nærəʊ'maɪndɪd] *adj*
ограни́ченный (ограни́чен).
narrowness ['nærəʊnɪs] *n* у́зость *f*.
NAS *n abbr* (*US*) = National Academy of Sciences.
NASA ['næsə] *n abbr* (*US*: = National Aeronautics
and Space Administration) НАСА.
nasal ['neɪzl] *adj* (*ANAT*) носово́й; (*tone, voice*)
гнуса́вый.
Nassau ['næsɔː] *n* Насса́у *m ind*.
nastily ['nɑːstɪlɪ] *adv* зло́бно.
nastiness ['nɑːstɪnɪs] *n* (*unpleasantness*)
проти́вность *f*; (*spitefulness*) зло́бность *f*.
nasturtium [nəs'təːʃəm] *n* насту́рция.
nasty ['nɑːstɪ] *adj* (*unpleasant*) проти́вный*
(проти́вен); (*malicious*) зло́бный* (зло́бен);
(*situation, wound*) скве́рный* (скве́рен); **to**
say ~ things about sb говори́ть (*impf*) га́дости
о ком-н; **to turn ~** (*situation*) принима́ть
(приня́ть* *perf*) скве́рный оборо́т; (*weather*)
де́латься (сде́латься *perf*) скве́рным;
(*person*) озлобля́ться (озло́биться* *perf*); **it's**
a ~ business э́то ме́рзкое де́ло.
NAS/UWT *n abbr* (*BRIT*) = National Association
of Schoolmasters/Union of Women Teachers.
nation ['neɪʃən] *n* (*POL*) на́ция; (*people*) наро́д;
(*state*) страна́, госуда́рство.
national ['næʃənl] *adj* национа́льный ♦ *n*
граждани́н*(-да́нка*).
national anthem *n* госуда́рственный гимн.
national curriculum *n* (*BRIT*) всеобщая
програ́мма (обуче́ния) (*в шко́лах*).
national debt *n* госуда́рственный долг*.
national dress *n* национа́льная оде́жда.

National Guard *n* (*US*) Национа́льная
гва́рдия.
National Health Service *n* (*BRIT*)
Госуда́рственная слу́жба здравоохране́ния.
National Insurance *n* (*BRIT*) госуда́рственное
страхова́ние.
nationalism ['næʃnəlɪzəm] *n* национали́зм.
nationalist ['næʃnəlɪst] *adj* националист-
и́ческий ♦ *n* национали́ст(ка*).
nationality [næʃə'nælɪtɪ] *n* (*status*)
гражда́нство; (*ethnic group*) наро́дность *f*.
nationalization [næʃnəlaɪ'zeɪʃən] *n*
национализа́ция.
nationalize ['næʃnəlaɪz] *vt* национализ-
и́ровать (*impf/perf*).
nationalized industry ['næʃnəlaɪzd-] *n*
национализи́рованная промы́шленность *f*.
nationally ['næʃnəlɪ] *adv* (*nationwide*) в
национа́льном всей страны́.
national park *n* национа́льный па́рк.
national press *n* национа́льная пре́сса.
National Security Council *n* (*US*) Сове́т
национа́льной безопа́сности.
national service *n* (*MIL: esp BRIT*) во́инская
пови́нность *f*.
National Trust *n* (*BRIT*) *организа́ция,*
занима́ющаяся охра́ной архитекту́рных
па́мятников и приро́дных запове́дников.
nationwide ['neɪʃənwaɪd] *adj* общенаро́дный
♦ *adv* по всей стране́.
native ['neɪtɪv] *n* (*local inhabitant*)
ме́стный(-ая) жи́тель(ница) *m(f)* ♦ *adj*
(*indigenous*) коренно́й, исконный; (*of one's*
birth) родно́й; (*innate*) врождённый; **a ~ of**
Russia уроже́нец(-нка*) Росси́и; **a ~ speaker**
of Russian носи́тель(ница) *m(f)* ру́сского
языка́.
Native American *n* *пото́мок коренно́го*
населе́ния Се́веро-Америка́нского
контине́нта.
native language *n* родно́й язы́к*.
Nativity [nə'tɪvɪtɪ] *n*: **the ~** Рождество́
Христо́во.
nativity play *n* Рожде́ственская мисте́рия
(*обы́чно разы́грываемая детьми́*).
NATO ['neɪtəʊ] *n abbr* (= North Atlantic Treaty
Organization) НАТО.
natter ['nætə'] (*BRIT*) *vi* трепа́ться* (*impf*) ♦ *n*: **to**
have a ~ трепа́ться* (потрепа́ться* *perf*).
natural ['nætʃrəl] *adj* (*behaviour*) есте́ственный
(есте́ствен); (*aptitude, materials*) приро́дный;
(*foods*) натура́льный; (*disaster*) стихи́йный;
to die of ~ causes умира́ть (умере́ть* *perf*)
есте́ственной сме́ртью.
natural childbirth *n* есте́ственные ро́ды *pl*.
natural gas *n* приро́дный газ.
natural history *n* естествозна́ние.
naturalist ['nætʃrəlɪst] *n* натурали́ст.
naturalize ['nætʃrəlaɪz] *vt*: **to become ~d**
(*person*) получа́ть (получи́ть* *perf*)
гражда́нство; (*plant*) акклиматизи́роваться

(impf/perf).

naturally ['nætʃrəlɪ] *adv* естественно; (*innately*) от природы; (*in nature*) в природе; ~, I **refused** естественно, я отказался.

naturalness ['nætʃrəlnɪs] *n* естественность *f*.

natural resources *npl* природные ресурсы *mpl*.

natural selection *n* (*BIO*) естественный отбор.

natural wastage *n* (*INDUSTRY*) естественная убыль* *f* (*рабочей силы*).

nature ['neɪtʃə'] *n* (*also:* **N~**) природа; (*character*) натура; (*sort*) характер; **by ~** (*person*) по натуре; (*event, thing*) по природе; **documents of a confidential ~** документы конфиденциального характера.

-natured ['neɪtʃəd] *suffix*: **ill-~** злобный по натуре.

nature reserve *n* (*BRIT*) заповедник.

nature trail *n* размеченная тропа, проходящая через сельскую местность, заповедник *итп*.

naturist ['neɪtʃərɪst] *n* нудист(ка*).

naught [nɔ:t] *n* = **nought**.

naughtiness ['nɔ:tɪnɪs] *n* (*see adj*) непослушание, озорство; пикантность *f*.

naughty ['nɔ:tɪ] *adj* (*child*) непослушный* (непослушен), озорной; (*story, film*) пикантный* (пикантен).

nausea ['nɔ:sɪə] *n* тошнота.

nauseate ['nɔ:sɪeɪt] *vt* (*also fig*) вызывать (вызвать* *perf*) тошноту в +*prp or* у +*gen*.

nauseating ['nɔ:sɪeɪtɪŋ] *adj* (*also fig*) тошнотворный* (тошнотворен).

nauseous ['nɔ:sɪəs] *adj* тошнотворный* (тошнотворен); **he's feeling ~** его тошнит.

nautical ['nɔ:tɪkl] *adj* морской.

naval ['neɪvl] *adj* военно-морской; (*battle, power*) морской.

naval officer *n* военно-морской офицер.

nave [neɪv] *n* неф.

navel ['neɪvl] *n* пупок*.

navigable ['nævɪgəbl] *adj* судоходный* (судоходен).

navigate ['nævɪgeɪt] *vt* (*NAUT, AVIAT*) управлять (*impf*) +*instr* ◆ *vi* определять (определить *perf*) маршрут; **to ~ a ship through/around** вести* (провести* *perf*) корабль через +*acc*/вокруг +*gen*.

navigation [nævɪ'geɪʃən] *n* (*science*) навигация; (*action*): ~ (**of**) управление (+*instr*).

navigator ['nævɪgeɪtə'] *n* штурман.

navvy ['nævɪ] *n* (*BRIT*) чернорабочий* *m adj*.

navy ['neɪvɪ] *n* военно-морской флот; **Department of the N~** (*US*) ≈ Министерство военно-морского флота.

navy(-blue) ['neɪvɪ('blu:)] *adj* тёмно-синий*.

Nazareth ['næzərɪθ] *n* Назарет.

Nazi ['nɑ:tsɪ] *n* нацист(ка*).

NB *abbr* = *nota bene*; (*note well!*) NB, нотабене; (*CANADA*) = *New Brunswick*.

NBA *n abbr* (*US*) = *National Basketball Association*; *National Boxing Association*.

NBC *n abbr* (*US*) = *National Broadcasting Company*.

NBS *n abbr* (*US*) = *National Bureau of Standards*.

NC *abbr* (*COMM etc*: = *no charge*) бесплатно; (*US*: *POST*) = *North Carolina*.

NCC *n abbr* (*BRIT*) = *Nature Conservancy Council*; (*US*) *National Council of Churches*.

NCCL *n abbr* (*BRIT*: = *National Council for Civil Liberties*) Национальный совет по гражданским правам.

NCO *n abbr* (*MIL*) = *noncommissioned officer*.

ND *abbr* (*US*: *POST*) = *North Dakota*.

NE *abbr* (*US*: *POST*) = *New England*; *Nebraska*.

NEA *n abbr* (*US*) = *National Education Association*.

neap [ni:p] *n* (*also*: ~ **tide**) квадратурный прилив.

Neapolitan [nɪə'pɔlɪtən] *adj* неаполитанский* ◆ *n* неаполитанец(-нка*).

near [nɪə'] *adj* близкий* (близок) ◆ *adv* близко ◆ *prep* (*also*: ~ **to**: *space*) возле +*gen*, около +*gen*; (: *time*) к +*dat*, около +*gen* ◆ *vt* приближаться (приблизиться* *perf*) к +*dat*; ~ **here/there** недалеко отсюда/оттуда; **£25,000 or ~est offer** (*BRIT*) цена £25.000 или по договорённости; **in the ~ future** в ближайшем будущем; ~**er (to) the time** около положенной даты; **to come ~ (to)** (*also fig*) приближаться (приблизиться* *perf*) (к +*dat*); **he was ~ to despair/victory** он был близок к отчаянию/победе; **the building is ~ing completion** строительство приближается к завершению.

nearby [nɪə'baɪ] *adj* близлежащий ◆ *adv* поблизости.

Near East *n*: **the ~ ~** Ближний* Восток.

nearer ['nɪərə'] *adj, adv* ближе.

nearly ['nɪəlɪ] *adv* почти; **I ~ fell** я чуть (было) не упал; **she was ~ crying** она почти плакала; **it's not ~ as easy as it looks** это отнюдь не так просто, как кажется; **the house is not ~ big enough** дом совсем мал.

near miss *n* (*failed attempt*): **that was a ~ ~!** промахнулся!; **we had a ~ ~ in the car today** мы сегодня чуть не попали в аварию.

nearness ['nɪənɪs] *n* близость *f*.

nearside ['nɪəsaɪd] *n* (*AUT*: *in Britain*) левая сторона; (: *in US, Europe etc*) правая сторона.

near-sighted [nɪə'saɪtɪd] *adj* близорукий* (близорук).

neat [ni:t] *adj* (*person, place*) опрятный* (опрятен); (*work*) аккуратный* (аккуратен);

---

* marks translations which have irregular inflections. The Russian-English side of the dictionary gives inflectional information.

(*clear: categories*) чёткий* (чёток); (*esp US: inf*) клáссный* (клáссен); (*alcohol*) неразбáвленный.

neatly ['ni:tlɪ] *adv* (*dress*) опрятно; (*work*) аккурáтно; (*sum up*) чётко.

neatness ['ni:tnɪs] *n* (*see adv*) опрятность *f*; аккурáтность *f*; чёткость *f*.

nebulous ['nɛbjuləs] *adj* (*concept, proposal*) тумáнный* (тумáнен).

necessarily ['nɛsɪsrɪlɪ] *adv* неизбéжно; **not** ~ не обязáтельно.

necessary ['nɛsɪsrɪ] *adj* необходúмый (необходúм); (*inevitable*) обязáтельный, неизбéжный; **if** ~ éсли необходúмо; **it's not** ~ э́то не обязáтельно; **it is** ~ **to/that** ... необходúмо +*infin*/чтóбы ....

necessitate [nɪ'sɛsɪteɪt] *vt* обуслóвливать (обуслóвить* *perf*).

necessity [nɪ'sɛsɪtɪ] *n* необходúмость *f*; **necessities** *npl* (*essentials*) предмéты *mpl* пéрвой необходúмости; **in case of** ~ в слýчае необходúмости.

neck [nɛk] *n* (*ANAT*) шéя; (*of garment*) вóрот; (*of bottle*) гóрлышко* ♦ *vi* (*inf*) миловáться (*impf*); ~ **and** ~ врóвень; **to stick one's** ~ **out** (*inf*) лезть* (*impf*) на рожóн; **to risk one's** ~ (*inf*) рисковáть (рискнýть *perf*) головóй.

necklace ['nɛklɪs] *n* ожерéлье.

neckline ['nɛklaɪn] *n* вырез.

necktie ['nɛktaɪ] *n* (*US*) гáлстук.

nectar ['nɛktə] *n* нектáр.

nectarine ['nɛktərɪn] *n* нектарúн.

NEDC *n abbr* (*BRIT*: = *National Economic Development Council*) Национáльный совéт экономúческого развúтия.

Neddy ['nɛdɪ] *n abbr* (*BRIT*: *inf*) = **NEDC**.

née [neɪ] *adj*: ~ **Scott** урождённая Скотт.

need [ni:d] *n* (*thing needed*) потрéбность *f*; (*deprivation*) нуждá; (*necessity*): ~ (**for**) нуждá (в +*prp*) ♦ *vt*: **I** ~ **time/money** мне нýжно врéмя/нужны дéньги; **there's no** ~ **to worry** нéзачем волновáться; **to be in** ~ **of, have** ~ **of** нуждáться (*impf*) в +*prp*; **in case of** ~ в слýчае необходúмости; **the** ~**s of industry** потрéбности промышленности; **£10 will meet my immediate** ~**s** £10 удовлетворят мои нýжды на дáнный момéнт; **I** ~ **to see him** мне нáдо *or* нýжно с ним увúдеться; **you don't** ~ **to leave yet** Вам ещё не порá идтú; **a signature is** ~**ed** трéбуется пóдпись.

needle ['ni:dl] *n* иглá, игóлка*; (*for knitting*) спúца ♦ *vt* (*fig: inf*) подкáлывать (подколóть *perf*).

needlecord ['ni:dlkɔ:d] *n* (*BRIT*) тóнкий* вельвéт.

needless ['ni:dlɪs] *adj* излúшний* (излúшен); ~ **to say** самó собóй разумéется.

needlessly ['ni:dlɪslɪ] *adv* напрáсно.

needlework ['ni:dlwə:k] *n* рукодéлие.

needn't ['ni:dnt] = **need not**; *see* **need**.

needy ['ni:dɪ] *adj* нуждáющийся; **the** ~ *npl* нуждáющиеся *pl adj*.

negation [nɪ'geɪʃən] *n* отрицáние.

negative ['nɛgətɪv] *adj* (*also ELEC*) отрицáтельный ♦ *n* (*LING*) отрицáние; (*PHOT*) негатúв; **to answer in the** ~ давáть* (дать* *perf*) отрицáтельный отвéт.

negative cash flow *n* отрицáтельный потóк налúчности.

negative equity *n* (*COMM*) отрицáтельная *or* негатúвная мáржа.

neglect [nɪ'glɛkt] *vt* (*child, work*) забрáсывать (забрóсить* *perf*); (*garden, area, health*) запускáть (запустúть* *perf*); (*duty*) пренебрегáть (пренебрéчь* *perf*) ♦ *n*: ~ (**of**) невнимáние (к +*dat*); (*duty*) пренебрежéние (+*instr*); **in a state of** ~ в запустéнии.

neglected [nɪ'glɛktɪd] *adj* (*animal, child*) забрóшенный (забрóшен).

neglectful [nɪ'glɛktful] *adj* небрéжный* (небрéжен); **to be** ~ **of sb** относúться* (*impf*) к комý-н без внимáния; **to be** ~ **of sth** пренебрегáть (пренебрéчь* *perf*) чем-н.

negligee ['nɛglɪʒeɪ] *n* пеньюáр.

negligence ['nɛglɪdʒəns] *n* халáтность *f*.

negligent ['nɛglɪdʒənt] *adj* халáтный* (халáтен); **to be** ~ **in** халáтно относúться* (*impf*) к +*dat*.

negligently ['nɛglɪdʒəntlɪ] *adv* (*irresponsibly*) халáтно; (*offhandedly*) небрéжно.

negligible ['nɛglɪdʒɪbl] *adj* ничтóжный* (ничтóжен).

negotiable [nɪ'gəʊʃɪəbl] *adj*: **the price/contract is** ~ цéну/контрáкт мóжно обсудúть; (*road*) проходúмый (проходúм); (*cheque, assets*): ~**/not negotiable** с прáвом/без прáва передáчи.

negotiate [nɪ'gəʊʃɪeɪt] *vt* (*treaty, transaction*) заключáть (заключúть *perf*); (*obstacle*) преодолевáть (преодолéть *perf*); (*bend in road*) огибáть (обогнýть *perf*) ♦ *vi*: **to** ~ (**with sb for sth**) вестú* (*impf*) переговóры (с кем-н о чём-н).

negotiating table [nɪ'gəʊʃɪeɪtɪŋ-] *n* стол* переговóров.

negotiation [nɪgəʊʃɪ'eɪʃən] *n* (*see vb*) заключéние; преодолéние; переговóры *mpl*; **to enter into** ~**s with sb** вступáть (вступúть* *perf*) в переговóры с кем-н.

negotiator [nɪ'gəʊʃɪeɪtə'] *n* учáстник переговóров.

Negress ['ni:grɪs] *n* негритянка*.

Negro ['ni:grəʊ] (*pl* ~**es**) *adj* негритянский* ♦ *n* (*old-fashioned*) негр(итянка*); (*pej*) чёрный(-ая) *m(f) adj*.

neigh [neɪ] *vi* ржать* (*impf*).

neighbor *etc* (*US*) = **neighbour** *etc*.

neighbour ['neɪbə'] (*US* **neighbor**) *n* сосéд*(ка*).

neighbourhood ['neɪbəhud] *n* (*place*) райóн; (*people*) сосéди *mpl*.

neighbourhood watch *n* *систéма, при котóрой сосéди договáриваются смотрéть*

за дома́ми друг дру́га.
neighbouring ['neɪbərɪŋ] *adj* сосе́дний*.
neighbourly ['neɪbəlɪ] *adj* доброcoсе́дский.
neither ['naɪðə'] *adj* ни тот, ни друго́й ♦ *conj*: **I didn't move and ~ did John** ни я, ни Джон не дви́нулись с ме́ста ♦ *pron*: **~ of them came** ни оди́н из них не пришёл, ни тот, ни друго́й не пришли́; **~ version is true** ни та, ни друга́я ве́рсия не верна́; **~ ... nor ...** ни ..., ни ...; **~ good nor bad** ни хорошо́, ни пло́хо.
neo... ['ni:əu] *prefix* нео....
neolithic [ni:əu'lɪθɪk] *adj* неолити́ческий.
neologism [nɪ'ɔlədʒɪzəm] *n* неологи́зм.
neon ['ni:ɔn] *n* нео́н.
neon light *n* нео́новый свет.
neon sign *n* нео́новая вы́веска.
Nepal [nɪ'pɔ:l] *n* Непа́л.
Nepalese [nɛpə'li:z] *adj* непа́льский*.
nephew ['nɛvju:] *n* племя́нник.
nepotism ['nɛpətɪzəm] *n* непоти́зм, кумовство́.
Neptune ['nɛptju:n] *n* (*planet*) Непту́н.
nerd [nə:d] *n* (*inf*) приду́рок*.
nerve [nə:v] *n* (*ANAT*) нерв; (*courage*) вы́держка; (*impudence*) на́глость *f*; **to have a fit of ~s** перене́рвничать (*perf*); **he gets on my ~s** он де́йствует мне на не́рвы; **she lost her ~** у неё сда́ли не́рвы.
nerve centre *n* (*ANAT*) не́рвный центр; (*fig*) мозгово́й центр.
nerve gas *n* не́рвный газ.
nerve-racking ['nə:vrækɪŋ] *adj* (*period*) не́рвный; (*situation*) нерво́зный* (нерво́зен).
nervous ['nə:vəs] *adj* не́рвный* (не́рвен); (*ANAT*) не́рвный; **to be** *or* **feel ~** не́рвничать (*impf*).
nervous breakdown *n* не́рвный срыв.
nervously ['nə:vəslɪ] *adv* не́рвно.
nervousness ['nə:vəsnɪs] *n* не́рвность *f*.
nervous wreck *n* (*inf*) комо́к не́рвов.
nervy ['nə:vɪ] *n* не́рвный*.
nest [nɛst] *n* гнездо́* ♦ *vi* гнезди́ться* (*impf*); **~ of tables** компле́кт сто́ликов (*вставля́ющихся один в друго́й*).
nest egg *n* зана́чка*.
nestle ['nɛsl] *vi* (*snuggle*) приюти́ться (*perf*).
nestling ['nɛstlɪŋ] *n* птене́ц*.
Net [nɛt] *n* (*inf*): **the ~** Сеть *f*.
net [nɛt] *n* (*fabric*) тюль *m*; (*netting, also SPORT*) се́тка*; (*for fish, game: also fig*) сеть* *f* ♦ *adj* (*COMM*) чи́стый ♦ *vt* (*fish*) лови́ть* (пойма́ть* *perf*) в сеть; (*profit*) приноси́ть* (принести́* *perf*); (*deal, sale*) повора́чивать (проверну́ть *perf*); **~ of tax** по́сле вы́чета нало́гов; **~ assets** не́тто-акти́вы; **he earns ten thousand ~ per year** он зараба́тывает чи́стыми де́сять ты́сяч в год.
netball ['nɛtbɔ:l] *n* нетбо́л.

net curtains *npl* тю́левые занаве́ски *fpl*.
Netherlands ['nɛðələndz] *npl*: **the ~** Нидерла́нды *pl*.
nett [nɛt] *adj* = **net**.
netting ['nɛtɪŋ] *n* се́тка*.
nettle ['nɛtl] *n* крапи́ва; **to grasp the ~** (*fig*) без промедле́ния взя́ться (*perf*) за де́ло.
network ['nɛtwə:k] *n* сеть* *f* ♦ *vt* (*RADIO, TV*) трансли́ровать (*impf/perf*) по разли́чным кана́лам; (*COMPUT*) подключа́ть (подключи́ть* *perf*) к систе́ме.
neuralgia [njuə'rældʒə] *n* невралги́я.
neurosis [njuə'rəusɪs] *n* невро́з.
neurological [njuərə'lɔdʒɪkl] *n* невролог-и́ческий.
neurotic [njuə'rɔtɪk] *adj* неврастени́чный* (неврастени́чен) ♦ *n* неврасте́ник.
neuter ['nju:tə'] *vt* (*cat etc*) кастри́ровать (*impf/ perf*) ♦ *adj* (*LING*): **~ noun** существи́тельное *nt adj* сре́днего ро́да.
neutral ['nju:trəl] *adj* нейтра́льный* (нейтра́лен) ♦ *n* (*AUT*) холосто́й ход*.
neutrality [nju:'trælɪtɪ] *n* нейтралите́т.
neutralize ['nju:trəlaɪz] *vt* нейтрализова́ть (*impf/perf*).
neutron ['nju:trɔn] *n* нейтро́н.
neutron bomb *n* нейтро́нная бо́мба.
Neva ['ni:və] *n*: **the ~** Нева́.
never ['nɛvə'] *adv* никогда́; **~ in my life** никогда́ в жи́зни; **~ again** бо́льше никогда́; **I ~ went** я не ходи́л; *see also* **mind**.
never-ending [nɛvər'ɛndɪŋ] *adj* несконча́емый (несконча́ем).
nevertheless [nɛvəðə'lɛs] *adv* тем не ме́нее.
new [nju:] *adj* (*brand new*) но́вый* (нов); (*recent*) неда́вний*; **I'm ~ to this business** я в э́том де́ле новичо́к; **as good as ~** совсе́м как но́вый.
New Age *adj* (*PHILOSOPHY*) *филосо́фская систе́ма, бази́рующаяся на ве́ре в альтернати́вную медици́ну, астроло́гию итп*; ~ **(music)** *тип му́зыки, включа́ющий элеме́нты джа́за, наро́дной и класси́ческой му́зыки*.
newborn ['nju:bɔ:n] *adj* новорождённый.
newcomer ['nju:kʌmə'] *n* новичо́к*.
newfangled ['nju:fæŋgld] *adj* (*pej*) новомо́дный* (новомо́ден).
new-found ['nju:faund] *adj* неда́вно обретённый.
Newfoundland ['nju:fənlənd] *n* Нью-фа́ундле́нд.
New Guinea *n* Но́вая Гвине́я.
newly ['nju:lɪ] *adv* неда́вно.
newlyweds ['nju:lɪwɛdz] *npl* новобра́чные *pl* .
new moon *n* молодо́й ме́сяц; (*time*) новолу́ние.
newness ['nju:nɪs] *n* новизна́.

New Orleans [-'ɔːliːənz] n Но́вый Орлеа́н.
news [njuːz] n (good, bad) но́вость* f, изве́стие; **a piece of** ~ но́вость*; **the** ~ (RADIO, TV) но́вости fpl; **what's the** ~? каки́е но́вости?; **financial** ~ фина́нсовые но́вости*.
news agency n информацио́нное аге́нтство.
newsagent ['njuːzeɪdʒənt] n (BRIT: also: ~'s) ≈ газе́тный кио́ск; (person) владе́лец*(-лица) газе́тного кио́ска.
news bulletin n сво́дка* новосте́й.
newscaster ['njuːzkɑːstəʳ] n ди́ктор (програ́ммы новосте́й).
newsdealer ['njuːzdiːləʳ] n (US) = newsagent.
newsflash ['njuːzflæʃ] n э́кстренное сообще́ние.
newsletter ['njuːzlɛtəʳ] n информацио́нный бюллете́нь m.
newspaper ['njuːzpeɪpəʳ] n газе́та; **daily/ weekly** ~ ежедне́вная/еженеде́льная газе́та.
newsprint ['njuːzprɪnt] n (paper) газе́тная бума́га.
newsreader ['njuːzriːdəʳ] n = newscaster.
newsreel ['njuːzriːl] n информацио́нный киножурна́л.
newsroom ['njuːzruːm] n (PRESS) отде́л новосте́й; (RADIO, TV) сту́дия новосте́й.
newsstand ['njuːzstænd] n газе́тный кио́ск.
newsworthy ['njuːzwəːði] adj досто́йный* (досто́ен) интере́са.
newt [njuːt] n трито́н.
new town n но́вый го́род*.
New Year n Но́вый год*; **Happy** ~~! С Но́вым го́дом!; **to wish sb a Happy** ~~ (for the festive season) поздравля́ть (поздра́вить* perf) кого́-н с Но́вым го́дом; (for the coming year) жела́ть (пожела́ть perf) кому́-н счастли́вого но́вого го́да.
New Year's Day n пе́рвое января́.
New Year's Eve n кану́н Но́вого го́да.
New York [-'jɔːk] n Нью-Йо́рк.
New Zealand [-'ziːlənd] n Но́вая Зела́ндия ◆ adj новозела́ндский*.
New Zealander [-'ziːləndəʳ] n новозела́ндец*(-дка*).
next [nɛkst] adj сле́дующий*; (neighbouring) сосе́дний* ◆ adv пото́м, зате́м ◆ prep: ~ **to** ря́дом с +instr, во́зле +gen; ~ **time** в сле́дующий раз; **the** ~ **day** на сле́дующий* день; **the** ~ **week** на сле́дующей неде́ле; **the week after** ~ че́рез неде́лю; ~ **year** в бу́дущем or сле́дующем году́; **in the** ~ **15 minutes** в ближа́йшие 15 мину́т; ~ **to nothing** почти́ ничего́; ~ **please!** сле́дующий, пожа́луйста!; **who's** ~? кто сле́дующий?; **"turn to the** ~ **page"** "переверни́те страни́цу"; **when do we meet** ~? когда́ мы сно́ва встре́тимся?
next door adv по сосе́дству, ря́дом ◆ adj (flat, house) сосе́дний*; ~~ **neighbour** ближа́йший* сосе́д*.
next of kin n ближа́йший* ро́дственник.

NF n abbr (BRIT: POL: = National Front) НФ= Национа́льный фронт ◆ abbr (CANADA) = Newfoundland.
NFL n abbr (US) = National Football League.
NG abbr (US) = **National Guard**.
NGO n abbr (US: = non-governmental organization) неправи́тельственная организа́ция.
NH abbr (US: POST) = New Hampshire.
NHL n abbr (US: = National Hockey League) НХЛ= Национа́льная хокке́йная ли́га.
NHS n abbr (BRIT) = **National Health Service**.
NI abbr = **Northern Ireland**; (BRIT) = **National Insurance**.
Niagara Falls [naɪ'ægərə-] npl: **the** ~~ Ниага́рский водопа́д msg.
nib [nɪb] n перо́*.
nibble ['nɪbl] vt надку́сывать (надкуси́ть* perf) ◆ vi: **to** ~ **at** (mice) грызть* (impf); (at grass) щипа́ть* (impf).
NICAM n abbr = near-instantaneous companding system: ~ **stereo** систе́ма стереозвуча́ния.
Nicaragua [nɪkə'rægjuə] n Никара́гуа f ind.
Nicaraguan [nɪkə'rægjuən] adj никарагуа́нский* ◆ n никарагуа́нец*(-нка*).
Nice [niːs] n Ни́цца.
nice [naɪs] adj прия́тный* (прия́тен), хоро́ший (хоро́ш); (attractive) симпати́чный* (симпати́чен); **to look** ~ хорошо́ вы́глядеть (impf); **that's very** ~ **of you** о́чень ми́ло с ва́шей стороны́.
nicely ['naɪslɪ] adv прия́тно, хорошо́; **that will do** ~ э́то вполне́ подойдёт.
niceties ['naɪsɪtɪz] npl то́нкости fpl.
niche [niːʃ] n (also fig) ни́ша.
nick [nɪk] n (in skin) поре́з; (in surface) зару́бка* ◆ vt (inf: steal) пере́ть* (спере́ть* perf); (: BRIT: arrest) ца́пать (сца́пать perf); (cut): **to** ~ **o.s.** поре́заться* (perf); **in the** ~ **of time** как раз во́время; **in good** ~ (BRIT: inf: condition) в хоро́шем состоя́нии.
nickel ['nɪkl] n ни́кель m; (US: coin) моне́та в 5 це́нтов.
nickname ['nɪkneɪm] n кли́чка*, про́звище ◆ vt прозыва́ть (прозва́ть* perf).
Nicosia [nɪkə'siːə] n Никоси́я.
nicotine ['nɪkətiːn] n никоти́н.
niece [niːs] n племя́нница.
nifty ['nɪftɪ] adj (inf: car, jacket) сти́льный* (сти́лен); (: gadget, tool) ло́вко приду́манный (приду́ман).
Niger ['naɪdʒəʳ] n Ни́гер.
Nigeria [naɪ'dʒɪərɪə] n Ниге́рия.
Nigerian [naɪ'dʒɪərɪən] adj нигери́йский* ◆ n нигери́ец*(-и́йка).
niggardly ['nɪgədlɪ] adj (person) ска́редный; (amount) ску́дный.
nigger ['nɪgəʳ] n (inf!) черномазый(-ая) m(f) adj (!)
niggle ['nɪgl] vt задева́ть (заде́ть* perf) ◆ vi (find fault) придира́ться (придра́ться* perf).

niggling [ˈnɪglɪŋ] *adj* (*trifling*) придирчивый (придирчив); (*annoying*) навязчивый (навязчив).

night [naɪt] *n* ночь* *f*; (*evening*) вечер*; **at ~, by ~** ночью; **all ~ long** всю ночь напролёт; **in** *or* **during the ~** ночью; **last ~** вчера ночью; (*evening*) вчера вечером; **the ~ before last** позапрошлой ночью; (*evening*) позавчера вечером.

nightcap [ˈnaɪtkæp] *n* (*drink*) стаканчик на ночь.

nightclub [ˈnaɪtklʌb] *n* ночной клуб.

nightdress [ˈnaɪtdrɛs] *n* ночная рубашка*.

nightfall [ˈnaɪtfɔːl] *n* сумерки* *pl*.

nightgown [ˈnaɪtgaun] *n* = **nightdress**.

nightie [ˈnaɪtɪ] *n* (*inf*) = **nightdress**.

nightingale [ˈnaɪtɪŋgeɪl] *n* соловей*.

nightlife [ˈnaɪtlaɪf] *n* ночная жизнь *f*.

nightly [ˈnaɪtlɪ] *adj* (*every night*) еженощный; (*by night*) ночной ♦ *adv* еженощно.

nightmare [ˈnaɪtmɛəʳ] *n* (*also fig*) кошмар.

nightmarish [ˈnaɪtmɛərɪʃ] *adj* кошмарный*.

night porter *n* ночной портье *m ind.*

night safe *n* ночной сейф (в банке).

night school *n* вечерняя школа.

nightshade [ˈnaɪtʃeɪd] *n*: **deadly ~** белладонна, красавка.

night shift *n* ночная смена.

night-time [ˈnaɪttaɪm] *n* ночное время* *nt*.

night watchman *n* ночной сторож*.

nihilism [ˈnaɪlɪzəm] *n* нигилизм.

nil [nɪl] *n* нуль* *m*; (*BRIT: SPORT*) ноль* *m* ♦ *cpd* нулевой.

Nile [naɪl] *n*: **the ~** Нил.

nimble [ˈnɪmbl] *adj* (*agile*) проворный* (проворен); (*alert*) сообразительный* (сообразителен).

nine [naɪn] *n* девять*; *see also* **five**.

nineteen [ˈnaɪnˈtiːn] *n* девятнадцать*; *see also* **five**.

nineteenth [ˈnaɪnˈtiːnθ] *adj* девятнадцатый; *see also* **fifth**.

ninetieth [ˈnaɪntɪɪθ] *adj* девяностый; *see also* **fifth**.

ninety [ˈnaɪntɪ] *n* девяносто*; *see also* **fifty**.

ninth [naɪnθ] *adj* девятый; *see also* **fifth**.

nip [nɪp] *vt* (*pinch*) щипать* (ущипнуть *perf*); (*bite*) кусать (*impf*) ♦ *n* (*pinch*) щипок*; (*bite*) укус; (*drink*) рюмочка* ♦ *vi* (*BRIT: inf*): **to ~ out** выскакивать (выскочить *perf*); **to ~ into a shop** заскакивать (заскочить* *perf*) в магазин.

nipple [ˈnɪpl] *n* (*ANAT*) сосок*; (*TECH*) ниппель* *m*.

nippy [ˈnɪpɪ] *adj* (*BRIT: inf*) проворный* (проворен); (: *weather*) холодноватый (холодноват).

nit [nɪt] *n* (*in hair*) гнида; (*BRIT: inf: idiot*) олух.

nit-pick [ˈnɪtpɪk] *vi* (*inf*) придираться (придраться* *perf*).

nitrogen [ˈnaɪtrədʒən] *n* азот.

nitroglycerin(e) [ˈnaɪtrəuˈglɪsəriːn] *n* нитроглицерин.

nitty-gritty [ˈnɪtɪˈgrɪtɪ] *n* (*inf*): **to get down to the ~** переходить* (перейти* *perf*) к сути дела.

nitwit [ˈnɪtwɪt] *n* (*inf*) олух.

Nizhni Novgorod [ˈniːʒnij ˈnɔvgərət] *n* Нижний Новгород.

NJ *abbr* (*US: POST*) = **New Jersey**.

NLF *n abbr* (= *National Liberation Front*) ФНО= *Фронт национального освобождения*.

NLQ *abbr* (*COMPUT, TYP*: = *near letter quality*) *повышенное качество печати*.

NLRB *n abbr* (*US*) = **National Labor Relations Board**.

NM *abbr* (*US: POST*) = **New Mexico**.

KEYWORD

no [nəu] (*pl* **noes**) *adv* (*opposite of "yes"*) нет; **are you coming? – no (I'm not)** Вы придёте? -нет(, не приду); **no thank you** нет, спасибо
♦ *adj* (*not any*): **I have no money/time/books** у меня нет денег/времени/книг; **there is no bread left** хлеб кончился; **there is no one here** здесь никого нет; **it is of no importance at all** это не имеет никакого значения; **no system is totally fair** никакая система не является полностью справедливой; **"no entry"** "вход воспрещён"; **"no smoking"** "не курить"
♦ *n*: **there were twenty noes** двадцать (человек) были "против".

no. *abbr* = **number**.

nobble [ˈnɔbl] *vt* (*BRIT: inf: bribe*) покупать (купить* *perf*); (: *to speak to*) подлавливать (подловить* *perf*); (: *RACING*) портить* (испортить* *perf*).

Nobel Prize [nəuˈbɛl-] *n* Нобелевская премия.

nobility [nəuˈbɪlɪtɪ] *n* (*social class*) знать *f*, дворянство; (*quality*) благородство.

noble [ˈnəubl] *adj* (*aristocratic*) дворянский; (*high-minded*) благородный* (благороден); (*impressive*) величавый (величав).

nobleman [ˈnəublmən] *irreg n* дворянин*.

noblewoman [ˈnəublwumən] *irreg n* дворянка*.

nobly [ˈnəublɪ] *adv* (*behave, act*) благородно.

nobody [ˈnəubədɪ] *pron* никто*.

no-claim(s) bonus [ˈnəukleɪmz-] *n* (*INSURANCE*) скидка со следующего страховой премии (*предоставляется страхователю в случае отсутствия страховых претензий в предыдущем году*).

nocturnal [nɔkˈtəːnl] *adj* ночной.

nod [nɔd] *vi* (*gesture*) кивать (*impf*); (*doze*) клевать* (*impf*) носом ♦ *n* кивок* ♦ *vt*: **to ~ one's head** кивать (*impf*) головой; **they ~ded their agreement** они кивнули в знак

---

* marks translations which have irregular inflections. The Russian-English side of the dictionary gives inflectional information.

согласия

▶ **nod off** vi задремать* (perf).

no-fly zone [nəu'flaɪ-] n запретная воздушная зона.

noise [nɔɪz] n шум.

noiseless ['nɔɪzlɪs] adj бесшумный* (бесшумен).

noisily ['nɔɪzɪlɪ] adv шумно.

noisy ['nɔɪzɪ] adj шумный* (шумен).

nomad ['nəumæd] n кочевник(-ица).

nomadic [nəu'mædɪk] adj кочевой.

no-man's-land ['nəumænzlænd] n (MIL) ничейная полоса; (fig) туманность f.

nominal ['nɔmɪnl] adj номинальный* (номинален); (value) номинальный.

nominate ['nɔmɪneɪt] vt (propose): **to ~ sb (for)** выставлять (выставить* perf) кандидатуру кого-н (на +acc); (appoint): **to ~ sb (to/as)** назначать (назначить perf) кого-н (на +acc/ +instr)

nomination [nɔmɪ'neɪʃən] n (see vb) выставление; назначение.

nominee [nɔmɪ'niː] n кандидат.

non... [nɔn] prefix не....

nonalcoholic [nɔnælkə'hɔlɪk] adj (drink) безалкогольный* (безалкоголен).

nonaligned adj неприсоединившийся.

nonbreakable [nɔn'breɪkəbl] adj небьющийся.

nonce word ['nɔns-] n окказионализм.

nonchalant ['nɔnʃələnt] adj беспечный* (беспечен).

noncommissioned officer [nɔnkə'mɪʃənd-] n унтер-офицер.

noncommittal [nɔnkə'mɪtl] adj уклончивый (уклончив).

nonconformist [nɔnkən'fɔːmɪst] n нонконформист(ка*); (BRIT: REL): **N~** нонконформист(ка) ♦ adj нонконформистский.

non-contributory pension scheme n пенсионные схемы, по которым работники не должны делать регулярных взносов.

noncooperation ['nɔnkəuэрə'reɪʃən] n отказ в сотрудничестве.

nondescript ['nɔndɪskrɪpt] adj (person, clothing) невзрачный* (невзрачен); (colour) небросский*.

none [nʌn] pron (person) никто*, ни один*; (thing) ничто*, ни один*; **~ of you** никто or ни один из Вас; **I've ~ left** у меня ничего не осталось; **~ at all** совсем ничего; **he's ~ the worse for it** ему от этого отнюдь не хуже.

nonentity [nɔ'nɛntɪtɪ] n ничтожество.

nonessential [nɔnɪ'sɛnʃl] adj (items) несущественный (несуществен) ♦ n: **~s** несущественные вещи fpl.

nonetheless ['nʌnðə'lɛs] adv тем не менее, всё же.

non-event [nɔnɪ'vɛnt] n бессмысленное мероприятие.

nonexecutive [nɔnɪg'zɛkjutɪv] adj: **~ director** директор* без распорядительных полномочий.

nonexistent [nɔnɪg'zɪstənt] adj несуществующий.

nonfiction [nɔn'fɪkʃən] n документальная литература.

nonflammable [nɔn'flæməbl] adj невоспламеняющийся*.

nonintervention ['nɔnɪntə'vɛnʃən] n невмешательство.

no-no ['nəunəu] n (inf) запретная тема.

non obst. abbr (notwithstanding: = non obstante) несмотря на +acc.

no-nonsense [nəu'nɔnsəns] adj деловой.

nonpayment [nɔn'peɪmənt] n неуплата.

nonplussed [nɔn'plʌst] adj ошеломлённый (ошеломлён).

non-profit-making [nɔn'prɔfɪtmeɪkɪŋ] adj: **~ organization** некоммерческая организация.

nonsense ['nɔnsəns] n (rubbish) ерунда, чепуха; **it is ~ to say that ...** говорить (сказать* perf), что ... -- просто глупость.

nonsensical [nɔn'sɛnsɪkl] adj бессмысленный* (бессмыслен).

nonshrink [nɔn'ʃrɪŋk] adj (BRIT): **nylon is (a) ~ (fabric)** нейлон не садится.

nonskid [nɔn'skɪd] adj нескользящий.

nonsmoker ['nɔn'sməukə'] n некурящий*(-ая) m(f) adj.

nonstarter [nɔn'stɑːtə'] n мёртвый номер no pl.

nonstick ['nɔn'stɪk] adj непригорающий.

nonstop ['nɔn'stɔp] adj (conversation) беспрерывный* (беспрерывен); (flight) беспосадочный; (train, bus) идущий без остановок ♦ adv (see adj) беспрерывно; без посадки; без остановок.

nontaxable [nɔn'tæksəbl] adj необлагаемый (необлагаем) налогом.

non-U adj abbr (BRIT: inf: = non-upper class) не принадлежащий к высшему (социальному) классу.

nonvolatile [nɔn'vɔlətaɪl] adj: **~ memory** (COMPUT) энергонезависимая память f.

nonvoting [nɔn'vəutɪŋ] adj: **~ shares/member** акции/член без права голосования.

non-white ['nɔn'waɪt] adj (person) цветной* ♦ n: **non-White** цветной*(-ая) m(f) adj.

noodles ['nuːdlz] npl вермишель fsg.

nook [nuk] n: **in every ~ and cranny** во всех углах.

noon [nuːn] n полдень* m.

no-one ['nəuwʌn] pron = **nobody**.

noose [nuːs] n петля*.

nor [nɔː'] conj = **neither** ♦ adv see **neither**.

Norf abbr (BRIT: POST) = **Norfolk**.

norm [nɔːm] n норма.

normal ['nɔːml] adj нормальный* (нормален) ♦ n: **to return to ~** возвращаться (вернуться perf) в нормальное состояние.

normality [nɔː'mælɪtɪ] n нормальность f.

normally ['nɔːmэlɪ] adv (usually) обычно; (properly) нормально.

Normandy ['nɔ:məndɪ] *n* Нормáндия.
north [nɔ:θ] *n* сéвер ♦ *adj* сéверный ♦ *adv* (*go*) на сéвер; (*be*) к сéверу.
North Africa *n* Сéверная Áфрика.
North African *adj* североафрикáнский ♦ *n* жи́тель(ница) *m(f)* Сéверной Áфрики.
North America *n* Сéверная Амéрика.
North American *adj* североамерикáнский ♦ *n* североамерикáнец*(-нка*).
Northants [nɔ:'θænts] *abbr* (*BRIT: POST*) = Northamptonshire.
northbound ['nɔ:θbaund] *adj* (*traffic, carriageway*) на сéвер; (*platform*) сéверного направлéния.
Northd *abbr* (*BRIT: POST*) = Northumberland.
northeast [nɔ:θ'i:st] *n* сéверо-востóк.
northerly ['nɔ:ðəlɪ] *adj* сéверный.
northern ['nɔ:ðən] *adj* сéверный.
northerner ['nɔ:ðənə'] *n* северя́нин*(-я́нка*).
Northern Ireland *n* Сéверная Ирлáндия.
North Korea *n* Сéверная Корéя.
North Pole *n* Сéверный пóлюс.
North Sea *n* Сéверное мóре.
North-Sea oil ['nɔ:θsi:-] *n* нефть *f* Сéверного мóря.
northward(s) ['nɔ:θwəd(z)] *adv* к сéверу.
northwest [nɔ:θ'wɛst] *n* сéверо-зáпад.
Norway ['nɔ:weɪ] *n* Норвéгия.
Norwegian [nɔ:'wi:dʒən] *adj* норвéжский* ♦ *n* норвéжец*(-жка*); (*LING*) норвéжский* язы́к*.
nos. *abbr* = numbers.
nose [nəuz] *n* нос*; (*sense of smell*) нюх, чутьё ♦ *vi*: to ~ forward осторóжно пробирáться (пробрáться* *perf*) вперёд; he has a ~ for danger/scandal у негó нюх на опáсность/скандáл; to pay through the ~ (for sth) (*inf*) платúть* (заплатúть* *perf*) втри́дорога (за что-н)
► **nose about** *vi* выню́хивать (вы́нюхать *perf*)
► **nose around** *vi* = nose about.
nosebleed ['nəuzbli:d] *n* носовóе кровотечéние.
nose dive *n* (крутóе) пики́рование.
nose drops *npl* кáпли *fpl* для нóса.
nosey ['nəuzɪ] *adj* (*inf*) = nosy.
nostalgia [nɔs'tældʒɪə] *n* ностальги́я.
nostalgic [nɔs'tældʒɪk] *adj* (*film, memory*) ностальги́ческий*; (*person*): to be ~ (for) испы́тывать (*impf*) ностальги́ю (по +*dat*).
nostril ['nɔstrɪl] *n* ноздря́*.
nosy ['nəuzɪ] *adj* (*inf*): to be ~ совáть* (*impf*) нос в чужи́е делá.

KEYWORD

not [nɔt] *adv* нет; (*before verbs*) не; he is not or isn't at home егó нет дóма; he asked me not to do it он попроси́л меня́ не дéлать э́того; you must not *or* you mustn't do that (*forbidden*) э́того нельзя́ дéлать; (*should not*)

Вы не должны́ э́то дéлать; it's too late, isn't it? уже́ сли́шком пóздно, да?; not that ... не то, чтóбы ...; not yet нет ещё, ещё нет; not now не сейчáс; see also all, only.

notable ['nəutəbl] *adj* примечáтельный* (примечáтелен).
notably ['nəutəblɪ] *adv* (*particularly*) осóбенно; (*markedly*) замéтно.
notary ['nəutərɪ] *n* (*also*: ~ public) нотáриус.
notation [nəu'teɪʃən] *n* (*MUS etc*) нотáция.
notch [nɔtʃ] *n* (*on the edge*) зазýбрина; (*on the surface*) вы́емка*
► **notch up** *vt* (*victory*) добивáться (доби́ться* *perf*) +*instr*; (*score*) набирáть (набрáть* *perf*).
note [nəut] *n* (*record*) зáпись *f*; (*letter*) запи́ска*; (*also*: **footnote**) примечáние; (*also*: **banknote**) банкнóта; (*MUS*) нóта; (*tone*) тон ♦ *vt* (*observe*) замечáть (замéтить* *perf*); (*also*: ~ **down**) запи́сывать (записáть* *perf*); of ~ примечáтельный (примечáтелен).
notebook ['nəutbuk] *n* записнáя кни́жка; (*exercise book*) тетрáдь *f*.
notecase ['nəutkeɪs] *n* (*BRIT*) бумáжник.
noted ['nəutɪd] *adj* извéстный* (извéстен).
notepad ['nəutpæd] *n* блокнóт.
notepaper ['nəutpeɪpə'] *n* пи́счая бумáга.
noteworthy ['nəutwə:ðɪ] *adj* достóйный* (достóен) внимáния; it is ~ that ... достóйно внимáния что ....
nothing ['nʌθɪŋ] *n* ничтó*; (*zero*) ноль *m*; he does ~ он ничегó не дéлает; there is ~ to do/be said дéлать/сказáть нéчего; ~ new/ much/of the sort ничегó нóвого/осóбенного/ подóбного; for ~ (*free*) дáром; (*in vain*) да́ром; think ~ of it! не за что!; it was ~! не за что!; ~ like as ... as ... совсéм не так ..., как ...; to say ~ of ... не говоря́ уже́ о +*prp* ...; it has ~ to do with you э́то Вас не касáется.
notice ['nəutɪs] *n* (*announcement*) объявлéние; (*official letter, circular*) уведомлéние; извещéние; (*warning*) предупреждéние; (*BRIT: review*) óтзыв ♦ *vt* замечáть (замéтить* *perf*); to take ~ of обращáть (обрати́ть* *perf*) внимáние на +*acc*; to bring sth to sb's ~ (*attention*) обращáть (обрати́ть* *perf*) внимáние когó-н на что-н; to escape *or* avoid ~ оставáться* (остáться* *perf*) незамéченным; it has come to my ~ that ... мне стáло извéстно, что ...; to hand in one's ~ подавáть* (подáть* *perf*) заявлéние об ухóде с рабóты; he was given 2 weeks ~ егó предупреди́ли, что он бýдет увóлен чéрез 2 недéли; advance ~ заблаговрéменное предупреждéние; without ~ без предупреждéния; at short ~ без предупреждéния; until further ~ впредь до дальнéйшего уведомлéния.

---

* marks translations which have irregular inflections. The Russian-English side of the dictionary gives inflectional information.

noticeable ['nəutɪsəbl] *adj* заме́тный*
(заме́тен).

notice board *n* (BRIT) доска́* объявле́ний.

notification [nəutɪfɪ'keɪʃən] *n* уведомле́ние.

notify ['nəutɪfaɪ] *vt*: **to ~ sb (of sth)** уведомля́ть
(уве́домить* *perf*) кого́-н (о чём-н).

notion ['nəuʃən] *n* (*idea*) поня́тие; (*opinion*)
представле́ние; **~s** *npl* (US: *haberdashery*)
галантере́я *fsg*.

notoriety [nəutə'raɪətɪ] *n* дурна́я сла́ва.

notorious [nəu'tɔ:rɪəs] *adj* (*criminal, liar*)
изве́стный* (изве́стен); (*place*) печа́льно
изве́стный* (изве́стен).

notoriously [nəu'tɔ:rɪəslɪ] *adv*: **she is ~
unreliable** у неё дурна́я сла́ва ненадёжного
челове́ка; **this word is ~ difficult to translate**
э́то сло́во изве́стно тем, что его́ тру́дно
перевести́.

Notts [nɔts] *abbr* (BRIT: POST) = **Nottinghamshire.**

notwithstanding [nɔtwɪθ'stændɪŋ] *adv* тем не
ме́нее ♦ *prep* несмотря́ на +*acc*.

nougat ['nu:gɑ:] *n* нуга́.

nought [nɔ:t] *n* ноль* *m*.

noun [naun] *n* (и́мя* *nt*) существи́тельное *nt adj*.

nourish ['nʌrɪʃ] *vt* (*feed*) пита́ть (*impf*); (*fig*:
foster) взра́щивать (взрасти́ть* *perf*).

nourishing ['nʌrɪʃɪŋ] *adj* пита́тельный*
(пита́телен).

nourishment ['nʌrɪʃmənt] *n* (*food*) пита́ние.

Nov. *abbr* = **November.**

Nova Scotia ['nəuvə'skəuʃə] *n* Но́вая
Шотла́ндия.

Novaya Zemlya ['nɔvəjə zɪm'lja] *n* Но́вая
Земля́.

novel ['nɔvl] *n* рома́н ♦ *adj* оригина́льный*
(оригина́лен).

novelist ['nɔvəlɪst] *n* романи́ст(ка*).

novelty ['nɔvəltɪ] *n* (*newness*) новизна́; (*object*)
нови́нка*.

November [nəu'vɛmbər] *n* ноя́брь* *m*; *see also*
July.

novice ['nɔvɪs] *n* новичо́к*; (REL)
послу́шник(-ица).

Novosibirsk [nɔvəsi'birsk] *n* Новосиби́рск.

NOW [nau] *n abbr* (US) = *National Organization
for Women.*

now [nau] *adv* тепе́рь, сейча́с ♦ *conj*: **~ (that)** ...
тепе́рь, когда́ ...; **right ~** пря́мо сейча́с; **by ~**
к настоя́щему вре́мени; **~ and then** *or* **again**
вре́мя от вре́мени; **from ~ on** впредь; **until ~**
до сих пор; **that's the fashion just ~** э́то
сейча́с в мо́де; **I saw her just ~** я то́лько что
её ви́дел; **in 3 days from ~** че́рез 3 дня;
between ~ and Monday ме́жду сего́дняшним
днём и понеде́льником; **that's all for ~** пока́
всё.

nowadays ['nauədeɪz] *adv* в на́ши дни.

nowhere ['nəuwɛər] *adv* (*be*) нигде́; (*go*)
никуда́; **~ else** (*be*) бо́льше нигде́; (*go*)
бо́льше никуда́; **I have ~ else to go** мне
бо́льше не́куда идти́.

no-win situation [nəu'wɪn-] *n*
безвы́игрышное положе́ние.

noxious ['nɔkʃəs] *adj* вредоно́сный; (*smell*)
проти́вный* (проти́вен).

nozzle ['nɔzl] *n* (TECH) сопло́*; (*of hose, vacuum
cleaner*) наса́дка*; (*of fire extinguisher*)
брандспо́йт.

NP *n abbr* (LAW) = **notary public.**

NS *abbr* (CANADA) = **Nova Scotia.**

NSC *n abbr* (US: = *National Security Council*)
Сове́т национа́льной безопа́сности.

NSF *n abbr* (US) = *National Science Foundation.*

NSPCC *n abbr* (BRIT) = *National Society for the
Prevention of Cruelty to Children.*

NSW *abbr* (AUSTRALIA) = *New South Wales.*

NT *n abbr* (BIBLE: = *New Testament*) Но́вый
заве́т.

nth [ɛnθ] *adj*: **for the ~ time** (*inf*) в э́нный раз.

nuance ['nju:ɑ:ns] *n* нюа́нс.

nubile ['nju:baɪl] *adj* (*woman*) зре́лый;
(*attractive*) прельсти́тельный.

nuclear ['nju:klɪə] *adj* я́дерный.

nuclear disarmament *n* я́дерное раз-
оруже́ние.

nuclear-free zone ['nju:klɪə'fri:-] *n* внея́дерная
зо́на.

nuclear reactor *n* я́дерный реа́ктор.

nuclei ['nju:klɪaɪ] *npl of* **nucleus.**

nucleus ['nju:klɪəs] (*pl* **nuclei**) *n* (*also fig*) ядро́*.

NUCPS *n abbr* (BRIT) = *National Union of Civil
and Public Servants.*

nude [nju:d] *adj* обнажённый (обнажён),
наго́й* (наг) ♦ *n* обнажённая фигу́ра; **in the
~** в обнажённом ви́де.

nudge [nʌdʒ] *vt* подта́лкивать (подтолкну́ть*
perf).

nudist ['nju:dɪst] *n* нуди́ст(ка*).

nudist colony *n* коло́ния нуди́стов.

nudity ['nju:dɪtɪ] *n* нагота́.

nugget ['nʌgɪt] *n* (*of gold*) саморо́док*; **~ of
information** це́нная информа́ция.

nuisance ['nju:sns] *n* (*state of affairs, thing*)
доса́да; (*person*) доку́чливый челове́к*; **what
a ~!** кака́я доса́да!; **that noise is a real ~** э́тот
шум си́льно раздража́ет; **he is a real ~** он
о́чень надое́дливый.

NUJ *n abbr* (BRIT) = *National Union of
Journalists.*

nuke [nju:k] *n* (*inf*) я́дерное ору́жие.

null [nʌl] *adj*: **to be ~ and void** потеря́ть (*perf*)
зако́нную си́лу.

nullify ['nʌlɪfaɪ] *vt* (*efforts*) своди́ть* (свести́*
perf) к нулю́; (LAW) аннули́ровать (*impf/perf*).

NUM *n abbr* (BRIT) = *National Union of
Mineworkers.*

numb [nʌm] *adj*: **~ (with)** онеме́вший (от +*gen*)
♦ *vt*: **the cold ~ed his fingers** его́ па́льцы
онеме́ли от хо́лода; **to go ~** онеме́ть (*perf*).

number ['nʌmbər] *n* но́мер*; (MATH) число́*;
(*written figure*) ци́фра; (*quantity*) коли́чество
♦ *vt* (*pages etc*) нумерова́ть (пронумерова́ть

perf); (*amount to*) насчи́тывать (*impf*); **a ~ of** не́сколько +*gen*; **in a ~ of cases** в ря́де слу́чаев; **they were ten in ~** их бы́ло де́сять; **you've got the wrong ~** (*TEL*) Вы не туда́ попа́ли; **he is ~ed among** ... его́ причисля́ют к +*dat* ...; **~ed (bank) account** номерно́й счёт в ба́нке.

numberplate ['nʌmbəpleɪt] *n* (*BRIT: AUT*) номерно́й знак.

Number Ten *n* (*BRIT: also:* ~ ~ **Downing Street**) но́мер 10 по Да́унинг Стри́т (*резиде́нция премье́р-мини́стра*).

numbness ['nʌmnɪs] *n* (*due to cold*) онеме́ние; (*due to fear, shock*) оцепене́ние.

numbskull ['nʌmskʌl] *n* (*inf*) тупи́ца *m/f*.

numeral ['nju:mərəl] *n* ци́фра.

numerate ['nju:mərɪt] *adj* (*BRIT*): **to be ~** знать (*impf*) арифме́тику.

numerical [nju:'mɛrɪkl] *adj* (*value*) числово́й; (*superiority*) чи́сленный; (*data*) цифрово́й; **in ~ order** по номера́м.

numerous ['nju:mərəs] *adj* многочи́сленный (многочи́слен); **on ~ occasions** многокра́тно.

nun [nʌn] *n* мона́хиня.

nunnery ['nʌnərɪ] *n* же́нский* монасты́рь *m*.

nuptial ['nʌpʃəl] *adj* бра́чный.

nurse [nəːs] *n* медсестра́*; (*also:* **male ~**) медбра́т; (*also:* **~maid**) ня́ня ◆ *vt* (*patient*) уха́живать (*impf*) за +*instr*; (*desire, also BRIT: cuddle*) леле́ять (взлеле́ять *perf*); (*grudge*) таи́ть (*impf*); (*US: suckle*) корми́ть* (*impf*) гру́дью; **to ~ a cold** сиде́ть* (*impf*) до́ма с просту́дой.

nursery ['nəːsərɪ] *n* (*institution*) я́сли* *pl*; (*room*) де́тская *f adj*; (*for plants*) пито́мник.

nursery rhyme *n* пе́сенка для дете́й.

nursery school *n* де́тский* сад*.

nursery slope *n* (*BRIT*) спуск для начина́ющих лы́жников.

nursing ['nəːsɪŋ] *n* (*profession*) профе́ссия

медсестры́; (*care*) ухо́д.

nursing home *n* ча́стный дом* (*для престаре́лых*).

nursing mother *n* корма́щая мать* *f*.

nurture ['nəːtʃə'] *vt* (*child, plant*) выра́щивать (вы́растить* *perf*).

NUS *n abbr* (*BRIT*) = *National Union of Students*.

NUT *n abbr* (*BRIT*) = *National Union of Teachers*.

nut [nʌt] *n* (*BOT*) оре́х; (*TECH*) га́йка; (*inf*) = **nutcase**.

nutcase ['nʌtkeɪs] *n* (*inf*) псих.

nutcrackers ['nʌtkrækəz] *npl* щипцы́* *pl* для оре́хов.

nutmeg ['nʌtmɛg] *n* муска́тный оре́х.

nutrient ['nju:trɪənt] *n* пита́тельное вещество́.

nutrition [nju:'trɪʃən] *n* (*diet*) пита́ние; (*nourishment*) пита́тельность *f*.

nutritionist [nju:'trɪʃənɪst] *n* дието́лог.

nutritious [nju:'trɪʃəs] *adj* пита́тельный* (пита́телен).

nuts [nʌts] (*inf*) *adj*: **he's ~** он чо́кнутый; **to be ~ about sb** с ума́ сходи́ть* (*impf*) по кому́-н.

nutshell ['nʌtʃɛl] *n* оре́ховая скорлупа́*; **in a ~** (*fig*) в двух слова́х.

nutty ['nʌtɪ] *adj* (*flavour*) похо́жий* (по вку́су) на оре́хи; (*inf: person*) чо́кнутый (чо́кнут); (*idea*) бредо́вый.

nuzzle ['nʌzl] *vi*: **to ~ up to** тере́ться* (потере́ться* *perf*) но́сом о +*acc*.

NV *abbr* (*US: POST*) = *Nevada*.

NWT *abbr* (*CANADA*) = *Northwest Territories*.

NY *abbr* (*US: POST*) = *New York*.

NYC *abbr* (*US: POST*) = *New York City*.

nylon ['naɪlɔn] *n* нейло́н ◆ *adj* нейло́новый; **~s** *npl* нейло́новые чулки́* *mpl*.

nymph [nɪmf] *n* (*MYTHOLOGY*) ни́мфа; (*ZOOL*) личи́нка*.

nymphomaniac ['nɪmfəu'meɪnɪæk] *n* нимфома́нка*.

NYSE *n abbr* (*US*) = *New York Stock Exchange*.

NZ *abbr* = *New Zealand*.

---

* marks translations which have irregular inflections. The Russian-English side of the dictionary gives inflectional information.

~ O, o ~

O, o [əu] *n* (*letter*) 15-ая бу́ква англи́йского алфави́та; (*number*: *TEL etc*) ноль* *m*.

O *abbr* = **outstanding**; (*US*: *SCOL*) ≈ отл.= отли́чно.

oaf [əuf] *n* чурба́н, дуби́на *m/f*.

oak [əuk] *n* дуб* ♦ *adj* дубо́вый.

O & M *n abbr* = **organization and method**.

OAP *n abbr* (*BRIT*) = **old age pensioner**.

oar [ɔ:ʳ] *n* весло́*; **to put** *or* **shove one's ~ in** (*fig*: *inf*) встрева́ть (встрять* *perf*).

oarsman ['ɔ:zmən] *n* гребе́ц*.

OAS *n abbr* = **Organization of American States**.

oases [əu'eɪsi:z] *npl of* **oasis**.

oasis [əu'eɪsɪs] (*pl* **oases**) *n* (*also fig*) оа́зис.

oath [əuθ] *n* (*promise*) кля́тва; (: *LAW*) прися́га; (*swear word*) прокля́тие; **on** (*BRIT*) **or under ~** под прися́гой; **to take the ~** принима́ть (приня́ть* *perf*) прися́гу.

oatmeal ['əutmi:l] *n* овся́ная мука́.

oats [əuts] *npl* овёс*.

OAU *n abbr* = **Organization of African Unity**.

obdurate ['ɔbdjurɪt] *adj* непрекло́нный* (непрекло́нен).

OBE *n abbr* (*BRIT*: = *Order of the British Empire*) о́рден Брита́нской импе́рии.

obedience [ə'bi:dɪəns] *n* повинове́ние, послуша́ние; **in ~ to** повину́ясь +*dat*.

obedient [ə'bi:dɪənt] *adj* послу́шный (послу́шен); **to be ~ to sb/sth** слу́шаться (послу́шаться *perf*) кого́-н/чего́-н.

obelisk ['ɔbɪlɪsk] *n* обели́ск.

obese [əu'bi:s] *adj* ту́чный* (ту́чен).

obesity [əu'bi:sɪtɪ] *n* ожире́ние, ту́чность *f*.

obey [ə'beɪ] *vt* подчиня́ться (подчини́ться *perf*) +*dat*, повинова́ться (*impf/perf*) +*dat* ♦ *vi* подчиня́ться (подчини́ться *perf*), повинова́ться (*impf*).

obituary [ə'bɪtjuərɪ] *n* некроло́г.

object [*n* 'ɔbdʒɪkt, *vi* əb'dʒɛkt] *n* (*thing*) предме́т; (*aim, purpose*) цель *f*; (*of affection, desires*) объе́кт; (*LING*) дополне́ние ♦ *vi*: **to ~** (**to**) возража́ть (возрази́ть* *perf*) (про́тив +*gen*); **expense is no ~** де́ньги – не пробле́ма; **what's the ~ of doing that?** для чего́ де́лать э́то?; **he ~ed that ...** он возрази́л, что ...; **I ~!** я возража́ю!; **do you ~ to my smoking?** Вы не возража́ете е́сли я бу́ду кури́ть?

objection [əb'dʒɛkʃən] *n* возраже́ние; **I have no ~ to ...** я не име́ю никаки́х возраже́ний

про́тив +*gen* ...; **if you have no ~** е́сли Вы не возража́ете; **to make** *or* **raise an ~** выдвига́ть (вы́двинуть *perf*) возраже́ние.

objectionable [əb'dʒɛkʃənəbl] *adj* (*language, conduct*) возмути́тельный* (возмути́телен); (*person*) неприя́тный* (неприя́тен).

objective [əb'dʒɛktɪv] *adj* объекти́вный* (объекти́вен) ♦ *n* (*aim, purpose*) цель *f*.

objectively [əb'dʒɛktɪvlɪ] *adv* объекти́вно.

objectivity [ɔbdʒɪk'tɪvɪtɪ] *n* объекти́вность *f*.

object lesson *n*: **an ~ ~ in** нагля́дный приме́р +*gen*.

objector [əb'dʒɛktəʳ] *n* протесту́ющий*(-ая) *m(f) adj*.

obligation [ɔblɪ'geɪʃən] *n* обяза́тельство; **we are under no ~ to them** мы им ниче́м не обя́заны; **we are under (an) ~ to give him what he needs** мы обя́заны дать ему́ всё, что потре́буется; **"without ~"** (*COMM*) „без обяза́тельств".

obligatory [ə'blɪgətərɪ] *adj* обяза́тельный* (обяза́телен).

oblige [ə'blaɪdʒ] *vt* (*do a favour for*) обя́зывать (обяза́ть *perf*); (*force*): **to ~ sb to do** обя́зывать (обяза́ть* *perf*) кого́-н +*infin*; **I'm much ~d to you for your help** (*grateful*) я о́чень обя́зан Вам за ва́шу по́мощь; **anything to ~!** (*inf*) (я весь) к ва́шим услу́гам!

obliging [ə'blaɪdʒɪŋ] *adj* (*helpful*) любе́зный* (любе́зен).

oblique [ə'bli:k] *adj* (*line*) накло́нный; (*comment, reference*) ко́свенный ♦ *n* (*BRIT*: *TYP*): **~ (stroke)** накло́нная черта́.

obliterate [ə'blɪtəreɪt] *vt* (*destroy*) уничтожа́ть (уничто́жить *perf*); (*from mind*) стира́ть (стере́ть* *perf*).

oblivion [ə'blɪvɪən] *n* забве́ние; **these events have sunk into ~** э́ти собы́тия пре́даны забве́нию.

oblivious [ə'blɪvɪəs] *adj*: **to be ~ of** *or* **to** не сознава́ть* (*impf*) +*gen*.

oblong ['ɔblɔŋ] *adj* продолгова́тый ♦ *n* продолгова́тый предме́т.

obnoxious [əb'nɔkʃəs] *adj* отврати́тельный* (отврати́телен).

o.b.o. *abbr* (*US*: *in classified ads*: = *or best offer*) и́ли по договорённости.

oboe ['əubəu] *n* гобо́й.

obscene [əb'si:n] *adj* непристóйный*
(непристóен).
obscenity [əb'sɛnɪtɪ] *n* непристóйность *f*.
obscure [əb'skjuə'] *adj* (*little known*) мало-
извéстный* (малоизвéстен); (*difficult to
understand*) неясный* (неясен), смýтный*
(смýтен) ◆ *vt* (*view, sun etc*) загорáживать
(загородить* *perf*); (*truth, meaning etc*)
затемнять (затемнить* *perf*).
obscurity [əb'skjuərɪtɪ] *n* (*see adj*) безвéстность
f; неясность *f*.
obsequious [əb'si:kwɪəs] *adj* подобо-
стрáстный* (подобострáстен).
observable [əb'zə:vəbl] *adj* наблюдáемый;
(*appreciable*) замéтный* (замéтен).
observance [əb'zə:vns] *n* (*of law, custom*)
соблюдéние; **religious ~s** религиóзные
обряды.
observant [əb'zə:vnt] *adj* наблюдáтельный*
(наблюдáтелен).
observation [ɔbzə'veɪʃən] *n* (*remark*)
замечáние; (*surveillance, also* MED)
наблюдéние.
observation post *n* наблюдáтельный пост* *or*
пункт.
observatory [əb'zə:vətrɪ] *n* обсерватóрия.
observe [əb'zə:v] *vt* (*watch*) наблюдáть (*impf*)
за +*instr*; (*comment*) замечáть (замéтить*
perf); (*abide by*) соблюдáть (соблюсти* *perf*).
observer [əb'zə:və'] *n* наблюдáтель *m*.
obsess [əb'sɛs] *vt* владевáть (владéть* *perf*);
you are ~ed by the idea Вы одержимы этой
идéей; **he is totally ~ed with this woman** он
совершéнно помéшан на этой жéнщине.
obsession [əb'sɛʃən] *n* навязчивая идéя; **she
has an ~ for cats** онá помéшана на кóшках.
obsessive [əb'sɛsɪv] *adj* одержимый
(одержим).
obsolescence [ɔbsə'lɛsns] *n* устарéлость *f*.
obsolete ['ɔbsəli:t] *adj* (*words*) устарéвший;
(*technology*) устарéлый.
obstacle ['ɔbstəkl] *n* (*also fig*) препятствие.
obstacle race *n* бег с препятствиями.
obstetrician [ɔbstə'trɪʃən] *n* врач-акушéр.
obstetrics [ɔb'stɛtrɪks] *n* акушéрство.
obstinacy ['ɔbstɪnəsɪ] *n* (*of person*) упрямство.
obstinate ['ɔbstɪnɪt] *adj* (*person, behaviour*)
упрямый (упрям); (*cold, pain*) упóрный.
obstruct [əb'strʌkt] *vt* (*road, path*)
загорáживать (загородить* *perf*); (*traffic,
progress*) препятствовать
(воспрепятствовать *perf*) +*dat*.
obstruction [əb'strʌkʃən] *n* (*action*)
препятствование; (: *of law*) обстрýкция;
(*object*) препятствие.
obstructive [əb'strʌktɪv] *adj* (*behaviour*)
обструкциóнный; **he is ~** он чинит
препятствия.

obtain [əb'teɪn] *vt* (*get hold of*) доставáть*
(достáть* *perf*); (*gain*) получáть (получить*
perf) ◆ *vi* (*formal: exist*) существовáть (*impf*); **to
~ sth (for o.s.)** добивáться (добиться* *perf*)
чегó-н (для себя).
obtainable [əb'teɪnəbl] *adj* достижимый
(достижим).
obtrusive [əb'tru:sɪv] *adj* навязчивый
(навязчив).
obtuse [əb'tju:s] *adj* (*person, remark*)
бестолкóвый (бестолкóв); (*матн*) тупóй.
obverse ['ɔbvə:s] *n*: **the ~** обрáтное *nt adj*.
obviate ['ɔbvɪeɪt] *vt* устранять (устранить*
perf).
obvious ['ɔbvɪəs] *adj* очевидный* (очевиден).
obviously ['ɔbvɪəslɪ] *adv* очевидно; (*of course*)
разумéется; **he was ~ not drunk** бы́ло
очевидно, что он не пьян; **he was not ~
drunk** он не был очевидным óбразом пьян;
~ not разумéется, нет.
OCAS *n abbr* = **Organization of Central American
States.**
occasion [ə'keɪʒən] *n* (*time*) раз*; (*case*)
слýчай; (*event*) собы́тие; (*opportunity*)
возмóжность *f* ◆ *vt* (*cause*) вызывáть
(вы́звать* *perf*); **on this ~** на этот раз; **on that
~** в тот раз; **to rise to the ~** окáзываться
(оказáться* *perf*) на высотé.
occasional [ə'keɪʒənl] *adj* рéдкий*, нечáстый.
occasionally [ə'keɪʒənəlɪ] *adv* врéмя от
врéмени, изрéдка; **very ~** óчень рéдко.
occasional table *n* запаснóй стóлик.
occult [ɔ'kʌlt] *n*: **the ~** оккýльтные наýки *fpl*.
occupancy ['ɔkjupənsɪ] *n* пребывáние.
occupant ['ɔkjupənt] *n* (*long-term*)
обитáтель(ница) *m(f)*; (*temporary*): **the ~s of
the car/room** находящиеся *pl adj* в машине/
кóмнате.
occupation [ɔkju'peɪʃən] *n* занятие;
(*occupancy*) пребывáние; (MIL) оккупáция;
unfit for ~ (*house*) непригóдный*
(непригóден) для жилья.
occupational accident [ɔkju'peɪʃənl-] *n*
произвóдственный несчáстный слýчай.
occupational guidance *n* (BRIT) консультáция
по пóиску мéста рабóты.
occupational hazard *n* произвóдственный
риск.
occupational pension scheme *n* пенсиóнный
план, по котóрому пенсиóнный фонд
формирýется за счёт взнóсов рабóтника и
егó работодáтеля.
occupational therapy *n* трудотерапия.
occupier ['ɔkjupaɪə'] *n* проживáющий(-ая) *m(f)
adj*; **"to the ~"** „проживáющему" (*обращéние
в письмé*).
occupy ['ɔkjupaɪ] *vt* занимáть (занять* *perf*);
(*country, attention*) захвáтывать (захватить*

---

* marks translations which have irregular inflections. The Russian-English side of the dictionary gives inflectional information.

perf); **to ~ o.s. (with sth)** занима́ться (заня́ться *perf*) (чем-н); **all of the rooms are occupied** все ко́мнаты за́няты; **he was occupied with his work** он был за́нят рабо́той.

occur [ə'kɔː'] *vi* (*take place*) происходи́ть* (произойти́* *perf*), случа́ться (случи́ться *perf*); (*exist*) встреча́ться (встре́титься *perf*); **to ~ to sb** приходи́ть* (прийти́* *perf*) кому́-н в го́лову.

occurrence [ə'kʌrəns] *n* (*event*) происше́ствие; (*existence*) слу́чай.

ocean ['əuʃən] *n* океа́н; **~s of** (*fig: inf*) мо́ре +*gen*.

ocean bed *n* дно* океа́на.

ocean-going ['əuʃəngəuiŋ] *adj* (*ship etc*) океа́нский.

Oceania [əuʃɪ'eɪnɪə] *n* Океа́ния.

ocean liner *n* океа́нский ла́йнер.

ochre ['əukə'] (*US* **ocher**) *adj* (*colour*) о́хровый.

o'clock [ə'klɔk] *adv*: **it is five ~** сейча́с пять часо́в.

OCR *n abbr* (*COMPUT*) = **optical character recognition, optical character reader**.

Oct. *abbr* = **October**.

octagonal [ɔk'tægənl] *adj* восьмиуго́льный.

octane ['ɔkteɪn] *n* окта́н; **high-~ petrol** *or* (*US*) **gas** бензи́н с высо́ким окта́новым число́м.

octave ['ɔktɪv] *n* окта́ва.

October [ɔk'təubə'] *n* октя́брь* *m*; *see also* **July**.

octogenarian ['ɔktəudʒɪ'nɛərɪən] *n*: **he is an ~** ему́ за во́семьдесят.

octopus ['ɔktəpəs] *n* осьмино́г.

odd [ɔd] *adj* (*strange*) стра́нный* (стра́нен), необы́чный* (необы́чен); (*uneven*) нечётный; (*not paired*) непа́рный; (*rare*) ре́дкий*; **60-~** шестьдеся́т с ли́шним; **at ~ times** вре́мя от вре́мени; **I was the ~ one out** я был ли́шний.

oddball ['ɔdbɔːl] *n* (*inf*) чуда́к*.

oddity ['ɔdɪtɪ] *n* (*thing*) дико́винка; (*person*) ре́дкость *f*; (*characteristic*) стра́нность *f*.

odd-job man [ɔd'dʒɔb-] *n* разнорабо́чий* *m adj*.

odd jobs *npl* случа́йные рабо́ты *fpl*.

oddly ['ɔdlɪ] *adv* (*strangely: behave, dress*) стра́нно; *see also* **enough**.

oddments ['ɔdmənts] *npl* оста́тки *mpl*.

odds [ɔdz] *npl* (*in betting*) ста́вки *fpl*; **the ~ are against him** обстоя́тельства про́тив него́; **to succeed against all the ~** добива́ться (доби́ться* *perf*) успе́ха напереко́р всему́; **it makes no ~** всё равно́; **to be at ~ (with)** быть* (*impf*) не в лада́х (с +*instr*).

odds and ends *npl* ме́лочи* *fpl*.

odds-on [ɔdz'ɔn] *adj* (*inf: favourite*) абсолю́тный; **he is ~ to win the election** он наверняка́ победи́т на вы́борах.

ode [əud] *n* о́да.

Odessa [əu'dɛsə] *n* Оде́сса.

odious ['əudɪəs] *adj* одио́зный* (одио́зен).

odometer [ɔ'dɔmɪtə'] *n* одо́метр.

odour ['əudə'] (*US* **odor**) *n* за́пах.

odourless ['əudəlɪs] *adj* без за́паха.

OECD *n abbr* = *Organization for Economic Cooperation and Development*.

oesophagus [iː'sɔfəgəs] (*US* **esophagus**) *n* пищево́д.

oestrogen ['iːstrəudʒən] (*US* **estrogen**) *n* эстроге́н.

KEYWORD

of [ɔv] *prep*: *1*: **the history of Russia** исто́рия Росси́и; **a friend of ours** наш друг*; **a boy of 10** ма́льчик десяти́ лет; **that was kind of you** это бы́ло о́чень любе́зно с ва́шей стороны́; **a man of great ability** челове́к больши́х спосо́бностей; **the city of New York** го́род Нью-Йо́рк; **south of London** к ю́гу от Ло́ндона

2 (*expressing quantity, amount, dates etc*): **a kilo of flour** килогра́мм муки́; **how much of this material do you need?** ско́лько тако́й тка́ни Вам ну́жно?; **there were three of them** (*people*) их бы́ло тро́е; (*objects*) их бы́ло три; **3 of us stayed** тро́е из нас оста́лись; **the 5th of July** 5-ое ию́ля; **on the 5th of July** 5-ого ию́ля

3 (*from, out of*) из +*gen*; **the house is made of wood** дом* сде́лан из де́рева.

KEYWORD

off [ɔf] *adv* *1* (*referring to distance, time*): **it's a long way off** это далеко́ отсю́да; **the city is five miles off** до го́рода пять миль; **the game is 3 days off** до игры́ оста́лось 3 дня

2 (*departure*): **to go off to Paris/Italy** уезжа́ть (уе́хать* *perf*) в Пари́ж/Ита́лию; **I must be off** мне пора́ идти́*

3 (*removal*): **to take off one's hat/coat/clothes** снима́ть (снять* *perf*) шля́пу/пальто́/оде́жду; **the button came off** пу́говица оторвала́сь; **10% off** (*COMM*) ски́дка в 10%

4: **to be off** (*on holiday*) быть (*impf*) в о́тпуске; **I'm off on Fridays** у меня́ выходно́й по пя́тницам; **he was off on Friday** в пя́тницу его́ не́ было на рабо́те; **I have a day off** у меня́ отгу́л; **to be off sick** не рабо́тать (*impf*) по боле́зни

♦ *adj* *1* (*not turned on*) вы́ключенный (вы́ключен); (: *tap*) закры́тый (закры́т); (*disconnected*) отключённый (отключён)

2 (*cancelled: meeting, match*) отменённый (отменён); (*agreement*) расто́ргнутый (расто́ргнут)

3 (*BRIT*): **to go off** (*milk*) прокиса́ть (проки́снуть* *perf*); (*cheese, meat*) по́ртиться (испо́ртиться *perf*); **the milk has gone off** молоко́ проки́сло:

4: **on the off chance** на вся́кий* слу́чай; **to have an off day** встава́ть* (встать* *perf*) с ле́вой ноги́

♦ *prep* *1* (*indicating motion, removal etc*) с +*gen*; **to fall off a cliff** упа́сть (*perf*) со скалы́

2 (*distant from*) от +*gen*; **it's just off the M1** это недалеко от автострады M1; **it's five km off the main road** это в пяти км от шоссе; **to be off meat** (*no longer eat it*) не есть* (*impf*) мясо; (*no longer like it*) разлюбить* (*perf*) мясо.

offal ['ɔfl] *n* потроха* *pl*.

offbeat ['ɔfbi:t] *adj* нетривиальный* (нетривиален).

off-centre [ɔf'sɛntə'] (*US* **off-center**) *adj* смещённый* (смещён) ♦ *adv* не по центру.

off colour *adj* (*BRIT*: *inf*): **I feel ~ ~** мне нездоровится.

offence [ə'fɛns] (*US* **offense**) *n* (*crime*) правонарушение; (*insult*) оскорбление; **to commit an ~** совершать (совершить *perf*) правонарушение; **to take ~ at** обижаться (обидеться* *perf*) на +*acc*; **to give ~ to** обижать (обидеть* *perf*), оскорблять (оскорбить* *perf*); **"no ~, but ..."** „не в обиду будет сказано, но ...".

offend [ə'fɛnd] *vt* (*person*) обижать (обидеть* *perf*); (*feelings*) оскорблять (оскорбить* *perf*) ♦ *vi*: **to ~ against** (*law, rule*) нарушать (нарушить *perf*).

offender [ə'fɛndə'] *n* правонарушитель(ница) *m(f)*.

offending [ə'fɛndɪŋ] *adj* соответствующий*.

offense [ə'fɛns] *n* (*US*) = **offence**.

offensive [ə'fɛnsɪv] *adj* (*remark, behaviour*) оскорбительный* (оскорбителен); (*smell etc*) отвратительный* (отвратителен) ♦ *n* (*MIL*) наступление; **~ weapon** орудие нападения.

offer ['ɔfə'] *n* предложение ♦ *vt* предлагать (предложить* *perf*); **to make an ~ for sth** предлагать (предложить* *perf*) цену за что-н; **to ~ sth to sb** предлагать (предложить* *perf*) кому-н что-н; **to ~ to do** предлагать (предложить* *perf*) +*infin*; **"on ~"** (*COMM*) „продаётся со скидкой".

offering ['ɔfərɪŋ] *n* (*also REL*) подношение.

offer price *n* цена продовца.

offhand [ɔf'hænd] *adj* (*unfriendly*) пренебрежительный* (пренебрежителен); (*easy-going*) непринуждённый* (непринуждён) ♦ *adv* сразу, не думая; **I can't tell you ~** я не могу Вам сказать сразу.

office ['ɔfɪs] *n* офис; (*room*) кабинет; (*position*) пост, должность *f*; **doctor's ~** (*US*) кабинет врача; **to take ~** (*person*) вступать (вступить* *perf*) в должность; (*political party*) приходить (прийти* *perf*) к власти; **through his good ~s** (*fig*) благодаря его услугам; **the O~ of Fair Trading** (*BRIT*) Управление добросовестной конкуренции.

office automation *n* автоматизация делопроизводства.

office bearer *n* должностное лицо*.

office block (*US* **office building**) *n* административное здание.

office boy *n* посыльный *m adj*.

office hours *npl* часы *mpl* работы; (*US: MED*) приёмные часы *mpl*.

office manager *n* начальник конторы.

officer ['ɔfɪsə'] *n* (*MIL*) офицер; (*also*: **police ~**) полицейский* *m adj*; (: *in Russia*) милиционер; (*of organization*) заведующий* *m adj*.

office work *n* канцелярская работа.

office worker *n* канцелярский*(-ая) or конторский*(-ая) служащий*(-ая) *m(f) adj*.

official [ə'fɪʃl] *adj* официальный ♦ *n* должностное лицо*; **government ~** официальное лицо*.

officialdom [ə'fɪʃldəm] *n* (*pej*) бюрократия.

officially [ə'fɪʃəlɪ] *adv* официально.

Official Receiver *n* (*COMM*) официальное лицо, *назначенное для проведения ликвидации неплатёжеспособной компании*.

official strike *n* официальная забастовка.

officiate [ə'fɪʃɪeɪt] *vi* распоряжаться (*impf*); (*REL*) совершать (совершить *perf*) богослужение; **to ~ as Mayor** исполнять (*impf*) обязанности мэра; **to ~ at a marriage** совершать (совершить *perf*) бракосочетание.

officious [ə'fɪʃəs] *adj* придирчивый.

offing ['ɔfɪŋ] *n*: **war is in the ~** война грядёт.

off-key [ɔf'ki:] *adj* (*MUS*) фальшивый.

off-licence ['ɔflaɪsns] *n* (*BRIT*) винный магазин.

off-limits [ɔf'lɪmɪts] *adj* (*esp US*) закрытый (закрыт).

off-line [ɔf'laɪn] *adj* (*COMPUT*) автономный, независимый ♦ *adv* (*COMPUT*) автономно, независимо; (: *switched off*) отключённо.

off-load ['ɔfləud] *vt* сваливать (свалить *perf*).

off-peak ['ɔf'pi:k] *adj* (*heating, electricity*) непиковый; (*train, ticket*) со скидкой.

off-putting ['ɔfputɪŋ] *adj* (*BRIT*) нерасполагающий.

off-season ['ɔf'si:zn] *adj* (*booking etc*) несезонный ♦ *adv* не в сезон.

offset ['ɔfsɛt] *irreg vt* уравновешивать (*impf*).

offshoot ['ɔfʃu:t] *n* (*fig*) ответвление; (: *of discussion*) последствие.

offshore [ɔf'ʃɔ:'] *adj* (*oilrig, fishing*) морской; **there was a gentle ~ breeze** на море дул лёгкий бриз.

offside ['ɔf'saɪd] *n* (*AUT: in Britain*) правая сторона ♦ *adj* (*SPORT*): **to be ~** быть* (*impf*) в офсайде.

offspring ['ɔfsprɪŋ] *n inv* отпрыск.

offstage [ɔf'steɪdʒ] *adv* (*sounds*) за сценой.

off-the-cuff [ɔfðə'kʌf] *adj* импровиз-ированный.

off-the-job ['ɔfðə'dʒɔb] adj: ~ **training**
обуче́ние с отры́вом от произво́дства.

off-the-peg ['ɔfðə'pɛg] (US **off-the-rack**) adj: ~
clothing гото́вая оде́жда.

off-the-rack ['ɔfðə'ræk] adj (US) = **off-the-peg**.

off-the-record ['ɔfðə'rɛkɔːd] adj
неофициа́льный* (неофициа́лен) ♦ adv
неофициа́льно.

off-white ['ɔfwaɪt] adj белова́тый.

Ofgas ['ɔfgæs] n (BRIT) управле́ние по
контро́лю за газоснабже́нием.

Oftel ['ɔftɛl] n (BRIT) управле́ние по контро́лю
за телефо́нной се́тью.

Ofwat ['ɔfwɔt] n (BRIT) управле́ние по
контро́лю за водоснабже́нием.

often ['ɔfn] adv ча́сто; **how ~ ...?** как ча́сто ...?;
more ~ than not ча́ще всего́; **as ~ as not**
дово́льно ча́сто; **every so ~** вре́мя от
вре́мени.

ogle ['əugl] vt глазе́ть (impf) на +acc.

ogre ['əugəʳ] n великан-людое́д.

OH abbr (US: POST) = Ohio.

oh [əu] excl о, а; **~ really!** да!; **~ no!** (о) нет!

ohm [əum] n (ELEC) ом.

OHMS abbr (BRIT: = On His/Her Majesty's
Service) на слу́жбе у Его́/Её Короле́вского
Вели́чества.

oil [ɔɪl] n (CULIN) ма́сло; (petroleum) нефть f;
(for heating) печно́е то́пливо ♦ vt (engine, gun
etc) сма́зывать (сма́зать* perf); **~s** npl (ART)
ма́сляные кра́ски fpl.

oilcan ['ɔɪlkæn] n маслёнка*.

oil change n (AUT) сме́на ма́сла (в мото́ре).

oilcloth ['ɔɪlklɔθ] n клеёнка*.

oilfield ['ɔɪlfiːld] n месторожде́ние не́фти.

oil filter n (AUT) ма́сляный фильтр.

oilfired ['ɔɪlfaɪəd] adj ма́сляный.

oil gauge n (AUT) индика́тор у́ровня ма́сла.

oil industry n нефтяна́я промы́шленность f.

oil painting n карти́на, напи́санная ма́слом.

oil refinery n нефтеперераба́тывающий
заво́д.

oil rig n нефтяна́я платфо́рма.

oilseed rape ['ɔɪlsiːd-] n рапс, суре́пка.

oilskins ['ɔɪlskɪnz] npl водонепроница́емая
оде́жда fsg.

oil slick n нефтяно́е пятно́*.

oil tanker n (ship) та́нкер; (truck) нефтево́з.

oil well n нефтяна́я сква́жина.

oily ['ɔɪlɪ] adj (rag) прома́сленный
(прома́слен); (substance) масляни́стый;
(food) жи́рный* (жи́рен).

ointment ['ɔɪntmənt] n мазь f.

OK abbr (US: POST) = Oklahoma.

O.K. ['əu'keɪ] excl (inf) хорошо́, ла́дно ♦ adj
(film, meal etc) сре́дний* ♦ vt (approve)
одобря́ть (одо́брить perf) ♦ n: **to give sth the
~** дава́ть (дать* perf) добро́ на что-н; **is it ~?**
(это) норма́льно?; **is everything ~?** всё в
поря́дке?; **are you (feeling) ~?** Вы себя́
норма́льно чу́вствуете?; **are you ~ for**

money? у Вас нет пробле́м с деньга́ми?; **it's
~ with** or **by me** я не про́тив.

okay ['əu'keɪ] excl = O.K..

old [əuld] adj (aged) ста́рый* (стар); (former)
ста́рый; **how ~ are you?** ско́лько Вам лет?;
he's 10 years ~ ему́ 10 лет; **~ man** стари́к; **~
woman** стару́ха; **~er brother** ста́рший*
брат*; **any ~ rag will do** сойдёт люба́я
тря́пка.

old age n ста́рость f.

old age pension n пе́нсия по ста́рости.

old age pensioner n (BRIT) пенсионе́р(ка*).

old-fashioned ['əuld'fæʃnd] adj старомо́дный*
(старомо́ден).

old hand n о́пытный челове́к.

old hat adj (inf): **this is very ~ ~** э́то ужа́сно
нено́во.

old maid n ста́рая де́ва.

old people's home n дом* для престаре́лых.

old-style ['əuldstaɪl] adj в стари́нном сти́ле.

old-time ['əuld'taɪm] adj (dancing)
старомо́дный.

old-timer ['əuld'taɪməʳ] n (inf) старожи́л(ка*).

old wives' tale n ба́бушкины ска́зки* fpl.

oleander [əulɪ'ændəʳ] n олеа́ндр.

O-level ['əulɛvl] n (formerly) ≈ экза́мены в
8-ом кла́ссе сре́дней шко́лы.

olive ['ɔlɪv] n (fruit) масли́на, оли́вка* ♦ adj
(also: ~-green) оли́вковый; **~ tree** оли́вковое
де́рево*; **to offer an ~ branch** (fig) предлага́ть
(предложи́ть* perf) переми́рие.

olive oil n оли́вковое ма́сло.

Olympic [əu'lɪmpɪk] adj олимпи́йский*.

Olympic Games npl: **the ~ ~** (also: **the
Olympics**) Олимпи́йские и́гры fpl.

OM n abbr (BRIT: = Order of Merit) о́рден "За
заслу́ги".

Oman [əu'maːn] n Ома́н.

OMB n abbr (US) = Office of Management and
Budget.

ombudsman ['ɔmbudzmən] n официа́льное
лицо́, рассма́тривающее жа́лобы ча́стных
лиц на госуда́рственные учрежде́ния.

omelet(te) ['ɔmlɪt] n омле́т; **ham/cheese ~**
омле́т с ветчино́й/сы́ром.

omen ['əumən] n предзнаменова́ние.

ominous ['ɔmɪnəs] adj злове́щий* (злове́щ).

omission [əu'mɪʃən] n про́пуск.

omit [əu'mɪt] vt пропуска́ть (пропусти́ть* perf)
♦ vi: **he ~ted to inform me of this** он не
проинформи́ровал меня́ об э́том.

omnipotent [ɔm'nɪpətnt] adj всемогу́щий*
(всемогу́щ).

omnivorous [ɔm'nɪvrəs] adj всея́дный
(всея́ден).

ON abbr (CANADA) = Ontario.

KEYWORD
---

on [ɔn] prep **1** (position) на +prp; (motion) на
+acc; **the book is on the table** кни́га на столе́;
to put the book on the table класть*
(положи́ть* perf) кни́гу на стол; **on the left**

слéва; **the house is on the main road** дом стои́т у шоссé

2 (*indicating means, method, condition etc*): **on foot** пешкóм; **on the train/plane** (*go*) на пóезде/ самолёте; (*be*) в пóезде/самолёте; **on the telephone/radio/television** по телефóну/ рáдио/телеви́зору; **she's on the telephone** онá разговáривает по телефóну; **to be on drugs** принимáть (*impf*) лекáрства; **to be on holiday/business** быть (*impf*) в óтпуске/ командирóвке

3 (*referring to time*): **on Friday** в пя́тницу; **on Fridays** по пя́тницам; **on June 20th** 20-ого ию́ня; **a week on Friday** чéрез недéлю, считáя с пя́тницы; **on arrival** по приéзде; **on seeing this** уви́дев э́то

4 (*about, concerning*) о +*prp*, по +*dat*; **information on train services** информáция о расписáнии поездóв; **a book on physics** кни́га по фи́зике

♦ *adv* **1** (*referring to dress*) в +*prp*; **to have one's coat on** быть (*impf*) в пальтó; **what's she got on?** во что онá былá одéта?; **she put her boots/gloves/hat on** онá надéла сапоги́/ перчáтки/шля́пу

2 (*further, continuously*) дáльше, дáлее; **to walk on** идти́* (*impf*) дáльше

♦ *adj* **1** (*functioning, in operation*) включённый (включён); (: *tap*) откры́тый (откры́т); **is the meeting still on?** (*in progress*) собрáние ещё идёт?; (*not cancelled*) собрáние не отмени́ли?; **there's a good film on at the cinema** в кинотеáтре идёт хорóший фильм

2: **that's not on!** (*inf: of behaviour*) так не пойдёт *or* не годи́тся!

ONC *n abbr* (*BRIT*: = *Ordinary National Certificate*) ≈ свидéтельство об окончáнии начáльной шкóлы.

once [wʌns] *adv* (*on one occasion*) (оди́н) раз; (*formerly*) когдá-то, однáжды ♦ *conj* (*immediately afterwards*) как тóлько; ~ **he had left** как тóлько он ушёл; **at** ~ (*immediately*) срáзу же; (*simultaneously*) вмéсте; **come here at** ~! сейчáс же подойди́ сюдá!; (**all**) **at** ~ все вмéсте; ~ **a week** (оди́н) раз в недéлю; ~ **more** ещё раз; ~ **and for all** раз и навсегдá; **I knew him** ~ я когдá-то был знакóм с ним; ~ **upon a time there lived** ... жил-был ....

oncoming [ˈɔnkʌmɪŋ] *adj* (*traffic etc*) встрéчный.

OND *n abbr* (*BRIT*: = *Ordinary National Diploma*) дипло́м о срéднем техни́ческом образовáнии.

---

one [wʌn] *n* оди́н* (*f* однá*, *nt* однó*, *pl* одни́*); **one hundred and fifty** сто пятьдеся́т; **one day there was a sudden knock at the door** однáжды неожи́данно раздáлся стук в дверь; **one by one** по одномý, оди́н за другáм; *see also* **five**

♦ *adj* **1** (*sole*) еди́нственный; **the one book which** еди́нственная кни́га, котóрая

2 (*same*) оди́н; **they all belong to the one family** они́ все из однóй семьи́

♦ *pron*: **1**: **I'm the one who did it** э́то я сдéлал; **this one** (*f* э́та, *nt* э́то); **that one** тот (*f* та, *nt* то); **I've already got one** у меня́ ужé есть:

2: **one another** друг дрýга; **do you two ever see one another?** Вы когдá-нибудь ви́дитесь?; **the boys didn't dare look at one another** мáльчики не смéли взгляну́ть друг на дрýга

3 (*impersonal*): **one never knows** никогдá не знáешь; **to cut one's finger** порéзать (*perf*) (себé) пáлец; **one needs to eat** нáдо *or* ну́жно есть.

---

one-day excursion [ˈwʌndeɪ-] *n* (*US*) обрáтный билéт (*действи́тельный в течéние одногó дня*).

One-hundred share index [ˈwʌnhʌndrəd-] *n* и́ндекс стá áкций (*публику́емый ежеднéвно и покáзывающий состоя́ние фóндовой би́ржи*).

one-man [ˈwʌnˈmæn] *adj* (*business*) индивидуáльный; (*canoe*) одномéстный.

one-man band *n* человéк-оркéстр.

one-off [wʌnˈɔf] *n* (*BRIT: inf*) едини́чный слýчай.

one-parent family [ˈwʌnpɛərənt-] *n* непóлная семья́*.

one-piece [ˈwʌnpiːs] *adj*: ~ **bathing suit** цéльный купáльник.

onerous [ˈɔnərəs] *adj* тя́гостный* (тя́гостен), обремени́тельный* (обремени́телен).

one's [wʌnz] *adj*: **to dry** ~ **hands** вытирáть (вы́тереть* *perf*) рýки; *see also* **my**.

oneself [wʌnˈsɛlf] *pron* (*reflexive*) себя́; (*emphatic*) сам; (*after prep: +acc, +gen*) самогó себя́; (: +*dat*) самомý себé; (: +*instr*) сами́м собóй; (: +*prp*) самóм себé; **to hurt** ~ ушибáться (ушиби́ться *perf*); **to keep sth for** ~ держáть* (*impf*) что-н при себé; **to talk to** ~ разговáривать (*impf*) с сами́м собóй.

one-shot [ˈwʌnˈʃɔt] *n* (*US*) = **one-off**.

one-sided [wʌnˈsaɪdɪd] *adj* односторóнний (односторóнен); (*contest*) нерáвный* (нерáвен).

one-time [ˈwʌntaɪm] *adj* бы́вший*.

one-to-one [ˈwʌntəwʌn] *adj* (*tuition etc*) индивидуáльный ♦ *adv* оди́н на оди́н.

---

one-upmanship [wʌn'ʌpmənʃɪp] *n*: **the art of** ~ умéние вы́делиться и показáть своё превосхóдство.

one-way ['wʌnweɪ] *adj* (*traffic*) одно-сторо́нний*; ~ **street** у́лица с односторо́нним движéнием.

ongoing ['ɒngəʊɪŋ] *adj* продолжáющийся.

onion ['ʌnjən] *n* лук*.

on-line ['ɒnlaɪn] (*COMPUT*) *adj* неавтонóмный; (*switched on*) подключённый ♦ *adv* неавтонóмно.

onlooker ['ɒnlʊkə*] *n* зри́тель(ница) *m(f)*.

only ['əʊnlɪ] *adv* тóлько ♦ *adj* еди́нственный ♦ *conj* (*but*) тóлько; **an** ~ **child** еди́нственный ребёнок*; **I** ~ **bought one bottle** я купи́л тóлько однý бутьíлку; **I saw her** ~ **yesterday** я тóлько вчерá ви́дел её; **I'd be** ~ **too pleased to help** я был бы óчень рад помóчь; **I would come,** ~ **I'm too busy** я бы пришёл, тóлько я сли́шком зáнят; **not** ~ **... but also** ... не тóлько ..., но и ....

o.n.o. *abbr* (*BRIT: in classified ads*) **= or near(est) offer.**

onset ['ɒnsɛt] *n* наступлéние.

onshore ['ɒnʃɔ:'] *adj*: ~ **wind** вéтер с мóря; (*oil rig, drilling*) назéмный.

onslaught ['ɒnslɔ:t] *n* нападéние.

on-the-job ['ɒnðə'dʒɒb] *adj*: ~ **training** обучéние без отры́ва от произвóдства.

onto ['ɒntu] *prep* **= on to.**

onus ['əʊnəs] *n*: **the** ~ **is on him to prove it** егó долг – доказáть э́то.

onward(s) ['ɒnwəd(z)] *adv* вперёд, дáльше; **from that time** ~ с тех пор.

onyx ['ɒnɪks] *n* óникс.

oops [ʊps] *excl* (*inf*) ой!

ooze [u:z] *vi* сочи́ться (*impf*) ♦ *vt*: **to** ~ **confidence** излучáть (*impf*) увéренность.

opacity [əʊ'pæsɪtɪ] *n* непрозрáчность *f*.

opal ['əʊpl] *n* опáл.

opaque [əʊ'peɪk] *adj* непрозрáчный* (непрозрáчен).

OPEC ['əʊpɛk] *n abbr* (= *Organization of Petroleum-Exporting Countries*) ОПÉК.

open ['əʊpn] *adj* (*also fig*) откры́тый; (*enemy, hostility*) откровéнный; (*vacancy*) свобóдный* ♦ *vt* открывáть (откры́ть* *perf*) ♦ *vi* открывáться (откры́ться* *perf*); (*flower*) раскрывáться (раскры́ться* *perf*); (*book, debate etc: commence*) начинáться (начáться* *perf*); **in the** ~ (**air**) на откры́том вóздухе; **the** ~ **sea** откры́тое мóре; ~ **ground** (*among trees*) поля́на; (*waste ground*) пусты́рь* *m*; **to have an** ~ **mind on sth** подходи́ть* (*impf*) к чемý-н без предубеждéния

▸ **open on to** *vt fus* (*subj: room, door*) выходи́ть* (*impf*) в/на +*acc*

▸ **open out** *vt* раскрывáть (раскры́ть* *perf*) ♦ *vi* раскрывáться (раскры́ться* *perf*)

▸ **open up** *vt* открывáть (откры́ть* *perf*) ♦ *vi*

открывáться (откры́ться* *perf*).

open-air [əʊpn'ɛə'] *adj* (*concert*) на откры́том вóздухе; (*swimming pool*) откры́тый.

open-and-shut ['əʊpnənʃ'ʌt] *adj*: ~ **case** элементáрное дéло.

open day *n* день* *m* откры́тых дверéй.

open-ended [əʊpn'ɛndɪd] *adj* (*fig: question*) откры́тый; (: *discussion*) незавершённый.

opener ['əʊpnə] *n* (*also*: **tin** *or* **can** ~) открывáлка*.

open-heart [əʊpn'hɑ:t] *adj*: ~ **surgery** откры́тая операция на сéрдце.

opening ['əʊpnɪŋ] *adj* (*speech, remarks etc*) вступи́тельный ♦ *n* (*gap, hole*) отвéрстие; (*start*) начáло; (*opportunity*) возмóжность *f*; (*job*) вакáнсия.

opening night *n* (*THEAT*) премьéра.

open learning *n* самообучéние (*по подготóвленным посóбиям*).

openly ['əʊpnlɪ] *adv* откры́то.

open-minded [əʊpn'maɪndɪd] *adj* (*person*) откры́тый; (*approach*) непредвзя́тый.

open-necked ['əʊpnnɛkt] *adj* расстёгнутый.

openness ['əʊpnnɪs] *n* (*frankness*) откры́тость *f*.

open-plan ['əʊpn'plæn] *adj*: ~ **office** óфис с откры́той планирóвкой.

open prison *n* тюрьмá свобóдного режи́ма.

open sandwich *n* бутербрóд.

open shop *n* (*TRADE UNIONS*) *предприя́тие, на котóрое нанимáют рабóчих незави́симо от члéнства в профсою́зе.*

Open University *n* (*BRIT*): **the** ~ ~ Откры́тый университéт.

open verdict *n* (*LAW*): **an** ~ ~ **was passed** объяви́ли, что причи́на смéрти неустанóвлена.

opera ['ɒpərə] *n* óпера.

opera glasses *npl* театрáльный бинóкль *msg*.

opera house *n* óперный теáтр.

opera singer *n* óперный(-ая) певéц*(-ви́ца).

operate ['ɒpəreɪt] *vt* управля́ть (*impf*) +*instr* ♦ *vi* дéйствовать (*impf*); (*drug*) дéйствовать (подéйствовать* *perf*); (*MED*): **to** ~ (**on sb**) опери́ровать (проопери́ровать* *perf*) (когó-н).

operatic [ɒpə'rætɪk] *adj* óперный.

operating costs *n* эксплуатациóнные затрáты *fpl*.

operating profit *n* при́быль *f* от произ-вóдственной дéятельности.

operating room ['ɒpəreɪtɪŋ-] *n* (*US*) операциóнная *f adj*.

operating statement *n* отчёт о при́были и убы́тках; (*esp US*) текýщий балáнс.

operating system *n* (*COMPUT*) операциóнная систéма.

operating table *n* операциóнный стол*.

operating theatre *n* операциóнная *f adj*.

operation [ɒpə'reɪʃən] *n* (*of machine: functioning*) рабóта; (: *controlling*) управле́ние; (*MED, MIL, COMM*) опера́ция; **to be in ~** де́йствовать (*impf*); **he had an ~** (*MED*) ему́ сде́лали опера́цию; **to perform an ~** (*MED*) де́лать (сде́лать *perf*) опера́цию.

operational [ɔpəˈreɪʃənl] *adj* (*working*) функциони́рующий; **the machine was ~** маши́на функциони́ровала.

operative [ˈɔpərətɪv] *adj* (*law etc*) де́йствующий; (*position*) операти́вный ♦ *n* (*in factory*) опера́тор; **the ~ word** ключево́е сло́во*.

operator [ˈɔpəreɪtə'] *n* (*TEL*) телефони́ст(ка*); (*of machine*) опера́тор.

operetta [ɔpəˈrɛtə] *n* опере́тта.

ophthalmic [ɔfˈθælmɪk] *adj* офтальмологи́ческий.

ophthalmic optician *n* окули́ст.

ophthalmologist [ɔfθælˈmɔlədʒɪst] *n* офтальмо́лог.

opinion [əˈpɪnjən] *n* мне́ние; **in my ~** по-мо́ему, по моему́ мне́нию; **to seek a second ~** запра́шивать (запроси́ть* *perf*) дополни́тельное мне́ние.

opinionated [əˈpɪnjəneɪtɪd] *adj* самоуве́ренный.

opinion poll *n* опро́с обще́ственного мне́ния.

opium [ˈəupɪəm] *n* о́пиум.

opponent [əˈpəunənt] *n* оппоне́нт, проти́вник(-ница); (*MIL, SPORT*) проти́вник.

opportune [ˈɔpətjuːn] *adj* подходя́щий*.

opportunism [ɔpəˈtjuːnɪsəm] *n* оппортуни́зм.

opportunist [ɔpəˈtjuːnɪst] *n* оппортуни́ст.

opportunity [ɔpəˈtjuːnɪtɪ] *n* возмо́жность *f*; **to take the ~ of doing** по́льзоваться (воспо́льзоваться *perf*) слу́чаем что́бы +*infin*.

oppose [əˈpəuz] *vt* проти́виться (воспроти́виться* *perf*) +*dat*; **to be ~d to sth** проти́виться (*impf*) чему́-н; **as ~d to b** в противополо́жность +*dat*.

opposing [əˈpəuzɪŋ] *adj* (*ideas, forces*) противополо́жный; **the ~ team** кома́нда проти́вника.

opposite [ˈɔpəzɪt] *adj* противополо́жный ♦ *adv* напро́тив ♦ *prep* напро́тив +*gen* ♦ *n*: **the ~** (*say, think, do etc*) противополо́жное *nt adj*; **the ~ sex** противополо́жный пол; "**see ~ page**" „см. на противополо́жной страни́це".

opposite number *n* (*person*) лицо́, занима́ющее соотве́тствующую до́лжность в друго́й организа́ции.

opposition [ɔpəˈzɪʃən] *n* оппози́ция; **the O~** (*POL*) оппозицио́нная па́ртия.

oppress [əˈprɛs] *vt* угнета́ть (*impf*).

oppression [əˈprɛʃən] *n* угнете́ние.

oppressive [əˈprɛsɪv] *adj* (*régime*) угнета́тельский; (*weather, heat*) гнету́щий*.

opprobrium [əˈprəubrɪəm] *n* (*formal*) осужде́ние.

opt [ɔpt] *vi*: **to ~ for** избира́ть (избра́ть* *perf*); **to ~ to do** реша́ть (реши́ть *perf*) +*infin*

▶ **opt out** *vi* (*school, hospital etc*) выходи́ть* (вы́йти* *perf*) из-под госуда́рственного контро́ля; **to ~ out of sth** выходи́ть* (вы́йти* *perf*) из чего́-н.

optical [ˈɔptɪkl] *adj* опти́ческий*.

optical character reader *n* (*COMPUT*) устро́йство опти́ческого считыва́ния си́мволов.

optical character recognition *n* (*COMPUT*) опти́ческое распознава́ние си́мволов.

optical fibre *n* опти́ческое волокно́.

optical illusion *n* опти́ческий* обма́н.

optician [ɔpˈtɪʃən] *n* окули́ст.

optics [ˈɔptɪks] *n* (*PHYS*) о́птика.

optimism [ˈɔptɪmɪzəm] *n* оптими́зм.

optimist [ˈɔptɪmɪst] *n* оптими́ст(ка*).

optimistic [ɔptɪˈmɪstɪk] *adj* оптимисти́чный* (оптимисти́чен).

optimum [ˈɔptɪməm] *adj* оптима́льный.

option [ˈɔpʃən] *n* (*choice*) вариа́нт; (*SCOL*) предме́т по вы́бору; (*COMM*) опцио́н; **to keep one's ~s open** оставля́ть (оста́вить* *perf*) за собо́й пра́во вы́бора; **I have no ~** у меня́ нет вы́бора.

optional [ˈɔpʃənl] *adj* (*also COMM*) необяза́тельный*; **~ extras** дополни́тельные, но необяза́тельные това́ры и́ли услу́ги.

opulence [ˈɔpjuləns] *n* бога́тство.

opulent [ˈɔpjulənt] *adj* (*person, society etc*) бога́тый.

OR *abbr* (*US: POST*) = Oregon.

or [ɔː'] *conj* и́ли; (*otherwise*): **~ (else)** а то, ина́че; (*with negative*): **he hasn't seen ~ heard anything** он ничего́ не ви́дел и не слы́шал.

oracle [ˈɔrəkl] *n* (*prophet*) ора́кул; (*prophecy*) прорица́ние.

oral [ˈɔːrəl] *adj* (*test, report*) у́стный; (*vaccine, medicine*) ора́льный ♦ *n* (*exam*) у́стный экза́мен.

orange [ˈɔrɪndʒ] *n* апельси́н ♦ *adj* (*colour*) ора́нжевый.

orangeade [ɔrɪndʒˈeɪd] *n* апельси́новый напи́ток*.

oration [ɔːˈreɪʃən] *n* торже́ственная речь *f*.

orator [ˈɔrətə'] *n* ора́тор.

oratorio [ɔrəˈtɔːrɪəu] *n* орато́рия.

orb [ɔːb] *n* шар*.

orbit [ˈɔːbɪt] *n* орби́та ♦ *vt* обраща́ться (*impf*) вокру́г +*gen*.

orchard [ˈɔːtʃəd] *n* сад* (*фрукто́вый*); **apple ~** я́блоневый сад*.

orchestra [ˈɔːkɪstrə] *n* орке́стр; (*US: seating*) парте́р.

orchestral [ɔːˈkɛstrəl] *adj* оркестро́вый; **~ musician** оркестра́нт(ка*).

---

* marks translations which have irregular inflections. The Russian-English side of the dictionary gives inflectional information.

orchestrate ['ɔ:kɪstreɪt] *vt* (*stage-manage*)
организо́вывать (организова́ть *perf*); (*MUS*)
оркестрова́ть (*impf/perf*).
orchid ['ɔ:kɪd] *n* орхиде́я.
ordain [ɔ:'deɪn] *vt* (*REL*) посвяща́ть (посвяти́ть*
perf) в сан; (*decide*) предпи́сывать
(предписа́ть* *perf*).
ordeal [ɔ:'di:l] *n* испыта́ние.
order ['ɔ:də'] *n* (*command*) прика́з; (*from shop,
company, in restaurant*) зака́з; (*sequence,
discipline*) поря́док* ♦ *vt* (*command*)
прика́зывать (приказа́ть* *perf*) +*dat*; (*from
shop, company, in restaurant*) зака́зывать
(заказа́ть* *perf*); (*also:* put in ~) располага́ть
(расположи́ть* *perf*) по поря́дку; **in ~** в
поря́дке; **in** (**working**) ~ испра́вный*
(испра́вен); **in ~ to do** для того́ чтобы +*infin*;
in ~ of size по разме́ру; **it is already on ~**
(*COMM*) э́то уже́ зака́зано; **out of ~** (*not in
sequence*) не по поря́дку; (*not working*)
неиспра́вный* (неиспра́вен); **to place an ~ for
sth with sb** зака́зывать (заказа́ть* *perf*) что-н
кому́-н; **made to ~** сде́лан на зака́з; **she is
under ~s to remain silent** ей прика́зано
молча́ть; **a point of ~** вопро́с о наруше́нии
регла́мента; **to the ~ of** (*BANKING*)
опла́чиваемый по ве́кселю на и́мя +*gen*; **to ~
sb to do** прика́зывать (приказа́ть* *perf*)
кому́-н +*infin*.
order book *n* кни́га зака́зов.
order form *n* бланк зака́за.
orderly ['ɔ:dəlɪ] *n* (*MIL*) ордина́рец*; (*MED*)
санита́р ♦ *adj* (*room*) опря́тный* (опря́тен);
(*person*) организо́ванный* (организо́ван);
(*system*) упоря́доченный* (упоря́дочен).
order number *n* но́мер* зака́за.
ordinal ['ɔ:dɪnl] *adj*: ~ **number** поря́дковое
числи́тельное *nt adj*.
ordinarily ['ɔ:dnrɪlɪ] *adv* обы́чно.
ordinary ['ɔ:dnrɪ] *adj* (*everyday, usual*)
обыкнове́нный* (обыкнове́нен), обы́чный*
(обы́чен); (*mediocre*) заура́дный*
(заура́ден); **out of the ~** (*exceptional*)
необыкнове́нный* (необыкнове́нен).
ordinary seaman *n* (*BRIT*) мла́дший* матро́с.
ordinary shares *npl* обыкнове́нные а́кции *fpl*.
ordination [ɔ:dɪ'neɪʃən] *n* (*REL*) посвяще́ние в
духо́вный сан.
ordnance ['ɔ:dnəns] *n* (*MIL*) ору́дие ♦ *adj*
(*factory, supplies*) оруже́йный.
Ordnance Survey *n* (*BRIT*) ≈ Госуда́рственное
Управле́ние по геоде́зии и картогра́фии.
ore [ɔ:'] *n* руда́*.
Orenburg ['ɔrənbə:g] *n* Оренбу́рг.
organ ['ɔ:gən] *n* (*ANAT*) о́рган; (*MUS*) орга́н.
organic [ɔ:'gænɪk] *adj* (*fertilizer*)
органи́ческий*; (*food*) вы́ращенный без
примене́ния хими́ка́та.
organism ['ɔ:gənɪzəm] *n* органи́зм.
organist ['ɔ:gənɪst] *n* органи́ст(ка).
organization [ɔ:gənaɪ'zeɪʃən] *n* организа́ция.

organization chart *n* организацио́нная
структу́ра.
organize ['ɔ:gənaɪz] *vt* организо́вывать
(организова́ть *perf*), устра́ивать (устро́ить
perf); **to get ~d** организо́вываться
(организова́ться *perf*).
organized crime *n* организо́ванная
престу́пность *f*.
organized labour *n* чле́ны *mpl* профсою́зов.
organizer ['ɔ:gənaɪzə'] *n* организа́тор,
устро́итель(ница) *m(f)*.
orgasm ['ɔ:gæzəm] *n* орга́зм.
orgy ['ɔ:dʒɪ] *n* о́ргия, разгу́л.
Orient ['ɔ:rɪənt] *n*: **the ~** Восто́к.
orient ['ɔ:rɪənt] *vt* ориенти́ровать
(сориенти́ровать *perf*).
oriental [ɔ:rɪ'ɛntl] *adj* восто́чный.
orientate ['ɔ:rɪənteɪt] *vt*: **to ~ o.s.** ориент-
и́роваться (сориенти́роваться *perf*).
orifice ['ɔrɪfɪs] *n* отве́рстие.
origin ['ɔrɪdʒɪn] *n* происхожде́ние; **country of ~**
ме́сто* рожде́ния.
original [ə'rɪdʒɪnl] *adj* (*new*) оригина́льный*
(оригина́лен); (*genuine*) по́длинный*
(по́длинен); (*imaginative: writer, artist etc*)
самобы́тный* (самобы́тен) ♦ *n* по́длинник,
оригина́л.
originality [ərɪdʒɪ'nælɪtɪ] *n* (*of artist etc*)
самобы́тность *f*, оригина́льность *f*.
originally [ə'rɪdʒɪnəlɪ] *adv* первонача́льно.
originate [ə'rɪdʒɪneɪt] *vi*: ~ **from**
происходи́ть* (произойти́* *perf*) от/из +*gen*;
to ~ in зарожда́ться (зароди́ться* *perf*) в
+*prp*.
originator [ə'rɪdʒɪneɪtə'] *n* созда́тель *m*.
Orkneys ['ɔ:knɪz] *npl*: **the ~** (*also:* the Orkney
Islands) Орке́йские острова́* *mpl*.
ornament ['ɔ:nəmənt] *n* (*decorative object*)
украше́ние; (*on building, dress etc*)
орна́мент.
ornamental [ɔ:nə'mɛntl] *adj* (*decorative:
garden, pond*) декорати́вный.
ornamentation [ɔ:nəmɛn'teɪʃən] *n* украше́ние.
ornate [ɔ:'neɪt] *adj* декорати́вный.
ornithologist [ɔ:nɪ'θɔlədʒɪst] *n* орнито́лог.
ornithology [ɔ:nɪ'θɔlədʒɪ] *n* орнитоло́гия.
orphan ['ɔ:fn] *n* сирота́* *m/f* ♦ *vt*: **to be ~ed**
оста́ться* (*perf*) сирото́й, осироте́ть (*perf*).
orphanage ['ɔ:fənɪdʒ] *n* де́тский дом*.
orthodox ['ɔ:θədɔks] *adj* (*also fig*)
ортодокса́льный* (ортодокса́лен); **the
Russian O~ Church** Ру́сская Правосла́вная
це́рковь.
orthodoxy ['ɔ:θədɔksɪ] *n* ортодокса́льные
воззре́ния *ntpl*.
orthopaedic [ɔ:θə'pi:dɪk] (*US* orthopedic) *adj*
ортопеди́ческий*.
OS *abbr* (*BRIT*) = **Ordnance Survey**; (*NAUT*) =
ordinary seaman; (*DRESS*) = **outsize**.
O/S *abbr* (*COMM*: = *out of stock*) нет в прода́же.
Oscar ['ɔskə'] *n* О́скар (*приз*).

oscillate ['ɔsɪleɪt] *vi* (*ELEC, PHYS*) колеба́ться* (*impf*), осцилли́ровать (*impf*); (*fig*) колеба́ться* (*impf*).

OSHA *n abbr* (*US*) = *Occupational Safety and Health Administration*.

Oslo ['ɔzləu] *n* О́сло *nt ind*.

ostensible [ɔs'tɛnsɪbl] *adj* мни́мый.

ostensibly [ɔs'tɛnsɪblɪ] *adv* я́кобы.

ostentation [ɔstɛn'teɪʃən] *n* показна́я ро́скошь *f*.

ostentatious [ɔstɛn'teɪʃəs] *adj* (*building, car*) бро́ский*; (*behaviour*) показно́й; **he is very ~** он выставля́ет себя́ напока́з.

osteopath ['ɔstɪəpæθ] *n* остеопа́т.

ostracize ['ɔstrəsaɪz] *vt* подверга́ть (подве́ргнуть* *perf*) остраки́зму.

ostrich ['ɔstrɪtʃ] *n* стра́ус.

OT *abbr* (*BIBLE*: = *Old Testament*) Ве́тхий* заве́т.

OTB *n abbr* (*US*: = *off-track betting*) внеипподро́мный тотализа́тор.

OTE *abbr* (*COMM*: = *on-target earnings*) *предполага́емый дохо́д*.

other ['ʌðə'] *adj* друго́й ◆ *pron*: **the ~ (one)** друго́й(-а́я) *m(f) adj*, тот (*f* та) ◆ *adv*: **~ than** кро́ме *+gen*; **~s** (*other people*) други́е *pl adj*; **the ~s** остальны́е *pl adj*; **the ~ day** на дня́х; **some ~ people have still to arrive** прие́дет ещё не́сколько челове́к; **some actor or ~** како́й-то из актёров; **somebody or ~** кто-нибу́дь, кто́-то; **it was none ~ than the prime minister** э́то был ни кто ино́й как премье́р-мини́стр.

otherwise ['ʌðəwaɪz] *adv* (*differently*) ина́че, по-друго́му; (*apart from that*) в остально́м ◆ *conj* а то, ина́че; **it is an ~ good piece of work** в остально́м э́то о́чень хоро́шая рабо́та.

OTT *abbr* (*inf*) = *over the top see* **top**.

Ottawa ['ɔtəwə] *n* Отта́ва.

otter ['ɔtə'] *n* вы́дра.

OU *n abbr* (*BRIT*) = *Open University*.

ouch [autʃ] *excl* ай, ой.

ought [ɔ:t] (*pt* **ought**) *aux vb*: **I ~ to do it** мне сле́довало бы э́то сде́лать; **this ~ to have been corrected** э́то сле́довало испра́вить; **he ~ to win** он до́лжен вы́играть; **you ~ to go and see this film** Вы обяза́тельно должны́ посмотре́ть э́тот фильм.

ounce [auns] *n* у́нция.

our ['auə'] *adj* наш; *see also* **my**.

ours [auəz] *pron* наш; (*referring to subject of sentence*) свой; *see also* **mine¹**.

ourselves [auə'sɛlvz] *pl pron* (*reflexive*) себя́; (*complement*) себя́; (*after prep: +acc, +gen*) себя́; (: *+dat*) себе́; (: *+instr*) собо́й; (: *+prp*) себе́; (*emphatic*) са́ми; (*alone*): (**all) by ~** са́ми; **let's keep it between ~** дава́йте оста́вим э́то ме́жду на́ми; *see also* **myself**.

oust [aust] *vt* изгоня́ть (изгна́ть* *perf*).

KEYWORD

out [aut] *adv* **1** (*not in*): **they're out in the garden** они́ в саду́; **out in the rain/snow** под дождём/ сне́гом; **out here** здесь; **out there** там; **to go out** выходи́ть* (вы́йти* *perf*); **out loud** гро́мко **2** (*not at home, absent*): **he is out at the moment** его́ сейча́с нет (до́ма); **let's have a night out on Friday!** дава́йте пойдём куда́-нибудь в пя́тницу ве́чером! **3** (*indicating distance*) в *+prp*; **the boat was 10 km out (from the shore)** кора́бль находи́лся в 10 км от бе́рега; **three days out from Plymouth** в трёх днях пла́вания от Пли́мута **4** (*SPORT*): **the ball is out** мяч за преде́лами по́ля; **out!** (*TENNIS etc*) а́ут!

◆ *adj*: **1**: **to be out** (*unconscious*) быть (*impf*) без созна́ния; (*out of game*) быть (*impf*) удалённым(-ой) с по́ля; (*have appeared: flowers*) распуска́ться (распусти́ться* *perf*); (: *news, secret*) станови́ться* (стать* *perf*) изве́стным(-ой); (*extinguished: fire, light, gas*) ту́хнуть* (поту́хнуть* *perf*), га́снуть* (пога́снуть* *perf*); (*fashion*): **to go out** выходи́ть* (вы́йти* *perf*) из мо́ды **2** (*finished*): **before the week was out** до оконча́ния неде́ли: **3**: **to be out to do** (*intend*) намерева́ться (*impf*) *+infin*; **to be out in one's calculations** (*wrong*) ошиба́ться (ошиби́ться* *perf*) в расчётах

◆ *prep* **1** (*outside, beyond*) из *+gen*; **to go out of the house** выходи́ть* (вы́йти* *perf*) из до́ма; **to be out of danger** (*safe*) быть (*impf*) вне опа́сности **2** (*cause, motive*): **out of curiosity** из любопы́тства; **out of fear** из стра́ха; **out of boredom** от or со ску́ки; **out of grief/joy** с го́ря/ра́дости; **out of necessity** по необходи́мости **3** (*from, from among*) из *+gen* **4** (*without*): **we are out of sugar/petrol** *etc* у нас ко́нчился са́хар/бензи́н *etc*.

---

outage ['autɪdʒ] *n* (*esp US: power failure*) отключе́ние электри́чества.

out-and-out ['autəndaut] *adj* отъя́вленный.

outback ['autbæk] *n* (*in Australia*): **the ~** необжиты́е райо́ны *mpl*.

outbid [aut'bɪd] *vt*: **to ~ sb** перебива́ть (переби́ть* *perf*) чью-н це́ну.

outboard ['autbɔ:d] *n* (*also: ~ motor*) подвесно́й мото́р.

outbreak ['autbreɪk] *n* (*of disease, violence*) вспы́шка*; (*of war*) нача́ло.

outbuilding ['autbɪldɪŋ] *n* надво́рная постро́йка*.

outburst ['autbə:st] *n* вспы́шка*, взрыв.

outcast ['autkɑ:st] *n* изго́й.

outclass [aut'klɑ:s] *vt* превосходи́ть*

(превзойти• *perf*).

outcome ['autkʌm] *n* исхо́д, результа́т.

outcrop ['autkrɔp] *n* (*of rock*) обнаже́ние.

outcry ['autkraɪ] *n* негодова́ние, проте́ст.

outdated [aut'deɪtɪd] *adj* (*customs, ideas*) отжи́вший; (*clothes*) старомо́дный•; (*technology*) устаре́лый.

outdo [aut'du:] *irreg vt* превосходи́ть• (превзойти́• *perf*).

outdoor [aut'dɔ:•] *adj* на откры́том во́здухе; (*swimming pool*) откры́тый; ~ **clothes** ве́рхняя оде́жда.

outdoors [aut'dɔ:z] *adv* на у́лице, на откры́том во́здухе.

outer ['autə•] *adj* нару́жный; ~ **suburbs** да́льние предме́стья; **the ~ office** кра́йний• кабине́т.

outer space *n* косми́ческое простра́нство.

outfit ['autfɪt] *n* (*set of clothes*) компле́кт (оде́жды); (*inf: organization*) компа́ния.

outfitter's ['autfɪtəz] *n* (BRIT) торго́вец• мужско́й оде́ждой.

outgoing ['autgəuɪŋ] *adj* (*extrovert*) общи́тельный• (общи́телен); (*president, mayor etc*) уходя́щий; (*mail etc*) исходя́щий•.

outgoings ['autgəuɪŋz] *npl* (BRIT) расхо́ды *mpl*.

outgrow [aut'grəu] *irreg vt* (*one's clothes*) выраста́ть (вы́расти• *perf*) из +*gen*; (*friends, habits*) перераста́ть (перерасти́• *perf*).

outhouse ['authaus] *n* надво́рная постро́йка•.

outing ['autɪŋ] *n* похо́д.

outlandish [aut'lændɪʃ] *adj* дико́винный.

outlast [aut'lɑ:st] *vt* пережива́ть (пережи́ть• *perf*).

outlaw ['autlɔ:] *n* челове́к вне зако́на ♦ *vt* объявля́ть (объяви́ть• *perf*) вне зако́на.

outlay ['autleɪ] *n* (*expenditure*) затра́ты *fpl*; (*investment*) вложе́ния *ntpl*.

outlet ['autlɛt] *n* (*hole*) выходно́е отве́рстие; (*pipe*) сток; (US: ELEC) розе́тка•; (COMM: *also*: **retail ~**) торго́вая то́чка•; (*for emotions*) вы́ход.

outline ['autlaɪn] *n* (*shape*) очерта́ния *ntpl*; (*sketch, explanation*) набро́сок• ♦ *vt* (*fig: theory, plan etc*) набра́сывать (наброса́ть *perf*).

outlive [aut'lɪv] *vt* пережива́ть (пережи́ть• *perf*).

outlook ['autluk] *n* (*attitude*) взгля́ды *mpl*, воззре́ния *ntpl*; (*prospects*) перспекти́вы *fpl*; (: *for weather*) прогно́з.

outlying ['autlaɪɪŋ] *adj* отдалённый.

outmanoeuvre [autmə'nu:və•] (US **outmaneuver**) *vt* перехитри́ть (*perf*).

outmoded [aut'məudɪd] *adj* устаре́вший.

outnumber [aut'nʌmbə•] *vt* превосходи́ть• (превзойти́• *perf*) число́м; **they were ~ed by 5 to 1** их бы́ло в пять раз ме́ньше.

out of bounds *adj*: **this area is** ~ ~ ~ э́та ме́сто явля́ется запре́тным.

out-of-court [autəv'kɔ:t] *adv*: **to settle** ~

приходи́ть• (прийти́• *perf*) к соглаше́нию без обраще́ния в суд.

out-of-date [autəv'deɪt] *adj* (*clothes etc*) немо́дный; (*dictionary*) устаре́вший; (*equipment*) устаре́лый; (*passport*) просро́ченный.

out-of-doors [autəv'dɔ:z] *adv* на у́лице, на откры́том во́здухе.

out-of-the-way ['autəvðə'weɪ] *adj* (*place*) глуби́нный; (*fig*) глухо́й.

out of touch *adj*: **to be** ~ ~ ~ отстава́ть• (отста́ть• *perf*) от вре́мени.

out-of-work ['autəvwə:k] *adj* безрабо́тный.

outpatient ['autpeɪʃənt] *n* амбулато́рный(-ая) больно́й(-а́я) *m(f) adj*.

outpouring ['autpɔ:rɪŋ] *n* (*of emotions*) излия́ние.

outpost ['autpəust] *n* аванпо́ст.

output ['autput] *n* (*production*) вы́работка; (COMPUT) выходны́е да́нные *pl adj* ♦ *vt* (COMPUT) выводи́ть• (вы́вести• *perf*) (*да́нные*).

outrage ['autreɪdʒ] *n* (*action: scandalous*) возмути́тельный посту́пок•; (: *violent*) акт наси́лия; (*emotion*) возмуще́ние ♦ *vt* (*shock, anger*) возмуща́ть (возмути́ть• *perf*); **his behaviour is an** ~ его́ поведе́ние про́сто возмути́тельно.

outrageous [aut'reɪdʒəs] *adj* возмути́тельный (возмути́телен).

outrider ['autraɪdə•] *n* (*on motorcycle, horse*) эско́рт.

outright [aut'raɪt] *adv* (*win, own*) абсолю́тно; (*refuse, deny*) наотре́з; (*ask*) пря́мо; (*kill*) наповал ♦ *adj* (*winner, victory*) абсолю́тный; (*refusal, hostility*) откры́тый; **to be killed** ~ погиба́ть (поги́бнуть *perf*) сра́зу.

outrun [aut'rʌn] *irreg vt* обгоня́ть (обогна́ть• *perf*), опережа́ть (опереди́ть• *perf*).

outset ['autsɛt] *n* нача́ло; **from the** ~ с са́мого нача́ла; **at the** ~ внача́ле.

outshine [aut'ʃaɪn] *irreg vt* (*fig*) затмева́ть (затми́ть *perf*).

outside [aut'saɪd] *n* нару́жная сторона́• ♦ *adj* нару́жный, вне́шний• ♦ *adv* (*be*) снару́жи; (*go*) нару́жу ♦ *prep* вне +*gen*, за преде́лами +*gen*; (*next to: building*) у +*gen*; (: *London etc*) под +*instr*; **at the** ~ (*with times*) са́мое по́зднее; (*of size*) са́мое бо́льшее; **an ~ chance** ничто́жный шанс; **it's cold** ~ на у́лице хо́лодно.

outside broadcast *n* (RADIO, TV) репорта́ж *or* трансля́ция с ме́ста собы́тий.

outside lane *n* (AUT: *in Britain*) пра́вый ряд; (: *in US, Europe*) ле́вый ряд.

outside left *n* (FOOTBALL) ле́вый кра́йний• напада́ющий• *m adj*.

outside line *n* (TEL) городско́й телефо́н; **dial "9" for an** ~ го́род – че́рез девя́тку.

outsider [aut'saɪdə•] *n* (*person not involved*) посторо́нний•(-яя) *m(f) adj*; (*in race etc*) аутса́йдер.

outside right *n* (FOOTBALL) пра́вый кра́йний* напада́ющий* *m adj*.

outsize ['autsaɪz] *adj*: ~ **clothes** оде́жда *fsg* больши́х разме́ров.

outskirts ['autskɜːts] *npl* окра́ины *fpl*.

outsmart [aut'smaːt] *vt* перехитри́ть *(perf)*.

outspoken [aut'spəukən] *adj* открове́нный* (открове́нен).

outspread [aut'sprɛd] *adj* (*wings*) распростёртый (распростёрт).

outstanding [aut'stændɪŋ] *adj* (*exceptional*) выдаю́щийся*; (*unfinished*) незако́нченный (незако́нчен); (*unpaid*) неопла́ченный (неопла́чен); **your account is still** ~ Вы до сих пор не уплати́ли по счёту.

outstay [aut'steɪ] *vt*: **to** ~ **one's welcome** заси́живаться (засиде́ться* *perf*) в гостя́х.

outstretched [aut'strɛtʃt] *adj* (*hand*) протя́нутый; (*arms*) вы́тянутый; (*body*) вытяну́вшийся.

outstrip [aut'strɪp] *vt* превосходи́ть* (превзойти́* *perf*).

out tray *n* корзи́на для исходя́щих докуме́нтов.

outvote [aut'vəut] *vt*: **to** ~ **sb by 3 votes** победи́ть *(perf)* кого́-н с переве́сом в 3 го́лоса.

outward ['autwəd] *adj* (*sign, appearances*) вне́шний*, нару́жный; **the** ~ **journey was much quicker** пое́здка туда́ намно́го быстре́е, чем пое́здка обра́тно.

outwardly ['autwədlɪ] *adv* вне́шне.

outweigh [aut'weɪ] *vt* переве́шивать (переве́сить* *perf*).

outwit [aut'wɪt] *vt* перехитри́ть *(perf)*.

ova ['əuvə] *npl of* **ovum**.

oval ['əuvl] *adj* ова́льный ♦ *n* ова́л.

ovarian [əu'vɛərɪən] *adj*: ~ **cyst** киста́ яи́чника; ~ **cancer** рак яи́чника.

ovary ['əuvərɪ] *n* яи́чник.

ovation [əu'veɪʃən] *n* ова́ция.

oven ['ʌvn] *n* (*domestic*) духо́вка*; (*baker's, industrial*) печь* *f*.

ovenproof ['ʌvnpruːf] *adj* жаросто́йкий, жаропро́чный*.

oven-ready ['ʌvnrɛdɪ] *adj* (*chicken, chips etc*) гото́вый для жа́рения в духо́вке.

ovenware ['ʌvnwɛə'] *n* жаросто́йкая *or* жаропро́чная посу́да.

KEYWORD

over ['əuvə'] *adv* **1** (*across*): **to cross over (to the other side of the road)** переходи́ть* (перейти́* *perf*) (на другу́ю сто́рону доро́ги); **over here** здесь; **over there** там; **to ask sb over** (*to one's house*) приглаша́ть (пригласи́ть* *perf*) кого́-н в го́сти *or* к себе́
2 (*indicating movement from upright*): **to knock/turn sth over** сбива́ть (сбить* *perf*)/

перевора́чивать (переверну́ть *perf*) что-н; **to fall over** па́дать (упа́сть* *perf*); **to bend over** нагиба́ться (нагну́ться *perf*)
3 (*finished*): **the game is over** игра́ око́нчена; **his life is over** его́ жизнь ко́нчена
4 (*excessively*) сли́шком, чересчу́р
5 (*remaining: money, food etc*): **there are 3 over** 3 оста́лось:
6: **all over** (*everywhere*) везде́, повсю́ду; **over and over** (*again*) сно́ва и сно́ва

♦ *prep* **1** (*on top of*) на +*prp*; (*above*) над +*instr*
2 (*on the other side of*) че́рез +*acc*; **the pub over the road** паб че́рез доро́гу; **he jumped over the wall** он перепры́гнул че́рез сте́ну
3 (*more than*) свы́ше +*gen*; **over and above** бо́льше (чем); **this is over and above what we have already ordered** э́то бо́льше, чем мы уже́ заказа́ли
4 (*in the course of*) в тече́ние +*gen*, за +*acc*; **over the winter** за зи́му, в тече́ние зимы́; **let's discuss it over dinner** дава́йте обсу́дим э́то за обе́дом; **the work is spread over two weeks** рабо́та рассчи́тана на две неде́ли.

---

over... ['əuvə'] *prefix* пере....

overact [əuvər'ækt] *vi* переи́грывать (переигра́ть *perf*).

overall ['əuvərɔːl] *adj* о́бщий* ♦ *adv* (*in general*) в це́лом *or* о́бщем; (*entirely*) целико́м ♦ *n* (BRIT: *child's, painter's etc*) хала́т; ~**s** *npl* (*clothing*) комбинезо́н *msg*.

overall majority *n* большинство́.

overanxious [əuvər'æŋkʃəs] *adj* весьма́ встрево́женный* (встрево́жен).

overawe [əuvər'ɔː] *vt* вызыва́ть (вы́звать* *perf*) благогове́ние в +*prp*.

overbalance [əuvə'bæləns] *vi* теря́ть (потеря́ть *perf*) равнове́сие.

overbearing [əuvə'bɛərɪŋ] *adj* вла́стный* (вла́стен).

overboard ['əuvəbɔːd] *adv*: **to fall** ~ па́дать (упа́сть* *perf*) за́ борт; **man** ~! челове́к за борто́м!; **to go** ~ (*fig*) переба́рщивать (переборщи́ть *perf*).

overbook [əuvə'buk] *vt*: **the play is** ~**ed** на пье́су прода́ли сли́шком мно́го биле́тов; **the hotel is** ~**ed** гости́ница перепо́лнена.

overcame [əuvə'keɪm] *pt of* **overcome**.

overcapitalize [əuvə'kæpɪtəlaɪz] *vt*: **to** ~ **a project** вкла́дывать (вложи́ть* *perf*) в прое́кт неопра́вданно большо́й капита́л.

overcast ['əuvəkɑːst] *adj* па́смурный (па́смурен), хму́рый (хмур).

overcharge [əuvə'tʃɑːdʒ] *vt* обсчи́тывать (обсчита́ть *perf*).

overcoat ['əuvəkəut] *n* пальто́ *nt ind*.

overcome [əuvə'kʌm] *irreg vt* (*opponent, enemy*) одолева́ть (одоле́ть *perf*);

---

* marks translations which have irregular inflections. The Russian-English side of the dictionary gives inflectional information.

(*difficulties, problems*) преодолева́ть (преодоле́ть *perf*) ♦ *adj*: ~ **by** (*fear, suspicion*) одолева́емый (одолева́ем) +*instr*; ~ **with** (*joy*) охва́ченный (охва́чен) +*instr*; **he was ~ with grief** он был уби́т го́рем.

overconfident [əuvə'kɔnfɪdənt] *adj* (*person*) самонаде́янный (самонаде́ян).

overcrowded [əuvə'kraudɪd] *adj* перепо́лненный (перепо́лнен).

overcrowding [əuvə'kraudɪŋ] *n* перенаселённость *f*; (*in bus*) теснота́.

overdo [əuvə'du:] *irreg vt* (*work, exercise*) перестара́ться (*perf*) в +*prp*; (*interest, concern*) утри́ровать (*impf*); (*overcook: boil*) перева́ривать (перевари́ть* *perf*); (: *fry, bake*) пережа́ривать (пережа́рить *perf*); **don't ~ it!** (*compliments etc*) не переусе́рдствуйте!; (*work etc*) не перестара́йтесь!

overdose ['əuvədəus] *n* передозиро́вка*.

overdraft ['əuvədra:ft] *n* (*COMM*) овердра́фт.

overdrawn [əuvə'drɔ:n] *adj*: **he is** *or* **his account is ~** он превы́сил креди́т своего́ теку́щего счёта.

overdrive ['əuvədraɪv] *n* (*AUT*) ускоря́ющая переда́ча.

overdue [əuvə'dju:] *adj* (*change, reform etc*) запозда́лый; (*account*) просро́ченный (просро́чен); **he/the bus is an hour ~** он/автобус опа́здывает на час; **these changes were long ~** э́тих переме́н давно́ жда́ли.

overemphasis [əuvər'ɛmfəsɪs] *n*: **~ on** изли́шнее ударе́ние на +*prp*.

overestimate [əuvər'ɛstɪmeɪt] *vt* переоце́нивать (переоцени́ть* *perf*).

overexcited [əuvərɪk'saɪtɪd] *adj* чрезме́рно возбуждённый* (возбуждён).

overexertion [əuvərɪg'zə:ʃən] *n* перенапряже́ние.

overexpose [əuvərɪk'spəuz] *vt* (*PHOT*) переде́рживать (передержа́ть* *perf*).

overflow [əuvə'fləu] *vi* (*river*) разлива́ться (разли́ться* *perf*); (*sink, vase etc*) перепо́лняться (перепо́лниться *perf*) ♦ *n* (*also:* ~ **pipe**) сливна́я труба́.

overfly [əuvə'flaɪ] *irreg vt* (*fly past*) пролета́ть (пролете́ть* *perf*).

overgenerous [əuvə'dʒɛnərəs] *adj* сли́шком ще́дрый* (щедр).

overgrown [əuvə'grəun] *adj* (*garden*) заро́сший; **he's just an ~ schoolboy** он про́сто переро́сток.

overhang ['əuvə'hæŋ] *irreg vt* нависа́ть (нави́снуть* *perf*) над +*instr* ♦ *vi* нависа́ть (нави́снуть* *perf*) ♦ *n* наве́с.

overhaul [əuvə'hɔ:l] *vt* (*engine, equipment*) производи́ть (произвести́* *perf*) по́лную прове́рку и ремо́нт +*gen* ♦ *n* по́лная прове́рка и ремо́нт.

overhead [*adv* əuvə'hɛd, *adj, n* 'əuvəhɛd] *adv* (*above*) наверху́, над голово́й; (*in the sky*) в не́бе ♦ *adj* (*lighting*) ве́рхний*; (*cable, railway*) надзе́мный ♦ *n* (*US*) = **overheads**; **~s** *npl* (*expenses*) накладны́е расхо́ды *mpl*.

overhear [əuvə'hɪə] *irreg vt* (*случайно*) подслу́шать* (*perf*).

overheat [əuvə'hi:t] *vi* перегрева́ться (перегре́ться *perf*).

overjoyed [əuvə'dʒɔɪd] *adj*: **to be ~ (at)** о́чень ра́доваться (обра́доваться *perf*) (+*dat*); **she was ~ to see him** она́ была́ о́чень ра́да его́ ви́деть.

overkill ['əuvəkɪl] *n* (*fig*): **it would be ~** э́то бу́дет я́вный перебо́р.

overland ['əuvəlænd] *adj* сухопу́тный ♦ *adv* (*travel*) по су́ше.

overlap [əuvə'læp] *vi* (*edges*) находи́ть* (*impf*) оди́н на друго́й; (*fig: ideas, activities etc*) части́чно совпада́ть (совпа́сть* *perf*).

overleaf [əuvə'li:f] *adv* на оборо́те.

overload [əuvə'ləud] *vt* (*also ELEC, fig*) перегружа́ть (перегрузи́ть* *perf*); **to ~ with work/problems** перегружа́ть (перегрузи́ть* *perf*) рабо́той/пробле́мами.

overlook [əuvə'luk] *vt* (*have view into*) выходи́ть* (*impf*) на +*acc*; (*fail to consider*) упуска́ть (упусти́ть* *perf*) из ви́ду; (*excuse*) закрыва́ть (закры́ть* *perf*) глаза́ на +*acc*.

overlord ['əuvələ:d] *n* повели́тель *m*.

overmanning [əuvə'mænɪŋ] *n* (*INDUSTRY*) избы́ток* рабо́чей си́лы.

overnight [əuvə'naɪt] *adv* (*for the night*) на́ ночь; (*during the night*) за́ ночь; (*fig: suddenly*) за́ день, сра́зу же ♦ *adj* (*train, journey*) ночно́й; **to travel ~** путеше́ствовать (*impf*) но́чью; **to stay ~** ночева́ть (переночева́ть *perf*); **he'll be away ~** он е́дет с ночёвкой.

overpass ['əuvəpa:s] *n* (*esp US*) путепрово́д.

overpay [əuvə'peɪ] *vt*: **to ~ sb by £50** перепла́чивать (переплати́ть* *perf*) кому́-н £50.

overplay [əuvə'pleɪ] *vt* преувели́чивать (преувели́чить *perf*) значе́ние +*gen*.

overpower [əuvə'pauə] *vt* переси́ливать (переси́лить *perf*).

overpowering [əuvə'pauərɪŋ] *adj* (*heat, stench*) невыноси́мый (невыноси́м).

overproduction ['əuvəprə'dʌkʃən] *n* перепроизво́дство.

overrate [əuvə'reɪt] *vt* переоце́нивать (переоцени́ть* *perf*).

overreach [əuvə'ri:tʃ] *vt*: **to ~ o.s.** перенапряга́ться (перенапря́чься* *perf*).

overreact [əuvəri:'ækt] *vi* горячи́ться (погорячи́ться *perf*).

override [əuvə'raɪd] *irreg vt* (*order, objection*) отверга́ть (отве́ргнуть* *perf*).

overriding [əuvə'raɪdɪŋ] *adj* (*importance*) первостепе́нный; (*factor, consideration*) реша́ющий*.

overrule [əuvə'ru:l] *vt* (*decision*) отменя́ть (отмени́ть* *perf*); (*objection*) отверга́ть

(отве́ргнуть* *perf*); **the judge ~d the defence**
судья́ отклони́л тре́бования защи́тника.
overrun [əuvə'rʌn] *irreg vt* (*country*) бы́стро
овладева́ть (овладе́ть *perf*) +*instr*; (*time limit*)
превыша́ть (превы́сить* *perf*) ♦ *vi* дли́ться*
(*impf*) до́льше поло́женного (вре́мени); **the
town is ~ with tourists** го́род наводнён
тури́стами.
overseas [əuvə'si:z] *adv* (*live, travel, work*) за
рубежо́м *or* грани́цей; (*to go*) за рубе́ж *or*
грани́цу ♦ *adj* (*market, trade*) вне́шний*;
(*student, visitor*) иностра́нный; **to trade ~**
торгова́ть (*impf*) с иностра́нными
госуда́рствами.
oversee [əuvə'si:] *vt* следи́ть* (*impf*) за +*instr*.
overseer ['əuvəsiə'] *n* (*in factory*) контролёр.
overshadow [əuvə'ʃædəu] *vt* (*place, building
etc*) возвыша́ться (*impf*) над +*instr*; (*fig*)
затмева́ть (затми́ть* *perf*).
overshoot [əuvə'ʃu:t] *irreg vt* проезжа́ть
(прое́хать* *perf*).
oversight ['əuvəsait] *n* недосмо́тр; **due to an ~**
по недосмо́тру.
oversimplify [əuvə'simplifai] *vt* сли́шком
упроща́ть (упрости́ть* *perf*).
oversleep [əuvə'sli:p] *irreg vi* просыпа́ть
(проспа́ть* *perf*).
overspend [əuvə'spɛnd] *irreg vi*
перерасхо́довать (*impf/perf*); **we have
overspent by 5,000 dollars** наш перерасхо́д
соста́вил 5,000 до́лларов.
overspill ['əuvəspil] *n* (*excess population*)
избы́точное населе́ние.
overstaffed [əuvə'stɑ:ft] *adj*: **this office is ~** в
э́том отде́ле сли́шком мно́го рабо́тников.
overstate [əuvə'steit] *vt* преувели́чивать
(преувели́чить *perf*).
overstatement [əuvə'steitmənt] *n* пре-
увеличе́ние.
overstay [əuvə'stei] *vt*: **to ~ one's welcome**
загости́ться* (*perf*).
overstep [əuvə'stɛp] *vt*: **to ~ the mark**
переходи́ть* (перейти́* *perf*) грани́цы.
overstock [əuvə'stɔk] *vt* затова́ривать
(затова́рить *perf*).
overstretched [əuvə'strɛtʃt] *adj* (*at work*)
перегру́женный (перегру́жен); (*funds*)
переизрасхо́дованный (переизрас-
хо́дован).
overstrike ['əuvəstraik] *irreg n* (*on printer*)
набо́р ли́шних си́мволов ♦ *vt* набира́ть
(набра́ть* *perf*) (*на клавиату́ре*).
oversubscribed [əuvəsəb'skraibd] *adj*: **this
product is ~** коли́чество зая́вок на э́тот
това́р превыша́ет предложе́ние.
overt [əu'və:t] *adj* открове́нный* (открове́нен).
overtake [əuvə'teik] *irreg vt* (*AUT*) обгоня́ть
(обогна́ть* *perf*); (*subj: event, change*)

застига́ть (засти́гнуть* *perf*) врасплох;
(: *emotion, weakness*) овладева́ть (овладе́ть
perf) +*instr*.
overtaking [əuvə'teikiŋ] *n* (*AUT*) обго́н.
overtax [əuvə'tæks] *vt* (*ECON*) облага́ть
(обложи́ть* *perf*) сли́шком высо́ким
нало́гом; (*strength, patience*) истоща́ть
(истощи́ть *perf*); **to ~ o.s.** перенапряга́ться
(перенапря́чься* *perf*).
overthrow [əuvə'θrəu] *irreg vt* сверга́ть
(све́ргнуть* *perf*).
overtime ['əuvətaim] *n* сверхуро́чное вре́мя*
nt; **to do** *or* **work ~** рабо́тать (*impf*) в
сверхуро́чное вре́мя.
overtime ban *n* запре́т на сверхуро́чную
рабо́ту.
overtone ['əuvətəun] *n* (*also:* **~s**): **~ of** намёк на
+*acc*.
overture ['əuvətʃuə'] *n* (*MUS*) увертю́ра; (*fig*)
подгото́вка*.
overturn [əuvə'tə:n] *vt* (*car, chair*) пере-
вора́чивать (переверну́ть *perf*); (*decision,
plan*) отверга́ть (отве́ргнуть *perf*);
(*government, system*) сверга́ть (све́ргнуть
perf) ♦ *vi* перевора́чиваться (переверну́ться
perf).
overview ['əuvəvju:] *n* (*summary*) обзо́р;
(*general understanding*) о́бщее
представле́ние.
overweight [əuvə'weit] *adj* (*person*) ту́чный*
(ту́чен); **your luggage is ~** у Вас переве́с.
overwhelm [əuvə'wɛlm] *vt* (*opponent, enemy
etc*) оде́рживать (одержа́ть *perf*) верх над
+*instr*; (*subj: feelings, emotions*) переполня́ть
(перепо́лнить *perf*).
overwhelming [əuvə'wɛlmiŋ] *adj* (*victory,
defeat*) по́лный*; (*majority*) подавля́ющий;
(*feeling, desire*) всепобежда́ющий*; (*heat*)
невыноси́мый (невыноси́м); **~ impression**
о́бщее впечатле́ние.
overwhelmingly [əuvə'wɛlmiŋli] *adv* (*vote,
win*) по́лностью; (*appreciative, generous etc*)
безграни́чно; (*predominantly: opposed etc*) в
основно́м.
overwork [əuvə'wə:k] *n* перегру́зка ♦ *vt*
(*person*) перегружа́ть (перегрузи́ть* *perf*);
(*cliché etc*) зата́скивать (затаска́ть *perf*) ♦ *vi*
(*person*) переутомля́ться (переутоми́ться*
perf).
overwrite [əuvə'rait] *vt* (*COMPUT*) пере-
пи́сывать (переписа́ть* *perf*).
overwrought [əuvə'rɔ:t] *adj* (*person*)
переутомлённый (переутомлён).
ovulate ['ɔvjuleit] *vi* овули́ровать (*impf/perf*).
ovulation [ɔvju'leiʃən] *n* овуля́ция.
ovum ['əuvəm] (*pl* **ova**) *n* яйцо́* (*АНАТ*).
owe [əu] *vt*: **she ~s me £500** она́ мне должна́
£500; **we ~ him our gratitude** мы должны́

---

* marks translations which have irregular inflections. The Russian-English side of the dictionary gives inflectional information.

быть* благода́рны ему́; **he ~s his talent/life to that man** он обя́зан свои́м тала́нтом/ свое́й жи́знью э́тому челове́ку.

owing to [ˈəʊɪŋ-] *prep* всле́дствие +*gen*.

owl [aul] *n* сова́*.

own [əʊn] *vt* владе́ть *(impf)* +*instr* ♦ *vi* (BRIT): **to ~ to sth** признава́ться* (призна́ться *perf*) в чём-н ♦ *adj* (*house, work, style etc*) со́бственный; **a room of one's ~** своя́ со́бственная ко́мната; **he lives on his ~** он живёт оди́н; **to come into one's ~** быть* *(impf)* в свое́й стихи́и; **to get one's ~ back** оты́грываться (отыгра́ться *perf*)

▶ **own up** *vi*: **to ~ up to sth** признава́ться* (призна́ться *perf*) в чём-н.

own brand *n* (COMM) това́р с ма́ркой продаю́щей его́ торго́вой компа́нии.

owner [ˈəʊnə] *n* владе́лец*(-ли́ца).

owner-occupier [ˈəʊnərˈɔkjupaɪə] *n* домо-владе́лец(-ли́ца).

ownership [ˈəʊnəʃɪp] *n*: **~ (of)** владе́ние (+*instr*); **under new ~** в но́вом владе́нии.

own goal *n* (SPORT): **to score an ~** ~ забива́ть (заби́ть* *perf*) гол в свои́ воро́та.

ox [ɔks] (*pl* **~en**) *n* бык*.

oxen [ˈɔksn] *npl of* **ox**.

Oxfam [ˈɔksfæm] *n abbr* (BRIT: = Oxford Committee for Famine Relief) О́ксфордский комите́т по́мощи голода́ющим.

Oxford [ˈɔksfəd] *n* О́ксфорд.

oxide [ˈɔksaɪd] *n* о́кись *f*, окси́д.

oxidize [ˈɔksɪdaɪz] *vi* окисля́ться (окисли́ться *perf*).

Oxon. [ˈɔksn] *abbr* (BRIT: POST) = Oxfordshire; (*in degree titles*) Oxoniensis.

oxtail [ˈɔksteɪl] *n*: **~ soup** суп из бы́чьего хвоста́.

oxyacetylene [ˈɔksɪəˈsetɪliːn] *adj* (*flame*) ацетиле́новый.

oxygen [ˈɔksɪdʒən] *n* кислоро́д.

oxygen mask *n* кислоро́дная ма́ска*.

oxygen tent *n* кислоро́дная пала́тка*.

oyster [ˈɔɪstəʳ] *n* у́стрица.

oz. *abbr* = **ounce**.

ozone [ˈəʊzəʊn] *n* озо́н.

ozone layer *n* озо́новый слой*.

ozonosphere [əʊˈzəʊnəsfɪəʳ] *n* озо́нный слой.

~ P, p ~

P, p [piː] n (letter) 16-ая буква английского алфавита.
P. abbr = **president, prince.**
p abbr (BRIT) = **penny, pence.**
p. abbr (= **page**) стр.= страница.
PA n abbr = **personal assistant, public-address system** ◆ abbr (US: POST) = **Pennsylvania.**
pa [pɑː] n (inf) папа.
p.a. abbr (= per annum) в год.
PAC n abbr (US) = political action committee.
pace [peɪs] n (step) шаг*; (speed) темп ◆ vi: **to ~ up and down** ходить* (impf) взад вперёд; **to keep ~ with** (person, events) идти* (impf) в ногу с +instr; **to set the ~** (also fig) определять (определить* perf); **I put him through his ~s** (fig) я посмотрел, на что он способен.
pacemaker ['peɪsmeɪkə'] n (MED) ритмизатор сердца; (SPORT) лидер.
Pacific [pə'sɪfɪk] n: **the ~ (Ocean)** Тихий* океан.
pacific [pə'sɪfɪk] adj (intentions etc) миролюбивый.
pacifier ['pæsɪfaɪə'] n (US: dummy) соска*(-пустышка*).
pacifist ['pæsɪfɪst] n пацифист(ка*).
pacify ['pæsɪfaɪ] vt умиротворять (умиротворить perf).
pack [pæk] n (packet) пачка*; (of hounds) свора*; (of wolves) стая; (of people) компания; (also: **backpack**) рюкзак*; (of cards) колода ◆ vt (fill) паковать or упаковывать (упаковать perf); (press down) уплотнять (уплотнить perf); (COMPUT) упаковывать (упаковать perf); (cram): **to ~ into** набивать (набить* perf) в +acc ◆ vi: **to ~ (one's bags)** паковать or упаковывать (упаковать perf) чемоданы; **to ~ sb off** отправлять (отправить* perf) кого-н; **to send sb ~ing** (inf) посылать (послать* perf) кого-н подальше
▶ **pack in** (BRIT: inf) vi (machine) разваливаться (развалиться perf) ◆ vt (boyfriend) завязывать (завязать* perf) с +instr; **~ it in!** прекрати!
▶ **pack off** vt отправлять (отправить* perf)
▶ **pack up** vi (BRIT: inf: machine) разваливаться

(развалиться perf); (: person) закругляться (закруглиться perf) ◆ vt паковать or упаковывать (упаковать perf).
package ['pækɪdʒ] n (parcel, also COMPUT) пакет; (also: ~ **deal**) пакет предложений ◆ vt паковать or упаковывать (упаковать perf).
package holiday n (BRIT) организованный отдых по путёвке.
package tour n (BRIT) туристическая поездка* по путёвке.
packaging ['pækɪdʒɪŋ] n упаковка.
packed [pækt] adj (crowded) набитый (набит).
packed lunch n (BRIT) завтрак в пакете.
packer ['pækə'] n упаковщик(-ица).
packet ['pækɪt] n (of cigarettes, washing powder etc) пачка*; (of crisps) пакет.
packet switching n (COMPUT) коммутация пакетов, пакетная коммутация.
pack ice ['pækaɪs] n пак, паковый лёд*.
packing ['pækɪŋ] n (act) упаковка; (material) прокладочный материал.
packing case n упаковочный ящик.
pact [pækt] n пакт.
pad [pæd] n (of paper) блокнот; (soft material) прокладка*; (for inking) подушечка*; (inf: home) (свой) угол* ◆ vt (cushion, soft toy etc) набивать (набить* perf); (shoulder, suit) подбивать (подбить* perf) ◆ vi: **to ~ about** ступать (impf).
padded cell ['pædɪd-] n палата, обитая войлоком (в психиатрической больнице).
padding ['pædɪŋ] n (material) набивочный материал, набивка; (in speech) вода*.
paddle ['pædl] n (oar) байдарочное весло*; (US: for table tennis) ракетка* ◆ vt (boat, canoe etc) управлять (impf) +instr ◆ vi (with feet) шлёпать (impf).
paddle steamer n колёсный пароход.
paddling pool ['pædlɪŋ-] n (BRIT) плескательный бассейн.
paddock ['pædək] n (field) выгон; (at racecourse) загон.
paddy field ['pædɪ-] n рисовое поле*.
padlock ['pædlɔk] n (висячий*) замок* ◆ vt запирать (запереть* perf) на висячий замок.
padre ['pɑːdrɪ] n (REL) падре m ind.

---

* marks translations which have irregular inflections. The Russian-English side of the dictionary gives inflectional information.

paediatrician [piːdɪəˈtrɪʃən] (*US* **pediatrician**) *n* педиа́тр, де́тский врач.
paediatrics [piːdɪˈætrɪks] (*US* **pediatrics**) *n* педиатри́я.
paedophile ['piːdəufaɪl] (*US* **pedophile**) *n* педофи́л.
paedophilia [piːdəuˈfɪlɪə] (*US* **pedophilia**) *n* педофили́я.
pagan ['peɪɡən] *adj* язы́ческий* ♦ *n* язы́чник(-ица).
page [peɪdʒ] *n* страни́ца; (*also:* ~**boy**) паж*; (: *at wedding*) ма́льчик, несу́щий шлейф неве́сты ♦ *vt* (*in hotel etc*) вызыва́ть (вы́звать* *perf*).
pageant ['pædʒənt] *n* театрализо́ванное представле́ние.
pageantry ['pædʒəntrɪ] *n* пы́шное зре́лище.
pageboy ['peɪdʒbɔɪ] *n see* **page**.
pager ['peɪdʒə'] *n портати́вное электро́нное устро́йство для вы́зова полице́йского, врача́ итп.*
page three girl *n де́вушка, снима́ющаяся в полуобнажённом ви́де для фотогра́фий в бульва́рных газе́тах.*
paginate ['pædʒɪneɪt] *vt* нумерова́ть* (пронумерова́ть* *perf*) страни́цы +*gen.*
pagination [pædʒɪˈneɪʃən] *n* нумера́ция страни́ц, пагина́ция.
pagoda [pəˈɡəudə] *n* па́года.
paid [peɪd] *pt, pp of* **pay** ♦ *adj* опла́чиваемый; **to put** ~ **to** (*BRIT*) класть* (положи́ть* *perf*) коне́ц +*dat.*
paid-in ['peɪdɪn] *adj* (*US*) = **paid-up**.
paid-up ['peɪdʌp] (*US* **paid-in**) *adj* (*COMM: shares*) опла́ченный; **he is a** ~ **member** он упла́тил чле́нский* взнос; ~ **capital** (*COMM*) опла́ченная часть объя́вленного акционе́рного капита́ла.
pail [peɪl] *n* ведро́*.
pain [peɪn] *n* (*also fig*) боль *f*; **to be in** ~ страда́ть (*impf*) от бо́ли; **to have a** ~ **in** чу́вствовать (*impf*) боль в +*prp*; **to take** ~**s to do** стара́ться (постара́ться *perf*) изо всех сил, что́бы +*infin*; **on** ~ **of death** под стра́хом сме́рти.
pained [peɪnd] *adj* оби́женный (оби́жен).
painful ['peɪnful] *adj* (*upsetting, unpleasant, laborious*) мучи́тельный* (мучи́телен); (*sore*): **my back is** ~ спина́ причиня́ет мне боль.
painfully ['peɪnfəlɪ] *adv* (*fig: very*) глубоко́*; (: *aware, familiar*) до бо́ли; (: *dull, obvious*) мучи́тельно.
painkiller ['peɪnkɪlə'] *n* болеутоля́ющее *nt adj* (сре́дство).
painless ['peɪnlɪs] *adj* безболе́зненный* (безболе́знен).
painstaking ['peɪnzteɪkɪŋ] *adj* кропотли́вый (кропотли́в).
paint [peɪnt] *n* кра́ска* ♦ *vt* (*wall, door, house etc*) кра́сить* (вы́красить* *or* покра́сить*

perf); (*picture, portrait*) рисова́ть (нарисова́ть *perf*); (*about artists*) писа́ть* (написа́ть* *perf*); (*fig*) изобража́ть (изобрази́ть* *perf*); **a tin of** ~ ба́нка* кра́ски; **to** ~ **the door blue** кра́сить* (вы́красить* *or* покра́сить* *perf*) дверь в голубо́й цвет; **to** ~ **in oils** писа́ть* (написа́ть* *perf*) ма́слом.
paintbox ['peɪntbɒks] *n* набо́р кра́сок.
paintbrush ['peɪntbrʌʃ] *n* кисть* *f*.
painter ['peɪntə'] *n* (*artist*) худо́жник(-ица); (*decorator*) маля́р*.
painting ['peɪntɪŋ] *n* (*activity: of artist*) жи́вопись *f*; (: *of decorator*) маля́рное де́ло; (*picture*) карти́на.
paint stripper *n* сре́дство для сня́тия кра́ски.
paintwork ['peɪntwəːk] *n* кра́ска.
pair [peə'] *n* па́ра; **a** ~ **of scissors** но́жницы *pl*; **a** ~ **of trousers** па́ра брюк
► **pair off** *vi*: **to** ~ **off with sb** объединя́ться (объедини́ться* *perf*) в па́ре с кем-н.
pajamas [pəˈdʒɑːməz] *npl* (*US*) пижа́ма *fsg*.
Pakistan [pɑːkɪˈstɑːn] *n* Пакиста́н.
Pakistani [pɑːkɪˈstɑːnɪ] *adj* пакиста́нский* ♦ *n* пакиста́нец*(-нка).
PAL *n abbr* (*TV:* = *phase alternation line*) ПАЛ.
pal [pæl] *n* (*inf*) ко́реш.
palace ['pæləs] *n* дворе́ц*.
palaeontology [pælɪɒnˈtɔlədʒɪ] *n* палеонтоло́гия.
palatable ['pælɪtəbl] *adj* (*food, drink*) вку́сный* (вку́сен); (*idea, fact*) прие́млемый.
palate ['pælɪt] *n* (*ANAT*) нёбо; (*fig*) вкус.
palatial [pəˈleɪʃəl] *adj* роско́шный* (роско́шен).
palaver [pəˈlɑːvə'] *n* (*inf*) суетня́.
pale [peɪl] *adj* бле́дный* (бле́ден) ♦ *vi* бледне́ть (побледне́ть *perf*) ♦ *n*: **his behaviour is beyond the** ~ (*unacceptable*) его́ поведе́ние перехо́дит все грани́цы; **to grow** *or* **turn** ~ бледне́ть (побледне́ть *perf*); ~ **blue** бле́дно-голубо́й; **to** ~ **into insignificance beside** бледне́ть (побледне́ть *perf*) пе́ред +*instr.*
paleness ['peɪlnɪs] *n* бле́дность *f*.
Palestine ['pælɪstaɪn] *n* Палести́на.
Palestinian [pælɪsˈtɪnɪən] *adj* палести́нский* ♦ *n* палести́нец*(-нка).
palette ['pælɪt] *n* (*ART*) пали́тра.
palings ['peɪlɪŋz] *npl* частоко́л *msg.*
palisade [pælɪˈseɪd] *n* крепостна́я огра́да.
pall [pɔːl] *n* (*cloud of smoke*) покро́в ♦ *vi* приеда́ться (прие́сться* *perf*).
pallet ['pælɪt] *n* (*for goods*) поддо́н.
palliative ['pælɪətɪv] *n* (*MED*) паллиати́вное сре́дство; (*fig*) полуме́ра.
pallid ['pælɪd] *adj* бле́дный* (бле́ден).
pallor ['pælə'] *n* бле́дность *f*.
pally ['pælɪ] *adj* (*inf*) сво́йский*.
palm [pɑːm] *n* (*also:* ~ **tree**) па́льма; (*of hand*) ладо́нь *f* ♦ *vt*: **to** ~ **sth off on sb** (*inf*) подсо́вывать (подсу́нуть *perf*) что-н кому́-н.

palmist ['pɑːmɪst] n хиромáнт(ка*).
Palm Sunday n ≈ Вéрбное воскресéнье.
palpable ['pælpəbl] adj ощутúмый (ощутúм).
palpitations [pælpɪ'teɪʃənz] npl (учащённое) сердцебиéние ntsg.
paltry ['pɔːltrɪ] adj (amount) ничтóжный* (ничтóжен).
pamper ['pæmpə'] vt баловáть (избаловáть perf).
pamphlet ['pæmflət] n (leaflet) брошюра; (: political, literary etc) памфлéт.
pan [pæn] n (also: **saucepan**) кастрюля; (also: **frying** ~) сковородá ♦ vi (CINEMA, TV) панорамúровать (impf/perf) ♦ vt (inf: book, film) разносúть* (разнестú* perf); **to** ~ **for gold** намывáть (намыть* perf) зóлото.
panacea [pænə'sɪə] n панацéя.
panache [pə'næʃ] n щегольствó.
Panama ['pænəmɑː] n Панáма.
panama n (also: ~ **hat**) панáма.
Panama Canal n: **the** ~ ~ Панáмский* канáл.
Panamanian [pænə'meɪnɪən] adj панáмский* ♦ n панáмец*(-мка).
pancake ['pænkeɪk] n (thin) блин*; (thick) олáдья.
Pancake Day n (BRIT) втóрник во врéмя мáсленицы, в котóрый пекýт блины.
pancake roll n блúнчик с начúнкой (свёрнутый в трýбочку).
pancreas ['pæŋkrɪəs] n поджелýдочная железá*.
panda ['pændə] n бамбýковый медвéдь m.
panda car n (BRIT) полицéйская машúна.
pandemonium [pændɪ'məʊnɪəm] n столпотворéние.
pander ['pændə'] vi: **to** ~ **to** потвóрствовать (impf) +dat.
p & h abbr (US: = postage and handling) почтóвые расхóды pl.
P & L abbr (= profit and loss) прúбыль f и убыток.
p & p abbr (BRIT: = postage and packing) почтóвые расхóды и упакóвка.
pane [peɪn] n: ~ **(of glass)** (in window) окóнное стеклó*.
panel ['pænl] n (of wood, metal, glass) панéль f; (of judges, experts) комúссия.
panel game n (BRIT: TV, RADIO) викторúна.
panelling ['pænəlɪŋ] (US **paneling**) n деревянная обшúвка.
panellist ['pænəlɪst] (US **panelist**) n (TV, RADIO) учáстник(-ица) прогрáммы.
pang [pæŋ] n: ~ **of jealousy** укóл рéвности; ~**s of conscience** укóры сóвести; ~ **of regret** мýки сожалéния; **hunger** ~**s** голóдные бóли.
panhandler ['pænhændlə'] n (US: inf) нúщий* m adj.
panic ['pænɪk] n пáника ♦ vi паниковáть (impf).

panic buying [-baɪɪŋ] n скýпка дефицúтных товáров.
panicky ['pænɪkɪ] adj (feeling, reaction) панúческий*; (person): **he is very** ~ он паникýет.
panic-stricken ['pænɪkstrɪkən] adj (person, crowd) охвáченный (охвáчен) пáникой.
pannier ['pænɪə'] n (on bicycle) корзúнка*-багáжник; (on animal) корзúна.
panorama [pænə'rɑːmə] n панорáма.
panoramic [pænə'ræmɪk] adj панорáмный.
pansy ['pænzɪ] n анютины глáзки mpl; (inf: pej) флунтяй.
pant [pænt] vi задыхáться (задохнýться perf).
pantechnicon [pæn'tɛknɪkən] n (BRIT: AUT) автофургóн для перевóзки мéбели or оборýдования.
panther ['pænθə'] n пантéра.
panties ['pæntɪz] npl трýсики pl.
pantihose ['pæntɪhəʊz] npl (US) колгóтки* pl.
panto ['pæntəʊ] n = **pantomime**.
pantomime ['pæntəmaɪm] n (BRIT) рождéственское представлéние для детéй; (: fig) фарс.
pantry ['pæntrɪ] n кладовáя f adj, кладóвка; (room) буфéтная f adj.
pants [pænts] npl (BRIT: underwear) трусы pl; (US: trousers) брюки pl.
pantsuit ['pæntsuːt] n (US) брючный костюм.
papacy ['peɪpəsɪ] n пáпство.
papal ['peɪpəl] adj пáпский.
paparazzi [pæpə'rætsiː] npl фотóграфы, гоняющиеся за знаменúтостями и фотографúрующие их для бульвáрной прéссы.
paper ['peɪpə'] n бумáга; (also: **newspaper**) газéта; (exam) пúсьменный экзáмен; (academic essay: at conference) доклáд; (: in journal) статья*; (also: **wallpaper**) обóи pl ♦ adj бумáжный ♦ vt (room) оклéивать (оклéить* perf) обóями; ~**s** npl (also: **identity** ~**s**) докумéнты mpl; **a piece of** ~ (odd bit) клочóк бумáги, бумáжка; (sheet) лист* бумáги; **to put** or **get sth down on** ~ запúсывать (записáть* perf) что-н на бумáге.
paper advance n (on printer) продвижéние бумáги.
paperback ['peɪpəbæk] n кнúга в мягкой облóжке ♦ adj: ~ **edition** издáние в мягкой облóжке.
paper bag n бумáжный пакéт.
paperboy ['peɪpəbɔɪ] n мáльчик-разнóсчик газéт.
paperclip ['peɪpəklɪp] n (канцелярская) скрéпка*.
papergirl ['peɪpəgəːl] n дéвочка-разнóсчица газéт.

---

paper hankie n бумáжный носовóй платóк*.
paper mill n бумáжная фáбрика.
paper profit n бумáжная or нереализóванная прúбыль f.
paper shop n ≈ газéтный кибск.
paperweight ['peɪpəweɪt] n пресс-папьé nt ind.
paperwork ['peɪpəwəːk] n канцелярская рабóта.
papier-mâché ['pæpɪeɪ'mæʃeɪ] n папьé-машé nt ind.
paprika ['pæprɪkə] n крáсный мóлотый пéрец*.
Pap smear ['pæp-] n мазóк* с шéйки мáтки.
Pap test n = Pap smear.
par [pɑː] n (equality of value) рáвенство; (GOLF) колúчество ударов, допустúмое для кáждой лýнки úли для всегó пóля; **to be on a ~ with** быть* (impf) на однóм ýровне с +instr; **at ~** (COMM) по номинáлу; **to feel below** or **under ~** чýвствовать (impf) себя невáжно.
parable ['pærəbl] n прúтча.
parabola [pə'ræbələ] n парáбола.
parachute ['pærəʃuːt] n парашют.
parachute jump n прыжóк* с парашютом.
parachutist ['pærəʃuːtɪst] n парашютúст(ка*).
parade [pə'reɪd] n (public procession) шéствие; (MIL) парáд ♦ vt (troops etc) выстрáивать (выстроить perf); (show off: wealth, knowledge etc) выставлять (выставить* perf) напокáз ♦ vi (MIL) идтú* (impf) стрóем; **fashion ~** покáз мод.
parade ground n (учéбный) плац*.
paradise ['pærədaɪs] n (also fig) рай*.
paradox ['pærədɒks] n парадóкс.
paradoxical [pærə'dɒksɪkl] adj парадоксáльный* (парадоксáлен).
paradoxically [pærə'dɒksɪklɪ] adv как это ни парадоксáльно.
paraffin ['pærəfɪn] n (BRIT: also: ~ oil) керосúн; **liquid ~** (BRIT) вазелúновое мáсло.
paraffin heater n (BRIT) обогревáтель m на твёрдом парафúне.
paraffin lamp n (BRIT) керосúновая лáмпа.
paragon ['pærəgən] n (of honesty, virtue etc) образéц*.
paragraph ['pærəgrɑːf] n абзáц; (of document) парáграф; **to begin a new ~** начинáть (начáть* perf) писáть с абзáца.
Paraguay ['pærəgwaɪ] n Парагвáй.
Paraguayan [pærə'gwaɪən] adj парагвáйский ♦ n парагвáец*(-áйка*).
parallel ['pærəlɛl] adj параллéльный* (параллéлен); (fig: similar) аналогúчный* (аналогúчен); (COMPUT) параллéльный ♦ n (GEO, fig) параллéль f; **to draw ~s between/with** проводúть* (провестú* perf) параллéль мéжду +instr/c +instr; **~ (with** or **to)** параллéльно (с +instr); **in ~** (ELEC) параллéльно.
paralyse ['pærəlaɪz] vt (BRIT: also fig) парализовáть (impf/perf); **he is ~d** (BRIT) он парализóван.

paralyses [pə'rælɪsiːz] npl of **paralysis**.
paralysis [pə'rælɪsɪs] (pl **paralyses**) n (MED) паралúч*.
paralytic [pærə'lɪtɪk] adj (MED) парализóванный (парализóван); (BRIT: inf: drunk) упúвшийся.
paralyze ['pærəlaɪz] vt (US) = **paralyse**.
paramedic [pærə'mɛdɪk] n парамéдик; **~s** комáнда скóрой пóмощи.
parameter [pə'ræmɪtə] n парáметр.
paramilitary [pærə'mɪlɪtərɪ] adj военизúрованный.
paramount ['pærəmaunt] adj первостепéнный.
paranoia [pærə'nɔɪə] n паранóйя.
paranoid ['pærənɔɪd] adj (person) паранóидный; (feeling) паранoúческий.
paranormal [pærə'nɔːml] adj не поддающúйся объяснéнию ♦ n: **the ~** явлéния ntpl, не поддающиеся объяснéнию.
parapet ['pærəpɪt] n парапéт.
paraphernalia [pærəfə'neɪlɪə] n (gear) принадлéжности fpl.
paraphrase ['pærəfreɪz] vt перефразúровать (impf/perf).
paraplegic [pærə'pliːdʒɪk] n страдáющий(-ая) m(f) adj параличóм нúжней чáсти тéла.
parapsychology [pærəsaɪ'kɔlədʒɪ] n парапсихолóгия.
parasite ['pærəsaɪt] n (also fig) паразúт.
parasol ['pærəsɒl] n зóнтик (защищáющий от сóлнца); (at café etc) тент.
paratrooper ['pærətruːpə] n десáнтник.
parcel ['pɑːsl] n (package) свёрток*; (sent by post) посылка* ♦ vt (also: ~ up) завёртывать (завернýть perf).
▶ **parcel out** vt раздавáть* (раздáть* perf).
parcel bomb n (BRIT) бóмба, спрятанная в пакéт.
parcel post n почтóво-посылочная слýжба.
parch [pɑːtʃ] vt (crops, land) выжигáть (выжечь* perf).
parched [pɑːtʃt] adj: **I'm ~** у меня пересóхло в гóрле.
parchment ['pɑːtʃmənt] n пергáмент.
pardon ['pɑːdn] n (LAW) помúлование ♦ vt прощáть (простúть* perf); (LAW) помúловать (perf); **~ me!, I beg your ~!** прошý прощéния!; **(I beg your) ~?, (US) ~ me?** (what did you say?) простúте, не расслышал.
pare [pɛə] vt (BRIT: nails) стричь* (острúчь* perf); (fruit) чúстить* (очúстить* perf); (costs) урéзывать or урезáть (урéзать* perf).
parent ['pɛərənt] n родúтель(ница) m(f); **~s** npl (mother and father) родúтели mpl.
parentage ['pɛərəntɪdʒ] n происхождéние; **she is of unknown ~** её происхождéние неизвéстно.
parental [pə'rɛntl] adj родúтельский*.
parent company n (COMM) матерúнская компáния.
parentheses [pə'rɛnθɪsiːz] npl of **parenthesis**.

parenthesis [pə'rɛnθɪsɪs] (*pl* **parentheses**) *n*
(*word*) вво́дное сло́во*; (*phrase*) вво́дное
предложе́ние; **in** ~ в ско́бках.
parenthood ['pɛərənthud] *n* (*motherhood*)
матери́нство; (*fatherhood*) отцо́вство.
parenting ['pɛərəntɪŋ] *n* воспита́ние.
Paris ['pærɪs] *n* Пари́ж.
parish ['pærɪʃ] *n* (*REL*) прихо́д; (*BRIT: civil*)
о́круг*.
parish council *n* (*BRIT*) прихо́дский* сове́т.
parishioner [pə'rɪʃənə'] *n* (*REL*)
прихожа́нин*(-а́нка*).
Parisian [pə'rɪzɪən] *adj* пари́жский* ♦ *n*
парижа́нин*(-нка*).
parity ['pærɪtɪ] *n* (*equality: of pay, conditions etc*)
парите́т.
park [pɑːk] *n* парк ♦ *vt* (*AUT*) ста́вить*
(поста́вить* *perf*), паркова́ть (припаркова́ть
perf) ♦ *vi* (*AUT*) паркова́ться (припаркова́ться
perf).
parka ['pɑːkə] *n* (*coat*) *стёганая ку́ртка на
меху́.*
parking ['pɑːkɪŋ] *n* (*of vehicle*) паркова́ние;
(*space to park*) стоя́нка*; "**no** ~" „стоя́нка
запрещена́''.
parking lights *npl* подфа́рники *mpl*.
parking lot *n* (*US*) (авто)стоя́нка.
parking meter *n* (*AUT*) счётчик на
(авто)стоя́нке.
parking offence *n* (*BRIT*) наруше́ние пра́вил
стоя́нки.
parking place *n* ме́сто* на автостоя́нке.
parking ticket *n* *штраф за наруше́ние пра́вил
паркова́ния.*
parking violation *n* (*US*) = **parking offence**
Parkinson's ['pɑːkɪnsənz] *n* (*also:* ~ **disease**)
боле́знь *f* Паркинсона.
parkway ['pɑːkweɪ] *n* (*US*) алле́я.
parlance ['pɑːləns] *n*: **in common/modern** ~
говоря́ обы́чным/совреме́нным языко́м.
parliament ['pɑːləmənt] *n* парла́мент.
parliamentary [pɑːlə'mɛntərɪ] *adj* парла́мент-
ский*.
parlour ['pɑːlə'] (*US* **parlor**) *n* гости́ная *f adj*.
parlous ['pɑːləs] *adj* бе́дственный.
Parmesan [pɑːmɪ'zæn] *n* (*also:* ~ **cheese**) сыр
пармеза́н.
parochial [pə'rəukɪəl] *adj* (*pej*) местечко́вый.
parody ['pærədɪ] *n* паро́дия ♦ *vt* пароди́ровать
(*impf/perf*).
parole [pə'rəul] *n*: **he is/was released on** ~ (*LAW*)
он освобождён/был освобождён под
че́стное сло́во.
paroxysm ['pærəksɪzəm] *n* (*also MED*)
парокси́зм.
parquet ['pɑːkeɪ] *n*: ~ **floor(ing)** парке́тный
пол*.
parrot ['pærət] *n* попуга́й.

parrot-fashion ['pærətfæʃən] *adv* как попуга́й.
parry ['pærɪ] *vt* (*blow*) отража́ть (отрази́ть*
perf); (*question*) пари́ровать (*impf/perf*).
parsimonious [pɑːsɪ'məunɪəs] *adj* (*person*)
скупо́й* (скуп).
parsley ['pɑːslɪ] *n* петру́шка.
parsnip ['pɑːsnɪp] *n* пастерна́к (посевно́й).
parson ['pɑːsn] *n* прихо́дский* свяще́нник;
(*Church of England*) па́стор.
part [pɑːt] *n* (*section, division*) часть* *f*;
(*component*) дета́ль *f*; (*role*) роль* *f*; (*episode*)
се́рия; (*MUS*) па́ртия; (*US: in hair*) пробо́р ♦
adv = **partly** ♦ *vt* разделя́ть (раздели́ть* *perf*);
(*hair*) расчёсывать (расчеса́ть* *perf*) на
пробо́р ♦ *vi* (*people*) расстава́ться
(расста́ться* *perf*); (*crowd*) расступа́ться
(расступи́ться *perf*); (*roads*) расходи́ться*
(разойти́сь* *perf*); **to take** ~ **in** принима́ть
(приня́ть* *perf*) уча́стие в +*prp*; **to take sth in
good** ~ не обижа́ться (обиде́ться* *perf*) на
что-н; **to take sb's** ~ (*support*) станови́ться*
(стать* *perf*) на чью-н сто́рону; **on his/for my**
~ с его́/мое́й стороны́; **for the most** ~
бо́льшей ча́стью; **for the better** ~ **of the day**
бо́льшую часть дня; **to be** ~ **and parcel of**
явля́ться (*impf*) неотъе́млемой ча́стью +*gen*;
~ **of speech** (*LING*) часть ре́чи
▸ **part with** *vt fus* (*money, possessions*)
расстава́ться* (расста́ться* *perf*) с +*infin*.
partake [pɑː'teɪk] *irreg vi* (*formal*): **to** ~ **of sth**
отве́дывать (отве́дать *perf*) чего́-н.
part exchange *n* (*BRIT: COMM*) *рассчёт, при
кото́ром де́нежный взнос сочета́ется с
обме́ном ста́рого това́ра на но́вый.*
partial ['pɑːʃl] *adj* (*not complete*) части́чный*;
(*biased*) пристра́стный* (пристра́стен); **I am**
~ **to chocolate** (*like*) я пристра́стен к
шокола́ду.
partially ['pɑːʃəlɪ] *adv* части́чно.
participant [pɑː'tɪsɪpənt] *n* уча́стник(-ица).
participate [pɑː'tɪsɪpeɪt] *vi*: **to** ~ **in** уча́ствовать
(*impf*) в +*prp*.
participation [pɑːtɪsɪ'peɪʃən] *n* уча́стие.
participle ['pɑːtɪsɪpl] *n* прича́стие.
particle ['pɑːtɪkl] *n* (*also PHYS*) части́ца.
particular [pə'tɪkjulə'] *adj* (*distinct, special*)
осо́бый; (*demanding*) приверёдливый
(приверёдлив); ~**s** *npl* (*specifics*) ча́стности
fpl; (*personal details*) да́нные *pl adj*; **he is very**
~ **about what he eats** он о́чень приверёдлив
в еде́; **in** ~ в ча́стности.
particularly [pə'tɪkjulərɪ] *adv* осо́бенно.
parting ['pɑːtɪŋ] *n* (*action*) разделе́ние;
(*farewell*) проща́ние; (*BRIT: in hair*) пробо́р ♦
adj (*words, gift etc*) проща́льный; ~ **shot**
проща́льное замеча́ние.
partisan [pɑːtɪ'zæn] *adj* (*politics, views*)
пристра́стный* (пристра́стен) ♦ *n* (*supporter*)

---

* marks translations which have irregular inflections. The Russian-English side of the dictionary gives inflectional information.

привéрженец*; (*resistance fighter*)
партизáн(ка*).

partition [pɑːˈtɪʃən] *n* (*wall, screen*)
перегорóдка*; (*of country*) раздéл ◆ *vt*
разделя́ть (раздели́ть* *perf*).

partly [ˈpɑːtlɪ] *adv* части́чно.

partner [ˈpɑːtnəʳ] *n* (*spouse*) супрýг(а);
(*girlfriend*) дéвушка*; (*boyfriend*) пáрень* *m*;
(*COMM, SPORT, CARDS*) партнёр ◆ *vt*: **I used to ~
him** я был его́ партнёром.

partnership [ˈpɑːtnəʃɪp] *n* (*COMM: company*)
товáрищество; (: *with person*) партнёрство;
(*POL*) сою́з; **to go into** *or* **form a ~ (with)**
устанáвливать (установи́ть* *perf*)
партнёрство (с +*instr*).

part payment *n* части́чная оплáта.

partridge [ˈpɑːtrɪdʒ] *n* (сéрая) куропáтка*.

part-time [ˈpɑːtˈtaɪm] *adj* (*work*) почасовóй;
(*staff*) зáнятый* (зáнят) непóлный рабóчий*
день* ◆ *adv*: **to work ~** быть* (*impf*) на
почасовóй стáвке; **to study ~** обучáться
(*impf*) по непóлной прогрáмме.

part-timer [pɑːtˈtaɪməʳ] *n* (*also*: **part-time
worker**) рабóтник*(-ица) на почасовóй
стáвке, почасови́к.

party [ˈpɑːtɪ] *n* (*POL*) пáртия; (*celebration:
formal*) вéчер*; (: *informal*) вечери́нка*;
(*group of people: surveying etc*) пáртия;
(: *rescue etc*) отря́д; (: *tourists etc*) грýппа;
(*LAW*) сторонá* ◆ *cpd* (*POL*) парти́йный;
dinner ~ звáнный обéд; **to give** *or* **throw a ~**
(*official*) устрáивать (устрóить* *perf*) вéчер;
we're having a ~ next Saturday в слéдующую
суббóту у нас вечери́нка; **birthday ~**
прáзднование дня рожде́ния; **he was (a) ~ to
the crime** он явля́лся соучáстником
преступле́ния.

party dress *n* вечéрнее плáтье*.

party line *n* (*TEL*) óбщая телефóнная ли́ния;
(*POL*) парти́йная ли́ния.

party piece *n* корóнный нóмер*.

party-political [ˈpɑːtɪpəˈlɪtɪkl] *adj* парти́йный.

party-political broadcast *n* реклáма
*полити́ческой пáртии по рáдио и
телеви́дению.*

pass [pɑːs] *vt* (*spend: time*) проводи́ть*
(провести́* *perf*); (*hand over*) передавáть*
(передáть* *perf*); (*go past: on foot*) проходи́ть*
(пройти́* *perf*); (: *by transport*) проезжáть
(проéхать* *perf*); (*overtake: vehicle*) обгоня́ть
(обогнáть* *perf*); (*fig: surpass*) превосходи́ть*
(превзойти́* *perf*); (*exam*) сдавáть* (сдать*
perf); (*approve: law, proposal*) принимáть
(приня́ть* *perf*) ◆ *vi* (*go past: on foot*)
проходи́ть* (пройти́* *perf*); (: *by transport*)
проезжáть (проéхать* *perf*); (*in exam*)
сдавáть* (сдать* *perf*) ◆ *n* (*permit*) прóпуск*;
(*membership card*) чле́нский биле́т*; (*GEO*)
перевáл; (*SPORT*) пас, передáча; (*SCOL: also*:
~ mark): **to get a ~** получáть (получи́ть *perf*)
зачёт; **to ~ sth through sth** просóвывать

(просýнуть *perf*) что-н че́рез что-н; **could you
~ the vegetables round?** передáйте,
пожáлуйста, о́вощи всем; **she could ~ for 25**
онá моглá бы сойти́ за 25-лéтнюю; **things
have come to a pretty ~** (*BRIT*) делá плóхи; **to
make a ~ at sb** (*inf*) приставáть* (пристáть*
perf) к комý-н

▶ **pass away** *vi* (*die*) скончáться (*perf*)

▶ **pass by** *vi* (*on foot*) проходи́ть* (пройти́*
perf); (*by transport*) проезжáть (проéхать*
perf) ◆ *vt* (*ignore*) не обращáть (обрати́ть*
perf) внимáния на +*acc*

▶ **pass down** *vt* (*customs, inheritance*)
передавáть* (передáть* *perf*)

▶ **pass on** *vt* передавáть* (передáть* *perf*);
(*price rises*) переклáдывать (переложи́ть*
perf) ◆ *vi* (*die*) скончáться (*perf*)

▶ **pass out** *vi* (*faint*) теря́ть (потеря́ть *perf*)
сознáние; (*BRIT: MIL*) успéшно проходи́ть*
(пройти́* *perf*) подготóвку

▶ **pass over** *vt* (*ignore*) оставля́ть (остáвить*
perf) без внимáния ◆ *vi* (*die*) скончáться (*perf*)

▶ **pass up** *vt* (*opportunity*) упускáть (упусти́ть*
perf).

passable [ˈpɑːsəbl] *adj* (*road*) проходи́мый
(проходи́м); (*acceptable: work*) снóсный*
(снóсен).

passage [ˈpæsɪdʒ] *n* (*also ANAT*) прохóд; (*in
book*) отры́вок*; (*act of passing*)
прохожде́ние; (*journey: on boat*)
путеше́ствие.

passenger [ˈpæsɪndʒəʳ] *n* пассажи́р*(ка*).

passer-by [pɑːsəˈbaɪ] (*pl* **passers-by**) *n*
прохóжий*(-ая) *m(f) adj*.

passers-by [pɑːsəzˈbaɪ] *npl of* **passer-by**.

passing [ˈpɑːsɪŋ] *adj* мимолётный*
(мимолётен) ◆ *n*: **in ~** мимохóдом; **to
mention sth in ~** замечáть (замéтить* *perf*)
что-н мимохóдом.

passing place *n* (*AUT*) расшире́ние на дорóге.

passion [ˈpæʃən] *n* (*also fig*) страсть* *f*; **she has
a ~ for history** у неё страсть к исто́рии.

passionate [ˈpæʃənɪt] *adj* страстный*
(стрáстен).

passion fruit *n* плод* страстоцвéта.

Passion play *n* мисте́рия, в которой
представля́ются стрáсти Госпóдни.

passive [ˈpæsɪv] *adj* пасси́вный (пасси́вен);
(*LING*) пасси́вный, страдáтельный ◆ *n* (*LING*):
the ~ страдáтельный залóг.

passive smoking *n* пасси́вное куре́ние.

passkey [ˈpɑːskiː] *n* отмы́чка*.

Passover [ˈpɑːsəuvəʳ] *n* евре́йская Пáсха.

passport [ˈpɑːspɔːt] *n* (*official document*)
пáспорт*; (*fig*) ключ*.

passport control *n* пáспортный контрóль
m.

password [ˈpɑːswɜːd] *n* парóль *m*.

past [pɑːst] *prep* (*in front of*) ми́мо +*gen*;
(*beyond*) за +*instr*; (*later than*) пóсле +*gen* ◆ *adj*
(*previous: government etc*) бы́вший*; (: *week,*

month etc) прошлый ♦ *n* прошлое *nt adj*;
(*LING*): **the ~ (tense)** прошедшее время* *nt* ♦
adv: **to run ~** пробегать (пробежать* *perf*)
мимо; **he's ~ forty** (*older than*) ему за сорок;
it's ~ midnight уже за полночь; **ten/quarter ~
eight** десять минут/четверть девятого; **he
ran ~ me** он пробежал мимо меня; **I'm ~
caring** мне уже всё равно; **he's ~ it** (*BRIT: inf*)
он выдохнулся; **for the ~ few/3 days** за
последние несколько дней/3 дня; **in the ~** в
прошлом; (*LING*) в прошедшем времени.
pasta ['pæstə] *n* макаронные изделия *ntpl*.
paste [peɪst] *n* (*wet mixture*) паста; (*glue*)
клейстер; (*jewellery*) страз; (*fish, meat paste*)
паштет ♦ *vt* (*paper etc*) наносить* (нанести*
perf) клей на +*acc*; **tomato ~** томатная паста;
to ~ sth onto sth наносить* (нанести* *perf*)
что-н на что-н.
pastel ['pæstl] *adj* (*colour*) пастельный.
pasteurized ['pæstʃəraɪzd] *adj* (*milk etc*)
пастеризованный.
pastille ['pæstl] *n* пастила.
pastime ['pɑ:staɪm] *n* (*hobby*) время-
препровождение.
past master *n* (*BRIT*) непревзойдённый
мастер.
pastor ['pɑ:stə'] *n* пастор.
pastoral ['pɑ:stərl] *adj* (*REL*) пасторский.
pastry ['peɪstrɪ] *n* (*dough*) тесто; (*cake*)
пирожное *nt adj*.
pasture ['pɑ:stʃə'] *n* пастбище.
pasty [*adj* 'peɪstɪ, *n* 'pæstɪ] *adj* (*complexion, face*)
бледный* (бледен) ♦ *n* пирожок*.
pat [pæt] *adj* (*answer, remark*) стандартный*
(стандартен) ♦ *vt* (*dog*) приласкать
perf) ♦ *n*: **to give sb/o.s. a ~ on the back** (*fig*)
хвалить* (похвалить* *perf*) кого-н/себя ♦ *adv*:
to know sth off ~, (*US*) **have sth down ~** знать
(*impf*) что-н назубок; **to ~ sb's back**
похлопывать (похлопать *perf*) кого-н по
спине.
patch [pætʃ] *n* (*piece of material*) заплата; (*also*:
eye ~) повязка*; (*area*: *damp, black etc*)
пятно*; (*repair*: *on tyre etc*) заплата,
заплатка*; (*of land*) участок ♦ *vt* (*clothes*)
латать (залатать *perf*); **to go through a bad ~**
попадать (попасть* *perf*) в полосу
невезения; **bald ~** лысина.
▶ **patch up** *vt* (*mend temporarily*) заделывать
(заделать *perf*); (*quarrel*) улаживать
(уладить* *perf*).
patchwork ['pætʃwə:k] *n* (*SEWING*) лоскутная
работа.
patchy ['pætʃɪ] *adj* (*uneven*: *colour*) пятнистый
(пятнист); (*incomplete*: *information,
knowledge etc*) отрывочный* (отрывочен).
pate [peɪt] *n*: **a bald ~** лысина на макуше.
pâté ['pæteɪ] *n* (*CULIN*) паштет.

patent ['peɪtnt] *n* (*COMM*) патент ♦ *vt* (*COMM*)
патентовать* (запатентовать* *perf*) ♦ *adj*
(*obvious*) явный* (явен).
patent leather *n* лакированная кожа.
patently ['peɪtntlɪ] *adv* (*obvious, wrong*)
очевидно.
patent medicine *n* патентованное лекарство.
Patent Office *n* патентное бюро *nt ind*.
patent rights *npl* патентное право *ntsg*.
paternal [pə'tə:nl] *adj* (*love, duty*) отцовский*;
(*grandmother etc*) по отцу.
paternalistic [pətə:nə'lɪstɪk] *adj* (*society,
attitudes*) патерналистический.
paternity [pə'tə:nɪtɪ] *n* отцовство.
paternity leave *n* отпуск отца по уходу за
ребёнком.
paternity suit *n* (*LAW*) установление
отцовства.
path [pɑ:θ] *n* (*trail, track*) тропа*, тропинка*;
(*concrete path, gravel path etc*) дорожка*;
(*trajectory*) путь *m* движения; (*fig*) путь*.
pathetic [pə'θetɪk] *adj* (*pitiful*: *sight, cries*)
жалостный* (жалостен); (*very bad*) жалкий*
(жалок).
pathological [pæθə'lɔdʒɪkl] *adj* (*liar, hatred*)
патологический*; (*MED*: *work*) в области
патологии.
pathologist [pə'θɔlədʒɪst] *n* (*MED*) патолог.
pathology [pə'θɔlədʒɪ] *n* (*MED*) патология.
pathos ['peɪθɔs] *n* патетика, горечь *f*.
pathway ['pɑ:θweɪ] *n* (*path*) тропа; (*route, fig*)
путь* *m*.
patience ['peɪʃns] *n* (*personal quality*)
терпение; (*BRIT*: *CARDS*) пасьянс; **to lose one's
~** терять (потерять *perf*) терпение.
patient ['peɪʃnt] *n* (*MED*) пациент(ка) ♦ *adj*
(*person*) терпеливый (терпелив); **he is ~ with
me** он терпелив со мной.
patiently ['peɪʃntlɪ] *adv* терпеливо.
patio ['pætɪəu] *n* патио *m ind*, внутренний
дворик.
patriot ['peɪtrɪət] *n* патриот(ка).
patriotic [pætrɪ'ɔtɪk] *adj* (*person*) патриотичный* (патриотичен); (*song, speech etc*)
патриотический, патриотичный*
(патриотичен).
patriotism ['pætrɪətɪzəm] *n* патриотизм.
patrol [pə'trəul] *n* (*MIL, POLICE*) патруль *m* ♦ *vt*
(*MIL, POLICE*: *city, streets etc*) патрулировать*
(*impf*); **to be on ~** быть* (*impf*) в дозоре;
(*POLICE*) быть* (*impf*) на дежурстве.
patrol boat *n* (*NAUT, MIL, CUSTOMS etc*)
сторожевой катер.
patrol car *n* (*POLICE*) полицейская патрульная
машина.
patrolman [pə'trəulmən] *irreg n* (*US*: *POLICE*)
дежурный полицейский *m adj*.
patron ['peɪtrən] *n* (*customer, client*)

---

* marks translations which have irregular inflections. The Russian-English side of the dictionary gives inflectional information.

(постоя́нный) клие́нт; (*benefactor: of charity*) спо́нсор, шеф; ~ **of the arts** покрови́тель(ница) *m(f)* иску́сств.

patronage ['pætrənɪdʒ] *n* (*of artist etc*) покрови́тельство; (*of charity*) спо́нсорство, ше́фство.

patronize ['pætrənaɪz] *vt* (*pej: look down on*) относи́ться* (отнести́сь* *perf*) свысока́; (*artist, writer*) покрови́тельствовать (*impf*) +*dat*; (*shop, club, firm*) постоя́нно посеща́ть (*impf*).

patronizing ['pætrənaɪzɪŋ] *adj* (*pej: person, tone, comment etc*) снисходи́тельный* (снисходи́телен).

patron saint *n* (*REL*) засту́пник(-ица).

patter ['pætə] *n* (*sound: of feet, rain*) топота́ние; (*of rain*) стук; (*sales talk etc*) речитати́в◆*vi* (*footsteps*) топота́ть (*impf*); (*rain*) бараба́нить (*impf*).

pattern ['pætən] *n* (*design*) узо́р; (*SEWING*) вы́кройка*; (*sample*) образе́ц*; **behaviour** ~s мане́ры *fpl* поведе́ния.

patterned ['pætənd] *adj* (*fabric, wallpaper, carpet etc*) узо́рчатый; ~ **with flowers** с узо́ром из цвето́в.

paucity ['pɔːsɪtɪ] *n* недоста́ток*.

paunch [pɔːntʃ] *n* брюшко́*.

pauper ['pɔːpə] *n* ни́щий*(-ая) *m(f) adj*; ~'**s grave** бедня́цкая моги́ла.

pause [pɔːz] *n* (*temporary halt*) переры́в; (*MUS*) па́уза ◆ *vi* (*stop temporarily*) де́лать (сде́лать *perf*) переры́в; (: *while speaking*) де́лать (сде́лать *perf*) па́узу; **to** ~ **for breath** переводи́ть* (перевести́* *perf*) дыха́ние; (*fig*) передохну́ть (*perf*).

pave [peɪv] *vt* (*street, yard etc*) мости́ть* (вы́мостить* *perf*); **to** ~ **the way for** (*fig*) прокла́дывать (проложи́ть* *perf*) путь к +*dat*.

pavement ['peɪvmənt] *n* (*BRIT: for pedestrians*) тротуа́р; (*US: roadway*) доро́жное покры́тие.

pavilion [pə'vɪlɪən] *n* (*SPORT*) павильо́н.

paving ['peɪvɪŋ] *n* (*material*) доро́жное покры́тие.

paving stone *n* брусча́тка*.

paw [pɔː] *n* (*of animal*) ла́па* ◆ *vt* (*animal*) тро́гать (потро́гать *perf*) ла́пой *или* ла́пами; (*horse, bull*) бить* (*impf*) копы́том *или* копы́тами; (*pej: touch*) ла́пать (*impf*).

pawn [pɔːn] *n* (*CHESS, fig*) пе́шка ◆ *vt* закла́дывать (заложи́ть* *perf*).

pawnbroker ['pɔːnbrəukə] *n* ростовщи́к(-и́ца).

pawnshop ['pɔːnʃɔp] *n* ломба́рд.

pay [peɪ] (*pt, pp* **paid**) *n* (*wage, salary etc*) зарпла́та ◆ *vt* (*sum of money, wage*) плати́ть* (заплати́ть* *perf*); (*debt, bill*) плати́ть* (уплати́ть* *perf*); (*be profitable to: also fig*) окупа́ть (окупи́ть* *perf*) ◆ *vi* (*be profitable*) окупа́ться (окупи́ться* *perf*); **how much did you** ~ **for it?** ско́лько Вы за него́/неё/э́то заплати́ли?; **I paid £5 for that record** я заплати́л £5 за ту пласти́нку; **to** ~ **one's way** обеспе́чивать (обеспе́чить *perf*) себя́; **to** ~ **dividends** (*fig*) вознагражда́ться (вознагради́ться* *perf*); **it won't** ~ **you to do that** э́то де́ло не принесёт вам успе́ха; **to** ~ **attention (to)** обраща́ть (обрати́ть* *perf*) внима́ние (на +*acc*); **to** ~ **sb a visit** наноси́ть* (нанести́* *perf*) кому́-н визи́т; **to** ~ **one's respects to sb** свиде́тельствовать* (засвиде́тельствовать* *perf*) кому́-н (своё) почте́ние.

▶ **pay back** *vt* (*money*) возвраща́ть (возврати́ть* *или* верну́ть *perf*); (*person*) отплати́ть* (*perf*).

▶ **pay for** *vt fus* (*purchases*) опла́чивать (оплати́ть* *perf*); (*fig*) поплати́ться* (*perf*) за +*acc*

▶ **pay in** *vt* (*money, cheque etc*) вноси́ть* (внести́* *perf*)

▶ **pay off** *vt* (*debt, creditor, mortgage*) распла́чиваться (расплати́ться* *perf*) с +*instr*; (*person*) рассчи́тывать (рассчита́ть *perf*) ◆ *vi* (*also fig*) окупа́ться (окупи́ться* *perf*); **to** ~ **sth off in instalments** расплачи́ваться (расплати́ться* *perf*) за что-н в рассро́чку

▶ **pay out** *vt* (*money*) выпла́чивать (вы́платить* *perf*); (*rope*) трави́ть* (потрави́ть* *perf*)

▶ **pay up** *vt* (*money*) выпла́чивать (вы́платить* *perf*) ◆ *vi* (*person, company etc*) рассчи́тываться (рассчита́ться *perf*) (сполна́).

payable ['peɪəbl] *adj* (*sum of money*) подлежа́щий упла́те; (*cheque*): ~ **to** подлежа́щий упла́те на и́мя +*gen*.

pay award *n* повыше́ние зарпла́ты.

payday ['peɪdeɪ] *n* день* *m* зарпла́ты.

PAYE *n abbr* (*BRIT*: = *pay as you earn*) *отчисле́ние подохо́дного нало́га из зарпла́ты.*

payee [peɪ'iː] *n* (*of cheque, postal order*) получа́тель(ница) *m(f)*.

pay envelope *n* (*US*) = **pay packet**.

paying guest *n* ['peɪɪŋ-] *n* постоя́лец(-лица).

payload ['peɪləud] *n* (*COMM*) поле́зная нагру́зка*.

payment ['peɪmənt] *n* (*act*) платёж*, упла́та; (*of bill*) опла́та; (*amount of money*) вы́плата; **advance** ~ (*part sum*) внесе́ние ава́нса; (*total sum*) платёж ава́нсом; **deferred** ~ отсро́ченный платёж; ~ **by instalments** платёж в рассро́чку; **monthly** ~ ме́сячный платёж; **in** ~ **for, in** ~ **of** в опла́ту за +*acc*; **on** ~ **of five pounds** по упла́те пяти́ фу́нтов.

pay packet *n* (*BRIT*) паке́т с зарпла́той.

payphone ['peɪfəun] *n* (*TEL*) телефо́н-автома́т.

payroll ['peɪrəul] *n* платёжная ве́домость *f*; **to be on a firm's** ~ быть* (*impf*) в спи́сочном соста́ве фи́рмы.

pay slip *n* (*BRIT*) извеще́ние о зарпла́те.

pay station *n* (*US*) телефо́н-автома́т.

PBS *n abbr* (*US*: = *Public Broadcasting Service*)

Госуда́рственная слу́жба радиовеща́ния.
PC n abbr (= **personal computer**) ПК=
  персона́льный компью́тер; (BRIT) = **police**
  constable ♦ adj abbr = **politically correct ♦** abbr
  (BRIT) = **Privy Councillor**.
pc abbr = **per cent, postcard**.
p/c abbr = **petty cash**.
PCB n abbr (ELEC, COMPUT: = printed circuit
  board) полихлори́рованный дифени́л.
  (= polychlorinated
  biphenyl) полихлори́рованный дифени́л.
pcm abbr (= per calendar month) в ме́сяц.
PD n abbr (US) = **police department**.
pd abbr = **paid**.
PDQ adv abbr (inf: = pretty damn quick)
  чертовски бы́стро.
PDSA n abbr (BRIT: = People's Dispensary for Sick
  Animals) благотвори́тельное о́бщество,
  организу́ющее ветерина́рную по́мощь
  живо́тным.
PDT abbr (US) = Pacific Daylight Time.
PE n abbr (SCOL) (= physical education)
  физкульту́ра= физи́ческая культу́ра ♦ abbr
  (CANADA) = Prince Edward Island.
pea [pi:] n (BOT, CULIN) горо́х no pl.
peace [pi:s] n (not war) мир; (calm: of place,
  surroundings) поко́й, споко́йствие;
  (: personal) поко́й; **to be at ~ with sb** быть*
  (impf) в ми́ре с кем-н; **to be at ~ with sth**
  смиря́ться (смири́ться* perf) с чем-н; **to keep**
  the ~ (policeman) подде́рживать
  (поддержа́ть* perf) споко́йствие; (citizen)
  соблюда́ть (impf) споко́йствие.
peaceable ['pi:səbl] adj миролюби́вый
  (миролюби́в).
peaceful ['pi:sful] adj (calm) ми́рный* (ми́рен).
peacekeeper ['pi:ski:pə'] n член ми́рных
  войск.
peacekeeping force ['pi:ski:piŋ-] n миро-
  тво́рческие си́лы fpl.
peace offering n задабривание.
peach [pi:tʃ] n пе́рсик.
peacock ['pi:kɔk] n павли́н.
peak [pi:k] n верши́на, пик; (of cap) козырёк*.
peak hours npl часы́ mpl пик.
peak period n пи́ковый пери́од.
peak rate n (TEL) расце́нки, применя́емые в
  пи́ковый пери́од.
peaky ['pi:ki] adj (BRIT: inf) до́хлый.
peal [pi:l] n (of bells) перезво́н; **~ of laughter**
  раска́т сме́ха.
peanut ['pi:nʌt] n ара́хис.
peanut butter n ара́хисовая па́ста.
pear [pɛə'] n гру́ша.
pearl [pə:l] n жемчу́жина; **~s** же́мчуг.
peasant ['pɛznt] n крестья́нин*(-нка*).
peat [pi:t] n торф.
pebble ['pɛbl] n га́лька* no pl.
peck [pɛk] vt (subj: bird) клева́ть* (impf); (: once)

клю́нуть (perf); (also: ~ at: food) поклева́ть*
  (impf) ♦ n (of bird) клево́к*; (kiss) чмо́канье.
pecking order ['pɛkiŋ-] n ста́ршинство́.
peckish ['pɛkiʃ] adj (BRIT: inf): **I'm feeling ~** мне
  хо́чется пожева́ть.
peculiar [pɪ'kju:lɪə'] adj (strange) свое-
  обра́зный* (своеобра́зен); (belonging
  exclusively): **~ to** сво́йственный* (сво́йствен)
  +dat.
peculiarity [pɪkju:lɪ'ærɪtɪ] n (strange habit)
  стра́нность f; (distinctive feature)
  осо́бенность f.
peculiarly [pɪ'kju:lɪəlɪ] adv (oddly) стра́нно;
  (distinctively) осо́бенно.
pecuniary [pɪ'kju:nɪərɪ] adj де́нежный.
pedal ['pɛdl] n педа́ль f ♦ vi крути́ть (impf)
  педа́ли.
pedal bin n (BRIT) му́сорное ведро́* с педа́лью.
pedant ['pɛdənt] n педа́нт(ка*).
pedantic [pɪ'dæntɪk] adj педанти́чный*
  (педанти́чен).
peddle ['pɛdl] vt (goods, drugs) торгова́ть
  (impf) +instr; (gossip) разноси́ть* (разнести́*
  perf).
peddler ['pɛdlə'] n: (drug) **~** торго́вец*
  нарко́тиками.
pedestal ['pɛdəstl] n пьедеста́л.
pedestrian [pɪ'dɛstrɪən] n пешехо́д ♦ adj
  пешехо́дный; (fig) ску́чный.
pedestrian crossing n (BRIT) пешехо́дный
  перехо́д.
pedestrian precinct n (BRIT) пешехо́дная
  зо́на.
pediatrics [pi:dɪ'ætrɪks] n (US) = **paediatrics**.
pedigree ['pɛdɪgri:] n (also fig) родосло́вная f
  adj ♦ cpd (animal) поро́дистый (поро́дист).
pee [pi:] vi (inf) пи́сать (попи́сать perf).
peek [pi:k] vi: **to ~ at/over** взгля́дывать
  (взгляну́ть* perf) на +acc/пове́рх +gen ♦ n: **to**
  have or **take a ~ (at)** взгля́дывать (взгляну́ть*
  perf) (на +acc); **to ~ into** загля́дывать
  (загляну́ть* perf) в +acc.
peel [pi:l] n кожура́ ♦ vt (vegetables, fruit)
  чи́стить* (почи́стить* perf), очища́ть
  (очи́стить* perf) ♦ vi (paint) лупи́ться*
  (облупи́ться* perf); (wallpaper) отстава́ть*
  (отста́ть* perf); (skin) шелуши́ться (impf)
  ▶ **peel back** vt оття́гивать (оттяну́ть* perf)
peeler ['pi:lə'] n (for potatoes etc) нож для
  очи́стки овоще́й и фру́ктов.
peelings ['pi:lɪŋz] npl очи́стки pl.
peep [pi:p] n (look) взгляд укра́дкой; (sound)
  писк ♦ vi взгля́дывать (взгляну́ть* perf); **to**
  have or **take a ~ (at)** взгля́дывать (взгляну́ть*
  perf) (на +acc)
  ▶ **peep out** vi (be visible) пока́зываться
  (показа́ться* perf), выгля́дывать (вы́глянуть*
  perf).

---

* marks translations which have irregular inflections. The Russian-English side of the dictionary gives inflectional information.

peephole ['pi:phəul] n глазо́к*.

peer [pɪəʳ] n (BRIT: noble) пэр; (equal) ро́вня m/f; (contemporary) рове́сник(-ица) ♦ vi: to ~ at всма́триваться (всмотре́ться* perf) в +acc.

peerage ['pɪərɪdʒ] n (title, position) пэ́рство; the ~ пэ́ры.

peerless ['pɪəlɪs] adj несравне́нный* (несравне́нен).

peeved [pi:vd] adj (inf) злой (зол).

peevish ['pi:vɪʃ] adj капри́зный* (капри́зен), сварли́вый (сварли́в).

peg [pɛg] n (for coat etc) крючо́к*; (BRIT: also: clothes ~) прище́пка*; (also: tent ~) ко́лышек* (для натяги́вания пала́тки) ♦ vt (clothes: on line) прикрепля́ть (прикрепи́ть* perf) прище́пками; (prices) замора́живать (заморо́зить* perf); off the ~ clothing гото́вая оде́жда.

pejorative [pɪ'dʒɔrətɪv] adj уничижи́тельный* (уничижи́телен).

Pekin [pi:'kɪn] n = **Peking**.

Pekinese [pi:kɪ'ni:z] n = **Pekingese**.

Peking [pi:'kɪŋ] n Пеки́н.

Pekingese [pi:kɪ'ni:z] n (dog) кита́йский* мопс.

pelican ['pɛlɪkən] n пелика́н.

pelican crossing n (BRIT) пешехо́дный перехо́д, на кото́ром переключе́ние светофо́ра регули́руется нажа́тием кно́пки.

pellet ['pɛlɪt] n (of paper, mud) ша́рик, ка́тышек*; (for shotgun) дроби́на.

pell-mell ['pɛl'mɛl] adv очертя́ го́лову.

pelmet ['pɛlmɪt] n ламбреке́н.

pelt [pɛlt] n (animal skin) шку́ра ♦ vi (rain: also: ~ down) лить* (impf) как из ведра́; (inf: run) проноси́ться* (пронести́сь* perf) ♦ vt: to ~ sb with sth забра́сывать (заброса́ть* perf) кого́-н чем-н.

pelvis ['pɛlvɪs] n таз* no pl.

pen [pɛn] n ру́чка*; (felt-tip) флома́стер; (enclosure) заго́н; (US: inf: prison) тюрьма́*; to put ~ to paper бра́ться* (взя́ться* perf) за перо́.

penal ['pi:nl] adj (colony, institution) исправи́тельный; (system) кара́тельный; ~ code уголо́вный ко́декс.

penalize ['pi:nəlaɪz] vt (also fig) нака́зывать (наказа́ть* perf); (SPORT) штрафова́ть (оштрафова́ть perf).

penal servitude [-'sə:vɪtju:d] n ка́торжные рабо́ты fpl.

penalty ['pɛnltɪ] n (punishment) наказа́ние; (fine) штраф; (RUGBY) штрафно́й m adj (уда́р); (FOOTBALL) штрафно́й (уда́р), пена́льти m ind.

penalty area n (BRIT: SPORT) штрафна́я f adj (площа́дка*).

penalty clause n (COMM) пункт, предусма́тривающий вид и разме́р штра́фа за наруше́ние усло́вий контра́кта.

penalty kick n (RUGBY) штрафно́й m adj (уда́р); (FOOTBALL) штрафно́й (уда́р), пена́льти m ind.

penalty shoot-out [-'ʃu:taut] n определе́ние кома́нды-победи́теля путём забива́ния се́рии штрафны́х уда́ров по́сле ма́тча око́нчившегося ничье́й.

penance ['pɛnəns] n ка́ра.

pence [pɛns] npl of **penny**.

penchant ['pɑ̃:ʃɑ̃:ŋ] n скло́нность f; to have a ~ for име́ть (impf) скло́нность к +dat.

pencil ['pɛnsl] n каранда́ш* ♦ vt: to ~ sth in впи́сывать (вписа́ть* perf) что-н карандашо́м; (fig) помеча́ть (поме́тить* perf) что-н.

pencil case n пена́л.

pencil sharpener n точи́лка.

pendant ['pɛndnt] n куло́н.

pending ['pɛndɪŋ] prep впредь до +gen, в ожида́нии +gen ♦ adj (lawsuit, exam etc) предстоя́щий*.

pendulum ['pɛndjuləm] n ма́ятник.

penetrate ['pɛnɪtreɪt] vt (subj: person, light) проника́ть (прони́кнуть* perf) в/на +acc.

penetrating ['pɛnɪtreɪtɪŋ] adj (sound, glance) пронзи́тельный* (пронзи́телен); (mind) проница́тельный* (проница́телен); (observation) глубо́кий*.

penetration [pɛnɪ'treɪʃən] n проникнове́ние.

pen friend n (BRIT) друг* (подру́га) по перепи́ске.

penguin ['pɛŋgwɪn] n пингви́н.

penicillin [pɛnɪ'sɪlɪn] n пеницилли́н.

peninsula [pə'nɪnsjulə] n полуо́стров*.

penis ['pi:nɪs] n пе́нис, мужско́й полово́й член.

penitence ['pɛnɪtns] n раска́яние.

penitent ['pɛnɪtnt] adj ка́ющийся.

penitentiary [pɛnɪ'tɛnʃərɪ] n (US) тюрьма́*.

penknife ['pɛnnaɪf] n перочи́нный нож*.

pen name n (литерату́рный) псевдони́м.

pennant ['pɛnənt] n (NAUT) сигна́льный флажо́к*.

penniless ['pɛnɪlɪs] adj без гроша́; she is ~ у неё нет ни гроша́.

Pennines ['pɛnaɪnz] npl: the ~ Пени́нские го́ры* fpl.

penny ['pɛnɪ] n (pl **pennies** or (BRIT) **pence**) n пе́нни nt ind, пенс; (US) цент.

pen pal n = **pen friend**.

penpusher ['pɛnpuʃəʳ] n занима́ющийся ну́дной пи́сьменной рабо́той/пи́сарь m.

pension ['pɛnʃən] n пе́нсия

▶ **pension off** vt отправля́ть (отпра́вить* perf) на пе́нсию.

pensionable ['pɛnʃnəbl] adj (age) пенсио́нный; (job) даю́щий пра́во на пе́нсию.

pensioner ['pɛnʃənəʳ] n (BRIT: also: old age ~) пенсионе́р(ка*).

pension fund n пенсио́нный фонд.

pensive ['pɛnsɪv] adj заду́мчивый (заду́мчив).

pentagon ['pɛntəgən] *n* пятиуго́льник; (*US*): the P~ Пентаго́н.
Pentecost ['pɛntɪkɔst] *n* (*Jewish*) пятидеся́тница; (*Christian*) Тро́ицын день* *m*.
penthouse ['pɛnthaus] *n* (*flat*) „пе́нтхаус" (*фешене́бельная кварти́ра, располо́женная на кры́ше*).
pent-up ['pɛntʌp] *adj* (*feelings*) сде́рживаемый.
penultimate [pɛ'nʌltɪmət] *adj* предпосле́дний*.
penury ['pɛnjurɪ] *n* нужда́, бе́дность *f*.
people ['pi:pl] *npl* (*persons*) лю́ди *pl*; (*nation, race*) наро́д; **old ~** старики́ *mpl*; **young ~** молодёжь *fsg*; **the ~** (*POL*) наро́д; **~ at large** лю́ди в ма́ссе свое́й; **a man of the ~** челове́к из наро́да; **several ~ came** пришло́ не́сколько челове́к; **the room was full of ~** в ко́мнате бы́ло полно́ наро́ду; **~ say that ...** говоря́т, что ....
pep [pɛp] (*inf*) *n* бо́дрость *f*
▶ **pep up** *vt* (*enliven*) оживи́ть* (*perf*); (*food*) де́лать (сде́лать *perf*) остре́е.
pepper ['pɛpə^r] *n* пе́рец* ♦ *vt* (*fig*): **to ~ with** забра́сывать (заброса́ть *perf*) +*instr*.
peppercorn ['pɛpəkɔːn] *n* перчи́нка*.
pepper mill *n* ме́льница для пе́рца.
peppermint ['pɛpəmɪnt] *n* (*sweet*) мя́тная конфе́та; (*plant*) мя́та пере́чная.
pepperoni [pɛpə'rəunɪ] *n* пеперо́ни *f ind* (*италья́нская колбаса́*).
pepper pot *n* пе́речница.
pep talk *n* (*inf*) нака́чка*.
per [pə:'] *prep* (*for each: of amounts*) на +*acc*; (: *of price*) за +*acc*; (: *of charge*) с +*gen*; **~ annum/day/hour** в год/день/час; **~ person** на челове́ка; **~ kilo** за килогра́мм; **as ~ your instructions** согла́сно ва́шим инстру́кциям; **as ~ usual** по обыкнове́нию.
per capita *adj*, *adv* (*income*) на ду́шу населе́ния.
perceive [pə'si:v] *vt* (*sound, light, idea*) воспринима́ть (восприня́ть* *perf*); (*realize*) понима́ть (поня́ть* *perf*).
per cent *n* проце́нт; **a twenty ~ ~ discount** двадцатипроце́нтная ски́дка.
percentage [pə'sɛntɪdʒ] *n* (*of income*) проце́нт; (*of immigrants etc*) до́ля; (*of substances*) (проце́нтное) содержа́ние; **on a ~ basis** на основа́нии проце́нтного отчисле́ния.
percentage point *n* проце́нт.
perceptible [pə'sɛptɪbl] *adj* ощути́мый (ощути́м).
perception [pə'sɛpʃən] *n* (*faculty*) восприя́тие; (*insight*) понима́ние *no pl*; (*opinion, understanding*) ощуще́ние.
perceptive [pə'sɛptɪv] *adj* проница́тельный* (проница́телен).
perch [pə:tʃ] *n* (*for bird*) насе́ст ♦ *n inv* (*fish*)

о́кунь* *m* ♦ *vi*: **to ~ (on)** (*bird*) сади́ться* (сесть* *perf*) (на +*acc*); (*person*) приса́живаться (присе́сть* *perf*) (на +*acc*).
percolate ['pə:kəleɪt] *vt* (*coffee*) вари́ть* (свари́ть* *perf*) в кофева́рке ♦ *vi* (*coffee*) вари́ться (свари́ться *perf*) в кофева́рке; (*idea, information, light etc*): **to ~ through/into** проса́чиваться (просочи́ться *perf*) сквозь +*acc*/в +*acc*.
percolator ['pə:kəleɪtə^r] *n* (*also:* **coffee ~**) кофева́рка.
percussion [pə'kʌʃən] *n* уда́рные инструме́нты *mpl*.
peremptory [pə'rɛmptərɪ] *adj* (*pej: person*) вла́стный* (вла́стен), категори́чный* (категори́чен); (: *order, instruction*) категори́ческий*.
perennial [pə'rɛnɪəl] *adj* (*plant*) многоле́тний*; (*fig: problem, feature etc*) ве́чный* (ве́чен) ♦ *n* (*BOT*) многоле́тнее *nt adj* (расте́ние).
perfect [*adj, n* 'pə:fɪkt, *vt* pə'fɛkt] *adj* (*person, behaviour etc*) безупре́чный* (безупре́чен); (*weather*) прекра́сный* (прекра́сен); (*utter: nonsense etc*) соверше́нный ♦ *n* (*also:* **~ tense**) перфе́кт ♦ *vt* (*technique*) соверше́нствовать (усоверше́нствовать *perf*); **he's a ~ stranger to me** он мне соверше́нно незнако́м.
perfection [pə'fɛkʃən] *n* соверше́нство.
perfectionist [pə'fɛkʃənɪst] *n* взыска́тельный* челове́к*.
perfective [pə'fɛktɪv] *n* (*also:* **~ aspect**) соверше́нный вид.
perfectly ['pə:fɪktlɪ] *adv* (*emphatic*) вполне́, соверше́нно; (*faultlessly*) безупре́чно; (*completely*) вполне́, прекра́сно; **I'm ~ happy with the situation** я вполне́ дово́лен положе́нием дел; **you know ~ well** Вы прекра́сно зна́ете.
perforate ['pə:fəreɪt] *vt* перфори́ровать (*impf/perf*).
perforated ulcer ['pə:fəreɪtəd-] *n* перфорати́вная я́зва желу́дка.
perforation [pə:fə'reɪʃən] *n* перфора́ция.
perform [pə'fɔ:m] *vt* (*task, operation*) выполня́ть (вы́полнить *perf*); (*ceremony, experiment*) проводи́ть* (провести́* *perf*); (*piece of music*) исполня́ть (испо́лнить *perf*); (*play*) игра́ть (сыгра́ть *perf*); (*subj: mechanism*) рабо́тать (*impf*) ♦ *vi* (*well, badly*) справля́ться* (*perf*).
performance [pə'fɔ:məns] *n* (*of actor, athlete etc*) выступле́ние; (*of musical work*) исполне́ние; (*of play, show*) представле́ние; (*of car, engine, company*) рабо́та; (*of economy*) эффекти́вность *f*; **the team put up a good ~** кома́нда хорошо́ вы́ступила.
performer [pə'fɔ:mə^r] *n* исполни́тель(ница)

---

* marks translations which have irregular inflections. The Russian-English side of the dictionary gives inflectional information.

m(f).

performing [pə'fɔːmɪŋ] *adj* (*animal*) дрессированный.

perfume ['pəːfjuːm] *n* духи *pl*; (*aroma*) аромат ♦ *vt* (*air, room etc*) ароматизировать (*impf/perf*).

perfunctory [pə'fʌŋktərɪ] *adj* (*kiss, remark etc*) небрежный* (небрежен).

perhaps [pə'hæps] *adv* может быть, возможно; ~ **he'll come** может быть, *or* возможно он придёт; ~ **so** может быть; ~ **not** может быть* и нет.

peril ['pɛrɪl] *n* опасность *f*.

perilous ['pɛrɪləs] *adj* опасный* (опасен).

perilously ['pɛrɪləslɪ] *adv*: **they came ~ close to being caught** они находились на грани разоблачения.

perimeter [pə'rɪmɪtəʳ] *n* периметр.

perimeter wall *n* стена по периметру.

period ['pɪərɪəd] *n* (*length of time*) период; (*SCOL*) урок; (*esp US*: *full stop*) точка*; (*MED*) менструация ♦ *adj* (*costume, furniture*) старинный; ~ **of validity** срок действия; **for a ~ of three weeks** (*go*) на три недели; (*be*) три недели; **the holiday ~** (*BRIT*) время* *or* период отпусков.

periodic [pɪərɪ'ɔdɪk] *adj* периодический*.

periodical [pɪərɪ'ɔdɪk] *n* (*magazine*) периодическое издание ♦ *adj* периодический*.

periodically [pɪərɪ'ɔdɪklɪ] *adv* периодически.

period pains *npl* (*BRIT*: *MED*) менструальные боли *fpl*.

peripatetic [pɛrɪpə'tɛtɪk] *adj* (*salesman*) бродячий; (*BRIT*: *teacher*) приходящий*.

peripheral [pə'rɪfərəl] *adj* (*also COMPUT*) периферийный ♦ *n* (*COMPUT*) периферия.

periphery [pə'rɪfərɪ] *n* периферия.

periscope ['pɛrɪskəup] *n* перископ.

perish ['pɛrɪʃ] *vi* (*person*) погибать (погибнуть* *perf*); (*fabric*) приходить* (прийти* *perf*) в негодность.

perishable ['pɛrɪʃəbl] *adj* (*food, goods*) скоропортящийся*.

perishables ['pɛrɪʃəblz] *npl* (*food*) скоропортящиеся продукты *mpl*.

perishing ['pɛrɪʃɪŋ] *adj* (*BRIT*: *inf*): **it's ~ (cold)** ужасно холодно.

peritonitis [pɛrɪtə'naɪtɪs] *n* перитонит.

perjure ['pəːdʒəʳ] *vt*: **to ~ o.s.** давать* (дать* *perf*) ложные показания.

perjury ['pəːdʒərɪ] *n* (*LAW*) лжесвидетельство.

perk [pəːk] *n* (*inf*) льгота.

perk up *vi* (*inf*) оживляться (оживиться* *perf*).

perky ['pəːkɪ] *adj* (*cheerful*) весёлый* (весел), бойкий* (боек).

perm [pəːm] *n* (*for hair*) перманент, химическая завивка* ♦ *vt*: **to have one's hair ~ed** делать (сделать *perf*) себе химическую завивку *or* химию.

permanence ['pəːmənəns] *n* постоянство.

permanent ['pəːmənənt] *adj* постоянный* (постоянен); (*job, position*) постоянный; (*dye, ink*) стойкий*; ~ **address** постоянное местожительство; **I'm not ~ here** я нахожусь здесь временно.

permanently ['pəːmənəntlɪ] *adv* постоянно.

permeable ['pəːmɪəbl] *adj* водопроницаемый (водопроницаем).

permeate ['pəːmɪeɪt] *vt* (*subj*: *liquid*) пропитывать (пропитать *perf*); (: *idea*) пронизывать (пронизать *perf*) ♦ *vi*: **to ~ into/through** проникать (проникнуть* *perf*) в +*acc*/сквозь +*acc*.

permissible [pə'mɪsɪbl] *adj* (*action, behaviour*) допустимый (допустим), позволительный (позволителен).

permission [pə'mɪʃən] *n* (*consent*) позволение; (*official authorization*) разрешение; **to give sb ~ to do** разрешать (разрешить *perf*) кому-н +*infin*.

permissive [pə'mɪsɪv] *adj* (*person*) терпимый (терпим); (*behaviour*) вольный* (волен); **the ~ society** общество вседозволенности.

permit [*vt* pə'mɪt, *n* 'pəːmɪt] *vt* (*allow*) позволять (позволить *perf*), разрешать (разрешить *perf*); (*make possible*) давать* (дать* *perf*) возможность +*dat* ♦ *n* (*official authorization*) разрешение; (*entrance pass*) пропуск*; **to ~ sb to do** разрешать (разрешить *perf*) кому-н +*infin*; **weather ~ting** если погода позволяет; **fishing ~** разрешение на рыбную ловлю.

permutation [pəːmju'teɪʃən] *n* (*MATH*) перестановка*; (*fig*) перемещение.

pernicious [pəː'nɪʃəs] *adj* (*attitude, influence etc*) пагубный* (пагубен); (*MED*) пернициозный.

pernickety [pə'nɪkɪtɪ] *adj* (*inf*) привередливый (привередлив).

perpendicular [pəːpən'dɪkjulə] *adj* (*line, surface*) перпендикулярный* (перпендикулярен); (*cliff, slope*) отвесный* (отвесен).

perpetrate ['pəːpɪtreɪt] *vt* совершать (совершить *perf*).

perpetual [pə'pɛtjuəl] *adj* (*motion, questions*) вечный* (вечен); (*darkness, noise*) постоянный* (постоянен).

perpetuate [pə'pɛtjueɪt] *vt* увековечивать (увековечить *perf*).

perpetuity [pəːpɪ'tjuːɪtɪ] *n*: **in ~** навсегда, навечно.

perplex [pə'plɛks] *vt* озадачивать (озадачить *perf*).

perplexing [pəː'plɛksɪŋ] *adj* запутанный* (запутан), сложный* (сложен).

perquisites ['pəːkwɪzɪts] *npl* (*formal*) льготы *fpl*.

per se [-seɪ] *adv* (*as such*) как таковой; (*in itself*) само по себе.

persecute ['pəːsɪkjuːt] *vt* преследовать (*impf*), подвергать (подвергнуть* *perf*) гонениям

+*dat.*

persecution [pə:sɪ'kju:ʃən] *n* пресле́дование.

perseverance [pə:sɪ'vɪərns] *n* насто́йчивость *f.*

persevere [pə:sɪ'vɪəʳ] *vi* упо́рно добива́ться *(impf).*

Persia ['pə:ʃə] *n* Пе́рсия.

Persian ['pə:ʃən] *adj:* **the (Persian) Gulf** Перси́дский* зали́в.

Persian cat *n* перси́дский*(-ая) кот* (ко́шка).

persist [pə'sɪst] *vi:* **to ~ (in doing)** наста́ивать (настоя́ть *perf*) (на том, что́бы +*infin*).

persistence [pə'sɪstəns] *n* упо́рство.

persistent [pə'sɪstənt] *adj (noise)* непрекраща́ющийся*; *(smell)* сто́йкий* (сто́ек); *(cough)* непроходя́щий; *(person)* упо́рный* (упо́рен); *(lateness)* постоя́нный* (постоя́нен); *(rain)* непреры́вный* (непреры́вен); **~ offender** рецидиви́ст(ка*).

persnickety [pə'snɪkɪtɪ] *adj (US: inf)* = **pernickety**.

person ['pə:sn] *n* челове́к*; **in ~** ли́чно; **to have sth on** *or* **about one's ~** *(weapon)* носи́ть* *(impf)* что-н при себе́; **~ to ~ call** *(TEL)* междугоро́дный телефо́нный разгово́р с вы́зовом абоне́нта.

personable ['pə:snəbl] *adj (adult)* представи́тельный* (представи́телен).

personal ['pə:snl] *adj* ли́чный; *(car)* персона́льный.

personal allowance *n (COMM)* ли́чные ски́дки *fpl* с подохо́дного нало́га.

personal assistant *n* ли́чный секрета́рь* *m.*

personal column *n* коло́нка* для ча́стных объявле́ний.

personal computer *n* персона́льный компью́тер.

personal details *npl* биографи́ческие да́нные *pl adj.*

personal effects *npl* ли́чные ве́щи *fpl or* принадле́жности *fpl.*

personal hygiene *n* ли́чная гигие́на.

personal identification number *n (BANKING)* ли́чный идентификацио́нный но́мер* *(владе́льца пла́стиковой ка́рточки);* *(COMPUT)* персона́льный *or* ли́чный идентификацио́нный но́мер*.

personality [pə:sə'nælɪtɪ] *n* хара́ктер; *(famous person)* знамени́тость *f.*

personal loan *n (COMM)* ли́чная ссу́да.

personally ['pə:snəlɪ] *adv* ли́чно; **to take sth ~** принима́ть (приня́ть* *perf*) что-н на свой счёт.

personal organizer *n* ежедне́вник.

personal property *n* ли́чное иму́щество.

personal stereo *n* персона́льное сте́рео *nt ind.*

personify [pə:'sɔnɪfaɪ] *vt* олицетворя́ть (олицетвори́ть *perf*), воплоща́ть (воплоти́ть* *perf*).

personnel [pə:sə'nɛl] *n* персона́л, штат; *(MIL)* ли́чный соста́в.

personnel department *n* отде́л ка́дров.

personnel management *n* руково́дство ка́драми.

personnel manager *n* нача́льник отде́ла ка́дров.

perspective [pə'spɛktɪv] *n (ARCHIT, ART)* перспекти́ва; *(way of thinking)* ви́дение; **to get sth into ~** *(fig)* смотре́ть* (посмотре́ть* *perf*) на что-н в и́стинном све́те.

Perspex® ['pə:spɛks] *n* плексигла́с.

perspicacity [pə:spɪ'kæsɪtɪ] *n* проница́тельность *f.*

perspiration [pə:spɪ'reɪʃən] *n* пот*.

perspire [pə'spaɪəʳ] *vi* поте́ть (вспоте́ть *perf*).

persuade [pə'sweɪd] *vt:* **to ~ sb to do** убежда́ть (убеди́ть* *perf*) *or* угова́ривать (уговори́ть *perf*) кого- н +*infin*; **to ~ sb of/that** убежда́ть (убеди́ть* *perf*) кого́-н в +*prp/*, что.

persuasion [pə'sweɪʒən] *n* убежде́ние; *(religious)* вероиспове́дание.

persuasive [pə'sweɪsɪv] *adj (argument)* убеди́тельный* (убеди́телен); *(person)* насто́йчивый* (насто́йчив).

pert [pə:t] *adj (impudent)* де́рзкий* (де́рзок); *(jaunty: hat etc)* коке́тливый.

pertaining [pə:'teɪnɪŋ]: **~ to** *prep* относя́щийся к +*dat*, каса́ющийся +*gen.*

pertinent ['pə:tɪnənt] *adj* уме́стный* (уме́стен).

perturb [pə'tə:b] *vt* трево́жить (встрево́жить *perf*).

Peru [pə'ru:] *n* Перу́ *f ind.*

perusal [pə'ru:zl] *n* прочте́ние.

peruse [pə'ru:z] *vt* просма́тривать (просмотре́ть* *perf*).

Peruvian [pə'ru:vjən] *adj* перуа́нский* ♦ *n* перуа́нец*(-нка*).

pervade [pə'veɪd] *vt (subj: smell, feeling)* наполня́ть (напо́лнить *perf*).

pervasive [pə'veɪzɪv] *adj (smell, influence, ideas)* всепроника́ющий; *(gloom)* прони́зывающий.

perverse [pə'və:s] *adj (contrary)* вре́дный* (вре́ден).

perversion [pə'və:ʃən] *n* извраще́ние.

perversity [pə'və:sɪtɪ] *n* вре́дность *f.*

pervert [*vt* pə'və:t, *n* 'pə:və:t] *vt (person, mind)* развраща́ть (разврати́ть* *perf*), растлева́ть (растли́ть *perf*); *(truth, sb's words)* извраща́ть (изврати́ть* *perf*) ♦ *n (also:* **sexual ~)** (полово́й) извраще́нец.

pessimism ['pɛsɪmɪzəm] *n* пессими́зм.

pessimist ['pɛsɪmɪst] *n* пессими́ст(ка*).

pessimistic [pɛsɪ'mɪstɪk] *adj* пессимисти́чный* (пессимисти́чен).

pest [pɛst] *n (insect)* вреди́тель *m*; *(fig: nuisance)* зану́да *m/f.*

---

pest control *n* борьба́ с вреди́телями.
pester ['pɛstə'] *vt* пристава́ть (приста́ть* *perf*) к +*dat*.
pesticide ['pɛstɪsaɪd] *n* пестици́д.
pestilence ['pɛstɪləns] *n* мор.
pestle ['pɛsl] *n* пе́стик.
pet [pɛt] *n* дома́шнее живо́тное *nt adj* ♦ *cpd* излю́бленный ♦ *vt* (*stroke*) ласка́ть (*impf*) ♦ *vi* (*inf: sexually*) обнима́ться (*impf*), целова́ться (*impf*); ~ **lion** *etc* ручно́й лев *etc*; **teacher's** ~ люби́мчик.
petal ['pɛtl] *n* лепесто́к*.
peter out ['pi:tə-] *vi* (*road*) исчеза́ть (исче́знуть* *perf*); (*stream, conversation*) иссяка́ть (исся́кнуть* *perf*); (*meeting*) зака́нчиваться (зако́нчиться *perf*).
petite [pə'ti:t] *adj* миниатю́рный* (миниатю́рен).
petition [pə'tɪʃən] *n* (*signed document*) пети́ция; (*LAW*) хода́тайство ♦ *vt* обраща́ться (обрати́ться* *perf*) с пети́цией к +*dat* ♦ *vi*: **to** ~ **for divorce** подава́ть* (пода́ть* *perf*) заявле́ние о разво́де.
pet name *n* (*BRIT*) ласка́тельное и́мя* *nt*.
petrified ['pɛtrɪfaɪd] *adj* (*fig*) оцепене́вший.
petrify ['pɛtrɪfaɪ] (*fig*) *vt* приводи́ть* (привести́* *perf*) в оцепене́ние.
petrochemical [pɛtrə'kɛmɪkl] *adj* нефтехими́ческий.
petrodollars ['pɛtrəudɔləz] *npl* (*COMM*) нефтедо́ллары *mpl*.
petrol ['pɛtrəl] *n* (*BRIT*) бензи́н; **two/four-star** ~ ни́зкоокта́новый/высо́коокта́новый бензи́н; **unleaded** ~ бензи́н не содержа́щий свинца́.
petrol bomb *n* ба́нка со взрывча́той сме́сью.
petrol can *n* (*BRIT*) кани́стра для бензи́на.
petrol engine *n* (*BRIT*) бензи́новый дви́гатель *m*.
petroleum [pə'trəuliəm] *n* нефть *f*.
petroleum jelly *n* вазели́н*.
petrol pump *n* (*BRIT: in garage*) бензо-коло́нка*; (: *in engine*) бензонасо́с.
petrol station *n* (*BRIT*) бензозапра́вочная ста́нция.
petrol tank *n* (*BRIT*) бензоба́к.
petticoat ['pɛtɪkəut] *n* (*full-length*) комбина́ция; (*waist slip*) ни́жняя ю́бка*.
pettifogging ['pɛtɪfɔgɪŋ] *adj* ме́лочный* (ме́лочен).
pettiness ['pɛtɪnɪs] *n* (*of actions*) ме́лочность *f*; (*of mind*) ограни́ченность *f*.
petty ['pɛtɪ] *adj* (*small, unimportant*) ме́лкий* (ме́лок); (*small-minded*) ограни́ченный* (ограни́чен).
petty cash *n* (*in office*) де́ньги *pl* на ме́лкие расхо́ды.
petty officer *n* старшина́ *m* (*во фло́те*).
petulant ['pɛtjulənt] *adj* оби́дчивый (оби́дчив).
pew [pju:] *n* скамья́* (*в це́ркви*).
pewter ['pju:tə'] *n* сплав о́лова со свинцо́м.

Pfc *abbr* (*US: MIL:* = *private first class*) рядово́й 1-го кла́сса.
PG *n abbr* (*CINEMA:* = *parental guidance*) фильм до 16-ти лет.
PGA *n abbr* = *Professional Golfers Association*.
PH *n abbr* (*US: MIL:* = *Purple Heart*) ≈ меда́ль *f* „За отва́гу".
pH *n abbr* (= *potential of hydrogen*) pH (*водоро́дный показа́тель*).
PHA *n abbr* (*US*) = *Public Housing Administration*.
phallic ['fælɪk] *adj* фалли́ческий.
phantom ['fæntəm] *n* фанто́м ♦ *adj* (*fig*) при́зрачный* (при́зрачен).
Pharaoh ['fɛərəu] *n* фарао́н.
pharmaceutical [fɑ:mə'sju:tɪkl] *adj* фармацевти́ческий ♦ *n*: ~**s** медикаме́нты *mpl*.
pharmacist ['fɑ:məsɪst] *n* фармаце́вт.
pharmacy ['fɑ:məsɪ] *n* (*profession*) фармаце́втика; (*shop*) апте́ка.
phase [feɪz] *n* фа́за ♦ *vt*: **to** ~ **sth in** поэта́пно вводи́ть* (ввести́* *perf*) что-н; **to** ~ **sth out** ликвиди́ровать (*impf/perf*) что-н.
PhD *n abbr* (= *Doctor of Philosophy*) до́ктор филосо́фии.
pheasant ['fɛznt] *n* фаза́н.
phenomena [fə'nɔmɪnə] *npl of* **phenom·** **on**.
phenomenal [fə'nɔmɪnl] *adj* феномена́льный* (феномена́лен).
phenomenon [fə'nɔmɪnən] (*pl* **phenomena**) *n* явле́ние, фено́мен.
phew [fju:] *excl* уф.
phial ['faɪəl] *n* скля́нка*.
philanderer [fɪ'lændərə'] *n* волоки́та *m*.
philanthropic [fɪlən'θrɔpɪk] *adj* филантроп-и́ческий.
philanthropist [fɪ'lænθrəpɪst] *n* филантро́п (ка*).
philatelist [fɪ'lætəlɪst] *n* филатели́ст(ка*).
philately [fɪ'lætəlɪ] *n* филатели́я.
Philippines ['fɪlɪpi:nz] *npl*: **the** ~ Филиппи́ны *pl*, Филиппи́нские острова́* *mpl*.
philosopher [fɪ'lɔsəfə'] *n* фило́соф.
philosophical [fɪlə'sɔfɪkl] *adj* филосо́фский.
philosophize [fɪ'lɔsəfaɪz] *vi* филосо́фствовать (*impf*).
philosophy [fɪ'lɔsəfɪ] *n* филосо́фия.
phlegm [flɛm] *n* (*MED*) мокро́та.
phlegmatic [flɛg'mætɪk] *adj* флегмати́чный* (флегмати́чен).
phobia ['fəubjə] *n* (*MED*) фо́бия, страх.
phone [fəun] *n* телефо́н ♦ *vt* звони́ть (позвони́ть *perf*) (по телефо́ну) +*dat*; **to be on the** ~ (*possess a phone*) име́ть (*impf*) телефо́н; (*be calling*) говори́ть (*impf*) по телефо́ну
▶ **phone back** *vt* перезва́нивать (перезвони́ть *perf*) +*dat* ♦ *vi* перезва́нивать (перезвони́ть *perf*)
▶ **phone up** *vt* звони́ть (позвони́ть *perf*) +*dat* ♦ *vi* звони́ть (позвони́ть *perf*).
phone book *n* телефо́нная кни́га.

phone booth *n* телефо́н-автома́т.
phone box *n* (*BRIT*) телефо́нная бу́дка*, телефо́н-автома́т.
phone call *n* телефо́нный звоно́к*.
phone-card ['fəʊnkɑːd] *n* телефо́нная ка́рточка (*испо́льзуется в автома́тах для безнали́чной опла́ты перегово́ров*).
phone-in ['fəʊnɪn] *n* (*BRIT: RADIO, TV*) програ́мма „звони́те-отвеча́ем".
phone tapping [-tæpɪŋ] *n* прослу́шивание телефо́нных разгово́ров.
phonetics [fə'nɛtɪks] *n* фоне́тика.
phoney ['fəʊnɪ] *adj* фальши́вый (фальши́в).
phonograph ['fəʊnəɡrɑːf] *n* (*US*) про-и́грыватель *m*.
phony ['fəʊnɪ] *adj* = **phoney**.
phosphate ['fɔsfeɪt] *n* фосфа́т.
phosphorus ['fɔsfərəs] *n* фо́сфор.
photo ['fəʊtəʊ] *n* фотогра́фия.
photo... ['fəʊtəʊ] *prefix* фото....
photocopier ['fəʊtəʊkɔpɪəʳ] *n* (*machine*) ксе́рокс, копирова́льная маши́на.
photocopy ['fəʊtəʊkɔpɪ] *n* ксероко́пия, фотоко́пия ♦ *vt* фотокопи́ровать (сфотокопи́ровать *perf*), ксерокопи́ровать (*impf/perf*).
photoelectric [fəʊtəʊɪ'lɛktrɪk] *adj* фото-электри́ческий; ~ **cell** фотоэлеме́нт.
photo finish *n* фотофи́ниш.
Photofit® ['fəʊtəʊfɪt] *n* фотобо́т.
photogenic [fəʊtəʊ'dʒɛnɪk] *adj* фотогени́чный* (фотогени́чен).
photograph ['fəʊtəɡræf] *n* фотогра́фия ♦ *vt* фотографи́ровать (сфотографи́ровать *perf*); **to take a ~ of sb** фотографи́ровать (сфотографи́ровать *perf*) кого́-н.
photographer [fə'tɔɡrəfəʳ] *n* фото́граф.
photographic [fəʊtə'ɡræfɪk] *adj* фото-графи́ческий.
photography [fə'tɔɡrəfɪ] *n* фотогра́фия.
photo opportunity *n* ситуа́ция, даю́щая возмо́жность знамени́тостям быть предста́вленным в вы́годном све́те на фотогра́фии.
Photostat® ['fəʊtəʊstæt] *n* фотоко́пия.
photosynthesis [fəʊtəʊ'sɪnθəsɪs] *n* (*BIO*) фотоси́нтез.
phrase [freɪz] *n* (*also LING, MUS*) фра́за ♦ *vt* формули́ровать (сформули́ровать *perf*); (*letter*) составля́ть (соста́вить* *perf*).
phrase book *n* разгово́рник.
physical ['fɪzɪkl] *adj* физи́ческий*; (*world, universe, object*) материа́льный* (материа́лен); ~ **examination** медосмо́тр= *медици́нский* осмо́тр; ~ **exercises** физи́ческие упражне́ния.
physical education *n* физи́ческое воспита́ние, физкульту́ра.

physically ['fɪzɪklɪ] *adv* физи́чески.
physician [fɪ'zɪʃən] *n* (*esp US*) врач*.
physicist ['fɪzɪsɪst] *n* фи́зик.
physics ['fɪzɪks] *n* фи́зика.
physiological ['fɪzɪə'lɔdʒɪkl] *adj* физиолог-и́ческий*.
physiology [fɪzɪ'ɔlədʒɪ] *n* физиоло́гия.
physiotherapist [fɪzɪəʊ'θɛrəpɪst] *n* физио-терапе́вт.
physiotherapy [fɪzɪəʊ'θɛrəpɪ] *n* физиотерапи́я.
physique [fɪ'ziːk] *n* (*build*) телосложе́ние; (*health*) физи́ческие да́нные *pl adj*.
pianist ['piːənɪst] *n* пиани́ст(ка*).
piano [pɪ'ænəʊ] *n* пиани́но, фортепья́но *nt ind*; **grand ~** роя́ль *m*.
piano accordion *n* (*BRIT*) аккордео́н.
piccolo ['pɪkələʊ] *n* пи́кколо *nt ind*.
pick [pɪk] *n* (*also:* ~**axe**) кирка́* ♦ *vt* (*select*) выбира́ть (вы́брать* *perf*); (*gather: fruit, flowers*) собира́ть (собра́ть* *perf*); (*pluck*) рвать* (*impf*); (*lock*) взла́мывать (взлома́ть *perf*); (*scab, spot*) сковы́ривать (сковырну́ть *perf*); **take your ~** выбира́йте; **the ~ of the bunch** (*best*) са́мое лу́чшее; **to ~ one's nose/teeth** ковыря́ть в носу́/зуба́х; **to ~ sb's brains** обраща́ться (обрати́ться* *perf*) к кому́-н за сове́том; **to ~ pockets** ла́зать (*impf*) карма́нам; **to ~ a quarrel (with sb)** иска́ть* (*impf*) по́вод для ссо́ры (с кем-н)
 ▸ **pick at** *vt fus* (*food*) ковыря́ть (*impf*)
 ▸ **pick off** *vt* (*planes*) методи́чно сбива́ть (сбить* *perf*); (*people*) методи́чно стреля́ть (*impf*) по +*dat*
 ▸ **pick on** *vt fus* (*criticize*) придира́ться (придира́ться* *perf*) к +*dat*; (*treat badly*) цепля́ться (*impf*) к +*dat*
 ▸ **pick out** *vt* (*distinguish*) разгляде́ть (*perf*); (*select*) выбира́ть (вы́брать* *perf*)
 ▸ **pick up** *vt* (*improve: health, economy*) улучша́ться (улу́чшиться *perf*) ♦ *vt* (*lift*) поднима́ть (подня́ть* *perf*); (*POLICE: arrest*) забира́ть (забра́ть* *perf*); (*collect: person: on foot*) заходи́ть* (зайти́* *perf*) за +*instr*; (*: with transport*) заезжа́ть (зае́хать* *perf*) за +*instr*; (*: parcel*) забира́ть (забра́ть* *perf*); (*AUT: passenger*) подбира́ть (подобра́ть* *perf*); (*inf: person: for sexual encounter*) подцепи́ть* (*perf*); (*language, skill etc*) усва́ивать (усво́ить *perf*); (*RADIO*) лови́ть* (пойма́ть *perf*); **to ~ up speed** набира́ть (набра́ть* *perf*) ско́рость; **to ~ o.s. up** (*after falling etc*) поднима́ться (подня́ться* *perf*); **we ~ed up where we left off** мы на́чали с того́ ме́ста, где останови́лись.
pickaxe ['pɪkæks] (*US* **pickax**) *n* кирка́*.
picket ['pɪkɪt] *n* (*in strike*) пике́т ♦ *vt* пикети́ровать (*impf*).
picketing ['pɪkɪtɪŋ] *n* пикети́рование.
picket line *n* ли́ния пике́тов.

---

* marks translations which have irregular inflections. The Russian-English side of the dictionary gives inflectional information.

pickings ['pɪkɪŋz] *npl*: **there are good ~ to be had here** на э́том мо́жно хорошо́ нажи́ться.

pickle ['pɪkl] *n* (*marinade*) марина́д; (*also:* ~s) соле́нья *ntpl*; (*fig: inf*) переде́лка* ◆ *vt* (*in vinegar*) маринова́ть (замаринова́ть *perf*); (*in salt water*) соли́ть* (засоли́ть* *perf*); **to be in a ~** (*fig: inf*) попада́ть (попа́сть* *perf*) в переде́лку.

pick-me-up ['pɪkmiːʌp] *n* тонизи́рующий* напи́ток*.

pickpocket ['pɪkpɔkɪt] *n* вор*-карма́нник.

pick-up ['pɪkʌp] *n* (*also:* ~ **truck** *or* **van**) пика́п; (*BRIT: on record player*) звукоснима́тель *m*.

picnic ['pɪknɪk] *n* пикни́к* ◆ *vi* устра́ивать (устро́ить *perf*) пикни́к.

picnicker ['pɪknɪkə'] *n* уча́стник(-ица) пикника́.

pictorial [pɪk'tɔːrɪəl] *adj* иллюстри́рованный (иллюстри́рован).

picture ['pɪktʃə'] *n* (*also fig*) карти́на; (*photograph*) фотогра́фия; (*TV*) изображе́ние; (*film*) (кино)карти́на ◆ *vt* (*imagine*) рисова́ть (нарисова́ть *perf*) карти́ну +*gen*; **the ~s** *npl* (*BRIT: inf*) кино́ *nt ind*; **to take a ~ of sb/sth** фотографи́ровать (сфотографи́ровать *perf*) кого́-н/что-н; **the overall ~** о́бщая карти́на; **to put sb in the ~** вводи́ть* (ввести́* *perf*) кого́-н в курс де́ла.

picture book *n* кни́га* с карти́нками.

picturesque [pɪktʃə'rɛsk] *adj* живопи́сный* (живопи́сен).

picture window *n* (*ARCHIT*) большо́е окно́, из кото́рого открыва́ется краси́вый вид.

piddling ['pɪdlɪŋ] *adj* (*inf*) пустя́чный*.

pidgin ['pɪdʒɪn] *adj*: **~ English** пи́джин-и́нглиш.

pie [paɪ] *n* пиро́г*; (*small*) пирожо́к*.

piebald ['paɪbɔːld] *adj* пе́гий* (пег).

piece [piːs] *n* (*portion, part*) кусо́к*; (*component*) дета́ль *f*; (*CHESS*) фигу́ра; (*DRAUGHTS*) ша́шка* ◆ *vt*: **to ~ together** (*information*) свя́зывать (связа́ть* *perf*); (*parts of a whole*) соединя́ть (соедини́ть *perf*); **a ~ of clothing** вещь* *f*; **a ~ of advice** сове́т; **in ~s** (*broken*) вдре́безги; (*not yet assembled*) разо́бранный (разо́бран); **to take to ~s** (*dismantle*) разбира́ть (разобра́ть* *perf*); **in one ~** в це́лости и сохра́нности; **to get back all in one** *(pl)* возвраща́ться (верну́ться *perf*) це́лым и невреди́мым; **a 10p ~** (*BRIT*) моне́та в 10 пе́нсов; **~ by ~** по частя́м; **a six-~ band** анса́мбль *m* из шести́ музыка́льных инструме́нтов; **to say one's ~** выска́зывать (вы́сказать* *perf*) своё мне́ние.

piecemeal ['piːsmiːl] *adv* понемно́гу.

piece rate *n* тари́ф *or* ста́вка за едини́цу вы́полненных рабо́т.

piecework ['piːswəːk] *n* сде́льная рабо́та.

pie chart *n* се́кторная диагра́мма.

pier [pɪə'] *n* пирс.

pierce [pɪəs] *vt* протыка́ть (проткну́ть *perf*), прока́лывать (проколо́ть* *perf*); **to have one's ears ~d** прока́лывать (проколо́ть* *perf*) у́ши.

piercing ['pɪəsɪŋ] *adj* (*cry, eyes, stare*) пронзи́тельный* (пронзи́телен); (*wind*) прони́зывающий.

piety ['paɪətɪ] *n* на́божность *f*.

piffling ['pɪflɪŋ] *adj* (*inf*) никчёмный* (никчёмен).

pig [pɪg] *n* (*also fig*) свинья́*.

pigeon ['pɪdʒən] *n* го́лубь* *m*.

pigeonhole ['pɪdʒənhəul] *n* (*in office, bureau*) яче́йка (*для корреспонде́нции*); (*fig*) ни́ша ◆ *vt* (*person*) накле́ивать (накле́ить *perf*) ярлыки́ на +*acc*.

pigeon-toed ['pɪdʒəntəud] *adj* косола́пый (косола́п).

piggy bank ['pɪgɪ-] *n* копи́лка*.

pig-headed ['pɪg'hɛdɪd] *adj* (*inf*) упря́мый (упря́м).

piglet ['pɪglɪt] *n* поросёнок*.

pigment ['pɪgmənt] *n* пигме́нт.

pigmentation [pɪgmən'teɪʃən] *n* пигмента́ция.

pigmy ['pɪgmɪ] *n* = **pygmy**

pigskin ['pɪgskɪn] *n* свина́я ко́жа.

pigsty ['pɪgstaɪ] *n* (*also fig*) свина́рник.

pigtail ['pɪgteɪl] *n* коси́чка*.

pike [paɪk] *n inv* (*fish*) щу́ка ◆ *n* (*spear*) пи́ка.

pilchard ['pɪltʃəd] *n* сарди́на.

pile [paɪl] *n* (*large heap*) ку́ча, гру́да; (*neat stack*) сто́пка*; (*pillar*) сва́я; (*of carpet, cloth*) ворс ◆ *vi*: **to ~ into** (*vehicle*) набива́ться (наби́ться* *perf*) в +*acc*; **in a ~** в ку́че; **to ~ out of** (*vehicle*) выва́ливаться (вы́валиться *perf*) из +*gen*

▶ **pile on** *vt*: **to ~ it on** (*inf*) переба́рщивать (переборщи́ть* *perf*)

▶ **pile up** *vt* (*objects*) сва́ливать (свали́ть* *perf*) в ку́чу ◆ *vi* громозди́ться* (*impf*); (*problems, work*) нака́пливаться (накопи́ться *perf*).

piles [paɪlz] *npl* (*MED*) геморро́й *msg*.

pile-up ['paɪlʌp] *n* (*AUT*) столкнове́ние нескольких маши́н.

pilfer ['pɪlfə'] *vti* ворова́ть (*impf*)

pilfering ['pɪlfərɪŋ] *n* ме́лкое воровство́.

pilgrim ['pɪlgrɪm] *n* пало́мник(-ица), пилигри́м.

pilgrimage ['pɪlgrɪmɪdʒ] *n* пало́мничество.

pill [pɪl] *n* табле́тка; **the ~** (*contraceptive*) противозача́точные *pl adj* (табле́тки); **to be on the ~** принима́ть (*impf*) противозача́точные табле́тки.

pillage ['pɪlɪdʒ] *n* грабёж*.

pillar ['pɪlə'] *n* (*ARCHIT*) столб*, коло́нна; **a ~ of society** (*fig*) столп о́бщества.

pillar box *n* (*BRIT*) почто́вый я́щик*.

pillion ['pɪljən] *n*: **to ride ~** (*on motorcycle*) éхать*/éздить* (*impf*) на за́днем сиде́нье мотоци́кла; (*on horse*) éхать*/éздить* (*impf*) верхо́м на ло́шади сза́ди вса́дника.

pillory ['pɪlərɪ] *vt* выставля́ть (вы́ставить* *perf*) на осмея́ние ◆ *n* позо́рный столб*.

pillow ['pɪləu] *n* поду́шка*.

pillowcase ['pɪləukeɪs] n на́волочка*.
pillowslip ['pɪləuslɪp] n = **pillowcase**.
pilot ['paɪlət] n (AVIAT) пило́т, лётчик; (NAUT) ло́цман ◆ cpd (scheme, study etc) эксперимента́льный ◆ vt (aircraft) управля́ть (impf) +instr; (fig: new law, scheme) апроби́ровать (impf/perf).
pilot boat n ло́цманский ка́тер*.
pilot light n запа́льник.
pimento [pɪ'mɛntəu] n души́стый пе́рец.
pimp [pɪmp] n сутенёр.
pimple ['pɪmpl] n прыщ*, пры́щик.
pimply ['pɪmplɪ] adj прыща́вый (прыща́в).
PIN n abbr = **personal identification number**.
pin [pɪn] n була́вка*; (TECH) штифт*; (BRIT: also: drawing ~) кно́пка*; (of grenade) чека́; (BRIT: ELEC: of plug) штырь* m ◆ vt прика́лывать (приколо́ть* perf); **~s and needles** (fig) колоть́е; **to ~ sb against** or **to** прижима́ть (прижа́ть* perf) кого́-н к +dat; **to ~ sth on sb** (fig) возлага́ть (возложи́ть* perf) на кого́-н вину́ за что-н
▶ **pin down** vt (fig): **to ~ sb down** припира́ть (припере́ть* perf) кого́-н к сте́нке; **there's something strange here but I can't quite ~ it down** что-то здесь не так, но не пойму́ что.
pinafore ['pɪnəfɔ:'] n (also: ~ **dress**) сарафа́н.
pinball ['pɪnbɔ:l] n кита́йский* билья́рд.
pincers ['pɪnsəz] npl (TECH) кле́щи pl; (of crab etc) клешни́ fpl.
pinch [pɪntʃ] n (small amount) щепо́тка* ◆ vt щипа́ть* (ущипну́ть perf); (inf: steal) стащи́ть* (perf) ◆ vi (shoe) жать* (impf); **at a ~** в кра́йнем слу́чае; **to feel the ~** (fig) ока́зываться (оказа́ться* perf) в стеснённых обстоя́тельствах.
pinched [pɪntʃt] adj (drawn) осу́нувшийся; **~ with cold** съёжившийся от хо́лода; **I am ~ for money** у меня́ ту́го с деньга́ми; **we're ~ for space here** у нас здесь ма́ло ме́ста.
pincushion ['pɪnkuʃən] n иго́льник.
pine [paɪn] n (tree, wood) сосна́* ◆ vi: **to ~ for** тоскова́ть (impf) по +dat
▶ **pine away** vi (gradually die) ча́хнуть* (зача́хнуть* perf).
pineapple ['paɪnæpl] n анана́с m no pl.
pine cone n сосно́вая ши́шка.
pine needles npl сосно́вые иго́лки fpl.
ping [pɪŋ] n (noise) звон.
Ping-Pong® ['pɪŋpɔŋ] n насто́льный те́ннис, пинг-по́нг.
pink [pɪŋk] adj ро́зовый ◆ n (colour) ро́зовый цвет*; (BOT) гвозди́ка.
pinking shears npl зу́бчатые но́жницы pl.
pin money n (BRIT) де́ньги pl на була́вки.
pinnacle ['pɪnəkl] n (of building) шпиц; (of mountain, also fig) верши́на.
pinpoint ['pɪnpɔɪnt] vt (discover) то́чно определя́ть (определи́ть perf); (explain) то́чно объясня́ть (объясни́ть perf); (position of sth) то́чно ука́зывать (указа́ть* perf).
pinstripe ['pɪnstraɪp] n поло́ска*; **~ suit** костю́м в поло́ску.
pint [paɪnt] n пи́нта.
pin-up ['pɪnʌp] n (picture) журна́льная вы́резка с изображе́нием краси́вых де́вушек.
pioneer [paɪə'nɪə'] n (initiator: of scheme, science, method) первооткрыва́тель m, нова́тор; (early settler, also fig) первопрохо́дец*, пионе́р ◆ vt (initiate) прокла́дывать (проложи́ть* perf) путь к +dat.
pious ['paɪəs] adj на́божный* (на́божен).
pip [pɪp] n (of grape, melon) ко́сточка*; (of apple, orange) зёрнышко*; **the ~s** npl (BRIT: RADIO) сигна́л msg (то́чного вре́мени).
pipe [paɪp] n (for water, gas) труба́*; (for smoking) тру́бка*; (MUS) ду́дка* ◆ vt (water, gas, oil) подава́ть (пода́ть* perf); **~s** npl (also: **bagpipes**) волы́нка* fsg
▶ **pipe down** vi (inf: be quiet) затыка́ться (заткну́ться perf).
pipe cleaner n ёршик (для тру́бки).
piped music [paɪpt-] n му́зыка из громкоговори́теля.
pipe dream n пусты́е мечты́ fpl.
pipeline ['paɪplaɪn] n трубопрово́д; **oil ~** нефтепрово́д; **gas ~** газопрово́д; **a new project is in the ~** (fig) дан ход но́вому прое́кту.
piper ['paɪpə'] n (bagpipe player) волы́нщик.
pipe tobacco n тру́бочный таба́к*.
piping ['paɪpɪŋ] adv: **~ hot** о́чень горя́чий*.
piquant ['pi:kənt] adj (also fig) пика́нтный* (пика́нтен).
pique [pi:k] n заде́тое самолю́бие.
piracy ['paɪərəsɪ] n пира́тство.
pirate ['paɪərət] n (sailor) пира́т ◆ vt (video tape, cassette) незако́нно распространя́ть (распространи́ть perf); (book) незако́нно переиздава́ть (переизда́ть* perf).
pirate radio n (BRIT): **~ ~ station** пира́тская радиоста́нция.
pirouette [pɪru'ɛt] n пируэ́т.
Pisces ['paɪsi:z] n (ASTROLOGY) Ры́бы; **he is ~** он – Ры́ба.
piss [pɪs] n (inf!) vi пи́сать (попи́сать perf) (!); **~ off!** пошёл ты! (!)
pissed [pɪst] adj (inf!: drunk) пья́ный* (пьян) в сте́льку (!)
pistol ['pɪstl] n пистоле́т.
piston ['pɪstən] n по́ршень* m.
pit [pɪt] n (in ground) я́ма; (in surface of sth) я́мка*; (also: **coal ~**) ша́хта; (also: **orchestra ~**) оркестро́вая я́ма; (quarry) карье́р ◆ vt: **to ~ one's wits against sb** состяза́ться (impf) в эруди́ции с кем-н; **~s** npl (in motor racing)

пункт *msg* ремо́нта и запра́вки; **to ~ sb against sb** направля́ть (напра́вить* *perf*) кого́-н на кого́-н.

pitapat ['pɪtə'pæt] *adv* (*BRIT: of heart*) тук-ту́к; (: *of rain*) кап-ка́п.

pitch [pɪtʃ] *n* (*BRIT: SPORT*) по́ле*; (*MUS*) высота́; (*fig: level, degree*) у́ровень *m*; (*tar*) смола́; (*also: sales ~*) речь *f*; (*NAUT*) килева́я ка́чка ♦ *vt* (*throw*) подава́ть* (пода́ть* *perf*), гнать* (погна́ть* *perf*); (*set: price*) устана́вливать (установи́ть* *perf*) ♦ *vi* (*fall*) па́дать (упа́сть* *perf*); (*NAUT*) испы́тывать (испыта́ть *perf*) килеву́ю ка́чку; **at this ~** (*fig*) на тако́м у́ровне; **to ~ a tent** ста́вить* (поста́вить* *perf*) пала́тку; **he was ~ed forward** его́ бро́сило вперёд.

pitch-black ['pɪtʃ'blæk] *adj* о́чень тёмный.

pitched battle [pɪtʃt-] *n* ожесточённая схва́тка*.

pitcher ['pɪtʃər] *n* (*jug*) кувши́н; (*US: BASEBALL*) пода́ющий *m adj*.

pitchfork ['pɪtʃfɔ:k] *n* ви́лы *pl*.

piteous ['pɪtɪəs] *adj* (*sound etc*) жа́лобный* (жа́лобен); (*sight*) несча́стный* (несча́стен).

pitfall ['pɪtfɔ:l] *n* (*difficulty, danger*) лову́шка, подво́дные ка́мни *mpl*.

pith [pɪθ] *n* (*of orange, lemon etc*) паренхи́ма*; (*of plant*) сердцеви́на; (*fig*) суть *f*.

pithead ['pɪthɛd] *n* (*BRIT*) копёр (*над ша́хтой*).

pithy ['pɪθɪ] *adj* (*saying etc*) содержа́тельный* (содержа́телен).

pitiable ['pɪtɪəbl] *adj* (*sight, person*) жа́лкий* (жа́лок).

pitiful ['pɪtɪful] *adj* жа́лкий* (жа́лок).

pitifully ['pɪtɪfəlɪ] *adv* жа́лобно; **it's ~ obvious** к несча́стью, э́то очеви́дно.

pitiless ['pɪtɪlɪs] *adj* безжа́лостный* (безжа́лостен).

pittance ['pɪtns] *n* гроши́ *mpl*.

pitted ['pɪtɪd] *adj*: **~ with** (*holes, acne*) изры́тый (изры́т) +*instr*; (*rust*) изъе́денный (изъе́ден) +*instr*.

pity ['pɪtɪ] *n* жа́лость *f* ♦ *vt* жале́ть (пожале́ть *perf*); **what a ~!** кака́я жа́лость!; **it is a ~ that you can't come** жа́лко, что Вы не смо́жете прийти́; **to have** *or* **take ~ on sb** сжа́литься (*perf*) над кем-н.

pitying ['pɪtɪŋ] *adj* жа́лостливый (жа́лостлив).

pivot ['pɪvət] *n* (*TECH: pin*) ось *f*; (: *point*) то́чка* враще́ния; (*fig*) центр ♦ *vi*: **to ~ on** (*balance*) держа́ться* (*perf*) на +*prp*; (*turn*) враща́ться (*impf*) вокру́г +*gen*; (*fig: depend on*) зави́сеть* (*impf*) от +*gen*.

pixel ['pɪksl] *n* (*COMPUT*) пи́ксель *m*, элеме́нт изображе́ния.

pixie ['pɪksɪ] *n* эльф.

pizza ['pi:tsə] *n* пи́цца.

placard ['plækɑ:d] *n* плака́т.

placate [plə'keɪt] *vt* (*person*) умиротворя́ть (умиротвори́ть *perf*); (*anger*) усмиря́ть (усмири́ть *perf*).

placatory [plə'keɪtərɪ] *adj* примири́тельный* (примири́телен).

place [pleɪs] *vt* (*put*) помеща́ть (помести́ть* *perf*); (*identify: person*) вспомина́ть (вспо́мнить *perf*) ♦ *n* ме́сто*; (*home*): **at his ~** у него́; (*in street names*): **Laurel P~** Ло́рел Плейс; **to ~ an order with sb for sth** (*COMM*) зака́зывать (заказа́ть* *perf*) что-н у кого́-н; **to be ~d** (*in race, exam*) быть* (*impf*) на како́м-н ме́сте; **how are you ~d next week?** как у Вас со сле́дующей неде́лей?; **to take ~** происходи́ть* (произойти́* *perf*); **from ~ to ~** с ме́ста на ме́сто; **all over the ~** повсю́ду; **out of ~** (*not suitable*) неуме́стный* (неуме́стен); **I feel out of ~ here** я чу́вствую себя́ не в свое́й таре́лке/не на ме́сте здесь; **in the first ~** (*first of all*) во-пе́рвых; **to put sb in his ~** (*fig*) ста́вить* (поста́вить* *perf*) кого́-н на ме́сто; **he's going ~s** он далеко́ пойдёт; **it's not my ~** э́то не моё де́ло; **to change ~s with sb** меня́ться (поменя́ться *perf*) места́ми с кем-н.

placebo [plə'si:bəu] *n* (*MED*) плаце́бо *nt ind*; (*fig*) успокои́тельное сре́дство.

place mat *n* подста́вка* (*для столо́вых прибо́ров*); (*in linen etc*) салфе́тка*.

placement ['pleɪsmənt] *n* (*action*) размеще́ние; (*job*) ме́сто*.

place name *n* географи́ческое назва́ние, топони́м.

placenta [plə'sɛntə] *n* плаце́нта.

place of birth *n* ме́сто* рожде́ния.

place setting *n* столо́вый прибо́р.

placid ['plæsɪd] *adj* споко́йный* (споко́ен); (*place*) ти́хий* (тих).

plagiarism ['pleɪdʒərɪzəm] *n* плагиа́т.

plagiarist ['pleɪdʒərɪst] *n* плагиа́тор.

plagiarize ['pleɪdʒəraɪz] *vt* красть* (укра́сть* *perf*), спи́сывать (списа́ть* *perf*).

plague [pleɪg] *n* (*MED*) чума́; (*fig: of locusts etc*) наше́ствие ♦ *vt* (*fig: subj: problems, difficulties*) осажда́ть (осади́ть* *perf*); **to ~ sb with questions** донима́ть (*impf*) кого́-н вопро́сами.

plaice [pleɪs] *n inv* ка́мбала.

plaid [plæd] *n* шотла́ндка* (*ткань*).

plain [pleɪn] *adj* (*simple, not beautiful*) просто́й* (прост); (*unpatterned*) гла́дкий* (гла́док); (*clear, easily understood*) я́сный* (я́сен), поня́тный* (поня́тен); (*frank*) прямо́й* (прям) ♦ *adv* (*wrong, stupid etc*) я́вно ♦ *n* (*GEO*) равни́на; (*KNITTING*) чуло́чная вя́зка; **to make sth ~ to sb** разъясня́ть (разъясни́ть *perf*) что-н кому́-н.

plain chocolate *n* го́рький* шокола́д.

plain-clothes ['pleɪnkləuðz] *adj*: **~ policeman** полице́йский* *m adj* в шта́тском.

plain flour *n* мука́ без дрожжевы́х доба́вок.

plainly ['pleɪnlɪ] *adv* я́сно.

plainness ['pleɪnnɪs] n (*simplicity*) простота́; (*clarity*) я́сность f.

plaintiff ['pleɪntɪf] n исте́ц*(-ти́ца).

plain speaking n прямота́.

plaintive ['pleɪntɪv] adj (*voice, look, song*) жа́лобный* (жа́лобен).

plait [plæt] n (*of hair*) коса́* ♦ vt (*hair*) заплета́ть (заплести́* perf); (*rope*) плести́* (сплести́* perf).

plan [plæn] n план ♦ vt плани́ровать (заплани́ровать perf); (*draw up plans for*) плани́ровать (*impf*) ♦ vi плани́ровать (*impf*); **to ~ to do** плани́ровать (заплани́ровать perf) +infin; **how long do you ~ to stay?** как до́лго Вы плани́руете пробы́ть здесь?; **to ~ for sth** (*anticipate*) рассчи́тывать (*impf*) на что-н.

plane [pleɪn] n (*AVIAT*) самолёт; (*MATH*) пло́скость f; (*fig: level*) план; (*tool*) руба́нок*; (*BOT*) плата́н ♦ vt (*wood*) строга́ть (вы́стругать perf) ♦ vi (*NAUT, AUT*): **to ~ across** скользи́ть* (*impf*) по +dat.

planet ['plænɪt] n плане́та.

planetarium [plænɪ'tɛərɪəm] n планета́рий.

plank [plæŋk] n доска́*; (*fig: of policy etc*) при́нцип.

plankton ['plæŋktən] n планкто́н.

planned economy ['plænd-] n пла́новая эконо́мика.

planner ['plænə'] n (*of towns*) планиро́вщик; (*of TV programme, project*) состави́тель m.

planning ['plænɪŋ] n (*of future, event*) плани́рование; (*of programme etc*) составле́ние; (*also: town ~*) планиро́вка.

planning permission n (*BRIT*) разреше́ние на строи́тельство.

plant [plɑːnt] n (*BOT*) расте́ние; (*factory*) заво́д; (*machinery*) устано́вка* ♦ vt (*seed, plant, garden*) сажа́ть (посади́ть* perf); (*field*) засе́ивать (засе́ять perf); (*bomb, evidence*) подкла́дывать (подложи́ть* perf); (*fig: kiss*) запечатлева́ть (запечатле́ть perf).

plantation [plæn'teɪʃən] n (*of tea, rubber, sugar etc*) планта́ция; (*of trees*) лесонасажде́ние.

plant pot n (*BRIT*) цвето́чный горшо́к*.

plaque [plæk] n (*on building etc*) мемори-а́льная доска́*; (*on teeth*) налёт.

plasma ['plæzmə] n пла́зма.

plaster ['plɑːstə'] n (*for walls*) штукату́рка*; (*also: ~ of Paris*) гипс; (*BRIT: also: sticking ~*) пла́стырь m ♦ vt (*wall, ceiling*) штукату́рить (оштукату́рить perf); (*cover*): **to ~ with** залепля́ть (залепи́ть* perf) +instr; **in ~** (*BRIT*) в ги́псе.

plasterboard ['plɑːstəbɔːd] n ги́псовые щиты́ (*для обши́вки стен и потолка́*).

plaster cast n (*MED*) гипс; (*model, statue*) ги́псовый слепо́к*.

plastered ['plɑːstəd] adj (*inf: drunk*): **he is ~** он

нажра́лся.

plasterer ['plɑːstərə'] n штукату́р.

plastic ['plæstɪk] n пластма́сса ♦ adj (*made of plastic*) пластма́ссовый; (*flexible*) пласти́чный*; (*art*) пласти́ческий*.

plastic bag n полиэтиле́новый мешо́к*.

plastic bullet n пластма́ссовая пу́ля*.

plastic explosive n синтети́ческая взрывча́тка консисте́нции пластили́на.

Plasticine® ['plæstɪsiːn] n пластили́н.

plastic surgery n (*science*) пласти́ческая хирурги́я; (*operation*) пласти́ческая опера́ция.

plate [pleɪt] n (*dish*) таре́лка*; (*metal cover: on building, machinery*) пласти́на; (*TYP*) печа́тная фо́рма; (*PHOT*) фотопласти́нка*; (*AUT: number plate*) но́мер*; (*in book*) вкладна́я иллюстра́ция; (*also: dental ~*) вставна́я че́люсть* f; (*on door*) табли́чка*; **gold ~** позоло́та; **silver ~** серебре́ние.

plateau ['plætəʊ] n (*pl ~s or ~x*) (*GEO, also fig*) плато́ nt ind.

plateaux ['plætəʊz] npl of **plateau**.

plateful ['pleɪtful] n: **a ~ of** таре́лка* +gen.

plate glass n (*for window, door*) зерка́льное стекло́.

platen ['plætən] n (*TYP*) ва́лик.

plate rack n суши́лка* (*для посу́ды*).

platform ['plætfɔːm] n (*at meeting*) трибу́на; (*at concert*) помо́ст; (*for landing, loading on etc*) площа́дка; (*RAIL, POL*) платфо́рма; (*BRIT: of bus*) подно́жка*; **the train leaves from ~ seven** по́езд отправля́ется с седьмо́го пути́.

platform ticket n (*BRIT: RAIL*) перро́нный биле́т.

platinum ['plætɪnəm] n пла́тина.

platitude ['plætɪtjuːd] n пло́скость f, бана́льность f.

platonic [plə'tɔnɪk] adj платони́ческий.

platoon [plə'tuːn] n взвод.

platter ['plætə'] n блю́до.

plaudits ['plɔːdɪts] npl похвала́ fsg.

plausible ['plɔːzɪbl] adj (*theory, excuse etc*) правдоподо́бный* (правдоподо́бен); (*person*) убеди́тельный*.

play [pleɪ] n пье́са ♦ vt (*subj: children: game*) игра́ть (*impf*) в +acc; (*sport, cards*) игра́ть (сыгра́ть perf) в +acc; (*opponent*) игра́ть (сыгра́ть perf) с +instr; (*part, role, piece of music*) игра́ть (сыгра́ть perf); (*instrument*) игра́ть (*impf*) на +prp; (*listen to: tape, record*) ста́вить (поста́вить* perf) ♦ vi игра́ть (*impf*); **a ~ on words** игра́* слов; **to bring** or **call into ~** вводи́ть* (ввести́* perf) в де́йствие; **to ~ a trick on sb** сыгра́ть (сыгра́ть perf) шу́тку над кем-н; **they're ~ing at soldiers** они́ игра́ют в солда́тики; **to ~ for time** тяну́ть (*impf*) вре́мя; **to ~ safe** де́йствовать (*impf*) осторо́жно; **to ~**

---

into sb's hands играть (сыграть *perf*) кому-н на руку
▶ **play about** *vi*: **to ~ about with** (*feelings*) играть (*impf*) +*instr*; (*object*) возиться (*impf*) с +*instr*
▶ **play along** *vi* (*fig*): **to ~ along with** (*person, plan, idea*) подыгрывать (подыграть *perf*) +*dat* ◆ *vt* (*fig*): **to ~ sb along** использовать (*impf*) кого-н в своих целях
▶ **play around** *vi* = **play about**
▶ **play back** *vt* (*recording*) проигрывать (проиграть *perf*) (*повторно*)
▶ **play down** *vt* не заострять (*impf*) внимание на +*prp*
▶ **play on** *vt fus* (*sb's feelings etc*) играть (*impf*) на +*prp*; **to ~ on sb's nerves** действовать (*impf*) кому-н на нервы
▶ **play up** *vi* (*machine*) барахлить (*impf*); (*children*) шалить (*impf*), прикидываться (*impf*).

play-act ['pleɪækt] *vi* делать (сделать *perf*) вид.
playboy ['pleɪbɔɪ] *n* хлыщ.
player ['pleɪə^r] *n* (*SPORT*) игрок*; (*MUS, THEAT*) исполни́тель(ница) *m(f)*.
playful ['pleɪful] *adj* (*person*) игри́вый (игри́в).
playgoer ['pleɪgəuə^r] *n* театрал.
playground ['pleɪgraund] *n* (*in park*) (детская) площадка*; (*in school*) (игровая) площадка*.
playgroup ['pleɪgruːp] *n* детская группа.
playing card ['pleɪɪŋ-] *n* игральная карта.
playing field *n* игровое поле*.
playmate ['pleɪmeɪt] *n* приятель(ница) *m(f)*.
play-off ['pleɪɔf] *n* (*SPORT*) игра за призовое место.
playpen ['pleɪpɛn] *n* (детский*) манеж.
playroom ['pleɪruːm] *n* детская *f adj*.
playschool ['pleɪskuːl] *n* = **playgroup**.
plaything ['pleɪθɪŋ] *n* игрушка*.
playtime ['pleɪtaɪm] *n* (*SCOL*) перемена.
playwright ['pleɪraɪt] *n* драматург.
plc *abbr* (*BRIT*: = *public limited company*) публичная компания с ограниченной ответственностью.
plea [pliː] *n* (*personal request*) мольба; (*public request*) призыв; (*LAW*) заявление; (*excuse*) предлог.
plea bargaining *n* признание виновности в обмен на более короткое тюремное заключение.
plead [pliːd] *vt* (*ignorance, ill health etc*) ссылаться (сослаться *perf*) на +*acc* ◆ *vi* (*LAW*) признавать* (признать* *perf*) себя; (*beg*): **to ~ with sb** умолять (*impf*) кого-н, молить (*impf*) кого-н; **to ~ sb's case** (*LAW*) защищать (*impf*) кого-н (*в суде*); **to ~ for sth** призывать (призвать* *perf*) к чему-н; **to ~ guilty/not guilty** признавать* (признать* *perf*) себя виновным(-ой)/невиновным(-ой).
pleasant ['plɛznt] *adj* приятный* (приятен).
pleasantly ['plɛzntlɪ] *adv* приятно.
pleasantries ['plɛzntrɪz] *npl* любезности *fpl*.

please [pliːz] *excl* пожалуйста ◆ *vt* угождать (угодить* *perf*) +*dat* ◆ *vi* (*give pleasure, satisfaction*) угождать (угодить* *perf*); **yes, ~** да, спасибо; **my bill, ~** получите (с меня), пожалуйста; **~ don't cry!** не плачь, пожалуйста!; **~ yourself!** (*inf*) как Вам угодно!; **do as you ~** делайте как хотите; **he is difficult/easy to ~** ему трудно/легко угодить (*perf*).
pleased [pliːzd] *adj*: **~ (with)** довольный* (доволен) (+*instr*); **~ to meet you** очень приятно; **we are ~ to inform you that ...** мы рады сообщить Вам, что ....
pleasing ['pliːzɪŋ] *adj* приятный* (приятен).
pleasurable ['plɛʒərəbl] *adj* радостный* (радостен).
pleasure ['plɛʒə^r] *n* удовольствие; **it's a ~** не стоит; **with ~** с удовольствием; **to take ~ in** получать (получить *perf*) удовольствие от +*gen*; **is this trip for business or ~?** эта поездка деловая или развлекательная?
pleasure boat *n* прогулочный катер.
pleasure cruise *n* круиз.
pleat [pliːt] *n* складка*.
plebiscite ['plɛbɪsɪt] *n* плебисцит.
plebs [plɛbz] *npl* (*pej*) плебеи *mpl*, плебс *msg*.
plectrum ['plɛktrəm] *n* плектр.
pledge [plɛdʒ] *n* (*promise*) обязательство ◆ *vt* (*promise: money, support, help*) обязаться (*perf*); **to ~ sb to secrecy** брать* (взять* *perf*) с кого-н слово молчать.
plenary ['pliːnərɪ] *adj*: **in ~ session** на пленарном заседании.
plentiful ['plɛntɪful] *adj* обильный* (обилен).
plenty ['plɛntɪ] *n* (*sufficient*) достаточное количество; **~ of** (*food, money etc*) много +*gen*; (*jobs, people, houses etc*) множество +*gen*; **we've got ~ of time to get there** у нас довольно времени, чтобы туда добраться.
plethora ['plɛθərə] *n*: **a ~ of** великое множество +*gen*.
pleurisy ['pluərɪsɪ] *n* плеврит.
Plexiglas® ['plɛksɪgla:s] *n* (*US*) плексиглас.
pliable ['plaɪəbl] *adj* (*material*) гибкий* (гибок); (*fig: person*) уступчивый (уступчив), податливый (податлив).
pliant ['plaɪənt] *adj* = **pliable**.
pliers ['plaɪəz] *npl* плоскогубцы* *pl*.
plight [plaɪt] *n* мучительное положение.
plimsolls ['plɪmsəlz] *npl* (*BRIT*) парусиновые туфли *pl*, кеды *pl*.
plinth [plɪnθ] *n* постамент.
PLO *n abbr* (= *Palestine Liberation Organization*) ООП= *Организация освобождения Палестины*.
plod [plɔd] *vi* (*walk, also fig*) тащиться* (*impf*).
plodder ['plɔdə^r] *n* (*pej: slow worker*) волокитчик; **he is a real ~** (*pej*) он такой медлительный.
plonk [plɔŋk] *n* (*inf: BRIT: wine*) дешёвое вино ◆ *vt* (*inf*): **to ~ sth down** бухать (бухнуть *perf*)

что-н.

plot [plɔt] *n* (*conspiracy*) за́говор; (*of story*) сюже́т; (*of land*) уча́сток* ♦ *vt* (*sb's downfall etc*) замышля́ть (*impf*); (*AVIAT, NAUT*) прокла́дывать (проложи́ть *perf*); (*MATH*) наноси́ть* (нанести́* *perf*) ♦ *vi* (*conspire*) составля́ть (соста́вить* *perf*) за́говор; **a vegetable ~** (*BRIT*) садо́вый уча́сток*, огоро́д.

plotter ['plɔtə'] *n* (*instrument*) графо-постро́итель *m*; (: *AVIAT, NAUT*) курсопрокла́дчик; (*COMPUT*) пло́ттер, графопостро́итель *m*.

plough [plau] (*US* **plow**) *n* плуг* ♦ *vt* паха́ть* (вспаха́ть* *perf*); **to ~ money into** вкла́дывать (вложи́ть *perf*) де́ньги в +*acc*
▸ **plough back** *vt* (*COMM*) реинвести́ровать (*impf/perf*)
▸ **plough through** *vt fus* (*crowd*) продира́ться (продра́ться* *perf*) сквозь +*acc*; (*snow etc*) пробира́ться (пробра́ться* *perf*) че́рез +*acc*.

ploughman ['plaumən] (*US* **plowman**) *irreg n* па́харь *m*.

ploughman's lunch ['plaumənz-] *n* (*BRIT*) ≈ крестья́нский* обе́д.

plow *etc* (*US*) = **plough** *etc*.

ploy [plɔɪ] *n* уло́вка*.

pluck [plʌk] *n* (*courage*) му́жество ♦ *vt* (*fruit, flower*) срыва́ть (сорва́ть *perf*); (*bird*) ощи́пывать (ощипа́ть* *perf*); (*eyebrows*) выщи́пывать (вы́щипать* *perf*); (*string instrument*): **to ~ (the strings of) sth** перебира́ть (*impf*) стру́ны чего́-н; **to ~ up courage** набира́ться (набра́ться* *perf*) хра́брости *or* му́жества.

plucky ['plʌkɪ] *adj* му́жественный* (му́жествен), отва́жный* (отва́жен).

plug [plʌg] *n* (*ELEC*) ви́лка*; (*in sink, bath*) про́бка*; (*AUT*: *also*: **spark(ing) ~**) свеча́ (зажига́ния*) ♦ *vt* (*hole*) затыка́ть (заткну́ть *perf*); (*inf*: *advertise*) реклами́ровать (разреклами́ровать *perf*); **to give sb/sth a ~** реклами́ровать (разреклами́ровать *perf*) кого́-н/что-н
▸ **plug in** *vt* (*ELEC*) включа́ть (включи́ть *perf*) в розе́тку ♦ *vi* включа́ться (включи́ться *perf*).

plughole ['plʌghəul] *n* (*BRIT*) сток.

plum [plʌm] *n* сли́ва* ♦ *cpd* (*inf*): **~ job** мирова́я рабо́та.

plumage ['plu:mɪdʒ] *n* опере́ние.

plumb [plʌm] *vt*: **to ~ the depths of** (*fig*) достига́ть (дости́чь* *perf*) глубин +*gen*
▸ **plumb in** *vt* (*washing machine*) подключа́ть (подключи́ть *perf*), подсоединя́ть (подсоедини́ть *perf*).

plumber ['plʌmə'] *n* водопрово́дчик.

plumbing ['plʌmɪŋ] *n* (*piping*) водопрово́д и канализа́ция; (*trade, work*) сле́сарное де́ло.

plumb line *n* отве́с.

plume [plu:m] *n* (*of bird*) перо́*; (*on helmet, horse's head*) плюма́ж; (*fig*): **~ of smoke** струя́* ды́ма.

plummet ['plʌmɪt] *vi*: **to ~ (down)** (*bird, aircraft*) ру́хнуть (*perf*); (*price, amount*) ре́зко па́дать (упа́сть* *perf*).

plump [plʌmp] *adj* (*adult*) по́лный*; (*child*) пу́хлый* (пухл) ♦ *vi*: **to ~ for** (*inf*) выбира́ть (вы́брать* *perf*)
▸ **plump up** *vt* взбива́ть (взбить* *perf*).

plunder ['plʌndə'] *n* (*activity*) грабёж*; (*stolen things*) награ́бленное *nt adj* ♦ *vt* гра́бить* (разгра́бить* *perf*).

plunge [plʌndʒ] *n* (*dive: of bird, person*) бросо́к*; (*fig: of prices, rates etc*) ре́зкое паде́ние ♦ *vt* (*knife*) мета́ть (метну́ть *perf*); (*hand*) выбра́сывать (вы́бросить* *perf*) ♦ *vi* (*fall: person, thing*) ру́хнуть (*perf*); (*dive: bird, person*) броса́ться (бро́ситься* *perf*); (*fig: prices, rates etc*) ре́зко па́дать (упа́сть* *perf*); **to take the ~** (*fig*) отва́живаться (отва́житься *perf*); **the room was ~d into darkness** ко́мната погрузи́лась во тьму.

plunger ['plʌndʒə'] *n* (*for sink*) плу́нжер.

plunging ['plʌndʒɪŋ] *adj*: **~ neckline** декольте́ *nt ind*.

pluperfect [plu:'pə:fɪkt] *n* плюсквамперфе́кт.

plural ['pluərl] *adj* мно́жественный ♦ *n* мно́жественное число́*.

plus [plʌs] *n, adj* плюс ind ♦ *prep*: **ten ~ ten is twenty** де́сять плюс де́сять – два́дцать; **ten/twenty ~** (*more than*) де́сять/два́дцать с ли́шним; **we discussed the ~es of the plan** (*fig*) мы обсужда́ли плю́сы прое́кта.

plus fours *npl* бри́джи *pl*.

plush [plʌʃ] *adj* шика́рный* (шика́рен), роско́шный* (роско́шен) ♦ *n* (*fabric*) плюш.

Pluto ['plu:təu] *n* (*planet*) Плуто́н.

plutonium [plu:'təunɪəm] *n* плуто́ний.

ply [plaɪ] *vt* (*a trade*) занима́ться (заня́ться* *perf*) +*instr*; (*tool*) ору́довать (*impf*) +*instr* ♦ *vi* (*ship*) курси́ровать (*impf*) ♦ *n* (*of wool, rope*) нить *f*; (*of wood*) слой*; **to ~ sb with sth** (*food, drink*) по́тчевать (*perf*) кого́-н чем-н; **to ~ sb with questions** засыпа́ть (засы́пать* *perf*) кого́-н вопро́сами; **two/three ~** двойна́я/ тройна́я нить.

Plymouth ['plɪməθ] *n* Пли́мут.

plywood ['plaɪwud] *n* фане́ра.

PM *abbr* (*BRIT*) = **Prime Minister**.

p.m. *adv abbr* (= *post meridiem*) по́сле полу́дня.

PMT *abbr* = **premenstrual tension**.

pneumatic [nju:'mætɪk] *adj* пневмати́ческий*.

pneumatic drill *n* пневмати́ческая дрель *f*.

pneumonia [nju:'məunɪə] *n* воспале́ние лёгких, пневмони́я.

Pnomh Penh [nɔm pɛn] *n* Пномпе́нь *m*.

PO *n abbr* = **Post Office**; (*MIL*) = **petty officer**.

---

p.o. *abbr* = postal order.
POA *n abbr* (*BRIT*) = Prison Officers' Association.
poach [pəʊtʃ] *vt* (*steal: fish etc*) охо́титься (*impf*) без лице́нзии на +*acc*; (*cook: fish*) вари́ть* (свари́ть* *perf*) ♦ *vi* (*steal*) охо́титься (*impf*) без лице́нзии; **to ~ an egg** вари́ть* (свари́ть* *perf*) яйцо́-пашо́т.
poached [pəʊtʃt] *adj*: ~ **egg** яйцо́-пашо́т *ind*.
poacher [ˈpəʊtʃəˈ] *n* браконье́р.
PO Box *n abbr* = Post Office Box.
pocket [ˈpɒkɪt] *n* (*on clothes*) карма́н; (*on suitcase, car door*) отделе́ние; (*fig: small area*) уголо́к* ♦ *vt* класть* (положи́ть* *perf*) себе́ в карма́н; **to be out of ~** (*BRIT*) быть* (*impf*) в убы́тке на чём-н.
pocketbook [ˈpɒkɪtbʊk] *n* (*US: wallet*) бума́жник; (*handbag*) (да́мская) су́мочка*; (*notebook*) записна́я кни́жка*.
pocket calculator *n* карма́нный калькуля́тор.
pocketknife [ˈpɒkɪtnaɪf] *n* перочи́нный нож*.
pocket money *n* карма́нные де́ньги* *pl*.
pocket-sized [ˈpɒkɪtsaɪzd] *adj* (*book*) карма́нный; (*nation*) кро́хотный.
pockmarked [ˈpɒkmɑːkt] *adj* рябо́й* (ряб).
pod [pɒd] *n* (*BOT*) стручо́к*.
podgy [ˈpɒdʒɪ] *adj* (*inf*) то́лстый* (толст).
podiatrist [pɔˈdiːətrɪst] *n* (*US*) ортопе́д.
podiatry [pɔˈdiːətrɪ] *n* (*US*) ортопеди́я.
podium [ˈpəʊdɪəm] *n* по́диум.
POE *n abbr* (= *port of embarkation*) порт вы́садки; (= *port of entry*) порт захо́да.
poem [ˈpəʊɪm] *n* (*short*) стихотворе́ние; (*long*) поэ́ма.
poet [ˈpəʊɪt] *n* (*male*) поэ́т; (*female*) поэте́сса.
poetic [pəʊˈɛtɪk] *adj* (*also fig*) поэти́ческий.
poetic justice *n* воздая́ние.
poetic licence *n* поэти́ческая во́льность *f*.
poet laureate *n* придво́рный поэ́т.
poetry [ˈpəʊɪtrɪ] *n* поэ́зия.
poignant [ˈpɔɪnjənt] *adj* жа́лостный* (жа́лостен).
point [pɔɪnt] *n* (*of needle, knife etc*) остриё*, ко́нчик; (*purpose*) цель *f*; (*significant part*) смысл; (*subject, idea*) предме́т; (*detail, aspect, quality*) аспе́кт; (*particular place or position*) то́чка*, ме́сто*; (*moment*) моме́нт; (*stage in development*) ста́дия; (*score: in competition, game, sport*) очко́*; (*ELEC: also:* **power** ~) розе́тка* ♦ *vt* (*show, mark*) ука́зывать (указа́ть* *perf*); (*gun etc*) ~ **to sth at sb** наце́ливать (наце́лить *perf*) что-н на кого́-н ♦ *vi*: **to ~ at** ука́зывать (указа́ть* *perf*) на +*acc*; ~**s** *npl* (*AUT*) конта́кты (зажига́ния); (*RAIL*) стре́лка* *fsg*; **good ~s** (*of person, plan*) досто́инства; **2 ~ 3 (2.3)** 2 и 3 деся́тых; **to be on the ~ of doing** собира́ться (*impf*) +*infin*; **I made a ~ of visiting him** я счёл необходи́мым посети́ть его́; **to get/miss the ~** понима́ть (поня́ть* *perf*)/не понима́ть (поня́ть* *perf*) суть; **to come to the ~**

доходи́ть* (дойти́* *perf*) до су́ти; **when it comes to the ~** когда́ дохо́дит до де́ла; **that's the whole ~!** в э́том-то и де́ло!; **that's beside the ~** не в э́том де́ло; **there's no ~ in doing** нет смы́сла +*infin*; **you've got a ~ there!** в э́том Вы пра́вы!; **in ~ of fact** на де́ле; ~ **of departure** (*also fig*) отправно́й пункт; ~ **of sale** (*COMM*) торго́вая то́чка*
▶ **point out** *vt* ука́зывать (указа́ть* *perf*) на +*acc*
▶ **point to** *vt fus* (*also fig*) ука́зывать (указа́ть* *perf*) на +*acc*.
point-blank [ˈpɔɪntˈblæŋk] *adv* (*refuse*) наотре́з; (*say, ask*) напрямик ♦ *adj*: **at ~ range** в упо́р.
point duty *n* (*BRIT*): **to be on** ~ ~ находи́ться* (*impf*) на посту́ регулиро́вщика.
pointed [ˈpɔɪntɪd] *adj* о́стрый* (остёр); (*fig: remark*) язви́тельный.
pointedly [ˈpɔɪntɪdlɪ] *adv* язви́тельно.
pointer [ˈpɔɪntəˈ] *n* (*on chart, machine*) стре́лка*; (*stick*) ука́зка*; (*fig*) намёк; (*dog*) по́йнтер.
pointing [ˈpɔɪntɪŋ] *n* (*CONSTR*) заме́на раство́ра в швах.
pointless [ˈpɔɪntlɪs] *adj* бессмы́сленный* (бессмы́слен).
point of order *n* вопро́с по поря́дку веде́ния.
point-of-sale advertising [ˈpɔɪntəvˈseɪl-] *n* рекла́ма в места́х соверше́ния поку́пок.
point of view *n* то́чка* зре́ния.
poise [pɔɪz] *n* (*composure, balance*) равнове́сие; (*of head, body*) оса́нка* ♦ *vt*: **to be ~d for** (*fig*) наце́ливаться (наце́литься *perf*) на +*acc*.
poison [ˈpɔɪzn] *n* яд, отра́ва ♦ *vt* отравля́ть (отрави́ть* *perf*).
poisoning [ˈpɔɪznɪŋ] *n* отравле́ние.
poisonous [ˈpɔɪznəs] *adj* ядови́тый (ядови́т); (*fig*) гну́сный* (гну́сен).
poison-pen letter [pɔɪznˈpɛn] *n* анони́мка*.
poke [pəʊk] *vt* (*with finger, stick etc*) ты́кать* (ткнуть *perf*); (*fire*) вороши́ть (*impf*), меша́ть (*impf*) ♦ *n* (*jab*) толчо́к*; (*to fire*) поме́шивание; **to ~ sth in(to)** (*put*) втыка́ть (воткну́ть *perf*) что-н в +*acc*; **to ~ one's head out of the window** высо́вываться (вы́сунуться *perf*) из окна́; **to ~ fun at sb** подка́лывать (подколо́ть* *perf*) кого́-н
▶ **poke about** *vi* ша́рить (поша́рить *perf*)
▶ **poke out** *vi* высо́вываться (вы́сунуть *perf*).
poker [ˈpəʊkəˈ] *n* кочерга́*; (*CARDS*) по́кер.
poker-faced [ˈpəʊkəˈfeɪst] *adj* невозмути́мый (невозмути́м).
poky [ˈpəʊkɪ] *adj* (*room, house*) убо́гий* (убо́г).
Poland [ˈpəʊlənd] *n* По́льша.
polar [ˈpəʊləˈ] *adj* поля́рный.
polar bear *n* бе́лый медве́дь* *m*.
polarize [ˈpəʊləraɪz] *vt* раска́лывать (расколо́ть* *perf*), поляризи́ровать (*impf/perf*).
Pole [pəʊl] *n* поля́к(-лька*).

pole [pəʊl] n (*stick, staff*) шест*; (*for flag*) дре́вко; (*telegraph pole*) столб; (*GEO, ELEC*) по́люс.

poleaxe ['pəʊlæks] n (*butcher's*) топо́р; (*HISTORY*) секи́ра ♦ vt (*hit*) тре́снуть (*perf*); (*surprise*) ошеломля́ть (ошеломи́ть *perf*).

pole bean n (*US*) стручко́вая фасо́ль f.

polecat ['pəʊlkæt] n (чёрный) хорёк*.

Pol. Econ. ['pɔlɪkɔn] n abbr (= *political economy*) политэконо́мия= *политическая экономия*.

polemic [pə'lɛmɪk] n поле́мика.

Pole Star n поля́рная звезда́*.

pole vault ['pəʊlvɔːlt] n прыжо́к* с шесто́м.

police [pə'liːs] npl поли́ция *fsg*; (*in Russia*) мили́ция *fsg* ♦ vt следи́ть* (*impf*) за поря́дком; **a large number of ~ were hurt** бы́ло ра́нено мно́го полице́йских.

police car n полице́йская маши́на.

police constable n (*BRIT*) полице́йский* m adj.

police department n (*US*) полице́йский* уча́сток*.

police force n поли́ция.

policeman [pə'liːsmən] irreg n полице́йский* m adj.

police officer n = police constable.

police record n: **to have a ~ ~** состоя́ть (*impf*) на учёте в поли́ции.

police state n полице́йское госуда́рство.

police station n полице́йский* уча́сток*; (*in Russia*) отделе́ние мили́ции.

policewoman [pə'liːswumən] irreg n (же́нщина-) полице́йский* m adj.

policy ['pɔlɪsɪ] n поли́тика; (*also:* **insurance ~**) по́лис; **to take out a ~** (*INSURANCE*) застрахо́вываться (застрахова́ться *perf*).

policyholder ['pɔlɪsɪ'həʊldəʳ] n (*INSURANCE*) держа́тель m страхово́го по́лиса.

policymaking ['pɔlɪsɪmeɪkɪŋ] n разрабо́тка страте́гии.

polio ['pəʊlɪəʊ] n полиомиели́т.

Polish ['pəʊlɪʃ] adj по́льский* ♦ n (*LING*) по́льский* язы́к*.

polish ['pɔlɪʃ] n (*for shoes*) гутали́н; (*for furniture*) лак*; (*for floors*) масти́ка; (*shine, also fig*) лоск ♦ vt (*shoes*) вычища́ть (вы́чистить* *perf*); (*floors*) натира́ть (натере́ть *perf*); (*furniture etc*) полирова́ть (отполирова́ть *perf*); (*fig: improve*) шлифова́ть (отшлифова́ть *perf*)
▶ **polish off** vt fus (*work, food*) поко́нчить (*perf*) с +instr.

polished ['pɔlɪʃt] adj (*person*) изы́сканный* (изы́скан); (*style*) отто́ченный (отто́чен).

polite [pə'laɪt] adj (*well-mannered*) ве́жливый (ве́жлив); (*socially superior: company, society*) све́тский*; **it's not ~ to do that** так де́лать не при́нято.

politely [pə'laɪtlɪ] adv ве́жливо.

politeness [pə'laɪtnɪs] n ве́жливость f.

politic ['pɔlɪtɪk] adj: **it would be ~ to ...** бы́ло бы благоразу́мно +infin ....

political [pə'lɪtɪkl] adj полити́ческий*; (*person*) полити́чески акти́вный, политизи́рованный (политизи́рован).

political asylum n полити́ческое убе́жище.

politically [pə'lɪtɪklɪ] adv полити́чески; **~ correct** полити́чески корре́ктный.

politician [pɔlɪ'tɪʃən] n поли́тик, полити́ческий* де́ятель m.

politics ['pɔlɪtɪks] n поли́тика; (*subject*) политоло́гия ♦ npl (*beliefs, opinions*) полити́ческие убежде́ния ntpl.

polka ['pɔlkə] n по́лька*.

poll [pəʊl] n (*also:* **opinion ~**) опро́с; (*election*) вы́боры mpl ♦ vt (*in opinion poll*) опра́шивать (опроси́ть* *perf*); (*number of votes*) набира́ть (набра́ть* *perf*); **to go to the ~s** (*voters*) голосова́ть (проголосова́ть *perf*) (*на выборах*); (*government*) объявля́ть (объяви́ть* *perf*) вы́боры.

pollen ['pɔlən] n пыльца́.

pollen count n содержа́ние пыльцы́ в во́здухе.

pollinate ['pɔlɪneɪt] vt (*BOT*) опыля́ть (опыли́ть *perf*).

polling booth ['pəʊlɪŋ-] n (*BRIT*) каби́на для голосова́ния.

polling day n (*BRIT*) день* m вы́боров.

polling station n (*BRIT*) избира́тельный уча́сток*.

pollster ['pəʊlstəʳ] n челове́к, производя́щий* опро́с обще́ственного мне́ния.

poll tax n (*BRIT: formerly*) поду́шный нало́г.

pollutant [pə'luːtənt] n загрязня́ющий аге́нт.

pollute [pə'luːt] vt загрязня́ть (загрязни́ть *perf*).

pollution [pə'luːʃən] n загрязне́ние; (*substances*) загрязни́тель m.

polo ['pəʊləʊ] n по́ло nt ind.

polo neck n (*also:* **~ ~ sweater** or **jumper**) сви́тер с кру́глым воротнико́м.

polo-necked ['pəʊləʊnɛkt] adj: **~ sweater** or **jumper** сви́тер с кру́глым воротнико́м.

poltergeist ['pɔːltəgaɪst] n полтерге́йст.

poly ['pɔlɪ] n abbr (*BRIT*) = **polytechnic**.

poly... ['pɔlɪ] prefix мно́го..., поли...

poly bag n полиэтиле́новый мешо́к* or паке́т.

polyester [pɔlɪ'ɛstəʳ] n (*CHEM*) сло́жный полиэфи́р; (*fabric*) полиэфи́рное воло́кно.

polygamy [pə'lɪgəmɪ] n многобра́чие, полига́мия.

polygraph ['pɔlɪgrɑːf] n дете́ктор лжи.

Polynesia [pɔlɪ'niːzɪə] n Полине́зия.

Polynesian [pɔlɪ'niːzɪən] adj полинези́йский* ♦ n полинези́ец*(-и́йка*).

polyp ['pɔlɪp] n (*MED*) поли́п.

polystyrene [pɔlɪ'staɪri:n] *n* пенопла́ст.
polytechnic [pɔlɪ'tɛknɪk] *n* (*college*) ≈
политехни́ческий* институ́т.
polythene ['pɔlɪθi:n] *n* полиэтиле́н.
polythene bag *n* полиэтиле́новый мешо́к* or
паке́т.
polyurethane [pɔlɪ'juərɪθeɪn] *n* полиурета́н.
pomegranate ['pɔmɪgrænɪt] *n* (*BOT*) грана́т.
pommel ['pɔml] *n* (*of saddle*) лука́; (*of sword*)
голо́вка* ♦ *vt* = **pummel**.
pomp [pɔmp] *n* пы́шность *f*.
pompom ['pɔmpɔm] *n* помпо́н.
pompous ['pɔmpəs] *adj* (*pej: person, style*)
напы́щенный* (напы́щен).
pond [pɔnd] *n* пруд*; (*stagnant*) за́водь *f*.
ponder ['pɔndə'] *vt* обду́мывать (обду́мать
perf) ♦ *vi* размышля́ть (*impf*).
ponderous ['pɔndərəs] *adj* (*style*) тяжело-
ве́сный* (тяжелове́сен); (*person*)
неповоро́тливый (неповоро́тлив).
pong [pɔŋ] (*BRIT: inf*) *n* вонь *f* ♦ *vi* воня́ть (*impf*).
pontiff ['pɔntɪf] *n* (*REL*) Па́па *m* ри́мский*.
pontificate [pɔn'tɪfɪkeɪt] *vi* (*fig*): **to ~ (about)**
разглаго́льствовать (*impf*) (о +*prp*).
pontoon [pɔn'tu:n] *n* (*floating platform*)
понто́н; (*CARDS*) два́дцать одно́.
pony ['pəunɪ] *n* по́ни *m ind.*
ponytail ['pəunɪteɪl] *n* (*hairstyle*) хвост*,
хво́стик; **to have one's hair in a ~** носи́ть*
(*impf*) хво́стик.
pony trekking *n* (*BRIT*) ко́нный похо́д.
poodle ['pu:dl] *n* пу́дель* *m*.
pooh-pooh [pu:'pu:] *vt* заши́кивать (заши́кать
perf).
pool [pu:l] *n* (*puddle*) лу́жа; (*pond*) пруд*; (*also:*
swimming ~) бассе́йн; (*fig: of light, paint*)
пятно́; (*SPORT, COMM*) пул; (*money at cards*)
банк ♦ *vt* (*money, knowledge, resources*)
объединя́ть (объедини́ть *perf*); **~s** *npl* (*also:*
football ~s) тотализа́тор; **typing ~**, (*US*)
secretary ~ машинопи́сное бюро́ *nt ind*; **to do
the (football) ~s** игра́ть (сыгра́ть *perf*) в
тотализа́тор.
poor [puə'] *adj* (*not rich*) бе́дный* (бе́ден); (*bad*)
плохо́й* (плох); **the ~** *npl* (*people*) беднота́
fsg; **~ in** (*resources etc*) бе́дный* (бе́ден) +*instr*.
poorly ['puəlɪ] *adv* пло́хо ♦ *adj*: **she is feeling ~**
она́ пло́хо себя́ чу́вствует.
pop [pɔp] *n* (*also: ~ music*) поп-му́зыка; (*inf:
fizzy drink*) лимона́д*; (: *US: father*) па́па,
оте́ц; (*sound*) хлопо́к* ♦ *vi* (*balloon*) ло́паться
(ло́пнуть *perf*); (*cork*) выстре́ливать
(вы́стрелить *perf*); (*fig: eyes*) тара́щиться
(вы́таращиться *perf*) ♦ *vt* (*put quickly*): **to ~
sth into/onto** *etc* забра́сывать (забро́сить*
perf) в +*acc*/на +*acc* *etc*; **she ~ped her head out
of the window** она́ вы́сунула го́лову из окна́
▸ **pop in** *vi* загля́дывать (загляну́ть* *perf*),
заска́кивать (заскочи́ть *perf*)
▸ **pop out** *vi* выска́кивать (вы́скочить *perf*).
▸ **pop up** *vi* вылеза́ть (вы́лезти *perf*).

popcorn ['pɔpkɔ:n] *n* возду́шная кукуру́за,
попко́рн.
pope [pəup] *n*: **the P~** Па́па *m* ри́мский*.
poplar ['pɔplə'] *n* то́поль* *m*.
poplin ['pɔplɪn] *n* попли́н.
popper ['pɔpə'] *n* (*BRIT: fastener*) кно́пка*.
poppy ['pɔpɪ] *n* мак.
poppycock ['pɔpɪkɔk] *n* (*inf*) вздор.
Popsicle® ['pɔpsɪkl] *n* (*US*) ≈ фрукто́вое
моро́женое *nt adj*.
pop star *n* поп-звезда́* *m/f*.
populace ['pɔpjuləs] *n*: **the ~** наро́д*.
popular ['pɔpjulə'] *adj* популя́рный*
(популя́рен); (*POL*) наро́дный; **to be ~ (with)**
(*person, belief*) по́льзоваться (*impf*)
популя́рностью (среди́ +*gen*); (*decision*)
по́льзоваться (*impf*) подде́ржкой (+*gen*); **a ~
song** популя́рная пе́сня*.
popularity [pɔpju'lærɪtɪ] *n* популя́рность *f*.
popularize ['pɔpjuləraɪz] *vt* (*pastime, fashion*)
де́лать (сде́лать *perf*) популя́рным; (*science,
ideas*) популяризи́ровать (*impf/perf*).
popularly ['pɔpjuləlɪ] *adv* (*generally*) обы́чно; **it
is ~ believed that ...** мно́гие полага́ют, что ....
population [pɔpju'leɪʃən] *n* населе́ние; (*of a
species*) популя́ция; **the civilian ~s**
гражда́нское населе́ние; **Britain has a prison
~ of 44 thousand** о́бщее коли́чество
заключённых в тю́рьмах Великобрита́нии
составля́ет 44 ты́сячи.
population explosion *n* демографи́ческий*
взрыв.
populous ['pɔpjuləs] *adj* густонаселённый.
porcelain ['pɔ:slɪn] *n* фарфо́р.
porch [pɔ:tʃ] *n* крыльцо́*; (*US*) вера́нда.
porcupine ['pɔ:kjupaɪn] *n* дикобра́з.
pore [pɔ:'] *n* по́ра ♦ *vi*: **to ~ over** погружа́ться
(погрузи́ться* *perf*) в +*acc*.
pork [pɔ:k] *n* свини́на.
pork chop *n* свина́я отбивна́я *f adj*.
porn [pɔ:n] *n* (*inf*) порногра́фия.
pornographic [pɔ:nə'græfɪk] *adj* порно-
графи́ческий*.
pornography [pɔ:'nɔgrəfɪ] *n* порногра́фия.
porous ['pɔ:rəs] *adj* по́ристый (по́рист).
porpoise ['pɔ:pəs] *n* бу́рый дельфи́н.
porridge ['pɔrɪdʒ] *n* овся́ная ка́ша.
port [pɔ:t] *n* (*harbour, also COMPUT*) порт*;
(*opening in ship*) люк; (*NAUT*) ле́вый борт*;
(*wine*) портве́йн ♦ *cpd* (*NAUT*) ле́вый; **to ~**
(*NAUT*) нале́во; **~ of call** порт* захо́да.
portable ['pɔ:təbl] *adj* портати́вный.
portal ['pɔ:tl] *n* порта́л.
portcullis [pɔ:t'kʌlɪs] *n* (*опускна́я*) решётка* (*в
воро́тах*).
portend [pɔ:'tɛnd] *vt* предвеща́ть (*impf*).
portent ['pɔ:tɛnt] *n* предзнаменова́ние,
предве́стник.
porter ['pɔ:tə'] *n* (*for luggage*) носи́льщик;
(*doorkeeper*) швейца́р, портье́ *m ind*; (: *in
offices*) вахтёр; (*US: RAIL*) проводни́к*(-и́ца).

portfolio [pɔːtˈfəuliəu] *n* (*also POL*) портфе́ль *m*; (*FINANCE*) портфе́ль це́нных бума́г; (*of artist*) па́пка*.
porthole [ˈpɔːthəul] *n* иллюмина́тор.
portico [ˈpɔːtikəu] *n* по́ртик.
portion [ˈpɔːʃən] *n* (*part*) часть* *f*; (*equal part*) до́ля*; (*helping of food*) по́рция.
portly [ˈpɔːtlɪ] *adj* доро́дный* (доро́ден).
portrait [ˈpɔːtreɪt] *n* портре́т.
portray [pɔːˈtreɪ] *vt* изобража́ть (изобрази́ть* *perf*).
portrayal [pɔːˈtreɪəl] *n* изображе́ние; (*representation*) о́браз.
Portsmouth [ˈpɔːtsməθ] *n* По́ртсмут.
Portugal [ˈpɔːtjugl] *n* Португа́лия.
Portuguese [pɔːtjuˈgiːz] *adj* португа́льский* ◆ *n inv* португа́лец*(-лка*); (*LING*) португа́льский* язы́к*.
Portuguese man-of-war [-mænəvˈwɔː] *n* (*ZOOL*) португа́льский* вое́нный кора́бль *m*.
pose [pəuz] *n* по́за ◆ *vt* (*question*) ста́вить* (поста́вить* *perf*); (*problem, danger*) создава́ть* (созда́ть* *perf*) ◆ *vi* (*pretend*): **to ~ as** выдава́ть* (вы́дать* *perf*) себя́ за +*acc*; **to strike a ~** принима́ть (приня́ть* *perf*) по́зу; **to ~ for** пози́ровать (*impf*) для +*gen*.
poser [ˈpəuzəʳ] *n* (*puzzle*) головоло́мка*; (*person*) = **poseur**.
poseur [pəuˈzɜːʳ] *n* (*pej*) позёр(ка*).
posh [pɔʃ] *adj* (*inf: hotel, restaurant etc*) фешене́бельный* (фешене́белен); (*: person, behaviour*) великосве́тский; **to talk ~** (*inf*) мане́рничать (*impf*).
position [pəˈzɪʃən] *n* положе́ние; (*of house, thing*) расположе́ние, ме́сто*; (*job*) до́лжность *f*; (*in race, competition*) ме́сто*; (*attitude*) пози́ция ◆ *vt* располага́ть (расположи́ть* *perf*); **to be in a ~ to do** име́ть (*impf*) возмо́жность +*infin*.
positive [ˈpɔzɪtɪv] *adj* (*affirmative*) положи́тельный* (положи́телен); (*certain*) уве́ренный* (уве́рен), убеждённый* (убеждён); (*definite: decision, action, policy*) несомне́нный* (несомне́нен), определённый* (определён); (*MATH, ELEC*) положи́тельный.
positive cash flow *n* положи́тельный пото́к нали́чности.
positively [ˈpɔzɪtɪvlɪ] *adv* (*for emphasis*) положи́тельно; (*definitely*) несомне́нно.
posse [ˈpɔsɪ] *n* (*US*) ко́нный отря́д доброво́льных помо́щников шери́фа при ло́вле престу́пника.
possess [pəˈzɛs] *vt* владе́ть (*impf*) +*instr*; (*quality, ability*) облада́ть (*impf*) +*instr*; (*subj: feeling, belief*) овладева́ть (овладе́ть* *perf*); **like one ~ed** как одержи́мый(-ая) *m(f) adj*; **whatever can have ~ed you?** и како́й чёрт тебя́ попу́тал?
possession [pəˈzɛʃən] *n* (*state*) владе́ние; **~s** *npl* (*belongings*) принадле́жности *fpl*; **to take ~ of** вступа́ть (вступи́ть* *perf*) во владе́ние +*instr*.
possessive [pəˈzɛsɪv] *adj* со́бственнический*; (*LING*) притяжа́тельный.
possessiveness [pəˈzɛsɪvnɪs] *n* (*of another person*) со́бственничество; **~ towards sb/sth** ревни́вое отноше́ние к кому́-н/чему́-н.
possessor [pəˈzɛsəʳ] *n* (*of property*) владе́лец*(-е́лица); (*of quality*) облада́тель(ница) *m(f)*.
possibility [pɔsɪˈbɪlɪtɪ] *n* возмо́жность *f*; **he's a ~ (for the part)** он возмо́жный кандида́т (на роль).
possible [ˈpɔsɪbl] *adj* возмо́жный* (возмо́жен); **it's ~** э́то не исключено́; **it is ~ to do it** э́то осуществи́мо; **as far as ~** наско́лько возмо́жно; **if ~** е́сли (э́то) возмо́жно; **as big as ~** са́мый большо́й.
possibly [ˈpɔsɪblɪ] *adv* (*perhaps*) возмо́жно; **if you ~ can** е́сли то́лько Вы мо́жете; **I cannot ~ come** я ника́к не смогу́ прийти́.
post [pəust] *n* (*BRIT: mail*) по́чта; (*pole*) столб*; (*job, situation, also MIL*) пост* ◆ *vt* (*BRIT: mail*) посыла́ть (посла́ть* *perf*), отправля́ть (отпра́вить* *perf*) (по по́чте); (*: MIL*) выставля́ть (вы́ставить* *perf*); (*: appoint*) откомандиро́вывать (откомандирова́ть *perf*); **by ~** (*BRIT*) по по́чте; **by return of ~** (*BRIT*) с обра́тной по́чтой; **trading ~** факто́рия; **to keep sb ~ed** держа́ть (*impf*) кого́-н в ку́рсе (дел).
post... [pəust] *prefix* пост..., по́сле...; **~1990** (*as adj*) в 90-е го́ды; (*as adv*) как 90-е го́ды.
postage [ˈpəustɪdʒ] *n* (*charge*) почто́вые расхо́ды *mpl*; **~ paid, (US) ~ prepaid** с предвари́тельно опла́ченными почто́выми расхо́дами.
postage stamp *n* почто́вая ма́рка*.
postal [ˈpəustl] *adj* почто́вый.
postal order *n* (де́нежный) почто́вый перево́д.
postbag [ˈpəustbæg] *n* (*BRIT: letters received*) по́чта, корреспонде́нция; (*: postman's*) су́мка* (*почтальо́на*).
postbox [ˈpəustbɔks] *n* (*BRIT*) почто́вый я́щик.
postcard [ˈpəustkɑːd] *n* (почто́вая) откры́тка*.
postcode [ˈpəustkəud] *n* (*BRIT*) почто́вый и́ндекс.
postdate [ˈpəustˈdeɪt] *vt* дати́ровать (*impf/perf*) бо́лее по́здним число́м.
poster [ˈpəustəʳ] *n* афи́ша, плака́т; (*for advertising*) по́стер.
poste restante [pəustrɛstɑ̃nt] *adv* (*BRIT*) до востре́бования.
posterior [pɔsˈtɪərɪəʳ] *n* зад.

---

* marks translations which have irregular inflections. The Russian-English side of the dictionary gives inflectional information.

posterity [pɔs'tɛrɪtɪ] *n* после́дующие поколе́ния *ntpl*, пото́мство.
poster paint *n* плака́тная тушь *f*.
post exchange *n* (*US: MIL*) военто́рг, гарнизо́нный магази́н.
post-free [pəust'fri:] *adj, adv* (*BRIT*) с предвари́тельно опла́ченными почто́выми расхо́дами.
postgraduate [ˈpəustˈɡrædjuət] *n* аспира́нт(ка*) ♦ *adj*: ~ **study** аспиранту́ра.
posthumous [ˈpɔstjuməs] *adj* посме́ртный.
posthumously [ˈpɔstjuməslɪ] *adv* посме́ртно.
posting [ˈpəustɪŋ] *n* (*job*) командиро́вка.
postman [ˈpəustmən] *irreg n* почтальо́н.
postmark [ˈpəustmɑːk] *n* почто́вый ште́мпель* *m*.
postmaster [ˈpəustmɑːstə] *n* нача́льник по́чты *or* почто́вого отделе́ния.
postmaster general *n* ≈ мини́стр свя́зи.
postmistress [ˈpəustmɪstrɪs] *n* нача́льник по́чты *or* почто́вого отделе́ния (*же́нщина*).
postmortem [pəustˈmɔːtəm] *n* (*MED*) вскры́тие, аутопси́я.
postnatal [ˈpəustˈneɪtl] *adj* послеродово́й.
post office *n* почто́вое отделе́ние, отделе́ние свя́зи; (*organization*): **the P~ O~** ≈ Министе́рство свя́зи.
Post Office Box *n* абоне́нтский я́щик.
post-paid [ˈpəustˈpeɪd] *adj* (*BRIT*) с опла́ченными почто́выми расхо́дами.
postpone [pəusˈpəun] *vt* откла́дывать (отложи́ть* *perf*).
postponement [pəusˈpəunmənt] *n* отсро́чка.
postscript [ˈpəustskrɪpt] *n* (*in letter*) постскри́птум.
postulate [ˈpɔstjuleɪt] *vt* постули́ровать (*impf/perf*).
posture [ˈpɔstʃə] *n* (*of body*) оса́нка; (*fig*) положе́ние ♦ *vi* (*pej*) пози́ровать (*impf*).
postwar [ˈpəustˈwɔː] *adj* послевое́нный.
posy [ˈpəuzɪ] *n* буке́тик.
pot [pɔt] *n* (*for cooking, flowers*) горшо́к*; (*also:* **teapot**) (зава́рочный) ча́йник; (*also:* **coffeepot**) кофе́йник; (*bowl, container*) ба́нка; (*inf: marijuana*) план ♦ *vt* (*plant*) сажа́ть (посади́ть* *perf*); **a ~ of tea** ча́йник ча́я; **to go to ~** (*inf: work, performance*) разва́ливаться (развали́ться* *perf*); ~**s of** (*BRIT: inf*) ку́ча +*gen*, у́йма +*gen*.
potash [ˈpɔtæʃ] *n* пота́ш.
potassium [pəˈtæsɪəm] *n* ка́лий.
potato [pəˈteɪtəu] (*pl* —**es**) *n* карто́фель *m no pl*, карто́шка *f no pl* (*разг*); (*single potato*) карто́фелина.
potato chips *npl* (*US*) = **potato crisps**.
potato crisps *npl* (*BRIT*) чи́псы *pl*.
potato flour *n* карто́фельная мука́.
potato peeler *n* картофелечи́стка.
potbellied [ˈpɔtbɛlɪd] *adj* (*from overeating*) пуза́тый (пуза́т*); (*from malnutrition*) со взду́тым живото́м.

potency [ˈpəutnsɪ] *n* си́ла; (*of drink*) кре́пость *f*.
potent [ˈpəutnt] *adj* (*weapon*) мо́щный; (*argument*) убеди́тельный* (убеди́телен); (*drink*) кре́пкий* (кре́пок); (*man*) облада́ющий сексуа́льной поте́нцией.
potentate [ˈpəutnteɪt] *n* властели́н, повели́тель *m*.
potential [pəˈtɛnʃl] *adj* потенциа́льный, возмо́жный ♦ *n* потенциа́л; **to have ~** облада́ть (*impf*) (доста́точным) потенциа́лом.
potentially [pəˈtɛnʃəlɪ] *adv* потенциа́льно; **it's ~ dangerous** э́то в при́нципе опа́сно.
pothole [ˈpɔthəul] *n* (*in road*) вы́боина; (*BRIT: underground*) прова́л.
potholing [ˈpɔthəulɪŋ] (*BRIT*) *n* спелеоло́гия; **to go ~** отправля́ться (отпра́виться *perf*) обсле́довать пеще́ры.
potion [ˈpəuʃən] *n* насто́йка; (*poison*) зе́лье.
potluck [pɔtˈlʌk] *n*: **to take ~** обе́дать (пообе́дать* *perf*) чем Бог посла́л.
potpourri [pəuˈpuːri] *n* аромати́ческая смесь из сухи́х лепестко́в; (*fig*) попурри́ *nt ind*.
pot roast *n* тушёное мя́со.
pot shot *n*: **to take ~** стреля́ть (вы́стрелить *perf*) навски́дку в +*acc*.
potted [ˈpɔtɪd] *adj* (*food*) консерви́рованный; (*plant*) ко́мнатный; (*account, biography*) кра́ткий*.
potter [ˈpɔtə] *n* (*pottery maker*) гонча́р* ♦ *vi*: **to ~ around, ~ about** (*BRIT*) вози́ться* (*impf*); **to ~ about (in) the garden** вози́ться* (*impf*) в саду́.
potter's wheel *n* гонча́рный круг*.
pottery [ˈpɔtərɪ] *n* кера́мика; (*factory*) заво́д керами́ческих изде́лий; (*workshop*) гонча́рная мастерска́я *f adj*; **a piece of ~** керами́ческое изде́лие.
potty [ˈpɔtɪ] *adj* (*inf: mad*) чо́кнутый ♦ *n* (*for child*) горшо́к* (ночно́й).
potty-training [ˈpɔtɪtreɪnɪŋ] *n* приуче́ние ребёнка к горшку́.
pouch [pautʃ] *n* (*for tobacco*) кисе́т; (*for coins*) кошелёк*; (*ZOOL*) су́мка*.
pouf(fe) [puːf] *n* пуф.
poultice [ˈpəultɪs] *n* припа́рка*.
poultry [ˈpəultrɪ] *n* (*birds*) дома́шняя пти́ца; (*meat*) пти́ца.
poultry farm *n* птицефе́рма.
poultry farmer *n* птицево́д.
pounce [pauns] *vi*: **to ~ on** набра́сываться (набро́ситься* *perf*) на +*acc*.
pound [paund] *n* (*money, weight*) фунт; (*for dogs*) живодёрня; (*for cars*) *стоя́нка для непра́вильно припарко́ванных автомаши́н, увезённых поли́цией* ♦ *vt* (*beat*) колоти́ть* (*impf*) по +*dat*; (*crush*) толо́чь* (растоло́чь* *perf*); (*with guns*) обстре́ливать (обстреля́ть *perf*) ♦ *vi* (*heart*) колоти́ться* (*impf*); **half a ~ of** полфу́нта +*gen*; **a five—note** банкно́та в пять фу́нтов; **my car has been taken to the ~** мою́ маши́ну арестова́ли.

pounding ['paundıŋ] n: **we took a ~** (SPORT) нас поби́ли; (fig) нас разнесли́.
pound sterling n фунт сте́рлингов.
pour [pɔː'] vt (liquid) налива́ть (нали́ть* perf); (dry substance) насыпа́ть (насы́пать* perf) ♦ vi (water, blood, sweat etc) ли́ться* (impf); (rain) лить* (impf); **to ~ sb some tea** налива́ть (нали́ть* perf) кому́-н чай; **it's ~ing with rain** льёт дождь
▶ **pour away** vt вылива́ть (вы́лить* perf)
▶ **pour in** vi (people) вали́ть* (повали́ть* perf); (news, letters etc) сы́паться* (impf)
▶ **pour into** vt fus устремля́ться (устреми́ться* perf) в +acc
▶ **pour off** vt слива́ть (слить* perf)
▶ **pour out** vi (people) вали́ть* (повали́ть* perf) ♦ vt (drink) налива́ть (нали́ть* perf); (fig: thoughts, feelings, etc) излива́ть (изли́ть* perf).
pouring ['pɔːrıŋ] adj: **~ rain** проливно́й дождь m.
pout [paut] vi надува́ть (наду́ть perf) гу́бы, ду́ться (наду́ться perf).
poverty ['pɔvətı] n бе́дность f, нищета́.
poverty line n черта́ бе́дности.
poverty-stricken ['pɔvətıstrıkn] adj впа́вший в нищету́, обнища́вший.
poverty trap n (BRIT) тиски́ pl бе́дности.
POW n abbr = **prisoner of war**.
powder ['paudə'] n порошо́к*; (also: **face ~**) пу́дра ♦ vt: **to ~ one's face** пу́дрить (напу́дрить perf) лицо́; **to ~ one's nose** (euphemism) помы́ть* (perf) ру́ки.
powder compact n пу́дреница.
powdered milk ['paudəd-] n сухо́е молоко́.
powder keg n порохова́я бо́чка.
powder puff n пухо́вка.
powder room n да́мская ко́мната.
power ['pauə'] n (authority) власть f; (ability, opportunity) возмо́жность f; (legal right) полномо́чие; (strength: of person, speech, thought) мощь f; (of explosion, engine) мо́щность f; (electricity) электроэне́ргия; (MATH) сте́пень f; **to do all in one's ~ to help** де́лать (сде́лать perf) всё что в свои́х си́лах, что́бы помога́ть (помо́чь* perf); **the world ~s** мировы́е держа́вы; **to be in ~** находи́ться* (impf) у вла́сти.
powerboat ['pauəbəut] n мото́рный ка́тер*.
power cut n (BRIT) отключе́ние электроэне́ргии.
powered ['pauəd] adj: **~ by** рабо́тающий на +prp; **nuclear-~ submarine** а́томная подво́дная ло́дка*.
power failure n остано́вка* пода́чи электроэне́ргии.
powerful ['pauəful] adj могу́чий* (могу́ч); (person, organization) могу́щественный*

(могу́ществен); (engine, argument) мо́щный; (smell, voice, emotion) си́льный* (си́лен); (evidence) ве́ский* (ве́сок).
powerhouse ['pauəhaus] n (person): **a ~ of ideas** генера́тор иде́й.
powerless ['pauəlıs] adj бесси́льный* (бесси́лен).
power line n ли́ния электропереда́чи.
power of attorney n (LAW) дове́ренность f.
power point n (BRIT) (штéпсельная) розéтка*.
power station n электроста́нция.
power steering n (AUT) рулево́й приво́д с усили́телем.
powwow ['pauwau] n совéт.
pp abbr = **per procurationem**; (by proxy) по дове́ренности.
pp. abbr = **pages**.
PPE n abbr (BRIT: SCOL) = **philosophy, politics and economics**.
PPS n abbr (= post postscriptum) второ́й постскри́птум; (BRIT = parliamentary private secretary) ли́чный парла́ментский секрета́рь мини́стра.
PQ abbr (CANADA) = **Province of Quebec**.
PR n abbr = **public relations**; (POL) = **proportional representation** ♦ abbr (US: POST) = **Puerto Rico**.
Pr. abbr = **prince**.
practicability [præktıkə'bılıtı] n осуществи́мость f.
practicable ['præktıkəbl] adj осуществи́мый (осуществи́м).
practical ['præktıkl] adj (not theoretical) практи́ческий*; (sensible, viable) практи́чный* (практи́чен); (good with hands) умéлый (умéл).
practicalities [præktı'kælıtı] n практи́чность f; **practicalities** npl (of situation etc) практи́ческая сторона́ fsg.
practical joke n ро́зыгрыш.
practically ['præktıklı] adv практи́чески.
practice ['præktıs] n (habit) привы́чка*; (of profession) пра́ктика; (REL) обы́чай; (exercise, training) пра́ктика, трениро́вка ♦ vti (US) = **practise**; **in ~** на пра́ктике; **I am out of ~** я давно́ э́того не де́лал; **it's common ~** э́то распространено́; **to put sth into ~** осуществля́ть (осуществи́ть* perf) что-н на пра́ктике; **target ~** учéбная стрельба́.
practice match n трениро́вочный матч.
practise ['præktıs] (US **practice**) vt (musical instrument) упражня́ться (impf) на +acc; (SPORT, piece of music, language) отраба́тывать (отрабо́тать perf); (custom) выполня́ть (вы́полнить perf); (craft) занима́ться (impf) +instr; (religion) испове́довать (impf) ♦ vi (on instrument) упражня́ться (impf); (SPORT) тренирова́ться (impf); (lawyer, doctor) практикова́ть (impf); **to**

---

* marks translations which have irregular inflections. The Russian-English side of the dictionary gives inflectional information.

~ **for a match** тренирова́ться *(impf)* пе́ред ма́тчем; **to** ~ **law/medicine** занима́ться *(impf)* адвока́тской/враче́бной пра́ктикой.

practised ['præktɪst] *adj (BRIT: person)* о́пытный; *(: performance)* иску́сный; *(: liar)* закоренéлый; **with a** ~ **eye** *(BRIT)* намётанным гла́зом.

practising ['præktɪsɪŋ] *adj (Christian etc)* ве́рующий*; *(doctor, lawyer)* практику́ющий*; *(homosexual)* веду́щий* акти́вную полову́ю жизнь.

practitioner [præk'tɪʃənəʳ] *n (MED)* терапе́вт.

pragmatic [præg'mætɪk] *adj (reason etc)* прагмати́ческий; *(person)* прагмати́чный* (прагмати́чен).

pragmatism ['prægmətɪzəm] *n* прагмати́зм.

Prague [prɑ:g] *n* Пра́га.

prairie ['prɛərɪ] *n* пре́рия; *(US):* **the** ~**s** пре́рии *fpl.*

praise [preɪz] *n (approval)* похвала́; *(admiration)* восхвале́ние ♦ *vt (see n)* хвали́ть* (похвали́ть* *perf);* восхваля́ть *(impf).*

praiseworthy ['preɪzwə:ðɪ] *adj* досто́йный* (досто́ен) похвалы́.

pram [præm] *n (BRIT)* дéтская коля́ска.

prance [prɑ:ns] *vi (horse)* гарцева́ть *(impf);* *(person):* **to** ~ **about** красова́ться *(impf).*

prank [præŋk] *n (practical joke)* ро́зыгрыш; *(tomfoolery)* проде́лка*.

prat [præt] *n (inf. pej: BRIT)* идио́т.

prattle ['prætl] *vi:* **to** ~ **on (about)** трепа́ться *(impf)* (о +*prp).*

prawn [prɔ:n] *n* креве́тка*.

pray [preɪ] *vi* моли́ться* (помоли́ться* *perf);* **to** ~ **for** моли́ться* *(impf)* за +*acc;* **to** ~ **that** моли́ться* *(impf)*, что́бы.

prayer [prɛəʳ] *n (activity)* моли́тва, моле́ние; *(words)* моли́тва.

prayer book *n* моли́твенник.

pre... ['pri:...] *prefix* до..., пред...; ~**1970** до 1970-го го́да.

preach [pri:tʃ] *vi (also fig)* пропове́довать *(impf)* ♦ *vt:* **to** ~ **a sermon** *(also fig)* произноси́ть* (произнести́* *perf)* про́поведь; **to** ~ **at sb** чита́ть *(impf)* про́поведа кому́-н.

preacher ['pri:tʃəʳ] *n* пропове́дник(-ица).

preamble ['pri:æmbl] *n* преа́мбула.

prearranged [pri:ə'reɪndʒd] *adj (зара́нее)* подгото́вленный (подгото́влен).

precarious [prɪ'kɛərɪəs] *adj* риско́ванный* (риско́ван).

precaution [prɪ'kɔ:ʃən] *n* предосторо́жность *f;* **to take** ~**s** принима́ть (приня́ть* *perf)* ме́ры предосторо́жности.

precautionary [prɪ'kɔ:ʃənrɪ] *adj (measure)* предупреди́тельный.

precede [prɪ'si:d] *vt* предше́ствовать *(impf)* +*dat;* *(person)* быть* *(impf)* впереди́ +*gen.*

precedence ['prɛsɪdəns] *n (priority)* первоочерёдность *f;* **to take** ~ **over** быть*

(impf) важнée, чем.

precedent ['prɛsɪdənt] *n* прецеде́нт; **to establish** *or* **set a** ~ создава́ть* (созда́ть* *perf)* прецеде́нт.

preceding [prɪ'si:dɪŋ] *adj* предыду́щий*, предше́ствующий*.

precept ['pri:sɛpt] *n* пра́вило.

precinct ['pri:sɪŋkt] *n (US: part of city)* райо́н, префекту́ра; *(round cathedral)* двор*; ~**s** *npl (of large building)* террито́рия *fsg;* **pedestrian** ~ *(BRIT)* пешехо́дная зо́на; **shopping** ~ *(BRIT)* торго́вый центр.

precious ['prɛʃəs] *adj (commodity, object)* це́нный* (це́нен); *(stone)* драгоце́нный; *(pej: person, behaviour)* мане́рный ♦ *adv (inf):* ~ **little** *or* **few** о́чень ма́ло; **your** ~ **dog** *(ironic)* Ва́ша драгоце́нная соба́ка.

precious stone *n (GEO)* драгоце́нный ка́мень* *m.*

precipice ['prɛsɪpɪs] *n* обры́в.

precipitate [*vb* prɪ'sɪpɪteɪt, *adj* prɪ'sɪpɪtɪt] *vt (hasten)* ускоря́ть (уско́рить *perf)* ♦ *adj* скоропали́тельный* (скоропали́телен).

precipitation [prɪsɪpɪ'teɪʃən] *n (rain)* оса́дки *mpl.*

precipitous [prɪ'sɪpɪtəs] *adj (steep)* круто́й* (крут), обры́вистый (обры́вист); *(hasty)* поспе́шный (поспе́шен).

précis ['preɪsi:] *(pl ~)* *n* конспе́кт.

precise [prɪ'saɪs] *adj* то́чный* (то́чен).

precisely [prɪ'saɪslɪ] *adv (accurately)* то́чно; *(exactly)* ро́вно; ~**!** вот и́менно!, соверше́нно ве́рно!

precision [prɪ'sɪʒən] *n* то́чность *f.*

preclude [prɪ'klu:d] *vt* предотвраща́ть (предотврати́ть* *perf);* **to** ~ **sb from doing** меша́ть (помеша́ть *perf)* кому́-н +*infin.*

precocious [prɪ'kəuʃəs] *adj (talent)* ра́но разви́вшийся; **a** ~ **child** не по года́м разви́той ребёнок.

preconceived [pri:kən'si:vd] *adj* предвзя́тый (предвзя́т).

preconception ['pri:kən'sɛpʃən] *n* предвзя́тое мне́ние.

precondition ['pri:kən'dɪʃən] *n* непреме́нное усло́вие, предпосы́лка*.

precursor ['pri:kə:səʳ] *n (person, thing)* предте́ча *m/f.*

predate ['pri:'deɪt] *vt* предше́ствовать *(impf)* +*dat.*

predator ['prɛdətəʳ] *n (also fig)* хи́щник.

predatory ['prɛdətərɪ] *adj (animal)* хи́щный; *(fig)* хи́щный* (хи́щен).

predecessor ['pri:dɪsɛsəʳ] *n* предше́ственник (-ица).

predestination [pri:dɛstɪ'neɪʃən] *n* предопределе́ние.

predetermine [pri:dɪ'tə:mɪn] *vt* предопределя́ть (предопредели́ть *perf).*

predicament [prɪ'dɪkəmənt] *n* затрудне́ние; **to be in a** ~ быть* *(impf)* в затрудне́нии.

predicate ['prɛdɪkɪt] n (LING) сказу́емое nt adj.
predict [prɪ'dɪkt] vt предска́зывать
(предсказа́ть* perf).
predictable [prɪ'dɪktəbl] adj предсказу́емый
(предсказу́ем).
predictably [prɪ'dɪktəblɪ] adv как и ожида́лось;
~ **she didn't arrive** как и ожида́лось, она́ не
пришла́.
prediction [prɪ'dɪkʃən] n предсказа́ние.
predispose ['pri:dɪs'pəuz] vt предрасполага́ть
(предрасположи́ть* perf).
predominance [prɪ'dɔmɪnəns] n пре-
облада́ние; (dominance) госпо́дство.
predominant [prɪ'dɔmɪnənt] adj
домини́рующий, преоблада́ющий
(преоблада́ющ); **to become** ~ станови́ться*
(стать* perf) преоблада́ющим(-ей).
predominantly [prɪ'dɔmɪnəntlɪ] adv
преиму́щественно.
predominate [prɪ'dɔmɪneɪt] vi преоблада́ть
(impf).
pre-eminent [pri:'ɛmɪnənt] adj выдаю́щийся*.
pre-empt [pri:'ɛmt] vt предупрежда́ть
(предупреди́ть* perf); **to** ~ **the issue**
предупрежда́ть (предупреди́ть* perf)
собы́тия.
pre-emptive [pri:'ɛmtɪv] adj: ~ **strike**
упрежда́ющий уда́р.
preen [pri:n] vt: **to** ~ **itself** (bird) чи́стить*
(почи́стить* perf) пёрышки; **to** ~ **o.s.**
прихора́шиваться (impf).
prefab ['pri:fæb] n сбо́рный дом*.
prefabricated [pri:'fæbrɪkeɪtɪd] adj сбо́рный.
preface ['prɛfəs] n (in book) предисло́вие ♦ vt:
to ~ **sth with** предпосыла́ть (предпосла́ть*
perf) чему́-н +acc.
prefect ['pri:fɛkt] n (BRIT: SCOL) ста́роста m/f.
prefer [prɪ'fə:'] vt предпочита́ть (предпоче́сть*
perf); (LAW): **to** ~ **charges against** выдвига́ть
(вы́двинуть perf) обвине́ние про́тив +gen; **to**
~ **doing** or **to do** предпочита́ть (предпоче́сть*
perf) +infin; **I** ~ **coffee to tea** я предпочита́ю
ко́фе ча́ю.
preferable ['prɛfrəbl] adj предпочти́тельный*
(предпочти́телен).
preferably ['prɛfrəblɪ] adv предпочти́тельно.
preference ['prɛfrəns] n (liking): **to have a** ~ **for**
предпочита́ть (impf); (priority): **to give** ~ **to**
отдава́ть* (отда́ть* perf) предпочте́ние +dat;
in ~ **to sth** вме́сто чего́-н.
preference shares npl (BRIT: COMM)
привилегиро́ванные а́кции fpl.
preferential [prɛfə'rɛnʃəl] adj: ~ **treatment**
осо́бое отноше́ние.
preferred stock [prɪ'fəd-] npl (US) = **preference
shares**.
prefix ['pri:fɪks] n приста́вка*, префикс.
pregnancy ['prɛgnənsɪ] n бере́менность f.

pregnancy test n ана́лиз на бере́менность.
pregnant ['prɛgnənt] adj бере́менная
(бере́менна); (remark, pause)
многозначи́тельный* (многозначи́телен);
she is 3 months ~ она́ на четвёртом ме́сяце
(бере́менности).
prehistoric ['pri:hɪs'tɔrɪk] adj доистори́ческий*.
prehistory [pri:'hɪstərɪ] n первобы́тная
исто́рия.
prejudge [pri:'dʒʌdʒ] vt предреша́ть
(предреши́ть perf).
prejudice ['prɛdʒudɪs] n (unreasonable dislike)
предрассу́док*; (bias in favour) предвзя́тость
f, предубежде́ние ♦ vt (harm) вреди́ть*
(повреди́ть* perf) +dat; **without** ~ **to** без
уще́рба для +gen; **to** ~ **sb in favour of**
располага́ть (расположи́ть* perf) кого́-н в
по́льзу +gen; **to** ~ **sb against** настра́ивать
(настро́ить perf) кого́-н про́тив +gen.
prejudiced ['prɛdʒudɪst] adj (biased against)
предубеждённый (предубеждён); (in favour)
располо́женный* (располо́жен); (view)
предвзя́тый (предвзя́т).
prelate ['prɛlət] n (REL) прела́т.
preliminaries [prɪ'lɪmɪnərɪz] npl
предвари́тельные мероприя́тия ntpl; (in
competition) предвари́тельный отбо́р msg.
preliminary [prɪ'lɪmɪnərɪ] adj
предвари́тельный.
prelude ['prɛljuːd] n (MUS, fig) прелю́дия.
premarital ['pri:'mærɪtl] adj добра́чный.
premature ['prɛmətʃuə'] adj
преждевре́менный* (преждевре́мен); (baby)
недоно́шенный* (недоно́шен); **you are being
a little** ~ Вы не́сколько поторопи́лись.
premeditated [pri:'mɛdɪteɪtɪd] adj
преднаме́ренный* (преднаме́рен).
premeditation [pri:'mɛdɪ'teɪʃən] n разду́мье.
premenstrual tension [pri:'mɛnstruəl-] n
предменструа́льный синдро́м.
premier ['prɛmɪə'] adj (best) лу́чший* ♦ n (POL)
премье́р-мини́стр.
première ['prɛmɪɛə'] n премье́ра.
premise ['prɛmɪs] n предпосы́лка*; ~**s** npl (of
business) помеще́ние ntsg; **on the** ~**s** в
помеще́нии.
premium ['pri:mɪəm] n (COMM, INSURANCE)
пре́мия; **to be at a** ~ (expensive) сто́ить (impf)
вы́ше номина́ла; (hard to get) по́льзоваться
(impf) больши́м спро́сом; **to sell at a** ~
(shares) продава́ть* (прода́ть* perf) по цене́
вы́ше номина́ла.
premium bond n (BRIT) премиа́льная
(сберега́тельная) облига́ция.
premium deal n (COMM) премиа́льная
сде́лка*.
premium gasoline n (US) высокоокта́новый
бензи́н.

premonition [prɛmə'nɪʃən] *n* предчу́вствие.
preoccupation [pri:ɔkju'peɪʃən] *n*: ~ **with** озабо́ченность *f* +*instr*.
preoccupied [pri:'ɔkjupaɪd] *adj* озабо́ченный* (озабо́чен).
prep [prɛp] *adj abbr*: ~ **school** = *preparatory school*; (*BRIT*) ча́стная нача́льная шко́ла; (*US*) сре́дняя шко́ла ◆ *n abbr* = *preparation*.
prep *n* (*homework*) дома́шнее зада́ние.
prepaid [pri:'peɪd] *adj* зара́нее опла́ченный (опла́чен); (*envelope*) с зара́нее опла́ченными почто́выми расхо́дами.
preparation [prɛpə'reɪʃən] *n* (*activity*) подгото́вка*; (*of food*) приготовле́ние; (*medicine, cosmetic*) препара́т; ~**s** *npl* (*arrangements*) приготовле́ния *ntpl*; **in** ~ **for sth** гото́вясь к чему́-н.
preparatory [prɪ'pærətərɪ] *adj* подготови́тельный; ~ **to doing** пре́жде чем +*infin*.
preparatory school *n* (*BRIT*) ча́стная нача́льная шко́ла; (*US*) сре́дняя шко́ла.
prepare [prɪ'pɛəʳ] *vt* (*plan, speech, room etc*) подгота́вливать (подгото́вить* *perf*); (*CULIN*) гото́вить* (*impf*), приготавливать (пригото́вить* *perf*) ◆ *vi*: **to** ~ **for** (*event, action etc*) гото́виться* (*impf*) *or* подгота́вливаться (подгото́виться* *perf*) к +*dat*.
prepared [prɪ'pɛəd] *adj* гото́вый (гото́в); **I am** ~ **to help you** (*willing*) я гото́в помо́чь Вам; ~ **for** (*ready*) гото́вый (гото́в) к +*dat*.
preponderance [prɪ'pɔndərns] *n* (*of people, things*) преоблада́ние.
preposition [prɛpə'zɪʃən] *n* (*LING*) предло́г.
prepossessing [pri:pə'zɛsɪŋ] *adj* привлека́тельный* (привлека́телен).
preposterous [prɪ'pɔstərəs] *adj* (*outrageous*) ди́кий*.
prep school *n* = **preparatory school**.
prerecorded ['pri:rɪ'kɔ:dɪd] *adj* предвари́тельно запи́санный.
prerequisite [pri:'rɛkwɪzɪt] *n* предпосы́лка*, непреме́нное усло́вие.
prerogative [prɪ'rɔgətɪv] *n* прерогати́ва.
Presbyterian [prɛzbɪ'tɪərɪən] *n* (*REL*) пресвитериа́нин*(-а́нка*) ◆ *adj* пресвитериа́нский.
presbytery ['prɛzbɪtərɪ] *n* пресвите́рия.
preschool [ˌpriː'skuːl] *adj* (*age, education*) дошко́льный; ~ **child** ребёнок дошко́льного во́зраста.
prescribe [prɪ'skraɪb] *vt* (*MED*) пропи́сывать (прописа́ть* *perf*); (*action, duty*) предпи́сывать (предписа́ть* *perf*); ~**d books** (*BRIT: SCOL*) рекомендо́ванные уче́бники.
prescription [prɪ'skrɪpʃən] *n* (*MED: slip of paper*) реце́пт; (*: medicine*) лека́рство (*назна́ченное врачо́м*); **to make up** *or* (*US*) **fill a** ~ приготовля́ть (пригото́вить* *perf*) лека́рство по реце́пту; **"only available on** ~" „прода́жа лека́рства то́лько по реце́птам".

prescription charges *npl* (*BRIT*) минима́льная цена́ за лека́рства, отпуска́емые по реце́пту.
prescriptive [prɪ'skrɪptɪv] *adj* нормати́вный* (нормати́вен).
presence ['prɛzns] *n* прису́тствие; (*fig*) нару́жность *f*; **in sb's** ~ в кого́-н прису́тствии.
presence of mind *n* прису́тствие ду́ха.
present [*adj, n* 'prɛznt, *vt* prɪ'zɛnt] *adj* (*current*) ны́нешний*, настоя́щий*; (*in attendance*) прису́тствующий ◆ *n* (*gift*) пода́рок*; (*LING: also*: ~ **tense**) настоя́щее вре́мя* *nt* ◆ *vt* представля́ть (предста́вить* *perf*); (*threat*) представля́ть (предста́вить* *perf*) собо́й; (*RADIO, TV*) вести́* (*impf*); (*give*): **to** ~ **sth to sb**, ~ **sb with sth** (*prize, award etc*) вруча́ть (вручи́ть* *perf*) что-н кому́-н; (*gift*) преподноси́ть* (преподнести́* *perf*) что-н кому́-н; (*formally introduce*): **to** ~ **sb (to)** представля́ть (предста́вить* *perf*) кого́-н (+*dat*); **to be** ~ **at** прису́тствовать (*impf*) на +*prp*; **those** ~ прису́тствующие; **the** ~ (*time*) настоя́щее вре́мя*; **at** ~ в настоя́щее вре́мя; **to give sb a** ~ дари́ть* (подари́ть* *perf*) кому́-н пода́рок.
presentable [prɪ'zɛntəbl] *adj* представи́тельный* (представи́телен), презента́бельный* (презента́белен).
presentation [prɛzn'teɪʃən] *n* (*of plan, report etc*) изложе́ние; (*appearance*) вне́шний* вид; (*also*: ~ **ceremony**) представле́ние, презента́ция; (*lecture, talk*) выступле́ние; **on** ~ **of** (*voucher etc*) по предъявле́нии +*gen*.
present-day ['prɛzntdeɪ] *adj* совреме́нный, ны́нешний*.
presenter [prɪ'zɛntəʳ] *n* (*RADIO, TV*) ди́ктор; (*: of news*) веду́щий*(-ая) *m(f) adj*.
presently ['prɛzntlɪ] *adv* вско́ре; (*now*) в да́нный моме́нт, в настоя́щее вре́мя.
present participle *n* прича́стие настоя́щего вре́мени.
preservation [prɛzə'veɪʃən] *n* (*act: of building, democracy*) сохране́ние; (*: of food*) хране́ние; (*state*) сохра́нность *f*.
preservative [prɪ'zə:vətɪv] *n* (*for food*) консерва́нт; (*for wood*) пропи́точный соста́в; (*for metal*) защи́тное сре́дство.
preserve [prɪ'zə:v] *vt* сохраня́ть (сохрани́ть* *perf*); (*food*) консерви́ровать (законсерви́ровать* *perf*); (*keep safe*) оберега́ть (*impf*), охраня́ть (*impf*) ◆ *n* (*often pl*: *jam*) варе́нье; (*for game, fish*) запове́дник; **a working class** ~ стихи́я рабо́чего кла́сса; **a male** ~ чи́сто мужско́е заня́тие.
preshrunk ['pri:'ʃrʌŋk] *adj*: ~ **fabric** ткань, проше́дшая предвари́тельную уса́дку.
preside [prɪ'zaɪd] *vi*: **to** ~ **(over)** председа́тельствовать (*impf*) (на +*prp*).
presidency ['prɛzɪdənsɪ] *n* президе́нтство.
president ['prɛzɪdənt] *n* (*POL, COMM*) президе́нт;

(*US: SCOL*) ре́ктор.

presidential [prɛzɪ'dɛnʃl] *adj* (*election, campaign etc*) президе́нтский; ~ **candidate** кандида́т в президе́нты; ~ **adviser** сове́тник президе́нта.

press [prɛs] *n* (*also:* **printing** ~) печа́тный стано́к*; (*of switch, button, bell*) кно́пка*; (*for wine*) пресс для виногра́да; (*crowd*) да́вка ♦ *vt* (*hold together*) прижима́ть (прижа́ть* *perf*); (*push*) нажима́ть (нажа́ть* *perf*); (*iron*) гла́дить* (погла́дить* *perf*); (*put pressure on: person*) наста́ивать (настоя́ть *perf*); (*squeeze*) выжима́ть (вы́жать* *perf*); (*pursue*) добива́ться (доби́ться* *perf*) +*gen* ♦ *vi* (*squeeze*) жать* (*impf*), дави́ть* (*impf*); **the** ~ (*newspapers, journalists*) пре́сса; **to go to** ~ идти́* (*impf*) в печа́ть; **to be in the** ~ (*being printed*) находи́ться* (*impf*) в печа́ти; (*in the newspapers*) быть* (*impf*) в газе́тах; **we are** ~**ed for time/money** у нас ма́ло вре́мени/ де́нег; **to** ~ **sth on sb** (*insist*) навя́зывать (навяза́ть* *perf*) что-н кому́-н; **to** ~ **sb to do** *or* **into doing** вынужда́ть (вы́нудить *perf*) кого́-н +*infin*; **to** ~ **sb for an answer** торопи́ть* (поторопи́ть* *perf*) кого́-н с отве́том; **to** ~ **charges against sb** выдвига́ть (вы́двинуть *perf*) обвине́ния про́тив кого́-н; **to** ~ **for** (*improvement, change etc*) наста́ивать (настоя́ть *perf*) на +*prp*

▶ **press ahead** *vi* приступа́ть (приступи́ть* *perf*) к де́лу

▶ **press on** *vi* продолжа́ть (*impf*).

press agency *n* аге́нтство печа́ти.

press clipping *n* газе́тная вы́резка.

press conference *n* пресс-конфере́нция.

press cutting *n* = **press clipping**.

press-gang ['prɛsgæŋ] *vt*: **to** ~ **sb into doing** наси́льно заставля́ть (заста́вить* *perf*) кого́-н +*infin*.

pressing ['prɛsɪŋ] *adj* (*urgent*) сро́чный* (сро́чен), неотло́жный* (неотло́жен).

press officer *n* сотру́дник(-ица) отде́ла информа́ции.

press release *n* сообще́ние для печа́ти.

press stud *n* (*BRIT*) оде́жная кно́пка*.

press-up ['prɛsʌp] *n* (*BRIT: SPORT*) отжима́ние, отжи́м.

pressure ['prɛʃə'] *n* давле́ние; (*stress*) напряже́ние ♦ *vt*: **to** ~ **sb (to do)** принужда́ть (прину́дить* *perf*) кого́-н (+*infin*); **to put** ~ **on sb (to do)** ока́зывать (оказа́ть* *perf*) давле́ние *or* нажи́м на кого́-н (+*infin*); **high/low** ~ высо́кое/ни́зкое давле́ние.

pressure cooker *n* скорова́рка*.

pressure gauge *n* мано́метр.

pressure group *n* инициати́вная гру́ппа.

pressurize ['prɛʃəraɪz] *vt*: **to** ~ **sb (to do** *or* **into doing)** ока́зывать (оказа́ть* *perf*) давле́ние на

кого́-н (+*infin*).

pressurized ['prɛʃəraɪzd] *adj* (*cabin, container, spacesuit*) гермети́чный.

Prestel® ['prɛstɛl] *n* Пре́стел.

prestige [prɛs'tiːʒ] *n* прести́ж.

prestigious [prɛs'tɪdʒəs] *adj* прести́жный* (прести́жен).

presumably [prɪ'zjuːməblɪ] *adv* наве́рно; ~ **he did it** наве́рно, э́то сде́лал он.

presume [prɪ'zjuːm] *vt*: **to** ~ **(that)** (*suppose*) предполага́ть (предположи́ть* *perf*)(, что); **to** ~ **to do** (*dare*) реша́ться (реши́ться *perf*) +*infin*.

presumption [prɪ'zʌmpʃən] *n* предположе́ние.

presumptuous [prɪ'zʌmpʃəs] *adj* самонаде́янный* (самонаде́ян).

presuppose [priːsə'pəuz] *vt* предполага́ть (предположи́ть* *perf*).

presupposition [priːsʌpə'zɪʃən] *n* предположе́ние.

pretax [priː'tæks] *adj* (*profit*) до вы́чета нало́гов.

pretence [prɪ'tɛns] (*US* **pretense**) *n* (*false appearance*) притво́рство; (*excuse*) предло́г; **under false** ~**s** под ло́жным предло́гом; **she is devoid of all** ~ **of helping** она́ соверше́нно лишена́ притво́рства; **he is making a** ~ **of helping** он де́лает вид, что помога́ет.

pretend [prɪ'tɛnd] *vi*: **to** ~ **that** притворя́ться (притвори́ться *perf*), что; **he** ~**ed to help** он притвори́лся, что помога́ет; **to** ~ **to sth** (*make claim*) претендова́ть (*impf*) на что-н.

pretense [prɪ'tɛns] *n* (*US*) = **pretence**.

pretentious [prɪ'tɛnʃəs] *adj* претенцио́зный* (претенцио́зен).

preterite ['prɛtərɪt] *n* прете́рит.

pretext ['priːtɛkst] *n* предло́г; **on** *or* **under the** ~ **of being busy/tired** под предло́гом за́нятости/уста́лости.

Pretoria [prɪ'tɔːrɪə] *n* Прето́рия.

pretty ['prɪtɪ] *adj* (*person*) хоро́шенький*; (*thing*) краси́вый (краси́в) ♦ *adv* (*quite*) дово́льно.

prevail [prɪ'veɪl] *vi* (*be current*) преоблада́ть (*impf*), превали́ровать (*impf*); (*gain influence*) оде́рживать (одержа́ть *perf*) верх; (*persuade*): **to** ~ **(up)on sb to do** убежда́ть (убеди́ть* *perf*) кого́-н +*infin*.

prevailing [prɪ'veɪlɪŋ] *adj* (*wind*) преобла́дающий; (*fashion, attitude*) превали́рующий.

prevalent ['prɛvələnt] *adj* (*belief, custom*) преобла́дающий; (*fashion*) превали́рующий; (*disease*) распространённый* (распространён).

prevaricate [prɪ'værɪkeɪt] *vi* извора́чиваться (*impf*).

prevarication [prɪværɪ'keɪʃən] *n* виля́ние.

---

* marks translations which have irregular inflections. The Russian–English side of the dictionary gives inflectional information.

prevent [prɪ'vɛnt] vt (accident etc) предотвращать (предотвратить* perf); **to ~ sb from doing** мешать (помешать perf) кому-н +infin; **this policy ~s inflation from rising** эта политика препятствует росту инфляции.

preventable [prɪ'vɛntəbl] adj предотвратимый (предотвратим).

preventative [prɪ'vɛntətɪv] adj = **preventive**.

prevention [prɪ'vɛnʃən] n предотвращение, предупреждение.

preventive [prɪ'vɛntɪv] adj (measures) предупредительный; (: POL) превентивный; (medicine) профилактический*.

preview ['pri:vju:] n (of film) (закрытый) просмотр; (fig) предварительная картина.

previous ['pri:vɪəs] adj предыдущий*; **I have a ~ engagement** это время у меня уже занято; **~ to** до +gen.

previously ['pri:vɪəslɪ] adv (before) ранее; (in the past) прежде; **I retired two years ~** я ушёл на пенсию двумя годами ранее.

prewar [pri:'wɔ:'] adj довоенный, предвоенный.

prey [preɪ] n добыча ♦ vi: **to ~ on** (animal: feed on) охотиться* (impf) на +acc; **it was ~ing on his mind** это терзало его.

price [praɪs] n (also fig) цена* ♦ vt (goods) оценивать (оценить* perf); **what is the ~ of ...?** сколько стоит ...?; **to go up** or **rise in ~** дорожать (вздорожать or подорожать perf); **to put a ~ on sth** назначать (назначить perf) цену чему-н; **Britain has been out of the market** Великобритания была вытеснена из рынка из-за завышения цен; **what ~ his promises now?** (BRIT) что стоят все его обещания сейчас?; **he regained his freedom, but at a ~** он получил свободу, но дорогой ценой.

price control n контроль m за ценами.

price cutting n снижение цен.

priceless ['praɪslɪs] adj бесценный* (бесценен); (inf: amusing) бесподобный* (бесподобен).

price list n прейскурант.

price range n диапазон цен; **it's within my ~ ~** это мне по карману.

price tag n ценник; (fig) цена*.

price war n война цен.

pricey ['praɪsɪ] adj (inf) дорогой.

prick [prɪk] n (short, sharp pain) укол; (ANAT: inf!) хуй (!) ♦ vt (make hole in) прокалывать (проколоть* perf); (cause pain to) уколоть* (perf); **to ~ up one's ears** (listen eagerly) навострить (perf) уши.

prickle ['prɪkl] n (of plant) шип*, колючка*; (sensation) покалывание.

prickly ['prɪklɪ] adj колючий* (колюч).

prickly heat n потница.

prickly pear n (BOT) опунция.

pride [praɪd] n гордость f; (pej: feeling of superiority) гордыня ♦ vt: **to ~ o.s. on** гордиться* (impf) +instr; **to take (a) ~ in** гордиться* (impf) +instr; **I take (a) ~ in working well** я горжусь тем что я работаю хорошо; **to have ~ of place** (BRIT) занимать (занять* perf) почётное место.

priest [pri:st] n священник; (non-Christian) жрец*.

priestess ['pri:stɪs] n (non-Christian) жрица.

priesthood ['pri:sthud] n священство.

prig [prɪg] n: **he's a** ~ он такая цаца.

prim [prɪm] adj чопорный* (чопорен).

primacy ['praɪməsɪ] n первенство.

prima-facie ['praɪmə'feɪʃɪ] adj: **to have a ~ case** (LAW) разбирать (impf) ясное судебное дело*.

primal ['praɪməl] adj (instinct) первичный*; (cause) изначальный; **~ scream** первый крик (младенца).

primarily ['praɪmərɪlɪ] adv в первую очередь.

primary ['praɪmərɪ] adj (first in importance) первостепенный* (первостепенен), первоочередной ♦ n (US: POL) предварительные выборы mpl; **~ education** начальное образование*; **~ teacher** учитель(ница) m(f) начальных классов.

primary colour n основной цвет*.

primary school n (BRIT) начальная школа.

primate ['praɪmɪt] n (ZOOL) примат; (REL) примас.

prime [praɪm] adj (most important) главный, основной; (best quality) первосортный ♦ n (of person's life) расцвет ♦ vt (wood, canvas) грунтовать (загрунтовать perf); (fig: person) подготавливать (подготовить* perf); (gun) заряжать (зарядить perf); (pump) заливать (залить* perf); **in the ~ of life** в расцвете сил, во цвете лет; **~ example** (typical) яркий* пример.

Prime Minister n премьер-министр.

primer ['praɪmə'] n (paint) грунтовка; (book) учебник-введение.

prime time n (RADIO, TV) лучшее эфирное время* nt.

primeval [praɪ'mi:vl] adj первобытный.

primitive ['prɪmɪtɪv] adj (early) первобытный; (unsophisticated: way of life, tool etc) примитивный* (примитивен).

primrose ['prɪmrəuz] n первоцвет.

primula ['prɪmjulə] n примула.

Primus® ['praɪməs] n (BRIT: also: **p~ stove**) примус.

prince [prɪns] n принц; (Russian) князь* m.

prince charming n прекрасный принц.

princess [prɪn'sɛs] n принцесса; (Russian) княгиня, княжна*.

principal ['prɪnsɪpl] adj главный, основной ♦ n (of school, college) директор*; (of university) ректор; (in play) ведущий*(-ая) актёр (-триса); (money) капитал.

principality [prɪnsɪ'pælɪtɪ] n княжество.

principally ['prɪnsɪplɪ] adv преимущественно, главным образом.

principle ['prɪnsɪpl] n принцип; (scientific law)

закóн; **in** ~ в прúнципе; **on** ~ из прúнципа.

print [prɪnt] *n* (*TYP*) шрифт*; (*ART*) эстáмп, гравю́ра; (*PHOT, fingerprint*) отпечáток*; (*footprint*) след*; (*fabric*) сúтец* ♦ *vt* (*book etc*) печáтать (напечáтать *perf*); (*cloth*) набивáть (набúть* *perf*); (*write in capitals*) писáть* (написáть* *perf*) печáтными бýквами; **this book is out of** ~ э́та кнúга распрóдана
▶ **print out** *vt* (*COMPUT*) распечáтывать (распечáтать *perf*), выводúть* (вы́йти* *perf*) на печáть.

printed circuit board ['prɪntɪd-] *n* (*ELEC*) печáтная схéма *or* плáта.

printed matter *n* печáтные материáлы *mpl*.

printer ['prɪntə'] *n* (*person*) печáтник; (*machine*) прúнтер; (*firm: also:* ~'**s**) типогрáфия.

printhead ['prɪnthɛd] *n* (*COMPUT*) печáтающая голóвка.

printing ['prɪntɪŋ] *n* (*act*) печáтание; (*art*) печáтное дéло.

printing press *n* печáтный станóк*.

print-out ['prɪntaʊt] *n* (*COMPUT*) распечáтка*.

print wheel *n* (*COMPUT*) печáтающее колесó*.

prior ['praɪə'] *adj* (*previous*) прéжний*; (*more important*) первоочереднóй ♦ *n* (*REL*) настоя́тель *m*, приóр; **without** ~ **notice** без предварúтельного предупреждéния; **to have** ~ **knowledge of sth** знать* (*impf*) о чём-н зарáнее; **to have a** ~ **claim to sth** имéть (*impf*) первоочереднóе *or* преимýщественное прáво на что-н; ~ **to** до +*gen*.

priority [praɪ'ɒrɪtɪ] *n* (*most urgent task*) первоочереднáя задáча; (*most important thing, task*) приоритéт; **to have** ~ **(over)** имéть (*impf*) преимýщество (пéред +*instr*).

priory ['praɪərɪ] *n* монастéрь* *m*.

prise [praɪz] *vt*: **to** ~ **open** взлáмывать (взломáть *perf*).

prism ['prɪzəm] *n* прúзма.

prison ['prɪzn] *n* тюрьмá* ♦ *cpd* тюрéмный.

prison camp *n* исправúтельно-трудовóй лáгерь* *m*.

prisoner ['prɪznə'] *n* (*in prison*) заключённый (-ая) *m(f) adj*; (*captured person*) плéнный(-ая) *m(f) adj*; **the** ~ **at the bar** подсудúмый(-ая) *m(f) adj*; **to take sb** ~ брать* (взять* *perf*) когó-н в плен.

prisoner of war *n* военноплéнный *m adj*.

prissy ['prɪsɪ] *adj* (*pej*) чóпорный.

pristine ['prɪstiːn] *adj* безупрéчный* (безупрéчен).

privacy ['prɪvəsɪ] *n* уединéние; **invasion of sb's** ~ вторжéние в чью-н чáстную жизнь.

private ['praɪvɪt] *adj* (*not public: property, industry*) чáстный; (: *discussion, club*) закры́тый; (*personal, confidential: belongings, life*) лúчный; (: *thoughts, plans*)

скры́тый; (*secluded: place*) уединённый (уединён); (*secretive, reserved*) зáмкнутый (зáмкнут); (*confidential*) конфиденциáльный* (конфиденциáлен) ♦ *n* (*MIL*) рядовóй *m adj*; "**private**" (*on envelope*) „лúчно"; (*on door*) „постороннним вход воспрещён"; **in** ~ конфиденциáльно; **in (his)** ~ **life** в (егó) лúчной жúзни; **he is a very** ~ **person** он óчень зáмкнутый человéк; **to be in** ~ **practice** имéть (*impf*) чáстную прáктику; ~ **hearing** (*LAW*) закры́тое слýшание.

private enterprise *n* (*economic activity*) чáстное предпринимáтельство.

private eye *n* чáстный сы́щик.

private limited company *n* (*BRIT*) чáстная акционéрная компáния.

privately ['praɪvɪtlɪ] *adv* (*discuss*) конфиденциáльно; (*act*) в чáстном поря́дке; (*within o.s.*) в душé.

private parts *npl* (*ANAT*) (нарýжные) половы́е óрганы *mpl*.

private property *n* чáстная сóбственность *f*.

private school *n* чáстная шкóла.

privation [praɪ'veɪʃən] *n* (*state*) лишéния *ntpl*.

privatize ['praɪvɪtaɪz] *vt* приватизúровать (*impf/perf*).

privet ['prɪvɪt] *n* (*BOT*) бирючúна.

privilege ['prɪvɪlɪdʒ] *n* привилéгия.

privileged ['prɪvɪlɪdʒd] *adj* привилегирóванный; **to be** ~ **to do** имéть (*impf*) честь +*infin*.

privy ['prɪvɪ] *adj*: ~ **to** посвящённый в +*acc*.

Privy Council *n* (*BRIT*) Тáйный Совéт.

Privy Councillor *n* (*BRIT*) Тáйный Совéтник.

prize [praɪz] *n* приз*; (*money*) прéмия ♦ *adj* (*first-class*) первоклáссный; (*example, idiot*) класси́ческий* ♦ *vt* (высокó) ценúть (*impf*).

prizefighter ['praɪzfaɪtə'] *n* профессионáльный боксёр.

prize-giving ['praɪzgɪvɪŋ] *n* церемóния вручéния нагрáд за хорóшую успевáемость.

prize money *n* призовы́е дéньги* *pl*.

prizewinner ['praɪzwɪnə'] *n* призёр, лауреáт.

prizewinning ['praɪzwɪnɪŋ] *adj* (*person*) удостóенный нагрáды; (*animal*) призовóй; (*novel, essay etc*) удостóенный прéмии.

PRO *n abbr* = **public relations officer**

pro [prəʊ] *n* (*SPORT: inf*) профессионáл ♦ *prep* (*in favour of*) за +*acc*; **the** ~**s and cons** (дóводы) „за" и „прóтив".

pro- [prəʊ] *prefix* про-.

proactive [prəʊ'æktɪv] *adj* дéйственный.

probability [prɔbə'bɪlɪtɪ] *n*: ~ **of/that** вероя́тность *f* +*gen*/что; **in all** ~ по всей вероя́тности.

probable ['prɔbəbl] *adj* вероя́тный* (вероя́тен); **it seems** ~ **that** ... представля́ется вероя́тным, что ....

---

* marks translations which have irregular inflections. The Russian-English side of the dictionary gives inflectional information.

probably ['prɔbəblɪ] *adv* вероя́тно.
probate ['prəubɪt] *n* утвержде́ние завеща́ния.
probation [prə'beɪʃən] *n*: **he is on** ~ (*LAW*) он
осуждён усло́вно; (*employee*) он прохо́дит
испыта́тельный срок; (*REL*) он отбыва́ет
по́слух.
probationary [prə'beɪʃənrɪ] *adj* (*period*)
испыта́тельный.
probationer [prə'beɪʃənə'] *n* (*LAW*) усло́вно
осуждённый.
probation officer *n до́лжностно́е лицо́,
осуществля́ющее надзо́р за усло́вно
осуждёнными.*
probe [prəub] *n* (*MED, SPACE*) зонд; (*enquiry*)
рассле́дование ◆ *vt* (*investigate*) рас-
сле́довать (*impf/perf*); (*poke*) прощу́пывать
(*impf*).
probity ['prəubɪtɪ] *n* че́стность *f*.
problem ['prɔbləm] *n* пробле́ма; **we are having**
~**s with the car** у нас непола́дки с маши́ной;
what's the ~? в чём де́ло?; **I had no** ~ **in
finding her** я нашёл её без труда́; **no** ~! нет
пробле́м!
problematic(al) [prɔblə'mætɪk(l)] *adj*
проблемати́чный* (проблемати́чен).
problem-solving ['prɔbləmsɔlvɪŋ] *n уме́ние
находи́ть вы́ход из тру́дного положе́ния.*
procedural [prə'si:djurəl] *adj* процеду́рный.
procedure [prə'si:dʒə'] *n* процеду́ра.
proceed [prə'si:d] *vi* (*subj: activity, event,
process: carry on*) продолжа́ться
(продо́лжиться *perf*); (*person: go*) дви́гаться
(дви́нуться *perf*); (*continue*): **to** ~ (**with**)
продолжа́ть (продо́лжить *perf*); **to** ~ **to do**
продолжа́ть (продо́лжить *perf*) +*infin*; **to** ~
against sb (*LAW*) возбужда́ть (возбуди́ть*
perf) де́ло про́тив кого́-н.
proceedings [prə'si:dɪŋz] *npl* (*organized
events*) собы́тия *ntpl*; (*LAW*) суде́бное
разбира́тельство *ntsg*; (*minutes*) протоко́л
msg.
proceeds ['prəusi:dz] *npl* поступле́ния *ntpl*.
process ['prəusɛs] *n* проце́сс ◆ *vt* (*also COMPUT*)
обраба́тывать (обрабо́тать *perf*) ◆ *vi* (*BRIT: go in
procession*) уча́ствовать (*impf*) в проце́ссии;
in ~ в проце́ссе; **we are in the** ~ **of moving
house** сейча́с мы переезжа́ем.
processed cheese ['prəusɛst-] (*US* **process
cheese**) *n* пла́вленый сыр*.
processing ['prəusɛsɪŋ] *n* (*PHOT*) обрабо́тка*.
procession [prə'sɛʃən] *n* проце́ссия.
pro-choice [prəu'tʃɔɪs] *adj защища́ющий пра́во
же́нщины на або́рт.*
proclaim [prə'kleɪm] *vt* провозглаша́ть
(провозгласи́ть* *perf*).
proclamation [prɔklə'meɪʃən] *n* провоз-
глаше́ние.
proclivity [prə'klɪvɪtɪ] *n* накло́нность *f*.
procrastinate [prəu'kræstɪneɪt] *vi* оття́гивать
(оттяну́ть *perf*).
procrastination [prəukræstɪ'neɪʃən] *n*
оття́гивание.
procreation [prəukrɪ'eɪʃən] *n* размноже́ние.
procurator fiscal ['prɔkjurətə-] *n* (*SCOTTISH:
LAW*) прокуро́р.
procure [prə'kjuə'] *vt* приобрета́ть
(приобрести́* *perf*).
procurement [prə'kjuəmənt] *n* приобрете́ние.
prod [prɔd] *vt* ты́кать* (ткнуть *perf*); (*fig:
remind*) подстёгивать (подстегну́ть *perf*) ◆ *n*
(*see vb*) тычо́к*; (*fig*) напомина́ние.
prodigal ['prɔdɪgl] *adj* блу́дный.
prodigious [prə'dɪdʒəs] *adj* огро́мный*
(огро́мен).
prodigy ['prɔdɪdʒɪ] *n* (*person*) тала́нт;
(*achievement*) успе́хи *mpl*; **child** ~
вундерки́нд.
produce [*vt* prə'dju:s, *n* 'prɔdju:s] *vt* (*object,
offspring, effect*) производи́ть* (произвести́*
perf); (*BIO, CHEM*) выраба́тывать (вы́работать
perf); (*evidence, argument*) представля́ть
(предста́вить* *perf*); (*bring or take out*)
предъявля́ть (предъяви́ть* *perf*); (*play, film*)
ста́вить* (поста́вить* *perf*) ◆ *n* (*AGR*)
проду́кция.
producer [prə'dju:sə'] *n* (*of film, play*)
режиссёр-постано́вщик, продю́сер; (*of
record*) продю́сер; (*country, company*)
производи́тель *m*.
product ['prɔdʌkt] *n* (*thing*) изде́лие; (*food,
result*) проду́кт.
production [prə'dʌkʃən] *n* (*process*)
произво́дство; (*amount produced*)
проду́кция; (*of electricity etc*) вы́работка*;
(*THEAT*) постано́вка*; **to put into** ~ (*goods*)
запуска́ть (запусти́ть* *perf*) в произво́дство.
production agreement *n* (*US*) соглаше́ние о
долево́м распределе́нии проду́кции.
production line *n* пото́чная ли́ния.
production manager *n* руководи́тель *m*
произво́дством.
productive [prə'dʌktɪv] *adj* (*also fig*)
производи́тельный* (производи́телен),
продукти́вный* (продукти́вен).
productivity [prɔdʌk'tɪvɪtɪ] *n* произ-
води́тельность *f*, продукти́вность *f*.
productivity agreement *n* (*BRIT*) догово́р о
производи́тельности труда́.
productivity bonus *n* пре́мия за высо́кую
производи́тельность труда́.
Prof. *n abbr* = **professor**.
profane [prə'feɪn] *adj* (*secular*) све́тский*;
(*language etc*) богоху́льный* (богоху́лен).
profess [prə'fɛs] *vt* (*claim*) претендова́ть (*impf*)
на +*acc*; (*express*) заявля́ть (заяви́ть* *perf*) о
+*prp*; (*REL*) испове́довать (*impf/perf*); **I do not** ~
to be an expert я не претенду́ю на роль
специали́ста.
professed [prə'fɛst] *adj* (*self-declared*)
открове́нный.
profession [prə'fɛʃən] *n* профе́ссия; **the** ~**s**
„профе́ссии с большо́й бу́квы" (*ЮР, МЕД,*

РЕЛ).

professional [prə'fɛʃənl] *adj*
профессиона́льный ♦ *n* (*doctor, lawyer,*
teacher etc) специали́ст; (*skilled person, also*
SPORT) профессиона́л; **he's a ~ man** он –
челове́к с образова́нием; **to take ~ advice**
получа́ть (получи́ть* *perf*) профессион-
а́льный сове́т.

professionalism [prə'fɛʃnəlɪzəm] *n*
профессионали́зм.

professionally [prə'fɛʃnəlɪ] *adv* (*also SPORT,*
MUS) профессиона́льно; **I only know him ~** я
зна́ю его́ то́лько по рабо́те.

professor [prə'fɛsə'] *n* (*BRIT*) профе́ссор; (*US*)
преподава́тель(ница) *m(f)*.

professorship [prə'fɛsəʃɪp] *n* профе́ссорство.

proffer ['prɔfə'] *vt* (*remark*) выска́зывать
(вы́сказать* *perf*); (*apologies*) приноси́ть*
(принести́* *perf*); (*one's hand*) протя́гивать
(протяну́ть* *perf*).

proficiency [prə'fɪʃənsɪ] *n* квалифика́ция,
уме́ние.

proficient [prə'fɪʃənt] *adj* уме́лый; **to be ~ at sth**
(*at sth mental*) быть* (*impf*) знатоко́м чем-н;
he is ~ at swimming он ма́стерски пла́вает.

profile ['prəufaɪl] *n* (*of face*) про́филь *m*; (*article*)
о́черк; **to keep a high ~** (*fig*) находи́ться*
(*impf*) в це́нтре (обще́ственного) внима́ния;
to keep a low ~ (*fig*) стара́ться (*impf*) не
выделя́ться.

profit ['prɔfɪt] *n* при́быль *f*, дохо́д ♦ *vi*: **to ~ by**
or **from** (*fig*) извлека́ть (извле́чь* *perf*) вы́году
из +*gen*; **~ and loss account** счёт при́былей и
убы́тков; **to make a ~** получа́ть (получи́ть*
perf) при́быль; **to sell (sth) at a ~** продава́ть*
(прода́ть* *perf*) (что-н) с вы́годой.

profitability [prɔfɪtə'bɪlɪtɪ] *n* при́быльность *f*.

profitable ['prɔfɪtəbl] *adj* при́быльный*
(при́былен); (*fig*) вы́годный* (вы́годен).

profit centre *n* (*COMM*) „центр получе́ния
при́были".

profiteering [prɔfɪ'tɪərɪŋ] *n* (*pej*) спекуля́ция.

profitmaking ['prɔfɪtmeɪkɪŋ] *adj* при́быльный*
(при́былен).

profit margin *n* ма́ржа при́быльности.

profit-sharing ['prɔfɪtʃɛərɪŋ] *n* уча́стие
(слу́жащих) в при́былях.

profits tax *n* (*BRIT*) нало́г с при́были.

profligate ['prɔflɪgɪt] *adj*: **~ (with)**
расточи́тельный* (расточи́телен) (в +*prp*).

pro forma ['prəu'fɔːmə] *adj*: **~ ~ invoice**
предвари́тельный счёт-факту́ра.

profound [prə'faund] *adj* глубо́кий* (глубо́к).

profuse [prə'fjuːs] *adj* оби́льный* (оби́лен).

profusely [prə'fjuːslɪ] *adv* оби́льно; (*apologize*)
горячо́.

profusion [prə'fjuːʒən] *n* оби́льность *f*.

progeny ['prɔdʒɪnɪ] *n* пото́мство.

prognoses [prɔg'nəusiːz] *npl of* **prognosis**.

prognosis [prɔg'nəusis] (*pl* **prognoses**) *n*
прогно́з.

program ['prəugræm] *n* (*COMPUT*) програ́мма ♦
vt (*COMPUT*) программи́ровать (запрограм-
ми́ровать* *perf*).

programme ['prəugræm] (*US* **program**) *n*
програ́мма ♦ *vt* программи́ровать
(запрограмми́ровать* *perf*).

programmer ['prəugræmə'] *n* (*COMPUT*)
программи́ст(ка*).

programming ['prəugræmɪŋ] (*US* **programing**)
n (*COMPUT*) программи́рование.

programming language *n* (*COMPUT*) язы́к*
программи́рования.

progress [*n* 'prəugrɛs, *vi* prə'grɛs] *n* (*advances,*
changes) прогре́сс; (*development*) разви́тие
♦ *vi* прогресси́ровать (*impf*); (*move up in rank*)
продвига́ться (продви́нуться *perf*) (по
слу́жбе); (*continue*) продолжа́ться
(продо́лжиться* *perf*); **the meeting/match is in**
~ сейча́с идёт собра́ние/матч; **to make ~**
де́лать (сде́лать *perf*) успе́хи; **as the match**
~ed по хо́ду ма́тча.

progression [prə'grɛʃən] *n* (*gradual*
development) продвиже́ние; (*series*) череда́;
(*MATH*) прогре́ссия.

progressive [prə'grɛsɪv] *adj* прогресси́вный*
(прогресси́вен); (*gradual*) постепе́нный.

progressively [prə'grɛsɪvlɪ] *adv*: **the work**
became ~ harder рабо́та станови́лась всё
трудне́е.

progress report *n* (*MED*) протоко́л о хо́де
боле́зни; (*ADMIN*) докла́д о хо́де дел.

prohibit [prə'hɪbɪt] *vt* запреща́ть (запрети́ть*
perf); **to ~ sb from doing** запреща́ть
(запрети́ть* *perf*) кому́-н +*infin*; **"smoking**
~ed" „кури́ть воспреща́ется".

prohibition [prəuɪ'bɪʃən] *n* запреще́ние,
запре́т; **P~** сухо́й зако́н.

prohibitive [prə'hɪbɪtɪv] *adj* (*price etc*)
недосту́пный* (недосту́пен).

project [*n* 'prɔdʒɛkt, *vb* prə'dʒɛkt] *n* (*large-scale*
plan, scheme) прое́кт; (*SCOL*) рабо́та ♦ *vt*
(*plan, estimate*) проекти́ровать (*impf*); (*film*)
демонстри́ровать (продемонстри́ровать
perf); (*light, picture*) проеци́ровать
(спроеци́ровать *perf*) ♦ *vi* (*stick out*)
выступа́ть (вы́ступить* *perf*).

projectile [prə'dʒɛktaɪl] *n* снаря́д.

projection [prə'dʒɛkʃən] *n* (*estimate*)
перспекти́вная оце́нка*; (*overhang*) вы́ступ;
(*CINEMA*) прое́кция.

projectionist [prə'dʒɛkʃənɪst] *n* (*CINEMA*)
киномеха́ник.

projection room *n* бу́дка киномеха́ника,
проекцио́нная каби́на.

projector [prə'dʒɛktə'] *n* (*CINEMA*)

---

* marks translations which have irregular inflections. The Russian-English side of the dictionary gives inflectional information.

кинопроéктор; (*also*: **slide** ~) проéктор.
proletarian [prəulɪ'tɛərɪən] *adj* пролетáрский*.
proletariat [prəulɪ'tɛərɪət] *n*: **the** ~
пролетариáт.
pro-life [prəu'laɪf] *adj выступáющий прóтив абóртов.*
proliferate [prə'lɪfəreɪt] *vi* распространя́ться
(распространи́ться *perf*).
proliferation [prəlɪfə'reɪʃən] *n* рас-
пространéние.
prolific [prə'lɪfɪk] *adj* плодови́тый (плодови́т).
prologue ['prəulɒg] (*US* **prolog**) *n* пролоѓ.
prolong [prə'lɒŋ] *vt* продлевáть (продли́ть
perf).
prom [prɒm] *n abbr* = **promenade**; (*MUS*) =
promenade concert; (*US*: *college ball*)
студéнческий* бал.
promenade [prɒmə'nɑːd] *n* променáд, мéсто*
для прогýлок.
promenade concert *n* (*BRIT*) променáдный
концéрт (*на котóром часть пýблики
стои́т*).
promenade deck *n* вéрхняя пáлуба.
prominence ['prɒmɪnəns] *n* (*of person*) ви́дное
положéние; (*of issue*) ви́дное мéсто.
prominent ['prɒmɪnənt] *adj* (*important, very
noticeable*) выдаю́щийся*; **he is** ~ **in the field
of** ... он извéстен в óбласти *+gen* ....
prominently ['prɒmɪnəntlɪ] *adv* замéтно; **he
figured** ~ **in the case** он игрáл замéтную
роль в э́том дéле.
promiscuity [prɒmɪs'kjuːɪtɪ] *n* распýщенность
f.
promiscuous [prə'mɪskjuəs] *adj* распýщенный.
promise ['prɒmɪs] *n* (*vow*) обещáние; (*talent*)
потенциáл; (*hope*) надéжда ◆ *vi* (*vow*)
давáть* (дать* *perf*) обещáние ◆ *vt*: **to** ~ **sb
sth,** ~ **sth to sb** обещáть (пообещáть *perf*)
что-н комý-н; **a young man of** ~ мно́го-
обещáющий* молодóй человéк*; **she shows**
~ онá подаёт надéжды; **to** ~ **(sb) to do/that**
обещáть (пообещáть *perf*) (комý-н) *+infin*/
что; **to** ~ **well** подавáть* (*impf*) больши́е
надéжды.
promising ['prɒmɪsɪŋ] *adj* многообещáющий*.
promissory note ['prɒmɪsərɪ-] *n* (простóй)
вéксель* *m*.
promontory ['prɒməntrɪ] *n* мыс*.
promote [prə'məut] *vt* (*employee*) повышáть
(повы́сить* *perf*) (в дóлжности); (*product,
pop star*) реклами́ровать (*impf*/*perf*); (*ideas*)
поддéрживать (поддержáть* *perf*); (*venture,
event*) содéйствовать (*impf*/*perf*) *+dat*; **the team
was** ~**d to the second division** (*BRIT*) комáнда
былá переведенá во вторýю ли́гу.
promoter [prə'məutə*] *n* (*of event*) агéнт*; (*of
cause, idea*) пропаганди́ст(ка*).
promotion [prə'məuʃən] *n* (*at work*)
повышéние (в дóлжности); (*of product,
event, idea*) реклами́рование; (*publicity
campaign*) реклáма.

prompt [prɒmpt] *adj* незамедли́тельный*
(незамедли́телен) ◆ *n* (*COMPUT*)
приглашéние ◆ *vt* (*cause*) побуждáть
(побуди́ть* *perf*); (*sb talking*) подскáзывать
(подсказáть* *perf*); (*THEAT*) суфли́ровать
(*impf*) *+dat* ◆ *adv*: **at 8 o'clock** ~ рóвно в 8
часóв; **they're very** ~ они́ óчень
пунктуáльны; **he was** ~ **to accept** он
немéдленно согласи́лся; **to** ~ **sb to do**
побуждáть (побуди́ть* *perf*) когó-н *+infin*.
prompter ['prɒmptə*] *n* (*THEAT*) суфлёр.
promptly ['prɒmptlɪ] *adv* (*immediately*)
незамедли́тельно; (*exactly*) тóчно.
promptness ['prɒmptnɪs] *n* незамедли́тель-
ность *f*.
promulgate ['prɒmʌlgeɪt] *vt* обнарóдовать
(*impf*).
prone [prəun] *adj*: **to lie** ~ лежáть (*impf*)
ничкóм; ~ **to** (*inclined to*) склóнный*
(склóнен) к *+dat*; **I am** ~ **to illness** у меня́
слáбое здорóвье; **he is** ~ **to colds** он
подвéржен простýдам; **she is** ~ **to burst into
tears if you shout at her** éсли на неё кричáть,
онá мóжет легкó разрыдáться.
prong [prɒŋ] *n* (*of fork*) зубéц*.
pronoun ['prəunaun] *n* местоимéние.
pronounce [prə'nauns] *vt* (*word*) произноси́ть*
(произнести́* *perf*); (*declaration, verdict*)
объявля́ть (объяви́ть* *perf*); (*opinion*)
выскáзывать (вы́сказать* *perf*) ◆ *vi*: **to** ~
(up)on выскáзываться (вы́сказаться* *perf*)
относи́тельно *+gen*; **they** ~**d him unfit to drive**
егó объяви́ли непригóдным к вождéнию
автомоби́ля.
pronounced [prə'naunst] *adj* отчётливый
(отчётлив).
pronouncement [prə'naunsmənt] *n*
объявлéние.
pronto ['prɒntəu] *adv* (*inf*) жи́во.
pronunciation [prənʌnsɪ'eɪʃən] *n* (*of word*)
произношéние; (*by person*) вы́говор.
proof [pruːf] *n* (*evidence*) доказáтельство;
(*TYP*) корректýра; (*test, PHOT*) прóбный
отпечáток*; (*of alcohol*) крéпость *f* ◆ *vt* (*BRIT*:
tent, anorak) дéлать (сдéлать *perf*)
водонепроница́емым ◆ *adj*: **this material is** ~
against water э́тот материáл не пропускáет
вóду; **this vodka is 70%** ~ э́то – семи́десяти-
процéнтная вóдка.
proofreader ['pruːfriːdə*] *n* корр éктор.
prop [prɒp] *n* (*support*) подпóрка*; (*fig*: *person*)
опóра ◆ *vt* (*also*: ~ **up**) подпирáть
(подпер éть* *perf*); (*lean*): **to** ~ **sth against**
прислоня́ть (прислони́ть* *perf*) что-н к *+dat*;
~**s** *npl* (*THEAT*) реквизи́т *msg*.
Prop. *abbr* (*COMM*) = **proprietor**.
propaganda [prɒpə'gændə] *n* пропагáнда.
propagate ['prɒpəgeɪt] *vt* (*idea, information*)
распространя́ть (распространи́ть *perf*);
(*plant*) разводи́ть* (развести́* *perf*).
propagation ◆ [prɒpə'geɪʃən] *n* (*see vt*)

распространение; разведение.

propel [prə'pɛl] *vt* (*vehicle, machine*) приводить* (привести* *perf*) в движение; (*fig: person*) толкать (толкнуть *perf*).

propeller [prə'pɛlə*] *n* пропеллер.

propelling pencil [prə'pɛlɪŋ-] *n* (*BRIT*) автоматический* карандаш*.

propensity [prə'pɛnsɪtɪ] *n*: **a ~ for/to do** расположенность *f* к +*dat*/+*infin*.

proper ['prɔpə*] *adj* (*real*) настоящий*; (*correct*) подходящий*, надлежащий*; (*socially acceptable*) приличный* (приличен); **he looked a ~ fool** (*inf*) он выглядел настоящим дураком; **the village ~** собственно деревня*; **to go through the ~ channels** проходить* (пройти* *perf*) через надлежащие каналы.

properly ['prɔpəlɪ] *adv* (*eat, study*) как следует; (*behave*) прилично, должным образом.

proper noun *n* имя* *nt* собственное.

property ['prɔpətɪ] *n* (*possessions*) собственность *f*; (*building and its land*) недвижимость *f*; (*quality*) свойство ♦ *cpd*: **~ developer** застройщик; **it's their ~** это их собственность; **~ market** рынок недвижимости; **~ tax** налог на собственности.

prophecy ['prɔfɪsɪ] *n* пророчество.

prophesy ['prɔfɪsaɪ] *vti* пророчить (напророчить *perf*).

prophet ['prɔfɪt] *n* пророк.

prophetic [prə'fɛtɪk] *adj* пророческий*.

proportion [prə'pɔːʃən] *n* (*part*) часть *f*, доля; (*ratio*) пропорция, соотношение; **his head is in perfect ~ to his body** голова его абсолютно пропорциональна его телу; **to be out of all ~ to** никак не соответствовать (*impf*) +*dat*; **to get sth in(to) ~** соизмерять (соизмерить *perf*) что-н; **to get sth out of ~** не соизмерять (соизмерить *perf*) что-н; **a sense of ~** чувство меры.

proportional [prə'pɔːʃənl] *adj*: **~ (to)** пропорциональный* (пропорционален) (+*dat*).

proportional representation *n* (*POL*) пропорциональное представительство.

proportionate [prə'pɔːʃənɪt] *adj*: **~ (to)** пропорциональный* (пропорционален) (+*dat*).

proposal [prə'pəuzl] *n* предложение.

propose [prə'pəuz] *vt* (*plan, toast*) предлагать (предложить* *perf*); (*motion*) выдвигать (выдвинуть *perf*) ♦ *vi* (*offer marriage*): **to ~ (to sb)** делать (сделать *perf*) предложение (кому-н); **to ~ sth/to do** *or* **doing** (*have in mind*) предполагать (*impf*) что-н/+*infin*.

proposer [prə'pəuzə*] *n* (*BRIT*): **the ~ of the motion** вносящий(-ая) *m(f)* *adj* предложение.

proposition [prɔpə'zɪʃən] *n* (*statement*)

утверждение; (*offer*) предложение; **to make sb a ~** делать (сделать *perf*) предложение кому-н.

propound [prə'paund] *vt* (*idea, argument*) выдвигать (выдвинуть *perf*).

proprietary [prə'praɪətərɪ] *adj* (*medicine*) патентованный; (*brand*) фирменный; (*behaviour*) собственнический*.

proprietor [prə'praɪətə*] *n* (*of hotel, shop, newspaper etc*) владелец(-лица).

propriety [prə'praɪətɪ] *n* пристойность *f*.

propulsion [prə'pʌlʃən] *n* движущая сила.

pro rata [prəu'rɑːtə] *adv* пропорционально ♦ *adj* пропорциональный* (пропорционален); **on a ~ ~ basis** на пропорциональной основе.

prosaic [prəu'zeɪk] *adj* (*person*) прозаичный* (прозаичен); (*piece of writing*) прозаический*.

Pros. Atty. *abbr* (*US*) = **prosecuting attorney**.

proscribe [prə'skraɪb] *vt* воспрещать (воспретить* *perf*).

prose [prəuz] *n* (*not poetry*) проза; (*SCOL*) отрывок* для перевода.

prosecute ['prɔsɪkjuːt] *vt* (*case*) вести* (*impf*); **to ~ sb** подавать* (подать* *perf*) на кого-н в суд.

prosecuting attorney ['prɔsɪkjuːtɪŋ-] *n* (*US*) обвинитель *m*.

prosecution [prɔsɪ'kjuːʃən] *n* (*LAW: action*) судебное преследование; (*: accusing side*) обвинение.

prosecutor ['prɔsɪkjuːtə*] *n* обвинитель *m*; (*also: public ~*) прокурор.

prospect ['prɔspɛkt] *n* перспектива ♦ *vi*: **to ~ for** разведывать (разведать *perf*) на +*acc*; **~s** *npl* (*for work etc*) перспективы *fpl*; **we are faced with the ~ of leaving** нас ожидает перспектива отъезда; **there's every ~ of an early victory** есть перспектива скорой победы.

prospecting ['prɔspɛktɪŋ] *n* разведка, изыскание.

prospective [prə'spɛktɪv] *adj* (*son-in-law*) будущий*; (*customer, candidate*) возможный.

prospectus [prə'spɛktəs] *n* проспект.

prosper ['prɔspə*] *vi* преуспевать (преуспеть *perf*).

prosperity [prɔ'spɛrɪtɪ] *n* преуспевание.

prosperous ['prɔspərəs] *adj* преуспевающий.

prostate ['prɔsteɪt] *n* (*also: ~ gland*) предстательная железа*.

prostitute ['prɔstɪtjuːt] *n* проститутка*.

prostitution [prɔstɪ'tjuːʃən] *n* проституция.

prostrate [*vt* prɔ'streɪt, *adj* 'prɔstreɪt] *vt*: **to ~ o.s. before** падать (упасть* *perf*) ниц перед +*instr* ♦ *adj* (*fig*) убитый; **to lie ~** лежать (*impf*)

---

* marks translations which have irregular inflections. The Russian-English side of the dictionary gives inflectional information.

ничко́м.

protagonist [prə'tægənɪst] *n* (*supporter*)
сторо́нник(-ица); (*leading participant*)
де́ятель *m*; (*THEAT*) (гла́вный) геро́й.

protect [prə'tɛkt] *vt* защища́ть (защити́ть*
perf).

protection [prə'tɛkʃən] *n* защи́та; **to be under
sb's ~** находи́ться* (*impf*) под защи́той
кого́-н.

protectionism [prə'tɛkʃənɪzəm] *n*
протекциони́зм.

protection racket *n* ра́кет.

protective [prə'tɛktɪv] *adj* (*clothing, layer,
gesture etc*) защи́тный; (*person*)
покрови́тельственный; **~ custody** (*LAW*)
опе́ка.

protector [prə'tɛktə'] *n* (*person*)
защи́тник(-ница); (*device*) защи́тное
устро́йство.

protégé ['prəutɛʒeɪ] *n* протеже́ *m ind*.

protégée ['prəutɛʒeɪ] *n* протеже́ *f ind*.

protein ['prəuti:n] *n* бело́к*, протеи́н.

pro tem [prəu'tɛm] *adv abbr = pro tempore*; (*for
the time being*) вре́менно.

protest [*n* 'prəutɛst, *vb* prə'tɛst] *n* проте́ст ♦ *vi*: **to
~ about/against** протестова́ть (*impf*) по
по́воду +*gen*/про́тив +*gen* ♦ *vt* (*insist*): **to ~
that** заявля́ть (заяви́ть* *perf*), что.

Protestant ['prɔtɪstənt] *n* протеста́нт(ка*) ♦ *adj*
протеста́нтский*.

protester [prə'tɛstə'] *n* протесту́ющий*(-ая)
m(f) adj.

protest march *n* марш проте́ста.

protestor [prə'tɛstə'] *n* = **protester**.

protocol ['prəutəkɔl] *n* протоко́л.

prototype ['prəutətaɪp] *n* прототи́п.

protracted [prə'træktɪd] *adj* затяну́вшийся.

protractor [prə'træktə'] *n* (*GEOM*) транспорти́р.

protrude [prə'tru:d] *vi* выдава́ться* (*impf*).

protuberance [prə'tju:bərəns] *n* вы́пуклость *f*.

proud [praud] *adj*: **~ (of)** го́рдый* (горд)
(+*instr*); **I am ~ to know him** я горжу́сь
знако́мством с ним *or* тем, что я знако́м с
ним; **to do sb ~** (*inf*) принима́ть (приня́ть*
perf) кого́-н на сла́ву; **to do o.s. ~** (*inf*) име́ть
(*impf*) основа́ния горди́ться.

proudly ['praudlɪ] *adv* (*say, smile*) го́рдо;
(*show*) с го́рдостью.

prove [pru:v] *vt* дока́зывать (доказа́ть* *perf*) ♦
vi: **to ~ (to be)** оказа́ться (*impf/perf*) +*instr*; **to ~
o.s.** проявля́ть (прояви́ть* *perf*) себя́; **he was
~d right in the end** в конце́ (концо́в) бы́ло
дока́зано, что он прав.

Provençal [prɔvɔn'sɑ:l] *adj* прованса́льский.

Provence [prɔ'vɑ:s] *n* Прова́нс.

proverb ['prɔvə:b] *n* посло́вица.

proverbial [prə'və:bɪəl] *adj* знамени́тый.

provide [prə'vaɪd] *vt* обеспе́чивать
(обеспе́чить *perf*) +*instr*; **to ~ sb with sth**
обеспе́чивать (обеспе́чить *perf*) кого́-н
чем-н; **to be ~d with** (*person*) быть* (*impf*)

обеспе́ченным(-ой); (*thing*) быть* (*impf*)
снабжённым(-ой).

▶ **provide for** *vt fus* (*person*) обеспе́чивать
(обеспе́чить *perf*); (*future event*)
предусма́тривать (предусмотре́ть* *perf*);
(*emergency*) забо́титься (позабо́титься *perf*)
о +*prp*.

provided (that) [prə'vaɪdɪd-] *conj* при усло́вии,
что.

Providence ['prɔvɪdəns] *n* провиде́ние.

providing [prə'vaɪdɪŋ] *conj* = **provided (that)**.

province ['prɔvɪns] *n* (*of country*) о́бласть *f*; (*of
person*) о́бласть *f*; **the ~s** *npl*: **in the ~s**
(*regions*) в провинции.

provincial [prə'vɪnʃəl] *adj* провинциа́льный*.

provision [prə'vɪʒən] *n* (*supplying*) обеспе́-
чение; (*supply*) снабже́ние; (*stipulation*)
усло́вие; (*of contract, agreement*) положе́ние;
~s *npl* (*food*) прови́зия *fsg*; **to make ~s for**
забо́титься (позабо́титься *perf*) о +*prp*;
there's no ~ for this in the contract в
контра́кте э́то не предусмо́трено.

provisional [prə'vɪʒənl] *adj* вре́менный
♦ *n*: **P~** (*IRISH: POL*) член Ирла́ндской
Республика́нской А́рмии.

provisional licence *n* (*BRIT: AUT*)
предвари́тельные води́тельские права́ *ntpl*.

provisionally [prə'vɪʒnəlɪ] *adv* вре́менно.

proviso [prə'vaɪzəu] *n* усло́вие; **with the ~ that
... с** усло́вием, что ....

Provo ['prɔvəu] *n abbr* (*IRISH: POL: inf*) =
Provisional.

provocation [prɔvə'keɪʃən] *n* провока́ция;
under ~ бу́дучи спровоци́рован.

provocative [prə'vɔkətɪv] *adj* (*remark, article,
gesture*) провокацио́нный*
(провокацио́нен), вызыва́ющий*
(вызыва́ющ); (*intellectually or sexually
stimulating*) возбужда́ющий*.

provoke [prə'vəuk] *vt* (*person*) задира́ться
(*impf*) к +*dat*; (*fight, argument etc*)
провоци́ровать (спровоци́ровать *perf*); **to ~
sb to sth/to do** *or* **into doing** провоци́ровать
(спровоци́ровать *perf*) кого́-н на что-н/+*infin*.

provost ['prɔvəst] *n* (*BRIT: of university*) ре́ктор;
(*SCOTTISH: POL*) мэр.

prow [prau] *n* (*NAUT*) нос*.

prowess ['prauɪs] *n* мастерство́; **his ~ as a
footballer** его́ мастерство́ футболи́ста.

prowl [praul] *vi* (*also*: **~ about**, **~ around**)
кра́сться* (*impf*) ♦ *n*: **to be on the ~ for**
охо́титься* (*impf*) на +*acc*.

prowler ['praulə'] *n* подозри́тельный тип.

proximity [prɔk'sɪmɪtɪ] *n* бли́зость *f*.

proxy ['prɔksɪ] *n*: **by ~** по дове́ренности.

PRP *abbr* (= *performance related pay*) *опла́та по
результа́там рабо́ты*.

prude [pru:d] *n* ханжа́* *m/f*.

prudence ['pru:dns] *n* благоразу́мие.

prudent ['pru:dnt] *adj* благоразу́мный*
(благоразу́мен).

prudish ['pru:dɪʃ] *adj* ха́нжеский.

prune [pru:n] *n* черносли́в* *m no pl* ◆ *vt* подреза́ть (подре́зать* *perf*).

pry [praɪ] *vi*: **to ~ (into)** сова́ть* (су́нуть *perf*) нос (в +*acc*).

PS *abbr* = **postscript**.

psalm [sɑ:m] *n* псало́м*.

PSAT *n abbr* (*US*) = **Preliminary Scholastic Aptitude Test.**

PSBR *n abbr* (*BRIT: ECON*: = **public sector borrowing requirement**) потре́бность госуда́рственного се́ктора в заёмных сре́дствах.

pseud [sju:d] (*BRIT: inf*) *n* (*intellectually*) псевдоинтеллектуа́л(ка*); (*socially*) позёр(ша).

pseudo- ['sju:dəu] *prefix* псе́вдо-.

pseudonym ['sju:dənɪm] *n* псевдони́м.

PST *abbr* (*US*) = **Pacific Standard Time.**

PSV *n abbr* (*BRIT*) = **public-service vehicle.**

psyche ['saɪkɪ] *n* пси́хика.

psychedelic [saɪkə'dɛlɪk] *adj* психодели́ческий.

psychiatric [saɪkɪ'ætrɪk] *adj* психиатри́ческий*.

psychiatrist [saɪ'kaɪətrɪst] *n* психиа́тр.

psychiatry [saɪ'kaɪətrɪ] *n* психиатри́я.

psychic ['saɪkɪk] *adj* (*person: also: ~al*) яснови́дящий*; (*of the mind*) психи́ческий*.

psycho ['saɪkəu] *n* (*inf*) псих.

psychoanalyse [saɪkəu'ænəlaɪz] *vt* подверга́ть (подве́ргнуть *perf*) психоана́лизу.

psychoanalysis [saɪkəuə'nælɪsɪs] *n* психоана́лиз.

psychoanalyst [saɪkəu'ænəlɪst] *n* психоанали́тик.

psychological [saɪkə'lɔdʒɪkl] *adj* психологи́ческий*.

psychologist [saɪ'kɔlədʒɪst] *n* психо́лог.

psychology [saɪ'kɔlədʒɪ] *n* психоло́гия.

psychopath ['saɪkəupæθ] *n* психопа́т(ка*).

psychoses [saɪ'kəusi:z] *npl of* **psychosis**.

psychosis [saɪ'kəusɪs] (*pl* **psychoses**) *n* психо́з.

psychosomatic ['saɪkəusə'mætɪk] *adj* психосомати́ческий.

psychotherapy [saɪkəu'θɛrəpɪ] *n* психотерапи́я.

psychotic [saɪ'kɔtɪk] *adj* психи́чески больно́й.

PT *n abbr* (*BRIT: SCOL*: = *physical training*) физкульту́ра= *физическая культу́ра*.

Pt *abbr* (*in place names*) = **Point.**

pt *abbr* = **pint**, **point.**

PTA *n abbr* (= *Parent-Teacher Association*) о́бщество по объедине́нию уси́лий шко́лы и роди́телей.

Pte *abbr* (*BRIT: MIL*) = **private.**

PTO *abbr* (= *please turn over*) смотри́ на оборо́те.

PTV *n abbr* (*US*: = *pay television*) *комме́рческое телеви́дение*; (= *public television*) *некомме́рческое (общеобразова́тельное) телеви́дение*.

pub [pʌb] *n* = **public house.**

pub crawl *n* (*inf*) похо́д по па́бам *or* ба́рам.

puberty ['pju:bətɪ] *n* полова́я зре́лость *f*.

pubic ['pju:bɪk] *adj* лобко́вый.

public ['pʌblɪk] *adj* обще́ственный; (*statement, action etc*) публи́чный ◆ *n*: **the ~** (*all people of country*) наро́д; (*particular set of people*) пу́блика; **the general ~** широ́кая обще́ственность; **this is ~ knowledge** э́то широко́ изве́стно; **to make ~** предава́ть* (преда́ть* *perf*) гла́сности; **to go ~** (*COMM*) выпуска́ть (вы́пустить* *perf*) а́кции на прода́жу че́рез би́ржу; **in ~** публи́чно.

public-address system [pʌblɪkə'drɛs-] *n* (ра́дио)трансля́ция.

publican ['pʌblɪkən] *n* содержа́тель(ница) *m(f)* пивно́го ба́ра *or* па́ба.

publication [pʌblɪ'keɪʃən] *n* публика́ция, изда́ние.

public company *n* (*COMM*) публи́чная компа́ния, компа́ния откры́того ти́па.

public convenience *n* (*BRIT*) обще́ственный туале́т.

public holiday *n* общенаро́дный пра́здник.

public house *n* (*BRIT*) паб, пивна́я *f adj*, пивно́й бар.

publicity [pʌb'lɪsɪtɪ] *n* (*information*) рекла́ма, па́блисити *nt ind*; (*attention*) шуми́ха.

publicize ['pʌblɪsaɪz] *vt* (*fact, event*) предава́ть* (преда́ть* *perf*) гла́сности.

public limited company *n* (*COMM*) публи́чная компа́ния с ограни́ченной отве́тственностью.

publicly ['pʌblɪklɪ] *adv* публи́чно; (*COMM*): **~ owned** госуда́рственный.

public opinion *n* обще́ственное мне́ние.

public ownership *n*: **to be taken into ~ ~** (*COMM*) переходи́ть* (перейти́* *perf*) в госуда́рственную *or* общенаро́дную со́бственность.

Public Prosecutor *n* ≈ генера́льный поркуро́р.

public relations *npl* свя́зи *fpl* с обще́ственностью.

public relations officer *n* сотру́дник отде́ла свя́зей с обще́ственностью.

public school *n* (*BRIT*) ча́стная шко́ла; (*US*) госуда́рственная шко́ла.

public sector *n*: **the ~ ~** госуда́рственный се́ктор.

public-service vehicle [pʌblɪk'sə:vɪs-] *n* (*BRIT*) обще́ственное тра́нспортное сре́дство.

public-spirited [pʌblɪk'spɪrɪtɪd] *adj* забо́тящийся об обще́ственных интере́сах.

public transport *n* обще́ственный тра́нспорт.

---

* marks translations which have irregular inflections. The Russian-English side of the dictionary gives inflectional information.

public utility n компа́ния, обеспе́чивающая
како́й-либо вид коммуна́льных услу́г.
public works npl обще́ственные сооруже́ния
ntpl.
publish ['pʌblɪʃ] vt (book, magazine) издава́ть*
(изда́ть* perf); (letter, article) публикова́ть
(опубликова́ть perf).
publisher ['pʌblɪʃə'] n (person) изда́тель m;
(company) изда́тельство.
publishing ['pʌblɪʃɪŋ] n (profession)
изда́тельское де́ло; (of a book) изда́ние,
публика́ция.
publishing company n изда́тельство.
puce [pjuːs] adj краснова́то-кори́чневый.
puck [pʌk] n (ICE HOCKEY) ша́йба.
pucker ['pʌkə'] vt мо́рщить (намо́рщить or
смо́рщить perf).
pudding ['pudɪŋ] n пу́динг; (BRIT: dessert)
сла́дкое nt adj; **rice** ~ ри́совый пу́динг; **black**
~, (US) **blood** ~ кровяна́я колбаса́*.
puddle ['pʌdl] n лу́жа.
puerile ['pjuəraɪl] adj ребя́ческий*.
Puerto Rico ['pwɔːtəu'riːkəu] n Пуэ́рто-Ри́ко f
ind.
puff [pʌf] n (of cigarette, pipe) затя́жка*; (gasp)
пыхте́ние; (of wind) дунове́ние; (of smoke)
клуб ◆ vi (breathe loudly) пыхте́ть* (impf) ◆ vt:
to ~ **one's pipe** затя́гиваться (затяну́ться*
perf)
▸ **puff out** vt (chest, cheeks) раздува́ть
(разду́ть perf); (smoke) выпуска́ть
(вы́пустить* perf).
puffed [pʌft] adj (inf: out of breath)
запыха́вшийся.
puffin ['pʌfɪn] n (ZOOL) ту́пик.
puff pastry (US **puff paste**) n слоёное те́сто.
puffy ['pʌfɪ] adj опу́хший*.
pugnacious [pʌg'neɪʃəs] adj задири́стый
(задири́ст).
pull [pul] n (of moon, magnet, the sea etc)
притяже́ние; (fig) тя́га ◆ vt тяну́ть*
(потяну́ть* perf); (trigger) нажима́ть (нажа́ть
perf) на +acc; (close: curtains, blind)
задёргивать (задёрнуть perf); (inf: people)
привлека́ть (привле́чь* perf); (pint of beer)
нака́чивать (накача́ть perf) ◆ vi (tug) тяну́ть*
(impf); **to give sth a** ~ (tug) тяну́ть* (потяну́ть*
perf); **to** ~ **a face** кро́ить (скро́ить perf)
грима́су; **to** ~ **to pieces** разрыва́ть
(разорва́ть* perf) на ча́сти; **to** ~ **one's**
punches дра́ться* (impf) вполси́лы; **he doesn't**
~ **his punches** (fig) он дерётся всерьёз; **to** ~
one's weight выполня́ть (вы́полнить perf)
свою́ часть рабо́ты; **to** ~ **o.s. together** взять*
(perf) себя́ в ру́ки; **to** ~ **sb's leg** (fig)
разы́грывать (разыгра́ть perf) кого́-н; **to** ~
strings (for sb) пуска́ть (пусти́ть* perf) в ход
все свя́зи (для кого́-н)
▸ **pull about** vt (BRIT: object, person) трепа́ть
(impf)
▸ **pull apart** vt разрыва́ть (разорва́ть* perf) на

куски́
▸ **pull back** vi отступа́ть (отступи́ть* perf)
▸ **pull down** vt (building) сноси́ть* (снести́*
perf); (tree) сруба́ть (сруби́ть* perf)
▸ **pull in** vt (money) загреба́ть (загрести́* perf);
(crowds, people) привлека́ть (привле́чь*
perf); (subj: police: suspect) сцапать (perf)
▸ **pull into** vt (AUT) подъезжа́ть (подъе́хать*
perf) к +dat
▸ **pull off** vt (clothes etc) стя́гивать (стяну́ть*
perf); (fig): **he managed to** ~ **it off** ему́ удало́сь
ски́нуть э́то с себя́
▸ **pull out** vt (extract) выта́скивать (вы́тащить
perf) ◆ vi: **to** ~ **out (from)** (AUT: from kerb)
отъезжа́ть (отъе́хать* perf) (от +gen); (RAIL)
отходи́ть* (отойти́* perf) (от +gen);
(withdraw): **to** ~ **out (of)** выходи́ть* (вы́йти*
perf) (из +gen)
▸ **pull over** vi (AUT) подъезжа́ть (подъе́хать*
perf) к кра́ю доро́ги
▸ **pull round** vi (unconscious person)
приходи́ть* (прийти́* perf) в себя́; (sick
person) поправля́ться (попра́виться* perf)
▸ **pull through** vi (MED) выкара́бкиваться
(вы́карабкаться perf)
▸ **pull up** vi (stop) остана́вливаться
(останови́ться* perf) ◆ vt (object, clothing)
подтя́гивать (подтяну́ть* perf); (plant)
вырыва́ть (вы́рвать* perf) (с ко́рнем); (chair)
пододвига́ть (пододви́нуть* perf)
pullback ['pulbæk] n отступле́ние.
pulley ['pulɪ] n шкив*.
pull-out ['pulaut] n (of forces etc) отхо́д ◆ cpd
(pages) вкладно́й; ~ **magazine** журна́л с
вкла́дками.
pullover ['puləuvə'] n пуло́вер.
pulp [pʌlp] n (of fruit) мя́коть f; (for paper)
бума́жная ма́сса; (pej: magazines, fiction)
чти́во; **to reduce sth to a** ~ превраща́ть
(преврати́ть* perf) что-н в мя́гкую ма́ссу or
пу́льпу.
pulpit ['pulpɪt] n ка́федра.
pulsate [pʌl'seɪt] vi пульси́ровать (impf);
(music) вибри́ровать (impf).
pulse [pʌls] n (ANAT) пульс; (of blood)
пульси́рование; (of heart) бие́ние; (rhythm)
такт ◆ vi пульси́ровать* (impf); ~s npl (BOT)
семена́ бобо́вых, употребля́емые в пи́щу;
(CULIN) бобо́вые pl adj; **to take** or **feel sb's** ~
нащу́пывать (нащу́пать perf) чей-н пульс.
pulverize ['pʌlvəraɪz] vt размельча́ть
(размельчи́ть perf); (fig: destroy)
изничтожа́ть (изничто́жить perf).
puma ['pjuːmə] n пу́ма.
pumice ['pʌmɪs] n (also: ~ **stone**) пе́мза.
pummel ['pʌml] vt колоти́ть* (impf).
pump [pʌmp] n насо́с; (also: **petrol** ~)
бензоколо́нка*; (shoe) паруси́новая ту́фля*
◆ vt кача́ть (impf); (extract: oil, water, gas)
выка́чивать (вы́качать perf); **to** ~ **sb for**
information выка́чивать (impf) из кого́-н

информа́цию
▶ **pump up** *vt* нака́чивать (накача́ть *perf*).
pumpkin ['pʌmpkɪn] *n* ты́ква.
pun [pʌn] *n* каламбу́р.
punch [pʌntʃ] *n* (*blow*) уда́р; (*fig*: *force*) заря́д; (*for making holes*) дыроко́л; (*drink*) пунш ◆ *vt* (*make a hole in*) пробива́ть (проби́ть* *perf*); (*hit*): **to ~ sb/sth** ударя́ть (уда́рить *perf*) кого́-н/что-н кулако́м; **to ~ a hole (in)** пробива́ть (проби́ть* *perf*) отве́рстие (в +*prp*)
▶ **punch in** *vi* (*US*) отмеча́ться (отме́титься* *perf*) (*приходя́ на рабо́ту*)
▶ **punch out** *vi* (*US*) отмеча́ться (отме́титься* *perf*) (*уходя́ с рабо́ты*).
Punch and Judy show *n* Панч и Джу́ди (*ку́кольное представле́ние*).
punch-drunk ['pʌntʃdrʌŋk] (*BRIT*) *adj* (*confused*) со сму́тным; **~ boxer** боксёр с травматологи́ческой энцефалопа́тией.
punch(ed) card *n* (*COMPUT*) перфока́рта.
punch line *n* изю́минка.
punch-up ['pʌntʃʌp] *n* (*BRIT*: *inf*) потасо́вка*.
punctual ['pʌŋktjuəl] *adj* пунктуа́льный* (пунктуа́лен).
punctuality [pʌŋktju'ælɪtɪ] *n* пунктуа́льность *f*.
punctually ['pʌŋktjuəlɪ] *adv* (*arrive*, *leave*, *deliver*) пунктуа́льно; **the film will start ~ at 6** фильм начнётся ро́вно в 6 часо́в.
punctuation [pʌŋktju'eɪʃən] *n* пунктуа́ция.
punctuation mark *n* знак препина́ния.
puncture ['pʌŋktʃər] *n* (*AUT*) проко́л ◆ *vt* прока́лывать (проколо́ть* *perf*); **I have a ~** у меня́ проко́лота ши́на.
pundit ['pʌndɪt] *n* до́ка *m/f*.
pungent ['pʌndʒənt] *adj* е́дкий* (е́док).
punish ['pʌnɪʃ] *vt* (*person*) нака́зывать (наказа́ть* *perf*); **to ~ sb for sth** нака́зывать (наказа́ть* *perf*) кого́-н за что-н; **this crime must be ~ed** э́то преступле́ние должно́ быть* нака́зано.
punishable ['pʌnɪʃəbl] *adj* наказу́емый (наказу́ем).
punishing ['pʌnɪʃɪŋ] *adj* (*fig*: *defeat*, *exercise*) изма́тывающий.
punishment ['pʌnɪʃmənt] *n* наказа́ние; **he took a lot of ~** (*inf*: *boxer*) ему́ си́льно доста́лось.
punitive ['pjuːnɪtɪv] *adj* кара́тельный.
Punjab [pʌn'dʒɑːb] *n* Пенджа́б.
Punjabi [pʌn'dʒɑːbɪ] *n* пенджа́бец*(-бка*); (*LING*) пенджа́бский* язы́к* ◆ *adj* пенджа́бский*.
punk [pʌŋk] *n* (*also*: **~ rocker**) панк; (*also*: **~ rock**) панк-рок; (*US*: *inf*: *thug*) громи́ла *m*.
punnet ['pʌnɪt] *n* корзи́ночка*.
punt [pʌnt] *n* (*boat*) плоскодо́нка* ◆ *vi* пла́вать/ плыть* (*impf*) на плоскодо́нке.
punter ['pʌntər] *n* (*BRIT*: *gambler*) (профессиона́льный) игро́к*; (*inf*: *customer*)

клие́нт(ка*); **the ~s** (*inf*) клиенту́ра *fsg*.
puny ['pjuːnɪ] *adj* хи́лый (хил).
pup [pʌp] *n* (*young dog*, *seal etc*) щено́к*.
pupil ['pjuːpl] *n* (*SCOL*) учени́к*(-и́ца); (*of eye*) зрачо́к*.
puppet ['pʌpɪt] *n* (*also fig*) марионе́тка*.
puppet government *n* марионе́точное прави́тельство.
puppy ['pʌpɪ] *n* (*young dog*) щено́к*.
purchase ['pəːtʃɪs] *n* поку́пка*; (*grip etc*) захва́т ◆ *vt* покупа́ть (купи́ть* *perf*); **to get a ~ on** ухва́тываться (ухвати́ться* *perf*) за +*acc*.
purchase order *n* зака́з на това́ры.
purchase price *n* заку́почная цена́*.
purchaser ['pəːtʃɪsər] *n* покупа́тель *m*.
purchase tax *n* нало́г на поку́пку.
purchasing power ['pəːtʃɪsɪŋ-] *n* покупа́тельная спосо́бность *f*.
pure [pjuər] *adj* чи́стый; (*water*, *air*, *woman*) чи́стый* (чист); **a ~ wool jumper** сви́тер из чи́стой ше́рсти; **~ and simple** про́сто-на́просто; **it's laziness ~ and simple** э́то про́сто-на́просто лень.
purebred ['pjuəbrɛd] *adj* чистопоро́дный, чистокро́вный.
purée ['pjuəreɪ] *n* пюре́ *nt ind*.
purely ['pjuəlɪ] *adv* чи́сто.
purgatory ['pəːgətərɪ] *n* (*REL*) чисти́лище; (*fig*) муче́ние.
purge [pəːdʒ] *n* (*POL*) чи́стка*; (*MED*) слаби́тельное *nt adj* ◆ *vt* (*thoughts*, *mind etc*) очища́ть (очи́стить* *perf*); (*organization*): **to ~ (of)** чи́стить (очи́стить* *perf*) (от +*gen*); (*extremists etc*): **to ~ from** вычища́ть (вы́чистить* *perf*) от +*gen*.
purification [pjuərɪfɪ'keɪʃən] *n* очи́стка*.
purify ['pjuərɪfaɪ] *vt* очища́ть (очи́стить* *perf*).
purist ['pjuərɪst] *n* пури́ст.
puritan ['pjuərɪtən] *n* пурита́нин*(-а́нка*).
puritanical [pjuərɪ'tænɪkl] *adj* пурита́нский*.
purity ['pjuərɪtɪ] *n* чистота́.
purl [pəːl] *n* изна́ночная вя́зка ◆ *vt* провя́зывать (провяза́ть *perf*) изна́ночной вя́зкой.
purloin [pəː'lɔɪn] *vt* присва́ивать (присво́ить *perf*).
purple ['pəːpl] *adj* фиоле́товый.
purport [pəː'pɔːt] *vi*: **he ~s to be an objective party** он притяза́ет на роль объекти́вного наблюда́теля; **he ~s to care about this** он утвержда́ет, что он обеспоко́ен э́тим.
purpose ['pəːpəs] *n* цель *f*; **on ~** наме́ренно; **for illustrative ~s** в ка́честве иллюстра́ции; **for the ~s of this meeting** пресле́дуя це́ли да́нного собра́ния; **to no ~** напра́сно.
purpose-built ['pəːpəs'bɪlt] *adj* (*BRIT*): **~ school** шко́ла целево́го назначе́ния.
purposeful ['pəːpəsful] *adj* целеустремлённый*

(целеустремлён).

purposely ['pə:pəslı] *adv* преднамеренно.

purr [pə:'] *vi* мурлыкать* (*impf*).

purse [pə:s] *n* (*BRIT*) кошелёк*; (*US: handbag*) сумка* ◆ *vt*: **to ~ one's lips** поджимать (поджать* *perf*) губы.

purser ['pə:sə'] *n* (*NAUT*) (судовой) казначей.

purse-snatcher ['pə:ssnætʃə'] *n* (*US*) вор, крадущий сумки.

pursue [pə'sju:] *vt* (*person, thing, aim*) преследовать (*impf*); (*fig: activity*) осуществлять (*impf*); (*: interest*) заниматься (*impf*) +*instr*; (*: plan*) следовать (*impf*) +*dat*.

pursuer [pə'sju:ə'] *n* преследователь(ница) *m(f)*.

pursuit [pə'sju:t] *n* (*of person, thing*) преследование; (*of happiness, wealth etc*) поиски *mpl*; (*pastime*) занятие; **scientific ~s** научные поиски; **in (the) ~ of sth** (*of wealth, fame*) в погоне за чем-н; (*of truth, knowledge*) в поисках чего-н.

purveyor [pə'veɪə'] *n* поставщик(-йца).

pus [pʌs] *n* гной.

push [puʃ] *n* (*of button etc*) нажатие; (*of car, door, person etc*) толчок*; (*fig: urgent demand*) требование* ◆ *vt* (*press*) нажимать (нажать* *perf*); (*shove*) толкать (толкнуть* *perf*); (*promote*) проталкивать (протолкнуть* *perf*) ◆ *vi* (*press*) нажимать (нажать* *perf*); (*shove*) толкаться (*impf*); (*fig*): **to ~ for** требовать (потребовать* *perf*) +*acc or* +gen; **at a ~** (*BRIT: inf*) при желании; **to ~ a door open** распахивать (распахнуть* *perf*) дверь; **to ~ a door shut** захлопывать (захлопнуть* *perf*) дверь; **"push"** (*on door*) „от себя"; (*on bell*) „нажмите"; **to be ~ed for time/money** иметь (*impf*) мало времени/ денег; **she is ~ing fifty** (*inf*) ей под пятьдесят

▶ **push aside** *vt* (*person, object*) отталкивать (оттолкнуть* *perf*); (*issue*) отметать (отмести* *perf*)

▶ **push in** *vi* влезать (влезть* *perf*)

▶ **push off** *vi* (*inf*) убираться (убраться* *perf*)

▶ **push on** *vi* (*continue*) двигаться (*impf*) дальше *or* вперёд

▶ **push over** *vt* опрокидывать (опрокинуть* *perf*)

▶ **push through** *vi* (*crowd etc*) проталкиваться (протолкнуться* *perf*) ◆ *vt* (*measure, scheme*) проталкивать (протолкнуть* *perf*)

▶ **push up** *vt* (*prices*) повышать (повысить* *perf*).

push-bike ['puʃbaɪk] *n* (*BRIT*) велосипед.

push-button ['puʃbʌtn] *adj* кнопка*.

pushchair ['puʃtʃɛə'] *n* (*BRIT*) (складная) коляска*.

pusher ['puʃə'] *n* (*drug pusher*) торговец* (-вка*) наркотиками.

pushover ['puʃəuvə'] *n* (*inf*): **it's a ~** это пара пустяков *or* пустяковое дело.

push-up ['puʃʌp] *n* (*US: press-up*) отжимание.

pushy ['puʃı] *adj* (*pej: person*) настырный*

(настырен).

puss [pus] *n* (*inf*) киска*.

pussy(cat) ['pusı(kæt)] *n* (*inf: female*) киска*; (*: male*) котик.

put [put] (*pt, pp* **put**) *vt* (*thing: horizontally*) класть* (положить* *perf*); (*: vertically*) ставить* (поставить* *perf*); (*person: in institution*) помещать (поместить* *perf*); (*: in prison, in situation*) сажать (посадить* *perf*); (*idea, remark etc*) говорить (сказать* *perf*); (*case, view*) излагать (изложить* *perf*); (*question, word, sentence*) ставить* (поставить* *perf*); (*estimate*) относить* (отнести* *perf*), ставить* (поставить* *perf*); **to ~ sb in a good mood** приводить* (привести* *perf*) кого-н в хорошее настроение; **to ~ sb in a bad mood** портить* (испортить* *perf*) кому-н настроение; **to ~ sb to bed** укладывать (уложить* *perf*) кого-н спать *or* в кровать; **to ~ sb to a lot of trouble** доставлять (доставить* *perf*) кому-н много хлопот; **how shall I ~ it?** как бы это сказать?; **to ~ a lot of time into sth** уделять (уделить* *perf*) много времени чему-н; **to ~ money on a horse** ставить* (поставить* *perf*) на лошадь; **the cost is now ~ at 2 billion pounds** сейчас стоимость оценивается в 2 миллиарда фунта; **I ~ it to you that ...** я говорю Вам, что ...; **to stay ~** оставаться* (остаться* *perf*)

▶ **put about** *vi* (*NAUT*) разворачиваться (развернуться* *perf*) ◆ *vt* (*rumour*) пускать (пустить* *perf*)

▶ **put across** *vt* (*ideas etc*) объяснять (объяснить* *perf*)

▶ **put around** *vt* = **put about**

▶ **put aside** *vt* откладывать (отложить* *perf*); (*idea*) отгонять (отогнать* *perf*)

▶ **put away** *vt* (*store*) убирать (убрать* *perf*); (*eat*) уминать (умять* *perf*); (*save*) откладывать (отложить* *perf*); (*imprison*) упрятать* (*perf*)

▶ **put back** *vt* (*replace*) класть* (положить* *perf*) на место; (*postpone*) откладывать (отложить* *perf*); (*delay*) задерживать (задержать* *perf*); **this will ~ us back 10 years** это отбросит нас на 10 лет назад

▶ **put by** *vt* откладывать (отложить* *perf*)

▶ **put down** *vt* (*place*) класть* (положить* *perf*), ставить* (поставить* *perf*); (*note down*) записывать (записать* *perf*); (*suppress, humiliate*) подавлять (подавить* *perf*); (*animal: kill*) умерщвлять (умертвить* *perf*); (*attribute*): **to ~ sth down to** объяснять (объяснить* *perf*) что-н +*instr*

▶ **put forth** *vt* объявлять (объявить* *perf*)

▶ **put forward** *vt* (*ideas, proposal*) выдвигать (выдвинуть* *perf*); (*date*) переносить* (перенести* *perf*); (*watch, clock*) переводить* (перевести* *perf*) вперёд

▶ **put in** *vt* (*application, complaint*) подавать* (подать* *perf*); (*time, effort*) вкладывать

(вложи́ть *perf*); (*gas, electricity*) проводи́ть*
(провести́* *perf*) ♦ *vi* (*NAUT*) заходи́ть* (зайти́*
perf) в порт; **the ship ~ in at Plymouth**
кора́бль* зашёл в Пли́мут
▶ **put in for** *vt fus* (*job, promotion*) подава́ть*
(пода́ть* *perf*) заявле́ние на +*acc*
▶ **put off** *vt* (*delay*) откла́дывать (отложи́ть*
perf); (*discourage*) отта́лкивать (оттолкну́ть
perf); (*switch off*) выключа́ть (вы́ключить *perf*)
▶ **put on** *vt* (*clothes*) надева́ть (наде́ть* *perf*);
(*make-up, ointment etc*) накла́дывать
(наложи́ть* *perf*); (*light etc*) включа́ть
(включи́ть* *perf*); (*play, kettle, record, dinner*)
ста́вить* (поста́вить* *perf*); (*brake*) жать*
(нажа́ть* *perf*) на +*acc*; (*extra bus, train etc*)
пуска́ть (пусти́ть* *perf*); (*assume: look*)
напуска́ть (напусти́ть* *perf*) на себя́;
(*behaviour*) принима́ть (приня́ть* *perf*); (*inf:
tease*) разы́грывать (разыгра́ть *perf*);
(*inform, indicate*): **to ~ sb on to sb** связа́ть*
(*perf*) кого́-н с кем-н; **to ~ sb on to sth**
выводи́ть* (вы́вести* *perf*) кого́-н на что-н;
to ~ on weight поправля́ться (попра́виться*
perf); **to ~ on airs** ва́жничать (*impf*)
▶ **put out** *vt* (*fire*) туши́ть* (потуши́ть* *perf*);
(*candle, cigarette*) гаси́ть* (погаси́ть* *perf*);
(*electric light*) выключа́ть (вы́ключить *perf*);
(*rubbish*) выноси́ть* (вы́нести* *perf*); (*cat*)
выпуска́ть (вы́пустить* *perf*); (*one's hand*)
вытя́гивать (вы́тянуть* *perf*); (*story*)
выду́мывать (вы́думать *perf*), пуска́ть
(пусти́ть* *perf*); (*BRIT: dislocate*) выви́хивать
(вы́вихнуть *perf*); (*inf*): **he was rather ~ out** он
был вы́бит из колеи́ ♦ *vi* (*NAUT*): **to ~ out to
sea** выходи́ть* (вы́йти* *perf*) в мо́ре; **to ~ out
from Plymouth** выходи́ть* (вы́йти* *perf*) из
Пли́мута
▶ **put through** *vt* (*person, call*) соединя́ть
(соедини́ть* *perf*); (*plan, agreement*)
выполня́ть (вы́полнить *perf*); **~ me through
to Miss Blair** соедини́те меня́ с мисс Блэр
▶ **put together** *vt* соединя́ть (соедини́ть* *perf*);
(*furniture, toys etc*) собира́ть (собра́ть* *perf*);
(*meal*) гото́вить* (пригото́вить* *perf*); (*plan,
campaign*) организова́ть (*impf/perf*)
▶ **put up** *vt* (*building, tent*) ста́вить*
(поста́вить* *perf*); (*umbrella*) раскрыва́ть
(раскры́ть* *perf*); (*hood*) надева́ть (наде́ть*
perf); (*poster, sign etc*) выве́шивать

(вы́весить* *perf*); (*price, cost*) поднима́ть
(подня́ть* *perf*); (*guest, visitor*) размеща́ть
(размести́ть* *perf*); (*opposition, resistance*)
подавля́ть (подави́ть* *perf*); (*incite*): **to ~ sb
up to sth** толка́ть (толкну́ть *perf*) кого́-н на
что-н; **to ~ sth up for sale** выставля́ть
(вы́ставить* *perf*) что-н на прода́жу
▶ **put upon** *vt fus*: **to be ~ upon: we are not
prepared to be ~ upon** мы не привы́кли,
чтобы на нас е́здили
▶ **put up with** *vt fus* терпе́ть (*impf*), мири́ться
(*impf*) с +*instr*.
putative [ˈpjuːtətɪv] *adj* предполага́емый.
putrid [ˈpjuːtrɪd] *adj* гнило́й.
putt [pʌt] *n* (*GOLF*) уда́р, загоня́ющий мяч в
лу́нку (в го́льфе).
putter [ˈpʌtəʳ] *n* (*GOLF*) коро́ткая клю́шка для
го́льфа ♦ *vi* (*US*) = **potter**.
putting green [ˈpʌtɪŋ-] *n* по́ле для го́льфа, на
кото́ром мяч прогоня́ется к лу́нками а не
поддаётся уда́рами.
putty [ˈpʌtɪ] *n* зама́зка.
put-up [ˈpʌtʌp] *n*: **~ job** (*BRIT: inf*) под-
стро́енное де́ло*.
puzzle [ˈpʌzl] *n* (*question, mystery*) зага́дка;
(*game, toy*) головоло́мка*; (*also*: **crossword
~**) кроссво́рд ♦ *vt* озада́чивать (озада́чить
perf) ♦ *vi* лома́ть (*impf*) го́лову
над чем-н; **to be ~d about sth** пребыва́ть
(*impf*) в недоуме́нии по по́воду чего́-н.
puzzling [ˈpʌzlɪŋ] *adj* запу́танный* (запу́тан).
PVC *n abbr* (= *polyvinyl chloride*) поливини́л-
хлори́д.
Pvt. *abbr* (*US: MIL*) = **private**.
PW *n abbr* (*US*) = **prisoner of war**.
p.w. *abbr* = *per week*.
PX *n abbr* (*US: MIL*) = **post exchange**.
pygmy [ˈpɪgmɪ] *n* пигме́й.
pyjamas [pɪˈdʒɑːməz] (*US* **pajamas**) *npl*: (**a pair
of**) **~** пижа́ма *fsg*.
pylon [ˈpaɪlən] *n* пило́н, опо́ра.
Pyongyang [ˈpjɔŋˈjæŋ] *n* Пхенья́н.
pyramid [ˈpɪrəmɪd] *n* (*ARCHIT, GEOM*) пирами́да;
(*pile*) гру́да.
Pyrenean [pɪrəˈniːən] *adj* пирене́йский.
Pyrenees [pɪrəˈniːz] *npl*: **the ~** Пирене́и *pl*.
Pyrex® [ˈpaɪrɛks] *n* пи́рекс ♦ *cpd*: **~ dish**
таре́лка пи́рекс.
python [ˈpaɪθən] *n* пито́н.

---

* marks translations which have irregular inflections. The Russian-English side of the dictionary gives inflectional information.

~ Q, q ~

Q, q [kjuː] *n* (*letter*) 17-ая бу́ква англи́йского алфави́та.

Qatar [kæ'tɑːʳ] *n* Ка́тар.

QC *n abbr* (*BRIT: LAW*: = **Queen's Counsel**) короле́вский* адвока́т (*адвока́тский ранг*).

QED *abbr* (= *quod erat demonstrandum*) что и тре́бовалось доказа́ть.

QM *n abbr* (*MIL*) = **quartermaster**.

q.t. *n abbr* (*inf*) = *quiet*: **on the ~.** тишко́м.

qty *abbr* (= **quantity**) коли́чество.

quack [kwæk] *n* кря́канье; (*doctor*) шарлата́н ♦ *vi* кря́кать (*impf*).

quad [kwɔd] *abbr* = **quadrangle, quadruplet**.

quadrangle ['kwɔdræŋgl] *n* (*courtyard*) двор*; (*MATH*) четырёхуго́льник.

quadrilateral [kwɔdrɪ'lætərəl] *n* четырёху-го́льник.

quadruped ['kwɔdrupɛd] *n* четвероно́гое *nt adj*.

quadruple [kwɔ'druːpl] *vt* увели́чивать (увели́чить *perf*) в четы́ре ра́за ♦ *vi* увели́чиваться (увели́читься *perf*) в четы́ре ра́за.

quadruplets [kwɔ'druːplɪts] *npl* четы́ре близнеца́.

quagmire ['kwægmaɪəʳ] *n* (*also fig*) тряси́на.

quail [kweɪl] *n* (*bird*) пе́репел(-пёлка*) ♦ *vi*: **to ~ at the thought of** содрога́ться (содрогну́ться *perf*) при мы́сли об +*prp*.

quaint [kweɪnt] *adj* (*house, village*) причу́д-ливый (причу́длив); (*ideas, customs*) своеобра́зный* (своеобра́зен).

quake [kweɪk] *vi* трепета́ть* (*impf*).

Quaker ['kweɪkəʳ] *n* ква́кер.

qualification [kwɔlɪfɪ'keɪʃən] *n* (*usu pl*: *academic, vocational*) квалифика́ция *no pl*; (*skill, quality*) ка́чество; (*reservation*) огово́рка*; **what are your ~s?** кака́я у Вас квалифика́ция?

qualified ['kwɔlɪfaɪd] *adj* (*trained*: *person*) квалифици́рованный (квалифици́рован); (*limited*: *approval etc*) небезусло́вный; **I'm not ~ to discuss/judge that** я не компете́нтен обсужда́ть/суди́ть об э́том; **the show was a ~ success** спекта́кль не по́льзовался осо́бым успе́хом; **he's not ~ for the job** у него́ нет необходи́мой квалифика́ции для э́той рабо́ты.

qualify ['kwɔlɪfaɪ] *vt* (*modify*: *make more specific*) уточня́ть (уточни́ть *perf*); (: *express reservation*) огова́ривать (оговори́ть *perf*); (*make competent*): **to ~ sb to do** позволя́ть (позво́лить *perf*) кому́-н +*infin* ♦ *vi*: **to ~ as an engineer** получа́ть (получи́ть* *perf*) квалифика́цию инжене́ра; (*be eligible*: *for benefit, grant*): **to ~ (for)** име́ть (*impf*) пра́во (на +*acc*); (*in competition*): **to ~ (for)** выходи́ть* (вы́йти* *perf*) (в +*acc*).

qualifying ['kwɔlɪfaɪŋ] *adj*: **~ exam** квалификацио́нный экза́мен; **~ round** отбо́рочное соревнова́ние.

qualitative ['kwɔlɪtətɪv] *adj* ка́чественный.

quality ['kwɔlɪtɪ] *n* (*standard, characteristic*) ка́чество; (*property*: *of wood, stone etc*) сво́йство ♦ *cpd* ка́чественный; **of good/poor ~** хоро́шего/плохо́го ка́чества.

quality control *n* контро́ль *m* ка́чества.

quality of life *n* у́ровень *m* жи́зни.

quality papers *npl* (*BRIT*): **the ~ ~** серьёзные газе́ты *fpl*.

qualm [kwɑːm] *n* сомне́ние; **to have ~s about** сомнева́ться (*impf*) в +*prp*.

quandary ['kwɔndərɪ] *n*: **to be in a ~** быть* (*impf*) в затрудне́нии.

quango ['kwæŋgəu] *n abbr* (*BRIT*: = *quasi-autonomous non-governmental organization*) *организа́ция, име́ющая распоряди́тельные и координацио́нные фу́нкции*.

quantifiable ['kwɔntɪfaɪəbl] *adj* измери́мый (измери́м).

quantitative ['kwɔntɪtətɪv] *adj* коли́чественный.

quantity ['kwɔntɪtɪ] *n* коли́чество; (*large amount*): **in ~** в большо́м коли́честве; **an unknown ~** зага́дка.

quantity surveyor *n* инжене́р-планови́к* (*на строи́тельных рабо́тах*).

quantum leap ['kwɔntəm-] *n* скачо́к*.

quarantine ['kwɔrntiːn] *n* каранти́н.

quark [kwɑːk] *n* кварк.

quarrel ['kwɔrl] *n* ссо́ра ♦ *vi*: **to ~ (with)** ссо́риться (поссо́риться *perf*) (с +*instr*); **to have a ~ with sb** поссо́риться* (*perf*) с кем-н; **I've no ~ with him** у меня́ нет прете́нзий к нему́; **I can't ~ with that** я не могу́ не согласи́ться с э́тим.

quarrelsome ['kwɔrəlsəm] *adj* вздо́рный* (вздо́рен).

quarry ['kwɔrɪ] *n* карье́р; (*for stone*)

каменоло́мня; (*hunted animal*) добы́ча ♦ *vt* добыва́ть (добы́ть* *perf*).

quart [kwɔːt] *n* ква́рта.

quarter ['kwɔːtəʳ] *n* че́тверть* *f*; (*of year, town*) кварта́л; (*US: coin*) два́дцать пять це́нтов ♦ *vt* дели́ть* (раздели́ть* *perf*) на четы́ре ча́сти; (*MIL: lodge*) квартирова́ть (раскварти́ровать *perf*); ~s *npl* (*living quarters*) помеще́ние *ntsg*; (: *MIL*) каза́рмы *fpl*; **a ~ of an hour** че́тверть* *f* ча́са; **it's a ~ to three,** *or* (*US*) **of three** сейча́с без че́тверти три; **it's a ~ past three,** *or* (*US*) **after three** сейча́с че́тверть четвёртого; **from all ~s** отовсю́ду; **at close ~s** вблизи́.

quarterback ['kwɔːtəbæk] *n* (*SPORT*) гла́вный напада́ющий* (*в америка́нском футбо́ле*).

quarterdeck ['kwɔːtədɛk] *n* (*NAUT*) квартерде́к.

quarterfinal ['kwɔːtə'faɪnl] *n* четвертьфина́л.

quarterly ['kwɔːtəlɪ] *adj* (*meeting*) (еже)кварта́льный; (*payment*) (по)кварта́льный ♦ *adv* (*meet*) ежекварта́льно; (*pay*) покварта́льно ♦ *n* кварта́льный журна́л.

quartermaster ['kwɔːtəmɑːstəʳ] *n* (*MIL*) квартирме́йстер.

quartet(te) [kwɔː'tɛt] *n* (*group*) кварте́т.

quarto ['kwɔːtəu] *n* (*book*) кни́га форма́та ин-ква́рто.

quartz [kwɔːts] *n* кварц ♦ *cpd* ква́рцевый.

quash [kwɔʃ] *vt* (*verdict, judgement*) отменя́ть (отмени́ть* *perf*).

quasi- ['kweɪzaɪ] *prefix* ква́зи-.

quaver ['kweɪvəʳ] *n* (*BRIT: MUS*) восьма́я *f adj* ♦ *vi* дрожа́ть (*impf*).

quay [kiː] *n* (*also:* ~**side**) при́стань* *f*.

quayside ['kiːsaɪd] *n* при́стань* *f*.

queasiness ['kwiːzɪnɪs] *n* тошнота́.

queasy ['kwiːzɪ] *adj*: **I feel a bit ~** меня́ немно́го мути́т.

Quebec [kwɪ'bɛk] *n* Квебе́к.

queen [kwiːn] *n* короле́ва; (*also:* ~ **bee**) пчели́ная ма́тка*; (*CARDS*) да́ма; (*CHESS*) ферзь* *m*, короле́ва.

queen mother *n* короле́ва-мать* *f*.

Queen's speech *n* (*at Christmas*) обраще́ние (короле́вы) к по́дданым; (*at opening of parliament*) тро́нная речь *f* (короле́вы).

queer [kwɪəʳ] *adj* стра́нный* (стра́нен); (*BRIT*): **I feel ~** мне ду́рно ♦ *n* (*pej: homosexual*) го́мик.

quell [kwɛl] *vt* подавля́ть (подави́ть* *perf*).

quench [kwɛntʃ] *vt*: **to ~ one's thirst** утоля́ть (утоли́ть *perf*) жа́жду.

querulous ['kwɛrʊləs] *adj* (*voice*) жа́лобный* (жа́лобен); (*child*) хны́кающий.

query ['kwɪərɪ] *n* вопро́с ♦ *vt* подверга́ть (подве́ргнуть *perf*) сомне́нию.

quest [kwɛst] *n* по́иск.

question ['kwɛstʃən] *n* вопро́с; (*doubt*) сомне́ние ♦ *vt* (*interrogate*) допра́шивать

(допроси́ть* *perf*); (*doubt*) сомнева́ться (*impf*) в +*prp*; **to ask sb a ~, put a ~ to sb** задава́ть (зада́ть* *perf*) кому́-н вопро́с; **to bring** *or* **call sth into ~** ста́вить* (поста́вить* *perf*) что-н под вопро́с *or* сомне́ние; **the ~ is** ... вопро́с в том, ...; **it's (just) a ~ of finding out** де́ло (то́лько) за тем, что́бы узна́ть; **there's some ~ as to whether** существу́ют не́которые сомне́ния в том, что; **beyond ~** бесспо́рно; **that's out of the ~** об э́том не мо́жет быть* и ре́чи.

questionable ['kwɛstʃənəbl] *adj* сомни́тельный* (сомни́телен).

questioner ['kwɛstʃənəʳ] *n* зада́вший(-ая) *m(f) adj* вопро́с.

questioning ['kwɛstʃənɪŋ] *adj* (*expression*) вопроси́тельный* (вопроси́телен); (*mind*) пытли́вый (пытли́в) ♦ *n* (*POLICE*) допро́с.

question mark *n* вопроси́тельный знак.

questionnaire [kwɛstʃə'nɛəʳ] *n* анке́та.

queue [kjuː] (*BRIT*) *n* о́чередь* *f* ♦ *vi* (*also:* ~ **up**) стоя́ть (*impf*) в о́череди; **to jump the ~** проходи́ть* (пройти́* *perf*) без о́череди.

quibble ['kwɪbl] *vi*: **to ~ about** *or* **over** спо́рить (поспо́рить *perf*) о +*prp*.

quiche [kiːʃ] *n* киш (*откры́тый пиро́г с овощно́й иͳп начи́нкой*).

quick [kwɪk] *adj* бы́стрый* (быстр); (*clever: person*) сообрази́тельный* (сообрази́телен); (: *mind*) живо́й; (*brief*) коро́ткий* (ко́роток) ♦ *adv* бы́стро ♦ *n*: **to cut to the ~** задева́ть (заде́ть* *perf*) за живо́е; **be ~!** бы́стро!, побыстре́е!; **to be ~ to act** бы́стро реаги́ровать (отреаги́ровать *perf*); **she was ~ to see that** ... она́ сра́зу заме́тила, что ...; **to have a ~ look** взгляну́ть (*perf*); **she has a ~ temper** она́ вспы́льчива.

quicken ['kwɪkən] *vt* ускоря́ть (уско́рить *perf*) ♦ *vi* ускоря́ться (уско́риться *perf*).

quick-fire ['kwɪkfaɪəʳ] *adj*: ~ **questions** град *msg* вопро́сов.

quicklime ['kwɪklaɪm] *n* негашёная и́звесть *f*.

quickly ['kwɪklɪ] *adv* бы́стро.

quickness ['kwɪknɪs] *n* быстрота́; (*of mind*) жи́вость *f*.

quicksand ['kwɪksænd] *n* зыбу́чий* песо́к*.

quickstep ['kwɪkstɛp] *n* куи́к-сте́п.

quick-tempered [kwɪk'tɛmpəd] *adj* вспы́льчивый (вспы́льчив).

quick-witted [kwɪk'wɪtɪd] *adj* сообрази́тельный* (сообрази́телен).

quid [kwɪd] *n inv* (*BRIT: inf*) фунт (сте́рлингов).

quid pro quo ['kwɪdprəu'kwəu] *n* услу́га за услу́гу.

quiet ['kwaɪət] *adj* (*not loud or noisy*) ти́хий* (тих); (: *engine*) бесшу́мный* (бесшу́мен); (*peaceful, not busy*) споко́йный* (споко́ен); (*without fuss: wedding etc*) скро́мный*

---

* marks translations which have irregular inflections. The Russian-English side of the dictionary gives inflectional information.

(скро́мен) ♦ *n* (*silence*) тишина́; (*peace*) поко́й ♦ *vti* (*US*) = **quieten; be** ~! ти́хо!; **I'll have a** ~ **word with him** я поговорю́ с ним наедине́; **business is** ~ **at this time of year** в э́то вре́мя го́да в дела́х зати́шье; **on the** ~ тайко́м.

quieten ['kwaɪətn] *vi* (*also:* ~ **down**) затиха́ть (зати́хнуть *perf*) ♦ *vt* (*also:* ~ **down**) успока́ивать (успоко́ить *perf*).

quietly ['kwaɪətlɪ] *adv* (*not loudly*) ти́хо; (*calmly*) споко́йно.

quietness ['kwaɪətnɪs] *n* (*silence*) тишина́; (*peacefulness*) поко́й.

quill [kwɪl] *n* перо́•; (*of porcupine*) игла́•.

quilt [kwɪlt] *n* (*covering*) стёганое покрыва́ло; (*also:* **continental** ~) стёганое одея́ло.

quilting ['kwɪltɪŋ] *n* (*quilt-making*) стёжка; (*material*) стёганая ткань *f*.

quin [kwɪn] *n abbr* (*BRIT*) = **quintuplet.**

quince [kwɪns] *n* айва́.

quinine [kwɪ'niːn] *n* хини́н.

quintessential [kwɪntɪ'senʃəl] *adj* показа́тельный.

quintet(te) [kwɪn'tet] *n* (*group*) квинте́т.

quintuplets [kwɪn'tjuːplɪts] *npl* пя́теро• близнецо́в.

quip [kwɪp] *n* остро́та ♦ *vt* остри́ть (состри́ть *perf*); ... **he** ~**ped** ... состри́л он.

quire ['kwaɪə] *n* (*of paper*) десть *f*.

quirk [kwəːk] *n* причу́да, при́хоть *f*; **by some** ~ **of fate** по при́хоти судьбы́.

quit [kwɪt] (*pt, pp* **quit** *or* **quitted**) *vt* броса́ть (бро́сить• *perf*); (*premises*) съезжа́ть (съе́хать• *perf*) с +*gen* ♦ *vi* (*give up*) сдава́ться• (сда́ться• *perf*); (*resign*) увольня́ться (уво́литься *perf*); **to** ~ **smoking** броса́ть (бро́сить• *perf*) кури́ть•; ~ **stalling!** (*US: inf*) переста́ньте ходи́ть вокру́г да о́коло!; **they were given 3 months notice to** ~ (*BRIT*) их предупреди́ли, что они́ должны́ освобо- ди́ть помеще́ние в трёхме́сячный срок.

quite [kwaɪt] *adv* (*rather*) дово́льно; (*entirely*) соверше́нно; (*following negative: almost*): **the flat's not** ~ **big enough** кварти́ра недоста́точно больша́я; **he's** ~ **right** он соверше́нно прав; **she's** ~ **pretty** она́ дово́льно симпати́чная; **I** ~ **understand** я вполне́ понима́ю; **I'm not** ~ **sure** я не совсе́м уве́рен; **not** ~ **as many as the last time** не так мно́го, как в про́шлый раз; **that lunch was** ~ **something!** вот э́то был обе́д!; ~ **a few** дово́льно мно́го; ~ (**so**)! ве́рно!

Quito ['kiːtəu] *n* Ки́то *m ind.*

quits [kwɪts] *adj*: **to be** ~ (**with**) быть• (*impf*) в расчёте (с +*instr*); **let's call it** ~ бу́дем кви́ты.

quiver ['kwɪvə] *vi* трепета́ть (*impf*).

quiz [kwɪz] *n* (*game*) викторина ♦ *vt* расспра́шивать (расспроси́ть• *perf*).

quizzical ['kwɪzɪkl] *adj*: **a** ~ **look** понима́ющий и насме́шливый взгляд.

quoits [kwɔɪts] *npl* игра́, заключа́ющаяся в мета́нии коле́ц в цель.

quorum ['kwɔːrəm] *n* кво́рум.

quota ['kwəutə] *n* кво́та.

quotation [kwəu'teɪʃən] *n* цита́та; (*estimate*) цена́ (продавца́); (*of shares etc*) котиро́вка•.

quotation marks *npl* кавы́чки *fpl.*

quote [kwəut] *n* (*from book, play etc*) цита́та; (*estimate*) цена́ ♦ *vt* цити́ровать (процити́ровать *perf*); (*figure, example*) приводи́ть• (привести́• *perf*); (*price*) назнача́ть (назна́чить *perf*); ~**s** *npl* (*quotation marks*) кавы́чки *fpl*; **to** ~ **for a job** устана́вливать (установи́ть• *perf*) сто́имость *f* рабо́ты; **in** ~**s** в кавы́чках; ~ ... **unquote** ... в кавы́чках.

quotient ['kwəuʃənt] *n* (*factor*) фа́ктор.

qv *abbr* = **quod vide**; (*which see*) см.= *смотри́.*

qwerty keyboard ['kwəːtɪ-] *n типи́чная англи́йская клавиату́ра печа́тной маши́нки и́ли компью́тера.*

~ R, r ~

R, r [ɑː'] n (letter) 18-ая бу́ква англи́йского алфави́та.

R. abbr = **right**;(= **river**) р.= река́; (= Réaumur (scale)) по шкале́ Реомю́ра; (US: CINEMA: = restricted) ≈ до 18-ти лет; (US: POL) = **republican**; (BRIT) = Rex; (BRIT) = Regina.

RA abbr (MIL) = **rear admiral** ♦ n abbr (BRIT) = Royal Academy; (BRIT) = Royal Academician.

RAAF n abbr (MIL) = Royal Australian Air Force.

Rabat [rə'bɑːt] n Раба́т.

rabbi ['ræbaɪ] n равви́н.

rabbit ['ræbɪt] n (male) кро́лик; (female) крольчи́ха ♦ vi: **to ~ (on)** (BRIT: inf) трещáть (impf).

rabbit hole n кро́личья нора́*.

rabbit hutch n кро́личья кле́тка*.

rabble ['ræbl] n (pej) чернь f.

rabid ['ræbɪd] adj (also fig) бе́шеный.

rabies ['reɪbiːz] n бе́шенство, водобоя́знь f.

RAC n abbr (BRIT: = Royal Automobile Club) Короле́вский автомоби́льный клуб (крупне́йшая автомоби́льная ассоциа́ция).

raccoon [rə'kuːn] n ено́т.

race [reɪs] n (species) ра́са; (competition: NAUT, AUT, SKIING etc) го́ньки* fpl; (: running) забе́г; (: swimming) заплы́в; (: horse race) ска́чки* fpl; (for power, control) борьба́ ♦ vi (horse) гнать* (impf); (pigeon) гоня́ть (impf); (car etc) вести́* (impf); (person) бежа́ть* (impf) наперегонки́ с +instr ♦ vi (compete) принима́ть (приня́ть* perf) уча́стие в го́нках/забе́ге/заплы́ве/ска́чках; (hurry) мча́ться (impf); (pulse) учаща́ться (участи́ться* perf); (engine) увели́чивать (увели́чить perf) оборо́ты; **the human ~** челове́чество, челове́ческий* род; **the arms ~** го́нка вооруже́ний; **he ~d across the road** он бы́стро перебежа́л че́рез доро́гу; **to ~ in(to)** влета́ть (влете́ть* perf) (в +acc); **to ~ out (of)** выска́кивать (вы́скочить perf) (из +gen).

race car n (US) = **racing car**.

race car driver n (US) = **racing driver**.

racecourse ['reɪskɔːs] n ипподро́м.

racehorse ['reɪshɔːs] n скакова́я ло́шадь* f.

race meeting n день m ска́чек.

race relations npl ра́совые отноше́ния ntpl.

racetrack ['reɪstræk] n (for people) бегова́я доро́жка*; (for cars) трек; (US) = **racecourse**.

racial ['reɪʃl] adj (discrimination, prejudice) ра́совый; **~ equality** ра́совое ра́венство.

racialism ['reɪʃlɪzəm] n раси́зм.

racialist ['reɪʃlɪst] adj (beliefs, attitudes) раси́стский* ♦ n раси́ст(ка*).

racing ['reɪsɪŋ] n (horse racing) ска́чки* fpl; (motor racing) го́нки* fpl.

racing car n (BRIT) го́ночный автомоби́ль m.

racing driver n (BRIT) го́нщик.

racism ['reɪsɪzəm] n раси́зм.

racist ['reɪsɪst] adj (statement, policy) раси́стский* ♦ n раси́ст(ка*).

rack [ræk] n (shelf) по́лка*; (also: **luggage ~**) бага́жная по́лка*; (also: **roof ~**) бага́жник (на кры́ше автомоби́ля); (also: **dish ~**) суши́лка* для посу́ды ♦ vt: **she was ~ed by pain** её терза́ла боль; **to ~ one's brains** лома́ть (impf) го́лову; **magazine ~** журна́льная по́лка; **toast ~** подста́вка для то́стов; **shoe ~** по́лка* для о́буви; **to go to ~ and ruin** (building) ветша́ть (обветша́ть perf); (business) разоря́ться (разори́ться perf).

racket ['rækɪt] n (SPORT) раке́тка*; (noise) шум; (swindle) жу́льничество; (organized crime) рэ́кет.

racketeer [rækɪ'tɪə'] n (esp US) рэкети́р.

racoon [rə'kuːn] n = **raccoon**.

racquet ['rækɪt] n (SPORT) раке́тка*.

racy ['reɪsɪ] adj (book) пика́нтный* (пика́нтен); (behaviour etc) экстравага́нтный* (экстравага́нтен).

RADA [rɑːdə] (BRIT) n abbr = Royal Academy of Dramatic Art.

radar ['reɪdɑː'] n рада́р, радиолока́тор ♦ cpd рада́рный, радиолокацио́нный.

radar trap n (AUT) радиолокацио́нная лову́шка.

radial ['reɪdɪəl] adj (also: **~ply**: tyre) радиа́льный.

radiance ['reɪdɪəns] n (glow) сия́ние.

radiant ['reɪdɪənt] adj (smile, person) сия́ющий*; (PHYS) лучи́стый.

radiate ['reɪdɪeɪt] vt (also fig) излуча́ть (impf) ♦ vi (lines) радиа́льно расходи́ться* (разойти́сь* perf).

---

* marks translations which have irregular inflections. The Russian-English side of the dictionary gives inflectional information.

radiation [reɪdɪ'eɪʃən] n (radioactive) радиа́ция, радиоакти́вное излуче́ние; (of heat, light) излуче́ние.
radiation sickness n лучева́я боле́знь f.
radiator ['reɪdɪeɪtə'] n (heater) радиа́тор, батаре́я; (AUT) радиа́тор.
radiator cap n кры́шка* радиа́тора.
radiator grill n (AUT) решётка* радиа́тора.
radical ['rædɪkl] adj (extreme) радика́льный* (радика́лен) ♦ n (person) радика́л.
radii ['reɪdɪaɪ] npl of **radius**.
radio ['reɪdɪəu] n (broadcasting) ра́дио nt ind; (device: for receiving broadcasts) радио-приёмник; (: for transmitting and receiving) радиопереда́тчик ♦ vt (person) свя́зываться (связа́ться* perf) по ра́дио с +instr; (information) передава́ть* (переда́ть* perf) по ра́дио ♦ vi: **to ~ to sb** ради́ровать (impf/perf) кому́-н; **on the ~** по ра́дио.
radio... ['reɪdɪəu] prefix ра́дио....
radioactive ['reɪdɪəu'æktɪv] adj радио-акти́вный* (радиоакти́вен).
radioactivity ['reɪdɪəuæk'tɪvɪtɪ] n радио-акти́вность f.
radio announcer n ди́ктор ра́дио.
radio-controlled ['reɪdɪəukən'trəuld] adj управля́емый при по́мощи радиосигна́лов.
radiographer [reɪdɪ'ɔgrəfə'] n рентгено́лог.
radiography [reɪdɪ'ɔgrəfɪ] n рентгеногра́фия, радиогра́фия.
radiologist [reɪdɪ'ɔlədʒɪst] n рентгено́лог, радио́лог.
radiology [reɪdɪ'ɔlədʒɪ] n рентгеноло́гия, радиоло́гия.
radio station n радиоста́нция.
radio taxi n радиофици́рованное такси́ nt ind.
radiotelephone ['reɪdɪəu'tɛlɪfəun] n радио-телефо́н.
radio telescope n радиотелеско́п.
radiotherapist ['reɪdɪəu'θɛrəpɪst] n радио-терапе́вт.
radiotherapy ['reɪdɪəu'θɛrəpɪ] n радиотерапи́я, рентгенотерапи́я.
radish ['rædɪʃ] n (one radish) реди́ска*; ~es реди́с msg, реди́ска fsg (разг).
radium ['reɪdɪəm] n ра́дий.
radius ['reɪdɪəs] (pl radii) n ра́диус; (ANAT) лучева́я кость* f; **within a ~ of 50 miles** в ра́диусе 50-ти миль.
RAF n abbr (BRIT) (= Royal Air Force) ≈ BBC= вое́нно-возду́шные си́лы.
raffia ['ræfɪə] n ра́фия.
raffish ['ræfɪʃ] adj разгу́льный* (разгу́лен).
raffle ['ræfl] n (вещева́я) лотере́я ♦ vt (prize) разы́грывать (разыгра́ть perf) в лотере́е.
raft [rɑːft] n плот*.
rafter ['rɑːftə'] n (CONSTR) стропи́ло.
rag [ræg] n тря́пка*; (pej: newspaper) газетёнка*; (SCOL: for charity) благотвор́и́тельное шу́точное студе́нческое представле́ние ♦ vt (BRIT: tease) те́шиться

(поте́шиться perf) над +instr; ~s npl (torn clothes) лохмо́тья* pl; **in ~s** (person) в лохмо́тьях; (clothes) изно́шенный* (изно́шен) до дыр.
rag-and-bone man [rægən'bəun-] irreg n (BRIT) старьёвщик.
ragbag ['rægbæg] n (fig: inf) вся́кая вся́чина.
rag doll n тря́пичная ку́кла*.
rage [reɪdʒ] n (fury) я́рость f, бе́шенство ♦ vi (person) свире́пствовать (impf); (storm, debate) бушева́ть (impf); **it's all the ~** (very fashionable) все помеша́лись на э́том; **to fly into a ~** приходи́ть* (прийти́* perf) в я́рость, свирепе́ть (рассвирепе́ть perf).
ragged ['rægɪd] adj (edge) зазу́бренный* (зазу́брен); (clothes) потрёпанный* (потрёпан), изо́рванный (изо́рван); (appearance) обо́рванный* (обо́рван).
raging ['reɪdʒɪŋ] adj (sea, storm) бушу́ющий; (pain, fever) свире́пый; ~ **toothache** свире́пая зубна́я боль; **in a ~ temper** в я́рости.
rag trade n (inf): **the ~** инду́стрия оде́жды.
raid [reɪd] n (MIL) рейд; (criminal) налёт; (by police) обла́ва, рейд ♦ vt (see n) соверша́ть (соверши́ть perf) рейд на +acc; соверша́ть (соверши́ть perf) налёт на +acc; устра́ивать (устро́ить perf) обла́ву или рейд на +acc.
rail [reɪl] n (on stairs, bridge etc) пери́ла pl; (of ship) борт*; ~s npl (RAIL) ре́льсы mpl; **by ~** по́ездом.
railing(s) ['reɪlɪŋ(z)] n(pl) (iron fence) решётка fsg.
railroad ['reɪlrəud] n (US) = **railway**.
railway ['reɪlweɪ] n (BRIT) желе́зная доро́га ♦ cpd железнодоро́жный.
railway engine n локомоти́в.
railway line n (BRIT) железнодоро́жная ли́ния.
railwayman ['reɪlweɪmən] irreg n (BRIT) железнодоро́жник.
railway station n (BRIT: large) железно-доро́жный вокза́л; (: small) железнодоро́жная ста́нция.
rain [reɪn] n дождь* m ♦ vi: **it's ~ing** идёт дождь ♦ vi: **it's ~ing cats and dogs** льёт как из ведра́; **in the ~** под дождём, в дождь; **it ~ed a lot last night** вчера́ но́чью шёл си́льный дождь.
rainbow ['reɪnbəu] n ра́дуга.
rain check n (US): **I'll take a ~** ~ я ещё немно́го поду́маю.
raincoat ['reɪnkəut] n плащ*.
raindrop ['reɪndrɔp] n дождева́я ка́пля*.
rainfall ['reɪnfɔːl] n оса́дки mpl; (measurement) коли́чество оса́дков.
rainforest ['reɪnfɔrɪst] n тропи́ческий* лес.
rainproof ['reɪnpruːf] adj непромока́емый (непромока́ем).
rainstorm ['reɪnstɔːm] n ли́вень* m.
rainwater ['reɪnwɔːtə'] n дождева́я вода́*.
rainy ['reɪnɪ] adj (day) дождли́вый (дождли́в); **Manchester is a ~ place** в Манче́стере ча́сто иду́т дожди́; **to save sth for a ~ day**

откла́дывать (отложи́ть* *perf*) что-н на
чёрный день.
raise [reɪz] *n* (*esp US*: *pay rise*) повыше́ние ♦ *vt*
(*lift, produce*) поднима́ть (подня́ть* *perf*);
(*end*: *siege, embargo*) снима́ть (снять* *perf*);
(*increase, improve*) повыша́ть (повы́сить*
perf); (*doubts*) выска́зывать (вы́сказать* *perf*);
(*rear*: *cattle*) разводи́ть* (развести́* *perf*);
(: *family*) воспи́тывать (воспита́ть* *perf*);
(*cultivate*: *crop*) выра́щивать (вы́растить*
perf); (*get together*: *army, funds*) собира́ть
(собра́ть* *perf*); (: *loan*) достава́ть* (доста́ть*
perf); **to ~ a glass to sb/sth** поднима́ть
(подня́ть* *perf*) бока́л за кого́-н/что-н; **to ~
one's voice** повыша́ть (повы́сить* *perf*)
го́лос; **to ~ one's hopes** обнадёживать
(обнадёжить *perf*); **to ~ a laugh/smile**
вызыва́ть (вы́звать* *perf*) смех/улы́бку.
raisin ['reɪzn] *n* (*one raisin*) изю́минка*; **~s**
изю́м* *m no pl*.
Raj [rɑːdʒ] *n*: **the ~** пери́од брита́нского
правле́ния в Инди́и.
rajah ['rɑːdʒə] *n* ра́джа.
rake [reɪk] *n* (*tool*) гра́бли* *pl*; (*person*) пове́са *m*
♦ *vt* (*garden*) разра́внивать (разровня́ть *perf*)
(гра́блями); (*leaves, hay*) сгреба́ть (сгрести́*
perf); (*with machine gun*) обстре́ливать
(обстреля́ть *perf*) ♦ *vi*: **to ~ through** (*search*)
ры́ться* (*impf*) в +*prp*.
rake-off ['reɪkɔf] *n* (*inf*) до́ля* при́были.
rally ['rælɪ] *n* (*POL etc*) ми́тинг; (*AUT*)
авторалли *nt ind*; (*TENNIS*) ра́лли *nt ind* ♦ *vt*
(*support*) спла́чивать (сплоти́ть* *perf*) ♦ *vi*
(*sick person*) оправля́ться (опра́виться* *perf*);
(*Stock Exchange*) оживля́ться (оживи́ться*
perf).
▶ **rally round** *vt fus* (*fig*: *give support to*)
спла́чиваться (сплоти́ться* *perf*) вокру́г +*gen*
♦ *vi* бра́ться* (взя́ться* *perf*) за де́ло вме́сте.
rallying point ['rælɪŋ-] *n* (*idea*) объедин-
я́ющая иде́я.
RAM [ræm] *n abbr* (*COMPUT*) (= **random access
memory**) ЗУПВ= запомина́ющее
устро́йство с произво́льной вы́боркой.
ram [ræm] *n* бара́н ♦ *vt* (*crash into*) тара́нить
(протара́нить *perf*); (*push*: *bolt*) задвига́ть
(задви́нуть *perf*); (: *fist*) дви́нуть (*perf*) +*instr*.
ramble ['ræmbl] *n* прогу́лка* ♦ *vi* (*walk*)
броди́ть* (*impf*); (*talk*: *also*: **~ on**) болта́ть
(*impf*).
rambler ['ræmblə] *n* (*walker*) тури́ст(ка)
(уча́стник пешехо́дной прогу́лки или
похо́да); (*BOT*) вью́щееся расте́ние.
rambling ['ræmblɪŋ] *adj* (*speech*) несвя́зный*
(несвя́зен); (*house*) беспоря́дочно
вы́строенный (вы́строен); (*BOT*) вью́щийся.
rambunctious [ræm'bʌŋkʃəs] *adj* (*US*) =
rumbustious.

RAMC *n abbr* (*BRIT*) = **Royal Army Medical Corps**.
ramification [ræmɪfɪ'keɪʃən] *n* сле́дствие.
ramp [ræmp] *n* (*incline*) скат, укло́н; (*in garage*)
па́ндус; **on ~** (*US*: *AUT*) въезд на автостра́ду;
off ~ (*US*: *AUT*) съезд с автостра́ды.
rampage [ræm'peɪdʒ] *n*: **to be on the ~**
бу́йствовать (*impf*) ♦ *vi*: **they went rampaging
through the town** они́ бу́йствовали по всему́
го́роду.
rampant ['ræmpənt] *adj*: **to be ~** (*crime*)
свире́пствовать (*impf*).
rampart ['ræmpɑːt] *n* крепостно́й вал*.
ram raid *n* ограбле́ние, совершённое при
по́мощи автомаши́на.
ramshackle ['ræmʃækl] *adj* ве́тхий* (ветх).
RAN *n abbr* = **Royal Australian Navy**.
ran [ræn] *pt of* **run**.
ranch [rɑːntʃ] *n* ра́нчо *nt ind*.
rancher ['rɑːntʃə] *n* (*owner*) владе́лец*(-лица)
ра́нчо; (*ranch hand*) рабо́тник на ра́нчо.
rancid ['rænsɪd] *adj* (*butter*) прого́рклый;
(*bacon*) ту́хлый*.
rancour ['ræŋkə] (*US* **rancor**) *n* зло́ба.
R & B *n abbr* (= *rhythm and blues*) ритм и блюз.
R & D *n abbr* (= *research and development*)
нау́чно-иссле́довательские и о́пытно-
констру́кторские рабо́ты.
random ['rændəm] *adj* (*arrangement, selection*)
случа́йный*; (*COMPUT, MATH*) случа́йный,
произво́льный ♦ *n*: **at ~** науга́д.
random access *n* (*COMPUT*) прямо́й *or*
произво́льный до́ступ.
random access memory *n* (*COMPUT*)
запомина́ющее устро́йство с произво́льной
вы́боркой.
R & R *n abbr* (*US*: *MIL*) = **rest and recreation**.
randy ['rændɪ] *adj* (*BRIT*: *inf*) похотли́вый
(похотли́в).
rang [ræŋ] *pt of* **ring**.
range [reɪndʒ] *n* (*series*: *of proposals, offers*)
ряд*; (: *of products*) ассортиме́нт *no pl*,
вы́бор *no pl*; (: *of colours*) га́мма; (*of
mountains*) цепь* (*цепи́*) дальность *f*,
ра́диус де́йствия; (*of voice*) диапазо́н; (*MIL*:
also: **shooting ~**) стре́льбище; (: *indoor*) тир;
(*also*: **kitchen ~**) ку́хонная плита́* ♦ *vt* (*place
in a line*) выстра́ивать (вы́строить *perf*) ♦ *vi*:
to ~ over (*extend*) простира́ться (*impf*); **price
~** диапазо́н цен; **do you have anything else in
this price ~?** у Вас есть что́-нибудь ещё в
преде́лах э́той цены́?; **within** (*firing*) **~** на
расстоя́нии вы́стрела; **~d right/left** (*text*) с
поля́ми спра́ва/сле́ва; **to ~ from ... to ...**
колеба́ться* (*impf*) от +*gen* ... до +*gen* ....
ranger ['reɪndʒə] *n* (*in forest*) лесни́чий* *m adj*,
лесни́к*; (*in park*) смотри́тель(ница) *m(f)*.
Rangoon [ræŋ'guːn] *n* Рангу́н.
rank [ræŋk] *n* (*row*) ряд*; (*MIL*) шере́нга;

(*status*) чин*, ранг; (*BRIT. also:* **taxi** ~) стоя́нка* такси́ ♦ *adj* (*stinking*) зловóнный* (зловóнен); (*injustice*) вопию́щий*; (*hypocrisy*) я́вный* (я́вен) ♦ *vt:* **to** ~ **among** чи́слиться (*impf*) среди́ +*gen* ♦ *vt:* **I** ~ **him sixth** я ста́влю его́ на шестóе мéсто; **the** ~**s** *npl* (*MIL*) рядовы́е *pl adj*, рядовóй состáв *msg;* **the** ~ **and file** (*fig*) рядовы́е члéны *mpl;* **to close** ~**s** (*MIL, also fig*) смыкáть (сомкнýть *perf*) ряды́.

rankle ['ræŋkl] *vi:* **to** ~ **with sb** терзáть (*impf*) когó-н.

rank outsider *n* совершéнно безнадёжный кандидáт, кандидáт без шáнсов на успéх.

ransack ['rænsæk] *vt* (*search*) перерыть* (*perf*); (*plunder*) грáбить* (разгрáбить* *perf*).

ransom ['rænsəm] *n* выкуп; **to hold to** ~ (*fig: nation, company, individual*) держáть (*impf*) в залóжниках.

rant [rænt] *vi:* **to** ~ **and rave** рвать* (*impf*) и метáть (*impf*).

ranting ['ræntɪŋ] *n* разглагóльствование.

rap [ræp] *n* стук; (*POETRY, MUS*) *стиль в мýзыке или поэ́зии, характеризýющийся отрывистым ри́тмом, испóльзованием речитати́ва* ♦ *vi:* **to** ~ **on a door/table** стучáть (постучáть *perf*) в дверь/по столý.

rape [reɪp] *n* изнаси́лование; (*BOT*) рапс ♦ *vt* (*woman*) наси́ловать (изнаси́ловать *perf*).

rape(seed) oil ['reɪp(siːd)-] *n* рáпсовое мáсло.

rapid ['ræpɪd] *adj* стреми́тельный* (стреми́телен).

rapidity [rə'pɪdɪtɪ] *n* стреми́тельность *f.*

rapidly ['ræpɪdlɪ] *adv* стреми́тельно.

rapids ['ræpɪdz] *npl* (*GEO*) стремни́на *fsg.*

rapist ['reɪpɪst] *n* наси́льник.

rapport [ræ'pɔː'] *n* взаимопонимáние.

rapprochement [ræ'prɒʃmɑːŋ] *n* сближéние.

rapt [ræpt] *adj* (*attention*) сосредотóченный* (сосредотóчен); **he was** ~ **in contemplation** он был погружён в раздýмья.

rapture ['ræptʃə'] *n* (*delight*) востóрг; **to go into** ~**s over** приходи́ть* (прийти́* *perf*) в востóрг от +*gen.*

rapturous ['ræptʃərəs] *adj* (*applause*) востóрженный* (востóржен).

rare [rɛə'] *adj* рéдкий* (рéдок); (*rare steak*) кровáвый*; **it is** ~ **to find** ... рéдко удаётся найти́ ....

rarebit ['rɛəbɪt] *n see* **Welsh rarebit.**

rarefied ['rɛərɪfaɪd] *adj* разрежённый* (разрежён).

rarely ['rɛəlɪ] *adv* рéдко, нечáсто.

raring ['rɛərɪŋ] *adj:* **he is** ~ **to go** (*inf: keen*) емý не тéрпится приступи́ть к дéлу.

rarity ['rɛərɪtɪ] *n* рéдкость *f.*

rascal ['rɑːskl] *n* негодя́й(ка*).

rash [ræʃ] *adj* опромéтчивый (опромéтчив) ♦ *n* (*MED*) сыпь *f no pl*; (*spate: of events, robberies*) ряд*, волнá*; **he came out in a** ~ у негó вы́ступила сыпь.

rasher ['ræʃə'] *n* (*of bacon*) лóмтик.

rashly ['ræʃlɪ] *adv* опромéтчиво.

rasp [rɑːsp] *n* (*tool*) рáшпиль *m* ♦ *vt* (*speak: also:* ~ **out**) хрипéть* (прохрипéть* *perf*).

raspberry ['rɑːzbərɪ] *n* мали́на *f no pl.*

rasping ['rɑːspɪŋ] *adj:* **a** ~ **noise** скрежéщущий звук; **a** ~ **voice** скрипýчий* гóлос.

rat [ræt] *n* (*also fig*) кры́са.

ratable ['reɪtəbl] *adj* = **rateable.**

ratchet ['rætʃɪt] *n* храповúк; ~ **wheel** храповóе колесó*.

rate [reɪt] *n* (*speed*) скóрость *f*; (: *of change, inflation*) темп; (*of interest*) стáвка; (*ratio*) ýровень *m*; (*price: at hotel etc*) расцéнка ♦ *vt* (*value*) оцéнивать (оцени́ть* *perf*); (*estimate*) расцéнивать (расцени́ть* *perf*); ~**s** *npl* (*BRIT: property tax*) налóг *msg* на недви́жимость; (*fees*) расцéнки *fpl*; **at a** ~ **of 60 kilometres an hour** со скóростью 60 киломéтров в час; ~ **of flow** скóрость потóка; ~ **of growth** темпы рóста; ~ **of return** стáвка дохóда (*от вложéния капитáла*); **pulse** ~ частотá пýльса; **to** ~ **sb as** считáть (*impf*) когó-н +*instr*; **to** ~ **sth as** расцéнивать (расцени́ть (*perf*)) что-н как; **to** ~ **sb/sth among** относи́ть* (отнести́* *perf*) когó-н/что-н к +*dat*; **to** ~ **sb/ sth highly** высóко цени́ть (*impf*) когó-н/ что-н.

rateable value ['reɪtəbl-] *n* (*BRIT: formerly*) *стóимость дóма на оснóве котóрой рассчи́тывается налóг на недви́жимость.*

ratepayer ['reɪtpeɪə'] *n* (*BRIT: formerly*) *лицó, выплáчивающее налóг на недви́жимость.*

rather ['rɑːðə'] *adv* (*quite, somewhat*) довóльно; (*to some extent*) нéсколько; (*more accurately*): **or** ~ вернéе сказáть; **it's** ~ **expensive** (*quite*) э́то довóльно дóрого; (*too*) э́то сли́шком дóрого; **there's** ~ **a lot** сли́шком мнóго; **I would** ~ **go** я, пожáлуй, пойдý; **I'd** ~ **not leave** я бы не хотéл уходи́ть; **I** ~ **think he won't come** я дýмаю, что, пожáлуй, он не придёт.

ratification [rætɪfɪ'keɪʃən] *n* ратификáция.

ratify ['rætɪfaɪ] *vt* ратифици́ровать (*impf/perf*).

rating ['reɪtɪŋ] *n* (*assessment*) оцéнка*, рéйтинг; (*NAUT: BRIT*) матрóс; ~**s** *npl* (*RADIO, TV*) рéйтинг *msg.*

ratio ['reɪʃɪəu] *n* отношéние, соотношéние; **in the** ~ **of one hundred to one** в отношéнии сто к одномý.

ration ['ræʃən] *n* (*allowance: of food*) рациóн, паёк*; (: *of petrol*) нóрма ♦ *vt* норми́ровать (*impf/perf*); ~**s** *npl* (*MIL*) рациóн *msg*; **to be on** ~**s** быть* (*impf*) на довóльствии.

rational ['ræʃənl] *adj* (*solution, reasoning*) рационáльный* (рационáлен); (*person*) разýмный* (разýмен).

rationale [ræʃə'nɑːl] *n* рационáльное *or* разýмное обоснованáние.

rationalization [ræʃnəlaɪ'zeɪʃən] *n* рационализáция.

rationalize ['ræʃnəlaɪz] *vt* (*justify*) давáть*

(дать* *perf*) рациона́льное объясне́ние +*dat*.
rationally ['ræʃnəlɪ] *adv* рациона́льно.
rationing ['ræʃnɪŋ] *n* нормирова́ние.
rat poison *n* крыси́ный яд.
rat race *n*: **the ~ ~** грызня́ за власть.
rattan [ræ'tæn] *n* рота́нг.
rattle ['rætl] *n* дребезжа́ние; (*of train, car*)
громыха́ние; (*baby's toy*) погрему́шка* ♦ *vi*
(*small objects*) дребезжа́ть (*impf*) ♦ *vt* (*shake
noisily*) греме́ть (прогреме́ть *perf*); (*fig:
unsettle*) нерви́ровать (*impf*), выводи́ть*
(вы́вести* *perf*) из себя́; **to ~ along** (*car, bus*)
прогромыха́ть (*impf*); **a cold November wind
~d the windows** от холо́дного ноя́брьского
ве́тра дребезжа́ли о́кна.
rattlesnake ['rætlsneɪk] *n* грему́чая змея́*.
ratty ['rætɪ] *adj* (*inf: person*) издёрганный*
(издёрган).
raucous ['rɔːkəs] *adj* оглуши́тельный*
(оглуши́телен).
raucously ['rɔːkəslɪ] *adv* оглуши́тельно.
raunchy ['rɔːntʃɪ] *adj* (*song*) распу́тный*
(распу́тен).
ravage ['rævɪdʒ] *vt* разоря́ть (разори́ть *perf*).
ravages ['rævɪdʒɪz] *npl* (*of time, weather*)
разруши́тельные после́дствия *ntpl*.
rave [reɪv] *vi* (*in anger*) беснова́ться (*impf*),
бушева́ть (*impf*); (*MED*) бре́дить (*impf*); (*with
enthusiasm*): **to ~ about** восторга́ться (*impf*)
+*instr* ♦ *cpd* (*inf*) восто́рженный.
raven ['reɪvən] *n* во́рон.
ravenous ['rævənəs] *adj* (*person*) голо́дный*
(го́лоден) как волк.
ravine [rə'viːn] *n* уще́лье*.
raving ['reɪvɪŋ] *adj*: **~ lunatic** бу́йно
поме́шанный(-ая) *m(f) adj*.
ravings ['reɪvɪŋz] *npl* бред *msg*.
ravioli [rævɪ'əʊlɪ] *n* равио́ли *ind* (*италья́нское
блю́до, напомина́ющее пельме́ни*).
ravishing ['rævɪʃɪŋ] *adj* (*beautiful*)
восхити́тельный* (восхити́телен).
raw [rɔː] *adj* (*uncooked*) сыро́й*; (*not processed:
cotton*) необрабо́танный* (необрабо́тан);
(: *unrefined sugar*) нерафини́рованный
(нерафини́рован); (*sore*) све́жий* (свеж);
(*inexperienced*) зелёный* (зе́лен); (*weather,
day*) промо́зглый.
raw deal *n* (*inf: bad bargain*) неуда́чная
сде́лка*; (: *unfair treatment*): **he got a ~ ~** с
ним пло́хо обошли́сь.
raw material *n* сырьё *nt no pl*.
ray [reɪ] *n* (*of light, sunshine*) луч*; (*of heat*)
пото́к*; **~ of hope** луч наде́жды.
rayon ['reɪɒn] *n* иску́сственный шёлк.
raze [reɪz] *vt* (*building, forest: also*: **~ to the
ground**) сровня́ть (*perf*) с землёй.
razor ['reɪzər] *n* бри́тва; **safety ~** безопа́сная
бри́тва; **electric ~** электробри́тва.

razor blade *n* ле́звие (бри́твы).
razzle(-dazzle) ['ræzl('dæzl)] *n* (*BRIT: inf*): **to go
on the ~** идти́ (*impf*) кути́ть.
razzmatazz ['ræzmə'tæz] *n* (*inf*) буффона́да.
RC *abbr* = **Roman Catholic**.
RCAF *n abbr* = *Royal Canadian Air Force*.
RCMP *n abbr* = *Royal Canadian Mounted Police*.
RCN *n abbr* = *Royal Canadian Navy*.
RD *abbr* (*US: POST*: = *rural delivery*) доста́вка
по́чты в се́льскую ме́стность.
Rd *abbr* = *road*.
RDC *n abbr* (*BRIT*: = *rural district council*)
райо́нный сове́т (*в се́льской ме́стности*).
RE *n abbr* (*BRIT: SCOL*: = *religious education*)
религио́зное воспита́ние; (*MIL*: = *Royal
Engineers*) ≈ инжене́рные войска́.
re [riː] *prep* (*with regard to*) относи́тельно +*gen*.
reach [riːtʃ] *n* (*scope: of imagination*) разма́х ♦
vt (*place, end, agreement*) достига́ть
(дости́гнуть* *or* дости́чь* *perf*) +*gen*; (:
conclusion, decision) приходи́ть* (прийти́*
perf) к +*dat*; (*be able to touch*) достава́ть*
(доста́ть* *perf*); (*by telephone*) свя́зываться
(связа́ться* *perf*) с +*instr* ♦ *vi*: **to ~ into** сова́ть
(су́нуть *perf*) в +*acc*; **within ~** в преде́лах
досяга́емости; **out of ~** вне досяга́емости;
within ~ of the shops/station недалеко́ от
магази́нов/вокза́ла; **within easy ~ of** (*place*)
недалеко́ от +*gen*; "**keep out of the ~ of
children**" „бере́чь от дете́й"; **upper ~es** (*of
river*) верхо́вья *ntpl*; **lower ~es** (*of river*)
низо́вья *ntpl*; **can I ~ you at your hotel?** мо́жно
ли связа́ться с Ва́ми в гости́нице?; **to ~ for**
протя́гивать (протяну́ть* *perf*) ру́ку к +*dat*; **to
~ up** протя́гивать (протяну́ть* *perf*) ру́ку
вверх
▶ **reach out** *vt* протя́гивать (протяну́ть* *perf*) ♦
vi вытя́гиваться (вы́тянуться *perf*); **to ~ out
for sth** протя́гивать (протяну́ть* *perf*) ру́ку за
чем-н.
react [riː'ækt] *vi* (*CHEM*): **to ~ (with)** вступа́ть
(вступи́ть* *perf*) в реа́кцию (с +*instr*); (*MED*): **to
~ (to)** реаги́ровать (*impf*) (на +*acc*); (*respond*)
реаги́ровать (отреаги́ровать *perf*) (на +*acc*);
(*rebel*): **to ~ (against)** восстава́ть* (восста́ть*
perf) (про́тив +*gen*).
reaction [riː'ækʃən] *n* (*CHEM*) реа́кция; (*also
MED, POL*): **~ (to/against)** реа́кция (на +*acc*/
про́тив +*gen*); **~s** *npl* (*reflexes*) реа́кция *fsg*.
reactionary [riː'ækʃənrɪ] *adj* реакцио́нный*
(реакцио́нен).
reactor [riː'æktər] *n* (*also*: **nuclear ~**) реа́ктор.
read[1] [rɛd] *pt, pp of* **read**[2].
read[2] [riːd] (*pt, pp* **read**) *vt* чита́ть (прочита́ть *or*
проч́есть* *perf*); (*mood*) определя́ть
(определи́ть* *perf*); (*meter, thermometer etc*)
снима́ть (снять* *perf*) показа́ния с +*gen*; (*subj:
instrument etc*) пока́зывать (*impf*); (*study: at*

---

* marks translations which have irregular inflections. The Russian-English side of the dictionary gives inflectional information.

university) изучать (*impf*) ♦ *vi* (*person*) читать (*impf*); (*text etc*) читаться (*impf*); **the notice ~s ...** в объявлении говорится ...; **it can be taken as ~ that ...** (*fig*) само собой разумеется, что ...; **do you ~ me?** (*TEL*) Вы слышите меня?

▶ **read out** *vt* зачитывать (зачитать *perf*)

▶ **read over** *vt* перечитывать (перечитать *perf*)

▶ **read through** *vt* (*quickly*) пролистывать (пролистать *perf*); (*thoroughly*) прочитывать (прочитать *perf*)

▶ **read up** *vt* много читать (*impf*)

▶ **read up on** *vt fus* много читать (*impf*) по +*dat*.

readable ['ri:dəbl] *adj* (*handwriting*) разборчивый (разборчив); (*book, author*) хорошо читающийся; **this book is very ~** эта книга хорошо читается.

reader ['ri:də'] *n* (*of book, newspaper etc*) читатель(ница) *m(f)*; (*book*) книга для чтения, хрестоматия; (*BRIT: at university*) ≈ доцент.

readership ['ri:dəʃɪp] *n* (*of newspaper etc*) круг читателей.

readily ['rɛdɪlɪ] *adv* (*willingly*) с готовностью; (*easily*) легко; (*quickly*) охотно.

readiness ['rɛdɪnɪs] *n* готовность *f*; **in ~** наготове, в состоянии готовности.

reading ['ri:dɪŋ] *n* (*of books, newspapers etc*) чтение; (*understanding*) толкование; (*as entertainment*) чтения *ntpl*; (*on meter, thermometer etc*) показание.

reading lamp *n* настольная лампа.

reading matter *n* материал для чтения.

reading room *n* читальный зал.

readjust [ri:ə'dʒʌst] *vt* (*alter: position*) переменить (*impf*); (: *knob, mirror*) поворачивать (повернуть *perf*); (*instrument*) подрегулировать (*perf*) ♦ *vi* (*adapt*): **to ~ (to)** приспосабливаться (приспособиться* *perf*) (к +*dat*).

readjustment [ri:ə'dʒʌstmənt] *n* (*adapting*) приспособление; (*alteration*) регулировка*.

ready ['rɛdɪ] *adj* готовый (готов); (*available*) готовый ♦ *n*: **at the ~** (*MIL*) в положении для стрельбы; (*fig*) наготове; **~ for use** готовый (готов) к употреблению; **I am ~ to help** я готов помочь; **to get ~** приготавливаться (приготовиться* *perf*); **to get sb/sth ~** подготавливать (подготовить* *perf*) кого-н/ что-н.

ready cash *n* наличные деньги* *pl*.

ready-cooked ['rɛdɪkukt] *adj* готовый.

ready-made ['rɛdɪ'meɪd] *adj* готовый.

ready-mix ['rɛdɪmɪks] *n* (*for cakes etc*) полуфабрикат; (*concrete*) товарный бетон.

ready money *n* наличные деньги* *pl*.

ready reckoner [-'rɛkənə'] *n* (*BRIT*) арифметические таблицы *fpl* готовых расчётов.

ready-to-wear ['rɛdɪtə'wɛə'] *adj* (*dress etc*) готовый.

reaffirm [ri:ə'fə:m] *vt* вновь подтверждать

(подтвердить* *perf*).

reagent [ri:'eɪdʒənt] *n*: **chemical ~** химический* реактив.

real [rɪəl] *adj* (*reason, interest, result etc*) настоящий*, реальный* (реален); (*leather*) натуральный*; (*gold, feeling*) настоящий* ♦ *adv* (*US: inf: very*) очень; **in ~ life** в действительности; **in ~ terms** реально; **a ~ idiot** (*for emphasis*) настоящий* идиот.

real estate *n* недвижимость *f* ♦ *cpd* (*US*): **~ ~ agency** агентство по продаже недвижимости.

realign [ri:ə'laɪn] *vt* перестраивать (перестроить *perf*).

realism ['rɪəlɪzəm] *n* реализм.

realist ['rɪəlɪst] *n* реалист(ка*).

realistic [rɪə'lɪstɪk] *adj* (*practical*) реалистичный* (реалистичен); (*true to life*) реалистический*.

reality [ri:'ælɪtɪ] *n* реальность *f*, действительность *f*; **in ~** на самом деле, в реальности.

realization [rɪəlaɪ'zeɪʃən] *n* (*understanding*) осознание; (*fulfilment: of hopes*) осуществление; (*of asset*) реализация.

realize ['rɪəlaɪz] *vt* (*understand*) осознавать* (осознать* *perf*); (*fulfil*) осуществлять (осуществить* *perf*); (*COMM: asset*) реализовать (*impf*/*perf*); **I ~ that ...** я осознаю, что ....

reallocate [rɪ'æləkeɪt] *vt* перераспределять (перераспределить *perf*).

really ['rɪəlɪ] *adv* (*very*) очень; (*actually*): **what ~ happened?** что произошло на самом деле?; **~?** (*indicating interest*) правда?, да?; (*expressing surprise*) неужели?, серьёзно?; **~!** (*indicating annoyance*) ну, знаете!

realm [rɛlm] *n* (*of monarch*) королевство; (*fig: area of activity or study*) область* *f*, сфера.

real-time ['ri:ltaɪm] *adj* (*COMPUT*) в реальном времени.

realtor ['rɪəltɔ:'] *n* (*US*) агент по продаже недвижимости.

ream [ri:m] *n* (*of paper*) стопа*; **~s of** (*fig: inf*) куча, масса; **she's written ~s!** у неё масса *or* куча написанного!

reap [ri:p] *vt* (*crop*) жать (сжать* *perf*); (*fig: benefits, rewards*) пожинать (пожать* *perf*).

reaper ['ri:pə'] *n* (*machine*) жатка*.

reappear [ri:ə'pɪə'] *vi* снова появляться (появиться* *perf*).

reappearance [ri:ə'pɪərəns] *n* новое появление.

reapply [ri:ə'plaɪ] *vi*: **to ~ for** повторно обращаться (обратиться* *perf*) за +*instr*.

reappoint [ri:ə'pɔɪnt] *vt* повторно назначать (назначить *perf*).

reappraisal [ri:ə'preɪzl] *n* переоценка*.

rear [rɪə'] *adj* задний* ♦ *n* (*back*) задняя часть* *f*; (*buttocks*) зад; (*MIL*) тыл* ♦ *vt* (*cattle, family*) выращивать (вырастить* *perf*) ♦ *vi* (*also: ~*

up) становиться (стать* *perf*) на дыбы.

rear admiral *n* контр-адмира́л.

rear-engined ['rɪər'ɛndʒɪnd] *adj* (*AUT*) с мото́ром в за́дней ча́сти.

rearguard ['rɪəgɑ:d] *n* (*MIL*) арьерга́рд.

rearm [ri:'ɑ:m] *vi* перевооружа́ться (перевооружи́ться *perf*) ♦ *vt* перевооружа́ть (перевооружи́ть *perf*).

rearmament [ri:'ɑ:məmənt] *n* перевооруже́ние.

rearrange [ri:ə'reɪndʒ] *vt* (*objects*) переставля́ть (переста́вить* *perf*); (*order*) изменя́ть (измени́ть* *perf*).

rear-view mirror ['rɪəvju:-] *n* (*AUT*) зе́ркало* за́днего ви́да *or* обзо́ра.

reason ['ri:zn] *n* (*cause*) причи́на; (*ability to think*) ра́зум, рассу́док*; (*sense*) смысл ♦ *vi*: **to ~ with sb** убежда́ть (*impf*) кого́-н; **the ~ for/why** причи́на для +*gen*/по кото́рой; **to have ~ to think that** ... име́ть (*impf*) основа́ние ду́мать; **it stands to ~ that** ... разуме́ется, что ...; **she claims with good ~ that** ... она́ не без причи́ны счита́ет, что ...; **all the more ~ why** ... тем бо́лее ....

reasonable ['ri:znəbl] *adj* разу́мный* (разу́мен); (*quality*) неплохо́й* (непло́х); (*price*) прие́млемый (прие́млем), уме́ренный (уме́рен); (*not bad*) сно́сный* (сно́сен); **be ~!** бу́дьте благоразу́мны!

reasonably ['ri:znəblɪ] *adv* (*sensibly*) разу́мно; (*fairly*) дово́льно; **one can ~ assume that** ... мо́жно справедли́во предположи́ть, что ....

reasoned ['ri:znd] *adj* (*argument*) обосно́ванный* (обосно́ван).

reasoning ['ri:znɪŋ] *n* рассужде́ние.

reassemble [ri:ə'sɛmbl] *vt* (*снова*) собира́ть (собра́ть* *perf*).

reassert [ri:ə'sə:t] *vt* (*authority, oneself*) сно́ва утвержда́ть (утверди́ть* *perf*).

reassurance [ri:ə'ʃuərəns] *n* подтвержде́ние; (*comfort*) подде́ржка.

reassure [ri:ə'ʃuə'] *vt* (*comfort*) утеша́ть (уте́шить *perf*); **to ~ sb of** заверя́ть (заве́рить *perf*) кого́-н в +*prp*.

reassuring [ri:ə'ʃuərɪŋ] *adj* (*smile, manner*) ободря́ющий.

reawakening [ri:ə'weɪknɪŋ] *n* пробужде́ние.

rebate ['ri:beɪt] *n* обра́тная вы́плата.

rebel [*n* 'rɛbl, *vi* rɪ'bɛl] *n* бунта́рь*(-рка*) *m(f)* ♦ *vi* восстава́ть* (восста́ть* *perf*).

rebellion [rɪ'bɛljən] *n* восста́ние.

rebellious [rɪ'bɛljəs] *adj* (*child, behaviour*) стропти́вый (стропти́в); (*troops*) мяте́жный*; (*factions*) бунту́ющий.

rebirth [ri:'bə:θ] *n* возрожде́ние.

rebound [*vi* rɪ'baund, *n* 'ri:baund] *vi*: **to ~ (off)** отска́кивать (отскочи́ть* *perf*) (от +*gen*) ♦ *n*: **on the ~** (*ball*) на отско́ке; **he married her on**

the **~** он жени́лся на ней по́сле разочарова́ния в любви́ к друго́й.

rebuff [rɪ'bʌf] *n* отпо́р ♦ *vt* (*suggestion*) ре́зко отклоня́ть (отклони́ть *perf*); (*person*) дава́ть* (дать* *perf*) отпо́р +*dat*.

rebuild [ri:'bɪld] *irreg vt* (*town, building etc*) перестра́ивать (перестро́ить *perf*); (*economy, confidence*) восстана́вливать (восстанови́ть* *perf*).

rebuke [rɪ'bju:k] *vt* упрека́ть (упрекну́ть *perf*), де́лать (сде́лать *perf*) вы́говор +*dat* ♦ *n* упрёк, вы́говор.

rebut [rɪ'bʌt] *vt* опроверга́ть (опрове́ргнуть* *perf*).

rebuttal [rɪ'bʌtl] *n* опроверже́ние.

recalcitrant [rɪ'kælsɪtrənt] *adj* непоко́рный* (непоко́рен).

recall [*vb* rɪ'kɔ:l, *n* 'ri:kɔl] *vt* вспомина́ть (вспо́мнить *perf*); (*parliament, ambassador etc*) отзыва́ть (отозва́ть* *perf*); (*COMPUT*) перевызыва́ть (перевы́звать *perf*), вызыва́ть (вы́звать *perf*) повто́рно ♦ *n* (*ability to remember*) па́мять *f*; (*of ambassador etc*) о́тзыв; **the event is beyond ~** собы́тие безвозвра́тно исче́зло из па́мяти.

recant [rɪ'kænt] *vi* отрека́ться (отре́чься* *perf*).

recap ['ri:kæp] *vt* (*summarize*) резюми́ровать (*impf/perf*) ♦ *vi* де́лать (сде́лать *perf*) резюме́ ♦ *n* резюме́ *nt ind*.

recapitulate [ri:kə'pɪtjuleɪt] *vti* = **recap**.

recapture [ri:'kæptʃə'] *vt* (*town, territory etc*) сно́ва захва́тывать (захвати́ть* *perf*); (*atmosphere, mood etc*) воссоздава́ть* (воссозда́ть* *perf*).

rec'd *abbr* (*COMM*) = **received**.

recede [rɪ'si:d] *vi* (*tide*) спада́ть (спасть* *perf*); (*lights*) угаса́ть (уга́снуть* *perf*); (*memory*) слабе́ть (ослабе́ть* *perf*); (*hair*) реде́ть* (пореде́ть *perf*).

receding [rɪ'si:dɪŋ] *adj* (*hair*) реде́ющий; (*chin*) сре́занный (сре́зан).

receipt [rɪ'si:t] *n* (*document*) квита́нция; (*act of receiving*) получе́ние; **~s** *npl* (*COMM*) де́нежные поступле́ния *ntpl*, платежи́ *mpl*; **to acknowledge ~ of** подтвержда́ть (подтверди́ть* *perf*) получе́ние +*gen*; **on ~** по получе́нии; **we are in ~ of** ... (*COMM*) мы получи́ли ....

receivable [rɪ'si:vəbl] *adj* (*COMM*) подлежа́щий получе́нию; (: *bill, account*) надлежа́щий упла́те.

receive [rɪ'si:v] *vt* получа́ть (получи́ть* *perf*); (*criticism*) встреча́ть (встре́тить* *perf*); (*visitor, guest*) принима́ть (приня́ть* *perf*); **"received with thanks"** (*formal*) „полу́чено с благода́рностью".

receiver [rɪ'si:və'] *n* (*TEL*) (телефо́нная) тру́бка*; (*RADIO*) (ра́дио-)приёмник; (*TV*) телеви́зор; (COMM) ликвида́тор (неплатё-жеспосо́бной компа́нии); ~ **of stolen goods** укрыва́тель(ница) m(f) кра́деного.

receivership [ɪɪ'siːvəʃɪp] n конфиска́ция иму́щества обанкро́тившейся компа́нии суде́бными исполни́телями в це́лях вы́платы долго́в кредито́рам.

recent ['riːsnt] adj (event, times) неда́вний*; **in** ~ **years** в or за после́дние го́ды.

recently ['riːsntlɪ] adv неда́вно; **until** ~ до неда́внего вре́мени; **as** ~ **as last year** ещё в про́шлом году́.

receptacle [rɪ'sɛptɪkl] n сосу́д.

reception [rɪ'sɛpʃən] n (in hotel) регистра́ция; (in office) приёмная f adj; (in hospital) регистрату́ра; (party, also RADIO, TV) приём; **we got a warm** ~ нам был ока́зан тёплый приём.

reception centre n (BRIT) приёмный пункт для размеще́ния бе́женцев, бездо́мных итп.

reception desk n (in hotel) стол регистра́ции; (in hospital, at doctor's) регистрату́ра; (in large building, offices) отде́л приёма посети́телей.

receptionist [rɪ'sɛpʃənɪst] n (in hotel, hospital) регистра́тор; (in firm) секрета́рь* m по приёму посети́телей.

receptive [rɪ'sɛptɪv] adj восприи́мчивый (восприи́мчив).

recess [rɪ'sɛs] n (in room) ни́ша; (secret place) тайни́к*; (POL etc: holiday) кани́кулы pl; (US: LAW: short break) переры́в; (: SCOL) больша́я переме́на.

recession [rɪ'sɛʃən] n (ECON) спад.

recharge [riː'tʃɑːdʒ] vt (battery) перезаряжа́ть (перезаряди́ть* perf).

rechargeable [riː'tʃɑːdʒəbl] adj переза-ряжа́ющийся.

recipe ['rɛsɪpɪ] n (also fig) реце́пт.

recipient [rɪ'sɪpɪənt] n получа́тель m.

reciprocal [rɪ'sɪprəkl] adj взаи́мный* (взаи́мен), обою́дный* (обою́ден).

reciprocate [rɪ'sɪprəkeɪt] vt (answer): (отве́тить* perf) на +acc ♦ vi (favour) отпла́чивать (отплати́ть* perf); (feeling) отвеча́ть (отве́тить* perf) взаи́мностью.

recital [rɪ'saɪtl] n (concert) со́льный конце́рт.

recitation [rɛsɪ'teɪʃən] n (of poetry) деклама́ция; (of prose) чте́ние.

recite [rɪ'saɪt] vt (poem) деклами́ровать (продеклами́ровать perf); (prose) чита́ть (impf) (вслух); (complaints, grievances etc) произноси́ть* (произнести́ perf).

reckless ['rɛkləs] adj безрассу́дный* (безрассу́ден).

recklessly ['rɛkləslɪ] adv безрассу́дно.

reckon ['rɛkən] vt (calculate) счита́ть (посчита́ть or сосчита́ть perf); (think): **I** ~ **that** ... я счита́ю, что ... ♦ vi: **he is somebody to be** ~**ed with** с таки́м челове́ком, как он, ну́жно счита́ться; **to** ~ **without sb** не счита́ться

(посчита́ться perf) с кем-н; **to** ~ **without sth** не учи́тывать (уче́сть* perf) чего́-н
▶ **reckon on** vt fus рассчи́тывать (impf) на +acc.

reckoning ['rɛknɪŋ] n (calculation) подсчёт, расчёт; **the day of** ~ час распла́ты.

reclaim [rɪ'kleɪm] vt (demand back) тре́бовать (потре́бовать perf) обра́тно; (land: from sea) отвоёвывать (отвоева́ть* perf); (: from forest etc) осва́ивать (осво́ить perf); (waste materials) перераба́тывать (перерабо́тать perf).

reclamation [rɛklə'meɪʃən] n (of land) освое́ние.

recline [rɪ'klaɪm] vi отки́дываться (отки́нуться perf).

reclining [rɪ'klaɪmɪŋ] adj (seat) отки́дыва-ющийся.

recluse [rɪ'kluːs] n затво́рник(-ица).

recognition [rɛkəg'nɪʃən] n призна́ние; (of person, place) узнава́ние; **in** ~ **of** в знак призна́ния +gen; **to gain** ~ получа́ть (получи́ть* perf) призна́ние; **he has changed beyond** ~ он измени́лся до неузнава́емости.

recognizable ['rɛkəgnaɪzəbl] adj: ~ **(by)** узнава́емый (по +dat).

recognize ['rɛkəgnaɪz] vt признава́ть* (призна́ть* perf); (person, place) узнава́ть* (узна́ть perf); (attitude, illness) распознава́ть* (распозна́ть* perf); **to** ~ **by** узнава́ть* (узна́ть perf) по +dat.

recoil [n 'riːkɔɪl, vb rɪ'kɔɪl] n (of gun) отда́ча ♦ vi (person): **to** ~ **from doing** в у́жасе отказа́ться (perf) +infin.

recollect [rɛkə'lɛkt] vt припомина́ть (припо́мнить perf), вспомина́ть (вспо́мнить perf).

recollection [rɛkə'lɛkʃən] n воспомина́ние, па́мять f; **to the best of my** ~ наско́лько мне по́мнится.

recommend [rɛkə'mɛnd] vt рекомендова́ть (порекомендова́ть perf); **she has a lot to** ~ **her** мно́гое говори́т в её по́льзу.

recommendation [rɛkəmɛn'deɪʃən] n рекоменда́ция; **on the** ~ **of** по рекоменда́ции +gen.

recommended retail price n (BRIT) рекоменду́емая ро́зничная цена́.

recompense ['rɛkəmpɛns] n компенса́ция.

reconcilable ['rɛkənsaɪləbl] adj (ideas) совмести́мый (совмести́м).

reconcile ['rɛkənsaɪl] vt (people) мири́ть (помири́ть perf); (facts, beliefs) примиря́ть (примири́ть perf); **to** ~ **o.s. to sth** смиря́ться (смири́ться perf) с чем-н.

reconciliation [rɛkənsɪlɪ'eɪʃən] n примире́ние.

recondite [rɪ'kɔndaɪt] adj зау́мный* (зау́мен).

recondition [riːkən'dɪʃən] vt (machine) ремонти́ровать (отремонти́ровать perf).

reconditioned [riːkən'dɪʃənd] adj от-ремонти́рованный (отремонти́рован).

reconnaissance [rɪ'kɔnɪsns] n (MIL) разве́дка,

рекогносциро́вка.

reconnoitre [rɛkə'nɔɪtəʳ] (*US* **reconnoiter**) *vt* (*MIL: enemy territory*) разве́дывать (разве́дать *perf*).

reconsider [ri:kən'sɪdəʳ] *vt* пересма́тривать (пересмотре́ть* *perf*) ♦ *vi* переду́мать (*perf*).

reconstitute [ri:'kɔnstɪtju:t] *vt* (*organization*) реорганизова́ть (*impf/perf*); (*food*) восстана́вливать (восстанови́ть* *perf*).

reconstruct [ri:kən'strʌkt] *vt* перестра́ивать (перестро́ить *perf*); (*event, crime*) воспроизводи́ть* (воспроизвести́* *perf*), реконструи́ровать (*impf/perf*).

reconstruction [ri:kən'strʌkʃən] *n* (*of building*) реконстру́кция; (*of country*) перестро́йка; (*of crime*) воспроизведе́ние.

reconvene [ri:kən'vi:n] *vi* возобновля́ть (возобнови́ть* *perf*) рабо́ту.

record [*vb* rɪ'kɔ:d, *n, adj* 'rɛkɔ:d] *vt* (*in writing, on tape*) запи́сывать (записа́ть* *perf*); (*register: temperature, speed etc*) регистри́ровать (зарегистри́ровать *perf*) ♦ *n* (*written account, also* COMPUT) за́пись *f*; (*of meeting*) протоко́л; (*of attendance*) учёт; (*file*) де́ло*; (MUS) пласти́нка*; (*history: of person, company*) репута́ция; (*also:* **criminal ~**) суди́мость *f*; (SPORT) реко́рд ♦ *adj*: **in ~ time** в реко́рдное вре́мя; **public ~s** архи́вные за́писи; **to keep a ~ of** вести́* (*impf*) учёт +*gen*; **to put the ~ straight** (*fig*) пока́зывать (показа́ть* *perf*) и́стинное положе́ние веще́й; **he is on ~ as saying that ...** изве́стно, что он сказа́л, что ...; **off the ~** (*statement*) неофициа́льный; (*speak*) неофициа́льно.

recorded delivery [rɪ'kɔ:dɪd-] *n* (BRIT) доста́вка с уведомле́нием (о вруче́нии).

recorder [rɪ'kɔ:dəʳ] *n* (MUS) англи́йская фле́йта; (LAW) реко́рдер.

record holder (SPORT) *n* рекордсме́н(ка).

recording [rɪ'kɔ:dɪŋ] *n* за́пись *f*.

recording studio *n* сту́дия звукоза́писи.

record library *n* фоноте́ка.

record player *n* прои́грыватель *m*.

recount [rɪ'kaunt] *vt* (*story*) передава́ть* (переда́ть* *perf*); (*event*) пове́дать (*perf*) о +*prp*.

re-count ['ri:kaunt] *n* (*of votes*) пересчёт ♦ *vt* пересчи́тывать (пересчита́ть *perf*).

recoup [rɪ'ku:p] *vt*: **to ~ one's losses** возвраща́ть (верну́ть *perf*) поте́рянное.

recourse [rɪ'kɔ:s] *n*: **to have ~ to** прибега́ть (прибе́гнуть* *perf*) к +*dat*.

recover [rɪ'kʌvəʳ] *vt* (*lost or stolen items*) получа́ть (получи́ть* *perf*) обра́тно; (*financial loss*) возмеща́ть (возмести́ть* *perf*) ♦ *vi* (*subj: country*) встава́ть (встать* *perf*) на́ ноги; (*: economy*) улучша́ться (улу́чшиться *perf*); (*get better*): **to ~ (from)** поправля́ться

(попра́виться* *perf*) (по́сле +*gen*).

re-cover [ri:'kʌvəʳ] *vt* (*chair etc*) перебива́ть (переби́ть* *perf*) (оби́вку).

recovery [rɪ'kʌvərɪ] *n* (*from illness, operation*) выздоровле́ние; (*in economy, finances*) подъём; (*of stolen items*) возвраще́ние; (*of lost items*) обнаруже́ние.

re-create [ri:krɪ'eɪt] *vt* воссоздава́ть* (воссозда́ть* *perf*).

recreation [rɛkrɪ'eɪʃən] *n* (*free time*) о́тдых; (*leisure activities*) развлече́ние.

recreational [rɛkrɪ'eɪʃənl] *adj*: **~ facilities** усло́вия *ntpl* для о́тдыха и развлече́ния.

recreational drug *n* нарко́тик, принима́емый для удово́льствия и не предполага́ющий наркоти́ческой зави́симости.

recrimination [rɪkrɪmɪ'neɪʃən] *n* взаи́мные обвине́ния *ntpl*.

recruit [rɪ'kru:t] *n* (MIL) новобра́нец*, призывни́к*; (*in company*) но́вый сотру́дник; (*in organization*) но́вый член ♦ *vt* (*into army, organization*) вербова́ть (завербова́ть *perf*); (*into company*) нанима́ть (наня́ть* *perf*).

recruiting office [rɪ'kru:tɪŋ-] *n* (MIL) вербо́вочный пункт.

recruitment [rɪ'kru:tmənt] *n* (MIL) вербо́вка; (*by company*) набо́р (*на рабо́ту*).

rectangle ['rɛktæŋgl] *n* прямоуго́льник.

rectangular [rɛk'tæŋgjuləʳ] *adj* прямоуго́льный.

rectify ['rɛktɪfaɪ] *vt* исправля́ть (испра́вить* *perf*).

rector ['rɛktəʳ] *n* (REL) прихо́дский* свяще́нник.

rectory ['rɛktərɪ] *n* (*house*) дом* прихо́дского свяще́нника.

rectum ['rɛktəm] *n* пряма́я кишка́*.

recuperate [rɪ'kju:pəreɪt] *vi* оправля́ться (опра́виться* *perf*).

recur [rɪ'kə:ʳ] *vi* повторя́ться (повтори́ться *perf*).

recurrence [rɪ'kə:rns] *n* повторе́ние.

recurrent [rɪ'kə:rnt] *adj* повторя́ющийся.

recurring [rɪ'kə:rɪŋ] *adj* (*problem*) постоя́нно возника́ющий; (*dream*) повторя́ющийся.

recycle [ri:'saɪkl] *vt* перераба́тывать (перерабо́тать *perf*).

red [rɛd] *n* кра́сный цвет; (*pej:* POL) кра́сный (-ая) *m(f) adj* ♦ *adj* кра́сный* (кра́сен); (*hair*) ры́жий*; (*wine*) кра́сный; **she was dressed in ~** она́ была́ в кра́сном; **to be in the ~** име́ть (*impf*) задо́лженность.

red alert *n* состоя́ние боево́й гото́вности.

red-blooded ['rɛd'blʌdɪd] *adj*: **~ male** саме́ц* (*перен*).

red-carpet treatment [rɛd'ka:pɪt-] *n* торже́ственный приём.

Red Cross *n* Кра́сный Крест*.

redcurrant ['rɛdkʌrənt] *n* кра́сная сморо́дина *f*

no pl.

redden ['rɛdn] *vi* краснéть (покраснéть *perf*) ♦ *vt* окрáшивать (окрáсить* *perf*) в крáсный цвет.

reddish ['rɛdɪʃ] *adj* красновáтый (красновáт); (*hair*) рыжевáтый (рыжевáт).

redecorate [ri:'dɛkəreɪt] *vt* ремонти́ровать (отремонти́ровать *perf*) ♦ *vi* дéлать (сдéлать *perf*) ремóнт.

redecoration [ri:dɛkə'reɪʃən] *n* ремóнт.

redeem [rɪ'di:m] *vt* (*situation, reputation*) спасáть (спасти́* *perf*); (*pawned item*) выкупáть (вы́купить* *perf*); (*debt*) выплáчивать (вы́платить* *perf*); (*REL*) искупáть (искупи́ть* *perf*); **to ~ o.s.** искупáть (искупи́ть* *perf*) свою́ вину́.

redeemable [rɪ'di:məbl] *adj* подлежáщий вы́купу.

redeeming [rɪ'di:mɪŋ] *adj*: **~ feature** подкупáющее кáчество.

redefine [ri:dɪ'faɪn] *vt* (*position, theory*) пересмáтривать (пересмотрéть* *perf*); (*word, concept*) давáть* (дать* *perf*) нóвое определéние +*dat*.

redemption [rɪ'dɛmpʃən] *n* (*REL*) искуплéние грехóв; **past** *or* **beyond ~** (*fig*) безнадёжный* (безнадёжен), без надéжды на спасéние.

redeploy [ri:dɪ'plɔɪ] *vt* (*resources*) перераспределя́ть (перераспредели́ть* *perf*); (*MIL*) передислоци́ровать (*impf/perf*).

redeployment [ri:dɪ'plɔɪmənt] *n* (*see vb*) перераспределéние; передислокáция.

redevelop [ri:dɪ'vɛləp] *vt* (*area*) перестрáивать (перестрóить *perf*).

redevelopment [ri:dɪ'vɛləpmənt] *n* перестрóйка.

red-handed [rɛd'hændɪd] *adj*: **he was caught ~** его́ поймáли с поли́чным.

redhead ['rɛdhɛd] *n* ры́жий*(-ая) *m(f) adj*.

red herring *n* (*fig*) отвлекáющий манёвр.

red-hot [rɛd'hɔt] *adj* (*metal*) раскалённый* (раскалён) докраснá.

redirect [ri:daɪ'rɛkt] *vt* (*mail*) переадресóвывать (переадресовáть *perf*).

rediscover [ri:dɪs'kʌvə'] *vt* зáново открывáть (откры́ть* *perf*).

redistribute [ri:dɪs'trɪbju:t] *vt* перераспределя́ть (перераспредели́ть *perf*).

red-letter day ['rɛdlɛtə-] *n* прáздничный день* *m*.

red light *n*: **to go through a ~ ~** (*AUT*) éхать* (поéхать* *perf*) на крáсный свет.

red-light district ['rɛdlaɪt-] *n* квартáл публи́чных домóв.

red meat *n* тёмное мя́со (*особенно говя́дина и барáнина*).

redness ['rɛdnɪs] *n* краснотá; (*of hair*) рыжинá*.

redo [ri:'du:] *irreg vt* передéлывать (передéлать *perf*).

redolent ['rɛdələnt] *adj* (*fig*) напоминáющий;

(*smell*): **~ of** (*unpleasant*) отдаю́щий +*instr*; (*pleasant*) пáхнущий +*gen*.

redouble [ri:'dʌbl] *vt*: **to ~ one's efforts** удвáивать (удвóить *perf*) свои́ уси́лия.

redraft [ri:'drɑ:ft] *vt* перепи́сывать (переписáть* *perf*).

redraw [ri:'drɔ:] *vt* изменя́ть (измени́ть* *perf*).

redress [rɪ'drɛs] *n* (*compensation*) возмещéние ♦ *vt* (*error, wrong*) исправля́ть (испрáвить* *perf*); **to ~ the balance** восстанáвливать (восстанови́ть* *perf*) равновéсие сил.

Red Sea *n*: **the ~ ~** Крáсное мóре.

red tape *n* (*fig*) волоки́та.

reduce [rɪ'dju:s] *vt* сокращáть (сократи́ть* *perf*); **to ~ sth by/to** сокращáть (сократи́ть* *perf*) что-н на +*acc*/до +*gen*; **to ~ sb to** (*tears*) доводи́ть* (довести́* *perf*) когó-н до +*gen*; **to ~ sb to silence** заставля́ть (застáвить* *perf*) когó-н замолчáть; **he was ~d to stealing** он дошёл до тогó, что стал воровáть; **"reduce speed now"** (*AUT*) "сбáвьте скóрость".

reduced [rɪ'dju:st] *adj* (*goods*) по сни́женным цéнам; (*ticket*) со ски́дкой; **at a ~ price** (*goods*) по сни́женной ценé; (*ticket*) со ски́дкой.

reduction [rɪ'dʌkʃən] *n* (*in price*) ски́дка; (*in numbers*) сокращéние.

redundancy [rɪ'dʌndənsɪ] (*BRIT*) *n* (*dismissal*) увольнéние (*при сокращéнии штáтов*); (*unemployment*) сокращéние штáтов; **compulsory ~** вы́нужденное увольнéние; **voluntary ~** увольнéние по сóбственному желáнию.

redundancy payment *n* (*BRIT*) выходнóе посóбие (*при сокращéнии штáтов*).

redundant [rɪ'dʌndnt] *adj* (*BRIT: unemployed*) увóленный (увóлен); (*useless*) изли́шний* (изли́шен); **he was made ~** его́ сократи́ли.

reed [ri:d] *n* (*BOT*) тростни́к*; (*MUS*) язычóк*.

re-educate [ri:'ɛdjukeɪt] *vt* перевоспи́тывать (перевоспитáть* *perf*).

reedy ['ri:dɪ] *adj* (*voice*) пронзи́тельный* (пронзи́телен).

reef [ri:f] *n* риф.

reek [ri:k] *vi*: **to ~ (of)** си́льно пáхнуть* (*impf*) (+*instr*).

reel [ri:l] *n* кату́шка*; (*of film, tape*) боби́на; (*dance*) рил (*нарóдный хоровóдный тáнец*) ♦ *vi* (*sway*) качáться (*impf*), шатáться (*impf*); **my head is ~ing** у меня́ кру́жится головá

▸ **reel in** *vt* (*line*) смáтывать (смотáть *perf*); (*fish*) вытáскивать (вы́тащить *perf*) (*при пóмощи спи́ннинга*)

▸ **reel off** *vt* (*say*) вы́палить (*perf*).

re-election [ri:ɪ'lɛkʃən] *n* (*event*) перевы́боры *pl*; (*of person*) переизбрáние.

re-enter [ri:'ɛntə'] *vt* вновь входи́ть* (войти́* *perf*).

re-entry [ri:'ɛntrɪ] *n* повтóрный вход.

re-examine [ri:ɪg'zæmɪn] *vt* пересмáтривать (пересмотрéть* *perf*).

re-export ['riːɪks'pɔːt] *vt* реэкспорти́ровать (*impf/perf*) ◆ *n* реэ́кспорт.

ref [rɛf] *n abbr* (*SPORT: inf*) = **referee**.

ref. *abbr* (*COMM*: = *with reference to*) ссыла́ясь на +*acc*.

refectory [rɪ'fɛktərɪ] *n* столо́вая *f adj*.

refer [rɪ'fəː'] *vt*: **to ~ sb to** (*book, source*) отсыла́ть (отосла́ть* *perf*) кого́-н к +*dat*; (*doctor*) направля́ть (напра́вить* *perf*) кого́-н к +*dat*; **to ~ sth to** (*pass on*) передава́ть* (переда́ть* *perf*) что-н к +*dat*; **he ~red me to the manager** он напра́вил меня́ к управля́ющему

▶ **refer to** *vt fus* (*mention*) упомина́ть (упомяну́ть* *perf*) о +*prp*; (*relate to*) относи́ться* (*impf*) к +*dat*; (*consult*) обраща́ться (обрати́ться* *perf*) к +*dat*; **~ring to your letter** ссыла́ясь на Ва́ше письмо́.

referee [rɛfə'riː] *n* (*SPORT*) рефери́ *m ind*, судья́* *m*; (*BRIT: for job application*) лицо́, даю́щее *рекоменда́цию* ◆ *vt* суди́ть* (*impf*).

reference ['rɛfrəns] *n* (*mention*) упомина́ние; (*in book, paper*) ссы́лка*; (*for job application: letter*) рекоменда́ция; (: *person*) лицо́, *даю́щее рекоменда́цию*; **with ~ to** (*in letter*) ссыла́ясь на +*acc*; **"please quote this ~"** (*COMM*) "сошли́тесь на э́тот спра́вочный но́мер".

reference book *n* спра́вочник.

reference library *n* спра́вочная библиоте́ка.

reference number *n* спра́вочный но́мер*.

referenda [rɛfə'rɛndə] *npl of* **referendum**.

referendum [rɛfə'rɛndəm] (*pl* **referenda**) *n* рефере́ндум.

referral [rɪ'fəːrəl] *n* направле́ние.

refill [*vb* riː'fɪl, *n* 'riːfɪl] *vt* (*glass*) сно́ва наполня́ть (напо́лнить *perf*); (*pen*) заправля́ть (запра́вить* *perf*) ◆ *n* (*for pen*) запасно́й сте́ржень* *m*.

refine [rɪ'faɪn] *vt* (*sugar*) рафини́ровать (*impf/ perf*); (*oil*) очища́ть (очи́стить* *perf*); (*theory, idea, task*) соверше́нствовать (усоверше́нствовать *perf*).

refined [rɪ'faɪnd] *adj* (*person, taste*) утончённый* (утончён); (*sugar*) рафини́рованный*; (*oil*) очи́щенный*.

refinement [rɪ'faɪnmənt] *n* (*of person*) утончённость *f*; (*of system*) усоверше́нствование.

refinery [rɪ'faɪnərɪ] *n* (*for oil*) нефтеперераба́тывающий заво́д.

refit [riː'fɪt] *n* (*NAUT*) переобору́дование ◆ *vt* (*ship*) переобору́довать (*impf/perf*).

reflate [riː'fleɪt] *vt*: **to ~ the economy** проводи́ть* (провести́* *perf*) рефля́цию.

reflation [riː'fleɪʃən] *n* рефля́ция.

reflationary [riː'fleɪʃənrɪ] *adj* рефляцио́нный.

reflect [rɪ'flɛkt] *vt* (*also fig*) отража́ть

(отрази́ть* *perf*) ◆ *vi* (*think*) размышля́ть (*impf*)

▶ **reflect on** *vt* (*discredit*) броса́ть (бро́сить* *perf*) тень на +*acc*.

reflection [rɪ'flɛkʃən] *n* (*also fig*) отраже́ние; (*thought*) размышле́ние; (*criticism*): **~ on** осужде́ние +*gen*; **on ~** по размышле́нии.

reflector [rɪ'flɛktə'] *n* (*on car, bicycle*) отража́тель *m*; (*for light, heat*) рефле́ктор.

reflex ['riːflɛks] *adj* (*action, gesture*) рефлекто́рный ◆ *n* рефле́кс.

reflexive [rɪ'flɛksɪv] *adj* (*LING*) возвра́тный.

reform [rɪ'fɔːm] *n* (*of law, system*) рефо́рма; (*of sinner, character*) преобразова́ние ◆ *vt* (*character*) преобразова́ть (*impf/perf*); (*system*) реформи́ровать (*impf/perf*).

reformat [riː'fɔːmæt] *vt* (*COMPUT*) переформати́ровать (*impf/perf*).

Reformation [rɛfə'meɪʃən] *n*: **the ~** Реформа́ция.

reformatory [rɪ'fɔːmətərɪ] *n* (*US*) исправ- и́тельное заведе́ние.

reformed [rɪ'fɔːmd] *adj* (*character, alcoholic*) испра́вившийся.

refrain [rɪ'freɪn] *n* (*of song*) припе́в ◆ *vi*: **to ~ from commenting/visiting** возде́рживаться (воздержа́ться* *perf*) от коммента́риев/ визи́та.

refresh [rɪ'frɛʃ] *vt* освежа́ть (освежи́ть *perf*).

refresher course [rɪ'frɛʃə-] *n* (*BRIT*) курс повыше́ния квалифика́ции.

refreshing [rɪ'frɛʃɪŋ] *adj* (*drink, sleep*) освеж- а́ющий (освежа́ющ); (*change, idea*) све́жий.

refreshment [rɪ'frɛʃmənt] *n* (*food*) заку́ска*; (*drink*) напи́ток*; **I am in need of (some) ~** мне на́до закуси́ть.

refreshments [rɪ'frɛʃmənts] *npl* заку́ски* *fpl* и напи́тки *mpl*.

refrigeration [rɪfrɪdʒə'reɪʃən] *n* (*low temperature*) охлажде́ние; (*in deep freeze*) замора́живание.

refrigerator [rɪ'frɪdʒəreɪtə'] *n* холоди́льник.

refuel [riː'fjuəl] *vi* направля́ться (запра́виться* *perf*) ◆ *vt* заправля́ть (запра́вить* *perf*).

refuelling [riː'fjuəlɪŋ] *n* запра́вка*.

refuge ['rɛfjuːdʒ] *n* (*shelter*) убе́жище; **to take ~ in** укрыва́ться (укры́ться* *perf*) в +*prp*.

refugee [rɛfju'dʒiː] *n* бе́женец*(-нка*); **a political ~** полити́ческий*(-ая) бе́женец (-нка*).

refugee camp *n* ла́герь* *m* бе́женцев.

refund [*n* 'riːfʌnd, *vb* rɪ'fʌnd] *n* возмеще́ние ◆ *vt* (*money*) возмеща́ть (возмести́ть* *perf*).

refurbish [riː'fəːbɪʃ] *vt* за́ново отде́лывать (отде́лать *perf*).

refurbishment [riː'fəːbɪʃmənt] *n* ремо́нт.

refurnish [riː'fəːnɪʃ] *vt* за́ново обставля́ть (обста́вить* *perf*).

---

* marks translations which have irregular inflections. The Russian-English side of the dictionary gives inflectional information.

refusal [rɪ'fjuːzəl] *n* отка́з; **first ~** (*option*) пра́во пе́рвого вы́бора.

refuse¹ [rɪ'fjuːz] *vt* (*offer, gift*) отка́зываться (отказа́ться* *perf*) от +*gen*; (*permission, consent*) отка́зывать (отказа́ть* *perf*) в +*prp* ◆ *vi* отка́зываться (отказа́ться* *perf*); (*horse*) упря́миться (заупря́миться *perf*); **to ~ to do** отка́зываться (отказа́ться* *perf*) +*infin*.

refuse² ['rɛfjuːs] *n* му́сор*.

refuse collection *n* убо́рка му́сора.

refuse disposal *n* (*by carting away*) вы́воз му́сора.

refusenik [rɪ'fjuːznɪk] *n* отка́зник.

refute [rɪ'fjuːt] *vt* опроверга́ть (опрове́ргнуть* *perf*).

regain [rɪ'geɪn] *vt* (*power, position*) вновь обрета́ть (обрести́* *perf*).

regal ['riːgl] *adj* короле́вский*.

regale [rɪ'geɪl] *vt*: **to ~ sb with sth** развлека́ть (развле́чь* *perf*) кого́-н чем-н.

regalia [rɪ'geɪlɪə] *n* рега́лии *fpl*.

regard [rɪ'gɑːd] *n* (*esteem*) уваже́ние ◆ *vt* (*consider*) счита́ть (*impf*); (*view, look on*): **to ~ with** относи́ться (*impf*) *or* рассма́тривать (*impf*) с +*instr*; **to give one's ~s to** передава́ть* (переда́ть* *perf*) приве́т +*dat*; **"with kindest ~s"** „с наилу́чшими пожела́ниями"; (*more formal*) „с уваже́нием"; **as ~s, with ~ to** что каса́ется +*gen*, относи́тельно +*gen*.

regarding [rɪ'gɑːdɪŋ] *prep* относи́тельно +*gen*.

regardless [rɪ'gɑːdlɪs] *adv* (*carry on, continue*) несмотря́ ни на что́; **~ of** не счита́ясь с +*instr*.

regatta [rɪ'gætə] *n* рега́та.

regency ['riːdʒənsɪ] *n* ре́гентство ◆ *adj*: **R~** (*furniture, style*) эпо́хи ре́гентства.

regenerate [rɪ'dʒɛnəreɪt] *vt* возрожда́ть (возроди́ть* *perf*) ◆ *vi* возрожда́ться (возроди́ться* *perf*).

regent ['riːdʒənt] *n* ре́гент.

reggae ['rɛgeɪ] *n* рэ́гги *m ind*.

regime [reɪ'ʒiːm] *n* (*system of government*) режи́м.

regiment ['rɛdʒɪmənt] *n* полк* ◆ *vt* подчиня́ть (подчини́ть *perf*) жёсткому контро́лю.

regimental [rɛdʒɪ'mɛntl] *adj* полково́й.

regimentation [rɛdʒɪmɛn'teɪʃən] *n* жёсткий* контро́ль *m*.

region ['riːdʒən] *n* (*area: of country*) райо́н, регио́н; (*ADMIN, ANAT*) о́бласть* *f*; **in the ~ of** (*fig: approximately*) в райо́не +*gen*.

regional ['riːdʒənl] *adj* (*organization, committee*) областно́й, региона́льный; (*characteristic of region*) ме́стный.

regional development *n* региона́льное разви́тие.

register ['rɛdʒɪstə*] *n* (*census, record*) за́пись *f*; (*SCOL*) журна́л; (*also: electoral ~*) спи́сок* избира́телей; (*MUS*) реги́стр ◆ *vt* регистри́ровать (зарегистри́ровать *perf*); (*subj: meter, gauge*) пока́зывать (показа́ть*

perf) ◆ *vi* регистри́роваться (зарегистри́роваться *perf*); (*as student*) запи́сываться (записа́ться* *perf*); (*make impression*) запечатлева́ться (запечатле́ться *perf*) в па́мяти; **to ~ for a course** запи́сываться (записа́ться* *perf*) на ку́рс; **to ~ a protest** выража́ть (вы́разить* *perf*) проте́ст.

registered ['rɛdʒɪstəd] *adj* (*letter*) заказно́й; (*nurse, addict*) зарегистри́рованный*.

registered company *n* зарегистри́рованная компа́ния.

registered nurse *n* (*US*) зарегистри́рованная медсестра́*.

registered office *n* зарегистри́рованный о́фис.

Registered Trademark *n* зарегистри́рованный това́рный знак.

registrar ['rɛdʒɪstrɑː*] *n* регистра́тор; (*BRIT: in hospital*) гла́вный врач*.

registration [rɛdʒɪs'treɪʃən] *n* регистра́ция; (*AUT: also: ~ number*) (регистрацио́нный) но́мер* маши́ны.

registry ['rɛdʒɪstrɪ] *n* регистрату́ра.

registry office *n* (*BRIT*) ≈ ЗАГС (*отде́л за́писей гражда́нского состоя́ния*).

regret [rɪ'grɛt] *n* (*sorrow*) сожале́ние ◆ *vt* сожале́ть (*impf*) о +*prp*; (*death*) опла́кивать (опла́кать* *perf*); **to ~ that ...** сожале́ть (*impf*), что ...; **we ~ to inform you that ...** мы с сожале́нием сообща́ем Вам, что ....

regretfully [rɪ'grɛtfəlɪ] *adv* (*unfortunately*) к сожале́нию.

regrettable [rɪ'grɛtəbl] *adj* (*unfortunate*) приско́рбный* (приско́рбен), досто́йный* (досто́ин) сожале́ния.

regrettably [rɪ'grɛtəblɪ] *adv* (*drunk, late*) огорчи́тельным о́бразом; **~, he ...** к сожале́нию, он ....

Regt *abbr* (*MIL*) = **regiment**.

regular ['rɛgjulə*] *adj* регуля́рный* (регуля́рен); (*even*) ро́вный* (ро́вен); (*symmetrical*) пра́вильный* (пра́вилен); (*usual: time*) определённый; (: *doctor, customer*) регуля́рный; (*LING*) пра́вильный; (*COMM: size*) сре́дний* ◆ *n* (*in cafe, restaurnat*) завсегда́тай; (*in shop*) клие́нт; **~ soldier** солда́т регуля́рной а́рмии.

regularity [rɛgju'lærɪtɪ] *n* (*frequency*) регуля́рность *f*.

regularly ['rɛgjuləlɪ] *adv* регуля́рно; (*symmetrically: shaped etc*) пра́вильно.

regulate ['rɛgjuleɪt] *vt* (*control, adjust*) регули́ровать (*impf*).

regulation [rɛgju'leɪʃən] *n* регули́рование; (*rule*) пра́вило.

regulatory [rɛgju'leɪtrɪ] *adj* регули́рующий.

rehabilitate [riːə'bɪlɪteɪt] *vt* (*criminal*) интегри́ровать (*impf/perf*); (*invalid, addict*) реабилити́ровать (*impf/perf*).

rehabilitation ['riːəbɪlɪ'teɪʃən] *n* (*of criminal*)

интегра́ция; (*of disabled, addict*)
реабилита́ция.
rehash [ri:'hæʃ] *vt* (*inf*) преподноси́ть*
(преподнести́* *perf*) в но́вом све́те.
rehearsal [rɪ'hɔːsəl] *n* репети́ция; **dress** ~
генера́льная репети́ция.
rehearse [rɪ'hɔːs] *vt* репети́ровать
(отрепети́ровать *perf*).
rehouse [riː'hauz] *vt* (*person*) переселя́ть
(пересели́ть *perf*).
reign [rem] *n* ца́рствование; (*fig*) госпо́дство ◆
vi (*monarch*) ца́рствовать (*impf*); (*fig*) цари́ть
(*impf*).
reigning ['remɪŋ] *adj* (*monarch*) ца́рствующий;
(*champion*) ны́нешний*.
reimburse [riːɪm'bɔːs] *vt* возмеща́ть
(возмести́ть* *perf*).
rein [rem] *n* (*for horse*) вожжа́*; **to give sb free** ~
(*fig*) дава́ть* (дать* *perf*) кому́-н свобо́ду
де́йствий.
reincarnation [riːɪnkɑː'neɪʃən] *n* (*belief*)
переселе́ние душ*.
reindeer ['remdɪə'] *n inv* се́верный оле́нь *m*.
reinforce [riːɪn'fɔːs] *vt* (*strengthen*) укрепля́ть
(укрепи́ть* *perf*); (*back up*) подкрепля́ть
(подкрепи́ть* *perf*).
reinforced concrete *n* железобето́н.
reinforcement [riːɪn'fɔːsmənt] *n* (*strengthening*)
укрепле́ние; (*action*) усиле́ние; **~s** *npl* (*MIL*)
подкрепле́ние *ntsg*.
reinstate [riːɪn'steɪt] *vt* восстана́вливать
(восстанови́ть* *perf*) в пре́жнем положе́нии.
reinstatement [riːɪn'steɪtmənt] *n*
восстановле́ние в пре́жнем положе́нии.
reissue [riː'ɪʃjuː] *vt* (*book*) переиздава́ть*
(переизда́ть* *perf*); (*film*) сно́ва выпуска́ть
(вы́пустить* *perf*).
reiterate [riː'ɪtəreɪt] *vt* повторя́ть (повтори́ть
perf).
reject [*vt* rɪ'dʒɛkt, *n* 'riːdʒɛkt] *vt* отклоня́ть
(отклони́ть* *perf*), отверга́ть (отве́ргнуть*
perf); (*political system*) отверга́ть
(отве́ргнуть* *perf*); (*candidate*) отклоня́ть
(отклони́ть* *perf*); (*coin*) не принима́ть
(приня́ть* *perf*); (*goods, fruit etc*) бракова́ть
(забракова́ть *perf*) ◆ *n* (*COMM: single item*)
брако́ванное изде́лие; ~**s** брак.
rejection [rɪ'dʒɛkʃən] *n* отклоне́ние; (*of
candidate*) отклоне́ние.
rejoice [rɪ'dʒɔɪs] *vi*: **to** ~ **at** *or* **over** ликова́ть
(*impf*) по по́воду +*gen*.
rejoinder [rɪ'dʒɔɪndə'] *n* (*retort*) возраже́ние,
отве́т.
rejuvenate [rɪ'dʒuːvəneɪt] *vt* (*person*)
омола́живать (омолоди́ть* *perf*);
(*organization, system etc*) обновля́ть
(обнови́ть* *perf*).
rekindle [riː'kɪndl] *vt* разжига́ть (разже́чь*

perf).
relapse [rɪ'læps] *n* (*MED*) рециди́в ◆ *vi*: **to** ~ **into**
(*depression*) (сно́ва) впада́ть (впасть* *perf*) в
+*acc*.
relate [rɪ'leɪt] *vt* (*tell*) переска́зывать
(пересказа́ть* *perf*); (*connect*): **to** ~ **sth to**
относи́ть* (отнести́* *perf*) что-н к +*dat* ◆ *vi*: **to**
~ **to** (*person*) сходи́ться* (*impf*) с +*instr*;
(*subject, thing*) относи́ться* (*impf*) к +*dat*.
related [rɪ'leɪtɪd] *adj*: ~ (**to**) (*person*) свя́занный
родство́м (с +*instr*); (*animal, language*)
ро́дственный* (ро́дствен) (с +*instr*); **they are**
~ они́ состоя́т в родстве́.
relating to [rɪ'leɪtɪŋ-] *prep* относи́тельно +*gen*.
relation [rɪ'leɪʃən] *n* (*member of family*)
ро́дственник(-ица); (*connection*) отноше́ние;
~**s** *npl* (*dealings*) сноше́ния *ntpl*; (*relatives*)
родня́ *fsg*; **diplomatic/international** ~**s**
дипломати́ческие/междунаро́дные
отноше́ния; **in** ~ **to** относи́тельно +*gen*; **to**
bear no ~ **to** не име́ть (*impf*) никако́го
отноше́ния к +*dat*.
relationship [rɪ'leɪʃənʃɪp] *n* (*between two
people, countries*) (взаимо-)отноше́ния *ntpl*;
(*between two things*) связь *f*; (*also*: **family** ~)
родство́; (*affair*) связь; **they have a good** ~ у
них хоро́шие (взаимо-)отноше́ния.
relative ['rɛlətɪv] *n* (*member of family*)
ро́дственник(-ица) ◆ *adj* (*comparative*)
относи́тельный* (относи́телен); (*connected*):
~ **to** относя́щийся к +*dat*.
relatively ['rɛlətɪvlɪ] *adv* относи́тельно.
relative pronoun *n* (*LING*) относи́тельное
местоиме́ние.
relax [rɪ'læks] *vi* (*person: unwind*) расслаб-
ля́ться (рассла́биться* *perf*); (: *calm down*)
успока́иваться (успоко́иться *perf*); (*muscle*)
расслабля́ться (рассла́биться* *perf*) ◆ *vt*
(*one's grip, rule*) ослабля́ть (осла́бить* *perf*);
(*mind, person*) расслабля́ть (рассла́бить*
perf); (*control*) ослабля́ть (осла́бить* *perf*).
relaxation [riːlæk'seɪʃən] *n* (*rest*) о́тдых; (*of
muscle*) расслабле́ние; (*of grip, rule, control
etc*) ослабле́ние; (*recreation*) о́тдых,
развлече́ние.
relaxed [rɪ'lækst] *adj* (*person, atmosphere*)
споко́йный* (споко́ен).
relaxing [rɪ'læksɪŋ] *adj* (*holiday, afternoon*)
расслабля́ющий*.
relay [*n* 'riːleɪ, *vt* rɪ'leɪ] *n* (*race*) эстафе́та ◆ *vt*
(*pass on: message etc*) передава́ть*
(переда́ть* *perf*); (*transmit*) трансли́ровать
(*impf/perf*).
release [rɪ'liːs] *n* (*from prison, obligation*)
освобожде́ние; (*of gas, water etc*) вы́пуск; (*of
film, book, record*) вы́пуск; (*device*) спусково́е
устро́йство, спуск ◆ *vt* (*prisoner*)
освобожда́ть (освободи́ть* *perf*); (*gas etc*)

выпускáть (вы́пустить* perf); (free: from wreckage etc) высвобождáть (вы́свободить* perf); (TECH: catch, spring etc) отпускáть (отпусти́ть* perf); (book, film) выпускáть (вы́пустить* perf); (report, news) передавáть (передáть* perf); **to ~ the clutch** (AUT) отпускáть (отпусти́ть* perf) сцеплéние; *see also* **press release**.

relegate ['rɛləgeɪt] vt понижáть (пони́зить* perf); (BRIT: SPORT): **to be ~d** переводи́ть* (перевести́* perf) в ни́зшую ли́гу.

relent [rɪ'lɛnt] vi (give in) уступáть (уступи́ть* perf).

relentless [rɪ'lɛntlɪs] adj (effort) неослáбный; (rain) продолжи́тельный* (продолжи́телен); (determined) неустáнный* (неустáнен).

relevance ['rɛləvəns] n (of remarks) умéстность f, релевáнтность f; (of information) актуáльность f; (of question) умéстность; **~ of sth to sth** умéстность чегó-н по отношéнию к чемý-н.

relevant ['rɛləvənt] adj (pertinent) актуáльный* (актуáлен), релевáнтный* (релевáнтен); (corresponding) соотвéтствующий*; **~ to** относя́щийся* к +dat.

reliability [rɪlaɪə'bɪlɪtɪ] n (see adj) надёжность f; достовéрность f.

reliable [rɪ'laɪəbl] adj надёжный* (надёжен); (news, information) достовéрный* (достовéрен).

reliably [rɪ'laɪəblɪ] adv: **to be ~ informed that** ... имéть (impf) достовéрную информáцию о том, что ....

reliance [rɪ'laɪəns] n: **~ (on)** (person, drugs) зави́симость f (от +gen).

reliant [rɪ'laɪənt] adj: **to be ~ on sth/sb** полагáться (положи́ться* perf) на когó-н/ чтó-н.

relic ['rɛlɪk] n (REL) мóщи pl; (of the past etc) рели́квия.

relief [rɪ'liːf] n облегчéние; (aid) пóмощь f; (ART, GEO) рельéф; **by way of light ~** для разря́дки напряжённости.

relief map n рельéфная кáрта.

relief road n объéзд (дорóга, отводя́щая трáнспорт).

relieve [rɪ'liːv] vt (pain, sufferings) облегчáть (облегчи́ть perf); (fear, worry) уменьшáть (умéньшить perf); (patient) освобождáть (освободи́ть* perf); (victims, refugees etc) окáзывать (оказáть* perf) пóмощь +dat; (colleague, guard) сменя́ть (смени́ть* perf); **to ~ sb of sth** освобождáть (освободи́ть* perf) когó-н от чегó-н; **to ~ o.s.** облегчáться (облегчи́ться perf).

relieved [rɪ'liːvd] adj: **to feel ~** почýвствовать (perf) облегчéние; **he is ~ that** ... он рад, что ...; **I'm ~ to hear it** я рад э́то слы́шать.

religion [rɪ'lɪdʒən] n рели́гия.

religious [rɪ'lɪdʒəs] adj религиóзный* (религиóзен).

religious education n религиóзное воспитáние.

religiously [rɪ'lɪdʒəslɪ] adv (scrupulously) неукосни́тельно.

relinquish [rɪ'lɪŋkwɪʃ] vt (authority) откáзываться (отказáться* perf) от +gen; (plan, habit) оставля́ть (остáвить* perf).

relish ['rɛlɪʃ] n (CULIN) припрáва; (enjoyment) наслаждéние ♦ vt (food, drink) наслаждáться (наслади́ться* perf) +instr; (idea, thought, prospect etc) наслаждáться (impf).

relive [riː'lɪv] vt (memory, pleasure, visit etc) вновь пережи́вáть (пережи́ть* perf).

reload [riː'ləud] vt (gun) перезаряжáть (перезаряди́ть* perf).

relocate [riː'ləu'keɪt] vt перемещáть (перемести́ть* perf) ♦ vi: **to ~ (in)** перемещáться (перемести́ться* perf) (в +acc).

reluctance [rɪ'lʌktəns] n неохóта, нежелáние.

reluctant [rɪ'lʌktənt] adj (acceptance) неохóтный* (неохóтен); (person): **he is ~ to go there** он идёт тудá неохóтно.

reluctantly [rɪ'lʌktəntlɪ] adv неохóтно.

rely [rɪ'laɪ] vt fus (be dependent on) полагáться (impf) на +acc; (trust) полагáться (положи́ться* perf) на +acc.

remain [rɪ'meɪn] vi (continue to be) остáвáться* perf); (survive) сохраня́ться (сохрани́ться perf); **to ~ silent** храни́ть (impf) молчáние; **I ~, yours faithfully** (BRIT: in letters) остаю́сь, и́скренне Ваш.

remainder [rɪ'meɪndər] n остáток*.

remaining [rɪ'meɪnɪŋ] adj сохрани́вшийся; (surviving) остáвшийся.

remains [rɪ'meɪnz] npl (of meal) остáтки mpl; (of building) развáлины fpl; (of corpse) остáнки mpl.

remand [rɪ'mɑːnd] n: **on ~** взя́тый под стрáжу ♦ vt: **he was ~ed in custody** он был взят под стрáжу.

remand home n (BRIT) исправи́тельная колóния для несовершеннолéтних.

remark [rɪ'mɑːk] n замечáние ♦ vt замечáть (замéтить* perf) ♦ vi: **to ~ on sth** дéлать (сдéлать perf) замечáние относи́тельно +gen; **to ~ that** замечáть (замéтить* perf), что.

remarkable [rɪ'mɑːkəbl] adj замечáтельный* (замечáтелен).

remarry [riː'mærɪ] vi вступáть (вступи́ть* perf) в повтóрный брак.

remedial [rɪ'miːdɪəl] adj (tuition, classes) исправи́тельный* (исправи́телен), корректи́вный*; (exercise) лечéбный.

remedy ['rɛmədɪ] n (cure) срéдство ♦ vt исправля́ть (испрáвить* perf).

remember [rɪ'mɛmbər] vt (call back to mind) вспоминáть (вспóмнить perf); (bear in mind) пóмнить (impf); (send greetings): **~ me to him** передáйте емý от меня́ привéт; **I ~ seeing her, I ~ having seen her** я пóмню, что я её ви́дел; **she ~ed to call me** онá не забы́ла позвони́ть мне.

remembrance [rɪ'mɛmbrəns] *n* па́мять *f*.

remind [rɪ'maɪnd] *vt*: **to ~ sb to do** напомина́ть (напо́мнить *perf*) кому́-н +*infin*; **to ~ sb of sth/sb** напомина́ть (напо́мнить *perf*) кому́-н о чём-н/ком-н; **that ~s me!** кста́ти!; **she ~s me of her mother** она́ напомина́ет мне свою́ мать.

reminder [rɪ'maɪndə^r] *n* напомина́ние.

reminisce [rɛmɪ'nɪs] *vi* вспомина́ть (вспо́мнить *perf*).

reminiscences [rɛmɪ'nɪsnsɪz] *npl* воспомина́ния *ntpl*.

reminiscent [rɛmɪ'nɪsnt] *adj*: **to be ~ of sth** напомина́ть (напо́мнить *perf*) что-н.

remiss [rɪ'mɪs] *adj* (*careless*) небре́жный* (небре́жен); **it was ~ of him** с его́ стороны́ э́то бы́ло небре́жностью.

remission [rɪ'mɪʃən] *n* (*cancelling: of debt, fee*) освобожде́ние; (*reduction: of prison sentence*) сокраще́ние; (*MED*) реми́ссия; (*REL*) отпуще́ние.

remit [rɪ'mɪt] *vt* (*send*) пересыла́ть (пересла́ть* *perf*).

remittance [rɪ'mɪtns] *n* (*payment*) де́нежный перево́д (*для опла́ты чего́-н*).

remnant ['rɛmnənt] *n* оста́ток*; **~s** *npl* (*COMM*) оста́тки *mpl*.

remonstrate ['rɛmənstreɪt] *vi*: **to ~ (with sb about sth)** выража́ть (вы́разить* *perf*) проте́ст (кому́-н по по́воду чего́-н).

remorse [rɪ'mɔːs] *n* раска́яние.

remorseful [rɪ'mɔːsful] *adj* по́лный* (по́лон) раска́яния.

remorseless [rɪ'mɔːslɪs] *adj* (*person*) неща́дный* (неща́ден); (*noise, pain*) невыноси́мый (невыноси́м).

remote [rɪ'məut] *adj* (*place, time*) отдалённый* (отдалён); (*person*) за́мкнутый (за́мкнут); (*possibility, chance*) незначи́тельный* (незначи́телен); **there is a ~ possibility that ...** существу́ет маловероя́тная возмо́жность, что ....

remote control *n* дистанцио́нное управле́ние.

remote-controlled [rɪ'məutkən'trəuld] *adj* с дистанцио́нным управле́нием.

remotely [rɪ'məutlɪ] *adv* отдалённо; **I'm not ~ interested** я нисколько не заинтересо́ван.

remoteness [rɪ'məutnɪs] *n* (*of place*) отдалённость *f*, (*of person*) за́мкнутость *f*.

remould ['riːməuld] *n* (*BRIT: tyre*) ши́на с восстано́вленным проте́ктором.

removable [rɪ'muːvəbl] *adj* (*detachable*) съёмный.

removal [rɪ'muːvəl] *n* (*also MED*) удале́ние; (*BRIT: of furniture*) перево́зка; (*dismissal*) отстране́ние.

removal man *irreg n* (*BRIT*) перево́зчик ме́бели.

removal van *n* (*BRIT*) автофурго́н для перево́зки ме́бели.

remove [rɪ'muːv] *vt* (*take away*) убира́ть (убра́ть* *perf*); (*clothing, bandage, employee*) снима́ть (снять* *perf*); (*stain, also MED*) удаля́ть (удали́ть *perf*); (*problem, doubt*) устраня́ть (устрани́ть *perf*); **first cousin once ~d** двою́родный(-ая) племя́нник(-ица).

remover [rɪ'muːvə^r] *n* (*for paint, varnish*) сре́дство для сня́тия; **stain ~** пятно-выводи́тель *m*; **paint/make-up ~** сре́дство для сня́тия кра́ски/макия́жа.

remunerate [rɪ'mjuːnəreɪt] *vt* вознагражда́ть (вознагради́ть* *perf*).

remuneration [rɪmjuːnə'reɪʃən] *n* вознагражде́ние.

Renaissance [rɪ'neɪsɑːs] *n*: **the ~** (*HISTORY*) Возрожде́ние.

renal ['riːnl] *adj* по́чечный.

renal failure *n* по́чечная недоста́точность *f*.

rename [riː'neɪm] *vt* переимено́вывать (переименова́ть *perf*).

rend [rɛnd] (*pt, pp* **rent**) *vt* (*subj: society*) раздира́ть (*impf*); **a whistle rent the air** свист рассёк во́здух.

render ['rɛndə^r] *vt* (*give: assistance*) ока́зывать (оказа́ть* *perf*); (*cause to become: harmless, useless*) де́лать (сде́лать *perf*) +*instr*; (*submit: account*) предъявля́ть (предъяви́ть* *perf*); **the blow ~ed him unconscious** уда́р привёл его́ в бессозна́тельное состоя́ние.

rendering ['rɛndərɪŋ] *n* (*MUS etc*) исполне́ние; (*CONSTR*) штукату́рка.

rendezvous ['rɔndɪvuː] *n* (*meeting*) свида́ние, рандеву́ *nt ind*; (*place*) ме́сто свида́ния ♦ *vi* встреча́ться (встре́титься* *perf*); **to ~ with sb** встреча́ться (встре́титься* *perf*) с кем-н.

rendition [rɛn'dɪʃən] *n* (*MUS*) исполне́ние.

renegade ['rɛnɪgeɪd] *n* ренега́т.

renew [rɪ'njuː] *vt* возобновля́ть (возобнови́ть* *perf*).

renewal [rɪ'njuːəl] *n* возобновле́ние.

renounce [rɪ'nauns] *vt* отка́зываться (отказа́ться* *perf*) от +*gen*; (*belief, throne*) отрека́ться (отре́чься* *perf*) от +*gen*; (*holy orders*) отверга́ть (отве́ргнуть *perf*).

renovate ['rɛnəveɪt] *vt* (*building, machine*) ремонти́ровать (отремонти́ровать *perf*); (*painting*) реставри́ровать (отреставри́ровать *perf*).

renovation [rɛnə'veɪʃən] *n* ремо́нт; (*of work of art*) реставра́ция.

renown [rɪ'naun] *n* сла́ва.

renowned [rɪ'naund] *adj* просла́вленный.

rent [rɛnt] *pt, pp of* **rend** ♦ *n* кварти́рная пла́та ♦ *vt* (*take for rent: house*) снима́ть (снять* *perf*);

---

* marks translations which have irregular inflections. The Russian-English side of the dictionary gives inflectional information.

(: *television, car*) брать* (взять* *perf*)
напрока́т; (*also*: ~ **out**: *house*) сдава́ть*
(сдать* *perf*) (внаём); (: *television, car*)
дава́ть* (дать* *perf*) напрока́т.
rental ['rɛntl] *n* (*for television, car*) пла́та за
прока́т.
rent strike *n* неупла́та жильца́ми аре́ндной
пла́ты с це́лью выраже́ния проте́ста.
renunciation [rɪnʌnsɪ'eɪʃən] *n* отка́з; (*of belief,
throne*) отрече́ние.
reopen [ri:'əupən] *vt* (*shop, restaurant etc*)
сно́ва открыва́ть (откры́ть* *perf*);
(*discussion, legal case etc*) возобновля́ть
(возобнови́ть* *perf*).
reopening [ri:'əupnɪŋ] *n* (*see vb*) откры́тие
(*по́сле ремо́нта итп*); возобновле́ние.
reorder [ri:'ɔ:də'] *vt* возобновля́ть
(возобнови́ть* *perf*) зака́з на +*acc*; (*rearrange*)
перестра́ивать (перестро́ить* *perf*).
reorganization ['ri:ɔ:gənaɪ'zeɪʃən] *n*
реорганиза́ция.
reorganize [ri:'ɔ:gənaɪz] *vt* реорганизо́вывать
(реорганизова́ть* *perf*).
rep [rɛp] *n abbr* (*COMM*) = **representative**; (*THEAT*)
= **repertory**.
Rep. *abbr* (*US: POL*) = **representative, republican**.
repair [rɪ'pɛə'] *n* ремо́нт ♦ *vt* (*clothes, shoes*)
чини́ть* (почини́ть* *perf*); (*car, engine*)
ремонти́ровать (отремонти́ровать *perf*); **in
good/bad** ~ в хоро́шем/плохо́м состоя́нии;
under ~ в ремо́нте.
repair kit *n* ремо́нтный компле́кт.
repairman [rɪ'pɛəmæn] *irreg n* ма́стер* по
ремо́нту.
repair shop *n* ремо́нтная мастерска́я *f adj*.
repartee [rɛpɑ:'ti:] *n* (*conversation*)
остроу́мная бесе́да; (*riposte*) остро́та.
repast [rɪ'pɑ:st] *n* тра́пеза.
repatriate [ri:'pætrɪeɪt] *vt* репатрии́ровать
(*impf/perf*).
repay [ri:'peɪ] *irreg vt* (*money, debt*)
выпла́чивать (вы́платить* *perf*); (*person*)
упла́чивать (уплати́ть* *perf*) +*dat*; (: *reward*)
вознагражда́ть (вознагради́ть* *perf*);
(*efforts*) возмеща́ть (возмести́ть* *perf*); **to** ~
sb (for sth) (*favour*) отпла́чивать (отплати́ть*
perf) кому́-н (за что-н).
repayment [ri:'peɪmənt] *n* вы́плата.
repeal [rɪ'pi:l] *n* отме́на ♦ *vt* отменя́ть
(отмени́ть* *perf*).
repeat [rɪ'pi:t] *vt* повторя́ть (повтори́ть* *perf*) ♦
vi повторя́ться (повтори́ться *perf*) ♦ *n* (*RADIO,
TV*) повторе́ние ♦ *cpd* (*performance, order etc*)
повто́рный; **to** ~ **a class** (*SCOL*) остава́ться*
(оста́ться* *perf*) на второ́й год.
repeatedly [rɪ'pi:tɪdlɪ] *adv* неоднокра́тно.
repel [rɪ'pɛl] *vt* (*drive away*) отбива́ть (отби́ть*
perf); (*disgust*) отта́лкивать (оттолкну́ть*
perf).
repellent [rɪ'pɛlənt] *adj* (*appearance, smell*)
отта́лкивающий*; (*idea, thought*) отврат-

и́тельный* (отврати́телен) ♦ *n*: **insect** ~
репелле́нт.
repent [rɪ'pɛnt] *vi*: **to** ~ (**of**) ка́яться (пока́яться
perf) (в +*prp*).
repentance [rɪ'pɛntəns] *n* покая́ние.
repercussions [ri:pə'kʌʃənz] *npl* после́дствия
ntpl.
repertoire ['rɛpətwɑ:'] *n* репертуа́р.
repertory ['rɛpətərɪ] *n* (*also*: ~ **theatre**)
репертуа́рный теа́тр.
repertory company *n* постоя́нная тру́ппа.
repetition [rɛpɪ'tɪʃən] *n* повторе́ние; (*of order,
in text*) повто́р.
repetitious [rɛpɪ'tɪʃəs] *adj* изоби́лующий
повто́рами.
repetitive [rɪ'pɛtɪtɪv] *adj* повторя́ющийся.
replace [rɪ'pleɪs] *vt* (*put back*: *vertically*) класть*
(положи́ть* *perf*) обра́тно; (: *horizontally*)
ста́вить* (поста́вить* *perf*) обра́тно; (*take the
place of*) заменя́ть (замени́ть* *perf*); **to** ~ **sth
with sth** заменя́ть (замени́ть* *perf*) что-н
чем-н; **"replace the receiver"** (*TEL*) „положи́те
тру́бку".
replacement [rɪ'pleɪsmənt] *n* заме́на.
replacement cost *n* изде́ржки* *pl*
возмеще́ния.
replacement part *n* запасна́я часть* *f*.
replacement value *n* (*INSURANCE*) сто́имость *f*
страхово́го возмеще́ния.
replay [*n* 'ri:pleɪ, *vb* ri:'pleɪ] *n* (*of match*)
переигро́вка*; (*of tape*) повто́рное
прои́грывание; (*of film*) повто́рный пока́з ♦
vt (*match, game*) переи́грывать (переигра́ть
perf); (*part of tape*) повто́рно прои́грывать
(проигра́ть *perf*).
replenish [rɪ'plɛnɪʃ] *vt* (*glass*) сно́ва наполня́ть
(напо́лнить *perf*); (*stock etc*) пополня́ть
(попо́лнить *perf*).
replete [rɪ'pli:t] *adj* (*well-fed*) насы́тившийся; ~
with загру́женный +*instr*; **I'm
quite** ~ я вполне́ насы́тился.
replica ['rɛplɪkə] *n* (*copy*) ко́пия.
reply [rɪ'plaɪ] *n* отве́т ♦ *vi* отвеча́ть (отве́тить*
perf); **to** ~ **to** в отве́т на +*acc*; **there's no** ~ (*TEL*)
не отвеча́ет.
reply coupon *n* бланк для отве́та.
reply-paid postcard *n* откры́тка* с
опла́ченным отве́том.
report [rɪ'pɔ:t] *n* (*account*) докла́д; (*PRESS, TV
etc*: *statement*) репорта́ж; (: *information*)
сообще́ние; (*BRIT*: *also*: **school** ~) отчёт об
успева́емости; (*of gun*) вы́стрел ♦ *vt*
сообща́ть (сообщи́ть *perf*) о +*prp*; (*event,
meeting*) докла́дывать (доложи́ть* *perf*) о
+*prp*; (*person*) доноси́ть* (донести́* *perf*) на
+*acc* ♦ *vi* (*make a report*) докла́дывать
(доложи́ть* *perf*); (*present o.s.*): **to** ~ (**to sb**)
явля́ться (яви́ться* *perf*) (к кому́-н); (*be
responsible to*): **to** ~ **to sb** (*impf*) под
нача́лом кого́-н; **to** ~ **that** сообща́ть
(сообщи́ть *perf*), что; **to** ~ **on** представля́ть

(предста́вить* *perf*) докла́д о +*prp*; **it is ~ed
that ...** сообща́ется, что ....
report card *n* (*US, SCOTTISH*) та́бель *m*
успева́емости.
reportedly [rɪ'pɔːtɪdlɪ] *adv*: **she is ~ living in
Spain** по сообще́ниям, она́ живёт в
Испа́нии; **he ~ ordered them to ...** сообща́ют,
что он приказа́л им +*infin* ....
reported speech *n* (*LING*) ко́свенная речь *f*.
reporter [rɪ'pɔːtəʳ] *n* репортёр.
repose [rɪ'pəuz] *n*: **in ~** (*face*) в поко́е.
repository [rɪ'pɔzɪtərɪ] *n* (*place*) храни́лище;
(*person*) храни́тель *m*.
repossess ['riːpə'zɛs] *vt* (*goods, building*)
изыма́ть (изъя́ть* *perf*) (*за неплатёж*).
reprehensible [rɛprɪ'hɛnsɪbl] *adj* (*behaviour*)
предосуди́тельный* (предосуди́телен).
represent [rɛprɪ'zɛnt] *vt* (*person, nation*)
представля́ть (предста́вить* *perf*); (*view,
belief*) излага́ть (изложи́ть* *perf*); (*constitute*)
представля́ть (*impf*) собо́й; (*idea, emotion*)
символизи́ровать* (*impf/perf*); (*describe*): **to ~
sth as** изобража́ть (изобрази́ть* *perf*) что-н
как; (*explain*): **to ~ to sb that** объясня́ть
(объясни́ть* *perf*) кому́-н, что.
representation [rɛprɪzɛn'teɪʃən] *n* (*state*)
представи́тельство; (*picture, statue*)
изображе́ние; (*petition*) заявле́ние; **~s** *npl*
(*protest*) представле́ния *ntpl*.
representative [rɛprɪ'zɛntətɪv] *n* пред-
стави́тель(ница) *m(f)*; (*of belief, also COMM,
POL*) представи́тель *m* ♦ *adj* (*group, survey,
cross-section*) представи́тельный*
(представи́телен); **~ of** характе́рный*
(характе́рен) для +*gen*.
repress [rɪ'prɛs] *vt* подавля́ть (подави́ть* *perf*).
repression [rɪ'prɛʃən] *n* подавле́ние.
repressive [rɪ'prɛsɪv] *adj* (*society, measures*)
репресси́вный* (репресси́вен).
reprieve [rɪ'priːv] *n* (*LAW*) отсро́чка (*в
исполне́нии пригово́ра*); (*fig: delay*)
переды́шка* ♦ *vt* (*LAW*): **he was ~d** он
получи́л отсро́чку.
reprimand ['rɛprɪmɑːnd] *n* вы́говор ♦ *vt* де́лать
(сде́лать* *perf*) вы́говор +*dat*.
reprint [*n* 'riːprɪnt, *vb* riː'prɪnt] *n* перепеча́тка ♦
vt перепеча́тывать (перепеча́тать *perf*).
reprisal [rɪ'praɪzl] *n* отве́тное де́йствие; **~s** *npl*
(*acts of revenge*) отве́тные де́йствия *ntpl*; **to
take ~s** мстить* (отомсти́ть* *perf*).
reproach [rɪ'prəutʃ] *n* упрёк ♦ *vt*: **to ~ sb for
sth/with sth** упрека́ть (упрекну́ть *perf*)
кого́-н за что-н/в чём-н; **his behaviour was
beyond ~** его́ поведе́ние бы́ло безупре́чно.
reproachful [rɪ'prəutʃful] *adj* (*look, remark*)
укори́зненный* (укори́знен).
reproduce [riːprə'djuːs] *vt* воспроизводи́ть*
(воспроизвести́* *perf*) ♦ *vi* размножа́ться

(размно́житься *perf*).
reproduction [riːprə'dʌkʃən] *n*
воспроизведе́ние; (*ART*) репроду́кция;
(*breeding*) воспроизведе́ние.
reproductive [riːprə'dʌktɪv] *adj* (*process*)
репродукти́вный; (*system*) полово́й.
reproof [rɪ'pruːf] *n* (*rebuke*) порица́ние;
(*disapproval*): **with ~** с уко́ром.
reprove [rɪ'pruːv] *vt* (*person*): **to ~ sb for sth**
осужда́ть (осуди́ть* *perf*) кого́-н за что-н.
reproving [rɪ'pruːvɪŋ] *adj* осужда́ющий.
reptile ['rɛptaɪl] *n* пресмыка́ющееся *nt adj*
(живо́тное).
Repub. *abbr* (*US: POL*) = **republican**.
republic [rɪ'pʌblɪk] *n* респу́блика.
republican [rɪ'pʌblɪkən] *adj* республика́нский*
♦ *n* (*US: POL*): **R~** республика́нец*(-нка*).
repudiate [rɪ'pjuːdɪeɪt] *vt* отверга́ть
(отве́ргнуть *perf*).
repudiation [rɪpjuːdɪ'eɪʃən] *n* отрица́ние,
отрече́ние; (*COMM*) отка́з от до́лга *or*
выполне́ния контра́кта.
repugnance [rɪ'pʌgnəns] *n* отвраще́ние.
repugnant [rɪ'pʌgnənt] *adj* отврати́тельный*
(отврати́телен).
repulse [rɪ'pʌls] *vt* (*drive back*) отража́ть
(отрази́ть* *perf*); (: *enemy*) отбра́сывать
(отбро́сить* *perf*); (*disgust*) отта́лкивать
(оттолкну́ть* *perf*).
repulsion [rɪ'pʌlʃən] *n* отвраще́ние.
repulsive [rɪ'pʌlsɪv] *adj* отврати́тельный*
(отврати́телен).
reputable ['rɛpjutəbl] *adj* (*person*) уважа́емый;
~ company etc компа́ния с хоро́шей
репута́цией.
reputation [rɛpju'teɪʃən] *n* репута́ция; **to have a
~ for** име́ть (*impf*) репута́цию +*gen*; **he has a ~
for being tactless** он изве́стен свое́й
беста́ктностью.
repute [rɪ'pjuːt] *n* до́брая сла́ва.
reputed [rɪ'pjuːtɪd] *adj* (*rumoured*) пред-
полага́емый; **he is ~ to be intelligent/rich**
счита́ется, что он умён/бога́т.
reputedly [rɪ'pjuːtɪdlɪ] *adv* по о́бщему мне́нию.
request [rɪ'kwɛst] *n* (*polite demand*) про́сьба;
(*formal demand*) зая́вка* ♦ *vt*: **to ~ sth of** *or*
from sb проси́ть* (попроси́ть* *perf*) что-н у
кого́-н; **at the ~ of** по про́сьбе +*gen*; (*formal*)
по зая́вке +*gen*; **"you are ~ed not to smoke"**
„про́сим не кури́ть".
request stop *n* (*BRIT*) остано́вка* по
тре́бованию.
requiem ['rɛkwɪəm] *n* (*REL*) панихи́да; (*MUS*)
ре́квием.
require [rɪ'kwaɪəʳ] *vt* (*person*) нужда́ться (*impf*)
в +*prp*; (*thing, situation*) тре́бовать (*impf*);
(*order*): **to ~ sth of sb** тре́бовать
(потре́бовать *perf*) что-н от кого́-н; **we ~ you**

to complete the task мы тре́буем, что́бы Вы заверши́ли рабо́ту; **if ~d** е́сли тре́буется; **what documents are ~d?** каки́е докуме́нты тре́буются?; **~d by law** тре́буемый зако́ном.

required [rɪ'kwaɪəd] *adj* необходи́мый.

requirement [rɪ'kwaɪəmənt] *n* (*need, want*) потре́бность *f*; (*condition*) тре́бование; **to meet sb's ~s** удовлетворя́ть (удовлетвори́ть *perf*) чьим-н тре́бованиям.

requisite ['rɛkwɪzɪt] *n* тре́бование ♦ *adj* необходи́мый.

requisition [rɛkwɪ'zɪʃən] *vt* (*MIL*) реквизи́ровать (*impf/perf*) ♦ *n*: ~ (**for**) зая́вка (на +*acc*).

reroute [ri:'ru:t] *vt* (*train etc*) изменя́ть (измени́ть* *perf*) маршру́т +*gen*.

resale [ri:'seɪl] *n* перепрода́жа; "**not for ~**" „перепрода́жа запрещена́".

resale price maintenance *n* поддержа́ние цен при перепрода́же това́ров.

reschedule [ri:'ʃɛdju:l] *vt*: ~ (**for**) переноси́ть* (перенести́* *perf*) (на +*acc*).

rescind [rɪ'sɪnd] *vt* (*law, judgement*) отменя́ть (отмени́ть* *perf*); (*contract, order etc*) аннули́ровать (*impf/perf*).

rescue ['rɛskju:] *n* спасе́ние ♦ *vt*: **to ~ (from)** спаса́ть (спасти́* *perf*) (от +*gen*); **to come to sb's ~** приходи́ть* (прийти́* *perf*) кому́-н на по́мощь.

rescue party *n* спаса́тельный отря́д, спаса́тельная па́ртия.

rescuer ['rɛskjuə] *n* спаса́тель(ница) *m(f)*.

research [rɪ'sə:tʃ] *n* иссле́дование ♦ *vt* иссле́довать (*impf/perf*) ♦ *vi* проводи́ть* (провести́* *perf*) иссле́дование *or* иссле́дования; **a piece of ~** (нау́чное) иссле́дование; **~ and development** нау́чно-иссле́довательские и о́пытно-констру́кторские рабо́ты.

researcher [rɪ'sə:tʃə] *n* иссле́дователь(ница) *m(f)*.

research work *n* нау́чно-иссле́довательская рабо́та.

research worker *n* нау́чный рабо́тник.

resell [ri:'sɛl] *irreg vt* перепродава́ть* (перепрода́ть* *perf*).

resemblance [rɪ'zɛmbləns] *n* схо́дство; **he bears a strong ~ to his father** он си́льно похо́дит на отца́; **this bears no ~ to ...** э́то не име́ет никако́го схо́дства с +*instr* ....

resemble [rɪ'zɛmbl] *vt* походи́ть* (*impf*) (на +*acc*); **he very much ~s his father** он о́чень похо́дит на отца́.

resent [rɪ'zɛnt] *vt* (*situation*) негодова́ть (*impf*) про́тив +*gen*; (*person*) негодова́ть (*impf*) на +*acc*.

resentful [rɪ'zɛntful] *adj* негоду́ющий*.

resentment [rɪ'zɛntmənt] *n* негодова́ние.

reservation [rɛzə'veɪʃən] *n* (*booking*) предвари́тельный зака́з; (*doubt*) сомне́ние; (*for tribe*) резерва́ция; **to make a ~ (in an hotel/on a**

plane) брони́ровать* (заброни́ровать* *perf*) (ме́сто в гости́нице/на самолёте); **with ~s** (*doubts*) с огово́рками.

reservation desk *n* (*US: in hotel*) стол* администра́тора.

reserve [rɪ'zə:v] *n* (*store*) резе́рв, запа́с; (*also*: **nature ~**) запове́дник; (*SPORT*) запасно́й игро́к*; (*restraint*) сде́ржанность *f* ♦ *vt* (*keep*: *money, food*) приберега́ть (прибере́чь* *perf*); (: *energy*) бере́чь* (сбере́чь* *perf*); (*seats, table etc*) брони́ровать (заброни́ровать *perf*); **~s** *npl* (*MIL*) запа́с *msg*; (*COMM*) резе́рвы *mpl*; **in ~** в резе́рве *or* запа́се.

reserve currency *n* резе́рвная валю́та.

reserved [rɪ'zə:vd] *adj* (*restrained*) сде́ржанный* (сде́ржан); (*seat*) заброни́рованный (заброни́рован).

reserve price *n* (*BRIT*) отправна́я *or* резерви́рованная цена́*.

reserve team *n* (*BRIT: SPORT*) запасна́я кома́нда.

reservist [rɪ'zə:vɪst] *n* резерви́ст.

reservoir ['rɛzəvwɑ:] *n* (*of water*) водохрани́лище; (*small: of ink etc*) резервуа́р; (*fig: of talent, strength*) храни́лище.

reset [ri:'sɛt] *irreg vt* вновь устана́вливать (установи́ть* *perf*); (*clock, watch*) переводи́ть* (перевести́* *perf*); (*COMPUT*) сбра́сывать (сбро́сить* *perf*), возвраща́ть (возврати́ть* *perf*) в исхо́дное положе́ние.

reshape [ri:'ʃeɪp] *vt* (*policy*) изменя́ть (измени́ть *perf*).

reshuffle [ri:'ʃʌfl] *n*: **Cabinet ~** перестано́вки *fpl* в кабине́те мини́стров.

reside [rɪ'zaɪd] *vi* (*live*) прожива́ть (*impf*).

residence ['rɛzɪdəns] *n* (*home*) резиде́нция; (*length of stay*) пребыва́ние; **to take up ~** поселя́ться (посели́ться *perf*); **to be in ~** (*queen etc*) пребыва́ть (*impf*); (*artist*) прожива́ть (*impf*) по ме́сту слу́жбы.

residence permit *n* (*BRIT*) вид на жи́тельство.

resident ['rɛzɪdənt] *n* (*of country, town*) (постоя́нный(-ая)) жи́тель(ница) *m(f)*; (*in hotel*) прожива́ющий(-ая) *m(f) adj* ♦ *adj*: ~ **population** постоя́нное населе́ние; ~ **doctor** врач*, живу́щий при больни́це.

residential [rɛzɪ'dɛnʃəl] *adj* (*area*) жило́й; (*course, college*) с прожива́нием.

residue ['rɛzɪdju:] *n* оста́ток*; (*CHEM, PHYS*) оса́док*.

resign [rɪ'zaɪn] *vi* (*from post*) оставля́ть (оста́вить* *perf*) ♦ *vt* (*one's post*) уходи́ть* (уйти́* *perf*) в отста́вку с +*gen*; **to ~ o.s. to** смиря́ться (смири́ться *perf*) с +*instr*.

resignation [rɛzɪg'neɪʃən] *n* отста́вка*; (*acceptance*) поко́рность *f*; **to tender one's ~** подава́ть* (пода́ть* *perf*) в отста́вку.

resigned [rɪ'zaɪnd] *adj* (*to situation etc*) смири́вшийся.

resilience [rɪ'zɪliəns] *n* (*of material*) упру́гость *f*;

(*of person*) сто́йкость f.
resilient [rɪ'zɪlɪənt] adj (*material*) упру́гий*
(упру́г); (*person*) сто́йкий* (сто́ек).
resin ['rɛzɪn] n смола́*.
resist [rɪ'zɪst] vt сопротивля́ться (*impf*) +dat;
(*temptation*) не поддава́ться* (подда́ться*
perf) +dat.
resistance [rɪ'zɪstəns] n (*opposition*)
сопротивле́ние; (*to illness, infection*)
сопротивля́емость f.
resistant [rɪ'zɪstənt] adj: **to be ~ to** (*opposing*)
сопротивля́ться (*impf*) +dat; (*immune*)
облада́ть (*impf*) усто́йчивостью к +dat.
resolute ['rɛzəlu:t] adj твёрдый* (твёрд).
resolution [rɛzə'lu:ʃən] n (*decision*) реше́ние;
(: *formal*) резолю́ция; (*determination*)
реши́мость f; (*of problem, difficulty*)
разреше́ние; **to make a ~** принима́ть
(приня́ть* *perf*) реше́ние.
resolve [rɪ'zɔlv] n реши́тельность f ◆ vt
(*problem, difficulty*) разреша́ть (разреши́ть
perf) ◆ vi: **to ~ to do** реша́ть (реши́ть *perf*)
+infin.
resolved [rɪ'zɔlvd] adj (*determined*)
реши́тельный* (реши́телен).
resonance ['rɛzənəns] n (*TECH*) резона́нс.
resonant ['rɛzənənt] adj (*voice*) зву́чный*
(зву́чен); (*place*) резони́рующий*.
resort [rɪ'zɔ:t] n (*town*) куро́рт; (*recourse*)
прибега́ние ◆ vi: **to ~ to** прибега́ть
(прибе́гнуть *perf*) к +dat; **seaside/winter
sports ~** морско́й/зи́мний* спорти́вный
куро́рт; **the last/only ~** после́дняя/
еди́нственная наде́жда; **in the last ~** в
кра́йнем слу́чае.
resound [rɪ'zaund] vi: **to ~ with** наполня́ться
(напо́лниться *perf*) +instr.
resounding [rɪ'zaundɪŋ] adj (*noise*) зву́чный*
(зву́чен); (*fig: success*) гро́мкий*.
resource [rɪ'sɔ:s] n (*raw material*) ресу́рс; **~s** npl
(*money, energy, coal etc*) ресу́рсы mpl; **natural
~s** приро́дные ресу́рсы; **he was left to his
own ~s** (*fig*) он мог положи́ться то́лько на
самого́ себя́.
resourceful [rɪ'sɔ:sful] adj изобрета́тельный*
(изобрета́телен).
resourcefulness [rɪ'sɔ:sfəlnɪs] n
изобрета́тельность f.
respect [rɪs'pɛkt] n уваже́ние ◆ vt уважа́ть
(*impf*); **~s** npl (*greetings*) почте́ние ntsg; **to have
or show ~ for sb/sth** относи́ться* (*impf*) к
кому́-н/чему́-н с уваже́нием; **out of ~ for** из
уваже́ния к +dat; **with ~ to, in ~ of** в
отноше́нии +gen; **in this ~** в э́том
отноше́нии; **in some ~s** в не́которых
отноше́ниях; **with (all) due ~** ... при всём
уваже́нии ....
respectability [rɪspɛktə'bɪlɪtɪ] n респекта́-

бельность f.
respectable [rɪs'pɛktəbl] adj прили́чный*
(прили́чен); (*morally correct*) респекта́-
бельный.
respected [rɪs'pɛktɪd] adj (*scholar, actor etc*)
при́знанный (при́знан).
respectful [rɪs'pɛktful] adj почти́тельный*
(почти́телен).
respectfully [rɪs'pɛktfəlɪ] adv почти́тельно.
respective [rɪs'pɛktɪv] adj (*policies, measures*)
соотве́тствующий*; **he drove them to their ~
homes** он отвёз их обо́их по дома́м.
respectively [rɪs'pɛktɪvlɪ] adv соотве́тственно;
France and Britain were 3rd and 4th ~
Фра́нция и Великобрита́ния бы́ли на 3-ем и
4-ом ме́сте соотве́тственно.
respiration [rɛspɪ'reɪʃən] n дыха́ние.
respirator ['rɛspɪreɪtəʳ] n (*MED*) аппара́т
иску́сственного дыха́ния.
respiratory ['rɛspərətərɪ] adj (*ANAT, MED*)
дыха́тельный, респирато́рный.
respite ['rɛspaɪt] n (*rest*) переды́шка*.
resplendent [rɪs'plɛndənt] adj блиста́тельный*
(блиста́телен).
respond [rɪs'pɔnd] vi (*answer*) отвеча́ть
(отве́тить* *perf*); (*react*): **to ~ (to)** (*to pressure,
criticism*) реаги́ровать (отреаги́ровать *perf*)
(на +acc); (*to treatment*) поддава́ться*
(подда́ться* *perf*) (+dat).
respondent [rɪs'pɔndənt] n (*LAW*) отве́тчик
(-ица).
response [rɪs'pɔns] n (*answer*) отве́т; (*reaction*)
реа́кция; **in ~ to (your letter)** в отве́т на
(Ва́ше письмо́).
responsibility [rɪspɔnsɪ'bɪlɪtɪ] n (*liability*)
отве́тственность f; (*duty*) обя́занность f; **to
take ~ for sth/sb** принима́ть (приня́ть* *perf*)
(на себя́) отве́тственность за что-н/кого́-н.
responsible [rɪs'pɔnsɪbl] adj отве́тственный*
(отве́тствен); **~ for** отве́тственный*
(отве́тствен) за +acc; **to be ~ to sb (for sth)**
отвеча́ть (отве́тить* *perf*) пе́ред кем-н (за
что-н).
responsibly [rɪs'pɔnsɪblɪ] adv отве́тственно.
responsive [rɪs'pɔnsɪv] adj (*child, nature*)
отзы́вчивый (отзы́вчив); (*gesture*)
отве́тный; **~ to demand/treatment**
восприи́мчивый (восприи́мчив) к
тре́бованиям/лече́нию.
rest [rɛst] n (*relaxation, pause*) о́тдых; (*MUS*)
па́уза; (*stand, support*) подста́вка* ◆ vi (*relax,
stop*) отдыха́ть (отдохну́ть *perf*) ◆ vt (*head,
eyes etc*) дава́ть* (дать* *perf*) о́тдых +dat;
(*lean*): **to ~ sth against** прислоня́ть
(прислони́ть* *perf*) что-н к +dat; **the ~**
(*remainder of sth*) остально́е nt adj; **the ~ of
them** остальны́е из них; **to set sb's mind at ~**
утеша́ть (уте́шить *perf*) кого́-н; **to ~ one's**

---

arms on облока́чиваться (облокоти́ться*
perf) на +*acc*; **to ~ sth on** опуска́ть (опусти́ть*
perf) на +*acc*; **to ~ on** (*weight*) опира́ться
(опере́ться* *perf*) на +*acc*; (*idea*) опира́ться
(*impf*) на +*acc*; (*object*) лежа́ть* (*impf*) на +*prp*;
(*hope*) наде́яться (*impf*) на +*acc*; **~ assured
that ...** бу́дьте уве́рены, что ...; **it ~s with him
to ...** на нём лежи́т +*infin* ...; **to ~ one's eyes** *or*
gaze on остана́вливать (останови́ть* *perf*)
(свой) взгляд на +*acc*.
restart [riː'stɑːt] *vt* (*engine*) вновь запуска́ть
(запусти́ть* *perf*); (*work*) возобновля́ть
(возобнови́ть* *perf*).
restaurant ['rɛstərɒŋ] *n* рестора́н.
restaurant car *n* (*BRIT*) ваго́н-рестора́н.
rest-cure ['rɛstkjuəʳ] *n* лече́ние поко́ем.
restful ['rɛstful] *adj* успока́ивающий.
rest-home ['rɛsthəum] *n* дом для
престаре́лых.
restitution [rɛstɪ'tjuːʃən] *n*: **to make ~ to sb for
sth** (*compensate*) возмеща́ть (возмести́ть*
perf) кому́-н что-н.
restive ['rɛstɪv] *adj* неспоко́йный* (неспоко́ен);
(*horse*) норови́стый (норови́ст).
restless ['rɛstlɪs] *adj* (*person, audience*)
беспоко́йный* (беспоко́ен); **to get ~**
проявля́ть (прояви́ть* *perf*) нетерпе́ние.
restlessly ['rɛstlɪslɪ] *adv* беспоко́йно.
restock [riː'stɔk] *vt* пополня́ть (попо́лнить
perf) запа́сы +*gen*; **to ~ a lake/river (with fish)**
пополня́ть (попо́лнить *perf*) о́зеро/ре́ку
ры́бой.
restoration [rɛstə'reɪʃən] *n* (*of building etc*)
реставра́ция; (*of order, health*)
восстановле́ние; (*of stolen property*)
возвраще́ние.
restorative [rɪ'stɔrətɪv] *adj* укрепля́ющий* ♦ *n*
укрепля́ющее сре́дство.
restore [rɪ'stɔːʳ] *vt* (*building, painting*)
реставри́ровать (отреставри́ровать *perf*);
(*order, health etc*) восстана́вливать
(восстанови́ть* *perf*); (*stolen property*)
возвраща́ть (возврати́ть* *perf*); (*to power*)
возвраща́ть (верну́ть *perf*).
restorer [rɪ'stɔːrəʳ] *n* (*ART etc*) реставра́тор; **hair
~** восстанови́тель *m* для воло́с.
restrain [rɪs'treɪn] *vt* уде́рживать (сдержа́ть*
perf); (*person*): **to ~ sb from doing** не дава́ть*
(дать* *perf*) кому́-н +*infin*.
restrained [rɪs'treɪnd] *adj* сде́ржанный*
(сде́ржан).
restraint [rɪs'treɪnt] *n* (*moderation*)
сде́ржанность *f*; (*restriction*) ограниче́ние;
wage ~ сде́рживание ро́ста за́работной
пла́ты.
restrict [rɪs'trɪkt] *vt* ограни́чивать (ограни́чить
perf).
restricted area *n* (*AUT*) райо́н ограни́ченной
ско́рости движе́ния.
restriction [rɪs'trɪkʃən] *n*: **~ (on)** ограниче́ние
(на +*acc*).

restrictive [rɪs'trɪktɪv] *adj* ограничи́тельный;
(*clothing*) стесня́ющий.
restrictive practices *npl* (*INDUSTRY*)
ограничи́тельная делова́я пра́ктика *fsg*.
rest room *n* (*US*) туале́т.
restructure [riː'strʌktʃəʳ] *vt* (*business, economy*)
перестра́ивать (перестро́ить *perf*).
result [rɪ'zʌlt] *n* результа́т ♦ *vi*: **to ~ in**
зака́нчиваться (зако́нчиться *perf*) +*instr*; **as a
~ of** в результа́те +*gen*; **as a ~ it is too
expensive** в результа́те э́то сли́шком
до́рого; **the fire ~ed from bombing** пожа́р
возни́к всле́дствие бомбёжки.
resultant [rɪ'zʌltənt] *adj*: **~ saving/problem**
вытека́ющая из э́того эконо́мия/пробле́ма.
resume [rɪ'zjuːm] *vt* (*work, journey*)
возобновля́ть (возобнови́ть* *perf*) ♦ *vi*
продолжа́ть (продо́лжить *perf*); **to ~ one's
seat** возвраща́ться (верну́ться *perf*) на
(своё) ме́сто.
résumé ['reɪzjuːmeɪ] *n* резюме́ *nt ind*; (*US:
curriculum vitae*) автобиогра́фия (*обычно
пи́шущаяся при поступле́нии на учёбу и́ли
рабо́ту*).
resumption [rɪ'zʌmpʃən] *n* возобновле́ние.
resurgence [rɪ'səːdʒəns] *n* (*of energy, activity*)
всплеск.
resurrection [rɛzə'rɛkʃən] *n* (*of hopes, fears*)
возрожде́ние; (*REL*): **the R~** Воскресе́ние.
resuscitate [rɪ'sʌsɪteɪt] *vt* (*MED*) приводи́ть*
(привести́* *perf*) в созна́ние; (*fig*) возвраща́ть
(возврати́ть* *perf*) к жи́зни.
resuscitation [rɪsʌsɪ'teɪʃən] *n* (*MED*)
приведе́ние в созна́ние; (*fig*) возвраще́ние к
жи́зни.
retail ['riːteɪl] *adj* ро́зничный ♦ *adv* в ро́зницу ♦
vt продава́ть* (прода́ть* *perf*) в ро́зницу ♦ *vi*:
to ~ at £5 продава́ться* (*impf*) по ро́зничной
цене́ в £5; **~ shop** магази́н ро́зничной
торго́вли.
retailer ['riːteɪləʳ] *n* ро́зничный торго́вец*.
retail outlet *n* ро́зничная торго́вая то́чка.
retail price *n* ро́зничная цена́*.
retail price index *n* (*BRIT*) и́ндекс ро́зничных
цен.
retain [rɪ'teɪn] *vt* (*keep*) сохраня́ть (сохрани́ть
perf), уде́рживать (удержа́ть *perf*).
retainer [rɪ'teɪnəʳ] *n* (*fee*) предвари́тельный
гонора́р.
retaliate [rɪ'tælɪeɪt] *vi*: **to ~ (against)** (*attack*)
наноси́ть* (нанести́* *perf*) отве́тный уда́р
(+*dat*); (*ill-treatment*) отпла́чивать
(отплати́ть* *perf*) (за +*acc*); **to ~ (on sb)**
предъявля́ть (предъяви́ть* *perf*) встре́чный
иск (кому́-н).
retaliation [rɪtælɪ'eɪʃən] *n* (*against attack*)
отве́тный уда́р; (*against ill-treatment*)
возме́здие; **in ~ for** в отве́т на +*acc*.
retaliatory [rɪ'tælɪətərɪ] *adj* отве́тный.
retarded [rɪ'tɑːdɪd] *adj* (*development, growth*)
заме́дленный* (заме́длен); (*also: mentally ~*:

person) ýмственно отсталый.

retch [rɛtʃ] *vi*: **the thought made him ~** от этой мысли его затошнило.

retention [rɪ'tɛnʃən] *n* удержание; (*of tradition, rights*) сохранение; (*MED: of fluid*) задержка.

retentive [rɪ'tɛntɪv] *adj*: **a ~ memory** цепкая память *f*.

rethink ['ri:'θɪŋk] *vt* (*proposal, policy*) пересматривать (пересмотреть* *perf*).

reticence ['rɛtɪsns] *n* скрытность *f*.

reticent ['rɛtɪsnt] *adj* сдержанный* (сдержан).

retina ['rɛtɪnə] *n* сетчатка.

retinue ['rɛtɪnju:] *n* свита.

retire [rɪ'taɪə'] *vi* (*give up work*) уходить (уйти* *perf*) на пенсию; (*withdraw*) удаляться (удалиться *perf*); (*go to bed*) удаляться (удалиться *perf*) на покой.

retired [rɪ'taɪəd] *adj*: **he is ~** он на пенсии.

retirement [rɪ'taɪəmənt] *n* выход *or* уход на пенсию; **we hope to enjoy a long and happy ~** мы надеемся жить долго и счастливо, выйдя на пенсию.

retirement age *n* пенсионный возраст.

retiring [rɪ'taɪərɪŋ] *adj* (*leaving*) уходящий на пенсию; (*shy*) застенчивый (застенчив).

retort [rɪ'tɔ:t] *vi* резко отвечать (ответить* *perf*) ♦ *n* резкий* ответ.

retrace [ri:'treɪs] *vt*: **to ~ one's steps** возвращаться (вернуться *perf*) тем же путём; (*fig*) восстанавливать (восстановить* *perf*).

retract [rɪ'trækt] *vt* (*statement, offer*) забирать (забрать* *perf*) назад; (*claws*) втягивать (втянуть* *perf*); (*undercarriage, aerial*) убирать (убрать* *perf*).

retractable [rɪ'træktəbl] *adj* (*TECH*) убирающийся.

retrain [ri:'treɪn] *vt* переподготавливать (переподготовить* *perf*), переквалифицировать (*impf/perf*) ♦ *vi* (*see vt*) пройти* (*perf*) переподготовку; переквалифицироваться (*impf/perf*).

retraining [ri:'treɪnɪŋ] *n* (*see vb*) переподготовка*; переквалификация.

retread ['ri:trɛd] *n* (*tyre*) шина с восстановленным протектором.

retreat [rɪ'tri:t] *n* (*place*) убежище; (*withdrawal*) уход; (*MIL*) отступление ♦ *vi* отступать (отступить* *perf*); **to go into ~** (*withdraw*) уйти* (*perf*) от мира; **to beat a hasty ~** поспешно отступать (отступить* *perf*).

retrial [ri:'traɪəl] *n* (*LAW*) повторное слушание дела.

retribution [rɛtrɪ'bju:ʃən] *n* возмездие.

retrieval [rɪ'tri:vəl] *n* восстановление; (*of error*) исправление; (*COMPUT*) поиск; (*by dog*) поиск (*дичи*).

retrieve [rɪ'tri:v] *vt* (*object*) брать* (взять* *perf*)

обратно; (*situation, honour, loss*) восстанавливать (восстановить* *perf*); (*error*) исправлять (исправить* *perf*); (*COMPUT*) отыскивать (отыскать* *perf*); (*subj: dog*) приносить* (принести* *perf*) (*убитую дичь*).

retriever [rɪ'tri:və'] *n* (*dog*) охотничья собака.

retroactive [rɛtrəu'æktɪv] *adj* имеющий обратное действие.

retrograde ['rɛtrəgreɪd] *adj* реакционный* (реакционен).

retrospect ['rɛtrəspɛkt] *n*: **in ~** в ретроспекции.

retrospective [rɛtrə'spɛktɪv] *adj* (*exhibition, view*) ретроспективный* (ретроспективен); (*law, tax*) имеющий обратную силу ♦ *n* (*ART*) ретроспективная выставка*.

return [rɪ'tə:n] *n* (*going or coming back*) возвращение; (*of sth stolen, borrowed, bought*) возврат; (*FINANCE: from land, shares etc*) доход; (*official report*) отчёт ♦ *cpd* (*journey, ticket*) обратный; (*match*) ответный ♦ *vi* возвращаться (вернуться *perf*) ♦ *vt* возвращать (вернуть* *perf*); (*LAW: verdict*) выносить* (вынести* *perf*); (*POL: candidate*) избирать (избрать* *perf*); (*ball*) отбивать (отбить* *perf*); **~s** *npl* (*COMM*) доходы *mpl*; **in ~ (for)** в ответ (на +*acc*); **by ~ of post** обратной почтой; **many happy ~s (of the day)!** с днём рождения!; **to ~ to** (*consciousness*) приходить (прийти* *perf*) в +*acc*; (*power*) возвращаться (вернуться *perf*) к +*dat*.

returnable [rɪ'tə:nəbl] *adj* (*bottle etc*) подлежащий возврату *or* обмену.

returning officer [rɪ'tə:nɪŋ-] *n* председатель *m* окружной комиссии.

return key *n* (*COMPUT*) клавиша "возврат каретки".

reunion [ri:'ju:nɪən] *n* (*reuniting*) воссоединение; (*party*) встреча.

reunite [ri:ju:'naɪt] *vt* воссоединять (воссоединить *perf*).

rev [rɛv] *n abbr* (*AUT*: = *revolution*) оборот.

Rev. *abbr* (*REL*) = **Reverend**.

revaluation [ri:vælju'eɪʃən] *n* (*of property, attitudes*) переоценка*; (*of currency*) ревальвация.

revamp [ri:'væmp] *vt* (*organization, system*) обновлять (обновить* *perf*).

rev counter *n* (*BRIT: AUT*) счётчик оборотов.

Revd. *abbr* (*REL*) = **Reverend**.

reveal [rɪ'vi:l] *vt* (*make known*) обнаруживать (обнаружить *perf*); (*make visible*) открывать (открыть* *perf*).

revealing [rɪ'vi:lɪŋ] *adj* (*action, statement*) показательный* (показателен); (*dress*) открытый.

reveille [rɪ'vælɪ] *n* (*MIL*) побудка*.

revel ['rɛvl] *vi*: **to ~ in sth** упиваться (*impf*)

чем-н; **to ~ in doing** обожа́ть (*impf*) +*infin*.
revelation [rɛvə'leɪʃən] *n* (*fact*) откры́тие; (*experience*) открове́ние.
reveller ['rɛvləʳ] *n* гуля́ка *m/f*.
revelry ['rɛvlrɪ] *n* кутёж.
revenge [rɪ'vɛndʒ] *n* месть *f* ♦ *vt* (*also*: **get one's ~ for**) мстить (отомсти́ть *perf*) за +*acc*; **to take ~ on, ~ o.s. on** мстить (отомсти́ть *perf*) +*dat*.
revengeful [rɪ'vɛndʒful] *adj* мсти́тельный (мсти́телен).
revenue ['rɛvənju:] *n* дохо́ды *mpl*; **~ account** счёт поступле́ний.
reverberate [rɪ'və:bəreɪt] *vi* (*also fig*) отдава́ться (отда́ться *perf*) э́хом.
reverberation [rɪvə:bə'reɪʃən] *n* (*of thunder*) раска́т; (*shock*) резона́нс.
revere [rɪ'vɪəʳ] *vt* (*person*) почита́ть (*impf*), чтить (*impf*).
reverence ['rɛvərəns] *n* (*feeling*) почте́ние.
Reverend ['rɛvərənd] *adj*: **the ~** его́ преподо́бие; **the ~ John Smith** его́ преподо́бие Джон Смит.
reverent ['rɛvərənt] *adj* (*behaviour etc*) почти́тельный (почти́телен).
reverie ['rɛvərɪ] *n* мечта́ние.
reversal [rɪ'və:sl] *n* радика́льное измене́ние; (*of roles*) переме́на.
reverse [rɪ'və:s] *n* (*opposite*) противополо́жность *f*; (*back: of cloth*) обра́тная сторона́; (: *of coin, medal*) оборо́тная сторона́; (: *of paper*) оборо́т; (*AUT: also*: **~ gear**) обра́тный ход; (*setback, defeat*) неуда́ча ♦ *adj* (*opposite*) обра́тный ♦ *vt* (*order, position*) по́лностью изменя́ть (измени́ть *perf*); (*direction*) изменя́ть (измени́ть *perf*); (*process, policy, decision*) кру́то изменя́ть (измени́ть *perf*); (*LAW: judgement*) отменя́ть (отмени́ть *perf*) ♦ *vi* (*BRIT: AUT*) дава́ть (дать *perf*) за́дний ход; **their fortunes went into ~** уда́ча отверну́лась от них; **in ~ order** в обра́тном поря́дке; **to ~ direction** изменя́ть (измени́ть *perf*) направле́ние на обра́тное; **to ~ a car** дава́ть (дать *perf*) за́дний ход; **to ~ roles** меня́ться (поменя́ться *perf*) места́ми.
reverse-charge call [rɪ'və:stʃɑ:dʒ-] *n* (*BRIT: TEL*) телефо́нный разгово́р за счёт принима́ющего абоне́нта.
reverse video *n* негати́вное изображе́ние на экра́не дисппле́я.
reversible [rɪ'və:səbl] *adj* (*garment, material*) двусторо́нний; (*procedure*) обрати́мый (обрати́м).
reversing lights [rɪ'və:sɪŋ-] *npl* (*BRIT: AUT*) фона́рь *msg* за́днего хо́да.
reversion [rɪ'və:ʃən] *n* (*ZOOL*) проявле́ние атави́зма; **~ to** возвраще́ние к +*dat*.
revert [rɪ'və:t] *vi*: **to ~ to** (*to former state*) возвраща́ться (возврати́ться *perf*) к +*dat*; (*LAW: money, property*) переходи́ть

(перейти́ *perf*) к +*dat*.
review [rɪ'vju:] *n* (*of situation, policy etc*) пересмо́тр; (*MIL*) смотр; (*of book, film etc*) реце́нзия; (*magazine*) обозре́ние ♦ *vt* (*situation, policy etc*) пересма́тривать (пересмотре́ть *perf*); (*MIL*) проводи́ть (провести́ *perf*) смотр +*gen*; (*book, film etc*) рецензи́ровать (отрецензи́ровать *perf*); **to come under ~** рассма́триваться (*impf*).
reviewer [rɪ'vju:əʳ] *n* (*of book, film etc*) рецензе́нт.
revile [rɪ'vaɪl] *vt* поноси́ть (*impf*).
revise [rɪ'vaɪz] *vt* (*manuscript*) перераба́тывать (перерабо́тать *perf*); (*opinion*) пересма́тривать (пересмотре́ть *perf*); (*price, procedure*) изменя́ть (измени́ть *perf*); (*SCOL: lesson, maths*) повторя́ть (повтори́ть *perf*); **~d edition** пересмо́тренное изда́ние.
revision [rɪ'vɪʒən] *n* (*amendment*) измене́ние; (*for exam*) повторе́ние.
revitalize [ri:'vaɪtəlaɪz] *vt* оживля́ть (оживи́ть *perf*).
revival [rɪ'vaɪvəl] *n* (*recovery*) оживле́ние; (*of interest, faith*) возрожде́ние; (*THEAT*) возобновле́ние.
revive [rɪ'vaɪv] *vt* (*person*) возвраща́ть (возврати́ть *perf*) к жи́зни; (*economy, industry*) оживля́ть (оживи́ть *perf*); (*tradition, hope, interest etc*) возрожда́ть (возроди́ть *perf*); (*play*) восстана́вливать (восстанови́ть *perf*) ♦ *vi* (*person: from faint*) приходи́ть (прийти́ *perf*) в созна́ние; (*activity, economy etc*) оживля́ться (оживи́ться *perf*); (*faith, hope, interest etc*) возрожда́ться (возроди́ться *perf*).
revoke [rɪ'vəuk] *vt* (*treaty, law, title etc*) отменя́ть (отмени́ть *perf*); (*promise, decision*) брать (взять *perf*) наза́д.
revolt [rɪ'vəult] *n* (*rebellion*) восста́ние ♦ *vi* (*rebel*) восстава́ть (восста́ть *perf*) ♦ *vt* вызыва́ть (вы́звать *perf*) отвраще́ние у +*gen*; **to ~ against sb/sth** восстава́ть (восста́ть *perf*) про́тив кого́-н/чего́-н.
revolting [rɪ'vəultɪŋ] *adj* (*disgusting*) отврати́тельный (отврати́телен).
revolution [rɛvə'lu:ʃən] *n* револю́ция; (*of wheel, earth etc*) оборо́т.
revolutionary [rɛvə'lu:ʃənrɪ] *adj* революцио́нный (революцио́нен) ♦ *n* революционе́р(ка).
revolutionize [rɛvə'lu:ʃənaɪz] *vt* (*industry, society etc*) революционизи́ровать (*impf/perf*).
revolve [rɪ'vɔlv] *vi* (*turn*) враща́ться (*impf*); (*fig*): **to ~ (a)round** враща́ться (*impf*) вокру́г +*gen*.
revolver [rɪ'vɔlvəʳ] *n* (*gun*) револьве́р.
revolving [rɪ'vɔlvɪŋ] *adj* (*chair etc*) враща́ющийся.
revolving door *n* враща́ющаяся дверь *f*.
revue [rɪ'vju:] *n* ревю́ *nt ind*.
revulsion [rɪ'vʌlʃən] *n* (*disgust*) отвраще́ние.
reward [rɪ'wɔ:d] *n* (*recompense: for work,*

service, merit) награ́да; *(sum of money)* пре́мия; (: *for capture of criminal, information etc)* вознагражде́ние ♦ *vt:* **to ~ (for)** *(effort)* вознагражда́ть (вознагради́ть* *perf)* (за +*acc*).

rewarding [rɪ'wɔːdɪŋ] *adj (fig):* **this work is very ~** э́та рабо́та прино́сит удовлетворе́ние; **financially ~** хорошо́ опла́чиваемый.

rewind [riː'waɪnd] *irreg vt (cassette)* перема́тывать (перемота́ть *perf) (наза́д).*

rewire [riː'waɪəʳ] *vt:* **to ~ a house** заменя́ть (замени́ть *perf)* прово́дку в до́ме.

reword [riː'wɜːd] *vt* перефрази́ровать *(impf/ perf).*

rework [riː'wɜːk] *vt* переде́лывать (переде́лать *perf).*

rewrite [riː'raɪt] *irreg vt (rework)* перепи́сывать (переписа́ть* *perf).*

Reykjavik ['reɪkjəviːk] *n* Рейкья́вик.

RFD *abbr (US: POST.* = *rural free delivery) беспла́тная доста́вка по́чты в се́льской ме́стности.*

Rh *abbr (MED.* = *rhesus)* ре́зус.

rhapsody ['ræpsədɪ] *n (MUS)* рапсо́дия.

rhesus negative *adj (MED)* с отрица́тельным ре́зусом.

rhesus positive *adj (MED)* с положи́тельным ре́зусом.

rhetoric ['rɛtərɪk] *n* рито́рика.

rhetorical [rɪ'tɔrɪkl] *adj* ритори́ческий.

rheumatic [ruː'mætɪk] *adj* ревмати́ческий*.

rheumatism ['ruːmətɪzəm] *n* ревмати́зм.

rheumatoid arthritis ['ruːmətɔɪd-] *n* ревмато́идный артри́т.

Rhine [raɪn] *n:* **the ~** Рейн.

rhinestone ['raɪnstəun] *n* фальши́вый бриллиа́нт.

rhinoceros [raɪ'nɔsərəs] *n* носоро́г.

Rhodes [rəudz] *n* Ро́дос.

Rhodesia [rəu'diːʒə] *n* Роде́зия.

Rhodesian [rəu'diːʒən] *adj* родези́йский ♦ *n* родези́ец*(-и́йка*).

rhododendron [rəudə'dɛndrn] *n* рододе́ндрон.

Rhone [rəun] *n:* **the ~** Ро́на.

rhubarb ['ruːbɑːb] *n* реве́нь* *m.*

rhyme [raɪm] *n* ри́фма; *(verse)* стихотворе́ние; *(in poetry)* разме́р ♦ *vi:* **to ~ (with)** рифмова́ться *(impf)* (с +*instr);* **without ~ or reason** ни с того́ ни с сего́.

rhythm ['rɪðm] *n* ритм.

rhythmic(al) ['rɪðmɪk(l)] *adj (sound)* ритми́ческий*, ритми́чный* (ритми́чен).

rhythmically ['rɪðmɪklɪ] *adv* ритми́чно.

rhythm method *n* есте́ственный *or* натура́льный ме́тод контраце́пции.

RI *n abbr (BRIT: SCOL.* = *religious instruction)* религио́зное воспита́ние ♦ *abbr (US: POST.)* = *Rhode Island.*

rib [rɪb] *n (ANAT)* ребро́* ♦ *vt (inf: mock)* подшу́чивать (подшути́ть* *perf)* над +*instr.*

ribald ['rɪbəld] *adj (laughter, jokes)* непристо́йный* (непристо́ен), скабрёзный* (скабрёзен); *(person)* гру́бый* (груб).

ribbed [rɪbd] *adj (shell)* ребри́стый (ребри́ст); **~ knitting** вяза́ние рези́нкой.

ribbon ['rɪbən] *n* ле́нта; **in ~s** *(torn)* в кло́чья.

rice [raɪs] *n* рис.

rice field *n* ри́совое по́ле*.

rice pudding *n* ри́совый пу́динг.

rich [rɪtʃ] *adj* бога́тый (бога́т); *(clothes, jewels)* роско́шный* (роско́шен); *(soil)* бога́тый; *(food, colour, life)* насы́щенный; *(voice)* густо́й (густ); *(abundant):* **~ in** бога́тый (бога́т) +*instr;* **the ~** *npl (rich people)* бога́тые *pl adj.*

riches ['rɪtʃɪz] *npl (wealth)* бога́тство *ntsg.*

richly ['rɪtʃlɪ] *adv (dressed, decorated)* роско́шно, бога́то; *(rewarded)* ще́дро; *(deserved, earned)* вполне́.

richness ['rɪtʃnɪs] *n* бога́тство.

rickets ['rɪkɪts] *n (MED)* рахи́т.

rickety ['rɪkɪtɪ] *adj (furniture etc)* ша́ткий* (ша́ток).

rickshaw ['rɪkʃɔː] *n* ри́кша.

ricochet ['rɪkəʃeɪ] *vi (bullet, stone)* рикошети́ровать *(impf)* ♦ *n* рикоше́т.

rid [rɪd] *(pt, pp rid) vt:* **to ~ sb of sth** избавля́ть (изба́вить* *perf)* кого́-н от чего́-н; **to get ~ of** избавля́ться (изба́виться* *perf) or* отде́лываться (отде́латься *perf)* от +*gen.*

riddance ['rɪdns] *n:* **good ~!** ска́тертью доро́га!

ridden ['rɪdn] *pp of* **ride.**

riddle ['rɪdl] *n (conundrum)* зага́дка*; *(mystery)* та́йна ♦ *vt:* **~d with** *(holes, bullets)* изрешечённый (изрешечён) +*instr;* *(guilt, doubts)* по́лный* (по́лон) +*gen;* *(corruption)* прони́занный (прони́зан) +*instr.*

ride [raɪd] *(pt* **rode,** *pp* **ridden)** *n* пое́здка*; *(track, path)* лесна́я доро́га, тропа́* ♦ *vi (as sport)* е́здить* *(impf)* верхо́м; *(go somewhere, travel)* е́хать*/е́здить* *(impf)* ♦ *vt (horse)* е́хать*/ е́здить* *(impf)* верхо́м на +*prp; (bicycle, motorcycle)* е́хать*/е́здить* *(impf)* на +*prp; (distance)* проезжа́ть (прое́хать* *perf);* **a 5 mile ~** пое́здка в 5 миль; **horse/car ~** пое́здка* верхо́м/на маши́не; **to go for a ~** пойти́* *(perf)* поката́ться; **to take sb for a ~** *(fig)* прокати́ть* *(perf)* кого́-н; **we rode all day/all the way** мы е́хали весь день/всю доро́гу; **to ~ at anchor** *(NAUT)* стоя́ть *(impf)* на я́коре; **can you ~ a bike?** Вы уме́ете е́здить на велосипе́де?

▶ **ride out** *vt:* **to ~ out the storm** *(fig)* выде́рживать (вы́держать *perf)* тру́дности.

rider ['raɪdəʳ] *n (on horse)* нае́здник(-ица),

вса́дник(-ица); (*on bicycle*)
велосипеди́ст(ка*); (*on motorcycle*)
мотоцикли́ст(ка*); (*in document*)
дополне́ние.

ridge [rɪdʒ] *n* (*of hill*) гре́бень *m*; (*of roof*) конёк*
(*крыши*); (*on material*) вы́ступ.

ridicule ['rɪdɪkjuːl] *n* насме́шка* ♦ *vt*
высме́ивать (вы́смеять *perf*); **an object of ~**
предме́т насме́шек.

ridiculous [rɪˈdɪkjuləs] *adj* смехотво́рный*
(смехотво́рен); **it's ~** э́то смешно́.

riding ['raɪdɪŋ] *n* верхова́я езда́.

riding school *n* шко́ла верхово́й езды́.

rife [raɪf] *adj*: **to be ~** (*bribery, corruption*)
процвета́ть (*impf*); **to be ~ with** (*rumours,
fears*) изоби́ловать (*impf*) +*instr*.

riffraff ['rɪfræf] *n* шу́шера.

rifle ['raɪfl] *n* (*MIL*) винто́вка*; (*for hunting*)
ружьё* ♦ *vt* (*steal from: pockets etc*) очи́стить*
(*perf*)
► **rifle through** *vt fus* (*papers, belongings*)
бы́стро перебира́ть (перебра́ть* *perf*).

rifle range *n* (*outdoor*) стре́льбище; (*indoor, at
fair*) тир.

rift [rɪft] *n* (*also fig*) тре́щина; (*in clouds*)
просве́т.

rig [rɪg] *n* (*also*: **oil ~**) бурова́я устано́вка*; (:
*on
land*) бурова́я вы́шка* ♦ *vt* (*election etc*)
подтасо́вывать (подтасова́ть *perf*)
результа́ты +*gen*
► **rig out** *vt* (*BRIT*): **to ~ out as/in** наряжа́ть
(наряди́ть *perf*) как/в +*acc*
► **rig up** *vt* на́скоро сооружа́ть (сооруди́ть*
perf).

Riga [ˈriːɡə] *n* Ри́га.

rigging ['rɪgɪŋ] *n* (*NAUT*) такела́ж.

right [raɪt] *adj* (*answer, solution, decision etc*)
пра́вильный* (пра́вилен); (*size*) ну́жный;
(*person, clothes, time*) подходя́щий*; (*morally
good, fair, just*) справедли́вый (справедли́в),
пра́вильный* (пра́вилен); (*not left*) пра́вый ♦
n справедли́вость *f*; (*entitlement*) пра́во*; (*not
left*) пра́вая сторона́ ♦ *adv* (*correctly*)
пра́вильно; (*properly, fairly*) справедли́во;
(*not on the left*) спра́ва; (*not to the left*)
напра́во ♦ *vt* (*ship*) выра́внивать (вы́ровнять
perf); (*car*) ста́вить* (поста́вить* *perf*) на
колёса; (*fault, situation*) исправля́ть
(испра́вить* *perf*); (*wrong*) устраня́ть
(устрани́ть *perf*) ♦ *excl* так, хорошо́; **the ~
time** (*precise*) то́чное вре́мя; (*not wrong*)
ну́жный *or* подходя́щий* моме́нт; **she's ~**
она́ пра́ва; **that's ~!** (*answer*) пра́вильно!; **is
that clock ~?** э́то то́чные часы́?; **to get sth ~**
де́лать (сде́лать *perf*) что-н как сле́дует; **let's
get it ~ this time!** дава́йте сде́лаем э́то как
сле́дует на э́тот раз; **you did the ~ thing** Вы
поступи́ли пра́вильно; **to put a mistake ~**
(*BRIT*) исправля́ть (испра́вить* *perf*) оши́бку;
on the ~ спра́ва; **you are in the ~** пра́вда за
Ва́ми; **by ~s** по справедли́вости; **~ and**

wrong пра́вильное и непра́вильное; **he
doesn't know the difference between ~ and
wrong** он не зна́ет ра́зницы ме́жду
пра́вильным и непра́вильным; **film ~s**
пра́во на экраниза́цию; **~ now** сейча́с же; **~
away** сра́зу же; **~ before/after** как раз пе́ред
+*instr*/по́сле +*gen*; **~ against the wall** пря́мо у
стены́; **~ ahead** пря́мо вперёд; **~ in the
middle** пря́мо посереди́не; **~ to the end of sth**
до са́мого конца́ чего́-н.

right angle *n* прямо́й у́гол*.

righteous ['raɪtʃəs] *adj* пра́ведный* (пра́веден).

righteousness ['raɪtʃəsnɪs] *n* пра́ведность *f*.

rightful ['raɪtful] *adj* зако́нный.

rightfully ['raɪtfəlɪ] *adv* (*yours etc*) зако́нно.

right-hand drive ['raɪthænd-] *n* право-
сторо́ннее управле́ние ♦ *adj* (*vehicle*) с
правосторо́нним управле́нием.

right-handed [raɪtˈhændɪd] *adj*: **he is ~** он
правша́.

right-hand man *n* пра́вая рука́* (*перен*).

right-hand side *n* пра́вая сторона́*.

rightly ['raɪtlɪ] *adv* (*with reason*) справедли́во; **if
I remember ~** (*BRIT*) е́сли я пра́вильно
по́мню.

right-minded [raɪtˈmaɪndɪd] *adj*
благоразу́мный* (благоразу́мен).

right of way *n* (*path etc*) пра́во* прохо́да;
(*AUT*) пра́во* прое́зда.

rights issue *n* (*STOCK EXCHANGE*) *вы́пуск а́кции
для прода́жи уже́ существу́ющим
акционе́рам по льго́тным це́нам*.

right wing *n* (*POL*) пра́вое крыло́*; (*MIL, SPORT*)
пра́вый фланг.

right-wing [raɪtˈwɪŋ] *adj* (*POL*) пра́вый.

right-winger [raɪtˈwɪŋə*] *n* (*POL*) челове́к
пра́вых взгля́дов, пра́вый(-ая) *m(f) adj*;
(*SPORT*) пра́вый напада́ющий* *m adj*.

rigid ['rɪdʒɪd] *adj* (*structure, principle*) жёсткий*
(жёсток); (*fig: attitude, views etc*) ко́сный*
(ко́сен); (: *principle, control etc*) стро́гий*
(строг).

rigidity [rɪˈdʒɪdɪtɪ] *n* (*of structure*) жёсткость *f*;
(*of attitude etc*) ко́сность *f*.

rigidly ['rɪdʒɪdlɪ] *adv* (*hold, fix etc*) про́чно;
(*control*) жёстко; (*behave*) ско́ванно.

rigmarole ['rɪɡmərəul] *n* (*procedure*) кани́тель
f.

rigor ['rɪɡə*] *n* (*US*) = **rigour**.

rigor mortis ['rɪɡə'mɔːtɪs] *n* тру́пное
окочене́ние.

rigorous ['rɪɡərəs] *adj* стро́гий* (строг);
(*training*) серьёзный.

rigorously ['rɪɡərəslɪ] *adv* (*test, assess etc*)
стро́го.

rigour ['rɪɡə*] (*US* **rigor**) *n* (*strictness*) стро́гость
f; (*severity*): **~s of life/winter** тру́дности *fpl*
жи́зни/зимы́.

rigout ['rɪɡaut] *n* (*BRIT: inf: clothes*) одея́ние.

rile [raɪl] *vt* раздража́ть (раздражи́ть *perf*).

rim [rɪm] *n* (*of glass, dish*) край*; (*of spectacles*)

ободо́к•; (*of wheel*) о́бод•.
rimless ['rɪmlɪs] *adj* (*spectacles*) без ободка́.
rimmed [rɪmd] *adj*: ~ **with** окаймлённый (окаймлён) +*instr*.
rind [raɪnd] *n* (*of bacon, cheese*) ко́рка; (*of lemon, orange etc*) кожура́.
ring [rɪŋ] (*pt* **rang**, *pp* **rung**) *n* (*of metal, smoke*) кольцо́•; (*of people, objects, light*) круг•; (*of spies, drug dealers etc*) сеть• *f*; (*for boxing*) ринг; (*bullring, also of circus*) аре́на; (*of doorbell, telephone*) звоно́к• ♦ *vi* звони́ть (позвони́ть *perf*); (*doorbell*) звони́ть (зазвони́ть *perf*); (*also:* ~ **out**: *voice, shot*) раздава́ться• (разда́ться• *perf*) ♦ *vt* (*BRIT: TEL*) звони́ть (позвони́ть *perf*) +*dat*; (*bell etc*) звони́ть (позвони́ть *perf*) в +*acc*; **to give sb a** ~ (*BRIT: TEL*) звони́ть (позвони́ть *perf*) кому́-н; **that has a** ~ **of truth about it** э́то звучи́т правдоподо́бно; **my ears are** ~**ing** у меня́ звени́т в уша́х; **to** ~ **the bell** звони́ть (*impf*) в звоно́к; (*doorbell*) звони́ть (позвони́ть *perf*) в дверь; **the name doesn't** ~ **a bell (with me)** э́то и́мя мне ни о чём не говори́т
▶ **ring back** (*BRIT*) ♦ *vt* перезва́нивать (перезвони́ть *perf*) +*dat* ♦ *vi* звони́ть (позвони́ть *perf*) (в отве́т)
▶ **ring off** *vi* (*BRIT*) ве́шать (пове́сить• *perf*) тру́бку
▶ **ring up** *vt* (*BRIT*) звони́ть (позвони́ть *perf*) +*dat*.
ring binder *n* скоросшива́тель *m*.
ring finger *n* безымя́нный па́лец•.
ringing ['rɪŋɪŋ] *n* (*of telephone, doorbell*) звоно́к•; (*of church bell, in ears*) звон.
ringing tone *n* (*BRIT: TEL*) дли́нные гудки́ *pl*.
ringleader ['rɪŋliːdə'] *n* (*of gang*) глава́рь• *m*.
ringlets ['rɪŋlɪts] *npl* ло́коны *mpl*.
ring road *n* (*BRIT*) кольцева́я доро́га.
rink [rɪŋk] *n* (*also:* **ice** ~, **roller skating** ~) като́к•.
rinse [rɪns] *n* (*process*) полоска́ние; (*dye: for hair*) кра́ска• для воло́с ♦ *vt* полоска́ть• (прополоска́ть• *perf*); (*clothes*) полоска́ть (вы́полоскать *perf*); **to give sth a** ~ ополя́скивать (ополосну́ть *perf*) что-н.
Rio (de Janeiro) ['riːəu(dədʒə'nɪərəu)] *n* Ри́о-де-Жане́йро *m ind*.
riot ['raɪət] *n* (*disturbance*) беспоря́дки• *mpl*, бесчи́нства *ntpl*; (*of colours, flowers*) бу́йство ♦ *vi* бесчи́нствовать (*impf*); **to run** ~ бу́йствовать• (*impf*).
rioter ['raɪətə'] *n* наруши́тель *m* поря́дка.
riot gear *n* защи́тное снаряже́ние поли́ции.
riotous ['raɪətəs] *adj* (*mob, behaviour, party*) бесчи́нствующий; (*living*) разгу́льный• (разгу́лен); (*welcome*) бу́рный• (бу́рен).
riotously ['raɪətəslɪ] *adv*: ~ **funny** неимове́рно смешно́й.

riot police *n* спецподразделе́ние поли́ции для подавле́ния беспоря́дков.
RIP *abbr* (= *rest in peace*) мир пра́ху твоему́.
rip [rɪp] *n* (*tear*) разры́в ♦ *vt* (*paper, cloth*) разрыва́ть• (разорва́ть• *perf*) ♦ *vi* (*see vt*) разрыва́ться• (разорва́ться• *perf*).
▶ **rip up** *vt* разрыва́ть (разорва́ть• *perf*).
ripcord ['rɪpkɔːd] *n* (*on parachute*) вытяжно́й трос.
ripe [raɪp] *adj* спе́лый• (спел), зре́лый• (зрел); (*cheese*) вы́держанный• (вы́держан).
ripen ['raɪpn] *vi* спеть• (поспе́ть• *perf*), зреть *or* созрева́ть (созре́ть *perf*) ♦ *vt*: **the sun will** ~ **them soon** они́ ско́ро созре́ют на со́лнце.
ripeness ['raɪpnɪs] *n* спе́лость *f*, зре́лость *f*.
rip-off ['rɪpɔf] *n* (*inf*): **it's a** ~! э́то обдира́ловка!
riposte [rɪ'pɔst] *n* нахо́дчивый отве́т.
ripple ['rɪpl] *n* (*wave: caused by wind, rain etc*) рябь *f no pl*; (: *caused by stone etc*) зыбь *f no pl*; (*of laughter, applause*) волна́•, гул *m no pl* ♦ *vt* (*water, sand*) поднима́ть (подня́ть• *perf*) зыбь на +*prp* ♦ *vi* (*water*) покрыва́ться (покры́ться• *perf*) ря́бью.
rise [raɪz] (*pt* **rose**, *pp* **risen**) *n* (*slope*) подъём; (*increase*) повыше́ние; (*fig: of state, leader*) возвыше́ние ♦ *vi* поднима́ться (подня́ться• *perf*); (*prices, numbers, voice*) повыша́ться (повы́ситься• *perf*); (*sun, moon*) всходи́ть• (взойти́• *perf*); (*sound*) нараста́ть (*impf*); (*also:* ~ **up**: *building*) возвыша́ться (*impf*); (: *rebels*) восстава́ть• (восста́ть• *perf*); (*in rank*) продвига́ться (продви́нуться *perf*); ~ **to power** прихо́д к вла́сти; **to give** ~ **to** вызыва́ть (вы́звать• *perf*); **to** ~ **to the occasion** оказыва́ться (оказа́ться• *perf*) на высоте́ положе́ния.
risen [rɪzn] *pp of* **rise**.
rising ['raɪzɪŋ] *adj* (*number, prices*) расту́щий; (*tide*) нараста́ющий; (*sun, moon*) восходя́щий.
rising damp *n* засоле́ние (*поднима́ющаяся вверх сы́рость*).
rising star *n* (*fig*) восходя́щая звезда́•.
risk [rɪsk] *n* риск ♦ *vt* (*endanger*) рискова́ть (*impf*) +*instr*; (*chance*) рискова́ть• (рискну́ть *perf*) +*instr*; **to take a** ~ рискова́ть (рискну́ть *perf*), идти́• (*impf*) на риск; **to run the** ~ **of doing** рискова́ть (*impf*) +*infin*; **at** ~ в опа́сной ситуа́ции; **to put sb/sth at** ~ подверга́ть (подве́ргнуть) кого́-н/что-н ри́ску; **at one's own** ~ на свой (страх и) риск; **at the** ~ **of sounding rude** ... рискуя́ показа́ться гру́бым(-ой) ...; **it's a fire** ~ с противопожа́рной то́чки зре́ния это опа́сно; **it's a health** ~ э́то опа́сно для здоро́вья; **I'll** ~ **it** я рискну́.
risk capital *n* „ри́сковый" *or* ве́нчурный

• marks translations which have irregular inflections. The Russian-English side of the dictionary gives inflectional information.

капита́л.

risky ['rɪskɪ] adj риско́ванный* (риско́ван).

risqué ['riːskeɪ] adj (joke) сомни́тельный* (сомни́телен).

rissole ['rɪsəʊl] n бито́к*.

rite [raɪt] n обря́д; **last ~s** после́днее прича́стие.

ritual ['rɪtjʊəl] adj ритуа́льный ♦ n (of religion) обря́д; (of procedure) ритуа́л.

rival ['raɪvl] n сопе́рник(-ица); (in business) конкуре́нт ♦ adj (competing: business) конкури́рующий; (competition) сопе́рничающий ♦ vt сопе́рничать (impf) с +instr; **to ~ sb/sth** сопе́рничать (impf) с кем-н/с чем-н в +prp; **~ team** кома́нда сопе́рника.

rivalry ['raɪvlrɪ] n (in sport, love) сопе́рничество; (in business) конкуре́нция.

river ['rɪvəʳ] n река́* ♦ cpd (port, traffic) речно́й; **up/down ~** вверх/вниз по реке́.

riverbank ['rɪvəbæŋk] n бе́рег* реки́.

riverbed ['rɪvəbed] n ру́сло реки́.

riverside ['rɪvəsaɪd] n бе́рег* реки́.

rivet ['rɪvɪt] n заклёпка* ♦ vt (fig) прико́вывать (прикова́ть perf).

riveting ['rɪvɪtɪŋ] adj (fig) захва́тывающий*.

Riviera [rɪvɪ'ɛərə] n: **the (French) ~** (францу́зская) Ривье́ра; **the Italian ~** италья́нская Ривье́ра.

Riyadh [rɪ'jɑːd] n Эр-Рия́д.

RN n abbr (BRIT) = Royal Navy; (US: = registered nurse) ≈ медсестра́= *медици́нская сестра́*.

RNA n abbr (= ribonucleic acid) РНК= *рибонуклеи́новая кислота́*.

RNLI n abbr (BRIT) = Royal National Lifeboat Institution.

RNZAF n abbr = Royal New Zealand Air Force.

RNZN n abbr = Royal New Zealand Navy.

road [rəʊd] n (also fig) путь* m, доро́га; (in town) доро́га; (motorway etc) шоссе́ nt ind; **~ accident** доро́жная ава́рия; **main ~** гла́вная доро́га; **major/minor ~** гла́вная/ второстепе́нная доро́га; **it takes 4 hours by ~** э́то 4 часа́ по доро́ге; **let's hit the ~** дава́йте вы́едем на доро́гу; **to be on the ~** (tramp) бродя́жничать (impf); (salesman) быть* (impf) в разъе́здах; (pop group) быть* (impf) на гастро́лях, гастроли́ровать* (impf); **on the ~ to success** на пути́ к успе́ху; **~ sense** чу́вство доро́ги; **~ junction** пересече́ние доро́г, перекрёсток*.

roadblock ['rəʊdblɔk] n доро́жное загражде́ние.

road haulage n доро́жная перево́зка.

road hog n лиха́ч.

road map n доро́жная ка́рта.

road rage n агресси́вное поведе́ние на автодоро́ге.

road safety n доро́жная безопа́сность f.

roadside ['rəʊdsaɪd] n обо́чина ♦ cpd придоро́жный; **~ verge** обо́чина; **by the ~** у обо́чины.

road sign n доро́жный знак.

road sweeper n (BRIT: person) дво́рник; (vehicle) подмета́льная маши́на.

road user n (driver) води́тель m.

roadway ['rəʊdweɪ] n (central part of road) прое́зжая часть* f (доро́ги).

road works npl доро́жно-ремо́нтные рабо́ты.

roadworthy ['rəʊdwəːðɪ] adj (car) приго́дный* (приго́ден) к эксплуата́ции.

roam [rəʊm] vi броди́ть* (impf), скита́ться (impf) ♦ vt броди́ть* (impf) по +dat.

roar [rɔːʳ] n (of animal) рёв m no pl; (of crowd, engine, wind) рёв; (of laughter) взрыв ♦ vi (animal, person) реве́ть (impf); (crowd, engine, wind) реве́ть (impf); **to ~ with laughter** хохота́ть (impf).

roaring ['rɔːrɪŋ] adj: **a ~ fire** я́рко пыла́ющий ками́н; **a ~ success** гро́мкий успе́х; **to do a ~ trade** вести́* (impf) бо́йкую торго́влю.

roast [rəʊst] n (of meat) жарко́е nt adj ♦ vt (meat, potatoes) жа́рить (зажа́рить perf); (coffee) жа́рить (поджа́рить perf).

roast beef n ро́стбиф, жа́реная говя́дина.

roasting ['rəʊstɪŋ] n (inf): **to give sb a ~** устра́ивать (устро́ить perf) кому́-н разно́с.

rob [rɔb] vt (person, house, bank) обкра́дывать (обокра́сть* perf); **to ~ sb of sth** красть* (укра́сть* perf) что-н у кого́-н; (fig) лиша́ть (лиши́ть perf) кого́-н чего́-н.

robber ['rɔbəʳ] n граби́тель m.

robbery ['rɔbərɪ] n (theft) ограбле́ние, грабёж.

robe [rəʊb] n (for ceremony etc) ма́нтия; (also: **bath ~**) ба́нный хала́т; (US) плед ♦ vt облача́ть (облачи́ть perf).

robin ['rɔbɪn] n (also: **~ redbreast**) заря́нка*.

robot ['rəʊbɔt] n ро́бот.

robotics [rə'bɔtɪks] n (ELEC, COMPUT) робототе́хника.

robust [rəʊ'bʌst] adj кре́пкий* (кре́пок).

rock [rɔk] n (substance) го́рная поро́да; (boulder) валу́н*; (cliff) скала́*; (US: small stone) ка́мешек*; (BRIT: sweet) леденцо́вая караме́ль в фо́рме дли́нных па́лочек; (MUS: also: **~ music**) рок ♦ vt (swing gently) кача́ть (impf); (shake) шата́ть (impf) ♦ vi (object) кача́ться (impf), шата́ться (impf); (person) кача́ться (impf); **on the ~s** (drink) со льдом; (marriage etc) на гра́ни распа́да; **the ship was smashed on the ~s** кора́бль разби́лся о ска́лы; **to ~ the boat** (fig) наруши́ть (perf) поко́й.

rock and roll n рок-н-ро́лл.

rock bottom n (fig) преде́льная ни́зкая черта́; **to reach or touch or hit ~** (price) достига́ть (дости́чь* perf) преде́льно ни́зкой черты́; (person) доходи́ть* (дойти́* perf) до крити́ческой то́чки.

rock-bottom ['rɔk'bɔtəm] adj (fig: prices) преде́льно ни́зкий*.

rock cake n ко́ржик с изю́мом.

rock climber n скалола́з.

rock climbing *n* скалола́зание.
rockery ['rɔkərɪ] *n* альпи́йский* сад*.
rocket ['rɔkɪt] *n* раке́та ◆ *vi* (*prices*) подска́кивать (подскочи́ть* *perf*).
rocket launcher *n* (*MIL*) пускова́я раке́тная устано́вка*.
rock face *n* пове́рхность *f* скалы́.
rock fall *n* камнепа́д.
rocking chair ['rɔkɪŋ-] *n* (кре́сло-)кача́лка*.
rocking horse *n* конь-кача́лка*.
rocky ['rɔkɪ] *adj* (*mountain*) скали́стый (скали́ст); (*path, soil*) камени́стый (камени́ст); (*unsteady, unstable*) ша́ткий* (ша́ток).
Rocky Mountains *npl*: the ~ ~ Скали́стые го́ры* *fpl*.
rod [rɔd] *n* прут*; (*TECH*) сте́ржень* *m*; (*also*: **fishing** ~) у́дочка*.
rode [rəud] *pt of* **ride**.
rodent ['rəudnt] *n* грызу́н*.
rodeo ['rəudɪəu] *n* (*US*) роде́о *nt ind*.
roe [rəu] *n* (*also*: ~ **deer**) косу́ля; (*of fish*): **hard** ~ икра́; **soft** ~ моло́ки *fpl*.
roe deer *n inv* косу́ля.
rogue [rəug] *n* (*dishonest person*) моше́нник, жу́лик.
roguish ['rəugɪʃ] *adj* (*mischevious*) плутова́тый (плутова́т).
role [rəul] *n* (*THEAT, fig*) роль* *f*.
role model *n* приме́р.
role play *n* ролевы́е игры́ *fpl*.
roll [rəul] *n* (*of paper, cloth etc*) руло́н; (*of banknotes*) сви́ток*; (*also*: **bread** ~) бу́лочка*; (*register, list*) спи́сок*; (*sound: of drums*) бой*; (: *of thunder*) раска́т ◆ *vt* (*ball, stone etc*) ката́ть/кати́ть* (*impf*); (*also*: ~ **up**: **string**) скру́чивать (скрути́ть* *perf*); (: *sleeves*) зака́тывать (заката́ть *perf*); (*cigarette*) свёртывать (сверну́ть *perf*); (*eyes*) зака́тывать (закати́ть* *perf*); (*also*: ~ **out**: *pastry*) раска́тывать (раската́ть *perf*); (*lawn, road etc*) ука́тывать (уката́ть *perf*) ◆ *vi* (*ball, stone etc*) кати́ться* (*impf*); (*drum*) греме́ть (*impf*); (*car. also*: ~ **along**) кати́ться* (*impf*); (*ship*) кача́ться (*impf*); **cheese/ham** ~ бу́лочка* с сы́ром/с ветчино́й
▶ **roll about** *vi* перека́тываться (перекати́ться* *perf*)
▶ **roll around** *vi* = **roll about**
▶ **roll by** *vi* (*time*) протека́ть (проте́чь* *perf*)
▶ **roll in** *vi* (*orders*) сы́паться* (*impf*); (*cash*) течь* (поте́чь* *perf*)
▶ **roll over** *vi* перевора́чиваться (переверну́ться *perf*)
▶ **roll up** *vi* (*inf: arrive*) подка́тывать (подкати́ть* *perf*) ◆ *vt* (*carpet, newspaper*) свора́чивать (сверну́ть *perf*); (*umbrella*) скла́дывать (сложи́ть* *perf*); **to** ~ **o.s. up into**

a ball свора́чиваться (сверну́ться *perf*) кала́чиком.
roll call *n* перекли́чка*.
roller ['rəulə*] *n* (*in machine*) ва́лик; (*wheel*) ро́лик; (*for lawn, road*) като́к*; (*for hair*) бигуди́ *pl ind*.
roller blind *n* што́ра на ро́ликах.
roller coaster *n* аттракцио́н "америка́нские го́ры" *fpl*.
roller skates *npl* ро́лики *mpl*, ро́ликовые коньки́ *mpl*.
rollicking ['rɔlɪkɪŋ] *adj* потряса́ющий* (потряса́ющ); **to have a** ~ **time** весели́ться (повесели́ться *perf*).
rolling ['rəulɪŋ] *adj* (*landscape*) холми́стый (холми́ст).
rolling mill *n* прока́тный стан.
rolling pin *n* ска́лка*.
rolling stock *n* (*RAIL*) подвижно́й соста́в.
roll-on/roll-off ferry *adj* (*BRIT*) паро́м, приспосо́бленный для въе́зда и вы́езда автомоби́лей.
roly-poly ['rəulɪ'pəulɪ] *n* (*BRIT: CULIN*) руле́т с варе́ньем.
ROM [rɔm] *n abbr* (*COMPUT*: = *read-only memory*) ПЗУ= *постоя́нное запомина́ющее устро́йство*.
Roman ['rəumən] *adj* ри́мский* ◆ *n* (*person*) ри́млянин(-нка).
Roman Catholic *adj* (ри́мско-)католи́ческий* ◆ *n* като́лик(-и́чка*).
romance [rə'mæns] *n* (*love affair, novel*) рома́н; (*charm*) рома́нтика; (*MUS*) рома́нс.
Romanesque [rəumə'nɛsk] *adj* рома́нский*.
Romania [rəu'meɪnɪə] *n* Румы́ния.
Romanian [rəu'meɪnɪən] *adj* румы́нский* ◆ *n* (*person*) румы́н(ка*); (*LING*) румы́нский язы́к*.
Roman numeral *n* ри́мская ци́фра.
romantic [rə'mæntɪk] *adj* романти́чный* (романти́чен); (*play, story etc*) романти́ческий.
romanticism [rə'mæntɪsɪzəm] *n* романти́зм.
Romany ['rɔmənɪ] *adj* цыга́нский* ◆ *n* цыга́н(ка*); (*LING*) цыга́нский* язы́к*.
Rome [rəum] *n* Рим.
romp [rɔmp] *n* возня́ ◆ *vi* (*also*: ~ **about**) вози́ться* (*impf*); **to** ~ **home** (*horse*) выи́грывать (вы́играть *perf*) ска́чки.
rompers ['rɔmpəz] *npl* ползунки́ *mpl*.
rondo ['rɔndəu] *n* ро́ндо *nt ind*.
roof [ru:f] (*pl* ~**s**) *n* кры́ша ◆ *vt* (*house*) настила́ть (настла́ть* *perf*) кры́шу +*gen or* на +*prp*; **the** ~ **of the mouth** нёбо.
roof garden *n* сад* на кры́ше.
roofing ['ru:fɪŋ] *n* кро́вельный материа́л; ~ **felt** руло́нный кро́вельный материа́л.
roof rack *n* (*AUT*) бага́жник (*на кры́ше*

автомобиля).

rook [ruk] *n* (*bird*) грач*; (*CHESS*) ладья*, тура ◆ *vt* (*inf*: *cheat*) надувать (надуть *perf*).

rookie ['ruki:] *n* (*US*: *inf*) новичок.

room [ru:m] *n* (*in house*) комната; (*in school*) класс; (*in hotel*) номер*; (*space*) место*; **~s** *npl* (*lodging*) квартира *fsg*; **"rooms to let"**, (*US*) **"rooms for rent"** „сдаются комнаты"; **single/ double** ~ (*in hotel*) одноместный/ двухместный номер*; **is there ~ for this?** это здесь поместится?; **to make ~ for sb** давать* (дать* *perf*) место кому-н; **there is ~ for improvement** кое-что можно улучшить; **there is still ~ for doubt** ещё есть основания сомневаться.

rooming house ['ru:mɪŋ-] *n* (*US*) мебелированные комнаты *fpl*.

roommate ['ru:mmeɪt] *n* сосед*(ка*) по комнате.

room service *n* обслуживание в номере.

room temperature *n* комнатная температура.

roomy ['ru:mɪ] *adj* (*building, car, garment*) просторный* (просторен); (*bag*) вместительный* (вместителен).

roost [ru:st] *vi* усаживаться (усесться* *perf*) на ночлег.

rooster ['ru:stə'] *n* (*esp US*) петух*.

root [ru:t] *n* корень* *m* ◆ *vi* (*plant, belief: also*: **take ~**) укореняться (укорениться *perf*); **~s** *npl* (*family origins*) корни* *mpl*; **the ~ of the problem is that ...** корень проблемы в том ...

▶ **root about** *vi* (*fig*) рыться* (*impf*)

▶ **root for** *vt fus* (*inf*: *support*) болеть* (*impf*) за +*acc*

▶ **root out** *vt* откопать (*perf*).

root beer *n* безалкогольный напиток из корней трав.

rope [rəup] *n* верёвка*, канат*; (*NAUT*) трос* ◆ *vt* (*area: also*: **~ off**) отгораживать (отгородить* *perf*) верёвкой; (*tie on*): **to ~ to** привязывать (привязать* *perf*) верёвкой к +*dat*; (*join*): **to ~ together** связывать (связать* *perf*) верёвкой; **to know the ~s** (*fig*) знать (*impf*), что к чему

▶ **rope in** *vt* (*fig*) втягивать (втянуть* *perf*).

rope ladder *n* верёвочная лестница.

ropey ['rəupɪ] *adj* (*inf*) дрянной*.

rosary ['rəuzərɪ] *n* чётки* *pl*.

rose [rəuz] *pt of* **rise** ◆ *n* роза; (*on watering can*) насадка* ◆ *adj* (*colour*) розовый (розов).

rosé ['rəuzeɪ] *n* (*wine*) розовое вино*.

rosebed ['rəuzbɛd] *n* клумба с розами.

rosebud ['rəuzbʌd] *n* бутон розы.

rosebush ['rəuzbuʃ] *n* розовый куст*.

rosemary ['rəuzmərɪ] *n* розмарин.

rosette [rəu'zɛt] *n* (*decoration*) розетка*.

ROSPA ['rɔspə] *n abbr* (*BRIT*) = Royal Society for the Prevention of Accidents.

roster ['rɔstə'] *n*: **duty ~** расписание дежурств.

rostrum ['rɔstrəm] *n* (*POL*) трибуна.

rosy ['rəuzɪ] *adj* (*colour*) розовый (розов); (*face, cheeks*) румяный (румян); (*situation*) радостный* (радостен); **a ~ future** радужное будущее.

rot [rɔt] *n* (*process*) гниение; (*result*) гниль *f*; (*fig*: *nonsense*) чушь *f* ◆ *vt* (*wood, fruit*) гноить (сгноить *perf*); (*teeth*) портить* (испортить* *perf*) ◆ *vi* гнить* (сгнить* *perf*); **to stop the ~** (*BRIT*: *fig*) навести* (*perf*) порядок; **dry/wet ~** сухая/мокрая гниль.

rota ['rəutə] *n* чередование; **on a ~ basis** чередуясь, поочерёдно.

rotary ['rəutərɪ] *adj* (*motion*) вращательный; (*machine*) ротационный, вращающийся; **~ engine** роторно-поршневой двигатель.

rotate [rəu'teɪt] *vt* вращать (*impf*); (*change round*: *crops, jobs*) чередовать (*impf*) ◆ *vi* вращаться (*impf*).

rotating [rəu'teɪtɪŋ] *adj* (*movement*) вращательный.

rotation [rəu'teɪʃən] *n* вращение; (*of crops*) севооборот; **in ~** поочерёдно.

rote [rəut] *n*: **to learn by ~** учить (*impf*) наизусть.

rotor ['rəutə'] *n* (*also*: **~ blade**) (несущий) винт* (*вертолёта*).

rotten ['rɔtn] *adj* (*fruit, wood, teeth*) гнилой*; (*meat, eggs*) тухлый*; (*fig*: *unpleasant*) мерзкий* (мерзок), отвратительный* (отвратителен); (*dishonest*) продажный* (продажен); (*inf*: *bad*) поганый*; **to feel ~** (*ill*) чувствовать (*impf*) себя погано.

Rotterdam ['rɔtədæm] *n* Роттердам.

rotund [rəu'tʌnd] *adj* (*person*) полный.

rouble ['ru:bl] (*US* **ruble**) *n* рубль* *m*.

rouge [ru:ʒ] *n* румяна *pl*.

rough [rʌf] *adj* грубый (груб); (*surface*) шероховатый (шероховат); (*terrain*) пересечённый; (*road*) ухабистый (ухабист); (*brusque: person, manner*) резкий* (резок); (*weather*) ненастный; (*sea*) бурный* (бурен); (*town, area*) опасный* (опасен); (*plan, sketch, work*) черновой; (*guess*) приблизительный* (приблизителен) ◆ *n* (*GOLF*): **in the ~** на нестриженной части поля ◆ *vt*: **to ~ it** обходиться* (обойтись* *perf*) без удобств ◆ *adv*: **to play ~** вести* (*impf*) жёсткую игру*; **the sea is ~ today** море сегодня штормит/ неспокойное; **we had a ~ time (of it)** нам пришлось туго; **~ estimate** грубая оценка* *or* смета; **to sleep ~** (*BRIT*) ночевать* (*impf*), где придётся; **to feel ~** (*BRIT*: *ill*) чувствовать (*impf*) себя плохо

▶ **rough out** *vt* (*draft*) набрасывать (набросать *perf*).

roughage ['rʌfɪdʒ] *n* грубая пища.

rough-and-ready ['rʌfən'rɛdɪ] *adj* дрянной*.

rough-and-tumble ['rʌfən'tʌmbl] *n* потасовка*.

roughcast ['rʌfkɑ:st] *n* (*for wall*) галечная штукатурка.

rough copy *n* черновик*.

rough draft *n* черновик*.
rough justice *n* жёсткий* суд.
roughly [ˈrʌflɪ] *adv* грубо; (*approximately*) приблизительно; ~ **speaking** грубо говоря.
roughness [ˈrʌfnɪs] *n* (*of surface*) шероховатость *f*; (*of manner*) грубость *f*.
roughshod [ˈrʌfʃɔd] *adv*: **to ride** ~ **over** не считаться (*impf*) с +*instr*.
roulette [ruːˈlɛt] *n* рулётка*.
Roumania *etc* = **Romania** *etc*.
round [raund] *adj* круглый* (кругл); (*figures, sum*) круглый ♦ *n* (*BRIT: of toast*) ломтик; (*duty: of policeman, doctor*) обход; (: *of milkman*) маршрут; (*game: of cards, golf*) партия; (*in competition*) тур; (*of ammunition*) патрон, комплект выстрела; (*of talks, also BOXING*) раунд ♦ *vt* огибать (обогнуть* *perf*) ♦ *prep* (*surrounding*): ~ **his neck/the table** вокруг его шеи/стола; (*approximately*): ~ **about three hundred** около трёхсот ♦ *adv*: **all** ~ кругом, вокруг; **in** ~ **figures** в круглых цифрах; **a** ~ **of applause** взрыв аплодисментов; **a** ~ **of drinks** по бокалу для всех; **the daily** ~ (*fig*) повседневные дела; **it's just** ~ **the corner** (*fig*) это как раз за углом; ~ **the clock** круглые сутки, круглосуточно; **to go** ~ **the back** обходить* (обойти* *perf*) сзади; **to walk** ~ **the room** ходить* (*impf*) по комнате; **to go** ~ **an obstacle** огибать (обогнуть *perf*) *or* обходить* (обойти* *perf*) препятствие; **the long way** ~ кружным путём; **all the year** ~ круглый год; **to ask sb** ~ приглашать (пригласить* *perf*) кого-н в гости; **I'll be** ~ **at 6 o'clock** я приду в 6 часов; **to go** ~ **to sb's (house)** идти*/ходить* (*impf*) к кому-н; **there's enough to go** ~ хватит на всех
▶ **round off** *vt* (*speech etc*) завершать (завершить *perf*)
▶ **round up** *vt* (*cattle, people*) сгонять (согнать* *perf*); (*price, figure*) округлять (округлить *perf*).
roundabout [ˈraundəbaut] *n* (*BRIT: AUT*) кольцевая транспортная развязка*; (: *at fair*) карусель *f* ♦ *adj* окольным путём.
rounded [ˈraundɪd] *adj* округлый (округл).
rounders [ˈraundəz] *n* английская лапта.
roundly [ˈraundlɪ] *adv* (*fig: criticize*) резко.
round robin *n* (*letter*) коллективное письмо*.
round-shouldered [ˈraundˈʃəuldəd] *adj* сутулый (сутул).
round trip *n* поездка* туда-обратно.
roundup [ˈraundʌp] *n* (*information*) сводка*; (*of animals*) загон; (*of criminals*) облава; **a** ~ **of the latest news** сводка последних новостей.
rouse [rauz] *vt* (*wake up*) будить* (разбудить* *perf*); (*stir up*) возбуждать (возбудить* *perf*).
rousing [ˈrauzɪŋ] *adj* (*cheer, welcome*) бурный*

(бурен).
rout [raut] *n* (*MIL*) разгром ♦ *vt* (*defeat*) громить* (разгромить* *perf*).
route [ruːt] *n* (*way*) путь* *m*, дорога; (*of bus, train, shipping*) маршрут; **the best** ~ **to London** лучший* путь в Лондон; **en** ~ **for** по пути в +*acc*; **en** ~ **from** ... **to** ... по пути из +*gen* ... в +*acc* ....
route map *n* (*BRIT*) маршрутная карта.
routine [ruːˈtiːn] *adj* (*work*) повседневный* (повседневен); (*procedure*) обычный* (обычен) ♦ *n* (*habits*) распорядок*; (*drudgery*) рутина; (*THEAT*) номер*; **daily** ~ распорядок* дня.
rove [rəuv] *vt* (*streets*) бродить* (*impf*) по +*dat*, скитаться (*impf*) по +*dat*.
roving reporter *n* разъездной репортёр.
row[1] [rəu] *n* ряд* ♦ *vi* (*in boat*) грести* (*impf*) ♦ *vt* (*boat*) управлять (*impf*) +*instr*; **in a** ~ (*fig*) подряд.
row[2] [rau] *n* (*noise*) шум; (*dispute*) скандал, ссора; (*inf: scolding*) нагоняй ♦ *vi* (*argue*) скандалить (поскандалить *perf*); **to have a** ~ ссориться (поссориться *perf*), поскандалить (*perf*).
rowboat [ˈrəubəut] *n* (*US*) гребная шлюпка*.
rowdiness [ˈraudɪnɪs] *n* буйство.
rowdy [ˈraudɪ] *adj* буйный* (буен).
rowdyism [ˈraudɪɪzəm] *n* буйство.
rowing [ˈrəuɪŋ] *n* гребля.
rowing boat *n* (*BRIT*) гребная шлюпка*.
rowlock [ˈrɔlək] *n* (*BRIT*) уключина.
royal [ˈrɔɪəl] *adj* королевский*.
Royal Air Force *n* (*BRIT*) Британские военно-воздушные силы.
royal-blue [ˈrɔɪəlbluː] *adj* ярко-синий*.
royalist [ˈrɔɪəlɪst] *adj* роялистский ♦ *n* роялист(ка*).
Royal Navy *n* (*BRIT*) Британский военно-морской флот.
royalty [ˈrɔɪəltɪ] *n* (*royal persons*) члены *mpl* королевской семьи; (*payment*) (авторский*) гонорар.
RP *n abbr* (*BRIT*: = *received pronunciation*) стандартное произношение.
rpm *abbr* (= *revolutions per minute*) оборотов в минуту.
RR *abbr* (*US*) (= **railroad**) ж.д., ж/д= железная дорога.
RRP *n abbr* (*BRIT*) (= **recommended retail price**) рекомендованная розничная цена.
RSA *n abbr* (*BRIT*) = *Royal Society of Arts*; *Royal Scottish Academy*.
RSI *n abbr* (*MED*: = *repetitive strain injury*) производственная травма, вызванная напряжением одной и той же группы мышц (*у машинисток итп*).
RSPB *n abbr* (*BRIT*) = *Royal Society for the*

---

* marks translations which have irregular inflections. The Russian-English side of the dictionary gives inflectional information.

Protection of Birds.

RSPCA n abbr (BRIT) = Royal Society for the Prevention of Cruelty to Animals.

RSVP abbr (= répondez s'il vous plaît) про́сьба отве́тить на приглаше́ние.

RTA n abbr = road traffic accident.

Rt Hon. abbr (BRIT: = Right Honourable) высокочти́мый.

Rt Rev. abbr (REL: = Right Reverend) высокопреподо́бный.

rub [rʌb] vt (part of body) тере́ть* (потере́ть* perf); (object: to clean) тере́ть* (impf); (: to polish) натира́ть (натере́ть* perf); (: to dry) вытира́ть (вы́тереть* perf); (hands: also: ~ together) потира́ть (потере́ть* perf) ◆ n: to give sth a ~ (polish) натира́ть (натере́ть* perf) что-н; to ~ one's hands (together) тере́ть* (потере́ть* perf) ру́ки; to ~ sb up or (US) ~ sb the wrong way раздража́ть (impf) кого́-н

▶ **rub down** vt обтира́ть (обтере́ть* perf)

▶ **rub in** vt (ointment) втира́ть (втере́ть* perf); don't ~ it in! (fig: inf) не ка́пай!

▶ **rub off** vi (paint) стира́ться (стере́ться* perf)

▶ **rub off on** vt fus передава́ться* (переда́ться* perf) +dat

▶ **rub out** vt стира́ть (стере́ть* perf).

rubber ['rʌbə'] n (substance) рези́на, каучу́к; (BRIT: eraser) рези́нка, ла́стик; (US: inf: condom) презервати́в.

rubber band n (кру́глая) рези́нка*.

rubber bullet n рези́новая пу́ля.

rubber plant n каучуконо́с, (каучуконо́сный) фи́кус.

rubber ring n надувно́й рези́новый круг*.

rubber stamp n штамп; (POST) штемпель m.

rubber-stamp [rʌbə'stæmp] vt (fig) штампова́ть (проштампова́ть perf).

rubbery ['rʌbərɪ] adj (material, substance) рези́новый; (meat, food) жёсткий* как рези́на.

rubbish ['rʌbɪʃ] n му́сор; (waste food) отбро́сы mpl; (junk) хлам; (fig: pej: nonsense) ерунда́, чушь f; (: junk) дрянь f ◆ vt (BRIT: inf) критикова́ть (impf); what you've just said is ~ то, что Вы то́лько что сказа́ли – ерунда́ or чепуха́ or чушь.

rubbish bin n (BRIT) му́сорное ведро́*.

rubbish dump n сва́лка*.

rubbishy ['rʌbɪʃɪ] adj (BRIT: inf) дрянно́й.

rubble ['rʌbl] n обло́мки mpl; (building material) бут.

ruble ['ru:bl] n (US) = rouble.

ruby ['ru:bɪ] n руби́н.

RUC n abbr (BRIT: = Royal Ulster Constabulary) североирла́ндская поли́ция.

rucksack ['rʌksæk] n рюкза́к*.

ructions ['rʌkʃənz] npl (protest) возмуще́ние ntsg; (quarrel) сканда́л msg.

rudder ['rʌdə'] n руль* m.

ruddy ['rʌdɪ] adj (face, complexion) румя́ный (румя́н); (glow) краснова́тый; (inf: damned) прокля́тый.

rude [ru:d] adj (impolite) гру́бый* (груб); (shocking) непристо́йный* (непристо́ен); (crudely made) гру́бо сде́ланный (сде́лан); he was ~ to me он был груб со мной; a ~ awakening глубо́кое разочарова́ние, неприя́тное откры́тие.

rudely ['ru:dlɪ] adv гру́бо.

rudeness ['ru:dnɪs] n (impoliteness) гру́бость f.

rudimentary [ru:dɪ'mɛntərɪ] adj (equipment, knowledge) элемента́рный* (элемента́рен).

rudiments ['ru:dɪmənts] npl осно́вы fpl.

rue [ru:] vt (action, decision) жале́ть (пожале́ть perf) o +prp; (day, hour etc) проклина́ть (прокля́сть* perf).

rueful ['ru:ful] adj (expression, person etc) печа́льный* (печа́лен).

ruffian ['rʌfɪən] n банди́т.

ruffle ['rʌfl] vt (hair) еро́шить (взъеро́шить perf); (clothes) гофрирова́ть (impf/perf); (water) ряби́ть* (impf); (fig: person) раздража́ть (impf).

rug [rʌg] n ко́врик; (BRIT: blanket) плед.

rugby ['rʌgbɪ] n (also: ~ football) ре́гби nt ind.

rugged ['rʌgɪd] adj (landscape) скали́стый (скали́ст); (features) гру́бый* (груб); (character) прямо́й (прям); (determination) непрекло́нный* (непрекло́нен), твёрдый* (твёрд).

rugger ['rʌgə'] n (BRIT: inf) ре́гби nt ind.

ruin ['ru:ɪn] n (destruction: of building, hopes, plans) разруше́ние; (: of hopes, plans) круше́ние; (downfall) ги́бель f; (bankruptcy) разоре́ние; (remains: of building) разва́лины fpl ◆ vt (building, hopes, plans) разруша́ть (разру́шить perf); (future, health, reputation) губи́ть* (погуби́ть* perf); (person: financially) разоря́ть (разори́ть perf); (spoil: clothes) по́ртить* (испо́ртить* perf); ~s npl (of building, castle etc) разва́лины fpl, руи́ны fpl; in ~s (building) в разва́линах or руи́нах; my life is in ~s моя́ жизнь загу́блена.

ruination [ru:ɪ'neɪʃən] n уничтоже́ние.

ruinous ['ru:ɪnəs] adj (interest) губи́тельный* (губи́телен); (expense) разори́тельный* (разори́телен).

rule [ru:l] n (norm, regulation) пра́вило; (government) правле́ние, власть f; (ruler) лине́йка ◆ vt (country, people) управля́ть (impf) +instr ◆ vi (leader, monarch etc) пра́вить* (impf), управля́ть (impf); to ~ in favour of/against выноси́ть* (вы́нести perf) реше́ние в по́льзу +gen/про́тив +gen; under British ~ (dominion) под брита́нским правле́нием; it's against the ~s э́то про́тив пра́вил; by ~ of thumb науга́д; as a ~ как пра́вило; to ~ that (umpire, judge etc) постановля́ть (постанови́ть* perf), что ...

▶ **rule out** vt (exclude) исключа́ть (исключи́ть perf); murder cannot be ~d out уби́йство не мо́жет быть* исключено́.

ruled [ruːld] *adj* (*paper*) линóваный.
ruler ['ruːləʳ] *n* прави́тель(ница) *m(f)*; (*for measuring*) лине́йка.
ruling ['ruːlɪŋ] *adj* (*party*) пра́вящий*; (*class*) госпóдствующий* ♦ *n* (*LAW*) постановлéние.
rum [rʌm] *n* ром ♦ *adj* (*BRIT: inf*) чуднóй.
Rumania *etc* = **Romania** *etc.*
rumble ['rʌmbl] *n* (*of traffic, thunder*) гул ♦ *vi* бубни́ть (*impf*); (*also: ~ along*) с гу́лом проезжа́ть (проéхать* *perf*); (*stomach, pipe*) бурча́ть (*impf*); (*thunder*) грохота́ть* (прогрохота́ть* *perf*).
rumbustious [rʌm'bʌstʃəs] *adj* бóйкий* (бóек).
ruminate ['ruːmɪneɪt] *vi* жева́ть* (*impf*) жва́чку; (*fig*) размышля́ть (*impf*).
rummage ['rʌmɪdʒ] *vi* (*search*) ры́ться (*impf*).
rummage sale *n* (*US*) благотвори́тельная распрода́жа поде́ржанных веще́й.
rumour ['ruːməʳ] (*US* **rumor**) *n* слух ♦ *vt*: **it is ~ed that** ... хóдят слу́хи, что ....
rump [rʌmp] *n* (*of horse*) круп; (*of cow*) за́дняя часть *f*; (*of group, political party*) оста́тки *mpl*.
rumple ['rʌmpl] *vt* (*clothes*) мять* (помя́ть* *or* измя́ть* *perf*).
rump steak *n* вы́резка* (*из за́дней ча́сти*).
rumpus ['rʌmpəs] *n* шум; **to kick up a ~** поднима́ть (подня́ть* *perf*) шум.
run [rʌn] (*pt* **ran**, *pp* **run**) *n* (*fast pace*) бег*; (*journey*) поéздка; (*distance travelled*) пробéг; (*SKIING*) тра́сса; (*CRICKET, BASEBALL*) очкó*; (*in tights, stockings*) спусти́вшиеся пéтли *fpl* ♦ *vt* (*race, distance*) пробега́ть (пробежа́ть* *perf*); (*operate: business, hotel*) управля́ть (*impf*) +*instr*; (*: competition, course*) устра́ивать (устрóить *perf*); (*: house*) вести́* (*impf*); (*COMPUT: program*) выполня́ть (вы́полнить *perf*); (*pass: hand, fingers*): **to ~ along** *or* **over** проводи́ть* (провести́* *perf*) +*instr* по +*dat*; (*water*) пуска́ть (пусти́ть* *perf*); (*bath*) наполня́ть (напóлнить *perf*); (*PRESS: feature*) печа́тать (напеча́тать *perf*) ♦ *vi* бéгать/бежа́ть* (*impf*); (*flee*) бежа́ть* (*impf*), сбега́ть (сбежа́ть* *perf*); (*work: machine*) рабóтать (*impf*); (*bus, train*) ходи́ть* (*impf*); (*continue: play, show*) идти́* (*impf*); (*: contract*) дли́ться (*impf*); (*in election*) баллоти́роваться (*perf*); (*river*) течь* (*impf*), протека́ть (*impf*); (*bath*) наполня́ться (напóлниться *perf*); (*colours, washing*) линя́ть (полиня́ть *perf*); (*nose*) течь* (*impf*); **to go for a ~** (*for exercise*) идти́* (пойти́* *perf*) побéгать; **to break into a ~** пуска́ться (пусти́ться* *perf*) бежа́ть; **a ~ of luck** перио́д уда́ч; **the play had a 6 week ~** пьéса шла 6 недéль; **to have the ~ of sb's house** имéть (*impf*) разрешéние пóльзоваться чьим-н дóмом; **there was a ~ on tickets** на билéты был большóй спрос; **in the long ~** в конéчном итóге; **in the short ~** на

какóе-то врéмя; **to make a ~ for it** убега́ть* (убежа́ть *perf*) со всех ног; **to be on the ~** скрыва́ться (*impf*); (*inf: to be busy*) быть* (*impf*) в бега́х; **I'll ~ you to the station** я подвезу́ Вас до ста́нции; **to ~ a risk** подверга́ться (подвéргнуться *perf*) ри́ску; **to ~ errands for sb** выполня́ть (*impf*) мéлкие поручéния для когó-н; **my car is very cheap to ~** моя́ маши́на экономи́чна; **to be ~ off one's feet** (*BRIT*) сби́ться* (*perf*) с ног; **the train ~s between Gatwick and Victoria** пóезд хóдит мéжду Га́твиком и Виктóрией; **the bus ~s every 20 minutes** автóбус хóдит ка́ждые 20 мину́т; **to ~ on petrol** *or* (*US*) **gas/on diesel/off batteries** рабóтать (*impf*) на бензи́не/на ди́зеле/на батарéйках; **to ~ for president** баллоти́роваться (*impf*) в президéнты; **their losses ran into millions** их потéри исчисля́лись миллиóнами
▸ **run about** *vi* бéгать (*impf*)
▸ **run across** *vt fus* (*find*) натыка́ться (наткну́ться *perf*) на +*acc*
▸ **run around** *vi* = **run about**
▸ **run away** *vi* убега́ть (убежа́ть* *perf*)
▸ **run down** *vt* (*production, industry*) сокраща́ть (сократи́ть* *perf*); (*AUT: hit*) сбива́ть (сбить* *perf*); (*criticize*) поноси́ть* (*impf*); **to be ~ down** (*person*) выбива́ться (вы́биться* *perf*) из сил; (*battery*) конча́ться (*impf*), иссяка́ть (*impf*)
▸ **run in** *vt* (*BRIT: car*) обка́тывать (обката́ть *perf*)
▸ **run into** *vt fus* (*meet: person*) ста́лкиваться (столкну́ться *perf*) с +*instr*; (*: trouble*) ната́лкиваться (натолкну́ться *perf*) на +*acc*; (*collide with*) вреза́ться (врéзаться* *perf*) в +*acc*; **to ~ into debt** залеза́ть (залéзть* *perf*) в долги́
▸ **run off** *vt* (*subj: water*) спуска́ть (спусти́ть* *perf*); (*copies*) дéлать (сдéлать *perf*), отсня́ть* (*perf*) ♦ *vi* (*person, animal*) сбега́ть (сбежа́ть* *perf*), убега́ть (убежа́ть* *perf*)
▸ **run out** *vi* (*person*) выбега́ть (вы́бежать* *perf*); (*liquid*) вытека́ть (вы́течь* *perf*); (*lease, visa*) истека́ть (истéчь* *perf*); (*money*) зака́нчиваться (закóнчиться *perf*); **my passport ~s out in July** срок дéйствия моегó па́спорта истека́ет в июле
▸ **run out of** *vt fus*: **I've ~ out of money/time/petrol** *or* (*US*) **gas** у меня́ кóнчились дéньги/ кóнчилось врéмя/кóнчился бензи́н
▸ **run over** *vt* (*AUT*) задави́ть* (*perf*) ♦ *vt fus* (*revise*) пробега́ть (пробежа́ть *perf*)
▸ **run through** *vt fus* пробега́ть (пробежа́ть *perf*); (*rehearse*) прогоня́ть (прогна́ть *perf*)
▸ **run up** *vt*: **to ~ up a debt** влеза́ть (влезть* *perf*) в долги́; **to ~ up against** (*difficulties*)

---

* marks translations which have irregular inflections. The Russian-English side of the dictionary gives inflectional information.

стáлкиваться (столкнýться *perf*) с +*instr*.
runabout ['rʌnəbaut] *n* (*AUT*) малолитрáжка*.
run around *n* (*inf*): **to give sb the ~~** водúть*
(*impf*) когó-н за нос.
runaway ['rʌnəweɪ] *adj* (*truck, horse etc*)
потерáвший управлéние; (*person*) бéглый;
(*inflation*) неуправлáемый.
rundown ['rʌndaun] *n* (*BRIT: of industry etc*)
сокращéние.
run-down [rʌn'daun] *adj* (*tired, ill*)
измождённый* (измождён).
rung [rʌŋ] *pp of* **ring ♦** *n* (*of ladder*) ступéнька*;
(*in organization*) ступéнь *m*.
run-in ['rʌnɪn] *n* (*inf*) стычка*.
runner ['rʌnə'] *n* (*in race: person*) бегýн*(ья);
(: *horse*) скакýн*; (*on sledge, for drawer etc*)
пóлоз*; (*carpet: in hall etc*) дорóжка*.
runner bean *n* (*BRIT*) стручкóвая фасóль *f no pl*.
runner-up [rʌnəg'ʌp] *n* финалúст (*занáвший
второе мéсто*).
running ['rʌnɪŋ] *n* (*sport*) бег*; (*of business,
organization*) руковóдство; (*of event*)
организáция; (*of machine etc*) эксплуатáция
♦ *adj* (*water*) текýщий*; (: *to house*)
водопровóдный; **he is in/out of the ~ for sth**
емý сулúт/не сулúт что-н; **6 days ~** 6 дней
подрáд.
running commentary *n* (*TV, RADIO*) прямóй
репортáж.
running costs *npl* (*of business*) операциóнные
издéржки *fpl*; (*of car*) содержáние *ntsg*.
running head *n* колонтúтул (*заголóвок,
печáтаемый на верхý кáждой странúцы*).
running mate *n* (*US: POL*) кандидáт на
дóлжность вице-президéнта.
runny ['rʌnɪ] *adj* (*honey, egg*) жúдкий*
(жúдок); (*nose*) соплúвый (соплúв); (*eyes*)
слезáщийся.
runoff ['rʌnɔf] *n* (*in contest, election*)
повтóрные вúборы *mpl*; (*extra race*)
повтóрный забéг.
run-of-the-mill ['rʌnəvðə'mɪl] *adj* срéдний*.
runt [rʌnt] *n* (*animal*) недомéрок*; (*pej: person*)
сморчóк*.
run-through ['rʌnθru:] *n* (*rehearsal*) прогóн.
run-up ['rʌnʌp] *n* перúод, предшéствующий
какóму-нибудь собútию.
runway ['rʌnweɪ] *n* взлётно-посáдочная
полосá*.
rupee [ru:'pi:] *n* рýпия.
rupture ['rʌptʃə'] *n* (*MED: hernia*) грúжа;
(*between people, groups*) разрúв **♦** *vt*: **to ~
o.s.** (*MED*) получáть (получúть *perf*) грúжу.
rural ['ruərl] *adj* сéльский*; (*accent*)
деревéнский*.
rural district council *n* (*BRIT*) сéльский*
райóнный совéт.
ruse [ru:z] *n* улóвка*, ухищрéние.

rush [rʌʃ] *n* (*hurry*) спéшка; (*COMM: sudden
demand*) большóй спрос; (*of water, current*)
потóк; (*of emotion*) прилúв; (*plant*) камúш*
♦ *vt* (*BRIT: inf: overcharge*) обсчúтывать
(обсчитáть *perf*) **♦** *vi* (*person*) бежáть* (*impf*);
(*air, water*) хлúнуть (*perf*); **is there any ~ for
this?** это спéшно?; **a ~ of orders** наплúв
закáзов; **I'm in a ~ (to do)** я спешý (+*infin*);
gold ~ золотáя лихорáдка; **to ~ one's meal/
work** второпáх есть (*impf*)/дéлать (*impf*)
рабóту; **don't ~ me!** не подгонáйте *or*
торопúте менá!; **to ~ sth off** (*do*) спéшно
дéлать (сдéлать *perf*) что-н; (*send*) спéшно
отправлáть (отпрáвить* *perf*) что-н; **she ~ed
to the door** онá брóсилась к двéри
► **rush through** *vt fus* дéлать (сдéлать *perf*) в
спéшке; (*meal*) проглáтывать (проглотúть*
perf); (*town*) носúться* (нестúсь* *perf*) по +*dat*.
rush hour *n* час пик.
rush job *n* рабóта, сдéланная наспéх.
rush matting *n* цинóвка*.
rusk [rʌsk] *n* (*biscuit*) ≈ сухáрь *m*.
Russia ['rʌʃə] *n* Россúя.
Russian ['rʌʃən] *adj* (*native Russian*) рýсский*;
(*belonging to Russian Federation*)
россúйский* **♦** *n* рýсский(-ая) *m(f) adj*; (*LING*)
рýсский* язúк*.
rust [rʌst] *n* (*also BOT*) ржáвчина **♦** *vi* ржавéть
(заржавéть *perf*).
rustic ['rʌstɪk] *adj* деревéнский* **♦** *n* (*pej*)
деревéнщина *m/f no pl*.
rustle ['rʌsl] *vi* шуршáть (*impf*), шелестéть*
(*impf*) **♦** *vt* шелестéть* (*impf*) +*instr*; (*US: steal*)
угонáть (угнáть* *perf*).
rustproof ['rʌstpru:f] *adj* (*metal*) нержавéющ-
ий*; (*car*) сдéланный (сдéлан) из
нержавéющего материáла.
rustproofing ['rʌstpru:fɪŋ] *n* обрабóтка
прóтив ржáвчины.
rusty ['rʌstɪ] *adj* ржáвый*; (*fig: skill*)
подзабútый.
rut [rʌt] *n* (*groove*) колеá, бороздá*; (*ZOOL:
season*) половáя охóта; **to get into a ~** (*fig*)
заходúть* (зайтú* *perf*) в тупúк, застревáть
(застрáть* *perf*).
rutabaga [ru:tə'beɪgə] *n* (*US*) рéпа.
ruthless ['ru:θlɪs] *adj* (*person, action*)
беспощáдный* (беспощáден),
безжáлостный* (безжáлостен).
ruthlessness ['ru:θlɪsnɪs] *n* беспощáдность *f*,
безжáлостность *f*.
RV *abbr* (*BIBLE*: = revised version) *испрáвленное
издáние Бúблии* **♦** *n abbr* (*US*) = **recreational
vehicle**.
Ryazan [rɪ'zanj] *n* Рязáнь *f*.
rye [raɪ] *n* рожь* *f*.
rye bread *n* ржанóй хлеб.

~ S, s ~

S, s [ɛs] n (letter) 19-ая бу́ква англи́йского
алфави́та; (US: SCOL: = satisfactory) ≈
удовлетвори́тельно.
S abbr (= south) Ю= юг; = small; (= saint) св=
свято́й.
SA abbr = **South Africa, South America.**
Sabbath ['sæbəθ] n (Jewish) суббо́та;
(Christian) воскресе́нье.
sabbatical [sə'bætɪkl] n (also: ~ **year**)
тво́рческий о́тпуск*.
sabotage ['sæbətɑːʒ] n сабота́ж ♦ vt (machine,
building) выводи́ть* (вы́вести* perf) из стро́я;
(plan, meeting) саботи́ровать (impf/perf).
sabre ['seɪbə*] n са́бля*.
sabre-rattling ['seɪbərætlɪŋ] n бряца́ние
ору́жием (перен).
saccharin(e) ['sækərɪn] n сахари́н.
sachet ['sæʃeɪ] n (of shampoo, sugar etc)
паке́тик.
sack [sæk] n (bag) мешо́к* ♦ vt (dismiss)
выгоня́ть (вы́гнать* perf) с рабо́ты; (plunder)
опустоша́ть (опустоши́ть perf); **to give sb the**
~ выгоня́ть (вы́гнать* perf) кого́-н (с
рабо́ты); **I got the ~** меня́ вы́гнали (с
рабо́ты).
sackful ['sækful] n: **a ~ of** мешо́к* +gen.
sacking ['sækɪŋ] n (dismissal) увольне́ние;
(material) мешкови́на.
sacrament ['sækrəmənt] n (rite) та́инство.
sacred ['seɪkrɪd] adj свяще́нный; (place)
свято́й; (music) духо́вный.
sacred cow n (fig) святы́ня.
sacrifice ['sækrɪfaɪs] n (offering)
жертвоприноше́ние; (thing or person offered)
же́ртва ♦ vt (animal) приноси́ть* (принести́*
perf) в же́ртву +dat; (fig) же́ртвовать
(поже́ртвовать perf) +instr; **to make ~s (for sb)**
же́ртвовать (поже́ртвовать perf) собо́й
(ра́ди кого́-н).
sacrilege ['sækrɪlɪdʒ] n святота́тство.
sacrosanct ['sækrəusæŋkt] adj (also fig)
свяще́нный.
sad [sæd] adj печа́льный* (печа́лен).
sadden ['sædn] vt печа́лить (опеча́лить perf).
saddle ['sædl] n седло́* ♦ vt (horse) седла́ть
(оседла́ть perf); **to ~ sb with sth** (inf)

наве́шивать (наве́сить* perf) что-н на кого́-н.
saddlebag ['sædlbæg] n (on bicycle) седе́льная
су́мка.
sadism ['seɪdɪzəm] n сади́зм.
sadist ['seɪdɪst] n сади́ст(ка*).
sadistic [sə'dɪstɪk] adj (person, behaviour)
сади́стский.
sadly ['sædlɪ] adv (unhappily) печа́льно,
гру́стно; (unfortunately) к сожале́нию;
(seriously: mistaken, neglected) серьёзно; **the**
school is ~ lacking in equipment шко́ла
испы́тывает серьёзный недоста́ток в
обору́довании.
sadness ['sædnɪs] n печа́ль f, грусть f.
sadomasochism [seɪdəu'mæsəkɪzəm] n
са́до-мазохи́зм.
sae abbr (BRIT) = **stamped addressed envelope;**
see **stamp.**
safari [sə'fɑːrɪ] n сафа́ри nt ind; **to go on ~**
проводи́ть* (провести́* perf) о́тпуск в
сафа́ри.
safari park n парк сафа́ри.
safe [seɪf] adj (place, subject) безопа́сный*
(безопа́сен); (return, journey)
благополу́чный* (благополу́чен); (bet,
appointment) надёжный* (надёжен) ♦ n сейф;
to be ~ находи́ться* (impf) в безопа́сности; **~**
from (attack) защищённый (защищён) от
+gen; **~ and sound** цел и невреди́м; **(just) to**
be on the ~ side на вся́кий слу́чай; **to play ~**
де́йствовать (impf) осторо́жно; **it is ~ to say**
that ... мо́жно с уве́ренностью сказа́ть, что
...; **~ journey!** счастли́вого пути́!; **~ seat** (POL)
парла́ментское ме́сто с гаранти́рованной
подде́ржкой избира́телей.
safe bet n ве́рное де́ло; **he is a ~ ~** на него́
мо́жно положи́ться.
safe-breaker ['seɪfbreɪkə*] n (BRIT) взло́мщик
се́йфов.
safe-conduct [seɪf'kɔndʌkt] n
неприкоснове́нность f.
safe-cracker ['seɪfkrækə*] n = **safe-breaker.**
safe-deposit ['seɪfdɪpɔzɪt] n храни́лище.
safeguard ['seɪfgɑːd] n гара́нтия ♦ vt (life,
interests) охраня́ть (impf); (future)
гаранти́ровать (impf/perf).

---

* marks translations which have irregular inflections. The Russian-English side of the dictionary gives inflectional information.

safe haven *n* зо́на безопа́сности.
safe house *n* конспирати́вная кварти́ра.
safekeeping ['seɪf'kiːpɪŋ] *n* сохра́нность *f*.
safely ['seɪflɪ] *adv* (*assume, say*) с
  уве́ренностью; (*drive, arrive*) благополу́чно;
  I can ~ say ... я могу́ с уве́ренностью сказа́ть
  ....
safe passage *n* безопа́сный путь* *m*.
safe sex *n* безопа́сный секс; **to practise ~ ~**
  испо́льзовать (*impf*) презервати́вы во вре́мя
  се́кса.
safety ['seɪftɪ] *n* безопа́сность *f*; **~ first!**
  соблюда́йте осторо́жность!
safety belt *n* привязно́й реме́нь *m*.
safety catch *n* (*on gun*) замо́к*; (*on window*)
  защёлка*.
safety net *n* (*also fig*) страхо́вочная сеть.
safety pin *n* англи́йская була́вка*.
safety valve *n* предохрани́тельный кла́пан.
saffron ['sæfrən] *n* шафра́н.
sag [sæg] *vi* (*breasts*) отвиса́ть (отви́снуть
  perf); (*roof, hem*) провиса́ть (прови́снуть
  perf); (*spirits, prices*) па́дать (упа́сть* *perf*).
saga ['sɑːgə] *n* са́га.
sage [seɪdʒ] *n* (*herb*) шалфе́й; (*wise man*)
  мудре́ц*.
Sagittarius [sædʒɪ'tɛərɪəs] *n* Стреле́ц*; **he is ~**
  он – Стреле́ц.
sago ['seɪgəu] *n* са́го *nt ind*.
Sahara [sə'hɑːrə] *n*: **the ~ (Desert)** Саха́ра.
Sahel [sæ'hɛl] *n* Сахе́ль *f*.
said [sɛd] *pt, pp of* **say**.
Saigon [saɪ'gɒn] *n* Сайго́н.
sail [seɪl] *n* па́рус* ♦ *vt* (*boat*) пла́вать/плыть*
  (*impf*) на +*prp* ♦ *vi* (*ship, passenger*) пла́вать/
  плыть* (*impf*); (*SPORT*) занима́ться (*impf*)
  па́русным спо́ртом; (*also:* **set ~**) отплыва́ть
  (отплы́ть* *perf*); **to go for a ~** е́хать* (пое́хать*
  perf) ката́ться на ло́дке; **they ~ed into**
  Copenhagen они́ приплы́ли в Копенга́ген
  ▸ **sail through** *vt fus* (*fig*): **to ~ through an**
  exam/interview с лёгкостью сдава́ть*
  (сдать* *perf*) экза́мен/проходи́ть* (пройти́*
  perf) собесе́дование.
sailboat ['seɪlbəut] *n* (*US*) = **sailing boat**.
sailing ['seɪlɪŋ] *n* (*SPORT*) па́русный спорт; **to**
  go ~ занима́ться (*impf*) па́русным спо́ртом.
sailing boat *n* па́русная ло́дка*.
sailing ship *n* па́русное су́дно*.
sailor ['seɪlə'] *n* моря́к*, матро́с.
saint [seɪnt] *n* (*also fig*) свято́й(-а́я) *m(f) adj*.
saintly ['seɪntlɪ] *adj* свято́й*.
sake [seɪk] *n*: **for the ~ of sb/sth, for sb's/sth's ~**
  ра́ди кого́-н/чего́-н; **arguing for arguing's ~**
  спор ра́ди спо́ра; **for the ~ of argument** в
  ка́честве предположе́ния; **for heaven's ~!**
  ра́ди Бо́га!
Sakhalin [səxa'lin] *n* Сахали́н.
salad ['sæləd] *n* сала́т; **tomato ~** сала́т из
  помидо́ров; **green ~** зелёный сала́т.
salad bowl *n* сала́тница.

salad cream *n* (*BRIT*) сала́тный со́ус.
salad dressing *n* припра́ва к сала́ту.
salami [sə'lɑːmɪ] *n* саля́ми *f ind*.
salaried ['sælərɪd] *adj* (*staff*) получа́ющий
  зарпла́ту.
salary ['sælərɪ] *n* зарпла́та (= *за́работная*
  пла́та).
salary scale *n* шкала́* за́работной пла́ты.
sale [seɪl] *n* (*act of selling*) прода́жа; (*at reduced*
  prices) распрода́жа; (*auction*) то́рги *mpl*; **~s**
  npl (*total amount sold*) объём прода́жи ♦ *cpd*
  (*campaign, conference*) рекла́мный; (*figures,*
  target) прода́жный; **"for ~"** „продаётся"; **on**
  ~ в прода́же; **these goods are on ~ or return**
  е́сли э́ти това́ры не бу́дут про́даны, они́
  бу́дут возвращены́ владе́льцу; **closing-down**
  or (US) **liquidation ~** ликвидацио́нная
  распрода́жа.
sale and lease back *n* (*COMM*) *прода́жа*
  со́бственности с усло́вием получе́ния её
  обра́тно в аре́нду на огово́рённый срок.
saleroom ['seɪlruːm] *n* торго́вый зал.
sales assistant [seɪlz-] (*US* **salesclerk**) *n* (*BRIT*)
  продаве́ц*(-вщи́ца).
salesclerk ['seɪlzklɑːrk] *n* (*US*) = **sales assistant**.
sales force *n* торго́вые аге́нты *mpl*.
salesman ['seɪlzmən] *irreg n* (*in shop*)
  продаве́ц*; (*also:* **travelling ~**) торго́вый
  аге́нт.
sales manager *n* (*in company*) нача́льник
  отде́ла сбы́та; (*in shop*) ста́рший*(-ая)
  продаве́ц*(-вщи́ца).
salesmanship ['seɪlzmənʃɪp] *n* уме́ние
  продава́ть.
sales tax *n* (*US*) нало́г на прода́жи
  (*упла́чивается потреби́телем при поку́пке*
  определённых това́ров).
saleswoman ['seɪlzwumən] *irreg n* (*in shop*)
  продавщи́ца; (*representative*) торго́вый
  аге́нт.
salient ['seɪlɪənt] *adj* суще́ственный.
saline ['seɪlaɪn] *adj* соляно́й.
saliva [sə'laɪvə] *n* слюна́.
sallow ['sæləu] *adj* (*complexion*) желту́шный.
sally forth ['sælɪ-] *vi* отправля́ться
  (отпра́виться* *perf*).
sally out *vi* = **sally forth**.
salmon ['sæmən] *n inv* (*ZOOL*) лосо́сь* *m*; (*CULIN*)
  лосо́сина.
salmon trout *n* тайме́нь *m*.
salon ['sælɒn] *n* сало́н; **beauty ~**
  космети́ческий* сало́н.
saloon [sə'luːn] *n* (*US: bar*) бар; (*BRIT: AUT*)
  седа́н; (*ship's lounge*) сало́н.
SALT [sɔːlt] *n abbr* (= *Strategic Arms Limitation*
  Talks/Treaty) перегово́ры *pl*/догово́р ОСВ
  = *об ограниче́нии стратеги́ческих*
  наступа́тельных вооруже́ний.
salt [sɔːlt] *n* соль *f* ♦ *vt* (*preserve*) заса́ливать
  (засоли́ть* *perf*); (*season*) соли́ть* (посоли́ть*

perf) ♦ *cpd* солёный; **the ~ of the earth** соль
земли́.
saltcellar ['sɔːltsɛlə'] *n* соло́нка*.
salt-free ['sɔːlt'friː] *adj* не содержа́щий со́ли.
salt mine *n* соляна́я ша́хта.
saltwater ['sɔːlt'wɔːtə'] *adj* живу́щий в
солёных во́дах.
salty ['sɔːltɪ] *adj* солёный* (со́лон).
salubrious [sə'luːbrɪəs] *adj* целе́бный*
(целе́бен); (*fig: district etc*) благода́тный*
(благода́тен).
salutary ['sæljutərɪ] *adj* поле́зный* (поле́зен).
salute [sə'luːt] *n* (MIL) салю́т; (*greeting*)
приве́тствие ♦ *vt* (MIL) отдава́ть* (отда́ть*
perf) честь +*dat*; (*fig*) приве́тствовать (*impf*).
salvage ['sælvɪdʒ] *n* (*saving*) спасе́ние; (*things
saved*) спасённые ве́щи *fpl* ♦ *vt* (*also fig*)
спаса́ть (спасти́* *perf*).
salvage vessel *n* спаса́тельное су́дно*.
salvation [sæl'veɪʃən] *n* спасе́ние.
Salvation Army *n* А́рмия Спасе́ния.
salver ['sælvə'] *n* подно́с.
salvo ['sælvəu] (*pl* ~**es**) *n* залп.
Samaritans [sə'mærɪtənz] *npl*: **the ~**
Самаритя́не* *mpl*.
same [seɪm] *adj* тако́й же; (*identical*)
одина́ковый ♦ *pron*: **the ~** тот же (са́мый) (*f*
та же (са́мая), *nt* то же (са́мое), *pl* те же
(са́мые); **the ~ book as** та же (са́мая) кни́га,
что и; **on the ~ day** в тот же день; **at the ~
time** (*simultaneously*) в э́то же вре́мя; (*yet*) в
то же вре́мя; **all** *or* **just the ~** всё равно́; **to do
the ~ (as sb)** де́лать (сде́лать *perf*) то же
(са́мое) (что и кто-н); **Happy New Year! - the
~ to you!** С Но́вым Го́дом! – Вас та́кже!;
you're a fool! - the ~ to you! ты дура́к! – сам
(ты) дура́к!; **I hate him - ~ here!** я ненави́жу
его́ – и я то́же!; **the company director and Mr
Smith are one and the ~** дире́ктор компа́нии
и Ми́стер Смит одно́ лицо́; **the books we're
talking about are one and the ~** мы говори́ли
об одно́й и то́йже кни́ге; **~ again!** (*in bar etc*)
повтори́те!
sample ['sɑːmpl] *n* (*of water*) про́ба; (*of work,
merchandise*) образе́ц* ♦ *vt* (*food, wine*)
про́бовать (попро́бовать *perf*); **to take a ~**
брать* (взять* *perf*) про́бу; **to take a blood/
urine ~** брать* (взять* *perf*) кровь/мочу́ для
ана́лиза; **free ~** беспла́тный образе́ц*.
sanatoria [sænə'tɔːrɪə] *npl of* **sanatorium**.
sanatorium [sænə'tɔːrɪəm] (*pl* **sanatoria** *or* ~**s**) *n*
(MED) санато́рий.
sanctify ['sæŋktɪfaɪ] *vt* освяща́ть (освяти́ть*
perf).
sanctimonious [sæŋktɪ'məunɪəs] *adj*
благочи́нный* (благочи́нен).
sanction ['sæŋkʃən] *n* (*approval*) са́нкция ♦ *vt*
(*give approval to*) санкциони́ровать (*impf*/

perf); **~s** *npl* (*severe measures*) са́нкции *fpl*; **to
impose economic ~s on** *or* **against** применя́ть
(примени́ть* *perf*) экономи́ческие са́нкции
про́тив +*gen*.
sanctity ['sæŋktɪtɪ] *n* свя́тость *f*.
sanctuary ['sæŋktjuərɪ] *n* (*for animals*)
запове́дник; (*for people*) убе́жище; (*in
church*) алта́рная часть *f*.
sand [sænd] *n* песо́к* ♦ *vt* (*also*: ~ **down**)
ошку́ривать (ошку́рить *perf*); *see also* **sands**.
sandal ['sændl] *n* санда́лия.
sandbag ['sændbæg] *n* мешо́к* с песко́м.
sandblast ['sændblɑːst] *vt* подверга́ть
(подве́ргнуть *perf*) пескостру́йной
обрабо́тке.
sandbox ['sændbɔks] *n* (US) песо́чница.
sand castle *n* песча́ный за́мок*.
sand dune *n* (песча́ная) дю́на.
sander ['sændə'] *n* ручно́й шлифова́льный
стано́к.
S & M *n abbr* (= *sadomasochism*)
садомазохи́зм.
sandpaper ['sændpeɪpə'] *n* нажда́чная бума́га,
шку́рка.
sandpit ['sændpɪt] *n* песо́чница.
sands [sændz] *npl* пески́ *mpl*.
sandstone ['sændstəun] *n* песча́ник.
sandstorm ['sændstɔːm] *n* песча́ная бу́ря.
sandwich ['sændwɪtʃ] *n* бутербро́д ♦ *vt*: ~**ed
between** зажа́тый ме́жду +*instr*; **cheese/ham
~** бутербро́д с сы́ром/ветчино́й.
sandwich board *n* (*notice*) рекла́мный щит*.
sandwich course *n* (BRIT) курс обуче́ния,
сочета́ющий тео́рию с пра́ктикой.
sandwich man *n irreg* челове́к, несу́щий на
себе́ рекла́мный щит.
sandy ['sændɪ] *adj* песча́ный; (*hair*) песо́чный.
sane [seɪn] *adj* разу́мный* (разу́мен).
San Francisco [sæn frən'sɪskəu] *n*
Сан-Франци́ско *m ind*.
sang [sæŋ] *pt of* **sing**.
sanguine ['sæŋgwɪn] *adj* оптимисти́чный*
(оптимисти́чен).
sanitaria [sænɪ'tɛərɪə] *npl* (US) *of* **sanitarium**.
sanitarium [sænɪ'tɛərɪəm] (*pl* **sanitaria** *or* ~**s**) *n*
(US) = **sanatorium**.
sanitary ['sænɪtərɪ] *adj* (*system, inspector*)
санита́рный; (*clean*) гигиени́чный*
(гигиени́чен).
sanitary towel (US **sanitary napkin**) *n*
гигиени́ческий* паке́т, же́нская прокла́дка.
sanitation [sænɪ'teɪʃən] *n* санитари́я.
sanitation department *n* (US) санита́рное
управле́ние.
sanity ['sænɪtɪ] *n* (*of person*) рассу́док*; (*of
suggestion etc*) разу́мность *f*.
sank [sæŋk] *pt of* **sink**.
San Marino ['sænmə'riːnəu] *n* Сан-Мари́но *nt*

---

* marks translations which have irregular inflections. The Russian-English side of the dictionary gives inflectional information.

ind.

Santa Claus [sæntə'klɔ:z] *n* (*in Britain, US etc*) Са́нта-Кла́ус; (*in Russia*) ≈ Дед Моро́з.
Santiago [sæntɪ'ɑ:gəu] *n* (*also:* ~ **de Chile**) Сантья́го *m ind.*
sap [sæp] *n* (BOT) сок* ♦ *vt* (*strength, confidence*) выса́сывать (вы́сосать *perf*).
sapling ['sæplɪŋ] *n* молодо́е де́ревце*, побе́г.
sapper ['sæpə'] *n* сапёр.
sapphire ['sæfaɪə'] *n* сапфи́р.
Sarajevo [særə'jeɪvəu] *n* Сара́ево.
sarcasm ['sɑ:kæzm] *n* сарка́зм.
sarcastic [sɑ:'kæstɪk] *adj* саркасти́чный* (саркасти́чен).
sarcophagi [sɑ:'kɔfəgaɪ] *npl of* **sarcophagus**.
sarcophagus [sɑ:'kɔfəgəs] (*pl* **sarcophagi**) *n* саркофа́г.
sardine [sɑ:'di:n] *n* сарди́на.
Sardinia [sɑ:'dɪnɪə] *n* Сарди́ния.
Sardinian [sɑ:'dɪnɪən] *adj* сарди́нский ♦ *n* сарди́нец*(-нка*); (LING) сарди́нский диале́кт.
sardonic [sɑ:'dɔnɪk] *adj* сардони́ческий.
sari ['sɑ:rɪ] *n* са́ри *nt ind.*
sartorial [sɑ:'tɔ:rɪəl] *adj*: ~ **elegance** уме́ние одева́ться.
SAS *n abbr* (BRIT: MIL: = *Special Air Service*) осо́бые возду́шно-деса́нтные войска́.
SASE *n abbr* (US) = *self-addressed stamped envelope*.
sash [sæʃ] *n* (*around waist*) куша́к*; (*over shoulder*) ле́нта; (*of window*) подъёмная ра́ма.
sash window *n* окно́* с подъёмной ра́мой.
SAT *n abbr* (US) = *Scholastic Aptitude Test*.
sat [sæt] *pt, pp of* **sit**.
Sat. *abbr* = **Saturday**.
Satan ['seɪtn] *n* Сатана́ *m.*
satanic [sə'tænɪk] *adj* сатани́нский.
satanism ['seɪtnɪzəm] *n* сатани́зм.
satchel ['sætʃl] *n* ра́нец*.
sated ['seɪtɪd] *adj* (*person*): **to be** ~ (**with**) пресыща́ться (пресы́титься* *perf*) (+*instr*).
satellite ['sætəlaɪt] *n* спу́тник; (POL: *country*) сателли́т; ~ **town** го́род-спу́тник.
satellite dish *n* спу́тниковая анте́нна.
satellite television *n* спу́тниковое телеви́дение.
satiate ['seɪʃɪeɪt] *vt* насыща́ть (насы́тить* *perf*).
satin ['sætɪn] *n* атла́с ♦ *adj* атла́сный; **with a** ~ **finish** с атла́сным отли́вом.
satire ['sætaɪə'] *n* сати́ра.
satirical [sə'tɪrɪkl] *adj* сатири́ческий*.
satirist ['sætɪrɪst] *n* сати́рик.
satirize ['sætɪraɪz] *vt* высме́ивать (вы́смеять *perf*).
satisfaction [sætɪs'fækʃən] *n* (*pleasure*) удовлетворе́ние; (*refund, apology etc*) возмеще́ние; **has it been done to your** ~? Вы удовлетворены́ тем, как э́то сде́лано?
satisfactorily [sætɪs'fæktərɪlɪ] *adv* удовле-

твори́тельно.
satisfactory [sætɪs'fæktərɪ] *adj* удовлетвор-и́тельный* (удовлетвори́телен).
satisfied ['sætɪsfaɪd] *adj* (*customer*) дово́льный* (дово́лен), удовлетворённый* (удовлетворён); **he is/was** ~ (**with sth**) он дово́лен/был дово́лен *or* удовлетворён/был удовлетворён (чем-н.).
satisfy ['sætɪsfaɪ] *vt* (*please, fulfil*) удовлетворя́ть (удовлетвори́ть *perf*); (*convince*) убежда́ть (убеди́ть* *perf*); **to** ~ **the requirements** удовлетворя́ть (удовлетвори́ть *perf*) тре́бованиям; **to** ~ **sb (that)** убежда́ть (убеди́ть* *perf*) кого́-н (в том, что); **to** ~ **o.s. of sth** удостоверя́ться (удостове́риться *perf*) в чём-н.
satisfying ['sætɪsfaɪŋ] *adj* прия́тный* (прия́тен).
satsuma [sæt'su:mə] *n* мандари́н.
saturate ['sætʃəreɪt] *vt*: **to** ~ (**with**) (*also fig*) насыща́ть (насы́тить* *perf*) (+*instr*).
saturated fat ['sætʃəreɪtɪd-] *n* насы́щенные жиры́ *mpl.*
saturation [sætʃə'reɪʃən] *n* (*process*) насыще́ние; (CHEM, *fig*) насы́щенность *f.*
Saturday ['sætədɪ] *n* суббо́та; *see also* **Tuesday**.
Saturn ['sætən] *n* Сату́рн.
sauce [sɔ:s] *n* со́ус.
saucepan ['sɔ:spən] *n* кастрю́ля.
saucer ['sɔ:sə'] *n* блю́дце*.
saucy ['sɔ:sɪ] *adj* (*inf*) по́шлый (пошл).
Saudi Arabia ['saudɪ-] *n* Сау́довская Ара́вия.
Saudi (Arabian) *adj* сау́довский*.
sauna ['sɔ:nə] *n* са́уна, фи́нская ба́ня.
saunter ['sɔ:ntə'] *vi* прогу́ливаться (*impf*).
sausage ['sɔsɪdʒ] *n* (*for cooking*) сарде́лька*, соси́ска*; (*cold meat*) колбаса́*.
sausage roll *n* (BRIT) пирожо́к* с соси́ской.
sauté ['səuteɪ] *adj* жа́реный ♦ *vt* жа́рить (пожа́рить *perf*).
savage ['sævɪdʒ] *adj* (*attack*) зве́рский*; (*voice*) я́ростный* (я́ростен); (*dog, criticism*) свире́пый* (свире́п); (*primitive: tribe*) ди́кий* ♦ *n* дика́рь*(-рка*) *m(f)* ♦ *vt* (*attack, also fig*) разрыва́ть (разорва́ть* *perf*) на ча́сти.
savagely ['sævɪdʒlɪ] *adv* (*attack, pull*) я́ростно; (*criticize*) свире́по.
savagery ['sævɪdʒrɪ] *n* свире́пость *f.*
save [seɪv] *vt* (*rescue*) спаса́ть (спасти́* *perf*); (*economize on: money, time*) эконо́мить* (сэконо́мить* *perf*); (*put by: food, money*) откла́дывать (отложи́ть* *perf*); (*receipts, also* COMPUT) сохраня́ть (сохрани́ть *perf*); (*avoid: work, trouble*) избавля́ть (изба́вить* *perf*) от +*gen*; (*keep: seat, place*) занима́ть (заня́ть* *perf*); (SPORT: *shot, ball*) отбива́ть (отби́ть* *perf*), отража́ть (отрази́ть* *perf*) ♦ *vi* (*also:* ~ **up**) копи́ть (скопи́ть* *perf*) де́ньги ♦ *prep* (*except*) поми́мо +*gen*; **it will** ~ **me an hour** я сэконо́млю на э́том час; **to** ~ **face** спасти́* (*perf*) свою́ репута́цию; **God** ~ **the Queen!**

Бóже храни корóлéву!; **that was a brilliant ~ (by the goalkeeper)** вратáрь прекрáсно отразил удáр.
saving ['seɪvɪŋ] *n* (*on price etc*) эконóмия ♦ *adj*: **the ~ grace of** спасéние +*gen*; **~s** *npl* (*money*) сбережéния *ntpl*; **to make ~s** отклáдывать (отложить* *perf*).
savings account *n* сберегáтельный счёт*.
savings bank *n* сберегáтельный банк.
saviour ['seɪvjə'] (*US* savior) *n* спаситель(ница) *m(f)*; (*REL*) Спаситель *m*.
savoir-faire ['sævwɑːfɛə'] *n* свéтскость *f*.
savour ['seɪvə'] (*US* savor) *vt* (*food, drink*) смаковáть (*impf*); (*experience*) наслаждáться (насладиться* *perf*) +*instr* ♦ *n* (*of food*) аромáт.
savoury ['seɪvərɪ] (*US* savory) *adj* (*dish*) неслáдкий* (неслáдок).
savvy ['sævɪ] *n* (*inf*) понимáние.
saw [sɔː] (*pt* sawed, *pp* sawed *or* sawn) *vt* пилить* (*impf*) ♦ *n* пилá* ♦ *pt of* see; **to ~ sth up** распиливать (распилить* *perf*) что-н.
sawdust ['sɔːdʌst] *n* опилки* *pl*.
sawed-off ['sɔːdɔf] *adj* (*US*) = sawn-off.
sawmill ['sɔːmɪl] *n* лесопильный завóд.
sawn [[sɔːn]] *pp of* saw.
sawn-off ['sɔːnɔf] (*US* sawed-off) *adj*: **~ shotgun** обрéз.
saxophone ['sæksəfəun] *n* саксофóн.
say [seɪ] (*pt, pp* said) *vt* говорить (сказáть* *perf*) ♦ *n*: **to have one's ~** выражáть (выразить* *perf*) своё мнéние; **to ~ yes** соглашáться (согласиться* *perf*); **to ~ no** отказываться (отказáться* *perf*); **could you ~ that again?** повторите, пожáлуйста; **she said (that) I was to give you this** онá сказáла, что я дóлжен отдáть это Вам; **my watch ~s 3 o'clock** мои часы покáзывают 3 часá; **shall we ~ Tuesday?** ну, скáжем, во вторник?; **that doesn't ~ much for him** это не говорит в его пóльзу; **when all is said and done** когдá всё (бýдет) оговóрено; **there is a lot to be said for ...** мнóгое мóжно сказáть в пóльзу +*gen* ...; **that is to ~** то есть; **that goes without ~ing** это сáмо собóй разумéется; **to ~ nothing of** не говоря ужé о +*prp*; **~ (that) you ...** ну, скáжем, Вы ...; **to have a** *or* **some ~ in sth** имéть (*impf*) прáво гóлоса в чём-н.
saying ['seɪŋ] *n* поговóрка*.
say-so ['seɪsəu] *n*: **to do sth on sb's ~** дéлать (сдéлать *perf*) что-н с чьегó-н соглáсия.
SBA (*US*) *n abbr* = **Small Business Administration.**
SC *n abbr* (*US*) = **Supreme Court** ♦ *abbr* (*POST*) = **South Carolina.**
s/c *abbr* = **self-contained.**
scab [skæb] *n* (*on wound*) струп*; (*inf: pej*) штрейкбрéхер.
scabby ['skæbɪ] *adj* (*pej: hands, skin*) покрытый

(покрыт) струпьями.
scaffold ['skæfəld] *n* (*for execution*) эшафóт.
scaffolding ['skæfəldɪŋ] *n* лесá* *pl*.
scald [skɔːld] *n* ожóг ♦ *vt* (*burn*) ошпáривать (ошпáрить *perf*).
scalding ['skɔːldɪŋ] *adj* (*also: ~ hot*) óчень горячий*.
scale [skeɪl] *n* шкалá*; (*usu pl: of fish*) чешуя *f no pl*; (*MUS*) гáмма; (*of map, model, project etc*) масштáб ♦ *vt* (*mountain, tree*) взбирáться (взобрáться* *perf*) на +*acc*; **~s** *npl* (*for weighing*) весы *pl*; **to draw sth to ~** чертить* (начертить* *perf*) что-н по масштáбу; **a small-~ model** умéньшенная модéль; **on a large ~** в широком масштáбе; **pay ~** тарифная сéтка* зарплáты; **~ of charges** шкалá* расцéнок
▸ **scale down** *vt* сокращáть (сократить* *perf*).
scaled down [skeɪld-] *adj* в умéньшенном масштáбе.
scale drawing *n* масштáбный рисýнок *or* чертёж*.
scallion ['skæljən] *n* (*shallot*) зелёный лук *m no pl*; (*US: leek*) лук-порéй *m no pl*.
scallop ['skɔləp] *n* (*ZOOL*) (морскóй) гребешóк*; (*in sewing etc*) фестóн.
scalp [skælp] *n* скальп ♦ *vt* скальпировать (*impf/perf*); **I have an itchy ~** у меня чéшется головá.
scalpel ['skælpl] *n* скáльпель *m*.
scalper ['skælpə'] *n* (*US: inf: ticket tout*) спекулянт(ка*).
scam [skæm] *n* (*inf*) жýльничество *nt no pl*.
scamp [skæmp] *n* (*inf*) безобрáзник(-ица).
scamper ['skæmpə'] *vi*: **to ~ away** *or* **off** ускакáть* (*perf*).
scampi ['skæmpɪ] *npl* (*BRIT*) панирóванные кревéтки* *fpl*.
scan [skæn] *vt* (*examine*) обслéдовать (*perf*); (*read quickly*) просмáтривать (просмотрéть* *perf*); (*TV*) разлагáть (*impf*) изображéние; (*RADAR*) сканировать (*impf*) ♦ *vi* (*poetry*) рифмовáться (*impf*) ♦ *n* (*MED*) сканирование; **ultrasound ~** ультразвýк.
scandal ['skændl] *n* (*shocking event*) скандáл; (*gossip*) сплéтни* *fpl*; (*fig: disgrace*) позóр.
scandalize ['skændəlaɪz] *vt* скандализировать (*impf/perf*).
scandalous ['skændələs] *adj* скандáльный (скандáлен); (*waste*) возмутительный* (возмутителен).
Scandinavia [skændɪ'neɪvɪə] *n* Скандинáвия.
Scandinavian [skændɪ'neɪvɪən] *adj* скандинáвский ♦ *n* скандинáв(ка*).
scanner ['skænə'] *n* (*RADAR, MED*) скáнер.
scant [skænt] *adj* (*attention*) повéрхностный; (*reward*) незначительный.
scantily ['skæntɪlɪ] *adv*: **she was ~ clad** *or*

---

* marks translations which have irregular inflections. The Russian-English side of the dictionary gives inflectional information.

dressed она была́ едва́ оде́та.
scanty ['skæntɪ] *adj* (*meal*) ску́дный* (ску́ден); **her underwear was ~** бельё едва́ прикрыва́ло её те́ло.
scapegoat ['skeɪpɡəʊt] *n* козёл* отпуще́ния.
scar [skɑ:] *n* (*on skin*) шрам; (*fig*) тра́вма ♦ *vt* (*also fig*) травми́ровать (*impf/perf*); **his face is ~red** у него́ на лице́ шрам.
scarce [skɛəs] *adj* ре́дкий* (ре́док); **to make o.s. ~** (*inf*) улизну́ть (*perf*).
scarcely ['skɛəslɪ] *adv* (*hardly*) едва́; (*with numbers: barely*) то́лько; **~ anybody** едва́ ли кто́-нибудь; **I can ~ believe it** я едва́ могу́ э́тому пове́рить; **that is ~ the point** едва́ ли в э́том де́ло.
scarcity ['skɛəsɪtɪ] *n* нехва́тка*, недоста́ток*; **~ value** (*COMM*) це́нность това́ра, определя́емая его́ дефици́тностью.
scare [skɛəʳ] *n* (*fright*) испу́г; (*public fear*) трево́га ♦ *vt* (*frighten*) пуга́ть (испуга́ть *or* напуга́ть *perf*); **to ~ sb stiff** (*inf*) пуга́ть (напуга́ть *perf*) кого́-н до́ смерти; **there was a bomb ~ at the station** опаса́лись, что на ста́нции подло́жена бо́мба
▶ **scare away** *vt* отпу́гивать (отпугну́ть *perf*).
▶ **scare off** *vt* = scare away.
scarecrow ['skɛəkrəʊ] *n* огоро́дное) чу́чело.
scared [skɛəd] *adj* испу́ганный (испу́ган), напу́ганный (напу́ган); **he was ~** он испуга́лся *or* был испу́ган.
scaremonger ['skɛəmʌŋɡəʳ] *n* паникёр.
scarf [skɑ:f] (*pl* **~s** *or* **scarves**) *n* шарф; (*also:* **headscarf**) плато́к*.
scarlet ['skɑ:lɪt] *adj* а́лый (ал).
scarlet fever *n* скарлати́на.
scarper ['skɑ:pəʳ] *vi* (*inf*) смыва́ться (смы́ться* *perf*).
scarred [skɑ:d] *adj* (*fig: person*) травми́рованный (травми́рован); **~ face** лицо́ в шра́мах.
scarves [skɑ:vz] *npl of* scarf.
scary ['skɛərɪ] *adj* стра́шный* (стра́шен).
scathing ['skeɪðɪŋ] *adj* уничтожа́ющий*; **to be ~ about sth** относи́ться* (отнести́сь* *perf*) к чему́-н с презре́нием.
scatter ['skætəʳ] *vt* (*papers, seeds*) разбра́сыва ть (разброса́ть *perf*); (*flock of birds, crowd*) разгоня́ть (разогна́ть* *perf*) ♦ *vi* (*crowd*) рассыпа́ться (рассы́паться* *perf*).
scatterbrained ['skætəbreɪnd] *adj* (*inf*) рассе́янный* (рассе́ян).
scattered ['skætəd] *adj* разбро́санный; **~ showers** преры́вистые ли́вни.
scatty ['skætɪ] *adj* (*BRIT: inf*) несо́бранный (несо́бран).
scavenge ['skævəndʒ] *vi*: **to ~ for food** ры́скать* (*impf*) в по́исках пи́щи.
scavenger ['skævəndʒəʳ] *n* (*person*) старьёвщик; (*animal, bird*) живо́тное *nt adj*, пита́ющееся па́далью, стервя́тник.
SCE *n abbr* = Scottish Certificate of Education.

scenario [sɪ'nɑ:ɪəʊ] *n* (*also fig*) сцена́рий.
scene [si:n] *n* (*THEAT, fig*) сце́на; (*of crime, accident*) ме́сто*; (*sight, view*) карти́на; **behind the ~s** (*also fig*) за кули́сами; **to make a ~** (*inf: fuss*) устра́ивать (устро́ить *perf*) сце́ну; **to appear on the ~** появля́ться (появи́ться* *perf*) на сце́не; **the political ~** полити́ческая аре́на.
scenery ['si:nərɪ] *n* (*THEAT*) декора́ции *fpl*; (*landscape*) пейза́ж.
scenic ['si:nɪk] *adj* живопи́сный* (живопи́сен).
scent [sɛnt] *n* (*smell*) за́пах; (*track, also fig*) след; (*perfume*) духи́* *pl*; **to put** *or* **throw sb off the ~** (*fig*) сбива́ть (сбить* *perf*) кого́-н со сле́да.
sceptic ['skɛptɪk] (*US* **skeptic**) *n* ске́птик.
sceptical ['skɛptɪkl] (*US* **skeptical**) *adj* (*person*) скепти́чный* (скепти́чен); (*remarks*) скепти́ческий*.
scepticism ['skɛptɪsɪzəm] (*US* **skepticism**) *n* скептици́зм.
sceptre ['sɛptəʳ] (*US* **scepter**) *n* ски́петр.
schedule ['ʃɛdju:l, (*US*) 'skɛdju:l] *n* (*timetable*) расписа́ние, гра́фик; (*list of prices, details etc*) пе́речень* *m* ♦ *vt* (*timetable*) распи́сывать (расписа́ть* *perf*); (*visit*) назнача́ть (назна́чить *perf*); **on ~** по расписа́нию *or* гра́фику; **as ~d** как (бы́ло) заплани́ровано; **we are working to a very tight ~** мы рабо́таем по пло́тному гра́фику; **everything went according to ~** всё прошло́ по гра́фику *or* расписа́нию; **to be ahead of ~** опережа́ть (опереди́ть* *perf*) гра́фик; **to be behind ~** отстава́ть (*impf*) от гра́фика.
scheduled ['ʃɛdju:ld, (*US*) 'skɛdju:ld] *adj* (*time, event*) заплани́рованный (заплани́рован); (*train, bus, stop*) обозна́ченный (обозна́чен) в расписа́нии.
scheduled flight *n* регуля́рный рейс.
schematic [skɪ'mætɪk] *adj* схемати́ческий*.
scheme [ski:m] *n* (*plan, idea*) за́мысел*; (*plot*) про́иски *pl*, ко́зни *pl*; (*pension plan etc*) програ́мма; (*arrangement*) план, схе́ма ♦ *vi* стро́ить (*impf*) ко́зни; **colour** *or* (*US*) **color ~** цветова́я га́мма.
scheming ['ski:mɪŋ] *adj* кова́рный ♦ *n* ко́зни *pl*, про́иски *pl*.
schism ['skɪzəm] *n* раско́л.
schizophrenia [skɪtsə'fri:nɪə] *n* шизофрени́я.
schizophrenic [skɪtsə'frɛnɪk] *adj* шизофрени́ческий ♦ *n* шизофре́ник(-и́чка*).
scholar ['skɔləʳ] *n* (*scholarship holder*) стипендиа́т; (*learned person*) учёный *m adj*.
scholarly ['skɔləlɪ] *adj* (*text, approach*) академи́ческий*; (*person*) учёный.
scholarship ['skɔləʃɪp] *n* (*academic knowledge*) учёность *f*; (*grant*) стипе́ндия.
school [sku:l] *n* шко́ла; (*US: inf*) университе́т; (*BRIT*) институ́т; (*of fish, whales*) ста́я ♦ *cpd* шко́льный.
school age *n* шко́льный во́зраст.

schoolbook ['sku:lbuk] *n* (шко́льный) учéбник.
schoolboy ['sku:lbɔɪ] *n* шко́льник.
schoolchildren ['sku:ltʃɪldrən] *npl* шко́льники *mpl.*
school days *npl* шко́льные дни *mpl.*
schooled [sku:ld] *adj:* ~ **(in)** обу́ченный (обу́чен) (+*dat*).
schoolgirl ['sku:lgə:l] *n* шко́льница.
schooling ['sku:lɪŋ] *n* шко́льное образова́ние.
school-leaver [sku:l'li:vəᵉ] *n* (*BRIT*) выпускни́к(-и́ца) шко́лы.
schoolmaster ['sku:lmɑ:stəᵉ] *n* учи́тель* *m.*
schoolmistress ['sku:lmɪstrɪs] *n* учи́тельница.
school report *n* (*BRIT*) та́бель *m* успева́емости.
schoolroom ['sku:lru:m] *n* класс, кла́ссная ко́мната.
schoolteacher ['sku:lti:tʃəᵉ] *n* (шко́льный(-ая)) учи́тель*(ница) *m(f).*
schoolyard ['sku:ljɑ:d] *n* (*US*) шко́льный двор*.
schooner ['sku:nəᵉ] *n* (*ship*) шху́на; (*BRIT: for sherry*) фуже́р (*для хе́реса*); (*US: for beer*) кру́жка* (*для пи́ва*).
sciatica [saɪˈætɪkə] *n* и́шиас.
science ['saɪəns] *n* (*study of natural things*) нау́ка; (*in school*) есте́ственные нау́ки *fpl*; **the ~s** есте́ственные и то́чные нау́ки.
science fiction *n* нау́чная фанта́стика.
scientific [saɪənˈtɪfɪk] *adj* нау́чный.
scientist ['saɪəntɪst] *n* учёный *m adj.*
sci-fi ['saɪfaɪ] *n abbr* (*inf*) (= **science fiction**) НФ= нау́чная фанта́стика.
Scillies ['sɪlɪz] *npl* = **Scilly Isles.**
Scilly Isles ['sɪlɪ'aɪlz] *npl:* **the ~ ~** острова́ *mpl* Си́лли.
scintillating ['sɪntɪleɪtɪŋ] *adj* (*fig: conversation, wit*) блестя́щий*; (*smile*) сия́ющий*.
scissors ['sɪzəz] *npl:* **(a pair of)** ~ но́жницы *pl.*
sclerosis [sklɪˈrəusɪs] *n* склеро́з.
scoff [skɔf] *vt* (*BRIT: inf: eat*) жрать* (сожра́ть* *perf*) ◆ *vi:* **to ~ (at)** (*mock*) насмеха́ться (*impf*) (над +*instr*).
scold [skəuld] *vt* брани́ть (вы́бранить *perf*), руга́ть (отруга́ть *perf*).
scolding ['skəuldɪŋ] *n* вы́говор.
scone [skɔn] *n* (*CULIN*) кекс.
scoop [sku:p] *n* (*measuring scoop: for flour etc*) сово́к*; (: *for ice-cream*) черпа́к; (*PRESS*) сенсацио́нное сообще́ние.
▶ **scoop out** *vt* выскреба́ть (вы́скрести* *perf*)
▶ **scoop up** *vt* зачёрпывать (зачерпну́ть *perf*).
scooter ['sku:təᵉ] *n* (*also:* **motor ~**) мопе́д; (*toy*) самока́т.
scope [skəup] *n* (*opportunity*) просто́р; (*of plan, undertaking*) масшта́б; (*of person*) компете́нция; **within the ~ of** в ра́мках +*gen*;

there is plenty of ~ **for improvement** (*BRIT*) есть просто́р для соверше́нствования; **it is well within his ~ to** ... ... в его́ компете́нции.
scorch [skɔ:tʃ] *vt* (*clothes*) сжига́ть (сжечь* *perf*); (*earth, grass*) выжига́ть (вы́жечь* *perf*).
scorched-earth policy [skɔ:tʃt'ə:θ-] *n* (*MIL*) поли́тика *or* та́ктика вы́жженой земли́.
scorcher ['skɔ:tʃəᵉ] *n* (*inf: hot day*) жари́ща.
scorching ['skɔ:tʃɪŋ] *adj* паля́щий.
score [skɔ:ᵉ] *n* (*number of points etc*) счёт; (*MUS*) партиту́ра; (*twenty*) два́дцать* ◆ *vt* (*goal*) забива́ть (заби́ть* *perf*); (*point*) набира́ть (набра́ть* *perf*); (*mark*) получа́ть (получи́ть* *perf*); (*cut: leather, wood etc*) цара́пать (поцара́пать *perf*); (*achieve: success*) завоёвывать (завоева́ть *perf*) ◆ *vi* (*in game*) набира́ть (набра́ть* *perf*) очки́; (*FOOTBALL etc*) забива́ть (заби́ть* *perf*) гол; (*keep score*) вести́* (*perf*) счёт; **to settle an old ~ with sb** (*fig*) своди́ть* (свести́* *perf*) с кем-н ста́рые счёты; **~s of** деся́тки +*gen*; **on that ~** на э́тот счёт; **to ~ well** набира́ть (набра́ть* *perf*) мно́го очко́в; **to ~ 6 out of 10** набира́ть (*perf*) 6 ба́ллов из 10; **to ~ (a point) over sb** превосходи́ть* (превзойти́* *perf*) кого́-н
▶ **score out** *vt* вычёркивать (вы́черкнуть *perf*).
scoreboard ['skɔ:bɔ:d] *n* табло́ *nt ind.*
scorecard ['skɔ:kɑ:d] *n* (*SPORT*) ка́рта, на кото́рую зано́сится счёт.
scoreline ['skɔ:laɪn] *n* счёт* на да́нный моме́нт.
scorer ['skɔ:rəᵉ] *n* (*FOOTBALL*) игро́к*, заби́вший гол; (*scorekeeper*) судья́*.
scorn [skɔ:n] *n* презре́ние ◆ *vt* презира́ть (*impf*).
scornful ['skɔ:nful] *adj* презри́тельный* (презри́телен).
Scorpio ['skɔ:pɪəu] *n* Скорпио́н; **he is ~** он – Скорпио́н.
scorpion ['skɔ:pɪən] *n* скорпио́н.
Scot [skɔt] *n* шотла́ндец*(-дка)
Scotch [skɔtʃ] *n* (*whisky*) (шотла́ндское) ви́ски *nt ind.*
scotch [skɔtʃ] *vt* (*end: rumour, plan*) пресека́ть (пресе́чь* *perf*).
Scotch tape® *n* кле́йкая ле́нта, "скотч" (*разг*).
scot-free [skɔt'fri:] *adv:* **to get off ~** легко́ отде́лываться (отде́латься *perf*).
Scotland ['skɔtlənd] *n* Шотла́ндия.
Scots [skɔts] *adj* шотла́ндский.
Scotsman ['skɔtsmən] *irreg n* шотла́ндец*.
Scotswoman ['skɔtswumən] *irreg n* шотла́ндка*.
Scottish ['skɔtɪʃ] *adj* шотла́ндский*; **the ~ National Party** Шотла́ндская национа́льная па́ртия; **the ~ Parliament** парла́мент Шотла́ндии, шотла́ндский парла́мент.
scoundrel ['skaundrl] *n* негодя́й.
scour ['skauəᵉ] *vt* (*search*) обы́скивать

---

* marks translations which have irregular inflections The Russian-English side of the dictionary gives inflectional information.

(обыска́ть* *perf*); (*clean*) выска́бливать (вы́скоблить* *perf*).

scourer ['skauərə'] *n* жёсткая моча́лка*.

scourge [skə:dʒ] *n* (*cause of trouble*) бич.

scout [skaut] *n* (*MIL*) разве́дчик; (*also:* **boy** ~) (бой)ска́ут; **girl** ~ (*US*) (де́вочка*-)ска́ут
▸ **scout around** *vi* ры́скать* (*impf*) в по́исках +*gen*.

scowl [skaul] *vi* хму́риться (нахму́риться *perf*); **to** ~ **at sb** хму́ро смотре́ть* (посмотре́ть* *perf*) на кого́-н.

scrabble ['skræbl] *vi* (*also:* ~ **around:** *search*) ша́рить (поша́рить *perf*); (*claw*): **to** ~ **at** цепля́ться (*impf*) (за +*acc*) ◆ *n*: **S~®** (игра́) Скрэбл *ind*; **to** ~ **about** *or* **around for sth** ша́рить (поша́рить *perf*) в по́исках чего́-н.

scraggy ['skrægɪ] *adj* то́щий* (тощ).

scram [skræm] *vi* (*inf*) смыва́ться (смы́ться* *perf*); ~! убира́йся!

scramble ['skræmbl] *n* (*climb: using hands*) кара́бканье; (*struggle, rush*) сва́лка ◆ *vi*: **to** ~ **out** выкара́бкиваться (вы́карабкаться *perf*) из +*gen*; **to** ~ **for** дра́ться* (подра́ться* *perf*) за +*acc*.

scrambled eggs ['skræmbld-] *n* яи́чница-болту́нья.

scrambling ['skræmblɪŋ] *n* (*SPORT*) мотокро́сс.

scrap [skræp] *n* (*of paper*) клочо́к*; (*of information*) обры́вок*; (*of material etc*) лоску́т*; (*fig: of truth*) крупи́ца; (*inf: fight*) потасо́вка; (*also:* ~ **metal**) металли́ческий* лом, металлоло́м ◆ *vt* (*discard: machines etc*) отдава́ть* (отда́ть* *perf*) на слом; (*fig: plans etc*) отка́зываться (отказа́ться* *perf*) от +*gen* ◆ *vi* (*fight*) дра́ться* (подра́ться* *perf*); **~s** *npl* (*of food*) объе́дки *mpl*; (*of material*) обре́зки *mpl*; **to sell sth for** ~ сдава́ть* (сдать* *perf*) в ути́ль.

scrapbook ['skræpbuk] *n* альбо́м для вы́резок.

scrap dealer *n* ути́льщик.

scrape [skreɪp] *vt* (*scrape off*) очища́ть (очи́стить* *perf*); (*scrape against*) цара́пать (поцара́пать *perf*), обдира́ть (ободра́ть* *perf*) ◆ *vi*: **to** ~ **through** (*exam etc*) пролеза́ть (проле́зть* *perf*) на +*prp* ◆ *n* (*fig*): **to get into a** ~ попада́ть (попа́сть* *perf*) в переде́лку
▸ **scrape together** *vt* (*money*) наскреба́ть (наскрести́* *perf*).

scraper ['skreɪpə'] *n* скребо́к*.

scrapheap ['skræphi:p] *n*: **on the** ~ (*fig*) на сва́лку.

scrap merchant *n* (*BRIT*) ути́льщик.

scrap metal *n* металлоло́м.

scrap paper *n* макулату́ра.

scrappy ['skræpɪ] *adj* (*piece of work*) дрянно́й.

scrap yard *n* сва́лка*.

scratch [skrætʃ] *n* цара́пина ◆ *cpd* импровизи́рованный ◆ *vt* цара́пать (поцара́пать *perf*); (*an itch*) чеса́ть* (почеса́ть* *perf*); (*COMPUT*) стира́ть (стере́ть* *perf*) ◆ *vi* чеса́ться* (почеса́ться* *perf*); **to start**

from ~ начина́ть (нача́ть* *perf*) с нуля́; **to be up to** ~ (*person, conditions, standard*) быть* (*impf*) на у́ровне.

scratch pad *n* (*US*) блокно́т.

scrawl [skrɔːl] *n* кара́кули *fpl* ◆ *vt* цара́пать (нацара́пать *perf*).

scrawny ['skrɔːnɪ] *adj* то́щий (тощ).

scream [skriːm] *n* вопль *m*, крик ◆ *vi* крича́ть (*impf*); **it's a real** ~ (*inf*) э́то пря́мо умора́; **to** ~ **at sb** крича́ть (*impf*) на кого́-н.

scree [skriː] *n* камени́стая о́сыпь *f*.

screech [skriːtʃ] *vi* визжа́ть (*impf*) ◆ *n* визг.

screen [skriːn] *n* (*CINEMA, TV, COMPUT*) экра́н; (*barrier, also fig: cover*) ши́рма; (*also:* **windscreen**) ветрово́е стекло́* ◆ *vt* (*protect, conceal*) заслоня́ть (заслони́ть* *perf*); (*show: film, programme*) выпуска́ть (вы́пустить* *perf*) на экра́н; (*check: candidates etc*) проверя́ть (прове́рить *perf*); **to** ~ **sb for sth** (*for illness*) проверя́ть (прове́рить *perf*) кого́-н на что-н.

screen editing *n* (*COMPUT*) экра́нное редакти́рование.

screening ['skriːnɪŋ] *n* (*MED*) профилакти́ческий* осмо́тр; (*of film*) выпуск на экра́н; (*for security*) прове́рка*.

screen memory *n* (*COMPUT*) экра́нная па́мять *f*, видеопа́мять *f*.

screenplay ['skriːnpleɪ] *n* сцена́рий.

screen test *n* кинопро́ба.

screw [skruː] *n* винт* ◆ *vt* (*fasten*) приви́нчивать (привинти́ть* *perf*); (*inf!: have sex with*) тра́хать (тра́хнуть *perf*) (*!*); **to** ~ **sth in** зави́нчивать (завинти́ть* *perf*) что-н; **to** ~ **sth to the wall** приви́нчивать (привинти́ть* *perf*) что-н к стене́; **he's got his head** ~**ed on** (*inf*) у него́ есть голова́ на плеча́х
▸ **screw up** *vt* (*paper etc*) ко́мкать (ско́мкать *perf*); (*inf: ruin*) порта́чить (напорта́чить *perf*); **to** ~ **up one's eyes** прищу́ривать (прищу́рить *perf*) глаза́.

screwdriver ['skruːdraɪvə'] *n* отвёртка*.

screwed-up ['skruːd'ʌp] *adj* (*paper*) ско́мканный (ско́мкан); (*inf: person*) закомплексо́ванный (закомплексо́ван).

screwy ['skruːɪ] *adj* (*inf*) с завихре́нием.

scribble ['skrɪbl] *n* кара́кули *mpl* ◆ *vt* черкну́ть (*perf*) ◆ *vi* исчёркивать (исчёркать *perf*); **to** ~ **sth down** запи́сывать (записа́ть* *perf*) что-н на́скоро.

scribe [skraɪb] *n* писе́ц*.

script [skrɪpt] *n* (*CINEMA etc*) сцена́рий; (*system of writing*) шрифт*; (*in exam*) конспе́кт.

scripted ['skrɪptɪd] *adj* (*RADIO, TV*) зара́нее подгото́вленный.

Scripture(s) ['skrɪptʃə'(-əz)] *n(pl)* Свяще́нное писа́ние.

scriptwriter ['skrɪptraɪtə'] *n* сцена́рист.

scroll [skrəul] *n* сви́ток* ◆ *vt* (*COMPUT*) прокру́чивать (прокрути́ть* *perf*), перемеща́ть (перемести́ть* *perf*).

scrotum ['skrəutəm] n (ANAT) мошо́нка*.
scrounge [skraundʒ] (inf) vt: **to ~ sth off** or **from sb** кля́нчить (вы́клянчить perf) что-н у кого́-н ◆ vi попроша́йничать (impf) ◆ n: **to be on the ~** быть* (impf) на мёли.
scrounger ['skraundʒəʳ] n (inf) попроша́йка* m/f.
scrub [skrʌb] n (land) куста́рник ◆ vt скрести́* (impf); (inf: reject) отбра́сывать (отбро́сить* perf).
scrubbing brush ['skrʌbɪŋ-] n жёсткая щётка*.
scruff [skrʌf] n: **by the ~ of the neck** за ши́ворот.
scruffy ['skrʌfɪ] adj потрёпанный*.
scrum(mage) ['skrʌm(ɪdʒ)] n (RUGBY) разы́грывание мяча́.
scruple ['skru:pl] n (usu pl) терза́ние; **to have no ~s about doing sth** де́лать (сде́лать perf) что-н без угрызе́ний со́вести.
scrupulous ['skru:pjuləs] adj (painstaking) тща́тельный* (тща́телен), скрупулёзный* (скрупулёзен); (fair-minded) щепети́льный* (щепети́лен).
scrupulously ['skru:pjuləslɪ] adv (behave, act) добросо́вестно; **he is ~ honest/fair/clean** он преде́льно че́стен/справедли́в/чистопло́тен.
scrutinize ['skru:tɪnaɪz] vt тща́тельно изуча́ть (изучи́ть perf) or рассма́тривать (рассмотре́ть* perf).
scrutiny ['skru:tɪnɪ] n тща́тельное изуче́ние or рассмотре́ние; **under sb's ~** под чьим-н наблюде́нием.
scuba ['sku:bə] n аквала́нг.
scuba diving n подво́дное погруже́ние.
scuff [skʌf] vt (feet) волочи́ть (impf); (mark: shoes) ста́птывать (стопта́ть perf).
scuffle ['skʌfl] n потасо́вка*.
scull [skʌl] n (on rowing boat) весло́*.
scullery ['skʌlərɪ] n (old) подсо́бное помеще́ние (при ку́хне).
sculptor ['skʌlptəʳ] n ску́льптор.
sculpture ['skʌlptʃəʳ] n скульпту́ра.
scum [skʌm] n пе́на; (inf: pej: people) подо́нки mpl; **the ~ of society** отбро́сы о́бщества.
scupper ['skʌpəʳ] vt (BRIT: inf: plan) срыва́ть (сорва́ть* perf).
scurrilous ['skʌrɪləs] adj (accusation, gossip etc) оскорби́тельный* (оскорби́телен).
scurry ['skʌrɪ] vi ю́ркнуть (perf).
▶ **scurry off** vi ры́сью убега́ть (убежа́ть perf).
scurvy ['skə:vɪ] n цинга́.
scuttle ['skʌtl] n (also: **coal ~**) ведро́* для угля́ ◆ vt (ship) топи́ть* (затопи́ть* or потопи́ть* perf) ◆ vi: **to ~ away** or **off** ры́сью убега́ть (убежа́ть perf).
scythe [saɪð] n серп*.
SD abbr (US: POST) = South Dakota.
SDI n abbr (US: MIL: = Strategic Defense Initiative) СОИ= *Стратегúческая оборóнная инициатúва.*

SDLP n abbr (BRIT: POL) = Social Democratic and Labour Party.
SDP n abbr (BRIT: POL: formerly) = Social Democratic Party.
sea [si:] n мо́ре* ◆ cpd морско́й; **by ~** (travel) мо́рем; **beside the ~** у мо́ря; **on the ~** (boat) в мо́ре; (town) на мо́ре; **to be all at ~** (fig) быть* (impf) в растёрянности; **out to ~**, **out at ~** в мо́ре; **to look out to ~** смотре́ть* (impf) на мо́ре; **heavy** or **rough ~(s)** бу́рное мо́ре; **a ~ of faces** мо́ре лиц.
sea anemone n морско́й анемо́н.
sea bed n морско́е дно.
seaboard ['si:bɔ:d] n побере́жье*.
seafarer ['si:fɛərəʳ] n морепла́ватель m.
seafaring ['si:fɛərɪŋ] adj морско́й; **~ people** морехо́ды mpl.
seafood ['si:fu:d] n ры́бные блю́да ntpl.
seafront ['si:frʌnt] n на́бережная f adj.
seagoing ['si:gəuɪŋ] adj морско́й.
seagull ['si:gʌl] n ча́йка*.
seal [si:l] n (ZOOL) тюле́нь m; (stamp) печа́ть f ◆ vt (close: envelope) запеча́тывать (запеча́тать perf); (: opening) заде́лывать (заде́лать perf); (decide: sb's fate) реша́ть (реши́ть* perf); (deal) заключа́ть (заключи́ть perf); **to give sth one's ~ of approval** официа́льно одобря́ть (perf) что-н
▶ **seal off** vt (area, street) огора́живать (огороди́ть* perf); (building) опеча́тывать (опеча́тать perf).
sea level n у́ровень* m мо́ря; **2,000 feet above/below ~ ~** 2000 фу́тов над у́ровнем мо́ря/ ни́же у́ровня мо́ря.
sealing wax ['si:lɪŋ-] n сургу́ч*.
sea lion n морско́й лев*.
sealskin ['si:lskɪn] n ко́тик (мех).
seam [si:m] n (of garment) шов*; (of coal) слой*; **the hall was bursting at the ~s** зал треща́л по швам.
seaman ['si:mən] irreg n матро́с, моря́к.
seamanship ['si:mənʃɪp] n судовожде́ние.
seamless ['si:mlɪs] adj без шва; (fig) це́лостный.
seamy ['si:mɪ] adj тёмный* (тёмен).
seance ['seɪɔns] n спирити́ческий сеа́нс.
seaplane ['si:pleɪn] n гидросамолёт.
seaport ['si:pɔ:t] n (морско́й) порт*.
search [sə:tʃ] n (for person) ро́зыск; (for thing) по́иски mpl; (COMPUT) по́иск; (inspection: of sb's home etc) о́быск ◆ vt (place, person) обы́скивать (обыска́ть* perf); (memory) ры́ться* (impf) в +prp ◆ vi: **to ~ for** иска́ть* (impf); **in ~ of** в по́исках +gen; **"search and replace"** (COMPUT) "по́иск и заме́на"
▶ **search through** vt fus переры́ть (perf).
searcher ['sə:tʃəʳ] n иска́тель(ница) m(f).

searching ['sə:tʃɪŋ] *adj* (*look*) пытли́вый (пытли́в); (*question*) наводя́щий*; (*examination*) тща́тельный* (тща́телен).

searchlight ['sə:tʃlaɪt] *n* проже́ктор*.

search party *n* поиско́вая гру́ппа; **to send out a** ~ ~ посыла́ть (посла́ть* *perf*) поиско́вую гру́ппу.

search warrant *n* о́рдер на о́быск.

searing ['sɪərɪŋ] *adj* (*heat, pain*) жгу́чий* (жгуч).

seashore ['si:ʃɔ:ʳ] *n* бе́рег* мо́ря; **on the** ~ на берегу́ мо́ря.

seasick ['si:sɪk] *adj*: **to be** ~ страда́ть (*impf*) морско́й боле́знью.

seasickness ['si:sɪknɪs] *n* морска́я боле́знь *f*.

seaside ['si:saɪd] *n* взмо́рье, примо́рье; **to go to the** ~ е́здить*/е́хать* (пое́хать* *perf*) на взмо́рье; **at the** ~ на взмо́рье.

seaside resort *n* примо́рский* куро́рт.

season ['si:zn] *n* (*of year*) вре́мя* *nt* го́да; (*for football, of films etc*) сезо́н ♦ *vi* (*food*) заправля́ть (запра́вить* *perf*); **the busy** ~ акти́вный сезо́н; **the open** ~ (*HUNTING*) охо́тничий сезо́н; **tomatoes are in** ~ сейча́с сезо́н помидо́ров.

seasonal ['si:znl] *adj* сезо́нный.

seasoned ['si:znd] *adj* (*traveller*) закалённый, запра́вский; (*wood*) вы́держанный; **a** ~ **campaigner** о́пытный агита́тор.

seasoning ['si:znɪŋ] *n* припра́ва.

season ticket *n* (*RAIL*) сезо́нный (проездно́й) биле́т; (*THEAT, SPORT*) абонеме́нт.

seat [si:t] *n* (*chair, place*) сиде́нье*; (*in theatre, in parliament*) ме́сто*; (*of trousers*) зад; (*of government*) резиде́нция; (*of learning etc*) центр ♦ *vt* (*place: guests etc*) рассади́ть (рассади́ть* *perf*), уса́живать (усади́ть* *perf*); (*subj: venue*) вмеща́ть (вмести́ть* *perf*); **are there any** ~**s left?** есть ещё места́?; **to take one's** ~ сади́ться (сесть* *perf*); **please be** ~**ed** пожа́луйста, сади́тесь; **to be** ~**ed** сиде́ть (*impf*); **this table** ~**s 10 people** за э́тим столо́м умеща́ется 10 челове́к.

seat belt *n* привязно́й реме́нь* *m*.

seating arrangements ['si:tɪŋ-] *npl* распределе́ние *ntsg* мест.

seating capacity *n* сидя́чие места́ *ntpl*; **the hall has a** ~ ~ **of 100** зал рассчи́тан на 100 сидя́чих мест.

SEATO ['si:təu] *n abbr* (= *Southeast Asia Treaty Organization*) СЕА́ТО.

sea urchin *n* морско́й ёж.

sea water *n* морска́я вода́.

seaweed ['si:wi:d] *n* во́доросли *fpl*.

seaworthy ['si:wə:ði] *adj* морехо́дный.

Sebastopol [sɪ'bæstəpəl] *n* Севасто́поль *m*.

SEC *n abbr* (*US*: = *Securities and Exchange Commission*) Коми́ссия по це́нным бума́гам и би́ржам.

sec. *abbr* = **second**.

secateurs [sɛkə'tə:z] *npl* садо́вые но́жницы *pl*, сека́тор *msg*.

secede [sɪ'si:d] *vi*: **to** ~ (**from**) отделя́ться (отдели́ться* *perf*) (от +*gen*).

secluded [sɪ'klu:dɪd] *adj* уединённый.

seclusion [sɪ'klu:ʒən] *n* уедине́ние; **in** ~ в уедине́нии.

second[1] [sɪ'kɔnd] *vt* (*BRIT: employee*) командирова́ть* (*impf*).

second[2] ['sɛkənd] *adj* второ́й ♦ *adv* (*come, be placed*) вторы́м; (*when listing*) во-вторы́х ♦ *n* (*unit of time*) секу́нда; (*AUT: also*: ~ **gear**) втора́я ско́рость *f*; (*COMM: imperfect*) дефе́ктное изде́лие; (*BRIT: SCOL: degree*) дипло́м второ́го кла́сса ♦ *vt* (*motion*) подде́рживать (поддержа́ть* *perf*); **Charles the S**~ Карл Второ́й; ~ **floor** (*BRIT*) тре́тий* эта́ж; (*US*) второ́й эта́ж; **just a** ~! секу́ндочку!; *see also* **fifth**.

secondary ['sɛkəndərɪ] *adj* втори́чный.

secondary education *n* сре́днее образова́ние.

secondary picketing [-'pɪkɪtɪŋ] *n* втори́чное пикети́рование.

secondary school *n* сре́дняя шко́ла.

second-best [sɛkənd'bɛst] *n* не са́мое лу́чшее *nt adj* ♦ *adj* (*hotel, room*) второ́й по ка́честву; (*pupil*) второ́й (по успева́емости); **as a** ~ за неиме́нием лу́чшего.

second-class ['sɛkənd'klɑ:s] *adj* (*citizen, standard etc*) второразря́дный; (*POST, RAIL*) второ́го кла́сса ♦ *adv* вторы́м кла́ссом.

second cousin *n* (*male*) трою́родный брат*; (*female*) трою́родная сестра́*.

seconder ['sɛkəndəʳ] *n*: **he is the** ~ **of the proposal** он поддержа́л предложе́ние.

second-guess ['sɛkənd'gɛs] *vt* предска́зывать (предсказа́ть* *perf*).

second hand *n* (*on clock*) секу́ндная стре́лка*.

second-hand ['sɛkənd'hænd] *adj* поде́ржанный ♦ *adv* (*buy*) с рук; **to hear sth** ~ узнава́ть* (узна́ть* *perf*) что-н из вторы́х рук.

second in command *n* (*MIL*) второ́й *m adj* по зва́нию; (*ADMIN*) второ́й *m adj* по до́лжности.

secondly ['sɛkəndlɪ] *adv* во-вторы́х.

secondment [sɪ'kɔndmənt] *n* (*BRIT*) командиро́вка*.

second-rate ['sɛkənd'reɪt] *adj* (*film etc*) посре́дственный* (посре́дствен); (*restaurant*) второразря́дный.

second thoughts *npl*: **to have** ~ ~ (**about doing**) начина́ть (нача́ть* *perf*) сомнева́ться (сле́дует ли +*infin*); **on** ~ ~ *or* (*US*) **thought** по зре́лом размышле́нии.

Second World War *n*: **the** ~ ~ ~ Втора́я мирова́я война́.

secrecy ['si:krəsɪ] *n* секре́тность *f*; **in** ~ в та́йне.

secret ['si:krɪt] *adj* секре́тный (секре́тен), та́йный; (*admirer*) та́йный ♦ *n* секре́т, та́йна; **to keep sth** ~ **from sb** держа́ть* (*impf*) что-н в секре́те *or* та́йне от кого́-н; **keep it** ~ держи́те э́то в секре́те *or* в та́йне; **in** ~ (*say, give*) по секре́ту; (*do, meet*) секре́тно; **to**

make no ~ of sth не де́лать *(impf)* секре́та из чего́-н.

secret agent *n* секре́тный *or* та́йный аге́нт.

secretarial [sɛkrɪ'tɛərɪəl] *adj* секрета́рский; **~ course** ку́рсы *mpl* секретаре́й.

secretariat [sɛkrɪ'tɛərɪət] *n* секретариа́т.

secretary ['sɛkrətərɪ] *n* секрета́рь* *m*; **S~ of State (for)** *(BRIT)* ≈ мини́стр *(+gen)*; **S~ of State** *(US)* Госуда́рственный секрета́рь* *m*.

secretary-general ['sɛkrətərɪ'dʒɛnərəl] *n* генера́льный секрета́рь *m*.

secrete [sɪ'kri:t] *vt* *(BIO)* выделя́ть (вы́делить *perf)*; *(hide)* пря́тать* (спря́тать* *perf)*.

secretion [sɪ'kri:ʃən] *n* *(substance)* выделе́ние, секре́ция.

secretive ['si:krətɪv] *adj* *(pej: person)* скры́тный* (скры́тен); **he is ~ about his plans** он де́ржит свои́ пла́ны в секре́те.

secretly ['si:krɪtlɪ] *adv* *(do, meet)* секре́тно; *(marry)* та́йно.

secret police *n* секре́тная поли́ция.

secret service *n* секре́тная слу́жба.

sect [sɛkt] *n* се́кта.

sectarian [sɛk'tɛərɪən] *adj* секта́нтский*.

section ['sɛkʃən] *n* *(part)* часть* *f*; *(of population, company)* се́ктор; *(in shop)* се́кция; *(of document, book)* разде́л; *(cross-section)* сече́ние, разре́з ♦ *vt* рассека́ть (рассе́чь* *perf)*; **the business** *etc* **~** *(PRESS)* разде́л би́знеса *etc*.

sectional ['sɛkʃənl] *adj:* **~ drawing** рису́нок в разре́зе, разре́з.

sector ['sɛktə^r] *n* *(part, also MIL)* се́ктор.

secular ['sɛkjulə^r] *adj* *(music, society)* све́тский*; *(priest)* мирско́й.

secure [sɪ'kjuə^r] *adj* *(safe: person, money, job)* надёжный* (надёжен); *(: building)* безопа́сный* (безопа́сен); *(firmly fixed, strong: rope, shelf)* про́чный* (про́чен); *(free from anxiety: person)* уве́ренный ♦ *vt* *(fix: rope, shelf etc)* (про́чно) закрепля́ть (закрепи́ть* *perf)*; *(get: job, contract etc)* обеспе́чивать (обеспе́чить *perf)*; *(COMM: loan)* обеспе́чивать (обеспе́чить *perf)*; **to make sth ~** про́чно *or* надёжно закрепля́ть (закрепи́ть* *perf)* что-н; **to ~ sth for sb** обеспе́чивать (обеспе́чить *perf)* для кого́-н что-н.

secured creditor [sɪ'kjuəd-] *n* кредито́р, получи́вший обеспе́чение.

securely [sɪ'kjuəlɪ] *adv* *(fasten)* про́чно; *(keep)* в надёжном ме́сте.

security [sɪ'kjuərɪtɪ] *n* *(protection)* безопа́сность *f*; *(for one's future)* обеспе́ченность *f*; *(FINANCE)* зало́г; **securities** *npl* *(COMM)* це́нные бума́ги *fpl*; **to increase** *or* **tighten ~** повыша́ть (повы́сить* *perf)* безопа́сность; **~ of tenure**

гаранти́рованное пра́во.

Security Council *n:* **the ~ ~** Сове́т безопа́сности.

security forces *npl* си́лы *fpl* безопа́сности.

security guard *n* охра́нник.

security risk *n:* **it's a ~ ~** *(for country)* э́то представля́ет угро́зу для безопа́сности страны́.

secy. *abbr* = **secretary**.

sedan [sə'dæn] *n* *(US: AUT)* седа́н.

sedate [sɪ'deɪt] *adj* *(person)* степе́нный* (степе́нен); *(pace)* разме́ренный* (разме́рен) ♦ *vt* *(MED)* дава́ть* (дать* *perf)* седати́вное *or* успокои́тельное сре́дство.

sedation [sɪ'deɪʃən] *n:* **to be under ~** находи́ться* *(impf)* под возде́йствием седати́вных *or* успокои́тельных средств.

sedative ['sɛdɪtɪv] *n* седати́вное *or* успокои́тельное сре́дство.

sedentary ['sɛdntrɪ] *adj* сидя́чий*.

sediment ['sɛdɪmənt] *n* оса́док*.

sedimentary [sɛdɪ'mɛntərɪ] *adj* оса́дочный.

sedition [sɪ'dɪʃən] *n* крамо́ла.

seduce [sɪ'dju:s] *vt* соблазня́ть (соблазни́ть *perf)*.

seduction [sɪ'dʌkʃən] *n* *(attraction)* собла́зн; *(act of seducing)* обольще́ние.

seductive [sɪ'dʌktɪv] *adj* *(look, voice)* обольсти́тельный* (обольсти́телен); *(offer)* соблазни́тельный* (соблазни́телен).

see [si:] *(pt saw, pp seen)* *vt* ви́деть* (уви́деть* *perf)*; *(understand)* понима́ть (поня́ть* *perf)* ♦ *vi* ви́деть *(impf)*; *(find out)* выясня́ть (вы́яснить *perf)* ♦ *n* епа́рхия; **to ~ sb to the door** *(accompany)* провожа́ть (проводи́ть* *perf)* кого́-н до двери́; **to ~ that** *(ensure)* следи́ть* (проследи́ть* *perf)*, что́бы; **there was nobody to be ~n** никого́ не́ было ви́дно; **let me ~** *(show me)* да́йте мне посмотре́ть; *(let me think)* да́йте мне поду́мать; **to go and ~ sb** навеща́ть (навести́ть* *perf)* кого́-н; **~ for yourself** *(suggestion)* убеди́тесь са́ми; **I don't know what she saw in him** я не зна́ю, что она́ в нём нашла́; **as far as I can ~** наско́лько я понима́ю; **~ you!** пока́!; **~ you soon!** до ско́рого!, пока́!

▶ **see about** *vt fus* *(deal with)* занима́ться (заня́ться* *perf)* +*instr*

▶ **see off** *vt* провожа́ть (проводи́ть* *perf)*

▶ **see through** *vt* доводи́ть (довести́* *perf)* до конца́ ♦ *vt fus* ви́деть *(impf)* наскво́зь

▶ **see to** *vt fus* забо́титься* (позабо́титься* *perf)* о +*prp*.

seed [si:d] *n* се́мя* *nt*; **~s** *(fig)* семена́* *ntpl*; **he is the number 2 ~** *(SPORT)* в ранжиро́вке спортсме́нов он второ́й; **to go to ~** *(plant)* пойти́* *(perf)* в семена́; *(fig)* сдать* *(perf)*.

seedless ['si:dlɪs] *adj* без ко́сточек.

---

seedling ['si:dlɪŋ] *n* рассáда *no pl*.
seedy ['si:dɪ] *adj* (*person*) потрёпанный*
(потрёпан); (*place*) захудáлый.
seeing ['si:ɪŋ] *conj*: ~ **(that)** поскóльку, так как.
seek [si:k] (*pt, pp* **sought**) *vt* искáть* (*impf*); **to** ~
advice/help from sb обращáться
(обратúться* *perf*) за совéтом/пóмощью к
комý-н
▸ **seek out** *vt* (*person*) разы́скивать
(разыскáть* *perf*).
seem [si:m] *vi* казáться* (показáться* *perf*);
there ~**s to be** ... кáжется, что имéется ...; **it**
~**s (that)** кáжется, (что); **what** ~**s to be the**
trouble? что у Вас за проблéма?
seemingly ['si:mɪŋlɪ] *adv* по-вúдимому.
seemly ['si:mlɪ] *adj* (*behaviour*) подобáющий*;
(*dress*) надлежáщий*.
seen [si:n] *pp of* **see**.
seep [si:p] *vi* просáчиваться (просочúться
perf).
seersucker ['sɪəsʌkə'] *n* (*fabric*) марлёвка.
seesaw ['si:sɔ:] *n* качéли *pl*.
seethe [si:ð] *vi* (*place*) кишéть* (*impf*); **to** ~ **with**
anger кипéть* (*impf*) от гнéва.
see-through ['si:θru:] *adj* прозрáчный*
(прозрáчен).
segment ['sɛgmənt] *n* (*of circle*) сегмéнт; (*of*
population) сéктор; (*of orange*) дóлька*.
segregate ['sɛgrɪgeɪt] *vt* разделя́ть
(раздели́ть* *perf*).
segregation [sɛgrɪ'geɪʃən] *n* (*racial*)
сегрегáция; (*SCOL*) раздéльное обучéние.
seismic ['saɪzmɪk] *adj* сейсмúческий*.
seize [si:z] *vt* хватáть (схватúть* *perf*); (*power,*
hostage, territory) захвáтывать (захватúть*
perf); (*opportunity*) пóльзоваться
(воспóльзоваться *perf*) +*instr*; (*LAW*)
конфисковáть (*impf/perf*)
▸ **seize up** *vi* (*TECH: engine*) глóхнуть*
(заглóхнуть* *perf*)
▸ **seize (up)on** *vt fus* ухвáтываться
(ухватúться* *perf*) за +*instr*.
seizure ['si:ʒə'] *n* (*MED*) прúступ; (*of power*)
захвáт; (*of goods*) конфискáция.
seldom ['sɛldəm] *adv* рéдко.
select [sɪ'lɛkt] *adj* (*school, area*) элитáрный;
(*pupils*) úзбранный; (*goods*) отбóрный ♦ *vt*
(*choose*) выбирáть (вы́брать* *perf*); (*SPORT*)
отбирáть (отобрáть* *perf*); **a** ~ **few** немнóгие
úзбранные *pl adj*.
selection [sɪ'lɛkʃən] *n* (*process*) отбóр; (*COMM:*
range available) вы́бор; (*medley*) подбóрка.
selection committee *n* отбóрочная
комúссия.
selective [sɪ'lɛktɪv] *adj* (*careful in choosing*)
разбóрчивый (разбóрчив); (*not general*)
избирáтельный.
selector [sɪ'lɛktə'] *n* (*person*) член отбóрочной
комúссии; (*TECH*) селéктор.
self [sɛlf] (*pl* **selves**) *n*: **he became his usual** ~
again он стал опя́ть самúм собóй; **my own** ~

моё сóбственное "я".
self... [sɛlf] *prefix* сáмо..., себя́....
self-addressed ['sɛlfə'drɛst] *adj*: ~ **envelope**
конвéрт, адресóванный на сóбственное
úмя.
self-adhesive [sɛlfəd'hi:zɪv] *adj* само-
приклéивающийся.
self-appointed [sɛlfə'pɔɪntɪd] *adj* самозвáный.
self-assertive [sɛlfə'sə:tɪv] *adj* увéренный*
(увéрен).
self-assurance [sɛlfə'ʃuərəns] *n* само-
увéренность *f*.
self-assured [sɛlfə'ʃuəd] *adj* самоувéренный*
(самоувéрен).
self-catering [sɛlf'keɪtərɪŋ] *adj* (*BRIT*): ~ **holiday**
путёвка, в котóрую включáется проéзд и
жильё с самообслýживанием.
self-centred [sɛlf'sɛntəd] (*US* **self-centered**) *adj*
эгоцентрúчный* (эгоцентрúчен).
self-cleaning [sɛlf'kli:nɪŋ] *adj* само-
очищáющийся.
self-confessed [sɛlfkən'fɛst] *adj* (*alcoholic etc*)
сознáвшийся.
self-confidence [sɛlf'kɔnfɪdns] *n* увéренность *f*
в себé.
self-confident [sɛlf'kɔnfɪdənt] *adj* увéренный*
(увéрен) в себé.
self-conscious [sɛlf'kɔnʃəs] *adj* (*nervous*)
застéнчивый (застéнчив).
self-contained [sɛlfkən'teɪnd] *adj* (*BRIT: flat*)
отдéльный, изолúрованный; (*society,*
person) незавúсимый.
self-control [sɛlfkən'trəul] *n* самооблáдание.
self-defeating [sɛlfdɪ'fi:tɪŋ] *adj* (*plan, action*)
пáгубный* (пáгубен).
self-defence [sɛlfdɪ'fɛns] (*US* **self-defense**) *n*
самозащúта, самооборóна; **in** ~ защищáя
себя́.
self-discipline [sɛlf'dɪsɪplɪn] *n* само-
дисциплúна.
self-employed [sɛlfɪm'plɔɪd] *adj* рабóтающий
на себя́.
self-esteem [sɛlfɪs'ti:m] *n* чýвство
сóбственного достóинства.
self-evident [sɛlf'ɛvɪdnt] *adj* самоочевúдный*
(самоочевúден).
self-explanatory [sɛlfɪks'plænətrɪ] *adj*: **this**
phrase is ~ э́та фрáза не трéбует
разъяснéний.
self-financing [sɛlffaɪ'nænsɪŋ] *n*
самофинансúрование.
self-governing [sɛlf'gʌvənɪŋ] *adj* (*organization,*
group) рабóтающий по прúнципу
самоуправлéния.
self-help ['sɛlf'hɛlp] *n* самопóмощь *f*.
self-importance [sɛlfɪm'pɔ:tns] *n* самомнéние.
self-indulgent [sɛlfɪn'dʌldʒənt] *adj*: **he is being**
~ он потвóрствует свои́м слáбостям.
self-inflicted [sɛlfɪn'flɪktɪd] *adj* (*injury*)
нанесённый (нанесён) самомý себé;
(*problems*) причинённый самомý себé.

self-interest [sɛlf'ɪntrɪst] *n* корысть *f*.

selfish ['sɛlfɪʃ] *adj* (*behaviour, attitude*) эгоисти́ческий*; (*person*) эгоисти́чный* (эгоисти́чен).

selfishly ['sɛlfɪʃlɪ] *adv* эгоисти́чно.

selfishness ['sɛlfɪʃnɪs] *n* (*of behaviour*) эгоисти́чность *f*; (*of person*) эгои́зм.

selfless ['sɛlflɪs] *adj* самоотве́рженный* (самоотве́ржен).

selflessly ['sɛlflɪslɪ] *adv* самоотве́рженно.

selflessness ['sɛlflɪsnɪs] *n* самоотве́рженность *f*.

self-made ['sɛlfmeɪd] *adj*: **he's a ~ man** он доби́лся всего́ свои́ми си́лами.

self-perpetuating [sɛlfpə'pɛtʃueɪtɪŋ] *adj* несконча́емый.

self-pity [sɛlf'pɪtɪ] *n* жа́лость *f* к (самому́) себе́.

self-portrait [sɛlf'pɔːtreɪt] *n* автопортре́т.

self-possessed [sɛlfpə'zɛst] *adj* хладнокро́вный* (хладнокро́вен).

self-preservation ['sɛlfprɛzə'veɪʃən] *n* самосохране́ние.

self-raising [sɛlf'reɪzɪŋ] (*US* **self-rising**) *adj* (*BRIT*): **~ flour** мука́ с разрыхли́телем.

self-reliant [sɛlfrɪ'laɪənt] *adj* (*person*) самостоя́тельный* (самостоя́телен).

self-respect [sɛlfrɪs'pɛkt] *n* самоуваже́ние.

self-respecting [sɛlfrɪs'pɛktɪŋ] *adj* уважа́ющий себя́.

self-righteous [sɛlf'raɪtʃəs] *adj* (*person*) убеждённый* в свое́й правоте́.

self-rising [sɛlf'raɪzɪŋ] *adj* (*US*) = **self-raising**.

self-sacrifice [sɛlf'sækrɪfaɪs] *n* самопоже́ртвование.

selfsame ['sɛlfseɪm] *adj* тот же са́мый.

self-satisfied [sɛlf'sætɪsfaɪd] *adj* самодово́льный* (самодово́лен).

self-sealing [sɛlf'siːlɪŋ] *adj* (*envelope*) самозакле́ивающийся.

self-service [sɛlf'səːvɪs] *adj*: **~ restaurant/shop** рестора́н/магази́н самообслу́живания.

self-styled ['sɛlfstaɪld] *adj* самозва́ный.

self-sufficient [sɛlfsə'fɪʃənt] *adj* самостоя́тельный* (самостоя́телен); **to be ~ in sth** по́лностью обеспе́чивать (*impf*) себя́ чем-н.

self-supporting [sɛlfsə'pɔːtɪŋ] *adj* само-окупа́ющийся.

self-tanning [sɛlf'tænɪŋ] *adj* спосо́бствующий зага́ру.

self-taught [sɛlf'tɔːt] *adj*: **~ artist/pianist** худо́жник-/пиани́ст-самоу́чка.

self-test ['sɛlftɛst] *n* (*COMPUT*) самопрове́рка*.

sell [sɛl] (*pt, pp* **sold**) *vt* продава́ть* (прода́ть* *perf*) ♦ *vi* продава́ться* (прода́ться* *perf*); **to ~ at** *or* **for 10 pounds** продава́ться* (прода́ться* *perf*) за 10 фу́нтов; **to ~ sb sth, ~ sth to sb** продава́ть* (прода́ть* *perf*) что-н кому́-н; **to ~ sb an idea** (*fig*) убежда́ть (убеди́ть* *perf*) кого́-н в иде́е

▶ **sell off** *vt* распродава́ть* (распрода́ть* *perf*)

▶ **sell out** *vi* (*book etc*) расходи́ться* (разойти́сь* *perf*); (*shop*): **to ~ out of sth** распродава́ть* (распрода́ть* *perf*) что-н; **the tickets are sold out** все биле́ты (рас)про́даны

▶ **sell up** *vi* продава́ть* (прода́ть* *perf*) всё иму́щество.

sell-by date ['sɛlbaɪ-] *n* срок го́дности.

seller ['sɛlə'] *n* продаве́ц*(-вщи́ца); **~'s market** "ры́нок продавцо́в" (*на кото́ром усло́вия дикту́ют продавцы́*).

selling price ['sɛlɪŋ-] *n* прода́жная цена́*.

Sellotape® ['sɛləuteɪp] *n* (*BRIT*) кле́йкая ле́нта.

sellout ['sɛlaut] *n* (*inf: betrayal*) преда́тельство; (*of tickets*): **the match was a ~** все биле́ты на матч бы́ли распро́даны.

selves [sɛlvz] *pl of* **self**.

semantic [sɪ'mæntɪk] *adj* семанти́ческий*.

semantics [sɪ'mæntɪks] *n* сема́нтика.

semaphore ['sɛməfɔː'] *n* семафо́р.

semblance ['sɛmblns] *n* ви́димость *f*.

semen ['siːmən] *n* се́мя* *nt*, спе́рма.

semester [sɪ'mɛstə'] *n* (*esp US*) семе́стр.

semi ['sɛmɪ] *n* = **semidetached (house)**.

semi... ['sɛmɪ] *prefix* полу....

semibreve ['sɛmɪbriːv] *n* (*BRIT*) це́лая но́та.

semicircle ['sɛmɪsəːkl] *n* полукру́г.

semicircular ['sɛmɪ'səːkjulə'] *adj* полукру́глый.

semicolon [sɛmɪ'kəulən] *n* то́чка* с запято́й.

semiconductor [sɛmɪkən'dʌktə'] *n* полу-проводни́к*.

semiconscious [sɛmɪ'kɔnʃəs] *adj* в полу-забы́тьи.

semidetached [sɛmɪdɪ'tætʃt-] *n* (*BRIT*: *also*: **~ house**) *дом, примыка́ющий к сосе́днему*.

semifinal [sɛmɪ'faɪnl] *n* полуфина́л.

seminar ['sɛmɪnɑː'] *n* семина́р.

seminary ['sɛmɪnərɪ] *n* семина́рия.

semiprecious [sɛmɪ'prɛʃəs] *adj*: **~ stone** полудрагоце́нный ка́мень* *m*, самоцве́т.

semiquaver ['sɛmɪkweɪvə'] *n* (*BRIT*) шестна́дцатая но́та.

semiskilled [sɛmɪ'skɪld] *adj* (*work, worker*) полуквалифици́рованный.

semiskimmed [sɛmɪ'skɪmd] *adj* полужи́рный, полуобезжи́ренный.

semitone ['sɛmɪtəun] *n* полуто́н*.

semolina [sɛmə'liːnə] *n* ма́нная крупа́, ма́нка (*inf*).

SEN *n abbr* (*BRIT*: = *State Enrolled Nurse*) медсестра́= *медици́нская сестра́*.

Sen. *abbr* (*US*) = **senator**; (*in names*) = **senior**.

sen. *abbr* = **Sen**.

senate ['sɛnɪt] *n* сена́т.

senator ['sɛnɪtə'] *n* (*US etc*) сена́тор.

send [sɛnd] (*pt, pp* **sent**) *vt* (*dispatch*) посыла́ть (посла́ть* *perf*), отправля́ть (отпра́вить* *perf*); (*transmit*) посыла́ть (посла́ть* *perf*); **to**

~ by post or *(US)* **mail** посыла́ть (посла́ть* *perf)* or отправля́ть (отпра́вить* *perf)* по по́чте; **to ~ sb for sth** посыла́ть (посла́ть* *perf)* кого́-н за чем-н; **to ~ word that ...** передава́ть* (переда́ть* *perf),* что ...; **she ~s (you) her love** она́ передаёт Вам приве́т; **to ~ sb to Coventry** *(BRIT)* объявля́ть (объяви́ть* *perf)* кому́-н бойко́т; **to ~ sb to sleep** нагоня́ть (нагна́ть* *perf)* на кого́-н сон; **to ~ sb into fits of laughter** смеши́ть (рассмеши́ть *perf)* кого́-н; **to ~ sth flying** рассе́ивать (рассе́ять *perf)* что-н в во́здухе

► **send away** *vt (letter, goods)* отправля́ть (отпра́вить* *perf),* отсыла́ть (отосла́ть* *perf);* *(unwelcome visitor)* прогоня́ть (прогна́ть* *perf)*

► **send away for** *vt fus* зака́зывать (заказа́ть* *perf)*

► **send back** *vt* посыла́ть (посла́ть* *perf)* обра́тно

► **send for** *vt fus (by post)* зака́зывать (заказа́ть* *perf);* *(person)* посыла́ть (посла́ть* *perf)* за +*instr*

► **send in** *vt (report)* представля́ть (предста́вить* *perf);* *(resignation, application)* подава́ть* (пода́ть* *perf)* заявле́ние о +*prp*

► **send off** *vt (goods)* отправля́ть (отпра́вить* *perf);* *(BRIT: SPORT: player)* удаля́ть (удали́ть* *perf)*

► **send on** *vt (BRIT: letter)* пересыла́ть (пересла́ть* *perf),* (: *luggage etc: in advance)* перепра́вливать (перепра́вить* *perf)*

► **send out** *vt (invitation)* рассыла́ть (разосла́ть* *perf);* *(heat, smell, light)* распространя́ть (распространи́ть *perf);* *(signal)* посыла́ть (посла́ть* *perf)*

► **send round** *vt (letter, document etc)* рассыла́ть (разосла́ть* *perf)*

► **send up** *vt (price, blood pressure)* поднима́ть (подня́ть* *perf);* *(astronaut)* запуска́ть (запусти́ть* *perf);* *(BRIT: parody)* высме́ивать (вы́смеять *perf).*

sender ['sɛndə'] *n* отправи́тель(ница) *m(f).*

sending-off ['sɛndɪŋˈɒf] *n* удале́ние с по́ля.

sendoff ['sɛndɒf] *n*: **a good send-off** хоро́шие про́воды *pl.*

send-up ['sɛndʌp] *n* паро́дия.

Senegal [sɛnɪ'gɔ:l] *n* Сенега́л.

Senegalese ['sɛnɪgə'li:z] *adj* сенега́льский ♦ *n inv* сенега́лец*(-лка*).

senile ['si:naɪl] *adj* маразмати́ческий.

senility [sɪ'nɪlɪtɪ] *n* ста́рческий мара́зм.

senior ['si:nɪə'] *adj (staff, officer)* ста́рший*;* *(manager, consultant)* гла́вный; *(of higher rank):* **to be ~ to sb** быть* *(impf)* вы́ше кого́-н по до́лжности; **the ~s** *npl (SCOL: at school)* старшекла́ссники *mpl;* (: *at college, university)* старшеку́рсники *mpl;* **he is 15 years his ~** она́ ста́рше его́ на 15 лет; **P. Jones ~** П. Джоунз ста́рший*.*

senior citizen *n (esp BRIT)* пожило́й челове́к*,*

челове́к* пенсио́нного во́зраста.

senior high school *n (US)* ≈ ста́ршие ку́рсы ко́лледжа.

seniority [si:nɪ'ɒrɪtɪ] *n* старшинство́.

sensation [sɛn'seɪʃən] *n (ability to feel)* чувстви́тельность *f;* *(feeling)* ощуще́ние; *(great success)* сенса́ция; **to cause a ~** вызыва́ть (вы́звать* *perf)* сенса́цию.

sensational [sɛn'seɪʃənl] *adj (wonderful)* потряса́ющий* (потрясающ); *(causing much interest)* сенсацио́нный* (сенсацио́нен).

sensationalize [sɛn'seɪʃnəlaɪz] *vt* де́лать (сде́лать *perf)* сенса́цию из +*gen.*

sense [sɛns] *vt (become aware of)* чу́вствовать (почу́вствовать *perf),* ощуща́ть (ощути́ть* *perf)* ♦ *n (feeling)* чу́вство, ощуще́ние; *(meaning of word)* смысл; *(also: good ~):* **it makes ~** в э́том есть смысл; **~s** *npl (sanity)* рассу́док* *msg;* **the ~s** пять чувств; **there is no ~ in that/in doing that** нет смы́сла в э́том/ де́лать э́то; **to come to one's ~s** образу́миться *(perf);* **to take leave of one's ~s** теря́ть (потеря́ть *perf)* рассу́док.

senseless ['sɛnslɪs] *adj (pointless)* бессмы́сленный* (бессмы́слен); *(unconscious)* без чувств.

sense of humour *(US* **sense of humor**) *n* чу́вство ю́мора.

sensibility [sɛnsɪ'bɪlɪtɪ] *n* чувстви́тельность *f.*

sensible ['sɛnsɪbl] *adj* разу́мный* (разу́мен); *(shoes)* практи́чный.

sensitive ['sɛnsɪtɪv] *adj* чувстви́тельный* (чувстви́телен); *(understanding)* чу́ткий* (чу́ток); *(issue)* щекотли́вый (щекотли́в); **~ to** чувстви́тельный* (чувстви́телен) к +*dat;* **he is very ~ about it** он отно́сится к э́тому о́чень боле́зненно.

sensitivity [sɛnsɪ'tɪvɪtɪ] *n (responsiveness)* чувстви́тельность *f;* *(understanding)* чу́ткость *f;* *(delicate nature: of issue etc)* щекотли́вость *f.*

sensual ['sɛnsjuəl] *adj (of the senses)* чу́вственный; *(sexual)* чу́вственный* (чу́вствен).

sensuous ['sɛnsjuəs] *adj (lips)* чу́вственный* (чу́вствен); *(material)* не́жный* (не́жен).

sent [sɛnt] *pt, pp of* **send.**

sentence ['sɛntns] *n (LING)* предложе́ние; *(LAW)* пригово́р ♦ *vt:* **to ~ sb to death/to five years in prison** пригова́ривать (приговори́ть* *perf)* кого́-н к сме́рти/к пяти́ года́м тюре́много заключе́ния; **to pass ~ on sb** выноси́ть* (вы́нести* *perf)* кому́-н пригово́р.

sentiment ['sɛntɪmənt] *n (tender feelings)* чу́вство; *(opinion)* мне́ние, настрое́ние.

sentimental [sɛntɪ'mɛntl] *adj* сентимента́льный* (сентимента́лен).

sentimentality ['sɛntɪmɛn'tælɪtɪ] *n* сентимента́льность *f.*

sentry ['sɛntrɪ] *n* часово́й *m adj,* карау́льный *m adj.*

sentry duty *n*: **to be on** ~ ~ нести* *(impf)* караўльную слўжбу.
Seoul [səul] *n* Сеўл.
separable ['sɛprəbl] *adj*: ~ **(from)** отделѝмый (отделѝм) (от +*gen*).
separate [*adj* 'sɛprɪt, *vb* 'sɛpəreɪt] *adj* отдѐльный; *(ways)* рѐзный ♦ *vt (split up: people)* разлучѐть (разлучѝть *perf*); (: *things*) разделѝть (разделѝть* *perf*); *(make a distinction between)* различѐть (различѝть *perf*) ♦ *vi* расходѝться* (разойтѝсь* *perf*); ~ **from** отдѐльно от +*gen*; **to ~ into** разделѝть (разделѝть* *perf*) на +*acc*; *see also* **separates**.
separately ['sɛprɪtlɪ] *adv* отдѐльно.
separates ['sɛprɪts] *npl (clothes)* предмѐты жѐнской одѐжды, не входѝщие в комплѐкт.
separation [sɛpə'reɪʃən] *n (being apart)* разлўка; *(LAW)* раздѐльное прожива́ние.
sepia ['si:pjə] *adj*: ~ **photograph** фотогра́фия, выполненная в те́хнике се́пии.
Sept. *abbr* = **September.**
September [sɛp'tɛmbəʳ] *n* сентя́брь* *m*; *see also* **July.**
septic ['sɛptɪk] *adj* заражённый* (заражён); **to go ~** заражѐться (заразѝться* *perf*).
septicaemia [sɛptɪ'si:mɪə] (*US* **septicemia**) *n* сѐпсис, септицемѝя.
septic tank *n* ≈ выгребна́я я́ма.
sequel ['si:kwl] *n* продолже́ние.
sequence ['si:kwəns] *n* послѐдовательность *f*; *(dance sequence)* комбина́ция; *(CINEMA)* эпизо́д; **in the correct ~** в пра́вильной послѐдовательности; ~ **of tenses** согласова́ние времён.
sequential [sɪ'kwɛnʃəl] *adj (process, link etc)* послѐдовательный* (послѐдователен); ~ **access** (*COMPUT*) послѐдовательный до́ступ.
sequestrate [sɪ'kwɛstreɪt] *vt* конфискова́ть (*impf/perf*).
sequin ['si:kwɪn] *n* блёстка*.
Serbia ['sə:bɪə] *n* Сѐрбия.
Serbian ['sə:bɪən] *n* серб(ка) ♦ *adj* сѐрбский*.
Serbo-Croat ['sə:bəu'krəuæt] *n* (*LING*) сербскохорва́тский язы́к*.
serenade [sɛrə'neɪd] *n* серена́да ♦ *vt* петь* (спеть* *perf*) серена́ду +*dat*.
serene [sɪ'ri:n] *adj* безмяте́жный* (безмяте́жен).
serenity [sə'rɛnɪtɪ] *n* безмяте́жность *f*.
sergeant ['sɑ:dʒənt] *n* сержа́нт.
sergeant major *n* = ста́рший сержа́нт.
serial ['sɪərɪəl] *n* (*TV*, *RADIO*) сериа́л; *(in magazine)* рома́н, печа́тающийся в не́скольких частя́х ♦ *adj* (*COMPUT*) послѐдовательный; ~ **printer** посимво́льно печа́тающее устро́йство.
serialize ['sɪərɪəlaɪz] *vt (story, book: in print)* тиражи́ровать (*impf*) частя́ми; (: *on TV*, *RADIO*)

ста́вить* (поста́вить* *perf*) сериа́л по +*prp*.
serial killer *n* манья́к *(совершивший многочисленные убийства).*
serial number *n* сери́йный но́мер*.
series ['sɪərɪz] *n inv* се́рия.
serious ['sɪərɪəs] *adj* серьёзный* (серьёзен); **are you ~ (about it)?** Вы (это) серьёзно?
seriously ['sɪərɪəslɪ] *adv* серьёзно; **to take sb/ sth ~** принима́ть (восприни́мать *perf*) кого́-н/что-н серьёзно.
seriousness ['sɪərɪəsnɪs] *n* серьёзность *f*.
sermon ['sə:mən] *n (also fig)* про́поведь *f*.
serrated [sɪ'reɪtɪd] *adj* зазу́бренный.
serum ['sɪərəm] *n* сы́воротка.
servant ['sə:vənt] *n (male)* слуга́ *m*; *(female)* служа́нка; *(fig)* слуга́*.
serve [sə:v] *vt (company, country)* служи́ть* *(impf)* +*dat*; *(customer: in shop, restaurant)* обслу́живать (обслужи́ть* *perf*); *(purpose)* служи́ть* (послужи́ть *(impf)*) +*dat*; *(food, goods: to sb)* подава́ть* (пода́ть* *perf*); (*subj: train etc*) обслу́живать *(impf)*; *(apprenticeship)* проходи́ть* (пройти́* *perf*); *(prison term)* отбыва́ть (отбы́ть* *perf*) ♦ *vi (at table)* прислу́живать *(impf)*; (*TENNIS*) подава́ть* (пода́ть* *perf*); *(soldier etc)* служи́ть* *(impf)* ♦ *n* (*TENNIS*) пода́ча; **are you being ~d?** Вас уже́ обслу́живают?; **it ~s my purpose** это мне подхо́дит; **it ~s him right** поде́лом ему́; **to ~ on a committee/jury** состоя́ть *(impf)* в комите́те/жюри́; **to ~ as/for** служи́ть* (послужи́ть *perf*) +*instr*/вме́сто +*gen*
▶ **serve out** *vt (food)* раскла́дывать (разложи́ть* *perf*)
▶ **serve up** *vi* = **serve out.**
service ['sə:vɪs] *n (help)* услу́га; *(in hotel)* обслу́живание, се́рвис; *(REL)* слу́жба; *(AUT)* техобслу́живание; *(TENNIS)* пода́ча; *(dinner set etc)* серви́з ♦ *vt (car, washing machine)* проводи́ть* (провести́* *perf*) техобслу́живание +*gen*; **the S~s** *npl (army, navy etc)* Вооружённые си́лы *fpl*; **military** *or* **national ~** вое́нная слу́жба; **train ~** железнодоро́жное сообще́ние; **postal ~** почто́вая связь; **how can I be of ~ (to you)?** чем могу́ быть* поле́зен?; **to do sb a ~** ока́зывать (оказа́ть* *perf*) кому́-н услу́гу; **to put one's car in for ~** отдава́ть* (отда́ть* *perf*) маши́ну на техобслу́живание.
serviceable ['sə:vɪsəbl] *adj* про́чный* (про́чен).
service area *n (on motorway)* се́рвисная ста́нция.
service charge *n (BRIT)* (рестора́нная) наце́нка.
service industry *n* сфе́ра услу́г.
serviceman ['sə:vɪsmən] *irreg n* вое́нно-служа́щий* *m adj*.
service station *n (AUT)* ста́нция

техобслу́живания.
serviette [sɔːvɪˈɛt] *n* (*BRIT*) салфе́тка*.
servile [ˈsɔːvaɪl] *adj* подобостра́стный*
(подобостра́стен).
session [ˈsɛʃən] *n* (*sitting*) се́ссия; (*SCOL*:
academic year) уче́бный год*; **recording ~**
за́пись *f*; **drinking ~** запо́й; **to be in ~** (*court
etc*) заседа́ть (*impf*).
session musician *n* музыка́нт, кото́рого
приглаша́ют на за́писи в ра́зные анса́мбли.
set [sɛt] (*pt, pp* **set**) *n* (*collection*) набо́р; (*of
saucepans, clothes*) компле́кт; (*of books*)
многото́мник; (*also*: **radio ~**)
радиоприёмник; (*also*: **television ~**)
телеви́зор; (*TENNIS*) сет; (*group of people*)
круг*, о́бщество; (*MATH*) мно́жество;
(*CINEMA, THEAT*: *stage*) сце́на; (: *scenery*)
(худо́жественное) оформле́ние; (*hairdo*)
укла́дка ♦ *adj* (*fixed*) устано́вленный; (*ready*)
гото́вый (гото́в) ♦ *vt* (*place*: *vertically*)
ста́вить* (поста́вить* *perf*); (: *horizontally*)
класть* (положи́ть* *perf*); (*table*) накрыва́ть
(накры́ть* *perf*); (*time*) назнача́ть (назна́чить
perf); (*price, rule, record*) устана́вливать
(установи́ть* *perf*); (*alarm, watch, task*)
ста́вить* (поста́вить* *perf*); (*exam*)
составля́ть (соста́вить* *perf*); (*TYP*) набира́ть
(набра́ть* *perf*) ♦ *vi* (*sun*) сади́ться* (сесть*
perf), заходи́ть* (зайти́* *perf*); (*jam*) густе́ть
(загусте́ть *perf*); (*jelly, concrete*) застыва́ть
(засты́ть* *perf*); (*bone*) вправля́ться
(впра́виться* *perf*); **a ~ of false teeth** вставны́е
зу́бы* *mpl*; **a ~ of dining-room furniture**
столо́вый гарниту́р; **a chess ~** ша́хматы *pl*;
to be ~ on doing настра́иваться
(настро́иться *perf*) +*infin*; **to be all ~ to do**
собира́ться (*impf*) +*infin*; **to be (dead) ~ against**
быть* (*impf*) (категори́чески) про́тив +*gen*;
he's ~ in his ways у него́ устоя́вшиеся
привы́чки; **the novel is ~ in Rome** де́йствие
рома́на происхо́дит в Ри́ме; **a ~ phrase**
усто́йчивое словосочета́ние; **to ~ to music**
класть* (положи́ть* *perf*) на му́зыку; **to ~ on
fire** поджига́ть (подже́чь* *perf*); **to ~ free**
освобожда́ть (освободи́ть* *perf*); **to ~ sth
going** приводи́ть* (привести́* *perf*) что-н в
де́йствие; **to ~ sail** отплыва́ть (отплы́ть*
perf)
▶ **set about** *vt fus* (*task*) приступа́ть
(приступи́ть* *perf*) к +*dat*; **to ~ about doing**
принима́ться (приня́ться* *perf*) +*infin*
▶ **set aside** *vt* (*money*) откла́дывать
(отложи́ть* *perf*); (*time*) выделя́ть (вы́делить
perf)
▶ **set back** *vt* (*progress*) заде́рживать
(задержа́ть* *perf*); (*cost*): **to ~ sb back £5**
обходи́ться* (обойти́сь* *perf*) кому́-н в £5; (*in
time*): **to ~ sb back (by)** заде́рживать
(задержа́ть* *perf*) кого́-н (на +*acc*); (*place*):
the house is ~ back from the road дом
нахо́дится в стороне́ от доро́ги

▶ **set in** *vi* (*infection*) внедря́ться (внедри́ться
perf); (*bad weather*) устана́вливаться
(установи́ться* *perf*); (*complications*)
начина́ться (нача́ться* *perf*); **the rain has ~ in
for the day** дождь заряди́л на весь день
▶ **set off** *vi* отправля́ться (отпра́виться* *perf*) ♦
vt (*bomb*) взрыва́ть (взорва́ть* *perf*); (*alarm*)
приводи́ть* (привести́* *perf*) в де́йствие;
(*chain of events*) вызыва́ть (вы́звать* *perf*);
(*show up well*) подчёркивать (*impf*)
▶ **set out** *vt* (*goods etc*) расставля́ть
(расста́вить* *perf*); (*arguments*) излага́ть
(изложи́ть* *perf*) ♦ *vi* (*depart*): **to ~ out (from)**
отправля́ться (отпра́виться* *perf*) (из +*gen*);
to ~ out to do намерева́ться (*impf*) +*infin*
▶ **set up** *vt* (*organization*) учрежда́ть
(учреди́ть* *perf*); (*monument*) устана́вливать
(установи́ть* *perf*); **to ~ up shop** (*fig*)
открыва́ть (откры́ть* *perf*) своё де́ло.
setback [ˈsɛtbæk] *n* (*hitch*) неуда́ча; (*in health*)
ухудше́ние.
set menu *n* ко́мплексное меню́ *nt ind*.
set square *n* уго́льник.
settee [sɛˈtiː] *n* дива́н.
setting [ˈsɛtɪŋ] *n* (*background*) обстано́вка*;
(*position*: *of controls*) положе́ние; (*of sun*)
зака́т, захо́д; (*of jewel*) опра́ва.
setting lotion *n* (*for hair*) лосьо́н для укла́дки
воло́с.
settle [ˈsɛtl] *vt* (*argument, problem*) разреша́ть
(разреши́ть* *perf*); (*matter*) ула́живать
(ула́дить* *perf*); (*accounts*) рассчи́тываться
(рассчита́ться *perf*) с +*instr*; (*colonize*: *land*)
заселя́ть (засели́ть *perf*) ♦ *vi* (*also*: **~ down**:
somewhere) обосно́вываться (*perf*); (: *live
sensibly*) остепеня́ться (*perf*); (*bird*) сади́ться*
(сесть* *perf*); (*dust, sediment*) оседа́ть
(осе́сть* *perf*); (*calm down*) успока́иваться
(успоко́иться *perf*); **to ~ one's stomach**
успока́ивать (успоко́ить *perf*) желу́док; **to ~
down to sth** уса́живаться (усе́сться* *perf*) за
что-н; **to ~ for sth** соглаша́ться
(согласи́ться* *perf*) на что-н; **to ~ on sth**
остана́вливаться (останови́ться* *perf*) на
чём-н
▶ **settle in** *vi* осва́иваться (осво́иться *perf*)
▶ **settle up** *vi*: **to ~ up with sb** рассчи́тываться
(рассчита́ться *perf*) с кем-н.
settlement [ˈsɛtlmənt] *n* (*payment*) упла́та;
(*agreement*) соглаше́ние; (*village, colony*)
поселе́ние; (*of conflict*) урегули́рование; **in ~
of our account** (*COMM*) для опла́ты на́шего
счёта.
settler [ˈsɛtləʳ] *n* поселе́нец*(-нка*).
setup [ˈsɛtʌp] *n* (*organization*) устро́йство;
(*situation*) положе́ние дел.
seven [ˈsɛvn] *n* семь*; *see also* **five**.
seventeen [sɛvnˈtiːn] *n* семна́дцать*; *see also*
five.
seventeenth [sɛvnˈtiːnθ] *adj* семна́дцатый; *see
also* **fifth**.

seventh ['sɛvnθ] *adj* седьмо́й; *see also* **fifth**.
seventieth ['sɛvntɪɪθ] *adj* семидеся́тый; *see also* **fifth**.
seventy ['sɛvntɪ] *n* се́мьдесят*; *see also* **fifty**.
sever ['sɛvə'] *vt* (*artery, pipe*) перереза́ть (перере́зать* *perf*); (*relations*) прерыва́ть (прерва́ть* *perf*); (*ties, connections*) обрыва́ть (оборва́ть* *perf*).
several ['sɛvərl] *adj* не́сколько +*gen* ♦ *pron* не́которые *pl adj*; ~ **of us** не́которые из нас; ~ **times** не́сколько раз.
severance ['sɛvərəns] *n* разры́в.
severance pay *n* выходно́е посо́бие (*при сокраще́нии шта́тов*).
severe [sɪ'vɪə'] *adj* (*shortage, pain, winter*) жесто́кий* (жесто́к); (*damage*) серьёзный (серьёзен); (*stern*) жёсткий* (жёсток); (*plain: dress*) стро́гий* (строг).
severely [sɪ'vɪəlɪ] *adv* (*punish*) жесто́ко; (*look*) жёстко; (*damaged*) серьёзно; (*wounded, ill*) тяжело́.
severity [sɪ'vɛrɪtɪ] *n* жесто́кость *f*; (*of damage*) серьёзность *f*; (*of illness*) тя́жесть *f*.
sew [səu] (*pt* **sewed**, *pp* **sewn**) *vti* шить* (*impf*)
▶ **sew up** *vt* (*clothes*) зашива́ть (заши́ть* *perf*); **it is all ~n up** (*fig*) де́ло на мази́.
sewage ['su:ɪdʒ] *n* (*waste*) сто́чные во́ды* *fpl*; ~ **system** канализа́ция.
sewage works *n* канализацио́нные очисти́тельные сооруже́ния *npl*.
sewer ['su:ə'] *n* канализацио́нная труба́*.
sewing ['səuɪŋ] *n* шитьё.
sewing machine *n* шве́йная маши́на.
sewn [səun] *pp of* **sew**.
sex [sɛks] *n* (*gender*) пол; (*lovemaking*) секс; **both ~es** о́ба по́ла; **to have ~ with sb** переспа́ть* (*perf*) с кем-н.
sex act *n* сексуа́льный акт.
sex appeal *n* сексопи́льность *f*, сексуа́льная привлека́тельность *f*; **he's got a lot of ~ ~** он о́чень сексопи́льный.
sex education *n* сексуа́льное воспита́ние.
sexism ['sɛksɪzəm] *n* предубежде́ние к ли́цам противополо́жного по́ла.
sexist ['sɛksɪst] *adj* сексистский ♦ *n* сексист.
sex life *n* полова́я *or* сексуа́льная жизнь *f*.
sex object *n* сексуа́льный объе́кт.
sextet [sɛks'tɛt] *n* (*group*) секстет.
sexual ['sɛksjuəl] *adj* (*reproduction, equality*) полово́й; (*attraction, relationship*) сексуа́льный* (сексуа́лен), полово́й; ~ **equality** ра́венство поло́в.
sexual assault *n* сексуа́льное посяга́тельство, нападе́ние с сексуа́льным моти́вом.

sexual harassment *n* сексуа́льное пресле́дование.
sexual intercourse *n* полово́й акт.
sexually ['sɛksjuəlɪ] *adv* (*attractive, attract*) сексуа́льно; (*segregated*) в зави́симости от по́ла; (*discriminate*) по полово́му при́знаку; (*reproduce*) половы́м путём.
sexual orientation *n* сексуа́льная ориента́ция.
sexy ['sɛksɪ] *adj* (*person, voice*) сексуа́льный* (сексуа́лен).
Seychelles [seɪ'ʃɛl(z)] *npl*: **the** ~ Сейше́льские острова́ *mpl*.
SF *n abbr* (= **science fiction**) НФ= *нау́чная фанта́стика*.
SG *n abbr* (*US*: *MIL*, *MED*: = *Surgeon General*) ≈ начмед= *нача́льник медици́нской слу́жбы*.
Sgt *abbr* (*POLICE*, *MIL*) = **sergeant**.
shabbiness ['ʃæbɪnɪs] *n* запу́щенность *f*.
shabby ['ʃæbɪ] *adj* (*person*) обтрёпанный; (*clothes*) потрёпанный (потрёпан); (*treatment, behaviour*) недосто́йный* (недосто́ен); (*building*) ве́тхий* (ветх).
shack [ʃæk] *n* лачу́га
▶ **shack up** *vi* (*inf*): **to ~ up (with sb)** нача́ть* (*perf*) сожи́тельствовать (с +*instr*).
shackles ['ʃæklz] *npl* (*also fig*) око́вы *pl*.
shade [ʃeɪd] *n* (*shelter*) тень* *f*; (*for lamp*) абажу́р; (*of colour*) отте́нок* (*US*: *also*: **window** ~) што́ра ♦ *vt* (*shelter*) затеня́ть (затени́ть *perf*); (*eyes*) заслоня́ть (заслони́ть* *perf*); **~s** *npl* (*inf*: **sunglasses**) тёмные очки́ *pl*; **in the** ~ в тени́; **a** ~ (*more/too large*) чу́точку (бо́льше/велика́т).
shadow ['ʃædəu] *n* тень* *f* ♦ *vt* (*follow*) ходи́ть* (*impf*) как тень за +*instr*; **without** *or* **beyond a** ~ **of a doubt** без тени сомне́ния.
shadow cabinet *n* (*BRIT*: *POL*) тенево́й кабине́т.
shadowy ['ʃædəuɪ] *adj* (*place*) тени́стый (тени́ст); (*figure, shape*) сму́тный* (смутен).
shady ['ʃeɪdɪ] *adj* (*place, trees*) тени́стый (тени́ст); (*fig: dishonest*) тёмный* (тёмен).
shaft [ʃɑ:ft] *n* (*of arrow, spear*) дре́вко*; (*AUT*, *TECH*) вал; (*of mine, lift*) ша́хта; (*of light*) сноп*; **ventilation** ~ вентиляцио́нная труба́*.
shag [ʃæg] *vt* (*inf!*) тра́хать (тра́хнуть *perf*) (*!*) ♦ *vi* (*inf!*) тра́хаться (тра́хнуться *perf*) (*!*) ♦ *n* (*also*: ~ **tobacco**) махо́рка; (*ZOOL*) длиннохво́стый бакла́н; (*inf!*): **to have a** ~ тра́хнуться (*perf*).
shaggy ['ʃægɪ] *adj* лохма́тый (лохма́т).
shake [ʃeɪk] (*pt* **shook**, *pp* **shaken**) *vt* трясти́* (*impf*); (*bottle*) взба́лтывать (взболта́ть *perf*); (*building*) сотряса́ть (сотрясти́* *perf*); (*weaken: beliefs, resolve*) пошатну́ть (*perf*); (*upset, surprise*) потряса́ть (потрясти́* *perf*) ♦ *vi* (*voice*) дрожа́ть (*impf*) ♦ *n* (*movement*)

---

* marks translations which have irregular inflections The Russian-English side of the dictionary gives inflectional information.

дрожа́ние; **to ~ one's head** кача́ть (покача́ть *perf*) голово́й; **to ~ hands with sb** жать* (пожа́ть* *perf*) кому́-н ру́ку; **to ~ with** +*gen*; трясти́сь* (*impf*) от +*gen*; **give the bottle a good ~** хорошо́ взболта́йте буты́лку
▶ **shake off** *vt* стря́хивать (стряхну́ть *perf*); (*fig: pursuer*) избавля́ться (изба́виться* *perf*) от +*gen*
▶ **shake up** *vt* (*ingredients*) взба́лтывать (взболта́ть *perf*); (*fig: organization*) встря́хивать (встряхну́ть *perf*).
shaken ['ʃeɪkn] *pp of* **shake**.
shake-out ['ʃeɪkaut] *n* перетря́ска.
shake-up ['ʃeɪkʌp] *n* встря́ска*.
shakily ['ʃeɪkɪlɪ] *adv* (*reply*) с дро́жью в го́лосе; (*walk*) шата́ясь; (*write*) дрожа́щей руко́й.
shaky ['ʃeɪkɪ] *adj* (*hand, voice*) дрожа́щий; (*table, knowledge*) ша́ткий* (ша́ток); (*memory*) непро́чный* (непро́чен); (*prospects, future*) неопределённый*; (*start*) неуве́ренный*; **his voice was ~** го́лос его́ дрожа́л.
shale [ʃeɪl] *n* сла́нец*.
shall [ʃæl] *aux vb*: **I ~ go** я пойду́; **~ I open the door?** (мне) откры́ть дверь?; **I'll get some, ~ I?** я принесу́ немно́го, да?
shallot [ʃə'lɔt] *n* (*BRIT*) лук-шало́т *no pl*.
shallow ['ʃæləu] *adj* (*water*) ме́лкий*; (*box*) неглубо́кий*; (*breathing, also fig*) пове́рхностный* (пове́рхностен).
sham [ʃæm] *n* притво́рство; (*jewellery, furniture*) подде́лка* ♦ *vt* притворя́ться (притвори́ться* *perf*) +*instr*.
shambles ['ʃæmblz] *n* неразбери́ха; **the economy is (in) a complete ~** в эконо́мике цари́т по́лная неразбери́ха.
shambolic [ʃæm'bɔlɪk] *adj* (*inf*) хаоти́чный* (хаоти́чен).
shame [ʃeɪm] *n* (*embarrassment*) стыд*; (*disgrace*) позо́р ♦ *vt* позо́рить (опозо́рить *perf*); **it is a ~ that/to do** жаль, что/+*infin*; **what a ~!** кака́я жа́лость!, как жаль!; **to put sb to ~** (*fig*) заставля́ть (заста́вить* *perf*) кого́-н устыди́ться; **your work puts mine to ~** моя́ рабо́та бледне́ет в сравне́нии с Ва́шей.
shamefaced ['ʃeɪmfeɪst] *adj* устыжённый*.
shameful ['ʃeɪmful] *adj* позо́рный* (позо́рен).
shameless ['ʃeɪmlɪs] *adj* бессты́дный* (бессты́ден).
shampoo [ʃæm'pu:] *n* шампу́нь *m* ♦ *vt* мыть* (помы́ть* *or* вы́мыть* *perf*) шампу́нем.
shampoo and set *n* мытьё и укла́дка воло́с.
shamrock ['ʃæmrɔk] *n* трили́стник, кисли́ца.
shandy ['ʃændɪ] *n* смесь пи́ва с лимона́дом.
shan't [ʃɑ:nt] = **shall not**.
shanty town ['ʃæntɪ-] *n* трущо́бы *fpl*.
SHAPE [ʃeɪp] *n abbr* (*MIL*: = *Supreme Headquarters Allied Powers, Europe*) Штаб верхо́вного главнокома́ндующего НАТО в Евро́пе.
shape [ʃeɪp] *n* фо́рма ♦ *vt* (*fashion, ideas,*

events) формирова́ть (сформирова́ть *perf*); (*clay*) лепи́ть* (слепи́ть* *perf*); (*statement*) оформля́ть (офо́рмить* *perf*); **to take ~** (*painting, plan etc*) обрета́ть (обрести́* *perf*) фо́рму; **I can't bear gardening in any ~ or form** я не выношу́ садо́водства ни в како́й фо́рме; **to get o.s. into ~** приводи́ть* (привести́* *perf*) себя́, входи́ть* (войти́* *perf*) в фо́рму
▶ **shape up** *vi* (*events*) скла́дываться (сложи́ться* *perf*); (*person*) формирова́ться (сформирова́ться *perf*).
-shaped [ʃeɪpt] *suffix*: **heart~** сердцеви́дный*.
shapeless ['ʃeɪplɪs] *adj* бесфо́рменный (бесфо́рмен).
shapely ['ʃeɪplɪ] *adj* (*woman*) хорошо́ сло́женный (сло́жен); (*legs*) краси́вый (краси́в).
share [ʃɛə'] *n* до́ля*; (*COMM*) а́кция ♦ *vt* (*books, cost*) дели́ть* (раздели́ть* *or* подели́ть* *perf*); (*toys*) дели́ться* (подели́ться* *perf*) +*instr*; (*features, qualities etc*) разделя́ть (*impf*); (*opinion, concern*) разделя́ть (раздели́ть* *perf*); **to ~ in** (*joy, sorrow*) дели́ться* (раздели́ться* *perf*); (*profits*) дели́ться* (подели́ться* *perf*); (*work*) уча́ствовать (*impf*) в +*prp*
▶ **share out** *vt* дели́ть* (раздели́ть* *perf*).
share capital *n* акционе́рный капита́л.
share certificate *n* сертифика́т а́кции.
shareholder ['ʃɛəhəuldə'] *n* акционе́р.
share index *n* (*COMM*) фо́ндовый и́ндекс.
share issue *n* (*COMM*) вы́пуск а́кции.
shareware ['ʃɛəwɛə'] *n* програ́ммное обеспе́чение о́бщего по́льзования.
shark [ʃɑ:k] *n* аку́ла.
sharp [ʃɑ:p] *adj* ре́зкий* (ре́зок); (*knife, teeth, nose*) о́стрый* (остр); (*curve, bend*) круто́й* (крут); (*MUS*) дие́з; (*dishonest: practice etc*) ло́вкий* (ло́вок) ♦ *n* (*MUS*) дие́з ♦ *adv* (*precisely*): **at 2 o'clock ~** ро́вно в два часа́; **he is very ~** у него́ о́чень о́стрый ум; **he was rather ~ with her** он был дово́льно ре́зок с ней; **look ~!** поторопи́тесь!; **C ~** (*MUS*) до-дие́з.
sharpen ['ʃɑ:pn] *vt* (*stick etc*) заостря́ть (заостри́ть *perf*); (*pencil, knife*) точи́ть* (поточи́ть* *perf*); (*fig: appetite*) уси́ливать (уси́лить *perf*).
sharpener ['ʃɑ:pnə'] *n* (*also*: **pencil ~**) точи́лка*; (*also*: **knife ~**) точи́ло.
sharp-eyed [ʃɑ:p'aɪd] *adj* (*person*) зо́ркий* (зо́рок).
sharpish ['ʃɑ:pɪʃ] *adv* (*inf*) бы́стренько.
sharply ['ʃɑ:plɪ] *adv* ре́зко.
sharp-tempered [ʃɑ:p'tɛmpəd] *adj* (*person*) вспы́льчивый (вспы́льчив).
sharp-witted [ʃɑ:p'wɪtɪd] *adj* (*person*) сообрази́тельный* (сообрази́телен).
shatter ['ʃætə'] *vt* (*vase, hopes*) разбива́ть (разби́ть* *perf*); (*fig: nerves*) надрыва́ть

(надорва́ть* *perf*); (: *person*) потряса́ть
(потрясти́* *perf*) ♦ *vi* би́ться* (разби́ться*
perf).

shattered ['ʃætəd] *adj* (*overwhelmed, grief-
stricken*) потрясённый (потрясён); (*inf*:
exhausted) разби́тый (разби́т).

shattering ['ʃætərɪŋ] *adj* (*experience*) тя́жкий*;
(*day*) утоми́тельный* (утоми́телен).

shatterproof ['ʃætəpru:f] *adj* небью́щийся.

shave [ʃeɪv] *vt* брить* (побри́ть* *perf*) ♦ *vi*
бри́ться* (побри́ться* *perf*) ♦ *n*: **to have a ~**
бри́ться* (побри́ться* *perf*).

shaven ['ʃeɪvn] *adj* бри́тый (брит).

shaver ['ʃeɪvə'] *n* (*also:* **electric ~**)
(электри́ческая) бри́тва.

shaver point *n* розе́тка* для бри́твы.

shaving ['ʃeɪvɪŋ] *n* бритьё; **~s** *npl* (*of wood etc*)
стру́жки* *fpl*.

shaving brush *n* ки́сточка* для бритья́,
помазо́к*.

shaving cream *n* крем для бритья́.

shaving foam *n* крем для бритья́.

shaving soap *n* крем для бритья́.

shawl [ʃɔ:l] *n* шаль *f*.

she [ʃi:] *pron* она́.

sheaf [ʃi:f] (*pl* **sheaves**) *n* (*of corn*) сноп*; (*of
papers*) сто́пка*.

shear [ʃɪə'] (*pt* **sheared**, *pp* **shorn**) *vt* (*sheep*)
стричь* (постри́чь* *or* остри́чь* *perf*)

▸ **shear off** *vi* (*bolt etc*) надла́мываться
(надломи́ться* *perf*).

shears ['ʃɪəz] *npl* (*for hedge*) садо́вые
но́жницы *pl*.

sheath [ʃi:θ] *n* (*of knife*) но́жны* *pl*;
(*contraceptive*) презервати́в.

sheathe [ʃi:ð] *vt* (*sword, knife etc*) вкла́дывать
(вложи́ть* *perf*) в но́жны.

sheath knife *n* фи́нка*.

sheaves [ʃi:vz] *npl of* **sheaf**.

shed [ʃed] (*pt, pp* **shed**) *n* сара́й; (*INDUSTRY, RAIL*)
наве́с ♦ *vt* (*skin, load*) сбра́сывать (сбро́сить*
perf); (*tears*) лить* (*impf*); (*blood*) пролива́ть
(проли́ть* *perf*); (*workers*) увольня́ть
(уво́лить* *perf*); **to ~ light on** пролива́ть
(проли́ть* *perf*) свет на +*acc*.

she'd [ʃi:d] = **she had**, **she would**.

sheen [ʃi:n] *n* лоск.

sheep [ʃi:p] *n inv* овца́*; (*male*) бара́н.

sheepdog ['ʃi:pdɔg] *n* овча́рка*.

sheep farmer *n* овцево́д.

sheepish ['ʃi:pɪʃ] *adj* ро́бкий* (ро́бок).

sheepskin ['ʃi:pskɪn] *n* овчи́на ♦ *cpd* (*jacket,
mittens*) овчи́нный; **~ coat** (*short*)
дублёный полушу́бок; (*long*) дублённая
шу́ба, дублёнка (*разг*).

sheer [ʃɪə'] *adj* (*utter*) су́щий*; (*steep*)
отве́сный; (*almost transparent*) сквозно́й ♦
adv (*straight up or down*) отве́сно; **by ~ chance**

по чи́стой случа́йности.

sheet [ʃi:t] *n* (*on bed*) простыня́*; (*of paper,
metal, glass*) лист*; (*of ice*) полоса́*.

sheet feed *n* (*on printer*) автопода́ча бума́ги.

sheet lightning *n* зарни́ца.

sheet metal *n* листово́й мета́лл.

sheet music *n* но́ты *fpl*.

sheik(h) [ʃeɪk] *n* шейх.

shelf [ʃelf] (*pl* **shelves**) *n* по́лка*.

shelf life *n* срок го́дности.

shell [ʃel] *n* (*of mollusc*) ра́ковина; (*of egg, nut*)
скорлупа́; (*explosive*) снаря́д; (*of building*)
карка́с; (*of ship*) ко́рпус ♦ *vt* (*peas*) лущи́ть
(облущи́ть* *perf*); (*MIL: fire on*) обстре́ливать
(обстреля́ть* *perf*)

▸ **shell out** *vt* (*inf*): **to ~ out (for)** выкла́дывать
(вы́ложить* *perf*) (на +*acc*).

she'll [ʃi:l] = **she will**, **she shall**.

shellfish ['ʃelfɪʃ] *n inv* (*crab etc*) рачки́ *pl*;
(*scallop etc*) моллю́ски *mpl*.

shellsuit ['ʃelsu:t] *n* спорти́вный костю́м
(*капро́новый на покла́дке*).

shelter ['ʃeltə'] *n* (*refuge*) прию́т; (*protection*)
укры́тие; (*also:* **air-raid ~**) бомбоубе́жище ♦
vt (*protect*) укрыва́ть (укры́ть* *perf*); (*give
lodging to*) дава́ть* (дать* *perf*) прию́т +*dat* ♦
vi укрыва́ться (укры́ться* *perf*); **to take ~
(from)** приюти́ться* (*perf*) (от +*gen*).

sheltered ['ʃeltəd] *adj* (*life*) беззабо́тный;
(*spot*) защищённый (защищён).

sheltered housing *n* жили́щный ко́мплекс,
специа́льно приспосо́бленный для нужд
престаре́лых, инвали́дов итп.

shelve [ʃelv] *vt* (*fig: plan*) класть* (положи́ть*
perf) под сукно́.

shelves ['ʃelvz] *npl of* **shelf**.

shelving ['ʃelvɪŋ] *n* (*shelves*) стелла́ж*.

shepherd ['ʃepəd] *n* пасту́х* ♦ *vt* (*guide*)
направля́ть (напра́вить* *perf*).

shepherdess ['ʃepədɪs] *n* пасту́шка*.

shepherd's pie *n* (*BRIT*) ≈ запека́нка* из мя́са и
карто́феля.

sherbet ['ʃə:bət] *n* шербе́т; (*US: water ice*)
фрукто́вое моро́женое *nt adj*.

sheriff ['ʃerɪf] *n* (*US*) шери́ф.

sherry ['ʃerɪ] *n* хе́рес*.

she's [ʃi:z] = **she is**, **she has**.

Shetland ['ʃetlənd] *n* (*also:* **the ~ Islands**)
Шетла́ндские острова́* *mpl*.

Shetland pony *n* шетла́ндский по́ни *m ind*.

shield [ʃi:ld] *n* (*protection, also MIL*) щит*;
(*trophy*) трофе́й ♦ *vt*: **to ~ (from)** заслоня́ть
(заслони́ть* *perf*) (от +*gen*).

shift [ʃɪft] *n* (*in direction, conversation*)
переме́на; (*in policy, emphasis*) сдвиг; (*at
work*) сме́на ♦ *vt* передвига́ть (передви́нуть*
perf), перемеща́ть (перемести́ть* *perf*); (*stain*)
выводи́ть* (вы́вести* *perf*) ♦ *vi* перемеща́ться

---

* marks translations which have irregular inflections. The Russian-English side of the dictionary gives inflectional information.

(перемести́ться* *perf*); **a ~ in demand** измене́ние в спро́се; **the wind has ~ed to the south** ве́тер перемени́лся к ю́гу.

shift key *n* реги́стровая кла́виша.

shiftless ['ʃɪftlɪs] *adj* (*person*) безде́йственный.

shiftwork ['ʃɪftwɜːk] *n* сме́нная рабо́та; **to do ~** рабо́тать (*impf*) посме́нно.

shifty ['ʃɪftɪ] *adj* (*person*) увёртливый (увёртлив); (*eyes*) бега́ющий.

Shiite ['ʃiːaɪt] *n* шии́т ♦ *adj* шии́тский.

shilling ['ʃɪlɪŋ] *n* (*BRIT*) ши́ллинг.

shillyshally ['ʃɪlɪʃælɪ] *vi* тяну́ть* (*impf*).

shimmer ['ʃɪmə'] *vi* мерца́ть (*impf*).

shimmering ['ʃɪmərɪŋ] *adj* мерца́ющий; (*satin etc*) перелива́ющийся.

shin [ʃɪn] *n* го́лень *f* ♦ *vi*: **to ~ up a tree** влеза́ть (влезть* *perf*) на де́рево; **to ~ down a tree** слеза́ть (слезть* *perf*) с де́рева.

shindig ['ʃɪndɪg] *n* (*inf*) сабанту́й.

shine [ʃaɪn] (*pt, pp* **shone**) *n* блеск ♦ *vi* (*sun, light*) свети́ть* (*impf*); (*eyes, hair*) блесте́ть* (*impf*); (*fig: person*) сия́ть (*impf*), свети́ться* (*impf*) ♦ *vt* (*polish*) (*pt, pp* **shined**) натира́ть (натере́ть* *perf*); **to ~ a torch on sth** свети́ть* (посвети́ть* *perf*) фонарём на что-н.

shingle ['ʃɪŋgl] *n* (*on beach*) га́лька; (*on roof*) кро́вельная дра́нка.

shingles ['ʃɪŋglz] *n* опоя́сывающий лиша́й*.

shining ['ʃaɪnɪŋ] *adj* блестя́щий*.

shiny ['ʃaɪnɪ] *adj* блестя́щий*.

ship [ʃɪp] *n* кора́бль* *m* ♦ *vt* (*transport*) перевози́ть* (перевезти́* *perf*) по мо́рю; (*send*) экспеди́ровать (*impf/perf*); (*water*) забира́ть (забра́ть* *perf*); **on board ~** на борту́ корабля́.

shipbuilder ['ʃɪpbɪldə'] *n* кораблестрои́тель *m*, судострои́тель *m*.

shipbuilding ['ʃɪpbɪldɪŋ] *n* кораблестрое́ние, судострое́ние.

ship canal *n* судохо́дный кана́л.

ship chandler [-'tʃɑːndlə'] *n* поставщи́к корабе́льного обору́дования.

shipment ['ʃɪpmənt] *n* (*goods*) па́ртия.

shipowner ['ʃɪpəunə'] *n* судовладе́лец*.

shipper ['ʃɪpə'] *n* отправи́тель *m*.

shipping ['ʃɪpɪŋ] *n* (*transport of cargo*) перево́зка; (*ships*) судохо́дство.

shipping agent *n* экспеди́тор.

shipping company *n* судохо́дная компа́ния.

shipping lane *n* морска́я тра́сса.

shipping line *n* = **shipping company**.

shipshape ['ʃɪpʃeɪp] *adj* (*house, boat etc*) ла́дный.

ship's manifest *n* деклара́ция судово́го гру́за.

shipwreck ['ʃɪprɛk] *n* (*event*) корабле-круше́ние; (*ship*) потерпе́вшее круше́ние су́дно ♦ *vt*: **to be ~ed** терпе́ть (потерпе́ть* *perf*) кораблекруше́ние.

shipyard ['ʃɪpjɑːd] *n* (судострои́тельная) верфь *f*.

shire ['ʃaɪə'] *n* (*BRIT*) гра́фство.

shirk [ʃɜːk] *vt* уви́ливать (увильну́ть* *perf*) от +*gen*.

shirt [ʃɜːt] *n* (*man's*) руба́шка*; (*woman's*) блу́зка*; **in (one's) ~ sleeves** в одно́й руба́шке.

shirty ['ʃɜːtɪ] *adj* (*BRIT: inf: person*) наду́тый (наду́т).

shit [ʃɪt] *excl* (*inf!*) чёрт.

shiver ['ʃɪvə'] *n* дрожь *f* ♦ *vi* дрожа́ть (*impf*).

shoal [ʃəul] *n* (*of fish*) кося́к*; (*fig: also:* **~s**) то́лпы *fpl*.

shock [ʃɔk] *n* (*start, impact*) толчо́к*; (*ELEC, MED*) шок; (*emotional*) потрясе́ние ♦ *vt* (*upset*) потряса́ть (потрясти́* *perf*); (*offend*) возмуща́ть (возмути́ть* *perf*), шоки́ровать (*impf/perf*); **to be suffering from ~** (*MED*) находи́ться* (*impf*) в состоя́нии шо́ка; **the news gave us a ~** э́та но́вость нас потрясла́; **it came as a ~ to hear that ...** мы бы́ли потрясены́, когда́ услы́шали, что ....

shock absorber *n* амортиза́тор.

shocker ['ʃɔkə'] *n* (*inf: film*) ужа́сник; (: *news*) ужаса́ющая но́вость *f*.

shocking ['ʃɔkɪŋ] *adj* (*outrageous*) возмути́тельный* (возмути́телен); (*dreadful*) кошма́рный* (кошма́рен).

shockproof ['ʃɔkpruːf] *adj* противоуда́рный.

shock therapy *n* шокотерапи́я.

shock treatment *n* = **shock therapy**.

shock wave *n* уда́рная волна́; (*fig*) чу́вство потрясе́ния.

shod [ʃɔd] *pt, pp of* **shoe** ♦ *adj*: **well-~** хорошо́ обу́тый (обу́т).

shoddy ['ʃɔdɪ] *adj* (*goods*) дрянно́й; (*workmanship*) куста́рный.

shoe [ʃuː] (*pt, pp* **shod**) *n* (*for person*) ту́фля*; (*for horse*) подко́ва; (*AUT: also:* **brake ~**) коло́дка ♦ *vt* (*horse*) подко́вывать (подкова́ть* *perf*); **~s** (*footwear*) о́бувь *fsg*.

shoebrush ['ʃuːbrʌʃ] *n* обувна́я щётка*.

shoehorn ['ʃuːhɔːn] *n* рожо́к* (*для о́буви*).

shoelace ['ʃuːleɪs] *n* шнуро́к*.

shoemaker ['ʃuːmeɪkə'] *n* сапо́жник.

shoe polish *n* гутали́н.

shoe shop *n* обувно́й магази́н.

shoestring ['ʃuːstrɪŋ] *n* (*fig*): **on a ~** на гроши́.

shoetree ['ʃuːtriː] *n* распо́рка* для о́буви.

shone [ʃɔn] *pt, pp of* **shine**.

shoo [ʃuː] *excl* вон; (*to cats*) брысь ♦ *vt* (*also:* **~ away, ~ off**) отгоня́ть (отогна́ть* *perf*).

shook [ʃuk] *pt of* **shake**.

shoot [ʃuːt] (*pt, pp* **shot**) *n* (*BOT*) росто́к*, побе́г; (*SPORT: event*) охо́та; (*CINEMA*) съёмка ♦ *vt* (*gun, arrow*) стреля́ть (*impf*) из +*gen*; (*kill: bird, robber etc*) застре́ливать (застрели́ть* *perf*); (*BRIT: game*) стреля́ть (*impf*); (*wound*) вы́стрелить (*perf*) в +*acc*; (*execute*) расстре́ливать (расстреля́ть* *perf*); (*film*) снима́ть (снять* *perf*) ♦ *vi*: **to ~ (at)** стреля́ть (вы́стрелить *perf*) (в +*acc*); (*FOOTBALL etc*) бить* (*impf*) (по +*dat*); **to ~ past** (*move*) проноси́ться* (пронести́сь* *perf*); **he shot through the door** он влете́л в дверь

▶ **shoot down** *vt* (*plane*) сбива́ть (сбить* *perf*)

▶ **shoot in** *vi* (*rush in*) стремгла́в вбега́ть (вбежа́ть* *perf*)

▶ **shoot out** *vi* (*rush out*) стремгла́в выбега́ть (вы́бежать* *perf*)

▶ **shoot up** *vi* (*fig: prices*) подска́кивать (подскочи́ть* *perf*); (*child*) вытя́гиваться (вы́тянуться *perf*).

shooting ['ʃuːtɪŋ] *n* (*shots, attack*) стрельба́; (*murder*) уби́йство; (*CINEMA*) съёмки* *fpl*; (*HUNTING*) охо́та.

shooting range *n* стре́льбище.

shooting star *n* па́дающая звезда́*.

shop [ʃɔp] *n* магази́н; (*also:* **workshop**) мастерска́я *f adj* ◆ *vi* (*also:* **go ~ping**) ходи́ть* (*impf*) по магази́нам, де́лать (*impf*) поку́пки; **repair ~** (ремо́нтная) мастерска́я; **to talk ~** (*fig*) говори́ть (*impf*) *or* разгова́ривать (*impf*) о рабо́те

▶ **shop around** *vi* (*also fig*) прице́ниваться (прицени́ться* *perf*).

shopaholic ['ʃɔpə'hɔlɪk] *n* (*inf*) *челове́к, поме́шанный на магази́нах.*

shop assistant *n* (*BRIT*) продаве́ц*(-вщи́ца).

shop floor *n* (*BRIT: INDUSTRY*) цех*.

shopkeeper ['ʃɔpkiːpəʳ] *n* владе́лец*(-лица) магази́на.

shoplifter ['ʃɔplɪftəʳ] *n* вор*(о́вка*) (*краду́щий в магази́нах*).

shoplifting ['ʃɔplɪftɪŋ] *n* кра́жа това́ров (*из магази́нов*).

shopper ['ʃɔpəʳ] *n* покупа́тель(ница) *m(f)*.

shopping ['ʃɔpɪŋ] *n* (*goods*) поку́пки* *fpl*.

shopping bag *n* хозя́йственная су́мка*.

shopping centre (*US* **shopping center**) *n* торго́вый центр.

shopping mall *n* (*esp US*) торго́вый центр.

shopsoiled ['ʃɔpsɔɪld] *adj* (*goods*) лежа́лый.

shop steward *n* (*BRIT: INDUSTRY*) цехово́й ста́роста *m*.

shop window *n* (*also fig*) витри́на.

shore [ʃɔːʳ] *n* бе́рег* ◆ *vt*: **to ~ (up)** подпира́ть (подпере́ть* *perf*); **on ~** на берегу́.

shore leave *n* (*NAUT*) увольне́ние на бе́рег.

shorn [ʃɔːn] *pp of* **shear** ◆ *adj*: **~ of** (*power, protection etc*) лишённый (лишён) +*gen*.

short [ʃɔːt] *adj* (*in length, time*) коро́ткий* (ко́роток); (*in height*) невысо́кий* (невысо́к); (*curt*) ре́зкий* (ре́зок); (*insufficient*) ску́дный ◆ *n* (*also:* **~ film**) короткометра́жный фильм; **we are ~ of milk** у нас ма́ло молока́; **I'm ten pence ~** мне не хвата́ет десяти́ пе́нсов; **in ~** коро́че говоря́; **water is in ~ supply** э́тот райо́н испы́тывает нехва́тку воды́; **it is ~ for ...** э́то сокраще́ние от +*gen* ...; **a ~ time ago**

неда́вно; **in the ~ term** в настоя́щее вре́мя; **to cut ~** (*speech, visit*) сокраща́ть (сократи́ть* *perf*); **everything ~ of ...** всё, кро́ме +*gen* ...; **~ of doing** остаётся то́лько +*infin* ...; **to fall ~ of** не выполня́ть (вы́полнить *perf*); **we're running ~ of time** у нас зака́нчивается вре́мя; **to stop ~** застыва́ть (засты́ть* *perf*) на ме́сте; **to stop ~ of doing** не осме́ливаться (осме́литься *perf*) +*infin*; *see also* **shorts**.

shortage ['ʃɔːtɪdʒ] *n*: **a ~ of** нехва́тка +*gen*, дефици́т +*gen*.

shortbread ['ʃɔːtbrɛd] *n* ≈ песо́чное пече́нье.

short-change [ʃɔːt'tʃeɪndʒ] *vt*: **to ~ sb** обсчи́тывать (обсчита́ть *perf*) кого́-н.

short circuit *n* коро́ткое замыка́ние.

shortcoming ['ʃɔːtkʌmɪŋ] *n* недоста́ток*.

short(crust) pastry ['ʃɔːt(krʌst)-] *n* (*BRIT*) песо́чное те́сто.

short cut *n* коро́ткий* путь* *m no pl*; (*fig*) эконо́мный путь*.

shorten ['ʃɔːtn] *vt* (*clothes*) укора́чивать (укороти́ть* *perf*); (*visit*) сокраща́ть (сократи́ть* *perf*).

shortening ['ʃɔːtnɪŋ] *n* (*CULIN*) жир*.

shortfall ['ʃɔːtfɔːl] *n* недоста́ток*.

shorthand ['ʃɔːthænd] *n* (*BRIT*) стеногра́фия; (*fig*) сокраще́ние; **to take sth down in ~** стенографи́ровать (застенографи́ровать *perf*) что-н.

shorthand notebook *n* (*BRIT*) стенограф-и́ческая тетра́дь *f*.

shorthand typist *n* (*BRIT*) стенографи́ст(ка*).

short list *n* (*BRIT*) спи́сок* оконча́тельных кандида́тов.

short-lived ['ʃɔːt'lɪvd] *adj* кратковре́менный* (кратковре́мен), недо́лгий* (недо́лог).

shortly ['ʃɔːtlɪ] *adv* вско́ре.

shorts [ʃɔːts] *npl*: **(a pair of)** ~ шо́рты *pl*.

short-sighted [ʃɔːt'saɪtɪd] *adj* (*BRIT: also fig*) близору́кий* (близору́к).

short-sightedness [ʃɔːt'saɪtɪdnɪs] *n* близору́кость *f*.

short-staffed [ʃɔːt'stɑːft] *adj*: **to be ~** испы́тывать (*impf*) нехва́тку персона́ла.

short story *n* расска́з.

short-tempered [ʃɔːt'tɛmpəd] *adj* вспы́льчивый (вспы́льчив).

short-term ['ʃɔːttəːm] *adj* (*effect*) кратко-вре́менный; (*borrowing*) краткосро́чный.

short time *n*: **to be on ~ ~** (*INDUSTRY*) быть* (*impf*) на сокращённой рабо́чей неде́ле.

short wave *n* (*RADIO*) коро́ткие во́лны* *fpl* ◆ *adj* (*RADIO*): **~ ~** коротково́лновый.

shot [ʃɔt] *pt, pp of* **shoot** ◆ *n* (*of gun*) вы́стрел; (*shotgun pellets*) дробь *f*; (*FOOTBALL etc*) уда́р; (*injection*) уко́л; (*PHOT*) сни́мок*; **to fire a ~ at sb/sth** вы́стрелить (*perf*) в кого́-н/что-н; **to**

have a ~ at sth попытáть *(perf)* удáчи в чём-н;
to have a ~ at doing *(try)* прóбовать
(попрóбовать *perf)* +*infin*; **to get ~ of sb/sth**
(inf) распрости́ться* *(perf)* с кем-н/чем-н; **a
big ~** *(inf)* большáя ши́шка* *m/f*; **a good/poor
~** *(person)* мéткий*/плохóй стрелóк*; **like a ~**
ми́гом.

shotgun ['ʃɔtgʌn] *n* дробови́к*.

should [ʃud] *aux vb*: **I ~ go now** я дóлжен идти́
тепéрь; **he ~ be there now** сейчáс он дóлжен
бы́ть там; **I ~ go if I were you** на Вáшем
мéсте я бы пошёл; **I ~ like to** я бы хотéл; **~
he phone ...** éсли он позвони́т ....

shoulder ['ʃəuldə'] *n* (ANAT) плечó* ♦ *vt* (*fig*:
responsibility, blame) принимáть (приня́ть*
perf) на себя́; **to look over one's ~** смотрéть*
(посмотрéть* *perf)* чéрез плечó; **to rub ~'s
with sb** (*fig*) вращáться *(impf)* с кем-н в одни́х
кругáх; **to give sb the cold ~** обходи́ться*
(обойти́сь* *perf)* с кем-н прохлáдно.

shoulder bag *n* сýмка* на дли́нном ремнé.

shoulder blade *n* лопáтка*.

shoulder strap *n* бретéлька*; (*on dungarees*)
ля́мка*; (*on bag*) ремéнь* *m*.

shouldn't ['ʃudnt] = **should not**.

shout [ʃaut] *n* крик ♦ *vt* выкри́кивать
(вы́крикнуть *perf)*; (*also*: **~ out**) кричáть
(impf); **to give sb a ~** кри́кнуть *(perf)* комý-н.

▶ **shout down** *vt* заглушáть (заглуши́ть *perf)*
кри́ками.

shouting ['ʃautɪŋ] *n* крик.

shouting match *n* (*inf*) крик, скандáл.

shove [ʃʌv] *vt* толкáть *(impf)*; (*inf*: *put*): **to ~ sth
in** затáлкивать (затолкáть *perf)* что-н,
запи́хивать (запихáть *or* запихнýть *perf)*
что-н ♦ *n*: **to give sb/sth a ~** пихáть (пихнýть
perf) когó-н/что-н; **he ~d me out of the way**
он отпихнýл меня́

▶ **shove off** (*inf*) *vi* отвáливать (отвали́ть*
perf).

shovel ['ʃʌvl] *n* лопáта; (*mechanical*) ковш ♦ *vt*
(*snow, coal, earth*) грести́* (сгрести́* *perf)*
(*лопáтой*).

show [ʃəu] (*pt* **showed**, *pp* **shown**) *n* (*of emotion*)
покáз; (*semblance*) подóбие; (*exhibition*)
вы́ставка*; (THEAT) спектáкль *m*; (TV)
прогрáмма, шоу *nt ind*; (CINEMA) сеáнс ♦ *vt*
покáзывать (показáть* *perf)*; (*courage etc*)
проявля́ть (прояви́ть* *perf)* ♦ *vi* (*be evident*)
проявля́ться (прояви́ться* *perf)*,
обнарýживаться (обнарýжиться *perf)*; (*inf*:
also: **~ up**) явля́ться (яви́ться* *perf)*; **to ~ sb to
his seat** проводи́ть* (провести́* *perf)* когó-н
на мéсто; **to ~ sb to the door** укáзывать
(указáть* *perf)* комý-н на дверь; **to ~ a profit/
loss** (COMM) демонстри́ровать *(impf/perf)*
при́быль/убы́тки; **it just goes to ~ that ...** э́то
прóсто покáзывает, что, ...; **to ask for a ~ of
hands** проси́ть* (попроси́ть* *perf)* подня́ть
рýки (*при голосовáнии*); **for ~** для ви́ду; **on ~**
(*exhibits etc*) на вы́ставке; **who's running the**

~ here? (*inf*) кто здесь заправля́ет?

▶ **show in** *vt* (*person*) проводи́ть* (провести́*
perf)

▶ **show off** *vi* хвáстаться (похвáстаться *perf)* ♦
vt (*display*) хвáстаться (похвáстаться *perf)*
+*instr*

▶ **show out** *vt* (*person*) провожáть
(проводи́ть* *perf)* к вы́ходу

▶ **show up** *vi* (*stand out*: *against background*)
виднéться *(impf)*; (: *fig*) обнарýживаться
(обнарýжиться *perf)*; (*inf*: *turn up*) явля́ться
(яви́ться* *perf)* ♦ *vt* (*uncover*: *imperfections
etc*) выявля́ть (вы́явить* *perf)*.

showbiz ['ʃəubiz] *n* (*inf*) = **show business**.

show business *n* шóу би́знес.

showcase ['ʃəukeɪs] *n* витри́на; (*fig*)
показáтельный примéр.

showdown ['ʃəudaun] *n*: **to have a ~** (**with**)
раскрывáть (раскры́ть* *perf)* кáрты (+*dat*).

shower ['ʃauə'] *n* (*also*: **~ bath**) душ; (*of rain*)
ли́вень *m*; (*of stones etc*) град; (US: *party*)
звáнный вéчер ♦ *vi* принимáть (приня́ть*
perf) душ ♦ *vt*: **to ~ sb with** (*gifts, abuse etc*)
осыпáть (осы́пать* *perf)* когó-н +*instr*;
(*missiles*) забрáсывать (заброcáть* *perf)*; **to
have** *or* **take a ~** принимáть (приня́ть* *perf)*
душ.

shower cap ['ʃauəkæp] *n* шáпочка* (*для
дýша*).

showerproof ['ʃauəpru:f] *adj* (*clothing*)
непромокáемый.

showery ['ʃauərɪ] *adj* дождли́вый.

showground ['ʃəugraund] *n* вы́ставка* (*на
откры́том вóздухе*).

showing ['ʃəuɪŋ] *n* (*of film*) покáз.

show jumping *n* конкýр.

showman ['ʃəumən] *irreg n* (*at fair, circus*)
ведýщий* *m adj*, конферансьé *m ind*; (*owner of
circus*) хозя́ин ци́рка; (*fig*) позёр.

showmanship ['ʃəumənʃɪp] *n* талáнт.

shown [ʃəun] *pp of* **show**.

show-off ['ʃəuɔf] *n* (*inf*) хвастýн(ья).

showpiece ['ʃəupi:s] *n* (*of exhibition etc*)
центрáльный экспонáт; **this is a ~ of ...** э́то
явля́ется блестя́щим образцóм +*gen* ....

showroom ['ʃəurum] *n* демонстрациóнный
зал.

show trial *n* показáтельный процéсс.

showy ['ʃəuɪ] *adj* брóский*.

shrank [ʃræŋk] *pt of* **shrink**.

shrapnel ['ʃræpnl] *n* шрапнéль *f*.

shred [ʃred] *n* (*usu pl*) клочóк*; (*fig*: *of truth,
evidence*) крупи́ца ♦ *vt* кроши́ть*
(накроши́ть* *perf)*; (CULIN) шинковáть
(нашинковáть *perf)*.

shredder ['ʃredə'] *n* (*also*: **vegetable ~**)
шинкóвка; (*also*: **document ~**) маши́на для
дезинтегрáции докумéнтов.

shrew [ʃru:] *n* (ZOOL) землерóйка*; (*pej*:
woman) змея́.

shrewd [ʃru:d] *adj* проницáтельный*
(проницáтелен).

shrewdness [ˈʃruːdnɪs] *n* проница́тельность *f*.
shriek [ʃriːk] *n* визг ♦ *vi* визжа́ть* (*impf*).
shrift [ʃrɪft] *n*: **to give sb short** ~ бы́стро отде́лываться (отде́латься *perf*) от кого́-н.
shrill [ʃrɪl] *adj* визгли́вый (визгли́в).
shrimp [ʃrɪmp] *n* (ме́лкая) креве́тка*.
shrimping [ˈʃrɪmpɪŋ] *n* ло́вля креве́ток.
shrine [ʃraɪn] *n* (*tomb*) ра́ка; (*place of worship, also fig*) святы́ня.
shrink [ʃrɪŋk] (*pt* **shrank**, *pp* **shrunk**) *vi* (*cloth*) сади́ться* (сесть* *perf*); (*profits, audiences*) сокраща́ться (сократи́ться* *perf*); (*also:* ~ **away**) отпря́нуть (*perf*) ♦ *vt*: **washing will** ~ **the dress** от сти́рки пла́тье сади́тся ♦ *n* (*inf: psychiatrist*) психоанали́тик; **to** ~ **from sth** ускользáть (ускользну́ть *perf*) от +*gen*.
shrinkage [ˈʃrɪŋkɪdʒ] *n* уса́дка.
shrink-wrap [ˈʃrɪŋkræp] *vt* (*goods etc*) упако́вывать (упакова́ть *perf*) в уса́дочную плёнку.
shrivel [ˈʃrɪvl] (*also:* ~ **up**) *vt* высу́шивать (вы́сушить *perf*) ♦ *vi* высыха́ть (вы́сохнуть *perf*).
shroud [ʃraud] *n* са́ван ♦ *vt*: ~**ed in mystery** оку́танный (оку́тан) та́йно.
Shrove Tuesday [ˈʃrəuv-] *n* вто́рник на ма́сленой неде́ле.
shrub [ʃrʌb] *n* куст*.
shrubbery [ˈʃrʌbərɪ] *n* куста́рник.
shrug [ʃrʌg] *n* пожима́ние (*плеча́ми*) ♦ *vi*: **to** ~ **(one's shoulders)** пожима́ть (пожа́ть* *perf*) плеча́ми
► **shrug off** *vt* отма́хиваться (отмахну́ться *perf*) от +*gen*.
shrunk [ʃrʌŋk] *pp of* **shrink**.
shrunken [ˈʃrʌŋkn] *adj* (*material*) се́вший; (*person, figure*) съёженный.
shudder [ˈʃʌdə'] *n* дрожь *f* ♦ *vi* содрога́ться (содрогну́ться *perf*).
shuffle [ˈʃʌfl] *vt* тасова́ть (стасова́ть *perf*) ♦ *vi*: **to** ~ **(one's feet)** волочи́ть (*impf*) но́ги.
shun [ʃʌn] *vt* избега́ть (*impf*) +*gen*.
shunt [ʃʌnt] *vt* (*train*) переводи́ть* (перевести́* *perf*) на друго́й путь ♦ *vi* (*RAIL*): **to** ~ **(to and fro)** маневри́ровать (*impf*/*perf*).
shunting yard [ˈʃʌntɪŋ-] *n* сортиро́вочная ста́нция.
shush [ʃuʃ] *excl* ш-ш.
shut [ʃʌt] (*pt, pp* **shut**) *vt* закрыва́ть (закры́ть* *perf*) ♦ *vi* закрыва́ться (закры́ться* *perf*)
► **shut down** *vt* закрыва́ть (закры́ть* *perf*); (*machine*) отключа́ть (отключи́ть *perf*) ♦ *vi* закрыва́ться (закры́ться* *perf*); (*machine*) отключа́ться (отключи́ться *perf*)
► **shut off** *vt* (*supply etc*) отключа́ть (отключи́ть *perf*)
► **shut out** *vt* (*person, cold, noise*) не пропуска́ть (пропусти́ть* *perf*); (*view,*

memory) заслоня́ть (заслони́ть *perf*)
► **shut up** *vi* (*inf: keep quiet*) заткну́ться (*perf*) ♦ *vt* (*close*) запира́ть (запере́ть* *perf*); (*silence*) затыка́ть (заткну́ть *perf*) рот +*dat*; ~ **up!** закни́сь!
shutdown [ˈʃʌtdaun] *n* (*temporary*) приостановле́ние; (*permanent*) закры́тие.
shutter [ˈʃʌtə'] *n* (*on window*) ста́вень* *m*; (*PHOT*) затво́р.
shuttle [ˈʃʌtl] *n*: ~ **plane** самолёт-челно́к; (*also: space* ~) шатл; (*also:* ~ **service**) челно́чный маршру́т; (*for weaving*) челно́к ♦ *vi*: **to** ~ **between** соверша́ть (*impf*) челно́чные ре́йсы ме́жду +*instr* ♦ *vt* (*passengers*) вози́ть* (*impf*) туда́ и обра́тно.
shuttlecock [ˈʃʌtlkɔk] *n* (*SPORT*) вола́н.
shuttle diplomacy *n* челно́чная диплома́тия.
shy [ʃaɪ] *adj* (*timid*) засте́нчивый (засте́нчив), стесни́тельный* (стесни́телен); (*reserved*) осторо́жен* (осторо́жен) ♦ *vi*: **to** ~ **away from doing** (*fig*) чужда́ться (*impf*) +*infin*; **to fight** ~ **of** избега́ть (*impf*) +*gen*; **to be** ~ **of doing** стесня́ться (постесня́ться *perf*) +*infin*.
shyly [ˈʃaɪlɪ] *adv* засте́нчиво.
shyness [ˈʃaɪnɪs] *n* (*see adj*) засте́нчивость *f*, стесни́тельность *f*; осторо́жность *f*.
Siamese [saɪəˈmiːz] *adj*: ~ **cat** сиа́мская ко́шка*; ~ **twins** сиа́мские близнецы́ *mpl*.
Siberia [saɪˈbɪərɪə] *n* Сиби́рь *f*.
sibling [ˈsɪblɪŋ] *n* (*brother*) родно́й брат; (*sister*) родна́я сестра́.
Sicilian [sɪˈsɪlɪən] *adj* сицили́йский ♦ *n* сицили́ец(-и́йка*).
Sicily [ˈsɪsɪlɪ] *n* Сици́лия.
sick [sɪk] *adj* (*ill*) больно́й* (бо́лен); (*humour*) пога́ный, скве́рный* (скве́рен); (*vomiting*): **he is/was** ~ его́ рвёт/вы́рвало; (*nauseated*): **I feel** ~ меня́ тошни́т; **to fall** ~ заболева́ть (заболе́ть *perf*); **to be** ~ (*impf*) на больни́чном; **a** ~ **person** больно́й челове́к*; **to be** ~ **of** (*of war etc*) смерте́льно уста́ть* (*perf*) от +*gen*; **I'm** ~ **of arguing/school** меня́ тошни́т от спо́ров/шко́лы.
sickbag [ˈsɪkbæg] *n* (*on airplane*) санита́рный паке́т.
sickbay [ˈsɪkbeɪ] *n* изоля́тор.
sickbed [ˈsɪkbɛd] *n* посте́ль *f* больно́го.
sick building *n* помеще́ние с нездоро́вым микрокли́матом.
sicken [ˈsɪkn] *vt* (*disgust*) вызыва́ть (вы́звать* *perf*) отвраще́ние у +*gen* ♦ *vi*: **to be** ~**ing for sth** заболева́ть (*impf*) чем-н.
sickening [ˈsɪknɪŋ] *adj* (*fig*) проти́вный (проти́вен).
sickle [ˈsɪkl] *n* серп*.
sick leave *n* о́тпуск по боле́зни.
sick list *n*: **to be on the** ~ ~ быть* (*impf*) на бюллете́не *or* больни́чном.

---

sickly ['sɪklɪ] *adj* (*child, plant*) хи́лый (хил); (*smell*) тошнотво́рный* (тошнотво́рен).
sickness ['sɪknɪs] *n* (*illness*) боле́знь *f*; (*vomiting*) рво́та.
sickness benefit *n* посо́бие по боле́зни.
sick note *n* бюллете́нь *m*, больни́чный лист*.
sick pay *n* опла́та по бюллете́ню *or* больни́чному листу́.
sickroom ['sɪkruːm] *n* ко́мната больно́го.
side [saɪd] *n* сторона́*; (*of body*) бок*; (*of paper*) страни́ца; (*team*) кома́нда; (*of hill*) склон ◆ *adj* (*door etc*) боково́й ◆ *vi*: **to ~ with sb** встава́ть* (встать* *perf*) на сторону́ кого́-н; **by the ~ of** у +*gen*; **by her** во́зле неё; **~ by ~** (*to walk*) ря́дом; (*to work*) бок о́ бок; **the right ~** (*of material*) лицо́; **the wrong ~** (*of material*) изна́нка; **we're on the wrong ~ of the road/ river** мы не на той стороне́ доро́ги/реки́; **they are on our ~** они́ на на́шей стороне́; **from ~ to ~** с бо́ку на́ бок; **from all ~s** со всех сторо́н; **to take ~s (with sb)** принима́ть (приня́ть* *perf*) (чью-н) сто́рону; **a ~ of beef** полови́на говя́жьей ту́ши.
sideboard ['saɪdbɔːd] *n* буфе́т; **~s** *npl* (*BRIT*) = **sideburns**.
sideburns ['saɪdbəːnz] *npl* бакенба́рды *pl*.
sidecar ['saɪdkɑːʳ] *n* (*AUT*) коля́ска* (*мотоци́кла*).
side dish *n* гарни́р.
side drum *n* ма́лый бараба́н.
side effect *n* побо́чное де́йствие.
sidekick ['saɪdkɪk] *n* (*inf*) подру́чный *m adj*.
sidelight ['saɪdlaɪt] *n* (*AUT*) боково́е освеще́ние.
sideline ['saɪdlaɪn] *n* (*SPORT*) боковáя ли́ния; (*fig: supplementary job*) побо́чная рабо́та; **to stand on the ~s** стоя́ть* (*impf*) в стороне́.
sidelong ['saɪdlɔŋ] *adj* косо́й; **to give sb a ~ glance** смотре́ть* (посмотре́ть* *perf*) на кого́-н и́скоса.
side plate *n* десе́ртная таре́лка.
side road *n* просёлочная доро́га.
side-saddle ['saɪdsædl] *adv*: **to ride ~** е́хать* (*impf*) в да́мском седле́.
sideshow ['saɪdʃəu] *n* аттракцио́н.
sidestep ['saɪdstɛp] *vt* (*fig*) обходи́ть* (обойти́* *perf*) ◆ *vi* отступа́ть (отступи́ть* *perf*).
side street *n* переу́лок*.
sidetrack ['saɪdtræk] *vt* уводи́ть* (увести́* *perf*) в сто́рону.
sidewalk ['saɪdwɔːk] *n* (*US*) тротуа́р.
sideways ['saɪdweɪz] *adv* (*go in, lean*) бо́ком; (*look*) и́скоса.
siding ['saɪdɪŋ] *n* (*RAIL*) запа́сный путь* *m*.
sidle ['saɪdl] *vi*: **to ~ up (to)** подходи́ть* (подойти́* *perf*) бочко́м (к +*dat*).
SIDS *n abbr* (*MED*: = *sudden infant death syndrome*) *синдро́м внеза́пной сме́рти вне́шне здоро́вого младе́нца*.
siege [siːdʒ] *n* оса́да; **to be under ~** быть* (*impf*) в оса́де; **to lay ~ to** осажда́ть (осади́ть* *perf*).

siege economy *n* засто́йная эконо́мика.
siege mentality *n* психоло́гия люде́й в оса́дном положе́нии.
Sierra Leone [sɪˈɛrəlɪˈəun] *n* Сье́рра-Лео́не.
siesta [sɪˈɛstə] *n* сие́ста.
sieve [sɪv] *n* (*CULIN*) си́то*; (*for garden*) решето́* ◆ *vt* просе́ивать (просе́ять *perf*).
sift [sɪft] *vt* (*flour, sand*) просе́ивать (просе́ять *perf*); (*also*: ~ **through**: *evidence etc*) просе́ивать (просе́ять *perf*).
sigh [saɪ] *n* вздох ◆ *vi* вздыха́ть (вздохну́ть *perf*).
sight [saɪt] *n* (*faculty*) зре́ние; (*spectacle*) вид; (*on gun*) прице́л ◆ *vt* замеча́ть (заме́тить* *perf*); **in ~** в по́ле зре́ния; **out of ~** из ви́да; **at ~** (*COMM*) по предъявле́нию; **at first ~** с пе́рвого взгля́да; **I know her by ~** я зна́ю её в лицо́; **to catch ~ of** замеча́ть (заме́тить* *perf*); **to lose ~ of sb/sth** теря́ть (потеря́ть *perf*) кого́-н/что-н из ви́ду; **to set one's ~s on sth** положи́ть* (*perf*) глаз на что-н; **to shoot sb on ~** стреля́ть (*impf*) в кого́-н на ме́сте.
sighted ['saɪtɪd] *adj* (*person*) зря́чий* (зряч); **partially ~** слабови́дящий.
sightseeing ['saɪtsiːɪŋ] *n* осмо́тр достопримеча́тельностей; **to go ~** осма́тривать (осмотре́ть* *perf*) достопримеча́тельности.
sightseer ['saɪtsiːəʳ] *n* тури́ст(ка*).
sign [saɪn] *n* (*notice*) вы́веска*; (*with hand*) знак; (*indication, evidence*) при́знак; (*also*: **road ~**) доро́жный знак ◆ *vt* (*document*) подпи́сывать (подписа́ть* *perf*); (*player*) нанима́ть (наня́ть* *perf*); **as a ~ of** в знак +*gen*; **it's a good/bad ~** э́то хоро́ший/плохо́й знак; **plus/minus ~** знак "плюс"/"ми́нус"; **there's no ~ of her changing her mind** нет никаки́х при́знаков того́, что она́ переду́мала; **he is showing ~s of improvement** у него́ видны́ при́знаки улучше́ния; **to ~ one's name** распи́сываться (расписа́ться* *perf*); **to ~ sth over to sb** передава́ть* (переда́ть* *perf*) что-н в дар кому́-н.
▶ **sign away** *vt* (*rights etc*) передава́ть (переда́ть* *perf*)
▶ **sign in** *vi* регистри́роваться (зарегистри́роваться *perf*)
▶ **sign off** *vi* зака́нчивать (зако́нчить *perf*)
▶ **sign on** *vi* (*MIL*) нанима́ться (наня́ться* *perf*); (*BRIT: as unemployed*) отмеча́ться (отме́титься* *perf*) как безрабо́тный; (*for course*) регистри́роваться (зарегистри́роваться *perf*) ◆ *vt* (*MIL: recruits*) набира́ть (набра́ть* *perf*); (*employee*) нанима́ть (наня́ть* *perf*)
▶ **sign out** *vi* выпи́сываться (вы́писаться* *perf*)
▶ **sign up** *vi* (*MIL*) нанима́ться (наня́ться* *perf*); (*for course*) регистри́роваться (зарегистри́роваться *perf*) ◆ *vt* (*player, recruit*) нанима́ть (наня́ть* *perf*).
signal ['sɪgnl] *n* сигна́л ◆ *vi* сигнализи́ровать

(*impf/perf*) ♦ *vt* (*person*) подава́ть* (пода́ть*
perf) знак +*dat*; (*message*) передава́ть*
(переда́ть* *perf*); **to ~ a right/left turn** (*AUT*)
дава́ть* (дать* *perf*) сигна́л пра́вого/ле́вого
поворо́та; **to ~ to sb (to do)** подава́ть*
(пода́ть* *perf*) знак кому́-н (+*infin*).
signal box *n* сигна́льная бу́дка*.
signalman [sɪɡnlmən] *irreg n* стре́лочник.
signatory ['sɪɡnətərɪ] *n* подписа́вшаяся
сторона́*.
signature ['sɪɡnətʃə'] *n* по́дпись *f*.
signature tune *n* музыка́льная ша́пка*.
signet ring ['sɪɡnət-] *n* кольцо́* с печа́ткой.
significance [sɪɡ'nɪfɪkəns] *n* значе́ние; **that is of
no ~** э́то не име́ет значе́ния.
significant [sɪɡ'nɪfɪkənt] *adj* (*amount, discovery
etc*) значи́тельный* (значи́телен); (*look,
smile*) многозначи́тельный*
(многозначи́телен); **it is ~ that** ... ва́жно,
что ....
significantly [sɪɡ'nɪfɪkəntlɪ] *adv* (*see adj*)
значи́тельно; многозначи́тельно.
signify ['sɪɡnɪfaɪ] *vt* (*subj: sign, gesture etc*)
означа́ть (*impf*); (: *person*) выража́ть
(вы́разить* *perf*).
sign language *n* язы́к* же́стов.
sign post *n* (*also fig*) указа́тель *m*.
Sikh [siːk] *n* сикх ♦ *adj* си́кхский.
silage ['saɪlɪdʒ] *n* (*fodder*) си́лос; (*method*)
силосова́ние.
silence ['saɪləns] *n* тишина́ ♦ *vt* заставля́ть
(заста́вить* *perf*) замолча́ть.
silencer ['saɪlənsə'] *n* (*BRIT*) глуши́тель *m*.
silent ['saɪlənt] *adj* (*place, person, prayer*)
безмо́лвный* (безмо́лвен); (*machine*)
бесшу́мный* (бесшу́мен); (*taciturn*)
молчали́вый (молчали́в); (*film*) немо́й; **to
remain ~** молча́ть* (*impf*).
silently ['saɪləntlɪ] *adv* мо́лча.
silent partner *n* (*COMM*) пасси́вный партнёр.
silhouette [sɪluː'ɛt] *n* силуэ́т ♦ *vt*: **to be ~d
against** вырисо́вываться (*impf*) на фо́не +*gen*.
silicon ['sɪlɪkən] *n* кре́мний.
silicon chip *n* кре́мниевый криста́лл,
кре́мниевая микропласти́нка.
silicone ['sɪlɪkəun] *n* силико́н.
Silicon Valley *n* зо́на скопле́ния предприя́тий,
занима́ющихся вы́пуском вычисли́тельной
те́хники.
silk [sɪlk] *n* шёлк ♦ *adj* шёлковый.
silky ['sɪlkɪ] *adj* шелкови́стый (шелкови́ст).
sill [sɪl] *n* (*also:* **window ~**) подоко́нник; (*of
door*) поро́г; (*AUT*) карни́з.
silly ['sɪlɪ] *adj* глу́пый* (глуп); **to do something
~** труть (сде́лать *perf*) глу́пость.
silo ['saɪləu] *n* (*on farm*) си́лосная ба́шня*; (*for
missile*) ста́ртовая ша́хта.
silt [sɪlt] *n* ил

▶ **silt up** *vi* заи́ливаться (заи́литься* *perf*) ♦ *vt*
засоря́ть (засори́ть *perf*).
silver ['sɪlvə'] *n* серебро́ ♦ *adj* серебряный.
silver foil *n* (*BRIT*) = **silver paper**.
silver paper *n* (*BRIT*) фольга́.
silver-plated [sɪlvə'pleɪtd] *adj* серебрёный.
silversmith ['sɪlvəsmɪθ] *n* серебряных дел
ма́стер.
silverware ['sɪlvəwɛə'] *n* серебро́.
silver wedding (anniversary) *n* серебряная
сва́дьба*.
silvery ['sɪlvrɪ] *adj* серебри́стый (серебри́ст);
(*sound*) серебри́стый, серебряный.
similar ['sɪmɪlə'] *adj*: **~ (to)** схо́дный* (схо́ден)
(с +*instr*), подо́бный* (подо́бен) (+*dat*).
similarity [sɪmɪ'lærɪtɪ] *n* схо́дство.
similarly ['sɪmɪləlɪ] *adv* (*in a similar way*)
подо́бным о́бразом; (*likewise*) таки́м же
о́бразом.
simile ['sɪmɪlɪ] *n* сравне́ние.
simmer ['sɪmə'] *vi* (*CULIN*) кипе́ть* (*impf*) на
ме́дленном огне́
▶ **simmer down** *vi* (*fig: inf*) остыва́ть (осты́ть*
perf).
simper ['sɪmpə'] *vi* жема́нничать (*impf*).
simpering ['sɪmprɪŋ] *adj* (*person, smile*)
жема́нный* (жема́нен).
simple ['sɪmpl] *adj* (*easy, plain*) просто́й*
(прост); (*foolish*) недалёкий* (недалёк); **the
~ truth** очеви́дная и́стина.
simple interest *n* просты́е проце́нты *mpl*.
simple-minded [sɪmpl'maɪndɪd] *adj*
простоду́шный* (простоду́шен).
simpleton ['sɪmpltən] *n* проста́к.
simplicity [sɪm'plɪsɪtɪ] *n* (*see adj*) простота́;
недалёкость *f*.
simplification [sɪmplɪfɪ'keɪʃən] *n* упроще́ние.
simplify ['sɪmplɪfaɪ] *vt* упроща́ть (упрости́ть*
perf).
simply ['sɪmplɪ] *adv* про́сто.
simulate ['sɪmjuleɪt] *vt* (*enthusiasm*)
симули́ровать (*impf/perf*); (*innocence*)
изобража́ть (изобрази́ть* *perf*).
simulated ['sɪmjuleɪtɪd] *adj* (*hair, fur*)
подде́льный; (*nuclear explosion*)
имити́рованный.
simulation [sɪmju'leɪʃən] *n* притво́рство.
simultaneous [sɪməl'teɪnɪəs] *adj*
одновре́менный.
simultaneously [sɪməl'teɪnɪəslɪ] *adv*
одновре́менно.
sin [sɪn] *n* грех* ♦ *vi* греши́ть (согреши́ть *perf*).
Sinai ['saɪneɪaɪ] *n* Сина́йский полуо́стров.
since [sɪns] *adv* с тех пор (*time*); как;
(*because*) так как ♦ *prep*: **~ July** с ию́ля;
~ then, ever ~ с тех пор; **it's two weeks ~ I
wrote** уже́ две неде́ли с тех пор, как я
написа́л; **~ our last meeting** со вре́мени

---

* marks translations which have irregular inflections. The Russian–English side of the dictionary gives inflectional information.

нашей последней встречи.
sincere [sɪn'sɪəʳ] *adj* и́скренний* (и́скренен).
sincerely [sɪn'sɪəlɪ] *adv* и́скренне; **Yours ~**
и́скренне Ваш.
sincerity [sɪn'sɛrɪtɪ] *n* и́скренность *f*.
sine [saɪn] *n* (*MATH*) си́нус.
sine qua non [sɪnɪkwɑː'nɔn] *n* необходи́мое
усло́вие.
sinew ['sɪnjuː] *n* сухожи́лие.
sinful ['sɪnful] *adj* гре́шный* (гре́шен).
sing [sɪŋ] (*pt* **sang**, *pp* **sung**) *vti* петь* (спеть*
perf).
Singapore [sɪŋgə'pɔː'] *n* Сингапу́р.
singe [sɪndʒ] *vt* пали́ть (опали́ть *perf*); (*clothes*)
подпа́ливать (подпали́ть *perf*).
singer ['sɪŋəʳ] *n* певе́ц*(-ви́ца).
Singhalese [sɪŋə'liːz] *adj* = **Sinhalese**.
singing ['sɪŋɪŋ] *n* пе́ние; (*in the ears*) звон.
single ['sɪŋgl] *adj* (*individual*) одино́кий*; (*man*)
холосто́й* (хо́лост); (*woman*) незаму́жняя;
(*not double*) одина́рный* (одина́рен) ♦ *n*
(*BRIT: also:* ~ **ticket**) биле́т в оди́н коне́ц;
(*record*) сорокопя́тка*; **not a ~ one was left**
ни одного́ не оста́лось; **every ~ day** ка́ждый
бо́жий день; **~ spacing** с интерва́лом в одну́
стро́чку
▶ **single out** *vt* (*choose*) отбира́ть (отобра́ть*
perf); (*distinguish*) выделя́ть (вы́делить *perf*).
single bed *n* односпа́льная крова́ть *f*.
single-breasted ['sɪŋglbrɛstɪd] *adj*
однобо́ртный.
Single European Market *n*: **the ~ ~ ~**
Еди́ный европе́йский* ры́нок*.
single file *n*: **in ~ ~** в коло́нку.
single-handed [sɪŋgl'hændɪd] *adv* без
посторо́нней по́мощи.
single-minded [sɪŋgl'maɪndɪd] *adj*
целеустремлённый* (целеустремлён).
single parent *n* (*mother*) мать-одино́чка*;
(*father*) оте́ц-одино́чка*.
single room *n* ко́мната на одного́.
singles ['sɪŋglz] *n* (*TENNIS*) оди́н на оди́н ♦ *npl*
(*single people*) несеме́йные *pl adj*.
singles bar *n* бар для несеме́йных.
single-sex [sɪŋgl'sɛks] *adj* разде́льный.
singly ['sɪŋglɪ] *adv* (*alone, one by one*) врозь, в
отде́льности.
singsong ['sɪŋsɔŋ] *adj* (*tone*) моното́нно
иду́щий то вверх, то вниз ♦ *n*: **to have a ~**
попе́ть* (*perf*) хо́ром.
singular ['sɪŋgjuləʳ] *adj* необыча́йный*
(необыча́ен); (*LING*) еди́нственный* ♦ *n* (*LING*)
еди́нственное число́; **in the feminine ~**
же́нского ро́да еди́нственного числа́.
singularly ['sɪŋgjuləlɪ] *adv* необыча́йно.
Sinhalese [sɪnhə'liːz] *adj* синга́льский ♦ *n inv*
синга́лец(-ка*); (*LING*) синга́льский язы́к*.
sinister ['sɪnɪstəʳ] *adj* злове́щий* (злове́щ).
sink [sɪŋk] (*pt* **sank**, *pp* **sunk**) *n* ра́ковина ♦ *vt*
(*ship*) топи́ть* (потопи́ть* *perf*); (*well*) рыть*
(вы́рыть* *perf*); (*foundations*) врыва́ть

(врыть* *perf*) ♦ *vi* (*ship*) тону́ть* (потону́ть*
perf); (*heart, spirits*) па́дать (упа́сть* *perf*);
(*ground*) оседа́ть (осе́сть* *perf*); (*also:* ~ **back,**
~ **down**) отки́дываться (отки́нуться *perf*); **to**
~ **sth into** (*teeth, claws etc*) вонза́ть (вонзи́ть*
perf) что-н в +*acc*; **he sank into a chair/the mud**
он опусти́лся на стул/провали́лся в грязь
▶ **sink in** *vi* (*fig*): **it took a long time for her**
words to ~ **in** потре́бовалось до́лгое вре́мя
что́бы до меня́ дошли́ её слова́.
sinking ['sɪŋkɪŋ] *adj* (*sun*) опуска́ющийся*;
(*ship*) то́нущий; **I had a ~ feeling** у меня́ всё
внутри́ опусти́лось.
sinking fund *n* (*COMM*) фонд погаше́ния.
sink unit *n* комбини́рованная *or* встро́енная
ра́ковина.
sinner ['sɪnəʳ] *n* гре́шник(-ица).
Sinn Féin *n* Шинн Фейн (*ирла́ндская*
полити́ческая па́ртия).
Sino- ['saɪnəu] *prefix* сино-, китае-.
sinuous ['sɪnjuəs] *adj* извива́ющийся.
sinus ['saɪnəs] *n* па́зуха.
SIPS *n abbr* (= *side impact protection system*)
систе́ма защи́ты автомоби́лей от боковы́х
уда́ров.
sip [sɪp] *n* ма́ленький* глото́к* ♦ *vt* пить*
(вы́пить* *perf*) ма́ленькими глотка́ми.
siphon ['saɪfən] *n* сифо́н
▶ **siphon off** *vt* выка́чивать (вы́качать *perf*).
sir [səʳ] *n* сэр, господи́н; **S~ John Smith** Сэр
Джон Смит; **yes ~** да, сэр; **Dear S~** (*in letter*)
Уважа́емый господи́н.
siren ['saɪərn] *n* сире́на.
sirloin ['səːlɔɪn] *n* (*also:* ~ **steak**) говя́жье филе́
nt ind.
sirocco [sɪ'rɔkəu] *n* сиро́кко *m ind.*
sisal ['saɪsəl] *n* сиза́ль *m.*
sissy ['sɪsɪ] *n* (*inf*) не́женка* *m/f.*
sister ['sɪstəʳ] *n* (*also REL*) сестра́*; (*BRIT: MED*)
(медици́нская *or* мед-) сестра́* ♦ *cpd:* ~
organization паралле́льная организа́ция; ~
ship однотипное су́дно*.
sister-in-law ['sɪstərɪnlɔː] *n* (*brother's wife*)
неве́стка*; (*husband's sister*) золо́вка*; (*wife's*
sister) свояче́ница.
sit [sɪt] (*pt, pp* **sat**) *vi* (*sit down*) сади́ться* (сесть*
perf); (*be sitting*) сиде́ть* (*impf*); (*assembly*)
заседа́ть (*impf*); (*for painter*) пози́ровать (*impf*)
♦ *vt* (*exam*) сдава́ть* (сдать* *perf*); **to** ~ **on a**
committee входи́ть* (*impf*) в комите́т; **to** ~
tight не принима́ть (*impf*) никаки́х
де́йствий
▶ **sit about** *vi* сиде́ть* (*impf*)
▶ **sit around** *vi* = **sit about**
▶ **sit back** *vi* (*in seat*) сиде́ть* (*impf*)
▶ **sit down** *vi* сади́ться* (сесть* *perf*); **to be**
~**ting down** сиде́ть* (*impf*)
▶ **sit in on** *vt fus* (*meeting*) прису́тствовать
(*impf*) в/на +*prp*
▶ **sit up** *vi* (*after lying*) приподнима́ться
(приподня́ться* *perf*); (*straight*)

выпрямля́ться (вы́прямиться* perf); (not go to bed) заси́живаться (засиде́ться* perf).

sitcom ['sɪtkɔm] n abbr (TV) = **situation comedy**.

sit-down ['sɪtdaun] adj: **a ~ strike** сидя́чая забасто́вка*; **a ~ meal** приём пи́щи, си́дя.

site [saɪt] n (place) ме́сто*; (also: **building ~**) строи́тельная площа́дка ♦ vt (factory, missiles) помеща́ть (помести́ть* perf).

sit-in ['sɪtɪn] n демонстрати́вное заня́тие помеще́ния.

siting ['saɪtɪŋ] n (location) расположе́ние.

sitter ['sɪtə^r] n (for painter) нату́рщик(-ица); (also: **baby-~**) приходя́щая ня́ня.

sitting ['sɪtɪŋ] n (of assembly etc) заседа́ние; (in canteen) сме́на.

sitting member n (POL) де́йствующий* депута́т парла́мента.

sitting room n гости́ная f adj.

sitting tenant n (BRIT) квартиросъёмщик (-ица).

situate ['sɪtjueɪt] vt располага́ть (расположи́ть* perf).

situated ['sɪtjueɪtɪd] adj располо́женный* (расположён); **to be ~** находи́ться* (impf).

situation [sɪtju'eɪʃən] n (state) ситуа́ция, положе́ние; (job) ме́сто*; (location) ме́сто*, положе́ние; **"situations vacant"** (BRIT) "вака́нтные места́".

situation comedy n коме́дия положе́ний.

six [sɪks] n шесть*; see also **five**.

six-pack ['sɪkspæk] n шестибуты́лочная упако́вка пи́ва.

sixteen [sɪks'tiːn] n шестна́дцать*; see also **five**.

sixteenth [sɪks'tiːnθ] adj шестна́дцатый; see also **fifth**.

sixth [sɪksθ] adj шесто́й ♦ n (fraction) одна́ шеста́я f adj, шеста́я часть f; **the upper/lower ~** (BRIT: SCOL) пе́рвая/втора́я ступе́нь выпускно́го кла́сса; see also **fifth**.

sixtieth ['sɪkstɪɪθ] adj шестидеся́тый; see also **fifth**.

sixty ['sɪkstɪ] n шестьдеся́т*; see also **fifty**.

size [saɪz] n разме́р*; (extent) величина́, масшта́б; (glue) клей*; **I take ~ 14** я ношу́ четы́рнадцатый разме́р; **the small/large ~** ма́ленького/большо́го разме́ра; **it's the ~ of ...** э́то разме́ром с +acc ...; **cut to ~** обре́занный согла́сно разме́рам +gen
► **size up** vt оце́нивать (оцени́ть* perf).

sizeable ['saɪzəbl] adj поря́дочный.

sizzle ['sɪzl] vi шипе́ть* (impf).

SK abbr (CANADA) = **Saskatchewan**.

skate [skeɪt] n (also: **ice ~**) конёк*; (also: **roller ~**) ро́ликовый конёк*, ро́лик; (fish: pl inv) скат ♦ vi ката́ться (impf) на конька́х
► **skate around** vt fus (problem, issue) обходи́ть* (обойти́* perf)
► **skate over** vt fus (problem, issue)

игнори́ровать (impf/perf).

skateboard ['skeɪtbɔːd] n ро́ликовая доска́*.

skater ['skeɪtə^r] n конькобе́жец*(-жка).

skating ['skeɪtɪŋ] n (for pleasure) ката́ние на конька́х; (SPORT) конькобе́жный спорт.

skating rink n като́к*.

skeleton ['skɛlɪtn] n (ANAT) скеле́т; (TECH) карка́с; (outline) набро́сок*, схе́ма.

skeleton key n отмы́чка*.

skeleton staff n минима́льный персона́л.

skeptic etc ['skɛptɪk] (US) = **sceptic** etc.

sketch [skɛtʃ] n (drawing) эски́з, набро́сок*; (outline) набро́сок*; (THEAT, TV) скетч ♦ vt (drawing) наброса́ть (perf); (also: **~ out**) обрисо́вывать (обрисова́ть* perf) в о́бщих черта́х.

sketchbook ['skɛtʃbuk] n альбо́м для зарисо́вок.

sketchpad ['skɛtʃpæd] n блокно́т для зарисо́вок.

sketchy ['skɛtʃɪ] adj пове́рхностный* (пове́рхностен).

skew [skjuː] n: **on the ~** (BRIT) ко́со, кри́во.

skewed [skjuːd] adj (idea, outlook) искажённый (искажён).

skewer ['skjuːə^r] n ве́ртел.

ski [skiː] n лы́жа ♦ vi ката́ться (impf) на лы́жах.

ski boot n лы́жный боти́нок*.

skid [skɪd] n (AUT) зано́с, юз ♦ vi скользи́ть* (impf); (AUT) идти́* (пойти́* perf) ю́зом; **the car went into a ~** маши́ну занесло́.

skid mark n тормозно́й след*.

skier ['skiːə^r] n лы́жник(-ица).

skiing ['skiːɪŋ] n (for pleasure) ката́ние на лы́жах; (SPORT) лы́жный спорт; **to go ~** идти́* (пойти́* perf) or е́хать (пое́хать* perf) ката́ться на лы́жах.

ski instructor n инстру́ктор по лы́жному спо́рту.

ski jump n (ramp) лы́жный трампли́н; (event) прыжки́ mpl на лы́жах с трампли́на.

skilful ['skɪlful] (US **skillful**) adj иску́сный* (иску́сен), уме́лый (уме́л).

ski lift n (лы́жный) подъёмник.

skill [skɪl] n (ability, dexterity) мастерство́; (computer skill etc) на́вык.

skilled [skɪld] adj (able) иску́сный* (иску́сен), уме́лый (уме́л); (worker) квалифиц-и́рованный.

skillet ['skɪlɪt] n (CULIN) неглубо́кая сковорода́*.

skillful ['skɪlful] adj (US) = **skilful**.

skil(l)fully ['skɪlfəlɪ] adv иску́сно, уме́ло.

skim [skɪm] vt (milk) снима́ть (снять* perf) сли́вки с +gen; (soup) снима́ть (снять* perf) на́кипь с +gen; (glide over) скользи́ть* (impf) над +instr ♦ vi: **to ~ through** пробежа́ть* (perf).

skimmed milk [skɪmd-] n обезжи́ренное

молоко́.

skimp [skɪmp] *vt* (*also:* ~ **on**: *work*)
манки́ровать (*impf/perf*) +*instr*; (: *cloth etc*)
эконо́мить* (*impf*) на +*prp*.

skimpy ['skɪmpɪ] *adj* ску́дный* (ску́ден); (*skirt*)
те́сный* (те́сен).

skin [skɪn] *n* (*of person*) ко́жа; (*of animal*)
шку́ра; (*of fruit, vegetable*) кожура́; (*of
grapes, tomatoes*) ко́жица ♦ *vt* (*fruit etc*)
снима́ть (снять* *perf*) кожуру́ с +*gen*,
чи́стить* (очи́стить* *perf*); (*animal*) снима́ть
(снять* *perf*) шку́ру с +*gen*, свежева́ть
(освежева́ть *perf*); **she is soaked to the** ~ она́
промо́кла до ни́тки.

skin cancer *n* рак ко́жи.

skin-deep ['skɪn'di:p] *adj* пове́рхностный*
(пове́рхностен).

skin-diver ['skɪndaɪvə'] *n* акваланги́ст(ка*).

skin diving *n* подво́дное пла́ванье.

skinflint ['skɪnflɪnt] *n* (*inf*) скря́га *m/f*.

skin graft *n* ко́жный транспланта́т.

skinhead ['skɪnhɛd] *n* бритоголо́вый(-ая) *m(f)*
adj.

skinny ['skɪnɪ] *adj* то́щий* (тощ).

skin test *n* ана́лиз ко́жи.

skintight ['skɪntaɪt] *adj* в обтя́жку.

skip [skɪp] *n* прыжо́к*, скачо́к*; (*BRIT: container*)
скип ♦ *vi* подпры́гивать (подпры́гнуть *perf*);
(*with rope*) скака́ть* (*impf*) ♦ *vt* (*miss out*)
пропуска́ть (пропусти́ть* *perf*); **to** ~ **school**
(*esp US*) прогу́ливать (прогуля́ть *perf*)
уро́ки.

ski pants *npl* лы́жные брю́ки *pl*.

ski pole *n* лы́жная па́лка*.

skipper ['skɪpə'] *n* (*NAUT*) шки́пер, капита́н;
(*SPORT*) капита́н ♦ *vt* быть* (*impf*) капита́ном
+*gen*.

skipping rope ['skɪpɪŋ-] *n* (*BRIT*) скака́лка*.

ski resort *n* лы́жная ба́за.

skirmish ['skə:mɪʃ] *n* сты́чка*.

skirt [skə:t] *n* ю́бка* ♦ *vt* обходи́ть* (обойти́*
perf).

skirting board ['skə:tɪŋ-] *n* (*BRIT*) пли́нтус.

ski run *n* лы́жня.

ski slope *n* лы́жный спуск.

ski suit *n* лы́жный костю́м.

skit [skɪt] *n* паро́дия.

ski tow *n* букси́рный подъёмник.

skittle ['skɪtl] *n* ке́гля*; ~**s** *npl* (*game*) ке́гли *fpl*.

skive [skaɪv] *vi* (*BRIT: inf*) сачкова́ть (*impf*).

skulk [skʌlk] *vi* (*hide*) пря́таться* (*impf*); (*prowl
about*) кра́сться* (*impf*).

skull [skʌl] *n* че́реп*.

skullcap ['skʌlkæp] *n* ермо́лка*.

skunk [skʌŋk] *n* (*animal*) скунс; (*fur*)
ску́нсовый мех*.

sky [skaɪ] *n* не́бо*; **to praise sb to the skies**
превозноси́ть* (превознести́* *perf*) кого́-н до
небе́с.

sky-blue [skaɪ'blu:] *adj* небе́сно-голубо́й,
лазу́рный.

skydiving ['skaɪdaɪvɪŋ] *n* свобо́дное паде́ние
(*при прыжка́х с парашю́том*).

sky-high ['skaɪ'haɪ] *adj* (*prices*) сумасше́дший*;
(*structure*) до небе́с; **to blow** ~ разноси́ть*
(разнести́* *perf*) вчисту́ю.

skylark ['skaɪlɑ:k] *n* жа́воронок*.

skylight ['skaɪlaɪt] *n* окно́* в кры́ше.

skyline ['skaɪlaɪn] *n* горизо́нт; (*of city*) силуэ́т.

skyscraper ['skaɪskreɪpə'] *n* небоскрёб.

slab [slæb] *n* (*of stone*) плита́*; (*of wood*)
пласти́на; (*of cake, cheese*) кусо́к*.

slack [slæk] *adj* (*rope*) прови́сший; (*trousers*)
вися́щий; (*discipline*) сла́бый* (слаб);
(*security*) плохо́й* (плох); (*market*) вя́лый;
(*demand*) небольшо́й ♦ *n* (*in rope etc*)
слабина́; ~**s** *npl* (*trousers*) сла́ксы *pl*;
business is ~ в дела́х засто́й.

slacken ['slækn] *vi* (*also:* ~ **off**: *demand, speed*)
па́дать (упа́сть* *perf*); (*rain*) переставать*
(переста́ть* *perf*) ♦ *vt* (*grip, clothing etc*)
ослабля́ть (осла́бить* *perf*); (*speed*) снижа́ть
(сни́зить* *perf*).

slacker ['slækə'] *n* (*inf*) ло́дырь *m*.

slag heap [slæg-] *n* шла́ковая гора́*.

slag off *vt* (*BRIT: inf*): **to slag sb off** перемыва́ть
(перемы́ть* *perf*) кому́-н ко́сточки.

slain [sleɪn] *pp of* **slay**.

slake [sleɪk] *vt*: **to** ~ **one's thirst** утоля́ть
(утоли́ть *perf*) жа́жду.

slalom ['slɑ:ləm] *n* сла́лом.

slam [slæm] *vt* (*door*) хло́пать (хло́пнуть *perf*)
+*instr*; (*throw*) швыря́ть (швырну́ть *perf*);
(*criticize*) раскритикова́ть (*perf*) ♦ *vi* (*door*)
захло́пываться (захло́пнуться *perf*); **to** ~ **on
the brakes** ре́зко тормози́ть* (затормози́ть*
perf).

slammer ['slæmə'] *n* (*inf*) куту́зка.

slander ['slɑ:ndə'] *n* клевета́ ♦ *vt* клевета́ть*
(наклевета́ть* *perf*) на +*acc*.

slanderous ['slɑ:ndrəs] *adj* клеветни́ческий*.

slang [slæŋ] *n* (*informal language*) сленг;
(*jargon*) жарго́н.

slanging match ['slæŋɪŋ-] *n* перебра́нка.

slant [slɑ:nt] *n* накло́н; (*fig: approach*) укло́н.

slanted ['slɑ:ntɪd] *adj* (*roof*) накло́нный,
пока́тый; (*eyes*) раско́сый.

slanting ['slɑ:ntɪŋ] *adj* = **slanted**.

slap [slæp] *n* шлепо́к* ♦ *vt* шлёпать (шлёпнуть
perf) ♦ *adv* (*directly*) пря́мо; **to** ~ **sb in the face**
дать* (*perf*) кому́-н пощёчину; **to** ~ **sth on sth**
(*paint etc*) ля́пать (наля́пать *perf*) что-н на
что-н; **it fell** ~ **in the middle** оно́ упа́ло пря́мо
посереди́не.

slapdash ['slæpdæʃ] *adj* небре́жный*
(небре́жен).

slapstick ['slæpstɪk] *n* фарс.

slap-up ['slæpʌp] *adj*: **a** ~ **meal** (*BRIT*)
роско́шный обе́д.

slash [slæʃ] *vt* ре́зать* (поре́зать* *perf*); (*fig:
prices*) ре́зко снижа́ть (сни́зить* *perf*).

slat [slæt] *n* пла́нка*.

slate [sleɪt] n (material) сла́нец*; (tile) ши́ферная пли́тка* ◆ vt (fig) разноси́ть* (разнести́* perf) в пух и прах.

slaughter ['slɔ:tə'] n (of animals) убо́й; (of people) резня́ ◆ vt (animals) забива́ть (заби́ть* perf); (people) ре́зать* (impf).

slaughterhouse ['slɔ:təhaus] n скотобо́йня.

Slav [slɑ:v] adj славя́нский* ◆ n славяни́н (-я́нка).

slave [sleɪv] n раб*(ы́ня) ◆ vi (also: ~ away) рабо́тать (impf) как раб; to ~ (away) at sth рабо́тать (impf) над чем-н как прокля́тый.

slave-driver ['sleɪvdraɪvə'] n (inf) де́спот.

slave labour n (also fig) ра́бский* труд*.

slaver ['slævə'] vi пуска́ть (impf) слюну́.

slavery ['sleɪvərɪ] n ра́бство.

Slavic ['slævɪk] adj славя́нский*.

slavish ['sleɪvɪʃ] adj ра́бский*; (copy) слепо́й.

slavishly ['sleɪvɪʃlɪ] adv по-ра́бски.

Slavonic [slə'vɔnɪk] adj славя́нский*.

slay [sleɪ] (pt **slew**, pp **slain**) vt поража́ть (порази́ть* perf).

SLD n abbr (BRIT. POL) = Social and Liberal Democratic Party.

sleazy ['sli:zɪ] adj (place) запу́щенный* (запу́щен).

sled [slɛd] n (esp US) = **sledge**.

sledge [slɛdʒ] n са́ни* pl; (for children) са́нки pl.

sledgehammer ['slɛdʒhæmə'] n кува́лда.

sleek [sli:k] adj (shiny, smooth: fur) лосня́щийся; (: hair) блестя́щий* и гла́дкий*; (car, boat etc) аэродинами́чный.

sleep [sli:p] (pt, pp **slept**) n сон* ◆ vi спать* (impf); (spend night) ночева́ть* (переночева́ть* perf) ◆ vt: **the house can** ~ **four** в до́ме мо́жно размести́ть четверы́х; **to go to** ~ засыпа́ть (засну́ть perf); **to have a good night's** ~ (хорошо́) вы́спаться* (perf); **to put to** ~ (animal) усыпля́ть (усыпи́ть* perf); **to** ~ **lightly** спать (impf) чу́тко; **to** ~ **with sb** спать* (impf) с кем-н

▸ **sleep around** vi спать* (impf) с кем попа́ло

▸ **sleep in** vi (oversleep) просыпа́ть (проспа́ть* perf); (lie late) отсыпа́ться (отоспа́ться* perf).

sleeper ['sli:pə'] n (RAIL: train) по́езд со спа́льными ваго́нами; (: carriage) спа́льный ваго́н; (: berth) спа́льное ме́сто*; (: BRIT: on track) шпа́ла; (person) спя́щий(-ая) m(f) adj.

sleepily ['sli:pɪlɪ] adv со́нно.

sleeping ['sli:pɪŋ] adj (person) спя́щий.

sleeping bag n спа́льный мешо́к*.

sleeping car n спа́льный ваго́н.

sleeping partner n (BRIT: COMM) = **silent partner**.

sleeping pill n снотво́рное nt adj, снотво́рная табле́тка*.

sleeping sickness n со́нная боле́знь f.

sleepless ['sli:plɪs] adj (night) бессо́нный.

sleeplessness ['sli:plɪsnɪs] n бессо́нница.

sleepwalk ['sli:pwɔ:k] vi ходи́ть* (impf) во сне.

sleepwalker ['sli:pwɔ:kə'] n луна́тик.

sleepy ['sli:pɪ] adj со́нный; **I feel** or **am** ~ мне хо́чется спать.

sleet [sli:t] n дождь m со сне́гом.

sleeve [sli:v] n (of jacket etc) рука́в*; (of record) конве́рт; **to have sth up one's** ~ име́ть (impf) ко́е-что на уме́.

sleeveless ['sli:vlɪs] adj без рукаво́в.

sleigh [sleɪ] n са́ни* pl.

sleight [slaɪt] n: ~ **of hand** ло́вкость f рук.

slender ['slɛndə'] adj (figure) стро́йный* (стро́ен); (means) ску́дный* (ску́ден); (majority) небольшо́й.

slept [slɛpt] pt, pp of **sleep**.

sleuth [slu:θ] n сы́щик.

slew [slu:] vi (BRIT. also: ~ **round**) кру́то повора́чивать (поверну́ть perf) ◆ pt of **slay**.

slice [slaɪs] n (of meat) кусо́к*; (of bread, lemon) ло́мтик; (also: **fish** ~) ры́бный нож; (also: **cake** ~) лопа́тка* для то́рта ◆ vt (bread, meat etc) нареза́ть (наре́зать* perf), ре́зать* (наре́зать* perf); ~**d bread** наре́занный хлеб.

slick [slɪk] adj (performance) гла́дкий*; (salesman, answer) бо́йкий* (бо́ек) ◆ n (also: **oil** ~) плёнка не́фти.

slid [slɪd] pt, pp of **slide**.

slide [slaɪd] (pt, pp **slid**) n (downward movement) скольже́ние; (in playground) де́тская го́рка*; (PHOT) слайд; (BRIT. also: **hair** ~) зако́лка*; (also: **microscope** ~) предме́тное стекло́*; (in prices) сниже́ние ◆ vt задвига́ть (задви́нуть perf), сова́ть* (су́нуть perf) ◆ vi скользи́ть* (скользну́ть perf); **to let things** ~ (fig) запуска́ть (запусти́ть* perf) дела́, пусти́ть (perf) дела́ самотёком.

slide projector n диапрое́ктор.

slide rule n логарифми́ческая лине́йка.

sliding door n задвижна́я дверь f.

sliding roof n (AUT) сдвига́ющийся верх.

sliding scale n скользя́щий* тари́ф.

slight [slaɪt] adj (slim: figure) то́нкий* (то́нок); (frail) хру́пкий* (хру́пок); (small, trivial) незначи́тельный; (error) небольшо́й; (accent) сла́бый*; (pain) несильный* ◆ n (insult) униже́ние; **the** ~**est** ма́лейший* шум; **I haven't the** ~**est idea** я поня́тия не име́ю; **not in the** ~**est** ниско́лько.

slightly ['slaɪtlɪ] adv немно́го, слегка́; ~ **built** хру́пкого сложе́ния.

slim [slɪm] adj (figure) стро́йный* (стро́ен); (chance) небольшо́й ◆ vi худе́ть (похуде́ть perf).

slime [slaɪm] n слизь f.

slimming ['slɪmɪŋ] n (losing weight) похуде́ние.

slimy ['slaɪmɪ] adj (pond) и́листый (и́лист); (covered with mud) ско́льзкий* и ли́пкий*;

---

* marks translations which have irregular inflections. The Russian-English side of the dictionary gives inflectional information.

(*fig: person*) гнусный.
sling [slɪŋ] (*pt, pp* **slung**) *n* (*MED*) перевязь *f*; (*for baby*) *приспособление, позволяющее носить ребёнка на спине или груди*; (*weapon*) праща, рогатка* ◆ *vt* (*throw*) швырять (швырнуть *perf*); **his arm is in a ~** у него рука на перевязи.
slingshot ['slɪŋʃɒt] *n* рогатка*.
slink [slɪŋk] (*pt, pp* **slunk**) *vi*: **to ~ away** *or* **off** уходить (уйти* *perf*) поджавши хвост*.
slinky ['slɪŋkɪ] *adj* в обтяжку.
slip [slɪp] *n* (*fall*) обвал; (*mistake*) промах; (*underskirt*) подъюбник; (*of paper*) полоска* ◆ *vt* совать* (сунуть *perf*) ◆ *vi* (*slide*) скользить* (скользнуть *f*); (*lose balance*) поскользнуться (*perf*); (*decline*) снижаться (снизиться* *perf*); (*move smoothly*): **to ~ into** (*room etc*) скользнуть (*perf*) в +*acc*; **to give sb the ~** ускользать (ускользнуть *perf*) от кого-н; **a ~ of the tongue** оговорка*; **to ~ sth on** надевать (надеть* *perf*) что-н; **to ~ sth off** сбрасывать (сбросить* *perf*) что-н; **to ~ out of** (*room etc*) выскользнуть (*perf*) из +*gen*; **to let a chance ~ by** упускать (упустить* *perf*) возможность; **the cup ~ped from her hand** чашка выскользнула из её рук
▶ **slip away** *vi* улизнуть (*perf*)
▶ **slip in** *vt* совать* (сунуть *perf*) ◆ *vi* (*errors*) закрадываться* (*perf*)
▶ **slip out** *vi* (*go out*) выскакивать (выскочить *perf*)
▶ **slip up** *vi* (*make mistake*) ошибаться (ошибиться* *perf*).
slip-on ['slɪpɒn] *adj* без пуговиц и застёжек; **~ shoes** туфли без шнурков и застёжек.
slipped disc [slɪpt-] *n* смещённый позвонок.
slipper ['slɪpə'] *n* тапочка*.
slippery ['slɪpərɪ] *adj* (*also fig*) скользкий*.
slippy ['slɪpɪ] *adj* (*inf*) скользский* (скользок).
slip road *n* (*BRIT: on to*) въезд на автостраду; (*off from*) съезд с автострады.
slipshod ['slɪpʃɒd] *adj* небрежный* (небрежен).
slipstream ['slɪpstriːm] *n* воздушный поток.
slip-up ['slɪpʌp] *n* ошибка*.
slipway ['slɪpweɪ] *n* (*NAUT*) стапель* *m*.
slit [slɪt] (*pt, pp* **slit**) *n* (*cut*) разрез; (*opening*) щель* *f*; (*tear*) разрыв ◆ *vt* разрезать (разрезать* *perf*); (*tear*) разрывать (разорвать* *perf*); **to ~ sb's throat** перерезать* (*perf*) кому-н горло.
slither ['slɪðə'] *vi* (*person*) скользить* (*impf*); (*snake*) извиваться (*impf*).
sliver ['slɪvə'] *n* (*of glass*) осколок*; (*of wood*) щепка*; (*of cheese etc*) кусочек*.
slob [slɒb] *n* (*inf*) олух*.
slog [slɒg] *vi* (*BRIT: work hard*) корпеть* (*impf*) ◆ *n*: **it was a hard ~** это была тяжёлая работа.
slogan ['sləʊgən] *n* лозунг*.
slop [slɒp] *vi* (*also: ~ over*) выплёскиваться (выплеснуться *perf*) ◆ *vt* выплёскивать (выплеснуть *perf*)

▶ **slop out** *vi* (*in prison etc*) выносить* (вынести* *perf*) парашу.
slope [sləʊp] *n* (*gentle hill*) уклон; (*side of mountain*) склон; (*ski slope*) спуск; (*slant*) наклон ◆ *vi*: **to ~ down** спускаться (*impf*); **to ~ up** подниматься (*impf*) под уклоном.
sloping ['sləʊpɪŋ] *adj* (*ground, roof*) покатый (покат); (*handwriting*) наклонный.
sloppy ['slɒpɪ] *adj* (*work*) небрежный* (небрежен), халтурный; (*appearance*) неряшливый (неряшлив); (*pej: film etc*) сентиментальный* (сентиментален).
slops [slɒps] *npl* помои *pl*.
slosh [slɒʃ] (*inf*) *vi*: **to ~ around** *or* **about** плескаться* (*impf*).
sloshed [slɒʃt] *adj* (*inf: drunk*) пьяный в дымину.
slot [slɒt] *n* (*in machine*) прорезь *f*, паз*; (*fig: in timetable*) окно*; (*RADIO, TV*) место* ◆ *vt*: **to ~ sth into** опускать (опустить* *perf*) что-н в +*acc* ◆ *vi*: **to ~ into** входить* (войти* *perf*) в +*acc*.
sloth [sləʊθ] *n* (*laziness*) лень *f*; (*ZOOL*) ленивец*.
slot machine *n* (*BRIT: vending machine*) торговый автомат; (*: fruit machine*) игральный автомат.
slot meter *n* (*BRIT*) счётчик.
slouch [slaʊtʃ] *vi* сутулиться (ссутулиться *perf*); **she was ~ed in a chair** она сидела на стуле, сгорбившись.
Slovakia [sləʊˈvækɪə] *n* Словакия.
Slovakian [sləʊˈvækɪən] *adj* словацкий* ◆ *n* (*person*) словак(-ачка).
Slovenia [sləʊˈviːnɪə] *n* Словения.
Slovenian [sləʊˈviːnɪən] *adj* словенский* ◆ *n* (*person*) словенец*(-нка); (*LING*) словенский* язык*.
slovenly ['slʌvənlɪ] *adj* неряшливый (неряшлив).
slow [sləʊ] *adj* медленный; (*not clever*) тупой* (туп) ◆ *adv* медленно ◆ *vt* (*also: ~ down, ~ up: vehicle*) притормаживать (притормозить* *perf*); (*: business*) приостанавливать (приостановить* *perf*) ◆ *vi* (*traffic*) замедляться (замедлиться *perf*); (*car, train etc*) сбавлять (сбавить* *perf*) ход; **at a ~ speed** на низкой скорости; **to be ~ to act/decide** быть* (*impf*) медлительным(-ой) в делах/в решениях; **my watch is (20 minutes) ~** мои часы отстают (на 20 минут); **business is ~** дела идут неважно; **"slow"** (*road sign*) "медленно"; **to go ~** (*driver*) двигаться (*impf*) медленно; (*BRIT: workers*) снижать (снизить* *perf*) темп работы.
slow-acting [sləʊˈæktɪŋ] *adj* замедленного действия.
slowly ['sləʊlɪ] *adv* медленно; **to drive ~** водить*/вести* (*impf*) машину медленно.
slow motion *n*: **in ~ ~** в замедленном действии.

slow-moving [slǝu'mu:vɪŋ] adj ме́дленно дви́жущийся, ме́дленный.
slowness ['slǝunɪs] n ме́дленность f.
sludge [slʌdʒ] n грязь f.
slue [slu:] vi (US) = **slew**.
slug [slʌg] n (ZOOL) слизня́к*; (bullet) пу́ля.
sluggish ['slʌgɪʃ] adj (stream) ме́дленно теку́щий*; (engine) пло́хо рабо́тающий; (person) медли́тельный* (медли́телен); (trading) вя́лый.
sluice [slu:s] n (gate) шлюз; (channel) жёлоб* ♦ vt: **to ~ down** or **out** промыва́ть (промы́ть* perf), ока́тывать (окати́ть* perf).
slum [slʌm] n трущо́ба.
slumber ['slʌmbǝʳ] n сон*.
slump [slʌmp] n (economic) спад; (in profits, sales) ре́зкое паде́ние ♦ vi (person) вали́ться* (повали́ться* perf); (prices) ре́зко па́дать (упа́сть* perf); **he was ~ed over the wheel** он сиде́л, упа́в на руль.
slung [slʌŋ] pt, pp of **sling**.
slunk [slʌŋk] pt, pp of **slink**.
slur [slǝːʳ] vt (words) произноси́ть* (произнести́* perf) нечленоразде́льно ♦ n (MUS) ли́га; (fig): ~ **(on)** пятно́ (на +prp); **to cast a ~ on** поро́чить (impf).
slurp [slǝːp] vt (гро́мко) хлеба́ть (хлебну́ть perf).
slurred [slǝːd] adj (speech, voice) невня́тный* (невня́тен).
slush [slʌʃ] n сля́коть f.
slush fund n (POL) фонд для по́дкупа госуда́рственных лиц.
slushy ['slʌʃɪ] adj (snow) мо́крый; (street) покры́тый сля́котью; (BRIT: fig) сентимента́льный* (сентимента́лен).
slut [slʌt] n (inf. pej) потаску́ха.
sly [slaɪ] adj хи́трый* (хитёр) ♦ n: **on the ~** тайко́м.
smack [smæk] n (slap) шлепо́к*; (on face) пощёчина; (inf. heroin) геройн ♦ vt хло́пать (хло́пнуть perf); (child) шлёпать (отшлёпать perf); (on face) дава́ть* (дать* perf) пощёчину +dat ♦ vi: **to ~ of** попа́хивать (impf) +instr ♦ adv (inf): **the ball fell ~ in the middle** мяч упа́л пря́мо посереди́не; **to ~ one's lips** чмо́кать (чмо́кнуть perf) губа́ми.
smacker ['smækǝʳ] n (inf: kiss) поцелу́й; (: BRIT: pound note) бума́жный фунт; (: US: dollar bill) бума́жный до́ллар.
small [smɔːl] adj ма́ленький*; (quantity, amount) небольшо́й ♦ n: **the ~ of the back** поясни́ца; **to get** or **grow ~er** уменьша́ться (уме́ньшиться perf); **to make ~er** (amount, income) снижа́ть (сни́зить* perf); (object, garment) уменьша́ть (уме́ньшить perf); **a ~ shopkeeper** ме́лкий(-ая) ла́вочник(-ица).
small ads npl (BRIT) ма́ленькие объявле́ния

ntpl (в газе́те о ку́пле-прода́же).
small arms npl (MIL) стрелко́вое ору́жие ntsg.
small business n ма́лое предприя́тие.
small change n ме́лочь* f.
small fry npl (fig) ме́лкая со́шка fsg.
smallholder ['smɔːlhǝuldǝʳ] n (BRIT) владе́лец небольшо́го земе́льного уча́стка.
smallholding ['smɔːlhǝuldɪŋ] n (BRIT) небольшо́е земе́льное владе́ние.
small hours npl: **in the ~ ~** в предрассве́тные часы́*.
smallish ['smɔːlɪʃ] adj небольшо́й, дово́льно ма́ленький*.
small-minded [smɔːl'maɪndɪd] adj ограни́ченный.
smallpox ['smɔːlpɔks] n о́спа.
small print n ме́лкий* шрифт.
small-scale ['smɔːlskeɪl] adj (map, model) ма́ленького масшта́ба; (business, farming) ме́лкий*.
small screen n: **the ~ ~** телеви́дение, ма́лый экра́н.
small talk n све́тская бесе́да.
small-time ['smɔːltaɪm] adj (farmer etc) ме́лький.
small-town ['smɔːltaun] adj провинциа́льный* (провинциа́лен).
smarmy ['smɑːmɪ] adj (BRIT: pej) вкра́дчивый (вкра́дчив).
smart [smɑːt] adj (neat, tidy) опря́тный* (опря́тен); (fashionable) мо́дный* (мо́ден); (clever) толко́вый (толко́в); (quick) бы́стрый* (быстр); (pej) наха́льный* (наха́лен) ♦ vi (also fig) жечь* (impf); **the ~ set** фешене́бельное о́бщество; **to look ~** вы́глядеть* (impf) элега́нтно; **my eyes are ~ing** у меня́ глаза́ щи́плет.
smart card n (for transactions) вид креди́тной ка́рточки с микропроце́ссором, испо́льзуемой в платёжных опера́циях.
smarten up ['smɑːtn-] vi приоде́ться* (perf), принаряди́ться (perf) ♦ vt (place) приводи́ть* (привести́* perf) в поря́док; (person) принаряжа́ть (perf).
smash [smæʃ] n (collision: also: ~-up) ава́рия; (sound) гро́хот; (TENNIS) смэш ♦ vt разбива́ть (разби́ть* perf); (SPORT: record) поби́ть* (perf) ♦ vi (break) разбива́ться (разби́ться* perf); (collide): **to ~ against** or **into** врeза́ться (вре́заться* perf) в +acc
▶ **smash up** vt (car) разбива́ть (разби́ть* perf); (room) громи́ть* (разгроми́ть* perf).
smash hit n шля́гер.
smashing ['smæʃɪŋ] adj (inf) потряса́ющий*.
smattering ['smætǝrɪŋ] n: **a ~ of** пове́рхностное зна́ние +gen.
smear [smɪǝʳ] n (trace) след*; (insult) клевета́; (MED) мазо́к* ♦ vt (spread) ма́зать*

---

* marks translations which have irregular inflections. The Russian-English side of the dictionary gives inflectional information.

(намáзать* *perf*); (*make dirty*) пáчкать
(испáчкать *perf*); **his hands were ~ed with
oil/ink** егó рýки бы́ли испáчканы мáслом/
черни́лами.
smear campaign *n* клеветни́ческая
кампáния.
smear test *n* (*BRIT: MED*) мазóк* для анáлиза.
smell [smɛl] (*pt, pp* **smelt** *or* **smelled**) *n* зáпах;
(*sense*) обонáние ♦ *vt* чýвствовать
(почýвствовать *perf*) зáпах +*gen* ♦ *vi*: **to ~ (of)**
(*unpleasant*) воня́ть (*impf*) (+*instr*); (*food etc*)
пáхнуть (*impf*) (+*instr*).
smelly ['smɛlɪ] *adj* воню́чий* (воню́ч).
smelt [smɛlt] *pt, pp of* **smell** ♦ *vt* (*ore*) плáвить*
(расплáвить* *perf*).
smile [smaɪl] *n* улы́бка* ♦ *vi* улыбáться
(улыбнýться *perf*).
smiling ['smaɪlɪŋ] *adj* улыбáющийся.
smirk [smə:k] *n* (*pej*) ухмы́лка*.
smithy ['smɪðɪ] *n* кýзница.
smitten ['smɪtn] *adj*: **he is ~ with her** он от неё
без умá.
smock [smɔk] *n* блýза; (*children's*) дéтское
плáтье в сбóрочку; (*US: overall*)
комбинезóн.
smog [smɔg] *n* смог.
smoke [sməuk] *n* дым ♦ *vi* (*person*) кури́ть*
(*impf*); (*chimney*) дыми́ться (*impf*) ♦ *vt*
(*cigarettes*) кури́ть* (вы́курить *perf*); **to have a
~** кури́ть* (покури́ть* *perf*); **to go up in ~**
сгорéть (*perf*); (*fig*) пойти́* (*perf*) прáхом; **do
you ~?** Вы кýрите?
smoked ['sməukt] *adj* (*bacon, fish*) копчёный;
(*glass*) ды́мчатый.
smokeless fuel ['sməuklɪs-] *n* бездь́мное
тóпливо.
smokeless zone *n* (*BRIT*) бездь́мная
городскáя зóна.
smoker ['sməukə'] *n* (*person*)
кури́льщик(-щица); (*RAIL*) вагóн для
куря́щих.
smoke screen *n* (*also fig*) дымовáя завéса.
smoke shop *n* (*US*) конти́нька.
smoking ['sməukɪŋ] *n* (*act*) курéние; "**no ~**" "не
кури́ть".
smoking compartment (*US* **smoking car**) *n*
вагóн для куря́щих.
smoking room *n* кури́тельная кóмната.
smoky ['sməukɪ] *adj* (*atmosphere, room*)
задымлённый (задь́млен); (*taste*) с
при́вкусом ды́ма.
smolder ['sməuldə'] *vi* (*US*) = **smoulder**.
smoochy ['smu:tʃɪ] *adj* (*inf: music*)
чýвственный.
smooth [smu:ð] *adj* глáдкий* (глáдок); (*sauce*)
без комкóв; (*sea*) спокóйный* (спокóен);
(*flavour*) мя́гкий* (мя́гок); (*movement*)
плáвный* (плáвен); (*flight*) рóвный; (*pej:
person*) лóвкий* (лóвок) ♦ *vt* (*also: ~* **out**)
разглáживать (разглáдить* *perf*); (*:
difficulties*) устраня́ть (устрани́ть *perf*)

▸ **smooth over** *vt*: **to ~ things over** (*fig*)
улáживать (улáдить* *perf*) делá.
smoothly ['smu:ðlɪ] *adv* (*easily*) без трудá;
everything went ~ всё прошлó глáдко.
smoothness ['smu:ðnɪs] *n* глáдкость *f*;
(*flavour*) мя́гкость *f*; (*movement*) плáвность
f.
smother ['smʌðə'] *vt* (*fire*) туши́ть*
(потуши́ть* *perf*); (*person*) души́ть*
(задуши́ть* *perf*); (*emotions*) подавля́ть
(подави́ть* *perf*).
smoulder ['sməuldə'] (*US* **smolder**) *vi* (*fire*)
тлеть* (*impf*); (*fig: anger, hatred*) зреть
(*impf*).
smudge [smʌdʒ] *n* пятнó* ♦ *vt* размáзывать
(размáзать* *perf*).
smug [smʌg] *adj* самодовóльный*
(самодовóлен).
smuggle ['smʌgl] *vt* (*goods*) провози́ть*
(провезти́* *perf*) контрабáндой; (*refugees*)
переправля́ть (перепрáвить* *perf*) тáйно; **to
~ in/out** (*goods etc*) ввози́ть* (ввезти́* *perf*)/
вывози́ть* (вы́везти* *perf*) контрабáндой.
smuggler ['smʌglə'] *n* контрабанди́ст(ка*).
smuggling ['smʌglɪŋ] *n* контрабáнда.
smut [smʌt] *n* (*soot*) сáжа *no pl*; (*in conversation
etc*) похáбщина.
smutty ['smʌtɪ] *adj* (*joke, book*) похáбный*
(похáбен).
snack [snæk] *n* закýска*; **to have a ~**
закýсывать (закуси́ть* *perf*), перекýсывать
(перекуси́ть* *perf*).
snack bar *n* закýсочная *f adj*.
snag [snæg] *n* (*problem*) загвóздка*,
затруднéние.
snail [sneɪl] *n* ули́тка*.
snake [sneɪk] *n* змея́*.
snap [snæp] *n* (*sound*) треск; (*photograph*)
сни́мок*; (*game*) снэп* ♦ *adj* (*decision etc*)
необдýманный* (необдýман) ♦ *vt* (*break*)
разлáмывать (разломи́ть* *perf*); (*fingers*)
щёлкать (щёлкнуть *perf*) +*instr* ♦ *vi* (*break*)
разлáмываться (разломáться *or*
разломи́ться* *perf*); (*fig: lose control*)
сломáться (*perf*); (*: speak sharply*) кричáть*
(*impf*); **to ~ at sb** (*subj: person*) кричáть* (*impf*)
на когó-н; **to ~ one's fingers at** (*fig*)
отмáхиваться (отмахнýться *perf*) от +*gen*; **a
cold ~** (*weather*) внезáпное рéзкое
похолодáние; **to ~ shut** (*trap, jaws etc*)
защёлкивать (защёлкнуть *perf*)
▸ **snap at** *vt fus* огрызáться (огрызнýться *perf*)
на +*acc*
▸ **snap off** *vi* отлáмывать (отломáть *or*
отломи́ть* *perf*)
▸ **snap up** *vt* (*bargains*) расхвáтывать
(расхватáть *perf*).
snap fastener *n* кнóпка*.
snappy ['snæpɪ] (*inf*) *adj* (*slogan*) брóский*;
(*answer*) бы́стрый; **make it ~!**
поторáпливайся!

snapshot ['snæpʃɒt] *n* сни́мок*.

snare [snɛəʳ] *n* лову́шка*, капка́н ♦ *vt* (*also fig*) зама́нивать (замани́ть* *perf*) в лову́шку.

snarl [snɑːl] *vi* (*animal, person*) рыча́ть (*impf*), ворча́ть (*impf*) ♦ *vt*: **to get ~ed up** (*plans*) пу́таться (запу́таться *perf*); **the traffic was ~ed up** произошёл зато́р в у́личном движе́нии.

snarl-up ['snɑːlʌp] *n* пу́таница.

snatch [snætʃ] *n* (*of conversation, song etc*) обры́вок* ♦ *vt* (*grab*) хвата́ть (схвати́ть* *perf*); (*handbag*) вырыва́ть (вы́рвать* *perf*); (*child etc*) красть* (укра́сть* *perf*); (*opportunity, look etc*) урыва́ть (урва́ть* *perf*) ♦ *vi*: **don't ~!** не хвата́й!; **to ~ a sandwich** перехва́тывать (перехвати́ть* *perf*) бутербро́д; **I managed to ~ some sleep** мне удало́сь немно́го поспа́ть
▸ **snatch up** *vt* схва́тывать (схвати́ть* *perf*).

snazzy ['snæzi] *adj* (*inf*) шика́рный* (шика́рен).

sneak [sniːk] *n* (*inf: informer*) я́беда *m/f* ♦ *vi*: **to ~ into/out of** незаме́тно проска́льзывать (проскользну́ть *perf*) в +*acc*/из +*gen* ♦ *vt*: **to ~ a look at sth** взгля́дывать (взгляну́ть* *perf*) украдко́й на что-н; **to ~ up on sb** я́бедничать (ная́бедничать *perf*) на кого́-н.

sneakers ['sniːkəz] *npl* кроссо́вки* *fpl*.

sneaking ['sniːkɪŋ] *adj*: **I have a ~ feeling** *or* **suspicion that ...** у меня́ закра́лось подозре́ние, что ....

sneaky ['sniːkɪ] *adj* (*pej: person*) хи́трый* (хитёр*); (*advantage, look*) незаме́тный* (незаме́тен).

sneer [snɪəʳ] *vi* (*laugh*) посме́иваться (*impf*); (*mock*): **to ~ at** глуми́ться* (*impf*) над +*instr*.

sneeze [sniːz] *n* чиха́нье ♦ *vi* чиха́ть (чихну́ть *perf*)
▸ **sneeze at** *vt fus*: **such things are not to be ~d at** таки́ми веща́ми не броса́ются.

snide [snaɪd] *adj* (*pej*) ехи́дный* (ехи́ден).

sniff [snɪf] *n* (*sound*) сопе́ние; (*smell: by dog, person*) обню́хивание ♦ *vi* шмы́гать (шмыгну́ть *perf*) но́сом; (*when crying*) всхли́пывать (*impf*) ♦ *vt* ню́хать (*impf*); (*glue, drugs*) вдыха́ть (*impf*), ню́хать (*impf*)
▸ **sniff at** *vt fus*: **such things are not to be ~ed at** таки́ми веща́ми не броса́ются.

sniffer dog ['snɪfə-] *n* (*POLICE*) соба́ка-ище́йка (*для обнаруже́ния нарко́тиков и взры́вчатых веще́ств*).

snigger ['snɪɡəʳ] *vi* хихи́кать (хихи́кнуть *perf*).

snip [snɪp] *n* (*cut*) надре́з; (*BRIT: inf: bargain*) нахо́дка* ♦ *vt* (*cut*) ре́зать (*impf*).

sniper ['snaɪpəʳ] *n* сна́йпер.

snippet ['snɪpɪt] *n* обры́вок*.

snivel ['snɪvl] *vi* хны́кать (*impf*).

snob [snɒb] *n* сноб.

snobbery ['snɒbərɪ] *n* сноби́зм.

snobbish ['snɒbɪʃ] *adj* сноби́стский*.

snog [snɒg] *vi* лиза́ться (*impf*) ♦ *n*: **to have a ~** лиза́ться (*impf*).

snooker ['snuːkəʳ] *n* сну́кер (*игра́ в билья́рд*) ♦ *vt* (*BRIT: inf: fig*): **we're completely ~ed** мы соверше́нно за́гнаны в у́гол.

snoop ['snuːp] *vi*: **to ~ about** шпио́нить (*impf*); **to ~ on sb** подгля́дывать (*impf*) за кем-н (в щёлочку).

snooper ['snuːpəʳ] *n* шпио́н.

snooty ['snuːtɪ] *adj* зади́ристый.

snooze [snuːz] *vi* прикорну́ть (*perf*), вздремну́ть (*perf*) ♦ *n*: **to have a ~** вздремну́ть (*perf*).

snore [snɔːʳ] *n* храп ♦ *vi* храпе́ть* (*impf*).

snoring ['snɔːrɪŋ] *n* храп.

snorkel ['snɔːkl] *n* тру́бка*.

snort [snɔːt] *n* фы́рканье ♦ *vi* (*animal*) фаркну́ть (*perf*); (*horse*) всхра́пывать (*impf*) ♦ *vt* (*inf: drugs*) ню́хать (*impf*).

snotty ['snɒtɪ] *adj* (*inf: handkerchief, nose*) сопли́вый; (: *pej: snobbish*) на́глый.

snout [snaut] *n* (*of pig*) ры́ло; (*of dog etc*) мо́рда.

snow [snəu] *n* снег* ♦ *vi*: **it's ~ing** идёт снег ♦ *vt*: **she is ~ed under with work** она́ зава́лена рабо́той.

snowball ['snəubɔːl] *n* снежо́к* ♦ *vi* (*fig: problem, campaign*) нараста́ть (*impf*) как сне́жный ком.

snowbound ['snəubaund] *adj* засы́панный сне́гом.

snowcapped ['snəukæpt] *adj* сне́жный.

snowdrift ['snəudrɪft] *n* сугро́б.

snowdrop ['snəudrɒp] *n* (*BOT*) подсне́жник.

snowfall ['snəufɔːl] *n* снегопа́д.

snowflake ['snəufleɪk] *n* снежи́нка*.

snow line *n* снегова́я ли́ния.

snowman ['snəumæn] *n irreg* сне́жная ба́ба, снегови́к.

snowplough ['snəuplau] (*US* **snowplow**) *n* снегоубо́рочный комба́йн.

snowshoes ['snəuʃuːz] *npl* снегосту́пы *mpl*.

snowstorm ['snəustɔːm] *n* бура́н, вьюга.

snowy ['snəuɪ] *adj* сне́жный; (*covered with snow*) засне́женный.

SNP *n abbr* (*BRIT: POL*) = *Scottish National Party*.

snub [snʌb] *vt* (*person*) пренебрежи́тельно обходи́ться* (обойти́сь* *perf*) с +*instr* ♦ *n* вы́зов.

snub-nosed [snʌb'nəuzd] *adj* курно́сый.

snuff [snʌf] *n* ню́хательный таба́к* ♦ *vt* (*also:~ out*) туши́ть* (потуши́ть* *perf*).

snuff movie *n* порнографи́ческий фильм, в кото́ром засня́то настоя́щее уби́йство.

snug [snʌg] *adj* (*place*) ую́тный* (ую́тен); (*well-fitting*) пло́тно облега́ющий*; **I'm very ~ here** мне здесь о́чень ую́тно; **the sweater is a ~ fit** сви́тер хорошо́ прилега́ет.

---

snuggle ['snʌgl] *vi*: to ~ up to sb прижима́ться (прижа́ться* *perf*) к кому́-н; to ~ down in bed забива́ться (заби́ться* *perf*) под одея́ло.

snugly ['snʌglɪ] *adv* ую́тно; to fit ~ (*object in pocket etc*) удо́бно помеща́ться (*impf*); the sweater fits ~ сви́тер хорошо́ прилега́ет.

SO *n abbr* (*COMM*) = **standing order**.

KEYWORD

so [səu] *adv* **1** (*thus, likewise*): so saying he walked away с э́тими слова́ми, он ушёл; while she was so doing, he ... пока́ она́ э́то де́лала, он ...; if so е́сли да; if this is so е́сли э́то так; I didn't do it – you did so! э́то не я (сде́лал) – нет, ты!; I like him – so do I мне он нра́вится – мне то́же; I'm still at school – so am I я ещё учу́сь в шко́ле – я то́же; he has a brother – so has David у него́ есть брат – у Дави́да то́же; so it is! да, действи́тельно!; I hope/think so наде́юсь/ду́маю, что да; so far I haven't had any problems пока́ что у меня́ не́ было пробле́м; how do you like the book so far? ну как, нра́вится Вам кни́га?

2 (*in comparisons etc*: +*adv*) насто́лько, так; (+*adj*) насто́лько, тако́й; so quickly (that) насто́лько *or* так бы́стро(, что); the house is so big (that) дом насто́лько *or* тако́й большо́й(, что); she's not so clever as her brother она́ не так умна́, как её брат; I'm so glad to see you я так рад Вас ви́деть;

3: I've got so much work у меня́ так мно́го рабо́ты; I love you so much я Вас так люблю́; thank you so much спаси́бо Вам большо́е; there are so many books I would like to read сто́лько есть книг, кото́рые я бы хоте́л проче́сть

4 (*phrases*): ten or so о́коло десяти́; so long! (*inf*: *goodbye*) пока́!

◆ *conj* **1** (*expressing purpose*): so as to do что́бы сде́лать (*perf*); I brought this wine so that you could try it я принёс э́то вино́, что́бы Вы могли́ его́ попро́бовать

2 (*expressing result*) так что; so I was right after all так что, я был всё-таки прав; so you see, I could have stayed так что ви́дите, я мог бы оста́ться; so, what shall we do now так, что тепе́рь бу́дем де́лать.

---

soak [səuk] *vt* (*drench*) промочи́ть* (*perf*); (*steep in water*) зама́чивать (замочи́ть* *perf*) ◆ *vi* (*washing, dishes*) отмока́ть (*impf*); to be ~ed through промо́кнуть (*perf*) наскво́зь
▶ **soak in** *vi* впи́тываться (впита́ться *perf*)
▶ **soak up** *vt* впи́тывать (впита́ть *perf*) (в себя́).

soaking ['səukɪŋ] *adj* (*also*: ~ wet) мо́крый наскво́зь.

so-and-so ['səuənsəu] *n* (*somebody*) не́кто*; Mr ~ Господи́н тако́й-то; you little ~! (*pej*) ах ты тако́й-ся́кой!

soap [səup] *n* мы́ло*; (*TV*: *also*: ~ opera) мы́льная о́пера.

soapbox ['səupbɔks] *n* (*container*) я́щик из-под мы́ла; (*platform*) импровизи́рованная трибу́на.

soap flakes *npl* мы́льные хло́пья *pl*.

soap opera *n* (*TV*) мы́льная о́пера.

soap powder *n* мы́льный порошо́к*.

soapsuds ['səupsʌdz] *npl* мы́льная пе́на *fsg*.

soapy ['səupɪ] *adj* мы́льный.

soar [sɔ:] *vi* (*bird, rocket*) взвива́ться (взви́ться* *perf*) в во́здух; (*price, production, temperature*) ре́зко подска́кивать (подскочи́ть* *perf*); (*building etc*) возвыша́ться (*impf*).

soaring ['sɔ:rɪŋ] *adj* (*prices, inflation*) неуправля́емый.

sob [sɔb] *n* рыда́ние ◆ *vi* рыда́ть (*impf*), всхли́пывать (*impf*).

s.o.b. *n abbr* (*US*: *inf*!: = son of a bitch) су́кин сын* (!)

sober ['səubə] *adj* тре́звый* (трезв); (*colour, style*) небро́ский*
▶ **sober up** *vt* протрезви́ть* (*perf*) ◆ *vi* трезве́ть (*impf*), протрезвля́ться (протрезви́ться* *perf*).

sobriety [sə'braɪətɪ] *n* тре́звость *f*.

sobriquet ['səubrɪkeɪ] *n* (*nickname*) про́звище.

sob story *n* душещипа́тельная исто́рия.

Soc. *abbr* = **society**.

so-called ['səu'kɔ:ld] *adj* так называ́емый.

soccer ['sɔkə] *n* футбо́л.

soccer pitch *n* футбо́льное по́ле*.

soccer player *n* футболи́ст.

sociable ['səuʃəbl] *adj* (*person*) общи́тельный* (общи́телен); (*behaviour*) све́тский*.

social ['səuʃl] *adj* (*history, structure etc*) обще́ственный, социа́льный; (*event*) све́тский*; (*sociable*: *animal*) ста́дный ◆ *n* (*party*) встре́ча, ве́чер*; he has a good ~ life он мно́го обща́ется с людьми́.

social class *n* социа́льный класс.

social climber *n* челове́к, *стремя́щийся заня́ть бо́лее высо́кое социа́льное положе́ние*.

social club *n* клуб обще́ния.

social democrat *n* (*POL*) социа́л-демокра́т.

social insurance *n* (*US*) социа́льное обеспе́чение *or* страхова́ние.

socialism ['səuʃəlɪzəm] *n* социали́зм.

socialist ['səuʃəlɪst] *n* социали́ст ◆ *adj* социалисти́ческий*.

socialite ['səuʃəlaɪt] *n* све́тский* челове́к*.

socialize ['səuʃəlaɪz] *vi*: to ~ (with) обща́ться (пообща́ться *perf*) (с +*instr*).

socially ['səuʃəlɪ] *adv*: to visit sb ~ зайти́* (*perf*) к кому́-н по-дру́жески; ~ acceptable социа́льно прие́млемый.

social science *n* (*SCOL*) обще́ственные нау́ки *fpl*.

social security (*BRIT*) *n* социа́льное обеспе́чение; Department of S~ S~ Министе́рство социа́льного обеспе́чения.

social services *npl* систе́ма *fsg* социа́льного обслу́живания.

social welfare *n* социа́льное обеспе́чение.

social work *n* социа́льная рабо́та.
social worker *n* социа́льный рабо́тник.
society [sə'saɪətɪ] *n* о́бщество ♦ *cpd* (*party*) све́тский*.
socioeconomic ['səʊsɪəʊɪkə'nɒmɪk] *adj* (*group, factor*) социа́льно-экономи́ческий*.
sociological [səʊsɪə'lɒdʒɪkl] *adj* (*study*) социологи́ческий.
sociologist [səʊsɪ'ɒlədʒɪst] *n* социо́лог.
sociology [səʊsɪ'ɒlədʒɪ] *n* социоло́гия.
sock [sɒk] *n* носо́к* ♦ *vt* (*inf*): **to ~ sb in the face** дава́ть* (дать* *perf*) кому́-н по физионо́мии; **to pull one's ~s up** (*fig*) подтяну́ться* (*perf*).
socket ['sɒkɪt] *n* глазни́ца; (*BRIT: ELEC: in wall*) розе́тка*; (: *for light bulb*) патро́н.
sod [sɒd] *n* (*of earth*) дёрн; (*BRIT: inf!*) дрянь *f* така́я (*!*)
► **sod off** *vi* (*inf!*): ~ **off** убира́йся отсю́да!, иди́ на́ фиг!
soda ['səʊdə] *n* (*CHEM*) со́да; (*also:* ~ **water**) со́довая *f adj*; (*US: also:* ~ **pop**) газиро́ванная вода́.
sodden ['sɒdn] *adj* прокля́тый.
sodium ['səʊdɪəm] *n* на́трий.
sodium chloride *n* хлори́д на́трия.
sofa ['səʊfə] *n* дива́н.
Sofia ['səʊfɪə] *n* Со́фия.
soft [sɒft] *adj* мя́гкий* (мя́гок); (*music*) негро́мкий* (негро́мок); **don't be ~!** (*inf: stupid*) не будь дурако́м!
soft-boiled ['sɒftbɔɪld] *adj*: ~ **egg** яйцо́* всмя́тку.
soft currency *n* неконверти́руемая валю́та.
soft drink *n* безалкого́льный напи́ток*, сок*.
soft drugs *npl* мя́гкие нарко́тики *mpl*.
soften ['sɒfn] *vt* смягча́ть (смягчи́ть *perf*) ♦ *vi* смягча́ться (смягчи́ться *perf*).
softener ['sɒfnəʳ] *n* (*also:* **water** ~) хими́ческое сре́дство, смягча́ющее во́ду; (*also:* **fabric** ~) смягча́ющее сре́дство для сти́рки.
soft fruit *n* (*BRIT*) я́годы *fpl*.
soft furnishings *npl* мя́гкая оби́вка *fsg*.
softhearted [sɒft'hɑ:tɪd] *adj* мягкосерде́чный* (мягкосерде́чен).
softly ['sɒftlɪ] *adv* (*gently*) мя́гко; (*quietly*) ти́хо.
softness ['sɒftnɪs] *n* мя́гкость *f*.
soft option *n* лёгкий путь* *m*.
soft sell *n* (*COMM*) мя́гкая та́ктика сбы́та проду́кции.
soft spot *n*: **to have a ~ ~ for sb** пита́ть (*impf*) к кому́-н сла́бость.
soft target *n* лёгкая добы́ча.
soft toy *n* мя́гкая игру́шка*.
software ['sɒftwɛəʳ] *n* (*COMPUT*) програ́ммное обеспе́чение.
software package *n* (*COMPUT*) паке́т програ́мм.

soft water *n* мя́гкая вода́.
soggy ['sɒgɪ] *adj* (*ground*) сыро́й; (*sandwiches*) размо́кший.
soil [sɔɪl] *n* (*earth*) по́чва; (*territory*) земля́* ♦ *vt* па́чкать *or* испа́чкать *perf*); (*fig*) мара́ть (замара́ть *perf*).
soiled [sɔɪld] *adj* испа́чканный (испа́чкан); (*COMM*) повреждённый.
sojourn ['sɒdʒə:n] *n* пребыва́ние.
solace ['sɒlɪs] *n* утеше́ние.
solar ['səʊləʳ] *adj* со́лнечный.
solaria [sə'lɛərɪə] *npl of* **solarium**.
solarium [sə'lɛərɪəm] (*pl* **solaria**) *n* соля́рий.
solar panel *n* со́лнечная батаре́я.
solar plexus [-'plɛksəs] *n* со́лнечное сплете́ние.
solar power *n* со́лнечная эне́ргия.
solar system *n* со́лнечная систе́ма.
solar wind *n* со́лнечная бу́ря.
sold [səʊld] *pt, pp of* **sell**.
solder ['səʊldəʳ] *vt* пая́ть (*impf*), спа́ивать (спая́ть *perf*) ♦ *n* припо́й.
soldier ['səʊldʒəʳ] *n* (*not officer*) солда́т*; (*in army*) вое́нный *m adj* ♦ *vi*: **to ~ on** не сдава́ться* (*impf*); **toy ~** солда́тик.
sold out *adj* распро́данный (распро́дан).
sole [səʊl] *n* (*of foot*) подо́шва; (*of shoe*) подо́шва, подмётка* ♦ *n inv* (*fish*) па́лтус ♦ *adj* (*unique*) еди́нственный; (*exclusive*) исключи́тельный; **the ~ reason** еди́нственная причи́на.
solely ['səʊllɪ] *adv* то́лько; **I will hold you ~ responsible** вся отве́тственность ля́жет то́лько на Вас.
solemn ['sɒləm] *adj* торже́ственный* (торже́ствен).
sole trader *n* (*COMM*) единоли́чный торго́вец*.
solicit [sə'lɪsɪt] *vt* (*request*) обраща́ться (обрати́ться* *perf*) с про́сьбой за +*instr* ♦ *vi* (*prostitute*) предлага́ть (*impf*) себя́.
solicitor [sə'lɪsɪtəʳ] *n* (*BRIT*) адвока́т.
solid ['sɒlɪd] *adj* (*not hollow*) це́льный; (*not liquid*) твёрдый; (*reliable*) непоколеби́мый (непоколеби́м); (*meal*) пло́тный; (*vote*) сплочённый; (*entire*) це́лый; (*gold*) чи́стый ♦ *n* (*solid object*) твёрдое те́ло*; ~**s** *npl* (*food*) твёрдая пи́ща *fsg*; (*for babies*) прико́рм *msg*; **to be on ~ ground** (*fig*) твёрдо стоя́ть (*impf*) на нога́х; **we waited two ~ hours** мы прожда́ли це́лых два часа́.
solidarity [sɔlɪ'dærɪtɪ] *n* солида́рность *f*.
solid fuel *n* твёрдое то́пливо.
solidify [sə'lɪdɪfaɪ] *vi* (*fat etc*) застыва́ть (засты́ть* *perf*); (*metal*) затвердева́ть (затверде́ть *perf*) ♦ *vt* де́лать (*impf*) твёрдым.
solidity [sə'lɪdɪtɪ] *n* твёрдость *f*.
solidly ['sɒlɪdlɪ] *adv* (*built*) кре́пко; (*respectable*) соли́дно; (*in favour*) по́лностью.

solid-state ['sɔlɪdsteɪt] adj (ELEC) твёрдый, в твёрдом состоянии.
soliloquy [sə'lɪləkwɪ] n монолог.
solitaire [sɔlɪ'tɛɑ'] n (gem) солитёр; (game) пасьянс.
solitary ['sɔlɪtərɪ] adj одинокий* (одинок); (isolated) уединённый; (single) единичный.
solitary confinement n одиночное заключение; **to be in ~ ~** находиться* (impf) в одиночном заключении.
solitude ['sɔlɪtjuːd] n одиночество, уединение; **to live in ~** жить* (impf) в уединении.
solo ['səuləu] n соло nt ind ◆ adv (fly) в одиночку; (play) соло.
soloist ['səuləuɪst] n солист*(ка).
Solomon Islands ['sɔləmən-] npl: **the ~ ~** Соломоновы острова mpl.
solstice ['sɔlstɪs] n солнцестояние.
soluble ['sɔljubl] adj растворимый.
solution [sə'luːʃən] n (answer) решение; (liquid) раствор.
solve [sɔlv] vt (puzzle) решать (решить perf); (problem) разрешать (разрешить perf); (mystery) раскрывать (раскрыть perf).
solvency ['sɔlvənsɪ] n платёжеспособность f.
solvent ['sɔlvənt] adj (COMM) платёжеспособный ◆ n (CHEM) растворитель m.
solvent abuse n токсикомания.
Som. abbr (BRIT: POST) = Somerset.
Somali [sə'mɑːlɪ] adj сомалийский ◆ n сомалиец*(-ийка*).
Somalia [sə'mɑːlɪə] n Сомали nt ind.
sombre ['sɔmbə'] (US **somber**) adj мрачный* (мрачен).

KEYWORD
---

some [sʌm] adj **1** (a certain amount or number of): **would you like some tea/biscuits?** хотите чаю/печенья?; **there's some milk in the fridge** в холодильнике есть молоко; **he asked me some questions** он задал мне несколько вопросов; **there are some people waiting to see you** Вас ждут какие-то люди; **I've got some money, but not much** у меня есть деньги, но немного
2 (certain: in contrasts) некоторый; **some people say that ...** некоторые говорят, что ...
3 (unspecified) какой-то; **some woman phoned you this afternoon** Вам сегодня днём звонила какая-то женщина; **we'll meet again some day** мы когда-нибудь опять встретимся; **shall we meet some day next week?** встретимся как-нибудь на той or следующей неделе?
◆ pron (a certain number: people) одни; **I've got some** у меня есть; **some took the bus, and some walked** одни поехали на автобусе, а другие пошли пешком, кто-то поехал на автобусе, кто-то пошёл пешком; **who would like a piece of cake? – I'd like some** кто хочет кусок торта? – я с удовольствием; **I've read some of the book** я прочёл часть книги
◆ adv: **some ten people** человек десять.

somebody ['sʌmbədɪ] pron = someone.
someday ['sʌmdeɪ] adv когда-нибудь.
somehow ['sʌmhau] adv (in some way) как-нибудь; (for some reason) почему-то, каким-то образом.
someone ['sʌmwʌn] pron (specific person) кто-то; (unspecified person) кто-нибудь; **I saw ~ in the garden** я видел кого-то в саду; **~ will help you** Вам кто-нибудь поможет.
someplace ['sʌmpleɪs] adv (US) = somewhere.
somersault ['sʌməsɔːlt] n (in the air) сальто nt ind; (on the ground) кувырок* ◆ vi кувыркаться (impf), перекувырнуться (perf).
something ['sʌmθɪŋ] pron (something specific) что-то; (something unspecified) что-нибудь; **there's ~ wrong with my car** у меня что-то случилось с машиной; **would you like ~ to eat/drink?** хотите чего-нибудь поесть/выпить?; **I have ~ for you** у меня кое-что для Вас есть.
sometime ['sʌmtaɪm] adv (in future) когда-нибудь; (in past): **~ last month** где-то в прошлом месяце; **I'll finish it ~** когда-нибудь я это закончу.
sometimes ['sʌmtaɪmz] adv иногда.
somewhat ['sʌmwɔt] adv несколько.
somewhere ['sʌmwɛɑ'] adv (be: somewhere specific) где-то; (: anywhere) где-нибудь; (go: somewhere specific) куда-то; (: anywhere) куда-нибудь; (come from) откуда-то; **it's ~ or other in Scotland** это где-то в Шотландии; **is there a post office ~ around here?** здесь где-нибудь есть почта?; **let's go ~ else** давайте поедем куда-нибудь в другое место.
son [sʌn] n сын*.
sonar ['səunɑː'] n (NAUT) гидролокатор, эхолот.
sonata [sə'nɑːtə] n соната.
song [sɔŋ] n песня*.
song book n сборник песен, песенник.
songwriter ['sɔŋraɪtə'] n (композитор-) песенник, (поэт-)песенник.
sonic ['sɔnɪk] adj звуковой.
son-in-law ['sʌnɪnlɔː] n зять* m.
sonnet ['sɔnɪt] n сонет.
sonny ['sʌnɪ] n (inf) сынок*.
soon [suːn] adv (in a short time) скоро; (early) рано; **~ (afterwards)** вскоре; **quite ~** довольно скоро; **how ~ can you do it/come back?** когда Вы сможете это сделать/вернуться?; **see you ~!** до скорого!; see also **as**.
sooner ['suːnə'] adv (time) скорее; (preference): **I would ~ do that** я бы скорее сделал это; **~ or later** рано или поздно; **the ~ the better** чем скорее, тем лучше; **no ~ said than done** сказано-сделано; **no ~ had we left than ...** не

успе́ли мы уйти́, как ....

soot [sut] *n* са́жа.

soothe [su:ð] *vt* успока́ивать (успоко́ить *perf*).

soothing ['su:ðɪŋ] *adj* (*ointment, drink, bath*) успокои́тельный; (*tone, words etc*) утеши́тельный* (утеши́телен).

SOP *n abbr* (= *standard operating procedure*) станда́ртная рабо́чая процеду́ра.

sop [sɔp] *n*: **that's only a** ~ э́то то́лько пода́чка.

sophisticated [sə'fɪstɪkeɪtɪd] *adj* изощрённый* (изощрён); (*woman*) изы́сканная (изы́скана).

sophistication [səfɪstɪ'keɪʃən] *n* (*see adj*) изощрённость *f*; изы́сканность *f*.

sophomore ['sɔfəmɔ:ʳ] *n* (*US: SCOL*) второку́рсник(-ица).

soporific [sɔpə'rɪfɪk] *adj* (*speech*) усыпля́ющий; (*drug*) снотво́рный ◆ *n* снотво́рное *nt adj*.

sopping ['sɔpɪŋ] *adj*: ~ (**wet**) (*hair, clothes etc*) промо́кший наскво́зь.

soppy ['sɔpɪ] *adj* (*pej*) душещипа́тельный, сентимента́льный.

soprano [sə'prɑ:nəu] *n* сопра́но *f ind*.

sorbet ['sɔ:beɪ] *n* (*CULIN*) фрукто́вое моро́женое *nt adj*.

sorcerer ['sɔ:sərəʳ] *n* колду́н*.

sordid ['sɔ:dɪd] *adj* (*place*) зага́женный (зага́жен); (*story etc*) гну́сный* (гну́сен).

sore [sɔ:ʳ] *n* я́зва, боля́чка* ◆ *adj* (*esp US: offended*) оби́женный* (оби́жен); (*painful*): **my arm is** ~, **I've got a** ~ **arm** у меня́ боли́т рука́; **it's a** ~ **point** (*fig*) э́то боле́зненный предме́т.

sorely ['sɔ:lɪ] *adv*: **I am** ~ **tempted (to)** у меня́ большо́е соблазн (+*infin*).

soreness ['sɔ:nɪs] *n* боль *f*.

sorrel ['sɔrəl] *n* щаве́ль* *m*.

sorrow ['sɔrəu] *n* (*regret*) печа́ль* *f*, грусть *f*; ~**s** *npl* (*troubles*) печа́ли *fpl*.

sorrowful ['sɔrəuful] *adj* печа́льный* (печа́лен).

sorry ['sɔrɪ] *adj* (*condition, excuse, sight*) плаче́вный* (плаче́вен); (*regretful*): **I'm** ~ мне жаль; ~! (*apology*) извини́те, пожа́луйста!; ~? (*pardon*) прости́те?; **I feel** ~ **for him** мне его́ жа́лко; **I'm** ~ **to hear that** ... мне гру́стно слы́шать, что ...; **to be** ~ **about sth** сожале́ть (*impf*) о чём-н.

sort [sɔ:t] *n* сорт*; (*of car etc*) тип ◆ *vt* (*also:* ~ **out:** *papers, mail, belongings*) разбира́ть (разобра́ть* *perf*); (: *problems*) разбира́ться (разобра́ться* *perf*) в +*prp*; (*COMPUT*) сортирова́ть (*impf*); **what** ~ **do you want?** како́й сорт Вы хоти́те?; **what** ~ **of car?** кака́я маши́на?; **I'll do nothing of the** ~! я не собира́юсь де́лать ничего́ подо́бного; **it's** ~ **of awkward** (*inf*) э́то как-то неудо́бно.

sortie ['sɔ:tɪ] *n* (*MIL: on the ground*) вы́лазка*; (: *by air*) вы́лет; (*fig*) вы́лазка*.

sorting office ['sɔ:tɪŋ-] *n* (*POST*) сортиро́вочное отделе́ние.

SOS *n abbr* (= *save our souls*) SOS.

so-so ['səusəu] *adv* так себе́.

soufflé ['su:fleɪ] *n* суфле́ *nt ind*.

sought [sɔ:t] *pt, pp of* **seek**.

sought-after ['sɔ:tɑ:ftəʳ] *adj* (*person, thing*) по́льзующийся спро́сом; **a much** ~ **item** вещь, по́льзующаяся больши́м спро́сом.

soul [səul] *n* душа́*; (*music*) (му́зыка) "соул"; **the poor** ~ **had nowhere to sleep** несча́стному не́где бы́ло спать; **I didn't see a** ~ я не ви́дел ни души́.

soul-destroying ['səuldɪstrɔɪŋ] *adj*: **this work is** ~ э́та рабо́та выма́тывает ду́шу.

soulful ['səulful] *adj* проникнове́нный.

soulless ['səullɪs] *adj* (*place*) мёртвый (мёртв); **this is a** ~ **task** э́то иссуша́ет ду́шу.

soul mate *n* родна́я душа́*.

soul-searching ['səulsə:tʃɪŋ] *n*: **after much** ~, **I decided** ... по́сле до́лгих душе́вных по́исков я реши́л ....

sound [saund] *adj* (*healthy*) здоро́вый; (*safe, not damaged*) про́чный* (про́чен), це́лый (цел); (*reliable, thorough*) солидный* (соли́ден); (*sensible: advice*) разу́мный* (разу́мен); (*valid: argument*) ве́ский*; (: *policy*) здравомы́слящий*; (: *claim*) основа́тельный ◆ *n* звук; (*GEO*) зонд ◆ *vt* (*alarm*) поднима́ть (подня́ть* *perf*) ◆ *vi*: звуча́ть (прозвуча́ть *perf*) ◆ *adv*: **he is** ~ **asleep** он кре́пко спит; **to be of** ~ **mind** быть* (*impf*) в здра́вом уме́; **I don't like the** ~ **of it** э́то мне не нра́вится; **to** ~ **one's horn** (*AUT*) сигна́лить (*impf*); **to** ~ **like** звуча́ть (прозвуча́ть *perf*) как (+*dat*); **it** ~**s like Russian** похо́же на ру́сский; **that** ~**s like them arriving** слы́шится, похо́же они́ прие́хали; **it** ~**s as if** ... похо́же, что ...; похо́же как бу́дто ...

▶ **sound off** *vi* (*inf*): **to** ~ **off (about)** вы́сказаться* (*perf*) (о +*prp*)

▶ **sound out** *vt* (*person, opinion*) зонди́ровать (прозонди́ровать *perf*).

sound barrier *n* звуково́й барье́р.

sound effects *npl* звуковы́е эффе́кты *mpl*.

sound engineer *n* звукорежиссёр.

sounding ['saundɪŋ] *n* (*NAUT etc*) проме́р глубины́.

sounding board *n* (*MUS*) де́ка: **to use sb as a** ~ ~ **for one's ideas** проверя́ть (прове́рить *perf*) свои иде́и на ком-н.

soundly ['saundlɪ] *adv* (*sleep*) кре́пко; (*beat etc*) здо́рово.

soundproof ['saundpru:f] *adj* звуконепроница́емый (звуконепроница́ем)

---

* marks translations which have irregular inflections The Russian-English side of the dictionary gives inflectional information.

♦ *vt* звукоизоли́ровать *(impf/perf)*.
sound system *n* (*TECH*) (звукова́я) систе́ма.
soundtrack ['saundtræk] *n* му́зыка (*из кинофи́льма*).
sound wave *n* звукова́я волна́*.
soup [su:p] *n* суп*; **to be in the** ~ (*fig*) попада́ть (попа́сть* *perf*) в передря́гу.
soup course *n* пе́рвое *nt adj*.
soup kitchen *n* столо́вая *f adj* для бе́дных, супова́я ку́хня.
soup plate *n* глубо́кая таре́лка*.
soupspoon ['su:pspu:n] *n* столо́вая ло́жка*.
sour ['sauə'] *adj* ки́слый; (*fig: bad-tempered*) неприя́зненный* (неприя́знен); **to go** *or* **turn** ~ скиса́ть (ски́снуть* *perf*); (*fig*) по́ртиться* (испо́ртиться* *perf*); **it's** ~ **grapes** (*fig*) э́то за́висть.
source [sɔ:s] *n* (*also fig*) исто́чник; **I have it from a reliable** ~ **that** ... у меня́ есть све́дения из надёжного исто́чника, что ....
south [sauθ] *n* юг *m* ♦ *adj* ю́жный ♦ *adv* (*go*) на юг; (*be*) на ю́ге; (**to the**) ~ **of** к ю́гу от +*gen*; **to travel** ~ е́хать*/е́здить* (*impf*) на юг; **the S** ~ **of France** Юг Фра́нции.
South Africa *n* Ю́жная А́фрика.
South African *adj* южноафрика́нский ♦ *n* южноафрика́нец*(-нка*).
South America *n* Ю́жная Аме́рика.
South American *adj* южноамерика́нский ♦ *n* южноамерика́нец*(-нка*).
southbound ['sauθbaund] *adj* (*traffic*) дви́жущийся в ю́жном направле́нии; (*train, carriageway*) ю́жного направле́ния.
southeast [sauθ'i:st] *n* ю́го-восто́к.
Southeast Asia *n* Ю́го-восто́чная А́зия.
southerly ['sʌðəlɪ] *adj* обращённый к ю́гу; (*wind*) ю́жный.
southern ['sʌðən] *adj* ю́жный; **a room with a** ~ **aspect** ко́мната, выходя́щая на юг; **the** ~ **hemisphere** ю́жное полуша́рие.
South Korea *n* Ю́жная Коре́я.
South Pole *n*: **the** ~ ~ Ю́жный по́люс.
South Sea Islands *npl*: **the** ~ ~ ~ острова́ *mpl* ю́жной ча́сти Ти́хого Океа́на.
South Seas *npl*: **the** ~ ~ ю́жная часть *f* Ти́хого Океа́на.
southward(s) ['sauθwəd(z)] *adv* на юг, в ю́жном направле́нии.
southwest [sauθ'wɛst] *n* ю́го-за́пад.
souvenir [su:və'nɪə'] *n* сувени́р.
sovereign ['sɔvrɪn] *n* (*ruler*) госуда́рь(-рыня) *m(f)*.
sovereignty ['sɔvrɪntɪ] *n* суверените́т.
Soviet ['səuvɪət] *adj* сове́тский* ♦ *n* (*person*) сове́тский* челове́к; **the** ~ **Union** Сове́тский* Сою́з.
sow¹ [sau] *n* (*pig*) свинья́*, свинома́тка*.
sow² [səu] (*pt* **sowed**, *pp* **sown**) *vt* (*also fig*) се́ять (посе́ять *perf*).
sown [səun] *pp of* **sow²**.
soya ['sɔɪə] (*US* **soy**) *n*: ~ **bean/sauce** со́евый

боб/со́ус.
sozzled ['sɔzld] *adj* (*inf*) под му́хой.
spa [spɑ:] *n* (*town*) куро́ртный го́род*; (*US: also:* **health** ~) лече́бно-оздорови́тельный куро́рт.
space [speɪs] *n* (*gap*) простра́нство; (*place: small*) ме́сто*; (: *large*) простра́нство; (*room*) ме́сто*; (*beyond Earth*) ко́смос; (*interval, period*) промежу́ток* ♦ *cpd* косми́ческий* ♦ *vt* (*also:* ~ **out**: *text*) разбива́ть (разби́ть* *perf*); (: *payments, visits*) распределя́ть (распредели́ть* *perf*); **to clear a** ~ **for sth** расчища́ть (расчи́стить* *perf*) ме́сто для чего́-н; **in a confined** ~ в ограни́ченном простра́нстве; **in a short** ~ **of time** в коро́ткий промежу́ток вре́мени; (**with**)**in the** ~ **of an hour** в тече́ние ча́са.
space-bar ['speɪsbɑ:'] *n* (*TYP*) интерва́л.
spacecraft ['speɪskrɑ:ft] *n* косми́ческий* кора́бль* *m*.
spaceman ['speɪsmæn] *irreg n* космона́вт.
spaceship ['speɪsʃɪp] *n* = **spacecraft**.
space shuttle *n* косми́ческий кора́бль многора́зового испо́льзования.
spacesuit ['speɪssu:t] *n* скафа́ндр.
spacewoman ['speɪswumən] *irreg n* же́нщина-космона́вт.
spacing ['speɪsɪŋ] *n* (*TYP*) промежу́тки *mpl*, интерва́лы *mpl*; **single/double** ~ (*TYP*) с одни́м/двойны́м интерва́лом.
spacious ['speɪʃəs] *adj* просто́рный* (просто́рен).
spade [speɪd] *n* (*tool*) лопа́та; (*child's*) лопа́тка*; ~**s** *npl* (*CARDS*) пи́ки *fpl*.
spadework ['speɪdwə:k] *n* (*fig*) черновая́ рабо́та.
spaghetti [spə'gɛtɪ] *n* спаге́тти *pl ind*.
Spain [speɪn] *n* Испа́ния.
span [spæn] *pt of* **spin** ♦ *n* (*of hand, wings*) разма́х; (*of bridge*) пролёт; (*in time*) промежу́ток* ♦ *vt* (*river*) переки́нуть (*perf*) че́рез +*acc*; (*fig: time*) охва́тывать (охвати́ть* *perf*).
Spaniard ['spænjəd] *n* испа́нец*(-нка*).
spaniel ['spænjəl] *n* спание́ль *m*.
Spanish ['spænɪʃ] *adj* испа́нский* ♦ *n* (*LING*) испа́нский* язы́к*; **the** ~ *npl* испа́нцы *mpl*; ~ **omelette** омле́т по-испа́нски.
spank [spæŋk] *vt* шлёпать (отшлёпать *perf*).
spanner ['spænə'] *n* (*BRIT*) га́ечный ключ*.
spar [spɑ:'] *n* (*pole*) шта́нга ♦ *vi* (*BOXING*) спаррингова́ть (*impf*).
spare [spɛə'] *adj* (*free: time, seat*) свобо́дный* (свобо́ден); (*surplus*) ли́шний*; (*reserve*) запасно́й ♦ *n* = **spare part** ♦ *vt* (*trouble, expense, effort*) избавля́ть (изба́вить* *perf*) от +*gen*; (*refrain from using: energy, water etc*) бере́чь* (сбере́чь* *perf*); (*make available: person, time, money*) выделя́ть (вы́делить *perf*); (*afford to give: money*) дава́ть* (дать* *perf*); (*refrain from hurting: person, city etc*)

щади́ть* (пощади́ть* *perf*); **to have some time to ~** име́ть (*impf*) свобо́дное вре́мя; **to have money to ~** име́ть (*impf*) ли́шние де́ньги; **these 2 are going ~** э́ти два – ли́шние; **to ~ no expense** не жале́ть (пожале́ть *perf*) средств; **can you ~ the time?** у Вас найдётся вре́мя?; **I've a few minutes to ~** у меня́ есть не́сколько мину́т; **there is no time to ~** у нас нет ли́шнего вре́мени; **can you ~ ten pounds?** у Вас не найдётся десяти́ фу́нтов?

spare part *n* запча́сть *f*= *запасна́я часть.*

spare room *n* свобо́дная ко́мната.

spare time *n* свобо́дное вре́мя* *nt.*

spare tyre *n* запасна́я ши́на.

spare wheel *n* запасно́е колесо́*.

sparing ['spɛərɪŋ] *adj*: **he is ~ with his money** он эконо́мен с деньга́ми; **he was ~ with his praise** он был скуп на похвалу́.

sparingly ['spɛərɪŋlɪ] *adv* эконо́мно.

spark [spɑːk] *n* (*also fig*) и́скра.

spark(ing) plug ['spɑːk(ɪŋ)-] *n* запа́льная свеча́*.

sparkle ['spɑːkl] *n* блеск ◆ *vi* (*diamonds, water*) сверка́ть (сверкну́ть *perf*); (*eyes*) блесте́ть* (*impf*); (*bubble*) шипе́ть* (*impf*).

sparkler ['spɑːklə'] *n* (*firework*) бенга́льский ого́нь* *m.*

sparkling ['spɑːklɪŋ] *adj* (*wine*) игри́стый; (*conversation, performance*) блестя́щий*.

sparring partner ['spɑːrɪŋ-] *n* (*BOXING*) партнёр для трениро́вок в бо́ксе.

sparrow ['spærəʊ] *n* воробе́й*.

sparse [spɑːs] *adj* ре́дкий* (ре́док).

spartan ['spɑːtən] *adj* спарта́нский.

spasm ['spæzəm] *n* (*MED*) спазм; (*of anger etc*) при́ступ.

spasmodic [spæz'mɔdɪk] *adj* (*fig*) спазмати́ческий.

spastic ['spæstɪk] *n* (*MED*) парали́тик ◆ *adj* (*MED*) спасти́ческий.

spat [spæt] *pt, pp of* **spit** ◆ *n* (*US*: *quarrel*) размо́лвка*.

spate [speɪt] *n* (*fig*): **a ~ of** пото́к* +*gen*; **the river is in ~** река́ вздула́сь.

spatial ['speɪʃl] *adj* простра́нственный.

spatter ['spætə'] *vt* бры́згать (бры́знуть *perf*) ◆ *vi* обры́згаться (обры́знуться *perf*).

spatula ['spætjʊlə] *n* (*MED*) шпа́тель *m*; (*CULIN*) лопа́тка*.

spawn [spɔːn] *vi* (*fish etc*) мета́ть* (*impf*) икру́ ◆ *vt* (*fig*) порожда́ть (породи́ть* *perf*) ◆ *n* икра́.

SPCA *n abbr* (*US*) = *Society for the Prevention of Cruelty to Animals.*

SPCC *n abbr* (*US*) = *Society for the Prevention of Cruelty to Children.*

speak [spiːk] (*pt* **spoke**, *pp* **spoken**) *vi* (*use voice*) говори́ть (*impf*); (*make a speech*) выступа́ть (вы́ступить* *perf*) ◆ *vt* (*truth*) говори́ть

(сказа́ть *perf*); **to ~ to sb** разгова́ривать (*impf*) с кем-н; **to ~ of** *or* **about** говори́ть (*impf*) о +*prp*; **he has no money to ~ of** у него́ о́чень немно́го де́нег; **~ up!** говори́те гро́мче!; **to ~ at a conference/in a debate** выступа́ть (вы́ступить* *perf*) на конфере́нции/в деба́тах; **to ~ Russian/several languages** говори́ть (*impf*) по-ру́сски/на не́скольких языка́х; **to ~ one's mind** выска́зывать (вы́сказать* *perf*) своё мне́ние

▶ **speak for** *vt fus*: **to ~ for sb** говори́ть (*impf*) за кого́-н; **that picture is already spoken for** (*already sold*) э́ту карти́ну уже́ сторгова́ли.

speaker ['spiːkə'] *n* (*in public*) ора́тор; (*also:* **loudspeaker**) громкоговори́тель *m*; (*POL*): **the S~** спи́кер; **are you a Welsh ~?** Вы говори́те по-уэ́льски?

speaking ['spiːkɪŋ] *adj* говоря́щий; **Italian-~ people** италогово́рящие *pl adj*; **we are no longer on ~ terms** мы бо́льше не обща́емся.

spear [spɪə'] *n* копьё* ◆ *vt* пронза́ть (пронзи́ть* *perf*) копьём.

spearhead ['spɪəhɛd] *vt* возглавля́ть (возгла́вить* *perf*).

spearmint ['spɪəmɪnt] *n* мя́та колосова́я.

spec [spɛk] *n* (*inf*): **on ~** (*buy, go etc*) науда́чу.

spec. *n abbr* (*TECH*: = **specification**) специфика́ция.

special ['spɛʃl] *adj* (*important*) осо́бый, осо́бенный; (*edition, adviser, school etc*) специа́льный ◆ *n* (*RAIL*) по́езд* специа́льного назначе́ния; **take ~ care** проявля́ть осо́бенную забо́ту; **nothing ~** ничего́ осо́бенного; **today's ~** (*at restaurant*) сего́дняшнее фи́рменное блю́до.

special agent *n* аге́нт по осо́бым поруче́ниям.

special correspondent *n* специа́льный корреспонде́нт.

special delivery *n* (*POST*): **by ~ ~** сро́чной доста́вкой.

special effects *npl* (*CINEMA*) специа́льные съёмочные эффе́кты *mpl.*

specialist ['spɛʃəlɪst] *n* специали́ст; **heart ~** специали́ст-кардио́лог.

speciality [spɛʃɪ'ælɪtɪ] *n* (*dish*) фи́рменное блю́до; (*subject*) специализа́ция.

specialize ['spɛʃəlaɪz] *vi*: **to ~ (in)** специализи́роваться (*impf/perf*) (в +*prp*).

specially ['spɛʃlɪ] *adv* (*especially*) осо́бенно; (*on purpose*) специа́льно.

special offer *n*: **the book is on ~ ~** кни́гу продаю́т по сни́женной цене́.

specialty ['spɛʃəltɪ] *n* (*esp US*) = **speciality**.

species ['spiːʃiːz] *n inv* вид.

specific [spə'sɪfɪk] *adj* определённый; **~ to** хара́ктерно для +*gen*.

specifically [spə'sɪfɪklɪ] *adv* (*exactly*)

---

* marks translations which have irregular inflections. The Russian-English side of the dictionary gives inflectional information.

определённо; (*specially*) специа́льно.
specification [spɛsɪfɪˈkeɪʃən] *n* (*TECH*)
специфика́ция; (*requirement*) тре́бование;
~s *npl* (*TECH*) техни́ческие усло́вия *ntpl*.
specify [ˈspɛsɪfaɪ] *vt* (*time, place, colour etc*)
уточня́ть (уточни́ть *perf*); **unless otherwise
specified** е́сли нет други́х указа́ний.
specimen [ˈspɛsɪmən] *n* (*example*) экземпля́р;
(*sample for testing*) образе́ц*; **a ~ of urine**
моча́ для ана́лиза.
specimen copy *n* образцо́вый экземпля́р.
specimen signature *n* образе́ц* по́дписи.
speck [spɛk] *n* (*of dirt*) пя́тнышко; (*of dust*)
кра́пинка*.
speckled [ˈspɛkld] *adj* (*hen, eggs*) пёстрый
(пёстр).
specs [spɛks] *npl* (*inf: glasses*) очки́ *pl*.
spectacle [ˈspɛktəkl] *n* (*scene, event*) зре́лище;
~s *npl* (*glasses*) очки́ *pl*.
spectacle case *n* (*BRIT*) футля́р для очко́в.
spectacular [spɛkˈtækjulə*] *adj* впечатля́ющий
(впечатля́ющ) ♦ *n* (*THEAT etc*) впечатля́ющее
зре́лище.
spectator [spɛkˈteɪtə*] *n* зри́тель(ница) *m(f)* ♦
cpd: **a ~ sport** зре́лищный спорт.
spectra [ˈspɛktrə] *npl of* **spectrum**.
spectre [ˈspɛktə*] (*US* **specter**) *n* (*also fig*)
при́зрак.
spectrum [ˈspɛktrəm] (*pl* **spectra**) *n* спектр.
speculate [ˈspɛkjuleɪt] *vi* (*COMM*) игра́ть (*impf*)
на би́рже; (*guess*): **to ~ about** стро́ить (*impf*)
дога́дки *or* размышля́ть (*impf*) о +*prp*.
speculation [spɛkjuˈleɪʃən] *n* (*see vb*) биржева́я
игра́; дога́дка, предположе́ние.
sped [spɛd] *pt, pp of* **speed**.
speech [spi:tʃ] *n* речь *f*; (*THEAT*) моноло́г, речь.
speech day *n* (*BRIT: SCOL*) а́ктовый день* *m*.
speech impediment *n* дефе́кт ре́чи.
speechless [ˈspi:tʃlɪs] *adj* безмо́лвный*
(безмо́лвен).
speech therapist *n* логопе́д.
speech therapy *n* логопе́дия.
speed [spi:d] (*pt, pp* **sped**) *n* (*rate*) ско́рость* *f*;
(*promptness*) быстрота́ ♦ *vi* (*AUT: exceed
speed limit*) превыша́ть (превы́сить* *perf*)
ско́рость; (*move*): **to ~ along/by** *etc* мча́ться*
(промча́ться* *perf*) по +*dat*/ми́мо +*gen etc*; **at ~**
(*BRIT*) на большо́й ско́рости; **at full** *or* **top ~**
на по́лной *or* преде́ле ско́рости; **at a ~ of
70km/h** со ско́ростью 70км в час; **shorthand/
typing ~** ско́рость* маши́нописи/
стенографи́рования; **a five-~ gearbox**
коро́бка* переда́ч с пятью́ скоростя́ми
▸ **speed up** (*pt, pp* **speeded up**) *vi* (*also fig*)
ускоря́ться (уско́риться* *perf*) ♦ *vt* (*also fig*)
ускоря́ть (уско́рить *perf*).
speedboat [ˈspi:dbəut] *n* быстрохо́дный
ка́тер*.
speedily [ˈspi:dɪlɪ] *adv* ско́ро.
speeding [ˈspi:dɪŋ] *n* (*AUT*) превыше́ние
ско́рости.

speed limit *n* (*AUT*) ограниче́ние ско́рости.
speedometer [spɪˈdɔmɪtə*] *n* (*AUT*) спидо́метр.
speed trap *n* (*AUT*) пост доро́жной поли́ции по
контро́лю за ско́ростью.
speedway [ˈspi:dweɪ] *n* (*sport: also:* ~ **racing**)
спидве́й; (*track*) го́ночный трек.
speedy [ˈspi:dɪ] *adj* (*fast: car*) бы́стрый (быстр);
(*prompt: reply, recovery, settlement*) ско́рый
(скор).
speleologist [spɛlɪˈɔlədʒɪst] *n* спелео́лог.
spell [spɛl] (*pt, pp* **spelt** (*BRIT*) *or* **spelled**) *n* (*also:*
magic ~) колдовство́; (*period of time*)
пери́од ♦ *vt* (*in writing*) объясня́ть
(объясни́ть *perf*) в дета́лях; (*also:* ~ **out**)
произноси́ть* (произнести́* *perf*) по бу́квам;
(*fig: advantages, difficulties*) разъясня́ть
(разъясни́ть *perf*) ♦ *vi*: **he can't ~** он не уме́ет
писа́ть без оши́бок; **to cast a ~ on sb**
околдо́вывать (околдова́ть *perf*) кого́-н;
how do you ~ your surname? как пи́шется
Ва́ша фами́лия?; **can you ~ it for me?** Вы
мо́жете произнести́ э́то по бу́квам?
spellbound [ˈspɛlbaund] *adj* зачаро́ванный
(зачаро́ван).
spelling [ˈspɛlɪŋ] *n* правописа́ние.
spelt [spɛlt] *pt, pp of* **spell**.
spend [spɛnd] (*pt, pp* **spent**) *vt* (*money*) тра́тить*
(истра́тить* *perf*); (*time, life*) проводи́ть*
(провести́* *perf*); (*devote*): **to ~ time/effort on
sth** тра́тить (потра́тить *perf*) вре́мя/си́лы на
что-н.
spending [ˈspɛndɪŋ] *n* расхо́ды *mpl*;
government ~ госуда́рственные расхо́ды
mpl.
spending money *n* карма́нные де́ньги* *pl*.
spending power *n* покупа́тельная
спосо́бность *f*.
spendthrift [ˈspɛndθrɪft] *n* расточи́тель(ница)
m(f).
spent [spɛnt] *pt, pp of* **spend** ♦ *adj* (*cartridge*)
пусто́й (пуст); (*bullets*) израсхо́дованный; ~
matches испо́льзованные *or* израсхо́до-
ванные спи́чки; **my patience is ~** моё
терпе́ние ко́нчилось.
sperm [spə:m] *n* спе́рма.
sperm bank *n* храни́лище до́норской
спе́рмы.
sperm whale *n* кашало́т.
spew [spju:] *vt* изрыга́ть (изрыгну́ть *perf*) ♦ *vi*
(*inf: vomit*) рвать (вы́рвать *perf*); **he ~ed** его́
вы́рвало.
sphere [sfɪə*] *n* сфе́ра.
spherical [ˈsfɛrɪkl] *adj* сфери́ческий*,
шарообра́зный* (шарообра́зен).
sphinx [sfɪŋks] *n* сфинкс.
spice [spaɪs] *n* спе́ция, пря́ность *f* ♦ *vt* (*food*)
приправля́ть (припра́вить* *perf*) спе́циями.
spick-and-span [ˈspɪkənˈspæn] *adj*: **to be ~**
сверка́ть (*impf*).
spicy [ˈspaɪsɪ] *adj* (*food*) о́стрый (остр).
spider [ˈspaɪdə*] *n* пау́к*; ~**'s web** паути́на.

spidery ['spaɪdərɪ] *adj* (*handwriting*) тóнкий* (тóнок) и небрéжный* (небрéжен).

spiel [spiːl] *n* (*inf*) стёб, говорúльня.

spike [spaɪk] *n* (*point*) острие; (*BOT: of flower*) соцвéтие; (: *of corn*) кóлос; (*ELEC*) штырь *m*; **~s** *npl* (*SPORT*) шипы *mpl*.

spike heel *n* (*US*) шпúлька*.

spiky ['spaɪkɪ] *adj* (*plant, animal*) колючий* (колюч).

spill [spɪl] (*pt, pp* **spilt** *or* **spilled**) *vt* (*liquid*) проливáть (пролúть* *perf*), разливáть (разлúть* *perf*) ♦ *vi* (*liquid*) проливáться (пролúться* *perf*), разливáться (разлúться* *perf*); **to ~ the beans** (*inf*) проболтáться (проболтáться *perf*)
► **spill out** *vi* выливáться (вылиться* *perf*)
► **spill over** *vi* (*liquid*) переливáться (перелúться* *perf*) (чéрез край); (*fig: crowd, conflict*) выливáться (вылиться* *perf*).

spillage ['spɪlɪdʒ] *n* (*of oil*) разлúв.

spilt [spɪlt] *pt, pp of* **spill**.

spin [spɪn] (*pt* **spun** *or* **span**, *pp* **spun**) *n* (*trip in car*) катáние; (*revolution of wheel*) поворóт, вращéние; (*AVIAT*) штóпор ♦ *vt* (*wool etc*) прясть* (спрясть* *perf*); (*top*) крутúть* (закрутúть* *perf*); (*wheel*) вращáть (вертéть* *perf*); (*BRIT: clothes*) выжимáть (выжать* *perf*) (в стирáльной машúне) ♦ *vi* (*make thread*) прясть* (*impf*); (*person, head*) кружúться* (закружúться* *perf*); (*car*) вращáться (*impf*); **let's go for a ~ in the car** поéдем покатáться на машúне; **to put ~ on a ball** закрýчивать (закрутúть* *perf*) мяч*; **to ~ a yarn** (*inf: story*) плестú* (наплестú* *perf*) небылúцы; **to ~ a coin** (*BRIT*) подбрáсывать (подбрóсить* *perf*) монéту
► **spin out** *vt* растягивать (растянýть* *perf*).

spina bifida ['spaɪnə'bɪfɪdə] *n* (*MED*) *расщеплéние остúстых отрóстков позвонóчника*.

spinach ['spɪnɪtʃ] *n* шпинáт.

spinal ['spaɪnl] *adj* спиннóй; **~ injury** повреждéние позвонóчника.

spinal column *n* (*ANAT*) позвонóчный столб*.

spinal cord *n* спиннóй мозг*.

spindly ['spɪndlɪ] *adj* длúнный* (длúнен) и тóнкий* (тóнок).

spin doctor *n* (*inf*) партúйный пропагандúст, спин-дóктор.

spin-dry ['spɪn'draɪ] *vt* (*clothes, washing*) выжимáть (выжать* *perf*) дóсуха (*в центрифýге*).

spin-dryer [spɪn'draɪə'] *n* (*BRIT*) центрифýга-сушúлка*.

spine [spaɪn] *n* (*ANAT*) позвонóчник; (*thorn*) колючка*, иглá*.

spine-chilling ['spaɪntʃɪlɪŋ] *adj* (*story, film*) жýткий* (жýток).

spineless ['spaɪnlɪs] *adj* (*fig*) бесхребéтный* (бесхребéтен).

spinner ['spɪnə'] *n* (*of thread*) прядúльщик(-щица), пряха *m/f*.

spinning ['spɪnɪŋ] *n* (*craft*) прядéние.

spinning top *n* волчóк*.

spinning wheel *n* прялка*.

spin-off ['spɪnɔf] *n* (*fig: by-product*) побóчный результáт.

spinster ['spɪnstə'] *n* (*unmarried woman*) стáрая дéва.

spiral ['spaɪərl] *n* спирáль *f* ♦ *vi* (*fig: prices etc*) рéзко возрастáть (возрастú* *perf*); **the inflationary ~** спирáль инфляции.

spiral staircase *n* винтовáя лéстница.

spire ['spaɪə'] *n* шпиль *m*.

spirit ['spɪrɪt] *n* дух; (*soul*) душá*; **~s** *npl* (*drink*) спиртнóе *ntsg adj*; **in good/low ~s** в хорóшем/ подáвленном настроéнии; **community ~**, **public ~** общéственный дух.

spirited ['spɪrɪtɪd] *adj* энергúчный* (энергúчен); (*performance*) воодушевлённый*; (*horse*) горячий* (горяч).

spirit level *n* ватерпáс.

spiritual ['spɪrɪtjuəl] *adj* духóвный* (духóвен) ♦ *n* (*also: Negro ~*) спúричуал.

spiritualism ['spɪrɪtjuəlɪzəm] *n* спиритúзм.

spit [spɪt] (*pt, pp* **spat**) *n* (*for roasting*) вéртел; (*saliva*) слюнá ♦ *vi* (*person*) плевáть* (плюнуть *perf*); (*fire, hot oil*) шипéть* (*impf*); (*inf: rain*) моросúть* (*impf*).

spite [spaɪt] *n* злóба, злость *f* ♦ *vt* досаждáть (досадúть* *perf*) +*dat*; **in ~ of** несмотря на +*acc*.

spiteful ['spaɪtful] *adj* злóбный* (злóбен).

spit roast *n* *мясо, зажáренное на вéртеле*.

spitting ['spɪtɪŋ] *n*: "**spitting prohibited**" "плевáть воспрещáется" ♦ *adj*: **he is the ~ image of his father** он вылитый отéц.

spittle ['spɪtl] *n* слюнá.

spiv [spɪv] *n* (*BRIT: inf: pej*) фрáйер, жýлик.

splash [splæʃ] *n* (*sound*) всплеск ♦ *excl*: **~!** плюх! ♦ *vt* брызгать* (брызнуть *perf*) ♦ *vi* (*also: ~ about*) плескáться* (*impf*); **a ~ of colour** цветовóе пятнó; **to ~ paint on the floor** забрызгивать (забрызгать* *perf*) пол крáской.

splashdown ['splæʃdaun] *n* (*SPACE*) приводнéние.

splayfooted ['spleɪfutɪd] *adj* *ступáющий пятками внутрь, носкáми врозь*.

spleen [spliːn] *n* (*ANAT*) селезёнка*.

splendid ['splendɪd] *adj* великолéпный* (великолéпен).

splendour ['splendə'] (*US* **splendor**) *n* великолéпие; **~s** *npl* (*features*) великолéпие *ntsg*.

---

* marks translations which have irregular inflections. The Russian-English side of the dictionary gives inflectional information

splice [splaɪs] *vt* соединя́ть (соедини́ть *perf*); (*tape, film*) скле́ивать (скле́ить *perf*).

splint [splɪnt] *n* ши́на.

splinter ['splɪntə'] *n* (*of wood*) ще́пка*; (*of glass*) оско́лок*; (*in finger*) зано́за * *vi* (*bone, wood, glass etc*) расщепля́ться (расщепи́ться* *perf*).

splinter group *n* отколо́вшаяся группиро́вка.

split [splɪt] (*pt, pp* **split**) *n* (*crack, tear*) тре́щина; (*POL, fig*) раско́л * *vt* (*divide*) расщепля́ть (расщепи́ть* *perf*); (*POL*) раска́лывать (расколо́ть* *perf*); (*share equally: work, profits*) разделя́ть (раздели́ть* *perf*) * *vi* (*divide*) расщепля́ться (расщепи́ться* *perf*), разделя́ться (раздели́ться* *perf*); (*glass, wood*) раска́лываться (расколо́ться* *perf*); (*cloth*) разрыва́ться (разорва́ться* *perf*); **let's ~ the difference** дава́йте сойдёмся на сре́дней ци́фре; **to do the ~s** де́лать (сде́лать *perf*) шпага́т

▸ **split up** *vi* (*couple*) расходи́ться* (разойти́сь* *perf*); (*group*) разделя́ться (раздели́ться* *perf*); (*meeting*) зака́нчиваться (зако́нчиться *perf*).

split-level ['splɪtlɛvl] *adj*: ~ **house** дом, постро́енный на ра́зных у́ровнях.

split peas *npl* ко́лотый горо́х *msg*.

split personality *n* раздвое́ние ли́чности.

split second *n* до́ля* секу́нды.

splitting ['splɪtɪŋ] *adj*: **I've got a ~ headache** у меня́ голова́ раска́лывается.

splutter ['splʌtə'] *vi* (*engine etc*) треща́ть* (*impf*); (*person*) бры́згать* (*impf*) слюно́й.

spoil [spɔɪl] (*pt, pp* **spoilt** *or* **spoiled**) *vt* (*damage, mar*) по́ртить* (испо́ртить* *perf*); (*indulge*) балова́ть (избалова́ть *perf*) * *vi*: **he's ~ing for a fight** он так и ле́зет в дра́ку.

spoils [spɔɪlz] *npl* (*also fig*) трофе́и *mpl*.

spoilsport ['spɔɪlspɔːt] *n* (*pej: person*): **don't be a ~** не отравля́й лю́дям настрое́ние.

spoilt [spɔɪlt] *pt, pp of* **spoil** * *adj* испо́рченный* (испо́рчен); (*child*) избало́ванный* (избало́ван).

spoke [spəʊk] *pt of* **speak** * *n* (*of wheel*) спи́ца.

spoken ['spəʊkn] *pp of* **speak**.

spokesman ['spəʊksmən] *irreg n* представи́тель *m*.

spokesperson ['spəʊkspɜːsn] *irreg n* представи́тель(ница) *m(f)*.

spokeswoman ['spəʊkswʊmən] *irreg n* представи́тельница.

sponge [spʌndʒ] *n* гу́бка*; (*also*: ~ **cake**) бискви́т * *vt* (*wash*) обтира́ть (обтере́ть* *perf*) гу́бкой * *vi*: **to ~ off** *or* **on sb** сиде́ть* (*impf*) на ше́е у кого́-н.

sponge bag *n* (*BRIT*) су́мочка* для туале́тных принадле́жностей.

sponger ['spʌndʒə'] *n* (*pej*) парази́т.

spongy ['spʌndʒɪ] *adj* гу́бчатый.

sponsor ['spɒnsə'] *n* спо́нсор; (*for application*) поручи́тель *m* * *vt* финанси́ровать (*impf/perf*), спонси́ровать (*impf/perf*); (*applicant*) поруча́ться (поручи́ться *perf*) за +*acc*; (*proposal, bill etc*) вноси́ть* (внести́* *perf*) на рассмотре́ние; **I ~ed him at twenty pence a mile** я поже́ртвовал ему́ два́дцать пе́нсов за ми́лю.

sponsorship ['spɒnsəʃɪp] *n* спо́нсорство.

spontaneity [spɒntə'neɪɪtɪ] *n* спонта́нность *f*.

spontaneous [spɒn'teɪnɪəs] *adj* (*gesture*) спонта́нный* (спонта́нен); (*demonstration*) стихи́йный; ~ **combustion** самовозгора́ние, самовоспламене́ние.

spoof [spuːf] (*inf*) *n* (*imitation*) паро́дия; (*joke*) ро́зыгрыш * *vt* (*imitate*) передра́знивать (*impf*).

spooky ['spuːkɪ] *adj* (*inf: place, atmosphere*) злове́щий*, жу́ткий*.

spool [spuːl] *n* (*for thread*) кату́шка*; (*for film, tape etc*) боби́на.

spoon [spuːn] *n* ло́жка*.

spoon-feed ['spuːnfiːd] *vt* (*baby, patient*) корми́ть* (*impf*) с ло́жки; (*fig: students*) всё разжёвывать (*impf*) +*dat*.

spoonful ['spuːnful] *n* (*по́лная*) ло́жка*.

sporadic [spə'rædɪk] *adj* споради́ческий*.

sport [spɔːt] *n* (*game*) спорт *m no pl*; (*person: also: good ~*) молодчи́на *m* * *vt* (*wear*) щеголя́ть (щегольну́ть *perf*) +*instr*; **indoor/ outdoor ~s** ви́ды спо́рта для закры́тых помеще́ний/на откры́том во́здухе.

sporting ['spɔːtɪŋ] *adj* (*event etc*) спорти́вный; (*generous*) ры́царский*; **to give sb a ~ chance** дава́ть* (дать* *perf*) кому́-н не́который шанс.

sport jacket *n* (*US*) = **sports jacket**.

sports car *n* спорти́вная маши́на.

sports centre *n* спорти́вный центр.

sports ground *n* спорти́вная площа́дка*.

sports jacket *n* (*BRIT*) спорти́вная ку́ртка* из тви́да.

sportsman ['spɔːtsmən] *irreg n* спортсме́н.

sportsmanship ['spɔːtsmənʃɪp] *n* спорти́вный дух; **he showed real ~** он показа́л себя́ как настоя́щий спортсме́н.

sports page *n* спорти́вная страни́ца.

sportswear ['spɔːtswɛə'] *n* спорти́вная оде́жда.

sportswoman ['spɔːtswʊmən] *irreg n* спортсме́нка*.

sporty ['spɔːtɪ] *adj* (*person*) спорти́вный* (спорти́вен).

spot [spɒt] *n* (*mark*) пятно́*; (*dot: on pattern*) кра́пинка*; (*on skin*) пры́щик; (*place*) ме́сто*; (*RADIO, TV*) рекла́мный переры́в; ~ **advertisement** рекла́мная ру́брика * *vt* (*notice*) замеча́ть (заме́тить* *perf*); **a ~ of bother** ма́ленькая неприя́тность *f*; **shall we have a ~ of lunch?** не переку́сить ли нам?; ~**s of rain** ка́пли дождя́; **on the ~** (*in that place*) на ме́сте; (*immediately*) в тот же моме́нт; **to put sb on the ~** ста́вить* (поста́вить* *perf*) кого́-н в затрудни́тельное положе́ние; **in a ~** (*in difficulty*) в затрудни́тельном положе́нии; **to come out in ~s** (*rash*) покрыва́ться (покры́ться* *perf*) сы́пью; (*blemishes*) покрыва́ться (покры́ться* *perf*) прыща́ми.

spot check *n* вы́борочная прове́рка*.

spotless ['spɒtlɪs] *adj* (*shirt, kitchen etc*) без пя́тнышка; (*reputation*) незапя́тнанный.

spotlight ['spɒtlaɪt] *n* (освети́тельный) прожёктор; **to be in the ~** (*fig*) быть* (*impf*) в це́нтре внима́ния.

spot-on [spɒt'ɒn] *adj* (*BRIT: inf*): **to be ~** попа́сть* (*perf*) в са́мую то́чку.

spot price *n* (*COMM*) цена́ при усло́виях неме́дленной опла́ты (нали́чными).

spotted ['spɒtɪd] *adj* (*pattern*) пятни́стый (пятни́ст); **~ with** запя́тнанный (запя́тнан) +*instr*.

spotty ['spɒtɪ] *adj* (*face, youth*) прыща́вый (прыща́в).

spouse [spaus] *n* супру́г(а).

spout [spaut] *n* (*of jug*) но́сик; (*of pipe*) выпускно́е отве́рстие; (*of liquid*) струя́* ◆ *vi* (*water etc*) бить* (*impf*) струёй; (*volcano*) изверга́ться (изве́ргнуться* *perf*).

sprain [spreɪn] *n* (*MED*) растяже́ние ◆ *vt*: **to ~ one's ankle/wrist** растя́гивать (растяну́ть* *perf*) щи́колотку/запя́стье.

sprang [spræŋ] *pt of* **spring**.

sprawl [sprɔ:l] *vi* (*person*) разва́ливаться (развали́ться* *perf*); (*place*) раски́дываться (раски́нуться *perf*) ◆ *n*: **urban ~** разраста́ние го́рода; **to send sb ~ing** сбива́ть (сбить* *perf*) кого́-н с ног.

spray [spreɪ] *n* (*drops of water*) бры́зги *pl*; (*hair spray*) аэрозо́ль *m*; (*garden spray*) разбры́згиватель *m*; (: *chemicals*) ядохимика́ты *mpl*; (*of flowers*) ве́точка* ◆ *vt* (*sprinkle*) обры́згивать (обры́згать *perf*); (*crops*) опры́скивать (опры́скать *perf*) ◆ *cpd*: **~ deodorant** дезодора́нт в аэрозо́льной упако́вке.

spread [sprɛd] (*pt, pp* **spread**) *n* (*range*) спектр; (*distribution*) распростране́ние; (*CULIN: paste*) па́ста; (: *margarine etc*) бутербро́дная маргари́н; (*inf. food*) оби́льное угоще́ние; (*PRESS, TYP: two pages*) разворо́т ◆ *vt* (*lay out*) расстила́ть (расстели́ть* *perf*); (*scatter*) разбра́сывать (разброса́ть* *perf*); (*butter, paste*) нама́зывать (нама́зать* *perf*); (*wings*) расправля́ть (распра́вить* *perf*); (*arms*) раскрыва́ть (раскры́ть* *perf*); (*sail*) развёртывать (разверну́ть *perf*); (*workload, wealth*) распределя́ть (распредели́ть *perf*); (*rumour, disease*) распространя́ть (распространи́ть *perf*); (*repayments*) распределя́ть (распредели́ть *perf*) ◆ *vi* (*disease, news*) распространя́ться (распространи́ться *perf*); (*also: ~* **out**)

расширя́ться (расши́риться *perf*); **middle-age ~** возрастна́я полнота́

▶ **spread out** *vi* (*move apart*) раздвига́ть (раздви́нуть *perf*).

spread-eagled ['sprɛdi:gld] *adj* распла́станный (распла́стан); **to be** *or* **lie ~** лежа́ть* (*impf*) плашмя́.

spreadsheet ['sprɛdʃi:t] *n* (*COMPUT*) электро́нная табли́ца.

spree [spri:] *n*: **to go on a ~** кути́ть (покути́ть* *perf*).

sprig [sprɪg] *n* (*BOT*) ве́точка*.

sprightly ['spraɪtlɪ] *adj* (*old person*) бо́дрый (бодр).

spring [sprɪŋ] (*pt* **sprang**, *pp* **sprung**) *n* (*coiled metal*) пружи́на; (*season*) весна́*; (*of water*) исто́чник, родни́к*; (*leap*) прыжо́к*; (*bounciness*) упру́гость *f* ◆ *vi* (*leap*) пры́гать (пры́гнуть *perf*) ◆ *vt*: **to ~ a leak** (*pipe etc*) дава́ть* (дать* *perf*) течь; **in ~** весно́й; **to walk with a ~ in one's step** ходи́ть*/идти́* (*impf*) упру́гой *or* пружи́нистой похо́дкой; **to ~ from sth** (*be the result of*) быть* (*impf*) вы́званным(-ой) чем-н; **he sprang the news on me** он вы́валил на меня́ э́ту но́вость; **to ~ into action** ри́нуться (*perf*) в де́ло

▶ **spring up** *vi* (*building, plant*) выраста́ть (вы́расти* *perf*).

springboard ['sprɪŋbɔ:d] *n* (*SPORT*) трампли́н; (*fig*): **to be the ~ for** служи́ть (послужи́ть *perf*) трампли́ном для +*gen*.

spring-clean(ing) [sprɪŋ'kli:n(ɪŋ)] *n* генера́льная убо́рка*.

spring onion *n* (*BRIT: BOT*) лук-баты́н *no pl*; (: *CULIN*) зелёный лук *no pl*.

spring roll *n* бли́нчик с начи́нкой, свёрнутый в тру́бочку.

springtime ['sprɪŋtaɪm] *n* весе́няя пора́.

springy ['sprɪŋɪ] *adj* упру́гий*.

sprinkle ['sprɪŋkl] *vt* (*salt, sugar*) посыпа́ть (посы́пать* *perf*) +*instr*; **to ~ water on sth, ~ sth with water** бры́згать (побры́згать *perf*) водо́й на что-н; **to ~ sugar on sth, ~ sth with sugar** посыпа́ть (посы́пать* *perf*) что-н са́харом; **~d with** (*fig*) усы́панный (усы́пан) +*instr*.

sprinkler ['sprɪŋklə'] *n* (*for lawn*) разбры́згиватель *m*; (*to put out fire*) спри́нклер.

sprinkling ['sprɪŋklɪŋ] *n* небольшо́е коли́чество; (*of salt, sugar*) го́рсточка, го́рстка.

sprint [sprɪnt] *n* (*race*) спринт ◆ *vi* (*run fast*) стреми́тельно бе́гать/бежа́ть* (*impf*); (*SPORT*) спринтова́ть (*impf*); **the 200 metres ~** спринт на 200-метро́вую диста́нцию.

sprinter ['sprɪntə'] *n* спри́нтер.

sprite [spraɪt] *n* эльф; (*fairy*) фе́я.

---

spritzer ['sprɪtsəʳ] n бе́лое вино́ с со́довой (водо́й).

sprocket ['sprɔkɪt] n (TECH) (цепна́я) звёздочка*.

sprout [spraut] vi (BOT) пуска́ть (пусти́ть* perf) ростки́.

sprouts [sprauts] npl (also: **Brussels** ~) брюссе́льская капу́ста fsg.

spruce [spru:s] n inv (BOT) ель f ◆ adj (neat) опря́тный* (опря́тен); (smart) наря́дный* (наря́ден)

▶ **spruce up** vt (smarten up: room etc) наводи́ть* (навести́* perf) гля́нец на +acc; **to ~ o.s. up** наводи́ть* (навести́* perf) на себя́ гля́нец.

sprung [sprʌŋ] pp of **spring**.

spry [spraɪ] adj (old person) бо́дрый (бодр).

SPUC n abbr (= Society for the Protection of Unborn Children) о́бщество, бо́рющееся про́тив дозволи́тельности або́ртов.

spud [spʌd] n (inf: potato) карто́шка*.

spun [spʌn] pt, pp of **spin**.

spur [spə:ʳ] n шпо́ра; (fig) сти́мул ◆ vt (also: ~ **on**) подстёгивать (подстегну́ть* perf); **to ~ sb on to** побужда́ть (побуди́ть* perf) кого́-н к +dat; **on the ~ of the moment** под влия́нием мину́ты.

spurious ['spjuərɪəs] adj подде́льный.

spurn [spə:n] vt (reject) отверга́ть (отве́ргнуть* perf).

spurt [spə:t] n (of blood etc) струя́; (of energy) поры́в ◆ vi хлы́нуть (perf); **to put on a ~** де́лать (сде́лать perf) рыво́к.

sputter ['spʌtəʳ] vi = **splutter**.

spy [spaɪ] n шпио́н ◆ vi: **to ~ on** шпио́нить (impf) за +instr ◆ vt (see) замеча́ть (заме́тить* perf) ◆ cpd (film, story) шпио́нский.

spying ['spaɪɪŋ] n шпиона́ж.

Sq. abbr (in address) (= square) пл. = пло́щадь.

sq. abbr = **square**.

squabble ['skwɔbl] vi вздо́рить (повздо́рить perf) ◆ n перебра́нка*.

squad [skwɔd] n (MIL, POLICE) кома́нда; (SPORT) кома́нда; **flying ~** (POLICE) отря́д бы́строго реаги́рования.

squad car n (BRIT: POLICE) дежу́рная полице́йская маши́на.

squaddie ['skwɔdɪ] n (inf) солда́т.

squadron ['skwɔdrn] n (MIL) эскадро́н; (AVIAT) эскадри́лья; (NAUT) эска́дра.

squalid ['skwɔlɪd] adj (conditions, room) убо́гий* (убо́г); (story etc) гря́зный (гря́зен).

squall [skwɔ:l] n (stormy wind) шквал.

squalor ['skwɔləʳ] n убо́гость f.

squander ['skwɔndəʳ] vt (money) прома́тывать (промота́ть perf); (chances) растра́чивать (растра́тить* perf).

square [skwɛəʳ] n (shape) квадра́т; (in town) пло́щадь f; (US: block of houses) кварта́л; (also: **set ~**) уго́льник; (inf: person) немо́дный, се́рый челове́к* ◆ adj

квадра́тный; (inf: ideas, tastes) немо́дный, се́рый ◆ vt (reconcile, settle) ула́живать (ула́дить* perf); (MATH) возводи́ть* (возвести́* perf) в квадра́т ◆ vi (agree) согласо́вываться (согласова́ться perf); **we are all ~** мы кви́ты; **a ~ meal** пло́тная трапе́за; **2 metres ~** 2 ме́тра длино́й и 2 ме́тра ширино́й; **2 ~ metres** 2 квадра́тных ме́тра; **I'll ~ it with him** (inf) я с ним э́то ула́жу; **can you ~ it with your conscience?** (reconcile) э́то согласу́ется с Ва́шей со́вестью?; **we're back to ~ one** мы верну́лись туда́, отку́да нача́ли

▶ **square up** vi (BRIT): **to ~ up with sb** поквита́ться (perf) с кем-н.

square bracket n (TYP) квадра́тная ско́бка*.

squarely ['skwɛəlɪ] adv пря́мо.

square root n квадра́тный ко́рень* m.

squash [skwɔʃ] n (BRIT: drink): **lemon/orange ~** лимо́нный/апельси́новой напи́ток* (пригото́вленный из концентра́та); (US) ты́ква; (SPORT) ракетбо́л ◆ vt дави́ть* (раздави́ть* perf).

squat [skwɔt] adj призе́мистый (призе́мист) ◆ vi (also: ~ **down**: position) сиде́ть* (impf) на ко́рточках; (: motion) сесть* (perf) на ко́рточки; (on property) незако́нно поселя́ться (посели́ться perf) в дом.

squatter ['skwɔtəʳ] n (in house) лицо́, самово́льно поселя́ющееся в чужо́м до́ме; (on land) сква́ттер.

squawk [skwɔ:k] vi (bird) клекота́ть* (impf).

squeak [skwi:k] vi (door) скрипе́ть* (скри́пнуть perf); (mouse) пища́ть* (пи́скнуть perf) ◆ n (of hinge, wheel etc) скрип.

squeaky-clean [skwi:kɪ'kli:n] adj (surface etc) чи́стый (чист) до скри́па; (fig) без пя́тнышка.

squeal [skwi:l] vi визжа́ть* (impf), взви́згивать (взви́згнуть perf).

squeamish ['skwi:mɪʃ] adj (person) брезгли́вый (брезгли́в).

squeeze [skwi:z] n (of hand) сжа́тие; (ECON) ограниче́ние; (also: **credit** ~) ограниче́ние креди́та ◆ vt сжима́ть (сжать* perf); (juice) выжима́ть (вы́жать* perf) ◆ vi: **to ~ past/ under sth** проти́скиваться (проти́снуться perf) че́рез что-н/под чем-н; **a ~ of lemon** не́сколько капе́ль лимо́нного со́ка

▶ **squeeze out** vt (juice etc) выжима́ть (вы́жать* perf); (fig: money etc) выжима́ть (вы́жать* perf).

squelch [skwɛltʃ] vi (mud etc) хлю́пать (хлю́пнуть perf).

squib [skwɪb] n (firework) пета́рда.

squid [skwɪd] n кальма́р.

squiggle ['skwɪgl] n загогу́лина.

squint [skwɪnt] vi (permanently) коси́ть* (impf); (in sunlight) щу́риться (impf), прищу́риваться (прищу́риться perf) ◆ n (MED) косогла́зие; **he has a ~** у него́ косогла́зие, он коси́т.

squire ['skwaɪə'] *n* (*BRIT*) помéщик; (*inf*) начáльник.

squirm [skwə:m] *vi* выгибáться (вы́гнуться *perf*); (*with embarrassment or shame*) поёживаться (поёжиться *perf*).

squirrel ['skwɪrəl] *n* бéлка*.

squirt [skwə:t] *vi* бры́згать* (бры́знуть *perf*) ◆ *vt* бры́згать* (бры́знуть *perf*) +*instr*.

Sr *abbr* (*in names*) = **senior**; (*REL*) = **sister**.

SRC *n abbr* (*BRIT*) = **Students' Representative Council**.

Sri Lanka [srɪ'læŋkə] *n* Шри-Лáнка.

SRN *n abbr* (*BRIT*: = **State Registered Nurse**) медсестрá= *медици́нская сестрá*.

SRO *abbr* (*US*: = **standing room only**) тóлько стоя́чие местá *ntpl*.

SS *abbr* = **steamship**.

SSA *n abbr* (*US*: = **Social Security Administration**) ≈ департáмент социáльного обеспéчения.

SST *n abbr* (*US*: = **supersonic transport**) сверхзвуковóй реакти́вный самолёт.

ST *abbr* (*US*) = **Standard Time**.

St *abbr* = **saint**; (= **street**) ул.= *у́лица*.

stab [stæb] *n* (*with knife etc*) удáр (*чем-н óстрым*); (*of pain*) укóл; (*inf: try*): **to have a ~ at doing** пытáться (попытáться *perf*) +*infin* ◆ *vt* наноси́ть* (нанести́* *perf*) удáр +*dat*; **to ~ sb to death** закáлывать (заколóть* *perf*) когó-н.

stabbing ['stæbɪŋ] *n*: **there's been a ~** здесь былá поножóвщина ◆ *adj* (*pain, ache*) рéзкий*.

stability [stə'bɪlɪtɪ] *n* (*of object*) усто́йчивость *f*; (*of government, economy etc*) стаби́льность *f*.

stabilization [steɪbəlaɪ'zeɪʃən] *n* стабилизáция.

stabilize ['steɪbəlaɪz] *vt* (*prices*) стабилизи́ровать (*impf/perf*) ◆ *vi* стабилизи́роваться (*impf/perf*).

stabilizer ['steɪbəlaɪzə'] *n* стабилизáтор.

stable ['steɪbl] *adj* стаби́льный* (стаби́лен), усто́йчивый (усто́йчив) ◆ *n* (*for horse*) коню́шня, стóйло; (*for cattle*) хлев*, стóйло; **riding ~s** (*school*) кóнно-спорти́вная шкóла.

staccato [stə'kɑ:təu] *adv* (*MUS*) стаккáто ◆ *adj* отры́вистый (отры́вист).

stack [stæk] *n* (*pile: of hay*) стог*, скирдá*; (*of wood*) штáбель *m*, полéнница; (*of papers*) ки́па, стóпка; (*of plates*) стопá* ◆ *vt* (*also:* **~ up**: *chairs etc*) склáдывать (сложи́ть* *perf*) в кýчу; (: *books, plates*) склáдывать (сложи́ть* *perf*) в стóпку; (*room, table etc*): **to ~ (with)** уставля́ть (устáвить* *perf*) стóпками; **there's ~s of time** (*BRIT: inf*) ещё есть кýча врéмени.

stadia ['steɪdɪə] *npl of* **stadium**.

stadium ['steɪdɪəm] (*pl* **stadia** *or* **~s**) *n* (*SPORT*) стадиóн.

staff [stɑ:f] *n* (*workforce*) рабóтники *pl*, штат; (*BRIT: SCOL: also:* **teaching ~**) штат учителéй, преподавáтельский состáв; (*servants*) штат;

(*MIL*) ли́чный состáв; (*stick*) пóсох ◆ *vt* укомплектóвывать (укомплектовáть *perf*).

staffroom ['stɑ:fru:m] *n* (*SCOL*) учи́тельская *f adj*.

Staffs *abbr* (*BRIT: POST*) = **Staffordshire**.

stag [stæg] *n* самéц олéня; (*BRIT: STOCK EXCHANGE*) спекуля́нт цéнными бумáгами.

stage [steɪdʒ] *n* (*in theatre*) сцéна; (*platform*) подмóстки *pl*; (*profession*): **the ~** сцéна; (*point, period*) стáдия ◆ *vt* (*play*) стáвить* (постáвить* *perf*); (*demonstration*) устрáивать (устрóить* *perf*); (*fig: recovery etc*) осуществля́ть (осуществи́ть* *perf*); **in ~s** поэтáпно, по этáпам; **he is going through a difficult ~** он пережива́ет трýдный перио́д; **in the early/final ~s** на рáнних/послéдних стáдиях *or* этáпах.

stagecoach ['steɪdʒkəutʃ] *n* почтóвый дилижáнс.

stage door *n* (*THEAT*) служéбный вход (*в меáтр*).

stage fright *n* волнéние пéред выступлéнием.

stagehand ['steɪdʒhænd] *n* рабóчий*(-ая) *m(f)* *adj* сцéны.

stage-manage ['steɪdʒmænɪdʒ] *vt* (*fig*) закули́сно руковóдить* (*impf*) +*instr*.

stage manager *n* дирéктор сцéны.

stagger ['stægə'] *vt* (*amaze*) потряса́ть (потрясти́* *perf*) ◆ *vi*: **he ~ed along the road** он шёл по дорóге, пошáтываясь; **the management has ~ed the workers' leave** администрáция состáвила грáфик отпускóв.

staggering ['stægərɪŋ] *adj* потряса́ющий*.

staging post ['steɪdʒɪŋ-] *n* (*on flight*) промежýточный аэродрóм.

stagnant ['stægnənt] *adj* (*water*) стоя́чий*; (*economy*) застóйный.

stagnate [stæg'neɪt] *vi* (*person*) заси́живаться (засидéться* *perf*); (*economy, business*) быть* (*impf*) в застóе.

stagnation [stæg'neɪʃən] *n* застóй; (*ECON*) стагнáция, застóй.

stag party *n* мальчи́шник.

staid [steɪd] *adj* (*person, attitudes*) степéнный* (степéнен).

stain [steɪn] *n* пятнó*; (*for wood*) мори́лка* ◆ *vt* (*mark*) пятнáть (запятнáть *perf*), пáчкать (запáчкать *perf*); (*wood*) мори́ть (замори́ть *perf*).

stained glass window [steɪnd-] *n* витрáж.

stainless steel ['steɪnlɪs-] *n* нержавéющая сталь *f*.

stain remover *n* пятновыводи́тель *m*.

stair [stɛə'] *n* (*step*) ступéнь *f*, ступéнька*; **~s** *npl* (*steps*) лéстница *fsg*; **on the ~s** на лéстнице.

staircase ['stɛəkeɪs] *n* лéстница.

---

* marks translations which have irregular inflections. The Russian-English side of the dictionary gives inflectional information.

stairway ['stɛəweɪ] = **staircase**.
stairwell ['stɛəwɛl] *n* лéстничная шáхта.
stake [steɪk] *n* (*post*) кол*; (*investment*) дóля*; (*wager*) стáвка*; (*horse race: usu pl*) скáчки* *fpl* ◆ *vt* (*wager: money, life, reputation*) стáвить* (постáвить* *perf*); (*also: ~ out: area*) огорáживать (огородúть* *perf*); (*fig*) очéрчивать (очертúть* *perf*) грани́цы +*gen*; **his reputation was at ~** егó репутáция былá постáвлена на кáрту; **he has a ~ in this business** он крóвно заинтересóван в э́том бизнесе; **to ~ a claim (to sth)** притязáть (*impf*) (на что-н).
stake out *n* (*US: inf*) засáда.
stalactite ['stæləktaɪt] *n* сталактúт.
stalagmite ['stæləgmaɪt] *n* сталагми́т.
stale [steɪl] *adj* (*bread*) чéрствый (чёрств); (*food, beer*) несвéжий* (несвéж); (*air, smell*) зáтхлый.
stalemate ['steɪlmeɪt] *n* (*CHESS*) пат; (*fig*) тупи́к.
stalk [stɔːk] *n* (*of flower*) стéбель *m*; (*of fruit*) черенóк* ◆ *vt* (*person, animal*) крáсться* (подкрáсться* *perf*) к +*dat* ◆ *vi*: **to ~ out/off** удалúться (удали́ться *perf*).
stall [stɔːl] *n* (*BRIT: in street*) ларёк*, киóск; (*in market*) прилáвок*; (*in stable*) стóйло ◆ *vt* (*fig: delay*) задéрживать (задержáть* *perf*) ◆ *vi* (*AUT*) глóхнуть (заглóхнуть* *perf*); (*fig: person*) мéшкать (помéшкать *perf*); **~s** *npl* (*BRIT: THEAT*) партéр *msg*; **watch you don't ~ the engine** смотри́, чтóбы у тебя́ мотóр не заглóх; **a seat in the ~s** мéсто *or* крéсло* в партéре; **a newspaper/flower ~** газéтный/ цветóчный ларёк.
stallholder ['stɔːlhəʊldə*] *n* (*BRIT*) владéлец* ларькá.
stallion ['stæljən] *n* жеребéц*.
stalwart ['stɔːlwət] *adj* (*worker, supporter, party member*) стóйкий*.
stamen ['steɪmɛn] *n* тычи́нка*.
stamina ['stæmɪnə] *n* вынóсливость *f*.
stammer ['stæmə*] *n* заикáние ◆ *vi* заикáться.
stamp [stæmp] *n* (*postage stamp*) мáрка*; (*rubber stamp*) печáть *f*, штамп; (*mark, also fig*) печáть* ◆ *vi* (*also: ~ one's foot*) тóпать* (тóпнуть *perf*) ногóй ◆ *vt* (*letter*) наклéивать (наклéить *perf*) мáрку на +*acc*; (*mark*) отти́скивать (отти́снуть *perf*); (*with rubber stamp*) стáвить* (постáвить* *perf*) печáть *or* штамп на +*acc*; **~ed addressed envelope** надпи́санный конвéрт с мáркой
▸ **stamp out** *vt* (*fire*) затáптывать (затоптáть* *perf*); (*crime*) уничтожáть (уничтóжить *perf*); (*opposition*) подавля́ть (подави́ть* *perf*).
stamp album *n* альбóм для мáрок.
stamp collecting *n* филатели́я.
stamp duty *n* (*BRIT*) гéрбовый сбор.
stampede [stæm'piːd] *n* (*also fig*) мáссовое бéгство.
stamp machine *n* автомáт по продáже

почтóвых мáрок.
stance [stæns] *n* (*also fig*) пози́ция.
stand [stænd] (*pt, pp* **stood**) *n* (*stall*) ларёк*, киóск; (*at exhibition*) стенд; (*SPORT*) трибýна; (*piece of furniture: for umbrellas*) подстáвка*; (: *for coats, hats*) вéшалка* ◆ *vi* (*be upright*) стоя́ть* (*impf*); (*rise*) вставáть* (встать* *perf*); (*remain: decision, offer*) оставáться* (остáться* *perf*) в си́ле; (*in election etc*) выставля́ть (вы́ставить* *perf*) свою́ кандидатýру, баллоти́роваться (*impf*); (*value, level, score etc*): (остáться* *perf*) на +*prp* ◆ *vt* (*place: object*) стáвить* (постáвить* *perf*); (*tolerate, withstand*) терпéть* (*impf*), выноси́ть* (вы́нести* *perf*); **to make a ~ against sth** окáзывать (оказáть* *perf*) сопротивлéние чемý-н; **to take a ~ on sth** занимáть (заня́ть* *perf*) твёрдую пози́цию по пóводу чегó-н; **take the ~** (*US: LAW*) занимáть (заня́ть* *perf*) мéсто свидéтеля; **to ~ for parliament** (*BRIT*) баллоти́роваться (*impf*) в парлáмент; **to ~ to gain/lose sth** имéть (*impf*) шанс обрести́/ потеря́ть что-н; **to ~ sb dinner** угощáть (угости́ть* *perf*) когó-н обéдом; **to ~ sb a drink** стáвить* (постáвить* *perf*) комý-н вы́пивку; **it ~s to reason** самó собóй разумéется; **as things ~** в э́той ситуáции; **I can't ~ him** я егó терпéть не могý
▸ **stand aside** *vi* (*fig*) стоя́ть (*impf*) в сторонé
▸ **stand by** *vi* (*be ready*) быть* наготóве ◆ *vt fus* (*opinion, decision*) не отступáть (не отступи́ть* *perf*) от +*gen*; (*person*) поддéрживать (поддержáть* *perf*)
▸ **stand down** *vi* (*withdraw*) уступáть (уступи́ть* *perf*) мéсто, уходи́ть* (уйти́* *perf*); (*LAW*) покидáть (поки́нуть *perf*) мéсто свидéтеля
▸ **stand for** *vt fus* (*signify*) обозначáть (*impf*); (*represent*) представля́ть (*impf*); **I won't ~ for it** я э́того не потерплю́
▸ **stand in for** *vt fus* (*replace*) замещáть (замести́ть* *perf*) +*acc*
▸ **stand out** *vi* (*be prominent*) выделя́ться (вы́делиться *perf*)
▸ **stand up** *vi* (*rise*) вставáть* (встать* *perf*)
▸ **stand up for** *vt fus* (*defend: rights etc*) отстáивать (отстоя́ть* *perf*); (: *person*) стоя́ть* (постоя́ть* *perf*) за +*acc*
▸ **stand up to** *vt fus* (*withstand: also fig*) выдéрживать (вы́держать* *perf*).
stand-alone ['stændələʊn] *adj* (*COMPUT*) автонóмный.
standard ['stændəd] *n* (*level*) ýровень* *m*; (*norm, criterion*) стандáрт; (*flag*) штандáрт ◆ *adj* (*normal: size etc*) стандáртный (стандáртен); (*text*) основнóй, (*practice*) общепри́нятый (общепри́нят); (*model, feature*) типи́чный* (типи́чен); **~s** *npl* (*morals*) нрáвы *mpl*; **to be** *or* **to come up to ~** быть* (*impf*) на соотвéтствующем ýровне; **to apply**

a double ~ испо́льзовать *(impf/perf)* двойну́ю мора́ль.

standardization [stændədaɪˈzeɪʃən] *n* стандартиза́ция.

standardize [ˈstændədaɪz] *vt* стандартиз-и́ровать *(impf/perf)*.

standard lamp *n (BRIT)* торше́р.

standard of living *n* у́ровень *m* жи́зни.

standard time *n* станда́ртное вре́мя* *nt*.

stand-by [ˈstændbaɪ] *n (reserve)* резе́рв, подмо́га ♦ *adj* запасно́й, резе́рвный; **to be on ~** *(doctor, crew, firemen etc)* быть* *(impf)* нагото́ве.

stand-by ticket *n (THEAT etc)* биле́т, ку́пленный пе́ред нача́лом представле́ния.

stand-in [ˈstændɪn] *n* замести́тель(ница) *m(f)*.

standing [ˈstændɪŋ] *adj (permanent)* постоя́нный; *(ovation)* стоя́чий* ♦ *n (status)* положе́ние; *(duration)*: **of 6 months' ~** 6-ти ме́сячной да́вности; **he received/was given a ~ ovation** ему́ аплоди́ровали стоя́; **he gave me a ~ invitation** он сказа́л, что́бы я приходи́л в любо́е вре́мя; **a man of some ~** челове́к с положе́нием; **promises of many years ~** многоле́тние обеща́ния.

standing committee *n* постоя́нный комите́т.

standing joke *n* дежу́рная шу́тка*.

standing order *n (BRIT: at bank)* прика́з о регуля́рных платежа́х.

standing room *n* стоя́чие места́ *ntpl*.

standoffish [stændˈɔfɪʃ] *adj* спеси́вый (спеси́в).

standpat [ˈstændpæt] *adj (US: person)* консервати́вный.

standpipe [ˈstændpaɪp] *n* напо́рная труба́*.

standpoint [ˈstændpɔɪnt] *n* то́чка* зре́ния.

standstill [ˈstændstɪl] *n*: **to be at a ~** *(also fig)* проста́ивать *(impf)*; **to come to a ~** остана́вливаться (останови́ться* *perf)*.

stank [stæŋk] *pt of* **stink**.

stanza [ˈstænzə] *n (of poem)* строфа́*.

staple [ˈsteɪpl] *n (for papers)* скобка*; *(chief product)* основно́й проду́кт ♦ *adj (food etc)* основно́й ♦ *vt (fasten)* сшива́ть (сшить* *perf)* сте́плером.

stapler [ˈsteɪplər] *n* сшива́тель *m*, сте́плер.

star [stɑːr] *n (also fig)* звезда́ ♦ *vi*: **to ~ in** игра́ть (сыгра́ть *perf)* гла́вную роль в +*prp* ♦ *vt (THEAT, CINEMA)*: **the film ~s my brother** гла́вную роль игра́ет в фи́льме мой брат; **the ~s** *npl (horoscope)* звёзды *fpl*; **4-~ hotel** четырёхзвёздочная гости́ница; **2-~/4-~ petrol** *(BRIT)* бензи́н с ни́зким/высо́ким окта́новым число́м.

star attraction *n* гвоздь* *m* програ́ммы.

starboard [ˈstɑːbəd] *n (NAUT)* пра́вый борт*; **to ~** впра́во руля́.

starch [stɑːtʃ] *n (also CULIN)* крахма́л.

starched [ˈstɑːtʃt] *adj (collar)* накрахма́ленный (накрахма́лен).

starchy [ˈstɑːtʃɪ] *adj (food)* содержа́щий крахма́л; *(pej: person)* чо́порный* (чо́порен).

stardom [ˈstɑːdəm] *n* сла́ва.

stare [stɛər] *n* при́стальный взгляд ♦ *vi*: **to ~ at** при́стально смотре́ть* *(impf)* на +*acc*.

starfish [ˈstɑːfɪʃ] *n* морска́я звезда́*.

stark [stɑːk] *adj (bleak)* го́лый* (гол); *(facts, reality)* го́лый; *(poverty)* соверше́нный; *(colour, contrast)* я́вный* (я́вен) ♦ *adv*: **~ naked** соверше́нно го́лый.

starkers [ˈstɑːkəz] *adj, adv* без всего́.

starlet [ˈstɑːlɪt] *n (CINEMA)* молода́я актри́са.

starlight [ˈstɑːlaɪt] *n*: **by ~** при све́те звёзд.

starling [ˈstɑːlɪŋ] *n* скворе́ц*.

starlit [ˈstɑːlɪt] *adj (night)* звёздный.

starry [ˈstɑːrɪ] *adj (night, sky)* звёздный.

starry-eyed [stɑːrɪˈaɪd] *adj (innocent)* наи́вный* (наи́вен); *(from wonder)* очаро́ванный.

Stars and Stripes *n*: **the ~ ~ ~** звёздно-полоса́тый *m adj (флаг США)*.

star sign *n* знак зодиа́ка.

star-studded [ˈstɑːstʌdɪd] *adj*: **this film has a ~ cast** в э́том фи́льме снима́ется мно́го звёзд.

START *n abbr (MIL: = Strategic Arms Reduction Talks)* перегово́ры *pl* о сокраще́нии стратеги́ческих вооруже́ний.

start [stɑːt] *n* нача́ло; *(SPORT)* старт; *(departure)* отправле́ние; *(sudden movement)* вздра́гивание; *(advantage)* преиму́щество ♦ *vt (begin)* начина́ть (нача́ть* *perf)*; *(cause)* вызыва́ть (вы́звать* *perf)*; *(found: business etc)* осно́вывать (основа́ть* *perf)*; *(engine)* заводи́ть (завести́* *perf)*, запуска́ть (запусти́ть* *perf)* ♦ *vi (begin)* начина́ться (нача́ться* *perf)*; *(begin moving)* отправля́ться (отпра́виться* *perf)*; *(engine, car)* заводи́ться (завести́сь* *perf)*; *(jump: with fright)* вздра́гивать (вздро́гнуть* *perf)*; **to ~ doing** *or* **to do** начина́ть (нача́ть* *perf)* +*impf infin*; **at the ~** в нача́ле; **for a ~** для нача́ла; **to make an early ~** ра́но начина́ть (нача́ть* *perf)*; **to ~ (off) with ...** *(firstly)* во-пе́рвых ...; *(at the beginning)* снача́ла

► **start off** *vi (begin)* начина́ться (нача́ться* *perf)*; *(begin moving, leave)* отправля́ться (отпра́виться* *perf)*

► **start out** *vi (leave)* отправля́ться (отпра́виться* *perf)*

► **start over** *vi (US)* начина́ть (нача́ть* *perf)* сно́ва

► **start up** *vi (business etc)* открыва́ться (откры́ться* *perf)*; *(engine, car)* заводи́ться (завести́сь* *perf)* ♦ *vt (business etc)* осно́вывать (основа́ть* *perf)*; *(engine, car)* заводи́ть (завести́* *perf)*, запуска́ть (запусти́ть* *perf)*.

---

starter ['sta:tə'] n (AUT, SPORT) стáртер; (runner, horse) учáстник(-ица) забéга; (BRIT: CULIN) закýска.

starting point ['sta:tɪŋ-] n (for journey) отправнóй пункт; (for discussion, idea etc) отправнáя тóчка*.

starting price n (at auction) начáльная or отправнáя цена*.

startle ['sta:tl] vt вспýгивать (вспугнýть perf).

startling ['sta:tlɪŋ] adj поразúтельный* (поразúтелен).

star turn n (BRIT) корóнный нóмер*.

starvation [sta:'veɪʃən] n гóлод; **to die of** or **from ~** умирáть (умерéть* perf) от гóлода.

starve [sta:v] vi (to death) умирáть (умерéть* perf) с гóлоду; (be very hungry) проголодáться (perf) ♦ vt (person, animal) морúть (заморúть perf) гóлодом; (fig: deprive): **to ~ sb of sth** лишáть (лишúть perf) когó-н чегó-н; **I'm starving** (inf) я умирáю от гóлода.

Star Wars n „Звёздные вóйны" fpl.

stash [stæʃ] vt (inf) припрятывать (припрятать perf), запасáться (запастúсь* perf) +instr.

state [steɪt] n (condition) состояние; (government) госудáрство ♦ vt (say, declare) констатúровать (impf/perf); **the S~s** npl (GEO) Соединённые Штáты mpl; **to be in a ~** быть* (impf) в пáнике; **~ of emergency** чрезвычáйное положéние; **~ of mind** душéвное состояние.

state control n госудáрственный контрóль m.

stated ['steɪtɪd] adj (aims, beliefs etc) устанóвленный.

State Department n (US) Госудáрственный департáмент.

state education n (BRIT) госудáрственное образовáние.

stateless ['steɪtlɪs] adj (person) не имéющий граждáнства.

stately ['steɪtlɪ] adj велúчественный* (велúчествен); **~ home** дом-усáдьба.

statement ['steɪtmənt] n (declaration) заявлéние; (FINANCE) отчёт, счёт; **official ~** официáльное заявлéние; **bank ~** выписка* с бáнковского счёта.

state of the art n послéднее слóво тéхники ♦ adj: **~-~-~** ультрасовремéнный.

state-owned ['steɪtəund] adj (industry etc) госудáрственный.

state school n (BRIT) госудáрственная шкóла.

state secret n госудáрственная тáйна.

statesman ['steɪtsmən] irreg n госудáрственный дéятель m.

statesmanship ['steɪtsmənʃɪp] n госудáрственная дéятельность f.

static ['stætɪk] n (RADIO, TV) (атмосфéрные) помéхи fpl ♦ adj (not moving) статúчный* (статúчен), неподвúжный* (неподвúжен).

static electricity n статúческое электрúчество.

station ['steɪʃən] n стáнция; (larger railway station) вокзáл; (also: police ~) полицéйский* учáсток ♦ vt (position: guards etc) выставлять (выставить* perf); (base: soldiers etc) дислоцúровать (impf/perf), размещáть (размести́ть* perf); **action ~s** сигнáл "все по местáм!"; **to get above one's ~** садúться* (сесть* perf) не в свои сáни.

stationary ['steɪʃnərɪ] adj (vehicle) неподвúжный.

stationer ['steɪʃənə'] n торгóвец* канцелярскими товáрами.

stationer's (shop) n магазúн канцелярских товáров.

stationery ['steɪʃnərɪ] n канцелярские принадлéжности fpl.

stationmaster ['steɪʃənma:stə'] n начáльник стáнции.

station wagon n (US) автомобúль-фургóн, пикáп.

statistic [stə'tɪstɪk] n статúстик.

statistical [stə'tɪstɪkl] adj (evidence, techniques) статистúческий*.

statistics [stə'tɪstɪks] n (science) статúстика.

statue ['stætju:] n стáтуя.

statuesque [stætju'ɛsk] adj (woman) стáтная (стáтна).

statuette [stætju'ɛt] n статуэтка*.

stature ['stætʃə'] n рост; (fig: reputation) положéние.

status ['steɪtəs] n стáтус; (importance) значéние; **the ~ quo** стáтус-кво m ind.

status line n (COMPUT) строкá* состояния.

status symbol n сúмвол положéния в общéстве.

statute ['stætju:t] n статýт, законодáтельный акт; **~s** npl (of club etc) устáв msg.

statute book n (LAW, POL): **the ~ ~** свод закóнов.

statutory ['stætjutrɪ] adj (powers, rights etc) устанóвленный закóном; **~ meeting** учредúтельное собрáние.

staunch [stɔ:ntʃ] adj (ally etc) прéданный ♦ vt останáвливать (остановúть* perf).

stave [steɪv] n (MUS) нóтный стан

▶ **stave off** vt (attack) отсрóчивать (отсрóчить perf); (threat) отводúть (отвестú* perf).

stay [steɪ] n пребывáние ♦ vi (remain) оставáться* (остáться* perf); (with sb, as guest) гостúть* (impf); (in place: spend some time) останáвливаться (останови́ться* perf); **~ of execution** (LAW) отсрóчка* исполнéния; **to ~ at home** сидéть* (impf) дóма; **to ~ in bed** лежáть* (impf) в постéли; **to ~ put** не двúгаться (двúнуться perf) с мéста; **to ~ with friends** останáвливаться (останови́ться* perf) or гостúть* (impf) у друзéй; **to ~ the night** (in a place) ночевáть (заночевáть* perf); (with sb) проводúть* (провести́* perf) ночь

▶ **stay behind** vi оставáться* (остáться* perf)

▶ **stay in** vi (at home) оставáться* (остáться*

perf) до́ма
▶ **stay on** *vi* оставáться* (остáться* *perf*)
▶ **stay out** *vi* (*of house*) отсу́тствовать (*impf*);
(*remain on strike*) продолжáть (*impf*)
бастовáть
▶ **stay up** *vi* (*at night*) не ложи́ться (*impf*) спать.
staying power ['stenŋ-] *n* выно́сливость *f*.
STD *n abbr* (*BRIT: TEL: = subscriber trunk dialling*)
≈ АМТС= *автомати́ческая междугоро́д-
ная телефо́нная связь*; (*MED: = sexually
transmitted disease*) *заболевáние,
передавáемое половы́м путём.*
stead [stɛd] *n*: **in sb's ~** вме́сто кого́-н; **to stand
sb in good ~** пригождáться (пригоди́ться*
perf) кому́-н.
steadfast ['stɛdfɑːst] *adj* (*person*) сто́йкий*
(сто́ек); (*refusal, support*) твёрдый.
steadily ['stɛdɪlɪ] *adv* (*firmly*) про́чно;
(*constantly, fixedly*) постоя́нно; (*walk:
decisively*) реши́тельно; (: *without stumbling*)
твёрдо.
steady ['stɛdɪ] *adj* (*constant*) стаби́льный*
(стаби́лен); (: *boyfriend, speed*) постоя́нный;
(*person, character*) уравнове́шенный*
(уравнове́шен); (*firm: hand etc*) твёрдый*
(твёрд); (*calm: look, voice*) ро́вный* (ро́вен) ◆
vt (*object*) придавáть* (придáть* *perf*) устóй-
чивость +*dat*; (*nerves, person*) успокáивать
(успокóить *perf*); (*voice*) придавáть*
(придáть* *perf*) рóвность +*dat*; **to ~ o.s. on** *or*
against sth опирáться (опере́ться* *perf*) о(бо)
что-н.
steak [steɪk] *n* (*beef*) бифште́кс; (*fish*) филе́ *nt
ind*; (*pork*) вы́резка*.
steakhouse ['steɪkhaus] *n* бифште́ксная *f adj*.
steal [stiːl] (*pt* **stole**, *pp* **stolen**) *vt* воровáть
(своровáть *perf*), красть* (укрáсть* *perf*) ◆ *vi*
(*thieve*) воровáть (*impf*); (*move secretly*)
крáсться* (*impf*)
▶ **steal away** *vi* незамéтно ускользáть
(ускользну́ть *perf*)
▶ **steal off** *vi* = **steal away**.
stealth [stɛlθ] *n*: **by ~** укрáдкой.
stealthy ['stɛlθɪ] *adj* (*movements, actions*)
тáйный.
steam [stiːm] *n* пар* ◆ *vt* (*CULIN*) вари́ть*
(свари́ть* *perf*) на пару́, пáрить (*impf*) ◆ *vi*
(*give off steam*) испускáть (испусти́ть* *perf*)
пар; **under one's own ~** (*fig*) свои́ми си́лами;
to run out of ~ (*fig: person*) выдыхáться
(вы́дохнуться *perf*); **to let off ~** (*fig: inf*)
выпускáть (вы́пустить* *perf*) пар
▶ **steam up** *vi* (*window*) запотевáть (запоте́ть
perf); **to get ~ed up about sth** (*fig: inf*)
кипяти́ться* (раскипяти́ться* *perf*) из-за
чего́-н.
steam engine *n* (*RAIL*) парово́з.
steamer ['stiːmə'] *n* парохо́д; (*CULIN*)

паровáрка*.
steam iron *n* утю́г* с отпáривателем.
steamroller ['stiːmrəʊlə'] *n* паровóй катóк*.
steamship ['stiːmʃɪp] *n* = **steamer**.
steamy ['stiːmɪ] *adj* (*room*) пóлный* (пóлон)
пáра; (*window*) запоте́вший*.
steed [stiːd] *n* конь *m*.
steel [stiːl] *n* сталь *f* ◆ *adj* стальнóй.
steel band *n* (*MUS*) кари́бский удáрный
оркéстр.
steel industry *n* сталелити́йная
промы́шленность *f*.
steel mill *n* сталели́тейный завóд.
steelworks ['stiːlwəːks] *n* сталели́тейный
завóд.
steely ['stiːlɪ] *adj* (*eyes, gaze*) стальнóй;
(*determination*) непреклóнный*.
steep [stiːp] *adj* крутóй* (крут); (*price*)
высóкий* (высóк) ◆ *vt* (*soak: food*)
вымáчивать (вы́мочить *perf*); (: *clothes*)
замáчивать (замочи́ть* *perf*); **a house ~ed in
history** (*fig*) дом* с истори́ческим прóшлым
овéянный истóрией.
steeple ['stiːpl] *n* шпиль *m*; (*belltower*)
колокóльня*.
steeplechase ['stiːpltʃeɪs] *n* стипль-чéз.
steeplejack ['stiːpldʒæk] *n* верхолáз.
steeply ['stiːplɪ] *adv* крýто.
steer [stɪə'] *vt* (*vehicle, person*) води́ть*/вести́*
(*impf*) ◆ *vi* (*manoeuvre*) маневри́ровать (*impf*)
◆ *n* кастри́рованный бык*; **to ~ clear of sb/
sth** (*fig*) избегáть (*impf*) когó-н/чегó-н.
steering ['stɪərɪŋ] *n* (*AUT*) управлéние.
steering column *n* рулевáя колóнка.
steering committee *n* комúссия по
вырабóтке реглáмента.
steering wheel *n* руль* *m*.
stellar ['stɛlə'] *adj* (*of stars*) звёздный.
stem [stɛm] *n* (*BOT: of plant*) ствол*, стéбель* *m*;
(*of leaf, fruit*) черешóк*; (*of glass*) нóжка*; (*of
pipe*) черенóк* ◆ *vt* (*stop*) останáвливать
(останови́ть* *perf*)
▶ **stem from** *vt fus* (*subj: condition, problem*)
происходи́ть* (произойти́* *perf*) от +*gen*; **their
aggressiveness ~med from fear** их
агресси́вность порождéна стрáхом.
stench [stɛntʃ] *n* (*pej*) вонь *f*.
stencil ['stɛnsl] *n* трафарéт ◆ *vt* (*letters, designs
etc*) дéлать (сдéлать *perf*) по трафарéту.
stenographer [stɛ'nɔɡrəfə'] *n* (*US*)
стенографи́ст(ка*).
stenography [stɛ'nɔɡrəfɪ] *n* (*US*) стенографи́я.
step [stɛp] *n* (*also fig*) шаг*; (*of stairs*) ступéнь *f*
◆ *vi*: **to ~ forward/back** ступáть (ступи́ть*
perf) вперёд/назáд; **~s** *npl* (*BRIT*) = **stepladder**;
~ by ~ (*also fig*) шаг за шáгом; **to be in/out of
~ (with)** идти́* (*impf*) в нóгу/не в нóгу (с
+*instr*); (*fig*) соотвéтствовать (*impf*)/не

---

* marks translations which have irregular inflections. The Russian–English side of the dictionary gives inflectional information.

соответствовать (*impf*) (+*dat*)
► **step down** *vi* (*fig: resign*) уходить* (уйти* *perf*) в отставку
► **step in** *vi* (*fig*) вмешиваться (вмешаться *perf*)
► **step off** *vt fus* сходить* (сойти* *perf*) с +*gen*
► **step on** *vt fus* (*walk on*) наступать (наступить* *perf*) на +*acc*
► **step over** *vt fus* переступать (переступить* *perf*) через +*acc*
► **step up** *vi* (*increase*) усиливать (усилить *perf*).

step aerobics *n* степ-аэробика (*с использованием особой ступеньки*).
stepbrother ['stɛpbrʌðə'] *n* сводный брат*.
stepchild ['stɛptʃaɪld] *n* (*boy*) пасынок*; (*girl*) падчерица.
stepdaughter ['stɛpdɔ:tə'] *n* падчерица.
stepfather ['stɛpfɑ:ðə'] *n* отчим.
stepladder ['stɛplædə'] *n* (*BRIT*) стремянка*.
stepmother ['stɛpmʌðə'] *n* мачеха.
stepping stone ['stɛpɪŋ-] *n* (*in river*) опорный камень *m*; (*fig*) ступенька.
step-reebok® [step'ri:bɔk] *n* ступенька, используемая при степ-аэробике.
stepsister ['stɛpsɪstə'] *n* сводная сестра*.
stepson ['stɛpsʌn] *n* пасынок*.
stereo ['stɛrɪəʊ] *n* (*system*) стереосистема; (*record player*) стереопроигрыватель *m* ♦ *adj* (*also:* ~**phonic**) стереофонический; **in** ~ стерео.
stereotype ['stɪərɪətaɪp] *n* стереотип ♦ *vt* воспринимать (*impf*) по стереотипу.
sterile ['stɛraɪl] *adj* (*also fig*) бесплодный* (бесплоден); (*free from germs*) стерильный* (стерилен).
sterility [stɛ'rɪlɪtɪ] *n* (*infertility*) бесплодие.
sterilization [stɛrɪlaɪ'zeɪʃən] *n* стерилизация.
sterilize ['stɛrɪlaɪz] *vt* стерилизовать (*impf*).
sterling ['stɜ:lɪŋ] *adj* (*efforts: noble*) благородный*; (: *excellent*) отменный ♦ *n* (*ECON*) фунт стерлингов; ~ **silver** серебро 925-ой пробы; **one pound** ~ один фунт стерлингов.
sterling area *n* стерлинговая зона.
stern [stɜ:n] *adj* строгий* (строг) ♦ *n* (*of boat*) корма.
sternum ['stɜ:nəm] *n* грудина.
steroid ['stɪərɔɪd] *n* стероид.
stet [stɛt] *n* корректирующий знак, отменяющий поправки ♦ *vi* оставить (*perf*) как было.
stethoscope ['stɛθəskəʊp] *n* стетоскоп.
stevedore ['sti:vədɔ:'] *n* портовый грузчик.
stew [stju:] *n* (*meat*) тушёное мясо ♦ *vt* (*meat*) тушить* (потушить* *pcrf*); (*fruit*) варить (сварить *perf*) ♦ *vi* (*meat*) тушиться* (потушиться* *perf*); (*fruit*) вариться (свариться *perf*); **vegetable** ~ тушёные овощи; ~**ed tea** перестоявшийся чай; ~**ed fruit** варёные фрукты.

steward ['stju:əd] *n* (*on ship, train*) стюард; (*on plane*) бортпроводник*; (*in club etc*) распорядитель *m*; (*also:* **shop** ~) цеховой староста.
stewardess ['stju:ədɛs] *n* (*on plane*) стюардесса, бортпроводница.
stewardship ['stju:ədʃɪp] *n* управление.
stewing steak ['stju:ɪŋ-] (*US* **stew meat**) *n* говядина для тушения.
St. Ex. *abbr* = **stock exchange**.
stg *abbr* = **sterling**.
stick [stɪk] (*pt, pp* **stuck**) *n* (*of wood*) палка*; (*of dynamite, chalk etc*) палочка*; (*walking stick*) трость *f* ♦ *vt* (*with glue etc*) клеить (приклеить *perf*); (*inf: put*) совать* (сунуть *perf*); (: *tolerate*) терпеть (вытерпеть *perf*); (*thrust*) втыкать (воткнуть *perf*) ♦ *vi* (*become attached*) приклеиваться (приклеиться *perf*); (*be unmoveable*) застревать (застрять* *perf*); (*in mind etc*) засесть* (*perf*); (*get jammed: door*) заедать (заесть* *perf*); (: *lift*) застревать (застрять* *perf*); **to get hold of the wrong end of the** ~ (*BRIT: fig*) совсем не так понимать (понять* *perf*); **he stuck a cigar in his mouth** он засунул сигару в рот; **to** ~ **to** (*become attached*) приклеиваться (приклеиться *perf*) к +*dat*; (*one's word, promise*) держать* (сдержать* *perf*); (*principles*) оставаться* (остаться* *perf*) верным(-ой) +*dat*
► **stick around** *vi* (*inf*) торчать (*impf*)
► **stick out** *vi* (*ears etc*) торчать (*impf*) ♦ *vi*: **to** ~ **it out** (*inf*) терпеть* (вытерпеть* *perf*)
► **stick up** *vi* (*hair etc*) торчать (*impf*)
► **stick up for** *vt fus* (*person*) заступаться (заступиться* *perf*) за +*acc*; (*principle*) отстаивать (отстоять *perf*).
sticker ['stɪkə'] *n* наклейка.
sticking plaster ['stɪkɪŋ-] *n* лейкопластырь *m*.
sticking point *n* (*in relationship*) точка преткновения.
stickleback ['stɪklbæk] *n* колюшка.
stickler ['stɪklə'] *n*: **to be a** ~ **for** настаивать (*impf*) на +*prp*.
stick shift *n* (*US: AUT*) переключатель *m* скоростей.
stick-up ['stɪkʌp] *n* (*inf*) вооружённое ограбление.
sticky ['stɪkɪ] *adj* (*hands etc*) липкий*; (*label*) клейкий*; (*fig: situation*) щекотливый (щекотлив).
stiff [stɪf] *adj* (*brush*) жёсткий* (жёсток); (*paste*) густой*; (*egg-white*) крутой*; (*person*) деревянный*; (*door, zip*) тугой* (туг); (*manner, smile*) натянутый (натянут); (*competition*) ожесточённый*; (*severe: sentence*) суровый* (суров); (*high: price*) высокий* (высок); (*strong: drink*) крепкий*; (: *breeze*) сильный* (силён) ♦ *adv* (*bored, worried, scared*) до смерти; **I am** *or* **feel** ~ **y** меня всё тело ноет; **I have a** ~ **neck** у меня свело шею; **to keep a** ~ **upper lip** (*BRIT: fig*)

сохранять (сохранить *perf*) хладнокровие.
stiffen ['stɪfn] *vi* (*body*) напрягаться
(напрячься* *perf*); (*joints, neck*) не сгибаться
(*impf*); **my muscles have ~ed** у меня свело
мышцы.
stiffness ['stɪfnɪs] *n* (*of joints*) неподвижность
f; (*of paper, cloth*) жёсткость *f*; (*in
consistency*) густота; (*in behaviour etc*)
натянутость *f*.
stifle ['staɪfl] *vt* (*yawn*) подавлять (подавить*
perf); (*opposition*) душить (задушить *perf*);
(*subj: heat*) душить (*impf*).
stifling ['staɪflɪŋ] *adj* (*heat*) удушливый
(удушлив).
stigma ['stɪgmə] *n* (*of failure, defeat etc*)
клеймо; (*BOT*) рыльце; (*MED*) стигма.
stile [staɪl] *n* перелаз.
stiletto [stɪ'lɛtəu] *n* (*BRIT: also: ~ heel*)
шпилька.
still [stɪl] *adj* тихий* (тих); (*BRIT: not fizzy*)
негазированный ◆ *adv* (*up to this time*) всё
ещё; (*even, yet*) ещё; (*nonetheless*) всё-таки,
тем не менее ◆ *n* (*CINEMA*) рекламный
фотокадр; **to stand ~** стоять* (*impf*)
неподвижно; **keep ~!** не шевелитесь!; **he ~
hasn't arrived** он всё ещё не пришёл.
stillborn ['stɪlbɔːn] *adj* (*baby*) мертво-
рождённый.
still life *n* (*ART*) натюрморт.
stilt [stɪlt] *n* (*pile*) свая; (*for walking on*)
ходуля*.
stilted ['stɪltɪd] *adj* (*behaviour, conversation*)
высокопарный* (высокопарен).
stimulant ['stɪmjulənt] *n* стимулирующее *or*
возбуждающее средство.
stimulate ['stɪmjuleɪt] *vt* стимулировать (*impf/
perf*).
stimulating ['stɪmjuleɪtɪŋ] *adj* вдохно-
вляющий.
stimulation [stɪmju'leɪʃən] *n* стимулирование.
stimuli ['stɪmjulaɪ] *npl of* **stimulus**.
stimulus ['stɪmjuləs] (*pl* **stimuli**) *n*
(*encouragement*) стимул; (*MED*) стимулятор;
(*BIO, PSYCH*) раздражитель *m*.
sting [stɪŋ] (*pt, pp* **stung**) *n* (*from insect*) укус;
(*from plant*) ожог; (*organ: of wasp etc*) жало;
(*inf: confidence trick*) мошенничество ◆ *vt*
(*also fig*) уязвлять (уязвить* *perf*) ◆ *vi* (*insect,
animal*) жалиться (*impf*); (*plant*) жечься* (*impf*);
(*eyes, ointment etc*) жечь* (*impf*); **my eyes are
~ing** мне жжёт глаза.
stingy ['stɪndʒɪ] *adj* (*pej: person*) скаредный*
(скареден).
stink [stɪŋk] (*pt* **stank**, *pp* **stunk**) *n* смрад, вонь *f*
◆ *vi* смердеть (*impf*).
stinker ['stɪŋkə'] (*inf*) *n* (*person*)
мерзавец*(-вка*); **it's a real ~ of a problem/
exam** это жуткая проблема/ужасный

экзамен.
stinking ['stɪŋkɪŋ] (*inf*) *adj* (*inf*) вонючий*
(вонюч); **a ~ cold** жуткая простуда; **~ rich**
жутко богатый.
stint [stɪnt] *n* период работы ◆ *vi*: **to ~ on**
(*work*) халтурить (*impf*) в +*prp*; (*ingredients*)
зажимать (зажать* *perf*).
stipend ['staɪpɛnd] *n* (*of vicar etc*) жалованье;
(*of student*) стипендия.
stipendiary [staɪ'pɛndɪərɪ] *adj*: **~ magistrate**
платный мировой судья.
stipulate ['stɪpjuleɪt] *vt* (*condition, amount etc*)
определять (определить *perf*).
stipulation [stɪpju'leɪʃən] *n* условие.
stir [stɜː'] *n* (*fig: agitation*) шум, сенсация ◆ *vt*
(*tea etc*) мешать (помешать *perf*); (*fig:
emotions*) волновать (взволновать *perf*) ◆ *vi*
(*move slightly*) шевелиться (пошевелиться
perf); **to give sth a ~** размешивать
(размешать *perf*) что-н; **to cause a ~**
вызывать (вызвать* *perf*) сенсацию
▶ **stir up** *vt* (*trouble*) вызывать (вызвать* *perf*).
stir-fry ['stɜː'fraɪ] *vt* быстро обжаривать
(обжарить *perf*).
stirring ['stɜːrɪŋ] *adj* (*speech, occasion*)
волнующий.
stirrup ['stɪrəp] *n* стремя* *nt*.
stitch [stɪtʃ] *n* (*SEWING*) стежок*; (*KNITTING*)
петля*; (*MED*) шов* ◆ *vt* (*sew*) шить* (сшить*
perf); (*MED: wound*) зашивать (зашить* *perf*); **I
have a ~ in my side** у меня колет в боку.
stoat [stəut] *n* горностай.
stock [stɔk] *n* (*supply*) запас; (*AGR*) поголовье;
(*CULIN*) бульон; (*descent, origin*)
происхождение; (*FINANCE*) ценные бумаги
fpl; (*COMM: of company*) акционерный
капитал; (*RAIL: also: rolling ~*) (подвижной)
состав ◆ *adj* (*fig: reply, excuse etc*)
шаблонный ◆ *vt* (*have in stock*) иметь (*impf*) в
наличии; **~s and shares** акции и ценные
бумаги; **to be in/out of ~** иметься (*impf*)/не
иметься (*impf*) в наличии; **a well-~ed shop**
магазин с большим ассортиментом
товаров; **to take ~ of** (*fig*) оценивать
(оценить* *perf*); **government ~**
правительственные акции
▶ **stock up** *vi*: **to ~ up with** запасаться
(запастись* *perf*) +*instr*.
stockade [stɔ'keɪd] *n* частокол.
stockbroker ['stɔkbrəukə'] *n* (*COMM*) фондовый
брокер.
stock control *n* (*COMM*) управление запасами.
stock cube *n* (*BRIT: CULIN*) бульонный кубик.
stock exchange *n* фондовая биржа.
stockholder ['stɔkhəuldə'] *n* (*COMM*) акционер.
Stockholm ['stɔkhəum] *n* Стокгольм.
stocking ['stɔkɪŋ] *n* чулок*.
stock in trade *n* (*COMM*) *запасы имеющиеся в*

наличии и предназначенные для продажи;
(*fig*): **it's his ~ ~ ~** это его обычное занятие.
stockist ['stɔkɪst] *n* (*BRIT*) стокист (*фирма,
имеющая запас какой-нибудь продукции*).
stock market *n* (*BRIT*) фондовая биржа.
stock phrase *n* клише *nt ind*.
stockpile ['stɔkpaɪl] *n* (*of weapons, food*) запас
◆ *vt* запасать (запасти* *perf*).
stockroom ['stɔkru:m] *n* (*COMM*) склад.
stocktaking ['stɔkteɪkɪŋ] *n* (*BRIT*: *COMM*)
инвентаризация.
stocky ['stɔkɪ] *adj* коренастый (коренаст).
stodgy ['stɔdʒɪ] *adj* (*food*) тяжёлый.
stoic ['stəʊɪk] *n* стоик.
stoical ['stəʊɪkl] *adj* (*person, behaviour*)
стойческий*.
stoke [stəʊk] *vt* (*fire*) поддерживать (*impf*);
(*boiler, furnace*) поддерживать (*impf*) огонь в
+*prp*.
stoker ['stəʊkə^r] *n* (*RAIL, NAUT etc*) кочегар.
stole [stəʊl] *pt of* **steal** ◆ *n* палантин.
stolen ['stəʊln] *pp of* **steal**.
stolid ['stɔlɪd] *adj* (*person, behaviour*)
бесстрастный* (бесстрастен).
stomach ['stʌmək] *n* (*ANAT*) желудок*; (*belly*)
живот* ◆ *vt* (*fig*) переносить* (*impf*).
stomachache ['stʌməkeɪk] *n* желудочные
боли *fpl*.
stomach pump *n* желудочный зонд.
stomach ulcer *n* язва желудка.
stomp [stɔmp] *vi*: **to ~ in/out** входить* (войти*
perf)/уходить* (уйти* *perf*) тяжёлыми
шагами.
stone [stəʊn] *n* (*also MED*) камень* *m*; (*pebble*)
камешек*; (*in fruit*) косточка*; (*BRIT*: *weight*)
стоун (*14 фунтов*) ◆ *adj* каменный ◆ *vt*
(*person*) закидывать (закидать *perf*)
камнями в +*acc*; (*fruit*) вынимать (вынуть
perf) косточки из +*gen*; **within a ~'s throw of
the school** в двух шагах от школы.
Stone Age *n*: **the ~ ~** каменный век.
stone-cold ['stəʊn'kəʊld] *adj* холодный* как
лёд.
stoned [stəʊnd] *adj* (*inf*: *drunk*) мертвецки
пьяный* (пьян); (: *on drugs*) обкурившийся.
stone-deaf ['stəʊn'dɛf] *adj* совершенно
глухой*.
stonemason ['stəʊnmeɪsn] *n* каменщик.
stonewall [stəʊn'wɔ:l] *vti* заниматься (*impf*)
процедурными задержками (*в
парламенте*).
stonework ['stəʊnwə:k] *n* (каменная) кладка.
stony ['stəʊnɪ] *adj* (*ground*) каменистый
(каменист); (*fig*: *glance, silence etc*)
холодный.
stood [stud] *pt, pp of* **stand**.
stooge [stu:dʒ] *n* (*inf*) порученец*, шестёрка;
(: *THEAT*) партнёр комика.
stool [stu:l] *n* табуретка*.
stoop [stu:p] *vi* (*also*: ~ **down**: *bend*)
наклоняться (наклониться* *perf*),

нагибаться (нагнуться *perf*); (*also*: **have a ~**)
сутулиться (*impf*); (*fig*): **to ~ to sth/doing**
унижаться (унизиться* *perf*) до чего-н/до
того, чтобы +*infin*.
stop [stɔp] *n* остановка*; (*in punctuation*: *also*:
full ~) точка* ◆ *vt* останавливать
(остановить* *perf*); (*prevent*: *also*: **put a ~ to**)
прекращать (прекратить* *perf*) ◆ *vi* (*person,
clock*) останавливаться (остановиться* *perf*);
(*rain, noise etc*) прекращаться
(прекратиться* *perf*); **to ~ sb (from) doing**
удерживать (удержать *perf*) кого-н от того,
чтобы +*infin*; **~ it!** прекратите!; **to ~ doing**
переставать* (перестать* *perf*) +*infin*; **the car
~ped dead** машина остановилась как
вкопанная
▸ **stop by** *vi* заходить* (зайти* *perf*)
▸ **stop off** *vi* останавливаться (остановиться*
perf)
▸ **stop up** *vt* (*hole*) заделывать (заделать *perf*).
stopcock ['stɔpkɔk] *n* запорный кран.
stopgap ['stɔpgæp] *n* (*person, thing*) временная
замена; (*also*: ~ **measure**) временная мера.
stop-go [stɔp'gəʊ] *adj* (*BRIT*: *ECON*): ~ **policy**
экономическая политика, чередующая
stoplights ['stɔplaɪts] *npl* (*AUT*) стоп-сигнал
msg.
stopover ['stɔpəʊvə^r] *n* остановка*; (*AVIAT*)
посадка*.
stoppage ['stɔpɪdʒ] *n* (*strike*) забастовка*;
(*blockage*) остановка*; (*of pay*)
прекращение.
stopper ['stɔpə^r] *n* пробка*.
stop press *n* экстренное сообщение.
stopwatch ['stɔpwɔtʃ] *n* секундомер.
storage ['stɔ:rɪdʒ] *n* хранение*; (*in house*)
кладовка*; (*COMPUT*) память *f*, накопитель
m.
storage capacity *n* ёмкость *f*.
storage heater *n* (*BRIT*) аккумулирующий
электрообогреватель *m*.
store [stɔ:^r] *n* (*stock, reserve*) запас*; (*depot*)
склад; (*BRIT*: *large shop*) универмаг*; (*esp US*)
магазин ◆ *vt* хранить (*impf*); ~**s** *npl*
(*provisions*) запасы *mpl*; **in** ~ в будущем; **who
knows what's in ~ for us?** кто знает, что нас
ждёт в будущем?; **to set great/little ~ by sth**
придавать* (придать* *perf*) большое/
маленькое значение чему-н
▸ **store up** *vt* (*food*) запасать (запасти* *perf*);
(*memories*) хранить (*impf*).
storehouse ['stɔ:haus] *n* (*US*: *COMM*) склад;
(*fig*) кладовая *f adj*.
storekeeper ['stɔ:ki:pə^r] *n* (*US*: *manager*)
управляющий*(-ая) *m(f) adj* магазином;
(*owner*) владелец*(-лица) магазина.
storeroom ['stɔ:ru:m] *n* кладовая *f adj*.
storey ['stɔ:rɪ] (*US* **story**) *n* этаж*.
stork [stɔ:k] *n* аист.
storm [stɔ:m] *n* (*also fig*) буря*; (*of criticism*)
волна*; (*of laughter*) взрыв; (*also*: **electric ~**)

гроза* ◆ *vi* (*fig: speak angrily*) крича́ть* (*impf*)
◆ *vt* (*attack: place*) штурмова́ть (*impf*).
storm cloud *n* грозова́я ту́ча.
storm door *n* нару́жная дверь* *f*.
stormy ['stɔ:mɪ] *adj* штормово́й; (*fig: debate, relations*) бу́рный; ~ **weather** нена́стье.
story ['stɔ:rɪ] *n* исто́рия; (*PRESS: article*) статья́*; (: *subject*) газе́тный материа́л; (*lie*) вы́думка*; (*US*) = **storey; short ~** расска́з.
storybook ['stɔ:rɪbuk] *n* сбо́рник расска́зов *or* ска́зок (*для дете́й*).
storyteller ['stɔ:rɪtɛlə'] *n* расска́зчик(-ица); (*inf: liar*) вру́н(ья).
stout [staut] *adj* (*strong: branch etc*) кре́пкий* (кре́пок); (*fat*) доро́дный* (доро́ден); (*resolute: friend, supporter*) надёжный (надёжен) ◆ *n* (*beer*) кре́пкий* по́ртер.
stove [stəuv] *n* (*for cooking*) плита́*; (: *small*) пли́тка*; (*for heating*) печь* *f*; **gas/electric ~** (*cooker*) га́зовая/электри́ческая плита́.
stow [stəu] *vt* (*also:* ~ **away**) убира́ть (убра́ть* *perf*).
stowaway ['stəuəweɪ] *n* безбиле́тник(-ница).
St Petersburg [sənt'pi:təzbə:g] *n* Санкт-Петербу́рг ◆ *adj* (санкт-) петербу́ргский*.
straddle ['strædl] *vt* (*chair, fence etc*) осёдла́ть (*perf*); (*fig*) охва́тывать (охвати́ть* *perf*).
strafe [strɑ:f] *vt* (*MIL: with bullets*) обстре́ливать (обстреля́ть *perf*); (*with bombs*) бомби́ть (*impf*).
straggle ['strægl] *vi* (*houses etc*) раски́дываться (раски́нуться *perf*); (*people*) разбреда́ться (разбрести́сь* *perf*).
straggler ['stræglə'] *n* (*person*) отста́вший(-ая) *m(f) adj*.
straggly ['stræglɪ] *adj* (*hair*) беспоря́дочно торча́щий.
straight [streɪt] *adj* прямо́й* (прям); (*simple: choice*) я́сный* (я́сен); (*THEAT: part, play*) серьёзный; (*inf: heterosexual*) гетеросексуа́льный* ◆ *adv* прямо ◆ *n*: **the ~** (*SPORT*) прямая *f adj*; **to put** *or* **get sth ~** (*make clear*) вноси́ть* (внести́* *perf*) я́сность во что-н; **let's get this ~** дава́йте внесём я́сность *or* определённость в э́то; **to set (all) ~** (*tidy*) быть* (*impf*) в (по́лном) поря́дке; (*clarified*) быть* (*impf*) я́сным(-ой); **10 ~ wins** 10 побе́д подря́д; **to go ~ home** идти́* (пойти́* *perf*) сра́зу домо́й; **to tell sb ~ out** говори́ть (сказа́ть* *perf*) кому́-н прямо; **to drink vodka ~** пить* (*impf*) неразба́вленную во́дку; ~ **away**, ~ **off** (*at once*) сра́зу.
straighten ['streɪtn] *vt* (*skirt, tie etc*) поправля́ть (попра́вить* *perf*); (*bed*) заправля́ть (запра́вить* *perf*)
▶ **straighten out** *vt* (*fig: problem etc*) ула́живать (ула́дить* *perf*).

straight-faced [streɪt'feɪst] *adj, adv* с серьёзным ви́дом; **to be ~** сохраня́ть (*impf*) серьёзный вид.
straightforward [streɪt'fɔ:wəd] *adj* (*simple*) просто́й* (прост); (*honest*) прямо́й.
straight sets *n*: **to win in ~ ~** (*men*) побежда́ть (победи́ть* *perf*) в трёх па́ртиях подря́д; (*women*) побежда́ть (победи́ть* *perf*) в двух па́ртиях подря́д.
strain [streɪn] *n* (*TECH*) натяже́ние; (*pressure*) нагру́зка*; (*MED: physical*) растяже́ние; (: *mental*) напряже́ние; (*of virus*) вид; (*breed*) поро́да ◆ *vt* (*back etc*) растя́гивать (растяну́ть* *perf*); (*friendship, marriage*) испы́тывать (*impf*); (*stretch: resources*) ударя́ть (уда́рить *perf*) по +*dat*; (*CULIN*) проце́живать (процеди́ть* *perf*); ~**s** *npl* (*MUS*) зву́ки *mpl*; **he's been under a lot of ~** у него́ был о́чень напряжённый пери́од.
strained [streɪnd] *adj* (*back, muscle*) растя́нутый (растя́нут); (*laugh, relations*) натя́нутый (натя́нут).
strainer ['streɪnə'] *n* (*for vegetables*) си́то; (*for tea*) си́течко.
strait [streɪt] *n* (*GEO*) проли́в; ~**s** *npl* (*fig*): **to be in dire ~s** находи́ться* (*impf*) *or* быть* (*impf*) в бе́дственном положе́нии.
straitjacket ['streɪtdʒækɪt] *n* смири́тельная руба́шка*.
strait-laced [streɪt'leɪst] *adj* (*person*) пурита́нский.
strand [strænd] *n* (*of thread*) ни́тка*; (*of wool*) волокно́*, нить *f*; (*of hair*) прядь *f*; (*fig: element of whole*) часть *f*.
stranded ['strændɪd] *adj* (*ship, sea creature etc*) вы́брошенный на бе́рег *or* мель; (*traveller, holidaymaker etc*): **to be ~** застрева́ть (застря́ть* *perf*).
strange [streɪndʒ] *adj* (*not known*) незнако́мый (незнако́м); (*foreign*) чужо́й; (*odd*) стра́нный (стра́нен).
strangely ['streɪndʒlɪ] *adv* (*act, laugh*) стра́нно; *see also* **enough**.
stranger ['streɪndʒə'] *n* (*unknown person*) незнако́мый челове́к*, посторо́нний(-яя) *m(f) adj*; **I'm a ~ here** я здесь чужо́й.
strangle ['strængl] *vt* (*also fig*) души́ть* (задуши́ть* *perf*).
stranglehold ['stræŋglhəuld] *n* (*SPORT*) мёртвая хва́тка; (*fig*) заси́лье.
strangulation [stræŋgju'leɪʃən] *n* (*also fig*) удуше́ние.
strap [stræp] *n* реме́нь* *m*; (*of slip, dress*) брете́лька*; (*of watch, on shoes*) ремешо́к* ◆ *vt* (*also:* ~ **on**) пристёгивать (пристегну́ть* *perf*).
straphanging ['stræphæŋɪŋ] *n*: **I hate ~** я ненави́жу стоя́ть в тра́нспорте.

strapless ['stræplɪs] adj (bra, dress) без бретёлек.

strapped [stræpt] adj (inf): **to be ~ for cash** сидёть* (impf) на мели.

strapping ['stræpɪŋ] adj дюжий, рослый.

Strasbourg ['stræzbɔ:g] n Страсбург.

strata ['strɑ:tə] npl of **stratum**.

stratagem ['strætɪdʒəm] n хитрость f.

strategic [strə'ti:dʒɪk] adj стратегический*.

strategist ['strætɪdʒɪst] n стратёг.

strategy ['strætɪdʒɪ] n (plan, also MIL) стратёгия.

stratosphere ['strætəsfɪəʳ] n стратосфёра.

stratum ['strɑ:təm] n (pl **strata**) n слой*.

straw [strɔ:] n солома; (drinking straw) соломинка*; **that's the last ~!** это послёдняя капля!

strawberry ['strɔ:bərɪ] n (cultivated) клубника f no pl; (wild) земляника f no pl.

stray [streɪ] adj (animal) бездомный, бродячий; (bullet) шальной; (scattered) отдёльный ♦ vi заблудиться* (perf); (thoughts) блуждать (impf).

streak [stri:k] n (stripe) полоса*; (in hair) прядь f; (fig: of madness etc) черта, склонность f ♦ vt пронизывать (пронизать* perf) ♦ vi: **to ~ past** мчаться* (промчаться* perf) мимо; **to have ~s in one's hair** имёть (impf) окрашенные пряди волос; **a winning/losing ~** полоса удач/неудач; **~ed with ...** с ... полосками.

streaker ['stri:kəʳ] n человёк, появляющийся голым пёред толпой.

streaky ['stri:kɪ] adj: **~ bacon** бекон с прожилками жира.

stream [stri:m] n (small river) ручёй*; (current) течёние; (of people, vehicles, questions) поток; (of smoke) струя* ♦ vt (SCOL) делить* (разделить* perf) на группы ♦ vi (liquid) течь (impf), литься (impf); **to ~ in/out** (people) валить* (повалить* perf) толпой в +acc/из +gen; **against the ~** против течёния; **to come on ~** (new power plant etc) вступать (вступить* perf) в строй.

streamer ['stri:məʳ] n (paper decoration) серпантин.

stream feed n (on photocopier etc) подача (страниц) потоком.

streamline ['stri:mlaɪn] vt придавать* (придать* perf) обтекаемую форму +dat; (fig) рационализировать (impf/perf).

streamlined ['stri:mlaɪnd] adj обтекаемый; (AVIAT, AUT) обтекаемой формы; (fig) упрощённый.

street [stri:t] n улица; **the back ~s** переулки mpl; **to be on the ~s** (homeless) быть* (impf) бездомным(-ой); (as prostitute) заниматься (impf) проституцией.

streetcar ['stri:tkɑ:ʳ] n (US) трамвай.

street cred [-krɛd] n (inf) имидж.

streetlamp ['stri:tlæmp] n уличный фонарь* m.

street lighting n уличное освещёние.

street map n план улиц.

street market n уличный рынок*.

street plan n план улиц.

streetwise ['stri:twaɪz] adj (inf) ушлый.

strength [strɛŋθ] n сила; (of girder, knot etc) прочность f, крёпость f; (of chemical solution, wine) крёпость; **on the ~ of** на основании +gen; **at full ~** во всём составе; **below ~** (not enough people) недоукомплектованный (недоукомплектован); (not all members present) не в полном составе.

strengthen ['strɛŋθn] vt укреплять (укрепить* perf); (muscle) развивать (impf); (fig: group) пополнять (пополнить perf); (: argument) подкреплять (подкрепить* perf).

strenuous ['strɛnjuəs] adj (exercise) энергичный* (энергичен); (efforts) напряжённый; (tiring) утомительный* (утомителен).

strenuously ['strɛnjuəslɪ] adv напряжённо; **she ~ denied the rumour** она усиленно отрицала слухи.

stress [strɛs] n (pressure, also TECH) давлёние; (mental strain) стресс; (LING: accent) ударёние; (emphasis) значёние ♦ vt (point, importance etc) подчёркивать (подчеркнуть perf); (syllable) ставить* (поставить* perf) ударёние на +acc; **to lay great ~ on sth** придавать* (придать* perf) особое значёние чему-н; **to be under ~** быть* (impf) под напряжёнием.

stressful ['strɛsful] adj (job) напряжённый* (напряжён); (situation) стрёссовый.

stretch [strɛtʃ] n (area: of sand, water etc) пространство; (of time) промежуток* ♦ vt (pull) натягивать (натянуть* perf); (fig: subj: job, task) утомлять (утомить* perf); (spread: resources) растягивать (растянуть* perf) ♦ vi (person, animal) потягиваться (потянуться* perf); (extend): **to ~ to** or **as far as** простираться (простерёться* perf) к +dat; (be enough): **to ~ (to)** хватать (хватить* perf) на +acc; **at a ~** подряд; **he's no hero by any ~ of the imagination** как ни старайтесь, его нельзя вообразить героем; **to ~ one's legs** разминать (размять* perf) ноги.

▶ **stretch out** vi растягиваться (растянуться* perf) ♦ vt (arm etc) протягивать (протянуть* perf); (spread) растягивать (растянуть* perf); **to ~ out for sth** тянуться* (потянуться* perf) за чем-н.

stretcher ['strɛtʃəʳ] n (MED) носилки* pl.

stretcher-bearer ['strɛtʃəbɛərəʳ] n санитар-носильщик.

stretchmarks ['strɛtʃmɑ:ks] npl слёды растягивания на кóже.

strewn [stru:n] adj: **~ with** усыпанный (усыпан) +instr.

stricken ['strɪkən] adj (person) сражённый; (city, industry etc) пострадавший; **~ with**

(*arthritis, disease*) поражённый +*instr*.

strict [strɪkt] *adj* (*severe, firm: person, rule*) стро́гий* (строг); (*precise: meaning*) то́чный* (то́чен); **in ~** *or* **in the ~est confidence** в строжа́йшей та́йне.

strictly [strɪktlɪ] *adv* (*severely*) стро́го; (*exactly*) то́чно; ~ **confidential** соверше́нно конфиденциа́льно *or* секре́тно; ~ **speaking** стро́го говоря́; ~ **between ourselves** то́лько ме́жду на́ми.

strictness [strɪktnɪs] *n* стро́гость *f*.

stridden [strɪdn] *pp of* **stride**.

stride [straɪd] (*pt* **strode**, *pp* **stridden**) *n* (*step*) широ́кий* шаг* ♦ *vi* шага́ть (*impf*); **to take sth in one's ~** (*fig: changes etc*) относи́ться* (*impf*) споко́йно к чему́-н.

strident [straɪdnt] *adj* (*voice, sound*) пронзи́тельный* (пронзи́телен); (*demands*) шу́мный.

strife [straɪf] *n* борьба́.

strike [straɪk] (*pt, pp* **struck**) *n* (*of workers*) забасто́вка*; (*MIL: attack*) уда́р; (*of oil etc*) откры́тие месторожде́ния ♦ *vt* (*hit: person, thing*) ударя́ть (уда́рить *perf*); (*fig: subj: disease, disaster*) поража́ть (порази́ть* *perf*); (*: idea, thought*) осеня́ть (осени́ть *perf*); (*oil etc*) открыва́ть (откры́ть* *perf*) месторожде́ние +*gen*; (*bargain, deal*) заключа́ть (заключи́ть *perf*); (*make: coin, medal*) чека́нить (отчека́нить *perf*) ♦ *vi* (*workers*) бастова́ть (*impf*); (*attack: soldiers*) напада́ть (напа́сть* *perf*); (*: disaster, illness*) приходи́ть* (прийти́ *perf*); (*clock*) бить* (проби́ть* *perf*); **to be on ~** (*workers*) бастова́ть (*impf*); **to ~ a balance** соблюда́ть (*impf*) равнове́сие; **to ~ a match** зажига́ть (заже́чь* *perf*) спи́чку

▶ **strike back** *vi* (*MIL, fig*) наноси́ть* (нанести́* *perf*) отве́тный уда́р

▶ **strike down** *vt* сража́ть (срази́ть* *perf*)

▶ **strike off** *vt* (*name from list*) вычёркивать (вы́черкнуть *perf*); (*: doctor etc*) лиша́ть (лиши́ть *perf*) пра́ва практикова́ть

▶ **strike out** *vt* (*word, sentence*) вычёркивать (вы́черкнуть *perf*)

▶ **strike up** *vt* (*MUS*) заигра́ть (*impf*); (*conversation, friendship*) завя́зывать (завяза́ть* *perf*).

strikebreaker [straɪkbreɪkə] *n* штрейкбре́хер.

strike pay *n* посо́бие бастую́щим.

striker [straɪkə] *n* (*person on strike*) забасто́вщик(-ица); (*SPORT*) напада́ющий* (-ая) *m(f) adj*.

striking [straɪkɪŋ] *adj* порази́тельный* (порази́телен).

strimmer [strɪmə] *n механи́ческое ручно́е приспособле́ние для стри́жки газо́нов в труднодосту́пных места́х*.

string [strɪŋ] (*pt, pp* **strung**) *n* верёвка*; (*row: of onions*) свя́зка*; (*: of islands*) цепь *f*; (*: of cars, people*) верени́ца; (*series: of disasters*) се́рия; (*: of excuses*) пото́к; (*COMPUT*) строка́, цепо́чка; (*MUS: for guitar etc*) струна́* ♦ *vt*: **to ~ together** свя́зывать (связа́ть* *perf*); **the ~s** *npl* (*MUS: section of orchestra*) стру́нные инструме́нты *mpl*; **to ~ out** растя́гивать (растяну́ть* *perf*); **a ~ of beads** бу́сы; **to pull ~s** (*fig*) испо́льзовать (*impf/perf*) свя́зи; **with no ~s attached** (*fig*) без дополни́тельных усло́вий.

string bean *n* стручко́вая фасо́ль *f*.

string(ed) instrument *n* стру́нный инструме́нт.

stringent [strɪndʒənt] *adj* (*rules, measures*) стро́гий* (строг).

string quartet *n* (*MUS*) стру́нный кварте́т.

strip [strɪp] *n* полоса́*; (*SPORT*): **the Rangers ~** фо́рма Ре́йнджерз ♦ *vt* (*undress*) раздева́ть (разде́ть* *perf*); (*paint*) обдира́ть (ободра́ть* *perf*), сдира́ть (содра́ть* *perf*); (*also: ~ down: machine*) разбира́ть (разобра́ть* *perf*) ♦ *vi* (*undress*) раздева́ться (разде́ться* *perf*).

strip cartoon *n* исто́рия в карти́нках.

stripe [straɪp] *n* поло́ска*; (*MIL, POLICE*) петли́ца.

striped [straɪpt] *adj* (*fabric, animal etc*) полоса́тый (полоса́т).

strip lighting *n* (*BRIT*) дневно́е освеще́ние.

stripper [strɪpə] *n* уча́стница стрипти́за.

strip-search [strɪpsɛtʃ] *n* ли́чный досмо́тр ♦ *vt* производи́ть* (произвести́* *perf*) ли́чный досмо́тр +*gen*.

striptease [strɪptiːz] *n* стрипти́з.

strive [straɪv] (*pt* **strove**, *pp* **striven**) *vi*: **to ~ for sth/to do** стреми́ться* (*impf*) к чему́-н/+*infin*.

striven [strɪvn] *pp of* **strive**.

strobe [strəʊb] *n* (*also: ~ light*) строб-и́мпульс, селе́кторный и́мпульс.

strode [strəʊd] *pt of* **stride**.

stroke [strəʊk] *n* (*also MED*) уда́р; (*SWIMMING*) стиль *m*; (*of piston*) ход, такт; (*of paintbrush*) мазо́к*; (*of pen etc*) штрих ♦ *vt* (*caress*) гла́дить (погла́дить* *perf*); **at a ~** одни́м ма́хом; **on the ~ of 5** ро́вно в 5; **a ~ of luck** уда́ча; **a 2-~ engine** двухта́ктный дви́гатель *m*.

stroll [strəʊl] *n* прогу́лка* ♦ *vi* прогу́ливаться (прогуля́ться *perf*), пройти́сь* (*perf*); **to go for a ~, have** *or* **take a ~** идти́* (пойти́* *perf*) прогуля́ться.

stroller [strəʊlə] *n* (*US: pushchair*) (складна́я) коля́ска.

strong [strɒŋ] *adj* си́льный* (силён); (*healthy, powerful*) кре́пкий* (кре́пок); (*object, material*) про́чный* (про́чен); (*imagination*) большо́й; (*drugs, chemicals*) си́льный; (*letters, measures*) ре́зкий* (ре́зок) ♦ *adv*: **to be going ~** занима́ть (*impf*) про́чные пози́ции;

---

they are 50 ~ их 50.
strong-arm ['strɔŋɑ:m] adj: ~ **methods** приёмы mpl сильной руки.
strongbox ['strɔŋbɔks] n сейф.
stronghold ['strɔŋhəuld] n район сопротивления; (fig) оплот, твердыня.
strongly ['strɔŋlɪ] adv (construct) крепко; (push, defend, believe) сильно; **I feel** ~ **about it** во мне это вызывает сильные эмоции.
strongman ['strɔŋmæn] irreg n силач, богатырь* m; (fig) сильная личность f.
strongroom ['strɔŋru:m] n сейф.
stroppy ['strɔpɪ] adj (inf) строптивый (строптив).
strove [strəuv] pt of **strive**.
struck [strʌk] pt, pp of **strike**.
structural ['strʌktʃrəl] adj структурный.
structurally ['strʌktʃrəlɪ] adv (sound) со структурной точки зрения.
structure ['strʌktʃə] n структура.
struggle ['strʌgl] n борьба; (difficulty) усилие ♦ vi (try hard) прилагать (impf) большие усилия; (fight) бороться* (impf); (: to free o.s.) сопротивляться (impf); **to have a** ~ **to do** делать (сделать perf) усилие +infin.
strum [strʌm] vt (guitar) играть (impf) на +prp.
strung [strʌŋ] pt, pp of **string**.
strut [strʌt] n (wood, metal) распорка* ♦ vi ходить*/идти* (пойти* perf) величественно.
strychnine ['strɪkni:n] n стрихнин.
stub [stʌb] n (of cheque, ticket etc) корешок*; (of cigarette) окурок* ♦ vt: **to** ~ **one's toe** больно спотыкаться (споткнуться perf).
▶ **stub out** vt (cigarette) гасить* (загасить* perf).
stubble ['stʌbl] n (AGR) жнивьё; (on chin) щетина.
stubborn ['stʌbən] adj (child, determination) упрямый (упрям), упорный (упорен); (stain) несмывающийся; (illness) плохо поддающийся лечению.
stubby ['stʌbɪ] adj (fingers, pencil) короткий*.
stucco ['stʌkəu] n (CONSTR) декоративная "каменная" штукатурка.
stuck [stʌk] pt, pp of **stick** ♦ adj: **to be** ~ застрять* (perf); **to get** ~ застревать (застрять* perf).
stuck-up [stʌk'ʌp] adj (inf) надутый (надут).
stud [stʌd] n (on clothing etc) кнопка*, заклёпка*; (collar stud) запонка*; (earring) серьга* со штифтом; (on sole of boot) шип*; (also: ~ **farm**) конный завод; (also: ~ **horse**) племенной конь* m ♦ vt (fig): ~**ded with** усыпанный +instr.
student ['stju:dənt] n (at university) студент(ка*); (at school) учащийся*(-аяся) m(f) ♦ adj (life, union) студенческий*; (nurse: female) медсестра-практикантка*; (: male) медбрат-практикант; **law/medical** ~ студент(ка*) юридического/медицинского факультета.

student driver n (US) ученик* автомобиля.
student loan n студенческий* заём.
students' union ['stju:dənts-] n (BRIT: association) студенческий* союз; (building) здание студенческого союза.
studied ['stʌdɪd] adj (expression, attitude) продуманный* (продуман).
studio ['stju:dɪəu] n студия.
studio flat (US **studio apartment**) n однокомнатная квартира.
studious ['stju:dɪəs] adj (person) усердный* (усерден); (careful: attention) тщательный* (тщателен).
studiously ['stju:dɪəslɪ] adv (carefully) тщательно.
study ['stʌdɪ] n (activity) учёба; (room) кабинет ♦ vt (learn about, examine) изучать (изучить* perf) ♦ vi учиться* (perf); **studies** npl (subjects studied) курсы pl; **to make a** ~ **of sth** исследовать (импфперф) что-н; **to** ~ **for one's exams** готовиться (impf) к экзаменам.
stuff [stʌf] n (things) вещи fpl; (substance) вещество* ♦ vt набивать (набить* perf); (CULIN) начинять (начинить perf), фаршировать (нафаршировать perf); (inf: push: object) запихивать (запихать perf); **my nose is** ~**ed up** у меня заложен нос; **get** ~**ed!** (inf!) пошёл ты!
stuffed toy [stʌft-] n мягкая игрушка*.
stuffing ['stʌfɪŋ] n набивка; (CULIN) начинка, фарш.
stuffy ['stʌfɪ] adj (room) душный* (душен); (person, ideas) чопорный* (чопорен).
stumble ['stʌmbl] vi спотыкаться (споткнуться perf); **to** ~ **across** or **on** (fig) натыкаться (наткнуться perf) на +acc.
stumbling block ['stʌmblɪŋ-] n камень* m преткновения.
stump [stʌmp] n (of tree) пень* m; (of limb) обрубок* ♦ vt озадачивать (озадачить perf); **he is** ~**ed** он озадачен.
stun [stʌn] vt (subj: news) ошеломлять (ошеломить* perf); (: blow on head) оглушать (оглушить* perf).
stung [stʌŋ] pt, pp of **sting**.
stunk [stʌŋk] pp of **stink**.
stunning ['stʌnɪŋ] adj (fig: news, event) ошеломительный* (ошеломителен); (: girl, dress) потрясающий* (потрясающ), изумительный* (изумителен).
stunt [stʌnt] n трюк.
stunted ['stʌntɪd] adj (trees) подрубленный; (growth) замедленный* (замедлен).
stuntman ['stʌntmæn] irreg n каскадёр.
stupefaction [stju:pɪ'fækʃən] n отупение; (surprise) остолбенение; **to my** ~ к моему изумлению.
stupefy ['stju:pɪfaɪ] vt приводить* (привести* perf) в отупение; (fig) изумлять (изумить* perf).
stupendous [stju:'pɛndəs] adj (large)

колосса́льный* (колосса́лен); (*impressive*)
изуми́тельный* (изуми́телен).
stupid ['stju:pɪd] *adj* (*person, question etc*)
глу́пый (глуп).
stupidity [stju:'pɪdɪtɪ] *n* глу́пость *f*.
stupidly ['stju:pɪdlɪ] *adv* (*say, look*) глу́по.
stupor ['stju:pǝ'] *n* сту́пор; **in a ~** в сту́поре.
sturdily ['stǝ:dɪlɪ] *adv* (*built*) про́чно, кре́пко.
sturdy ['stǝ:dɪ] *adj* (*person, thing*) кре́пкий*
(кре́пок).
sturgeon ['stǝ:dʒǝn] *n* (*ZOOL*) осётр*.
stutter ['stʌtǝ'] *n* заика́ние ♦ *vi* заика́ться (*impf*).
Stuttgart ['stutgɑ:t] *n* Шту́ттгарт.
sty [staɪ] *n* (*for pigs*) свина́рник.
stye [staɪ] *n* ячме́нь *m*.
style [staɪl] *n* стиль *m*; **in the latest ~** по
после́дней мо́де; **hair ~** причёска*.
styli ['staɪlaɪ] *npl of* **stylus**.
stylish ['staɪlɪʃ] *adj* шика́рный* (шика́рен).
stylist ['staɪlɪst] *n* (*also:* **hair ~**)
парикма́хер-модельёр; (*literary stylist*)
стили́ст.
stylized ['staɪlaɪzd] *adj* (*picture, account*)
стилизо́ванный* (стилизо́ван).
stylus ['staɪlǝs] (*pl* **styli** *or* **~es**) *n* (*of record
player*) игла́*, иго́лка*.
Styrofoam® ['staɪrǝfǝum] *n* (*US*)
синтети́ческий упако́вочный материа́л.
suave [swɑ:v] *adj* (*person, manners etc*)
еле́йный* (еле́ен).
sub [sʌb] *n abbr* (*NAUT*) (= **submarine**)
подло́дка= *подво́дная ло́дка*; (*ADMIN*) =
subscription; (*PRESS*: = **sub-editor**) помо́щник
or замести́тель *m* реда́ктора.
sub... [sʌb] *prefix* суб..., под....
subcommittee ['sʌbkǝmɪtɪ] *n* подкомите́т.
subconscious [sʌb'kɔnʃǝs] *adj* (*desire etc*)
подсозна́тельный* (подсозна́телен).
subcontinent [sʌb'kɔntɪnǝnt] *n*: **the (Indian) ~**
(инди́йский*) субконтине́нт.
subcontract [*vt* sʌbkǝn'trækt, *n* 'sʌb'kɔntrækt] *vt*
заключа́ть (заключи́ть *perf*) субподря́д с
+*instr* ♦ *n* субподря́д.
subcontractor ['sʌbkǝn'træktǝ'] *n*
субподря́дчик.
subdivide [sʌbdɪ'vaɪd] *vt* подразделя́ть
(подраздели́ть *perf*).
subdivision ['sʌbdɪvɪʒǝn] *n* подразделе́ние.
subdue [sǝb'dju:] *vt* подавля́ть (подави́ть*
perf).
subdued [sǝb'dju:d] *adj* (*light*) приглушённый
(приглушён); (*person*) пода́вленный*
(пода́влен).
sub-editor ['sʌb'ɛdɪtǝ'] *n* (*BRIT: PRESS*)
помо́щник *or* замести́тель *m* реда́ктора.
subject [*n* 'sʌbdʒɪkt, *vt* sǝb'dʒɛkt] *n* (*topic*) те́ма;
(*SCOL*) предме́т; (*of kingdom*) по́данный(-ая)
m(f) adj; (*LING*) подлежа́щее *nt adj* ♦ *vt*: **to ~ sb**

to sth подверга́ть (подве́ргнуть* *perf*) кого́-н
чему́-н; **to be ~ to** (*tax*) подлежа́ть (*impf*) +*dat*;
(*law*) подчиня́ться (*impf*) +*dat*; **he is ~ to heart
attacks** он подве́ржен серде́чным
при́ступам; **this is ~ to confirmation in writing**
э́то подлежи́т пи́сьменному
подтвержде́нию; **to change the ~** меня́ть
(поменя́ть *perf*) те́му (разгово́ра).
subjection [sǝb'dʒɛkʃǝn] *n* (*of women, enemy
etc*) подчине́ние.
subjective [sǝb'dʒɛktɪv] *adj* субъекти́вный*
(субъекти́вен).
subject matter *n* (*content*) те́ма.
sub judice [sʌb'dju:dɪsɪ] *adj*: **the case is ~ ~ по
да́нным моме́нт э́то де́ло рассма́тривается
судо́м.
subjugate ['sʌbdʒugeɪt] *vt* (*people*) покоря́ть
(покори́ть *perf*).
subjunctive [sǝb'dʒʌŋktɪv] *n* сослага́тельное
наклоне́ние.
sublet [sʌb'lɛt] *vt* (*property*) передава́ть*
(переда́ть* *perf*) в субаре́нду.
sublime [sǝ'blaɪm] *adj* возвы́шенный; **from the
~ to the ridiculous** от вели́кого до
смешно́го.
subliminal [sʌb'lɪmɪnl] *adj* (*memory*)
подсозна́тельный; (*advertising*)
де́йствующий* на подсозна́ние.
submachine gun ['sʌbmǝ'ʃi:n-] *n* автома́т.
submarine [sʌbmǝ'ri:n] *n* подво́дная ло́дка*.
submerge [sǝb'mǝ:dʒ] *vt* погружа́ть
(погрузи́ть* *perf*) (в во́ду) ♦ *vi* (*submarine, sea
creature*) погружа́ться (погрузи́ться* *perf*) (в
во́ду).
submersion [sǝb'mǝ:ʃǝn] *n* погруже́ние.
submission [sǝb'mɪʃǝn] *n* (*state*) подчине́ние,
повинове́ние; (*of plan etc*) пода́ча; (*to
committee etc*) представле́ние.
submissive [sǝb'mɪsɪv] *adj* поко́рный*
(поко́рен).
submit [sǝb'mɪt] *vt* (*proposal, application etc*)
представля́ть (предста́вить* *perf*) на
рассмотре́ние ♦ *vi*: **to ~ to sth** подчиня́ться
(подчини́ться *perf*) чему́-н.
subnormal [sʌb'nɔ:ml] *adj* (*backward: child etc*)
отста́лый*; **~ temperatures** температу́ры *fpl*
ни́же норма́льных.
subordinate [sǝ'bɔ:dmǝt] *adj* (*position, rank*): **to
be ~ to sb** подчиня́ться (*impf*) кому́-н; (*LING:
clause*) прида́точный ♦ *n* подчинённый(-ая)
m(f) adj.
subpoena [sǝb'pi:nǝ] *n* (*LAW*) пове́стка* ♦ *vt*
(*LAW: witness etc*) вызыва́ть (вы́звать* *perf*) в
суд.
subroutine [sʌbru:'ti:n] *n* (*COMPUT*)
подпрогра́мма.
subscribe [sǝb'skraɪb] *vi* подпи́сываться
(подписа́ться* *perf*); **to ~ to** (*opinion, fund*)

поддерживать (**поддержать*** *perf*); (*magazine etc*) **подписываться** (**подписаться*** *perf*) на +*acc*; **~d capital** подписной акционерный капитал.

subscriber [səb'skraɪbə*] *n* (*to periodical*) подписчик; (*to telephone*) абонент.

subscript ['sʌbskrɪpt] *n* (*TYP*) подстрочный знак.

subscription [səb'skrɪpʃən] *n* (*to magazine etc*) подписка*; (*membership dues*) (членский*) взнос; **to take out a ~ to** подписываться (подписаться* *perf*) на +*acc*.

subsequent ['sʌbsɪkwənt] *adj* последующий*; **~ to** вслед +*dat*.

subsequently ['sʌbsɪkwəntlɪ] *adv* впоследствии.

subservient [səb'sə:vɪənt] *adj* (*person, behaviour*) подобострастный* (подобострастен); (*less important: policy etc*) подвластный* (подвластен); **he is ~ to ...** он подвластен +*dat* ....

subside [səb'saɪd] *vi* (*feeling, wind*) утихать (утихнуть* *perf*); (*flood*) убывать (убыть* *perf*).

subsidence [səb'saɪdns] *n* (*in road etc*) оседание.

subsidiarity [səbsɪdɪ'ærɪtɪ] *n* (*POL*) уровень* *m* зависимости.

subsidiary [səb'sɪdɪərɪ] *adj* (*question, details*) второстепенный* (второстепен); (*BRIT: SCOL: subject*) факультативный ◆ *n* (*also: ~ company*) дочерняя компания.

subsidize ['sʌbsɪdaɪz] *vt* (*education, industry etc*) субсидировать (*impf/perf*).

subsidy ['sʌbsɪdɪ] *n* субсидия, дотация.

subsist [səb'sɪst] *vi*: **to ~ on sth** существовать (*impf*) за счёт чего-н.

subsistence [səb'sɪstəns] *n* (*ability to live*) существование; (*food*) пропитание.

subsistence allowance *n* аванс (*перед первой зарплатой*).

subsistence level *n* прожиточный минимум.

substance ['sʌbstəns] *n* (*product, material*) вещество; (*fig: essence*) суть* *f*; **a man of ~** солидный мужчина; **the essay lacks ~** в сочинении нет стержня.

substance abuse *n* токсикомания.

substandard [sʌb'stændəd] *adj* (*goods*) некачественный; (*housing*) непригодный* (непригоден) для жилья.

substantial [səb'stænʃl] *adj* (*solid*) прочный* (прочен), основательный* (основателен); (*fig: reward, meal*) значительный* (значителен), солидный* (солиден).

substantially [səb'stænʃəlɪ] *adv* (*by a large amount*) значительно; (*in essence*) существенно, основательно; **~ bigger** значительно больше.

substantiate [səb'stænʃɪeɪt] *vt* (*claim, story, statement etc*) обосновывать (обосновать* *perf*).

substitute ['sʌbstɪtju:t] *n* (*person*) замена; (: *FOOTBALL etc*) запасной *m adj* (игрок*); (*thing*) заменитель *m* ◆ *vt*: **to ~ A for B** заменять (заменить* *perf*) А на Б.

substitute teacher *n* (*US*) замещающий(-ая) учитель(ница) *m(f)*.

substitution [sʌbstɪ'tju:ʃən] *n* (*act of substituting*) замена.

subterfuge ['sʌbtəfju:dʒ] *n* уловка*.

subterranean [sʌbtə'reɪnɪən] *adj* (*passage*) подземный.

subtitle ['sʌbtaɪtl] *n* (*CINEMA*) субтитр.

subtle ['sʌtl] *adj* (*change*) тонкий*, едва уловимый; (*person*) искусный (искусен).

subtlety ['sʌtltɪ] *n* (*small detail*) тонкость *f*; (*of person*) искусность *f*.

subtly ['sʌtlɪ] *adv* (*change, vary*) едва уловимо; (*different*) слегка; (*criticize, persuade*) искусно.

subtotal [sʌb'təʊtl] *n* суммарное число*.

subtract [səb'trækt] *vt* вычитать (вычесть* *perf*).

subtraction [səb'trækʃən] *n* вычитание.

subtropical [sʌb'trɔpɪkl] *adj* субтропический.

suburb ['sʌbə:b] *n* пригород; **the ~s** *npl* (*area*) пригород *msg*.

suburban [sə'bə:bən] *adj* пригородный.

suburbia [sə'bə:bɪə] *n* пригород.

subvention [səb'vɛnʃən] *n* (*subsidy*) дотация, субсидия.

subversion [səb'və:ʃən] *n* подрывная деятельность *f*.

subversive [səb'və:sɪv] *adj* (*activities, literature*) подрывной.

subway ['sʌbweɪ] *n* (*US: underground railway*) метро *nt ind*, подземка*; (*BRIT: underpass*) подземный переход.

sub-zero [sʌb'zɪərəʊ] *adj*: **~ temperatures** температуры *fpl* ниже нуля.

succeed [sək'si:d] *vi* (*plan etc*) удаваться* (удаться* *perf*), иметь (*impf*) успех; (*person: in career etc*) преуспевать (преуспеть *perf*) ◆ *vt* (*in job, order*) сменять (сменить* *perf*); **he ~ed in finishing the article** ему удалось закончить статью.

succeeding [sək'si:dɪŋ] *adj* (*following*) последующий*; **~ generations** последующие поколения.

success [sək'sɛs] *n* (*achievement*) успех, удача; (*hit*): **the book was a ~** книга имела успех; **he was a ~** он добился успеха.

successful [sək'sɛsful] *adj* (*venture*) успешный* (успешен); **he was ~ in convincing her** ему удалось убедить её.

successfully [sək'sɛsfəlɪ] *adv* (*complete, do*) успешно.

succession [sək'sɛʃən] *n* (*series*) череда, ряд; (*to throne etc*) наследование; **in ~** подряд; **3 years in ~** три года подряд.

successive [sək'sɛsɪv] *adj* (*governments*) следующий* один за другим; **3 ~ days/**

attempts три дня/попы́тки подря́д.
successor [sək'sɛsəˈ] *n* прее́мник(-ица); (*to throne*) насле́дник(-ица).
succinct [sək'sɪŋkt] *adj* (*explanation*) сжа́тый (сжат).
succulent ['sʌkjulənt] *adj* (*fruit, meat*) со́чный* (со́чен) ♦ *n* (*BOT*): ~s суккуле́нты *pl.*
succumb [sə'kʌm] *vi* (*to temptation*) поддава́ться* (подда́ться* *perf*); **he ~ed to illness** боле́знь оконча́тельно его́ победи́ла.
such [sʌtʃ] *adj* тако́й; (*emphasizing similarity*) подо́бный, тако́й ♦ *adv*: ~ **a long trip** така́я дли́нная пое́здка; ~ **a book** така́я кни́га; ~ **books** таки́е кни́ги; ~ **a lot of** тако́е мно́жество +*gen*; **making ~ a noise that ...** создава́я тако́й шум, что ...; ~ **as** (*like*) таки́е как; ~ **books as I have** таки́е кни́ги, как у меня́; **I said no ~ thing** я ничего́ подо́бного *or* тако́го не говори́л; **as ~** как таково́й.
such-and-such ['sʌtʃənsʌtʃ] *adj* тако́й-то и тако́й-то.
suchlike ['sʌtʃlaɪk] *pron* (*inf*): **and ~** и им подо́бные.
suck [sʌk] *vt* соса́ть* (*impf*); (*subj: pump, machine*) вса́сывать (всоса́ть *perf*).
sucker ['sʌkəˈ] *n* присо́ска*; (*BOT*) корнево́й побе́г; (*inf*) о́лух.
suckle ['sʌkl] *vt* корми́ть* (*impf*) (гру́дью), дава́ть* (дать* *perf*) грудь +*dat*; (*subj: animal*) корми́ть* (*impf*).
sucrose ['su:krəuz] *n* сахаро́за.
suction ['sʌkʃən] *n* вса́сывание.
suction pump *n* вса́сывающий насо́с.
Sudan [su'dɑ:n] *n* Суда́н.
Sudanese [su:də'ni:z] *adj* суда́нский ♦ *n inv* суда́нец*(-ка*).
sudden ['sʌdn] *adj* внеза́пный* (внеза́пен); **all of a ~** (*unexpectedly*) внеза́пно, вдруг.
sudden death *n* (*in competition*) дополни́тельный матч (*по́сле ничьи́*).
suddenly ['sʌdnlɪ] *adv* (*unexpectedly*) внеза́пно, вдруг.
suds [sʌdz] *npl* (мы́льные) пузыри́ *mpl.*
sue [su:] *vt* предъявля́ть (предъяви́ть* *perf*) иск +*dat*, возбужда́ть (возбуди́ть* *perf*) де́ло про́тив +*gen* ♦ *vi*: **to ~ (for)** суди́ться (*impf*) (за +*acc*); **to ~ for divorce** возбужда́ть (возбуди́ть* *perf*) де́ло о разво́де; **to ~ sb for damages** предъявля́ть (предъяви́ть* *perf*) иск кому́-н о компенса́ции.
suede [sweid] *n* за́мша ♦ *cpd* за́мшевый.
suet ['suit] *n* жир.
Suez ['su:iz] *n*: **the ~ Canal** Суэ́цкий* кана́л.
Suff. *abbr* (*BRIT: POST*) = Suffolk.
suffer ['sʌfəˈ] *vt* (*hardship etc*) переноси́ть* (перенести́* *perf*); (*pain, rudeness*) страда́ть (*impf*) от +*gen* ♦ *vi* (*person, results etc*) страда́ть (пострада́ть *perf*); **to ~ from** (*illness*

etc) страда́ть (*impf*) +*instr*; **to ~ the effects of alcohol/a fall** страда́ть (пострада́ть *perf*) от возде́йствия алкого́ля/от после́дствий паде́ния.
sufferance ['sʌfərns] *n*: **she hadn't wanted him to go, so he was only there on ~** она́ не хоте́ла отпуска́ть его́, он был там, причиня́я ей страда́ния.
sufferer ['sʌfərəˈ] *n* (*MED*) страда́ющий(-ая) *m(f) adj.*
suffering ['sʌfərɪŋ] *n* (*hardship*) страда́ние.
suffice [sə'faɪs] *vi* (*be enough*): **this ~s ...** э́того доста́точно, ...
sufficient [sə'fɪʃənt] *adj* доста́точный* (доста́точен); ~ **money** доста́точное коли́чество де́нег.
sufficiently [sə'fɪʃəntlɪ] *adv* (*recover, provide*) доста́точно; (*powerful, enthusiastic*) в доста́точной ме́ре.
suffix ['sʌfɪks] *n* (*LING*) су́ффикс.
suffocate ['sʌfəkeɪt] *vi* задыха́ться (задохну́ться *perf*); (*have difficulty breathing*) задыха́ться (*impf*); (*die*) задохну́ться (*impf*) ♦ *vt* (*gas etc*) удуша́ть (удуши́ть *perf*).
suffocation [sʌfə'keɪʃən] *n* удушье.
suffrage ['sʌfrɪdʒ] *n* (*right to vote*) избира́тельное пра́во.
suffragette [sʌfrə'dʒɛt] *n* суфражи́стка*.
suffused [sə'fju:zd] *adj*: ~ **with** (*light, colour*) погружённый (погружён) в +*prp*; (*tears*) зали́тый (зали́т) +*instr*.
sugar ['ʃugəˈ] *n* са́хар* ♦ *vt* (*tea etc*) сласти́ть* (посласти́ть* *perf*).
sugar beet *n* са́харная свёкла.
sugar bowl *n* са́харница.
sugar cane *n* са́харный тростни́к.
sugar-coated ['ʃugə'kəutɪd] *adj* (*sweet*) заса́харенный.
sugar lump *n* кусо́к* са́хара.
sugar refinery *n* сахарорафина́дный заво́д.
sugary ['ʃugərɪ] *adj* сла́дкий* (сла́док), сахари́стый (сахари́ст); (*fig*) слаща́вый (слаща́в).
suggest [sə'dʒɛst] *vt* (*propose*) предлага́ть (предложи́ть* *perf*); (*indicate*) предполага́ть (предположи́ть* *perf*); **what do you ~ I do?** что Вы предлага́ете мне де́лать?
suggestion [sə'dʒɛstʃən] *n* (*proposal*) предложе́ние; (*indication*) предположе́ние.
suggestive [sə'dʒɛstɪv] *adj* (*pej: remarks, looks*) неприли́чный* (неприли́чен).
suicidal [suɪ'saɪdl] *adj* (*person*) стоя́щий на гра́ни самоуби́йства; (*act*) само-уби́йственный.
suicide ['suɪsaɪd] *n* (*death*) самоуби́йство; (*person*) самоуби́йца *m/f; see also* **commit**.
suicide attempt *n* попы́тка* самоуби́йства.
suicide bid *n* попы́тка* самоуби́йства.

suit [su:t] n костю́м; (LAW) иск; (CARDS) масть f
♦ vt (be convenient, appropriate) подходи́ть*
(подойти́* perf) +dat; (colour, clothes) идти́*
(impf) +dat; (adapt): **to ~ sth to**
приспоса́бливать (приспосо́бить* perf) что-н
к +dat; **he was ~ed to lead the party** он
хорошо́ подходи́л на роль ли́дера па́ртии;
to bring a ~ against sb предъявля́ть
(предъяви́ть* perf) иск кому́-н; **to follow ~**
(fig) сле́довать (после́довать perf) приме́ру;
they are well ~ed (couple) они́ хорошо́ друг
дру́гу подхо́дят.
suitability [su:tə'bɪlɪtɪ] n приго́дность f.
suitable ['su:təbl] adj подходя́щий*; **would**
tomorrow be ~? за́втра Вам подойдёт or Вас
устро́ит?; **we found somebody ~** мы нашли́
подходя́щего челове́ка.
suitably ['su:təblɪ] adv надлежа́щим о́бразом.
suitcase ['su:tkeɪs] n чемода́н.
suite [swi:t] n (of rooms) апартаме́нты mpl;
(MUS) сюи́та; (furniture): **bedroom/dining**
room ~ спа́льный/столо́вый гарниту́р; **a**
three-piece ~ мя́гкая ме́бель f.
suitor ['su:tə'] n: **he is her ~** он и́щет её руки́.
sulfate ['sʌlfeɪt] n (US) = **sulphate**.
sulfur ['sʌlfə'] n (US) = **sulphur**.
sulfuric [sʌl'fjuərɪk] (US) = **sulphuric**.
sulk [sʌlk] vi быть* (impf) в дурно́м
настрое́нии.
sulky ['sʌlkɪ] adj (child, mood) су́мрачный*
(су́мрачен).
sullen ['sʌlən] adj (person, silence) угрю́мый
(угрю́м).
sulphate ['sʌlfeɪt] (US **sulfate**) n сульфа́т.
sulphur ['sʌlfə'] (US **sulfur**) n се́ра.
sulphur dioxide (US **sulfur dioxide**) n
дву́о́кись f се́ры, серни́стый ангидри́д.
sulphuric [sʌl'fjuərɪk] (US **sulfuric**) adj: ~ **acid**
се́рная кислота́.
sultan ['sʌltən] n султа́н.
sultana [sʌl'tɑ:nə] n (CULIN) кишми́ш.
sultry ['sʌltrɪ] adj (weather) ду́шный* (ду́шен).
sum [sʌm] n (calculation) арифме́тика,
вычисле́ние; (amount) су́мма
▶ **sum up** vt (describe) сумми́ровать (impf/perf);
(evaluate rapidly) вычисля́ть (вы́числить
perf) ♦ vi (summarize) подводи́ть* (подвести́*
perf) ито́г.
Sumatra [su'mɑ:trə] n Сума́тра.
summarize ['sʌməraɪz] vt сумми́ровать (impf/
perf).
summary ['sʌmərɪ] n (of essay etc) кра́ткое
изложе́ние ♦ adj (justice) поспе́шный;
weather/news ~ сво́дка пого́ды/новосте́й.
summer ['sʌmə'] n (season) ле́то ♦ adj (dress,
school) ле́тний*; **in ~** ле́том.
summer camp n (US) ле́тний* ла́герь* m.
summer holidays npl ле́тние кани́кулы pl.
summerhouse ['sʌməhaus] n (in garden)
бесе́дка*.
summertime ['sʌmətaɪm] n (season) ле́то,

ле́тний* пери́од.
summer time n ле́тнее вре́мя* nt.
summery ['sʌmərɪ] adj (day, dress) ле́тний*.
summing-up [sʌmɪŋ'ʌp] n (LAW) кра́ткое
изложе́ние де́ла (обращённое к
прися́жным).
summit ['sʌmɪt] n (of mountain) верши́на, пик;
(also: ~ **conference**) конфере́нция на
вы́сшем у́ровне; (also: ~ **meeting**) встре́ча
на вы́сшем у́ровне.
summon ['sʌmən] vt вызыва́ть (вы́звать* perf);
(help) звать* (позва́ть* perf) на +acc
▶ **summon up** vt собира́ть (собра́ть* perf).
summons ['sʌmənz] n (LAW) пове́стка; (fig)
приказа́ние ♦ vt (LAW) вызыва́ть (вы́звать*
perf); **to serve a ~ on sb** посыла́ть (посла́ть*
perf) кому́-н пове́стку.
sumo ['su:məu] n (also: ~ **wrestling**) су́мо ind
(япо́нская борьба́).
sump [sʌmp] n (BRIT: AUT) ма́сляный поддо́н.
sumptuous ['sʌmptjuəs] adj (meal, costume)
роско́шный* (роско́шен), великоле́пный*
(великоле́пен).
sun [sʌn] n со́лнце; **in the ~** на со́лнце; **to catch**
the ~ слегка́ загоре́ть (perf); **everything under**
the ~ всё в ми́ре.
Sun. abbr = **Sunday**.
sunbathe ['sʌnbeɪð] vi загора́ть (impf).
sunbeam ['sʌnbi:m] n со́лнечный луч*.
sunbed ['sʌnbɛd] n шезло́нг; (with sun lamp)
устро́йство с ква́рцевой ла́мпой для
получе́ния иску́сственного зага́ра.
sunburn ['sʌnbə:n] n (painful) со́лнечный
ожо́г.
sunburned ['sʌnbə:nd] adj = **sunburnt**.
sunburnt ['sʌnbə:nt] adj (tanned) загоре́лый;
(painfully) обожжённый (со́лнцем).
sun-cream ['sʌnkri:m] n солнцезащи́тный
крем.
sundae ['sʌndeɪ] n моро́женое nt adj с
фру́ктами.
Sunday ['sʌndɪ] n воскресе́нье; see also
Tuesday.
Sunday paper n воскре́сная газе́та.
Sunday school n воскре́сная шко́ла.
sundial ['sʌndaɪəl] n со́лнечные часы́ pl.
sundown ['sʌndaun] n зака́т, захо́д (со́лнца).
sundries ['sʌndrɪz] npl (miscellaneous items)
ра́зное nt adj.
sundry ['sʌndrɪ] adj (various) ра́зного ро́да; **all**
and ~ все подря́д.
sunflower ['sʌnflauə'] n (BOT) подсо́лнечник.
sunflower oil n (CULIN) подсо́лнечное ма́сло.
sung [sʌŋ] pp of **sing**.
sunglasses ['sʌnglɑ:sɪz] npl солнцезащи́тные
очки́* pl.
sunk [sʌŋk] pp of **sink**.
sunken ['sʌŋkn] adj (rock, ship) затону́вший;
(cheeks) впа́лый; (eyes) вва́лившийся; (bath)
встро́енный в углубле́ние.
sunlamp ['sʌnlæmp] n ультрафиоле́товая or

sunlight ['sʌnlaɪt] n сóлнечный свет.
sunlit ['sʌnlɪt] adj освещённый (освещён) сóлнцем.
sunny ['sʌnɪ] adj (weather, day, place) сóлнечный; (fig) свéтлый; **it is ~** сóлнечно.
sunrise ['sʌnraɪz] n восхóд (сóлнца).
sun roof n (AUT) раздвижнáя панéль f (в крыше автомобиля).
sunscreen ['sʌnskriːn] n солнцезащи́тный крем.
sunset ['sʌnsɛt] n захóд (сóлнца), закáт.
sunshade ['sʌnʃeɪd] n зóнтик.
sunshine ['sʌnʃaɪn] n сóлнечный свет; **we sat in the ~** мы сидéли на сóлнце.
sunspot ['sʌnspɔt] n (ASTRONOMY) сóлнечное мéсто*.
sunstroke ['sʌnstrəuk] n сóлнечный удáр.
suntan ['sʌntæn] n загáр.
suntan lotion n лосьóн для загáра.
suntanned ['sʌntænd] adj (body, person) загорéлый.
suntan oil n мáсло для загáра.
suntrap ['sʌntræp] n сóлнечный островóк*.
super ['suːpə'] adj (inf) потрясáющий*.
superannuation [suːpərænjuˈeɪʃən] n ежегóдный пенсиóнный вклад.
superb [suːˈpəːb] adj великолéпный* (великолéпен).
Super Bowl n (US) финáльный матч америкáнского чемпионáта по футбóлу.
supercilious [suːpəˈsɪlɪəs] adj (disdainful, haughty) высокомéрный* (высокомéрен).
superconductor [suːpəkənˈdʌktə'] n сверхпроводни́к.
superficial [suːpəˈfɪʃəl] adj повéрхностный* (повéрхностен); (wound) лёгкий* (лёгок).
superficially [suːpəˈfɪʃəlɪ] adv повéрхностно.
superfluous [suːˈpəːfluəs] adj изли́шный, ненýжный.
superglue ['suːpəgluː] n сýперклей.
superhuman [suːpəˈhjuːmən] adj (effort, strength) сверхчеловéческий.
superimpose ['suːpərɪmˈpəuz] vt: **to ~ (on)** накла́дывать (наложи́ть* perf) (на +acc).
superintend [suːpərɪnˈtɛnd] vt надзирáть (impf) за +instr; **to be ~ed by** быть* (impf) под надзóром +gen.
superintendent [suːpərɪnˈtɛndənt] n (of place) завéдующий*(-ая) m(f)adj; (of activity) руководи́тель(ница) m(f); (POLICE) начáльник, надзирáтель m.
superior [suːˈpɪərɪə'] adj (better) превосходя́щий; (more senior) стáрший*; (smug) высокомéрный ♦ n начáльник(-ица); **Mother S~** (REL) настоя́тельница.
superiority [suːpɪərɪˈɔrɪtɪ] n превосхóдство.
superlative [suːˈpəːlətɪv] n прилагáтельное или

наречие превосхóдной стéпени.
superman ['suːpəmæn] irreg n супермéн, сверхчеловéк m no pl.
supermarket ['suːpəmɑːkɪt] n универмáг, универсáм; (in Europe, US etc) супермáркет.
supermodel ['suːpəmɔdl] n супермодéль f.
supernatural [suːpəˈnætʃərəl] adj (creature, force etc) сверхъестéственный ♦ n: **the ~** сверхъестéственные си́лы fpl.
supernova [suːpəˈnəuvə] n взрывáющаяся нóвая звездá.
superpower ['suːpəpauə'] n (POL) сверхдержáва.
superscript ['suːpəskrɪpt] n (TYP) надстрóчные знáки mpl.
supersede [suːpəˈsiːd] vt сменя́ть (смени́ть* perf).
supersonic ['suːpəˈsɔnɪk] adj (flight, aircraft) сверхзвуковóй.
superstar ['suːpəstɑː'] n (CINEMA, SPORT etc) суперзвездá*.
superstition [suːpəˈstɪʃən] n суевéрие.
superstitious [suːpəˈstɪʃəs] adj суевéрный* (суевéрен).
superstore ['suːpəstɔː'] n (BRIT: COMM) универмáг, супермáркет.
supertanker ['suːpətæŋkə'] n (NAUT) супертáнкер.
supertax ['suːpətæks] n дополни́тельный подохóдный налóг.
supervise ['suːpəvaɪz] vt (person, activity) следи́ть (impf) или наблюдáть (impf) за +instr.
supervision [suːpəˈvɪʒən] n руковóдство, надзóр; **under medical ~** под наблюдéнием врачá.
supervisor ['suːpəvaɪzə'] n (of workers) начáльник(-ица); (of students) наýчный(-ая) руководи́тель(ница) m(f).
supervisory ['suːpəvaɪzərɪ] adj (role) руководя́щий*; (staff) контроли́рующий.
supine ['suːpaɪn] adj лежáщий на спинé ♦ adv лёжа на спинé.
supper ['sʌpə'] n ýжин; **to have ~** ýжинать (поýжинать perf).
supplant [səˈplɑːnt] vt (person, thing) приходи́ть* (прийти́* perf) на смéну +dat.
supple ['sʌpl] adj (person, body) ги́бкий* (ги́бок); (leather) мя́гкий* (мя́гок).
supplement ['sʌplɪmənt] n (vitamins etc) добáвка; (of book, newspaper etc) приложéние ♦ vt (diet) добаᴠ́ать (impf) к +dat; (income) подрабáтывать (impf).
supplementary [sʌplɪˈmɛntərɪ] adj (question) дополни́тельный.
supplementary benefit n (BRIT: formerly) пособие для малоимýщих в Великобритáнии.
supplier [səˈplaɪə'] n (COMM: person, firm)

---

* marks translations which have irregular inflections. The Russian-English side of the dictionary gives inflectional information.

поставщи́к*.

supply [sə'plaɪ] n (*stock*) запа́с, запа́сы mpl; (*supplying*) поста́вка*; (*TECH*) обеспе́чение ♦ vt (*need*) удовлетворя́ть (удовлетвори́ть perf); (*provide*): **to ~ sth (to sb)** поставля́ть (поста́вить* perf) что-н (кому́-н); **supplies** npl (*food*) запа́сы mpl (продово́льствия); (*MIL*) боеприпа́сы mpl (и продово́льствие); **office supplies** конто́рские принадле́жности; **water is in short ~** э́тот райо́н испы́тывает нехва́тку воды́; **the electricity ~** снабже́ние электроэне́ргии; **the water ~** водоснабже́ние; **the gas ~** снабже́ние га́зом; **~ and demand** спрос и предложе́ние; **to ~ sb with sth** снабжа́ть (снабди́ть* perf) кого́-н чем-н; (*system, machine*) обору́довать (impf/ perf) кого́-н чем-н; **it comes supplied with an adaptor** поставля́ется с ада́птером.

supply teacher n (*BRIT*) замеща́ющий(-ая) учи́тель(ница) m(f).

support [sə'pɔ:t] n (*moral, financial etc*) подде́ржка; (*TECH*) опо́ра, подпо́рка* ♦ vt (*football team etc*) боле́ть (impf) за +acc; (*financially: family etc*) содержа́ть (impf); (*TECH: hold up*) подде́рживать (impf); (*sustain: theory etc*) подтвержда́ть (подтверди́ть* perf); **they stopped work in ~ of** они́ прекрати́ли рабо́ту в подде́ржку +gen; **to ~ o.s.** (*financially*) зараба́тывать (impf) (самому́) себе́ на жизнь.

support buying n (*COMM*) заку́пка в це́лях пониже́ния цен.

supporter [sə'pɔ:tə'] n (*POL etc*) сторо́нник(-ица); (*SPORT*) боле́льщик(-ица).

supporting [sə'pɔ:tɪŋ] adj второстепе́нный; **~ actor** актёр второ́го пла́на.

supportive [sə'pɔ:tɪv] adj: **to be ~ of sb** подде́рживать (поддержа́ть* perf) кого́-н.

suppose [sə'pəuz] vt полага́ть (impf); **he was ~d to do it** (*duty*) он до́лжен был э́то сде́лать; **it was worse than she'd ~d** э́то оказа́лось ху́же, чем она́ предполага́ла; **I don't ~ she'll come** я полага́ю, она́ не придёт; **he's about sixty, I ~** я полага́ю, ему́ лет шестьдеся́т; **he's ~d to be an expert** счита́ется, что он в э́том разбира́ется.

supposedly [sə'pəuzɪdlɪ] adv по иде́е.

supposing [sə'pəuzɪŋ] conj предположи́м, допу́стим.

supposition [sʌpə'zɪʃən] n предположе́ние, допуще́ние.

suppository [sə'pɔzɪtrɪ] n (*MED*) свеча́*.

suppress [sə'prɛs] vt подавля́ть (подави́ть* perf); (*scandal*) замя́ть* (perf); (*publication*) запреща́ть (запрети́ть* perf).

suppression [sə'prɛʃən] n подавле́ние.

suppressor [sə'prɛsə'] n (*ELEC etc*) глуши́тель m.

supremacy [su'prɛməsɪ] n (*MIL, POL etc*) госпо́дство.

supreme [su'pri:m] adj (*in titles: court etc*) Верхо́вный; (*effort, achievement*) велича́йший.

Supreme Court n (*US*) Верхо́вный Суд.

supremo [su'pri:məu] n (*BRIT: inf*) верхо́вный or гла́вный нача́льник.

Supt. abbr (*POLICE*) = **superintendent**.

surcharge ['sə:tʃɑ:dʒ] n (*extra cost*) дополни́тельный сбор, дополни́тельная пла́та.

sure [ʃuə'] adj (*definite, convinced*) твёрдый* (твёрд); (*aim, friend, remedy*) ве́рный* (ве́рен) ♦ adv (*inf: esp US*): **that ~ is pretty, that's ~ pretty** э́то пра́вда ми́ло; **to make ~ of sth/that** удостове́риться (perf) в чём-н/, что; **~!** (*of course*) безусло́вно!; **~ enough** и пра́вда or впра́вду; **I'm not ~ how/why/when** я не уве́рен, как/почему́/когда́; **to be ~ of o.s.** не сомнева́ться (impf) в себе́.

sure-fire ['ʃuəfaɪə'] adj (*inf*) ве́рный.

sure-footed [ʃuə'futɪd] adj (*animal, person*) твёрдо держа́щийся на нога́х.

surely ['ʃuəlɪ] adv (*certainly*) наверняка́; **~ you don't mean that!** наверня́ка, Вы э́то несерьёзно!

surety ['ʃuərətɪ] n (*money*) зало́г; **to go** or **stand ~ for sb** брать* (взять* perf) кого́-н на пору́ки.

surf [sə:f] n (*waves*) прибо́й; (*foam*) бара́шки mpl.

surface ['sə:fɪs] n пове́рхность f ♦ vt (*road*) покрыва́ть (покры́ть* perf) ♦ vi (*fish, person in water*) пока́зываться (показа́ться* perf) на пове́рхности; (*fig: news, feeling*) всплыва́ть (всплы́ть* perf); (: *person in bed*) объявля́ться (объяви́ться* perf); **on the ~** (*fig*) с ви́ду.

surface area n пло́щадь f пове́рхности.

surface mail n обы́чная по́чта.

surface-to-surface ['sə:fɪstə'sə:fɪs] adj: **~ missile** раке́та ти́па "земля́-земля́".

surfboard ['sə:fbɔ:d] n аквапла́н.

surfeit ['sə:fɪt] n: **a ~ of** переизбы́ток* +gen.

surfer ['sə:fə'] n челове́к* занима́ющийся сёрфингом.

surfing ['sə:fɪŋ] n сёрфинг.

surge [sə:dʒ] n (*increase*) прито́к*; (*fig: of emotion*) прили́в; (*ELEC*) и́мпульс ♦ vi (*water*) вздыма́ться (impf), нахлыну́ть (perf); (*people, vehicles*) ри́нуться (perf); (*ELEC: power*) ре́зко увели́чиваться (увели́читься perf); **to ~ forward** ри́нуться (perf) or броса́ться (бро́ситься* perf) вперёд; **relief ~d through her** она́ почу́вствовала прили́в облегче́ния.

surgeon ['sə:dʒən] n (*MED*) хиру́рг.

Surgeon General n (*US: MED, MIL*) нача́льник медици́нского управле́ния.

surgery ['sə:dʒərɪ] n (*treatment*) хирурги́ческое вмеша́тельство; (*BRIT: room*) кабине́т врача́; (: *of MP, doctor etc*) приём; **to undergo ~** переноси́ть* (перенести́* perf) опера́цию.

surgical ['sə:dʒɪkl] adj хирурги́ческий*.

surgical spirit n (*BRIT*) медици́нский* спирт.

surly ['sɜːlɪ] *adj* (*person, behaviour*) неприве́тливый.

surmise [sə'maɪz] *vt*: **to ~ that** выска́зывать (вы́сказать° *perf*) предположе́ние, что.

surmount [sə'maunt] *vt* (*fig: problem, difficulty*) преодолева́ть (преодоле́ть *perf*).

surname ['sɜːneɪm] *n* фами́лия.

surpass [sɜː'pɑːs] *vt* (*person, thing*) превосходи́ть (превзойти́° *perf*).

surplus ['sɜːpləs] *n* избы́ток°, изли́шек°; (*of trade, payments*) акти́вное са́льдо *nt ind* ♦ *adj* (*stock, grain*) ли́шний°; **it is ~ to our requirements** э́то превыша́ет на́ши тре́бования.

surprise [sə'praɪz] *n* удивле́ние ♦ *vt* (*astonish*) удивля́ть (удиви́ть° *perf*); (*catch unawares*) застава́ть (заста́ть° *perf*) враспло́х; **to take by ~** застига́ть (засти́гнуть *perf*) враспло́х.

surprising [sə'praɪzɪŋ] *adj* (*situation, announcement*) неожи́данный° (неожи́дан); **it is ~ how/that** удиви́тельно как/что.

surprisingly [sə'praɪzɪŋlɪ] *adv* удиви́тельно; (*somewhat*) ~, **he agreed** как ни удиви́тельно, он согласи́лся.

surrealism [sə'rɪəlɪzəm] *n* сюрреали́зм.

surrealist [sə'rɪəlɪst] *adj* сюрреалисти́ческий.

surrender [sə'rɛndəʳ] *n* капитуля́ция ♦ *vi* (*army, hijackers etc*) сдава́ться° (сда́ться° *perf*) ♦ *vt* (*claim, right*) отка́зываться (отказа́ться° *perf*) от +*gen*.

surrender value *n* (INSURANCE) сто́имость *страхово́го по́лиса при возвра́те его́ страхово́му о́бществу.*

surreptitious [sʌrəp'tɪʃəs] *adj* скры́тый.

surrogate ['sʌrəgɪt] *n* (*substitute*) замени́тель *m* ♦ *adj* замеща́ющий.

surrogate mother *n* суррога́тная мать° *f*.

surround [sə'raund] *vt* (*subj: walls, hedge etc*) окружа́ть (*impf*); (MIL, POLICE *etc*) окружа́ть (окружи́ть *perf*).

surrounding [sə'raundɪŋ] *adj* (*countryside*) близлежа́щий.

surroundings [sə'raundɪŋz] *npl* окре́стности *fpl*.

surtax ['sɜːtæks] *n* доба́вочный подохо́дный нало́г.

surveillance [sɜː'veɪləns] *n* патрули́рование.

survey [*vt* sɜː'veɪ, *n* 'sɜːveɪ] *vt* (*land*) де́лать (сде́лать *perf*) топографи́ческие съёмки +*gen*; (*house*) производи́ть° (произвести́° *perf*) осмо́тр +*gen*; (*scene, work etc*) осма́тривать (осмотре́ть° *perf*) ♦ *n* (*of land*) топографи́ческая *or* геодези́ческая съёмка; (*of house*) инспе́кция *or* (*of habits etc*) иссле́дование; (*of situation etc*) оце́нка°.

surveying [sə'veɪɪŋ] *n* (*of land*) геоде́зия, топографи́ческие съёмки° *fpl*.

surveyor [sə'veɪəʳ] *n* (*of land*) топо́граф; (*of house*) инспе́ктор.

survival [sə'vaɪvl] *n* (*continuation of life*) выжива́ние; (*relic*) пережи́ток° ♦ *cpd*: ~ **kit** неприкоснове́нный запа́с; ~ **course** обуче́ние выжива́нию в экстрема́льных усло́виях.

survive [sə'vaɪv] *vi* (*person, thing*) уцеле́ть (*perf*), выжива́ть (вы́жить° *perf*); (*custom etc*) сохраня́ться (сохрани́ться *perf*), уцеле́ть (*perf*) ♦ *vt* (*person*) пережи́ть° (*perf*).

survivor [sə'vaɪvəʳ] *n* (*of illness, accident*) пережи́вший(-ая) *m(f)* adj; **an accident** оста́вшиеся в живы́х по́сле ава́рии.

susceptible [sə'sɛptəbl] *adj*: ~ (**to**) (*heat*) чувстви́тельный° (чувстви́телен) (к +*dat*); (*injury*) подве́рженный° (подве́ржен) (+*dat*); (*flattery, pressure*) подда́ющийся (на +*acc*).

suspect [*vb* səs'pɛkt, *n, adj* 'sʌspɛkt] *vt* (*person*) подозрева́ть (*impf*), заподо́зрить (*perf*); (*think*) подозрева́ть (*impf*); (*doubt*) не доверя́ть (*impf*) ♦ *n* подозрева́емый(-ая) *m(f)* adj ♦ *adj* подозри́тельный° (подозри́телен).

suspected [səs'pɛktɪd] *adj* подозрева́емый (подозрева́ем).

suspend [səs'pɛnd] *vt* (*hang*) подве́шивать (подве́сить° *perf*); (*delay, stop*) приостана́вливать (приостанови́ть° *perf*); (*from employment*) отстраня́ть (отстрани́ть *perf*) от до́лжности.

suspended animation [səs'pɛndid-] *n* вре́менное замора́живание (*живо́го органи́зма*).

suspended sentence *n* усло́вный пригово́р.

suspender belt [səs'pɛndəʳ-] *n* (*же́нский°*) по́яс°.

suspenders [səs'pɛndəz] *npl* (BRIT) рези́нки° *fpl*; (US) подтя́жки° *fpl*.

suspense [səs'pɛns] *n* (*uncertainty*) трево́га ожида́ния; (*in film etc*) напряже́ние; **to keep sb in** ~ держа́ть° (*impf*) кого́-н в подве́шенном состоя́нии.

suspension [səs'pɛnʃən] *n* (*from job, team*) отстране́ние от до́лжности; (AUT) амортиза́тор; (*of driving licence*) изъя́тие; (*of payment*) прекраще́ние.

suspension bridge *n* подвесно́й *or* вися́чий° мост°.

suspicion [səs'pɪʃən] *n* (*distrust*) подозре́ния *ntpl*; (*bad feeling*) подозре́ние; (*trace*) намёк, след; **to be under** ~ находи́ться° (*impf*) под подозре́нием; **arrested on** ~ **of murder** аресто́ванный по подозре́нию в уби́йстве.

suspicious [səs'pɪʃəs] *adj* подозри́тельный° (подозри́телен); **to be ~ of** *or* **about sb/sth** относи́ться° (отнести́сь° *perf*) подозри́тельно *or* с подозре́нием к кому́-н/чему́-н.

suss out [sʌs-] (BRIT: *inf*) *vt* (*discover*) разобра́ться° (*perf*) в +*prp*; (*understand*)

---

* marks translations which have irregular inflections. The Russian-English side of the dictionary gives inflectional information.

раскуси́ть* (perf); **I've sussed him out** я его́ раскуси́л.

sustain [səs'teɪn] vt подде́рживать (поддержа́ть* perf); (injury) понести́* (perf).

sustainable [səs'teɪnəbl] adj (economy, development) жизнеспосо́бный.

sustained [səs'teɪnd] adj (effort, attack) неослабева́ющий.

sustenance ['sʌstɪnəns] n пропита́ние.

suture ['suːtʃə'] n (MED) шов*.

SW abbr (RADIO) (= short wave) КВ= коро́ткие во́лны.

swab [swɔb] n (MED) тампо́н ♦ vt (also: ~ down) мыть* (вы́мыть* perf) (шва́брой).

swagger ['swægə'] vi расха́живать (impf) с ва́жным ви́дом.

swallow ['swɔləu] n (ZOOL) (дереве́нская) ла́сточка*; (of food) кусо́чек*; (of drink) глото́к* ♦ vt (food, pills, insult) глота́ть (impf), прогла́тывать (проглоти́ть* perf); (fig: story) купи́ться* (perf) на +acc; (one's pride, one's words) подавля́ть (подави́ть* perf)

▶ **swallow up** vt (savings etc) съеда́ть (съесть* perf).

swam [swæm] pt of **swim**.

swamp [swɔmp] n боло́то ♦ vt (with water etc) залива́ть (зали́ть* perf); (fig: person) зава́ливать (завали́ть* perf).

swampy ['swɔmpɪ] adj (ground) боло́тистый.

swan [swɔn] n ле́бедь* m.

swank [swæŋk] vi (inf: talk boastfully) хва́стать (impf); (: show off) рисова́ться (impf).

swansong ['swɔnsɔŋ] n (fig) лебеди́ная песнь f.

swap [swɔp] n обме́н ♦ vt: **to ~ (for)** (exchange (for)) меня́ть (обменя́ть perf) (на +acc); (replace (with)) сменя́ть (смени́ть perf) (на +acc).

SWAPO n abbr (= South-West Africa People's Organization) СВАПО (Наро́дная организа́ция Ю́го-За́падной А́фрики).

swarm [swɔːm] n (of bees) рой ♦ vi (bees) рои́ться (impf); (people) толо́читься* (impf); (place): **to be ~ing with** кише́ть (impf) +instr.

swarthy ['swɔːðɪ] adj (person, complexion, face) сму́глый, тёмный.

swashbuckling ['swɔʃbʌklɪŋ] adj (film) залихва́тский; (role, hero) удало́й.

swastika ['swɔstɪkə] n сва́стика.

swat [swɔt] vt (insect) прихло́пнуть (perf) ♦ n (BRIT: also: fly ~) хлопу́шка*.

swathe [sweɪð] vt: **to ~ in** (blankets) заку́тывать (заку́тать perf) в +acc; (bandages) обма́тывать (обмота́ть perf) +instr.

swatter ['swɔtə'] n (also: fly ~) хлопу́шка*.

sway [sweɪ] vi (person, tree) кача́ться (качну́ться perf) ♦ vt (influence) склоня́ть (склони́ть* perf) ♦ n: **to hold ~ (over sb)** по́льзоваться* (impf) непререка́емым авторите́том (у кого́-н).

Swaziland ['swɑːzɪlænd] n Свазиле́нд.

swear [swɛə'] (pt **swore**, pp **sworn**) vi (curse) руга́ться (вы́ругаться perf) ♦ vt (promise) торже́ственно дава́ть* (дать* perf); **to ~ an oath** дава́ть* (дать* perf) кля́тву

▶ **swear in** vt (person) приводи́ть* (привести́* perf) к прися́ге.

swearword ['swɛəwəːd] n руга́тельство.

sweat [swɛt] n пот* ♦ vi поте́ть (вспоте́ть perf), пропоте́ть (perf); **in a ~** в поту́.

sweatband ['swɛtbænd] n повя́зка*.

sweater ['swɛtə'] n сви́тер*.

sweatshirt ['swɛtʃəːt] n хлопчатобума́жный спорти́вный сви́тер*.

sweatshop ['swɛtʃɔp] n (pej) предприя́тие, где существу́ет потого́нная систе́ма.

sweaty ['swɛtɪ] adj (clothes) пропоте́вший; (hands) по́тный.

Swede [swiːd] n швед(ка*).

swede [swiːd] n (BRIT) брю́ква.

Sweden ['swiːdn] n Шве́ция.

Swedish ['swiːdɪʃ] adj шве́дский* ♦ n (LING) шве́дский язы́к*; **the ~** npl шве́ды.

sweep [swiːp] (pt, pp **swept**) n (act of sweeping) подмета́ние; (curve) изги́б; (range) разма́х; (also: chimney ~) трубочи́ст ♦ vt (brush) мести́* or подмета́ть (подмести́* perf); (with arm) сма́хивать (смахну́ть* perf); (subj: current) смыва́ть (смыть* perf) ♦ vi (hand, arm) дви́гаться (impf); (wind) бушева́ть (impf)

▶ **sweep away** vt смета́ть (смести́* perf), уноси́ть* (унести́* perf)

▶ **sweep past** vi проноси́ться* (пронести́сь* perf) ми́мо

▶ **sweep up** vi подмета́ть (подмести́* perf).

sweeper ['swiːpə:] n (also: carpet ~) щётка для ковра́; (FOOTBALL) ли́беро nt ind.

sweeping ['swiːpɪŋ] adj (gesture) широ́кий* (широ́к); (changes, reforms) всеобъе́млющий*; (statement) огу́льный.

sweepstake ['swiːpsteɪk] n пари́ nt ind на ска́чках.

sweet [swiːt] n (candy) конфе́та; (BRIT: CULIN) сла́дкое nt adj no pl ♦ adj сла́дкий* (сла́док); (kind, attractive) ми́лый* (мил) ♦ adv: **to smell ~** сла́дко па́хнуть (impf); **to taste ~** име́ть (impf) сла́дкий вкус; **~ and sour** ки́сло-сла́дкий*.

sweetbread ['swiːtbrɛd] n (CULIN) "сла́дкое мя́со" (поджелу́дочная железа́).

sweet corn n кукуру́за.

sweeten ['swiːtn] vt добавля́ть (доба́вить* perf) са́хар к +dat; (temper) смиря́ть (смири́ть perf).

sweetener ['swiːtnə'] n замени́тель m са́хара; (fig) подслащённая пилю́ля.

sweetheart ['swiːthɑːt] n возлю́бленный(-ая) m(f) adj; (term of affection) дорого́й(-а́я) m(f) adj.

sweetness ['swiːtnɪs] n (amount of sugar) сла́дость f; (kindness) прия́тность f.

sweet pea n души́стый горо́шек*.

sweet potato *n* ямс.
sweet shop *n* (*BRIT*) конди́терская ла́вка.
sweet tooth *n*: **he/she has a ~ ~** он/она́ сластёна.
swell [swɛl] (*pt* **swelled**, *pp* **swollen** *or* **swelled**) *n* (*of sea*) волне́ние ♦ *adj* (*US*: *inf*: *excellent*) мирово́й ♦ *vi* (*numbers*) расти́* (вы́расти* *perf*); (*sound, feeling*) расти́* (*impf*); (*also*: ~ **up**: *face, ankle etc*) опуха́ть (опу́хнуть *perf*).
swelling ['swɛlɪŋ] *n* (*MED*) о́пухоль *f*.
sweltering ['swɛltərɪŋ] *adj* ду́шный.
swept [swɛpt] *pt, pp of* **sweep**.
swerve [swə:v] *vi* ре́зко виля́ть (вильну́ть *perf*).
swift [swɪft] *n* (*bird*) стриж* ♦ *adj* стреми́тельный* (стреми́телен).
swiftly ['swɪftlɪ] *adv* стреми́тельно.
swiftness ['swɪftnɪs] *n* стреми́тельность *f*.
swig [swɪg] *n* (*inf*: *drink*) глото́к*.
swill [swɪl] *vt* (*also*: ~ **out**, ~ **down**) спола́скивать (сполосну́ть *perf*) ♦ *n* (*for pigs*) по́йло.
swim [swɪm] (*pt* **swam**, *pp* **swum**) *vi* пла́вать/ плыть* (*impf*); (*as sport*) пла́вать (*impf*); (*head*) идти́* (пойти́* *perf*) кру́гом; (*room*) плыть* (поплы́ть* *perf*) ♦ *vt* (*the Channel*) переплыва́ть (переплы́ть* *perf*); (*a length*) проплыва́ть (проплы́ть* *perf*); **to go ~ming**, **go for a ~** ходи́ть*/идти́* (пойти́* *perf*) пла́вать.
swimmer ['swɪmə'] *n* пловец́*(-вчи́ха).
swimming ['swɪmɪŋ] *n* пла́вание.
swimming baths *npl* (*BRIT*) пла́вательный бассе́йн *msg*.
swimming cap *n* рези́новая ша́почка* (*для пла́вания*).
swimming costume *n* (*BRIT*) купа́льный костю́м.
swimmingly ['swɪmɪŋlɪ] *adv* как по ма́слу; **everything's going ~** всё идёт как по ма́слу.
swimming pool *n* пла́вательный бассе́йн.
swimming trunks *npl* пла́вки* *pl*.
swimsuit ['swɪmsu:t] *n* купа́льник.
swindle ['swɪndl] *n* моше́нничество ♦ *vt* надува́ть (наду́ть* *perf*).
swindler ['swɪndlə'] *n* жу́лик.
swine [swaɪn] *n* (*inf!*) свинья́* *m/f* (!)
swing [swɪŋ] (*pt, pp* **swung**) *n* (*in playground*) каче́ли *pl*; (*movement*) кача́ние; (*change: in opinions etc*) колеба́ние; (*MUS, rhythm*) свинг ♦ *vt* (*arms*) разма́хивать (*impf*) +*instr*; (*legs*) болта́ть (*impf*) +*instr*; (*also*: ~ **round**: *vehicle etc*) развора́чивать (разверну́ть *perf*) ♦ *vi* кача́ться (*impf*); (*also*: ~ **round**: *vehicle etc*) свора́чивать (сверну́ть *perf*); **a ~ to the left** (*POL*) крен вле́во; **to get into the ~ of things** входи́ть* (войти́* *perf*) в ритм; **to be in full ~** (*party etc*) быть* (*impf*) в по́лном разга́ре; **the road ~s south** доро́га свора́чивает на юг.

swing bridge *n* разводно́й мост*.
swing door (*US* **swinging door**) *n* дверь, открыва́ющаяся в о́бе сто́роны.
swingeing ['swɪndʒɪŋ] *adj* (*BRIT*: *blow, attack*) сокруши́тельный* (сокруши́телен); (: *cuts*) беспоща́дный.
swinging ['swɪŋɪŋ] *adj* кача́ющийся; (*fig*) весёлый.
swipe [swaɪp] *vt* (*hit*) ударя́ть (уда́рить *perf*) с разма́ху; (*inf*: *steal*) тащи́ть (стащи́ть* *perf*).
swirl [swə:l] *vi* (*water, smoke, leaves*) кружи́ться (*impf*) ♦ *n* (*of water*) водоро́т; (*of leaves*) круже́ние.
swish [swɪʃ] *vi* (*tail*) маха́ть* (*impf*); (*clothes*) шелесте́ть* (*impf*), шурша́ть (*impf* ♦ *n* свист ♦ *adj* (*inf*) шика́рный.
Swiss [swɪs] *adj* швейца́рский* ♦ *n inv* швейца́рец*(-рка*).
Swiss French *adj* фра́нко-швейца́рский* ♦ *n* (*person*) франкоговоря́щий(-ая) швейца́рец(-рка); (*LING*) швейца́рский* диале́кт францу́зского языка́.
Swiss German *adj* неме́цко-швейца́рский* ♦ *n* (*person*) немецкоговоря́щий(-ая) швейца́рец(-рка); (*LING*) швейца́рский* диале́кт неме́цкого языка́.
swiss roll *n* руле́т с варе́ньем.
switch [swɪtʃ] *n* (*for light, radio etc*) выключа́тель *m*; (*change*) переключе́ние ♦ *vt* (*change*) переключа́ть (переключи́ть *perf*); (*exchange*) переменя́ть* (*perf*); **to ~ (round** *or* **over)** меня́ть (поменя́ть *perf*) места́ми
► **switch off** *vt* выключа́ть (вы́ключить *perf*)
► **switch on** *vt* включа́ть (включи́ть *perf*).
switchback ['swɪtʃbæk] *n* (*BRIT*) доро́га иду́щая то вверх, то вниз.
switchblade ['swɪtʃbleɪd] *n* (*also*: ~ **knife**) нож с заменя́ющимися ле́звиями.
switchboard ['swɪtʃbɔ:d] *n* (*TEL*) коммута́тор.
switchboard operator *n* (*TEL*) телефони́ст(ка*).
Switzerland ['swɪtsələnd] *n* Швейца́рия.
swivel ['swɪvl] *vi* (*also*: ~ **round**) верте́ться* (*impf*).
swollen ['swəʊlən] *pp of* **swell** ♦ *adj* (*ankle*) опу́хший*; (*lake*) перепо́лнившийся.
swoon [swu:n] *vi* замира́ть (замере́ть *perf*).
swoop [swu:p] *n* (*by police etc*) налёт; (*of bird etc*) стреми́тельное паде́ние ♦ *vi* (*also*: ~ **down**: *bird, plane*) стреми́тельно па́дать (*impf*).
swop [swɔp] = **swap**.
sword [sɔ:d] *n* шпа́га, меч*.
swordfish ['sɔ:dfɪʃ] *n* меч-ры́ба.
swore [swɔ:'] *pt of* **swear**.
sworn [swɔ:n] *pp of* **swear** ♦ *adj* (*statement, evidence*) под прися́гой; (*enemy*) закля́тый.
swot [swɔt] *vi* зубри́ть (*impf*) ♦ *n* (*pej*: *of person*)

---

* marks translations which have irregular inflections. The Russian-English side of the dictionary gives inflectional information

зубри́ла *m/f*
▶ **swot up** *vi*: **to ~ up (on)** зазу́бривать (зазубри́ть *perf*).
swum [swʌm] *pp of* **swim**.
swung [swʌŋ] *pt, pp of* **swing**.
sycamore ['sɪkəmɔː'] *n* я́вор.
sycophant ['sɪkəfænt] *n* подхали́м.
sycophantic [sɪkə'fæntɪk] *adj* подхали́мский*.
Sydney ['sɪdnɪ] *n* Сидне́й.
syllable ['sɪləbl] *n* слог*.
syllabus ['sɪləbəs] *n* програ́мма; **on the ~** входя́щий* в програ́мму.
symbol ['sɪmbl] *n* (*sign, also* MATH) знак; (*representation*) си́мвол.
symbolic(al) [sɪm'bɔlɪk(l)] *adj* символи́ческий*; **to be symbolic of sth** символизи́ровать (*impf*) что-н.
symbolism ['sɪmbəlɪzəm] *n* символи́зм.
symbolize ['sɪmbəlaɪz] *vt* символизи́ровать (*impf*).
symmetrical [sɪ'mɛtrɪkl] *adj* симметри́чный* (симметри́чен).
symmetry ['sɪmɪtrɪ] *n* симме́трия.
sympathetic [sɪmpə'θɛtɪk] *adj* (*person*) сочу́вствующий*; (*remark*) сочу́вственный; (*likeable: character*) прия́тный* (прия́тен); (*showing support*): **~ to(wards)** благоскло́нно настро́енный по отноше́нию к +*dat*; **to be ~ to sth** (*well-disposed*) сочу́вственно относи́ться* (отнести́сь* *perf*) к чему́-н.
sympathetically [sɪmpə'θɛtɪklɪ] *adv* сочу́вственно.
sympathize ['sɪmpəθaɪz] *vi*: **to ~ with** (*person*) сочу́вствовать* (*impf*) +*dat*, проявля́ть (прояви́ть* *perf*) сочу́вствие к +*dat*; (*feelings, cause*) сочу́вственно относи́ться* (отнести́сь* *perf*) к +*dat*.
sympathizer ['sɪmpəθaɪzə'] *n* (POL) симпатизи́рующий(-ая) *m(f) adj*.
sympathy ['sɪmpəθɪ] *n* (*pity*) сочу́вствие; **sympathies** *npl* (*support, tendencies*) симпа́тии *fpl*; **with our deepest ~** прими́те на́ши глубоча́йшие соболе́знования; **to come out in ~** (*workers*) бастова́ть (*impf*) в знак солида́рности.
symphonic [sɪm'fɔnɪk] *adj* симфони́ческий*.
symphony ['sɪmfənɪ] *n* симфо́ния.
symphony orchestra *n* симфони́ческий* орке́стр.
symposia [sɪm'pəuzɪə] *npl of* **symposium**.
symposium [sɪm'pəuzɪəm] (*pl* **~s** *or* **symposia**) *n* симпо́зиум.
symptom ['sɪmptəm] *n* (MED) симпто́м; (*indicator*) при́знак.
symptomatic [sɪmptə'mætɪk] *adj*: **~ of** симптомати́чный* при́знак +*gen*.

sync [sɪŋk] *n* (*inf: watches etc*): **out of ~** в разнобо́й.
synagogue ['sɪnəgɔg] *n* синаго́га.
synchromesh [sɪŋkrəu'mɛʃ] *n* синхрониза́тор.
synchronize ['sɪŋkrənaɪz] *vt* (*watches*) сверя́ть (све́рить *perf*); (*sound, movements*) синхронизи́ровать (*impf/perf*) ♦ *vi*: **to ~ with** совпада́ть (совпа́сть* *perf*) (по вре́мени) с +*instr*.
synchronized swimming ['sɪŋkrənaɪzd-] *n* синхро́нное пла́вание.
syncopated ['sɪŋkəpeɪtɪd] *adj* (*rhythm, beat*) синкопи́рованный.
syndicate ['sɪndɪkɪt] *n* (*of people, businesses*) синдика́т; (*of newspapers*) аге́нтство печа́ти.
syndrome ['sɪndrəum] *n* (*also* MED) синдро́м.
synonym ['sɪnənɪm] *n* сино́ним.
synonymous [sɪ'nɒnɪməs] *adj* (*fig*): **~ (with)** равноси́льный* (равноси́лен) (+*dat*).
synopses [sɪ'nɒpsiːz] *npl of* **synopsis**.
synopsis [sɪ'nɒpsɪs] (*pl* **synopses**) *n* кра́ткое изложе́ние.
syntactic [sɪn'tæktɪk] *adj* синтакси́ческий*.
syntax ['sɪntæks] *n* си́нтаксис.
syntax error *n* (COMPUT) синтакси́ческая оши́бка*.
syntheses ['sɪnθəsiːz] *npl of* **synthesis**.
synthesis ['sɪnθəsɪs] (*pl* **syntheses**) *n* (*of ideas, styles*) слия́ние, си́нтез.
synthesizer ['sɪnθəsaɪzə'] *n* синтеза́тор.
synthetic [sɪn'θɛtɪk] *adj* (*materials*) синтети́ческий*, иску́сственный ♦ *n* иску́сственный материа́л; (TEXTILES) синте́тика, иску́сственный материа́л; **~s** *npl* (*man-made fabrics*) синте́тика *fsg*, синтети́ческие тка́ни *fpl*.
syphilis ['sɪfɪlɪs] *n* си́филис.
syphon ['saɪfən] = **siphon**.
Syria ['sɪrɪə] *n* Си́рия.
Syrian ['sɪrɪən] *adj* сири́йский* ♦ *n* сири́ец*(-и́йка).
syringe [sɪ'rɪndʒ] *n* шприц*.
syrup ['sɪrəp] *n* (*juice*) сиро́п; (*also*: **golden ~**) (све́тлая *or* жёлтая) па́тока.
syrupy ['sɪrəpɪ] *adj* (*liquid*) густо́й* (густ); (*pej: quality*) слаща́вый (слаща́в).
system ['sɪstəm] *n* систе́ма; **it was a shock to his ~** э́то яви́лось для него́ потрясе́нием.
systematic [sɪstə'mætɪk] *adj* (*methodical*) системати́ческий*.
systems analyst ['sɪstəmz-] *n* (COMPUT) систе́мный анали́тик, системоте́хник.
systems disk *n* (COMPUT) систе́мный диск.

~ T, t ~

T, t [tiː] *n* (*letter*) 20-ая бу́ква англи́йского алфави́та.

TA *n abbr* (*BRIT*: = Territorial Army) территориа́льная а́рмия.

ta [tɑː] *excl* (*BRIT*: *inf*) спаси́бо.

tab [tæb] *n abbr* = **tabulator**.

tabby ['tæbɪ] *n* (*also*: ~ **cat**: *male*) полоса́тый кот; (*female*) полоса́тая ко́шка.

tabernacle ['tæbənækl] *n* (*REL*) ски́ния.

table ['teɪbl] *n* (*piece of furniture*) стол; (*MATH, CHEM etc*) табли́ца ◆ *vt* (*BRIT*: *motion etc*) выноси́ть* (вы́нести* *perf*) на обсужде́ние; **to lay** *or* **set the** ~ накрыва́ть (накры́ть* *perf*) на стол; **to clear the** ~ убира́ть (убра́ть* *perf*) со стола́; **league** ~ (*BRIT*: *FOOTBALL, RUGBY*) ли́говая табли́ца; ~ **of contents** оглавле́ние.

tablecloth ['teɪblklɔθ] *n* ска́терть *f*.

table d'hôte [[tɑːbl'dəut]] *adj*: ~ ~ **menu** табльдо́т.

table lamp *n* насто́льная ла́мпа.

tablemat ['teɪblmæt] *n* подста́вка.

table salt *n* столо́вая соль *f*.

tablespoon ['teɪblspuːn] *n* столо́вая ло́жка.

tablet ['tæblɪt] *n* (*MED*) таблётка*; (*for writing*) доще́чка* (для письма́); (*of stone*) доска́*; ~ **of soap** (*BRIT*) кусо́к* мы́ла.

table tennis *n* насто́льный те́ннис.

table wine *n* столо́вое вино́.

tabloid ['tæblɔɪd] *n* (*newspaper*) малоформа́тная газе́та, табло́ид; **the ~s** жёлтая *or* бульва́рная пре́сса.

taboo [tə'buː] *n* табу́ *nt ind* ◆ *adj* запрещённый.

tabulate ['tæbjuleɪt] *vt* (*data, figures*) своди́ть* (свести́* *perf*) в табли́цу.

tabulator ['tæbjuleɪtə'] *n* колонкоустанови́тель *m*; (*on typewriter*) табуля́тор.

tachograph ['tækəgraːf] *n* (*AUT*) тахо́граф (*для регистра́ции режи́ма движе́ния автомоби́ля*).

tachometer [tæ'kɔmɪtə'] *n* (*AUT*) тахо́метр, счётчик числа́ оборо́тов.

tacit ['tæsɪt] *adj* (*agreement, approval etc*) молчали́вый.

taciturn ['tæsɪtəːn] *adj* (*person*) молчали́вый

(молчали́в).

tack [tæk] *n* (*nail*) гвоздь *m* с широ́кой шля́пкой; (*fig*) путь *m* ◆ *vt* (*nail*) прибива́ть (приби́ть* *perf*); (*stitch*) смётывать (смета́ть* *perf*) ◆ *vi* (*NAUT*) идти́* (пойти́* *perf*) га́лсами; **on the wrong** ~ (*fig*) на ло́жном пути́; **to** ~ **sth on to (the end of) sth** прикрепля́ть (прикрепи́ть* *perf*) что-н к чему́-н.

tackle ['tækl] *n* (*for fishing etc*) снасть *f*; (*for lifting*) сло́жный блок; (*FOOTBALL, RUGBY*) блокиро́вка ◆ *vt* (*difficulty*) справля́ться (спра́виться* *perf*) с +*instr*; (*grapple with*) схвати́ться* (*perf*) с +*instr*; (*FOOTBALL, RUGBY*) блоки́ровать (*impf*/*perf*).

tacky ['tækɪ] *adj* (*sticky*) ли́пкий*; (*pej: of poor quality*) дешёвый.

tact [tækt] *n* такт, такти́чность *f*.

tactful ['tæktful] *adj* такти́чный (такти́чен); **she is very** ~ она́ о́чень такти́чна.

tactfully ['tæktfəlɪ] *adv* такти́чно.

tactical ['tæktɪkl] *adj* (*also MIL*) такти́ческий*; ~ **error** такти́ческая оши́бка.

tactician [tæk'tɪʃən] *n* та́ктик.

tactics ['tæktɪks] *npl* та́ктика *fsg*.

tactless ['tæktlɪs] *adj* беста́ктный* (беста́ктен).

tactlessly ['tæktlɪslɪ] *adv* беста́ктно.

tadpole ['tædpəul] *n* голова́стик.

taffy ['tæfɪ] *n* (*US: toffee*) ири́ска*, тяну́чка*.

tag [tæg] *n* (*label*) этике́тка*, ярлы́к*; **price** ~ це́нник; **name** ~ би́рка*.

▶ **tag along** *vi* сле́довать (*impf*) по пята́м.

Tahiti [tɑː'hiːtɪ] *n* Таи́ти *m ind*.

tail [teɪl] *n* (*of animal, plane*) хвост*; (*of shirt*) коне́ц*; (*of coat*) пола́* ◆ *vt* (*follow*) сади́ться* (сесть* *perf*) на хвост +*dat*; ~**s** *npl* (*formal suit*) фрак *msg*; **to turn** ~ броса́ться (бро́ситься* *perf*) наутёк; *see also* **head**

▶ **tail away** *vi* (*voice, wind*) затиха́ть (зати́хнуть *perf*).

▶ **tail off** *vi* = **tail away**.

tailback ['teɪlbæk] *n* (*BRIT: AUT*) хвост.

tail coat *n* фрак.

tail end *n* (*of train etc*) хвост; (*of meeting etc*) коне́ц.

tailgate ['teɪlgeɪt] *n* (*AUT*) за́дняя дверь *f*.

taillight ['teɪlaɪt] *n* (*US: AUT*) за́дняя фа́ра.

---

* marks translations which have irregular inflections. The Russian-English side of the dictionary gives inflectional information.

tailor ['teɪlə'] n (мужско́й) портно́й m adj ◆ vt: **to ~ sth (to)** приспоса́бливать (приспосо́бить perf) что-н (к +dat); **~'s shop** портня́жная мастерска́я f adj.

tailoring ['teɪlərɪŋ] n (cut) покро́й; (craft) портня́жное де́ло.

tailor-made ['teɪlə'meɪd] adj (suit) сши́тый на зака́з; (fig); **she is ~ for the job** она́ идеа́льно подхо́дит для э́той рабо́ты.

tailwind ['teɪlwɪnd] n хвостово́й or попу́тный ве́тер.

taint [teɪnt] vt (meat, food) по́ртить (испо́ртить perf); (fig) пятна́ть (запятна́ть perf).

tainted ['teɪntɪd] adj (food) испо́рченный; (air, water) загрязнённый (загрязнён); (fig) запя́тнанный.

Taiwan ['taɪ'wɑːn] n Тайва́нь m.

Tajik ['tɑːdʒɪk] n таджи́к(-и́чка).

Tajiki [tɑː'dʒɪkɪ] adj таджи́кский ◆ n таджи́кский язы́к.

Tajikistan [tɑːdʒɪkɪ'stɑːn] n Таджикиста́н.

take [teɪk] (pt **took**, pp **taken**) vt брать (взять perf); (photo, measures) снима́ть (снять perf); (shower, decision, drug) принима́ть (приня́ть perf); (notes) де́лать (сде́лать perf); (grab: sb's arm etc) хвата́ть (схвати́ть perf); (require: courage, time) тре́бовать (потре́бовать perf); (pain etc) переноси́ть (перенести́ perf); (hold: passengers etc) вмеща́ть (вмести́ть perf); (person: on foot) отводи́ть (отвести́ perf); (thing: on foot) относи́ть (отнести́ perf); (person, thing: by transport) отвози́ть (отвезти́ perf); (exam) сдава́ть (сдать perf); (conduct: meeting) вести́ (impf) ◆ vi (fire) занима́ться (заня́ться perf); (dye) впи́тываться (впита́ться perf); (plant, injection) принима́ться (приня́ться perf) ◆ n (CINEMA) дубль m; **to ~ sth from** (drawer etc) вынима́ть (вы́нуть perf) что-н из +gen; (steal from: person) брать (взять perf) что-н у +gen; **I ~ it that ...** как я понима́ю, ...; **I took him for a doctor** я при́нял его́ за врача́; **to ~ sb's hand** брать (взять perf) кого́-н за́ руку; **to ~ for a walk** (child, dog) брать (взять perf) на прогу́лку; **to be ~n ill** заболева́ть (заболе́ть perf); **to ~ it upon o.s. to do** бра́ться (взя́ться perf) +infin; **~ the first (street) on the left** пе́рвый поворо́т нале́во; **to ~ Russian at university** изуча́ть (impf) ру́сский язы́к в университе́те; **it won't ~ long** э́то не займёт мно́го вре́мени; **I was quite ~n with her** (attracted) она́ произвела́ на меня́ большо́е впечатле́ние.

▶ **take after** vt fus (resemble) пойти́ (perf) в +acc

▶ **take apart** vt разбира́ть (разобра́ть perf)

▶ **take away** vt (remove) убира́ть (убра́ть perf); (carry off) забира́ть (забра́ть perf); (MATH) отнима́ть (отня́ть perf) ◆ vi: **to ~ away from** отнима́ть (отня́ть perf) от +gen

▶ **take back** vt (return: thing) относи́ть

(отнести́ perf) обра́тно; (: person) отводи́ть (отвести́ perf) обра́тно; (one's words) брать (взять perf) наза́д.

▶ **take down** vt (building) сноси́ть (снести́ perf); (scaffolding) разбира́ть (разобра́ть perf); (picture) снима́ть (снять perf); (write down: letter etc) запи́сывать (записа́ть perf)

▶ **take in** vt (deceive) обма́нывать (обману́ть perf); (understand) воспринима́ть (восприня́ть perf); (include) включа́ть (включи́ть perf); (lodger, orphan) брать (взять perf); (dress, waistband) ушива́ть (уши́ть perf)

▶ **take off** vi (AVIAT) взлета́ть (взлете́ть perf); (go away) улета́ть (улете́ть perf) ◆ vt (remove) снима́ть (снять perf); (imitate) копи́ровать (скопи́ровать perf)

▶ **take on** vt (work, employee) брать (взять perf); (opponent) сража́ться (срази́ться perf) с +instr

▶ **take out** vt (invite) води́ть (повести́ perf); (remove) вынима́ть (вы́нуть perf); (licence) оформля́ть (офо́рмить perf); **to ~ sth out of sth** (drawer, pocket etc) вынима́ть (вы́нуть perf) что-н из чего́-н; **don't ~ it out on me!** вымеща́й э́то на мне!

▶ **take over** vt (business, country) принима́ть (приня́ть perf) руково́дство +instr ◆ vi: **to ~ over from sb** сменя́ть (смени́ть perf) кого́-н

▶ **take to** vt fus (activity) пристрасти́ться (perf) к +dat, занима́ться (заня́ться perf) +instr; (form habit of): **to ~ to doing** пристрасти́ться (perf) +infin; **she took to him at once** он ей сра́зу понра́вился

▶ **take up** vt (hobby, sport, job) заня́ться (perf) +instr; (idea, suggestion, story) подхва́тывать (подхвати́ть perf); (time, space) занима́ть (заня́ть perf); (garment) подшива́ть (подши́ть perf) ◆ vi: **to ~ up with sb** сходи́ться (сойти́сь perf) с кем-н; **to ~ sb up on sth** (offer, suggestion) воспо́льзоваться (perf) +instr; **I'll ~ you up on that!** ловлю́ Вас на сло́ве!

takeaway ['teɪkəweɪ] n (BRIT) магази́н или рестора́н, где продаётся горя́чая еда́ на вы́нос; (food) горя́чая еда́ на вы́нос.

take-home pay ['teɪkhəum-] n чи́стый за́работок.

taken ['teɪkən] pp of **take**.

takeoff ['teɪkɔf] n (AVIAT) взлёт.

takeout ['teɪkaut] (US) n = **takeaway**.

takeover ['teɪkəuvə'] n (COMM) поглоще́ние; (of country) захва́т вла́сти.

takeover bid n (COMM) попы́тка поглоще́ния.

takings ['teɪkɪŋz] npl (COMM) вы́ручка fsg.

talc [tælk] n тальк.

talcum powder ['tælkəm-] n = **talc**.

tale [teɪl] n (story, account) расска́з, сказа́ние; **to tell ~s** (fig: to teacher, parents etc) я́бедничать (ная́бедничать perf).

talent ['tælnt] n тала́нт.

talented ['tæləntɪd] adj (person, actor etc) тала́нтливый (тала́нтлив).

talent scout n (THEAT, SPORT) челове́к, занима́ющийся по́иском молоды́х дарова́ний.

talisman ['tælɪzmən] n талисма́н.

talk [tɔːk] n (a (prepared) speech) докла́д; (conversation, interview) бесе́да; (gossip) слух ♦ vi (speak) разгова́ривать (impf); ~**s** npl (POL etc) перегово́ры pl; **to give a** ~ де́лать (сде́лать perf) докла́д; **to** ~ **about** расска́зывать (рассказа́ть perf) о +prp; ~**ing of films, have you seen** ...? кста́ти о фи́льмах, вы ви́дели ...?; **to** ~ **sb into doing** угова́ривать (уговори́ть perf) кого́-н +infin; **to** ~ **sb out of sth** отгова́ривать (отговори́ть perf) кого́-н от чего́-н; **to** ~ **shop** говори́ть (impf) о дела́х

▶ **talk over** vt (problem etc) обгова́ривать (обговори́ть perf).

talkative ['tɔːkətɪv] adj (person) разгово́рчивый (разгово́рчив).

talker ['tɔːkə'] n: **she is a good** ~ она́ хоро́ший ора́тор; (pej) болту́н(-у́шка); **he is a fast** ~ он красноречи́в.

talking point ['tɔːkɪŋ-] n те́ма для разгово́ра.

talking-to ['tɔːkɪŋtu] n: **to give sb a good** ~ отчи́тывать (отчита́ть perf) кого́-н как сле́дует.

talk show n (TV, RADIO) ток-шо́у ind.

tall [tɔːl] adj высо́кий* (высо́к); **he is 6 feet** ~ его́ рост – 6 фу́тов; **how** ~ **are you?** како́й у Вас рост?

tallboy ['tɔːlbɔɪ] n (BRIT) высо́кий* комо́д.

Tallin(n) ['tælɪn] n Та́ллин(н).

tallness ['tɔːlnɪs] n высота́.

tall story n небыли́ца.

tally ['tælɪ] n (of marks, amounts of money etc) счёт ♦ vi: **to** ~ **(with)** (subj: figures, stories etc) сходи́ться* (сойти́сь* perf) (с +instr); **to keep a** ~ **of sth** вести́* (impf) счёт чего́-н.

talon ['tælən] n (of eagle, owl etc) ко́готь* m.

tambourine [tæmbə'riːn] n (MUS) тамбури́н, бу́бен.

tame [teɪm] adj (animal, bird) ручно́й; (fig: story, style) вя́лый (вял).

tamper ['tæmpə'] vi: **to** ~ **with sth** пыта́ться (попыта́ться perf) измени́ть что-н.

tampon ['tæmpɔn] n тампо́н.

tan [tæn] n (also: **suntan**) зага́р ♦ vi (person) загора́ть (загоре́ть perf); (skin) загора́ть (perf) ♦ vt дуби́ть* (вы́дубить* perf) ♦ adj (colour) рыжева́то-кори́чневый; **to get a** ~ загора́ть (загоре́ть perf).

tandem ['tændəm] n (cycle) танде́м; **in** ~ (together) совме́стно, вме́сте.

tandoori [tæn'duərɪ] n инди́йский ме́тод приготовле́ния мя́са и лепёшек в гли́няной печи́.

tang [tæŋ] n си́льный за́пах.

tangent ['tændʒənt] n (MATH) каса́тельная f adj; **to go off at a** ~ (fig) сбива́ться (сби́ться* perf).

tangerine [tændʒə'riːn] n (fruit) мандари́н; (colour) я́рко-ора́нжевый цвет.

tangible ['tændʒəbl] adj (proof, benefits) ощути́мый (ощути́м); ~ **assets** реа́льный акти́в.

Tangier [tæn'dʒɪə'] n Танже́р.

tangle ['tæŋgl] n пу́таница; **to get in(to) a** ~ (also fig) запу́тываться (запу́таться perf).

tango ['tæŋgəu] n та́нго nt ind.

tank [tæŋk] n (water tank) бак; (: large) цисте́рна; (PHOT) ва́нна; (for fish) аква́риум; (MIL) танк.

tankard ['tæŋkəd] n (for beer) пивна́я кру́жка.

tanker ['tæŋkə'] n (ship) та́нкер; (truck, RAIL) цисте́рна.

tanned [tænd] adj загоре́лый.

tannin ['tænɪn] n тани́н.

tanning ['tænɪŋ] n (of leather) дубле́ние.

Tannoy® ['tænɔɪ] n (BRIT) громкоговори́тель m; **over the** ~ по громкоговори́телю.

tantalizing ['tæntəlaɪzɪŋ] adj (smell, possibility) дразня́щий*.

tantamount ['tæntəmaunt] adj: ~ **to** равноси́льный* (равноси́лен) +dat.

tantrum ['tæntrəm] n исте́рика; **to throw a** ~ устра́ивать (устро́ить perf) исте́рику.

Tanzania [tænzə'nɪə] n Танза́ния.

Tanzanian [tænzə'nɪən] adj танзани́йский* ♦ n танзани́ец(-и́йка).

tap [tæp] n кран; (gentle blow) стук ♦ vt (hit gently) стуча́ть (постуча́ть perf) по +dat; (resources) испо́льзовать (impf/perf); (telephone, conversation) прослу́шивать (impf); **to be on** ~ (fig: resources) находи́ться* (impf) под руко́й; (beer) в разли́в.

tap-dancing ['tæpdɑːnsɪŋ] n чечётка.

tape [teɪp] n (also: **magnetic** ~) плёнка; (cassette) кассе́та; (sticky tape) кле́йкая ле́нта; (for tying) ле́нта ♦ vt (record) запи́сывать (записа́ть perf); (stick with tape) закле́ивать (закле́ить perf) кле́йкой ле́нтой; **on** ~ (song etc) на кассе́те.

tape deck n кассе́тный магнитофо́н.

tape measure n сантиме́тр.

taper ['teɪpə'] n (candle) то́нкая восковая свеча́ ♦ vi (narrow) сужа́ться (су́зиться* perf).

tape recorder n магнитофо́н.

tape recording n магнитофо́нная за́пись f.

tapered ['teɪpəd] adj (skirt) сужа́ющийся.

tapering ['teɪpərɪŋ] adj (fingers) то́нкий*.

tapestry ['tæpɪstrɪ] n (object) гобеле́н; (art) иску́сство гобеле́на.

tapeworm ['teɪpwəːm] n ленте́ц*, ле́нточный червь m.

---

* marks translations which have irregular inflections. The Russian-English side of the dictionary gives inflectional information.

tapioca [tæpɪ'əukə] *n* тапио́ка.
tappet ['tæpɪt] *n* (*AUT*) толка́тель *m* кла́пана.
tar [tɑ:] *n* дёготь *m*; **low/middle ~ cigarettes** сигаре́ты с ни́зким/сре́дним содержа́нием никоти́на.
tarantula [tə'ræntjulə] *n* тара́нтул.
tardy ['tɑ:dɪ] *adj* (*reply, development*) запозда́лый.
target ['tɑ:gɪt] *n* цель *f*; **to be on ~** (*project*) идти́* (*impf*) согла́сно пла́ну.
target audience *n* потенциа́льные клие́нты *mpl*.
target market *n* целево́й ры́нок*.
target practice *n* уче́бная стрельба́.
tariff ['tærɪf] *n* (*tax on goods*) тари́ф; (*BRIT: in hotels, restaurants*) прейскура́нт.
tariff barrier *n* (*COMM*) тари́фный барье́р.
tarmac ['tɑ:mæk] *n* (*BRIT: on road*) асфа́льт; (*AVIAT*) лётное по́ле; (: *runway*) взлётная полоса́ ◆ *vt* (*BRIT: road, drive etc*) асфальти́ровать (заасфальти́ровать *perf*).
tarn [tɑ:n] *n* ка́ровое о́зеро.
tarnish ['tɑ:nɪʃ] *vt* (*silver, brass etc*) де́лать (сде́лать *perf*) ту́склым; (*fig: reputation etc*) броса́ть (бро́сить* *perf*) тень на +*acc*.
tarot ['tærəu] *adj*: **~ cards** гада́льные ка́рты *fpl*.
tarpaulin [tɑ:'pɔ:lɪn] *n* брезе́нт.
tarragon ['tærəgən] *n* (*herb*) эстраго́н.
tart [tɑ:t] *n* (*CULIN: large*) пиро́г; (: *small*) пиро́жное *nt adj*; (*BRIT: inf: prostitute*) шлю́ха ◆ *adj* (*flavour*) го́рький*
▶ **tart up** (*BRIT: inf*) ◆ *vt* (*object etc*) принаряжа́ть (принаряди́ть* *perf*); **to ~ o.s. up** принаряжа́ться (принаряди́ться* *perf*); (*pej*) нама́зываться (нама́заться* *perf*), выря́живаться (вы́рядиться* *perf*).
tartan ['tɑ:tn] *n* шотла́ндка (*ткань*) ◆ *adj* (*rug, scarf etc*) кле́тчатый.
tartar ['tɑ:təʳ] *n* (*on teeth*) (зубно́й) ка́мень *m*; (*pej: person*) сте́рва.
tartar(e) sauce ['tɑ:tə-] *n* со́ус с лу́ком и ка́персами.
Tashkent [tæʃ'kɛnt] *n* Ташке́нт.
task [tɑ:sk] *n* зада́ча; **to take sb to ~** отчи́тывать (отчита́ть *perf*) кого́-н.
task force *n* (*MIL, POLICE*) операти́вная гру́ппа.
taskmaster ['tɑ:skmɑ:stəʳ] *n*: **he's a hard ~** он настоя́щий* надсмо́трщик.
Tasmania [tæz'meɪnɪə] *n* Тасма́ния.
tassel ['tæsl] *n* ки́сточка; **~s** бахрома́ *fsg*.
taste [teɪst] *n* вкус; (*sample*) про́ба; (*fig: glimpse, idea*) представле́ние ◆ *vt* про́бовать (попро́бовать *perf*) ◆ *vi*: **the fish ~s of or like** рыба́ име́ет вкус +*gen*; **what does the fish ~ like?** какова́ рыба́ на вкус?; **you can ~ the garlic (in the dish)** (в блю́де) чу́вствуется чесно́к; **to have a ~ of sth** про́бовать (попро́бовать *perf*) чего́-н; **to have a ~ for sth** име́ть (*impf*) вкус к чему́-н; **in good/bad ~** в хоро́шем/дурно́м вку́се.
taste bud *n* (*ANAT*) вкусово́й буго́р.

tasteful ['teɪstful] *adj* (*furnishings*) элега́нтный.
tastefully ['teɪstfəlɪ] *adv* (*decorated, furnished etc*) со вку́сом.
tasteless ['teɪstlɪs] *adj* безвку́сный* (безвку́сен).
tasty ['teɪstɪ] *adj* (*food*) вку́сный* (вку́сен).
tattered ['tætəd] *adj* (*clothes, paper etc*) изо́рванный (в кло́чья); (*fig: hopes etc*) разби́тый (разби́т).
tatters ['tætəz] *npl*: **in ~** (*clothes*) изо́рванный (изо́рван) в кло́чья.
tattoo [tə'tu:] *n* (*on skin*) татуиро́вка; (*spectacle*) вое́нный смотр ◆ *vt* (*name, design*) татуи́ровать (вытатуи́ровать *perf*).
tatty ['tætɪ] *adj* (*BRIT: inf*) потрёпанный.
taught [tɔ:t] *pt, pp of* **teach**.
taunt [tɔ:nt] *n* издева́тельство ◆ *vt* (*person*) издева́ться (*impf*) над +*instr*.
Taurus ['tɔ:rəs] *n* (*ASTROLOGY*) Теле́ц*; **he is ~** он – Теле́ц.
taut [tɔ:t] *adj* (*thread etc*) туго́й (туг); (*skin*) упру́гий* (упру́г).
tavern ['tævən] *n* (*old*) таве́рна.
tawdry ['tɔ:drɪ] *adj* (*jewellery etc*) безвку́сный* (безвку́сен).
tawny ['tɔ:nɪ] *adj* желтова́то-кори́чневый.
tawny owl *n* нея́сыть *f*.
tax [tæks] *n* нало́г ◆ *vt* (*earnings, goods etc*) облага́ть (обложи́ть *perf*) нало́гом; (*fig: memory, patience*) испы́тывать (испыта́ть *perf*); **before ~** до вы́чета нало́гов; **after ~** за вы́четом нало́гов; **free of ~** не облага́емый нало́гом.
taxable ['tæksəbl] *adj* (*income*) облага́емый (облага́ем) нало́гом.
tax allowance *n* нало́говая ски́дка.
taxation [tæk'seɪʃən] *n* (*system*) налогообложе́ние; (*money paid*) разме́р нало́га.
tax avoidance *n* оптимиза́ция нало́говой поли́тики.
tax collector *n* сбо́рщик нало́гов.
tax disc *n* (*BRIT: AUT*) свиде́тельство об упла́те подоро́жного нало́га, кото́рое прикрепля́ется к ветрово́му стеклу́.
tax evasion *n* уклоне́ние от нало́гов.
tax exemption *n* освобожде́ние от нало́гов.
tax exile *n* челове́к с высо́ким дохо́дом, кото́рый живёт за грани́цей с це́лью минимиза́ции свои́х нало́гов.
tax-free ['tæksfri:] *adj* (*goods, services*) необлага́емый нало́гом.
tax haven *n* нало́говое убе́жище (*страна́ с ни́зкими нало́гами*).
taxi ['tæksɪ] *n* такси́ *nt ind* ◆ *vi* (*AVIAT: plane*) выру́ливать (вы́рулить *perf*).
taxidermist ['tæksɪdə:mɪst] *n* наби́вщик чу́чел.
taxi driver *n* води́тель *m* такси́, такси́ст.
tax inspector *n* (*BRIT*) нало́говый инспе́ктор.
taxi rank *n* (*BRIT*) стоя́нка такси́.
taxi stand *n* = **taxi rank**.

taxpayer ['tækspeɪə'] *n* налогоплате́льщик (-щица).

tax rebate *n* возвра́т нало́га.

tax relief *n* ски́дка с нало́га.

tax return *n* поступле́ния *ntpl* от нало́гов; (*form*) нало́говая деклара́ция.

tax shelter *n* нало́говая защи́та (*че́рез вложе́ния в це́нные бума́ги*).

tax year *n* нало́говый год*.

TB *n abbr* = **tuberculosis**.

Tbilisi [dbɪ'li:sɪ] *n* Тбили́си *m ind*.

TD *n abbr* (*US*) = **Treasury Department**; (: *FOOTBALL*) = **touchdown**.

tea [ti:] *n* (*drink*) чай; (*BRIT*: *meal*) у́жин; **afternoon** ~ чай (с бутербро́дами и пиро́жными); **high** ~ (*BRIT*) (по́здний*) обе́д.

tea bag *n* чай в паке́тике.

tea break *n* (*BRIT*) переры́в.

teacake ['ti:keɪk] *n* (*BRIT*) сдо́бная бу́лка с изю́мом.

teach [ti:tʃ] (*pt,pp* **taught**) *vi* (*be a teacher*) преподава́ть* (*impf*) ♦ *vt*: **to** ~ **sb sth**, ~ **sth to sb** учи́ть (научи́ть *perf*) кого́-н чему́-н; (*in school*) преподава́ть* (*impf*) что-н; **it taught him a lesson** (*fig*) э́то послужи́ло ему́ хоро́шим уро́ком.

teacher ['ti:tʃə'] *n* (*in secondary school*) учи́тель(ница) *m(f)*, преподава́тель(ница) *m(f)*; (*in primary school*) учи́тель(ница); **Russian** ~ учи́тель(ница) *or* преподава́тель(ница) ру́сского.

teacher training college *n* (*for primary schools*) педагоги́ческое учи́лище; (*for secondary schools*) педагоги́ческий* институ́т.

teaching ['ti:tʃɪŋ] *n* (*work of teacher*) преподава́ние.

teaching aids *npl* уче́бные посо́бия *ntpl*.

teaching hospital *n* (*BRIT*: *MED*) ≈ клини́ческая больни́ца.

teaching staff *n* (*BRIT*) преподава́тельский соста́в.

tea cosy *n* ≈ "ба́ба" на ча́йник.

teacup ['ti:kʌp] *n* ча́йная ча́шка*.

teak [ti:k] *n* тик.

tea leaves *npl* зава́рка *fsg*.

team [ti:m] *n* (*of people*) кома́нда; (*of animals*) упря́жка

▶ **team up** *vi*: **to** ~ **up (with)** объединя́ть (объедини́ть *perf*) уси́лия (с +*instr*).

team games *npl* кома́ндные и́гры *fpl*.

team spirit *n* дух това́рищества, кома́ндный дух.

teamwork ['ti:mwə:k] *n* коллекти́вная рабо́та.

tea party *n* чаепи́тие, чай.

teapot ['ti:pɔt] *n* (зава́рочный) ча́йник.

tear¹ [tɛə'] (*pt* **tore**, *pp* **torn**) *n* (*hole*) дыра́*, ды́рка* ♦ *vt* (*rip*) рвать* (порва́ть* *perf*) ♦ *vi* (*become torn*) рва́ться* (порва́ться* *perf*); **to** ~ **to pieces** *or* **to bits** *or* **to shreds** (*also fig*) разрыва́ть (разорва́ть* *perf*) на ме́лкие клочки́

▶ **tear along** *vi* (*rush*) нести́сь* (понести́сь* *perf*)

▶ **tear apart** *vt* (*also fig*) разрыва́ть (разорва́ть* *perf*) на ча́сти

▶ **tear away** *vt*: **to** ~ **o.s. away (from sth)** (*fig*) отрыва́ться (оторва́ться* *perf*) (от чего́-н)

▶ **tear out** *vt* (*sheet of paper, cheque*) вырыва́ть (вы́рвать* *perf*)

▶ **tear up** *vt* разрыва́ть (разорва́ть* *perf*).

tear² [tɪə'] *n* слеза́; **in** ~**s** в слеза́х; **to burst into** ~**s** распла́каться (*perf*), разрыда́ться (*perf*).

tearaway ['tɛərəweɪ] *n* (*inf*: *person*) сорвиголова́ *m/f*.

teardrop ['tɪədrɔp] *n* слези́нка*.

tearful ['tɪəful] *adj* запла́канный* (запла́кан).

tear gas *n* слезоточи́вый газ.

tearing ['tɛərɪŋ] *adj*: **to be in a** ~ **hurry** быть* (*impf*) в безу́мной спе́шке.

tearoom ['ti:ru:m] *n* ча́йная *f adj*.

tease [ti:z] *vt* дразни́ть (*impf*); (*unkindly*) дразни́ть (задразни́ть *perf*) ♦ *n* (*person*) насме́шник.

tea set *n* ча́йный серви́з.

teashop ['ti:ʃɔp] *n* (*BRIT*) = **tearoom**.

Teasmade® ['ti:zmeɪd] *n* приспособле́ние для зава́ривания ча́я, приводи́мое в де́йствие буди́льником.

teaspoon ['ti:spu:n] *n* ча́йная ло́жка.

tea strainer *n* ча́йное си́течко.

teat [ti:t] *n* (*of bottle*) со́ска.

teatime ['ti:taɪm] *n* у́жин.

tea towel *n* (*BRIT*) полоте́нце для посу́ды.

tea urn *n* тита́н с ча́ем.

tech [tɛk] *n abbr* (*inf*) = **technology**, **technical college**) ≈ ПТУ = *профессиона́льно-техни́ческое учи́лище*.

technical ['tɛknɪkl] *adj* (*terms, advances*) техни́ческий*.

technical college *n* (*BRIT*) техни́ческий* ко́лледж, те́хникум.

technicality [tɛknɪ'kælɪtɪ] *n* (*point of law*) техни́ческая то́нкость *f*; (*detail*) форма́льность *f*; **on a (legal)** ~ из-за юриди́ческой форма́льности.

technically ['tɛknɪklɪ] *adv* (*strictly speaking*) техни́чески, форма́льно; (*regarding technique*) с техни́ческой то́чки зре́ния.

technician [tɛk'nɪʃən] *n* те́хник.

technique [tɛk'ni:k] *n* те́хника.

techno ['tɛknəu] *n* (*MUS*) стиль поп му́зыки.

technocrat ['tɛknəkræt] *n* технокра́т.

technological [tɛknə'lɔdʒɪkl] *adj* (*development*,

knowledge) техни́ческий*.
technologist [tɛk'nɔlədʒɪst] *n* те́хник; (*in particular field*) техно́лог.
technology [tɛk'nɔlədʒɪ] *n* те́хника; (*in particular field*) техноло́гия.
teddy (bear) ['tɛdɪ(-)] *n* (плю́шевый *or* игру́шечный) ми́шка.
tedious ['ti:dɪəs] *adj* (*work, discussions etc*) ну́дный* (ну́ден), ску́чный.
tedium ['ti:dɪəm] *n* ску́ка.
tee [ti:] *n* ме́тка для ша́ра (*в го́льфе*)
▶ **tee off** *vi* де́лать (сде́лать *perf*) пе́рвый уда́р.
teem [ti:m] *vi*: **the city is ~ing with** (*visitors, tourists etc*) го́род киши́т +*instr*; **it is ~ing (with rain)** льёт как из ведра́.
teenage ['ti:neɪdʒ] *adj* (*fashions etc*) подростко́вый; **~ children** подро́стки *mpl*.
teenager ['ti:neɪdʒə'] *n* подро́сток*, тинэ́йджер.
teens [ti:nz] *npl*: **to be in one's ~** быть* (*impf*) в подростко́вом во́зрасте.
tee shirt *n* = T-shirt.
teeter ['ti:tə'] *vi* (*also fig*) колеба́ться (*impf*).
teeth [ti:θ] *npl of* tooth.
teethe [ti:ð] *vi*: **she is teething** (*baby*) у неё ре́жутся зу́бы.
teething ring ['ti:ðɪŋ-] *n* кольцо́.
teething troubles *npl* (*fig*) боле́зни *fpl* ро́ста.
teetotal ['ti:'təutl] *adj* тре́звый, не пью́щий*.
teetotaller ['ti:'təutlə'] (*US* teetotaler) *n* тре́звенник.
TEFL ['tɛfl] *n abbr* = Teaching of English as a Foreign Language.
Teflon® ['tɛflɔn] *n* Тефло́н.
Teheran [tɛə'rɑ:n] *n* Тегера́н.
tel. *abbr* (= telephone) тел.= *телефо́н*.
Tel Aviv ['tɛlə'vi:v] *n* Тель Ави́в.
telecast ['tɛlɪkɑ:st] *vt* передава́ть* (переда́ть* *perf*) по телеви́дению.
telecommunications ['tɛlɪkəmju:nɪ'keɪʃənz] *n* телекоммуника́ции *fpl*.
teleconferencing ['tɛlɪkɔnfərənsɪŋ] *n* организа́ция телеконфере́нций.
telegram ['tɛlɪgræm] *n* телегра́мма.
telegraph ['tɛlɪgrɑ:f] *n* (*system*) телегра́ф.
telegraphic [tɛlɪ'græfɪk] *adj* (*equipment*) телеграфи́ческий.
telegraph pole *n* телегра́фный столб.
telegraph wire *n* телегра́фные провода́ *mpl*.
telepathic [tɛlɪ'pæθɪk] *adj* телепати́ческий.
telepathy [tə'lɛpəθɪ] *n* телепа́тия.
telephone ['tɛlɪfəun] *n* телефо́н ♦ *vt* (*person*) звони́ть (позвони́ть *perf*) +*dat*; (*message*) сообща́ть (сообщи́ть *perf*) (по телефо́ну); **on the ~** (*talking*) по телефо́ну; **are you on the ~?** (*possessing phone*) у Вас есть телефо́н?
telephone booth (*BRIT* telephone box) *n* телефо́нная бу́дка.
telephone call *n* телефо́нный звоно́к*; **there is a ~~ for Peter** Пи́тера про́сят к телефо́ну.
telephone directory *n* телефо́нный спра́вочник.

telephone exchange *n* телефо́нная ста́нция.
telephone number *n* но́мер* телефо́на.
telephone operator *n* телефони́ст(ка).
telephone tapping *n* прослу́шивание телефо́на.
telephonist [tə'lɛfənɪst] *n* (*BRIT*) телефони́ст(ка).
telephoto ['tɛlɪ'fəutəu] *adj*: **~ lens** телефотообъекти́в.
teleprinter ['tɛlɪprɪntə'] *n* телета́йп.
Teleprompter® ['tɛlɪprɔmptə'] *n* (*US*) телесуфлёр, телете́кст.
telesales ['tɛlɪseɪlz] *n* (*COMM*) прода́жа по телефо́ну.
telescope ['tɛlɪskəup] *n* телеско́п ♦ *vi* (*fig*: *vehicles*) ста́лкиваться (столкну́ться *perf*) ♦ *vt* раскла́дывать (разложи́ть* *perf*).
telescopic [tɛlɪ'skɔpɪk] *adj* (*lens*) телескопи́ческий*; (*legs, aerial*) складно́й.
Teletext® ['tɛlɪtɛkst] *n* телете́кст, веща́тельная видеогра́фия.
telethon ['tɛlɪθɔn] *n* благотвори́тельный телемарафо́н.
televangelist [tɛlɪ'vændʒəlɪst] *n* телепропове́дник(-ица).
televise ['tɛlɪvaɪz] *vt* передава́ть* (переда́ть* *perf*) по телеви́дению.
television ['tɛlɪvɪʒən] *n* телеви́дение; (*set*) телеви́зор; **on ~** по телеви́дению.
television licence *n* (*BRIT*) телевизио́нная лице́нзия.
television programme *n* телевизио́нная програ́мма.
television set *n* телеви́зор.
telex ['tɛlɛks] *n* те́лекс ♦ *vt* свя́зываться (связа́ться* *perf*) по те́лексу с +*instr*; (*message*) передава́ть (переда́ть* *perf*) по те́лексу ♦ *vi* посыла́ть (посла́ть* *perf*) те́лекс.
tell [tɛl] (*pt,pp* told) *vt* (*say*) говори́ть (сказа́ть* *perf*); (*relate*) расска́зывать (рассказа́ть* *perf*); (*distinguish*): **to ~ sth from** отлича́ть (отличи́ть *perf*) что-н от +*gen* ♦ *vi* (*talk*): **to ~ of** расска́зывать (рассказа́ть* *perf*) о +*prp*; (*have an effect*): **to ~ (on)** ска́зываться (сказа́ться* *perf*) (на +*prp*); **to ~ sb to do** говори́ть (сказа́ть* *perf*) кому́-н +*infin*; **to ~ sb about sth** расска́зывать (рассказа́ть* *perf*) кому́-о чём-н; **he told me what happened** он рассказа́л мне, что случи́лось; **to ~ the time** (*know how to*) определя́ть (определи́ть *perf*), кото́рый час; **can you ~ me the time?** Вы не ска́жете, кото́рый час?; **(I) ~ you what ... вот что: ...; I can't ~ them apart** я не могу́ их различи́ть
▶ **tell off** *vt*: **to ~ sb off** отчи́тывать (отчита́ть *perf*) кого́-н
▶ **tell on** *vt fus* (*inform on*) жа́ловаться (нажа́ловаться *perf*) на +*acc*.
teller ['tɛlə'] *n* (*in bank*) касси́р.
telling ['tɛlɪŋ] *adj* (*remark, detail*) показа́тельный* (показа́телен).
telltale ['tɛlteɪl] *adj* (*sign*) многозначи́тельный

♦ *n* (*pej: child*) я́беда *m/f*.

telly ['tɛlɪ] *n abbr* (*BRIT: inf*) (= **television**) те́лик.

temerity [tə'mɛrɪtɪ] *n* де́рзость *f*.

temp [tɛmp] *n abbr* (*BRIT: inf.* = *temporary office worker*) вре́менный секрета́рь *m* ♦ *vi* вре́менно рабо́тать (*impf*) секретарём.

temper ['tɛmpə'] *n* (*nature*) нрав; (*mood*) настрое́ние; (*fit of anger*) гнев ♦ *vt* (*moderate*) смягча́ть (смягчи́ть *perf*); **to be in a** ~ быть* (*impf*) в гне́ве; **to lose one's** ~ выходи́ть* (вы́йти *perf*) из себя́; **to keep one's** ~ сде́рживаться (сдержа́ться* *perf*).

temperament ['tɛmprəmənt] *n* темпера́мент.

temperamental [tɛmprə'mɛntl] *adj* темпера́ментный* (темпера́ментен); (*fig*) капри́зный.

temperate ['tɛmprət] *adj* (*climate, zone, behaviour*) уме́ренный* (уме́рен); ~ **country** страна́ с уме́ренным кли́матом.

temperature ['tɛmprətʃə'] *n* температу́ра; **he has** *or* **is running a** ~ у него́ температу́ра.

temperature chart *n* температу́рный гра́фик.

tempered ['tɛmpəd] *adj* (*steel*) отпу́щенный.

tempest ['tɛmpɪst] *n* бу́ря.

tempestuous [tɛm'pɛstjuəs] *adj* (*time, relationship*) бу́рный* (бу́рен); (*person*) бу́йный* (бу́ен).

tempi ['tɛmpiː] *npl of* **tempo**.

template ['tɛmplɪt] *n* шабло́н.

temple ['tɛmpl] *n* (*REL*) храм; (*ANAT*) висо́к*.

templet ['tɛmplɪt] *n* = **template**.

tempo ['tɛmpəu] (*pl* ~**s** *or* **tempi**) *n* (*MUS, also fig*) темп.

temporal ['tɛmpərl] *adj* (*non-religious*) све́тский*; (*relating to time*) временно́й.

temporarily ['tɛmpərərɪlɪ] *adv* вре́менно.

temporary ['tɛmpərərɪ] *adj* вре́менный* (вре́менен).

temporize ['tɛmpəraɪz] *vi* ме́длить (*impf*).

tempt [tɛmpt] *vt* соблазня́ть (соблазни́ть *perf*), искуша́ть (искуси́ть* *perf*); **to** ~ **sb into doing** соблазня́ть (соблазни́ть *perf*) *or* искуша́ть (искуси́ть* *perf*) кого́-н +*infin*; **I was** ~**ed to call you** у меня́ бы́ло искуше́ние позвони́ть Вам.

temptation [tɛmp'teɪʃən] *n* собла́зн, искуше́ние.

tempting ['tɛmptɪŋ] *adj* (*offer*) соблазни́тельный* (соблазни́телен).

ten [tɛn] *n* де́сять*; ~**s of thousands** деся́тки ты́сяч; *see also* **five**.

tenable ['tɛnəbl] *adj* здра́вый (здрав); **the position of Chairman is** ~ **for three years** пост председа́теля закреплён за ним на три го́да.

tenacious [tə'neɪʃəs] *adj* насто́йчивый (насто́йчив).

tenacity [tə'næsɪtɪ] *n* насто́йчивость *f*.

tenancy ['tɛnənsɪ] *n* (*possession of room, land etc*) владе́ние на усло́виях аре́нды; (*period of possession*) срок аре́нды *or* на́йма.

tenant ['tɛnənt] *n* съёмщик(-мщица).

tend [tɛnd] *vt* (*crops, sick person*) уха́живать (*impf*) за +*instr* ♦ *vi*: **to** ~ **to do** име́ть (*impf*) скло́нность +*infin*; **he** ~**s to do everything in a hurry** он скло́нен к тому́, что́бы де́лать всё в спе́шке.

tendency ['tɛndənsɪ] *n* (*habit*) скло́нность *f*; (*trend*) тенде́нция.

tender ['tɛndə'] *adj* не́жный* (не́жен); (*sore*) чувстви́тельный* (чувстви́телен) ♦ *n* (*COMM: offer*) предложе́ние ♦ *vt* (*offer*) подава́ть* (пода́ть* *perf*); (*apology*) приноси́ть* (принести́* *perf*); **to put in a** ~ (**for**) подава́ть* (пода́ть* *perf*) зая́вку (на +*acc*); **to put sth out to** ~ (*BRIT*) объявля́ть (объяви́ть* *perf*) то́рги на что-н; **legal** ~ (*money*) зако́нное платёжное сре́дство; **to** ~ **one's resignation** пода́ть* (*perf*) в отста́вку.

tenderize ['tɛndəraɪz] *vt* (*meat*) отбива́ть (отби́ть* *perf*).

tenderly ['tɛndəlɪ] *adv* не́жно.

tenderness ['tɛndənɪs] *n* не́жность *f*.

tendon ['tɛndən] *n* сухожи́лие.

tendril ['tɛndrɪl] *n* (*BOT*) у́сик; (*of hair*) прядь *f*.

tenement ['tɛnəmənt] *n* многокварти́рный дом* (*сдава́емый внаём*).

Tenerife [tɛnə'riːf] *n* Тенери́фе *m ind*.

tenet ['tɛnət] *n* основополага́ющий при́нцип.

tenner ['tɛnə'] *n* (*BRIT: inf: ten pounds*) ≈ деся́тка*.

tennis ['tɛnɪs] *n* те́ннис.

tennis ball *n* те́ннисный мяч*.

tennis club *n* те́ннисный клуб.

tennis court *n* те́ннисный корт.

tennis elbow *n* (*MED*) те́ннисный ло́коть *m*, лучеплечево́й бурси́т.

tennis match *n* те́ннисный матч.

tennis player *n* тенниси́ст(ка*).

tennis racket *n* те́ннисная раке́тка*.

tennis shoes *npl* те́ннисные ту́фли* *fpl*.

tenor ['tɛnə'] *n* (*MUS*) те́нор*; (*of speech etc*) смысл.

tenpin bowling ['tɛnpɪn-] *n* (*BRIT*) ке́гли *pl*.

tense [tɛns] *adj* (*person, muscle, period*) напряжённый* (напряжён); (*smile*) натя́нутый (натя́нут) ♦ *n* (*LING*) вре́мя* *nt* ♦ *vt* напряга́ть (напря́чь* *perf*).

tenseness ['tɛnsnɪs] *n* напряжённость *f*.

tension ['tɛnʃən] *n* (*nervousness*) напряжённость *f*; (*between ropes etc*) натя́нутость *f*.

tent [tɛnt] *n* пала́тка*.

tentacle ['tɛntəkl] *n* щу́пальце*.

tentative ['tɛntətɪv] *adj* (*person, smile*)

осторо́жный* (осторо́жен); (*conclusion, plans*) предвари́тельный* (предвари́телен).

tentatively ['tɛntətɪvlɪ] *adv* (*suggest*) предвари́тельно; (*wave*) осторо́жно.

tenterhooks ['tɛntəhuks] *npl*: **on ~** как на иго́лках.

tenth [tɛnθ] *adj* деся́тый ♦ *n* (*fraction*) деся́тая часть *f*, одна́ деся́тая *f adj*; *see also* **fifth**.

tent peg *n* ко́лышек* для пала́тки.

tent pole *n* столб* для пала́тки.

tenuous ['tɛnjuəs] *adj* (*hold, links etc*) сла́бый* (слаб).

tenure ['tɛnjuə'] *n* (*of land, buildings etc*) срок аре́нды; (*of office*) побыва́ние в до́лжности; **to have ~** име́ть (*impf*) постоя́нную рабо́ту.

tepid ['tɛpɪd] *adj* (*tea, pool etc*) теплова́тый (теплова́т); (*reaction, applause*) прохла́дный* (прохла́ден).

Ter. *abbr* = **Terrace**.

term [tə:m] *n* (*word, expression*) те́рмин; (*period in power etc*) срок*; (*SCOL: in school*) че́тверть *f*; (: *at university*) триме́стр ♦ *vt* (*call*) называ́ть (назва́ть* *perf*); **~s** *npl* (*conditions*) усло́вия *ntpl*; **in abstract ~s** в абстра́ктных выраже́ниях; **~ of imprisonment** срок заключе́ния; **"easy ~s"** (*COMM*) "льго́тные усло́вия"; **in the short ~** в настоя́щее вре́мя; **in the long ~** в перспекти́ве; **to be on good ~s with sb** подде́рживать (*impf*) хоро́шие отноше́ния с кем-н; **to come to ~s with** примиря́ться (примири́ться *perf*) с +*instr*.

terminal ['tə:mɪnl] *adj* неизлечи́мый (неизлечи́м) ♦ *n* (*ELEC*) кле́мма, зажи́м; (*COMPUT, COMM*) термина́л; (*also*: **air ~**) аэровокза́л; (*BRIT: also*: **coach ~**) авто́бусная ста́нция.

terminate ['tə:mɪneɪt] *vt* прекраша́ть (прекрати́ть* *perf*) ♦ *vi*: **to ~ in** зака́нчиваться (зако́нчиться *perf*) +*instr*.

termination [tə:mɪ'neɪʃən] *n* прекраще́ние.

termini ['tə:mɪnaɪ] *npl of* **terminus**.

terminology [tə:mɪ'nɒlədʒɪ] *n* терминоло́гия.

term insurance *n* страхова́ние на определённый срок.

terminus ['tə:mɪnəs] (*pl* **termini**) *n* (*for buses*) коне́чная остано́вка*; (*for trains*) коне́чная ста́нция.

termite ['tə:maɪt] *n* терми́т.

term paper *n* (*US: at university*) ≈ курсова́я *f adj*.

Terr. *abbr* = **Terrace**.

terrace ['tɛrəs] *n* терра́са; (*BRIT: row of houses*) ряд примыка́ющих друг к дру́гу однотипных домо́в; (*in street names*): **Rose T~** Ро́уз Те́рес; **the ~s** *npl* (*BRIT: standing areas*) трибу́ны *fpl*.

terraced ['tɛrəst] *adj* (*garden*) терра́сный; **~ house** дом в ряду́ примыка́ющих друг дру́гу однотипных домо́в.

terracotta ['tɛrə'kɒtə] *n* (*clay*) террако́та; (*colour*) террако́товый цвет ♦ *adj* террако́товый.

terrain [tɛ'reɪn] *n* ландша́фт.

terrible ['tɛrɪbl] *adj* ужа́сный* (ужа́сен).

terribly ['tɛrɪblɪ] *adv* ужа́сно.

terrier ['tɛrɪə'] *n* терье́р.

terrific [tə'rɪfɪk] *adj* (*thunderstorm, speed etc*) колосса́льный* (колосса́лен); (*time, party etc*) потряса́ющий*.

terrify ['tɛrɪfaɪ] *vt* ужаса́ть (ужасну́ть *perf*); **to be terrified (of)** быть (*impf*) в у́жасе (от +*gen*).

terrifying ['tɛrɪfaɪɪŋ] *adj* ужаса́ющий*.

territorial [tɛrɪ'tɔ:rɪəl] *adj* территориа́льный ♦ *n* (*BRIT: MIL*) военнослу́жащий* *m adj* территориа́льной а́рмии.

Territorial Army *n* (*BRIT: MIL*): **the ~ ~** территориа́льная а́рмия.

territorial waters *npl* территориа́льные во́ды *fpl*.

territory ['tɛrɪtərɪ] *n* террито́рия; (*fig*) о́бласть *f*.

terror ['tɛrə'] *n* у́жас.

terrorism ['tɛrərɪzəm] *n* террори́зм.

terrorist ['tɛrərɪst] *n* террори́ст(ка*) ♦ *adj* террористи́ческий.

terrorize ['tɛrəraɪz] *vt* терроризи́ровать (*impf/perf*).

terse [tə:s] *adj* сжа́тый (сжат), кра́ткий* (кра́ток).

tertiary ['tə:ʃərɪ] *adj* (*system*) трети́чный; (*third in order, importance*) тре́тий*; **~ education** (*BRIT*) вы́сшее образова́ние.

Terylene® ['tɛrɪli:n] *n* териле́н.

TESL ['tɛsl] *n abbr* = Teaching of English as a Second Language.

TESSA ['tɛsə] *abbr* (*BRIT*: = Tax Exempt Special Savings Account*) безнало́говый сберега́тельный счёт.

test [tɛst] *n* (*trial, check*) прове́рка, тест; (*of courage etc*) испыта́ние; (*MED*) ана́лиз; (*CHEM*) о́пыт; (*SCOL*) контро́льная рабо́та, тест; (*also*: **driving ~**) экза́мен на води́тельские права́ ♦ *vt* проверя́ть (прове́рить *perf*); (*courage*) испы́тывать (испыта́ть *perf*); (*MED*) анализи́ровать (*impf/perf*); **to put sth to the ~** подверга́ть (подве́ргнуть* *perf*) что-н прове́рке; **to ~ sth for sth** проверя́ть (прове́рить *perf*) что-н на что-н.

testament ['tɛstəmənt] *n* свиде́тельство; **the Old/New T~** Ве́тхий*/Но́вый заве́т.

test ban *n* (*also*: **nuclear ~ ~**) запреще́ние испыта́ний я́дерного ору́жия.

test card *n* (*TV*) телевизио́нная табли́ца.

test case *n* (*LAW, fig*) про́бное *or* прецеде́нтное де́ло.

testes ['tɛsti:z] *npl* (*ANAT*) яи́чки *ntpl*.

test flight *n* испыта́тельный полёт.

testicle ['tɛstɪkl] *n* яи́чко*.

testify ['tɛstɪfaɪ] *vi* (*LAW*) дава́ть* (дать* *perf*) показа́ния; **to ~ to sth** свиде́тельствовать (*impf*) о чём-н.

testimonial [tɛstɪ'məunɪəl] *n* (*BRIT: reference*) рекоменда́ция.

testimony ['tɛstɪmənɪ] n (LAW: statement)
показа́ние, свиде́тельство; (clear proof): **to
be (a) ~ to** явля́ться (яви́ться* perf)
свиде́тельством +gen.
testing ['tɛstɪŋ] adj (situation, period)
испыта́тельный.
test match n (CRICKET, RUGBY)
междунаро́дный матч.
testosterone [tɛs'tɔstərəun] n тестостеро́н.
test paper n (SCOL) экзаменацио́нный биле́т.
test pilot n лётчик-испыта́тель m.
test tube n проби́рка*.
test-tube baby ['tɛsttju:b-] n ребёнок из
проби́рки.
testy ['tɛstɪ] adj (person, comment)
невы́держанный* (невы́держан).
tetanus ['tɛtənəs] n (disease) столбня́к*.
tetchy ['tɛtʃɪ] adj (person, behaviour)
раздражи́тельный* (раздражи́телен).
tether ['tɛðəʳ] vt (animal) привя́зывать
(привяза́ть* perf) ♦ n: **at the end of one's ~** на
гра́ни срыва.
Texas ['tɛksəs] n Теха́с.
text [tɛkst] n текст.
textbook ['tɛkstbuk] n уче́бник.
textiles ['tɛkstaɪlz] npl (fabrics) тексти́льные
изде́лия ntpl; (TECH) тексти́ль msg; (textile
industry) тексти́льная промы́шленность
fsg.
textual ['tɛkstjuəl] adj: **~ analysis** ана́лиз
те́кста.
texture ['tɛkstʃəʳ] n (of cloth, soil) строе́ние;
(feel: of cloth, silk) факту́ра; (of skin)
ка́чество.
TGWU n abbr (BRIT) = Transport and General
Workers' Union.
Thai [taɪ] adj тайла́ндский ♦ n таила́ндец*
(-дка*).
Thailand ['taɪlænd] n Таила́нд.
thalidomide [θə'lɪdəmaɪd] n талидоми́д.
Thames [tɛmz] n: **the ~** Те́мза.
than [ðæn] conj (in comparisons): **you have more
~ ten** у Вас бо́льше десяти́; **I have more/less
work ~ you/Paul** у меня́ бо́льше/ме́ньше
рабо́ты, чем у Вас/у Па́вла; **she is older ~
you think** она́ ста́рше, чем Вы ду́маете; **more
~ once** не раз; **more ~ three times** бо́лее or
бо́льше трёх раз.
thank [θæŋk] vt благодари́ть (поблагодари́ть
perf); **~ you (very much)** (большо́е) спаси́бо;
~ God! сла́ва Бо́гу!
thankful ['θæŋkful] adj: **~ (for)** благода́рный*
(благода́рен) (за +acc); **~ that** (relieved)
благода́рный за то, что.
thankfully ['θæŋkfəlɪ] adv к сча́стью; **~ there
were few victims** к сча́стью, жертв бы́ло
ма́ло.
thankless ['θæŋklɪs] adj неблагода́рный*.

thanks [θæŋks] npl благода́рность fsg ♦ excl
спаси́бо; **many ~, ~ a lot** большо́е спаси́бо;
~ to благодаря́ +dat.
Thanksgiving (Day) ['θæŋksgɪvɪŋ(-)] n (US)
День* m благодаре́ния.

KEYWORD
---

that [ðæt] (pl **those**) adj (demonstrative) тот*;
that man тот мужчи́на; **which book would
you like? – that one over there** каку́ю кни́гу
Вы хоти́те? – вон ту, пожа́луйста; **I like this
film better than that one** мне э́тот фильм
нра́вится бо́льше, чем тот
  ♦ pron **1** (demonstrative: in questions): **who's/
what's that?** кто/что э́то?; **is that you?** э́то
Вы?; **we talked of this and that** мы говори́ли
о том о сём; **that's how ...** вот как ...; **that's
what he said** так он сказа́л; **what happened
after that?** а что пото́м произошло́?; **that is
(to say)** то́ есть
  2 (direct object) кото́рый (f кото́рую, nt
кото́рое, pl кото́рые); (indirect object)
кото́рому (f кото́рой, pl кото́рым); (after
prep: +acc) кото́рый (f кото́рую, nt кото́рое,
pl кото́рые); (: +gen) кото́рого (f кото́рой, pl
кото́рых); (: +dat) кото́рому (f кото́рой, pl
кото́рым); (: +instr) кото́рым (f кото́рой, pl
кото́рыми); (: +prp) кото́ром (f кото́рой, pl
кото́рых); **the theory that we discussed last
week** тео́рия, кото́рую мы обсужда́ли на
про́шлой неде́ле; **all (that) I have** всё, что у
меня́ есть
  3 (of time) когда́; **the day (that) he died** день,
когда́ он у́мер
  ♦ conj что; (introducing purpose) что́бы; **he
thought that I was ill** он ду́мал, что я был
бо́лен; **she suggested that I phone you** она́
предложи́ла, что́бы я Вам позвони́л
  ♦ adv (demonstrative): **I can't work that much**
я не могу́ так мно́го рабо́тать; **it can't be
that bad** ну не так уж всё пло́хо; **I have drunk
that much** я вы́пил вот сто́лько; **the wall's
about that high and that thick** стена́
приме́рно вот тако́й высоты́ и вот тако́й
толщины́.

thatched [θætʃt] adj соло́менный.
Thatcherism ['θætʃərɪzəm] n тэтчери́зм.
Thatcherite ['θætʃəraɪt] n сторо́нник(-ица)
поли́тики Тэ́тчер.
thaw [θɔ:] n о́ттепель f ♦ vi (ice) та́ять
(раста́ять perf); (food) отта́ивать (отта́ять
perf) ♦ vt (food: also: **~ out**) отта́ивать
(отта́ять perf); **it's ~ing today** сего́дня та́ет.

KEYWORD
---

the [ði:] def art: **1**: **the books/children are in the
library** кни́ги/де́ти в библиоте́ке; **the rich and
the poor** бога́тые pl adj и бе́дные pl adj; **to
attempt the impossible** пыта́ться

---

* marks translations which have irregular inflections. The Russian-English side of the dictionary gives inflectional information.

(попыта́ться *perf*) сде́лать невозмо́жное
2 (*in titles*): **Elizabeth the First** Елизаве́та Пе́рвая
3 (*in comparisons*): **the more I think about it the more I like it** чем бо́льше я ду́маю об э́том, тем бо́льше мне э́то нра́вится.

theatre ['θɪətə'] (*US* **theater**) *n* теа́тр; (*also:* **lecture ~**) лекцио́нный зал; (*MED: also:* **operating ~**) операцио́нная *f adj*.
theatregoer ['θɪətəgəʊə'] *n* театра́л(ка•).
theatrical [θɪ'ætrɪkl] *adj* театра́льный; (*gestures*) театра́льный• (театра́лен); **~ company** театра́льная тру́ппа.
theft [θɛft] *n* кра́жа.
their [ðɛə'] *adj* их; (*referring to subject of sentence*) свой.
theirs [ðɛəz] *pron* (*see adj*) их; свой; *see also* **mine**¹.
them [ðɛm] *pron* (*direct*) их; (*indirect*) им; (*after prep: +gen, +prp*) их; (: *+dat*) им; (: *+instr*) и́ми; (*referring to subject of sentence*) свой; **a few of ~ are going to the cinema** не́которые из них иду́т в кино́; **give me a few of ~** да́йте мне их немно́го; *see also* **me**.
theme [θiːm] *n* те́ма.
theme park *n парк, стилизо́ванный под определённую эпо́ху и́ли те́му*.
theme song *n* пе́сня из кинофи́льма.
theme tune *n* мело́дия из кинофи́льма.
themselves [ðəm'sɛlvz] *pl pron* (*reflexive*) себя́; (*emphatic*) са́ми; (*after prep: +gen*) себя́; (: *+dat, +prp*) себе́; (: *+instr*) собо́й; (*alone*): (**all**) **by ~** одни́; **they shared the money between ~** они́ раздели́ли де́ньги ме́жду собо́й; *see also* **myself**.
then [ðɛn] *adv* пото́м; (*at that time*) тогда́ ♦ *conj* (*therefore*) тогда́ ♦ *adj*: **the ~ president** тогда́шний• президе́нт; **from ~ on** с тех пор; **by ~** (*past*) к э́тому *or* тому́ вре́мени; **we should know by ~** к тому́ вре́мени мы уже́ бу́дем знать; **if ... ~ ...** е́сли ... то ...; **before ~** до э́того *or* того́ вре́мени; **until ~** до тех пор; **and ~ what?** и что пото́м?; **what do you want me to do ~?** (*afterwards*) что Вы мне де́лать пото́м?; (*in that case*) что Вы мне де́лать тогда́?
theologian [θɪə'ləʊdʒən] *n* богосло́в, тео́лог.
theological [θɪə'lɒdʒɪkl] *adj* теологи́ческий•, богосло́вский.
theology [θɪ'ɒlədʒɪ] *n* теоло́гия, богосло́вие.
theorem ['θɪərəm] *n* теоре́ма.
theoretical [θɪə'rɛtɪkl] *adj* теорети́ческий•.
theorize ['θɪəraɪz] *vi* теоретизи́ровать (*impf*).
theory ['θɪərɪ] *n* тео́рия; **in ~** теорети́чески, в тео́рии.
therapeutic(al) [θɛrə'pjuːtɪk(l)] *adj* терапевт-и́ческий.
therapist ['θɛrəpɪst] *n* врач.
therapy ['θɛrəpɪ] *n* терапи́я.

KEYWORD

there [ðɛə'] *adv*: **1**: **there is some milk in the fridge** молоко́ в холоди́льнике; **there is someone in the room** в ко́мнате кто́-то есть; **there will be a lot of people at the concert** на конце́рте бу́дет мно́го наро́ду; **there was a book/there were flowers on the table** на столе́ лежа́ла кни́га/стоя́ли цветы́; **there has been an accident** произошла́ ава́рия
2 (*referring to place: position*) там; (: *motion*) туда́; **there he is!** вот он!:
3: **there, there** (*esp to child*) ну, ничего́, ничего́.

thereabouts ['ðɛərə'baʊts] *adv* (*place*) побли́зости; (*amount*) о́коло э́того.
thereafter [ðɛər'ɑːftə'] *adv* с того́ вре́мени.
thereby ['ðɛəbaɪ] *adv* таки́м о́бразом.
therefore ['ðɛəfɔː'] *adv* поэ́тому.
there's ['ðɛəz] = **there is, there has**.
thereupon [ðɛərə'pɒn] *adv* (*at that point*) вслед за тем; (*formal: on that subject*) в свя́зи с э́тим.
thermal ['θəːml] *adj* (*springs*) горя́чий•; (*energy*) терми́ческий•; (*underwear*) утеплённый•; (*paper, printer*) термографи́ческий.
thermodynamics ['θəːmədaɪ'næmɪks] *n* термодина́мика.
thermometer [θə'mɒmɪtə'] *n* термо́метр, гра́дусник.
thermonuclear ['θəːməʊ'njuːklɪə'] *adj* термоя́дерный.
Thermos® ['θəːməs] *n* (*also:* **~ flask**) те́рмос.
thermostat ['θəːməʊstæt] *n* термоста́т.
thesaurus [θɪ'sɔːrəs] *n* теза́урус.
these [ðiːz] *pl adj, pron* э́ти.
theses ['θiːsiːz] *npl of* **thesis**.
thesis ['θiːsɪs] (*pl* **theses**) *n* (*SCOL*) диссерта́ция; (*theory*) те́зис.
they [ðeɪ] *pron* они́; **~ say that ...** говоря́т, что ....
they'd [ðeɪd] = **they had, they would**.
they'll [ðeɪl] = **they shall, they will**.
they're [ðɛə'] = **they are**.
they've [ðeɪv] = **they have**.
thick [θɪk] *adj* (*in shape*) то́лстый (толст); (*in consistency*) густо́й (густ); (*inf: stupid*) тупо́й (туп) ♦ *n*: **in the ~ of the battle** в са́мой гу́ще би́твы; **the wall is 20 cm ~** толщина́ стены́ – 20 см.
thicken ['θɪkn] *vi* (*fog etc*) сгуща́ться (сгусти́ться• *perf*); (*plot*) усложня́ться (усложни́ться• *perf*) ♦ *vt* (*sauce etc*) де́лать (сде́лать *perf*) гу́ще.
thicket ['θɪkɪt] *n* за́росли *fpl*.
thickly ['θɪklɪ] *adv* (*spread*) гу́сто; (*cut*) то́лсто; **~ populated** густонаселённый.
thickness ['θɪknɪs] *n* (*size*) толщина́; (*layer*) слой•.
thickset [θɪk'sɛt] *adj* корена́стый (корена́ст).
thick-skinned [θɪk'skɪnd] *adj* (*fig*) толсто-

ко́жий*.

thief [θi:f] (*pl* **thieves**) *n* вор(о́вка).

thieves [θi:vz] *npl of* **thief**.

thieving ['θi:vɪŋ] *n* воровство́.

thigh [θaɪ] *n* бедро́*.

thighbone ['θaɪbəʊn] *n* (*ANAT*) бе́дренная кость* *f.*

thimble ['θɪmbl] *n* напёрсток*.

thin [θɪn] *adj* то́нкий* (то́нок); (*person, animal*) худо́й (худ); (*soup, sauce*) жи́дкий* (жи́док); (*hair, crowd*) ре́дкий*; (*fog*) лёгкий* (лёгок) ◆ *vt:* **to ~ (down)** (*sauce, paint*) разбавля́ть (разба́вить* *perf*); (*hair: at hairdresser's*) разре́живать (*impf*) ◆ *vi* (*fog*) рассе́иваться (рассе́яться *perf*); (*also:* **~ out:** *crowd*) реде́ть (пореде́ть *perf*); **his hair is ~ning** у него́ реде́ют во́лосы.

thing [θɪŋ] *n* вещь* *f;* **~s** *npl* (*belongings*) ве́щи* *fpl;* **first ~ (in the morning)** пе́рвым де́лом (с утра́); **last ~ (at night), he** ... напосле́док (но́чью) он ...; **the ~ is** ... де́ло в том, что ...; **for one ~** во-пе́рвых; **she's got a ~ about mice** она́ не выно́сит мыше́й; **don't worry about a ~** ни о чём не беспоко́йтесь; **you'll do no such ~!** попро́буй то́лько!; **poor ~** бедня́жка* *m/f;* **the best ~ would be to** ... са́мое лу́чшее бы́ло бы +*infin* ...; **how are ~s?** как дела́?

think [θɪŋk] (*pt,pp* **thought**) *vt* (*reflect, believe*) ду́мать (*impf*); (*imagine*) предполага́ть (предположи́ть* *perf*) ◆ *vi* ду́мать (поду́мать *perf*) о +*prp;* (*remember*) вспомина́ть (вспо́мнить *perf*); (*consider*) приводи́ть* (привести́* *perf*); **what did you ~ of them?** что Вы о них ду́маете?; **to ~ about sth/sb** ду́мать (поду́мать *perf*) о чём-н/ком-н; **I'll ~ about it** я поду́маю (об э́том); **I am ~ing of starting a business** я ду́маю нача́ть би́знес; **I ~ so/not** я ду́маю, что да/нет; **to ~ well of sb** хорошо́ о ком-н ду́мать (*impf*); **to ~ aloud** ду́мать (*impf*) вслух; **~ again!** поду́майте ещё раз!

▶ **think out** *vt* (*plan, solution*) обду́мывать (обду́мать *perf*), проду́мывать (проду́мать *perf*)

▶ **think over** *vt* обду́мывать (обду́мать *perf*); **I'd like to ~ things over** я хочу́ всё обду́мать

▶ **think through** *vt* проду́мывать (проду́мать *perf*) до конца́

▶ **think up** *vt* приду́мывать (приду́мать *perf*).

thinking ['θɪŋkɪŋ] *n* мышле́ние; **to my way of ~** на мой взгляд.

think-tank ['θɪŋktæŋk] *n* мозгово́й центр.

thinly ['θɪnlɪ] *adv* то́нко.

thinness ['θɪnnɪs] *n* то́нкость *f.*

third [θə:d] *adj* тре́тий* ◆ *n* (*fraction*) треть *f,* одна́ тре́ть *f adj;* (*AUT: also:* **~ gear**) тре́тья ско́рость *f;* (*BRIT: SCOL: degree*) дипло́м

тре́тьей и́ли ни́зшей сте́пени; **a ~ of** треть +*gen,* тре́тья часть +*gen; see also* **fifth.**

third-degree burns ['θə:ddɪgri:-] *npl* (*MED*) ожо́ги *mpl* тре́тьей сте́пени.

thirdly ['θə:dlɪ] *adv* в-тре́тьих.

third party insurance *n* (*BRIT*) страхова́ние в по́льзу тре́тьей стороны́.

third-rate ['θə:d'reɪt] *adj* (*pej: performance, actor etc*) третьесо́ртный* (третьесо́ртен).

Third World *n:* **the ~ ~** Тре́тий* мир.

thirst [θə:st] *n* (*also fig*) жа́жда.

thirsty ['θə:stɪ] *adj:* **to be ~** (*person, animal*) хоте́ть* (*impf*) пить; **I am ~** я хочу́ *or* мне хо́чется пить; **gardening is ~ work** рабо́та в саду́ вызыва́ет жа́жду.

thirteen [θə:'ti:n] *n* трина́дцать*; *see also* **five.**

thirteenth [θə:'ti:nθ] *adj* трина́дцатый; *see also* **fifth.**

thirtieth ['θə:tɪθ] *adj* тридца́тый; *see also* **fifth.**

thirty ['θə:tɪ] *n* три́дцать*; *see also* **fifty.**

KEYWORD

this [ðɪs] (*pl* **these**) *adj* (*demonstrative*) э́тот; **this man** э́тот мужчи́на; **which book would you like? – this one please** каку́ю кни́гу Вы хоти́те? – вот э́ту, пожа́луйста

◆ *pron* (*demonstrative*) э́тот (*f* э́та, *nt* э́то); **who/what is this?** кто/что э́то?; **this is where I live** вот здесь я живу́; **this is what he said** вот, что он сказа́л; **this is Mr Brown** э́то ми́стер Бра́ун

◆ *adv* (*demonstrative*): **this high/long** *etc* тако́й высоты́/длины́ *etc;* **the dog was about this big** соба́ка была́ приме́рно тако́го разме́ра *or* тако́й величины́; **we can't stop now we've gone this far** мы не мо́жет тепе́рь останови́ться, ведь мы так далеко́ ушли́.

---

thistle ['θɪsl] *n* чертополо́х.

thong [θɒŋ] *n* реме́нь* *m.*

thorn [θɔ:n] *n* шип, колю́чка*.

thorny ['θɔ:nɪ] *adj* (*plant, tree*) колю́чий* (колю́ч); (*problem*) нелёгкий*.

thorough ['θʌrə] *adj* (*search, wash*) тща́тельный* (тща́телен); (*knowledge, research*) основа́тельный* (основа́телен); (*person*) скрупулёзный* (скрупулёзен).

thoroughbred ['θʌrəbrɛd] *n* чистокро́вная *or* чистопоро́дная ло́шадь *f.*

thoroughfare ['θʌrəfɛə'] *n* гла́вная арте́рия (го́рода), тра́нспортная магистра́ль *f;* **"no ~"** (*BRIT*) "Прое́зда нет".

thoroughgoing ['θʌrəgəʊɪŋ] *adj* доскона́льный* (доскона́лен), тща́тельный* (тща́телен).

thoroughly ['θʌrəlɪ] *adv* (*fully*) тща́тельно; (*very*) вполне́; **he ~ agreed** он по́лностью согласи́лся.

thoroughness ['θʌrənɪs] *n* тща́тельность *f.*

---

those [ðəuz] *pl adj, pron* те.

though [ðəu] *conj* хотя ◆ *adv* впрочем, однако; **even ~** ... хотя и ...; **it's not easy, ~** впрочем *or* однако это не просто.

thought [θɔ:t] *pt, pp of* **think** ◆ *n* (*idea, intention*) мысль *f*; (*reflection*) размышление; (*opinion*) соображение; **after much ~** после долгих размышлений; **I've just had a ~** мне только что пришла в голову мысль; **to give sth some ~** обдумывать (обдумать *perf*) что-н.

thoughtful ['θɔ:tful] *adj* (*deep in thought*) задумчивый (задумчив); (*serious*) глубокий*; (*considerate*) внимательный* (внимателен).

thoughtfully ['θɔ:tfəlɪ] *adv* (*pensively*) задумчиво; (*considerately*) внимательно.

thoughtless ['θɔ:tlɪs] *adj* бездумный* (бездумен), неосмотрительный* (неосмотрителен).

thoughtlessly ['θɔ:tlɪslɪ] *adv* бездумно, неосмотрительно.

thoughtlessness ['θɔ:tlɪsnɪs] *n* бездумность *f*, неосмотрительность *f*.

thought-out [θɔ:t'aut] *adj* продуманный* (продуман).

thought-provoking ['θɔ:tprəvəukɪŋ] *adj* провоцирующий на мысли.

thousand ['θauzənd] *n* тысяча*; **two ~** две тысячи; **five ~** пять тысяч; **about a ~** около тысячи; **people came in their ~s** *or* **by the ~** пришли тысячи людей; **~s of** тысячи +*gen*.

thousandth ['θauzəntθ] *adj* тысячный.

thrash [θræʃ] *vt* (*beat*) пороть* (выпороть* *perf*); (*inf: defeat*) побивать (побить* *perf*).
► **thrash about** *vi* метаться* (*impf*)
► **thrash around** *vi* = **thrash about**
► **thrash out** *vt* (*problem*) прорабатывать (проработать *perf*).

thrashing ['θræʃɪŋ] *n*: **to give sb a ~** пороть* (выпороть* *perf*) кого-н.

thread [θrɛd] *n* (*yarn*) нить *f*, нитка*; (*of screw*) резьба ◆ *vt* (*needle*) продевать (продеть* *perf*) нитку в +*acc*; **to ~ one's way between** пробираться (пробраться* *perf*) через *or* сквозь +*acc*.

threadbare ['θrɛdbɛə'] *adj* потёртый (потёрт), потрёпанный* (потрёпан).

threat [θrɛt] *n* (*also fig*) угроза; **to be under ~ of** быть* (*impf*) под угрозой +*gen*.

threaten ['θrɛtn] *vi* (*storm, danger*) грозить* (*impf*) ◆ *vt*: **to ~ sb with** угрожать (*impf*) *or* грозить* (*impf*) кому-н +*instr*; **to ~ to do** угрожать (*impf*) *or* грозить* (*impf*) +*infin*.

threatening ['θrɛtnɪŋ] *adj* угрожающий*.

three [θri:] *n* три*; (*collective*) трое*; *see also* **five**.

three-dimensional [θri:dɪ'mɛnʃənl] *adj* (*object*) трёхмерный; (*film, picture, image*) стереоскопический.

threefold ['θri:fəuld] *adv*: **to increase ~** увеличиваться (увеличиться *perf*) в три раза.

three-piece suit ['θri:pi:s-] *n* (костюм)-тройка *m*.

three-piece suite *n* мягкая мебель *f*.

three-ply [θri:'plaɪ] *adj* трёхслойный.

three quarters *npl* три* четверти; **~ ~ full** полный* на три четверти.

three-wheeler (car) [θri:'wi:lə'(-)] *n* трехколёсная машина.

thresh [θrɛʃ] *vt* молотить* (*impf*).

threshing machine ['θrɛʃɪŋ-] *n* (*old*) молотилка*.

threshold ['θrɛʃhəuld] *n* (*also fig*) порог; **to be on the ~ of** (*fig*) быть* (*impf*) на пороге +*gen*.

threshold agreement *n* (*ECON*) *способ приведения в соответствие заработной платы работников со стоимостью жизни*.

threw [θru:] *pt of* **throw**.

thrift [θrɪft] *n* бережливость *f*.

thrifty ['θrɪftɪ] *adj* бережливый (бережлив).

thrill [θrɪl] *n* трепет ◆ *vi* трепетать* (*impf*) ◆ *vt* (*person, audience*) восхищать (восхитить* *perf*); **to be ~ed** быть* (*impf*) в восторге; **I am ~ed** я в восторге.

thriller ['θrɪlə'] *n* остросюжетный фильм, триллер.

thrilling ['θrɪlɪŋ] *adj* захватывающий*.

thrive [θraɪv] (*pt* **thrived** *or* **throve**, *pp* **thrived**) *vi* (*child, animal, business*) процветать (*impf*); (*plant*) разрастаться (разрастись* *perf*); **to ~ on sth** процветать (*impf*) на чём-н.

thriving ['θraɪvɪŋ] *adj* процветающий.

throat [θrəut] *n* горло; **I have a sore ~** у меня болит горло.

throb [θrɔb] *n* (*of heart*) биение; (*of wound*) пульсация; (*of engine*) вибрация ◆ *vi* (*heart*) биться* (*impf*); (*with pain: arm*) ныть* (*impf*); (*machine: vibrate*) вибрировать* (*impf*); **my head is ~bing** у меня гудит голова.

throes [θrəuz] *npl*: **in the ~ of** (*war, moving house etc*) в лихорадке +*gen*; **death ~** смертельные муки.

thrombosis [θrɔm'bəusɪs] *n* тромбоз.

throne [θrəun] *n* трон.

throng ['θrɔŋ] *n* толпа* ◆ *vt* заполнять (заполнить *perf*).

throttle ['θrɔtl] *n* (*AUT*) дроссель *m* ◆ *vt* (*strangle*) душить* (задушить* *perf*).

through [θru:] *prep* (*space*) через +*acc*; (*water etc*) в +*acc*; (*time*) в течение +*gen*; (*by means of*) через +*acc*, посредством +*gen*; (*owing to*) из-за +*gen* ◆ *adj* (*ticket, train*) прямой ◆ *adv* насквозь; **he is absent ~ illness** он отсутствовал по болезни; **(from) Monday ~ Friday** (*US*) с понедельника по пятницу; **to put sb ~ to sb** (*TEL*) соединять (соединить *perf*) кого-н с кем-н; **to be ~ with sb/sth** поканчивать (покончить *perf*) с кем-н/чем-н; **"no ~ road"** (*BRIT*) "нет сквозного проезда"; **"no ~ traffic"** (*US*) "нет сквозного

движе́ния"; **to let sb ~** пропуска́ть
(пропусти́ть* *perf*) кого́-н.
throughout [θru:'aut] *prep* (*place*) по +*dat*;
(*time*) в тече́ние +*gen* ♦ *adv* везде́, повсю́ду.
throughput ['θru:put] *n* пропускна́я
спосо́бность *f*; (*COMPUT*) производи́тель-
ность *f*.
throve [θrəuv] *pt of* **thrive**.
throw [θrəu] (*pt* **threw**, *pp* **thrown**) *n* бросо́к* ♦
vt (*object*) броса́ть (бро́сить* *perf*); (*rider*)
сбра́сывать (сбро́сить* *perf*); (*fig: person*)
сбива́ть (сбить* *perf*) с то́лку; (*pottery*)
обраба́тывать (обрабо́тать *perf*) на
гонча́рном кру́ге; **to ~ a party** устра́ивать
(устро́ить *perf*) ве́чер; **to ~ open** (*doors,
windows*) распа́хивать (распахну́ть *perf*);
(*competition, race etc*) открыва́ть (откры́ть*
perf)
► **throw about** *vt* (*litter etc*) разбра́сывать
(разброса́ть *perf*)
► **throw around** *vt* = **throw about**
► **throw away** *vt* (*rubbish*) выбра́сывать
(вы́бросить* *perf*); (*money*) броса́ть (*impf*) на
ве́тер
► **throw off** *vt* сбра́сывать (сбро́сить* *perf*)
► **throw out** *vt* (*rubbish, person*) выбра́сывать
(вы́бросить* *perf*); (*idea*) отверга́ть
(отве́ргнуть* *perf*)
► **throw together** *vt* (*clothes, meal etc*)
сооружа́ть (сооруди́ть* *perf*); (*essay*)
набра́сывать (наброса́ть *perf*)
► **throw up** *vi* (*vomit*) рвать* (вы́рвать* *perf*);
he threw up его́ вы́рвало.
throwaway ['θrəuəweɪ] *adj* (*toothbrush etc*)
одноразовый; (*line, remark*) ска́занный
невзнача́й.
throwback ['θrəubæk] *n*: **it's a ~ to** э́то возвра́т
к +*dat*.
throw-in ['θrəuɪn] *n* (*FOOTBALL*) вбра́сывание.
thrown [θrəun] *pp of* **throw**.
thru [θru:] (*US*) = **through**.
thrush [θrʌʃ] *n* (*ZOOL*) дрозд*; (*MED*)
моло́чница.
thrust [θrʌst] (*pt, pp* **thrust**) *n* (*TECH*) дви́жущая
си́ла; (*push*) толчо́к*; (*main idea*)
направле́ние ♦ *vt* толка́ть (толкну́ть *perf*).
thud [θʌd] *n* глухо́й стук.
thug [θʌg] *n* (*criminal*) головоре́з*; (*pej*)
банди́т.
thumb [θʌm] *n* (*ANAT*) большо́й па́лец* (*руки́*)
♦ *vt*: **to ~ a lift** (*inf*) голосова́ть* (*impf*); **to give
sb/sth the ~s up** (*approve*) одобря́ть
(одо́брить *perf*) кого́-н/что-н; **to give sth the
~s down** отверга́ть (отве́ргнуть *perf*) что-н
► **thumb through** *vt fus* перели́стывать
(перелиста́ть *perf*).
thumb index *n* бу́квенный указа́тель *m* (*на
обре́зе кни́ги*).

thumbnail ['θʌmneɪl] *n* но́готь* *m* (*большо́го
па́льца руки́*).
thumbnail sketch *n* набро́сок*.
thumbtack ['θʌmtæk] *n* (*US*) кно́пка*.
thump [θʌmp] *n* (*blow*) уда́р; (*sound*) глухо́й
стук ♦ *vt* (*person*) сту́кнуть (*perf*) ♦ *vi* (*heart
etc*) стуча́ть (*impf*).
thumping ['θʌmpɪŋ] *adj* (*inf: majority, victory
etc*) грома́дный; (: *headache, cold*) жу́ткий*.
thunder ['θʌndə'] *n* гром ♦ *vi* (*shout*) реве́ть
(*impf*); (*train etc*): **to ~ past** громыха́ть
(прогромыха́ть *perf*) ми́мо; **it's ~ing** греми́т
гром.
thunderbolt ['θʌndəbəult] *n* уда́р мо́лнии.
thunderclap ['θʌndəklæp] *n* раска́т гро́ма.
thunderous ['θʌndrəs] *adj* (*applause*)
оглуши́тельный; (*crash*) громово́й.
thunderstorm ['θʌndəstɔ:m] *n* гроза́*.
thunderstruck ['θʌndəstrʌk] *adj* (*fig*): **I was ~** я
был потрясён.
thundery ['θʌndərɪ] *adj* грозово́й.
Thur(s). *abbr* = **Thursday**.
Thursday ['θə:zdɪ] *n* четве́рг*; *see also* **Tuesday**.
thus [ðʌs] *adv* таки́м о́бразом.
thwart [θwɔ:t] *vt* (*person*) чини́ть (*impf*)
препя́тствия +*dat*; (*plans*) расстра́ивать
(расстро́ить *perf*).
thyme [taɪm] *n* тимья́н.
thyroid ['θaɪrɔɪd] *n* (*also*: ~ **gland**) щитови́дная
железа́.
tiara [tɪ'ɑ:rə] *n* тиа́ра.
Tiber ['taɪbə'] *n*: **the ~** Тибр.
Tibet [tɪ'bet] *n* Тибе́т.
Tibetan [tɪ'betən] *adj* тибе́тский* ♦ *n*
тибе́тец*(-е́тка*); (*LING*) тибе́тский* язы́к*.
tibia ['tɪbɪə] *n* большеберцо́вая кость* *f*.
tic [tɪk] *n* тик.
tick [tɪk] *n* (*sound: of clock*) ти́канье; (*mark*)
га́лочка*; (*ZOOL*) клещ* *m*; (*clock*) ти́кать
(*impf*) ♦ *vt* отмеча́ть (отме́тить* *perf*)
га́лочкой; **to put a ~ against sth** ста́вить* (по-
ста́вить* *perf*) га́лочку ря́дом с чем-н; **in a ~**
(*BRIT: inf*) мину́точку; **to buy sth on ~** (*BRIT:
inf*) покупа́ть (купи́ть* *perf*) что-н в креди́т
► **tick off** *vt* (*item on list*) отмеча́ть (отме́тить*
perf) га́лочкой; (*person*) отчи́тывать
(отчита́ть *perf*)
► **tick over** *vi* (*engine*) рабо́тать (*impf*) на
холосто́м ходу́; (*fig: business*) идти́* (*impf*)
свои́м чередо́м.
ticker tape ['tɪkəteɪp] *n* ти́керная ле́нта, ти́кер;
(*US: in celebrations*) *серпанти́н из ти́керной
ле́нты*.
ticket ['tɪkɪt] *n* биле́т; (*price tag*) этике́тка*;
(*from cash register*) чек; (*also*: **parking ~**)
штраф за наруше́ние пра́вил паркова́ния;
(*US: POL*) спи́сок* кандида́тов па́ртии.
ticket agency *n* (*THEAT*) театра́льная ка́сса.

---

* marks translations which have irregular inflections. The Russian-English side of the dictionary gives inflectional information.

ticket collector *n* контролёр.
ticket holder *n* владе́лец(-лица) биле́та.
ticket inspector *n* контролёр.
ticket office *n* биле́тная ка́сса.
tickle ['tɪkl] *vt* щекота́ть* (пощекота́ть* *perf*) ◆ *vi* щекота́ть* (*impf*).
ticklish ['tɪklɪʃ] *adj* (*problem*) щекотли́вый (щекотли́в); (*blanket*) колю́чий* (колю́ч); (*cough*) перша́щий; (*person*): **to be ~** боя́ться* (*impf*) щеко́тки.
tidal ['taɪdl] *adj* (*force*) прили́вный; (*estuary*) прили́вно-отли́вный.
tidal wave *n* прили́вная волна́*.
tidbit ['tɪdbɪt] *n* (*US*) = **titbit**.
tiddlywinks ['tɪdlɪwɪŋks] *n* бло́шки *pl*.
tide [taɪd] *n* прили́в и отли́в; (*fig: of events*) волна́; (*of fashion, opinion*) направле́ние; **high ~** по́лная вода́*, вы́сшая то́чка прили́ва; **low ~** ма́лая вода́*, ни́зшая то́чка отли́ва
▶ **tide over** *vt* (*help out*): **this money will ~ me over till Monday** на э́ти де́ньги я смогу́ продержа́ться до понеде́льника.
tidily ['taɪdɪlɪ] *adv* (*dress*) опря́тно; (*arrange*) аккура́тно.
tidiness ['taɪdɪnɪs] *n* опря́тность *f*; (*of person*) аккура́тность *f*.
tidy ['taɪdɪ] *adj* опря́тный* (опря́тен); (*person, mind*) аккура́тный* (аккура́тен) ◆ *vt* (*also: ~ up*) прибира́ть (прибра́ть* *perf*); **to ~ o.s. up** приводи́ть* (привести́* *perf*) себя́ в поря́док.
tie [taɪ] *n* (*string etc*) шнуро́к*; (*BRIT: also: necktie*) га́лстук; (*fig: link*) связь *f*; (*SPORT: game, match*) игра́ вничью́; (*: draw*) ничья́; (*US: RAIL*) шпа́ла ◆ *vt* завя́зывать (завяза́ть* *perf*) ◆ *vi* (*SPORT etc*) игра́ть (сыгра́ть* *perf*) вничью́; **"black/white ~"** *пара́дный костю́м*; **family ~s** семе́йные у́зы; **to ~ sth in a bow** завя́зывать (завяза́ть* *perf*) что-н ба́нтом; **to ~ a knot in sth** завя́зывать (завяза́ть* *perf*) что-н узло́м
▶ **tie down** *vt* (*fig: person*) свя́зывать (связа́ть* *perf*)
▶ **tie in** *vi*: **to ~ in with** (*correspond*) увя́зываться (*impf*) с +*instr*
▶ **tie on** *vt* (*BRIT: label etc*) привя́зывать (привяза́ть* *perf*)
▶ **tie up** *vt* (*dog, boat*) привя́зывать (привяза́ть* *perf*); (*prisoner, parcel*) свя́зывать (связа́ть* *perf*); (*arrangements*) организова́ть (*impf/perf*); **I'm ~d up at the moment** (*busy*) я сейча́с о́чень за́нят.
tie-break ['taɪbreɪk] *n* (*TENNIS*) *реша́ющий гейм по́сле ниче́йного сче́та*; (*in quiz*) дополни́тельный реша́ющий* вопро́с.
tiebreaker ['taɪbreɪkə'] *n* = **tie-break**.
tie-on ['taɪɔn] *adj* (*BRIT: label*) привязно́й.
tiepin ['taɪpɪn] *n* (*BRIT*) була́вка* для га́лстука.
tier [tɪə'] *n* (*of stadium etc*) я́рус; (*of cake*) слой*.
Tierra del Fuego [tɪ'ɛrədɛl'fweɪgəu] *n* О́гненная Земля́*.

tie tack *n* (*US*) = **tiepin**.
tiff [tɪf] *n* размо́лвка*.
tiger ['taɪgə'] *n* тигр.
tight [taɪt] *adj* (*firm: rope*) туго́й; (*narrow: shoes, bend, clothes*) у́зкий* (у́зок); (*strict: security*) стро́гий*; (*schedule, budget*) жёсткий* ◆ *adv* (*hold, squeeze*) кре́пко; (*shut*) пло́тно; **money is ~** у меня́ ту́го с деньга́ми; **he is ~** (*inf: drunk*) он навеселе́; **the suitcase is packed ~** чемода́н ту́го наби́т; **everybody hold ~!** все держи́тесь кре́пко!
tighten ['taɪtn] *vt* (*rope*) натя́гивать (натяну́ть* *perf*); (*screw*) подтя́гивать (подтяну́ть* *perf*); (*grip*) кре́пче сжима́ть (сжать* *perf*); (*security*) уси́ливать (уси́лить* *perf*) ◆ *vi* (*grip*) кре́пче сжима́ться (сжа́ться* *perf*); (*rope*) натя́гиваться (натяну́ться* *perf*).
tightfisted [taɪt'fɪstɪd] *adj* прижи́мистый (прижи́мист).
tight-lipped ['taɪt'lɪpd] *adj* скры́тный* (скры́тен); (*fig: through anger*) с поджа́тыми губа́ми.
tightly ['taɪtlɪ] *adv* (*grasp*) кре́пко.
tightrope ['taɪtrəup] *n* натя́нутый кана́т; **to be on** *or* **walking a ~** (*fig*) ходи́ть* (*impf*) по острию́ ножа́.
tightrope walker *n* канатохо́дец*.
tights [taɪts] *npl* (*BRIT*) колго́тки* *pl*.
tigress ['taɪgrɪs] *n* тигри́ца.
tilde ['tɪldə] *n* (*LING*) ти́льда.
tile [taɪl] *n* (*on floor*) черепи́ца; (*on wall*) ка́фельная пли́тка* ◆ *vt*: **to ~ the floor/bathroom** выкла́дывать (вы́ложить* *perf*) пол/ва́нную пли́ткой; **~s** (*on wall*) ка́фель *m*; **to ~ the roof** крыть* (покры́ть* *perf*) кры́шу черепи́цей.
tiled [taɪld] *adj* (*see n*) черепи́чный; пли́точный; ка́фельный.
till [tɪl] *n* (*in shop etc*) ка́сса ◆ *vt* (*land*) возде́лывать (возде́лать* *perf*) ◆ *prep, conj* = **until**.
tiller ['tɪlə'] *n* (*NAUT*) ру́мпель *m*.
tilt [tɪlt] *vt* наклоня́ть (наклони́ть* *perf*); (*head*) склоня́ть (склони́ть* *perf*) ◆ *vi* наклоня́ться (наклони́ться* *perf*) ◆ *n* (*slope*) накло́н; **to wear one's hat at a ~** носи́ть* (*impf*) шля́пу набекре́нь; **(at) full ~** во весь дух.
timber ['tɪmbə'] *n* (*material*) древеси́на; (*trees*) лес.
time [taɪm] *n* вре́мя* *nt*; (*epoch: often pl*) времена́* *pl*, вре́мя*; (*occasion, also MATH*) раз; (*MUS*) разме́р, темп ◆ *vt* (*measure time of: race etc*) засека́ть (засе́чь* *perf*) вре́мя +*gen*; (*fix moment for: visit etc*) выбира́ть (вы́брать* *perf*) вре́мя для +*gen*; **a long ~** до́лго; **for the ~ being** пока́; **4 at a ~** по четы́ре; **from ~ to ~** вре́мя от вре́мени; **~ after ~, time and again** сно́ва и сно́ва; **at ~s** времена́ми; **in ~** (*eventually*) со вре́менем; (*MUS: be*) в та́кте; (*: play*) в такт; **in a week's ~** че́рез неде́лю; **in no ~** в два счёта; **any ~** в любо́е вре́мя; **on ~** во́время;

to be 30 mins behind/ahead of ~ опа́здывать
(опозда́ть *perf*)/опережа́ть (опереди́ть* *perf*)
на 30 мину́т; **by the** ~ **he arrived** к тому́
вре́мени, когда́ он пришёл; **five** ~**s five**
пя́тью пять; **what** ~ **is it?** кото́рый час?; **to
have a good** ~ хорошо́ проводи́ть*
(провести́* *perf*) вре́мя; **we had a hard** ~ нам
бы́ло о́чень тяжело́; ~**'s up!** вре́мя истекло́!;
I've no ~ **for it** (*fig*) меня́ э́то не интересу́ет;
he'll do it in his own (good) ~ (*without being
hurried*) он сде́лает э́то не торопя́сь; **he'll do
it in** *or* (*US*) **on his own** (*out of working hours*)
он сде́лает э́то в свобо́дное (в нерабо́чее)
вре́мя*; **to be behind the** ~**s** отстава́ть*
(отста́ть* *perf*) от вре́мени; **to** ~ **sth well/
badly** выбира́ть (вы́брать* *perf*) подходя́щее/
неподходя́щее вре́мя для чего́-н; **the bomb
was** ~**d to go off 5 minutes later** часово́й
механи́зм бо́мбы до́лжен был срабо́тать
че́рез 5 мину́т.
time and motion study *n* ана́лиз
эффекти́вности рабо́ты.
time bomb *n* бо́мба с часовы́м механи́змом;
(*fig*) бо́мба заме́дленного де́йствия.
timecard ['taɪmkɑːd] *n* хронока́рта.
time clock *n* (*in factory etc*) часы́-та́бель *m*.
time-consuming ['taɪmkənsjuːmɪŋ] *adj*
отнима́ющий мно́го вре́мени.
time difference *n* ра́зница во вре́мени.
time frame *n*: **within a broad/narrow** ~ ~ в
тече́ние продолжи́тельного/коро́ткого
отре́зка вре́мени.
time-honoured ['taɪmɔnəd] (*US* **time-honored**)
adj освящённый века́ми.
timekeeper ['taɪmkiːpə^r] *n* судья́*-
хронометри́ст; **she's a very good** ~ она́
о́чень пунктуа́льная.
time-lag ['taɪmlæg] *n* (*BRIT*) (временно́й)
промежу́ток вре́мени.
timeless ['taɪmlɪs] *adj* ве́чный* (ве́чен).
time limit *n* преде́льный срок.
timely ['taɪmlɪ] *adj* своевре́менный*
(своевре́менен).
time off *n* свобо́дное вре́мя* *nt*.
timer ['taɪmə^r] *n* (*time switch*) та́ймер.
timesaving ['taɪmseɪvɪŋ] *adj* (*gadget, method
etc*) эконо́мящий вре́мя.
timescale ['taɪmskeɪl] *n* (*BRIT*) вре́мя* *nt*,
пери́од вре́мени.
time-share ['taɪmʃɛə^r] *n* жильё в куро́ртной
зо́не, находя́щееся в совме́стном владе́нии
не́скольких лиц.
time sharing *n* (*COMPUT*) разделе́ние вре́мени,
режи́м разделе́ния вре́мени.
time sheet *n* = **timecard**.
time signal *n* (*RADIO*) сигна́л вре́мени.
time switch *n* та́ймер, выключа́тель *m* с
часовы́м механи́змом.

timetable ['taɪmteɪbl] *n* расписа́ние.
time zone *n* часово́й по́яс*.
timid ['tɪmɪd] *adj* ро́бкий* (ро́бок).
timidity [tɪ'mɪdɪtɪ] *n* ро́бость *f*.
timing ['taɪmɪŋ] *n* (*SPORT*) хронометра́ж; **the** ~
of his resignation was unfortunate вы́бор
вре́мени его́ отста́вки был неуда́чен.
timing device *n* (*on bomb*) часово́й
механи́зм.
timpani ['tɪmpəni] *npl* лита́вры *fpl*.
tin [tɪn] *n* (*material*) о́лово; (*also:* ~ **plate**) бе́лая
жесть *f*; (*container*) (жестяна́я) ба́нка*; (: *for
baking*) про́тивень* *m*; (: *BRIT*: **can**)
консе́рвная ба́нка*; **we'll need 2** ~**s of paint**
(*quantity*) нам ну́жно бу́дет 2 ба́нки кра́ски.
tinfoil ['tɪnfɔɪl] *n* фольга́.
tinge [tɪndʒ] *n* отте́нок* ♦ *vt*: ~**d with** с
отте́нком +*gen*.
tingle ['tɪŋgl] *vi* пока́лывать (*impf*); **I was
tingling with excitement** я горе́л от
возбужде́ния.
tinker ['tɪŋkə^r] *n* (*gipsy*) бродя́чий луди́льщик
► **tinker with** *vt fus* вози́ться* (*impf*) с +*instr*.
tinkle ['tɪŋkl] *vi* звя́кать (звя́кнуть *perf*) ♦ *n*
(*inf*): **to give sb a** ~ (*TEL*) звя́кнуть (*perf*)
кому́-н.
tin mine *n* оловя́нный рудни́к*.
tinned [tɪnd] *adj* (*BRIT*) консерви́рованный.
tinnitus ['tɪnɪtəs] *n* звон в уша́х.
tinny ['tɪnɪ] *adj* (*pej: sound*) металли́ческий*;
(: *car etc*) как консе́рвная ба́нка.
tin-opener ['tɪnəupnə^r] *n* (*BRIT*) консе́рвный
нож*.
tinsel ['tɪnsl] *n* мишура́.
tint [tɪnt] *n* отте́нок*; (*for hair*) кра́ска ♦ *vt* (*hair*)
кра́сить* (покра́сить* *perf*).
tinted ['tɪntɪd] *adj* (*hair*) кра́шеный; (*spectacles,
glass*) ды́мчатый.
tiny ['taɪnɪ] *adj* кро́шечный* (кро́шечен).
tip [tɪp] *n* (*of pen etc*) ко́нчик; (*on umbrella etc*)
наконе́чник; (*gratuity*) чаевы́е *pl adj*; (*BRIT*: *for
rubbish*) сва́лка*; (: *for coal*) гора́*; (*advice*)
сове́т ♦ *vt* (*waiter*) дава́ть* (дать* *perf*) на чай
+*dat*; (*tilt*) наклоня́ть (наклони́ть* *perf*); (*also:*
~ **over**) опроки́дывать (опроки́нуть *perf*);
(*also:* ~ **out**) выва́ливать (вы́валить *perf*);
(*winner etc*) уга́дывать (угада́ть *perf*); (*for a
job etc*) про́чить (*impf*); **he** ~**ped out the
contents of the box** он вы́валил содержи́мое
я́щика
► **tip off** *vt* предупрежда́ть (предупреди́ть*
perf).
tip-off ['tɪpɔf] *n* предупрежде́ние.
tipped [tɪpt] *adj* (*BRIT*: *cigarette*) с фи́льтром;
steel-~ со стальны́м наконе́чником.
Tipp-Ex® ['tɪpɛks] *n* ≈ штрих®, Ти́пекс.
tipple ['tɪpl] (*BRIT*) *vi* выпива́ть (*impf*) ♦ *n*: **to
have a** ~ выпива́ть (вы́пить* *perf*) по

ма́ленькой.

tipster ['tɪpstə'] *n* жучо́к* (*на ска́чках*).

tipsy ['tɪpsɪ] *adj* (*inf*) хмельно́й* (хмелён).

tiptoe ['tɪptəu] *n*: **on** ~ на цы́почках.

tiptop ['tɪptɔp] *adj*: **in** ~ **condition** в прекра́сном состоя́нии.

tirade [taɪ'reɪd] *n* тира́да.

Tirana [tɪ'rɑːnə] *n* Тира́на.

tire ['taɪə'] *n* (*US*) = **tyre** ♦ *vt* (*make tired*) утомля́ть (утоми́ть* *perf*) ♦ *vi* устава́ть* (уста́ть* *perf*)

▶ **tire out** *vt* (*exhaust*) выма́тывать (вы́мотать *perf*).

tired ['taɪəd] *adj* уста́лый (уста́л); **I am** ~ я уста́л; **he feels** ~ он чу́вствует себя́ уста́вшим; **you look** ~ Вы вы́глядите уста́лым; **to be** ~ **of sth** устава́ть* (уста́ть* *perf*) от чего́-н.

tiredness ['taɪədnɪs] *n* уста́лость *f*.

tireless ['taɪəlɪs] *adj* (*worker, efforts*) неутоми́мый (неутоми́м).

tiresome ['taɪəsəm] *adj* надое́дливый (надое́длив).

tiring ['taɪərɪŋ] *adj* утоми́тельный* (утоми́телен).

tissue ['tɪʃuː] *n* (*handkerchief*) бума́жная салфе́тка*; (*ANAT, BIO*) ткань *f*.

tissue paper *n* папиро́сная *or* то́нкая обёрточная бума́га.

tit [tɪt] *n* (*ZOOL*) сини́ца; (*inf: breast*) си́ська*; **to give** ~ **for tat** отпла́чивать (отплати́ть* *perf*) зуб за зуб.

titanium [tɪ'teɪnɪəm] *n* тита́н.

titbit ['tɪtbɪt] (*US* **tidbit**) *n* (*food*) ла́комый кусо́чек*; (*news*) пика́нтная но́вость* *f*.

titillate ['tɪtɪleɪt] *vt* (*person, senses*) возбужда́ть (возбуди́ть* *perf*).

titivate ['tɪtɪveɪt] *vt* (*oneself*) прихора́шиваться (*impf*); (*place*) украша́ть (украси́ть* *perf*).

title ['taɪtl] *n* (*of book, play etc*) назва́ние; (*rank, BOXING etc*) ти́тул; (*LAW*): ~ **to** пра́во* на +*acc*.

title deed *n* (*LAW*) докуме́нт, подтвержда́ющий пра́во со́бственности.

title page *n* ти́тульный лист*.

title role *n* (*in play, film*) гла́вная роль *f*.

title track *n* назва́ние пе́сни или музыка́льной пье́сы, кото́рое та́кже явля́ется назва́нием пласти́нки, альбо́ма, плёнки *итп*.

titter ['tɪtə'] *vi* хихи́кать (хихи́кнуть *perf*).

tittle-tattle ['tɪtltætl] *n* (*inf*) болтовня́.

tizzy ['tɪzɪ] *n*: **to be in a** ~ волнова́ться (разволнова́ться *perf*) по пустяка́м.

T-junction ['tiː'dʒʌŋkʃən] *n* (*AUT*) Т-обра́зный перекрёсток*.

TM *abbr* = **trademark, transcendental meditation**.

TN *abbr* (*US: POST*) = **Tennessee**.

TNT *n abbr* (= *trinitrotoluene*) троти́л.

┌─────────────┐
│ **KEYWORD** │
└─────────────┘

to [tuː] *prep* **1** (*direction*) в/на +*acc*; **to drive to school/the station** е́хать*/е́здить* (пое́хать*

perf) в шко́лу/на ста́нцию; **the road to Edinburgh** доро́га в Эдинбу́рг; **to the left** нале́во; **to the right** напра́во

2 (*as far as*) до +*gen*; **from Paris to London** от Пари́жа до Ло́ндона; **to count to ten** счита́ть (посчита́ть *perf*) до десяти́

3 (*with expressions of time*): **a quarter to five** без че́тверти пять

4 (*for, of*): **a letter to his wife** письмо́ жене́; **the key to the front door** ключ от входно́й две́ри; **she is secretary to the director** она́ секрета́рь дире́ктора

5 (*expressing indirect object*): **to give sth to sb** дава́ть* (дать* *perf*) что-н кому́-н; **to talk to sb** разгова́ривать (*impf*) *or* говори́ть (*impf*) с кем-н; **what have you done to your hair?** что Вы сде́лали с свои́ми волоса́ми

6 (*in relation to*) к +*dat*; **A is to B as C is to D** "А" отно́сится к "Б", как "В" отно́сится к "Г"; **three goals to two** три два; **X miles to the gallon** Х ли́тров на киломе́тр; **1500 roubles to the dollar** 1500 рубле́й за до́ллар

7 (*purpose, result*) к +*dat*; **to my surprise** к моему́ удивле́нию; **to come to sb's aid** приходи́ть* (прийти́* *perf*) кому́-н на по́мощь

♦ *with vb* **1** *перево́дится неопределённой фо́рмой глаго́ла*; **to want/try to do** хоте́ть* (захоте́ть* *perf*)/пыта́ться (попыта́ться *perf*) +*infin*; **he has nothing to lose** ему́ не́чего теря́ть; **ready to use** гото́в к употребле́нию; **too old/young to ...** сли́шком стар/мо́лод, что́бы +*infin* ...

2 (*with vb omitted*): **I don't want to** я не хочу́; **I don't feel like going – you really ought to** мне не хо́чется идти́ – нет, Вы должны́

3 (*purpose, result*) что́бы +*infin*; **I did it to help you** я сде́лал э́то, что́бы помо́чь Вам

♦ *adv*: **push/pull the door to** закрыва́ть (закры́ть* *perf*) дверь.

toad [təud] *n* (*ZOOL*) жа́ба.

toadstool ['təudstuːl] *n* (*BOT*) пога́нка*.

toady ['təudɪ] *vi* (*pej*): **to** ~ **to sb** подхали́мничать (*impf*) пе́ред кем-н.

toast [təust] *n* (*CULIN*) тост; (*drink, speech*) тост ♦ *vt* (*CULIN: bread etc*) поджа́ривать (поджа́рить *perf*); (*drink to*) пить* (вы́пить* *perf*) за +*acc*; **a piece** *or* **slice of** ~ ло́мтик то́ста.

toaster ['təustə'] *n* то́стер.

toastmaster ['təustmɑːstə'] *n* тамада́ *m*.

toast rack *n* подста́вка для то́стов.

tobacco [tə'bækəu] *n* таба́к*; **pipe** ~ тру́бочный таба́к*.

tobacconist [tə'bækənɪst] *n* торго́вец*(-вка*) таба́чными изде́лиями.

tobacconist's (shop) [tə'bækənɪsts-] *n* таба́чная ла́вка.

Tobago [tə'beɪgəu] *n see* **Trinidad**.

toboggan [tə'bɔgən] *n* (*child's*) са́нки *pl*.

today [tə'deɪ] *adv*, *n* сегодня; **what day is it** ~? какой сегодня день?; **what date is it** ~? какое сегодня число?; ~ **is the 4th of March** сегодня 4-ое марта; **a week ago** ~ ровно неделю назад.

toddle ['tɔdl] (*inf*) *vi*: **to** ~ **in** проковылять (*perf*); **to** ~ **along** *or* **off** приковылять (*impf*).

toddler ['tɔdlə'] *n* малыш*.

to-do [tə'du:] *n* (*fuss*) шум.

toe [təu] *n* (*of foot*) палец* (*ноги*); (*of shoe, sock*) носок*; **to** ~ **the line** (*fig*) подчиняться (*impf*) официальной линии; **big** ~ большой палец* (*ноги*); **little** ~ мизинец* (*ноги*).

TOEFL *n abbr* = *Teaching of English as a Foreign Language.*

toehold ['təuhəuld] *n* (*in climbing*) точка опоры; (*fig*): **to get** *or* **gain a** ~ находить* (найти* *perf*) точку опоры.

toenail ['təuneɪl] *n* ноготь* *m* (*на пальце ноги*).

toffee ['tɔfɪ] *n* ириска*, тянучка*.

toffee apple *n* (*BRIT*) яблоко на палочке, глазированное ирисом.

toga ['təugə] *n* тога.

together [tə'gɛðə'] *adv* вместе; (*at same time*) одновременно; ~ **with** вместе с +*instr*.

togetherness [tə'gɛðənɪs] *n* близость *f*.

toggle switch ['tɔgl-] *n* (*COMPUT*) тумблер, переключатель *m*.

Togo ['təugəu] *n* Того *m ind*.

togs [tɔgz] *npl* (*inf*: *clothes*) одежды *fpl*.

toil [tɔɪl] *n* тяжёлый труд* ♦ *vi* работать (*impf*) в поте лица.

toilet ['tɔɪlət] *n* унитаз; (*BRIT*: *room*) туалет ♦ *cpd* (*kit, accessories etc*) туалетный; **to go to the** ~ ходить* (сходить* *perf*) в туалет.

toilet bag *n* (*BRIT*) туалетная сумочка.

toilet bowl *n* унитаз.

toilet paper *n* туалетная бумага.

toiletries ['tɔɪlətrɪz] *npl* туалетные принадлежности *fpl*.

toilet roll *n* рулон туалетной бумаги.

toilet soap *n* туалетное мыло.

toilet water *n* туалетная вода.

toing and froing ['tu:ɪŋən'frəuɪŋ] *n* (*BRIT*: *on foot*) ходьба туда-обратно; (: *by transport*) езда туда-обратно.

token ['təukən] *n* (*sign, souvenir*) знак; (*substitute coin*) жетон ♦ *adj* (*strike, payment etc*) символический*; **by the same** ~ (*fig*) по той же причине; **book/gift** ~ (*BRIT*) книжный/подарочный талон; **record** ~ (*BRIT*) талон на пластинку.

tokenism ['təukənɪzəm] *n* видимость *f*.

Tokyo ['tɔkjəu] *n* Токио *m ind*.

told [təuld] *pt*, *pp of* **tell**.

tolerable ['tɔlərəbl] *adj* (*bearable*) терпимый (терпим); (*fairly good*) сносный* (сносен).

tolerably ['tɔlərəblɪ] *adv*: ~ **good** довольно

хорошо.

tolerance ['tɔlərns] *n* (*patience*) терпимость *f*; (*also TECH*) допуск.

tolerant ['tɔlərnt] *adj*: ~ (*of*) терпимый (терпим) (к +*dat*).

tolerate ['tɔləreɪt] *vt* терпеть* (*impf*).

toleration [tɔlə'reɪʃən] *n* терпимость *f*.

toll [təul] *n* (*of casualties, deaths*) число; (*tax, charge*) плата ♦ *vi* (*bell*) звонить (*impf*); **the accident** ~ **on the roads** число жертв на дорогах.

toll bridge *n* (*AUT*) платный мост*.

toll call *n* (*US*) междугородный телефонный звонок*.

toll-free [təul'fri:] *adj* (*US*) бесплатный.

toll road *n* (*AUT*) платная дорога.

tomato [tə'mɑ:təu] (*pl* ~**es**) *n* помидор.

tomato purée *n* томатная паста.

tomb [tu:m] *n* склеп, гробница.

tombola [tɔm'bəulə] *n* лотерея.

tomboy ['tɔmbɔɪ] *n* (*girl*) сорванец*.

tombstone ['tu:mstəun] *n* надгробная плита*.

tomcat ['tɔmkæt] *n* кот*.

tome [təum] *n* том*.

tomorrow [tə'mɔrəu] *adv*, *n* (*also fig*) завтра; **the day after** ~ послезавтра; **a week** ~/**on Monday** через неделю, считая с завтрашнего дня/с понедельника; ~ **morning** завтра утром.

ton [tʌn] *n* (*BRIT*) длинная тонна; (*US*: *also*: **short** ~) короткая тонна; (*also*: **metric** ~) метрическая тонна; (*NAUT*: *also*: **register** ~) регистровая тонна; ~**s of** (*inf*) тонны +*gen*.

tonal ['təunl] *adj* тональный.

tone [təun] *n* тон*; (*TEL*) гудок* ♦ *vi* (*colours*: *also*: ~ **in**) сочетаться (*impf*)

▶ **tone down** *vt* (*colour, criticism, demands*) смягчать (смягчить* *perf*); (*sound*) уменьшать (уменьшить *perf*)

▶ **tone up** *vt* (*muscles*) укреплять (укрепить* *perf*).

tone-deaf [təun'dɛf] *adj* без слуха.

toner ['təunə'] *n* (*for photocopier*) чернила.

Tonga [tɔŋə] *n* Тонга.

tongs [tɔŋz] *npl* щипцы *pl*.

tongue [tʌŋ] *n* язык*; ~ **in cheek** (*speak, say*) в шутку.

tongue-tied ['tʌŋtaɪd] *adj* (*fig*): **he was** ~ он лишился дара речи.

tongue twister [-twɪstə'] *n* скороговорка.

tonic ['tɔnɪk] *n* (*MED*) тонизирующее средство; (*also*: ~ **water**) тоник; (*MUS*) тоника.

tonight [tə'naɪt] *adv* (*this evening*) сегодня вечером; (*this night*) сегодня ночью ♦ *n* (*see adv*) сегодняшний вечер; сегодняшняя ночь *f*; (**I'll**) **see you** ~! до вечера!

tonnage ['tʌnɪdʒ] *n* (*NAUT*) тоннаж.

tonne [tʌn] *n* (*BRIT*: *metric ton*) тонна.

---

* marks translations which have irregular inflections. The Russian-English side of the dictionary gives inflectional information.

tonsil ['tɒnsl] *n* (*gen pl*) минда́лина; **to have one's ~s out** удаля́ть (удали́ть *perf*) минда́лины.

tonsillitis [tɒnsɪ'laɪtɪs] *n* тонзилли́т.

too [tu:] *adv* (*excessively*) сли́шком; (*also: referring to subject*) та́кже, то́же; (: *referring to object*) та́кже; **the tea is ~ sweet** чай сли́шком сла́дкий; **I went ~** я то́же пошёл; **~ much, ~ many** сли́шком мно́го; **~ bad!** о́чень жаль!

took [tuk] *pt of* **take**.

tool [tu:l] *n* инструме́нт; (*fig: person*) ору́дие.

tool box *n* я́щик для инструме́нтов.

tool kit *n* набо́р инструме́нтов.

toot [tu:t] *n* (*of horn*) гудо́к*; (*of whistle*) свисто́к* ♦ *vi* (*with car horn*) сигна́лить (просигна́лить *perf*).

tooth [tu:θ] (*pl* **teeth**) *n* (*ANAT*) зуб*; (*TECH*) зубе́ц*; **to have a ~ out** *or* (*US*) **pulled** удаля́ть (удали́ть *perf*) *or* вырыва́ть (вы́рвать* *perf*) зуб; **to brush one's teeth** чи́стить* (почи́стить* *perf*) зу́бы; **by the skin of one's teeth** (*fig*) чу́дом.

toothache ['tu:θeɪk] *n* зубна́я боль *f*; **I have ~** у меня́ боли́т зуб.

toothbrush ['tu:θbrʌʃ] *n* зубна́я щётка.

toothpaste ['tu:θpeɪst] *n* зубна́я па́ста.

toothpick ['tu:θpɪk] *n* зубочи́стка*.

tooth powder *n* зубно́й порошо́к*.

top [tɒp] *n* (*of mountain*) верши́на; (*of tree*) верху́шка*; (*of head*) маку́шка; (*of ladder*) верх*; (*of page, list etc*) нача́ло*; (*of cupboard, table, box*) ве́рхняя пове́рхность *f*; (*lid: of box, jar*) кры́шка*; (: *bottle*) про́бка*; (*AUT: also: ~ gear*) са́мая вы́сшая ско́рость *f*; (*also: spinning ~*) юла́, волчо́к*; (*blouse etc*) верх ♦ *adj* (*shelf, step*) ве́рхний*; (*marks*) вы́сший*; (*salesman etc*) веду́щий*; (*best*) отме́нный ♦ *vt* (*poll, vote*) лиди́ровать (*impf*) в +*prp*; (*list*) возглавля́ть (возгла́вить* *perf*); (*exceed: estimate etc*) превыша́ть (превы́сить* *perf*); **the ~ of the milk** (*BRIT*) сли́вки *pl* (на молоке́); **at the ~ of the stairs/page** на верху́ ле́стницы/страни́цы; **at the ~ of the street** в да́льнем конце́ у́лицы; **on ~ of** (*above: be*) на +*prp*; (: *put etc*) на +*acc*; (*in addition to*) сверх +*gen*; **put the book on ~ of the table** положи́те кни́гу на стол; **from ~ to bottom** све́рху до́низу; **from ~ to toe** (*BRIT*) с головы́ до ног *or* до пят; **at the ~ of the list** пе́рвый по спи́ску; **at the ~ of one's voice** во весь го́лос; **at ~ speed** на максима́льной ско́рости; **over the ~** (*inf: behaviour etc*) сверх ме́ры.

▸ **top up** (*US* **top off**) *vt* (*bottle*) долива́ть (доли́ть* *perf*); (*salary*) прибавля́ть (приба́вить* *perf*).

topaz ['təupæz] *n* топа́з.

top-class ['tɒp'klɑ:s] *adj* вы́сшего кла́сса.

topcoat ['tɒpkəut] *n* ве́рхний* слой*.

top floor *n* ве́рхний* эта́ж*.

top hat *n* цили́ндр, котело́к*.

top-heavy [tɒp'hɛvɪ] *adj*: **~ object** предме́т с утяжелённым ве́рхом; **~ bureaucracy** бюрократи́ческий аппара́т с гро́моздким ве́рхним эшело́ном.

topic ['tɒpɪk] *n* те́ма.

topical ['tɒpɪkl] *adj* актуа́льный* (актуа́лен).

topless ['tɒplɪs] *adj* обнажённый по по́яса.

top-level ['tɒplɛvl] *adj* на вы́сшем у́ровне.

topmost ['tɒpməust] *adj* (*branch etc*) са́мый ве́рхний *or* бли́жний к верху́шке.

topography [tə'pɒgrəfɪ] *n* топогра́фия.

topping ['tɒpɪŋ] *n* (*CULIN*): **with a ~ of** с ве́рхом из +*gen*.

topple ['tɒpl] *vt* (*government, leader*) ски́дывать (ски́нуть *perf*) ♦ *vi* (*person, object*) опроки́дываться (опроки́нуться *perf*).

top-ranking ['tɒprænkɪŋ] *adj* (*official*) высокопоста́вленный.

top-secret ['tɒp'si:krɪt] *adj* сверхсекре́тный* (сверхсекре́тен).

top-security ['tɒpsə'kjuərɪtɪ] *adj* (*BRIT*) под уси́ленной охра́ной.

topsy-turvy ['tɒpsɪ'tɜ:vɪ] *adj* переёрнутый ♦ *adv* вверх нога́ми.

top-up ['tɒpʌp] *n*: **would you like a ~?** Вам ещё подли́ть?

top-up loan *n* (*BRIT*) доба́вочная ссу́да.

torch [tɔ:tʃ] *n* (*with flame*) фа́кел; (*BRIT: electric*) фона́рь* *m*.

tore [tɔ:ʳ] *pt of* **tear**.

torment [*n* 'tɔ:mɛnt, *vt* tɔ:'mɛnt] *n* муче́ние ♦ *vt* му́чить* (*impf*).

torn [tɔ:n] *pp of* **tear**[1] ♦ *adj*: **she is ~ between ...** она́ разрыва́ется ме́жду +*instr* ....

tornado [tɔ:'neɪdəu] (*pl* ~**es**) *n* смерч.

torpedo [tɔ:'pi:dəu] (*pl* ~**es**) *n* торпе́да.

torpedo boat *n* торпе́дный ка́тер.

torpor ['tɔ:pəʳ] *n* оцепене́ние.

torrent ['tɒrnt] *n* (*also fig*) пото́к.

torrential [tɒ'rɛnʃl] *adj* (*rain*) проливно́й.

torrid ['tɒrɪd] *adj* (*weather*) зно́йный* (зно́ен); (*love affair*) бу́рный.

torso ['tɔ:səu] *n* ту́ловище, торс.

tortoise ['tɔ:təs] *n* черепа́ха.

tortoiseshell ['tɔ:təʃɛl] *adj* черепа́ховый; (*cat*) с тигро́вым окра́сом.

tortuous ['tɔ:tjuəs] *adj* (*path*) изви́листый (изви́лист); (*argument, mind*) зау́мный* (зау́мен).

torture ['tɔ:tʃəʳ] *n* (*also fig*) пы́тка* ♦ *vt* пыта́ть (*impf*); (*fig*) му́чить (*impf*).

torturer ['tɔ:tʃərəʳ] *n* пала́ч*, мучи́тель *m*.

Tory ['tɔ:rɪ] (*BRIT: POL*) *adj* консервати́вный ♦ *n* (*POL*) то́ри *m/f indecl*, консерва́тор.

toss [tɒs] *vt* (*throw*) подки́дывать (подки́нуть *perf*), подбра́сывать (подбро́сить* *perf*); (*one's head*) отки́дывать (отки́нуть *perf*); (*salad*) меша́ть (*impf*) ♦ *vi*: **to ~ and turn** (*in bed*) воро́чаться (*impf*) ♦ *n*: **with a ~ of her head, she...** отки́нув го́лову, она́ ...; **to ~ a**

coin подбра́сывать (подбро́сить* *perf*) моне́ту; **to ~ up to do** подбра́сывать (подбро́сить* *perf*) моне́ту, что́бы +*infin*; **to win/lose the ~** выи́грывать (вы́играть *perf*)/ прои́грывать (проигра́ть *perf*) подбра́сывание моне́ты.

tot [tɔt] *n* (*drink*) глото́к*; (*child*) малы́ш*
▶ **tot up** *vt* (*BRIT*: *figures*) подсчи́тывать (подсчита́ть *perf*).

total ['təutl] *adj* (*number, workforce etc*) о́бщий*; (*failure, wreck etc*) по́лный ♦ *n* о́бщая су́мма ♦ *vt* (*add up*) скла́дывать (сложи́ть *perf*); (*add up to*) составля́ть (соста́вить* *perf*); **in ~** в о́бщей сло́жности.

totalitarian [təutælɪ'tɛərɪən] *adj* (*POL*) тоталита́рный.

totality [təu'tælɪtɪ] *n* полнота́.

totally ['təutəlɪ] *adv* по́лностью; (*unprepared*) соверше́нно.

tote bag [təut-] *n* сума́.

totem pole ['təutəm-] *n* тоте́мный столб*.

totter ['tɔtər] *vi* (*person*) ходи́ть*/идти́* (*impf*) шата́ясь *or* ша́ткой похо́дкой; (*fig*: *government*) занима́ть (*impf*) ша́ткую пози́цию.

touch [tʌtʃ] *n* осяза́ние; (*approach*) мане́ра; (*detail*) штрих; (*contact*) прикоснове́ние ♦ *vt* (*with hand, foot*) каса́ться (косну́ться *perf*) +*gen*, тро́гать (тро́нуть *perf*); (*tamper with*) тро́гать (*impf*); (*make contact with*) прикаса́ться (прикосну́ться *perf*) к +*dat*, дотра́гиваться (дотро́нуться *perf*) до +*gen*; (*emotionally*) тро́гать (тро́нуть *perf*); **the personal ~** индивидуа́льность *f*; **to put the finishing ~es to sth** вноси́ть* (внести́* *perf*) после́дние штрихи́ в что-н; **there's been a ~ of frost** подморо́зило; **in ~ with** в конта́кте с +*instr*; **to get in ~ with sb** связа́ться* (*perf*) с кем-н; **I'll be in ~ with you** я свяжу́сь с Ва́ми; **to lose ~** (*friends*) теря́ть (потеря́ть *perf*) связь; **to be out of ~ with events** быть* (*impf*) не в ку́рсе собы́тий
▶ **touch on** *vt fus* каса́ться (косну́ться *perf*) +*gen*
▶ **touch up** *vt* (*paint*) подкра́шивать (подкра́сить* *perf*).

touch-and-go ['tʌtʃən'gəu] *adj* нея́сный* (нея́сен); **it was ~ whether we'd succeed** бы́ло нея́сно, вы́шло ли э́то у нас.

touchdown ['tʌtʃdaun] *n* (*of rocket, plane*) поса́дка*; (*US*: *FOOTBALL*) гол.

touched [tʌtʃt] *adj* тро́нутый (тро́нут).

touching ['tʌtʃɪŋ] *adj* (*scene, photograph etc*) тро́гательный* (тро́гателен).

touchline ['tʌtʃlaɪn] *n* (*SPORT*) бокова́я ли́ния.

touch-sensitive ['tʌtʃ'sensɪtɪv] *adj* сраба́тывающий на прикоснове́ние.

touch-type ['tʌtʃtaɪp] *vi* печа́тать (*impf*) слепы́м ме́тодом.

touchy ['tʌtʃɪ] *adj* (*person*) оби́дчивый (оби́дчив); (*subject*) больно́й; **he is ~** его́ легко́ заде́ть.

tough [tʌf] *adj* (*strong, hard-wearing*: *material*) кре́пкий* (кре́пок), про́чный* (про́чен); (*meat, policies, negotiations*) жёсткий*; (*person*: *physically*) выно́сливый (выно́слив); (: *mentally*) сто́йкий* (сто́ек); (*task, problem, journey*) тяжёлый (тяжёл); (*rough*) опа́сный* (опа́сен); **~ luck!** не везёт!

toughen ['tʌfn] *vt* закаля́ть (закали́ть *perf*).

toughness ['tʌfnɪs] *n* про́чность *f*; (*of person*) сто́йкость *f*.

toupee ['tu:peɪ] *n* (*wig*) пари́к*.

tour ['tuər] *n* (*journey*) пое́здка*; (*also*: **package ~**) туристи́ческая пое́здка*; (*of town, factory, museum*) экску́рсия; (*by pop group etc*) турне́ *nt ind*, гастро́ли *fpl* ♦ *vt* (*country, city*) объезжа́ть (объе́хать* *perf*); (*factory*) обходи́ть* (обойти́* *perf*); **to go on a ~ of** (*museum, region*) осма́тривать (осмотре́ть* *perf*); **to go on ~** (*band*) е́здить*/е́хать* (*impf*) на гастро́ли.

touring ['tuərɪŋ] *n* гастро́ли *fpl*.

tourism ['tuərɪzm] *n* (*business*) тури́зм.

tourist ['tuərɪst] *n* тури́ст*(ка*) ♦ *cpd* (*attractions, season*) тури́стский*; **the ~ trade** инду́стрия тури́зма.

tourist class *n* (*NAUT, AVIAT*) второ́й класс.

tourist information centre *n* (*BRIT*) туристи́ческое бюро́ *nt ind*.

tourist office *n* туристи́ческое бюро́ *nt ind*.

tournament ['tuənəmənt] *n* турни́р, состяза́ние.

tourniquet ['tuənɪkeɪ] *n* жгут, турнике́т.

tour operator *n* (*BRIT*) рабо́тник туристи́ческой фи́рмы; (*company*) туристи́ческая фи́рма.

tousled ['tauzld] *adj* (*hair*) взъеро́шенный (взъеро́шен).

tout [taut] *n* (*also*: **ticket ~**) спекуля́нт*(ка*) ♦ *vi*: **to ~ for** (*business*) добива́ться (*impf*) +*gen*, выбива́ть (*impf*) ♦ *vt*: **to ~ sth (around)** (*BRIT*) спекули́ровать* (*impf*) чем-н.

tow [təu] *vt* (*vehicle, caravan, trailer*) везти́*/ вози́ть* (*impf*) на букси́ре ♦ *n*: **to give sb a ~** (*AUT*) брать* (взять* *perf*) кого́-н на букси́р; **"on** *or* (*US*) **in ~"** (*AUT*) "на букси́ре".

toward(s) [tə'wɔ:d(z)] *prep* к +*dat*; (*attitude*) по отноше́нию к +*dat*; (*purpose*): **~ doing** с тем что́бы +*infin*; **towards noon/the end of the year** к полу́дню/концу́ го́да; **to feel friendly ~ sb** относи́ться* (*impf*) дружелю́бно к кому́-н.

towel ['tauəl] *n* (*also*: **hand ~**) полоте́нце* для рук; (*also*: **bath ~**) ба́нное полоте́нце*; **to throw in the ~** (*fig*) сдава́ться* (сда́ться* *perf*).

towelling ['tauəlɪŋ] *n* (*fabric*) махро́вая ткань.

towel rail (*US* **towel rack**) *n* ве́шалка* для

---

* marks translations which have irregular inflections The Russian-English side of the dictionary gives inflectional information

полоте́нец.

tower ['tauə[r]] n ба́шня* ♦ vi (building, mountain) возвыша́ться (impf); **to ~ above** or **over sb/sth** возвыша́ться (impf) над кем-н/чем-н.

tower block n (BRIT) ба́шня*, высо́тный дом*.

towering ['tauərɪŋ] adj возвыша́ющийся.

towline ['təʊlaɪn] n букси́рный трос.

town [taun] n го́род*; **to go to ~** ходи́ть*/идти́* (impf) в го́род; (fig) разоря́ться (разори́ться perf); **in ~** в го́роде; **to be out of ~** (person) быть* (impf) в отъе́зде.

town centre n це́нтр (го́рода).

town clerk n гла́вный делопроизводи́тель m городско́го сове́та.

town council n городско́й сове́т.

town crier [-'kraɪə[r]] n глаша́тай.

town hall n ра́туша.

townie ['taunɪ] n (inf) городско́й(-а́я) m(f) adj.

town plan n план го́рода.

town planner n градостро́итель m, плани́ровщик.

town planning n городско́е плани́рование, градострои́тельство.

township ['taunʃɪp] n (in South Africa) негритя́нский* при́город; (in America) городско́й райо́н.

townspeople ['taunzpi:pl] npl горожа́не mpl.

towpath ['təʊpɑ:θ] n (of canal) тропи́нка.

towrope ['təʊrəup] n букси́рный трос.

tow truck n (US) авари́йная маши́на.

toxic ['tɔksɪk] adj токси́чный* (токси́чен).

toxic waste n ядови́тые отхо́ды mpl.

toxin ['tɔksɪn] n токси́н.

toy [tɔɪ] n игру́шка*

► **toy with** vt fus (object) игра́ть (impf) +instr; (food) вози́ться* (impf) с +instr; (idea) игра́ть (impf) с +instr.

toy shop n магази́н игру́шек.

trace [treɪs] n след ♦ vt (draw) переводи́ть* (перевести́* perf); (follow) просле́живать (проследи́ть* perf); (locate) устана́вливать (установи́ть* perf); **without ~** бесслéдно, без следа́; **there was no ~ of him** он исче́з без следа́.

trace element n микроэлемéнт.

tracer ['treɪsə[r]] n (also: ~ **bullet**) трасси́рующий снаря́д.

trachea [trə'kɪə] n трахе́я.

tracing paper ['treɪsɪŋ-] n ка́лька.

track [træk] n ·   ед*; (path) тропа́*; (of bullet etc) траекто́рия; (RAIL) (железнодоро́жный) путь* m; (on tape, record, also SPORT) доро́жка* ♦ vt (follow: animal, person) идти́* (impf) по слéду +gen; **to keep ~ of** следи́ть* (impf) за +instr; **to be on the right ~** (fig) быть* (impf) на ве́рном пути́

► **track down** vt (prey) высле́живать (вы́следить* perf); (sth lost) оты́скивать (отыска́ть* perf).

tracked [trækt] adj (AUT) гу́сеничный.

tracker dog ['trækə-] n (BRIT) соба́ка-ище́йка.

track events npl соревнова́ния ntpl по лёгкой атле́тике.

tracking station ['trækɪŋ-] n пульт управле́ния полётом.

track meet n (SPORT) соревнова́ния ntpl по атле́тике.

track record n: **to have a good ~ ~** (fig) име́ть (impf) хоро́шую репута́цию.

tracksuit ['træksu:t] n трениро́вочный костю́м.

tract [trækt] n (GEO) простра́нство; (pamphlet) тракта́т; respiratory ~ (ANAT) дыха́тельные пути́ mpl; **digestive ~** желу́дочно-кише́чный тракт.

traction ['trækʃən] n (power) тя́га; (AUT: grip) си́ла сцепле́ния; (MED): **~ in** в вытяже́нии.

traction engine n тяга́ч*.

tractor ['træktə[r]] n тра́ктор.

trade [treɪd] n (activity) торго́вля; (skill, job) род заня́тий ♦ vi (do business) торгова́ть* (impf) ♦ vt: **to ~ sth (for sth)** обме́нивать (обменя́ть perf) что-н (на что-н); **to ~ with/in** торгова́ть* (impf) с +instr/+instr; **foreign ~** вне́шняя торго́вля; **Department of T~ and Industry** (BRIT) Министе́рство торго́вли и промы́шленности

► **trade in** vt (old car etc) предлага́ть (предложи́ть* perf) для встре́чной прода́жи.

trade barrier n торго́вый барье́р.

trade deficit n торго́вый дефици́т.

Trade Descriptions Act n (BRIT: LAW, COMM) положе́ние о торго́вле.

trade discount n торго́вая ски́дка* (о́птовым торго́вцам).

trade fair n торго́вая я́рмарка*.

trade figures npl показа́тель msg товарооборо́та.

trade-in ['treɪdɪn] n: **to take as a ~** принима́ть (приня́ть* perf) как встре́чную прода́жу.

trade-in price n цена́* с учётом встре́чной прода́жи.

trademark ['treɪdmɑ:k] n това́рный знак.

trade mission n торго́вое представи́тельство.

trade name n торго́вое назва́ние.

trade-off ['treɪdɔf] n компроми́сс.

trade price n торго́вая цена́.

trader ['treɪdə[r]] n торго́вец*.

trade reference n информа́ция о состоя́нии дел фи́рмы.

trade secret n промы́шленный секре́т.

tradesman ['treɪdzmən] irreg n рабо́тник; (shopkeeper) торго́вец*, ла́вочник.

trade union n профсою́з= профессиона́льный сою́з.

trade unionist [-'ju:njənɪst] n член профсою́за.

trade wind n (GEO) пасса́т.

trading ['treɪdɪŋ] n торго́вля.

trading account n счёт расчётов.

trading estate n (BRIT) промы́шленная зо́на.

trading stamps npl бума́жные ма́рки с

объявленной стоимостью.
tradition [trə'dɪʃən] *n* традиция.
traditional [trə'dɪʃənl] *adj* (*also fig*)
традиционный*.
traditionally [trə'dɪʃnəlɪ] *adv* традиционно.
traffic ['træfɪk] *n* (*of people, vehicles*) движение;
(*of drugs etc*) нелегальная торговля ♦ *vi*: **to** ~
in (*liquor, drugs*) нелегально торговать*
(*impf*) +*instr*.
traffic circle *n* (*US*) кольцевая транспортная
развязка*.
traffic island *n* островок* безопасности.
traffic jam *n* пробка*.
trafficker ['træfɪkə'] *n* (*also:* **drug** ~)
наркокурьер.
traffic lights *npl* светофор *msg*.
traffic offence *n* (*BRIT*) нарушение правил
дорожного движения.
traffic sign *n* дорожный знак.
traffic violation *n* (*US*) = **traffic offence**.
traffic warden *n* (*BRIT*) регулировщик
парковании машин на улицах города.
tragedy ['trædʒədɪ] *n* трагедия.
tragic ['trædʒɪk] *adj* трагический*.
tragically ['trædʒɪkəlɪ] *adv* трагически.
trail [treɪl] *n* (*path*) дорожка*, тропинка*;
(*track*) след; (*of smoke, dust*) хвост* ♦ *vt* (*drag*)
волочить* (*impf*); (*follow: person, animal*)
следовать (*impf*) по пятам за +*instr* ♦ *vi* (*hang
loosely*) волочиться* (*impf*); (*in game, contest*)
волочиться* (*impf*) в хвосте, отставать*
(*impf*); **to be on sb's** ~ устраивать (устроить
perf) слежку за кем-н
▶ **trail away** *vi* (*sound, voice*) затихать
(затихнуть *perf*)
▶ **trail behind** *vi* (*lag*) волочиться* (*impf*) в
хвосте
▶ **trail off** *vi* = **trail away**.
trailer ['treɪlə'] *n* (*AUT*) прицеп; (*US: caravan*)
автоприцеп; (*CINEMA*) кинореклама, анонс.
trailer tent *n* прицеп с палаткой.
trailer truck *n* (*US*) грузовик* с прицепом.
train [treɪn] *n* поезд*; (*of dress*) шлейф ♦ *vt*
(*apprentice, doctor etc*) учить* (обучить* *perf*);
(*athlete, mind*) тренировать (*impf*); (*dog*)
дрессировать (выдрессировать *perf*); (*plant*)
приучать (приучить* *perf*) ♦ *vi* (*learn a skill*)
учиться* (обучиться* *perf*); (*SPORT*)
тренироваться (*impf*); **one's** ~ **of thought** ход
чьих-н мыслей; ~ **of events** цепь *f* событий;
to go by ~ ездить*/ехать* (*impf*) поездом *or* на
поезде; **to** ~ **sb to do** обучать (обучить* *perf*)
кого-н +*impf infin*; **to** ~ **sb as** учить* (*impf*)
кого-н на +*acc*; **to** ~ **on** (*camera etc*)
направлять (направить* *perf*) на +*acc*.
train attendant *n* (*US*) проводник.
trained [treɪnd] *adj* (*worker, teacher*)
подготовленный*; (*animal*) тренированный;

(*eye*) натренированный* (натренирован).
trainee [treɪ'ni:] *n* (*hairdresser*) ученик*; ~
teacher студент(ка*) практикант.
trainer ['treɪnə'] *n* (*coach*) тренер; (*of animals*)
дрессировщик(-щица); ~**s** *npl* (*sports shoes*)
кроссовки *fpl*.
training ['treɪnɪŋ] *n* (*for occupation*) обучение,
подготовка*; (*SPORT*) тренировка; **to be in** ~
(*SPORT*) тренироваться (*impf*).
training college *n* (*for teachers*)
педагогический* институт.
training course *n* курс профессиональной
подготовки.
traipse [treɪps] *vi*: **to** ~ **through**
притаскиваться (притащиться* *perf*).
trait [treɪt] *n* черта.
traitor ['treɪtə'] *n* предатель(ница) *m(f)*.
trajectory [trə'dʒɛktərɪ] *n* траектория.
tram [træm] *n* (*BRIT*) трамвай.
tramcar ['træmkɑ:'] *n* (*BRIT*) = **tram**.
tramline ['træmlaɪn] *n* трамвайная линия.
tramp [træmp] *n* (*person*) бродяга *m/f*; (*inf: pej:
woman*) шлюха ♦ *vi* бродить* (*impf*) ♦ *vt*
(*town, streets*) бродить*/брести* (*impf*) по
+*dat*.
trample ['træmpl] *vt*: **to** ~ (**underfoot**)
растаптывать (растоптать* *perf*) ♦ *vi* (*fig*): **to**
~ **on** растаптывать (растоптать* *perf*).
trampoline ['træmpəli:n] *n* батут.
trance [trɑ:ns] *n* (*also fig*) транс; **to go into a** ~
входить* (войти* *perf*) в транс.
tranquil ['træŋkwɪl] *adj* безмятежный*
(безмятежен).
tranquillity [træŋ'kwɪlɪtɪ] (*US* **tranquility**) *n*
безмятежность *f*.
tranquillizer ['træŋkwɪlaɪzə'] (*US* **tranquilizer**) *n*
(*MED*) транквилизатор.
transact [træn'zækt] *vt* (*business*) вести* (*impf*).
transaction [træn'zækʃən] *n* (*piece of business*)
операция; **cash** ~ оплата наличными.
transatlantic ['trænzət'læntɪk] *adj*
трансатлантический.
transcend [træn'sɛnd] *vt* (*boundaries, loyalties
etc*) выходить* (выйти* *perf*) за пределы
+*gen*.
transcendental [trænsɛn'dɛntl] *adj*: ~
meditation трансцендентная медитация.
transcribe [træn'skraɪb] *vt* переписывать
(переписать* *perf*), транскрибировать (*impf/
perf*).
transcript ['trænskrɪpt] *n* (*typed*) печатная
копия; (*hand-written*) рукописная копия.
transcription [træn'skrɪpʃən] *n* транскрипция.
transept ['trænsɛpt] *n* трансепт.
transfer ['trænsfə'] *n* перевод; (*POL*) передача;
(*SPORT*) переход; (*picture etc*) переводная
картинка ♦ *vt* (*employees, money etc*)
переводить* (перевести* *perf*); (*POL, SPORT*)

---

* marks translations which have irregular inflections. The Russian-English side of the dictionary gives inflectional information.

передава́ть• (переда́ть• *perf*); **to ~ the charges**
(*BRIT: TEL*) звони́ть (позвони́ть *perf*) по
колле́кту; **by bank ~** по ба́нковскому
перево́ду.
transferable [trænsˈfəːrəbl] *adj* (*ticket*)
перево́дный, с пра́вом переда́чи; "**not ~**"
"без пра́ва переда́чи".
transfix [trænsˈfɪks] *vt* (*person, animal*)
пронза́ть (пронзи́ть• *perf*); (*fig*): **~ed with fear**
пронзённый стра́хом.
transform [trænsˈfɔːm] *vt* (*person, situation etc*)
преобража́ть (преобрази́ть• *perf*).
transformation [trænsfəˈmeɪʃən] *n*
преобразова́ние, перевоплоще́ние.
transformer [trænsˈfɔːmər] *n* трансформа́тор.
transfusion [trænsˈfjuːʒən] *n* (*also*: **blood ~**)
перелива́ние кро́ви.
transgress [trænsˈɡrɛs] *vt* преступа́ть
(преступи́ть• *perf*) грани́цы +*gen*.
transient [ˈtrænzɪənt] *adj* мимолётный•
(мимолётен).
transistor [trænˈzɪstər] *n* (*ELEC*) транзи́сторное
устро́йство; (*also*: **~ radio**) транзи́стор.
transit [ˈtrænzɪt] *n*: **in ~** (*people, things*)
транзи́том.
transit camp *n* перева́лочный пункт.
transition [trænˈzɪʃən] *n* перехо́д.
transitional [trænˈzɪʃənl] *adj* перехо́дный.
transitive [ˈtrænzɪtɪv] *adj* (*LING*) перехо́дный.
transit lounge *n* зал транзи́тных
пассажи́ров.
transitory [ˈtrænzɪtərɪ] *adj* преходя́щий•.
transit visa *n* транзи́тная ви́за.
translate [trænzˈleɪt] *vt*: **to ~** (*from/into*)
переводи́ть• (перевести́• *perf*) (с +*gen*/на
+*acc*).
translation [trænzˈleɪʃən] *n* перево́д; (*SCOL*: *as
opposed to prose*) перево́д на родно́й язы́к.
translator [trænzˈleɪtər] *n* перево́дчик(-ица).
translucent [trænzˈluːsnt] *adj* (*object, quality*)
прозра́чный• (прозра́чен),
просве́чивающий.
transmission [trænzˈmɪʃən] *n* переда́ча; (*AUT*)
коро́бка переда́ч, приво́д.
transmit [trænzˈmɪt] *vt* передава́ть• (переда́ть•
perf).
transmitter [trænzˈmɪtər] *n* (*equipment*)
переда́тчик.
transparency [trænsˈpɛərnsɪ] *n* (*of glass etc*)
прозра́чность *f*; (*BRIT: PHOT*) диапозити́в.
transparent [trænsˈpærnt] *adj* прозра́чный•
(прозра́чен).
transpire [trænsˈpaɪər] *vi* (*turn out*) выясня́ться
(вы́ясниться *perf*); (*happen*) происходи́ть•
(произойти́• *perf*); **it finally ~d that ...** наконе́ц
вы́яснилось, что ....
transplant [*n* ˈtrænsplɑːnt, *vt* trænsˈplɑːnt] *n*
переса́дка• ♦ *vt* (*MED, seedlings*)
переса́живать (пересади́ть• *perf*); **he had a
heart ~** ему́ сде́лали переса́дку се́рдца.
transport [*n* ˈtrænspɔːt, *vt* trænsˈpɔːt] *n*

тра́нспорт; (*moving people, goods*)
перево́зка• ♦ *vt* (*carry*) перевози́ть•
(перевезти́• *perf*); **public ~** обще́ственный
тра́нспорт; **Department of T~** (*BRIT*)
Министе́рство тра́нспорта.
transportation [ˈtrænspɔːˈteɪʃən] *n* (*transport*)
транспортиро́вка•, перево́зка•; (*means of
transport*) тра́нспорт; **Department of T~** (*US*)
Министе́рство тра́нспорта.
transport café *n* (*BRIT*) доро́жное кафе́ *nt ind*.
transpose [trænsˈpəuz] *vt* перемеща́ть
(перемести́ть• *perf*).
transsexual [trænzˈsɛksuəl] *n* транссексуа́л.
transverse [ˈtrænzvəːs] *adj* (*beam etc*)
попере́чный.
transvestite [trænzˈvɛstaɪt] *n* трансвести́т.
trap [træp] *n* западня́, лову́шка; (*carriage*)
двуко́лка• ♦ *vt* лови́ть• (пойма́ть *perf*) в
лову́шку *or* западню́; (*confine*) запира́ть
(запере́ть• *perf*); (*immobilize*) ско́вывать
(скова́ть *perf*); (*jam*) защемля́ть (защеми́ть•
perf); **to set** *or* **lay a ~** (**for sb**) расставля́ть
(расста́вить• *perf*) лову́шку *or* западню́
(кому́-н); **to shut one's ~** (*inf*) затыка́ть
(заткну́ть *perf*) свою́ гло́тку; **to ~ one's finger
in the door** защемля́ть (защеми́ть• *perf*) себе́
па́лец.
trap door *n* люк.
trapeze [trəˈpiːz] *n* трапе́ция.
trapper [ˈtræpər] *n* ловец•.
trappings [ˈtræpɪŋz] *npl* атрибу́ты *mpl*.
trash [træʃ] *n* (*rubbish: also pej*) сор, му́сор;
(: *nonsense*) чушь *f*.
trash can *n* (*US*) му́сорное ведро́•.
trashy [ˈtræʃɪ] *adj* (*inf*) дрянно́й.
trauma [ˈtrɔːmə] *n* тра́вма.
traumatic [trɔːˈmætɪk] *adj* травмати́ческий.
traumatize [ˈtrɔːmətaɪz] *vt* травми́ровать•
(*impf/perf*).
travel [ˈtrævl] *n* (*travelling*) путеше́ствия *ntpl* ♦
vi (*for pleasure*) путеше́ствовать (*impf*);
(*commute*) е́здить• (*impf*); (*move*)
передвига́ться (*impf*); (*news, sound*)
распространя́ться (распространи́ться *perf*);
(*wine, food*) сохраня́ться (*impf*) при
перево́зке ♦ *vt* (*distance: by transport*)
проезжа́ть (прое́хать• *perf*); (: *on foot*)
проходи́ть• (пройти́• *perf*); **~s** *npl* (*journeys*)
путеше́ствия *ntpl*.
travel agency *n* туристи́ческое аге́нтство.
travel agent *n* рабо́тник туристи́ческого
аге́нтства.
travel brochure *n* рекла́мная брошю́ра для
тури́стов.
traveller [ˈtrævlər] (*US* **traveler**) *n*
путеше́ственник(-ица); (*COMM*)
коммивояжёр.
traveller's cheque (*US* **traveler's check**) *n*
доро́жный чек.
travelling [ˈtrævlɪŋ] (*US* **traveling**) *n* (*for
pleasure*) путеше́ствия *ntpl*; (*from necessity*)

переéзды *mpl* ◆ *cpd* (*circus, exhibition*) передвижнóй; (*bag, clock, expenses*) дорóжный.

travel(l)ing salesman *irreg n* коммивояжёр.

travelogue ['trævəlɔg] *n* (*book*) кни́га о путешéствиях.

travel-sickness ['trævlsɪknɪs] *n* (*on ship*) морскáя болéзнь *f*; **he suffers from travel sickness** (*in car*) егó укáчивает в маши́не.

traverse ['trævəs] *vt* пересекáть (пересéчь* *perf*).

travesty ['trævəstɪ] *n* парóдия.

trawler ['trɔ:lə'] *n* трáулер.

tray [treɪ] *n* (*for carrying*) поднóс; (*on desk*) корзи́нка.

treacherous ['trɛtʃərəs] *adj* (*person*) вероло́мный* (вероло́мен); (*look, action*) предáтельский*; (*ground, tide*) ковáрный* (ковáрен); **road conditions are ~** склáдывается слóжная дорóжная обстанóвка.

treachery ['trɛtʃən] *n* предáтельство, вероло́мство.

treacle ['tri:kl] *n* (*black treacle*) пáтока; (*golden syrup*) свéтлая *or* очи́щенная пáтока.

tread [trɛd] (*pt* **trod**, *pp* **trodden**) *n* (*step*) похóдка; (*sound*) пóступь *f*; (*of stair*) ступéнь *f*; (*of tyre*) протéктор ◆ *vi* ступáть (*impf*)
▸ **tread on** *vt fus* наступáть (наступи́ть* *perf*) на +*acc*.

treadle ['trɛdl] *n* (*on sewing machine etc*) педáль *f*.

treas. *abbr* = **treasurer**.

treason ['tri:zn] *n* измéна.

treasure ['trɛʒə'] *n* сокрóвище ◆ *vt* (*object*) храни́ть (*impf*) как зени́цу óка; (*friendship*) высóко цени́ть* (*impf*); (*memory*) свя́то храни́ть (*impf*); (*thought*) лелéять (*impf*); (*store*) храни́ть (*impf*); **~s** *npl* (*art treasures etc*) сокрóвища *ntpl*.

treasure hunt *n* пóиски *mpl* сокрóвищ.

treasurer ['trɛʒərə'] *n* казначéй.

treasury ['trɛʒən] *n*: **the T~**, (*US*) **the T~ Department** Госудáрственное Казначéйство.

Treasury bill *n* (*BRIT*) казначéйский вéксель *m*.

treat [tri:t] *n* (*present*) удовóльствие ◆ *vt* (*person, object*) обращáться (*impf*) с +*instr*; (*patient, illness*) лечи́ть* (*impf*); (*TECH: coat*) обрабáтывать (обрабóтать *perf*); **it was a ~** э́то бы́ло наслаждéние; **to ~ sth as a joke** относи́ться* (отнести́сь *perf*) к чемý-н несерьёзно; **to ~ sb to sth** угощáть (угости́ть* *perf*) когó-н чем-н.

treatment ['tri:tmənt] *n* (*attention, handling*) обращéние; (*MED*) лечéние; **to have ~ for sth** проходи́ть* (пройти́* *perf*) курс лечéния от чегó-н.

treaty ['tri:tɪ] *n* соглашéние.

treble ['trɛbl] *adj* (*triple*) тройнóй; (*MUS: voice, part*) дискáнтный, сопрáно *ind*; (: *instrument*) сопрáно ◆ *n* (*MUS*) дискáнт, сопрáно *m ind*; (*on hi-fi, radio etc*) высóкие частóты *fpl* ◆ *vt* утрáивать (утрóить *perf*) ◆ *vi* утрáиваться (утрóиться *perf*); **to be ~ the size of sth** быть* (*impf*) бóльше чегó-н втрóе.

treble clef *n* скрипи́чный ключ*.

tree [tri:] *n* дéрево*.

tree-lined ['tri:laɪnd] *adj* усáженный дерéвьями.

treetop ['tri:tɔp] *n* верхýшка дéрева.

tree trunk *n* ствол дéрева.

trek [trɛk] *n* (*long difficult journey*) похóд, перехóд ◆ *vi* (*as holiday*) идти́* (пойти́* *perf*) в похóд.

trellis ['trɛlɪs] *n* шпалéра.

tremble ['trɛmbl] *vi* дрожáть (*impf*).

trembling ['trɛmblɪŋ] *n* дрожáние ◆ *adj* (*hand, voice etc*) дрожáщий.

tremendous [trɪ'mɛndəs] *adj* (*enormous*) огрóмный* (огрóмен); (*excellent*) великолéпный* (великолéпен).

tremendously [trɪ'mɛndəslɪ] *adv* чрезвычáйно; **he enjoyed it ~** он получи́л огрóмное удовóльствие от э́того.

tremor ['trɛmə'] *n* (*trembling*) дрожь *f*, содрогáние; (*also*: **earth ~**) толчóк* (землетрясéния).

trench [trɛntʃ] *n* канáва; (*MIL*) траншéя, окóп.

trench coat *n* тёплая полушинéль *f*.

trench warfare *n* окóпная войнá*.

trend [trɛnd] *n* (*tendency*) тендéнция; (*of events, fashion*) направлéние; **~ towards sth** тендéнция к чемý-н; **~ away from sth** отхóд от чегó-н; **to set the ~** задавáть* (задáть* *perf*) направлéние; **to set a ~** задавáть* (задáть* *perf*) тон.

trendy ['trɛndɪ] *adj* мóдный (мóден).

trepidation [trɛpɪ'deɪʃən] *n* (*apprehension*) трéпет; **in ~** в трéпете.

trespass ['trɛspəs] *vi*: **to ~ on** (*private property*) вторгáться (вто́ргнуться *perf*) в +*acc*; "**no ~ing**" "вход воспрещён".

trespasser ['trɛspəsə'] *n* вторгáющийся(-ая) *m(f) adj* в чáстные владéния; "**trespassers will be prosecuted**" "ли́ца, вторгáющиеся на дáнную террито́рию бýдут преслéдоваться закóном".

tress [trɛs] *n* (*of hair*) косá*.

trestle ['trɛsl] *n* кóзлы *pl*.

trestle table *n* стол* на кóзлах.

trial ['traɪəl] *n* (*LAW*) процéсс, суд*; (*test: of machine etc*) испытáния *ntpl*; (*worry*) переживáние; **~s** *npl* (*unpleasant experiences*) перипети́и *fpl*; **horse ~s** соревновáния *ntpl* по вы́ездке; **~ by jury** суд* прися́жных; **to be**

---

* marks translations which have irregular inflections. The Russian-English side of the dictionary gives inflectional information.

sent for ~ предава́ть° (преда́ть° *perf*) суду́; **on** ~ (*LAW*) под судо́м; **by** ~ **and error** ме́тодом проб и оши́бок.

trial balance *n* (*COMM*) про́бный бала́нс.

trial basis *n*: **on a** ~~ на испыта́тельный срок.

trial period *n* испыта́тельный срок.

trial run *n* прого́н.

triangle ['traɪæŋgl] *n* (*MATH, MUS*) треуго́льник.

triangular [traɪ'æŋgjuləʳ] *adj* треуго́льный.

tribal ['traɪbl] *adj* (*warrior, warfare, dance*) племенно́й.

tribe [traɪb] *n* пле́мя° *nt*.

tribesman ['traɪbzmən] *irreg n* тузе́мец°.

tribulations [trɪbju'leɪʃənz] *npl* злоключе́ния *ntpl*.

tribunal [traɪ'bju:nl] *n* трибуна́л.

tributary ['trɪbjutərɪ] *n* (*of river*) прито́к°.

tribute ['trɪbju:t] *n* (*compliment*) дань *f*; **to pay** ~ **to** отдава́ть° (отда́ть° *perf*) дань +*dat*.

trice [traɪs] *n*: **in a** ~ ми́гом.

trick [trɪk] *n* (*magic trick*) фо́кус; (*prank, joke*) подво́х; (*skill, knack*) уло́вка, приём; (*CARDS*) взя́тка° ◆ *vi* проводи́ть° (провести́° *perf*); **to play a** ~ **on sb** разы́грывать (разыгра́ть *perf*) кого́-н; **to** ~ **sb into doing** обма́ном заставля́ть (заста́вить° *perf*) кого́-н +*infin*; **to** ~ **sb out of sth** выма́нивать (вы́манить *perf*) что-н у кого́-н; **a** ~ **of the light** игра́° све́та, опти́ческий° обма́н; **that should do the** ~ э́то должно́ срабо́тать.

trickery ['trɪkərɪ] *n* моше́нничество.

trickle ['trɪkl] *n* (*of water etc*) стру́йка ◆ *vi* (*water, rain etc*) струи́ться (*impf*); (*people*) стека́ться (*impf*).

trick question *n* хи́трый вопро́с.

trickster ['trɪkstəʳ] *n* моше́нник.

tricky ['trɪkɪ] *adj* (*job*) непросто́й; (*business*) хи́трый; (*problem*) заковы́ристый.

tricycle ['traɪsɪkl] *n* трёхколёсный велосипе́д.

trifle ['traɪfl] *n* (*small detail*) пустя́к°; (*CULIN*) *десе́рт из ке́кса, фрукто́вого желе́ и сли́вок* ◆ *adv*: **a** ~ **long** чуть длиннова́т ◆ *vi*: **to** ~ **with sb/sth** шути́ть° (*impf*) с кем-н/чем-н.

trifling ['traɪflɪŋ] *adj* пустяко́вый.

trigger ['trɪgəʳ] *n* (*of gun*) куро́к°
► **trigger off** *vt* (*reaction, riot*) спровоци́ровать (*perf*), вызыва́ть (вы́звать° *perf*).

trigonometry [trɪgə'nɔmətrɪ] *n* тригономе́трия *f*.

trilby ['trɪlbɪ] *n* (*BRIT: also:* ~ **hat**) фе́тровая шля́па.

trill [trɪl] *vi* (*birds*) залива́ться (зали́ться *perf*) ◆ *n* (*MUS*) трель *f*.

trilogy ['trɪlədʒɪ] *n* трило́гия *f*.

trim [trɪm] *adj* (*house, garden*) ухо́женный; (*figure*) подтя́нутый ◆ *n* отде́лка ◆ *vt* (*cut*) подра́внивать (подровня́ть° *perf*); (*NAUT*) ста́вить° (поста́вить° *perf*) по́ ветру; (*decorate*): **to** ~ (**with**) отде́лывать (отде́лать *perf*) (+*instr*); **to give sb a** ~ подра́внивать

(подровня́ть *perf*) во́лосы кому́-н; **to keep in** (**good**) ~ держа́ть° (*impf*) (в хоро́шей) фо́рме.

trimmings ['trɪmɪŋz] *npl* (*CULIN*) потроха́ *mpl*; (*cuttings*) обре́зки *mpl*.

Trinidad and Tobago ['trɪnɪdæd-] *n* Тринида́д и Тоба́го.

trinity ['trɪnɪtɪ] *n* (*group*) тро́йка; (*REL*): **the** (**Holy**) **T**~ Тро́ица.

trinket ['trɪŋkɪt] *n* (*ornament*) безделу́шка°; (*jewellery*) побряку́шка°.

trio ['tri:əu] *n* тро́йка; (*MUS*) три́о *nt ind*.

trip [trɪp] *n* (*journey*) пое́здка°; (*outing*) прогу́лка° ◆ *vi* (*stumble*) спотыка́ться (споткну́ться *perf*); (*go lightly*) идти́° (*impf*) лёгкой похо́дкой; **on a** ~ на экску́рсии
► **trip up** *vi* (*stumble*) ста́вить° (поста́вить° *perf*) подно́жку ◆ *vt* (*person*) подставля́ть (подста́вить° *perf*) подно́жку.

tripartite [traɪ'pɑːtaɪt] *adj* трёхсторо́нний°.

tripe [traɪp] *n* (*CULIN*) требуха́; (*pej: rubbish*) чушь *f*.

triple ['trɪpl] *adj* тройно́й ◆ *adv*: ~ **the distance/ the speed** тройно́е расстоя́ние/тройна́я ско́рость, в три ра́за да́льше/бы́стрее.

triple jump *n* тройно́й прыжо́к (в длину́).

triplets ['trɪplɪts] *npl* тройня́шки *fpl*.

triplicate ['trɪplɪkət] *n*: **in** ~ в трёх экземпля́рах.

tripod ['traɪpɔd] *n* трено́га.

Tripoli ['trɪpəlɪ] *n* Три́поли *m ind*.

tripper ['trɪpəʳ] *n* (*BRIT*) тури́ст(ка°).

tripwire ['trɪpwaɪəʳ] *n* *замаскиро́ванная про́волока, свя́занная с капка́ном и́ли взрывча́ткой*.

trite [traɪt] *adj* (*pej*) изби́тый.

triumph ['traɪʌmf] *n* (*satisfaction*) торжество́; (*great achievement*) триу́мф ◆ *vi*: **to** ~ (**over**) торжествова́ть (восторжествова́ть *perf*) (над +*instr*).

triumphal [traɪ'ʌmfl] *adj* (*arch, return*) триумфа́льный.

triumphant [traɪ'ʌmfənt] *adj* (*team, wave*) торжеству́ющий; (*return*) побе́дный.

triumphantly [traɪ'ʌmfəntlɪ] *adv* (*shout, look etc*) торжеству́юще.

trivia ['trɪvɪə] *npl* (*pej*) тривиа́льности *fpl*, тривиа́льные ве́щи *fpl*.

trivial ['trɪvɪəl] *adj* (*unimportant*) незначи́тельный° (незначи́телен); (*commonplace*) тривиа́льный° (тривиа́лен).

triviality [trɪvɪ'ælɪtɪ] *n* ме́лочи *fpl*.

trivialize ['trɪvɪəlaɪz] *vt* упроща́ть (упрости́ть° *perf*).

trod [trɔd] *pt of* **tread**.

trodden [trɔdn] *pp of* **tread**.

trolley ['trɔlɪ] *n* теле́жка°; (*also:* ~ **bus**) тролле́йбус.

trollop ['trɔləp] *n* (*pej*) лаху́дра.

trombone [trɔm'bəun] *n* тромбо́н.

troop [tru:p] *n* (*of people*) отря́д, гру́ппа; (*of monkeys*) ста́до ◆ *vi*: **to** ~ **in/out** входи́ть°

(войти* *perf*)/выходи́ть* (вы́йти* *perf*)
стро́ем; ~s *npl* (*MIL*) войска́ *ntpl*; a ~ of
children ста́йка ребяти́шек.
troop carrier *n* (*plane*) тра́нспортно-
деса́нтный самолёт; (*NAUT*: *also*: **troopship**)
тра́нспорт для перево́зки войск.
trooper ['tru:pə*'] *n* (*MIL*: *in cavalry*) кавалери́ст;
(: *in armoured regiment*) солда́т*; (*US*:
policeman) ко́нный полице́йский* *m adj*.
trooping the colour ['tru:pɪŋ-] *n* (*BRIT*:
ceremony) внос зна́мени.
troopship ['tru:pʃɪp] *n* тра́нспорт для
перево́зки войск.
trophy ['trəufɪ] *n* трофе́й.
tropic ['trɔpɪk] *n*: ~s тро́пики *mpl*; in the ~s в
тро́пиках; T~ of Cancer/Capricorn Тро́пик
Ра́ка/Козеро́га.
tropical ['trɔpɪkl] *adj* (*rain forest, climate etc*)
тропи́ческий*.
trot [trɔt] *n* рысь *f* ♦ *vi* (*horse*) идти́* (*impf*)
ры́сью; (*person*) бежа́ть* (*impf*) рысцо́й; on
the ~ (*BRIT*: *fig*) подря́д
▶ **trot out** *vt* (*excuse, reason*) приводи́ть*
(привести́* *perf*); (*names, facts*) сы́пать (*impf*)
+*instr*.
trouble ['trʌbl] *n* (*difficulty*) затрудне́ние,
неприя́тность *f*; (*worry, unrest*)
беспоко́йство; (*bother, effort*) хло́поты *pl* ♦ *vt*
(*worry*) беспоко́ить (*impf*); (*person: disturb*)
беспоко́ить (побеспоко́ить *perf*) ♦ *vi*: to ~ to
do побеспоко́иться (*perf*); ~s *npl*
(*personal, POL etc*) бе́ды *fpl*; to be in ~ име́ть
(*impf*) неприя́тности; (*ship, climber etc*) быть*
(*impf*) в беде́; to have ~ doing с трудо́м мочь
(*impf*) +*infin*; to go to the ~ of doing
забо́титься* (позабо́титься* *perf*) о том,
что́бы +*infin*; it's no ~! э́то ника́к не
затрудни́т меня́!; it's too much ~ сли́шком
мно́го хлопо́т; please don't ~ yourself
пожа́луйста, не беспоко́йтесь; the ~ is ...
беда́ в том, что ...; what's the ~? (*with broken
television etc*) где непола́дка?, в чём там
де́ло?; (*MED*) что Вас беспоко́ит?; stomach ~
больно́й желу́док.
troubled [trʌbld] *adj* (*person*) в постоя́нной
трево́ге; (*country*) бе́дствующий; (*life, era*)
беспоко́йный.
trouble-free ['trʌblfri:] *adj* (*period, campaign
etc*) без происше́ствий.
troublemaker ['trʌblmeɪkə*'] *n* смутья́н; (*child*)
прока́зник.
troubleshooter ['trʌblʃu:tə*'] *n* (*in conflict*)
*уполномо́ченный, выявля́ющий недоста́тки
в рабо́те компа́нии*.
troublesome ['trʌblsəm] *adj* (*child*)
прока́зливый.
trouble spot *n* (*MIL*) горя́чая то́чка*.
troubling ['trʌblɪŋ] *adj* трево́жный.

trough [trɔf] *n* (*also*: **drinking** ~) коры́то; (*also*:
feeding ~) корму́шка*; (*channel*) жёлоб; (*low
point*) впа́дина; a ~ of low pressure
(*METEOROLOGY*) фронт ни́зкого давле́ния.
trounce [trauns] *vt* (*defeat*) разбива́ть
(разби́ть* *perf*).
troupe [tru:p] *n* тру́ппа.
trouser press ['trauzə-] *n* приспособле́ние для
гла́жки брюк.
trousers ['trauzəz] *npl* брю́ки *mpl*; short ~
штаны́ *mpl*.
trouser suit *n* (*BRIT*) брю́чный костю́м.
trousseau ['tru:səu] (*pl* ~x *or* ~s) *n* прида́ное *nt
adj*.
trousseaux ['tru:səuz] *npl of* **trousseau**.
trout [traut] *n inv* (*ZOOL*) форе́ль *f*.
trowel ['trauəl] *n* (*garden tool*) сово́к*; (*builder's
tool*) мастеро́к*.
truant ['truənt] *n* (*BRIT*): to play ~ прогу́ливать
(прогуля́ть *perf*).
truce [tru:s] *n* переми́рие.
truck [trʌk] *n* (*lorry*) грузови́к*; (*RAIL*) откры́тая
това́рная платфо́рма; (*for luggage*)
теле́жка*, вагоне́тка*.
truck driver *n* води́тель *m* грузовика́.
trucker ['trʌkə*'] *n* води́тель *m* грузовика́.
truck farm *n* (*US*) овощево́дческая фе́рма.
trucking ['trʌkɪŋ] *n* (*esp US*) грузова́я
транспортиро́вка*.
trucking company *n* (*US*) грузово́е
тра́нспортное аге́нтство.
truculent ['trʌkjulənt] *adj* (*person*) свире́пый
(свире́п).
trudge [trʌdʒ] *vi* (*also*: ~ along) плести́сь*
(*impf*), тащи́ться (*impf*).
true [tru:] *adj* (*real, genuine*) настоя́щий*,
и́стинный; (*accurate: likeness*) то́чный;
(*faithful: friend*) настоя́щий*; (*wall*) прямо́й;
(*beam, wheel*) центри́рованный; to come ~
сбыва́ться (сбы́ться* *perf*); ~ to life
жи́зненный.
truffle ['trʌfl] *n* трю́фель *m*.
truly ['tru:lɪ] *adv* (*really*) по-настоя́щему;
(*truthfully*) и́скренне; yours ~ (*in letter*)
и́скренне Ваш.
trump [trʌmp] *n* (*also*: ~ card: *also fig*) ко́зырь
m; to turn up ~s (*fig*) подава́ть* (пода́ть* *perf*)
ру́ку по́мощи.
trumped-up [trʌmpt'ʌp] *adj* (*pej*)
сфабрико́ванный.
trumpet ['trʌmpɪt] *n* труба́.
truncated [trʌŋ'keɪtɪd] *adj* (*object*)
обре́занный; (*message*) сокращённый.
truncheon ['trʌntʃən] *n* (*BRIT*) дуби́нка*.
trundle ['trʌndl] *vt* (*push slowly*) кати́ть*
(*impf*) ♦ *vi*: to ~ along (*person*) брести́*
(*impf*); (*vehicle*) кати́ться* (*impf*).
trunk [trʌŋk] *n* (*of tree*) ствол*; (*of person*)
ту́ловище; (*of elephant*) хо́бот; (*case*)

---

* marks translations which have irregular inflections. The Russian-English side of the dictionary gives inflectional information.

доро́жный сунду́к; (*US: AUT*) бага́жник; **~s**
npl (*also:* **swimming ~s**) пла́вки* *pl*.
trunk call *n* (*BRIT: TEL*) междугоро́дные
переговоры *mpl*, междугоро́дный звоно́к*.
trunk road *n* (*BRIT*) магистра́ль *f*.
truss [trʌs] *n* (*MED*) грыжево́й банда́ж
▶ **truss (up)** *vt* (*CULIN*) перетя́гивать
(перетяну́ть* *perf*) бечёвкой; (*person*)
свя́зывать (связа́ть* *perf*).
trust [trʌst] *n* (*faith*) дове́рие; (*responsibility*)
долг*; (*LAW*) *управле́ние иму́ществом по*
дове́ренности; (*COMM*) трест ♦ *vt* (*rely on,*
have faith in) доверя́ть (*impf*) +*dat*; (*hope*): **to ~**
(that) полага́ть (*impf*)(, что); (*entrust*): **to ~ sth**
to sb доверя́ть (дове́рить *perf*) что-н кому́-н;
to take sth on ~ принима́ть (приня́ть* *perf*)
что-н на ве́ру; **in ~** (*LAW*) управля́емый по
дове́ренности.
trust company *n* (*COMM*) трест.
trusted ['trʌstɪd] *adj* (*friend, servant*)
пре́данный.
trustee [trʌs'tiː] *n* (*also LAW*) попечи́тель *m*.
trustful ['trʌstful] *adj* (*person, nature, smile*)
дове́рчивый (дове́рчив).
trust fund *n* (*COMM*) фонд тре́ста.
trusting ['trʌstɪŋ] *adj* (*person, nature*)
дове́рчивый (дове́рчив).
trustworthy ['trʌstwəːðɪ] *adj* (*person, report*)
надёжный, заслу́живающий дове́рия.
trusty ['trʌstɪ] *adj* испы́танный.
truth [truːθ] (*pl* **~s**) *n* пра́вда; (*universal*
principle) и́стина.
truthful ['truːθful] *adj* правди́вый (правди́в).
truthfully ['truːθfəlɪ] *adv* (*answer*) правди́во.
truthfulness ['truːθfəlnɪs] *n* правди́вость *f*.
try [traɪ] *n* (*attempt*) попы́тка*; (*RUGBY*) прохо́д
с мячо́м ♦ *vt* (*test*) пробовать (попробовать
perf); (*LAW: person*) суди́ть* (*impf*); (*strain:*
patience) испыты́вать (*impf*); (*attempt*): **to ~**
to do стара́ться (*impf*) *or* пыта́ться (*impf*) +*infin*
♦ *vi* (*make effort, attempt*) стара́ться (*impf*),
пыта́ться (*impf*); **to have a ~** пробовать
(попробовать *perf*); **I tried a different key** я
пыта́лся откры́ть други́м ключо́м; **to ~**
one's (very) best *or* **one's (very) hardest**
стара́ться (постара́ться *perf*) изо́ всех сил
▶ **try on** *vt* (*dress etc*) ме́рить (поме́рить *perf*),
примеря́ть (приме́рить *perf*); **to ~ it on** (*fig*)
вести́* (*impf*) себя́ на́гло
▶ **try out** *vt* пробовать (попробовать *perf*).
trying ['traɪɪŋ] *adj* (*person, experience*)
утоми́тельный* (утоми́телен).
tsar [zɑː] *n* царь* *m*.
T-shirt ['tiːʃəːt] *n* футбо́лка*.
T-square ['tiːskwɛə] *n* (*TECH*) рейсши́на.
TT *adj abbr* (*BRIT: inf*) = **teetotal** ♦ *abbr* (*US: POST*)
= *Trust Territory*; = *telegraphic transfer*
телегра́фный де́нежный перево́д.
tub [tʌb] *n* (*container*) бо́чка*; (*bath*) ва́нна.
tuba ['tjuːbə] *n* ту́ба.
tubby ['tʌbɪ] *adj* упи́танный.

tube [tjuːb] *n* (*pipe*) тру́бка*; (*container*)
тю́бик; (*BRIT: underground*) метро́ *nt ind*; (*for*
tyre) ка́мера; (*inf: television*): **the ~** те́лик.
tubeless ['tjuːblɪs] *adj* бескаме́рный.
tuber ['tjuːbə] *n* клу́бень *m*.
tuberculosis [tjubəːkjuˈləusɪs] *n* туберкулёз.
tube station *n* (*BRIT*) ста́нция *f* метро́.
tubing ['tjuːbɪŋ] *n* шланг тру́бки; **a piece of ~**
тру́бка*.
tubular ['tjuːbjuləʳ] *adj* (*furniture, metal*)
тру́бчатый.
TUC *n abbr* (*BRIT*): = *Trades Union Congress*
Конгре́сс (брита́нских) тред-юнио́нов.
tuck [tʌk] *vt* (*put*) подбира́ть (подобра́ть* *perf*)
♦ *n* (*SEWING*) вы́кладка
▶ **tuck away** *vt* (*money*) припря́тывать
(припря́тать* *perf*); (*building*): **to be ~ed away**
приткну́ться (*perf*)
▶ **tuck in** *vt* (*clothing*) заправля́ть (запра́вить*
perf); (*child*) укрыва́ть (укры́ть* *perf*) ♦ *vi* (*eat*)
умина́ть (умя́ть* *perf*)
▶ **tuck up** *vt* (*invalid, child*) укрыва́ть (укры́ть*
perf).
tuck shop *n* буфе́т.
Tue(s). *abbr* = **Tuesday**.
Tuesday ['tjuːzdɪ] *n* вто́рник; **it is ~ 23rd March**
(сего́дня) вто́рник 23-его ма́рта; **on ~** во
вто́рник; **on ~s** по вто́рникам; **every ~**
ка́ждый вто́рник; **every other ~** ка́ждый
второ́й вто́рник; **last/next ~** в про́шлый/
сле́дующий вто́рник; **the following ~** в
сле́дующий вто́рник; **~'s newspaper** газе́та
за вто́рник; **a week/fortnight on ~** во
вто́рник че́рез неде́лю/че́рез две неде́ли; **the**
~ before last позапро́шлый вто́рник; **the ~**
after next во вто́рник че́рез неде́лю; **~**
morning/lunchtime/afternoon/evening во
вто́рник у́тром/в обе́д/днём/ве́чером; **we'll**
spend ~ night in Rome во вто́рник мы
проведём ночь в Ри́ме.
tuft [tʌft] *n* (*of hair*) пучо́к*.
tug [tʌg] *n* (*ship*) букси́р ♦ *vt* тяну́ть* (*impf*).
tug of war *n* перетя́гивание кана́та; (*fig*)
тя́жба.
tuition [tjuːˈɪʃən] *n* (*BRIT*) обуче́ние; (: *private*
tuition) ча́стные уро́ки *mpl*, дома́шнее
обуче́ние; (: *US: school fees*) пла́та за
обуче́ние.
tulip ['tjuːlɪp] *n* тюльпа́н.
tumble ['tʌmbl] *n* (*fall*) паде́ние ♦ *vi* (*fall:*
person) па́дать (упа́сть* *perf*); (: *water*)
журча́ть (*impf*); (*somersault*) ска́тываться
(скати́ться* *perf*); **to ~ to sth** (*inf*) набрести́*
(*perf*) на что-н.
tumbledown ['tʌmbldaun] *adj* (*building*)
полуразру́шенный.
tumble dryer *n* (*BRIT*) суши́лка* для белья́.
tumbler ['tʌmbləʳ] *n* бока́л.
tummy ['tʌmɪ] *n* (*inf*) пу́зо *nt no pl*.
tummy tuck *n* *пласти́ческая опера́ция по*
ушива́нию живота́.

tumour ['tju:məʳ] (*US* tumor) *n* (*MED*) óпухоль *f*.
tumult ['tju:mʌlt] *n* шум, суматóха.
tumultuous [tju:'mʌltjuəs] *adj* бýрный.
tuna ['tju:nə] *n inv* (*also:* ~ **fish**) тунéц*.
tune [tju:n] *n* (*melody*) мотúв ♦ *vt* (*MUS, RADIO, TV*) настрáивать (настрóить *perf*); (*AUT*) налáживать (налáдить* *perf*); **the guitar is in/out of** ~ гитáра настрóена/расстрóена; **to sing in** ~ петь* чúсто; **to sing out of** ~ фальшúвить* (*impf*); **to be in/out of** ~ **with** (*fig*) быть* (*impf*) в ладý/не в ладý с +*instr*; **she was robbed to the** ~ **of £10,000** (*fig*) её ограбили на цéлых £10 000
▶ **tune in** *vi* (*RADIO, TV*): **to** ~ **in** (**to**) настрáиваться (настрóиться *perf*) (на +*acc*)
▶ **tune up** *vi* (*musician*) настрáивать (настрóить *perf*) инструмéнт; (*orchestra*) настрáивать (настрóить *perf*) инструмéнты.
tuneful ['tju:nful] *adj* (*music*) мелодúчный* (мелодúчен).
tuner ['tju:nəʳ] *n* (*radio set*) блок настрóйки; **piano** ~ настрóйщик фортепьяно.
tuner amplifier *n* резонáнсный усилúтель *m*.
tungsten ['tʌŋstn] *n* вольфрáм.
tunic ['tju:nɪk] *n* тýника.
tuning fork ['tju:nɪŋ-] *n* камертóн.
Tunis ['tju:nɪs] *n* Тунúс.
Tunisia [tju:'nɪzɪə] *n* Тунúс.
Tunisian [tju:'nɪzɪən] *adj* Тунúсский* ♦ *n* тунúсец*(-ска*).
tunnel ['tʌnl] *n* (*passage*) туннéль *m*; (*in mine*) штóльня ♦ *vi* проклáдывать (проложúть* *perf*) туннéль.
tunnel vision *n* ýзость *f* зрéния; (*fig*) трýбочное зрéние.
tunny ['tʌnɪ] *n* тунéц*.
turban ['tə:bən] *n* чалмá, тюрбáн.
turbid ['tə:bɪd] *adj* (*water*) мýтный* (мýтен); (*air*) пыльный* (пылен).
turbine ['tə:baɪn] *n* (*TECH*) турбúна.
turbo ['tə:bəu] *n* турбúна.
turbojet [tə:bəu'dʒɛt] *n* (*AVIAT*) турбо-реактúвный самолёт.
turboprop [tə:bəu'prɔp] *n* (*engine*) турбо-винтовóй мотóр.
turbot ['tə:bət] *n inv* белокóрый пáлтус.
turbulence ['tə:bjuləns] *n* встрéчные потóки *mpl* вóздуха.
turbulent ['tə:bjulənt] *adj* (*also fig*) бýрный.
tureen [tə'ri:n] *n* (*for soup*) сýпница; (*for vegetables*) глубóкое блюдо с крышкой.
turf [tə:f] *n* (*grass*) дёрн; (*clod*) торф ♦ *vt* (*area*) покрывáть (покрыть* *perf*) дёрном; **the T**~ (*course*) скаковáя дорóжка; (*horse-racing*) скáчки *mpl*
▶ **turf out** *vt* (*inf: person*) выставлять (выставить* *perf*).
turf accountant *n* (*BRIT*) букмéкер.

turgid ['tə:dʒɪd] *adj* (*speech*) напыщенный.
Turin ['tjuə'rɪn] *n* Турúн.
Turk [tə:k] *n* тýрок* (турчáнка*).
Turkey ['tə:kɪ] *n* Тýрция.
turkey ['tə:kɪ] *n* индéйка.
Turkish ['tə:kɪʃ] *adj* турéцкий* ♦ *n* (*LING*) турéцкий* язык*.
Turkish bath *n* турéцкие бáни *fpl*.
Turkish delight *n* рахáт-лукýм.
Turkmen ['tə:kmɛn] *n,adj* туркмéнский*; (*person*) туркмéн(ка*); (*LING*) туркмéнский* язык*.
Turkmenia [tə:k'mi:nɪə] *n* Туркмéния.
turmeric ['tə:mərɪk] *n* (*CULIN*) куркýма.
turmoil ['tə:mɔɪl] *n* смятéние; **in** ~ в смятéнии.
turn [tə:n] *n* поворóт; (*performance*) нóмер*; (*chance*) óчередь *f*; (*inf: MED*) вывих ♦ *vt* поворáчивать (повернýть* *perf*); (*collar*) отворáчивать (отвернýть* *perf*); (*change: wood, metal*) обтáчивать (обточúть* *perf*) ♦ *vi* (*object*) поворáчиваться (повернýться *perf*); (*person: look back*) оборáчиваться (обернýться *perf*); (*reverse direction: in car*) развора́чиваться (развернýться *perf*); (: *wind*) переменяться (переменúться *perf*); (*milk*) скисáть (скúснуть *perf*); (*change*) изменяться (изменúться *perf*); (*become*): **he's** ~**ed forty** емý испóлнилось сóрок; **a good/bad** ~ дóбрая/плохáя услýга; **it gave me quite a** ~ э́то меня сúльно испугáло; **"no left** ~**"** (*AUT*) "нет лéвого поворóта"; **it's your** ~ твоя óчередь; **in** ~ по óчереди; **to take** ~**s at sth** дéлать (*impf*) что-н по óчереди; **at the** ~ **of the century** на рубежé вéка; **at the** ~ **of the year** под конéц гóда; **to take a** ~ **for the worse** (*situations, events*) принимáть (принять* *perf*) дурнóй оборóт; **his health** *or* **he has taken a** ~ **for the worse** емý сдéлалось хýже; **to** ~ **sth into sth** (*change*) превращáть (превратúть* *perf*) что-н в что-н; **to** ~ **nasty** озлобляться (озлобúться* *perf*)
▶ **turn about** *vi* поворáчиваться (повернýться *perf*)
▶ **turn away** *vi* отворáчиваться (отвернýться *perf*) ♦ *vt* (*business, applicant*) отклонять (отклонúть* *perf*)
▶ **turn back** *vi* поворáчивать (повернýть *perf*) назáд ♦ *vt* (*person*) вернýть (*perf*); (*vehicle*) развора́чивать (развернýть *perf*); (*clock*) переводúть* (перевестú* *perf*) назáд; **to** ~ **back the clock** (*fig*) повернýть (*perf*) врéмя вспять
▶ **turn down** *vt* (*request*) отклонять (отклонúть* *perf*); (*heating*) уменьшáть (уменьшúть* *perf*); (*bedclothes*) отворáчивать (отвернýть *perf*)
▶ **turn in** *vi* (*inf: go to bed*) идтú* (пойтú* *perf*) на боковýю ♦ *vt* (*fold*) сворáчивать

---

* marks translations which have irregular inflections. The Russian–English side of the dictionary gives inflectional information.

(сверну́ть *perf*)
▶ **turn off** *vi* (*from road*) свора́чивать (сверну́ть *perf*) ♦ *vt* выключа́ть (вы́ключить *perf*)
▶ **turn on** *vt* включа́ть (включи́ть *perf*)
▶ **turn out** *vt* (*light, gas*) выключа́ть (вы́ключить *perf*); (*produce*) выпуска́ть (вы́пустить* *perf*) ♦ *vi* (*troops, doctor, voters*) прибыва́ть (прибы́ть* *perf*); **to ~ out to be** (*prove to be*) ока́зываться (оказа́ться* *perf*) +*instr*
▶ **turn over** *vi* (*person*) перевора́чиваться (переверну́ться *perf*) ♦ *vt* (*object, page*) перевора́чивать (переверну́ть *perf*); (*funds, production etc*): **to ~ over to** передава́ть* (переда́ть* *perf*) +*dat*
▶ **turn round** *vi* (*person, vehicle*) развора́чиваться (разверну́ться *perf*); (*rotate*) повора́чиваться (*impf*)
▶ **turn up** *vi* (*person*) объявля́ться (объяви́ться* *perf*); (*lost object*) находи́ться* (найти́сь* *perf*) ♦ *vt* (*collar*) поднима́ть (подня́ть* *perf*); (*radio*) де́лать (сде́лать *perf*) гро́мче; (*heater*) де́лать (сде́лать *perf*) вы́ше.
turnabout ['tə:nəbaut] *n* (*fig*) поворо́т на 180 гра́дусов.
turnaround ['tə:nəraund] *n* (*fig*) = **turnabout**.
turncoat ['tə:nkəut] *n* ренега́т, отсту́пник.
turned-up ['tə:ndʌp] *adj* (*nose*) вздёрнутый, курно́сый.
turning ['tə:nɪŋ] *n* (*in road*) поворо́т; **the first ~ on the right** пе́рвый поворо́т напра́во.
turning circle *n* (*BRIT: AUT*) окру́жность *f* поворо́та.
turning point *n* (*fig*) поворо́тный пункт, перело́мный моме́нт.
turning radius *n* (*US*) = **turning circle**.
turnip ['tə:nɪp] *n* (*BOT, CULIN*) ре́па.
turnout ['tə:naut] *n* (*of voters etc*) число́.
turnover ['tə:nəuvə²] *n* (*COMM*) оборо́т; (: *of staff*) теку́честь *f*; (*CULIN*): **apple ~** я́блочная сло́йка; **there is a rapid ~ in staff** больша́я теку́честь ка́дров.
turnpike ['tə:npaɪk] *n* (*US*) магистра́ль *f*, шоссе́ *nt ind*.
turnstile ['tə:nstaɪl] *n* турнике́т.
turntable ['tə:nteɪbl] *n* (*on record player*) верту́шка*, прои́грыватель *m*.
turn-up ['tə:nʌp] *n* (*BRIT: on trousers*) манже́та, отворо́т; **that's a ~ for the books!** вот неожи́данность!
turpentine ['tə:pəntaɪn] *n* (*also:* **turps**) скипида́р.
turquoise ['tə:kwɔɪz] *n* (*stone*) бирюза́ ♦ *adj* (*colour*) бирюзо́вый.
turret ['tʌrɪt] *n* ба́шенка*.
turtle ['tə:tl] *n* черепа́ха.
turtleneck (sweater) ['tə:tlnɛk(-)] *n* водола́зка*.
Tuscany ['tʌskənɪ] *n* Тоска́нь *f*.
tusk [tʌsk] *n* (*of elephant*) би́вень* *m*; (*of boar*)

клык*.
tussle ['tʌsl] *n* (*fight, scuffle*) схва́тка*.
tutor ['tju:tə²] *n* (*SCOL*) преподава́тель(ница) *m(f)*; (*private tutor*) репети́тор.
tutorial [tju:'tɔ:rɪəl] *n* (*SCOL*) семина́р.
tuxedo [tʌk'si:dəu] *n* (*US*) смо́кинг.
TV [ti:'vi:] *n abbr* (= **television**) ТВ= *телеви́дение*; **~ dinner** пищево́й полуфабрика́т, го́дный к потребле́нию по́сле разогре́ва.
twaddle ['twɔdl] *n* (*inf*) чепуха́.
twang [twæŋ] *n* (*of instrument*) протя́жный звук; (*of voice*) гну́сость *f* ♦ *vi* протя́жно звене́ть (зазвене́ть *perf*) ♦ *vt* (*guitar*) бренча́ть* (*impf*) на +*prp*.
tweak [twi:k] *vt* дёргать (дёрнуть *perf*) за +*acc*.
tweed [twi:d] *n* твид ♦ *adj* (*jacket, skirt*) тви́довый.
tweezers ['twi:zəz] *npl* пинце́т *msg*.
twelfth [twɛlfθ] *adj* двена́дцатый; *see also* **fifth**.
Twelfth Night *n* Двена́дцатая ночь *f*.
twelve [twɛlv] *n* двена́дцать*; **at ~** (*o'clock*) (*midday*) в двена́дцать (дня); (*midnight*) в двена́дцать (но́чи); *see also* **five**.
twentieth ['twɛntɪɪθ] *adj* двадца́тый; *see also* **fifth**.
twenty ['twɛntɪ] *n* два́дцать*; *see also* **fifty**.
twerp [twə:p] *n* (*inf*) крети́н.
twice [twaɪs] *adv* два́жды; **~ as much** вдво́е бо́льше; **~ a week** два ра́за в неде́лю; **she is ~ your age** она́ вдво́е *or* в два ра́за ста́рше Вас.
twiddle ['twɪdl] *vt* тереби́ть* (*impf*) ♦ *vi*: **to ~ with sth** тереби́ть* (*impf*) что-н; **to ~ one's thumbs** (*fig*) бить* баклу́ши.
twig [twɪg] *n* ве́тка* ♦ *vi* (*inf*) смекну́ть (*perf*).
twilight ['twaɪlaɪt] *n* су́мерки *mpl*; (*morning*) (предрассве́тные) су́мерки; **in the ~** в су́мерках.
twill [twɪl] *n* (*cloth*) твил, са́ржа.
twin [twɪn] *adj* (*towers*) па́рный ♦ *n* близне́ц*, двойня́*; (*room in hotel etc*) двойно́й но́мер* ♦ *vt* (*towns etc*) де́лать (сде́лать *perf*) побрати́мами; **~ sister** сестра́-близне́ц*; **~ brother** брат-близне́ц*.
twin-bedded room ['twɪn'bɛdɪd-] *n* но́мер с двумя́ односпа́льными крова́тями.
twin beds *npl* две односпа́льные крова́ти *fpl*.
twin-carburettor ['twɪnkɑ:bju'rɛtə²] *adj* двухкарбюра́торный.
twine [twaɪn] *n* бечёвка ♦ *vi* (*plant*) ви́ться* (*impf*).
twin-engined [twɪn'ɛndʒɪnd] *adj* (*aircraft*) с двумя́ дви́гателями.
twinge [twɪndʒ] *n* (*of pain*) при́ступ; (*of conscience, regret*) уко́л.
twinkle ['twɪŋkl] *vi* (*star, light*) мерца́ть (*impf*); (*eyes*) мига́ть (*impf*), подми́гивать (*impf*) ♦ *n* мерца́ние.
twin town *n* го́род-побрати́м.
twirl [twə:l] *vt* верте́ть* (*impf*) ♦ *vi* крути́ться*

(*impf*) ◆ *n* поворо́т.

twist [twɪst] *n* (*action*) закру́чивание; (*in road, coil, flex*) изги́б; (*in story*) поворо́т ◆ *vt* (*turn*) изгиба́ть (изогну́ть *perf*); (*injure: ankle etc*) вывихивать (вы́вихнуть *perf*); (*weave*) сплета́ть (сплести́* *perf*); (*fig: meaning, words*) искажа́ть (исказить* *perf*) ◆ *vi* (*road, river*) извива́ться (*impf*).

twisted ['twɪstɪd] *adj* (*wire, rope*) скру́ченный; (*ankle, wrist*) вы́вихнутый; (*fig: logic, mind*) извращённый.

twit [twɪt] *n* (*inf*) недоу́мок*.

twitch [twɪtʃ] *n* (*pull*) рыво́к*; (*nervous*) подёргивание ◆ *vi* (*muscle, body*) подёргиваться (*impf*).

two [tu:] *n* два* *m/nt* (*f* две*); ~ **by** ~, **in** ~**s** па́рами; **to put** ~ **and** ~ **together** (*fig*) сложи́ть (*perf*) два и два; *see also* **five**.

two-bit [tu:'bɪt] *adj* (*esp US: inf*) расхо́жий.

two-door [tu:'dɔ:'] *adj* (*AUT*) двухдве́рный.

two-faced [tu:'feɪst] *adj* (*pej: person*) двули́чный* (двули́чен).

twofold ['tu:fəuld] *adj* (*increase*) двойно́й; (*reply*) дво́йственный ◆ *adv*: **to increase** ~ вдво́е.

two-piece (suit) ['tu:pi:s-] *n* (костю́м) дво́йка.

two-piece swimsuit *n* разде́льный купа́льник.

two-ply ['tu:plaɪ] *adj* (*wool*) двойно́й; (*tissues*) двухсло́йный* (двухсло́ен).

two-seater car [tu:'si:tə-] *n* двухме́стный автомоби́ль *m*.

twosome ['tu:səm] *n* (*people*) па́ра.

two-stroke ['tu:strəuk] *n* (*also:* ~ **engine**) двухта́ктный дви́гатель *m* ◆ *adj* двухта́ктный.

two-tone ['tu:'təun] *adj* (*in colour*) двухцве́тный.

two-way ['tu:weɪ] *adj*: ~ **traffic** двусторо́ннее движе́ние; ~ **radio** приёмно-передаю́щая радиоста́нция.

TX *abbr* (*US: POST*) = *Texas*.

tycoon [taɪ'ku:n] *n*: (**business**) ~ магна́т.

type [taɪp] *n* (*category, model, example*) тип; (*TYP*) шрифт ◆ *vt* (*letter etc*) печа́тать (напеча́тать *perf*); **what** ~ **do you want?** како́й вид Вы бы хоте́ли?; **in bold** ~ жи́рным шри́фтом; **in italic** ~ курси́вом шри́фтом.

typecast ['taɪpkɑ:st] *adj* (*actor*) одноти́пных роле́й.

typeface ['taɪpfeɪs] *n* шрифт.

typescript ['taɪpskrɪpt] *n* машинопи́сный текст.

typeset ['taɪpsɛt] *vt* набира́ть (набра́ть* *perf*).

typesetter ['taɪpsɛtə'] *n* набо́рщик(-и́ца).

typewriter ['taɪpraɪtə'] *n* пи́шущая маши́нка*.

typewritten ['taɪprɪtn] *adj* машинопи́сный, напеча́танный (напеча́тан) (на маши́нке).

typhoid ['taɪfɔɪd] *n* брюшно́й тиф.

typhoon [taɪ'fu:n] *n* тайфу́н.

typhus ['taɪfəs] *n* сыпно́й тиф.

typical ['tɪpɪkl] *adj* (*behaviour, weather etc*): ~ (**of**) типи́чный* (типи́чен) (для +*gen*); **that's** ~! (*pej*) вот так всегда́!

typify ['tɪpɪfaɪ] *vt* явля́ться (яви́ться* *perf*) типи́чным приме́ром +*gen*.

typing ['taɪpɪŋ] *n* машинопись *f*.

typing error *n* опеча́тка*.

typing pool *n* (*BRIT*) машинопи́сное бюро́ *nt ind*.

typist ['taɪpɪst] *n* машини́стка*.

typo ['taɪpəu] *n abbr* (*inf.* = *typographical error*) типогра́фская опеча́тка*.

typography [tɪ'pɔgrəfɪ] *n* полигра́фия.

tyranny ['tɪrənɪ] *n* тирани́я, деспоти́зм.

tyrant ['taɪərnt] *n* тира́н, де́спот.

tyre ['taɪə'] (*US* **tire**) *n* ши́на.

tyre pressure *n* давле́ние в ши́не.

Tyrol [tɪ'rəul] *n* Тиро́ль *m*.

Tyrolean [tɪrə'li:ən] *adj* тиро́льский ◆ *n* тиро́лец*.

Tyrolese [tɪrə'li:z] = **Tyrolean**.

Tyrrhenian Sea [tɪ'ri:nɪən-] *n*: **the** ~~ Тирре́нское мо́ре.

tzar [zɑ:'] *n* = **tsar**.

---

* marks translations which have irregular inflections. The Russian-English side of the dictionary gives inflectional information.

~ U, u ~

U, u [ju:] *n* (*letter*) 21-ая бу́ква англи́йского алфави́та.

U *n abbr* (*BRIT: CINEMA:* = *universal*) фильм, приго́дный для пока́за всем возрастны́м гру́ппам.

UAW *n abbr* (*US*) = *United Automobile Workers*.

UB40 *n abbr* (*BRIT:* = *unemployment benefit form 40*) бланк, заполня́емый при получе́нии посо́бия по безрабо́тице.

U-bend ['ju:bɛnd] *n* (*in pipe*) двойно́й изги́б.

ubiquitous [ju:'bɪkwɪtəs] *adj* вездесу́щий* (вездесу́щ).

UCCA ['ʌkə] *n abbr* (*BRIT:* = *Universities Central Council on Admissions*) организа́ция, координи́рующая приём в университе́ты.

UDA *n abbr* (*BRIT:* = *Ulster Defence Association*) военизи́рованная организа́ция, бо́рющаяся за сохране́ние Се́верой Ирла́ндии как ча́сти Великобрита́нии.

UDC *n abbr* (*BRIT:* = *Urban District Council*).

udder ['ʌdəʳ] *n* вы́мя* *nt*.

UDI *n abbr* (*BRIT: POL:* = *unilateral declaration of independence*) односторо́ннее провозглаше́ние незави́симости.

UDR *n abbr* (*BRIT:* = *Ulster Defence Regiment*) ча́сти брита́нской а́рмии, размещённые в Се́верной Ирла́ндии.

UEFA [ju:'eɪfə] *n abbr* (= *Union of European Football Associations*) УЕФА́.

UFO ['ju:fəu] *n abbr* (= *unidentified flying object*) НЛО= неопо́знанный лета́ющий объе́кт.

Uganda [ju:'gændə] *n* Уга́нда.

Ugandan [ju:'gændən] *adj* уга́ндский ♦ *n* уга́ндец*(-дка*).

UGC *n abbr* (*BRIT:* = *University Grants Committee*) комите́т, координи́рующий финанси́рование университе́тов.

ugh [ə:h] *excl* фу.

ugliness ['ʌglɪnɪs] *n* уро́дство

ugly ['ʌglɪ] *adj* (*person, dress etc*) уро́дливый (уро́длив), безобра́зный* (безобра́зен); (*dangerous: situation*) опа́сный* (опа́сен).

UHF *abbr* (= *ultra-high frequency*) УВЧ= ультравысо́кая частота́.

UHT *abbr* = *ultra heat treated* ♦ *adj abbr*: ~ **milk** молоко́, проше́дшее обрабо́тку сверх-высо́кой температу́рой.

UK *n abbr* = **United Kingdom**.

Ukraine [ju:'kreɪn] *n* Украи́на.

Ukrainian [ju:'kreɪnɪən] *adj* украи́нский ♦ *n* украи́нец*(-нка); (*LING*) украи́нский* язы́к*.

Ulan Bator *n* [u'lɑ:n'bɑ:tɔ:'] Ула́н-Ба́тор.

ulcer ['ʌlsəʳ] *n* я́зва.

Ulster ['ʌlstəʳ] *n* О́льстер.

ulterior [ʌl'tɪərɪəʳ] *adj*: ~ **motive** скры́тый моти́в.

ultimata [ʌltɪ'meɪtə] *npl of* **ultimatum**.

ultimate ['ʌltɪmət] *adj* (*final*) оконча́тельный*, коне́чный; (*greatest*) преде́льный* ♦ *n*: **the ~ in luxury** преде́л ро́скоши.

ultimately ['ʌltɪmətlɪ] *adv* в конце́ концо́в.

ultimatum [ʌltɪ'meɪtəm] (*pl* ~**s** *or* **ultimata**) *n* ультима́тум.

ultrasonic [ʌltrə'sɔnɪk] *adj* (*sound*) сверхзвуково́й, ультразвуково́й.

ultrasound ['ʌltrəsaund] *n* ультразву́к.

ultraviolet ['ʌltrə'vaɪəlɪt] *adj* (*light etc*) ультрафиоле́товый.

umbilical cord [ʌm'bɪlɪkl-] *n* пупови́на.

umbrage ['ʌmbrɪdʒ] *n*: **to take ~** обижа́ться (оби́деться* *perf*).

umbrella [ʌm'brɛlə] *n* зо́нтик, зонт*; (*fig*): **under the ~ of** под защи́той +*gen*.

umlaut ['umlaut] *n* у́мляут.

umpire ['ʌmpaɪəʳ] *n* (*TENNIS, CRICKET*) судья́* *m*, рефери́ *m ind* ♦ *vt* (*game*) суди́ть* (*impf*).

umpteen [ʌmp'ti:n] *adj* (*inf*) бесчи́сленный; ~ **stories** бесконе́чное коли́чество исто́рии.

umpteenth [ʌmp'ti:nθ] *adj* (*inf*): **for the ~ time** в э́нный *or* со́тый раз.

UMW *n abbr* = *United Mineworkers of America*.

UN *n abbr* = **United Nations**.

unabashed [ʌnə'bæʃt] *adj*: **she seemed ~** она́ каза́лось не была́ возмути́мой.

unabated [ʌnə'beɪtɪd] *adj* (*enthusiasm, excitement*) неосла́бный* (неосла́бен) ♦ *adv*: **to continue ~** продолжа́ться (продо́лжиться *perf*) с то́й же си́лой.

unable [ʌn'eɪbl] *adj* неспосо́бный*; **he is ~ to pay** он не спосо́бен заплати́ть.

unabridged [ʌnə'brɪdʒd] *adj* (*novel etc*) несокращённый

unacceptable [ʌnək'sɛptəbl] *adj* неприе́млемый (неприе́млем).

unaccompanied [ʌnə'kʌmpənɪd] *adj* (*child, luggage*) не сопровожда́емый; (*song*) без аккомпанеме́нта.

unaccountably [ʌnə'kauntəblɪ] *adv* необъясни́мо.

unaccounted [ʌnə'kauntɪd] *adj*: **several people are still ~ for** не́скольких люде́й недосчита́лись.

unaccustomed [ʌnə'kʌstəmd] *adj*: **he is ~ to …** он не привы́чен к +*dat* ....

unacquainted [ʌnə'kweɪntɪd] *adj*: **he is ~ with these ideas** он не знако́м с э́тими иде́ями.

unadulterated [ʌnə'dʌltəreɪtɪd] *adj* настоя́щий*; (*wine*) чи́стый*.

unaffected [ʌnə'fɛktɪd] *adj* (*person, behaviour*) есте́ственный* (есте́ствен); **~ by** (*emotionally*) безуча́стный (безуча́стен) к +*dat*.

unafraid [ʌnə'freɪd] *adj* незапу́ганный.

unaided [ʌn'eɪdɪd] *adv* без по́мощи.

unanimity [ju:nə'nɪmɪtɪ] *n* единоду́шие, единогла́сие.

unanimous [ju:'nænɪməs] *adj* единоду́шный* (единоду́шен), единогла́сный* (единогла́сен).

unanimously [ju:'nænɪməslɪ] *adv* единоду́шно, единогла́сно.

unanswered [ʌn'ɑ:nsəd] *adj* оста́вшийся без отве́та.

unappetizing [ʌn'æpɪtaɪzɪŋ] *adj* (*food etc*) неаппети́тный* (неаппети́тен).

unappreciative [ʌnə'pri:ʃɪətɪv] *adj* неблаго-да́рный* (неблагода́рен).

unarmed [ʌn'ɑ:md] *adj* безору́жный* (безору́жен); (*combat*) без ору́жия.

unashamed [ʌnə'ʃeɪmd] *adj* бессты́дный* (бессты́ден).

unassisted [ʌnə'sɪstɪd] *adj*, *adv* без посторо́нней по́мощи.

unassuming [ʌnə'sju:mɪŋ] *adj* (*person, manner*) непритяза́тельный* (непритяза́телен).

unattached [ʌnə'tætʃt] *adj* (*person*) одино́кий* (одино́к); (*part etc*) неприкреплённый*.

unattended [ʌnə'tɛndɪd] *adj* оста́вленный (оста́влен) без присмо́тра.

unattractive [ʌnə'træktɪv] *adj* непривлек-а́тельный* (непривлека́телен).

unauthorized [ʌn'ɔ:θəraɪzd] *adj* неразреш-ённый*.

unavailable [ʌnə'veɪləbl] *adj* (*article, room etc*) недосту́пный* (недосту́пен); (*person*) недосяга́емый (недосяга́ем).

unavoidable [ʌnə'vɔɪdəbl] *adj* (*delay*) неизбе́жный* (неизбе́жен).

unavoidably [ʌnə'vɔɪdəblɪ] *adv* (*delayed etc*) неизбе́жно.

unaware [ʌnə'wɛə'] *adj*: **to be ~ of** не подозрева́ть (*impf*) о +*prp*.

unawares [ʌnə'wɛəz] *adv* враспло́х.

unbalanced [ʌn'bælənst] *adj* (*report*) односторо́нний*; (*mentally*) неуравнове́шенный* (неуравнове́шен).

unbearable [ʌn'bɛərəbl] *adj* невыноси́мый (невыноси́м).

unbeatable [ʌn'bi:təbl] *adj* (*team*) непобеди́мый (непобеди́м); (*price, quality*) непревзойдённый* (непревзойдён).

unbeaten [ʌn'bi:tn] *adj* (*person*) непобеди́мый (непобеди́м); (*record*) непревзойдённый* (непревзойдён).

unbecoming [ʌnbɪ'kʌmɪŋ] *adj* (*language, behaviour*) неподоба́ющий (неподоба́ющ); (*garment*) не иду́щий к лицу́; **that dress is ~ on you** Вам не идёт э́то пла́тье.

unbeknown(st) [ʌnbɪ'nəun(st)] *adv*: **~ to me** без моего́ ве́дома.

unbelief [ʌnbɪ'li:f] *n* неве́рие.

unbelievable [ʌnbɪ'li:vəbl] *adj* невероя́тный* (невероя́тен).

unbelievably [ʌnbɪ'li:vəblɪ] *adv* невероя́тно.

unbend [ʌn'bɛnd] *irreg vi* (*relax*) расслабля́ться (расслаби́ться* *perf*) ♦ *vt* (*wire*) выпрямля́ть (вы́прямить* *perf*).

unbending [ʌn'bɛndɪŋ] *adj* непреклонный* (непрекло́нен).

unbias(s)ed [ʌn'baɪəst] *adj* (*report*) непредвзя́тый (непредвзя́т); (*person*) беспристра́стный* (беспристра́стен).

unblemished [ʌn'blɛmɪʃt] *adj* незапя́тнанный (незапя́тнан).

unblock [ʌn'blɔk] *vt* (*pipe*) прочища́ть (прочи́стить* *perf*).

unborn [ʌn'bɔ:n] *adj* (ещё) не рождённый.

unbounded [ʌn'baundɪd] *adj* безграни́чный* (безграни́чен).

unbreakable [ʌn'breɪkəbl] *adj* небью́щийся.

unbridled [ʌn'braɪdld] *adj* необу́зданный* (необу́здан).

unbroken [ʌn'brəukən] *adj* (*seal*) це́лый* (цел); (*silence, series*) непре́рванный; (*window*) неразби́тый, це́лый* (цел); (*SPORT: record*) непоби́тый.

unbuckle [ʌn'bʌkl] *vt* (*belt, shoe*) расстёгивать (расстегну́ть* *perf*).

unburden [ʌn'bə:dn] *vt*: **to ~ o.s. (to sb)** излива́ть (изли́ть* *perf*) ду́шу (кому́-н).

unbusinesslike [ʌn'bɪznɪslaɪk] *adj* неделово́й.

unbutton [ʌn'bʌtn] *vt* расстёгивать (расстегну́ть* *perf*).

uncalled-for [ʌn'kɔ:ldfɔ:'] *adj* неуме́стный* (неуме́стен).

uncanny [ʌn'kænɪ] *adj* (*resemblance, knack*) необъясни́мый (необъясни́м); (*silence*) жу́ткий* (жу́ток).

unceasing [ʌn'si:sɪŋ] *adj* (*misery, flow etc*) беспреры́вный (беспреры́вен); (*search*) неуста́нный* (неуста́нен).

unceremonious [ʌnsɛrɪ'məunɪəs] *adj* (*abrupt, rude*) бесцеремо́нный* (бесцеремо́нен).

uncertain [ʌn'sə:tn] *adj* (*hesitant*)

---

* marks translations which have irregular inflections. The Russian-English side of the dictionary gives inflectional information.

неуве́ренный* (неуве́рен), нереши́тельный* (нереши́телен); (*unsure*): ~ **about** неуве́ренный* (неуве́рен) относи́тельно +*gen*; **in no ~ terms** без обиняко́в.
uncertainty [ʌnˈsəːtntɪ] *n* (*not knowing*) неопределённость *f*; (*often pl: doubt*) сомне́ние.
unchallenged [ʌnˈtʃælɪndʒd] *adj* не вызыва́ющий* возраже́ний; **to go ~** не вызыва́ть (вы́звать* *perf*) возраже́ний.
unchanged [ʌnˈtʃeɪndʒd] *adj* (*condition*) неизмени́вшийся; **my orders remain ~** мои́ прика́зы остаю́тся неизме́нными.
uncharitable [ʌnˈtʃærɪtəbl] *adj* немилосе́рдный* (немилосе́рден).
uncharted [ʌnˈtʃɑːtɪd] *adj* (*land, sea*) не отме́ченный на ка́рте.
unchecked [ʌnˈtʃɛkt] *adv* беспрепя́тственно.
uncivil [ʌnˈsɪvɪl] *adj* грубый* (груб).
uncivilized [ʌnˈsɪvɪlaɪzd] *adj* (*country, people*) нецивилизо́ванный (нецивилизо́ван); (*fig: behaviour etc*) ди́кий* (дик); **at an ~ hour** ни свет, ни заря́.
uncle [ˈʌŋkl] *n* дя́дя* *m*.
unclear [ʌnˈklɪəʳ] *adj* нея́сный* (нея́сен); **I'm still ~ about what I'm supposed to do** мне всё ещё нея́сно, что мне на́до де́лать.
uncoil [ʌnˈkɔɪl] *vt* разма́тывать (размота́ть *perf*) ♦ *vi* разма́тываться (размота́ться *perf*).
uncomfortable [ʌnˈkʌmfətəbl] *adj* (*physically*) неудо́бный* (неудо́бен); (*uneasy*) неудо́бный* (неудо́бен), нело́вкий* (нело́вок); (*unpleasant*) трево́жный* (трево́жен).
uncomfortably [ʌnˈkʌmfətəblɪ] *adv* (*sit*) неудо́бно; (*smile*) нело́вко; (*tall, shy*) до нело́вкого.
uncommitted [ʌnkəˈmɪtɪd] *adj* нейтра́льный* (нейтра́лен).
uncommon [ʌnˈkɔmən] *adj* (*rare, unusual*) необы́чный* (необы́чен).
uncommunicative [ʌnkəˈmjuːnɪkətɪv] *adj* необщи́тельный* (необщи́телен).
uncomplicated [ʌnˈkɔmplɪkeɪtɪd] *adj* несло́жный* (несло́жен).
uncompromising [ʌnˈkɔmprəmaɪzɪŋ] *adj* бескомпроми́ссный.
unconcerned [ʌnkənˈsəːnd] *adj* (*person*) беззабо́тный* (беззабо́тен); ~ **about** равноду́шный* (равноду́шен) к +*dat*.
unconditional [ʌnkənˈdɪʃənl] *adj* (*acceptance, obedience*) безусло́вный* (безусло́вен); (*discharge, surrender*) безогово́рочный* (безогово́рочен).
uncongenial [ʌnkənˈdʒiːnɪəl] *adj* (*surroundings*) чу́ждый* (чужд), неприя́тный* (неприя́тен).
unconnected [ʌnkəˈnɛktɪd] *adj* (*unrelated*): ~ **(with)** несвя́занный (с +*instr*).
unconscious [ʌnˈkɔnʃəs] *adj* без созна́ния; (*unaware*): ~ **of** не сознаю́щий* +*gen* ♦ *n*: **the ~** подсозна́ние; **he was knocked ~** он упа́л

без созна́ния.
unconsciously [ʌnˈkɔnʃəslɪ] *adv* (*unawares*) подсозна́тельно.
unconsciousness [ʌnˈkɔnʃəsnɪs] *n* бессозна́тельное состоя́ние.
unconstitutional [ˈʌnkɔnstɪˈtjuːʃənl] *adj* неконституцио́нный* (неконституцио́нен).
uncontested [ʌnkənˈtɛstɪd] *adj* (*champion*) неоспори́мый* (неоспори́м); ~ **election** вы́боры, на кото́рых баллоти́руется (лишь) оди́н кандида́т.
uncontrollable [ʌnkənˈtrəuləbl] *adj* (*child, animal*) неуправля́емый (неуправля́ем); (*temper*) неукроти́мый (неукроти́м); (*laughter*) неудержи́мый (неудержи́м).
uncontrolled [ʌnkənˈtrəuld] *adj* безу́держный* (безу́держен).
unconventional [ʌnkənˈvɛnʃənl] *adj* нетрадицио́нный (нетрадицио́нен).
unconvinced [ʌnkənˈvɪnst] *adj*: **to be** *or* **remain ~** остава́ться* (оста́ться* *perf*) неубеждённым(-ой).
unconvincing [ʌnkənˈvɪnsɪŋ] *adj* неубеди́тельный* (неубеди́телен).
uncork [ʌnˈkɔːk] *vt* (*bottle*) отку́поривать (отку́порить *perf*).
uncorroborated [ʌnkəˈrɔbəreɪtɪd] *adj* неподтверждённый.
uncouth [ʌnˈkuːθ] *adj* неотёсанный* (неотёсан).
uncover [ʌnˈkʌvəʳ] *vt* открыва́ть (откры́ть* *perf*); (*plot, secret*) раскрыва́ть (раскры́ть* *perf*).
unctuous [ˈʌŋktjuəs] *adj* еле́йный* (еле́ен).
undamaged [ʌnˈdæmɪdʒd] *adj* (*goods*) неповреждённый*; (*fig: reputation*) незапя́тнанный (незапя́тнан).
undaunted [ʌnˈdɔːntɪd] *adj* (*person*) неустраши́мый* (неустраши́м); ~, **she struggled on** она́ неустраши́мо продолжа́ла свои́ стара́ния.
undecided [ʌndɪˈsaɪdɪd] *adj* (*person*) нереши́тельный* (нереши́телен); (*question*) нерешённый.
undelivered [ʌndɪˈlɪvəd] *adj* (*goods, letters*) недоста́вленный; **if ~ return to sender** е́сли не доста́влено, верну́ть отправи́телю.
undeniable [ʌndɪˈnaɪəbl] *adj* (*fact, evidence*) неоспори́мый* (неоспори́м).
undeniably [ʌndɪˈnaɪəblɪ] *adv* несомне́нно.
under [ˈʌndəʳ] (*go, fly etc*) вниз ♦ *prep* (*position*) под +*instr*; (*motion*) под +*acc*; (*less than: in price*) ни́же +*gen*; (*according to: law, agreement etc*) по +*dat*; (*during: sb's leadership*) при +*prp*; (*in age*): **children ~ 16** де́ти до 16-ти лет; **from ~ sth** из-под чего́-н; ~ **there** там внизу́; **in ~ 2 hours** ме́ньше, чем за 2 часа́; ~ **anaesthetic** под нарко́зом; ~ **discussion** в проце́ссе обсужде́ния; ~ **repair** в ремо́нте; ~ **the circumstances** при сложи́вшихся обстоя́тельствах.

under... ['ʌndə'] *prefix* недо....

underage [ʌndər'eɪdʒ] *adj* (*person*) несовершеннолетний*; ~ **smoking/drinking** курение/потребление алкоголя несовершеннолетними.

underarm ['ʌndərɑːm] *adv* (*bowl*) снизу ♦ *adj* (*deodorant*) для подмышек; ~ **throw** бросок* снизу.

undercapitalized ['ʌndə'kæpɪtəlaɪzd] *adj* (*project, industry*) недостаточно капитализированный.

undercarriage ['ʌndəkærɪdʒ] *n* (*BRIT*) шасси *nt ind*.

undercharge [ʌndə'tʃɑːdʒ] *vt* назначать (назначить *perf*) слишком низкую цену +*dat*.

underclass ['ʌndəklɑːs] *n* неимущий* класс.

underclothes ['ʌndəkləuðz] *npl* нижнее бельё *ntsg*.

undercoat ['ʌndəkəut] *n* (*paint*) грунтовка*.

undercover [ʌndə'kʌvə'] *adj* тайный.

undercurrent ['ʌndəkʌrnt] *n* (*fig*) затаённое чувство.

undercut [ʌndə'kʌt] *irreg vt* (*prices*) сбивать (сбить* *perf*); **he can ~ his competitors** он может продавать товары по более низкой цене, чем его конкуренты.

underdeveloped ['ʌndərdɪ'vɛləpt] *adj* (*country, region*) слаборазвитый (слаборазвит).

underdog ['ʌndədɔg] *n*: **the ~** (*in society*) обездоленный *m adj*; (*in team competition*) слабая команда.

underdone [ʌndə'dʌn] *adj* (*fried, roasted food*) недожаренный; (*boiled food*) недоваренный.

underemployment ['ʌndərɪm'plɔɪmənt] *n* неполная занятость *f*.

underestimate ['ʌndər'ɛstɪmeɪt] *vt* недооценивать (недооценить* *perf*).

underexposed ['ʌndərɪks'pəuzd] *adj* (*PHOT*) недодержанный.

underfed [ʌndə'fɛd] *adj* недокормленный.

underfoot [ʌndə'fut] *adv* (*crush, trample*) под ногами.

underfunded ['ʌndə'fʌndɪd] *adj* плохо финансируемый.

undergo [ʌndə'gəu] *irreg vt* (*repair*) проходить* (пройти* *perf*); (*operation*) переносить* (перенести* *perf*); (*change*) подвергаться (подвергнуться* *perf*) +*dat*; **the car is ~ing repairs** машина проходит ремонт.

undergraduate [ʌndə'grædjuɪt] *n* студент(ка) ♦ *cpd*: ~ **courses** университетские курсы *mpl*.

underground ['ʌndəgraund] *adv* (*work*) под землёй ♦ *adj* (*car park*) подземный; (*newspaper, activities*) подпольный ♦ *n*: **the ~** (*BRIT: railway*) метро *nt ind*; (*POL*) подполье; **to go ~** (*fig*) уходить* (уйти* *perf*) в подполье.

undergrowth ['ʌndəgrəuθ] *n*: **the ~** подлесок*.

underhand(ed) [ʌndə'hænd(ɪd)] *adj* (*fig: behaviour, method etc*) закулисный.

underinsured [ʌndərɪn'ʃuəd] *adj* неполностью застрахованный*.

underlay [ʌndə'leɪ] *n* подкладка*.

underlie [ʌndə'laɪ] *irreg vt* (*fig*) лежать (*impf*) в основе +*gen*; **the underlying cause** причина, лежащая в основе.

underline [ʌndə'laɪn] *vt* (*also fig*) подчёркивать (подчеркнуть* *perf*).

underling ['ʌndəlɪŋ] *n* (*pej*) мелкая сошка*.

undermanning [ʌndə'mænɪŋ] *n* недостаток* в рабочей силе.

undermentioned [ʌndə'mɛnʃənd] *adj* нижеупомянутый.

undermine [ʌndə'maɪn] *vt* (*confidence, authority*) подрывать (подорвать* *perf*).

underneath [ʌndə'niːθ] *adv* внизу ♦ *prep* (*position*) под +*instr*; (*motion*) под +*acc*.

undernourished [ʌndə'nʌrɪʃt] *adj* недокормленный.

underpaid [ʌndə'peɪd] *adj* (*person*) не получающий должной оплаты, низкооплачиваемый (низкооплачиваем).

underpants ['ʌndəpænts] *npl* (*men's*) трусы *pl*.

underpass ['ʌndəpɑːs] *n* (*BRIT*) туннель *m*, тоннель *m*.

underpin [ʌndə'pɪn] *vt* (*argument, case*) подкреплять (подкрепить* *perf*).

underplay [ʌndə'pleɪ] *vt* (*BRIT*) преуменьшать (преуменьшить* *perf*).

underpopulated [ʌndə'pɔpjuleɪtɪd] *adj* малонаселённый* (малонаселён).

underprice [ʌndə'praɪs] *vt* занижать (занизить* *perf*) слишком низкую цену на +*acc*.

underprivileged [ʌndə'prɪvɪlɪdʒd] *adj* (*family*) неимущий*.

underrate [ʌndə'reɪt] *vt* недооценивать (недооценить* *perf*).

underscore [ʌndə'skɔː'] *vt* (*word*) подчёркивать (подчеркнуть* *perf*).

underseal [ʌndə'siːl] *vt* (*BRIT: AUT*) наносить* (нанести* *perf*) антикоррозийное покрытие (*на днище автомобиля*) ♦ *n* (*AUT*) антикоррозийное покрытие (*днища автомобиля*).

undersecretary ['ʌndə'sɛkrətərɪ] *n* (*POL*) заместитель *m* министра.

undersell [ʌndə'sɛl] *irreg vt* (*competitors*) продавать* (продать* *perf*) дешевле +*gen*.

undershirt ['ʌndəʃəːt] *n* (*US*) нижняя рубашка*.

undershorts ['ʌndəʃɔːts] *npl* (*US*) трусы *pl*.

underside ['ʌndəsaɪd] *n* нижняя сторона*.

undersigned ['ʌndəsaɪnd] *adj* (*document*) подписанный ниже ♦ *n* нижеподписавшийся*(-аяся) *m(f) adj*; **we the ~ agree**

---

* marks translations which have irregular inflections. The Russian–English side of the dictionary gives inflectional information.

that ... мы, нижеподписа́вшиеся,
догова́риваемся, что ....
underskirt ['ʌndəskə:t] n (BRIT) ни́жняя ю́бка*.
understaffed [ʌndə'stɑ:ft] adj (project etc)
неукомплекто́ванный ка́драми.
understand [ʌndə'stænd] (irreg: like stand) vt
понима́ть (поня́ть* perf); (believe): **to ~ that**
полага́ть (impf), что ...; **to make o.s.**
understood объясня́ться (объясни́ться perf).
understandable [ʌndə'stændəbl] adj
поня́тный* (поня́тен).
understanding [ʌndə'stændɪŋ] adj (kind)
понима́ющий ♦ n понима́ние; (agreement)
взаимопонима́ние; **to come to an ~ with sb**
достига́ть (дости́чь* perf) взаимопонима́ния
с кем-н; **on the ~ that** ... при усло́вии, что ....
understate [ʌndə'steɪt] vt преуменьша́ть
(преуме́ньшить perf).
understatement ['ʌndəsteɪtmənt] n (quality)
преуменьше́ние; **that's an ~l** э́то сли́шком
мя́гко ска́зано!
understood [ʌndə'stud] pt, pp of **understand** ♦
adj (agreed) согласо́ванный* (согласо́ван);
(implied) подразумева́емый
(подразумева́ем).
understudy ['ʌndəstʌdɪ] n дублёр.
undertake [ʌndə'teɪk] (irreg: like take) vt (task,
duty) брать* (взять* perf) на себя́; **to ~ to do**
обя́зываться (обяза́ться* perf) +infin.
undertaker ['ʌndəteɪkə*] n владе́лец*
похоро́нного бюро́.
undertaking ['ʌndəteɪkɪŋ] n (job) предприя́тие;
(promise) обяза́тельство.
undertone ['ʌndətəun] n (of criticism etc)
отте́нок*; (speak): **in an ~** вполго́лоса.
undervalue [ʌndə'vælju:] vt недооце́нивать
(недооцени́ть* perf).
underwater [ʌndə'wɔ:tə*] adv (use, swim etc)
под водо́й ♦ adj (exploration, camera etc)
подво́дный.
underwear ['ʌndəwɛə*] n ни́жнее бельё.
underweight [ʌndə'weɪt] adj ве́сящий ни́же
но́рмы.
underworld ['ʌndəwə:ld] n (of crime)
престу́пный мир.
underwrite [ʌndə'raɪt] vt (FINANCE) гаран-
ти́ровать (impf/perf) размеще́ние +gen;
(COMM) брать* (взять* perf) на себя́
финанси́рование +gen; (INSURANCE)
принима́ть (приня́ть* perf) на себя́
страхово́й риск.
underwriter ['ʌndəraɪtə*] n (INSURANCE)
андеррайтер, принима́ющий m adj на себя́
страхово́й риск.
undeserving [ʌndɪ'zə:vɪŋ] adj: **to be ~ of** не
заслу́живать (impf) +gen.
undesirable [ʌndɪ'zaɪərəbl] adj нежела́тель-
ный* (нежела́телен).
undeveloped [ʌndɪ'vɛləpt] adj (land) незастро́-
енный; (resources) неразрабо́танный.
undies ['ʌndɪz] npl (inf) (ни́жнее) бельё ntsg.

undiluted ['ʌndaɪ'lu:tɪd] adj (substance, liquid)
неразба́вленный; (emotion) чи́стый.
undiplomatic ['ʌndɪplə'mætɪk] adj
недипломати́чный* (недипломати́чен).
undischarged ['ʌndɪs'tʃɑ:dʒd] adj: **~ bankrupt**
не восстано́вленный в права́х банкро́т.
undisciplined [ʌn'dɪsɪplɪnd] adj недисциплин-
и́рованный (недисциплини́рован).
undiscovered ['ʌndɪs'kʌvəd] adj (island)
неоткры́тый; (fact) необнару́женный;
(situation) неиссле́дованный.
undisguised ['ʌndɪs'gaɪzd] adj я́вный* (я́вен).
undisputed ['ʌndɪs'pju:tɪd] adj неоспори́мый
(неоспори́м).
undistinguished ['ʌndɪs'tɪŋgwɪʃt] adj
посре́дственный* (посре́дствен).
undisturbed ['ʌndɪs'tə:bd] adj (uninterrupted)
безмяте́жный* (безмяте́жен); **to leave ~** не
волнова́ть (impf).
undivided [ʌndɪ'vaɪdɪd] adj: **can I have your ~**
attention? я прошу́ Ва́шего неразде́льного
внима́ния.
undo [ʌn'du:] (irreg: like do) vt (unfasten: laces,
strings) развя́зывать (развяза́ть* perf);
(: buttons) расстёгивать (расстегну́ть* perf);
(spoil) губи́ть* (погуби́ть* perf).
undoing [ʌn'du:ɪŋ] n (downfall) ги́бель f.
undone [ʌn'dʌn] pp of **undo**; (unfastened): **my**
lace has come ~ у меня́ развяза́лся шнуро́к.
undoubted [ʌn'dautɪd] adj несомне́нный*
(несомне́нен), бесспо́рный* (бесспо́рен).
undoubtedly [ʌn'dautɪdlɪ] adv несомне́нно,
бесспо́рно.
undress [ʌn'drɛs] vt раздева́ть (разде́ть* perf) ♦
vi раздева́ться (разде́ться* perf).
undrinkable [ʌn'drɪŋkəbl] adj (poisonous)
непригóдный* для питья́; (unpalatable): **this**
wine is ~ э́то вино́ невозмо́жно пить. ·
undue [ʌn'dju:] adj изли́шний*.
undulating ['ʌndjuleɪtɪŋ] adj холми́стый*.
unduly [ʌn'dju:lɪ] adv изли́шне.
undying [ʌn'daɪɪŋ] adj бессме́ртный*.
unearned [ʌn'ə:nd] adj незарабо́танный; **~**
income нетрудовы́е дохо́ды mpl.
unearth [ʌn'ə:θ] vt выка́пывать (вы́копать
perf); (fig) раска́пывать (раскопа́ть perf).
unearthly [ʌn'ə:θlɪ] adj: **at an ~ hour** ни свет,
ни заря́.
unease [ʌn'i:z] n нело́вкость f.
uneasy [ʌn'i:zɪ] adj (feeling) трево́жный*
(трево́жен); (peace, truce) напряжённый*;
(person): **he is** or **feels ~** он неспоко́ен; **I feel**
~ about taking his money я неспоко́ен, когда́
беру́ у него́ де́ньги.
uneconomic(al) ['ʌni:kə'nɔmɪk(l)] adj
неэконо́мный*.
uneducated [ʌn'ɛdjukeɪtɪd] adj (person)
необразо́ванный*.
unemployed [ʌnɪm'plɔɪd] adj (worker)
безрабо́тный ♦ npl: **the ~** безрабо́тные pl adj.
unemployment [ʌnɪm'plɔɪmənt] n

безрабóтица.
unemployment benefit *n* пособие по безрабóтице.
unemployment compensation *n* (*US*) = **unemployment benefit**.
unending [ʌn'ɛndɪŋ] *adj* нескончáемый.
unenviable [ʌn'ɛnvɪəbl] *adj* незавúдный* (незавúден).
unequal [ʌn'iːkwəl] *adj* нерáвный* (нерáвен); **to feel ~ to** чýвствовать (*impf*) себя неспосóбным отвечáть трéбованиям +*gen*.
unequalled [ʌn'iːkwəld] (*US* **unequaled**) *adj* несравнúмый (несравнúм).
unequivocal [ʌnɪ'kwɪvəkl] *adj* (*answer, person*) недвусмýсленный*.
unerring [ʌn'əːrɪŋ] *adj* безошúбочный* (безошúбочен).
UNESCO [ju:'nɛskəu] *n abbr* (= *United Nations Educational, Scientific and Cultural Organization*) ЮНÉСКО.
unethical [ʌn'ɛθɪkl] *adj* неэтúчный* (неэтúчен).
uneven [ʌn'iːvn] *adj* нерóвный*.
uneventful [ʌnɪ'vɛntful] *adj* без осóбых событий.
unexceptional [ʌnɪk'sɛpʃənl] *adj* заурядный* (заурядень).
unexciting [ʌnɪk'saɪtɪŋ] *adj* (*news, film*) неинтерéсный* (неинтерéсен).
unexpected [ʌnɪks'pɛktɪd] *adj* неожúданный* (неожúдан).
unexpectedly [ʌnɪks'pɛktɪdlɪ] *adv* неожúданно.
unexplained [ʌnɪks'pleɪnd] *adj* необъяснённый.
unexploded [ʌnɪks'pləudɪd] *adj* (*bomb*) невзорвáвшийся.
unfailing [ʌn'feɪlɪŋ] *adj* неизмéнный* (неизмéнен).
unfair [ʌn'fɛə'] *adj*: ~ (**to**) несправедлúвый (к +*dat*); **it's ~ that** ... несправедлúво, что ....
unfair dismissal *n* незакóнное увольнéние.
unfairly [ʌn'fɛəlɪ] *adv* (*treat*) несправедлúво; (*dismiss*) незакóнно.
unfaithful [ʌn'feɪθful] *adj* невéрный* (невéрен).
unfamiliar [ʌnfə'mɪlɪə'] *adj* незнакóмый (незнакóм); **he is ~ with the accent** он незнакóм с акцéнтом.
unfashionable [ʌn'fæʃnəbl] *adj* немóдный* (немóден).
unfasten [ʌn'fɑːsn] *vt* (*undo*) расстёгивать (расстегнýть *perf*); (*open*) открывáть (открыть* *perf*).
unfathomable [ʌn'fæðəməbl] *adj* (*mystery*) непостижúмый (непостижúм).
unfavourable [ʌn'feɪvrəbl] (*US* **unfavorable**) *adj* неблагоприятный* (неблагоприятен).
unfavourably [ʌn'feɪvrəblɪ] (*US* **unfavorably**) *adv* (*compare, review*) неблагоприятно; **to**

look ~ on (*suggestion etc*) смотрéть* (*impf*) неблагосклóнно на +*acc*.
unfeeling [ʌn'fiːlɪŋ] *adj* бесчýвственный* (бесчýвствен).
unfinished [ʌn'fɪnɪʃt] *adj* незакóнченный.
unfit [ʌn'fɪt] *adj* (*physically*): **she is ~** онá в плохóй спортúвной фóрме; **he is ~ for the job** он непригóден к рабóте.
unflagging [ʌn'flægɪŋ] *adj* неослáбный* (неослáбен).
unflappable [ʌn'flæpəbl] *adj* невозмутúмый (невозмутúм).
unflattering [ʌn'flætərɪŋ] *adj* (*remark*) нелéстный* (нелéстен); (*garment*) не идýщий к лицý; **that dress is ~ on you** Вам не идёт э́то плáтье.
unflinching [ʌn'flɪntʃɪŋ] *adj* неустрашúмый (неустрáшим).
unfold [ʌn'fəuld] *vt* (*sheets, map*) разворáчивать *or* развёртывать (развернýть *perf*) ♦ *vi* (*situation*) разворáчиваться (развернýться *perf*).
unforeseeable [ʌnfɔ:'siːəbl] *adj* непредвúдимый* (непредвúден).
unforeseen ['ʌnfɔ:'siːn] *adj* непредвúденный.
unforgettable [ʌnfə'gɛtəbl] *adj* незабывáемый (незабывáем).
unforgivable [ʌnfə'gɪvəbl] *adj* непростúтельный* (непростúтелен).
unformatted [ʌn'fɔ:mætɪd] *adj* (*COMPUT*) бесформáтный, неформатúрованный.
unfortunate [ʌn'fɔ:tʃənət] *adj* (*person, event*) несчáстный*; (*remark*) неудáчный*; **he's been very ~** емý óчень не повезлó; **it is ~ that** ... как неудáчно, что ....
unfortunately [ʌn'fɔ:tʃənətlɪ] *adv* к сожалéнию.
unfounded [ʌn'faundɪd] *adj* необоснóванный*.
unfriendly [ʌn'frɛndlɪ] *adj* недружелюбный* (недружелюбен).
unfulfilled [ʌnful'fɪld] *adj* (*ambition, prophecy, desire*) неосуществлённый; (*promise, terms*) невыполненный; (*person*) нереализовáвшийся.
unfurl [ʌn'fɔ:l] *vt* разворáчивать *or* развёртывать (развернýть *perf*).
unfurnished [ʌn'fɔ:nɪʃt] *adj* немеблирóванный.
ungainly [ʌn'geɪnlɪ] *adj* нелóвкий*.
ungodly [ʌn'gɔdlɪ] *adj*: **at an ~ hour** не свет, ни заря.
ungrateful [ʌn'greɪtful] *adj* неблагодáрный* (неблагодáрен).
unguarded [ʌn'gɑ:dɪd] *adj*: **in an ~ moment** в момéнт неосторóжности.
UNHCR *n abbr* (= *United Nations High Commission for Refugees*) *управлéние верхóвного комиссáра ООН по делáм*

---

* marks translations which have irregular inflections. The Russian-English side of the dictionary gives inflectional information.

бе́женцев.

unhappily [ʌnˈhæpɪlɪ] adv несчастли́во; (*unfortunately*) к несча́стью or сожале́нию.

unhappiness [ʌnˈhæpɪnɪs] n несча́стье.

unhappy [ʌnˈhæpɪ] adj (*sad*) гру́стный* (гру́стен); (*unfortunate*) несча́стный* (несча́стен); I am ~ with (*dissatisfied*) я недово́лен +*instr*.

unharmed [ʌnˈhɑːmd] adj неповреждённый.

unhealthy [ʌnˈhɛlθɪ] adj (*also fig*) нездоро́вый (нездоро́в).

unheard-of [ʌnˈhəːdɔv] adj (*event, situation*) неслы́ханный* (неслы́хан); (*person*) неизве́стный*.

unhelpful [ʌnˈhɛlpful] adj бесполе́зный*.

unhesitating [ʌnˈhɛzɪteɪtɪŋ] adj (*loyalty*) непоколеби́мый (непоколеби́м); (*reply, offer*) реши́тельный* (реши́телен).

unholy [ʌnˈhəulɪ] adj поро́чный* (поро́чен); (*dreadful*) безобра́зный.

unhook [ʌnˈhuk] vt расстёгивать (расстегну́ть perf) крючки́ +*gen*.

unhurt [ʌnˈhəːt] adj невреди́мый (невреди́м).

unhygienic [ˈʌnhaɪˈdʒiːnɪk] adj негигиени́чный* (негигиени́чен).

UNICEF [ˈjuːnɪsɛf] n abbr (= United Nations International Children's Emergency Fund) ЮНИСЕ́Ф.

unicorn [ˈjuːnɪkɔːn] n единоро́г.

unidentified [ʌnaɪˈdɛntɪfaɪd] adj (*body*) неопо́знанный; (*source, person*) анони́мный; *see also* **UFO**.

unification [juːnɪfɪˈkeɪʃən] n (*POL etc*) объедине́ние, унифика́ция.

uniform [ˈjuːnɪfɔːm] n фо́рма ♦ adj (*length, width etc*) единообра́зный* (единообра́зен); (*temperature*) постоя́нный* (постоя́нен).

uniformity [juːnɪˈfɔːmɪtɪ] n единообра́зие.

unify [ˈjuːnɪfaɪ] vt объединя́ть (объедини́ть perf).

unilateral [juːnɪˈlætərəl] adj (*disarmament etc*) односторо́нний* (односторо́нен).

unimaginable [ʌnɪˈmædʒɪnəbl] adj невообрази́мый (невообрази́м).

unimaginative [ʌnɪˈmædʒɪnətɪv] adj (*person*) лишённый воображе́ния; (*design*) прозаи́чный* (прозаи́чен).

unimpaired [ʌnɪmˈpɛəd] adj непострада́вший.

unimportant [ʌnɪmˈpɔːtənt] adj нева́жный* (нева́жен).

unimpressed [ʌnɪmˈprɛst] adj: I was ~ by his explanation его́ объясне́ние меня́ не убеди́ло.

uninhabited [ʌnɪnˈhæbɪtɪd] adj необита́емый (необита́ем).

uninhibited [ʌnɪnˈhɪbɪtɪd] adj раско́ванный* (раско́ван).

uninjured [ʌnˈɪndʒəd] adj непострада́вший.

uninspiring [ʌnɪnˈspaɪərɪŋ] adj не вдохновля́ющий.

unintelligent [ʌnɪnˈtɛlɪdʒənt] adj (*person*)

невеже́ственный* (невеже́ствен).

unintentional [ʌnɪnˈtɛnʃənəl] adj неумы́шленный* (неумы́шлен).

unintentionally [ʌnɪnˈtɛnʃnəlɪ] adv неумы́шленно.

uninvited [ʌnɪnˈvaɪtɪd] adj незва́ный.

uninviting [ʌnɪnˈvaɪtɪŋ] adj (*food*) неаппети́тный* (неаппети́тен), несоблазни́тельный* (несоблазни́телен); (*place*) непривлека́тельный* (непривлека́телен).

union [ˈjuːnjən] n (*unification*) объедине́ние; (*also: trade* ~) профсою́з ♦ cpd (*activities, leader etc*) профсою́зный; **the U~** (*US*) Соединённые Шта́ты mpl.

unionize [ˈjuːnjənaɪz] vt (*employees, industry*) объединя́ть (объедини́ть perf) в профсою́зы.

Union Jack n (*BRIT*) госуда́рственный флаг Соединённого Короле́вства.

Union of Soviet Socialist Republics n (*formerly*) Сою́з Сове́тских Социалисти́ческих Респу́блик.

union shop n предприя́тие, на кото́ром мо́гут рабо́тать то́лько чле́ны профсою́за.

unique [juːˈniːk] adj (*object etc*) уника́льный* (уника́лен); (*ability, performance etc*) исключи́тельный* (исключи́телен); **these problems are not** ~ **to** ... э́ти пробле́мы каса́ются не то́лько +*gen* ....

unisex [ˈjuːnɪsɛks] adj для обо́их поло́в.

unison [ˈjuːnɪsn] n: **in** ~ (*say*) в оди́н го́лос; (*sing*) в унисо́н.

unissued capital [ʌnˈɪʃuːd-] n невы́пущенный акционе́рный капита́л.

unit [ˈjuːnɪt] n (*single whole*) це́лое nt adj; (*measurement*) едини́ца; (*section: of furniture etc*) се́кция; (*team, squad*) подразделе́ние; **production** ~ едини́ца проду́кции; **kitchen** ~ ку́хонная се́кция.

unitary [ˈjuːnɪtrɪ] adj едини́чный* (едини́чен).

unit cost n (*COMM*) сто́имость f едини́цы проду́кции.

unite [juːˈnaɪt] vt объединя́ть (объедини́ть perf) ♦ vi объединя́ться (объедини́ться perf).

united [juːˈnaɪtɪd] adj объединённый*; (*effort*) совме́стный.

United Arab Emirates npl: the ~ ~ ~ Объединённые Ара́бские эмира́ты mpl.

United Kingdom n Соединённое Короле́вство.

United Nations (Organization) n Организа́ция Объединённых На́ций.

United States of America n Соединённые Шта́ты mpl Аме́рики.

unit price n (*COMM*) цена́* за едини́цу, шту́чная цена́*.

unit trust n (*BRIT: COMM*) (довери́тельный) паево́й трест.

unity [ˈjuːnɪtɪ] n еди́нство.

Univ. abbr = **university**.

universal [ju:nɪ'vɜ:sl] *adj* универсáльный*
(универсáлен).

universe ['ju:nɪvɜ:s] *n* вселéнная *f adj*.

university [ju:nɪ'vɜ:sɪtɪ] *n* университéт ♦ *cpd*
(*education, year*) университéтский*; ~
student/professor студéнт(ка*)/профéссор
университéта.

university degree *n* университéтская
стéпень *f*.

unjust [ʌn'dʒʌst] *adj* несправедлúвый
(несправедлúв).

unjustifiable ['ʌndʒʌstɪ'faɪəbl] *adj*
неопрáвданный* (неопрáвдан).

unjustified [ʌn'dʒʌstɪfaɪd] *adj* (*belief, action*)
неопрáвданный* (неопрáвдан); (*text*)
невы́равненный.

unkempt [ʌn'kɛmpt] *adj* (*appearance*)
неопря́тный* (неопря́тен); (*hair, beard*)
растрёпанный* (растрёпан).

unkind [ʌn'kaɪnd] *adj* (*person, comment etc*)
злой; (*behaviour*) злóбный* (злóбен).

unkindly [ʌn'kaɪndlɪ] *adv* недоброжелáтельно.

unknown [ʌn'nəun] *adj* неизвéстный*
(неизвéстен); ~ **to me** без моегó вéдома; ~
quantity (*MATH*) неизвéстная величинá; (*fig*)
загáдка.

unladen [ʌn'leɪdn] *adj* (*ship*) порóжний*; ~
weight вес порожняком.

unlawful [ʌn'lɔ:ful] *adj* незакóнный*
(незакóнен).

unleaded petrol ['ʌn'lɛdɪd-] *n* бензúн не
содержáщий свинцá.

unleash [ʌn'li:ʃ] *vt* (*fig*) давáть* (дать* *perf*)
вóлю +*dat*.

unleavened [ʌn'lɛvnd] *adj* прéсный*.

unless [ʌn'lɛs] *conj* éсли не; ~ **he comes** éсли
он не придёт; ~ **otherwise stated** éсли не
бýдут даны́ другúе указáния; ~ **I am
mistaken** éсли я не ошибáюсь.

unlicensed [ʌn'laɪsnst] *adj* (*BRIT: restaurant*) не
имéющий лицéнзии на продáжу спиртны́х
напúтков.

unlike [ʌn'laɪk] *adj* (*not alike*) непохóжий*
(непохóж) ♦ *prep* (*different from*) в отлúчие
от +*gen*; **Russian is grammatically** ~ **English** с
граммáтической тóчки зрéния рýсский не
похóж на англúйский.

unlikelihood [ʌn'laɪklɪhud] *n* неправдо-
подóбие.

unlikely [ʌn'laɪklɪ] *adj* (*not likely*) мало-
вероя́тный* (маловероя́тен); (*unexpected*)
невероя́тный* (невероя́тен); **in the** ~ **event of**
при маловероя́тном слýчае +*gen*; **in the** ~
event that ... в том маловероя́тном слýчае,
когдá ....

unlimited [ʌn'lɪmɪtɪd] *adj* (*travel, wine etc*)
неогранúченный.

unlisted ['ʌn'lɪstɪd] *adj* (*US: TEL*) не

включённый (включён) в телефóнный
спрáвочник; (*STOCK EXCHANGE*) не
котúрующийся.

unlit [ʌn'lɪt] *adj* (*room*) неосвещённый.

unload [ʌn'ləud] *vt* (*box, car*) разгружáть
(разгрузúть* *perf*).

unlock [ʌn'lɔk] *vt* отпирáть (отперéть* *perf*).

unlucky [ʌn'lʌkɪ] *adj* (*person*) невезýчий
(невезýч); (*object, number*) несчастлúвый; **he
is** ~ емý не везёт.

unmanageable [ʌn'mænɪdʒəbl] *adj* (*tool,
vehicle*) труднокотролúруемый; (*situation*)
неуправля́емый (неуправля́ем).

unmanned [ʌn'mænd] *adj* (*spacecraft etc*)
автоматúчески управля́емый.

unmarked [ʌn'mɑ:kt] *adj* (*unstained*) чúстый*
(чист); ~ **police car** полицéйская машúна без
опознавáтельных знáков.

unmarried [ʌn'mærɪd] *adj* (*man*) неженáтый
(неженáт), холостóй* (хóлост); (*woman*)
незамýжняя.

unmarried mother *n* мать* *f*-одинóчка.

unmask [ʌn'mɑ:sk] *vt* (*thief etc*) разоблачáть
(разоблачúть* *perf*).

unmatched [ʌn'mætʃt] *adj* непревзойдённый*
(непревзойдён).

unmentionable [ʌn'mɛnʃnəbl] *adj* (*topic*)
запрéтный* (запрéтен); (*word*)
неприлúчный* (неприлúчен).

unmerciful [ʌn'mə:sɪful] *adj* безжáлостный*
(безжáлостен).

unmistak(e)able [ʌnmɪs'teɪkəbl] *adj* (*voice,
sound*) характéрный*.

unmistak(e)ably [ʌnmɪs'teɪkəblɪ] *adv* я́вно.

unmitigated [ʌn'mɪtɪgeɪtɪd] *adj* пóлный*.

unnamed [ʌn'neɪmd] *adj* (*nameless*)
безымя́нный; (*anonymous*) не назвáвший
себя́.

unnatural [ʌn'nætʃrəl] *adj* неестéственный*
(неестéствен); (*against nature*)
противоестéственный* (противоестéствен).

unnecessarily [ʌn'nɛsəsrɪlɪ] *adv* излúшне.

unnecessary [ʌn'nɛsəsərɪ] *adj* излúшний*
(излúшен).

unnerve [ʌn'nə:v] *vt* тревóжить (встревóжить*
perf).

unnoticed [ʌn'nəutɪst] *adj* незамéченный.

UNO ['ju:nəu] *n abbr* (= *United Nations
Organization*) ОÓН= *Организáция
Объединённых Нáций*.

unobservant [ʌnəb'zə:vnt] *adj* (*person*)
ненаблюдáтельный* (ненаблюдáтелен).

unobtainable [ʌnəb'teɪnəbl] *adj*: **this book is** ~
э́ту кнúгу нельзя́ достáть; **this number is** ~
э́тот нóмер не функционúрует.

unobtrusive [ʌnəb'tru:sɪv] *adj* (*person*)
ненавя́зчивый (ненавя́зчив); (*engine*)
бесшýмный* (бесшýмен).

---

* marks translations which have irregular inflections. The Russian-English side of the dictionary gives inflectional information.

unoccupied [ʌn'ɔkjupaɪd] *adj* (*also* MIL) неза́нятый.

unofficial [ʌnə'fɪʃl] *adj* неофициа́льный* (неофициа́лен).

unopened [ʌn'əupənd] *adj* (*letter*) нераспеча́танный; (*tin, bottle etc*) неоткры́тый.

unopposed [ʌnə'pəuzd] *adj* не встре́тивший сопротивле́ния.

unorthodox [ʌn'ɔ:θədɔks] *adj* (*treatment*) неортодокса́льный* (неортодокса́лен); (*REL*) неортодокса́льный.

unpack [ʌn'pæk] *vi* распако́вываться (распакова́ться *perf*) ♦ *vt* распако́вывать (распакова́ть *perf*).

unpaid [ʌn'peɪd] *adj* (*bill*) неопла́ченный; (*time off*) неопла́чиваемый; (*work*) неопла́чиваемый; (*worker*) беспла́тный.

unpalatable [ʌn'pælətəbl] *adj* (*meal*) невку́сный* (невку́сен); (*truth*) го́рький* (го́рек).

unparalleled [ʌn'pærəlɛld] *adj* несравни́мый (несравни́м).

unpatriotic ['ʌnpætrɪ'ɔtɪk] *adj* (*person*) непатриоти́чески настро́енный; (*speech, attitude*) непатриоти́чный* (непатриоти́чен).

unplanned [ʌn'plænd] *adj* (*visit, baby*) незаплани́рованный.

unpleasant [ʌn'plɛznt] *adj* неприя́тный* (неприя́тен).

unplug [ʌn'plʌg] *vt* отключа́ть (отключи́ть* *perf*) от се́ти.

unpolluted [ʌnpə'lu:tɪd] *adj* (*river, water etc*) незагрязнённый.

unpopular [ʌn'pɔpjulə'] *adj* (*person, decision etc*) непопуля́рный* (непопуля́рен); **to make o.s. ~ (with)** теря́ть (потеря́ть *perf*) популя́рность (у +*gen*).

unprecedented [ʌn'prɛsɪdəntɪd] *adj* беспрецеде́нтный* (беспрецеде́нтен).

unpredictable [ʌnprɪ'dɪktəbl] *adj* непредска́зуемый (непредска́зуем).

unprejudiced [ʌn'prɛdʒudɪst] *adj* (*not biased*) непредвзя́тый; (*having no prejudices*) непредубеждённый*.

unprepared [ʌnprɪ'pɛəd] *adj* (*person, speech*) неподгото́вленный.

unprepossessing ['ʌnpriː'pɔ'zɛsɪŋ] *adj* нераполага́ющий.

unpretentious [ʌnprɪ'tɛnʃəs] *adj* непретенцио́зный* (непретенцио́зен).

unprincipled [ʌn'prɪnsɪpld] *adj* (*person*) беспринци́пный* (беспринци́пен).

unproductive [ʌnprə'dʌktɪv] *adj* (*land*) неплодоро́дный* (неплодоро́ден); (*discussion*) непродукти́вный* (непродукти́вен); (*labour*) непроизводи́тельный* (непроизводи́телен).

unprofessional [ʌnprə'fɛʃənl] *adj* непрофессиона́льный (непрофессиона́лен)*.

unprofitable [ʌn'prɔfɪtəbl] *adj* невы́годный* (невы́годен).

unprotected ['ʌnprə'tɛktɪd] *adj* незащищённый; **~ sex** секс без контрацепти́вов.

unprovoked [ʌnprə'vəukt] *adj* (*attack*) неспровоци́рованный.

unpunished [ʌn'pʌnɪʃt] *adj*: **to go ~** остава́ться* (оста́ться* *perf*) безнака́занным(-ой).

unqualified [ʌn'kwɔlɪfaɪd] *adj* (*teacher, nurse etc*) неквалифици́рованный; (*disaster, success*) соверше́нный.

unquestionably [ʌn'kwɛstʃənəblɪ] *adv* бесспо́рно.

unquestioning [ʌn'kwɛstʃənɪŋ] *adj* беспрекосло́вный* (беспрекосло́вен).

unravel [ʌn'rævl] *vt* (*ball of string*) распу́тывать (распу́тать *perf*); (*mystery*) разга́дывать (разгада́ть *perf*).

unreal [ʌn'rɪəl] *adj* (*not real*) нереа́льный* (нереа́лен); (*peculiar*) фантасти́ческий.

unrealistic ['ʌnrɪə'lɪstɪk] *adj* (*person, project*) нереалисти́чный* (нереалисти́чен).

unreasonable [ʌn'riːznəbl] *adj* (*person, attitude, demand*) неразу́мный* (неразу́мен); (*length of time*) нереа́льный* (нереа́лен).

unrecognizable [ʌn'rɛkəgnaɪzəbl] *adj* неузнава́емый (неузнава́ем).

unrecognized [ʌn'rɛkəgnaɪzd] *adj* (*also* POL) непри́знанный*.

unreconstructed ['ʌnriː:kən'strʌktɪd] *adj* (*US*) неисправи́мый (неисправи́м).

unrecorded [ʌnrə'kɔ:dɪd] *adj* (*piece of music etc*) незапи́санный; (*incident, statement*) незафикси́рованный.

unrefined [ʌnrə'faɪnd] *adj* (*petroleum*) неочи́щенный; (*sugar*) нерафини́рованный.

unrehearsed [ʌnrɪ'hə:st] *adj* (THEAT) неотрепети́рованный; (*spontaneous*) неподгото́вленный.

unrelated [ʌnrɪ'leɪtɪd] *adj* (*incident*) отде́льный; **to be ~** (*people*) не состоя́ть (*impf*) в родстве́.

unrelenting [ʌnrɪ'lɛntɪŋ] *adj* неумоли́мый (неумоли́м).

unreliable [ʌnrɪ'laɪəbl] *adj* ненадёжный* (ненадёжен).

unrelieved [ʌnrɪ'li:vd] *adj* (*monotony*) невыноси́мый (невыноси́м).

unremitting [ʌnrɪ'mɪtɪŋ] *adj* неосла́бный* (неосла́бен).

unrepeatable [ʌnrɪ'pi:təbl] *adj* (*offer*) неповтори́мый; (*comment*) неприли́чный* (неприли́чен).

unrepentant [ʌnrɪ'pɛntənt] *adj* нераска́явшийся.

unrepresentative ['ʌnrɛprɪ'zɛntətɪv] *adj*: **~ (of)** нетипи́чный* (нетипи́чен) (для +*acc*).

unreserved [ʌnrɪ'zə:vd] *adj* (*seat*) незаброни́рованный; (*approval, admiration*) по́лный*.

unreservedly [ʌnrɪ'zə:vɪdlɪ] *adv* по́лностью.

unresponsive [ʌnrɪs'pɔnsɪv] *adj* без-

529

unrest ~ unsure

разли́чный* (безразли́чен).
unrest [ʌnˈrɛst] n волне́ния ntpl.
unrestricted [ʌnrɪˈstrɪktɪd] adj (power, time) неограни́ченный*; **to have ~ access to** име́ть (impf) неограни́ченный до́ступ к +dat.
unrewarded [ʌnrɪˈwɔːdɪd] adj (efforts) безуспе́шный* (безуспе́шен).
unripe [ʌnˈraɪp] adj незре́лый (незре́л).
unrivalled [ʌnˈraɪvəld] (US **unrivaled**) adj непревзойдённый* (непревзойдён).
unroll [ʌnˈrəʊl] vt развёртывать (разверну́ть perf).
unruffled [ʌnˈrʌfld] adj (person) невозмути́мый (невозмути́м); (hair) гла́дкий*.
unruly [ʌnˈruːlɪ] adj непослу́шный* (непослу́шен).
unsafe [ʌnˈseɪf] adj опа́сный* (опа́сен); (machine, bridge, car etc) ненадёжный* (ненадёжен); (method) риско́ванный; **~ to eat/drink** неприго́дный* (неприго́ден) для еды́/питья́.
unsaid [ʌnˈsɛd] adj: **to leave sth ~** не упомина́ть (impf) о чём-н.
unsaleable [ʌnˈseɪləbl] (US **unsalable**) adj неходово́й.
unsatisfactory [ˈʌnsætɪsˈfæktərɪ] adj неудовлетвори́тельный* (неудовлетвори́телен).
unsatisfied [ʌnˈsætɪsfaɪd] adj неудовлетворённый.
unsavoury [ʌnˈseɪvərɪ] (US **unsavory**) adj (fig) сомни́тельный* (сомни́телен).
unscathed [ʌnˈskeɪðd] adj невреди́мый (невреди́м).
unscientific [ˈʌnsaɪənˈtɪfɪk] adj ненау́чный* (ненау́чен).
unscrew [ʌnˈskruː] vt отви́нчивать (отвинти́ть* perf).
unscrupulous [ʌnˈskruːpjuləs] adj бессо́вестный*.
unseat [ʌnˈsiːt] vt (from office) смеща́ть (смести́ть* perf).
unsecured [ˈʌnsɪˈkjuəd] adj: **~ creditor** незастрахо́ванный кредито́р; **~ loan** необеспе́ченный заём*.
unseemly [ʌnˈsiːmlɪ] adj непристо́йный* (непристо́ен).
unseen [ʌnˈsiːn] adj (person) неви́димый (неви́дим); (danger) скры́тый (скрыт).
unselfish [ʌnˈsɛlfɪʃ] adj бескоры́стный* (бескоры́стен).
unsettled [ʌnˈsɛtld] adj (person) беспоко́йный* (беспоко́ен); (future) нея́сный* (нея́сен); (question) нерешённый; (weather) неусто́йчивый (неусто́йчив).
unsettling [ʌnˈsɛtlɪŋ] adj трево́жный* (трево́жен).
unshak(e)able [ʌnˈʃeɪkəbl] adj непоколеби́мый (непоколеби́м).

unshaven [ʌnˈʃeɪvn] adj небри́тый (небри́т).
unsightly [ʌnˈsaɪtlɪ] adj непригля́дный* (непригля́ден).
unskilled [ʌnˈskɪld] adj (worker, work) неквалифици́рованный*.
unsociable [ʌnˈsəʊʃəbl] adj (person) необщи́тельный* (необщи́телен); (way of life) за́мкнутый (за́мкнут).
unsocial [ʌnˈsəʊʃl] adj: **~ hours** сверхуро́чные часы́.
unsold [ʌnˈsəʊld] adj (goods) непро́данный.
unsolicited [ʌnsəˈlɪsɪtɪd] adj (advice) непро́шенный; (goods) незатре́бованный.
unsophisticated [ʌnsəˈfɪstɪkeɪtɪd] adj бесхи́тростный* (бесхи́тростен); (method, device) просто́й* (прост).
unsound [ʌnˈsaʊnd] adj (health) сла́бый* (слаб); (floor, foundations) непро́чный* (непро́чен); (policy) ша́ткий* (ша́ток); (advice) ненадёжный* (ненадёжен).
unspeakable [ʌnˈspiːkəbl] adj отврати́тельный* (отврати́телен).
unspoken [ʌnˈspəʊkn] adj (word) невы́сказанный; (agreement, approval) молчали́вый.
unstable [ʌnˈsteɪbl] adj (piece of furniture) неусто́йчивый (неусто́йчив); (government) нестаби́льный* (нестаби́лен); (person: mentally) неуравнове́шенный* (неуравнове́шен).
unsteady [ʌnˈstɛdɪ] adj (step) нетвёрдый (нетвёрд); (voice, hands, legs) дрожа́щий; (ladder) неусто́йчивый (неусто́йчив), ша́ткий* (ша́ток).
unstinting [ʌnˈstɪntɪŋ] adj (support) огро́мный* (огро́мен); (generosity) бесконе́чный* (бесконе́чен).
unstuck [ʌnˈstʌk] adj: **to come ~** (label etc) откле́иваться (откле́иться perf); (plan, idea etc) расстра́иваться (расстро́иться perf).
unsubstantiated [ˈʌnsəbˈstænʃɪeɪtɪd] adj (rumour) неподтверждённый; (accusation) необоснованный.
unsuccessful [ʌnsəkˈsɛsful] adj (attempt) безуспе́шный* (безуспе́шен); (writer) посре́дственный* (посре́дствен); (proposal, marriage) неуда́чный* (неуда́чен); **to be ~ in sth** терпе́ть* (потерпе́ть* perf) неуда́чу в +prp; **your application was ~** Ва́ше заявле́ние не при́нято.
unsuccessfully [ʌnsəkˈsɛsfəlɪ] adv безуспе́шно.
unsuitable [ʌnˈsuːtəbl] adj неподходя́щий*.
unsuited [ʌnˈsuːtɪd] adj: **to be ~ for** or **to** не подходи́ть* (impf) для +gen.
unsung [ˈʌnsʌŋ] adj незаме́ченный.
unsure [ʌnˈʃuə] adj (uncertain) неуве́ренный* (неуве́рен); **he is ~ of himself** он неуве́рен в себе́.

---

* marks translations which have irregular inflections. The Russian-English side of the dictionary gives inflectional information.

unsuspecting [ʌnsəs'pɛktɪŋ] *adj* ничего не подозревающий.

unsweetened [ʌn'swiːtnd] *adj* неподслащённый.

unswerving [ʌn'swəːvɪŋ] *adj* непоколебимый (непоколебим).

unsympathetic ['ʌnsɪmpə'θɛtɪk] *adj* равнодушный* (равнодушен); (*unlikeable*) несимпатичный* (несимпатичен); ~ **to** *or* **towards** равнодушный +*dat*.

untangle [ʌn'tæŋgl] *vt* распутывать (распутать *perf*).

untapped [ʌn'tæpt] *adj* (*resources*) неиспользованный.

untaxed [ʌn'tækst] *adj* не облагаемый (облагаем) налогом.

unthinkable [ʌn'θɪŋkəbl] *adj* немыслимый (немыслим).

unthinking [ʌn'θɪŋkɪŋ] *adj* бездумный* (бездумен).

untidy [ʌn'taɪdɪ] *adj* неопрятный* (неопрятен); (*work, writing*) неаккуратный* (неаккуратен).

untie [ʌn'taɪ] *vt* (*lace, person*) развязывать (развязать* *perf*); (*dog, horse etc*) отвязывать (отвязать* *perf*).

until [ən'tɪl] *prep* до +*gen*; (*after negative*) пока ♦ *conj* пока не; ~ **he comes** пока он не придёт; ~ **now/then** до сих/тех пор; **from morning** ~ **night** с утра до ночи.

untimely [ʌn'taɪmlɪ] *adj* (*inopportune: moment*) неподходящий*; (: *arrival*) несвоевременный* (несвоевременен); (*death*) безвременный.

untold [ʌn'təuld] *adj* (*story*) нерассказанный; (*joy, suffering*) невыразимый; (*wealth*) несметный.

untouched [ʌn'tʌtʃt] *adj* (*not used etc*) нетронутый (нетронут); (*safe*) невредимый (невредим); ~ **by** (*unaffected*) нетронутый (нетронут) +*instr*.

untoward [ʌntə'wɔːd] *adj* (*events*) скверный* (скверен); (*effects*) отрицательный* (отрицателен).

untrained ['ʌn'treɪnd] *adj* нетренированный.

untrammelled [ʌn'træmld] *adj* раскованный* (раскован).

untranslatable [ʌntrænz'leɪtəbl] *adj* непереводимый.

untried [ʌn'traɪd] *adj* (*policy, remedy*) неиспытанный; (*prisoner*) не подвергавшийся суду.

untrue [ʌn'truː] *adj* ложный* (ложен).

untrustworthy [ʌn'trʌstwəːðɪ] *adj* ненадёжный* (ненадёжен).

unusable [ʌn'juːzəbl] *adj* непригодный* (непригоден).

unused[1] [ʌn'juːzd] *adj* (*not used*) неиспользованный*.

unused[2] [ʌn'juːst] *adj*: **he is** ~ **to it** он к этому не привык; **she is** ~ **to flying** она не привыкла летать.

unusual [ʌn'juːʒuəl] *adj* (*strange*) необычный* (необычен); (*rare*) редкий* (редок); (*exceptional, distinctive*) необыкновенный* (необыкновенен).

unusually [ʌn'juːʒuəlɪ] *adv* (*large, high etc*) необыкновенно.

unveil [ʌn'veɪl] *vt* (*statue*) открывать (открыть* *perf*).

unwanted [ʌn'wɒntɪd] *adj* (*clothing etc*) ненужный; (*child, pregnancy*) нежеланный.

unwarranted [ʌn'wɔrəntɪd] *adj* необоснованный*.

unwary [ʌn'wɛərɪ] *adj* неосторожный* (неосторожен).

unwavering [ʌn'weɪvərɪŋ] *adj* (*faith*) твёрдый* (твёрд), непоколебимый (непоколебим); (*gaze*) пристальный* (пристален).

unwelcome [ʌn'wɛlkəm] *adj* (*guest*) непрошенный* (непрошен); (*news*) неприятный* (неприятен); **to feel** ~ чувствовать (*impf*) себя лишним.

unwell [ʌn'wɛl] *adj*: **to feel** ~ чувствовать (*impf*) себя плохо; **he is** ~ ему нездоровится, он нездоров.

unwieldy [ʌn'wiːldɪ] *adj* громоздкий* (громоздок).

unwilling [ʌn'wɪlɪŋ] *adj*: **to be** ~ **to do** не хотеть* (*impf*) +*infin*.

unwillingly [ʌn'wɪlɪŋlɪ] *adv* неохотно.

unwind [ʌn'waɪnd] *irreg vt* (*undo*) разматывать (размотать *perf*) ♦ *vi* (*relax*) расслабляться (расслабиться* *perf*).

unwise [ʌn'waɪz] *adj* неблагоразумный* (неблагоразумен).

unwitting [ʌn'wɪtɪŋ] *adj* невольный.

unworkable [ʌn'wəːkəbl] *adj* неосуществимый (неосуществим).

unworthy [ʌn'wəːðɪ] *adj* недостойный* (недостоен); **to be** ~ **of sth/to do** быть* (*impf*) недостойным(-ой) чего-н/+*infin*; **that remark is** ~ **of you** Вам не пристало это говорить.

unwrap [ʌn'ræp] *vt* разворачивать (развернуть *perf*).

unwritten [ʌn'rɪtn] *adj* (*law, agreement*) неписаный.

unzip [ʌn'zɪp] *vt* расстёгивать (расстегнуть *perf*) на молнию.

KEYWORD

up [ʌp] *prep*: **he went up the stairs/the hill** он поднялся по лестнице/на гору; **the cat was up a tree** кошка была на дереве; **they live further up the street** они живут дальше на этой улице; **he has gone up to Scotland** он поехал в Шотландию

♦ *adv* **1** (*upwards, higher*): **up in the sky/the mountains** высоко в небе/в горах; **put the picture a bit higher** повесьте картину немного повыше; **up there** (*up above*) там наверху; **there's a village and up above, on the hill, a monastery** там есть деревня, а над ней,

на холме́ – монасты́рь
2: **to be up** (*out of bed*) встава́ть* (встать*
perf); (*prices, level*) поднима́ться (подня́ться*
perf); **the tent is up** пала́тка поста́влена
3: **up to** (*as far as*) до +*gen*); **I've read up to page
five** я дочита́л до пя́той страни́цы; **up to
now** до сих пор
4: **to be up to** (*depending on*) зави́сеть* (*impf*)
от +*gen*; **it's not up to me to decide** не мне
реша́ть; **it's up to you** э́то ва́ше де́ло
5: **to be up to** (*inf: be doing*) затева́ть (*impf*);
he's not up to the job он не тя́нет на э́ту
рабо́ту; **his work is not up to the required
standard** его́ рабо́та не соотве́тствует
тре́буемым станда́ртам; **what is he up to?**
что он затева́ет?; **what's she up to these
days?** а что она́ тепе́рь поде́лывает?
♦ *n*: **ups and downs** (*in life, career*) взлёты *mpl*
и паде́ния *ntpl*.

up-and-coming [ʌpənd'kʌmɪŋ] *adj*
перспекти́вный* (перспекти́вен).
upbeat [ʌpbiː't] *n* (*MUS*) сла́бая до́ля та́кта;
(*ECON*) подъём ♦ *adj* (*optimistic*)
оживлённый* (оживлён).
upbraid [ʌp'breɪd] *vt* упрека́ть (упрекну́ть
perf).
upbringing ['ʌpbrɪŋɪŋ] *n* воспита́ние.
upcoming ['ʌpkʌmɪŋ] *adj* (*forthcoming*)
предстоя́щий*, гряду́щий.
update [ʌp'deɪt] *vt* (*records, information*)
вноси́ть* (внести́* *perf*) измене́ния и
дополне́ния.
upend [ʌp'ɛnd] *vt* перевора́чивать
(переверну́ть *perf*) (вверх нога́ми).
upfront [ʌp'frʌnt] *adj* (*inf: frank*) откры́тый
(откры́т) ♦ *adv* (*pay*) вперёд.
upgrade [ʌp'greɪd] *vt* (*improve: house*)
модернизи́ровать (*impf/perf*); (: *job*)
усложня́ть (усложни́ть *perf*); (*employee*)
повыша́ть (повы́сить* *perf*) в до́лжности;
(*COMPUT*) нара́щивать (нарасти́ть* *perf*)
вычисли́тельные возмо́жности,
модернизи́ровать (*impf/perf*).
upheaval [ʌp'hiːvl] *n* переворо́т.
uphill [ʌp'hɪl] *adj* (*fig: task*) тяжёлый* (тяжёл) ♦
adv (*face, look*) вверх; (*go, move*) в го́ру; **to go
~** поднима́ться (*impf*) в го́ру.
uphold [ʌp'həʊld] (*irreg: like* **hold**) *vt*
подде́рживать (поддержа́ть* *perf*).
upholstery [ʌp'həʊlstərɪ] *n* оби́вка.
upkeep ['ʌpkiːp] *n* содержа́ние.
up-market [ʌp'mɑːkɪt] *adj* (*product*) дорого́й;
(*area*) элита́рный.
upon [ə'pɔn] *prep* (*position*) на +*prp*; (*motion*) на
+*acc*.
upper ['ʌpə'] *adj* ве́рхний* ♦ *n* (*of shoe*) верх.
upper class *n*: **the ~ ~** вы́сший* класс.
upper-class ['ʌpə'klɑːs] *adj* (*families, accent*)

аристократи́ческий*; (*district*) элита́рный.
uppercut ['ʌpəkʌt] *n* (*BOXING*) апперко́т.
upper hand *n*: **to have the ~ ~** контрол-
и́ровать (*impf*).
Upper House *n* (*BRIT*) Пала́та Ло́рдов.
uppermost ['ʌpəməʊst] *adj* вы́сший*; **what was
~ in my mind** что бо́льше всего́ занима́ло
мои́ мы́сли.
Upper Volta [-'vɔltə] *n* Ве́рхняя Во́льта,
Бурки́на-Фасо́ *nt ind*.
upright ['ʌpraɪt] *adj* (*straight, honest*) прямо́й*
(прям); (*vertical*) вертика́льный*
(вертика́лен) ♦ *n* (*CONSTR*) вертика́льная
сто́йка*.
uprising ['ʌpraɪzɪŋ] *n* восста́ние.
uproar ['ʌprɔː'] *n* (*protests*) возмуще́ние;
(*shouts*) шум.
uproarious [ʌp'rɔːrɪəs] *adj* (*people*)
хохо́чущий; (*play etc*) ужа́сно смешно́й
(смешо́н).
uproot [ʌp'ruːt] *vt* (*tree*) вырыва́ть (вы́рвать
perf) с ко́рнем; (*fig: people*) снима́ть (снять*
perf) с ме́ста.
upset [*vb, adj* ʌp'sɛt, *n* 'ʌpsɛt] (*irreg: like* **set**) *vt*
(*glass etc*) опроки́дывать (опроки́нуть *perf*);
(*routine*) наруша́ть (нару́шить *perf*); (*plan,
person*) расстра́ивать (расстро́ить *perf*);
(*person: offend*) оскорбля́ть (оскорби́ть*
perf) ♦ *adj* расстро́енный* (расстро́ен) ♦ *n* (*to
plan etc*) наруше́ние; **to get ~** (*sad*)
расстра́иваться (расстро́иться *perf*);
(*offended*) оскорбля́ться (оскорби́ться* *perf*);
to have a stomach ~ (*BRIT*) страда́ть (*impf*)
расстро́йством желу́дка.
upset price ['ʌpsɛt-] *n* (*US, SCOTTISH*) ни́зшая
отправна́я цена́ на аукцио́не.
upsetting [ʌp'sɛtɪŋ] *adj* (*annoying*) доса́дный.
upshot ['ʌpʃɔt] *n* результа́т; **the ~ of it all was
that ...** ко́нчилось всё тем, что ....
upside down ['ʌpsaɪd-] *adv* (*hang, hold*) вверх
нога́ми; (*turn*) вверх дном; **to turn a place ~
~** (*fig*) переверну́ть (*perf*) всё вверх дном.
upstairs [ʌp'stɛəz] *adv* (*be*) наверху́; (*go*)
наве́рх ♦ *adj* (*window, room*) ве́рхний* ♦ *n*
ве́рхний* эта́ж*; **there's no ~** здесь нет
ве́рхнего этажа́.
upstage ['ʌp'steɪdʒ] *vt* затмева́ть (затми́ть*
perf).
upstart ['ʌpstɑːt] *n* (*pej: person*) вы́скочка* *m/f*.
upstream [ʌp'striːm] *adv* про́тив тече́ния ♦ *adj*
вверх по тече́нию.
upsurge ['ʌpsəːdʒ] *n* (*of enthusiasm etc*)
подъём.
uptake ['ʌpteɪk] *n*: **to be quick/slow on the ~**
бы́стро/ме́дленно сообража́ть (*impf*).
uptight [ʌp'taɪt] *adj* (*inf*) натя́нутый (натя́нут).
up-to-date ['ʌptə'deɪt] *adj* (*information*)
после́дний*; (*person*) совреме́нный*

---

* marks translations which have irregular inflections. The Russian-English side of the dictionary gives inflectional information.

(совреме́нен).

upturn ['ʌptə:n] *n* (*in economy*) подъём.

upturned ['ʌptə:nd] *adj* (*nose*) курно́сый (курно́с), вздёрнутый (вздёрнут).

upward ['ʌpwəd] *adj*: ~ **movement/glance** движе́ние/взгляд вверх ♦ *adv* = **upwards**.

upwardly mobile ['ʌpwədlɪ-] *adj* преуспева́ющий; **a new ~~ generation** но́вое поколе́ние преуспева́ющих люде́й.

upwards ['ʌpwədz] *adv* (*move, glance*) вверх; (*more than*): ~ **of** свы́ше +*gen*.

URA *n abbr* (*US*: = *Urban Renewal Administration*) *правительственная организа́ция, координи́рующая рабо́ты по обновле́нию и улучше́нию устро́йства городо́в*.

Ural Mountains ['juərəl-] *npl*: **the** ~~ (*also*: **the Urals**) Ура́л *msg*, Ура́льские го́ры *fpl*.

uranium [juə'reɪnɪəm] *n* ура́н.

Uranus [juə'reɪnəs] *n* Ура́н.

urban ['ə:bən] *adj* городско́й.

urbane [ə:'beɪn] *adj* учти́вый (учти́в).

urbanization ['ə:bənaɪ'zeɪʃən] *n* урбаниза́ция.

urchin ['ə:tʃɪn] *n* (*pej*) беспризо́рник(-ица).

Urdu ['uədu:] *n* язы́к* урду́.

urge [ə:dʒ] *n* (*need, desire*) потре́бность *f* ♦ *vt*: **to ~ sb to do** настоя́тельно сове́товать (*impf*) кому́-н +*infin*; **to ~ caution** сове́товать (посове́товать *perf*) быть* осторо́жным(-ой)
▶ **urge on** *vt* подгоня́ть (*impf*).

urgency ['ə:dʒənsɪ] *n* (*of task etc*) неотло́жность *f*, безотлага́тельность *f*; (*of tone*) насто́йчивость *f*.

urgent ['ə:dʒənt] *adj* (*need, message*) сро́чный* (сро́чен); (*voice*) насто́йчивый (насто́йчив).

urgently ['ə:dʒəntlɪ] *adv* сро́чно.

urinal ['juərɪnl] *n* (*building*) мужско́й туале́т; (*vessel*) писсуа́р.

urinate ['juərɪneɪt] *vi* мочи́ться* (помочи́ться* *perf*).

urine ['juərɪn] *n* моча́.

urn [ə:n] *n* (*container*) у́рна; (*also*: **tea** ~) бак.

Uruguay ['juərəgwaɪ] *n* Уругва́й.

Uruguayan [juərə'gwaɪən] *adj* уругва́йский* ♦ *n* уругва́ец*(-а́йка*).

US *n abbr* = **United States**.

us [ʌs] *pron* (*direct*) нас; (*indirect*) нам; (*after prep*: +*gen*, +*prp*) нас; (: +*dat*) нам; (: +*instr*) на́ми; (*referring to subject of sentence*) свой; **a few of ~ are going to the cinema** не́которые из нас иду́т в кино́; *see also* **me**.

USA *n abbr* (= *United States of America*) США= *Соединённые Шта́ты Аме́рики*; (*MIL*) = *United States Army*.

usable ['ju:zəbl] *adj* приго́дный* (приго́ден).

USAF *n abbr* = *United States Air Force*.

usage ['ju:zɪdʒ] *n* (*LING*) употребле́ние.

USCG *n abbr* = *United States Coast Guard*.

USDA *n abbr* = *United States Department of Agriculture*.

USDAW ['ʌzdɔ:] *n abbr* (*BRIT*) = *Union of Shop,*

Distributive and Allied Workers.

USDI *n abbr* (= *United States Department of the Interior*) ≈ Министе́рство вну́тренних дел.

use [*vt* ju:z, *n* ju:s] *vt* (*object, tool*) испо́льзовать (*impf/perf*); (*phrase*) употребля́ть (употреби́ть* *perf*) ♦ *n* (*using*) испо́льзование, употребле́ние; (*usefulness*) по́льза; (*purpose*) примене́ние; **she ~d to do it** она́ когда́-то занима́лась э́тим; **what's this ~d for?** для чего́ э́то употребля́ется?; **to be ~d to** быть* (*impf*) привы́чным(-ой) к +*dat*; **to get ~d to** привыка́ть (привы́кнуть* *perf*) к +*dat*; **to be in ~** употребля́ться (*impf*), быть* (*impf*) в употребле́нии; **to be out of ~** не употребля́ться (*impf*); **to be of ~** быть* (*impf*) поле́зным(-ой); **to make ~ of sth** испо́льзовать (*impf/perf*) что-н; **it's no ~** э́то бесполе́зно; **to have the ~ of** по́льзоваться (*impf*) +*instr*
▶ **use up** *vt* (*food, leftovers*) испо́льзовать (*impf/perf*); (*money*) расхо́довать (израсхо́довать *perf*).

used [ju:zd] *adj* (*object*) бы́вший* в употребле́нии; (*car*) поде́ржанный.

useful ['ju:sful] *adj* поле́зный* (поле́зен); **to come in ~** пригоди́ться* (*perf*).

usefulness ['ju:sfəlnɪs] *n* по́льза.

useless ['ju:slɪs] *adj* (*unusable*) непригодный* (непригоден); (*pointless, hopeless*) бесполе́зный* (бесполе́зен).

user ['ju:zə'] *n* по́льзователь *f*; (*of petrol, gas etc*) потреби́тель *m*.

user-friendliness ['ju:zə'frɛndlɪnɪs] *n* простота́ в испо́льзовании.

user-friendly ['ju:zə'frɛndlɪ] *adj* просто́й (прост) в испо́льзовании.

USES *n abbr* (= *United States Employment Service*) *управле́ние по размеще́нию и регули́рованию рабо́чей си́лы*.

usher ['ʌʃə'] *n* (*at wedding*) распоряди́тель *m* ♦ *vt*: **to ~ sb into** проводи́ть* (провести́* *perf*) кого́-н в +*acc*.

usherette [ʌʃə'rɛt] *n* билете́рша.

USIA *n abbr* (= *United States Information Agency*) ЮСИА (*Информацио́нное аге́нтство США*).

USM *n abbr* (= *United States Mint*) Моне́тный двор США; (= *United States Mail*) По́чта США.

USN *n abbr* = *United States Navy*.

USPHS *n abbr* = *United States Public Health Service*.

USPO *n abbr* = *United States Post Office*.

USS *abbr* = *United States Ship*.

USSR *n abbr* (*formerly*: = *Union of Soviet Socialist Republics*) СССР = *Сою́з Сове́тских Социалисти́ческих Респу́блик*.

usu. *abbr* = **usually**.

usual ['ju:ʒuəl] *adj* (*time, place etc*) обы́чный; **as ~** как обы́чно.

usually ['ju:ʒuəlɪ] *adv* обы́чно.

usurer ['juːʒərəʳ] *n* ростовщи́к*.
usurp [juːˈzəːp] *vt* узурпи́ровать *(impf/perf)*.
usury ['juːʒʊrɪ] *n* ростовщи́чество.
UT *(US: POST) abbr = Utah.*
utensil [juːˈtɛnsl] *n* инструме́нт; **kitchen ~s** ку́хонные принадле́жности.
uterus ['juːtərəs] *n* ма́тка*.
utilitarian [juːtɪlɪˈtɛərɪən] *adj* утилита́рный* (утилита́рен).
utility [juːˈtɪltɪ] *n (usefulness)* поле́зность *f*; **public utilities** коммуна́льные услу́ги *fpl*.
utility room *n* подсо́бная ко́мната, подсо́бка* *(разг)*.
utilization [juːtɪlaɪˈzeɪʃən] *n* утилиза́ция.
utilize ['juːtɪlaɪz] *vt* утилизи́ровать *(impf/perf)*; *(information)* находи́ть (найти́* *perf)* примене́ние +*dat*.

utmost ['ʌtməʊst] *adj* велича́йший ♦ *n*: **to do one's ~** де́лать (сде́лать *perf)* всё возмо́жное; **of the ~ importance** велича́йшей ва́жности.
utter ['ʌtəʳ] *adj (amazement)* по́лный; *(conviction)* глубо́кий*; *(rubbish)* соверше́нный ♦ *vt (sounds)* издава́ть* (изда́ть* *perf)*; *(words)* произноси́ть* (произнести́* *perf)*.
utterance ['ʌtərəns] *n* выска́зывание.
utterly ['ʌtəlɪ] *adv* соверше́нно.
U-turn ['juːˈtəːn] *n (AUT)* разворо́т на 180 гра́дусов; *(fig)* коренно́е измене́ние.
Uzbek ['ʌzbɛk] *n (person)* узбе́к(-е́чка*); *(LING)* узбе́кский* язы́к* ♦ *adj* узбе́кский*.
Uzbekistan [ʌzbɛkɪˈstɑːn] *n* Узбекиста́н.

---

* marks translations which have irregular inflections. The Russian-English side of the dictionary gives inflectional information.

~ V, v ~

V, v [vi:] n (letter) 22-ая буква английского алфавита.

v. abbr (= **verse, versus**; (= **volt**) В= вольт; (see: = vide) см. смотри.

VA (US: POST) abbr = Virginia.

vac [væk] n abbr (BRIT: inf) = **vacation**.

vacancy ['veɪkənsɪ] n (BRIT: job) вакансия; (room in hotel etc) свободный номер*; "no vacancies" „мест нет"; **have you any vacancies?** (hotel) у Вас есть свободные номера?; (office) у Вас есть вакансии?

vacant ['veɪkənt] adj (room, seat, toilet) свободный* (свободен); (look, expression) отсутствующий*; (job) вакантный.

vacant lot n (US) пустырь* m; (: for sale) участок*.

vacate [və'keɪt] vt освобождать (освободить* perf).

vacation [və'keɪʃən] n (esp US: holiday) отпуск*; (BRIT: SCOL) каникулы pl; **to take a ~** брать* (взять* perf) отпуск; **on ~** в отпуске.

vacation course n лётние курсы mpl.

vaccinate ['væksɪneɪt] vt: **to ~ sb (against sth)** делать (сделать perf) прививку кому-н (от чего-н).

vaccination [væksɪ'neɪʃən] n прививка*.

vaccine ['væksi:n] n вакцина.

vacuum ['vækjum] n (empty space) вакуум ♦ vt пылесосить (пропылесосить perf).

vacuum cleaner n пылесос.

vacuum flask n (BRIT) термос.

vacuum-packed ['vækjum'pækt] adj герметично упакованный (упакован).

Vaduz [fa'duts] n Вадуц.

vagabond ['vægəbɔnd] n бродяга m/f.

vagary ['veɪgərɪ] n: **the vagaries of the weather** капризы mpl погоды.

vagina [və'dʒaɪnə] n влагалище.

vagrancy ['veɪgrənsɪ] n бродяжничество.

vagrant ['veɪgrənt] n бродяга m/f.

vague [veɪg] adj (blurred: memory, outline) смутный* (смутен); (uncertain) неопределённый; (look) рассеянный; (idea, instructions) расплывчатый (расплывчат); (evasive: answer) уклончивый (уклончив); **he was ~ about it** (evasive) он не сказал ничего определённого об этом; **I haven't the ~st idea** я не имею ни малейшего представления.

vaguely ['veɪglɪ] adv (promise, say, plan) неопределённо; (look) рассеянно; (suspect) смутно; **they were ~ amused** они слегка развеселились; **it looks ~ like yours** это немножко напоминает Ваш.

vagueness ['veɪgnɪs] n неопределённость f.

vain [veɪn] adj (conceited) тщеславный* (тщеславен); (useless: attempt, action) тщётный (тщётен); **in ~** напрасно.

vainly ['veɪnlɪ] adv тщётно.

valance ['væləns] n (for bed) подзор.

valedictorian [vælɪdɪk'tɔ:rɪən] n (US: SCOL) "лучший* выпускник" (в двенадцатом классе средней школы).

valedictory [vælɪ'dɪktərɪ] adj (speech, remarks) прощальный.

valentine ['væləntaɪn] n (also: ~ card) (анонимное) любовное послание в день Св. Валентина (14 февраля).

valet ['vælɪt] n камердинер.

valet parking n припарковка автомобилей клиентов, например в гостиницах.

valet service n (for clothes) служба по уходу за одеждой клиентов; (for car) обслуживание автомобилей – мойка, заправка итп.

valiant ['vælɪənt] adj (attempt, effort) отважный* (отважен).

valid ['vælɪd] adj (ticket, document) действительный* (действителен); (reason) вёский* (вёсок); (argument) убедительный* (убедителен).

validate ['vælɪdeɪt] vt (contract, document) утверждать (утвердить* perf); (argument, claim) подтверждать (подтвердить perf).

validity [və'lɪdɪtɪ] n (see adj) действительность f; вёскость f; убедительность f.

valise [və'li:z] n саквояж.

Valletta [və'lɛtə] n Валлетта.

valley ['vælɪ] n долина.

valour ['vælə'] (US valor) n доблесть f.

valuable ['væljuəbl] adj ценный; (time) драгоценный.

valuables ['væljuəblz] npl (jewellery etc) ценности fpl.

valuation [vælju'eɪʃən] n оценка*.

value ['vælju:] n ценность f ♦ vt (fix price or worth of) оценивать (оценить* perf); (appreciate) ценить* (impf); **~s** npl (principles, beliefs) це́нности *fpl*; **you get good ~ (for money) in that shop** в э́том магази́не вы́годно покупа́ть; **to lose (in)** ~ па́дать (упа́сть* *perf*) в цене́; **to gain (in)** ~ поднима́ться (подня́ться* *perf*) в цене́; **to be of great ~ to sb** *(fig)* представля́ть *(impf)* для кого́-н большу́ю це́нность.

value-added tax [væljuː'ædɪd-] *n (BRIT)* нало́г на доба́вленную сто́имость.

valued ['væljuːd] *adj (customer, advice)* це́нный.

valuer ['væljuəʳ] *n* оце́нщик.

valve [vælv] *n (also MED)* кла́пан.

vampire ['væmpaɪəʳ] *n* вампи́р.

van [væn] *n (AUT)* фурго́н; *(BRIT: RAIL)* бага́жный ваго́н.

V and A *n abbr (BRIT)* = **Victoria and Albert Museum**.

vandal ['vændl] *n*ванда́л.

vandalism ['vændəlɪzəm] *n* вандали́зм.

vandalize ['vændəlaɪz] *vt (damage)* бессмы́сленно уро́довать (изуро́довать *perf)*; *(destroy)* бессмы́сленно разруша́ть (разру́шить *perf)*.

vanguard ['vænɡɑːd] *n (fig)*: **in the ~ of** в аванга́рде +*gen*.

vanilla [və'nɪlə] *n* вани́ль *f*.

vanilla ice cream *n* ≈ сли́вочное моро́женое *nt adj*.

vanish ['vænɪʃ] *vi* исчеза́ть (исче́знуть *perf)*.

vanity ['vænɪtɪ] *n (of person)* тщесла́вие.

vanity case *n* космети́чка*.

vantage point ['vɑːntɪdʒ-] *n* наблюда́тельный пункт; **from our 20th century ~ ~** *(fig)* с пози́ции на́шего 20-го ве́ка.

vapor *etc (US)* = **vapour** *etc*.

vaporize ['veɪpəraɪz] *vt (liquid)* выпа́ривать (вы́парить *perf)* ♦ *vi* испаря́ться (испари́ться *perf)*.

vapour ['veɪpəʳ] *(US* **vapor**) *n (gas, mist, steam)* пар*.

vapour trail *n (AVIAT)* след* самолёта.

variable ['vɛərɪəbl] *adj (likely to change: mood, quality, weather)* изме́нчивый (изме́нчив); *(able to be changed: temperature, height, speed)* переме́нный ♦ *n* фа́ктор; *(MATH)* переме́нная *f adj*.

variance ['vɛərɪəns] *n*: **to be at ~ with** расходи́ться* *(impf)* (с +*instr)*; *(facts)* противоре́чить *(impf)* +*dat*.

variant ['vɛərɪənt] *n* вариа́нт.

variation [vɛərɪ'eɪʃən] *n (in level, amount, quantity)* измене́ние; *(of plot, musical theme etc)* вариа́ция.

varicose veins ['værɪkəus-] *npl (MED)* варико́зное расшире́ние *ntsg* вен.

varied ['vɛərɪd] *adj* разнообра́зный* (разнообра́зен).

variety [və'raɪətɪ] *n* разнообра́зие; *(type)* разнови́дность *f*; **a wide ~ of** ... большо́е разнообра́зие +*gen* ...; **for a ~ of reasons** по ря́ду причи́н.

variety show *n (THEAT)* варьете́ *nt ind*.

various ['vɛərɪəs] *adj (different)* разли́чный; *(several)* ра́зный; **at ~ times** в ра́зное вре́мя.

varnish ['vɑːnɪʃ] *n (product)* лак; *(also:* **nail ~**) лак для ногте́й ♦ *vt (wood, piece of furniture etc)* покрыва́ть (покры́ть* *perf)* ла́ком; *(nails)* кра́сить (накра́сить* *perf)*.

vary ['vɛərɪ] *vt (routine, diet)* вноси́ть* (внести́* *perf)* разнообра́зие в +*acc* ♦ *vi (be different: sizes, colours)* различа́ться *(impf)*; *(become different)*: **to ~ with** *(weather, season etc)* меня́ться *(impf)* в зави́симости от +*gen*; **to ~ (according to** *or* **with)** меня́ться *(impf)* в соотве́тствии с +*instr*).

varying ['vɛərɪŋ] *adj (amount, opinions etc)* разли́чный* (разли́чен).

vase [vɑːz] *n* ва́за.

vasectomy [væ'sɛktəmɪ] *n (MED)* вазектоми́я.

Vaseline® ['væsɪliːn] *n* вазели́н.

vast [vɑːst] *adj (knowledge)* обши́рный* (обши́рен); *(expense)* грома́дный* (грома́ден); *(area)* необъя́тный* (необъя́тен).

vastly ['vɑːstlɪ] *adv* кра́йне.

vastness ['vɑːstnɪs] *n* необъя́тность *f*.

VAT [væt] *n abbr (BRIT)* (= **value-added tax**) НДС= *нало́г на доба́вленную сто́имость*.

vat [væt] *n* ка́дка.

Vatican ['vætɪkən] *n*: **the ~** Ватика́н.

vatman ['vætmæn] *n (BRIT: inf)* чино́вник, *собира́ющий нало́г на доба́вленную сто́имость*.

vaudeville ['vəudəvɪl] *n (THEAT)* водеви́ль *m*.

vault [vɔːlt] *n (of roof)* свод; *(tomb)* склеп; *(in bank)* храни́лище; *(jump)* опо́рный прыжо́к ♦ *vt (also:* **~ over**) перепры́гивать (перепры́гнуть *perf)* (че́рез +*acc)*.

vaunted ['vɔːntɪd] *adj*: **much-~** восхваля́емый.

VC *n abbr* = **vice-chairman**; *(BRIT:* = **Victoria Cross**) "Крест Викто́рии" *(вы́сшая вое́нная награ́да)*.

VCR *n abbr* = **video cassette recorder**.

VD *n abbr* = **venereal disease**.

VDU *n abbr (COMPUT)* = **visual display unit**.

veal [viːl] *n (CULIN)* теля́тина.

veer [vɪəʳ] *vi (vehicle)* свора́чивать (сверну́ть *perf)*; *(wind)* меня́ть (применя́ть *perf)* направле́ние.

veg. [vɛdʒ] *n abbr (BRIT: inf)* = **vegetable(s)**.

vegan ['viːɡən] *n* вегетариа́нец, *не употребля́ющий моло́чных проду́ктов* ♦ *adj* расти́тельный.

vegeburger ['vɛdʒɪbəːɡəʳ] *n* вегетариа́нская котле́та.

---

* marks translations which have irregular inflections. The Russian-English side of the dictionary gives inflectional information.

vegetable ['vɛdʒtəbl] n (BOT) о́вощ ♦ adj (oil etc) расти́тельный; (dish) овощно́й; ~ **garden** огоро́д.

vegetarian [vɛdʒɪ'tɛərɪən] n (person) вегетариа́нец*(-а́нка*) ♦ adj (diet, restaurant etc) вегетариа́нский*.

vegetate ['vɛdʒɪteɪt] vi (person) прозяба́ть (impf).

vegetation [vɛdʒɪ'teɪʃən] n (plants) расти́тельность f.

vegetative ['vɛdʒɪtətɪv] adj (BIO) вегетати́вный; (fig) расти́тельный.

veggieburger ['vɛdʒɪbə:gə'] n = **vegeburger**.

vehemence ['vi:məns] n я́рость f.

vehement ['vi:mənt] adj (attack, denial) я́ростный* (я́ростен); (passions) нейстовый (нейстов).

vehicle ['vi:ɪkl] n автотра́нспортное сре́дство; (fig: means of expressing) сре́дство.

vehicular [vɪ'hɪkjulə'] adj (AUT): "**no ~ traffic**" „движе́ние автотра́нспорта запрещено́".

veil [veɪl] n вуа́ль f ♦ vt скрыва́ть (скрыть* perf); **under a ~ of secrecy** (fig) под покро́вом та́йны.

veiled [veɪld] adj (fig: threat) скры́тый.

vein [veɪn] n (of leaf) жи́лка*; (ANAT) ве́на; (of ore) жи́ла; (fig: of mood, style) тон.

Velcro® ['vɛlkrəu] n липу́чка.

vellum ['vɛləm] n (writing paper) веле́невая бума́га.

velocity [vɪ'lɔsɪtɪ] n ско́рость f.

velour [və'luə'] n велю́р.

velvet ['vɛlvɪt] n ба́рхат ♦ adj ба́рхатный.

vendetta [vɛn'dɛtə] n венде́тта.

vending machine ['vɛndɪŋ-] n автома́т по прода́же сигаре́т, шокола́да итп.

vendor ['vɛndə'] n (of house, land) продаве́ц; **street ~** у́личный(-ая) торго́вец(-вка).

veneer [və'nɪə'] n (on furniture) фанеро́вка; (fig: of person, place) личи́на.

venerable ['vɛnərəbl] adj (person) почте́нный; (building etc) дре́вний*; (REL) преподо́бный.

venereal disease [vɪ'nɪərɪəl-] n венери́ческое заболева́ние.

Venetian [vɪ'ni:ʃən] adj венециа́нский* ♦ n венециа́нец(-а́нка*).

Venetian blind n жалюзи́ pl.

Venezuela [vɛnɛ'zweɪlə] n Венесуэ́ла.

Venezuelan [vɛnɛ'zweɪlən] adj венесуэ́льский* ♦ n венесуэ́лец*(-лка).

vengeance ['vɛndʒəns] n возме́здие; **with a ~** (fig) с лихво́й.

vengeful ['vɛndʒful] adj мсти́тельный* (мсти́телен).

Venice ['vɛnɪs] n Вене́ция.

venison ['vɛnɪsn] n олени́на.

venom ['vɛnəm] n (of snake, insect) яд; (bitterness, anger) зло́ба.

venomous ['vɛnəməs] adj (snake, insect) ядови́тый (ядови́т); (look, stare) зло́бный* (зло́бен).

vent [vɛnt] n (also: **air ~**) вентиляцио́нное отве́рстие; (in jacket) разре́з ♦ vt (fig) дава́ть* (дать* perf) вы́ход +dat.

ventilate ['vɛntɪleɪt] vt (room, building) прове́тривать (прове́трить perf).

ventilation [vɛntɪ'leɪʃən] n вентиля́ция.

ventilation shaft n вентиляцио́нная ша́хта.

ventilator ['vɛntɪleɪtə'] n (TECH, MED) вентиля́тор.

ventriloquist [vɛn'trɪləkwɪst] n чревовеща́тель (ница) m(f).

venture ['vɛntʃə'] n (risky undertaking) сме́лое предприя́тие ♦ vt (opinion) осме́ливаться (осме́литься perf) вы́сказать ♦ vi (dare to go) осме́ливаться (осме́литься perf); **business ~** предприя́тие; **to ~ to do** отва́живаться (отва́житься perf) +infin.

venture capital n (COMM) ве́нчурный капита́л.

venue ['vɛnju:] n (place fixed for sth) ме́сто* проведе́ния.

Venus ['vi:nəs] n (planet) Вене́ра.

veracity [və'ræsɪtɪ] n правди́вость f.

veranda(h) [və'rændə] n вера́нда.

verb [və:b] n глаго́л.

verbal ['və:bl] adj (spoken: skills, translation etc) у́стный; (of a verb) глаго́льный.

verbally ['və:bəlɪ] adv (communicate, transmit) на слова́х.

verbatim [və:'beɪtɪm] adj досло́вный ♦ adv досло́вно.

verbose [və:'bəus] adj (person, writing) многосло́вный.

verdict ['və:dɪkt] n (LAW) пригово́р; (fig: opinion) заключе́ние; **to bring in a ~ of guilty/ not guilty** выноси́ть* (вы́нести* perf) обвини́тельный/оправда́тельный пригово́р.

verge [və:dʒ] n (BRIT: of road) обо́чина; "**soft ~s**" (BRIT: AUT) незаасфальти́рованная, грунтова́я обо́чина; **to be on the ~ of sth** быть* (impf) на гра́ни чего́-н

▶ **verge on** vt fus (panic etc) грани́чить (impf) с +instr.

verger ['və:dʒə'] n (REL) церко́вный служи́тель m.

verification [vɛrɪfɪ'keɪʃən] n (see vb) подтвержде́ние; прове́рка.

verify ['vɛrɪfaɪ] vt (confirm) подтвержда́ть (подтверди́ть* perf); (check) проверя́ть (прове́рить perf).

veritable ['vɛrɪtəbl] adj (for emphasis: real) настоя́щий*.

vermin ['və:mɪn] npl (animals) вреди́тели mpl; (fleas, lice etc) парази́ты mpl.

vermouth ['və:məθ] n ве́рмут.

vernacular [və'nækjulə'] n (language) национа́льный язы́к*; (local language) ме́стный диале́кт.

versatile ['və:sətaɪl] adj (person) разно-сторо́нний*; (substance, machine, tool etc) универса́льный* (универса́лен).

versatility [vəːsəˈtɪlɪtɪ] n (see adj) разносторо́нность f; универса́льность f.
verse [vəːs] n (poetry, in Bible) стих; (one part of a poem) строфа́*; **in** ~ в стиха́х.
versed [vəːst] adj: **(well-)~ in** све́дущий* (све́дущ) в +prp.
version [ˈvəːʃən] n (form: of design, production) вариа́нт; (account: of events, accident etc) ве́рсия.
versus [ˈvəːsəs] prep про́тив +gen.
vertebra [ˈvəːtɪbrə] (pl ~e) n (ANAT) позвоно́к*.
vertebrae [ˈvəːtɪbriː] npl of **vertebra**.
vertebrate [ˈvəːtɪbrɪt] n позвоно́чное nt adj (живо́тное).
vertical [ˈvəːtɪkl] adj вертика́льный* (вертика́лен) ◆ n вертика́ль f.
vertically [ˈvəːtɪklɪ] adv вертика́льно.
vertigo [ˈvəːtɪgəu] n головокруже́ние; **to suffer from** ~ страда́ть (impf) от головокруже́ний.
verve [vəːv] n (vivacity) воодушевле́ние.
very [ˈvɛrɪ] adv о́чень ◆ adj: **the** ~ **book which** та са́мая кни́га, кото́рая; ~ **well/little** о́чень хорошо́/ма́ло; **thank you** ~ **much** большо́е спаси́бо; ~ **much better** гора́здо лу́чше; **I much hope so** я о́чень наде́юсь на э́то; **the** ~ **thought (of it) alarms me** сама́ мысль (об э́том) пуга́ет меня́; **at the** ~ **end** в са́мом конце́; **the** ~ **last** са́мый после́дний*; **at the** ~ **least** как ми́нимум.
vespers [ˈvɛspəz] npl (REL) вече́рня fsg.
vessel [ˈvɛsl] n (NAUT) су́дно*; (container) сосу́д; see also **blood**.
vest [vɛst] n (BRIT: underwear) ма́йка; (US: waistcoat) жиле́т ◆ vt: **to** ~ **sb with sth,** ~ **sth in sb** наделя́ть (надели́ть* perf) кого́-н чем-н.
vested interest [ˈvɛstɪd-] n (COMM) заинтересо́ванность f; **to have a** ~ ~ **in sth** быть* (impf) заинтересо́ванным(-ой) в чём-н.
vestibule [ˈvɛstɪbjuː] n (in building) вестибю́ль m.
vestige [ˈvɛstɪdʒ] n оста́ток*.
vestment [ˈvɛstmənt] n (REL) ри́за.
vestry [ˈvɛstrɪ] n (of church) ри́зница.
Vesuvius [vɪˈsuːvɪəs] n Везу́вий.
vet [vɛt] n abbr (BRIT) = **veterinary surgeon**.
veteran [ˈvɛtərn] n (of war) ветера́н ◆ adj: **she's a** ~ **campaigner for** ... она́ ста́рый ветера́н движе́ния за +acc ....
veteran car n (BRIT) маши́на ста́рой ма́рки.
veterinarian [vɛtrɪˈnɛərɪən] n (US) ветерина́р.
veterinary [ˈvɛtrɪnərɪ] adj (practice, care etc) ветерина́рный.
veterinary surgeon n (BRIT) ветерина́р.
veto [ˈviːtəu] (pl ~es) n ве́то nt ind ◆ vt (proposal etc) налага́ть (наложи́ть* perf) ве́то на +acc; **to put a** ~ **on** налага́ть (наложи́ть* perf) ве́то на +acc.
vetting [ˈvɛtɪŋ] n (of person) прове́рка (на

благонадёжность).
vex [vɛks] vt (irritate, upset) досажда́ть (досади́ть* perf).
vexed [vɛkst] adj (question) досажда́ющий.
VFD n abbr (US) = volunteer fire department.
VG n abbr (BRIT: SCOL etc) = very good.
VHF abbr (RADIO: = very high frequency) ОВЧ= о́чень высо́кая частота́.
VI abbr (US: POST) = Virgin Islands.
via [ˈvaɪə] prep (through, by way of) че́рез +acc.
viability [vaɪəˈbɪlɪtɪ] n жизнеспосо́бность f; (of product) конкурентоспосо́бность f.
viable [ˈvaɪəbl] adj (company) конкурентоспосо́бный; (project) осуществи́мый.
viaduct [ˈvaɪədʌkt] n виаду́к.
vial [ˈvaɪəl] n (for medicine) пузырёк; (for perfume) флако́н.
vibes [vaɪbz] npl (inf: atmosphere) флюи́ды mpl.
vibrant [ˈvaɪbrnt] adj (lively) по́лный* (по́лон) жи́зни; (light) я́ркий* (я́рок); (colour) со́чный* (со́чен); (full of emotion: voice) насы́щенный.
vibraphone [ˈvaɪbrəfəun] n вибрафо́н.
vibrate [vaɪˈbreɪt] vi (house, machine etc) вибри́ровать* (impf); (resound) отдава́ться* (impf).
vibration [vaɪˈbreɪʃən] n вибра́ция.
vibrator [vaɪˈbreɪtəʳ] n вибра́тор.
vicar [ˈvɪkəʳ] n (REL) свяще́нник.
vicarage [ˈvɪkərɪdʒ] n дом* свяще́нника.
vicarious [vɪˈkɛərɪəs] adj (pleasure, experience) опосре́дованный (опосре́дован).
vice [vaɪs] n (moral fault) поро́к; (TECH) тиски́ pl.
vice- [vaɪs] prefix (president) ви́це-.
vice-chairman [vaɪsˈtʃɛəmən] irreg n замести́тель m председа́теля.
vice chancellor n (BRIT: of university) ви́це-ка́нцлер.
vice president n ви́це-президе́нт.
viceroy [ˈvaɪsrɔɪ] n короле́вский* наме́стник.
vice squad n (POLICE) отде́л в поли́ции, кото́рый име́ет де́ло с преступле́ниями, свя́занными с порногра́фией, проститу́цией, нарко́тиками итп.
vice versa [ˈvaɪsɪˈvəːsə] adv наоборо́т.
vicinity [vɪˈsɪnɪtɪ] n (area): **in the** ~ **(of)** в окре́стностях (+gen).
vicious [ˈvɪʃəs] adj (attack, blow) жесто́кий* (жесто́к); (words, look, dog) злой* (зол); (horse) норови́стый (норови́ст).
vicious circle n поро́чный круг.
viciousness [ˈvɪʃəsnɪs] n зло́ба.
vicissitudes [vɪˈsɪsɪtjuːdz] npl превра́тности fpl.
victim [ˈvɪktɪm] n же́ртва; **to be the** ~ **of** быть* (impf) же́ртвой +gen.
victimization [ˈvɪktɪmaɪˈzeɪʃən] n пресле́дование.

---

* marks translations which have irregular inflections The Russian-English side of the dictionary gives inflectional information

victimize ['vɪktɪmaɪz] *vt* (*strikers etc*)
преследовать* (*impf*/*perf*).
victor ['vɪktə'] *n* победитель(ница) *m(f)*.
Victorian [vɪk'tɔːrɪən] *adj* викторианский.
victorious [vɪk'tɔːrɪəs] *adj* (*team*)
победоносный; (*shout*) победный.
victory ['vɪktərɪ] *n* победа; **to win a ~ over sb**
одержать* (*perf*) победу над кем-н.
video ['vɪdɪəu] *cpd* видео *ind* ♦ *n* (*also:* ~ **film**)
видеофильм; (*also:* ~ **cassette**)
видеокассета; (*also:* ~ **cassette recorder**)
видеомагнитофон; (*also:* ~ **camera**)
видеокамера.
videodisc ['vɪdɪəudɪsk] *n* видеодиск.
video game *n* видеоигра.
video nasty *n* видеофильм со сценами
насилия.
videophone ['vɪdɪəufəun] *n* видеотелефон.
video recorder *n* видеомагнитофон.
video recording *n* видеозапись *f*.
video tape *n* видеолента.
vie [vaɪ] *vi*: **to ~ with sb/for sth** соперничать
(*impf*) с кем-н/в чём-н.
Vienna [vɪ'ɛnə] *n* Вена.
Viennese [vɪə'niːz] *adj* венский ♦ *n inv*
житель(ница) *m(f)* Вены.
Vietnam ['vjɛt'næm] *n* Вьетнам.
Viet Nam ['vjɛt'næm] *n* = **Vietnam**.
Vietnamese [vjɛtnə'miːz] *adj* вьетнамский* ♦ *n*
inv (*person*) вьетнамец*(-мка*); (*LING*)
вьетнамский* язык*.
view [vjuː] *n* (*sight, outlook*) вид; (*opinion*)
взгляд ♦ *vt* (*look at: also fig*) рассматривать
(рассмотреть *perf*); (*situation*) оценивать
(оценить *perf*); (*house*) осматривать
(осмотреть *perf*); **to be on ~** (*in museum etc*)
выставляться (*impf*); **in full ~ (of)** на виду (у
+*gen*); **in ~ of the weather/the fact that** ввиду
плохой погоды/того, что; **in my ~** на мой
взгляд; **an overall ~ of the situation** общая
картина положения; **with a ~ to doing** с тем,
чтобы +*infin*.
Viewdata® ['vjuːdeɪtə] *n* (*BRIT. COMPUT*)
видеотекст; (*TEL*) телекоммуникационная
система, позволяющая клиентам делать
заказы на товары или услуги прямо из
дома.
viewer ['vjuː'] *n* (*person*) зритель *m*.
viewfinder ['vjuːfaɪndə'] *n* (*PHOT*) видо-
искатель *m*.
viewpoint ['vjuːpɔɪnt] *n* (*attitude*) точка
зрения; (*place*) место* обозрения.
vigil ['vɪdʒɪl] *n* бдение; **to keep ~** дежурить
(подежурить *perf*).
vigilance ['vɪdʒɪləns] *n* бдительность *f*.
vigilance committee *n* (*US*) "комитет
бдительности" (*организация линчевателей*).
vigilant ['vɪdʒɪlənt] *adj* бдительный.
vigilante [vɪdʒɪ'læntɪ] *n* самодеятельный
блюститель порядка, считающий действия
полиции недостаточными.

vigor ['vɪgə'] (*US*) *n* = **vigour**.
vigorous ['vɪgərəs] *adj* (*action, campaign*)
мощный; (*plant*) сильный.
vigour ['vɪgə'] (*US* **vigor**) *n* (*energy: of person*)
сила; (: *of campaign*) мощь *f*.
vile [vaɪl] *adj* (*evil*) гнусный; (*unpleasant*)
мерзкий*; ♦ **language** сквернословие.
vilify ['vɪlɪfaɪ] *vt* (*person*) поносить* (*impf*).
villa ['vɪlə] *n* вилла.
village ['vɪlɪdʒ] *n* деревня.
villager ['vɪlɪdʒə'] *n* деревенский*(-ая)
житель(ница) *m(f)*.
villain ['vɪlən] *n* (*scoundrel*) негодяй; (*in novel
etc*) злодей; (*BRIT: criminal*) преступник.
Vilnius ['vɪlnɪəs] *n* Вильнюс.
VIN *n abbr* (*US*) = *vehicle identification number*.
vinaigrette [vɪneɪ'grɛt] *n* (*salad dressing*)
заправка для салата (*из уксуса и
растительного масла*).
vindicate ['vɪndɪkeɪt] *vt* (*person: free from
blame*) доказывать (доказать* *perf*) правоту
+*gen*; (*action: justify*) оправдывать
(оправдать *perf*).
vindication [vɪndɪ'keɪʃən] *n*: **in ~ of sb/sth** в
оправдание кого-н/чего-н.
vindictive [vɪn'dɪktɪv] *adj* мстительный*
(мстителен).
vine [vaɪn] *n* (*BOT: with grapes*) виноградная
лоза; (: *climbing plant*) вьющееся растение;
(: *in jungle*) лиана.
vinegar ['vɪnɪgə'] *n* уксус.
vineyard ['vɪnjɑːd] *n* виноградник.
vintage ['vɪntɪdʒ] *n* (*year*) год изготовления
вина ♦ *cpd* (*classic: comedy, performance etc*)
классический*; **the 1970 ~** (*of wine*) урожая
1970 года.
vintage car *n* машина старой марки.
vintage wine *n* выдержанное вино.
vinyl ['vaɪnl] *n* винил.
viola [vɪ'əulə] *n* (*MUS*) альт*.
violate ['vaɪəleɪt] *vt* нарушать (нарушить *perf*);
(*graveyard*) осквернять (осквернить *perf*).
violation [vaɪə'leɪʃən] *n* (*of agreement etc*)
нарушение; **in ~ of** в нарушение +*gen*.
violence ['vaɪələns] *n* (*brutality*) насилие;
(*strength*) сила.
violent ['vaɪələnt] *adj* (*behaviour*) жестокий*;
(*death*) насильственный; (*debate, criticism*)
яростный; **a ~ dislike of sb/sth** резкая
неприязнь к кому-н/чему-н.
violently ['vaɪələntlɪ] *adv* (*dislike*) сильно; (*ill,
angry*) очень.
violet ['vaɪələt] *adj* фиолетовый ♦ *n* (*colour*)
фиолетовый цвет; (*plant*) фиалка*.
violin [vaɪə'lɪn] *n* (*MUS*) скрипка*.
violinist [vaɪə'lɪnɪst] *n* скрипач*(ка*).
VIP *n abbr* (= *very important person*) очень
важное лицо.
viper ['vaɪpə'] *n* гадюка.
viral ['vaɪərəl] *adj* вирусный.
virgin ['vəːdʒɪn] *n* (*person*) девственница;

(: *religious etc*) де́ва ♦ *adj* (*snow, forest etc*) де́вственный; **the Blessed V~** пресвята́я де́ва Мари́я; (*in Orthodox Church*) Богоро́дица.
virgin birth *n* рожде́ние от де́вственницы.
virginity [vəˈdʒɪnɪtɪ] *n* (*of person*) де́вственность *f*.
Virgo [ˈvəːgəu] *n* Де́ва; **he is ~** он – Де́ва.
virile [ˈvɪraɪl] *adj* вери́льный.
virility [vɪˈrɪlɪtɪ] *n* (*sexual power*) вери́льность *f*; (*fig: masculine qualities*) му́жественность *f*.
virtual [ˈvəːtjuəl] *adj* факти́ческий*; (*COMPUT, PHYS*) виртуа́льный; (*in effect*): **it's a ~ impossibility** э́то практи́чески *or* факти́чески невозмо́жно.
virtually [ˈvəːtjuəlɪ] *adv* (*almost*) факти́чески, практи́чески; **it is ~ impossible** э́то факти́чески *or* практи́чески невозмо́жно.
virtual reality *n* систе́ма трёхмерного телеви́дения.
virtue [ˈvəːtjuː] *n* (*moral correctness*) доброде́тель *f*; (*advantage*) преиму́щество; (*merit*) досто́инство; **by ~ of** благодаря́ +*dat*.
virtuosi [vəːtjuˈəuzɪ] *npl of* **virtuoso**.
virtuosity [vəːtjuˈɔsɪtɪ] *n* виртуо́зность *f*.
virtuoso [vəːtjuˈəuzəu] (*pl* **~s** *or* **virtuosi**) *n* виртуо́з.
virtuous [ˈvəːtjuəs] *adj* (*displaying virtue*) доброде́тельный.
virulence [ˈvɪruləns] *n* (*see adj*) ядови́тость *f*; смерте́льность *f*; не́нависть *f*.
virulent [ˈvɪrulənt] *adj* (*poison*) ядови́тый; (*disease*) смерте́льный; (*actions, feelings*) по́лный* (по́лон) не́нависти.
virus [ˈvaɪərəs] *n* (*MED*) ви́рус.
visa [ˈviːzə] *n* (*for travel*) ви́за.
vis-à-vis [viːzəˈviː] *prep* по отноше́нию к +*dat*.
viscose [ˈvɪskəus] *n* виско́за.
viscount [ˈvaɪkaunt] *n* вико́нт.
viscous [ˈvɪskəs] *adj* (*liquid, substance*) вя́зкий* (вя́зок).
vise [vaɪs] *n* (*US: TECH*) = **vice**.
visibility [vɪzɪˈbɪlɪtɪ] *n* ви́димость *f*.
visible [ˈvɪzəbl] *adj* (*able to be seen or recognized*) ви́димый (ви́дим); (*results, growth*) очеви́дный* (очеви́ден); **~ exports/imports** (*ECON*) ви́димый э́кспорт/и́мпорт.
visibly [ˈvɪzəblɪ] *adv* (*upset, nervous, damaged*) я́вно.
vision [ˈvɪʒən] *n* (*sight*) зре́ние; (*foresight*) предви́дение; (*in dream*) виде́ние.
visionary [ˈvɪʒənrɪ] *n* (*person*) прови́дец.
visit [ˈvɪzɪt] *n* (*to person, place*) посеще́ние; (*stay*) пребыва́ние ♦ *vt* (*person*) идти́ (прийти́* *perf*) *or* ходи́ть* (приходи́ть* *perf*) в го́сти к +*dat*; (*elderly, disabled person*) навеща́ть (навести́ть* *perf*); (*place*) посеща́ть (посети́ть* *perf*); **on a private/official ~** с ча́стным/официа́льным визи́том.

visiting [ˈvɪzɪtɪŋ] *adj* (*speaker*) прие́хавший по приглаше́нию; **~ team** кома́нда госте́й.
visiting card *n* визи́тная ка́рточка*.
visiting hours *npl* (*in hospital etc*) часы́ *mpl* посеще́ния.
visiting professor *n* профе́ссор, прие́хавший по приглаше́нию.
visitor [ˈvɪzɪtə] *n* (*person visiting*) гость(я) *m(f)*; (*in public place, museum etc*) посети́тель (ница) *m(f)*; (*tourist: in town etc*) прие́зжий*(-ая) *m(f) adj*.
visitors' book [ˈvɪzɪtəz-] *n* кни́га посети́телей.
visor [ˈvaɪzə] *n* (*of helmet etc*) щито́к.
VISTA [ˈvɪstə] *n abbr* (= *Volunteers in Service to America*) доброво́льная организа́ция по оказа́нию по́мощи бе́дным.
vista [ˈvɪstə] *n* (*view*) перспекти́ва.
Vistula [ˈvɪstjulə] *n*: **the ~** Ви́сла.
visual [ˈvɪzjuəl] *adj* (*image*) зри́тельный.
visual aid *n* (*SCOL*) нагля́дное посо́бие.
visual arts *npl* изобрази́тельное иску́сство и кино́.
visual display unit *n* (*COMPUT*) устро́йство визуа́льного изображе́ния *or* диспле́й.
visualize [ˈvɪzjuəlaɪz] *vt* (*picture, imagine*) представля́ть (предста́вить* *perf*) мы́сленно; (*foresee*) представля́ть (предста́вить* *perf*) себе́.
visually [ˈvɪzjuəlɪ] *adv*: **~ appealing** привлека́тельный на вид; **~ handicapped** со зри́тельным дефе́ктом.
vital [ˈvaɪtl] *adj* (*essential, important, crucial*) жи́зненно необходи́мый (необходи́м); (*full of life: person*) живо́й, жизнеспосо́бный* (жизнеспосо́бен); (*necessary for life: organ*) жи́зненно ва́жный* (ва́жен); **of ~ importance (to sb/sth)** жи́зненно ва́жно (для кого́-н/чего́-н).
vitality [vaɪˈtælɪtɪ] *n* (*liveliness*) жи́вость *f*.
vitally [ˈvaɪtəlɪ] *adv*: **~ important** жи́зненно ва́жный* (ва́жен).
vital statistics *npl* (*of woman*) габари́ты *mpl*; (*of population*) демографи́ческая стати́стика *fsg*.
vitamin [ˈvɪtəmɪn] *n* витами́н.
vitiate [ˈvɪʃieɪt] *vt* (*spoil*) по́ртить (испо́ртить* *perf*); **to ~ sb's efforts** своди́ть* (свести́* *perf*) на нет чьи-н уси́лия.
vitreous [ˈvɪtrɪəs] *adj* стеклови́дный.
vitriolic [vɪtrɪˈɔlɪk] *adj* (*fig: language*) ядови́тый (ядови́т); (: *behaviour*) зло́бный* (зло́бен).
viva (voce) [ˈvaɪvə(ˈvəutʃɪ)] *n* (*SCOL*) у́стный экза́мен.
vivacious [vɪˈveɪʃəs] *adj* (*person*) живо́й.
vivacity [vɪˈvæsɪtɪ] *n* жи́вость *f*.
vivid [ˈvɪvɪd] *adj* (*description, colour, light*) я́ркий*; (*memory*) отчётливый; (*imagination*)

---

* marks translations which have irregular inflections. The Russian-English side of the dictionary gives inflectional information.

живой.
vividly ['vɪvɪdlɪ] *adv* (*describe*) в живых
деталях; (*remember*) отчётливо.
vivisection [vɪvɪ'sɛkʃən] *n* вивисекция.
vixen ['vɪksn] *n* самка* лисицы; (*pej: woman*)
мегера.
viz [vɪz] *abbr* (*namely*: = *videlicet*) а именно.
Vladivostok [vlædɪ'vɒstɒk] *n* Владивосток.
VLF *abbr* (*RADIO*: = *very low frequency*) ОНЧ=
очень низкая частота.
V-neck ['viːnɛk] *n* (*also*: ~ **jumper** *or* **pullover**)
джемпер *or* пуловер с вырезом.
VOA *n abbr* (= *Voice of America*) "Голос
Америки".
vocabulary [vəu'kæbjulərɪ] *n* (*words known*)
словарный запас.
vocal ['vəukl] *adj* (*of the voice: in singing*)
вокальный; (*articulate*) звучный* (звучен); **to
be ~ for/against** поднять (*perf*) голос в
пользу +*gen*/против +*gen*.
vocal cords *npl* голосовые связки *fpl*.
vocalist ['vəukəlɪst] *n* вокалист(ка*).
vocals ['vəuklz] *npl* вокальная партия *fsg*.
vocation [vəu'keɪʃən] *n* призвание.
vocational [vəu'keɪʃənl] *adj* (*training, guidance
etc*) профессиональный.
vociferous [və'sɪfərəs] *adj* (*protesters,
demands*) громогласный.
vodka ['vɒdkə] *n* водка.
vogue [vəug] *n* мода; **in ~** в моде.
voice [vɔɪs] *n* голос ♦ *vt* (*opinion*) высказывать
(высказать* *perf*); **in a loud/soft** ~ громким/
тихим голосом; **to give ~ to sth** выражать
(выразить* *perf*) что-н.
voice mail *n* голосовая почта.
voice-over ['vɔɪsəuvə'] *n* голос за кадром.
void [vɔɪd] *n* (*emptiness*) пустота; (*hole*)
пробел ♦ *adj* (*invalid*) недействительный*
(недействителен); ~ **of** (*empty*) лишённый
(лишён) +*gen*.
voile [vɔɪl] *n* (*fabric*) вуаль *f*.
vol. *abbr* (= **volume**) т. = *том*.
volatile ['vɒlətaɪl] *adj* (*situation, person*)
изменчивый (изменчив); (*liquid*) летучий*.
volcanic [vɒl'kænɪk] *adj* (*rock, eruption*)
вулканический.
volcano [vɒl'keɪnəu] (*pl ~es*) *n* вулкан.
Volga ['vɒlgə] *n*: **the ~** Волга.
Volgograd ['vɒlgəgræd] *n* Волгоград.
volition [və'lɪʃən] *n*: **of one's own ~** по своей
воле.
volley ['vɒlɪ] *n* (*of gunfire*) залп; (*of stones etc*)
град; (*of questions etc*) поток; (*TENNIS etc*)
удар с лёта.
volleyball ['vɒlɪbɔːl] *n* (*SPORT*) волейбол.
volt [vəult] *n* (*ELEC*) вольт.
voltage ['vəultɪdʒ] *n* (*ELEC*) напряжение; **high/
low** ~ высокое/низкое напряжение.
volte-face ['vɒlt'fɑːs] *n inv* резкая перемена.
voluble ['vɒljubl] *adj* (*person, speech*)
многословный.

volume ['vɒljuːm] *n* (*space*) объём; (*amount*)
количество; (*book*) том; (*sound level*)
громкость *f*; ~ **one/two** (*book*) том первый/
второй; **his expression spoke ~s** выражение
его лица говорило красноречивее всяких
слов.
volume control *n* (*RADIO, TV*) громкость *f*.
volume discount *n* (*COMM*) скидка за покупку
крупной партии товара.
voluminous [və'luːmɪnəs] *adj* (*clothes*)
просторный; (*correspondence, notes*)
пространный.
voluntarily ['vɒləntrɪlɪ] *adv* (*willingly*) добро-
вольно.
voluntary ['vɒləntərɪ] *adj* (*willing: exile*)
добровольный*; (*unpaid: work, worker*)
общественный.
voluntary liquidation *n* (*COMM*)
добровольная ликвидация.
voluntary redundancy *n* (*BRIT*) увольнение по
собственному желанию.
volunteer [vɒlən'tɪə'] *n* (*unpaid helper*)
волонтёр; (*to army etc*) доброволец,
волонтёр ♦ *vt* (*information*) предлагать
(предложить* *perf*) ♦ *vi* (*for army etc*) идти*
(пойти* *perf*) добровольцем; **to ~ to do**
вызываться (вызваться* *perf*) +*infin*.
voluptuous [və'lʌptjuəs] *adj* (*movement, body,
feeling*) сладострастный*.
vomit ['vɒmɪt] *n* рвота ♦ *vi*: **he ~ed** его
вырвало; **she began to ~** её начало рвать.
voracious [və'reɪʃəs] *adj* жадный* (жаден); **he
is a ~ reader** он с жадностью читает.
vote [vəut] *n* (*indication of choice, opinion*)
голосование; (*votes cast*) голос; (*right to
vote*) право голоса ♦ *vi* (*in election etc*)
голосовать (проголосовать* *perf*) ♦ *vt*
(*elect*): **he was ~d chairman** он был избран
председателем; (*propose*): **to ~ that**
предлагать (предложить* *perf*), чтобы; **to put
sth to the ~, take a ~ on sth** ставить*
(поставить* *perf*) что-н на голосование; ~ **of
censure** выражение порицания; ~ **of thanks**
благодарственная речь *f*; **to pass a ~ of
confidence/no confidence** выражать
(выразить* *perf*) вотум доверия/недоверия;
to ~ for *or* **against** голосовать*
(проголосовать* *perf*) за +*acc*/против +*gen*; **to
~ Labour** голосовать* (проголосовать* *perf*)
за Лейбористскую партию.
voter ['vəutə'] *n* избиратель *m*.
voting ['vəutɪŋ] *n* голосование.
voting paper *n* (*BRIT*) избирательный
бюллетень *m*.
voting right *n* право голоса.
vouch [vautʃ] *vt fus*: **to ~ for** (*person, quality etc*)
ручаться (поручиться* *perf*) за +*acc*.
voucher ['vautʃə'] *n* (*for meal: also: luncheon ~*)
талон на обед; (*with petrol, cigarettes etc*)
ваучер; (*receipt*) расписка.
vow [vau] *n* клятва ♦ *vt*: **to ~ to do/that**

клясться* (поклясться* *perf*) +*infin*/, что; **to take** *or* **make a ~ to do** давать* (дать* *perf*) обет +*infin*.

vowel ['vauəl] *n* (*LING*) гласный *m adj*.

voyage ['vɔɪdʒ] *n* (*by ship*) плавание; (*by spacecraft*) полёт.

voyeur [vwɑː'jəː'] *n человек, получающий сексуальное удовольствие от тайного созерцания людей во время полового акта.*

voyeurism [vwɑː'jəːrɪzəm] *n* процесс созерцания других людей во время полового акта.

VP *n abbr* = **vice president**.

vs *abbr* = **versus**.

V-sign ['viːsam] *n* (*BRIT: as insult*) грубый жест; (*in victory*) знак победы.

VSO *n abbr* (*BRIT:* = *Voluntary Service Overseas*) *благотворительное общество,оказывающее помощь нуждающимся за рубежом.*

VT *abbr* (*US: POST*) = *Vermont*.

vulgar ['vʌlgə'] *adj* (*remarks, gestures, graffiti*) вульгарный; (*decor, ostentation*) пошлый*.

vulgarity [vʌl'gærɪtɪ] *n* (*rudeness*) вульгарность *f*; (*ostentation*) пошлость *f*.

vulnerability [vʌlnərə'bɪlɪtɪ] *n* (*see adj*) уязвимость *f*; ранимость *f*.

vulnerable ['vʌlnərəbl] *adj* (*position*) уязвимый*; (*person*) ранимый*; **he is ~ to** он подвержен +*dat*.

vulture ['vʌltʃə'] *n* гриф; (*fig: pej*) стервятник.

vulva ['vʌlvə] *n* вульва.

---

* marks translations which have irregular inflections. The Russian-English side of the dictionary gives inflectional information.

~ W, w ~

W, w ['dʌblju:] n (letter) 23-ая бу́ква
англи́йского алфави́та.

W abbr (= west) З= за́пад; (ELEC: = watt) Вт=
ватт.

WA abbr (US: POST) = Washington.

wad [wɔd] n (of cotton wool) комо́к*; (of
banknotes, paper) па́чка*.

wadding ['wɔdɪŋ] n упако́вочный материа́л.

waddle ['wɔdl] vi ходи́ть*/идти́* (impf)
вперева́лку.

wade [weɪd] vi: to ~ through (water)
пробира́ться (пробра́ться* perf) че́рез +acc;
(book) одолева́ть (одоле́ть* perf).

wafer ['weɪfə'] n (biscuit) ва́фля*.

wafer-thin ['weɪfə'θɪn] adj тонча́йший.

waffle ['wɔfl] n (CULIN) ва́фля*; (empty talk)
трёп ♦ vi (in speech, writing) трепа́ться (impf).

waffle iron n ва́фельница.

waft [wɔft] vt доноси́ть* (донести́* perf) ♦ vi
доноси́ться (донести́сь* perf).

wag [wæg] vt (head) кача́ть (impf) +instr ♦ vi
(tail) виля́ть (impf); the dog ~ged its tail
соба́ка виля́ла хвосто́м; to ~ one's finger at
sb грози́ть* (погрози́ть* perf) кому́-н
па́льцем.

wage [weɪdʒ] n (also: ~s) зарпла́та=
за́работная пла́та ♦ vt: to ~ war вести́* (impf)
войну́; a day's ~s дневно́й зарабо́ток*.

wage claim n тре́бование увеличе́ния
за́работной пла́ты.

wage differential n дифференциа́льные
ста́вки fpl за́работной пла́ты.

wage earner [-ə:nə'] n лицо́*, рабо́тающее по
на́йму; (in the family) корми́лец*(-лица).

wage freeze n заморо́живание за́работной
пла́ты.

wage packet n конве́рт с зарпла́той.

wager ['weɪdʒə'] n пари́* nt ind ♦ vt ста́вить*
(поста́вить* perf); (reputation) ста́вить*
(поста́вить* perf) на ка́рту.

waggle ['wægl] vt (ears, eyebrows etc)
шевели́ть (пошевели́ть perf) +instr ♦ vi (head)
пока́чиваться (impf).

wag(g)on ['wægən] n (horse-drawn) пово́зка*;
(BRIT: RAIL) това́рный ваго́н.

wail [weɪl] n вопль m; (of siren) вой ♦ vi
(person) вопи́ть* (impf); (siren) выть* (impf).

waist [weɪst] n та́лия.

waistcoat ['weɪskəut] n (BRIT) жиле́т.

waistline ['weɪstlaɪn] n ли́ния та́лии.

wait [weɪt] vi ждать* (подожда́ть* perf) ♦ n: we
had a long ~ for the bus мы до́лго жда́ли
авто́буса; to keep sb ~ing заставля́ть
(заста́вить* perf) кого́-н ждать; I can't ~ to go
home/meet my new boss (fig) мне не
те́рпится пойти́ домо́й/встре́титься с мои́м
но́вым нача́льником; to ~ for sb/sth ждать*
(подожда́ть* perf) кого́-н/чего́-н; ~ a minute!
подожди́те мину́тку!; "repairs while you ~"
„ремо́нт в прису́тствии зака́зчика"; to lie in
~ for поджида́ть (impf) +gen.

▶ **wait behind** vi заде́рживаться
(задержа́ться* perf)

▶ **wait on** vt fus (serve) обслу́живать
(обслужи́ть* perf)

▶ **wait up** vi: don't ~ up for me не жди́те меня́,
ложи́тесь спать.

waiter ['weɪtə'] n официа́нт.

waiting ['weɪtɪŋ] n: "no ~" (BRIT: AUT)
„остано́вка запрещена́".

waiting list n спи́сок* очереднико́в.

waiting room n (in surgery) приёмная f adj; (in
station) зал ожида́ния.

waitress ['weɪtrɪs] n официа́нтка*.

waive [weɪv] vt (rule) отменя́ть (отмени́ть*
perf).

waiver ['weɪvə'] n отка́з.

wake [weɪk] (pt woke or waked, pp woken or
waked) vt (also: ~ up) буди́ть* (разбуди́ть*
perf) ♦ vi (also: ~ up) просыпа́ться
(просну́ться* perf) ♦ n бде́ние у гро́ба; (NAUT)
кильва́тер; to ~ up to danger/threat
осозна́ть* (perf) опа́сность/угро́зу; in the ~ of
(fig) всле́дствие +gen; he followed in his
father's ~ (fig) он пошёл по стопа́м отца́.

waken ['weɪkn] vti = wake.

Wales [weɪlz] n Уэ́льс; the Prince of ~ принц
Уэ́льский.

walk [wɔːk] n (hike) похо́д; (shorter)
прогу́лка*; (gait) похо́дка; (path) доро́жка*,
тропа́ ♦ vi (go on foot) ходи́ть*/идти́* (impf)
(пешко́м); (baby) ходи́ть* (impf); (for pleasure,
exercise) гуля́ть (impf) ♦ vt (distance)
проходи́ть* (пройти́* perf); (dog) выгу́ливать
(вы́гулять perf); 10 minutes' ~ from here в
10-ти мину́тах ходьбы́ отсю́да; to go for a ~
ходи́ть*/идти́* (impf) гуля́ть or на прогу́лку;
at a quick ~ бы́стрым ша́гом; to ~ in one's

sleep ходи́ть* (impf) во сне́; **I'll ~ you home** я провожу́ Вас домо́й; **people from all ~s of life** лю́ди из всех слоёв о́бщества

▶ **walk out** vi (audience) демонстрати́вно покида́ть (поки́нуть perf) зал; (workers) бастова́ть (impf)

▶ **walk out on** vt fus (inf: family etc) броса́ть (бро́сить* perf).

walkabout ['wɔːkəbaut] n (queen, politician etc): **to go (on a) ~** проха́живаться (пройти́сь* perf) ми́мо толпы́.

walker ['wɔːkə'] n (hiker) тури́ст(ка).

walkie-talkie ['wɔːkɪ'tɔːkɪ] n переносна́я ра́ция.

walking ['wɔːkɪŋ] n ходьба́; **to be fond of ~** люби́ть* (impf) ходи́ть (пешко́м); **the university is within ~ distance** до университе́та мо́жно дойти́ пешко́м.

walking boots npl боти́нки mpl для ходьбы́.

walking holiday n похо́д.

walking stick n трость f.

Walkman® ['wɔːkmən] n пле́йер.

walk-on ['wɔːkɔn] adj: **~ part** второстепе́нная роль* f.

walkout ['wɔːkaut] n забасто́вка*.

walkover ['wɔːkəuvə'] n (inf) лёгкая побе́да.

walkway ['wɔːkweɪ] n пешехо́дная доро́жка*.

wall [wɔːl] n стена́*; **to go to the ~** (fig) терпе́ть (потерпе́ть perf) крах

▶ **wall in** vt обноси́ть* (обнести́* perf) стено́й.

wall cupboard n встро́енный шкаф*.

walled [wɔːld] adj (city) окружённый крепостно́й стено́й; (garden) обнесённый стено́й.

wallet ['wɔlɪt] n бума́жник.

wallflower ['wɔːflauə'] n желтофио́ль f; **to be a ~** (fig) быть* (impf) незаме́тным(-ой).

wall hanging n насте́нный ковёр*.

wallop ['wɔləp] vt (BRIT: inf) дуба́сить* (отдуба́сить perf).

wallow ['wɔləu] vi (in mud) валя́ться (impf); (in water) бара́хтаться (impf); (in guilt, sentiment) упива́ться (impf); **to ~ in one's grief** упива́ться (impf) свои́м го́рем.

wallpaper ['wɔːlpeɪpə'] n обо́и pl ◆ vt (room) окле́ивать (окле́ить perf) обо́ями.

wall-to-wall ['wɔːltə'wɔːl] adj: **~ carpeting** ковро́вое покры́тие для всей пло́щади по́ла.

wally ['wɔlɪ] n (inf) дурачо́к*.

walnut ['wɔːlnʌt] n (nut) гре́цкий* оре́х; (tree) оре́ховое де́рево*; (wood) оре́х.

walrus ['wɔːlrəs] (pl ~ or ~es) n морж*.

waltz [wɔːlts] n вальс ◆ vi (dancers) вальси́ровать (impf), танцева́ть (impf) вальс.

wan [wɔn] adj изнурённый* (изнурён); **~ complexion** боле́зненная бле́дность f.

wand [wɔnd] n (also: **magic ~**) волше́бная па́лочка*.

wander ['wɔndə'] vi (person) броди́ть* (impf); (mind, thoughts) блужда́ть (impf); (river) извива́ться (impf) ◆ vt броди́ть* (impf) по +dat.

wanderer ['wɔndərə'] n стра́нник(-ица), скита́лец*(-лица).

wandering ['wɔndrɪŋ] adj (tribe) кочево́й; (minstrel, actor) бродя́чий; (path, river) изви́листый; (glance, mind) блужда́ющий.

wane [weɪn] vi (moon) убыва́ть (убы́ть* perf); (enthusiasm, influence etc) ослабева́ть (ослабе́ть* or осла́бнуть perf).

wangle ['wæŋgl] vt (BRIT: inf) пробива́ть (проби́ть* perf), добива́ться (доби́ться* perf) +gen.

wanker ['wæŋkə'] n (BRIT: inf!) муда́к (!)

want [wɔnt] vt (wish for) хоте́ть* (impf) +gen; (need) нужда́ться (impf) в +prp ◆ n: **for ~ of** за недоста́тком +gen; **~s** npl (needs) ну́жды fpl; **to ~ to do** хоте́ть* (impf) +infin; **I ~ you to apologize** я хочу́, что́бы Вы извини́лись; **you're ~ed on the phone** Вас к телефо́ну; **a ~ of foresight** отсу́тствие предви́дения.

want ads npl (US) объявле́ния под ру́брикой "Куплю́", "Ищу́ рабо́ту" итп.

wanted ['wɔntɪd] adj (criminal etc) разы́скиваемый; "**cook ~**" "тре́буется по́вар".

wanting ['wɔntɪŋ] adj: **he was found ~** он оказа́лся не на высоте́ положе́ния; **he is ~ in common sense** ему́ недостаёт здра́вого смы́сла.

wanton ['wɔntn] adj (gratuitous) беспричи́нный* (беспричи́нен); (promiscuous) распу́тный* (распу́тен).

war [wɔː'] n война́*; **to go to ~** вступа́ть (вступи́ть* perf) в войну́; **to be at ~ with** воева́ть* (impf) с +instr; **to declare ~ (on)** (also fig) объявля́ть (объяви́ть* perf) войну́ (+dat).

warble ['wɔːbl] n (of bird) трель f ◆ vi издава́ть (impf) тре́ли.

war crime n вое́нное преступле́ние.

war cry n боево́й клич.

ward [wɔːd] n (MED) пала́та; (BRIT: POL) о́круг; (LAW) ребёнок, находя́щийся под опе́кой

▶ **ward off** vt (attack, enemy) отража́ть (отрази́ть* perf); (danger, illness) отвраща́ть (отврати́ть* perf).

warden ['wɔːdn] n (of park, game reserve) смотри́тель(ница) m(f); (of prison) нача́льник; (of youth hostel) коменда́нт; (BRIT: of college) ре́ктор; (: also: **traffic ~**) ≈ инспе́ктор* ГАИ.

warder ['wɔːdə'] n (BRIT) надзира́тель(ница) m(f), тюре́мщик(-ица).

wardrobe ['wɔːdrəub] n платяно́й шкаф, гардеро́б; (clothes) гардеро́б; (CINEMA, THEAT) костюме́рная f adj.

---

* marks translations which have irregular inflections. The Russian-English side of the dictionary gives inflectional information.

warehouse ['wɛəhaus] *n* склад.
wares [wɛəz] *npl* товáры *mpl*.
warfare ['wɔ:fɛə'] *n* воéнные *или* боевы́е
дéйствия *ntpl*.
war game *n* воéнная игрá*.
warhead ['wɔ:hɛd] *n* боеголóвка*.
warily ['wɛərɪlɪ] *adv* осторóжно,
насторóженно.
Warks *abbr* (*BRIT*: *POST*) = Warwickshire.
warlike ['wɔ:laɪk] *adj* войнственный*
(войнствен).
warm [wɔ:m] *adj* тёплый*; (*thanks, supporter,
heart*) горя́чий*; (*person*) сердéчный*; **it's ~
today** сегóдня теплó; **I'm ~** мне теплó; **to
keep sth ~** (*hands, feet etc*) держáть (*impf*)
что-н в теплé; (*soup etc*) держáть (*impf*) что-н
тёплым(-ой); **with my ~est thanks** с горя́чей
or сердéчной благодáрностью; **please accept
my ~est congratulations** примúте мой
сердéчные поздравлéния
► **warm up** *vi* (*person, room*) согревáться
(согрéться *perf*); (*water*) нагревáться
(нагрéться *perf*); (*athlete*) разминáться
(размя́ться *perf*) ♦ *vt* (*food*) разогревáть
(разогрéть *perf*), подогревáть (подогрéть
perf); (*engine*) разогревáть (разогрéть *perf*);
the weather ~ed up на у́лице потеплéло.
warm-blooded [wɔ:m'blʌdɪd] *adj* тепло-
крóвный* (теплокрóвен).
war memorial *n* воéнный обелúск.
warm-hearted [wɔ:m'hɑ:tɪd] *adj* сердéчный*
(сердéчен).
warmly ['wɔ:mlɪ] *adv* (*applaud*) горячó; (*dress,
welcome*) теплó.
warmonger ['wɔ:mʌŋgə'] *n* (*pej*) поджигáтель
(ница) *m(f)* войны́.
warmongering ['wɔ:mʌŋgrɪŋ] *n* (*pej*)
разжигáние войны́.
warmth [wɔ:mθ] *n* теплó.
warm-up ['wɔ:mʌp] *n* размúнка*.
warn [wɔ:n] *vt*: **to ~ sb (not) to do/of/that**
предупреждáть (предупредúть *perf*) когó-н
(не) +*infin*/о +*prp*/, что.
warning ['wɔ:nɪŋ] *n* предупреждéние; **without
(any) ~** (*suddenly*) неожúданно; (*without
notifying*) без предупреждéния; **gale ~**
штормовóе предупреждéние.
warning light *n* предупредúтельный
световóй сигнáл.
warning triangle *n* аварúйный треугóльник
(*знак, предупреждáющий о том, что
стоя́щая на дорóге машúна слóмана*).
warp [wɔ:p] *vi* (*wood etc*) корóбиться*
(покорóбиться* *perf*) ♦ *vt* (*fig*) коверкáть
(исковеркáть *perf*) ♦ *n* (*TEXTILES*) оснóва.
warpath ['wɔ:pɑ:θ] *n*: **he is on the ~** (*fig*) он
настрóен войнственно.
warped [wɔ:pt] *adj* (*wood*) покорóбленный
(покорóблен); (*fig*) исковеркáнный
(исковеркáн).
warrant ['wɔrnt] *n* (*document*) гарáнтия; (*LAW*)
óрдер ♦ *vt* (*justify*) опрáвдывать (оправдáть
perf); (*merit*) гарантúровать (*impf/perf*); **search
~** óрдер на óбыск.
warrant officer *n* (*MIL*) ≈ старшинá* *m*; (*NAUT*)
мúчман.
warranty ['wɔrəntɪ] *n* гарáнтия; **under ~** с
гарáнтией; **the car was still under ~** у
машúны ещё не истёк гарантúйный срок.
warren ['wɔrən] *n* (*of rabbits*) мéсто, где
вóдятся крóлики; (*fig*) лабирúнт.
warring ['wɔ:rɪŋ] *adj* воюющий; (*interests etc*)
непримирúмый (непримирúм).
warrior ['wɔrɪə'] *n* вóин.
Warsaw ['wɔ:sɔ:] *n* Варшáва.
warship ['wɔ:ʃɪp] *n* воéнный корáбль* *m*.
wart [wɔ:t] *n* бородáвка*.
wartime ['wɔ:taɪm] *n*: **in ~** в воéнное врéмя.
wary ['wɛərɪ] *adj* (*person*) осторóжный*
(осторóжен), насторóженный*
(насторóжен); **to be ~ of sth**
относúться* (*impf*) к чему́-н насторóженно;
to be ~ about doing остерегáться (*impf*) +*infin*.
was [wɔz] *pt of* **be**.
wash [wɔʃ] *n* мытьё; (*clothes etc*) стúрка;
(*washing programme*) режúм стúрки (*в
стирáльной машúне*); (*of ship*) пéнистый
след ♦ *vt* (*hands, body*) мыть* (помы́ть* *perf*);
(*clothes*) стирáть (постирáть *perf*); (*face*)
умывáть (умы́ть* *perf*); (*sweep away*)
смывáть (смыть* *perf*) ♦ *vi* (*person*) мы́ться*
(помы́ться* *perf*); (*sea etc*): **to ~ over sth**
перекáтываться (*impf*) чéрез что-н; **to have a
~** помы́ться* (*perf*); **to give sth a ~** помы́ть*
(*perf*) что-н; (*clothes*) постирáть (*perf*) что-н;
the sea ~ed the body ashore мóре вы́несло
тéло на бéрег; **he was ~ed overboard** егó
смы́ло волнóй зá борт
► **wash away** *vt* смывáть (смыть* *perf*)
► **wash down** *vt* (*wall, path, car*) мыть*
(вы́мыть* *perf*); (*food*) запивáть (запúть* *perf*)
► **wash off** *vi* отмывáться (отмы́ться* *perf*);
(*out of clothes*) отстúрываться (отстирáться
perf)
► **wash up** *vi* (*BRIT*) мыть* (вы́мыть* *perf*)
посу́ду; (*US*) мы́ться* (помы́ться* *perf*).
washable ['wɔʃəbl] *adj* (*wallpaper etc*)
мóющийся; **acrylic blankets are ~** акрúловые
одея́ла мóжно стирáть.
washbasin ['wɔʃbeɪsn] *n* (умывáльная)
рáковина.
washbowl ['wɔʃbəul] *n* (*US*) (умывáльная)
рáковина.
washcloth ['wɔʃklɔθ] *n* (*US: face cloth*)
салфéтка для лицá (*из махрóвой ткáни*).
washer ['wɔʃə'] *n* (*TECH*) шáйба.
washing ['wɔʃɪŋ] *n* (*dirty*) стúрка; (*clean*)
стúраные вéщи *fpl*.
washing line *n* (*BRIT*) бельевáя верёвка*.
washing machine *n* стирáльная машúна.
washing powder *n* (*BRIT*) стирáльный
порошóк.

Washington ['wɔʃɪŋtən] *n* Вашингто́н.

washing-up [wɔʃɪŋˈʌp] *n* (гря́зная) посу́да; **to do the ~** мыть* (вы́мыть* *perf*) посу́ду.

washing-up liquid *n* (BRIT) жи́дкое сре́дство для мытья́ посу́ды.

wash-out ['wɔʃaut] *n* (*inf*) прова́л.

washroom ['wɔʃrum] *n* (US) убо́рная *f adj*.

wasn't ['wɔznt] = **was not**.

WASP [wɔsp] *n abbr* (US: *inf*: = *White Anglo-Saxon Protestant*) америка́нец англо-саксо́нского происхожде́ния и протеста́нтского вероиспове́дания.

Wasp [wɔsp] *n abbr* = **WASP**.

wasp [wɔsp] *n* оса́*.

waspish ['wɔspɪʃ] *adj* (*person*) раздражи́тельный* (раздражи́телен).

wastage ['weɪstɪdʒ] *n* (*waste*) растра́та; (ECON: *loss*) убы́ток*; **natural ~** есте́ственная у́быль *f*.

waste [weɪst] *n* (*act*) растра́та; (*rubbish*) отхо́ды *mpl*; (*also*: **household ~**) дома́шние отбро́сы *mpl*; (*unwanted: energy, heat*) изли́шек* ♦ *adj* (*material: rejected, damaged*) брако́ванный* (брако́ван); (*unwanted: energy, heat*) изли́шний* (изли́шен); (*left over*) отрабо́танный* (отрабо́тан); (*also*: ~ **land**: *in city*) пусты́рь* *m* ♦ *vt* растра́чивать (растра́тить* *perf*); (*opportunity*) упуска́ть (упусти́ть* *perf*); ~**s** *npl* (*area of land*) пусты́ня *fsg*; **it's a ~ of money/time** э́то пуста́я тра́та де́нег/вре́мени; **to go to ~** пропада́ть (пропа́сть* *perf*); **to lay ~** (*destroy*) уничтожа́ть (уничто́жить *perf*); ~ **paper** испо́льзованная бума́га

▶ **waste away** *vi* (*person*) истоща́ть (истощи́ть *perf*) себя́.

wastebasket ['weɪstbɑ:skɪt] *n* (US) = **wastepaper basket**.

waste disposal unit *n* (BRIT) устро́йство для удале́ния отхо́дов (*в ку́хонной ра́ковине*).

wasteful ['weɪstful] *adj* (*person*) расточи́тельный* (расточи́телен); (*process*) неэконо́мный* (неэконо́мен).

waste ground *n* (BRIT) пусты́рь* *m*.

wasteland ['weɪstlənd] *n* пу́стошь *f*; (*in town*) пусты́рь* *m*; (*fig*) пусты́ня.

wastepaper basket ['weɪstpeɪpə-] *n* корзи́на для (ненужных) бума́г.

waste pipe *n* сливна́я труба́*.

waste products *npl* отхо́ды *pl* произво́дства.

waster ['weɪstə*'] *n* (*inf*) безде́льник(-ица).

watch [wɔtʃ] *n* (*also*: **wristwatch**) (нару́чные) часы́ *pl*; (*act of watching*) наблюде́ние; (MIL, NAUT: *group of guards*) патру́ль* *m*; (NAUT: *spell of duty*) ва́хта ♦ *vt* (*look at*) наблюда́ть (*impf*) за +*instr*; (*match, programme*) смотре́ть* (посмотре́ть* *perf*); (*events, weight, language*) следи́ть* (*impf*) за +*instr*; (*be careful of: person*) остерега́ться (*impf*) +*gen*; (*look after*) смотре́ть (*impf*) за +*instr* ♦ *vi* (*take care*) смотре́ть (*impf*); (*keep guard*) дежу́рить (*impf*); **to keep a close ~ on sb/sth** внима́тельно следи́ть* (*impf*) за кем-н/чем-н; ~ **what you're doing** смотри́, что ты де́лаешь; ~ **how you drive** внима́тельно веди́те маши́ну

▶ **watch out** *vi* остерега́ться (остере́чься* *perf*).

watchband ['wɔtʃbænd] *n* (US) ремешо́к* для часо́в.

watchdog ['wɔtʃdɔg] *n* сторожева́я соба́ка; (*fig*) наблюда́тель *m*.

watchful ['wɔtʃful] *adj* бди́тельный* (бди́телен).

watchmaker ['wɔtʃmeɪkə*'] *n* часовщи́к*.

watchman ['wɔtʃmən] *irreg n see* **night watchman**.

watchstrap ['wɔtʃstræp] *n* ремешо́к* для часо́в.

watchword ['wɔtʃwə:d] *n* ло́зунг.

water ['wɔ:tə*'] *n* вода́* ♦ *vt* (*plant, garden*) полива́ть (поли́ть* *perf*) ♦ *vi* (*eyes*) слези́ться (*impf*); **a glass of ~** стака́н воды́; **in British ~s** в брита́нских во́дах; **to pass ~** (*urinate*) мочи́ться* (помочи́ться* *perf*); **my mouth is ~ing** у меня́ теку́т слю́нки

▶ **water down** *vt* разбавля́ть (разба́вить* *perf*) (водо́й); (*fig*) смягча́ть (смягчи́ть* *perf*).

water biscuit *n* ≈ гале́та.

water cannon *n* брандспо́йт.

water closet *n* (BRIT) туале́т.

watercolour ['wɔ:təklə*'] (US **watercolor**) *n* (*picture*) акваре́ль *f*; ~**s** *npl* (*paints*) акваре́льные кра́ски* *fpl*.

water-cooled ['wɔ:təku:ld] *adj* (*engine*) с водяны́м охлажде́нием.

watercress ['wɔ:təkrɛs] *n* кресс водяно́й.

waterfall ['wɔ:təfɔ:l] *n* водопа́д.

waterfront ['wɔ:təfrʌnt] *n* (*seafront: street*) на́бережная *f adj*; (: *piece of land*) берегова́я ли́ния; (*at docks*) райо́н по́рта.

water heater *n* кипяти́льник.

water hole *n* исто́чник (*для водопо́я в пусты́не*).

water ice *n* фрукто́вое моро́женое *nt adj*.

watering can ['wɔ:tərɪŋ-] *n* ле́йка*.

water level *n* у́ровень* *m* воды́.

water lily *n* кувши́нка*.

waterline ['wɔ:təlaɪn] *n* (NAUT) ватерли́ния.

waterlogged ['wɔ:təlɔgd] *adj* (*ground*) заболо́ченный* (заболо́чен), зато́пленный (зато́плен).

water main *n* водопрово́дная магистра́ль *m*.

watermark ['wɔ:təma:k] *n* (*on paper*) водяно́й знак; (*level of water*) отме́тка у́ровня воды́.

watermelon ['wɔ:təmɛlən] *n* арбу́з.

waterproof ['wɔ:təpru:f] *adj* непромока́емый

(непромока́ем).

water-repellent ['wɔːtəri'pɛlnt] *adj* (*cloth etc*)
водооттáлкивающий*.

watershed ['wɔːtəʃɛd] *n* (*also fig*) водоразде́л.

water-skiing ['wɔːtəskiːɪŋ] *n* воднолы́жный
спорт.

water softener *n* сре́дство для смягче́ния
воды́.

water tank *n* резервуáр для воды́; (*smaller*)
бак для воды́.

watertight ['wɔːtətaɪt] *adj*
водонепроница́емый (водонепроница́ем);
(*fig: argument*) неопровержи́мый
(неопровержи́м); (: *excuse*) ве́ский; (: *case,
agreement*) я́сный* (я́сен); (: *story*)
правдоподо́бный* (правдоподо́бен).

water vapour *n* (водяно́й) пар*.

waterway ['wɔːtəweɪ] *n* (*canal, river*) во́дный
путь* *m*; (*at sea*) ватерве́йс.

waterworks ['wɔːtəwɔːks] *n* (*building*)
гидротехни́ческое сооруже́ние; (*inf: ANAT*)
по́чки *fpl*.

watery ['wɔːtərɪ] *adj* (*coffee, soup etc*)
водяни́стый (водяни́ст); (*eyes*) слезя́щийся.

watt [wɔt] *n* ватт.

wattage ['wɔtɪdʒ] *n* мо́щность *f* в вáттах.

wattle ['wɔtl] *n* (*CONSTR*) плете́нь* *m*.

wattle and daub *n* пру́тья и гли́на (*материáл
для постро́йки мáзанки*).

wave [weɪv] *n* волнá*; (*of hand*) взмах; (*in hair*)
зави́вка ♦ *vi* (*signal*) махáть* (*impf*); (*branches*)
качáться (*impf*); (*grass*) волновáться (*impf*);
(*flag*) развевáться (*impf*) ♦ *vt* махáть* (*impf*)
+*instr*; (*stick, gun, sword*) размáхивать (*impf*)
+*instr*; (*hair*) завивáть (зави́ть* *perf*); **short/
medium/long** ~ коро́ткие/сре́дние/дли́нные
во́лны *fpl*; **the new** ~ (*CINEMA, MUS*) но́вая
волнá; **he** ~**d us over to his table** он знако́м
подозвáл нас к своему́ столу́; **to** ~ **goodbye
to sb** махáть* (помахáть* *perf*) кому́-н на
прощáние

▸ **wave aside** *vt* (*person*) отстраня́ть
(отстрани́ть *perf*); (*fig*) отмáхиваться
(отмахну́ться *perf*) от +*gen*

▸ **wave away** *vt* = **wave aside**.

waveband ['weɪvbænd] *n* диапазо́н волн.

wavelength ['weɪvlɛŋθ] *n* (*RADIO*) длинá
волны́; **they are on the same** ~ (*fig*) они́
одинáково смо́трят на ве́щи.

waver ['weɪvə'] *vi* (*voice*) дро́гнуть (*perf*);
(*person, faith*) колебáться* (поколебáться*
perf).

wavy ['weɪvɪ] *adj* волни́стый (волни́ст).

wax [wæks] *n* (*polish*) воск; (*for skis*) мазь *f*;
(*for sealing*) сургу́ч*; (*in ear*) се́ра ♦ *vt* (*floor*)
вощи́ть (навощи́ть *perf*), натирáть
(натере́ть* *perf*) во́ском; (*car*) натирáть
(натере́ть* *perf*) во́ском; (*skis*) мáзать
(намáзать* *perf*) мáзью ♦ *vi* (*moon*)
прибывáть (*impf*).

waxed [wækst] *adj* вощёный.

waxen [wæksn] *adj* (*face*) восково́й; ~
complexion восково́й цвет лицá.

waxworks ['wækswəːks] *npl* (*models*)
восковы́е фигу́ры *fpl* ♦ *n* (*place*) галере́я
восковы́х фигу́р.

way [weɪ] *n* (*route*) путь* *m*, доро́га; (*path,
access*) путь*; (*manner, method*) спо́соб; (*usu
pl: habit*) привы́чка; **which** ~**? – this** ~ кудá? –
сюдá; **is it a long** ~ **from here?** э́то далеко́
отсю́да?; **which** ~ **do we go now?** кудá нам
тепе́рь идти́?; **on the** ~ (*en route*) по пути́ *or*
доро́ге; **to be on one's** ~ быть* (*impf*) в пути́;
I'd better be on my ~ мне уже́ порá идти́; **to
fight one's** ~ **through a crowd** продирáться
(продрáться* *perf*) сквозь толпу́; **to lie one's
~ out of the situation** выходи́ть* (вы́йти* *perf*)
из положе́ния за счёт лжи; **to keep out of sb's
~** держáться* (*impf*) от кого́-н подáльше; **it's
a very long ~ away** э́то о́чень далеко́; **the
village is rather out of the** ~ дере́вня
нахо́дится дово́льно далеко́ в стороне́; **to
go out of one's** ~ **to do** старáться
(постарáться *perf*) изо всех сил +*infin*; **to be in
sb's** ~ (*also fig*) стоя́ть (*impf*) на чьей-н
доро́ге; **to be in the** ~ мешáть (помешáть
perf); **to lose one's** ~ заблуди́ться* (*perf*); **the
plan is under** ~ план осуществля́ется; **to
make** ~ (**for sb/sth**) уступáть (уступи́ть* *perf*)
ме́сто (кому́-н/чему́-н); **to get one's own** ~
де́лать (сде́лать *perf*) по-сво́ему; **to put sth
the right** ~ **up** (*BRIT*) стáвить* (постáвить*
perf) что-н нáдо *or* прáвильно; **to be the
wrong** ~ **round** быть* (*impf*) задо́м наперёд;
he's in a bad ~ его́ делá пло́хи; **that's a funny
~ to show your affection** э́то стрáнная
манéра выражáть свою́ привя́занность; **in a
~** в изве́стном смы́сле; **in some** ~**s** в
не́которых отноше́ниях; **no** ~**!** (*inf*) ни в
ко́ем слу́чае!; **by the** ~ ... ме́жду про́чим ...;
"way in" (*BRIT*) „вход"; **"way out"** (*BRIT*)
„вы́ход"; **the** ~ **back** обрáтный путь*,
обрáтная доро́га; **this** ~ **and that** тудá-сюдá;
"give ~**"** (*BRIT: AUT*) „уступи́те доро́гу".

waybill ['weɪbɪl] *n* накладнáя *f adj*.

waylay ['weɪleɪ] (*irreg: like* lay) *vt* подстерегáть
(подстере́чь* *perf*); **I got waylaid** (*fig*) меня́
перехватáли по пути́.

wayside ['weɪsaɪd] *adj* придоро́жный ♦ *n*
обо́чина; **to fall by the** ~ (*fig*) выбывáть
(вы́быть* *perf*) из стро́я.

way station *n* (*US: RAIL*) полустáнок*; (: *fig*)
промежу́точный э́тап.

wayward ['weɪwəd] *adj* своенрáвный*
(своенрáвен).

WC *n abbr* (*BRIT*) = **water closet**.

WCC *n abbr* = **World Council of Churches**.

we [wiː] *pron* мы.

weak [wiːk] *adj* слáбый* (слаб); (*morally*)
слабохарáктерный* (слабохарáктерен); **to
grow** ~ ослабевáть *or* слабе́ть (ослабе́ть
perf).

weaken ['wi:kn] *vi* ослабева́ть *or* слабе́ть
(ослабе́ть *perf*); (*resolve, person*) смягча́ться
(смягчи́ться *perf*) ♦ *vt* (*person, government*)
ослабля́ть (осла́бить* *perf*).
weak-kneed ['wi:k'ni:d] *adj* (*fig*) мало-
ду́шный* (малоду́шен).
weakling ['wi:klıŋ] *n* слаба́к*.
weakly ['wi:klı] *adv* сла́бо.
weakness ['wi:knıs] *n* сла́бость *f*; **to have a ~
for** име́ть (*impf*) сла́бость к +*dat*.
wealth [wɛlθ] *n* (*money, resources*) бога́тство;
(*of details, knowledge etc*) оби́лие.
wealth tax *n* иму́щественный нало́г.
wealthy ['wɛlθı] *adj* состоя́тельный*
(состоя́телен).
wean [wi:n] *vt* (*baby*) отнима́ть (отня́ть* *perf*)
от груди́.
weapon ['wɛpən] *n* ору́жие*.
wear [wɛəˈ] (*pt* **wore**, *pp* **worn**) *n* (*use*) изно́с;
(*damage*) изно́шенность *f*; (*clothing*) оде́жда
♦ *vi* (*last*) носи́ться* (*impf*); (*rub through*)
изна́шиваться (износи́ться* *perf*) ♦ *vt* (*put on*)
надева́ть (наде́ть* *perf*); (*beard*) носи́ть*
(*impf*); (*damage*) изна́шивать (износи́ть* *perf*);
(*clothes*): **he was ~ing his new shirt** на нём
была́ его́ но́вая руба́шка; **evening ~** (*for
ladies*) вече́рнее пла́тье*; (*for men*) вече́рний*
костю́м; **to ~ a hole in sth** протира́ть
(протере́ть* *perf*) дыру́ в чём-н
▶ **wear away** *vt* стира́ть (стере́ть* *perf*) ♦ *vi*
стира́ться (стере́ться* *perf*)
▶ **wear down** *vt* (*heels*) сна́шивать (сноси́ть*
perf); (*resistance, strength*) сломи́ть (*perf*)
▶ **wear off** *vi* (*pain etc*) постепе́нно проходи́ть*
(пройти́* *perf*)
▶ **wear on** *vi* тяну́ться* (*impf*)
▶ **wear out** *vt* (*shoes, clothing*) изна́шивать
(износи́ться* *perf*); (*person, strength*)
изма́тывать (измота́ть* *perf*).
wearable ['wɛərəbl] *adj* приго́дный*
(приго́ден) для но́ски.
wear and tear [-tɛəˈ] *n* изно́с.
wearer ['wɛərəˈ] *n* владе́лец*(-лица).
wearily ['wıərılı] *adv* уста́ло.
weariness ['wıərınıs] *n* утомле́ние.
wearisome ['wıərısəm] *adj* (*tiring*)
утоми́тельный* (утоми́телен); (*boring*)
надое́дливый (надое́длив).
weary ['wıərı] *adj* (*tired*) утомлённый
(утомлён); (*dispirited*) уста́лый ♦ *vi*: **to ~ of**
утомля́ться (утоми́ться* *perf*) от +*gen*.
weasel ['wi:zl] *n* (*ZOOL*) ла́ска*.
weather ['wɛðəˈ] *n* пого́да ♦ *vt* (*storm, crisis*)
переноси́ть* (перенести́* *perf*), выде́рживать
(вы́держать *perf*) (*of wood*) подверга́ться
(подве́ргнуться* *perf*) атмосфе́рным
влия́ниям; **what's the ~ like today?** кака́я
сего́дня пого́да?; **I am under the ~** мне

нездоро́вится.
weather-beaten ['wɛðəbi:tn] *adj* (*face, skin*)
обве́тренный* (обве́трен); (*building, stone*)
повреждённый непого́дой.
weathercock ['wɛðəkɔk] *n* флю́гер*.
weather forecast *n* прогно́з пого́ды.
weatherman ['wɛðəmæn] *irreg n* (*inf*)
сино́птик.
weatherproof ['wɛðəpru:f] *adj* (*garment*)
защища́ющий от непого́ды; (*building*)
погодоусто́йчивый (погодоусто́йчив),
утеплённый* (утеплён).
weather report *n* сообще́ние о пого́де.
weather vane [-veın] *n* = **weathercock**.
weave [wi:v] (*pt* **wove**, *pp* **woven**) *vt* (*cloth*)
ткать* (сотка́ть* *perf*); (*basket*) плести́*
(сплести́* *perf*) ♦ *vi* (*pt, pp* **weaved**; *fig*)
лави́ровать (*impf*).
weaver ['wi:vəˈ] *n* ткач*(и́ха).
weaving ['wi:vıŋ] *n* (*craft*) тка́чество; (*of
baskets*) плете́ние.
web [wɛb] *n* (*of spider*) паути́на; (*on duck's
foot*) перепо́нка*; (*also fig*) сеть* *f*.
webbed ['wɛbd] *adj* перепо́нчатый.
webbing ['wɛbıŋ] *n* (*on chair*) тка́ный реме́нь.
website ['wɛbsaıt] *n* веб-сайт, сайт.
wed [wɛd] (*pt,pp* **wedded**) *vt* (*marry*) венча́ться
(обвенча́ться *perf*) с +*instr* ♦ *vi* венча́ться
(обвенча́ться *perf*) ♦ *n*: **the newly-~s**
новобра́чные *pl adj*.
Wed. *abbr* = **Wednesday**.
we'd [wi:d] = **we had, we would**.
wedded ['wɛdıd] *pt, pp* of **wed** ♦ *adj*: **he is ~ to**
(*idea, policy etc*) он пре́дан +*dat*.
wedding [wɛdıŋ] *n* сва́дьба*; (*in church*)
венча́ние; **silver/golden ~** сере́бряная/
золота́я сва́дьба.
wedding day *n* день* *m* сва́дьбы.
wedding dress *n* сва́дебное *or* подвене́чное
пла́тье*.
wedding present *n* сва́дебный пода́рок*.
wedding ring *n* обруча́льное кольцо́*.
wedge [wɛdʒ] *n* клин*; (*of cake*) кусо́к* ♦ *vt*
закрепля́ть (закрепи́ть* *perf*) кли́ном; (*pack
tightly*): **to ~ in** вти́скивать (вти́снуть *perf*) в
+*acc*.
wedge-heeled shoes ['wɛdʒhi:ld-] *npl* ту́фли*
pl на танке́тке.
wedlock ['wɛdlɔk] *n* супру́жество.
Wednesday ['wɛdnzdı] *n* среда́*; *see also*
Tuesday.
wee [wi:] *adj* (*SCOTTISH: little*) кро́шечный*.
weed [wi:d] *n* сорня́к* ♦ *vt* (*garden*) поло́ть*
(вы́полоть *perf*)
▶ **weed out** *vt* устраня́ть (устрани́ть *perf*).
weedkiller ['wi:dkılə'] *n* сре́дство от
сорняко́в.
weedy ['wi:dı] *adj* (*man*) худосо́чный*

---

* marks translations which have irregular inflections. The Russian-English side of the dictionary gives inflectional information.

(худосо́чен).

week [wi:k] *n* неде́ля; **once/twice a ~** раз/два
ра́за в неде́лю; **in two ~s' time** че́рез две
неде́ли; **a ~ today** че́рез неде́лю, a week on
Friday, в сле́дующую пя́тницу.

weekday ['wi:kdeɪ] *n (Monday to Friday)*
бу́дний *or* рабо́чий* день* *m*; **on ~s** в бу́дни.

weekend [wi:k'ɛnd] *n* выходны́е *pl adj* (дни),
суббо́та и воскресе́нье, уик-э́нд; **this/next/
last ~** в э́ти/сле́дующие/про́шлые выходны́е
(дни); **what are you doing at the ~?** что Вы
де́лаете в выходны́е?; **open at ~s** откры́то
по суббо́там и воскресе́ньям *or* по
выходны́м дням.

weekly ['wi:klɪ] *adv* еженеде́льно ♦ *adj*
еженеде́льный ♦ *n* еженеде́льник.

weep [wi:p] *(pt,pp* **wept)** *vi (person)* пла́кать*
(impf); *(wound)* сочи́ться *(impf)*.

weeping willow ['wi:pɪŋ-] *n* плаку́чая и́ва.

weepy ['wi:pɪ] *adj* слезли́вый (слезли́в),
плакси́вый (плакси́в) ♦ *n (inf: film)*
душещипа́тельный фильм.

weft [wɛft] *n* уто́к*.

weigh [weɪ] *vt* взве́шивать (взве́сить* *perf)* ♦ *vi*
ве́сить* *(impf)*; **to ~ anchor** поднима́ть
(подня́ть* *perf)* я́корь
► **weigh down** *vt* отягоща́ть (отяготи́ть* *perf)*;
(fig) тяготи́ть* *(impf)*, отягоща́ть *(impf)*
► **weigh out** *vt* отве́шивать (отве́сить* *perf)*
► **weigh up** *vt* взве́шивать (взве́сить* *perf)*; **to
~ up all the pros and cons** взве́шивать
(взве́сить* *perf)* все "за" и "про́тив".

weighbridge ['weɪbrɪdʒ] *n* мостовы́е весы́ *pl.*

weighing machine ['weɪŋ-] *n* автомат-
и́ческие весы́ *pl.*

weight [weɪt] *n (for scales)* ги́ря; *(heaviness)*
вес* ♦ *vt*: **to be ~ed in favour of**
предоставля́ть (предоста́вить* *perf)*
преиму́щество +*dat*; **sold by ~** продаётся на
вес; **to lose ~** худе́ть (похуде́ть* *perf)*; **to put
on ~** поправля́ться (попра́виться* *perf)*; **W~s
and Measures Office** Пала́та мер и весо́в.

weighting ['weɪtɪŋ] *n (allowance)* надба́вка.

weightlessness ['weɪtlɪsnɪs] *n* невесо́мость *f.*

weightlifter ['weɪtlɪftəʳ] *n* штанги́ст.

weight limit *n* преде́л ве́са.

weight training *n* силова́я гимна́стика.

weighty ['weɪtɪ] *adj (heavy: object)* тяжёлый
(тяжёл); (: *person)* гру́зный* (гру́зен); (:
important) весо́мый (весо́м).

weir [wɪəʳ] *n (in river)* запру́да.

weird [wɪəd] *adj (strange)* стра́нный*
(стра́нен); *(eerie)* таи́нственный*
(таи́нственен).

weirdo ['wɪədəu] *n (inf)* чуда́к.

welcome ['wɛlkəm] *adj* жела́нный* (жела́нен)
♦ *n (hospitality)* приём; *(greeting)*
приве́тствие ♦ *vt (also:* **bid ~)**
приве́тствовать *(impf)*; **to make sb ~**
ока́зывать (оказа́ть* *perf)* кому́-н раду́шный
приём; **you're ~ to try** пожа́луйста,

попро́буйте; **thank you – you're ~!** спаси́бо –
пожа́луйста!

welcoming ['wɛlkəmɪŋ] *adj (person, smile etc)*
раду́шный* (раду́шен); *(room)* прия́тный*
(прия́тен); *(speech)* приве́тственный.

weld [wɛld] *n* сварно́й шов ♦ *vt* сва́ривать
(свари́ть* *perf)*.

welder ['wɛldəʳ] *n* сва́рщик.

welding ['wɛldɪŋ] *n* сва́рка*.

welfare ['wɛlfɛəʳ] *n (well-being)* благополу́чие;
(US: social aid) социа́льное посо́бие.

welfare state *n* госуда́рство всео́бщего
благосостоя́ния.

welfare work *n* социа́льная по́мощь *f.*

well [wɛl] *n (for water)* коло́дец*; *(also:* oil ~)
(нефтяна́я) сква́жина ♦ *adv* хорошо́ ♦ *excl*
(anyway) ну; *(so)* ну вот ♦ *adj*: **he is ~** он
здоро́в; **I don't feel ~** я пло́хо себя́ чу́вствую;
to think ~ of sb быть* *(impf)* хоро́шего
мне́ния о ком-н; **as ~** та́кже; **oh ~ ...** ну что
же ...; **you might as ~ tell me** уж лу́чше ты
скажи́ мне; **he played as ~ as he could** он
сыгра́л как смог; **I woke ~ before dawn** я
просну́лся задо́лго до рассве́та; **I've brought
my anorak as ~ as a jumper** кро́ме пуло́вера я
привёз ещё и анора́к; **~, as I was saying ...** ну,
как я уже́ говори́л ...; **~ done!** молоде́ц!; **get
~ soon!** поправля́йтесь скоре́е; **he is doing ~
at school** в шко́ле он успева́ет; **the business is
doing ~** би́знес процвета́ет
► **well up** *vi (tears)* наверну́ться *(perf)*.

we'll [wi:l] = **we will, we shall.**

well-behaved ['wɛlbɪ'heɪvd] *adj* воспи́танный*
(воспи́тан).

well-being ['wɛl'bi:ɪŋ] *n* благополу́чие.

well-bred ['wɛl'brɛd] *adj (person)*
воспи́танный* (воспи́тан),
благовоспи́танный (благовоспи́тан).

well-built ['wɛl'bɪlt] *adj* хорошо́ сложённый
(сложён), кре́пкий* (кре́пок).

well-chosen ['wɛl'tʃəuzn] *adj (remarks, words)*
хорошо́ подо́бранный (подо́бран).

well-deserved ['wɛldɪ'zə:vd] *adj* заслу́ж-
енный* (заслу́жен).

well-developed ['wɛldɪ'vɛləpt] *adj* с
ра́звитыми фо́рмами.

well-disposed ['wɛl'dɪspəuzd] *adj*: **~ to(wards)**
благожела́тельный* (благожела́телен) к
+*dat.*

well-dressed ['wɛl'drɛst] *adj* хорошо́ оде́тый
(оде́т).

well-earned ['wɛl'ə:nd] *adj* заслу́женный*
(заслу́жен).

well-groomed ['wɛl'gru:md] *adj (person)*
ухо́женный* (ухо́жен).

well-heeled ['wɛl'hi:ld] *adj (inf)* де́нежный*

well-informed ['wɛlɪn'fɔ:md] *adj (about
something)* хорошо́ информи́рованный*
(информи́рован); *(in general)* зна́ющий*.

Wellington ['wɛlɪŋtən] *n* Веллингто́н.

wellingtons ['wɛlɪŋtənz] *npl (also:* **wellington**

boots) резиновые сапоги* *mpl*.
well-kept ['wɛl'kɛpt] *adj* (*house, grounds*)
ухоженный (ухожен); (*secret*) полный.
well-known ['wɛl'nəun] *adj* (*famous*)
известный* (известен).
well-mannered ['wɛl'mænəd] *adj*
воспитанный* (воспитан).
well-meaning ['wɛl'miːnɪŋ] *adj*: **he is very ~** он
действует из наилучших побуждений.
well-nigh ['wɛl'naɪ] *adv*: **~ impossible** почти
невозможно.
well-off ['wɛl'ɔf] *adj* состоятельный*
(состоятелен).
well-read ['wɛl'rɛd] *adj* начитанный*
(начитан).
well-spoken ['wɛl'spəukn] *adj* (*words*)
учтивый (учтив); **she was ~** она говорила
правильным языком.
well-stocked ['wɛl'stɔkt] *adj* (*shop*) хорошо
снабжаемый.
well-timed ['wɛl'taɪmd] *adj* своевременный*
(своевременен).
well-to-do ['wɛltə'duː] *adj* обеспеченный
(обеспечен), состоятельный* (состоятелен).
well-wisher ['wɛlwɪʃəʳ] *n* (*friend, admirer*)
доброжелатель(ница) *m(f)*; **scores of ~s had
gathered** собрались десятки
доброжелателей; **letters from ~s** письма от
доброжелателей.
well-woman clinic ['wɛlwumən-] *n* ≈ женская
консультация.
Welsh [wɛlʃ] *adj* уэльский ♦ *n* (*LING*) уэльский*
or валлийский язык*; **the ~ Assembly**
Ассамблея Уэльса; **the ~** *npl* (*people*)
уэльсцы *mpl*, валлийцы *mpl*.
Welshman ['wɛlʃmən] *irreg n* уэльсец*,
валлиец*.
Welsh rarebit *n* гренок* с сыром.
Welshwoman ['wɛlʃwumən] *n irreg* валлийка*,
жительница Уэльса.
welter ['wɛltəʳ] *n*: **a ~ of** хаос +*gen*.
went [wɛnt] *pt of* **go**.
wept [wɛpt] *pt, pp of* **weep**.
were [wəːʳ] *pt of* **be**.
we're [wɪəʳ] = **we are**.
weren't [wəːnt] = **were not**.
werewolf ['wɪəwulf] (*pl* **werewolves**) *n*
человек-волк.
werewolves ['wɪəwulvz] *npl of* **werewolf**.
west [wɛst] *n* запад ♦ *adj* западный ♦ *adv* на
запад; **the W~** (*POL*) Запад.
westbound ['wɛstbaund] *adj* (*carriageway,
traffic*) западного направления.
West Country *n*: **the ~ ~** (*BRIT*) западная
Англия.
westerly ['wɛstəlɪ] *adj* западный.
western ['wɛstən] *adj* (*also POL*) западный ♦ *n*
(*CINEMA*) вестерн.

westerner ['wɛstənəʳ] *n* западный человек*.
westernized ['wɛstənaɪzd] *adj* ориентир-
ованный (ориентирован) на Запад.
West German *adj* (*formerly*)
западногерманский ♦ *n* житель(ница) *m(f)*
Западной Германии.
West Germany *n* (*formerly*) Западная
Германия.
West Indian *adj* вест-индийский* ♦ *n*
житель(ница) *m(f)* Вест-Индии.
West Indies [-'ɪndɪz] *npl*: **the ~ ~** Вест-Индия.
Westminster ['wɛstmɪnstəʳ] *n* Вестминстер.
westward(s) ['wɛstwəd(z)] *adv* на запад, к
западу.
wet [wɛt] *adj* (*damp, rainy*) влажный*
(влажен), сырой* (сыр); (*soaking*) мокрый*
(мокр) ♦ *n* (*BRIT: POL*) "умеренный(-ая)" *m(f)*
adj ♦ *vt*: **to ~ one's pants** *or* **o.s.** мочить
(намочить *perf*) штаны; **to get ~** промокать
(промокнуть* *perf*); **"~ paint!"** "осторожно,
окрашено!"; **he is a ~ blanket** (*fig: pej*) он –
зануда.
wetness ['wɛtnɪs] *n* влажность *f*, сырость *f*.
wetsuit ['wɛtsuːt] *n* гидрокостюм.
we've [wiːv] = **we have**.
whack [wæk] *vt* давать* (дать* *perf*) затрещину
+*dat*.
whacked [wækt] *adj* (*BRIT: inf*) разбитый
(разбит).
whale [weɪl] *n* кит*.
whaler ['weɪləʳ] *n* (*ship*) китобойное судно.
whaling ['weɪlɪŋ] *n* китобойный промысел.
wharf [wɔːf] (*pl* **wharves**) *n* пристань* *f*.
wharves [wɔːvz] *npl of* **wharf**.

KEYWORD

what [wɔt] *adj* **1** (*interrogative: direct, indirect*)
какой; **what size is the dress?** какого размера
это платье?; **what books do you need?** какие
книги Вам нужны?
2 какой; **what a lovely day!** какой чудесный
день!; **what a mess!** (*room etc*) ну и
беспорядок!; (*fig*) что за неразбериха!; **what
a fool I am!** какой же я дурак!
  ♦ *pron* **1** (*interrogative*) что; **what are you
doing?** что Вы делаете?; **what are you talking
about?** о чём Вы говорите?; **what is it called?**
как это называется?; **what about me?** а (как
же) я?; **what about doing ...?** как насчёт того,
чтобы +*infin* ...?
2 (*relative*) что; **I saw what you did/was on the
table** я видел, что Вы делали/было на
столе; **is that what happened?** так это то, что
случилось?; **tell me what you're thinking
about** скажите мне, о чём Вы думаете; **what
you say is wrong** то, что Вы говорите,
неверно
  ♦ *excl* (*disbelieving*) что; **I've crashed the car –
what!** я разбил машину – что!

---

* marks translations which have irregular inflections. The Russian-English side of the dictionary gives inflectional information.

whatever [wɔt'ɛvəʳ] *adj:* ~ **book** люба́я кни́га ♦ *pron:* **do** ~ **is necessary/you want** де́лайте всё, что необходи́мо/хоти́те; ~ **happens** что бы ни случи́лось; **no reason** ~ *or* **whatsoever** нет никако́й причи́ны; **nothing** ~ совсе́м ничего́.

whatsoever [wɔtsəu'ɛvəʳ] *adj see* **whatever**.

wheat [wi:t] *n* пшени́ца.

wheatgerm ['wi:tdʒə:m] *n* заро́дыш пшени́чного зерна́.

wheatmeal ['wi:tmi:l] *n пшени́чная мука́ гру́бого помо́ла.*

wheedle ['wi:dl] *vt:* **to** ~ **sb into doing** угова́ривать (уговори́ть *perf*) кого́-н ле́стью +*infin*; **to** ~ **sth out of sb** выма́нивать (вы́манить *perf*) что-н у кого́-н.

wheel [wi:l] *n (of vehicle etc)* колесо́•; *(also:* **steering** ~) руль• *m*; *(NAUT)* штурва́л ♦ *vt (pram etc)* ката́ть/кати́ть• *(impf)* ♦ *vi (birds)* кружи́ться *(impf)*; *(also:* ~ **round:** *person)* кру́то повора́чиваться (поверну́ться *perf*).

wheelbarrow ['wi:lbærəu] *n* та́чка•.

wheelbase ['wi:lbeɪs] *n* колёсная ба́за.

wheelchair ['wi:ltʃɛəʳ] *n* инвали́дное кре́сло•.

wheel clamp *n (AUT)* блокира́тор *(для блокиро́вки рулево́го колеса́)*.

wheeler-dealer ['wi:lə'di:ləʳ] *n (pej)* махина́тор.

wheelie-bin ['wi:lɪbɪn] *n му́сорное ведро́ на колёсиках.*

wheeling ['wi:lɪŋ] *n:* ~ **and dealing** *(pej)* махина́ции *fpl.*

wheeze [wi:z] *vi (person)* хрипе́ть• *(impf)* ♦ *n (idea, joke etc)* остроу́мная иде́я, зате́я.

wheezy ['wi:zɪ] *adj* хрипя́щий, сипя́щий.

when [wɛn] *adv, conj* когда́; ~ **you've read the book, tell me what you think** когда́ Вы прочита́ете кни́гу, скажи́те мне что Вы ду́маете; **you said I was wrong** ~ **in fact I was right** Вы сказа́ли, что я был непра́в, когда́ на са́мом де́ле я был прав.

whenever [wɛn'ɛvəʳ] *adv* в любо́е вре́мя ♦ *conj (any time)* когда́ то́лько; *(every time that)* ка́ждый раз, когда́; **I go** ~ **I can** я пойду́, как то́лько смогу́.

where [wɛəʳ] *adv (place)* где; *(direction)* куда́; *(from where)* отку́да ♦ *conj* где; **this is** ~ ... э́то там, где ...; ~ **possible** где возмо́жно; ~ **have you come from?** отку́да Вы прие́хали?

whereabouts [*adv* wɛərə'bauts, *n* 'wɛərəbauts] *adv* где; *(motion)* куда́ ♦ *n:* **nobody knows his** ~ никто́ не зна́ет его́ местонахожде́ния.

whereas [wɛər'æz] *conj* тогда́ *or* в то вре́мя как.

whereby [wɛə'baɪ] *adv (formal)* посре́дством чего́.

whereupon [wɛərə'pɔn] *adv* по́сле *or* всле́дствие чего́.

wherever [wɛər'ɛvəʳ] *conj (no matter where: position):* ~ **he was** где бы он ни́ был; (: *motion):* ~ **he goes** куда́ бы он ни шёл; *(not knowing where):* ~ **that is** где бы то ни́ было

♦ *adv (interrogative):* ~ **have you been?** где же Вы бы́ли?; **let's go away -** ~ **to?** дава́йте уйдём отсю́да – куда́ же?; **sit** ~ **you like** сади́тесь, где хоти́те.

wherewithal ['wɛəwɪðɔ:l] *n:* **the** ~ **(to do)** сре́дства *ntpl* (+*infin*).

whet [wɛt] *vt (appetite)* возбужда́ть (возбуди́ть• *perf*); *(tool)* точи́ть• (наточи́ть• *perf*).

whether ['wɛðəʳ] *conj:* **I doubt** ~ **she loves me** я сомнева́юсь, лю́бит ли она́ меня́; **I don't know** ~ **to accept this proposal or not** я не зна́ю, приня́ть ли э́то предложе́ние и́ли нет; ~ **you go or not** пойдёте Вы и́ли нет.

whey ['weɪ] *n* сы́воротка.

KEYWORD
---

which [wɪtʃ] *adj* **1** *(interrogative: direct, indirect)* како́й *(f* кака́я, *nt* како́е?); **which picture would you like?** каку́ю карти́ну Вы хоти́те?; **which books are yours?** каки́е кни́ги Ва́ши?; **which one?** како́й? *(f* кака́я?, *nt* како́е?); **I've got two pens, which one do you want?** у меня́ есть две ру́чки, каку́ю Вы хоти́те?; **which one of you did it?** кто из вас э́то сде́лал?

2: in which case в тако́м слу́чае; **by which time** к тому́ вре́мени

♦ *pron* **1** *(interrogative)* како́й *(f* кака́я, *nt* како́е, *pl* каки́е); **there are several museums, which shall we visit first?** здесь есть не́сколько музе́ев, в како́й мы пойдём снача́ла?; **which do you want, the apple or the banana?** что Вы хоти́те – я́блоко и́ли бана́н?; **which of you are staying?** кто из вас остаётся?

2 *(relative)* кото́рый *(f* кото́рая, *nt* кото́рое, *pl* кото́рые); **the apple which you ate/which is on the table** я́блоко, кото́рое Вы съе́ли/кото́рое лежи́т на столе́; **the news was bad, which is what I had feared** ве́сти бы́ли плохи́е, как я и боя́лся; **I had lunch, after which I decided to go home** я пообе́дал, по́сле чего́ я реши́л пойти́ домо́й; **I made a speech, after which nobody spoke** я вы́ступил с ре́чью, по́сле кото́рой никто́ не произнёс ни сло́ва.

---

whichever [wɪtʃ'ɛvəʳ] *adj:* **take** ~ **book you prefer** возьми́те любу́ю кни́гу, каку́ю предпочтёте; ~ **book you take** каку́ю бы кни́гу Вы ни взя́ли.

whiff [wɪf] *n* дунове́ние; **to catch a** ~ **of sth** ула́вливать (улови́ть *perf*) почу́ять за́пах чего́-н.

while [waɪl] *n (period of time)* вре́мя• *nt* ♦ *conj* пока́, в то вре́мя как; *(although)* хотя́, несмотря́ на то, что; **for a** ~ ненадо́лго; **in a** ~ ско́ро; **all the** ~ всё вре́мя; **we promise to make it worth your** ~ мы обеща́ем, что Вы не оста́нетесь в про́игрыше

▸ **while away** *vt:* ~ **away the time** корота́ть (скорота́ть *perf*) вре́мя.

whilst [waɪlst] *conj* = **while**.

whim [wɪm] n при́хоть f.
whimper ['wɪmpə'] n хны́канье ♦ vi хны́кать*
(*impf*); (*dog*) скули́ть (*impf*).
whimsical ['wɪmzɪkl] adj причу́дливый
(причу́длив).
whine [waɪn] n вой ♦ vi (*person, animal*)
скули́ть (*impf*); (*engine, siren*) выть* (*impf*).
whip [wɪp] n кнут*, хлыст*; (*POL: person*)
организа́тор парла́ментской фра́кции ♦ vt
(*person, animal*) хлеста́ть* (*impf*); (*cream,
eggs*) взбива́ть (взбить* *perf*); (*move quickly*):
to ~ sth out выхва́тывать (вы́хватить* *perf*)
что-н; **to ~ sth away** вырыва́ть (вы́рвать*
perf) что-н
▶ **whip up** vt (*cream*) взбива́ть (взбить* *perf*);
(*inf: meal*) де́лать (сде́лать* *perf*) на ско́рую
ру́ку; (*support, emotion*) возбужда́ть
(возбуди́ть* *perf*).
whiplash ['wɪplæʃ] n (*also: ~ injury*)
поврежде́ние ше́и, вы́званное ре́зким
движе́нием головы́ вперёд и наза́д,
наприме́р, при автомоби́льной ава́рии.
whipped cream [wɪpt-] n взби́тые сли́вки* pl.
whipping boy ['wɪpɪŋ-] n (*fig*) ≈ козёл
отпуще́ния.
whip-round ['wɪpraund] n (*BRIT*) скла́дчина.
whirl [wə:l] vt враща́ть (*impf*), верте́ть* (*impf*) ♦
vi кружи́ться* (*impf*), враща́ться (*impf*) ♦ n
круже́ние; **my mind is in a ~** у меня́ голова́
идёт кру́гом; **~ of social engagements**
водоворо́т or вихрь све́тской жи́зни.
whirlpool ['wə:lpu:l] n водоворо́т.
whirlwind ['wə:lwɪnd] n вихрь m.
whirr [wə:'] vi (*insects*) стрекота́ть (*impf*);
(*motor etc*) треща́ть (*impf*).
whisk [wɪsk] n (*CULIN*) ве́нчик ♦ vt (*cream, eggs*)
взбива́ть (взбить* *perf*); **to ~ sb away** or **off**
отгоня́ть (отогна́ть* *perf*).
whiskers ['wɪskəz] npl (*of animal*) усы́ mpl; (*of
man*) бакенба́рды fpl.
whisky ['wɪskɪ] (*US, IRELAND* **whiskey**) n ви́ски nt
ind.
whisper ['wɪspə'] n шёпот ♦ vi шепта́ться*
(*impf*) ♦ vt шепта́ть* (*impf*); **to ~ sth to sb**
шепта́ть* (*impf*) что-н кому́-н.
whispering ['wɪspərɪŋ] n перешёптывание.
whist [wɪst] n (*BRIT*) вист.
whistle ['wɪsl] n (*sound*) свист; (*object*)
свисто́к* ♦ vi свисте́ть* (*impf*), сви́стнуть (*perf*)
♦ vt: **to ~ a tune** насви́стывать (*impf*)
мело́дию.
whistle-stop ['wɪslstɔp] adj: **to make a ~ tour of**
(*POL*) объезжа́ть (объе́хать* *perf*) с
агитацио́нными це́лями.
Whit [wɪt] n Тро́ицын день* m.
white [waɪt] adj бе́лый* (бел) ♦ n (*colour*)
бе́лый цвет; (*person*) бе́лый(-ая) m(f) adj; (*of
egg, eye*) бело́к*; **to turn** or **go ~** беле́ть

(побеле́ть *perf*); **the ~s** (*washing*) бе́лое
бельё; **tennis/cricket ~s** те́ннисная/
крике́тная фо́рма.
whitebait ['waɪtbeɪt] n снето́к*.
white coffee n (*BRIT*) ко́фе m ind с молоко́м.
white-collar worker ['waɪtkɔlə-] n
слу́жащий*(-ая) m(f) adj.
white elephant n (*fig*) изли́шняя ро́скошь f.
white goods npl (*appliances*) бытовы́е
электротова́ры mpl; (*linen etc*) белошве́йные
това́ры mpl.
white-hot [waɪt'hɔt] adj раскалённый*
(раскалён) добела́.
white lie n безоби́дная ложь* f.
whiteness ['waɪtnɪs] n белизна́.
white noise n (*RADIO, ELEC etc*) „бе́лый шум"
(поме́хи в радиоэфи́ре).
whiteout ['waɪtaut] n бе́лая мгла.
white paper n (*POL*) "Бе́лая кни́га"
(докуме́нт, излага́ющий поли́тику
прави́тельства по тем и́ли ины́м вопро́сам).
whitewash ['waɪtwɔʃ] n (*paint*) известко́вый
раство́р (*для побе́лки*); (*inf: SPORT*) "сухая́" ♦
vt (*building*) бели́ть* (побели́ть* *perf*); (*fig:
incident, reputation*) обеля́ть (обели́ть* *perf*).
white water n: **~~ rafting** пла́вание на
плота́х по го́рным ре́кам.
whiting ['waɪtɪŋ] n инв хек.
Whit Monday n ≈ Ду́хов день* m.
Whitsun ['wɪtsn] n ≈ Тро́ицын день* m,
Тро́ица.
whittle ['wɪtl] vt: **to ~ away** or **down** (*costs*)
уменьша́ть (уме́ньшить *perf*).
whizz [wɪz] vi: **to ~ past** or **by** проноси́ться*
(пронести́сь* *perf*) ми́мо.
whizz kid n (*inf*) вундерки́нд.
WHO n abbr (= World Health Organization)
ВОЗ= Всеми́рная организа́ция
здравоохране́ния.

KEYWORD

who [hu:] pron **1** (*interrogative*) кто*; **who is it?,
who's there?** кто э́то or там?; **who did you see
there?** кого́ Вы там ви́дели?
2 (*relative*) кото́рый (f кото́рая, nt кото́рое);
the woman who spoke to me же́нщина,
кото́рая говори́ла со мно́й; **those who can
swim** те, кто уме́ют пла́вать.

whodunit [hu:'dʌnɪt] n (*inf*) детекти́в.
whoever [hu:'evə'] pron: **~ finds him ...** тот, кто
найдёт его́ ...; кто бы ни нашёл его́ ...; **ask ~
you like** спроси́те, кого́ хоти́те; **~ told you
that?** кто Вам э́то сказа́л?; **come out, ~ you
are!** вы́ходи, кто бы ты ни был!
whole [həul] adj це́лый (цел) ♦ n (*entire unit*)
це́лое nt adj; (*all*): **the ~ of Europe** вся Евро́па;
the ~ lot (of it) всё (э́то); **the ~ lot (of them)**
все pl (они́); **the ~ of the time** всё вре́мя; **~**

---

* marks translations which have irregular inflections. The Russian-English side of the dictionary gives inflectional information.

villages were destroyed це́лые дере́вни бы́ли разру́шены; **the ~ of the town** весь го́род; **on the ~, as a ~** в це́лом.

wholefood(s) ['həulfu:d(z)] *n(pl)* натура́льные проду́кты *mpl*.

wholefood shop *n* магази́н натура́льных проду́ктов.

wholehearted [həul'hɑ:tɪd] *adj* (*agreement etc*) и́скренний*; (*support*) горя́чий*.

wholeheartedly [həul'hɑ:tɪdlɪ] *adv* (*see adj*) и́скренне; горячо́.

wholemeal ['həulmi:l] *adj* (*BRIT*): **~ flour** мука́ гру́бого помо́ла; **~ bread** хлеб из муки́ гру́бого помо́ла.

whole note *n* (*US*) це́лая но́та.

wholesale ['həulseɪl] *n* опто́вая торго́вля ◆ *adj* (*price*) опто́вый; (*destruction*) ма́ссовый ◆ *adv* (*buy, sell*) о́птом.

wholesaler ['həulseɪlə*] *n* оптови́к*; (*insitution*) опто́вое предприя́тие.

wholesome ['həulsəm] *adj* здоро́вый.

wholewheat ['həulwi:t] *adj* = **wholemeal**.

wholly ['həulɪ] *adv* по́лностью, целико́м.

whom [hu:m] *pron* **1** (*interrogative: +acc, +gen*) кого́; (: *+dat*) кому́; (: *+instr*) кем; (: *+prp*) ком; **whom did you see there?** кого́ Вы там ви́дели?; **to whom did you give the book?** кому́ Вы кни́гу отда́ли?

2 (*relative: +acc*) кото́рого (*f* кото́рую, *pl* кото́рых); (: *+gen*) кото́рого (*f* кото́рой, *pl* кото́рых); (: *+dat*) кото́рому (*f* кото́рой, *pl* кото́рым); (: *+instr*) кото́рым (*f* кото́рой, *pl* кото́рыми); (: *+prp*) кото́ром (*f* кото́рой, *pl* кото́рых); **the man whom I saw/to whom I spoke** челове́к, кото́рого я ви́дел/с кото́рым я говори́л.

whooping cough ['hu:pɪŋ-] *n* коклю́ш.

whoosh [wuʃ] *n* свист ◆ *vi*: **to ~ past** *etc* просвисте́ть* (*perf*) ми́мо *etc*; **the skiers ~ed past, skiers came by with a ~** лы́жники со сви́стом пронесли́сь ми́мо.

whopper ['wɔpə*] *n* (*inf: lie*) чудо́вищная ложь* *f*; (*large thing*) грома́дина.

whopping ['wɔpɪŋ] *adj* (*inf: big*) грома́дный* (грома́ден).

whore [hɔ:*] *n* (*inf: pej*) шлю́ха.

whose [hu:z] *adj* **1** (*possessive: interrogative*) чей*; **whose book is this?, whose is this book?** чья э́то кни́га?

2 (*possessive: relative*) кото́рый; **the woman whose son you rescued** же́нщина, сы́на кото́рой Вы спасли́

◆ *pron* чей (*f* чья, *nt* чьё, *pl* чьи); **whose is this?** э́то чьё?; **I know whose it is** я зна́ю, чьё э́то.

Who's Who ['hu:z'hu:] *n* Кто есть кто (*спра́вочник*).

why [waɪ] *adv, conj* почему́; **why is he always late?** почему́ он всегда́ опа́здывает?; **why not?** почему́?; **why not do it now?** почему́ бы не сде́лать э́то сейча́с?; **I wonder why he said that** интере́сно, почему́ он э́то сказа́л; **that's not why I'm here** я здесь во́все не поэ́тому; **that's why** вот почему́; **there is a reason why I want to see him** у меня́ есть причи́ны для встре́чи с ним

◆ *excl*: **why, it's you!** о, неуже́ли э́то Вы?; **why, it's obvious/that's impossible!** но ведь э́то же очеви́дно/невозмо́жно!

WI *n abbr* (*BRIT*: = *Women's Institute*) ассоциа́ция же́нщин, интересу́ющихся вопро́сами домово́дства ◆ *abbr* = *West Indies*; (*US: POST*) *Wisconsin*.

wick [wɪk] *n* фити́ль* *m*; **he gets on my ~** (*inf*) он де́йствует мне на не́рвы.

wicked ['wɪkɪd] *adj* зло́бный* (зло́бен), злой*; (*mischievous: smile*) лука́вый, плутовско́й; (*terrible: prices, weather*) жу́ткий*.

wicker ['wɪkə*] *adj* плетёный.

wickerwork ['wɪkəwə:k] *adj* плетёный ◆ *n* плете́ние.

wicket ['wɪkɪt] *n* (*CRICKET: stumps*) воро́тца* *pl*; (: *grass area*) кон ме́жду двумя́ воро́тцами.

wicket-keeper ['wɪkɪtki:pə*] *n* игро́к, охраня́ющий воро́тца.

wide [waɪd] *adj* широ́кий* (широ́к) ◆ *adv*: **to open ~** широ́ко открыва́ть (откры́ть* *perf*); **to shoot ~** стреля́ть (*impf*) ми́мо це́ли; **the bridge is 3 metres ~** ширина́ моста́ – 3 ме́тра.

wide-angle lens ['waɪdæŋgl-] *n* (*PHOT*) широкоуго́льная ли́нза.

wide-awake [waɪdə'weɪk] *adj*: **I feel ~** у меня́ сна ни в одно́м глазу́.

wide-eyed [waɪd'aɪd] *adj* (*fig*) наи́вный* (наи́вен); **she sat there ~** она́ сиде́ла с широко́ раскры́тыми глаза́ми.

widely ['waɪdlɪ] *adv* (*believed, known*) широко́; (*travelled*) мно́го; (*differing*) значи́тельно; **he is ~ read** (*author*) его́ мно́го чита́ют; (*reader*) он о́чень начи́тан.

widen ['waɪdn] *vt* расширя́ть (расши́рить *perf*) ◆ *vi* расширя́ться (расши́риться *perf*).

wideness ['waɪdnɪs] *n* широта́.

wide open *adj* широко́ раскры́тый (раскры́т).

wide-ranging [waɪd'reɪndʒɪŋ] *adj* (*survey, report*) всесторо́нний* (всесторо́нен); (*interests*) широ́кий*.

widespread ['waɪdsprɛd] *adj* (*belief etc*) распространённый* (распространён).

widow ['wɪdəu] *n* вдова́*.

widowed ['wɪdəud] *adj* овдове́вший.

widower ['wɪdəuə*] *n* вдове́ц*.

width [wɪdθ] *n* ширина́; **the street is 7 metres in ~** ширина́ у́лицы – 7 ме́тров.

widthways ['wɪdθweɪz] *adv* в ширину́.

wield [wi:ld] *vt* (*sword*) владе́ть (*impf*) +*instr*;

(*power*) по́льзоваться* (*impf*) +*instr*.
wife [waɪf] (*pl* **wives**) *n* жена́*.
wig [wɪg] *n* пари́к*.
wigging ['wɪgɪŋ] *n* (*BRIT: inf*) разно́с.
wiggle ['wɪgl] *vt* (*hips*) пока́чивать (*impf*) +*instr*; (*ears*) шевели́ть (*impf*) +*instr*.
wiggly ['wɪglɪ] *adj* волни́стый* (волни́ст).
wigwam ['wɪgwæm] *n* вигва́м.
wild [waɪld] *adj* (*animal, plant*) ди́кий*; (*weather, sea*) бу́рный* (бу́рен); (*person, behaviour*) бу́йный* (бу́ен); (*idea, guess*) ди́кий; (*enthusiastic: applause*) бу́рный ♦ *n*: **the ~** (*natural surroundings*) ло́но приро́ды *ntpl*; **the ~s** *npl* (*remote area*) ди́кие места́ *ntpl*; **in the ~s of Taiga** в де́брях тайги́; **I am ~ about her/this film** я без ума́ от неё/э́того фи́льма.
wild card *n* (*COMPUT*) универса́льный си́мвол.
wildcat ['waɪldkæt] *n* ди́кая ко́шка*.
wildcat strike *n* неофициа́льная забасто́вка*.
wilderness ['wɪldənɪs] *n* ди́кая ме́стность *f*; (*desert*) пусты́ня.
wildfire ['waɪldfaɪə'] *n*: **to spread like ~** распространя́ться (распространи́ться *perf*) с быстрото́й огня́.
wild-goose chase [waɪld'gu:s-] *n* (*fig*) бессмы́сленная зате́я.
wildlife ['waɪldlaɪf] *n* ди́кая приро́да.
wildly ['waɪldlɪ] *adv* (*behave*) бу́йно, ди́ко; (*applaud*) бу́рно; (*hit, happy*) нейстово; (*guess*) наобу́м.
wiles [waɪlz] *npl* уло́вки* *fpl*.
wilful ['wɪlful], (*US* **willful**) *adj* (*obstinate*) своенра́вный* (своенра́вен); (*deliberate*) умы́шленный*.

KEYWORD
---

will [wɪl] *aux vb* **1** (*forming future tense*): **I will finish it tomorrow** я зако́нчу э́то за́втра; **I will be working all morning** я бу́ду рабо́тать всё у́тро; **I will have finished it by tomorrow** к за́втрашнему дню я э́то зако́нчу; **I will always remember you** я бу́ду по́мнить тебя́ всегда́; **will you do it? – yes, I will/no, I won't** Вы сде́лаете э́то? – да, сде́лаю/нет, не сде́лаю; **the car won't start** маши́на ника́к не заво́дится

2 (*in conjectures, predictions*): **he will** *or* **he'll be there by now** он, наве́рное, уже́ там; **mistakes will happen** оши́бки неизбе́жны

3 (*in commands, requests, offers*): **will you be quiet!** а ну́-ка поти́ше!; **will you help me?** Вы мне не помо́жете?; **will you have a cup of tea?** не хоти́те ли ча́шку ча́я?; **I won't put up with it!** я э́того не потерплю́!;

♦ (*pt,pp* **willed**) *vt*: **I willed him to win** я хоте́л всели́ть в него́ дух побе́ды

♦ *n* (*volition*) во́ля; (*testament*) завеща́ние.

willful ['wɪlful] *adj* (*US*) = **wilful**.
willing ['wɪlɪŋ] *adj* (*agreed*) согла́сный* (согла́сен); (*enthusiastic*) усе́рдный* (усе́рден); **he's ~ to do it** он гото́в э́то сде́лать; **to show ~** проявля́ть (прояви́ть* *perf*) гото́вность.
willingly ['wɪlɪŋlɪ] *adv* охо́тно.
willingness ['wɪlɪŋnɪs] *n* гото́вность *f*.
will-o'-the wisp ['wɪləðə'wɪsp] *n* (*also fig*) неулови́мое *nt adj*.
willow ['wɪləu] *n* (*tree*) и́ва; (*wood*) ивня́к.
willpower ['wɪl'pauə'] *n* си́ла во́ли.
willy-nilly ['wɪlɪ'nɪlɪ] *adv* во́лей-нево́лей.
wilt [wɪlt] *vi* поника́ть (пони́кнуть* *perf*).
Wilts [wɪlts] *abbr* (*BRIT: POST*) = **Wiltshire**.
wily ['waɪlɪ] *adj* хи́трый* (хитёр).
wimp [wɪmp] (*inf: pej*) *n* хлю́пик ♦ *vi*: **to ~ out** стру́сить* (*perf*).
wimpish ['wɪmpɪʃ] *adj* (*inf: pej*) хлю́пкий* (хлю́пок).
win [wɪn] (*pt,pp* **won**) *n* побе́да ♦ *vt* выи́грывать (вы́играть *perf*); (*support, popularity*) завоёвывать (завоева́ть* *perf*) ♦ *vi* побежда́ть (победи́ть* *perf*), выи́грывать (вы́играть *perf*)
▶ **win over** *vt* (*person*) покоря́ть (покори́ть *perf*)
▶ **win round** *vt* (*BRIT*) = **win over**.
wince [wɪns] *vi* мо́рщиться (помо́рщиться *perf*).
winch [wɪntʃ] *n* лебёдка*, во́рот.
Winchester disk ['wɪntʃɪstə-] *n* (*COMPUT*) винче́стерский диск.
wind[1] [wɪnd] *n* ве́тер*; (*MED*) га́зы *mpl*; (*breath*) дыха́ние ♦ *vt*: **the blow ~ed him** от уда́ра у него́ захвати́ло дух; **the ~s** *npl* (*MUS*) духовы́е инструме́нты *mpl*; **into** *or* **against the ~** про́тив ве́тра; **he got the ~ of the news** (*fig*) до него́ дошла́ но́вость; **to break ~** де́лать (сде́лать *perf*) отры́жку.
wind[2] [waɪnd] (*pt, pp* **wound**) *vt* (*roll: thread, rope*) мота́ть (смота́ть *perf*); (*rotate*) верте́ть* (*impf*), крути́ть* (*perf*); (*bandage*) завора́чивать (заверну́ть* *perf*); (*clock, toy*) заводи́ть* (завести́* *perf*) ♦ *vi* (*road, river*) ви́ться* (*impf*)
▶ **wind down** *vt* (*car window*) опуска́ть (опусти́ть* *perf*); (*production, business*) свора́чивать (сверну́ть* *perf*)
▶ **wind up** *vt* (*clock, toy*) заводи́ть* (завести́* *perf*); (*debate*) заверша́ть (заверши́ть *perf*).
windbreak ['wɪndbreɪk] *n* бурело́м; (*plants*) ветрозащи́тная лесополоса́.
windbreaker ['wɪndbreɪkə'] *n* (*US*) = **windcheater**.
windcheater ['wɪndtʃi:tə'] *n* штормо́вка*.
winder ['waɪndə'] *n* (*BRIT: on watch*) (заводно́й) ключ*.

---

* marks translations which have irregular inflections. The Russian-English side of the dictionary gives inflectional information.

windfall ['wɪndfɔ:l] n (money) неожиданные деньги pl; (apple etc) паданец*.

winding ['waɪndɪŋ] adj извилистый (извилист); ~ **staircase** витая лестница.

wind instrument ['wɪnd-] n духовой инструмент.

windmill ['wɪndmɪl] n ветряная мельница.

window ['wɪndəu] n (in house, vehicle) окно*; (in shop) витрина; (also:~ **pane**) оконное стекло*.

window box n наружный ящик для цветов.

window cleaner n мойщик(-ица) окон.

window dresser n оформитель(ница) m(f) витрин.

window envelope n конверт с прозрачным прямоугольником, через который виден адрес, напечатанный на письме.

window frame n оконная рама.

window ledge n наружный подоконник.

window pane n оконное стекло*.

window-shopping ['wɪndəuʃɔpɪŋ] n: **to go ~** рассматривать (impf) витрины.

windowsill ['wɪndəusɪl] n подоконник.

windpipe ['wɪndpaɪp] n (ANAT) трахея.

wind power ['wɪnd-] n сила ветра.

windscreen ['wɪndskri:n] n ветровое стекло*.

windscreen washer n стеклоомыватель m.

windscreen wiper [-waɪpə'] n дворник, стеклоочиститель m.

windshield ['wɪndʃi:ld] n (US) = **windscreen**.

wind surfing ['wɪnd-] n виндсёрфинг.

windswept ['wɪndswɛpt] adj (place) незащищённый от ветра; (person, hair) растрёпанный* (растрёпан).

wind tunnel ['wɪnd-] n аэродинамическая труба*.

windy ['wɪndɪ] adj ветреный* (ветрен); **it's ~** сегодня ветрено.

wine [waɪn] n вино* ♦ vt: **to ~ and dine sb** поить*-кормить* (impf) кого-н.

wine bar n винный бар.

wine cellar n винный погреб*.

wine glass n бокал.

wine grower n виноградарь m.

wine growing n виноградарство ♦ adj: ~~ **region** виноградарский район.

wine list n карта вин.

wine merchant n виноторговец*.

wine tasting [-teɪstɪŋ] n дегустация вин.

wine waiter n официант, ведающий винами.

wing [wɪŋ] n (also AUT) крыло*; ~**s** npl (THEAT) кулисы fpl.

winger ['wɪŋə'] n (FOOTBALL, RUGBY) крайний* нападающий* m adj.

wing mirror n (BRIT) боковое зеркало*.

wing nut n крыльчатая гайка*.

wingspan ['wɪŋspæn] n размах крыла.

wingspread ['wɪŋsprɛd] n размах крыла.

wink [wɪŋk] n подмигивание ♦ vi (with eye) подмигивать (подмигнуть perf); (light etc) мигать (мигнуть perf).

winkle [wɪŋkl] n береговая or морская улитка*.

winner ['wɪnə'] n победитель(ница) m(f).

winning ['wɪnɪŋ] adj (team, competitor) победивший, выигравший; (shot, goal) решающий; (smile) обаятельный* (обаятелен), покоряющий; see also **winnings**.

winning post n финишный столб*.

winnings ['wɪnɪŋz] npl выигрыш msg.

winsome ['wɪnsəm] adj привлекательный* (привлекателен).

winter ['wɪntə'] n (season) зима* ♦ vi (birds) зимовать (перезимовать perf); **in ~** зимой.

winter sports npl зимние виды mpl спорта.

wintry ['wɪntrɪ] adj зимний*.

wipe [waɪp] n: **to give sth a ~** протирать (протереть* perf) что-н ♦ vt (rub) вытирать (вытереть* perf); (erase) стирать (стереть* perf); **to ~ one's nose** вытирать (вытереть* perf) нос

► **wipe off** vt стирать (стереть* perf)

► **wipe out** vt (debt) ликвидировать (impf/perf); (memory) стирать (стереть* perf); (city, population) стирать (стереть* perf) с лица земли

► **wipe up** vt (mess) подтирать (подтереть* perf).

wire ['waɪə'] n проволока; (ELEC) провод*; (telegram) телеграмма ♦ vt (fence) скреплять (скрепить* perf) проволокой; (ELEC: also:~ **up**) подключать (подключить* perf); **to ~ a house** делать (сделать perf) проводку в доме; **to ~ sb** телеграфировать (impf/perf) кому-н.

wire brush n проволочная щётка*.

wire cutters npl кусачки* pl.

wireless ['waɪəlɪs] n (BRIT) радио nt ind.

wire netting n проволочная сеть f.

wire service n (US) агентство новостей.

wire-tapping ['waɪə'tæpɪŋ] n подслушивание телефонных разговоров.

wiring ['waɪərɪŋ] n (ELEC) электропроводка.

wiry ['waɪərɪ] adj (person) жилистый (жилист); (hair) жёсткий* (жёсток).

wisdom ['wɪzdəm] n мудрость f.

wisdom tooth n зуб* мудрости.

wise [waɪz] adj мудрый* (мудр); **I'm none the ~r** я всё равно ничего не понимаю

► **wise up** vi (inf): **to ~ up to sth** осознавать* (осознать* perf) что-н.

...wise [waɪz] suffix: **timewise** etc в отношении времени etc.

wisecrack ['waɪzkræk] n шпилька*.

wisely ['waɪzlɪ] adv мудро.

wish [wɪʃ] n желание ♦ vt желать (пожелать perf); **best ~es** (for birthday etc) всего наилучшего; **with best ~es** (in letter) с наилучшими пожеланиями; **give her my best ~es** передайте ей мой наилучшие пожелания; **to ~ sb goodbye** прощаться (попрощаться perf) с кем-н; **he ~ed me well** он пожелал мне всего хорошего; **to ~ to do**

хоте́ть* *(impf)* +*infin*; **I ~ him to come** я хочу́, чтобы он пришёл; **to ~ for** жела́ть (пожела́ть *perf)* +*acc or* +*gen*; **to ~ sth on sb** навя́зывать (навяза́ть* *perf*) что-н кому́-н.

wishbone ['wɪʃbəʊn] *n* счастли́вая ду́жка (*грудна́я кость пти́цы, разла́мывая кото́рую, зага́дывают жела́ние*).

wishful ['wɪʃfʊl] *adj*: **it's ~ thinking** э́то – приня́тие жела́емого за действи́тельное.

wishy-washy ['wɪʃɪ'wɒʃɪ] *adj* (*inf: colour*) му́тный; (*ideas, person*) вя́лый (вял).

wisp [wɪsp] *n* (*of grass, hair*) клочо́к*; (*of smoke*) стру́йка*.

wistful ['wɪstfʊl] *adj* тоскли́вый (тоскли́в).

wit [wɪt] *n* (*wittiness*) остроу́мие; (*intelligence: also*: ~**s**) ум*, ра́зум; (*person*) остря́к* (-яка́*); (*presence of mind*) сообрази́тельность *f*; **to be at one's ~s' end** (*fig*) быть* (*impf*) в отча́янии; **to have one's ~s about one** не теря́ться (растеря́ться *perf*); **to ~ a** и́менно.

witch [wɪtʃ] *n* ве́дьма.

witchcraft ['wɪtʃkrɑːft] *n* колдовство́.

witch doctor *n* зна́харь(-рка*) *m(f)*.

witch-hunt ['wɪtʃhʌnt] *n* (*fig*) охо́та за ве́дьмами.

KEYWORD

with [wɪð] *prep* **1** (*accompanying, in the company of*) с +*instr*; **I spent the day with him** я провела́ с ним день; **we stayed with friends** мы остана́вливались у друзе́й; **I'll be with you in a minute** я освобожу́сь че́рез мину́ту; **would you like chips with your steak?** Вы хоти́те жа́реную карто́шку к бифште́ксу?; **I'm with you** (*I understand*) я Вас понима́ю; **she is really with it** (*inf: fashionable*) она́ о́чень совреме́нная деви́ца; (: *aware*) она́ всё сообража́ет

2 (*descriptive*) с +*instr*; **a girl with blue eyes** де́вушка с голубы́ми глаза́ми; **a skirt with a silk lining** ю́бка на шёлковой подкла́дке

3 (*indicating manner*) с +*instr*; (*indicating cause*) от +*gen*; (*indicating means*): **to write with a pencil** писа́ть* (*impf*) карандашо́м; **with tears in her eyes** со слеза́ми на глаза́х; **red with anger** кра́сный от гне́ва; **you can open the door with this key** Вы мо́жете откры́ть дверь э́тим ключо́м; **to fill sth with water** наполня́ть (наполни́ть *perf*) что-н водо́й.

---

withdraw [wɪθ'drɔː] (*irreg: like draw*) *vt* (*object*) извлека́ть (извле́чь* *perf*); (*offer, remark*) брать* (взять* *perf*) наза́д ♦ *vi* (*troops, person*) уходи́ть* (уйти́* *perf*); **to ~ into o.s.** уходи́ть* (уйти́* *perf*) в себя́; **to ~ money from an account** снима́ть (снять* *perf*) де́ньги со счёта.

withdrawal [wɪθ'drɔːəl] *n* (*of offer, remark,*

participation) отка́з; (*of troops*) вы́вод; (*of services*) отме́на; (*of money*) сня́тие.

withdrawal symptoms *npl* (*MED*) синдро́м *msg* отме́ны *or* абстине́нтный синдро́м *msg* (*при отвыка́нии от лека́рств, нарко́тиков итп*).

withdrawn [wɪθ'drɔːn] *pp of* **withdraw** ♦ *adj* за́мкнутый (за́мкнут).

wither ['wɪðə'] *vi* (*plant*) вя́нуть (завя́нуть *perf*), со́хнуть (засо́хнуть *perf*).

withered ['wɪðəd] *adj* (*plant*) увя́дший*, засо́хший; (*limb*) вы́сохший*.

withhold [wɪθ'həʊld] (*irreg: like hold*) *vt* (*money*) уде́рживать (удержа́ть* *perf*); (*permission*) не дава́ть* (дать* *perf*); (*information*) ута́ивать (утаи́ть *perf*).

within [wɪð'ɪn] *prep* (*inside: of place, time, distance*) внутри́ +*gen*, в преде́лах +*gen* ♦ *adv* внутри́; ~ **reach** в преде́лах досяга́емости; ~ **sight (of)** в по́ле зре́ния (+*gen*); **the finish is ~ sight** коне́ц не за гора́ми; ~ **the week** в преде́лах неде́ли; ~ **a mile of** в преде́лах ми́ли от +*gen*; ~ **an hour of** че́рез час по́сле +*gen*; ~ **the law** в ра́мках зако́на.

without [wɪð'aʊt] *prep* без +*gen*; ~ **a coat** без пальто́; ~ **saying a word** не говоря́ ни сло́ва; ~ **looking** не гля́дя; **to go ~ sth** обходи́ться* (обойти́сь* *perf*) без чего́-н.

withstand [wɪθ'stænd] (*irreg: like stand*) *vt* выде́рживать (вы́держать* *perf*).

witness ['wɪtnɪs] *n* (*person, also LAW*) свиде́тель(ница) *m(f)* ♦ *vt* (*event*) быть* (*impf*) свиде́телем(-льницей) +*gen*; (*document*) заверя́ть (заве́рить *perf*); **to bear ~ to** (*fig*) свиде́тельствовать (*impf*) о +*prp*; ~ **for the prosecution/defence** свиде́тель обвине́ния/ защи́ты; **to ~ to sth** засвиде́тельствовать (*perf*) факт чего́-н; **I can ~ to having seen ...** я могу́ засвиде́тельствовать, что я ви́дел ....

witness box *n* свиде́тельское ме́сто*.

witness stand (*US*) = **witness box**.

witticism ['wɪtɪsɪzəm] *n* остро́та.

witty ['wɪtɪ] *adj* остроу́мный* (остроу́мен).

wives [waɪvz] *npl of* **wife**.

wizard ['wɪzəd] *n* волше́бник.

wizened ['wɪznd] *adj* (*person*) морщи́нистый (морщи́нист); (*fruit, vegetable*) смо́рщенный* (смо́рщен).

wk *abbr* = **week**.

Wm. *abbr* = **William**.

WO *n abbr* (*MIL*: = **warrant officer**) ≈ пра́порщик.

wobble ['wɒbl] *vi* (*legs*) трясти́сь* (*impf*); (*jelly*) колыха́ться* (*impf*); (*chair*) шата́ться (*impf*).

wobbly ['wɒblɪ] *adj* (*hand, voice*) дрожа́щий; (*table, chair*) ша́ткий* (ша́ток).

woe [wəʊ] *n* го́ре.

woeful ['wəʊfʊl] *adj* (*sad*) печа́льный* (печа́лен); (*awful*) вопию́щий.

---

wok [wɔk] *n* глубо́кая сковорода́ (*в кита́йской ку́хне*).
woke [wəuk] *pt of* **wake**.
woken ['wəukn] *pp of* **wake**.
wolf [wulf] (*pl* **wolves**) *n* волк.
wolves [wulvz] *npl of* **wolf**.
woman ['wumən] (*pl* **women**) *n* же́нщина; ~ **friend** подру́га; ~ **teacher** учи́тельница; **young** ~ молода́я же́нщина; **women's page** (*PRESS*) страни́ца для же́нщин.
woman doctor *n* же́нщина-врач.
womanize ['wumənaɪz] *vi* (*pej*) вести́* (*impf*) распу́тную жизнь.
womanizer ['wumənaɪzə'] *n* женолю́б, ба́бник (*разг*).
womanly ['wumənlɪ] *adj* (*virtues etc*) же́нский*; (*figure*) же́нственный.
womb [wu:m] *n* ма́тка*.
women ['wɪmɪn] *npl of* **woman**.
women's lib ['wɪmɪnz-] *n* (*inf*) эмансипа́ция же́нщин.
Women's (Liberation) Movement *n* движе́ние за эмансипа́цию же́нщин.
won [wʌn] *pt, pp of* **win**.
wonder ['wʌndə'] *n* (*miracle*) чу́до; (*feeling*) изумле́ние ◆ *vi*: **I ~ whether you could tell me** ... не мо́жете ли Вы сказа́ть мне ...; **I ~ why he is late** интере́сно, почему́ он опозда́л; **to ~ at** (*marvel at*) удивля́ться (*impf*) +*dat*; **to ~ about** разду́мывать* (*impf*) о +*prp*; **it's no ~ (that)** не удиви́тельно(, что).
wonderful ['wʌndəful] *adj* (*excellent*) замеча́тельный* (замеча́телен); (*astonishing*) удиви́тельный (удиви́телен).
wonderfully ['wʌndəfəlɪ] *adv* (*see adj*) замеча́тельно; удиви́тельно.
wonky ['wɔŋkɪ] *adj* (*BRIT: inf*) ша́ткий* (ша́ток).
wont [wəunt] *adj*: **he is ~ to** ... он име́ет обыкнове́ние +*infin* ...; **as is my ~** по обыкнове́нию.
won't [wəunt] = **will not**.
woo [wu:] *vt* (*woman*) добива́ться (доби́ться *perf*) расположе́ния +*gen*; (*audience etc*) заи́грывать* (*impf*) с +*instr*.
wood [wud] *n* (*timber*) де́рево; (*forest*) лес ◆ *cpd* (*house*) деревя́нный; (*shed*) дровяно́й; ~**pile** штабель *n* дров.
wood carving *n* (*act*) резьба́ по де́реву; (*object*) резьба́ (по де́реву).
wooded ['wudɪd] *adj* (*slopes, area*) леси́стый.
wooden ['wudn] *adj* (*object*) деревя́нный; (*fig: performance, actor*) дубо́вый.
woodland ['wudlənd] *n* леси́стая ме́стность *f*.
woodpecker ['wudpekə'] *n* дя́тел*.
wood pigeon *n* лесно́й го́лубь *m*.
woodwind ['wudwɪnd] *n* деревя́нный духово́й инструме́нт; **the ~** деревя́нные духовы́е *pl adj* инструме́нты.
woodwork ['wudwə:k] *n* (*skill*) столя́рное де́ло.
woodworm ['wudwə:m] *n* (*larvae*) личи́нка

древото́чца.
woof [wuf] *n* лай ◆ *vi* ла́ять (*impf*); ~, ~**!** гав, гав!
wool [wul] *n* (*material, yarn*) шерсть *f*; **to pull the ~ over sb's eyes** (*fig*) ве́шать (*impf*) лапшу́ на́ уши.
woollen ['wulən] (*US* **woolen**) *adj* шерстяно́й.
woollens ['wulənz] *npl* шерстяны́е ве́щи *fpl*.
woolly ['wulɪ] (*US* **wooly**) *adj* шерстяно́й; (*fig: ideas*) расплы́вчатый (расплы́вчат); (: *person*) вя́лый (вял) ◆ *n* шерстяно́й сви́тер* *m*.
woozy ['wu:zɪ] *adj* (*inf*) окосе́вший.
Worcs *abbr* (*BRIT: POST*) = **Worcestershire**.
word [wə:d] *n* сло́во; (*news*) слух ◆ *vt* (*letter, message*) формули́ровать (сформули́ровать* *perf*); ~ **for ~** (*repeat*) сло́во в сло́во; (*translate*) досло́вно; **what's the ~ for "pen" in French?** как (бу́дет) по-францу́зски (сло́во) "ру́чка"?; **to put sth into ~s** выража́ть (вы́разить* *perf*) что-н слова́ми; **in other ~s** други́ми слова́ми; **to break/keep one's ~** наруша́ть (нару́шить *perf*)/держа́ть (сдержа́ть* *perf*) своё сло́во; **to have ~s with sb** име́ть (*impf*) кру́пный разгово́р с кем-н; **to have a ~ with sb** поговори́ть (*perf*) с кем-н; **I'll take your ~ for it** я пове́рю Вам на́ сло́во; **to send ~ of** извеща́ть (извести́ть* *perf*) о +*prp*; **to leave ~ (with sb/for sb) that** ... передава́ть* (переда́ть* *perf*) (че́рез кого́-н/кому́-н), что ....
wording ['wə:dɪŋ] *n* формулиро́вка*; (*in card*) поздрави́тельный текст.
word of mouth *n*: **by** *or* **through ~ ~ ~** из уст в уста́; **I found out about it by ~ ~ ~** я об э́том услы́шал от кого́-то.
word-perfect ['wə:d'pə:fɪkt] *adj*: **to be ~** (*person*) знать (*impf*) ка́ждое сло́во; **the speech was ~** речь была́ прекра́сно подгото́влена.
word processing *n* обрабо́тка *or* подгото́вка те́кстов.
word processor [-prəusɛsə'] *n* те́кстовый проце́ссор.
wordwrap ['wə:dræp] *n* (автомати́ческий*) перехо́д (*на но́вую стро́ку*).
wordy ['wə:dɪ] *adj* многосло́вный* (многосло́вен).
wore [wɔ:'] *pt of* **wear**.
work [wə:k] *n* рабо́та; (*ART, LITERATURE*) произведе́ние ◆ *vi* рабо́тать (*impf*); (*medicine etc*) де́йствовать (поде́йствовать *perf*) ◆ *vt* (*clay*) рабо́тать (*impf*) с +*instr*; (*wood, metal, land*) обраба́тывать (обрабо́тать *perf*); (*mine*) разраба́тывать (разрабо́тать *perf*); (*machine*) управля́ть (*impf*) +*instr*; (*effect, miracle*) твори́ть (сотвори́ть* *perf*); **to go to ~** ходи́ть*/идти́* (*impf*) на рабо́ту; **to start** *or* **set to ~** принима́ться (приня́ться* *perf*) за рабо́ту; **to be at ~ (on sth)** рабо́тать

(impf) (над чем-н); **he has been out of ~ for three months** у него́ уже́ три ме́сяца нет рабо́ты; **to ~ hard** мно́го рабо́тать *(impf)*; **to ~ loose** *(part)* расша́тываться (расшата́ться *perf)*; *(knot)* сла́бнуть (осла́бнуть *perf)*

▶ **work on** *vt fus (task)* рабо́тать *(impf)* над +*instr*; *(person)* рабо́тать *(impf)* с +*instr*; *(principle)* опира́ться *(impf)* на +*acc*; **he's ~ing on his car** *(repairing)* он чи́нит маши́ну; *(doing up)* он рабо́тает над свое́й маши́ной

▶ **work out** *vi (plans etc)* удава́ться* (уда́ться* *perf)*; *(SPORT)* занима́ться *(impf)* физи́ческими упражне́ниями ♦ *vt (problem)* реша́ть (реши́ть *perf)*; *(plan)* разраба́тывать (разрабо́тать *perf)*; **it ~s out at £100** *(cost)* получа́ется £100

▶ **work up** *vt:* **to get ~ed up (about sth)** разне́рвничаться *(perf)* (из-за чего́-н).

workable ['wɔːkəbl] *adj (solution)* осуществи́мый (осуществи́м), выполни́мый (выполни́м).

workaholic [wɔːkə'hɒlɪk] *n:* **he is a ~** он не мо́жет жить без рабо́ты.

workbench ['wɔːkbɛntʃ] *n* верста́к*.

worker ['wɔːkəʳ] *n (in factory)* рабо́чий*(-ая) *m(f) adj*; *(in community etc)* рабо́тник(-ница); **office ~** конто́рский* слу́жащий*(-ая) *m(f) adj*.

workforce ['wɔːkfɔːs] *n* рабо́чая си́ла.

work-in ['wɔːkɪn] *n (BRIT)* "уо́рк-ин" *(вид забасто́вки)*.

working ['wɔːkɪŋ] *adj (day, tools etc)* рабо́чий*; **~ conditions** усло́вия *ntpl* рабо́ты; **~ partner** делово́й партнёр; **~ population** за́нятая часть населе́ния; **a ~ knowledge of English** практи́ческое зна́ние англи́йского языка́.

working capital *n* оборо́тный капита́л.

working class *n* рабо́чий* класс.

working-class ['wɔːkɪŋ'klɑːs] *adj* рабо́чий*.

working man *n* рабо́тающий мужчи́на.

working order *n:* **in ~** в рабо́чем состоя́нии.

working party *n (BRIT)* рабо́чая гру́ппа.

working relationship *n* деловы́е отноше́ния.

working week *n* рабо́чая неде́ля.

work-in-progress ['wɔːkɪn'prəugrɛs] *n (COMM: products)* объём проду́кции, вы́пущенной к настоя́щему моме́нту; *(: value)* сто́имость проду́кции, вы́пущенной к настоя́щему моме́нту.

workload ['wɔːkləud] *n* нагру́зка*.

workman ['wɔːkmən] *irreg n* (квалифици́рованный) рабо́чий* *m adj*.

workmanship ['wɔːkmənʃɪp] *n (skill)* мастерство́; *(quality)* ка́чество рабо́ты; **good/poor ~** то́нкая/гру́бая рабо́та.

workmate ['wɔːkmeɪt] *n* това́рищ по рабо́те.

workout ['wɔːkaut] *n* размя́нка.

work permit *n* разреше́ние на рабо́ту.

works [wɔːks] *n (BRIT: factory)* заво́д, фа́брика ♦ *npl (of clock, machine)* механи́зм *msg*.

worksheet ['wɔːkʃiːt] *n* рабо́чая ка́рта.

workshop ['wɔːkʃɒp] *n (at home, in factory)* мастерска́я *f adj*, цех; *(practical session)* семина́р, практи́ческие заня́тия *ntpl*; *(THEAT, MUS)* сту́дия.

work station *n часть большо́го о́фиса, отделённая для рабо́ты одного́ слу́жащего*; *(COMPUT)* рабо́чая ста́нция.

work study *n ≈* нау́чная организа́ция труда́.

worktop ['wɔːktɒp] *n* рабо́чая пове́рхность *f*.

work-to-rule ['wɔːktə'ruːl] *n (BRIT)* "рабо́та по пра́вилам" *(вид забасто́вочной борьбы́)*.

world [wɔːld] *n* мир ♦ *cpd (tour)* кругосве́тный; *(war, record)* мирово́й; **~ champion** чемпио́н, чемпио́н ми́ра; **~ power** мирова́я держа́ва; **all over the ~** во всём ми́ре; **to think the ~ of sb** быть* *(impf)* о́чень высо́кого мне́ния о ком-н; **what in the ~ are you doing?** ты сообража́ешь, что ты де́лаешь?; **to do sb a ~ of good** приноси́ть* (принести́* *perf)* кому́-н огро́мную по́льзу; **W~ War One/Two** пе́рвая/втора́я мирова́я война́; **out of this ~** неземно́й.

World Cup *n:* **the ~ ~** *(FOOTBALL)* Ку́бок *or* чемпиона́т ми́ра.

world-famous [wɔːld'feɪməs] *adj* всеми́рно изве́стный* (изве́стен).

worldly ['wɔːldlɪ] *adj (not spiritual)* земно́й; *(knowledgeable)* иску́шенный.

world music *n* му́зыка наро́дов ми́ра.

World Series *n:* **the ~ ~** *(US: BASEBALL)* ку́бковые соревнова́ния *ntpl*.

worldwide ['wɔːld'waɪd] *adj* всеми́рный ♦ *adv* во всём ми́ре.

World Wide Web *n* (Всеми́рная) Сеть, Повсеме́стно Протя́нутая Паути́на.

worm [wɔːm] *n (ZOOL)* червь *m*

▶ **worm out** *vt:* **to ~ sth out of sb** выта́гивать (вы́тянуть *perf)* что-н из кого́-н.

worn [wɔːn] *pp of* **wear** ♦ *adj (carpet)* потёртый (потёрт); *(shoe)* поно́шенный* (поно́шен).

worn-out ['wɔːnaut] *adj (object)* изно́шенный* (изно́шен); *(teddy)* потрёпанный* (потрё пан); *(person)* измо́танный (измо́тан).

worried ['wʌrɪd] *adj* обеспоко́енный (обеспоко́ен), встрево́женный (встрево́жен); **she is ~ about it** она́ обеспоко́ена э́тим.

worrier ['wʌrɪəʳ] *n:* **she is a natural ~** она́ всегда́ чем-то обеспоко́ена.

worrisome ['wʌrɪsəm] *adj* вызыва́ющий беспоко́йство, трево́жный.

worry ['wʌrɪ] *n (anxiety)* беспоко́йство, волне́ние ♦ *vi (person)* беспоко́иться *(impf)*, волнова́ться *(impf)* ♦ *vt (person)* беспоко́ить *(impf)*, волнова́ть (взволнова́ть *perf)*; **to ~**

about *or* **over sth/sb** беспоко́иться *(impf)* за
что-н/кого́-н.

worrying ['wʌrɪɪŋ] *adj* трево́жный*
(трево́жен).

worse [wəːs] *adj* ху́дший* ♦ *adv* ху́же ♦ *n*
ху́дшее *nt adj*; **to get ~** ухудша́ться
(уху́дшиться *perf*); **a change for the ~**
ухудше́ние; **he is none the ~ for it** ему́ не
ста́ло от э́того ху́же; **so much the ~ for you!**
тем ху́же для Вас!

worsen ['wəːsn] *vt* ухудша́ть (уху́дшить *perf*) ♦
vi ухудша́ться (уху́дшиться *perf*).

worse off *adj* (*financially*) бедне́е; (*fig*): **you'll be
~ ~ this way** Вам так бу́дет ху́же; **he is now
~ ~ than before** его́ положе́ние тепе́рь ху́же,
чем ра́ньше.

worship ['wəːʃɪp] *n* поклоне́ние, преклоне́ние
♦ *vt* поклоня́ться *(impf) +dat*, преклоня́ться
(impf) пе́ред *+instr*; **Your W~** (*BRIT: to mayor,
judge*) Ва́ша ми́лость.

worshipper ['wəːʃɪpə'] *n* (*REL*) моля́щийся
(-аяся) *m(f) adj*, прихожа́нин*(-нка); (*fig*)
покло́нник(-ница).

worst [wəːst] *adj* наиху́дший* ♦ *adv* ху́же всего́
♦ *n* наиху́дшее *nt adj*; **at ~** в ху́дшем слу́чае; **if
the ~ comes to the ~** на худо́й коне́ц, в
са́мом ху́дшем слу́чае.

worst-case scenario ['wəːstkeɪs-] *n* ху́дший*
вариа́нт.

worsted ['wustɪd] *n*: (**wool**) **~** гребенна́я
шерсть *f*.

worth [wəːθ] *n* (*value*) сто́имость *f* ♦ *adj*: **to be
~** сто́ить *(impf)*; **how much is it ~?** ско́лько
э́то сто́ит?; **50 pence ~ of apples** я́блок на 50
пе́нсов; **an hour's ~ of work** рабо́та на час;
it's ~ it э́то того́ сто́ит.

worthless ['wəːθlɪs] *adj* никчёмный* (никчё
мен).

worthwhile ['wəːθ'waɪl] *adj* сто́ящий*; **a ~
book** сто́ящая кни́га.

worthy [wəːðɪ] *adj* досто́йный; **~ of**
досто́йный* (досто́ин) *+gen*.

KEYWORD

would [wud] *aux vb* **1** (*conditional tense*): **I
would tell you if I could** я бы сказа́л Вам, е́сли
бы мог; **if you asked him he would do it** е́сли
Вы его́ попро́сите, (то) он э́то сде́лает; **if
you had asked him he would have done it** е́сли
бы Вы попроси́ли его́, (то) он бы э́то
сде́лал

2 (*in offers, invitations, requests*): **would you
like a biscuit?** не хоти́те (ли) пече́нья?; **would
you ask him to come in?** пригласи́те его́
войти́?; **would you open the window please?**
откро́йте, пожа́луйста, окно́

3 (*in indirect speech*): **I said I would do it** я
сказа́л, что сде́лаю э́то; **he asked me if I
would stay with him** он попроси́л меня́
оста́ться с ним; **he asked me if I would resit
the exam if I failed** он спроси́л меня́, бу́ду ли
я пересдава́ть экза́мен, е́сли я провалю́сь

4 (*emphatic*): **it WOULD have to snow today!**
именно сего́дня до́лжен был пойти́ снег!;
you WOULD say that, wouldn't you! Вы,
коне́чно, э́то ска́жете!

5 (*insistence*): **she wouldn't behave** она́ ника́к
не хоте́ла хорошо́ себя́ вести́

6 (*conjecture*): **it would have been midnight**
должно́ быть, была́ по́лночь; **it would seem
so** должно́ быть, так; **it would seem that ...**
похо́же, что ...

7 (*indicating habit*): **he would always come
here on Mondays** он всегда́ приходи́л сюда́
по понеде́льникам; **he would spend every day
on the beach** он проводи́л ка́ждый день на
пля́же.

would-be ['wudbiː] *adj* (*pej*): **~ writer** челове́к*,
вообража́ющий себя́ писа́телем.

wouldn't ['wudnt] = **would not**.

wound[1] [waund] *pt, pp of* **wind**[2].

wound[2] [wuːnd] *n* ра́на ♦ *vt* ра́нить *(impf/perf)*;
~ed in the leg ра́неный в но́гу.

wove [wəuv] *pt of* **weave**.

woven ['wəuvn] *pp of* **weave**.

WP *n abbr* = **word processing**, **word processor** ♦
abbr (*BRIT: inf.* = **weather permitting**) е́сли
позво́лит пого́да.

WPC (*BRIT*) *n abbr* = **woman police constable**.

wpm *abbr* = **words per minute**.

WRAC *n abbr* (*BRIT*) = **Women's Royal Army
Corps**.

WRAF *n abbr* (*BRIT*) = **Women's Royal Air Force**.

wrangle ['ræŋgl] *n* пререка́ние ♦ *vi*: **to ~ with
sb over sth** пререка́ться *(impf)* с ке́м-н по
по́воду чего́-н.

wrap [ræp] *n* (*shawl*) широ́кий* шарф; (*cape*)
наки́дка* ♦ *vt* (*also*: **~ up**) завора́чивать
(заверну́ть *perf*); (*wind*): **to ~ sth round sth**
(*tape etc*) обора́чивать (оберну́ть *perf*) что-н
вокру́г чего́-н; **to keep sth under ~s** (*fig*)
скрыва́ть *(impf)* что-н.

wrapper ['ræpə'] *n* (*on chocolate*) обёртка;
(*BRIT: of book*) обло́жка*.

wrapping paper ['ræpɪŋ-] *n* обёрточная
бума́га.

wrath [rɔθ] *n* гнев.

wreak [riːk] *vt*: **to ~ havoc (on)** наноси́ть*
(нанести́* *perf*) уще́рб (*+dat*); **to ~ vengeance**
or **revenge on sb** отомсти́ть* (*perf*) кому́-н.

wreath [riːθ] (*pl* **~s**) *n* (*at funeral*) вено́к*.

wreck [rɛk] *n* (*vehicle*) ава́рия; (*ship*)
круше́ние; (*sea disaster*) кораблекруше́ние;
(*pej: person*) разва́лина ♦ *vt* (*car etc*)
разбива́ть (разби́ть* *perf*); (*stereo*) лома́ть
(слома́ть *perf*); (*fig: weekend, relationship*)
по́ртить* (испо́ртить* *perf*); (: *life, health*)
губи́ть* (погуби́ть* *perf*).

wreckage ['rɛkɪdʒ] *n* обло́мки *pl*; (*of building*)
разва́лины *fpl*.

wrecker ['rɛkə'] *n* (*US: breakdown van*)
авари́йная маши́на.

Wren [rɛn] *n* (*BRIT: MIL*) же́нщина, слу́жащая в
вое́нно-морско́м фло́те.
wren [rɛn] *n* крапи́вник.
wrench [rɛntʃ] *n* (*TECH*) га́ечный ключ*; (*tug*)
рыво́к*; (*fig*) щемя́щая тоска́ ♦ *vt* (*twist*)
выве́ртывать (вы́вернуть *perf*); **to ~ sth from
sb** вырыва́ть (вы́рвать *perf*) что-н у кого́-н.
wrest [rɛst] *vt*: **to ~ sth from sb** вырыва́ть
(вы́рвать *perf*) что-н у кого́-н.
wrestle ['rɛsl] *vi*: **to ~ (with sb)** боро́ться* (*impf*)
(с кем-н); **to ~ with a problem** му́читься (*impf*)
над пробле́мой.
wrestler ['rɛslə'] *n* боре́ц*.
wrestling ['rɛslɪŋ] *n* борьба́; (*also:* **all-in ~**)
кетч (*вид борьбы́*).
wrestling match *n* соревнова́ния *ntpl* по
борьбе́.
wretch [rɛtʃ] *n* негодя́й; **little ~!** него́дник!
wretched ['rɛtʃɪd] *adj* несча́стный*
(несча́стен).
wriggle ['rɪgl] *vi* (*also:* **~ about:** *person, snake
etc*) извива́ться (*impf*) ♦ *n* выгиба́ние.
wring [rɪŋ] (*pt,pp* **wrung**) *vt* (*wet clothes*)
выжима́ть (вы́жать* *perf*); (*hands*) лома́ть
(*impf*); (*bird's neck*) свора́чивать (сверну́ть
perf); (*fig*): **to ~ sth out of sb** выжима́ть
(вы́жать* *perf*) что-н из кого́-н.
wringer ['rɪŋə'] *n* пресс для отжима́ния белья́.
wringing ['rɪŋɪŋ] *adj* (*also:* **~ wet**): **he is ~ (wet)**
с него́ течёт (вода́).
wrinkle ['rɪŋkl] *n* (*on skin*) морщи́на; (*on paper
etc*) скла́дка* ♦ *vt* (*nose, forehead etc*)
мо́рщить (смо́рщить *perf*) ♦ *vi* (*skin etc*)
мо́рщиться (смо́рщиться *perf*); (*paint*)
покрыва́ться (покры́ться* *perf*) тре́щинами.
wrinkled ['rɪŋkld] *adj* (*fabric, paper*) мя́тый*;
(*surface*) смо́рщенный* (смо́рщен); (*skin*)
морщи́нистый (морщи́нист).
wrinkly ['rɪŋklɪ] *adj* = **wrinkled**.
wrist [rɪst] *n* (*ANAT*) запя́стье.
wristband ['rɪstbænd] *n* (*BRIT: of shirt*)
манже́та; (*of watch: leather*) ремешо́к*;
(: *metal*) брасле́т.
wristwatch ['rɪstwɔtʃ] *n* нару́чные часы́ *pl*.
writ [rɪt] *n* (*LAW*) о́рдер; **to issue a ~ against sb**
выдава́ть* (вы́дать* *perf*) о́рдер на чей-н
аре́ст; **to serve a ~ on sb** посыла́ть (посла́ть*
perf) кому́-н пове́стку в суд.
write [raɪt] (*pt* **wrote**, *pp* **written**) *vt* (*letter, novel
etc*) писа́ть* (написа́ть* *perf*); (*cheque, receipt,
prescription*) выпи́сывать (вы́писать* *perf*) ♦
vi писа́ть* (*impf*); **to ~ to sb** писа́ть*
(написа́ть* *perf*) кому́-н
▶ **write away** *vi*: **to ~ away for** (*information*)
запра́шивать (запроси́ть* *perf*) о(б) +*prp*;
(*goods*) посыла́ть (посла́ть* *perf*)
пи́сьменный зака́з на +*acc*
▶ **write down** *vt* (*note*) писа́ть* (написа́ть*

perf); (*put in writing*) запи́сывать (записа́ть*
perf)
▶ **write off** *vt* (*debt*) спи́сывать (списа́ть* *perf*);
(*plan, project*) аннули́ровать (*impf/perf*); (*car
etc*) спи́сывать (списа́ть* *perf*) ♦ *vi* = **write
away**
▶ **write out** *vt* (*put in writing*) излага́ть
(изложи́ть* *perf*) пи́сьменно; (*cheque, receipt
etc*) выпи́сывать (вы́писать* *perf*); (*copy:
address etc*) спи́сывать (списа́ть* *perf*)
▶ **write up** *vt* приводи́ть* (привести́* *perf*) в
поря́док.
write-off ['raɪtɔf] *n* (*inf*): **the car is a ~** маши́не
коне́ц.
write-protect ['raɪtprə'tɛkt] *vt* (*COMPUT*)
защища́ть (защити́ть* *perf*) от за́писи.
writer ['raɪtə'] *n* писа́тель *m*.
write-up ['raɪtʌp] *n* (*review*) реце́нзия.
writhe [raɪð] *vi* извива́ться (*impf*).
writing ['raɪtɪŋ] *n* (*words written*) на́дпись *f*;
(*also:* **handwriting**) по́черк; (*of author*)
рабо́та, произведе́ние; **~ is his favourite
occupation** бо́льше всего́ он лю́бит писа́ть;
in ~ в пи́сьменном ви́де; **in my own ~**
напи́санный мое́й руко́й.
writing case *n* пена́л.
writing desk *n* пи́сьменный стол*.
writing paper *n* пи́счая бума́га.
written ['rɪtn] *pp of* **write**.
WRNS *n abbr* (*BRIT*) = **Women's Royal Naval
Service**.
wrong [rɔŋ] *adj* непра́вильный* (непра́вилен);
(*information*) неве́рный; (*immoral*) дурно́й ♦
adv непра́вильно; (*informed*) неве́рно ♦ *n*
(*injustice*) несправедли́вость *f*; (*evil*) зло ♦ *vt*
(*treat unfairly*) нехорошо́ поступа́ть
(поступи́ть* *perf*) с +*instr*; **the answer was ~**
отве́т был непра́вильный *or* оши́бочный; **he
is ~ in saying that ...** он непра́в, когда́ он
говори́т, что ...; **you are ~ to do it** э́то
нехорошо́ с Ва́шей стороны́; **it's ~ to steal,
stealing is ~** воровать – нехорошо́; **you are ~
about that, you've got it ~** Вы непра́вы; **who
is in the ~?** чья э́то вина́?; **what's ~?** в чём
де́ло?; **there's nothing ~** всё в поря́дке; **to go
~** (*plan*) не удава́ться (уда́ться* *perf*);
(*machine*) лома́ться (слома́ться* *perf*); **right
and ~** хоро́шее и дурно́е.
wrong-doer ['rɔŋdu:ə'] *n* правонаруши́тель *m*.
wrong-foot [rɔŋ'fut] *vt* (*SPORT*) застига́ть
(засти́гнуть *perf*) враспло́х; (*fight*) лови́ть*
(пойма́ть* *perf*) кого́-н на́ слове.
wrongful ['rɔŋful] *adj* (*imprisonment,
dismissal*) несправедли́вый (несправедли́в).
wrongly ['rɔŋlɪ] *adv* непра́вильно; (*unjustly*)
несправедли́во.
wrong number *n*: **you have a ~ ~** (*TEL*) Вы не
туда́ попа́ли.

---

wrong side *n*: the ~~ (*of material*) изна́нка*.
wrote [rəut] *pt of* **write**.
wrought [rɔːt] *adj*: ~ **iron** ко́ваное желе́зо.
wrung [rʌŋ] *pt, pp of* **wring**.
WRVS *n abbr* (*BRIT*) = *Women's Royal Voluntary Service*.
wry [raɪ] *adj* (*humour, expression*) лука́вый (лука́в); (*smile*) криво́й* (крив).

wt. *abbr* = **weight**.
WV *abbr* (*US: POST*) = *West Virginia*.
WWW *abbr* = **World Wide Web**.
WY *abbr* (*US: POST*) = *Wyoming*.
WYSIWYG ['wɪzɪwɪg] *abbr* (*COMPUT*: = *what you see is what you get*) режи́м по́лного соотве́тствия (*в те́кстовых проце́ссорах и изда́тельских систе́мах*).

X, x [ɛks] n (letter) 24-ая бу́ква англи́йского
алфави́та; (BRIT: CINEMA: formerly)
свиде́тельство " X ", кото́рое разреша́ет
пока́з кинофи́льма с элеме́нтами эро́тики
и́ли карти́нами наси́лия.
Xerox® ['zɪərɔks] n (also: ~ **machine**) ксе́рокс;
(photocopy) ксероко́пия ♦ vt де́лать (сде́лать
perf) ко́пию +gen, ксерокопи́ровать
(отксерокопи́ровать perf).
XL abbr = extra large.

Xmas ['ɛksməs] n abbr = **Christmas**.
X-rated ['ɛks'reɪtɪd] adj (US: film) для
взро́слых.
X-ray [ɛks'reɪ] n (ray) рентге́новские лучи́ mpl;
(photo) рентге́новский сни́мок* ♦ vt
просве́чивать (просвети́ть* perf)
(рентге́новскими луча́ми); **to have an** ~
де́лать (сде́лать perf) рентге́н.
xylophone ['zaɪləfəun] n ксилофо́н.

~ Y, y ~

Y, y [waɪ] *n* (*letter*) 25-ая буква английского алфавита.

Y2K *abbr* (= *year two thousand*) двухтысячный год.

yacht [jɔt] *n* яхта.

yachting ['jɔtɪŋ] *n* парусный спорт.

yachtsman ['jɔtsmən] *irreg n* яхтсмен.

yam [jæm] *n* (*vegetable*) ямс, батат.

Yank [jæŋk] *n* (*pej*) янки *m ind*.

yank [jæŋk] *vt* дёргать (дёрнуть *perf*) ♦ *n* рывок*.

Yankee ['jæŋkɪ] *n* (*pej*) = **Yank**.

yap [jæp] *vi* (*dog*) тявкать (*impf*).

yard [jɑːd] *n* (*of house etc*) двор; (*US: garden*) сад*; (*measure*) ярд; **builder's ~** строительная площадка.

yardstick ['jɑːdstɪk] *n* (*fig*) мерило, критерий.

yarn [jɑːn] *n* (*thread*) пряжа; (*tale*) байка.

yawn [jɔːn] *n* зевок* ♦ *vi* зевать (зевнуть *perf*).

yawning ['jɔːnɪŋ] *adj* (*gap*) зияющий.

yd *abbr* = **yard**.

yeah [jɛə] *adv* (*inf*) да, ага.

year [jɪəʳ] *n* год*; (*at school*) класс; (*at university*) курс; **every ~** каждый год; **this ~** в этом году; **a** *or* **per ~** в год; **~ in, ~ out** из года в год; **school/academic ~** учебный/академический год; **he is eight ~s old** ему восемь лет; **an eight-~-old child** восьмилетний* ребёнок*.

yearbook ['jɪəbuk] *n* ежегодник.

yearling ['jɪəlɪŋ] *n* годовалое животное *nt adj*; (*racehorse*) стригунок*.

yearly ['jɪəlɪ] *adj* ежегодный ♦ *adv* ежегодно; **twice ~** два раза в год.

yearn [jɔːn] *vi*: **to ~ for sth** тосковать (*impf*) по чему-н; **to ~ to do** жаждать (*impf*) +*infin*.

yearning ['jɔːnɪŋ] *n*: **to have a ~ to do** иметь (*impf*) страстное желание +*infin*; **to have a ~ for** жаждать (*impf*) +*gen*.

yeast [jiːst] *n* дрожжи *pl*.

yell [jɛl] *n* вопль *m* ♦ *vi* вопить* (*impf*).

yellow ['jɛləu] *adj* жёлтый (жёлт) ♦ *n* (*colour*) жёлтый цвет.

yellow fever *n* жёлтая лихорадка.

yellowish ['jɛləuɪʃ] *adj* желтоватый (желтоват).

Yellow Pages® *n* „Жёлтые страницы" *fpl* (*телефонный справочник*).

Yellow Sea *n*: **the ~~** Жёлтое море.

yelp [jɛlp] *n* визг ♦ *vi* взвизгнуть (*perf*).

Yemen ['jɛmən] *n* Йемен.

Yemeni ['jɛmənɪ] *adj* йеменский ♦ *n* (*person*) йеменец*(-нка*).

yen [jɛn] *n* (*currency*) иена; (*craving*): **~ for** страсть *f* к +*dat*; **~ to do** страстное желание +*infin*.

yeoman ['jəumən] *irreg n* (*BRIT*): **~ of the guard** лейб-гвардеец* (*королёвской стражи*).

yes [jɛs] *particle* да; (*in reply to negative*) нет ♦ *n* (*POL*) проголосовавший(-ая) *m(f)* *adj* „за"; **to say ~** говорить (сказать* *perf*) да; **to answer ~** отвечать (ответить* *perf*) согласием.

yes man *irreg n* (*pej*) подпевала *m/f*.

yesterday ['jɛstədɪ] *adv* вчера ♦ *n* вчерашний* день *m*; **~ morning/evening** вчера утром/вечером; **the day before ~** позавчера; **all day ~** вчера весь день.

yet [jɛt] *adv* ещё, до сих пор ♦ *conj* однако, и всё же; **the work is not finished ~** работа ещё не окончена; **must you go just ~?** Вам уже пора идти?; **the best ~** самый лучший на сегодняшний день; **as ~** ещё, до настоящего момента; **a few days ~** ещё несколько дней; **~ again** ещё раз.

yew [juː] *n* (*tree*) тисовое дерево*; (*wood*) тис.

Y-fronts® ['waɪfrʌnts] *npl* мужские трусы *pl* (*с ширинкой*).

YHA *n abbr* (*BRIT*: = *Youth Hostels Association*) Ассоциация молодёжных гостиниц.

Yiddish ['jɪdɪʃ] *n* идиш.

yield [jiːld] *n* (*AGR*) урожай *m*; (*COMM*) доход ♦ *vt* (*surrender*) сдавать* (сдать* *perf*); (*produce*) приносить* (принести* *perf*) ♦ *vi* (*surrender*) отступать (отступить* *perf*); (*US: AUT*) уступать (уступить* *perf*) дорогу; **a ~ of five percent** пятипроцентный доход.

YMCA *n abbr* = *Young Men's Christian Association*; (*organization*) ИМКА; (*hostel*) общежитие ИМКА.

yob(bo) ['jɔb(əu)] *n* (*BRIT*: *inf*: *pej*) шпана.

yodel ['jəudl] *vi* петь* (*impf*) и йодлером.

yoga ['jəugə] *n* йога.

yog(h)ourt ['jəugət] *n* йогурт.

yog(h)urt ['jəugət] *n* = **yog(h)ourt**.

yoke [jəuk] *n* (*also fig*) ярмо* ♦ *vt* (*also*: **~ together**: *oxen etc*) запрягать (запрячь* *perf*).

yolk [jəuk] *n* желток*.

yonder ['jɔndəʳ] *adv* вон там.

yonks [jɔŋks] *n* (*inf*): **for ~** давным-давно.

Yorks [jɔ:ks] *abbr* (*BRIT: POST*) = Yorkshire.

| KEYWORD |

you [ju:] *pron* **1** (*subject: familiar*) ты; (*: polite*) Вы; (*: 2nd person pl*) вы; **you French enjoy your food** вы, французы, знаете толк в еде; **you and I will stay here** мы с тобой/Вами останемся здесь

2 (*direct: familiar*) тебя́; (*: polite*) Вас; (*: 2nd person pl*) вас

3 (*indirect: familiar*) тебе́; (*: polite*) Вам; (*: 2nd person pl*) вам; **I love you** я тебя́/Вас люблю́; **I'll give you a present** я тебе́/Вам что́-нибудь подарю́

4 (*after prep: +gen: familiar*) тебя́; (*: polite*) Вас; (*: 2nd person pl*) вас; (*: +dat: familiar*) тебе́; (*: polite*) Вам; (*: 2nd person pl*) вам; (*: +instr: familiar*) тобо́й; (*: polite*) Ва́ми; (*: 2nd person pl*) ва́ми; (*: +prp: familiar*) тебе́; (*: polite*) Вас; (*: 2nd person pl*) вас; **they've been talking about you** они́ говори́ли о тебе́/Вас

5 (*after prep: referring to subject of sentence: +gen*) себя́; (*: +dat, +prp*) себе́; (*: +instr*) собо́й; **will you take the children with you?** Вы возьмёте дете́й с собо́й?; **close the door behind you** закро́йте за собо́й дверь; **she's younger than you** она́ моло́же Вас *or* моло́же, чем Вы

6 (*impersonal: one*): **you never know what can happen** никогда́ не зна́ешь, что мо́жет случи́ться; **you never know!** тру́дно предсказа́ть!; **you can't do that!** так нельзя́ (де́лать)!; **fresh air does you good** све́жий во́здух поле́зен (для здоро́вья).

you'd [ju:d] = **you had, you would.**

you'll [ju:l] = **you shall, you will.**

young [jʌŋ] *adj* молодо́й (мо́лод); (*child*) ма́ленький ♦ *npl* (*of animal*) молодня́к *msg*; (*people*): **the ~** молодёжь *f*; **a ~ man** молодо́й челове́к; **a ~ lady** де́вушка*.

younger [jʌŋɡə^r] *adj* мла́дший*; **the ~ generation** мла́дшее поколе́ние.

youngish [ˈjʌŋɪʃ] *adj* моложа́вый (моложа́в).

youngster [ˈjʌŋstə^r] *n* молодо́й челове́к*; (*child*) ребёнок*; **the ~s of today**

сего́дняшняя молодёжь.

your [jɔ:^r] *adj* (*polite*) Ваш; (*familiar*) твой; (*2nd person pl*) ваш; *see also* **my.**

you're [juə^r] = **you are.**

yours [jɔ:z] *pron* (*familiar*) твой; (*polite*) Ваш; (*2nd person pl*) ваш; (*referring to subject of sentence*) свой; **is this ~?** э́то твоё/Ва́ше?; **~ sincerely, ~ faithfully** и́скренне Ваш; *see also* **mine**[1].

yourself [jɔ:ˈsɛlf] *pron* (*reflexive*) себя́; (*after prep: +gen*) себя́; (*: +dat, +prp*) себе́; (*: +instr*) собо́й; (*emphatic*) сам (*f* сама́, *pl* са́ми); (*alone*): **(all) by ~** оди́н; **you ~ told me** Вы са́ми говори́ли мне; *see also* **myself.**

yourselves [jɔ:ˈsɛlvz] *pl pron* (*reflexive*) себя́; (*after prep: +gen*) себя́; (*: +dat, +prp*) себе́; (*: +instr*) собо́й; (*emphatic*) са́ми; (*alone*): **(all) by ~** одни́; **talk amongst ~ for a moment** посовеща́йтесь ме́жду собо́й пока́; *see also* **myself.**

youth [ju:θ] *n* (*young days*) мо́лодость *f*, ю́ность *f*; (*pl ~s; young man*) ю́ноша *m*; **in my ~** в мо́лодости *or* ю́ности.

youth club *n* молодёжный клуб.

youthful [ˈju:θful] *adj* ю́ношеский*; (*person, looks*) ю́ный.

youthfulness [ˈju:θfəlnɪs] *n* мо́лодость *f*.

youth hostel *n* молодёжная гости́ница.

youth movement *n* молодёжное движе́ние.

you've [ju:v] = **you have.**

yowl [jaul] *n* (*of person, animal*) вой.

yr *abbr* = **year.**

Yugoslav [ˈju:ɡəuslɑ:v] *adj* югосла́вский ♦ *n* югосла́в(ка*).

Yugoslavia [ˈju:ɡəuˈslɑ:vɪə] *n* Югосла́вия.

Yugoslavian [ˈju:ɡəuˈslɑ:vɪən] *adj* югосла́вский.

yule log [ju:l-] *n* большо́е поле́но, сжига́емое в сочельник.

yuppie [ˈjʌpɪ] *n* (*inf*) молодо́й челове́к из сре́днего кла́сса, сде́лавший карье́ру.

YWCA *n abbr* = **Young Women's Christian Association**; (*organization*) же́нский христиа́нский сою́з молодёжи; (*hostel*) общежи́тие же́нского христиа́нского сою́за молодёжи.

---

* marks translations which have irregular inflections. The Russian-English side of the dictionary gives inflectional information.

~ Z, z ~

Z, z [zɛd, (US) ziː] n (letter) 26-ая буква
английского алфавита.
Zagreb ['zɑːgrɛb] n Загреб.
Zaire [zɑːˈiːəʳ] n Заир.
Zambia ['zæmbɪə] n Замбия.
Zambian ['zæmbɪən] adj замбийский* ♦ n
замбиец(-ийка).
zany ['zeɪnɪ] adj (ideas, sense of humour)
забавный* (забавен).
zap [zæp] vt (COMPUT) стирать (стереть* perf).
zeal [ziːl] n рвение.
zealot ['zɛlət] n фанатик.
zealous ['zɛləs] adj ревностный* (ревностен).
zebra ['ziːbrə] n зебра.
zebra crossing n (BRIT) „зебра", пешеходный
переход.
zenith ['zɛnɪθ] n (also fig) зенит.
zero ['zɪərəu] n ноль m, нуль m ♦ vi: to ~ in (on
target) пристреливаться (пристреляться
perf); **5 degrees below** ~ 5 градусов ниже
нуля or ноля.
zero hour n (fig) решительный час.
zero option n нулевой вариант.
zero-rated ['ziːrəureɪtɪd] adj (BRIT)
освобождённый от уплаты налогов.
zest [zɛst] n (for life) вкус; (of orange) цедра.
zigzag ['zɪgzæg] n зигзаг ♦ vi делать (impf)
зигзаги.
Zimbabwe [zɪmˈbɑːbwɪ] n Зимбабве ind.
Zimbabwean [zɪmˈbɑːbwɪən] adj: ~
government/people правительство/народ
Зимбабве.
zimmer frame® ['zɪmə-] n ходунки mpl
Зиммера.
zinc [zɪŋk] n цинк.
Zionism ['zaɪənɪzəm] n сионизм.
Zionist ['zaɪənɪst] adj сионистский ♦ n сионист.
zip [zɪp] n (also:~ fastener) молния ♦ vt (also:~
up) застёгивать (застегнуть perf) на
молнию.
zip code n (US) почтовый индекс.
zipper ['zɪpəʳ] n (US) = zip.
zither ['zɪðəʳ] n цитра.
zodiac ['zəudɪæk] n зодиак.
zombie ['zɔmbɪ] n (fig) зомби ind.
zone [zəun] n зона.
zonked [zɔŋkt] adj (inf): I'm completely ~
(exhausted) я совершенно одуревший.
zoo [zuː] n зоопарк.
zoological [zuəˈlɔdʒɪkl] adj зоологический*.
zoologist [zuˈɔlədʒɪst] n зоолог.
zoology [zuːˈɔlədʒɪ] n зоология.
zoom [zuːm] vi: to ~ past промелькнуть (perf)
мимо; to ~ in (on sth/sb) (PHOT, CINEMA)
давать* (дать* perf) крупный план (чего-н/
кого-н).
zoom lens n объектив с переменным
фокусным расстоянием.
zucchini [zuːˈkiːnɪ] n(pl) (US: courgette(s))
кабачок*.
Zulu ['zuːluː] adj зулусский ♦ n зулус(ка).
Zürich ['zjuərɪk] n Цюрих.

ПРИЛОЖЕНИЯ

APPENDICES

Английские Неправильные Глаголы

present	pt	pp	present	pt	pp
arise	arose	arisen	**dwell**	dwelt	dwelt
awake	awoke	awaked	**eat**	ate	eaten
be (am, is,	was,	been	**fall**	fell	fallen
are; being)	were		**feed**	fed	fed
bear	bore	born(e)	**feel**	felt	felt
beat	beat	beaten	**fight**	fought	fought
become	became	become	**find**	found	found
begin	began	begun	**flee**	fled	fled
behold	beheld	beheld	**fling**	flung	flung
bend	bent	bent	**fly (flies)**	flew	flown
beseech	besought	besought	**forbid**	forbade	forbidden
beset	beset	beset	**forecast**	forecast	forecast
bet	bet, betted	bet, betted	**forget**	forgot	forgotten
bid	bid, bade	bid, bidden	**forgive**	forgave	forgiven
bind	bound	bound	**forsake**	forsook	forsaken
bite	bit	bitten	**freeze**	froze	frozen
bleed	bled	bled	**get**	got	got, (*US*)
blow	blew	blown			gotten
break	broke	broken	**give**	gave	given
breed	bred	bred	**go (goes)**	went	gone
bring	brought	brought	**grind**	ground	ground
build	built	built	**grow**	grew	grown
burn	burnt, burned	burnt, burned	**hang**	hung, hanged	hung, hanged
burst	burst	burst	**have (has;**	had	had
buy	bought	bought	**having)**		
can	could	(been able)	**hear**	heard	heard
cast	cast	cast	**hide**	hid	hidden
catch	caught	caught	**hit**	hit	hit
choose	chose	chosen	**hold**	held	held
cling	clung	clung	**hurt**	hurt	hurt
come	came	come	**keep**	kept	kept
cost	cost	cost	**kneel**	knelt, kneeled	knelt, kneeled
creep	crept	crept	**know**	knew	known
cut	cut	cut	**lay**	laid	laid
deal	dealt	dealt	**lead**	led	led
dig	dug	dug	**lean**	leant, leaned	leant, leaned
do (*3rd***	did	done	**leap**	leapt, leaped	leapt, leaped
***person*: he/**			**learn**	learnt, learned	learnt, learned
she/it/does)			**leave**	left	left
draw	drew	drawn	**lend**	lent	lent
dream	dreamed,	dreamed,	**let**	let	let
	dreamt	dreamt	**lie (lying)**	lay	lain
drink	drank	drunk	**light**	lit, lighted	lit, lighted
drive	drove	driven	**lose**	lost	lost

present	pt	pp	present	pt	pp
make	made	made	speed	sped, speeded	sped, speeded
may	might	—	spell	spelt, spelled	spelt, spelled
mean	meant	meant	spend	spent	spent
meet	met	met	spill	spilt, spilled	spilt, spilled
mistake	mistook	mistaken	spin	spun	spun
mow	mowed	mown, mowed	spit	spat	spat
must	(had to)	(had to)	split	split	split
pay	paid	paid	spoil	spoiled, spoilt	spoiled, spoilt
put	put	put	spread	spread	spread
quit	quit, quitted	quit, quitted	spring	sprang	sprung
read	read	read	stand	stood	stood
rid	rid	rid	steal	stole	stolen
ride	rode	ridden	stick	stuck	stuck
ring	rang	rung	sting	stung	stung
rise	rose	risen	stink	stank	stunk
run	ran	run	stride	strode	stridden
saw	sawed	sawn	strike	struck	struck, stricken
say	said	said			
see	saw	seen	strive	strove	striven
seek	sought	sought	swear	swore	sworn
sell	sold	sold	sweep	swept	swept
send	sent	sent	swell	swelled	swollen, swelled
set	set	set			
shake	shook	shaken	swim	swam	swum
shall	should	—	swing	swung	swung
shear	sheared	shorn, sheared	take	took	taken
shed	shed	shed	teach	taught	taught
shine	shone	shone	tear	tore	torn
shoot	shot	shot	tell	told	told
show	showed	shown	think	thought	thought
shrink	shrank	shrunk	throw	threw	thrown
shut	shut	shut	thrust	thrust	thrust
sing	sang	sung	tread	trod	trodden
sink	sank	sunk	wake	woke, waked	woken, waked
sit	sat	sat	wear	wore	worn
slay	slew	slain	weave	wove, weaved	woven, weaved
sleep	slept	slept			
slide	slid	slid	wed	wedded, wed	wedded, wed
sling	slung	slung	weep	wept	wept
slit	slit	slit	win	won	won
smell	smelt, smelled	smelt, smelled	wind	wound	wound
sow	sowed	sown, sowed	wring	wrung	wrung
speak	spoke	spoken	write	wrote	written

TABLES OF RUSSIAN IRREGULAR FORMS

Nouns

Table 1			мать
		Singular	*Plural*
	Nom	мать	ма́тери
	Acc	мать	матере́й
	Gen	ма́тери	матере́й
	Dat	ма́тери	матеря́м
	Instr	ма́терью	матеря́ми
	Prp	о ма́тери	о матеря́х

Table 2			дочь
		Singular	*Plural*
	Nom	дочь	до́чери
	Acc	до́чь	дочере́й
	Gen	до́чери	дочере́й
	Dat	до́чери	дочеря́м
	Instr	до́черью	дочерьми́
	Prp	о до́чери	о дочеря́х

Table 3			путь
		Singular	*Plural*
	Nom	путь	пути́
	Acc	путь	пути́
	Gen	пути́	путе́й
	Dat	пути́	путя́м
	Instr	путём	путя́ми
	Prp	о пути́	о путя́х

Table 4			время
		Singular	*Plural*
	Nom	вре́мя	времена́
	Acc	вре́мя	времена́
	Gen	вре́мени	времён
	Dat	вре́мени	времена́м
	Instr	вре́менем	времена́ми
	Prp	о вре́мени	о времена́х

(NB. Similarly with nouns like и́мя, пле́мя etc)

Pronouns

Personal Pronouns

Table 5a

Nom	я	ты	он	она́	оно́
Acc/Gen	меня́	тебя́	его́	её	его́
Dat	мне	тебе́	ему́	ей	ему́
Instr	мной	тобо́й	им	ей	им
Prp	обо мне	о тебе́	о нём	о ней	о нём

Table 5b

Nom	мы	вы	они́
Acc/Gen	нас	вас	их
Dat	нам	вам	им
Instr	на́ми	ва́ми	и́ми
Prp	о нас	о вас	о них

(NB. The instrumental forms мной, тобо́й, ей have alternatives мно́ю, тобо́ю and е́ю respectively. The reflexive personal pronoun себя́ declines like тебя́)

Interrogative Pronouns

(The alternatives given at the accusative are animate forms which are identical with the genitive.)

Table 6

Nom	кто	что
Acc	кого́	что
Gen	кого́	чего́
Dat	кому́	чему́
Instr	кем	чем
Prp	о ком	о чём

(NB. Similarly with никто́, ничто́ etc)

Table 7

	m	*f*	*nt*	*pl*
Nom	чей	чья	чьё	чьи
Acc	чей/чьего́	чью	чьё	чьи/чьих
Gen	чьего́	чьей	чьего́	чьих
Dat	чьему́	чьей	чьему́	чьим
Instr	чьим	чьей	чьим	чьи́ми
Prp	о чьём	о чьей	о чьём	о чьих

(NB. The instrumental form чьей has the alternative чье́ю.)

Possessive Pronouns

Table 8

	m	*f*	*nt*	*pl*
Nom	мой	моя́	моё	мои́
Acc	мой/моего́	мою́	моё	мои́/мои́х
Gen	моего́	мое́й	моего́	мои́х
Dat	моему́	мое́й	моему́	мои́м
Instr	мои́м	мое́й	мои́м	мои́ми
Prp	о моём	о мое́й	о моём	о мои́х

(NB. твой declines like мой, as does the reflexive possessive pronoun свой. The instrumental form мое́й has the alternative мое́ю)

Table 9

	m	*f*	*nt*	*pl*
Nom	наш	на́ша	на́ше	на́ши
Acc	наш/на́шего	на́шу	на́ше	на́ши/на́ших
Gen	на́шего	на́шей	на́шего	на́ших
Dat	на́шему	на́шей	на́шему	на́шим
Instr	на́шим	на́шей	на́шим	на́шими
Prp	о на́шем	о на́шей	о на́шем	о на́ших

(NB. ваш declines like наш. The instrumental form на́шей has the alternative на́шею. The possessive pronouns его́, её and их are invariable)

Demonstrative Pronouns

Table 10

	m	*f*	*nt*	*pl*
Nom	э́тот	э́та	э́то	э́ти
Acc	э́тот/э́того	э́ту	э́то	э́ти/э́тих
Gen	э́того	э́той	э́того	э́тих
Dat	э́тому	э́той	э́тому	э́тим
Instr	э́тим	э́той	э́тим	э́тими
Prp	об э́том	об э́той	об э́том	об э́тих

(NB. the instrumental form э́той has the alternative э́тою)

Table 11

	m	*f*	*nt*	*pl*
Nom	тот	та	то	те
Acc	тот/того́	ту	то	те/тех
Gen	того́	той	того́	тех
Dat	тому́	той	тому́	тем
Instr	тем	той	тем	те́ми
Prp	о том	о той	о том	о тех

(NB. The instrumental form той has the alternative то́ю)

Table 12

	m	*f*	*nt*	*pl*
Nom	сей	сия́	сие́	сии́
Acc	сей/сего́	сию́	сие́	сии́/сих
Gen	сего́	сей	сего́	сих
Dat	сему́	сей	сему́	сим
Instr	сим	сей	сим	си́ми
Prp	о сём	о сей	о сём	о сих

(NB. The instrumental form сей has the alternative се́ю)

Table 13

	m	*f*	*nt*	*pl*
Nom	весь	вся	всё	все
Acc	весь/всего́	всю	всё	все/всех
Gen	всего́	всей	всего́	всех
Dat	всему́	всей	всему́	всем
Instr	всем	всей	всем	все́ми
Prp	обо всём	обо всей	обо всём	обо всех

(NB. The instrumental form всей has the alternative все́ю)

Verbs

Table 14			дать	
		Present	*Past*	*Imperative*
	я	дам	дал/дала́	
	ты	дашь	дал/дала́	
	он	даст	дал	
	она́	даст	дала́	
	оно́	даст	да́ло	
	мы	дади́м	да́ли	
	вы	дади́те	да́ли	
	они́	даду́т	да́ли	
				да́й(те)

(NB. Similarly with verbs such as переда́ть, изда́ть, отда́ть, разда́ть etc)

Table 15			есть	
		Present	*Past*	*Imperative*
	я	ем	ел/е́ла	
	ты	ешь	ел/е́ла	
	он	ест	ел	
	она́	ест	е́ла	
	оно́	ест	е́ло	
	мы	еди́м	е́ли	
	вы	еди́те	е́ли	
	они́	едя́т	е́ли	
				е́шь(те)

(NB. Similarly with verbs such as съесть, пое́сть, переéсть etc)

Table 16			хоте́ть	
		Present	*Past*	
	я	хочу́	хоте́л/хоте́ла	
	ты	хо́чешь	хоте́л/хоте́ла	
	он	хо́чет	хоте́л	
	она́	хо́чет	хоте́ла	
	оно́	хо́чет	хоте́ло	
	мы	хоти́м	хоте́ли	
	вы	хоти́те	хоте́ли	
	они́	хотя́т	хоте́ли	

(NB. Similarly with verbs such as расхоте́ть, захоте́ть etc)

Table 17			**чтить**	
		Present	*Past*	*Imperative*
	я	чту	чтил/чти́ла	
	ты	чтишь	чтил/чти́ла	
	он	чтит	чтил	
	она́	чтит	чти́ла	
	оно́	чтит	чти́ло	
	мы	чтим	чти́ли	
	вы	чти́те	чти́ли	
	они́	чтут/чтят	чти́ли	
				чти́(те)

(NB. Similarly with verbs such as почти́ть etc)

Table 18			**идти́**	
		Present	*Past*	*Imperative*
	я	иду́	шёл/шла	
	ты	идёшь	шёл/шла	
	он	идёт	шёл	
	она́	идёт	шла	
	оно́	идёт	шло	
	мы	идём	шли	
	вы	идёте	шли	
	они́	иду́т	шли	
				иди́(те)

(NB. Similarly with verbs such as прийти́, уйти́, отойти́, зайти́ etc)

Table 19			**éхать**	
		Present	*Past*	*Imperative*
	я	éду	éхал/éхала	
	ты	едешь	éхал/éхала	
	он	éдет	éхал	
	она́	éдет	éхала	
	оно́	éдет	éхало	
	мы	éдем	éхали	
	вы	éдете	éхали	
	они́	éдут	éхали	
				поезжа́й(те)

(NB. Similarly with verbs such as прие́хать, перее́хать, уе́хать, въе́хать)

Table 20			бежа́ть		
		Present	*Past*	*Imperative*	
	я	бегу́	бежа́л/бежа́ла		
	ты	бежи́шь	бежа́л/бежа́ла		
	он	бежи́т	бежа́л		
	она́	бежи́т	бежа́ла		
	оно́	бежи́т	бежа́ло		
	мы	бежи́м	бежа́ли		
	вы	бежи́те	бежа́ли		
	они́	бегу́т	бежа́ли		
				беги́(те)	

(NB. Similarly with verbs such as побежа́ть, убежа́ть, прибежа́ть etc)

Table 21			быть		
		Future	*Past*	*Imperative*	
	я	бу́ду	был/была́		
	ты	бу́дешь	был/была́		
	он	бу́дет	был		
	она́	бу́дет	была́		
	оно́	бу́дет	бы́ло		
	мы	бу́дем	бы́ли		
	вы	бу́дете	бы́ли		
	они́	бу́дут	бы́ли		
				бу́дь(те)	

(NB. Not used in present tense, except есть in certain cases)

Numerals

Cardinal Numbers

(NB. The alternatives given at the accusative are animate forms which are identical with the genitive)

Table 22

	m	f	nt	pl
Nom	оди́н	одна́	одно́	одни́
Acc	оди́н/одного́	одну́	одно́	одни́/одни́х
Gen	одного́	одно́й	одного́	одни́х
Dat	одному́	одно́й	одному́	одни́м
Instr	одни́м	одно́й	одни́м	одни́ми
Prp	об одно́м	об одно́й	об одно́м	об одни́х

(NB. The instrumental form одно́й has the alternative одно́ю)

Table 23

	m	f	nt
Nom	два	две	два
Acc	два/двух	две/двух	два/двух
Gen	двух	двух	двух
Dat	двум	двум	двум
Instr	двумя́	двумя́	двумя́
Prp	о двух	о двух	о двух

Table 24		три
	Nom	три
	Acc	три/трёх
	Gen	трёх
	Dat	трём
	Instr	тремя́
	Prp	о трёх

Table 25		четы́ре
	Nom	четы́ре
	Acc	четы́ре/четырёх
	Gen	четырёх
	Dat	четырём
	Instr	четырьмя́
	Prp	о четырёх

Table 26		о́ба	о́бе
		m/nt	f
	Nom	о́ба	о́бе
	Acc	о́ба/обо́их	о́бе/обе́их
	Gen	обо́их	обе́их
	Dat	обо́им	обе́им
	Instr	обо́ими	обе́ими
	Prp	об обо́их	об обе́их

Table 27		пять
	Nom	пять
	Acc	пять
	Gen	пятѝ
	Dat	пятѝ
	Instr	пятью̀
	Prp	о пятѝ

Table 28		со́рок
	Nom	со́рок
	Acc	со́рок
	Gen	сорока́
	Dat	сорока́
	Instr	сорока́
	Prp	о сорока́

(NB. The numerals шесть to два́дцать plus
три́дцать decline like пять)

Table 29		пятьдеся́т
	Nom	пятьдеся́т
	Acc	пятьдеся́т
	Gen	пятѝдесяти
	Dat	пятѝдесяти
	Instr	пятью̀десятью
	Prp	о пятѝдесяти

Table 30		сто
	Nom	сто
	Acc	сто
	Gen	ста
	Dat	ста
	Instr	ста
	Prp	о ста

(NB. Similarly with шестьдеся́т and
се́мьдесят)

(NB. Similarly with девяно́сто)

Table 31		две́сти
	Nom	две́сти
	Acc	две́сти
	Gen	двухсо́т
	Dat	двумста́м
	Instr	двумяста́ми
	Prp	о двухста́х

Table 32		три́ста
	Nom	три́ста
	Acc	три́ста
	Gen	трёхсо́т
	Dat	трёмста́м
	Instr	тремяста́ми
	Prp	о трёхста́х

Table 33		четы́реста
	Nom	четы́реста
	Acc	четы́реста
	Gen	четырёхсо́т
	Dat	четырёмста́м
	Instr	четырьмяста́ми
	Prp	о четырёхста́х

Table 34		пятьсо́т
	Nom	пятьсо́т
	Acc	пятьсо́т
	Gen	пятисо́т
	Dat	пятиста́м
	Instr	пятьюста́ми
	Prp	о пятиста́х

(NB. Similarly with шестьсо́т, семьсо́т,
восемьсо́т and девятьсо́т)

Table 35		ты́сяча	
		Singular	*Plural*
Nom		ты́сяча	ты́сячи
Acc		ты́сячу	ты́сячи
Gen		ты́сячи	ты́сяч
Dat		ты́сяче	ты́сячам
Instr		ты́сячей	ты́сячами
Prp		о ты́сяче	о ты́сячах

(NB. The instrumental singular form ты́сячью also exists)

Collective Numerals

The following tables shows how collective numerals 2-7 decline:

Table 36a

Nom	дво́е	тро́е	че́тверо
Acc	дво́е/двои́х	тро́е/трои́х	че́тверо/четверы́х
Gen	двои́х	трои́х	четверы́х
Dat	двои́м	трои́м	четверы́м
Instr	двои́ми	трои́ми	четверы́ми
Prp	о двои́х	о трои́х	о четверы́х

Table 36b

Nom	пя́теро	ше́стеро	се́меро
Acc	пя́теро/пятеры́х	ше́стеро/шестеры́х	се́меро/семеры́х
Gen	пятеры́х	шестеры́х	семеры́х
Dat	пятеры́м	шестеры́м	семеры́м
Instr	пятеры́ми	шестеры́ми	семеры́ми
Prp	о пятеры́х	о шестеры́х	о семеры́х

(NB. The alternatives given at the accusative are animate forms and identical with the genitive. Other collective numerals decline like че́тверо)

NUMBERS

КОЛИЧЕСТВЕННЫЕ ЧИСЛИТЕЛЬНЫЕ		CARDINAL NUMBERS
оди́н (одна́, одно́, одни́)	1	one
два (две)	2	two
три	3	three
четы́ре	4	four
пять	5	five
шесть	6	six
семь	7	seven
во́семь	8	eight
де́вять	9	nine
де́сять	10	ten
оди́ннадцать	11	eleven
двена́дцать	12	twelve
трина́дцать	13	thirteen
четы́рнадцать	14	fourteen
пятна́дцать	15	fifteen
шестна́дцать	16	sixteen
семна́дцать	17	seventeen
восемна́дцать	18	eighteen
девятна́дцать	19	nineteen
два́дцать	20	twenty
два́дцать оди́н (одна́, одно́ одни́)	21	twenty-one
два́дцать два (две)	22	twenty-two
три́дцать	30	thirty
со́рок	40	forty
пятьдеся́т	50	fifty
шестьдеся́т	60	sixty
се́мьдесят	70	seventy
во́семьдесят	80	eighty
девяно́сто	90	ninety
сто	100	a hundred
сто оди́н (одна́, одно́, одни́)	101	a hundred and one
две́сти	200	two hundred
две́сти оди́н (одна́, одно́, одни́)	201	two hundred and one
три́ста	300	three hundred
четы́реста	400	four hundred
пятьсо́т	500	five hundred
ты́сяча	1 000	a thousand
миллио́н	1 000 000	a million

СОБИРАТЕЛЬНЫЕ ЧИСЛИТЕЛЬНЫЕ

COLLECTIVE NUMERALS

двóе
трóе
чéтверо
пя́теро
шéстеро
сéмеро

ПОРЯДКОВЫЕ ЧИСЛИТЕЛЬНЫЕ

ORDINAL NUMBERS

пéрвый	1-ый	first	1st
вторóй	2-óй	second	2nd
трéтий	3-ий	third	3rd
четвёртый	4-ый	fourth	4th
пя́тый	5-ый	fifth	5th
шестóй	6-óй	sixth	6th
седьмóй	7-óй	seventh	7th
восьмóй	8-óй	eighth	8th
девя́тый	9-ый	ninth	9th
деся́тый	10-ый	tenth	10th
оди́ннадцатый		eleventh	
двенáдцатый		twelfth	
тринáдцатый		thirteenth	
четы́рнадцатый		fourteenth	
пятнáдцатый		fifteenth	
шестнáдцатый		sixteenth	
семнáдцатый		seventeenth	
восемнáдцатый		eighteenth	
девятнáдцатый		nineteenth	
двадцáтый		twentieth	
двáдцать пéрвый		twenty-first	
двáдцать вторóй		twenty-second	
тридцáтый		thirtieth	
сороковóй		fortieth	
пятидеся́тый		fiftieth	
восьмидеся́тый		eightieth	
девянóстый		ninetieth	
сóтый		hundredth	
сто пéрвый		hundred-and-first	
ты́сячный		thousandth	
миллиóнный		millionth	

ДРОБИ

полови́на	½
треть (*f*)	⅓
че́тверть (*f*)	¼
одна́ пя́тая	⅕
три че́тверти	¾
две тре́ти	⅔
полтора́ (полторы́)	1½
ноль це́лых (и) пять деся́тых	0·5
три це́лых (и) четы́ре деся́тых	3·4
шесть це́лых (и) во́семьдесят де́вять со́тых	6·89
де́сять проце́нтов	10%
сто проце́нтов	100%

FRACTIONS

a half	½
a third	⅓
a quarter	¼
a fifth	⅕
three quarters	¾
two thirds	⅔
one and a half	1½
(nought) point five	0·5
three point four	3·4
six point eight nine	6·89
ten per cent	10%
a hundred per cent	100%

TIME AND DATE

ВРЕМЯ

который час?
сейчас 5 часов
в какое время?
в +*acc* ...
в час дня

полночь (*f*)
десять минут первого

десять минут второго, час десять
четверть второго, час пятнадцать
полвторого, половина второго, час
тридцать
без четверти два, час сорок пять
без десяти два, час пятьдесят
полдень (*m*)
полпервого, половина первого,
двенадцать тридцать
час дня

семь часов вечера

девять тридцать вечера
без четверти двенадцать, одиннадцать
сорок пять

через двадцать минут
двадцать минут назад
в ближайшие двадцать минут
за двадцать минут
спустя двадцать минут
сейчас двадцать минут четвёртого

полчаса
четверть часа
полтора часа
час с четвертью

через час
каждый час
через час, каждый час
через час

разбудите меня в семь часов
уже начало пятого
с девяти до пяти

TIME

what time is it?
it is *or* it's 5 o'clock
at what time?
at ...
at one p.m.

00.00 midnight
00.10, ten past midnight, ten past twelve
a.m.
01.10, ten past one, one ten
01.15, a quarter past one, one fifteen
01.30, half past one, one thirty

01.45, a quarter to two, one forty-five
01.50, ten to two, one fifty
12.00, midday
12.30, half past twelve, twelve thirty p.m.

13.00, one (o'clock) (in the afternoon), one
p.m.
19.00, seven (o'clock) (in the evening),
seven p.m.
21.30, nine thirty (p.m. *or* at night)
23.45, a quarter to twelve, eleven forty-five
p.m.

in twenty minutes
twenty minutes ago
in the next twenty minutes
within twenty minutes
after twenty minutes
it's twenty after three (*US*)

half an hour
quarter of an hour
an hour and a half
an hour and a quarter

in an hour's time
every hour, on the hour
hourly
in an hour from now

wake me up at seven
it's just gone four
from nine to five

с двух до трех (часо́в)	between two and three (o'clock)
сего́дня с девяти́ утра́	since nine o'clock this morning
до десяти́ часо́в ве́чера	till ten o'clock tonight
о́коло трёх часо́в дня	at about three o'clock in the afternoon
три часа́ по Гри́нвичу	three o'clock GMT

ДАТЫ

DATE

сего́дня	today
за́втра	tomorrow
вчера́	yesterday
сего́дня у́тром	this morning
за́втра днём/ве́чером	tomorrow afternoon/night
позавчера́ ве́чером, позапро́шлой но́чью	the night before last
позавчера́	the day before yesterday
вчера́ ве́чером, прошлой но́чью	last night
послеза́втра	the day after tomorrow
два дня́/шесть лет наза́д	two days/six years ago
ка́ждый день/вто́рник	every day/Tuesday
в сре́ду	on Wednesday
он хо́дит туда́ по сре́дам	he goes there on Wednesdays
"закры́то по пя́тницам"	"closed on Fridays"
с понеде́льника до пя́тницы	from Monday to Friday
к четвергу́	by Thursday
как-то в ма́рте, в суббо́ту	one Saturday in March
че́рез неде́лю	in a week's time
во вто́рник на сле́дующей неде́ле	a week on *or* next Tuesday
в воскресе́нье на про́шлой неде́ле	a week last Sunday
че́рез понеде́льник	Monday week
на э́той/сле́дующей/про́шлой неде́ле	this/next/last week
че́рез две неде́ли	in two weeks *or* a fortnight
в понеде́льник че́рез две неде́ли	two weeks on Monday
в э́тот день шесть лет наза́д	six years to the day
пе́рвая/после́дняя пя́тница ме́сяца	the first/last Friday of the month
сле́дующий ме́сяц	next month
про́шлый год	last year
в конце́ ме́сяца	at the end of the month
два ра́за в неде́лю/ме́сяц/год	twice a week/month/year
како́е сего́дня число́?	what's the date?, what date is it today?
сего́дня 28-ое	today's date is the 28th, today is the 28th
пе́рвое января́	the first of January, January the first
ты́сяча девятьсо́т шестьдеся́т пя́тый год	1965, nineteen (hundred and) sixty-five
роди́лся в 1967-ом году́	I was born in 1967

у него день рождения 5 июня

18-го августа 1992

с 19-го до 3-го

в 89-ом году
весна 87-го года
в 1930-ых годах
в 1940-ых годах
в 2006-ом году
в 13-ом веке
4 год до н.э.
70 год н.э.

his birthday is on June 5th (*BRIT*) *or* 5th June (*US*)
on 18th August (*BRIT*) *or* August 18th 1992 (*US*)
from the 19th to the 3rd

in '89
the Spring of '87
in (*or* during) the 1930s
in 1940 something
in the year 2006
in the 13th century
4 BC
70 AD

[eɪ]	**A,**	**a**
[bi:]	**B,**	**b**
[si:]	**C,**	**c**
[di:]	**D,**	**d**
[i:]	**E,**	**e**
[ɛf]	**F,**	**f**
[dʒi:]	**G,**	**g**
[eɪtʃ]	**H,**	**h**
[aɪ]	**I,**	**i**
[dʒeɪ]	**J,**	**j**
[keɪ]	**K,**	**k**
[ɛl]	**L,**	**l**
[ɛm]	**M,**	**m**
[ɛn]	**N,**	**n**
[əu]	**O,**	**o**
[pi:]	**P,**	**p**
[kju:]	**Q,**	**q**
[ɑ:*]	**R,**	**r**
[ɛs]	**S,**	**s**
[ti:]	**T,**	**t**
[ju:]	**U,**	**u**
[vi:]	**V,**	**v**
[ˈdʌblju]	**W,**	**w**
[ɛks]	**X,**	**x**
[waɪ]	**Y,**	**y**
[zɛd, (US) zi:]	**Z,**	**z**

А, а	[ɑʒ]
Б, б	[be]
В, в	[ve]
Г, г	[ge]
Д, д	[de]
Е, е	[je]
Ё, ё	[jɔ]
Ж, ж	[ʒe]
З, з	[ze]
И, и	[i]
Й, й	[iˈkratkɔje]
К, к	[ka]
Л, л	[ɛl]
М, м	[ɛm]
Н, н	[ɛn]
О, о	[ɔ]
П, п	[pe]
Р, р	[ɛr]
С, с	[ɛs]
Т, т	[te]
У, у	[u]
Ф, ф	[ɛf]
Х, х	[xa]
Ц, ц	[tse]
Ч, ч	[tʃe]
Ш, ш	[ʃa]
Щ, щ	[ʃta]
Ъ, ъ	[ˈtɣɔrd+ znak]
Ы, ы	[+]
Ь, ь	[ˈm̩akk+ znak]
Э, э	[ɛ]
Ю, ю	[ju]
Я, я	[ja]